To Bernard
with the affectionate regards
of his old friend
Clarence

March 17, 1960

The New Century

HANDBOOK OF ENGLISH LITERATURE

The New Century
HANDBOOK OF ENGLISH
LITERATURE

Edited by CLARENCE L. BARNHART

with the assistance of
WILLIAM D. HALSEY

APPLETON-CENTURY-CROFTS, INC.
New York

PREFACE

The New Century Handbook of English Literature seeks to answer those questions about English writers, works of literature, characters from works of literature, and various related (but not necessarily English) items which are most likely to be raised by modern American readers of English literature. It is intended to add to the enjoyment of the vast number of people in every walk of life who read primarily for pleasure, and whose reading tastes have been influenced by college courses in literature. Students, teachers, editors, writers, librarians, lawyers, and clergymen who want to check a literary allusion or confirm a reference will find it a rewarding source of information. *The New Century Handbook of English Literature* opens doors to new reading pleasure for the casual reader. For the professional user it offers a quantity and variety of information now available in no other single work.

In order to establish a basis for the entries to include in a work of this scope we have consulted the most recent editions of such standard college textbooks as *A Literary History of England*, edited by Albert C. Baugh (with Tucker Brooke, Samuel C. Chew, Kemp Malone, and George Sherburn), *A History of English Literature*, edited by Hardin Craig (with George K. Anderson, Joseph Warren Beach, and Lewis I. Bredvold), *History of English Literature*, by William M. Moody and Robert M. Lovett (in the edition revised under Fred B. Millett), and other works of a more specialized nature. Of the more than 14,000 entries in the entire book, approximately 4,000 have been selected as a result of a detailed analysis of these standard textbooks. These 4,000 represent a basic list of items, especially from the standpoint of the American reader.

A book of such wide range and comprehensiveness as this must of necessity be produced by many minds embracing different studies, interests, and backgrounds. Very fortunately, the work of many of the hundreds of scholars and specialists who aided in the making of *The New Century Cyclopedia of Names* has also been available in the preparation of this book. Their special knowledge and scholarship have been widely and gratefully used in an effort to make *The New Century Handbook of English Literature* not only an authoritative work, but one which rests on a broad scholarly basis.

On a basis of the authors and periods which the standard textbooks jointly indicated to be the most important we were able to conclude how many separate entries (and thus indirectly how much space) should be assigned to the chief titles and principal characters of the most important authors. In certain instances this led to a most comprehensive coverage of the writings of a single author. For example, in the case of Shakespeare, the reader will find that *The New Century Handbook of English Literature* includes a short stage history and plot summary of each of the plays, and articles (each in its own alphabetical position, and ranging in length from the short essays under such major names as Iago, Gloucester, and Hamlet to simple identification of very minor figures) on every character in these plays. Other writers for whom coverage in comparable detail has been provided include, to name only a few over the great span of English letters, Chaucer (all of whose known works and major characters are separately listed, with the various tales in the *Canterbury Tales* each being assigned a separate article in its proper alphabetical position), Milton, Dickens, Thackeray, Shaw, and H. G. Wells.

To increase the effectiveness of *The New Century Handbook of English Literature* as a reference tool for modern Americans, we have included the great Irish writers. For the same reason, it seemed desirable to include the more important of what might be called the "Anglo-Americans" (for example, Henry James and Logan Pearsall Smith), as well as those

Canadian, Australian, and South African writers who have become important to a considerable number of American readers. Other areas in which important, if supplementary, aspects of English literature are involved include the geography of Great Britain, as well as some aspects of English history and political (as distinguished from "literary") biography, plus also, to a limited extent, that of Europe. Many items from classical mythology have played an important part in English letters, and it has therefore been necessary to include a carefully evaluated selection of these in our list of articles. Finally, there are what might be called the descriptive and technical terms of the writer's craft ("essay," "mystery story," "sonnet," and so on), including some which may now seem to be of purely historical importance (for example, "beast fable"); although most of these are hardly unique to English literature, it seemed to us that brief articles on the more important of them would be very helpful to many users of the book.

In the matter of contemporary novelists, dramatists, poets, and so on, we have sought to rest our selection on reviews and articles in the leading newspapers and literary journals of this country and Great Britain. Although posterity must render the final judgment on many of these names and works, for the purposes of this book great current popularity and widespread critical acclaim has seemed to us adequate reason for including entries of contemporary literary interest.

For many American readers, the pronunciation of English names and titles is, in some instances, extremely difficult. For example, "Wriothesley" (pronounced "rot'sli") and "Beauchamp" (pronounced "bē'cham") are perhaps as simple as Smith and Jones for British readers; many Americans, on the other hand, would be utterly unfamiliar with the pronunciations given to them in English literature. And when one is dealing with works or characters from the Old English or Middle English periods, the difficulties of pronunciation are further compounded. For this reason we have shown pronunciations for every item of main entry in the book, except for a relatively small number of common nouns (such as "verse," "poem," and the like), which are, from a pronunciation standpoint, actually dictionary items, and which cannot conceivably present any difficulties to any user. The pronunciations are indicated immediately after the main entry form, in the key which will already be familiar to many users through its use in *The New Century Dictionary* and *The New Century Cyclopedia of Names*. I am especially indebted to Professor Allan F. Hubbell of New York University for his careful check of the pronunciations of difficult names.

Every entry in *The New Century Handbook of English Literature* has been arranged in a single alphabetical list; it is not necessary to look through tables or special sections at the back or front to obtain information wanted. Moreover, the alphabetical convention followed is in our opinion the simplest and most effective, being based on that used in *The New Century Cyclopedia of Names*, and represents a combination of the systems employed in the telephone directory (and thus certainly one of the most familiar to most Americans of any system in existence) and the leading American dictionaries. Particular attention has been paid also to cross references; for example, any character from a work of fiction entered in *The New Century Handbook of English Literature* who has more than one name (as "Uriah Heep") will have his main article under the surname (at "Heep, Uriah"), but cross reference is made in every such case also from the prename, so that the reader will be directed to the full article.

In closing, it would seem desirable to make some mention of our gratitude to the staff which helped in making this book. Writers and editors whose contributions have been particularly outstanding are Florette Henri, Barbara Fairberg, Judith Scherer, Elise Simpkins, Roger Wiehe, Jane Pope, Margaret Rose, and Pamela Shortall. Last, but by no means least, should be mentioned Frances Murlin, whose work as copy editor often went far beyond that which a copy editor is ordinarily expected to do. If *The New Century Handbook of English*

Literature serves it users as an effective and comprehensive aid to the enjoyment and greater knowledge of what is perhaps the greatest and most inspiring body of literature in history, we know that they will feel, as will Mr. Halsey and I, that the time and effort devoted to its preparation have been well spent.

CLARENCE L. BARNHART

The New

CENTURY HANDBOOK

OF

English Literature

A

Aaron (ār'ọn). In Shakespeare's *Titus Andronicus*, the Moorish lover of the Gothic queen, Tamora. He arranges the elaborate murders of Bassianus, Quintus, and Martius, and the mutilation of Titus and Lavinia. His remarkable villainy has caused some scholars to suspect a definite link in authorship between this character and Barabas in Marlowe's *Jew of Malta*, and to attribute the tragedy for this reason to Marlowe, but it is also a fact that a very similar character appears in Shakespeare's *Richard III*, which tends to contradict this attribution. In the play, Aaron is ruthlessly punished by Lucius, the new emperor, for his treachery and cruelty on behalf of Tamora against Titus's family.

Aaron. fl. c15th–16th centuries B.C. In the Old Testament, the first high priest of the Israelites and companion of Moses on the Exodus from Egypt. From Aaron and his tribe (the Levites), by tradition, are descended the priests of Israel. The most important Old Testament references to him are found in Exodus, Numbers, and Deuteronomy.

Aaron's Rod. In the Old Testament, the rod of Aaron which turned into a serpent (Aaron's Serpent). Later Aaron's Rod was one of the 12 rods of the 12 tribes of Israel. Representing the tribe of Levi, it was the only one that sprouted, budded, flowered, and bore ripe almonds, as a sign of the endowment of the priesthood upon Aaron and his descendants (Num. xvii. 8).

Aaron's Rod. A novel (1922) by D. H. Lawrence, written in Italy, partly Italian in setting.

Aaron's Serpent. In the Old Testament, the serpent which the rod of Aaron, high priest of Israel, turned into (Ex. vii. 10). Aaron was competing before Pharaoh with the Egyptian magicians, and when they also turned their rods into serpents, his swallowed theirs: "Hence one master-passion in the breast, like Aaron's serpent, swallows up the rest" (Pope, *Essay on Man*).

Abaddon (ạ.bad'ọn). **1.** The place of destruction; the depth of hell: "In all her gates Abaddon rues thy bold attempt" (Milton, *Paradise Regained*). **2.** The destroyer personified; the angel of the bottomless pit. In literature he is more commonly referred to by his name in its Greek form, Apollyon (Rev. ix. 11).

Abaelard or **Abailard** (ab'ẹ.lärd), **Peter.** See **Abelard, Peter.**

Abana (ab'ạ.nạ, ạ.bā'nạ). Biblical name of the river in Syria, flowing through the plain and city of Damascus, now known as the Barada. In Biblical times, as the Abana, it was famous (with the river Pharphar) for the sacredness of its waters. 2 Kings, v. 12.

Abaris (ab'ạ.ris). [Called **"the Hyperborean."**] A mythical Greek sage, assigned by Pindar to the 6th century B.C., by Eusebius to the 7th. According to these writers and to Herodotus, Apollo gave him a magic arrow ("the dart of Abaris") on which he rode through the air and which he gave to Pythagoras in exchange for instruction in the latter's philosophy. He was believed to have worked miraculous cures, and was widely invoked by the ancient Greeks in oracles and charms.

Abbassides (ạ.bas'īdz, ab'ạ.sīdz). [Also: **Abbasids** (ab'ạ.sidz), **Abbasides.**] A dynasty (750–1258) of 37 caliphs at Baghdad. The most famous of the Abbassides was Harun al-Rashid (caliph 786–809), during whose reign many of the tales of the *Arabian Night's Entertainments* are supposed to have happened.

Abberville (ab'ėr.vil), **Lord.** The principal character in the sentimental comedy *The Fashionable Lover* (1772), by Richard Cumberland.

Abbeville (ȧb.vēl; Anglicized, ab'ẹ.vil), **Treaty of.** A treaty concluded (1259) between Henry III of England and Louis IX of France, formalizing the

fat, fāte, fär, ȧsk, fāre; net, mē, hėr; pin, pīne; not, nōte, mȯve, nôr; up, lūte, pu̇ll; ᴛʜ, then; ḍ, d or j; ṣ, s or sh; ṭ, t or ch; ẓ, z or zh; o, F. cloche; ü, F. menu; ċh, Sc. loch; ń, F. bonbon.

end of England's claims to Anjou, Poitou, Normandy, Touraine, and Maine, and acceptance of Guienne as a fief of the French throne.

Abbey of the Holy Ghost. An anonymous religious prose work (c1350), telling of the victory of the Holy Ghost in driving evil out of a place of virtue.

Abbey of Thélème (tā.lem'). See **Thélème, Abbey of.**

Abbey Theatre (ab'i). An Irish company of actors and the theater at Dublin which was used by them. The company was founded in 1904 as a development of an earlier group, the Irish Literary Theatre (1899 *et seq.*), on a subsidy from Mrs. A. E. F. Horniman, who also enabled the group at that time to use the Dublin theater building from which the name of the modern company is derived. On Dec. 27, 1904, the theater first opened its doors with performances of *On Baile's Strand* by W. B. Yeats and *Spreading the News* by Lady Gregory. This building, bought by the company in 1910, was destroyed by fire on July 18, 1951. Plans for rebuilding the theater on the old site and two adjoining sites were approved by the Government of the Irish Republic in December, 1954. Prominent among the members of the original group were Lady Gregory, J. M. Synge, and W. B. Yeats (who was director until his death in 1939), all of whom wrote plays first produced by the Abbey Theatre; other playwrights whose works have been brought to the public through the Abbey Theatre include Padraic Colum, Sean O'Casey, Lord Dunsany, James Stephens, and Paul Vincent Carroll. In addition to giving plays at Dublin, the company has on several occasions toured the U.S. and other countries.

Abbo of Fleury (ab'ō; flė.rē'). [Also: **Abbon of Fleury** (à.bôṅ').] b. near Orléans, France, c945; d. at La Réole, France, Nov. 13, 1004. A French theologian. His *Lives* of the saints and of the Popes were used as sources by Ælfric.

Abbot (ab'ọt), **George.** b. at Guildford, Surrey, England, Oct. 29, 1562; d. at Croydon, Surrey, Aug. 4, 1633. An English prelate, archbishop of Canterbury (1611–33), and one of the translators of the New Testament in the Authorized (or King James) Version of the Bible; brother of Robert Abbot. A militant Protestant, he was influential in state affairs during the reign of James I, but was largely deprived of his power under Charles I.

Abbot, George. [Called **"the Puritan."**] b. at Easington, Yorkshire, England, 1603; d. 1649. An English scholar, lay writer on religious subjects, and member of the Long Parliament. Author of the *Whole Book of Job Paraphrased* (1640), which had a simplicity of style in striking contrast to that of other commentators then living, of *Vindiciae Sabbathi* (1641), which was influential in the Sabbatarian controversy, and others.

Abbot, Robert. b. at Guildford, Surrey, England, c1560; d. March 2, 1617. An English prelate, bishop of Salisbury (1615–17); brother of George Abbot (1562–1633), archbishop of Canterbury. A vigorous opponent of Roman Catholicism and supporter of Calvinism as against Arminianism in the Anglican Church, he was in great favor with James I for such works as the *Mirror of Popish*

Subtleties (1594), *Antichristi Demonstratio* (1603), *Defence of the Reformed Catholike of Mr. William Perkins* (1606–09), and others.

Abbot, The. A historical novel by Sir Walter Scott, published in 1820. It is a sequel to *The Monastery*, and was avowedly intended by Scott to redeem the careless work and supernatural absurdities which had marred that novel. The historical background is the imprisonment of Mary, Queen of Scots, in Lochleven Castle, her escape, her defeat at the battle of Langside, and her flight into England. The fictional framework is provided by the impetuous Roland Graeme (a foundling educated by Lady Avenel, later revealed as heir of the house of Avenel) and his love for Catherine Seyton, one of the Queen's ladies-in-waiting. In aiding the Queen's escape from Lochleven, Graeme is given the part which belonged historically to William Douglas. The study of the Queen is considered one of Scott's most brilliant pieces of historical portraiture. The Abbot is Father Ambrose, of the monastery of Kennaquhair (for his descriptions of which Scott drew upon his knowledge of the famous Melrose Abbey on the Tweed) and brother of the knight of Avenel.

Abbot of Misrule. [Also: **Lord of Misrule, King of Misrule,** and (in Scotland) **Abbot of Unreason.**] The personage who took the principal part in the Christmas revels of the populace before the Reformation. In Sir Walter Scott's *The Abbot*, Adam Woodcock, the English falconer at Avenel Castle, plays this part at one point in the story.

Abbotsford (ab'ọts.fọrd). The residence (1812 *et seq.*) of Sir Walter Scott, on the Tweed ab. 3 mi. from Melrose, Scotland. A 100-acre farm nicknamed Clarty ("Muddy") Hole when he bought it in 1811, it was enlarged and renamed by Scott, who built on it in 1817 a mansion in baronial style.

Abbotsford Club. A club founded in 1834 by W. B. D. D. Turnbull which published (1835–64) historical books connected with the works of Sir Walter Scott, and was named for his home.

Abbott (ab'ọt), **Claude Colleer.** b. 1889—. An English scholar and poet. He has been a professor (1932 *et seq.*) at Durham University and editor (1939 *et seq.*) of the Durham University *Journal*. His discovery (1930–31, although formal announcement was not made until 1936) in Scotland of some 1,600 previously unknown letters and other papers written by, or to, Samuel Johnson, James Boswell, and other figures of note in 18th-century English letters, has been of great value to specialists in the field of literary history. Author of *Poems* (1921), *Early Medieval French Lyrics* (1932), and *The Sand Castle and other Poems* (1946).

Abbott, Edwin Abbott. b. at London, 1838; d. 1926. An English clergyman, educator, and Shakespeare scholar, notable as headmaster (1865–89) of the City of London School. Author of *A Shakespearian Grammar* (1870), *Bacon and Essex* (1877), *Francis Bacon* (1885), *The Kernel and the Husk* (1887), *The Anglican Career of Newman* (1892), and works of New Testament criticism (1900–17).

A.B.C., An. A minor poem by Chaucer, designed as a prayer to the Virgin Mary, and possibly the earliest of his surviving works. Voicing conven-

---

fat, fāte, fär, ȧsk, fāre; net, mē, hėr; pin, pīne; not, nōte, möve, nôr; up, lūte, pull; ᴛʜ, then;

tional sentiments, it contains 23 stanzas (there are none beginning with J, U, or W) beginning in each case with a different letter of the alphabet. It is a loose translation from a French original by Guillaume de Deguilleville, a Cistercian monk who died c1360.

Abdaldar (abd.al'där). One of the three great magicians who are Thalaba's opponents (Lobaba and Mohareb are the other two) in *Thalaba the Destroyer*, by Robert Southey.

Abdalla (ab.dal'ạ). In Dryden's tragedy *Don Sebastian*, the Mufti.

Abdalla (äb.däl'ạ), **Baba.** See **Baba Abdalla.**

Abdelazar (äb.del.ä'zạr). A tragedy derived by Aphra Behn from the play *Lust's Dominion*, first acted in 1676, and published the next year. It is notable for inclusion of the song *Love in fantastic triumph sat.*

Abdemon (ab'dẹ.mọn). A Tyrian who is said to have answered all Solomon's riddles and in turn proposed insoluble ones.

Abdera (ab.dir'ạ). In ancient geography, a maritime city in Thrace, on Cape Balastra, opposite the island of Thasos in NE Greece. It was thought in ancient times that the air of the region caused people to become dull, and from this came a folk belief among the ancient Greeks that all Abderites were stupid. This conviction (which may be compared to the English traditions and stories about the people of the village of Gotham, near Nottingham) persisted despite the fact that a number of famous men, including Protagoras and Democritus, were either born at or residents of Abdera.

Abdias (ab.dī'ạs). See **Obadiah.**

Abdiel (ab'di.el). A seraph in Milton's *Paradise Lost* (v. 896), the only seraph who remained loyal when Satan stirred up the angels to revolt. He is mentioned also by the Jewish cabalists.

Abdulla (ab.dul'ạ). In Conrad's novels *Outcast of the Islands* and *Almayer's Folly*, a Malay trader who competes with the trader Almayer.

Abdullah (ab.dul'ạ), **Achmed.** b. (probably) at Yalta, in the Crimea, May 12, 1881; d. at New York, May 12, 1945. A novelist and short-story writer. Educated at Eton, Oxford, the University of Paris, and elsewhere, he served with the British army in the Near East, India, China, and France before becoming a writer. He produced a vast amount of superficial but quick-moving and colorful fiction, and also contributed works to the stage and, during his later years, to the films.

à Becket (ạ bek'ẹt), **Thomas.** See **Thomas à Becket.**

à Beckett (ạ bek'ẹt), **Arthur William.** b. 1844; d. 1909. A British playwright, journalist, and lawyer; son of Gilbert Abbott à Beckett. Author of *The À Becketts of Punch* (1903).

à Beckett, Gilbert Abbott. b. at London, Jan. 9, 1811; d. at Boulogne, France, Aug. 30, 1856. A British lawyer, journalist, playwright, and humorist. He was educated at Westminster School, founded the journal *Figaro in London*, and wrote for *Punch* and the London *Times*. Many of his stories are about a young lawyer, *Mr. Briefless*, his most successful character. He is the author of *Comic History of England* (1848), *Comic History of*

Rome (1852), and *The Comic Blackstone* (1844–64), esteemed by collectors for their color plates by George Cruikshank.

à Beckett, Gilbert Arthur. b. 1837; d. 1891. A British playwright and journalist, a member (1879 *et seq.*) of the staff of *Punch*; son of Gilbert Abbott à Beckett. In addition to his contributions to *Punch*, he wrote works for the stage, most notably *The Happy Land* (1873), in collaboration with W. S. Gilbert.

Abednego (ạ.bed'nẹ.gō). In the Old Testament, one of the three Hebrews (Shadrach and Meshach were the others) cast by Nebuchadnezzar into the fiery furnace. By intervention of an angel, all three were miraculously delivered unharmed from the flames.

Abeilard (ab'ẹ.lärd), **Peter.** See **Abelard, Peter.**

Abel (ā'bel). In the Old Testament, the second son of Adam, slain by his brother Cain. Gen. iv. 1–8.

Abel, Mr. The narrator and chief male character of *Green Mansions*, by William Henry Hudson.

Abelard (ab'ẹ.lärd), **Peter.** [French, **Pierre Abélard** (ä.bā.lär); Latinized, **Petrus Abelardus;** older spellings, **Abaelard, Abailard, Abeilard.**] b. of a noble family at Pallet (Palais) near Nantes, France, 1079; d. at the abbey of St. Marcel near Châlons-sur-Saône, April 21, 1142. A French logician, philosopher, theologian, and teacher. At the age of twenty-two he opened a school of his own at Melun. Finally, he reached Paris where he finished his work in logic and taught there with considerable success. Employed by Fulbert, a canon of Paris, to supervise the education of his niece Héloïse, Abelard fell in love with his pupil and seduced her. Her uncle eventually learned of the affair and forced Abelard to marry her. Abelard tried to keep the marriage secret and persuaded Héloïse to hide herself in a convent. Fearing that Abelard planned to repudiate Héloïse, Fulbert hired some ruffians who broke into Abelard's house at night and castrated him. Abelard then took refuge in monastic life at St. Denis. Cited (1121) before the Synod of Soissons on a charge of disseminating Sabellianism (explanation of the doctrine of the Trinity on philosophical principles) and compelled to burn his *Introductio ad Theologiam*, he retired to Nogent-sur-Seine, where he was sought out by devoted students who built for him the Oratory of the Paraclete. Abbot of St. Gildas, Brittany, from 1125 to c1134, he was accused (1140) of heresy at the Council of Sens by Bernard of Clairvaux (who believed that faith must be mystical and intuitive rather than rationalistic) and was condemned by the Council in 1141, and, finally, in Rome by the Pope in 1142. Abelard was buried at the Paraclete and in 1164 Héloïse was buried there also at the side of her lover. They are now supposed to be buried in the Père Lachaise, Paris, where their tomb is shown to visitors. Abelard's connection with English literature is sentimental rather than theological. The love letters attributed to him and Héloïse have had more readers than his treatises; among the works directly inspired by them are Alexander Pope's poetic epistle *Eloisa to Abelard* (1717) and George Moore's novel *Héloïse and Abelard* (1921).

Abel Drugger (ā'bel drug'ėr). See **Drugger, Abel.**

Abell (ā'bẹl), **Thomas.** [Also, **Abel.**] Executed at Smithfield, London, July 30, 1540. A Roman Catholic clergyman, a rector at Bradwell, Essex, and chaplain to Catherine of Aragon, wife of Henry VIII. He actively supported the queen in her endeavor to prevent the divorce sought by Henry, and was thereupon condemned and executed on a charge of concealing the alleged treason of Elizabeth Barton, called the "Nun of Kent." Author of *Invicta veritas* (c1532).

Abel Magwitch (ā'bẹl mag'wich). See **Magwitch, Abel.**

Abencerrages (ạ.ben'sẹ.räj.iz). A Moorish family in Granada, famous in Spanish romance. The tale of the struggle of the Abencerrages with the family of the Zegris is used as the basis of the plot in Dryden's play *The Conquest of Granada* (1670).

Aber (ab'ẻr). An element in many place names of ancient British origin, signifying "a confluence of waters," either of two rivers or of a river with the sea, as in Aberdeen, Aberdour, Abergavenny, Aberystwyth, and others.

Abercrombie (ab'ẻr.krom.bi, -krum.bi), **Lascelles.** b. at Ashton-on-Mersey, Cheshire, England, Jan. 9, 1881; d. at London, Oct. 27, 1938. An English poet, critic, playwright, and professor. He taught English literature at the universities of Leeds (1922–29) and London (1929–35). Abercrombie did not attempt to sever himself completely from the Victorian tradition; there are, in fact, many signs of Browning's influence on him. He made frequent use of the dialogue form in his verse, which included *Interludes and Poems* (1908), *Emblems of Love* (1912), and *Twelve Idylls* (1928). Of his six plays from *The Adder* (1913) to *Phoenix* (1923), the best-known and the best-liked was *Deborah* (1913). Perhaps *The Sale of Saint Thomas* (published in part in 1911 but not entire till 1930) is the most memorable. His reputation was academic rather than popular, and his hold upon the intellectuals was strengthened by his work in criticism and aesthetics: *An Essay towards a Theory of Art* (1922), *Principles of English Prosody* (1923), *The Idea of Great Poetry* (1925), *Romanticism* (1926), and *Principles of Literary Criticism* (1932).

Aberdeen (ab.ẻr.dēn'), **The University of.** A university at Aberdeen, Scotland, incorporated under this name in 1860 as a union of King's College (founded in 1494) and Marischal College (founded in 1593). Conjointly with the universities of St. Andrews, Edinburgh, and Glasgow, it sent, until after World War II, the "Scottish Universities" members to Parliament.

Aberfoyle (ab.ẻr.foil'). A civil parish in C Scotland, in Perthshire, situated on the river Forth, ab. 8 mi. SW of Callander, ab. 462 mi. N of London by rail. It figures in Scott's novel *Rob Roy.*

Abergavenny (ab″ẻr.gạ.ven'i). A municipal borough and market town in W England, in Monmouthshire, situated at the confluence of the rivers Gavenny and Usk, ab. 20 mi. N of Newport, ab. 153 mi. W of London by rail. It was involved constantly in the border struggles of the Middle Ages and was burned (1404) by Owen Glendower. It has the ruins of a Norman castle, and also an ancient priory church containing the tombs and effigies of the lords of Bergavenny, once owners of the castle.

Abergavenny (ab″ẻr.gen'i), **Lord.** In Shakespeare's *Henry VIII*, a baron who adheres to Buckingham's cause against Wolsey and is sent to the Tower with Buckingham.

Abershaw (ab'ẻr.shô), **Louis Jeremiah** (or **"Jerry"**). b. c1773; d. 1795. An English highwayman. He was for several years able to exact tribute from travelers by coach and horseback on the roads from London to Kingston and Wimbledon, which were then some ten miles SW of the city proper. He was a favorite character of Robert Louis Stevenson, who was planning a book about him at the time of his death.

Abessa (ạ.bes'ạ). In Spenser's *Faerie Queene*, the personification of superstition and ecclesiastical corruption, particularly in abbeys and convents.

Abhorson (ab.hôr'sọn). In Shakespeare's *Measure for Measure*, an executioner who thinks of his job as a "mystery" (i.e., a skilled craft).

Abide with Me. A hymn (1847) by Henry Francis Lyte.

Abigail (ab'i.gāl). In the Old Testament, the wife of Nabal, and after his death, of David. She called herself the handmaid of David. 1 Sam. xxv.

Abigail. A lady's maid in Beaumont and Fletcher's *Scornful Lady,* and in various other plays, presumably after the Abigail of the Bible, who called herself (1 Sam. xxv. 24) the handmaid of David. This Elizabethan usage later caused the name to become a literary synonym for lady's maid.

Abigail. In Christopher Marlowe's play *The Jew of Malta,* the daughter of Barabas. The dialogue between father and daughter is in some ways very close to that between Shylock and Jessica in Shakespeare's *Merchant of Venice.*

Abigor (ab'i.gôr). In medieval demonology, a demon of high degree, grand duke in the infernal regions.

Abingdon (ab'ing.dọn), **4th Earl of.** Title of **Bertie, Willoughby.**

Abingdon Law. An act of summary justice, whereby the accused is "hanged first and tried later." It derives from the ruthless action of Major General Sir Richard Browne, one of Cromwell's generals, who invoked the "Abingdon Law" in order to stamp out all opposition to the Puritan cause in the area of Oxford, England, in 1644. Abingdon is a small town near Oxford where most of the hangings took place. It is comparable to "lynch law" in the United States, and to "Jeddart justice" in the Border country between England and Scotland.

Abington (ab'ing.tọn), **Frances.** [Maiden name, **Barton.**] b. at London, 1737; d. there, March 4, 1815. An English actress. From flower girl and street singer, she rose to a position of eminence on the stage. She first appeared as Miranda in Susannah Centlivre's *The Busybody* (1755) at the Haymarket Theatre, then went to the Drury Lane to join Mrs. Clive and Mrs. Pritchard. After marrying a Mr. Abingdon, she spent five years in Dublin, returning then to London and resuming her career at the Drury Lane. She was Garrick's leading lady at the Drury Lane for 18 years. She played Betty Modish in Cibber's *The Careless Husband,* Miss

Prue in Congreve's *Love for Love* and was the first to play Lady Teazle in Sheridan's *The School for Scandal*. In 1782 she went to Covent Garden, from which she retired in 1790.

Aboan (ạ.bō′ạn). A slave in the play *Oroonoko*, adapted by Thomas Southerne from the novel by Aphra Behn. Though of secondary importance in the play, the part was for many years esteemed by critics.

Abora (ạb′ọ.rạ). A mountain mentioned in Coleridge's *Kubla Khan*. By some scholars it is identified with the Abyssinian Mount Amara mentioned by Milton in *Paradise Lost*.

Ab′-o′-th′-Yate (ab″ọ.тнẹ.yāt′). Pseudonym of **Brierley, Benjamin.**

Abou ben Adhem (ä′bö ben ä′dem). A short poem (1834) by Leigh Hunt in which Abou ben Adhem discovers, from an angel who appears to him, that his name is not listed in the golden book of those who love the Lord. He thereupon prays that he may at least be listed as one who loves his fellow men, and discovers on the following night that he is therefore entered as the first of those who love the Lord.

Abou Hassan (ä′bö has′ạn). [Also, **Abu-Hassan.**] In the story "The Sleeper Awakened" in *The Arabian Nights' Entertainments*, a citizen of Baghdad who, while entertaining the disguised caliph, expresses a wish to "be caliph for one day." The wish is granted by having Abou Hassan conveyed while in a drunken slumber to the palace of Harun al-Rashid, where the attendants act as though he were the caliph, to the great amusement of the real caliph, who in the end makes him his companion and favorite. Shakespeare has adopted this idea, from an older play, in the deception practiced on Christopher Sly, the tinker, in the induction to *The Taming of the Shrew*.

Aboukir (ä.bö.kēr′), **Bay of.** See **Abukir, Bay of.**

Abou-Klea (ä′bö.klä′ạ). See **Abu Klea.**

Abra (ab′rạ). A favorite concubine of Solomon, notable in Matthew Prior's *Solomon on the Vanity of the World* for her docility:

"Abra was ready ere I called her name;
And, though I called another, Abra came."

abracadabra (ab″rạ.kạ.dab′rạ). A cabalistic word used in incantations, occurring first in a poem (*Praecepta de Medicina*) by Q. Serenus Sammonicus, in the second century. When written in a manner similar to that shown in the accompanying

```
A B R A C A D A B R A
  A B R A C A D A B R
    A B R A C A D A B
      A B R A C A D A
        A B R A C A D
          A B R A C A
            A B R A C
              A B R A
                A B R
                  A B
                    A
```

diagram, so as to be read in different directions, and worn as an amulet, it was supposed to cure certain ailments.

Abraham (ā′brạ.ham). [Also, **Abram.**] The first of the patriarchs, father of Isaac, and founder of the Hebrew people. Through his son Ishmael, he is the traditional ancestor of the Arabs. The question of the date of his life is a difficult one, but the 14th chapter of Genesis contains enough specific references to identifiable contemporary historical figures to suggest a tentative dating between 1550 and 1450 B.C. Abraham is equally revered by Jews, Christians, and Mohammedans. We are told that he was buried in the cave of Machpelah (the double cave) at Hebron, now said to be enclosed by the Great Mosque (Haram) of that place. Gen. xi–xxv.

Abraham, Plains of. An elevated plain SW of the city of Quebec, above the St. Lawrence River, on which was fought (Sept. 13, 1759) the deciding battle of the French and Indian War in its last phase. The British were led by General James Wolfe and the French by the Marquis de Montcalm; both commanders were killed in the battle. The British victory in this battle was one of the chief factors in determining that the further development of North America would rest primarily with the English rather than the French. A portion of the area is now preserved by the Canadian government as a national park.

Abraham Adams (ad′ạmz). See **Adams, Parson.**

Abraham Lincoln (ling′kọn). A historical play (1918) in six episodes by John Drinkwater. It was first produced at the Birmingham Repertory Theatre and was staged at London in 1919. Its theme of the great leader slain at the moment of victory had topical importance for those who saw a possible parallel between the problems of the Reconstruction period in the U.S. and the problem then faced by the Allies of what to do with Germany and Austria.

Abraham-man (ā′brạ.hạm.man″). [Also, **Abraman.**] A name originally applied to a mendicant lunatic from London's Bethlehem (Bedlam) Hospital, notably one from the ward named after the patriarch Abraham. On certain days of the year, patients from this ward were permitted to beg on the London streets, wearing a distinctive badge and becoming known in time as "Abraham-men." Their success as beggars led others to wear the badge, and to feign lunacy, until the term came to mean any imposter who sought alms under pretense of madness. The once common term "to sham Abraham," in the sense of pretending sickness, derives from this usage.

Abraham's Oak. An ancient tree which stood on the plain of Mamre, near Hebron, Syria, and was believed to be that under which Abraham pitched his tent.

Abrahen (ab′rạ.hen). The second son of the caliph in George Chapman's tragedy *Revenge for Honor*.

Abram (ā′brạm). In Shakespeare's *Romeo and Juliet*, a servant of Montague.

Abram. See also **Abraham.**

Absalom (ab′sạ.lọm). In the Old Testament, the third son of David, king of Israel. He slew his brother Amnon for the rape of his sister Tamar, and thereupon fled the wrath of David. He subsequently returned and was accepted by his father,

---

ḍ, d or j; ṣ, s or sh; ṭ, t or ch; ẓ, z or zh; *o*, F. cloche; ü, F. menu; ċh, Sc. loch; ṅ, F. bonbon.

but later rebelled (with David's counselor Ahithophel) against him, and was defeated and slain in the forest of Ephraim. 2 Sam. xiii–xix.

Absalom. An undutiful son, intended to represent the Duke of Monmouth, in John Dryden's satirical *Absalom and Achitophel.*

Absalom and Achitophel (ạ.kit′ọ.fel). A political satire in heroic couplets by John Dryden, published in 1681. After the excitement of the Popish Plot (1678) there had been repeated attempts to force a bill through Parliament excluding Catholics (and thus the legitimate heir, the duke of York) from the throne of England. The villain in these attempts was the Whig leader, the earl of Shaftesbury, who in the summer of 1681 was under arrest charged with high treason. At the suggestion of the King, *Absalom and Achitophel* was written and its publication timed to fall just a week before Shaftesbury's fruitless arraignment. The poem makes use of biblical story to suggest how Achitophel (Shaftesbury) is tempting to rebellion Absalom (the duke of Monmouth, illegitimate son of Charles II and the Whig candidate to succeed his father). Since Monmouth had not yet rebelled, the poem lacks action, but not tenseness. It consists largely of satirical portraits and of eloquent argumentative speeches in Dryden's epical style. A second part, chiefly written by Nahum Tate, but revised by Dryden and containing 200 lines written by him, was published in 1682 against the lesser figures in the conspiracy. The name "Achitophel" was taken from the Vulgate Bible, and corresponds to the "Ahithophel" of the King James version. The poem, which still ranks as one of the leading political satires in English verse, had an immediate success, and was to a large extent responsible for the quick waning of the Shaftesbury cabal.

Absentee, The. A short novel by Maria Edgeworth, included in the second series (1812) of her *Tales of Fashionable Life.* Generally regarded as the author's masterpiece, it deals with London society, the Irish gentry, and the evils of absentee landlordism.

Absent-Minded Beggar, The. A poem (1899) written by Rudyard Kipling for the benefit of the families of reservists called into service in the Boer War (1899–1902). It was set to music by Sir Arthur Sullivan.

Absolon (ab′sọ.lọn). In Chaucer's *Miller's Tale,* an amorous parish clerk who comes to grief in his wooing of the carpenter's wife.

Absolute (ab′sọ.löt), **Captain Jack.** In Richard Brinsley Sheridan's comedy *The Rivals,* the son of Sir Anthony Absolute. He is a spirited soldier and persistent lover who appears as the impecunious Ensign Beverley (and is thus his own rival) to win the affections of the romantic Lydia Languish. She, in turn, scorns a match with one so suitable as the son of Sir Anthony Absolute, but falls in love with him, unknowingly, as Ensign Beverley, and is thereby persuaded to accept him when his real identity becomes known.

Absolute, Sir Anthony. In Richard Brinsley Sheridan's comedy *The Rivals,* an obstinate, passionate, self-willed, but generous old man.

Absolute Unlawfulness of the Stage-Entertainment. A tract (1726) by William Law, attacking the drama. It was answered by John Dennis in *The Stage Defended* (1726).

Absyrtus (ab.sèr′tus). In Greek legend, the brother of Medea, who cut him into pieces and cast the fragments into the sea to delay her father's pursuit as she fled with Jason.

Abt Vogler (fō′glèr). A poem by Robert Browning, published (1864) in *Dramatis Personae.* The work is written in the form of a dramatic monologue from the mouth of a certain "Abbé (or Abt) Vogler," in real life Georg Joseph Vogler (1749–1814), court chaplain at Mannheim, Germany, notable for devising various improvements in the organ. In the poem, Vogler at first expresses his sorrow that the beautiful musical structure which he has just extemporized on the organ should disappear with the sound that brought it into being, but is then heartened to recall that nothing beautiful or true can ever really be lost: God hears or knows it, and it thus acquires an existence transcending human understanding.

Abu-Hassan (ä′bö.has′ạn). See **Abou Hassan.**

Abukir (ä.bö.kèr′), **Bay of.** [Also, **Bay of Aboukir.**] A bay N of Egypt, between Abukir and the Rosetta mouth of the Nile, the scene of the Battle of the Nile (Aug. 1–2, 1798), in which an English fleet under Nelson defeated the French fleet under Brueys, who lost 13 out of 17 vessels and some 9,000 men.

Abu Klea (ä′bö klā′ạ). [Also, **Abou-Klea.**] Wells in the Nubian desert in the bend of the Nile on the route between Korti and Shendi, where, on Jan. 17, 1885, the Mahdists attacked the British, and were repulsed with severe losses on both sides.

Abul-Hassan Ali ebn Bekar (ä′böl.has′ạn ä′lē eb′n be′kär). In *The Arabian Nights' Entertainments,* the lover of the caliph's favorite.

Abus (ā′bus). Latin name of the **Humber.**

Abuses Stript and Whipt. A long moralistic poem (1613) by George Wither, divided into two books, critical of the weaknesses of man, especially as exemplified by the practices of the court and the nobility. The popularity of the work was great (it went through four editions in the year of publication), but its publication resulted in Wither's imprisonment in Marshalsea prison.

Abydos (ạ.bī′dọs). In ancient geography, a town in Mysia, Asia Minor, on the Hellespont, noted in the legend of Hero and Leander, in Byron's *Bride of Abydos,* and as the location of the famous bridge of boats by which the Persians, under Xerxes, crossed from Asia into Europe in their assault on Greece.

Abydos, The Bride of. See **Bride of Abydos, The.**

Abyla (ab′i.lạ). In ancient geography, a promontory in Africa, the modern Jebel Musa, opposite the ancient Calpe (the modern Gibraltar). The two together constitute the famous "Pillars of Hercules" of the ancient geographers.

Academus (ak.ạ.dē′mus). In Greek mythology, the hero responsible for revealing to Castor and Pollux the place in Athens where Theseus had hidden their sister Helen, thus enabling them to rescue her.

academy (ạ.kad'ẹ.mi). An association of adepts for the promotion of literature, science, or art, established sometimes by government, and sometimes by the voluntary union of private individuals. The members (academicians), who are usually divided into ordinary, honorary, and corresponding members, either select their own departments or follow those prescribed by the constitution of the society, and at regular meetings communicate the results of their labors in papers, of which the more important are afterward printed. Among the most noted institutions of this name are the five academies composing the National Institute of France (the French Academy, the Academy of Inscriptions and Belles-Lettres, the Academy of the Fine Arts, the Academy of Moral and Political Sciences, and the Academy of Sciences), the Royal Academy of Arts in London, The Royal Spanish Academy, The British Academy, and the Accademia della Crusca. The chief object of the French Academy, as also of the celebrated Italian Academy della Crusca and of the Spanish Academy, is to regulate and purify the vernacular tongue.

Academy. [Also: **Academe** (ak'ạ.dēm); Greek, **Akademeia, Akademia.**] A public pleasure-ground on the Cephissus, about one mile NW of ancient Athens, on land said to have belonged, in the time of the Trojan war, to the hero Academus. It was surrounded with a wall by Hipparchus and further adorned by Cimon, the son of Miltiades, who bequeathed it to the citizens of Athens. It was the resort of Plato, who taught in its groves for nearly 50 years.

Academy. A term applied to the Platonic school of philosophy down to the time of Cicero; so called from the pleasure-ground of the same name. It is commonly divided into the Old, the Middle, and the New Academy. The chief representatives of the first were, in addition to Plato himself, Speusippus, Xenocrates of Chalcedon, Polemo, Crates, and Crantor. The Middle Academy was founded by Arcesilaus ab. 244 B.C., and the New Academy by Carneades ab. 160 B.C. Sometimes the academies of Philo and Antiochus are spoken of as the Fourth Academy and the Fifth Academy, respectively.

Academy, British. See **British Academy.**

Academy, French. See **French Academy.**

Academy, Italian. See **Accademia della Crusca.**

Academy, Royal. See **Royal Academy.**

Academy, The. A periodical established (1869) at London by Charles Edward Cutts Birch Appleton, and through most of its history a weekly review of life and letters. Early contributors included Matthew Arnold and T. H. Huxley; at the close of the century, under the editorship of Lewis Hind, its most famous reviewer was Francis Thompson. It ceased publication in 1909.

Academy, The Della Crusca. See **Accademia della Crusca.**

Academy Notes. Criticisms of the exhibitions of the Royal Academy of Art, published annually (1855–59) by John Ruskin.

Acasto (ạ.kas'tō). In Thomas Otway's play *The Orphan*, a nobleman, the father of Polydore and Castalio, retired from the court and living on his estates.

Acastus (ạ.kas'tus). In Greek legend, one of the Argonauts, the father of Laodamia.

acatalectic verse (a.kat.ạ.lek'tik, ā-). In prosody, a verse which has the complete number of syllables in the last foot.

Accademia della Crusca (äk.kä.dā'myä del'lä krös'kä). An academy founded at Florence in 1582 by the poet Grazzini, with the object of purifying the Italian language and literature. It published in 1612 the first edition of the *Vocabolario degli Accademici della Crusca*, long the standard dictionary of the Italian language. It was the first dictionary to contain quotations from standard authors to illustrate the various senses of a word and it greatly influenced the plan of succeeding national dictionaries, including the French dictionary and Johnson's dictionary. Accademia della Crusca means "academy of the bran" and is a fanciful name alluding to the Academy's professed object of sifting or purifying the Italian language.

Acca Larentia (ak'a lạ.ren'shi.ạ). In Roman legend, a shepherd's wife, nurse of Romulus and Remus; according to some, an earth goddess, mother of the Lares.

accentual feet, meters, etc. Those in which the rhythmical beat or ictus coincides with the syllabic accent or stress, as in modern poetry: opposed to quantitative feet, meters, etc., in which the ictus falls upon syllables literally long or prolonged in time, as in ancient Greek and Latin poetry.

Accolon (ak'ọ.lon). In Malory's *Morte d'Arthur*, a knight of Gaul, celebrated for his combat with King Arthur. In this combat the latter sought to regain his enchanted sword and scabbard, of which Accolon had gained possession through the aid of Morgan le Fay.

Accoramboni (äk''kō.räm.bô'nē), **Vittoria.** [Title, Duchess of **Bracciano.**] b. at Rome, c1557; d. at Padua, Dec. 22, 1585. An Italian beauty, whose tragic story has been used by numerous writers in the centuries since her death. Her first husband, Francesco Peretti, was murdered (1581) at the instigation of Paolo Giordano Orsini, Duke of Bracciano, whom she subsequently married. On his death (1585) she became involved in litigation with Lodovic Orsini concerning the inheritance, and was murdered by him. These events were adapted in Webster's tragedy *The White Devil, or Vittoria Corombona* (1612).

Account of Corsica (kôr'si.kạ), **An.** A narrative (1768) by James Boswell, written as a result of a visit to Corsica in 1765. In it Boswell clearly reveals his sympathy for the Corsicans in their lengthy period of rebellion (1729–68) against control by Genoa. The book was published in the year that Corsica was sold by Genoa to France.

Account of the English Dramatick Poets, An. A collection of brief biographies (1691) by Gerard Langbaine, revised in 1698 by Charles Gildon as *Lives and Characters of the English Drama*. Langbaine's contempt for the practice of borrowing material from older playwrights is evident throughout the original version, in which he repeatedly censures his contemporaries for plagiarism (although it was a generally accepted custom during the Restoration to use 17th-century French and

ḍ, d or j; ṣ, s or sh; ṭ, t or ch; ẓ, z or zh; o, F. cloche; ü, F. menu; ċh, Sc. loch; ṅ, F. bonbon.

earlier Jacobean and Elizabethan plays as source material with varying degrees of imitation).

Account of the European Settlements in America, An. A historical essay, published in two volumes (1757), written by Edmund Burke in collaboration with his kinsman, William Burke.

Aceldama (a.sel′da̱.ma̱). A field said to have been situated south of Jerusalem, the Potter's Field, purchased with the bribe which Judas took for betraying Jesus (whence the name, meaning "field of blood" in Aramaic). It was later appropriated to the burial of strangers, and it was from this use that the term "potter's field" came to mean a burying ground for paupers. Mat. xxvii. 8; Acts, i. 19.

Acestes (a̱.ses′tēz). In Greek legend, a son of the Sicilian river-god Crimisus and Egesta (Segesta), a Trojan woman. He figured in the Trojan War, and was introduced by Vergil in the *Aeneid*.

Achates (a̱.kā′tēz). The faithful companion (whence *fidus Achates*) of Aeneas, and thus in literary usage often used to mean any follower, adherent, or companion of great loyalty.

Achelous (ak.e.lō′us). In Greek mythology, a river god, defeated by Hercules in a struggle over Deianira.

Acheron (ak′e̱.ron). In Greek mythology, one of the five rivers surrounding Hades, the river of woe. The souls of the dead had to bathe in it or cross it. Later it became synonymous with the lower world in general.

Acherusia Palus (ak.e̱.rö′s̲i.a̱ pā′lus). In ancient geography, the name of several small lakes supposed to be connected with the lower world; notably, the modern Lago del Fusaro, west of Naples.

Achilles (a̱.kil′ēz). In Greek legend, a great warrior, one of the chief heroes of the Trojan War. He is said to have been the son of Peleus and Thetis, the grandson of Aeacus, and chief of the Myrmidons, a Thessalian tribe. According to the legend of his life, he was educated by the centaur Chiron. He is the central hero of Homer's *Iliad*, which is largely occupied with his quarrel with Agamemnon, leader of the Greek host, and with his martial exploits. He was the slayer of Hector, and was himself slain by Paris, who pierced his heel, Achilles' only vulnerable spot (all other portions of his body had been rendered invulnerable when his mother, holding him by the heel, had immersed him as a child in the river Styx). Symonds in *Studies of the Greek Poets* says:

"In Achilles, Homer summed up and fixed forever the ideal of the Greek character. He presented an imperishable picture of their national youthfulness, and of their ardent genius, to the Greeks. The "beautiful human heroism" of Achilles, his strong personality, his fierce passions controlled and tempered by divine wisdom, his intense friendship and love that passed the love of women, above all, the splendor of his youthful life in death made perfect, hovered like a dream above the imagination of the Greeks, and insensibly determined their subsequent development. At a later age, this ideal was destined to be realized in Alexander."

Achilles. In Shakespeare's *Troilus and Cressida*, a Greek commander who is aroused from his moody inactivity in the war by the death in battle of his friend, Patroclus. To avenge his friend, he attacks Hector (who is resting unarmed) and orders his Myrmidons to murder him.

Achilles. A comic drama (1733) by John Gay. It is a burlesque of the classical story, and also a satire on contemporary English politics.

Achitophel (a̱.kit′ō̱.fel). A character in Dryden's poem *Absalom and Achitophel*, intended to represent the Earl of Shaftesbury, who was called by this name by his contemporaries, implying a treacherous friend and adviser. The name is intended, of course, to suggest the counselor of David, in the Old Testament, who joined Absalom in his revolt against his father. Dryden took his spelling from the Vulgate Bible; the King James Bible shows "Ahithophel," which is now the spelling most commonly used for the Old Testament character, but Dryden's character retains the Vulgate spelling.

Acis (ā′sis). In classical mythology, a beautiful Sicilian shepherd, beloved by Galatea and slain by his rival Polyphemus.

Acis and Galatea (ā′sis; gal.a̱.tē′a̱). A pastoral opera by John Gay, with music by Handel, first performed in 1721. Gay included verses by Dryden and Pope, and spiritedly burlesqued one of Ovid's *Metamorphoses*.

Ackermann (ak′ėr.man), **Rudolph.** b. at Schneeberg, Saxony, April 20, 1764; d. at Finchley, Middlesex, England, March 30, 1834. A German art publisher and bookseller at London (1795 *et seq.*). A one-time coach-builder and harness-maker, he patented (1801) a method of making cloth and paper waterproof, which had considerable value to publishers of books. He himself published (1817–28) the monthly *Repository of Arts, Literature, Fashions, etc.* and travel books, illustrated with lithographs by Rowlandson and others. The establishment of lithography as a fine art in England is often credited to him.

Ackland (ak′land), **Rodney.** b. 1908—. An English playwright. His *Strange Orchestra* (1932) was much admired at London, but failed after a single performance at New York. Other plays include *The Old Ladies* (1935), an adaptation of Sir Hugh Walpole's novel about three aged gentlefolk, and the Chekhovian *After October* (1936) and *Remembrance of Things Past* (1938). He also adapted (1949) *Crime and Punishment* for the stage.

Acontius (a̱.kon′shi.us, -shus). Principal character in the tale of Acontius and Cydippe, told by Aristaenetus and by Ovid. "Acontius gathered an orange in the garden of Venus, and having written on the rind the words, 'By Artemis, I will marry Acontius,' threw it in Cydippe's way. She took it in her hand, read out the inscription, and threw it from her. But Artemis heard the vow, and brought about the marriage." William Morris took the legend for the subject of one of his poems in *The Earthly Paradise*.

Acrasia (a̱.krā′zi.a̱). In Spenser's *Faerie Queene* (Book II), a beautiful woman, the personification of intemperance in all things, living in the "Bower of Bliss," which contains everything to delight the senses. She was suggested originally by Circe and, more directly, by the Alcina of Ariosto. Milton alludes to her and her bower in his *Areopagitica*.

---

fat, fāte, fär, a̱sk, fãre; net, mē, hėr; pin, pīne; not, nōte, mȯve, nôr; up, lūte, pu̇ll; ᴛʜ, then;

Acrates (a̱.krā′tēz). In Spenser's *Faerie Queene* (Book II), a male character personifying the intemperate love of pleasure.

Acre (ā′kẻr, ä′kẻr). [French, **St.-Jean-d'Acre** (so named by the Knights of St. John).] A city and seaport in Palestine, in NW Israel, ab. 9 mi. NE of Haifa. Once a leading port and trading center of the E Mediterranean, Acre has in modern times lost much of its economic importance through the development of feeder rail-lines to other cities and ports. Although it was in the territory assigned to the tribe of Asher (Judges, i. 31.), Acre was never conquered in Biblical times by the Israelites. Its kings were reckoned next in importance to those of Tyre and Sidon. It was conquered by the Assyrian king Sennacherib, and again by his grandson, Assurbanipal, who sacked it. Subsequently it was captured by the Arabs (638), by the Crusaders (1104), by Saladin (1187), and again by the Crusaders (1191). It was thereafter held by the Knights of St. John until 1291, being the last Palestinian stronghold to be held by the Christians of western Europe. It was taken by Turkey in 1517, who held it against various attacks (including one by Napoleon in 1799), until it was absorbed (1832) as part of Syria into Egypt, falling again (with British help) to the Turks in 1840. In World War I the British captured it from the Turks in 1918, and administered it thereafter until 1948.

Acres (ā′kẻrz), **Bob.** In Richard Brinsley Sheridan's comedy *The Rivals*, an awkward and simple country gentleman changed into a boasting coward by the sudden excitement of high society at fashionable 18th-century Bath, England. His bragging, his ludicrous vanity, and his assurance are combined with a comic trepidation and an uneasy gaiety.

Acrisius (a̱.kris′i.us). In Greek mythology, a king of Argos, father of Danaë.

Across the Plains. A series of essays and sketches by Robert Louis Stevenson, originally published (1883) in *Longman's Magazine* and expanded into book form in 1892.

acrostic (a̱.kros′tik). **1.** A composition in verse, in which the first, or the first and last, or certain other letters of the lines, taken in order, form a name, title, motto, the order of the alphabet, etc.
2. A Hebrew poem in which the initial letters of the lines or stanzas were made to run over the letters of the alphabet in their order. Twelve of the Psalms are of this character, of which Psalm 119 is the best example.

Actaeon (ak.tē′o̱n). In Greek mythology, a hunter, who, having seen Artemis (Diana) bathing, was changed by her into a stag and (according to the most usual account of his death) torn to pieces by his own dogs.

Acta Sanctorum (sangk.tō′rum). [Eng. trans., "*Acts of the Saints.*"] A title that may be applied to all collections of accounts of saints and martyrs, both of the Roman and Greek churches; specifically, the great Roman Catholic work begun (1643) by the Bollandists, a society of Jesuits. It now consists of more than 60 folio volumes, including an index published in 1875.

Actes and Monuments. See **Book of Martyrs.**

Actions and Reactions. A volume of short stories (1909), by Rudyard Kipling. The most famous story in the collection is "An Habitation Enforced."

Actium (ak′shi.um, -ti.um). In ancient geography, a promontory on the NW coast of Acarnania, in Greece. The ancient *peribolos* or sacred enclosure, rectangular in plan and built in *opus reticulatum*, the seat of the famous Actian games of Augustus, still remains. Modern excavations have laid bare extensive ruins of several successive temples, one of the latest of which is that dedicated by Augustus after the victory of 31 B.C. A famous naval battle was fought (Sept. 2, 31 B.C.) near Actium between Octavius and Mark Antony and Cleopatra. It was decided by the flight of Cleopatra, Mark Antony's land forces thereupon surrendering to Octavius. The victory secured for Octavius supreme rule over the Roman dominion.

Acton (ak′to̱n), Lord. [Full name, **John Emerich Edward Dalberg-Acton**; title, 1st Baron **Acton of Aldenham.**] b. at Naples, Italy, Jan. 10, 1834; d. at Tegernsee, in Bavaria, June 19, 1902. An English historian. He succeeded his father as eighth baronet in 1837, and was successively member of Parliament for Carlow (1859–65) and for Bridgenorth (1865–66). He was a Liberal and a close friend of Gladstone, who obtained his elevation to the peerage in 1869. He was appointed regius professor of modern history at Cambridge University in 1895 and held that post until his death in 1902. His famous historical library of about 60,000 volumes was purchased by Andrew Carnegie, who, after Acton's death, gave it to John Morley, who presented it to the University of Cambridge. He was a leader of liberal British Roman Catholics in opposing the doctrine of papal infallibility, but accepted it when it was promulgated officially. He published *Lecture on the Study of History* (1895), and outlined the plan of the *Cambridge Modern History* (which was completed, however, by others after his death, except for the first volume). His famous *Lectures on the French Revolution*, edited by J. Neville Figgis and Reginald Vere Laurence, were published in 1910.

Acton, Eliza. b. at Battle, England, April 17, 1799; d. at Hampstead, England, Feb. 13, 1859. An English poet and prose writer, now chiefly remembered, however, as the author of *Modern Cookery* (1845).

Acton, Sir Francis. The enemy of Sir Charles Mountford, and would-be seducer of Mountford's sister Susan, in Thomas Heywood's tragedy *A Woman Killed with Kindness.*

Actors' Vindication, The. See under **Apology for Actors, An.**

Acunha (dä.kön′ya̱), **Teresa D'.** The evil maidservant of the Countess of Glenallan, mother of the hero, in Sir Walter Scott's novel *The Antiquary.*

Ada Clare (ā′da̱ klār). See **Clare, Ada.**

Adah (ā′da̱). The wife of Cain, a character in *Cain,* by Byron.

Adair (a̱.dār′), **Robin.** See **Robin Adair.**

Adam (ad′a̱m). The first man; the father of all humanity, according to the account of the creation in Genesis. In its etymology, the word "Adam" derives from a Babylonian term meaning "man" in

d̤, d or j; ş, s or sh; ṯ, t or ch; z̧, z or zh; o, F. cloche; ü, F. menu; c̆h, Sc. loch; ṅ, F. bonbon.

the general sense, and is found used in this sense in both Hebrew and Assyrian. Adam may therefore be taken to refer to both "mankind" and to the specific and particular individual of the male sex from one of whose ribs was derived Eve, and from whom mankind is said to have descended.

Adam. A 12th-century Anglo-Norman drama dealing with the fall and expulsion of Adam and Eve from Paradise and Cain and Abel, to which is appended an incomplete play about the Prophets. It is the earliest mystery play composed in England and was used in the medieval churches to illustrate the sermon on Christ's nativity and is a good example of the religious forerunners of English drama.

Adam. In Shakespeare's *As You Like It*, the old servant who faithfully follows the exiled Orlando, leaving the service of Orlando's elder brother, Oliver. There is a late tradition, based on a statement (1750) of William Oldys, that Shakespeare himself acted this part.

Adam, Jean. b. near Greenock, Scotland, 1710; d. at Glasgow, 1765. A Scottish poetess and schoolmistress, now remembered chiefly as the author of *Poems* (1734), a collection of religious verse. She died in a poorhouse after a life of extreme hardship.

Adam, Robert. b. at Kirkcaldy, Scotland, 1728; d. at London, March 3, 1792. A British architect, furniture designer, and landscape painter. Impressed during travels (c1754) in Italy and Dalmatia by the architecture of the ancient Romans, he patterned much of his work, as architect (1762–68) to King George III, upon it. He was assisted in virtually all his work (perhaps most notably in connection with London's famous Adelphi terrace) by his brother, James (1730–94). Adam's architecture, with its delicate and graceful interior designs, probably influenced him in the selection of the wreaths, paterae, honeysuckle, and fan ornaments which are the characteristic marks of his furniture style.

Adamastor (ad.am.as'tor). A phantom of the Cape of Good Hope in the *Lusiad*, a terrible spirit described by Camões as appearing to Vasco da Gama and prophesying the misfortunes which would befall other expeditions to India.

Adamastor. A volume of poems (1930) by Roy Campbell, South African poet.

Adam Bede (ad'am bēd). A novel (1859) by George Eliot. It was her first full-length work, and in many respects her finest. The story opens in the village of Hayslope in the summer of 1799. Adam Bede and his brother Seth are carpenters. Adam loves pretty, frivolous Hetty Sorrel, but Hetty is seduced by Arthur Donnithorne, son of the local squire. Arthur deserts her; she finds herself pregnant; sets out in agonized and fruitless pursuit of her lover; is convicted of the murder of her child, and sentenced to penal transportation. Adam ultimately marries Dinah Morris, a young Methodist preacher whom Seth has loved in vain. Notable among the minor characters are the rector, Mr. Irwine, Bartle Massey, the schoolmaster, and, above all, Mrs. Poyser, one of finest rustic characters in English fiction. In *Adam Bede* George Eliot produced "the first realistic pastoral novel. She did for the novel what Wordsworth had done for poetry more than fifty years earlier."

Adam Bede. See also **Bede, Adam.**

Adam Bell (bel). See **Bell, Adam.**

Adam Bell, Clym of the Cloughe, and Wyllyam of Cloudeslee (klim; cluf; wil'yam; kloudz'li). An old ballad of outlaw life printed (c1550) by William Copland, and in the collections of both Thomas Percy and Joseph Ritson. The 19th-century American scholar Francis James Child repeated it from Ritson, with some variations from an edition older than Copland's recovered by Payne Collier. The three outlaws are supposed to have lived in the forest of Englewood, near Carlisle. Clym of the Cloughe figures in Ben Jonson's play *The Alchemist*.

Adam Blair (blār). A novel of Scottish life (1822), by John Gibson Lockhart.

Adam Cast Forth. A dramatic poem (1908) in 30,000 lines on the expulsion of Adam and Eve from Eden, by Charles Montagu Doughty.

Adam Craigdallie (krāg.dal'i). See **Craigdallie, Adam.**

Adam Cupid (ad'am kū'pid). In Shakespeare's *Romeo and Juliet*, a nickname of Cupid.

Adam Hartley (härt'li), **Dr.** See **Hartley, Dr. Adam.**

Adam in Moonshine. A satiric novel (1927), by J. B. Priestley.

Adamites (ad'am.īts). A sect which originated in N Africa during the 2nd century A.D. and claimed to have attained the primitive innocence of Adam. They spurned marriage and, in their assemblies or "paradises," made a rite of nudity. The sect reappeared in the 14th and 15th centuries and the 18th and 19th centuries and then vanished as a religious group.

Adamnan (ad'am.nan) or **Adomnan**, Saint. b. in Ulster, Ireland, c625; d. at Iona, Scotland, 704. An Irish ecclesiastic, abbot of Iona (679–704). He is generally considered to be the author of *Vita Columbae*, the life of St. Columba, and of *De Locis Sanctis*, an account of Palestine and other countries.

Adam of Murimuth (mur'i.muth). b. in Oxfordshire, England, c1274; d. 1347. An English chronicler. He was educated at Oxford, where he became a doctor of civil law in 1312 or soon before. From c1312–18 and even later he spent much time at Avignon, representing the archbishop of Canterbury or the king, and defending English ecclesiastical interests before the curia. By 1323, he was canon at Hereford, and he held other ecclesiastical offices at Exeter and London. Having observed that the chronicles of Exeter did not extend beyond 1302 and those of Westminster beyond 1305, he decided to write a "continuatio ex visu et auditu mei temporis." This work, entitled *Continuatio chronicorum*, covers the period from 1303 to 1347. He began to write it c1325 and worked at it until the last year of his life. The information for the years 1303–37 is quite meager; for the last ten years the material is more abundant, although he never wrote in great detail. This part of the chronicle is of particular value for the account of the English campaigns in France and of the negotiations between the two countries. The chronicle is of special interest from the ecclesiastical point of view. There is an anonymous continuation down to 1380.

---

fat, fāte, fär, ȧsk, fāre; net, mē, hėr; pin, pīne; not, nōte, mȯve, nôr; up, lūte, půll; ŦH, then;

Adam Overdoo (ŏ'vẽr.dö). See **Overdoo, Adam.**

Adams (ad'ạmz), **Clement.** b. at Buckington, Warwickshire, England, c1519; d. Jan. 9, 1587. An English writer and teacher, schoolmaster to the royal "henchmen" (pages) at Greenwich. His transcription of Richard Chancellor's narrative of the journey to Moscow (1553) is the first written account of the earliest Anglo-Russian contact. It was published by Richard Hakluyt in his *Collections* (1589).

Adams, Joseph Quincy. b. at Greenville, S. C., March 23, 1881; d. Nov. 10, 1946. An American Shakespeare scholar, professor of English at Cornell University (1919–31) and director of the Folger Shakespeare Library (1931–46) at Washington. Author of *Shakespearean Playhouses* (1917); editor of *Chief Pre-Shakespearean Dramas* (1924), *The Adams Shakespeare* (1929), *The Passionate Pilgrim* (1939); and general editor of *The New Variorum Shakespeare.*

Adams, Parson. [Also, **Abraham Adams.**] In Fielding's novel *Joseph Andrews,* a poor curate whose amusing adventures in the company of Joseph Andrews and his betrothed, Fanny, constitute a large part of the book. Usually considered to be a portrait of Fielding's friend William Young (a classical scholar with whom Fielding had collaborated on a translation of Aristophanes' *Plutus*), he is a good-natured but naïve scholar. As a character in fiction, he is ranked by many authorities with Oliver Goldsmith's "Vicar" and Laurence Sterne's "Uncle Toby." Fielding in *Joseph Andrews* says: "Mr. Abraham Adams was an excellent scholar. He was a perfect master of the Greek and Latin languages: to which he added a great share of knowledge in the Oriental tongues and could read and translate French, Italian, and Spanish. He had applied many years to the most severe study, and had treasured up a fund of learning rarely to be met with in a university: he was, besides, a man of good sense, good parts, and good nature; but was, at the same time, as entirely ignorant of the ways of this world as an infant just entered into it could possibly be. As he had never any intention to deceive, so he never suspected such a design in others. He was generous, friendly, and brave, to an excess; but simplicity was his characteristic: he did, no more than Mr. Colley Cibber, apprehend any such passions as malice and envy to exist in mankind; which was indeed less remarkable in a country parson, than in a gentleman who has passed his life behind the scenes;—a place which has been seldom thought the school of innocence; and where a very little observation would have convinced the great apologist that those passions have a real existence in the human mind."

Adams, Sarah Flower. b. at Great Harlow, Essex, England, Feb. 22, 1805; d. in August, 1848. An English poet, now remembered chiefly as the author of the hymn *Nearer, My God, to Thee* (1840). She also wrote a dramatic poem about the early Christians, *Vivia Perpetua* (1841).

Adams, William Henry Davenport. b. at London, May 5, 1828; d. at Wimbledon, near London, Dec. 30, 1891. An English author, editor, compiler, private tutor, and French translator. He founded (1870) and edited (1870–78) the *Scottish Guardian,* later editing several volumes in the *Whitefriars Library of Wit and Humor.* Author of *Memorable Battles in English History* (1862), *The Bird World* (1877), *Good Queen Anne* (1886), and a *Concordance to the Works of Shakespeare* (1886).

Adamson (ad'ạm.sọn), **Robert.** b. 1852; d. 1902. A Scottish philosophical writer, professor of philosophy at Owens College, Manchester, and of logic and rhetoric at Glasgow (1895–1902). Author of *Roger Bacon: the Philosophy of Science in the Middle Ages* (1876), *On the Philosophy of Kant* (1879), *Fichte* (1881), and others.

Adam Warner (wôr'nẽr). See **Warner, Adam.**

Adam Woodcock (wŭd'kok). See **Woodcock, Adam.**

Addison (ad'i.sọn), **Joseph.** b. at Milston, Wiltshire, England, May 1, 1672; d. at Holland House, London, June 17, 1719. An English essayist, poet, and statesman. He was educated at the Charterhouse (where he first met Richard Steele) and at Queen's College, Oxford (where he won high praise for his Latin verse), and where he took his M.A. degree in 1693. In 1698 he obtained a fellowship which he held until 1711. A Latin poem which he published in 1697 on the Peace of Ryswick brought him a pension of 300 pounds, and he proceeded to qualify himself for the diplomatic service of the government by travel and study on the Continent (1699–1703), visiting France, Italy, Austria, Germany, and Holland. He was under-secretary of state (1706–08); chief secretary to the lord lieutenant of Ireland, Wharton (1709–10); secretary to the lords justices on the death of Queen Anne (1714); secretary for Ireland under the Earl of Sunderland (1715); a commissioner for trade and the colonies (1716); and secretary of state (April, 1717 to March, 1718). On Aug. 3, 1716, he married the Countess of Warwick. His principal works are his *Letter from Italy,* a poem written as he was crossing the Alps in 1701, printed in 1703; *Campaign,* a poem published in 1704; *Remarks on Italy,* published in 1705; *Fair Rosamond,* an opera, published anonymously in 1707; *Cato,* a classical tragedy, produced at the Drury Lane on April 14, 1713, and an immediate success partly because of its political implications; *The Drummer,* a play, published anonymously in 1716 (acted in 1715); and contributions to the *Whig Examiner* in 1710 (five papers); contributions to the *Tatler* from 1709 to 1711 (41 papers were by Addison alone, 34 by Addison and Steele together); and 274 *Spectators* from 1711 to 1712: these last were all signed by one of the letters of the word C.L.I.O. (Clio). His most famous character is that of Sir Roger de Coverley, originally sketched by Steele. He contributed to the *Guardian* in 1713 (51 papers), and also others to a new *Spectator* in 1714. From Dec., 1715 to June, 1716, he contributed 55 papers to *The Free-Holder.*

Addison of the North. See **Mackenzie, Henry.**

Addison's Walk. A walk in the grounds of Magdalen College, Oxford, said to have been a favorite promenade of Joseph Addison, who in 1689 held a demyship (foundation scholarship) in that college.

Addled Parliament, The. A nickname of the second Parliament of James I (April-June, 1614), which was dissolved without having passed any acts, on

ḍ, d or j; ṣ, s or sh; ṭ, t or ch; ẓ, z or zh; o, F. cloche; ü, F. menu; ċh, Sc. loch; ṅ, F. bonbon.

its refusal to grant supplies until the king's imposition of customs and the restoration of the nonconforming clergy ejected from the Anglican Church in 1604 had been considered.

Address of the Soul to the Body, The. See **Soul and Body.**

Address to the Deil (dēl). A satiric poem (1786) by Robert Burns, in which he ridicules traditional concepts of the Devil, and urges Satan to take thought and mend his ways.

Address to the Irish People, An. A prose pamphlet by Percy Bysshe Shelley, printed in Dublin in 1812, urging redress of the social wrongs under which Ireland suffered.

Address to the Unco Guid or **Rigidly Righteous** (un'kō güd). A satiric poem (1786) by Robert Burns, in which the poet begs the rigidly righteous to show more Christian charity in judging the sins and shortcomings of other people. "O ye, wha are sae guid yoursel, Sae pious and sae holy, Ye've nought to do but mark and tell Your neebour's fauts and folly."

Adela (ad'e.la). b. c1062; d. 1137. The fourth daughter of William the Conqueror. She was the wife of Stephen, earl of Blois and Chartres, and mother of Stephen, king of England, whose claim to the throne derived through her.

Adelaide (ad'e.lād). [Full name, **Amelia Adelaide Louise Theresa Caroline.**] b. Aug. 13, 1792; d. Dec. 2, 1849. Princess of Saxe-Coburg-Meiningen and queen of England; wife of the Duke of Clarence (later William IV), whom she married on July 18, 1818.

Adelard of Bath (ad'e.lärd; bàth). b. at Bath, England; fl. c1116 to c1142. An English mathematician, scientist, philosophical writer, and traveler, known for his knowledge of Arabic learning, and considered to have been the greatest in his field before Grosseteste and Bacon. He studied at Tours and Laon, and then traveled in Italy, Sicily, Greece, Asia Minor, and Africa, returning to England in the reign of Henry I. Before 1116 he wrote a philosophical treatise on identity and difference (*De eodem et diverso*), and before 1137 (probably much earlier) a dialogue (*Questiones naturales*) divided into 76 chapters, each of which treats of a scientific question, the whole purporting to expound Arabic knowledge on these questions. In chapter 51, apropos of an experiment carefully described by him, he explains the impossibility of a vacuum by a theory of universal continuity (developed later by Roger Bacon). The *De eodem et diverso* is a dialogue explaining Platonic views similar to those of the School of Chartres and opposing exaggerated Realism: genera and species are nothing but individuals considered from different points of view. This attitude has been regarded as preparing Abelard's conceptualism. He introduced Moslem trigonometry, and more specifically the sine and tangent functions, into the Latin world. He translated Euclid's works from the Arabic, this being the earliest Latin translation known to us, though he would seem to have made use of an earlier version from the Greek. He was probably instrumental in introducing some knowledge of Moslem music into the West.

Adeline (ad'e.līn), **Lady.** The wife of Lord Henry Amundeville, in Byron's *Don Juan*, who is described in Canto XIII as

The fair most fatal Juan ever met,
Although she was not evil nor meant ill.

Adeliza (ad.e.lī'za). d. in March, 1151. The second queen of Henry I of England; daughter of Godfrey (Barbatus) of Louvain, duke of Brabant or Lower Lotharingia, and a descendant, in the male line, of Charlemagne. She was married to Henry I on Jan. 24, 1120 (or 1121), and after his death married William de Albini.

Adelphi (a.del'fī, -fē). A section in W central London, in Westminster metropolitan borough, comprising several streets on the S side of the Strand, on the approximate site (now occupied by office buildings) of the Adelphi terrace, facing the river. The name was given from the Greek *adelphoi* ("brothers") from the fact that the terrace which formerly occupied it was designed (c1768) by the Adam brothers.

Adelphi Theatre. A theater on the Strand, London, first built in 1806, and rebuilt and enlarged in 1858.

Adeste fideles (a.des'tā fē.dā'lās). [English, **O Come, All Ye Faithful.**] A hymn, originally in Latin, beginning with these words. It has been ascribed to Bonaventura (1221–74), but is more probably of the 17th or 18th century and of French or German authorship. The familiar arrangement, commencing "O come, all ye faithful, joyfully triumphant," first appeared in Murray's *Hymnal* in 1852 and is an adaptation of the translation made by the Reverend Frederick Oakeley in 1841. It has also been published in many other translations. The tune is ascribed to John Reading (1677–1764), organist, and was at first called the "Portuguese Hymn" in England because it was sung at the chapel of the Portuguese embassy in 1797.

Adicia (a.dish'i.a). In Spenser's *Faerie Queene* (Book V), the wife of the Soldan, an unrighteous woman, transformed into a raging tiger. She typifies injustice and wrong.

Aditi (a'di.ti). A term used in the Vedas as an adjective to mean "unbound," "free," "limitless," "infinite," "exhaustless," and, as a noun, to mean "freedom," "security," and then "infinity," in particular that of heaven in contrast with the finitude of earth and its spaces. The last conception personified is the goddess Aditi, the mother of the Adityas.

Adityas (a'dit.yaz). [Eng. trans., *"Sons of Aditi."*] In the Vedic literature, the seven gods of the heavenly light.

Admetus (ad.mē'tus). In Greek mythology, a Thessalian king delivered from death by the voluntary sacrifice of his wife Alcestis (who was thereupon rescued from Hades by Hercules). He took part in the expedition of the Argonauts and in the chase of the Calydonian boar.

Admirable Bashville (bash'vil), **The.** A drama (1901) by George Bernard Shaw. It is based on *Cashel Byron's Profession*, written by Shaw in 1882 and generally considered to be the best of his five novels.

---

fat, fāte, fär, àsk, fâre; net, mē, hèr; pin, pīne; not, nōte, mōve, nôr; up, lūte, pùll; ᴛʜ, then;

Admirable Crichton (krī′tọn), **The.** A dramatic work (1902) by J. M. Barrie. Crichton is the butler in a wealthy household whose head, Lord Loam, likes to pretend that class distinctions are actually meaningless, and who accordingly once a year entertains his servants at tea. Believing firmly that such an arrangement violates the laws of nature, Crichton resists, but without avail until during a yachting trip the family is wrecked on a desert island and left there for two years. Now the situation is different, and the laws of nature clearly dictate that the most competent member of the party (obviously Crichton) shall be the leader. He cheerfully assumes the responsibility, and accepts all the prerogatives of an absolute master: the others are reduced to the status of slaves, and he proposes to marry his former master's daughter. However, when rescue comes and the party returns to England, Crichton punctiliously returns to his original menial rank, and life goes on as it had before the shipwreck except for one important difference: Crichton's point about the relative positions of master and servant has now been clearly driven home to Lord Loam. In real life, there was a man actually called "the Admirable Crichton" (a Scottish scholar and adventurer of the late 16th century, named James Crichton) whose accomplishments were comparable in their variety (although not in kind) to those of Barrie's character.

"Admirable Doctor," The. See **Bacon, Roger.**

Admiral Guinea (gin′i). A drama written (c1885) by Robert Louis Stevenson in collaboration with William Ernest Henley. It failed of production during Stevenson's lifetime; experimental productions after his death were not successful.

Admiral Hosier's Ghost (hō′zhĕrz). A ballad by Richard Glover, on the capture of Portobelo (Porto Bello) by Admiral Edward Vernon in 1739. The ghost of Admiral Francis Hosier (1673–1727) is represented as saying in effect that he could have done all that Vernon did, and more, had he not been hampered by orders which kept him idle till most of his crews were dead of fever and his own heart was broken. It is a partisan poem, with little relation to the historical facts, included by Percy in his *Reliques.*

Admirals All. The title poem of a volume (1897) of verse, mainly patriotic, by Sir Henry Newbolt (1862–1937).

Admiral's Men. See **Lord Admiral's Men.**

Adolphus Tetterby (ạ.dol′fus tet′ẽr.bi). See **Tetterby, Adolphus.**

Adomnan (ad′ọm.nạn, ạ.dom′nạn), Saint. See **Adamnan**, Saint.

Adonai (ad.ọ.nā′ī, ạ.dō′nī). A name substituted by the Hebrews in place of the ineffable name YHWH (the tetragrammaton from which, with greater or lesser error, Yahweh and Jehovah were derived) wherever it occurs in the Scriptures. The term "Adonai" means "my lord" in Hebrew.

Adonais (ad.ọ.nā′is). An elegy by Percy Bysshe Shelley, commemorating the death of John Keats, published in 1821, and generally considered to rank with Milton's *Lycidas*, Arnold's *Thyrsis*, and Tennyson's *In Memoriam* among English elegies. The name was coined by Shelley probably to hint at an analogy between Keats's fate and that of Adonis.

Adonbeck al Hakim (ad′ọn.bek al hak′ēm). In Sir Walter Scott's *The Talisman*, a Saracen doctor who turns out to be Saladin in disguise.

Adonis (ạ.don′is, ạ.dō′nis). In ancient Greek mythology, a beautiful youth who was loved by Aphrodite. He died, according to the usual account, from the wound of a boar's tusk, received while hunting. Acceding partly to the entreaties of Aphrodite that he be restored to life, Zeus thereupon decreed that he should pass half the year in the upper and half in the lower world.

Adonius (ạ.don′i.us). [Also, **Adonic verse** (ạ.don′ik).] A verse consisting of a dactyl and a spondee or trochee, as *rārǎ jǔvĕntūs*, and on account of its animated movement is adapted to gay and lively poetry. It is seldom used by itself, but is joined with other kinds of verse. It is said to have been devised by Sappho and is so called because it was used in songs sung at the festival of Adonis.

Adosinda (ad.ọ.sin′dạ). The daughter of the Gothic governor of the Spanish town of Auria, in Robert Southey's *Roderick, the Last of the Goths* (1814).

Adramelech (ạ.dram′ẹ.lek). In Milton's *Paradise Lost*, one of the fallen angels.

Adrastus (ạ.dras′tus). In Greek legend, a king of Argos, leader and only survivor of the original expedition of the "Seven against Thebes." Some ten years later he led the sons of the Seven in a successful campaign to avenge their fathers, and on this occasion was able to capture Thebes.

Adrian (ā′dri.ạn). In Shakespeare's *Coriolanus*, a Volscian.

Adrian. In Shakespeare's *Tempest*, a lord who attends Alonso and is shipwrecked with him.

Adrian IV. [Also: **Hadrian**; original name, **Nicholas Breakspear.**] b. at Langley, near St. Albans, in Hertfordshire, England, before 1100; d. at Anagni, Italy, 1159. Pope from 1154 to 1159, the only Englishman ever to occupy the papal chair. Created cardinal-bishop of Albano (1146) by Pope Eugenius III, he was legate to Denmark and Norway (1152–54). As pope, he is said to have bestowed (c1156) Irish sovereignty on Henry II of England (this point has long been a center of controversy among historians, but it is now generally agreed that it is true and that the documents supporting it are genuine). He also opened the great conflict between the papacy and the Hohenstaufens by his firm assertion of papal prerogatives against the emperor Frederick I (Frederick Barbarossa).

Adriana (ā.dri.ā′nạ). In Shakespeare's *Comedy of Errors*, the wife of Antipholus of Ephesus. She confuses her husband with his twin, Antipholus of Syracuse.

Adrian de Castello (ā′dri.ạn dẹ kas.tel′ō). [Also, **Adrian de Corneto** (dē kôr.net′ō).] b. at Corneto, Tuscany, Italy, c1460; d. c1521. An Italian ecclesiastic and scholar, nuncio of Pope Innocent VIII in Scotland in 1488, agent at Rome of Henry VII of England, collector of Peter's pence in England, and papal prothonotary. He obtained in 1492 the prebend of Ealdland in Saint Paul's

Cathedral, and the rectory of Saint Dunstan-in-the-East, but returned to Rome on the death of Innocent VIII. He was made bishop of Hereford in 1502, bishop of Bath and Wells in 1504, and cardinal in 1503. In 1517 he was implicated in the conspiracy of Cardinals Petrucci, De Sauli, and Riario to poison Pope Leo X, and was deprived of his cardinalate (1518) and of his dignities in England. He was probably assassinated. He wrote *Venatio*, a poem (1505), *De Vera Philosophia* (1507), *De Sermone Latino et modo Latine Loquendi* (1513), and others.

Adrian Harley (här′li). See **Harley, Adrian.**

Adriano de Armado (ä.dri.ä′nō dä är.mä′dō), **Don.** See **Armado, Don Adriano de.**

Adullam (ạ.dul′ạm), **Cave of.** In the Old Testament, the stronghold to which David withdrew from Gath. 1 Sam. xxii.

Advancement of Learning, The. A treatise (1605) by Francis Bacon that discusses both the good and evil aspects of the intellectual life of the time, the different branches of learning, and proposes new classifications for the arts and sciences. In contrast to the Aristotelians, Bacon's theories are based not merely on a description of nature but on an attempt to change and adjust it to the needs of man. A somewhat expanded Latin version of the treatise appeared in 1623, under the title *De Augmentis Scientiarum.*

Advent, The. See under **Ascension, The.**

Adventurer, The. A periodical issued every Tuesday and Saturday from Nov. 7, 1752 to March 9, 1754 at London under the editorship of John Hawkesworth, who wrote 70 of the 140 essays. Both Samuel Johnson and Joseph Warton were contributors to it.

Adventures. For titles beginning with this word, and not entered or cross referred immediately below, as *Adventures of Sherlock Holmes*, see under the first key element, as **Sherlock Holmes.**

Adventures of a Black Girl in Search of God. A novel by George Bernard Shaw, published in 1932.

Adventures of a Guinea. See **Chrysal, or the Adventures of a Guinea.**

Adventures of an Atom, The. A political satire by Tobias Smollett, published in 1769, in which he used the idea, also employed a few years earlier by Charles Johnstone in *Chrysal, or the Adventures of a Guinea*, of having an inanimate object tell the story. An Atom relates his experiences while in the body of a Japanese, Japan representing England. The Japanese characters in the tale are easily recognizable as satirical portraits of prominent political figures in England during the early part of the reign of George III. The work is an extremely coarse and virulent satire on both political issues and persons.

Adventures of Arthur at the Tarn Wadling (är′thẻr; tärn wäd′ling). See **Awntyrs of Arthure at the Terne Wathelyne.**

Adventures of a Younger Son, The. A novel by Edward John Trelawny, published in 1831. It is the partially autobiographical story of a youth whose character has been twisted by the harshness of a father's treatment. The young man deserts from the navy and becomes a pirate in the Indian Ocean. His exotic exploits are probably exaggerations of the author's own experiences.

Adventures of Brown, Jones, and Robinson, The. See **Brown, Jones, and Robinson, The Adventures of.**

Adventures of Caleb Williams (kā′lẹb wil′yạmz), **The.** See **Caleb Williams.**

Adventures of Master F. J., The. A story by George Gascoigne, published in 1573. The hero, F. J., is a guest at the country estate who does not return the affection of Frances, the daughter of the host. Instead, he has an affair with Elinor, the daughter-in-law. Elinor jilts him for another lover, F. J. leaves, and Frances returns placidly to her former life. The social events and customs of the day are presented with some realism, and the work is often considered an ancestor of the novels of Richardson and Meredith.

Adventures of Mr. Verdant Green, An Oxford Freshman, The. A novel by Edward Bradley, published in 1853. It tells the story of the pranks played upon Verdant while he is a freshman, and goes on to describe how he later used the same tricks on new boys.

Adventures of Philip (fil′ip), **The.** A novel by W. M. Thackeray, published in 1862. It was the last of Thackeray's novels to be published in his lifetime, and is considered by most critics to reflect a waning of the novelist's creative power.

Adventures of Ulysses (ụ.lis′ēz), **The.** A volume of tales for children (1808), by Charles Lamb. It is a retelling of the *Odyssey* of Homer, based very closely on the Chapman translation.

Advocates' Library. The great public library in Edinburgh, since 1925 the National Library of Scotland. Founded by Sir George Mackenzie of Rosehaugh (1636–91), it was opened in 1689, and was maintained by the Faculty of Advocates until 1924, when it was presented to the nation. Under British copyright law, it is one of the libraries entitled to receive a copy of every book published in Great Britain.

Æ. See **Russell, George William.**

Aeacus (ē′ạ.kus). In Greek mythology, the son of Zeus and Aegina, the grandfather of Achilles, and a judge in the lower world.

Aedhan (ad′han), **Saint.** See **Saint Aidan.**

Aëdon (ā.ē′dọn). In Greek legend, a daughter of Pandareus of Ephesus. According to Homer she was the wife of Zethus, king of Thebes, and the mother of Itylus. Inspired by envy of Niobe, the wife of her brother Amphion, who had six sons and six daughters, she formed the design of killing Niobe's eldest son, but by mistake destroyed her own son Itylus. To relieve her grief she was changed by Zeus into a nightingale.

Aeëtes (ẹ.ē′tēz). In Greek mythology, a king of Colchis, father of Medea, and custodian of the Golden Fleece.

Aegaeon (ē.jē′ọn). See **Briareus.**

Aegeon (ē.jē′on). In Shakespeare's *Comedy of Errors*, a merchant of Syracuse, husband of Aemilia, and the father of the Antipholus twins.

---

fat, fāte, fär, ȧsk, fāre; net, mē, hẻr; pin, pīne; not, nōte, mȯve, nôr; up, lūte, pụll; ᴛʜ, then;

Aegeria (ẹ.jir′i.ạ). See **Egeria**.

Aegeus (ē′jẹ.us, -jös). In Greek legend, the father of Theseus, and king of Athens. He is said to have drowned himself in what is now called the Aegean Sea (whence, according to one tradition, its name) out of grief at the supposed killing of his son by the Minotaur.

Aegiale (ẹ.jī′ạ.lē). In George Chapman's *The Blind Beggar of Alexandria*, the wife of the King of Egypt.

Aegidius of Assisi (ẹ.jid′i.us; ạ.sē′zē). [Also, Blessed **Giles**.] d. 1262. A friar, philosopher, and companion of Saint Francis of Assisi, by whom he was called "the Knight of our Round Table." His aphorisms were collected and printed as the *Dicta* after his death; an English translation of this was made by Paschal Robinson under the title *The Golden Words of the Blessed Brother Giles* (1906).

Aeginetan Marbles (ej.i.nē′tạn). A name given to an important collection of ancient Greek sculptures from the temple of Athena at Aegina, now the property of a museum at Munich. Discovered in 1811, these sculptures consist for the most part of the remains of the series of statues from both pediments of the temple. Five figures survive from the eastern pediment, and 10 from the western, which is probably complete. Both groups represent the exploits of Greek heroes in the Trojan War, with Athena as the central figure.

Aegir (ā′gir, ē′jir). In Old Norse mythology, the god of the ocean. He was the principal water-demon and by race a giant, but personifies the more propitious characteristics of the sea. His wife is Ran.

Aegisthus (ẹ.jis′thus). In Greek legend, a son of Thyestes and cousin of Agamemnon. According to the older accounts, he seduced Clytemnestra, and procured the murder of Agamemnon, although in the *Agamemnon* of Aeschylus it is Clytemnestra, incited to the act by Aegisthus, who commits the murder.

Aeglamour (ē′glạ.mör). The "Sad Shepherd" in Ben Jonson's play of that name. He grieves at the reported drowning of the shepherdess Earine.

Aegle (eg′lē). In Greek mythology: **1.** A naiad, mother of the Graces.
2. One of the Hesperides.

Aegydius (ẹ.jid′i.us), Saint. See Saint **Giles**.

Aegyptus (ẹ.jip′tus). In Greek mythology, a son of Belus and twin brother of Danaüs. He received from Belus the sovereignty of Arabia and conquered Egypt. It is from his name, by one tradition, that the name "Egypt" is derived.

Ælfheah (alf′he″ạch), Saint. [Also: **Alphege, Elphege**.] b. 954; d. 1012. An Anglo-Saxon bishop of Winchester (984) and archbishop of Canterbury (1006). He obtained a peace promise from the Danes in 994, but was later (1011) captured by them and slain (1012).

Ælfled (al′fled). See **Ethelfleda**.

Ælfred (alf′rād). Old English spelling of **Alfred**.

Ælfric (al′frik). [Called **Grammaticus**.] b. c955; d. c1020. Abbot of Eynsham in Oxfordshire, participant in and chief literary figure of the Benedictine reform of the 10th century. He wrote two series of homilies, a Latin grammar adapted from Priscian,

a *Heptateuch* (a translation of and commentary on extensive portions of the first seven books of the Bible), a treatise on the Old and New Testaments, a volume of saints' lives, and other works. His style, elaborate but controlled, fluent, often rhythmical and alliterative, represents the highest achievement in prose during the Old English period.

Ælfthryth (alf′thrith). See **Elfrida**.

Ælfwine (alf′win.e). A character in *Widsith*, representing the actual historical figure Alboin, an early king of the Lombards.

Aelius Donatus (ē′li.us dọ.nā′tus). See **Donatus, Aelius**.

Ælla (al′ạ), **Songe to**. See **Songe to Ælla**.

Aëllo (ā.el′ō). In Greek mythology, one of the Harpies.

Aelred (al′red), Saint. See Saint **Ethelred**.

Aemilia (ẹ.mil′i.ạ). In Spenser's *Faerie Queene* (Book IV), a lovely lady "rapt by greedie lust," into the power of a cannibal giant who held Amoret also captive. She is saved by Belphoebe.

Aemilia. In Shakespeare's *Comedy of Errors*, the wife of Aegeon and mother of the Antipholus twins. When she is separated from her family she becomes an abbess at the convent of Ephesus, where she later harbors Antipholus of Syracuse when he is thought to be a lunatic.

Aemilius (ẹ.mil′i.us). In Shakespeare's *Titus Andronicus*, a Roman who asks Titus's brother Marcus to present Lucius as emperor in the final scene.

Aemilius Lepidus (lep′i.dus), **Marcus**. See **Lepidus, M. Aemilius**.

Aeneas (ẹ.nē′ạs). In classical legend, a Trojan prince, son of Anchises, king of Dardanus, and Aphrodite. The accounts of his life and achievements vary considerably, depending on the period of their writing. According to Homer, having been robbed of his cattle by Achilles, he took sides, with his Dardanians, against the Greeks, played an important part in the Trojan War, and after the sack of Troy, and the extinction of the house of Priam, reigned (as did also his descendants) in Troas (or the Troad, as the territory in the vicinity of Troy was known). In post-Homeric accounts he is sometimes represented as absent from the sack of Troy, sometimes as seeking refuge, on the admonition of Aphrodite, on Mount Ida, and carrying his father thither on his shoulders (with other variations), and as settling in the peninsula of Pallene, or in the Arcadian Orchomenos. Most of the accounts, however (including that in Vergil's *Aeneid*), represent him as landing in Italy, and becoming the ancestral hero of the Romans.

Aeneas. In Shakespeare's *Troilus and Cressida*, a Trojan commander who informs Troilus of the exchange of Cressida for the Trojan warrior Antenor, a prisoner of the Greeks.

Aeneid (ẹ.nē′id). An epic poem, in 12 books, by Vergil, recounting one version of the adventures of Aeneas after the fall of Troy, founded on the Roman tradition that Aeneas settled in Latium and became the ancestral hero of the Roman people. The hero, driven by a storm onto the coast of Africa, is hospitably received by Dido, queen of Carthage, to whom he relates the fall of Troy and his wanderings.

ḍ, d or j; ṣ, s or sh; ṭ, t or ch; ẓ, z or zh; *o*, F. cloche; ü, F. menu; ċh, Sc. loch; ṅ, F. bonbon.

An attachment between them is broken by the departure of Aeneas in obedience to the will of the gods, and the suicide of Dido follows. After a visit to Sicily, Aeneas lands at Cumae at Italy. In a descent to the infernal regions he sees his father, Anchises, and has a prophetic vision of the glorious destiny of his race as well as of the future heroes of Rome. He marries Lavinia, daughter of Latinus, king of the Latini, and a contest with Turnus, king of the Rutuli, the rejected suitor, follows, in which Turnus is slain. The poem is a glorification of Rome and of the emperor Augustus, who, as a member of the Julian gens, traced his descent from Julus (sometimes identified with Ascanius), the grandson of Aeneas. The poem was completed, but not finally corrected, at the death of the author in 19 B.C. Among the more noteworthy English translations of the poem into English are those by Gavin Douglas (in rhyme, 1512–13), by Henry Howard, called by courtesy "the earl of Surrey" (whose translation in the middle of the 16th century is believed to mark the first appearance of blank verse in English poetry), by John Dryden (1697), and by William Morris (a translation notable more for the fact that it was done (1876) by Morris than for its quality).

Aeolus (ē'ọ.lus, ẹ.ō'lus). In Greek mythology:
1. The god of the winds, which he confined in a cavern.
2. The son of Hellen, and the eponymic founder of the division of the ancient Greek people known as the Aeolians.

Aeschylus (es'ki.lus). b. at Eleusis, Greece, 525 B.C.; d. at Gela, Sicily, 456 B.C. An Athenian tragic dramatist. He was a soldier of Athens in the war against the Persians, and is believed by many to have been at the battles of Marathon, Artemisium, Salamis, and Plataea (490–479). In his career as a playwright, he entered the annual Athenian competition of tragic drama more than 20 times (499–458), winning first prize on the first occasion in 484 and last in 458, being defeated by Sophocles in 468. Of his approximately 90 plays, seven survive: *The Suppliants, The Persians, The Seven against Thebes, Prometheus Bound* (sole surviving drama of his Promethean trilogy), and the Orestean trilogy, consisting of *Agamemnon, Choëphoroe,* and *Eumenides.*

Aesculapius (es.kụ.lā'pi.us). [Also, **Asclepius.**] In Greek mythology, the god of medicine; son of Apollo and Coronis. He was killed with a thunderbolt by Zeus, because Pluto complained that, through his efforts, Hades was being depopulated. At the request of Apollo, he was, after death, placed among the stars. He is commonly represented as an old man with a beard, his usual attribute being a staff with a serpent coiled around it. The common offering to him was a cock.

Aesir (ē'sèr, ā'sir). A collective name for the gods of the Scandinavian mythology. There were 12 gods and 26 goddesses, dwellers in Asgard.

Aeson (ē'son). In Greek legend, the father of Jason, and stepbrother of Pelias, who excluded him from his share of the kingdom of Thessaly. One account has it that when Pelias, on the reported return of the Argonauts, attempted to kill him, he committed suicide. According to Ovid, he was rejuvenated by Medea after the return of the Argonauts.

Aesop (ē'sop). [Also, **Esop.**] According to tradition, a Greek fabulist of the 6th century B.C., represented as a dwarf and originally a slave. Samos and other places claimed the honor of being his birthplace. After obtaining his freedom he visited Lydia and Greece. Of the so-called fables of Aesop there have been several editions, but they are all considered to be spurious. Indeed, Aesop was probably not an actual historical personage. Several of the fables which he is popularly supposed to have written have been traced to sources which considerably antedate his own alleged period of life; some, in fact, may be found in Egyptian materials dating from approximately the 14th century B.C. He was represented in later art as deformed, "perhaps to indicate his nearer approach to the lower animals and his peculiar sympathy for their habits."

Aesthetic Movement. A body of literary and artistic attitudes, convictions, and techniques that developed in the late 19th century in opposition to the belief that art must be "useful" or serve an explicitly moral purpose. This movement sought to establish art as an end in itself. Walter Pater, influenced by Ruskin's esteem of the Middle Ages, is generally considered to have been the leading figure of the movement. Behind Pater's well-known phrase, to "burn with a hard gem-like flame," is his belief in the importance of intense individual moments of sensation and aesthetic experience. However, the studied and impudent vagaries of some adherents of the movement, as in the behavior of Oscar Wilde and some others, aroused indignation and, without consideration for their literary intentions and contributions, the appearance and manner of these men were ridiculed (as in Gilbert and Sullivan's operetta *Patience*) to such an extent that the movement rapidly lost whatever vestige of popular support it had ever had.

Æthelburh (ath'ẹl.bòrch), Saint. See Saint **Ethelburga.**

Æthelflaed (ath'ẹl.flad). See **Ethelfleda.**

Æthelred (ath'ẹl.red). See **Ethelred.**

Æthelstan (ath'ẹl.stan). See **Athelstan.**

Æthelweard (ath'ẹl.werd; Old English, aᴛн'el.-wa.ȧrd). See **Ethelwerd.**

Æthelwold (ath'ẹl.wōld; Old English, aᴛн'el.wold), Saint. [Also, **Ethelwold.**] b. at Winchester, England, c908; d. 984. Bishop of Winchester, who with Dunstan, Archbishop of Canterbury, and Oswald, Bishop of Worcester, fostered the reform of the Church and the revival of learning in England early in the 10th century. He translated (c960) the *Rule of Saint Benedict* into English. His *Regularis Concordia,* a commentary on Benedictine customs and education, describes the method of performance of the *Quem Quaeritis* trope in the Easter service.

Aether (ē'thèr). In Greek mythology, the son of Chaos and Darkness, and the brother of Night, Day, and Erebus; in the Orphic hymns, the soul of the world and source of life; later, the expanse of heaven or abode of the gods.

Aethiopica (ē.thi.op'i.kạ). See **Theagenes and Chariclea.**

Aethra (ē'thrạ). In Greek mythology, the mother of Theseus: an attendant of Helen at Troy.

---

fat, fāte, fär, ȧsk, fāre; net, mē, hèr; pin, pīne; not, nōte, mõve, nôr; up, lūte, pùll; ᴛн, then;

Aetion (ē'shi.ọn, ā.ē'-). A character in Spenser's *Colin Clout's Come Home Again*, thought by some critics to represent Shakespeare.

Aetolus (ẹ.tō'lus). In Greek mythology, a son of Endymion and founder of the kingdom of Aetolia.

Affery (af'ẹ.ri). In Dickens's *Little Dorrit*, the wife of Flintwinch.

afreet (ạ.frēt', af'rēt) or **afrite** (af.rit', af.rīt'). In Arabian mythology, a powerful evil demon or monster.

> We first behold the feet,
> Then the huge, grasping hands; at last the frown
> On what should be the face of this Afreet.
>
>   (R. H. Stoddard, *Guests of the State*.)

After Many a Summer Dies the Swan. A novel by Aldous Huxley, published in 1940.

Afterwards. A poem by Thomas Hardy.

Agada (ag'ạ.dạ). [Also, **Haggadah**.] The name given in Aramaic to one of the two great divisions of post-Biblical Hebrew literature. The spelling of the name here shown is the one preferred by most authorities in the field, but the spelling "Haggadah" is also common and the term "Haggadist" is generally used to describe a Talmudic scholar who concerns himself chiefly with this division of Hebrew literature. It denotes that portion of the Talmudic literature not devoted to religious law; thus the exegetical and homiletical portions, fables, proverbs, the ethics, as well as everything relating to natural science and history, are included under the Agada, which is thus complementary to the Halacha, the legal portions.

Agag (ā'gag). A character in John Dryden's *Absalom and Achitophel*, generally believed to be a satirical portrait of Sir Edmund Berry Godfrey, a magistrate who received the declaration of Titus Oates. His mutilated body was found in a country ditch shortly thereafter, which led Dryden to the allusion:

> "And Corah might for Agag's murder call
>   In terms as coarse as Samuel used to Saul."

The name "Corah" applies, of course, to Titus Oates.

Agamemnon (ag.ạ.mem'non). In Greek legendary history, the son of Atreus, king of Mycenae, and the most powerful ruler in Greece. He led the Greek expedition against Troy and on his return was slain, according to Homer, by Aegisthus, and according to Aeschylus, by his wife Clytemnestra, who was incited to the deed partly by jealousy of Cassandra, and partly through fear on account of her adultery with Aegisthus.

Agamemnon. A tragic drama by Aeschylus, considered by some to have been his greatest. The scene is laid in Argos, in the palace of Agamemnon, at the time of the king's return from the capture of Troy. The catastrophe is the murder (behind the scenes) of Agamemnon and Cassandra (whom he has brought captive with him) by the queen Clytemnestra urged on by her paramour Aegisthus.

Agamemnon. In Shakespeare's *Troilus and Cressida*, the Greek general. He opens the discussion with Nestor, Ulysses, and Menelaus, on the ill fortunes of the Greeks in the war with Troy (I.iii), and is present in many of the following scenes.

Agamemnon. A translation (1936) by Louis MacNeice of the drama of that name by Aeschylus.

Agamemnon of Aeschylus, The. A translation (1877) by Robert Browning of the Greek play by Aeschylus. Many critics consider that Browning attempted deliberately to reproduce in this work the harshness and obscurity of the original Greek in order to increase, by comparison, the stature of Euripides (whom Browning greatly admired) at the expense of Aeschylus (who was receiving at that time a degree of acclaim which seemed to Browning a reflection on Euripides).

Aganippe (ag.ạ.nip'ẹ). In ancient geography, a fountain near Mount Helicon, in Boeotia, Greece, sacred to the Muses. It was believed to inspire those who drank of it, and it gave the name "Aganippides" to the Muses.

Agape (ag'ạ.pē). In Spenser's *Faerie Queene*, a fay (or fairy), the mother of three knights, Diamond, Priamond, and Triamond, for whom she obtained the gift that if one were killed his strength would pass into the remaining brothers or brother.

Agard or **Agarde** (ạ.gärd'), **Arthur.** b. at Foston, Derbyshire, England, 1540; d. at London, Aug. 22, 1615. An English antiquary, clerk in the British Exchequer, and (1603) deputy chamberlain. He prepared catalogues of state papers, compiled a list of all the leagues, treaties of peace, "intercourses," and marriages arranged between England and other countries down to the end of the 16th century, and wrote a Latin treatise on the Doomsday Book. He bequeathed his numerous manuscripts partly to the Exchequer and partly to his friend Robert Cotton. Most of them are now in the British Museum.

Agate (ā'gạt), **James Evershed.** b. at Manchester, England, 1877—. A British critic and author. He served as dramatic critic of the London *Sunday Times*, film critic of *The Tatler* and literary critic of the London *Daily Express*. He was also the author of the *Ego* autobiographical volumes, most lately *Ego 7* (1945).

Agathon (ag'ạ.thon). An unknown author referred to by Chaucer in the Prologue to *The Legend of Good Women*.

Agave (ạ.gā'vē). In Greek legend, the daughter of Cadmus and mother of Pentheus.

Agdistes (ag.dis'tēz). In Spenser's *Faerie Queene*, the menial guardian of the Bower of Bliss.

"Aged P." In Dickens's *Great Expectations*, John Wemmick's name for his deaf old father.

Agelaus (aj.ẹ.lā'us). In Greek mythology: **1.** A son of Hercules, and ancestor of Croesus.
2. A servant of Priam. He exposed Paris on Mount Ida.
3. The bravest of Penelope's suitors, and the last to be slain by Ulysses.

Age of Anxiety, The. A long poem (1946) by W. H. Auden, set in dramatic form, involving three men and a woman meeting in a bar in time of war. The metrical pattern is a close approximation of Old English stressed alliterative meter. The title has attained a certain vogue as a byword for mid-20th-century culture. A ballet with music by Leonard Bernstein was inspired by the poem, subtitled by Auden "A Baroque Eclogue."

Age of Reason, The. A treatise on religion by Thomas Paine, published at Paris, in two parts (Part I, 1794; Part II, 1796). Shortly after the publication of the first part, the author was arrested. Part I asserts the existence of God, suggests that the Word of God is contained in His creation, and deprecates the machinery of national churches. Part II endeavors to point out the fallibility of the Bible by presenting examples of its inconsistency. The work was in its time regarded as revolutionary and has been called "the atheist's bible."

Ager (ā'gėr), **Captain.** In Middleton and Rowley's play *A Fair Quarrel*, a soldier of delicate and noble nature who is faced with the choice of perjuring himself or being considered a coward on the field of honor.

Agib (ā'gib). In *The Arabian Nights' Entertainments:* **1.** The third Calender in *The Three Calenders.*
2. A son of Bedreddin Hassan and the Queen of Beauty.

Agincourt (aj'in.kōrt; French, à.zhaṅ.kȯr). A village in N France, near which the English bowmen under Henry V defeated a very much larger force of heavily armed French knights under the Constable d'Albret on Oct. 25, 1415. This battle forms the background of some of the principal scenes in Shakespeare's *Henry V*.

Aglaia (a.glā'a). In Greek mythology, one of the three Graces.

Aglaura (a.glô'ra). A tragedy by Sir John Suckling, acted in 1637–38 and printed in 1646.

Agnes (ag'nes), Saint. fl. probably in middle of 3rd century. A virgin and child martyr, said to have been beheaded at the age of 12 or 13 after being cast into a brothel. She is the patron saint of young maidens, and the source of the legend that on Saint Agnes's Eve (Jan. 20) a girl might perform a certain ritual and discover the visage of her future husband, a superstition important in Keats's *Eve of St. Agnes*. It is also used by Tennyson in *St. Agnes' Eve*. The date of her martyrdom is very uncertain. The *Acts* of Agnes are regarded as spurious, and the latest studies suggest that she did not suffer under Diocletian (304), but during a persecution just after or before the reign of Decius (251).

Agnes Fleming (flem'ing). See **Fleming, Agnes.**

Agnes Grey (grā). A novel by Anne Brontë, published (1847) under the pseudonym Acton Bell. It is to a considerable extent autobiographical, being based on Anne Brontë's experiences as a governess in various well-to-do middle-class families, and describing in some detail the pettiness and snobbery she found there.

Agnes Wickfield (wik'fēld). See **Wickfield, Agnes.**

Agni (ag'ni). In Hindu mythology, the god of fire, one of the three chief divinities of the Vedas.

Agora (ag'ō.ra), **The.** A large irregular area near the Acropolis in ancient Athens, used as forum and marketplace.

Agravaine (ag'ra.vān), **Sir.** In medieval romance, a knight of the Round Table, surnamed "the Proud" (*L'Orgueilleux*).

Agreeable Surprise, The. An operatic farce by John O'Keeffe, produced in 1781.

Agricola (a.grik'ō.la), **Gnaeus Julius.** b. at Forum Julii (now Fréjus, France), 37 A.D.; d. at Rome, 93 A.D. A Roman soldier and politician; father-in-law of Tacitus. Quaestor in Asia (63) under Salvius Titianus; made commander (70) of the XXth Legion in Britain by Vespasian; governor of Aquitania (74–78); elected consul (78) and assigned to southern Britain, where in seven campaigns (78–84) he extended Roman law to the northern boundary of Perth and Argyll. He may have been poisoned by agents of the emperor. Tacitus' *Agricola*, an account of his life and accomplishments, is generally considered to be an outstanding example of good classical biography.

Agrippa (a.grip'a). In Shakespeare's *Antony and Cleopatra*, a friend of Octavius who suggests that Antony marry Octavia, the sister of Octavius.

Agrippa. See also **Herod Agrippa I.**

Agrippa, Menenius. See **Menenius Agrippa.**

Aguecheek (ā'gū.chēk), **Sir Andrew.** In Shakespeare's *Twelfth Night*, a timid, silly, but amusing country squire. He is the friend of Sir Toby Belch.

Aguilar (a.gwil'ar, ä.gē.lär'), **Grace.** b. at London, 1816; d. at Frankfort on the Main, 1847. An English writer on Jewish history, best known for *The Spirit of Judaism* (1842). She also wrote several novels, including *Home Influence* (1847) and *The Vale of Cedars* (1850).

Ahania (a.hā'ni.a). A female character in Blake's mystical poems, *The Book of Ahania* (1795) and *The Song and Book of Los* (1795). She is a symbol of physical desire and is thus an opposing force to Urizen, the symbol of reason and morality.

Ahasuerus (a.has.ū.ē'rus). Biblical name of **Xerxes I.**

Ahasuerus. A name sometimes given to the legendary Wandering Jew.

Ahmed (ä'med), **Prince.** A character in the story "Prince Ahmed and the Fairy Peri-Banou," in the *Arabian Nights' Entertainments*. He is one of three brothers who must acquire some marvelous object before the king will choose which of them is to marry the princess. Ahmed does not win, but finds a wonderful apple that cures all disease, discovers the fairy Peri-Banou, and marries her.

Ahithophel (a.hith'ō.fel). In the Old Testament, a counselor of King David and, later, of Absalom in his revolt against his father. He was famous for his political wisdom, and his defection caused David great apprehension. His advice, however, was rejected by Absalom, and he thereupon retired to his home, set his affairs in order, and hanged himself. He is thought to have been the grandfather of Bathsheba. Ahithophel is spelled **Achitophel** in the Vulgate and Douay Bibles. It was from the latter spelling that John Dryden derived the spelling used in his satiric poem *Absalom and Achitophel*.

Aholah and **Aholibah** (a.hō'la; a.hō'li.ba). In the Old Testament, two harlots who personify Samaria and Jerusalem. Ezekiel, xxiii.

Aholibah. A poem (1866) by Algernon Charles Swinburne, included in *Poems and Ballads: First Series* (called *Laus Veneris, and Other Poems and Ballads* in the United States).

fat, fāte, fär, ȧsk, fāre; net, mē, hėr; pin, pīne; not, nōte, mōve, nôr; up, lūte, pùll; ᴛʜ, then;

Aholibamah (a̯.hol.i.bā′ma̯). In Byron's *Heaven and Earth,* the proud, ambitious granddaughter of Cain.

Ahriman (ä′ri.ma̯n). In the Zoroastrian religion, the spirit or principle of evil.

Ahuramazda (ä′hö.rä.mäz′dä). [Also: **Ormazd, Ormuzd.**] The Good Spirit in the dual system of Zoroaster. He is in perpetual conflict with Ahriman, the "spiritual enemy."

Aidan (ā′da̯n). d. 606. King of Scottish Dalriada. In 575, at the council of Drumceat, he declared the independence of his kingdom, which had been formed in the 5th century by emigrants from Irish Dalriada, and which had hitherto been treated as an Irish dependency.

Aidan, Saint. [Also, **Aedhan.**] d. 651. An Irish monk, first bishop of Lindisfarne, and founder of the church in Northumbria, to which he was sent by the monks of Hii or Iona in answer to a request by King Oswald that someone be dispatched to his realm in order to convert his heathen subjects. After the defeat (642) of Oswald by Penda, Aidan joined Oswin, king of the Deirans.

Aïdé (à.ē.dā′, ī.dā′), **Hamilton.** b. at Paris, c1829; d. 1906. An English novelist and poet. Son of an Armenian father and English mother, he was for a time (1845–52) an officer in the British army. His poetic works include *Eleanore and Other Poems* (1856), *The Romance of the Scarlet Leaf* (1865), and *Songs Without Music* (1882); his novels include *Rita* (1859), *The Marstons* (1868), *Passages in the Life of a Lady* (1887), and others.

Aids to Reflection. A miscellany (1825) by Samuel Taylor Coleridge, containing essays discussing various aspects of philosophy, religion, and literary criticism. It reflects Coleridge's deep interest in contemporary German idealistic metaphysics.

Aikin (ā′kin), **John.** b. at Kibworth, England, Jan. 15, 1747; d. at Stoke Newington, England, Dec. 7, 1822. An English physician and writer. Author of *General Biography* (1799–1815), *Evenings at Home* (1792–95), written in conjunction with his sister, Anna Letitia Barbauld), and others.

Aikin, Lucy. b. at Warrington, Lancashire, England, Nov. 6, 1781; d. at Hampstead, England, Jan. 29, 1864. An English writer; daughter of John Aikin (1747–1822). Author of *Memoirs of the Court of Queen Elizabeth* (1818), *Memoirs of the Court of James I* (1822), *Memoirs of the Court of Charles I* (1833), *Life of Addison* (1843), and others.

Ailred (āl′red), Saint. See **Saint Ethelred.**

Ailred of Rievaulx (rē.vō′). b. c1109; d. c1166. Abbot of the Cistercian monastery Rievaulx, in Yorkshire, and author of a rule for recluses, a historical chronicle, and other works of a historical and religious nature.

Aimon (ā′mo̯n). See **Aymon.**

Aimwell (ām′wel″). In James Shirley's play *The Witty Fair One,* the lover of Violetta. He closely resembles the Thomas Aimwell who appears in Farquhar's *The Beaux' Stratagem.*

Aimwell, Thomas. The young hero of Farquhar's *The Beaux' Stratagem,* a young gentleman of a romantic temperament, who has dissipated his fortune and who, with his cooler-headed friend

Archer disguised as his servant, impersonates a rich lord, with a view to retrieving their losses by a rich marriage for either or both, making a journey from one town to another, and taking turns in being master and man. The stratagem is successful at the end of the play.

Ainger (ān′jèr), **Alfred.** b. at London, Feb. 9, 1837; d. at Darley Abbey, Derbyshire, England, Feb. 8, 1904. An English clergyman, author, and editor. He wrote biographies of Lamb (1882) and of Crabbe (1903), and published annotated editions of Lamb's *Essays of Elia* (1883), of Lamb's *Letters* (1888), and of Hood's *Poems,* with a biographical memoir (1897).

Ainslie (ānz′li), **Douglas.** [Original full name, **Douglas Ainslie Grant Duff.**] b. at Paris, 1865—. An English poet, critic, and diplomat. Translated works of Benedetto Croce into English; author of *Chosen Poems* (1928), *The Conquest of Pleasure* (1942), and others.

Ainsworth (ānz′wèrth), **William Harrison.** b. at Manchester, England, 1805; d. at Reigate, England, 1882. An English editor, publisher, and writer. He was editor (1840 *et seq.*) of *Bentley's Miscellany, Ainsworth's Magazine,* and the *New Monthly.* His novel *Rookwood* (1834) established him as a successful writer, and by 1881 he had published 39 novels, including *Crichton* (1837), *Jack Sheppard* (1839), *Tower of London* (1840), *Old St. Paul's* and *Guy Fawkes* (both 1841), *Windsor Castle* (1843), *The Flitch of Bacon,* and others. Seven of his novels were illustrated by Cruikshank.

Aintree (ān′trē). A small area in W England, in Lancashire, ab. 5 mi. N of Liverpool, comprising a racecourse over which the steeplechase known as the Grand National is run in March of each year. The racecourse, which was founded over 100 years ago, is ab. 4½ mi. long and notable as one of the most difficult for riders in the world.

Aircastle (ãr′kàs″l). A character in Samuel Foote's comedy *The Cozeners,* originally played in an amusingly prolix and digressive manner by Foote himself, burlesquing Gahagan, a highly educated young Irish gentleman who was hanged (1749) for "filing or diminishing the current coin of the realm."

Airy (ãr′i), **Sir George.** The successful lover of Miranda in Susannah Centlivre's comedy *The Busybody.*

Ajax (ā′jaks). In Greek legend, one of the leading Greek heroes in the Trojan War, famous for his size and physical strength and beauty; son of Telamon and half-brother of Teucer. According to Homer he was, next to Achilles, the bravest of the Greek warriors. He engaged several times in victorious single combat with Hector, and was always a source of terror to the Trojans. There are various accounts of his exploits after the war and of his death. According to the common poetical tradition, he died by his own hand. The decision of Agamemnon (on the advice of Athena) to award the arms of Achilles to Odysseus drove Ajax mad, and, according to Sophocles, in his insanity he furiously attacked and slew the sheep of the Greeks, imagining them to be his enemies. Shame for this conduct drove him to suicide. According to other accounts he was murdered. From his blood was said to have sprung up a purple flower bearing on its leaves the letters *ai*, which were the first letters of his name in Greek and also an exclamation of woe. His story was dramatized by Sophocles.

Ajax. A Locrian legendary king, son of Oïleus, and one of the heroes in the Trojan War. Having incurred the displeasure of Athena, he was shipwrecked and drowned on his return from the war. He is often called the "Lesser Ajax."

Ajax. In Shakespeare's *Troilus and Cressida*, a Greek commander who is praised beyond his worth by the other leaders in order that Achilles, who has refused to go to battle, will become indignant and return to the wars. Alexander, Cressida's serving-man, compares him to the lion, the bear, and the elephant, says that he has every virtue and every vice, and that he is "all eyes and no sight" (I.ii).

Akbar (ak'bär). b. at Amarkote, India, 1542; d. at Agra, India, 1605. The greatest of India's Mogul emperors; reigned 1556–1605. He instituted laws against extortion, a uniform system of weights and measures, banned child marriage below a certain age, and compelled toleration of religious diversity.

Akeman Street (āk'man). An ancient Roman road in Britain, from Bath to London.

Akenside (ā'ken.sīd), **Mark.** b. at Newcastle, England, 1721; d. at London, 1770. An English poet and physician, author of *The Pleasures of the Imagination* (1757), in blank verse, and of various minor poems and odes. *Hymn to the Naiads* (1746) is perhaps the best known of his lesser poems.

Alabaster (al'a.bas.tèr), **William.** [Also, **Arblastier.**] b. at Hadleigh, Suffolk, England, 1567; d. 1640. An English clergyman and writer of verse in Latin. He wrote a tragedy, *Roxana*, which was performed in 1632, and began an epic poem in praise of Queen Elizabeth. He also wrote minor poems including *Upon the Crucifix* and *On the Reed of Our Lord's Passion*.

Aladdin (a.lad'in). In the story of "Aladdin or the Wonderful Lamp," in *The Arabian Nights' Entertainments*, the son of a poor widow in China, who becomes possessed of a magic lamp and ring, which command the services of two powerful jinns. Learning the magic power of the lamp by accidentally rubbing it, Aladdin becomes rich and marries the Princess of Cathay through the agency of the "slave of the lamp," who also builds in a night a palace for her reception. One window of this palace is left unfinished, and no one can complete it to match the others. Aladdin therefore directs the jinns to finish it, which is done in the twinkling of an eye (hence the phrase "to finish Aladdin's window"; that is, to attempt to finish something begun by a greater man). After many years the original owner of the lamp, a magician, in order to recover it, goes through the city offering new lamps for old. The wife of Aladdin, tempted by this idea, exchanges the old and rusty magic lamp for a new and shining useless one (hence the phrase "to exchange old lamps for new"), and the magician transports both palace and princess to Africa, but the ring helps Aladdin to find them. He kills the magician, and, possessing himself of the lamp, transports the palace to Cathay, and at the sultan's death succeeds to the throne.

Alaham (al'a.ham). A tragedy by Sir Fulke Greville, published posthumously in 1633 and dealing in didactic, neoclassic style with the political results of Alaham's dethroning of King Ormus, his father. Certain obvious likenesses in theme to *A Mirror for Magistrates* probably caused Lamb's remark that it was better to refer to it as a political treatise than as a play.

Alan Breck (al'an brek). See **Breck, Alan.**

Alan Fairford (fār'fôrd, -fòrd). See **Fairford, Alan.**

Alarbus (a.lär'bus). In Shakespeare's *Titus Andronicus*, the eldest son of Tamora. When he is sacrificed by the sons of Titus, Tamora is provided with the motive for her various acts of cruel and bloody vengeance.

Alarum Against Usurers, An. A prose satire (1584) by Thomas Lodge, directed against the hypocrisies and selfishness of contemporary society.

Al Asnam (äl äs'näm), **Prince Zayn.** [Also, **Alasnam.**] The chief character of a story in *The Arabian Nights' Entertainments*. He acquires eight rare and precious statues through the help of a sheikh, and is told that he will find one more valuable than any of them if he finds the missing occupant of the ninth pedestal. To do this he uses a magic mirror that shows flaws in human character, finds a perfect woman, and falls in love with her. When he returns to his statues he finds that the woman belongs on the empty pedestal, and he marries her.

Alastor (a.las'tor). In Greek mythology, a surname of Zeus in his capacity of avenger.

Alastor. In medieval demonology, a spirit of evil who carries out the sentences of the king of hell.

Alastor. A poem by Shelley, published in 1816, named from its chief character, "Alastor or the Spirit of Solitude." It is usually considered to have been Shelley's first major work.

Alba (al'ba). A poem (1598) by Robert Tofte. It is remembered now chiefly for its allusion to Shakespeare's play *Love's Labour's Lost.*

Alban (ôl'ban, al'-), Saint. Killed at Verulamium (now St. Albans, Hertfordshire, England), c304. A Roman soldier and first martyr of Britain, executed for sheltering a Christian priest. He is said to have been a native of the town where he was killed. The famous monastery of Saint Alban was founded in his honor by King Offa c795. His festival is celebrated in the Roman Catholic Church on June 22, and in the Anglican Church on June 17.

Albania (al.bā'ni.a) or **Albany** (ôl'ba.ni). An ancient name of the Scottish Highlands, fancifully derived from the mythical Albanact, son of Brute.

Albanius (al.bā'ni.us). See **Albion and Albanius.**

Albany (ôl'ba.ni), **Duke of.** In Shakespeare's *King Lear*, the husband of Goneril, Lear's eldest daughter. He is a kindly man who accuses Goneril and Regan of being unnatural in their treatment of Lear. At the death of Lear, the kingdom becomes his.

Albany, The. A residence (bachelors' quarters) in Piccadilly, occupied at different times by Byron, Bulwer-Lytton, Macaulay, and Matthew ("Monk") Lewis, as well as other literary notables.

---

fat, fāte, fär, àsk, fāre; net, mē, hèr; pin, pīne; not, nōte, möve, nôr; up, lūte, púll; ᴛн, then;

Albemarle (al'bẹ.märl), 6th **Earl of.** Title of **Keppel, George Thomas.**

Alberich (äl'bẹ.riċh). In the Middle High German *Nibelungenlied*, the dwarf responsible for guarding the hoard of the Nibelungs, which was eventually seized by Siegfried. In medieval legend, Alberich is later developed into Oberon, the king of the fairies.

Albert (al'bėrt), Prince. [Full name, **Albert Francis Charles Augustus Emmanuel of Saxe-Coburg-Gotha.**] b. at the Rosenau, near Coburg, Germany, 1819; d. at Windsor Castle, 1861. The husband of Queen Victoria and prince consort of England; second son of the Duke of Saxe-Coburg-Gotha. He first met Queen Victoria in 1836; after their marriage (1840) he managed to overcome the initial distrust of the English people by his tact and diligent interest in the arts and scientific development; the great Exhibition of 1851 was successful largely through his efforts. He was given the formal title of Prince Consort in 1857.

Albert (al'bėrt). [Title, **Count of Geierstein** (gī'ėr.stīn).] In Sir Walter Scott's novel *Anne of Geierstein*, a restless intriguer and head of the Vehmgericht. Pursued by Charles the Bold, he takes refuge in a monastery, whence he becomes known as the "Black Priest of St. Paul's." By order of the Vehmgericht he kills Charles in battle.

Albert Memorial. A monument in London, erected to the memory of Prince Albert, Queen Victoria's husband, on the S side of Kensington Gardens, built from the designs of Sir Gilbert Scott. It consists of a colossal bronze statue of the prince, seated, beneath an ornate spired canopy which rises to a height of 175 ft. Statue and canopy rest on a basement bearing reliefs of artists of all countries and times. At the angles four pedestals project with groups of statuary representing Agriculture, Commerce, Engineering, and Manufacture. Steps descend on all sides in pyramidal form, and at the lower angles are placed sculptures personifying Europe, America, Asia, and Africa.

Albert Peter Smallways (pē'tėr smôl'wāz). See **Smallways, Albert Peter.**

Albertus Magnus (al.bėr'tus mag'nus), Saint. [Called **"Albert the Great," "Doctor Universalis";** hereditary title, Count **von Bollstädt.**] b. at Lauingen, Swabia, c1193 (or 1205); d. at Cologne, Prussia, 1280. A German scholastic philosopher, member (1223 *et seq.*) of the Dominican order, and teacher at Paris, Cologne, Strasbourg, and elsewhere. He was noted as one of the foremost scholars of his time by Roger Bacon, his contemporary, and was named by later writers the most powerful expositor of the intellectual efforts of the 13th century. Chiefly known for his interest in Aristotle, whose works he endeavored to free from Arabic interpolations, he was excelled in his pioneering efforts to reconcile the study of Aristotelian logic and philosophy with Catholic theology by his favorite pupil, Thomas Aquinas. He was, however, without a rival in his day, preëminently successful as a teacher in interpreting and making comprehensible to his contemporaries the Aristotelian works in natural philosophy. Raised (1260) to the bishopric of Ratisbon, he retired two years later in order to continue his teaching at Cologne. His sci-

entific studies based on the Aristotelian method and plan were supplemented by his own observations of the animal and plant life around him, and by his visits to the mines, mineral deposits, and the laboratories of alchemists in the vicinity of his residence at Cologne. He was canonized (1932) by Pope Pius XI.

Albigenses (al.bi.jen'sēz). A collective name for the members of several anti-sacerdotal sects in the S part of France in the 12th and 13th centuries; so called after Albi, in Languedoc, where they were dominant. They revolted against the established church, were charged with Manichaean errors, and were so vigorously persecuted that, as sects, they had in great part disappeared by the end of the 13th century. A crusade against them was preached by Pope Innocent III in 1208, and was led by Arnold of Citeaux and Simon de Montfort. The war of extermination, which lasted for several years, was one of the bloodiest in history. Their doctrines are now known chiefly from the writings of their orthodox enemies.

Albinus (al.bī'nus). See **Alcuin.**

Albion (al'bi.ọn). An ancient name of Britain, specifically, England. The Romans associated the term with *albus*, "white," and identified it with the Dover chalk cliffs.

Albion and Albanius (al.bā'ni.us). An operatic entertainment by Dryden, produced in 1685, allegorically representing the chief events of King Charles II's reign (he is Albion) and also his successor, James II, who came to the throne just as it was about to be performed (he is Albanius). It contains several notable lyrics, as "See the God of Seas attends Thee" (a welcome to James).

Albion Knight. An anonymous play, probably printed in 1566, of which only a fragment is now extant. It belongs to the category of political moralities.

Albion's England. A popular Elizabethan verse chronicle by William Warner, in twelve books, printed in 1586. It relates mythological "history" from Noah to the legendary early British kings, then takes up the chronology of actual events to the reign of Elizabeth (with many fictional digressions). The work is based on Hall's *Chronicle* and attempts to show by the evidence of "history" that Henry VII had been established on the throne by divine providence to unify the country. It was later continued to 1606.

Alboin (al'bọ.in). See under **Ælfwine.**

Al Borak (äl bō'räk). A legendary animal, white in color, between a mule and an ass in size, with two wings and of great swiftness, on which Mohammed is said to have made a nocturnal journey to the seven heavens, conducted by the angel Gabriel.

Albovine (al'bọ.vīn). A tragedy by Sir William D'Avenant, printed in 1629 and possibly never produced. It is a court play similar to those of Shirley and in its chief characters presents the theme of Platonic love, much enjoyed by the consort of Charles I (Queen Henrietta). The same plot was used by Middleton in *The Witch* and by Swinburne in *Rosamund, Queen of the Lombards.*

Albumazar (äl.bọ.mä'zär). b. at Balkh, Turkestan, 805; d. at Wasid, in central Asia, 885. An Arab

d̦, d or j; ș, s or sh; ț, t or ch; z̦, z or zh; o, F. cloche; ü, F. menu; ċh, Sc. loch; ṅ, F. bonbon.

astronomer and astrologer at Baghdad, who made important contributions to the study of tides. A prolific writer, he compiled astronomical tabulations based on the Persian system, differentiating it from the Jewish. He predicted the end of the world in his *De magnis conjunctionibus*. He was used as a prototype of a knavish astrologer in Gian Battista del Porta's play *L'Astrologo* (1606), on which were based Thomas Tomkis's *Albumazar*, played (1614) before James I, revived by Dryden (1748) and Garrick, and Ralph's *The Astrologer* (1734). He was the author of some 50 works including *Flores astrologici* (Augsburg, 1488), *De magnis conjunctionibus* (Augsburg, 1489), and *Introductorium in astronomiam* (Venice, 1506).

Albumazar (al.bū.maz'ạr). A tragedy (acted 1614, printed 1615) by Thomas Tomkis.

Alcaeus (al.sē'us) or **Alkaios** (-kī'os). fl. in Mytilene, c611–580 B.C. A Greek poet whose lyrics in Aeolic dialect, known through fragments, are thought to have been a prototype of Sappho's. He was the probable inventor of alcaics, a meter much used by later classical poets.

Alcaeus. In Greek legend, a son of Perseus and Andromeda, and an ancestor of Hercules.

alcaic verse (al.kā'ik). A line written in the measures invented by Alcaeus. The most important one of these consists of an anacrusis, a trochee, a spondee, and two dactyls. A second consists of a catalectic iambic pentameter, of which the third foot is always a spondee, and the first may be. A third consists of two dactyls followed by two trochees. Two lines of the first, followed by one of the second and one of the third, constitute the alcaic strophe, the commonest arrangement of alcaics. The following is an example from Tennyson of an alcaic strophe:

> O might-mouth'd inventor of harmonies,
> O skill'd to sing of Time or Eternity,
>   God-gifted organ-voice of England,
>   Milton, a name to resound for ages.

Alceste (ȧl.sest). The principal character in Molière's comedy *The Misanthrope;* an upright but tactless man who scorns the excessive civilities of courtly life and the shams of society. Wycherley took him as the model for his rude and brutal Manly in *The Plain Dealer.*

Alceste (al.sest'). The wife of the God of Love in Chaucer's prologue to *The Legend of Good Women.*

Alcestis (al.ses'tis) or **Alceste** (-tē). In Greek legend, the daughter of Pelias and wife of Admetus, king of Pherae in Thessaly. When her husband was stricken with a mortal sickness she sacrificed her life for him, in accordance with the promise of Apollo that by this means he should be saved. According to one form of the legend she was allowed to return to the upper world by Persephone; according to another she was rescued by Hercules. She is the subject of a play by Euripides.

Alchemist, The. A comedy by Ben Jonson, first acted in 1610. It is a satire on avarice as shown in the foolish quest for love, power, and wealth by means of the philosopher's stone. The crafty alchemist, Subtle, and his accomplice, Dol Common, establish themselves in Lovewit's empty house with the aid of his servant, Face. They pro-

ceed to dupe Sir Epicure Mammon, an old voluptuary, Drugger, a loutish tobacconist, Dapper, a lovesick lawyer's clerk, and Kastril, seeking to find a good match for Dame Pliant, his over-romantic sister. Two ambitious Puritan fanatics, Tribulation Wholesome and Ananias, also fall to the lure of unlimited power. Surly, recognizing their intentions, pretends to be a Spanish nobleman and deceives the scheming Dol by his romantic actions. Subtle, aware of his true identity, will only allow him to go on deceiving Dol if he consents to woo Dame Pliant in the same disguise. The unexpected return of Lovewit touches off a merry round of trickery before Subtle and Dol make off, leaving Face to meet his master. He resourcefully marries Lovewit to Dame Pliant amidst the general recognition by the victims that their greed has made them foolishly gullible. Garrick's version of the play made Drugger the star character. Jonson's version is one of the finest examples of classical unity of time (a single day in autumn, 1610), place (Lovewit's house in Blackfriars), and action (rigid division into scenes and acts). Coleridge considered the plot as one of the three most perfect ever planned. Jonson drew on contemporary lives as well as Plautus's *Mostellaria* and *Panulus* for the characterizations.

Alchfrith (älch'frith). Son of Oswui, king of the Northumbrians, and Eanflæd, daughter of Eadwine. He married Cyneburh, daughter of Penda, king of the Mercians. He was created under-king of the Deirans by his father, whom he joined in the defeat (655) of Penda, near the river Winwæd. Later he waged an unsuccessful war against his father, and probably fled to Mercia.

Alcibiades (al.si.bī'ạ.dēz). In Shakespeare's *Timon of Athens*, an Athenian captain who is banished for speaking hotly before the Senate when its members refuse to pardon one of his friends. Timon aids him toward the capture of Athens and thus they get revenge on their common enemy.

Alcibiades. A tragedy by Thomas Otway, produced in 1675 at the Drury Lane. It is done in rhyming couplets and is in the heroic style.

Alcida, or Greene's Metamorphosis (al'si.dạ). A pamphlet by Robert Greene, licensed in 1588, probably published in 1589. It consists of stories exposing the evils of women's pride and vanity. The narrator is supposedly shipwrecked on the island of Taprobane in the Antarctic.

Alcides (al'si.dēz). A patronymic of Hercules, who was a descendant of Alcaeus.

Alcinous (al.sin'ọ̄.us). In Greek legend, a king of the Phaeacians, in the island of Scheria, mentioned in the *Odyssey*. A considerable part of the poem (Books VI–XIII) is devoted to the events of Odysseus's stay in his dominions.

Alciphron (al'si.fron). A character in Thomas Moore's romance *The Epicurean*, published in 1827. Moore also wrote a poem with this title, published in 1839.

Alciphron, or the Minute Philosopher. A philosophical dialogue by Bishop Berkeley, written to expose the weakness of infidelity. It was composed while Berkeley was at Newport, R. I., and was published in 1732.

---

fat, fāte, fär, ȧsk, fãre; net, mē, hėr; pin, pīne; not, nōte, mȯve, nôr; up, lūte, půll; ᴛн, then;

Alcmaeon (alk.mē′ǫn). In Greek legend, the son of Amphiaraus and Eriphyle and the leader of the Epigoni in the expedition against Thebes. In accordance with the command of his father, given when he joined the first expedition against Thebes, and the advice of the oracle, he slew his mother, and was driven mad and pursued by the Furies in consequence. Having, under false pretenses, obtained from Phegeus the Arcadian the necklace and robe of Harmonia for his wife Callirrhoe, he was waylaid and slain by Phegeus's order.

Alcman or **Alkman** (alk′mạn) or **Alcmaeon** (alk.mē′ǫn). b. at Sardis, Lydia; fl. middle of the 7th century B.C. A Greek poet, founder of the Doric school. Formerly a slave, he was freed and made a citizen of Sparta. He is often considered the inventor of lyric poetry; he wrote, especially for choral performance, hymns, paeans, processionals, and *parthenia* (maidens' songs); one of the latter was discovered (1855) on an Egyptian papyrus.

Alcmene or **Alkmene** (alk.mē′nē). In Greek mythology, the wife of Amphitryon and mother, by Zeus, of Hercules.

Alcofribas Nasier (àl.ko.frē.bàs nà.zyā). An anagrammatic pseudonym of François Rabelais, once or twice shortened to the first word only.

Alcor (al′kôr). A fifth-magnitude star very near to Mizar (ʒ Ursae Majoris). It is easily seen with the naked eye if the eye is normal, but not otherwise: hence sometimes used as a test of vision. It is called Aliore in the Latin version of the *Almagest*.

Alcoran (al.kǭ.rän′, al′kǭ.rạn). The sacred book of the Mohammedans, better known in English as the Koran, consisting of revelations delivered orally by Mohammed and taken down in writing, being collected after his death.

Alcuin (al′kwin). [Also: **Albinus, Ealhwine.**] b. at York, England, 735; d. at Tours, France, 804. An English prelate and scholar, a leader in the medieval revival of learning in Europe. He made no direct contribution to English scholarship or literature, except as his activities on the Continent were reflected in a cultural framework that included England. At Charlemagne's invitation, he settled at Aix-la-Chapelle (Aachen); he served as abbot of Ferrières and Troyes, as head of the palace school, and as mentor for the Frankish educational and ecclesiastical reform that took place in his day. As abbot of Tours (796–804), he conducted the foremost school of Carolingian Europe. The value of Alcuin's services to Western culture can hardly be exaggerated; he was the main instrument in the transmission to the ignorant Franks of the relatively high culture which had been attained in English monasteries under Bede's guidance.

Alcyone (al.sī′ǭ.nē). In ancient Greek mythology, the daughter of Aeolus and wife of Ceyx. One version of their story contends that after the loss of her husband she cast herself into the sea and was changed into a kingfisher (halcyon).

Alcyone. In classical mythology, a Pleiad, daughter of Atlas and Pleione.

Aldabella (àl.dạ.bel′ạ). In Henry Hart Milman's play *Fazio*, a handsome, shameless woman who beguiles Fazio when he becomes rich, and after his execution is condemned to imprisonment in a nunnery for life through the interposition of Bianca, the wife of Fazio.

Aldebaran (al.deb′ạ.rạn). The standard first-magnitude orange star α Tauri, in the northern constellation Taurus ("the Bull"), in the eye of the animal; most conspicuous member of the group known as the Hyades. Its diameter is 50 times that of the sun. One of the stars with which Halley discovered the proper motion of stars (1718); known to Hesiod and Homer. It is also often called Palilicium.

Alderney (ôl′dėr.ni). [French, **Aurigny;** ancient names, **Aurinia, Riduna.**] One of the Channel Islands, situated ab. 23 mi. NE of Guernsey and ab. 7 mi. W of the Cap de la Hague, France: noted for its breed of cattle. The island, a British possession, is politically a dependency of the bailiwick of Guernsey, but has its own government, vested in a judge, 6 jurats, and 12 representatives. Both English and Norman-French are spoken, the latter being the official language. Capital, St. Anne; length, ab. 4 mi.; greatest width, ab. 1 mi.; area, ab. 3 sq. mi.

Aldersgate (ôl′dėrz.gāt). A gate in old London wall, which stood in the reëntering angle of the old city between Newgate and Cripplegate and at the junction of Aldersgate Street and St. Martin's Lane. It is called Ealdred's gate in the laws of Ethelred.

Aldfrith (äld′frith). [Also: **Eahfrith, Ealdfrith.**] d. 705. King of the Northumbrians, an illegitimate son of Oswiu, and brother of Ecgfrith, whom he succeeded in 685.

Aldgate (ôld′gāt). A gate in the old London wall, situated near the junction of Leadenhall Street, Houndsditch, Whitehall, and the Minories. It must have been one of the seven double gates mentioned by Fitz Stephens (who died 1191), not one of the Roman gates. The great road to Essex by which provisions were brought to the Roman city crossed the Lea at Old-ford and entered the city by way of Eormine (Ermine) Street, not at Aldgate but at Bishopsgate. Aldgate may have been opened in the reign of King Eadgar, or that of Edward the Confessor, but probably dates from the first years of Henry I, at which time Bow Bridge across the Lea at Stratford is supposed to have been built by his queen, Matilda.

Aldhelm (ôld′helm). [Also, **Ealdhelm.**] b. c640; d. at Doulting, England, 709. An English scholar and cleric; abbot of Malmesbury (675–709) and first bishop of Sherborne (705–709). A student of the classics, he is believed to have been the first Englishman to write Latin verse. He was also the author of *Epistola ad Acircium*, a treatise on Latin prosody which included 101 riddles in Latin hexameters; *De laude virginitatis sive virginitate sanctorum* (c705), a commemorative treatise on the saints; and of Old English poems and songs, but these very early examples of English literature have not survived (presumably because Aldhelm considered them trivial items, undeserving of notice compared to his works in Latin). Aldhelm was later canonized, his feast falling on May 25.

Aldiborontephoscophornio (al″di.bǭ.ron″tẹ.fos″kǭ.fôr′ni.ō). A character in Henry Carey's burlesque

Chrononhotonthologos. It was given as a nickname to James Ballantyne the printer, on account of the solemn pomposity of his manner, by Sir Walter Scott.

Aldine Press (ôl′dĕn, al′dīn). The press established (c1490) at Venice by Aldus Manutius.

Aldingar (al′ding.gär). The prior of St. Cuthbert's Abbey in Sir Walter Scott's poem *Harold the Dauntless.*

Aldingar (ôl′ding.gär), **Sir.** See **Sir Aldingar.**

Aldington (ôl′ding.ton), **Richard.** b. in Hampshire, England, 1892—. An English poet and novelist; leader of the Imagist school of English verse writing. He was for a short time in 1919 a staff member of the London *Times* literary supplement after service (1916–18) in World War I. He lived until the outbreak of World War II in Switzerland, Italy, France, and elsewhere, becoming in 1939 a resident of the U.S. He was married (1913–37) to the American poet Hilda Doolittle ("H.D."), and since 1937 has been married to Netta McCulloch. Author of *Images Old and New* (1915), *War and Love* (1918), *Images of Desire* (1919), *A Fool i' the Forest* (1925), *Collected Poems* (1928), and many other volumes of verse; his novels include *Death of a Hero* (1929), *The Colonel's Daughter* (1931), *All Men Are Enemies* (1933), *Very Heaven* (1937), *Rejected Guest* (1939), and others. He has also written the autobiographical *Life for Life's Sake* (1941), as well as a play, several short stories, and a number of translations from Greek, Latin, Italian, and French.

Aldo (al′dō), **Father.** In John Dryden's play *Limberham, or the Kind Keeper,* an abandoned but kind-hearted old debauchee.

Aldrovand (al′drō̩.vand), **Father.** A Dominican friar, the warlike chaplain of Eveline Berenger in Sir Walter Scott's novel *The Betrothed.*

Aldus Manutius (ôl′dus, al′-; ma̩.nū′shi.us, -shus). See **Manutius, Aldus.**

Aldwych (ôld′wich). A street in W London, in Westminster metropolitan borough. It is a crescent (100 ft. wide) extending ab. ¼ mi. from its intersection with the Strand at St. Clement's to intersect again with the Strand at the S end of Catherine Street. The Gaiety Theatre, Bush House, and Australia House are on Aldwych.

Alecto (a̩.lek′tō). In Greek mythology, one of the Furies.

Alectryon (a̩.lek′tri.o̩n). In Greek mythology, a youth responsible to Ares for keeping watch while the god made clandestine visits to Aphrodite. One time he fell asleep while on guard, and Helios discovered the affair and reported it to Hephaestus (Aphrodite's husband). Ares punished Alectryon by changing him into a cock (henceforth to crow and give warning of the day's beginning).

Alençon (a̩.len′so̩n), **Duke of.** In Shakespeare's *Henry V,* a French noble, the father of the Duke of Alençon in *1 Henry VI,* who is mentioned as having been killed in battle by Henry. Henry gives Williams's glove to Fluellen, saying it is Alençon's, in order to be amused by the two men challenging and attacking each other.

Alençon, Duke of. In Shakespeare's *1 Henry VI,* a French nobleman who speaks contemptuously of

Englishmen's habits, but admires their bravery in battle; he also praises Joan of Arc.

Alexander (al.eg.zan′dėr). In Greek legend, another name for Paris.

Alexander. A middle English prose romance (1430–40) in the Thornton manuscript.

Alexander. In Shakespeare's *Troilus and Cressida,* a servant of Cressida.

Alexander III. [Original name, **Orlando** (or **Rolando Ranuci**) **Bandinelli.**] b. at Siena, Italy; d. 1181. Pope from 1159 to 1181, successor of Adrian IV. A champion of ecclesiastical independence, he carried out the policy of Hildebrand in opposition to Frederick Barbarossa (whom he excommunicated) and Henry II of England. Three antipopes, Victor IV, Pascal III, and Calixtus III (elected 1159, 1164, and 1168, respectively) were confirmed by Frederick, and disputed the authority of Alexander, who was compelled to take refuge (1162–65) in France and again (1167) at Venice and elsewhere. His struggle with Henry II, who had murdered (1173) Thomas à Becket, most outspoken English supporter of papal claims of supremacy, ended in the penance (1174) of the king and the canonization of Thomas. His contest with the emperor ended in decisive defeat of the latter at the battle of Legnano (1176), reconciliation (1177) at Venice, and the abdication (1178) of antipope Calixtus III. At the third Lateran Council (1179), he established the law of papal succession.

Alexander, Mrs. Pseudonym of **Hector, Annie.**

Alexander, Romance of. One of the most famous romances of the Middle Ages. Callisthenes, a companion of Alexander the Great, wrote an account of the Asiatic expedition of Alexander, but it is lost. His name, however, is attached to a fabulous account which is supposed to have been written in Alexandria in the early part of the 3rd century. There are three Latin translations of this pseudo-Callisthenes: one by Julius Valerius, before 340; the *Itinerarium Alexandri;* and the *Historia de preliis,* by Archpresbyter Leo. Later translations or versions are based on these. It was translated into Syriac and Armenian in the 5th century. The Persians and Arabs made use of the myth, and in the 11th century Simeon Seth, keeper of the imperial wardrobe at the Byzantine court, translated it back from the Persian into the Greek. In the 11th century it entered into French literature as a troubadour poem; the earliest extant form of this is in fragments by Aubry or Alberic of Besançon. Lamprecht, a priest, translated the French into German, and called it the *Alexanderlied,* in the 12th century. In England it was celebrated as *King Alisaunder,* an 8,000-line poem written c1300. The *Alexandreis* of the Austrian Siegfried was written c1350. In the 15th century Alexander again appeared as the hero of prose romances in Germany. Alexander myths are to be found in many other of the old French poems, and he becomes a knightly conqueror surrounded by 12 paladins. The poems do not properly form a cycle, as they are quite independent of one another.

Alexander, The Buik of. A Scottish poem written c1438. The version published in Scotland in 1580 is the only one now extant. The work is based on two

---

French poems, their translation being attributed by some scholars to the author of *The Bruce*.

Alexander, Sir William. [Title, Earl of **Stirling**.] b. c1567; d. at London, Sept. 12, 1640. A Scottish poet and statesman, tutor to Prince Henry and adherent of King James I of England. He is the author of four tragedies, *Darius*, published in 1603, *Croesus*, published in 1604, *The Alexandrean Tragedy*, published in 1607, and *Julius Caesar*, published in 1607, and called collectively *Monarchicke Tragedies*; a poem to Prince Henry, *Paraenesis to the Prince* (1604); an epic poem, *Doomesday* (first part, 1614); and other works, including a number of sonnets published as *Aurora* in 1604. He received on Sept. 21, 1621, the grant of New Scotland (Nova Scotia and New Brunswick), which was transferred to De la Tour in 1630. In 1626 he was appointed secretary of state for Scotland.

Alexander A and Alexander B. Names given by scholars to two fragments of Middle English alliterative verse, written in the middle of the 14th century. The first fragment, of about 450 lines, deals with the conquests of Philip of Macedon and is based on the Latin of Orosius. The second fragment is composed of an exchange of letters between Alexander and Dindimus discussing the Brahmin way of life.

Alexander and Campaspe (kam.pas'pē). A prose comedy by John Lyly, printed in 1584, and reprinted as *Campaspe* in that year and in 1591. The theme of the comedy is the renunciation of Alexander the Great, who resigns his claim to the Theban captive when he discovers that she loves Apelles.

Alexander Court (kōrt). See **Court, Alexander**.

Alexander Iden (ĭ'den). See **Iden, Alexander**.

Alexander Manette (ma.net'), **Doctor**. See **Manette, Doctor Alexander**.

Alexander of Hales (hālz). [Also: **Alexander Halensis**; called **Doctor Irrefragabilis**.] b. at Hales, Gloucestershire, England, c1175; d. 1245. An English scholastic philosopher and theologian. He lectured (c1220) at Paris, and in 1222 joined the Franciscan order. He wrote *Summae Universae Theologiae* (printed 1475), the first amalgamation of Augustinian Christian doctrine with the Aristotelian system and Arabian thought; this work was much used by Thomas Aquinas and others.

Alexander's Feast. [Also, **Ode for Saint Cecilia's Day**.] An Ode by John Dryden, written in 1697, in honor of Saint Cecilia's Day. It is sometimes confused with the *Song for Saint Cecilia's Day*, written ten years earlier.

Alexander the Great. [Also, **Alexander III** (of Macedonia)]. b. at Pella, Macedonia, 356 B.C.; d. at Babylon, June 13, 323 B.C. A Macedonian ruler, conqueror of the civilized world. Legend has it that he inherited his military ability from his father, Philip II of Macedonia, a rough mountain king of genius, while from Olympias, the Epirote princess who was his mother, came his mysticism and impetuousness. He was educated by Aristotle. He was a handsome man, whose temper was his greatest enemy; contrary to legend, he rarely drank. With Philip, he defeated (338) the armies of Greek city-

states at Chaeronea. In 336 Philip was murdered, and Alexander became king of Macedonia and leader of the Greeks in war against the predatory Persian empire. Two years were spent pacifying tribes to his rear; rebellious Thebes was destroyed. His highly professional army, which was devoted to him, consisted of 30,000 heavy- and light-armed infantry and 5,000 cavalry, with a superior siege train, commissary, and intelligence service. In 334 he crossed to Asia, defeated the Persians at the Granicus River and the following year at Issus. Taking Tyre en route, he continued (332) to Egypt, where he built Alexandria, the first of 70 communities founded by him which became powerful forces for the Hellenization of the non-Greek world. With the eastern Mediterranean coasts now in his possession, he turned inland and at Gaugamela (at the battle sometimes called the Battle of Arbela) overwhelmed (331) the armies of Darius III. Alexander's march next carried him across Iran to India (326). When his men refused to follow him farther, he returned by way of the Indus Valley and Baluchistan to Babylon. Here, not yet 33 years of age, he died from fatigue and disease. Napoleon called him the greatest general in history. Alexander strongly believed in the fusion of races; both of his wives, Roxane and Barsine, were eastern princesses. His life altered the course of history, for he created a new world society based on a common Greek culture. He became after his death a legendary figure to medieval Europe and to the Orient of all periods.

Alexandra (al.eg.zan'dra). [Full prename, **Alexandra Caroline Marie Charlotte Louisa Julia**.] b. at Copenhagen, Dec. 1, 1844; d. 1925. Queen of England; daughter of Christian IX of Denmark and wife of Edward VII, king of England, whom she married on March 10, 1863. Her second son subsequently became King George V of England. "Alexandra Day" was instituted (1913) in her honor.

Alexandra. See also **Cassandra**.

Alexandrian Library (al.eg.zan'dri.an). A library in Alexandria, founded by Ptolemy I of Egypt and made into an important and valuable collection by his son Ptolemy II. At one time it was said to have contained 700,000 volumes. Part of the library was burnt when Julius Caesar laid siege to Alexandria. Marcus Antonius presented a collection of manuscripts through Cleopatra and the library flourished again until 641 A.D. when Alexandria was taken by the Moslems, under the caliph Omar. The Alexandrian Library was probably the largest collection of manuscripts before printing.

Alexandrine (al.eg.zan'drin, -drēn). In prosody, a line consisting of six iambic feet. It is the line used in French heroic verse, and is also the last line of the typical Spenserian stanza. It is so called because of the 12th- and 13th-century French poems dealing with the life of Alexander the Great that were written in this form. French Alexandrines are written in couplets, alternately acatalectic with masculine rhymes and hypercatalectic with feminine rhymes. French tragedies are generally composed in Alexandrines. The cesura occurs at the end of the third foot. The second line of the following extract is an example:

---

d, d or j; s̩, s or sh; t̩, t or ch; z̩, z or zh; o, F. cloche; ü, F. menu; c̀h, Sc. loch; ǹ, F. bonbon.

A needless Alexandrine ends the song,
That, like a wounded snake, drags its
    slow length along.
       (Pope, *Essay on Criticism.*)

Alexas (a.lek′sas). In Shakespeare's *Antony and Cleopatra*, an attendant of Cleopatra who, as Enobarbus relates, deserts Antony, only to be hanged by Octavius.

Aleyn (a.lān′, al′in). One of the Cambridge students (clerks of Cantebregge) in Chaucer's *Reeve's Tale.*

Aleyn (al′in), **Charles.** d. 1640. A minor English poet, author of *The Battailes of Crescey and Poictiers* (1631).

Alfheim (älf′hīm). In Old Norse mythology, the abode of the light elves. It was conceived to be near the sacred well of the Norns, at the foot of the ash Yggdrasil.

Alford (ôl′fọrd), **Henry.** b. at London, 1810; d. at Canterbury, England, 1871. An English Biblical scholar. Graduate (1832) and fellow (1834) of Trinity College, Cambridge; dean of Canterbury (1857–71). He was the first editor (1866–70) of the *Contemporary Review.* His publications include an important critical edition of the Greek Testament (1849–61), *A Plea for the Queen's English* (1866), *New Testament for English Readers* (1867), poems, hymns, and others.

Alfred (al′frẹd). [Also: **Ælfred;** called **Alfred the Great.**] b. at Wantage, in Berkshire, England, 849; d. Oct. 28, 899. A king of England (871–899). He encouraged and, to a considerable extent, himself participated in the creation of the first considerable body of English scholarly literature intended explicitly for English readers. Having himself been partly reared abroad (he had been to Rome, and had spent time at the French court), he reached young manhood with a most unusual (for his time and position in life) interest in scholarly and literary matters, but the recurring threat of Danish conquest made it impossible for him to give them any great attention until c880. He fought against the Danes in the defensive campaign of 871, serving under his brother Ethelred at Ashdown, Basing, and Merton, and commanded as king at Wilton. In 878 he withdrew before the Danes to Athelney, but later obtained a decisive victory over them at Ethandun. By the treaty of Wedmore, which followed, the Danish Guthrum consented to receive baptism and to retire north of Watling Street. Alfred fortified London in 886, and carried on a defensive war (892–896) with the Danes, which ended in the withdrawal of the invaders, and in which, by the aid of ships of improved model, the English for the first time gained a decisive naval advantage over the Vikings. His success against the Danes was due largely to his reform of the national *fyrd* or militia, by which half the force of each shire was always ready for military service. His administration was also marked by judicial and educational reforms. He compiled a code of laws, rebuilt the schools and monasteries, and invited scholars to his court. *Literary and Scholarly Significance.* A complete and authoritative bibliography of the works written or translated by Alfred himself has never been and probably never will be produced. The five most important works with which his name has been linked are the translations of the *Consolations*

of Philosophy by Boethius, the *Epitome of Universal History* by Paulus Orosius, the *Pastoral Rule* of Pope Gregory the Great (which we know Alfred translated himself, from his own statement in the preface), Bede's *Ecclesiastical History*, and a work based on the *Soliloquies* of Saint Augustine. There is reason to believe that his participation in the translation of the first two of these was very considerable; by his own words, he was responsible for the third; but it is not clear to what extent he may have contributed personally to the translation into the vernacular of the last two. In addition to this, however, he encouraged and guided the initial work on the *Anglo-Saxon Chronicle*, and some authorities have felt that they could detect evidence of his actual participation in certain parts of this very extensive work. By any standard, and viewed with whatever degree of caution, his contributions as a writer and scholar entitle him to a high place in the history of English letters; when we bear in mind that this was only one aspect of a life in which military and political activities could never be ignored for long, and when we recall that the mere ability to read and write was lacking in more than a few rulers of the day, we cannot but concede the justice of the name given to him by posterity: "Alfred the Great." But in recognizing his greatness, posterity also made him the central figure of many tales and legends without historical foundation, and these tales have entered in a very real sense into the great body of English literature. Perhaps the best known of these is the famous story which has Alfred sitting by the fire in a peasant hut, supposedly watching the baking of oatmeal cakes on the hearth, but actually lost in thought about weightier matters; the cakes burn, and Alfred, the greatest Englishman of the age, meekly accepts the indignant reproval of the wife of the peasant who is sheltering him. Apocryphal though such tales as this may be, they are nonetheless one part of the whole story of Alfred's place in English literature.

Alfred. A masque (1740) by James Thomson, containing the well-known "Rule Britannia."

Alfred, Proverbs of. See **Proverbs of Alfred.**

Alfred Jingle (jing′gl). See **Jingle, Alfred.**

Alfred Lammle (lam′l). See **Lammle, Alfred.**

Alfred Polly (pol′i). See **Polly, Alfred.**

Alfred the Great. A historical play by J. Sheridan Knowles, produced in 1831.

Alftruda (alf′trö′′da). In Charles Kingsley's *Hereward the Wake*, the second wife of Hereward.

Algarsife (al′gär.sīf). In Chaucer's *Squire's Tale*, a son of King Cambuscan.

Algernon Percy Deuceace (al′jẹr.nọn pẹr′si dūs′äs), **The Honourable.** See **Deuceace, The Honourable Algernon Percy.**

Algrind (al′grind). An anagram of Edmund Grindal, archbishop of Canterbury, used in Spenser's *Shepherd's Calendar.*

Alhambra (al.ham′bra; Spanish, ä.läm′brä). A Moslem fortress and palace, with additional buildings, at Granada, Spain, built chiefly (1248–1354) by the king Mohammed Ibn Al Ahmar and his successors; the outstanding example of Moslem architecture

---

fat, fāte, fär, àsk, fāre; net, mē, hėr; pin, pīne; not, nōte, mōve, nôr; up, lūte, pùll; ᴛʜ, then;

and decoration in Spain. Damaged after the expulsion (1492) of the Moslems from Spain and by the emperor Charles V (Charles I of Spain), who replaced part of the old structure with a Renaissance palace in the 16th century, it was extensively restored in the 19th century. Standing on a plateau about 35 acres in area and surrounded by heavy brick walls, the buildings are composed mainly of small rooms laid out around open courtyards which contain the fountains and rich gardens characteristic of Moslem landscape architecture. Most noted of these is the Court of Lions, in which a covered passage, or arcade, of tall arches on 124 paired or grouped white marble columns surrounds a paved patio with the Fountain of Lions in the center. The interior and exterior decoration, in the style known as Arabesque, consists of infinitely varied interwoven patterns of foliage-like forms, Arabic script in gold on blue background, and geometric tracery, done in majolica tiles, carved wood, pressed plaster and stucco, and pierced stone heightened with brilliant colors; ceilings and doorways present the intricate repetition of geometrical forms resulting in what is known as "honeycomb" and "stalactite" vaulting.

Ali Baba (ä′lē bä′bä). A character in *The Arabian Nights' Entertainments*, in the story "Ali Baba and the Forty Thieves." He is a poor woodcutter who, concealed in a tree, sees a band of robbers enter a secret cavern, and overhears the magic words "open sesame," which open its door. After the departure of the thieves he repeats the spell and the door opens, disclosing a room full of treasures with which he loads his donkeys and returns home. His brother Cassim Baba, who discovers his secret, enters the cave alone, forgets the word "sesame," and is found, killed, and dismembered by the robbers. The thieves, discovering that Ali Baba knows their secret, resolve to kill him, but are outwitted by Morgiana, Ali Baba's slave.

Alice (al′is). The wife of Bath in Chaucer's tale of that name. Her "gossib," to whom she alludes, has the same name.

Alice. In Shakespeare's *Henry V*, a lady in attendance on Princess Katherine. She gives the Princess a lesson in English (III.iv).

Alice. The principal female character in *The Tragedy of Mr. Arden of Feversham*, a play of unknown authorship which was first published in 1592. She murders her husband, Mr. Arden.

Alice. The little girl who dreams the fantastic adventures in *Alice's Adventures in Wonderland* and *Through the Looking-Glass* by Charles Lutwidge Dodgson (Lewis Carroll). In real life, "Alice" was Alice Liddell, daughter of the classical scholar Henry George Liddell.

Alice Brand (brand). A ballad in Canto Four of Scott's *Lady of the Lake*. It tells how Alice Brand removed the curse from Urgen, the dwarf, and revealed him to be actually her brother, Ethert Brand.

Alice Bridgenorth (brij′nôrth″). See **Bridgenorth, Alice.**

Alice-for-Short. A novel (1907) by William De Morgan, the story of a child rescued from the slums.

Alice Frankford (frangk′fọrd). See **Frankford, Alice.**

Alice in Wonderland. See **Alice's Adventures in Wonderland.**

Alice Lee (lē). See **Lee, Alice.**

Alice, or The Mysteries. A novel by Edward Bulwer-Lytton, published in 1838 as a sequel to *Ernest Maltravers*. Ernest Maltravers, a man of wealth and position, is saved from robbery and murder by Alice Darvil, daughter of a cut-throat. Ernest is touched by the helplessness and beauty of the uneducated girl, and takes her under his protection. He finally acknowledges his love for her and Alice remains faithful to him in spite of the fact that circumstances separate them for many years. Finally Ernest and Alice are reunited and married, after the murder of Ernest's unscrupulous enemy, Lumley Ferrers.

Alice's Adventures in Wonderland. A story for children by Charles Lutwidge Dodgson (writing under the pseudonym of Lewis Carroll), published in 1865. The heroine, Alice, falls asleep while her sister is reading to her, and dreams that a White Rabbit passes her, looking at his watch with great concern. As he goes rushing along, she follows him down a large rabbit hole, but she loses sight of him in a long passageway. She comes to a door too small for her to pass through, but magic potions that she drinks make her change size, becoming either very small (so that she may pass through the door) or extremely large (so that she fills the entire passage). She finally manages to achieve a pleasant and comfortable size, and wanders along until she meets a philosophical caterpillar, with whom she enters into conversation. Alice then finds the house of the Duchess, where babies turn into pigs and the Cheshire Cat disappears, but leaves his grin behind him. She is further amazed and confused at a tea-party given by the March Hare, the Mad Hatter, and the Dormouse, each character equally ridiculous. The Duchess takes her to the castle of the King and Queen of Hearts, where she enters into a game of croquet in which the mallets are live flamingoes and the balls are hedgehogs. A trial ensues when the Queen's tarts are stolen, and the Queen orders that Alice's head be cut off when she accidentally upsets the jury box. Alice wakes up just as a deck of cards begins to fly at her. The book has been variously interpreted by 20th-century critics as a straightforward satire on some aspects of Victorian England or as a Freudian allegory. The story was followed (1871) by a continuation, *Through the Looking-Glass*.

Alicia (a.lish′ạ). One of the principal female characters in Nicholas Rowe's tragedy *Jane Shore*, a woman of strong passions who by her jealousy ruins her former friend Jane Shore. The name was given by Lillo in his *Arden of Feversham* to the Alice of the earlier (and anonymous) *The Tragedy of Mr. Arden of Feversham*.

Alicia Kavanagh (kav′ạ.nä, -nô, -nạ). See **Kavanagh, Alicia.**

Aliena (ā.li.ē′nạ). In Shakespeare's *As You Like It*, the name assumed by Celia when, disguised as a shepherdess, she follows Rosalind.

Alifánfaron (ä.lē.fän′fä.rōn). The emperor of the Island of Trapoban, mentioned by Cervantes' *Don Quixote*. When he sees two flocks of sheep coming

---

ḍ, d or j; ṣ, s or sh; ṭ, t or ch; ẓ, z or zh; o, F. cloche; ü, F. menu; ċh, Sc. loch; ṅ, F. bonbon.

toward him Don Quixote says of one of them: "Know, friend Sancho, that yonder army before us is commanded by the Emperor Alifánfaron, sovereign of the Island of Trapoban. . . ."

Alígero Clavileño (ä.lē′gä.rō klä.ᴮē.lä′nyō), **El**. See **Clavileño, El Alígero.**

Alinda (ạ.lin′dạ). A character in Lodge's *Rosalynde*, the source of Shakespeare's *As You Like It*. She corresponds to Celia.

Alinda. The name assumed by young Archas when disguised as a woman, in John Fletcher's *Loyal Subject*.

Alinda. The daughter of Alphonso in John Fletcher's *Pilgrim*.

Alisaunder (al.i.sôn′dėr), **King.** See **King Alisaunder.**

Alison (al′i.sọn). See under **Miller's Tale, The.**

Alison, Sir Archibald. b. at Kenley, Shropshire, England, Dec. 29, 1792; d. at Glasgow, May 23, 1867. A British historian.

Alison Wilson (wil′sọn), **Mrs.** See **Wilson, Mrs. Alison.**

Alithea (al.i.thē′ạ). One of the principal characters in William Wycherley's comedy *The Country Wife*, a woman of the world, brilliant and cool.

Alla (al′ạ), **King.** The king in "The Man of Law's Tale," one of Chaucer's *Canterbury Tales*, who marries Constance, the heroine of the tale.

Allan-a-Dale (al″ạn.ạ.dāl′). See **Allen-a-Dale.**

Allan Quatermain (al′ạn kwä′tėr.mạn). A novel (1887) by Henry Rider Haggard.

Allan Woodcourt (al′ạn wûd′kôrt). See **Woodcourt, Allan.**

All Day I Hear. A short poem by James Joyce, included in his volume of verse, *Chamber Music* (1907).

allegory (al′ē.gọ.ri). A narrative or description, in verse or prose, usually didactic, in which the literal sense stands for one or more additional meanings which are parallel, but distinct. The two most famous examples in English literature are probably Spenser's *The Faerie Queene* and Bunyan's *Pilgrim's Progress*. Taken literally, the former is a chivalric romance; it does, however, embody moral, religious, social, and political meanings in the accounts of the adventures of the knights serving the Faerie Queene, who represents both glory and Queen Elizabeth. *Pilgrim's Progress*, a more personal allegory with fewer levels of meaning, describes the efforts of a Christian man to achieve a godly life and to overcome inner obstacles to his faith which are outwardly symbolized by such places as the Slough of Despond and the Castle of Despair.

Allegra (ạ.lä′grạ). The daughter of Byron and Claire Clairmont, born in Switzerland in 1817, who died at the age of five in a convent near Ravenna.

Allegro (ä.lā′grō), **L'.** See **L'Allegro.**

Allemaine (al.ẹ.mān′). An early English name of Germany.

Allen (al′ẹn), **Arabella.** In Charles Dickens's *Pickwick Papers*, a young lady, afterward Mrs. Nathaniel Winkle.

Allen, Benjamin. In Charles Dickens's *Pickwick Papers*, "a coarse, stout, thick-set" young surgeon,

"with black hair cut rather short and a white face cut rather long."

Allen, Grant. [Full name, **Charles Grant Blairfindie Allen**; pseudonyms: **Cecil Power** and **J. Arbuthnot Wilson.**] b. at Kingston, Ontario, Canada, Feb. 24, 1848; d. at Hindhead, Surrey, England, Oct. 25, 1899. An English novelist, poet, essayist, scientist, and philosopher. Author of *Strange Stories* and *Philistia* (both 1884), *The Devil's Die* (1888), *The Woman Who Did* (1895; his best-known work and a sensation in its day because of its then startlingly frank discussion of freedom in sex), *The British Barbarians* (1896), *An African Millionaire* (1897), and other novels; of *The Lower Slopes* (1894), poetry; *Falling in Love* (1889) and *Postprandial Philosophy* (1894), collected essays; and of scientific and philosophical works including *Physiological Aesthetics* (1877; dedicated to Herbert Spencer), *Color Sense* (1879), *Vignettes from Nature, An Evolutionist at Large,* and *Anglo-Saxon Britain* (all 1881), *Colors of Flowers* (1882), *Colin Clout's Calendar: The Record of a Summer* and *Flowers and Their Pedigrees* (both 1883; the former highly praised by Huxley and Darwin), *Force and Energy* (1888), and *Evolution of the Idea of God* (1897).

Allen, Ralph. b. 1694; d. at Bath, England, June 20, 1764. An English philanthropist, known chiefly as a friend of Fielding, Pope, and the elder Pitt. He acquired a fortune by devising (1720) a postal system for England and Wales. He is said to have been the original of Squire Allworthy in Fielding's *Tom Jones.*

Allen-a-Dale (al″ẹn.ạ.dāl′). [Also, **Allan-a-Dale.**] In the Robin Hood tales, a brave, gaily dressed, and musical youth whom Robin Hood assisted to elope with his bride who was to be married against her will to an old knight. He is usually introduced as "chaunting a round-de-lay." He appears as Robin Hood's minstrel in Scott's *Ivanhoe.*

Alleyn (al′in), **Edward.** [Also: **Alleyne;** called **Ned Allen.**] b. at London, Sept. 1, 1566; d. Nov. 25, 1626. An English actor; son-in-law of Philip Henslowe and later, by a second marriage, of John Donne. He was the founder (1613) and director (1619–26) of Dulwich College (the College of God's Gift), at London. Rated by Jonson, Nash, and others as the foremost actor, especially of tragedy, of his time, he was a member of the Earl of Worcester's Men (1586 *et seq.*), head of the Lord Admiral's (Earl of Nottingham's) Men (c1592), and owner-manager, with Henslowe, of various London theaters including the Rose and the Fortune (built in 1600), and of a bearbaiting house at Paris Garden (1594–1626). He played leads in Marlowe's *Jew of Malta, Tamburlaine,* and *Doctor Faustus,* his acting mannerisms being parodied by Shakespeare in the character of Pistol in *2 Henry IV.* His last known appearance was at a reception address to James I (c1604).

Alleyn, Ellen. Pseudonym of **Rossetti, Christina Georgina.**

All Fools' Day. See **April Fools' Day.**

All Fools, or All Fools but the Fool. A dramatic work by George Chapman, printed in 1605. It was first called *The World on Wheels*, and registered in 1599. It is considered by some to be the best

---

fat, fāte, fär, àsk, fâre; net, mē, hėr; pin, pīne; not, nōte, möve, nôr; up, lūte, pùll; ᴛʜ, then:

of his comedies. Valerio has married a poor gentle-woman and his friend, Fortunio, is in love with Valerio's sister. Fortunio's younger brother, Rinaldo, disillusioned by an unhappy love affair, tricks Valerio's father, Gostanzo, into the belief that Fortunio is the one who has married. He persuades Gostanzo to take the two into his house and thus starts a series of misunderstandings which end when all have been made fools. There is also a sub-plot concerning a young man's jealousy of his young wife. This play is in the vein of Roman comedy (it is based on works by Terence) and the characters are like those found in the Roman comedy: the opinionated and foolish fathers, the gay sons, and the mischievous servant (in this case, the younger brother, Rinaldo).

All For Love, or A Sinner Well Saved. A poem (1829) by Robert Southey, based on the life of Saint Basil. It tells of a man, Eleëmon, who sells his soul to Satan for love, but when the bargain is revealed, Eleëmon, repentant, goes to Saint Basil. The Saint orders him to do penance and defends him against Satan when the latter comes to claim his soul.

All for Love, or the World Well Lost. A heroic tragedy by John Dryden, produced in 1677. It is based largely upon Shakespeare's *Antony and Cleopatra*, and a number of lines or passages were taken from others of Shakespeare's plays, including *Hamlet, Othello,* and *As You Like It.* The style, however, is plainly Dryden's and the structure adheres carefully to the classical unities. The action follows the dictum of Rymer and the French dramatists Corneille and Racine that true tragedy reflects a conflict of love and honor. Therefore, Antony must choose between the illicit passion offered by Cleopatra and the honorable love of Octavia. It is considered by some critics as one of the best Restoration tragedies, although the action is often impeded by long arguments in blank verse over the merits of love or honor. In the Preface the playwright answered some of the critics of heroic drama and noted that he himself preferred the scene in Act I between Ventidius and Antony to anything he had written of this kind.

All-Hallows Day (ôl''hal'ōz). See **All Saints Day.**

Allingham (al'ing.ạm), **Margery.** b. at London, 1904—. An English writer of detective stories. Her best-known character is the mild Albert Campion.

Allingham, William. b. at Ballyshannon, Ireland, 1824; d. at London, 1889. An Irish poet, editor (1874–79) of *Fraser's Magazine.* He was a friend of Dante Gabriel Rossetti (who illustrated some of his books), Tennyson, Thomas Carlyle, and Leigh Hunt.

All Is True. A play, perhaps by Shakespeare, important as an earlier form of *Henry VIII.* The manuscript was destroyed (1613) when the Globe theater burned down.

alliteration (a.lit.ẹ.rā'shọn). The repetition of initial letters or sounds within a line of verse. The repetition of the same letter or sound at the beginning of two or more words in close or immediate succession; the recurrence of the same initial sound in the first accented syllables of words; initial rime: as, *many men, many minds.* It was the predominant

form of versification in Old English poetry. During the middle of the 14th century it was revived in English literature in such poems as *Sir Gawayne and The Green Knight.* In modern poetry it has been used to some extent by Swinburne, and more recently by W. H. Auden.

All Men Are Enemies. A satirical novel, inspired by his experiences in World War I, by Richard Aldington, published in 1933.

Allott (al'ọt), **Robert.** [Also, **Allot.**] fl. 1600. An English anthologist and editor. He is the probable compiler of *England's Parnassus* (1600), which contains extracts from the works of Spenser, Shakespeare, Michael Drayton, George Chapman, and numerous other writers.

All Our Yesterdays. A novel by H. M. Tomlinson, published in 1930, dealing with World War I.

Alloway Kirk (al'ọ.wä). A ruined church in Ayr, Scotland, near the river Doon. Burns rendered it famous in *Tam o' Shanter.*

All Religions Are One. A critical work (c1789) by William Blake. It was printed in booklet form as an experiment in "illuminated printing" (which means that the text as well as the illustrations were engraved, and that each copy was then colored by hand).

All Saints Day. [Former name, **All-Hallows Day.**] A Christian feast day, marked by church services in memory of all the saints on the various religious calendars. Originally, the feast was celebrated on May 1, but since 834 A.D. the Western world has observed it on November 1.

All's Lost by Lust. A play by William Rowley, a leading English comic actor of his day. Resembling in many ways what is now called melodrama, it was first performed in 1633.

All Souls. A poem (c1911) by Katharine Tynan Hinkson.

All Souls College. A college of Oxford University, England, founded in 1437 by Archbishop Henry Chichele, to provide masses for the souls of the departed, especially those killed in the Hundred Years' War. The first quadrangle, with its fine gate, remains substantially as when first built; the chapel possesses beautiful fan tracery and reredos. The second quadrangle, with its two towers, was built in 1720. The statutes of the college were formally issued on April 2, 1443.

All Souls' Day. A Roman Catholic holy day for the liturgical commemoration of the souls of the faithful dead still in Purgatory. It falls on November 2. The observance is believed to date from the 9th century, when it was introduced at the monasteries of Cluny.

All's Well That Ends Well. A comedy by Shakespeare, played as early as c1596. Portions of this play were written not later than 1593, but the play as we have it was probably written in large part in the period 1602–04. It was first printed in the folio of 1623. The plot is from "Giletta of Narbonne" in Painter's *Palace of Pleasure*; Painter took it in 1566 from the *Decameron* of Boccaccio. The story is followed closely, but the countess, the clown, Lafeu, and Parolles are Shakespeare's own.

The Story. Helena, the daughter of a famous

ḍ, d or j; ṣ, s or sh; ṭ, t or ch; ẓ, z or zh; o, F. cloche; ü, F. menu; ċh, Sc. loch; ṅ, F. bonbon.

physician, Gerard de Narbon, cures the King of France of a supposedly incurable disease, and as a reward asks that Bertram, the young Count of Rossillion, marry her. This Bertram does reluctantly, and leaves immediately for the wars at the suggestion of the coward and braggart Parolles, one of Shakespeare's most amusing comic characters. Bertram sends a message to Helena that "When thou canst get the ring upon my finger which never shall come off, and show me a child begotten of thy body that I am father to, then call me husband." Passing through Florence on a pilgrimage, Helena discovers that Bertram is engaged in dalliance with Diana, the daughter of her hostess. She arranges to have Bertram informed that she (Helena) is dead, and to replace Diana in bed. Bertram gets her with child and she exchanges her ring (that the King had given her) for Bertram's. When Bertram returns home, the King notices the ring, and accuses Bertram of killing Helena. Helena arrives in time to explain and to demand that Bertram accept her as his wife now that the conditions in his letter have been met.

All-the-Talents Administration. A name given ironically to the English ministry of 1806–07. Among the leading members were William Wyndham Grenville (prime minister), Charles James Fox (foreign secretary), Thomas Erskine (1st Baron Erskine of Restormel), William Wentworth Fitzwilliam (2nd Earl Fitzwilliam), Henry Addington (1st Viscount Sidmouth), and Edmund Law (1st Baron Ellenborough).

All the Year Round. A periodical established and conducted by Charles Dickens. Its first issue appeared in 1859. It was a successor to Dickens's earlier family-magazine, *Household Words*.

Allwit (ôl′wit″). A cuckolded husband, whose wife's amour with the licentious Sir Walter Whorehound forms the subplot of Thomas Middleton's comedy *A Chaste Maid in Cheapside*. When Whorehound, believing himself near death, reveals the state of affairs, Allwit and his wife run him out of their house, and thence he goes to jail.

Allworth (ôl′wèrth), **Lady.** A rich widow in Philip Massinger's play *A New Way to Pay Old Debts*.

Allworth, Tom. In Philip Massinger's play *A New Way to Pay Old Debts*, a young gentleman, page to Lord Lovell.

Allworthy (ôl′wèr″ᴛʜi), **Bridget.** In Henry Fielding's novel, *Tom Jones*, the unmarried sister of Squire Allworthy. She is eventually revealed as the mother (through a youthful indiscretion) of Tom Jones.

Allworthy, Squire. [Also, **Thomas Allworthy.**] In Henry Fielding's novel *Tom Jones*, a squire of large fortune, the foster father of the foundling Tom Jones. He is depicted as a man of the most upright and attractive character, a sharp contrast to Squire Western. He is generally considered to have been a portrait of Fielding's friend Ralph Allen.

Alma (al′mạ). In Edmund Spenser's *Faerie Queene*, the Queen of Body Castle, the personification of the soul.

Almack's (ôl′maks). Famous assembly rooms built by William Almack in 1764, and opened on Feb. 20, 1765, in King Street, St. James, London. It re-

mained a popular gathering place until the middle of the 19th century. These rooms were later also called "Willis's," after the next proprietor.

Almagest (al′mạ.jest). **1.** A scientific treatise, in 13 books, by Ptolemy. The title, from the Arabic translation of Ptolemy's Greek *Syntaxis*, means "the greatest synthesis"; the work embodies Ptolemy's astronomic theories, establishing a geocentric universe, and, by his own system of eccentrics and epicycles, fixing the length of the year at 365¼ days. The work also gives a modified list of Hipparchus's catalogue of stars. The translation of this work into Latin was unquestionably one of the most important events in European astronomy before the Renaissance. Actually, there were two translations, both made in the 12th century. The first was made by anonymous scholars in Sicily about 1160 from a Greek manuscript brought to Sicily from the library of one of the Byzantine rulers. The second was made at Toledo, in Spain, from an Arabic manuscript some 15 years after the first. However, the first translation (from the Greek), remained practically unknown (despite the fact that most scholars consider that it was probably the superior of the two), and the Almagest became known in Europe chiefly through the translation from Arabic. In this translation, it remained the standard astronomic authority of Europe until the time of Copernicus.
2. (*l.c.*) Any book or collection of the same general nature as that drawn up by Ptolemy; and so named by the Arabs because it was reckoned the greatest work on these subjects.

> Cross, and character, and talisman,
> And almagest, and altar.
> (Scott, *Lay of the Last Minstrel*.)

Almahide (al′mạ.hĭd). The Queen of Granada in John Dryden's *The Conquest of Granada*. The name was taken from Madeleine de Scudéry's novel *Almahide*.

Almanach de Gotha (àl.mà.nàk dẹ go.tà). See **Gotha, Almanach de.**

Almanzor (al.man′zọr). The Caliph of Arabia in George Chapman's *Revenge for Honour*.

Almanzor. The heroic general in John Dryden's *The Conquest of Granada* who falls in love with Almahide, a Moorish princess. He is described as "Vast in his courage, boundless in his mind, Rough as a storm, and humorous [i.e., erratic] as wind: Honor's the only idol of his eyes."

Almanzor and Almahide (al′mạ.hĭd). See **Conquest of Granada, The.**

Alma: or, the Progress of the Mind (al′mạ). A poem (1716) by Matthew Prior. It is written in tetrameter couplets in the form of a dialogue between Prior and his friend, Richard Shelton, and mocks all philosophies (Prior's misanthropic frame of mind doubtless derived at least in part from the fact that he was in jail when he wrote the poem).

Almayer's Folly (ôl′mī.èrz). A novel (1895) by Joseph Conrad. It is set in remote jungle trading-posts on the Malay peninsula.

Almeria (al.mir′i.ạ). In Congreve's play *The Mourning Bride*, the supposedly widowed bride of Alphonso, prince of Valentia. It is she who utters

(Act 1, Scene 1) the familiar words: "Music hath charms to soothe a savage breast, To soften rocks, or bend a knotted oak."

Almesbury (ämz'ber''i, -bėr.i). A town in Wiltshire, England (the modern **Amesbury**) where Guinevere sought sanctuary and where she died.

Almond for a Parrot. An essay (1590) probably by Robert Greene in reply to the Martin Marprelate pamphlets. Some literary historians believe that Thomas Nash may have been its actual author.

Alnaschar (al.nash'ạr, -nas'kär). The "Barber's Fifth Brother" in *The Arabian Nights' Entertainments*. He invests his inheritance in glassware. While awaiting customers he fancies himself already a millionaire, and an incautious movement upsets his basket, breaking its contents and destroying all his prospects (hence the phrase "visions of Alnaschar," that is, counting one's chickens before they are hatched; daydreams).

A. L. O. E. Pseudonym of **Tucker, Charlotte Maria.**

Aloeus (ạ.lō'ūs). In Greek mythology, the son of Poseidon and husband of Iphimedia, the mother of the Aloidae.

Aloidae (al.ọ.ī'dē) or **Aloadae** (ạ.lō'ạ.dē) or **Aloiadae** (al.ọ.ī'ạ.dē). In Greek mythology, the two giant sons of Poseidon, slain by Apollo for attempting to scale the heavens by piling Ossa on Olympus and Pelion on Ossa.

Alonso (ạ.lon'zō). In Shakespeare's *Tempest*, the King of Naples, who has helped Antonio to usurp Prospero's dukedom. On a return voyage from Tunis he is shipwrecked on Prospero's island and is made to repent his action. His son, Ferdinand, marries Miranda.

Alonzo (ạ.lon'zō). In Beaumont and Fletcher's *The Custom of the Country*, a young Portuguese gentleman, the enemy of Duarte.

Alonzo. In Richard Brinsley Sheridan's translation of Kotzebue's *Pizarro*, the commander of the army of Ataliba, king of Quito.

Alonzo the Brave and the Fair Imogine (im'ọ.jin). A ballad (1796) by M. G. ("Monk") Lewis, contained in his novel *The Monk*.

Alph (alf). A sacred underground river in Xanadu, in Coleridge's poem *Kubla Khan*.

Alpha of the Plough. Pseudonym of **Gardiner, Alfred George.**

Alphege (al'fej), Saint. See Saint **Ælfheah.**

Alpheus (al.fē'us, al'fẹ.us). River in Greece, in the Peloponnesus, flowing generally NW from S Greece into the Ionian Sea. The plain of Olympia touches its N bank, and its name is mentioned repeatedly in the legend and history of Greece. In more modern times, it occurs in English literature as the original of Coleridge's river Alph, mentioned in *Kubla Khan*. In Greek mythology, it was the river diverted by Hercules in order to clean the Augean stables. It flows at one point under the ground, and was for this reason believed by the ancient Greeks actually to flow under the sea to Sicily.

Alphonso (al.fon'zō, -sō). The hero of Sir William Davenant's *The Siege of Rhodes*. He loves Ianthe, and finally wins her after various trials involving him in debates about the choice between love and honor.

Alphonsus, King of Aragon (al.fon'sus; ar'ạ.gon). [Full title, **The Comical History of Alphonsus, King of Aragon.**] A tragedy (produced c1587) by "R.G.," who is probably Robert Greene, in imitation of Marlowe's *Tamburlaine*.

Alpiew (al'pū). In Susannah Centlivre's comedy *The Basset-Table*, Lady Reveller's waiting-woman, a pert, adroit soubrette. The name is taken from "alpieu," a term in the once popular game of basset implying the continuance of the bet on a card that has already won.

Alsatia (al.sā'shạ). Formerly a cant name (Alsace being a debatable ground or scene of frequent contests) for Whitefriars, a district in London between the Thames and Fleet Street, and adjoining the Temple, which possessed certain privileges of sanctuary derived from the convent of the Carmelites, or White Friars, founded there in 1241. The locality became the resort of libertines and rascals of every description, whose abuses and outrages, and especially the riot in the reign of Charles II, led in 1697 to the abolition of the privilege and the dispersion of the Alsatians. The term "Alsatia" was later applied offensively to the English stock-exchange, because of the supposedly questionable character of some of its proceedings. The name first occurs in Shadwell's plays *The Woman Captain* (1680) and *The Squire of Alsatia* (1688).

Alsemero (al.sẹ.mir'ō). In Thomas Middleton and William Rowley's play *The Changeling*, the young man loved by Beatrice.

Al Sirat (äl si.rät'). The bridge over which must pass all who enter the Mohammedan paradise. It is of inconceivable narrowness, finer than the edge of a razor; hence those burdened by sins are sure to fall off and are dashed into hell, which lies below the bridge. A somewhat similar conception has occurred at various times in other theologies, most notably the Jewish and that of the Zoroastrians.

Altamont (al'tạ.mont). In Nicholas Rowe's play *The Fair Penitent*, the forgiving husband of Calista.

Altamont. In W. M. Thackeray's *Memoirs of Mr. C. J. Yellowplush*, a young man who mysteriously disappears each day in order to sweep a crossing.

Altamont, Colonel Jack. In W. M. Thackeray's novel *Pendennis*, the name assumed by the returned convict Amory. He is the first husband of Lady Clavering and father of the emotional Blanche Amory.

Altar of Righteousness, The. A poem by Algernon Charles Swinburne. The burden of this poem is Swinburne's belief in his later years that there is no star to guide a man "save his own soul." It is probably now considered notable not so much for its subject matter as for being Swinburne's last poem before his death in 1909.

Altar of the Dead, The. A story (1895) by Henry James.

Altar-Piece, The. A novel by Naomi Royde-Smith, published in 1939.

Altar Steps, The. A novel by Compton Mackenzie, published in 1922. The first of a trilogy, it deals with the spiritual development of Mark Lidderdale, an

---

Anglican minister. His story is continued in *The Parson's Progress* (1923) and *The Heavenly Ladder* (1924).

Althaea or **Althea** (al.thē'a). In Greek legend, a daughter of Thestius, wife of Oneus, king of Calydon, and mother of Tydeus, Meleager, and Deïaneira. See **Meleager.**

Althea (al.thē'a). A name by which Richard Lovelace poetically addressed a woman, supposed to have been Lucy Sacheverell, whom he also celebrated by the name of Lucasta.

Altisidora (äl''tē.sē.dō'rä). A character in the "Curious Impertinent," an episode in Cervantes' *Don Quixote*. An attendant of the duchess, she torments Don Quixote by pretending to be in love with him.

Altofronto (al.tọ.fron'tọ), **Giovanni.** The name of the Duke of Genoa in John Marston's *The Malcontent.* He pretends to be Malevole, the malcontent.

Alton Locke (ôl'tọn lok). [Full title, **Alton Locke, Tailor and Poet.**] A novel by Charles Kingsley, published in 1850. Alton Locke, a talented young poet and an ardent Chartist, is befriended by Saunders Mackaye, an old Scottish bookseller, and a benevolent dean, with the daughter of whom Alton presently falls in love. Spurned by the taunts of his Chartist friends, Alton becomes involved in a riot and is sentenced to three years in prison. On his release he finds that Lillian, the dean's daughter, is engaged to his prosperous cousin. He falls ill with typhus and is nursed by Lillian's cousin, Eleanor, who persuades him of the value of Christian ideals to replace the revolutionary creed of Chartism. He then emigrates to America, but dies on the voyage.

Alvan (al'van), **Sigismund.** In George Meredith's novel *The Tragic Comedians* (1880), the fictional name of Ferdinand Lassalle, a well-known 19th-century German socialist.

Alvarez (dal'va.rez), **Count D'.** See **D'Alvarez, Count.**

Alysoun (al'i.sọn). A Middle English love poem, by an unknown author.

Amadas (am'a.das), **Sir.** See **Sir Amadas.**

Amadis of Gaul (am'a.dis). [French, **Amadis de Gaule** (à.mà.dēs dẹ gōl); Spanish, **Amadís de Gaula** (ä.mä.ᴛʜēs' dä gou'lä).] The legendary and titular hero of a famous medieval romance of chivalry, the center of a cycle of romances. He is the oldest of the heroes of chivalry. He is represented as the illegitimate son of Perion, king of Gaul, and Elisena, princess of Brittany. His mother abandoned him soon after his birth, putting him, in his cradle, in the sea. Rescued by a Scottish knight, he was educated at the court of the king of Scotland, and fell in love with, and eventually married, Oriana, daughter of Lisuarte, king of England. After being knighted he returned to Gaul, and during the rest of his life performed there and elsewhere a number of impressive exploits. It is believed that the *Amadis* was originally translated by the Spaniard Montalvo from a lost Portuguese original of the 14th century. There is no trace of a French original, the existence of which has been assumed by French critics. The first known edition was prepared by Garcia Ro-

dríguez de Montalvo in Spanish and published at Saragossa, Spain, in 1508. It contained four books and stated that the first three had not been originally written by him. The authorship of the romance is a controversial matter. It has been ascribed to the Portuguese Vasco de Lobeira (d. c1403) by some scholars; to João de Lobeira (13th century), also a Portuguese, by others; still others have ascribed one part (the third book) to the former and another part (the first two books) to the latter. References to the first three books of the romance are often found in the literature of the 14th century. In 1540, Nicholas d' Herberay des Essarts undertook to give a French version of it. His version, in turn, had sequels, but none which equaled the popularity or power of his work. The book became immensely popular in France. It had, moreover, a great influence on the heroic romances of the early 17th century.

Amadis of Greece. A continuation of the seventh book of *Amadis of Gaul.* It was in Spanish, and said to be by Feliciano de Silva. It relates the exploits of the son of Lisuarte of Greece who was the son of Esplandian, the son of Amadis of Gaul.

Amaimon (a.mā'mon). [Also: **Amaymon, Amoymon.**] In medieval demonology, one of the four kings of hell, of which he governed the eastern portion. Asmodeus was his lieutenant and first prince of his realm. Shakespeare alludes to Amaimon in *The Merry Wives of Windsor.*

Amalthaea or **Amalthea** (am.al.thē'a). In Greek mythology, the nurse of Zeus, in most versions a goat.

Amalthaea. In Roman legend, the Sibyl who sold the Sibylline books to Tarquin.

Amanda (a.man'da). The faithful wife of the libertine, Loveless, in Colley Cibber's *Love's Last Shift* and Vanbrugh's sequel, *The Release.*

Amara (am'a.ra), **Mount.** A mountain in Abyssinia (Ethiopia), referred to by Milton in Book IV of *Paradise Lost.* Johnson refers to it as Amhara in *Rasselas.*

Amarant (am'a.rant). In English legend, a giant killed in the Holy Land by Guy of Warwick.

Amaranta (am.a.ran'ta). In Beaumont and Fletcher's *Spanish Curate,* the wife of Bartolus, "as cunning as she's sweet."

Amaranth (am'a.ranth), **Lady.** A character in John O'Keeffe's farce *Wild Oats.*

Amaryllis (am.a.ril'is). A shepherdess or country maiden in the *Idyls* of Theocritus and the *Eclogues* of Vergil.

Amaryllis. In Edmund Spenser's *Colin Clout's Come Home Again,* a personage described with adulation, intended to represent Alice Spenser, Countess of Derby, with whose family Spenser claimed an alliance. It was for Alice Spenser that Milton wrote his *Arcades.*

Amaryllis. In John Fletcher's pastoral *The Faithful Shepherdess,* a shepherdess who is in love with Perigot, and uses foul means to part him from Amoret.

Amaryllis. In *The Rehearsal,* by George Villiers, Duke of Buckingham, with aid from Thomas Sprat, Martin Clifford, Samuel Butler, and possibly others, a female character intended to ridicule Polydama in Dryden's *Marriage à la Mode*. Ann Reeve, whose supposed intrigue with Dryden is alluded to, took the role.

Amaurote (am′ô.rōt). In Thomas More's *Utopia*, the capital city.

Amaury (ạ.mô′ri), **Giles**. The grand master of the Knights Templars in Sir Walter Scott's tale *The Talisman*. He conspired against King Richard and was killed by Saladin.

Amaymon (ạ.mā′mon). See **Amaimon**.

Amazing Marriage, The. A novel (1895) by George Meredith, now generally considered to be one of the author's less successful works.

Amazons (am′ạ.zonz). In Greek legend, a race of women supposed to have dwelt on the coast of the Black Sea and in the Caucasus Mountains. The Amazons and their contests were a favorite theme in Grecian art and story. They were represented as forming a state from which men were excluded, as devoting themselves to war and hunting, and as being often in conflict with the Greeks in the heroic age.

Ambassadors, The. A novel by Henry James, published in 1903. Lambert Strether, a middle-aged American editor, is sent by Mrs. Newsome, to whom he is engaged, to reclaim her son Chad from his attachment to Paris. Strether finds that Chad has not only succumbed to the fascination of Continental life but is also presumably the lover of the Countess de Vionnet. Strether himself begins to surrender to the color and tone of Europe, and all but abandons his original mission. Mrs. Newsome hears news of Strether's changed attitude, and sends a new ambassador, her daughter, Mrs. Pocock, to reclaim both Chad and Strether. Mrs. Pocock finally convinces Strether that he must conform to convention and return to Woollett, Mass., giving up his mild flirtation with Maria Gostrey. Before he leaves, however, Strether advises Chad to remain in Paris, to live life to the fullest.

Amberley (am′bèr.li), **Viscount**. A title of **Russell, Lord John**.

Amber Witch, The. An opera in four acts by W. V. Wallace, words by Henry Fothergill Chorley, first produced at London, on Feb. 28, 1861. It was founded on a popular German romance by Johann Wilhelm Meinhold, published in 1843.

Ambitioso (am.bi.shyō′sō). The son of the Duchess in Cyril Tourneur's *The Revenger's Tragedy*.

Ambitious Statesman, or The Loyal Favorite, The. A tragedy by John Crowne, acted in 1679.

Ambitious Stepmother, The. A tragedy by Nicholas Rowe, acted and printed in 1700. It is a drama of palace intrigue, with echoes of Otway's heroic tragedies (particularly *The Orphan*) that had been popular during the Restoration.

Ambler (am′blèr), **Eric**. b. 1909—. An English writer of fiction especially of novels of suspense. His novels include *Background to Danger* (1937), *Epitaph for a Spy* (1938), *Cause for Alarm* (1939), *A Coffin for Dimitrios* (1939), *Journey Into Fear* (1940), *Judgment on Deltchev* (1951), and *The Schirmer Inheritance* (1953).

Ambois (dän.bwȧ), **Bussy d'**. The partly arrogant, partly noble hero of Chapman's *Bussy d'Ambois*.

Amboyna, or The Cruelties of the Dutch to the English Merchants (am.boi′nạ). A tragedy by John Dryden, produced in 1673. Part of the plot was taken from one of the Italian novels in the *Hecatommithi* of Giovanni Battista Giraldi (known as Cinthio), and part has reference to occurrences of the time.

Ambree (am′brē), **Mary**. A woman who is said to have fought against the Spanish at the siege of Ghent in 1584 to revenge her lover's death. She is frequently mentioned in old ballads, and is the subject of one preserved by Thomas Percy. Ben Jonson refers to her in the *Epicoene*, *The Tale of a Tub*, and in *The Fortunate Isles*, where he quotes the words of this ballad. John Fletcher also mentions her in *The Scornful Lady*. The ballad in Percy's *Reliques* is often quoted by the writers of Jonson's time, and, like him, they frequently gave the name of Mary Ambree to any remarkable woman who adopted man's attire.

Ambrose (am′brōz), **Saint**. [Latinized, **Ambrosius**.] b. at what is now Trier, Germany, c340; d. at Milan, Italy, 397. One of the fathers of the Roman Church; bishop of Milan (374–397). As consular prefect (c369) in upper Italy, he demonstrated his interest in public welfare; he was elected (374), though a layman and unbaptized, bishop of Milan. A champion of Catholics against paganism and heresy, he resisted the Arianism of the empress Justina and accomplished the deposition of the Arian prelates Palladius and Secundianus by persuading the emperor Gratian to limit the synod of Aquileia (381) to western bishops. Sent twice under Valentinian II to dissuade Maximus from invading Italy, he succeeded on the first occasion but failed on the second. Remaining in Milan under Gallic occupation, he melted down church vessels for the relief of the poor; after the reconquest by Theodosius, Emperor of the East, Ambrose forced penance on him for the massacre in Thessalonica. Forced to flee at the time of the assassination of Valentinian II, he returned to intercede with Theodosius (who again reconquered the West in 394) for the Arian supporters of the usurper Eugenius. Following the doctrine of Saint Basil of Caesarea and other Greeks, but with a characteristically western emphasis on divine grace and individual faith, he was, with Paul, a main precursor of Augustine. Author of commentaries on early Old Testament narratives of Hexaëmeron, Abraham, and others, of hymns such as *Deus Creator Omnium* and *Veni redemptor gentium*, and of treatises including *De Spiritu Sanctu*, *De mysteriis*, *De officiis ministrorum*.

Ambrose, Father. The abbot of St. Mary's at Kennaquhair, Edward Glendinning, in Sir Walter Scott's novel *The Abbot*.

Ambrose's Tavern. An old tavern in Edinburgh, now destroyed, the scene of John Wilson's *Noctes Ambrosianae*.

Ambrosio (am.brō′zhō). The hero of *The Monk*, a novel by M. G. ("Monk") Lewis, published in 1796.

Ambrosius Aurelianus (am.brō′zhus ô.rē.li.ā′nus). [Welsh, **Emrys**.] fl. c440 A.D. Roman emperor of

Britain, Gaul, and Spain under Honorius; leader of the Britons against the Saxon invasion; said by some chroniclers to have been a son of Constantine. He drove back the Saxons, and, as king of Britain, defeated the opposition of Hengist. He was poisoned at Winchester by a Saxon.

Amelia (ạ.mēl′yạ). A character in Thomson's *The Seasons*. She figures in the section "Summer," in the story of Celadon and Amelia.

Amelia. A novel by Henry Fielding, published in December, 1751. William Booth, a penniless young officer, is unjustly thrown into prison as a result of an attempt to help a stranger. There he meets an old friend, Miss Matthews, who has also been unjustly imprisoned. Booth tells her how he eloped with the beautiful Amelia Harris, whose mother originally opposed the marriage, and how through a series of misfortunes they have become destitute, Amelia's mother having died and left her money to Amelia's sister Elizabeth. Miss Matthews is very sympathetic, and bribes the jailer to let Booth move into her private room in the prison. When they are released from prison, Miss Matthews, who has fallen in love with Booth, pursues him in reproachful letters, while Amelia is pursued by a designing nobleman. The couple's difficulties are further complicated by the arrest of Booth for debt through a misunderstanding on the part of their old friend and curate, Dr. Harrison, and by Booth's unsuccessful gambling with money lent him by friends. Everything is finally resolved when Miss Matthews agrees to leave Booth in peace, Amelia thwarts the plans of the nobleman and forgives her husband his infidelity, and Booth gives up gambling. It is next discovered that the will by which Elizabeth inherited the money was one she and a lawyer have forged, and that Amelia is her mother's real heiress. Fielding, who was a justice of the peace, presented in this, his last novel, a picture of the scandalous conditions then prevailing in English prisons, the injustices practiced in the name of justice, and the cruelties inflicted on people in their charge by servants of the law, in order (the novelist hoped) that the public might be aroused to demand reforms.

Amelia Booth (bŏth). See under **Amelia**; see also **Booth, Amelia.**

Amelia Sedley (sed′li). See **Sedley, Amelia.**

Amen (ä′men). [Also: **Ammon, Amon, Amun, Hammon.**] In Egyptian mythology, a deity variously represented as a ram with large curving horns, as a being with a ram's head and a human body, and as a man enthroned or standing erect. In art his figure is colored blue. On his head he wears the royal symbol and two long feathers, and in one hand he carries a scepter and in the other the sign of life. His chief temple and oracle were on an oasis in the Libyan desert near Memphis. Later he became identified with the sun god Ra and was worshiped as Amen-Ra, the chief deity of Egypt.

Amends for Ladies. A comedy by Nathan Field, in the first production of which (c1612) the author himself played a part.

Amenities of Literature, The. Three volumes (1841) of a projected history of literature, by Isaac D'Israeli.

American (ạ.mer′i.kạn), **The.** A novel by Henry James, published in 1877. Christopher Newman, a wealthy American, falls in love with a Parisian lady, Claire de Cintré. Newman, a fairly direct and sincere individual, is appalled by the subtleties of European life and particularly by the contrivings of Claire's family, who succeed in breaking the couple's engagement. Newman learns that Claire's mother and brother were instrumental in the death of her father, but instead of revealing this information he destroys the evidence and surrenders the opportunity for revenge.

Amery (ā′mėr.i), **Leopold Charles Maurice Stennett.** b. at Gorakhpur, India, 1873; d. at London, Sept. 16, 1955. An English politician and journalist. After serving on the staff of the London *Times* (1899–1909), he was elected (1911) to Parliament from a Birmingham constituency. He served in the army (1914–16) and as War Cabinet secretary (1917–18); thereafter he held numerous cabinet posts, becoming in 1940 secretary of state for India and Burma, which post he surrendered in 1945 after the victory of the Labour party at the polls. Author of the seven-volume *Times History of the South African War* (1909), as well as of numerous works pertaining to empire and international affairs.

Amesbury (āmz′ber′′i, -bėr.i). A town in S England, in Wiltshire, ab. 8 mi. N of Salisbury. It is probably now chiefly known outside of England as being the community closest to Stonehenge, but it is important also as the site of a portion of one of England's largest military training centers. At the time of King Arthur Amesbury was called **Almesbury.**

Amexia (ạ.meks′i.ạ). The "Indian Queen" in Dryden and Howard's tragicomedy of that name. She is the mother of Montezuma and the true Queen of Mexico, dethroned for the moment by the villainous Zempoalla.

Amhara (am.har′ạ). See under **Amara, Mount.**

Amherst (am′ėrst), **Jeffrey.** [Title, Baron **Amherst.**] b. at Sevenoaks, Kent, England, Jan. 29, 1717; d. there, Aug. 4, 1797. A British field marshal, commander against the French in North America. He served under Ligonier and Cumberland in Europe in the War of the Austrian Succession. Sent (1758) by William Pitt to take Louisburg from the French, he was victorious there, at Crown Point and Ticonderoga (1759), and at Montreal (1760), securing British control of Canada. He was appointed (1761) governor-general of British North America, but returned (1763) to England after an unsuccessful campaign against the Indians. He later acted as an adviser to the British government during the American Revolution. For his services, he was made a baron (1787), commander in chief of the army (1793), and a field marshal (1796).

Amidas and Bracidas (am′i.dạs; bras′i.dạs). The twin brothers whom Artegall reconciles in Book V of Edmund Spenser's *Faerie Queene.*

Amideo (am.i.dē′ō). See under **Angelina.**

Amie (ā′mi). In Ben Jonson's *Sad Shepherd,* a gentle shepherdess.

Amiel (ā′mi.el). In John Dryden's *Absalom and Achitophel,* a character supposed to have been

fat, fāte, fär, ȧsk, fāre; net, mē, hėr; pin, pīne; not, nōte, mŏve, nôr; up, lūte, pull; ᴛн, then;

intended for Edward Seymour, speaker of the House of Commons, who was an adherent of William of Orange and the head of the house of Seymour.

Amiel (à.myel), **Henri Frédéric.** b. at Geneva, Switzerland, Sept. 27, 1821; d. there, May 11, 1881. A Swiss philosopher and poet. After studying philosophy at Berlin 1844–48, he served as professor of aesthetics and French literature (1849 *et seq.*) and of moral philosophy (1854) at the academy at Geneva. Author of *Fragments d'un journal intime*, published after his death (2 volumes, 1883), translated (1885) by Mrs. Humphry Ward and praised by Matthew Arnold.

Amiens (am'i.ęnz). In Shakespeare's *As You Like It*, one of the lords attending the banished father of Rosalind. His cheerfulness is a foil to the melancholy cynicism of the other lord, Jaques. It is Amiens who sings the well-known "Under the greenwood tree" and "Blow, blow, thou winter wind."

Amiens, Mise of. An award pronounced on Jan. 23, 1264, by Louis IX of France, to whom the question as to the obligation of Henry III to observe the Provisions of Oxford had been referred on Dec. 16, 1263. By this award the King of France entirely annulled the Provisions of Oxford, and all obligations made under them.

Amiens, Treaty of. A peace concluded at Amiens, March 27, 1802, between Great Britain on one side, and France, Spain, and the Batavian republic on the other. England restored all conquests except Ceylon and Trinidad, the Ionian republic was acknowledged, the French were to abandon Rome and Naples, and Malta was to be restored to the Knights of St. John.

Aminadab (ą.min'ą.dab). A name often used by the English dramatists of the 18th century to designate a Quaker.

Aminadab Sleek (slēk). See **Sleek, Aminadab.**

Aminta (ą.min'tą). The heroine of Meredith's *Lord Ormont and His Aminta.*

Amintor (ą.min'tôr). The fiancé of Aspatia in Beaumont and Fletcher's *The Maid's Tragedy.* Convinced that a subject must obey the commands of his ruler, even though they run counter to his best interest, he marries Evadne instead of Aspatia when the King orders him to. However, his faith in royal honor receives a crushing blow when Evadne confesses that he is merely a screen for her love affair with the King, and that he will enjoy no rights as a husband.

Amis et Amiloun (ä.mēs ā ä.mē.lǫn). [Also, **Amys and Amyloun.**] An Anglo-Norman metrical romance, dating probably from the 12th century, and probably of French origin. It tells the story of two perfect friends, born the same day and alike in beauty, courage, and devotion. Amiloun saves the honor of Amis in a trial by combat, and is punished with leprosy. Amis in true devotion cures Amiloun with the blood of his own children. As reward for such perfect friendship the children are restored to life.

Amlet (am'lęt), **Dick** (or **Richard**). In Vanbrugh's comedy *The Confederacy*, a gamester, the son of a garrulous old woman who sells paint, powder, and toilet luxuries to ladies. He attempts with her assistance to pass himself off as a fine gentleman, but fails.

Amleth (am'lęth). See under **Hamblet.**

Ammon or **Amon** (am'ǫn, ä'mǫn). See **Amen.**

amoebaeum (am.ē.bē'um). A poem in which persons are represented as speaking alternately, as in the third and seventh eclogues of Vergil.

Amor (ā'môr). See **Cupid.**

Amores (am'ǫ.rēz). A volume of poetry (1916) by D. H. Lawrence.

Amoret (am'ǫ.ret). The twin sister of Belphoebe in Edmund Spenser's *Faerie Queene.* Her mother is the nymph Chrysogone.

Amoret. In John Fletcher's *Faithful Shepherdess*, a shepherdess in love with, and loved by, Perigot, and enduring many trials with sweetness and constancy.

Amoretti (am.ǫ.ret'i). A group of sonnets (1595) by Edmund Spenser. They are largely autobiographical, and give an account of his wooing of Elizabeth Boyle, who had come to Ireland with her brother and settled in County Cork, near Youghal, on the coast.

Amorous Bigotte (big'ǫt), **The.** A comedy (1690) by Thomas Shadwell. Many of the incidents and characters of the play were conceived with the deliberate intent of pleasing the Whigs (in his political sympathies, Shadwell was a "true-blue" Whig), and this fact won the work considerable partisan popularity.

Amorous Complaint Made at Windsor, An. A poem attributed to Chaucer.

Amorous La Foole (lä föl'), **Sir.** See **La Foole, Sir Amorous.**

Amorous Widow, The. A comedy by Thomas Betterton, produced in 1670 and based upon Molière's *George Dandin.*

Amorphus (ą.môr'fus). In Jonson's *Cynthia's Revels*, an affected braggart who arbitrates others' quarrels but is himself no fighter.

Amory (ā'mǫ.ri), **Blanche.** In Thackeray's novel *Pendennis*, a pretty, worldly, frivolous, and selfish girl, whose real name is Betsy. She is the daughter of Lady Clavering and the returned convict who calls himself Altamont. She encourages any man, even the French cook, and, while posing as a tender, delicate flower, makes everyone about her as uncomfortable as possible. "For this young lady was not able to carry out any emotion to the full; but had a sham enthusiasm, a sham hatred, a sham love, a sham taste, a sham grief, each of which flared and shone very vehemently for an instant, but subsided and gave place to the next sham emotion." (Thackeray, *Pendennis*.)

Amory, Thomas. b. c1691; d. Nov. 25, 1788. An English writer, author of *Memoirs Containing the Lives of Several Ladies of Great Britain* (1755), *The Life of John Buncle, Esq.* (1756–66), and others. Likened to Rabelais and Dickens, he included in his books an extraordinary combination of theology, amorous adventure, scenic description, and autobiography.

ḍ, d or j; ş, s or sh; ṭ, t or ch; ẓ, z or zh; o, F. cloche; ü, F. menu; ċh, Sc. loch; ṅ, F. bonbon.

Amoryus and Cleopes (a̤.môr′yus; klē′o̤.pēz). A Middle English verse work written (1448–49) by John Metham, a Norfolk author, for Sir Miles Stapleton and his wife. A poem of 2,200 lines in rime royal, it deals with a variant of the Pyramus and Thisbe theme loosely associated with the story of Alexander the Great.

Amos Barton (ā′mo̤s bär′to̤n). [Full title: **The Sad Fortunes of the Reverend Amos Barton.**] A short story (1857) by George Eliot. Originally published in *Blackwood's*, it was one of her first works of fiction.

Amoymon (a̤.moi′mon). See **Amaimon.**

Amphialus (am.fī′a̤.lus). In Sir Philip Sidney's *Arcadia*, the valiant and virtuous son of the wicked Cecropea, and the lover of his cousin Philoclea.

Amphiaraus (am′′fī.a̤.rā′us). In Greek mythology, brother-in-law of Adrastus: a seer who foresaw the disastrous outcome of the expedition of the Seven against Thebes.

amphibology (am.fi.bol′o̤.ji). In logic, a sentence which is ambiguous from uncertainty with regard to its construction, but not from uncertainty with regard to the meaning of the words forming it. A good example of amphibology is the answer of the oracle to Pyrrhus: "Aio te Romanos vincere posse." Here *te* and *Romanos* may either of them be the subject or object of *vincere posse*, and the sense may be either, "you can conquer the Romans," or, "the Romans can conquer you." The English language seldom admits of amphibology:

> An amphibolous sentence is one that is capable of two meanings, not from the double sense of any of the words, but from its admitting a double construction; as, . . . "The duke yet lives that Henry shall depose."
> (Whately, *Logic.*)

amphibrach (am′fi.brak). In prosody, a foot of three syllables, the middle one long, the first and last short: as, *hăbērĕ*, in Latin: the opposite of *amphimacer.*

Amphictyonic League (am.fik.ti.on′ik), **The.** A powerful federation of Greek peoples which assumed charge of the temple of Apollo at Delphi and of the Pythian games. Formed near the beginnings of Greek history, it outlasted Greek independence.

amphigory (am′fi.go̤.ri). A meaningless rigmarole, as of nonsense verses or the like; a nonsensical parody.

amphimacer (am.fim′a̤.sèr). In prosody, a foot of three syllables, the middle one short and the others long, as in Latin *cāstĭtās;* the opposite of *amphibrach.*

Amphion (am.fī′on, am′fi.o̤n). In Greek mythology, a skillful musician; son of Zeus and Antiope, twin brother of Zethus, and husband of Niobe. The brothers slew Dirce, who had ill-treated their mother, by causing her to be dragged to death by a bull. They took possession of Thebes, and when the walls were building, the stones moved of their own accord to their places under the influence of Amphion's lyre.

Amphitryon (am.fit′ri.o̤n). In Greek legend, the husband of Alcmene and father of Iphicles. To secure Alcmene (who would not wed him until the death of her brothers had been avenged) he undertook, for his uncle Creon, to catch a ravaging fox, which by a decree of fate could not be captured, with the help of an Athenian dog which fate had decreed should catch every animal it might pursue. This conflict was resolved when both animals were turned into stone. He attacked the Taphians, but could not overcome them so long as the chief, Pterelaus, who was rendered immortal by one golden hair, continued to live. Comaetho, daughter of Pterelaus, cut off this hair for love of Amphitryon, and Pterelaus perished. The application, in later literature, of the name Amphitryon to a host is from that part of the story where Jupiter assumes the former's shape in order to visit Alcmene. He gives a feast and is interrupted by the real Amphitryon. This gives rise (in Molière's comedy) to a dispute which is settled by the phrase "Le véritable Amphitryon est l'Amphitryon où l'on dine" (translatable as, "he who gives the feast is the host").

Amphitryon. A play by Plautus. A comedy founded on the fable of Jupiter and Alcmene, it has been adapted or imitated by Molière, John Dryden, and many others. Its source is uncertain, but it is possibly from Archippus, a writer of the old comedy (415 B.C.)

Amphitryon (äṅ.fē.trē.ôṅ). A comedy by Molière, produced in 1668; a version of Plautus's play.

Amphitryon, or The Two Socias (am.fit′ri.o̤n; sō′shạz). A comedy by John Dryden, performed in 1690. It is substantially an English version, with various alterations, of Molière's *Amphitryon* (which is itself based on Plautus).

Amphitryon 38 (French, äṅ.fē.trē.ôṅ tränt.wēt). A philosophical comedy (1929; Eng. trans., 1938) on the ancient theme, in French, by the French writer Jean Giraudoux (1889–1944). The figure in the title indicates the author's surmise that there have been 37 previous treatments.

Amram (am′ram). The father of Moses. Milton refers to the "son of Amram" in *Paradise Lost.* Ex. vi, 20.

Amrita (am.rē′ta̤). In Hindu mythology, the beverage of immortality.

Amun (ä′mön). See **Amen.**

Amundeville (a̤.mun′de̤.vil), **Lord Henry.** In Byron's *Don Juan*, one of Juan's hosts, who is described in Canto XIII as

> A man known in the councils of the nation, Cool, and quite English, imperturbable.

Amyas (am′i.a̤s). In Edmund Spenser's *Faerie Queene*, the captive lover of Aemilia, a squire of low degree.

Amyas Leigh (lē). See **Leigh, Amyas.**

Amy Dorrit (ā′mi dor′it). See **Dorrit, Amy.**

Amymone (a̤.mī′mo̤.ne̤). One of the Danaïdes, or daughters of Danaus, referred to by Milton in *Paradise Regained.*

Amynta (a̤.min′ta̤). A character in Thomas D'Urfé's romance *Astrea.*

Amyntas (a̤.min′tạs). A character in Spenser's *Colin Clout's Come Home Again.* He represents Thomas Watson, English poet and translator.

---

fat, fāte, fär, àsk, fãre; net, mē, hèr; pin, pīne; not, nōte, mŏve, nôr; up, lūte, pùll; ᴛʜ, then;

Amyntas, or The Impossible Dowry. A pastoral drama of the Italian type by Thomas Randolph, first printed in 1638, and performed before Charles I and Queen Henrietta at Whitehall, in London.

Amyot (à.myō), **Jacques.** b. at Melun, France, Oct. 30, 1513; d. at Auxerre, France, Feb. 6, 1593. A French prelate and classical scholar whose translations of ancient writers, especially Plutarch, had a great influence on later writers. Tutor to Charles IX and Henry III of France, he was also bishop of Auxerre (1570–93). His version of Plutarch's *Lives*, entitled *Vies des hommes illustres de Plutarque* (1559–65), as translated (1579) into English by Sir Thomas North, was the source on which Shakespeare drew for his Roman plays. He also produced *Théagène et Chariclée* (1547 *et seq.*, after Heliodorus), *Daphnis et Chloé* (1559, after Longus), *Oeuvres morales de Plutarque* (1572, from *Opera Moralia*), and others.

Amy Robsart (ā′mi rob′särt). See **Robsart, Amy.**

Amys and Amyloun (a′mis; ā′mi.lọn). See **Amis et Amiloun.**

ana (ā′nạ, an′ạ). A general term for books recording miscellaneous sayings, anecdotes, and gossip about a particular person or subject; the sayings and anecdotes themselves:

> But, all his vast heart sherris-warm'd,
>   He flash'd his random speeches;
> Ere days, that deal in ana, swarm'd
>   His literary leeches.
>
>   (Tennyson, *Will Waterproof.*)

-ana. A suffix of Latin origin, in modern use with a euphonic variant, *-i-ana*, to form collective plurals, as *Scaligerana, Johnsoniana*, etc., applied to a collection of sayings of Scaliger, of Johnson, etc., or of anecdotes or gossip concerning them; also sometimes appended to common nouns, as *boxiana* (annals of pugilism); more recently extended to all the literature of a subject, as *Americana, Shakespeariana*, etc. Hence, sometimes used as an independent word.

Anabasis (ạ.nab′ạ.sis). An account by Xenophon, in seven books, of the campaign of the Persian prince Cyrus (the Younger) against his brother Artaxerxes II of Persia, and of the retreat (401–399) of the 10,000 Greeks who had fought under Cyrus, after his death at Cunaxa. Xenophon himself, a volunteer soldier, was one of those who led the 10,000 and, after a long and arduous march through Armenia and Georgia, brought them to the sea at Trebizond (now Trabzon).

anacoluthon (an″ạ.kọ.lū′thon). In grammar and rhetoric, a construction characterized by a want of grammatical sequence. For example: "And he charged him to tell no man: but go and shew thyself to the priest." Luke, v. 14. "He that curseth father or mother, let him die the death." Mat. xv. 4. As a figure of speech it has propriety and force only so far as it suggests that the emotion of the speaker is so great as to make him forget how he began his sentence, as in the following example:

> "If thou beest he—But, O, how fall'n! how changed!"
>
>   (Milton, *Paradise Lost.*)

Anacreon (ạ.nak′rẹ.ọn). b. at Teos, in Asia Minor, c563 B.C.; d. there, c478 B.C. A Greek lyric poet, whose work concerns itself chiefly with love and wine. He was widely imitated in the Alexandrian period, and later, in a form of verse called, from him, Anacreontics. He is supposed to have been driven from Teos by the invasion (545) of Cyrus the Great, to have fought briefly in the resisting army, and to have been tutor to Polycrates of Samos, at whose court he became a favorite. He was called to Athens on Polycrates' death by Hipparchus, the patron of Simonides and other literary figures; he probably returned to Teos after Hipparchus was assassinated (514). Pliny's account, probably mythical, of his death by choking on a grapeseed, gives the key to his reputation as a celebrator of the gay and leisurely life, though various writers attest to his sobriety. Although only fragments of his work are now extant, imitations, from the pseudocollection by Stephens (1554) to Thomas Moore (1800), demonstrate the popularity of his short, facile lyrics.

anacrusis (an.ạ.krö′sis). In prosody, an upward beat at the beginning of a verse, consisting of either one or two unaccented syllables, regarded as separate from and introductory to the remainder of the verse.

Anadyomene (an″ạ.di.om′ẹ.nē). In Greek mythology, an epithet ("rising from the sea") of the seaborn Aphrodite.

anagram (an′ạ.gram). A transposition of the letters of a word or sentence, to form a new word or sentence: thus, *Galenus* is an anagram of *angelus*. Charles Burney's anagram of *Horatio Nelson* is one of the happiest, *Honor est a Nilo* (Honor is from the Nile).

Anaides (ạ.nā′dēz). In Ben Jonson's *Cynthia's Revels*, an impudent ruffian. Thomas Dekker imagined that in this character he was caricatured.

analecta (an.ạ.lek′tạ). Selected passages from the writings of an author or of different authors; a title for a collection of choice extracts.

Analogy of Religion. [Full title, **The Analogy of Religion, Natural and Revealed, to the Constitution and Course of Nature.**] A religious treatise by Joseph Butler, published in 1736, defending Christian theology against the attacks of the deists by means of rationalism, supposedly the deists' own chief weapon. He rests his case on an assumption made by (or at least acceptable to) both sides, that there is in the universe a governing force and author of life. From this basis he is able to assert that Providence does exist, and that there is in fact a harmony between the teachings of religion and the observable functioning and phenomena of the natural world.

Analysis of the Human Mind. A prose work (1829) by James Mill. It was one of the earliest works in English to concern itself explicitly with something approaching what is now called psychology (the word, in its modern sense, was virtually never used in Mill's day, but his theory of "associationism" was nevertheless a pioneering effort in an area of science then still almost unknown).

Ananias (an.ạ.nī′ạs). In the New Testament: **1.** An early Christian of Jerusalem who with his wife Sapphira was struck dead for lying. (Acts v.) His name has since become a generally used term for one who lies.

2. An early Damascene Christian and friend of Paul.

3. A Jewish high priest (48–59 A.D.) and friend of the Romans before whom Paul was tried.

Ananias. In Ben Jonson's comedy *The Alchemist*, a hypocritical Puritan deacon resident in Amsterdam.

anapest or **anapaest** (an'ạ.pest). In prosody, a foot consisting of three syllables, the first two short or unaccented, the last long or accented: the reverse of the *dactyl*.

> And the sheen of their spears was like stars on the sea
> Where the blue waves roll nightly o'er deep Galilee.
> (Byron, *Descent of Sennacherib*.)

anaphora (an.af'ọ.rạ). In rhetoric, a figure consisting in the repetition of the same word or words at the beginning of two or more succeeding verses, clauses, or sentences.

Anarchy, The Masque of. See **Masque of Anarchy, The.**

Anastasia Veneering (vẹ.nir'ing). See **Veneering, Anastasia.**

Anastasius (an.ạs.tā'zhus). [Full title, **Anastasius, or Memoirs of a Greek.**] A picaresque novel by Thomas Hope, published in 1819. The story is told in the form of an autobiography and concerns the adventures of a Greek from Chios. He is a strange mixture of generosity and greed, of profligacy and sentiment. His travels take him to Constantinople, Egypt, Smyrna, and Arabia. The author introduces a considerable body of authentic (but obscure) historical fact, drawn in large part from notebooks made during his travels.

anastrophe (a.nas'trọ.fẹ). In rhetoric and grammar, an inversion of the usual order of words: as, "echoed the hills" for "the hills echoed."

Anatomy of Absurdity, The. A prose satire by Thomas Nash, published in 1589, attacking the cheats and scoundrels of his age.

Anatomy of Abuses, The. A curious account (1583) of the social customs of the period, by Philip Stubbes.

Anatomy of Art, The. See **Meaning of Art, The.**

Anatomy of Melancholy, The. A famous work by Robert Burton (1577–1640), published in 1621 under the pseudonym "Democritus Junior," and frequently republished and abridged. The sixth edition is the last which contains changes by the author; it was published, shortly after his death, from an annotated copy. It is divided into three parts which treat (1) of the causes and symptoms of melancholy, (2) of its cure, and (3) of erotic and religious melancholy. It is certainly one of the best-organized works in English literature, being divided into detailed, carefully thought out sections and subsections, and comprises essays covering almost every aspect of human nature, learning, scientific method, and social thought. In the preface, "Democritus Jr. to the Reader," the author suggests that the work may make possible a kind of

Utopia, in which man can be cured of all sadness and evil, in spite of his inbred melancholy.

Anatomy of the World, An. A poem (1611) by John Donne, subtitled "The First Anniversary" and written in commemoration of the death of Elizabeth Drury. For approximately 100 lines the poem is a paean of praise of Elizabeth Drury but, after that, Donne turns to matters of philosophy, and especially metaphysics, expressing his doubt of the new science and wondering about the future of the world.

Anatomy of Wit. See **Euphues.**

Anaxarete (an.ak.sar'ẹ.tē). In Greek legend, a maiden of Cyprus whose desperate lover hanged himself at her door. For her coldness she was changed by Venus into a statue.

Ancaeus (an.sē'us). In Greek classical legend, a son of Poseidon. He was told by a seer that he would not live to enjoy the wine from a vineyard which he had planted. He lived, however, to have wine from his own grapes, and, in scorn of the prophet, raised a cup of it to his mouth. The seer replied, "There is many a slip between the cup and the lip," and at the same instant a tumult arose over a wild boar in the vineyard. Ancaeus put down the cup, and was killed in an attempt to destroy the animal.

Ancaeus. In Greek classical legend, a son of the Arcadian Lycurgus, and one of the Argonauts. He was killed in the Calydonian boar hunt.

Anchises (an.kī'sēz, ang-). In Greek legend, a prince of the royal house of Troy, father (by Aphrodite) of Aeneas.

Ancient Mariner, The Rime of the. A poem by Samuel Taylor Coleridge, published in the *Lyrical Ballads* in 1798 as his principal contribution to the book. The narrative of the poem is told for the most part by the Ancient Mariner himself, as he stops a man bound for a wedding. The mariner is doomed by a curse to go through the world teaching universal love through the recounting of his own awful deed, which consisted in the heartless killing of a storm-tossed albatross.

Ancrene Riwle (angk'rẹn röl; Middle English, ängk'rẹ.nẹ rü'lẹ), **The.** Term meaning "the rule of anchoresses," used as the name of a specific work on the rules and duties of monastic life. It was written, probably first in Middle English and afterward in Latin and French, for three sisters who had just become anchoresses. The names of the sisters, the place of composition, and the identity of the author are unknown, but many conjectures have been made about all these questions. It was probably composed c1200, and contains eight books of advice on the manners, observances, and devotional ritual that the young ladies should adopt in their life of religious seclusion. It is perhaps the most remarkable piece of vernacular prose between King Alfred and Malory because of the frank, generous, and bold treatment. Five manuscripts are extant; the work was edited for the Camden Society by James Morton in 1853 and by R. M. Wilson for Oxford University Press in 1954.

And Death Shall Have No Dominion. A lyric poem (1943) by Dylan Thomas, consisting of four stanzas which deal with the all-embracing and limitless

---

fat, fāte, fär, ȧsk, fāre; net, mē, hėr; pin, pīne; not, nōte, möve, nôr; up, lūte, půll; ᴛʜ, then;

qualities of death. In addition to the conventional images of death, it is marked by a variety of unusual imagery (the unicorn, the sea, waves, and gulls).

Anderida (an.der'i.da). A Roman encampment in England, generally identified with Pevensey. It was destroyed (491) by the South Saxons.

Andersen (an'der.sen; Danish, än'ner.sen), **Hans Christian.** b. at Odense, Denmark, April 2, 1805; d. at Copenhagen, Aug. 4, 1875. A Danish poet and novelist, best known for fairy tales. Son of a poverty-stricken shoemaker, he went (1819) to Copenhagen to become an actor; a failure in the theater, he nevertheless won friends in the musical and dramatic world, and attracted the attention of King Frederick VI, who sent him to school. He achieved his first success with a curious work entitled *A Journey on Foot from Holmen's Canal to the East Point of Amager* (1829), which was followed by a volume of verse. Critical approval began to come his way with his first novel, *Improvisatoren* (The Improvisator, 1835), and was further stimulated by the first volume of fairy tales, under the title *Eventyr*, published the same year. Thereafter, until 1872, he averaged a volume of these tales a year, establishing himself not only as Denmark's best-known author, but as one of the leading story-tellers of history. Included among his best-known fairy tales are *The Fir Tree, The Tinder Box, The Ugly Duckling, The Red Shoes,* and *The Emperor's New Clothes.*

Anderson (an'der.son), **Anthony.** The Presbyterian minister in George Bernard Shaw's *The Devil's Disciple*, a stern, unforgiving New Englander.

Anderson, Judith. The wife of Anthony Anderson in George Bernard Shaw's *The Devil's Disciple*.

And Even Now. A volume of essays (1920) by Max Beerbohm.

And Now Goodbye. A novel by James Hilton, published in 1931.

Andouillets (än.dwē.yā'), **Abbess of.** The chief figure of one of the episodes in Sterne's *Tristram Shandy* (volume 7).

André (än.drä), **Bernard.** [Also, **Andreas** (an-drē'as).] fl. in the second half of the 15th century. A French poet and historian, poet laureate of England in the reign of Henry VII (the first laureate appointed by an English king), tutor of Arthur, prince of Wales, and royal historiographer. In spite of blindness he attained a high degree of scholarship. He wrote a life of Henry VII.

André, Petit. See **Petit André.**

Andrea del Sarto (än'drē.a del sär'tō). A poem (1855) by Robert Browning, included in the volume *Men and Women*. It is written in the form of a dramatic monologue in which the painter Andrea del Sarto addresses his wife, Lucrezia. Despite his reputation as "the faultless painter," he speaks of his unworthiness and his shortcomings, and of how he is barred from any truly great achievement by his devotion to his wife (a devotion which, we are given to understand, she does not actually merit).

Andrea Ferrara (fe.rä'ra). A sword or swordblade of a kind greatly esteemed in Scotland toward the end of the 16th century and later.

Andrea of Hungary (än'drē.a; hung'ga.ri). One of a trilogy of plays (*Giovanna of Naples* and *Fra Rupert* were the other two) by Walter Savage Landor. The first two were published in 1839, the third in 1840.

Andreas (än'drā.as, an'dri.as). An Old English poem, ascribed to Cynewulf and preserved in the *Vercelli Book*, of approximately 1,722 lines. It tells of the rescue of Saint Matthew from savage cannibals by Saint Andrew at the behest of God. Saint Andrew, by calling forth a miraculous flood, subdues the savages and persuades them to renounce heathen error and accept the Christian faith. The poem ends with the cannibals singing in praise of God.

Andrew Aguecheek (an'drö ā'gū.chēk), **Sir.** See **Aguecheek, Sir Andrew.**

Andrew Dinmont (din'mont, -mont). See **Dinmont, Dandie.**

Andrewes (an'dröz), **Lancelot.** b. at Barking, England, 1555; d. at London, Sept. 25, 1626. An English prelate, leader and spokesman of the High Church (Anglican) party against Roman Catholics and Puritans, respected even by his opponents for his scholarship, high principles, and brilliant preaching. He was chaplain to Elizabeth, James I, and Charles I; dean of Westminster (1601); bishop of Chichester (1605), Ely (1609), and Winchester (1619); privy councillor for England (1609) and Scotland (1617); and one of the translators (1607–11) of the Bible into the King James Version. Author of *Tortura Torti* (1609), an anti-Catholic defense of James I, manuals of devotions and prayers (1648), and others.

Andrew Fairservice (an'drö fär'ser"vis). See **Fairservice, Andrew.**

Andrew Freeport (frē'pōrt), **Sir.** See **Freeport, Sir Andrew.**

Andrew of Wyntoun (win'tun). See **Wyntoun, Andrew of.**

Andrews (an'dröz), **James Pettit.** b. near Newbury, England, c1737; d. at London, Aug. 6, 1797. An English antiquary and historian. He was the author of translations, satires, and two histories of Great Britain (1794–95 and 1796).

Andrews, Joseph. In Fielding's *Joseph Andrews*, a handsome footman, represented as the brother of Richardson's Pamela, whose trials Fielding burlesques by subjecting the virtue of Joseph to parallel temptations by his employer, Lady Booby.

Andrews, Pamela. The heroine of Samuel Richardson's *Pamela*, whose unyielding virtue is eventually rewarded by marriage to Mr. B., her master.

Androcles and the Lion (an'drō.klēz). A comedy (1912) by George Bernard Shaw. The plot is based initially upon the story of Androclus (or Androcles), a slave who befriended a lion by removing a thorn from his paw, for which he had his reward when the animal later refused to attack him in the Roman arena. In this play, Shaw may be said to have outlined a martyrology, but of a type uniquely Shavian in its emphasis on the not always very admirable but always extremely human characteristics of its chief figures. His ideal of saintliness would appear to be Androcles, the kindly, gentle, and witty tailor

---

d, d or j; s, s or sh; t, t or ch; z, z or zh; o, F. cloche; ü, F. menu; ch, Sc. loch; ṅ, F. bonbon.

who, without sentimentality or false piety, is capable of Christian good will. On a lower level of sainthood is Lavinia, willing to face martyrdom, but incapable of the utter selflessness of Androcles. Ranked below them are others who avow a desire to follow their Christian faith to the bitter end, but are rendered incapable by their natures of doing so. One of them (Spintho) completely lacks courage; Shaw shows him becoming so terrified at the thought that he will really have to die for his belief that he runs off blindly and blunders into the lion's cage (thus obtaining martyrdom, but only on a technicality). Another is Ferrovius, a great brute of a man seeking to become a gentleman, and hoping that Christian humility (of which he is finally incapable) may be the means to this end.

Androclus (an'drọ.klus) or **Androcles** (-klēz). fl. 1st century A.D. A Roman slave noted for his friendship with a lion, subject of Shaw's play *Androcles and the Lion.* According to Aelian and Aulus Gellius, Androclus, escaping from his master in Africa, hid in a cave and there removed a thorn from a lion's foot; years later the animal, remembering him, refused to harm him in the arena.

Andromache (an.drom'ạ.kẹ). In Greek legend, the wife of Hector, and, after his death, of Neoptolemus, son of Achilles; later the wife of Helenus, brother of Hector. She was the daughter of the king of Thebae in Cilicia, who, with his seven sons, was slain by Achilles when he captured Thebae.

Andromache. In Shakespeare's *Troilus and Cressida,* the wife of Hector. She, the prophetess Cassandra, and Hector's father, Priam, the King of Troy, plead with Hector not to go into battle, because they feel certain that he will be killed, as he is.

Andromeda (an.drom'ẹ.dạ). In Greek legend, the daughter of Cepheus and Cassiopeia. Poseidon, angered by boasts that there were women more beautiful than the Nereids, sent against the country a sea monster which could only be appeased by the sacrifice of the king's daughter. Andromeda was consequently offered to the monster, but was rescued by Perseus. The legend states that Andromeda, Perseus, and the monster were all three changed into constellations upon their deaths.

Andromeda. A poem (1858) by Charles Kingsley. This work, in hexameters, is Kingsley's most ambitious undertaking in verse, although not so well known as his *The Sands of Dee.*

Andronicus (an.dron'i.kus, an.drọ.nī'kus), **Marcus.** See **Marcus Andronicus.**

Andronicus, Titus. See **Titus Andronicus.**

Andrugio (än.drö'jō). In John Marston's *Antonio and Mellida,* the noble but turbulent Duke of Genoa. He utters the speech beginning, "Why, man, I never was a prince till now."

Andvaranaut (änd'vä.rä.nôt''). The last ring of Andvari's treasure, bearing the curse of destruction to each of its owners: ultimately, the Ring of the Nibelungs.

Andvari (änd'vä.rē). In Old Norse mythology, a dwarf who lived in the water in the form of a pike. He was caught by Loki and forced to give up his

treasure, ultimately called from its possessors the Nibelung Hoard. On the last ring, the Andvaranaut, later the Ring of the Nibelungs, he laid the curse of destruction to all who should own it.

anecdote (an'ek.dōt). A short narrative of a particular or detached incident or occurrence of an interesting nature; a biographical incident; a single passage of private life.

Anecdotes of Painting in England. A prose work (4 vols., 1763–71) by Horace Walpole. It was based on the notebooks of the engraver George Vertue, which Walpole had purchased from Vertue's widow, and has led many scholars to consider Walpole an authentic pioneer in the history of English painting.

Anecdotes of the Late Samuel Johnson. A volume of reminiscences by Mrs. Thrale (Hester Salusbury), published in 1786.

Aneirin (ä'nī.rẹn). See **Aneurin.**

Anelida and Arcite (ạ.nel'i.dạ; är'sīt). An unfinished poem (c1373–86) by Chaucer. It was among those printed by Caxton, and is mentioned in both Lydgate's and Thynne's lists of Chaucer's works. In the latter it is mentioned as "Of Queen Anelida and False Arcite." There are passages in it from Boccaccio's *Il Teseida,* and the *Thebaid* of Statius was also drawn upon. Elizabeth Barrett Browning wrote a modernized version of the poem about the middle of the 19th century. In the poem is included "The Complaint of Anelida the Queen upon False Arcite," occasioned by the fact that the Theban knight (who is not the true Arcite of *The Knight's Tale*) deserted her for another. After a double invocation, the meagerly developed story is carried on for about 200 lines and does little more than introduce the "Complaint," which is a polished and metrically elaborate example of this genre. A single stanza of the narrative follows and the poem then breaks off.

Aneurin (an'ū.rin, ä'nī.rẹn). [Also: **Aneirin, Neurin.**] fl. c600 A.D. A Welsh bard, author of *Gododin,* an epic of the struggle between Britons and Saxons, one of the oldest works in Welsh literature. Son of a chief (Caw ab Geraint or Gildas) of the Otadini or Gododin, a sea-coast tribe living south of the Firth of Forth, he is variously thought to have been Gildas the historian or his son.

Angelica (an.jel'i.kạ). The principal female character in William Congreve's play *Love for Love,* a witty and piquant woman, and the author's favorite character. She saves her lover, Valentine, from disinheritance after tormenting him by her plot to pretend affection for his father.

Angelica. A character in George Farquhar's comedy *The Constant Couple* and also in its sequel *Sir Harry Wildair.*

"Angelical Salutation." See **Ave Maria.**

Angelicus (an.jel'i.kus), **Doctor.** An epithet of **Aquinas,** Saint **Thomas.**

Angelina (an.jẹ.lī'nạ). In John Dryden's tragicomedy *The Rival Ladies,* a sister of Don Rhodorigo, in love with Gonsalvo. She disguises herself as a man and goes by the name of Amideo.

Angelina. The heroine of Oliver Goldsmith's ballad *The Hermit, or Edwin and Angelina.*

---

fat, fāte, fär, ȧsk, fāre; net, mē, hėr; pin, pīne; not, nōte, möve, nôr; up, lūte, pull; ᴛн, then;

Angel in the House, The. A poem (1854) by Coventry Patmore. Its theme of wedded love may be traced, for its inspiration, to Patmore's own relationship with his wife (whose beauty was so great as to attract the comment also of many of Patmore's fellow Pre-Raphaelites). It was published in four parts: *The Betrothal* (published anonymously in 1854), *The Espousals* (1856), *Faithful Forever*, a poem of disappointed love (1860), and *The Victories of Love*, a poem of bereavement (1862).

Angell (ăn'jĕl), Sir **Norman.** [Original name, **Ralph Norman Angell Lane.**] b. at Holbeach, England, Dec. 26, 1874—. An Anglo-American economist, pacifist, journalist, and author. He received his early education at St.-Omer, France, and Geneva, Switzerland, and lived in the western U.S. as a rancher, prospector, and newspaperman, becoming a citizen before his return (1898) to Europe as a newspaper correspondent. He was general manager of the Paris edition of the London *Daily Mail* (1905–14) and editor of *Foreign Affairs* (1928–31). A Labour member of Parliament (1929–31), he was awarded (1934) the Nobel peace prize for 1933. He is also the inventor of "The Money Game" which utilizes cards to teach economic principles of currency and banking. Author of *The Great Illusion* (1910), *The Great Illusion, 1933* (1933), *America's Dilemma* (1940), *Let the People Know* (1943), *After All* (1952, autobiography), and others.

Angelo (an'jĕ.lō). In Shakespeare's *Comedy of Errors*, a goldsmith.

Angelo. In Shakespeare's *Measure for Measure*, the Duke's deputy who is granted full administrative powers in Vienna when the Duke pretends to leave. He condemns Claudio to death for unchastity, but agrees to pardon him if his sister, Isabella, will yield herself to him (Angelo). When the Duke resumes his own guise, Angelo is punished and is forced to marry Mariana (to whom he had been engaged).

Angelo Cyrus Bantam (sī'rus ban'tăm). See **Bantam, Angelo Cyrus.**

Angels of Mons (monz; French, môns), **The.** A war legend (1915) by Arthur Machen.

Angevin (an'jĕ.vin). A dynastic name sometimes applied to the Plantagenet rulers of England. The term, taken from French, is a derivative of "Anjou," from which French house the Plantagenets were descended; the first three Plantagenets (Henry II, Richard I, and John) were actually counts of Anjou as well as kings of England, and the Plantagenets (or Angevins) are ordinarily listed as a separate and rightful house under the counts of Anjou.

Angles (ang'glz). [Latin, **Angli.**] A Germanic tribe which in the earliest period of their recorded history dwelt in the neighborhood of the district of Germany now called Angeln, in the region of Schleswig (said to be so named from *angel, angul,* or *ongul,* a hook, in reference to its shape). In the 5th century, from c449, accompanied by kindred peoples, the Saxons and Jutes (and possibly some Frisians), they crossed over to Britain as conquerors and colonizers. The Angles were originally the most numerous of these settlers, and founded the three kingdoms of East Anglia, Mercia, and Northumbria. It was in Northumbria, which remained until c750

the most powerful of these and even exercised an intermittent hegemony over the chief kingdoms of the Saxons (Wessex) and of the Jutes (Kent), that a literature first appeared, and it was from the Northumbrians, as the initially dominant Angles, that the entire country derived its modern name of England, in Old English *Engla land,* "land of the Angles."

Anglesey or **Anglesea** (ang'gl.si). An island and county in N Wales, lying NW of the mainland, from which it is separated by Menai Strait; the strait is crossed by a famous suspension bridge, reconstructed in 1940. The surface of Anglesey is generally flat, the highest elevation being Holyhead Hill (703 ft.). Anglesey was an ancient seat of the Druids, was conquered by the Romans under Suetonius Paulinus in 61 A.D., and by Agricola in 78, and later became a Welsh stronghold. Length, ab. 28 mi.; width, ab. 20 mi.; area of county, ab. 276 sq. mi.

Angleterre (än.glĕ.ter). The French name of England.

Anglia (ang'gli.ạ). A Latin name of England; specifically, that part of England which was settled by the Angles.

Anglian (ang'gli.ạn). The name most often used for the dialect spoken by the Angles. It is used also, but less often, as an ethnic term for one of the people who spoke this dialect.

Anglican Church (ang'gli.kạn). See **Church of England.**

Anglicism (ang'gli.sizm). 1. An idiom of the English language.
2. A word or an expression used particularly in England, and not in use, or in good use, in the United States.

Anglicus (ang'gli.kus), **Bartholomaeus.** See **Bartholomaeus Anglicus.**

Anglo-Latin (ang'glō.lat'in). Middle or medieval Latin as written in England in the Middle Ages: the ordinary language of the church and the courts until the modern period. It is characterized by the liberal inclusion and free Latinizing of technical and vernacular English and Norman or Anglo-French terms.

Anglo-Saxon (ang'glō.sak'sọn). A member of the English people of Germanic stock or speech or both, particularly with reference to the period before the Norman Conquest; also, the English language during this period. As an adjective, the term is primarily applied to the English people in times before the Norman Conquest, their culture and institutions, language, and the like. Although occasionally used before 1066, the term Anglo-Saxon has been current chiefly in Modern English, having been revived in the late 16th century. In the Old English period the usual vernacular terms were *Engle* for the people (it had at first been applied to the Angles only), *Englisc* for the language, and *Angelcynn* for the country or the people. Many scholars today prefer to use Old English to designate the language of Anglo-Saxon England, because it parallels the terms Middle and Modern English and does not give rise to the misconception that the Conquest marked a breach in the continuity of linguistic development. This practice is followed in the present work.

Anglo-Saxon Chronicle, The. A name applied to a group of manuscripts that serve as chief source for the history and literature of England during the 10th, 11th, and part of the 12th centuries. The "chronicle" (some modern scholars prefer "Old English *Annals*" as a more descriptive title) is actually clearly divisible into several distinct units, which are nevertheless ordinarily treated as parts of the same overall series of annals, and the earlier portions of which comprise the oldest considerable example of English prose yet known. Work on this earliest portion was probably commenced (c892) by monks at Winchester, almost certainly at the behest of (and possibly with the actual editorial aid of) Alfred the Great. Certain parts of the work contain material from Bede and other earlier writers, but the greater portion of the chronicle consists of entries about events that took place at approximately the time of writing. The annals come to a close some years after the Norman conquest, at about the middle of the 12th century. Seven manuscript versions are now known to exist (all seven versions are in England), and range in their coverage from a final date of 977 to one of 1154.

Angus (ang'gus). In Shakespeare's *Macbeth*, a Scottish thane who eventually supports Malcolm against Macbeth.

Angus, 5th Earl of. Title of **Douglas, Archibald** (c1449–1514).

Anima Poetae (an'i.mạ pō'ẹ.tē). A volume of comments, criticisms, and miscellaneous literary observations compiled from notebook materials left by Samuel Taylor Coleridge at his death. It was published by Ernest Coleridge in 1895.

Animula (ạ.nim'ụ.lạ). A poem by T. S. Eliot, usually grouped with the six-poem sequence *Ash-Wednesday* (1930), and dealing, like it, primarily with the difficulty and cost of attaining the religious life, and also with its paradoxical nature. The poem *Animula* specifically expresses the perplexities of the soul projected into an existence from which it shrinks.

Anjou (an'jö; French, äṅ.zhö). A medieval countship and duchy of France. By the marriage of Geoffrey IV (Geoffrey Plantagenet) with Matilda, heiress of Henry I of England, the way was opened for the eventual joining of Anjou, England, and Normandy under an English ruler. This step took place in 1154 when Geoffrey's son, Henry, already in possession of the French territories, ascended the English throne as Henry II, and founded the Plantagenet (or Angevin) house of English rulers. Anjou was conquered (c1204) by Philip Augustus of France and was subsequently united with Naples and Provence. It was annexed finally and formally to the French crown in 1480 by Louis XI.

Anjou, Duke of. See **Reignier, Duke of Anjou.**

Ann (an). A young woman who seeks to marry Tanner, her extremely rational guardian, in Shaw's *Man and Superman.*

Anna (an'ạ). One of the principal female characters in John Home's play *Douglas.*

Annabel (an'ạ.bel). A character in John Dryden's *Absalom and Achitophel*, intended as a satirical portrait of the Duchess of Monmouth.

Annabella (an.ạ.bel'ạ). In John Ford's tragedy *'Tis Pity She's a Whore*, the sister of Giovanni, with whom she is carrying on an incestuous love affair. She marries Soranzo in an effort to escape from the consequences of it (she is carrying her brother's child), but her husband, discovering this, plans to be revenged upon the pair. She is killed in the end, however, by Giovanni, who is driven by his warped love to stab her just before the banquet planned by her husband as the scene of his revenge on both brother and sister.

Annabella, Queen. In Sir Walter Scott's novel *The Fair Maid of Perth*, the wife of King Robert III and mother of Rothsay.

Anna Comnena (kom.nē'nạ). b. at Constantinople, Dec. 1, 1083; d. c1150. A Byzantine princess and historian; daughter of Alexius I Comnenus. Having unsuccessfully conspired against her brother, John II, she retired to a convent where she wrote the *Alexiad*. She is a character in Scott's *Count Robert of Paris.*

Annajanska, the Bolshevik Empress (an.ạ.jan'skạ). A play (1918) by George Bernard Shaw, included by most critics among his lesser plays.

Anna Karenina (än'nạ kä.rä'nyi.nạ). A novel by Leo Tolstoy, published in 1855–57. The book, which has as its theme the nature of marriage, is set in the Russian society of the middle 19th century. The titular heroine, unhappy in her marriage to the much older Alexis Karenin, finds an affinity in Count Vronski; the rules of society, however, so far prevent the two from enjoying any happiness together that Anna, driven to desperation, commits suicide by throwing herself under a train after Vronski has rejoined his regiment.

Anna Livia Plurabelle (an'ạ liv'i.ạ plö'rạ.bel). The heroine of James Joyce's *Finnegans Wake*. She exemplifies, on a local scale, the River Liffey, and, on a broader scale, the whole female principle; concretely, she appears as Maggie Earwicker, the publican's wife. Her initials, ALP, are woven through the narrative, juxtaposed against those of the hero (HCE, for Humphrey Chimpden Earwicker).

Annals of the Parish. A novel by John Galt, published in 1821. In it, the events touching the simple lives of the parishioners of Dalmailing in Ayrshire are told with unconscious humor and realism by the Rev. Micah Balwhidder, against a background description of the rising industrialism of the period between 1760 and 1810.

Anna Matilda (an'ạ mạ.til'dạ). The name adopted by Mrs. Hannah Cowley, dramatist and poet, in a poetical correspondence with Robert Merry (who called himself "Della Crusca"). With two others of her school (the "Della Cruscans") she was held up to scorn by the critic William Gifford in his *Baviad and Maeviad*, and the name "Anna Matilda" acquired considerable usage as a synonym for namby-pamby verse and sentimental fiction.

Anna of the Five Towns (an'ạ). A novel by Arnold Bennett, published in 1902. A study of a young middle-class woman, it is the first volume in the first "Five Towns" trilogy, which also contains *Leonora*

(1903) and *Sacred and Profane Love* (1905; revised, 1911, as *The Book of Carlotta*). The "Five Towns" comprised a district in Staffordshire known as "the Potteries," a grimy and unlovely locality. Bennett himself came from one of the towns and his affectionate knowledge of it made him one of the foremost of the regionalists.

Anna St. Ives (an'ạ sānt ῑvz'). A novel (1792) by Thomas Holcroft. In it the revolutionary program of "perfectibility" is put into the form of fiction. The idealistic hero confounds the machinations of the aristocratic villain and in the end converts him to a better view of life.

Anne (an). b. at London, Feb. 6, 1665; d. at Kensington, England, Aug. 1, 1714. Queen of Great Britain and Ireland (1702–14); daughter of James II of England and Anne Hyde, and wife of Prince George of Denmark (married 1683). She was for much of her reign under the influence of the Duke and Duchess of Marlborough, and later of Mrs. Abigail Masham. She sided with William of Orange (who, as William III, was king of England from 1689 to 1702) in the English revolution that unseated her father, James II. Among the notable events of her reign were the War of the Spanish Succession and the union of England and Scotland. Her name is given to the graceful style of interior decoration associated with the early 18th century.

Anne, Lady. In Shakespeare's *Richard III*, the historical Anne Neville, daughter of Warwick "the Kingmaker" and widow of Edward, Prince of Wales. She curses Richard for the murder of her husband, but he wins and marries her. Later she admits that he has never slept well and that she regrets marrying him. Richard gives order for her close confinement when he plans to marry Elizabeth, and she dies under unexplained circumstances. Her ghost appears to Richard before the battle of Bosworth.

Anne Boleyn (bŭl'in). A tragedy by Henry Hart Milman, produced in 1821.

Anne Boleyn or **Bullen** (bŭl'ẹn). See also **Boleyn, Anne,** and **Bullen, Anne.**

Anne Elliot (el'i.ọt, el'yọt). See **Elliot, Anne.**

Anne of Bohemia (bō.hē'mi.ạ). b. at Prague, Bohemia (in what is now Czechoslovakia), May 11, 1366; d. June 7, 1394. Queen of England; daughter of the emperor Charles IV and wife of Richard II of England. It was while she was queen that Richard, infuriated because its bankers refused his request for a loan, revoked the rights of the City of London, and it was largely through the persuasive efforts of Anne that Richard was prevailed upon to restore them.

Anne of Cleves (klēvz). b. at Cleves, Germany, 1515; d. in England, 1557. Queen of England; daughter of the Duke of Cleves and fourth wife of Henry VIII. She was selected for Henry by Thomas Cromwell, for political reasons. She was married in January, 1540, and divorced in July of the same year. Having agreed to live in England for the rest of her life, she died there, and is buried in Westminster Abbey.

Anne of Denmark. b. at Skanderborg, Denmark, Dec. 12, 1574; d. March 2, 1619. Queen of England and Scotland; daughter of Frederick II of Denmark and wife of James VI of Scotland (James I of England). She was interested in elaborate entertainments, personally taking part in masques by Ben Jonson and Thomas Dekker.

Anne of Geierstein (gī'ẽr.shtῑn, -stῑn). A romance by Sir Walter Scott, published in 1829. This is one of the works that Scott wrote during the last seven years of his life, when he was burdened by debt and forced himself to unremitting toil to satisfy his creditors. The scene is set mainly in Switzerland at the time of the reign of Edward IV of England. The Earl of Oxford and his son, Arthur de Vere, are exiled from England after the Yorkist victory at Tewkesbury and, disguised as the merchants Philipson, are travelling to see Charles the Bold, Duke of Burgundy, in the interests of the Lancastrian party. While in the mountains of Switzerland they are entertained by Arnold Biederman and his niece, the Countess Anne of Geierstein. Oxford and his son decide to accompany Biederman and other Swiss delegates who wish to protest against certain proceedings of Charles the Bold, as they must see the duke. They are captured en route by the wicked and cruel Archibald of Hagenbach, who is the governor of a stronghold of the duke's, and escape death only by the rising of the citizens against Hagenbach. Their plans for negotiations with Charles the Bold are brought to an end by the defeat of the duke at Granson and Morat by the Swiss and his subsequent death at Nancy. Oxford and his son return to Geierstein, where Arthur marries Anne. Interesting elements of the book include the secret tribunal of the Vehmgericht (based at least partially on Goethe's *Götz von Berlichingen*), the picture of Charles the Bold, and the description of the court of René, the king of Troubadours.

Anne Page (pāj). See **Page, Anne.**

Anne Severn and the Fieldings (sev'ẽrn; fēl'dingz). A novel by May Sinclair, published in 1922.

Annesley (anz'li), **James.** b. 1715; d. Jan. 5, 1760. An English claimant to nobility, the subject of Charles Reade's *Wandering Heir*. His legitimacy as son of Lord Altham (d. 1727) being disputed, he was sent into slavery (1728–40) in America by his uncle who also claimed the title. His subsequent lawsuit to establish his claim was used in part in Smollett's *Peregrine Pickle* and Scott's *Guy Mannering*.

Annie Laurie (an'i lô'ri). A song written by William Douglas of Kirkcudbright and widely popular in Great Britain, the U. S., and other English-speaking countries.

Anniversary, The. A poem (1633) by John Donne, celebrating the eternal and ever-present quality of love.

Ann Lovely (an luv'li). See **Lovely, Ann.**

Annot Lyle (an'ọt lῑl'). See **Lyle Annot.**

Ann Pornick (an pôr'nik). See **Pornick, Ann.**

annual (an'ū.ạl). A literary production published annually; especially, an illustrated work issued near Christmas of each year. The name is more especially applied to certain publications handsomely bound, illustrated with plates, and containing prose, tales, poems, etc., which were formerly very popular, but are now no longer issued. The first one published in London appeared in 1822, and the last in 1856.

Annual Register, The. A periodical founded in 1758 and published by Robert Dodsley, a fashionable bookseller of the time and the leading publisher of English poetry. Edmund Burke was the first contributor. Each annual volume contained a retrospective account of the year, even including reviews of a few chosen books. Somewhat imitative in concept of early registers, such as John Meres's *Historical Register* for the years 1714–38, it surpassed its predecessors by being more inclusive and more literary. Burke remained the principal conductor of this undertaking, of which he made an enormous success, for over 31 years.

Annunciation, Feast of the. [Also, **Lady Day.**] A Roman Catholic holy day observed on March 25. It commemorates the Annunciation (the announcement to the Virgin Mary by the angel Gabriel that she was to be the mother of Christ).

Annus Mirabilis (an'us mi.rab'i.lis). [Eng. trans., "*The Year of Wonders.*"] A poem (published 1667) by John Dryden, descriptive of the Dutch war and the London fire of 1666. Dryden regards his material as historical rather than epic, but insists on the lofty heroic quality of the events, and he makes them majestic both by the sound of the verse and by the use of grandiose imagery. Many critics feel that the poem is on the whole less interesting than its preface, in which Dryden sets forth his notion of poetic imagination.

Ann Veronica (an' vẹ.ron'i.kạ). [Full title, **Ann Veronica: A Modern Love Story.**] A novel by H. G. Wells, published in 1909. This is the story of a girl who decides that she will break away from the security and confinement of her home and discover what life really is, and quickly learns that she is restricted by lack of money and that this is a man's world. She joins the Woman's Suffrage movement in her determination to change woman's place in society and is put into prison. She later falls in love with Capes, a married man, and they go abroad together; eventually they are able to get married and return to England.

Another Time. A collection of poems (1940) by W. H. Auden, including biographical poems on Housman, Edward Lear, Rimbaud, Melville, Pascal, Voltaire, Matthew Arnold, Yeats, Ernst Toller, and Freud. The poems "The Novelist," "Musée des Beaux Arts," and "The Composer" show an increased interest by Auden in the problems of creative expression as subject matter for poetry. Seven of the poems in this collection are sonnets, and there is little of Auden's usual experimentation with forms except in the songs, which include several ballads and a madrigal.

Anselm (an'selm), Saint. b. at Aosta, Italy, 1033; d. at Canterbury, England, 1109. A Burgundian prelate who became archbishop of Canterbury; forerunner of the great medieval scholastic philosophers. In 1060 he became a monk at Bec, in Normandy; he studied under Lanfranc and succeeded him as prior (1063–78) of Bec, in the latter year becoming abbot. Made archbishop of Canterbury in 1093 by William II of England (William Rufus), he accepted reluctantly, with the stipulation that church rule of prelates, rather than royal sanction (inaugurated by Gregory VII), be observed, thus beginning a long struggle with William (1087–1100) and with Henry I (1100–35) over the right of investiture, ending in compromise (1107) with Henry. An expositor of Augustinian doctrine and of the priority of faith over reason, he anticipated the thought of later scholastics, though he was not accepted by them because he wrote tracts and dialogues (as distinguished from treatises) on separate questions. He is now most noted for his ontological proof of the existence of God, which states that the concept of perfection encompasses all desirable traits, including real existence. Immanuel Kant, among others, attempted a refutation of this reasoning, but it remains nevertheless one of the most often cited of arguments in support of the existence of God. He was the author of *Monologion* and *Proslogion* (on God) and *Cur Deus Homo* (on atonement). He was canonized (1494) by Pope Alexander VI.

Anson (an'sọn), Sir **William Reynell.** b. at Walberton, Sussex, England, 1843; d. 1914. An English jurist, university official, and member of Parliament. He was vice-chancellor of Oxford (1898–99) and Liberal Unionist member of Parliament (1899 *et seq.*). Author of *Principles of the English Law of Contract* (1879), the two-volume *Law and Custom of the Constitution* (1886, 1892), and others.

Anster (an'stẹr), **John.** b. at Charleville, County Cork, Ireland, 1793; d. at Dublin, June 9, 1867. An Irish scholar and poet, regius professor of civil law at Dublin (1850–67). He translated Goethe's *Faust* (1835, 1864), works by Schiller, La Motte-Fouqué, and others. Author of biographies (in the *North British Review*, 1847 *et seq.*) of Shelley, Swift, and others.

Anster Fair. A poem (1812) by William Tennant. It is notable chiefly for the fact that it served to introduce the Italian mock-heroic style into English literature.

Anstey (an'sti), **Christopher.** b. at Brinkley, England, Oct. 31, 1724; d. at Chippenham, England, Aug. 3, 1805. An English satirical poet. He was a fellow (1745) of King's College, Cambridge, where he wrote Latin verses and was refused the degree of master of arts because of his opposition to regulations. Author of *New Bath Guide* (1766) and *The Election Ball* (1776), letters in varied verse poking fun at Bath society, the first of which was in its day enormously popular.

Anstey, F. Pseudonym of **Guthrie, Thomas Anstey.**

Antaeus (an.tē'us). In Greek mythology, a Libyan giant and wrestler, son of Poseidon, god of the sea, and Gaea, the earth. He was invincible so long as he remained in contact with his mother. He compelled strangers in his country to wrestle with him, and built a house to Poseidon of their skulls. Hercules discovered the source of his strength, and, lifting him into the air, crushed him.

Antenor (an.tē'nọr). In Greek legend, a Trojan, according to Homer the wisest of the elders. He was the host of Menelaus and Odysseus when they visited Troy, and strongly advised the Trojans to surrender Helen. His friendliness toward the Greeks in the end amounted, from the Trojan point of view, to treason.

Antenor. In Shakespeare's *Troilus and Cressida*, a Trojan commander who is captured by the Greeks and exchanged for Cressida.

Anteros (an'tē.ros). In Greek mythology, a brother of Eros: god of mutual love and avenger of love unrequited.

anthology (an.thol'ọ.ji). A collection of writings, either poetry or prose, usually by various authors. Selections in an anthology are commonly grouped on a basis of some particular subject or interest, as that of publishing the best prose or verse of a particular literature, period, or group of authors. Some anthologies may focus upon a relatively narrow aspect of a subject, whereas others, by the arrangement of selections, may attempt to instruct the reader in a general appreciation of literature. One important function of some anthologies is to publish and bring to the attention of the public contemporary, unknown writers. Anthologies date back to the *Stephanos* ("Wreath") of Meleager (c90 B.C.), a collection of epigrams by some 50 Greek poets. This was gradually enlarged and eventually became part of the *Anthologia Palatina*, a collection of Greek poems and epigrams, made about 925 by a Byzantine, Constantine Cephalas. Similar collections were made of Latin poetry, as well as of Arabic writings. Both the Bible and the Koran may be considered types of anthologies. In English literature, *Tottel's Miscellany*, published in 1559 and including the major works of Wyatt and Surrey, was one of the earliest of numerous anthologies. Among the important subsequent anthologies in English are *England's Helicon* (1602; containing works of Sidney and Spenser); Percy's *Reliques of Ancient English Poetry* (1765); and Palgrave's *Golden Treasury* (1861), a collection of standard works of English poets.

anticlimax (an.ti.klī'maks). A figure or fault of style, consisting in an abrupt descent from stronger to weaker expressions, or from the mention of more important to that of less important things.

Anthony (an'thọ.ni, -tọ-). Entries on literary characters having this prename will be found under the surnames Absolute, Anderson, Bonthron, Branville, Chuzzlewit, Denny, Foster, and Wybrow.

Anthony, C. L. Pseudonym of **Smith, Dodie.**

Antic Hay. Novel (1923) by Aldous Huxley.

Anticleia (an.ti.klē'ạ). In Greek legend, the mother of Odysseus. She died of grief at his prolonged absence.

Antigone (an.tig'ọ.nē). In Greek legend, a daughter of Oedipus by his mother Jocasta. She accompanied Oedipus, as a faithful daughter, in his wanderings until his death at Colonus; she then returned to Thebes. According to Sophocles, Haemon, the son of Creon (who in other accounts was then dead), fell in love with her. Contrary to the edict of Creon, she buried the body of her brother Polynices, who had been slain in single combat with his brother Eteocles, and (according to Sophocles) was shut up in a cave where she perished by her own hand. Haemon also slew himself. Various other accounts of her life and death are given.

Antigone. A tragedy by Sophocles, of uncertain date.

Antigonus (an.tig'ọ.nus). In Shakespeare's *Winter's Tale*, a lord of Sicilia and husband of Paulina. He is sent by Leontes to abandon Perdita in a "desert place," takes her to the "seacoast of Bohemia," and there is killed by a bear.

Antigonus. In John Fletcher's *Humorous Lieutenant*, an old and licentious king.

Anti-Jacobin (an.ti.jak'ọ.bin), **The.** An English periodical issued weekly (1797–98) founded by George Canning and others that attacked the philosophy of the French Revolution and its English sympathizers, edited by William Gifford.

Anti-Jacobin Review, The. A monthly (1798–1821) started by John Gifford as a successor to *The Anti-Jacobin.*

Antilla (an.til'ạ) or **Antillia** (-til'i.ạ). See under **Seven Cities, Island of the.**

antimasque (an'ti.màsk). [Also, **antimask.**] A secondary or lesser masque, of a ludicrous character, introduced between the acts of a serious masque by way of lightening it; a ludicrous interlude.

Antinoüs (an.tin'ọ.us). b. in Bithynia, Asia Minor; fl. c110–130 A.D. The page, attendant, and favorite of the emperor Hadrian. After he was drowned in the Nile during a trip to Egypt, Hadrian established a cult to deify him, named cities in his honor, and commissioned statues which portray him as an ideal of youthful beauty.

Antiochus (an.tī'ọ.kus). In Shakespeare's *Pericles*, the King of Antioch. He tries to poison Pericles, who has discovered his incestuous relationship with his daughter. Fire from heaven finally destroys him.

Antiochus. In Philip Massinger's *Believe as You List*, the king of Lower Asia, a fugitive. His patient suffering at the hands of the cruel Roman ambassador, Flaminius, in his insistence upon his right, secures him considerable sympathy wherever he goes, but no assistance.

Antiope (an.tī'ọ.pē). In Greek legend, a daughter of the Boeotian river-god Asopus, and mother, by Zeus, of Amphio and Zethus.

Antiope. In Greek legend, the sister or daughter of Hippolyte, queen of the Amazons, and wife of Theseus.

Antipholus of Ephesus (an.tif'ọ.lus; ef'ẹ.sus) and **Antipholus of Syracuse** (sir'ạ.kūs). In Shakespeare's *Comedy of Errors*, twin brothers, the first of a violent and the latter of a mild nature. They are the sons of Aegeon, a merchant of Syracuse, and his wife, Aemilia. Their identical appearance and opposite natures furnish the plot complications, as each is mistaken for the other.

antiphrasis (an.tif'rạ.sis). In rhetoric, the use of a word in a sense opposite to its proper meaning, or when its opposite should have been used; irony, used either in sarcasm or in humor. "You now find no cause to repent that you never dipt your hands in the bloody high courts of justice, so called only by antiphrasis." (Robert Southey.)

Antiquary, The. A comedy (c1635) by Shakerley Marmion, characterized by a display of classical erudition and Jonsonian humor.

ḍ, d or j; ṣ, s or sh; ṭ, t or ch; ẓ, z or zh; *o*, F. cloche; ü, F. menu; ċh, Sc. loch; ṅ, F. bonbon.

Antiquary, The. A novel by Sir Walter Scott, published in 1816. A young officer, known as Major Neville, falls in love with Isabella Wardour, but her father makes her refuse the major's advances because he is supposed to be illegitimate. Under the assumed name of Lovel, the major follows Isabella to Scotland, where he becomes friendly with Jonathan Oldbuck, laird of Monkbarns and an antiquary. Lovel saves the life and fortune of Sir Arthur Wardour, Isabella's father, and it is finally revealed that he is the son and heir of the Earl of Glenallan (a repetition of the missing-heir plot which Scott had already used in *Guy Mannering*). The character of Oldbuck the antiquary, who, according to Scott, is drawn from a friend of his, George Constable, is far more interesting than the hero, as is the king's beadsman (licensed beggar), Edie Ochiltree.

Antisthenes (an.tis′thẹ.nēz). b. at Athens, c444 B.C.; d. there, after 371 B.C. An Athenian philosopher, founder of the school of the Cynics. He was a pupil of Socrates and taught in a gymnasium at Athens.

antistrophe (an.tis′trọ.fẹ). **1.** A part of an ancient Greek choral ode corresponding to the strophe, which immediately precedes it, and identical with it in meter. It was sung by the chorus when returning from left to right, they having previously sung the strophe when moving from right to left. The strophe, antistrophe, and epode (the last sung by the chorus standing still), in this sequence, were the last three divisions of a larger choral passage, which in its turn was treated as a unit and might be used once or repeated a number of times. This structure was occasionally imitated in Latin, and has sometimes been used in modern poetry. **2.** In rhetoric: (a) The reciprocal conversion of the same words in consecutive clauses or sentences: as, "the master of the servant, the servant of the master." (b) The turning of an adversary's plea against him: as, "Had I killed him as you report, I had not stayed to bury him."

antithesis (an.tith′ẹ.sis). A literary or rhetorical technique in which opposite or contrasting ideas or statements, usually of similar grammatical construction, are brought into close association.

Oh thoughtless Mortals! ever blind to Fate,
Too soon dejected, and too soon elate.
(Alexander Pope.)

Antoninus Pius (an.tọ.nī′nus pī′us). b. near Lanuvium, Italy, Sept. 19, 86 A.D.; d. at Lorium, Italy, March 7, 161 A.D. Emperor of Rome (138–161 A.D.). He was consul and proconsul in Asia under Hadrian, and was adopted by Hadrian in 138. His reign was marked by general internal peace and prosperity. The Wall of Antoninus was a wall from the Clyde to the Forth consisting of an earthen rampart and a ditch with watchtowers and stations to protect Britain from invasions by barbarians from the north.

Antonio (an.tō′ni.ō). In Shakespeare's *Merchant of Venice*, the princely merchant who gives the play its name. He is of a sensitive, melancholy nature, with a presentiment of evil and danger. Being obliged to borrow money from Shylock to meet the needs of Bassanio, his friend, he is induced to sign a bond agreeing to forfeit a pound of flesh if he does not repay the money within a specified time. Not being able to pay, he nearly loses his life to satisfy the demands of Shylock, but is saved by Portia who, disguised as a lawyer, points out to Shylock the impossibility of taking the flesh—his legal right—without spilling a drop of blood—a criminal act.

Antonio. In Shakespeare's *Much Ado About Nothing*, the aged brother of Leonato, Governor of Messina. When Leonato's daughter Hero has her reputation impugned by Claudio, he tries to comfort Leonato, and himself challenges Claudio.

Antonio. In Shakespeare's *Tempest*, the usurping Duke of Milan, and Prospero's brother, who is wrecked on the island where Prospero landed 12 years before. By Prospero's use of magic he is made to repent, and restores the dukedom to its rightful ruler.

Antonio. In Shakespeare's *Twelfth Night*, a sea captain devoted to Sebastian. He lends his purse to Sebastian and later (upon arriving in Illyria) mistakes Viola for Sebastian. Upon being arrested by the officers of Duke Orsino for fighting in defense of the supposed Sebastian, he demands the purse from her.

Antonio. In Shakespeare's *Two Gentlemen of Verona*, the father of Proteus.

Antonio. The chief male character of John Marston's double tragedy, *Antonio and Mellida* and *Antonio's Revenge*. Antonio is in love with Mellida, but has to overcome the opposition of her father, Piero, Doge of Venice. This he succeeds in doing by pretending that he is dead and having a promise made by Piero to give his daughter if it "would but redeem one minute of his death." In *Antonio's Revenge* Piero has poisoned Antonio's father (who has been exiled from Genoa), and now marries Antonio's mother and prevents the wedding of Antonio and Mellida. In despair over a false report of Antonio's suicide, Mellida kills herself. Antonio together with Pandulpho (whose son has been killed through Piero's machinations), appear in a masque at the Venetian court in disguise, and kill Piero. In the course of the action comprising the second part, the ghost of Antonio's father appears twice in a fashion quite similar to that of Hamlet's father in Shakespeare's *Hamlet*.

Antonio. In Thomas Tomkis's comedy *Albumazar*, an old gentleman, supposedly drowned, who returns in time to frustrate the schemes of the thievish Albumazar.

Antonio. In Thomas Middleton and William Rowley's play *The Changeling*, a secondary character who pretends for his own purposes to be an idiot or a changeling; it is from this that the play takes its name.

Antonio. In John Webster's tragedy *The Duchess of Malfi*, the steward of the household of the duchess, and, secretly, her husband. He is killed by Bosola, henchman of the Duchess' two vengeful brothers.

Antonio. In Thomas Otway's play *Venice Preserv'd*, a foolish speechmaker and senator whose buffooneries were probably intended to ridicule the first earl of Shaftesbury. As a comic role it does not harmonize well with the rest of the play.

fat, fāte, fär, ȧsk, fãre; net, mē, hėr; pin, pīne; not, nōte, mŏve, nôr; up, lūte, púll; ᴛʜ, then;

Antonio. In John Dryden's tragedy *Don Sebastian*, a young Portuguese nobleman, a slave at the time the play begins. Dorax, another character in the same play, calls him "The amorous airy spark, Antonio."

Antonio. A young man in love with Louisa in Sheridan's *The Duenna*.

Antonio and Mellida (an.tō′ni.ō; mel′i.dạ). [Full title, **The History of Antonio and Mellida.**] The first part of a two-part play (the second part being *Antonio's Revenge*), by John Marston, printed in 1602. It uses the conventional Italian setting and verse lines which Marston liked and had been played in 1601 prior to its printing. Antonio loves Mellida, the daughter of Piero, the Doge of Venice, who forbids their marriage and favors the son of the Duke of Florence. Indeed, the Doge has set a price upon the heads of both Antonio and his father, the Duke of Genoa, after the Venetian navy has defeated the Genoese. Antonio comes in the disguise of an Amazon to Venice and arranges to flee with Mellida, but is discovered and returns to his father. The Duke of Genoa now decides to present himself before the Doge of Venice to offer his head as the price of Mellida's bestowal upon Antonio. A coffin is borne in before the Venetian court, supposedly containing Antonio's body, and the Doge promises both his life and his daughter if Antonio can be brought back to life again. Antonio leaps up quite alive and the play ends happily. Marston gave freedom to his wish in the prologue that "our Muse . . . with a strain of fresh invention . . . might press out the rarity of art" by introducing such words as "glibbery" (applied to love, ice, and an urchin), "sliftered paunch" (of a wave), "chawn" (of a chasm in the earth), and phrases like "erect your gracious symmetry" (a suitor urges this of Mellida), "put all thy wits In wimble action" (a friend urges Antonio to do this). This play was ridiculed by Ben Jonson in *The Poetaster* and possibly in *Cynthia's Revels*.

Antonio Balladino (bal.ạ.dē′nō). See **Balladino, Antonio.**

Antonio's Revenge. The second (and tragic) part of a two-part play (the first part being *Antonio and Mellida*), by John Marston, printed in 1602. Piero, Doge of Venice, who has graciously yielded his daughter, Mellida, to Antonio in *Antonio and Mellida*, appears at the beginning covered with blood. In the interval between the two parts he has poisoned the Duke of Genoa, father of Antonio, and stabbed Feliche, who has supposedly committed adultery with Mellida. Feliche's father, Pandulpho, and Antonio are eager to be revenged. There is a similarity of situation to Shakespeare's *Hamlet* when Piero confesses that he has poisoned the Duke of Genoa to marry his widow, Maria. Mellida is now also forbidden to wed Antonio (her father now again wishes her to marry the son of the Duke of Florence). Antonio pretends to be mad and even takes the garb of a professional fool so that he may accomplish the revenge to which his father's ghost incites him. Meanwhile, Mellida kills herself upon hearing a false story of his suicide. In the final scene Antonio and Pandulpho appear in a masque which is presented at the Venetian court. In the course of this masque they murder Piero while the ghost of Antonio's father exults over the spectacle.

Antonius (an.tō′ni.us), **Marcus.** See **Mark Antony.**

Antony (an′tọ.ni). In Shakespeare's *Antony and Cleopatra*, the hero. See also **Mark Antony.**

Antony and Cleopatra (klē.ọ.pā′trạ, -pat′rạ, -pä′trạ). [Full title, **The Tragedy of Antony and Cleopatra.**] A tragedy by Shakespeare, written and produced c1607, entered on the Stationers' Register in 1608 and printed in 1623. It was founded on North's translation of Plutarch's *Lives* and in it Shakespeare followed history more closely than in any other of his plays. The subject was used by John Dryden in *All for Love* (1678), and by John Fletcher and Philip Massinger in *The False One*, but the character of Mark Antony is incomparably stronger in Shakespeare's play than in the others. Dryden makes him a weak voluptuary entirely given up to his passion for Cleopatra, whereas Shakespeare shows him as brave and noble. However, Dryden's play was acted more often than Shakespeare's for a century. It was not until 1849 that the Shakespeare play was produced in its original form, being mixed with scenes from Dryden until that time. The play is noted for its rich imagery and J. Middleton Murry has pointed out the close relationship between these images and the theme of the play, a powerful exposition of the beauty and strength of love.

The Story. In Alexandria, Antony luxuriates in the love of Cleopatra and the sybaritic life of the Egyptian court but, hearing of the death of his wife, Fulvia, and Pompey's uprising, he reluctantly departs for Rome. There he quarrels with Octavius, one of the Triumvirate with Lepidus and Antony, and in order to heal the breach between them Antony agrees to marry Octavius's sister, Octavia. Cleopatra, meanwhile, longs for Antony, and when the news of his marriage reaches her she almost kills the messenger in jealous wrath. Meanwhile, in Rome, the antagonism between the two men resumes and, unable to stay away from Cleopatra longer, Antony returns to Egypt. Octavius imprisons Lepidus, renews the war against Pompey, and begins a campaign against Antony. In Egypt, Octavius challenges Antony to a sea battle and Antony accepts, although his forces would have proved superior on land. During the battle at Actium, Cleopatra suddenly orders her fleet to retreat and Antony follows, thus losing both the battle and his honor. He tries to make peace with Octavius, requesting to be allowed to live in Rome, but Octavius refuses and sends a messenger to try to persuade Cleopatra to renounce Antony. Relations are tense between the two lovers, and as Antony's followers desert him, including his friend Enobarbus, doom seems imminent. Antony sends his friend's belongings after him, and Enobarbus, doubly stricken by his own betrayal in the face of this magnanimity on the part of Antony, dies of a broken heart. A land battle commences, but once more Cleopatra's retreat decides the victory in favor of Octavius. Antony determines to kill Cleopatra for her supposed treachery, and she, in terror, flees to her tomb and sends word to Antony that she has killed herself. Antony, believing the news, falls on his own sword, but lives long enough to be carried to Cleopatra, and the two reaffirm their eternal love. Cleopatra thereupon procures her own death with the bite of an asp.

Anubis (ạ.nū′bis). In Egyptian mythology, the son of Osiris, often identified by the Greeks with Hermes. He is represented with a jackal's head, and was the ruler of graves and supervisor of the burial of the dead.

Anville (an′vil), **Miss.** A false name assumed by the heroine of Fanny Burney's *Evelina*. She uses the name until she is recognized by her father, Sir John Belmont.

Anything for a Quiet Life. A play by Thomas Middleton, printed c1621.

Aonia (ā.ō′ni.ạ). In ancient geography, a district in Boeotia, Greece. The name is often used as synonymous with Boeotia.

Apaturia (ap.ạ.tū′ri.ạ). In Greek antiquity, the solemn annual meeting of the phratries for registering the free-born children born during the preceding year.

Apelles (ạ.pel′ēz). b. in Ionia; fl. 4th century B.C. A Greek painter, considered one of the great ancient artists. His style is described as a blend of Ionian and Dorian elements. He was celebrated particularly for his portraits, including one of Alexander with the thunderbolts of Zeus, and those of such other Macedonian notables as Archelaus, Clitus, and Antigonus. He also painted a procession of the high priest of Artemis, Artemis and her nymphs, and the *Aphrodite Anadyomene* (Aphrodite wringing out her hair as she rises from the sea), painted for the temple of Aesculapius at Cos. This last was probably his most noted work. None of his pictures are preserved. The nearest to a copy remaining is Raphael's drawing (now in the collection of the Louvre), from Lucian's description, of the allegory *Calumny*.

Apelles. In John Lyly's *Alexander and Campaspe*, a painter who falls in love with the slave girl, Campaspe.

Apemantus (ap.ẹ.man′tus). In Shakespeare's *Timon of Athens*, a cynical and churlish philosopher who warns Timon about his false friends. When Timon becomes a recluse, and even more misanthropic, he drives even Apemantus away from his cave.

apheresis (a.fer′e.sis). [Also, **aphaeresis**.] In grammar, the omission of a letter or an unaccented syllable from the beginning of a word. Examples in English are *round*, adv., for *around*, *vantage* for *advantage*, *squire* for *esquire*, *'mid* for *amid*, *'pon* for *upon*, etc.

aphorism (af′ọ.rizm). **1.** A definition or concise statement of a principle:

The aphorism . . . formulated by Linnaeus in regard to plants.
(Quatrefages, *Human Species*, trans.).

2. A precept or rule expressed in few words; a detached sentence containing some important truth: as, the *aphorisms* of Hippocrates, or of the civil law.

The three ancient commentators on Hippocrates . . . have given the same definition of an aphorism, i.e., "a succinct saying, comprehending a complete statement," or a saying poor in expression, but rich in sentiment. (Fleming.)

Aphrodite against Artemis (af.rọ.dī′tẹ; är′tẹ.mis). A play (1901) by Thomas Sturge Moore.

Apicata (ap.i.kā′tạ). In Ben Jonson's play *The Fall of Sejanus*, the wife of Sejanus.

Apis (ā′pis). In Egyptian mythology, the sacred bull of Memphis, worshiped by the ancient Egyptians. He was believed to be the incarnation of Osiris, and was the sacred emblem of that god. Sometimes he is portrayed as a man with a bull's head.

Apius and Virginia (ap′i.us; vėr.jin′yạ). An interlude (printed in 1575 and written c1563) by R.B., whom the 19th-century scholar, Fleay, thought was Richard Bower. It deals with the story of Appius and Virginia, which may be found in its original form in the works of Dionysius of Halicarnassus, but the plot of the decemvir, Appius, against Virginia is here suggested by Haphazard, who is a medieval vice in the morality tradition. As a vice he actually is turned into a "humour" character (i.e., with a particular bias of temperament) rather than being an evil principle.

Apocalypse. An autobiographical work (1932) by D. H. Lawrence. It was published posthumously.

Apocalypse, The. The book of Revelation, the last book of the New Testament.

Apocrypha (ạ.pok′ri.fạ). A collection of 14 books subjoined to the canonical books of the Old Testament in the authorized version of the Bible, as originally issued, but now generally omitted. They do not exist in the Hebrew Bible, but are found with others of the same character scattered through the Septuagint and Vulgate versions of the Old Testament. They are: First and Second Esdras (otherwise Third and Fourth Esdras, reckoning Nehemiah as Second Ezra or Esdras), Tobit or Tobias, Judith, the Rest of Esther, Wisdom of Solomon, Ecclesiasticus, Baruch (as joined to Jeremiah), parts of Daniel (namely, Song of the Three Children, the History of Susanna, the Destruction of Bel and the Dragon), the Prayer of Manasses, and First and Second Maccabees. Most of these are recognized by the Roman Catholic Church as canonical, though theologians of that church often distinguish them as deutero-canonical, on the ground that their place in the canon was decided later than that of the other books, limiting the name Apocrypha to the two books of the Esdras and the Prayer of Manasses, and other books not in the above collection, namely, Third and Fourth Maccabees, a book of Enoch, an additional or 151st Psalm of David, and 18 Psalms of Solomon. With these sometimes are included certain pseudepigraphic books, such as the Apocalypse of Baruch and the Assumption of Moses. The name Apocrypha is also occasionally made to embrace the Antilegomena of the New Testament. The Greek Church makes no distinction among the books contained in the Septuagint.

apodosis (a.pod′ọ.sis). In grammar, the concluding part of a conditional sentence; the consequent which results from or is dependent on the protasis, or condition; the conclusion. Thus, in the sentence, "If it rains, I shall not go," the first clause is the protasis, the second the apodosis. When the protasis is introduced by such conditional conjunctions as *notwithstanding*, *though*, *although*, the apodosis predicates something opposite to what might have been looked for: as, "Although we were few in numbers [protasis], we overthrew the enemy [apodosis]." By some grammarians the term is not restricted to conditional sentences, but is extended to others similarly constructed: thus, in a simile the apodosis is the application or latter part.

Apollo (a.pol'ō). In Greek and later in Roman mythology, one of the great Olympian gods, the son of Zeus and Leto, representing the light- and life-giving influence, as well as the deadly power, of the sun, and often identified with the sun-god Helios. He was the leader of the Muses, god of music, poetry, and healing, and patron of these arts; a mighty protector from evil, all-seeing, and hence the master of prophecy; also the destroyer of the unjust and insolent, and ruler of pestilence. In art he was represented in the full majesty of youthful manhood, usually unclothed or only lightly draped, and usually characterized by the bow and arrows, the laurel, the lyre, the oracular tripod, the serpent, or the dolphin. He was the father of Aesculapius, to whom he granted his art of healing. Apollo was honored, both locally and generally, under many special titles, of which each had its particular type in art and literature: as, *Apollo Citharoedus* (Apollo who sings to the accompaniment of the lyre), equivalent to *Apollo Musagetes*, the conductor of the Muses; *Apollo Chresterios* (the Apollo of oracles), *Apollo Sauroktonos* (the lizard-killer), and others. In Roman mythology he was primarily a god of healing.

Apollo Belvedere (bel.vẹ.dir'; Italian, ä.pôl'lō bel.vä-dā'rä). The most famous extant statue of Apollo, a marble figure carved during the early Roman empire, now in the collection of the Belvedere, Vatican, Rome, discovered (1485) at Antium (now Anzio, Italy). It was copied from a Greek original in bronze. Just over life size, it depicts a vigorous, youthful god wearing a chlamys around the neck and over the extended left arm. The left hand, one of the parts restored by Montorsoli, a pupil of Michelangelo, holds part of an object variously thought to have been an aegis, a bow from which he has shot an arrow, or another weapon. The original may have been a commemorative figure erected at Delphi to celebrate the expulsion of the Gauls (279 B.C.) from the temple of Apollo.

Apollo Club, The. A 17th-century club meeting at the Devil Tavern, near Temple Bar, London. Jonson and Herrick were members.

Apollonius (ap.ọ.lō'ni.us). See under **Pericles.**

Apollonius of Tyre (tīr), **The History of.** A Greek romance, of which the earliest known version is in Latin prose. It was much translated in the Middle Ages, and is the source of one of the tales in Gower's *Confessio Amantis* and in part of Shakespeare's *Pericles.*

Apollonius Rhodius (rō'di.us). [Also, **Apollonius of Rhodes** (rōdz).] fl. at Alexandria and Rhodes 3rd century B.C. A Greek epic poet, author of *Argonautica*, on the legend of the Golden Fleece, an imitation of Homer which was in turn used by Vergil, Marianus, and others. He is known to have been, for a time, librarian at Alexandria.

Apollyon (a.pol'yọn). The angel of destruction, who is introduced by Bunyan as Christian's antagonist in *Pilgrim's Progress.* The name is a Greek rendering of Abaddon, the Hebrew term which originally meant the bottomless pit of which Apollyon is the keeper (Rev. ix. 11).

Apollyonists, The. A poem (1627) by Phineas Fletcher, an English paraphrase of his Latin poem, *Locustae, vel Pietas Jesuitica*, prompted by the Gun Powder Plot of 1605. The poem is an allegorical representation of the Gun Powder Plot, showing how the fallen angels under Satan work their revenge on God. Fletcher's conception of Satan as a very strong figure and the representation of Sin as the porter of Hell greatly influenced Milton in *Paradist Lost.*

Apologia pro Vita Sua (ap.ọ.lō'gi.a prō vī'ta sū'a). An autobiographical treatise (1864) by Cardinal Newman.

Apologie for Poetrie, An. [Also, **Defence of Poesie.**] A short prose work by Sir Philip Sidney, published in 1595 and again in 1598 as *Defence of Poesie.* It was written (c1579) in answer to Stephen Gosson's *The School of Abuse*, which attacked poetry and drama. Sidney considers all forms of creative writing to be poetry and upholds them as an entertaining means of useful instruction. He discusses the various forms of poetry and their relation to history, gives an outline of English literature from the time of Chaucer, and explains his ideas on the principles of drama.

apologue (ap'ọ.log). A story or relation of fictitious events intended to convey useful truths; a moral fable; an allegory. An *apologue* differs from a *parable* in that the latter is drawn from events which occur among mankind, and is therefore supported by probability, while the former may be founded on supposed actions of brutes or inanimate things, and therefore does not require to be supported by probability. Aesop's fables are good examples of apologues.

Apology for Actors, An. Work in three books by Thomas Heywood, published in 1612, and reprinted in 1658 by William Cartwright, with some alterations, under the title of *The Actors' Vindication.* It is one of the most successful apologias in English, and, though it opens with a sharp rebuke of "the sundry exclamations of many seditious sectists in this age, who in the fatness and rankness of a peaceable commonwealth grow up like unsavory tufts of grass," it proceeds with modesty and common sense.

apophasis (a.pof'a.sis). In rhetoric, denial of an intention to speak of something which is at the same time hinted or insinuated.

aposiopesis (ap''ō.sī.ọ.pē'sis). In rhetoric, sudden reticence; the suppression by a speaker or writer of something which he seemed to be about to say; the sudden termination of a discourse before it is really finished. The word is also applied to the act of speaking of a thing while pretending to say nothing about it, or of aggravating what one pretends to conceal by uttering a part and leaving the remainder to be understood: as, "His character is such—but it is better I should not speak of *that*."

Apostate, The. A tragedy by Richard Lalor Sheil, produced in 1817.

apostrophe (a.pos′trō.fē). In rhetoric, a digressive address; the interruption of the course of a speech or writing, in order to address briefly a person or persons (present or absent, real or imaginary) individually or separately; hence, any abrupt interjectional speech. Originally the term was applied only to such an address made to one present.

apothegm (ap′ō.them). [Also, **apophthegm**.] A short, pithy, instructive saying; a terse remark, conveying some important truth; a sententious precept or maxim.

apparatus (ap.ạ.rā′tus). A collection of materials for any literary work: as, critical *apparatus* for the study of the Greek text of the New Testament.

Apperley (ap′ėr.li), **Charles James.** [Pseudonym, **Nimrod**.] b. at Plasgronow, Wales, 1777; d. at London, May 19, 1843. An English writer on sporting matters, author of *The Life of a Sportsman* (1842), and others, popular with collectors, as well as sportsmen, for their illustrations by Henry Alken and others.

Appian Way (ap′i.ạn). The most famous of the ancient Roman highways. It ran from Rome to Brundisium (now called Brindisi), and is probably the first great Roman road which was formally undertaken as a public work. It was begun in 312 B.C. by Appius Claudius Caecus, the censor, who carried it as far as Capua. The next stage of the work extended it to Beneventum (Benevento), and it probably did not reach Brundisium until 244 B.C., when a Roman colony was inaugurated there. At present the Appian Way, for a long distance after it leaves Rome, forms one of the most notable memorials of antiquity in or near Rome, bordered as it is by tombs and the ruins of monumental buildings. Long stretches of the pavement remain perfect, and show that the width of the roadway proper was only 15 ft. Length, ab. 350 mi.

Appius (ap′i.us) or **Appius Claudius** (klô′di.us). See under **Physician's Tale, The.**

Appius and Virginia (vėr.jin′yạ). A tragedy attributed to John Webster and Thomas Heywood, printed in 1654 as by Webster alone. No one knows exactly when it was written, and opinion varies as to the scenes by each playwright. The story, based on earlier versions by Dionysius of Halicarnassus and Livy, forms the first novel of the 19th day in the *Pecorone di Giovanni Fiorentino* (1378), and was reproduced in Painter's *Palace of Pleasure* (1st ed., 1566) two centuries later. There is a version of it in the *Roman de la Rose*. Chaucer tells it in *The Physician's Tale*, and Gower embodied it in his *Confessio Amantis*. John Dennis also wrote a tragedy with this name in 1709. See also **Apius and Virginia.**

Apple Cart, The. A play (1929) by George Bernard Shaw. The writing of the play was largely a result of Shaw's indignant repudiation of the British Socialist leader, Ramsay MacDonald. Shaw created in the play a mythical Socialist government led by Prime Minster Proteus, but actually controlled by an industrial combine called Breakages Limited.

Appreciations. A collection of miscellaneous essays by Walter Pater, published in 1889, and including the famous "Essay on Style."

Appuleius (ap.ū.lē′us), **Lucius.** See **Apuleius, Lucius.**

April Fools' Day. [Also, **All Fools' Day**.] April 1, the day for playing practical jokes on unsuspecting victims.

Apsley House (aps′li). The name of what was at one time the residence of the Duke of Wellington, at Hyde Park Corner in London. It was built for Lord Bathurst (whose family name was Apsley) in 1785, purchased by the government in 1820, and presented to the Duke of Wellington as part of the national reward for his services.

Apuleius (ap.ū.lē′us), **Lucius.** [Also, **Lucius Appuleius**.] b. in Numidia (or, according to some authorities, at what is now Bône, Algeria), c125 A.D.; fl. chiefly at Carthage. A Roman rhetorician and Platonic sophist, notable as a clever and versatile writer with an encyclopedic range of interests. He is probably now best known for his *Metamorphoses*, or *The Golden Ass*, one of the few Latin romances still extant. The extraordinary adventures (including metamorphosis into the shape of an ass) attributed by Apuleius to the hero of this fictional work were later freely adapted and used by Fielding, Smollett, Boccaccio, and Cervantes. However, Apuleius is also of some considerable importance, although less well known, for his scientific writings. His most important work in this field (particularly for the historian of medicine) was his book on magic (*De magia* or *Apologia*), which dealt with various matters not unrelated to those which were the concern of the first alchemists, and thus historically linked to what was later to emerge as modern science. All of his other scientific writings, including a translation of an early text on arithmetic, have now been lost, except for *De mundo* (*On the World*), and some scholars have even questioned the authenticity of extant copies of this.

Aquae Calidae (ak′wē kal′i.dē; ā′kwē) or **Aquae Solis** (sō′lis) or **Sulis** (sö′lis). Latin names of **Bath,** England.

Aquarius (ạ.kwār′i.us). A zodiacal constellation supposed to represent a man standing with his left hand extended upward, and with his right pouring out of a vase a stream of water which flows into the mouth of the Southern Fish. Its symbol is designed to represent a stream of water.

Aquilo (ak′wi.lō). A Latin personification of the north wind (Boreas).

Aquinas (ạ.kwī′nạs), Saint **Thomas.** [Called **Doctor Angelicus**, **"Father of Moral Philosophy,"** and (in fun by his schoolmates) the **"Dumb Ox."**] b. at Rocca Secca, near Aquino, Italy, c1225; d. at Fossanuova, Italy, 1274. Italian theologian, leading scholastic philosopher, ranked with the fathers of the Latin Church. He was educated at Monte Cassino and Naples, and joined (c1243) the Dominican order. A student at Paris (1245–48) under Albertus Magnus, he followed him to Cologne (1248), where he began teaching. His great fame was attained at Paris (1252–56 and 1268–72) and Rome (1259–68). At Paris he engaged in a great controversy with Siger de Brabant and the Averroists over the interpretation of Aristotle, which ended in a triumph for scholasticism. Founder of the philosophical system now called Thomism, and synthesizer of the theology which was pronounced (1879) as official for the Roman Catholic Church, he was a great medieval scholar in breadth of scope and brilliance of logic. He was the author of a *Mass for Corpus Christi* (1264), containing hymns considered among the finest in the Christian church and examples of masterful Latin prosody; also of a body of writing leading up to his *Summa Theologica*, chiefly a commentary (1254–56) on the *Sentences* of Peter Lombard, a work following Albertus Magnus and Augustinianism; commentaries (1265–73) on the *Physics*, *Metaphysics*, *De anima*, *Ethics*, and other works of Aristotle; and the *Summa de Veritate Catholicae Fidei contra Gentiles* (1258–60), an attempt to persuade non-Christians by distinguishing and reconciling reason and faith. The *Summa Theologica* (1267–73) a three-part work dealing with God, Man, and Christ, and intended to summarize all learning and to demonstrate his fundamental belief in the compatibility of faith and intellect, is still studied as one of the greatest philosophical works of all time. It was not, however, completed by him.

Aquitaine (ak.wi.tān′, ak′wi.tān; French, à.kē.ten). A medieval division of SW France, lying between the Garonne and Loire rivers. A Visigothic kingdom was founded there in the first part of the 5th century. It was conquered (507) by Clovis, became (c700) a duchy, and was conquered by Charlemagne and made a kingdom (including all S Gaul and the Spanish March) for his son Louis. In 838 Neustria was united to it, and it became soon after a duchy and one of the great fiefs of the French crown. Gascony was united to it in 1052. In 1137 it passed temporarily to France, by the marriage of Eleanor of Aquitaine with Louis VII of France, but in 1152 was united (by the marriage of Eleanor with Henry II of England) to Normandy and Anjou, and in 1154 to England, which retained it under John. It became (c1258) nominally a French fief, but was freed from French vassalage and granted to Edward III of England in 1360. Part of it was recovered from the English in the reign of Charles V of France, but was won back for England by Henry V. It was finally conquered by the French in 1451–53. It included (as Guienne) properly Bordelais, Rouergue, Périgord, Quercy, Agénois, and Bazadois, and comprised nearly the modern departments of Gironde, Dordogne, Lot, Lot-et-Garonne, and Aveyron.

Arabella (ar.a.bel′a). A character in David Garrick's play *The Male Coquette*.

Arabella. The romantic heroine of Charlotte Lennox's novel *The Female Quixote; or, the Adventures of Arabella* (2 vols., 1752).

Arabella Allen (al′en). See **Allen, Arabella.**

Arabella Briggs (brigz), **Miss.** See **Briggs, Miss Arabella.**

Arabella Transome (tran′sǫm), **Mrs.** See **Transome, Mrs. Arabella.**

Arabella Zeal (zēl). See **Zeal, Arabella.**

Arabia Deserta (a.rā′bi.a dē.zėr′ta). [Eng. trans., "*desert*," or "*uninhabited*," *Arabia*.] In ancient geography, the N and C portions of Arabia.

Arabia Deserta, Travels in. A prose work (1888) by C. M. Doughty.

Arabia Felix (fē′liks). [Eng. trans., "*flourishing*," or "*happy*," *Arabia*.] In ancient geography, the region in the SE and S parts of Arabia, or perhaps the peninsula proper.

Arabia Felix. A prose work (1932) by Bertram Thomas.

Arabian Nights' Entertainments, The. [Also, **A Thousand and One Nights.**] Collection of tales, originally in Arabic, of which the plan and name are very ancient. The source of some of the stories has been traced, others are traditional. In 943 al-Masudi speaks of a Persian work *A Thousand Nights and a Night*. In the course of centuries passages were added and taken from it, and in 1450 it was reduced to its present form in Egypt, probably at Cairo. The tales show their Persian, Indian, and Arabian origin. The stories are separate from each other in plot and the work as a whole is held together by the device of Scheherazade, the supposed teller of the tales. She is supposedly under sentence of death from her husband, but postpones her execution night after night by telling him a story almost to the end, but withholding the climax until the following night. The modern editions are Antoine Galland's, from the oldest known manuscript (1548), published in French at Paris, in 1704–17, in 12 volumes, an inaccurate translation; E. W. Lane's English scholarly translation, published in 1840; Payne's English translation, 1882–84; and Sir Richard Burton's English translation, printed (1885 *et seq.*) by the Kamashastra Society, for subscribers only, at Benares. Lady Burton issued an expurgated edition for popular reading, at London, 1886–88, in six volumes. One of the most recent editions is that by Pourys Mathers, from the French (4 vols., 1937).

Arabia Petraea (a.rā′bi.a pē.trē′a). [Eng. trans., "*stony*" *Arabia*.] In ancient geography, the NW part of Arabia.

Arabin (ar′a.bin), **Francis.** In *Barchester Towers* by Anthony Trollope, a clergyman and protégé of Dr. Grantly who later marries Mrs. Bold.

Arachne (a.rak′nē). In Greek legend, a Lydian maiden who challenged Athena to a contest in weaving, and was changed by her into a spider.

Arafat (ä.rä.fät′). A sacred mountain of the Mohammedans in W Arabia, situated ab. 15 mi. SE of Mecca. 1,980 ft.

Aragon (ar′a.gon). A medieval kingdom, subsequently a province of Spain, bordering on France. See also **Arragon.**

Aram (ār′am), **Eugene.** An English schoolmaster who was tried and executed for murder in 1759. He is the chief character in Bulwer-Lytton's novel, *Eugene Aram* (published 1832) and the subject of Hood's ballad, *The Dream of Eugene Aram*. See **Eugene Aram.**

Araminta (ar.a.min′ta). A wealthy young lady in William Congreve's comedy *The Old Bachelor* who finally marries the dissolute Vainlove.

Araminta. In John Vanbrugh's comedy *The Confederacy*, the wife of Moneytrap, an extravagant,

---

d̞, d or j; ṣ, s or sh; ṭ, t or ch; ẓ, z or zh; o, F. cloche; ü, F. menu; ċh, Sc. loch; ñ, F. bonbon.

luxurious woman with a marked leaning toward "the quality."

Aramis (à.rà.mēs). One of the "Three Musketeers," in the novel *The Three Musketeers*, by the elder Alexandre Dumas.

Aran Islands (ar'ạn). Three islands at the entrance of Galway Bay, in Connacht province, in the Irish Republic, included in County Galway. The islands form a chain ab. 15 mi. long, stretching from NW to SE. The largest, Inishmore, is ab. 9 mi. long; the others are Inishmaan and Inisheer.

Ara Vos Prec (ar'ạ vōs prek). A volume of poems (1919) by T. S. Eliot.

Arbaces (är'bạ.sēz, är.bā'-). In Beaumont and Fletcher's *King and No King*, the king of Iberia, whose nature is a compound of vainglory and violence.

Arbaces. In Byron's *Sardanapalus*, the governor of Media, who became, in place of Sardanapalus, the king of Nineveh and Assyria.

Arbaces. In Bulwer-Lytton's *Last Days of Pompeii*, the villainous guardian of the young and beautiful heroine, Ione.

Arbasto, the Anatomie of Fortune (är.bas'tō). Prose narrative (1584) by Robert Greene. It is a romantic tale about Arbasto, king of Denmark, who, while warring against the French king, fell in love with his daughter, Doralicia. She scorned him, but her sister Myrania loved him, released him from prison, fled with him to Denmark, and there died of a broken heart because of his indifference. Doralicia then repented and offered love, but was rebuffed and she too died. Arbasto's subjects revolted and banished him, and he found content as a hermit.

Arber (är'bėr), **Edward.** b. at London, Dec. 4, 1836; killed by a London taxicab, Nov. 23, 1912. An English admiralty clerk, professor, and research scholar. He edited a series of works of tremendous value to students and scholars, including *Arber's English Reprints* (39 vols., 1868–80), *An English Garner: Ingatherings from Our History and Literature* (10 vols., 1877–96, usually called *Arber's English Garner*), *English Scholar's Library* (16 vols., 1878–84), *Transcript of the Registers of the Company of Stationers of London, 1554–1640* (5 vols., 1875–94), *Term Catalogues 1668–1709* (3 vols., 1903–06).

Arber's English Garner. Ten volumes of modernized selections of English prose and poetry (1402–1715) edited by Edward Arber, 1877–96.

Arber's English Reprints. Thirty-nine volumes of textually exact reprints of English prose and poetry (1516–1712) issued by Edward Arber, 1868–80.

Arblastier (är.blas'tyėr), **William.** See **Alabaster, William.**

Arblay (där'blā), Madame d'. See **Burney, Fanny.**

Arbor of Amorous Devices, The. An anthology of poetry (1597) issued by Richard Jones under Nicholas Breton's name. Breton is not the sole author of these poems, although a good many are his. There was an edition of the *Arbor* in 1594, but no copy is known still to exist.

Arbuthnot (är.buth'nọt, är'buth.not), **Alexander.** b. in Kincardineshire, Scotland, 1538; d. 1583. A

Scottish poet, Protestant divine, and lawyer. Author of three short poems (*The Praises of Women, The Miseries of a Pure Scholar,* and *On Love*), a Latin work on the origin and dignity of the law, and a manuscript history, also in Latin, of his family.

Arbuthnot, John. b. at Arbuthnot, Scotland, 1667; d. at London, 1735. A British physician, wit, and man of letters. He was physician extraordinary (1705), and later (1709) in ordinary to Queen Anne. The Tory ministry employed him as a political writer. He joined Jonathan Swift, Alexander Pope, John Gay, and Thomas Parnell to form (c1713) the Scriblerus Club, and was a friend of Philip Dormer Stanhope, 4th Earl of Chesterfield, William Congreve, Swift, who mentions him frequently in *Journal to Stella*, and Pope, who dedicated to him the *Epistle to Dr. Arbuthnot* (1735). Author of satirical pamphlets, chiefly *Law is a Bottomless Pit, exemplified in the case of Lord Strutt, John Bull, Nicholas Frog, and Lewis Baboon, who spent all they had in a lawsuit* (1712), later known as *The History of John Bull,* a lively attack on Whig war policy which established (though it did not invent) the popular character of John Bull as the symbol personified of Great Britain; and the entertaining *Art of Political Lying* (1712), which recommended, among other suggestions, that a lie could best be countered with another lie. The *Memoirs of Martinus Scriblerus,* published (1741) in Pope's works but mainly written by Arbuthnot, is a satire of contemporary pedantry and antiquarianism.

Arc (ärk), **Joan of.** See **Joan of Arc.**

Arcades (är'kạ.dēz). A masque by John Milton, acted shortly after *Comus* in 1634, and printed in 1645.

Arcadia (är.kā'di.ạ). In ancient geography, a region in Greece, in the heart of the Peloponnesus, bounded by Achaea on the N, by Argolis on the E, by Laconia and Messenia on the S, and by Elis on the W. All but isolated by mountains and intersected by them, it was proverbial for its rural simplicity. Its cities Tegea, Mantinea, and others formed a confederation c370–360 B.C.

Arcadia. [Full title, **The Countess of Pembroke's Arcadia.**] A pastoral prose romance by Sir Philip Sidney, published in 1590, but written in 1580–81. It concerns the trials of the two pairs of lovers, Musidorus and Pamela, and Pyrocles and Philoclea. Abundant use is made of the devices of disguise and mistaken identity.

Arcadia. A romance by Robert Greene, published in 1589. It is modeled on Sir Philip Sidney's celebrated pastoral of the same name, which, although not printed until after the publication of Greene's *Arcadia,* had actually been written several years before it.

Arcadia. A pastoral play possibly by James Shirley, acted in 1639 and printed in 1640. It is a dramatization of Sir Philip Sidney's pastoral romance of the same name.

archaism (är'kạ.izm). **1.** The quality of being archaic; antiquity of style, manner, or use, as in art or literature. "A select vocabulary corresponding (in point of archaism and remoteness from ordinary use) to our Scriptural vocabulary." (De Quincey.)

2. That which is archaic; especially, an antiquated or obsolete word, expression, pronunciation, or idiom. "Doubtless the too free use of archaisms is an abuse." (G. P. Marsh, *Lectures on Eng. Lang.*)

Archas (är'kạs). The person in John Fletcher's *The Loyal Subject* whose character gives the play its name. He is a general of the Muscovites whose loyalty is pictured as being of the kind that bears all kinds of outrage from an unworthy king. Young Archas, the son of the general, disguises himself as a woman, and takes the name of Alinda.

Archer (är'chẽr), **Francis.** In George Farquhar's comedy *The Beaux' Stratagem*, a friend of Aimwell who pretends to be his servant in order to further the success of the stratagem. He carries on various lively adventures on his own account.

Archer, Isabel. In Henry James's novel, *The Portrait of a Lady* (1881), the heroine, a New England woman who inherits a fortune in England.

Archer, William. b. at Perth, Scotland, 1856; d. 1924. A British drama critic and playwright; translator and popularizer of Ibsen in England. Newspaper work in Scotland, Australia, and London was followed by the translation of Ibsen's *Pillars of Society*, the production of which (1880) at the Gaiety Theatre gave the London public its first taste of Ibsen. He edited *Ibsen's Prose Dramas* (5 vols., 1890–91). His own works included *English Dramatists of Today* (1882), *Henry Irving* (1883), *Masks or Faces* (1888), *Study and Stage* (1899), *The Old Drama and the New* (1923) and, with Granville-Barker, *A National Theatre* (1907), as well as several plays, including *The Green Goddess* (1923), a melodrama successful on both sides of the Atlantic.

Archibald, Earl of Douglas (är'chi.bôld; dug'lạs). See **Douglas, Archibald,** (4th) **Earl of.**

Archibald Campbell, (8th) **Earl of Argyll** (kam'bẹl, kam'ẹl; är.gīl'). See **Argyll.**

Archibald of Hagenbach (hä'gẹn.bäch). In Sir Walter Scott's novel *Anne of Geierstein*, a cruel follower of Charles the Bold.

Archidamus (är.ki.dā'mus). In Shakespeare's *Winter's Tale*, a Bohemian lord.

Archilochus (är.kil'ọ.kus). b. at Paros, in the Cyclades; fl. c700–650 B.C. A Greek lyric poet, probable inventor of iambic and trochaic meters. Embittered by poverty and by the refusal of a fellow townsman to give him his daughter in marriage, he became a wanderer and soldier, being eventually killed in battle. He used iambics in satires praised by Horace and Hadrian, among others. Author also of hymns (one of which was sung in the Olympics), elegies, and lampoons; he used the trochee in his serious works, and was the first to alternate long and short verses in the form called epode.

Archimage (är'ki.māj). [Also, **Archimago** (är.ki.mä'gō).] The personification of Hypocrisy in Edmund Spenser's *Faerie Queene*, a magician and a compound of deceit and credulity. He deceives Una by assuming the appearance of the Red Cross Knight, but his falsehood is exposed. The whole story is taken from Ariosto's *Orlando Furioso*.

Archimedes (är.ki.mē'dēz). b. at Syracuse, Sicily, c287 B.C.; killed there, 212 B.C. A Greek mathematician, engineer, and physicist, now usually considered to have been in each of these fields the outstanding figure of the ancient world. He was the discoverer of principles and the author of treatises basic to the subsequent study of geometry and calculus, particularly on the dimensions of the circle, sphere, cylinder, and parabola; in physics, developer of the displacement theory known as Archimedes' principle, and supposedly also of that of the lever (of which, according to tradition, he said, "Give me the place to stand, and I will move the world"); in mechanics he was the inventor of the Archimedean screw and various machines of war. The son of an astronomer, he was a student at Alexandria, and was probably associated with Conon of Samos. He spent much of his life at the court of Hiero II of Syracuse (who is said to have been his relative). Given the problem of analyzing the gold content of Hiero's crown, he is supposed to have cried "Eureka!" ("I have found [it]"), as, stepping into his bath, he discovered the relationship between weight and displacement of water, the principle now applied to determining the displacement of ships and specific gravity. His engines of war, which struck terror among the Romans and held them off for three years in their siege of Syracuse (214–212 B.C.), were considered unimportant by him. According to one tradition he was killed at the fall of Syracuse while drawing geometrical figures in the sand, though the Roman commander had ordered him spared for his great learning.

Archipropheta (är.ki.prof'ẹ.tạ). A tragedy (c1547) written in Latin by Nicholas Grimald.

Archon (är'kon). In John Dryden's poem *Albion and Albanius*, a character intended to represent George Monck.

Archy MacSarcasm (mak.sär'kaz.ẹm), **Sir.** See **MacSarcasm, Sir Archy.**

Arcite (är'sīt). A character in Chaucer's *Knight's Tale* (q. v.), and also a (different) character in his *Anelida and Arcite*. See also **Palamon and Arcite.**

Arcite. In *The Two Noble Kinsmen*, one of the principal characters, the cousin of Palamon.

Arden (är'dẹn), **Alice.** See **Arden of Feversham, Tragedy of Mr.;** see also under **Alice.**

Arden, Forest of. An English forest which in former times extended through Warwickshire and other midland counties of England. Many scholars of Shakespeare have held that the Forest of Arden of *As You Like It* was the Forest of Ardennes in French Flanders. Wherever the scene of the play was laid, it is likely from the allusions to Robin Hood and the bits of description that it is the English forest that Shakespeare meant, though some of the characters have French names. A comparatively small wooded area in N Warwickshire is all that remains today of the original forest. In the long topographical poem *Polyolbion* Drayton had it extending from the Severn to the river Trent.

Ardennes (är.den'), **Wild Boar of.** See **Marck, William de la.**

Arden of Feversham (är'den; fev'ẽr.shạm). A tragedy, published by George Lillo in 1736, founded on the earlier *Tragedy of Mr. Arden of Feversham*, and played first in 1759. It was unfinished when Lillo died in 1739, and was thereafter completed by other hands. It was considerably altered and revised by Dr. John Hoadley in 1762, and was produced in this form in 1790.

Arden of Feversham, Tragedy of Mr. A tragedy first printed (anonymously) in 1592, sometimes attributed to Shakespeare, and dramatized from Raphael Holinshed's account of the murder of a leading citizen of Feversham (now Faversham) in Kent in 1551. The play offers a vivid and fairly realistic picture of English middle-class life of the time. The plot, which has the wife, Alice, and her paramour, Masby, murdering the husband, Arden, suggests Clytemnestra and Aegisthus in the *Agamemnon* of Aeschylus. According to Frederick Gard Fleay, who dates it 1585, there is some ground for attributing it to Thomas Kyd. Ludwig Tieck translated it into German as Shakespeare's work.

Ardoch (är'doch). A parish in S Perthshire, Scotland, ab. 12 mi. N of Stirling. It has noted Roman military antiquities (the best-preserved Roman camp in Great Britain), and is the probable site of the victory of Agricola over the North Britons in 84 A.D.

Ardven (ärd'ven). In the poems of Ossian, a name given to a region on the W coast of Scotland.

Areopagitica (ar''ē.ọ.pạ.jit'i.kạ). [Full title, **Areopagitica, or Speech for the Liberty of Unlicensed Printing**.] A pamphlet by John Milton, published in 1644. It is an argument in behalf of liberty of conscience and freedom of the press. It is one of the first and most famous of English works on this subject. Milton appeals to Parliament to repeal the licensing of the press, saying that art must be unrestricted or it will perish. He urges an attitude that would view books as living things, so that to burn them is to destroy life itself.

Areopagus (ar.ē.op'ạ.gus). [Eng. trans., *"Hill of Mars"* (Ares).] A low rocky hill at Athens, Greece, continuing westward the line of the Acropolis, from which it is separated by a depression of ground. On the S side near the top there is a flight of 15 rock-cut steps, and portions of the summit are hewn smooth to form platforms, doubtless for altars. Upon this hill sat the famous court of the same name, which originally exercised supreme authority in all matters, and under the developed Athenian constitution retained jurisdiction in cases of life and death and in religious concerns, and exercised a general censorship. From the slopes of the Areopagus Saint Paul delivered his address to the Athenians (Acts, xvii.), who were probably assembled on the border of the Agora below.

Ares (ār'ēz). In Greek mythology, the god of war (son of Zeus and Hera), typical particularly of the violence, brutality, confusion, and destruction it calls forth. The corresponding Roman deity was Mars. Ares is the subject of a poem by Chaucer, *The Complaint of Mars*, written probably c1379.

Arete (ạ.rē'tē). The companion of Cynthia, in Ben Jonson's *Cynthia's Revels*, a dignified, grave lady, personifying Virtue or Reasonableness.

Arethusa (ar.ē.thū'sạ). A name of various springs in ancient Greece, especially of one on the island of Ortygia in the harbor of Syracuse. With it was connected the legend that Arethusa, a nymph of Elis, while bathing in the Alpheus, was surprised by a lover, the river god, and fled from him to Ortygia; he followed under the sea and overtook her.

Arethusa. In Beaumont and Fletcher's play *Philaster*, a princess, a woman of the greatest self-abnegation and womanly devotion.

Aretino (ä.rä.tē'nō), **Pietro.** [Called the **"Scourge of Princes"**; original surname, **Bacci**.] b. at Arezzo, Italy, April 20, 1492; d. at Venice, Oct. 21, 1556. An Italian writer of poems, satires, comedies, letters, and dialogues. Born of plebeian parents, he left home at 14 to become an art student and then a vagabond. In 1516, he took a menial position with the Roman banker, Agostino Chigi, whence he attracted the attention of Pope Leo X with a mordant satire. Thereafter, as a hired wit and literary bravo, he served Leo, the marquis of Mantua, Pope Clement VII, and the Medici warrior, Giovanni delle Bande Nere, until a threat against his life caused him, in 1527, to take refuge at Venice, where he remained until his death. There, living like a magnifico in a palace filled with great art and rowdy hangers-on, he discovered that by having many employers, he could dispense with subservience to one patron. By 1537, his pen had earned him 10,000 crowns, and he had become friend and adviser to Titian (whose portrait of Aretino is now in the Metropolitan Museum at New York). The Emperor Charles V was but one of many who paid him tribute money. Most of his voluminous writings were published during his Venetian stay, including his lively comedy *La Cortegiana*, his vivid, but pornographic *Ragionamenti*, and the six volumes of his "Letters." Once neglected, the latter are now widely regarded as his most important work. With their variety of subject matter and their colorful, informal style, they have established his present-day reputation as the father of journalism.

Argalus (är'gạ.lus). In Sir Philip Sidney's romance *Arcadia*, the husband of Parthenia. He was killed by Amphialus in single combat.

Argalus and Parthenia (pär.thē'ni.ạ). A tragedy (1629) by Francis Quarles. It was based on Sir Philip Sidney's *Arcadia* and attained equal popularity in its day.

Argante (är.gan'tē). A giantess in Spenser's *Faerie Queene*, the personification of Licentiousness.

Argentile and Curan (är'jen.til; kùr'ạn). A story in verse in William Warner's *Albion's England*, printed about 1586. Curan is the son of a Danish prince who disguises himself as a kitchen helper in order to woo Princess Argentile, but she rejects him and he leaves to become a shepherd. Argentile now also flees, to become a neatherd's maid, and the two meet in these roles, fall in love, and marry. Curan thereafter rules the kingdom and kills the evil guardian of Argentile, King Edel.

Argonautica (är.gọ.nô'ti.kạ). An epic poem by Apollonius of Rhodes. It deals with Jason's legendary voyage in search of the Golden Fleece.

Argonauts (är′gō.nôts). In Greek legend, the heroes who sailed to Colchis in the ship *Argo* to carry off the Golden Fleece. The expedition took place not long after the Trojan War. Jason was its leader, and it included demigods and heroes from all parts of Greece.

Argurion (är.gū′ri.ǫn). A semiallegorical personification of Money, in Ben Jonson's *Cynthia's Revels*. The character is afterward expanded in *The Staple of News* as Lady Pecunia.

Argus (är′gus). In Greek legend, the guardian of Io. Slain by Hermes, he is said to have had one hundred eyes, which were rendered useless when Hermes, through a charm, caused him to fall asleep.

Argyll (är.gïl′), Duchess of. A title of **Gunning, Elizabeth.**

Argyll or **Argyle** (är.gïl′), **Archibald Campbell,** (8th) **Earl of.** In Scott's *Legend of Montrose*, a Scottish nobleman, the rival of the Earl of Montrose.

Argyll or **Argyle, John Campbell,** (2nd) **Duke of.** In Scott's *Heart of Midlothian*, the Scottish nobleman who obtains an interview with Queen Caroline for Jeanie Deans.

Ariadne (ar.i.ad′nē). In Greek mythology, the daughter of Minos, king of Crete. She gave Theseus the unwinding strand by means of which he retraced his steps out of the Labyrinth after killing the Minotaur. She then went with Theseus to the island of Naxos, where, according to the common account, she was abandoned by him, and became the wife of Dionysus. She is the subject of Chaucer's "Legend of Ariadne" in *The Legend of Good Women* and of various other literary works including Elizabeth Barrett Browning's *Paraphrase on Nonnus* and M. Hewlett's *Ariadne Forsaken*.

Arians (ār′i.ǫnz). The followers of Arius, a deacon of Alexandria, who in the 4th century A.D. maintained, in opposition to both Sabellianism and Tritheism, that the Son is of a nature similar to (not the same as) the Father, and is subordinate to him. The tendency of these doctrines, in the eyes of orthodox theologians, was toward the denial of the divinity of Christ. The Arian discussion raged fiercely in the 4th century, and though Arianism was condemned by the Council of Nicaea (325), the heresy long retained great importance, both theological and political. The strongholds of the Arians were in the East and among the Goths and other barbarians who were converted by Arian missionaries.

Ariel (ār′i.ęl, ā′ri.ęl). "An airy spirit" in Shakespeare's *Tempest*, employed by Prospero. Ariel has been imprisoned by the witch, Sycorax, in a cloven pine, from which Prospero frees him on promise that he assist his plans, which Ariel does with the utmost ingenuity and good will. At the close of the play, after Ariel presents a charming masque before the lovers, Ferdinand and Miranda, Prospero dismisses him. The well-known lyrics "Come unto these yellow sands," "Full fathom five," and "Where the bee sucks" are sung by Ariel.

Ariel. One of the rebel angels in John Milton's *Paradise Lost*.

Ariel. A sylph, guardian of Belinda, in Alexander Pope's *Rape of the Lock*. This particular spirit was the chief of those whose

"Humbler province is to tend the fair . . .
To save the powder from too rude a gale,
Nor let the imprison'd essences exhale . . .
    . . . to curl their waving hairs,
Assist their blushes and inspire their airs."

Ariel. A biography of Shelley (1924) by André Maurois.

Arimanes (ar.i.mä′nēz). In Byron's *Manfred*, a form of Ahriman, the name of the personification of evil in the Zoroastrian system.

Arioch (ar′i.ok). In Milton's *Paradise Lost*, one of the rebellious angels overthrown by Abdiel.

Arion (ạ.rī′on). b. on the island of Lesbos, in the Aegean Sea; fl. c700–625 B.C. A Greek musician and poet at the court of Periander of Corinth, subject of a legend made famous by Herodotus. He is represented among constellations by his lyre and the dolphin which, according to tradition, saved him from robbers at sea. He has been credited with the first literary use of the dithyramb.

Arion. In Greek legend, a fabulous horse. It was said to be the offspring of Poseidon by Demeter (or, in other accounts, Gaea or a harpy) who to escape him had metamorphosed herself into a mare. It was successively owned by Copreus, Oncus, Hercules, and Adrastus. It possessed marvelous powers of speech, and its right feet were those of a man.

Ariosto (ä.rē.ôs′tō), **Lodovico** or **Ludovico.** [Called "Divino Lodovico."] b. at Reggio, Italy, Sept. 8, 1474; d. at Ferrara, Italy, June 6, 1533. An Italian poet, author of *Orlando Furioso*, an epic of Roland considered one of the masterpieces of Renaissance literature. A student of law, then of the classics, he was early connected with the court at Ferrara. He began (c1495) to write comedies, among which *La Cassaria* and *I Suppositi* (performed c1512) found him a patron in Cardinal Ippolito d'Este. He was poorly paid for missions to Pope Julius II and other diplomatic services, and for his epic, which he had begun (1503) with the aim of completing Matteo Maria Boiardo's *Orlando Innamorato*. He dedicated the first version (1516) to Cardinal Ippolito. Ariosto left (c1517) the cardinal's service for that of his brother Alfonso d'Este, duke of Ferrara. Rewarded only with the governorship (1522–25) of the bandit-ridden Italian district of Garfagnana, he retired (1525) to write comedies and revise *Orlando* (final version, 1532). Besides those mentioned, his works include comedies such as *Il Negromante*, satires in the manner of Horace, Latin poems, and sonnets; only his Italian lyrics and his epic receive unmixed acclaim; *Orlando Furioso* has been widely translated, and was used by Cervantes, Spenser, Scott, Byron, and others.

Ariosto of the North (ar.i.os′tō). In Byron's *Childe Harold's Pilgrimage*, the epithet used as a name for Sir Walter Scott.

Aristaeus (ar.is.tē′us). In Greek mythology, a beneficent deity, protector of husbandmen and shepherds. He is especially considered the patron of beekeeping. According to Vergil, his swarms

ḍ, d or j; ş, s or sh; ṭ, t or ch; z̧, z or zh; o, F. cloche; ü, F. menu; ċh, Sc. loch; ṅ, F. bonbon.

of bees were destroyed by the nymphs after he had unintentionally brought death on Euridyce, but on his offering a penitential sacrifice, his bees were restored to him.

Aristarchus of Samos (sā'mos). fl. c280–264 B.C. A Greek astronomer and mathematician of the Alexandrian school. According to Archimedes and Copernicus, he was the first to maintain the heliocentric theory of the universe and the rotation of the earth on its axis.

Aristarchus of Samothrace (sam'ō.thrās). fl. at Alexandria, c217–c145 B.C.; d. on Cyprus. A Greek grammarian and critic, a leading Homeric scholar of antiquity, now considered to have been one of the greatest philologists of the ancient world. A student of Aristophanes of Byzantium, and his successor (c180) as librarian at Alexandria, he was the founder of a school of philology known as Aristarcheans. A prolific commentator on and editor of Hesiod, Pindar, Aeschylus, Sophocles, and other Greeks, his version of the Homeric language and the arrangement into 24 books of the *Iliad* and *Odyssey* is a basis of many modern texts.

Aristides (ar.is.tī'dēz). [Surnamed **"the Just."**] b. c530 B.C.; d. probably at Athens, c468 B.C. An Athenian statesman and general. One of the ten Greek generals at Marathon (490), he is said to have ensured victory over the Persians by persuading his colleagues to give full command to Miltiades. He served (489–488) as chief archon of Athens. A conservative, he advocated land power for Athens in opposition to the naval policy of Themistocles; he was ostracized in c483 as a result of this conflict. Returning under the amnesty of 480 to help the defense of Athens against the Persians under Xerxes, he served (480–479 and 479–478) as strategus, took part in the victory of Salamis (480) by capturing Psyttaleia from the Persians, was a commander at Plataea (479) and Byzantium (c478), and succeeded Pausanius as admiral after the Ionian revolt. He was in charge of taxation for the Delian League (c477) and thereafter influential in Athenian affairs. An administrator of ability and integrity, he was probably not the great democrat he has been called.

Aristippus (ar.is.tip'us). b. at Cyrene, Africa; fl. c435–386 B.C. A Greek philosopher; pupil of Socrates, and founder of the Cyrenaic school. Starting with the Socratic principles of virtue and happiness, he based his ethics on the pursuit of pleasure, tempered with prudence in order to avoid pain. Little is known of his life, and it is uncertain how much of his theory actually originated with him, and how much was developed by his followers.

Aristippus, or The Jovial Philosopher. A comedy (1630) by Thomas Randolph.

Aristogiton (a.ris.tō.jī'ton, ar''is.tō-). See **Harmodius.**

Aristophanes (ar.is.tof'a.nēz). b. between c450 and 446 B.C.; d. c380 B.C. An Athenian writer of Greek comedies. Out of the buffoonery of Greek comic plays Aristophanes created an artistic comedy. A conservative and passionate believer in the good old days of Marathon, he attacked with triumphant vigor "progressive" education (Socrates), new ideas in philosophy (the Sophists), melodrama,

rhetorical claptrap, and bizarre musical innovations in contemporary tragedy (Euripides), and above all demagoguery and corruption in politics (Cleon and Hyperbolus). His criticism of the tragedies of Aeschylus and Euripides in *The Frogs* is the earliest and one of the best pieces of literary criticism in existence. His comedies are characterized by a wealth of imagination, a freshness of wit, a pungency of satire, and bursts of pure lyric poetry that can be found in no other comedies except perhaps those of Shakespeare. He took the role of public critic seriously and his political satire was so effective that he was awarded by the Athenian state a crown of wild olive for the good advice he had given the city. Of his many comedies these eleven survive: *The Acharnians* (425), *The Knights* (424), *The Clouds* (423), *The Wasps* (422), *The Peace* (421), *The Birds* (414), *Lysistrata* (411), *The Thesmophoriazusae* (411), *The Frogs* (405), *The Ecclesiazusae* (c393), and *The Plutus* (388).

Aristophanes' Apology. A poem by Robert Browning, published in 1875. It is the sequel to *Balaustion's Adventure* and sets forth a defense of Euripides against the detractions current at the time, as well as a statement of Browning's own poetic faith and practice.

Aristotle (ar'is.tot.l). [Sometimes called the **"Stagirite."**] b. at Stagira (whence the name above), on the NW Aegean coast, 384 B.C.; d. at Chalcis, in Euboea, 322 B.C. A Greek philosopher, one of the greatest thinkers of antiquity, and a continuing influence on philosophic speculation. He was the son of Nicomachus, the personal physician of Amyntas II of Macedonia, and probably spent part of his childhood at the Macedonian court. When he was 17 he went to Athens and attended the academy of Plato, where he remained until Plato's death. He then went to Assos as the guest (348–347) of Hermias, the ruler of Atarneus and Assos, and married Hermias's niece, Pythias. After the death of Hermias in 345, he went to Mytilene, and there carried on zoölogical studies. In 343–42 Philip of Macedonia invited him to Pella to act as the tutor of his son, Alexander. In 335, after Philip's death, he returned to Athens and founded outside the city a school which took its name (the Peripatetic School) from a covered court, or *peripatos*, in the garden of the school. The school had a communal life and an extensive library, and was a center of research in every field of contemporary knowledge. When Alexander died there was an outbreak of feeling against the Macedonians, and Aristotle was charged with impiety. He left Athens and went to Chalcis, and there died in 322 of a digestive disease. His works were of three kinds: (1) early writings in the form of Platonic dialogues, and Platonic in spirit, which survive only in fragments, e.g. the *Protrepticus;* (2) later didactic works in which he moved away from Platonism towards his more mature views, and which also survive only in fragments, e.g. the *Theodectea;* and (3) the works of his maturity, many of which still survive. The body of his surviving works does contain some which are spurious, but for the most part the works are genuine. The extant writings may be conveniently divided into the classes used by the ancient editors: (1) the *Organon*, or group of logical writings, which includes the *Prior* and *Posterior Analytics;* (2) the works on natural science which include the *Physics, On the Soul,* and the *History of Animals;* (3) miscellaneous writings, which include the *Problems;* (4) the work on primary philosophy, called the *Metaphysics;* (5) the works on moral philosophy, which include the *Nicomachean Ethics* and the *Politics;* and (6) the works on art, the *Rhetoric,* and the *Poetics.* To these must be added one historical work, the *Constitution of Athens,* written on papyrus and discovered in Egypt in the latter part of the 19th century. Aristotle has been the philosopher *par excellence* of the western world, and his influence is still significant. He was primarily a philosopher of moderation and common sense. In metaphysics he believed in both matter and mind, in both the natural and the supernatural. In ethics he believed in both physical well-being and spiritual contemplation. In political theory he believed in both constitutional government and a leadership of merit. Aristotle's philosophy is an inspired common sense governed by a critical insight into the meaning of human experience.

Arkell (är′kĕl, är.kel′), **Reginald.** b. at Lechlade, Gloucestershire, England, 1882—. An English journalist, librettist, and playwright. His musical comedies include an adaptation (1935) of *1066 and All That;* among his other works are *Colombine and Other Verses* (1912), *Tragedy of Mr. Punch* (1920), *Green Fingers* (1934), *War Rumours* (1939), *Green Fingers Again* (1942), and *Old Herbaceous* (1951). Editor (1946 *et seq.*) of *Men Only* and *London Opinion.*

Arliss (är′lis), **George.** b. at London, 1868; d. there, 1946. An English actor. He made his stage debut (1887) as an extra at the Elephant and Castle, London, after a short career in his father's printing and publishing office; in 1901 he arrived in the U. S. with Mrs. Patrick Campbell for an appearance in Sir Arthur Wing Pinero's *The Second Mrs. Tanqueray.* Thereafter he appeared in a series of plays including *Disraeli* (1911), which was written particularly for him, and in which he toured the U. S. from 1912 to 1915. He began his film career in 1920, and after 1929 completely forsook the legitimate stage. His films include many of his earlier stage successes as well as such biographical productions as *Voltaire, Cardinal Richelieu,* and others. His autobiography, *Up the Years from Bloomsbury,* was published in 1927.

Armada (är.mä′dạ, -mä′-), **Spanish.** [Also, **Invincible Armada.**] A great fleet sent by Philip II of Spain against England in 1588. It consisted of 129 (or more) vessels, with an estimated 19,295 soldiers and 8,460 sailors, and was commanded by the Duke of Medina Sidonia. It was met and defeated by an English fleet of about 80 vessels, under Charles Howard, in the English Channel and Strait of Dover, in August, 1588. The best-known English captains serving under Howard were Sir Francis Drake, Sir Martin Frobisher, and Sir John Hawkins.

Armada, The. A poem by Thomas Babington Macaulay.

Armadale (är′mạ.dāl). A novel by Wilkie Collins, published in 1866.

Armado (är.mä′dō), **Don Adriano de.** In Shakespeare's *Love's Labour's Lost,* a fantastical Spaniard who speaks with elaborate language, and contends with Costard for Jaquenetta. He is a satire of the popular literary figure of the melancholy lover and is thought by some scholars to caricature Sir Walter Raleigh.

Armageddon (är.mạ.ged′ọn). A name used in Rev. xvi. 16, and signifying "the mountain of Megiddo." The reference in the passage in Revelation is probably to Megiddo, but some refer it to the plain of Esdraelon in Galilee and Samaria, famous as a battlefield.

Armagh (är.mä′). An urban district in Ulster, Northern Ireland, county seat of County Armagh, situated near the river Callan, ab. 33 mi. SW of Belfast: customs station. It is the seat of an Anglican archbishop (primate of Ireland) and a Roman Catholic archbishop. Armagh was the ancient metropolis of Ireland and a center of learning. Saint Patrick founded his church here in 432 A.D. The cathedral (Protestant) of Armagh, the metropolitan church of the primate of Ireland, is a late Gothic structure which was well restored some years ago. The town was sacked by Shane O'Neill in 1564.

Armellina (är.mẹ.lī′nạ). The shrewd maidservant of Antonio, in Thomas Tomkis's comedy *Albumazar.* She is loved and finally won by Trincalo.

Armin (är′min), **Robert.** [Nicknamed **Robin.**] d. 1615. An English actor and playwright, probable successor in 1599 to Will Kempe as actor, in the Lord Chamberlain's company of players, of Shakespearian clowns and fools. Shakespeare may have created the role of the Fool in *King Lear* for him. He also played in Ben Jonson's *The Alchemist* (1610), and was the author of *Nest of Ninnies* (1608) and other plays. He is mentioned in the lists of the Lord Chamberlain's company in 1603, 1604, and 1610.

Armine (är′min). The hero of Benjamin Disraeli's *Henrietta Temple.* He is loved, to his considerable embarrassment, by two women.

Arminius (är.mē′nẹ.ůs), **Jacobus.** [Original name, **Jacob Harmensen, Hermanns,** or **Hermansz.**] b. at Oudewater, in South Holland, Oct. 10, 1560; d. at Leiden, Oct. 19, 1609. A Dutch theologian, founder of the anti-Calvinist Dutch reformed movement in Protestant theology known as Arminianism. His doctrines became the basis of the Arminian, or Remonstrant, sect in Holland, and are evident today in Methodist and certain other Protestant theologies. He studied at Geneva (1582 *et seq.*), served as a minister (1588–1603) at Amsterdam, and was a professor of theology (1603–09) at Leiden. His early acceptance of the Calvinist doctrine of predestination was modified as a result of studies undertaken when he was selected to defend the belief against its opponents; the reversal in his point of view brought on bitter controversy (1604 *et seq.*) with Franciscus Gomarus, a leading Calvinist also on the faculty at Leiden. The Arminian doctrine of ultimate redemption and predestination mitigated by divine prescience was

ḍ, d or j; ṣ, s or sh; ṭ, t or ch; ẓ, z or zh; o, F. cloche; ü, F. menu; ċh, Sc. loch; ṅ, F. bonbon.

carried even further by his followers in the five articles called *The Remonstrance* (1610), which precipitated internecine strife between the Calvinist House of Orange and the allegedly republican Arminian Remonstrants.

Armour Wherein He Trusted. An unfinished novel by Mary Webb, published in 1929. The time of the story is the First Crusade (1096).

Arms and the Man. A play (1894) by George Bernard Shaw, included in his *Plays, Pleasant and Unpleasant* (1898). It is a satirical treatment of the traditional high regard for martial prowess, which seemed barbaric to Shaw. The scene is set in Bulgaria, and the leading character is the Swiss Bluntschli, an unwilling soldier. He expresses his preference for a supply of chocolate rather than bullets when he goes into battle, thus clearly indicating his (and Shaw's) skepticism about the heroics of soldiering. This view of warfare is not accepted at first by the romantic Raina, nor later by her fiancé, Sergius, who, in keeping with his ideas about military glory, charges the enemy line at risk of sudden death, but is saved because someone has forgotten to provide proper ammunition. Both Sergius and Raina come to realize that such heroics are ridiculous, and Raina accepts her "chocolate soldier." Sergius, his glory deflated, falls prey to the designing servant girl, Louka. The well-known operetta, *The Chocolate Soldier*, uses the same plot and characters.

Armstrong (ärm′strông), **Archibald.** [Called **Archie** or **Archy.**] b. in Cumberland, England, or in S Scotland; d. 1672. A jester to James I and Charles I (of England), discharged, after attaining considerable power, for ridiculing William Laud. He is the original of a character in Sir Walter Scott's novel *The Fortunes of Nigel.*

Armstrong, John. [Called **Johnie** (or **Johnnie**) **Armstrong of Gilnockie.**] Killed c1528. A Scottish freebooter, subject of many Scottish and English ballads. Chief of a band of over 150 men, he is supposed to have levied tribute from the English almost as far south as Newcastle, though tradition has it that he never harmed a Scot. When James V (of Scotland) undertook (c1528) to suppress the turbulent border marauders, Armstrong, one of the most notorious, appeared before him with 36 of his band and offered his services; the king had them all hanged on trees near Hawick (or, according to other accounts, killed them in a bloody battle, or had them ambushed). This, and the rest of the legend, became the material for *Armstrong's Good-Night, Johnie Armstrong,* and other popular ballads.

Armstrong, John. b. in Roxburghshire, Scotland, 1709; d. at London, 1779. A British physician, poet, and essayist. He was the author of the blank verse *Art of Preserving Health* (1744). At one time a close friend of John Wilkes (who is believed by some to have obtained for him a post as physician to the army in Germany), he severed the relationship as the result of disputes arising from the publication (c1761) by Wilkes of his verse *Day.*

Armstrong, Martin Donisthorpe. b. at Newcastle, England, 1882—. An English poet and short-story writer. Educated at Cambridge as a mechanical

engineer, he forsook science for a literary career two years after his graduation. Author of *Exodus, and Other Poems* (1912), *The Puppet Show* (1922), *Sir Pompey and Madame Juno* (1927), *Lover's Leap* (1932), *General Buntop's Miracle* (1934), *The Butterfly* (1941), *Chichester Concert* (1944), *Said the Cat to the Dog* (1945), and others.

Armstrong, William. [Called "Kinmont Willie."] fl. c1587. A Scottish marauder on the border between Scotland and England. Captured in 1587, he escaped and continued his depredations until again imprisoned (1596) by the English; his subsequent rescue by the Scotch led almost to a break in relations between England and Scotland. He should not be confused with the more famous Scottish freebooter and border raider, John Armstrong.

Arne (ärn), **Michael.** b. at London, 1741; d. there, Jan. 14, 1786. An English harpsichordist and composer; son of Thomas Augustine Arne (1710–78). He wrote music for David Garrick's *Cymon* (1767), Hannah Cowley's *The Belle's Stratagem* (1780), and other plays, and popular songs such as *The Highland Laddie.*

Arne, Thomas Augustine. b. at London, March 12, 1710; d. there, March 5, 1778. An English composer of songs, especially for Shakespearean plays, and of oratorios and operas. In his first production, a setting of Addison's *Rosamund* (1733), the lead was played by his sister, Susanna Maria Cibber; in *Opera of Operas* (1733), based on Fielding's *Tragedy of Tragedies*, his brother played Tom Thumb. His most noteworthy works include music for John Milton's *Comus* (1738) and for James Thomson and David Mallet's masque *Alfred* (1740), the finale of which is now known as *Rule Britannia;* music for *Under the Greenwood Tree* and other songs in Shakespeare's *As You Like It* (1740), and for *Where the Bee Sucks*, among others, in *The Tempest* (1746); and the oratorios *Abel* (1744) and *Judith* (1764), a performance (1773) of the latter using female voices in an oratorio chorus for the first time. He also composed the operas *Artaxerxes* (1762) and *Love in a Village* (1762), and others.

Arnim (är′nim), **Countess von.** See **Russell, Elizabeth Mary.**

Arnold (är′nọld). In Byron's unfinished drama, *The Deformed Transformed*, an ugly hunchback who, tempted by the devil, chooses to be transformed into the form of Achilles.

Arnold, Sir Arthur. b. at Gravesend, Kent, England, May 28, 1833; d. at London, May 20, 1902. An English editor, reformer, and novelist; brother of Sir Edwin Arnold.

Arnold, Sir Edwin. b. at Gravesend, Kent, England, June 10, 1832, d. at London, March 24, 1904. An English poet, journalist, educator, Oriental student and translator, and author of *The Light of Asia;* brother of Sir Arthur Arnold. He was educated at King's College, Rochester, King's College, London, and University College, Oxford, winning the Newdigate prize (1852) with his poem, *Belshazzar's Feast.* Thereafter he taught at Birmingham at the King Edward's School, and was principal (1856–61) of the Deccan Government

College at Poona, Bombay. Returning to England in 1861, he joined the staff of the London *Daily Telegraph*, serving as editorial writer (until 1873) and as chief editor from 1873 until his death. He traveled in Japan (marrying a Japanese woman as his third wife) and along the U. S. Pacific coast (1889), and traveled and lectured elsewhere in the U. S. (1891). Author of *Poems Narrative and Lyrical* (1853), *Griselda* (1856), *The Wreck of the Northern Belle* (1857), *The Light of Asia* (1879), an epic poem on the life of Buddha, once his best-known and most popular work, but now little read; *Pearls of the Faith* (1883), *Secret of Death* (1885), *Lotus and Jewel* (1887), *The Light of the World* (1891), the last of which dealt with Christ in somewhat the same fashion as *The Light of Asia* did with Buddha. His other poetry includes *Potiphar's Wife* (1892), *The Tenth Muse* (1895), and *The Voyage of Ithobal* (1901). History, travel books, and comment include *History of the Marquis of Dalhousie's Administration* (2 vols., 1862–65), *India Revisited* (1886), *Seas and Lands* (1891), *Japonica* (1892), *Wandering Words* (1894), and *East and West* (1896). He also translated poetry by Victor Hugo and Giuseppe Garibaldi, *Poets of Greece* (1869), the *Hero and Leander* (1873) of Musaeus, several volumes of Indian poetry, and wrote (1877) a Turkish grammar.

Arnold, Matthew. b. at Laleham, England, Dec. 24, 1822; d. at Liverpool, England, April 15, 1888. An English critic, poet, and essayist; son of Thomas Arnold (1795–1842), headmaster of Rugby. Educated at Winchester, Rugby, and Balliol College, Oxford, Matthew became a fellow of Oriel College, Oxford, in 1845, and secretary to the marquis of Lansdowne in 1847; he was lay inspector of schools (1851–83) and professor of poetry at Oxford (1857–67). His teaching at Oxford prompted him to devote the greater part of his interest, over a period of years, to criticism in the widest sense and the formulation of his own standards in the evaluation of literature and literary techniques. This was first evident in his own poem on Wordsworth, Byron, and Goethe in *Empedocles on Etna and Other Poems* (1852) and in his preface to *Poems by Matthew Arnold* (1853). In the latter work he included his *Requiescat*, *The Scholar-Gipsy*, and *Sohrab and Rustum* (which last was taken from the works of the Persian epic poet, Firdausi, and which embodied Arnold's own standard of unity). This interest in critical writing was again apparent in *Merope* (1858), which was intended as a poetical manifesto and was, at least partly for this reason, not successful as a tragedy. Most modern critics consider that his poetry from this date on lacked the power of his earlier work, with certain notable exceptions such as the elegies *Rugby Chapel* (1857) on his father, *A Southern Night* (1859) on his brother, *Thyrsis* (1861) on Arthur Hugh Clough, and *Westminster Abbey* (1881) on Arthur Penrhyn Stanley, the dean of Westminster Abbey. His critical works, on which his fame as a master of clear and felicitous English may be said chiefly to rest, include published lectures *On Translating Homer* (1861–62) and *On the Study of Celtic Literature* (1867); two volumes of *Essays in Criticism* (1865, 1888), the first of which contains the essay depicting Heine as a great intellectual liberator, such as

Arnold himself wanted very intensely to be; and *Culture and Anarchy* (1869), reprinted from the *Cornhill Magazine*, in which Arnold put forth his so-called "sweetness and light" theory. His other works include theological studies such as *Literature and Dogma* (1873), and such works of essays as *Discourses in America* (1885) and *Civilization in the United States* (Boston, 1888), both based on his American lecture tours (1883–84 and 1886).

Arnold, Thomas. [Called "Arnold of Rugby."] b. at West Cowes, on the Isle of Wight, June 13, 1795; d. at Rugby, England, June 12, 1842. An English educator and historian, headmaster of Rugby (1828–42); father of Matthew Arnold. Educated at Winchester and at Corpus Christi College, Oxford, he was a fellow (1815–19) at Oriel College, Oxford. Ordained deacon in 1818, he settled (1819) at Laleham, where he tutored young men for universities. At Rugby, he set the modern pattern for the English public-school system. His leadership was widely recognized, in spite of outspoken criticism by certain elements of the clergy, and he was given an appointment (1841) as regius professor of modern history at Oxford. His works include a collection of sermons (1829–34), an edition of Thucydides (1830–35), *History of Rome* (3 vols., 1838–43), and *Lectures on Modern History* (1842).

Arnold, Thomas. b. at Laleham, England, 1823; d. at Dublin, 1900. An English scholar; son of Thomas Arnold (1795–1842) and brother of Matthew Arnold. Inspector of schools in Tasmania (1850–56), he joined (1856) the Roman Catholic Church. He was professor of English literature at Dublin, appointed by Newman to New Catholic University there, and later at St. Stephen's Green. Author of *Manual of English Literature, Historical and Critical* (1862), of editions of Wycliffe (1869–71), *Beowulf* (1876), and others; also of *Passages in a Wandering Life* (1900), containing much material on Newman and the Tractarian (now better known as the Oxford) Movement.

Arnold, William Thomas. b. at Hobart, Tasmania, Sept. 18, 1852; d. at London, May 29, 1904. An English historian, journalist, and editor; grandson of Thomas Arnold (1795–1842) and son of Thomas Arnold (1823–1900). He was author of a *Manual of English Literature*, and an inspector of schools in Tasmania. Educated at Rugby and at University College, Oxford, he was on the staff of the *Manchester Guardian* for many years. Author of *The Roman System of Provincial Administration to the Accession of Constantine the Great* (1879), a standard work in its field, and *Studies in Roman Imperialism* (1906). In 1886, he edited his grandfather's *History of Rome: The Second Punic War*. Matthew Arnold was his uncle, and Mary Arnold, better known as Mrs. Humphry Ward (1851–1920), the novelist, was his sister.

Arnold Biedermann (bē'dĕr.män). See **Biedermann, Arnold.**

Arnold of Brescia (är'nold; brä'shä). b. at Brescia, Italy, c1100; executed at Rome, 1155. An Italian religious reformer and political agitator. Possibly a student of Abelard at Paris, he excoriated the corruption of the clergy and the power they exercised through ownership of the land. He was banished (1139) by Pope Innocent II for arousing the people against the bishop of Brescia; in France, he probably reprimanded Saint Bernard of Clairvaux, whose measures against him, including condemnation (with Abelard) by the Council of Sens (1140), drove him to Zurich and thence (1143 or 1145) to Italy, where he did penance to Pope Eugene III (but soon afterward took leadership of the republican faction at Rome which drove Eugene into exile). Though excommunicated (1148) by Eugene, Arnold remained powerful until the accession (1154) of Pope Adrian IV who, supported by the emperor Frederick I (Barbarossa), laid an interdict (1155) on Rome, driving out the republicans and reëstablishing papal power.

Arnulf (är′nŭlf). See **Ernulf.**

Arod (ā′rod). In the second part of *Absalom and Achitophel* (which was written in the main by Nahum Tate and revised by John Dryden), a character intended for Sir William Waller.

Arondight (ā′ron.dīt). The sword of Sir Lancelot of the Lake.

Arpasia (är.pā′zhạ). In Nicholas Rowe's tragedy *Tamerlane*, a Greek princess.

A.R.P.M. A pseudonym of John Galsworthy; see under **Burning Spear, The.**

Arragon (ar′ạ.gon), **Prince of.** In Shakespeare's *Merchant of Venice*, the second of Portia's suitors. He chooses the silver casket as the one containing her portrait; it doesn't, and he thus fails to win her.

Arragon, Prince of. See also **Pedro, Don.**

Arraignment of a Lover. A poem by George Gascoigne.

Arraignment of Paris (par′is), **The.** A play, combining the elements of a pageant and a masque, which was published anonymously in 1584 and probably staged also in that year. It is thought to have been written by George Peele. It is written in varied lyrical measures, with about 200 lines of blank verse, considered by some critics to be the loveliest written before those of Marlowe. It deals with the quarrel of the three goddesses, Juno, Pallas (Athena), and Venus, over a golden ball which the handsome Paris has been asked to award to the fairest. He chooses Venus, and Diana resolves the ensuing squabble by delivering the ball, with the unanimous consent of the three competing goddesses "to the Queen's own hands" (the flattery to Queen Elizabeth could hardly have been more fulsome, but it was not for this reason any less welcome). The setting is pastoral, on the slopes of Ida, where Paris tends his flocks.

Arria (ar′i.ạ). d. 42 A.D. A Roman woman whose husband, Caecina Paetus, was condemned to death for conspiracy against the emperor Claudius. As he hesitated to destroy himself, she stabbed herself and handed him the dagger with the words "*Paete, non dolet*" ("Paetus, it does not pain me").

Arrow of Gold, The. A novel (1919) by Joseph Conrad. It is a reworking of his earlier *The Mirror of the Sea.* Both books draw upon his own experiences when (1874) he made his way to Marseilles, where he was involved in gun-running adventures for the Spanish Carlists.

Arrowpoint (ar′ọ.point), **Catharine.** In George Eliot's novel *Daniel Deronda*, a girl accomplished to a point of exasperating thoroughness, but possessing much good sense.

arsis (är′sis). In prosody: **1.** Originally, the metrically unaccented part of a foot, as opposed to the *thesis* or part which receives the ictus or metrical stress.

2. In prevalent modern usage, that part of a foot which bears the ictus or metrical accent, as opposed to the metrically unaccented part, called the *thesis*. According to the original Greek usage, *arsis* denoted the raising of the foot in dancing or beating time, and therefore the accented part of the prosodial foot. Latin writers show great confusion in the application of these terms, sometimes employing them in conformity with Greek usage, sometimes interchanging their meaning, sometimes assigning still other meanings to them. Some modern writers have employed them with their original Greek significations, as given above under **1,** but the meanings given under **2,** and believed to be supported by the Latin writers, are those generally adopted at the present time.

Artagnan (där.tȧ.nyäṅ; Anglicized, där.tan′yạn), **D'.** See **D'Artagnan.**

Artegal (är′tẹ.gạl). One of the chief characters in *Artegal and Elidure*, a poem by William Wordsworth. The story is taken from Geoffrey of Monmouth, where it is related that Artegal, son of Gorbonian, was a legendary king of Britain who regained his throne after years of exile due to crimes he had earlier committed. During this time his brother, Elidure, was king.

Artegall (är′tẹ.gạl), **Sir.** [Also: **Arthegall, Artegal, Arthegal.**] In Edmund Spenser's *Faerie Queene*, a knight errant, the personification of Justice, supposed to have been intended to represent Arthur Grey, 14th Baron Grey de Wilton, Spenser's patron.

Artemidorus (är″tẹ.mi.dō′rus). In Shakespeare's *Julius Caesar*, a teacher of rhetoric who tries to save Caesar by a note of warning. However, Caesar refuses to read the note.

Artemis (är′tẹ.mis). [Latin, **Diana.**] In Greek mythology, one of the Olympian deities; daughter of Zeus and Leto, and twin sister of Apollo. She may be regarded as a feminine counterpart of Apollo. She chastised evil with her keen shafts and with deadly sickness, and also protected mortals from danger and pestilence. Unlike Apollo, she was not connected with poetry or divination, but, like him, she was a deity of light, and to her was attributed authority over the moon, which belonged more particularly to her kinswomen Hecate and Selene. In art Artemis is represented as a young woman of noble and severe beauty, tall and majestic, and generally bearing bow and quiver as the huntress or mountain goddess. She was identified by the Romans with their Diana, an original Italian divinity. Literature about Artemis includes E. Arnold's *Hymn of the Priestess of Diana*, E. W. Gosse's *The Praise of Artemis*, Ben Jonson's *Hymn to Cynthia*, and Shelley's *Homer's Hymn to the Moon.*

Artemis. A court lady in John Dryden's comedy *Marriage à la Mode.*

---

fat, fāte, fär, ȧsk, fãre; net, mē, hėr; pin, pīne; not, nōte, mŏve, nôr; up, lūte, pùll; ᴛʜ, then;

Arte of English Poesie. A treatise by George Puttenham, published in 1589. It is a manual of Elizabethan poetry, discussing new forms and authors.

Artesius (är.tē′zhus). In *The Two Noble Kinsmen*, an Athenian captain.

Artevelde (är′tẹ.vel.dẹ), **Philip van.** See **Philip van Artevelde.**

"Artful Dodger," the. See **Dawkins, John.**

Arthegall or **Arthegal** (är′tẹ.gạl), **Sir.** See **Artegal, Sir.**

Arthur (är′thẹr). The central character in the great Arthurian Cycle of medieval romances. Possibly in origin a historical figure, a British leader who in the early 6th century led armies against the invading Saxons. He was first celebrated as an actual person by the Welsh chronicler Nennius (c796), according to whom Arthur defended the Christian cause against the pagan Saxons in many battles, including the great victory at Mount Badon (c516). Later historians add his death (537) at the battle of Camlan (*Annales Cambriae*, c956) and burial at Glastonbury (Giraldus Cambrensis, c1195). It is probable that the Arthurian stories were first elaborated in Wales, Cornwall, and Brittany by the addition of all sorts of elements from folk literature, but they have not survived in this form. In the 12th century they were given currency throughout much of western Europe by Geoffrey of Monmouth's *Historia Regum Britanniae* (1147) and the romances of Chrétien de Troyes (c1160–90). According to tradition he was the illegitimate son of Uther Pendragon, and demonstrated his royalty by drawing a sword from a stone when a boy; he fought with the miraculous sword Excalibur given him by the Lady of the Lake, and was the leader of the Knights of the Round Table at Camelot (variously identified, possibly Caerleon, in Monmouthshire). It is chiefly through the continuing popularity of Malory's *Morte d' Arthur* that the Arthurian stories were preserved for later generations of readers and writers. Dryden wrote an opera entitled *King Arthur* with music by Purcell, Sir Richard Blackmore an epic poem called *Prince Arthur*, and Bulwer-Lytton a poem, *Prince Arthur*. In the modern period the stories have been treated by such poets as Tennyson, William Morris, and, in America, E. A. Robinson.

Arthur. Entries on literary characters having this prename will be found under the surnames Clarington, Clennam, De Vere, Donnithorne, Gride, Huntingdon, Kipps, Pendennis, and Wardour.

Arthur or **Arthure** (är′thẹr), **Adventures (or Awntyrs) of.** See **Awntyrs of Arthure at the Terne Wathelyne.**

Arthur, King. In Henry Fielding's burlesque *Tom Thumb the Great*, a "passionate sort of king," husband to Dollallolla (of whom he is afraid) and in love with Glumdalca.

Arthur, Prince. In Edmund Spenser's *Faerie Queene*, the personification of "Magnificence." His important adventures are the slaying of Gerioneo and the Soudan. It has been suggested that Prince Arthur represents the Earl of Leicester.

Arthur and Merlin (mẻr′lin). A Middle English verse romance of nearly 10,000 lines written c1300.

Among other things, it deals with the childhood of Merlin, who is revealed as a great prophet. Merlin's discovery of the identity of Arthur, who is alone able to draw the magic sword Excalibur from the stone in which it is set, is also described. The work is probably based on a French version.

Arthur, Duke of Britain (brit′ạn). In Shakespeare's *King John*, the historical Arthur of Brittany, son of Constance of Brittany and (posthumously) of Geoffrey Plantagenet, John's elder brother. Thus Arthur should therefore have been king, but John was chosen by the Great Council. Arthur serves as a rallying point for the discontented English nobles and John orders him put to death. Spared by the chamberlain, Hubert de Burgh, Arthur escapes, but in doing so falls to his death in such a way as to make it appear that murder has been committed.

Arthurian Cycle of Romances (är.thū′ri.ạn), **The.** A series of romances relating to the exploits of Arthur and his knights. See also under **Arthur.**

Arthur's (är′thẹrz). A London club established in 1765. It was named from the former keeper of White's Chocolate House, who died in 1761.

Arthur's Seat. A hill in S Scotland, in Midlothian, in the SE quarter of the city of Edinburgh. It has an extensive view of the city. 822 ft.

Arthur's Show. A representation, principally an exhibition of archery, by 58 city worthies who called themselves by the names of the Knights of the Round Table, referred to in Shakespeare's *2 Henry IV.*

Arundel (ar′un.dẹl). The horse of Sir Bevis of Hampton in some versions of the Arthurian legend and in Michael Drayton's *Polyolbion.*

Arundel, Thomas. [Family surname, **Fitzalan.**] b. 1353; d. 1414. An English prelate. He was archbishop of Canterbury (1396–97, 1399–1412), and was involved, with his brother Richard Fitzalan, the 4th Earl of Arundel, in the struggle between Richard II and Parliament. As bishop of Ely (1374–88), he was instrumental in inducing the king to submit to Parliament, which set up a council of regency (that included his brother), made Thomas chancellor in 1386, and imposed sentences of treason on the king's advisers. He became archbishop of York in 1388. Declaring himself of age, the king deprived Thomas of the chancellorship in 1389, and later (1397) secured his impeachment and banishment for complicity in the regency of 1386. A year before this happened, Thomas had been made archbishop of Canterbury, but his occupancy of this office was now interrupted. Returning with Henry of Lancaster in 1399, Thomas conspired with him to prevent Richard's escape, crowned him Henry IV, was restored by him to Canterbury and the chancellorship (1399, 1407, 1412). He played a chief role in the execution of Sir John Oldcastle and other Lollards.

Arundel Club. [Original name, **Arundel Society.**] An English society for the promotion of art, founded at London in 1849. It was known as the Arundel Society until 1897, when for a period of some seven years it became inactive, and reappeared in the first decade of the 20th century as the Arundel Club.

Arundel House. A house belonging to the earls of Arundel (in the Howard line), which formerly stood near Highgate, London. Francis Bacon died there in 1626.

Arundel House. A mansion belonging to the earls of Arundel (in the Howard line) which formerly stood on the Strand, London, where Arundel, Norfolk, Surrey, and Howard streets now are. In its gardens were originally placed the Arundel Marbles.

Arundell (ar'un.dẹl), **Thomas.** [Title, 1st Baron Arundell of Wardour.] b. 1562; d. at Oxford, England, 1639. An English soldier of fortune. He was made a count of the Holy Roman Empire by the emperor Rudolph II for his service (1595) against the Turks in Hungary. He was said to have been a great favorite of Queen Elizabeth, and was created baron Arundell of Wardour by James I in 1605.

Arundel (or Oxford) Marbles. Part of a group of ancient sculptures and antiquities collected by Thomas Howard, 14th Earl of Arundel, presented to the University of Oxford in 1667. It includes the Parian Chronicle, a marble slab detailing events in Greek history.

Arviragus (är.vir'a.gus) or **Arveragus** (-ver'-). Knight, the husband of Dorigen, in *The Franklin's Tale*, by Geoffrey Chaucer.

Arviragus. In Shakespeare's *Cymbeline*, the son of Cymbeline, brought up as Cadwal, the son of Belarius, a banished lord, who is disguised as Morgan.

Asaph (ā'saf). The name under which Nahum Tate wrote of John Dryden in the second part of *Absalom and Achitophel* (the part which was written originally almost entirely by Tate and edited by Dryden).

Asa Trenchard (ā'sạ tren'chạrd). See **Trenchard, Asa.**

Asbru (äs'brö). See **Bifrost.**

Ascalon (as'kạ.lon). The sword of Saint George, in the collection of medieval tales known as the *Seven Champions of Christendom*.

Ascanio (as.kä'ni.ō). A page in Philip Massinger's play *The Bashful Lover*.

Ascanio. The son of Don Henriques, in John Fletcher and Philip Massinger's play *The Spanish Curate*. He is a modest, affectionate boy of great tenderness.

Ascanio. A page in John Dryden's play *The Assignation*.

Ascanius (as.kā'ni.us). In classical legend, the son of Aeneas and (in the Roman version) the ancestor of the Roman Julii.

Ascension, The. [Also, **Christ B.**] An Old English poem by Cynewulf, one of the four works signed by the poet. It is for the most part a versification of a homily on the Ascension by Gregory the Great. The title *Christ* is sometimes given to this together with the poem which precedes it in the *Exeter Book*, both of which were formerly considered the work of Cynewulf; the first of the pair is now generally entitled *The Advent*, is thought to be by a different author, and is sometimes designated also *Christ A*, the second being called *Christ B*.

Ascent of F.6, The. A play (1936) by W. H. Auden and Christopher Isherwood about the scaling of a mountain, which operation here symbolizes modern imperialism, and is used by the authors as a means of criticizing certain aspects of modern society.

Ascham (as'kạm), **Roger.** b. at Kirby Wiske, Yorkshire, England, 1515; d. at London, 1568. An English classical scholar and author. At St. John's College, Cambridge (B.A., 1534), then a center of humanism, he became an accomplished Greek scholar. As tutor (1548–50) to Elizabeth Tudor (later to be Queen Elizabeth of England), he can probably be held responsible for her great interest in the classics. He was subsequently secretary (1550–53) to Sir Richard Morysin, ambassador to the emperor Charles V, and Latin secretary (1553–68) to both Mary and Elizabeth. His chief works are *Toxophilus* (1545), a treatise in dialogue form on archery, an early masterpiece of modern English prose, and *The Scholemaster* (1570), highly valued for its method of teaching Latin.

Asclepiades of Samos (as.klẹ.pī'ạ.dēz; sā'mos). fl. early 3rd century B.C. A Greek lyric poet and epigrammatist. He is the earliest, and considered by some the most important, of his school; some scholars believe that the type of verse known as Asclepiadic is so named from him.

Asem the Man Hater (ā'sẹm). A tale (1759) by Oliver Goldsmith. It appeared in *The Bee*, a periodical of the day, which was issued on eight Saturdays in October and November, 1759. The figure of Asem is a center for a fantasy of Goldsmith's favorite ideas. Asem is taught the necessity of having the life of pure reason stimulated by emotion and he is cured of his misanthropy by means of regenerated social emotions.

As Far As Thought Can Reach. See under **Back to Methuselah.**

Asgard (as'gärd). The realm of the gods and goddesses in Old Norse mythology. It was apparently located in the heavens above the earth. Asgard contained different regions as well as separate abodes. The principal of these was Valhalla, the assembling-place of the gods and heroes.

Ash (ash), **John.** b. in Dorsetshire, England, c1724; d. 1779. An English lexicographer and author. His works include a grammar and a two-volume *New and Complete Dictionary of the English Language* (1775), based on both those of Samuel Johnson and Nathan Bailey, and including the latter's vocabulary of cant, plus provincial words.

Ashanti War (ä.shän'tē). A war (1873–74) between Great Britain and the Ashanti, in W Africa. Ashanti was invaded by a British army under Garnet Joseph Wolseley, who conquered and burned Kumasi in February, 1874, and exacted from the Ashanti a treaty that prepared the way for a British protectorate some 22 years later.

Ashby-de-la-Zouch (ash'bi.del.ạ.zöch'). An urban district in C England, in Leicestershire, situated on the river Mease, ab. 16 mi. NW of Leicester, ab. 120 mi. N of London by rail. It contains a ruined castle in which Mary Stuart was confined (1569).

Ashby-Sterry (ash'bi.ster'i), **Joseph.** b. at London; d. June 1, 1917. An English journalist and author. He studied painting and actually began a career as an illustrator illustrating for *Punch*, but soon gave this up for writing. He was the author of *Nutshell*

Novels (1890), *Lazy Minstrel* (1892), *Naughty Girl* (1893), *A Tale of the Thames in Verse* (1896), *Sketches in Song* (1903), and *River Poems* (1909). He also created and wrote (1890–1909) the popular "Bystander" column in the London *Graphic*, and was art critic (1891–1907) for the London *Daily Graphic*.

Ashcroft (ash'kroft), **Peggy.** [Full name, **Edith Margaret Emily Ashcroft.**] b. 1907—. An English actress. She made her debut (1926) as Margaret in James Barrie's *Dear Brutus* with the Birmingham Repertory Theatre; later she played Desdemona to Paul Robeson's *Othello* (1930), and appeared in a revival of *The Importance of Being Earnest* (1942), and in *The Duchess of Malfi* (1944). In 1950 she appeared at Stratford-on-Avon opposite John Gielgud. Her film appearances include *The Wandering Jew*, *The 39 Steps*, and others.

Ashenden (ash'ęn.dęn). [Full title, **Ashenden, or the British Agent.**] A novel by W. Somerset Maugham, published in 1928. It is based on the author's experiences with the British secret service during World War I.

Ashestiel (ash'ęs.tēl). A house on the Tweed, near Selkirk, occupied by Sir Walter Scott 1804–11. His autobiography to 1792 (*The Ashestiel Memoir*) was written there.

Ashford (ash'fǫrd), **Margaret Mary.** [Pen name, **Daisy Ashford.**] An English child author known for works written at the age of eight and earlier; she was introduced to English readers by Sir James M. Barrie, and to the American public by Irvin S. Cobb. She was the author of *The Young Visiters, or Mr. Salteena's Plan* (published 1919, written when she was nine), *Daisy Ashford: Her Book* (published in the U. S. in 1920), containing *A Short History of Love and Marriage* (written when she was eight and dictated by her to her father), *The True History of Leslie Woodcock* (when she was eleven), *Where Love Lies Deepest* (when she was twelve), and *The Hangman's Daughter* (when "about thirteen"). An earlier manuscript, *Mr. Chapmer's Bride*, was lost. The stories, published as originally written, owed their popularity and appeal to a combination of childish wisdom, ignorance, imagination, sentence structure, spelling, and punctuation. Barrie's preface to the 1919 volume, as Daisy Ashford gladly admitted, played a large part in securing favorable attention to her work. One English reviewer expressed the opinion that *The Young Visiters* was a literary hoax, having been written by Barrie himself; though entirely without foundation, this theory gained a certain credence, and made the book something of a literary curiosity.

Ashley (ash'li), Baron or Lord. See **Shaftesbury.**

Ashmole (ash'mōl), **Elias.** b. at Lichfield, England, May 23, 1617; d. at London, May 18, 1692. An English antiquary, founder of the Ashmolean Museum at Oxford. He was a Royalist (1642 *et seq.*) and subsequently an official under Charles II. He took up mathematics, alchemy, botany, and other studies. Author of *Institutions, Laws, and Ceremonies of the Order of the Garter* (1672).

Ashmolean Museum (ash.mō'lę.ąn). A museum at Oxford University, founded (c1679) by Elias Ashmole. The original building was designed and built by Sir Christopher Wren in the period 1682–83. The museum collections have been removed from the Old Ashmolean Museum (Broad Street), which is now occupied in part by the Bodleian Library, to the New Ashmolean Museum, on Beaumont Street. The museum contains some of the Arundel marbles, the Cretan antiquities discovered by Sir Arthur Evans, and others.

Ashton (ash'tǫn); **Helen Rosaline.** b. at London, 1891—. An English novelist. She is perhaps best known for *Doctor Serocold* (1930), which was a choice of the Book of the Month Club, and also wrote *A Lot of Talk* (1927), *Bricks and Mortar* (1932), *Family Cruise* (1934), *People in Cages* (1937), *The Swan of Usk* (1939), *Tadpole Hall* (1941), *Parson Austen's Daughter* (1949), *Footman in Powder* (1954), and others. Her *William and Dorothy* (1938) is a fictionalized biography of the Wordsworths.

Ashton, Henry. In Sir Walter Scott's *Bride of Lammermoor*, the youngest child of Sir William and Lady Ashton, who succeeds to his father's estates. He is the last of the Ashtons.

Ashton, Lady. The wife of Sir William and mother of Lucy, the "bride of Lammermoor," in Sir Walter Scott's novel of that name.

Ashton, Lucy. The "bride of Lammermoor" in Sir Walter Scott's novel of that name, the daughter of Sir William and Lady Ashton. Betrothed to Edgar Ravenswood, she is forced by her mother to marry Frank Hayston. Grief makes her insane and she dies on her wedding night. The leading characters of this novel also appear, with slightly altered names, in Gaetano Donizetti's opera *Lucia di Lammermoor*, and in several dramas founded upon the incidents of the story.

Ashton, Sir William. In Sir Walter Scott's novel *The Bride of Lammermoor*, the Lord Keeper of Scotland, father of Lucy Ashton, the heroine.

Ashton, Winifred. See **Dane, Clemence.**

Ashtoreth (ash'tǫ.reth). See **Astarte.**

Ashur (ash'ėr). See **Assur.**

Ash Wednesday. A Christian holy day marking the beginning of Lent and occurring seven weeks before Easter. In some churches, notably the Roman Catholic, the day, which is one of repentance and of sorrowing for human sinfulness, is marked by the symbolic application of ash to the forehead.

Ash Wednesday. A six-poem sequence by T. S. Eliot, published in 1930, and consisting of "Because I Do Not Hope to Turn Again," "Lady, Three White Leopards Sat under a Juniper-Tree," "At the First Turning of the Second Stair," "Who Walked between the Violet and the Violet," "If the Word Is Lost, If the Word Is Spent," "Although I Do Not Hope to Turn Again."

As I Walked Out One Evening. A poem by W. H. Auden, included in his collection *Another Time* (1940). It employs a light, rapid ballad meter to deal with such subjects as the relationship of personal passion to impersonal time.

Aske (ask), **Robert.** Executed at York, England, 1537. An English lawyer, leader of the Yorkshire Catholic insurrection called the "Pilgrimage of Grace."

ḍ, d or j; ş, s or sh; ţ, t or çh; ẓ, z or zh; *o*, F. cloche; ü, F. menu; çh, Sc. loch; ṅ, F. bonbon.

As Kingfishers Catch Fire, Dragonflies Draw Flame. A poem by Gerard Manley Hopkins, concerned with the idea that man is determined by what he does, particularly as this is evidence of his submission to God: "[man] Acts in God's eye what in God's eye he is."

Aslaugas Ritter (äs.lou′gäs rit′ẹr). [Eng. trans., "*Aslauga's Knight.*"] A German story (1814) by Baron de La Motte-Fouqué, translated into English in Carlyle's *German Romance.* Aslauga is a spirit chosen by the Knight in preference to any earthly ladylove. She appears to him at important moments in his career, and he dies fancying himself clasped in her arms and shrouded in her wonderful golden hair.

Asmodai (as′mọ.dī). A rebel angel in Milton's *Paradise Lost* (Book IV), defeated by the good angel, Raphael. He is based on Asmodeus (or Ashmodai), the evil spirit who figures in the Book of Tobit.

Asmodeus (as.mọ.dē′us, as.mō′dẹ.us). In Jewish demonology, a destructive spirit of whom many stories are told. Le Sage used him in *Le Diable Boiteux,* whence Foote's play (1768) *The Devil upon Two Sticks.*

Asolando (as.ọ.lan′dō). A volume of poems by Robert Browning, published in London on Dec. 12, 1889, the day on which the poet died at Venice. It is a collection of love lyrics, versified anecdotes, and philosophical pronouncements. It closes with the *Epilogue* in which Browning describes himself as

> "One who never turned his back but marched
>   breast forward,
>   Never doubted clouds would break,
> Never dreamed, though right were worsted,
>   wrong would triumph,
> Held we fall to rise, are baffled to fight better,
>   Sleep to wake."

Asparagus Gardens. In 16th and 17th century England, a place of public entertainment, not far from Pimlico (which is now a district of London near Westminster). It is to this that Richard Brome refers in his *Sparagus Garden* (1635).

Aspasia (as.pā′zhạ). b. at Miletus, in Ionia; fl. c440 B.C. A Greek courtesan, renowned for her wisdom, beauty, and wit. She was for many years the mistress of Pericles, who was so attracted to her that he left his wife and would have married her except for his own law of 451 B.C., which forbade Athenians to take foreign wives. Her brilliance made her house a center of Athenian literary and philosophical life. Accused of impiety, she was saved from death by Pericles' eloquence; her son, by Pericles, was legitimized under his father's name by a special Athenian decree.

Aspatia (as.pā′shạ). The heroine of Beaumont and Fletcher's *The Maid's Tragedy.* She is betrothed to Amintor and is deserted by him. Heartbroken, she seeks her death by disguising herself as a man and challenging Amintor to a duel in which he kills her.

Aspects of Modern Poetry. A critical work by Edith Sitwell, published in 1934.

Aspects of the Novel. A critical work (1927) by Edward Morgan Forster giving the author's opinions on the art of novel writing.

Asper (as′pėr). In Ben Jonson's *Every Man Out of His Humour,* a rather bitter commentator upon the other characters in the loose succession of scenes comprising the action. He is believed to represent Jonson himself.

Asper. A pseudonym of Samuel Johnson in the *Rambler.* It was under this name that he launched his attacks on David Garrick.

Asquith (as′kwith), **Elizabeth.** [Married name, Princess **Bibesco.**] b. 1897; d. at Bucharest, Rumania, April 8, 1945. An English novelist, dramatist, and poet; daughter of Herbert Henry and Margot Asquith. She was the author of *I Have Only Myself to Blame* (1921), *Balloons* (1923), *The Fir and the Palm* (1924), *There Is No Return* (1927), *Portrait of Caroline* (1931), and *The Romantic* (1940), all fiction; *The Painted Swan* and *Points of View* (both 1926), three-act plays; and *Poems* (1927).

Asquith, Herbert. b. March 11, 1881—. An English novelist, poet, soldier, and lawyer; son of Herbert Henry Asquith, 1st Earl of Oxford and Asquith, and brother of Elizabeth Asquith. He saw service (1915–18) in France and Flanders in World War I. Author of poetry including *The Volunteer* (1915), *A Village Sermon* (1920), *Pillicock Hill, Poems 1912–1933* (1934), and *Youth in the Skies* (1940); of the novels *Wind's End, Young Orland* (1927), *Roon* (1929), and *Mary Dallon;* and of *Moments of Memory: Recollections and Impressions* (1937).

Assandun (ạ.san′dun). A locality, identified with Ashingdon, Essex, England, where Edmund Ironsides was defeated (1016) by Canute.

Assassin, The. A novel by Liam O'Flaherty, published in 1928.

Assassination Plot. The name given to a conspiracy against the life of William III of England, by Sir George Barclay and Robert Charnock, detected in 1696.

Assassins. A military and religious order in Syria, founded (c1090) in Persia by Hasan ibn-al-Sabbah. A colony migrated from Persia to Syria, settled in various places, with their chief seat on the mountains of Lebanon, and became notorious for their secret murders in blind obedience to the will of their chief. Their religion was a compound of Magianism, Judaism, Christianity, and Mohammedanism. One article of their creed was that the Holy Spirit resided in their chief and that his orders proceeded from God himself. The chief of the sect was best known by the denomination "old man of the mountain" (in Arabic, *sheik al-jebal,* meaning "chief of the mountains"). These chieftains and their followers spread terror among nations far and near for almost two centuries. In the time of the Crusades they totaled some 50,000, and presented a formidable obstacle to the arms of the Christians. They were eventually subdued by the Mongols about 1256. Their name is derived from the Arabic word for the drug hashish, which they are generally believed to have used to prepare themselves for their terroristic assignments.

Assembly of Fowls, The. See **Parliament of Fowls, The.**

Assembly of Ladies, The. A poem once attributed to Chaucer, but now considered the work of a later and inferior poet. In it a number of ladies are summoned to appear before Lady Loyaltè, to whom they present "bills" complaining of broken pledges and disappointed love.

Asser (as'ẽr). d. at Sherborne, England, c909 A.D. A Welsh monk, bishop of Sherborne (c900 *et seq.*); tutor and companion of Alfred the Great. Author of a life of Alfred (c893), containing also a history of England (849–87), which was used by later chroniclers.

Assignation, The. [Full title, **The Assignation, or, Love in a Nunnery.**] A comedy (1672) by John Dryden, now generally considered to be one of his poorer works.

Assize of Clarendon (klar'ẹn.dọn). An English ordinance, issued in 1166, which introduced important changes in the administration of English justice.

Assize of Northampton (nôrth.amp'tọn). An English ordinance, a reissue and expansion of the Assize of Clarendon, issued at Northampton in 1176, drawn up in the form of instructions to the judges. The new articles relate to tenure, reliefs, dower, and other matters.

Associated Counties. In English history, a name given to the counties of Norfolk, Suffolk, Essex, Hertford, Cambridge, Huntingdon, and Lincoln, because they combined (1642–46) to join the Parliamentary side in the English Civil War, and to keep their territory free from invasion.

assonance (as'ọ.nạns). In prosody, a species of imperfect rhyme, or rather a substitute for rhyme, especially common in Spanish poetry, consisting in using the same vowel sound with different consonants and requiring the use of the same vowels in the assonant words from the last accented vowel to the end of the word. Thus, *man* and *hat, penitent* and *reticence*, are examples of assonance in English. "There are some traces of the employment of rhyme and assonance in mere popular literature at a very remote period." (G. P. Marsh, *Lects. on Eng. Lang.*)

Assur (as'ẽr). [Also: **Asur, Ashur.**] The ancient national god of Assyria. The names of both the country and the people are derived from his name.

Astarte (as.tär'tē). [Also, **Ashtoreth.**] The Semitic goddess of fecundity and love, among the Phoenicians equivalent to the Ishtar of the Assyro-Babylonians; often considered to be an equivalent of the Greek Aphrodite. She is the female counterpart of Baal, with whom she held the first place in the Phoenician pantheon. Baal was identified with the sun, and Astarte with the moon, and she is often represented under the symbol of the crescent. The chief seat of her worship was at Sidon. The pomegranate and the dove were sacred to her. The favorite places of her worship were sacred groves, and she herself was often adored under the symbol of a tree, the *asherah* (translated "grove") often denounced in the Old Testament. Her cult in later times was combined with orgiastic celebration.

Astarte. A woman guiltily beloved by Manfred (in Byron's *Manfred*), and because of whom he suffers an undying remorse.

Astell (as'tẹl), **Mary.** b. at Newcastle, England, 1668; d. 1731. An English writer. She was the author of *A Serious Proposal to Ladies*, published anonymously (1694–97) suggesting the construction of a home for religious and academic retirement, to be conducted under the rules of the Church of England, a scheme which was attacked as "popish," particularly in the *Tatler* (Nos. 32, 59, and 63), where she was called Madonella and Platonne. Among her other works, also controversial and also published anonymously, were *The Christian Religion* (1705) and *Occasional Communion* (1705).

Asteria (as.tir'i.ạ). An ancient name of **Delos.**

Astle (as'l), **Thomas.** b. at Yoxall, England, Dec. 22, 1735; d. at Battersea Rise (now part of London), Dec. 1, 1803. An English paleographer and antiquary. He was keeper of records in the Tower of London (1783 *et seq.*), and a notable collector in his own right of books and manuscripts. He was the author of *The Origin and Progress of Writing* (1784), containing a valuable study of medieval handwriting, and others.

Astley (ast'li), **Philip.** b. at Newcastle-under-Lyme, England, 1742; d. at Paris, 1814. An English horsetrainer, equestrian, and theater manager. A cabinet-maker during his youth, he joined a regiment of light horse in Holland as a rough-rider (1759), and opened an exhibition of horsemanship at Lambeth, in London. He subsequently developed a prosperous business as proprietor of circuses there and elsewhere. His first circus and hippodrome (opened in 1770), known as "Astley's," became Astley's Royal Amphitheatre in 1798, under the patronage of the Prince of Wales and the Duke of York.

Astolat (as'tọ.lat). A place in the Arthurian romances sometimes identified with Guildford, in Surrey. It is the home of Elaine in Tennyson's *Lancelot and Elaine* (1859): the same as Shalott in *The Lady of Shalott.*

Astolfo or **Astolpho** (as.tol'fō). An important character in the Charlemagne romances and in the *Orlando Innamọrato* and *Orlando Furioso*: a noble, kindhearted, and eccentric English knight. The most notable of his knightly feats and adventures is his journey to the moon, where he enters the Valley of Lost Things, and among a mass of broken resolutions, lovers' tears, days lost by idlers, and similar items, finds Orlando's lost wits in a vessel larger than all the others (he also finds his own wits in another vase). He is permitted to take Orlando's back to their original owner (and also to have back his own). Alexander Pope, in the *Rape of the Lock*, speaking of the same place, says:

"Where the heroes' wits are kept in ponderous vases,
And beaux' in snuff boxes and tweezer cases."

Astolfo was also the possessor of a wonderful horn which spread universal terror when it was sounded.

Aston Hall (as'tọn). An old mansion (1618–35) near Birmingham, England, said to be the original of Irving's *Bracebridge Hall*. It is now a museum belonging to Birmingham.

Astraea or **Astrea** (as.trē'ạ). In classical mythology, the goddess of justice.

Astraea Redux (rē'duks). [Eng. trans., *Astraea Returned.*] A poem by John Dryden celebrating the restoration of Charles II, first published in 1660.

ḍ, d or j; ṣ, s or sh; ṭ, t or ch; ẓ, z or zh; *o*, F. cloche; ü, F. menu; čh, Sc. loch; ṅ, F. bonbon.

Astrolabe (as'trō.lăb), **The Treatise on the.** [Also, **The Conclusions of the Astrolabe.**] An unfinished prose work by Chaucer, written by him for the instruction of his son Lewis, then ten years old. It is inferred that it was written in 1391. This is not proved, however; and of the child nothing more is known than that in the introduction to this treatise Chaucer mentions him by name and gives his reasons for the "enditing" of the work for him. It contains some very slight autobiographical allusions, but is essentially a translation and adaptation of the work of an Arab astronomer, Messahala (8th century), from a Latin version. It has been described as "the oldest work written in English upon an elaborate scientific instrument."

Astrologer's Song, An. A poem by Rudyard Kipling, first published in the volume *Rewards and Fairies* (1909).

Astrophel (as'trō.fel). The name assumed by Sir Philip Sidney in the series of sonnets entitled *Astrophel and Stella*, often considered to have been his greatest literary work. These sonnets, 110 in number, chronicle the growth of Sidney's love for Stella (the name by which he alluded to Penelope Devereux, sister of the Earl of Essex, afterward Lady Rich). It contains about one-third of Sidney's extant poetry.

Astrophel. An elegy written by Edmund Spenser in 1586, lamenting the death of Sir Philip Sidney. It was printed in the same volume as *Colin Clout's Come Home Again* and was the first of a group of poems by various authors on Sidney's death.

Astrophel. A collection of poems (1894) by Algernon Charles Swinburne.

Astyanax (as.tī'a.naks). In Greek legend, the young son of Hector and Andromache, thrown from the walls of Troy by the victorious Greeks.

As You Find It. A comedy by Charles Boyle, 4th Earl of Orrery, produced in 1703.

As You Like It. A comedy by Shakespeare. Some scholars believed it was produced in 1599, but no copy of it is known to exist earlier than the folio of 1623. During the 18th century it was frequently performed, such actors as Macklin, Kitty Clive, Peg Woffington, Charles Kean, and Mrs. Siddons taking principal roles. It was founded on Thomas Lodge's romance *Rosalynde*, based upon a pseudo-Chaucerian *Tale of Gamelyn*, in which the servant, Adam, and the characters of Rosader (Orlando) and Saladyne (Orlando's brother, Oliver) also appear. In the comedy the characters of Touchstone, Audrey, and Jaques are Shakespeare's; otherwise he has followed Lodge quite closely. The main setting is the Forest of Arden. Touchstone, the clown, and Jaques, the cynical, melancholy philosopher, furnish moments of comedy considered by many to be among the best in Shakespeare.
The Story. Orlando, the son of the late Sir Rowland de Boys, objects to cruel treatment by his brother, Oliver, in whose charge he has been left, whereupon Oliver plans that Orlando will be killed during a wrestling match sponsored by Frederick, usurper of the dukedom of his elder brother, the Duke Senior. The latter has had to flee with his followers, including the melancholy Jaques, to the Forest of Arden, leaving behind his daughter Rosalind with her cousin and friend, Celia, the daughter of Frederick. During the wrestling match, Orlando and Rosalind fall in love, and when Orlando defeats his opponent he escapes from Oliver to the Forest of Arden, accompanied by the old family servant, Adam. There they fall in with the banished Duke and his attendants. Frederick, meanwhile, banishes Rosalind, who disguises herself as a boy called Ganymede, and with Celia, now posing as Aliena, sister of the supposed boy Ganymede, also seeks refuge in the Forest of Arden. Their jester, Touchstone, goes with them. There Rosalind meets Orlando, who, thinking she is the boy Ganymede, accepts her suggestion that he should court her as if she were his beloved Rosalind. Oliver arrives in pursuit of Orlando, but is saved from a lion and, repentant, falls in love with Celia. Ganymede promises Orlando that by magic Rosalind will appear in time for the wedding the following day, and at that time Rosalind reveals herself. These two couples, plus two more (Audrey and Touchstone, Phebe and Silvius), are gathered for the ceremonies, when Orlando's second brother, Jaques de Boys, arrives with the news that Frederick has left for a monastery and restored the dukedom to his elder brother.

Atala (à.tà.là). A romance by François René Auguste de Chateaubriand which first appeared (1801) in the newspaper *Le Mercure de France*. It is the story of a young Red Indian, Chactas, and an Indian maiden, Atala.

Atalanta (at.a.lan'ta) or **Atalante** (-tē). In Greek legend, a maiden whose story appears in two versions: In the Arcadian version, she is a daughter of Zeus by Clymene, exposed by her father in infancy, suckled by a bear, and brought up by a party of hunters, under whose care she develops into a beautiful and swift huntress. She takes part in the Calydonian boar hunt, is the first to strike the boar, and receives from Meleager the head and skin as prize of victory. She is also connected with the expedition of the Argonauts, and marries Milanion. In the Boeotian version, she is a daughter of Schoeneus, son of Athamas, of great beauty and very swift of foot. She is warned by an oracle not to marry, and rids herself of her suitors by challenging them to a race, and smiting them with a spear in the back on overtaking them. Hippomenes, however, overcomes her by throwing before her in the race three golden apples given to him by Aphrodite, which she stoops to pick up; she is thus tricked into pausing long enough to lose the race to Hippomenes. (However, because Hippomenes fails to give thanks to Aphrodite, the goddess subsequently changes the pair into lions.) Literature includes: Dryden, "Meleager and Atalanta" (from Ovid's *Metamorphoses*); Walter Savage Landor, *Hippomenes and Atalanta;* William Morris, "Atalanta's Race" in *Earthly Paradise;* Swinburne, *Atalanta in Calydon.*

Atalanta in Calydon (kal'i.don). A tragedy based on the classical theme of Atalanta and the Calydonian boar hunt, by Algernon Charles Swinburne, published in 1865. The choruses, especially the "Hymn to Artemis," are the portion of the work now chiefly remembered.

Ate (ā'tē). In Greek mythology, a daughter of Zeus (according to Homer) or of Eris, strife (according to Hesiod); the goddess of mischief and discord.

Ate. In Edmund Spenser's *Faerie Queene*, a hag, a liar and slanderer; friend of Duessa.

Athanasian Creed (ath.a.nā'zhan). One of the three great creeds of the Christian church, supposed at one time to have been composed by Athanasius, a Greek bishop and a father of the early church. The name was probably given to it during the Arian controversy in the 6th century, Athanasius having been the chief upholder of the system of doctrine opposed to the Arian system. It is included in the Greek, Roman, and English services, but is not retained in the Book of Common Prayer most commonly used in the U. S. It is also called *Quicunque vult*, after its first words.

Athanasius (ath.a.nā'shus), Saint. b. at Alexandria, c298; d. there, 373. A Greek bishop and father of the church, notable as a defender of orthodoxy against Arianism. His stubborn advocacy of his own beliefs throughout his life brought him the epithet "*contra mundum*" and led to his exile on five occasions.

Atharva-Veda (a.tär'va.vā'da). See under **Vedas.**

Atheist, or The Second Part of The Souldier's Fortune, The. A comedy by Thomas Otway, first acted in 1684.

Atheist's Tragedy; or the Honest Man's Revenge, The. A tragedy by Cyril Tourneur, published in 1611 and composed c1606. Presumably the plot is original; certainly no source has been located, but there are allusions to Shakespeare's *Hamlet* and *King Lear*. The play deals with the failure of an atheist's beliefs and the abandonment of the position taken by Edmund in *King Lear:* "Nature, thou art my goddess."

Athelney (ath'el.ni), **Isle of.** A place, once surrounded by marsh, near Taunton, Somersetshire, England, the refuge of Alfred the Great in 878. He founded (888) a Benedictine abbey here.

Athelstan (ath'el.stan). [Also, **Æthelstan;** surnamed **"the Glorious."**] b. 895; d. 940. King of the West Saxons and Mercia (924–940); a son of Edward the Elder and grandson of Alfred. He defeated the Danes and Celts at Brunanburh in 937, thus making himself ruler over all of England. Through the marriage of his sisters, he was brother-in-law to Charles III (Charles the Simple), king of the West Franks; Louis, king of Lower Burgundy; Hugh, the "Great Duke" of the French; and the emperor Otto the Great. He is the hero of the Old English poem *The Battle of Brunanburh.*

Athelstane (ath'el.stān). In Sir Walter Scott's novel *Ivanhoe*, the Thane of Coningsburgh, suitor of Rowena, called "The Unready," from the slowness of his mind.

Athelston (ath'el.ston). A Middle English verse romance (c1350) of unknown authorship. In its approximately 800 lines a purely fictitious story is told about a king who comes into conflict with three of his courtiers with whom he has previously sworn brotherhood. As one of them is the Archbishop of Canterbury, the parallel with the story of Henry II and Thomas à Becket is obvious. The

poem, which is full of scraps of history, legend, folklore, and commonplaces of romance, manages to weave Saint Edmund into the plot as the nephew and heir of the king, a touch entirely inaccurate historically, as Saint Edmund lived a century before the historical King Athelstan, and King Edmund was Athelstan's younger brother, not nephew.

Athena (a.thē'na) or **Athene** (-nē). [Also, **Pallas Athena.**] In Greek mythology, the goddess of knowledge, arts, sciences, and righteous war. She was particularly the tutelary deity of Athens, and was identified by the Romans with Minerva. She personified the clear upper air as well as mental clearness and acuteness, embodying the spirit of truth and divine wisdom, and was clothed with the aegis, symbolizing the dark storm-cloud, and armed with the resistless spear (the shaft of lightning). According to myth, she sprang full-grown from the forehead of Zeus. In English literature, she figures in Byron's *The Curse of Minerva*, Kingsley's *Pallas in Olympus*, and Shelley's *Homer's Hymn to Minerva.*

Athenae Oxoniensis (a.thē'nē ok.sō.ni.en'sis). [Full title, **Athenae Oxoniensis: an Exact History of All the Writers and Bishops Who Have Had Their Education in the University of Oxford from 1500 to 1690.**] Biographical sketches of some of the graduates of Oxford University, in three volumes, by Anthony Wood, two volumes of which were printed (1691–92) before his death. The third, which he prepared, appeared in the second edition in 1721.

Athenaeum (ath.e.nē'um). A famous school or university at Rome, founded by the emperor Hadrian. It was named for Athens, and was situated on the Capitoline Hill.

Athenaeum, The. A London club established in 1824. It was designed for the "association of individuals known for their scientific or literary attainments, artists of eminence in any class of the Fine Arts, and noblemen and gentlemen distinguished as liberal patrons of Science, Literature, or the Arts."

Athenian Captive, The. A tragedy (1838) in classical style, by Thomas N. Talfourd. It was written expressly for the actor Macready, but never played by him.

Athenian Gazette: or Casuistical Mercury, The. A periodical published from 1691 to 1697. It was a project of the eccentric bookseller John Dunton, whose staff included Richard Sault, John Norris, Samuel Wesley, and others. These men composed an "Athenian Society" and undertook to answer questions on all topics in the *Mercury.*

Athens (ath'enz, -inz), **Duke of.** See **Theseus.**

Athens: an Ode. A poem by Algernon Charles Swinburne. It is a patriotic poem in which Swinburne draws a parallel between Greece and England.

"Athens of the North." A title sometimes applied to Edinburgh, both from its topography and as a seat of learning.

Atherstone (ath'er.ston), **Edwin.** b. at Nottingham, England, April 17, 1788; d. at Bath, England, Jan. 29, 1872. An English author of romances and of epic poems such as *The Last Days of Herculaneum* (1821), *The Fall of Nineveh* (30 books, 1828–68), and others.

Atherton Moor (ath'ẽr.tọn), **Battle of.** A victory gained in the English Civil War near Bradford, England, in 1643, by the Royalists under the Earl of Newcastle over the Parliamentarians under Ferdinando Fairfax.

Athos (ā'thos; French, à.tos). One of the "three Musketeers" in the novel *The Three Musketeers*, by the elder Alexandre Dumas.

Atkins (at'kinz), **Tommy.** See **Tommy.**

Atkinson (at'kin.sọn), **John Christopher.** b. at Eddhangor, England, 1814; d. 1900. An English clergyman and antiquary, remembered chiefly for *Forty Years in Moorland Parish* (1891), a collection of local legends and traditions. He received his bachelor's degree from Cambridge University in 1838, served as vicar (1847–1900) of Danby, Yorkshire, and became prebendary of York in 1891. He published minor antiquarian works, and books for children.

Atkinson, Sergeant. In Fielding's novel *Amelia*, the foster brother of Amelia, whose devotion to her and her husband and self-sacrificing generosity prove invaluable in their misfortunes.

Atkyns (at'kinz), **Richard.** b. 1615; d. at London, 1677. An English writer on the history of printing. He was the author of *The Origin and Growth of Printing, etc.* (1664).

Atlantis (at.lan'tis). A legendary island in the Atlantic Ocean, NW of Africa, referred to by Plato and other ancient writers, which with its inhabitants (who had achieved, according to most accounts, a high degree of civilization) was said to have disappeared in a convulsion of nature. The belief in the possibility of such a place has continued to exist even into modern times, and many writers (including Francis Bacon in his work *The New Atlantis*) have taken the name as an equivalent for a utopian state.

Atlas (at'lạs). In Greek mythology, a Titan, brother of Prometheus and Epimetheus; son of Iapetus and Clymene (or Asia), and father (by Pleione) of the Pleiades and (by Aethra) of the Hyades, and also (in Homer) of Calypso. According to Hesiod he was condemned by Zeus, for his part in the battle of the Titans, to stand at the western extremity of the earth, near the habitation of the Hesperides, upholding the heavens with his shoulders and hands. His station was later said to be in the Atlas Mountains in Africa. According to some accounts he was the father of the Hesperides; also a king to whom the garden of the Hesperides belonged. The details of the myth vary greatly.

Atli (ät'lē). In the *Volsunga Saga*, the name of Attila, king of the Huns, who married Gudrun.

Atli. In William Morris's epic poem *Sigurd the Volsung*, a barbarian chieftain (the name is a variant of Attila).

Atom, The Adventures of an. See **Adventures of an Atom, The.**

Atossa (ạ.tos'ạ). The poetical name given to Sarah (Jennings) Churchill, the first Duchess of Marlborough, by Alexander Pope in his *Moral Essays.*

Atreus (ā'trẹ.us, -trös). In Greek legend, a king of Mycenae; son of Pelops and father of Agamemnon. He brought upon himself the curse of his brother Thyestes when, to revenge himself for the seduction, by Thyestes, of his wife, Atreus killed three of Thyestes' sons, and served them at a meal as meat to their father. Aegisthus, the only surviving son of Thyestes, subsequently slew Atreus.

Atridae (ạ.trī'dē). Agamemnon and Menelaus, the sons of Atreus.

Atrides (ạ.trī'dēz). A son of Atreus: usually Agamemnon, occasionally Menelaus.

Atropos (at'rọ.pos). In Greek mythology, that one of the three Fates who severs the thread of human life.

Attaché; or Sam Slick in England, The. Humorous sketches by Thomas Chandler Haliburton, published (1843, 1844) under the pseudonym Sam Slick, in two series. Sam is a Yankee peddler of clocks.

Atterbury (at'ẽr.ber.i, -bẽr.i), **Francis.** b. at Milton, Buckinghamshire, England, March 6, 1662; d. at Paris, Feb. 15, 1732. An English prelate, politician, and controversialist. He was appointed bishop of Rochester and dean of Westminster in 1713. From his tutorship at Christ Church a pamphleteer (1687 *et seq.*) against the Reformation, he was celebrated in Swift's *Battle of the Books* as leader of the attack on Richard Bentley. Involved in the plot (1721) to restore the Stuart pretender to the throne, he was imprisoned (1722) and banished (1723) as a Jacobite.

Atteridge (at'ẽr.ij), **Andrew Hilliard.** b. at Liverpool, England—. An English author, journalist, correspondent, and specialist on military and naval subjects. Educated at London and Louvain universities, he later served as an assistant editor of the London *Month*, correspondent for the London *Daily Chronicle*, and war correspondent (1896) in Kitchener's Anglo-Egyptian Dongola campaign. He wrote *Popular History of the Boer War* (1901), *Napoleon's Brothers* (1909), *Modern Battles from Alma to Mukden* (1910), *The First Phase* and *The Second Phase of the Great War* (1914, 1915), and *The World-Wide War* (1915). Author also of articles on "Sir Henry Hawkins," "The Irish in South Africa," and "English Catholic Periodical Literature" in the *Catholic Encyclopedia* (vols. 7, 8, 11).

Attic Boy, the. In Milton's *Il Penseroso*, an epithet used for Cephalus, the husband of Procris, who is loved by Aurora.

Attic dialect. The dialect of Greek used by the ancient Athenians, and regarded as the standard of the language. It was a subdivision of the Ionic, but is often spoken of as a coordinate dialect. It is distinguished from the Ionic by a more frequent retention of an original *a* (α) sound, and by its avoidance of hiatus, especially through contraction. Its chief literature belongs to the 5th and 4th centuries B.C. As written during the greater part of the former century it is known as *old Attic*; in its transition to the next century, as *middle Attic*; and during the greater part of the 4th century, as *new Attic*. It passed after this into the *Koinê* or common dialect, the general Greek of the Alex-

fat, fāte, fär, ȧsk, fāre; net, mē, hẽr; pin, pīne; not, nōte, mȯve, nôr; up, lūte, pu̇ll; ᴛн, then;

andrine and Roman periods, departing more or less from its former classic standard.

Attic style. A pure, chaste, and elegant style.

Attila (at'i.lạ, ạ.til'ạ). d. 453 A.D. A famous king of the Huns; surnamed the "Scourge of God" by medieval writers, on account of the ruthless and widespread destruction wrought by his arms. He became sole ruler and extended his sway over German as well as Slavonic nations. He laid waste the provinces of the Eastern Empire south of the Danube in the period 442–447, exacting from Theodosius II a tribute of six thousand pounds of gold, and establishing the annual subsidy at two thousand pounds. He laid claim to one half of the Western Empire as the betrothed husband of Honoria, the sister of Valentinian, who years previously had secretly sent him her ring and the offer of her hand in marriage; having been refused his demands, he invaded Gaul in 451, in alliance with Genseric, king of the Vandals, and was defeated in the same year by the Roman general Aëtius with the aid of the Visigothic king Theodoric at Châlons-sur-Marne. He led (452) an army into Italy, destroying Aquileia, but retired without attacking Rome, having been, according to legend, dissuaded from sacking that city by Pope Leo I; and died, probably from the rupture of a blood vessel, on the night of his marriage with the Gothic Ildico or Hilda. He appears in German legend, notably in the *Nibelungenlied*, as Etzel, who, in his turn, is the Atli of the heroic lays of the older *Edda*. Between Etzel and Atli there are differences as well as correspondences. According to the *Edda*, Atli, who married Gudrun, the widow of Sigurd (the Siegfried of the *Nibelungenlied*), possessed a kingdom in the south. He is, however, nowhere called a king of the Huns. "Hunaland," located in the south of Germany, is here a possession of Sigurd's ancestors, the Volsungs, and he himself is frequently called the "Hunnish." In the *Nibelungenlied* the land of the Huns is located in the east, and belongs to Etzel as king. In the later legend, as in this case, the whole external circumstances of Attila have been transferred to Etzel, and the historical and legendary person are regarded as one. Atli, in the Icelandic *Volsunga Saga*, was the husband of Gudrun and brother of Brynhild.

Auber (ō'bėr), **Harriet.** b. at London, Oct. 4, 1773; d. at Hoddesdon, Hertfordshire, England, Jan. 20, 1862. An English poetess. She was the author of several hymns published (1829) in *The Spirit of the Psalms. Hasten Lord, the glorious time* and *Our blest Redeemer ere he breathed* are two of her best-known hymns.

Aubrey (ō'bri). In Richard Cumberland's play *The Fashionable Lover*, the father of Augusta Aubrey. He rewards those who have befriended her.

Aubrey, Augusta. The principal female character in Richard Cumberland's *Fashionable Lover*, persecuted by Lord Abberville, but finally married to Francis Tyrrel.

Aubrey, John. b. in Wiltshire, England, 1626; d. at Oxford, in June, 1697. An English antiquary. Reduced to poverty by various lawsuits and amorous adventures, he was commissioned (1671) to make surveys of antiquities, which he described in *Per-*

ambulation of Surrey and other manuscripts published after his death. Supported mainly by wealthy friends, he collected anecdotes of such notables as Francis Bacon, John Milton, Thomas Hobbes, and Sir Walter Raleigh, which he contributed to the historian Anthony à Wood, as *Minutes of Lives* (first published separately in 1813; called *Brief Lives* in 20th-century editions), for his *Athenae Oxonienses* (1690). Author also of *Miscellanies* (1696), a collection of ghost stories and dreams.

Aubrey, Mr. The principal character in Samuel Warren's novel *Ten Thousand a Year*.

Auburn (ô'bėrn). The name of a village which figures in Oliver Goldsmith's *Deserted Village*. It is thought by some to be based upon the village of Lissoy, near Athlone in Ireland, but this conjecture has been rejected by the majority of critics.

Aucassin et Nicolette (ō.kȧ.san̄ ā nē.ko.let). A French romance of the 13th century, named after its hero and heroine. Aucassin, the son of the count of Beaucaire, falls in love with Nicolette, a captive Saracen maiden, who is in reality a king's daughter. After overcoming many obstacles the two are finally united.

Auchinleck (ô.ċhin.lek', ô.kin-). A civil parish and village in S Scotland, in Ayrshire, situated on Lugar Water, ab. 13 mi. E of Ayr, ab. 376 mi. N of London by rail. Here was the country estate of Alexander Boswell, Lord Auchinleck, the father of James Boswell.

Auchinleck, Lord. Title of **Boswell, Alexander.**

Auctioneer, The. A play (1901) by Charles Klein.

Auden (ô'den), **Wystan Hugh.** b. at York, England, Feb. 21, 1907—. An English poet, playwright, and critic, resident in the U. S. since 1939 and an American citizen since 1946. He was an early member of the group including Stephen Spender, Christopher Isherwood, and C. Day Lewis which oriented itself at that time to the left politically and against established conventions in writing technique. He collaborated with Isherwood on the plays *The Dog beneath the Skin* (1935), *The Ascent of F. 6* (1936), and *On the Frontier* (1938), as well as on *Journey to a War* (1939), a prose record of experiences in China; in collaboration with Louis MacNeice he wrote *Letters from Iceland* (1937). Editor of *The Oxford Book of Light Verse* (1938), and others. His volumes include *Poems* (1930), *The Orators* (1932), *The Dance of Death* (1933), *Look Stranger* (1936), *The Double Man* (1941), *For the Time Being* (1944), *The Age of Anxiety* (1947), for which he was awarded the Pulitzer prize for poetry in 1948, *Nones* (1951), and *The Shield of Achilles* (1955). A collection of his poems was published in 1945. Auden's use of common words and metaphors in preference to the poetic language of 19th-century romanticism is characteristic of his style both in his lyrics and in his longer, didactic poems. He has also written the libretto to *The Rake's Progress* (1951), an opera by Igor Stravinsky. He was the recipient of the 1953 Bollingen prize in poetry of the Yale University Library.

Audhumla (ou.ᴛʜum'lä). The cow, in the Old Norse cosmogony, from whose udders flowed the milk which nourished the first created being, the giant

---

ḍ, d or j; ṣ, s or sh; ṭ, t or ch; ẓ, z or zh; o, F. cloche; ü, F. menu; c̄h, Sc. loch; ṅ, F. bonbon.

Ymir, and his race. She licked out of the salty ice a being whose son was the father of Odin.

Audrey (ô'dri). In Shakespeare's *As You Like It*, an awkward country girl. Touchstone discovers her in the Forest of Arden and eventually marries her.

Audrey or **Awdrey** (ô'dri). The bride, in Ben Jonson's *Tale of a Tub*, a bright and perverse little person.

Aufidius (ô.fid'i.us), **Tullius**. In Shakespeare's *Coriolanus*, the general of the Volscians. He accepts the offer of his old enemy, Coriolanus, who has been banished from Rome, to lead the Volscian army against Rome. When Coriolanus spares Rome, the Volscians kill him.

Augeas (ô'jē.as, ô.jē'as). In Greek mythology, a son of Helios (or of Phorbas) and Hermione, king of the Epeians in Elis, and one of the Argonauts. He was the owner of a herd of 3,000 oxen, including 12 white bulls sacred to the sun, which he kept in a stable that had not been cleaned for 30 years. The task of cleaning this stable was deemed impracticable, but Hercules accomplished it in a single day by channeling the waters of two rivers through it. Augeas was slain by Hercules.

Aughrim (ôg'rim). A town in Connacht province, Irish Republic, in County Galway, ab. 4 mi. SW of Ballinasloe. Here, on July 12, 1691, the English forces of William III under Ginkel defeated the Irish and French forces of James II under Saint-Ruth.

Augsburg Confession (ôgz'bėrg; German, ouks'bûrk). The chief Lutheran creed, prepared by Melanchthon, approved by Luther, and read before the Diet of Augsburg on June 25, 1530.

Augusta (ô.gus'ta). **1.** A title of honor conferred upon the women of the Roman imperial house.
2. The name of some seventy Roman towns, one of which was on the site of modern London.

Augusta. See also **Guster.**

Augusta Aubrey (ô'bri). See **Aubrey, Augusta.**

Augustan age (ô.gus'tan). The Augustan age (31 B.C. to A.D. 14; the reign of the Emperor Augustus) was the most brilliant period in Roman literature. Hence the phrase has been applied by analogy to similar periods in the literary history of other countries. Thus the reign of Louis XIV has been called the Augustan age of French literature, while that of Queen Anne (the period of Pope, Addison, and Steele) has received this distinction in English.

Augusta of Berkely (ô.gus'ta; bėrk'li, bärk'li), **Lady.** The heroine of Sir Walter Scott's novel *Castle Dangerous.*

Augustine (ô'gus.tēn, ô.gus'tin), Saint. b. at Tagaste (now Souk-Ahras), in Numidia, 354; d. at Hippo (now Bône, Algeria), in Numidia, 430. An early Christian philosopher and father of the church. He was bishop of Hippo (396 *et seq.*), and defender of orthodoxy against the Pelagians, Donatists, and Manichaeans, of which last group he was himself for nine years a member. Despite his Christian parents, his early years were marked by skepticism, which continued during the period (384 *et seq.*) he spent as lecturer at Milan, but was ended by a mystic experience which was followed by baptism (387) at the hands of Ambrose, bishop of Milan, with whom Augustine had already conversed. Returned to the family property at Tagaste, he was thrust forward in 391 by the congregation at the nearby town of Hippo for ordination as a priest. His growing fame led to his consecration (395) as bishop, with the provision that he would succeed to the see of Hippo when it became vacant. His occupancy of the bishopric was marked by brilliant and voluminous correspondence defending orthodoxy against the heresies of his day. He was the author of the great *De Civitate Dei* (completed in 22 books by 426; Eng. trans., *City of God*), the *Confessiones*, and others.

Augustine of Canterbury (kan'tėr.ber.i, -bėr.i), Saint. [Also: **Austin;** called **"Apostle of the English."**] d. at Canterbury, England, c604 or 613. A Roman Benedictine monk chosen (595 or 596) by Pope Gregory I to head a group of 40 missionaries to the English. He was received (597) by the powerful and tolerant King Ethelbert of Kent, whose wife Bertha was a Christian, and installed at his capital, Canterbury. Probably with Bertha's aid, he converted the king. Made archbishop of the English at Arles, he baptized ten thousand converts in 597. Created first archbishop of Canterbury (601), he set up the dioceses of London, Rochester, York, and others, but failed to reconcile differences of practice, such as the date of Easter, with the Celtic bishops. He consecrated Christ Church, Canterbury, in 603, which was replaced by the present cathedral (begun by Lanfranc in 1070).

Augustus (ô.gus'tus). [Original name, **Gaius Octavius;** called later **Caius Julius Caesar Octavianus.**] b. at Velitrae, in Latium, or at Rome, Sept. 23, 63 B.C.; d. at Nola, Campania (now in Italy), Aug. 19, 14 A.D. The first Roman emperor, son of Caius Octavius by Attia, daughter of Julia, the sister of Julius Caesar whose chief heir he became. After Caesar's death he went from Epirus to Rome in the spring of 44 B.C. There he gained the influence of Cicero, the senate, and the people against Mark Antony. He was reconciled with Antony, and formed with him and Lepidus the second triumvirate in 43. He took part in the proscription of 43, and in the victory over Brutus and Cassius at Philippi in 42. He carried on the Persian war in the period 41–40. He became more closely allied with Antony in 40, and was ruler over the West. In 37 he renewed the triumvirate. In 36 he subdued Sextus Pompey. His defeat of Antony and Cleopatra at Actium in 31 left him sole ruler of the Roman dominion. In 28 he was made princeps senatus, and received the title of "Augustus" in 27. Augustus preserved the republican forms, but united in his own person the consular, tribunician, proconsular, and other powers. His generals carried on various wars in Spain, Africa, Germany, and elsewhere, but the Roman advance in the last-named country received a definite setback through the defeat of Varus by Arminius in 9 A.D. Under Augustus Roman literature reached its highest point, and the temple of Janus was closed, indicating world peace. The birth of Jesus Christ occurred during his reign.

Augustus Does His Bit. A play (1917) by George Bernard Shaw, included by most critics among his lesser works.

Augustus Snodgrass (snod'grȧs), **Mr.** See **Snodgrass, Mr. Augustus.**

Auld Lang Syne (ŏld' lang' zīn'). A song by Robert Burns, written c1789. Burns stated that the tune was not original with him, but was the first written version of an old folk melody which he had heard. It begins: "Should auld acquaintance be forgot, And never brought to min'?"

Auld Licht Idylls (lĭcht). A play (1888) by Sir James M. Barrie. It is a Scottish regional play.

"Auld Reekie" (rē'ki). A nickname of Edinburgh, so called because it was generally smoky.

Auld Robin Gray (rob'in grā'). A ballad by Lady Anne Barnard, published in 1772. It was written to an old Scottish tune, "The Bridegroom grat," which was later superseded by an English air. It begins: "When the sheep are in the fauld, and the kye a' at hame."

Aumerle (ô.mėrl'), **Duke of.** See under **York,** (2nd) **Duke of.**

Aumonier (ô.mon'yä), **Stacy.** b. 1887; d. in Switzerland, Dec. 21, 1928. An English novelist, short-story writer, landscape painter, and society entertainer. He began his career as an entertainer in 1908, and began writing in 1913. Author of *Three Bars' Interval* (1917), *The Querrils* (1919), *One After Another* (1920), and *Heartbeat* (1922), all novels, and *Fifteen Tales* (1924), a collection of short stories.

Aungerville (än'jėr.vil), **Richard.** [Also: **Aungervyle;** called **Richard de Bury** (de ber'i).] b. at Bury St. Edmunds, Suffolk, England, 1287; d. 1345. An English cleric, bibliophile, and writer. He was appointed tutor to young Edward of Windsor and was involved in the plotting that brought about the deposition of Edward II, and the accession of his pupil to the throne as Edward III; he was favored thereafter with rapid promotion. Twice (1330, 1333) ambassador to the papal court, he was appointed in the latter year to the bishopric of Durham, and was also made (1334) lord treasurer and lord chancellor. Known throughout Europe as a bibliophile, Aungerville left an account of his book-collecting in his *Philobiblon* (trans. 1888).

Aunt Grizzle (griz'l). See **Grizzle, Aunt.**

Aunt Margaret's Mirror (mär'gȧ.rẹts). A short novel by Sir Walter Scott, published in 1828 in the second series of the *Chronicles of the Canongate.*

Aurelia (ô.rē'li.ạ, -rē'lyạ). In John Marston's *The Malcontent*, the duchess, a dissolute, proud woman. She marries the usurping Pietro, but is almost immediately unfaithful to him by having two lovers, Ferneze and Mendoza. She now hopes to be the wife of Mendoza as the next Duke of Genoa, after he procures Malevole to kill Pietro. Her expectation is betrayed, however, when Mendoza actually does obtain the throne upon receiving news from the 'Hermit' (really Pietro in disguise) that Pietro is dead, and he banishes her so that he may marry another woman.

Aurelia. A pretty but impertinent and affected coquette in John Dryden's comedy *An Evening's Love, or The Mock Astrologer.*

Aurelius (ô.rē'li.us, -rēl'yus). The amorous squire in Geoffrey Chaucer's *Franklin's Tale.*

Aureng-Zebe (ô'rung.zeb'). [Full title, **Aureng-Zebe, or The Great Mogul.**] The last rhymed tragedy by John Dryden, produced in 1675. It has a very intricate plot involving the numerous trials of two lovers, Indamora and Aureng-Zebe.

Aurora (ô.rō'rạ). [Greek, **Eos.**] In Roman mythology, the goddess of the dawn. The poets represented her as rising out of the ocean in a chariot, her rosy fingers dropping gentle dew.

Aurora Leigh (lē). A narrative poem by Elizabeth Barrett Browning, published in 1857, named from its heroine.

Austen (ôs'tẹn), **Jane.** b. at Steventon, Hampshire, England, 1775; d. at Winchester, England, 1817. An English novelist; seventh and youngest child of George Austen, rector of Deane and Steventon. Unmarried, she lived with her family, writing apparently chiefly for their amusement, at Steventon, Bath (1801), Southampton (1805), Chawton (1809), and Winchester (1817), making a humorous, ironical study of middle-class society for which she is unrivaled. Her first novel to be sent to a publisher, *Susan* (afterwards *Northanger Abbey*), was sold in 1802 but did not appear till after her death. About this time she also began a novel, *The Watsons*, which she never finished. However, *Sense and Sensibility*, published in 1811, brought her immediate recognition. It was followed by *Pride and Prejudice* (1813; its original title when she began it in 1794 was *First Impressions*), *Mansfield Park* (1814), and *Emma* (1816). Her last, and many think her best, novel, *Persuasion*, did not appear till a year after her death, when it was published with *Northanger Abbey*. In her lifetime she was conceded rank possibly equal to that of Fanny Burney or Maria Edgeworth; later appreciation of her peculiar gifts of proportion and composition (which she called those of a miniaturist), began probably with Richard Whately and Sir Walter Scott, and was seconded enthusiastically by George Henry Lewes, Samuel Taylor Coleridge, Thomas Babington Macaulay, and others. Published writing by her, in addition to the novels already cited, includes various shorter and unfinished works, recently reissued as curiosities, and two volumes of her letters. Critical studies of her life and works include *Memoir of Jane Austen* (1926) by J. E. Austen Leigh, *Jane Austen: Facts and Problems* (1948) by R. W. Chapman, *Jane Austen: Irony as Defense and Discovery* (1952) by Marvin Mudrick, and *Jane Austen's Novels: A Study in Structure* (1954) by Andrew H. Wright.

Austin (ôs'tin), **Alfred.** b. at Headingley, Leeds, England, May 30, 1835; d. at Ashford, Kent, England, June 2, 1913. An English poet, essayist, and novelist. He was named poet laureate in 1896, although most critics consider his abundant verse of little worth. His critical views are indicated by the fact that he attacked Tennyson, Robert Browning, Matthew Arnold, Algernon Charles Swinburne, William Morris, Arthur Hugh Clough, and Victor Hugo as inferior poets in his *Poetry of the Period* (1870), and Wordsworth in his *The Bridling of Pegasus* (1910), a volume of collected essays.

Austin, Frederick Britten. b. May 8, 1885; d. at Weston-super-Mare, Somerset, England, March 12,

ḏ, d or j; ṣ, s or sh; ṭ, t or ch; ẓ, z or zh; o, F. cloche; ü, F. menu; ċh, Sc. loch; ṅ, F. bonbon.

1941. An English novelist, short-story writer, dramatist, and scenarist. Author of *The Shaping of Lavinia* (1911), *A Saga of the Sea* (1928), *The Road to Glory* (1935), novels; *The Thing That Matters* (1921), a drama; *On the Borderland* (1923), a collection of stories; *When Mankind Was Young* (1927), a fictional picture of prehistoric man; and *The Red Flag* (1934), an account of revolutions from Spartacus to Lenin (published 1933 in Spanish as *La Bandera Roja*).

Austin, John. b. at Creeling Mill, Suffolk, England, March 3, 1790; d. at Weybridge, Surrey, England, in December, 1859. An English lawyer and writer on jurisprudence. He has been praised for his work in establishing definitions of legal ideas and terms, and credited with laying a scientific foundation for legal analysis and a modern philosophy of law. He was a professor of jurisprudence (1826–32) at University College, London, where John Stuart Mill was his student; in 1834 he was royal commissioner on criminal law. Author of *Province of Jurisprudence Determined* (1832), *A Plea for the Constitution* (1859, a pamphlet against Charles Grey's proposal of parliamentary reform), *Lectures on Jurisprudence* (1869), and others.

Austin, Sarah. [Maiden name, **Taylor.**] b. at Norwich, Norfolk, England, 1793; d. at Weybridge, Surrey, England, Aug. 8, 1867. An English writer; wife of John Austin (1790–1859). Besides editions of her husband's lectures (1861–63), she was the author of painstaking translations from German and French, of which the best known are *Characteristics of Goethe from the German of Falk, Von Müller, and Others* (1833), Friedrich Wilhelm Carové's *Story Without an End* (1834), Leopold von Ranke's *History of the Popes* (1840), *History of the Reformation in Germany* (1845), and Guizot's *Causes of the Success of the English Revolution* (1850).

Austin, William. b. 1587; d. Jan. 16, 1634. An English lawyer and writer. His works include *Devotionis Augustinianae Flamma, or Certayne Devout, Godly, and Lerned Meditations* (1635), *Haec Homo, wherein the Excellency of the Creation of Woman is described by way of an Essay* (1637), and a translation of Cicero's *Cato Major*.

Austin Friars. The monastery of the Friars Eremite of the order of Saint Augustine, on the north side of Broad Street, Old London: founded in 1253 by Humphrey Bohun.

Austin of Canterbury (kan′tėr.ber.i, -bėr.i), Saint. See **Augustine of Canterbury,** Saint.

Australia Felix (ôs.trāl′yạ fē′liks). A novel by Henry Handel Richardson (pseudonym of Mrs. Henrietta Robertson), published in 1917. It is the first volume of the trilogy *The Fortunes of Richard Mahony* (1930), and deals with goldminers in Australia.

Austria (ôs′tri.ạ), **Duke of.** [Also, **Lymoges.**] In Shakespeare's *King John*, an ally of Philip and the Dauphin, supposed to have killed Richard I (the Lion-Hearted). The Bastard, Philip Faulconbridge, kills him in battle (III.ii).

Author, The. A comedy by Samuel Foote, produced and printed in 1757.

Authoress of the Odyssey (od′i.si), **The.** A prose work (1897) by Samuel Butler. Butler's reputation

as an ironist led many to take this for a hoax, but he actually was convinced that the *Odyssey* had been written at Trapani in Sicily and by a woman.

Author's Farce, The. [Full title, **The Author's Farce, and the Pleasures of the Town.**] A play by Henry Fielding, originally produced in 1730 and revived in 1734. It contains humorous portraits of Colley Cibber and his son Theophilus, and has such figures as Dr. Orator, Monsieur Pantomime, Mrs. Novel (satirizing the publisher, Bookweight), Don Tragedio, Sir Farcical Comick (Cibber), Opera, and the Goddess Nonsense (who takes Opera for her very own).

autobiography. A biography or memoir of a person written by himself.

Autocracy of Mr. Parham (pär′ạm), **The.** A novel (1930) by H. G. Wells. It is one in a series of his Utopian novels.

Autolycus (ô.tol′i.kus). In Greek legend, a son of Hermes (or Daedalion) and Chione, and father of Anticleia, the mother of Odysseus. He was a famous thief, and possessed the power of making himself and the things that he stole invisible, or of giving them new forms.

Autolycus. In Shakespeare's *Winter's Tale*, a witty thieving peddler, a "snapper up of unconsidered trifles." He indulges in grotesque self-raillery and droll soliloquizing on his own sins. He quite possibly derives from the amusing rogues of comic Italian epics, such as Morgante in Pulci's *Il Morgante Maggiore* and Margute in Ariosto's *Orlando Furioso*.

Automedon (ô.tom′ẹ.don). In Greek legend, the son of Diores, and, according to Homer, the comrade and charioteer of Achilles. In another account, he had an independent command of ten ships in the Trojan War. Vergil makes him the companion in arms of Pyrrhus, son of Achilles.

Autonoë (ô.ton′ọ.ē). In Greek mythology, the daughter of Cadmus, wife of Aristaeus, and mother of Actaeon.

Autumn Journal. A volume of poetry (1939) by Louis MacNeice.

Auvergne (ō.vėrn′), **Countess of.** In Shakespeare's *1 Henry VI*, a French noblewoman. She tries but fails to trap Talbot. He shows her that his power lies in his army, not himself.

Avallenau (ä.väl′ẹ.nou), **The.** A Welsh poem ascribed to the ancient Merlin. It is thought to have been written in the latter part of the reign of Owain Gwynedd, and to contain distinct historical allusion to affairs of the years 1165–70. The title means "of the apple trees."

Avalon (av′ạ.lon). [Also: **Avallon, Avelion, Avilion, Vale of Avalon.**] In medieval, and especially Arthurian, legend, the Land of the Blessed, or Isle of Souls, an earthly paradise in the western seas. The great heroes, such as Arthur and Ogier the Dane, are supposed to have been carried there at death, and Morgan le Fay (or the fairy Morgana) holds her court there.

Ave Atque Vale (ā′vē at′kwẹ vā′lẹ). In literature, originally a poem by Catullus written in memory of his brother (the phrase means "hail and farewell" in Latin), used subsequently by various English writers, most notably by Swinburne and Tennyson (in the poem *Frater Ave Atque Vale*).

Ave atque Vale. A poem (1867) by Algernon Charles Swinburne. It is a tribute to Baudelaire.

Avebury (āv′bẻr.i, ā′bẻr.i), 1st Baron. Title of Lubbock, Sir John.

Ave Imperatrix (ā′vē im.pẹ.rā′triks). A poem by Rudyard Kipling included among his *Schoolboy Lyrics* (1881). It is significant in that it strikes for the first time the authentic Kipling note of service to the British Empire.

Avelion (av′ẹl.yọn). See **Avalon**.

Ave Maria (ä′vä mä.rē′ä). [Also: the **"Angelical Salutation"**; English, **Hail Mary**.] Among Roman Catholics, the prayer most frequently addressed to the Virgin Mary. It is often known as the Hail Mary, from the meaning of the first two words in English. The words of the prayer as used today are, in English: "Hail, Mary, full of grace, the Lord is with Thee; blessed art thou among women, and blessed is the fruit of thy womb, Jesus. Holy Mary, Mother of God, pray for us sinners, now and at the hour of our death. Amen." The words up to and including "women" are the salutation of the angel Gabriel to Mary at the Annunciation, as given in Luke, i. 28 (Douay Version), with the name of Mary inserted; the next phrase is that spoken to Mary by Saint Elizabeth, according to Luke, i. 42, with the addition of the name Jesus. Beginning in the 6th century or earlier the prayer evolved through popular usage and the approval of various popes until its inclusion in its present form in the Roman Breviary, in 1568.

Avenel (āv′nẹl), **Julian.** The usurper of Avenel Castle and the uncle of Mary Avenel in Sir Walter Scott's novel *The Monastery*.

Avenel, Mary. One of the principal characters in Sir Walter Scott's novel *The Monastery*, the wife of Halbert Glendinning. She reappears in *The Abbot*.

Aventine Hill (av′ẹn.tīn). The southernmost of the seven hills of ancient Rome, rising on the left bank of the Tiber, S of the Palatine. Below it to the N lay the Circus Maximus, and to the E the thermae of Caracalla.

Averno (ä.ver′nō), **Lake.** [Latin, **Lacus Avernus** (lā′kus ạ.vẻr′nus).] A small lake in Campania, Italy, ab. 9 mi. W of Naples, anciently believed to be the entrance to the infernal regions. Circumference, ab. 2 mi.; depth, ab. 200 ft.

Avesta (ạ.ves′tạ). The bible of Zoroastrianism and the Parsis. The name comes from the Pahlavi *avistak*, which possibly means "knowledge." The name *Zendavesta* arose by mistake from inverting the Pahlavi phrase *Avistak va Zand*, "Avesta and Zend," or "the Law and Commentary," *Zend*, "knowledge, explanation," referring to the later version and commentary in Pahlavi.

Avianus (ā.vi.ā′nus), **Flavius.** fl. c4th century A.D. A Roman writer of fables. He wrote 42 fables in elegiac meter, which were, as a collection, once much used as a schoolbook.

Avice Caro (ā′vis kär′ō). In Hardy's *The Well-Beloved*, the mother, daughter, and granddaughter.

Each bears the name, and each is loved in turn by Jocelyn Pierston.

Avilion (av′il.yọn). See **Avalon**.

Avisa (ạ.vī′sạ). [Full title, **Willobie his Avisa, or the True Picture of a Modest Maid and of a Chast and Constant Wife.**] A poem by an English writer named Henry Willoughby (or Willobie). It was first printed in 1594, and prefixed to the second edition in 1596 are some verses which allude to Shakespeare's *Rape of Lucrece*. The parts of the work exemplify the character of a chaste woman resisting all the temptations to which her life exposes her. This is the earliest known work to make printed mention of Shakespeare's name.

Avoca (ạ.vō′kạ) or **Ovoca** (ọ-). A river and valley in the E part of the Irish Republic, in County Wicklow, ab. 43 mi. S of Dublin, formed by the union of the small rivers Avonmore and Avonbeg. The Avoca flows SW to the Irish Sea at Arklow. Thomas Moore celebrated the "Sweet Vale of Avoca" in his song *The Meeting of the Waters*.

Avon (ā′vọn, av′ọn), **the Swan of.** See **Swan of Avon, the.**

Avowals and Denials. A prose work by G. K. Chesterton, published during the decade 1925–35.

Awdelay or **Awdeley** (ôd′lā), **John.** [Also called **Sampson Awdelay** and **John Sampson.**] fl. 1559–77. An English printer and writer. He is best known for his *Fraternitye of Vacabondes* (1565), a detailed account of beggars and their organizations in the 16th century.

Awdrey (ô′dri). See **Audrey**.

Awkward Age, The. A novel by Henry James, published in 1899. It is the story of Nanda Brookenham, an English society girl, during the period between adolescence and marriage. She and her mother both compete for the love of Vanderbank, and she is forced to contend with various plots and schemes of various other older women. However, Vanderbank does not marry either woman, and the temporarily disillusioned Nanda goes to live in the country with Mr. Longdon, a man who had once loved her grandmother.

Awntyrs of Arthure at the Terne Wathelyne (oun′tirs; tern wäᴛн′lin). [Or, modernized, **Adventures of Arthur at the Tarn Wadling.**] A Middle English verse romance (14th century), written in the alliterative line. It deals with two adventures which happened while Arthur was hunting at the Tarn Wadling, in Cumberland. Gawain figures in both incidents.

Axel Heyst (ak′sẹl hīst). See **Heyst, Axel**.

Ayala's Angel (ā.yä′lạz). A novel by Anthony Trollope, published in 1881. It is the story of Lucy and Ayala Dormer, who are left orphaned and penniless after having grown up in a home of wealth and culture. Lucy goes to the home of her uncle, a man of modest means, and very quickly becomes bored with the drabness of life there. Ayala goes into the home of her aunt Emmeline, married to the millionaire, Sir Thomas Tringle. However, Ayala fails to display the worship of money that dominates this family, and the two sisters decide to exchange households. Lucy falls in love with a poor artist and Ayala has three suitors, Tom

Tringle, Captain Batsby, and Colonel Jonathan Stubbs, of whom, after first refusing them all, she eventually chooses Stubbs (her "Angel").

Ayenbite of Inwit (a̯.yen′bīt; in′wit), **The.** [Also, **The Remorse of Conscience.**] A Middle English version of the religious treatise *Somme le Roi* (or *Somme des Vices et Vertues*), translated in 1340. The title may be put into modern English, more or less literally, as "the again-biting of the inner wit" (whence the variant title above). Chaucer was familiar with it, and also with the French from which it was taken, as is evidenced by parts of *The Parson's Tale.*

Ayesha (ä′ye̯.shä). [Also: **Aisha, Ayeshah;** called (by Mohammedans) **Ummu al-Muminin,** meaning "Mother of the Believers."] b. at Medina, Arabia, c611; d. c678. Daughter of Abu-Bakr, first Moslem caliph; child-wife and favorite of Mohammed. She opposed Ali, Mohammed's cousin and the husband of his daughter Fatima, in his dispute with Abu-Bakr over the caliphate. When Ali took office after the death of Othman (656), she raised an army against him, but was defeated and taken prisoner by him at the "Battle of the Camel."

Aylmer (āl′mėr), **John.** b. at Tivetshall St. Mary, Norfolk, England, 1521; d. at Fulham (now part of London), June 3, 1594. An English prelate, bishop of London (1576–94) under Queen Elizabeth. He served as chaplain to Henry Grey, the duke of Suffolk, and tutor (1541) to his daughter Lady Jane Grey. Deprived of an archdeaconship for his opposition to Mary's restoration of the Roman Catholic Mass, he fled to Switzerland, where he remained during her reign (1553–58) and where he collaborated on John Foxe's translation of the *Acts of the Martyrs.* A relentless opponent of Roman Catholicism and Puritanism alike, he was bitterly attacked in the Martin Marprelate tracts (1588) and is supposed to be "Morrell" ("the proude and ambitious pastour") of Edmund Spenser's *Shepherd's Calendar.*

Aylwin (āl′win). A romance (1898) by Walter Theodore Watts-Dunton. It caused a momentary sensation because of the recognizable portraits of Rossetti and other celebrities it contained.

Aymer de Valence (ā′mėr de̯ val′e̯ns). [Title, Earl of **Pembroke.**] b. c1265; d. 1324. An English soldier and statesman; a half brother of Henry III of England. He succeeded to the earldom of Pembroke in 1296; led (as "Guardian of Scotland") the van of the English forces in the attack on Robert I ("the Bruce") in 1306, in the defeat of the Scots at Methven; and was himself defeated (1307) by Robert at Loudon Hill. Under Edward II he was one of the chief opponents of Gaveston, favorite and foster brother of Edward.

Aymer De Valence, Sir. See **Valence, Sir Aymer De.**

Aymon (ā′mọn). [Also: **Aimon, Haimon, Haymon;** title, **Count of Dordogne.**] fl. early 8th century. A French nobleman, much of whose story is based on legend rather than verifiable fact. He appears in the old French romances, a prince of Ardennes, possibly of Saxon origin, who took the title of Duke of Dordogne. He was the father of Renaud (Rinaldo), Guiscard (Guicciardo), Alard (Alardo), and Richard (Richardetto), the "four sons of Aymon"

whose adventures were written in a *chanson de geste* of the 13th century (first printed in 1493), supposed to be by Huon de Villeneuve, under the title of *Les Quatre Fils d'Aymon.* The brothers appear in Torquato Tasso's *Gerusalemme Liberata (Jerusalem Delivered)*, Luigi Pulci's *Morgante Maggiore*, Matteo Maria Boiardo's *Orlando Innamorato*, Lodovico Ariosto's *Orlando Furioso*, and other French and Italian romances.

Aymon, Foure Sonnes of. See **Foure Sonnes of Aymon.**

Ayr (ār). A royal burgh and seaport in S Scotland, county seat of Ayrshire, situated on the Firth of Clyde, at the mouth of the river Ayr, ab. 18 mi. NE of Girvan, ab. 406 mi. N of London by rail. The town has manufactures of woolens and other items, and exports coal. It is famous as the center of the Robert Burns country, Burns's birthplace being at Alloway, on the outskirts of the town. The "Auld Brig" mentioned by Burns (for 500 years the only bridge in town) still stands in the center of the town.

Ayres (ārz), **Ruby Mildred.** b. 1883; d. at Weybridge, England, Nov. 14, 1955. An English novelist. Her novels, published serially in London newspapers and elsewhere, brought her an enormous audience. Among her numerous works are *Richard Chatterton, V.C., The Remembered Kiss, The Scar, The Bachelor Husband, The Big Fellah, Compromise, Sunrise for Georgie,* and *The Lady from London.* Her play *Silver Wedding* was produced in 1932.

Ayrshire Legatee (ār′shir), **The.** A satirical sketch (1820) by John Galt. It is written in the form of letters to friends in Scotland by a Scottish minister who has gone to London with his family to obtain a legacy.

Ayscough (as′kū), **John.** Pseudonym of **Bickerstaffe-Drew, Francis Browning Drew.**

Ayton or **Aytoun** (ā′tọn), **Sir Robert.** b. near St. Andrews, Scotland, 1570; d. at London, in February, 1638. A Scottish poet at the court of James I of England. One of the first Scots to use English as a literary language, he was also a friend of Ben Jonson. Besides Latin poems including a panegyric on the accession (1603) of James I and an elegy on the death of Buckingham (1628), he wrote lyrics such as *Inconstancy Upbraided* and, probably, *I Do Confess Thou'rt Smooth and Fair.*

Aytoun (ā′tọn), **William Edmonstoune.** b. at Edinburgh, June 21, 1813; d. near Elgin, Scotland, Aug. 4, 1865. A Scottish poet and humorist. Though called to the Scottish bar in 1840, he had been more interested in writing than in law since the publication of his first book, *Poland, Homer, and Other Poems* (1832), and did virtually nothing to further his career as a barrister. He became a contributor to *Blackwood's Magazine* (in 1836, and later served on the staff), especially of satirical articles on politics and contemporary affairs. He was also a popular lecturer as professor (1845–65) of rhetoric and belles-lettres at Edinburgh. Author of *Lays of the Scottish Cavaliers* (1848), *Firmilian, a Spasmodic Tragedy* (1852, a satire on contemporary writers); with Sir Theodore Martin, of *The Bon Gaultier Ballads* (1855, reprinted from *Blackwood's*), a series of parodies imitated by W. S. Gilbert (*Bab Ballads*) and others; translated, with Martin, *Poems and*

Ballads of Goethe (1858); and collected and annotated *Ballads of Scotland* (1858).

Azariah (az.a.rī′a) or **Azarias** (az.a.rī′as). An Old English poem, preserved in part in the *Exeter Book*, dealing with the three youths (Azariah is another name for Shadrach) cast into the fiery furnace by Nebuchadnezzar. Part of it also appears as an interpolation in the poem *Daniel*, in the *Junius Manuscript*.

Azazel (a.zā′zel, az.a.zel′). [Arabic, **Azazil** (ä.zä′-zil).] A name which occurs in the ritual of the Day of Atonement, Lev. xvi. 8, 10–26. The high priest had among other ceremonies to cast lots upon two goats. One lot was inscribed "for Yahveh" (Jehovah), the other "for Azazel." The goat upon which the lot "for Yahveh" fell was offered as a sacrifice, while on the goat upon which the lot "for Azazel" had fallen the high priest laid his hands and confessed all the sins of the people. The goat was then led by a man into the desert, "unto a land not inhabited," and was there let loose. The authorized version of the Old Testament renders Azazel on the margin by "scape-goat"; the revised version has Azazel in the text and "or dismissal" on the margin. Arabic writers describe Azazel as one of the jinn who for transgression were taken prisoners by the angels. Azazel was their chief, until he refused to prostrate himself before Adam, when he became father of the Shaitans (evil spirits). This is reëchoed in Milton's *Paradise Lost*, where Azazel is represented as the standard-bearer of the infernal hosts, cast out from heaven and becoming the embodiment of despair. The identification of Azazel with Satan is also met in some of the church fathers.

Azaziel (a.zā′zi.el). A seraph in Byron's *Heaven and Earth*, who loves a mortal.

Azim (ä′zim). The lover of Zelica in "The Veiled Prophet of Khorassan," one of the tales in Thomas Moore's *Lalla Rookh* (1817). He kills her by mistake for Lalla Rookh.

Azo (ä′zō). In Byron's *Parisina*, the Marquis of Este, who orders the execution of his wife, Parisina, and his illegitimate son, Hugo, when he learns of the love affair between them.

Azrael (az′rā.el). In certain writings of Judaism and Islam, the angel who separates the soul from the body at the moment of death, for which he watches.

B

B., Mr. In Samuel Richardson's *Pamela*, the heroine's employer and eventual husband. His persistent and sometimes ludicrously inept efforts to seduce her are recounted in detail in various of Pamela's letters (the novel is cast in the form of a series of letters by its heroine). When, at last, he is able to possess her, it is on her terms, as his lawfully wedded wife, and during the years following she completely reforms him by her display of virtue. To Henry Fielding (and many other readers since) it has seemed that Pamela uses her "virtue" cleverly and coldly to secure Mr. B. as husband, and that he falls into her trap convinced that he has obtained something beyond price when, in fact, he has simply met the price set by Pamela. Perhaps for this reason, in Fielding's *Joseph Andrews*, begun as a satire on *Pamela*, Mr. B. is called Squire Booby, and later editions of *Pamela* tried to avoid the implication of ridicule by calling Mr. B. Mr. Boothby.

Baal (bā′al). [Plural, **Baalim** (bā′a.lim).] The name specifically of the supreme god of the Phoenicians and the Canaanites. The word derives through Hebrew from Assyro Babylonian (Akkadian), the oldest of the Semitic languages, and had originally a common language meaning of "owner" or "lord." It is cognate with the Babylonian "Bel." In those theologies of which he was the chief male god, Baal was conceived of as the productive power of generation and fertility, his female counterpart Astarte (Ashtoreth or Ishtar) being the receptive. His statue was placed on a bull, the symbol of generative power, and he was usually represented with bunches of grapes and pomegranates in his hands. He was also worshiped as the sun god, and was in this conception represented with a crown of rays. His cult was attended by wild and licentious orgies. Baal-worship came to Israel under Ahab and his wife, who was a Phoenician princess. Thus in Hos. ii.16 the name applied to Jehovah himself, while *Baal-berith* (the covenant-lord) was the god of the Shechemites, and *Baal-Zebub* (the fly-god) the idol of the Philistines at Ekron. *Baal-peor* (lord of the opening) was a god of Moab and Midian, probably the same as Chemosh. The word enters into the composition of many Hebrew, Phoenician, and Carthaginian names of persons and places, as *Jerubbaal*, *Hasdrubal* (help of Baal), *Hannibal* (grace of Baal), *Baal-Hammon*, *Baal-Thamar*, etc.

Bab (bab). [Full form, **Bab ed-Din**, meaning "Gate of Faith"; original name, **Ali Mohammed.**] b. at Shiraz, in what is now Iran, 1819; executed at Tabriz, in what is now Iran, July 9, 1850. The religious leader who founded (May 23, 1844) at Shiraz the sect known as Babism. Although his beliefs were in many respects basically those of the Shiite Moslems who were (and are) the dominant religious group in Iran, and although one of his aims was simply to achieve a degree of moral reform within the traditional framework of Islam, he also assumed the role of a prophet, equal in stature to Mohammed himself, and proclaimed the imminence of a Messiah. His success in persuading his followers to accept him in this role was so great as to threaten the established religious framework of the country, and to become a source of rebellion even against the civil authority of the state itself. As a result, after sentence by leading figures of the Shiite Moslem faction, he was shot by soldiers of the government and his sect was repressed with a

d, d or j; ş, s or sh; ţ, t or ch; z̧, z or zh; o, F. cloche; ü, F. menu; ċh, Sc. loch; ṅ, F. bonbon, degree of ruthlessness considered by some authorities to have been as great as any in the history of religious persecution (some estimates of the number of his followers who were killed have run as high as 20,000). Belief remained alive, however, in the 19-year interval (1844–63) which he had forecast before arrival of the Messiah, and in 1863 Baha Ullah was accepted by surviving Babists as the "Manifestation" prophesied by the Bab. Thereafter Babism, as such, disappeared, being replaced by Bahaism (although modern Bahaists reckon both Baha Ullah and the Bab as founders of their sect).

Baba (bä′bä), **Ali.** The hero of "Ali Baba and the Forty Thieves," a tale in *The Arabian Nights' Entertainments*. See **Ali Baba.**

Baba, Cassim. The brother of Ali Baba. He discovers the secret of the robbers' magic cave, and enters it alone, hoping to obtain the treasure for himself. However, he forgets the password "Open, Sesame" (although he remembers that it involves the name of a grain, and desperately tries such various others as "Open, Oats," etc.), and is unable to get out, wherefor he is found by the robbers, who kill and dismember him.

Baba, Hajji. The principal character in a novel by James Justinian Morier, *The Adventures of Hajji Baba of Ispahan*, published in 1824.

Baba, Mustapha. The shoemaker who stitches together the body of Cassim Baba, which has been cut into four pieces by the robbers and hung on the door of the magic cave.

Baba Abdalla (äb.däl′ä). The blind man, in a story in *The Arabian Nights' Entertainments*, who becomes rich through the kindness of a dervish. His covetousness makes him demand also a box of magic ointment which, when applied to the left eye, reveals all hidden treasures, but when used on the right produces total blindness. Doubting this, he applies it to both, and loses both sight and riches.

Babalatchi (bab.ä.lat′chi). The chief adviser of the rajah in Conrad's *Outcast of the Islands.*

Babar (bä′bar). The little elephant who is the hero of a series of children's books (which have recently, in English translations, gained a considerable audience in the U. S.) written and illustrated by the French author Jean de Brunhoff (1899–1937).

Babar (bä′bar). See also **Baber.**

Bab Ballads (bab), **The.** A volume of humorous verse by W. S. Gilbert, published at London in 1868. The poems in the collection appeared originally in the magazine *Fun.*

Babbie (bab′i). The heroine of J. M. Barrie's novel *The Little Minister.*

Babel (bä′bel, bab′el), **Tower of.** In the Old Testament, a tower built in the valley of Shinar by the descendants of Noah, who sought by this means to reach the heavenly realm above the earth. Displeased at their temerity, God thereupon threw their language into a multitude of languages, which made it impossible for the builders of the tower to understand each other or work together, and thus halted construction of the tower. Many scholars have interpreted this Biblical account (Gen. xi. 1–9)

as a primitive explanation of the diversity of the world's languages.

Baber, Babar, or **Babur** (bä′bẽr). [Mongol surname (meaning the "Tiger") of **Zahir ud-Din Mohammed.**] b. Feb. 4, 1483; d. Dec. 28, 1530. An Indian ruler, notable as the founder of the Mogul empire in India; great-grandson of Tamerlane. He wrote in the Tartar language memoirs afterward translated into Persian and from that into various Western languages.

Babes in the Wood, The. See **Children in the Wood, The.**

Babieça (bä.вyä′thä). See **Bavieça.**

Babington (bab′ing.tọn), **Anthony.** b. at Dethick, Derbyshire, England, in October, 1561; executed Sept. 20, 1586. An English Roman Catholic conspirator. He was page for a time to Mary Queen of Scots during her imprisonment at Sheffield, and became chief (under the guidance of various Catholic priests, particularly of John Ballard) of a conspiracy for the murder of Elizabeth, the release of Mary, and a general rising of the Catholics. The plot was discovered, and he was sentenced to death for high treason.

Babism (bäb′iz.ẹm). The Persian sect from which developed modern Bahaism. It was called "Babism" from its founder, Bab, who took his name from *bab*, meaning "gate." He claimed that no one could come to know God except through him, and hence called himself, in full, "Bab ed-Din," which means "Gate of Faith." The sect of Babism was, essentially, a pantheistic offshoot of Mohammedanism, tinctured with Gnostic, Buddhistic, and Jewish ideas. It inculcated a high morality, discountenanced polygamy, forbade concubinage, asceticism, and mendicancy, recognized the equality of the sexes, and encouraged the practice of charity, hospitality, and abstinence from intoxicants of all kinds.

Babley (bab′li), **Richard.** See **Dick, Mr.**

Baboon (ba.bön′), **Lewis** and **Philip.** Characters in John Arbuthnot's *History of John Bull*, representing, respectively, Louis XIV of France and Philip of Bourbon, Duc d'Anjou.

babu (bä′bö). [Also, **baboo.**] A Hindu title of address, equivalent to *sir* or *Mr.*, given to gentlemen, clerks, etc.: formerly applied in some parts of Hindustan to certain persons of distinction. "In Bengal and elsewhere, among Anglo-Indians, it is often used with a slight savor of disparagement, as characterizing a superficially cultivated but too often effeminate Bengali; and from the extensive employment of the class to which the term was applied as a title in the capacity of clerks in English offices, the word has come often to signify 'a native clerk who writes English.'" (Yule and Burnell, *Anglo-Ind. Gloss.*)

Babur (bä′bẽr). See **Baber.**

Babylon (bab′i.lọn). [Biblical, **Babel.**] In ancient geography, a city in Mesopotamia, the capital of Babylonia, situated on both sides of the Euphrates River, above the modern city of Hilla, S central Iraq, ab. 50 mi. S of Baghdad. The etymology of the name is, as ascertained by many passages in the cuneiform inscriptions, *Bab-Ili* (meaning "Gate of

God"), from *bab* (meaning "gate") and *ilu* (meaning "god"). Babylon was one of the oldest cities of Mesopotamia (compare Gen. x. 10), and was the undisputed capital of Babylonia at the time of the Elamite conquest, in the third millennium B.C. As capital of the country it shared in all its vicissitudes, and was the principal aim of the Assyrian invasions. Sennacherib sacked it (690 B.C.), and completely razed it to the ground. His son and successor Esarhaddon undertook, 11 years later, the restoration of the city. But it was under Nabopolassar (625–604 B.C.), the founder of the new Babylonian empire, and especially under his successor Nebuchadnezzar (605–562 B.C.) that it became "Babylon the Great." Sloping toward the river were the **Hanging Gardens,** one of the seven wonders of the world, the location of which is in the N mound of ruins, Babil. The temple described by Herodotus is that of Nebo in Borsippa, not far from Babylon, which Herodotus included under Babylon, and which also in the cuneiform inscriptions is called "Babylon the second." This temple, which in the mound of Birs Nimrud represents the most imposing ruin of Babylonia, is termed in the inscriptions *Ezida* ("the eternal house"), an ancient sanctuary of Nebo (Assyrian, *Nabu*), and was restored with great splendor by Nebuchadnezzar. It represents in its construction a sort of pyramid built in seven stages, whence it is sometimes called "temple of the seven spheres of heaven and earth," and it has been assumed that the narrative of the Tower of Babel in Gen. xi. may have been connected with this temple. Concerning Babylon proper Herodotus mentions that it had wide streets lined with houses of three and four stories. In the Apocalypse, Babylon is used for the city of the Antichrist.

Babylonian Captivity or **Exile.** A term applied to the period of the exile of the Jews in Babylon; usually reckoned as 70 years, although the actual period from the destruction of the temple and capture of Jerusalem to the return was not more than 50 years. In 586 the city was captured after a siege, and the city and temple were burned. A considerable part of the population, including the city's most prosperous and influential citizens, were carried off to Babylonia. Nearly 50 years later (c538), the Persian king Cyrus, after capturing Babylon, granted the exiles permission to return, and a group of more than 42,000 persons is said to have availed itself of the opportunity. Jerusalem at this time once more became for the Jews both a national and religious center, and rebuilding of the temple was at once undertaken. With its completion (c516) the 70 years of the scriptural prophecy were completed.

Babylonian Captivity. A term often applied to that period in Roman Catholic history when the popes lived at Avignon, France. During this period of some 70 years beginning in 1308 the popes (all of whom were French) were subject, in greater or lesser degree, to direct political control by the French throne. The term derives from the original Babylonian Captivity, of the Jews in the 6th century B.C., which is traditionally reckoned also as having lasted for 70 years.

Baca (bā′kạ), **Valley of.** A valley referred to in the Old Testament (Ps. lxxxiv. 6), probably the later El-Bakei'a, between Jerusalem and Bethlehem. The Biblical reference ("valley of weeping" in the King James Version) is clearly allegorical, and has been suggested as the probable source of the phrase "vale of tears."

Bacbuc (băk.bük). The priestess of the temple in François Rabelais' *Pantagruel.*

Bacchae (bak′ē) or **Bacchantes** (bạ.kan′tēz). [Also, **Maenads.**] In ancient Greece and Italy, female worshipers of the god of wine, generally called by the Greeks Dionysus, and by the Romans Bacchus.

Bacchae (bak′ē), **The.** A tragedy by Euripides, usually assigned to a late period in the life of the dramatist.

Bacchanalia (bak.ạ.nā′li.ạ). In Roman antiquity, a festival in honor of Bacchus. Introduced into Rome from the Greek communities in S Italy, the Bacchanalia (the name is a Latin translation of the Greek *Dionysia*) originally consisted of secret rites practiced by women only (the Bacchae or Bacchantes) on three days of the year. Later the rites were opened to men and were celebrated five days each month; they became drunken orgies, at which it was supposed that crimes were plotted and conspiracies were hatched, and the Roman Senate by decree in 186 B.C. prohibited them throughout Italy, under penalty of severe punishments.

bacchius (ba.kī′us). In prosody, a metric foot composed of one short and two long syllables, with the ictus on the first long, as in ăvā′rī, ăbōve′bōard.

Bacchus (bak′us). In classical mythology, a name of Dionysus, the son of Zeus (Jupiter) and Semele, and the god of wine, personifying both its good and its bad qualities. It was the current name of this god among the Romans. The orgiastic worship of Bacchus was especially characteristic of Boeotia, where his festivals were celebrated on the slopes of Mount Cithaeron, and extended to those of the neighboring Parnassus. In Attica the rural and somewhat savage cult of Bacchus underwent a metamorphosis, and reached its highest expression in the choragic literary contests in which originated both tragedy and comedy, and for which were written most of the masterpieces of Greek literature. Bacchus was held to have taught the cultivation of the grape and the preparation of wine. In early art, and less commonly after the age of Phidias, Bacchus is represented as a bearded man of full age, usually completely draped. After the time of Praxiteles he appears almost universally, except in archaistic examples, in the type of a beardless youth, of graceful and rounded form, often entirely undraped or very lightly draped. Among his usual attributes are the vine, the ivy, the thyrsus, the wine cup, and the panther.

Bacchylides (bạ.kil′i.dēz). b. on the island of Ceos (now Keos), in the Aegean Sea; fl. 5th century B.C. A Greek lyric poet; nephew and pupil of Simonides and a contemporary and rival of Pindar. He lived for a time at the court of Hiero I of Syracuse.

Bach (bäċh), **Johann Sebastian.** b. at Eisenach, Germany, March 21, 1685; d. at Leipzig, Germany, July 28, 1750. A German composer and instrumentalist, noted also as one of the foremost musicians of all time. He became totally blind in 1749 after an unsuccessful operation to restore his failing sight. He composed both secular and religious music for

ḍ, d or j; ṣ, s or sh; ṭ, t or ch; ẓ, z or zh; o, F. cloche; ü, F. menu; ċh, Sc. loch; ṅ, F. bonbon.

solo performance and for diverse vocal and instrumental combinations. His 48 preludes and fugues for *"Das wohl-temperierte Klavier"* ("The Well-tempered Clavier") represented the first whole-hearted use of the equally tempered scale throughout all keys. He was master of counterpoint, and his many organ preludes and fugues are still often played, both in their original form and in orchestral transcriptions. Of his secular instrumental works the best-known are the six Brandenburg Concertos (so called because they were composed at the request of the elector of Brandenburg) for chamber orchestra. Of his vocal works, the sacred cantatas and oratorios are the most important; outstanding among them are the *St. John's Passion* and the *St. Matthew Passion*. He also composed over 30 secular cantatas, and set over 300 of Luther's hymns to music. New sources on Bach have come to light and a new complete edition of his works is being issued by Bärenreiter-Verlag of Kassel and Basle under the direction of an international editorial board. The English members of the board are Professor Westrup and Dr. Alfred Dürr.

Bacis (bā′sis) or **Bakis** (-kis). In Greek legend, a name given to several seers or prophets, the most celebrated of whom was the Boeotian Bacis, whose oracles were delivered at Heleon in Boeotia.

Backbite (bak′bīt), **Sir Benjamin.** A slanderer in Richard Brinsley Sheridan's comedy *The School for Scandal.*

"Back Kitchen." In Thackeray's novel *Pendennis*, a part of a London tavern set off for entertainment and drinking late at night and often visited by Pendennis and his friends. It is now generally believed that Thackeray's model for it was the "Cyder Cellars," on Maiden Lane adjoining the stage door of the Adelphi theater, a place once very popular with Dickens and various other prominent literary figures of the day.

Back to Methuselah (mẹ.thö′zẹ.lạ). A cycle of five plays by George Bernard Shaw, published in 1921. The work is a satirical treatment of the theme of purposive evolution and the perfectibility of man. The separate parts, set in the Garden of Eden, England, and in the future, are entitled *In the Beginning*, *Gospel of the Brothers Barnabas*, *The Thing Happens*, *Tragedy of an Elderly Gentleman*, and *As Far As Thought Can Reach.*

Backwater. A novel by Dorothy M. Richardson, published in 1916. It is the second section of *Pilgrimage*, a novel sequence in 12 parts (published collectively in 1938), employing the stream-of-consciousness technique.

Backwell (bak′wel), **Edward.** d. 1683. A London goldsmith and alderman who played an important part in state financial affairs under Oliver Cromwell and Charles II of England. He is regarded as a chief founder of the modern English system of banking.

Bacon (bā′kọn), **Delia Salter.** b. at Tallmadge, Ohio, Feb. 2, 1811; d. Sept. 2, 1859. An American writer and lecturer. Her best-known work is *The Philosophy of the Plays of Shakespeare unfolded by Delia Bacon* (1857), in which she attempted to prove that the plays attributed to Shakespeare are the work of Francis Bacon and others. She wrote

the book in England, after abandoning a successful career as a lecturer in the U. S., conducting her researches at London and elsewhere for three years before making her literary contribution.

Bacon, Francis. [Titles: 1st Baron **Verulam of Verulam,** Viscount **St. Albans.**] b. Jan. 22, 1561; d. April 9, 1626. An English essayist, philosopher, jurist, and statesman; son of Sir Nicholas Bacon, Lord Keeper of the Great Seal, and related through his mother to the Cecils, a family politically powerful in the reigns of Elizabeth and James I. Bacon studied at Cambridge (1573–75) and at Gray's Inn (1576 *et seq.*). He was admitted to the bar in 1582, and entered Parliament in 1584. As a learned counsel under Elizabeth he was commissioned to prosecute his erstwhile friend and benefactor Robert Devereux, 2nd Earl of Essex, for treason. Under James I he was knighted in 1603. In 1607 he became solicitor-general, in 1608 secretary to the Council of the Star Chamber (this office he had formerly held by reversion), in 1612 a judge of the Court of the Verge, in 1613 attorney general, in 1617 Lord Keeper, and in 1618 Lord Chancellor. He was created Baron Verulam of Verulam in 1618, and Viscount St. Albans in 1621. From his boyhood he lived close to the court. He was an "adviser" of James in a continuous battle waged between king, court, and lords on the one side and the House of Commons and courts of common law on the other. At the instigation of his political enemies, he was tried in 1621 for bribery, condemned, fined, and deprived of office. He had accepted, after a fashion of the time, presents from litigants in the courts over which he presided. He called the verdict just, and contended, probably in all sincerity, that no gift had ever influenced him in his reaching judicial decisions.

Quest for Knowledge. Bacon pursued high place and power largely to obtain control of foundations, such as colleges, and of collectors of scientific data for the inauguration and perpetuation of a "new learning." He sought to encompass all scientific information and set out to be a "second Aristotle." He hoped that his new method of investigation (*novum organum*) would supplant the organon of that influential Greek thinker. He called his purported reform of learning the Great Instauration. This included a "refutation" of all previous opinions and theories, especially those of Aristotle; a freeing of the human mind from its predispositions to error, which he called Idols (false images); a new method of investigation; and a naturalistic philosophy to be based on conclusions reached through an inductive collecting and observing of the data of natural history. His logic he designed as a "machine" which was to keep the intellect from soaring in "speculation" and would at the same time enlighten the senses. His philosophy was materialistic. He gave over to revealed theology questions concerning God's nature, the rational soul and its processes, and the basic rules of morality.

Influence on Later Thought. Bacon's influence became considerable about the middle of the 17th century when many members of the Royal Society professed to be his followers. By the end of the century speculative opponents regarded him as a "dictator" in English philosophy. His followers were in the main naturalistic thinkers who refused to accept any opinion, those of revealed theology excepted, which could not be "proven" by "observation and experiment." Few of them were materialists. Bacon himself made no appreciable discoveries, but he did much to implement an inductive investigation of nature. He was instrumental in founding a philosophical tradition in which systematic thought became identified with generalized and organized conclusions obtained in the empirical sciences. He construed the purpose of human knowledge as the control of nature for the relief of human misery, and he gave prominence to a doctrine of education which rejected textual study as "useless" and identified "sound" and "solid" learning with technical information and skill gained in the practice of the pure and applied sciences.

Written Works. His most important works are *Essays* (1597, 1612, 1625), *Advancement of Learning* (1605), *De Sapientia veterum* (1609), *Novum Organum* (1620), *Phenomena universi* (1622), *De dignitate et augmentis scientiarum* (1623), and the following pieces published posthumously: *Cogitationes de rerum natura, Valerius Terminus, Delineatio et argumentum, Cogitata et visa, Redargutio philosophiarum, New Atlantis, De principiis atque originibus,* and *Sylva Sylvarum.* Most of his Latin writings are translated in his *Works,* edited by Robert Leslie Ellis, James Spedding, and Douglas Denon Heath. His *Life* has been written with painstaking care by Spedding.

Bacon, Mr. In Thackeray's novel *Pendennis,* a publisher, formerly a partner in Bacon & Bungay. He is now the bitter enemy of his erstwhile friend and business associate, Mr. Bungay. Supposedly, the animosity between the two originated in the rivalry of their wives (whose enmity for each other may be considered somewhat odd in view of the fact that Mrs. Bungay is the sister of Mr. Bacon, and Mrs. Bacon is the sister of Mr. Bungay).

Bacon, Phanuel. b. at Reading, England, Oct. 13, 1700; d. at Balden, Oxfordshire, England, Jan. 10, 1783. An English divine, comic dramatist, and poet. He received degrees in art (1719, 1722) and divinity (1731, 1735) from Oxford University; served as vicar of Bramber, Sussex, and rector of Balden. He was the author of *The Kite* (1719), a mock-heroic poem; *The Snipe,* a humorous ballad; and *A Song of Similies.* The latter two appeared in the *Oxford Sausage* (1764), a collection of college verse. He also wrote five comedies, all dated 1757, published in one volume, *Humorous Ethics.*

Bacon, Roger. [Called **Doctor Mirabilis,** Anglicized as the "**Admirable Doctor.**"] b. at or near Ilchester, Somersetshire, England, c1214; d. probably at Oxford, England, in 1294. English philosopher and scientist. He was educated at Oxford and Paris (whence he appears to have returned (c1250) to England), and joined the Franciscan order. In 1257 he was sent by his superiors to Paris where he was kept in close confinement for several years. He was invited (1266) by Pope Clement IV to write a general treatise on the sciences, in answer to which he composed his chief work, the *Opus majus.* He was in England in 1268. In 1278 his writings were condemned as heretical by a council of his order, in consequence of which he was again placed in confinement. He was at liberty in 1292. Besides the

Opus majus, his most notable works are *Opus minus, Opus tertium,* and *Compendium philosophiae.*

General Appreciation. Bacon was essentially an encyclopedist; that is, he was tormented with the idea of the unity of knowledge, and his life consistently reflected an effort better to grasp and to explain that unity. He denounced violently the evils of scholasticism (too violently, in fact, to obtain practical results within his own age). He realized the urgent need for philosophers and theologians to enlarge their basis of knowledge; they were not acquainted with available scientific data, and their mathematical and linguistic equipment was utterly inadequate. His greatest title to fame, however, was his vindication of the experimental spirit. He was not himself an experimenter any more than he was a mathematician, but he saw better than anyone else in his time that without experimentation and without mathematics, natural philosophy is very soon reduced to verbiage. He also realized the utility of knowledge, and this was even more remarkable than to realize its unity, for the latter had been done instinctively by almost every philosopher. In the *Opus majus* and the *Opus tertium* he insists upon that utility repeatedly. This double point of view, unity (to be discovered experimentally and proved with the help of mathematics) and utility, led him to entirely new conceptions of knowledge, of learning, and of education. His accomplishments fell considerably short of his visions. Yet visions are very important, and we need seers as well as inventors. Bacon made few if any experiments, and no invention, not even gunpowder, can be definitely ascribed to him. He seems to have vaguely foreseen fundamental discoveries and inventions: the possibility of circumnavigating the world, of propelling boats by mechanical means, of flying, of utilizing the explosive property of powder, and of improving sight by the proper adjustment of lenses. It is true that, as opposed to a dogmatic system like Thomism, Bacon's thoughts seem (and are) disconnected, but one should not confuse dogmatism with originality. Bacon's thought was less systematic, but on the whole more original than that of his great contemporaries. And the best proof of this is that he was a true harbinger of modern civilization, while Saint Thomas Aquinas (not to speak of the other great scholastics of the Continent) was destined to become virtually a symbol of medievalism. Bacon founded no schools, but the majority of modern scientists feel more genuinely attracted to him than to any other medieval personality.

Baconian Legends. The experiments suggested by Bacon failed to be appreciated for a considerable time, and there emerged gradually the legend of "Friar Bacon, the wonderworker." All sorts of magical powers were ascribed to him. This legend can be traced back to the 14th century; by 1385 it was already known on the W coast of the Adriatic Sea, in Dalmatia. It was finally established by a play of Robert Greene (*The Honorable Historie of Frier Bacon and Frier Bongay,* played with various "magical" properties; printed 1594 *et seq.*) and by a London chapbook dating from about the same time: "The famous historie of Frier Bacon containing the wonderful things that he did in his life, also the manner of his death with the lives and

ḍ, d or j; ṣ, s or sh; ṭ, t or ch; ẓ, z or zh; o, F. cloche; ü, F. menu; ċh, Sc. loch; ṅ, F. bonbon.

deaths of the two conjurers Bungey [sic] and Van-
dermast" (reprinted 1627, 1638, *et seq.*). This aspect
of the Baconian legend has been recently reinforced
by the discovery "in an ancient castle in Southern
Europe" of a manuscript written in cipher and
ascribed to Bacon. If it were authentic, Bacon
should be credited with the invention and actual
use of telescope and compound microscope, and
with the discovery of seminiferous tubes, cells with
nuclei, spermatozoa, and so forth. Such inventions
and discoveries in Bacon's time would have been
remarkable indeed, but unfortunately the manuscript cannot possibly be ascribed with any authenticity to Bacon. An entirely different legend dating
from comparatively modern times represents Bacon
as a martyr of science and of the freedom of thought.
This is doubly misleading, for Bacon was a scientist
but not a free thinker, as this phrase is generally
understood. A very original thinker and a forerunner of modern science, he was both outspoken
and incautious, but he was also very orthodox and,
in many ways, a fundamentalist. Granted that he
suffered for the originality of his mind and the
eccentricities of his character, his "martyrdom"
is nevertheless not established, and he was not in
any sense a forerunner of the modern rationalists.
For him, theology was still the crown of all knowledge, and the Bible its repository.

Bacon & Bungay (bung′gā). In Thackeray's novel
Pendennis, a firm of publishers which has existed
prior to the time of the events recounted in the
story, and the two members of which are now bitter
enemies.

Baconian theory. A theory (dating from the late
18th century and still having its adherents) that
the works of Shakespeare were actually written
by Francis Bacon. The body of scholars specializing
in the drama of the Elizabethan and Jacobean
periods has found the evidence offered on its behalf
fragmentary and inconclusive at best (and, at its
worst, absurd). Indeed, modern research in the field
has tended to make Shakespeare a more solid figure
than he was in the last century. It is true (and no
reputable scholar denies) that the Stationers' Register in Shakespeare's day (which by government
order recorded all plays licensed by the censor) lists
several plays by Shakespeare which are certainly
or probably not his. However, the register is demonstrably sometimes inaccurate in certain other
connections, and the fact that a number of plays
were erroneously listed there as Shakespeare's does
not mean that all its attributions to Shakespeare
are wrong. Freely granting that he had collaborators on several plays (for example, Fletcher probably participated very largely in the writing of
Henry VIII and *The Two Noble Kinsmen*), the
leading scholars in the field nevertheless remain
convinced that Shakespeare did in fact write the
great body of works associated with his name. However, supporters of the Baconian theory (and various other theories, which differ from it chiefly in
that they attribute the works to people other than
Bacon, such as Edward de Vere, Roger Manners,
and William Stanley, three eminent peers of Shakespeare's day) continue vigorously to support their
opposing view. The origin of the Baconian hypothesis may probably be traced to 1769, when a

certain Herbert Lawrence suggested that Shakespeare was an unschooled country bumpkin who
could not possibly have written the plays attributed
to him (Lawrence did not, however, propose Bacon
as their author). Lawrence's point was picked up
nearly eight decades later by an American, Joseph
C. Hart, who urged its validity in *The Romance of
Yachting* (1848) and an article published in 1852 in
Chambers' Journal. The specific suggestion of
Francis Bacon as the writer of the plays was first
made in 1856 (some sources indicate 1857) by an
Englishman, William Henry Smith, thus permitting
the theory to assume approximately the outline it
holds to this day (and answering the chief question
which had hampered the theory up to that time:
If Shakespeare didn't write the plays, who did?).
Meanwhile, an American, Delia Bacon, went
further in an article in *Putnam's Monthly* (1856)
and *The Philosophy of the Plays of Shakespeare unfolded by Delia Bacon* (1857), attempting to prove
that the wide knowledge evident in Shakespeare's
plays did not fit the facts of his known education,
but could better suggest Bacon, Edmund Spenser,
or Sir Walter Raleigh. Mrs. Henry Pott, an Englishwoman, now edited Bacon's commonplace book
and demonstrated similarities between his method
of expression and that found in the plays (to which
the anti-Baconians quickly replied by pointing out
that the same characteristics are found in virtually
every Elizabethan playwright, as well as in Burton's *Anatomy of Melancholy* and John Florio's
translation of Montaigne). American supporters of
the theory continued to multiply: Nathaniel
Holmes, a justice of the Missouri supreme court,
published a two-volume work on it in 1866 (the
work reached a 4th edition by 1886); a year later,
in 1867, Ignatius Donnelly proposed the crypto-
graphic method that has since been most often
used to support the theory. His *The Great Crypto-
gram: Francis Bacon's Cypher in the so-called
Shakespeare Plays* inspired Mrs. E. W. Gallup to
find further pro-Bacon clues in the plays. Sir Edwin
Durning-Lawrence found in the word "honorificabilitudinitatibus" in *Love's Labour's Lost* an alleged
Latin anagram meaning "These plays, F. Bacon's
offspring, are preserved for the world."

Bad Child's Book of Beasts, The. A humorous prose
work (1896) by Hilaire Belloc. It was his first book
and had several sequels.

Baddeley (bad′li), **Robert.** b. c1733; d. 1794. An
English actor. He was originally cook for Samuel
Foote, the playwright and actor; went on the stage
himself sometime before 1761. He was the original
Moses in *The School for Scandal*. In his will he left
the revenue of his house in Surrey for the support
of an asylum for aged and impoverished actors,
and also, from the interest, one hundred pounds a
year to provide wine and cake for the actors of the
Drury Lane Theatre on Twelfth Night.

Badebec (bàd.bek). The wife of Gargantua in
Rabelais's *Pantagruel*. She was the mother of
Pantagruel.

Badge of Ulster (ul′stẻr). [Sometimes called
"bloody hand of Ulster."] In heraldry, the ancient
distinctive ensign of the order of baronets. It is
the ancient badge of the Irish kingdom of Ulster,
and is thus blazoned: arg., a sinister hand ap-

paumée, couped at the wrist, gules. This may be borne upon a canton or an inescutcheon, and on that part of the bearer's armorial shield which is most convenient.

Badham (bad'ạm), **Charles.** b. at London, April 17, 1780; d. there, Nov. 10, 1845. An English physician, traveler, and classical scholar. Author of medical works, miscellaneous verse, and translator (1814) of Juvenal's *Satires.*

Badinguet (bȧ.dań.gȧ). [Later name, **Radot.**] d. 1883. A workman in whose clothes Napoleon III is said to have escaped (1846) from the fortress of Ham; hence, a nickname of Napoleon III.

Badman (bad'man), **The Life and Death of Mr.** See **Life and Death of Mr. Badman, The.**

Badminton (bad'min.tọn). The residence of the dukes of Beaufort, in Gloucestershire, England, 15 mi. NE of Bristol. Because of its comparative safety, Queen Mary, mother of King George VI, was sent here from London during World War II to escape heavy bombing raids.

Badminton. A London sporting club, founded 1876.

Badon (bā'dọn), **Mount.** The scene of a battle said to have been gained (c520) by King Arthur over the Saxon invaders: variously identified with Badbury Rings (in Dorsetshire), a hill near Bath, and Bouden Hill (near Linlithgow).

Badoura (bạ.dö'rạ). A principal character in the story of the "Amours of Prince Camaralzaman and the Princess Badoura," in *The Arabian Nights' Entertainments.*

Badroulboudour (bạ.dröl'bö.dör). The wife of Aladdin in the story of "Aladdin or the Wonderful Lamp," in *The Arabian Nights' Entertainments.*

Baducing (bäd'ú.king), **Biscop.** See **Benedict Biscop,** Saint.

Baeda (bē'dạ). See **Bede.**

Baedeker (bā'dẹ.kėr), **Karl.** b. at Essen, Germany, Nov. 3, 1801; d. at Koblenz, Germany, Oct. 4, 1859. A German publisher, noted as the founder of the series of guidebooks which bears his name.

Baerlein (bär'līn), **Henry.** b. at Manchester, England, April 1, 1875—. An English writer. Author of *Rimes of the Diables Bleus* (1917), poetry; *The Raft of Love* (1923), a three-act masque; *The House of the Fighting Cocks* (1923), *Mariposa* (1924), *Here are Dragons* (1925), and *Dreamy Rivers* (1930), novels; and *Mexico, the Land of Unrest* (1913), *Over the Hills of Ruthenia* (1923), *In Search of Slovakia* (1929), *Bessarabia and Beyond* (1935), *Travels Without a Passport* (1st series, 1941; 2nd series, 1942), and *Baltic Paradise* (1943), books of description and travel.

Baffin (baf'in), **William.** b. c1584; d. Jan. 23, 1622. An English navigator and explorer. He was pilot of the *Discovery,* commanded by Robert Bylot, which was dispatched (1615) by the Muscovy Company (of London) to North America in search of the Northwest Passage. The expedition resulted in the discovery (1616) of the bay between Greenland and Canada which has since received the name of Baffin Bay. An account of the expedition, written by Baffin, was printed by Samuel Purchas, who, however, took great liberties with the text. The original manuscript, with map, is in the British

Museum, and was edited first for the Hakluyt Society in 1849 (published in *Narratives of Voyages toward the North-west*) and later (1881) by Clements Markham. Baffin was killed while serving in the allied English and Persian armies on the island of Qishm, in the Persian Gulf.

Bage (bāj), **Robert.** b. at Darley, England, Feb. 29, 1728, d. at Tamworth, England, Sept. 1, 1801. An English novelist. He was a paper manufacturer by trade, and did not begin to publish until the age of 53. Author of *Mount Henneth* (1781), *Barham Downs* (1784), *Hermsprong, or Man as he is not* (1796), and others.

Bagehot (baj'ọt), **Walter.** b. at Langport, Somersetshire, England, Feb. 3, 1826; d. there, March 24, 1877. An English economist, publicist, social scientist, and journalist. He was graduated (1846) from the University of London, was called to the bar in 1852, later serving (1860–77) as editor of the *Economist* (and is considered by most modern authorities to have been one of the greatest, if not indeed the very greatest, of the brilliant editors who have served that publication during the past century). His published works covered a great diversity of subjects, and were written in a prose style which has caused him to be by many critics among the most admired of English 19th-century writers. His description, and at the same time painstakingly scientific analysis, of the British political system in *The English Constitution* (1867), and of the methods and history of the British banking system in *Lombard Street* (1873), remain even today among the standard works in these fields. The relationship of types of science to one another was enormously interesting to him, and in his *Physics and Politics* (1869) he made what is generally considered to have been a pioneer effort in the application of the theories of natural science (specifically, of evolution) to the working of a social science. His other works include *Literary Studies* (1879), *Economic Studies* (1880), and *Biographical Studies* (1881).

Bagford (bag'fọrd), **John.** b. at Blackfriars, London, 1650; d. at Charterhouse, London, May 15, 1716. An English bibliophile and shoemaker, collector of *Bagford Ballads,* two volumes of broadside ditties.

Bagheera (bä.gēr'ạ). In Rudyard Kipling's Mowgli stories, the great black panther who is one of Mowgli's friends.

Bagimont's Roll (baj'i.monts). A list of the benefices of Scotland, with their valuation, in the late Middle Ages.

Bagnell (bag'nẹl), **Mrs.** In Meredith's *Lord Ormont and his Aminta,* the aunt of the heroine, Aminta Farrell.

Bagnet (bag'net), **Mr.** and **Mrs. Joseph.** Characters in Charles Dickens's novel *Bleak House.* Bagnet is an ex-artilleryman, devoted to the bassoon. He has a notably high regard for Mrs. Bagnet, a large and indomitable woman, but never says so in her presence, as "discipline must be maintained." Their children Malta, Quebec, and Woolwich are named from the posts of the British army where they were born.

Bagnold (bag'nọld), **Enid.** An English novelist, poet, and author of books for children; married

(1920) to Sir Roderick Jones, chairman of Reuter's News Agency. Author of *A Diary Without Dates* (1917), *Serena Blandish, or the Difficulties of Getting Married* (1925; published anonymously), also a success as a play, and *National Velvet* (1937), a story about horses, later filmed; *Sailing Ships* (1918), poems; *Alice and Thomas and Jane* (1930), a story for children; *The Loved and Envied* (1950), a novel; and *The Girl's Journey* (1954; consisting in part of two short novels, *The Happy Foreigner*, a war story written in 1920, and *The Squire*, a story that was published in 1938 under the title *Door of Life*).

Bagot (bag'ọt). In Shakespeare's *Richard II*, a parasitic follower of King Richard. He is imprisoned after Richard's deposition and informs against Aumerle.

Bagstock (bag'stok), **Major Joe.** "A wooden-featured, blue-faced" officer, a friend of Mr. Dombey, in Charles Dickens's novel *Dombey and Son*.

Baia (bä'yä). [Ancient name, **Baiae** (bā'ē).] A seaport in SW Italy, in the *compartimento* (region) of Campania, near Cape Misenum on the Gulf of Pozzuoli, W of Naples. It was formerly a great seaport and the leading Roman watering-place, especially in the times of Horace, Nero, and Hadrian. It was famous for its luxury, and contained the villas of many celebrated Romans.

Bailey (bā'li), **Harry.** [Also: **Baillie, Bailly.**] The Host of the Tabard, in Chaucer's *Canterbury Tales.* It is he who suggests the telling of tales by each member of the company, and he goes along on the pilgrimage, acting as master of ceremonies. His comments on the stories, and exhortations or remarks to the narrators, interpolated between the tales, constitute not only a highly successful transitional device but one of Chaucer's happiest characterizations. He is a shrewd, bold, manly, well-informed fellow with a blabbing shrew for a wife. He is sometimes called "Henry Bailif."

A semely man our hoste was with-alle
For to han been a marshal in an halle;
A large man he was with eyen stepe,
A fairer burgeys is ther noon in Chepe:
Bold of his speche, and wys, and wel y-taught,
And of manhod him lakkede right naught.
Eek therto he was right a mery man . . . .

Bailey, Henry Christopher. b. at London, Feb. 1, 1878—. An English author of historical novels and detective stories; noted as creator of two fictional detectives: Reggie Fortune and Joshua Clunk. Among his historical novels are *My Lady of Orange* (1901), *The Plot* (1922), and *Bonaventure* (1927). His detective books include *Call Mr. Fortune* (1920), *Mr. Fortune's Practice* (1922), *Clunk's Claimant* (1937), and *Mr. Clunk's Text* (1939).

Bailey, Nathan or **Nathaniel.** d. at Stepney (now part of London), June 27, 1742. An English lexicographer, the most important before Johnson, and schoolmaster, author of *An Universal Etymological English Dictionary*, first published in 1721. Bailey emphasized etymologies and included expressions from Spenser, Chaucer, Shakespeare, and other authors. He also placed accents on each word to indicate their "true Pronunciation." A supple-

ment appeared in 1727, and a folio edition in 1730, with the title *Dictionarium Britannicum, collected by several hands . . . revised and improved with many thousand additions by N. Bailey.* The dictionary, based on the works of John Kersey, Elisha Coles, Edward Phillips, Thomas Blount, and others, was often republished, and served as a foundation for other works of the kind, including (to some extent) Samuel Johnson's.

Bailey, Old. See **Old Bailey Court.**

Bailey, Philip James. b. at Nottingham, England, April 22, 1816; d. there, Sept. 6, 1902. An English poet. Bailey was the author of a version of the Faust story, *Festus* (composed 1836–39, published anonymously in the latter year; subsequently revised and expanded; 2nd ed., 1845, 11th ed., 1889); his other works include *The Angel World* (1850), *The Mystic* (1855), *The Age* (1858), *The Universal Hymn* (1867), *Nottingham Castle* (1878), and other poems. With Sydney Dobell, Alexander Smith, and others, Bailey belonged to what W. E. Aytoun called the "spasmodic school."

Bailif (bā'li), **Henry.** See **Bailey, Harry.**

Bailiff's Daughter of Islington (iz'ling.tọn), **The.** A Middle English ballad, included in Percy's *Reliques*. It tells of two lovers (a squire's son and a bailiff's daughter) who, after a separation of seven years, are happily reunited.

Baillie (bā'li), **Lady Grizel.** b. at Redbraes Castle, Berwickshire, Scotland, Dec. 25, 1665; d. Dec. 6, 1746. A Scottish poet; daughter of Sir Patrick Hume, Scottish patriot, to whom she supplied food when he was in hiding from the English. She was in exile (1686–88) with her parents at Utrecht. One of her best-known songs is *And werena my heart licht I wad dee.*

Baillie, Harry. See **Bailey, Harry.**

Baillie, Joanna. b. at Bothwell, Lanarkshire, Scotland, Sept. 11, 1762; d. at Hampstead, England, Feb. 23, 1851. A Scottish dramatist and poet. She wrote *Plays on the Passions* (3 vols., 1798, 1802, and 1812), in which she delineates the principal passions of the mind, each passion being made the subject of a tragedy and a comedy; among them are *De Montfort* (1800) and *Family Legend* (1810). She was the author also of the poems *Lines to Agnes Baillie on her Birthday*, *The Kitten*, and *To a Child*.

Baillie, Robert. b. at Glasgow, Scotland, 1599; d. in July, 1662. A Scotch Presbyterian divine and controversialist, chiefly remembered as the author of *Letters and Journals, 1637–62.* This work is of historical value, especially in relation to the assembly of 1638 and the assembly of Westminster.

Bailly (bā'li), **Harry.** See **Bailey, Harry.**

Bain (bān), **Alexander.** b. at Aberdeen, Scotland, June 11, 1818; d. there, Sept. 18, 1903. A Scottish philosopher, psychologist, professor, editor, and biographer. He was educated at the Glasgow Mechanics' Institute and at Marischal College (part of Aberdeen University), graduating with honors in 1840. He visited London in 1842 and 1848, meeting Thomas Carlyle, John Stuart Mill, George Henry Lewes, and George Grote (1794–1871), whose *Aristotle* and other works he later edited, and lecturing at the Bedford College for Women (founded 1849); he was appointed (1860) professor of logic and English at Aberdeen University (a post he held until 1881), after being rejected for many positions because of his liberal religious views; he served as lord rector of the University in the period 1880–87. During Bain's lifetime psychology changed from a philosophical subject to an experimental subject. His psychological texts, *Senses and Intellects* (1855; rev. eds., 1860, 1868, 1894), *Emotions and the Will* (1859; rev. eds., 1865, 1875, 1899), and the combined version of these two books, *Mental and Moral Science* (1868), were the outstanding British texts in the field for 50 years. In 1876 he founded *Mind*, the first psychological journal in any language. He explicitly stated a doctrine of psychophysical parallelism, thus holding a physiological orientation toward psychology, restated the doctrine of association in terms of contiguity and similarity, and answered the problem of will in terms of experience of effort. Author also of *The Study of Character, Including an Estimate of Phrenology* (1861), *Logic* (1870), *Mind and Body* (1872), *Education as a Science* (1879, long a popular volume in the well-known "International Scientific Series"), *James Mill, John Stuart Mill*, biographies (both 1882); his own *Autobiography* appeared in 1904. In addition to these works, Bain also wrote several excellent and once-popular, but now no longer used, texts (1863, 1866, 1872, 1874) on grammar and rhetoric.

Baines (bānz). The surname of the two sisters, Constance and Sophia, whose lives provide the story of Arnold Bennett's *The Old Wives' Tale* (1908).

Bairam (bī.räm'). [Also, **Beiram**.] The name of two Mohammedan feasts. The great Bairam forms the concluding ceremony of the pilgrimage to Mecca, and is celebrated on the tenth day of the 12th month. Each householder who is able to do so sacrifices a sheep, the flesh of which is divided into three portions, one for the family, one for relatives, and one for the poor. The lesser Bairam is celebrated at the termination of the fast of the month of Ramadan (the ninth month). It is a season of great rejoicing at which presents and visits are exchanged.

Bait, The. A poem (1633) by John Donne. The pastoral theme and simple form of Christopher Marlowe's familiar *The Passionate Shepherd to His Love* is here reworked by Donne with "metaphysical wit":

> Come live with me and be my love,
> And we will some new pleasures prove,
> Of golden sands and crystal brooks
> With silken lines and silver hooks.

Bajazet (baj.a.zet'). In Christopher Marlowe's tragedy *Tamburlaine*, the mightiest of Tamburlaine's foes, later his captive. Tamburlaine uses him as a footstool and puts him in a cage. Despite the pleas of Bajazet's queen, Zabina, Tamburlaine humiliates him to such an extent that finally Bajazet and Zabina dash out their brains against the cage in desperation. Marlowe uses him to comment on Tamburlaine's relentless ambition: "We may curse his power, The heavens may frown, the earth for anger quake, But such a star hath influence in his sword, As rules the skies and countermands the gods. . . ." Marlowe based this char-

acter very little on the real sultan of Turkey, Bajazet I.

Bajazet I. b. 1347; d. 1403. A Turkish sultan (1389–1403); son of Murad I. He conquered Bulgaria and a great part of Asia Minor, Macedonia, Serbia, and Thessaly, defeated the allied Hungarians, Poles, and French at Nicopolis in 1396, but was defeated (1402) by Tamerlane at Angora, and held prisoner by him until his death.

Baker (bā'kėr), Sir **Richard**. b. at Sissinghurst, Kent, England, 1568; d. at London, in the Fleet Prison, Feb. 18, 1645. An English writer, author of *Chronicle of the Kings of England* (1643), and of various devotional and other works.

Baker, Sir Samuel White. b. at London, June 8, 1821; d. at Newton Abbot, England, Dec. 30, 1893. English traveler. He founded (1848) a settlement and sanatorium at Ceylon, was in the Turkish railway service, and left Cairo for the sources of the Nile in 1861. He explored (1861–62) the Blue Nile region and, starting from Khartoum in 1862, discovered (March 14, 1864) Lake Albert. Subsequently he commanded (1869–73) an Egyptian expedition in C Africa for the suppression of the slave trade and annexation of territory to Egypt, and traveled in Cyprus, Syria, India, and elsewhere. Author of *The Rifle and the Hound in Ceylon* (1854), *Eight Years' Wanderings in Ceylon* (1855), *The Albert Nyanza* (1866), *The Nile Tributaries of Abyssinia* (1867), *Ismaïlia* (1874), *Cyprus as I Saw It in 1879*, and *Wild Beasts and Their Ways* (1890).

Baker, Thomas. fl. 1700–09. A British playwright. He was the author of five now nearly forgotten comedies: *Humor of the Age* (1701), *Tunbridge Walks, or the Yeoman of Kent* (1703), *An Act at Oxford* (1704), *Hampstead Heath* (1705), an alteration of the previous play, which was banned by Oxford University authorities, and *The Fine Lady's Airs* (1709), all produced at Drury Lane and Covent Garden theaters in London. He may have been the author of the *Female Tatler* (1709), one of the many periodicals that attempted to duplicate the success of the *Spectator* and the *Tatler*. Baker, who did not like Sir Richard Steele, ridiculed him in issue No. 72; Steele retaliated with the character of Nick Doubt (*Tatler*, No. 91, Tuesday, Nov. 8, 1709).

Bakis (bā'kis). See **Bacis**.

Balaam (bā'lam). In the Bible, a prophet of Pethor, in Mesopotamia, mentioned in the Book of Numbers. The Moabite king Balak sent for him to curse the Israelites, who had already conquered Bashan and the land of King Sihon, and were threatening Moab. In the course of his journey, Balaam was rebuked by the ass on which he rode, and upon arriving among the Israelites, blessed them with a favorable prophecy. Num. xxii, xxiii.

Balaam. A character in John Dryden's satire *Absalom and Achitophel*, intended for the Earl of Huntingdon.

Balaam, Sir. In Pope's *Moral Essays* (*Epistle III, To Allen Lord Bathurst*), an originally simple and religious man, corrupted by Satan who "tempts by making rich, not making poor."

Balaclava (bal.a.klä'va). See **Balaklava**.

d, d or j; s, s or sh; t, t or ch; z, z or zh; o, F. cloche; ü, F. menu; ćh, Sc. loch; ṅ, F. bonbon.

Balade of Charitie, An Excelente. See **Excelente Balade of Charitie, An.**

Balafré (bả.là.frā), **Le.** See **Lorraine, Henri de** (1550–88).

Balak (bā'lak). A character in the satire *Absalom and Achitophel*, intended as a caricature of Dr. Burnet. It is in the second section, which was edited by John Dryden but largely written by Nahum Tate.

Balaklava (bal.ạ.klä'vạ). [Also, **Balaclava.**] A small seaport in the U.S.S.R., in the Crimean *oblast* (region) of the Russian Soviet Federated Socialist Republic, ab. 8 mi. SE of Sevastopol. Established in ancient times by Greek colonists, it was long an important Black Sea trading center. Its rulers have included (in addition to the Greeks) the Romans, the Genoese, the Turks, and the Russians. A Greek colony was settled here in comparatively modern times by Catherine II of Russia. It was a headquarters of the coalition (England, France, Turkey, and Sardinia) against Russia in the Crimean War, and the site in late October, 1854, of a series of engagements in the initial phase of the campaign to wrest Sevastopol from the Russians. However, its chief renown (and it is perhaps the most widely known of the battle sites of the Crimean War) stems not from its strategic importance but from the gallant (and unnecessary) British cavalry charge immortalized by Tennyson in *The Charge of the Light Brigade.*

Balan (bā'lan). In the *Morte d' Arthur*, the brother of Balin.

Balance (bal'ạns), **Justice.** The father of Sylvia in George Farquhar's comedy *The Recruiting Officer*, one of the principal characters.

Balaustion's Adventure (bạ.lôs'ti.ọnz). A poem by Robert Browning, published in 1871. Balaustion is a Greek girl of Rhodes. Her story is continued in *Aristophanes' Apology* (1875).

Balboa (bal.bō'ạ; Spanish, bäl.bō'ä), **Vasco Núñez de.** b. at Jerez de los Caballeros, or at Badajoz, Spain, c1475; d. at Acla, on the Isthmus of Panama (Darien), Jan. 12, 1519. A Spanish conquistador and soldier of fortune, discoverer of the "South Sea," later renamed the Pacific Ocean by Ferdinand Magellan. In one of his best-known poems, however, John Keats mistakenly credits the discovery to "stout Cortez." In 1500 he came to America with the expedition of Rodrigo de Bastidas. Balboa made numerous explorations into the interior of the Isthmus of Panama from the first Spanish settlement on the N coast, usually succeeding in keeping on good terms with the Indians, and later even married the daughter of a native chieftain. From the Indians he also learned that there was a large body of water to the S of the Isthmus, and that the S coast (of the Isthmus) was very rich in gold. Determined to discover if this were true, he set out from Santa María with part of his force on Sept. 1, 1513, and after an adventurous journey reached on Sept. 25 a mountain from which he first saw the Pacific. The shore itself was attained on Sept. 29, and Balboa, entering the water, took possession in the name of King Ferdinand of Spain. He returned to Santa María on Jan. 19, 1514. In the same year (June 29) Pedrarias Dávila (Pedro Arias de Ávila) arrived from Spain as governor of the colony. The relations of the two men were unfriendly. Nevertheless, Pedrarias granted Balboa permission to explore the South Sea. Cutting the timbers for his ships on the Caribbean side, Balboa transported them with immense labor across the Isthmus, and had launched two vessels when he was arrested by Pedrarias on a charge of treason against the king, and beheaded.

Balcarres (bal.kar'is, -iz), 10th Earl of. A title of **Lindsay, David Alexander Edward.**

Balchristie (bal.kris'ti), **Jenny.** In Sir Walter Scott's novel *The Heart of Midlothian*, the housekeeper to the laird of Dumbiedikes. "A fat, red-faced old dame of seventy or thereabouts, fond of her place, and jealous of her authority." Chapter xxvi.

Balclutha (bal.klö'ᴛHạ). A town in the Ossianic poem *Carthon*, actually written by the Scottish poet and literary forger James Macpherson.

Balcony, A. A play in three acts by Naomi Royde-Smith, published in 1926.

Baldassarre Calvo (bäl.däs.sä'rä käl'vō). See **Calvo, Baldassarre.**

Balder (bôl'dėr). [Also: **Baldur**; Old Norse, **Baldr** (bäl'dr).] In old Norse mythology, a son of Odin, and one of the principal gods. Balder's characteristics are those of a sun god. He is the "whitest" of the gods, and so beautiful and bright that a light emanates from him. His dwelling is Breidablik (Old Norse, *Breidhablik*). His wife is Nanna. He is finally slain, at the instigation of Loki, by a twig of mistletoe (the only material free from oath not to injure Balder) in the hands of the blind god Hoder (Old Norse, *Höndhr*). One of William Morris's best-known poems is "The Funeral of Balder," in *The Lovers of Gudrun.*

Balder. A poem by Sydney Dobell, published in 1854.

Balder Dead. A poem by Matthew Arnold.

Balderstone (bôl'dėr.stōn), **Caleb.** In Sir Walter Scott's novel *The Bride of Lammermoor*, the old butler of the Master of Ravenswood, who resorts to fantastic expedients to conceal his master's poverty.

Balderstone, Thomas. [Called **"Uncle Tom."**] In Charles Dickens's tale *Mrs. Joseph Porter*, the uncle of Mrs. Gattleton.

Baldur (bôl'dėr). See **Balder.**

Baldwin I. [French, **Baudouin.**] b. c1058; d. in Egypt, in March, 1118. A king of Jerusalem. He was a brother of Godfrey of Bouillon, whom he accompanied on the first Crusade (1096–99), and whom he succeeded as king of Jerusalem. He conquered Acre in 1104, Beirut in 1109, and Sidon in 1110.

Baldwin II. [French, **Baudouin.**] d. Aug. 21, 1131. Count of Edessa and King of Jerusalem (1118–31). In his reign the military orders of Saint John and the Templars were established for the defense of the Holy Land. He was succeeded by Fulc V of Anjou, his son-in-law.

Baldwin III. [French, **Baudouin.**] b. c1130; d. at Tripolis, Feb. 10, 1162. A king of Jerusalem

(1143–62). He lost Edessa to the Moslem ruler of Mosul in 1144, an event which gave rise to the second Crusade (1147–49).

Baldwin IV. [French, **Baudouin**; called **"Baldwin the Leper."**] A king of Jerusalem (1173–83); son of Amalric I. He gained a signal victory over Saladin on the plain of Ramah, on Nov. 25, 1177, and again near Tiberias in the early summer of 1182. He was succeeded by his nephew Baldwin V, who died in 1185.

Baldwin, Count. The father of Biron and Carlos in Thomas Southerne's *Fatal Marriage*, an unyielding, self-willed man.

Baldwin, Stanley. [Title, 1st Earl **Baldwin of Bewdley**.] b. Aug. 3, 1867; d. Dec. 14, 1947. A British statesman and writer, remembered for his service in settlement of war debts with the U. S. after World War I and for his association with the abdication of Edward VIII (the Duke of Windsor) in 1936. A Conservative member of Parliament from 1908, he became prime minister in 1923, succeeding Bonar Law. Though succeeded (1924) by Ramsay MacDonald in a short-lived Labour government, he was again prime minister in the period 1924–29 (during which term in office occurred (1926) the general strike). During his third term (1935–37) as prime minister arose the crisis (1936) over the marriage and abdication of Edward VIII. After Baldwin's retirement (1937) from public office, a peerage was bestowed on him. He was chancellor of Cambridge University (1930–47). Author of *The Classics and the Plain Man* (1926), *On England and Other Essays* (1926), *Our Inheritance* (speeches, 1928), *This Torch of Freedom* (1935), *Peace and Goodwill in Industry* (1935), *Service of Our Lives* (1937), and *An Interpreter of England* (1939).

Baldwin, William. d. c1564. An English divine, schoolmaster, philosopher, and poet. Author of *A Treatise of Moral Philosophy* (1547), *Canticles or Balades of Salomon* (1549, a verse translation of part of the Scriptures), *The Funeralles of King Edward the Sixt* (1560, an elegy), and *Beware the Cat* (1561, a satirical poem). He was associated with George Ferrers in publishing the famous Elizabethan collection of poems on the fall of great men *A Mirror for Magistrates* (1559; numerous subsequent editions). Baldwin's own work in the *Mirror* consists of four poems on Richard, the earl of Cambridge, Thomas Montague, the earl of Salisbury, William de La Pole, the duke of Suffolk, and Jack Cade.

Bale (bāl), **John.** b. at Cove, near Dunwich, Suffolk, England, Nov. 21, 1495; d. at Canterbury, England, 1563. English Protestant (originally Roman Catholic) prelate, bishop of Ossory (1558–1563). He was the author of morality plays of which *King John*, considered a valuable link between the earlier morality plays and the later historical plays, is probably his best. He was the compiler of a chronological catalogue of British writers, *Illustrium Majoris Britanniae Scriptorum Summarium* (1548). Among the works he wrote are *The Chief Promises of God, Comedy Concerning Three Laws, John Baptist*, and *The Temptation*.

Balfour (bal'för), **Alexander.** b. at Monikie, Forfarshire, Scotland, March 1, 1767; d. Sept. 12, 1829. A Scottish poet and novelist. He wrote *Campbell, or the Scottish Probationer* (1819), *Contemplation and other Poems* (1820), *Farmer's Three Daughters* (1822), *The Foundling of Glenthorn, or the Smuggler's Cave* (1823), and *Highland Mary* (1827).

Balfour, Arthur James. [Title, 1st Earl of **Balfour**.] b. July 25, 1848; d. March 19, 1930. A British Conservative statesman, known as the author of The Balfour Declaration; nephew of Robert Arthur Talbot Gascoyne-Cecil, the 3rd Marquis of Salisbury. He was president of the Local Government Board (1885–86), secretary for Scotland (1886–87), chief secretary for Ireland (1887–91), first lord of the treasury and leader of the House of Commons (1891–92, 1895–1900, and 1900–06), and prime minister (1902–05). He served as member of Parliament for the eastern division of Manchester (1885–1906), and for the City of London (1906–11). He succeeded (1915) Winston Churchill as first lord of the admiralty. During a term (1916–19) as foreign secretary, he framed (1917) the Balfour Declaration favoring limited Jewish settlements in Palestine; this set the official British attitude on the mandate of Palestine for the next 30 years. He served as chief British delegate (1921–22) to the disarmament conference at Washington. Author of *A Defence of Philosophic Doubt* (1879), *Essays and Addresses* (1893, 1905), *The Foundations of Belief* (1895), *Economic Notes on Insular Free Trade* (1903), *Reflections Suggested by the New Theory of Matter* (1904), *Speeches (1880–1905) on Fiscal Reform* (1906), *Criticism and Beauty* (Romanes lecture, 1909), and others.

Balfour, Clara Lucas. [Maiden name, **Liddell**.] b. in the New Forest, Hampshire, England, Dec. 21, 1808; d. at Croydon, England, July 3, 1878. An English writer. She lectured on temperance and other topics, and was the author of numerous works designed chiefly to promote the temperance cause.

Balfour, David. The young hero of Robert Stevenson's novels *Kidnapped* and *Catriona*.

Balfour, Sir James. b. 1600; d. 1657. A Scottish antiquary and historian, author of *Annals of the History of Scotland from Malcolm III to Charles II*.

Balfour of Burley (bėr'li), **John.** A Covenanter, a character in Sir Walter Scott's novel *Old Mortality*, historically taken from a real John Balfour of Kinloch, but by Scott confused with John Balfour of Burleigh (d. 1688). The latter was not a Covenanter.

Balgownie (bal.gou'ni), **Brig o'.** A high, wide-pointed arch spanning the river Don, at Aberdeen, Scotland; built about 1320.

Balibari (bal.i.bar'i), **Chevalier de.** [Title of **Cornelius Barry**.] In Thackeray's novel *Barry Lyndon*, the uncle of Barry Lyndon.

Balin (bā'lin) and **Balan** (-lan). In Malory's *Morte d'Arthur*, two brothers, born in Northumberland, each renowned for valor. Balin was called "Le Sauvage." They finally slew each other "by mishap," and were buried in one tomb. Their story

---

ḍ, d or j; ṣ, s or sh; ṭ, t or ch; ẓ, z or zh; o, F. cloche; ü, F. menu; c̣h, Sc. loch; ṅ, F. bonbon.

is one of those told by Tennyson in the *Idylls of the King*.

Balin and Balan. The last of the *Idylls of the King* by Alfred Tennyson. Although written about 1870 it was not published until 1885, when it rounded out the cycle to twelve.

Baliol (bāl'yọl, bā'li.ọl), (Mrs.) **Bethune.** The friend of Chrystal Croftangry who tells him the stories included in Sir Walter Scott's *Chronicles of the Canongate.*

Baliol, Edward de. [Also, **Balliol.**] d. 1363. A claimant to the throne of Scotland; eldest son of John de Baliol and Isabel, daughter of John de Warenne, the earl of Surrey. He landed in Scotland in 1332, and after a brilliant campaign of seven weeks was crowned at Scone on Sept. 24, but three months later was surprised at Annan by Archibald Douglas, and driven across the border. He was restored by Edward III of England, through whose assistance he won the battle of Halidon Hill, on July 19, 1333. After 1338, Edward being occupied in war with the French, Baliol maintained a nominal footing in Scotland until the return of David Bruce in 1341.

Baliol, John de. [Also, **Balliol.**] d. c1269. The founder of Balliol College, Oxford. He was a regent of Scotland during the minority of Alexander III, until deprived of the post, on a charge of treason, in 1255, through the influence of Henry III, with whom he sided in the barons' war (1263–65). He gave (c1263) the first lands for the endowment of the college which bears his name, an endowment which was increased by his will, and also by the gifts of his widow Devorguilla.

Balkis (bal'kis). An Arabic name, used in the Koran, of the Queen of Sheba.

Ball (bôl), **John.** [Called the **"Mad Priest."**] d. at St. Albans, England, July 15, 1381. An English priest who took a prominent part in Wat Tyler's rebellion in 1381. He accepted, in the main, the doctrines of John Wycliffe, modified by views of his own, and made himself popular, especially by preaching the equality of gentry and villeins. He was several times committed to the archbishop of Canterbury's prison, and was excommunicated by the archbishop Simon Islip. He was committed, probably about the end of April, 1381, to the archbishop's prison at Maidstone, and one of the first acts of the insurgents was to set him at liberty. He preached at Blackheath on the text "When Adam dalf [delved], and Eve span, Who was thanne [then] a gentilman?" After the death of Wat Tyler at Smithfield (now part of London), he fled to the midland counties, but was taken at Coventry, and executed at St. Albans in the presence of the king.

Ball, The. A comedy published as being by James Shirley and George Chapman, licensed in 1632 and published in 1639. It is very possibly the work only of Shirley, as there are no traces in it of Chapman's style. It was intended to satirize Court personalities; its plot involves the game of tennis, and the golden tennis ball then presented to the female president after the masque following the game.

ballad. A short narrative poem, often partly epic and partly lyric. The form derives from a type of poem especially adapted for singing and, as applied to the minstrelsy of the border country between England and Scotland, and of Scandinavia and Spain, the ballad is a sort of minor epic, reciting in verse more or less rude the exploits of warriors, the adventures of lovers, and the mysteries of fairyland, designed to be rehearsed in musical recitative accompanied by the harp. Popular ballads flourished, as a type of vernacular literature, in 14th and 15th-century England. Upwards of 300 of these (in some 1,300 versions) have survived, and may be found in Percy's *Reliques* and other similar collections. They fall into two main classes: first, the folk ballad, which often deals with tragic love or some other highly emotional theme, and was commonly written in brief stanzas, each one followed by a refrain; second, the minstrel ballad, which was generally the work of a single person (although his name may not be known), as exemplified by the various Robin Hood ballads. This latter type may offer a relatively extended narrative, and displays a relatively more sophisticated verse technique than the former. It characteristically contains four-line stanzas, written in iambics, with the second and fourth lines rhyming (*abcb*). The rhyming lines are usually six syllables long; the other lines are usually eight syllables long. It was this type of ballad form that provided a model for such later writers as Rossetti (*The King's Tragedy*) and Keats (*La Belle Dame sans Merci*).

ballade. **1.** A poem consisting of one or more triplets each formed of stanzas of seven or eight lines, the last line being a refrain common to all the stanzas.
2. A poem divided into stanzas having the same number of lines, commonly seven or eight.

ballade royal. A ballade in which each line consists of ten syllables.

Balladino (bal.ạ.dē'nō), **Antonio.** In Ben Jonson's comedy *The Case is Altered*, a "pageant poet" intended to ridicule Anthony Munday.

Ballad of Bouillabaisse (böl.yạ.bās'), **The.** See **Bouillabaisse, The Ballad of.**

Ballad of Chevy Chase (chev'i chās), **The.** See **Chevy Chase.**

Ballad of Otterbourne (ot'ẻr.bẻrn), **The.** See **Otterbourne.**

Ballad of Reading Gaol (red'ing jāl), **The.** A poem (1898) by Oscar Wilde. It was written, as evidenced by Wilde's letters, under the impulse of intense emotion and is moving in its expression of sympathy for outcasts from society. Inspired by a term of imprisonment which he served during his later life, the poem is now generally considered to be Wilde's best.

Ballad of St. Barbara (bär'bạ.rạ), **The.** A volume of verse (1922) by G. K. Chesterton.

Ballad of the Scottish King. A ballad by John Skelton. It was based on the battle of Flodden (1513) and is thought to have been the earliest printed English ballad.

Ballad of the White Horse, The. A long poem (1911) by G. K. Chesterton. It is a narrative ballad, thought by some critics to be his best work.

ballad opera. A form of musical drama devised in England during the last years of the Restoration and reaching its high point in John Gay's *The Beggar's Opera* (1728). The use of songs in plays was not new on the English stage, since they had frequently been used in plays written for the boys' companies at the end of the reign of Elizabeth and the first few years of the reign of James I, and later in plays written for courtly audiences, particularly the masques. However, these songs had a lyrical quality, usually related in mood to the dramas they accompanied but having no essential dramatic function. The Italian opera brought to the English stage dramas in which the singing conveyed the plot, ideas, and sentiments of the individual characters. The number of musical entertainments based either upon Italian opera (or shorter forms such as musical burlettas, interludes and after-pieces) increased steadily through the opening years of the 18th century; the influence may be noted in the many references to Italian singers and musical ventures in contemporary drama. Rather than turning entirely to musical means for drama, however, the English resorted to songs inserted in the play. In Gay's opera the songs are satirical, comprising solo arias, duets, or choral pieces. The form used for these songs was the popular English ballad, dating back to the Middle English period.

Ballads and Lyrics. A collection of poems (1891) by Katharine Tynan.

Ballads and Lyrics of Old France. A volume of poems (1872) by Andrew Lang.

Ballads and Other Poems. A volume of poems (1880) by Alfred Tennyson.

Ballads and Poems of Tragic Life. A volume of poems (1887) by George Meredith.

Ballads and Songs. A volume of poems (1894) by John Davidson.

Ballads and Sonnets. A volume of poems (1881) by Dante Gabriel Rossetti. It was his last published work.

Ballantine (bal'ạn.tīn), **James.** b. at Edinburgh, Scotland, 1808; d. there, in December, 1877. A Scottish poet, painter on glass, and manufacturer of stained glass. He wrote *The Gaberlunzie's Wallet* (1843), *The Miller of Deanhaugh* (1845), *Essay on Ornamental Art* (1847), *Poems* (1856), and others.

Ballantyne (bal'ạn.tīn), **James.** b. at Kelso, Scotland, 1772; d. Jan. 17, 1833. A Scottish publisher; friend and business associate of Sir Walter Scott. He printed the first two volumes of the *Border Minstrelsy* and subsequently published other works by Scott, who became his secret partner in 1805. He was ruined financially in 1826; he later edited the *Weekly Journal.*

Ballantyne, John. b. at Kelso, Scotland, 1774; d. at Edinburgh, Scotland, June 16, 1821. A Scottish writer and publisher; brother of James Ballantyne (1772–1833). He was an associate of his brother in the Edinburgh publishing and bookselling establishment of John Ballantyne and Company, publishers of novels by Sir Walter Scott.

Ballantyne, John. See also **Bellenden, John.**

Ballantyne, Robert Michael. b. at Edinburgh, Scotland, April 24, 1825; d. 1894. A British writer of juveniles. He was in the service (1841–47) of the Hudson's Bay Company. Among his 80 volumes are *Hudson's Bay* (1848), *Ungava* (1857), and *The Gorilla Hunters* (1862). He was also the author of *Personal Recollections* (1893).

Ballantyne, Thomas. b. at Paisley, Scotland, 1806; d. at London, Aug. 30, 1871. A Scottish editor, journalist, and social reformer, active in London. He was the editor at various times of the Bolton *Free Press,* Manchester *Guardian,* Manchester *Examiner,* Liverpool *Journal, Mercury,* the London *Leader,* the London *Statesman* (which he founded), and *Old St. James's Chronicle.* Interested in social and political questions, he associated himself with Richard Cobden and John Bright during the 1840's in agitating for repeal of the Corn Laws. Author of various papers; compiler of *Passages Selected from the Writings of Thomas Carlyle, with a Biographical Memoir* (1855, 1870); author of *Ideas, Opinions, and Facts* (1865) and *Essays in Mosaic* (1870). As part of his propaganda activity he wrote the *Corn Law Repealer's Handbook* (1841).

Ballenden (bal'ẹn.dẹn), **John.** See **Bellenden, John.**

Balliol (bal'yọl, bā'li.ọl). See also **Baliol.**

Balliol College. A college of Oxford University, England, founded between 1263 and 1268 through a gift of land from John de Baliol and his wife Devorguila. The oldest of the existing buildings dates from the 15th century.

Balmawhapple (bal.mạ.hwap'l). In Sir Walter Scott's novel *Waverley,* an obstinate Scottish laird, a Jacobite; in fuller form, his name is Falconer of Balmawhapple.

Balmoral Castle (bal.mor'ạl). The favorite residence of Queen Victoria in Aberdeenshire, Scotland, situated on the river Dee ab. 45 mi. W of Aberdeen. The property was purchased in 1852, and the castle was built (1853–55) in Scottish baronial style. It remains today a favorite residence in Scotland of the British royal family.

Balnibarbi (bal.ni.bär'bi). A land "occupied by projectors," visited by Gulliver in Swift's *Gulliver's Travels.* It is subject to Laputa, the flying island, and symbolizes Ireland.

Baloo (bä.lö'). In Rudyard Kipling's Mowgli stories, the brown bear who is one of Mowgli's teachers.

Balthasar (bal.thạ.zär'). Chaucer's name for Belshazzar in "The Monk's Tale," one of *The Canterbury Tales.*

Balthasar (bal.thạ.zär', -tạ-; bal.thaz'ạr, -taz'-; *in the 16th century the* th *represented* t *and some modern actors so pronounce the name*). In Shakespeare's *Merchant of Venice,* a servant of Portia. The name is assumed by Portia in her guise as a lawyer.

Balthasar. In Shakespeare's *Much Ado About Nothing,* a servant of Don Pedro. He sings the song "Sigh no more, ladies."

Balthasar. In Shakespeare's *Romeo and Juliet*, Romeo's servant who bears the word to Romeo in Mantua of Juliet's supposed death and returns with him to Verona. When Romeo enters the tomb, he threatens Balthasar with death if he follows or watches.

Balthazar or **Balthasar** (bal.thä′zạr). One of the three Magi who came from the East to worship the infant Jesus.

Balthazar (bal.thạ.zär′, -tạ-; bal.thaz′ạr, -taz′-). [Also, **Balthasar.**] In Shakespeare's *Comedy of Errors* (III.i), a merchant who is accompanying Antipholus of Ephesus to dinner when the latter's wife has locked him out. He convinces Antipholus that to break down the door would reflect on the character of his wife.

Baltic (bôl′tik), **The Battle of the.** The naval battle of Copenhagen (1801). Campbell has a poem *Battle of the Baltic* (1805).

Balwhidder (bal.hwid′ẽr), **Micah.** The Scottish Presbyterian minister of Dalmailing in John Galt's *Annals of the Parish.* He is one of the most famous clergymen in literature.

Balzac (bȧl.zȧk; Anglicized, bôl′zak), **Honoré de.** b. at Tours, France, May 20, 1799; d. at Paris, Aug. 18, 1850. A French novelist. His father, a lawyer and minor government official, was an eccentric whose ambition was to live to a great age, and who, in middle life, married a highly-strung young Parisienne, who so little cared for Honoré that she placed him in a monastic school at Vendôme, and utterly neglected him for years. Balzac described his school life in his autobiographical novel *Louis Lambert.* He was a refractory pupil, who for punishment was daily imprisoned in the school library, where he read every book it contained. His health failing, he joined his family near Paris and became a lawyer's clerk, but detesting law, determined to become an author. This intention was strongly opposed by his parents, who to discourage it installed him in a Paris attic on meager rations; despite this, Balzac recalled those days of privation as the happiest of his life: he was free in Paris, spent most of his time in the Arsenal Library, and composed a tragedy, *Cromwell*, which received only disapproval from his family. Undaunted, "to get his hand in," he wrote at least a dozen novels, under various pseudonyms, all rather mediocre, but with flashes of genius; these brought little money, and were never openly acknowledged by him. To earn more, he determined to be his own publisher, and engaged in business as a printer and type founder, having borrowed capital from relatives and friends; the concern, under Balzac's mismanagement, failed, and he was burdened with debt for the whole of his life. To recoup his losses, he resumed his pen, resolved to succeed as an author, and in 1829 wrote *Les Chouans*, the first work to bear his name Honoré Balzac (the particle *de* he added later). This success was followed by *Physiologie du mariage* (1830) and *La Peau de chagrin* (1831); both created a furor, and his position as writer was secure. Then followed a strenuous career in Parisian journalism, to which Balzac contributed a large number of novels, short stories, and articles.

This period is vividly revealed in the second part of his *Illusions perdues: Un grand homme de province à Paris.* Nearly all his work appeared first in periodicals, then in book form with titles and text changed. Nearly 100 works compose the *Comédie humaine* written between 1830 and 1857. In addition, Balzac wrote six plays: *Vautrin* (1840), *Les Ressources de Quinola* (1842), *Paméla Giraud* (1843), *La Marâtre* (1848), *Le Faiseur (Mercadet)* (1851), and *L'École des ménages* (1839, published 1907). Only one, *Mercadet*, was successful. In 1834 Balzac first conceived the idea of uniting his works by means of reappearing characters, and in 1842 he named the series *La Comédie humaine*, in a memorable *Avant-propos* (foreword). Balzac's ventures as an editor were financial failures; *La Chronique de Paris* (1835) lived but one year; *La Revue parisienne* (1840) ended with the third number. The complete total of Balzac's writings amounts to more than 350 titles. On March 14, 1850, he married a rich widow, Countess Evelina Hanska, of a noble Polish family, with whom he had corresponded since 1833, and whom he had subsequently met at Geneva, Vienna, and St. Petersburg. He died in Paris, three months after his return from the wedding trip. Balzac is among the greatest novelists who ever lived. In his *Comédie humaine* he succeeds in giving a panorama of the whole of French society in the first half of the 19th century. Through his device of reappearing characters (about 2,000, and as many as 155 in one novel), he gives an impression of comprehensiveness and reality to his fictional world.

Bamboccio (bäm.bôt′chō), **Il.** See **Laar** or **Laer, Pieter van.**

Bamford (bam′fọrd), **Samuel.** b. at Middleton, Lancashire, England, Feb. 28, 1788; d. at Harpurhey, Lancashire, England, April 13, 1872. An English weaver and poet, imprisoned (1819) for agitating for repeal of the Corn Laws. Author of *The Weaver Boy, or Miscellaneous Poetry* (1819), *Homely Rhymes* (1843), *Passages in the Life of a Radical* (1840–44), *The Dialect of South Lancashire* (1854), and *Early Days* (1849).

Bampton (bamp′tọn), **John.** b. c1689; d. 1751. An English divine, and the founder at Oxford of the "Bampton Lectures" on divinity. The first lecturer was chosen in 1779.

Ban (ban). In the Arthurian cycle of romances, a king of Brittany and father of Sir Lancelot.

Banastaire (ban′ạs.tẽr), **Humfrey.** In Thomas Sackville's poem *The Complaint of Buckingham*, a dependent of the Duke of Buckingham who betrays him to the king.

Banbury (ban′bėr.i). A municipal borough and market town in S England, in Oxfordshire, situated on the river Cherwell ab. 22 mi. N of Oxford, ab. 68 mi. NW of London by rail: manufactures farm machinery. An iron-ore field is in the vicinity. The ancient Banbury cross, noted in nursery rhyme, was destroyed in the latter part of the reign of Elizabeth. The town was famous until recent years for its ale and cakes, and for its cheese which was proverbially regarded as consisting of nothing but "parings." It is from this that we have the allusions in Shakespeare and other writers to persons thin as a Banbury cheese. Insurgents were defeated here by troops of Edward IV in 1469. It was twice besieged in the civil war.

Banbury Cross. A cross famous in nursery rhyme, at Banbury, Oxfordshire. It was destroyed in the reign of Elizabeth.

Banbury Man. A Puritan; from Banbury, Oxfordshire, in the 17th century a Puritan community.

Bancroft (bang'krôft, ban'-), Sir **Squire.** [Original surname, **Butterfield.**] b. 1841; d. 1926. English actor, theater manager, and writer. He dropped his family name of Butterfield for his original second name of Bancroft at the time of his marriage. After his first appearance on the stage at Birmingham in 1861 he played the provinces until 1865, when he made his London debut in Wooler's play *A Winning Hazard* under the direction of Marie Effie Wilton. They had taken over an old theater for their own productions, giving it the name (1865) of the Prince of Wales's Theatre. He became this popular actress's leading man and, in 1868, her husband; thereafter they were billed as "The Bancrofts." Jointly they managed the Prince of Wales's Theatre until 1879, specializing in producing and acting in the plays of Thomas William Robertson. At a time when the British stage was largely dominated by plays of a bombastic and oratorical character, the Bancrofts are credited with restoring the vogue of light comedy, realistic in theme and simple in diction. They introduced higher wages for leading players, used three-sided room sets, and were themselves noted for their roles in comedy, including *Masks and Faces*, Boucicault's *London Assurance*, and Bulwer's *Money*. In 1879 the Bancrofts moved to the Haymarket Theatre, where for many years they continued to produce and act in modern drama, including Sardou's *Odette* (in which they starred Helena Modjeska), Sardou's *Fedora*, W. S. Gilbert's *Sweethearts*, and Pinero's *Lords and Commons*. Squire Bancroft was knighted in 1897. He was the author, in collaboration with his wife, of *On and Off the Stage* (1888) and *Recollections of Sixty Years* (1909); in 1925, after his wife's death, he published *Empty Chairs*.

Bandello (bän.del'lō), **Matteo.** b. at Castelnuovo, Piedmont, Italy, 1480; d. at Agen, France, 1565. An Italian prelate (bishop of Agen 1550) and novelist. His tales (1554–73) furnished subjects for Shakespeare, Philip Massinger, and others.

Bangorian Controversy (bang.gō'ri.an). A controversy stirred up by a sermon preached before George I (of England) on March 31, 1717 by Benjamin Hoadley, Bishop of Bangor, in Wales, from the text "My kingdom is not of this world." He argued that Christ had not delegated judicial and disciplinary powers to the Christian ministry. Supporters of ecclesiastical authority in the Church of England sharply disputed Hoadley's points, and hundreds of pamphlets were published on both sides of the question during the ensuing several years.

Banim (bā'nim), **John.** b. at Kilkenny, Ireland, April 3, 1798; d. near Kilkenny, Aug. 13, 1842. An Irish novelist, dramatist, and poet. He wrote the tragedies *Damon and Pythias* (produced 1821) and *The Prodigal*, the *Tales of the O'Hara Family* (somber stories of Irish peasant life, written in collaboration with his brother Michael), *The Nowlans* (a novel), and others.

Banim, Michael. b. at Kilkenny, Ireland, Aug. 5, 1796; d. at Booterstown, near Dublin, Ireland, Aug. 30, 1874. An Irish novelist; brother of John Banim (1798–1842). He collaborated with his brother in writing the *Tales of the O'Hara Family* (6 vols., 1825–26), a work portraying in grim colors the life of the Irish peasantry. Author of *The Ghost Hunter* (1833), *Father Connell* (1842), and *The Town of the Cascades* (2 vols., 1864).

Bankette of Sapience, The. [Also, **The Banquet of Sapience.**] A collection of wise and moral sayings by Sir Thomas Elyot. It was printed as "newely augmented" in 1539, and was popular enough to have had at least five editions.

Bank of England. [Called the **"Old Lady of Threadneedle Street."**] The principal bank in Great Britain, since 1946 formally owned by the British government, originally a private joint-stock institution incorporated by charter on July 27, 1694. Formed at the outset for the purpose of advancing a loan of 1,200,000 pounds to the government, it still has the management of the national debt, acts as the government's banker, and administers the exchange-control regulations. It also acts as banker for many leading British banks, and has branches in various parts of the country. It enjoys the monopoly of issuing paper currency, popularly known as Bank of England notes. The Bank of England was formally nationalized (March 1, 1946) under the Labour government of Clement R. Attlee by the terms of legislation passed in the previous year. Its building in London stands on Threadneedle Street opposite the Mansion House; hence it is often called the "Old Lady of Threadneedle Street."

Bankrupt, The. A comedy by Samuel Foote, produced in 1773.

Banks (bangks), **George Linnaeus.** b. at Birmingham, England, March 2, 1821; d. at London, May 3, 1881. An English editor, song writer, dramatist, and social reformer; husband of Isabella Banks, the novelist and poet. He was the author of *The Slave King*, written for the Negro tragedian Ira Frederick Aldridge, and two burlesques, *Old Maids and Mustard*, and *Ye Doleful Wives of Windsor*. He also wrote *What I Live For*, a humanitarian poem, *Dandy Jim of Caroline*, a Negro song, and *Warwickshire Will*, a song in tribute to Shakespeare. He edited (1848–64) the Harrogate *Advertiser*, Birmingham *Mercury*, Dublin *Daily Express*, Durham *Chronicle*, Sussex *Mercury*, and other journals. Author also of a life of Blondin, the famous French tightrope walker, published in 1862.

Banks, Isabella. [Often called **Mrs. Linnaeus Banks**; maiden name, **Varley.**] b. at Manchester, England, March 25, 1821; d. at Dalston, England, May 5, 1897. An English novelist and poet; married (1864) George Linnaeus Banks. Her works include the novels *God's Providence House* (1865), *Stung to the Quick* (1867), and *The Manchester*

Man (1876); also the collection of poems entitled *Ripples and Breakers* (1878).

Banks, John. b. c1652; d. 1706. An English dramatist of the period of the Restoration. He wrote *The Rival Kings* (1677), *The Destruction of Troy* (acted 1678, printed 1679), *The Unhappy Favorite* (1682), *The Innocent Usurper* (1683, published 1694), *The Island Queens* (1684, acted 1704 as *The Albion Queens*), *Virtue Betrayed* (1692), and *Cyrus the Great* (1695). He is ranked by one authority next to Otway in his type of tragedy; his plays, while having an affinity to heroic tragedy, generally look forward to the sentimental dramas of domestic life popular in the early 18th century.

Banks, Sir Joseph. b. at London, Feb. 13, 1743; d. at Isleworth, England, June 19, 1820. An English naturalist (especially known as a botanist) and patron of science. He equipped the ship *Endeavour*, and accompanied Cook's first expedition (1768–71), visited Iceland (1772), and served as president of the Royal Society (1778–1820). His herbarium and library became after his death the property of the British Museum. He wrote *A Short Account of the Causes of the Disease called the Blight, Mildew, and Rust* (1805) and others.

Bankside (bangk′sīd). The south bank of the Thames between the Blackfriars and Waterloo bridges, London. In the time of the Tudors it consisted of a single row of houses, built on a dike, or levee, higher both than the river at high tide and the ground behind the bank. At one end of "Bank Side" (as it was then spelled) stood the Clink Prison, Winchester House, and Saint Mary Overies Church. A little to the W of the Clink and behind the houses stood the Globe Theatre. The Festival of Britain (1951) was situated on this area.

Banks's Horse (bangk′siz). A celebrated trick horse named Morocco, exhibited at London about 1590–1600.

Bannatyne (ban′a.tīn), **George.** b. in Scotland, 1545; d. c1608. A collector of early Scottish poetry. His manuscript collection was printed in part by Allan Ramsay and David Dalrymple, Lord Hailes, and completely by the Hunterian Club; the manuscripts relate to the poetry of the 15th and 16th centuries.

Bannatyne, John. See **Bellenden, John.**

Bannatyne Club. A Scottish literary club, named for George Bannatyne (1545–c1608), founded under the presidency of Sir Walter Scott in 1823, and dissolved in 1859. It was devoted to the publication of works on Scottish history and literature.

Bannockburn (ban′ok.bėrn). A town in C Scotland, in Stirlingshire, ab. 3 mi. SE of Stirling, ab. 415 mi. N of London by rail. Here, on June 24, 1314, the Scots (ab. 30,000) under Robert the Bruce totally defeated the English (ab. 100,000) under Edward II. The loss of the English was ab. 30,000. At Sauchieburn, in the vicinity, James III of Scotland was defeated and slain by rebellious nobles in 1488.

Bannockburn. See also **Scots Wha Hae wi' Wallace Bled.**

Banquet of Sapience, The. See **Bankette of Sapience, The.**

Banquo (bang′kwō). In Shakespeare's *Macbeth*, the Thane of Lochaber. He is a general in the king's army, with the same rank as Macbeth, and with the same ambitions, but is of a quieter nature and more discretion. The Witches (or Weird Sisters), who appear to Macbeth and Banquo, prophesy the crown for Macbeth, but promise Banquo that his offspring shall reign thereafter. Macbeth, in an effort to avert this prophecy, sends murderers to kill Banquo and his only son, Fleance. The boy, however, escapes. In one of the most powerful scenes of the play Banquo's ghost appears to the guilty Macbeth, unseen by the others, at a banquet, and Macbeth's horror arouses the suspicions of these other nobles. Although Holinshed mentions him, Banquo is not a historical figure.

Banshee and Other Poems, The. A volume of poems (1888) by John Todhunter.

Bantam (ban′tam), **Angelo Cyrus.** In Dickens's *Pickwick Papers*, the Grand Master of the Ceremonies at Bath. He is a man who considers that he has a very important job indeed, and expects others to share his own high opinion of his position.

Baphomet (baf′ō.met). An imaginary idol or symbol which the Templars were accused of worshiping. This speculation has never had the general acceptance of scholars. Indeed, the word may be simply a manipulated form of "Mahomet," a name which took strange shapes in the Middle Ages.

Baps (baps), **Mr.** In Charles Dickens's novel *Dombey and Son*, a dancing-master, "a very grave gentleman."

Baptista Minola (bap.tis′ta min′ō.la). In Shakespeare's *Taming of the Shrew*, a rich gentleman of Padua, the father of Katherina (the "Shrew") and the gentle Bianca. He will not allow the latter to wed until Katherina has a husband.

Barabas (ba.rab′as). In Christopher Marlowe's *The Jew of Malta*, a scheming Machiavellian villain whose ambition is to gain and hold wealth by any means. When he is deprived of some of this wealth, he turns against his Christian neighbors.

Barabbas (ba.rab′as). [Also, **Barrabas.**] In the Bible, a robber and insurrectionary leader whose release from prison instead of that of Jesus was demanded of Pilate by the Jews.

Barada (bä.rä′dä). [Also: **Amana**; Biblical name, **Abana**; Greek, **Chrysorrhoas.**] A small river in Syria, flowing through the plain and city of Damascus. In modern times, it has been important in irrigation, but in Biblical times it was probably chiefly known, in conjunction with the river Pharphar, for the sacredness of its waters. 2 Kings, v. 12.

Barbara Allen's Cruelty. An old ballad, included in Percy's *Reliques*, relating the cruelty to her lover, and subsequent remorse, of Barbara Allen. There is another version called *Bonny Barbara Allan*, or simply *Barbara Allan*, which was also included in Percy's collection.

Barbara Yellowley (yel'ọ.li). See **Yellowley, Barbara.**

barbarism. 1. An offense against purity of style or language; originally, the mixing of foreign words and phrases in Latin or Greek; hence, the use of words or forms not made according to the accepted usages of a language. Barbarism is limited by some modern writers on rhetoric to an offense against the accepted rules of derivation or inflection, as *hisn* or *hern* for *his* or *her*, *gooses* for *geese*, *goodest* for *best*, *pled* for *pleaded*, *proven* for *proved*. 2. A word or form so used; an expression not made in accordance with the proper usages of a language. "The Greeks were the first that branded a foreign term in any of their writers with the odious name of *barbarism*." (G. Campbell.) "A barbarism may be in one word; a solecism must be of more." (Johnson.)

Barbarossa (bär.bạ.ros'ạ), **Frederick.** See **Frederick I** (of the *Holy Roman Empire*).

Barbary (bär'bạ.ri), **Roan.** See **Roan Barbary.**

Barbason (bär'bạ.son). A fiend referred to in Shakespeare's *Henry V* (II.i) and *Merry Wives of Windsor* (II.ii).

Barbauld (bär'bôld), **Anna Letitia.** [Maiden name, **Aikin.**] b. at Kibworth-Harcourt, Leicestershire, England, June 20, 1743; d. at Stoke Newington (now part of London), March 9, 1825. An English poet and essayist. She wrote *Poems* (1773), *Hymns in Prose for Children* (1781), *The Female Spectator* (1811), *Eighteen Hundred and Eleven* (1812), and others.

Barbican (bär'bi.kạn). A locality in London, so named from its former watchtower. Milton lived here 1646–47.

Barbour (bär'bėr), **John.** b. c1316; d. March 13, 1395. Scottish poet, archdeacon of Aberdeen, and auditor of the exchequer. His chief poem is *The Bruce* (c1375; edited by Skeat, 1870–89; edited by Mackenzie, 1909) on the subject of Robert I (Robert the Bruce) of Scotland. In Wyntoun's *Orygynale Cronykil* (c1420), he is said to have also written *The Brut* and a genealogical poem on the Stuarts, neither of which has survived. His authorship of *The Buik of Alexander*, the Scottish *Legends of the Saints*, and a fragmentary version of the Troy legend has been both asserted and denied.

Barbox Brothers (bär'boks), and **Barbox Brothers and Co.** A story and its sequel by Charles Dickens, included in "Mugby Junction," an extra Christmas number of Dickens's own magazine, *All the Year Round*, in 1866.

Barbusse (bȧr.büs), **Henri.** b. at Asnières, France, 1873; d. at Moscow, 1935. A French editor, novelist, and poet. Although the protégé and son-in-law of Catulle Mendès, he remained relatively unknown until, having left (1914) a Swiss tuberculosis sanatorium to enlist in the French army, he quit the army to write the disillusioned *Le Feu* (1916; Eng. trans., *Under Fire*, 1917). Earlier he had worked on the *Siècle* and other papers, edited the *Je sais tout* magazine, and published a collection of poems, *Pleureuses* (1895), and two novels, *Les Suppliants* (1903) and *L'Enfer* (1908; Eng.

trans., *The Inferno*, 1917). After the success of *Le Feu* he devoted himself largely to social problems and antiwar propaganda.

Barchester Novels (bär'chẹs.tėr). See **Barsetshire.**

Barchester Towers. A novel by Anthony Trollope, published in 1857. It is the second in the so-called Barsetshire series of six novels, all dealing with the inhabitants of the imaginary cathedral town of Barchester in the imaginary county of Barsetshire. The bishop's chaplain, the hypocritical Mr. Slope, schemes to obtain the deanery of Barchester; his opponent in this attempt is the wife of Dr. Proudie, the new bishop of Barchester. The disposal of the wardenship of Hiram's Hospital is also hotly contested by Mr. Harding, the former warden, and Mr. Quiverful, father of 14 children, who is supported by Mrs. Proudie. Mrs. Proudie obtains the wardenship for Mr. Quiverful, and is able to administer another setback to Mr. Slope when she learns that he has been courting both Eleanor Bold, Mr. Harding's widowed daughter, and the Signora Vesey-Neroni, daughter of Canon Stanhope. The situation turns in the favor of the High Churchmen when the deanery of Barchester is awarded to Mr. Arabin. The sly maneuvers of Mr. Slope are now fully exposed and he is forced out of his sinecure as the bishop's chaplain. Mrs. Bold later marries Mr. Arabin. One of the best-known portions of the novel is that describing the party given by the Proudies for the people of Barchester.

Barclay (bär'kli), **Alexander.** b. probably in Scotland, c1475; d. at Croydon, England, 1552. A British poet, author of *The Shyp of Folys* (The Ship of Fools), regarded as being in part a translation of, and in part an imitation of, the *Narrenschiff* of Sebastian Brant; he was the author also of *Égloges* (Eclogues), among the earliest eclogues in English. He was a monk of Ely and Canterbury, priest at the College of Ottery St. Mary, vicar of Much Badew in Essex, and rector of All Hallows, Lombard Street, London.

Barclay, Florence Louisa. [Maiden name, **Charlesworth.**] b. in Surrey, England, Dec. 2, 1862; d. at Norfolk, England, March 10, 1921. An English novelist and lecturer. In 1909 she visited the U. S., lecturing on Palestine, and again visited the U. S. in 1910. Author of religious and sentimental novels, including *The Wheels of Time* (1908), *The Rosary* (1909, her best-known and most successful work, over a million copies having been sold before she died), *The Mistress of Shenstone* (1910; also popular as a moving picture), *The Following of the Star* (1911), *Through the Postern Gate* (1912), *The Broken Halo* (1913), *My Heart's Right There* (1914), and *The White Ladies of Worcester* (1917).

Barclay, John. b. at Pont-à-Mousson, France, Jan. 28, 1582; d. Aug. 15, 1621. A Scottish poet. His verse, which is satirical in nature, is exemplified in the *Satyricon* (1603; second part, 1607). He also wrote *Sylvae* (Latin poems; 1606), *Apologia* (1611), *Icon Animorum* (1614), and the *Argenis* (1621).

Barcynska (bär.sin'skạ), **Countess.** See **Sandys, Oliver.**

bard. 1. A poet and singer among the ancient Celts; one whose occupation was to compose and sing verses in honor of the heroic achievements of princes and brave men, and on other subjects, generally to the accompaniment of the harp. The Welsh bards formed a hereditary order regulated by laws, and held stated festivals for competition, called *eisteddfods,* which after a long suspension were revived in the 18th century. There was also a hereditary guild of bards in Ireland, many of whom attained great skill. "There is amongest the Irish a certayne kind of people called *Bards,* which are to them insteede of poetts, whose profession is to sett foorth the prayses and disprayses of men in theyr poems and rimes." (Spenser, *State of Ireland.*)
2. Formerly, in Scotland, a strolling musician; a minstrel. They were classed with vagabonds, as an object of penal laws. "All vagabundis, fulis [fools], *bardis,* scudlaris, and siclike idill pepill, sall be brint in the cheek." (Kenneth's Stat., in Sir J. Balfour's *Practick.*)
3. In modern use, a poet: as, the *bard* of Avon (Shakespeare); the Ayrshire *bard* (Burns).

Bard, The. A poem by Thomas Gray, published in 1758, beginning with the phrase "Ruin seize thee, ruthless King." It is a Pindaric ode, based on a medieval legend.

Bardell (bär.del'), **Mrs. Martha.** In Charles Dickens's *Pickwick Papers,* an accommodating landlady who let lodgings to Mr. Pickwick, construed some remarks of his as a proposal of marriage, and brought a suit for breach of promise against him.

Bardi (bär'dē), **Bardo di.** In George Eliot's novel *Romola,* a blind Florentine scholar, the father of Romola.

Bardolph (bär'dolf). In Shakespeare's *1* and *2 Henry IV,* a sharper and hanger-on, one of Falstaff's dissolute and amusing companions, called the "Knight of the Burning Lamp" by Falstaff on account of his red face. He is characterized also in *Henry V* "white livered and red-faced, by means whereof 'a faces it out and fights not." As a military man his exploits in *Henry V* are limited to robbing a church, wherefore he is hanged, unjustly as Pistol sees it. In *The Merry Wives of Windsor,* he is a tapster (bartender) at the Garter Inn, having been cast off by Falstaff.

Bardolph, Lord. In Shakespeare's *2 Henry IV,* a supporter of Northumberland who brings false news of Hotspur's victory over Prince Hal at Shrewsbury. He discusses the uprising with Archbishop Scroop, and Lords Hastings and Mowbray, and later (IV.iv) news is brought to the King that he has been defeated with Northumberland.

Bareacres (bār'ā''kèrz), **Lord and Lady.** In Thackeray's *Vanity Fair,* the Earl and Countess of Bareacres, an impoverished couple notable for extreme snobbery.

Barebone's Parliament (bār'bōnz). See **Little Parliament.**

Baretti (bä.rät'tē), **Giuseppe Marc' Antonio.** b. at Turin, April 25, 1719; d. at London, May 6, 1789. An Italian writer and lexicographer. He lived for many years at London, where he was a friend of David Garrick, Samuel Johnson, and Edmund Burke. He wrote *Lettere famigliari* (1762), and compiled an English-Italian and Italian-English dictionary (1760), a Spanish-English dictionary (1778), and others.

Bargrave (bär'grāv), **Mrs.** The woman to whom the ghost of Mrs. Veal appears in Daniel Defoe's narrative of *The True Relation of the Apparition of One Mrs. Veal* (1706).

Barham (bär'am), **Richard Harris.** [Pseudonym, **Thomas Ingoldsby.**] b. at Canterbury, England, Dec. 6, 1788; d. at London, June 17, 1845. English clergyman and poet. He wrote *The Ingoldsby Legends* (1840), a collection of burlesque poems originally published (1837 *et seq.*) in *Bentley's Miscellany;* a second series was published in 1847, and a third, edited by his son, in the same year. His other works include *Baldwin* (1819) and *My Cousin Nicholas* (1841).

Baring (bār'ing), **Maurice.** b. at London, April 27, 1874; d. at Beaufort Castle, Beauly, Scotland, Dec. 14, 1945. An English novelist, essayist, dramatist, poet, war correspondent, traveler, and diplomat; a member of the Baring family of financial and commercial note. Educated at Eton, in Germany and Italy, where he studied languages, and at Trinity College, Cambridge, he served (1893–1904) in the British diplomatic service at Paris, Copenhagen, Rome, and London. He spent several years in Russia, covering the Russo-Japanese War and writing weekly articles (1904–12) for the *Morning Post;* as a special correspondent (1912) for the London *Times,* he covered the First Balkan War. Author of the novels *Passing By* (1921), *A Triangle* (1923), *C* (1924), *Cat's Cradle* (1925), *Daphne Adeane* (1926), *Tinker's Leave* (1927), *Friday's Business* (1933), *The Lonely Lady of Dulwich* (1934), and *Darby and Joan* (1936), many of which have been translated into several European languages; *Poems* (1899; several eds., 1905–30), *Pastels* (1891), *Triolets* (1893), *The Black Prince* (1903), *Sonnets* (1914), and *Fifty Sonnets* (1915); the dramas *Gaston de Foix* (1903), *Mahasena* (1905), *The Grey Stocking* (1911), and *Manfroy* (1920); essays on Russian literature (1910, 1914) and on French literature (1927). *The Puppet Show of Memory* (1922) is an autobiography.

Baring-Gould (bār'ing.gōld'), **Sabine.** b. at Exeter, England, 1834; d. Jan. 2, 1924. An English clergyman and writer. His works include *Iceland* (1861), *The Book of Werewolves* (1865), *Post-Medieval Preachers* (1865), *Curious Myths of the Middle Ages* (1866–68), *The Origin and Development of Religious Belief* (1869–70), *Lives of the Saints* (1872–77), *Some Modern Difficulties* (1874), and *Mehalah* (1880), *John Herring* (1883), and other novels. He also wrote the hymn *Onward Christian Soldiers* which was subsequently set to music by Sir Arthur Sullivan.

Barker (bär'kèr), **Ernest.** b. at Woodley, Cheshire, England, Sept. 23, 1874—. An English historian. He was successively a fellow and lecturer (1898–1905) of Merton College at Oxford, and a lecturer at Wadham College (1899–1909), lecturer at St. John's College (1909–13), at New College (1913–

fat, fāte, fär, åsk, fāre; net, mē, hèr; pin, pīne; not, nōte, mōve, nôr; up, lūte, pùll; ᴛʜ, then;

20), principal (1920–27) of King's College at London, and a professor (1928–39) of political science at Cambridge. Author of *The Political Thought of Plato and Aristotle* (1906, revised as *Greek Political Theory*, 1915), *Political Thought in England from Herbert Spencer to Today* (1915), *The Crusades* (1923), *National Character* (1927), *Oliver Cromwell and the English People* (1927), *Ideas and Ideals of the British Empire* (1941), *Britain and the British People* (1942), and essays collected in *Church, State, and Study* (1930) and *The Citizen's Choice* (1937).

Barker, Harley Granville Granville-. See **Granville-Barker, Harley Granville.**

Barker, Matthew Henry. b. at Deptford, England, 1790; d. June 29, 1846. An English journalist and novelist, best known for his sea tales. He wrote *Land and Sea Tales* (1836), *Topsail-sheet Blocks* (1838), *Life of Nelson* (1836), *The Victory, or the Wardroom Mess* (1844), and others.

Barkis (bär′kis), **Mr.** In Charles Dickens's *David Copperfield*, a bashful carrier who marries Peggotty. He conveys his intentions to her by sending her, by David, the message "Barkis is willin'."

Barksteed (bärk′stēd) or **Barksted** (-sted), **William.** fl. c1611. An English actor and poet. His name appears instead of John Marston's on some copies of *The Insatiate Countess*. He was the author of *Hiren, or the Faire Greeke* (1611).

Barlaam and Josaphat (bär′lȧ.ȧm; jos′ȧ.fat). A romance, sometimes attributed to Saint John of Damascus (a Syrian monk of the 8th century), translated into Latin before the 13th century. It recounts the adventures of Barlaam, a monk of the wilderness of Sinai, in his successful attempt to convert Josaphat (or Joasaph), the son of a king of India, to Christianity and asceticism. The incidents of the story were probably taken from an Indian source. That part of the plot of Shakespeare's *Merchant of Venice* which relates to the choosing of the casket is said to have come originally from this romance, through the *Speculum Historiale* of Vincent of Beauvais (c1290), the *Cento Novelle Antiche* (65th tale), Boccaccio's *Decameron*, the *Golden Legend*, and the *Gesta Romanorum*. An English translation of this was printed (c1510–15) by Wynkyn de Worde, which contained the "Story of the Three Caskets." It is considered probable that Shakespeare read one of Richard Robinson's reissues (there were six between 1577 and 1601). Rudolf von Ems wrote a poem of the same name and subject in the 13th century, probably based on the original.

Barley (bär′li), **Clara.** In Charles Dickens's novel *Great Expectations*, a pretty girl who marries Herbert Pocket.

Barley, Old Bill. A drunken and gouty old man, the father of Clara Barley, in Charles Dickens's novel *Great Expectations*.

Barleycorn (bär′li.kôrn), **John** (or **Sir John**). A personification of malt liquor, as being made from barley. There is an English ballad in which he appears as a person.

Barlow (bär′lō), **George.** b. at London, June 19, 1847; d. in January, 1914. An English poet. He was educated at Harrow and at Exeter College,

Oxford. Author of *Poems and Sonnets* (3 vols., 1871), *A Life's Love* (1873), *Under the Dawn* (1874), and *Pageant of Life* (1888). At the invitation of Charles François Gounod, who was in London during the Franco-Prussian War, Barlow added English words to the French composer's *Ave Maria*.

Barlow, Jane. b. at Clontarf, Ireland, Oct. 17, 1860; d. April 17, 1917. An Irish novelist and poet. Among her works, which deal mainly with peasant life in Ireland, are *Bogland Studies* (1892), *Irish Idylls* (1892), *Kerrigan's Quality* (1893), *The End of Elfintown* (1894), *Strangers at Lisconnel* (1895), *A Creel of Irish Stories* (1897), *At the Back of Beyond* (1902), *By Beach and Bog Land* (1905), *Irish Neighbors* (1907), *Irish People in Irish Places* (1909), and *Flaws* (1911).

Barmecides (bär′me̯.sīdz). A family of the Persian nobility, established under the Abbasside caliphate. The family gained great wealth and influence. Khaled ibn-Barmak rose to be a member of the government of Abu-al-Abbas, and his son was vizier to the caliph al-Mahdi. The son, Yahya, was also tutor to Harun al-Rashid, later becoming his friend, as did his two sons. However, Harun al-Rashid so feared the power of this family that he had them all assassinated, only one child escaping. The Barmecides figure largely in several tales in *The Arabian Nights' Entertainments.*

Barnaby-bright (bär′na̯.bi.brīt″). [Also, **Barnaby Day.**] The day of Saint Barnabas, the 11th of June, which in old style was the day of the summer solstice.

> Barnaby-bright, the longest day and the shortest night. (Old rhyme.)

> This day the sunne is in his chiefest hight,
> With Barnaby the bright.
> (Spenser, *Epithalamion*.)

Barnaby Brittle (bär′na̯.bi brit′l). See **Brittle, Barnaby.**

Barnaby Bunch (bunch). See **Bunch, Barnaby.**

Barnaby Rudge (ruj). A novel by Charles Dickens which came out in parts, and was published in book form in 1841. It is based on the anti-Catholic riots of the London populace in June, 1780, which were instigated and abetted by Lord George Gordon. Barnaby Rudge, the half-witted son of a villainous murderer, is ignorantly and innocently involved in the riots, and is sentenced to death, but is pardoned on the scaffold. Meanwhile, his father has murdered the brother of Geoffrey Haredale, a country gentleman and a Roman Catholic, but is discovered and pays for his crime. Haredale's private battles with the villainous Sir John Chester comprise a large part of the plot, and the two men join forces for a while in order to prevent Emma, the niece of Haredale, from marrying Edward, the son of Chester. The marriage plans finally win Haredale's consent only after Edward saves the lives of Emma and her uncle during the Gordon Riots. The most interesting part of the work for many modern readers is Dickens's description of these riots, and it may be seen how closely Dickens has followed Scott's account of the Porteous Riots by a comparison of

ḍ, d or j; ṣ, s or sh; ṭ, t or ch; ż, z or zh; o, F. cloche; ü, F. menu; ċh, Sc. loch; ṅ, F. bonbon.

the riot scenes in *The Heart of Midlothian* and *Barnaby Rudge.*

Barnacle (bär′na̱.kl), **Lord Decimus Tite.** A pompous and windy peer, with a high position in the Circumlocution Office, in Charles Dickens's *Little Dorrit.* Clarence, an empty-headed youth, and Ferdinand, a well-dressed and agreeable young man, his sons, are also employed in the office.

Barnacle, Young and Old. The names of a rich uncle and his studious nephew in James Shirley's comedy *The Gamester.* Old Barnacle, in the hope of converting his nephew into a spirited young man, bribes Hazard to let Young Barnacle seem to win out in a public fight. This false triumph has the effect of converting the young man into a conceited gallant who gambles, roisters about taverns, and runs about with the latest gossip. His uncle, Old Barnacle, finding that he has succeeded beyond his desires as well as his expectations, now bribes Hazard to "unblade" the young man. This is done, and the young man regains his rightful place in his uncle's affections.

Barnard (bär′na̱rd), **Lady Anne.** [Maiden name, **Lindsay.**] b. Dec. 8, 1750; d. May 6, 1825. A Scottish poet; daughter of James Lindsay, the fifth Earl of Balcarres; married (1793) to Andrew Barnard, a British colonial official in South Africa. She wrote the ballad *Auld Robin Gray* (1772) and a sequel to it.

Barnard, Charlotte Alington. [Pseudonym, "**Claribel.**"] b. Dec. 23, 1830; d. at Dover, England, Jan. 30, 1869. An English ballad composer. Many of her songs, such as *Come back to Erin,* were very popular in the 19th century.

Barnardine (bär′na̱r.din). In Shakespeare's *Measure for Measure,* a savage and sullen prisoner who torpidly "apprehends death no more dreadfully but as a drunken sleep." His execution is ordered by the Duke of Vienna in place of Claudio, which sentence has been ordered by the Duke's deputy, Angelo (Barnardine refuses, however, to die on that particular day and eventually is pardoned).

Barnardo (bär.när′dō), **Thomas John.** b. in Ireland, 1845; d. at Surbiton, England, Sept. 19, 1905. A British philanthropist, noted for his labors in rescuing and training destitute children. He began his work in London, c1866, established a home for destitute children in 1867, founded a village for girls at Ilford in 1873 and a hospital for sick waifs in 1887, and formed the "Young Helpers' League" in 1891. About 150 branch schools (now generally known as "Dr. Barnardo's Homes") were opened at London and in the provinces. The institutions were incorporated in 1899 as "The National Institution for the Reclamation of Destitute Waif Children."

Barnard's Inn (bär′na̱rdz). One of the inns of Chancery in Holborn, London. The society is of very great antiquity; the hall itself was certainly in existence in 1451, and probably much earlier. The house began to be used as an inn of Chancery c1454. In 1894 the Mercers' Company erected two buildings here for the Mercers' Schools. The old hall of the inn was preserved as a dining-room for the boys. The area suffered considerable damage in World War II.

Barnavelt (bär′na̱.velt), **Sir John Van Olden.** See **Sir John Van Olden Barnavelt.**

Barnes (bärnz), **Barnabe.** b. in Yorkshire, England, c1569; d. 1609. An English poet. In 1593 he published a collection of love poems, sonnets, and madrigals, entitled *Parthenophil and Parthenophe.* He also wrote a book of sonnets (1595) and *The Divil's Charter* (1607), a tragedy.

Barnes, Juliana. See **Berners** or **Bernes, Juliana.**

Barnes, Ronald Gorell. [Title, 3d Baron **Gorell of Brampton.**] b. April 16, 1884—. An English poet, editor, journalist, and soldier. He was educated at Winchester, Harrow, and Oxford. He wrote (1910–15) for the London *Times* and saw service in World War I, attaining the rank of major; he held industry and government posts after the war. He edited (1933–39) the *Cornhill Magazine,* and produced several volumes of verse, including *Babes in the African Wood* (1911), *Love Triumphant* (1913), *Days of Destiny* (1917), *Pilgrimage* (1920), *Many Mansions* (1926), *Unheard Melodies* (1934), *In the Potter's Field* (1936), and *Last of the English* (1939); his *London to Paris by Air* is considered one of his best poems.

Barnes, Thomas. b. 1785; d. May 7, 1841. An English journalist. He was editor (1817–41) of the London *Times.*

Barnes, William. b. in Dorsetshire, England, Feb. 22, 1800; d. at Winterbourne Came, England, in October, 1886. An English poet, philologist, and clergyman. He is best known for his three series of *Poems of Rural Life in the Dorsetshire Dialect* (1844, 1847, and 1862). He wrote also various philological works, including a *Philological Grammar* (1854).

Barnes Newcome (nū′kum). See **Newcome, Barnes.**

Barney (bär′ni). In Charles Dickens's novel *Oliver Twist,* a waiter, with a cold in his head, at the "Three Cripples."

Barnfield (bärn′fēld), **Richard.** b. at Norbury, Shropshire, England, 1574; d. 1627. An English poet. Author of *The Affectionate Shepherd* (1594), *Cynthia* (1595), and *Poems in Divers Humors* (1598). In the last are the poems "If Music and Sweet Poetry Agree" and "As it Fell Upon a Day," which were long thought to be by Shakespeare.

Barnivelt (bär′ni.velt), **Esdras, Apothecary.** A pseudonym under which a key to *The Rape of the Lock* was published shortly after the poem itself. It was attributed to Alexander Pope, and also to John Arbuthnot.

Barnwell (bärn′wel, -wel), **George.** The apprentice hero of George Lillo's tragedy *The London Merchant, or George Barnwell.*

Barons' Wars, The. A historical poem in six cantos, by Michael Drayton. It was first published in 1596 under the title *Mortimeriados,* and republished with many alterations in 1603 under its present title.

baroque. In architecture and allied arts, a term applied to a style of decoration which prevailed in Europe during a great part of the 18th century, and may be considered to have begun toward the close of the 17th century. It is nearly equivalent to the French style of the time of Louis XV and is distinguished by its exuberant, sometimes (to some tastes) clumsy forms, particularly in church architecture, and its contorted ornamentation, made up in great part of scrolls and shellwork. It is also called, sometimes, the "Jesuit style," from the many examples supplied by churches founded by the Jesuit order.

Barr (bär), **Robert.** [Pseudonym, **Luke Sharp.**] b. at Glasgow, Scotland, Sept. 16, 1850; d. at Woldingham, Surrey, England, Oct. 21, 1912. A British novelist and editor. He was educated at Toronto, Canada, and taught in Canada until 1876, when he joined the editorial staff of the Detroit *Free Press.* He established the weekly English edition of the *Free Press* at London in 1881, and in 1892 founded, with Jerome K. Jerome, the *Idler* magazine, of which he was coeditor until 1895. Among his works are *In a Steamer Chair* (1892), *From Whose Bourne* (1893), *In the Midst of Alarms* (1894, 1900), *The Face and the Mask* (1895), *The Countess Tekla* (1899), *The Strong Arm* (1900), *The Unchanging East* (1900), *Over the Border* (1903), *The O'Ruddy* (1904; with Stephen Crane), *The Woman Wins* (1904), *A Chicago Princess* (1904), *Speculations of John Steele* (1905), *The Triumph of Eugene Valmont* (1906), *A Rock in the Baltic* (1907), *Cardillac* (1909), and *The Swordmaker* (1910).

Barrabas (ba̱.rab'a̱s). See **Barabbas.**

Barrack-Room Ballads. A volume of poems (1892) by Rudyard Kipling. They were published originally by W. E. Henley in *The National Observer,* and in their collected form added greatly to the fame which had come to Kipling in 1886 with the publication of *Departmental Ditties.* The volume includes "Gunga Din," "Fuzzy Wuzzy," "Danny Deever," and "The Road to Mandalay."

Barrès (bà.res), **Maurice.** b. at Charmes, in Lorraine, France, Sept. 22, 1862; d. at Neuilly, France, Dec. 4, 1923. A French novelist, journalist, and nationalist politician. Author of *Sous l'oeil des barbares* (1888), *Un homme libre* (1889), *Le Jardin de Bérénice* (1891), *Du Sang, de la volupté et de la mort* (1894), *Les Deracinés* (1897), *L'Appel au soldat* (1900), *Leurs figures* (1902), *Amori et dolori sacrum* (1903), *Colette Baudoche* (1909; Eng. trans., 1918), *La Colline inspirée* (1913; Eng. trans., *The Sacred Hill,* 1929) and others. His early work records a period of intense egocentrism and lyricism, followed by a middle period of discovery that the self meant to him little apart from the selves of other Frenchmen, and eventually by complete commitment to the doctrines of French nationalism, which he did much to elaborate. Elected deputy from Nancy in 1889, he remained prominent in politics from then until his death, favoring the dictatorship during the Boulanger campaign, the anti-Dreyfus party during the Dreyfus affair, ,and the strong-army, anti-German *revanchards* of the years before World War I. His literary following, originally very large, dwindled after 1918.

Barrett (bar'e̱t), **Wilson.** [Original name, **William Henry Barrett.**] b. at Chelmsford, Essex, England, Feb. 18, 1846; d. at London, July 22, 1904. An English actor, manager, and dramatist. He made his first appearance (1864) at the Halifax Theatre

Royal; in 1866 he married Caroline Heath (1835–87), an actress, with whom he traveled and acted until her health forced her to give up the stage. He operated several theaters at Hull, Leeds, and London, and played throughout England, in Australia (1898, 1902), and in the U. S., which he visited six times. He introduced the Polish actress Helena Modjeska to English audiences, playing Mercutio to her Juliet in Shakespeare's *Romeo and Juliet.* Some of his outstanding successes were as Hamlet, Othello, Wilfred Denver in Herman's *The Silver King,* Lemuel in *Daughters of Babylon,* Pete in *The Manxman,* Tom Robinson in *It's Never Too Late To Mend,* and roles in *East Lynne, Lights o' London, The Romany Rye,* and in his own popular success *The Sign of the Cross* (1895), in which he portrayed a Roman patrician converted to Christianity. Author of the plays *Nowadays* (1889), *Daughters of Babylon* (1897), *Quo Vadis?* (1900; from the novel by Henryk Sienkiewicz), *Lucky Durham* (1905); coauthor of *Hoodman Blind* (1885), *Lord Harry* (1886), both with Henry Arthur Jones; *Sister Mary* (1886), with Clement Scott; *Clito* (1886), with Sydney Grundy; *The Golden Ladder* (1887), with George Robert Sims; *Ben-My-Chree* (1888), *The Good Old Times* (1889), both with Hall Caine; *The People's Idol* (1890), with Victor Widnell; and *Man and His Makers* (1899), with Louis N. Parker.

Barri (bar'i), **Giraldus (or Gerald) de.** See **Giraldus Cambrensis.**

Barrie (bar'i), Sir **James Matthew.** b. at Kirriemuir, Forfarshire, Scotland, May 9, 1860; d. June 19, 1937. A Scottish playwright and novelist, noted for his deft use of whimsy to illustrate the value of simple emotions. His most popular work is now probably *Peter Pan* (1904), a fairy-tale play in which Maude Adams, Jean Arthur, Mary Martin, and others have appeared with great success in America. His other plays include *The Professor's Love Story* (1895), *Quality Street* (1902), *The Admirable Crichton* (1903), *Alice Sit-by-the-Fire* (1905), *What Every Woman Knows* (1908), *The Twelve-Pound Look* (1910), *Der Tag* (1914), *The Old Lady Shows Her Medals* (1917), *Dear Brutus* (1917), *Mary Rose* (1920), and *Shall We Join the Ladies?* (1922); outstanding among his prose works are *The Little Minister* (1891), which he also adapted (1897) for the stage, *A Window in Thrums* (1889), *Sentimental Tommy* (1896), the biographical *Margaret Ogilvie* (1896), *Tommy and Grizel* (1900), and *Peter and Wendy* (1911).

Barrington (bar'ing.to̱n), **Daines.** b. 1727; d. March 14, 1800. An English lawyer, naturalist, and antiquary; fourth son of John Shute Barrington. He wrote *Observations on the Statutes* (1766), *The Naturalist's Calendar* (1767), and others.

Barrington, E. A pseudonym of **Beck, Lily Adams.**

Barrington, George. [Original name, **George Waldron.**] b. at Maynooth, Ireland, May 14, 1755; d. c1840. An Irish writer on Australian topics. He was transported to Australia as a pickpocket in 1790, and emancipated in 1792. His most notable exploit as a thief was the robbing of one of the Russian princes of the Orlov family, at Covent Garden Theatre, of a snuffbox said to be worth

d̶, d or j; ṣ, s or sh; ṭ, t or ch; ẓ, z or zh; o, F. cloche; ü, F. menu; c̶h, Sc. loch; ṅ, F. bonbon.

about 150 thousand dollars. When the play *The Revenge*, by Edward Young, was presented at Sydney by a group of actors most of whom were convicts, it was probably Barrington who wrote the prologue containing the lines: "True patriots we, for be it understood, we left our country for our country's good." He also wrote *A Voyage to Botany Bay* (1801), *The History of New South Wales* (1802), *The History of New Holland* (1808), and other works.

Barrington, John Shute. [Title, 1st Viscount **Barrington**.] b. at Theobalds, Hertfordshire, England, 1678; d. at Becket, Berkshire, England, Dec. 14, 1734. An English lawyer and polemical writer; father of Daines Barrington. He was created Baron Barrington and Viscount Barrington (in the Irish peerage) in 1720. As a result of his favoring civil rights for Protestant dissenters he was sent to Scotland to gain Presbyterian backing for the union of Scotland with England. In 1723 he was expelled from the House of Commons for his connection with a lottery. His expulsion was thought by many to have been the result of personal malice on the part of Robert Walpole. He wrote *The Rights of Protestant Dissenters* (1704; second part 1705), *A Dissuasive to Jacobitism* (1713), *Miscellanea Sacra* (1725), and others.

Barrington, Sir Jonah. b. in Ireland, 1760; d. at Versailles, France, April 8, 1834. An Irish judge. He was the author of *Personal Sketches* (1827; 3rd vol., 1832), *Historic Memoirs of Ireland* (1832), and *The Rise and Fall of the Irish Nation* (1833).

Barrow (bar'ō), **Isaac.** b. at London, 1630; d. there, in April, 1677. An English theologian, classical scholar, and mathematician; a teacher of Isaac Newton. He was educated at Cambridge (scholar of Trinity, 1647, and fellow, 1649), traveled on the Continent (1655–59), was appointed professor of geometry at Gresham College, and in 1663 became the first Lucasian professor of mathematics at Cambridge (a post from which he resigned in 1669 in favor of Newton). He served as chaplain to Charles II; in 1672 he became master of Trinity College. Among his works are *Lectiones Opticae et Geometricae* (1669, 1670–74) and the posthumously published *Treatise on the Pope's Supremacy* (1680). The best edition of his theological works is that of Alexander Napier (1859).

Barrow, Sir John. b. near Ulverston, Lancashire, England, June 19, 1764; d. at Camden Town, now part of London, Nov. 23, 1848. An English writer, geographer, and traveler. He was secretary to the British ambassador to China (1792–94) and to the governor of the Cape of Good Hope (1796–98). While in Africa he was sent on missions into the interior and secured valuable information on that area. Following his return to England in 1803 he was second secretary of the admiralty (1804–06, 1807–45). He was a promoter of Arctic exploration (Barrow Straits, Cape Barrow, and Point Barrow were named for him), and a chief founder of the Royal Geographical Society. He was made a baronet in 1835. Among his works are *Travels in South Africa* (1801–04), *Travels in China* (1804), *Voyage to Cochin-China* (1806), *History of Arctic Voyages* (1818), *Voyages of Discovery and Research*

Within the Arctic Regions (1846), an autobiography, and others.

Barry (bar'i), **Ann.** [Maiden name, **Street.**] b. at Bath, England, 1734; d. Nov. 29, 1801. An English actress; wife of Spranger Barry. When very young she married an actor named Dancer, and first appeared (c1756) on the stage under his name. She married Barry in 1768. After his death she remained on the stage until 1798, marrying in 1778 a Mr. Crawford. She was considered good in tragedy and superb in comedy as in her playing of Millamant in Congreve's *Way of the World*. She is buried near her husband in the cloisters of Westminster Abbey.

Barry, Cornelius. See **Balibari, Chevalier de.**

Barry (bar'i; French, bȧ.rē), Comtesse **du.** See **du Barry.**

Barry, Elizabeth. b. 1658; d. Nov. 7, 1713. An English actress. She went on the stage under the patronage of the poet John Wilmot, 2nd Earl of Rochester, and was the creator of more than 100 roles, mostly those of tragedy. She inspired Thomas Otway to create the roles of Monimia (in *The Orphan*) and Belvidera (in *Venice Preserved*), which made her her highest reputation; another of her popular parts was the comic one of Lady Brute in *The Provoked Wife* by John Vanbrugh. She retired from the stage in 1710, and was buried at Acton, now part of London. She was usually known as "the great Mrs. Barry" (as distinguished from Ann Barry).

Barry, Giraldus (or **Gerald**) **de.** See **Giraldus Cambrensis.**

Barry, Spranger. b. at Dublin, Ireland, 1719; d. at London, Jan. 10, 1777. An Irish actor, a rival of David Garrick; husband of Ann Barry. He first appeared on the stage in 1743, in Dublin, in the role of Othello. He was generally considered one of the best actors of his time, and excelled in tragedy, though he occasionally played in comedy. Among his roles were Hamlet and Macbeth (in which he alternated with Garrick), Romeo (with Mrs. Cibber, the wife of Theophilus Cibber, as Juliet), and Othello (the part in which he made his London debut, at the Drury Lane Theatre). He is buried, near his wife, in the cloisters of Westminster Abbey.

Barry Leroy (lē.roi'). A historical novel by Henry Christopher Bailey, published in 1919. It is set in England and on the Continent, and takes place in the period 1793–1800.

Barry Lyndon (lin'don), **Memoirs of.** A novel by William Makepeace Thackeray, first published serially in *Fraser's Magazine*, beginning in 1844, as *The Luck of Barry Lyndon*. It was probably modeled on Fielding's *Jonathan Wild the Great*. In it Redmond Barry, an Irish rascal, tells the story of his own adventures. He flees Ireland because he believes he has killed his opponent in a duel, serves in the English and Prussian armies, and then acquires some money and a reputation as a man of fashion. He marries a wealthy widow, the Countess of Lyndon, whose name he takes, but treats her unmercifully, squanders her fortune, and finally ends his life in the Fleet Prison.

Barsad (bär'sad), **John.** See **Pross, Solomon.**

fat, fāte, fär, åsk, fāre; net, mē, hèr; pin, pīne; not, nōte, mōve, nôr; up, lūte, půll; ŦH, then;

Barsetshire (bär′sĕt.shir). The imaginary county in S England which is the scene of six novels by Anthony Trollope (*The Warden*, 1855; *Barchester Towers*, 1857; *Doctor Thorne*, 1858; *Framley Parsonage*, 1861; *The Small House at Allington*, 1864; *The Last Chronicle of Barsetshire*, 1867), collectively known as *The Chronicles of Barsetshire*, and sometimes also called the Barchester Novels or Cathedral Novels. Barsetshire resembles parts of the counties of Southampton in S England and Somersetshire in SW England, but its county seat, Barchester, is usually identified with Winchester in the county of Southampton. The 20th-century English novelist Angela Margaret Thirkell has used this same region as the scene of some of her novels.

Bartas (bär.tàs), **Guillaume de Salluste, Seigneur du.** b. at Montfort, near Auch, France, 1544; d. 1590. A French poet, familiar to the courts of Queen Elizabeth and James VI of Scotland (later James I of England). He wrote *La Semaine* (1578), an epic poem on the creation of the world which was translated into English and said to have influenced Spenser, Donne, and Milton.

Barthélemy (bär.tàl.mē), **Jean Jacques.** b. at Cassis, near Marseilles, Jan. 20, 1716; d. at Paris, April 30, 1795. A French antiquary and man of letters.

Bartholomaeus Anglicus (bär.thol.ọ̄.mē′us ang′glikus), or **Bartholomew the Englishman** (bär.thol′-ọ̄.mū). fl. 1230–50. An English Franciscan friar, and professor of theology at Paris and later in Saxony. He is frequently confused with another English Franciscan, Bartholomew de Glanville, who lived in the next century. He is noted as the author of *De Proprietatibus Rerum*, an encyclopedia widely used and translated throughout Europe, and still current in the late 16th century. Shakespeare is believed to have been well acquainted with it. This work, remarkably comprehensive and methodical, was translated from Latin into Italian (1309), into French (1372), into Provençal (before 1391), and into Spanish (sometime in the 15th century). An English translation was made in 1398 by John de Trevisa.

Bartholomew (bär.thol′ọ̄.mū), Saint. One of the 12 apostles, probably identical with Nathaniel (Mat. x.3). His day, in the Roman Catholic and Anglican churches, is Aug. 24.

Bartholomew, Massacre of Saint. See **Saint Bartholomew, Massacre of.**

Bartholomew Cokes (kōks). See **Cokes, Bartholomew.**

Bartholomew Fair. A fair formerly (1133–1855) held at Smithfield, London, beginning Aug. 24.

Bartholomew Fair. A comedy by Ben Jonson, produced 1614 at the Hope Theatre. It is laid against a background of a famous English fair. Various keepers of stalls are characterized: Ursula, a pig-woman of gross size; Mooncalf, her tapster; Joan Trash, a gingerbread seller; Knock'hum, a horse-bettor; Edgeworth, a pickpocket; Nightingale, his accomplice, who lulls the visitors by songs while he robs them; Lantern Leatherhead, a seller of musical instruments and toys and also a puppet-show manager (possibly a satire on Inigo Jones);

and John Littlewit, a proctor who issues marriage licenses (possibly a satire on Samuel Daniel and his wedding masques). Littlewit wishes to see the fair, but meets opposition from his mother-in-law, Mistress Purecraft, who is a Puritan. Mistress Purecraft is comically satirized, as is her suitor, formerly a baker, but now a prophet and church elder, Rabbi Zeal-of-the-Land Busy. Winwife is a rival of Busy, and eventually wins the widow Purecraft when Busy is placed in the stocks for upsetting booths in his zealous indignation.

Bartholomew pig. Pork sold at Bartholomew Fair (formerly held at Smithfield, London) and specifically mentioned in Jonson's comedy *Bartholomew Fair*, wherein one of the characters operates a booth dispensing this delicacy to fair-goers. The epithet "little tidy Bartholomew boar-pig" is applied endearingly to Falstaff by Doll Tearsheet in Shakespeare's *2 Henry IV* (II.iv).

Bartholomew's Hospital. A hospital at Smithfield, London, founded in 1123.

Bartholomew-the-Great, Saint. A church at Smithfield, London, founded in 1123, and chiefly Norman in its style. It shares with the chapel of the Tower of London a claim to be the oldest church in the city. The existing church (which was not damaged in World War II) consists of the choir, transepts, and one bay of the nave; the remainder of the nave, which was probably later, was destroyed by Henry VIII. The handsome Lady chapel in decorated Gothic style was long used as a factory, but was later restored. The church was founded by Rahere, a jester of Henry I of England, who became a monk. His tomb, on the north side of the sanctuary, is of a later date than his effigy, which is placed upon it.

Bartimeus (bär.ti.mē′us). Pseudonym of **Ritchie, Sir Lewis Anselm.**

Bartle Massey (bär′tl mas′i). See **Massey, Bartle.**

Bartlett (bärt′lĕt), **Vernon.** b. at Westbury, Wiltshire, England, April 30, 1894—. An English novelist and radio broadcaster. A special correspondent (1919–22) for the London *Times*, and a regular broadcaster (1928–34) on foreign affairs, he is known as the founder and publisher of the *World Review*. Author of *Mud and Khaki* (1916), *Topsy Turvy* (1927), *No Man's Land* (1930), *If I Were Dictator* (1935), *This is My Life* (1938), and *Tomorrow Always Comes* (1943).

Bartoline Saddletree (bär′tọ.lin sad′l.trē). See **Saddletree, Bartoline.**

Bartolus (bär′tọ.lus). In John Fletcher and Philip Massinger's play *The Spanish Curate*, a greedy, unprincipled lawyer, the husband of Amaranta. He is duped by Lopez, the curate, who pretends to leave him a large fee for writing up his bogus will, and by Leandro, a young gallant, who cuckolds him.

Barton (bär′tọn), **Andrew.** d. Aug. 2, 1511. Scottish naval commander in the service of James IV of Scotland. He announced his success in clearing the Scottish coast of Flemish pirates by sending the monarch three barrels filled with pirates' heads. He obtained letters of marque (documents authorizing him to capture and confiscate vessels) against the Portuguese, but, as his capture of Portuguese

ḍ, d or j; ṣ, s or sh; ṭ, t or ch; ẓ, z or zh; *o*, F. cloche; ü, F. menu; ċh, Sc. loch; ṅ, F. bonbon.

merchantmen inflicted damage on the trade of London, he was attacked by Sir Thomas Howard and Sir Edward Howard, acting for Henry VIII of England, and killed in an engagement in the Downs, in the English Channel off the coast of Kent. The incident is celebrated in the ballad *Sir Andrew Barton.*

Barton, Bernard. [Called the **"Quaker Poet."**] b. at Carlisle, England, Jan. 31, 1784; d. at Woodbridge, England, Feb. 19, 1849. An English poet, known as a friend of Charles Lamb. Author of *Metrical Effusions* (1812), *Poems by an Amateur* (1818), and *Poems and Letters* (1849).

Barton, Elizabeth. [Called the **"Nun of Kent,"** the **"Maid of Kent."**] b. c1506; executed at Tyburn, London, April 20, 1534. An English religious figure and mystic. In 1525, while in domestic service at Aldington, Kent, she was stricken with what appeared to be a nervous illness, accompanied by religious mania and trances. She was admitted to the priory of St. Sepulchre, at Canterbury, in 1527, and began to make prophecies regarding political questions and to denounce the opponents of the Roman Catholic Church, gaining great influence even in high quarters. She inveighed against the marriage of Henry VIII with Anne Boleyn, and after the marriage declared that, like Saul in the Old Testament, Henry was no longer king in the sight of God. This caused her arrest in 1533, and she was executed at Tyburn with Edward Bocking, a Roman Catholic priest, and several others convicted of "treasonable conspiracy."

Barton, Mary. See **Mary Barton.**

Baruch (bā'ruk, bär'uk). In the Bible: **1.** A Jew who repaired a part of the wall of Jerusalem. Neh. iii.20.
2. The amanuensis and friend of Jeremiah (Jer. xxxii.13), and nominal author of the Book of Baruch in the Apocrypha.

Baruch, Book of. An apocryphal book of the Old Testament bearing the name of the friend and amanuensis of Jeremiah. It is assigned by some critics to the latter part of the Maccabean period.

Barzillai (bär.zil'ạ.ī, bär.zil'ī). The name given to the character representing James Butler, 1st Duke of Ormonde, the friend of Charles II, in John Dryden's *Absalom and Achitophel.*

Bas (bas), **William.** See **Basse** or **Bas, William.**

Bashan (bā'shạn). In Biblical geography, a district of Palestine, E of the Jordan, reaching from the river Arnon in the S to Mount Hermon on the N. At the time of the entrance of the Israelites into Canaan the whole of this region was inhabited by the Amorites. It was famous for its sheep and oxen. The fertility of the country is proverbially mentioned in the Old Testament (Deut. xxxii.14, Ps. xxii. 12, Jer. 1. 19, Micah vii. 14).

Bashaw (bạ.shô'). In Thomas Heywood's tragicomedy *The Fair Maid of the West*, a Moroccan who offers his own life to assure the escape of Spencer.

Bashford (bash'fọrd), **Henry Howarth.** b. at London, 1880—. An English novelist and physician. He was a medical officer (1933–43) with the Eng-

lish post office department, and medical adviser (1943–45) to the treasury. Author of *The Corner of Harley Street*, *The Happy Ghost*, *The Harley Street Calendar*, *Lodgings for Twelve*, and *Fisherman's Progress.*

Bashful Lover, The. A play by Philip Massinger, licensed in 1636.

Bashkirtsev (bäsh.kēr'tsif), **Marie.** b. at Gavrontsi, in the government of Poltava, Russia, Nov. 23, 1860; d. at Paris, Oct. 31, 1884. A Russian artist and author. A member of a wealthy family of the nobility, she studied painting at Paris, where she became widely known in French society. She left many studies and some finished pictures, some of which show the influence of her teacher and close friend, Jules Bastien-Lepage. Parts of her *Journal* were published in 1887 (Eng. trans., 1890), and evoked wide interest. Her *Letters* (a correspondence with Guy de Maupassant) were published in 1891.

Basilikon Doron (bạ.sil'i.kon dō'ron). [Also, **Basilicon Doron.**] A work on the divine right of kings, written by James I of England. The work, which was written by James while he was king of Scotland (as James VI), but before he ascended the throne of England, was designed to instruct his son Henry in effective methods of kingly rule, and reflects James's great irritation with what he considered to be improper assumption of authority by his ministers (hence the emphasis on "divine right" and, by extension, absolute rule by the king). The work was published in 1599; Henry, to whom it was addressed, died in 1612, before his father, and therefore never ruled.

Basilisco (bas.i.lis'kō). A boastful character in the old play *Soliman and Perseda*, by Thomas Kyd, referred to in Shakespeare's *King John.*

Basilius (bạ.sil'i.us). The Prince of Arcadia, in love with Zelmane, in Sir Philip Sidney's pastoral romance *Arcadia.*

Basilius. The lover of Quiteria in Miguel de Cervantes' *Don Quixote.* He gets her away from Camacho by a stratagem.

Basille (bä'zil), **Theodore.** Pseudonym of **Becon, Thomas.**

Basing House (bā'zing). A former residence of the Marquis of Winchester, east of Basingstoke, Southampton, England. It was destroyed (1645) by Cromwell, after a long defense by the royalists.

Baskerville (bas'kēr.vil), **John.** b. at Wolverly, Worcestershire, England, Jan. 28, 1706; d. at Birmingham, Jan. 8, 1775. An English printer and type founder. In early life he followed various pursuits (footman, stonecutter, calligrapher, teacher, and maker of japanned ware), but about 1750 he turned his attention to typography and printing, and was elected (1758) printer to the University of Cambridge for ten years. His type faces were based on those of William Caslon, then universally accepted as the best; Baskerville's designs made a distinction in thickness between upstrokes and downstrokes, and refined the serifs. In his day, although subjected to considerable ridicule, they nevertheless also found immediate supporters among thoughtful users of type, and served as models for many later innovations in type design. His fonts were sold, after his death, to Pierre Augustin Caron Beaumarchais, who used them to print a 70-volume edition of the works of Voltaire. Baskerville's own first work was a famous edition of Vergil (1757); other noted specimens of his art are editions of Milton (1758 and 1759), the Prayer-Book (1760; four editions, and others in subsequent years), Juvenal (1761), Horace (1762), the Bible (1763), and a series of Latin authors (1772–73).

Baskett (bas.ket'), **John.** d. 1742. An English printer, now chiefly remembered for his editions of the Book of Common Prayer and of the Bible (2 volumes, 1716–17; comprising the edition nicknamed the "Vinegar Bible"). The latter was so marred by typographical errors that it was promptly dubbed "a basketful of errors."

"Basketmaker," the. See **Miller, Thomas.**

Bassae (bas'ē). A place in Arcadia, Greece, near Phigalia. It is noted for its ruined temple of Apollo Epicurius, built in the second half of the 5th century B.C., probably by Ictinus, the architect of the Parthenon. It is a Doric peripteros of 6 by 15 columns, in plan 41 by 125 ft., the cella with pronaos and opisthodomos of two columns *in antis*. In the interior of the cella six piers project from each side wall, their faces formed by Ionic three-quarter columns. A portion toward the back of the cella has no piers, and has a door in the side wall facing the east; it is probable that this was the cella proper, and that the main part of the cella was merely a monumental court, open to the sky—a unique arrangement. The famous frieze, ab. 2 ft. high (often called the Phigalian Marbles; since 1814 in the British Museum), surrounded the interior of the cella, above the architrave; it is in high relief, and represents combats of Greeks with Amazons and of Lapithae with Centaurs.

Bassanes (bas'ạ.nēz). A jealous nobleman in John Ford's tragedy *The Broken Heart*. He exhibits traces of basic strength and shrewdness through a cloud of indecision and weak raving. His jealousy over Penthea, his wife, is finally resolved into a pensive understanding of the power of love.

Bassanio (bạ.sä'ni.ō). In Shakespeare's *Merchant of Venice*, a Venetian nobleman, the friend of Antonio, and Portia's successful suitor. It is on Bassanio's account that Antonio obligates himself to woo Portia.

Basse or **Bas** (bas), **William.** d. c1653. An English poet, best known for his *Epitaph on Shakespeare*, a sonnet first attributed to John Donne. His *Angler's Song* is quoted by Izaac Walton in *The Compleat Angler*.

Basset (bas'ẹt). In Shakespeare's *1 Henry VI*, a supporter of the Lancastrian (or Red Rose) faction, who quarrels with Vernon, who is on the Yorkist (or White Rose) side.

Basset. A swindler in Colley Cibber's *Provoked Husband.*

Basset-Table (bas'ẹt.tä''bl), **The.** A comedy by Susannah Centlivre, first acted in 1705, and published the next year. It is a witty treatment of the fashionable gambling habit of the day. Lady

Reveller is a gamester loved by Lord Worthy, and her imitator on a lower level is Mrs. Sago, a merchant's wife.

Bassianus (bas.i.ā'nus). In Shakespeare's *Titus Andronicus*, a brother of Saturninus and son of the late emperor of Rome. He marries Lavinia, but is murdered by Tamora's sons.

Bassino (ba.sē'nō). "The perjured husband" in Susannah Centlivre's play of that name.

Bassiolo (bas.i.ō'lō). The "gentleman usher" in George Chapman's tragicomedy of that name. In his affectations of speech, dress and the "overweening thought of his own worth" he is like Malvolio, in Shakespeare's *Twelfth Night.*

Bastard, Philip the. See **Faulconbridge, Philip.**

Bastard, The. A poem (1728) by Richard Savage, addressed by the poet to the woman he supposed to be his mother.

Bastard, William the. A name of William I (William the Conqueror), from the fact that he was born out of wedlock to a tanner's daughter. His father (by whom he was acknowledged) was Robert, Duke of Normandy.

Bastard of Orleans (ôr.lēnz'). In Shakespeare's *1 Henry VI*, the historical Jean Dunois, bastard son of Louis, Duc d'Orléans. Persuaded that Joan of Arc may be able to save France from the English, he arranges a meeting between her and the Dauphin (I.ii).

Bastille (bas.tēl'). A celebrated prison at Paris. The first stone is said to have been laid on April 22, 1370; Hugh Aubriot, provost of Paris under Charles V, is generally considered to have been the original builder. There were at first only two round towers 75 ft. high, flanking the city gate. Afterward two more were added to the north and south and a parallel line was built to the west; four others were afterward added to these. These towers were united by walls of the same height and a moat dug around the whole, forming a quadrangle, the inner court of which was 162 ft. long and 72 ft. wide. The terrors of the Bastille as a state prison reached a culmination during the ministry of Richelieu (1624–42), when François Le Clerc du Tremblay (usually referred to as Father Joseph) was commandant. In the reign of Louis XI cages of iron had been constructed, and the vaults beneath the towers, being on a level with the water in the moat, were especially dreaded. From the beginning of the French Revolution the Bastille was an especial mark for the fury of the populace. On July 14, 1789, it was attacked by a mob which, after several unsuccessful attempts, forced it to surrender. The Commandant, Bernard René Jordan de Launay, was disarmed and conducted toward the Hôtel de Ville; at the Place de Grève he was killed and his head mounted on a pike. After the first anniversary of the fall of the Bastille (July 14, 1790) the old building was razed (demolition completed May 21, 1791).

Baston (bas'tọn), **Robert.** b. near Nottingham England, toward the close of the 13th century; date of death not known. An English poet. He was a Carmelite monk, and prior of the abbey of Scarborough. He followed Edward II on a campaign to Scotland, and was captured. Author of *Metra de Illustri de Bannockburn*, a panegyric upon Robert I (Robert the Bruce) of Scotland, written at the request of the Scots.

Batavia (ba̤.tā′vi.a̤). In ancient geography, originally a name for the island of the Batavi (Insula Batavorum), then the entire region inhabited by the Batavi; later, Holland, and then the kingdom of the Netherlands.

Batchelor's Banquet, The. A pamphlet by Thomas Dekker, first published in 1603, and four or five times reprinted. It is based on an old French satire of the 15th century, *Les Quinze Joyes de Mariage*, but is so treated as to be almost an original work.

Bates (bāts), **Charley.** A cheerful young thief in the employ of Fagin, in Charles Dickens's novel *Oliver Twist*.

Bates, H. E. [Full name, **Herbert Ernest Bates.**] b. at Rushden, England, May 16, 1905—. An English novelist and author of many widely anthologized short stories. His novels include *The Two Sisters* (1926), *Charlotte's Row*, *The Poacher*, *A House of Women* (all 1936), *Spella Ho* (1938), *Fair Stood the Wind for France* (1944), and *The Scarlet Sword* (1951).

Bates, Henry Walter. b. at Leicester, England, Feb. 18, 1825; d. at London, Feb. 16, 1892. An English naturalist and traveler. In 1848 he went to the Amazon with A. R. Wallace; at first with him, and afterward alone, he traveled over all parts of the Brazilian Amazon. Returning to England in 1859, with some 8,000 new species, he published *The Naturalist on the River Amazon* (1863). He also wrote a handbook of Central and South America, and others.

Bates, John. In Shakespeare's *Henry V*, an English soldier who talks with the disguised King before the battle of Agincourt. Although wishing he were at home in England, he determines to fight bravely for the King and adjures his friend, Williams, to stop arguing with another Englishman (the disguised King) since they all will be fighting the French soon.

Bates, Miss. In Jane Austen's novel *Emma*, an old maid who loves to talk.

Bath (bàth). [Latin, **Aquae Solis** (or **Sulis**) meaning "Springs," or "Baths, of the Sun"; sometimes **Aquae Calidae**, meaning "Hot Springs."] A city and county borough in SW England, in Somersetshire, situated on the river Avon, ab. 12 mi. SE of Bristol, ab. 107 mi. W of London by rail. It is an ancient health resort, one of the leading spas of England, noted for its saline and chalybeate hot springs. In the Roman period it was an important watering place, noted for its splendid buildings, its temples, its buildings for public amusement, and still more so for its medicinal baths. Remains of the Roman bathing-houses have been discovered in the course of modern excavations. It was the site of a magnificent temple dedicated to Minerva, who is supposed to have been the patron goddess of the place. The Roman town was destroyed by the Saxons. The redevelopment of Bath in the 17th and especially in the 18th century came about in part through the influence of Richard ("Beau") Nash. The city engaged in cloth manufacture in the Middle Ages, during

which time its function as a health resort was interrupted. One of Chaucer's most noted female characters is the Wife of Bath, and the cloth industry of Bath is referred to in Chaucer's description of her in the Prologue to *The Canterbury Tales:* "Of clooth-making she hadde swiche a haunt, She passed hem of Ypres and of Gaunt." The abbey church of Bath, an excellent example of the Perpendicular style, was begun c1500. It has been called "the Lantern of England," from the number and size of its traceried windows. The plan presents a square chevet and narrow transepts. The W window is considered noteworthy, as is the restored fan-vaulting of the interior. The church is 225 ft. long, the central tower 162 ft. high. Of the Roman *thermae* five large halls remain, one of them 68 by 110 ft., and several smaller ones, with the arrangements for heating beneath the floors. One of the *piscinae* (basins) retains its ancient lining of lead.

Bath, Colonel. An inflexibly punctilious but kind-hearted character in Fielding's novel *Amelia*.

Bath, Order of the. An order of British knighthood, now conferred for outstanding services either military or civil. The "most honourable Order of the Bath" was established by George I in 1725, ostensibly as a revival of an order supposedly originated by Henry IV at his coronation in 1399. The Order of the Bath is now limited in membership to the sovereign, the royal princes, distinguished foreigners, and 55 military and 27 civil knights of the grand cross (G.C.B.), 145 military and 108 civil knights commanders (K.C.B.), and 705 military and 298 civil companions (C.B.). The officers of the Order are the dean, who is the Dean of Westminster, the Bath King of Arms, the registrar, and the usher of the Scarlet Rod. In the gradations of knighthood in Great Britain, the Order of the Bath yields precedence only to the Order of the Garter.

Bath, Wife of. See **Wife of Bath's Tale, The.**

bathos. A ludicrous descent from the elevated to the commonplace or ridiculous in writing or speech; a sinking; anticlimax. "In his fifth sonnet he [Petrarch] may, I think be said to have sounded the lowest chasm of the *Bathos*." (Macaulay, *Petrarch*.)

Bathsheba (bath.shē′ba̤, bath′shē.ba̤). In the Bible, the wife of Uriah the Hittite, loved by David; later, David's wife and the mother of Solomon. 2 Sam. xi, xii.

Bathsheba. A character in John Dryden's *Absalom and Achitophel*, intended to represent Louise Keroualle, Duchess of Portsmouth, a favorite of Charles II of England.

Bathsheba Everdene (ev′ẽr.dēn). See **Everdene, Bathsheba.**

Batrachomyomachia (bat″ra̤.ko̤.mī″o̤.mā′ki.a̤). [English, **The Battle of the Frogs and Mice.**] An ancient Greek mock epic, in hexameters, of which 316 lines are extant. Although its authorship is, at best, a matter of conjecture, it was formerly attributed to Homer, and by some critics to Pigres, brother of Artemisia, queen of Caria. It tells the story of a war between frogs and mice.

Battersea Park (bat′ĕr.sē). A modern London park, facing Chelsea Hospital. It is on the Surrey side of the Thames.

Battle (bat′l), **Mrs. Sarah.** A whist-playing old lady in Charles Lamb's *Essays of Elia.*

Battle Bridge. In old London, a locality marked by a bridge across the upper Fleet or Holborn, at what is now King's Cross; the supposed scene of a battle between Suetonius and Boadicea, or between Alfred and the Danes.

Battle of Alcazar (al.kaz′ạr), **The.** A play by George Peele, acted c1589 and printed in 1594. Under this title Peele writes of a battle fought in Barbary between Sebastian, king of Portugal, and Abdelmelek, king of Morocco, which really took place on Aug. 4, 1578, at what is now the city of Alcázarquivir, in Spanish Morocco.

Battle of Blenheim (blen′ẹm), **The.** A poem (1798) by Robert Southey (1774–1843).

Battle of Brunanburh (brö′än.bÿrċh), **The.** See **Brunanburh.**

Battle of Dorking (dôr′king), **The.** A prose work (1871) by Sir George Chesney. It was a warning, published in pamphlet form, of the German threat and possible invasion of England after the victory of Prussia over France in 1870–71. The alarm it created soon subsided and the traditional enmity with France again loomed larger than any other in the contemporary British consciousness, if only because of the intense rivalry then existing between France and England in Africa.

Battle of Hastings (hås′tingz). A tragedy written by Richard Cumberland, produced in 1778.

Battle of Hastings, The. A poem by Thomas Chatterton, written c1768. He wrote two poems of this name, the first of which he acknowledged, but perversely insisted that the second and very much longer one was by Thomas Rowley, a fictitious 15th-century monk created as a by-product of Chatterton's own imagination.

Battle of Lake Regillus (rẹ.jil′us), **The.** A poem in Macaulay's *Lays of Ancient Rome.*

Battle of Life, The. A story by Charles Dickens, published in 1846.

Battle of Maldon (môl′dẹn), **The.** See **Maldon.**

Battle of Otterbourne (ot′ẽr.bẽrn), **The.** See **Otterbourne.**

Battle of the Books. A satirical work by Jonathan Swift, written in 1697. It is his contribution to the Bentley and Boyle controversy, and his first prose composition. The literary dispute began when Charles Boyle, 4th Earl of Orrery, published *Epistles of Phalaris,* supposedly an ancient work, which Sir William Temple praised extravagantly; but Richard Bentley proved the spuriousness of the manuscript and ridiculed Temple for his admiration of the work. Swift uses satire in a mock-heroic epic to point out the foolishness of the entire issue. The ancients are challenged by the moderns, who demand that they relinquish their peaks on Parnassus, and a battle ensues in the Royal Library, where all the books are assembled. One of the outcome is conclusive for neither side. One of Swift's most famous scenes is found here, in which a spider, representing the moderns, engages in a

dispute with a bee, representing the ancients. The spider is proud because he draws all his material from his own body, while the bee gathers honey from the flowers (like scholars who draw from the ancient learning), and produces sweetness and light.

Battle of the Frogs and Mice, The. See **Batrachomyomachia.**

Battle of the Horizons, The. A novel by Sylvia Thompson, published in 1928.

Battle of the Spurs. [Also, **Battle of the Golden Spurs.**] A battle (1302) near Courtrai, Belgium, between an army representing the Flemish cities and the forces of Philip IV of France. The name derived from the quantity of gilt spurs found on the field after the struggle (which is therefore sometimes also called the Battle of the Golden Spurs). The historical background of the battle was that the Flemish weavers, being dependent on supplies of wool from England, had constrained Guy of Dampierre, who became Count of Flanders in 1280, to enter an alliance with Edward I, king of England, against the French. Philip IV (Philip the Fair) of France thereupon overran Flanders, making prisoners of Guy, his sons, and numerous nobles. The harshness of French rule caused the Flemings to rebel, and after they had massacred the French garrison at Bruges on May 19, 1302, Philip led a large punitive force into the country, but was disastrously defeated on July 11. Nevertheless, when peace was concluded in 1305, the French were able to impose severe terms because they held Count Guy and the other captives at their mercy.

Battle of the Summer Islands, The. A mock-epic poem by Edmund Waller (1606–87). It is about an ineffectual attempt by the Bermudians to capture two stranded whales.

Battles of Crescey and Poictiers (kres′i; pwä′tyā), **The.** A narrative poem (1631) by Charles Aleyn.

Baucis (bô′sis). In Greek legend, a Phrygian woman who, with her husband Philemon, showed hospitality to Zeus and Hermes when everyone else had refused them admission. They were saved from an inundation with which the country was visited by the gods, and were made priests in the temple of Zeus. Wishing to die together, they were changed at the same moment into trees. Goethe wrote a poem on this subject.

Baucis and Philemon (fi.lē′mọn, fī-). A poem by Jonathan Swift, published in 1707. It is a poetic rendering, in a new style, of Ovid's *Baucis and Philemon.* There is a savage undertone in his attitude towards the village "Pack of churlish Boors," who may be thought to represent Swift's evaluation of the bulk of mankind.

Baudelaire (bōd.ler), **Charles Pierre.** b. at Paris, April 9, 1821; d. there, Aug. 31, 1867. A French poet and critic. His only volume of verse, *Les Fleurs du Mal* (1857), exerted an influence perhaps without parallel in French literature, first on the French symbolists and later on such modern poets as Paul Valéry and T. S. Eliot. His earliest works were brochures on the art salons of 1845 and 1846, followed by brilliant essays on Eugène Delacroix, Honoré Daumier, Constantin Guys, and other artists little appreciated or completely unknown at the time. He was an ardent and early champion of Richard Wagner's music (*R. Wagner et Tannhaeuser à Paris*, 1861). His literary criticism, including articles on Victor Hugo, Théophile Gautier, and Gustave Flaubert, was collected posthumously, together with his art criticism, under the titles of *Art Romantique* and *Curiosités esthétiques* (1868–69). A treatise on excitants (*Paradis artificiels*, 1860) is, in part, an adaptation of De Quincey's *Confessions of an English Opium Eater*. Baudelaire is considered to have created a literary genre with his *Petits Poèmes en Prose* (*Spleen de Paris*), collected posthumously in 1869. His translation of the more important prose works of Edgar Allan Poe (5 vols., 1856–65) did much to establish that author's European reputation. *Fusées* and *Mon Coeur mis à nu*, often referred to under the factitious title of *Journaux intimes*, first appeared in 1887. The standard modern edition of his works is that of Jacques Crépet (Paris, 1922–50).

Baudouin (bō.dwaṅ; Anglicized, bōd'win). French form of **Baldwin**. See **Baldwin I, II, III,** and **IV.**

Baviad (bā'vi.ad), **The.** A satire on the so-called Della Cruscans, a group of English poets, by William Gifford, published in 1794, and republished (1797) with Gifford's *The Maeviad* (originally published 1795). The latter also attacked some of the minor dramatists of the time. The titles of these works have allusion to the Roman poets Bavius and Maevius, both of whom wrote against Vergil and Horace.

Bavieça (bä.вyä'thä). [Also, **Babieça.**] The favorite horse of the Cid, Spanish hero.

Bawd. In Shakespeare's *Pericles*, the wife of the Pander who keeps the brothel in Mytilene.

Bax (baks), **Clifford.** b. July 13, 1886—. An English playwright and poet. His plays include *Shakespeare* (1921, with H. F. Rubenstein), *Polly* (1923), *Mr. Pepys* (1926), *The Venetian* (1930), *The House of Borgia* (1935), and *The King and Mistress Shore* (1936). Author also of *Twenty-five Chinese Poems* (1910), *Many a Green Isle* (1927), *Pretty Witty Nell* (1932) concerning Nell Gwyn, *Farewell My Muse* (1932), *Ideas and People* (1936), and *Golden Eagle* (1946).

Baxter (baks'tėr), **Richard.** b. at Rowton, Shropshire, England, Nov. 12, 1615; d. at London, Dec. 8, 1691. An English nonconformist divine. He was ordained in 1638, was chosen lecturer at Kidderminster in 1641, and became (c1645) a chaplain in Cromwell's army. He subsequently favored the Restoration, and on the accession of Charles II in 1660 was appointed chaplain to the king, but left the Church of England on the passage of the Act of Uniformity in 1662, when he retired to Acton. In May, 1685, he was tried by George Jeffries on the charge of libeling the established church, and was fined a considerable sum, for nonpayment of which he was detained in prison until November, 1686. His chief works are *The Saint's Everlasting Rest* (1650), *A Call to the Unconverted* (1657), *Methodus Theologiae* (1674), and *Reliquiae Baxterianae* (1696).

Bayard (bā'ạrd; French, bả.yàr). A legendary horse given by Charlemagne to the four sons of Aymon. He possessed magical powers, including the remarkable facility of being able to lengthen himself so as to accommodate all four of his masters at once. He is, according to French legend, still alive in the Forest of Ardennes, where he can be heard neighing on Midsummer Day.

Bayard, Chevalier **de.** [Original name, **Pierre Terrail.**] b. near Grenoble, France, c1475; killed at the river Sesia, Italy, April 30, 1524. A French national hero, called *le chevalier sans peur et sans reproche* ("the knight without fear and without reproach"), who distinguished himself in the Italian campaigns of Charles VIII, Louis XII, and Francis I. He was especially renowned for his bravery at the battles of Guinegate (1513) and Marignano (1515), and in the defense of Mézières (1521).

Bayazid (bä.yä.zēd'). See **Bajazet I.**

Bayes (bāz). A character in the farce *The Rehearsal*, by George Villiers, 2nd Duke of Buckingham, Samuel Butler, and others. A dramatic coxcomb, the character was at first called Bilboa, and was intended to ridicule Sir Robert Howard, in the 1663 version. But the piece was laid aside for several years, and Sir Robert meanwhile became a very good friend of Buckingham. John Dryden now became the chief object of the satirical characterization, although Howard and D'Avenant, producers of heroic "operas," were also included as objects of Buckingham's ridicule. The name "Bayes" is a play on words in reference to the poet laureateship, which Dryden received in 1670 (the laureate being crowned in Greek times with bay, a type of laurel). The satirical portrait of Monmouth which Dryden made so important a part of his *Absalom and Achitophel* (1681) is usually considered to have been inspired in large part by his resentment of this satirical treatment.

Bayes's Troops, Like. A phrase referring to the foot-soldiers and hobby-horses who fight a battle in *The Rehearsal* (1671), by George Villiers, 2nd Duke of Buckingham, Samuel Butler, and others. When all are killed it is a question of how they are to go off the stage. Bayes suggests, "as they came on, upon their legs." Whereupon they are obliged to revive and walk off.

Bayeux Tapestry (bả.yė'). A strip of linen about 230 ft. long and 20 in. wide, preserved in the Museum at Bayeux, France, embroidered with episodes of the Norman conquest of England from the visit of Harold II to the Norman court until his death at Senlac, each with its title in Latin. The work is of great archaeological interest from its details of costume and arms. It is traditionally ascribed to Matilda, wife of William I (the Conqueror), but is believed by many experts to be of a somewhat later date.

Bayham (bā'ạm), **Frederick.** In Thackeray's *The Newcomes*, a young newspaperman.

Bayle (bel), **Pierre.** b. at Carlat, in Foix, France, Nov. 18, 1647; d. at Rotterdam, Dec. 28, 1706. A French rationalist philosopher and critic. He was appointed professor of philosophy at Sedan in 1675, and at the Protestant academy of Rotterdam in 1681, and was removed (because his skeptical opinions seemed to the authorities dangerously close to religious unbelief) from his professorship in 1693. He is generally considered to have been the progenitor of 18th-century rationalistic philosophy, and is known as the compiler of the famous *Dictionnaire historique et critique* (1697), in which that point of view found clear expression. Among his other works are *Cogitationes rationales de Deo, anima, et malo, Pensées sur la comète, écrites à un docteur de la Sorbonne* (1682), and *Commentaire philosophique sur ces paroles de l'Évangile* (1686). In 1684 he established a sort of journal of literary criticism, *Nouvelles de la république des lettres*, which was maintained for several years.

Bayly (bā′li), **Ada Ellen.** [Pseudonym, **Edna Lyall.**] b. at Brighton, England; d. at Eastbourne, England, Feb. 8, 1903. An English novelist. Among her works are *Won by Waiting* (1879), *Donovan* (1882), *Autobiography of a Slander* (1887), *Knight Errant* (1887), and *A Hardy Norseman* (1889).

Bayly, Thomas Haynes. b. at Bath, England, Oct. 13, 1797; d. at Cheltenham, England, April 22, 1839. An English songwriter, dramatist, and novelist. He wrote *Perfection* (1830) and other plays, many popular songs (among them *The Soldier's Tear, I'd be a Butterfly, We met—'twas in a Crowd*), and such novels as *The Aylmers* and *A Legend of Killarney*.

Baynard's Castle (bā′nardz). A strong fortification on the Thames just below Blackfriars, London, founded by Baynard, a follower of William I (the Conqueror), and forfeited to the crown by one of his successors. It was burned in the London fire of 1666.

Bayne (bān), **Peter.** b. at Fodderty, Scotland, Oct. 19, 1830; d. Feb. 12, 1896. A Scottish author and journalist. He edited newspapers at Edinburgh, Glasgow, and London. Among his works are *Christian Life* (1855), *Hugh Miller* (1871), and *Luther* (1887).

Baynes (bānz), **Charlotte.** In Thackeray's novel *The Adventures of Philip*, the daughter of General Charles Baynes and Mrs. Baynes. She is an attractive and affectionate girl, deeply in love with Philip (to whom, despite Mrs. Baynes's objections, she is eventually married).

Baynes, General Charles. In Thackeray's novel *The Adventures of Philip*, a retired officer (formerly with the British Army in India) who is the custodian of Philip's fortune, and through whose ineptitude it is lost.

Baynes, Mrs. In Thackeray's novel *The Adventures of Philip*, the domineering and socially ambitious wife of General Charles Baynes.

Baynes, Thomas Spencer. b. at Wellington, Somersetshire, England, March 24, 1823; d. at London, May 30, 1887. A British philosophical writer, appointed professor of logic, rhetoric, and metaphysics at the University of St. Andrews in 1864. He was assistant editor of the London *Daily News*, and editor of the ninth edition (1873–87) of the *Encyclopaedia Britannica*.

Bayswater (bāz′wô″tėr). That part of London lying immediately N of Kensington Gardens, in W London, in Kensington and Paddington metro-

politan boroughs. The original Bayswater was a hamlet near what is now Gloucester Terrace.

Bazzard (baz′ard). In Dickens's unfinished novel *The Mystery of Edwin Drood*, the confidential clerk of Mr. Grewgious, over whom he is able in some unexplained way to exercise very considerable power.

B.B.C. The British Broadcasting Corporation, a public corporation established by royal charter Jan. 1, 1927 to prepare, supervise, and transmit all radio programs in Great Britain. Television programs are under the Independent Television Authority established in 1954. The best B.B.C. programs are printed in *The Listener*, a weekly publication.

Beaconsfield (bē′konz.fēld), 1st Earl of. Title of **Disraeli, Benjamin.**

Beadle (bē′dl), **Harriet.** See **Tattycoram.**

Beagle (bē′gl). The ship in which Darwin made his voyage as a naturalist. She was a 10-gun brig of 235 tons, commanded by Captain Robert Fitzroy. She sailed from England on Dec. 27, 1831, and returned almost five years later, on Oct. 2, 1836, having in the meantime circumnavigated the globe. The vessel had previously been used in surveying work along the South American coast. The scientific results of the expedition given in Darwin's diary of the voyage were published as Volume III of the official *Voyage of H.M.'s Ships Adventure and Beagle*, edited by Robert Fitzroy (1839). It was issued separately later in the same year. The zoölogy and botany of the expedition were published by Darwin and assistants in eight volumes (1840–46). The definitive edition is *Charles Darwin's Diary of the Voyage of H.M.S. "Beagle,"* edited by Nora Barlow (1934).

Beagle, Sir Harry. A fox-hunting English squire in the elder George Colman's comedy *The Jealous Wife*.

Bealby (bēl′bi). A novel (1915) by H. G. Wells.

Bealtaine (bal′toin). See **Beltane.**

Beamish (bē′mish), **Beau.** In Meredith's short story *The Tale of Chloe*, one of the principal characters.

Bean (bēn), **Alice.** In Sir Walter Scott's novel *Waverley*, the daughter of Donald Bean Lean, and a person who befriends Waverley in his time of need.

Bean Lean (bēn lēn), **Donald.** In Sir Walter Scott's novel *Waverley*, a Scottish robber and Jacobite partisan. He tried in every way to compel Waverley to support the Jacobite cause, but without success. His life was ended by the hangman's noose.

Beardsley (birdz′li), **Aubrey Vincent.** b. at Brighton, England, Aug. 24, 1872; d. at Menton, France, March 16, 1898. English illustrator (in black and white) and draftsman. He had little special training and at first divided his time between business and an architect's office. From this he turned to book illustration, in which he found extensive employment. His work is full of caprices which suggest Pre-Raphaelitism, the Japanese convention, and the French art of the 18th century. Among the works which he illustrated were *Volpone*, Oscar Wilde's *Salomé*, the *Rape of the Lock*,

d̦, d or j; ş, s or sh; ţ, t or ch; ẓ, z or zh; o, F. cloche; ü, F. menu; čh, Sc. loch; n̂, F. bonbon,

and *Morte d'Arthur*. He became the art editor of the *Yellow Book* in 1894.

Bear Fell Free, The. A novel by Graham Greene, published in 1935.

beast fable. [Also: **beast epic, beast tale;** in the Middle Ages, **bestiary.**] A short tale in verse using animals for characters. In this genre, animals may take all parts or the chief parts, and are used as a medium for moral or satirical comment on human affairs. The beast fable is an ancient form. Hermogenes, in a 2nd-century Greek manual on writing, explained that beast fables were good to set before the young, to lead their minds to better measures. They should be plausible, said Hermogenes, assigning to the animals characters, qualities, and actions that befit them. If beauty is to be represented, he said, let a peacock be the symbol; if wisdom, use a fox; if animals are to imitate the actions of men in the story, choose monkeys. Aesop, the great source of animal stories, is said by Herodotus to have lived in the 6th century and to have been a slave. But the fables attributed to him are now known certainly to have been compiled from many sources. Marie de France translated them c1180, and other "Ysopets" (little Aesops) followed in French after 1200, some possibly by Anglo-Norman writers. Walter of England produced the *Anonymus Neveleti* in the late 12th century. These collections became source materials for such writers as Walter Map, in whose Latin notebooks animal stories appear. The clergy in general relied heavily on the animal allegory for sermon material, as an interesting way of pointing a moral while keeping the congregation awake.

In the Middle Ages. One of the most extraordinary creations of the medieval mind was *Le Roman du Renart* (Reynard the Fox). There were several collections of animal stories, or bestiaries, by that name brought forth in France in the 13th century. The Fox here symbolizes the clever man who deludes society, is brought to judgment, but escapes by cunning. The beast fable was current in England, too, in the 13th century. A Middle English *Bestiary* dates from about 1225, describing the habits of various animals, and applying them symbolically to various aspects of Christian doctrine. This type of animal tale produced thousands of metaphors based on a questionable zoology, which later, in the Renaissance, filled the ink-pots of the Euphuists. A beast epic that survives from the Middle English period is *The Fox and the Wolf* (c1260). Chaucer's "Nun's Priest's Tale" from *The Canterbury Tales* is a beast fable, telling of a fox who beguiled a cock by praising his father's singing, and who was himself in turn beguiled into letting the cock escape. The Scottish Chaucerian, Robert Henryson, wrote verse fables such as "The Upon-landis Mous and the Burges Mous," "The Lyoun and the Mous," and "The Wolf and the Lamb."

In Modern Times. The beast fable, amusing and useful for social or political comment, crops up over and over again in English literature. It is still a favorite type of story for children. Kipling's *Jungle Books* and *Just So Stories* have run through enough editions to testify to the longevity of the animal story. Brer Fox and Brer Rabbit of the Uncle Remus tales, animal characters thought to have a mixed African Negro and American Indian heritage, prove how popular and wide-spread is this type of tale. Occasionally a major satirical work based on animal fable still appears in English, such as the late George Orwell's amusing and terrifying barnyard fantasy, *Animal Farm*.

Beatrice (bā.ä.trē′chä). In Dante's *Vita Nuova* and *Divina Commedia*, a symbolic figure developed from the lady of Dante's love on earth, usually identified with Beatrice Portinari.

Beatrice (bē′ạ.tris). In Shakespeare's *Much Ado About Nothing*, the gay and wayward niece of Leonato, and rebellious lover of Benedick. She is a person of intrigue, gaiety, and wit. Her affair with Benedick is actually a subplot, but her character overshadows those in the main action, particularly in the scene (IV.i) where, having previously revealed her love for him to the audience, she encounters Benedick and they admit their love for each other in some of the play's best lines. She then demands with ringing indignation that Benedick kill Claudio for his false accusation of Hero (but she is the only one with enough sensitivity to see at once the falseness of the charge).

Beatrice. In John Marston's play *The Dutch Courtezan*, an innocent, modest girl, the antithesis of her gay sister Crispinella. However, her maidenly perfection is such that she is rather colorless and a chief issue of the play (namely, the contrast between the illicit love of Franceschina and the marital love of Beatrice) is blunted.

Beatrice-Joanna (bē′ạ.tris.jō.an′ạ). The heroine of Thomas Middleton and William Rowley's play *The Changeling*. She is a headstrong, unscrupulous, unobservant girl, intent on putting an unwelcome lover out of the way. She induces De Flores, whom she loathes, to murder him (expecting thus to become free to marry Alsemero, whom she loves), and is astounded when her maidenly virtue is demanded as a reward instead of money. Unable to escape De Flores, she yields. In the meantime, her wedding with Alsemero has been arranged; Beatrice-Joanna induces her maid Diaphanta to take her place on the wedding night; De Flores, intent on removing any witnesses to his crime, kills Diaphanta. When the double crime is discovered, De Flores kills Beatrice-Joanna and himself.

Beatrice Justice (bē′ạ.tris jus′tis). See **Justice, Beatrice.**

Beatrice of Venice (bē′ạ.tris). A historical novel by Sir Max Pemberton, published in 1904. Set in Venice and Verona in 1796, it includes among its characters Napoleon I, his secretary Andoche Junot, and General Jean Victor Moreau.

Beatrice Portinari (bā.ä.trē′chä pōr.tē.nä′rē). b. 1266; d. June 9, 1290. An Italian lady, celebrated by Dante chiefly in his *Vita Nuova* and also in the *Divina Commedia* (Divine Comedy). Dante first saw her, in Florence, when he was nine years old; she represented to him ideal beauty and goodness. She married Simone de' Bardi, a Florentine, sometime before 1287.

Beatrix (bē′a̦.triks). The maid and confidante of the two sisters Theodosia and Jacintha in John Dryden's comedy *An Evening's Love, or The Mock Astrologer.*

Beatrix Esmond (ez′mo̦nd). See **Esmond, Beatrix.**

Beattie (bā′ti), **James.** b. at Laurencekirk, Kincardineshire, Scotland, Oct. 23, 1735; d. at Aberdeen, Scotland, Aug. 18, 1803. A Scottish poet, essayist, and philosophical writer. He was professor of moral philosophy and logic at Marischal College, Aberdeen. An opponent of David Hume, he advocated a philosophy of common sense. He wrote *Original Poems and Translations* (1761), *Judgment of Paris* (1765), *The Minstrel* (1771–74), *Essay on the Nature and Immutability of Truth* (1770), *Dissertations* (1783), and *Elements of Moral Science.*

Beau and the Lady, The. One of five historical narratives in *The Gallants* (1927), by Lily Adams Beck, writing under the pseudonym E. Barrington.

Beau Beamish (bē′mish). See **Beamish, Beau.**

Beau Brummell (brum′e̦l). See **Brummell, George Bryan.**

Beau Brummel, the King of Calais (ka.lā′). A play by William Blanchard Jerrold, produced at the Lyceum Theatre, on April 11, 1859. A play called *Beau Brummell* by Clyde Fitch was also produced at New York in 1891 by Richard Mansfield. George Bryan Brummell, called "Beau" Brummell, was a celebrated London dandy of the 18th century.

Beauchamp (bē′cha̦m), **Richard de.** See under **Warwick, Earl of.**

Beauchamp, Viscount. A title given by the Jacobites to Sir Frederick Vernon in Sir Walter Scott's novel *Rob Roy.*

Beauchamp's Career. A novel by George Meredith, serialized in 1875 and published in book form in 1876. A work with a political theme, it deals with the career of Nevil Beauchamp, whose radical views and love affairs furnish the chief interest of the novel. He was drawn from one of Meredith's friends, and the program of state control, universal suffrage, limitation of private wealth, and provision for future generations is that of the radicals of the period.

Beau Didapper (bō dī′dap.e̦r). See **Didapper, Beau.**

Beaufort (bō′fo̦rt). The family name of a number of historical figures who appear in Shakespeare's plays. For the two Edmund Beauforts, 2nd and 4th Dukes of Somerset, and for John Beaufort, Earl of Somerset, see the entries at **Somerset;** for Henry Beaufort, who was Bishop of Winchester and a cardinal, see **Winchester;** for Sir Thomas Beaufort, Duke of Exeter, see **Exeter.**

Beaugard (bō′gärd), **Captain.** The principal character in Thomas Otway's *The Soldier's Fortune* and its sequel *The Atheist.*

Beaugard, Old. A wild, extravagant man, father of Captain Beaugard in *The Atheist,* by Thomas Otway.

Beau Geste (bō′ zhest′). A novel by P. C. Wren, published in 1924. It deals with the adventures in the French Foreign Legion of a dashing young Englishman and his brothers, accused of a crime which they did not commit, but loyal to each other and to their family to the end. It has been widely popular as a book, play, and film.

Beau Ideal (bō ī.dē′a̦l). A novel by P. C. Wren, published in 1928. Like its predecessor, *Beau Geste* (which it never approached in popularity), it is a story of adventure in the French Foreign Legion.

Beaujeu (bō.zhė̇). A historical novel by Henry Christopher Bailey, published in 1905. It is set against a background of London and Oxford in the late 17th century.

Beaumains (bō.mānz′). In Malory's *Morte d'Arthur,* the sobriquet of Sir Gareth, given to him by Sir Kay because of the size of his hands.

Beaumanoir (bō.ma.nwär′), **Sir Lucas de.** In Sir Walter Scott's novel *Ivanhoe,* the grand master of the Knights Templar. He seizes Rebecca and tries her as a witch.

Beaumarchais (bō.mär.shā′; French, bō.mȧr.she), **Pierre Augustin Caron de.** b. at Paris, Jan. 24, 1732; d. there, May 18, 1799. A French polemic writer and dramatist. He was the seventh child of Charles Caron, a master clockmaker. After an elementary schooling, he joined his father in the trade. Subsequently he assumed the name of Beaumarchais, in accordance with a usage prevalent in France during that century. His claim to the invention of a new escapement in clockwork being disputed, young Caron appealed to the Academy of Sciences and to public opinion, thereby attracting also the attention of the court. On the death in 1770 of the financier Duverney, who had taken Beaumarchais into partnership, a question of inheritance occasioned litigation. Beaumarchais conducted his own case, and to vindicate himself published (1774–75) four *Mémoires* replete with wit and eloquence, which made him famous. In the meantime, his attempts to write for the stage, *Eugénie* and *Les Deux Amis, ou le négociant de Lyon,* had been failures. Moreover, *Le Barbier de Séville* (which was to bring him fame as a dramatist) waited two years to be presented to the public, and the first performance, on Feb. 23, 1775, was not very successful. He subsequently altered and greatly improved it. *Le Mariage de Figaro,* begun in 1775 and completed in 1778, was suppressed for four years by the censure of Louis XVI. It was given for the first time on April 27, 1784, and was immediately successful. During the war of American independence, Beaumarchais sent to the U. S. a fleet of his own, carrying a cargo of weapons and ammunition for the American colonists. His poverty during the latter part of his life was largely due to the difficulty he experienced in recovering payment for this from the U. S. He also spent a great deal of money in the publication of a 70-volume edition of the works of Voltaire, which he brought out in 1785–90. Beaumarchais is the hero of one of Goethe's plays, *Clavigo.*

Beaumelle (bō.mel′). In *The Fatal Dowry* by Nathaniel Field and Philip Massinger, the daughter of Rochfort, the chief justice of Dijon, and wife of Charalois. When she commits adultery, her husband has her brought before her blindfolded father to receive sentence, and he unknowingly orders death, which Charalois inflicts upon her.

d̦, d or j; ș, s or sh; ț, t or ch; z̦, z or zh; o, F. cloche; ü, F. menu; c̆h, Sc. loch; n̦, F. bonbon.

Beaumont (bō′mont). In Shakespeare's *Henry V*, a French lord.

Beaumont, Francis. b. at Grace-Dieu, Leicestershire, England, c1584; d. March 6, 1616. An English dramatist and poet. He was educated at Broadgates Hall, Oxford, but took no degree and entered (1600) the Inner Temple, where apparently he did not pursue his legal studies. In 1602 he published *Salmacis and Hermaphroditus*, a poem after Ovid. His most important non-dramatic poem, an epistle to the Countess of Rutland written in 1612, appeared after his death. His connection with the stage began c1606, possibly through Michael Drayton. His first play *The Woman Hater* was in the style of Jonson and, according to Dryden, he submitted all his writings to Jonson's censure. From 1607 to 1611 his commendatory poems were prefixed to several of Jonson's plays. His close personal and literary intimacy with John Fletcher dated from 1608 or 1609. Actually the famous collaboration covered some half dozen plays, as far as can be proven, but the folios of 1647 and 1679 had the names of both men on 53 plays, in which the greater part was work by Fletcher alone or with only minor portions by Beaumont. In 1613 Beaumont produced *A Masque for the Inner Temple*, and about that time he married Ursula, daughter of Henry Isley of Sundridge in Kent. Beaumont is buried in Westminster Abbey.

Beaumont, Sir John. b. probably at Grace-Dieu, Leicestershire, England, 1583; d. April 19, 1627. An English poet; brother of Francis Beaumont. He wrote poetical works including *Metamorphosis of Tobacco* (1602) and *Bosworth Field* (1629).

Beau Nash (bō′ nash′). A three-act comedy in prose by Douglas Jerrold, produced at the Haymarket Theatre, London, and published in 1825. Richard Nash, called "Beau" Nash, was in real life an 18th-century dandy, master of ceremonies at Bath.

Beau Nash. See also **Nash, Richard.**

Beaurepaire (bō′rẹ.pār). In Arthurian legend, the castle where Blanchefleur, imprisoned, is delivered by Sir Perceval.

Beau Sabreur (bō′ sa.brẻr′). A novel by P. C. Wren, published in 1926. It is a sequel to his popular *Beau Geste* (1924).

Beau's Duel, or A Soldier for the Ladies, The. A comedy by Susannah Centlivre, produced and printed in 1702. It was in part based on Jasper Mayne's *City Match*.

Beau Tibbs (bō′ tibz′). See **Tibbs, Beau.**

Beauties of English Poesy, The. A compilation (2 vols., 1767) by Oliver Goldsmith.

Beautiful Years, The. An autobiographical novel by Henry Williamson, published in 1921. It is the first volume of a tetralogy under the general title *The Flax of Dream.*

Beauty and the Beast. [French title, **La Belle et la bête** (là bel ā là bet).] A story in which a daughter (Beauty), Zémire, to save her father's life, becomes the guest of a monster (Azor, or the Beast), who, by his kindness and intelligence, wins her love, whereupon he regains his original form, that of a handsome young prince. The original French version was published in 1757. It probably derived its plot from Giovanni Straparola's *Piacevoli Notti*, a collection of the Italian stories published in 1550. There have been many English versions, of which one of the most noteworthy is that by Anne Isabella Ritchie, daughter of W. M. Thackeray. The story gave Grétry the subject for his opera *Zémire and Azor* and was recently the subject (although so greatly altered from the original as to be virtually unrecognizable) for Jean Cocteau's film *La Belle et la bête.*

Beaux' Stratagem, The. A comedy by George Farquhar, produced March 8, 1707. Considered by many to be his best play, it tells its story with ease and high spirits. The fortune hunters, Archer and Aimwell, win the audience's sympathies and their success, though somewhat accidental, is most pleasing. Lady Bountiful, with relatively few lines, lives perfectly as a type, and so do other minor persons. In style it is close to Congreve, although the characters of Archer and Aimwell show a tendency toward sentimental comedy.

Beazley (bēz′li), **Samuel.** b. at London, 1786; d. at Tunbridge Castle, Kent, England, Oct. 12, 1851. An English architect and dramatist, noted as a designer of theaters, including the St. James, the City of London, part of the Adelphi, and the colonnade of the Drury Lane. He wrote a number of comic operas, operettas, farces, and one melodrama, *Ivanhoe* (1820), based on Scott's novel.

Beck (bek), **Lily Adams.** [Pseudonyms: **E. Barrington** and **Louis Moresby**.] d. at Kyoto, Japan, Jan. 3, 1931. English romantic novelist, traveler, and mystic; daughter and granddaughter of two British admirals, John Moresby and Sir Fairfax Moresby. Before 1919 she traveled with her father in India, Ceylon, China, Java, Egypt, Japan, and Burma; from 1919 to 1930, she lived in Canada, and resided in Japan from 1930 until her death. Writing under three names, she was the author of a large body of miscellaneous work; as Louis Moresby she wrote works on the East, *The Treasure of Ho* (1924), *The Glory of Egypt* (1926), *Rubies* (1927), and *Captain Java* (1928); as L. Adams Beck she was the author of *The Ninth Vibration and Other Stories* and *The Key of Dreams* (both 1922), *Perfume of the Rainbow* (1923), *Dreams and Delights* (1926), *Story of Oriental Philosophy* (1928), *Joyous Story of Astrid* (1931), and *A Beginner's Book of Yoga* (1937); as E. Barrington she wrote a series of historical romantic novels and stories, among them *The Ladies!* (1922, which includes the tales "My Lady Mary," "The Golden Vanity," and "A Bluestocking at Court"), *The Chaste Diana* (1923), *The Divine Lady* (1924), *Glorious Apollo* (1925), *The Exquisite Perdita* (1926), *The Thunderer* (1927), *The Gallants* (1927, a volume of historical tales, including "The King and the Lady," "Her Majesty's Godson," "The Prince's Pawns," "The Pious Coquette," and the "Beau and the Lady"), *The Empress of Hearts* (1928), *The Laughing Queen* (1929), *The Irish Beauties* (1931), and *Anne Boleyn* (1932).

Beck, Madame. One of the principal characters in Charlotte Brontë's novel *Villette.*

Becket (bek′ẹt). A tragedy (1879) by Alfred Tennyson. It was the last in a series of three, the other two being *Queen Mary* (1875) and *Harold* (1877), in which Tennyson sought to dramatize the story of "the Making of England." Of these plays, only *Becket* had a successful run and then only after it had been much revised by Sir Henry Irving.

Becket, Thomas à.   See **Thomas à Becket.**

Beckford (bek'fọrd), **Peter.** b. at Stapleton, Dorsetshire, England, 1740; d. there, Feb. 18, 1811. An English sportsman, author of hunting treatises, and student of classical and modern literature. His works include *Thoughts upon Hare and Fox Hunting: also an Account of the most Celebrated Dog Kennels in the Kingdom* (1781), historically important as the first English work to give a complete and accurate account of the sport, *Essays on Hunting, containing a Philosophical Inquiry into the Nature and Properties of Scent, on Different Kinds of Hounds, Hares, etc., with an Introduction describing the Method of Hare-hunting among the Greeks* (1781), and *Familiar Letters from Italy to a Friend in England* (2 vols., 1805), an account of his travels in 1787, during which he met Voltaire, Jean Jacques Rousseau, and Laurence Sterne.

Beckford, William. b. at Fonthill, Wiltshire, England, Sept. 29, 1759; d. May 2, 1844. An English man of letters, connoisseur, and collector. He was for many years a member of Parliament, but is best known as the author of *Vathek* (1784), an Oriental tale written in French. He wrote also *Letters* (1834), and two burlesques, *The Elegant Enthusiast* (1796) and *Amezia* (1797). His villa at Fonthill, upon which he expended more than a million dollars, was famous in its day as an instance of eccentric extravagance and fanciful splendor.

Becky Sharp (bek'i shärp').   See **Sharp, Becky.**

Becon (bē'kon), **Thomas.** [Pseudonym, *Theodore Basille.*] b. in Norfolk, England, c1511; d. at London, 1567. An English ecclesiastic and writer. He was for a time a supporter of the Reformation in books written under the name of Theodore Basille, the doctrines of which, however, he was obliged to recant. He was chaplain to Lady Jane Seymour and to Thomas Cranmer under Edward VI, and rector of Saint Stephen's, Wallbrook. His best-known work is *The Governaunce of Vertue.*

Beddoes (bed'ŏz), **Thomas Lovell.** b. at Clifton, England, July 20, 1803; d. at Basel, Switzerland, Jan. 26, 1849. An English poet and physician and anatomist. His early poems *The Improvisatore* (1821) and *The Bride's Tragedy* (1822), which he published while an Oxford undergraduate, met with no success. Isolated from English literary society and influenced by a profound melancholy which made him skeptical of the value of literary effort, he published no more works. His most famous work, *Death's Jest-Book, or the Fool's Tragedy* (1850), was begun about 1825 and for almost a quarter of a century he tinkered with it, revising, deleting, and expanding. A selection from the mass of Beddoes' writings (*Poems*) was published (1851) posthumously by a devoted friend, Thomas Kelsall. In youth Beddoes was one of the earliest admirers of Shelley. Beddoes' fondness for sinister and spectral imagery probably owes some-

thing to Shelley but he was also influenced by tales of terror and Jacobean tragedies, for Beddoes was at the very center of the Elizabethan revival. Beddoes was aware of the new scientific speculation and experiment in the dim regions of physiology and psychology. He was the first among the English poets to use the discoveries of paleontology as material for poetry and there are passages in his poetry that suggest that he believed in the evolution of the species. Beddoes is memorable for scattered lines and passages, cadences of haunting beauty, and images of arresting grandeur.

Bede (bēd). [Also: **Baeda, Beda** (bē'da̧); called "**Baeda Venerabilis,**" meaning the "**Venerable Bede.**"] b. at or near Jarrow, Durham, England, c673; d. there, May 26, 735. An English historian, theologian, and scientist, considered to have been the greatest master of chronology in the Middle Ages. Probably the most learned Western European scholar of his period, he is generally assumed to have been the father of English history. He was educated at the monastery of Saint Peter's (at Wearmouth, now called Sunderland) and that of Saint Paul's (at Jarrow), where he spent the rest of his life. (Both Wearmouth and Jarrow were small towns in the NE part of England, near to Newcastle and to each other; some sources, for this reason, and because Bede's own statement in the matter is anything but explicit, cite Wearmouth as Bede's place of birth.) He was ordained a deacon in his 19th year, and became a priest 11 years later. The greater part of his life, however, was spent in teaching and writing rather than in carrying out what are now ordinarily thought of as priestly duties (this was not unusual, of course, in the time of Bede, when virtually all of European scholarship was confined to the monasteries). He understood Greek and had some acquaintance with Hebrew (in addition, obviously, to Latin). His main work, *Historia ecclesiastica gentis Anglorum* (The Ecclesiastical History of the English People), has been for centuries invaluable to historians concerned with the sequence of events in England between the latter part of the 6th century and 731 (the year in which Bede completed it). The work actually covers a much greater span of time than this, going back to the conquest by the Romans (Pliny and other Roman authorities, as well as such earlier British scholars as Gildas, are drawn upon as sources), but modern historiographers discount its worth in these earlier portions because of Bede's credulity with regard to legend, visions, unauthenticated miracles, and the like. As a piece of literature this work is also important; the story (*The Conversion of Edmund*) of the likening by a Northumbrian convert to Christianity of a man's life to the flight of a small bird from darkness and cold through a warm, lighted hall and thence again into darkness was later to be the subject of a sonnet by Wordsworth and to have its echo in Tennyson ("From the great deep to the great deep he goes"). His other historical and biographical works include *Historia abbatum*, concerning the abbots of the monasteries at Wearmouth and Jarrow, and biographies of various outstanding figures in the Church. His *De natura rerum* is concerned with the physical sciences, as they were understood in his day, and

ḍ, d or j; ṣ, s or sh; ṭ, t or ch; ẓ, z or zh; o, F. cloche; ü, F. menu; ċh, Sc. loch; ṅ, F. bonbon.

is based chiefly on Pliny and Isidore of Seville. It deals with various phenomena, which are referred to natural causes; for example, the earth is a sphere surrounded by a watery heaven. The *De loquela per gestum digitorum* (or *De indigitatione*) is our main source for the study of medieval finger-reckoning or symbolism. One of the most important of Bede's works on arithmetic and chronology is *De temporum ratione*. This work contains a remarkable theory of tides based upon Pliny, and also upon personal observation (Bede was curiously close to modern science and scholarship in the matter of making actual observations, where possible, and of citing his sources). The first collected edition of Bede's writings appeared at Paris in 1544–45, and was reprinted in 1554. Both of these editions are now extremely rare. The latest edition is in two volumes, edited by Charles Plummer, and published in 1896. English translations have appeared often in the past several centuries, one of the most recent having been made in 1870.

Bede, Adam. The principal character in George Eliot's novel of the same name, a young carpenter, a keen and clever workman, somewhat sharp-tempered, and with a knowledge of some good books. He has an alert conscience, good common sense, and "well-balanced shares of susceptibility and self-control." He loves Hetty Sorrel, but finally marries Dinah Morris. He is said to be in part a portrait of George Eliot's father.

Bede, Cuthbert. Pseudonym of **Bradley, Edward.**

Bede, Lisbeth. The mother of Adam and Seth in George Eliot's novel *Adam Bede.*

Bede, Seth. The tender-hearted brother of Adam, in George Eliot's novel *Adam Bede.* He loves Dinah Morris, but yields her to his brother.

Bede's Death Song. See **Death Song.**

Bedford (bed′fọrd), **Duke of.** See under **Lancaster, Prince John of.**

Bedford Coffee House. A coffee house which formerly stood in Covent Garden, London, a resort of David Garrick, Samuel Foote, Henry Fielding, and others.

Bedford House. A mansion formerly standing in Belgrave Square, London: the residence of the Duke of Bedford.

Bedivere (bed′i.vir), **Sir.** In the Arthurian cycle of romance, a knight of the Round Table. It was he who brought the dying Arthur to the barge which bore him to Avalon.

Bedlam (bed′lạm). The hospital of Saint Mary of Bethlehem (slurred in popular usage in Middle English to "Bethlem" or "Bedlem," and thence to "Bedlam") at London, originally a priory (founded c1247), but afterward used as an asylum for lunatics. Mention is made of it in Dekker and Middleton's *The Honest Whore.* It has been known in modern times as the Bethlehem Royal Hospital, and its facilities were moved (1930) from their original location in Lambeth, a densely populated borough of London, to the suburban community of Croydon.

Bed of Roses, A. A novel by W. L. George, published in 1911. It shows the same heightened interest in sex and its problems that marks his *Second Blooming* (1914) and *Blind Alley* (1919).

Bedouin Tribes of the Euphrates (bed′ö.in; ū.frā′tēz). A travel book (1879) by Lady Anne Blunt. In it she recounts the journeys on which she accompanied her husband, Wilfrid Scawen Blunt.

Bedreddin Hassan (bed.red.dēn′ has′ạn). The son of Noureddin Ali in *The Arabian Nights' Entertainments.* His identity is discovered by the superiority of the cheesecakes which he makes.

Bee, The. An English periodical which first appeared on Oct. 6, 1759; only eight weekly numbers were published. Oliver Goldsmith was the author of nearly all the essays.

Beeding (bē′ding), **Francis.** [Joint pseudonym of the English authors **John Palmer** and **Hilary Aidan St. George Saunders.**] Under this name they wrote many mystery and adventure novels, including *The Seven Sleepers* (1925), *The Little White Hag* (1926), *The Six Proud Walkers* (1928), *Pretty Sinister* (1929), *The Three Fishers* (1931), *Death Walks in Eastrepps* (1931), *The Nine Waxed Faces* (1936), *The Ten Holy Horrors* (1939), *Eleven Were Brave* (1941), and *Twelve Disguises* (1942).

Beefeaters or **Beef Eaters.** In English history, a name given to the Yeomen of the Guard, whose function it has been, ever since 1485, when they first appeared in the coronation procession of Henry VII, to attend the sovereign at banquets and other state occasions. The warders of the Tower of London are also sometimes called Beefeaters, 15 having been sworn in as Yeomen Extraordinary of the Guard during the reign of Edward VI. The uniform differs slightly, the Tower warders having no cross-belt; both groups wear flat hats, red, frogged coats, and breeches.

Beefington (bē′fing.tọn), **Milor.** A fictitious English nobleman exiled by royal tyranny before the granting of the Magna Charta. He is introduced in *The Rovers,* a verse printed in the *Anti-Jacobin,* a periodical established in 1797 by George Canning with the purpose of ridiculing the French Revolution, its doctrines, and its sympathizers in England.

Beefsteak Club. An English club founded in the reign of Queen Anne (it was called a "new society" in 1709), believed to be the earliest club with this name. It was composed of the "chief wits and great men of the nation" and its badge was a gridiron. The "Society of Beefsteaks," established some years later, which has been confused with this, scorned being called a club: they designated themselves "the Steaks." "The Sublime Society of the Steaks" was founded at Covent Garden Theatre in 1735. It is said to have originated in a dinner taken by Charles Mordaunt, 3rd Earl of Peterborough, with John Rich, the manager, in his private room at the theater. The latter cooked a beefsteak so appetizingly that Lord Peterborough proposed repeating the entertainment the next Saturday at the same hour. After the fire at Covent Garden in 1808 the Sublime Society met at the Bedford Coffee House, whence they removed to the Old Lyceum in 1809. When this was burned in 1830, they returned to the Bedford. When the Lyceum Theatre was rebuilt in 1838, a magnificent and appropriate room was provided for them, and

fat, fāte, fär, àsk, fāre; net, mē, hèr; pin, pīne; not, nōte, mŏve, nôr; up, lūte, pùll; ₮H, then;

they met there until 1867, when the dwindling society was dissolved. A Beefsteak Club was established (c1749) at the Theatre Royal, at Dublin, by Richard Brinsley Sheridan, with Peg Woffington as its president. There were also other clubs of the kind, one of the most recent being that founded by J. L. Toole, an English actor, in 1876.

Beelzebub (bē̱.el′zē̱.bub). [Also, **Belzebub**.] A name given to a god of the Philistines, who had a famous temple at Ekron. The name is ordinarily explained as having been a compound of "Baal" with "zebub," to mean, literally, "lord of flies." For obvious political as well as theological reasons, his worship was abhorrent to the Jews, and it was probably originally through them that the name became one of the appellations of the Devil.

Beelzebub. In demonology, one of the Gubernatores (rulers) of the Infernal Kingdom, under Lucifer.

Beelzebub. In Milton's *Paradise Lost*, one of the fallen angels, second only to Satan himself.

Beerbohm (bir′bōm), Sir **Max.** b. at London, Aug. 24, 1872; d. at Rapallo, Italy, May 20, 1956. An English writer, critic, and caricaturist. He studied at Oxford, living later (1910 *et seq.*) at Rapallo, Italy. He was successor (1898) to George Bernard Shaw as dramatic critic on the *Saturday Review*, at London. His caricature portraits of contemporary literary and political figures have been collected in *Twenty-five Gentlemen* (1896), *The Poet's Corner* (1904), *Rossetti and His Circle* (1922), and *Observations* (1925). He was knighted in 1939. His first publication was *The Works of Max Beerbohm* (1896). His only novel, *Zuleika Dobson* (1911), is a satirical account of a visit to Oxford University by a beautiful woman, and her effect upon the students; in *A Christmas Garland* (1912) he presents a series of parodies of contemporary writers; his essay collections include *The Happy Hypocrite* (1897), *More* (1899), *And Even Now* (1920), *Variety of Things* (1928), and *Mainly on the Air* (1947). Author also of *Seven Men* and *The Dreadful Dragon of Hay Hill*.

Beersheba (bir.shē′ba̱, bir′shē̱.ba̱). A town at the southern extremity of Palestine. Neh. xi.27. See **Dan.**

Beethoven (bā′tō.ve̱n), **Ludwig van.** b. at Bonn, Prussia, probably Dec. 16, 1770 (although through some confusion in the birth registry, Beethoven himself believed for a time that he was born in 1772); d. at Vienna, March 26, 1827. A German composer, considered by many to have been the greatest composer in the history of music. He was the eldest surviving son of a tenor singer attached to the chapel of the electoral archbishop of Cologne, in a family which may be traced to a 17th century origin in a village near Louvain, Belgium (hence the "van" in his name; it is not a sign of nobility, as some have thought). The father had some knowledge of both violin and piano, and gave Ludwig lessons on both. In 1778 the teaching was taken over by the court organist, in 1779 by a singer (and friend of his father) newly arrived from Berlin, and some two years after this by Christian Gottlieb Neefe, successor as court organist to Beethoven's first teacher. Neefe was a very competent musician, composer, and director; that he recognized the talent of his young pupil is evidenced by a statement he published in 1783: "This young genius deserves help, to enable him to travel. He will certainly be a second Mozart, if he goes on as he has begun." From this time until 1792 Beethoven filled various positions, including that of teacher, court organist, and (in orchestra rehearsals) a place at the piano which was equivalent at that time to the position of conductor today. In November, 1792, Beethoven was sent at the elector's expense to study music under Haydn at Vienna. It was in this city, in 1795, that he may be said to have begun what is often called "the First Period" of his career as a composer, and from that time on each year brought wider recognition of his greatness. In 1802 his deafness, which had caused him some trouble since c1798, began to be really serious. In 1814 lawsuits and other anxieties commenced, and these difficulties on top of his deafness (which was by that time total), clouded all his later years. An attempt to conduct in 1822 proved a complete failure, and in 1824 occurred one of the most pathetic and moving incidents in the history of any composer's life: at the close of the first performance of his great Ninth Symphony, the audience broke into a storm of applause which shook the concert hall; however, Beethoven, who had shared the platform with the conductor, was now so deaf he could not hear it, and had to be turned around to see with his eyes the acclaim his ears could no longer detect. Two years later, on Dec. 2, 1826, his last illness began.

The First Period. This span of Beethoven's career as a composer is generally accepted as extending from 1795, the year of the three Trios dedicated to Haydn, until the end of 1802, when the *Pastoral* Sonata and the String Quintet (Op. 29) appeared, and the Violin Sonatas (Op. 30) were in course of publication. Beethoven still showed at the beginning of this period little indication of the enormous impact he was to have on music; the first unmistakable revelation of the revolutionary Beethoven is found in the *Sonate Pathétique*. Familiarity has blinded many of us to the originality of this work, but at the time of its composition this was evident to all. With the six String Quartets (Op. 18) we see a sureness and imagination so obvious that there can no longer be question of dependence on the past, and the certainty of mind which he had now acquired gave him the courage to attempt the more crucial task of writing a symphony. In the First Symphony (Op. 21) we have the first of those nine universally acclaimed works which provide the surest evidence of Beethoven's greatness.

The Second Period. This period is usually considered to have begun with Op. 31. It includes by far the greater volume of his whole work, and represents him at the very height of his confidence in his revolutionary principles of music. The Second Symphony (Op. 36) was finished before the end of 1802 and belongs to the period of transition, but the Third Symphony (the *Eroica*, Op. 55), finished in August, 1804, is wholly representative not only of the second period but of the prophet of the new faith. (It is this symphony which was, according to most accounts, originally dedicated to Napoleon. The story is told that when Beethoven heard that Napoleon had so completely surrendered his democratic ideals as to have himself proclaimed emperor, he (Beethoven) tore off the title page in a fury, saying: "He is no better than other men.") The Fourth Symphony (Op. 60), completed in 1806, is one of the most serene of Beethoven's works, but now also one of the least popular of his symphonies with most listeners. The Fifth Symphony (Op. 67), which was begun in 1805 and finished in 1808, is unquestionably the most popular orchestral work ever written. So far as it may be characterized in the few words which space here permits, it may be said that it represents a more kinetic, affirmative sense of exalted human purpose even than the *Eroica*. (It gained in modern times, during World War II, even greater currency through the use of its opening phrase as a radio signal used by the Allies to reach the various underground movements on the Continent.) The *Pastoral* Symphony (Op. 68) is the sixth of Beethoven's symphonic works, and expresses his deep love of nature. The Seventh Symphony (Op. 92), completed in 1812, is perhaps the most enigmatic of Beethoven's symphonic works. It is now generally considered to indicate the changing mental attitude of the composer in the year of its composition, and this is confirmed to some extent by the Eighth Symphony (Op. 93), which was also written in 1812, and which reveals a subject or idea clearly no longer epic in breadth.

The Third Period. In 1812 there occurred a very definite change in Beethoven's creative activity, which may be attributable in large part to personal difficulties of various kinds. However, it was in this third and last period that he produced the Ninth Symphony (Op. 125), employing some six years (1817–23) to complete what was for the composer perhaps the most important project of his life. The *Finale* of this work, for the first time since the symphony had become a purely instrumental form, employs a chorus; and the text is that of Schiller's *Ode to Joy*, which Beethoven had determined many years before, while still a boy at Bonn, to set someday to music. The first three movements are in the nature of a prologue to this imposing *Finale*. There has been much debate as to the success of this last movement. Undoubtedly Beethoven demands too much of the voices; undoubtedly the movement is too long. But when all is said and done, the symphony remains still the most colossal effort of its kind in the 19th century, and an eloquent revelation of the undying human sympathies of its creator. However, many critics believe that the noblest music of all is to be found in the last Quartets (Op. 130 to 135), in which the whole later development of 19th-century music seems to be foreshadowed. That freedom of form toward which Beethoven was striving in the last Piano Sonatas seems in these works to be fully attained. Each idea seems to create its own form; and while the listener's effort in adjusting his expectations to a constantly changing musical order is at first so great that the music seems hardly intelligible, repeated experience only increases our certainty that in these Quartets Beethoven has attained

the highest ambition of the creative artist: to make form and thought indissoluble.

Beetle (bē'tl). In Rudyard Kipling's *Stalky and Co.*, one of the three boys about whom the stories revolve. He is generally considered to be an autobiographical portrait of the author during his school days (Kipling spent several years in a school in Devon during his boyhood).

Befana (bā.fä'nä), **the.** In Italian folklore, an old woman who is a sort of Santa Claus, but sometimes also a means of frightening children who have misbehaved. She is the good fairy who fills the children's stockings with presents on Twelfth Night, or the feast of the Epiphany, Jan. 6. If the children have been naughty she fills the stockings with ashes or coals; but she is compassionate, and will sometimes relent and return to comfort the little penitents with gifts. Tradition says that she was too busy sweeping to come to the window to see the Three Wise Men of the East when they passed by on their way to offer homage to the newborn Saviour, but said she could see them when they came back. For this lack of reverence she was duly punished, as they went back another way and she has been watching ever since. At one time her effigy was carried about the streets on the eve of the Epiphany, but the custom has now fallen into disuse. She has also sometimes been used as a bugbear by Italian mothers. The name is a corruption of *Epiphania* (Epiphany), the feast on which she makes her appearance.

Before the Bombardment. A novel by Sir Osbert Sitwell, published in 1926.

Beg (beg), **Callum.** A minor character in Sir Walter Scott's novel *Waverley*, the foot-page of Fergus MacIvor, in the service of Waverley.

Begbie (beg'bi), **Harold.** [Pseudonym, **A Gentleman With a Duster.**] b. at Fornham St. Martin, Suffolk, England, 1871; d. Oct. 8, 1929. An English novelist, journalist, and biographer. He was at various times on the staffs of the *Daily Chronicle*, *Globe*, *Times*, and *Daily Mail*. Author of *The Handy Man* (1900), *The Fall of the Curtain* (1901), *Master Workers* (1905), *The Priest* (1906), *The Cage* (1909), *Broken Earthenware* (1909; American title, *Twice-Born Men*, 1910), *Souls in Action* (1911), *The Distant Lamp* (1912), *The Ordinary Man and the Extraordinary Thing* (1912), *The Rising Dawn* (1913), *The Ways of Laughter* (1921), *Punishment and Personality* (1927), *Black Rent* (1928), and biographies of Kitchener (1915) and William Booth (1920). Other novels by him are *The Vigil* (1907), *The Challenge* (1911), *Millstone* (1915), and *The Convictions of Christopher Sterling* (1919); as "A Gentleman With a Duster" he wrote *Mirrors of Downing Street* (1920), *The Glass of Fashion* (1921), *The Conservative Mind* (1924), *The Great World* (1925), *The Howling Mob* (1927), an attack on democracy, and two novels, *Julius* (1927) and *The Laslett Affair* (1928). *Fighting Lines* (1914) is a volume of poetry, and *Painted Windows* (1922) contains studies of contemporary religious figures.

Beggar of Bethnal Green (beth'nạl), **The.** A comedy by J. Sheridan Knowles, produced in 1834. It was abridged from *The Beggar's Daughter of*

Bethnal Green (1828), which was based on a popular ballad.

Beggar's Bush, The. A tragicomedy by John Fletcher and Philip Massinger, performed at court in 1622 and printed in 1647. It was long popular. Several alterations have appeared: one, *The Royal Merchant*, an opera, in 1767, and another in 1815, under the title of *The Merchant of Bruges*. Its source is J. F. Petit's *Generall Historie of All the Netherlands* (Grimestone's translation), and it is based upon an actual episode of history. Florez, unaware that he is the son of Gerrard, the consort of the Countess of Flanders, has gone from the corrupt life at court to the forest, where he meets a tribe of beggars, led by Clause, who is actually Gerrard in disguise. The usurping earl, Wolfort, attempts with the aid of his henchman, Hempskirke, to kill Florez and Gerrard, but they are foiled by a good old lord, Hubert, who puts Florez on the throne. While dwelling with the beggars, Florez has fallen in love with Bertha, who is found to be Gertrude, the daughter of the Duke of Brabant, and therefore a fit spouse for the new ruler. The play is a combination of romance and pastoral, but the pastoral element, the camp of beggars, outlaws, and petty thieves, is comic rather than sentimental, and its speech is in large part drawn from the argot of the thieving fraternity of London. Coleridge said of this play that he could read it from morning to night.

Beggar's Daughter of Bethnal Green (beth'nạl), **The.** A popular ballad preserved in Thomas Percy's *Reliques*, in *Ancient Poems*, and in other collections of old ballads. It is the story of "pretty Bessee," the daughter of "the Blind Beggar." The latter is in reality Henry, the son of Simon de Montfort, who assumes this disguise to escape the spies of King Henry III. Bessee is wooed by a merchant, an innkeeper, a gentleman, and a knight; all but the knight, however, say farewell to her on learning that her father is a beggar. The knight marries her, and her father reveals his true fortune and character at the wedding.

Beggar's Opera, The. An opera by John Gay, first produced at Lincoln's Inn Fields, London, on Jan. 29, 1728. It is said to have been suggested by a remark of Jonathan Swift to Gay "that a Newgate pastoral might make . . . a pretty sort of thing." Gay was also said to have been induced to produce this opera from spite at having been offered an unacceptable appointment at court. It was intended as a satire on the elaborate operatic style recently imported from Italy, and also, on a more personal level, as a political satire directed at Sir Robert Walpole, the prime minister. Its great success led a wit to remark that the work had "made Gay rich, and Rich, gay" (John Rich was manager of the theater at Lincoln's Inn Fields). The songs were written for popular English and Scottish tunes, and were arranged and scored by John Christopher Pepusch, who composed the overture. The characters are highwaymen, pickpockets, and their gaolers. The satire was blunt enough so that there was some danger that *The Beggar's Opera* might be closed by Walpole. *The Beggar's Opera* served as the basis for the modern *Dreigroschen Oper* by Bert Brecht and Kurt Weill,

Beggar's Holiday by John Latouche and Duke Ellington, and has itself recently been revived.

The Story. Peachum is a receiver of goods stolen by pickpockets and highwaymen, especially Captain Macheath, who wins the heart of his pretty daughter, Polly. When he discovers that Macheath and Polly have been married, thus destroying his hopes of using her in his business (a satire upon marriages of convenience), he decides to inform upon Macheath and collect the reward money while bereaving Polly. Macheath is sentenced to Newgate, the keeper of which is Lockit, a venal man in league with Peachum. His daughter, Lucy, falls in love with Macheath, and procures his escape, but not before he's had a somewhat exhausting scene between his wife and Lucy, each claiming his attention. This causes altercations between Peachum and Lockit, who had hoped to split the Captain's estate (symbolizing Walpole's fight with his brother-in-law, Lord Townshend). Eventually Macheath is captured again, and taken to Tyburn, where the opera (being performed at Newgate from a beggar's score) suddenly dissolves, since it is manifestly impossible that such a fine hero should die (a satire on sentimental tragedy).

Beggar's Ride, The. A tragedy in six scenes, by Edward Shanks, published in 1926.

Beguines (beg'inz). [Also, **Beguins.**] A name given to the members of various religious communities of women who, professing a life of poverty and self denial, went about in coarse gray clothing (of undyed wool), reading the Scriptures and exhorting the people. They originated in the 12th or 13th century, and flourished for centuries in Germany, the Netherlands, France, and Italy. Communities of the type (called *beguinages*) still exist in Belgium and the Netherlands.

Behind the Veil. A volume of poems (1863) by Roden B. W. Noel. In his poems Noel expresses the transition from pessimistic realism to religious faith.

Behistun (bā.his.tön'). [Also: **Bisitun, Bisutun;** ancient name, **Baghistan.**] A town in W Iran, ab. 23 mi. E of the city of Kermanshah: a trading center. It is the site of a monument of Darius the Great, called the "Rosetta Stone of Asia," consisting of bas-reliefs and trilingual inscriptions on the face of a high cliff. The inscriptions, deciphered (c1840) by Sir Henry Rawlinson, provided the first key to ancient Assyrian writings.

Behn (bān), **Aphra** or **Afra** or **Aphara.** [Maiden name, **Johnson.**] b. at Wye, Kent, England, 1640; d. at London, April 16, 1689. An English dramatic writer and novelist. She was the daughter of a barber, John Johnson, and wife of a Dutch merchant named Behn, who died before 1666. After her husband's death she served as a spy for the British government, at Antwerp; later, far from being rewarded by her government, she was imprisoned for debt. In her youth she spent several years in Surinam (Dutch Guiana), in N South America, where she made the acquaintance of the chieftain who served as the model of her famous romance *Oroonoko, or The Royal Slave* (c1678). She wrote much, and is said to have been the first female writer who lived by her pen in England.

Her writings are generally regarded as gay and witty, but marked by the earthy vulgarity, if not actual coarseness, of the period. Among her 15 dramatic works are *The Forc'd Marriage* (1671), *The Amorous Prince* (1671), *The Dutch Lover* (1673), *Abdelazar* (1677), *The Rover* (1677), *The Debauchee* (1677), *The Town Fop* (1677), and *The False Count* (1682). She also published *Poems* (1684).

Beiram (bī.räm'). See **Bairam.**

Beith (bēth), **John Hay.** [Pseudonym, **Ian Hay.**] b. at Manchester, England, April 17, 1876; d. at Petersfield, England, Sept. 22, 1952. An English novelist and playwright. He served in the Argyll and Sutherland Highlanders with the British Expeditionary Force in World War I; he was also director (1938–41) of public relations at the British War Office during the early part of World War II. His early novels are *Pip* (1907), *The Right Stuff* (1908), *A Man's Man* (1909), and *A Safety Match* (1911), but he is better known for *Carrying On* (1917), *The Last Million* (1918), and *Paid, with Thanks* (1925); among his plays are *Tilly of Bloomsbury* (1919), *The Happy Ending* (1922), *Housemaster* (1936), and *Little Ladyship* (1939).

Bel and the Dragon (bel). One of the books of the Apocrypha.

Belarius (be.lār'i.us). In Shakespeare's *Cymbeline,* a banished lord disguised under the name of Morgan. He steals Arviragus and Guiderius, Cymbeline's sons, out of revenge, passing them off, under false names, as his own sons. When Cymbeline is made prisoner by the Roman general, Belarius comes to his rescue, is reconciled, and restores the princes.

Belch (belch), **Sir Toby.** In Shakespeare's *Twelfth Night,* the uncle of Olivia. He is a roistering knight, fond of drinking and singing. In his enjoyment of Maria's plot against Malvolio, he decides to marry her.

Beleaguered City, A. A novel (1880) by Margaret Oliphant. It is a story of the occult.

Belfield (bel'fēld). A character in Fanny Burney's *Cecilia,* said to have been drawn from the "animated, ingenious, and eccentric Percival Stockdale."

Belfond (bel'fond). A courteous, good-tempered, and accomplished gentleman in Thomas Shadwell's comedy *The Squire of Alsatia.* He is extremely dissipated and nearly ruined by women. His elder brother is a vicious, obstinate, and clownish boor.

Belford (bel'ford). The intimate friend and correspondent of Lovelace in Samuel Richardson's novel *Clarissa Harlowe.*

Belfry, The. American title of **Tasker Jevons.**

Belgae (bel'jē). The personification of Holland in Edmund Spenser's *Faerie Queene.* She has 17 sons (the 17 provinces of Holland).

Belgarde (bel.gärd'). A poor and proud captain, in Philip Massinger's play *The Unnatural Combat,* who, when told not to appear at the governor's table in his shabby clothes, arrives in full armor.

Belgrave Square (bel'grāv). A square in Belgravia, London.

Belgravia (bel.grā'vi.a). A fashionable district in the West End of London, adjoining Hyde Park.

Belial (bē'li.al, bēl'yal). In the Bible, the spirit of evil personified; the devil; Satan; in Milton's *Paradise Lost,* one of the fallen angels, distinct from Satan. In *Faust's Book of Marvels* (1469) he is called the Viceroy of the Infernal Kingdom under Lucifer or Satan.

Believe as You List. A play by Philip Massinger. It was licensed for performance at London on May 7, 1631 and printed in 1631. This play and a later one, *The Maid of Honor* (c1632), introduced propaganda in behalf of the unfortunate brother-in-law of Charles I, the elector Frederick V of the Palatinate, briefly (1619–20) king of Bohemia, who was one of the outstanding victims of Spanish diplomacy and of the Thirty Years' War (1618–48).

Believe Me, if All Those Endearing Young Charms. A song by Thomas Moore, one of his *Irish Melodies* (published intermittently between 1807 and 1834). It is still often sung (as a tenor solo).

Belinda (be.lin'da). In John Vanbrugh's comedy *The Provok'd Wife,* the niece of Lady Brute.

Belinda. In Charles Shadwell's comedy *The Fair Quaker of Deal,* a rich woman.

Belinda. The principal character in Alexander Pope's mock-heroic poem *The Rape of the Lock.*

Belinda. In Arthur Murphy's comedy *All in the Wrong,* a proud but tender-hearted girl in love with Beverley.

Belinda. A novel by Maria Edgeworth, published in 1801.

Belinda. See also **Bellinda.**

Belisarius (bel.i.sār'i.us). b. in Illyria, or possibly Dardania, c505; d. March 13, 565. A Byzantine soldier, perhaps the greatest general of the Eastern Roman Empire. He was commander, under Justinian I, of the eastern armies in the period, 529–532, and rescued Justinian by the suppression of the "Green" faction at Constantinople in 532. He overthrew the Vandal kingdom in Africa in 533–534, won famous victories over the Goths in Italy in 534–540, conquered Sicily in 535, and S Italy in 536–537, and conquered Ravenna in 540. He conducted the war against the Persians in the period 541–542, and again took command against the Goths in Italy in 544, but was superseded by Narses in 548. In 559 he rescued Constantinople from northern (Bulgarian) invaders. He was imprisoned (c563) for a short time by Justinian. The tale that in old age he was blind and obliged to beg his bread from door to door is believed to be untrue.

Beliza (be.lē'za). In John Dryden's comedy *Marriage à la Mode,* the waiting-woman of Doralice.

Bell (bel), **Acton.** Pseudonym of Anne Brontë; see **Brontë Family.**

Bell, Adam. An English outlaw, celebrated for his skill in archery, said to have lived in the time of Robin Hood's father. About him nothing certain is known. He is the hero of several old ballads, notably *Adam Bell, Clym of the Cloughe, and Wyllyam of Cloudeslee,* printed without date by William Copland c1550. There are several allusions to him in dramatic literature. Shakespeare alludes to him in *Much Ado about Nothing* and in *Romeo and Juliet*, as does William Davenant in a poem called *A Long Vacation in London*. Ben Jonson speaks of Clym o' the Clough in *The Alchemist*. Thomas Percy and Joseph Ritson both adhere mainly to Copland's text, and Francis James Child reprints from Ritson with some improvements. However, the real person or persons of the name were thought by Child to have no connection with the hero of the ballads.

Bell, Aubrey FitzGerald. b. at Muncaster, Cumberland, England, Aug. 20, 1881—. An English writer and critic, a specialist in Spanish and Portuguese literature. Among his works are *The Magic of Spain* (1912), *Portuguese Literature and Bibliography* (1922), *Contemporary Spanish Literature* (1925), and *Cervantes* (1947). Editor of the *Oxford Book of Portuguese Verse* (1925).

Bell, Charles Frederic Moberly. b. at Alexandria, Egypt, April 2, 1847; d. at London, April 5, 1911. An English journalist, correspondent, and publisher. He began (1865) his career as a journalist in Egypt, as correspondent (1865–90) for the London *Times;* he founded (1880) the *Egyptian Gazette,* and returned (1890) to London to become manager of the *Times.* During the period 1897–1901 he conducted, as a special section of the paper, *Literature,* which later became the *Times Literary Supplement;* thereafter he served as managing editor (1908–11) of the *Times.* Author, during his residence in Egypt, of *Khedives and Pashas* (1884), *Egyptian Finance* (1887), and *From Pharaoh to Fellah* (1889); publisher of the *Times Atlas* (1895), the *Encyclopaedia Britannica* (9th ed., 1898), and *History of the South African War* (9 vols., 1900–09).

Bell, Clive. [Full name, **Arthur Clive Howard Bell.**] b. 1881—. An English art critic and writer; husband of Vanessa Bell, and father of Julian Bell. The publication of his *Art* (1914) is now considered to have been an event of considerable importance in winning wide recognition of "modern art" defined as the work of the post-impressionists, cubists, futurists, *fauves,* and other innovators since the 1880's. Bell maintained that form and design are the important matters in painting and sculpture, and that some people have a special sensitiveness to these characteristics, while others do not. The effect of this doctrine was virtually to eliminate subject matter and realism from among the criteria of excellence in a work of art. Bell's *Since Cézanne* (1922), *Landmarks in Nineteenth-Century Painting* (1929), and *An Account of French Painting* (1932) further argued the case for modernism. Bell's command of an excellent English prose style was a contributing factor to the influence of his books. He is also the author of *Peace at Once* (1915), *Pot Boilers* (1918), *The Legend of Monte della Sibilla* (1920), *Poems* (1921), *On British Freedom* (1923), *Civilization* (1928), *Proust* (1929), and *Enjoying Pictures* (1934).

Bell, Currer. Pseudonym of Charlotte Brontë; see **Brontë Family.**

Bell, Ellis. Pseudonym of Emily Brontë; see **Brontë Family.**

Bell, George. b. 1814; d. at Hampstead, London, Nov. 27, 1890. An English publisher, founder of the London firm of G. Bell and Sons. Educated at Richmond (Yorkshire) Grammar School, he went (1820) to London, later entering the employ of Whitaker and Company; in 1838 he established his own business, and was associated with J. R. Daldy, and with Deighton and Company, publishers for Cambridge University Press. The firm founded by him was originally known as Bell and Daldy; in 1864 he purchased the business and the *Libraries* of H. G. Bohn, an outstanding figure in the history of English publishing. Bell is remembered especially for his editions, in many volumes, of the English poets. After his death, the business was carried on by his son Edward Bell (1844–1926).

Bell, Henry Glassford. b. at Glasgow, Nov. 8, 1803; d. there, Jan. 7, 1874. A Scottish lawyer and poet, ardent defender of the name and reputation of Mary Stuart (Queen of Scots). He founded (1828) and edited the *Edinburgh Literary Journal* for three years. He was the author of *Summer and Winter Hours* (1830), poetry, and *My Old Portfolio* (1832), prose selections, of which two stories, "The Dead Daughter" and "The Living Mummy" are sometimes believed to have inspired Edgar Allan Poe.

Bell, John Joy. b. May 7, 1871; d. 1934. A Scottish journalist, humorist, and dramatist. Educated at Scottish academies and Glasgow University; the author of humorous stories and novels of simple Scottish life, told in dialect, he is best known for his creation of the character of Wee Macgreegor. His works are *New Noar's Ark* (1898), *Wee Macgreegor* (1902; dramatized in 1912), *Mistress McLeerie* (1903), *Wee Macgreegor Again* (1904), *Mr. Pennycook's Boy* (1905), *Clyde Songs* (1906–11), *Oh Christina Coortin' Christina* (1913), *A Kingdom of Dreams* (1914), *Wee Macgreegor Enlists* (1915), *Johnny Pryde* (1918), *Secret Cards* (1922), *The Invisible Net* (1924), *Mr. and Mrs. Craw* (1926), *Exit Mrs. McLeerie, Betty* (1927), and *Hoots!* (1929).

Bell, Julian. [Full name, **Julian Heward Bell.**] b. 1908; d. 1937. An English poet and pacifist; son of Clive Bell. He wrote *Winter Movement* (1930) and *Work for the Winter* (1936), both volumes of poetry. He was killed during the Spanish Civil War while driving an ambulance for the Loyalists; like his father, he was a confirmed pacifist. He edited, with an introduction, *We Did Not Fight, 1914–18. Experiences of War Resisters* (1935), a collection of essays by prominent English pacifists.

Bell, Laura. In Thackeray's *Pendennis,* the heroine. She saves Arthur and his mother from financial ruin, and eventually marries Arthur.

Bell, Mackenzie. [Full name, **Henry Thomas Mackenzie Bell.**] b. at Liverpool, England, March 2, 1856; d. at Bayswater, London, Dec. 13, 1930. An English biographer, poet, and traveler. He studied in France, Italy, Spain, and Portugal. He was the author of biographical and critical studies, including *A Forgotten Genius: Charles Whitehead* (1884) and *Christina Rossetti* (1898); he also wrote *Pictures of Travel and Other Poems* (1898), *Poems* (1909), and *Poetical Pictures of the Great War* (1917).

ḍ, d or j; ş, s or sh; ṭ, t or ch; ż, z or zh; o, F. cloche; ü, F. menu; ch, Sc. loch; ń, F. bonbon.

Bell, Neil. A pseudonym of **Southwold, Stephen.**

Bell, Paul. Pseudonym of **Chorley, Henry Fothergill.**

Bell, Sir Robert. b. at Cork, Ireland, Jan. 16, 1800; d. at London, April 12, 1867. A British journalist, compiler, and general writer. His chief work is an *Annotated Edition of the British Poets* (24 vols., 1854–67), covering poets from Geoffrey Chaucer to William Cowper. He contributed to Dionysius Lardner's *Cabinet Cyclopaedia.*

Bell, The. An Inn at Edmonton, in Middlesex, not far from London. It was to this spot that John Gilpin pursued his mad career in Cowper's ballad *John Gilpin.*

Bell, The. A noted old inn in Warwick Lane, London.

Bell, Vanessa. [Maiden name, **Stephen.**] An English woman of letters; eldest daughter of Sir Leslie Stephen (1832–1904), sister of Virginia Woolf (1882–1941), wife (1907 *et seq.*) of Clive Bell, and mother of the poet Julian Bell (1908–37).

Bellafront (bel'a.frunt). The principal female character in John Middleton and Thomas Dekker's *Honest Whore.* She is the "honest whore" who is recommended to Hippolito by Matheo, falls in love with Hippolito (who, however, has only love for the supposedly dead Infelice), and turns toward virtue when Hippolito shows her the loathsomeness of her occupation.

Bellair (bel.ãr'), **Count.** A character originally in George Farquhar's *The Beaux' Stratagem,* a French officer, a prisoner at Lichfield. This part was cut out by the author after the first night's representation, and the words added to the part of Foigard.

Bellair, Old. An amorous old man who imagines he disguises his love for women, in George Etherege's comedy *The Man of Mode, or Sir Fopling Flutter.*

Bellair, Young. In *The Man of Mode, or Sir Fopling Flutter,* the son of Old Bellair, a well-bred, polite youth of the period; a character in which the author, George Etherege, is said to have drawn his own portrait.

Bellamira, her Dream, or the Love of Shadows (bel.a.mē'ra). A tragicomedy in two parts by Thomas Killigrew. It is in the folio edition of his works published in 1664.

Bellamira, or The Mistress. A comedy by Sir Charles Sedley, produced in 1687. The play was partly founded on the *Eunuchus* of Terence; in it Sedley mirrored the frailty of Barbara Villiers, Countess of Castlemaine, and what he considered to be the bullying and braggart temperament of John Churchill, 1st Duke of Marlborough.

Bellamour (bel'a.mōr). The lover of Bellinda, in William Congreve's comedy *The Old Bachelor.*

Bellamy (bel'a.mi). In John Dryden's play *An Evening's Love, or the Mock Astrologer,* a young, lively gallant, a friend of Wildblood. He disguises himself as an astrologer, and thus gives the sub-title to the play.

Bellamy, George Anne. b. at Fingal, Ireland, c1727; d. at London, cFeb. 16, 1788. An English actress. She was the illegitimate daughter of a Mrs. Bellamy and James O'Hara, 2nd Baron Tyrawley, who acknowledged her and supported her. She first appeared on the stage in *Love for Love* at Covent Garden (1742) and later as Monimia in *The Orphan* (1744). In 1750 she played Juliet to David Garrick's Romeo, while Mrs. Cibber and Spranger Barry were playing the same roles in a rival performance. She was best in romantic and tragic parts, and her success was due chiefly to youth and beauty. In 1785 her *Apology* was brought out in five volumes, to which a sixth was later added. Alexander Bicknell is believed to have written it from her material. The name George Anne was given her, apparently by mistake for Georgiana, in her certificate of birth.

Bellamy, Lord. A character in Thomas Shadwell's comedy *Bury Fair.*

Bellaria (be.lãr'i.a). The wife of Pandosto in Robert Greene's *Pandosto.* She is the character on which is based Hermione in Shakespeare's *Winter's Tale.*

Bellario (be.lãr'i.ō). In Beaumont and Fletcher's play *Philaster,* a page. She is Euphrasia in disguise, who follows the fortunes of Philaster with romantic tenderness and fidelity.

Bellario, Doctor. In Shakespeare's *Merchant of Venice,* an erudite lawyer of Padua, as whose substitute Portia appears in the trial scene. He makes no stage appearance.

Bellarmine (bel'ar.min). An impertinent fine gentleman, in Henry Fielding's novel *Joseph Andrews.* He is the mercenary lover of Leonora.

Bellarmine, Robert Francis Romulus. [Italian, **Roberto Francesco Romolo Bellarmino** (bel.lär-mē'nō).] b. at Montepulciano, Tuscany, Oct. 4, 1542; d. at Rome, Sept. 17, 1621. An Italian cardinal, and Jesuit theologian and controversialist. His theological disputes with James I of England and the Scottish theologian William Barclay, over the power of the Pope in political (as opposed to religious) spheres, were famous in their day. He was professor at Louvain and in the Roman College, and archbishop of Capua. His works include *Disputationes de Controversiis, fidei . . .* (1581), *Tractatus de potestate summi pontificis in rebus temporalibus,* and *Christianae doctrinae applicatio* (1603).

Bellaston (bel'as.ton), **Lady.** The fashionable cousin of Sophia in Fielding's novel *Tom Jones.* She is a sensual, profligate, and imperious woman.

Bella Wilfer (bel'a wil'fėr). See **Wilfer, Bella.**

Belle Berners (bel bėr'nėrz). See **Berners, Belle.**

Belle Dame Sans Merci (bel dàm sän mer.sē), **La.** [Eng. trans., "*The Fair Lady without Mercy.*"] A French poem by Alain Chartier. It was translated into English by Sir Richard Ros, and not by Geoffrey Chaucer, although the translation has been attributed to him. Perhaps the best-known poem of this title, however, is the ballad (1819) by John Keats. The Keats poem uses much of the medieval imagery of the French original: a knight, a pale lady, elfin grottoes.

Bellenden (bel'en.den), **Edith.** The heiress of Tillietudlem and heroine of Sir Walter Scott's novel *Old Mortality.*

Bellenden, John. [Also: **Ballantyne, Ballenden, Bannatyne.**] b. at Haddington (or Berwick), Scotland, c1490; d. perhaps at Rome, in 1550 or 1587. A Scottish poet, scholar, clergyman, and translator. Educated at the universities of St. Andrews and Paris, he received his Doctor of Divinity degree from the latter. He was attached to the court of King James V of Scotland, at whose suggestion he translated into Scots the Latin chronicle-history of Hector Boece, *Historia Gentis Scotorum* (1527), for which he received 78 pounds. His translation (1530–33) was published at Edinburgh in 1536. He also translated the first five books of Livy's Roman history, for which he received 36 pounds. This work, however, was not published until 1822. Bellenden was also the author of two poems, *Proem of the Cosmographie* and *Proem of the History*, and a prose *Epistle*, all of which were published in 1536. Bellenden was archdeacon of Moray and canon of Ross; opposed to the Reformation, he is said to have fled to Rome and to have died there in 1550, but Thomas Maitland, Lord Dundrennan, who edited Bellenden's Livy, declared that he was living in 1587.

Bellerophon (bẹ.ler'ọ.fon) or **Bellerophontes** (bẹ.ler-ọ.fon'tēz). In Greek legend, a son of Glaucus, king of Corinth (or, in some accounts, of Poseidon) and grandson of Sisyphus. He was the rider of Pegasus, the slayer of the monster Chimera, and a conqueror of the fabulous Amazons. His exploits gained for him the daughter and one half the kingdom of Iobates, king of Lycia, but he later fell under the displeasure of the gods. According to Pindar his pride so increased with his good fortune that he attempted to mount to heaven on Pegasus, but Zeus maddened the horse with a gadfly, and Bellerophon fell and perished. He was worshiped as a hero at Corinth.

Bellerophon. The name of two famous British war vessels: **1.** British line-of-battle ship of 74 guns and 1,613 tons. She served in the Channel squadron of 1793 and 1794, and was disabled at the battle of the Nile, Aug. 1, 1798, but was repaired and fought in the battle of Trafalgar, Oct. 21, 1805. It was on this vessel, ten years later, that Napoleon gave himself up to the English. **2.** One of the first armored warships, built according to the designs of Sir Edward James Reed, chief constructor of the British navy, and launched in 1866. Length, 300 ft.; breadth, 56 ft.; draught, 26.7 ft.

Bellerus (be.lē'rus). A Cornish giant in old English legend. Belerium was the name given to Lands End, supposed to be his home.

Belle Savage. See **Bell Savage.**

belles-lettres. Polite or elegant literature: a word of somewhat indefinite application, including poetry, fiction, and other imaginative literature, and studies and criticism connected therewith; literature regarded as a form of fine art.

Belle's Stratagem, The. A comedy by Hannah Cowley, produced in 1780.

Bellicent (bel'i.sent). The half sister of King Arthur, in the Arthurian romances. Tennyson also tells her story, in somewhat altered form, in "Gareth and Lynette," one of the *Idylls of the King*.

Bellinda (bẹ.lin'dạ). One of the principal characters in George Etherege's comedy *The Man of Mode*.

Bellinda. In William Congreve's comedy *The Old Bachelor*, the fair young lady in love with Bellamour.

Bellisant (bel'i.sant). In the Charlemagne cycle of romances, the mother of Valentine and Orson. She was banished by her husband Alexander, emperor of Constantinople, for supposed infidelity, and her sons were born in a wild forest.

Bellisant (bel'i.sant). One of the principal female characters in Philip Massinger's *The Parliament of Love*.

Bellman (bel'man), **The.** A literary review (1906–19) published by William C. Edgar.

Bellman of London, The. See **Belman of London, The.**

Bellman of Paris, The. A play by Thomas Dekker and John Day, licensed in 1623, but not printed. It is known only from a licensing entry of the Lord Chamberlain.

Belloc (bel'ok), **Hilaire.** [Full name, **Joseph Hilaire Pierre Belloc.**] b. at St.-Cloud, Paris, July 27, 1870; d. at Guildford, Surrey, England, July 16, 1953. An English essayist, historian, novelist, journalist, and poet. He was educated at the Oratory School, Edgbaston, England, and at Balliol College, Oxford. He became a naturalized British subject (1902) and was a member (1906–10) of the House of Commons for Salford. He published *The Bad Child's Book of Beasts* (1896), *More Beasts for Worse Children* (1897), *The Modern Traveller* (1898), *Danton* (1899), *Robespierre* (1901), *The Path to Rome* (1902), *Caliban's Guide to Letters* (1903), *Esto Perpetua* (1906), *The Historic Thames* (1907), *On Nothing* (1908), *The Pyrenees* (1909), *Hills and the Sea* (1910), *Pongo and the Bull* (1910), *The Servile State* (1912), *The Book of the Bayeux Tapestry* (1913), *Europe and the Faith* (1920), *The Jews* (1922; 2nd ed., 1937), *History of England* (4 vols., 1925–31), *Many Cities* (1928), *Belinda* (1928), *The Missing Masterpiece* (1929), *Richelieu* (1930), *Wolsey* (1930), *A Conversation with a Cat* (1931), *Napoleon* (1932), *Charles I* (1933), *Cromwell* (1934), *Characters of the Reformation* (1936), *The Great Heresies* (1938), and *The Last Rally* (1940).

Bellona (bẹ.lō'nạ). In Roman mythology, the goddess of war, regarded sometimes as the wife and sometimes as the sister of Mars. She was, probably, originally a Sabine divinity, and her worship appears to have been introduced at Rome by a Sabine family, the Claudii. She is represented as armed with shield and lance.

Bell Rock. [Also: **Inchcape Rock, Inch Cape.**] A rock in the North Sea, off the Firth of Tay (E Scotland), ab. 11 mi. SE of Arbroath. It is marked by a lighthouse.

Bells, The. A dramatization by Leopold Lewis from Erckmann-Chatrian's novel *Le Juif Polonais*; produced in 1871. Henry Irving created and was successful in the role of Mathias, the leading character.

ḑ, d or j; ṣ, s or sh; ṯ, t or ch; ẓ, z or zh; o, F. cloche; ü, F. menu; ċh, Sc. loch; ṅ, F. bonbon.

Bells and Pomegranates. A series of eight pamphlets by Robert Browning, published between 1841 and 1846. They contained many of his famous poems, as well as six dramas, including *Pippa Passes, Dramatic Lyrics, A Blot in the 'Scutcheon,* and *Dramatic Romances.*

Bell Savage or **Belle Sauvage** (bel sav'ạj). [Also, **Belle Savage.**] A London tavern which formerly stood on Ludgate Hill. Its inn yard was one of those used in the 16th century as a theater and for bearbaiting and other spectacles. A printing house later occupied the site.

Bells of Shoreditch (shōr'dich″), The. A novel by Ethel Sidgwick, published in 1928.

"Bell-the-Cat." A nickname of **Douglas, Archibald** (c1449–1514). At a deliberation of the nobles for the purpose of effecting the removal of Robert Cochrane, Earl of Mar, James III's obnoxious favorite, their predicament was compared to that of the mice which determined to hang a bell around the cat's neck, and the question was asked who would be brave enough to perform the act. To this Douglas replied: "I will bell the cat."

Belman (or **Bellman**) **of London, The.** A satirical work by Thomas Dekker, published in 1608. It is founded on the *Ground Work of Coney Catching,* which some believe to have been also written by Dekker. The latter was taken largely from Harman's *Caveat for Cursitors.* In the same year Dekker published a second part called *Lanthorne and Candlelight, or The Belman's Second Night's Walke.* In 1612 a fourth or fifth edition of the second part appeared, called *O per se O, or a new cryer of Lanthorne and Candlelight, Being an addition or lengthening of the Belman's Second Night's Walke.* A number of editions of the second part were published before 1648, all with differences. They are amusing descriptions of London rogues.

Belmont (bel'mont). In Shakespeare's *Merchant of Venice,* Portia's estate.

Belmont, Charles. A rakish young fellow in Edward Moore's play *The Foundling.* The part was played with great success by David Garrick.

Beloe (bē'lō), **William.** b. at Norwich, England, 1756; d. at London, April 11, 1817. An English clergyman and writer. He was a founder (1793) with Robert Nares of the *British Critic.* He became rector of All Hallows, at London, in 1796, and was keeper (1803–06) of printed books in the British Museum. He wrote *The Sexagenarian, or Recollections of a Literary Life* (1817).

Beloved Vagabond, The. A novel by William John Locke, published in 1906. Its central character, the "vagabond" of the title, is Berzelius Nibbidard Paragot, a Quixotic hero, one of the author's favorite types. He wanders about Europe as a musician with Anticot, an adopted waif, and Blanquette, a country lass.

Belphegor (bel'fẹ.gôr). An archdemon who undertook an earthly marriage, but who fled, daunted, from the horrors of female companionship. His name derives from the Baal-peor mentioned in the Bible. The story in its modern form, with merely a difference of names, was originally told in an old Latin manuscript, which is now lost, but which, till the period of the civil wars in France, remained in the library of Saint Martin de Tours. There has been some dispute as to whether Brevio or Niccolò Machiavelli (who spelled the name "Belfagor") first exhibited the tale in an Italian garb. It was printed by Brevio during his life, and under his own name, in 1545; and with the name of Machiavelli in 1549, which was about 18 years after that historian's death. It is believed that both writers borrowed the incidents from the Latin manuscript. Jean de La Fontaine treated this subject in one of his *Contes,* and Arthur Wilson printed an English tragicomedy called *Belphegor, or the Marriage of the Devil* in 1691.

Belphegor. A translation and adaptation of *Palliasse,* a French play by Adolphe Philippe Dennery and Marc Fournier, made (1856) by Charles Webb.

Belphoebe (bel.fē'bē). A huntress in Edmund Spenser's *Faerie Queene,* intended to represent Queen Elizabeth as a woman, as Gloriana represented her as a queen. She is the twin sister of Amoret and the daughter of the nymph Chrysogone.

Belsham (bel'shạm), **William.** b. at Bedford, 1752; d. near Hammersmith, now part of London, Nov. 17, 1827. An English historian and political essayist. He was the author of numerous works supporting the Whigs.

Belshazzar (bel.shaz'ạr). [Babylonian, **Bel-sharuzur** (bel.shär'ō'zör).] d. 538 B.C. In the Bible, according to the book of Daniel (v.), the son of Nebuchadnezzar, and the last king of Babylonia. According to the cuneiform inscriptions this was Nabonidus, while Belshazzar was his eldest son. He was governor of southern Babylonia and chief of the army in the last struggle, and coregent with his father. When the latter fled to Borsippa, after being defeated by Cyrus, Belshazzar assumed the command in Babylonia, and was killed in the sack of the city by Cyrus. According to the scriptural narrative he was warned during a feast of his coming doom by handwriting on the wall, which was interpreted by Daniel (Dan. v., vii. 1, viii. 1; Bar. i. 11, 12). Byron has a poem on the *Vision of Belshazzar* (1815).

Belshazzar. A tragedy by Henry Hart Milman, published in 1822.

Beltane (bel'tạn). | [Also, **Bealtaine.**] **1.** The first day of May (O.S.); old May day, one of the four quarter days (the others being Lammas, Hallowmas, and Candlemas) anciently observed in Scotland.
2. An ancient Celtic festival or anniversary formerly observed on Beltane or May day in Scotland, and in Ireland on June 21. Bonfires were kindled on the hills, all domestic fires having been previously extinguished, only to be relighted from the embers of the Beltane fires. This custom is supposed to derive its origin from the worship of the sun, or fire in general, which was formerly in vogue among the Celts as well as among many other heathen nations.

Belteshazzar (bel.tẹ.shaz'ạr). The Babylonian name for Daniel. Dan. i. 7, etc.

Belton Estate, The (bel'tọn), **The.** A novel (1866) by Anthony Trollope. Charles, the son of Mr. Amedroz, commits suicide, and as the Belton property in Somerset is to pass from Amedroz into the hands of Will Belton, a distant cousin, on his death, Belton comes to the estate to put affairs in order. Clara, Amedroz's daughter, will be left penniless when her father dies, and the confident, generous Belton proposes marriage to her. Belton is at first rejected because Clara is in love with the self-centered Captain Aylmer, but she soon realizes his true character, breaks her engagement to him, and marries Belton.

Belvedere (bel.vẹ.dir'; Italian, bel.vä.dā'rā). A portion of the Vatican Palace at Rome. Its *Apollo* and the *Laocoön* are among the best-known pieces in its valuable collection of classical art.

Belvidera (bel.vẹ.dā'rạ). The gentle daughter of Priuli, the Venetian senator, and the wife of Jaffier, the conspirator, in Thomas Otway's tragedy *Venice Preserv'd*. She is affronted by her husband's placing her in the power of a lustful fellow-conspirator, and in her chaste innocence brings about the ruin of Jaffier, his friend Pierre, and the other conspirators. Belvidera, on learning the result of her interference, goes mad and dies. The part was a favorite one with the English actresses of the Restoration and 18th century.

Belville (bel'vil). The lover of Peggy in David Garrick's *The Country Girl*, an adaptation of William Wycherley's *The Country Wife*.

Belvoir Castle (bē'vėr). In English history, the seat of the dukes of Rutland, in Leicestershire, England.

Belzebub (bel'zẹ.bub). See **Beelzebub**.

Ben (ben). A gay, simple, but somewhat incredible sailor in William Congreve's comedy *Love for Love*. He is supposedly destined to marry Miss Prue, but declares his independence. The realism of his role, despite its jarring note in a comedy of manners, probably accounted for part of the success of the play.

Ben, Big. See **Big Ben**.

Benaiah (bẹ.nā'ạ). In the Bible, a valiant warrior of David. 2 Sam. xxiii. 20.

Benaiah. A character in John Dryden and Nahum Tate's second part of *Absalom and Achitophel*, intended for George Edward Sackville, who was called General Sackville and was a devoted adherent of the Duke of York. See 1 Kings, ii. 35 for the Biblical character.

Benavente y Martínez (bä.nä.ʙen'tä ē mär.tē'neth), **Jacinto.** b. at Madrid, 1866; d. there, July 14, 1954. A Spanish playwright, called the leader of the "generation of 1898." Influenced by the works of other European writers, his plays were a departure from the Spanish dramatic school; they depend on social satire, characterization, and clever dialogue rather than powerful plots. In 1922 he received the Nobel prize for literature. His plays have been translated into many languages and have been produced in many countries. *La Malquerida* (The Passion Flower) and *Los Intereses creados* (The Bonds of Interest) have been presented successfully in Spain.

Benbow (ben'bō), **John.** b. at Shrewsbury, England, March 10, 1653; d. at Port Royal, Jamaica, Nov. 4, 1702. A British admiral. He early ran away to sea, served in various merchant and government vessels, and after 1689 was continuously in the royal navy. He became captain in 1689, rear admiral in 1696, and vice-admiral in 1701. In 1692 and 1693 he was engaged in various unsuccessful attacks on the French coast; in 1696 he served as squadron commander at Dunkerque; in 1699 and again in 1701 he commanded squadrons in the West Indies. From Aug. 19 to Aug. 24, 1702, he had a running fight with a section of the French fleet. On the last day his leg was shattered by a ball, but he continued to direct the battle. Benbow claimed that his failure to capture this fleet was the result of the poor conduct of his officers, much of his squadron having deserted him.

Bendemeer (ben'dẹ.mir). A river in Thomas Moore's poem *Lalla Rookh*.

Bending of the Bough, The. An adaptation by George Moore of *The Tale of a Town* (1902) by Edward Martyn.

Bendish: A Study in Prodigality (ben'dish). A historical novel by Maurice Hewlett, published in 1913. It is set against a background of London in the 1830's.

Bend-the-Bow (bend'ᴛʜẹ.bō'). An English archer in Sir Walter Scott's novel *Castle Dangerous*.

Benedick (ben'ẹ.dik). In Shakespeare's *Much Ado About Nothing*, a young gentleman of Padua, of inexhaustible humor, wit, and raillery, a ridiculer of love. He engages in much spirited bickering with Beatrice, and avows again and again his determination to die a bachelor, but through the maneuvering of Claudio and Don Pedro they are brought together. Benedick does not appear in the novel by Bandello from which the main plot is taken, but is Shakespeare's own creation, and is tied into the Claudio-Hero plot by Beatrice's demand that he kill his friend Claudio for impugning the virtue of her cousin Hero. His name has become a byword for a supposedly confirmed bachelor who marries, and in this connection is frequently written Benedict.

Benedict (ben'ẹ.dikt). d. 1193. An English ecclesiastic, abbot of Peterborough (1177–93). He wrote a history of the passion, and another of the miracles of Saint Thomas à Becket, but is probably not, as has been commonly supposed, the author of the *Gesta Regis Henrici Secundi*.

Benedict Biscop (bis'kọp), **Saint.** [Also called **Biscop Baducing** (bäd'ú.king).] b. c628; d. at Wearmouth, England, Jan. 12, 690. English ecclesiastic, the founder of the monasteries of Wearmouth (674) and of Jarrow (682). He is noteworthy as the guardian of Bede, who when only seven years old was placed under his charge.

Benedictines (ben.ẹ.dik'tinz, -tēnz, -tīnz). Roman Catholic monastic order. Saint Benedict of Nursia about the year 500 turned from the luxury and corruption of Rome to become a hermit. Other religious devotees gathered around his cave at Subiaco, and in this manner the precursor of the Benedictine monastery came into existence. In c529 Benedict established the celebrated monastery at Monte Cassino. When this was sacked by the Lombards, about 580, Pope Pelagius II estab-

ḍ, d or j; ş, s or sh; ṭ, t or ch; ẓ, z or zh; o, F. cloche; ü, F. menu; ċh, Sc. loch; ṅ, F. bonbon.

lished the monks at Rome, where for 140 years they had their principal house, and from which numerous missionaries went out to all parts of Western Europe and to England. The Christianization of the Germans in particular is credited largely to the "black monks," as Benedictines are often called from the color of their habit. Where the "black monks" established themselves in regions already partly Christianized by Irish and other Celtic missionaries, the very strict Celtic monasticism in many cases was softened by adaptation to the milder "Rule of Saint Benedict," which in the 8th century largely prevailed throughout Western Europe. Charlemagne patronized the Benedictines, and in 817 his son Louis the Pious caused minute regulations in conformity with the Benedictine Rule to be imposed on all monasteries in the newly revived Holy Roman Empire, but this attempt at compulsory uniformity in all details was not very successful. Benedictine monasticism took no root in eastern Europe, except in parts of Poland, Bohemia, Bavaria, and Austria. It is generally supposed that Saint Benedict had no intention of founding an order, but the increasing numbers of religious who put themselves under his guidance and the multiplication of monastic establishments on the model of Monte Cassino caused him, about the year 530, to commit to writing the Rule which thereafter guided this first monastic order of the Western Church. The Benedictine Order is probably unique in that it has never had an actual centralized authority and no general superior but the Pope. As Benedictine houses multiplied, they became grouped in so-called congregations, each administratively autonomous, united only by allegiance to the Rule, with considerable latitude, however, for modification of that Rule to meet conditions peculiar to a particular congregation or house. Union of individual houses in congregations was positively directed by the Fourth Lateran Council in 1215, which also ordered that the abbots of all houses in a congregation should meet every three years with power to pass regulations binding on all such houses. During the next century this directive was seriously followed only in England, but following publication of the Bull *Benedictina* of Pope Benedict XII in 1336, this reform was generally effected, and almost all Benedictine monasteries today are grouped in congregations. During the early years of the Reformation, most Benedictine establishments in Protestant countries were suppressed. Today, however, the Benedictine Order is flourishing, with houses in most parts of the world including the U. S. While Saint Benedict was at Monte Cassino his sister Scholastica presided over a religious community of women nearby. It is surmised that this community was under Benedict's spiritual direction and that such regulations as he made for them must have conformed closely to those which he embodied in his Rule.

Benengeli (ben.en.gä'lē; Spanish, bä.nen.нä'lē), **Cid Hamet.** See **Cid Hamet Benengeli.**

Benevolus (bẹ.nev'ọ.lus). See **Benlowes, Edward.**

Benger (beng'gẻr), **Elizabeth Ogilvy.** b. at Wells, Somersetshire, England, 1778; d. at London, Jan. 9, 1827. An English author. She wrote novels in-

cluding *Marian* and *The Heart and the Fancy*, and poems and dramas. She is chiefly known as the compiler of memoirs, among which are those of Elizabeth Hamilton, John Tobin, Anne Boleyn, Mary Queen of Scots, and Elizabeth of Bohemia.

Benham (ben'am), Sir **William Gurney.** b. 1859; d. 1944. An English compiler, and author of guide and travel books. The author of *A Pilgrimage to Cymbeline's Town and Constable's Country* (1903), *Elmstead Parish Church—Its Monuments and Relics* (1931), *Colchester—A History and a Guide* (1946), and many similar works, he is also widely known for *Cassell's Book of Quotations, Proverbs, and Household Words* (1907, 1913, 1914, 1936) and *Cassell's Classified Quotations* (1921), both of which he compiled.

Benjamin (ben'ja.min). In the Old Testament, the youngest son of Jacob; ancestor of one of the 12 tribes of Israel. He was named Benoni (meaning "son of my sorrow") by his mother, Rachel, who died in giving him birth, but this was changed to Benjamin (meaning "son of the right hand") by Jacob. The tribe of Benjamin occupied a territory ab. 26 mi. long and 12 mi. wide between Ephraim (on the N) and Judah, containing Jerusalem and Jericho. Gen. xlii. 4, xliv. 20.

Benjamin, Lewis Saul. [Pseudonym, **Lewis Melville.**] b. at London, March 30, 1874; d. 1932. An English author, editor, biographer, and actor. After a short career (1896–1901) on the London stage, he turned to writing, producing a large number of books in various fields of literary and state history, and biography. Among his works are lives of W. M. Thackeray (1909), Laurence Sterne (1911), William Cobbett (1913), and Tobias Smollett (1926). He was the author also of *Victorian Novelists* (1906), *Farmer George* (2 vols., 1907), *Beaux of the Regency* (1908), *Some Aspects of Thackeray* (1911), *Memoirs of Lady Craven* (1913), *London Scene* (1926), *Stage Favorites* (1928–29), and an edition (1901–07) of the works of Thackeray. He also wrote *The First Gentleman of Europe* (1906), *Bath Under Beau Nash* (1907), *Brighton—Its History, Follies, and Fashions* (1909), *Beau Brummell* (1924), *Famous Duels and Assassinations* (1929), and *Horace Walpole* (1930).

Benjamin Allen (al'ẹn). See **Allen, Benjamin.**

Benjamin Backbite (bak'bīt), **Sir.** See **Backbite, Sir Benjamin.**

Benjamin Britain (brit'an). See **Britain, Benjamin.**

Benjamin of Tudela (tö.dä'lä). d. 1173. A Jewish rabbi, scholar, and traveler. His fame now rests chiefly on an account he wrote in Hebrew of his travels over a period of some 13 years, which took him to France, Italy, Sicily, Greece, Constantinople, Egypt, Palestine, and Assyria. (By some authorities he is said to have gone still further east, through Persia and even into China. If this is true, he was probably the first traveler of the Middle Ages to reach China, but most modern historians believe that his accounts of the regions east of Baghdad are based on hearsay rather than his own knowledge from first-hand experience.) It has been translated into Latin (1575), into French (1734), and on several occasions into English. The most recent English translation of his writings is a critical edition, by Marcus Nathan Adler, published in 1907.

Benjamin Suddlechop (sud'l.chop). See **Suddle-chop, Benjamin.**

Ben Jochanan (ben jō.kä'nan). In the second part of *Absalom and Achitophel*, by John Dryden and Nahum Tate, a character intended for Samuel Johnson (1649–1703), a clergyman who upheld the right of private judgment and was persecuted therefor.

Benlowes (ben'lōz), **Edward.** [Called **Benevolus.**] b. in Essex, England, c1603; d. at Oxford, England, Dec. 18, 1676. An English poet. In 1620 he matriculated at St. John's College, Cambridge. He inherited his father's estate, and squandered it in foolish generosity (whence the name by which he was called, Benevolus, almost an anagram of his own name). He was the author of many poems in Latin, including *Theophila, or Love's Sacrifice, a Divine Poem* (1652, in 13 cantos, setting forth the victorious struggle of Theophila, the Soul, against sin) and *The Summary of Divine Wisdom* (1657). Samuel Butler, Alexander Pope (in his *Dunciad*), and Bishop William Warburton ridiculed Benlowes and his work.

Bennaskar (ben.nas'kar). A magician in Ridley's *Tales of the Genii.*

Bennet (ben'et), **Elizabeth.** The heroine of Jane Austen's novel *Pride and Prejudice*. The second in a family of five daughters, her intelligence is constantly required to cope with problems created by her mother's single-minded matchmaking, her older sister Jane's sentimental helplessness, and her younger sister Lydia's wild precociousness. Her pride comes in conflict with that of Fitzwilliam Darcy; she is turned against him by his imperiousness at a local ball, and by stories that have reached her of his ruthlessness; he, on the other hand, is irritatingly conscious of the superiority of his social position as compared to hers. Nevertheless, they are strongly attracted to each other, and Darcy makes Elizabeth a proposal, which she rejects absolutely. He then lets her know that the rumors against him have been completely untrue, thus disabusing Elizabeth of her prejudice against his moral character. Finally, in spite of his arrogant aunt, Lady Catherine de Bourgh, Darcy comes to realize that Elizabeth is in every way his equal, and his second proposal to her is accepted.

Bennet, Jane. A sister of Elizabeth Bennet, a character in Jane Austen's novel *Pride and Prejudice*. She is in love with Charles Bingley, but is separated from him by the design of Bingley's sisters, who consider Jane too vulgar to marry into their family. At the end of the book, however, the lovers are happily reunited.

Bennet, Kitty. A sister of Elizabeth Bennet, a character in Jane Austen's *Pride and Prejudice*. She shares with her sister Lydia the quality of a mind "more vacant than their sisters."

Bennet, Lydia. A sister of Elizabeth Bennet, a character in Jane Austen's novel *Pride and Prejudice*. Her high spirits and emotional susceptibility get her into various difficulties, which are all, however, righted in the end.

Bennet, Mary. A sister of Elizabeth Bennet, a character in Jane Austen's *Pride and Prejudice*. She is considered to be a great reader, and has the appearance of someone who wishes to say something very sensible, but can't quite decide what it should be.

Bennet, Mr. The father of Elizabeth Bennet, a character in Jane Austen's *Pride and Prejudice*.

Bennet, Mrs. The mother of Elizabeth Bennet, a character in Jane Austen's *Pride and Prejudice*. Her principal object in life is to get her daughters married.

Bennett (ben'et), **Arnold.** [Full name, **Enoch Arnold Bennett.**] b. in Staffordshire, May 27, 1867; d. March 27, 1931. An English novelist. He studied law, but turned to journalism, serving (1893–1900) as assistant editor and subsequently editor of *Woman*. He resigned his editorial post to devote his full time to writing. Besides several plays and miscellaneous writings he published a number of novels. He is best known for *The Old Wives' Tale* and his "Five Towns" books, all set against his native pottery-making region of the five towns which form now, together with a sixth, the county borough of Stoke-on-Trent, England. *Anna of the Five Towns* (1902), *Leonora* (1903), and *Sacred and Profane Love* (1905; revised ed., *The Book of Carlotta*, 1911) comprise the first "Five Towns" trilogy; the second—sometimes also called the "Clayhanger" series—consists of *Clayhanger* (1910), *Hilda Lessways* (1911), and *These Twain* (1916), brought out collectively as *The Clayhanger Family* (1925). His other works include *A Man from the North* (1898), *The Grand Babylon Hotel* (1902), *Buried Alive* (1908), *Your United States* (1912), *The Pretty Lady* (1918), *The Roll-Call* (1919), *Lilian* (1922), *Riceyman Steps* (1923), *Lord Raingo* (1926), *Accident* (1929), and *Imperial Palace* (1930). *The Great Adventure* (1913) was a dramatization of his *Buried Alive;* he collaborated with Edward Knoblock on the play *Milestones* (1912).

Benoît de Sainte-Maure (be.nwà de sant.mōr). [Also, **Sainte-More.**] b. at Sainte-Maure, in Touraine, France; fl. in the 12th century. A French trouvère. Little is known of his life beyond the brief autobiographical notices contained in his works. His royal patron, Henry II of England (1154–89), charged him to write the history of the Normans. Benoît accordingly composed *La Chronique des ducs de Normandie*, a poem of 45,000 lines, written c1180. He is better known for his *Roman de Troie*, a poem of over 30,000 lines, written c1160 and dedicated to Eleanor of Aquitaine, wife of Henry II of England. Two other works are sometimes ascribed to him: *Aeneas*, a poem of some 10,000 verses, and *Le Roman de Thèbes*, in 15,000 lines.

Bensley (benz'li), **Robert.** b. c1738; d. 1817. An English actor. He appeared at the Drury Lane in 1765 and later at Covent Garden, retiring from the latter theatre in 1796. He played few new parts, but was known for the role of Malvolio in *Twelfth Night*, Pierre in Otway's *Venice Preserv'd*, and Evander in *The Grecian Daughter* (which he played opposite Mrs. Siddons). He was much admired by Charles Lamb.

Benson (ben'son), **Arthur Christopher.** b. April 24, 1862; d. June 17, 1925. An English educator and author; brother of Edward Frederic Benson. He was a fellow and lecturer of Magdalene College, Cambridge, and a master at Eton College (1885–1903). Appointed (1911) professor of English fiction at the Royal Society of Literature, at London, he became (1915) a master of Magdalene College. He published *Archbishop Laud* (1887), *Rossetti* (1904), *The Upton Letters* (1905), *Walter Pater* (1906), *From a College Window* (1906, critical writings on Rossetti, FitzGerald, and Pater), *Selections from the Correspondence of Queen Victoria* (edited, with Viscount Esher, 1907), *The Silent Isle* (1910), *Ruskin, a Study in Personality, The Leaves of the Tree*, and others.

Benson, Edward Frederic. b. in Berkshire, England, July 24, 1867; d. Feb. 29, 1940. An English novelist; brother of Arthur Christopher Benson. He was the author of *Dodo* (1893), *The Babe* (1897), *Mammon and Co.* (1900), *Scarlet and Hyssop* (1902), *The Challoners* (1904), *The Angel of Pain* (1906), *The Blotting Book* (1908), *The Climber* (1908), *The Osbornes* (1910), *Mezzanine* (1926), and *Final Edition* (1940), an autobiography. Best known among his novels are the series of gentle satires centered around the heroine Lucia.

Benson, Sir Frank (or Francis) Robert. b. at Alresford, Hampshire, England, Nov. 4, 1858; d. Dec. 31, 1939. An English actor; nephew of Edward White Benson and brother of Godfrey Rathbone Benson, 1st Baron Charnwood. While at Oxford he superintended the production of Greek plays at that university. In 1882 he appeared at the Lyceum at London under the management of Henry Irving, and in 1889 undertook the production at the Globe theater, London, of Shakespearian plays by a specially selected company of his own. From 1887 he superintended the staging of the annual Shakespearian performance at Stratford-on-Avon.

Benson, Stella. b. at Much Wenlock, Shropshire, England, Jan. 6, 1892; d. in China, Dec. 6, 1933. An English novelist, short-story writer, poet, and dramatist; wife (1921 *et seq.*) of John C. O'Gorman Anderson. Author of the novels *I Pose* (1915), *This Is the End* (1917), *Living Alone* (1919), *The Poor Man* (1922), *Goodbye, Stranger* (1926), *The Far-Away Bride* (1930; published in England as *Tobit Transplanted*, 1931; awarded the 1931 Femina-Vie Heureuse Prize); *The Awakening* (1925), *The Man Who Missed the 'Bus* (1928), *Hope Against Hope* (1931), *Christmas Formula* (1932), collections of short stories; *The Little World* (1925) and *Worlds Within Worlds* (1928), travel books, both illustrated by herself; *Kwan-Yin* (1922), a play; and *Twenty* (1918) and *Poems* (1935), volumes of poetry.

Bentham (ben'thạm), **Jeremy.** b. at London, Feb. 4, 1748; d. there, June 6, 1832. An English reformer and utilitarian philosopher. He took the degree of B.A. at Queen's College, Oxford, in 1763, and of A.M. in 1766, and was subsequently admitted to the bar at Lincoln's Inn. He shortly gave up the practice of law in order to devote himself wholly to publishing and correspondence directed to the accomplishment of reform, and to the development of philosophical, political, and legal theories found necessary to that end. In this he was aided by a corps of zealous disciples, both in England and

abroad, whose names included many of the most famous of the era. Bentham's accomplishments were so great, in all fields of government and law, that it may be said that the total body of English law existing in 1875 bore a closer resemblance to Bentham's proposals than it did to the body of law existing a century earlier, before he commenced publication. He advocated the principles of associationist psychology, and was the first to formulate the theory of utilitarianism in ethics. The inaccessibility and unreadability of his later works, and the literary vogue of John Stuart Mill (his indirect disciple) and his associates, caused Bentham's philosophical merits and his practical achievements to be almost forgotten until a revival of interest which started about a century after his death. Bentham's chief works are *Introduction to the Principles of Morals and Legislation* (1789), *Fragment on Government* (1776), *Theory of Legislation* (1802), *Rationale of Judicial Evidence* (1825), and *Constitutional Code* (1830).

Bentinck's Act (ben'tingks). An English statute (1845) restricting gambling.

Bentley (bent'li), **Edmund Clerihew.** b. at London, July 10, 1875; d. there, March 30, 1956. An English writer of detective fiction; father of Nicolas Clerihew Bentley. He devised a form of witty quasi-biographical verse, sometimes called clerihews, consisting of four lines of unequal length, short ones alternating with long ones, and rhyming as couplets. Author of *Biography for Beginners* (1905), *Trent's Last Case* (1912), *Trent Intervenes* (1938), *Those Days* (1940), and *Elephant's Work* (1950).

Bentley, Nicolas Clerihew. b. at London, June 14, 1907–. An English humorous writer and illustrator; son of Edmund Clerihew Bentley. His works include *Die? I Thought I'd Laugh* (1936), *Ballet Hoo* (1937), *Le Sport* (1939), *Second Thoughts* (1939), and *Animal, Vegetable, and South Kensington* (1940). He has also written the detective stories *The Tongue-tied Canary* (1949) and *The Floating Dutchman* (1951).

Bentley, Phyllis. [Full name, **Phyllis Eleanor Bentley.**] b. at Halifax, Yorkshire, England, Nov. 19, 1894–. An English novelist, best known for works set against a Yorkshire background. She has done much lecturing in the U. S. and in the Netherlands. She was employed (1942–44) in the American division of the Ministry of Information during World War II. Author of *The World's Bane* (1918), *Pedagomania* (1918), *The Spinner of the Years* (1928), *The Partnership* (1928), *Carr* (1929), *Trio* (1930), *Inheritance* (1932), *A Modern Tragedy* (1934), *Freedom, Farewell!* (1936), *Take Courage* (1940), *Manhold* (1941), *The Rise of Henry Morcar* (1946), and *Quorum* (1951).

Bentley, Richard. b. at Oulton, near Wakefield, Yorkshire, England, Jan. 27, 1662; d. July 14, 1742. An English cleric, classical scholar, and critic. He received the B.A. degree at St. John's College, Cambridge, in 1680, and was appointed master of Trinity College, Cambridge, in 1700, after taking orders in 1690. Although generally conceded to have been one of the greatest of all English classical scholars, he is perhaps more vividly remembered for the violence of his temper and the tyranny of his administration of Trinity College (which last

fat, fāte, fär, åsk, fâre; net, mē, hėr; pin, pīne; not, nōte, mōve, nôr; up, lūte, pull; ᴛʜ, then;

resulted in trial and near-expulsion by his fellow scholars). He was the author of scholarly works including *Epistola ad Millium* (*Letter to Dr. John Mill*, 1691), on the Greek writer Malelas, which first won him note as a classical scholar; *Boyle Lectures* (1692), which he delivered at Oxford; and *Dissertation on the Epistles of Phalaris* (1697, 1699), in which he proved these epistles a forgery (precipitating the literary Battle of the Books).

Bentley, Richard. b. at London, 1794; d. at Ramsgate, Kent, England, Sept. 10, 1871. An English printer and publisher. He learned the printing business from his uncle John Nichols, author of *History and Antiquities of Leicester*, and entered (1819) a printing establishment owned by his brother Samuel; in 1829 he entered into partnership with Henry Colburn, publisher of novels, continuing the business after Colburn withdrew in 1832. He founded (1837) *Bentley's Miscellany* (with Charles Dickens as editor) in which *Oliver Twist* first appeared (January, 1837–March, 1839). He also published the works of R. H. Barham, T. C. Haliburton, Isaac and Benjamin D'Israeli, George Cruikshank, and many others, and brought out 127 volumes in the *Library of Standard Novels*.

Benvolio (ben.vō′li.ō). In Shakespeare's *Romeo and Juliet*, a friend of Romeo and nephew of Montague. His actions contribute to the tragic outcome of the play, for it is his fight with Tybalt in the opening scene that leads to the decree that street brawling is a capital offense, and it is he who persuades Romeo to attend Capulet's ball, where Romeo meets Juliet. He is present at Mercutio's death and at the time of Romeo's revenge against Tybalt for this.

Benzayda (ben.zā′dạ). In John Dryden's play *The Conquest of Granada*, the daughter of the sultan. She loves Ozwy, the son of her father's deadliest foe, and exhibits heroic courage and endurance while following her lover through the hardships and perils of civil war.

Beowulf (bā′ọ.wŭlf). An Old English epic poem composed in the 8th century, and generally conceded to be the greatest literary work of the Old English period. It has survived in a manuscript (Manuscript Cotton Vitellius A xv, now in the British Museum) dating from c1000, in 3,182 lines of alliterative verse. One of the best editions in English is that of F. Klaeber (1922; 3rd edition, 1936). A good comprehensive study is that of R. W. Chambers, published in 1921 (2nd edition, 1932). A recent and good verse translation is that of C. W. Kennedy, published in 1940.

The Story. The poem contains two major episodes, in each of which Beowulf displays his great courage and his might: first, his killing of the monster Grendel and then of Grendel's mother; second, his defense of his kingdom against a dragon many years later, an encounter which results in the vanquishing of the dragon, but in which Beowulf himself is also fatally wounded. The first part opens with a description of the setting: the Danish king Hrothgar has built a magnificent hall, Heorot, in which for a short time he and his thanes are able to pass their days according to the custom of the time, undisturbed in their mead drinking and entertained by the singing of scops. But this happy

interval is broken when the monstrous Grendel comes from the moor one night to slay 30 of the Danes in their sleep. For 12 years Grendel returns, to kill again, or to sleep in the hall, and not even the most stalwart of Hrothgar's subjects is able to slay him. Word of Hrothgar's plight reaches Beowulf, nephew of the king of Geatland (thought conjecturally to have been an actual place at the southern end of the Scandinavian peninsula), and with 14 companions Beowulf sets forth for Hrothgar's court, where he pleads that he may be permitted to rid the hall of its monstrous interloper. Then follows an account of his entertainment by Hrothgar, during which he tells at length the true story of a daring swimming contest in which he was victorious. Finally the Danes withdraw from the hall, leaving Beowulf and his companions to await the coming of Grendel. The monster arrives, smashing through a door held shut by "fire-hardened bands" to enter the hall. He slays one of Beowulf's companions, and is engaged in combat by Beowulf (whose surviving companions strive to aid him, but futilely, as mortal steel is useless against Grendel). However, Beowulf begins to gain the advantage, and presently Grendel tears himself from the fray, having an arm wrenched from his shoulder in the process, and flees the hall to die. Jubilation reigns on the following day, but in the evening Grendel's mother comes to the hall to wreak vengeance, and bears the body of one of the Danes off to her cave beneath the waters of a lake in the fenland. The next day Beowulf proceeds to the lake, dives to the bottom, and engages Grendel's mother in a long and desperate struggle in the cave. Beowulf's own sword is useless against the dreadful creature who spawned Grendel, and in the end he slays her only by a magic blade which he snatches up in her lair. With this he also cuts off the head of Grendel (whose corpse he finds in the cave), but so potent is Grendel's blood that it dissolves the metal even of this blade, and Beowulf is able to carry back with him only its hilt, in addition to the great head of his vanquished foe. His companions, who have feared that he was slain, rejoice and he receives the grateful thanks of Hrothgar and the Danes. Then the Geats depart for their own land. The second episode of the work takes place many years later, when Beowulf has reigned as king of Geatland for 50 years. Then a great dragon, enraged because a slave has stolen a jeweled cup from his hoard, begins to ravage Beowulf's kingdom by night and finally burns his royal hall to the ground. Again Beowulf goes forth to battle a creature too powerful for ordinary men, and again he succeeds in slaying it, but this time he himself receives a mortal hurt. As he is dying, he instructs his loyal thane, Wiglaf, to bring forth the dragon's treasure for the enrichment of his people, and he dies with his eyes resting upon this fabulous hoard.

Sources, Background, and Comment. The author of *Beowulf* (his identity is not known, but it has been conjectured that he was a Danish cleric living in England) was unquestionably a Christian (internal evidence clearly indicates that he was familiar with the Vulgate Bible), but he was also aware of his heritage from the heroic age of Germanic courtly culture, in the Scandinavia of the 5th and 6th centuries, and it is unmistakably from this that

---

ḍ, d or j; ṣ, s or sh; ṭ, t or ch; ẓ, z or zh; o, F. cloche; ü, F. menu; ċh, Sc. loch; ṅ, F. bonbon.

the chief characters and basic theme of the work are derived. In one significant aspect a parallel with Vergil's *Æneid* (with which the author of *Beowulf* is believed to have had some familiarity) may be drawn: both works draw upon the tradition and lore of a greatly cherished past for subject matter, but impart to this basic material, in the process of literary creation, important aspects of another and more sophisticated culture (Hellenism, in the case of the *Æneid;* Christian Rome, in the case of *Beowulf*). The result, in the character of Beowulf himself, is a hero disposed to gentleness and even forbearance, who nevertheless, in contending with monstrous embodiments of hideous evil, battles in a fashion which would have been warmly admired by the author's heathen forebears. The work is marked also by numerous very interesting digressions and allusions. Some of these, such as the touching on the subject of Finnsburg (*q.v.*), probably reflect the author's own recognition of and desire to use good story material, whether or not it had direct bearing on the subject of his particular work. Others, such as the very complete discussions of courtly manners and customs, clearly point up the author's deep feeling for his own cultural heritage.

"Beowulf Manuscript." See **Manuscript Cotton Vitellius A XV.**

Beppo (bep'ō). [Full title, **Beppo; A Venetian Story.**] A poem by Byron, written at Venice in 1817 and published in 1818. It is in mock-heroic style, relating the happy reconciliation of Beppo with his wife after a long absence.

Berchtesgaden (berċh'tęs.gä.dęn). A town in S Germany, in the *Land* (state) of Bavaria, American Zone, in the *Kreis* (district) of Upper Bavaria, situated on the Achen River, ab. 15 mi. S of Salzburg: a summer resort in the Bavarian Alps. Adolf Hitler had a summer residence on top of the nearby Obersalzberg, where he frequently held conferences of great political importance; he directed from here the annexation of Austria in 1938. Berchtesgaden and Obersalzberg were subjected to bombardment in March, 1945, and occupied by Allied troops on May 7 of the same year. A great part of the adjoining region was set aside as a recreation area for U. S. occupation troops after the end of the war, and the ruins of Hitler's residence became a much visited point of tourist interest for soldiers and civilians.

Berenger (ber'ęn.jėr), **Eveline.** The resolute, somewhat impatient heroine of Sir Walter Scott's novel *The Betrothed.*

Berenice (ber.ę.nī'sē). b. c28 A.D.; d. after 79 A.D. A Jewish princess; daughter of Herod Agrippa I, king of Judea (41–44 A.D.). A woman of remarkable beauty (events from her life provide the theme of Racine's *Bérénice*), she married, as her second husband, her uncle Herod, king of Chalcis in Lebanon. After his death she lived with her brother Herod Agrippa II (the possibility, or probability, of an incestuous relationship was generally accepted by many of her contemporaries). She subsequently married Polemon, king of Cilicia, but abandoned him soon and returned to her brother. Josephus Flavius declares that she endeavored to stop the cruelties of Florus, the last and worst of the Roman

governors in Judea (*Jewish Wars*, II. 15, 1). However, in the last struggle of her country she, like her brother, was on the side of Rome. She played some part in Roman politics, supporting the elevation of Vespasian as emperor. For some time Titus was attracted by her beauty and grace, and it was believed that he would marry her. She followed the conqueror of her country to Rome, but Titus was compelled, by the low repute in which Jews were held among the Romans, to repudiate her. In the New Testament she is mentioned as coming with her brother to welcome Festus at Caesarea, and as being present at the audience which Paul had with this governor (Acts, xxv. 13, 23; xxvi. 30).

Berenice II (of *Cyrene*). fl. 3rd century B.C. An Egyptian princess; wife of Ptolemy III (Euergetes). She is said to have dedicated her hair in the temple of Arsinoë at Zephyrium for the safe return of her husband from an expedition to Syria. The astronomer Conon of Samos reported that her hair had been transformed into the constellation called *Coma Berenices.*

Beresford (ber'ęz.ford), **John Davys.** b. at Castor, England, March 7, 1873; d. 1947. An English novelist and architect. He first achieved prominence with a trilogy dealing with the life of an architect, the separate volumes of which were entitled *The Early History of Jacob Stahl* (1911), *A Candidate for Truth* (1912), and *The Invisible Event* (1915). Author also of *The Mountains of the Moon* (1915), *God's Counterpoint* (1918), *The Monkey Puzzle* (1925), *Love's Illusion* (1930), *Cleo* (1937), *Snell's Folly* (1939), *Strange Rival* (1940), *A Common Enemy* (1942), *The Riddle of the Tower* (1944), and *The Prisoner* (1945).

Beresford-Hope (ber'ęz.ford.hōp'), **Alexander James.** See **Hope, Alexander James Beresford.**

Bergerac (ber.zhę.ràk), **Cyrano de.** See **Cyrano de Bergerac.**

Bergomask (bėr'gō.mask). [Also, **Bergamask** (-gà-).] A dance parodying what the people of Elizabethan England considered the ridiculous antics of the peasants of Bergamo, an Italian province formerly in the state of Venice. In Shakespeare's *Midsummer Night's Dream*, Bottom asks the audience if they would like "to hear a Bergomask" instead of the Epilogue (V.i).

Bergson (bėrg'sǫn; French, berg.sôṅ), **Henri Louis.** b. at Paris, Oct. 18, 1859; d. there, Jan. 4, 1941. A French philosopher, a professor at the Collège de France from 1900 to 1921. Bergson became a member of the Academy of Moral and Political Science in 1901, and received (1927) the Nobel prize for literature (but world renown had already come to him with the publication of *L'Évolution créatrice* in 1907). Published in English in 1911, under the title *Creative Evolution*, this book, according to William James, marked "one of the great turning-points in the history of thought. . . . It tells of reality itself . . . new horizons loom on every page." The reason for Bergson's influence lay in the originality of his attack on mechanistic materialism. Reality, he argued, cannot be revealed by intelligence alone, since concepts are always relative to practical needs. Philosophy must begin with the intuitions of the inmost reality of consciousness, which is experienced time, or duration, as evidenced, for example, in the phenomenon of memory. In human personality is found the freest expressions of what Bergson terms the *élan vital*, the creative force operative in nature, through the process of evolution. Other important works include *Essai sur les données immédiates de la conscience* (1889; Eng. trans., 1910), *Matière et mémoire* (1897; Eng. trans., 1929), *Le Rire* (1900; Eng. trans., 1911), and *Les Deux Sources de la morale et de la religion* (1932; Eng. trans., 1935).

Beringhen (ber'ing.gĕn), **De.** A gourmand in Edward Bulwer-Lytton's *Richelieu;* he is banished by the cardinal.

Berinthia (bė.rin'thi.a̤). A young and dissolute widow in Sir John Vanbrugh's comedy *The Relapse;* she also appears in Richard Brinsley Sheridan's adaptation, *A Trip to Scarborough.* It is she who, in the former play, lures Loveless away from the habits of marital fidelity which he has for a short time maintained.

Berinthia. [Called "Berry."] The niece of Mrs. Pipchin in Charles Dickens's novel *Dombey and Son;* she is much afflicted with boils on her nose.

Berkeley (bẽrk'li, bärk'li). In Shakespeare's *Richard III*, a gentleman attendant on the Lady Anne.

Berkeley, Elizabeth. b. 1750; d. at Naples, Italy, Jan. 13, 1828. An English writer. Her autobiography was published in 1825 and *Letters to the Margrave of Anspach* (her second husband) in 1814.

Berkeley, George. b. at Dysert Castle, in County Kilkenny, Ireland, March 12, 1685; d. at Oxford, England, Jan. 14, 1753. An Irish prelate (of English descent) of the established church (Church of England), known for his philosophical writings. He is especially famous for his theory of vision, the foundation of the later psychophysiological investigation of that subject, and for the extreme subjective idealism of his metaphysical views, his major tenet being expressed in *Three Dialogues between Hylas and Philonous* (1713), Socratic discussions in which Berkeley sets out to prove the nonexistence of matter except as it is perceived (and thus, of course, finally to confirm the existence of God). He was graduated from Trinity College, Dublin, where he held (1707–24) various offices; in the period 1713–20 he traveled in England and on the Continent. He became dean of Derry in 1724, and bishop of Cloyne in 1734. In 1725 he obtained the patent for a college in Bermuda, of which he was appointed first president, but which was never established; he sailed for Newport, R. I., on Sept. 4, 1728, landing there in January, 1729, and remaining in America until the end of 1731. In 1752 he retired. His other works include *Essay toward a New Theory of Vision* (1709; 3rd edition bound with *Alciphron* in 1732), *A Treatise concerning the Principles of Human Knowledge* (1710 and 1734), *Alciphron, or the Minute Philosopher* (1732), and *Siris, a Chain of Philosophical Reflections and Inquiries concerning the Virtues of Tar-water* (1744; the title *Siris* was first used in the edition of 1746). He was an enthusiastic advocate of the use of tar water as an almost universal remedy. His firm belief in the desirability of settlement in America is reflected in his poem containing the familiar line "Westward the course of Empire takes its way."

Berkeley, George Charles Grantley Fitzhardinge. b. Feb. 10, 1800; d. at Poole, Dorsetshire, England, Feb. 23, 1881. An English writer and sportsman. He was a member of Parliament from 1832 to 1852. He wrote *Berkeley Castle*, a novel (1836), *Sandron Hall, or the Days of Queen Anne* (1840), *The English Sportsman on the Western Prairies* (1861), *Anecdotes of the Upper Ten Thousand* (1867), and *Tales of Life and Death* (1870).

Berkeley, Lord. In Shakespeare's *Richard II*, a minor character who appears once to ask Bolingbroke why he has returned, armed, to England.

Berkeley Castle. A Norman castle between Bristol and Gloucester, England, founded soon after the Conquest: the scene of the murder (1327) of Edward II.

Berkeley Square. A three-act play (1928) by J. C. Squire and John L. Balderston. The central character, in the 1920's, gets his wish to live back in the 18th century; he takes the place of an earlier namesake, but cannot altogether fit himself into the older pattern of life.

Berkenhead (bẽr'kĕn.hed), Sir **John.** See **Birkenhead**, Sir **John.**

Berlin Decree (bėr.lin'). Decree issued (November, 1806), by Napoleon I at Berlin, prohibiting commerce and correspondence with Great Britain, which was declared to be in a state of blockade. The decree also declared all English property forfeited, and all Englishmen in a state occupied by French troops prisoners of war.

Bermoothes (bėr.mö'ᴛʜez). An old name for Bermuda. It is the name of the island in Shakespeare's *Tempest.*

Bermuda (bėr.mū'da̤). [Also: **Bermuda Islands, Bermudas;** former names, **Bermoothes, Somers** (or **Summers** or **Summer**) **Islands.**] Group of islands in the Atlantic Ocean, extending over a distance of 22 mi., ab. 650 mi. SE of Cape Hatteras, N. C., and ab. 700 mi. SE of New York: a British colony. The chief islands are Bermuda (or Great Bermuda), Somerset, Ireland, and St. George. The islands were discovered by Juan Bermudez before 1515, and settled by the English about 100 years later. The shipwreck (1609) here of Sir George Somers and a group of colonists may have been used by Shakespeare as material for *The Tempest.*

Bermudas (bėr.mū'da̤z). A name given to a group of alleys and courts between the bottom of St. Martin's Lane, Half Moon, and Chandos Street, in London; a resort and refuge of thieves, fraudulent debtors, and prostitutes in the 16th and 17th centuries. The area was also called (in the 17th century) the Streights and the Caribbee (corrupted into Cribbee) Islands, and the names were often applied to other localities of similar character.

Bermudas. A poem (1681) by Andrew Marvell. It is a song of praise to God, written as though it were sung by the English religious exiles who were the original colonists of Bermuda.

Bern (bern), **Dietrich von.** See **Dietrich von Bern.**

Bernard (bėr'na̤rd, bėr.närd'), **Saint.** See **Saint Bernard of Clairvaux.**

Bernard (bėr.närd'). An old man in *The Waves*, by Virginia Woolf.

---

d̟,⁻ d or j; ṣ, s or sh; ṭ, t or ch; z̧, z or zh; o, F. cloche; ü, F. menu; c̓h, Sc. loch; ṅ, F. bonbon.

Bernardo (bĕr.när′dō). In Shakespeare's *Hamlet*, a Danish officer. It is he, with Marcellus, who first sees the murdered king's Ghost.

Bernardo del Carpio (ber.när′dō del kär′pyō). fl. 9th century. A legendary Spanish hero. A nephew of Alfonso II (the Chaste), he is said to have fought with great distinction against the Moors, and, according to one tradition, defeated Roland at Roncesvalles. His exploits are celebrated in many Spanish ballads, and form the subject of several dramas by Lope de Vega.

Bernard of Clairvaux (bĕr′nạrd, bĕr.närd′; French, ber.nàr; kler.vō′), Saint. b. at Fontaines, near Dijon, France, 1090; d. at Clairvaux, France, Aug. 20, 1153. A French monastic reformer, scholar, and Doctor of the Church (so named by Pope Pius VIII). He entered the Cistercian monastery of Cîteaux in 1113, and in 1115 became abbot of Clairvaux, near Langres, which post he continued to fill until his death. Refusing all offers of preferment, he nevertheless exercised a profound influence on the ecclesiastical politics of Europe, and was the chief instrument in prevailing upon France and England to recognize Innocent II as Pope in opposition to the rival claimant, Cardinal Peter of León. He procured the condemnation of Abelard's writings at the Council of Sens in 1140.

Bernard of Cluny or **of Morlaix** (klö′ni; môr.lā′). fl. 12th century. A French Benedictine monk, author of a famous Latin poem *De Contemptu Mundi*, written in a remarkable metrical form, rhymed dactylic hexameter couplets with an additional internal rhyme in every line. The poem is popularly known through John Mason Neale's translations of passages from it in the three hymns: *The World Is Very Evil*, *Jerusalem the Golden*, and *For Thee, O Dear, Dear Country*.

Berners (bĕr′nĕrz), 2nd Baron. Title of **Bourchier, John**.

Berners, Belle. [Also, **Isopel Berners**.] In George Borrow's *Lavengro*, one of the principal female characters. Lavengro falls in love with her (she is his second in a duel with the Flaming Tinman), but she refuses to marry him because she realizes that it would ruin his happiness.

Berners (bĕr′nĕrz) or **Bernes** (bĕrnz), **Juliana**. [Also, **Barnes**.] b. c1388; date of death not known. An Englishwoman, according to a late and improbable tradition the prioress of Sopwell Nunnery, near St. Albans, and reputed author of a treatise on hunting contained in *The Boke of St. Albans* (printed 1486; 2nd ed., 1496).

Bernhardt (bĕrn′härt; French, ber.nàr), **Sarah**. [Original name, **Rosine Bernard**; called "the Divine Sarah."] b. at Paris, 1844; d. there, March 26, 1923. A French actress. Born of a Dutch and Jewish family which had embraced Catholicism, she was brought up in a convent. At 13 she began her theatrical training at the Paris Conservatoire and made her debut at the Comédie Française in 1862. She soon left the company to try her career in burlesque, but failed because she could not sing in tune. Her first success came six years later at the Odéon in Jean Racine's *Athalie*. During the Franco-Prussian War, while the theaters were closed, she worked as an ambulance nurse. She returned to the Odéon in 1872 and played Cordelia in Shakespeare's *King Lear* and the Queen in Victor Hugo's *Ruy Blas*. Two years later, she went back to the Comédie Française and scored a triumph in Racine's *Phèdre;* three years later she won acclaim with her playing of Doña Sol in Hugo's *Hernani*. She made a first American tour in 1880 and five more by 1906. She found some of her most successful roles in Victorien Sardou's *Tosca*, *Froufrou* by Henri Meilhac and Ludovic Halévy, and the younger Alexandre Dumas's *La Dame aux Camélias;* she also played the male leads in Edmond Rostand's *L'Aiglon* and in *Hamlet*. In 1912, she made a short film, *Queen Elizabeth*, and became the first great actress to appear in the at that time infant medium of the motion picture. In 1915 one of her legs was amputated because of an old stage injury, but she went on acting, even going to the front to play for the French soldiers in World War I. Her final American tour was in 1918, and her last continental tour was in 1922.

Berni (ber′nē), **Francesco**. [Also: **Berna** (-nä), **Bernia** (-nē.ä).] b. at Lamporecchio, in Tuscany, c1497; d. at Florence, May 26, 1535. An Italian poet, author of *Rime burlesche*, and a *rifacimento* (new version) of the *Orlando Innamorato* by Matteo Maria Boiardo (1541). His poetry is marked by a tone of "light and elegant mockery," for which his name has furnished the descriptive adjective "bernesque."

Bernicia (bĕr.nish′i.ạ). See under **Northumbria**.

Bernstein (bern′stīn), **Baron**. In Thackeray's novel *The Virginians*, the man Beatrix Esmond marries after the death of Tusher. He is a man of unsavory character, whose title cannot alter the fact that he was once a valet at Munich.

Bernstein, Baroness. In Thackeray's novel *The Virginians*, Beatrix Esmond, who has remarried after the death of Tusher, her first husband, and survived her second husband. She has long since lost the beauty of her youth, but retains her wicked wit.

Berosus (bẹ.rō′sus) or **Berossus** (-ros′us). fl. early 3rd century B.C. A Babylonian priest and historian, author of a history of Babylonia (in Greek), fragments of which have been preserved by later writers, including Eusebius and Josephus.

Berowne (bi.rön′). [Also, **Biron**.] In Shakespeare's *Love's Labour's Lost*, one of the three lords attending the King of Navarre at his rural academy. In order to get wisdom they swear to study at the academy for three years and to avoid the sight of women. Berowne is a somewhat unwilling partner to the agreement because he realizes the folly of it. Shortly after the Princess of France and her ladies, including the volatile Rosaline, appear on the scene, each of the lords and the King find that the vow has been broken by their falling in love. As the others play the part of ridiculously affected wooers, Berowne himself confesses the powers of Rosaline in a speech about the torments of love (IV, iii).

"Berry" (ber′i). See **Berinthia**.

Berry, Agnes. b. at Kirkbride, Yorkshire, England, 1764; d. 1852. An English literary figure; sister, and close companion for 48 years, of Mary

Berry (1763–1852). Horace Walpole bequeathed (1797) to the sisters a building on his famous estate of Strawberry Hill (at Twickenham, England), volumes of his published works, and manuscripts of his unpublished works.

Berry, Mary. b. at Kirkbridge, Yorkshire, England, March 16, 1763; d. at London, Nov. 20, 1852. An English literary figure. She and her sister Agnes (1764–1852) were friends of Horace Walpole, and she was one of his literary executors. Her chief work is *Social Life in England and France, 1660–1830* (2 vols., 1828, 1831).

Bertha (bėr'thạ). [Known as **Gertrude.**] The daughter of the Duke of Brabant in *The Beggar's Bush*, a comedy by John Fletcher and Philip Massinger.

Bertha, Big. See **Big Bertha.**

Bertha Plummer (plum'ėr). See **Plummer, Bertha.**

Bertie (bär'ti), **Willoughby.** [Title, 4th Earl of **Abingdon.**] b. Jan. 16, 1740; d. Sept. 26, 1799. An English liberal statesman and political writer. He opposed his country's participation in the Revolutionary War, and the policy which led to it, and sympathized with the French Revolution. He wrote *Thoughts of Mr. Burke's Letter to the Sheriffs of Bristol on the Affairs of America* (1777) and others.

Bertram (bėr'tram). In Shakespeare's *All's Well That Ends Well*, the young Count of Rossillion, who is loved by Helena and forced to marry her. He refuses to treat her as his wife unless she fulfills certain apparently impossible conditions; these she meets by means of a ruse, and Bertram agrees (in the event, happily) to live with her.

Bertram. A tragedy by Charles Robert Maturin, produced in 1816. The character of Bertram is an incarnation of a burning desire for revenge combined with passionate love, but with a considerable element of pathos. Edmund Kean created the part.

Bertram. An aged minstrel who is the companion and protector of Lady Augusta of Berkely in Sir Walter Scott's novel *Castle Dangerous.*

Bertram, Charles. [Pseudonym, **Charles Julius.**] b. at London, 1723; d. 1765. An English literary figure, a professor of English at the Royal Marine Academy, grammarian, and literary forger. He pretended, somewhat like James Macpherson and Thomas Chatterton, to have discovered an old manuscript on Roman antiquities which he claimed was by Richard of Cirencester, a 14th-century monk and chronicler; he deceived William Stukeley, an eminent antiquary of the day, and many others, who accepted his work as genuine, a reputation it generally held until 1866, when it was completely exposed as a forgery by Benjamin B. Woodward in the *Gentleman's Magazine.* Stukeley published Bertram's work in good faith in 1757, and Bertram himself published it at Copenhagen in the same year. His other works, all published at Copenhagen, are *An Essay on the Excellency of the English Tongue* (1749), *Rudimenta Grammaticae Anglicanae* (1750), *Ethics from Various Authors* (1751), *Royal English-Danish Grammar* (1753), *On the Great Advantages of a Godly Life* (1760, trans. from English into Danish), and other works in both German and Danish.

Bertram, Godfrey. The laird of Ellangowan in Sir Walter Scott's novel *Guy Mannering.* He is a man of weak character, anxious for political preferment, plundered and ruined by Glossin.

Bertram, Harry. The son of Godfrey Bertram in Sir Walter Scott's novel *Guy Mannering;* one of the principal characters, and the lover of Julia Mannering.

Bertram, Lucy. The daughter of Godfrey Bertram in Sir Walter Scott's novel *Guy Mannering.*

Bertram, Sir Thomas. In Jane Austen's novel *Mansfield Park,* the owner of the estate Mansfield Park.

Bertram Risingham (riz'ing.ạm). See **Risingham, Bertram.**

Bertrand of Brittany (bėr'trạnd; brit'ạ.ni). A historical novel by Warwick Deeping, published in 1908. It deals with the adventures of Bertrand Du Guesclin (c1320–80), who, as a constable of France, won himself the epithet "Eagle of Brittany" with his exploits against the English at Rennes (1356–57) and elsewhere.

"Bert" Smallways (smôl'wāz). See **Smallways, Albert Peter.**

Berwick (bėr'wik), **Mary.** Pseudonym of **Procter, Adelaide Ann.**

Beryn (ber'in), **History of.** A late Middle English poem formerly ascribed to Chaucer as *The Merchant's Second Tale,* but no longer considered to be his. The author is unknown.

Berzelius Nibbidard Paragot (bėr.zē'li.us nib'i.därd par'ạ.got). See **Paragot, Berzelius Nibbidard.**

Besant (bez'ạnt), **Annie.** [Maiden name, **Wood.**] b. at London, Oct. 1, 1847; d. Sept. 20, 1933. An English political radical, theosophist, and writer on philosophical topics. In 1867 she married Frank Besant, a clergyman, and was legally separated from him in 1873. She was influential in the radical free-thought movement represented by Charles Bradlaugh, and in 1877 was tried with him on charges of immorality, as a result of their joint publication of a pamphlet explaining and advocating birth control. In 1889 she became prominent as a pupil of Madame Helena Petrovna Blavatsky and a member of the Theosophical Society. By her long residence (1889 *et seq.*) in India, and her championship of the cause of home rule for India, she became an outstanding figure in Indian political life. She was equally renowned for her extensive writings and lectures on religious and philosophical subjects and was instrumental in acquainting English readers with Hindu philosophical speculation and thought. Her early efforts in India were dedicated to establishing (1898) a Hindu university, the Central Hindu College at Benares; her later career was devoted to agitation for home rule for India within the framework of the British Commonwealth. Among her best-known works on religion and philosophy are *Karma* (1895), *Four Great Religions* (1897), *Theosophy and the New Psychology* (1904), and *Wisdom of the Upanishads* (1906); among her other writings are *Autobiography* (1893), *How India Wrought for Freedom* (1915), and *India, Bond or Free* (1926).

ḍ, d or j; ṣ, s or sh; ṭ, t or ch; ẓ, z or zh; o, F. cloche; ü, F. menu; ch, Sc. loch; ṅ, F. bonbon,

Besant (bĕ.zant′), Sir **Walter.** b. Aug. 14, 1836; d. June 9, 1901. An English novelist, knighted in 1895. He was appointed a professor at the Royal College of Mauritius, but returned to England on account of ill health. From 1871 to 1882 he wrote in collaboration with James Rice, producing such novels as *Ready-Money Mortiboy* (1872) and *The Seamy Side* (1881). It was due to his novel *All Sorts and Conditions of Men* (1882), that the "People's Palace," a public hall in the East End of London, was built. Among his other works are *French Humorists* (1873), and an autobiography (1902).

Bess (bes). [Also: **Besse**; full name, **Bess Bridges.**] The tavern maid who is the heroine of Thomas Heywood's *Fair Maid of the West.*

Besselia (be.sē′li.ạ). The sweetheart of Captain Crowe, in Tobias Smollett's novel *Sir Launcelot Greaves.*

Bess of the Woods (bes). A novel by Warwick Deeping, published in 1906. It is a story of English rustic life in the middle of the 18th century.

Bessus (bes′us). fl. 331–330 B.C. A Persian soldier and satrap of Bactria. He commanded the left wing of the Persian army at the battle of Arbela in 331 B.C. He murdered Darius III in 330, but was captured shortly thereafter by Alexander the Great, and delivered to Oxathres, the brother of Darius, by whom he was executed.

Bessus. A blustering, swaggering coward in Beaumont and Fletcher's play *A King and No King.*

Bestiary (bes′ti.er.i). A Middle English poem (c1250). It is a poem of some 800 short lines made up of descriptions (all more or less fabulous) of the lion, eagle, serpent, ant, hart, fox, spider, whale, mermaid, elephant, turtle-dove, panther, and the culver (or dove), followed in each case by a Christian application or moral. See also **beast fable.**

Betham (beth′ạm), Sir **William.** b. at Stradbrooke, Suffolk, England, May 22, 1779; d. Oct. 26, 1853. An English antiquary, Ulster king-of-arms. His works include *Irish Antiquarian Researches* (1827), *Origin and History of the Constitution of England, and of the early Parliaments of Ireland* (1834; a reissue, with a new title, of an earlier work), and *The Gael and the Cymbri* (1834).

Betham-Edwards (beth′ạm.ed′wạrdz), **Matilda Barbara.** b. at Westerfield, Suffolk, England, March 4, 1836; d. at Hastings, Essex, England, Jan. 4, 1919. An English novelist, poet, editor, autobiographer, and author of books on France. She was educated chiefly by travel in France and Germany. A prolific author, she wrote the novels *The White House by the Sea* (1857), *John and I* (1862), *Dr. Jacob* (1864), *Kitty* (1869), *A Dream of Millions* (1891), *Lord of the Harvest* (1899), *A Suffolk Courtship* (1900), *Barham Brockleband, M.D.* (1904). *The Golden Bee* (1806), poetry published by Dickens in his periodical, *All the Year Round*, and *Poems* (1885 and 1907) are included in her verse works. *France of To-Day* (1892–94), *The Roof of France, or Travels in Lozère* (1899), *East of Paris* (1902), *Home Life in France* (1905), *Literary Rambles in France* (1907), *French Men, Women, and Books* (1910), *In French Africa* (1913), *Hearts of Alsace* (1916), and *Twentieth Century France* (1917) give

evidence of her interest in France. Her autobiographical works include *Reminiscences* (1898), *Anglo-French Reminiscences* (1899), and *Mid-Victorian Memories* (1919). In 1889 and 1898, respectively, she edited Arthur Young's *Travels in France* and *Autobiography and Correspondence.*

Bethany (beth′ạ.ni). In the Bible, a place southeast of the Mount of Olives, near Jerusalem: the dwelling place of Lazarus. Mat. xxi. 17, etc.

Beth-arbel (beth.är′bẹl). In the Bible, the scene of a massacre by Shalman: probably the modern Irbid. Hos. x. 14.

Bethel (beth′ẹl). In the Bible, a town 12 miles north of Jerusalem: the resting place of the ark of the covenant. 1 Sam. vii. 16.

Bethgelert (beth.gel′ẹrt). See under **Gellert.**

Beth-horon (beth.hō′rọn), **Nether** and **Upper.** In the Bible, two villages about 12 miles west of Jerusalem. Between them Joshua smote the Amorites. Josh. x. 10.

Bethlehem (beth′lẹ.ẹm). In the Bible, the birthplace of David and of Jesus, 6 miles south of Jerusalem. Mat. ii. 1.

Bethlehem Royal Hospital. See under **Bedlam.**

Bethnal Green (beth′nạl). A metropolitan borough in E London, in the County of London, situated on the N bank of the river Thames, ab. 1 mi. NE of Liverpool Street station. It forms a part of the East End of London and is among the smallest of the London boroughs in area. It is noted as the locality mentioned in the old ballad *The Beggar's Daughter of Bednal Green.* The beggar's house is still shown. The Bethnal Green Museum is a branch of the Victoria and Albert Museum, and was opened in 1872 in Victoria Park Square, Cambridge Road, for the inhabitants of East London. The district was heavily bombed (1940–41) during World War II.

Bethphage (beth′fạ.jē, beth′fāj). In the Bible, a village near Bethany, on the Mount of Olives. Mark, xi. 1.

Bethsaida (beth.sā′i.dạ). In the Bible, a place on the shore of the Sea of Galilee, probably between Capernaum and Magdala. John, i. 44.

Bethune Baliol (bē′tun bāl′yọl, bā′li.ọl), (Mrs.). See **Baliol**, (Mrs.) **Bethune.**

Betrothal, The. See under **Angel in the House, The.**

Betrothed, The. A novel (1825) by Sir Walter Scott, classed as one of the *Tales of the Crusaders.* It should not be confused with *The Betrothed* by Alessandro Manzoni, the English title of *I Promessi Sposi.* The novel is laid against a background of the Welsh Marches (the border country between England and Wales) during the reign of Henry II.

Betsey Prig (bet′si prig′). See **Prig, Betsey.**

Betsey Trotwood (trot′wụd). See **Trotwood, Betsey.**

Betteredge (bet′rij), **Gabriel.** In Wilkie Collins's novel *The Moonstone*, Lady Verinder's steward (earlier her bailiff), by whom much of the story is told, and who plays a part finally in solving the mystery. He is a devoted reader of *Robinson Crusoe*, to which work he frequently alludes.

Betterton (bet′ẹr.tọn), Mrs. d. 1711. An English actress. She apparently first joined Sir William

Davenant's company at Lincoln's Inn Fields Theatre c1661, later becoming attached to the acting group headed by Thomas Betterton, whom she presently married. She was known as Mrs. Saunderson (or Sanderson) at the time of her first stage appearance. She was noted, like her husband, for her Shakespearian roles, and as one of the first women to act in Shakespeare's plays may have contributed toward their popularity in the first years of the Restoration (previously female roles were taken by men or boys). Among the licentious careers of most Restoration actresses, hers is remarkable for its good reputation.

Betterton, Thomas. b. at London, c1635; d. there, April 28, 1710. An English actor and dramatist; son of an under-cook of Charles I. He was apprenticed to a bookseller, but other than this little is known of his early life. It is supposed that he began to act in 1659 or 1660, and it is known that he joined Sir William Davenant's company at the Lincoln's Inn Fields Theatre in 1661. Samuel Pepys, who saw him at the beginning of his career, and Alexander Pope, who saw him at the end, spoke of him as the best actor they had ever seen. After Davenant's death, Betterton headed the acting company, and with it moved (1671) to a different theater. He joined his company with that of the Theatre Royal, but broke with this group in 1695. Thereafter he reopened the Lincoln's Inn Fields Theatre with a production of William Congreve's *Love for Love*, and remained there until 1705, when he moved to the Haymarket Theatre, a new house especially constructed for him by John Vanbrugh. Although active in roles from Restoration drama, he excelled in Shakespearian roles, both comic and tragic, including Hamlet, Mercutio, Sir Toby Belch, and Macbeth. He wrote several plays based upon Elizabethan and Jacobean models. He was intimate with John Dryden and with many other notable men of his time.

Bettris (bet′ris). A country girl who loves the titular hero in the play *George-a′-Greene, The Pinner of Wakefield*, attributed to Robert Greene.

Betty (bet′i), **William Henry West.** [Called "Master Betty" and the "Young Roscius."] b. at Shrewsbury, England, Sept. 13, 1791; d. at London, Aug. 24, 1874. An English actor, especially famous for his precocity. He made his first appearance, on Aug. 19, 1803, as Oswyn in *Zara*, and played Douglas, Rolla, Romeo, Tancred, and Hamlet within two years with great success. At the height of his popularity, the younger William Pitt got a motion passed in the House of Commons that an adjournment should be made to allow the members of that body to attend a performance of Betty as Hamlet (for a time, indeed, he actually surpassed the great Kemble and Mrs. Siddons in popularity). His popularity, however, faded as quickly as it had grown; he left the stage in 1808 to attend Cambridge, returned to it in 1812, and finally abandoned it in 1824.

Betty Higden (hig′den), **Mrs.** See **Higden, Mrs. Betty.**

Betty Modish (mō′dish), **Lady.** See **Modish, Lady Betty.**

Between the Acts. A novel (1941) by Virginia Woolf. It was published posthumously (the author had died earlier in the same year) and represents a return to the essentially poetic technique which had marked *To the Lighthouse* (1927) and *The Waves* (1931). The work centers around a pageant produced by Miss La Trobe, which is in verse. As in some of the author's other works, time is not a sequence of events but a merging of past and present, and it is brought together in the pageant, which reviews the history of England. The central figures are Giles and Isabella Oliver, Mrs. Swithin, and her brother Bartholemew.

Beulah (bū′la). In the Old Testament, the name of the land of Israel when it shall be "married." Isa. lxii. 4.

Beulah. A land of rest, "where the sun shineth night and day," in John Bunyan's *Pilgrim's Progress*. The Pilgrims stay here till the time comes for them to go across the river of Death to the Celestial City.

Beuves d'Hantone (bėv dän′ton). A French *chanson de geste* (12th century), concerned with the adventures of Bevis of Hampton.

Beverley (bev′ėr.li). The titular hero of Edward Moore's tragedy *The Gamester*. David Garrick first played the part. Mrs. Beverley was a favorite character with the actresses of the time.

Beverley. The jealous lover of Belinda in Arthur Murphy's play *All in the Wrong*.

Beverley, Cecilia. The heroine of Fanny Burney's novel *Cecilia*.

Beverley, Constance de. A perjured nun in Scott's poem *Marmion*. She loves Marmion, and

> ". . . bows her pride
> A horseboy in his train to ride."

She is walled alive in the dungeons of a convent as a punishment for her broken vows.

Beverley, Ensign. The character assumed by Captain Absolute, in Richard Brinsley Sheridan's comedy *The Rivals*, to win the love of the romantic Lydia, who will not marry any one so suitable as the son of Sir Anthony Absolute.

Beverly (bev′ėr.li), **Thomas.** See under **Mayor of York.**

Bevil (bev′il). A character in Thomas Shadwell's comedy *Epsom Wells*.

Bevil. The model of everything becoming an 18th-century gentleman, in Richard Steele's play *The Conscious Lovers*.

Bevis (bē′vis). The horse of Lord Marmion in Sir Walter Scott's poem *Marmion*.

Bevis, George. In Shakespeare's *2 Henry VI*, a supporter of Jack Cade.

Bevis Marks. A thoroughfare in St. Mary Axe, near Houndsditch, London. It is referred to in Charles Dickens's *Old Curiosity Shop*.

Bevis of Hampton (hamp′ton). [Also, **Sir Southhampton.**] A knight whose bravery and adventures are celebrated in Arthurian romance and by Michael Drayton in *Polyolbion*. A Middle English verse romance on Bevis was in the 15th or 16th century turned into a prose romance and printed c1650. He was originally called Beuves d'Antone, from the Italian *Buovo d'Antona*, a name adapted as *d'Hantone* in French and *Hampton* in English.

---

d̦, d or j; ṣ, s or sh; ț, t or ch; z̦, z or zh; o, F. cloche; ü, F. menu; ċh, Sc. loch; ṅ, F. bonbon.

Bewick (bū′ik), **Thomas.** b. at Cherryburn, near Newcastle, England, in August, 1753; d. at Gateshead, near Newcastle, Nov. 8, 1828. An English wood engraver. He was apprenticed at the age of 14 to Ralph Bielby, a copperplate engraver at Newcastle; after 1770 he did most of Bielby's wood-engraving business. At the expiration of his apprenticeship he went to London, but returned shortly to Newcastle, where he entered into partnership with Bielby and occupied his old shop in Saint Nicholas Churchyard until a short time before his death. Among his chief works are the illustrations for John Gay's *Fables* (1779), *Select Fables* (1784), a *General History of Quadrupeds* (1790), and his best-known work, which was never completely finished, *The History of British Birds* (2 vols., 1797–1804), in which he showed the knowledge of a naturalist combined with the skill of an artist. His best-known (and perhaps his finest) single block is *The Chillingham Bull* (1789), after a painting by Landseer. His last complete work was the illustrations for *Aesop's Fables* (1818), upon which he was engaged six years. He was assisted by his son Robert Elliot Bewick, and by some of his pupils.

Beyle (bāl), **Marie Henri.** See **Stendhal.**

Bezaleel (bḙ.zal′ḙ.ḙl). In the Bible, the artificer who executed the works of art on the Hebrew tabernacle. Ex. xxxi. 2–6.

Bezaliel (bḙ.zal′i.el). In the second part of the satire *Absalom and Achitophel* by John Dryden and Nahum Tate, a character meant for Henry Somerset, Marquis of Worcester, afterward Duke of Beaufort. He was noted for his devotion to learning.

Bezonian (bḙ.zō′ni.ạn). A name given to a beggar; a mean, low person. According to John Florio a *bisogno* was "a new leuied souldier such as comes needy to the war." Randle Cotgrave defines *bisongne* as "a filthie knave, or clowne, a raskall, a bisonian, basehumoured scoundrel." Its original sense is a raw recruit; hence, as a term of contempt, a beggar, a needy person. The word is used by Shakespeare in *2 Henry IV* and derives from the Italian noun *bisogno* (need).

Bhagavad-Gita (bä″gạ.vạd.gē′tä). A Sanskrit dramatic poem of the 1st or 2nd century, in which Krishna (Bhagavat) is identified with the Supreme Being.

Bhagavata-Purana (bä″gạ.vạ.tạ.pö̤.rä′nạ). The most popular of the puranas. Its best-known book, the tenth, is the history of Krishna. It is ascribed to the grammarian Vopadeva, of about the 13th century.

Bianca (bi.ang′kạ). In Shakespeare's *Othello*, a woman of Cyprus, and the mistress of Cassio. He asks her to do some sewing on a handkerchief which he has found in his lodging. This handkerchief, a love token from Othello to Desdemona, has been planted by Iago, who contrives that Othello shall see Bianca return it to Cassio and thus be led to assume that Desdemona has betrayed their love and given it to Cassio. Cassio's talk about Bianca is also misconstrued deliberately by Iago, when Othello is present, as referring to Desdemona.

Bianca. In Shakespeare's *Taming of the Shrew*, the gentle sister of Katherina (the "Shrew"). She is wooed by Hortensio and Gremio, but is won by Lucentio.

Bianca. A pathetic and beautiful girl, the titular heroine of *The Fair Maid of the Inn*, by Philip Massinger, William Rowley, and John Fletcher.

Bianca. In Thomas Middleton's *Women Beware Women*, the young wife of Leantio.

Bianca. The Duchess of Pavia, in John Ford's play *Love's Sacrifice;* a gross and profligate woman who has the art of appearing innocent by denying the favors she means to grant.

Bianchi (byäng′kē). A political faction which arose in Tuscany c1300. The Guelph family of the Cancellieri at Pistoia having banished the Ghibelline family of the Panciatichi, a feud for power arose between two distantly related branches of the former, who were distinguished from each other by the names of Bianchi and Neri (the whites and the blacks). In the period 1296–1300, the two factions became so violent that Florence, in order to bring peace to Pistoia, required that city to banish the whole family of the Cancellieri, but at the same time opened its own gates to them. In Florence the Neri allied themselves with Corso Donati and the violent Guelphs, and the Bianchi with Vieri de' Cerchi and the moderate Guelphs, and subsequently with the Ghibellines and the Panciatichi. Pope Boniface VIII espoused the party of the Neri, and sent, nominally to bring about a reconciliation, Charles de Valois to Florence in 1301, with the result that the Bianchi, among whom was Dante, were exiled.

Bianco (byäng′kō), **Margery.** [Maiden name, **Williams.**] b. at London, July 22, 1881; d. at New York, Sept. 6, 1944. An English novelist and author of books for children. Educated in the U. S., where she lived for many years, she also resided in France, Italy, and England. Author of *The Late Returning* (1902), *The Price of Youth* (1904), *The Bar* (1906), novels; and books for children, including *The Velveteen Rabbit* (1922), *Poor Cecco* (1925), *The Little Wooden Doll* (1925) and *The Skin Horse* (1927), the latter two illustrated by her daughter, Pamela, *The Adventures of Andy* (1927), *Candlestick*, and *All About Pets* (both 1929).

Bible. 1. The Book, or rather the Books, by way of eminence; the Scriptures of the Old and New Testaments. The word *bible* is not found in the English version, but the Greek word occurs frequently, being always translated "book" or "books," sometimes indicating the books of the Old Testament. The Bible consists of two parts: the Old Testament, written in Hebrew, containing the Law, the Prophets, and the sacred writings, or Hagiographa; and the New Testament, written in Greek, consisting of the four Gospels, the Book of Acts, the Epistles of Paul and other apostolic writers, and the Apocalypse or Book of Revelation, the only strictly prophetic book which it contains. Roman Catholic writers accept, in addition to these, most of the books contained in the Apocrypha of the King James version, which occur in the Septuagint (see below) and Vulgate, distributed among the other books of the Old Testament. The principal ancient versions of the Bible, or of portions of it, are the *Targums,* a Chaldee or Aramaic paraphrase or in-

terpretation of the more ancient Hebrew Scriptures; the *Samaritan Pentateuch*, a Hebrew version of the first five books of the Old Testament, ancient in its character, and preserved with jealous care among the Samaritans; the *Septuagint*, a Greek version of the Old Testament prepared by Jewish scholars at Alexandria under the Ptolemies, principally in the 3rd century B.C.; the *Vulgate*, a Latin version of both Old Testament and New Testament, prepared by Jerome at the close of the 4th century A.D.; and the *Peshito*, a Syriac version of the Old Testament and the major part of the New Testament, probably prepared in the 2nd century A.D. Translations were early made into the principal languages of Christendom. The first complete translation into English was that of Wycliffe, about 1383; and the first printed English versions were those of Tyndale and Coverdale, 1524–35. Other important versions are the *Lutheran*, in the German, by Martin Luther, 1521–34 (the basis of the Swedish, Danish, Icelandic, Dutch, and Finnish versions); the *Authorized* or *King James*, prepared by a special commission of scholars in England under James I, 1604–11; the *Douay*, a popular name given to a translation into English prepared by Roman Catholic divines, the Old Testament at Douay (1609–10), the New Testament at Reims (1582); and the *Revised*, a recension of the King James Bible prepared by a committee of British and American Protestant divines, the New Testament appearing in 1881, and the Old Testament in 1885. Roman Catholics and Protestants differ in the degree of authority which they attach to the Bible. The Roman Catholic Church "receives with piety and reverence all the books of the Old and New Testaments, since one God is the Author of each" (Council of Trent); but "at the same time it maintains that there is an unwritten word of God over and above Scripture" (Cath. Dict.). Protestants generally hold that "the Supreme Judge, by which all controversies of religion are to be determined, and all decrees of councils, opinions of ancient writers, and private spirits are to be examined, and in whose sentence we are to rest, can be no other but the Holy Spirit speaking in Scripture" (Westminster Conf. of Faith).
Hence—**2.** Any book or collection of religious writings received by its adherents as a divine revelation: as, the Koran is the *Bible* of the Mohammedans; the Mormon *Bible.*
3. Any great book.

> To tellen all wold passen any *bible,*
> That owher [anywhere] is.

(Chaucer, Prologue to *Canon's Yeoman's Tale.*)

Bible in Spain, The. A travel narrative by George Borrow, published in 1843. The author gives accounts of the people of Spain and tells of his adventures there during the Carlist disturbances. One cannot tell how many of the incidents described here are based on experience, for Borrow mixed much fiction in his accounts of the wanderer's adventures in a foreign country.

Bible of Amiens (am'i.ẹnz; French, à.myaṅ), **The.** A prose work (1885) by John Ruskin.

Bible of Forty-two Lines, The. A Gutenberg Bible (1450–55), with 42 lines to the column.

Bible of Thirty-six Lines, The. Perhaps the oldest printed edition of the Latin Bible. A copy was given by Gutenberg to a monastery near Mainz. The two-column pages have 36 lines to the column.

Biblia Pauperum (bib'li.ạ pô'pẹ.rum) or **Bible of the Poor.** A popular manuscript Bible of the Middle Ages, which existed in many copies. It is supposed to have consisted first of pictures entirely.

bibliography. **1.** The writing of books.
2. The science which treats of books, their materials, authors, typography, editions, dates, subjects, classification, history, etc. "*Bibliography* . . . being the knowledge of books, which now is not confined to an 'erudition of title-pages,' but embraces the subject-division of all the branches of human learning." (J. C. Van Dyke, *Books and How to Use Them.*)
3. A classified list of authorities or books on any theme: as, the *bibliography* of political economy.

bibliomania. Book-madness; a rage for collecting and possessing books, especially rare and curious ones.

bibliophile. A lover of books.

bibliopole. A bookseller, now especially a dealer in rare and curious books.

bibliotheca (bib''li.ọ.thē'kạ). **1.** A library; a place to keep books; a collection of books. "Cairo was once celebrated for its magnificent collection of books. Besides private libraries, each large mosque had its *bibliotheca*." (Sir Richard Burton, *El-Medinah.*)
2. The Bible. "It is a *bibliotheca*, or a copy of the Bible of the large size folio, and now bound up into several large volumes." (Rock, *Church of our Fathers.*)

Bibliothèque Nationale (bē.blē.o.tek nà.syo.nàl). A vast library in the Rue de Richelieu, Paris. Its history goes back farther than that of printing. Henry II made obligatory the deposit of a copy of each book published in the kingdom.

Bickerdyke (bik'ẹr.dĭk), **John.** Pseudonym of **Cook, Charles Henry.**

Bickerstaff (bik'ẹr.stàf), **Isaac, Astrologer.** A pseudonym adopted by Jonathan Swift in 1708 during his controversy with the cobbler John Partridge, and borrowed (1709) by Richard Steele for his use as editor of *The Tatler.* The Swift-Partridge encounter began when Partridge published astrological predictions in an almanac; Swift, to prove these nonsensical, retorted with the parody *Predictions for the ensuing year, by Isaac Bickerstaff;* in this pamphlet he foretold Partridge's death on March 29; on March 30, he published a fulsome account of Partridge's demise; when the cobbler protested vigorously, Swift published a *Vindication*, in which he purported to prove Partridge's death beyond doubt. The joke became very popular, and when Steele wanted a pseudonym for himself, he adopted the name of Bickerstaff, as did Benjamin West (1730–1813).

Bickerstaffe (bik'ẹr.stàf), **Isaac.** b. in Ireland, 1735; d. 1812. A British dramatist. As a boy he was one of the pages to Lord Chesterfield, at that time lord lieutenant of Ireland. He attained an honorable position in the society of men of letters, but in 1772

ḍ, d or j; ṣ, s or sh; ṭ, t or ch; ẓ, z or zh; o, F. cloche; ü, F. menu; ċh, Sc. loch; ṅ, F. bonbon.

was suspected of a capital crime, and fled to St.-Malo, France, where he lived under an assumed name in poverty for many years. He wrote among other works, *Leucothoe*, a tragic opera (1756), *Love in a Village*, a comic opera, based on Charles Johnson's *The Village Opera* and acted with great success in 1762 (printed in 1763), *The Maid of the Mill* (1765) based on Richardson's novel, *Pamela*, *The Hypocrite* (1769), an adaptation of Colley Cibber's *The Non-Juror*, and *Lionel and Clarissa* (1769). He was a rival of Gay in musical comedy.

Bickerstaffe-Drew (bik′ẽr.stȧf.drö′), Monsignor Count **Francis Browning Drew.** [Pseudonym, **John Ayscough.**] b. at Headingly, Leeds, England, Feb. 11, 1858; d. at London, July 3, 1928. English novelist, essayist, and Roman Catholic priest. He was educated at Lichfield, at St. Chad's College, Denstone, and at Oxford University. The son of a Church of England clergyman, he became a Roman Catholic in 1879 and added his mother's maiden name, Drew, to his own name, in 1897; ordained in 1884, he was acting Catholic chaplain (1886–92) and chaplain (1892–99) to the British forces at Plymouth, and served (1914–15) in World War I; he was made a papal count in 1909. Under his pseudonym he wrote several novels, tales, and collections of essays, among them *Marotz* (1908), *Dromina and San Celestino* (1909), *Mezzogiorno* (1910), *Hurdcott* (1911), *Faustula* (1912), *Gracechurch* (1913), *Monksbridge* (1914), *French Windows* (1917), *Jacqueline* (1918), *Abbotscourt* (1919), *First Impressions in America* (1921), *Pages from the Past* (1922), and *Dobachi* (1923).

Bickersteth (bik′ẽr.steth), **Edward Henry.** b. Jan. 25, 1825; d. May 16, 1906. An English clergyman and poet. He was the author of *Yesterday, To-day, and For Ever* (1866) and others. He became bishop of Exeter in 1885.

Biddy (bid′i). Mr. Wopsle's "great-aunt's granddaughter," in Charles Dickens's *Great Expectations;* an orphan who for a time is in love with Pip, she is afterward married to Joe Gargery.

Biddy, Miss. A comic character in David Garrick's farce *Miss in her Teens.*

Biddy Tipkin (tip′kin). See **Tipkin, Biddy.**

Bidpai (bid′pī). See **Kalilah and Dimnah.**

Biedermann (bē′dẽr.män), **Arnold.** In Sir Walter Scott's novel *Anne of Geierstein*, the principal public official of the canton of Unterwalden. He has surrendered his claim to the countship of Geierstein to his brother, preferring the simple life of a shepherd, but is summoned thence by his fellow citizens to serve as one of their most respected officials.

Bifrost (biv′rost). [Also: **Asbru**; Old Norse, **Ásbrú.**] In Norse mythology, the rainbow, the bridge of the gods which reached from heaven to earth. Every day the gods rode over it to their judgment-place under the tree Yggdrasil, near the sacred well of the Norns.

Big Ben (ben). The bell in the clock tower of the houses of Parliament, London. It was cast in 1856 and is said to have been the largest bell to that date in England. It is the second of the name, the first having been defective. During World War II, the sound of Big Ben was made a symbol of British resistance, and its striking was broadcast nightly at 9 P.M. over the British Broadcasting network.

Big Bertha (bẽr′thạ). A name popularly applied to a type of long-range 8.26-inch gun used by the Germans in shelling Paris in the spring of 1918, during the latter part of World War I. The name was derived from that of Bertha Krupp von Bohlen, heiress of the Krupp works at Essen, Germany, where the gun was manufactured. (The name was originally coined as "Die dicke Bertha" by German soldiers; it was picked up in translation by members of the Allied forces.)

Big Brother. The legendary head of the Party, presumably now dead (if indeed he ever existed), in George Orwell's novel *1984.*

Big-endians (big′en′di.ạnz). In Jonathan Swift's *Gulliver's Travels*, a religious sect (intended to satirize the Catholic party) of Lilliput, who considered it a matter of duty to break eggshells at the big end. They were considered heretics by the Little-endians (intended for the Protestants), who broke their eggshells in what was for them the orthodox manner, at the little end.

Bigg (big), **John Stanyan.** b. at Ulverston, Lancashire, England, July 14, 1828; d. there, May 19, 1865. An English poet, dramatist, novelist, and journalist. Editor of the Ulverston *Advertiser* and later, during his stay in Ireland, of the *Downshire Protestant*, he was finally editor and proprietor (1860 *et seq.*) of the *Advertiser*. His works are *The Sea King* (1828), a metrical tale; *Night and the Soul* (1854), a poetic drama; *Shifting Scenes and other Poems* (1862); and *Alfred Staunton* (1860), a novel. With Gerald Massey, Alexander Smith, Sydney Dobell, and Philip James Bailey, Bigg was a member of what William E. Aytoun called the "spasmodic school" of English writers.

Big House, The. A play, with the subtitle *Four Scenes in its Life*, by Lennox Robinson, produced in 1926 and published in 1928.

Bigot (big′ọt), **Lord.** In Shakespeare's *King John*, a noble who joins the French after Arthur's death, but later returns to England.

Bildad (bil′dad). [Called **"Bildad the Shuhite."**] In the Old Testament, one of the three friends of Job. He is called the "Shuhite," after a territory identified by some with the Sakaia of Ptolemy, E of Bashan, by others with Suhu of the cuneiform inscriptions, situated on the Euphrates S of Carchemish.

"Biler," The. See **Toodle, Mr.**

Bilioso (bil.i.ō′sō). A comic diplomat, in John Marston's play *The Malcontent.*

Bill Barley (bil bär′li), **Old.** See **Barley, Old Bill.**

Billickin (bil′i.kin), **Mrs.** A keeper of lodgings in Charles Dickens's *Mystery of Edwin Drood*. Her distinguishing characteristics are "personal faintness and an overpowering personal candor."

Billingsgate (bil′ingz.gāt). A gate, wharf, and fish-market in London, on the N bank of the Thames, near London Bridge. There may have been a water gate here from the earliest times. The market was established in 1559, in the reign of Queen Elizabeth, and was made a free market in 1699. It was at first a general landing place for merchandise of all kinds.

fat, fāte, fär, ȧsk, fāre; net, mē, hẽr; pin, pīne; not, nōte, möve, nôr; up, lūte, púll; ᴛʜ, then;

It was burned down in 1715 and rebuilt. In 1852 new buildings were erected, and again in 1856. The present buildings were finished in 1874. The coarse language once used by the fishwives and others in the neighborhood gave the name of billingsgate to such speech. "Satire is nothing but ribaldry and *billingsgate*." (Addison, *Papers*.)

Bill of Rights. The name applied to one of the most important of the statutes which, taken collectively and with a considerable body of tradition, may be said to comprise the constitution of what is now the United Kingdom of Great Britain and Northern Ireland. When William of Orange and his consort Mary were offered the crown of England, the tender was conditional upon their acceptance of the Declaration of Rights of 1688. This Declaration, with the addition of an article barring the crown to Roman Catholics, was given the force of law by enactment as the Bill of Rights in 1689, the full title being "An Act declaring the Rights and Liberties of the Subject, and settling the Succession to the Crown." The Bill declares in effect: that laws and their execution cannot be suspended or dispensed with by royal authority without the consent of Parliament; that commissions and courts to deal with ecclesiastical issues, and all commissions and courts of like nature, are illegal; that levying money for use of the crown without grant of Parliament or for other use or longer time than granted by Parliament, is illegal; that subjects have the right to petition the king and shall not be committed or prosecuted for so doing; that raising or keeping a standing army within the kingdom in time of peace, without the consent of Parliament, is illegal; that Protestant subjects may keep arms for their defense; that "elections of members of Parliament ought to be free"; that speech, debate, and proceedings in Parliament should not be impeached or questioned anywhere outside of Parliament; that excessive bail should not be required, nor excessive fines imposed, nor cruel and unusual punishments be inflicted; that "jurors should be duly empanelled and returned" and jurors in trials for high treason should be freeholders; "that all grants and promises of fines and forfeitures" of particular persons before conviction are illegal and void; and that Parliament should be convened "frequently." The spirit, if not always the letter, of this statute has influenced the constitutional development and framework of law in every country in the British Commonwealth of Nations, as well as in the U. S., and (with the Magna Charta) it is often cited as part of the political heritage of the world's English-speaking democracies.

Bill Sikes (sīks). See **Sikes, Bill.**

Billy Taylor (bil'i tā'lọr). An old ballad in *Oliver's Comic Songs* (c1825). Billy Taylor is a sailor who is followed to sea by his sweetheart, disguised as a sailor. When she learns that he has been unfaithful to her, she kills him.

Bingham (bing'ạm), **Joseph.** b. at Wakefield, England, in September, 1668; d. at Havant, near Portsmouth, England, Aug. 17, 1723. An English divine and writer on church history. His chief work is *Origines Ecclesiasticae or Antiquities of the Christian Church* (1708–22).

Bingley (bing'li). [Full name, **Charles Bingley.**] In Jane Austen's novel *Pride and Prejudice*, an eligible young gentleman who falls in love with Jane, the eldest Bennet sister.

Binyon (bin'yọn), **Laurence.** b. at Lancaster, England, Aug. 10, 1869; d. 1943. An English poet and Orientalist. He served (1893–95) as assistant in the department of printed books of the British Museum, and in the museum's department of prints and drawings (1895 *et seq.*), where he became (1913) chief of Oriental works. Among his publications are *Lyric Poems* (1894), *Poems* (1895), *London Visions* (1895, 1898), *The Praise of Life* (1896), *Porphyrion and Other Poems* (1898), *Odes* (1900), *The Death of Adam* (1903), *Penthesilea* (1905), *Paris and Oenone* (1906), and *Attila* (1907). He also wrote a number of works on art, including *Painting in the Far East* (1908) and *The Drawings and Engravings of William Blake* (1922), compiled a catalogue of English drawings in the British Museum, and translated the first two parts of Dante's *Divine Comedy*.

Biographia Literaria (bī.ọ.graf'i.ạ lit.ẹ.rār'i.ạ). A prose work (2 vols., 1817) by Samuel Taylor Coleridge. It contains essays on literary criticism and develops the author's theory as to the distinction between fancy and imagination: fancy is simply a mode of memory and produces only the sensational, while imagination transcends time and establishes contact with a higher reality. In this work Coleridge also offers a distinction between reason and understanding, gives an excellent critical analysis of Wordsworth's poetry, and discusses in some detail various portions of the philosophies of Kant, Schelling, and Fichte.

biography. 1. The history of the life of a particular person. "There is no heroic poem in the world but is at bottom a *biography*, the life of a man." (Carlyle, *Essays*.)
2. Biographical writings in general, or as a department of literature. "This, then, was the first great merit of Montesquieu that he effected a complete separation between *biography* and history, and taught historians to study, not the peculiarities of individual character, but the general aspect of the society in which the peculiarities appeared." (Buckle, *Civilization*.)

Bion (bī'ọn). b. at Phlossa, near Smyrna, Asia Minor; fl. c280 B.C. (or, according to some authorities, in the 2nd century B.C.). A Greek bucolic poet. His chief extant poem is the *Epitaphios Adōnidos* ("Lament for Adonis").

Biondello (bē.on.del'ō). In Shakespeare's *Taming of the Shrew*, a servant to Lucentio.

Birch (bėrch), **Thomas.** b. at London, Nov. 23, 1705; d. near London, Jan. 9, 1766. An English writer on history and biography. He wrote nearly all the English biographies in the *General Dictionary, Historical and Critical* (1734–41), edited *Thurloe's State Papers* (1742), and compiled *Memoirs of the Reign of Queen Elizabeth* (1754).

Bird (bėrd), **James.** b. at Earl's Stonham, Suffolk, England, Nov. 10, 1788; d. at Yoxford, Suffolk, England, 1839. An English poet and dramatist. An unsuccessful miller from 1814 to 1820, and a stationer from 1820 until his death, he began to write before he was 16, some of his juvenile efforts later

ḍ, d or j; ṣ, s or sh; ṭ, t or ch; ẓ, z or zh; o, F. cloche; ü, F. menu; ċh, Sc. loch; ṅ, F. bonbon.

appearing in the *Suffolk Chronicle*. Author of *The Vale of Slaughden* (1819), a narrative of the Danish invasion of East Anglia; *The White Hats* (1819), a mock-heroic satire on radicals; *Machin, or the Discovery of Madeira* (1821), *Dunwich, a Tale of the Splendid City* (1828), *Framlingham, a Narrative of the Castle* (1831), and *The Emigrant's Tale* (1833), poems; and the dramas *Cosmo, Duke of Florence* (1822) and *The Smuggler's Daughter* (1836).

Bird, Theophilus. The hero of William John Locke's novel *The Kingdom of Theophilus* (1927).

Birdcage Walk. A walk on the S side of St. James's Park, London. It is so named from the aviaries which were ranged along its side as early as the time of the Stuarts.

Birdlime (bẽrd'līm). A disreputable character in John Webster and Thomas Dekker's *Westward Hoe*.

Bird of Dawning. A novel (1933) by John Masefield. It is considered by most critics to be one of his best novels.

Birds, Beasts and Flowers. A collection (1923) of poems by D. H. Lawrence.

Birds in London. A prose work (1898) by W. H. Hudson. Although Hudson is, and unquestionably will continue to be, best known as the author of the novel *Green Mansions*, he had a considerable knowledge of ornithology, and his writings on the subject still maintain a reputation among people interested in birds (Hudson's own great interest in the subject is clearly reflected even in his fiction; it is more than coincidence that the heroine of *Green Mansions* should be capable of what is virtually metamorphosis between woman and bird).

Birkenhead (bẽr'kẹn.hed), Sir **John.** [Also, **Berkenhead.**] b. near Northwich, Cheshire, England, March 24, 1616; d. at London, Dec. 4, 1679. An English satirist and journalist. He was the editor of the *Mercurius Aulicus* during the English Civil War.

Birmingham (bẽr'ming.ạm), **George A.** Pseudonym of **Hannay, James Owen.**

Birnam Wood (bẽr'nạm). In Shakespeare's *Macbeth*, a forest near Dunsinane, the seat of the Scottish kings. The witches prophesy that Macbeth will not be vanquished until Birnam Wood shall come to Dunsinane Hill against him. The prophecy is fulfilled when Macduff's army takes the branches from the woods for concealment as they march against Macbeth.

Biron (bī'rọn). The husband of Isabella in Thomas Southerne's play *The Fatal Marriage*. Supposedly killed in battle, he returns after seven years to find his wife married to another as the result of the machinations of his younger brother Carlos. He is killed in a fray instigated by Carlos.

Biron (bi.rön'). See also **Berowne.**

Birrell (bir'ẹl), **Augustine.** b. at Wavertree, near Liverpool, England, Jan. 19, 1850; d. Nov. 20, 1933. An English essayist, lecturer, and statesman. He studied at Cambridge before being admitted to the bar in 1875, and sat in Parliament as Liberal member for Fifeshire West (1889–1900) and for Bristol North (1906–18), also serving as professor of law at University College, London, in the period

1896–99. In 1903 he was a bencher of the Inner Temple; he was president of the board of education, with a seat in the cabinet, from December, 1905, to 1907, when he was appointed chief secretary for Ireland, a post he held until after the Easter Rebellion of 1916.

Birth of Merlin, or The Child Has Lost a Father (mẽr'lin), **The.** A tragicomedy published in 1662, then attributed to Shakespeare and William Rowley. It is now thought to be a refashioning by Rowley of an old play. The present title is Rowley's; the original author is unknown.

Biscop (bis'kọp) or **Biscop Baducing** (bäd'ú.king), Saint **Benedict.** See Saint **Benedict Biscop.**

Bishop (bish'ọp), **Isabella Lucy.** [Maiden name, **Bird.**] b. at Boroughbridge Hall, Yorkshire, England, Oct. 15, 1831; d. at Edinburgh, Oct. 7, 1904. An English traveler, travel writer, and founder of hospitals. She traveled in America and Canada (1854), Australia and New Zealand (1872), the Hawaiian Islands, and the Rocky Mountains (1873), Japan (1878), various parts of India and Armenia (1889–90), and in Japan, Korea, and China (1894–97). In China and India she founded five hospitals and an orphanage in memory of her parents, her sister, and her husband. Elected (1892) a fellow of the Royal Geographical Society, she was the first woman to be so honored. Author of *The Englishwoman in America* (1856), *Notes on Old Edinburgh* (1869), *The Hawaiian Archipelago* (1875), *A Lady's Life in the Rocky Mountains* (1879), *Unbeaten Tracks in Japan* (1880), *Journeys in Persia and Kurdistan* (1891), *Among the Tibetans* (1894), *Korea and Her Neighbors* (1898), and *The Yangtze Valley and Beyond* (1899).

Bishop Blougram's Apology (blog'rạmz). A dramatic monologue in verse by Robert Browning, published in *Men and Women* (1855).

Bishop Hatto (hat'ō, hät'o). See **Hatto.**

Bishopsgate (bish'ọps.gāt). The principal entrance through the N wall of old London. The only entrance in the N wall of Roman times was near this point. Near here Ermyn Street and the Vicinal Way entered the city. Bishopsgate Street is the street which goes over the site of the old gate, and is divided into "Bishopsgate within" and "Bishopsgate without." The gate was destroyed in the reign of George II. The foundations of the old Roman gate have been found.

Bismarck (biz'märk; German, bis'-) or **Bismarck-Schönhausen** (-shẽn'hou.zẹn), Prince **Otto Eduard Leopold von.** [Sometimes called the "**Iron Chancellor.**"] b. at Schönhausen, Prussia, April 1, 1815; d. at Friedrichsruh, Prussia, July 30, 1898. A Prussian statesman, famous as the creator and first chancellor of the German Empire. He studied at the Universities of Göttingen and Berlin. In the Prussian United Diet in 1847 and in the House of Representatives in the period 1849–51, he became known as an outspoken opponent of liberal and of German national measures, and a vigorous supporter of a reactionary Prussian monarchy. In 1851 he was appointed Prussian ambassador to the Diet of the Germanic Confederation at Frankfort on the Main, where he matured from a narrow *Junker* to a statesman of European vision and caliber. In 1859 he was sent as minister to Russia and in 1862 as ambassador to France. He became president of the Council of Ministers on Sept. 22, 1862, and took over the foreign office as well on Oct. 8 of the same year. He continued the conflict with the House of Representatives over the reorganization of the army and successfully maintained the prerogatives of the crown. To the budget committee, he declared that the great questions of the time are settled "not by speeches and majority votes . . . but by iron and blood." His foreign policy, amoral but successful, was simple in its aims but dazzlingly versatile in execution. It led to victorious war in 1864, in alliance with Austria, against Denmark for the possession of Schleswig-Holstein; in 1866, in alliance with Italy, against Austria for supremacy in Germany; and in the period 1870–71, in alliance with the south German states, against France (called the Franco-Prussian War).

Formation of the German Empire. After the war of 1866, Prussian territory was rounded out by the annexation of Hanover, Hesse-Cassell, Frankfort, and Schleswig-Holstein. The North German Confederation, formed in 1867 under Prussian dominance and with Bismarck as chancellor, became the German Empire in 1871 with the entry of the south German states and the annexation of Alsace-Lorraine. After this, Bismarck considered Germany one of the "saturated" states. Although he did give the colonial movement some support in the 1880's and secured colonies in Africa and the South Seas, his primary aim was not to expand, but to consolidate and safeguard, his creation. Until 1878 he worked in general harmony with the National Liberal Party and engaged in the *Kulturkampf*, a protracted struggle with the "Ultramontanes" (organized politically in the Center Party) which resulted from fear that the Roman Catholic doctrine of papal infallibility represented a threat of interference in German domestic and foreign affairs by the Catholic Church. After 1878 he gradually broke off the conflict, in part because the rise of the Socialist Party seemed a greater threat to state and society, and in part because he wanted the support of the powerful Center Party when the National Liberals were unwilling to accept tariff protection for industry and agriculture.

Later Years. In the 1880's he continued his policies of economic and social reform, especially in the enactment of the first comprehensive system of workmen's insurance against the disabilities of sickness, accident, and old age. To isolate France and thus to protect Germany against a war of revenge for 1870–71, Bismarck built up a complicated system of alliances, at first informal, but after the Congress of Berlin of 1878 (over which he presided) formal and written in treaties. The German-Austrian alliance (1879–1918) against Russia was followed by the "Three Emperors' Alliance" (1881–87) of Germany, Austria, and Russia, the Triple Alliance (1882–1915) of Germany, Austria, and Italy, later joined by Rumania, and the German-Russian "reinsurance" treaty (1887–90). In consequence of differences with the young Emperor William II, especially over foreign and social policy, Bismarck gave up office in March, 1890. He had been raised to the rank of count in 1865, that of prince in 1890, and was made Duke

of Lauenburg in 1890, a title which did little to console him for his loss of power. His 80th birthday (April 1, 1895) was made the occasion for extraordinary ovations in his honor, in which the emperor joined.

Bitzer (bit'sẽr). A schoolboy under Mr. M'Choakum, brought up on the Gradgrind system, in Charles Dickens's story *Hard Times*.

Black (blak), **John.** b. near Dunse, Berwickshire, Scotland, 1783; d. at Scotland, near Maidstone, Kent, England, June 15, 1855. A Scottish reporter, journalist, editor, and translator. He was a pupil at the Dunse parish school, and attended classes at the University of Edinburgh while serving as a clerk in an accountant's office. In 1810 he went to London and became a reporter, and translator of foreign correspondence, on the *Morning Chronicle*, of which he became editor in 1817. Requested to resign in 1843, he spent the rest of his life in retirement. Author of essays on Italian and German literature, contributions (1807–09) to the London *Universal Magazine*, and *Life of Tasso* (1810).

Black, William. b. at Glasgow, in November, 1841; d. at Brighton, England, Dec. 10, 1898. A British novelist and journalist. In 1864 he went to London, and was attached to the staff of the London *Morning Star* in 1865. He was also for some years assistant editor of the London *Daily News*. His works include *In Silk Attire* (1869), *A Daughter of Heth* (1871), *The Strange Adventures of a Phaeton* (1872), *A Princess of Thule* (1873), *The Maid of Killeena, and other Stories* (1876), *Three Feathers* (1875), *Madcap Violet* (1876), *Lady Silverdale's Sweetheart, and other Stories* (1876), *Green Pastures and Piccadilly* (1877), *Macleod of Dare* (1878), *White Wings* (1880), *Sunrise* (1880), *White Heather* (1885), and *In Far Lochaber* (1888).

Blackacre (blak'ā''kẽr), **Jerry.** In William Wycherley's *The Plain Dealer*, a raw booby, not of age and still under his mother's care, trained by her to the law, or at least to a glib use of its terms.

Blackacre, Widow. In William Wycherley's *The Plain Dealer*, a petulant, litigious woman, always with a law case on hand. She is considered one of the author's best and most amusing characters, and is taken from the countess in Jean Baptiste Racine's *Les Plaideurs.*

"Black Agnes" (ag'nẹs). See **Dunbar, Agnes.**

Black Bateman of the North (bāt'mạn). A play (1598) by Thomas Dekker, in collaboration with Michael Drayton and others. No copies of it have been preserved.

Black Bess (bes). The famous mare of Dick Turpin.

Black Book, The. A prose satire by Thomas Middleton, a coarse, humorous attack on the vices and follies of the time, published in 1604. It was suggested by Thomas Nash's *Pierce Pennilesse.*

Black Book of Carmarthen or **Caermarthen** (kär-mär'ᴛнen, kạr-), **The.** A manuscript (12th century) containing several examples of ancient Welsh poetry. It is interesting for the early allusions to King Arthur.

Black Brunswickers (brunz'wik.ẽrz). [Also, **Death's Head Corps.**] A corps of 2,000 horsemen equipped by Frederick William, Duke of Brunswick, to oper-ate against Napoleon I in Germany. It vainly attempted to coöperate with the Austrians in 1809.

Black Country. The mining and manufacturing region about Birmingham, England.

Black Death. In European history, the name given to the epidemic which swept across the world in the middle of the 14th century and is considered by many to have been probably the most terrible calamity in the recorded annals of mankind. There had been earlier plagues (the earliest one of this nature was almost certainly not the one described by Thucydides as occurring at Athens in the period 430–425 B.C., but there were many outbreaks of disease in Europe during the ten centuries immediately preceding the 14th which was unquestionably of the same type as the Black Death), but the Black Death was enormously more disastrous than any of the others. There can be no doubt as to its nature; it was the true Oriental plague, whether bubonic or pulmonary (indeed, axillary, inguinal, and pulmonary lesions were witnessed and duly recorded). The Black Death, so far as we can ascertain, began in India in 1332; epidemics occurring in Russia in 1341 and in Styria in 1342 may have been its forerunners in Europe. By the latter part of 1347 it had progressed, via Constantinople, as far as Sicily, Naples, and Genoa. Venice was visited by the pestilence early in 1348, and from that great commercial center it spread rapidly (one of the reasons for its severity may have been, indeed, that international commerce had vastly increased over early centuries and thus multiplied the chances of contagion, while there had been no corresponding development in scientific means of combating it). It reached its climax in central Europe and England in 1349, and in Russia in 1352 (which was a recurrence, if the epidemic of 1341 had been, indeed, the Black Death). The climax in each region lasted from about four to six months. If it broke out during the winter, it assumed the pulmonary form, and kept it or became the bubonic type in the spring. We now know that the disease was spread by fleas and rats, but nobody suspected that at the time, and the prophylactic measures were therefore irrelevant (except insofar as cleanliness tended to keep down every sort of parasite, and segregation restricted contagion). It is impossible to estimate with any precision how many people were its victims, although some have thought that a quarter of the population of the civilized world was wiped out. In any case, it had enormous social, political, moral, and religious impact. For example, probably because they were more exposed to contagion than the wealthy and powerful, there was a very high incidence of deaths among the poor, and this led to a shortage of labor which, in turn, gave rise in all probability to an atmosphere more favorable to the laborer than had ever before been possible. One particularly hideous consequence of the plague was that a great many people threw the responsibility for the common miseries upon the Jews, whom they accused of having poisoned wells in order to destroy Christians. This terrible delusion became very prevalent in central Europe, particularly in Germany. In fact, violent anti-Semitism reached such a point in that country that there were left in Germany, by the end of the 15th century, only three considerable Jewish communities. It is perhaps a relief, in view of crimes so unspeakable, to turn to Pope Clement VI, who sought vigorously to show the absurdity of the accusation made against the Jews, and took them under his own protection. It is even possible that the plague may have been felt in the field of linguistics, in that it favored the diffusion of the European vernaculars over Latin. It is certain that the diffusion of English (in England) as opposed to French increased materially during the second half of the 14th century. It is possible, even probable, that the Black Death had something to do with this, for it delivered such a formidable blow to the whole of society that everything was affected by it.

"Black Douglas" (dug'lạs), **the.** See **Douglas, Archibald,** and **Douglas, Sir James.**

Black Dwarf, The. A novel by Sir Walter Scott, published in 1816. It is in the first series of *Tales of My Landlord.* "The Black Dwarf" was a name given in parts of Scotland to a most malicious, uncanny creature considered responsible for all mischief done to flocks and herds; hence the name was applied in the novel to the deformed and gnomish-looking Scottish recluse, also known as Elshender or Canny Elshie. He lives in retirement until Grace Armstrong is carried away from the farmer she loves by a robber. The dwarf intervenes and saves her. He then helps Isabella Vere thwart her father's plan to have her marry Sir Frederick Langley, whom she does not love. At the end it is revealed that the dwarf is the wealthy Sir Edward Mauley, once in love with Isabella's mother.

Black-eyed Susan. [Full name, **Sweet William's Farewell to Black-eyed Susan.**] A ballad by John Gay, published in 1720 in a collection of his poems. The music to it was written by Richard Leveridge.

Black-eyed Susan, or All in the Downs. A comedy by Douglas Jerrold, produced on June 8, 1829. It was played 400 times in that year alone.

Blackfriars (blak'frī.ạrz). A name given to the locality at the SW angle of old London city, on the Fleet, from its association with the "Black Friars," or mendicant monks of the Dominican order. Members of this order made their appearance in London in 1221 under the patronage of Hubert de Burgh, and were located in Holborn. In 1285 they moved to the site of the old Montfichett tower, which had been given them for a monastery. The tower itself was destroyed and the material used in building the church. From Ludgate to the river the city wall was pulled down and moved W to the Fleet, all the added space being devoted to the monastery. The original site was given by Gregory Rokesley "in a street of Baynard Castle." The monastery was endowed with a privilege of asylum, which attached itself to the locality even after the dissolution.

Blackfriars Theatre. A private playhouse in use from 1576 to 1584, and reopened in 1596, formed from a Dominican priory originally built in 1275. One portion of this priory passed to the Master of the Revels after the suppression of the monasteries in 1538, then to Sir William More in 1559. This part of the priory was a series of two-story buildings along the west side of the cloisters. A chamber in the priory 125 feet by 25 feet was leased in 1576 to Richard Farrant, Master of the Children of the Chapel, for public performances by the Children preceding their Court appearances. After Farrant's death the performances continued under William Hunnis and Henry Evans. The Children of the Chapel and of Paul's performed Lyly's plays there (1582–84). More recovered the chamber in 1584. The second theater was formed from buildings bought by James Burbage in 1596. A hall, 66 feet by 46 feet, it had a stage, galleries, and seats. It was leased (1600) to Henry Evans and Nathaniel Giles for performances by the Children of the Chapel, who were now competing with adult companies. The King's Men obtained the theater in 1608 when a syndicate was formed of Richard Burbage, Cuthbert Burbage, Shakespeare, Heminge, Condell, Sly, and Thomas Evans. Since it was an enclosed theater with somewhat different arrangements from the public playhouses, the style of acting was different. Shakespeare's romantic comedies with their masques and scenic requirements were written for this theater or ones like it, and musical background, as in the plays of Marston, was often used. The theater was also well suited to the exotic settings of Beaumont and Fletcher's tragedies. The building was torn down in 1655.

Black Hambleton (ham′el.ton). A historic racecourse in England.

Blackheath (blak′hēth). A common in Kent, England: the scene of a Danish defeat (1011), of the risings of Wat Tyler (1381) and Jack Cade (1450), and of the defeat of the Cornish rebels (1497).

Black Hole of Calcutta (kal.kut′a). A garrison strongroom, or "black hole," at Calcutta, measuring ab. 18 ft. square, in which 146 British prisoners were confined, on June 20, 1756, during the Sepoy Rebellion in India. The next morning all but 23 were dead.

Blackie (blak′i), **John Stuart.** b. at Glasgow, in July, 1809; d. at Edinburgh, March 2, 1895. A Scottish philologist and poet, professor of Greek at Edinburgh from 1852 to 1882. He translated the works of Aeschylus in 1850, and later *Faust*, and the *Iliad*, and wrote *Four Phases of Morals* (1871), *Lays of the Highlands* (1872), *Horae Hellenicae* (1874), and others.

Black Knight. In early romances, the son of Oriana and Amadis of Gaul.

Black Knight. The disguise under which, in Sir Walter Scott's *Ivanhoe*, Richard Coeur de Lion wanders in Sherwood Forest, performs feats of valor, and feasts with Friar Tuck.

Black Lamb and Grey Falcon. A prose work (1941) by Rebecca West. It is an account of a visit to Yugoslavia in 1937, two and a half years after the assassination, at Marseilles, of Alexander I of Yugoslavia, and two years before the outbreak of World War II. It is written in a style that appears at first to be rambling, if not actually casual (as one critic has put it, the book has "divagations anthropological, cultural, literary, philosophical, and emotional"), and was greeted even before publication in book form in the U. S. (it was partly serialized in the *Atlantic Monthly* in 1940) as Rebecca West's greatest achievement.

Blacklock (blak′lok), **Thomas.** b. at Annan, Scotland, Nov. 10, 1721; d. at Edinburgh, July 7, 1791.

A Scottish poet. Having lost his sight at the age of six months through an attack of smallpox, he was given an education, including a course at the University of Edinburgh, by Dr. Stevenson, a physician of Edinburgh, and was licensed to preach in 1759. He became (c1762) minister of Kirkcudbright, but resigned in 1764. He enjoyed the friendship and patronage of David Hume and Joseph Spence. An edition of his poems appeared in 1756, with an introduction by Spence.

Black Michael (mī′kel). In Anthony Hope's novel *The Prisoner of Zenda*, the king's wicked brother, whom the English hero of the story finally succeeds in overcoming.

Black Mischief. A satirical novel by Evelyn Waugh, published in 1932. Its hero, Basil Seal, goes to Azania, there to help the local king (with whom he had been at Oxford) modernize his country. The locale is thought to be based on Ethiopia (Abyssinia).

Blackmore (blak′mōr), **Sir Richard.** b. at Corsham, Wiltshire, England, c1650; d. at Boxsted, Essex, England, Oct. 9, 1729. An English physician, poet, and prose writer, physician in ordinary to William III. His best-known work is *The Creation* (1712).

Blackmore, Richard Doddridge. b. at Longworth, Berkshire, England, June 7, 1825; d. at Teddington, Middlesex, England, Jan. 20, 1900. An English novelist, poet, and translator, best known as the author of *Lorna Doone* (1869). Educated at Blundell's School at Tiverton, in Devonshire, and at Exeter College, Oxford, he tried teaching and the practice of law for a time, but gave up both on coming into an inheritance. Author of *Poems by Melanter* (1853), *Epullia* (1853), *The Bugle of the Black Sea* (1855), *The Fate of Franklin* (1860), and *Fringilla* (1895), all poetry, he also translated the *Hero and Leander* of Musaeus, the *Georgics* of Vergil, and the *Idylls* of Theocritus. He is remembered for the novel *Lorna Doone: A Romance of Exmoor* (1869); his other novels include *Clara Vaughan* (1864), *Cradock Nowell* (1866), *The Maid of Sker* (1872), *Alice Lorraine* (1875), *Erema, or My Father's Sin* (1877), *Mary Anerley* (1880), *Christowell* (1882), *The Remarkable History of Tommy Upmore* (1884), *Springhaven* (1887), *Kit and Kitty* (1889), *Perlycross* (1894), and *Dariel* (1897).

Blackpool (blak′pōl), **Stephen.** In Charles Dickens's *Hard Times*, a power-loom weaver of upright character tied to a miserable, drunken wife. He cannot see the propriety of living with her and giving up a better woman whom he loves, and in his own words "'t is a' a muddle." He dies a lingering death from a fall into an abandoned mine, and it appears that his goodness and integrity have met with a poor return in this world.

Black Prince, The. A tragedy by Roger Boyle, 1st Earl of Orrery, acted in 1667. The plot is concerned with a widow and the conflicting claims of four lovers. There are a number of scenes where the playwright tried to imitate French heroic tragedy, particularly Corneille.

Black Rod. The title of a gentleman usher, with special duties, in the English houses of Lords and Commons. He carries a black rod of office surmounted with a gold lion.

d, d or j; ş, s or sh; t, t or ch; z, z or zh; o, F. cloche; ü, F. menu; ch, Sc. loch; ṅ, F. bonbon.

Black Rood (rŏd), **the.** See **Rood, the Black.**

Black Roses. A novel by Francis Brett Young, published in 1929. It is set in Italy during the latter part of the 19th century. The hero is Paul Ritchie, an artist, son of an English father and an Italian mother.

Black Soul, The. A novel by Liam O'Flaherty, published in 1924.

Blackstone (blak'stōn, -stǫn), Sir **William.** b. at London, July 10, 1723; d. there, Feb. 14, 1780. An English teacher, judge, and writer on common law whose famous work, *Commentaries on the Laws of England* (4 vols., 1765–69), has exerted more influence than any other treatise on law in the English language. Of humble parentage and educated at Oxford and the Middle Temple, he attracted attention through his lectures on the common law at Oxford, where he subsequently held the first Vinerian professorship. His fame as a legal scholar led to a successful law practice in London and to election (1761) to Parliament, where he supported George III. In 1770 he was appointed to the Court of King's Bench and knighted. Most of his time as judge was devoted to appeals and he became an advocate of prison reform. The *Commentaries* rescued English common law from Latin and provided a convenient means for its transmission to the British colonies. Some 35 editions and numerous abridgments of the work have been published, and it has been translated into several foreign languages. The first American edition was published at Philadelphia (1771–72). For more than a century after Blackstone's death the *Commentaries* were widely read by law students, and they are still cited by courts and writers of legal history.

Black Swan, The. A novel by Rafael Sabatini, published in 1933.

Black Watch. A body of Scotch Highlanders employed by the English government to watch the Highlands in 1725, and enrolled as a regiment in the regular army in 1739. The adjectival epithet "black" is occasioned by their dark (but not actually black) tartan uniform.

Blackwell (blak'wel), **Thomas.** b. at Aberdeen, Scotland, 1701; d. at Edinburgh, 1757. A Scottish classical scholar and educator. He took (1718) an M.A. degree at Marischal College, Aberdeen, where he later was professor of Greek (1723–57) and principal (1748–57). His chief works are *An Enquiry Into the Life and Writings of Homer* (1735) and *Memoirs of the Court of Augustus* (1753–55); the third volume of these memoirs was published posthumously (1764).

Blackwood (blak'wud), **Adam.** b. at Dunfermline, Scotland, 1539; d. 1613. A Scottish writer, and champion of Mary Stuart, Queen of Scots. He studied, taught, and wrote at Paris, dedicating (1612) a volume of Latin didactic poetry to Mary Stuart; during her captivity, he continued to pay her visits and homage. He published *De Vinculo* (1575) and another work condemning heretics. His work denouncing John Knox and Queen Elizabeth of England, *Martyre de la Royne d'Escosse, Douairiere de France*, was printed at Paris (1587) and Antwerp (1588 and 1589), and appears in Jebb's collection (1725); he also wrote eulogies of Charles

IX of France and James VI of Scotland, and pious prose and verse.

Blackwood, Algernon. b. in Kent, England, 1869; d. Dec. 10, 1951. An English author known for tales of the weird and supernatural. Before he began (1906) his writing career, he was a farmer in Canada, operated a Toronto hotel, was on the staff of the New York *Sun* and *Times*, and worked in the dried-milk industry. Author of *The Empty House* (1906), *The Listener* (1907), *John Silence* (1908), *The Human Chord* (1910), *The Centaur* (1911), *The Wave* (1916), *The Bright Messenger* (1921), *The Fruit-Stoners* (1934), *Shocks* (1935), and *The Doll and One Other* (1946).

Blackwood, John. b. at Edinburgh, Dec. 7, 1818; d. at Strathtyrum, near St. Andrews, Scotland, Oct. 29, 1879. A Scottish publisher who brought out the works of George Eliot; son of William Blackwood (1776–1834), and friend of W. M. Thackeray. Manager (1840–45) of the London branch of Blackwood's Edinburgh firm, he was subsequently editor (1845–79) of *Blackwood's Magazine* and head (1852 et seq.) of Blackwood's, both of which were founded by his father. The first to recognize George Eliot's genius, he published (1857) her first work, *Scenes of Clerical Life*, in his magazine. Until his death he was her friend, critic, and publisher.

Blackwood, William. b. at Edinburgh, Nov. 20, 1776; d. there, Sept. 16, 1834. A Scottish publisher and bookseller; father of John Blackwood. He was the founder (1817) and editor of *Blackwood's Edinburgh Magazine*, later *Blackwood's Magazine*, and founder (c1816) of the publishing firm of William Blackwood and Sons.

Bladud (blā'dud). A mythical British king, reputed founder of the city of Bath, England.

Blair (blār), **Eric.** See **Orwell, George.**

Blair, Hugh. b. at Edinburgh, April 7, 1718; d. there, Dec. 27, 1800. A Scottish Presbyterian divine and author. He was a lecturer on rhetoric and belles-lettres at Edinburgh in the period 1762–83. He wrote *Sermons* (1777), *Lectures on Rhetoric* (1783), and others.

Blair, Robert. b. at Edinburgh, 1699; d. at Athelstaneford, East Lothian, Scotland, Feb. 4, 1746. A Scottish clergyman and poet. His best-known poem is *The Grave* (1743), a lengthy work in blank verse. It was illustrated by William Blake.

Blake (blāk), **Franklin.** The hero of Wilkie Collins's novel *The Moonstone.*

Blake, George. b. at Greenock, Scotland, Oct. 28, 1893—. A British novelist and journalist. He served as an editorial staff member of *John o' London's Weekly* (1924–28) and of the *Strand Magazine* (1928–30). His novels include *Vagabond Papers* (1922), *The Shipbuilders* (1935), *David and Joanna* (1936), *Late Harvest* (1938), *The Valiant Heart* (1940), *The Westering Sun* (1946), and *The Five Arches* (1947).

Blake, Nicholas. Pseudonym of **Lewis, Cecil Day.**

Blake, William. b. at London, Nov. 28, 1757; d. at London, Aug. 12, 1827. An English poet, engraver, painter, and mystic. His works are noted for their lyrical and metaphysical power. Many of them are based on a mythological structure evolved by Blake.

Apprenticed (1771) to an engraver, he later illustrated his own works with copperplate engravings colored by hand. He was the author of *Poetical Sketches by W. B.* (1783), *Songs of Innocence* (1789), *Songs of Experience* (1794), and the so-called "Prophetical Books," including *The Book of Thel* (1789), *The Marriage of Heaven and Hell* (1790), *The Gates of Paradise* (1793), *The Vision of the Daughters of Albion* (1793), *The Song and Book of Los* (1795), and *The Book of Ahania* (1795); he also wrote *Jerusalem* (1804), *The Emanation of the Giant Albion* (1804), and *Milton* (1804). He illustrated works by Mary Wollstonecraft (1791), Edward Young's *Night Thoughts* (1793–1800), Robert Blair's *The Grave* (1805), and the Book of Job (1826).

Blaker (blā'kẻr), **Richard.** b. in India, March 4, 1893; d. at Santa Monica, Calif., Feb. 19, 1940. English novelist. His works include *But Beauty Vanishes* (1936), *Here Lies a Most Beautiful Lady* (1935), and *The Voice in the Wilderness* (1925).

Blameless Prince, The. A narrative poem (1869) by Edmund C. Stedman. It is a Tennysonian tale of the secret love of a prince for a lady of lesser degree.

Blamire (blạ.mīr'), **Susanna.** [Called the "Muse of Cumberland."] b. at Cardew Hall, near Carlisle, Cumberland, England; d. at Carlisle, April 5, 1794. An English poet and song writer. Her poems and songs appeared, unsigned, in various magazines; no collection of her work appeared until almost half a century after her death, when Henry Lonsdale, a Carlisle physician and man of letters, published her *Poetical Works* (1842). Her first poem, *Written in a Churchyard on Seeing a Number of Cattle Grazing in It*, composed when she was 19, shows the influence of Thomas Gray. *Stoklewath, or the Cumbrian Village* is suggestive of Oliver Goldsmith's *Deserted Village.* Her *Epistle to Friends at Gartmore* is a picture of the simple life she led with her aunt and of her physical suffering from rheumatic attacks. *What Ails this Heart o'Mine?*, *The Nabob*, *And Ye Shall Walk in Silk Attire*, *The Traveller's Return*, and *The Waefu' Heart*, all in Scottish dialect, are regarded as some of her loveliest songs.

Blanchard (blan'chạrd), **Edward Litt Laman.** b. at London, Dec. 11, 1820; d. there, Sept. 4, 1889. An English journalist, dramatist, critic, novelist, and author of pantomimes, songs, and variety entertainments. He edited (1841) the *London Journal*, before establishing and editing (1845) *The Astrologer and Oracle of Destiny.* Author of travel and railway guides and of two novels, *Temple Bar* and *Brave Without a Destiny*, for 37 years he wrote pantomimes for Drury Lane and for other theaters at London and elsewhere; he was also engaged as a dramatic critic for the *Sunday Times*, the *Weekly Dispatch*, the *Illustrated Times*, the London *Figaro*, the *Observer*, and the *Daily Telegraph.*

Blanchard, Samuel Laman. b. at Great Yarmouth, England, May 15, 1804; d. at London, Feb. 15, 1845. An English poet and journalist. He was acting editor of the *Monthly Magazine* (1831), editor of *The True Sun* (1832), *The Constitutional* (1836), *The Court Journal* (1837), *The Courier* (1837–39), and other periodicals, and author of *Lyric Offerings* and *Sonnets.*

Blanche Amory (blanch ā'mọ.ri). See **Amory, Blanche.**

Blanche of Devan (dev'ạn). The name of the demented Lowland bride in Sir Walter Scott's poem *The Lady of the Lake.*

Blanch of Spain (blanch). In Shakespeare's *King John*, the historical Blanche of Castile, daughter of the King of Castile and the niece of John. She is married to the French Dauphin to seal the truce between John and the French, but her loyalties are soon strained when Pandulph excommunicates John and the French fight him. She follows the Dauphin.

Bland (bland), **Edith Nesbit.** [Pen name, **E. Nesbit.**] b. at London, Aug. 19, 1858; d. May 4, 1924. An English writer; wife of Hubert Bland. A founder (1883) of the Fellowship of New Life, a predecessor of the Fabian Society, she is now, however, chiefly remembered as a writer of books for children. Her original contribution was the use as characters in her books of realistic young people behaving like ordinary youngsters, in place of the previously traditional heroes or moral dummies. Author of *The Would-be Goods* (1901) *Five Children and It* (1902), *The Red House* (1903), and others.

Bland, Hubert. d. 1914. An English socialist writer; husband of Edith Nesbit Bland.

Bland, Lizzie. See **Neilson, Lilian Adelaide.**

Blandamour (blan'dä.mör), **Sir.** A fickle and vainglorious knight, in Edmund Spenser's *The Faerie Queene.* He was defeated by Britomart, and won the false Florimel from Paridel.

Blandois (blän.dwà). See **Rigaud.**

Blane (blān), **Niel.** The popular landlord of the Howff, in Sir Walter Scott's novel *Old Mortality.* He is also town piper.

Blanketeers (blang.kẹ.tirz'). A name given to a body of Manchester mill-workers who met at St. Peter's Field, Manchester, England, on March 10, 1817. Each man was provided with provisions and a blanket, and their purpose was to walk to London to petition for some legislative remedy against what they conceived to be the willful injustices imposed upon them by their employers, and also for the great panacea of parliamentary reform. The leaders of the group were seized and imprisoned, as were some of their followers. The marchers never reached London.

blank verse. Unrhymed verse, particularly, that form of unrhymed heroic verse which is commonly employed in English dramatic and epic poetry. It was introduced by Henry Howard, Earl of Surrey (d. 1547), in his translation of the second and fourth books of the *Aeneid.* It was first employed in the drama in Sackville and Norton's tragedy *Gorboduc* (printed 1565), but it was not until Marlowe adopted it in his play *Tamburlaine* that it became the form regularly employed in the metrical drama, which it has since with only occasional intervals remained. After Milton's use of it in *Paradise Lost*, it was widely extended to many other classes of composition.

Blank Verse. A collection of poems by Charles Lamb in collaboration with Charles Lloyd, a Quaker. This contains Lamb's best-known poem,

"Old Familiar Faces," which in its gentle pathos and nostalgia for the past is characteristic of the author.

Blarney (blär'ni). A town in Munster province, Irish Republic, in County Cork, situated on the Blarney stream, ab. 5 mi. NW of Cork. It contains a noted castle built in 1446 by Cormac McCarthy, and now forming a picturesque ivy-clad ruin centered about a high, square, battlemented and machicolated keep. The fame of the castle is due to its possession of the Blarney Stone, a block bearing a Latin inscription that includes the name of the castle's builder and the date, originally built into the S angle of the keep ab. 20 ft. below the top. It is now possible for a tourist to kiss the stone by leaning head down over the parapet while someone holds his feet. An iron grating is provided as a safeguard.

Blarney, Lady. In Oliver Goldsmith's *Vicar of Wakefield*, one of the two town ladies, or rather ladies of the town, who make the acquaintance of the vicar's innocent family under false pretenses. The other lady is named Miss Carolina Wilhelmina Skeggs.

Blatant Beast, The. In Edmund Spenser's *Faerie Queene*, the personification of slander. He is a foul monster with a hundred tongues.

Blatchford (blach'ford), **Robert.** b. at Maidstone, Kent, England, March 17, 1851; d. in Sussex, England, Dec. 17, 1943. An English journalist, socialist, and author. A soldier (1871–78), and later a clerk at Northwich, he went into journalism, joining the staff of Bell's *Life* in 1884 and serving (1885–91) on the *Sunday Chronicle;* in 1891 he founded and edited *The Clarion*, which he published as a Socialist organ until World War I. He was the author of *God and My Neighbor* (1903), *Not Guilty: A Plea for the Bottom Dog* (1905), *My Life in the Army*, *Shadow Shapes*, and *My Eighty Years* (1931), but is best known for two propaganda works, *Merrie England*, which sold several million copies, both in England and the U. S., swelling the ranks of the Socialist movement, and *Britain for the British*. In 1910 he contributed several papers to the London *Daily Mail*, in which he was one of the first to call attention to the evil of German militarism and its danger to England.

Blathers and Duff (blaᴛʜ'ẽrz; duf). Bow-street officers in Charles Dickens's *Oliver Twist*.

Blattergowl (blat'ẽr.goul). A prosy Scotch minister, in Sir Walter Scott's novel *The Antiquary*.

Blavatsky (blạ.vat'ski), Madame **Helena Petrovna Hahn-Hahn.** [Often called **Madame Blavatsky.**] b. at Ekaterinoslav (now Dnepropetrovsk), Russia, 1831; d. at London, May 8, 1891. A Russian theosophist and traveler in the U. S., the East and elsewhere; one of the chief founders at New York of the Theosophical Society in 1875. The daughter of a German nobleman and granddaughter of the Russian Princess Dolgorouki, she went to Tibet and to India, where she was active in exhibiting her alleged supernatural powers. These psychic demonstrations were deemed unsatisfactory by the Society for Psychical Research. She wrote *Isis Unveiled* (1876), *The Secret Doctrine* (1888), *Key to Theosophy* (1889), and others.

Bleak House. A novel by Charles Dickens, published in the period 1852–53 in 20 monthly numbers. It was named from a dreary-looking house which was his summer residence at Broadstairs. The work, which is generally considered one of the most impressive of Victorian novels, sharply criticizes the English courts of Chancery for seemingly endless procrastination in the settling of legacies (the criticism was more than justified, and the novel played a considerable part in bringing about a reform). Richard Carstone and his cousin, Ada Clare, are wards of Chancery and await the settlement of an estate which is the object of the case of Jarndyce vs. Jarndyce. They are taken to live at Bleak House, with a kind and benevolent elderly relative, John Jarndyce, until the case is settled. There they fall in love, and soon are secretly married. Richard, a weak young man who is lured by his vision of wealth upon the final settlement of the estate, is unable to stick to any occupation and eventually sinks to financial ruin and dies. The law case, which has now gone on so long that it has become a joke among all the people professionally engaged on it, is finally brought to an end and it is discovered that the estate has been completely absorbed by the legal costs of settling it. Meanwhile, with Ada at Bleak House is Esther Summerson, a supposed orphan, who is a paragon of sweet generosity, sound advice, and common sense, and actually the daughter of the lovely but haughty Lady Dedlock. Before Lady Dedlock's marriage she had been in love with a Captain Rawdon, and had a daughter by him. She believes that the child is dead and that Rawdon died at sea, until she learns by the sight of his handwriting on a legal document that he is in England. She traces him through the help of Little Jo, a crossing-sweeper, only to find that he has just died. The sly and heartless lawyer, Tulkinghorn, discovers Lady Dedlock's secret and threatens to expose her to her husband, but is murdered by the Lady's maid before he can do this. The detective, Bucket, also uncovers the secret in his attempts to solve the lawyer's murder, and reveals all to Sir Leicester Dedlock. When his wife learns this, she flees in despair. She is pursued by her husband and Esther Summerson, who has learned that Lady Dedlock is her mother, but they reach her too late, and she is found dead near the grave of her former lover. Esther then accepts a proposal of marriage made to her by Jarndyce, not from love but through gratitude for all his kindness. When Jarndyce discovers that she really loves the young doctor, Woodcourt, who nursed her through smallpox, he releases her and she marries her doctor. Among the many excellent minor characters in *Bleak House* are Jo, the crossing-sweeper; Krook, who dies of spontaneous combustion; Mrs. Jellyby, who neglects her family because of her preoccupation with various missions and philanthropies; Miss Flite, a demented little old spinster who haunts Chancery; Skimpole, selfish and debonair; and William Guppy, a law clerk.

Bleeding Heart Yard. A name applied to a part of London not far distant from the lower end of Fleet Street. It was once the property of the family of Sir Christopher Hatton, a member of the government under Queen Elizabeth. About the origin of its title there are various traditions. It was intro-

---

fat, fāte, fär, ȧsk, fãre; net, mē, hẽr; pin, pīne; not, nōte, mŏve, nôr; up, lūte, púll; ᴛʜ, then;

duced by Charles Dickens in *Little Dorrit* as the residence of the Plornishes, Daniel Doyce, and others.

Blefuscu (ble.fus′kū). An island described in Jonathan Swift's *Gulliver's Travels*. It was separated from Lilliput by a channel, and was intended to satirize France. The inhabitants were pygmies, like those of Lilliput. Gulliver waded across the channel and carried off the entire fleet of Blefuscu.

Bleise (blēz). [Also, **Bleys**.] In Malory's *Morte d'Arthur*, the master of Merlin. He also figures in Tennyson's *Idylls of the King*.

Blemyes or **Blemmyes** (blem′i.ēz). In ancient history, a nomadic Ethiopian tribe, inhabiting Nubia and Upper Egypt. They were frequently at war with the Romans, and were defeated under Aurelian, Probus, and Diocletian. They were the subjects of fabulous accounts by early writers, who represented them as headless and as having their eyes, noses, and mouths in their breasts.

Blenerhasset (blen.ėr.has′ęt), **Thomas.** b. c1550; d. c1625. An English poet and historian. His best-known work is *The Second Parte of the Mirrour for Magistrates* (1578).

Blenheim (blen′im). A historical work by George Macaulay Trevelyan, published in 1930. It is the first part of his three-volume *England under Queen Anne* (1930–34; the other two are *Ramelies and the Union with Scotland* and *The Peace and the Protestant Succession*); the work as a whole is now generally recognized as one of the standard references for English history in that period.

Blenheim, The Battle of. See **Battle of Blenheim, The.**

Blenheim Palace. A Palladian mansion at Woodstock, Oxfordshire, England, built for John Churchill, the 1st Duke of Marlborough, by John Vanbrugh at the national expense in the period 1705–16. Located on an estate given by Queen Anne to the victor of the Battle of Blenheim, it measures ab. 320 ft. east and west, and ab. 190 ft. north and south. The chief façade presents a projecting entrance-portico between two prominent wings, whose inner faces sweep in a curve toward the entrance. The columns are so large as almost to dwarf even the enormous building. The park façade and the two lesser façades are of interest; each has a large bow-window in the middle, and is flanked by end pavilions. The interior has many large rooms.

Blessed Damozel, The. A poem (1847–48) by Dante Gabriel Rossetti. In it he resolved the conflict between the early Pre-Raphaelite realism and the visionary world of dreams (into which latter, of course, the poet moved ever more deeply during the rest of his life). The poem was one of those which were circulated in manuscript and which established Rossetti as a new force in poetry long before he became generally known to the public.

Blessington (bles′ing.ṭọn), **Marguerite, Countess of.** [Original name, **Marguerite Power.**] b. near Clonmel, County Tipperary, Ireland, Sept. 1, 1789; d. at Paris, June 4, 1849. An Irish beauty and woman of letters. Born Marguerite Power, the daughter of a small farmer, she was married at the age of 14 to an army officer, Maurice St. Leger Farmer, whose intemperance and bad temper caused her to leave

him. Farmer was killed in 1817, and the following year his widow became the wife of Charles John Gardiner, the 1st Earl of Blessington, a widower. He was wealthy and fond of lavish living, a taste which his second wife fully shared. Their house at London became a gathering place for the intellect, wit, and fashion of the day. In 1822 the count d'Orsay became an intimate of the family, and in 1827 married Blessington's daughter by his first wife (it was probably a loveless, and certainly an unsuccessful, marriage; separation came a few years later). Blessington died in 1829, and in 1831 his widow took a house in Mayfair. In 1833 she began her literary career as a means of adding to an income which, though large, was not sufficient to sustain the extravagant scale of living to which she had become accustomed. In 1836 she acquired Gore House, where d'Orsay lived with her for the next 13 years, during which her activity in the intellectual and fashionable worlds continued. In April, 1849, d'Orsay fled to avoid arrest at the demand of his creditors. Marguerite followed him to Paris in May, where she died less than a month later. Her novels include *The Two Friends* (1835), *Confessions of an Elderly Gentleman* (1836), *Confessions of an Elderly Lady* (1838), *The Governess* (1839), *Lottery of Life* (1842), *Strathern* (1843), *Memoirs of a Femme de Chambre* (1846), and *Marmaduke Herbert* (1847). She and Blessington had become well acquainted with Byron in 1823, and in 1834 she published what is now her best-known book, *Conversations with Lord Byron.* For a time after 1834 she edited *The Book of Beauty,* and from 1841 to the year of her death she was editor of *The Keepsake.*

Bleys (blēz). See **Bleise.**

Blickling Homilies (blik′ling). A collection of 19 sermons recorded on manuscript c970 and named by modern scholars after the English village of Blickling, the former home of the manuscript. They antedate the homilies of Ælfric and Wulfstan, and are considered to be more significant for their antiquity than for their literary merit.

Blifil (blī′fil). [Also, **Master Blifil.**] The son of Bridget, Squire Allworthy's sister, and Captain Blifil in Henry Fielding's novel *Tom Jones.* He is a smooth and hypocritical villain who tries to have Tom disinherited and hanged for murder.

Blifil, Captain John. In Henry Fielding's novel *Tom Jones,* a hypocritical coxcomb, of "pinchbeck professions and vamped up virtues," the husband of Squire Allworthy's sister Bridget.

Blifil, Doctor. The elder brother of Captain John Blifil, in Henry Fielding's novel *Tom Jones.*

Bligh (blī), **William.** b. at Tyntan, Cornwall, England, 1754; d. at London, Dec. 7, 1817. An English admiral. He was appointed commander of H.M.S. *Bounty* in 1787; after a mutiny of his crew, he and 18 others were cast adrift (1789) near the Friendly Islands in an open boat; they reached Timor after sailing close to 4,000 mi. He later served as governor of New South Wales; there he antagonized the soldiers, and was arrested by them. In 1814 he became a vice-admiral. He is an important figure in the novels *Mutiny on the Bounty* (1932) and its sequel *Men Against the Sea* (1933) by James Norman Hall and Charles Bernard Nordhoff. He published his own narrative of the mutiny in 1790.

ḍ, d or j; ṣ, s or sh; ṭ, t or ch; ẓ, z or zh; o, F. cloche; ü, F. menu; ċh, Sc. loch; ṅ, F. bonbon.

Blight (blīt), **Young.** Mr. Mortimer Lightwood's office-boy in Charles Dickens's novel *Our Mutual Friend.* He is of a peculiarly depressing aspect.

Blimber (blim'ẽr), **Cornelia.** The daughter of Doctor Blimber in Charles Dickens's *Dombey and Son.* She wore short hair and spectacles and was "dry and sandy with working in the graves of deceased languages."

Blimber, Doctor. The principal of the boarding school, in Charles Dickens's *Dombey and Son,* to which little Paul Dombey is sent. He is an unimpassioned, grave man with an appearance of learning, who crams his pupils with undigested facts.

Blind (blīnd), **Mathilde.** b. at Mannheim, Germany, March 21, 1841; d. at London, Nov. 26, 1896. An English poet. She published *Poems by Claude Lake* (1867), *The Prophecy of Saint Oran* (1881), *The Heather on Fire* (1886), *The Ascent of Man* (1888), *Dramas in Miniature* (1891), *Songs and Sonnets* (1893), and *Birds of Passage* (1895). She translated Strauss's *The Old Faith and the New* (1873–74) and *The Journal of Marie Bashkirtseff* (1890), and wrote biographies of George Eliot (1883) and Madame Roland (1886).

Blind Alley. A novel by W. L. George, published in 1919, and similar in its theme and purpose to his *Bed of Roses* (1911) and *Second Blooming* (1914).

Blind Beggar of Alexandria, The. A comedy by George Chapman, first acted in 1595, and printed in 1598 in an apparently imperfect version, since two of the chief characters have unaccountably disappeared at the close of the main plot.

Blind Beggar of Bednal Green, with the Merry Humours of Tom Stroud (bed'nạl; stroud), **The.** A play by Henry Chettle and John Day, written in 1600, but not printed till 1659. It was based on the popular ballad called *The Beggar's Daughter of Bednal Green.*

Blinder (blin'dẽr), **Mrs.** The keeper of a chandler's shop in Charles Dickens's *Bleak House.* She has "a dropsy or an asthma, or perhaps both."

Blind Fireworks. A volume of poems (1929) by Louis MacNeice.

Blind Harry (or **Hary**). [Also, **Henry the Minstrel.**] d. c1492. A Scottish minstrel, putative author of a long poem, immensely popular and influential in Scotland, on Sir William Wallace. The only known manuscript, dated 1488, is a copy made by John Ramsay. The poem, in rhyming couplets, extends to more than 11,000 lines, and recounts the heroic deeds of the Scottish patriot who was finally captured and executed by the English in 1305. It is difficult to believe that this rather aureate poem, full of literary borrowings, was written by a humble minstrel, blind from birth, and scholars have conjectured that it is, at least in part, the work of a later poet.

Blind Man, The. A short story by D. H. Lawrence. Considered by most critics to be one of Lawrence's finest short stories, it appeared in *England, My England* (1922).

Bliss (blis). A volume of short stories by Katherine Mansfield, published in 1920. Among the stories are "The Escape," "The Little Governess," "Psy-

chology," "Pictures," and "Prelude," as well as the title story, a delicate study of moods.

Blister (blis'tẽr). An apothecary in Henry Fielding's *Old Man Taught Wisdom, or The Virgin Unmasked.*

Blockade, The. An unpublished play by John Burgoyne, British general and dramatist. It was performed at Boston during the Revolutionary War, in the period of British occupation.

Blockheads or the Affrighted Officers, The. A prose farce (1776), of unknown authorship. Erroneously attributed at one time to Mercy Warren, it was a retort to General John Burgoyne's *The Blockade.*

Blocksberg (bloks'bẽrk). See **Brocken.**

Blome (blōm), **Richard.** d. 1705. An English publisher and compiler of many books said to have been written by impoverished authors for a pittance, and for which he obtained subscriptions from wealthy persons. Among these are a large work on heraldry, and two books relating to the British colonies in America.

Blondel (blon'dẹl; French, blôṅ.del). [Also, **Blondel de Nesle** (dẹ nel).] b. at Nesle, Picardy, France; fl. in the second half of the 12th century. A French trouvère; attendant and friend of Richard Coeur de Lion. According to the traditional account, probably legendary, he discovered the presence of the imprisoned Richard in the castle of Dürrenstein by singing a song which the two had composed, and to which the king responded.

Blood (blud), **Thomas.** [Called "Colonel Blood."] b., probably in Ireland, c1618; d. Aug. 24, 1680. An Irish adventurer. He is now chiefly remembered for his remarkable (and nearly successful) attempt to steal the crown jewels of England, which were then guarded with a casualness that seems unbelievable today. His scheme entailed an elaborate preliminary campaign to win the friendship and confidence of the keeper of the jewels (some accounts have it that he posed as a clergyman), and he had actually almost reached safety when he was caught with the royal crown under his coat. He then demanded, and got, an interview with Charles II of England, who appears to have pardoned him and even to have shown him royal preferment (some historians have suggested that the sheer audacity of Blood's scheme aroused Charles's admiration and amusement). In his earlier life, Blood had been the leader in an unsuccessful attempt to seize (1663) Dublin Castle and the person of James Butler, the 1st duke of Ormonde, who was then lord lieutenant of Ireland under Charles II. Blood escaped capture, and remained for a time in Ireland, but finally fled to Holland. He later made his way to England, where he joined the Fifth Monarchy men (a religious group that became prominent in England during the middle of the 17th century. Its members believed in the imminent return of Christ to rule the earth as the world's fifth great monarchy, in succession to the empires of Assyria, Persia, Greece, and Rome. Their objections to the established church and their readiness to assert their views by force, if necessary, caused the civil authorities to hang or imprison many of them.) Blood forsook this group to go to Scotland, where he associated himself with the Covenanters, remaining with them

fat, fāte, fär, àsk, fāre; net, mē, hẽr; pin, pīne; not, nōte, mŏve, nôr; up, lūte, pŭll; ṭн, then;

until their defeat on Pentland Hills, on Nov. 27, 1666; he then revisited England and Ireland. In 1670 he led another assault on Ormonde, and in 1671 made his famous attempt to steal the crown jewels from the Tower of London. Sir Walter Scott introduces him in *Peveril of the Peak*.

Bloody Assizes. A popular name for the trials for participation in the rising (1685) by which the Duke of Monmouth (the illegitimate son of Charles II) sought to take the throne of England from James II. The trials were held in the western counties of England and presided over by George Jeffreys, 1st Baron Jeffreys of Wem. Over 300 persons are supposed to have been executed, and Jeffrey's name has ever since been a byword for extreme or unnecessary brutality in a court of law.

Bloody Brother, The. [Full title, **The Bloody Brother, or Rollo, Duke of Normandy.**] A tragedy by John Fletcher, Philip Massinger, and possibly others (including John Chapman) printed in 1639 and produced c1616.

Bloody Claverse (klav′ĕrz, klä′vĕrz). See **Graham, John.**

"bloody hand of Ulster" (ul′stĕr). See **Badge of Ulster.**

Bloody Mary. See **Mary I.**

Bloody Tenent yet More Bloody, The. A tract by Roger Williams, published at London in 1652. It is a sequel to his *The Bloudy Tenent of Persecution* and reaffirms the position of religious tolerance for which Williams is now chiefly remembered, and which so greatly infuriated the Puritans of his day.

Bloom (blŏm), **Leopold.** A Dublin Jew, the central character of James Joyce's novel *Ulysses*. An advertising solicitor for a newspaper, he represents a combination of man and myth. The book takes Bloom through the 24 hours of an ordinary day, and parallels all his encounters with events in the travels of Ulysses; this correspondence is worked chiefly by implication. Bloom is sought out as a father symbol by Stephen Dedalus, who corresponds to Telemachus, while Molly, Bloom's wife, is comparable to Penelope. Bloom also appears as a counterpart of the Wandering Jew.

Bloom, Milly. In James Joyce's novel *Ulysses*, the daughter of Leopold and Molly Bloom. She never appears in the book, but is the subject of many thoughts and conversations.

Bloom, Molly. In James Joyce's novel *Ulysses*, the wife of Leopold Bloom. Although presented as unfaithful to her husband, she is yet made to correspond to Penelope in the *Odyssey*, and is presented as the embodiment of the elemental and the feminine. The stream-of-consciousness section which closes the novel voices her thoughts in a single, unbroken sentence (which is perhaps the longest in all recorded English literature).

Bloom, Ursula. b. at Chelmsford, Essex, England. An English writer. She married (1916) Arthur Brownlow Denham-Cookes and, after his death (1918), became (1925) the wife of Charles Gower Robinson. Author of *The Great Beginning* (1924), *Vagabond Harvest* (1925), *The Driving of Destiny* (1925), *Tarnish* (1929), *Pastoral* (1934), *These Roots Go Deep* (1939), *The Flying Swans* (1940),

No Lady with a Pen (1946), *Four Sons* (1946), and *Adam's Daughter* (1947).

Bloomfield (blŏm′fēld), **Robert.** b. at Honington, Suffolk, England, Dec. 3, 1766; d. at Shefford, Bedfordshire, England, Aug. 19, 1823. An English poet and shoemaker. His best-known work is *The Farmer's Boy* (1800). He also wrote *Rural Tales* (1802) and *The Banks of the Wye* (1811).

Bloomsbury (blōmz′bĕr.i). A ward of Holborn metropolitan borough, in W central London, in the County of London. The district, which is chiefly residential, lies N of Oxford Street between Euston Road, Gray's Inn Road, and Tottenham Court Road, and contains the British Museum. A favorite residential section with artists and writers, Bloomsbury gave its name to an intellectual group of the 1920's and 1930's which included Virginia Woolf, Clive Bell, Roger Fry, and Lytton Strachey.

Bloomsbury Square. A square in London, N of Oxford Street, and E of the British Museum.

Blostman (blōst′män). [Meaning, in Modern English, "Blossoms."] A prose work (c898) by King Alfred of England (Alfred the Great). The selections in it were taken chiefly from the *Soliloquies* of Saint Augustine.

Blot in the 'Scutcheon, A. A tragedy by Robert Browning, brought out in England in 1843, and part of a series called *Bells and Pomegranates*. The cause of a bitter quarrel between Browning and the actor William Charles Macready, it was afterward produced in America by Lawrence Barrett. The plot (a melodramatic quarrel between two noble houses in the 18th century) is of Browning's invention, but it has points of resemblance to *Romeo and Juliet*.

Bloudy Tenent of Persecution (blud′i), **The.** A tract by Roger Williams, published at London in 1644, arguing the cause of freedom of conscience.

Blougram (blog′ram), **Bishop.** The narrator of Robert Browning's *Bishop Blougram's Apology*.

Blount (blunt), **Charles.** b. at Upper Holloway, England, April 27, 1654; d. a suicide, in August, 1693. An English deist and pamphleteer. He wrote against the censorship of the press, and, having fallen in love with his deceased wife's sister, published a defense of marriage between persons so connected (at that time proscribed in England). He wrote *Anima mundi* (1679), *The Two Books of Philostratus, or the Life of Apollonius of Tyanaeus, from the Greek* (1680), and others.

Blount or **Blunt** (blunt), **Edward.** fl. 1588–1632. An English printer, publisher, and translator. He was an intimate friend of Christopher Marlowe, whose *Hero and Leander* he published (1598). He also issued John Florio's translation of Montaigne's *Essays*, translated Lorenzo Ducci's *Ars Aulica, or the Courtier's Arte*, published (1620) Thomas Shelton's first English translation of *Don Quixote*, and produced (1623) with Isaac Jaggard, under the direction of John Heming and Henry Condell, the first great folio of Shakespeare's works. He made (1632) the first collection of John Lyly's *Sixe Court Comedies;* in the same year Blount translated *Christian Police* from the Spanish of Juan de Santa Maria.

d̥, d or j; ş, s or sh; t̥, t or ch; z̥, z or zh; o, F. cloche; ü, F. menu; c̆h, Sc. loch; ṅ, F. bonbon.

Blount, Harry. Lord Marmion's page, in Sir Walter Scott's poem *Marmion.*

Blount, Martha. b. probably near Reading, England, June 15, 1690; d. in Berkeley Row, Hanover Square, London, 1762. An Englishwoman, an intimate friend of Alexander Pope. He left her by his will 1,000 pounds, many books, all his household goods, and made her residuary legatee. He had previously dedicated to her his *Epistle on Women.*

Blount, Thomas. b. at Bordesley, Worcestershire, England, 1618; d. at Orleton, Herefordshire, England, Dec. 26, 1679. An English writer on law. He studied law at the Inner Temple, and was admitted to the bar, but as a Roman Catholic in a country at that time strongly anti-Catholic, he found it difficult to practice his profession; he retired to his estate at Orleton, and continued his study of the law as an amateur. His most famous work is *Glossographia* (1656), the first English dictionary to include etymologies and to list the authorities consulted. In making the *Glossographia,* Blount utilized freely the English dictionary of Bullokar (1616) and the Latin-English dictionaries of Thomas Thomas and Francis Holyoke. However, Blount introduced new words into the dictionary and defended the practice by citing their use by current authors. The *Glossographia* was not a complete dictionary of English as native words and words from "poetical stories" were omitted, but the dictionary went through five editions (1656, 1661, 1670, 1674, 1681) and must have been fairly popular. Among his other works are the *Academie of Eloquence* (1654), *A Law Dictionary* (1670), and *Fragmenta Antiquitatis, Ancient Tenures of Land* (1679).

Blount, Sir Walter. See under **Blunt, Sir Walter.**

Blowzelinda (blou.ze̯.lin′da̯) or **Blowsalinda** (-za̯-). A country girl in John Gay's pastoral poem *The Shepherd's Week.* She is not the traditional rustic maiden of such poetry, but a physically strong, approximately true-to-life milkmaid, who feeds the hogs and does other necessary (but unromantic) chores.

blue. Applied to women, learned; pedantic. "Some of the ladies were very blue and well informed." (Thackeray.)

Bluebeard (blö′bird). [French, **Barbe-Bleue;** German, **Blaubart.**] A nickname of the chevalier Raoul (an imaginary personage), celebrated for his cruelty. The historic origin was, perhaps, Gilles de Laval, Baron de Retz (b. 1396; d. 1440). He is the subject of works by Charles Perrault, André Ernest Modeste Grétry, Jacques Offenbach, Ludwig Tieck, and others. In Perrault's story, he is a rich man who, in spite of his hideous blue beard, has had six wives and marries a seventh, a young girl named Fatima. He leaves the keys of the castle with her while he goes on a journey, telling her that she may enter any room but one. She disobeys, enters the forbidden chamber, and discovers the bodies of his former wives. A bloodstain on the key reveals her disobedience, and her husband gives her five minutes to prepare for death. Her sister Anne mounts to the top of the castle to watch for aid, and at last sees their brothers coming. They arrive and kill Bluebeard as he is about to dispatch Fatima. Perrault's story was written (c1697) in French, and translated into English in the 18th century.

Blue Beard, or Female Curiosity. A melodrama by the younger George Colman, produced in 1798.

Blue Coat School. See **Christ's Hospital.**

Blue Knight. In Arthurian legend, Sir Persaunt of India, overthrown by Sir Gareth. He is described in Thomas Malory's *Morte d' Arthur* and in Tennyson's idyll *Gareth and Lynette.*

Blue-Mantle. The English pursuivant-at-arms.

Bluestocking at Court, A. One of three historical tales in *The Ladies!* (1922), by Lily Adams Beck, published under the pseudonym E. Barrington. Its central character is Fanny Burney.

Bluestocking Clubs. A name applied to assemblies held in London c1750 at the houses of Elizabeth Montagu and other ladies, in which literary conversation and other intellectual enjoyments were substituted for cards and gossip. These meetings were characterized by a studied plainness of dress on the part of some of the guests. Among these was Benjamin Stillingfleet, who always wore blue stockings (rather than white ones, as would have been more usual on a formal occasion in that day), and in reference to whom the coterie was called in derision the "Bluestocking Society" or the "Bluestocking Club." The members, especially the ladies, were called "bluestockingers," "bluestocking ladies," and later simply "bluestockings" or "blues." The term "bluestocking" came later to be applied, usually derisively, to any woman who gave evidence of an affected (rather than real) interest in intellectual or literary matters.

Bluestring (blö′string), **Robin.** A nickname of **Walpole, Sir Robert.**

Bluff or **Bluffe** (bluf), **Captain.** In Congreve's comedy *The Old Bachelor,* a blustering braggart, constantly alluding to his great valor as a soldier.

Bluff, Colonel. A character in Henry Fielding's *The Intriguing Chambermaid.*

Blundell (blun′del), Mrs. **Francis.** [Pseudonym, **Mary E. Francis;** maiden name, **Sweetman.**] b. at Dublin, Ireland; d. in North Wales, March 9, 1930. An English writer of children's books, dramatist, and novelist. She wrote stories of North Lancashire and Dorset life and character. Author of *Whither* (1892), *In a North Country Village* (1893), *The Song of Dan* (1894), *Town Mice in the Country* (1894), *Daughter of the Soil* (1895), *Among the Untrodden Ways* (1896), *The Duenna of a Genius* (1898), *Pastorals of Dorset* (1901), *The Manor Farm* (1902), *Dorset Dear* (1905), *Simple Annals* (1906), *Margery o' the Mill* (1907), *Galatea of the Wheatfield* (1909), *Molly's Fortunes* (1914), *Dark Rosaleen* (1915), *A Maid o' Dorset* (1917), and many others, popular in America as well as England. Her plays include *The Widow Woos* (1904) and *The Third Time of Asking* (1906).

Blundell, Peter. b. at Tiverton, Devonshire, England; d. 1601. An English merchant and founder (1604) of Blundell's School. Of humble origin, he accumulated great wealth as a merchant and manufacturer in the kersey trade, and bequeathed his fortune toward the establishment and endowment of Blundell's School, near Tiverton, and the benefaction of London hospitals, and various institutions of the Devonshire cities of Tiverton and Exeter. Blundell's School is mentioned in Richard

---

fat, fāte, fär, ȧsk, fãre; net, mē, hér; pin, pīne; not, nōte, mõve, nôr; up, lūte, pùll; ᴛʜ, then;

Doddridge Blackmore's novel *Lorna Doone*, as the place where its hero was educated.

Blunden (blun′den), **Edmund Charles.** b. at London, Nov. 1, 1896—. An English poet and critic. He served as professor (1924–27) of English literature at Tokyo University, and fellow and tutor (1931–43) in English literature at Merton College, Oxford. He published *Poems 1914–1930* and *Poems 1930–40*; his prose works include *The Bonadventure* (1922), *Undertones of War* (1928), *Life of Leigh Hunt* (1930), *The Face of England* (1932), *Charles Lamb and his Contemporaries* (1934), *The Mind's Eye* (1934), *Keats's Publisher* (1936), and *Shelley, a Life-Story* (1946).

Blunderbore (blun′der.bor). A giant in the *Jack the Giant Killer* cycle of folk tales, who imprisoned Jack. Jack threw a noose out the window and strangled him. In another version, Jack scuttled his boat, and he was drowned.

Blunderstone Rookery (blun′der.stōn rūk′er.i). The residence of David Copperfield, senior, in Charles Dickens's novel *David Copperfield*.

Blunt (blunt). In Shakespeare's *2 Henry IV*, an officer in the royal army who is ordered by John of Lancaster to guard the rebel, Colevile (IV.iii).

Blunt, Colonel. A character in Sir Robert Howard's *The Committee*. Like Benedick, in Shakespeare's *Much Ado About Nothing*, he was a confirmed bachelor.

Blunt, Edward. See **Blount, Edward.**

Blunt, Major-General. An old cavalier, rough but honest, in Thomas Shadwell's play *The Volunteers*.

Blunt, Sir James. In Shakespeare's *Richard III*, a supporter of Richmond.

Blunt, Sir Walter. In Shakespeare's *1 Henry IV*, the historical Sir Walter Blount, a supporter of King Henry. He acts as intermediary between the King and the rebels before the battle of Shrewsbury. Later Douglas kills him thinking he is King Henry.

Blunt, Wilfrid Scawen. b. at Crawley, Sussex, England, in August, 1840; d. at London, Sept. 10, 1922. An English poet, prose writer, diplomat, traveler, and anti-imperialist. The son of a wealthy Roman Catholic family, he was educated at Stonyhurst and St. Mary's College, Oscott. His diplomatic duties (1858–70) took him to Greece, Turkey, France, Spain, Germany, and South America; a strong defender of freedom for minority national groups within the British empire, he frequently attacked his government's Eastern policies; he also favored Egyptian, Indian, and Irish independence, being sent to prison (1888) for advocating the latter. He was the author of *Future of Islam* (1882), *Ideas About India* (1885), *India Under Ripon* (1909), *Gordon at Khartoum* (1911), *The Land War in Ireland* (1912), *My Diaries* (1919–20; it created a sensation and was taken off the market by the publisher because it revealed state secrets), and of *Love Sonnets of Proteus* (1880), *The Wind and the Whirlwind* (1883), *Esther* (1892), *Stealing of the Mare* (1892), *Griselda* (1893), *Seven Golden Odes of Pagan Arabia* (1905), and other volumes of poetry. *On the Shortness of Time*, *The Two Highwaymen*, *The Desolate City*, *Farewell*, and *Laughter and Death* are some of his best-known short poems.

Bluntschli (blunch′lē), **Captain.** In George Bernard Shaw's *Arms and the Man*, the hero, an eminently practical man (by Shaw's standards) who prefers to take chocolates rather than ammunition when he goes to war.

Blurt, Master Constable (blėrt). A play by Thomas Middleton, produced in 1602. "Blurt, Master Constable," is equivalent to "A fig for Master Constable," and is a proverbial phrase. Blurt is also the name of the constable in the play; he is a sort of Dogberry, imbued with a tremendous sense of his own and his master the duke's importance.

Boabdelin (bō.ab′de.lin), **Mahomet.** The last king of Granada in John Dryden's play *The Conquest of Granada*. He is betrothed to Almahide, but eventually loses her to the heroic Almanzor.

Boaden (bō′den), **James.** b. at Whitehaven, Cumberland, England, May 23, 1762; d. Feb. 16, 1839. An English dramatist and biographer. He was briefly the editor of a newspaper, *The Oracle*. His works include *The Secret Tribunal* (1795), *An Italian Monk* (1797), *Aurelio and Miranda* (1798), and lives of the actresses Sarah Siddons (1827), Dorothea Jordan (1831), and of the great actor John Philip Kemble (1825). In one of his works he exposed (1796) the Ireland Shakespeare forgeries, and in an edition (1837) of Shakespeare's *Sonnets*, he sought to identify W. H., to whom they had been dedicated, with William Herbert, 3rd Earl of Pembroke.

Boadicea (bō″a.di.sē′a). [Also, **Boudicca**.] d. 62 A.D. A queen of ancient Britain; wife of Prasutagus, king of the Iceni, a tribe in eastern Britain. Thinking to secure his kingdom and family from molestation, Prasutagus, who died c60 A.D., bequeathed his great wealth to his daughters jointly with the Roman emperor. However, the will was used by the Roman officials as a pretext for appropriating the whole property. Boadicea was flogged, her daughters subjected to various outrages and indignities, and other members of the royal family treated as slaves, with the result that the Iceni joined the Trinobantes in a revolt under Boadicea against the Romans, in 62 A.D., which was put down by Suetonius Paulinus. Boadicea thereupon killed herself by taking poison. She has been made the subject of a tragedy by John Fletcher (see *Bonduca*). Richard Glover produced a play on the subject in 1735, and William Mason also wrote one, called *Caractacus*, in 1759. Both William Cowper and Tennyson have made Boadicea the subject of poems.

Boanerges (bō.a.nėr′jēz). In the New Testament, a surname, explained as meaning "sons of thunder," given to James and John, the sons of Zebedee. Mark, iii. 17.

Boar of Ardennes (är.den′), **the Wild.** See **Marck, William de la.**

Boar's Head. A tavern in Eastcheap, London, celebrated by Shakespeare as the scene of Falstaff's carousals in *1 and 2 Henry IV*. Actually the tavern is not explicitly mentioned in the original text, but is inferred from remarks made by Falstaff and others. It was destroyed in the great fire of London (September, 1666), afterward rebuilt, and again demolished to make room for one of the approaches to London Bridge.

Boas (bō'az), **Frederick S.** b. at Belfast, Ireland, July 24, 1862—. An English literary historian. He was professor (1901–05) of history and English literature at Queen's College, Belfast, before serving as inspector (1905–27) for the London County Council education department. His works include *Shakespeare and his Predecessors* (1896), *University Drama in the Tudor Age* (1914), *Shakespeare and the Universities* (1922), *Richardson to Pinero* (1936), *Marlowe and his Circle* (1929), and *An Introduction to Stuart Drama* (1946).

Boaz (bō'az). In the Bible, a Bethlehemite who, marrying Ruth the Moabitess, became an ancestor of David. Ruth, ii., iii., iv.

Boaz. In the Old Testament, the name of one of the two brazen pillars erected in the porch of Solomon's temple. The other was Jachin. 1 Kings, vii. 21.

Bob (bob). Entries on literary characters having this prename will be found under the surnames Acres, Brierly, Cratchit, Jakin, and Sawyer.

Bobadill (bob'ạ.dil), **Captain.** In Ben Jonson's *Every Man in His Humour*, a Paul's man (that is, a man who lounged in the middle aisle of London's old Saint Paul's Cathedral, which was destroyed in the great fire of 1666. In Jonson's day the middle aisle of this cathedral was the resort of sharpers, gulls, and loafers of every kind.) His cowardice and bragging are made comic by his intense gravity and the serious manner in which he regards himself.

Bobs Bahadur (bobz bạ.hä'dûr). A nickname applied to the English general Frederick Sleigh Roberts (1832–1914). It originated with the soldiers who served under his command in India ("bahadur" is an epithet of great respect in Hindustani), and is the name by which he is referred to by Terence Mulvaney, Learoyd, and Ortheris in Kipling's *Plain Tales from the Hills*.

Bocardo (bō.kär'dō). An old north gate of Oxford, over which was a room used as a prison. It was destroyed in 1771.

Boccaccio (bọ.kä'chẹ.ō; Italian, bōk.kät'chō), **Giovanni.** b. at Paris, 1313; d. at Certaldo, near Florence, Italy, Dec. 31, 1375. An Italian writer and humanist. Brought as a youth to Florence by his father, a merchant of that city, he was sent during the late 1320's to Naples in order to learn the trade of a merchant. Commercial work proved extremely distasteful to him (as did also canonical law, to which he turned for a time), and he was persuaded by his great affection for learning and literature that he should devote his life to study and writing. In the early 14th century, Naples was a city of active life, rich, cheerful, and gay, and Boccaccio seems to have entered wholeheartedly into the pleasures of youth. His one great love was for Maria d'Aquino, daughter of Robert, the king of Naples, and wife of a Neapolitan nobleman; it was this woman to whom Boccaccio gave the name Fiammetta in his imaginative writing. There was a real enough love affair, in which Fiammetta yielded to his desires fairly soon, but she proved inconstant and as unfaithful to her lover as she had been to her husband. Boccaccio's disillusionment and bit-

terness was great, and found reflection in various of his works. This affair with Fiammetta is usually placed in the middle 1330's, and from this Neapolitan period and immediately thereafter date most of his lesser works in Italian. Economic reverses suffered by his father at the end of the decade made it necessary for Boccaccio to return to Florence, and from 1340 onward his permanent base was at that city.

Middle Years. Our information about Boccaccio's life in the 1340's is extremely scanty, and nearly all that can be said is that he lived in obscurity and apparently in considerable want and discomfort. He seems to have traveled at least somewhat in central Italy in this decade, and more in the 1350's. He became a fervent admirer of Petrarch, whose works he read and with whom he perhaps corresponded in the 1340's; he met Petrarch in 1350, when the latter passed through Florence, and saw him again several times afterwards. In the 1350's Boccaccio began to emerge from obscurity, and was sent on several occasions as Florentine ambassador to Avignon and Ravenna. It is doubtful whether Boccaccio was in Florence in 1348, when the Black Death reached that city, although he graphically describes its effects in the introduction to the *Decameron*. During this time, he was gradually turning away from his youthful dissipations to a more serious and ascetic attitude. He never married; his youthful excesses had given him an antipathy towards marriage and towards the female sex in general, which found its expression especially in the *Corbaccio*. In his mature years, Boccaccio devoted more and more time to the study of the Latin classics and of Dante; in his old age, he took up the study of Greek, for which he succeeded in having a chair established at the University of Florence.

Later Years. Despite increasing recognition, Boccaccio's financial position was still precarious, and he apparently entertained hopes of returning to a happier situation at Naples. Finally, in 1362, he did return, hoping to find a home with a former friend who had risen to the position of grand seneschal to the king of Naples; however, Boccaccio was treated as a mere mendicant and hanger-on, and soon returned, in disgust, to Florence. In following years he took further trips, to visit Petrarch at Venice in 1367, and again to Naples in 1370–71. Boccaccio's poverty eventually excited some degree of public sympathy and a willingness to render assistance, and he was granted a professorship at Florence in 1373 for the public reading and exposition of Dante. However, his poor health forced him to end his lectures in 1374, and he died in the following year.

Written Works and Evaluation. Boccaccio's first long novel, *Il Filocolo*, was written at the request of Fiammetta; and his early lyrics as well as his two long poems in *ottava rima*, the *Filostrato* and the *Teseida*, make use of this early experience in "polite" love, as do also his *Elegy of Madonna Fiammetta*, the *Ameto*, and the *Amorosa Visione*. Some of these works were finished at Florence, shortly after his recall to that city from Naples by his father in 1340. It was at Florence that he wrote his mythological poem *Il Ninfale Fiesolano*, in which are already evident a new objectivity and a freedom from autobiographical themes pointing to the full maturity of his narrative art. This was realized in the *Decameron*, his very famous collection of 100 tales written (according to most authorities) between 1348 and 1353. His works of erudition in Latin, all compiled in the last years of his life, include *De casibus virorum illustrium*, *De claris mulieribus*, and *De genealogiis deorum gentilium*. Any estimate of Boccaccio's personality must depend entirely upon what can be deduced from his written works. He must obviously have been a man of considerable intellectual ability, both in the extent of his learning and in his observation of the life of his times. That Boccaccio had a very keen understanding of human psychology is evident from the tales of the *Decameron*. His nature must have been intensely emotional and strongly sexed, as we can tell both from the history of his youth and his earlier works, and from his later ascetic revulsion against his youthful excesses. It is an error, however, to regard the bulk of his stories, particularly those in the *Decameron*, as essentially lascivious, if not actually immoral; it was his intent simply to represent the world as it was. It is also certainly true that Boccaccio did not have as complicated a personality as either Dante or Petrarch, having neither the ability of the former to analyze and organize, nor the latter's wide range of emotional perception and forward-looking attitude toward knowledge, particularly of the Latin classics. In his studies, Boccaccio was essentially a man of the Middle Ages, accepting and assimilating traditional knowledge without broadening its horizon or making new discoveries or interpretations; his originality consisted primarily in bringing new content and new technique to vernacular literature. In this content there was much that stimulated English writers. Chaucer's *Troilus and Criseyde* was based chiefly on Boccaccio's *Filostrato*, and the *Teseida* was used by Chaucer; likewise the Clerke's story of Grisilda in Chaucer's *Canterbury Tales* had been told by Boccaccio. However, it is almost certain that Chaucer never saw the *Decameron*, but derived his material indirectly through Petrarch's Latin prose version. By the 16th century Boccaccio's stories were widely translated and used as plots for stories and plays. So well known were Boccaccio's tales that they were sometimes used by writers who were ignorant of their source, as in the case of Thomas Deloney, an English silk-weaver who wrote popular fiction. Shakespeare borrowed from Boccaccio in *All's Well that Ends Well*. Later Dryden borrowed from the same source in *The Fables*, and Keats based his narrative poem "Isabella" on a tragic story of Boccaccio's. Tennyson and other English poets also read his tales, and found them not without value as a source of inspiration.

Bodleian Library (bod.lē'ạn, bod'lẹ.ạn). A library of Oxford University, England, which was originally established in 1445 and actually opened in 1488. Reëstablished by Sir Thomas Bodley in the period 1597–1602 (it had been destroyed during the troubled reign of Edward VI), it was formally reopened on Nov. 8, 1603, and in 1604 James I of England granted letters of patent styling it by Bodley's name. The library (which has had a new building since 1946) later absorbed the quadrangle and buildings of the old Examination Schools,

whose Jacobean entrance tower, with its columns of all five classical orders, remains to this day one of the chief architectural curiosities of Oxford. The library contains almost two million volumes and ab. 40,000 manuscripts, as well as many portraits, models of ancient buildings, literary antiquities, and coins.

Bodley (bod'li), Sir **Thomas**. b. at Exeter, England, March 2, 1545; d. at London, Jan. 28, 1613. An English diplomat and scholar. He is now chiefly remembered for his reëstablishment of the library at Oxford, now universally known as the Bodleian Library.

Bodley Homilies. A prose collection of religious material from the Middle English period, probably c1200, composed chiefly of homilies by Ælfric, his *Lives of the Saints*, and homilies by Wulfstan and others.

Boece (bō.ēs') or **Boethius** (bō.ē'thi.us) or **Boetius** (bō.ē'shus), **Hector**. [Also: **Bois, Boyce, Boyis**.] b. at Dundee, Scotland, c1465; d. at Aberdeen, Scotland, c1536. A Scottish humanist and historian. His family name was *Boyce* (also spelled *Boys, Bois, Boyis*), *Boyis* being an adaptation of *Boetius* (corresponding to the later *Boice*, and the modern *Boyce*). He studied and later taught at Paris, where he attracted the interest and friendship of Erasmus, and subsequently served as a chief adviser to William Elphinstone, bishop of Aberdeen, in the founding of the University of Aberdeen. He was appointed (c1498) to be the first principal of the university, and is known to have been at the university when lectures were given for the first time in 1500. The work for which he is now best known is a history of Scotland (which had the full title *Scotorum Historiae a prima gentis origine cum aliarum et rerum et gentium illustratione non vulgari*) first published in 17 books in 1527 (a later edition, published in 1574, contains an 18th book and part of a 19th). Boece's primary purpose in this work was not to prepare a chronicle of events, but to tell the story of the Scottish people as reflected in their legends (despite the obviousness of which, many historians on the Continent and England used it as a source of what they took to be actual facts. Holinshed took much from it, and thus, coincidentally, provided Shakespeare (who read Holinshed) with the plot for *Macbeth*.) During the 16th century the work was twice translated from its original Latin: first, into Scottish verse, and later (between 1530 and 1533) by John Bellenden into Scottish prose. An edition of the latter of these versions was last published during the first quarter of the 19th century. Boece also wrote a Latin account of the lives of two Scottish bishops (one of whom was William Elphinstone, of Aberdeen) which was first published at Paris in 1522.

Boeotia (bē.ō'shạ). In ancient times, a district in C Greece, bounded by the land of the Locri Opuntii on the N, Attica and the strait of Evripos on the E, Attica, Megaris, and the Gulf of Corinth on the S, and Phocis on the W. Its surface was generally level, forming a basin in which was Lake Copais, now drained. According to ancient Greek tradition, the inhabitants of this district were all extremely stupid (but this, like most other Greek traditions, has come down to us through Athenian sources,

---

ḍ, d or j; ṣ, s or sh; ṭ, t or ch; ẓ, z or zh; o, F. cloche; ü, F. menu; c̆h, Sc. loch; n̈, F. bonbon.

and the Athenians had little love for the people or cities of Boeotia). The chief city of Boeotia was Thebes, which with other cities formed the Boeotian League.

Boethius (bō.ē′thi.us). A translation by King Alfred of the famous treatise *De Consolatione Philosophiae* (On the Consolation of Philosophy), by Anicius Manlius Severinus Boethius. It is generally considered from the literary point of view to have been King Alfred's major work.

Boethius, Anicius Manlius Severinus. b. c480 A.D.; d. 524 or 525 A.D. A medieval philosopher, sometimes described as a transmitter of classical thought and also as the first of the scholastics. His greatest work is the essay in five books of prose and verse, *De Consolatione Philosophiae*, written when he was facing death at Pavia. Here, in a dialogue with Lady Philosophy, who sets him straight about the ways of the goddess Fortuna, he uses material from Aristotle, Plato, and the Neoplatonists, to discuss the problem of moral responsibility. The essay had a profound influence on Dante, and was translated by King Alfred, Geoffrey Chaucer, Queen Elizabeth, and others. It was often imitated, and its material has been borrowed by countless writers.

Boffin (bof′in), **Nicodemus.** [Called "Noddy" or the "Golden Dustman."] In Charles Dickens's *Our Mutual Friend*, a faithful retainer of the elder Mr. Harmon. He is a simple-hearted, illiterate old man who has inherited the estate ("Boffin's Bower") of his late employer, a miserly dustman.

Boffin's Bower. The residence of the Boffins, in Charles Dickens's *Our Mutual Friend*. Mrs. Boffin, not liking its former name, Harmon's Jail, given it from its late owner's habits of life, gave it this cheerful appellation. Miss Jennie Collins established a successful charity for working-girls at Boston in 1870 under this name.

Boggley Wallah (bog′li wäl′a). In Thackeray's novel *Vanity Fair*, a place in India of which Joseph Sedley has served as "Collector."

Bogomils (bog′ọ.milz). [Also, **Bogomilians** (bog.ọ-mil′yanz).] A heretical sect of the 10th–15th centuries, thought by some to have been founded by Basil, a monk of Philippopolis, who was put to death at Constantinople in 1118. They were held to be Manichaean and Docetist in their doctrine, and were probably an offshoot of the Paulician sect. They flourished in Bulgaria, and spread thence to Bosnia and Serbia.

Bog of Stars, The. A collection (1893) of short stories by Standish James O'Grady.

Bohan (bō′an). A cynical humorist in an interlude in Robert Greene's comedy *James IV*, who perhaps inspired Shakespeare's Jaques in *As You Like It*.

Bohème (bo.em), **La.** An opera in four acts by Giacomo Puccini, with a libretto by Giuseppe Giacosa and Illica based on Henri Murger's *Scènes de la vie de Bohème*, first produced at Turin on Feb. 1, 1896.

Bohemia (bọ.hē′mi.a), **seacoast of.** In Shakespeare's *Winter's Tale*, the place where Antigonus abandons Perdita. Since Bohemia (now part of Czechoslovakia) has no coast, this has been often cited as an example of a mistake on Shakespeare's part. In

view of the generally unrealistic nature of the play itself, however, it is quite likely that this is a deliberate confusion.

Bohort (bō′hôrt), **Sir.** See **Bors, Sir.**

Bohun (bō′hun), **Edmund.** b. at Ringsfield, Suffolk, England, March 12, 1645; d. in Carolina, Oct. 5, 1699. An English publicist and miscellaneous writer, appointed chief justice of the colony of Carolina c1698. His chief work is *Geographical Dictionary* (1688).

Bohun (bön, bō′un), **Eleanor de.** See under **Gloucester, Duchess of.**

Bois (bois), **Hector.** See **Boece.**

Bois, Jaques de. See **Jaques.**

Bois-Guilbert (bwä′gēl.ber′), **Brian de.** A Knight Templar, a preceptor of the order, in Sir Walter Scott's novel *Ivanhoe*. Having fallen in love with Rebecca and been repulsed by her, he carries her off to his preceptory. Compelled to accuse her of witchcraft, he meets her defender Ivanhoe in the lists, and falls dead at the beginning of the encounter.

Bokenham or **Bokenam** (bok′en.am), **Osbern.** b. possibly at Bokeham (or Bookham), Surrey, England, Oct. 6, 1393; d. c1447. An English poet and member of the Augustinian order. He was the author of a collection of 13 saints' lives in verse, entitled *Legendys of Hooly Wummen* (c1445). Bokenham was familiar with Greek and Latin authors and was influenced by Chaucer and Lydgate. His work, important as an example of 15th-century Suffolk dialect, was published (1835) by the Roxburghe Club.

Boke of the Duchesse, The. See **Book of the Duchess, The.**

Bokerly Dyke (bō′kér.li). Ruins of Roman entrenchments near Farnham, England.

Bold (bōld), **John.** In Anthony Trollope's novel *The Warden*, a young surgeon in love with Eleanor Harding. It is he who brings suit to require an accounting of the money received and spent on behalf of Hiram's Hospital (and is therefore violently attacked by Dr. Grantly); however, because of the effect of the suit on Eleanor's father he finally withdraws it.

Boldrewood (bōl′dér.wud), **Rolf.** Pseudonym of **Browne, Thomas Alexander.**

Bold Stroke for a Husband, A. A comedy by Hannah Cowley, brought out in 1783.

Bold Stroke for a Wife, A. A comedy of amorous intrigue by Susannah Centlivre, produced in 1718. It shows the style of Congreve in its deft handling of the outwitting of four temperamental guardians by the heroine. The play was a great contemporary success. One of the characters, Simon Pure, is impersonated until the last act, when he arrives on stage as "the real Simon Pure," thus giving rise to use of the phrase as a standard of genuineness.

Boleyn (bul′in), **Anne.** b. c1507; beheaded at London, May 19, 1536. English queen; second wife of Henry VIII of England, whom she married on or about Jan. 25, 1533, and mother by him of Queen Elizabeth. She was the daughter of Sir Thomas Boleyn, later earl of Wiltshire and Ormond, and was Henry's acknowledged mistress for some time before he gained his divorce from Catherine of Aragon. She was condemned to death on a charge of adultery and incest, and decapitated. It is now generally believed that she was certainly not guilty of all the crimes of which she was accused, but her entire innocence has never been established. She has been the subject of various works of literature, including in recent times Maxwell Anderson's play *Anne of the Thousand Days* (1948).

Boleyn, Anne. See also **Bullen, Anne.**

Bolgolam (bol'gọ.lam). A character in David Garrick's play *Lilliput.*

Bolingbroke (bol'ing.brŭk), Viscount. [Title of **Henry St. John.**] b. 1678; d. 1751. An English statesman, active in politics as a Tory under Queen Anne (by whom he was ennobled) but thrust from office on the accession of George I (at whose behest he was attainted). He thereafter served James, the Stuart Pretender to the English throne, until 1716, when James also found it expedient to dispense with his services. He was pardoned and returned to England in 1723, and was thereafter again active in British politics. His literary works, many of them directed against the Whigs, were concerned with various political and historical subjects.

Bolingbroke, Henry. In Shakespeare's *Richard II,* the usurper of the throne; in *1* and *2 Henry IV,* the King of England (i.e., Henry IV himself). He is the Duke of Hereford, son of John of Gaunt, and, after the latter's death, Duke of Lancaster. In *Richard II,* he and Mowbray are banished for their mutual accusations of treason. When Richard leaves for the Irish wars, having confiscated Bolingbroke's estates, Bolingbroke returns to England with an army and is joined by a number of disaffected noblemen. Richard returns, and is confronted by Bolingbroke, who ostensibly demands only his rights as Duke of Lancaster, but is also preparing to maneuver Richard's deposition. Bolingbroke, a practical and ambitious man, then replaces the weak, poetic, and much more charming Richard on the throne. In *1 Henry IV,* he is a less dynamic personality. Factions around the kingdom are in rebellion, and he sorrows over his wild son, Prince Hal, wishing him more like the brave and chivalrous Hotspur. In *2 Henry IV,* he has become yet more weary and anxious about the fate of his kingdom, which he got through violence and has kept only at the price of constant vigilance.

Bolingbroke, Roger. In Shakespeare's *2 Henry VI,* a conjurer. He summons a prophetic spirit for Eleanor, Duchess of Gloucester, who aspires to the throne. York discovers them and arrests them as traitors.

Bolitho (bọ.li'thō), **Hector.** [Full name, **Henry Hector Bolitho.**] b. at Auckland, New Zealand, May 28, 1898—. An English writer of fiction and biography. He is the author of *The Islands of Wonder* (1920), *Thistledown and Thunder* (1928), *The New Zealanders* (1928), *The New Countries* (1929), *The Glorious Oyster* (1929), *Albert the Good* (1932), *The Prince Consort and his Brother* (1934), *Victoria, the Widow and her Son* (1934), *Older People* (1935), *The House in Half Moon Street* (1936), *Edward VIII* (1937), *Royal Progress* (1937), *George VI* (1937), *Victoria*

and Albert (1938), *A Century of British Monarchy* (1951), and the novels *Solemn Boy* (1927) and *Judith Silver* (1929).

Bolitho, William. [Full name, **William Bolitho Ryall.**] b. at Capetown, South Africa, 1890; d. at Avignon, France, June 2, 1930. An English newspaper correspondent, columnist, and author. During his service in World War I, he was the only one of a group of 16 who survived a mine explosion on the Somme front; after recovering, he became Paris correspondent for the Manchester *Guardian,* and European correspondent for the New York *World.* He was the author of political and biographical studies including *Leviathan* (1924), *Italy Under Mussolini* (1926), *Murder for Profit* (1926), and *Twelve Against the Gods* (1929). He also wrote a play, *Overture* (produced after his death), essays published in *Camera Obscura* (1931), and an unfinished novel, published by his wife, Sybil Bolitho, in her own novel, *My Shadow As I Pass.*

Bolt Court (bōlt). The name of a short alley at London, ab. $\frac{1}{16}$ mi. long, leading N off Fleet Street into Gough Square. Dr. Samuel Johnson passed the last years of his life here, dying at Number 8, in 1784.

Bolton or **Boulton** (bōl'tọn), **Edmund.** b. c1575; d. c1633. English historian and poet who was a fellow-contributor (1600) with Sir Philip Sidney, Edmund Spenser, and Sir Walter Raleigh to *England's Helicon.* He formulated a scheme (1617) for a royal academy of letters and science, which, although favorably received by James I, was never carried out. Among his writings are *Elements of Armouries* (1610), *Life of King Henry II* (originally intended for Speed's *Chronicle,* but rejected as too favorable to Thomas à Becket), *The Roman Histories of Lucius Iulius Florus* (translated 1618), *Hypercritica* (c1618), *Nero Caesar* (1624), *An Historical Parallel* (at the end of some copies of *Nero Caesar*), *Commentaries Roial,* and Latin verses prefacing William Camden's *Britannia* and Ben Jonson's *Volpone* (1605). He was once thought to be the "E.B." who first published Christopher Marlowe's *Hero and Leander,* but it is now generally accepted that these initials identify Edward Blount.

Bolton, Fanny. In Thackeray's novel *Pendennis,* the pretty daughter of the porter of the Shepherd's Inn. Pendennis is in love with her for a short time.

Bolton Castle. A castle in the West Riding of Yorkshire: the scene of the imprisonment (1568–69) of Mary, Queen of Scots.

Bolus (bō'lus), **Dr.** The apothecary of the younger George Colman's poem *The Newcastle Apothecary,* published in a volume of humorous verse entitled *Broad Grins.* It was Dr. Bolus's practice to write his prescriptions in rhyme, one of which ("When taken, To be well shaken") was too literally applied to the patient instead of to the dose.

Bomba (bōm'bä), **King.** A nickname given in Italy to Ferdinand II, king of the Two Sicilies, from his bombardment of Messina and other cities during the revolutionary troubles of 1849.

Bombardinian (bom.bär.din'i.ạn), **General.** The general of the king's forces in Henry Carey's burlesque *Chrononhotonthologos.* He has become proverbial for burlesque bombast.

---

d, d or j; ş, s or sh; ţ, t or ch; ẓ, z or zh; o, F. cloche; ü, F. menu; ċh, Sc. loch; ṅ, F. bonbon.

bombast. High-sounding words; inflated or extravagant language; fustian; speech too big and high-sounding for the occasion. "Bombast is commonly the delight of that audience which loves poetry, but understands it not." (Dryden, *Criticism in Tragedy*.)

Bombastes Furioso (bom.bas′tĕz fū.ri.ō′sō). A burlesque opera by William Barnes Rhodes, produced in 1790. It takes its name from the principal character, a victorious general, who returns from the wars with his army, which consists of four unprepossessing warriors. He discovers his king, Artaxominous, visiting Distaffina, his betrothed, and resolves to go mad. His howling, despairing, bombastic rant caused his name to become proverbial. He fights and kills his king for a pair of jackboots which he had hung up as a challenge, and is in his turn killed by Fusbos, the minister of state. The farce is a burlesque of Lodovico Ariosto's *Orlando Furioso.*

Bomby (bom′bi), **Hope-on-High.** A Puritan, in John Fletcher's play *Women Pleased*, intended to ridicule the sect to which he belonged. He denounces worldly pleasures, but joins in them.

Bona (bō′na̤). In Shakespeare's *3 Henry VI*, the sister of the Queen of France who has agreed to marry Edward IV at Warwick's suggestion but finds that he has taken Lady Grey instead. She urges King Lewis (Louis) to support Margaret in her fight against Edward and is joined by Warwick, who has been made a fool by the secret marriage.

Bonaparte (bō′na̤.pärt; French, bo.na̤.pȧrt), **Napoleon.** See **Napoleon I.**

Bonassus (bǫ.nas′us). An imaginary beast with whom the Scottish poet James Hogg (called the "Ettrick Shepherd") pretended in one of his works to have had an adventure.

Bonaventura (bon″a̤.ven.tū′ra̤). In John Ford's play *'Tis Pity She's a Whore*, a friar of a kindly, pliable nature, obviously modeled on Shakespeare's Friar Laurence in *Romeo and Juliet.*

Bond Street (bond). A thoroughfare between Oxford Street and Piccadilly, at London. It was formerly a popular promenade, and is now filled with fashionable shops. Laurence Sterne, Jonathan Swift, and James Boswell at one time or other all lived on this street. The section near Piccadilly is known as Old Bond Street, while New Bond Street is the end nearest Oxford Street.

Bondman, The. A tragedy by Philip Massinger, licensed in 1623, and first acted in 1624. It was dedicated to Philip Herbert, 1st Earl of Montgomery. The plot is partly based upon Plutarch's *Life of Timoleon*, although the portion about the rising of the slaves may have come from various works, since several Greek, Roman, and Renaissance historians mention it. Timoleon is possibly Prince Maurice of Orange, and the play quite obviously hits at certain abuses of the government of James I (so much so that it is rather strange no censorship was applied to the play before it was presented at Whitehall). Timoleon upon arriving at Syracuse (England) indicts private graft, lack of military preparation, and particularly the scandalous state of the navy. When Timoleon goes off to fight Carthage (Spain) another Greek leader, Pisander, disguised as a bondman (i.e. a slave) incites the Sicilian slaves to mutiny, using a variation of Stoic argument, namely that tyrants have enslaved men by disturbing the original equality. There is a scene in which the slaves turn upon their masters, and it probably called for impressive mob effects upon the stage. Pisander explains to Timoleon upon the latter's return that it was tyranny which caused the uprising and that rulers have forgotten the filial affection they ought to bear toward their people. Timoleon menaces the slaves with whips as they charge and their spirit is broken. When Pisander reveals himself, Timoleon pardons him and his followers.

Bonduca (bon.dū′ka̤). A tragedy by John Fletcher, written between 1609 and 1614, and printed in 1639. An alteration of Fletcher's play was brought out in 1696 by George Powell, an actor, and another alteration by the elder George Colman was acted in 1778. A third alteration, made by J. R. Planché and acted in 1837, was called *Caractacus.* The title character of the play is the British queen now usually known as Boadicea, the name Bonduca being an early variant of her name. The source was Book IV of Tacitus's *Annals.*

Bon Gaultier Ballads (bȯn gō.tyä′). A series of poems by W. E. Aytoun and Theodore Martin, parodying some of the mid-19th-century poets, including Tennyson, Elizabeth Barrett Browning, and Macaulay. The poems appeared in *Blackwood's Magazine* and other periodicals of the day and were published in book form in 1855.

Boniface (bon′i.fās), Saint. [Called the **"Apostle of Germany"**; original name, **Winfrid, Winfrith, Wynfrith.**] b. at Kirton, or Crediton, Devonshire, England, c680; d. near Dokkum, Friesland, June 5, c755. An English missionary. From 716 he labored among the Friesians and among the German tribes. He was made a bishop in 723, and archbishop in 732. He founded (c743) the abbey of Fulda, where his remains were later laid. From 746 to 754 he occupied the see of Mainz. He was murdered in 755. He is said to have enforced his missionary teaching by cutting down with his own hand the sacred oak at Geismar, in what is now Hesse, Germany. According to the most generally accepted account of this exploit, Boniface not only felled the oak (thus demonstrating the utter powerlessness of the god to whom it was sacred) but also used its wood to build a Christian chapel. There can be no doubt that this story, in its main outlines, is substantially true, and its effectiveness in converting the people of the area to Christianity was enormous. His festival is celebrated in the Roman and Anglican churches on June 5.

Boniface, Abbot. The head of the monastery in Sir Walter Scott's novel *The Monastery.*

Boniface, Will. The landlord of the inn at Lichfield in George Farquhar's *The Beaux' Stratagem.* He was in league with the highwaymen, and prided himself on his diet of ale. From him the name has been applied to innkeepers in general.

Bonivard (bo.nē.vȧr), **François de.** See **Bonnivard.**

bon mot (bôn mō). A witticism; a clever or witty saying; a witty repartee. "Some of us have written down several of her sayings, or what the French call bons mots, wherein she excelled beyond belief." (Swift, *Death of Stella.*) "You need not hurry when the object is only to prevent my saying a bon-mot, for there is not the least wit in my nature." (Jane Austen, *Mansfield Park.*)

"Bonnie Prince Charlie." See **Stuart, Charles Edward.**

Bonnivard or **Bonivard** (bo.nē.vȧr), **François de.** b. at Seyssel, Switzerland, c1493; d. at Geneva, 1570. A Swiss prelate and politician, the hero of Byron's poem *The Prisoner of Chillon.* He became (1514) prior of St. Victor, Switzerland, and was a conspicuous opponent of Charles III, Duke of Savoy, who endeavored to obtain control of Geneva. He was largely instrumental in bringing about an alliance (1518) between Geneva and Fribourg, and in 1519 was captured by the duke and imprisoned for 20 months. In 1530 he obtained a safe-conduct from the duke to visit his aged parents at Seyssel, but was arrested (May 26, 1530) at Lausanne, and confined in the castle of Chillon, where, after a visit (1532) from the duke, he was placed in a subterranean dungeon and, according to the local tradition, fastened to a pillar. He was liberated (March 29, 1536) upon the capture of Chillon by the Bernese. He was the author of *Les Chroniques de Genève* (edited by Dunant, Geneva, 1831), which was written at the instance of the magistracy of Geneva.

Bonny Dundee (dun.dē′). See **Graham, John.**

Bonthron (bon′thron), **Anthony.** In Sir Walter Scott's novel *The Fair Maid of Perth,* a henchman of Sir John Ramorny who is ordered to murder Henry Smith and the Duke of Rothsay.

Bon Ton (bôṅ tôṅ). A comedy by John Burgoyne, produced in 1760. David Garrick shortened it, and produced it in 1775 as *Bon Ton, or High Life above Stairs.*

Booby (bö′bi), **Lady.** In Henry Fielding's novel *Joseph Andrews,* a woman no longer young, but with unabated interest in carnal pleasure, who tries to seduce Joseph Andrews, her footman. She dismisses him when he refuses her advances.

Boojum (bö′jum). In Lewis Carroll's *The Hunting of the Snark,* the name of the snark.

Book of Common Order. The liturgy of the Church of Scotland, taken from the liturgy of the English church at Geneva. It was introduced in 1562.

Book of Common Prayer. [Popularly called the **Prayer Book.**] The service book of the Church of England, or a similar book authorized by one of the other branches of the Anglican Church. The first Book of Common Prayer was issued in 1549. It was almost entirely taken from medieval liturgical books. English was substituted for Latin, and a uniform use was established for the whole Church of England. Revisions were made in 1552, 1559, and 1662. The American Prayer Book was authorized in 1789; a revision was begun in 1880, and issued in 1892. Another revision was issued in 1928.

Book of Faith, The. A Middle English treatise (c1456) by Reginald Pecock. In it Pecock defends the authority of the Church even though he admits that she can err.

Book of Kells (kelz). See under **Kells.**

Book of Margery Kempe (kemp), **The.** An autobiography by Margery Kempe (d. c1438). The manuscript of this work was discovered in 1934, a modernized version was published in 1936, and the original text in 1940. Both as a human document and for its many glimpses of medieval life, it has great interest for students of English literature and history.

Book of Martyrs, The. [Original title, **Actes and Monuments.**] A history of the persecution of various Protestant reformers in England, by John Foxe. It was finished in 1559, and was written in Latin. It was published on March 20, 1563. Foxe himself translated it into English from the Latin in which he originally wrote it. It gives the lives of the martyrs from earliest times to Savonarola, painting lurid pictures for Protestant readers of the supposedly villainous efforts of the Papacy to quell the Protestant Reformation. In later sections he describes the persecutions in England under the Catholic Queen Mary ("Bloody Mary").

Book of Nonsense, The. A collection (1848) of humorous verse by Edward Lear.

Book of Snobs, The. A series of sketches by William Makepeace Thackeray on one of his favorite subjects, snobbery in all its branches. The sketches first came out (1843) in *Punch* as "The Snob Papers."

Book of St. Albans (sȧnt ôl′banz). A rhymed treatise on hawking, hunting, and similar sports, printed in English in 1486. It was reprinted by Wynkyn de Worde in 1496. It has been attributed to Juliana Berners, and some of it was certainly written by her. The second edition contains the popular *Treatyse on Fysshynge with an Angle.* It was reprinted many times. The original edition was reprinted in facsimile by Eliot Stock in 1881.

Book of the Duchess, The. [Also: **The Book** (or **Boke**) **of the Duchesse; The Death of Blanche the Duchess.**] An elegiac poem by Chaucer. The earliest of Chaucer's original poems of any length, it was written near the end of 1369, as Blanche, the wife of John of Gaunt, died on Sept. 12, 1369 (and it is thus that this poem, alone of the poet's major works, can be dated with something approaching confidence). The poem represents the inconsolable grief of the duke, and embodies the story of Ceyx and Alcyone from Ovid's *Metamorphoses.* Cast in the form of a love-vision, here adapted to the purposes of elegy, it is much indebted to the French poets of Chaucer's century and particularly to Guillaume de Machault.

Book of the Dun Cow. See under **Tain Bo Cuailgne.**

Book of the Glory and Perfection of the Saints. See **Melum Contemplativorum.**

Book of Thel (thel), **The.** A work in free verse by William Blake, published in 1789. The first of his so-called Prophetical Books, it is a mystical treatment of vanity, death, and redemption.

Book of Vices and Virtues, The. A Middle English translation in the East Midland dialect of *Somme le Roi.*

Book of Wisdom or **Book of the Wisdom of Solomon** (sol′ọ.mon). See **Wisdom of Solomon.**

Book of Wonder, The. A narrative (1912) by Lord Dunsany. Like many of his other stories, it is a

---

fantasy laid against a background of the mythology which he had himself invented.

Books and Characters. A prose work (1922) by Lytton Strachey. It contains a miscellaneous collection of articles originally printed in various periodicals as well as some brilliant sketches of various French personages of the 18th century.

Boötes (bọ̄.ō'tēz). A northern constellation, containing the first-magnitude star Arcturus, situated behind the Great Bear. It is supposed to represent a man holding a crook and driving the Bear. In modern times the constellation of the Hounds has been interposed between Boötes and the Bear.

Booth (bŏth). The husband of Amelia, a prominent character in Henry Fielding's novel *Amelia*. Fielding intended, in this character, partly to represent his own follies, improvidence, and weakness.

Booth, Amelia. The heroine of Henry Fielding's novel *Amelia* (published 1751), a virtuous and devoted wife, said to be a portrait of Fielding's own wife. She is represented as having suffered an injury to her nose (like Mrs. Fielding), which impaired her popularity among Fielding's readers. Thackeray considered her "the most charming character in English fiction."

Booth, Barton. b. in Lancashire, England, 1681; d. at London, May 10, 1733. An English tragedian noted for Shakespearian parts. He first appeared at London in 1700, having previously played in Ireland. He played with Thomas Betterton and with Robert Wilks.

Booth, Maud Ballington. [Maiden name, **Charlesworth.**] b. at Limpsfield, Surrey, England, Sept. 13, 1865; d. at Great Neck, N. Y., Aug. 26, 1948. An English writer and welfare worker; wife of Ballington Booth, and his successor as president of the Volunteers of America. She served with the Y.M.C.A. in France and Germany during World War I, and was a founder of the Parent-Teachers Association. Author of *Branded* (1897), *Look Up and Hope*, *Sleepy Time Stories* (1889), *After Prison —What?* (1905), and others.

Booth, William. [Called "**General Booth.**"] b. at Nottingham, England, April 10, 1829; d. near London, Aug. 20, 1912. An English preacher, founder of the Salvation Army. He became a minister of the Methodist New Connexion in 1850, and organized (1865) the Christian Revival Association which, when it had become a large organization formed on military lines, was renamed (1878) the Salvation Army. He established (1880) the *War Cry*, and published *In Darkest England* (1890).

Borachia (bō.rä'chạ). A woman given to drink, a comic but unwholesome character, in the play *A Very Woman*, ascribed to Philip Massinger.

Borachio (bō.rä'chi.ō). In Shakespeare's *Much Ado About Nothing*, a follower of Don John. He has the incriminating conversation with Margaret (who pretends to be Hero) that persuades Claudio of Hero's infidelity. He is arrested and confesses the scheme under Dogberry's cross-examination. The name also is used by other Elizabethan dramatists for a drunkard, alluding to the Spanish word for a large leather bag used for wine.

Borachio. The agent of D'Amville in his various plots to procure his family an inheritance and

successors in Cyril Tourneur's *The Atheist's Tragedy*.

Boraq (bō'räk), **al-.** See **Al Borak.**

Border Antiquities of England and Scotland, The. A prose work (1817) by Sir Walter Scott. It describes the scenery and architecture of the region known as the Border.

Borderers, The. A play by William Wordsworth. Written in the period 1796–97, it was not published until 1842, and no early draft exists to show how much it may have been revised in the meantime (although a preface, long believed to be lost, has now been recovered). The work is of slight moment as a drama but of great importance as a milestone in Wordsworth's life both as a poet and as a person who had taken more than a passing interest in the rationalist philosophies of 18th-century France; this play clearly reflects the transition in Wordsworth's point of view which took place in the autumn of 1795, when he began to turn away from France and Godwinism to a political philosophy more in harmony with Burke, and to the loveliness of the natural world. Its story of the villain Oswald who, after committing a crime, banishes remorse by condemning all human feeling as weakness, and thus becomes a malignant moral skeptic, is intended to demonstrate that though the attempt to live by the light of reason may be a noble aspiration, yet to discard affections and "prejudices" leaves not reason but the passions supreme.

Boreas (bō'rẹ.ạs). In Greek mythology, the personification of the north wind. He was a son either of Aeolus or of Astraeus and Eos, and brother of Hesperus, Zephyrus, and Notus. He was identified by the Romans with their Aquilo.

Borgia (bôr'jä). A noble family of Spanish origin, which acquired eminence in Italy after 1455, when one of its members became Pope Calixtus III.

Borgia, Cesare. [Title, Duke of **Valentinois.**] b. c1476; killed before the castle of Viana, Spain, March 12, 1507. An Italian ruler; natural son of Rodrigo Lenzuoli Borgia (Pope Alexander VI). He was created (1492) a cardinal by his father. In 1497 he procured the murder of his brother Giovanni Borgia, Duke of Gandia. Having resigned (1497) the cardinalate, he was invested (1498) with the duchy of Valentinois by Louis XII, and married (1499) Charlotte d'Albret, daughter of Jean d'Albret, king of Navarre. He was created (1501) duke of Romagna by his father, after having reduced by force and perfidy the cities of Romagna, which were ruled by feudatories of the Papal See; with the assistance of his family, he endeavored to found an independent hereditary power in central Italy, including Romagna, Umbria, and the Marches. His father having died in 1503, he was detained in captivity by Pope Julius II (1503–04) and by Ferdinand of Aragon (1504–06), until he escaped to the court of Jean d'Albret of Navarre, in whose service he fell before the castle of Viana. Handsome in person, educated, eloquent, a patron of learning, and an adept in the cruel and perfidious politics in vogue in his day, his methods are described with approval by Machiavelli in his *Principe*.

Borgia, Lucrezia. [Title, Duchess of **Ferrara.**] b. 1480; d. June 24, 1519. Daughter of Pope Alexander

VI, and sister of Cesare Borgia. She married Giovanni Sforza, lord of Pesaro, in 1493. This marriage was annulled by Alexander, who found (1498) a more ambitious match for her in Alfonso of Aragon, a natural son of Alfonso II of Naples. Alfonso having been murdered by Cesare Borgia in 1500, she married (1501) Alfonso of Este, who subsequently succeeded to the duchy of Ferrara. She was a woman of great beauty and ability, a patron of learning and the arts. She was long accused of the grossest crimes, but later writers have cleared her reputation of the worst charges brought against her.

Born in Exile. A novel (1892) by George Gissing. In it Gissing tells of the efforts of a young man to rise above his own social class.

Boron (bo.rôn). See **Robert de Boron.**

Borough (bur′ọ), **Stephen.** [Also: **Borrows, Burrough, Burrowe.**] b. at Northam, Devonshire, England, Sept. 25, 1525; d. July 12, 1584. An English navigator. He was master of one of several English ships which set out to reach Russia by the northern route. The vessels became separated and the *Edward Bonaventure,* under Borough's command, alone completed the voyage in 1553. It was thus the first English ship to round the North Cape, to which Borough gave its English name. Thereafter English merchant adventurers formed the Muscovy Company, in whose service Borough sailed in 1556–57, reaching Novaya Zemlya and the passage south of it into the Kara Sea. In 1560 he was in command of three English merchantmen which may be credited with having actually initiated direct maritime commerce between England and Russia. Accounts of some of Stephen Borough's voyages appear in Richard Hakluyt's *The Principal Navigations, Voyages, and Discoveries of the English Nation.*

Borough, The. A poem by George Crabbe, published in 1810.

Borrioboola-gha (bor″i.ọ.bö′lạ.gä′). An imaginary place in Africa, on the left bank of the Niger River, selected by Mrs. Jellyby (in Charles Dickens's *Bleak House*) as a field for her missionary philanthropic exertions, to the neglect of all home duties.

Borrow (bor′ō), **George.** b. at East Dereham, Norfolk, England, in July, 1803; d. at Oulton, Suffolk, England, in July, 1881. An English philologist, traveler, and novelist, noted for his works on Gypsies and the Romany language. He was an agent for the Bible Society in Spain and Russia, and used experiences from his travels in many of his novels. His works include *Targum, or Metrical Translations from thirty Languages* . . . (1835), *The Bible in Spain* (1843), *The Zincali, or an Account of the Gypsies* (1841), *Lavengro, the Scholar, the Gypsy, and the Priest* (1851), *The Romany Rye, a sequel to Lavengro* (1857), *Wild Wales* . . . (1862), and *Romano Lavo-Lil, or Word-book of the Romany* (1874).

Borrows (bor′ōz, bur′-), **Stephen.** See **Borough, Stephen.**

Bors (bôrs, bôrz). In Arthurian legend, a king of Gaul; uncle of Sir Lancelot. He and his brother went to King Arthur's assistance when he first mounted the throne.

Bors. In Arthurian legend, a natural son of King Arthur.

Bors, Sir. [Also, **Sir Bors de Ganis** (dẹ gā′nis), **Sir Bohort** (bō′hôrt), **Sir Bort** (bôrt).] A knight of the Round Table in Arthurian legend. He figures in Malory's *Morte d'Arthur* as the nephew of Sir Lancelot and as a participant in the quest for the Holy Grail.

Boscobel (bos′kọ.bel). A farmhouse near Shiffnal, in Shropshire, England, noted in connection with the escape of Charles II of England, in September, 1651. The "Royal Oak" (in which Charles hid) was in the vicinity.

Bosola (bo.sō′lạ). A character in John Webster's tragedy *The Duchess of Malfi.* An ex-galley slave, he is hired by the Duchess's brothers to spy on their sister while ostensibly in her employ. He betrays her, and joins with her brother Ferdinand in torturing her and, finally, in murdering her, after killing her lover Antonio. He turns remorseful and kills the cardinal, the other brother, and is himself killed by Ferdinand.

Bosporus (bos′pọ.rus). [Also: **Bosphorus** (bos′fọ.rus); Turkish, **Karadeniz Boğazi**; ancient name, **Bosporus Thracius** (thrā′shi.us), **Thracian Bosporus.**] A strait which connects the Black Sea and Sea of Marmara, and separates Europe from Asia. The name means "ox-ford": so named from the legend that Io, transformed into a heifer, swam across it. Length, ab. 20 mi.; greatest width, ab. 2½ mi.; narrowest, ab. 800 yds.

Boston (bôs′ton, bos′-), **Thomas.** b. at Dunse, Scotland, March 17, 1677; d. at Ettrick, Scotland, May 20, 1732. A Scottish Presbyterian divine. He wrote *Human Nature in Its Fourfold State* (1720) and other works. He was one of 12 clergymen known as "Marrow Men" because they based their views on a book (written anonymously) entitled *The Marrow of Modern Divinity.*

Bostonians, The. A novel by Henry James, published in 1866.

Boston Tea Party. A demonstration by colonial patriots at Boston, Mass., on Dec. 16, 1773, as a protest against the attempted importation of tea into the colonies. A large popular assembly met at the Old South Church to voice their grievances. As their protest was ineffectual, the same evening a body of about 50 men, disguised more or less as Indians, boarded the three British tea-ships in the harbor, and threw 342 chests of tea (valued at 18,000 pounds) into the water. The incident marked the rising influence of the radical wing in the colonies, and helped initiate the open break between Great Britain and the American colonists.

Boswell (boz′wel, -wẹl), **Alexander.** [Title, Lord Auchinleck.] b. 1706; d. 1782. A Scottish judge; father of James Boswell (1740–95). Appointed (1754) lord of session, he served in that capacity until his death, while also serving (1755–80) as lord justiciary. His son, in *Journal of A Tour to the Hebrides,* tells of Samuel Johnson's visit to him at Auchinleck.

Boswell, Sir Alexander. b. at Auchinleck, Scotland, 1775; d. of a collarbone wound inflicted in a duel, at Balmuto, Scotland, 1822. A Scottish antiquary and poet; son of James Boswell. After an education at

---

ḍ, d or j; ş, s or sh; ţ, t or ch; ẓ, z or zh; o, F. cloche; ü, F. menu; čh, Sc. loch; ṅ, F. bonbon.

Oxford, he settled (1795) at the family home at Auchinleck. In 1818 and 1820 he represented Plympton, Devonshire, in Parliament. At his home he established a private press and issued series of reprints of old poems, entitled *Frondes Caducae* (1816–18). He originated the idea of erecting a monument to Robert Burns on the banks of Doon, published poetical and antiquarian writings and edited several reprints of ancient works, and was poet laureate of the Harveian Society of Edinburgh.

Boswell, James. b. at Edinburgh, Scotland, Oct. 29, 1740; d. at London, May 19, 1795. An English man of letters, notable as a diarist and biographer of Dr. Samuel Johnson. He was the son of Alexander Boswell, a judge of the Court of Session at Edinburgh, who took the style of Lord Auchinleck from the ancient estate of the Boswell family in Ayrshire. James Boswell was admitted to the Scots bar in 1766, succeeded to Auchinleck in 1782, was called to the English bar in 1786 (removing his family to London in that year), and was elected Recorder of Carlisle in 1788. For upwards of 20 years he practiced law with complete regularity and a fair degree of assiduity; had plenty of business so long as he remained in Scotland, but never won distinction in his profession. In 1765, while traveling on the Continent, he went to Corsica, then in a state of armed revolt from the Republic of Genoa, and established an intimacy with General Paoli. This adventure he exploited in 1768 in *An Account of Corsica, the Journal of a Tour to that Island, and Memoirs of Pascal Paoli*, a book which had a considerable contemporary success in England and America, and was widely translated. In 1763 he made the acquaintance at London of Dr. Johnson, whom he accompanied on a journey to the Hebrides in 1773, and whom he managed to attend at London nearly every year during the vacations of the Scots courts. He began keeping a private journal as early as 1758. From this he drew the most valuable portion of his book on Corsica; and in 1785, a year after Johnson's death, he published a particularly brilliant segment as *The Journal of a Tour to the Hebrides with Samuel Johnson, LL.D.* In 1791 appeared his famous *Life of Samuel Johnson*. The journal again furnished the parts of the work that make it unique—Johnson's casual conversations, dramatically rendered. Boswell's voluminous papers, which for a century were supposed to have perished, became (1950) the property of Yale University. Though Boswell was vain and had the more serious weaknesses of incontinence and intemperance, he was a wellborn, cultured, and intelligent man, and in his own special fields of self-analysis and the imaginative recording of familiar history, especially as revealed in conversation, he stands without a peer in English letters. The standard biographies are *Young Boswell* (1922), by C. B. Tinker, and *A New Portrait of Boswell* (1927), by C. B. Tinker and F. A. Pottle; see also *The Hooded Hawk* (1947), by D. B. Wyndham Lewis.

Bosworth (boz'wĕrth). See **Market Bosworth.**

Bosworth Field. A battlefield in C England, in W Leicestershire, ab. 13 mi. N of Coventry, the site of the last battle in the Wars of the Roses, in 1485, when Richard III was killed and the crown passed to Henry VII (Henry Tudor).

Botany Bay (bot'ạ.ni). An inlet in SE Australia, ab. 6 mi. S of the center of Sydney, opening E to the Pacific Ocean. Captain Cook made the first landing in Australia here in 1770, and the settlement of Australia was begun here in 1788. The suburban areas of the city of Sydney have grown out to reach the bay. In English and Australian history, its name has long been connected with the penal colony which once existed in Australia (and which was actually situated on the site of what is now Sydney). Length, ab. 10 mi.; greatest width, ab. 6 mi.

Botany Bay Eclogues. A series of verse monologues and dialogues (1794) by Robert Southey, written while he was still attending Oxford.

Bothie of Tober-na-Vuolich (bŏ'ᴛʜi; tŏ'bĕr.nạ.vwô'-lich), **The.** A verse novelette (1848) in hexameters by Arthur Hugh Clough, one of his three principal poems.

Bothwell (both'wel, -wel; boᴛʜ'-), 4th Earl of. [Title of **James Hepburn.**] b. c1536; d. 1578. A Scottish noble, husband of Mary, Queen of Scots. He took no part in the murder of Rizzio, and aided Mary, after that event, in her flight from Holyrood, and was her chief supporter. He was the principal in the assassination of Darnley, was tried for the murder, under circumstances which made his conviction practically impossible, and was acquitted. On April 24, 1567, while the queen was returning to Edinburgh, she was met by Bothwell, who, with a show of force, carried her to his castle of Dunbar. He obtained a divorce from his wife early in May, and married the queen soon after (May 15, 1567). They were divorced in 1570. He became a pirate and died insane.

Bothwell. A tragedy by Algernon Charles Swinburne, published in 1874. It is the second part of a trilogy on Mary, Queen of Scots.

Bothwell, Sergeant. [Family name, **Francis Stuart.**] In Sir Walter Scott's novel *Old Mortality*, a descendant (through an illegitimate line) of James I of England (James VI of Scotland). He is an imposing, very haughty man, and serves as a non-commissioned officer in the Life Guards.

Botolph (bọ.tolf') or **Botolphus** (-tol'fus), Saint. [Also, Saint **Botulf.**] fl. 7th century. An English monk. According to Old English chronicles, he founded (654) a monastery at Ikanho in Lincolnshire, which is now called Boston (contracted from Botolphstown). He instituted the rule of Saint Benedict there. His death is commemorated on June 17.

Bo Tree (bō). See under **Buddha.**

Botticelli (bŏt.tē.chel'lē), **Sandro.** [Original name, **Alessandro di Mariano dei Filipepi.**] b. at Florence, c1444; d. there, May 17, 1510. An Italian painter. He was a pupil of Filippo Lippi, and was influenced by Antonio Pollaiuolo and Andrea Castagno. Among his earliest works is *Fortitude*, a series of circular pictures in the Uffizi at Florence, and madonnas now in the collection of the Uffizi and at London. In 1478 he painted, for the Villa di Castello, *Spring* and *Birth of Venus* (both in the Uffizi). Among his notable pictures is a reconstruction of the *Calumny* of Apelles from the description of Lucian. For Pier Francesco de' Medici he made a series of illustrations to the *Divina Commedia* of

Dante, 84 of which were later acquired by the Kaiser Friedrich Museum at Berlin, and eight of which were acquired by the Vatican. In 1482 he was invited by Pope Sixtus IV to assist in the decoration of the Sistine Chapel. He became one of the followers of Savonarola, and changed the subject-matter and style of his work to conform to his new religious attitude.

Bottom (bot′ǫm), **Nick.** In Shakespeare's *Midsummer Night's Dream*, an Athenian weaver who plays the part of Pyramus in the interpolated play. He is ambitious and enthusiastic, and in his eagerness wants to take all the parts in the play. While rehearsing the play in the forest, he has an ass's head put on him by Puck. In this guise he meets Titania; she has been put under a spell by Oberon to love the first person she sees on waking; when this is Bottom with his ass's head, she is deluded into thinking him beautiful, until Oberon releases her from the magic.

Bottome (bo.tōm′), **Phyllis.** b. at Rochester, England, May 31, 1884—. An English novelist; daughter of an American clergyman; wife (1917 *et seq.*) of Ernan Forbes Dennis. She published *Raw Material*, her first novel, in 1905, and used her experiences as a relief worker (1919 *et seq.*) at Vienna in *Old Wine.* Her other works include *Wind in His Fists* (1931), *Private Worlds* (1934), *Level Crossing* (1936), *The Mortal Storm* (1937), *Danger Signal* (1939), *London Pride* (1941), *Within the Cup* (1943), *From the Life* (1944), *Life-Line* (1946), and *Under the Skin* (1950).

Bottomley (bot′ǫm.li), **Gordon.** b. at Keighley, Yorkshire, England, 1874; d. 1948. An English poet and dramatist, noted for his revival of verse drama. He began with one-act plays, following these with *The Riding to Lithend* (1909), *King Lear's Wife* (1915), *Gruach* (1921), and *Britain's Daughter* (1921). The last two are generally acknowledged to be his best. His earlier work, characterized by the volume *Poems at White Nights* (1899), showed signs of what some critics considered to be an oversweetness of style, but influenced by Yeats, this vanished. Among his later poems are the verses collected in the two series of *Chambers of Imagery* (1907, 1912), *A Vision of Giorgione* (1910), and *Poems of Thirty Years* (1925).

Bottom the Weaver (bot′ǫm), **The Merry Conceited Humours of.** Farce made from the comic scenes of *A Midsummer Night's Dream*, published in 1672, attributed to Robert Cox, a comedian of the time of Charles I of England.

Botulf (bǫ.tulf′), **Saint.** See Saint **Botolph.**

Boucher (bou′chèr), **Jonathan.** b. at Blencogo, near Wigton, Cumberland, England, March 12, 1738; d. at Epsom, England, April 27, 1804. An English clergyman and writer. He collected materials for a *Glossary of Archaic and Provincial Words*, a part of which (the letter A) was published in 1807, and another part (as far as "Blade") in 1832; it was originally planned as a supplement to Samuel Johnson's dictionary.

Boucicault (bö′sę̄.kō), **Dion.** [Also: **Bourcicault;** original name, **Dionysius Lardner Boursiquot.**] b. at Dublin, Dec. 26, 1820 (some sources say 1822); d. at New York, Sept. 18, 1890. An American drama-

tist, manager, and actor. Existing accounts of his early life reveal a considerable amount of confusion, both as to dating and to actual episodes. However, he is now usually believed to have been only nominally the son of Boursiquot, the French refugee who was married to his mother; a certain Dionysius Lardner, who boarded in their house, is held to have been his actual father, and this is given some credence both by the similarity in names and by the fact that Lardner is known to have paid for Boucicault's education at London. He was first married to Agnes Robertson, the adopted daughter of Charles Kean, who was herself an actress of some note. (Some accounts have it that he separated from her many years later, declaring that he had never been legally married.) He toured extensively in the U. S. His plays include *London Assurance* (1841), *Old Heads and Young Hearts* (1843), *Colleen Bawn* (1860), *Arrah-na-Pogue* (1865), a version of *Rip Van Winkle* (1865), and *The Shaughraun* (1874).

Boudicca (bö.dik′a). See **Boadicea.**

Bouillabaisse (bö.yà.bes′), **The Ballad of.** A ballad by William Makepeace Thackeray celebrating the charms of a type of fish chowder (called bouillabaisse) which has long been identified with Marseilles and adjoining coastal regions in the S part of France.

Bouillon (bö.yôṅ′), **Godfrey of** (or **Godefroy de**). See **Godfrey of Bouillon.**

Boult (bōlt). In Shakespeare's *Pericles*, a servant to the Pander in Mytilene.

Boulton (bōl′tǫn), **Edmund.** See **Bolton.**

Bouncer (boun′sèr), **Mr.** A friend of Mr. Verdant Green in Edward Bradley's novel *Verdant Green.* He is a good-hearted little fellow, whose dogs Huz and Buz are a feature of the book.

Bounderby (boun′dèr.bi), **Josiah.** In Charles Dickens's *Hard Times*, "a rich man, banker, merchant, manufacturer, and what not . . . a self-made man . . . the Bully of humility." He marries Mr. Gradgrind's daughter, Louisa.

Bountiful, Lady. In George Farquhar's comedy *The Beaux' Stratagem*, a kind-hearted country gentlewoman. Her name has become proverbial for a charitable woman.

Bounty. An English ship whose crew, after leaving Tahiti, mutinied on April 28, 1789, under the lead of Fletcher Christian. The captain, William Bligh, and 18 of the crew were set adrift in a small boat and made their way over approximately 4,000 mi. of open sea to Timor, whence (by way of Batavia) they were able to make their way back to England. Of the mutineers, one group returned to Tahiti, on which island some of them were later captured; another group, under the leadership of John Adams (or possibly Fletcher Christian), settled on Pitcairn Island. Here, according to some accounts, they mingled with the natives, and eventually formed a curiously isolated but civilized community, in sharp contrast to the earlier violence of their mutiny; according to other accounts, they were all killed by the natives, except for one man (and it is true that at the beginning of 1829, only John Adams was left alive out of the original group). A fictional trilogy (but based on facts, so far as these could be

d̦, d or j; s̩, s or sh; t̩, t or ch; z̧, z or zh; o, F. cloche; ü, F. menu; c̓h, Sc. loch; ṅ, F. bonbon.

ascertained) was written by James Norman Hall and Charles Nordhoff about the *Bounty* and the various members of its crew.

Bounty of Sweden, The. An essay (1925) by William Butler Yeats. It was inspired by the award of the Nobel prize for literature to Yeats in 1923.

Bourbon (bŏr′bọn; French, bôr.bôṅ). A French family which held royal and ducal power in France, Spain, and Italy. The historical record of the family begins with Adhemar or Aimar, who late in the 9th century became baron of Bourbon l'Archambault in central France. Four centuries later, Beatrix, a Bourbon heiress, became the wife of Robert, Count of Clermont, a son of Louis IX, king of France, and their son Louis in 1327 was given the title of Duke of Bourbon. In 1505 Suzanne, heiress of this line, was married to Charles of the Montpensier branch of the family, who assumed the ducal title in 1505, was named constable of France in 1515, plotted with the emperor Charles V and with Henry VIII of England against his sovereign Francis I, and was killed while leading an army of Germans and Spaniards against Rome in 1527. It was another branch of the family, however, which eventually came to the throne of France. Antoine de Bourbon (Anthony of Bourbon) in 1548 married Jeanne d'Albret, of the house of Navarre, and became king of Navarre in 1554. The son of this union was the renowned Henry of Navarre, who became Henry IV of France, reigning from 1589 to 1610. The later Bourbon kings of France were Louis XIII (b. 1601; d. 1643), Louis XIV (b. 1638; d. 1715), Louis XV (b. 1710; d. 1774), Louis XVI (b. 1754; d. 1793), Louis XVIII (b. 1755; d. 1824), Charles X (b. 1757; d. 1836), and Louis-Philippe (of the Orléans branch of the family, b. 1773; d. 1850). The son of Louis XVI, reputedly put to death in childhood by the revolutionists, was to royalists nominally Louis XVII. The revolutionary and Napoleonic eras intervened between the execution of Louis XVI in 1793 and the resumption of the throne by Louis XVIII in 1814.

The Spanish and Italian Bourbons. King Charles II of Spain, dying in 1700, named as his successor the duke of Anjou, who as Philip V was the first Bourbon to wear the Spanish crown; he was also a Hapsburg. The Bourbon (or Borbón) line ruled in Spain until 1931 when, the Spanish people having voted for a republic, Alfonso XIII abdicated (claimants are his sons, Jaime and Juan de Borbón y Battenberg). Philip V succeeded in placing his son Charles on the throne of Naples and Sicily, where he reigned from 1735 to 1759, when he became Charles III of Spain, while his son Ferdinand succeeded him in Naples and Sicily, and changed the name of that kingdom to the Two Sicilies. The last Bourbon monarch of this kingdom was dethroned in 1861 by the revolution which made the Two Sicilies part of a united Italy. In 1748 Philip, youngest son of Philip V of Spain, became ruler of the duchy of Parma and Piacenza. In Napoleon's rearrangement of Italian affairs, this duchy was annexed to France in 1801, its Bourbon ruler, Duke Louis, being made king of Etruria. This title Louis' son Charles Louis had to surrender in 1807, but in 1815 the Congress of Vienna gave him the duchy of Lucca. A later Bourbon-Parma,

also named Charles Louis, in 1847 ceded Lucca to Tuscany but was restored to the throne of Parma and Piacenza. This was finally abolished in 1859, in the course of the unification of Italy. The Bourbons are now probably remembered by many people chiefly for the luxurious and extravagant mode of living of Louis XIV and Louis XV, and for their alleged stubborn resistance to political progress, which gave rise to the saying that "a Bourbon never learns and never forgets."

Bourbon (bŭr′bọn), **Duke of.** In Shakespeare's *Henry V*, a leader in the French army who is captured at Agincourt after urging on the French forces to the attack.

Bourchier (bou′chêr), **Cardinal.** In Shakespeare's *Richard III*, the Archbishop of Canterbury. Gloucester persuades him to take the young Duke of York from his mother, Queen Elizabeth, so that Gloucester can imprison him, with his brother Edward, Prince of Wales, in the Tower, on the pretext that they there await the coronation.

Bourchier (bŭr′chi.êr), **John.** [Title, 2nd Baron Berners.] b. 1467; d. at Calais, France, March 16, 1533. An English statesman and author. He was chancellor of the exchequer in 1516. He translated Froissart's *Chronicle* (1523–25), and *Arthur of Lytell Brytayne, Huon of Burdeux, The Castell of Love,* and others.

Bourdillon (bọr.dil′yọn), **Francis William.** b. March 22, 1852; d. Jan. 13, 1921. An English poet. He wrote *Among the Flowers, and other Poems* (1878), *Ailes d'Alouette* (1890), *A Lost God* (1891), *Sursum Corda* (1893), *Nephelé* (1896), *Minuscula* (1897), *Preludes and Romances* (1908), and others. Bourdillon also edited and translated *Aucassin and Nicolette* (1887).

Bourne (bŏrn, bōrn, bôrn), **Vincent.** b. 1695; d. Dec. 2, 1747. An English writer of Latin verse. He was the author of *Poemata . . .* (1734) and other works.

Bovary (bo.và.rē), **Emma.** The title character of Flaubert's *Madame Bovary* (1857). She is a provincial apothecary's wife who, weary of her dull life, seeks distraction with lovers, falls in debt, and finally poisons herself.

Bow Church (bō). See **Saint Mary le Bow.**

Bowdler (boud′lêr, bōd′-), **Thomas.** b. at Ashley, near Bath, England, July 11, 1754; d. at Rhyddings, near Swansea, Wales, Feb. 24, 1825. An English editor of Shakespeare. He published *The Family Shakespeare* (1818), and his method of expurgating the text (he deleted or altered those sections which he considered too coarse or vulgar for the eyes of the women and children of the typical English home) gave rise to the term "bowdlerize." He prepared, on similar lines, an edition of Edward Gibbon's *History of the Decline and Fall of the Roman Empire* (completed 1825 and published 1826).

bowdlerize (boud′lêr.īz, bōd′-). To expurgate in editing by expunging words or passages considered offensive or indelicate.

Bowen (bō′ẹn), **Elizabeth** (**Dorothea Cole**). b. at Dublin, June 7, 1899—. A British novelist and short-story writer; wife (married 1923) of Alan

---

fat, fāte, fär, àsk, fāre; net, mē, hėr; pin, pīne; not, nōte, mŏve, nôr; up, lūte, pùll; ᵺн, then;

Charles Cameron. Her novels include *The Hotel* (1927), *To the North* (1932), *The House in Paris* (1935), *The Death of the Heart* (1938), and *The Heat of the Day* (1949). Among her collections of short stories are *The Cat Jumps* (1934), *Look At All Those Roses* (1941), *Ivy Gripped the Steps* (1946), and *Early Stories* (1950). Author also of a family biography, *Bowen's Court* (1942), *The Shelbourne Hotel* (1951), and essays published in *Collected Impressions* (1950).

Bowen, Marjorie. A pseudonym of **Long, Gabrielle Margaret Vere.**

Bower of Bliss, The. The enchanted home of Acrasia, in Edmund Spenser's *Faerie Queene.*

Bowge of Court (böj), **The.** A poem (c1499) by John Skelton. Like Skelton's *Garland of Laurel,* it is a dream allegory in rime royal. In it, the hazards of one who lives at court are powerfully pictured in the growing terror of a young man, Dread, who believes himself at sea with a gang of ruffians and awakes at the moment when he is about to leap overboard to escape their malign whisperings.

Bowles (bōlz), **William Lisle.** b. at King's Sutton, Northamptonshire, England, Sept. 24, 1762; d. at Salisbury, England, April 7, 1850. An English poet, antiquary, and clergyman. He was vicar of Bremhill in Wiltshire, and became canon residentiary of Salisbury in 1828. His works include *Fourteen Sonnets* (1789), which brought praise from Samuel Taylor Coleridge, William Wordsworth, and Robert Southey, *Coombe Ellen* (1798), *St. Michael's Mount* (1798), *Battle of the Nile* (1799), *Sorrows of Switzerland* (1801), *The Picture* (1803), *The Spirit of Discovery* (1804), *Ellen Gray* (1823), and various prose works, including *Hermes Britannicus* (1828). His assertion, in an edition (1806) of Alexander Pope's works, that Pope was an inferior writer led to a heated controversy with Byron.

Bowley (bou'li), **Sir Joseph.** In Charles Dickens's story *The Chimes,* a very stately gentleman, "the poor man's friend," with a very stately wife.

Bowling (bō'ling), **Lieutenant Tom.** In *Roderick Random,* a novel by Tobias Smollett, a sailor, uncle of Roderick, the hero of the novel.

Bowling, Tom. The hero of a famous song by Dibdin.

Bows (bōz). A little old humpbacked violin player, the family friend of the Costigans, in William Makepeace Thackeray's *Pendennis.* He has taught the actress "the Fotheringay" (Emily Costigan) all she knows, and loves her devotedly, although he knows her to be self-centered and heartless.

Bow Street (bō). A street in London, by Covent Garden, forming the connecting link between Long Acre and Russell Street, in which is located one of the principal police courts of the city, established there in 1749. In the 17th and 18th centuries it was a fashionable quarter, and was the site of "Will's" also called the "Wits' Coffee House."

Bowyer (bō'yėr), **William.** [Called the **"Learned Printer."**] b. at Gowell Court, Whitefriars, London, Dec. 19, 1699; d. there, Nov. 18, 1777. An English printer, classical scholar, author, editor,

and translator. Made a partner (1722) in his father's business, he took charge of the editorial and scholarly work involved in publishing. He served as printer for both houses of Parliament, for the Royal Society, and for the Society of Antiquaries. Author of many papers and pamphlets on classical subjects, and editor of Jonathan Swift's works, he is best known for his edition (1763) of the New Testament in Greek, and for his own work, *The Origin of Printing, in Two Essays* (1774). His edition of Bentley's *Phalaris* and a reprint of the famous *Domesday Book* were not published until after his death.

Bowzybeus (bou.zi.bē'us). A musical Silenus in John Gay's *The Shepherd's Week.*

Box and Cox. A play (1847) by John M. Morton. The chief characters are two men with these names who occupy the same room, though neither knows it, one being employed all night, the other all day. This play should not be confused with the operetta on the same theme by Sir Arthur Sullivan and Sir Francis Cowley Burnand, entitled *Cox and Box.*

Boy. See under **Page to Falstaff.**

Boy and the Mantle, The. An old ballad, included in Percy's *Reliques.* The story tells of a boy who tested the chastity of the ladies of King Arthur's court by means of a boar's head, a golden horn, and a mantle. The mantle, called the "Mantle of Fidelity," turned different colors if the lady "was not leal." The only one to pass the test was the wife of Sir Cradock. The story is used by Spenser in *The Faerie Queene* in the episode of Florimel's girdle.

Boy at Mugby (mug'bi), **The.** A story by Charles Dickens, originally published (1866) as the third part of a special Christmas issue of *All the Year Round* entitled "Mugby Junction." It satirizes, by a comparison with facilities available in France, the refreshment counters of English railway stations: "French refreshmenting comes to this; and, oh, it comes to a nice total! First, eatable things to eat, and drinkable things to drink. . . ."

Boyce (bois), **Hector.** See **Boece.**

Boycott (boi'kot, -ḳǫt), **Charles Cunningham.** b. 1832; d. 1897. An English army officer. He is, however, known in history not for his military exploits but for the events that took place during his service (after retirement from the army) as agent for the owner of a large estate in County Mayo, Ireland. In 1880, when he refused to accept rents lower than those to which his employer was legally entitled, he was subjected to an organized campaign of abuse and calculated ostracism (his servants left him, and efforts were even made to prevent him from getting food. Some idea of the intensity of local feeling against him may be obtained from the fact that when the time arrived for harvesting his employer's crops, some 600 British soldiers had to be brought in to protect the harvesters— who were themselves imported from the north of Ireland.) From his experience, the word "boycott" has come to have very wide usage, as both verb and noun, to describe a policy or practice of abstention, as a punitive or retaliatory measure,

---

ḍ, d or j; ṣ, s or sh; ṭ, t or ch; ẓ, z or zh; o, F. cloche; ü, F. menu; ċh, Sc. loch; ṅ, F. bonbon.

from commerce of any sort with a person, group, or country.

Boyd's (boidz). A name given to a tavern at Edinburgh, formally called the White Horse Inn, in Boyd's Close, St. Mary's Wynd, Canongate. The tavern and most of the buildings in the immediate vicinity were later demolished. Samuel Johnson stopped at this inn on his arrival (1773) at Edinburgh.

Boyer (bwå.yā'), **Abel.** b. at Castres, France, June 24, 1667; d. at Chelsea, London, Nov. 16, 1729. An English lexicographer and historical writer. He compiled (1702) a French-English dictionary which had many subsequent editions.

Boyet (boi.et'; French, bwå.yā). In Shakespeare's *Love's Labour's Lost*, a mocking, mirthful lord attending on the Princess of France. He informs the Princess and her ladies that the Muscovite masquers are the King of Navarre and his lords.

Boyis (bois), **Hector.** See **Boece.**

Boyle (boil), **Charles.** [Titles: 4th Earl of **Orrery,** 1st Baron **Marston.**] b. at Chelsea, London, 1676; d. Aug. 28, 1731. An English statesman, soldier, and author; grandson of Roger Boyle (1621–79) and father of John Boyle (1707–62). He edited (c1695) the *Epistles of Phalaris,* which the classicist Richard Bentley proved spurious, and thus became involved in a controversy leading to Jonathan Swift's *Battle of the Books.* After fighting at Malplaquet, he was appointed (1709) a major general, and subsequently took part in preliminary negotiations for the Treaty of Utrecht (1713). He was imprisoned (1721) for his connection (which Swift denied) with Layer's Jacobite Plot. An astronomical instrument, the orrery, was named after him (in gratitude for his patronage) by George Graham, the instrument's inventor.

Boyle, John. [Titles: 5th Earl of **Cork,** 5th Earl of **Orrery.**] b. Jan. 2, 1707; d. at Marston, Somerset, England, Nov. 16, 1762. A British nobleman; son of Charles Boyle, 4th Earl of Orrery. He published *Remarks on the Life and Writings of Jonathan Swift* (1751), and others.

Boyle, Roger. [Titles: Baron **Broghill,** 1st Earl of **Orrery.**] b. at Lismore, Ireland, April 25, 1621; d. Oct. 16, 1679. A British statesman, soldier, and dramatist; grandfather of Charles Boyle (1676–1731). He was created Baron Broghill in 1627, and 1st Earl of Orrery in 1660. Though a Royalist, he served under Oliver Cromwell in the conquest of Ireland, and continued to support him and his son Richard. His dramatic works include the tragedies *Henry V* (acted in 1664, published in 1668), *Mustapha* (acted in 1665), *The Black Prince* (acted in 1667), *Tryphon* (acted in 1668); his comedies are *Guzman* (acted in 1669) and *Mr. Anthony* (published in 1690). He also wrote a number of poems and a romance, *Parthenissa* (1654), in the style of Mlle. de Scudéry. He was the earliest writer of English heroic dramas (dramas with romantic incidents from Spanish and French novels, magnificent heroes from the French tragedies of Corneille, Racine, and Quinault, blank or rimed verse, action motivated by problems of love or honor, exotic settings and spectacular characterizations, and complicated plots). This

refined and sometimes pompous style of drama excited contemporary ridicule, but gave Dryden some useful hints for his tragedies.

Boyle Lectures. A course of eight lectures in defense of Christianity, delivered annually at the church of Saint Mary le Bow, London. They were instituted in 1692.

Boyne (boin). [Irish, **Boinn.**] A river in Leinster province, in the Irish Republic. It rises near the County Kildare-County Meath boundary, in the Bog of Allen, and flows generally NE to Drogheda Bay, ab. 4 mi. E of Drogheda. It is the largest river in Leinster province. On its banks, ab. 3 mi. W of Drogheda, on July 1, 1690, was fought the Battle of the Boyne in which the army of William III (36,000) defeated that of James II (26,000). The loss of William was 500; that of James, 1,500. Length, ab. 70 mi.

Boys (bois), **Jaques de.** See **Jaques.**

Boythorn (boi'thôrn), **Lawrence.** A boisterously energetic and handsome old man of sterling qualities, whose bark is worse than his bite, a friend of Mr. Jarndyce, in Charles Dickens's *Bleak House.* The character was intended as a portrait of Walter Savage Landor.

Boz (bŏz, boz). The pseudonym assumed by Charles Dickens in his *Sketches by Boz,* first published together in 1836. He first used the name in the second part of "The Boarding House," which appeared in *The Monthly Magazine* (August, 1834). He himself says: "Boz was the nickname of a pet child, a younger brother (Augustus), whom I had dubbed Moses in honour of the Vicar of Wakefield; which being facetiously pronounced through the nose became Bōses, and being shortened became Bōz." Through ignorance of the derivation, the pronunciation boz, based on the nearest analogy, sprang up, and is now very widely heard.

Bozzy and Piozzi (boz'i; pi.oz'i). A poem (1768) by John Wolcot, written in the form of a dialogue between Bozzy (James Boswell) and Piozzi (Mrs. Thrale, known also as Hester Lynch Piozzi) as they reminisce about Samuel Johnson.

Brabantio (brạ.ban'shi.ō). In Shakespeare's *Othello,* a Venetian senator, father of Desdemona. He violently denounces Othello for his marriage with the latter.

Brabourne (brā'bẽrn), **1st Baron.** Title of **Knatchbull-Hugessen, Edward Hugessen.**

Bracegirdle (brās'gẽr''dl), **Anne.** b. c1663; d. at London, 1748. English actress. It was said at one time that she played the page in Otway's *The Orphan* before she was six years old, but *The Orphan* was not produced until 1680. She was on the stage till 1707, when a trial of skill with Mrs. Anne Oldfield took place, both playing the part of Mrs. Brittle in Thomas Betterton's *The Amorous Widow* on alternate nights. The preference was given to Mrs. Oldfield, and Mrs. Bracegirdle (in disgust, according to some accounts) left the stage. (However, she played once more, in 1709, at Thomas Betterton's benefit.) Both William Rowe and William Congreve were devoted to her, and she was suspected of being married to the latter.

---

fat, fāte, fär, ȧsk, fãre; net, mē, hėr; pin, pīne; not, nōte, mŏve, nôr; up, lūte, pull; ᴛн, then;

Brachiano (brä.chẹ.ä′nō), **Duke of.** In John Webster's tragedy *The White Devil*, the husband of Isabella and the lover of the "white devil," Vittoria Corombona. He kills his wife, and, having rescued Vittoria from prison, marries her. He is killed by the duke of Florence, Isabella's brother.

Bracidas (bras′i.dạs). See **Amidas and Bracidas**.

Bracton (brak′tọn) or **Bratton** (brat′ọn) or **Bretton** (bret′ọn), **Henry de.** d. 1268. An English ecclesiastic and jurist. In 1264 he was named chancellor of the cathedral of Exeter. He was the author of *De legibus et consuetudinibus Angliae* (printed in part in 1567, and entire in 1569), the first systematic and practical treatment of the body of English law. With regard to most of the facts of his life there is great uncertainty.

Bracy (brā′si), **Maurice de.** In Sir Walter Scott's novel *Ivanhoe*, a handsome and not ungenerous mercenary, a follower of Prince John. He carries off Rowena, but she is soon rescued.

Braddon (brad′ọn), **Mary Elizabeth.** [Married name, **Maxwell**; pseudonym, **Babington White**.] b. at London, Oct. 4, 1837; d. at Richmond, Surrey, England, Feb. 4, 1915. An English novelist, dramatist, poet, and editor; wife (1874 *et seq.*) of John Maxwell, a London publisher. She was educated at home by private tutors, and began to write while still in her teens, contributing to *Punch*, *The World*, the Paris *Figaro*, to the Christmas issues of various periodicals, and to *Robin Goodfellow* and the *Sixpenny Magazine;* she edited *Temple Bar*, *Belgravia*, and other magazines. She was the author of 80 novels, including *Three Times Dead, or the Secret of the Heath* (1856; rev. ed., 1861, as *The Trail of the Serpent*), *The Lady Lisle* (1861), *Lady Audley's Secret* (1862, her best-known work, a sensational murder-story, immensely popular in its own day and still popular almost a century later), *Aurora Floyd* (1863), *John Marchmont's Legacy* (1863), *Henry Dunbar* (1864), *The Doctor's Wife* (1864), *Birds of Prey* (1867), *Charlotte's Inheritance* (1868), *Robert Ainsleigh* (1872), *Strangers and Pilgrims* (1873), *Dead Men's Shoes* (1876), *Joshua Haggard's Daughter* (1876), *Vixen* (1879), *Asphodel* (1881), *Mount Royal* (1882), *Phantom Fortune* (1883), *Ishmael* (1884), *All Along the River* (1893), *Sons of Fire* (1895), *London Pride* (1896), *Rough Justice* (1896), *The Rose of Life* (1905), and *The Green Curtain* (1911); she also wrote short stories, plays, and *Garibaldi and Other Poems* (1861).

Bradley (brad′li), **Andrew Cecil.** b. at Cheltenham, Gloucestershire, England, March 26, 1851; d. Sept. 2, 1935. An English lecturer, professor, and Shakespearian critic; brother of Francis Herbert Bradley (1846–1924). He was educated at Cheltenham College, and at Balliol College, Oxford, of which he was made a fellow (1874) and at which he lectured (1876–81). He was later professor of modern literature (1881–89) at Liverpool, of English language and literature (1889–1900) at Glasgow, and of poetry (1901–06) at Oxford. Author of *Utopias—Ancient and Modern* (1875), *Commentary on Tennyson's In Memoriam* (1901), and *Oxford Lectures on Poetry* (1909). He is remembered chiefly for his *Shakespearean Tragedy* (1904, and many subsequent editions), criticism dealing with the nature of tragedy in general and especially with *Hamlet*, *Othello*, *Lear*, and *Macbeth*.

Bradley, Arthur Granville. b. Nov. 11, 1850; d. 1943. An English historian and writer. Among his publications are *Life of Wolfe* (1895), *Highways and Byways of North Wales* (1898), *Highways and Byways of the English Lake District* (1901), *Owen Glyndwr* (1901), *Highways and Byways of South Wales* (1903), *Marches of South Wales* (1905), and *The Romance of Northumberland* (1908).

Bradley, Edward. [Pseudonym, **Cuthbert Bede**.] b. at Kidderminster, England, 1827; d. 1889. An English author. He was rector of Denton, Huntingtonshire (1859–71) and of Stretton, Rutlandshire (1871–83), and became vicar of Lenton in 1883. He wrote *Adventures of Mr. Verdant Green, An Oxford Freshman* (1853), *The Curate of Cranston* (1861), *A Tour in Tartanland* (1863), *The Rook's Garden* (1865), and *Matins and Muttons* (1866).

Bradley, Francis Herbert. b. at Glasbury, Brecknockshire, South Wales, Jan. 30, 1846; d. at Oxford, England, Sept. 18, 1924. An English philosopher; brother of Andrew Cecil Bradley (1851–1935). Educated at Cheltenham and Marlborough, and at University College, Oxford, he won a fellowship at Merton College (1876) which he held until his death. He contributed many articles to the psychological quarterly *Mind*, and was the author of *Presuppositions of Critical History* (1874), *Ethical Studies* (1876), *Mr. Sidgwick's Hedonism* (1877), *The Principles of Logic* (1883, a criticism of, and a reply to, John Stuart Mill), and *Essays on Truth and Reality* (1914); his outstanding work, *Appearance and Reality* (1893), aroused keen interest and was hailed as "the greatest thing since Kant" by the Scottish philosopher Edward Caird. An opponent of utilitarianism, Bradley expounded a philosophy of absolute idealism.

Bradley, Henry. b. at Manchester, England, Dec. 3, 1845; d. at Oxford, England, May 23, 1923. An English lexicographer, historian, and philologist. He was educated at Oxford and Heidelberg, and was employed as a clerk and foreign correspondent at Sheffield until 1884, when he moved to London. He was president of the Philological Society in the periods 1891–93 and 1900–03. In 1889 he became joint editor with James Augustus Henry Murray of *The New English Dictionary* (which was later renamed *The Oxford English Dictionary*), and in 1915 succeeded to the post of editor in chief. His publications include *The Story of the Goths* (1888) and *The Making of English* (1904). He was made a fellow of the British Academy in 1907.

Bradley, Katherine Harris. [Pseudonym (with Edith Emma Cooper), **Michael Field**.] b. at Birmingham, England, Oct. 27, 1848; d. at Richmond, Surrey, England, Sept. 26, 1914. An English dramatic and lyric poet; aunt of Edith Emma Cooper. From the ages of 16 and 3, respectively, to their deaths nine months apart in 1914, aunt and niece lived, traveled, and subsequently worked together. The collaboration under the name Michael Field, which began in 1879, was so close that it is impossible to distinguish the work of one from the other. It resulted in eight volumes of poetry, 27 poetic tragedies, a masque, and a journal and letters. Under the joint pseudonym they wrote *Long Ago* (1889, imitations of Sappho), *Sight and Song* (1892), *Underneath the Bough* (1893), *Wild Honey* (1908), *Poems of Adoration* (1912), *Mystic Trees* (1913), all poetry; and the dramas *Calirrhoe* (1884), *Fair Rosamund* (1884), *The Father's Tragedy* (1885), *William Rufus* (1886), *Canute the Great* (1887), *The Tragic Mary Queen of Scots* (1890), *Borgia* (1905), and *The Accuser and Other Plays* (1911).

Bradley Headstone (hed'stōn). See **Headstone, Bradley.**

Bradshaw (brad'shô), **George.** b. near Pendleton, Lancashire, England, July 29, 1801; d. 1853. An English printer and engraver, notable as the originator of a type of railway timetable now standard throughout Great Britain and much of Europe. As a boy he was apprenticed to an engraver, and in time became proprietor of his own printing and engraving shop, specializing in maps. His first venture was the publication of *Bradshaw's Maps of Inland Navigation*, but he perceived the growing importance of railways, and in 1839 gave England and the world the first railway timetables. In 1841 he began issuing timetables every month under the name of *Bradshaw's Monthly Railway Guide*, and in 1847 he extended his service beyond the shores of England with the publication of *The Continental Railway Guide*. Subsequently a collocation of American timetables was undertaken, but the Bradshaw technique of combining timetables has never won wide public acceptance in the U. S. (although monthly guides not unlike those of Bradshaw may be found in most U. S. travel agencies and railroad ticket offices).

Bradshaw, Henry. b. at Chester, England, c1450; d. 1513. An English Benedictine monk and poet. He wrote *De Antiquitate et Magnificentia Urbis Cestriae*, and a life of Saint Werburgh, in English verse, mainly a translation of a Latin work by an unknown author.

Bradshaw, Henry. b. 1831; d. 1886. An English scholar, antiquary, and librarian who was prominent in exposing (1863) Simonides' forgeries. At Cambridge, he became a B.A. (1854), and fellow (1853), and served as assistant in the university library (1856–58), supervisor of manuscripts and early printed books (1859), and university librarian (1867–86). He published treatises of typographical and antiquarian interest, some describing original discoveries. The Henry Bradshaw Society for editing rare liturgical texts was established (1890) in his memory.

Bradwardine (brad'wạr.dēn), **Baron.** In Sir Walter Scott's *Waverley*, an old man, the master of Tully Veolan. He was a scholar, and of a very ancient family, a circumstance of which he was inordinately proud. He had been trained for the bar, and had served in the army. He had been in arms for the Stuarts, and was in concealment after the rebellion of 1745 till released by pardon.

Bradwardine, Rose. In Sir Walter Scott's *Waverley*, the daughter of Baron Bradwardine; "the Rose of Tully Veolan." She saves Waverley's life, and he marries her.

Brady (brā'di), **Nicholas.** b. at Bandon, County Cork, Ireland, Oct. 28, 1659; d. at Richmond,

Surrey, England, May 20, 1726. An English divine and poet. He collaborated with Nahum Tate in *New Version of the Psalms of David* (1696).

Braeme (brām), **Charlotte Monica.** See under **Clay, Bertha M.**

Braggadocchio (brag.ạ.dō'chi.ō). In Edmund Spenser's *Faerie Queene*, a big bragging fool. He personifies Cowardice, and is the comic element in the book. It is thought that he was taken from Martano, a similar character in Lodovico Ariosto's *Orlando Furioso.*

Bragi (brä'gē). In Old Norse mythology, a son of Odin, and the god of poetry. He is Odin's principal skald, or poet, in Valhalla. His wife is Idun.

Brahma (brä'mạ). One of the major gods of the Hindu pantheon, "the creator." Although Brahma is believed to be the creator of the universe, he is rarely worshiped, and there are only a few temples to him. He is portrayed as having four arms, holding a sceptre, a bow, beads, and the scripture called *Veda*. His vehicle is a swan or a goose.

Brahms (brämz; German, bräms), **Johannes.** b. at Hamburg, Germany, May 7, 1833; d. at Vienna, April 3, 1897. A German composer. He was the son of a jolly, sturdy, not particularly cultured double-bass player, and it was taken for granted that Johannes would become a musician, in the footsteps of his father, but there was no parental dreaming about the child's genius. However, of all the instruments, the boy loved the piano best, and he was sent to one Otto Friedrich Willibald Cossel, a man with a passion and a genius for teaching, who guided with a sure hand the astonishingly rapid development of the boy's talent both for playing and for composition. Although he had appeared but three times in public by the time he was ten, his playing had attracted the attention of musical circles at Hamburg, and a proposal was made that the boy be taken on a concert tour which might even extend to America. Cossel, aghast at this proposed exploitation of one so young, and whom he already believed to be a genius, sent Johannes to the most eminent of Hamburg teachers and theorists, Eduard Marxsen, whose reluctant acceptance of the pupil put a stop to the project of the tour. Marxsen, a thorough classicist, would have nothing to do with such "adventurers" as Schumann and Chopin, and gave his pupil only the music of Bach and Beethoven. Brahms, susceptible to the romantic fever of the day, continued his lessons with Cossel; but he was also a docile follower of Marxsen's precepts, and learned from him what many of his contemporaries never learned: the real purport and substance of the classical style. When Mendelssohn died in 1847, Marxsen was bold enough to say: "A master of the art has gone; a greater arises in Brahms." By all this labor, Brahms acquired an extraordinary power of self-discipline. Playing for pittances in cafés and bars, giving poorly paid lessons, he yet managed to read extensively and to compose, without thought of publication, inordinate quantities of music (he set, for instance, almost the whole of Heine's *Buch der Lieder* to music, and this, with all the rest of his work of the period, he one day complacently consigned to the furnace). None

---

fat, fāte, fär, ȧsk, fãre; net, mē, hėr; pin, pīne; not, nōte, mõve, nôr; up, lūte, púll; ᴛʜ, then;

but a great mind could have preserved its elasticity under such discipline, but Brahms's survived.

First Ventures into the World, and Schumann's Prophecy. In 1853 Brahms joined Edouard Reményi, a noted Hungarian violinist, on a concert tour, and it was through an introduction by Reményi that Brahms met the violinist Joseph Joachim, whose friendship was to be so enormously valuable to Brahms during the rest of his life. It was through Joachim that Brahms met Schumann, whose enthusiasm for the young man's work was so great (and who may also have sensed the tragic end which was so immediately in store for himself) that he wrote an article for the *Neue Zeitschrift* which contained the words "[here was] one who would not show us his mastery in a gradual development, but like Athene, would spring fully armed from the head of Zeus." This article was published in October, 1853, and its effect was unfortunate indeed: an unknown young man was exalted above older and more experienced artists; his actual production was too meager to support the contention made in his behalf; and by implication the whole "futuristic" movement of Liszt and Wagner was condemned. Brahms turned at once to the task of mastering the classics; the strong romantic impulse apparent in the works which he had submitted to Schumann he now set himself not wholly to suppress, but to curb. The next few years were difficult ones: they saw Schumann's suicide in 1854, the need to sustain (and the self-imposed impossibility of marrying) Schumann's widow, and the actual hissing (in January, 1859) of Brahms's own first major appearance, at Leipzig. Nevertheless, Brahms had completed, by 1860, three piano sonatas, the *Scherzo* in E flat minor, four *Ballades*, three sets of variations (all for piano), two *Serenades* for orchestra, the piano concerto in D minor, and several other works.

The Choral Decade, and the German Requiem. The decade 1860–70 saw more disappointments and also a measure of deep sorrow following the death (1865) of his mother. In some measure, however, the fruit of this sorrow was the *German Requiem*, a work which soon established the truth of Schumann's prophecy. Also, several other large choral works were completed during this decade: *Rinaldo* (a cantata, set to Goethe's text), the *Harzreise Rhapsodie* for alto solo, male chorus, and orchestra, the *Song of Destiny* (to a poem by Hölderlin), and finally the *Triumphlied* (1870, after the great victory of the Germans over the French at Sedan in the Franco-Prussian War). At the end of the decade, as recognition increased, his life also gained a degree of happiness which had hitherto been lacking.

The Symphonies and Last Works. Brahms approached the composition of the symphony, compositional music for full orchestra, with some trepidation; he had a vast respect for the symphony, little use for the symphonic attempts of some of his contemporaries, and the memory that his first attempt at a symphony had ended as a piano concerto. However, in the C-minor symphony, which finally appeared in 1876, he triumphed over his doubts. In this gnarled structure (as rigid in its logic as any Bach fugue) there is to be seen the very essence of Brahms's philosophy

up to this time—his utter rejection of all triviality; his conscientious devotion to the fundamentals of art as he understood them; and (in the last movement) a strong sense of the final achievement of his goal. The symphony that appeared in the following year is in strong contrast to the first, but its structure is equally perfect; it may be taken as a kind of pastoral symphony, but without the literalness of Beethoven's, in its suggestion of the well-being that comes from true contact with nature. In 1883 appeared the third symphony, and in 1884–85 came the contrast to it—the wonderful E-minor symphony, under whose quiet exterior many hearers believe they finally come to find more suggestion of mature feeling than is perhaps to be found in any other symphonic work. In this period also, Brahms produced the contrasting *Academic Festival Overture* and *Tragic Overture*, his two very popular *Rhapsodies* (Op. 76), and a great body of chamber music (which was perhaps his chief passion, as it had finally been Beethoven's).

Brailsford (brāls'fǒrd), **Henry Noel.** b. at Mirfield, Yorkshire, England, 1873—. An English journalist and author. A member (1913) of the Carnegie International Commission in the Balkans, he was later (1922–26) editor of *The New Leader*, and became a staff member of *The New Republic*. His books include *Macedonia* (1906), *How the Soviet Works* (1927), *Rebel India* (1932), *Property or Peace?* (1934), *Voltaire* (1935), *America Our Ally* (1940), and *Our Settlement With Germany* (1944).

Brainworm (brān'wèrm). In Ben Jonson's *Every Man in His Humour*, a servant of old Knowell, witty and shrewd, whose various disguises contribute to the perplexities and elaboration of the plot.

Brakelonde or **Brakelond** (brāk'lǒnd), **Jocelin de.** See **Jocelin de Brakelonde.**

Brakenbury (brak'en.ber.i, -bėr.i), **Sir Robert.** In Shakespeare's *Richard III*, the Lieutenant of the Tower who surrenders Clarence to the two murderers sent by Gloucester. He presumably surrenders the two young Princes later to Tyrrel.

Bramah (brä'mạ), **Ernest.** [Full name, **Ernest Bramah Smith.**] b. c1869; d. in Somersetshire, England, June 27, 1942. An English author of detective stories, and an expert on medals. He was the author of short stories in which he created two original characters, Kai Lung, a Chinese storyteller, and Max Carrados, a blind detective. His works include *The Wallet of Kai Lung* (1900), *The Mirror of Kung Ho* (1905), *Kai Lung's Golden Hours* (1922; dramatized 1931), *Kai Lung Unrolls His Mat* (1928), *The Moon of Much Gladness* (1932; American title, *The Return of Kai Lung*), and *Kai Lung Beneath the Mulberry-Tree* (1940). In the second series are *Max Carrados* (1914), *The Eyes of Max Carrados* (1923), and *Max Carrados Mysteries* (1927). Bramah also wrote a humorous autobiography, *English Farming and Why I Turned It Up* (1894), and *Guide to the Varieties and Rarity of English Regal Copper Coins: Charles II–Victoria* (1929), a standard work in its field, as well as publishing *Short Stories of Today and Yesterday* (1929).

Bramble (bram'bl), **Frederick.** In the younger George Colman's play *The Poor Gentleman*, the nephew of Sir Robert Bramble. He is generous and enthusiastic; he insults Emily's abductor "with all the civility imaginable," and saves her.

Bramble, Matthew. In Tobias Smollett's novel *Humphry Clinker*, a hot-tempered, kind-hearted, gouty squire, whose opinions are supposed to represent Smollett's.

Bramble, Sir Robert. In the younger George Colman's play *The Poor Gentleman*, a kindly but choleric squire.

Bramble, Tabitha. In Tobias Smollett's novel *Humphry Clinker*, the sister of Matthew Bramble. She is a prying and ugly old maid, "exceedingly starched, vain and ridiculous," who finally ensnares "the immortal Lismahago," an argumentative Scottish officer who has had romantic adventures among the Indians.

Brampton (bramp'tọn), **Lady.** In Richard Steele's play *The Funeral*, a scheming widow whose activities cause much trouble for her wards and their lovers, until her supposedly dead husband appears and compels her to mend her ways.

Bran (bran). The name of Fionn mac Cumhail's (Finn MacCool's) dog.

Bran. [Called **"The Blessed."**] In Brythonic mythology, a son of Llyr, the sea, and a king of Britain whose head was buried outside London, facing France, to protect the country from invasion. Later he was regarded as a saint.

Brandan (bran'dạn), **Saint.** See **Brendan** or **Brenainn,** Saint.

Brandon (bran'dọn). In Shakespeare's *Henry VIII,* an officer who arrives with the sergeant-at-arms to arrest Buckingham and Abergavenny on charges of high treason.

Brandon, Charles. See under **Suffolk,** (1st) **Duke of.**

Brandon, Colonel. In Jane Austen's novel *Sense and Sensibility*, the admirer who eventually marries Marianne Dashwood.

Brandon, Mrs. [Called **"the Little Sister"**; original name, **Caroline Gann.**] In Thackeray's novel *The Adventures of Philip*, a sweet and gentle nurse. The same character appears in *A Shabby Genteel Story* as Caroline Gann, betrayed (through the trick of a sham marriage) by Dr. Firmin (who is then using the name George Brandon).

Brandon, Richard. d. at London, 1649. The English executioner of Charles I and of his followers. He received thirty pounds for decapitating the king. His father, Gregory Brandon, had been hangman of London.

Brandon, Samuel. fl. 1598. An English dramatist. He wrote the play *Tragicomedy of the Virtuous Octavia*.

Brandon, Sir William. In Shakespeare's *Richard III*, a follower of the Earl of Richmond. He is the father of Charles Brandon, Duke of Suffolk, who appears in *Henry VIII*.

Brandt (bränt), **Margaret.** The heroine of Charles Reade's novel *The Cloister and the Hearth*.

Branford (bran'fọrd), **Frederick Victor.** b. at London, 1892—. An English poet, editor, and soldier. He lived in Scotland during his childhood, and has

been resident there since 1918; he was educated at the universities of Edinburgh and Leiden. He served in World War I as an officer in the air force, and was wounded. Founder of the magazine *Voices*, he is also the author of *Titans and Gods* (1922), *Five Poems* (1923), and *The White Stallion: Poems* (1924). "Any Daisy" and two sonnets, "Shakespeare" and "Secret Treaties," are anthology favorites.

Brangtons (brang'tọnz), **The.** In Fanny Burney's novel *Evelina*, a family of the middle class. Their name became proverbial for vulgar, malicious jealousy.

Brangwaine or **Brangwayne** (brang'wān) or **Brengwin** (breng'win). The confidante of Isolde (Iseult) in the romance of *Tristram and Isolde*.

Branville (bran'vil), **Sir Anthony.** In Frances Sheridan's play *The Discovery*, a pedantic and solemn lover. He talks most passionately, without showing a spark of meaning in his action or features, and has made love in this manner to eight women in 13 years. David Garrick first played the part.

Brasenose College (brāz'nōz). A college of Oxford University, England, founded (c1509) by Bishop William Smith of Lincoln and Sir Richard Sutton, upon the site of an old academical institution named Brasenose Hall (it is thought from its door-knocker, in the shape of a brass nose). The foundation stone was laid on June 1, 1509, and the charter was granted in 1512. The quadrangle is very picturesque; the Tudor gate tower and hall remain unaltered. The library and chapel are of a later period.

Brass (bràs). In John Vanbrugh's comedy *The Confederacy*, the knavish companion of Dick Amlet, passing for his servant; a clever valet.

Brass, Sally. The sister and partner of Sampson Brass in Charles Dickens's *Old Curiosity Shop*. She has a very red nose and suspicions of a beard, and devotes herself "with uncommon ardor to the study of the law."

Brass, Sampson. A harsh-voiced "attorney of no very good repute," in Charles Dickens's *Old Curiosity Shop*; the legal adviser of Quilp.

Brathwaite or **Brathwait** or **Brathwayte** (brath'wāt), **Richard.** [Pseudonym, **Corymbaeus.**] b. at Burneside, near Kendal, Westmorland, England, c1588; d. at East Appleton, Catterick, Yorkshire, England, May 4, 1673. An English poet and satirist. He studied at Oxford and Cambridge before going to London to devote himself to literature. He returned to Westmorland in 1610, after his father's death, and became justice of the peace for the county after his brother's death in 1618. Among his works are *The Golden Fleece* (1611), poetry; *The Poet's Willow* (1614), *The Prodigal's Tears* (1614), *The Scholar's Medley* (1614), and *A Strappado for the Devil* (1615), satires, derived from George Wither's *Abuses Stript and Whipt*; and *Essays upon the Five Senses* (1620). His most important work, *Barnabae Itinerarium, or Barnabee's Journall* (1638), a combination of Latin and English doggerel, is a lively account of Barnaby's four journeys to the north of England, and was published under the pseudonym of Corymbaeus.

---

fat, fāte, fär, àsk, fāre; net, mē, hėr; pin, pīne; not, nōte, mõve, nôr; up, lūte, pùll; ᴛʜ, then;

Bratton (brat'ọn), **Henry de.** See **Bracton.**

Brave New World. A novel (1932) by Aldous Huxley. In it Huxley seeks, through his portrayal of a nightmarish utopia, to depict the futility of scientific "progress." The scene is a scientist's utopia, a world of nonhuman perfection in which men and women live as much as possible like machines. If a specifically human state recurs in one of them he is made unconscious by a drug called soma until he has recovered a suitable equilibrium.

Brawne (brôn), **Fanny.** See under **Keats, John.**

Bray (brā). A parish in Berkshire, England, ab. 26 mi. W of London. A vicar of Bray, Simon Alleyn, is said to have been twice a Roman Catholic and twice a Protestant in the course of the reigns of Henry VIII, Edward VI, Mary, and Elizabeth, but always vicar of Bray: hence the modern application of the title to a turncoat.

Bray, Anna Eliza. [Maiden name, **Kempe.**] b. at Newington, Surrey, England, Dec. 25, 1790; d. at London, Jan. 21, 1883. An English novelist. She wrote *De Foix* (1826), *The Borders of the Tamar and the Tavy* (1836), *Trelawney of Trelawney* (1837), *Courtenay of Walreddon* (1844), and others.

Bray, Madeline. A young lady of singular beauty in Charles Dickens's *Nicholas Nickleby*, the slave of a profligate father. She becomes the wife of Nicholas Nickleby.

Bray, Vicar of. See under **Bray,** England.

Brazen (brā'zẹn), **Captain.** A rival recruiting officer to Captain Plume, an impudent, ignorant braggart, in George Farquhar's comedy *The Recruiting Officer.*

Brazenhead the Great (brā'zẹn.hed). A historical novel by Maurice Hewlett, published in 1911. It deals with the rebellion (1450) led by Jack Cade.

Brazil (brạ.zil'). [Also, the **Brazils.**] A mythical island which appeared on maps of the Atlantic as early as the 14th century, and long remained on them. It was placed at first apparently in the Azores, and also appeared as W of Ireland, whence, in literature the "Island of the Blest." It is alluded to by Gerald Griffin in the poem *O' Brazil, the Island of the Blest.*

Breadwinner, The. A play (1932) by W. Somerset Maugham. In it he attacked what he considered to be the spoiled arrogance of young people in the generation following World War I.

Breakfast in Bed. A novel by Sylvia Thompson, published in 1934.

Breck (brek), **Alan.** [In full, **Alan Breck Stewart.**] In Robert Louis Stevenson's *Kidnapped,* a recklessly courageous, but not too scrupulous supporter of the exiled Stuart claimant to the English throne. He is picked up from a sinking boat (run down in the fog by the ship on which David Balfour, the young hero of the book, is being transported to the Carolinas), and after the shipwreck journeys across Scotland with David. His real surname is Stewart (or Stuart), a fact of which he is fiercely proud ("I bear the name of a king"). He appears also in *Catriona.*

Breeches Bible, The. A name given to the Geneva Bible (New Testament, 1557; Old Testament, 1560) because of its rather quaint rendering of Genesis, iii. 7: "Then the eyes of them both were opened, and they knew that they were naked, and they sewed figtree leaves together and made themselves breeches." The Breeches Bible was the first Bible to have the now familiar numbering of the verses for each chapter.

Brendan (bren'dạn) or **Brenainn** (bren'in), **Saint.** [Also: **Brandan** or **Borondon.**] b. at Tralee, County Kerry, Ireland, 484; d. 577. An Irish monk, a contemporary of Saint Brendan of Birr, who was a friend of Saint Columba, and sometimes called "son of Finnloga" or Saint Brendan of Clonfert to distinguish him. After completing his studies at Tuam he set forth on the expedition known as the "Navigation of Saint Brendan." According to the legendary account of his travels, he set sail with others to seek the terrestrial paradise which was supposed to exist in an island of the Atlantic. Various miracles are related of the voyage, but they are always connected with the great island where the monks are said to have landed. The legend was current in the time of Christopher Columbus and long after, and many connected Saint Brendan's island with the newly discovered America. He is commemorated on May 16.

Brenda Troil (bren'dạ troil'). See under **Troil, Magnus.**

Brendle (bren'dl). A novel by Marmaduke Pickthall, published in 1905.

Brengwin (breng'win). See **Brangwaine.**

Brenhilda (bren.hil'dạ). The wife of Robert in Sir Walter Scott's novel *Count Robert of Paris.*

Brennoralt, or The Discontented Colonel (bren.ôr'alt). A tragedy by Sir John Suckling, an expansion of *The Discontented Colonel,* written c1639, printed in 1646.

Brennus (bren'us). fl. c389 B.C. The Roman name of the leader of the Gauls who pillaged Rome after defeating (c389 B.C.) Marcus Manlius Capitolinus. The Romans took refuge in the capitol, where the Gauls besieged them until a ransom of 1,000 pounds of gold was paid. A legend relates that the Romans charged the Gauls with using false weights, and that Brennus threw his sword into the scale and exclaimed "Vae victis" (that is, "Woe to the vanquished," conveying, although in reverse, approximately the same meaning as, in more modern times, "to the victor belong the spoils").

Brentford (brent'fọrd), **the Two Kings of.** Two burlesque characters who always appear together and act identically in *The Rehearsal,* by Buckingham and others.

Brereley (brir'li), **Roger.** [Also, **Brierley.**] b. at Marland, Lancashire, England, Aug. 4, 1586; d. at Burnley, Lancashire, England, June, 1637. An English clergyman and poet, now remembered chiefly as the founder of a small religious group known as the Grindletonians, from the name of the town and chapel of which he was curate. The Grindletonians were linked to the religious community known as Familists, a sect of the 16th and 17th centuries which sought to attain sympathy and love, and paid little heed to formal doctrines.

---

d̦, d or j; ș, s or sh; ț, t or ch; z̦, z or zh; o, F. cloche; ü, F. menu; ċh, Sc. loch; ǹ, F. bonbon.

Brereley was the author of sermons (published at Edinburgh, 1670, and at London, 1677), and of a few poems included in the latter edition of the sermons.

Breton (bret'ǫn), **Nicholas.** [Also: **Brittaine, Britton.**] b. at London, c1545; d. c1626. An English poet and prose writer; a stepson of George Gascoigne (c1525–77). Breton was a member of the group, almost a cult, at Oxford associated with the memory of Sir Philip Sidney and having the patronage of his sister, the Countess of Pembroke. In 1592, Breton published at Oxford two long allegories which he inscribed to the countess: *The Pilgrimage to Paradise* and *Joined with the Countess of Pembroke's Love*. He was the author also of the pastoral *The Passionate Shepheard* (1604), *The Honour of Valour* (1605), and *The Fantasticks* (1626).

Breton lays. Rhymed stories popular in England in the 14th century. The name originates from the French tales, particularly those of Marie de France. Chaucer's Franklin speaks of the old Bretons who rhymed their tales and either sang them to the accompaniment of musical instruments or read them. *Sir Landeval* and the *Lay de Freine* are two notable examples in English literature.

Brett (bret), **Reginald Baliol.** See **Esher,** 2nd Viscount.

Bretton (bret'ǫn), **Henry de.** See **Bracton.**

Bretton, John. In Charlotte Brontë's *Villette*, the English doctor in the school at Brussels.

Breval (brev'ạl), **John Durant.** [Pseudonym, **Joseph Gay.**] b. c1680; d. at Paris, in January, 1738. An English writer. He wrote much under the name of Joseph Gay. He attacked Alexander Pope under this pseudonym, and was in return held up to ridicule in Pope's *Dunciad*.

Brewer (brö'ẻr), **Antony.** fl. 1655. An English dramatic writer. He wrote *The Love-sick King* (1655), which was reprinted as *The Perjured Nun*. He is possibly better known, however, from the fact that *Lingua, or the Combat of the Five Senses* (1607), and *The Merry Devil of Edmonton* (1608), were formerly ascribed to him. *The Country Girl* (1647), signed *T.B.*, was also at one time erroneously identified as his.

Brewer, Ebenezer Cobham. b. 1810; d. 1897. An English clergyman, schoolmaster, and miscellaneous writer; brother of John Sherren Brewer (1809–79). Graduated from Cambridge (1835), he was ordained a priest in the following year. His best-known work is *Dictionary of Phrase and Fable* (1870).

Brewer, John Sherren. b. at Norwich, England, 1809; d. in Essex, England, 1879. An English historical writer and scholar; brother of Ebenezer Cobham Brewer (1810–97).

Briana (brī.ā'nạ). In Edmund Spenser's *Faerie Queene*, the owner of a strong castle, who could not obtain the love of Crudor unless she made him a mantle of "beards of knights and locks of ladies." No one was allowed to pass her domain without paying this toll.

Brian Boroimhe, or The Maid of Erin (brī'ạn bǫ.rö'). A play (1811) by James Sheridan Knowles, adapted

from an earlier work of the same name. ("Brian Boroimhe" is the Irish king and national hero more usually spelled in English as "Brian Boru.")

Brian Boru (brī'ạn bǫ.rö'). [Also: **Brian Boroimhe** or **Borumha.**] b. 926; killed at Clontarf, Ireland, on Good Friday, 1014. An Irish king and one of the principal national heroes of Ireland. He became sovereign of Munster c978, and principal king of Ireland in 1002. Many times victorious over the Danes, he was murdered (either by a Dane, or by one of the Irish allies of the Danes) in his tent after his victory (April 23, 1014) at Clontarf, near Dublin, had ended for all time the possibility of Scandinavian dominance in Ireland.

Brian de Bois-Guilbert (brē.än' dẹ bwä'gēl.ber'). See **Bois-Guilbert, Brian de.**

Briareus (brī.ār'ẹ.us). [Also, **Aegaeon.**] In Greek mythology, a monster with a hundred arms, a son of Uranus and Ge.

Brick (brik), **Jefferson.** In Charles Dickens's *Martin Chuzzlewit*, a correspondent for a New York journal. He is of excessively mild and youthful aspect, but bloodthirsty in the extreme in his political views.

Bricks and Mortar. A novel by Helen Ashton, published in 1932.

Bridal of Triermain (trī.ẻr.mān'), **The.** A poem by Sir Walter Scott, published in 1813. It is the first experiment by a 19th-century poet with the King Arthur legend. In it Scott tells as an Arthurian story the tale of the Sleeping Beauty (and thus crosses different strains of folklore with the easy license usually associated with medieval, rather than modern, romancers).

Bride (brīd), **Saint.** See Saint **Brigid.**

Bridehead (brīd'hed), **Sue.** In Hardy's *Jude the Obscure*, the young schoolteacher who leaves her husband to live with Jude, but is finally forced by social pressure and her own conscience to return to her husband.

Bride of Abydos (ạ.bī'dos), **The.** A poem by Byron, a Turkish tale, published in 1813. A melodrama adapted from the poem was produced c1819.

Bride of Lammermoor (lam'ẻr.mör), **The.** A novel by Sir Walter Scott, published in 1819. It is in the third series of *The Tales of My Landlord* and was written when Scott was so ill that he is said not to have recalled one scene when he reread it. Several plays have been written on the subject, notably one by J. W. Cole under the pseudonym John William Calcraft, also called *The Bride of Lammermoor*. The opera *Lucia di Lammermoor*, by Gaetano Donizetti, is also based on this novel. The titular heroine of the novel is Lucy Ashton. She is in love with, and loved by, Edgar, the Master of Ravenswood, an impoverished laird who regards Lucy's father as the cause of his family's ruin. However, under the influence of Lucy's affection, his wrath softens; nevertheless, although Lucy's father consents to the match, her mother forbids it, ordering her daughter instead to marry Frank Hayston, the Laird of Bucklaw. Lucy's letter to Ravenswood, apprising him of the situation, is intercepted, so that he remains for too long ignorant of the circumstances, and returns to Lucy just as the wedding

---

fat, fāte, fär, ȧsk, fâre; net, mē, hėr; pin, pīne; not, nōte, mȯve, nôr; up, lūte, pu̇ll; ᴛʜ, then;

ceremony with Bucklaw is ended. Ravenswood immediately challenges Lucy's brother and husband to a duel for the next day; but before this event can take place, Lucy, on her wedding night, stabs her husband to death, and is found in a state of hopeless insanity. Ravenswood dies when he is sucked into a quicksand on his way to the duel.

Brideshead Revisited (brīdz'hed). A novel by Evelyn Waugh, published in 1945.

Bridewell (brīd'wel). A London prison, or house of detention, most of which had been demolished by 1864. It was founded upon a favorite palace of Henry VIII, which stood at the mouth of the Fleet between Blackfriars and Whitefriars, and figures in Dekker and Middleton's *The Honest Whore.* There was a royal residence here as early as the reign of Henry III, if not that of John. Henry VIII is said to have rebuilt the palace, and he and Catherine of Aragon lived there when the cardinals convened to rule on their divorce in Blackfriars opposite. In 1553 Edward VI gave his father's palace of Bridewell to the city of London for a workhouse, and formulated a system of municipal charity. It later became a temporary prison or house of detention, with which use its name is especially familiar. In old views and maps it appears as a castellated building of some architectural pretensions. The name has become a generic term for a house of correction or jail.

Bridge (brij), **Ann.** An English novelist and short-story writer. The name "Ann Bridge" is a pseudonym; the writer's actual identity (and such vital statistics as the date and place of her birth) remain a secret known only to a few. Her books include *Peking Picnic* (1932), *The Ginger Griffin* (1934), *Illyrian Spring* (1935), *Enchanter's Nightshade* (1937), *Four-Part Setting* (1939), *Frontier Passage* (1942), *Singing Waters* (1945), and *The Dark Moment* (1952).

Bridgenorth (brij'nôrth), **Alice.** The principal female character in Sir Walter Scott's *Peveril of the Peak.*

Bridge of Sighs. A bridge in Venice which spans the Rio della Paglia, and connects the ducal palace with the Carceri, or prisons. The bridge dates from 1597; it is an elliptical arch, ab. 32 ft. above the water, enclosed at the sides and arched overhead. It contains two separate passages, through which prisoners were led for trial or judgment (and it was from their plaints at this circumstance that the bridge gained its name).

Bridge of Sighs, The. A poem by Thomas Hood, composed in 1844.

Bridges (brij'ez), **Bess.** See **Bess.**

Bridges, Robert. [Full name, **Robert Seymour Bridges.**] b. at Walmer, England, Oct. 23, 1844; d. 1930. An English poet and essayist, appointed poet laureate in 1913. Educated at Eton and Oxford, he subsequently traveled widely in Egypt, Syria, and Germany. He also served as a physician in various London hospitals until 1881, when he gave up the practice of medicine. His first book, *Poems by Robert Bridges,* was published in 1873. Further volumes of poetry appeared from time to time, and in 1929 was published *The Testament of Beauty,* his swan song and greatest poetical work.

Bridges wrote several plays, as follows: *Prometheus the Firegiver* (1883), *Nero* (Parts I, 1885, and II, 1894), *The Feast of Bacchus, Palicio, The Return of Ulysses* (1890), *The Christian Captives, Achilles in Scyros, The Humours of the Court,* and *Demeter.* He was deeply interested in prosody, and in addition to his own unusual experiments in English versification, he wrote of the prosody of John Milton (1893; final revision, 1921) and John Keats. His publication, in 1918, of the poems of his friend Gerard Manley Hopkins first brought that poet before the general public. He wrote hymns, odes which were set to music, and edited the *Yattendon Hymnal.* He was greatly interested in the history of the English language and its present-day use, including its pronunciation and spelling. In 1913, with Logan Pearsall Smith, Walter Raleigh, and others, he founded the Society for Pure English, and wrote and contributed to many of the Society's tracts. He was much concerned with the physical appearance of his published writings. After 1887 most of his books were printed and published by the Oxford University Press. Later in life Bridges developed a phonetic spelling, and a phonetic alphabet which was cast in a face based on Blado italic. Before his death this alphabet contained 39 characters, and was later expanded to 54 by his widow.

Bridget (brij'et), Saint. See Saint **Brigid.**

Bridget Credulous (kred'ū.lus). See **Credulous, Justice** and **Mrs. Bridget.**

Bridgewater House (brij'wô"ter, -wot"ẽr). The town residence of the Earls of Ellesmere, built in London in 1847–49, on the site of Cleveland House.

Bridgewater Treatises. A series of treatises written in compliance with the terms of the will of Francis Henry Egerton, 8th Earl of Bridgewater, who died in 1829. He left 8,000 pounds to be paid to the author of the best treatise on "The Goodness of God as manifested in the Creation." Those with whom the selection of the author was left decided to give the subject to eight persons for separate treatises. These were *The Adaptation of External Nature to the Moral and Intellectual Constitution of Man* (Thomas Chalmers, 1833), *Chemistry, Meteorology, and Digestion* (William Prout, 1834), *History, Habits, and Instincts of Animals* (Kirby, 1835), *Geology and Mineralogy* (Dean Buckland, 1836), *The Hand, as evincing Design* (Sir Charles Bell, 1833), *The Adaptation of External Nature to the Physical Condition of Man* (J. Kidd, M.D., 1833), *Astronomy and General Physics* (William Whewell, 1833), and *Animal and Vegetable Physiology* (P. M. Roget, M.D., 1834).

brief. A short or concise writing; a short statement or account; an epitome.

I shall make it plain as far as a sum or brief can make a cause plain. (Francis Bacon.)

And she told me, In a sweet verbal brief.
(Shakespeare, *All's Well That Ends Well.*)

Out of your gentleness, please you to consider
The brief of my petition, which contains
All hope of my last fortunes.
(John Ford, *The Fancies Chaste and Noble.*)

Brierley (brī'ẽr.li), **Benjamin.** [Pseudonym, **Ab'-o'-th'-Yate.**] b. at Failsworth, near Manchester,

ḍ, d or j; ṣ, s or sh; ṭ, t or ch; ẓ, z or zh; o, F. cloche; ü, F. menu; ċh, Sc. loch; ṅ, F. bonbon.

England, June 26, 1825; d. at Harpurhey, Manchester, England, Jan. 18, 1896. An English weaver, poet, dramatist, and short-story writer in Lancashire dialect. The son of a weaver, he was himself a weaver from the age of six to 38. Beginning his literary career with articles and essays in the *Oddfellows' Magazine* and the *Manchester Spectator*, he became (1863) subeditor of the *Oldham Times*, and founded and edited (April, 1869–Dec., 1891) *Ben Brierley's Journal;* he also dramatized some of his short stories and acted in them. His main works are *A Day's Out* (1856), *The Layrock of Langleyside* (1856, story and play), *Marlocks of Merriton* (1867), *Cotters of Mossburn* (1871), *Home Memories* (1886, an autobiography), and *Spring Blossoms and Autumn Leaves* (1893, poetry).

Brierley (brir'li), **Roger.** See **Brereley, Roger.**

Brierly (brī'ėr.li), **Bob.** The titular hero of the play *Ticket-of-Leave Man* by Tom Taylor.

Brieux (brė.ė), **Eugène.** b. at Paris, Jan. 19, 1858; d. at Nice, France, Dec. 7, 1932. A French dramatist. He worked as journalist on the Paris periodicals *La Patrie*, *Le Figaro*, and *Le Gaulois*. His first play, *Bernard Palissy*, written in collaboration with Gaston Salandri, was produced in 1880. André Antoine produced his *Ménage d'artistes* at the Théâtre Libre in 1890. This was followed by *Blanchette* (1892), *Les Bienfaiteurs* (1896), *Les Trois filles de M. Dupont* (1897), *Les Avariés* (1901, produced in the U. S. as *Damaged Goods*), *Les Hannetons* (1906), *Simone* (1908), and others. His purpose was to depict social evils, with a view to their reform.

Briffault (brė'fō), **Robert Stephen.** b. at London, 1876; d. in England, 1948. An English novelist, surgeon, and anthropologist. He practiced medicine (1894 *et seq.*) in New Zealand, and served as an army surgeon during World War I; thereafter he retired from his medical practice, and lived in France. His writings on anthropology include *The Making of Humanity* (1919), *The Mothers* (1927), *Sin and Sex* (1931), and *The Decline and Fall of the British Empire* (1938). Among his novels are *Europa* (1935), *Europa in Limbo* (1937), and *New Life of Mr. Martin* (1946).

Brigadore (brig'a.dōr). The horse of Sir Guyon in Edmund Spenser's *Faerie Queene.*

Brigantes (bri.gan'tēz). A confederation of tribes of Britain which in the 1st century A.D. occupied the region north of the river Humber.

Briget Elia (brij'ęt ē'li.ą). See under **Elia.**

Briggs (brigz), **Miss Arabella.** In Thackeray's novel *Vanity Fair*, the "companion" of Miss Crawley and the object of much ridicule (which Miss Crawley greatly enjoys) by Becky Sharp. Miss Crawley leaves her a small legacy, which presently disappears through the efforts of Becky.

Brighouse (brig'hous), **Harold.** b. at Eccles, Lancashire, England, July 26, 1882—. An English novelist and playwright. His plays include *Lonesome-Like* (1911), *Hobson's Choice* (1916), *Mary's John* (1924), and *London Front* (1941). He is the author of the novels *Fossie for Short* (1917), *The Marbeck Inn* (1920), and *The Wrong Shadow* (1923).

Bright (brīt), **John.** b. at Greenbank, near Rochdale, Lancashire, England, Nov. 16, 1811; d. there, March 27, 1889. An English Liberal statesman and orator. He was one of the chief agitators for the Anti-Corn-Law League in the period 1838–46, having first entered Parliament in 1843. He opposed the Crimean War, and favored the North in the American Civil War. He served as president of the Board of Trade (1868–70), and chancellor of the duchy of Lancaster (1873–74 and 1880–82), and became lord rector of the University of Glasgow in 1883. Author of *Speeches on Parliamentary Reform* (1867), *Speeches on Questions of Public Policy* (1869), and *Speeches on Public Affairs* (1869).

Brighton Rock (brī'ton). A novel by Graham Greene, published in 1938.

Bright Star. A sonnet (1819) by John Keats, often miscalled his "Last Sonnet."

Brigid (brij'id), Saint. [Also: **Bridget, Brigit** (brij'it), or **Bride.**] b. at Faughart, near Dundalk, Ireland, 451 or 452; d. at Kildare, Ireland, Feb. 1, 525. A patron saint of Ireland. According to an ancient Irish account of her life, she was born at Fochart (now Faugher or Faughart), and was the daughter of a Leinster chieftain by his bondmaid. She is said to have obtained her freedom through the intervention of the King of Leinster, who was impressed by her piety, and became the founder of a convent, in the shadow of which the present town of Kildare sprang up. Following close on Saint Patrick, whom she met before his death, Brigid is regarded as a patron of Ireland.

Brig o' Balgownie (bal.gou'ni). See **Balgownie, Brig o'.**

Brigs of Ayr (ār), **The.** A poem by Robert Burns, published in *Poems from the Edinburgh Edition* (1787). It refers to both the new and old bridges which spanned the river Ayr.

Brillat-Savarin (brė.yȧ.sȧ.vȧ.raṅ), **Anthelme.** b. at Belley, Ain, France, April 1, 1755; d. at Paris, Feb. 2, 1826. A French lawyer and authority on gastronomy. A political emigré (1793–95) during the latter part of the French Revolution, he traveled in Switzerland, the Netherlands, and the U. S. Author of *Physiologie du goût* (1825; Eng. trans., *Physiology of Taste*, 1925; rev. ed., 1948), and other works.

Briseis (brī.sē'is). In the *Iliad*, a name given to Hippodameia, a beautiful slave girl captured by Achilles and taken by Agamemnon, indirectly the cause of the quarrel between Achilles and Agamemnon.

Brisk (brisk), **Fastidious.** In Ben Jonson's comedy *Every Man Out of His Humour*, a pert, petulant, and lively fop. He is devoted to the life of the court, and overly fashionable.

Bristol Boy (bris'tol), **the.** A name given to Thomas Chatterton because of the poems and documents he published that purported to be the works of various inhabitants of 15th-century Bristol (notable among these are the so-called Rowley poems) which, in fact, were written by Chatterton himself.

Bristowe (Bristol) Merchant (bris'tō; bris'tol), **The.** A play possibly by John Ford and Thomas Dekker, licensed in 1624, probably an alteration of another play on the same theme by John Day. No copy of it is now extant.

---

fat, fāte, fär, ȧsk, fāre; net, mē, hėr; pin, pīne; not, nōte, mӧve, nôr; up, lūte, pull; ᴛн, then;

Bristowe Tragedy, or the Death of Sir Charles Bawdin (bô′din), **The.** A poem by Thomas Chatterton, written in 1768 and printed in 1772.

Britain (brit′ạn). **1.** Great Britain; the island comprising England, Scotland, and Wales.
2. In Arthurian romance, Little Britain, or Brittany, in France.

Britain, Arthur, Duke of. See **Arthur, Duke of Britain.**

Britain, Benjamin (or **Little**). In Charles Dickens's story *The Battle of Life*, at first a servant, and afterward landlord, of the Nutmeg Grater Inn. He is very small, and announces himself as knowing and caring for absolutely nothing.

Britain, Duke of. See **Arthur, Duke of Britain.**

Britain's Daughter. A play (1921) by Gordon Bottomley. It is considered one of his finest dramas.

Britain's Pastorals. A work of pastoral verse (2 vols., 1613–16) by William Browne. A third volume was left incomplete in manuscript form. Begun before the age of 20, it is Browne's largest and most Spenserian work.

Britain's Remembrancer. A narrative verse (1628) by George Wither. It is an eye-witness account of the London plague of 1625.

Britanni (bri.tan′ī). A Celtic people of northwest Gaul (modern Brittany, or Bretagne). They are supposed to have been driven out of southwestern Britain by the Anglo-Saxons.

Britannia (bri.tan′i.ạ). In ancient geography (after the time of Caesar), the name of the island of Great Britain, and specifically of the S part of the island; in modern times, a poetical name of the United Kingdom of Great Britain and Northern Ireland. Under the Romans Britannia Prima, the first province, was the district S of the river Thames, the Saxon Wessex under Egbert; Flavia Caesariensis, between the river Severn and the sea, was the Mercian kingdom of Offa; Britannia Secunda, W of the Severn, comprised Wales and the Welsh Marches; Maxima Caesariensis, between the rivers Humber and Tyne, is the Northumbrian province of Deira; and Valentia, whose N boundary was between the Firth of Forth and the river Clyde, embraced the Lowlands of Scotland and Northumberland.

Britannia. A historical work (1586) by William Camden. Written originally in Latin, it was translated into English in 1610.

Britannia Illustrata (i.lus′trạ.tạ). A prose work (1707–08) by Johannes Kip. In it Kip describes, with an obvious element of national pride, the Restoration houses and gardens of 18th-century England.

Britannia Triumphans (bri.tan′i.ạ trī.um′fanz). A masque by William D'Avenant (1638), with scenery by Inigo Jones.

British Academy. [Full name, **The British Academy for the Promotion of Historical, Philosophical, and Philological Studies.**] An association incorporated by royal charter, on Aug. 8, 1902. Its formation was due to a suggestion made at the assembling of the International Association of Academies at Wiesbaden, Germany, in 1899, and a consequent meeting of representative scholars at the British Museum in 1901.

"British Amazon," the. See **Talbot, Mary Anne.**

British Critic, The. A periodical published (1793–1826) in England. It was a leading conservative review of the day, edited by William Beloe and Robert Nares.

British Museum. A museum and library in Great Russell Street, Bloomsbury, London, founded in 1753. It contains collections of antiquities, drawings, prints, and a library of more than five million volumes, over 57,000 manuscripts, and 85,000 charters and rolls. The growth of the museum after its original establishment was very rapid: Montague House was first employed in 1754 when room was needed for Sir Hans Sloane's library and collections, which were bought for the nominal price of 20,000 pounds, being part of the funds raised by a lottery. The collection was opened to the public on Jan. 15, 1759. The Harleian manuscripts, the royal library presented in 1757, and 65,000 volumes transferred by George IV, raised the library to a position of world importance. The new building, designed by Sir Robert Smirke and completed by his brother Sydney Smirke, was begun soon after the beginning of the 19th century. The main building, completed in 1847, is in the Classic style. In 1816 the Elgin marbles were bought for the sum of 35,000 pounds. The first great Egyptian acquisition consisted of the objects taken with the French army in 1801. In 1802 the Rosetta Stone was deposited in the museum. Subsequently the collection of Sir Gardiner Wilkinson was added. The museum has an extensive collection of Egyptian papyri, and 2,700 Greek and Latin papyri. The Assyrian, Babylonian, coin, and Greek vase collections are considered the best in any contemporary museum. The natural history collections have been removed to the Museum of Natural History at South Kensington. Modern English publications are added free of expense by a privilege, shared with three universities, of receiving gratis a copy of every copyrighted book. The files of newspapers are housed in a special department at Colindale, London.

Britomart (brit′ọ.märt). In Edmund Spenser's *Faerie Queene*, a female knight personifying chastity.

Britomartis (brit.ọ.mär′tis). In Greek mythology, a Cretan divinity of hunters and fishermen. The legends concerning her are various. According to one, to escape from the pursuit of Minos she threw herself among the fishermen's nets in the sea, and was rescued and made a deity by Artemis.

Briton (brit′ọn), **The.** A historical tragedy (1722) by Ambrose Philips.

Brittain (brit′ạn), **Vera.** b. at Newcastle-under-Lyme, Staffordshire, England, c1896–. An English novelist, poet, and journalist. She served as a volunteer nurse (1915–19) at London, Malta, and France, and lectured in America (1934, 1937, 1940, 1946), the Netherlands (1936), Scandinavia (1945), and Germany (1947). Her works include *Verses of a V.A.D* (1918), *Not Without Honour* (1924), *Testament of Youth* (1933), *Poems of the War and After* (1934), *A Testament of Friendship* (1940), *Seed of Chaos* (1944), *On Becoming a Writer* (1947), *Born 1925: A Novel of Youth* (1948), and *Valiant Pilgrim* (1950).

Brittaine (brit′an), **Nicholas.** See **Breton, Nicholas.**

Brittle (brit′l), **Barnaby.** In Thomas Betterton's play *The Amorous Widow*, the husband of Mrs. Brittle. A character not unlike Molière's George Dandin, he was played by Charles Macklin at Covent Garden.

Brittle, Mrs. A character in Thomas Betterton's play *The Amorous Widow*. The part was chosen (1707) by Anne Bracegirdle and Anne Oldfield as a means of testing their relative popularity with the London public of the day. They played the part on alternate nights, and Anne Oldfield was better liked (whereupon Anne Bracegirdle is said to have retired in disgust from the stage).

Britton (brit′on), **Colonel.** The lover of Isabella in Susannah Centlivre's comedy *The Wonder, a Woman Keeps a Secret*. It is to keep the secret of Colonel Britton and Isabella that Violante nearly loses her own lover.

Britton, Nicholas. See **Breton, Nicholas.**

Britton's Bower of Delights. An anthology (1591, 1597), issued by Richard Jones under Nicholas Breton's name (in one of its various spellings). Breton disclaimed responsibility for it, except the long opening poem on Sir Philip Sidney's death entitled *Amoris Lachrimae*, and "one or two other toys."

Broadbottom (brôd′bot.om), **Geffery.** Pseudonym of **Stanhope, Philip Dormer.**

Broadhurst (brôd′hèrst), **George Howells.** b. June 3, 1866; d. at Santa Barbara, Calif., Jan. 31, 1952. An English playwright. In 1882 he came to the U. S., where his outstanding stage successes were *The Man of the Hour* (1907) and *Bought and Paid For* (1913). He returned to England in 1926 and devoted himself to writing fiction.

broadside (brôd′sīd). A sheet printed on one side only, and without arrangement in columns; especially, such a sheet containing some item of news, or an attack upon some person, etc., and designed for distribution. "Van Citters gives the best account of the trial. I have seen a broadside which confirms his narrative." (Macaulay, *History of England*.)

Brobdingnag (brob′ding.nag) or **Brobdignag** (-dig-). A country described in Jonathan Swift's *Gulliver's Travels*, in which the inhabitants and all objects were of gigantic size.

Brocken (brok′en; German, brok′en) or **Blocksberg** (bloks′berk). [Latin, **Mons Bructerus.**] The chief summit of the Harz Mountains, and the highest mountain in N Germany, situated in the *Land* (state) of Saxony-Anhalt, between Blankenburg and Clausthal. It is the traditional meeting place of the witches on Walpurgis Night, and is famous for the optical phenomenon called the "specter of the Brocken." 3,747 ft.

Brogan (brō′gan), **Denis William.** b. in Scotland, Aug. 11, 1900—. A British political scientist and author, especially noted in the U. S. for such studies of American culture as *The American Political System* (1933), *The American Character* (1944), *American Themes* (1949), and *Government of the People*. Educated at Glasgow, Oxford, and Harvard universities, he taught at the University of London and at the London School of Economics, and was professor of political science at Cambridge. His other books include *French Personalities and Problems* (1946), *The English People, The Free State*, and *The Price of Revolution* (1952).

Broghill (brog′hil), **Baron.** A title of **Boyle, Roger.**

Broke or **Brooke** (brük), **Arthur.** d. 1563. An English translator, who wrote *The Tragicall Historye of Romeus and Iulieit* (1562), one of the first English versions of that famous tragedy of love. This is probably the version used by Shakespeare as the source for the plot of his *Romeo and Juliet*. Broke translated freely from the French version of Matteo Bandello's Italian version of the story, published in the *Histoires tragiques* (Paris, 1559). George Turberville's "On the Death of Maister Arthur Brooke, drownde in passing to New Haven," in his *Epitaphes and other Poems* (1567), describes Broke as a young man.

Broken Heart, The. A tragedy by John Ford, acted at the Blackfriars Theatre, London, in 1629, printed in 1633.

Broken Soil. A play (1903) by Padraic Colum. A pioneering example of realistic drama, it was later rewritten by Colum as *The Fiddler's House*.

Brome (brōm), **Alexander.** b. 1620; d. June 30, 1666. An English attorney and royalist poet. He wrote *Songs and Poems* (1661; 2nd ed., enlarged, 1664) and a comedy, *The Cunning Lovers* (1654). He edited two volumes of Richard Brome's plays, but is not known to have been related to him.

Brome, Richard. d. c1652. English dramatist, in his early years the servant of Ben Jonson. Of his life and death little is known. Among his numerous plays are *The City Wit, or the Woman Wears the Breeches, The Northern Lass* (printed 1632), *The Sparagus Garden* (acted 1635, printed 1640), *The Antipodes* (acted 1638, printed 1640), and *A Jovial Crew, or the Merry Beggars* (acted 1641, printed 1652).

Bromia (brō′mi.a). In John Dryden's *Amphitryon*, the scolding, ill-tempered wife of Sosia, who is slave of Amphitryon.

Brompton (bromp′ton). A district of London, S.W., between Kensington and Pimlico, south of Hyde Park.

Brontë Family (bron′tä). An English family, originally of Irish descent, which produced three of the most important English novelists of the 19th century: Charlotte Brontë, Emily Brontë, and Anne Brontë. Their father, Patrick Brontë (b. at Emdale, County Down, Ireland, 1777; d. at Haworth, England, 1861) was the son of Hugh Brunty, an Irish farmer. At 25 he entered St. John's College, Cambridge, signing himself Patrick Brontë, a spelling borrowed from the title recently bestowed on Horatio Nelson, Duke of Bronte (in Sicily). He took orders in 1806, and from Cambridge went to a curacy in Essex. Three years later he removed to Yorkshire as curate of Heartshead-cum-Clifton. On Dec. 29, 1812, he married, in Guiseley Church, Maria Branwell, of Penzance, Cornwall, who was at that time staying with an uncle and aunt, the John Fennells, governor and governess of Woodhouse Grove Wesleyan Academy. At Heartshead were born two daughters, Maria (1813–25) and

Elizabeth (1815–25). In 1815 the Brontës exchanged the living of Heartshead for that of Thornton, where were born four more children: Charlotte (1816–55), Patrick Branwell (1817–48), Emily Jane (1818–48), and Anne (1820–49). Early in 1820 Patrick Brontë became perpetual curate of Haworth. The family had been but 18 months in their more commodious home when Mrs. Brontë died of cancer, and her sister, Elizabeth Branwell, thereupon came from Penzance to take charge of the household. When Maria was ten years old, she with Elizabeth, Charlotte, and Emily, were entered in the Clergy's Daughters' School at Cowan Bridge. It was there that Maria and Elizabeth contracted the tuberculosis which brought their death shortly thereafter. For the next six years the four remaining children were at home, Branwell having regular lessons with his father, and the three girls learning domestic arts from their aunt, at the same time picking up a strange assortment of knowledge from wide and varied reading. For their further amusement, they made up games or plays of imagination. Around their toys, particularly Branwell's wooden soldiers, they created a clearly defined country having its capital at the mouth of the Niger River, in Africa. Called originally Glasstown or Verdopolis, it developed in the course of years into a vast African empire known as Angria, and ruled by Arthur Wellesley, elder son of the Duke of Wellington. Its heroes not only performed great deeds, but, turning artists and authors, perpetuated them in diminutive booklets of supposed proportions to their authors, the wooden soldiers, executed in minute hand printing and illustrated with pen and ink drawings. The African game, now five years old, and having outgrown the wooden soldiers, was interrupted in January, 1835, when Charlotte departed for Miss Wooler's school at Roe Head. Emily and Anne seized this opportunity to set up a play of their own, centered in "Gondal, an island in the North Pacific," and "Gaaldine, a newly discovered island in the South Pacific." But when Charlotte returned after a year and a half, she rejoined Branwell in the old play, infusing into it new life and color drawn from her reading of Byron and Scott. A goodly number of play books by Charlotte and Branwell have survived, but none by Emily and Anne. Such creative writing absorbed and satisfied the girls, and, though Branwell kept pace with Charlotte in number of Angrian "books," he found himself hopelessly outdistanced by her genius in turning his crude inventions into literature. For compensation he sought the admiration of village lads and men who gathered for drink and conversation in the nearby Black Bull Inn. To break this association, it was decided in family council that he should enter the Royal Academy, and to help provide the necessary funds for his instruction, Charlotte accepted Miss Wooler's offer of a teaching position in her school. With her went Emily to enroll as a pupil. However, if Branwell went to London, he did not enter the Royal Academy, and Emily at Roe Head became so homesick that she was allowed to return home. After two years Charlotte herself broke in health. Since work away from home was virtually impossible for the girls, they hit upon the plan of a school of their own in the

parsonage, and Aunt Elizabeth advanced the money for Charlotte and Emily to improve their French by a term in a Brussels school for girls. They were making rapid progress when the death of Miss Branwell called them home. The small legacy she left them relieved the immediate need for employment. Anne went back to her post as governess, Charlotte returned to Brussels, and Emily settled down at home to look after her father.

First Published Work. It was in 1846, when the three were together in the parsonage, that they ventured to publish at their own cost a joint volume of poems, using pseudonyms to fit their true initials: Currer Bell (for Charlotte), Ellis Bell (for Emily), and Acton Bell (for Anne). The book was a failure, only two copies being sold. Undeterred, the three sisters, still using their earlier pseudonyms, soon had a novel each making the round of publishing houses. Emily's *Wuthering Heights* and Anne's *Agnes Gray* found early acceptance by Thomas Cautley Newby, but Charlotte's *The Professor* came back so many times that she retired the manuscript and pushed hard to finish a second novel called *Jane Eyre*. When completed, this manuscript was sent directly to Smith, Elder and Company, who accepted it enthusiastically, and put it into immediate printing. It was a phenomenal success from the first, while *Wuthering Heights* and *Agnes Gray* were received but coolly. Yet Anne persisted in her writing, publishing *The Tenant of Wildfell Hall* the next year. In the meanwhile, Branwell, whose dissipations had gone from bad to worse, died in September, 1848. Emily, taking cold at his funeral, followed him in December. In the following May, Anne died at Scarborough, where Charlotte had taken her, hoping she would benefit by the sea air. Charlotte in loneliness and grief turned again to her interrupted novel, *Shirley*. It, too, was well received, and its use of local setting betrayed the identity of Currer Bell to the public. In 1853, she completed *Villette*, the last written and generally considered to be the best of her four novels. *The Professor* was published posthumously. In all her novels Charlotte adapted to realistic English and Belgian settings characters and incidents from her Angrian stories, and there is considerable evidence that Emily's *Wuthering Heights* has it origin in lost Gondal stories. Anne wrote from real life. In June, 1853, Charlotte married her father's curate, Arthur Bell Nicholls. On March 31, 1854, she died. Her father lived on in the parsonage, cared for by Arthur Nicholls, until his death in 1861. Though Patrick Brontë never attained literary recognition, a list of his publications casts some light on the genius of his children: *Cottage Poems* (1811), *The Rural Minstrel* (1813), *The Cottage in the Woods* (1815), and *The Maid of Killarney* (1818), as well as tracts and sermons to the number of five.

Brontes (bron'tēz). One of the Cyclops.

Bronze Age, The. A play by Thomas Heywood, printed in 1613, founded on Ovid's *Metamorphoses*.

Brooch of Thebes (thēbz), **The.** [Also, **The Brooch of Vulcan.**] A name given to Chaucer's *Complaint of Mars* in one of its manuscript versions. Lydgate refers to the same poem as "the broche which that Vulcanus at Thebes wrouhte."

ḍ, d or j; ṣ, s or sh; ṭ, t or ch; ẓ, z or zh; o, F. cloche; ü, F. menu; ċh, Sc. loch; ṅ, F. bonbon.

Brook (brŭk), **Master.** In Shakespeare's *Merry Wives of Windsor*, the name assumed by Ford for the purpose of fooling Falstaff, who is seeking an affair with Ford's wife. Falstaff, all unaware of Brook's true identity, boasts to him of progress in his pursuit of Mistress Ford.

Brooke (brŭk), 1st Baron. Title of **Greville, Sir Fulke.**

Brooke, Arthur. See **Broke** or **Brooke, Arthur.**

Brooke, Celia. In George Eliot's novel *Middlemarch*, the sister of Dorothea Brooke. She is a pretty, practical girl whose common sense protests against the somewhat ideal philanthropy of Dorothea.

Brooke, Dorothea. The heroine of George Eliot's novel *Middlemarch*. Her temperament leads her to seek expression in work which shall be of permanent benefit to others. From admiration, she mistakenly marries a dried-up pedant, Casaubon, who hinders instead of helps her; after his death she abandons her high but vague ideal and marries a man who satisfies the common yearning of humanity for sympathy and love. She thereupon sinks into a happy obscurity.

Brooke, Emma Frances. d. 1926. An English novelist and Fabian Socialist. She studied at Cambridge University, and went to London in the early 1880's; attracted to socialism, she joined the Fabian Society. She was the author of *A Superfluous Woman* (1894), *Transition* (1895), *Life the Accuser* (1896), *The Confession of Stephen Whapshare* (1898), *The Engrafted Rose* (1900), *Sir Elyot of the Woods* (1907), and *The House of Robershaye* (1912), all novels, and *A Tabulation of the Factory Laws of European Countries In So Far as They Relate to . . . Women, Young Persons, and Children* (1898).

Brooke, Frances Moore. b. 1724; d. at Sleaford, Lincolnshire, England, Jan. 23 or 26, 1789. An English novelist, poet, and dramatist. She was the wife of John Brooke, rector of Colney, Norfolk, and chaplain to the garrison at Quebec, where for a time they resided. Her works include *The History of Lady Julia Mandeville* (1763), *History of Emily Montagu* (1769), and *The Excursion* (1777).

Brooke, Henry. b. at Rantavan, County Cavan, Ireland, c1703; d. at Dublin, Oct. 10, 1783. An Irish novelist, dramatist, and poet. He wrote *Universal Beauty* (a poem, 1735), *Gustavus Vasa* (a drama, 1739), and *The Fool of Quality* (a novel, 1766–68).

Brooke, Rupert. [Full name, **Rupert Chawner Brooke.**] b. at Rugby, Warwickshire, England, Aug. 3, 1887; d. of blood poisoning in a hospital on the Greek island of Skyros, April 23, 1915. An English poet, essayist, and soldier. Educated at Rugby School and at King's College, Cambridge, where he became a fellow, he traveled in Germany, Italy, America, Canada, and the South Seas (1913), and saw service (1914) in Belgium. He sailed for, but never reached, the Dardanelles. He was the author of *The Bastille* (1905, a prize poem), *Poems* (1911), *1914 and Other Poems* (1915), and *Lithuania* (1915, a one-act play), and also wrote *Puritanism in the Early English Drama* (1910, a prize essay), *John Webster and the Elizabethan Drama*

(1916, his fellowship thesis), and *Letters from America* (1916). He is remembered for his sonnet *The Soldier*, and for the poems *Dust, The Hill, Heaven, The Busy Heart, Dining-Room Tea, The Old Vicarage, Grantchester, The Great Lover*, and *The Dead.*

Brooke, Stopford. [Full name, **Stopford Augustus Brooke.**] b. at Letterkenny, County Donegal, Ireland, Nov. 14, 1832; d. at Ewhurst, Surrey, England, March 18, 1916. An English clergyman, critic, biographer, and anthologist. Educated at Trinity College, Dublin, where he won several prizes for poetry, he was ordained in 1857, and held various church posts at London. He served (1863–64) at Berlin as chaplain to the British embassy, was chaplain to Queen Victoria from 1872 until 1880, when he left the Church of England to become a Unitarian, and was later an independent preacher. He lectured on English poets and poetry (1900–05) at London University College. Author of *Theology in the English Poets* (1874), dealing with William Cowper, Samuel Taylor Coleridge, William Wordsworth, and Robert Burns, he also wrote *A Primer of English Literature* (1876), *History of Early English Literature* (1894), *Tennyson: His Art and Relation to Modern Life* (1894), *The Poetry of Browning* (1902), *Ten Plays of Shakespeare* (1905), and *Studies in Poetry* (1907). Among his other works are *Life and Letters of the Late Frederick W. Robertson* (1865), *Riquet of the Tuft* (1880), a verse drama, and *Poems* (1888); he edited the anthology *A Treasury of Irish Poetry in the English Tongue* (1900).

Brookfield (brŭk'fēld), **William Henry.** b. at Sheffield, England, 1809; d. 1874. An English educator and clergyman who was a friend of Tennyson, Thackeray, and Arthur Hallam. He received an M.A. degree at Cambridge in 1836, and was named a curate at Southampton (1840) and of St. Luke's, Berwick Street, London (1841). In 1848 he was appointed inspector of schools and was also at one time chaplain in ordinary to Queen Victoria. He is believed to have been the original in real life of Frank Whitestock in Thackeray's *Curate's Walk.*

Brook Kerith (brŭk ker'ith), **The.** [Full title, **The Brook Kerith: A Syrian Story.**] A life of Christ in the form of fiction, by George Moore, published in 1916. Adopting the rationalistic theory that Jesus did not die on the cross but was taken down by Joseph and secretly nursed back to health, the story rises to its climax when the fanatical missionary Paul comes face to face with the man whose resurrection and divinity he has proclaimed, while Jesus, thinking better of what he now considers to have been madness, wants only to live out his life in an atmosphere of personal charity and philosophic calm.

Brooks of Sheffield (shef'ēld). In Charles Dickens's *David Copperfield*, an imaginary person named by Mr. Murdstone, David's cruel stepfather, when speaking of David Copperfield in his presence, and hence since used for some person spoken of whose name it is not convenient to mention.

Brooks's (brŭk'sęz). A Conservative club at London established in 1764 by the Duke of Roxborough, the Duke of Portland, and others. It was formerly ə gaming-house kept by William Almack, which was afterward kept by "Brooks, a wine merchant and money-lender," for whom it was named.

Broome (brōm), **William.** b. at Haslington, Cheshire, England, in May, 1689; d. at Bath, England, Nov. 16, 1745. An English poet and divine. He assisted, as an accomplished Greek scholar, in Alexander Pope's translation of Homer. Having remained silent in respect to the indictment of Pope's originality implied by John Henley, he was ridiculed in the *Dunciad.*

Brophy (brō'fi), **John.** b. at Liverpool, England, Dec. 6, 1899—. An English novelist. Educated at Liverpool and Durham universities, he served in World War I. He was coeditor with Eric Partridge of *Songs and Slang of the British Soldier: 1914–1918* (1930). His first novel, *The Bitter End* (1928), was followed by *Fanfare* (1930), *Flesh and Blood* (1931), *Waterfront* (1934), *The World Went Mad* (1934), *The Ramparts of Virtue* (1936), *The Ridiculous Hat* (1939), *Gentleman of Stratford* (1939), *Green Glory* (1940), *Immortal Sergeant* (1942), *The Woman from Nowhere* (1946), *City of Departures* (1946), *Body and Soul* (1947), and *Sarah* (1948). He also wrote *The Human Face* (1945).

Brothers, The. A play by James Shirley, licensed for public performance in 1626, published in 1652.

Brothers, The. A political club of wits and statesmen established at London in 1713. Jonathan Swift was its treasurer. In 1714 it was merged in the Scriblerus Club.

Brothers, The. A tragedy by Edward Young, produced in 1753.

Brothers, The. A comedy by Richard Cumberland, produced in 1769. Like most of the fashionable comedies of the day, it has a complicated plot, a deep-dyed villain contrasting with a completely virtuous younger brother, a secret marriage, and a quarrelsome married couple.

Brothers, The. A novel by L. A. G. Strong, published in 1932, and issued in America under the title *Brothers.*

Brother Sam. A comedy by John Oxenford from a German play, altered by E. A. Sothern and J. B. Buckstone, produced in 1874. Brother Sam is the brother of Lord Dundreary, and the part was written for Sothern. The play is a kind of sequel to Tom Taylor's *Our American Cousin.*

Brough (bruf), **John.** In Thackeray's *The Great Hoggarty Diamond,* the business promoter and speculator who controls the Independent West Diddlesex. He leaves Sam Titmarsh to take the blame for the failure of this enterprise.

Brough, Robert Barnabas. b. at London, April 10, 1828; d. at Manchester, England, June 26, 1860. An English author of burlesques, humorous verse, novels, short stories, and essays. Among his many works are a novel, *Miss Brown* (1860), and *Which is Which?*, a romance (1860). With his brother, William Brough, and by himself, he wrote many burlesque plays; he adapted plays from the French, and translated the poetry of Victor Hugo and some of the prose works of Alphonse Karr.

Brougham (brōm, brō'ăm), **Henry Peter.** [Title, Baron **Brougham and Vaux** (vôks, vōz).] b. at

Edinburgh, Sept. 19, 1778; d. at Cannes, France, May 7, 1868. A British statesman, orator, jurist, and scientist. He was one of the founders of the *Edinburgh Review* in 1802. Having entered Parliament in 1810, he was counsel for Queen Caroline in the period 1820–21, and was lord chancellor of England in the period 1830–34.

Broughton (brô'tọn), **Rhoda.** b. near Denbigh, North Wales, Nov. 29, 1840; d. at Headington Hill, near Oxford, England, June 5, 1920. An English novelist of country life. She was educated by her father, Delves Broughton (d. 1863), a clergyman. Author of *Cometh Up as a Flower* (1867), *Not Wisely But Too Well* (1867), *Red as a Rose is She* (1870), *Good-bye, Sweetheart* (1872), *Nancy* (1873), *Joan* (1876), *Belinda* (1883), *Dr. Cupid* (1886), *Dear Faustina* (1897), *Foes-in-Law* (1900), *A Waif's Progress* (1905), *The Devil and the Deep Sea* (1910), *Between Two Stools* (1912), and many others.

Broughton, Thomas. b. at London, July 5, 1704; d. at Bedminster, England, Dec. 21, 1774. An English divine and miscellaneous writer. He wrote the lives marked *T* in the original edition of the *Biographia Britannica*, was the author of *An Historical Dictionary of all Religions from the Creation of the World to the Present Time* (1742), and furnished the words to the musical drama *Hercules*, by George Frederick Handel.

Broughton de Gyfford (brô'tọn dẹ gif'ọrd), **Baron.** Title of **Hobhouse, John Cam.**

Browdie (brou'di), **John.** In Charles Dickens's *Nicholas Nickleby,* a big, good-natured Yorkshireman. He marries Matilda Price.

Brown (broun), **Charles Armitage.** b. 1786; d. in New Zealand, 1842. An English man of letters; a close friend of John Keats. He conducted (c1805–10) his merchant brother's business at St. Petersburg; after the business collapsed (1810), he returned to England, ruined, and remained penniless until an inheritance enabled him to devote himself to literature. He traveled (1818) in Scotland with Keats (whom he had met before 1817), and, for two years, made him an intimate of his house at Hampstead, where he introduced him to Fanny Brawne. In Italy (1822–25), where he became intimate (1824) with Walter Savage Landor, he lectured on Keats and Shakespeare. In 1841 he went to New Zealand for reasons of health. Richard Monckton Milnes, 1st Baron Houghton, in his biography of Keats, includes many of Brown's papers about the poet. Brown's most important work is *Shakespeare's Autobiographical Poems* (1838), a personal interpretation of the sonnets.

Brown, Father. A Roman Catholic priest who solves crime by his own highly intuitive methods in G. K. Chesterton's detective stories.

Brown, Ford Madox. b. at Calais, France, April 16, 1821; d. at London, Oct. 6, 1893. An English painter, associated with the Pre-Raphaelites; father of Oliver Madox Brown (1855–74). At Manchester, England, he executed a series of murals depicting great events in that city's history. His other works include *Wyclif* (1849), *King Lear* (1849), *Chaucer Reciting His Poetry at the Court of Edward II* (1851), and *Christ Washing Peter's Feet* (1852).

ḍ, d or j; ṣ, s or sh; ṭ, t or ch; ẓ, z or zh; *o,* F. cloche; ü, F. menu; ċh, Sc. loch; ṅ, F. bonbon.

Brown, George Douglas. [Pseudonym, **George Douglas.**] b. at Ochiltree, Ayrshire, Scotland, Jan. 26, 1869; d. at London, Aug. 28, 1902. A Scottish novelist. He was educated at Glasgow University and at Balliol College, Oxford, winning scholarships, prizes, and medals at both. He went to London in 1895, where he wrote for the metropolitan newspapers and was a publisher's reader. Under his pseudonym he wrote *The House with the Green Shutters* (1901), a realistic study of Scottish life.

Brown, John. b. at Rothbury, Northumberland, England, Nov. 5, 1715; committed suicide, Sept. 23, 1766. An English clergyman and writer. He was the author of *An Estimate of the Manners and Principles of the Times* (1757), and others.

Brown, John. b. at Carpow, Perthshire, Scotland, 1722; d. at Haddington, East Lothian, Scotland, June 19, 1787. A Scottish Biblical scholar. His works include *A Dictionary of the Bible* (1769), *The Self-interpreting Bible* (1778), and *A Compendious History of the British Churches* (1784; new edition, 1823).

Brown, John. b. at Biggar, Lanarkshire, Scotland, in September, 1810; d. May 11, 1882. A Scottish physician and author. His chief work is *Horae Subsecivae* (1858, 1861, 1882), containing "Our Dogs," and "Rab and his Friends"; the latter was first published in 1859. He also wrote *John Leech and Other Papers* (1882).

Brown, John. The lifelong, faithful Scottish attendant of Queen Victoria. His position was more that of major domo and personal friend than of a humble servant, and dated from her girlhood at Balmoral Castle. He figures in many of the books written about her, perhaps most importantly in Lytton Strachey's highly interpretive biography, *Queen Victoria.*

Brown, Lancelot. [Called **"Capability" Brown.**] b. at Harle-Kirk, Northumberland, England, 1715; d. Feb. 6, 1783. An English landscape gardener. He was considered by Humphrey Repton the founder of the modern or English style of landscape gardening, superseding the geometric style which had been perfected at Versailles in the early 17th century. Although the true founder of the modern style is more often considered to have been William Kent, Brown had worked independently with the aim of bringing out the undulating lines of natural landscape. He also served (1770) as high sheriff of Huntingdonshire.

Brown, Mr. Pseudonym of William Makepeace Thackeray, under which he wrote (1849) letters to a young man about town, in *Punch.*

Brown, Oliver Madox. b. at Finchley, London, Jan. 20, 1855; d. there, Nov. 5, 1874. English painter, poet, and novelist; son of Ford Madox Brown (1821–93).

Brown, Thomas. [Called **Tom Brown.**] b. at Shifnal, Shropshire, England, 1663; d. at London, June 16, 1704. An English satirical poet and prose writer. A collected edition of his works was published in the period 1707–08. Perhaps the best-known of his many verses is the quatrain beginning *I Do Not Love Thee, Dr. Fell.*

Brown, Thomas. b. at Kilmabreck, Kirkcudbrightshire, Scotland, Jan. 9, 1778; d. at Brompton, near London, April 2, 1820. A Scottish physician, philosopher, and poet; a colleague (1810 *et seq.*) of Dugald Stewart. He is chiefly notable from his support of David Hume's theory of causation. His works include *Poems* (1804), *Paradise of Coquettes* (1814), *The War-fiend* (1816), *An Inquiry into the Relation of Cause and Effect* (1818), *Agnes* (1818), *Emily* (1819), and *Lectures on the Physiology of the Human Mind* (1820).

Brown, Thomas Edward. b. at Douglas, on the Isle of Man, May 5, 1830; d. at Clifton, Gloucestershire, England, Oct. 30, 1897. An English poet, curate, and schoolmaster. Educated at King William's College on the Isle of Man and at Christ Church, Oxford, he was elected (1854) a fellow of Oriel College, Oxford. He served as vice-principal (1855–61) of King William's College, headmaster (1861–63) of the Crypt School in Gloucester, master (1863–92) of Clifton College, and curate (1884–93) at St. Barnabas, Bristol. He was the author of *Betsey Lee* (1873), *Fo'c's'le Yarns* (1881), *The Doctor* (1887), *The Manx Witch* (1889), and *Old John* (1893), narrative and lyric poetry, much of it in Manx dialect; his *Collected Poems* and his *Letters* were published in 1900. Among his best-known poems are "Vespers," "Disguises," "An Autumn Trinket," "Juventa Perennis," and "The Schooner."

Brown, Tom. The typical healthy British schoolboy and youth in *Tom Brown's School Days* and *Tom Brown at Oxford*, by Thomas Hughes.

Brown Bess. A popular name of the English regulation flintlock musket toward the end of the 18th century.

Browne (broun), **Hablot Knight.** [Pseudonym, **Phiz.**] b. at Kennington, Surrey, England, June 15, 1815; d. at West Brighton, England, July 8, 1882. An English artist, noted especially as a caricaturist. He is best known for his illustrations of the novels of Charles Dickens, Charles Lever, and Harrison Ainsworth. In 1836 he began his association with Dickens, with the illustrations to *Pickwick Papers;* thereafter, he supplied pictures for the first book editions of many later works by Dickens.

Browne, Isaac Hawkins. b. at Burton-on-Trent, England, Jan. 21, 1705; d. at London, Feb. 14, 1760. An English poet. His chief work was a Latin poem, *De animi immortalitate* (1754).

Browne, James. b. at Whitefield, Scotland; d. near Edinburgh, 1841. A Scottish journalist and historian. After brief service as a minister of the Church of Scotland, he settled (c1827) at Edinburgh as a journalist. He was an editor of the *Scots Magazine* and the *Caledonian Mercury*, assistant editor of the seventh edition of the *Encyclopædia Britannica*, and author of *History of the Inquisition* (1817), *History of the Highlands* (1835), and other historical studies.

Browne, Matthew. A pseudonym of **Rands, William Brighty.**

Browne, Sir Thomas. b. at London, Oct. 19, 1605; d. at Norwich, England, Oct. 19, 1682. An English physician and author. He studied at Winchester and Oxford (at Broadgate Hall, now Pembroke College). Upon completion of his classical education, he spent several years in medical studies at

Montpellier, Padua, and Leiden (where he was made a doctor of medicine c1633). His first book, *Religio Medici* (A Doctor's Religion), written in a Yorkshire village, was the product of the vacant period after his return to England and before he settled into active practice. In 1637 he established himself at Norwich, and spent the rest of his long life as a provincial doctor there. He was knighted in September, 1671. *Religio Medici* is the author's private journal in which he attempts to read his own mind; it was not printed in an authorized edition until 1643, although two unauthorized editions by Andrew Croke appeared in 1642. Written in a solemn and sonorous style, the book is a fusion of the author's mystical acceptance of Christianity and his half-credulous skepticism. Enormously popular, there were nine English editions before 1660, and five in Latin. Before Browne's death it had also been translated into Dutch, French, and German. Browne's longest work is the *Pseudodoxia Epidemica, or Enquiries into Very Many Received Tenets and Commonly Presumed Truths*, which appeared in a folio volume in 1646 and reached its sixth edition in 1672. The spread of subject matter in this work is enormous and the author utilizes not only the quasi-scientific data compiled by Aristotle, Pliny, and their learned followers, but also the impressively large amount of accurate observation that he had made himself in botany, natural history, and medicine. In this book, Browne confutes dozens of false ideas which some educated persons have even today not thought of questioning. The style is less conscious than *Religio Medici*, but it marks the author's growing taste for elaborately periodic sentences and for Latin words. Emphasis on style is more conspicuous in the two shorter works which followed: *Hydriotaphia, or Urn Burial* and *The Garden of Cyrus: or the Quincuncial Lozenge*, printed together in 1658. *Hydriotaphia*, in part a scientific report on 40 or 50 Roman funeral urns which had then recently been exhumed near Norwich, becomes a disquisition on burial customs in general. *Miscellany Tracts* and *Christian Morals* were published posthumously.

Browne, Thomas Alexander. [Pseudonym, **Rolf Boldrewood.**] b. at London, Aug. 6, 1826; d. at Melbourne, Australia, March 11, 1915. An Australian novelist; son of one of the founders of Melbourne. He was educated at the University of Sydney, New South Wales. His experiences as a farmer, squatter, magistrate, and gold prospector gave him material for more than 30 novels of adventure and excitement. Under his pseudonym he wrote *Old Melbourne Memories* (1884), *Robbery Under Arms* (1888), *The Miner's Right* (1890), *A Colonial Reformer* (1890), *The Squatter's Dream* (1890), *A Sydney-Side Saxon* (1891), *Nevermore* (1892), *A Modern Buccaneer* (1894), *A Canvas Town Romance* (1898), *The Babes in the Bush* (1900), *In Bad Company* (1901), and *Ghost Camp* (1902).

Browne, William. b. at Tavistock, Devonshire, England, c1591; d. c1643. An English poet. Among his works are *Britannia's Pastorals* (1613–16) and *Shepherd's Pipe* (1614, written in collaboration).

Browning (broun'ing), Lady. Title of **Du Maurier, Daphne.**

Browning, Elizabeth Barrett. [Maiden name originally **Moulton,** subsequently **Barrett.**] b. at Coxhoe Hall, Durham, England, March 6, 1806; d. at Florence, Italy, June 30, 1861. An English poet. She was the eldest daughter of Edward Moulton (who took the name of Barrett on succeeding to an estate); married (1846) Robert Browning, and resided in Italy, chiefly at Florence, during the remainder of her life. An accident at 15 made her a partial invalid for many years. She was the author of *Prometheus Bound* (translation, 1833), *The Seraphim, and Other Poems* (1838), *Poems* (1844), *Poems* (including *Sonnets from the Portuguese*, 1850), *Casa Guidi Windows* (1851), *Aurora Leigh* (1857), *Poems before Congress* (1860), and *Last Poems* (1862, edited by her husband). Her prose works consist of *The Greek Christian Poets* (1842, 1862) and several volumes of *Letters*. Her best-known work is probably *Sonnets from the Portuguese*, a series of love poems addressed to Robert Browning, which include the popular "How do I love thee? Let me count the ways" and "If thou must love me, let it be for naught."

Browning, Oscar. b. at London, Jan. 17, 1837; d. at Rome, Oct. 6, 1923. An English historian, biographer, and professor. Educated at Eton and at King's College, Cambridge, he was classical master (1860–75) at Eton, and professor of history and political science (1876–1909) at Cambridge; later he served as principal of the Cambridge University Training College for Teachers. A prolific writer in many fields, he was the author of *The Netherlands in the 16th Century* (1869), *The Thirty Years' War* (1870), *Modern England* (1879), *History of Educational Theories* (1881), *England and Napoleon in 1803* (1889), *History of England* (4 vols., 1890), *Life of George Eliot* (1890), *Life of Peter the Great* (1890), *Dante: His Life and Works* (1891), *Wars of the 19th Century* (1899), *History of Europe: 1814–1843* (1901), *Guelphs and Ghibellines* (1903), *Napoleon: The First Phase* (1905), *The Fall of Napoleon* (1907), *History of the Modern World: 1815–1910* (1912), *General History of the World* (1913), *History of Medieval Italy: 586–1530* (1914), and *General History of Italy* (1915). He also wrote *Memories of Sixty Years at Eton, Cambridge, and Elsewhere* (1910) and *Memories of Later Years* (1923).

Browning, Robert. b. at Camberwell, London, May 7, 1812; d. in the Palazzo Rezzonico, at Venice, Dec. 12, 1889. An English poet. The son of a clerk in the Bank of England, Browning was privately educated and published his first work of verse, *Pauline*, in 1833. Copies of this later became among the most valuable first editions in English poetry. In 1846 Browning married Elizabeth Barrett and they resided at Pisa and later in the Casa Guidi at Florence until her death in 1861. One son, Robert Wiedemann Barrett Browning, was born to them in 1849. After his wife's death, Browning left Florence and lived thereafter mainly at London and Venice. With *The Ring and the Book* (1868–69) he reached his climax of popularity, and secured finally the recognition which he had sought for 50 years. This work is based upon an old manuscript telling the story of a "Roman Murder Case" which Browning picked up in the Square of San

Lorenzo at Florence for a sum approximating 14 cents in modern currency. This poem established him as one of the greatest of English poets; its sections entitled "Caponsacchi," "Pompilia," and "The Pope" are considered to contain some of the finest blank verse in the English language. Browning's other chief works are *Paracelsus* (1835), *Bells and Pomegranates* (1841–46; in eight parts, including *Pippa Passes, A Blot in the 'Scutcheon,* and *Luria*), *Christmas Eve and Easter Day* (1850), *Men and Women* (1855), *Dramatis Personae* (1864), *Aristophanes' Apology* (1875), *The Agamemnon of Aeschylus,* a translation (1877), *Dramatic Idyls* (1879–80), and *Asolando* (1889). Among his best-known separate poems and dramatic monologues are *De Gustibus, Saul, The Guardian Angel, My Last Duchess, The Pied Piper of Hamelin, A Grammarian's Funeral, An Epistle of Kharshish, Andrea del Sarto, Abt Vogler, Rabbi Ben Ezra, A Death in the Desert, Prospice,* and *An Epilogue to Asolando.*

Brown, Jones, and Robinson, The Adventures of. A series of illustrated articles by Richard Doyle, begun in *Punch* and completed for book publication in 1854. It is a satire on the manners of the middle-class Englishman abroad or on his travels. Anthony Trollope published in 1862 *The Struggles of Brown, Jones, and Robinson,* a story illustrated by John Everett Millais.

Brownlow (broun'lō), **Mr.** In Charles Dickens's novel *Oliver Twist,* a kind-hearted and benevolent old gentleman, the protector of Oliver Twist.

Brownrigg Papers (broun'rig), **The.** A collection of essays and sketches by Douglas Jerrold, published in 1860.

Brown the Younger, Thomas. A pseudonym of Thomas Moore, under which he wrote *Intercepted Letters, or the Twopenny Post Bag,* in 1813.

Bruce (brös), **James.** b. at Kinnaird, Scotland, Dec. 14, 1730; d. there, April 27, 1794. A Scottish traveler in Africa. He explored Syria, the Nile valley, and Ethiopia (1768–73), reaching the source of the Blue Nile. His *Travels to Discover the Sources of the Nile,* in five volumes, appeared in 1790.

Bruce, Michael. b. at Kinnesswood, Kinross-shire, Scotland, March 27, 1746; d. there, July 5 or 6, 1767. A Scottish poet and schoolteacher. His *Poems* were published by John Logan in 1770.

Bruce, The. [Also, **The Brus.**] A poem (c1375) by John Barbour, on the subject of King Robert I (Robert the Bruce) of Scotland. It relates in more than 13,000 lines the story of the warfare between Robert and the English. Barbour described his work as a romance, but nevertheless intended the narrative to be taken as history and some critics believe that in many places authentic tradition has been embodied in the poem.

Bruin (brö'in). The bear in *Reynard the Fox.*

Bruin. In Samuel Foote's play *The Mayor of Garratt,* a rough, overbearing man. He is a contrast to the henpecked Jerry Sneak. Mrs. Bruin is roughly treated by him.

Brulgruddery (brul.grud'ẽr.i), **Dennis.** In the younger George Colman's comedy *John Bull,* an eccentric, whimsical Irishman, the host of the Red Cow.

Brumaire (brü.mer). The name adopted in 1793 by the National Convention of the first French Republic for the second month of the year. In the years 1, 2, 3, 5, 6, and 7 it began on Oct. 23, and ended on Nov. 20; in the years 4, 8, 9, 10, 11, 13, and 14 it began on Oct. 23, and ended on Nov. 21; and in the year 12 it began on Oct. 24, and ended on Nov. 22.

Brumaire, the 18th. In French history, Nov. 9, 1799, when the coup d'état by which the Directory was overthrown was commenced. It was completed on the 19th Brumaire.

Brummagem (brum'a.jem). A variant name of the city of Birmingham, England, which, from the large manufacture there of cheap metal articles and of coins, came to be used to mean something showy but cheap, or something counterfeit.

Brummell (brum'el), **George Bryan.** [Called **Beau Brummell.**] b. at London, June 7, 1778; d. at Caen, France, March 30, 1840. An English gentleman famous as a leader in the fashionable society of the early 19th century at London. He was an intimate friend of the prince regent (later George IV), who is said to have wept when Brummell, who was admired in his dress not as a fop but for his studied moderation, disapproved of one of his coats. Losses at the gaming table forced him to retire to Calais in 1816. In 1830 he was appointed consul at Caen; was imprisoned for debt in 1835, and after 1837 sank into a condition of imbecility, if not actual insanity, and died in an asylum.

Brunanburh (brun'an.bûrch). [Also: **Brunanburg;** full title, **The Battle of Brunanburh.**] An Old English poem of 73 lines describing the battle at Brunanburh, probably in Northumbria, in which King Athelstan defeated a Scandinavian king from Ireland, Anlaf, and his ally Constantine of Scotland. The poem, a song in praise of Athelstan and his brother Edmund, is inserted into the *Anglo-Saxon Chronicle.*

Brünhild (brün'hilt). [Also, **Brünnehilde** (brün-e.hil'de).] In the *Nibelungenlied,* a famous legendary queen of Island (Iceland), the wife of King Gunther, for whom she is won by Siegfried. She takes vengeance on Siegfried for the trick played on her by having him murdered. See also **Brynhild.**

Brunton (brun'ton), **Louisa.** b. 1779; d. 1860. An English actress. She married William Craven, 1st Earl of Craven, in 1807, when she left the stage. She was remarkable for her beauty and for her success in the leading roles of various comedies of the day.

Brunton, Mary. [Maiden name, **Balfour.**] b. at Barra, in the Orkney Islands, Nov. 1, 1778; d. at Edinburgh, Dec. 19, 1818. An English novelist. She wrote *Self Control* (1810) and *Discipline* (1814).

Brus (brös), **The.** See **Bruce, The.**

Brushwood Boy, The. A short story (published originally in December, 1895, in the *Century Magazine*) by Rudyard Kipling. It is now generally included on lists of Kipling's more outstanding efforts, and represents one of that author's relatively few ventures into the realm of the love story. It tells the story of a young man home on leave from India and of the girl to whom he is introduced by his mother. When she idly sings a song containing the refrain "We must go back with Policeman Day—Back from the City of Sleep!" he realizes that she is the girl who has been recurring in a series of very vivid dreams which he has been subject to since childhood (these dreams are unusual in a number of respects, not the least of which is that she grows up into young womanhood in them). It develops that she, too, has been subject to the dreams, and the two are very shortly deeply in love. The story provides an excellent portrait of Kipling's idea of young manhood, although the characterization of the girl has been held by some to be blurred by sentimentality.

Brut (bröt). A Middle English amplified paraphrase (c1205) by Layamon of Wace's Norman French *Roman de Brut*. Written in alliterative verse, with the frequent introduction of rhyme, it is the first long poem in Middle English with any claim to literary quality and also marks the first appearance of the Arthurian story in English. In 30,000 lines, it tells the story of Britain from its founding by a mythical Brutus, a descendant of Aeneas, down to the year 689. King Arthur and many of the stories that concern him, Lear, Cymbeline, and other legendary kings of Britain play a large part in the work.

Brute (bröt) or **Brutus** (brö′tus). The legendary first king of the Britons and founder of the British nation. According to Geoffrey of Monmouth he was the son of Silvius, the grandson of Ascanius and the great-grandson of Aeneas. After inadvertently killing his father, he went with a small band of Trojans to Britain and founded the city of Troynovant (New Troy), which was later to be London. He was the ancestor of the line of British kings including Bladud, Gorboduc, Ferrex, Porrex, Lud, and Cymbeline.

Brute, Sir John. In John Vanbrugh's comedy *The Provok'd Wife*, a drunken, roistering, rough fellow. He passes through every phase of riot and debauchery, and is unbearably insolent to his "provok'd wife," though too much of a coward to resent her consequent actions.

Brutus (brö′tus), **Decius.** In Shakespeare's *Julius Caesar*, one of the conspirators, who succeeds in bringing Caesar to the Capitol by interpreting Calpurnia's dreams in a hopeful fashion. This is probably the historical Decimus Junius Brutus, who was put to death by Antony in 43 B.C.

Brutus, Junius. In Shakespeare's *Coriolanus*, a tribune who, together with Sicinius, so arouses the Romans against Coriolanus that the latter is banished. Upon Coriolanus's return with the Volscian army, they deny responsibility and ask Menenius to stop his advance.

Brutus, Lucius Junius. fl. in the 6th century B.C. Roman consul in 509 B.C. According to unhistorical legend, he feigned idiocy (whence the name *Brutus*, stupid; probably an erroneous etymology) to avoid exciting the fear of his uncle Tarquin the Proud, who had put to death the elder brother of Brutus to possess himself of their wealth. Tarquin, alarmed at the prodigy of a serpent appearing in the royal palace, sent his sons Titus and Aruns to consult the oracle at Delphi. They took with them for amusement Brutus, who propitiated the priestess

with a hollow staff filled with gold. When the oracle, in response to an inquiry of Titus and Aruns as to who should succeed to the throne, replied, "He who first kisses his mother," Brutus stumbled to the ground and kissed mother earth. After the outrage on Lucretia, Brutus threw off his pretence of idiocy, expelled the Tarquins, and established (c510 B.C.) the republic. While consul he condemned his own sons Titus and Tiberius to death for having conspired to restore Tarquin. He led (c507) an army against Tarquin, who was returning to Rome. Brutus and Aruns fell in the battle, pierced by each other's spears.

Brutus, Marcus. In Shakespeare's *Julius Caesar*, the historical Marcus Junius Brutus, the chief assassin. The conspirators appeal to his love of Rome and its traditional freedoms in order to obtain his aid in their plot against Caesar as the embodiment of tyranny. When the deed is done, Brutus's presence calls forth the shocked "Et tu Brute, Then die Caesar" from the fallen Caesar. Brutus is a man of scrupulous honor, who may be said to meet his subsequent downfall because he is unable to understand the practical aspects of politics or war. In spite of Cassius's warning he permits Antony to make his inflammatory address to the people over Caesar's body; he nearly alienates Cassius by censuring his levy of funds from their supporters; and finally he loses the struggle with Antony and Octavius by choosing to fight on the plains of Philippi instead of withdrawing as Cassius advises. When the battle is lost, he kills himself.

Brutus, Marcus Junius. [Adoptive name, **Quintus Caepio Brutus**.] b. c85 B.C.; d. near Philippi, Macedonia, 42 B.C. A Roman politician and general, remembered as Caesar's chief assassin. Originally an adherent of Pompey, he went over to Caesar after the battle of Pharsalia in 48. He was governor of Cisalpine Gaul in 46, and *praetor urbanus* in 44. Induced by Cassius, he joined in the assassination of Caesar, on March 15, 44 B.C. He gathered troops in Macedonia, with which he joined Cassius in Asia Minor in 42, and defeated Octavianus in the first battle of Philippi in 42. Cassius was defeated by Antony and committed suicide, and Brutus defeated in a second battle 20 days later, and fell upon his sword. His (second) wife Portia, daughter of Cato Uticensis, on receiving news of his death, committed suicide by swallowing live coals.

Bryan (brī′ạn), **Sir Francis.** d. at Clonmel, Ireland, Feb. 2, 1550. An English poet, soldier, and diplomat. He went on missions to Rome and France in the service of Henry VIII. Some of his poetry appeared in *Tottel's Miscellany*. A cousin of Anne Boleyn, he was given the nickname "the vicar of hell" because of his acquiescence to her execution.

Bryant (brī′ạnt), **Arthur Wynne Morgan.** b. at Dersingham, England, Feb. 18, 1899—. An English historian and columnist. A lecturer (1925–26) at Oxford, he produced pageants at Cambridge, Oxford, Wisbech, and Greenwich. On the death of G. K. Chesterton, he took over (1936) the writing of the column "Our Note Book" in the *Illustrated London News*. He is the author of *King Charles II* (1931), *Samuel Pepys, the Man in the Making*

ḍ, d or j; ṣ, s or sh; ṭ, t or ch; ẓ, z or zh; o, F. cloche; ü, F. menu; ċh, Sc. loch; ṅ, F. bonbon.

(1933), *The National Character* (1934), *The American Ideal* (1936), *The Years of Endurance* (1942), *Years of Victory* (1944), and *The Age of Elegance* (1951).

Bryce (brīs), **James.** [Title, Viscount **Bryce of Dechmont.**] b. at Belfast, Ireland, May 10, 1838; d. at Sidmouth, Devonshire, England, Jan. 22, 1922. An English diplomat, statesman, historian, and professor. Educated at the universities of Glasgow, Oxford (Trinity College, B.A., 1862), and Heidelberg, he was elected a fellow (1862) of Oriel College, Oxford. He was called to the bar in 1867, and engaged in law practice until 1882, as well as being regius professor of civil law (1870–93) at Oxford. A Liberal member of Parliament (1880–1907), he became undersecretary of foreign affairs in 1886, chancellor of the duchy of Lancaster in 1892, president of the board of trade in 1894, and served as chief secretary for Ireland (1905–06). From 1907 to 1913 he was British ambassador to the U. S. Awarded the Order of Merit, in 1907, he was created a viscount in 1914. He was one of the founders of the League of Nations. Among his works are *Two Centuries of Irish History; 1691–1870* (1888), *Impressions of South Africa* (1897), *William Ewart Gladstone* (1898), *Studies in History and Jurisprudence* (1901), *Studies in Contemporary Biography* (1903), *Hindrances to Good Citizenship* (1909), *South American Observations and Impressions* (1912), *Essays and Addresses in War Time* (1918), *Modern Democracies* (1921), *International Relations* (1922), *The Study of American History* (1922), and *Memories of Travel* (1923). His best-known writings are *The Holy Roman Empire* (1862, originally a prize essay) and *The American Commonwealth* (1888), considered a classic in its field.

Bryce Snailsfoot (snālz'fút). See **Snailsfoot, Bryce.**

Brydges (brij'ęz), Sir **Samuel Egerton.** b. at Wooton House, Kent, England, Nov. 30, 1762; d. near Geneva, Switzerland, Sept. 8, 1837. An English lawyer, miscellaneous writer, and genealogist, a member of Parliament from 1812 to 1818. He was the author of poems, novels, *Censura Literaria* (1805–09), *British Bibliographer* (1810–14), *Res Literariae* (1821–22), *Autobiography* (1834), and others.

Brynhild (brin'hild). In the *Volsunga Saga*, one of the Valkyries; a daughter of Odin, by whom she was put into a fire-encircled sleep for her disobedience in giving victory to the wrong warrior. Sigurd passed through the flame and wakened her, and they became lovers. In the kingdom of the Nibelungs, Sigurd forgot Brynhild, married Gudrun, and, in Gunnar's guise, helped Gunnar, the king, win Brynhild for his wife. When Brynhild learned of the deception, she had Sigurd murdered and took her own life.

Bryskett (bris'kęt), **Lodowick** or **Lewis.** b. c1545; d. c1612. An English poet and translator; a friend of Sir Philip Sidney and Edmund Spenser. Educated at Cambridge (1559), he served as clerk of the council in Ireland (c1571), clerk of chancery (succeeded by Spenser, c1581), and in other Irish offices until 1600, and was reputedly the holder of large estates at Dublin, Cavan, and Cork. He

accompanied Sidney on a continental tour (1572–75), and studied Greek under Spenser (1582). His poems include two elegies contributed to Spenser's *Astrophel* (1586; published with *Colin Clout*). His chief original work was a translation from Baptista Giraldo's philosophical treatise, which he entitled *A Discourse of Civil Life* (published in 1606, written 20 years earlier).

Brython (brith'on). A name applied to themselves by the Celts of southern Britain who successfully resisted the Teutonic invaders in the mountainous regions of the western coast, and whose language, or languages, Brythonic, was subsequently found in Wales, Cumbria, and parts of Devon and Cornwall. The name is sometimes used interchangeably with Cymry (Cumbri).

Bubble (bub'l). In John Cooke's comedy *Greene's Tu Quoque, or The Citie Gallant* (published in 1614), a servant. He becomes rich and endeavors to deceive people into believing that he is a gentleman by using the affectations of society, particularly the phrase "tu quoque," which is ever in his mouth. The character was played by a favorite actor named Greene (hence the title of the play).

Buccaneers. A name applied originally to a gang of adventurers and pirates which, in the 17th century, attained an almost national importance in the West Indies and on the coasts of South America. It had its nucleus in the English, French, and Dutch smugglers who carried on a clandestine trade with the Spanish island of Santo Domingo (now Hispaniola); they hunted the wild cattle there, drying the meat over fires. Gradually they formed regular settlements, not only on Santo Domingo, but on many of the smaller islands. As they became stronger they began to prey on Spanish commerce. In 1630 they seized the island of Tortuga and made it their headquarters. In 1655 they aided the English in the conquest of Jamaica, and this became another center; and in 1664 they settled the Bahamas. Under their leader Sir Henry Morgan, they ravaged the coasts of the Gulf of Mexico and the Caribbean Sea, and made expeditions inland; Portobelo was sacked; in 1671 Morgan crossed the isthmus and burned Panama, and from that year to 1685 the Buccaneers practically commanded the West Indian seas. Their immense spoils were divided equally, only the captain of a ship taking a larger share; French, Dutch, English, and Germans were banded together, their only bond being a common interest in spoils and a deep hatred of the Spaniards. In 1680 they again crossed the isthmus, seized some Spanish ships in the Pacific, and for several years raided the western coasts of Mexico, Peru, and Chile. After 1690 the war between France and England tended to separate the pirates of these two nations, and the impoverished coasts could no longer support their depredations. They gradually returned to the West Indies and Europe, and were drawn into the armies and navies of different powers.

Bucentaur (bū.sen'tôr). The state ship of the Venetian Republic, used in the annual ceremony of wedding the Adriatic, which was enjoined upon the Venetians by Pope Alexander III to commemorate the victory of the Venetians under Doge Sebastiano Ziani over the fleet of Frederick Barbarossa, in the 12th century. On Ascension day of each year a ring was dropped from the *Bucentaur* into the Adriatic, with the words "We espouse thee, Sea, in token of true and lasting dominion." The ceremony was attended by the entire diplomatic corps. The ship perhaps took her name from the figure of a bucentaur (head of a man and body of a bull) in her bows. Three of the name were built. The last was destroyed by the French in 1798.

Bucephalus (bū.sef′ạ.lus). The favorite horse of Alexander the Great which, after accompanying its master through his principal campaigns, died (326 B.C.) at the age of 30. Alexander buried the horse with great pomp on the banks of the Hydaspes River (now the Jhelum), in India, and built at the site the city of Bucephala, traces of which exist across the river from the modern town of Jhelum, in Pakistan.

Buchan (buk′ạn, buċh′-), **Sir John.** [Title, 1st Baron **Tweedsmuir.**] b. at Perth, Scotland, Aug. 26, 1875; d. at Montreal, Canada, Feb. 11, 1940. A Scottish government official, novelist, essayist, biographer, and historian. Educated at Glasgow University and at Brasenose College, Oxford, he was called to the bar in 1901. During World War I, he served (1915) in France as a war correspondent, was a member (1916–17) of the British headquarters staff in France, and served (1917 *et seq.*) with the British information department. After serving (1927–35) as a member of Parliament for the Scottish universities, he was governor-general of Canada (1935–40). He was the author of *John Burnet of Barns* (1898), *A Lodge in the Wilderness* (1906), *Prester John* (1910), *Salute to Adventurers* (1915), *The 39 Steps* (1915), *Greenmantle* (1916), *The Path of the King* (1921), *The Three Hostages* (1924), *The Blanket of the Dark* (1931), *The Gap in the Curtain* (1932), and many other adventure novels and tales, several of which have for their hero Richard Hannay. He wrote biographies of Sir Walter Raleigh (1911), Lord Minto (1924), Julius Caesar (1932), Sir Walter Scott (1932), and Oliver Cromwell (1934). Author also of histories of Brasenose College (1898), the battle of Jutland (1917), the battle of the Somme (1917), South African forces in France (1920), World War I (4 vols., 1921–22), the British Empire in World War I (1923), and others, of volumes of essays (1896, 1908, 1935), of *Poems—Scots and English* (1917), and of the autobiographical *Pilgrim's Way* (1940).

Buchan, Peter. b. at Peterhead, Aberdeenshire, Scotland, 1790; d. at London, Sept. 19, 1854. A Scottish poet, printer, dramatist, and collector and publisher of ballads. He opened a printing office (1816) at Peterhead, having learned the technique of printing in ten days, and devised (1819) a press worked by foot to take the place of the hand press. He collected and published *Ancient Ballads and Songs of the North of Scotland* (2 vols., 1828), containing many ballads never before printed and new versions of previously published ones, and also compiled *Scottish Traditional Versions of Ancient Ballads* (1845), which was published by the Percy Society. At his death he left two volumes of unpublished ballad material, now housed in the British Museum. He was the author also of *The Recreation of Leisure Hours, being Songs and Verses in the Scottish Dialect* (1814), *Annals of Peterhead* (1819), *Treatise proving that Brutes have Souls and are Immortal* (1824), *The Peterhead Smugglers of the Last Century, or William and Annie* (1834, a three-act melodrama), *Account of the Chivalry of the Ancients* (1840), and other works, many of them printed on his own Peterhead press.

Buchanan (bū.kan′ạn, bu-), **Dugald.** [Called the "Cowper of the Highlands."] b. at Ardoch, Balquhidder Parish, Perthshire, Scotland, 1716; d. at Rannoch, Perthshire, Scotland, July 2, 1768. A Scottish Gaelic schoolmaster, preacher, hymnist, and religious poet. He taught school in his native parish, and was schoolmaster and preacher (1755 *et seq.*) at Kinloch Rannoch in Fortingale. He was the author of *Spiritual Hymns* (1767), Gaelic poems, of which "The Day of Judgment," "The Skull," "The Dream," and "The Winter" are considered among his best. His poetry has been translated into English by various authors.

Buchanan, George. b. at Killearn, Stirlingshire, Scotland, in February, 1506; d. at Edinburgh, Sept. 29, 1582. A Scottish historian and scholar; tutor (1570) of James VI of Scotland. He taught at Bordeaux (1540–43), Paris (1544–47), and St. Andrews (1566–70). In 1571 he published *Detectio Mariae Reginae*, a violent attack on Mary, Queen of Scots, whom he held responsible for the murder of Darnley. Among his other works are *De jure regni apud Scotos* (1579), *Rerum Scoticarum historia* (1582), a version of the Psalms, translations of the *Medea* and *Alcestis*, and the dramas *Baptistes*, and *Jephthes.*

Buchanan, Robert Williams. b. at Caverswall, Staffordshire, England, Aug. 18, 1841; d. at Streatham, London, June 10, 1901. A Scottish poet, dramatist, and novelist. Educated at the University of Glasgow, he went to London at the age of 19, and wrote for the *Athenaeum*, *All the Year Round*, and other journals. He coined the phrase "the fleshly school of poetry," which he used as the title of an article (in the *Contemporary Review*, 1871), attacking Swinburne, Rossetti, and the Pre-Raphaelite leaders. The controversy lasted for ten years (1866–76); he sued Swinburne, and won, but later dedicated one of his novels, *God and the Man* (1881), to Rossetti. He was the author of *Undertones* (1863), *London Poems* (1866), *North Coast* (1867), *White Rose and Red* (1873), *Balder the Beautiful* (1877), *Ballads of Life, Love, and Humor* (1882), and other books of poetry. His novels include *The Shadow of the Sword* (1876), *A Child of Nature* (1881), and *Father Anthony* (1898). *A Nine Days' Queen* (1880), *Lady Clare* (1883), *Storm-Beaten* (1883), *Alone in London* (1884; with his sister-in-law, Harriet Jay), *A Man's Shadow* (1889), *The Charlatan* (1894), and *The Strange Adventures of Miss Brown* (1895) are all plays. He also dramatized Henry Fielding's *Tom Jones* as *Sophia* (1886), and the same author's *Joseph Andrews* as *Joseph's Sweetheart* (1888).

Bucket (buk′ęt), **Mr. Inspector.** In Charles Dickens's *Bleak House*, a detective officer. A character of great affability, but sagacious and extraordinarily persevering in carrying out his duties, he is said to have been based on Inspector Field of the London police force, whom Dickens knew well.

ḍ, d or j; ṣ, s or sh; ṭ, t or ch; ẓ, z or zh; o, F. cloche; ü, F. menu; ċh, Sc. loch; ṅ, F. bonbon.

Buckhurst (buk'herst), **Baron.** A title of **Sackville, Charles,** and of **Sackville, Thomas.**

Buckingham (buk'ing.am, -ham), **1st Duke of.** [Title of **George Villiers.**] b. in Leicestershire, England, Aug. 28, 1592; assassinated at Portsmouth, England, Aug. 23, 1628. An English nobleman, close adviser to James I and Charles I, noted in English history for unstable and impulsive policies that led to continual trouble with Parliament, with France and Spain, and to various military and naval disasters. James I was early attracted to Villiers by the youth's good looks. Created (1616) Baron Villiers, he was appointed (1617) lord high admiral. Urged James to defend Frederick, elector Palatine; later reversed this policy and made overtures to Spain's Gondomar; involved in an unpleasantness over monopolies; defended Bacon; accused by Hugh Spencer of threatening Spencer in order to force him to uphold certain monopolies; but remained a close friend of the king; failed (1623) in his attempt to marry Charles to Maria of Spain; created (1623) Duke of Buckingham; urged James to make war on Spain, and was upheld by Parliament; to demonstrate to the world his power in the court, he ordered the impeachment of Middlesex; unable to prosecute the war because of lack of funds; an expedition (1625) under Mansfield to the Palatinate failed; alienated the French by his unseemly behavior at court; and another expedition (1625) to Cadiz under Sir Edward Cecil failed. Charged (1625) with neglect, the first time since the reign of the Lancasters that the House had held an officer responsible for his actions; but Charles raised him to higher honors. All Buckingham's schemes for carrying on the war against France and Spain failed, and Parliament drew up a final remonstrance, but Charles stood by his courtier. While attempting to negotiate with Charles Portsmouth over raising the siege of the Protestants on the island of Rochelle, he was assassinated (1628) by John Felton.

Buckingham, 2nd Duke of. [Title of **George Villiers.**] b. at London, Jan. 30, 1627; d. at Kirkby Moorside, Yorkshire, England, April 17, 1688. An English politician, courtier, and writer; son of the 1st Duke of Buckingham. He was a privy councilor (1662–67), and organized the "Cabal" in 1670. His collected works were published in 1704.

Buckingham, (1st) **Duke of.** In Shakespeare's *2 Henry VI,* the historical Humphrey Stafford, one of the nobles who cause Gloucester's downfall. He persuades the followers of the rebel, Jack Cade, to disperse and later supports Henry in the war with the Yorkists. In *3 Henry VI,* his death is reported at the battle of St. Albans (1455); Shakespeare was actually compressing history to fit his play, since the historical personage was killed at Northampton in 1460.

Buckingham, (2nd) **Duke of.** In Shakespeare's *Richard III,* the historical Henry Stafford, the accomplice of Richard (Gloucester) in his conspiracy and crime. Buckingham arrests the relatives of Edward IV's widow (Rivers, Grey, and Dorset), and then helps to betray the unsuspecting Hastings on a trumped-up charge of conspiring in witchcraft against Richard. He then stages for the citizens of London the spectacle of Richard studying piously in the company of clergymen and refusing the kingship which Buckingham would thrust upon him. This obtains the throne for Richard, but Richard further demands that he kill the two sons of Edward IV. At this Buckingham at last has scruples, and thus becomes useless to Richard. His request for some property is refused by Richard, and he goes with foreboding to join Richmond's army, but is put to death before reaching it. His ghost appears to Richard on the night before the battle at Bosworth warning him of impending doom.

Buckingham, (3rd) **Duke of.** In Shakespeare's *Henry VIII,* the historical Edward Stafford, son of the Buckingham who was executed by Richard III. He is an enemy of Wolsey, whom he sees as dangerous to England. Arrested by Wolsey on a charge of threatening Henry's life, he defends himself at the place of execution (in a speech probably written by Fletcher).

Buckingham, James Silk. b. at Flushing, near Falmouth, England, Aug. 25, 1786; d. at London, June 30, 1855. An English traveler and man of letters. He wrote *Travels in Palestine* (1822), *Travels in Mesopotamia* (1827), *Travels in Assyria, Media, and Persia* (1829), and others.

Buckingham and Normanby (nôr'man.bi), **1st Duke of.** A title of **Sheffield, John.**

Buckingham Palace. The London residence of the British sovereign, situated at the W end of St. James's Park. It was settled by act of Parliament in 1775 upon Queen Charlotte, and was hence first known as the "queen's house." It was remodeled under George IV; the eastern façade, ballroom, and some other portions were added by Queen Victoria, who began to occupy it in 1837, since which time it has served as the official royal residence at London. The chief façade, which was added in 1847, is ab. 360 ft. long. The state apartments are magnificently adorned and furnished, the grand staircase, the throne room, and the state ballroom being especially notable. There is a collection of French buhl and other furniture, and the picture gallery contains a number of old and modern masterpieces. No permanent damage was sustained by the building during World War II.

Buckland (buk'land), **Francis Trevelyan.** b. at Oxford, England, Dec. 17, 1826; d. at London, Dec. 19, 1880. An English naturalist, noted for researches in fish culture. He wrote *Curiosities of Natural History* (1857), *Natural History of British Fishes* (1881), and others.

Bucklaw (buk'lô), **Laird of.** In Sir Walter Scott's novel *The Bride of Lammermoor,* Frank Hayston, the dissipated but good-natured suitor of Lucy Ashton. He is married to her by her mother's machinations.

Buckle (buk'l), **George Earle.** b. at Tiverton-on-Avon, near Bath, England, June 10, 1854; d. at London, March 12, 1935. A British editor and biographer. He was editor (1884–1912) of the London *Times.* He wrote volumes three to six (1914–20) of *Life of Disraeli,* a continuation of the two volumes published (1910–12) by W. F. Moneypenny, and edited a three-volume collection of

---

fat, fāte, fär, ȧsk, fāre; net, mē, hèr; pin, pīne; not, nōte, mȯve, nôr; up, lūte, pṳll; ŦH, then;

letters (1862–95), upon the authority of King George V, of Queen Victoria.

Buckle, Henry Thomas. b. at Lee, Kent, England, Nov. 24, 1821; d. at Damascus, Syria, May 29, 1862. An English historian. His health in early youth was delicate, on which account he was educated at home, chiefly by his mother. In 1840, on the death of his father, a wealthy shipowner at London, he inherited an ample fortune which enabled him to devote himself wholly to literary pursuits. In 1857 he published the first volume of his *History of Civilization in England.* The appearance of this volume, which is characterized by vigor of style and boldness of thought, produced a sensation in Europe and America, and raised the author from obscurity to fame. The special doctrine which it sought to uphold was that climate, soil, food, and the aspects of nature are the determining factors in intellectual progress. A second volume, considered by some critics inferior in execution and interest, appeared in 1861.

Buckstone (buk′stọn), **John Baldwin.** b. at Hoxton, London, Sept. 14, 1802; d. at Sydenham, London, Oct. 31, 1879. An English comedian and dramatist. Among his 200 melodramas and farces are *Married Life* (1834), *Single Life* (1839), and *The Flowers of the Forest* (1847).

bucolic (bū.kol′ik). A pastoral poem, representing rural affairs, or the life, manners, and occupation of shepherds, as the bucolics of Theocritus and Vergil. "The first modern Latin bucolics are those of Petrarch." (Thomas Warton, *History of English Poetry.*)

Bucolic Comedies. A volume of poems by Edith Sitwell, published in 1923.

Bud (bud), **Miss Rosa.** [Called **Rosebud.**] In Charles Dickens's *The Mystery of Edwin Drood,* an extremely pretty young lady, an orphan under the guardianship of Mr. Grewgious. A close friendship between their respective fathers has led to her betrothal, at a very tender age, to Edwin, but the two decide in later years to break off an engagement which was not of their wishing and to be thereafter as "brother and sister" to each other. Drood disappears soon afterward and is presumed to have been murdered. Many readers consider that, if Dickens had lived to complete the story, Rosa would have married Mr. Tartar.

Buddha (būd′ạ, bō′dạ). [Family name, **Gautama** or (in Pali) **Gotama;** hence also, **Gautama** (or **Gotama**) **Buddha;** called also at various times, **Siddhartha** (or **Siddharta**), **Sakyamuni, Tathagata.**] b. at Kapilavastu (in what is now the S part of Nepal, India), c563 B.C.; d. at Kusinagara (also in what is now Nepal), c483 B.C. An Indian philosopher and religious leader, founder of Buddhism. The various facts relating to his life are now so heavily encrusted with legend that it is possible to ascertain only approximately even such points as the dates of his birth and death: he is generally assumed to have died when he was 80 years old, and from a 4th-century Pali chronicle of the Indian kings which gives 218 years as the period intervening between the time of his death and the year when Asoka mounted the throne (a known date in history), recent scholars are in fairly general agreement on 483 B.C., or thereabouts, as the year of his death. From this, if he lived to the age of 80, 563 B.C. may be inferred as the year of his birth. However, it should be remembered that these dates are, at best, only informed guesses, and that various other dates have been and will continue to be advanced (for example, the Buddhist scholars of Ceylon reckon 544 B.C. as the date of Buddha's death). In the matter of Buddha's names there is also some degree of confusion: the name "Buddha" means, in Sanskrit, the "Enlightened," and was acquired only after Buddha had attained enlightenment under the famous Bo Tree in the village of Buddh Gaya, about 7 mi. S of the city of Gaya, in what is now the NE part of the Union of India. Prior to this enlightenment he was, in the terminology of Buddhist philosophy, simply a Bodhisattva, or potential Buddha; in the fashion in which names are most commonly used in the West, he would have been called Prince Gautama (or Gotama), of the Sakya clan. He is also called Sakyamuni (which means "sage of the Sakyas"), Siddhartha or Siddharta (which means "he who has accomplished his purpose"), and Tathagata (which means "he who has arrived at the truth" or the "Perfect One"). His father was the ruler of the Sakyas, but in the sense in which the word "king" is now most generally used he was perhaps more of a great and wealthy landowner than a king. Buddha's early years were spent at his father's "court" in circumstances which were, for that age and place, opulent indeed, and was married at the age of 16. At the age of 29, in accordance with a prophecy which had been made at the time of his conception, he saw an old man, a sick man, and a corpse, and realized for the first time that age, illness, and death were a part of life. It was this realization which led him to forsake his family and wife, and to seek truth, and truth alone, as a recluse (according to most accounts, it was because of his knowledge of this prophecy, and his desire that it should not come to pass, that Buddha's father reared him in sheltered and luxurious circumstances). Some six (or seven) years later, under the Bo Tree (which is the pipal, or sacred fig tree, of India, and except for this particular tree, not spelled, of course, with capital letters) at Buddh Gaya, he attained the perfect enlightenment which made him "the Buddha." For 49 (or 28) days thereafter he underwent various temptations, the most important of which was perhaps whether selfishly to keep for himself the great knowledge he had attained, or to share it. However, love triumphed, and for the rest of his life he sought to open the path to enlightenment for as many people as he could reach by his preaching (for some 44 years he preached in the area of Benares and Bihar). He formed an order of monks, and subsequently of nuns, and won the adherence of Ananda (who may be called, in a sense, the Saint John of Buddhism). He is said to have died of an illness contracted by eating spoiled, or improperly prepared, pork, and actually to have passed away in the arms of his devoted follower Ananda.

Budgell (buj′ẹl), **Eustace.** b. at St. Thomas, near Exeter, England, Aug. 19, 1686; committed suicide by drowning in the Thames, near London, May 4,

1737. An English miscellaneous writer. He was called to the bar, but his association with his cousin Joseph Addison induced him to turn his attention to literature. He contributed 37 papers to the *Spectator* in Addison's style. He wrote many pamphlets of a political nature, and in 1733 started *The Bee*, a weekly periodical which ran for about two years. He filled a number of positions after the accession of George I, when Addison became secretary to the lord lieutenant of Ireland, being at various times chief secretary to the lords justices, deputy clerk of the council, accountant-general, and a member of the Irish House of Commons. He fell into money difficulties, and after a scandal, connected with the disappearance of some bonds belonging to the estate of Matthew Tindal, he took his own life. He left a natural daughter, Anne Eustace, who became an actress.

Buffle (buf′l), **Sir Raffle.** In various of the works of Anthony Trollope, but most prominently in *The Small House at Allington* and *The Last Chronicle of Barset,* a pompous government official. His resemblance to an actual official of the British government evoked Trollope's assurance in his autobiography that he had "never seen the man with whom I am supposed to have taken the liberty."

Buffone (bö.fō′nä), **Carlo.** In Ben Jonson's *Every Man Out of His Humour,* an impudent, gluttonous jester. He is identified by some critics with John Marston; others think he was meant for Thomas Dekker.

Bugbears, The. An English comedy (c1565) of unknown authorship, based on Grazzini's *La Spiritata.*

Buik of Alexander, The. See **Alexander, The Buik of.**

Builder of Bridges, The. A four-act play (1909) by Alfred Sutro.

Bulbeck (bul′bek), **Lord.** See **Vere, Edward de.**

Bulgarian Horrors and the Question of the East, The. A prose work (1876) by William Ewart Gladstone, published in pamphlet form. It very eloquently fanned the indignation engendered at the time in England by the Turkish treatment of their subject Christian populations in the Balkans.

Bull (bul), **John.** b. in Somersetshire, England, 1563; d. at Antwerp, March 12, 1628. An English composer and organist. The song *God Save the King* was wrongly attributed to him. He became (1591) organist of the chapel royal, and was named (1596) professor of music at Gresham College. Having left England in 1613, he was organist (1617–28) of Antwerp Cathedral.

Bull, John. See also **John Bull.**

Bullcalf (bul′kaf), **Peter.** In Shakespeare's *2 Henry IV,* a recruit.

Bullein (bul′in), **William.** d. 1576. An English writer, author of *Dialogue against the Fever Pestilence* (1564–65).

Bullen (bul′en), **Anne.** In Shakespeare's *Henry VIII,* the historical Anne Boleyn, second wife of the King and former lady-in-waiting of Katherine, his first wife. Wolsey's downfall is brought about by the discovery of his plan to prevent the King from divorcing Katherine and marrying Anne. She is the mother of Elizabeth.

Bullen, Arthur Henry. b. at London, Feb. 9, 1857; d. at Stratford-on-Avon, England, Feb. 29, 1920. An English literary critic, scholar, biographer, editor, and poet. Educated at the City of London School and at Worcester College, Oxford, he contributed many articles to the *Dictionary of National Biography,* and founded the "Muses' Library" and the Shakespeare Head Press at Stratford, from which he published his "Stratford Town Shakespeare" in ten volumes. He was the author of *Weeping Cross* (1921), and *Elizabethans* (1924), essays, and edited the works (1881) of John Day, *Old English Plays* (1882–84), *Poems of Michael Drayton* (1883), *Carols and Poems from the 15th Century* (1884), *Lyrics from Elizabethan Song Books* (1886), the works of Thomas Campion (1889), *Speculum Amantis: Love Poems of the 17th Century* (1902), and other works. His edition of Campion, considered a major contribution to literary scholarship, was a virtual rediscovery of the genius of that poet.

Bullet (bul′et), **Gerald.** b. at London, Dec. 30, 1893—. An English fiction writer, anthologist, and critic. His works include *The Baker's Cart* (1925), *Modern English Fiction* (1926), *Helen's Lovers* (1932), *Eden River* (1934), *Judgment in Suspense* (1946), and *George Eliot, Her Life and Books* (1947).

Bullokar (bul′ọ.kär), **William.** fl. 1586. An English educator and phonetist who translated (1585) *Aesop's Fables* from Latin. Service in the army (1557) called him away from teaching (1550–57), but after an interim of study of law and agriculture, he returned (1573) to it. He advocated spelling reform (the addition of 14 letters to the alphabet) in a pamphlet (1575), and in a book (1580), and issued an English grammar, *Bref Grammar* (1586), which was called by Warton "the first grammar that ever waz, except . . . *Grammar at Large.*"

Bulls and Bears. A farce by Colley Cibber, produced in 1715.

Bulmer (bul′mėr), **Valentine.** In Sir Walter Scott's novel *St. Ronan's Well,* the titular Earl of Hetherington. He substitutes himself for his supposed bastard brother Francis Tyrrel, the real earl, in a clandestine marriage with Clara Mowbray, and later endeavors to rob Tyrrel of the proofs of the latter's right to his title.

Bulstrode (bul′strōd), **Mr.** In George Eliot's novel *Middlemarch,* a rich and powerful man, who pretends to an attitude of devout Christian goodness.

Bulstrode, Sir Richard. b. 1610; d. at St.-Germain, France, Oct. 3, 1711. An English Royalist soldier, diplomat, poet, and historical writer, knighted (1675) by Charles II of England. He was the author of a poem (written and published while he was a student at Pembroke College, Cambridge) on the birth of the duke of York, and of the posthumously published *Original Letters Written to the Earl of Arlington* (1712, written in 1674), *Life of James II* (1712), *Essays* (1715), and *Memoirs and Reflections upon the Reign and Government of King Charles I and King Charles II . . . wherein the Character of the Royal Martyr and of Charles II are Vindicated*

---

fat, fāte, fär, ȧsk, fāre; net, mē, hėr; pin, pīne; not, nōte, mōve, nôr; up, lūte, pûll; ᴛʜ, then;

from Fanatical Aspersions (1721). After passing his 80th birthday he wrote 185 Latin poems, some of which are included in the *Letters*.

Bultitude (bul′ti.tūd), **Mr.** In T. A. Guthrie's *Vice Versa*, a man who is magically transformed into the physical form of his son (Dick Bultitude).

Bulwer-Lytton (bŭl′wer.lit′on), **Edward George Earle Lytton.** [Title, 1st Baron **Lytton of Kneb-worth.**] b. at London, May 25, 1803; d. at Torquay, England, Jan. 18, 1873. An English novelist, poet, dramatist, politician, and orator. He graduated at Cambridge (B.A., 1826), served as member of Parliament (1831–41, 1852–66), was colonial secretary (1858–59), and was raised to the peerage in 1866. He wrote *Falkland* (1827), *Pelham, or the Adventures of a Gentleman* (1828), *The Disowned* (1829), *Devereux* (1829), *Paul Clifford* (1830), *Eugene Aram* (1832), *Godolphin* (1833), *England and the English* (1833), *Pilgrims of the Rhine* (1834), *The Last Days of Pompeii* (1834), *Rienzi* (1835), *The Student and The Crisis* (1835), *Ernest Maltravers* (1837), *Athens, its Rise and Fall* (1837), *Alice, or the Mysteries* (1838), *Leila* (1838), *Night and Morning* (1841), *Zanoni* (1842), *Last of the Barons* (1843), *Lucretia, or the Children of the Night* (1846), *Harold* (1848), *The Caxtons* (1850), *My Novel, or Varieties of English Life* (1853), *What will He do with it?* (1858), *A Strange Story* (1861), *Caxtoniana* (1863), *The Coming Race* (1871), *Kenelm Chillingly* (1873), *The Parisians* (1873), and *Pausanias*, an unfinished romance, edited by his son (1876). Among his poems are *Poems and Ballads of Schiller* (translation, 1844), *The New Timon* (1847), *King Arthur* (1849), *St. Stephens* (1860), *Lost Tales of Miletus* (1866), and a translation of Horace's *Odes* (1869). Among his dramas are *The Lady of Lyons* (1838), *Richelieu* (1839), *Money* (1840), *Cromwell* (1842), *Not so Bad as we Seem* (1852), and *The Rightful Heir* (1869).

Bulwer-Lytton, Edward Robert Lytton. See **Meredith, Owen.**

Bumble (bum′bl). In Charles Dickens's *Oliver Twist*, a fat and officious beadle. From his arrogant self-importance and magnifying of his parochial office the word "bumbledom" has come to have a place in the language.

Bumper (bum′pėr), **Sir Harry.** A character in Richard Brinsley Sheridan's *The School for Scandal.*

Bunce (buns), **John.** A pirate in Sir Walter Scott's novel *The Pirate.*

Bunch (bunch), **Barnaby.** In John Webster's play *The Weakest Goeth to the Wall*, a comic character, an English botcher, or mender of old clothes.

Bunch, Mother. In Thomas Dekker's *Satiromastix*, a derisive name given by Tucca to Mistress Miniver, an alewife. The name was used for the hypothetical author of various books of jests in 1604 and 1760, and for *Mother Bunch's Fairy Tales.*

Buncle (bung′kl), **John.** The chief character in Thomas Amory's novel *Life of John Buncle, Esq.*

Bungay (bung′gā), **Mr.** In Thackeray's novel *Pendennis*, a publisher, formerly a partner in Bacon & Bungay.

Bungay, Thomas. [Called **Friar Bungay.**] fl. c1290. An English Franciscan monk, who lectured at Oxford and Cambridge. He was popularly supposed to have been a magician, and figures as such in later literature. In Robert Greene's play *The Honourable History of Friar Bacon and Friar Bungay* (1592), the character is based on that presented in an anecdotal pamphlet of the day which contains legends about Roger Bacon and Thomas Bungay; in both of these he appears as Bacon's assistant in necromancy. Edward Bulwer-Lytton introduces a character based on Bungay in his novel *The Last of the Barons.*

Bungay & Bacon (bā′kon). See **Bacon & Bungay.**

Bunsby (bunz′bi), **Captain John.** In Dickens's *Dombey and Son*, a good friend and boon companion of Captain Cuttle.

Bunthorne (bun′thôrn). In Gilbert and Sullivan's opera *Patience*, an extremely commonplace youth who adopts the most extravagantly esthetic and lackadaisical style. The character was intended to satirize Oscar Wilde and his followers.

Bunthorne, Edna. In H. G. Wells's novel *The War in the Air*, the sweetheart, and eventually the wife, of the hero, Albert Peter ("Bert") Smallways.

Bunyan (bun′yan), **John.** b. at Elstow, near Bedford, England, baptized Nov. 30, 1628; d. at London, Aug. 31, 1688. An English writer and preacher. The son of a tinker, he received a meager education. He adopted his father's trade, served as a soldier in the parliamentary army from 1644 to 1646, and married in 1648 or 1649. In 1653 he joined a nonconformist body at Bedford, settling there c1655. He was appointed a preacher by his coreligionists in 1657, and as such traveled throughout all the midland counties. As a Puritan he led the resistance of dissenters against the Stuart effort to compel uniformity of worship and religious opinion, braving a long imprisonment as "a common upholder of unlawful meetings and conventicles" rather than compromise his spiritual liberty. He was arrested in 1660 near Bedford, under the statutes against nonconformists, and, except for a brief interval in 1666, was detained in prison at Bedford until 1672, when those statutes were suspended by Charles II. In these 12 years he wrote many of his books, and also studied the Bible and Foxe's *Book of Martyrs* intensely. He was licensed (May 9, 1672) to preach by the Crown, and during the remainder of his life was pastor of the nonconformist congregation at Bedford. In 1675 he was again imprisoned for a few months, and during this imprisonment he wrote his celebrated allegory *Pilgrim's Progress*, which appeared in 1678. This book, more widely read for over 200 years than any other except the Bible, is a picture of "the practick part of religion." Its second part ("safe arrival at the desired country"), written later, appeared in 1684. Among his other published and unpublished writings, over 40 in number, are *Some Gospel Truths Opened* (1656), in which Bunyan takes his stand on the literal interpretation of the gospels, as against the mystical approach of the Quakers, *Grace Abounding* (1666), self-portrait of a distracted and divided soul, the battleground of scruples versus tastes, *The Holy City, or the New Jerusalem* (1666), *A Confession of my Faith, and a Reason of my Practice* (1671), *The Life and Death*

ḍ, d or j; ṣ, s or sh; ṭ, t or ch; ẓ, z or zh; o, F. cloche; ü, F. menu; ċh, Sc. loch; ṅ, F. bonbon.

of Mr. Badman (1680), and *The Holy War* (1682), called by Thomas Babington Macaulay "the greatest allegory in the language if Pilgrim's Progress had not been written." One poem from his pen is remembered, which extols the steadfastness, "come wind, come weather," of a valiant pilgrim.

Burbage (bėr'bāj), **James.** d. 1597. An English actor, and the first builder of a theater in England; father of Richard Burbage. He was originally a joiner. In the period 1576–77 he erected the first English building specially intended for plays. It was "between Finsbury Fields and the public road from Bishopsgate and Shoreditch," in what is now part of London. It was of wood, and was called "The Theatre." The material was removed to the Bankside in 1598 and was rebuilt as the Globe Theatre. The Curtain Theatre was put up near The Theatre soon after the latter was opened, and Burbage was instrumental in the conversion of a large house at Blackfriars into Blackfriars Theatre, probably in November, 1596.

Burbage, Richard. b. c1567; d. 1619. An English actor; son of James Burbage. He made his fame at the Blackfriars and Globe theaters of which, with his brother and sister, he was proprietor, and played the leading parts in all the best plays produced at the time. Shakespeare was a member of the Lord Chamberlain's Company, playing at Blackfriars at the same time, and had some part in the profit of the house, as also a little later in the Globe; but Burbage apparently had the lion's share. There is no authentic account of any intimacy with Shakespeare till after 1594. Burbage seems to have been the original Hamlet, Lear, and Othello. He excelled in tragedy, and was held in the very highest esteem by authors and public; he was even sometimes introduced into plays in his own proper person. Many poems and tributes were written in his memory. Besides his fame as an actor he was known as a painter. In 1613, when the Globe theater burned down, he narrowly escaped with his life.

Burbon (bėr'bọn). In Edmund Spenser's *Faerie Queene*, a knight, representing Henry IV of France. He is assailed by a mob, but escapes and also rescues his mistress.

Burchell (bėr'chel), **Mr.** In Oliver Goldsmith's novel *The Vicar of Wakefield*, the name under which Sir William Thornhill dispenses joys and sorrows as a being from another sphere.

Burgh (bėrg), **Hubert de.** See **Hubert de Burgh.**

Burgh (bur'ọ), **James.** b. at Madderty, Perthshire, Scotland, 1714; d. Aug. 26, 1775. A Scottish miscellaneous writer. He wrote *Britain's Remembrancer* (1745), *Dignity of Human Nature* (1754), and others.

Burghley (bėr'li), 1st Baron. Title of **Cecil, William.**

Burgin (bėr'jin), **George Brown.** b. 1856; d. in June, 1944. An English novelist and writer of memoirs. He was the author of the novels *Gascoigne's Ghost* (1896), *Fortune's Footballs* (1897), *Tomalyn's Quest* (1897), *Shutters of Silence, the Romance of a Trappist* (1908), *Slaves of Allah* (1909), *The King of Four Corners* (1910), *The Girl Who Got Out* (1916), *The Throw-Back* (1918),

A Gentle Despot (1919), *A Rubber Princess* (1919), *The Young Lobell* (1924), and *The Lord of Little Laughton, A Modern Romance* (1925). He also wrote the autobiographical *Memoirs of a Clubman* (1921), *Many Memories* (1922), *More Memoirs and Some Travels* (1922), and *Some More Memoirs* (1925).

Burgoyne (bėr.goin'), **John.** b. 1722; d. at London, June 4, 1792. An English lieutenant general and dramatist. He commanded the British army which invaded New York in 1777, was defeated at Stillwater, on Sept. 19 and Oct. 7, 1777, and surrendered with 5,791 troops to Horatio Gates at Saratoga, on Oct. 17, 1777. In 1782 he was made commander in chief in Ireland, and in 1787 was one of the managers of the impeachment of Warren Hastings. He wrote satires directed against the administration of the elder William Pitt (the greater part of *Westminster Guide*), *The Lord of the Manor* (1780, the libretto of a comic opera), *The Heiress* (1786, a comedy which was very successful), and others.

Burgundy (bėr'gun.di), **Duke of.** In Shakespeare's *Henry V*, the French noble who arranges the terms of peace between the French and English. In a long, elaborate speech (V.ii) he compares war-torn France to a dying and uncared-for garden. In *1 Henry VI*, he fights at first on the English side but, in a speech much like his own in *Henry V*, Joan of Arc persuades him to return to the French (III.iii).

Burgundy, Duke of. In Shakespeare's *King Lear*, a rival of the King of France for the hand of Cordelia. He refuses to marry her when she is left without a dowry.

Burial of Sir John Moore. A poem (1816) by Charles Wolfe, published in a collection of his works in 1825.

Burial of the Dead. The first of five sections of T. S. Eliot's long poem *The Waste Land* (1922). The line "Those were pearls that were his eyes" is from Ariel's song in Shakespeare's *Tempest*, which foreshadows the rat's alley and bones image of *A Game of Chess*. It presents, through this imagery, both the past and the present, and the never-ending cycle of seasons from which the moral, spiritual, and human wasteland springs.

Buridan (bür'i.dạn; French, bü.rē.dän'), **Jean.** b. at Béthune, in Artois, France; d. after 1358. A French nominalist philosopher. He studied under William of Occam, and lectured on philosophy at the University of Paris, of which he became rector. He was a noted logician, and is popularly but probably incorrectly regarded as the author of the sophism known as "Buridan's Ass," which was used by the schoolmen to demonstrate the inability of the will to act between two equally powerful motives. According to this sophism an ass placed between two equidistant and equally attractive bundles of hay would starve to death for want of a reason to determine its choice between the two bundles.

Buried Alive. A novel (1908) by Arnold Bennett. Bennett made a play out of it under the title of *The Great Adventure* (1913), from which the motion picture *Holy Matrimony* was made.

Burke (bẽrk), **Edmund.** b. at Dublin, probably on Jan. 12, 1729; d. at Beaconsfield, England, July 9, 1797. A British parliamentarian, orator, and writer. The son of an Irish attorney, who was a Protestant, and of a Catholic mother, he was brought up and remained a Protestant, and was graduated (1748) from Trinity College in his native city before going to London, where he began his law studies in 1750. In 1756 he published *A Vindication of Natural Society*, a subtle satire of its supposed thesis, and in the same year an *Inquiry into the Sublime and the Beautiful*, which, despite some thought-provoking passages, left no permanent imprint on aesthetic theory in England. In 1759 he began publication of the *Annual Register*, a summary of the events of the preceding year seen within the framework of large trends and movements. In 1765 he became private secretary to the marquis of Rockingham when the latter became prime minister. Rockingham thereafter remained his firm friend and contributed to his financial support. In 1765 also Burke entered the House of Commons as member for Wendover, and the first of the many memorable speeches which he was to make there dealt, significantly enough, with a question involving the American colonies. Firmly attached to the Whig interests, from this time forward he made many vehement attacks upon the Tories. In 1768 he was affluent enough to acquire a large estate at Beaconsfield, where he lived with dignity but not ostentation, a patron of letters and art. In 1774 he became a member of Parliament for Bristol upon the invitation of citizens of that city, who probably supported his stand for compromise with the rebellious Americans, which had been made evident by his famous speeches (*On American Taxation*, in 1774, and the even better known *On Conciliation With the Colonies*, in 1775), but in 1780 they withdrew their support because of Burke's advocacy of free trade for Ireland, and of removal of the political restrictions then still imposed on Catholics in England. He reëntered Parliament in 1781 for the constituency of Malton in Yorkshire, and, by his attacks on the conduct of the war in America (particularly the use of Indians against the colonists), had a main part in bringing about the fall of Lord North's ministry. In the Whig government of 1782, and the coalition government which succeeded it, he was paymaster to the British forces and privy councilor. At this time also he began to take an interest in the conduct of the East India Company, and brought about the impeachment of Warren Hastings, governor general of India, during whose long trial (1786–94) in Parliament he delivered what some have considered to be his most forceful orations. (The full period of Burke's concern with Hastings may be said to have extended from 1781, when a committee report was made on Hastings's activities in India, to 1795, when Hastings was acquitted. Burke not only made a formal opening speech in the trial, but also delivered a nine-day reply to the defense in 1794.) Burke strongly supported Wilberforce in urging (1788–89) an end to the slave trade. The outbreak (1789) of the French Revolution brought to the fore all his love of order, temperance, tradition, and respect for authority, and led to his several books dealing with that world-shaking event. In November, 1790, he published his *Reflections on the Revolution in France* (which is the title now most often used; however, the full original title provides an interesting clue to the extent of his domestic concern: *Reflections on the Revolution in France, and on the proceedings in certain societies in London relative to that event*). As an almost inevitable corollary of his opposition to the French Revolution, his name became a rallying point for the forces not only of counterrevolution but of conservatism in general, and hence, by extension, of opposition to parliamentary reform, which led to separation (1791) from Charles James Fox and the bulk of the Whigs in Parliament. However, the intensity of Burke's opposition to the French Revolution actually increased during the next few years, and reached its highest point in the period 1795–97, when he published his four *Letters on a Regicide Peace*. In 1794 he retired from Parliament, and formally withdrew from political life in 1795, with a pension from the government. Burke's orations are among the greatest in any language in respect to their substance and logic, and although he was scarcely an original thinker, he may almost be said to have epitomized the liberalism of the 18th century. Some have suggested that, being an Irishman, his reverence for rank and royalty surpassed that of his liberal English confreres; he spoke for justice, but he abhorred radicalism. As a writer, he must be ranked among the masters of all who have ever written in English, having perfect command of a style that could be at one time the perfection of gravity, again the instrument of sentimentality, and yet again the portrayer of violence and horror.

Burke, John. b. 1787; d. 1848. An Irish genealogist. In 1826 he published the *Genealogical and Heraldic Dictionary of the Peerage and Baronetage of the United Kingdom*, the first comprehensive and systematic compilation in that field. Since 1847 this work has been published annually and is widely known as *Burke's Peerage*. In 1833 he began the publication of a similar reference book entitled *Burke's Landed Gentry*, dealing with the principal landholding families not included in the peerage or baronetage.

Burke, Thomas. b. 1886; d. at London, Sept. 22, 1945. An English writer of fiction and essays, who created the character of Quong Lee, Chinatown philosopher, in *Limehouse Nights* (1916). With this book and others he popularized the Limehouse district of London. His other works include the autobiographical novel *The Wind and the Rain* (1924), and *Flower of Life* (1929), *The English Inn* (1930), *The Real East End* (1932), *Night Pieces* (1935), and *Travel in England* (1943).

Burke, William. b. in the parish of Orrery, County Cork, Ireland, 1792; hanged Jan. 28, 1829. An Irish criminal, a partner of William Hare, who was keeper of a lodging house at Edinburgh. His criminal deeds started with the accidental death of an old pensioner at the lodging house; the corpse was sold to Dr. Robert Knox, a surgeon, for the purpose of dissection, at the price of seven pounds, ten shillings. This high price led the partners to deliberate murder of obscure wayfarers. In several months, assisted by their wives, they murdered at least 15 persons, all sold at similar prices for dissection, until the suspicions of neighbors were aroused. Burke was prosecuted, while Hare turned Crown witness.

Burleigh (bẽr′li), 1st Baron. See **Cecil, William.**

Burleigh, Lord. In Richard Brinsley Sheridan's *The Critic*, a character in Mr. Puff's play-within-a-play *The Spanish Armada*. He has not a word to say, but confines himself to the memorable nod by which, according to Mr. Puff, he expresses volumes.

burlesque (bẽr.lesk′). **1.** A burlesque literary or dramatic composition; travesty, caricature.

Burlesque is therefore of two kinds: the first represents mean persons in the accoutrements of heroes; the other describes great persons acting and speaking like the basest among the people. (Addison, *Spectator*, No. 249.)

2. A piece composed in burlesque style; a travesty; in modern use often specifically a theatrical piece, a kind of dramatic extravaganza, usually based upon a serious play or subject, with more or less music in it.

burletta (bẽr.let′a). A comic opera; a musical farce.

Burlington Arcade (bẽr′ling.ton). A covered pathway in London, between Piccadilly and Burlington Gardens, parallel with Old Bond Street. It has shops on each side for all kinds of small wares. The Gardens, now a park, once adjoined Burlington House, seat of the Earls of Burlington, built in the 17th century; Handel once stayed (1715) in a room of this house which at that time overlooked the gardens and the open country outside of London.

Burlington Gardens. See under **Burlington Arcade.**

Burlington House. A house, originally built about 1665 for the first Earl of Burlington, between Bond Street and Sackville Street, London: in 1868 handed over to the Royal Academy.

Burnaby (bẽr′na.bi), **Frederick Gustavus.** b. 1842; d. at Abu Klea, Sudan, Jan. 17, 1885. An English soldier and traveler. Sent at the end of 1874 to join Charles George Gordon in the Sudan as a correspondent of the London *Times*, he traveled up the Nile. In 1875 he made a 300-mile horseback journey across the Russian steppes in winter, and in 1876 made a five-month journey across Armenia and Asia Minor for the purpose of studying the Turks. He was killed by a spear wound while serving as a brigadier general during a Nile expedition to relieve Khartoum. His publications include *Ride to Rhiva* (1876), which was translated into several foreign languages, and *On Horseback through Asia Minor* (1876), which had seven editions.

Burnand (bẽr.nand′), Sir **Francis Cowley.** b. Nov. 29, 1836; d. 1917. An English editor, author, and playwright. He produced many plays, chiefly burlesques and comedies (among which are *Black-eyed Susan, Ixion,* and *The Colonel*), and wrote two light operas (*Contrabandista* and *The Chieftain*) in collaboration with Arthur Sullivan, with whom he also wrote *Cox and Box,* a musical version of John Maddison Morton's farce *Box and Cox*. He was a member (c1862 *et seq.*) of the editorial staff of *Punch* and one of its principal contributors, and

was its editor in chief in the period 1880–1906. He also wrote *Mokeanna,* several series of *Happy Thoughts, New Light on Darkest Africa, Eccentric Guide to the Isle of Thanet,* and a volume of reminiscences (1904).

Burne-Jones (bẽrn′jōnz′), Sir **Edward Coley.** b. at Birmingham, England, Aug. 28, 1833; d. at London, June 17, 1898. An English Pre-Raphaelite painter. He was a student at Exeter College, Oxford, at the same time as William Morris and Algernon Charles Swinburne, the latter of whom dedicated to him his first volume of poems. He went to London in 1856, and became a pupil of Dante Gabriel Rossetti, whose manner he imitated for several years. He soon formed, however, a style of his own, reminiscent of that of Botticelli, and inclining more to idealism and abstract beauty than to realism, and became one of the chief exponents in England of the romantic school. From 1857 to 1858 he was associated with Rossetti, Morris, and others in painting the Arthurian legends at Oxford. In 1861 he was one of the originators of the house of Morris and Company, and he made many designs for stained-glass windows and other decorative work. He was an associate of the Royal Academy in the period 1885–93. In 1894 he was made a baronet. Among his best-known works are *King Cophetua and the Beggar Maid, The Golden Stairs,* and *The Depths of the Sea.*

Burnell (bẽr.nel′), **Arthur Coke.** b. at St. Briavels, Gloucestershire, England, 1840; d. at West Stratton, Hampshire, England, Oct. 12, 1882. An English Sanskrit scholar and authority on the languages and literature of India. He was educated at King's College, London. Having entered the Indian Civil Service in 1857, he lived in India (except for terms of leave) from 1860 to 1880. His most important work, *Classified Index to the Sanskrit MSS. in the Palace at Tanjore,* was printed for the Madras government in 1880. He also published *Handbook of South Indian Palaeography* (1874), *The Aindra School of Sanskrit Grammarians* (1875), and translations from the Sanskrit. *Hobson Jobson, being a Glossary of Anglo-Indian Colloquial Words and Phrases,* a work which he compiled with Sir Henry Yule, was published in 1886.

Burnellus (bẽr.nel′us). [English, **Burnell** (bẽr′nel′).] In Nigel Wireker's *Speculum Stultorum* (*The Mirror of Fools,* c1180), the ass who goes to Salerno and Paris to study in the hope of getting a longer tail. He has many adventures and ends by losing his tail completely. The ass is intended to represent an ambitious monk. One of the episodes in this poem is referred to by Chaucer in *The Nun's Priest's Tale.*

Burnet (bẽr′net), **Gilbert.** b. at Edinburgh, Sept. 18, 1643; d. at London, March 17, 1715. A British prelate, historian, and theologian. He accompanied William III from Holland to England in 1688 as his chaplain, and was made bishop of Salisbury in 1689. His chief works are *History of the Reformation of the Church of England* (1679, 1681, 1715), *Exposition of the Thirty-nine Articles* (1699), and *A History of My Own Times* (edited by his son, 1723, 1734).

Burnet, Thomas. b. at Croft, Yorkshire, England, c1635; d. at London, Sept. 27, 1715. An English

---

fat, fāte, fär, àsk, fãre; net, mē, hẽr; pin, pīne; not, nōte, mõve, nôr; up, lūte, pùll; ᴛʜ, then;

author. He became a fellow of Christ's College in 1657, and master of the Charterhouse School in 1685. He is noted chiefly as the author of *Telluris Theoria Sacra* (1681), remarkable for its vivid imagery and pure Latinity, in which he attempts to prove that the earth originally resembled an egg, that at the deluge the shell was crushed and the waters rushed out, that the fragments of the shell formed the mountains and that the equator was diverted from its original coincidence with the ecliptic.

Burnett (bér.net'), **James.** See **Monboddo**, Lord.

Burney (bér'ni), **Fanny.** [Married name, Madame **d'Arblay**; original name, **Frances Burney.**] b. at King's Lynn, Norfolk, England, June 13, 1752; d. at Bath, England, Jan. 6, 1840. An English novelist. Her first book, the epistolary novel in the manner of Richardson, *Evelina, or a Young Lady's Entrance into the World* (1778), which she published anonymously, was well received and drew praise from Samuel Johnson. When her authorship of it was revealed, she was welcomed into the leading literary sets of her day, and was given, through the intervention of friends, a post at the court of Queen Charlotte, which she held from 1786 to 1791. In 1793 she married General Alexandre d'Arblay, a political refugee from the French Revolution. Her detailed journals and letters are a valuable source of information on contemporary court life, as well as furnishing anecdotes about Dr. Johnson's circle. Her other works include *Cecilia, or Memoirs of an Heiress* (1782), *Edwy and Elvina* (a tragedy, acted March 21, 1795), *Camilla, or a Picture of Youth* (1796), *Love and Fashion* (a comedy, 1800), *The Wanderer* (1814), *Memoirs of Dr. Burney* (1832), and *Letters and Diaries* (5 vols., 1842; 2 vols., 1846).

Burney, Sarah Harriet. b. c1770; d. at Cheltenham, Gloucestershire, England, Feb. 8, 1844. An English novelist; sister of Fanny Burney. She was the author of *Clarentine* (1796; published anonymously), *Geraldine Fauconberg* (1808; 2nd ed., 1813), *Traits of Nature* (1812), *Tales of Fancy* (1815), and *Romance of Private Life* (1839), novels and short narratives.

Burnham (bér'năm), **1st Baron.** [Title of **Edward Levy-Lawson**; original surname, **Levy.**] b. at London, Dec. 28, 1833; d. there, Jan. 9, 1916. An English newspaper owner, fund raiser, and social reformer; son of Joseph Moses Levy (1812–88), who in 1855 made the *Daily Telegraph* the first London penny paper; the son added Lawson to his name in 1875. Educated at London University College, he was drama critic (1851–55) on his father's *Sunday Times*, of which he was later (1855 *et seq.*) editor. Active in raising funds for hospitals, widows and orphans of soldiers and sailors, and similar causes, he also promoted the scientific researches and explorations of Henry Morton Stanley in Africa, George Smith in Assyria, and Sir Harry Johnston in East Africa. He served as vice-president and president (1867, 1908–16) of the Newspaper Press Fund, and president (1892) of the Institute of Journalists. He was created a baronet in 1892 and became Baron Burnham in 1903.

Burnham, 1st Viscount. [Title of **Harry Lawson Webster Lawson.**] b. at London, Dec. 18, 1862;

d. there, July 20, 1933. An English editor and newspaper proprietor who succeeded (1903) his father, the 1st Baron Burnham, as director of conduct and policy of the London *Daily Telegraph.* The newspaper was later (December, 1927) sold to Sir William Berry, James Gower Berry, and Edward Iliffe. Burnham served (1885–92, 1893–95, 1905–06) as a Liberal member of Parliament, and later (1910–16) as a Unionist member of Parliament. A member of the committee which drafted the Representation of the People Act, known as the Reform Act of 1918, he also presided over committees making an award on new scales of payment ("Burnham" scales) to teachers in Great Britain. He was president (1921, 1922, 1926) of the International Labor Conference at Geneva, and president (1916–28) of the Empire Press Union. In 1929 he was appointed president of Birkbeck College, University of London.

Burning Babe, The. A poem by Robert Southwell. It is the best known of Southwell's religious lyrics, which were written in prison and published in the year of his execution (1595).

Burning Cactus, The. A volume of short stories by Stephen Spender, published in 1936.

Burning Spear, The. A novel by John Galsworthy, published in 1921 under the pseudonym A. R. P. M., and reissued under the author's name in 1923. John Lavender, a quixotic hero with a touch of madness, is the central character in this satirical novel.

Burns (bérnz), **Robert.** b. at Alloway, Ayrshire, Scotland, Jan. 25, 1759; d. at Dumfries, Scotland, July 21, 1796. A Scottish poet. He was the son of a farmer and nurseryman, whose family name was variously spelled Burnes or Burness. Born to poverty, he grew up with little schooling but much hard work (so much, in fact, that before he reached his majority his health was impaired by it, and he had contracted a fondness for Scotch whisky which remained with him to the end of his life). During his minority the family moved more than once, always hoping, but in vain, that a different farm would bring better fortune; and in 1784 Robert and a brother rented Mossgiel, a farm of 118 acres near Mauchline. Mossgiel proved no better a way to wealth than the previous holdings, and in 1786 Robert made arrangements to take a clerical position in the British West Indies. In the hope of raising money for the expenses of this emigration, he published in that year, at Kilmarnock, a book entitled *Poems, Chiefly in the Scottish Dialect* which, although it is said to have netted him at that time only 20 pounds, changed his destiny, influenced the future development of the art of poetry, and gave him a place in the hearts of his countrymen as great as or greater than that of any of their kings or heroes. It was in connection with this publication that he shortened the family name to Burns. It is said that ploughboys and servant girls were eager to spend the hard-earned wages they needed for food and clothing to possess the book, while the gentry and the intellectuals of Edinburgh invited him to the capital, where as Sir Walter Scott wrote, he "was much caressed . . . but the efforts made for his relief were extremely trifling." He could dine with lords and ladies and charm a salon with his wit and natural dignity, but had to sleep in the cheapest lodgings. In 1787, however, two additional printings of his poems were published, bringing him some 500 pounds, whereupon he bought a farm at Ellisland and formally married (1788) Jean Armour, by whom he already had had children. (Burns's sexual activities were promiscuous as well as fruitful. Jean Armour bore him twins in 1786 and again in 1788; in the former year, Burns is said to have been involved simultaneously in affairs with Jean Armour, Elizabeth Patron, and Mary Campbell ("Highland Mary"). His decision to emigrate stemmed at least partly from the complications created by his intimacies with these lasses, and he apparently had decided to marry Mary Campbell and leave Scotland, when Mary died in childbirth.) In 1789 his Edinburgh friends secured for him a post as exciseman at Dumfries, at a salary of 70 pounds per annum, and it was here that a third edition of his poems was printed in 1793. Meanwhile, he contributed to Edinburgh and London magazines and newspapers, but his enthusiasm for the principles of the French Revolution cooled the friendship of his aristocratic patrons. He wrote or adapted some 200 songs for James Johnson's *Scots Musical Museum*, and about 100 for George Thompson's *Select Collection of Original Scottish Airs*. In 1794 he became alarmed at the threat of a French invasion of Britain, and joined the Dumfriesshire Volunteers, who gave him a military funeral when, his constitution weakened by excesses, he died in what should have been his middle years. His lyrics are diverse in mood and method. His songs of wooing range from the tender in *Mary Morison* to archness in *Tam Glen*, to a jocose treatment of bashfulness in *Duncan Gray*, and to uproarious delight in the story of *Last May a Braw Wooer*. Absence, though not his common theme, is sweetly treated in *Of a' the Airts*, and the elegiac tone of *Banks o' Doon* and *Highland Mary* expresses beautifully the tragedy of lost love. *Tam o' Shanter* alone would prove that Burns had superlative gifts in poetic narrative, but in his songs he seldom relies on story for substance. In *Auld Rob Morris, Open the Door*, and *Tam Glen*, however, story is exquisitely implied. The lover at parting perhaps protests too much in *Ae Fond Kiss*, but in the fervidly hyperbolic *Red, Red Rose* we surely have authentic passion if ever words conveyed it. His more "public" songs, such as the reworked *Auld Lang Syne, Is there for Honest Poverty*, and above all the battle song of *Scots Wha Hae wi' Wallace Bled*, are in their respective modes supremely eloquent.

Burnt Norton. First of the *Four Quartets* by T. S. Eliot, published in 1939, opening with the famous lines: "Time present and time past/ Are both perhaps contained in time future,/ And time future contained in time past." Thus Eliot poses the eternal quality of time and the universe which stretches beyond our human comprehension. The worlds within the universe are reached through memories, but "that which is only living/ Can only die" and so again we are faced with the eternal barrier.

Burrough or **Burrowe** (bur'ọ̄), **Stephen.** See **Borough, Stephen.**

Burton (bêr'tọn), Lady **Isabel.** [Maiden name, Arundell.] b. 1831; d. 1896. An English author and traveler, who wrote a biography of her author husband (whom she had married in 1861), Sir Richard Francis Burton (1821–90). She shared her husband's life of travel and literature, and after his death issued a memorial edition of his works and his biography. She also published *Inner Life of Syria* (1875) and *Arabia, Egypt, and India* (1879).

Burton, John Hill. b. at Aberdeen, Scotland, Aug. 22, 1809; d. at Morton House, near Edinburgh, Aug. 10, 1881. A Scottish historian and jurist. His chief works are a life of David Hume (1846), *A History of Scotland from Agricola's Invasion to the Rebellion of 1745* (1853–70), and *A History of the Reign of Queen Anne* (1880).

Burton, Sir Richard Francis. b. at Barham House, Hertfordshire, England, March 19, 1821; d. at Trieste, Oct. 20, 1890. An English explorer and Orientalist, author of travel books; husband (married 1861) of Lady Isabel Burton. After serving in the East Indian army he went in 1853 to Mecca. His *First Footsteps in Eastern Africa* (1856) described travels made in 1854, when, disguised as an Arab, he accompanied John Speke to Harar, in Ethiopia. In 1858 he was again in East Africa with Speke, and discovered Lake Tanganyika, while Speke discovered Lake Victoria. In 1861 he was in West Africa as British consul at Fernando Po, in Spanish Guinea; he ascended Cameroon Mountain, and spent three months at the court of Dahomey. To the end of his life he continued in the consular service: at Santos, Brazil (1865–69), at Damascus (1869–71), and at Trieste (1872–90), where he died. Of the more than 30 volumes published by him, the principal ones are *Personal Narrative of a Pilgrimage to El Medinah and Meccah* (1855), *Lake Regions of Central Africa* (1860), *A Mission to the King of Dahomey* (1864), *Explorations of the Highlands of Brazil* (1868), and a literal version of *The Arabian Nights' Entertainments*. His biography and a memorial edition of his works were published after his death by his wife.

Burton, Robert. [Pseudonym, **Democritus Junior.**] b. at Lindley, Leicestershire, England, Feb. 8, 1577; d. Jan. 25, 1640. An English writer and clergyman. He entered the University of Oxford in 1593, became a student of Christ Church College in 1599, and became rector of Segrave, in Leicestershire, in 1630. He was the author of *The Anatomy of Melancholy* (1621). In this work, which is the quintessence of the spirit of the late Renaissance in England, he expounded, with some wit and with a wealth of learned quotations, the causes and symptoms of melancholy, and its cures. The work went through several revisions before Burton's death, and had a lasting influence on much later English writing.

Bury (bėr'i), **Richard de.** See **Aungerville, Richard.**

Bury Fair. A play by Thomas Shadwell, produced c1689 at the Drury Lane. It is in its first part an imitation of Molière's *Le Misanthrope*, and also borrows from *Le Bourgeois Gentilhomme* and (in the character of La Roche in particular) from *Les Précieuses Ridicules*.

---

fat, fāte, fär, ȧsk, fāre; net, mē, hėr; pin, pīne; not, nōte, mȯve, nôr; up, lūte, pu̇ll; ᴛн, then;

Bury Saint Edmunds (ber'i sănt ed'mundz). [Also, **Bury St. Edmunds.**] A municipal borough and small manufacturing town in E England, in West Suffolk, situated on the river Lark ab. 28 mi. E of Cambridge, ab. 85 mi. NE of London by rail. It contains the ruins of a Benedictine abbey founded (c630) by Canute, the abbey gateway, Norman tower, and several churches. The grave of Mary Tudor is here. The Roman Villa Faustini was probably here. It was the capital of East Anglia, and has been the seat of several parliaments. According to tradition it was the scene of the martyrdom of Saint Edmund (Edmund the Martyr), a king of East Anglia who refused after a defeat by the Danes to renounce Christianity and was therefore beheaded by them in 870. During the first decade of the 10th century (c903, according to some accounts) his remains were placed in the Benedictine abbey which had been founded by Canute.

Busby (buz'bi), **Richard.** b., probably at Sutton, Lincolnshire, England, Sept. 22, 1606; d. April 6, 1695. An English teacher. He was made headmaster of the Westminster School in 1638.

Bushy (bùsh'i). In Shakespeare's *Richard II*, a follower of the King.

Busirane (bū'si.rān). In Edmund Spenser's *Faerie Queene*, an enchanter, the symbol of illicit love. He imprisoned Amoret, keeping her in torment until she was released by Britomarte.

Busiris (bụ.sī'ris). A mythical king of Egypt who, to insure the cessation of a famine, each year sacrificed to the gods one stranger who had set foot on his shores. Hercules was seized by him, and would have fallen a victim had he not broken his bonds and slain Busiris with his club. In *Paradise Lost* John Milton, who follows other writers, gives the name Busiris to the Pharaoh who was drowned in the Red Sea.

Busiris. A tragedy by Edward Young, author of *Night Thoughts.* It was produced in 1719.

buskin (bus'kin). **1.** A half-boot or high shoe strapped or laced to the ankle and the lower part of the leg.

> The hunted red-deer's undressed hide
> Their hairy buskins well supplied.
> (Sir Walter Scott, *Marmion.*)

2. A similar boot worn by the ancients; the cothurnus, particularly as worn by actors in tragedy.

> How I could reare the Muse on stately stage,
> And teache her tread aloft in Buskin fine.
> (Spenser.)

3. Hence tragedy or the tragic drama, as opposed to comedy.

> He was a critic upon operas, too,
> And knew all niceties of the sock and buskin.
> (Byron, *Beppo.*)

Bussy D'Ambois (bü.sē' dän.bwà'). A tragedy by George Chapman, published in 1607 and probably written in 1604. The allusions in it to the knights of James I, and to Elizabeth as an "old queen," forbid a date earlier than 1603; and the statement in Act I, Scene 2, " 'Tis Leap Year," which must apply to the date of production, appears to set the first presentation at 1604. Thomas D'Urfey produced a play, adapted from Chapman's, with this title in 1691. No definite source is known for the play but Marlowe's *The Massacre at Paris* deals with the same period in French history. The principal character in Chapman's play is a self-confident and arrogant adventurer who possesses some genuine loftiness of character. The plot is based on an actual incident involving a man named Louis de Bussy-d'Amboise at the court of Henry III of France. In the play Bussy D'Ambois is killed by the machinations of Monsieur, the king's brother, because of jealousy over the wife of the count of Montsurry. Bussy is akin in many respects to young Mortimer in Marlowe's *Edward II.*

Bussy D'Ambois, The Revenge of. A play by George Chapman, a sequel to *Bussy D'Ambois;* it was published in 1613, and composed between 1609 and 1612. The hero of this drama is Clermont D'Ambois, Bussy's brother, who tries to avenge his brother's slaying with an honorable duel. Clermont unlike Bussy, was not a historical figure. However, Chapman drew an actual incident concerning a Count d'Auvergne who was arrested by agents of the French king while reviewing troops. Clermont is substituted for the real d'Auvergne and is made into a procrastinating figure like Hamlet.

Busy (biz'i), **Zeal-of-the-Land.** [Called **Rabbi Busy.**] In Ben Jonson's play *Bartholomew Fair*, an unctuous, gormandizing Puritan, grossly ignorant and a scorner of culture.

Busybody, The. [Also, **The Busie Body.**] A comedy by Susannah Centlivre, produced and printed in 1709. In this play the character of Marplot is first introduced. The plot is partly from Ben Jonson's *The Devil is an Ass.* A second part, called *Marplot, or the Second Part of the Busybody*, was produced by Susannah Centlivre in 1710. Henry Woodward altered it and called it *Marplot in Lisbon.*

Busybody, The. A pseudonym of **Franklin, Benjamin.**

Butcher, Dick the. See **Dick the Butcher.**

Butcher (bùch'ẻr), **Samuel Henry.** b. at Dublin, April 16, 1850; d. at London, Dec. 29, 1910. An Irish classical scholar and teacher, translator of Homer. Educated at Marlborough School and at Trinity College, Cambridge, of which he was a fellow, he taught at Eton, at Trinity, and at University College, Oxford (1875–82), and was professor of Greek (1882–1903) at Edinburgh. In 1904 he visited the U. S. and lectured at Harvard. A Unionist member of Parliament (1906–10) for Cambridge University, he was also president of the English Classical Association and of the British Academy of Letters. He was the author of *Demosthenes* (1881), *Some Aspects of the Greek Genius* (1891), *Aristotle's Theory of Poetry and Fine Art* (1895), *Greek Idealism in the Common Things of Life* (1901), and *Harvard Lectures on Greek Subjects* (1904), and editor of the *Orationes* of Demosthenes (1903, 1907). His name is most familiar to students and readers as translator (with Andrew Lang) of a prose translation (1879–1887, 1889) of Homer's *Odyssey.*

Bute (būt), 3rd Marquis of. Title of **Stuart, John Patrick Crichton-.**

Bute Crawley (krô'li), **Rev.** and **Mrs.** See under Crawley.

Butler (but'lėr), **Alban.** b. at Appletree, Northamptonshire, England, 1710; d. at St.-Omer, France, May 15, 1773. An English Roman Catholic hagiographer. He wrote *Lives of the Fathers, Martyrs, and Other Principal Saints* (4 vols., 1756–59) and others.

Butler, Arthur John. b. at Putney, London, June 21, 1844; d. at Weybridge, Surrey, England, Feb. 26, 1910. An English scholar and teacher, translator of Dante. Educated at Eton and at Trinity College, Cambridge, he was an examiner (1870–87) for the London Board of Education, a partner (1887–94) in the Rivington publishing house, and professor of Italian (1898–1910) at London University College. An enthusiastic mountain climber from his early boyhood, he was a member (1886 *et seq.*) of the Alpine Club and editor (1890–93) of the *Alpine Journal.* He was the author of *Dante: His Times and his Work* (1895) and *The Forerunners of Dante* (1910), and editor (1899–1910) of *Calendars of Foreign State Papers.* A translator also of many works from French and German, he is best known for his translations of Dante's *Purgatory* (1880), *Paradise* (1885), and *Hell* (1892).

Butler, Joseph. b. at Wantage, Berkshire, England, May 18, 1692; d. at Bath, England, June 16, 1752. An English prelate and theologian, made bishop of Bristol in 1738, and of Durham in 1750. His most noted work is *Analogy of Religion, Natural and Revealed, to the Constitution and Course of Nature* (1736).

Butler, Reuben. In Sir Walter Scott's novel *The Heart of Midlothian*, a weak and sensitive minister of the Scottish Church, who marries Jeanie Deans.

Butler, Samuel. b. at Strensham, Worcestershire, England, in February, 1612; d. at London, Sept. 25, 1680. An English poet of the Restoration period, now perhaps best known for his mock-heroic *Hudibras* (1663–78). After serving as an attendant (c1628) to Elizabeth, Countess of Kent, he was employed in the families of various gentlemen, including the Presbyterian Sir Samuel Luke. It is generally, but probably erroneously, thought that Luke served as the model for Hudibras. The poem itself, in heroic couplets, satirizes Puritanism; its hero is something of a quixotic knight, though his arguments with his attendant are more biting than the ones conducted by Cervantes's hero. The poem, which abounds in burlesque and travesty, was well received; since most of Butler's other writings were published posthumously, his contemporary reputation was based almost entirely on *Hudibras.*

Butler, Samuel. b. at Langar, Nottinghamshire, England, Dec. 4, 1835; d. at London, June 18, 1902. An English novelist, satirist, Homeric scholar, and translator. Educated at Shrewsbury School and at St. John's College, Cambridge, he was a sheep-farmer (1860–64) in New Zealand. A man of many interests, scientific and artistic, Butler was a painter (some of his pictures being in the Royal Academy, the British Museum, and the Tate Gallery), wrote on topography and evolution, and composed musical pieces in various forms. He was

the author of *The Humor of Homer* (1892) and *The Authoress of the Odyssey* (1897, expounding his firm conviction that the *Odyssey* was written by a woman). Other literary theories are presented in *Shakespeare's Sonnets Reconsidered* (1899) and *Essays on Life, Art, and Science* (1904). *Life and Habit* (1877), *Evolution: Old and New* (1879), *Unconscious Memory* (1880), and *Luck or Cunning?* (1886) are scientific works. He also wrote several theological studies and translated the *Iliad* (1898) and the *Odyssey* (1900) into prose. However, the works by which he is best remembered are the autobiographical novel *The Way of All Flesh* (1903), *Erewhon* (1872), a Utopian romance satirizing Darwinism and orthodox Christianity, and its sequel, *Erewhon Revisited* (1901).

But Not for Love. A novel by Beatrice Kean Seymour, published in 1930.

Butter (but'ėr), **Nathaniel.** d. Feb. 22, 1664. An English printer and journalist. He issued, at London, pamphlets describing murders and plays (1605–39), weekly editions of foreign news-letters (1622–39), and half-yearly volumes of foreign news (1630–40). His newssheets were the forerunners of the modern newspaper. Ben Jonson ridiculed him under the name of Cymbal in his *Staple of News* (1625), and John Fletcher and James Shirley also referred to him in their works.

Butts (buts), **Doctor.** In Shakespeare's *Henry VIII*, the King's physician, the historical Sir William Butts.

Buzfuz (buz'fuz), **Serjeant.** In Charles Dickens's *Pickwick Papers*, the pompous and brutal counsel for Mrs. Bardell in the Bardell-Pickwick breach-of-promise suit.

Buzzard (buz'ạrd), **Mr. Justice.** In Henry Fielding's novel *Amelia*, a character whose "ignorance of law is as great as his readiness to take a bribe."

B. V. Pseudonym of **Thomson, James** (1834–82).

Bye Plot. The less important of two conspiracies (1603) to seize the person of James I of England and thereby to extort certain religious concessions. The other was the Main Plot.

Byng (bing), **John.** b. 1704; executed in Portsmouth harbor, England, March 14, 1757. A British admiral. He was unsuccessful in an expedition during the Seven Years' War to relieve Minorca, which was invaded by a French expedition under the Duc de Richelieu (a grandnephew of Cardinal Richelieu) in 1756. Although his failure aroused a considerable degree of public ire, it was probably largely at the instance of the British ministry then in power (which was controlled by the Duke of Newcastle and his brother Pelham), whose ineffectual war policy had rendered it unpopular, that he was tried by a court-martial, and found guilty of neglect of duty. He was shot in spite of the unanimous recommendation to mercy by the court, which deplored that the article of war under which he was condemned admitted of no mitigation of punishment, even if the crime were committed through a mere error of judgment.

Byrne (bėrn), **Donn.** See **Donn-Byrne, Brian Oswald.**

Byrom (bī'rọm), **John.** b. at Kersall Cell, Broughton, near Manchester, England, Feb. 29, 1692;

d. Sept. 26, 1763. An English poet. He studied at Trinity College, Cambridge, of which he became a fellow in 1714. He invented a system of shorthand which was published in 1767 under the title *The Universal English Shorthand.* A collective edition of his poems, among the most notable of which are "Colin to Phoebe," "Three Black Crows," and "Figg and Sutton," appeared at Manchester in 1773.

Byron (bī'rọn). An essay (1830) by Thomas Babington Macaulay.

Byron, Augusta Ada. See **Lovelace,** Countess of.

Byron, Duke of. The hero of George Chapman's tragedy *The Conspiracy and Tragedy of Charles, Duke of Byron.*

Byron, George Gordon Noel. [Title, 6th Baron **Byron of Rochdale** (roch'dāl.)] b. at London, Jan. 22, 1788; d. at Missolonghi, Greece, April 19, 1824. An English poet. The poet's profligate father, Captain John Byron, died in France in 1791, and the boy was brought up by his widowed mother, Catherine. At Harrow (1801–05) and at Trinity College, Cambridge (1805–08), he divided his time between wide reading and the acquisition of irregular habits, and was notably successful in both pursuits. He left Cambridge with an M.A., and having come into his great-uncle's title and estates, including Newstead Abbey, in 1798, took (1809) his seat in the House of Lords, but only to depart shortly afterwards with J. C. Hobhouse on the Mediterranean tour which took him all the way from Spain to the Near East. His crippled foot, the result of an early infantile paralysis, hardly impeded his vigorous living; he explored the Albanian wilderness and even, fired by the legend of Leander, swam the Hellespont. More important, in these travels he picked up what was to be material for some of his finest poetry. He had been writing since his Cambridge days, when his *Hours of Idleness* (1807) had been pilloried by a reviewer in the *Edinburgh Review;* Byron had, in turn, blasted the *Review* with his *English Bards and Scotch Reviewers* (1809), which left no doubt of his competence or virulence as a satirist. Following his return (1811) from abroad he published *Childe Harold,* Cantos I and II (1812), *The Giaour* and *The Bride of Abydos* (both 1813), and *The Corsair* and *Lara* (both 1814). His social success, which had been brilliant during the first few months after his return to England, was seriously compromised when, in 1813, gossip was heard of his liaison with his half sister, Augusta Leigh, and was dissipated completely within the year after his marriage (Jan. 2, 1815) to Annabella Milbanke, when that affluent and attractive heiress bore Byron a daughter but failed to render their marriage tolerable to her mercurial husband. Papers of separation were filed and public opinion unhesitatingly assigned the blame to the poet, even though knowledge of the details was not available and did not become so until the publication of Lord Lovelace's heavily documented account, *Astarte,* in 1905. Ostracized, but noteworthily unrepentant and violently blaming the English public for his mistreatment, Byron quit England (1816) for good. He traveled up the Rhine, joined the Shelleys near the Lake of Geneva, figured in a liaison with Clare Clairmont (their

daughter, Allegra, died at the age of five in a convent near Ravenna), and in November of 1816 arrived in Venice in the company of his friend Hobhouse. The tortured Italy of the *Risorgimento* was his home for the next six years, and the cause of liberty found him a stout, if somewhat erratic, friend. No less intense was his devotion to the last of his great loves, Teresa, Countess Guiccioli, separated (by papal decree) wife of an elderly husband who had made a private peace with the Austrian overlords and lived quietly in his palace in Ravenna while Teresa moved about Italy according to the political fortunes of her own family, the Gambas. Byron met her in 1819, when she was 17, and followed her from Venice to Ravenna, to Pisa, and on to Genoa. Much of the enthusiasm for Italy that runs through his later work is attributed by critics to her influence. In 1822 he was associated with Leigh Hunt in editing the short-lived *Liberal* but the collapse of the Carbonari movement left them without a cause. In the same year Shelley was drowned near Viareggio and the remaining members of his group, which for some months had included Byron, E. J. Trelawney, and Hunt, were herded (September, 1822) into Genoa by the Austrians. The time was ripe for the London Greek Committee to persuade Byron to transfer his fight for liberty from Italy to Greece. He outfitted a 120-ton brig, said a final farewell to his friends and Teresa, and with her brother and Trelawney sailed from Genoa in July, 1823. He got near enough the scene of action for his presence to encourage the Greek leaders, but his health had been failing for some time; he was stricken by fever at Missolonghi and died there in January, 1824. His body was given full military honors and taken back to England for burial at Hucknall Torkard Church, near Newstead.

Mature Works. Neither his amatory nor his political adventures could interrupt the flow of Byron's work. *Childe Harold,* Canto III, and *The Prisoner of Chillon* (both 1816) reflect the mood of his retreat from England after the early successes. *Manfred* (1817) and *Childe Harold,* Canto IV, reach the heights of Romantic exaltation. *Don Juan,* his satiric medley (begun 1818, published 1819–24 but never completed), is less stagily Romantic, certainly more adult, and at times self-critical; the mood changes from the pathos which had succeeded the heroics of the earlier, "strenuous," poems, to a sometimes pained but invariably open-eyed irony. Other poems of the period include *Beppo* (1818), *The Lament of Tasso* (1817), *The Prophecy of Dante* (1821), and *The Island* (1823). Less successful were the dramas, to which he devoted himself more and more as time went on: *Cain, Marino Faliero, Sardanapalus, The Two Foscari* (all 1821), *Werner* (1823), and *Heaven and Earth* (1824). He also had time to defend Pope and his school against the attacks of Bowles, and to answer an attack by Southey, in *The Vision of Judgment* (1822).

Reputation and Influence. In spite of Byron's great technical virtuosity, his manifest cleverness, and his astounding facility in rhyming, Anglo-Saxon critics have been less attracted to his work than to the serener poetry of Wordsworth and the admittedly richer writing of Keats. He has struck

ḍ, d or j; ş, s or sh; ṭ, t or ch; ẓ, z or zh; o, F. cloche; ü, F. menu; ċh, Sc. loch; ṅ, F. bonbon.

them as "shallow" in comparison, and they have at times doubted his sincerity. The scandals attached to him made him more often the subject of sermons than of critical encomiums, especially among the Victorians, and the turn of taste toward earlier poetry and especially toward the "School of Donne" has delayed a revival of interest in him in the 20th century. On the other hand, Continental readers have always esteemed him above his English contemporaries. Goethe admired *Manfred* and incorporated its hero in *Faust;* the Frenchman Lamartine attempted a final Canto of his own for *Childe Harold;* Musset imitated him extensively. In France generally, he is considered one of the fountainheads of Romanticism, and his poetry is frequently placed near, though perhaps not quite on a par with, the prose of Chateaubriand in this respect: *le byronisme* is an honored rubric in histories of French literature. His influence entered Spanish literature through poets like the Romantic Zorilla. The bibliography about him is extensive; important biographies include those by Galt (1830), Thomas Moore (1831), Mayne (1912), and Bellamy (1924); Trelawney's *Recollections* (1858) and Lord Ernle's collection of Byron's *Letters* (6 vols., 1898–1901) are essential material; and Harriet Beecher Stowe's *Lady Byron Vindicated* (1870) has special interest for American readers.

Byron, Harriet. In Samuel Richardson's epistolary novel *Sir Charles Grandison*, a supposed orphan, attached to Sir Charles Grandison and the principal writer of the letters. It is between her (the nice English girl) and Lady Clementina della Porretta (beautiful and exotic, but also an Italian and a Catholic, and hence, to 18th-century English readers, although possibly exciting, hardly capable of being a good wife) that Sir Charles Grandison wavers in his affections, and thus provides Richardson with the theme of his novel.

Byron, John. [Called **"Foul-weather Jack."**] b. Nov. 8, 1723; d. April 10, 1786. An English naval officer; grandfather of George Gordon Noel Byron. He entered the navy when a boy, and in 1740 was a midshipman on the *Wager* in George Anson's squadron which was wrecked near Cape Horn. He wrote an account of the disaster, and it is believed that this narrative was used by his grandson as the basis of several episodes in *Don Juan.* From 1764 to 1766 he commanded two vessels in a voyage of exploration around the world; but beyond certain curious observations on the Indians of Patagonia and the discovery of some small islands in the Pacific, he accomplished little. He was governor of Newfoundland (1769–72), became a vice-admiral in 1778, and on July 6, 1779, had an engagement with the French fleet of Jean Baptiste Charles Henri d'Estaing off Grenada, West Indies, but was defeated.

Byron's Conspiracy and **Byron's Tragedy.** See **Conspiracy and Tragedy of Charles, Duke of Byron.**

By Still Waters. A book of lyrical poems by George William Russell, published (1906) under his pseudonym "Æ."

By the Ionian Sea. A travel book (1901) by George Gissing. It was inspired by his wanderings in Calabria, in S Italy, in 1897.

Bywater (bī'wô''tẽr, -wot''ẽr), **Hector Charles.** b. at London, Oct. 21, 1884; d. Aug. 17, 1940. An English journalist, author, and expert on naval affairs. From 1898 to 1914 he lived in Canada, in the U. S., and on the Continent. During World War I he was engaged in intelligence work. He was European naval correspondent (1921–30) for the Baltimore *Sun,* and held the same post (1923–28) for the London *Daily News* and *Observer.* He was the author of *Sea Power in the Pacific* (1921, a study of the American-Japanese naval problem), *Navies and Nations* (1927, a survey of naval development since World War I), *Cruisers in Battle* (1939), and many articles in *Nineteenth Century and After,* the *Engineer, Atlantic Monthly,* and *Round Table.* His volume, *The Great Pacific War—A History of the American-Japanese Campaign of 1931–33* (1925), a fictitious account, was published (1942) with an added subtitle, *A Prophecy Now Being Fulfilled,* and an introduction by Hanson W. Baldwin.

Bywater, Ingram. b. at London, in June, 1840; d. there, Dec. 17, 1914. An English classical scholar and teacher, editor, and translator of Aristotle. He was educated at University College School and King's College School at London, and at Queen's College, Oxford, where he studied under Benjamin Jowett and was a friend of Algernon Charles Swinburne and Walter Pater, and was a fellow, Greek tutor (1863–84), and reader in Greek (1883–1908) at Exeter College. He was editor (1879–1914) of the *Journal of Philology,* to which he also contributed, and president (1883–1908) of the Oxford Aristotelian Society. He edited *Fragments of Heraclitus* (1877), *Works of Priscianus Lydus* (1886), Aristotle's *Nicomachean Ethics* (1890), and *Contributions to the Textual Criticism of the Ethics* (1892), wrote *The Erasmian Pronunciation of Greek and Its Precursors* (1908), and translated and edited with notes and commentary Aristotle's *Art of Poetry* (1909).

Byzantine Empire (biz'ạn.tēn, -tīn, bi.zan'tin). [Also: **Eastern Empire, Eastern Roman Empire, Greek Empire, Lower Empire.**] Name usually given to the empire formally established in 330 A.D. when the Roman emperor Constantine I gave the name Constantinople to the city he had built on the site of the ancient Byzantium (now Istanbul) and established it as his capital. From the standpoint of geography Constantine's empire was co-extensive (and indeed, in his eyes, identical) with the Roman Empire, but the disagreements between his successors led finally to an actual separation of East and West, the former comprising at first approximately half of the Roman Empire; from the standpoint of history after Sept. 4, 476, when the last ruler of the Roman Empire in the West was deposed, it was the sole remaining political unit which could, by its unbroken historical link to the earliest days of Roman conquest in the Mediterranean, claim to be the "Roman Empire." Between 951 and 1057 this empire reached the height of its power. Crete, Cyprus, Cilicia, and the N portion of Syria were recaptured from Islam, part of Armenia was conquered, a great Russian invasion was repulsed, the strong Bulgarian kingdom was overthrown, and Roman territory was once more extended to the Danube. Thereafter the empire waned in size and power, and in 1204 it fell an easy prey to the Venetians and their allies of the Fourth Crusade, who maintained it as a seat of empire, but oriented it toward the West in religion and culture (under their control, the Byzantine Empire became once again a Latin, or Western, Empire). The empire was thereafter maintained, often precariously, until the Ottoman Turks captured Constantinople in 1453 A.D., at which time the Byzantine Empire, as a continuation of the Roman Empire, came finally to an end. At its greatest extent it had included all or most of SE Europe, W Asia, N Africa, part of Italy, and various islands in the Mediterranean and Black Sea.

Byzantine Historians. A collective term for the Greek historians of the Byzantine Empire. Among the most important were Zosimus, Procopius, Agathias, Anna Comnena, Joannes Cinnamus, and Nicetas Acominatus.

Byzantium (bi.zan′shi.um, -ti-). A poem (1930) by William Butler Yeats, contrasting that which is human and transitory with that which is eternal: "A starlit or a moonlit dome disdains/ All that man is." The central image is of a "superhuman," synthesizing death and life, perceived by the poet only for that brief moment when he is able to transcend the mundane world. Some critics think that this poem, which is one of Yeats's most important later works, baffles analysis because of the private and esoteric nature of its images ("dolphin's mire" and "gong-tormented sea" are typical).

C

Caaba (kä′bạ). See **Kaaba**.

Cabal (kạ.bal′). In English history, an influential group at the court of Charles II, consisting of Clifford (Thomas Clifford, 1st Baron Clifford of Chudleigh), Ashley (Anthony Ashley Cooper, 1st Baron Ashley and 1st Earl of Shaftesbury), Buckingham (George Villiers, 2nd Duke of Buckingham), Arlington (Henry Bennet, 1st Earl of Arlington), and Lauderdale (John Maitland, 1st Duke of Lauderdale), the initials of whose names happened to compose the word. Although the group as a whole never formally comprised a British ministry, one or more of its members belonged to every ministry that existed between 1667 and 1674, and there was no question at any time during this period as to the power of the members of the Cabal, whether in or out of the government. The members of the group were guilty, individually and collectively, of intrigues and cynical corruption remarkable even in a day when public office was viewed by many as simply a means to power and wealth, and never hesitated to act accordingly. By coincidence, the initialism "Cabal" happened to be identical in spelling with the word "cabal," derived indirectly from the word "cabala," "cabbala," or "kabbala," which was the name of a medieval system of theosophy based on a mystical interpretation of Scriptures. "Cabala" had long been popularly associated with black magic and various secret rites, and the word "cabal" was therefore reinforced in its invidious connotations by the activities of the members of the Cabal. Since that time, in political usage, the term has been applied to many secret or conspiratorial cliques in both British and American history.

Cabot (kab′ọt), **John.** [Italian, **Giovanni Caboto** (jō.vän′nē kä.bō′tō); Spanish, **Gaboto**.] b. probably at Genoa, Italy, 1450; d. 1498. An Italian navigator in the English service on whose discoveries were based English claims in North America; father of Sebastian Cabot. He was probably a native of Genoa or its neighborhood, and in 1476 became a citizen of Venice after a residence there of 15 years. He subsequently removed (c1484) to Bristol, England. Believing that a northwest passage would shorten the route to India, he determined to undertake an expedition in search of such a passage, and in 1496 obtained from Henry VII of England a patent for the discovery, at his own expense, of unknown lands in the eastern, western, or northern seas. He set sail from Bristol in May, 1497, in company with his sons, and returned in the same year. The expedition resulted in the discovery of what is probably Cape Breton Island and Nova Scotia. In the spring of 1498 he made a second voyage, reaching Greenland and Baffin Island, and exploring the coast as far south as the 38th parallel.

Cabot, Sebastian. b. at Venice, Italy, c1476; d. 1557. An explorer; son of John Cabot. He accompanied his father on the voyage of 1497, when the shore of North America was discovered (his name appears with his father's in the petition to Henry VII), and it is probable that he was with him also on the voyage of 1498. In the period 1508–09, it is said, he went in search of a northwest passage, touching the coast of Labrador and possibly entering Hudson Bay. Invited by Charles V to Spain, he was made (1519) grand pilot of Castile but gave up the post to take command of four ships which left San Lucar on April 3, 1526, to sail to the Moluccas by the Strait of Magellan. Lacking provisions, he landed on the coast of Brazil, where he had some encounters with the Portuguese; thence he sailed southward, discovered the river Uruguay, and erected a fort there. He discovered and ascended the Paraná River, and explored the lower Paraguay to the present site of Asunción. Convinced of the importance of this region, and joined by Diego Garcia, he relinquished the voyage to the Moluccas and despatched a ship for reinforcements; meanwhile he established himself at the fort of Espírito Santo on the Paraná. Not receiving aid, he returned in 1530, leaving a garrison at Espírito Santo. Cabot was subsequently in the service of Spain until c1547, when he returned to England. He was interested (1553–56) in explorations in the Baltic, as a founder and (after 1555) life governor

ḍ, d or j; ṣ, s or sh; ṭ, t or ch; ẓ, z or zh; o, F. cloche; ü, F. menu; ċh, Sc. loch; ṅ, F. bonbon.

of the Merchant Adventurers, a company whose search for a northeast passage to the Orient opened the routes for trade with Russia. A map of the world published in 1544 is ascribed to him.

Cacafogo (kak.ạ.fō′gō). In John Fletcher's play *Rule a Wife and Have a Wife*, a cowardly, bullying, and rich usurer. He has been said to be a direct copy of Shakespeare's character Falstaff, but his lack of courage is the only resemblance.

cacodemon (kak.ọ.dē′mọn). In Shakespeare's *Richard III*, an evil spirit mentioned by Margaret. She calls Gloucester "Thou cacodemon!" (I.iii).

cacophony (ka.kof′ọ.ni). In rhetoric, a faulty choice or arrangement of words, producing inharmonious or discordant combinations of sounds, or too great frequency of such combinations as are for any reason unpleasant to the ear; also, the uncouth or disagreeable sound so produced: the opposite of euphony.

The Lancashire folk speak quick and curt, omit letters, or sound three or four words all together: thus I wou'didd'n, or I woudyedd'd, is a cacophony which stands for I wish you would!

    (Isaac D'Israeli, *Amenities of Literature*.)

Cacus (kā′kus). In Roman mythology, a giant and son of Vulcan, living near the spot on which Rome was built. He stole from Hercules some of the cattle of Geryon, dragging them backward into his cave under the Aventine, so that their footprints would not show the direction in which they had gone; but Hercules found them by their lowing, and slew the thief.

Cade (kād), **Jack**. In Shakespeare's *2 Henry VI*, the rebel leader, the historical John Cade. York, planning to usurp the throne, encourages Cade to stir up a rebellion in England. Cade assumes the name Mortimer and claims the throne himself. He captures London Bridge, but his followers desert him, he flees, and is killed by Alexander Iden.

Cade, John. [Called **Jack Cade**.] b. probably in Ireland; killed near Heathfield, Sussex, England, July 12, 1450. English rebel, the leader in Cade's Rebellion, a rising chiefly of Kentishmen, in May and June, 1450. The rebels defeated the royal forces at Sevenoaks on June 27, and entered London on July 2. On July 3, they killed Henry IV's lord chamberlain, James Fiennes, Baron of Saye and Sele, but within a few days their rebellion was suppressed. Cade is said to have been regarded by his cohorts as a cousin of the Duke of York.

cadence (kā′dẹns). **1.** A fall of the voice in reading or speaking, as at the end of a sentence; also, the falling of the voice in the general modulation of tones in reciting.
2. A regular and agreeable succession of measured sounds or movements; rhythmic flow, as the general modulation of the voice in reading or speaking, or of natural sounds.

    To make bokes, songes, dytees,
    In ryme, or elles in *cadence*.
        (Chaucer, *House of Fame*.)

    Blustering winds, which all night long
Had roused the sea, now with hoarse *cadence* lull
Sea-faring men.   (Milton, *P. L.*, ii. 287.)

    The preacher's *cadence* flow'd,
Softening thro' all the gentle attributes
Of his lost child. (Tennyson, *Aylmer's Field*.)

Cadenus (kạ.dē′nus). The name by which Jonathan Swift calls himself in his poem *Cadenus and Vanessa* (1726). The name is an anagram of *decanus*, meaning "dean" in Latin (Swift was Dean of St. Patrick's Cathedral, at Dublin, from 1713).

Cadenus and Vanessa (vạ.nes′ạ). A poem by Jonathan Swift. Considered one of Swift's best poems, it was written in 1712 or 1713 to cure Esther Vanhomrigh of a passion for Swift, and appeared in 1726, three years after her death.

Cadmus (kad′mus). In Greek legend, a son of Agenor, king of Phoenicia, and Telephassa. He was the reputed founder of Thebes in Boeotia, and the introducer of the letters of the Greek alphabet. The particular legendary episode for which he is now probably best known is that which has him sowing the teeth of a dragon, which he had killed, and from each of which there immediately grew a warrior, fully armed and accoutered. It was these men who were the ancestors of the people of Thebes. However, because the dragon had been sacred to Ares, the god of war, the descendants of Cadmus himself were involved by Ares, in punishment for Cadmus's deed, in various tragedies.

Cadwal (kad′wạl). In Shakespeare's *Cymbeline*, the name under which Arviragus is raised from infancy. As Cadwal, Arviragus believes himself to be the son of Morgan (who is actually Belarius).

Cadwalader or **Cadwallader** (kad.wol′ạ.dėr). [Called "The Blessed."] d. c664. A British king. He was the son of Caedwalla, king of Gwynedd (North Wales), whom he succeeded in 634.

Cadwallader (kad.wol′ạ.dėr). A character in Samuel Foote's play *The Author*. This play was stopped by the lord chamberlain at the request of a Mr. Aprice, a friend of Foote, who was imitated and ridiculed in this part, especially in a habit he had of sucking his wrist as he talked.

Cadwallader, Rev. Mr. In George Eliot's novel *Middlemarch*, the rector of the parish. He exasperates his wife, a clever, keen, epigrammatic woman, by his good temper.

Cadwallader Crabtree (krab′trē). See **Crabtree, Cadwallader.**

Cadwallon (kad.wol′ọn). In Sir Walter Scott's novel *The Betrothed*, a minstrel of Gwenwyn, the Welsh prince who is besieging the castle of Eveline Berenger. He disguises himself as Renault Vidal to prosecute a revenge, for which he is executed.

Caedmon (kad′mọn). [Also, **Cedmon**.] fl. c670. An early English poet, the reputed author of metrical paraphrases of the Old Testament. He was the earliest Christian poet in the history of English letters. He became late in life an inmate of the monastery at Whitby, under the abbess Hild. According to the account given by Bede, he was an unlearned cowherd, especially lacking in poetical talent, until he was commanded in a dream to sing of "the beginning of created things." A nine-line poem, known as Caedmon's *Hymn* and preserved in several manuscripts, is recognized as the first product of Caedmon's versification. The miraculous gift thus bestowed upon him was fostered by Hild, and he is thought to have produced metrical paraphrases of Genesis and other parts of the Bible. He is generally regarded as a saint. The

fat, fāte, fär, ȧsk, fāre; net, mē, hėr; pin, pīne; not, nōte, mōve, nôr; up, lūte, pull; ᴛʜ, then;

poems in the Junius Manuscript were once attributed to Caedmon, but no one today believes that they were all written by him or that any part of them is in the form he dictated.

Caelia (sēl′yạ). A variant spelling of Celia. See especially the **Celia** of Spenser's *Faerie Queene.*

Caelica (sē′li.kạ). See **Coelica.**

Caerleon (kär.lē′ọn). [Also: **Caerleon-on-Usk;** Latin, **Isca** or **Isca Silurum.**] An urban district in W England, in Monmouthshire, situated on the river Usk, ab. 3 mi. NE of Newport. It was an important city in the Roman period, being the headquarters of the Second (Augustan) Legion, and known for its theater, temples, and palaces; part of the massive walls remain. Caerleon has a museum containing many interesting Roman relics found in the vicinity. It is one of several places identified as the traditional seat (Camelot) of King Arthur's court.

Caermarthen (kär.mär′ᴛʜẹn, kạr-), **The Black Book of.** See **Black Book of Carmarthen, The.**

Caesar (sē′zạr). In ancient Rome, a patrician family of the Julian gens, of which the origin was fancifully traced to a legendary Julius, son of Aeneas. The first Caesar actually to be noted in the annals was Sextus Julius, who was a praetor in 208 B.C. Lucius Julius Caesar, consul in 90 B.C., had an important part in shaping Roman institutions by securing the enactment of the law granting Roman citizenship to such of the Italian allies as had not fought against Rome in the Social War or who had laid down their arms at once. Lucius Julius Caesar was killed in 87 B.C., during the civil war, and with him his brother Gaius Julius Caesar Strabo Vopisius, whom Cicero numbered among the Roman orators. A son of Lucius Julius Caesar, bearing the same name, served in Gaul under that other Gaius Julius Caesar (c100 B.C.–44 B.C.) who made the family name one of the most noted in history. This younger Lucius Julius Caesar accompanied his great relative in the campaign which secured for the latter mastery of the Roman world, and after his assassination, joined the avenging forces of Mark Antony, whose mother, Julia, was a sister of Lucius. He quarrelled with Antony, however, and was saved from proscription only by Julia's intervention.

Caesar, Don. In Hannah Cowley's *A Bold Stroke for a Husband,* the father of Olivia.

Caesar, Julius. In Shakespeare's *Julius Caesar,* the dictator of Rome, whom the conspirators, led by Brutus and Cassius, assassinate (on the part of Brutus solely, and on the part of Cassius at least partly, for fear that he would abridge the traditional Roman freedoms). Critical opinions have varied about this character: some critics find Caesar a weak man, others find him a noble figure (taking his words about his fearlessness literally). While portraying him as somewhat of an egotist, Shakespeare seems to have treated Caesar's fatalism sympathetically and to have injected references to his physical weakness as a means of completing the character.

Caesar, Octavius. See **Octavius Caesar.**

Caesar and Cleopatra. A play by George Bernard Shaw included in the volume *Three Plays for Puritans* (1901). It is a vindication of the character of Julius Caesar against the aspersions of Shakespeare's Roman heroes, and a revelation of what Shaw takes to be the great man's genuine intellectual processes. Shaw's Caesar is witty, and he never glosses over his actions with large, loose phrases designed to justify them on moral grounds. He is also used by Shaw to sharpen his satire of those aspects of middle-class English character which continued to infuriate him, as exemplified by the provincial Apollodorus, and Brittanus, a hidebound, unbending individual who looks upon himself with self-satisfied smugness.

Caesar and Luath (lö′ath). In Robert Burns's poem *Twa Dogs,* the two dogs whose conversation provides the substance of the poem. Caesar is a gentleman's dog, and tends toward arrogance; Luath is a simple farmer's collie.

Caesar and Pompey (pom′pi), **The Tragedy of.** A tragedy by George Chapman, published in 1631 and written c1613. Although Chapman in the dedicatory epistle stated that it had never appeared on the stage, an edition published in 1653 claimed that it was acted at the Blackfriars Theatre and its detailed stage directions suggest printing from a prompter's copy. The material of this play came from Plutarch's *Lives* and *Morals.*

Caesar in Egypt. A tragedy by Colley Cibber, produced at the Drury Lane Theatre, London, on Dec. 9, 1724, and published in 1728. It was taken from Philip Massinger and John Fletcher's *The False One* and Pierre Corneille's *La Mort de Pompée.* The plot deals with the defeat of Pompey by Caesar, the latter's love for Cleopatra, Ptolemy's attempted treachery, and Antony's attachment to Cleopatra as a result of his wooing her for Caesar.

Caesarion (sē.zär′i.ọn). b. 47 B.C.; d. 30 B.C. An Egyptian ruler; son of Cleopatra and (probably) Julius Caesar. He was executed by order of Augustus. As Ptolemy XIV (or XVI) he was, with his mother, a nominal ruler of Egypt from c44 B.C. to the time of his death.

Cagliostro (kä.lyôs′trō), Count **Alessandro di.** [Assumed name of **Giuseppe Balsamo.**] b. at Palermo, Sicily, June 2, 1743; d. at San Leone, Urbino, Italy, Aug. 26, 1795. An Italian adventurer, notorious for his activities in Russia, Paris, the East, and elsewhere. Among other adventures he was involved in the "Diamond Necklace Affair" at Paris, and was imprisoned in the Bastille, but escaped. He visited England, and was there imprisoned in the Fleet. On emerging he went to Rome, where he was arrested and condemned to death, but his sentence was commuted to imprisonment in the fortress of San Leone, where he died.

Cain: A Mystery (kān). A long dramatic poem (1821) by Byron. It challenges submissive orthodoxy and proclaims the right and duty of man to use his reason freely. It is a mystery play in title only, having little connection with the Biblical story of Cain and Abel. Lucifer, the tempter of Cain, is not unlike Satan in Milton's *Paradise Lost,* a relatively sympathetic character. Lucifer shows Cain the potentiality of his intellectual being, and Cain is enraged at "the author of Life" for his limitations in "encumbering clay."

cain-coloured. Yellowish red, the supposed color of Cain's hair. Shakespeare in *The Merry Wives of Windsor* (I.iv) refers to a "cain-coloured beard."

ḍ, d or j; ş, s or sh; ṭ, t or ch; ẕ, z or zh; o, F. cloche; ü, F. menu; ch, Sc. loch; ṅ, F. bonbon.

Caine (kān), Sir **Hall.** [Full name, **Thomas Henry Hall Caine.**] b. at Runcorn, Cheshire, England, 1853; d. Aug. 31, 1931. An English novelist, best known for his descriptions of life on the Isle of Man; brother of William Ralph Hall Caine (1865–1939). Among his works are *Sonnets of Three Centuries* (1882), *The Shadow of a Crime* (1885), *The Deemster* (1887), *The Manxman* (1894), *The Christian* (1897), *The Eternal City* (1901), *Drink* (1907), *My Story* (1909), *The White Prophet* (1909), *The Woman Thou Gavest Me* (1913), and *Master of Man* (1921). *Recollections of Rossetti* (1882) is an account of Caine's friendship with Dante Gabriel Rossetti. *The Bondman* was dramatized in 1907, *Pete* (with Louis N. Parker) in 1908, *The Bishop's Son* in 1910, and *The Eternal Question* in 1910.

Caine, William Ralph Hall. b. 1865; d. Jan. 14, 1939. An English journalist, editor, anthologist, and author of works on the Isle of Man; brother of Hall Caine (1853–1931). He was a writer for the Liverpool *Mercury*, and editor of the *Court Circular*, the *Family Churchman*, and *Household Words*. Author of *The Isle of Man* (1909), *The Kingdom of Man and the Isles* (1919), *The Story of Sodor and Man* (1925), and *Annals of the Magic Isle* (1926); editor of two anthologies, *Humorous Poems of the Century* (1890) and *Love Songs of England* (1893).

Ça ira (sà ē.rà). The first popular song (c1789) to grow out of the French Revolution. The music was that of a contredanse which was extremely popular under the name *Carillon national*, composed by a drummer in the orchestra of the opera, and was a great favorite with Marie Antoinette. The words are thought to have been suggested by Lafayette to Ladré, a street singer; he remembered them from hearing Benjamin Franklin say at various stages of the American Revolution, when asked for news, "Ça ira, Ça ira." There are five verses with different refrains, the words becoming more ferocious as the Revolution progressed. The best-known refrain is:

> Ah! ça ira, ça ira, ça ira!
> Les aristocrates à la lanterne!

Cairbar (kār′bär). In one of the Ossianic poems by the Scottish poet Macpherson, a rebel against King Ormac. He is slain by Ossian's son Oscar (who is himself killed in the next moment by Cairbar).

Caird (kärd), **Alice Mona.** [Pseudonym, **G. Noel Hatton**; maiden name, **Hector.**] b. on the Isle of Wight, 1858; d. Feb. 4, 1932. An English feminist and novelist. She is noted for what at the time were considered to be radical ideas on questions relating to sex, marriage, and morality. Under her pseudonym she wrote her earliest novels, *Whom Nature Leadeth* (1883) and *One That Wins* (1887). She was the author also of *The Wing of Azrael* (1889), *A Romance of the Moors* (1891), *The Daughters of Danaus* (1894), *Beyond the Pale* (1896), *The Pathway of the Gods* (1898), and *The Stones of Sacrifice* (1915). Her other works include *The Morality of Marriage and Other Essays* (1897), and *The Romantic Cities of Provence* (1906).

Caird, Edward. b. at Greenock, Scotland, March 22, 1835; d. at Oxford, England, Nov. 1, 1908. A Scottish philosopher and professor; brother of John Caird (1820–98). He was educated at Glasgow and St. Andrews universities, and at Balliol College, Oxford, of which he was subsequently (1893–1907) master. From 1866 to 1893 he was professor of moral philosophy at Glasgow. His works include *The Philosophy of Kant* (1878), *Hegel* (1883), *The Social Philosophy and Religion of Comte* (1885), *Critical Account of the Philosophy of Kant* (1889), *Essays in Literature and Philosophy* (1892), *Evolution of Religion* (1893), and *Evolution of Theology in the Greek Philosophers* (1904).

Caird, John. b. at Greenock, Scotland, Dec. 15, 1820; d. at Oxford, England, July 30, 1898. A Scottish philosopher, teacher, and theologian; brother of Edward Caird (1835–1908). Educated (1840–45) at Glasgow University, with which he was later associated as professor of theology and vicechancellor (1862–73) and principal (1873–98), he also held parishes (1845–57) at Newton-on-Ayr, at Edinburgh, and in Perthshire. He was the author of *Introduction to the Philosophy of Religion* (1880), *Spinoza* (1888), *University Sermons* (1899), *University Addresses* (1899), and *The Fundamental Ideas of Christianity* (1900, originally delivered in the period 1895–96 as the Gifford Lectures). He was popular for his sermon *Religion in Common Life* (1857), which he had delivered (1855) with great success before Queen Victoria.

Cairnes (kârnz), **John Elliott.** b. at Castle Bellingham, County Louth, Ireland, Dec. 26, 1823; d. near London, July 8, 1875. A British political economist, a follower of the theories of utilitarianism as laid down by John Stuart Mill. In 1866 he was appointed professor of political economy at University College, London. In a work entitled *The Slave Power* (1862) he discussed the basic weaknesses in any society which derived a major portion of its productive effort from slavery, and thereby was enabled accurately to forecast the eventual downfall of the Confederacy. The significance of this work, which had a marked effect on a considerable body of influential English opinion, was very great indeed; it dealt a blow to the hopes of the Confederacy for British alliance, and persuaded many Englishmen that their best interests would be served finally by Northern victory. His other works include *Character and Logical Method of Political Economy* (1857), *Essays in Political Economy* (1873), *Political Essays* (1873), and *Some Leading Principles of Political Economy, Newly Expounded* (1874).

Caithness (kāth′nes, kāth.nes′). In Shakespeare's *Macbeth*, a Scottish thane.

Caius (kā′us). In Shakespeare's *King Lear*, the assumed name of Kent.

Caius. In Shakespeare's *Titus Andronicus*, a kinsman of Titus.

Caius. See also **Gaius.**

Caius, Dr. In Shakespeare's *Merry Wives of Windsor*, a French doctor in love with Anne Page. Despite an arrangement with Mistress Page to carry off Anne and marry her, he loses her through a substitution arranged by Fenton and the Host of the Garter Inn.

Caius College (kēz). See **Gonville and Caius College.**

Caius Gracchus (kā′us grak′us). A tragedy by James Sheridan Knowles, produced in 1815 at

Belfast. He afterward revised it, and the new version was produced by William Charles Macready at Covent Garden in 1823.

Caius Lucius (lō'shus). See **Lucius, Caius.**

Caius Marcius (mär'shus). See under **Coriolanus.**

Caius Marius (mār'i.us), **The History and Fall of.** A tragedy (1679) in blank verse by Thomas Otway, an adaptation of Shakespeare's *Romeo and Juliet.*

Cakes, Land of. Scotland, famous for its oatmeal cakes.

Cakes and Ale. A novel by W. Somerset Maugham, published in 1930. A biting account of the life of a noted but not very talented English author, its central character has been variously identified as Thomas Hardy and Hugh Walpole (usually the latter, who is said by some who knew him to have been absolutely convinced that he was Maugham's target).

Calais (ka.lā', kal'ā; in Shakespeare, kal'is; French, ka.le). A city in N France, in the department of Pas-de-Calais, situated on the narrowest part of the Strait of Dover, between Dunkerque and Cap Gris Nez. It was formerly strongly fortified and had a number of historical monuments such as the Cathedral of Notre Dame, the old city hall, and the Porte de Guise, but much of the city was destroyed in World War II. In former times, Calais was much contested between the English and the French, and was under British rule from 1347 to 1558.

Calamities of Authors. A work by Isaac D'Israeli, published in 1812.

Calandrino (kä.län.drē'nō). The subject of a story in Giovanni Boccaccio's *Decameron.* He is very unfortunate and very amusing.

Calantha (ka.lan'tha). In John Ford's tragedy *The Broken Heart,* the daughter of Amyclas, the king of Laconia. She drops dead of a broken heart after placing a wedding ring upon the hand of her dead lover, Ithocles. This follows an extraordinary scene in a ballroom during which, with apparent calm and while continuing her dance, she listens to the announcement of the deaths, one after another, of her father, lover, and brother.

Calaynos (kä.lī'nōs). A tragedy by George Henry Boker. His first play, it was produced at London at the Sadler's Wells Theatre, May 10, 1849, without Boker's consent, by the actor Samuel Phelps. It was first played in the U. S. at the Walnut Street Theatre, Philadelphia, Jan. 20, 1851, with James E. Murdoch taking the part of Calaynos. The main theme of the tragedy is the complex racial friction between the Spaniards and Moors, and the consequent horror felt by the Spaniards for what they deem the "taint" of Moorish blood. Its importance rests not so much upon the plot as upon the creation of lofty standards of race and conduct, the atmosphere of inevitable tragedy, and the distinction of its blank verse.

Calchas (kal'kas). In Greek legend, a soothsayer who advised the sacrifice of Iphigenia. According to prophecy, he died when he met, in Miopsus, his superior in divination.

Calchas. In Shakespeare's *Troilus and Cressida,* a Trojan priest who becomes a traitor to his native city and joins the Greeks. He requests that his daughter Cressida (whom he has left in Troy) be exchanged for Antenor, a Trojan held prisoner by the Greeks. He does not object to Diomedes's seduction of his daughter.

Calcraft (kal'kräft), **John William.** Pseudonym of **Cole, John William.**

Calcutta (kal.kut'a). [Hindustani, **Kalikata**; original name, probably **Kalighat,** referring to a shrine of the goddess Kali in the vicinity.] The capital and principal seaport of West Bengal state, Union of India, on the Hooghly River, ab. 120 mi. above the Bay of Bengal: the chief commercial center of Asia, served by several railroads and by national and international air and steamship lines. It was founded as a British East India Company factory c1690, was fortified in 1696, and was originally called Fort William. It was the scene of the tragedy of the Black Hole. It was retaken by Clive in 1757, and became the capital of British India in 1773. The seat of government was transferred to Delhi in 1912.

Calderon (kôl'dėr.on), **George.** b. 1868; d. 1915. An English dramatist and scholar, known for his studies in Slavonic linguistics. His plays include *The Fountain* (1909), *The Little Stone House* (1911), and *Revolt* (1912).

Calderón de la Barca (käl.dā.rōn' dä lä bär'kä), **Pedro.** b. at Madrid, Jan. 17, 1600; d. there, May 25, 1681. A Spanish dramatist and poet. He was educated first by the Jesuits and then at Salamanca, being graduated from the latter university in 1619. He had at that time already some reputation as a dramatist. His extraordinary popularity continued until his death. He himself made a list of 111 plays and 70 (or 73) sacramental *autos* which forms the basis for a proper knowledge of his works. His *comedias de capa y espada* (comedies of the cloak and sword) are peculiarly characteristic, and about 30 of these can be enumerated. Among them are *La Dama duende* (The Fairy Lady), *Mejor está que estaba* (It is Better than it Was), *Peor está que estaba* (It is Worse than it Was), and *Astrologo fingido* (The Mock Astrologer); John Dryden used this last in his *An Evening's Love, or The Mock Astrologer.* Among his other plays are *El Mágico prodigioso* (The Wonder-working Magician), *La Devoción de la cruz* (The Devotion of the Cross), *El Principe constante* (The Constant Prince), *La Vida es sueño* (Life is a Dream), *El Mayor encanto amor* (No Magic like Love), and *Las Armas de la hermosura* (The Weapons of Beauty).

Calderon the Courtier. A historical novel based on events in Spanish history, by Edward Bulwer-Lytton, published in 1838.

Caleb (kā'leb). A character in John Dryden's satire *Absalom and Achitophel.* He is intended for Lord Grey of Wark, one of the adherents of the Duke of Monmouth.

Caleb Balderstone (bôl'dėr.stōn). See **Balderstone, Caleb.**

Caleb Garth (gärth). See **Garth, Caleb.**

Caleb Plummer (plum'ėr). See **Plummer, Caleb.**

Caleb Quotem (kwōt'em). See **Quotem, Caleb.**

Caleb Williams (wil'yamz). [Full title, **The Adventures of Caleb Williams, or Things as They**

Are.] A novel by William Godwin, published in 1794. In it Godwin sharply contrasts the power possessed by the privileged and the helplessness of the lowly. Caleb Williams, secretary to Ferdinando Falkland, discovers that the master he has so much admired is the killer of the arrogant and wicked Barnabas Tyrrel, for whose murder two innocent men have been executed. In spite of the fact that Caleb does not propose to reveal Falkland's secret, his master has him imprisoned on a false charge of theft. Caleb escapes from prison, but is hunted by agents of Falkland and finally, in desperation, publicly accuses Falkland, who is forced to confess. Caleb, however, is overcome by remorse that he should have been the person to bring about his master's downfall.

Caledonia (kal.ẹ.dō′ni.ạ). A Roman name for the N part of the island of Britain, comprising all of present-day Scotland N of the Firth of Forth and the Firth of Clyde. Although the Romans made numerous expeditions against the tribes of Caledonia between the 1st and 3rd centuries A.D., the region was never subjugated. The name Caledonia is often used in literature to mean Scotland.

Calenders (kal′ẹn.dẽrz), **the Three.** Three princes disguised as "Calenders" (begging dervishes) in *The Arabian Nights' Entertainments.*

Calepine (kal′ẹ.pēn), **Sir.** In Edmund Spenser's *Faerie Queene,* a knight who saves a child from a bear by squeezing the latter to death.

Calepino (kä.lā.pē′nō), **Ambrogio.** b. at Calepio, near Bergamo, Italy, June 6, 1435; d. there, Nov. 30, 1511. An Italian lexicographer. He compiled a Latin-Italian dictionary, originally entitled *Cornucopiae* (1502), which passed through many editions, and became, after successive enlargements, in 1590 a polyglot of 11 languages. Jacopo Facciolati reduced this number to seven in his edition (1718).

Caliban (kal′i.ban). In Shakespeare's *Tempest,* a deformed and repulsive slave. The son of the witch Sycorax, who ruled the island before Prospero's shipwreck on it, he becomes a reluctant captive to Prospero's magic powers. He grumbles at his lot, and wishes to break free, allying himself with Stephano and Trinculo for that purpose. After Prospero's rescue, Caliban is left the sole inhabitant of the island.

Caliban. A novel by W. L. George, published in 1920. It is a study of newspaper life.

Caliban by the Yellow Sands. A play (1916) by Percy MacKaye. It was written for the Shakespeare tercentenary.

Caliban upon Setebos; or, Natural Theology in the Island (set′ẹ.bos). A poem by Robert Browning, published in *Dramatis Personae* (1864). The poem reflects Browning's keen interest in the Darwinian hypothesis, which was a new, very much publicized, and extremely controversial issue at that time. Although the link between Browning's Caliban and the Caliban of Shakespeare is clear enough, Browning's use of the character to epitomize human superstition, vindictiveness, and abject terror at the thought that certain natural phenomena (such as thunderstorms) are measures taken by Setebos (who is Caliban's god) to punish human impudence is far more complex than Shakespeare's. A

clue to Browning's purpose in the poem may be obtained from the line taken from the Fiftieth Psalm which immediately follows the title: "Thou thoughtest that I was altogether such a one as thyself." In other words, Caliban (and by extension, man) cannot think of the Deity except as being a more powerful extension of himself, and Caliban attributes to Setebos, indeed, all the aches, pains, appetites, and irresponsibility which mark his own character. Caliban's musing, at the very beginning of the poem, as to the manner and fashion of the Creation makes this clear, and also establishes in a few lines what may be called the flavor and direction of the poem as a whole:

> Setebos, Setebos, and Setebos!
> 'Thinketh, He dwelleth i' the cold o' the moon.
> 'Thinketh He made it, with the sun to match,
> But not the stars; the stars came otherwise;
> Only made clouds, winds, meteors, such as that:
> Also this isle, what lives and grows thereon,
> And snaky sea which rounds and ends the same.
> 'Thinketh, it came of being ill at ease:
> He hated that He cannot change His cold,
> Nor cure its ache.

Caliburn (kal′i.bẽrn). See **Excalibur.**

Calidore (kal′i.dōr), **Sir.** A knight in Edmund Spenser's *Faerie Queene,* the personification of chivalric courtesy. He is modeled upon Sir Philip Sidney.

Caligula (kạ.lig′ū.lạ). [Original name, **Gaius Caesar.**] b. at Antium, Italy, Aug. 31, 12 A.D.; killed at Rome, Jan. 24, 41. A Roman ruler, the third emperor of Rome (37–41 A.D.); youngest son of Germanicus and Agrippina. He succeeded Tiberius, whose death he had caused or accelerated. The beginning of his reign was marked by great moderation, but, after he had undergone an illness, the rest of his life was marked by cruelty and licentiousness little short of madness. He is said to have exclaimed in a fit of vexation, "Would that the Roman people had only one head!" with the clear implication that this would considerably simplify their beheading. He is also reputed to have had himself worshiped as a god, and to have raised his horse to the consulship. He invaded Gaul in 40. He was assassinated by Cassius Chaerea, Cornelius Sabinus, and others.

Caligula. A tragedy by John Crowne, printed in 1698.

Caliphate. A term used to describe the position held by the successors of Mohammed, the word "caliph" meaning "successor," "lieutenant," "vice-regent," or "deputy." At the peak of its power, the Caliphate wielded a degree of temporal and spiritual might which had no rival in Islam. Theoretically, each caliph was vested with absolute authority in all matters of state, both civil and religious, as long as he ruled in conformity with the law of the Koran and the traditions of Islam. The caliph had to be a male, an adult, sane, a free man, a learned divine, a powerful ruler, a just person, and one of the Koreish (the Arab tribe to which Mohammed himself belonged). The Shiites (the schismatics of Islam) also demanded that he should be a descendant of Mohammed's family through Ali, who was the fourth caliph and Mohammed's nephew. The first five caliphs were Abu-Bakr,

Omar I, Othman, Ali, and Hasan, Ali's son. The last-named caliph ruled only nominally, because actual power had already passed into the hands of Muawiyah, who was to be the first Ommiad caliph, as a result of Ali's assassination in 661. Nevertheless, he is included in all tables of the caliphs. Among the Shiites his brother, Husain, is also reckoned as a caliph, as successor (680) to Muawiyah. According to some authorities, only the first five listed above have actual right to the title of caliph, all others being merely amirs or governors. The power of the Caliphate passed in 661 to the Ommiads, who, 14 in number, reigned until 750 at Damascus. They were succeeded by the Abbassides, with 37 caliphs reigning from 750 to 1258 at Baghdad (and hence sometimes called the Caliphate of Baghdad). After their temporal power had been overthrown by the Mongols in 1258, descendants of the Abbassides resided for almost three centuries in Egypt, and asserted their claim to the spiritual power. In 1517 their claim to the Caliphate passed over through one descendant of the Abbassides to Selim I, the ninth of the Ottoman dynasty of Turkish sultans. In this line, the Caliphate thereafter remained in the hands of the rulers of Turkey, until it was formally abolished in 1924. The Caliphate was also claimed at various times in history by descendants of an Ommiad who managed to escape the slaughter of his family by the Abbassides in 750 and established the Arab emirate at Córdoba, Spain. This came to be known as the Caliphate of Córdoba, or the Western Caliphate. Still another claim to the Caliphate existed from the early 10th century to the latter part of the 12th century, in North Africa, among various descendants (Fatimites) of Fatima, Mohammed's daughter and Ali's wife.

Calipolis (ka.lip'o̲.lis). In George Peele's play *The Battle of Alcazar*, the wife of Muly Mahamet. During a famine her husband presents her with a bit of meat, stolen from a lioness, on his bloody sword, with these words: "Feed then and faint not, fair Calipolis." Pistol ridicules this line in Shakespeare's *Henry IV*, Part II, Act II, scene 4.

Calista (ka.lis'ta̲). One of the principal characters in Philip Massinger's *The Guardian*.

Calista. In John Fletcher and Philip Massinger's play *The Lover's Progress*, the faithful wife of Cleander. Her struggle with her unfortunate passion for Lysander affords a powerful scene.

Calista. In Nicholas Rowe's *The Fair Penitent*, the titular heroine. She is the proud, fierce wife of a forgiving husband, Altamont, and loves "that haughty gallant, gay Lothario," who has seduced her. After the latter's death her sense of guilt induces her to kill herself, though Johnson remarks that she was more pained at being discovered than sorry for what had happened.

Calista. In Sir Walter Scott's novel *The Talisman*, the queen's woman. She is wily and intriguing.

Calisto and Melibea (ka.lis'tō; mel.i.bē'a̲). An interlude printed c1529, probably by John Rastell and based on Mabbe's translation of the Spanish romance, *Celestina*.

Calisto and Meliboea (mel.i.bē'a̲), **The Tragicomedy of.** See **Celestina**.

Call, The. A poem (c1630) by George Herbert, affirming the poet's faith by listing the needs of the soul for this faith. Each request that he calls for emerges from the one before:

> Come, my Light, my Feast, my Strength:
>> Such a light as shows a feast,
>> Such a feast as mends in length
>> Such a strength as makes his guest!

Callcott (kôl'kot), **Maria.** [Maiden name, **Dundas**.] b. at Papcastle, near Cockermouth, England, 1785; d. at Kensington, London, Nov. 21, 1842. An English writer. She wrote *Little Arthur's History of England* (1835).

Callimachus (ka.lim'a̲.kus). b. at Cyrene, in North Africa; d. c240 B.C. A Greek critic, grammarian, and poet, chief librarian of the Alexandrian library. Best known as a poet, he also compiled the *Pinakes*, an annotated catalogue of books which can be regarded as a literary history. He is known to have produced some 800 works, few of which are extant, and to have been a potent influence on Roman poets including Ovid, Catullus, and others.

Calliope (ka.lī'o̲.pē) In Greek mythology, the Muse of epic poetry and eloquence. She was the mother of Orpheus.

Callirrhoë (ka.lir'o̲.ē). In Greek legend, the wife of Alcmaeon. She persuaded her husband to procure for her the peplum and necklace of Harmonia, and thus caused his death, which was avenged by his sons.

Callista (ka.lis'ta̲). A novel set against a background of early Christianity, by John Henry Newman, published in 1856.

Callisthenes (ka.lis'the̲.nēz). b. at Olynthus, Macedonia, c360 B.C.; d. c328 B.C. A Greek philosopher; a cousin and pupil of Aristotle, and a companion of Alexander the Great in Asia. He incurred Alexander's ill will by his criticism of Alexander's adoption of Oriental customs, and was probably put to death by Alexander's order.

Callisto (ka.lis'tō). In Greek mythology, an Arcadian huntress, a companion of Artemis, beloved of Zeus and transformed either by him or by Artemis into a she bear. In this form she was slain by Artemis in the chase. She was placed among the stars as the constellation Ursa Major.

Callum Beg (kal'um beg). See **Beg, Callum**.

Calpe (kal'pē). An ancient name of the rock of Gibraltar. It and Abyla, as the facing promontory on the coast of Africa was then called, constituted the Pillars of Hercules.

Calphurnia (kal.fėr'ni.a̲). In Shakespeare's *Julius Caesar*, the historical Calpurnia, wife of Caesar. She is fearful for her husband's safety because of dreams she has had, and tries to persuade him not to go to the Capitol.

Calprenède (kàl.prḙ.ned). See **La Calprenède**.

Calvary (kal'va̲.ri). A word occurring in the New Testament (Luke, xxiii. 33), adopting the *calvaria* by which the Vulgate translates the Greek *kranion*, which itself is the rendering of the Aramean *golgotha*, skull; it was not in its original sense a proper name. The popular name "Mount Calvary" is not warranted by any statement in the gospels as being that of the place of the Crucifixion. Traditionally, however, Christ was crucified at the place now

d̲, d or j; s̲, s or sh; t̲, t or ch; z̲, z or zh; o, F. cloche; ü, F. menu; ch, Sc. loch; n̲, F. bonbon.

known as Calvary, outside the ancient Jerusalem. Golgotha is also often written with a capital letter, used as a variant of Calvary, and thought of as a place.

Calverley (kal'vėr.li). In *A Yorkshire Tragedy*, once attributed to Shakespeare, a ruined gamester, brutally cruel to his wife and children. The story is based on that of a real person of that name.

Calverley, Charles Stuart. b. at Martley, Worcestershire, England, Dec. 22, 1831; d. at London, Feb. 17, 1884. An English poet and parodist.

Calves' Head Club. A club said to have been instituted in ridicule of the memory of Charles I. It is first noticed in a tract reprinted in the *Harleian Miscellany*, called "The Secret History of the Calves' Head Club," undertaking to show how this club met for some years (1693–97) on the anniversary of the king's death. An ax was reverenced, and a dish of calves' heads represented the king and his friends. It seems to have met in secret after the Restoration and until 1734, when some ill feeling was excited against it, and riots are said to have ensued. In 1735 it was suppressed.

Calvin (kal'vin), **John.** [Original name, **Jean Chauvin** (or **Cauvin** or **Caulvin**); German, **Johann Calvin**; Italian, **Giovanni Calvino**; Latinized, **Johannes Calvinus.**] b. at Noyon, in Picardy, France, July 10, 1509; d. at Geneva, Switzerland, May 27, 1564. A Protestant reformer and theologian. He studied at Paris, Orléans, and Bourges. Having embraced the Reformation (c1528), he was driven (1533) from Paris, published (1536) *Institutes of the Christian Religion* at Basel, and went (1536) to Geneva. The extreme nature of the reforms which Calvin, with Guillaume Farel, attempted to carry out there, caused (1538) their banishment. Calvin returned to Geneva in 1541, however. He had a controversy with Bolsec in 1551, and with Servetus in 1553, causing Servetus to be burned at the stake. He founded the Academy of Geneva in 1559.

Calvo (käl'vō), **Baldassarre.** One of the principal characters in George Eliot's novel *Romola*.

Calydon (kal'i.dọn). In ancient geography, a city of Aetolia, in C Greece, situated near the river Evenus. It is the legendary scene of the hunt of the Calydonian boar.

Calydon. A great forest, supposed to be in the north of England, celebrated in Arthurian romance.

Calypso (kạ.lip'sō). In Homer's *Odyssey*, a nymph living in the island of Ogygia, who detained Ulysses for seven years. She promised him perpetual youth and immortality if he would remain with her.

Cam (kam). [Also, **Granta.**] A river in E central England, in Cambridgeshire, rising near Ashwell and flowing NE past Cambridge to its confluence with the river Ouse, ab. 4 mi. S of Ely. The names Cam and Granta have both appeared in literature and on maps of the region. Length, ab. 40 mi.; navigable to Cambridge.

Camacho (kä.mä'chō). In one of the episodes in Cervantes' *Don Quixote*, a rich but unfortunate man. He is cheated out of his bride, Quiteria, just as he has provided a great feast for his wedding; hence the phrase "Camacho's wedding" has been used to signify great but useless show and expenditure.

Camaralzaman (kam.ạ.ral'zạ.man), **Prince.** The hero of the tale "Amours of Prince Camaralzaman and the Princess Badoura" in *The Arabian Nights' Entertainments*.

Camballo (kam'bạ.lō). In Chaucer's "Squire's Tale," in *The Canterbury Tales*, the second son of Cambuscan. He is introduced by Edmund Spenser, who calls him Cambell, in *The Faerie Queene*.

Cambell (kam'bẹl) or **Camballo** (kam.bal'ō). A character in Edmund Spenser's *Faerie Queene*, taken from Chaucer's *Canterbury Tales*, where he appears as Camballo, a son of King Cambuscan.

Cambina (kam.bī'nạ). A daughter of the fairy Agape in Edmund Spenser's *Faerie Queene*. She has magic powers, and in the end marries Cambell.

Cambises (or **Cambyses**), **King of Persia** (kam.bī'sēz). [Full title, **A Lamentable Tragedy mixed full of Mirth, containing the Life of Cambises, King of Persia.**] An interlude by Thomas Preston, written as early as 1561.

Cambrensis (kam.bren'sis), **Giraldus.** See **Giraldus Cambrensis.**

Cambria (kam'bri.ạ). An ancient name of Wales.

Cambridge (kām'brij). [Middle English, **Cambrigge, Cambrig, Cantebrigge**; earlier, **Grantebrigge, Grauntebrigge**; Old English, **Grantabrycg, Grantanbrycg,** meaning "bridge of (the river) Granta"; Latin, **Cantabrigia.**] A municipal borough in E central England, the county seat of Cambridgeshire, situated on the river Cam ab. 56 mi. NE of London by rail. It is located in the Fens, a marshy district SW of the Wash. Cambridge is the seat of the University of Cambridge. It is probably on the site of an ancient British town and of the Roman Camboricum or Camboritum. It had a castle (now destroyed), founded by William the Conqueror; the round Church of the Holy Sepulchre dates from the Norman period.

Cambridge, Earl of. In Shakespeare's *Henry V*, the historical Richard, Earl of Cambridge, a conspirator who plots with Scroop and Grey to murder the King. The plot is discovered and the King hands them death warrants in place of the expected commissions for his French campaign. In *Richard II*, he is a son of the Duke of York and brother of Aumerle. His son is the York appearing in *1, 2*, and *3 Henry VI*.

Cambridge, Richard Owen. b. at London, Feb. 14, 1717; d. at Twickenham, England, Sept. 17, 1802. An English poet, satirist, essayist, and historian. He is known as the author of *The Scribleriad* (1751), a mock-heroic poem in the style of Alexander Pope, verse satires in imitation of Horace, and *History of the War upon the Coast of Coromandel* (1761). He contributed 21 essays (Nos. 50–51, 54–56, 65, 70–72, 76, 99, 102, 104, 106–108, 116, 118–119, 123, and 206) to the *World* (1753–56), one of the many imitators of the *Tatler* and *Spectator*. He entertained Samuel Johnson, Sir Joshua Reynolds, Thomas Gray, William Pitt, and many others at Twickenham, and is mentioned frequently in James Boswell's writings.

Cambridge, University of. [Also, **Cambridge University.**] A university at Cambridge, England. The town was a center of learning in the 12th century, and in 1231 Henry III issued writs for the regulation of Cambridge "clerks." It contains the following colleges: St. Peter's (Peterhouse), founded as a hospital in 1257, converted into a college by Hugh de Balsham (charter, 1284); Clare, by Richard Badew in 1326 as University Hall, refounded by the Countess of Clare in 1359; Pembroke, by the Countess of Pembroke in 1347; Gonville and Caius, by Gonville in 1348 and Caius in 1558; Trinity Hall, by Bateman in 1350; Corpus Christi, or Benet College, by Cambridge guilds in 1352; King's, by Henry VI in 1441; Queens', by Margaret of Anjou in 1448 and Elizabeth Woodville in 1465; St. Catherine's, by Woodlark in 1473; Jesus, by Alcock in 1496; Christ's, by William Bingham as a school in 1439, refounded by Margaret Beaufort, mother of Henry VII, in 1505; St. John's, founded as a hospital c1210, refounded in 1511 by Margaret Beaufort; Magdalene, established as a hostel for students in 1428, given to Lord Audley who founded it as a college in 1519; Trinity, by Henry VIII in 1546 on several earlier foundations; Emmanuel, by Mildmay in 1584; Sidney Sussex, by the will of the Countess of Sussex (d. 1589) in 1594; Downing, by Sir George Downing (d. 1749; charter in 1800); Ayerst Hall, founded in 1884, "to provide an economical education for theological students and others," closed 1896; Cavendish College, in 1873, by an association, for younger students, closed 1891; Selwyn College (a hostel), in 1882 in memory of George Augustus Selwyn. It has two women's colleges: Girton (established 1869) and Newnham (established 1875; originally founded, 1873, as a hall of residence). The university library contains some 1,500,000 volumes, more than 12,000 manuscripts, and 250,000 maps.

Cambridge History of English Literature. A survey history of English literature from its beginnings to the end of the 19th century, each section written by a notable expert scholar in that field, and edited by A. W. Ward and A. R. Waller. The work, published in 14 volumes from 1907 to 1927, now is published in 15 volumes, the separate indexes for each volume having been combined in a general index.

Cambuscan (kam.bus.kan´, kam´bus.kan). [Also, **Cambyuskan** (-byus-).] In Chaucer's "Squire's Tale," in *The Canterbury Tales*, a Tartar king who has extraordinary magical possessions: a ring, a glass, a sword, and a brazen horse. He is the father of Canace, Camballo, and Algarsife.

Cambyses (kam.bĭ´sēz). A tragicomedy (1671) by Elkanah Settle. It combined all the then-fashionable elements of heroic tragedy and had been issued in four editions before 1700.

Camden (kam´den), **William.** b. at London, May 2, 1551; d. at Chislehurst, Kent, England, Nov. 9, 1623. An English historian and antiquary, noted for his study of Elizabethan times, *Annales rerum Anglicarum et Hibernicarum regnante Elizabetha* (1615). He was an usher (1575–93) and headmaster (1593–97) of the Westminster School, London, leaving there to take up an appointment as Clarenceux king-of-arms. He spent many years on writing and revising *Britannia* (1st ed., 1586), a survey of the British islands; written in Latin, it was first translated into English in 1610. He also compiled a Greek grammar (1597), and published various editions of historical works. The Camden Society, founded in 1838 for the purpose of publishing historical documents, was named for him.

Camden Farebrother (fār´bruꝮ.ėr), **Rev.** See **Farebrother, Rev. Camden.**

Camden Society. An English historical society formed in 1838 for the publication of documents relating to English history. It was named for William Camden.

Cameliard (kam´el.yärd). In Malory's *Morte d'Arthur*, the kingdom of Leodegrance, Guinevere's father.

Camelon (kam´e.lon). A *quoad sacra* (i.e., ecclesiastical) parish in Falkirk parliamentary burgh, in E central Scotland, in Stirlingshire, situated on the Firth of Forth. It is said to be the site of the battle that ended the career of the historical King Arthur, in 537.

Camelot (kam´e.lot). A legendary spot in England or Wales where King Arthur was said to have had his palace and court, and where the Round Table was. Shakespeare alludes to it in *King Lear:*

Goose, if I had you upon Sarum plain,
I'd drive ye cackling home to Camelot.

This is supposed to be in allusion to the fact that great quantities of geese were bred on the moors at Queens Camel, Somersetshire. In Geoffrey of Monmouth, Camelot was, or was near, Winchester; other writers locate it in Monmouthshire, at Caerleon; still others identify it with Camelford, in Cornwall.

Cameron (kam´ėr.on), **Richard.** b. at Falkland, Fifeshire, Scotland; killed near Aird's Moss, Ayrshire, Scotland, July 20, 1680. A Scottish Presbyterian minister, a leader of the Covenanters. His followers, a sect of Scottish dissenters, were called Cameronians, later taking the name Reformed Presbyterians. A field preacher, he refused to submit to the authority of Charles II. A group of his followers were the nucleus of the Cameronian regiment of the British army.

Cameron of Lochiel (loċh.ēl´), **Donald.** [Called "the Gentle Lochiel."] b. c1695; d. 1748. A Scottish chieftain and soldier. In 1719 he became chief of the Clan Cameron. He arrived (Aug. 19, 1745) with 800 clansmen to support Prince Charles Edward, a move which rallied other support for the Pretender. He captured Edinburgh (Sept. 17, 1745), fought at Prestonpans, where the Camerons distinguished themselves, and was wounded while taking Falkirk. A leader at Culloden (April 16, 1746), he opposed the night attack, during which he was severely wounded. He escaped with Prince Charles Edward, arriving (Sept. 29, 1746) on the coast of Brittany.

Camilla (ka.mil´a). In Greek legend, a virgin warrior queen of the Volscians. She figures in Vergil's *Aeneid* as being killed by the Trojans.

Camilla. In John Lyly's *Euphues*, a lady with whom Philautus falls in love.

Camilla. [Full title, **Camilla, or a Picture of Youth.**] A novel by Fanny Burney, published in 1796.

Camille (kà.mēl). The name, and heroine, of the English version of *La Dame aux camélias*, a play by the younger Dumas.

Camillo (kạ.mil'ō). In John Webster's tragedy *The White Devil*, the husband of Vittoria Corombona.

Camillo. In Shakespeare's *Winter's Tale*, a Sicilian noble. He saves Polixenes and induces Leontes to protect Florizel and Perdita.

Camillo. A character in John Dryden's play *The Assignation*.

Camisards (kam'i.zärdz). A name given to a group of French Protestants in the Cévennes who revolted (1702–10) against the persecution which followed the revocation (1685) of the Edict of Nantes. They were probably so called from the blouses worn in night raids by the peasants, who were the chief participants in the insurrection. Inspired by prophecies of the fall of Babylon (the Roman Catholic Church), the Camisards burned churches and drove away many priests. With their religious fervor and strong sense of injustice and their knowledge of their own country, which had few roads, they were able to hold out against the large forces sent against them. On the offer of certain concessions to the Protestants, one of their leaders, Jean Cavalier, who had been successful in many guerrilla raids, submitted in 1704, and many of the Camisards disbanded, but scattered revolt continued until 1710.

Camlan (kam'lạn), **Battle of.** A legendary battle variously said to have taken place in Cornwall or (by Malory) near Salisbury, in which both King Arthur and his nephew Modred fell in single combat. See also **Camelon.**

Camões (kạ.moinsh'), **Luiz (Vaz) de.** [English, **Camoëns** (kam'ō.ẹnz, kạ.mō'ẹnz).] b. in Portugal, c1524; d. at Lisbon, June 10, 1580. A Portuguese poet, the most celebrated in that language, author of the epic poem *Os Lusíadas* (The Portuguese, 1572; commonly called the *Lusiads*), on the discovery of the sea route to India by the Portuguese navigator Vasco da Gama. Camões came of a family of the minor nobility and was educated at Coimbra, which he is believed to have left for Lisbon in the early 1540's. For about two years he lived in Ceuta, Africa, where he served in the army and lost the sight of his right eye, probably in a battle. At Lisbon, he was imprisoned (1552) for having wounded one of the king's equerries in a street fracas. He was pardoned (1553) on the condition of his immediate embarkation for India. He arrived in Goa in September of the same year, and went to Macao a few years later. About 1560 he was back in Goa. He embarked there for Portugal in 1567, but was left in Mozambique. At last he landed at Lisbon at the end of 1569 or the beginning of 1570, after about 17 years of exile. His lyric production is of extreme literary value, his sonnets being thought by many to have been unsurpassed. The most reliable edition of his lyrics is considered to be *Lírica de Camões*, a scholarly work published at Coimbra in 1932 by José Maria Rodrigues and Afonso Lopes Vieira, which contains all the lyric poems actually written by Camões, omitting those that for centuries had been unduly attributed to him. He also wrote three comedies in verse: *El-Rei Seleuco*, *Anfitriões*, and *Filodemo.*

Camorra (kạ.môr'ạ). A secret terroristic society that first became prominent (c1830) in the S part of Italy. Its ultimate origin is not known, although some have suggested a borrowing from Spain (from the Spanish word *camorra*, meaning "quarrel"). In Italy it had what might be considered a comparatively respectable origin as a mutual aid society of inmates and former inmates of the prisons of the Kingdom of the Two Sicilies, most of whom were political prisoners or otherwise victims of Bourbon tyranny. Its power spread, especially at Naples, as liberated prisoners perceived that in the chaotic conditions then prevailing in S Italy a living could most easily be made by thuggery, extortion, and the organization of what later came to be called rackets. Apprising each other by means of secret signs and signals of the approach of likely victims or, on the other hand, of the police, the *camorristi*, as the members were called, roamed the streets in bands. Smuggling was soon added to highway robbery as a major source of emolument, and merchants were easily induced to hire camorristi to afford, to their goods in transit and at their warehouses, protection which the police were impotent to give. The police, indeed, often sought the aid of the Camorra in the solution of crimes. The society evolved its own code and ranks of officers, and settled its problems before its own tribunals. First coming to public notice during the third decade of the 19th century, before long it had acquired such power as to be, in fact if not by law, the government of Naples. From 1848 to 1860 the Camorra supported the Italian movement for independence, and if it had been dissolved after this succeeded it might appear in history in a relatively favorable light. It continued, however, as a purely criminal organization, taking toll of prostitution, gambling, and other activities of the underworld, and buying immunity by bribing police, government officials, and even members of the clergy. In 1877 an attempt at suppression was made, without effect. In 1900, however, facts came out in the course of a lawsuit which caused the Italian government to set aside the municipal government of Naples and to institute a searching inquiry. In 1901 an Honest Government League was formed in the city, which began to bring the Camorra under control, and in 1911, following a murder traced to the society, 20 of its leaders (of whom the reputed chief was extradited from the U. S.) were tried, convicted, and heavily sentenced, and the organization fell apart.

Campagna di Roma (käm.pä'nyä dē rō'mä). A large plain in C Italy, surrounding Rome, lying between the Mediterranean Sea and the Sabine and Alban mountains. It corresponds in great part to the ancient Latium. It is of volcanic formation, and has been for centuries noted for its malarial climate, though in antiquity it was covered with villas and towns and was brought to a high state of cultivation. It has been largely reclaimed.

Campaign, The. A poem by Joseph Addison celebrating the battle of Blenheim, published in 1704.

"Campaigner," the. In Thackeray's novel *The Newcomes*, an epithet of Mrs. Mackenzie.

Campaspe (kam.pas'pē). In John Lyly's comedy *Alexander and Campaspe*, a beautiful slave girl, captured by Alexander the Great.

fat, fāte, fär, ȧsk, fāre; net, mē, hėr; pin, pīne; not, nōte, möve, nôr; up, lūte, pŭll; ᴛʜ, then;

Campaspe, Alexander and. A prose comedy by John Lyly, printed in 1584, and reprinted as *Campaspe* in that year and in 1591. The story is from Pliny's *Natural History*. The plot concerns the love of Alexander the Great for his Theban captive, Campaspe, whom he surrenders to Apelles, a painter hired to do a portrait of Campaspe, when he discovers their love. It was performed at Court before Queen Elizabeth in 1584 with scenery made of painted wooden frames.

Campbell (kam'bẹl, kam'ẹl). The family name of the earls of Argyll (or Argyle), subject of the popular ballad *The Campbells Are Coming*. See also **Argyll.**

Campbell, Archibald. [Title, 2nd Earl of **Argyll.**] Killed at Flodden, Northumberland, England, 1513. A Scottish soldier. He became master of the royal household in 1494, and shared with Matthew Stewart, Earl of Lennox, the command of the right wing of the Scottish army at the battle of Flodden, on Sept. 9, 1513, in which engagement he was killed.

Campbell, James Dykes. b. 1838; d. 1895. A Scottish merchant, and biographer of Samuel Taylor Coleridge. He entered (1854) a pottery business at Glasgow, and was a partner (1873–81) in the firm of Ireland, Fraser and Company, in Mauritius. His biography of Coleridge was prefixed to an 1893 edition of Coleridge's poetical works, but appeared in a separate volume the following year.

Campbell, Joseph. [Irish, **Seosamh MacCathmhaoil.**] b. at Belfast, Ireland, 1879; d. at Lackan, County Wicklow, Ireland, 1944. An Irish poet and artist (he illustrated some of his own poetry). He also wrote a play *Judgement* (1912). His volumes of poetry are *Rushlight* (1906), *Mountainy Singer* (1909), *Irishry* (1913), and *Earth of Cualann* (1917).

Campbell, Lewis. b. at Edinburgh, Scotland, Sept. 3, 1830; d. at Alassio, Italy, Oct. 25, 1908. A Scottish teacher, translator of Sophocles and Aeschylus. Educated at Edinburgh Academy, Glasgow University, and at Trinity and Balliol colleges, Oxford, winning medals, prizes, and fellowships, he was professor of Greek (1863–92) and Gifford Lecturer (1894–95) at St. Andrews University. He edited Plato and Sophocles, finished Benjamin Jowett's translation of Plato's *Republic*, and translated the extant tragedies of Sophocles and Aeschylus into English verse (1883 and 1890; both published 1906, and many times reprinted, in the *World's Classics* series). He was the author of *Life of James Clerk Maxwell* (1882), *Guide to Greek Tragedy* (1891), *Life of Jowett* (1897), *Religion in Greek Literature* (1898; Gifford Lectures), and *Tragic Drama in Aeschylus, Sophocles, and Euripides* (1904).

Campbell, Mrs. Patrick. [Maiden name, **Beatrice Stella Tanner.**] b. at London, 1865; d. April 9, 1940. An English actress. She made her debut in 1888, at Liverpool, and thereafter toured with Ben Greet's company; following her first appearance at London she was engaged by Sir Arthur Wing Pinero to play Paula, the title role in *The Second Mrs. Tanqueray*. Thereafter she became to some extent identified with the modern drama of ideas; she made a success as Rita in Henrik Ibsen's *Little Eyolf*, and as Magda in Hermann Sudermann's play of that name, and originated the part of Eliza in George Bernard Shaw's *Pygmalion*, which he had written expressly for her. She also appeared in a number of Shakespearian parts, including Rosalind in *As You Like It*, Ophelia in *Hamlet*, Lady Macbeth, and Juliet. With Sarah Bernhardt she appeared in an original version of Maurice Maeterlinck's *Pelléas et Mélisande*, which she also presented in an English version. Among her modern parts was also that of Anastasia Rakonitz in Gladys Bronwyn Stern's *The Matriarch*. She toured widely in England and Ireland, and appeared in the U. S. in the title role of *Magda* by Sudermann.

Campbell, Robert. In Scottish history, one of the names of the actual person now best known as the Rob Roy of Sir Walter Scott's novel. Rob's clan name was Macgregor (he was actually the chief of the clan), but the Macgregors had been proscribed as a Scottish clan by order of the British crown for their participation in various risings against the English, and Rob took his mother's clan name of Campbell.

Campbell, Thomas. b. at Glasgow, Scotland, July 27, 1777; d. at Boulogne, France, June 15, 1844. A British poet and critic. He was lord rector (1826–29) of the University of Glasgow. His works include *The Pleasures of Hope* (1799), *Gertrude of Wyoming* (1809), and *Specimens of the British Poets* (1819). Among his short lyrics are *Lochiel's Warning*, *Hohenlinden*, *Mariners of England*, and *Battle of the Baltic*. He is buried in Westminster Abbey.

Campeius (kam.pē'us), **Cardinal.** In Shakespeare's *Henry VIII*, a papal legate, who, with Wolsey, considers the question of the King's divorce from Katherine.

Camperdown (kam'pẹr.doun). [Dutch, **Kamperduin.**] A dune in W Netherlands, in the province of North Holland, near the village of Kamp (or Camp), NW of Alkmaar. On Oct. 11, 1797 a British fleet under Duncan defeated the Dutch in a naval battle in the North Sea near here.

Campian (kam'pi.ạn), **Theodora.** In Benjamin Disraeli's novel *Lothair*, a beautiful woman who fights for Italian freedom.

Campian, Thomas. See **Campion, Thomas.**

Campion (kam'pi.ọn), **Edmund.** b. at London, Jan. 25, 1540; executed at Tyburn (now Marble Arch, in Hyde Park, London), Dec. 1, 1581. An English Jesuit and scholar, remembered as one of the leading Jesuit missionaries in England. Although already subject to Roman Catholic leanings, he became (c1568) a deacon in the Church of England after having attended Oxford University. Having fled to France, he joined the Catholic Church, and in 1573 became a member of the Jesuit order. When the missionary movement to England was initiated (1580), he was among the first group to go there; his preaching was marked by a large number of conversions, although carried on illegally and therefore necessarily clandestinely. He wrote and distributed *Decem rationes*, a pamphlet listing his objections to the Anglican Church, which was so influential that the government's efforts to apprehend him were increased. Taken captive on July 14, 1581, he was taken to London where a recantation was sought from him; in spite of inducements by Queen Elizabeth, and three rackings,

ḍ, d or j; ṣ, s or sh; ṭ, t or ch; ẓ, z or zh; o, F. cloche; ü, F. menu; c̣h, Sc. loch; ṅ, F. bonbon.

he stood firm, and expounded his views brilliantly at Protestant councils. He was finally found guilty of conspiracy and sedition, and condemned to death. His life forms the subject of a monograph (1935) by Evelyn Waugh.

Campion, Thomas. [Also, **Campian.**] b. at London, Feb. 12, 1567; d. there, March 1, 1620. An English poet, physician, musician, song-writer, critic, and writer of masques. He was the author of *Poemata* (1595, Latin verses), *A Booke of Ayres* (1601), *Observations on the Art of English Poesie* (1602), and *Two Bookes of Ayres* (c1613). His *Songs of Mourning,* occasioned by the death of Prince Henry, was published in 1612; between 1607 and 1617 he wrote several elaborate court masques. His *New Way of Making Foure Parts in Counterpoint* (1617) was an important work in musical theory. Among his best-known poems are *Cherry Ripe, Of Corinna's Singing, Come, Cheerful Day, Now Winter Nights Enlarge, When Thou Must Home, Chance and Change,* and *There Is a Garden in Her Face.*

Camulodunum (kam″ū.lọ.dū′num). Latin name of Colchester, England.

Canaan's Calamity (kā′nanz). A versified work (1618) by Thomas Dekker. It is the story of the destruction of Jerusalem by Titus.

Canace (kan′a.sē). In Greek legend, a daughter of Aeolus, put to death on account of her illicit love for her brother. Chaucer refers to the story in the introduction to "The Man of Law's Tale" in *The Canterbury Tales.*

Canace. The daughter of Cambuscan in Chaucer's "Squire's Tale," in the *Canterbury Tales.*

Cancer (kan′sẽr). A constellation and also a sign of the zodiac, represented by the form of a crab, and showing the limits of the sun's course northward in summer; hence, the sign of the summer solstice.

Candace (kan′da.sē). The hereditary appellation of the ancient Ethiopian queens of Meroë, in Upper Nubia (now part of Anglo-Egyptian Sudan), like the name *Pharaoh* applied to the older Egyptian kings; specifically:
1. According to an old tradition, the Queen of Sheba who visited Solomon.
2. A queen of Meroë who invaded Egypt in 22 B.C. and captured Elephantine, Syene (modern Aswan), and Philae. She was defeated by the Roman general Petronius, renewed the attack, and was again defeated by him.
3. In Biblical history, the queen of Ethiopia whose high treasurer was converted to Christianity by Philip, in 30 A.D. Acts, viii. 27.

Candaules (kan.dô′lēz) or **Myrsilus** (mẽr.sī′lus). fl. in the 8th or 7th century B.C. The last Heracleid king of Lydia. He was slain by Gyges, who succeeded him.

Candida (kan′di.da). A play (1897) by George Bernard Shaw, included in *Plays, Pleasant and Unpleasant* (1898). It deals with the choice the titular heroine must make between her husband, James Morrell, who is a stern and ascetic clergyman, and Eugene Marchbanks, a young poet who adores her. While Marchbanks freely confesses his weakness of character, Candida discerns that

her undemanding husband needs her more deeply, and makes her decision accordingly. Rejected, the poet departs, to learn to find strength in himself. Candida is the type of person Nora, in Ibsen's *A Doll's House,* wished to become: a woman with a sense of her own mind, a willingness to consult her own wishes rather than convention, and the ability to choose wisely in terms of human needs. She decides to stay with Morrell not because she bows to convention, but because she discerns that she would be better as a wife to him than as a substitute mother to Marchbanks.

Candidate for Truth, A. A novel by John Davys Beresford, published in 1912, the second volume of the Jacob Stahl trilogy. Its companion volumes are *The Early History of Jacob Stahl* (1911) and *The Invisible Event* (1915).

Candide (kän.dēd; Anglicized, kan.dēd′). [Full title, **Candide, ou L'Optimisme.**] A philosophical novel by Voltaire, published in 1759, a satire on the optimism of Leibnitz and his followers. Its titular hero bears all the worst ills of life, including such catastrophes as the Lisbon earthquake of 1755, in naïve puzzlement while his tutor Pangloss assures him that Leibnitz is right, all is for the best. The book ends with the exhortation to the hero, and by implication to the reader, "Let us cultivate our garden," that is, apply common sense to everyday problems and stop worrying over the metaphysical problems we cannot solve.

Candido (kan′di.dō). A long-suffering linen draper in Dekker and Middleton's *The Honest Whore.*

Candish (kan′dish), **Thomas.** See **Cavendish** or **Candish, Thomas.**

Candlemas (kan′dl.mas). A Roman Catholic and Anglican feast day in commemoration of the presentation of Christ in the Temple, and the purification of the Virgin Mary. It falls annually on February 2.

Candle of Vision, The. An autobiographical fragment (1918) by Æ (George W. Russell).

Candour (kan′dor), **Mrs.** A slanderous woman with an affectation of frank amiability, in Richard Brinsley Sheridan's comedy *The School for Scandal.*

Can Grande (kän grän′dā). See **Scala, Cane Grande della.**

Canidia (ka.nid′i.a). fl. in the 2nd half of the 1st century B.C. A Neapolitan hetaera, loved by Horace. She deserted him, and he reviled her as a sorceress. Her real name is said by some authorities to have been Gratidia.

Canidius (ka.nid′i.us). In Shakespeare's *Antony and Cleopatra,* the chief lieutenant of Antony. He withholds his forces from the sea battle and, when he sees that Antony is losing, joins Octavius.

Canmore (kan′mōr), **Malcolm.** See **Malcolm III.**

Cannae (kan′ē). In ancient geography, a town in Apulia, Italy, situated S of the river Aufidus. Near here (and N of the river), Hannibal with a Carthaginian force of ab. 50,000 men virtually annihilated (216 B.C) the Roman army of ab. 80,000–90,000 under Varro and Aemilius Paulus. It was one of the greatest military disasters ever suffered by the ancient Romans, and the site is still called locally the "Field of Blood" (Italian, *Campo di Sangue*).

fat, fāte, fär, ȧsk, fāre; net, mē, hẽr; pin, pīne; not, nōte, mȯve, nôr; up, lūte, pu̇ll; ᴛʜ, then·

The Battle of Cannae remains even to this day of interest to military historians from the fact that it provides (with the earlier victory at Lake Trasimeno) clear evidence of Hannibal's military genius (his use of cavalry at Cannae is still studied by professional soldiers). Carthaginian fortunes were at their peak after Cannae, but lack of support from Carthage made it impossible for Hannibal to press his advantage and led finally to the defeat (201 B.C.) of Carthage by Rome in the Second Punic War.

Cannan (kan'an), **Gilbert.** b. at Manchester, England, June 25, 1884—. An English novelist, playwright, and critic. Educated at the University of Manchester and at Cambridge University, he was admitted to the bar in 1908, but never practiced. He served as drama critic (1909–10) on the London *Star*, and was a founder of the Manchester Repertory Theatre. His novels include *Peter Homunculus* (1909), *Devious Ways* (1910), *Little Brother* (1912), *Round the Corner* (1913), *Old Mole* (1914), *Mendel* (1916), *The Stucco House* (1918), *Mummery* (1918), *Pugs and Peacocks* (1920), *Sembal* (1922), and *The House of Prophecy* (1924). Among his plays are *Miles Dixon* (1910), *James and John* (1911), *Mary's Wedding* (1912), *The Perfect Widow* (1912), *Everybody's Husband* (1917), and *The Release of the Soul* (1920).

Canning (kan'ing), **George.** b. at London, April 11, 1770; d. at Chiswick, near London, Aug. 8, 1827. An English Liberal statesman and orator. He first entered Parliament in 1793, and served during his subsequent political career as secretary for foreign affairs (1807–09, 1822–27), president of the board of control for India (1816–20), and prime minister (1827). He attended Eton and Christ Church, Oxford, where he formed a debating club (and managed to achieve some renown for opposition to the aristocracy). However, in spite of this, after having come to London in 1792 he formed a friendship with the younger William Pitt, with whom he shared a horror of the results of the French Revolution. He made his maiden speech in Parliament in 1794, and soon became known as a brilliant orator. Under the aegis of Pitt, he held (1793–1801) several government posts, including the undersecretaryship for foreign affairs (1791 *et seq.*), in which he took an active part in the peace negotiations (1797) at Lille, France; during this period he also contributed to the *Anti-Jacobin*, an antiradical weekly. After Pitt's retirement (1801), Canning went through a period (1801–09) of alternate opposition and support of the government; but took at all times a great interest in the maintenance of an aggressive military policy toward Napoleon I (he was a firm supporter of the joint Anglo-Spanish campaigns in Spain under the Duke of Wellington now usually called the Peninsular War, and had a chief part in planning the naval operation which resulted (1807) in the capture of the Danish fleet at Copenhagen). From 1809 to 1822, he was comparatively inactive in major political affairs (at least partly because he could not stomach what he considered to be the unjustified attack of most leading figures in the British government on Queen Caroline), but in 1822, with his second appointment as secretary for foreign affairs, he entered on the period of his greatest influence, becoming one of the foremost statesmen of his time. His foreign policy was one of nonintervention in the liberal movements of the Continent in those years. The waning of any British inclination to support the reactionary policies of the Holy Alliance (Russia, Austria, and Prussia), despite the fact that Great Britain, through the Quadruple Alliance of 1814, was committed to a considerable interest in European affairs, is usually said to have reached a decisive point in Canning's protest at the Congress of Verona (1822) against the sending of a French army to put down a Spanish revolution. This protest had an enormously important significance on the course of American history through the fact that it, plus the recognition by Great Britain of South American independence of Spain, made very clear indeed to the powers of Europe that Great Britain (and hence the British navy) would not take part in enabling Spain, or anyone else, to regain lost overseas colonies. Most historians now consider that it was this which actually made the Monroe Doctrine possible. He was also well known for his advocacy of greater political and social freedom for Roman Catholics in England.

Canny Elshie (el'shi). See **Elshender.**

canon. The books of the Holy Scripture accepted by the Christian church as containing an authoritative rule of religious faith and practice. With the exception of the books called *antilegomena*, the canonicity of which was not at first universally recognized, the canon of the New Testament has always consisted of the same books. The books comprised in the Hebrew Bible, and constituting the Hebrew canon, that is to say, the books of the Old Testament as given in the authorized version from Genesis to Malachi inclusive, are universally recognized as canonical. The canonical character of the books not found in the Hebrew, but contained in the Septuagint or Vulgate; and although they are received without distinction by the Greek Church, and, with the exception of some among the number, by the Roman Catholic Church, they are not accounted canonical by the Anglican Church (which, however, treats them as *ecclesiastical books*, that is, books to be read in the church), nor by any of the Protestant churches.

Canongate (kan'on.gāt). A principal thoroughfare in the Old Town of Edinburgh. The little burgh of the Canongate grew around the abbey of Holyrood, which is about a mile E of the castle, in the 12th century, soon after the founding of the abbey. The street runs from that point, bearing different names at various parts of its course. Sir Walter Scott laid the scene of his *Chronicles of the Canongate* there.

Canonization, The. A poem by John Donne in which the poet speaks of his love. He first asks to be excused from routine worries so that he may love, then in the third stanza he proclaims his love, particularly through the symbol of the phoenix (who figures often in metaphysical poetry): "We die and rise the same, and prove/ Mysterious by this love." The canonization or blessing that he wants in order to sanctify his love is expressed in

ḍ, d or j; ṣ, s or sh; ṭ, t or ch; ẓ, z or zh; o, F. cloche; ü, F. menu; ċh, Sc. loch; ṅ, F. bonbon.

the last two stanzas. It need not be the conventional sort of canonization; immortality in poetry would suffice: "And by these hymns all shall approve/ Us canonized for love."

Canon's Yeoman's Tale, The. One of Chaucer's *Canterbury Tales*. It exposes the tricks of the alchemists. Elias Ashmole, in a work entitled *Theatrum Chemicum*, quotes the whole poem, with the prologue, under the impression, apparently, that Chaucer was an adept in the art, and wrote in its favor. The Canon, a ragged alchemist who has no gold but what he gets by trickery, with his disgruntled Yeoman joins the Canterbury pilgrims at Boughton-under-Blee. When the Yeoman begins to tell of the Canon's practices, the latter flees "for verry sorwe and shame." Then the Yeoman describes his life with the alchemist and tells of a canon (not his master, he protests) who practiced alchemy and of how he cheated a gullible priest.

Canopus (ka̱.nō'pus). The second brightest star in the sky. It is one magnitude brighter than Arcturus, and only half a magnitude fainter than Sirius; α Argus or α Carinae. It is situated in one of the steering paddles of Argo Navis, about 35 degrees S of Sirius and about the same distance E of Achernar. It is yellow, and is conspicuous in Florida during the winter.

Canossa (kä.nôs'sä; Anglicized, ka̱.nos'a̱). A village and ruined castle SW of Reggio nell' Emilia, Italy. It is celebrated as the scene of the penance of the emperor Henry IV before Pope Gregory VII, in January, 1077, to rescind the excommunication imposed by the Pope as a result of Henry's having made lay appointments to several sees. It is said that Henry stood for three days in the snow outside the castle where Gregory was the guest of Matilda of Tuscany, before the Pope would grant absolution.

cant. **1.** A whining or singing manner of speech; specifically, the whining speech of beggars, as in asking alms.
2. The language or jargon spoken by gypsies, thieves, professional beggars, or the like, and containing many words different from ordinary English; a kind of slang or argot.
3. The words and phrases peculiar to or characteristic of a sect, party, or profession; the dialect of a class, sect, or set of people: used in an unfavorable sense.

Of all the *cants* which are canted in this canting world, though the *cant* of hypocrites may be the worst, the *cant* of criticism is the most tormenting. (Sterne, *Tristram Shandy.*)

4. A pretentious or insincere assumption, in speech, of a religious character; an ostentatious or insincere use of solemn or religious phraseology.

That he [Richard Cromwell] was a good man, he evinced by proofs more satisfactory than deep groans or long sermons, by humility and suavity when he was at the height of human greatness, and by cheerful resignation under cruel wrongs and misfortunes; but the cant then common in every guard-room gave him a disgust which he had not always the prudence to conceal. (Macaulay, *Hist. Eng.*, i.)

Cantab. or **cantab** (kan'tab). **1.** An abbreviation of the Latin adjective *Cantabrigiensis:* as, John Jones, M.A. *Cantab.* (that is, Master of Arts of the University of Cambridge).
2. A member or graduate of the University of Cambridge. "The rattle-pated trick of a young cantab." (Sir Walter Scott.)

Canterbury (kan'tẽr.ber.i, -bẽr.i). [Middle English, also, **Cauntirbyry**; Old English, **Cantwaraburh**; Latin, **Durovernum.**] A city and county borough in SE England, in Kent, situated on the river Stour ab. 60 mi. SE of London by rail: principal archiepiscopal see of the Church of England. Part of Canterbury's importance is due to its position in the water gap of the river Stour through the North Downs. Canterbury is located on the edge of the East Kent coal field. It has little industry, but has a good commerce in malt, hops, and grain. Flowers and vegetables for the London market are grown in the neighborhood. During World War II, considerable numbers of military personnel were billeted in the city and vicinity. Canterbury's buildings of interest are the cathedral (where Thomas à Becket was murdered in 1170), Saint Martin's Church, Saint Dunstan's Church, remains of the castle, the monastery of Saint Augustine, and many old houses. Air-raid damage during World War II revealed some fine examples of Roman mosaic pavements. Canterbury is one of the oldest cities in the country; it is on the site of a British village, and was a Roman military station and a Kentish town. Augustine became the first archbishop here in 600. It was sacked by the Danes in 1011. 27, 778 (1951).

Canterbury Churches. The cathedral was founded in the 11th century. The existing choir was built by William of Sens (France) after 1174, and the Perpendicular nave, transepts, and great central tower date from the 15th century. In plan the cathedral is long and narrow, with double transepts. The interior is light and impressive. The choir is raised several feet, and separated from the nave by a sculptured 15th-century screen. The columns, arcades, vaulting, and chevet are very similar in character to those of the cathedral of Sens, which supplied the model. Some of the glass of the deambulatory is of the 13th century. The portion of the choir behind the altar contains several fine altar-tombs of early archbishops, and the tombs of Henry IV and the Black Prince. At the extreme E end is a beautiful circular chapel called the Corona. The crypt is very large, and early Norman in style. The Perpendicular cloisters are ornate and picturesque. The dimensions of the cathedral are 514 by 71 ft.; the height of the nave-vaulting 80 ft., and of the central tower 235 ft. Saint Martin's is called the "Mother Church of England." The original foundation was no doubt pre-Saxon, and there are Roman bricks in the lower parts of the walls. The upper parts of the long, low, quaint, ivy-clad structure are much later.

Canterbury, Archbishop of. In Shakespeare's *Henry V*, a counsellor to the King, who, in hopes that a war with France will deter the King from confiscating church property, proves at length that the old Salic Law, forbidding the succession of women and their descendants to the throne, would not apply to France, and that Henry's genealogy entitles him to claim French lands.

Canterbury, Archbishop of. See also under **Bourchier, Cardinal,** and under **Cranmer.**

Canterbury College. A former college of Oxford University, England. It was founded by Simon Islip, archbishop of Canterbury, in 1361 or 1362. John Wycliffe was its second warden. It was disbanded in the reign of Henry VIII, and the last remains of its buildings were demolished in 1775.

Canterbury Pilgrims, The. A play (1903) by Percy MacKaye. A Chaucerian revival, it is an adaptation of an old literary theme to modern dramatic presentation.

Canterbury Tales, The. A work (c1387–1400) by Geoffrey Chaucer. At the Tabard Inn, Southwark, Chaucer joins some 29 pilgrims bound for the shrine of Saint Thomas à Becket at Canterbury. The Prologue describes the vividly individualized pilgrims, ranging from an eminent jurist and a worthy knight to a plowman and a dishonest miller. The Host of the Tabard, Harry Bailey, suggests that on the journey each pilgrim tell four stories, the best to be rewarded by a supper on their return. Of the projected series of 120 tales, Chaucer completed only 22 (or 24, if one includes *The Rime of Sir Thopas* and the concluding sermon on the Seven Deadly Sins by the Parson). Most are in heroic couplets, a few in stanzas, and two in prose. First the Knight recounts a romance of fighting, love, and pageantry, condensed from Boccaccio's *Il Teseida*. The Host next calls upon the Monk, but Robin the Miller, already drunk, insists on his turn. With brilliant characterization he vitalizes a clever fabliau plot of an old uxorious carpenter deceived by an Oxford undergraduate, who in turn is tricked by a parish clerk. Osewold, the "sclendre colerik" Reeve, formerly a carpenter, takes personal offense and retaliates with a fabliau of a thieving miller deceived by two Cambridge students. Then Roger of Ware, the uncleanly London Cook, starts a story of low London life (unfinished). The Man of Law retells the tale of the long-suffering Constance from the Anglo-Norman *Chronicle* of Nicholas Trivet. After the Shipman's fabliau comes the Prioress's miracle of a boy's devotion to the Virgin Mary; then Chaucer attempts the doggerel rime of Sir Thopas, a romance so "drasty" that the Host makes him stop. Chaucer tries again with the long prose allegory of Melibeus and his wife Prudence, a humanitarian document against the evils of war and the perversion of justice, originally by Albertano of Brescia. The Monk is not allowed to finish his "tragedies" of the falls of the great; the Nun's Priest satirically retells the barnyard beast-epic of Chauntecleer and Pertelote. Alice of Bath, looking for a sixth husband, defends her marriages, tells how she has handled her husbands, and recounts the folk tale of an old hag who becomes a beautiful maiden when her husband promises obedience. After Friar Huberd and the Summoner have chastised each other with fabliaux, the Clerk of Oxenford retells Petrarch's story of patient Griselda, who submits to her husband's every whim. The disillusioned Merchant, two months wed, bitterly tells of old January deceived by his young wife May; then the gay Squire starts

an Eastern romance (unfinished). The country gentleman, the Franklin, tells of a perfect marriage based on truth and generosity. The Physician retells the old Roman "geste" of Appius and Virginia. The Pardoner shows how he wins money by preaching on "the root of all evil" and by telling his impressive exemplum of how avarice brought death to three revellers. After the second Nun's legend of the martyred Saint Cecilia, the Canon's Yeoman exposes his master's alchemical deceptions; the Manciple retells Ovid's story of Phoebus and the Crow; and as the company nears Canterbury, the Parson gives his prose sermon on Penance and the Seven Deadly Sins. The 83 complete or fragmentary manuscripts of *The Canterbury Tales* have been critically edited by John M. Manly and Edith Rickert, *The Text of the Canterbury Tales* (8 vols., 1940). The text in F. N. Robinson's edition of Chaucer's complete works is based on one of the best manuscripts, the Ellesmere, which is in the Huntington Library at San Marino, Calif. The exact order of the tales, as Chaucer intended them, is not certain; in fact, it is doubtful if he ever got as far as deciding upon a definite arrangement of those he had written. The sequence shown in the following table is one often followed in modern editions and the titles those most commonly used. For information about the individual tales, see these entries:

1. The Knight's Tale.	14. The Summoner's Tale.
2. The Miller's Tale.	15. The Clerk's Tale.
3. The Reeve's Tale.	16. The Merchant's Tale.
4. The Cook's Tale.	17. The Squire's Tale.
5. The Man of Law's Tale.	18. The Franklin's Tale.
6. The Shipman's Tale.	19. The Physician's Tale.
7. The Prioress's Tale.	20. The Pardoner's Tale.
8. The Rime of Sir Thopas.	21. The Second Nun's Tale.
9. The Tale of Melibeus.	22. The Canon's Yeoman's Tale.
10. The Monk's Tale.	23. The Manciple's Tale.
11. The Nun's Priest's Tale.	24. The Parson's Tale.
12. The Wife of Bath's Tale.	
13. The Friar's Tale.	

Canticles. See **Song of Solomon.**

canto. A part or division of a poem of some length, as the six cantos of *The Lady of the Lake*.

Canton (kan'tọn), **William.** b. on Chu Shan island, in the East China Sea, Oct. 27, 1845; d. at Hendon, Middlesex, England, May 2, 1926. An English poet, teacher, journalist, and historian. He was engaged in teaching and journalistic work at London (1867–76) and at Glasgow (1876–91). Among his books are *Through the Ages—the Legend of a Stone Axe* (1873), *A Lost Epic and Other Poems* (1887), *The Invisible Playmate* (1894), *W. V. Her Book* (1896), *A Child's Book of Saints* (1898), *In Memory of W. V.* (1901), and *The Story of Saint Elizabeth of Hungary* (1912). Some of his best-known short poems are *The Comrades, L'Alouette, The Lost Brother, The Story of the Rheinfrid* and *The Ancient Gods Pursuing*. His most ambitious

ḍ, d or j; ṣ, s or sh; ṭ, t or ch; ẓ, z or zh; o, F. cloche; ü, F. menu; ċh, Sc. loch; ṅ, F. bonbon.

work is *History of the British and Foreign Bible Society* (5 vols., 1903–10), an authority in its field.

Cantwell (kant'wel), **Dr.** The hypocrite in Isaac Bickerstaffe's play *The Hypocrite.*

Canute (ka̤.nūt'). [Also: **Cnut, Knut;** called **"Canute the Great."**] b. c994; d. at Shaftesbury, England, Nov. 12, 1035. King of England, Denmark, and Norway; younger son of Sweyn, king of Denmark. He was baptized before 1013, receiving the baptismal name of Lambert. In 1013 he was with his father in the invasion of England, succeeding him in February, 1014 (by election of the Danish peers) as king of England, his brother Harold ascending the Danish throne. Defeated by Ethelred the Unready, who was recalled from Normandy by the English *witan* or national council, he returned to Denmark in the same year. In 1015 he again invaded England with a large force; he besieged (May, 1016) London, and defeated the English under Edmund Ironside (who had succeeded his father Ethelred) at Assandun. At a conference held on the isle of Olney in the river Severn, he divided the kingdom with Edmund, retaining the northern part of the kingdom and leaving Wessex to Edmund. After Edmund's death, he was chosen (1017) sole king of England. Putting aside his first wife, Aelfgifu, he married Emma, the widow of Ethelred, who bore him Harthacanute. He visited (1019–20) Denmark, made (1026–27) a pilgrimage to Rome, and conquered (1028) Norway. His early career was marked by great barbarity, but after the conquest of England was completed his reign was that of a statesman and patriot, and he became one of the wisest as well as mightiest rulers of his age.

Canute, The Song of. See **Song of Canute, The.**

Can You Forgive Her? A novel (1864) by Anthony Trollope.

canzone (kän.tsō'nä). A particular variety of lyric poetry in the Italian style, and of Provençal origin, which closely resembled the madrigal.

Capability Brown. A nickname given to Lancelot Brown, an English landscape-gardener (1715–73).

Cape of Storms. [Portuguese, **Cabo Tormentoso** (kä'bö tôr.män.tō'zö).] The name first given by the Portuguese navigator Dias, in 1486, to the Cape of Good Hope.

Caper (kā'pėr). A "high fantastical" character in Allingham's comedy *Who Wins, or The Widow's Choice.*

Capern (kā'pėrn), **Edward.** b. at Tiverton, Devonshire, England, Jan. 21, 1819; d. at Braunton, near Bideford, Devonshire, England, June 4, 1894. An English poet, lace-factory worker, and postman. He began his literary career by contributing to the "Poet's Corner" of the *North Devon Journal;* his work soon became popular, and was praised by Walter Savage Landor, Charles Kingsley, Charles Dickens, and Tennyson. He was the author of *Poems by Edward Capern, Rural Postman of Bideford, Devon* (1856; later editions), *Ballads and Songs* (1858), *Devonshire Melodist* (1862), and *Wayside Warbles* (1865).

Capet (kā'pet, kap'et; French, kȧ.pe). A surname of the kings of France, commencing with Hugh Capet, who ascended the throne in 987.

Capgrave (kap'grāv), **John.** b. at Lynn, Norfolk, England, April 21, 1393; d. there, Aug. 12, 1464. An English historian, provincial of the Augustinian order in England. He wrote *Chronicle of England* (in English), *Liber de Illustribus Henricis* (Book of the Illustrious Henrys), *A Guide to the Antiquities of Rome,* and other historical and theological works in Latin. He is best known for *Nova legenda Angliae,* the first important collection of English saints' lives.

Caphis (kā'fis). In Shakespeare's *Timon of Athens,* a servant of one of Timon's creditors.

Capitol (kap'i.tol). In ancient Roman history, that part of the Capitoline Hill which was occupied by the Temple of Jupiter Capitolinus.

Capitoline Hill (kap'i.tō.līn). One of the seven hills of ancient Rome, NW of the Palatine, on the left bank of the Tiber. It constituted the citadel of the city after the construction of the Servian wall. Its SW summit was the famed Tarpeian Rock; on its NE summit rose the temple of Jupiter Capitolinus. The modern Capitol stands between the two summits. From the Capitoline the Forum Romanum extends its long, narrow area toward the SE, skirting the N foot of the Palatine.

Caponsacchi (käp.on.säk'ē), **Giuseppe.** In Browning's *The Ring and the Book,* the young priest who protects Pompilia in her flight to Rome.

Capricornus (kap.ri.kôr'nus). An ancient zodiacal constellation between Sagittarius and Aquarius; also, one of the 12 signs of the zodiac, the winter solstice. It is represented on ancient monuments by the figure of a goat, or a figure having the fore part like a goat and the hind part like a fish.

Captain, The. A play attributed to John Fletcher and another, produced c1612 at Court, and printed in the folios of 1647 and 1679.

Captain, The. A bragging, coarse ruffian in Thomas Middleton's play *The Phoenix.*

Captain Blood (blud). A romantic novel by Rafael Sabatini, published in 1922.

Captain Bottell (bot'el). A novel by James Hanley, published in 1933.

Captain Brassbound's Conversion (brȧs'boundz). A play by George Bernard Shaw, included in his volume *Three Plays for Puritans* (1901). It deals with the pirate Brassbound, a man hungry for vengeance, whose feelings are finally softened by the shrewd Lady Cicely Waynflete.

Captain Car (kär). A Middle English ballad, telling the story of a border feud.

Captain Margaret (mär'ga.ret). A historical novel by John Masefield, published in 1908. It is set in South Devon, Cornwall, and the Spanish Main in the period 1685–88.

Captains Courageous. A novel (1897) by Rudyard Kipling. It is the story of the redemption of a spoiled child of the rich who, falling overboard from a liner, learns courage and self-sacrifice among the fishermen of Newfoundland. A motion picture has been made from the book.

Captain's Doll, The. A novelette by D. H. Lawrence, published under this title in America in 1923. It was issued in England as *The Ladybird.* It is the story of an Englishman, Captain Hepburn, his Austrian mistress, Countess von Rassentlow, who makes dolls for a living, and the captain's wife, who dies, thus clearing the way for the marriage of the captain and the countess.

Captain Singleton (sing′gl.tọn). [Full title, **Adventures of Captain Singleton**.] A fictional narrative by Daniel Defoe, published in 1720. Typical of Defoe's narratives in its loose structure, it tells of a journey across the African continent, and of a career of piracy ending with the hero's repentance. One of the best characters is Quaker William, the pious adviser of the pirates.

Captain Thomas Stukeley (stūk′li). A play (1605) based on English history, of unknown authorship, but sometimes attributed to Thomas Heywood.

Captives, The. A novel by Hugh Walpole, published in 1920. It draws a picture of a religious community. The work won the James Tait Black memorial prize.

Captives, or The Lost Recovered, The. A tragicomedy tentatively identified as being written by Thomas Heywood. The Lord Chamberlain entered it as licensed for performance in 1624 and it had apparently been written shortly before. The plot is based on Plautus's *Rudens*. There is also a subplot based upon a short novel by Masuccio di Salerno, which Marlowe also used in *The Jew of Malta*.

Capuchin (kap′ụ.chin), **The.** A play by Samuel Foote, produced in 1776. It was an alteration of *A Trip to Calais*, which had been stopped by the public censor. The character of Lady Kitty Crocodile in *A Trip to Calais* was offensive to the duchess of Kingston, and was eliminated in *The Capuchin*.

Capuchins. A Roman Catholic order of mendicant Franciscan monks, founded (c1528) in Italy by Matteo di Bascio, and named from the long pointed capuche, or hood, which is the distinguishing mark of their dress. According to the statutes of the order, drawn up in 1529, the monks were to live by begging; they were not to use gold or silver or silk in the decoration of their altars, and the chalices were to be of pewter.

Capucius (kạ.pū′shus). In Shakespeare's *Henry VIII*, an ambassador from Charles V to the dying Katherine.

Capulet (kap′ụ.lẹt). In Shakespeare's *Romeo and Juliet*, a coarse, jovial old man with a passionate temper, the father of Juliet. Ignorant of her marriage to Romeo, he insists that she take Paris as her husband.

Capulet, Lady. In Shakespeare's *Romeo and Juliet*, Juliet's mother. She urges her daughter to marry Paris and, in an elaborate figure of speech, likens him to a beautiful book (I.iii).

Carabas (kar′ạ.bas), **Marquis of.** The master for whom Puss in Boots wins great wealth and a beautiful princess in Perrault's tale *Le Chat Botté* (now best known in English as *Puss in Boots*). The name has since been used allusively for a pretentious aristocrat who refuses to go along with his age. The Marquis of Carabas in Disraeli's *Vivian Grey* (1826) is intended to represent the Marquis of Clanricarde (Ulick John de Burgh, who had been made 1st marquis of Clanricarde, in a second creation, in 1825).

Caractacus (kạ.rak′tạ.kus) or **Caratacus** (-rat′ạ-). [Latinized name of **Caradoc**.] fl. c50 A.D. A British king, son of Cunobeline (who gave his name, in its variant form of Cymbeline, to a tragedy by Shakespeare), king of the Trinobantes. His capital was Camulodunum (Colchester). He was chief of the Catuvellauni, and resisted the Romans (under Aulus Plautius, Ostorius Scapula, and, for a short time, the emperor Claudius) for about nine years. Finally defeated, he took refuge among the Brigantes, but was delivered by Cartismandua, their queen, to the Romans, and was sent to Rome. Claudius granted him his life and his family. Caradoc, son of the legendary Brythonic Bran, is sometimes identified with this Caractacus.

Caractacus. A dramatic poem by William Mason, with music by Dr. Thomas Arne, published in 1759 and produced in Dublin in 1764. It follows the British story of Caractacus, in its general outline, and is modeled strictly upon the classical Greek tragic form, thus combining two traditions. However, in an age which was becoming increasingly fond of sentimental comedy, it was able to achieve little popular success.

Caractacus. A tragedy by J. R. Planché, an alteration of John Fletcher's tragedy *Bonduca;* in which, as in this, a principal character is based on the historical Caractacus. It was produced in 1837.

Caradoc (kạ.rad′ọk, kar′ạ.dok). [Also: **Cradock, Craddocke**.] A knight of the Round Table, in the Arthurian cycle of romance. The story goes that one day a boy arrived at King Arthur's court with a mantle which could not be worn by an unchaste woman. Of all the ladies of the court only Caradoc's wife could wear it. The tale is told in "The Boy and the Mantle," ballad 29 of F. J. Child's *English and Scottish Popular Ballads.* There is a version also in Thomas Percy's *Reliques of Ancient English Poetry.*

Caradoc. See also **Caractacus.**

Caradog (kạ.rad′ọg). [Called **Caradog of Llancarvan.**] d. c1247. A Welsh historian. His continuation of the *History* of his friend Geoffrey of Monmouth, though the original text is lost, is included in later Welsh chronicles.

Caran d'Ache (kà.rän′ dàsh). [Pseudonym of **Emmanuel Poiré.**] b. at Moscow, 1858; d. at Paris, Feb. 26, 1909. A French illustrator and caricaturist. His pseudonym derives from the Russian word *karandash*, which means "pencil." He was the grandson of a soldier in Napoleon's army, and was educated at Moscow. Having moved to Paris, he was first an attaché in the ministry of war and afterward became an illustrator of popular journals. His fame rests largely on his caricatures which appeared in *Tout Paris, La Vie Parisienne, Chat Noir*, and others. *Album Caran d'Ache* and *Bric-à-brac* are among well-known collections of his work.

Carathis (kar′ạ.this). The mother of Vathek, titular hero of William Beckford's *Vathek* (1786). She was a renowned sorceress and helped her son, who wished to behold the wonders of the underworld, to sell his soul to the devil in return for this and other favors.

Caravan. A collection (1925) of 50 short stories by John Galsworthy. The volume contains stories taken from five previously published collections: *A Sheaf* (1916), *Another Sheaf, Five Tales* (both 1919), *The Burning Spear* and *Captures* (both 1923). Some of the best-known stories in it are "The First and the Last," "A Stoic," "The Apple Tree," "The Juryman," "A Feud," "Timber," "Santa Lucia," and "A Stroke of Lightning."

Carbonari (kär.bō.nä′rē). A secret society formed in the kingdom of Naples during the reign of Murat (1808–15) by republicans and others dissatisfied with the French rule. They were originally refugees among the mountains of the Abruzzi provinces, and took their name from the mountain charcoal-burners. Their aim was to free their country from foreign domination. After having aided the Austrians in the expulsion of the French, the organization spread over all Italy as the champions of the National Liberal cause against the reactionary governments. At one time the Carbonari numbered several hundred thousand adherents. They were concerned in the various revolutions of the times until crushed by the Austrian power in Italy, and absorbed into the subsequent Risorgimento movement. They spread (c1820) into France, and played an important part in French politics until the revolution of 1830.

Carbonaro (kär.bō.nä′rō). See **Napoleon III.**

Card, The. A realistic novel (1911), one of the Five Towns group, by Arnold Bennett. It is entitled *Denry the Audacious* in the American edition, after the chief quality of its lucky hero, who finally becomes mayor.

Card Castle. A novel by the English novelist Alec Waugh, published in 1924.

Cardenio (kär.dā′ni.ō; Spanish, kär.тнä′nyō). An intellectual madman, crazed by disappointed love, but with lucid intervals, who appears in Miguel de Cervantes's *Don Quixote.* His love is finally restored to him. He is introduced in the younger George Colman's *The Mountaineers,* where he is called Octavian, and also in Thomas D'Urfey's *The Comical History of Don Quixote* (1694 and 1696).

Cardenio, The History of. A play entered on the Stationers' Register in 1653 as by John Fletcher and Shakespeare. Scholars are not certain beyond any possible doubt that Shakespeare did not have a hand in the play, but it seemed probable to Lounsbury in *The First Editors of Shakespeare* that Lewis Theobald, the Shakespearean scholar who published it in 1728 as *The Double Falsehood,* was the real author, even though he claimed it was "written originally by W. Shakespeare, and now revised and adapted to the stage by Mr. Theobald."

Cardinal, The. A tragedy by James Shirley, produced in 1641. It was doubtless independently suggested by the contemporary career of Richelieu in France, but suffers by resemblance to and comparison with the finer *Duchess of Malfi,* by John Webster. The ambitious Cardinal schemes to marry his nephew Columbo, a general, to the widowed Duchess Rosaura, and gains the consent of the king of Navarre, whose daughter-in-law she is. The Duchess, however, loves the young Count D'Alvarez, and during Columbo's absence gains the king's consent to this marriage also. However, on their

wedding night Alvarez is murdered by the returned Columbo. A series of murders follows, ending with the poisoning of the Duchess by the Cardinal and the murder of the Cardinal himself. At the end of the play, as in *Hamlet,* almost all the main characters are dead. *The Cardinal* is considered Shirley's best play, and he himself thought it "the best of my flock."

Cardinal, The. The cruel and haughty brother of the Duchess of Malfi in John Webster's tragedy of that name. He and his brother, Ferdinand, employ Bosola to kill the Duchess for her marriage with her steward, Antonio.

Cardinal College. See **Christ Church.**

Cardinal Wolsey (wûl′zi). See **Wolsey, Thomas, Cardinal.**

Carducci (kär.döt′chē), **Giosuè.** b. at Valdicastello, Tuscany, Italy, July 27, 1835; d. at Bologna, Italy, Feb. 16, 1907. An Italian poet, awarded (1906) the Nobel prize for literature, and generally numbered among the leading Italian poets of all time. From 1860 he taught literature at Bologna, and was also known as a critic and patriot. He was leader of a new classical school which sought its vitality in the cultures of the ancient world itself rather than in any neoclassic formulas. In his nature poems he expresses a pantheism not unlike that of Victor Hugo. Especially characteristic of this poet are the three collections of his *Odi barbare* (1877, 1882, 1889) and *Rime e ritmi* (1891 *et seq.*). His collected works were issued (1889–1924) in 20 volumes. Among his single poems are *Inno a Satano, Il Bove,* and *La Chiesa di polenta.*

Careless (kār′les). The friend of Mellefont in William Congreve's *The Double Dealer,* a gay gallant who makes love to Lady Pliant.

Careless. A suitor of Lady Dainty in Colley Cibber's *The Double Gallant.*

Careless. The friend of Charles Surface in Richard Brinsley Sheridan's *The School for Scandal.* It is he who says of the portrait of Sir Oliver in the auction scene: "An unforgiving eye, and a damned disinheriting countenance."

Careless, Colonel. The gay, light-hearted lover of Ruth in Sir Robert Howard's play *The Committee.* The play was slightly altered and produced by T. Knight as *The Honest Thieves.* The character of Careless is the same in both plays.

Careless Good Fellow, The. A drinking song by John Oldham, English Juvenalian poet of the Restoration period. Scholars are inclined to believe, on the basis of this song, that a number of anonymous Restoration ballads may well also be his work.

Careless Husband, The. A comedy by Colley Cibber, produced in 1704 and printed in 1705. In the last act a wife, through a casual act of kindness, shames the heart of a moderately shameless husband.

Careless Lovers, The. A Restoration farce-comedy (1672) by Edward Ravenscroft. Like virtually all his work it is not original, being actually nothing more than an adaptation from Molière.

Carew (ka̤.rō′), **Bamfylde Moore.** b. at Bickley, near Tiverton, England, in July, 1693; d. c1770.

---

fat, fāte, fär, a̤sk, fāre; net, mē, hėr; pin, pīne; not, nōte, mȯve, nôr; up, lūte, pu̇ll; тн, then;

An English vagabond. He ran away from school, joined a band of gypsies, and was eventually chosen king of the gypsies. Convicted of vagrancy, he was transported to Maryland, whence he escaped and returned to England. He is said to have accompanied Charles Edward Stuart (the Young Pretender) to Carlisle and Derby.

Carew, Richard. b. at East Antony, Cornwall, England, July 17, 1555; d. there, Nov. 6, 1620. An English poet and antiquary. He was high sheriff of Cornwall (1586), a member of Parliament, and the author of *Survey of Cornwall* (1602) and others.

Carew, Thomas. b. c1595; d. probably at London, c1639. An English poet. He studied (but was not graduated) at Oxford, and afterward led a wandering life, serving for a time as secretary to Sir Dudley Carleton, ambassador at Venice and Turin, and later about the court of Charles I. He wrote *Coelum Britannicum* (1634), a masque, and the love poem *The Rapture*. A disciple of Ben Jonson, he was one of the Cavalier Poets.

Carey (kār′i), **George Saville.** [Pseudonym, **Paul Tell-Truth.**] b. 1743; d. at London, 1807. An English poet; son of Henry Carey (d. 1743). He was a printer by trade, and for a time an actor. He wrote *The Inoculator*, a comedy (published 1766), *Liberty Chastized, or Patriotism in Chains* (1768), *Shakespeare's Jubilee, a Masque* (1769), *The Nut-Brown Maid* (1770), *The Old Women Weatherwise, an Interlude* (1770), and *Balnea, or History of all the Popular Watering-places of England* (1799).

Carey, Henry. b. c1687; d. (probably by his own hand) at London, Oct. 4, 1743. An English poet and composer of musical farces; said to have been the illegitimate son of George Saville, Marquis of Halifax; father of George Saville Carey (1743–1807). He was the reputed author of *God Save the King*, and author of the ballad *Sally in our Alley.* He wrote *Namby-Pamby*, *The Contrivances* (acted 1715), *Hanging and Marriage, or, The Dead-Man's Wedding* (1722, a farce), *Poems* (1727), *Amelia* (1732 an opera), *Teraminta* (1732, also an opera), *The Tragedy of Chrononhotonthologos* (acted Feb. 22, 1734, a burlesque), and *A Musical Century, or a hundred English Ballads.*

Carey, Philip. The hero of W. Somerset Maugham's realistic novel *Of Human Bondage* (1915). Philip, a shy, sensitive youth afflicted with a clubfoot, studies accounting and art, gives up both for medicine, and finally, after many hardships, becomes a doctor. His love affair with Mildred Rogers, a London waitress, is one of the most memorable portions in the book.

Carey, Rosa Nouchette. b. at London, 1840; d. there, July 19, 1909. An English novelist, whose stories for girls attained wide popularity. Among them are *Nellie's Memories* (1868), *Wee Wifie* (1869), *Heriot's Choice* (1879), *Not Like Other Girls* (1884), *The Old, Old Story* (1894), *Herb of Grace* (1901), *The Household of Peter* (1905), and *The Angel of Forgiveness* (1907).

Carfax (kär′faks). At Oxford, England, the junction of Cornmarket Street, Queen Street, St. Aldgate's, and High Street.

caricature. A representation, pictorial or descriptive, in which beauties or favorable points are concealed or perverted and peculiarities or defects exaggerated, so as to make the person or thing represented ridiculous, while a general likeness is retained.

Now and then, indeed, he [Dryden] seizes a very coarse and marked distinction, and gives us, not a likeness, but a strong caricature, in which a single peculiarity is protruded, and everything else neglected. (Macaulay, *Dryden*.)

Carino (kä.rē′nō). The father of Zenocia in John Fletcher and Philip Massinger's *The Custom of the Country.*

Carinthia Jane (ka̤.rin′thi.a̤ jān). The heroine of George Meredith's novel *The Amazing Marriage.* Her marriage to Fleetwood is the chief matter dealt with in the book.

Carisbrooke Castle (kar′iz.bruk). An ancient castle in the Isle of Wight, England, the place of captivity (1647–48) of Charles I.

Caritat (kȧ.rē.tȧ), **Marie Jean Antoine Nicolas.** See **Condorcet**, Marquis de.

Carker (kär′kẽr), **James.** The manager in the offices of Dombey and Son, in Charles Dickens's novel of that name. He is "sly of manner, sharp of tooth, soft of foot, watchful of eye, oily of tongue, cruel of heart, nice of habit." He induces Edith, the second wife of Dombey, to elope with him, to revenge herself on her husband. He is killed by a train while trying to escape from Dombey.

Carlell (kär.lel′), **Lodowick.** b. 1602; d. 1675. An English dramatist. He is the reputed author of *The Deserving Favourite*, a tragicomedy (1629), *Arviragus and Philicia*, a tragicomedy (1636), *The Passionate Lovers* (1638), *The Fool would be a Favourite, or the Discreet Lover* (1657), *Osmund, the Great Turk*, a tragedy (1657), *Heraclius, Emperor of the East* (1664), and *The Spartan Ladies* (lost).

Carleton (kärl′ton), **George.** The hero and supposed author of Daniel Defoe's *Memoirs of Captain George Carleton*, published in 1728. Attempts have been made to identify Carleton as a real soldier or to establish Jonathan Swift as the author, and historians often cite the work as a source, but it is now known to be one of Defoe's historical romances.

Carleton, Mary. b. c1642; d. 1673. An English criminal, cheat, bigamist, thief, and actress. She called herself "the German Princess," a title to which she had no claim, and she actually appeared in a play of that name, written at her request, at the Duke's House, in Lincoln's Inn Fields, in 1664. She succeeded in convincing a trusting soul, a Mrs. King, that she had a fortune close to 80,000 pounds a year, and in April, 1663 she married John Carleton, Mrs. King's brother, without taking the trouble to divorce another husband, John Stedman. She was sent to prison (where Pepys, who had seen her on the stage, visited her), and was tried at the Old Bailey on June 4, 1663, but defended herself with such skill that she was acquitted. Her luck, however, did not hold out, and when she was charged with a series of thefts in December, 1672, she was found guilty. The sentence at that time for her crimes was death, and she was hanged on Jan. 22, 1673 at Tyburn. She was supposed to be the daughter of Henry van Wolway, Lord of Holmstein, or of the Duke of Oundenia, but she admitted just before her death that she was simply Mary Moders, the daughter of a Canterbury Cathedral chorister. She was the subject of many books, both during her life and after her execution, of which a typical example is *The Counterfeit Lady Unveiled. Being a Full Account of the Birth, Life, Most Remarkable Actions, and Untimely Death of that Famous Cheat, Mary Carleton, Known by the Name of the German Princess* (1673), by Francis Kirkman.

Carleton, William. b. at Prillisk, County Tyrone, Ireland, March 4, 1794; d. at Dublin, Jan. 30, 1869. An Irish novelist, a delineator of Irish character and life. He wrote *Traits and Stories of the Irish Peasantry* (1830–33), *Tales of Ireland* (1834), *Fardorougha the Miser* (1839), *Valentine McClutchy* (1845), and others.

Carlile (kär.lĭl′, kär′lĭl), **Richard.** b. in Devonshire, England, 1790; d. at London, 1843. An English freethinker and reformer; follower of Thomas Paine. He sold (1817) prohibited papers and wrote and printed free-thought pamphlets. For publishing (1818) Paine's works, he was imprisoned (1819–26) at Dorchester; while there, he supervised the publication of *The Republican*, a journal. In 1830 he opened a hall at London to promote free speech. He was again (1830–33 and 1834–35) imprisoned for his refusal to pay church rates. He wrote many controversial papers and serials. Emperor Alexander of Russia thought it necessary to forbid the report of his trial (1819) from being brought into his territory.

Carling (kär′ling), **Walter.** A sentimental character in *Point Counterpoint* (1928), a novel by Aldous Huxley dealing satirically with social and intellectual life at London in the decade following World War I.

Carlion (kär.lĭ′on). In Malory's *Morte d'Arthur*, the city where King Arthur was crowned, possibly Caerleon, in Monmouthshire.

Carlisle (kär.lĭl′), 5th Earl of. Title of **Howard, Frederick.**

Carlisle, Bishop of. In Shakespeare's *Richard II*, a loyal supporter of Richard. He strenuously protests Bolingbroke's ascension to the throne and direly predicts that "The blood of English shall manure the ground and future ages groan for this foul act" (IV.i). He is arrested for treason, but pardoned by Bolingbroke.

Carlo Buffone (kär′lō bö.fō′nä). See **Buffone, Carlo.**

Carlos (kär′los, -lōs), Don. b. at Valladolid, Spain, July 8, 1545; d. at Madrid, July 24, 1568. A Spanish prince; eldest son of Philip II of Spain and Maria of Portugal. He was engaged to be married to Elizabeth of Valois, before she married his father, Philip II. He received the homage of the estates of Castile as crown prince (Prince of the Asturias) in 1560. In 1567, angered by the appointment of the Duke of Alva to the governorship of the Netherlands, he struck at the duke with a poniard in the presence of the king. Having laid plans to escape from Spain, he was apprehended by his father on Jan. 18, 1568, and a commission was appointed to

investigate his conduct. He died in prison a few months after, the manner of his death being involved in mystery to this day. Tragedies with Don Carlos as subject have been written by Thomas Otway (1676), Jean Galbert de Campistron (1683), Vittorio Alfieri (1783), Schiller (1787), André Chénier (1789), and others.

Carlos. An apathetic pedant in Colley Cibber's comedy *Love Makes a Man.* He is transformed by love into an enthusiastic and manly fellow.

Carlos. The treacherous younger brother of Biron in Thomas Southerne's play *Isabella* (a reworking of the same author's *The Fatal Marriage*).

Carlos, Don. The extravagant and profligate husband of Victoria in Hannah Cowley's comedy *A Bold Stroke for a Husband.*

Carlovingian (kär.lō.vin′ji.an). See **Carolingian.**

Carlton Club (kärl′ton). A London club established in 1832. A political club, strictly Conservative, it was founded by the Duke of Wellington.

Carlton House. A house formerly standing in what became Carlton House Terrace, London. It was built for Henry Boyle, Lord Carlton, in 1709, and in 1732 was occupied by the Prince of Wales, and afterward by the prince regent (who was later George IV). It was torn down in 1827 when Waterloo Place was built.

Carlyle (kär.lĭl′), **Alexander.** b. in Dumfriesshire, Scotland, Jan. 26, 1722; d. at Inveresk, near Edinburgh, Aug. 25, 1805. A Scottish clergyman, minister at Inveresk, Midlothian, from 1748 until his death, and leader of the moderate section of the Church of Scotland. He wrote an autobiography (edited by John Hill Burton, 1860) as well as some political and other pamphlets. He was a man of genial character, and an intimate friend of Hume, Smollett, and other Scottish men of letters. In appearance he was so impressive that he was nicknamed "Jupiter Carlyle." His patronage of the theater was a cause of scandal in the Church of Scotland.

Carlyle, Jane Baillie. [Maiden name, **Welsh.**] b. at Haddington, Scotland, July 14, 1801; d. while driving in Hyde Park, London, April 21, 1866. An English writer; the daughter of John Welsh, a surgeon of Haddington. She was noted for her wit and beauty. She married Thomas Carlyle at Templand on Oct. 17, 1826. Her letters and memoirs were first edited by J. A. Froude in 1883, and there have been several editions by various other scholars since.

Carlyle, Thomas. [Called the "Sage of Chelsea."] b. at Ecclefechan, Dumfriesshire, Scotland, Dec. 4, 1795; d. at London, Feb. 4, 1881. Scottish essayist and historian; son of a stonemason. Educated at Annan Academy and the University of Edinburgh (which he entered in 1809); taught mathematics at Annan (1814–16) and at Kircaldy, under Edward Irving (1816–18); gave up teaching and went to Edinburgh to study law (1819), which was soon abandoned in disgust. Wrote articles for *New Edinburgh Review* and for Brewster's *Edinburgh Encyclopedia*, and did translating and tutoring, all with little financial success; became a victim of dyspepsia and despair. Began (1820) a study of German literature; wrote *Life of Schiller* (published in *London Magazine*, 1823–24; separately, 1825) and translated Goethe's *Wilhelm Meister* (*Apprenticeship*, 1824; *Travels*, 1827); so gained reputation and learned to know writings of his first hero, of whom he wrote "the sight of such a man was to me a Gospel of Gospels." In 1824–25 visited Paris and London, where he met Coleridge, Lamb, Hazlitt, and other literary men; married Jane Welsh (1826); moved to Edinburgh and was admitted by Jeffrey, at that time the editor, to the *Edinburgh Review* with a short essay on Richter. Left Edinburgh to live at Craigenputtock, a solitary farmstead in Dumfriesshire (1828–34), where he wrote essays on Burns, Voltaire, Diderot, Goethe, and other subjects; *Signs of the Times* (1829), *Characteristics* (1831). He wrote also at this time his first original book, *Sartor Resartus* ("The Tailor Retailored") which was published in *Frazer's Magazine* (1833–34), separately at Boston (1835), and at London (1838). This work combines spiritual autobiography in fictional form and speculation on life (mainly German transcendentalism), according to which all material things and all conventions, creeds, customs of mankind are thought of as *clothes*, i.e., symbols of an immaterial, eternal reality beyond the reach of sense perception. In 1834, still seeking "bread and work," Carlyle settled at Cheyne Row, Chelsea, London, which was to be his home till death. *The French Revolution* (1837) established his reputation. Delivered four series of lectures (1837–40), the last of which, *Heroes and Hero-Worship*, he published in 1841. In *Chartism* (1839), *Past and Present* (1843), *Latter-Day Pamphlets* (1850), he attacked materialistic tendencies, corruptions, and shams of society in the spirit of a modern Elijah calling down punishment upon a world gone mad after strange gods. History and biography occupied Carlyle for about 20 years: *Oliver Cromwell's Letters and Speeches* (1845), *Life of John Sterling* (1851); *History of Frederick the Great* (6 vols., 1858–65), journeying twice to Germany (1852, 1858) for research, and visiting all the battlefields of Frederick. Carlyle conceived of history as a record and an interpretation of the past for the guidance of mankind in the present and future, as much less a chain of events (though it was that) than a revelation, through great leaders, of the operation of eternal justice in human society. Many critics consider that no other historian surpasses him in vividness of portraiture. Elected lord rector of Edinburgh University (1865); received the Prussian Order of Merit (1874). After death of wife (1866) wrote *Reminiscences* (2 vols., 1881); his last work, *Early Kings of Norway* (1875), composed by dictation because of palsied right hand. Carlyle's *Letters* published at various times in ten volumes; complete works in *People's Edition* (37 vols., 1871–74) and in *Centenary Edition* (30 vols., 1896–99). See *Life of Carlyle*, by J. A. Froude (4 vols., 1882–84), *Life of Carlyle*, by D. A. Wilson (6 vols., 1923–34), *Carlyle* (1953), an anthology compiled by G. M. Trevelyan, and *Thomas Carlyle* (1954), a collection of Carlyle's letters to his wife Jane, edited by Trudy Bliss.

Carmarthen (kär.mär′ᴛнᴇn, kạr-), **The Black Book of.** See **Black Book of Carmarthen, The.**

Carmathians (kär.mā′thi.ạnz). See **Karmathians.**

Carmelites (kär′mẹ.līts). One of the four principal orders of mendicant friars of the Roman Catholic Church. Traditionally the order originated on Mount Carmel in Palestine under the leadership of the prophet Elias; actually (and the dispute about these dates and facts aroused so great a storm that an official silence was decreed on the controversy in 1698) it seems to have begun there, in the middle of the 12th century, as an eremitical grouping under Saint Berthold. During the 13th century, after the failure of the armies of the Crusaders in the East, the order moved its base to Cyprus (c1240) and spread thence throughout Europe to England and (in later centuries) to the New World, Persia, India, and China. Under Saint Simon Stock (fl. 1247–65) the change from eremitic to mendicant life occurred, including the change of habit from the mantle with black and white rays (from which the friars were known as *Fratres barrati* or *virgulati* or *de pica*) to one of pure white wool (from which came their English appellation of White Friars). The Carmelites were royal confessors to the Lancastrian line in England, but were suppressed under Henry VIII, never again reaching the height of popular appeal they had previously attained there. Under the Spanish Saint Teresa of Ávila and Saint John of the Cross, the Carmelites again expanded in the 16th century, undergoing at the same time a split into two groups: the Calced (so-called because they wore shoes) or older group, and the Discalced (who wore sandals) or reform group, who tended to return to the more austere tradition. The latter was recognized (1593) as a separate order and is now the more prominent of the two orders. The Carmelite sisterhood began about 1450 when several orders of Beguines joined the Carmelite order (from their ranks came Saint Teresa). The present convent of the order on Mount Carmel was built in the period from 1827 to 1853, replacing an earlier building (built 1720) blown up (1821) by the Turks.

Carmilhan (kär′mil.han). A ghostly ship which is doomed, according to legend, to voyage endlessly through the seas near the Cape of Good Hope. Like the legendary Flying Dutchman, she is a portent of disaster to all ships that sight her.

Carmina Burana (kär′mi.nạ bū.ran′ạ). A manuscript of some 300 medieval songs from the 12th and 13th centuries, composed by *goliards*, i.e., wandering students. Most of the songs are in Latin, some in German, and some in a mixture of the two. They are satirical, roisterous, amorous, seldom serious. The name *Burana* derives from the Abbey of Benediktbeuren where the manuscript was found.

Carnahan (kär′nạ.han), **Peachey.** One of the two heroes in Rudyard Kipling's short story "The Man Who Would Be King." He is the companion (originally the servant) of the other hero, Daniel Dravot, "the man who would be king" (the country is never precisely located, but is somewhere beyond the Khyber Pass). When it is discovered that he is not a god, as he has succeeded in making the natives believe, but an ordinary man, Daniel is killed. Peachey, who lives to tell the tale, is crucified but manages to make his way back to India, mentally

ḍ, d or j; ṣ, s or sh; ṭ, t or ch; ẓ, z or zh; o, F. cloche; ü, F. menu; ċh, Sc. loch; ṅ, F. bonbon.

broken if not actually insane, carrying the head of Dravot as evidence of his story. The story is included in *The Phantom Rickshaw* (1889).

Caro (kär'ō), **Avice.** See **Avice Caro.**

carol. A kind of circular dance. It is often difficult to tell from the context whether carol is the dance or the song that seems to have been sung as an accompaniment to it; but in Chaucer it usually means simply the dance:

    Festes, instruments, caroles, daunces.
                (Chaucer, *Knight's Tale*.)

Carolina: or a Description of the Present State of that Country (kar.ọ.lī'nạ). A prose pamphlet (1682) by Thomas Ash printed at London. It sings the praises of Carolina in the hope of enticing hopeful fortune hunters. Like much such material of the colonial period, it is perhaps now chiefly important to students of history rather than literature.

Carolina Wilhelmina Amelia Skeggs (wil.hel.mē'nạ ạ.mēl'yạ skegz'). See **Skeggs.**

Caroline (kar'ọ.lin, -lin). Belonging to or characteristic of the times of Charles I and II of England. "He discovers that this venerable clergyman of the Caroline age had no idea of his own language." (*The Churchman* (New York).)

Caroline, Queen. In Sir Walter Scott's novel *The Heart of Midlothian*, the wife (known in history as Caroline of Anspach) of George II, who intercedes for Effie Deans, on the request of Jeanie.

Caroline Gann (gan). See **Brandon, Mrs.**

Caroline of Anspach (anz'pak, äns'päk). [Full name, **Wilhelmina Caroline of Brandenburg-Anspach.**] b. March 1, 1683; d. Nov. 20, 1737. Queen of Great Britain and Ireland; wife of George II and daughter of John Frederick, margrave of Brandenburg-Ansbach (Anglicized in his daughter's name to "Anspach"). She married George, then electoral prince of Hanover, on Sept. 2, 1705. She went to England on the accession (1714) of George I. She took an active part in politics, after her coronation in 1727, was a firm supporter of Robert Walpole, and several times acted as regent during the absence of the king. Her bitter hostility toward her eldest son, Frederick Louis, Prince of Wales, was notorious. As princess and as queen she was a patroness of learning; Pope and Chesterfield were members of her circle. She is introduced by Sir Walter Scott in *The Heart of Midlothian*, where Jeanie Deans has an interview with her at Richmond.

Caroline of Brunswick (brunz'wik). [Full name, **Amelia Elizabeth Caroline of Brunswick-Wolfenbüttel.**] b. May 17, 1768; d. Aug. 7, 1821. Queen of George IV of England; second daughter of Charles William Ferdinand, Duke of Brunswick, and Augusta, sister of George III of England. She married George, then prince of Wales, on April 8, 1795. Formally separated from the prince in 1796, she lived in retirement until 1813, and traveled abroad in the period 1813–20, her manner of living being much talked of. Returning to England on July 5, 1820, she was accused of adultery and tried before the House of Lords, in August, 1820. The trial was abandoned on Nov. 10, 1820, be-

cause of public disapproval. Her domestic troubles and trial played an important part in English politics (George IV, never a tremendously popular monarch, was considered by many of his subjects to have behaved with unforgivable cruelty in his treatment of her). Throughout she had strong popular support. After her forcible exclusion from the coronation of her husband in Westminster Abbey (July 29, 1821), she died within a month.

Carolingian (kar.ọ.lin'ji.ạn) or **Carlovingian** (kär-lọ.vin'ji.ạn). [French, **Carlovingien**; German, **Karolinger.**] A royal house descended from Frankish lords in Austrasia in the 17th century. It furnished the second dynasty of French kings (751–987) following the Merovingian dynasty, a dynasty of German emperors and kings (752–911), and a dynasty of Italian sovereigns (774–961). The Carolingian house began with Pepin the Short and attained its highest point with his son Charlemagne.

carpe diem (kär'pē dī'em). Enjoy the present day; take advantage of, or make the most of, the present: a maxim of the Epicureans.

Carpenter (kär'pen.tėr), **Edward.** b. at Brighton, England, Aug. 29, 1844; d. at Guildford, Surrey, England, June 28, 1929. An English poet, essayist, mystic, and social reformer; disciple of Walt Whitman. For much of his life he made his living by lecturing on music and science and by selling the products of his small Sheffield farm. While traveling in India, he became interested in Indian systems of philosophy. In 1884 Carpenter made a journey to the U. S., where he visited and became attached to Whitman. His works of poetry include *Narcissus* (1873), *Moses, a Drama* (1875), *Towards Democracy* (1883–1905), and *Sketches from Life in Town and Country* (1908). *Religious Influence of Art* (1870), *Prisons, Police, and Punishment* (1905), *Days with Walt Whitman* (1906), *Intermediate Types among Primitive Folk* (1914), and *My Days and Dreams* (1916) are all autobiographical. *Towards Industrial Freedom* (1918) and *Pagan and Christian Creeds* (1920) are among his other prose works. His best contributions are considered to be *England's Ideal* (1887), *Civilization—Its Cause and Cure* (1889), *Love's Coming of Age* (1896), *The Intermediate Sex* (1908), and *The Healing of Nations* (1915).

Carpio (kär'pyō), **Bernardo del.** See **Bernardo del Carpio.**

Carrasco (kạ.ras'kō; Spanish, kär.räs'kō), **Samson.** [Spanish, **Sansón.**] A bachelor or licentiate in Miguel de Cervantes's *Don Quixote*, a specialist in practical jokes.

Carrion Comfort. A poem (c1885) by Gerard Manley Hopkins, thought to be the poem referred to by Hopkins in a letter to Robert Bridges as the sonnet "written in blood." In the poem, the poet asserts his religious conviction that he will not give in to despair, that there is always hope. But he recalls how his soul once, divided against itself, struggled with God. Now, however, he reaffirms his faith:

    . . . That night, that year
Of now done darkness I wretch lay wrestling with
    (my God!) my God.

---

fat, fāte, fär, ȧsk, fāre; net, mē, hėr; pin, pīne; not, nōte, mȯve, nôr; up, lūte, pu̇ll; ŦH, then;

Carroll (kar′ol), **Lewis.** Pseudonym of **Dodgson, Charles Lutwidge.**

Carroll, Paul Vincent. b. at Dundalk, Ireland, July 10, 1900—. An Irish playwright. A teacher (1921–37) in the state schools in Scotland, he was cofounder and director of the Glasgow Citizens' Theatre. His works include *The Things That Are Caesar's* (1932, in collaboration with Teresa Deevy; it won the Abbey Theatre Prize), *Shadow and Substance* (1934), *The White Steed* (1939), *Kindred* (1939), *Plays for My Children* (1939), *The Wise Have Not Spoken* (1947), *Plays for Young and Old* (1947), and *The Wayward Saint* (acted on the New York stage in 1955). He also wrote the screen play for the film *Saints and Sinners* (c1950).

Carruthers (kạ.ruᴛʜ′ẽrz), **Robert.** b. at Dumfries, Scotland, Nov. 5, 1799; d. at Inverness, Scotland, May 26, 1878. A Scottish journalist and man of letters, editor and proprietor of the Inverness *Courier*. He was the biographer and editor of Alexander Pope, and the compiler, with Robert Chambers, of *Chambers's Cyclopedia of English Literature*, and others.

Carstone (kär′stōn, -stọn), **Richard.** One of the two wards of Chancery in Dickens's *Bleak House*. He dies as a result of the long and futile waiting for the case to be settled.

Carswell (kärz′wel, -wẹl), **Catherine Roxburgh.** [Maiden name, **Macfarlane**.] b. at Glasgow, Scotland, March 27, 1879; d. 1946. A Scottish novelist, biographer, and literary and dramatic critic; wife (married 1915) of Donald Carswell. Educated at Glasgow University and in Germany, where she studied music, she was dramatic and literary critic (1907–15) for the Glasgow *Herald*. Her works include the novels *Open the Door* (1920) and *The Camomile* (1922), and *Life of Robert Burns* (1930), *Savage Pilgrimage—A Narrative of D. H. Lawrence* (1932), *The Scots Week-End* (1936; with Donald Carswell), and *Tranquil Heart—A Portrait of Giovanni Boccaccio* (1937).

Carswell, Donald. b. at Glasgow, Scotland, 1882; d. in January, 1940. An English newspaperman, lawyer, soldier, and author; husband (married 1915) of Catherine Roxburgh Carswell. Educated at Glasgow University (M.A., 1904), he was associated (1904–12) with the Glasgow *Herald* and was a staff member (1912–17) of the London *Times*. He was the author of *The Trial of Ronald Tree* (1925), *Brother Scots* (1927), and *The Trial of Guy Fawkes* (1934), and collaborated with his wife in writing *The Scots Week-End* (1936).

Carte (kärt), **Thomas.** b. at Clifton-upon-Dunsmore, Warwickshire, England, in April, 1686; d. near Abingdon, Berkshire, England, April 2, 1754. An English scholar and historian. He was the author of *Life of James, Duke of Ormonde* (1736), an important history of England to 1654 (1747–55), and others. He was a strong Jacobite.

Carter (kär′tẽr), **Elizabeth.** b. at Deal, England, Dec. 16, 1717; d. at London, Feb. 19, 1806. An English poet and translator. She is best known for her friendship for Dr. Samuel Johnson which lasted for 50 years, and was also the friend of Horace Walpole and Edmund Burke. Her letters to Elizabeth Vesey, Elizabeth Montagu, and Catherine Tal-

bot were collected and printed in seven volumes (1809–17). She translated Epictetus, contributed to the *Gentleman's Magazine*, and published collections of poetry.

Carteret (kär′tẽr.ẹt), **Lionel.** The youthful hero of Henry Arthur Jones's problem play *Mrs. Dane's Defence* (1900). He wishes to marry Mrs. Dane, a woman with a past, but his foster father, a clever lawyer, forces her, under a merciless cross-examination, to confess to an old love affair on the Continent. Ruled by arguments that he cannot answer, the chivalrous Lionel gives up Mrs. Dane, and the audience is given to understand that he will marry a "nice" Scottish girl after he has recovered from the shock of losing his first love.

Carthage (kär′thạj). [Latin, **Carthago**; Phoenician, **Karthadasht,** meaning "New Town."] An ancient city and state in N Africa, situated on the Mediterranean, a few mi. NE of modern Tunis, and not far from the ancient city of Utica. It was founded by Phoenicians about the middle of the 9th century B.C. (According to tradition, Dido founded the city, having bought as much land as could be circumscribed by a buffalo hide; this she cut in strips with which, laid end to end, she encircled a sizable piece of ground and on it built the citadel called Byrsa, from the Greek word "hide.") It was a great commercial and colonizing center as early as the 6th century B.C., and was one of the largest cities of antiquity. It had two harbors, a naval and a mercantile. Its first treaty with Rome was made in 509 B.C. It was defeated at Himera in Sicily in 480, but overthrew Selinus and other Sicilian cities c400. It was the rival of Syracuse under Dionysius, Agathocles, and others. At the height of its power it had possessions in Sicily, Corsica, Sardinia, N Africa, and Spain. Its wars with Rome have the following dates: First Punic War, 264–241; Second Punic War, 218–201; Third Punic War, 149–146. It was recolonized as a Roman city by Gaius Gracchus and successfully by Augustus c29 B.C., was taken by the Vandals in 439 A.D., and was retaken by Belisarius in 533. It was an important center of Latin Christianity. The Saracens destroyed it c697. At present some cisterns, broken arches of an aqueduct, the Roman Catholic monastery of Saint Louis, and a museum mark the site of the former great rival of Rome.

Carthon (kär′thọn). A poem (1760) by the Scottish poet Macpherson, a retelling of the legend of the father (Clessammor) who unknowingly kills his son (Carthon) in battle and dies of grief upon discovering his victim's identity.

Carthusians (kär.thū′zhạnz). A monastic order of the Roman Catholic Church, founded (1084) by Saint Bruno (of Cologne) at La Grande Chartreuse, in SE France. The rule of the order, originally written in 1130, was put into its present form in 1681. The monks live an extremely austere and contemplative life, meeting together only at public worship and at stated meals. They are tonsured and beardless. Their isolation, in cells built to be completely separate from each other, has evoked the style of building known in English as the charterhouse, a cloister surrounded by separate houses. No woman, except a ruling queen, is permitted within the Carthusian monastery. The order is noted for the liqueur, chartreuse, made by it in France from a secret formula, the sale of which now brings its principal revenue. A globe with a cross and seven stars around it is the badge of the order.

Carton (kär′tọn), **Sydney.** In Charles Dickens's *A Tale of Two Cities*, a character whose real abilities and worth have been largely sacrificed to careless dissipation, but whose love for Lucy Manette leads him finally to an act of self-sacrifice which many readers consider to be among the noblest in English fiction: Carton substitutes himself for Charles Darnay, Lucy's husband, on the guillotine. (A remarkably close resemblance between the two men makes the substitution possible.) Carton's last thought as the blade of the guillotine drops has taken its place among the best-known lines in Dickens's works (and, indeed, in world literature): "It is a far, far better thing that I do than I have ever done: it is a far, far better rest that I go to than I have ever known."

Cartwright (kärt′rīt), **William.** b. at Northway, near Tewkesbury, England, c1611; d. at Oxford, England, Nov. 29, 1643. An English clergyman, dramatist, and poet. He was the son of an innkeeper at Cirencester, a student at Christ Church, Oxford, a member of the Council of War in 1642, and a proctor of the university in 1643. He wrote *The Ordinary*, *The Royal Slave, a Tragi-Comedy*, *The Lady-Errant, a Tragi-Comedy*, and *The Siege, or Love's Convert*. His poems include *No Platonique Love*, *On a Virtuous Young Gentlewoman that Died Suddenly*, a poem on Jonson in *Jonsonus Virbius*, and *Corinna's Tomb*, suggestive of the nature fantasy of William Collins. His plays and poems were collected in 1651.

Caruso (kạ.rö′sō; Italian, kä.rö′zō), **Enrico.** b. at Naples, Italy, Feb. 25, 1873; d. there, Aug. 2, 1921. An Italian dramatic tenor, noted for the outstanding power and control of his voice. He made his debut in a small theater near Naples, and was not brought into prominence until 1896, when he sang at the Fondo Theater at Naples. In 1898 he sang at Milan. In 1903 he began a series of engagements at New York, where, as a member of the Metropolitan Opera Company, he sang more than 30 roles, that brought him great popularity and world renown. Among his vehicles were *Rigoletto* and *Pagliacci*. He also made phonograph records of operatic excerpts and folk songs.

Carvell (kär′vẹl), **Nicholas.** d. 1566. An English poet, reputed author of two poems in *The Mirror for Magistrates*.

Cary (kār′i), **Henry Francis.** b. at Gibraltar, Dec. 6, 1772; d. at London, Aug. 14, 1844. An English poet and scholar, chiefly known as a translator of Dante.

Cary, Joyce. [Full name, **Arthur Joyce Lunel Cary.**] b. at Londonderry, Ireland, Dec. 7, 1888—. A British novelist. Author of *Aissa Saved* (1930), *The African Witch* (1936), *Castle Corner* (1938), *Mister Johnson* (1939), a trilogy comprising *Herself Surprised* (1941), *To Be a Pilgrim* (1942), and *The Horse's Mouth* (1944), *The Moonlight* (1946), *A Fearful Joy* (1949), *Prisoner of Grace* (1952), and other novels. He has also written *Marching Soldier* (1945) and *The Drunken Sailor* (1947), poetry;

and *Power in Men* (1937), *The Case for African Freedom* (1941), and other politico-philosophical works.

Cary, Lucius. See **Falkland,** 2nd Viscount.

Casabianca (kä.sạ.byäng′kạ). A narrative poem (1829) by Felicia Dorothea Hemans (1793–1835), the work for which she is chiefly remembered. It tells the story of a brave ten-year-old boy, Giacomo Jocante Casabianca, the son of a French naval officer, Louis Casabianca (c1752–98), who stays with his father's ship, *L'Orient*, until it is blown up and he dies, with his father, in carrying out the command to watch the ship. The poem has the frequently quoted opening line "The boy stood on the burning deck."

Casabianca (kä.sạ.byäng′kạ; French, kà.zà.byäṅ-kà), **Louis.** b. at Bastia, Corsica, c1752; killed off Abukir, Egypt, Aug. 1, 1798. A French naval officer. In company with his son, Giacomo Jocante Casabianca, he perished with his ship *L'Orient* (rather than leave the burning vessel, as he might have done) at the battle of the Nile. This event is the subject of the poem *Casabianca* by Felicia Hemans.

Casa Guidi Windows (kä′sä gwē′dē). A poem by Elizabeth Barrett Browning, published in 1851. It is named from the Casa Guidi, a house in Florence where the author resided during the composition of the poem, which was inspired by Mrs. Browning's enthusiasm for Italian freedom.

Casanova de Seingalt (kä.sä.nô′vä dẹ saṅ.gàl′; Anglicized, kaz.ạ.nō′vạ, kas-), **Giovanni Giacomo** (or **Jacopo**). b. at Venice, April 2, 1725; d. at Dux, in Bohemia, June 4, 1798. An Italian adventurer, notorious, through his own writings, as a libertine. His parents were actors, but they entrusted his education to others while they traveled. At the age of 16 Casanova entered a seminary at Venice; he was soon expelled for misconduct, served briefly as secretary to Cardinal Acquaviva, became a soldier in the Venetian service, and thereafter lived by his wits, turning his not inconsiderable abilities to any rewarding course that came to hand. He was a violinist in a theater orchestra, a preacher, a gambler, an alchemist, a thaumaturgist, and above all a rogue with a glib tongue whose attractiveness to women helped him alternately to positions of eminence and disgrace; he traveled through Europe. was imprisoned (1755) for magic and freemasonry at Venice, made a daring escape, and fled to Paris. There he used the story of his adventure to push himself forward and became, through the influence of Marie Antoinette, director of the state lottery; it was in this period that he adopted the style "Chevalier de Seingalt." His large fortune and his position of importance did not remain with him for long; Casanova's restless spirit soon caused him to travel again and in 1759 he left Paris, eventually passing through almost every European court from St. Petersburg to Madrid, from London to Rome. He became acquainted with Voltaire, Cagliostro, Catherine the Great, Madame Pompadour, Albrecht von Haller, and other notables, but in the long run he attained so dubious a reputation because of his immorality and charlatanism that his welcome was worn out. After 1774 he served as a police spy at Venice, but in 1782 had to leave the city when he angered a powerful Venetian personage by his writing. He settled (1785) as librarian at Count Waldstein's castle of Dux in Bohemia, where he spent the rest of his life. Casanova's latter years were spent in writing his *Mémoires écrits par lui-même* (published in 12 volumes, 1826–38, but as yet never printed in full), sensational, highly colored as to his personal adventures, but well written and an excellent source for the history and manners of the period.

Casaubon (ka.sô′bon; French, kȧ.zō.bôṅ), **Isaac.** b. at Geneva, Switzerland, Feb. 18, 1559; d. at London, July 12, 1614. A French classical scholar and Protestant theologian. He was professor of Greek at Geneva (1582–96) and of languages at Montpellier (1596–1600), librarian to Henry IV of France at Paris (1601–10), and from 1610 until his death a prebendary of Canterbury and a pensioner of James I of England. He published commentaries on Athenaeus, Theophrastus (with a Latin translation), and Suetonius, and *Ephemerides,* a journal of his studies.

Casaubon (ka.sô′bon), **Rev. Edward.** In George Eliot's *Middlemarch,* the husband of Dorothea Brooke. She marries him in the belief that his high and noble ideals will raise her into a broad and generous intellectual life, but finds him to be only a timid, self-absorbed pedant.

Casby (kaz′bi), **Christopher.** In Dickens's novel *Little Dorrit,* an avaricious landlord of various dwellings in Bleeding Heart Yard, utterly ruthless in exacting rents from his tenants. However, these unfortunate people think of him as the soul of kindly generosity, blaming his agent Pancks for the treatment they receive. He is the father of Flora Finching.

Casby, Flora. See **Finching, Flora.**

Casca (kas′ka). In Shakespeare's *Julius Caesar,* a conspirator against Caesar. Described as "a blunt fellow" of "quick mettle," his belief that Caesar has overstepped himself makes him willing to assist in the assassination. He plays no further part in the play after that event.

Case Is Altered, The. A comedy of intrigue by Ben Jonson, acted 1598, based on two plays by Plautus, *Aulularia* and *Captivi.* He developed their classic themes into a comedy of Italy in his own day.

Case Is Altered, The. A novel by William Plomer, published in 1932.

Caseldy (kas′el.di). In George Meredith's short romance *The Tale of Chloe,* the unscrupulous young man whom Chloe rescues.

Case of Rebellious Susan, The. A comedy (1894) by Henry Arthur Jones. The heroine, Susan, dissatisfied with her placid existence, decides to leave her husband, but quickly returns to her home when it appears that he will turn to another woman.

Case of the Roman Catholics of Ireland, The. A prose work (1760) by Henry Brooke, an Irishman, who is much better known for his famous sentimental novel *The Fool of Quality, or the History of Henry, Earl of Moreland.*

Cashel Byron's Profession (kash′el bī′ronz). A novel by George Bernard Shaw. Considered the best of his five novels, it was written in 1882, published 1885–86, and dramatized by him in blank verse as *The Admirable Bashville* (1901). It is the story of Cashel Byron, a pugilist, who loves, and finally marries, the wealthy Lydia Carew. He gives up boxing, enters politics, is elected as a Conservative, and has a large family. In his preface, Shaw declares "I never think of Cashel Byron's Profession without a shudder at the narrowness of my escape from becoming a successful novelist at the age of twenty-six." In its original stage version, the prizefighter James J. ("Gentleman Jim") Corbett had a considerable success as the fighting hero.

Caslon (kaz′lon), **William.** b. at Cradley, Worcestershire, England, 1692; d. at Bethnal Green, London, Jan. 23, 1766. A London type founder, famous for his skill as a designer and type cutter. His simple "old-style" type faces are still used extensively. He established an important business which was carried on in partnership with his son William, and after his death by the latter alone.

Caspar (kas′par). See **Gaspar.**

Cassandra (ka.san′dra). [Also, **Alexandra.**] In Greek legend, a Trojan princess; daughter of Priam and Hecuba. Apollo taught her the gift of prophecy, but when she refused his advances he cursed her by commanding that, though her divinations should always be true, they should never be believed. In vain did she thereafter warn her countrymen of various impending disasters, including the coming of the wooden horse. After the Trojan War she was made a slave by Agamemnon, and was later killed by Clytemnestra. Her character, with its tragic element of impotent wisdom, has been variously introduced into later literature.

Cassandra. In Shakespeare's *Troilus and Cressida,* a prophetess, daughter of King Priam of Troy, who foretells Troy's destruction and Hector's death.

Cassandra. A narrative poem (1595) by Richard Barnfield, dealing with Priam's unfortunate daughter, Cassandra, who had the gift of prophecy but was punished by never being believed. The author, Richard Barnfield, wrote an ode, "As it fell upon a day," and a sonnet, "If music and sweet poetry agree," of such high quality that they were long thought to be by Shakespeare.

Cassell (kas′el), **John.** b. at Manchester, England, 1817; d. at Regent's Park, London, April 2, 1865. An English temperance advocate, merchant, author, and publisher. He went to London in 1836 as a carpenter, began a tea and coffee business in 1847, and undertook the publishing of educational works in 1850 with *The Working Man's Friend and Family Instructor.* This was followed by *Cassell's Popular Educator* and *Cassell's Magazine* (1852), *Cassell's Family Paper* (1853), *The Freeholder,* supporting a free land movement, *The Pathway,* a religious journal, and *The Quiver* (1861). In addition to these periodicals, he also published, in book form or as serials, such works as *Don Quixote, Pilgrim's Progress, Robinson Crusoe,* and *Gulliver's Travels,* as well as dictionaries, histories, and other works, all designed for the education and improvement of working people. In 1859 he founded the publishing firm that was to become the famous London house of Cassell and Company.

ḍ, d or j; ṣ, s or sh; ṭ, t or ch; ẓ, z or zh; o. F. cloche; ü, F. menu; ċh, Sc. loch; ṅ, F. bonbon.

Cassibelan (ka.sib′ḝ.lan). In Shakespeare's *Cymbeline*, the historical Cassivellaunus, a British prince captured by Caesar, mentioned in the play.

Cassilis Engagement (kạ.sil′is), **The.** A satirical play (1905) by St. John Hankin. It is considered his best play, and was one of his most popular, being successful at London, Liverpool, Manchester, and Glasgow. It was published with "The Return of the Prodigal," and "The Charity That Began at Home," under the cynical title *Three Plays with Happy Endings* (1907). All Hankin's work illustrates his conviction that drama should "represent life, not argue about it."

Cassim Baba (kas′im bä′bä). See **Baba, Cassim.**

Cassio (kash′i.ō), **Michael.** In Shakespeare's *Othello*, a lieutenant of Othello. A somewhat weak but honorable man, he becomes, by the devices of Iago, the innocent object of Othello's jealousy.

Cassiopeia (kas″i.ọ.pē′ạ) or **Cassiepeia** (kas″i.ẹ-). In classical mythology, the wife of Cepheus, an Ethiopian king, and mother of Andromeda. She was transferred to the heavens as a constellation.

Cassiterides (kas.i.ter′i.dēz). In ancient geography, the "tin islands," generally identified with the Scilly Isles, off Cornwall, England, though by some thought to have been the islands near Vigo in Spain.

Cassius (kash′us, kash′i.us). In Shakespeare's *Julius Caesar*, the historical Gaius Cassius Longinus, one of the chief members of the conspiracy against Caesar, motivated partly by fear of the threat to Rome's traditional freedoms, but also by jealousy. He is an extremely realistic man who, however, reveres Brutus and gives way to his plans even when these seem ill-advised. After the Battle of Philippi, believing that Brutus had already been captured, he kills himself. It is he whom Caesar describes as having "a lean and hungry look, He thinks too much."

Castabella (kas.tạ.bel′ạ). The daughter of wealthy Lord Belforest, married against her will to Rousard, the puny son of D'Amville, in Cyril Tourneur's *The Atheist's Tragedy*. When Rousard dies, she is nearly raped by her father-in-law, so desperate is he in his desire for an heir. However, her lover, Charlemont, who has gone off to the Dutch wars, returns in time to save her.

Castalides (kas.tal′i.dēz). A poetical name for the Muses.

Castalio (kas.tā′li.ō). In Thomas Otway's tragedy *The Orphan*, the quiet, virtuous brother of Polydore, and husband of Monimia.

Castara (kas.tār′ạ). A collection of poems in praise of Lucy Herbert, issued anonymously by William Habington in 1634. He had married Lucy sometime between 1630 and 1633. A subsequent edition (1640) also included some religious poems.

Castaway, The. A lyric by William Cowper. It was written in 1799, the last year of his life, and was his last poem. The lyric is intensely personal and reflects the deep despair of which Cowper was a victim the greater part of his unhappy life. The basis of the poem derives from *A Voyage Round the World* (1748) by the English admiral George

Anson (1697–1762), who actually went through the experience so vividly described in the lyric. Cowper, who felt that he was eternally damned, regarded himself as a "castaway" in the sense that he was forgotten by God.

Caste. A social comedy (1867) by T. W. Robertson.

Castell of Pleasure (kås′l), **The.** A dream poem by William Neville. It was printed in 1518 by Hary Pepwell, and later by Wynkyn de Worde. A quarto copy is in the British Museum. The abstract characters are Desire and Beauty, to whom Desire makes passionate love in the Garden of Affection, and Pity and Disdain, who become involved in a lively quarrel.

Casterbridge (kås′tėr.brij), **The Mayor of.** See **Mayor of Casterbridge, The.**

Castiglione (käs.tē.lyō′nä), **Baldassare,** Conte. b. at Casantico, near Mantua, Italy, 1478; d. at Toledo, Spain, Feb. 7, 1529. An Italian courtier, diplomat, and writer. As a youth he served at the ducal court of Milan, but when Duke Lodovico Sforza was taken captive by the French, he became attached to Guidobaldo Malatesta, duke of Urbino, who employed him in diplomatic business with Henry VII of England. Guidobaldo's successor, Francesco della Rovere, brought Castiglione to the favorable notice of Pope Clement VII, who sent him to Spain to arbitrate the contentions of the papacy and the emperor Charles V. Charles made much of him and he remained in Spain as a Spanish subject. When in 1527 the emperor's army led by the Constable Bourbon attacked Rome and made the Pope captive, Castiglione was suspected of having played a treacherous role, but it is considered equally likely that he was tricked by Charles. Castiglione wrote shrewd and graceful letters and distinguished poetry in Latin and Italian, but his most memorable work is *Il Cortegiano* (*The Courtier*), one of the great books of the Italian Renaissance, being the mirror of the ideal conduct of the nobility and knightly class who thronged the courts and served the royal and ducal sovereigns of that time.

Castiza (kas′ti.zạ). In Cyril's Tourneur's *The Revenger's Tragedy*, the chaste and upright sister of Vendice and Hippolita.

Castle (kås′l), **Agnes.** [Maiden name, **Sweetman.**] b. in Queen's County (now County Laoighis), Ireland; d. at Genoa, Italy, April 30, 1922. An English novelist; wife of Egerton Castle (1858–1920). She was coauthor, with her husband, of many romantic and sentimental novels, including *The Pride of Jennico* (1898; also a play), *The Bath Comedy* (1900; a great dramatic success as *Sweet Kitty Bellairs*, *The Secret Orchard* (1901; dramatized, 1901), *The Star Dreamer* (1903), *The Incomparable Bellairs* (1904), *Rose of the World* (1905), *French Nan* (1905), *If Youth But Knew* (1906), *My Merry Rockhurst* (1907), *Flower o' the Orange and Other Stories* (1908), *The Ways of Miss Barbara* (1914), *Forlorn Adventurers* (1915), *The Black Office and other Chapters of Romance* (1917), *Wolf Lure* (1917), *New Wine* (1919), and *Pamela Pounce* (1921). Before her collaboration with Castle, she wrote *My Little Lady Anne* (1896), and, after his death, *Kitty and Others* (1922).

Castle, Egerton. b. at London, March 12, 1858; d. 1920. An English novelist, short-story writer, and dramatist. He was the author of *Schools and Masters of Fence* (1884), *Consequences* (1891), *English Book-plates* (1892), *The Jerningham Letters* (1896), *Young April* (1899), and *Marshfield, the Observer* (1900). Books which he wrote with his wife include *The Pride of Jennico* (1898), *The Bath Comedy* (1900; dramatized as *Sweet Kitty Bellairs*), *The Secret Orchard* (1901; dramatized, 1901), *The Star Dreamer* (1903), *The Incomparable Bellairs* (1904), *Rose of the World* (1905), *French Nan* (1905), *The Heart of Lady Anne* (1905), *If Youth But Knew* (1906), *My Merry Rockhurst* (1907), *Flower o' the Orange and Other Stories* (1908), *Panther's Cub* (1910) and *New Wine* (1919).

Castle Dangerous. A novel by Sir Walter Scott, published in 1831. It was published together with *Count Robert of Paris* as the fourth series of *Tales of My Landlord* (1832). Sir John de Walton and the young knight, Aymer de Valence, are holding Douglas Castle for the English against Robert Bruce (Robert I of Scotland) and Sir James Douglas in 1306. Lady Augusta of Berkely, a beautiful young Englishwoman, offers her hand and fortune to the man who can hold the castle for a year and a day, and goes in disguise to the castle, accompanied by her aged minstrel Bertram. There she is almost taken for a spy before Sir John recognizes her. She is then captured by the forces of Douglas and is offered in exchange for the castle. Sir John is ordered to surrender the castle, whereupon Lady Augusta is returned unharmed to him.

Castlemaine (kàs'l.mān), Earl of. Title of **Palmer, Roger.**

Castle of Indolence, The. A poem by James Thomson, published in 1748.

Castle of Otranto (ō.trän'tō), **The.** [Full title, **The Castle of Otranto, a Gothic Story.**] A romance by Horace Walpole, published in 1764. The book influenced the subsequent fashion for tales of terror and the supernatural (called, from the title of Walpole's book, "Gothic romances"). Manfred, the usurping prince of Otranto, is warned by a prophecy that he will retain the castle only as long as it is large enough to hold its rightful owner and while the usurper has male descendants. Shortly thereafter Manfred's son is killed by a giant helmet which falls on his head on the eve of his wedding to the beautiful Isabella. Manfred, realizing that he is unlikely to have any more male heirs by his wife, thereupon decides to take Isabella himself. Isabella flees from him and is aided in her escape by Theodore, a young peasant who bears a strong resemblance to the portrait of the dead Alonso, the original true owner of the castle. Manfred is going to have Theodore executed, but is forced to spare him when the ghost of Alonso, having grown too large for the castle, tears it down and announces that Theodore is his descendant and the rightful heir to Otranto. Theodore and Isabella then marry.

Castle of Perseverance, The. An early example (c1405) of the English morality play, and the longest (it contains over 3,600 lines), possibly first performed at Lincoln. It traces the spiritual history of man from birth to death and to final judgment. The characters who struggle for possession of man's soul are the Good Angel and the Bad Angel and the Virtues and Vices that accompany them. The themes typifying moralities are all present: the conflict between vice and virtue, the debate of the heavenly graces (in this case, the Four Daughters of God), the summons of death, the debate between Body and Soul, and a fight between virtues and vices.

Castle Perilous. In Malory's *Morte d'Arthur*, the castle of Lionês.

Castle Rackrent (rak'rent). A novel by Maria Edgeworth, published in 1800. The story is told by Thady Quirk, the steward to the Rackrent family. He explains how the landlords in this vicious family have oppressed their Irish tenants in order to get money, and how they have nevertheless lost their fortunes and estates through reckless living. Sir Patrick is a hard-drinking man who had the "finest funeral ever held." Sir Murtagh, the lawyer who is married to a woman of the Skinflint family, is followed by the next landlord, Sir Kit, who kept his Jewish wife locked up for seven years because she would not turn over her jewels to him. Sir Condy spends the rest of the family money and dies from excessive drinking. The property eventually falls into the hands of Attorney Quirk, Thady's cunning son.

Castlereagh (kàs'l.rā), Viscount. See **Stewart, Robert** (1769–1822).

Castle Spectre, The. A play by Matthew Gregory Lewis, produced in 1797.

Castlewood (kàs'l.wùd), **Colonel Francis Esmond, Lord.** The second Lord Castlewood in William Makepeace Thackeray's novel *Henry Esmond*, the father of Beatrix and Francis. He is a drunken sensualist who ill-treats and insults his wife, spoils his children, gambles away his property, and is killed in a duel.

Castlewood, Lady. The mother of Beatrix Esmond, and wife of the second Lord Castlewood, in Thackeray's *Henry Esmond*. She afterward marries Henry Esmond.

Castor (kas'tọr). In Greek and Roman mythology, the twin brother of Pollux, noted for his skill in the management of horses. He is regarded as the son of Zeus and Leda, wife of Tyndareus, king of Sparta, or of Tyndareus and Leda. According to one version of the legend, Zeus assumed the form of a swan. Two eggs were produced by Leda from one of which came Castor and Clytemnestra, from the other Pollux and Helen. The Dioscuri (Castor and Pollux) were the heroes of many adventures, and were worshiped as divinities, particularly by Dorians and at Rome. They were placed in the heavens as a constellation.

Castor and Pollux (pol'uks). The two principal stars of the zodiacal constellation Gemini, the Twins. Castor, α Geminorum, 1.6 magnitude, is 4 degrees NW of Pollux; β Geminorum, the brighter star, has a magnitude of 1.2.

Casuals of the Sea. A novel (1916) by William McFee.

Catacombs of Rome. Catacombs at Rome lying for the most part within a circle of three miles from the modern walls. The length of the galleries is estimated at ab. 600 miles. The vast network of subterranean passages and chambers is now held to have been formed, chiefly between the 2nd and the 6th century, expressly for the burial of Christians. Many of the chambers were later used as chapels. The Catacombs are the source of many sculptures, paintings, and inscriptions of high importance in early Christian art and archaeology.

Cataian (ka.tā′an). A Cathaian or inhabitant of Cathay (China), used by the Elizabethans (in reference to the supposed thieving habits of the Chinese) for a sharper. Shakespeare uses the term in *The Merry Wives of Windsor.*

catalectic (kat.a.lek′tik). In prosody: **1.** Wanting part of the last foot: opposed to acatalectic. In the following couplet the second line is catalectic, the first acatalectic:

Tell me / not, in / mournful / numbers, /
Life is / but an / empty / dream! /

Verses consisting of feet of three or more syllables are described as catalectic in a syllable, a disyllable, or a trisyllable, according to the number of syllables in the last or incomplete foot.
2. In a wider sense, wanting part of a foot or measure.

catalexis (kat.a.lek′sis). In prosody, incompleteness of the last foot or measure of a verse. In a wider sense, incompleteness of any foot in a verse. Catalexis is not the suppression of any rhythmical element, but the want of a corresponding syllable or syllables in the words to fill out a time or times necessary to the metrical completeness of the line. This space is filled out by a pause—in the quantitative poetry of the Greeks and Romans, either by a pause or by prolonging the preceding syllable.

Catalina (kat.a.lī′na). A novel by W. Somerset Maugham, published in 1948. It is set in Spain during the Inquisition.

Catalogue of the Royal and Noble Authors of England, The. A prose work (2 vols., 1758) by Horace Walpole. It is a compilation of literary and antiquarian gossip, and was published by the author on his own private printing press (the Strawberry Hill Press).

Cataract of Lodore (lō.dōr′), **The.** A poem (1820) by Robert Southey.

catastrophe. The arrangement of actions or interconnection of causes which constitutes the final event of a dramatic piece; the unfolding and winding up of the plot, clearing up difficulties, and closing the play; the dénouement. The ancients divided a play into the protasis, epitasis, catastasis, and catastrophe; that is, the introduction, continuance, heightening, and development or conclusion.

Pat, he comes, like the catastrophe of the old comedy. (Shakespeare, *King Lear.*)

All the actors must enter to complete and make up the catastrophe of this great piece.
(Sir T. Browne, *Religio Medici.*)

The Catastrophe of the Poem is finely presaged on this occasion. (Addison, *Spectator*, No. 327.)

Caterina Sarti (kä.tä.rē′nä sär′tē). See **Sarti, Caterina.**

Catesby (kāts′bi), **Sir William.** In Shakespeare's *Richard III*, a follower of Richard.

Catharine Arrowpoint (kath′a.rin ar′ō.point). See **Arrowpoint, Catharine.**

Catharine Coldstream (kōld′strēm), **Lady.** See **Coldstream, Lady Catharine.**

Cathay (ka.thā′). A literary designation for China, used in Western literature since the time of Marco Polo. The word survives in Russian as *Kitaí,* and derives from Chinese *Ch'i-tan* (or *Kitan* or *Khitan*), the name of a tribe which established authority over what is now Manchuria and Mongolia, and ruled N China for two centuries before 1125 A.D., hence the reference to China. See *History of Chinese Society: Liao 907–1125* by Karl A. Wittfogel and Feng Chia-sheng.

Cathedral, The. A novel (1923) by Hugh Walpole, analyzing the personality and the family relations of a church official.

Cathedral Novels. An occasional name for the series of novels (1855–67) by Anthony Trollope dealing with the society of a cathedral town in the north of England. See **Barsetshire.**

Catherine (kath′e.rin). [Full title, **Catherine. A Shabby Genteel Story.**] A novel (published 1839–40 in *Fraser's Magazine*, and in book form in 1840) by William Makepeace Thackeray. It tells the story of a vicious woman who murdered her husband in 1726 and was burned at Tyburn for her crime. The "Catherine" of the novel is drawn from Mrs. Catherine Hayes (1690–1726), who did in real life what Thackeray portrays in his pages. It was Thackeray's aim to ridicule the contemporary literary fashion of picturing criminals as heroes, as in the narratives of William Harrison Ainsworth and Edward Bulwer-Lytton. The novel first appeared under one of his many pen names, Ikey Solomons, Esq., Junior.

Catherine and Petruchio (pē.trö′ki.ō). A play condensed and adapted from Shakespeare's *Taming of the Shrew* by David Garrick, produced in 1756.

Catherine De Bourgh (de bérg), **Lady.** See **De Bourgh, Lady Catherine.**

Catherine Glover (gluv′ér). See **Glover, Catherine.**

Catherine Herself. A novel by James Hilton, published in 1920.

Catherine Morland (môr′land). See **Morland, Catherine.**

Catherine of Alexandria (al.eg.zan′dri.a), Saint. According to tradition, a Christian martyr of the 4th century, tortured on the wheel and beheaded at Alexandria by order of the emperor Maximian. According to some accounts the torture was prevented by a miracle. The wheel became her symbol. She is commemorated on Nov. 25.

Catherine of Aragon (ar′a.gon). See **Katherine** (in Shakespeare's *Henry VIII*).

Catherine of Valois (val′wä, và.lwà). See **Katherine** (in Shakespeare's *Henry V*).

Catherine Seyton (sē′ton). See **Seyton, Catherine.**

Cathleen ni Houlihan (kath.lēn′ ni hö′li.han). A one-act prose play (1902) by William Butler Yeats, published in his *Plays for an Irish Theatre* (1904). Considered by many to be the best of Yeats's serious plays, it is a dramatization of a story of 1798 (when the Irish, with French help, sought to

fat, fāte, fär, àsk, fāre; net, mē, hér; pin, pīne; not, nōte, mȯve, nôr; up, lūte, pull; ᴛʜ, then;

achieve independence) and noteworthy for its symbolic Irish nationalism. A poor old woman appears to Michael Gillane and urges him off to the wars. Despite his plans to marry and his duties at home, Michael follows this personification of patriotism out of the village. Not until the end of the play does anyone on the stage become aware that the old woman is the ancient queen of Ireland in disguise. Michael's sacrifice renews the old woman's youth and she goes off with him with "the walk of a Queen."

Catholic Majesty. A title of the kings of Spain, assumed at times after the Council of Toledo, and permanently after the time of Ferdinand the Catholic (1474–1516).

Catiline's Conspiracies (kat'i.lĭnz). A play by Stephen Gosson, written before 1579. It was acted, but not printed.

Catiline's Conspiracies. A tragedy (1598) by Robert Wilson and Henry Chettle, perhaps a revised version of Gosson's play.

Catiline's Conspiracy. A tragedy by Ben Jonson, produced in 1611. Catiline is made inhumanly ferocious in this play.

Cato (kā'tō). A tragedy by Joseph Addison, produced at the Drury Lane Theatre, London, in 1713, but probably written for the most part ten years before. At the time it was produced, its popularity was partly due to a political situation: the Whigs identified Cato with the Duke of Marlborough; the Tories identified Marlborough with Caesar, the would-be dictator. Hence, but for different reasons, both parties were loud in their praise of the play, while Addison protested his innocence of any political intention. It marked the emergence of a new form of English tragedy: neo-classical tragedy wherein the emphasis was upon rules of construction and decorum, particularly on the Aristotelian unities of time, place, and action. It did much to raise Continental appreciation of English drama; indeed, it was the British answer to the neo-classicism of Racine and Corneille. The plot is taken from history. Cato, holding Caesar, the aspiring general at bay, is betrayed by Sempronius and Syphax, both rather conventional villains. He is supported by Juba. When it is clear that further resistance is useless, Cato helps Juba and his supporters to escape, then commits suicide.

Cato, Dionysius. The reputed author of a famous collection of precepts. Nothing is known about him except that he is supposed to have gathered and arranged the morally edifying apothegms known as *Dionysii Catonis disticha de moribus ad filium*, much admired, and widely used in the schools, during the Middle Ages.

Cato, Marcus Porcius. [Called "Cato the Elder" and "Cato the Censor"; surnamed **Priscus**.] b. at Tusculum, Italy, 234 B.C.; d. 149 B.C. A Roman statesman, general, and writer. He was quaestor under Scipio in 204, served as consul in 195, served in Spain in 194 and against Antiochus in 191, was censor in 184, and was ambassador to Carthage in 150. He sought to restore the integrity of morals and the simplicity of manners prevalent in the early days of the republic, his severity as a censor earning him the epithet "Censorius." The prosper-

ity of Rome's old enemy Carthage led him to advocate a third Punic war, in his effort to incite to which he for years closed every speech in the senate with the words, "Ceterum censeo Carthaginem esse delendam" ("Furthermore, I am of the opinion that Carthage ought to be destroyed"). He wrote *De agri cultura*, also called *De re rustica* (edited by Keil, 1882) and *Origines* (extant in fragments).

Cato, Young. In Shakespeare's *Julius Caesar*, a friend of Brutus and Cassius who appears briefly at the Battle of Philippi.

Cato's Letters. A collection (4 vols., 1724) of essays by John Trenchard and Thomas Gordon They originally appeared in *The London Journal*, founded by Trenchard and Gordon in 1719. They presented the Whig viewpoint, and demanded the punishment of the promoters of the South Sea Bubble. Trenchard attacked standing armies, and superstition. Gordon, who translated Tacitus and Sallust, is supposed to be the Silenus of Pope's *Dunciad*.

Cato Street Conspiracy (kā'tō). [Also, **Thistlewood Conspiracy**.] In British history, a conspiracy under the lead of Arthur Thistlewood, which aimed to assassinate Robert Stewart, Viscount Castlereagh, and other cabinet officers. The plot was discovered on Feb. 23, 1820, and came to nothing.

Catriona (ka.trē'o.na). A romantic novel (1893) by Robert Louis Stevenson. It deals with the adventures of David Balfour, who also appears in *Kidnapped*, and with his love for Catriona Drummond, the daughter of James More Drummond, a rascal and a renegade. After much misunderstanding, David and Catriona are happily married.

Cattermole (kat'ėr.mōl), **George.** b. at Dickleborough, Norfolk, England, Aug. 8, 1800; d. at Clapham, London, July 24, 1868. An English painter, one of the earliest English water-colorists. He illustrated Sir Walter Scott's *Waverley Novels*. His subjects were chiefly medieval.

Cattle Raid of Cooley (kö'lē). See **Tain Bo Cuailgne.**

Catullus (ka.tul'us), **Gaius Valerius.** b. at Verona, Italy, c84 B.C.; d. c54 B.C. A Roman poet. Particularly effective in simple short lyric poems, he is ranked by many with Sappho and Shelley. Coming to Rome he became acquainted with the most celebrated men of his day, including Julius Caesar (whom he attacked in his verses but to whom he later was reconciled), Cicero, Asinius Pollio, Cornelius Nepos, and Calvus. His love poems are addressed to Lesbia, whose real name, according to Apuleius, was Clodia, the beautiful and fascinating wife of Caecilius Metellus and the sister of the demagogue Clodius, Cicero's enemy. This identification is now generally accepted. The stormy love affair (which gave to some of the poems a bitterness not usually found in lyric verse) ended in unhappiness for Catullus. The extant poems number 113, and include lyrics, epigrams, elegies, and even a short epic of 408 lines about the marriage of Peleus and Thetis. They fall into three groups: short lyrics, four longer poems (including two wedding hymns and the epic), and a group of epigrams and elegies. The themes of some of his most famous and charming poems are the death of Lesbia's pet sparrow, the "thousand kisses," the dinner invitation, the homecoming to Sirmio, the love of Acme and Septimius, the marriage of Torquatus, the death of a brother. The Attis, in galloping galliambics, is a metrical tour de force of extraordinary effectiveness. Catullus greatly influenced Horace in his *Odes*, Vergil in the *Aeneid*, Ovid and the other elegists, and the epigrammatist Martial.

Catuvellauni (kat″ū.ve̩.lô′nī). An ancient British people who lived in the region of what is now Herefordshire and Bedfordshire.

Cauchon (kō′shon). The Roman Catholic churchman in Shaw's *Saint Joan* who asserts the final authority of the Church as the sole instrument of mediation between God and the individual.

caudate rhyme. See end-rhyme.

Caudine Forks (kô′dīn). [Latin, **Furculae Caudinae**.] Two passes in the mountains of ancient Samnium, Italy, leading to an enclosed valley, between Capua and Benevento. Here the Romans under the consuls Spurius Postumius Albinus and T. Veturius were forced (321 B.C) to surrender to the Samnites under Pontius. The Romans were forced to swear to a treaty of peace, and to give 600 Roman *equites* (knights) as hostages, while the whole Roman army was sent under the yoke (thus symbolizing their collective submission). Infuriated by this last humiliation, which was one of the worst ever accepted by a Roman military force, the Roman senate refused to approve the treaty, and delivered the consuls to the Samnites, who refused to accept them.

Caudle (kô′dl), **Mrs.** The lecturing wife in *Mrs. Caudle's Curtain Lectures*, by Douglas Jerrold.

Cauline (kô′lĭn), **Sir.** A character in a ballad in Percy's *Reliques*, a young knight in love with Christabelle, the daughter of the king. The king banishes him when he discovers the lovers together, but Cauline returns secretly, in time to kill a horrible suitor for Christabelle's hand. But after the fight he dies from the wounds he has received, and Christabelle dies for sorrow.

Caution, Mrs. The aunt of Hippolita in William Wycherley's *The Gentleman Dancing-Master*.

Cautionary Tales. A volume of humorous verses (c1900) by Hilaire Belloc, ostensibly for children, but more generally read by adults. Some of the characters he introduces here and in the subsequent *New Cautionary Tales* include Henry King, Godolphin Horne, and Peter Goole ("who ruined his father and mother by extravagance").

Cavalcade. A play (1931) by Noel Coward. It traces the fortunes of an English family, the Marryots, from 1899 to 1930. Coward's aim is to glorify the English spirit during that period, which includes the last years of Victoria's reign, that of Edward VII, World War I, and the greater part of the reign of George V. The screen version duplicated the success of the stage play.

Cavaliers. A name given to the supporters of the Stuart kings of England, particularly under the reign of Charles I. Some of them came to the Virginia colony after 1647, but until recently their influence upon the life and culture of that area was highly exaggerated.

Cavall (ka̩.val′). King Arthur's dog.

Cave (kāv), **Anne** (**Estella Sarah Penfold**). [Title, Countess **Cave of Richmond**; maiden name, **Mathews**.] d. Jan. 7, 1938. An English author of travel books and memoirs. She was awarded the Medal of Queen Elizabeth of the Belgians. Her works include *Memories of Old Richmond* (1922), *Three Journeys* (1928), and *Odds and Ends of My Life* (1929).

Cave, Edward. b. at Newton, Warwickshire, England, Feb. 27, 1691; d. at London, Jan. 10, 1754. An English printer and bookseller. In 1731 he started a printing office at London under the name of R. Newton, and founded the *Gentleman's Magazine* which he edited under the pseudonym of Sylvanus Urban, Gent. He began in 1732 the publication of regular reports of parliamentary debates, based on the memory of reporters who had listened to the speeches, and put in proper literary shape by William Guthrie and, after him, for several years by Samuel Johnson. This publication of these reports brought upon him the censure of Parliament.

Caveat or Warning for Common Cursitors, Vulgarly Called Vagabones, A. A prose work (1566) by Thomas Harman, a country gentleman living at Crayford, Kent. He examined thieves, tramps, beggars, and other undesirable characters, who came to his door to beg. The knowledge thus obtained he used in the work by which he is remembered. It was dedicated to his neighbor, Elizabeth, Countess of Shrewsbury, and contains 24 essays, on different underworld types, examples of underworld slang, and some realistic woodcuts.

Cavendish (kav′e̩n.dish), **George.** b. 1500; d. c1561. An English biographer and constant attendant of Cardinal Wolsey. He served as an usher (1526–30) to Wolsey, retiring to Glensford, in Suffolk, after the cardinal's death. His *Life of Cardinal Wolsey*, written in 1557, was withheld from publication during Elizabeth's reign and, as a result, only abridged or garbled versions were in circulation until the definitive edition of S. W. Singer in the early 19th century.

Cavendish, Henry. b. at Nice, France, Oct. 10, 1731; d. at London, March 10, 1810. An English chemist and physicist. He studied at Cambridge in the period 1750–53, but did not take a degree. He discovered nitric acid, and was the first who, by inductive experiments, combined oxygen and hydrogen into water. He also anticipated several later discoveries concerning the nature of electricity. He published numerous scientific papers, including "Experiments on Air, by Henry Cavendish, Esq.," in the *Philosophical Transactions* of the Royal Society, of which he became a member in 1760.

Cavendish, Margaret. [Title, Duchess of **Newcastle**.] b. at St. John's, near Colchester, Essex, England, 1624; d. at London, Jan. 7, 1674. An English court lady, dramatist, poet, and biographer of her husband. In 1643 she was maid of honor to Queen Henrietta Maria, with whom she went to Paris, where she met and married (as his second wife) William Cavendish, 1st Duke of Newcastle. She wrote *Philosophical Fancies*, *Philosophical* *and Physical Opinions, Grounds of Natural Philosophy, A True Relation of My Birth, Breeding, and Life, Sociable Letters,* and several plays and poems, but she is best remembered for her enthusiastic life of her husband, written while he was still living, *The Life of the Thrice Noble, High and Puissant Prince, William Cavendish, Duke, Marquis, and Earl of Newcastle, Earl of Ogle, Viscount Mansfield, and Baron of Bolsover, of Ogle, Bothal, and Hepple* . . . (1667; another edition came out in 1675, and a Latin translation, in 1668, all published at London). Her plays appeared in 2 folio volumes (1662 and 1668), but were never produced. Charles Lamb praised her, but Samuel Pepys, who called her *Humorous Lovers* "a silly play," thought she was "a mad, conceited, ridiculous woman." She is buried in Westminster Abbey.

Cavendish (kav′ẹn.dish, kan′dish) or **Candish** (kan′dish), **Thomas.** b. in the parish of Trimlay St. Martin, Suffolk, England, c1555; d. at sea in the South Atlantic, in June, 1592. An English navigator and freebooter. In 1585 he commanded a ship in the fleet of Richard Grenville, sent by Raleigh to Virginia. On July 21, 1586, he sailed from Plymouth with three small vessels, the *Desire,* the *Content,* and the *Hugh Gallant* (which was sunk in the Pacific). He touched at Africa and Brazil, and passed the Strait of Magellan in January, 1587, ravaged the shores of Spanish South America and Mexico, taking many vessels, and on Nov. 14, 1587, captured a ship from the Philippines with an immense booty. He then crossed the Pacific, and returned by way of the Cape of Good Hope, reaching England on Sept. 10, 1588. This was the third circumnavigation of the world. Cavendish undertook a similar voyage in 1591 with five ships; but, after enduring great hardships, he was unable to pass the Strait of Magellan. His ships were scattered, and he died while attempting to return. Only a few of his crew ever reached England.

Cavendish College. A college of the University of Cambridge, founded in 1873.

Cave of Adullam (ạ.dul′ạm). See **Adullam, Cave of.**

"Cave of Harmony." In *The Newcomes* and various others of Thackeray's works, a coffee house popular as a gathering place after the theater. It is probably based upon Evans's, an establishment in Covent Garden, with some details taken from the "Coal Hole," a tavern on the Strand.

Cave of Mammon (mam′ọn). See **Mammon, Cave of.**

Cavour (kä.vör′), **Camillo Benso, Conte di.** b. at Turin, Italy, Aug. 10, 1810; d. there, June 6, 1861. An Italian statesman, a leading figure in the Italian Risorgimento movement. He entered the Sardinian parliament in 1848, was a member of Azeglio's cabinet (1850–52), and became prime minister of Sardinia in 1852. He joined the alliance of the western powers and Turkey against Russia in 1855 and in the same year sent a contingent of 15,000 Sardinian troops under La Marmora to the Crimea. In 1856 he represented Sardinia at the Congress of Paris; he formed an alliance with Napoleon III against Austria at Plombières in 1858, and carried on, with the assistance of the French, a successful war against Austria in 1859. In the same year he

resigned the premiership, dissatisfied with the terms of peace imposed by Napoleon at Villafranca di Verona. He resumed the premiership in 1860, secretly supported the expedition of Garibaldi against Sicily in the same year, and achieved the unification of Italy, except Venice and the Patrimonium Petri (a division of the Papal States), under the scepter of Victor Emmanuel II in 1861.

Cawdor (kô′dọr), **Thane of.** In Shakespeare's *Macbeth,* a prosperous gentleman whose rank was promised to Macbeth by the witches. No sooner had the prophecy been made than Macbeth learned that Cawdor was to be executed by order of Duncan for treason. He dies nobly ("nothing in his life became him like the leaving it"), and Macbeth succeeds to his rank. It has sometimes been said that his behavior corresponds in almost every circumstance with that of the unfortunate Earl of Essex beheaded by Queen Elizabeth. The Thane of Cawdor does not appear upon the stage at all.

Caxon (kak′sọn), **Jacob.** The hairdresser employed by the antiquary in Sir Walter Scott's novel of that name.

Caxton (kaks′tọn), **William.** b. in Kent, c1422; d. at Westminster, London, 1491. The first English printer. He was first apprenticed to a London mercer, Robert Large (Lord Mayor of London in 1439–40), and after his master's death (1441) went to Bruges, where he served out the remainder of his apprenticeship (1446), and then established himself as a mercer, becoming in 1463 governor of the English Association of Merchant Adventurers in that city. In 1469 he began a translation from French which he called *The Recuyell of the Historyes of Troye* (completed in 1471 at Cologne), and to supply the great demand for copies of the book set himself to learn the art of printing. He established a press at Bruges in partnership with Colard Mansion; from it in 1475 was issued *The Recuyell* as the first book ever printed in English. Another of his translations, *The Game and Playe of the Chesse,* and several French works were also printed there. He left Bruges in 1476, and set up his press at Westminster (the exact site is uncertain), from that time until his death being constantly engaged in translating and printing with several assistants, among whom was Wynkyn de Worde, his successor. It was here that he printed Chaucer's *Canterbury Tales* (before 1480; 2nd ed. between 1483 and 1485) and Malory's *Morte d'Arthur* (1485).

Caxtons, The. A novel by Edward Bulwer-Lytton, first published anonymously in *Blackwood's Magazine* in 1848 and brought out in book form in 1850.

Cayley (kā′li), **Charles Bagot.** b. near St. Petersburg, July 9, 1823; d. at London, Dec. 6, 1883. An English poet. He is known chiefly as a translator of Dante, and also translated Homer, Petrarch, and Aeschylus.

Cebes (sē′bēz). fl. at Thebes, Boeotia, in the 5th century B.C. A Greek philosopher; a friend and pupil of Socrates. He is one of the interlocutors in Plato's *Phaedo.* Three works were ascribed to him, probably erroneously, one of which, *Tabula,* is a philosophical explanation of a table symbolically representing the dangers and vicissitudes of life.

Cecil (ses'il, sis'il), Lord **David**. [Full name, Lord **Edward Christian David Gascoyne Cecil**.] b. April 9, 1902—. An English literary critic. He is the author of *Life of Cowper* (1929), *Sir Walter Scott* (1933), *Early Victorian Novelists* (1934), *Jane Austen* (1935), and *Hardy, the Novelist* (1943). He wrote a comprehensive biography of William Lamb (Lord Melbourne), *Melbourne* (1954), the first part of which was originally published in 1939 as *The Younger Melbourne*.

Cecil, William. [Title, 1st Baron **Burghley** (or **Burleigh**.)] b. at Bourn, Lincolnshire, England, Sept. 13, 1520; d. at London, Aug. 4, 1598. An English statesman who occupied a position of great power in the government of Elizabeth of England. From 1535 to 1541 he attended Cambridge University; subsequently he served under Edward Seymour, the protector, until named (1550) a secretary of state. He did not hold this office under Mary Tudor, but with the accession of Elizabeth he again held office. As Elizabeth's chief minister, he took the responsibility for the execution (1587) of Mary, Queen of Scots. He served (1558–72) as chief secretary of state, and in this position organized (1570) a vigilant group against potential papist plots. In 1572 he was made lord high treasurer, a position he held until his death.

Cecilia (sē.sil'yạ), Saint. d. at Rome, probably c230. A Christian martyr. According to the legend, she was compelled, in spite of a vow of celibacy, to marry a young nobleman, Valerian. She succeeded in converting him to her views and also to Christianity, for which they suffered death. She has generally been considered the patron saint of music, particularly church music, and is represented in art as singing and playing on some musical instrument, or as listening to the music of an angel who has been drawn from heaven by her harmony. Dryden alludes to this in his *Ode for Saint Cecilia's Day*. Her story is also told by Chaucer in the "Second Nun's Tale," one of the *Canterbury Tales*. In the Roman and Anglican calendars her feast is celebrated on Nov. 22.

Cecilia, or Memoirs of an Heiress. A novel by Fanny Burney, published in 1782. Cecilia Beverley has inherited a large fortune on the condition that the man she marries must take her name. She lives at different times with her three guardians, Harrel, Briggs, and Delvile. She falls in love with the son of Delvile, but his father refuses the match because he will not have his son change his name. The two young people thereupon contrive a plan by which Cecilia renounces her fortune and Mortimer Delvile keeps his name, but this is checked by the maneuvers of Monckton, a scheming man who hopes to win Cecilia for himself. However, Monckton's plots are exposed and Cecilia and Mortimer are married.

Cecropia (sē.krō'pi.ạ). The widow of the younger brother of King Basilius in Sir Philip Sidney's romance *Arcadia*.

Cecrops (sē'krops). In Greek mythology, the founder and first king of Athens, the introducer of civilization into Greece. He was regarded as autochthonous, and as a being whose upper half was human and the lower half reptile. He was

believed to have given the people their institutions of marriage, burial, and writing.

Cedmon (kad'mọn). See **Caedmon**.

Cedric of Rotherwood or **Cedric the Saxon** (sed'rik, sē'drik; roTH'ẹr.wud). The guardian of Rowena in Sir Walter Scott's novel *Ivanhoe*.

Ceiriog (kī'ri.ôg). Pseudonym of **Hughes, John Ceiriog**.

Ceix and Alceone (sēs; al'sē.ọn). A story related by Gower in his *Confessio Amantis*.

Celadon (sel'ạ.don). A generic name in English pastoral poetry for a rustic lover, as Chloe is for the maid he loves.

Celadon. A witty, inconstant gallant in John Dryden's play *Secret Love, or The Maiden Queen*. He marries the flirt Florimel, with the understanding that they may each have their own way after marriage.

Celadon. A character in James Thomson's *The Seasons*.

Celaeno (se.lē'nō). In Greek mythology, one of the Harpies; also, a Pleiad, a daughter of Atlas and Pleione.

Celestial City, the. In Bunyan's *Pilgrim's Progress*, the goal of the journey, the heavenly Jerusalem.

Celestial Elegies. A group of sonnets (1598) by Thomas Rogers. They differ from the conventional sonnet sequences, as their title suggests, in dealing not with love but with funeral lamentations.

Celestial Omnibus, The. A short story of a bus that goes to Heaven, by Edward Morgan Forster. It is the third in a collection of six, not the first, although the volume (1911) is named after it. The other stories are "The Story of a Panic," "The Other Side of the Hedge," "Other Kingdom," "The Curate's Friend," and "The Road from Colonus."

Celestina (thä.les.tē'nä). [Original full name, **The Tragicomedy of Calisto and Meliboea**.] A Spanish prose drama in 21 acts, or parts. From its length and structure, it is apparent that it could never have been played on the stage, but its dramatic spirit and movement have left their mark on the national drama ever since. The first act, which is much the longest, is believed by some to have been written by Rodrigo Cota, of Toledo, c1480. The entire book is more commonly ascribed to Fernando de Rojas.

Celia (sēl'yạ). [Also, **Caelia**.] In Edmund Spenser's *Faerie Queene*, the mother of Faith, Hope, and Charity. She lived in the hospice called Holiness.

Celia. In Shakespeare's *As You Like It*, the cousin and devoted friend of Rosalind, and daughter of Frederick, the usurping duke. She is the companion of Rosalind in the Forest of Arden, in the disguise of Aliena, a shepherdess. She falls in love with and marries Oliver, older brother to Orlando.

Celia. The wife of Corvino in Ben Jonson's *Volpone*.

Celia. A straightforward, affectionate English girl, with no squeamishness, in Beaumont and Fletcher's play *The Humorous Lieutenant*, made love to by both Antigonus and his son Demetrius. She disguises herself as Enanthe.

fat, fāte, fär, àsk, fãre; net, mē, hèr; pin, pīne; not, nōte, möve, nôr; up, lūte, pùll; ₸H, then;

Celia. A very young girl in William Whitehead's *School for Lovers.* The part was written for Susannah Cibber, then nearly 50 years old.

Celia Brooke (brŭk). See **Brooke, Celia.**

Celibates. A group (1895) of short stories by George Moore, dealing with abnormal and neurotic people. The collection was later published as *In Single Strictness* (1922) and as *Celibate Lives* (1927).

Célimène (sā.lē.men). An artificial, coquettish, but charming and sparkling lady in Molière's comedy *Le Misanthrope.* She makes Acaste and Clitandre both believe she loves them, but finally consents to marry the "misanthrope," Alceste, though declining to seclude herself from the world with him, whereupon he rejects her. Her name is sometimes applied proverbially to a coquette.

Cellini (chel.lē′nē), **Benvenuto.** b. at Florence, Nov. 1, 1500; d. Feb. 14, 1571. An Italian sculptor, goldsmith, and silversmith, now probably best known for his colorful and detailed autobiography. He studied with Michelangelo Bandinelli, father of the sculptor Bandinelli, and with Marcone the goldsmith. From 1516 to 1517 he worked at Pisa. In 1517 he returned to Florence, where he met Torregiano, who tried to secure him for his work in England. Benvenuto's loyalty to Michelangelo, however, prevented the engagement. From 1523 to 1540 he was at Rome under the patronage of Popes Clement VII and Paul III, occupied entirely with his work as goldsmith. In May, 1527, occurred the siege and sack of Rome by the troops of the Constable de Bourbon, in which Cellini assisted in the defense of the Castle of Sant'Angelo, and claimed to have killed Bourbon and wounded the Prince of Orange. At the instigation of Pier Luigi Farnese, illegitimate son of Pope Paul III, he was imprisoned in the Castle of Sant'Angelo in October, 1538. The account of his escape, in December, 1539, is one of the most sensational exploits told in his sensational autobiography. From 1540 to 1544 he lived in France at the court of Francis I. He had his atelier in the Petit Nesle. At this time his first attempts at sculpture were made, the chief being the *Nymph of Fontainebleau,* now in the collection of the Louvre. From 1544 to his death in 1571 he served Cosimo I and the Medici family at Florence. His well-known statue in bronze of *Perseus with the Head of Medusa* was made in this period for the Loggia dei Lanzi at Florence; perhaps the best-known example of his work in gold is a large saltcellar, made for Francis I. His autobiography, one of the most famous of Italian classics, circulated in manuscript until it was printed in 1730. It was translated into German by Goethe. The standard English translation is by J. A. Symonds.

Celt and Saxon (selt; sak′sọn). A fragment of a novel by George Meredith. It was published in 1910, a year after his death. The date of composition is unknown, but it seems to be an early work overlaid with later, highly mannered, revision. A conversation piece, it breaks off with no indication of the author's final intention as to the plot.

Celtic Twilight, The. A volume (1893) of stories and sketches by William Butler Yeats. Its subtitle, "Men and Women, Ghouls and Faeries," indicates that the material is based upon folklore and suggests the mystical strain of the Irish in their belief in the spirit world. The title of the work is also used, sometimes with a slight degree of irony, to mean the literary movement known as the Irish Renaissance, of which Yeats was a recognized leader.

Celts (selts, kelts). [Also, **Kelts.**] Name at first vaguely applied to a Western people, afterward the regular designation of the peoples which speak languages akin to those of Wales, Ireland, the Highlands of Scotland, and Brittany, and constitute a branch or principal division of the Indo-European language family. Formerly, these people occupied, partly or wholly, France, Spain, northern Italy, the western part of Germany, and the British islands. Of the remaining Celtic languages there are two chief divisions: the Goidelic, comprising the Highlands of Scotland, the Irish, and the Manx; and the Cymric, comprising Welsh, and Breton; the Cornish of Cornwall, related to the latter, is functionally extinct, but still survives as a literary language cultivated by some bilingual speakers of Cornish and English.

Cenci (chen′chē), **The.** A drama in verse by Percy Bysshe Shelley, published in 1819. Count Cenci, head of a noble Roman family during the Renaissance, turns upon his daughter, Beatrice, with an incestuous lust. Beatrice thereupon plots with her step-mother, Lucretia, and her brother, Bernardo, to hire assassins to kill the Count as he goes to his castle. However, the circumstances of the murder arouse suspicion, and under torture by the Inquisition, the three are forced to reveal their guilt. There is much beautiful poetry in the play, but the motivations are not always clear (for example Beatrice inspires compassion, but her actions are sometimes rather puzzling, and some of her speeches can be fully understood only by referring elsewhere in Shelley's work).

centaur (sen′tôr). In Greek myth, a monster, half man and half horse, descended from Ixion and Nephele, the cloud. The myth is probably of Eastern origin. The centaurs, supposed to have inhabited Thessaly, were rude and savage beings, embodying the destructive and ungovernable forces of nature. Chiron, the wise instructor of Achilles, and Pholus, the friend of Hercules, were beneficent centaurs. In art the centaur was originally represented as a complete man, to whose body were attached, behind, the barrel and hind quarters of a horse; later this ungainly combination was abandoned, and was universally replaced by the form in which the human body to the waist took the place of the head and neck of the horse. Examples of the primitive type of centaur survive on archaic painted vases, in a few small bronzes, terra cottas, etc., among the reliefs from the temple of Assos, and in certain wall paintings.

> Come, come, be every one officious
> To make this banquet, which I wish may prove
> More stern and bloody than the *Centaurs'* feast.
>   (Shak., *Tit. And.,* V.ii.)

Centaur, The. A novel (1911) by Algernon Blackwood.

Centlivre (sent.liv′ẻr, -lē′vẻr), **Susannah.** b. c1667; d. at London, Dec. 1, 1723. An English actress and

d, d or j; ṣ, s or sh; ṭ, t or ch; ẓ, z or zh; o, F. cloche; ü, F. menu; ċh, Sc. loch; ṅ, F. bonbon.

dramatist. She is said to have been the daughter of a man named Freeman, of Lincolnshire, who removed to Ireland shortly before her birth. About 1706 she married Joseph Centlivre, chief cook to Queen Anne and George I. Among her 19 plays are *The Platonic Lady* (acted 1706), *The Busybody* (acted 1709), *The Wonder! A Woman Keeps a Secret* (1714), which furnished David Garrick with one of his best roles, *A Gotham Election* (published 1715; 2nd ed., 1737, entitled *Humours of Elections*), *A Wife Well Manag'd* (acted 1715), and *A Bold Stroke for a Wife* (acted 1718) in which one of the characters, Simon Pure, after being impersonated, arrives in the last act as "the real Simon Pure." This is the origin of the popular reference to Simon Pure as a standard of genuineness.

Cent Nouvelles Nouvelles (sôn nö.vel nö.vel). An old French collection of 100 prose tales, from a manuscript of 1456.

Cento Novelle Antiche (chen'tō nō.vel'lä än.te'kä). A collection of 100 tales from ancient and medieval history, the romances of chivalry, and the fabliaux of the trouvères, made in Italy about the end of the 13th century.

Cephalus (sef'a.lus). In ancient Greek mythology, the son of Deion, and the husband of Procris whom he accidentally slew while hunting. Eos, the goddess of the dawn, had a liaison with him and suggested that he test Procris's fidelity. He disguised himself and managed to seduce her. She fled, returned in disguise, seduced him, and presented him with a never-failing spear in token of their reconciliation. But her jealousy led her to spy on him as he hunted and when she made an involuntary movement on hearing him invoke the breeze to cool him (she thought he uttered a woman's name) he threw the spear and killed her.

Cephissus (se.fis'us). [Also: **Cephisus, Kephisos.**] In ancient geography, a river in Attica, Greece, flowing through the plain of Athens into the Saronic Gulf.

Cerberus (sêr'bêr.us). In Greek mythology, the watchdog at the entrance to Hades, the infernal regions. Offspring of Typhon and Echidna, he was usually represented as having three heads, a serpent's tail, and a mane made of serpent's heads. Hercules, as one of his labors, brought Cerberus up from Hades. As one of their burial customs, the Greeks buried with the corpse a honey cake, with which the spirit was to quiet Cerberus so that it might pass the monster-dog on its way to Elysium; thence the expression "a sop to Cerberus."

Cerdic (cher'dich, sêr'dik). d. c534. A Saxon ealdorman who founded a settlement on the coast of Hampshire, England, in 495 A.D., assumed the title of King of the West Saxons in 519, and became ancestor of the English royal line. He defeated the Britons at Charford (in Hampshire) in 519, was himself defeated at Mount Badon (or Badbury, in Dorsetshire) in 520, and conquered the Isle of Wight in 530.

Ceres (sir'ēz, sē'rēz). In ancient Italian mythology, the goddess of grain and harvest, later identified by the Romans with the Greek Demeter. Her cult was quite old; one of the *flamens* (15 priests, each

assigned to one god and his cult observance) was the *flamen Cerealis.*

Ceres. In Shakespeare's *Tempest*, a spirit summoned by Prospero to celebrate the vows of Ferdinand and Miranda. She also addresses her blessings to the audience (probably referring to the Elector Palatine and Princess Elizabeth, before whom the play was first given).

Cerimon (ser'i.mon). In Shakespeare's *Pericles*, a lord of Ephesus who revives Thaisa. He sends her to the temple of Diana, where she becomes one of the vestals.

Certaine Tragicall Discourses. [Full title, **Certaine Tragicall Discourses written oute of French and Latine by Geffraie Fenton.**] Thirteen tales by Bandello translated into English by Geoffrey Fenton in 1567. His sources were the French versions of Boisteau and Belleforest.

Cervantes (sêr.van'tēz; Spanish, ther.ɐän'täs), **Miguel de.** [Full surname, **Cervantes Saavedra** (sä.ä.ɐä'тнrä).] b. at Alcalá de Henares, Spain, possibly on Oct. 9, 1547; d. at Madrid, April 23, 1616. A Spanish novelist, poet, and dramatist. His lineage was good, but the family was poverty stricken. Except that for a time he went to school at Madrid (ab. 20 mi. from his birthplace), where he published some verses (1568), nothing is known of his youth or education. In 1569 he went to Rome as the chamberlain of Cardinal Acquaviva. For the next five years he served in the Spanish army, based in Italy. In the naval battle of Lepanto (1571) he received the "beautiful" wounds that crippled his left hand and arm. En route home in 1575 he was captured by pirates and held at Algiers for five years, where his tireless bravery is well documented. After a brief turn with the army in Portugal he settled down to writing; but a number of plays brought neither fame nor wealth, nor did the pastoral *La Galatea* (1585). In 1584 he married a farmer's daughter. They had no children, but his household for long included two sisters, an illegitimate daughter, and a niece. A position as a government collector, first of grain and then of taxes, took him to Seville in 1587. His work yielded valuable knowledge of Andalusians, respectable and criminal, but his bad bookkeeping put him in jail at least twice. For a while he sojourned at Valladolid, then ended his days at Madrid (1608–16), "old, a soldier and gentleman, but poor." He had a considerable acquaintance among the writers of his day but no great reputation. The popular success of the first part of *Don Quixote* (Madrid, 1605) was a great surprise to his publisher, and probably to Cervantes. However, he dallied over the second part, first publishing the *Novelas Exemplares* (Twelve Instructive or Moral Tales, 1613) and the long poem *Viaje del Parnaso* (Journey to Parnassus, 1614). Aroused by the appearance of the spurious sequel to *Don Quixote* in 1614, he hurried his own second part to completion in 1615. In the same year he brought out his *Ocho Comedias* (Eight Comedies). He died of dropsy on April 23, 1616, and was buried, no one knows where, by the Franciscans, of whose Tertiary Order he was a member. *Persiles y Sigismunda*, a long prose romance, appeared posthumously in 1617. Though the beautiful dedication to this work was written only four days before his death, the book may well be largely early work. To the end of his life he was full of plans for other writings. Considering his age, illness, and financial worries, the productivity of his declining years is phenomenal.

Cervantes's Influence on English Literature. Before the appearance of *Don Quixote* some popular works of prose fiction (often picaresque tales) had been produced by such English writers as Thomas Deloney, Robert Greene, and Thomas Nash, but undoubtedly Cervantes's success gave impetus to the novel form. By the end of the 17th century, prose fiction was a flourishing form in England as elsewhere, including long romances, picaresque stories, and short domestic novels. In the 17th-century English theater John Fletcher was a distinguished borrower from Cervantes, using the *Novelas Exemplares* and *Persiles y Sigismunda* to provide plots for his plays; Fletcher's *Knight of the Burning Pestle,* produced a few years after the publication of the first part of *Don Quixote,* may have been inspired by Cervantes's story. In the next century the English novelist Smollett edited *Don Quixote,* and wrote a picaresque novel of his own called *Sir Launcelot Greaves,* the story of an eighteenth century Don Quixote; Smollett's *Roderick Random,* too, and others of his novels derive from Cervantes, both directly and through Cervantes's influence on the French writer LeSage, author of *Gil Blas.* The picaresque manner of *Don Quixote* is evident also in the novels of Fielding and Defoe.

Cesare Borgia (chä′zä.rä bôr′jä). A play (1920) by Arthur Symons.

Cesario (sẹ.zä′ri.ō). In Shakespeare's *Twelfth Night,* the name Viola takes when in disguise.

caesura or **cesura.** In prosody, a division made in a line by the termination of a word, especially when this coincides with a pause in delivery or recitation. Strictly, caesura is the division made by the termination of a word within a foot, the division occasioned by the concurrence of the end of a word with the end of a foot being called *dieresis.* This distinction of terms is not, however, generally observed in treating of modern poetry. A *masculine caesura* is one which immediately follows a syllable bearing the ictus or metrical accent; a *feminine caesura* is one which succeeds a metrically unaccented syllable. A caesura is called *trithemimeral, penthemimeral,* or *hephthemimeral,* according as it occurs in the middle of the second, third, or fourth foot. In the dactylic hexameter the caesura after the first of the two short syllables of the dactyl is called the *trochaic caesura* or *caesura after the trochee* (of the second, third, or fourth foot, as the case may be). In the same kind of verse a division at the end of the fourth foot is called a *bucolic caesura,* more accurately a *bucolic dieresis.* In the following examples the caesura is marked by a dagger (†), the dieresis by a parallel (‖). Thus, in the lines of English heroic verse (iambic pentapody) given below there is a dieresis after the third foot of the first line, and a caesura in the fourth and third feet of the second and third lines respectively:

Bĕfōre | thĕ hĭlls | ăppēar'd, ‖ ŏr fōun | taĭn flōw'd,
Thŏu wĭth | Ētĕr | năl Wĭs | dŏm † dĭdst | cŏn-
vērse,

Wĭsdōm | thy̆ sĭs | tĕr, † ănd | wĭth hĕr | dĭdst | plā̆y.
(Milton, P. L., vii. 8.)

A caesura occurs in the fourth foot of this iambic hexapody (trimeter):

Tŏ dēath's | bĕnūm | mĭng ō | pĭŭm † ās | my̆ ōn | ly̆ cūre.
(Milton, S. A., l. 630.)

Ceyx (sē′iks). In ancient Greek mythology, the husband of Alcyone, daughter of Aeolus. The pair were arrogant enough to style themselves Zeus and Hera, and were accordingly changed by Zeus into birds of their own names, respectively a diver and a kingfisher. Another myth dwelt on the tender love of the pair for each other. Ceyx was drowned at sea, and Alcyone found his body cast upon his native shore. The gods took pity on her grief, and changed the husband and wife into kingfishers (alcyones), whose affection for each other in the mating season was proverbial. Their story is introduced into Chaucer's *Book of the Duchess.*

Chabot, Admiral of France (shȧ.bō′). [Full title, **The Tragedy of Chabot, Admiral of France.**] A tragedy by George Chapman, with revisions (1637) by James Shirley. It was licensed in 1635 and printed in 1639. In this play Chapman was studying the conflict of character between a King and the greatest of his subjects, Chabot, who has been falsely accused. The historical information was obtained from Pasquier's *Les Recherches de la France* and concerned the historical Chabot, who was created Admiral of France but lost his position through the plotting of his enemies at court.

Chadband (chad′band), **Rev. Mr.** A fat and hypocritical minister, much given to platitudes, in Charles Dickens's *Bleak House.* He is "in the ministry," but is "attached to no particular denomination." He has "a general appearance of having a good deal of train-oil in his system."

Chad Newsome (chad nū′sọm). See **Newsome, Chad.**

Chaereas and Callirrhoe (kē′rē.ạs; kạ.lir′ọ.ē). An early Greek romance by Chariton Aphrodisiensis, only a part of which is extant.

Chaffanbrass (chaf′ạn.bras), **Mr.** In Anthony Trollope's *The Three Clerks, Orley Farm,* and *Phineas Redux,* a criminal lawyer of great skill, but of a singularly unprepossessing appearance. It is said of him that "no barrister living or dead ever rescued more culprits from the fangs of the law."

Chaikovski (chī.kôf′ski). See **Tchaikovsky.**

Chaldea (kal.dē′ạ). [Also, **Chaldaea**; in the Old Testament, **Kasdim**; Assyrian, **Kaldu, Kashdu.**] In Biblical geography, middle Babylonia, the tract S of the city of Babylon in the direction toward the Persian Gulf; other portions of the country included Akkad and Sumer. Later the name Kaldu (like "Land of Kasdim" in Jer. xxiv. 5, Ezek. xii. 13) was extended to the whole country of Babylonia, i.e., the territory bounded on the N by Assyria, on the S by the Syrian desert and the Persian Gulf, on the E by Elam, and on the W by Syria. The origin of the Chaldeans is uncertain, but some have supposed that they were a mixed people composed of Babylonians and Cosseans.

ḍ, d or j; ṣ, s or sh; ṭ, t or ch; ẓ, z or zh; o, F. cloche; ü, F. menu; ċh, Sc. loch; ṅ, F. bonbon.

Chalkhill (chôk'hĭl), **John.** fl. 1600. An English poet. He was the author of *Thealma and Clearchus, a Pastoral History in smooth and easie Verse,* not published until 1683. The work was brought out by Izaak Walton, who had known Chalkhill as a young man. That Chalkhill was an imaginary person, that his name was a pseudonym for Walton, or that Walton was the author, are theories no longer held. Chalkhill is also the author of two songs, "O, the Sweet Contentment" and "O, the Gallant Fisher's Life," included in the *Compleat Angler* (1653). George Saintsbury rescued Chalkhill's reputation from neglect by including him in his anthology (1905–06) of Caroline poets.

Chalkstone (chôk'stōn), **Lord.** A character in David Garrick's play *Lethe.* Garrick himself played the part.

Challenge. A novel by V. Sackville-West, published in 1923.

Challenge for Beauty, A. A tragicomedy by Thomas Heywood, printed in 1636, and acted at the Blackfriars and Globe theaters.

Challenger Expedition. A British scientific expedition (1872–76), under the direction of Charles Wyville Thomson, for the exploration of the deep sea, undertaken on board the British vessel *Challenger.* The expedition was undertaken at the suggestion of the Royal Society, which drew up a complete scheme of instructions. George Nares was in command (1872–74). The ship sailed for a year in the Atlantic, reached Capetown in October, 1873, and Kerguelen island, in the Indian Ocean, in January, 1874. She was the first steamship to cross the Antarctic Circle. The expedition made researches in the Pacific, reached Hong Kong, recrossed the ocean to Valparaíso, and, passing through the Strait of Magellan, reached the dockyard at Sheerness, Kent, in May, 1876. The *Challenger* report was published in 50 volumes (1880–95).

Chalmers (chä'mẽrz), **Alexander.** b. at Aberdeen, Scotland, March 29, 1759; d. at London, Dec. 10, 1834. A Scottish biographer, editor, and miscellaneous writer. He is best known as the editor of the *General Biographical Dictionary* (1812–14), based on the *New and General Biographical Dictionary* of Tooke, Nares, and Beloe.

Chamberlain (chām'bẽr.lin). In Shakespeare's *1 Henry IV,* an attendant at the inn at Rochester who tells Gadshill about some wealthy guests and is promised a share in the plunder.

Chamberlain, Lord. See **Lord Chamberlain.**

Chamberlain's Men. See **Lord Chamberlain's Men.**

Chamberlayne (chām'bẽr.lān, -lin), **Edward.** b. at Odington, Gloucestershire, England, Dec. 13, 1616; d. at Chelsea, London, in May, 1703. An English writer; father of John Chamberlayne. He was a graduate of Oxford (B.A., 1638; M.A., 1641), tutor of Henry Fitzroy (illegitimate son of Charles II) and Prince George of Denmark, and one of the founders of the Royal Society. He was the author of *Angliae notitiae, or the Present State of England* (1669, anonymous; the 21st ed., 1708, bears the title *Magnae Britanniae notitia*), a handbook of English society and politics, *England's Wants* (1667), and others.

Chamberlayne, John. b. 1666; d. 1723. An English writer; younger son of Edward Chamberlayne. He continued his father's *Magnae Britanniae notitia* and translated Brandt's *History of the Reformation in the Low Countries.*

Chamberlayne, William. b. 1619; d. Jan. 11, 1689. An English poet, physician, and Royalist soldier. He saw action at the second battle of Newbury, on Oct. 27, 1644. He was the author of *Love's Victory* (1658), a tragicomedy, *Pharonnida* (1659), his chief work, a heroic romance in 14,000 lines consisting of five books of five cantos each, and *England's Jubilee: A Poem on the Happy Return of His Sacred Majesty Charles II* (1660).

Chamber Music. A volume of poetry by James Joyce, published in 1907. The poems are written in the manner of the Elizabethan poets. They tell the story of the rise and gradual decline of a love in the course of a year. Included in this volume are "All Day I Hear," "I Hear an Army," and "Bright Cap and Streamers."

Chambers (chām'bẽrz), **Sir Edmund Kerchever.** b. in Berkshire, England, March 16, 1866; d. Jan. 21, 1954. An English literary scholar. Entering the service of the Board of Education in 1892, and for some years holding the post of an assistant secretary of that official body, he pursued those studies in English literature of earlier periods which resulted in a series of books considered important contributions to critical scholarship. These include *The Medieval Stage* (1903), *The Elizabethan Stage* (1923), *Shakespeare: A Survey* (1925), *Arthur of Britain* (1927), *William Shakespeare* (1930), *The English Folk-Play* (1933), *Sir Henry Lee* (1936), *Samuel Taylor Coleridge* (1938), and *A Sheaf of Studies* (1942). He also prepared editions of Donne, Vaughan and other poets.

Chambers, Ephraim. b. at Kendal, England, c1680; d. at London, May 15, 1740. An English writer, compiler of *Cyclopaedia, or Universal Dictionary of Arts and Sciences* (1728), the first of its kind in English. It was used by Diderot and his coworkers as a basis of the French *Encyclopédie.*

Chambers, Robert. b. at Peebles, Scotland, July 10, 1802; d. at St. Andrews, Scotland, March 17, 1871. A Scottish publisher and author. He wrote *Illustrations of the Author of Waverley* (1822), *Traditions of Edinburgh* (1823), *Walks in Edinburgh* (1825), *History of the Rebellion of 1745* (1828), *Biographical Dictionary of Eminent Scotsmen* (1832–34), *Book of Days* (1862–64), and the anonymously published *Vestiges of the Natural History of Creation* (1844). The last-named work, the authorship of which was not discovered until 1884, was an exposition of a theory of evolutionary development, and quickly became famous through both the criticism and the praise which its heterodox views aroused. He was founder (1832) and joint editor of *Chambers's Journal,* and a member of the Edinburgh publishing firm of W. and R. Chambers.

Chamier (sham'yẽr), **Frederick.** b. at London, 1796; d. at Waltham Abbey, Essex, England, in October, 1870. An English naval captain and historian, and novelist of the sea. He entered the Royal Navy in 1809, retired in 1827, and was made a captain in 1856, 23 years after his retirement. He was the author of *Life of a Sailor* (1832), *Ben Brace the Last of Nelson's Agamemnons* (1835), *The Saucy Arethusa* (1836), *Jack Adams* (1838), *Tom Bowling* (1841), and other novels of life at sea. Chamier also edited (1837) *Naval History of Great Britain from the Declaration of War by France in 1793 to the Accession of George IV* (1822–24), by William James, and extended the narrative to 1827. In Paris in 1848, he produced as a result *Review of the French Revolution* (1849), and his continental travels were recorded in *An Unsentimental Journey through France, Switzerland, and Italy* (1855).

Chamont (cham'ǫnt). A rough and extremely fiery young soldier of fortune, the brother of Monimia, the titular heroine of Thomas Otway's blank-verse tragedy *The Orphan* (1680).

Champeaux (shäṅ.pō), **Guillaume de** (or **William of**). See **Guillaume de Champeaux.**

Champion, The. A journal which first appeared in 1739, written and edited by Henry Fielding with the American poet and pamphleteer James Ralph. It was based on the model of the *Spectator* and *Tatler*, and combined literature and politics. Two volumes of the paper were republished in 1741. It ridiculed the Jacobite party.

Chance. A novel by Joseph Conrad, published in 1913. It deals with the effect of greed upon character.

Chancellor (chán'sẹ.lǫr), **Lord.** See **Lord Chancellor.**

Chancellor, Richard. d. Nov. 10, 1556. An English navigator. He accompanied Roger Bodenham on a journey to Candia (Crete) and Chios in 1550. In 1553 he became captain of the *Edward Bonaventure* and pilot-general of the expedition which set out in that year under the command of Sir Hugh Willoughby in search of a northeast passage to India. Becoming separated from the other ships of the expedition in a gale off the Lofoten Islands, he pushed on alone into the White Sea and Arkhangelsk, whence he made his way overland to Moscow. He obtained valuable trade concessions from the Russian court in behalf of the English, which led to the organization of the Muscovy Company on his return to England in 1554. He made a second visit to Moscow in 1555, and was shipwrecked off Pitsligo, on the coast of Aberdeenshire, on the return voyage. A narrative of his first visit to Moscow, written by Clement Adams, was published in Hakluyt's *Navigations*, and is the first considerable account of the Russian people in the English language.

Chancery Lane (chán'sẹ.ri). A street in London leading from Fleet Street to Holborn.

Chances, The. A comedy by John Fletcher. It was published in 1647, but had been acted at Court in 1624. The plot is from *La Señora Cornelia*, a "novel" by Miguel de Cervantes. George Villiers, 2nd Duke of Buckingham, produced an alteration of it in 1682, and David Garrick brought out a second alteration in 1773. In 1821 a musical drama founded on it, called *Don John, or the Two Violettas,* was produced.

Change Alley. An alley in Cornhill, London. It was the chief center of money transactions in 18th-century London.

Changeling, The. A play by Thomas Middleton and William Rowley, acted in 1623, published in 1653.

chanson (shäṅ.sôṅ). A song. **a.** Originally, a short poem in a simple, natural style, in stanzas called couplets, each usually accompanied by a refrain, intended to be sung. **b.** Later, any short lyric poem, and the music to which it is set.

The first row of the pious chanson will show you more. (Shakespeare, *Hamlet*.)

These [Christmas carols] were festal chansons for enlivening the merriments of the Christmas celebrity. (T. Warton, *History of English Poetry*.)

chanson de geste (shäṅ.sôṅ dẹ zhest). In French literature, a type of epic poem of the 9th to the 12th centuries dealing with the feats of historical or legendary knights. Many of the more than 100 *chansons de geste* deal with Charlemagne (and these are usually referred to collectively as the Charlemagne cycle); the most famous of these is the *Chanson de Roland*. A considerable number of them, including various stories from the Ferumbras and Otuel groups of the Charlemagne cycle, were translated or adapted into Middle English. The *chansons de geste* were usually written in lines of ten syllables, rhyming by assonance, and were intended to be sung with musical accompaniment by the *jongleurs* (minstrels) who roamed over the countryside. They differed from the medieval romances which followed them by their emphasis on martial exploits and the relatively insignificant role allotted to romantic love (or, indeed, to women in any role).

Chanson de Roland (ro.läṅ). [Also, **Chanson de Roncevaux,** meaning in English, "Song of Roncevaux."] A *chanson de geste*, ascribed to Théroulde or Turoldus, an unidentified Norman who probably lived in the 11th century. It was paraphrased c1450 in Middle English. The Oxford manuscript gives its earliest form in French. The text of this manuscript is probably that of the end of the 11th century; the date of the manuscript probably the middle of the 12th. It contains ab. 4,000 lines, and is the story of the death of Roland with the peers of Charlemagne at Roncevaux or Roncesvalles in the Pyrenees, and of Charlemagne's vengeance. The treason of Ganelon and his miserable death and the refusal of Roland to blow his horn to summon aid until his friend Oliver has been killed are the best-known of the incidents related in the poem.

chantey (shan'ti). A sailors' song. "Then give us one of the old chanteys . . . Why, the mere sound of those old songs takes me back forty years." (W. C. Russell, *Jack's Courtship*.)

Chanticleer (chan'ti.klir). See **Chauntecleer.**

Chantrey (chán'tri), Sir **Francis Legatt.** b. near Norton, Derbyshire, England, April 7, 1781; d. Nov. 25, 1841. An English portrait sculptor and painter. He is known chiefly for his portrait sculpture, his sitters including many of the most distinguished men of his time. The greater part of his property was left to the Royal Academy to estab-

ḍ, d or j; ṣ, s or sh; ṭ, t or ch; ẓ, z or zh; o, F. cloche; ü, F. menu; ċh, Sc. loch; ṅ, F. bonbon.

lish a fund for the purchase of the most meritorious work in sculpture and painting executed in Great Britain by artists of any nation.

chapbook or **chap-book** (chap′bu̇k). One of a class of tracts upon homely and miscellaneous subjects which at one time formed the chief popular literature of Great Britain and the American colonies. They consisted of lives of heroes, martyrs, and wonderful personages, stories of roguery and broad humor, of giants, ghosts, witches, and dreams, histories in verse, songs and ballads, theological tracts, etc. They emanated principally from the provincial press, and were hawked about the country by chapmen or peddlers. "Such a dream-dictionary as servant-maids still buy in penny chap-books at the fair." (E. B. Tylor, *Prim. Culture.*) "No chap-book was so poor and rude as not to have one or two prints, however inartistic." (*North American Review*, CXXXIX.)

Chapman (chap′man), **George.** b. near Hitchin, Hertfordshire, England, c1559; buried at London, in the parish of St. Giles-in-the-Fields, May 12, 1634. An English poet and dramatist, chiefly celebrated for his translation of Homer. He is said to have studied at Oxford and afterward at Cambridge. He lived, according to report, in straitened circumstances, but was intimate with Ben Jonson, John Fletcher, and other prominent figures of the time. Among his dramatic works are *The Blind Beggar of Alexandria* (produced in 1595, printed in 1598), *All Fools* (produced c1598, printed in 1605), *An Humorous Day's Mirth* (printed in 1599), *Eastward Ho!* with Jonson and John Marston (printed 1605) which, because of its satire on the Scottish nobility surrounding James I, caused the authors' imprisonment, *The Gentleman-Usher* (printed 1606), *Monsieur d'Olive* (printed 1606), *Bussy d'Ambois* (printed 1607), *May Day* (produced c1600, printed in 1611), *The Revenge of Bussy d'Ambois* (printed 1613), *The Conspiracy and Tragedy of Charles, Duke of Byron* (printed 1608; a play in two parts), *The Widow's Tears* (printed 1612), *Caesar and Pompey* (printed 1631), and *Chabot, Admiral of France* with James Shirley (printed 1639). He completed Marlowe's fragment of *Hero and Leander* in 1598. The first part of his translation of the *Iliad* was published in 1598; the whole was not issued before 1609 (entered on the Stationers' Register in 1611). The translation of the *Odyssey* was entered on the Stationers' Register in 1614. Finally, the *Iliad* and *Odyssey* were issued together with the date 1616 on Chapman's portrait prefixed. He translated also the Homeric hymns, Petrarch, Musaeus, Hesiod, and Juvenal.

Chapone (sha̤.pōn′), **Hester.** b. 1727; d. 1801. An English amateur of letters, a member of the "Bluestocking Club." She published verses and tales (1750–53) and essays (1773–77), and wrote part of No. 10 of *The Rambler.* Her *Letters on the Improvement of the Mind, Addressed to a Young Lady* (1773) brought her a reputation as a writer. Her *Works* and *Posthumous Works* appeared in 1807.

Chapter Coffee House. A London coffee house, noted in the 18th century as the resort of men of letters.

character. An account or statement of the qualities or peculiarities of a person or thing; specifi-

cally, an oral or a written statement with regard to the standing or qualifications of anyone, as a servant or an employee.

It was your character that first commended
Him to my thought. (Shirley, *Hyde Park.*)

Mr. Seldon was a Person whom no Character can flatter, or transmit in any Expressions equal to his Merit and Virtue.
(Clarendon, *Autobiography.*)

Character of a Happy Life, The. A poem by Sir Henry Wotton, published with his other writings in *Reliquiae Wottonianae* in 1651, celebrating the person who practices the virtues of truth and honest thought, who is master of his passions, and who is submissive to the will of God.

Charalois (chä.rä.lwä′). In Philip Massinger and Nathaniel Field's comedy *The Fatal Dowry* (c1618), the principal character, who goes to prison to release the body of his father who died in debt. He marries Rochfort's daughter, discovers her to be dishonest, and kills her when she is condemned by her father.

Charge of the Light Brigade. A poem (1854) by Alfred Tennyson, written in the same meter as Michael Drayton's *The Battle of Agincourt.* It commemorates the heroic charge at Balaklava during the Crimean War, and contains the well-known lines:

> Theirs not to reason why,
> Theirs but to do or die. . .
> Into the jaws of death,
> Into the mouth of hell,
> Rode the six hundred.

The situation on October 25, 1854, when this charge took place, was that certain fortified positions commanding the causeway to Balaklava's port (which was being used by the British for debarkation of men and supplies) were taken from a small force of approximately 250 Turks by a Russian force estimated to number some 12,000. A counter-attack by the English Heavy Brigade, under James Yorke Scarlett, deflected the Russian blow, but at the same time this was taking place, and through a tragic misunderstanding of orders, the Light Brigade, under the 7th earl of Cardigan, was sent against the Russian artillery at the end of the northern valley in the plain of Balaklava. The description in Tennyson's poem of the situation faced by the Light Brigade is probably as good as any that can be given:

> Cannon to right of them,
> Cannon to left of them,
> Cannon in front of them
> Volleyed and thundered.

Nevertheless, the charge was not repulsed; the Light Brigade broke through the Russian guns, routed the cavalry behind the gunners, and returned to their starting point "through the jaws of Death, back from the mouth of Hell." Of some 670 horsemen (Tennyson says 600), only 198 are known to have returned from the charge.

Chariclea (kar.i.klē′a̤). The heroine of Heliodorus's novel *Theagenes and Chariclea* (also called *Aethiopica*).

fat, fāte, fär, a̤sk, fāre; net, mē, hėr; pin, pīne; not, nōte, mȯve, nôr; up, lūte, pu̇ll; ᴛʜ, then;

Charing Cross (chär'ing krôs'). A place at Westminster, London, S of Trafalgar Square at the junction of Whitehall Street and the Strand. Charing Cross railways terminal is located here. The space took its name from the circumstance that one of the crosses to the memory of Eleanor of Castile stood here. It was demolished (1647) by the Long Parliament. A copy was erected (1865) by the South Eastern Railway Company. In traveling N to join her husband (Edward I of England) in Scotland, Eleanor was seized with a fever at Hardeby, near Grantham in Lincolnshire, and died there on Nov. 29, 1290. Edward followed her corpse in person during a 13 days' progress from Grantham to Westminster Abbey, and wherever the royal bier rested, at the end of each stage, a memorial cross was erected. Thirteen of these monuments once existed.

Chariot Wheels. A novel by Sylvia Thompson, published in 1929.

Charitable Grinders. In Dickens's novel *Dombey and Son*, an institution supported by private charity for the care and education of the children of the poor. Rob the Grinder (Robin Toodles) attended it.

Charity Pecksniff (pek'snif). See under **Pecksniff.**

Charlemagne (shär'lẹ.mān; French, shår.lẹ.mȧny'). [Also: **Charles I; Charles the Great;** German, **Karl der Grosse;** Italian, **Carlo Magno;** Latin, **Carolus Magnus.**] b. c742; d. Jan. 28, 814. King of the Franks and emperor of the Romans. He was the son of Pepin the Short, king of the Franks, on whose death in 768 he acceded to the throne conjointly with a brother, Carloman. He usurped the entire government on the death of the latter in 771. In 772 he began a war against the Saxons, the most notable events of which were the storming of Eresburg, the destruction of the Saxon idol Irminsul (Irmensäule), the May-field at Paderborn (777), and the submission of the Saxon leader Wittekind (785), and which resulted in 804 in the complete subjugation and Christianization of Saxony. In 773, at the instance of Pope Adrian I, he made war upon Desiderius, king of the Lombards, who had occupied the Pentapolis (the five cities of Rimini, Ancona, Fano, Pesaro, and Senigallia) and was threatening Rome. He captured the Lombard capital, Pavia, in 774, and the same year incorporated the kingdom of the Lombards with that of the Franks. In 778 he made an expedition against the Arabs in Spain, which terminated in the destruction of the Frankish rear guard under Roland at Roncevaux. He subdued Bavaria in 788, conquered the Avars (791–796), was crowned emperor at Saint Peter's, Dec. 25, 800, and in 808–810 defeated the Danes, whom he compelled to retire behind the Eider River. His kingdom, for the protection of which he erected in the border districts the so-called marks or margravates, extended at the close of his reign from the Ebro River in N Spain to the Raab in Austria, and from the Eider in what is now Schleswig-Holstein to the Garigliano, which is nearly 100 miles below Rome. He resided chiefly at Aix-la-Chapelle (Aachen), and by his patronage of letters attracted to his court the scholars Eginhard, Paul Warnefried, and Alcuin, the last-mentioned of whom wrote an account of his life entitled *Vita Caroli Magni*. He was buried at Aix-la-Chapelle.

Charlemagne cycle. A series of medieval romances, of war and adventure, grouped around the venerable figure of Charlemagne. See also under **chanson de geste.**

Charlemont (chärl'mont). The lover of Castabella in Cyril Tourneur's *The Atheist's Tragedy.*

Charles (chärlz). In Shakespeare's *As You Like It*, a wrestler hired by Duke Frederick and defeated by Orlando.

Charles. Entries on literary characters having this prename will also be found under the surnames Baynes, Belmont, Bingley, Coldstream, Darnay, Easy, Egremont, Gould, Grandison, Gripe, Heath, Honeyman, Marlow, Mountford, Oakly, Primrose, Strickland, and Surface.

Charles I (of *England*). b. at Dunfermline, Scotland, Nov. 19, 1600; d. at London, Jan. 30, 1649. King of England; second son of James I of England. He became prince of Wales in 1616, and in 1623, accompanied by George Villiers, 1st Duke of Buckingham, presented in person an ineffectual suit at the court of Madrid for the hand of the infanta Maria. He acceded to the throne on the death of his father in 1625, and in the same year married the Catholic Henrietta Maria of France. He retained in office the Duke of Buckingham, his father's unpopular minister, in consequence of which he became involved in a dispute with Parliament amounting in substance to a question of sovereignty. He granted the Petition of Right, on June 7, 1628. On the assassination of the Duke of Buckingham in August, 1628, he made William Laud and Thomas Wentworth his chief advisers. He governed without Parliament from 1629 to 1640, meeting the expenses of government by forced loans, the taxation known as poundage and tonnage, ship-money, and other extraordinary means of revenue. His ecclesiastical policy, which looked, among other things, to the introduction of the Episcopal liturgy in Scotland, provoked the adoption by the Scots of the Solemn League and Covenant, on Feb. 28, 1638, and the outbreak of a civil war, which terminated without a battle in the pacification of Berwick, on June 18, 1639. The war having broken out anew in 1640, he was compelled to summon a parliament, which met on Nov. 3, 1640. This parliament, the so-called Long Parliament (in contrast to one Charles had called earlier in the same year and which had broken up after a short sitting, called the Short Parliament), impeached Laud and Wentworth (who had been created Earl of Strafford), and proceeded to the redress of grievances. The House of Commons having ordered the publication of the Grand Remonstrance, on Dec. 14, 1641, Charles replied by impeaching and attempting to arrest (Jan. 4, 1642) five of the Parliamentary leaders, failing in which he left London, on Jan. 10, 1642, the English Civil War being now in full action. He raised the royal standard at Nottingham on Aug. 22, 1642, suffered a decisive defeat at the hands of the Parliamentary forces under Fairfax at Naseby on June 14, 1645, delivered himself to the Scottish army at Newark on May 5, 1646, and was surrendered to Parliament on Jan. 30, 1647. Tried for treason

ḍ, d or j; ṣ, s or sh; ṭ, t or ch; ẓ, z or zh; o, F. cloche; ü, F. menu; c̣h, Sc. loch; ṅ, F. bonbon.

by the so-called Rump Parliament, in the period Jan. 20-27, 1649, he was executed at Whitehall, London. The members of the court which judged his case came to be known as the Regicides.

Charles II (of *England*). b. at St. James's Palace, London, May 29, 1630; d. there, Feb. 6, 1685. King of England; son of Charles I of England. He was appointed to the command of the Royalist forces in the western counties of England in the Civil War, and after the decisive victory of the Parliamentary army at Naseby left England on March 2, 1646, living during his exile chiefly in France and the Netherlands. He was proclaimed king at Edinburgh on Feb. 5, 1649, arrived in the Firth of Cromarty on June 16, 1650, and was crowned at Scone on Jan. 1, 1651. Totally defeated by Oliver Cromwell at Worcester on Sept. 3, 1651, after an attempt to march into England, Charles escaped, after numerous adventures, to Fécamp, in Normandy, on Oct. 16, 1651. Owing to the influence of General Monck and the effect of Charles's Declaration of Breda, he was proclaimed king at Westminster on May 8, 1660, entered London on May 29, 1660, and was crowned on April 23, 1661. He married Catherine of Braganza on May 20, 1662. He assented at his restoration to the abolition of the feudal rights of knight service, wardship, and purveyance, in consideration of a yearly income to the crown of 1,200,000 pounds, and to an act of indemnity for all political offenses committed between Jan. 1, 1637, and June 24, 1660, from the operation of which act, however, the Regicides (those responsible for the condemnation and execution of Charles I) were excluded. During his reign the Dutch wars continued, colonization in America and India flourished, and the Great Fire of London (1666) took place shortly after the great plague of London (1665). The power of Parliament increased during the period, and the Rye House Plot against Charles was foiled. Charles is remembered for his immoral and pleasure-loving life; of his various mistresses the best known is the actress Nell Gwynn.

Charles VI. In Shakespeare's *Henry V*, the King of France. He makes the Treaty of Troyes whereby his daughter Katherine is to marry Henry and the latter to inherit France after his death. This follows an episode in the life of the real Charles (1368–1422).

Charles, Elizabeth. [Maiden name, **Rundle.**] b. 1828; d. March 29, 1896. An English novelist. Her works include *Chronicles of the Schönberg-Cotta Family* (1863), *Diary of Mrs. Kitty Trevylyan* (1864), *Draytons and Davenants* (1866), *Winifred Bertram* (1866), *Against the Stream* (1873), *Lapsed but not Lost* (1881), and *Our Seven Homes* (1897).

Charles Cheeryble (chir′i.bl). One of the **Cheeryble Brothers.**

Charles d'Orléans (shärl dôr.lā.äṅ). See **Orleans, Duke of.**

Charles Fitz Marshall (chärlz fits mär′sh*ạ*l). See **Jingle, Alfred.**

Charles Grandison (gran′di.s*ọ*n), **Sir.** See **Sir Charles Grandison.**

Charles Julius (jöl′yus). Pseudonym of **Bertram, Charles.**

Charles O'Malley (ọ.mal′i). A novel of adventure (1840) by Charles Lever.

Charles's Wain. See **Wain, Charles's.**

Charles the Bold. [French, **Charles le Téméraire** (shàrl lẹ tā.mā.rer); early title, Comte de **Charolais.**] b. at Dijon, France, Nov. 10, 1433; killed at Nancy, France, Jan. 5, 1477. Duke of Burgundy (1467–77); son of Philip the Good. He married Margaret, sister of Edward IV of England. An opponent of Louis XI of France, he joined in defeating him. He conquered Lorraine in 1475 but was defeated by the Swiss at Grandson (March 2, 1476), at Morat (June 22, 1476), and finally at Nancy (Jan. 5, 1477).

Charles, the Dauphin. In Shakespeare's *1 Henry VI*, the son of Charles VI (historically not, as Shakespeare makes him, the Dauphin). When Joan of Arc arrives to request troops, she impresses him with her prowess by overcoming him in a duel and he falls in love with her. He attributes the French victories to her, and when she is captured, he becomes viceroy under Henry.

Charley Bates (chär′li bāts′). See **Bates, Charley.**

Charley's Aunt (chär′liz). A popular farce by Brandon Thomas, produced first in 1892 and since then a nearly perennial favorite on the English stage.

Charlotte (shär′l*ọ*t). In Colley Cibber's comedy *The Refusal, or The Ladies' Philosophy*, the daughter of Sir Gilbert Wrangle and sister of Sophronia. She is courted by Frankly, with whom she is in love.

Charlotte. In Henry Fielding's *The Mock Doctor*, the daughter of Sir Jasper, who pretends to be dumb so as to avoid a marriage with Dapper. Her prototype in Molière's *Le Médecin Malgré Lui* is called Lucinde.

Charlotte. In Isaac Bickerstaffe's *The Hypocrite*, a lively, giddy girl who finally marries Darnley, though she has been promised to Cantwell, the titular hero. In Molière's *Tartuffe*, on which the play is based, the equivalent character is called Marianne.

Charlotte Baynes (bānz). See **Baynes, Charlotte.**

Charlotte Temple (tem′pl). [Full title, **Charlotte Temple: or, a Tale of Truth.**] Sentimental novel by Susanna Rowson, published in England in 1791 and in the U. S. in 1794. It has been many times republished. The heroine, an innocent 15-year-old school-girl, is induced to come to America by Montraville, a lieutenant in the British service, on his promise of marriage upon arrival. This promise is not fulfilled; he deserts her, and she dies after giving birth to a child. A grave marked by a tombstone bearing the name of "Charlotte Temple," erected by a sexton in the eighteenth century, lies in the graveyard of Old Trinity Church at New York. The author in her preface states that the tale is a true one, "yet I have substituted names and places according to my own fancy." The real name of Charlotte Temple is said to have been Stanley.

Charmian (chär′mi.*ạ*n). In Shakespeare's *Antony and Cleopatra*, Cleopatra's favorite waiting-woman. She kills herself after Cleopatra's death. She also appears in Dryden's *All for Love*.

fat, fāte, fär, ȧsk, fãre; net, mē, hėr; pin, pīne; not, nōte, mȯve, nôr; up, lūte, pu̇ll; ᴛʜ, then;

Charmond (shär'mǫnd), **Felice.** In Thomas Hardy's *The Woodlanders*, a wealthy and amorous widow, the seductress of Grace's husband.

charms. See **spells.**

Charon (kār'ǫn). In Greek mythology, the ferryman, a son of Erebus, who transported the souls of the dead (whose bodies had been buried) over the river Styx to the lower world. His fee was an obolus or other coin, and this was placed for him in the mouth of the dead at the time of burial.

Charterhouse (chär'tẽr.hous). Originally a Carthusian monastery, later a hospital, and then a school for boys, at London, founded in 1371 by Sir Walter Manny and the bishop of Northburgh. At the dissolution of the monasteries, the Charter House was given by Henry VIII to Sir Thomas Audley, and passed through various hands to Sir Thomas Sutton, who in 1611 endowed it as a charity under the name of the Hospital of King James. This foundation long existed as a hospital for the aged and a school for boys. The school was transferred to Godalming, Surrey, in 1872, and the premises were occupied by the school of the Merchant Taylors' Company.

Charteris (chär'tẽr.is), **Sir Evan.** b. Jan. 29, 1864; d. at Jesmond Hill, Pangbourne, Berkshire, England, Nov. 16, 1940. An English art connoisseur and writer. He served in World War I. Among the posts he filled were those of chairman of trustees (1928 *et seq.*) of the National Portrait Gallery, chairman (1934–40) of the Tate Gallery, and trustee (1932–39) of the National Gallery. His writings include *William Augustus, Duke of Cumberland* (1913), *John Sargent* (1927), and *The Life and Letters of Sir Edmund Gosse* (1931).

Charteris, Leslie. b. 1907—. An English novelist, creator of "the Saint," a fictional criminal-detective who has also been featured in films, comic strips, and on the radio. He studied at Cambridge, and was a contributor to *Cosmopolitan, American,* and other magazines, as well as serving as a Hollywood scenarist. He is the author of *Meet the Tiger* (1928), *Follow the Saint* (1938), *The Saint Goes West* (1942), *The Saint Sees it Through* (1946), *Call for the Saint* (1948), and *Saint Errant* (1948).

Charteris, Sir Patrick. In Sir Walter Scott's novel *The Fair Maid of Perth,* the provost of Perth.

Chartists (chär'tists). [Also, **Charterists.**] A body of political reformers (chiefly workingmen) that sprang up in England c1838 in protest against the Reform Bill of 1832 which had not given the vote to workingmen. The Chartists advocated as their leading principles universal manhood suffrage, the abolition of the property qualification for a seat in Parliament, annual election of parliaments, equal representation, payment of members of Parliament, and vote by ballot, all of which demands were set forth in the People's Charter, of which William Lovett was a coauthor. The members of the extreme section of the party, under Feargus O'Connor, which favored an appeal to arms or popular risings if the charter could not be obtained by legitimate means, were called "physical-force men," whereas the more conservative section was known as the "party of moral force." The Chartists disappeared as a party after 1849.

Charwoman's Daughter, The. A novel by James Stephens, published in 1912. It was issued in the U. S. under the title *Mary, Mary.*

Charybdis (kạ.rib'dis). In Greek mythology, a sea monster which three times a day sucks in the sea and discharges it again in a terrible whirlpool; depicted as a maiden with the tail of a fish begirt with hideous dogs. Opposite her was the other monster Scylla. In later times they were located in the Straits of Messina, Scylla being identified with a projecting rock on the Italian side, Charybdis with a whirlpool facing it.

Charyllis (kạ.ril'is). In Edmund Spenser's *Colin Clout's Come Home Again,* a character intended for Lady Anne Compton, one of the six daughters of Sir John Spenser of Althorpe.

Chase, The. A poem (1735) by William Somervile, written in blank verse. It is concerned with various aspects of the outdoor life of a country gentleman, chiefly the pleasures of the hunt.

Chassé (shä.sä'), **General.** A pseudonym of **Dixon, Henry Hall.**

Chaste Diana, The. A historical novel by Lily Adams Beck, published in 1923 under the pseudonym E. Barrington. It deals with the beautiful 18th-century actress Lavinia Fenton.

Chastelard (shas'tẹ.lärd). A tragedy by Algernon Charles Swinburne, published in 1865. It is based on the life of Pierre de Boscosel de Chastelard, a French poet who was executed at Edinburgh for his love of Mary, Queen of Scots. It is the first of a trilogy, the other dramas being *Bothwell* (1874) and *Mary Stuart* (1881).

Chaste Maid in Cheapside, A. A play by Thomas Middleton, produced c1613 and printed in 1630. The plot of this play concerns the enforced wedding of Moll, daughter of Yellowhammer and his wife, Maudlin, two unsavory characters, to Sir Walter Whorehound, whom the dramatist imbues with all of the qualities suggested by his name. Moll is in love with Touchwood, a young gentleman, and after two attempts to escape from the clutches of Whorehound, Touchwood attacks him and both lovers then play dead, the illusion being assisted by an elaborate double funeral. They suddenly rise from the coffins to be united by the attending clergyman. There is a subplot concerning the wooing of Moll's brother, Timotheus, just down from Cambridge, who is induced to pay court to Whorehound's mistress, disguised as a Welsh heiress (the Welsh were often the butt of Elizabethan humor). Further complications are provided by the Allwits, husband and wife, the latter cuckolding the former by an amour with Whorehound.

Chateaubriand (shà.tō.brē.äṅ), **François René, Vicomte de.** b. at St.-Malo, France, Sept. 4, 1768; d. at Paris, July 4, 1848. A French author and statesman. He entered the army in 1786, traveled in America (1791–92), served in the royalist army at Thionville in September, 1792, and subsequently emigrated to England, where in 1797 he published *Essai historique, politique, et moral sur les révolutions anciennes et modernes.* He returned to France in 1800; and, having been converted by the death of his mother to the Roman Catholic faith, published in 1802 a eulogy of Christianity, entitled

Le Génie du christianisme. In 1803 he was appointed by Napoleon secretary of legation at Rome, and in the same year became minister to the republic of Valais, a post which he resigned on the execution of the Duke of Enghien in 1804. In 1814 he supported the Bourbons in a pamphlet entitled *De Buonaparte et des Bourbons.* He was created a peer of France in 1815, was ambassador at London in 1822, and was minister of foreign affairs (1823–24). Other works by him include *Atala* (1801), *René* (1802), *Les Martyrs* (1809), *Itinéraire de Paris à Jérusalem* (1811), *Les Natchez* (1826), *Les Aventures du dernier des Abencérages* (1826), and *Mémoires d'outre-tombe* (1849–50, an autobiography). Chateaubriand is considered one of the first and leading writers of the Romantic Movement, and his influence on subsequent French literature was considerable, especially through *Le Génie du christianisme. Atala* and *René*, both of which had originally been written as episodes in the religious work, gained immense success on their separate publication as novels. In *Atala* he tells the story of an American Indian girl who becomes converted to Christianity. In this, as in other works, he drew on his travels in America for romantic descriptions of nature; it is thought now that to some extent these were invented, his travels never having extended beyond Pittsburgh, although he gives accounts of further regions. *René*, also a work with a religious moral, has for its hero an introspective young man, considered to have been to some extent autobiographical, who became the prototype of the Romantic hero.

Château Gaillard (gȧ.yȧr). A celebrated ruin of a castle built in 1197 by Richard I (Richard the Lion-Hearted), near Les Andelys, Eure, France.

Chatham (chat'ạm), 1st Earl of. Title of **Pitt, William** (1708–78).

Chatillon (sha.til'yọn, sha.til'i.on; French, shä.tē-yôṅ). In Shakespeare's *King John*, an ambassador from France sent by Philip to demand that John give up the throne to Arthur.

Chatrian (shȧ.trē.äṅ), **Louis Gratien Charles Alexandre.** See **Erckmann-Chatrian.**

Chatsworth (chats'wèrth). The seat of the dukes of Devonshire, situated on the river Derwent ab. 3½ mi. NE of Bakewell, Derbyshire, England. Chatsworth House, the Renaissance-style palace, c500 ft. long, was begun in 1688. The interior is rich in painting and sculpture, and contains an extensive collection of drawings, some fine old and modern paintings, a *Venus* by Thorvaldsen, and Canova's *Napoleon, Madame Létitia,* and *Endymion.* The formal gardens are also famous. They contain elaborate fountains and fine conservatories.

Chatterton (chat'ėr.tọn), **Edward Keble.** b. at Sheffield, England, 1878; d. 1944. An English soldier, journalist, and author of books on naval subjects. Educated at Sheffield and Oxford, he saw service in World War I. His works include *Sailing Ships* (1909), *Story of the British Navy* (1911), *Britain's Record: What She Has Done For the World* (1911), *Romance of Piracy* (1914), *Ship Models* (1923), *Whalers and Whaling* (1925), *Battles by Sea* (1925), *Chats on Naval Prints* (1926), *Brotherhood*

of the Sea (1927), *Captain John Smith* (1927), *Daring Deeds of Sea Rovers . . . From the Phoenicians . . . down to the Present Day* (1929), *England's Greatest Statesman, a Life of William Pitt* (1930), *The Sea Raiders* (1931), *Danger Zone* (1934), *Dardanelles Dilemma* (1935), *Amazing Adventure: A Biography of Commander Geoffrey Herbert* (1935), *Leaders of the Royal Navy* (1940), *The Epic of Dunkirk* (1940), and *Fighting the U-Boats* (1942). He also wrote the novels *Sea Spy* (1937) and *Secret Ship* (1939).

Chatterton, Thomas. b. at Bristol, England, Nov. 20, 1752; committed suicide at London, Aug. 24, 1770. An English poet, perhaps chiefly noted for his literary hoaxes (works written in a pseudo-medieval style and purporting to be the long-lost literary remains of a 15th-century monk). From his seventh year on, he became interested in the study of literary antiquities; his first pseudo-antique work was "Elinoure and Juga" (written 1764; published in the *Town and Country Magazine,* 1769), followed by a pseudo-archaic account (1768) of the opening (1248) of Bristol Bridge. He also fabricated pedigrees, claiming, as in the instance of his other literary frauds, to have discovered and be in possession of the original documents. His most famous hoax involved a number of poems which he represented as the work of Thomas Rowley, an imaginary 15th-century monk and poet. In 1769 he succeeded in temporarily deceiving Horace Walpole, to whom he sent a "transcript" of a prose work he attributed to Rowley, *The Ryse of Peyneteyne yn Englande, wroten by T. Rowleie, 1469, for Mastre Canynge.* Impressed, Walpole sent a letter of thanks to Chatterton, who responded with a number of "manuscript" poems which, upon being shown to Gray and Mason, were characterized by them as forgeries. The fraud was exposed by Thomas Tyrwhitt in 1777 and 1778, but the authenticity of the Rowley poems became the subject of a controversy which lasted for 80 years, until W. W. Skeat showed conclusively (in his 1871 edition of *Chatterton*) that there was no doubt that the archaic English of the Rowley works came from the hand of Chatterton. Chatterton, who left Bristol for London in 1770, also wrote squibs, political essays, letters after the style of Junius, and other works, including *Excelente Balade of Charitie.* After a brief period of literary success, he became impoverished and is thought to have been reduced to starvation. Locking himself in his garret, he ended his life by taking arsenic, at the age of 17. Among his other works are a satire, *Apostate Will* (1764), and *The Revenge* (1770), a burlesque opera. His literary hoaxes are distinguished by an undeniable poetic genius and lyric power.

Chaucer (chô'sėr), **Geoffrey.** b. c1344; d. at London, Oct. 25, 1400. An English poet, generally conceded to have been the greatest writer of the Middle English period and one of the greatest in the entire history of English literature. He was almost certainly born around 1344, although most older sources still carry 1340 or thereabouts. His father was a wealthy London vintner, John Chaucer, whose family had long been wholesale importers and merchants of wine, and collectors of the king's customs. Chaucer was early in a courtly environment, probably as a page; our first certain record, dated London, May, 1357, reveals him in the service of Elizabeth, Countess of Ulster and wife of Prince Lionel, son of King Edward III. At Christmas he was in her train at Hatfield, Yorkshire, where John of Gaunt, Lionel's younger brother, was visiting. In the same household records appears a lady-in-waiting, "Philippa, daughter of Pan'," probably the Philippa, daughter of Sir Paneto de Roet of Hainaut, who later served the queen and whom Chaucer had married by 1366. In the winter of 1359–60 Chaucer was with the English army invading France, was taken prisoner near Reims, and was then ransomed. Late in 1360 he carried letters from Lionel to England. From 1361 through 1366 Lionel served as the king's lieutenant in Ireland, but his very full records do not mention Chaucer. Perhaps during this period Chaucer obtained legal training at the Inns of Court. There is a convincing tradition that he studied at the Inner Temple, which offered a liberal education sufficiently broad to prepare Chaucer for his later career at court and in business. In 1367 Chaucer was a yeoman in the King's Household (*dilectus vallectus noster*) with a pension of 20 marks for life, and the following year was listed as "esquire." In 1369 he was with an English army raiding in France, probably under John of Gaunt, by that time Duke of Lancaster. Later that year John's wife, the Duchess Blanche, died of the pestilence, and Chaucer wrote his first long poem, *The Book of the Duchess*, an elegy in the form of a conventional French love-vision, praising Blanche and consoling the bereaved duke. From 1368 on, Chaucer undertook seven or more diplomatic missions to the Continent, to arrange for commercial treaties, for a marriage for Prince Richard, for help in the French war, and on secret business. He was envoy in 1373 to Genoa and Florence, and in 1378 to Milan; and though he probably met neither Petrarch nor Boccaccio, he came to know their writings and those of Dante, and Italian influences appear in his next poems, such as *The House of Fame* and *The Parliament of Fowls*. From 1374 through 1384 he was actively controller of the customs on wool, skins, and hides, for the Port of London, and lived rent-free in the house over Aldgate in the city wall. He had many business affairs, and often appointed a deputy in the customs. In these years Philippa Chaucer was in the favor of John of Gaunt's second duchess, Constance; while Philippa's sister Katherine was governess of John's children, and his mistress until she became his third duchess in 1396 (from this union was finally descended Henry VII, first Tudor king of England, and thus deviously, for those interested in genealogy, may Chaucer be linked to the English crown). In 1377 the new king, Richard II, confirmed the annuities from Edward III to both Geoffrey and Philippa Chaucer; but no payment of Philippa's annuity is recorded after June, 1387, and she must have died within the year. In 1385 Chaucer had a permanent deputy in the customs, and became justice of the peace for Kent; in 1386 he became a member of Parliament for Kent, and his customs position officially terminated. Chaucer's move from London to the countryside (probably Greenwich) and his

new activities apparently afforded him leisure to bring to completion two long narratives based on poems by Boccaccio, *Troilus and Criseyde* and the story of Palamon and Arcite (later *The Knight's Tale*). Soon he started *The Legend of Good Women* and also *The Canterbury Tales*. From 1389 to 1391 he was clerk of the king's works, in charge of building and repairs for the Tower of London, Westminster Palace, and eight other royal residences scattered from Surrey to Worcester. From 1391 until 1398 Chaucer was deputy forester of North Petherton Forest, Somersetshire, and probably lived chiefly in the Park House, where he may have composed most of *The Canterbury Tales*. In 1391 he composed *The Treatise on the Astrolabe* for his "little son Lewis." (Another son, Thomas Chaucer, became prominent in the next century.) In 1395–96 at London Chaucer seems to have been briefly in attendance upon Henry of Derby, son of John of Gaunt, who was later crowned Henry IV. As king, in 1399, he renewed the annuity to Chaucer and added another of 40 marks, and the poet leased a house in the garden of St. Mary's Chapel, Westminster Abbey. The traditional date of his death is Oct. 25, 1400, and he was buried in that part of the Abbey which has become the Poets' Corner. The most recent and authoritative edition of his works is *The Complete Works of Geoffrey Chaucer* (often called the "Cambridge Edition"), by F. N. Robinson in 1933. An earlier edition still valued for its glossary and notes is *The Complete Works of Geoffrey Chaucer* (often called the "Oxford Edition"), by Walter W. Skeat in seven volumes (1894–97). *The Book of the Duchess* (c1369) shows Chaucer's familiarity with Roman poetry (especially Ovid) and his intense preoccupation with courtly writings: the *Roman de la Rose* (of which he translated at least part), and poems by Deschamps, Froissart, and Machaut (poets whose lyrics and complaints he imitated). After 1373 come *The House of Fame*, *Anelida and Arcite*, and *The Parliament of Fowls*, which show a continued admiration of Roman poetry and courtly conventions, but also a new handling of detail and sensuous imagery learned from Dante and Boccaccio, and, in the latter two poems, a transition from French octosyllabics to the rime royal, which he invented. He translated the *De Consolatione Philosophiae* of Boethius, whose ideas are reflected in *Troilus and Criseyde* (c1385) and the story of Palamon and Arcite (later *The Knight's Tale*), poems retelling long romances by Boccaccio. The *Troilus* excels in characterization; *The Knight's Tale* and *The Legend of Good Women* show growth of narrative power, and mastery of the decasyllabic couplet, which he was the first to use in English. *The Canterbury Tales* (c1387–1400) reveal wider reading, freedom from earlier conventionalism, and greater control over materials. Among Chaucer's minor works are *An A.B.C.*, *Complaint of Mars*, *Complaint of Venus*, *Complaint to His Empty Purse*, and *Complaint Unto Pity*. A recent investigation has led to the contention that Chaucer responsible for a work heretofore attributed to Simon Bredon, an astronomer. *The Equatorie of the Planetis* (1955), edited by Derek J. Price, is a 14th-century manuscript describing the use of an instrument for calculating the positions of the planets.

The date 1392 (Bredon died in 1372) appears often throughout the text, linguistic analysis points strongly to Chaucer (the text is in Middle English), and Chaucer is known as the author of a similar work (*The Treatise on the Astrolabe*); it is therefore thought quite possible that he is responsible for this holograph. If this is true, it is the first example we have of his prose written entirely in his own hand, without the help of scribes.

Chaucer's Dream. A name at one time given by some to *The Book of the Duchess*, from the fact that the poet pretends, in writing it, to be recounting a dream.

Chaucer's Dream. A name given to an independent poem, first printed by Thomas Speght in the 1597 edition of the works of Geoffrey Chaucer. Speght prefixed to it a note saying: "That which heretofore hath gone under the name of his Dreame, is the book of the Duchesse: on the death of Blanche, Duchesse of Lancaster." This poem is not, however, now assigned to Chaucer.

Chaucer Society. A society founded by F. J. Furnivall in 1868 for the purpose of furnishing to scholars material (manuscripts, early texts, and others) relating to Chaucer which was not accessible to the public, and of facilitating collation.

Chauntecleer or **Chanticleer** (chan'tẹ.klir). The cock who is the hero of "The Nun's Priest's Tale" in Chaucer's *Canterbury Tales*. The same name is also given to the cock in the medieval stories dealing with Reynard the Fox.

Chauvin (shō.van), **Nicolas.** b. at Rochefort, France; fl. in the 18th and early 19th century. A French soldier of the Republic and the Empire. He was severely wounded and mutilated in the wars of Napoleon and received as reward for his services a saber of honor, a red ribbon, and a pension of 200 francs. His enthusiasm for the emperor was so demonstrative that it won for him the ridicule of his comrades and gave rise to the term "chauvinism." The word has come to denote blind and excessive nationalism.

Cheapside (chēp'sīd). [Former name, **Chepe**.] The central east-and-west thoroughfare of the City of London, originally a large open common in the course of Watling Street (one of the great Roman roads of ancient Britain) where the markets and public assemblies were held. Different kinds of wares were sold separately, and the names were perpetuated in the streets which were built up where the old booths had stood. In the Middle Ages Chepe was the great street of the retail trade. It was built with the finest houses in the city, and well supplied with churches (the principal one being the original Saint Mary-le-Bow, burned in the Great Fire of 1666, and so called from its great vault or bow, on the S side). On the S side of the street also was the stone gallery from which royalty reviewed the tournaments which were held here. There were two crosses in Chepe; the principal one was one of the 12 erected by Edward I to mark the resting places of the coffin containing the body of his wife, Eleanor of Castile, in its progress from the place of her death in E England to the site of its burial at London. The highway ran through the S portion of the market place, and became known as Cheapside. Before the Great Fire of London in 1666 it was twice as wide as the present street, and was lined with houses five stories high, each story projecting over the one below, and with high gables. Many of the shops were destroyed and Saint Mary-le-Bow Church (the modern one, built by Christopher Wren after the Great Fire) was severely damaged in World War II. Cheapside is 59 ft. above tidewater.

Cheats, The. A comedy by John Wilson, written in 1662. This play was temporarily suppressed, it is thought on account of its ridicule of some prominent nonconformist in the part of Scruple.

Cheats of Scapin (skä.pan'), **The.** A farce by Thomas Otway, acted in 1676 and translated from Molière's *Les Fourberies de Scapin*.

Cheddar (ched'ạr). A village in SW England, in NE Somersetshire, ab. 19 mi. by road SW of Bristol. Just NE of the village, in the Mendip Hills, are caverns, and the Cheddar Gorge, with cliffs 450 ft. high. Manufacture of the well-known Cheddar cheese began in this area in the 17th century.

Cheddar Cliffs. A picturesque group of limestone cliffs in the Mendip Hills, Somersetshire, England.

Cheeryble (chir'i.bl), **Frank.** The nephew of the Cheeryble Brothers in Charles Dickens's novel *Nicholas Nickleby*. He marries Kate Nickleby.

Cheeryble Brothers. Twin brothers, merchants, named separately Charles and Edwin, in Charles Dickens's novel *Nicholas Nickleby*. They are liberal, simple-minded, and noble-hearted, and are friends and patrons of Nicholas Nickleby. The originals of these characters are said to have been the Grant brothers, cotton-spinners, near Manchester.

Cheggs (chegz), **Mr.** A market-gardener in Charles Dickens's *Old Curiosity Shop*, the successful rival of Dick Swiveller in the affections of Sophy Wackles.

Cheiron (kī'ron). See **Chiron**.

Cheke (chēk), **Sir John.** b. at Cambridge, England, June 16, 1514; d. at London, Sept. 13, 1557. An English scholar of Greek, tutor to the Prince of Wales (later Edward VI of England). He studied at Cambridge (St. John's College), was professor of Greek there in the period 1540–51, was appointed tutor to Prince Edward in 1544, was knighted in 1552, and became a chamberlain of the exchequer in August, 1552, and a secretary of state in June, 1553. He was a zealous Protestant and partisan of Lady Jane Grey, and on Mary Tudor's accession was accused of treason and committed (July 27, 1553) to the Tower of London, but pardoned (Sept. 13, 1554) and permitted to travel abroad. In 1556 he was arrested near Antwerp, brought to England, and again thrown into the Tower, where he was induced to renounce his Protestant beliefs. He wrote numerous works in Latin and English.

Chekhov (che'họf; Anglicized, chek'ọf), **Anton Pavlovich.** [Also: **Chekov, Tchehov, Tchekhov**.] b. at Taganrog, Russia, Jan. 17, 1860; d. at Badenweiler, Germany, in July, 1904. A Russian dramatist and short-story writer, considered one of the foremost and most influential of the Russian writers of the late 19th century. By profession a doctor, he seldom practiced medicine, devoting almost his entire career to writing. Ill health forced him to live (1897 *et seq.*) in the Crimea except for periods spent at other health resorts. While still at the university he began to contribute short humorous stories to the magazines. In 1886 he published his first collection of stories and came under the patronage of Suvorin, who encouraged him. Later he became a friend of Tolstoi and Gorki, and relinquished his membership in the Russian Academy in 1902 in protest against its barring of Gorki. A journey to a convict island (1890) resulted in a book discussing contemporary penal conditions; in 1888 he wrote his first play, *Ivanov;* otherwise his output consisted almost entirely of short stories until c1897, when he began to devote himself chiefly to writing for the theater. In 1896 his second play, known in English as *The Sea-Gull,* was produced at St. Petersburg, but was not a success; a revival (1898) of it, however, by Stanislavsky's Moscow Art Theatre proved immensely popular, and thereafter all of Chekhov's plays were performed by the same group. The plays have all been acclaimed since, and have been widely translated and performed. The remaining ones are *Uncle Vanya* (first performed in 1900), *The Three Sisters* (first performed in 1901), and *The Cherry Orchard* (first performed in 1904). Even more popular than the plays were the short stories, which have exerted a profound influence on subsequent writing in that medium, notably in England (on the work of Katherine Mansfield, for example). They take for their protagonists little people, peasants, or intellectuals, and deal chiefly with an isolated and superficially minor experience in their lives. They all succeed, however, in conveying the theme of the frustrations and difficulties with which the individual sensitive life is beset, and in many cases show the gradual breaking of the human spirit. Imbued as they are, however, with gentle humor and great sympathy, these stories cannot be called wholly pessimistic. The plays as well as the stories portray the corroding stagnation that pervaded some sections of Russian life in his day. Chekhov's works are available in English in the translations of Constance Garnett (*The Tales of Tchekhov,* 13 vols., 1916–22; *The Plays of Tchehov,* 2 vols., 1923), and other partial collections, and in numerous anthologies.

Chelsea (chel'si). [Former spelling, **Chelsey**; Middle English, **Chelchith**; Old English, **Celchyth.**] Metropolitan borough in SW London, in the County of London, situated on the N bank of the river Thames, ab. 3 mi. SW of Saint Paul's. The borough has all types of residential development: large mansions, 17th-century houses, workmen's cottages, and large blocks of modern apartment houses. It has been the residence of many celebrated people, including Sir Thomas More, Elizabeth, Steele, Swift, the painters Turner and Whistler, Walpole, Dante Gabriel Rossetti, George Eliot, and Carlyle (who is sometimes called the "Sage of Chelsea"); Carlyle's house in Cheyne Row escaped bomb damage in World War II and is maintained as a museum. It contains the Chelsea Hospital for invalid soldiers, designed by Wren, built between 1682 and 1690, which sustained heavy war damage. Chelsea is the fourth smallest borough in London.

"Chelsea, Sage of." See **Carlyle, Thomas.**

Chemosh (kē'mosh). In the Old Testament, the principal deity, or Baal, of the Moabites. In Judges, xi. 24, Chemosh also appears as the national god of Ammon. His worship was introduced in Judah under Solomon, but was abolished by Josiah (1 Kings, xi. 7; 2 Kings, xxiii. 13).

Chenevix (chen'e.viks), **Richard.** b. in Ireland, 1774; d. April 5, 1830. An English chemist, mineralogist, and man of letters. He was named a fellow of the Royal Society in 1801, and received the Copley medal in 1803. Besides numerous scientific papers, he wrote *Mantuan Revels* (a comedy), *Henry the Seventh* (a tragedy), and poems.

Cherry (cher'i). The daughter of the landlord Boniface in George Farquhar's play *The Beaux' Stratagem* (1707).

Cherry and Merry (mer'i). In Charles Dickens's *Martin Chuzzlewit,* Pecksniff's daughters, Charity and Mercy. See also under **Pecksniff.**

Cherry Orchard, The. A drama (1904) by Anton Chekhov. An English adaptation of it is to be found in G. B. Shaw's *Heartbreak House.*

Cheshire Cat (chesh'ir). A cat with a most wonderful grin who can (and does) disappear at will in Lewis Carroll's (Charles L. Dodgson's) *Alice's Adventures in Wonderland.*

Chesney (ches'ni, chez'ni), Sir **George Tomkyns.** b. at Tiverton, Devonshire, England, April 30, 1830; d. at London, March 31, 1895. British general, engineer, and author. Having entered the army in 1848, he served during the Indian mutiny. He was president of the engineering college at Calcutta, the first president (1871–80) of the Royal Indian Civil Engineering College, Cooper's Hill, Staines, near London, secretary (1880–86) to the military department of the Indian government, and military member (1886–91) of the governor's council. He was knighted in 1890, and was elected a Conservative member of Parliament for Oxford in 1892. In 1871 he published anonymously in *Blackwood's Magazine* "The Battle of Dorking, or Reminiscences of a Volunteer," an account of an imaginary German assault upon England which attracted much attention. He also published *Indian Polity* (1868), *The True Reformer* (1874), and *The Dilemma* (1876), all novels dealing with army affairs, and *The Lesters, or a Capitalist's Labor* (1893).

Chesson (ches'on), **Nora Hopper.** b. at Exeter, England, 1871; d. 1906. An English poet, author of *Ballads in Prose* (1894) and *Under Quickened Boughs* (1896). Her work shows a considerable influence by Irish folklore.

Chester (ches'tèr), **Mr.** [Later, **Sir John Chester.**] A polished but unprincipled character in Charles Dickens's *Barnaby Rudge.* In order to avoid an alliance which will add nothing to his prestige and wealth, he attempts, without success, to avert the match between his son Edward and the worthy (but poor) Emma Haredale. Dickens based the character of Mr. Chester on what he knew of Philip Dormer Stanhope (Lord Chesterfield).

Chester, Thomas. See **Chestre, Thomas.**

ḍ, d or j; ṣ, s or sh; ṭ, t or ch; z̧, z or zh; o, F. cloche; ü, F. menu; ċh, Sc. loch; ṅ, F. bonbon.

Chesterfield (ches′tėr.fĕld), 4th Earl of. Title of **Stanhope, Philip Dormer.**

Chester Plays (ches′tėr). A cycle of 25 mystery plays formerly presented by the guilds of Chester, England, at Whitsuntide. They were commonly played during three days. Tradition ascribes part of their authorship to the 14th-century chronicler Ranulf Higden, and it is certainly true that whoever wrote them was a man of sophistication with some flair for comedy and some slight ability to create characters. A complete publication (1843) of them was edited for the Shakespeare Society by Thomas Wright.

Chesterton (ches′tėr.ṭon), **Ada Elizabeth.** [Maiden name, **Jones.**] b. at London, 1888—. An English newspaper writer, social worker, and dramatist; sister-in-law of G. K. Chesterton. She traveled in Russia, Poland, China, and Japan as a correspondent for the London *Daily Express.* Her works include *In Darkest London* (1926), *Women of the Underworld* (1930), *My Russian Venture* (1931), *Young China and New Japan* (1933), *What Price Youth* (1939), and *Salute the Soviet* (1942), works on social and international problems. In collaboration with Ralph Neale, she wrote the plays *The Man Who Was Thursday* (a dramatization of G. K. Chesterton's novel of the same name) and *The Love Game.* Interested in improving the living conditions of working girls and homeless women, she established homes (Cecil Houses) and a club (Cecil Residential Club for Working Girls) for their comfort and convenience.

Chesterton, G. K. [Full name, **Gilbert Keith Chesterton.**] b. at Campden Hill, London, May 29, 1874; d. at Beaconsfield, England, June 14, 1936. An English poet, journalist, novelist, and critic. He was educated at St. Paul's School and at the Slade School of Art. For a time he worked for book-publishing houses, and then turned to journalism. His writing was stylistically brilliant and made a great point of paradox. Among his literary creations is the Roman Catholic priest-detective Father Brown, drawn after Chesterton's friend Father O'Connor. Received (July, 1922) into the Roman Catholic Church, he defended Catholicism in his subsequent writings. He was the author of *The Wild Knight and Other Poems* (1900), *Greybeards at Play* (1900), *Robert Browning* (1903), *G. F. Watts* (1904), *The Napoleon of Notting Hill* (1904), *Charles Dickens* (1906), *The Man Who Was Thursday* (1908), *All Things Considered* (1908), *Orthodoxy* (1909), *George Bernard Shaw* (1910), *What's Wrong with the World* (1910), *William Blake* (1910), *Alarms and Discursions* (1910), *Appreciations and Criticisms of the Works of Charles Dickens* (1911), *The Innocence of Father Brown* (1911), *A Short History of England* (1917), *St. Francis of Assisi* (1923), *The Everlasting Man* (1925), *The Secret of Father Brown* (1927), *William Cobbett* (1925), *The Resurrection of Rome* (1930), *Chaucer* (1932), *Autobiography* (1936), and *The Paradoxes of Mr. Pond* (1936).

Chestre (ches′tėr), **Thomas.** [Also, **Chester.**] fl. 1430. An English poet of whom very little is known. He was the author of *Sir Launfal,* a metrical romance about the Arthurian knight, probably written c1430.

Chettle (chet′l), **Henry.** b. c1560; d. c1607. An English dramatist and pamphleteer, son of a dyer of London, and a stationer by trade. He was in a printing partnership from 1589 to 1591, but after that no book of his publication has been found. However, Nash's *Strange News* (1592) and *Terrors of the Night* (1594) came from the press of a former associate of Chettle's and a letter by Chettle printed in another Nash work refers to himself as "old compositor." He was the author or joint author of a large number of plays. *The Tragedy of Hoffman* (1602) is the only play now extant that is attributed to Chettle. By 1598 he was writing for the stage, and is mentioned by Francis Meres in his *Palladis Tamia* (1598) as "best for Comedy among us." In the period from 1598 to 1603 he collaborated on about 48 plays. He is also remembered for editing Greene's *Groatsworth of Wit* and for his eulogy on Queen Elizabeth, *England's Mourning Garment* (1603).

Chetwood (chet′wŭd), **William Rufus.** d. March 3, 1766. An English dramatist, bookseller, and prompter at the Drury Lane Theatre, London. He was the author of *General History of the Stage* (1749), several dramatic pieces, and others.

Chevalier, the Young. See **Stuart, Charles Edward Louis Philip Casimir.**

"Chevalier de St. George." See **Stuart, James Francis Edward.**

"Chevalier Strong" (strông), **the.** See **Strong, Captain Edward.**

Chevelere Assigne (shev′.lėr à.sēny′). [Full title, **Chevelere Assigne, or the Knight of the Swan.**] A Middle English alliterative romance of about 400 lines. It is the only piece in English verse that treats of Godfrey de Bouillon, leader of the First Crusade.

Cheverel (shev′e̱.re̱l), **Sir Christopher** and **Lady.** Two of the principal characters in George Eliot's novel *Mr. Gilfil's Love-Story.*

Chevy Chase (chev′i chās). [Full title, **The Ballad of Chevy Chase.**] An English ballad, probably from the 15th century, which recounts the incidents of the battle of Otterburn between the Scots and the English.

Chichevache (chē′che̱.väch; French, shēsh.vȧsh). A fabulous beast which devoured patient and submissive wives. The fable, of Old French origin, became a favorite with Middle English writers, who made the beast a lean cow, and ascribed her leanness to the scarcity of her peculiar diet. They added another beast named Bicorne or Bycorne (literally, "two-horned"), who lived only on patient and submissive husbands, and was in consequence always fat. Lydgate wrote a poem called *Bycorne and Chichevache.*

Chick (chik), **Mrs. Louisa.** Mr. Dombey's sister in Charles Dickens's *Dombey and Son,* a weak and self-satisfied woman who urged the fading Mrs. Dombey to "make an effort."

Chickenstalker (chik′e̱n.stô.kėr), **Mrs.** An old shopkeeper in Charles Dickens's story *The Chimes.*

"Chickweed" (chik′wēd). See under **Smallweed, Grandfather.**

Chief Justice. See **Lord Chief Justice.**

Chief Promises of God, The. A religious interlude by John Bale, written c1538.

Chiffinch (chif'inch), **Master Thomas.** A drinking and intriguing minister to the pleasures of King Charles II, in Sir Walter Scott's novel *Peveril of the Peak.*

Child (chĭld), **Francis James.** b. at Boston, Feb. 1, 1825; d. Sept. 11, 1896. An American philologist. He was educated at Harvard College, and was professor of rhetoric and oratory there from 1851 to 1876, when he became professor of English literature. His best-known work is an edition of *English and Scottish Ballads,* which he first brought out in the period 1857–58 in 8 volumes, and which was followed by *English and Scottish Popular Ballads* (5 vols., 1883–98). He also published *Poetical Works of Edmund Spenser* (5 vols., 1855; a critical edition) and "Observations on the Language of Chaucer" (in *Memoirs of the American Academy of Arts and Sciences,* 1863).

Childe Harold's Pilgrimage (chĭld har'ŏldz). A poem by Byron, of which the first and second cantos were published in 1812, the third in 1816, and the fourth in 1818. The poem, written in Spenserian stanzas, takes its hero, a romantically melancholy young man, on travels through Portugal, Spain, the Ionian islands, Albania, Greece, Belgium, and the Alps. In the fourth canto the device of the hero is abandoned, and the poem is a straight description of Italian cities and their artistic and historic associations. Appealing to the popular taste of the day for descriptions of foreign places, the poem made Byron famous.

Childe Morrice (or **Maurice**) (chĭld mor'is). See **Gil Morrice.**

Childe of Elle (chĭld; el). In a ballad in Percy's *Reliques,* a young man who runs away with his beloved, Emeline, and after various adventures is accepted once again by her father.

Childermas Day (chĭl'dẽr.mạs). [Also, **Feast of the Holy Innocents.**] A Christian holy day celebrated on December 28 in commemoration of Herod's wholesale slaughter of male infants after the birth of Christ.

Childe Roland to the Dark Tower Came (chĭld rō'lạnd). A poem by Robert Browning, included in *Dramatic Romances,* published in *Men and Women* (1855). It tells of a knight who attempts a journey to the "dark tower," a journey which all before have failed to complete. Arriving at the tower, he sees his companions, the lost adventurers:

There they stood, ranged along the hillsides, met
    To view the last of me, a living frame
    For one more picture! in a sheet of flame
I saw them and I knew them all. And yet
Dauntless the slug horn to my lips I set,
    And blew.

The title and theme of the poem are taken from the lines "sung" by Edgar in Shakespeare's *King Lear,* Act III, Scene 4. See also **Child Rowland.**

Childe Waters (chĭld wô'tẽrz). An old ballad, included in Percy's *Reliques,* telling of the constant Ellen's love for Childe Waters, a cruel knight who degrades her in every possible way, but who finally takes pity on her and marries her.

Child of Nature, The. A play by Elizabeth Inchbald, produced at Covent Garden Theatre, London, on Nov. 28, 1788. It is based on a work by Madame de Genlis.

Children in the Wood. A novel by Naomi Royde-Smith, published in 1928. Its American title is *In the Wood.*

Children in the Wood, The. [Also, **Babes in the Wood.**] An early English ballad, of unknown authorship, preserved in Ritson's, Percy's, and other collections. The ballad was entered in the Stationers' Register in 1595. In 1601 a play was published "of a young child murthered in a wood by two ruffins with the consent of his unkle."

Children of No Man's Land. A novel by G. B. Stern, published in 1919. It was issued under the American title *Debatable Ground* (1921).

Children of Paul's (pôlz). See **Paul's Boys.**

Children of the Abbey, The. A story by Regina Maria Roche, published in 1798.

Children of the Chapel. [Also, at various times: **Children of the Revels, Children of Blackfriars, Children of the Queen's Revels.**] An Elizabethan and Jacobean company of child actors, comprising the choir boys of the Chapel (or Chapel Royal), a part of the royal household which presented interludes with adult actors in the early 16th century. William Cornish was Master of the Children from 1509 until 1523, and actually formed the acting company. The company continued during the rest of the century under such masters as Edwards, Farrant, Hunnis, and Giles, and played, at various times, at the Blackfriars Theatre. The Children of the Chapel, and a similar group, Paul's Boys, competed with adult companies, and are disparaged by Hamlet in the "player scene." A number of the King's Men were once child actors with this company. They lost favor at Court, became the Children of the Revels, and finally, in 1606, the Children of Blackfriars. In 1608, they left Blackfriars Theatre and moved to Whitefriars, where they remained until 1610, when they again came under royal patronage, as the Children of the Queen's Revels. When Nathan Field left them about 1616 the company fell into obscurity.

Children of the King's Revels. A Jacobean company of child actors. It was formed (c1606) possibly from the company known as Paul's Boys, but lasted only until 1609, when disagreement among the members of the founding group led to its dispersal. A company of the same name played later (c1615) in the provinces.

Children of the Mist. A band of Highland outlaws in Sir Walter Scott's *Legend of Montrose.* There is also a painting with this title by Landseer.

Children of the Mist, The. A novel (1898) by Eden Phillpotts.

Children of the Nile, The. A novel by Marmaduke Pickthall, published in 1908.

Children of the Sea, The. A title once used in America for Conrad's *The Nigger of the Narcissus.*

Child Rowland (chĭld rō'lạnd). In Shakespeare's *King Lear* (III.iv) Edgar utters snatches from old ballads, one being "Child Rowland to the dark tower came." The words come from an old Scotch ballad wherein a young man rescues his sister from an elf's castle ("child" or "childe" means a squire or young lord who has not yet won his knightly spurs).

Child's Garden of Verses, A.   A collection of poems for children by Robert Louis Stevenson, published in 1885. It includes verses on the seasons ("Winter Time"), on children's games, and on children's fantasies.

Chillingly (chil'ing.li), **Kenelm.   See Kenelm Chillingly.**

Chillingworth (chil'ing.wèrth), **William.**   b. at Oxford, England, in October, 1602; d. at Chichester, England, Jan. 30, 1644. An English divine and controversialist. The most famous of his works is *The Religion of Protestants, a Safe Way to Salvation* (1637).

Chillip (chil'ip), **Mr.**   A mild and gentle little doctor who attended Mrs. Copperfield, in Charles Dickens's *David Copperfield*.

Chillon (shi.lon'; French, shē.yôn).   A castle in Vaud, Switzerland, on Lake Geneva: famous in literature, especially as the prison of Bonnivard (1530–36).

Chiltern Hundreds (chil'tèrn).   The three hundreds of Stoke, Desborough, and Bodenham, in Buckinghamshire. The stewardship of the Chiltern Hundreds (originally an office charged with the suppression of the robbers who infested the Chiltern Hills) is a nominal office, conferred upon a member of Parliament who wishes to resign his seat, such resignation being impossible unless the member is disqualified by the acceptance of a place of honor and profit under the crown, or by some other cause. The place is the gift of the chancellor of the exchequer.

Chimaera (ki.mir'a̦, kī-).   [Also, **Chimera.**]   In Greek mythology, a fire-breathing monster of divine origin (according to Hesiod, a daughter of Typhaon and Echidna). It was often shown in art as having a goat's head in the middle of the back and a dragon's head at the end of the tail. It dwelt in Lycia, and was slain by Bellerophon.

Chimène (shē.men).   The faithful daughter of Don Gomès in Pierre Corneille's tragedy *Le Cid*.

Chimes, The.   Charles Dickens's Christmas story for 1844. It is one of his most sociological narratives: a bitter attack upon the political economy of Victorian England.

Chios (kī'os).   [Also: **Khios**; Italian, **Scio**; Turkish, **Saki-Adasi, Saki-Adassi.**]   A Greek island in the Aegean Sea, situated W of Asia Minor. The surface is hilly and rocky. The island has been noted in ancient and modern times for wine and fruit. It was settled by Ionians, passed to Persian rule in the 6th century B.C., and was a member of the original Confederacy of Delos until 412 B.C. It was noted in the ancient world as a center of art and literature, particularly for its school of epic poets, and claim was made that it was the birthplace of Homer. Chios was part of the Macedonian, Roman, and other dominions in the area. The Genoese took the island in the 14th century; it was conquered by the Turks in 1566, and was lost by them to, and retaken from, the Florentines and Venetians during the

16th and 17th centuries. It was the scene of a terrible massacre of its inhabitants by the Turks in 1822, and was ravaged by earthquakes in 1881 and 1882. Chios forms a *nomos* (department) of modern Greece, of which it became a part in 1912.

Chippendale (chip'ęn.dāl), **Thomas.**   b. in Yorkshire, England, c1718; d. at London, 1779. An English furniture maker. His business was carried on at London. His work is heavier in design than that of Sheraton and other later cabinetmakers. He added to the common style of the early 18th century several details adapted from French rococo (Louis Quinze), Gothic, and Chinese. His work nearly always is in dark mahogany, and in this material he designed and built chairs and tables, desks and bookcases, cabinets and settees, his designs, emphasizing carving to give a light effect to the heavy material and solid construction, being so good that his work was quickly imitated in England and the U. S., and his name given to the entire style. He published *Gentleman and Cabinet-Maker's Director* (1754), a catalogue of various pieces turned out by his workshop.

Chirol (chir'ǫl), Sir **Valentine.**   [Full name, **Ignatius Valentine Chirol.**]   b. May 23, 1852; d. at London, Oct. 22, 1929. An English journalist, author, and traveler. Educated in France and Germany, he graduated from the University of Paris. He served (1872–76) as a British foreign office clerk, later (1876–92) traveling in the Far and Near East. From 1892 to 1899 he was Berlin correspondent of the London *Times*, on which he served (1899–1912) as foreign editor. He was a member (1912–16) of the Indian Royal Commission, and was knighted in 1912. Author of *'Twixt Greek and Turk* (1881), *The Far Eastern Question* (1896), *The Middle Eastern Question* (1903), *Indian Unrest* (1910), and the two autobiographical volumes *Fifty Years in a Changing World* (1927) and *With Pen and Brush in Eastern Lands* (1929).

Chiron or **Cheiron** (kī'ron).   In Greek mythology, a centaur; son of Kronos and one of the Oceanids. Chiron was the pupil of Apollo and Artemis, the friend and protector of Peleus, and the instructor of Achilles, Aesculapius, Hercules, Jason, and many other legendary Greek heroes. He was renowned for his wisdom and skill in medicine, hunting, music, and prophecy. Chiron lived on Mount Pelion. During Hercules's fight with the centaurs, one of the Hydra-poisoned arrows of the hero accidentally struck Chiron. Knowing that his immortality doomed him to unending pain from the venom, Chiron asked to die, giving his immortality to Prometheus. On his death he was placed by Zeus among the stars, where he may be seen as Sagittarius, the Archer.

Chiron (kī'ron).   In Shakespeare's *Titus Andronicus*, a son of Tamora. He and his brother Demetrius are guilty of various wicked crimes; Titus kills both by cutting their throats, and then bakes them in a pie to serve to their mother.

Chisholm (chiz'ǫm), **Hugh.**   b. at London, Feb. 22, 1866; d. there, Sept. 29, 1924. An English journalist and editor. Educated at Felsted and at Corpus Christi College, Oxford, from which he received his M.A. in 1888, he was called to the bar in 1892. He was assistant editor (1892–97) and editor

(1897–99) of the *St. James's Gazette*, resigning in order to write for *The Standard*. In 1900 he became a staff member of the London *Times*, and was that paper's city and financial editor from 1913 to 1920. He was also coeditor of the tenth edition (1902), and editor of the 11th (1910–11) and 12th (1922) editions of the *Encyclopaedia Britannica*.

chivalry. 1. Knighthood; the medieval system of military privileges, with its peculiar honorary titles and aristocratic limitations of honorable position to the possessors of those titles, founded upon the several degrees of military service rendered on horseback.

The age of *Chivalry* has gone. An age of Humanity has come. The Horse, whose importance, more than human, gave the name to that early period of gallantry and war, now yields his foremost place to Man. (Sumner, *Orations*.)

Chivalry [may be considered] as embodying the Middle-Age conception of the ideal life of the only class outside the clergy who had any real power, the knights. (Stillé, *Stud. Med. Hist.*)

2. That which pertains to knighthood; the usages and customs pertaining to the order of knighthood; the ideal qualifications of a knight, collectively, as courtesy, generosity, valor, and dexterity in arms; the ideal of knighthood.

The glory of our Troy doth this day lie
On his fair worth, and single *chivalry*.
(Shakespeare, *Troilus and Cressida*.)

The *chivalry*
That dares the right, and disregards alike
The yea and nay o' the world.
(Browning, *Ring and Book*, II. 202.)

Chivery (chiv'ĕr.i), **John.** "The sentimental son of a turnkey" in Charles Dickens's *Little Dorrit*. He passed his time in composing heartbreaking epitaphs. He was very weak and small, but "great of soul, poetical, expansive, faithful," and in love with Little Dorrit.

Chloe (klō'ē̞). A country maiden in love with Daphnis, in the Greek pastoral romance *Daphnis and Chloe*, attributed to Longus, a 3rd-century Greek poet.

Chloe. A shepherdess in Sir Philip Sidney's *Arcadia*.

Chloe. The ambitious wife of an honest, commonplace citizen in Ben Jonson's comedy *The Poetaster*.

Chloe. [Also, **Cloe.**] A wanton shepherdess in John Fletcher's *The Faithful Shepherdess*, intended as a contrast to the chaste Clorin, the faithful shepherdess.

Chloris (klō'ris). A character in the farce *The Rehearsal* by George Villiers, 2nd Duke of Buckingham, Samuel Butler, and others. She drowns herself because Prince Prettyman marries old Joan.

Choice, The. A four-act play (1919) by Alfred Sutro.

Choke (chōk), **General Cyrus.** In Charles Dickens's *Martin Chuzzlewit*, an American, "one of the most remarkable men in the country," encountered by Martin Chuzzlewit.

Choleric Man, The. A comedy by Richard Cumberland, produced in 1774.

Chollup (chol'up), **Major Hannibal.** In Charles Dickens's *Martin Chuzzlewit*, an American, a worshiper of freedom, lynch-law, and slavery.

Cholmondeley (chum'li), **Mary.** [Pseudonym, **Pax.**] b. at Hodnet, Shropshire, England; d. July 5, 1925. An English novelist. Among her best-known works are *The Danvers Jewels* (1887; written under the pseudonym Pax), *Diana Tempest* (1893), *Red Pottage* (1899), *Prisoners* (1906), *The Lowest Rung* (1908), *Hand on the Latch* (1909), and *Under One Roof* (1918).

Chopin (sho.pan̂), **Frédéric François.** b. at Zelazowa-Wola, near Warsaw, Poland, Feb. 22, 1810; d. at Paris, Oct. 17, 1849. A composer and pianist, noted for his piano works. His father was French, his mother a Pole. His earliest compositions included dances, mazurkas, and polonaises. His masters were a Bohemian, Zwyny, and Elsner, the director of the school of music at Warsaw. At 19 he was considered a finished virtuoso. He began at this age, with his two concertos and some smaller works, to give concerts at Vienna, Munich, and Paris. In the latter place he settled. About 1837 began a romantic connection with George Sand. In 1838 she took him to Majorca for his health, and nursed him there. She left him after a friendship of eight years, and he lived in retirement, giving lessons and composing. His works include two concertos for piano and orchestra, 27 études, 52 mazurkas, many preludes, nocturnes, rondos, and 16 Polish songs. His romantic, patriotic compositions enjoy wide popularity.

Chorley (chôr'li), **Henry Fothergill.** [Pseudonym, **Paul Bell.**] b. at Blackley Hurst, Lancashire, England, Dec. 15, 1808; d. at London, Feb. 16, 1872. An English journalist, novelist, dramatist, and poet, music critic and reviewer for the London *Athenaeum*. His works include *Modern German Music* (1854) and *Thirty Years' Musical Recollections* (1862). He also wrote a number of unsuccessful novels, including *Roccabella* which was published under the pseudonym Paul Bell, and several dramas, among them *Old Love and New Fortune*.

chorus. In ancient Greek drama: **a.** A dance performed by a number of persons in a ring, in honor of Bacchus, accompanied by the singing of the sacred dithyrambic odes. From this simple rite was developed the Greek drama. **b.** In continuation of the early tradition, a company of persons, represented as of age, sex, and estate appropriate to the play, who took part through their leader, the coryphaeus, with the actors in the dialogue of a drama, and sang their sentiments at stated intervals when no actor was on the stage. The chorus occupied in the theater a position between the stage and the auditorium, and moved or danced in appropriate rhythm around the sacred thymele or altar of Bacchus, which stood in the middle of the area allotted to the chorus.

Ham. This is one Lucianus, nephew to the king.
Oph. You are as good as a chorus, my lord.
(Shakespeare, *Hamlet*.)

c. One of the songs executed by the chorus.

Chouans (shö'ạnz; French, shwän). During the French Revolution, a name given to the royalist

d, d or j; s, s or sh; t, t or ch; z, z or zh; o, F. cloche; ü, F. menu; ch, Sc. loch; n̂, F. bonbon.

insurgents of Brittany. The name is sometimes thought to be derived from the appellation *chat-huant* (meaning "screechowl") given to their leader Jean Cottereau.

Chrétien (or Chrestien) de Troyes (krā.tyaṅ dẹ trwä). fl. c1150–90. The most famous of the medieval French writers of metrical romances, whose long poems dealing with King Arthur and the knights of the Round Table are the earliest which have survived and possibly the earliest which were written. Chrétien's works are (in chronological order): (1) translations of Ovid's *Ars Amatoria* and *Remedia Amoris* and of parts of the *Metamorphoses* (all now lost); (2) a story about Mark and Isolt (also lost, but probably a version of the Tristan romance); (3) *Erec et Enide* (the earliest Arthurian romance in French); (4) *Cligés* (an Arthurian romance which mingles Celtic and Byzantine themes); (5) *Lancelot, ou le Chevalier de la Charrette;* (6) *Guillaume d'Angleterre* (of uncertain date and attribution; not an Arthurian romance, but a romanticized saint's life); (7) *Yvain, ou le Chevalier au Lion* (his masterpiece from the point of view of composition and style); (8) *Perceval, ou le Conte du Graal* (the first appearance of the Holy Grail in literature; left unfinished by Chrétien, but continued by four other versifiers who wrote at intervals over a period of about 50 years, spinning the story out to a total of more than 60,000 lines). The *Erec et Enide* and the *Cligés* were written before 1164; the *Yvain* and the *Lancelot* after 1164, but before 1172; and the *Perceval* before 1191, probably about 1180–81. Chrétien wrote his *Perceval* earlier than Robert de Boron, who also composed an early verse romance on the subject of the Holy Grail (associating it for the first time with the vessel of the Last Supper and with the legend of Joseph of Arimathea), but there is no evidence of any connection between the two writers. The works of both Chrétien and Robert de Boron were, in the early years of the 13th century, used as the basis of voluminous romances in French prose, which also drew from other sources and which in turn served as the sources of inspiration for Malory, and through him for Tennyson and Swinburne.

Christ, Christ A, and **Christ B.** See under **Ascension, The.**

Christabel (kris'tạ.bel). The heroine of Samuel Taylor Coleridge's poem of that name, published in 1816. The gentle and pious daughter of Sir Leoline, she is induced by a powerful spell to bring into her father's castle the enchantress who calls herself the Lady Geraldine.

Christ and Satan. The name generally given to the concluding poem of the *Junius Manuscript*, a sequence of some 730 lines giving an account, notable for the freedom and imagination with which the Biblical narrative is treated, of the fall of the angels, Christ's harrowing of hell, Christ's life, resurrection, and ascension, the last judgment, and the temptation. The poem, of unknown authorship, was written in the 8th or early in the 9th century.

Christ Church. [Original name, **Cardinal College.**] One of the largest colleges of Oxford University, England, founded in 1525 by Cardinal Wolsey as Cardinal College, remodeled as King Henry VIII's

College in 1532, and refounded as Christ Church by Henry VIII in 1546. The gateway, in Perpendicular Gothic style, to the great quadrangle ("Tom Quad"), which is the largest in Oxford, opens beneath the Tom Tower, whose upper stage was built by Wren in 1682. On the south side of the quadrangle is the beautiful Perpendicular Gothic hall, ab. 115 by ab. 40 ft., and ab. 50 ft. high to the carved oak ceiling. It possesses many fine old and modern portraits.

Christian (kris'chạn). The hero of John Bunyan's *Pilgrim's Progress.*

Christian, Edward. In Sir Walter Scott's novel *Peveril of the Peak*, the hanger-on at court who tries to bring Alice Bridgenorth to the king's attention in order that she may become his (the king's) mistress.

Christian, Fletcher. fl. in the last half of the 18th century. An English seaman, master's mate and leader of the mutineers of the ship *Bounty*. After the ship reached Tahiti, what became of Christian is not known; according to Adams, the surviving mutineer found on Pitcairn Island, he was murdered by the Tahitians. It is possible that he escaped and returned to England. The founding of the colony on Pitcairn Island is variously attributed to Adams and Christian.

Christiana (kris.ti.an'ạ). The wife of Christian, and the chief female character in the second part of John Bunyan's *Pilgrim's Progress*. She also left the City of Destruction after Christian's flight.

Christian Custance (kus'tạns), **Dame.** See **Custance, Dame Christian.**

Christian Hero, The. A work by Richard Steele, published in 1701. Steele here strives to prove that only through Christianity may a man gain enough moral strength to become a hero (in opposition particularly to Stoicism, with its pagan morality). The man of Virtue, says Steele, should be guided by the Bible, which has triumphed over the older systems of philosophy.

Christian Observer, The. A periodical edited (1802–16) by Zachary Macaulay (1768–1838), father of Thomas Babington Macaulay. It was a chief organ of the English abolitionist movement and devoted itself to constant attacks on British participation in the slave-trade and on the continuing existence of slavery in some colonial areas within the British Empire or under British influence. Macaulay had gained a first-hand knowledge of this problem during his service (1793–99) as governor (under a private company) of Sierra Leone, on the W coast of Africa, which was then being settled in large part by liberated slaves under the sponsorship of antislavery elements in Great Britain.

Christian Year, The. A volume of sacred poems (1827) by the English poet John Keble, who was for many years a professor of poetry at Oxford, and was also a chief initiator of the Oxford (or Tractarian) Movement. Published anonymously, with the subtitle *Thoughts in Verse for the Sundays and Holy Days Throughout the Year*, it became immensely popular and has retained a considerable body of readers even to this day. Some of the best-known selections in the book are "Evening Hymn,"

"Sun of My Soul," "Thou Saviour Dear," and "The Voice that Breathed O'er Eden."

Christie (kris'ti), **Agatha.** [Full name, **Agatha Mary Clarissa Christie;** maiden name, **Miller.**] b. at Torquay, Devonshire, England,—. An English author of detective fiction and creator of the highly successful character of the Belgian detective Hercule Poirot. Her very successful career was begun with *The Mysterious Affair at Styles* (1920), which she wrote to disprove her sister's belief that it was practically impossible to write a detective story in which the reader could not guess who committed the crime. Her other works include *The Murder on the Links* (1923), *Poirot Investigates* and *The Man in the Brown Suit* (both 1924), *The Secret of Chimneys* (1925), *The Murder of Roger Ackroyd* (1926), which is regarded not only as one of her best works but as one of the best detective novels of the 20th century, *The Big Four* (1927), *The Mystery of the Blue Train* (1928), *The Seven Dials Mystery* (1929), *The Mysterious Mr. Quin* and *Murder at the Vicarage* (both 1930), *The Sittaford Mystery* (1931; American title, *Murder at Hazlemoore*), *Peril at End House* (1932), *The Thirteen Problems* (1933; American title, *The Tuesday Club Murders*), *Lord Edgeware Dies* (1933; American title, *Thirteen at Dinner*), *Murder in the Calais Coach* and *Murder in Three Acts* (both 1934), *Death in the Air* and *Boomerang Clue* (both 1935), *The ABC Murders* (1936), *Cards on the Table, Dead Man's Mirror, Death on the Nile, Poirot Loses a Client* (all 1937), *Appointment with Death* (1938), *The Regatta Mystery* and *Murder for Christmas* (both 1939), *Ten Little Niggers* (1940; American title, *And Then There Were None*), which was successful on both the stage and screen, *The Sad Cypress* (1940), *The Patriotic Murders, N or M,* and *Evil Under the Sun* (all 1941), *The Body in the Library* and *Murder in Retrospect* (both 1942), *Triple Threat* (1943), *Death Comes as the End* (1944), *Sparkling Cyanide* (1945), *The Hollow* (1946), and *They Came to Baghdad* (1951). Her most recent work includes the plays, *The Mouse Trap* (1952), *Witness for the Prosecution* (1953), and *The Spider's Web* (1954).

Christie, James. b. 1730; d. 1803. An English auctioneer; father of James Christie (1773–1831) and grandfather of Sir William Henry Mahoney Christie (1845–1922). In 1766 he opened Christie's, a world-famous auction room at London which was carried on after his death by his son.

Christie, James. b. at London, 1773; d. 1831. An English antiquarian, auctioneer, and author of works on Etruscan and Greek vases; son of James Christie (1730–1803).

Christie Johnstone (jon'ston, -son). A novel by Charles Reade, published in 1853. Christie, the simple Scottish girl who is the heroine, proves herself in every way worthy to marry the artist, Charles Gatty, and finally wins the agreement of his mother to the match when she saves him from drowning.

Christie's (kris'tiz). An auction-room at London. On Dec. 5, 1766, James Christie (1730–1803) held his initial public auction on the site of the United Service Club in Pall Mall, London. The business was at first general, but the picture sales soon became the chief attraction. The "private view-day" was especially popular with the prominent people of the time. Christie was succeeded by his son James Christie (1773–1831), who in 1824 moved to 8 King Street; after his death the business was carried on by his two sons. The firm name of Christie, Manson, and Woods was adopted in 1859, but the establishment has remained generally known even to this day simply as "Christie's." Many of the world's leading private art collections, including some of the most famous paintings in the history of Western art, have "gone under the hammer" at Christie's.

Christina (kris.tē'na). A romantic young girl in love with Valentine in Wycherley's *Love in a Wood.*

Christina Alberta's Father (al.bėr'taz). A novel (1925) by H. G. Wells, dealing with the theme (a favorite one with Wells, as it has been with many other 20th-century authors) of sexual conflict, and the unhappiness which this causes. In this book Wells presented views which were, for his time, both advanced and controversial, but which conveyed his idea as to possible methods of improving the relationship between men and women. It hinges on the fantastic story of a laundryman who imagines himself the reincarnation of Sargon, King of Kings.

Christina Light (līt'). See **Light, Christina.**

Christis Kirk on the Green (krīs'tis kėrk). A Scottish ballad found in the Bannatyne manuscript and edited by Allan Ramsay, who added two cantos. It describes the activities at a village festival.

Christmas Carol, A. [Full title, **A Christmas Carol in Prose; Being a Ghost Story of Christmas.**] A Christmas story in prose (December, 1843), by Charles Dickens. It is regarded as one of the best and is certainly one of the best known, examples of the "dream-and-reformation" type of story, familiar in English drama and poetry as well as fiction. Dickens states his aim in writing it in his short Preface: "I have endeavored," he says, "in this ghostly little book, to raise the Ghost of an Idea, which shall not put my readers out of humour with themselves, with each other, with the season, or with me. May it haunt their houses pleasantly, and no one wish to lay it!" The story is told in five staves (a term belonging to poetry rather than prose): I. Marley's Ghost, II. The First of the Three Spirits, III. The Second of the Three Spirits, IV. The Last of the Spirits, V. The End of It. The chief characters are Ebenezer Scrooge, his dead partner Jacob Marley, who appears as a ghost; Scrooge's happy (although poorly paid) clerk Bob Cratchit, his equally happy wife, and their son Tiny Tim, a pathetic little cripple. By means of a visit from Marley's ghost, and by visits from the Spirits of Christmas Past, Present, and Future, Scrooge is made to realize that he has never known the meaning of Christmas and that his will be a horrible end unless he changes his ways before it is too late. The dream visits take place on Christmas Eve, after Scrooge has returned from his office in a nasty, uncharitable mood, and he wakes up on Christmas morning, after a night of terror, a changed man, eager and anxious to observe Christmas as it should be observed, and with his heart full of friendliness for his fellows. The story is famous for its opening sentence, "Marley was dead, to begin with," and for the frequent cry of Tiny Tim, which closes it, "God bless us, every one!" Although less than a novel, it is something more than a short story, occupying, as it does, at least a hundred pages (more, in some editions). Dickens's classic has found equal popularity on the stage, on the screen, and on the air, and there are several phonographic recordings. The character of Scrooge has been interpreted by Alastair Sim, Eustace Wyatt, Basil Rathbone, Lionel Barrymore, and Ronald Colman.

Christmas Eve and Easter Day. Two poems by Robert Browning, published (1850) under one title. They were written while Browning was in Italy, and probably inspired by his critical examination of the Catholic ritual and his sympathy for the English dissenters. Its main argument involves the question of faith versus reason.

Christmas Garland, A. A collection of burlesques on contemporary authors (1912) by Max Beerbohm.

Christopher (kris'tọ.fẻr), Saint. fl. c3rd century. An early Christian martyr. Virtually nothing is known about him except that somewhere in Asia Minor, perhaps in Syria, and probably in the 3rd century, there was a pious man who took or was given the name (in Latin) "Christophorus," meaning "Christ-Bearer," and that he was martyred for his faith. As early as the 6th century at least one church and one monastery are known to have been dedicated to him. The significance of his name is supposed at first to have been that he bore Christ in his heart, but from an early time the legend as we know it today began to take form. According to this account, Christopher was a man of giant stature and prodigious strength, who vowed to serve only the strongest master. He bound himself first to Satan and then to an earthly king, but found neither of them really strong; he was then persuaded by a hermit that God is the strongest master, and he was baptized and entered the service of God. He would not undertake to pray and fast, but offered to carry across a certain raging torrent all Christian pilgrims who came that way. One day he started carrying a child across the stream, but the child's weight increased at every step, so that the giant porter was barely able to reach the other bank. There the child revealed himself as Christ, and said "Marvel not, for with me thou hast borne the sins of all the world." Then, at the Christ-child's bidding, he struck his staff into the ground, where overnight it grew into a palm tree. News of this miracle caused many conversions, which enraged the ruler of that land, who thereupon caused Christopher to be seized, tortured, and beheaded. Saint Christopher, who usually appears in art bearing the Christ-child and the staff, has been adopted as patron by a number of cities and by various classes of artisans and workers, including mariners and ferrymen; in modern times he has become a patron of travelers in general, and medals with his image are frequently affixed to automobiles or carried by motorists, while his name has been given to a number of shrines and churches located on much-traveled highways.

Christopher. Entries on literary characters having this prename will also be found under the surnames Casby, Cheverel, Corporate, Sly, and Urswick.

Christopher Robin (rob'in). The small boy in A. A. Milne's *Winnie the Pooh* and *The House at Pooh Corner*, also the hero of various children's poems in Milne's *When We Were Very Young* and *Now We Are Six*. He is taken to represent the author's son, Christopher Milne, for whom these stories and poems were written.

Christ's College. A college of Cambridge University, England, founded in 1505 by Margaret Beaufort, Countess of Richmond. The Tudor arms remain over the gateway, but the buildings were renovated in the 18th century. The gardens are celebrated for their beauty.

Christ's Hospital. A school, formerly in Newgate Street, London, known as the Blue Coat School from the ancient dress of the scholars, which is still retained. It was founded by Edward VI on the site of the monastery of Grey Friars, given by Henry VIII to the city near the end of his reign for the relief of the poor. The school was moved to Horsham, Sussex, in 1902. Charles Lamb and Samuel Taylor Coleridge attended this school.

Christ's Teares Over Jerusalem. A prose religious tract (1593) by the Elizabethan satirist Thomas Nash. In it the author turns to Christ's prophecy of the fall of Jerusalem in order to drive home, by implying a parallel fate, the moral degradation evidenced by the sinful life led by many London citizens in his day.

Christ's Victorie and Triumph. A poem (1610) by the younger Giles Fletcher. It is written in an eight-line stanza and divided into four books. The books are *Christ's Victory in Heaven*, *Christ's Victory on Earth*, *Christ's Triumph Over Death*, and *His Triumph after Death*, dealing with the themes of the redemption of man, the temptation, the Crucifixion, and the Resurrection.

Christy Mahon (kris'ti mạ.hön', -hön'). See **Mahon, Christy.**

Chronica (kron'i.kạ). A Latin prose work by Ethelwerd, an Anglo-Latin chronicler who died toward the end of the 10th century. It is a history of the world from the beginning to 973, and is in four books. The work was first edited in 1596 by Sir Henry Savile, and was translated from Latin into English by Giles in his *Six Old English Chronicles*.

Chronica. A Latin prose work by the English chronicler Roger of Hoveden, which is particularly important for its account of the closing years of the 12th century.

Chronica Majora (mạ.jō'rạ). A prose chronicle in Latin by Matthew Paris, covering events from the creation of the world to the year 1259. Down to 1235 it is a modified transcription of an earlier work, entitled *Flores Historiarum*, begun by John de Cella and completed by Roger of Wendover; from 1235 to 1259 it was compiled exclusively from original sources.

chronicle. A historical record or recounting of events or personages (chronicles in Latin were particularly common in England in the period after the Norman Conquest). These works, often compiled at monasteries, generally covered the time from the Anglo-Saxon period, or sometimes even from the Creation, until the writer's own day. In addition to historical events, a chronicle might include poems, legends, and details of daily life. The works of such men as Geoffrey of Monmouth and William of Malmesbury are examples of 12th-century chronicles. See also **Anglo-Saxon Chronicle.**

Chronicle of England. A prose work by John Capgrave, unfinished at the author's death in 1464. It begins with the Creation and concludes at the year 1417.

Chronicle of Scotland. See **Original Chronicle of Scotland, The.**

Chronicles of Barsetshire (bär′sęt.shir), **The.** See **Barsetshire.**

Chronicles of England, Scotland, and Ireland, The. [Called **Holinshed's Chronicles.**] A prose historical work (published 1577, in two folio volumes, and a second edition in three volumes in 1587) by Raphael Holinshed, with the assistance of William Harrison, Richard Stanyhurst, Edward Campion and others. The tremendous literary importance of the work is due partly to the fact that Shakespeare drew much from it for his *Cymbeline, Richard II, Richard III,* and all his *Henry* (IV, V, VI, VIII) plays.

Chronicles of the Canongate (kan′ọn.gāt). A collection of stories by Sir Walter Scott. The first series, published in 1827, includes *The Highland Widow, The Two Drovers,* and *The Surgeon's Daughter.* The second series, published in 1828, consists primarily of *The Fair Maid of Perth,* but also includes *Aunt Margaret's Mirror.* The tales are supposed to be narrated by Mr. Chrystal Croftangry, to whom they are told by Mrs. Bethune Baliol.

Chronicles of the House of Borgia. A prose historical work (1901) by a contributor to *The Yellow Book,* an English novelist, musician, and photographer with the cumbersome name of Frederick William Serafino Austin Lewis Mary Rolfe (who, it is not surprising to learn, preferred to be called "Baron Corvo"). The *Chronicles,* a remarkable combination of scholarship, fantasy, and tricks of style, is considered one of Rolfe's best works, although he is perhaps better remembered for his autobiographical romance *Hadrian the Seventh* (1904).

Chronicles of the Schönberg-Cotta Family (shĕn′-bĕrk.kot′ạ). A historical novel by Elizabeth Charles, published in 1863.

Chronicon ex Chronicis (kron′i.kon eks kron′i.sis). A Latin prose work by Florence of Worcester.

Chrononhotonthologos (krō.non″hō.ton.thol′ọ.gos). A burlesque by Henry Carey, "the most tragical tragedy ever yet tragedized," first performed in 1734. It was imitated to some degree from Henry Fielding's play *Tom Thumb.* Chrononhotonthologos is the King of Queerummania. His name is occasionally used as a nickname for any particularly bombastic and inflated talker.

Chrysal, or the Adventures of a Guinea (kris′ạl). A novel by Charles Johnstone, published serially in 1760–65. Chrysal is an elementary spirit whose abode is in a piece of gold converted into a guinea. In that form the spirit passes from man to man, and takes accurate note of the different scenes of which it becomes a witness. It describes the famous Hellfire Club, a notorious club which met at Medmenham Abbey under the slogan *Fay ce que voudras* ("Do what you will"), taken from Rabelais, and to which a number of the leading political figures of the day, such as John Wilkes, belonged.

Chrysaor (krī.sā′ôr, kris′ạ.ôr). In classical mythology, a son of Poseidon and Medusa, and father (by Callirrhoe) of the three-headed Geryon and Echidna. He sprang forth from the head of Medusa when Perseus cut it off.

Chrysaor. The sword of Sir Artegall, in Edmund Spenser's *Faerie Queene.* It represents justice.

Chryseis (krī.sē′is). In Homeric legend, Astynome, the daughter of Chryses, seized as a slave by Agamemnon. When the king refused to give her up, Chryses prayed to Apollo for vengeance, and the god sent a plague upon the camp of the Greeks, which was not stayed until the maiden was taken back to her father by Odysseus.

Chryses (krī′sēz). In Homeric legend, a priest of Apollo at Comana (Chryse), in Asia Minor; father of Chryseis.

Chrystal Croftangry (kris′tạl krôf′tang.gri). See **Croftangry, Chrystal.**

Chubb (chub), **Thomas.** b. at East Harnham, near Salisbury, England, Sept. 29, 1679; d. at Salisbury, England, Feb. 8, 1746. An English deist and religious writer.

Chucks (chuks), **Mr.** In Frederick Marryat's novel *Peter Simple,* a boatswain who longs to be a gentleman. His desire is fulfilled at the end of the story, when he is revealed to be really Count Shucksen.

Chuffey (chuf′i). The superannuated clerk who saves the life of old Anthony Chuzzlewit in Charles Dickens's *Martin Chuzzlewit.*

Church (chėrch), **Richard.** b. at London, March 26, 1893—. An English poet, novelist, and critic. His published verse includes *Flood of Life* (1917), *Hurricane* (1919), *Philip* (1923), *The Dream* (1927), *Twelve Noon* (1936), *The Solitary Man* (1941), and *The Lamp* (1946). Among his prose works are *Mary Shelley* (1928), *Oliver's Daughter* (1930), *The Prodigal Father* (1933), *The Porch* (1937), *The Stronghold* (1939), *Calling for a Spade* (1939), *Plato's Mistake* (1941), *The Sampler* (1942), and *Kent* (1948).

Church, Richard William. b. at Lisbon, Portugal, April 25, 1815; d. at Dover, England, Dec. 9, 1890. An English clergyman and writer, dean of Saint Paul's in the period 1871–90. He lived at Florence (1818–28), was graduated from Oxford in 1836, was a fellow of Oriel College (1838–52), was ordained a priest in 1852, and received the living of Whatley in Somerset in the same year. While a student at Oxford, he became a friend of Newman. During his subsequent career, he was a leader in the High Church movement. He was select preacher at Oxford in 1868 and in the periods 1876–78 and 1881–82. He wrote *Anselm* (1843: enlarged, 1870), *Dante* (1850), *Spenser* (1879), *Bacon* (1884), *A History of the Oxford Movement* (1891), and others.

ḏ, d or j; ṣ, s or sh; ṭ, t or ch; ẓ, z or zh; o, F. cloche; ü, F. menu; ċh, Sc. loch; ṅ, F. bonbon

Churches Quarrel Espoused, The. A polemical writing by John Wise, published in 1710.

Church History of Britain, The. A prose work (1655) by Thomas Fuller. A huge work, a folio volume of 1300 pages, it is an attempt to continue the work of Bede.

Churchill (chèrch'il), **Charles.** b. in Vine Street, at Westminster, London, in February, 1731; d. of fever at Boulogne, France, Nov. 4, 1764. English satirical poet, clergyman, teacher, and friend of John Wilkes. He was educated (1739–48) at Westminster School, London, but did not go to Christ Church, Oxford, or to Trinity College, Cambridge, as most Westminster boys did. He became a clergyman in 1756, and held curacies in Somersetshire, at Rainham, in Essex, and at Westminster (1758–63), as his father (also Charles) had done before him. At 17, he made an unwise marriage with a Westminster girl, named Scot, from whom he separated in 1761. He made a poor living by opening a school at Rainham, or Westminster, and taught in a girls' school kept by a Mrs. Dennis. He loved John Wilkes, hated all enemies of Wilkes, and detested Alexander Pope. He was generous in many ways, was free with his money, when he had it, and helped those whose need was greater than his. He left an annuity of 60 pounds to his wife, and of 50 pounds to his mistress, but did not leave any property to cover the annuities. Johnson thought him "a shallow fellow." but Byron visited his grave before his last departure from England, and wrote a poem on the occasion. His works are *The Rosciad* (1761), in which he bitterly satirizes practically every leading actor of the day, with the exception of Mrs. Cibber, Mrs. Clive, Mrs. Pritchard, and Garrick, *The Apology: Addressed to the Critical Reviewers* (1761), in which he attacked Smollett and warned Garrick, whom he had praised in the *Rosciad*, to be careful, *The Ghost* (1763), ridiculing Johnson for his investigation of the Cock Lane Ghost mystery, *The Prophecy of Famine: a Scots Pastoral* (1763), a satire on Bute, *The Duellist* (1763), defending Wilkes, who was wounded in a duel with Samuel Martin, and attacking all who opposed Wilkes, *The Author* (1763), another attack on Smollett, *Gotham* (1764), a political philosophy in verse in three books, and *The Candidate* (1764), attacking Lord Sandwich, who is satirized as Jemmy Twitcher, a character in Gay's *Beggar's Opera*. A minor work, a verse epistle to his friend Robert Lloyd, entitled *Night* (1762), is an attack on the *Day* of John Armstrong. *Independence* (September, 1764) has a special interest in that it gives us a portrait of the author as he saw himself. In a short writing life, Churchill produced a considerable amount of material, but his reputation rests largely on *The Rosciad*, which ranks with Pope's *Dunciad* and Byron's *English Bards and Scotch Reviewers*, on *The Duellist*, which brought him 450 pounds, a large sum in his time, and on *Gotham*, which was enthusiastically praised by Cowper (born in the same year as Churchill), who remembered him, 17 years after his death, as "the great Churchill."

Churchill, Frank. A handsome, lively young man in the novel *Emma* by Jane Austen. Emma picks him out as a very suitable match for her protégée, Harriet Smith, only to find that he is already secretly engaged to Jane Fairfax.

Churchill, Sir Winston. [Full name: **Winston Leonard Spencer Churchill.**] b. at Blenheim Palace, Oxfordshire, England, Nov. 30, 1874—. An English statesman, prime minister (1940–45) during World War II and again in 1951, journalist and author, originator or popularizer of slogans and phrases like "blood, toil, tears and sweat" and the "V for victory" finger gesture; a descendant of John Churchill, 1st Duke of Marlborough, and son of Randolph Henry Spencer Churchill and the American Jennie Jerome.

Early Years. Churchill was educated at Harrow and was a cavalry cadet at the Royal Military College at Sandhurst. He entered the army, took leave to fight on the side of the Spanish forces in Cuba in 1895, fought in India (1897) and in the Sudan (1898), where he was decorated for services at the battle of Khartoum. In 1899 he was sent to South Africa to cover the Boer War as correspondent for the London *Morning Post*. He was captured there by Louis Botha but escaped after a month's imprisonment and thereafter participated actively in the military campaigns. In 1900 he was elected a Conservative member of Parliament, then joined the Liberal Party and served (1905–08) as undersecretary for the colonies under Henry Campbell-Bannerman, promoting the establishment of self-government in the Transvaal and Orange River Colony in South Africa. He was a member of the Asquith cabinet as president of the board of trade (1908–10) and home secretary (1910–11). In 1911 he became first lord of the admiralty, to carry out Asquith's program of readying the fleet for possible international conflict. He drove forward the building program, established a naval war staff (thereby creating an upheaval in settled English naval customs) to coöperate with the war office on strategy.

World War I. When war came in 1914, the Royal Navy was so well prepared that it was able at once to confine the German fleet, except for submarines and a few raiders, to its own home ports (the Battle of Jutland was the only instance in World War I when a major German naval force ventured within reach of the Royal Navy, and although this battle can hardly be said to have resulted in a clear-cut British victory on the pattern of Trafalgar, it did serve to convince the German naval staff of the inadvisability of an all-out test of strength between the two fleets. For this reason, the bulk of the German surface navy was thereafter held close to the German coast, and was thus unable to play a decisive part in the war. It was this, among other factors, which led the Germans more and more into a reliance upon the submarine as their major weapon on the high seas.) It was under Churchill's ministry also that the Royal Air Force (originally the Royal Flying Corps) was established. He directed the naval campaign against Antwerp and espoused the Dardanelles (Gallipoli) campaign. When the latter failed dismally, Churchill resigned (1915) and was succeeded by Arthur James Balfour. In 1916 he was a lieutenant-colonel on active service in France, but resigned his commission to accept the post of minister of munitions in the Lloyd George cabinet. He was (1918–21) secretary of state for war and for air, during which time occurred the clash with Lloyd George over Churchill's use of British troops in an attempt to put down the new Bolshevist regime in Russia. When the opportunity came to appoint a new chancellor of the exchequer, Lloyd George appointed Sir Robert Horne instead of Churchill, who was expected to get the appointment. Churchill was secretary of state for the colonies in 1921–22. In 1924 he was elected to Parliament from Epping, which he represented until 1945. In the second Baldwin cabinet he was (1924–29) chancellor of the exchequer. From 1929 to 1939, he held no cabinet posts but increasingly made it clear that he expected another war to occur, and that he considered his country to be taking woefully few measures to prepare for it. He fought the Neville Chamberlain policy of appeasement of Germany, and, on the outbreak of war in September, 1939, he was given the post of first lord of the admiralty in response to a general desire to see Churchill in the cabinet.

World War II. After the complete failure of British arms in Norway, the Chamberlain government fell and on May 10, 1940, Churchill became prime minister. In his first speech following his appointment, he said he had nothing to offer but "blood, toil, tears and sweat" to the English. In August, 1941, he met at sea off Newfoundland with President Franklin Roosevelt and together they issued the statement of international policy known as the Atlantic Charter. This was followed by numerous conferences on strategy, war aims, conciliation, and planning with the heads of the countries fighting Germany and Japan: at Washington in 1942 and 1943 with Roosevelt; at Moscow in 1942 and 1944 with Stalin; at Casablanca, Morocco, in 1943, when Churchill and Roosevelt agreed that only the unconditional surrender of Germany would be acceptable as an end to the war; at Quebec, Canada, in 1943 and 1944; at Cairo in 1943 with Chiang Kai-shek and Roosevelt, and at Tehran, Iran, the following month with Stalin and Roosevelt; at Yalta in the Crimea in 1945 with Stalin and Roosevelt; at Potsdam, Berlin, Germany, in 1945 with Stalin and President Truman, Churchill himself being replaced during the conference by the new prime minister, Clement Attlee. Churchill had, after the German defeat, removed from the cabinet its Labour members and thus enabled a general election. In July, 1945, the Conservatives were defeated and Clement Attlee became prime minister.

Later Years. Churchill now became leader of the opposition in Parliament. In 1946, in a speech at Westminster College in Fulton, Mo., he denounced Russian aggrandizement and asked for strong ties to bind the U. S. and Great Britain closely, describing the borders of Russian-held territory as being an "iron curtain." In February, 1950, his Conservative Party came very close to beating the Labour Party in a general election, and in October, 1951, it succeeded in ousting the Labour Party, Churchill again becoming prime minister. He was a constant supporter of the idea of a federal union of Western European states as a preventive measure against further wars. Churchill has several times refused to be elevated to the peerage, but was made a Knight of the Garter in 1953. Among

his books are *Life of Lord Randolph Churchill* (1906), *My African Journey* (1908), *Liberalism and the Social Problem* (1909), a four-volume history of World War I, *The World Crisis* (1923–29; abridged and revised in one volume, 1931), *My Early Life* (1930), *Marlborough, his Life and Times* (4 volumes, 1933–38), and *The Second World War*, a six-volume series on World War II, comprising *The Gathering Storm* (Vol. I; 1948), *Their Finest Hour* (Vol. II; 1949), *The Grand Alliance* (Vol. III; 1950), *The Hinge of Fate* (Vol. IV; 1950), *Closing the Ring* (Vol. V; 1952), and *Triumph and Tragedy* (Vol. VI; 1954). His recent work includes a book of his speeches in 1951 and 1952, *Stemming The Tide* (1954), and in 1955 he announced that he has in preparation a multi-volume work, *A History of the English Speaking Peoples*. See *Churchill, By His Contemporaries* (1954), edited by Charles Eade, and *A Churchill Reader* (1954), edited by Colin R. Coote with P. D. Bunyan

Church of England. [Sometimes also called the **Anglican Church.**] The established church of England. Its titular head is the king (or queen) of England, and it is guided in all major ecclesiastical matters by two archbishops (the archbishop of Canterbury, who is the "Primate of All England," and the archbishop of York, who is the "Primate of England") and by 31 bishops. Canterbury, alone, has the power to crown the monarch. The bishops have the power to ordain, to confirm, to dedicate churches, and to consecrate their fellow bishops. The lower orders of the church consist of deacons and priests. The creeds employed are the Apostles' Creed (c200), the Nicene (325), and the Athanasian (c420–430). Its doctrines are expressed in the Book of Common Prayer, the Thirty-Nine Articles, the Catechism, and the Books of Homilies. Divisions of thought and practice within the church are represented by the High Church party, which emphasizes ritual observances, the Low Church, or Evangelical party, which advocates simplicity, and the Broad Church party, which attempts to steer a path between these two extremes. Points on which all branches agree are justification by faith, predestination, and original sin. About 70 percent of the church-going population in England belongs to the established church, but less than 4 percent in Scotland, which favors Presbyterianism. The position of the monarch as head of the Church of England goes back to the time of Henry VIII.

Churchyard (chẽrch′yärd), **Thomas.** b. at Shrewsbury, England, c1520; d. at London, April 4, 1604. An English poet, page to Henry Howard, Earl of Surrey, vagrant, hanger-on at court, and soldier. Between 1560 and 1603 he wrote a considerable amount of prose and poetry, much of it of autobiographical interest and referring to current happenings. Some of his works are *The Worthines of Wales* (1587), a long historical poem, *Shore's Wife*, a tragedy (in the 1563 enlarged edition of *A Mirror for Magistrates*), the story of Cardinal Wolsey (in the 1587 edition of the same work) and a volume of prose and poetry, *Churchyard's Challenge* (1593). As a soldier he saw service in Scotland, France, Ireland, and the Low Countries, and he drew on his own military experience in *Wofull Warres in Flaunders* (1578) and *General Rehearsal* (1579).

ḍ, d orj; ş, s or sh; ţ, t or ch; ẓ, z or zh; o, F. cloche; ü, F. menu; ċh, Sc. loch; ṅ, F. bonbon.

Specimens of his verse are to be found in volumes with such curious titles as *Churchyard's Chips, Churchyard's Chance, Churchyard's Charge,* and *Churchyard's Good Will,* and he is represented in the famous Elizabethan anthologies *Tottel's Miscellany,* the *Paradise of Dainty Devices,* and a *Gorgeous Gallery of Gallant Inventions.* In Spenser's *Colin Clout's Come Home Again* Churchyard is Old Palemon "that sang so long until quite hoarse he grew." He wrote to the very end of his long life, which included the reigns of Henry VIII, Edward VI, Mary, Elizabeth, and James I, and in his last years he dedicated *The Wonders of the Ayre, the Trembling of the Earth, and the Warnings of the World Before the Judgement Day* (1602) to a new patron, Dr. (later Sir) Julius Caesar, expressing gratitude to him "for the little that I live upon and am likely to die withall." He was buried in Saint Margaret's Church at Westminster, London.

Chuzzlewit (chuz'l.wit), **Anthony.** The shrewd and cunning father of Jonas, in Charles Dickens's *Martin Chuzzlewit.*

Chuzzlewit, Jonas. An unscrupulous, selfish, and overreaching fellow, the cousin of Martin and son of Anthony Chuzzlewit, in Charles Dickens's *Martin Chuzzlewit.* His slyness, selfish ignorance, and brutality finally culminate in murder.

Chuzzlewit, Martin. The grandfather of Martin Chuzzlewit, in Charles Dickens's novel of that name.

Chuzzlewit, Martin. A young architect, the principal character in Charles Dickens's novel of that name. At first dissipated, he is reformed by dint of many hard knocks from fortune, especially in his dreary American adventures with Mark Tapley in search of wealth, and eventually becomes the heir of his rich grandfather. (The section of the book dealing with Martin's travels in the U. S., from his arrival at New York and subsequent emigration to a settlement on the frontier, clearly reveals Dickens's distaste for certain aspects of 19th-century American culture, and led at the time of its first publication to a tremendous amount of resentment among his readers in the U. S.)

Cibber (sib'ẽr), **Colley.** b. at London, Nov. 6, 1671; d. there, Dec. 12, 1757. An English comic actor, dramatist, and theater manager. He was the son of Caius Gabriel Cibber (or Cibert, 1630–1700), a sculptor who was born in Flensborg, Holstein, and he was the father of Theophilus Cibber, like himself an actor and a dramatist. He was educated in Lincolnshire, at the Grantham Free School. He began his stage career about 1690, as a member of Betterton's company, and in 1691 he was acting minor roles in the London Theatre Royal. He was attacked, on grounds of immorality and indecency, by Jeremy Collier, in his famous *Short View of the Immorality and Profaneness of the English Stage,* and, on literary and artistic grounds, by Fielding. From 1711–32, he was, with Wilks and Doggett, one of the managers of London's famous Drury Lane Theatre. In 1730, he was made poet laureate, an appointment that was severely attacked by his fellow writers, Pope in the *Dunciad* (where he is enthroned as King of Dullness), being only one of many who belittle him. Cibber was an inferior poet, probably one of the worst to hold the office, and he frankly admitted that the post was given to him as a reward for being a good Whig. He made his first stage success in 1692 as the Chaplain in Otway's tragedy *The Orphan,* and his last, on Feb. 15, 1745, as Pandulph in his own *Papal Tyranny in the Reign of King John,* a "wretched version" of Shakespeare's *King John.* As an actor he was at his best in eccentric parts, but he failed as a tragedian, being more than once hissed off the stage. Some of the roles associated with him are Don Manuel in his own *She Would and She Would Not* (1702), the title role in Crowne's *Sir Courtly Nice* (1703), Sir Fopling Flutter in *The Man of Mode* (1706) of Etherege, Ben in Congreve's *Love for Love* (1708), Gloucester in his own version of *King Lear,* Iago in *Othello,* Sparkish in Wycherley's *Country Wife,* Fondlewife in Congreve's *Old Bachelor,* Tinsel in Addison's *The Drummer* (1716), Barnaby Brittle in *The Amorous Widow* of Betterton, Bayes in *The Rehearsal,* Shallow in Betterton's version of *Henry IV,* Jaques in *Love in a Forest,* an alteration of *As You Like It,* Dr. Wolf in his own play *The Non-juror* (1717), Wolsey in *Henry VIII,* and Lord Richly in *The Modern Husband* of Fielding (1732). Perhaps his most successful role was that of Sir Novelty Fashion, newly created Lord Foppington, in Vanbrugh's *The Relapse, or Virtue in Danger* (1696), which was a sequel to Cibber's own *Love's Last Shift, or the Fool in Fashion* (1696). Some of the many plays he wrote, either original or adaptations of other works, English or Continental, are *Woman's Wit: or, The Lady in Fashion* (1697); *Xerxes* (1699), a tragedy whose first performance, at Lincoln's Inn Fields, was its last; his version of *Richard III* (produced 1699), which still holds the stage today; *Love Makes the Man, or the Fop's Fortune* (1700, a combination of two plays, *The Custom of the Country* and *The Elder Brother,* by Beaumont and Fletcher); *The Careless Husband* (1704), a comedy of intrigue; *Perolla and Izadora* (1705), a tragedy; *The Comical Lovers* (1707), combining two plays by Dryden; *The Double Gallant: or, The Sick Lady's Cure* (1707), a comedy; *The Rival Fools* (1709), altered from Beaumont and Fletcher; *Venus and Adonis* (1715), a masque; *Ximena, or the Heroick Daughter* (1712), a tragedy based partly on the *Cid;* also *The Refusal; or, The Ladies' Philosophy* (1721), from *Les Femmes savantes* of Molière; *Caesar in Egypt* (1724) (based on *The False One* of Beaumont and Fletcher and a French play, *The Death of Pompey,* by Corneille); *The Provok'd Husband; or, A Journey to London* (1728), a completed version of Sir John Vanbrugh's unfinished comedy, *A Journey to London* (in which Cibber appeared as Sir Francis Wronghead, a country gentleman, who is called Headpiece in Vanbrugh's fragment), *The Rival Queans, with the Humours of Alexander the Great* (produced 1710, printed 1729), a comical tragedy, *Love in a Riddle* (1729, 1719 being a printer's error), a pastoral that was met with hisses, an imitation of Gay's *Beggar's Opera,* and *Damon and Phillida* (1729), a ballad opera which was simply *Love in a Riddle* in a converted form and which was immediately successful and for a long time after. He wrote his autobiography, called *Apology for the Life of Mr. Colley Cibber, Comedian* (1740), which is valuable for its comments on the Restoration and early

18th-century theater. Its modest self-confidence aroused Fielding to attack it in his burlesque, *Tom Thumb the Great.*

Cibber, Susannah Maria. [Maiden name, **Arne.**] b. at London, in February, 1714; d. at Westminster, London, Jan. 30, 1766. An English actress and singer; wife of Theophilus Cibber and sister of Thomas Arne. Her first appearance was at the Haymarket in 1732, in the opera *Amelia* by Lumpé, and her reputation was for several years chiefly founded upon her singing. Handel wrote leading parts for her in some of his oratorios. In 1736 she made her debut as a tragic actress in the part of Zara, in Hill's version of Voltaire's *Zaïre,* and rapidly became famous.

Cibber, Theophilus. b. Nov. 26, 1703; perished in a shipwreck in the Irish Channel, in October, 1758. An English actor and dramatist; son of Colley Cibber and husband of Susannah Maria Cibber. He wrote *The Lover* (1730, a comedy), *Patie and Peggy, or the Fair Foundling* (1730, a ballad opera), *The Harlot's Progress, or the Ridotto al' Fresco* (1733, a pantomime), *The Auction* (1757, a farce), and others. He also published an alteration of Shakespeare's *Henry VI.* His wife abandoned him a few years after their marriage; Cibber was said to be a man of unsavory reputation.

Cicely Homespun (sis'ẹ.li hōm'spun). See **Homespun, Zekiel** and **Cicely.**

Cicero (sis'ẹ.rō). In Shakespeare's *Julius Caesar,* a Roman senator, who is not asked to join the conspiracy.

Cicero, Marcus Tullius. [Formerly called **Tully.**] b. at Arpinum (now Arpino), Italy, Jan. 3, 106 B.C.; assassinated near Formiae (now Formia), Italy, Dec. 7, 43 B.C. A Roman orator, philosopher, and statesman; brother of Quintus Tullius Cicero. He served in the Social War in 89, traveled in Greece and Asia in the period 79–77, and was quaestor in Sicily in 75. On behalf of the Sicilians, he accused (70) Verres, who had been propraetor in Sicily, of criminal extortions; his orations were so effective that Verres left Rome and was found guilty in his absence. Cicero was aedile in 69, served as praetor in 66, and as consul suppressed Catiline's conspiracy to kill the consuls in 63. Cicero was banished in 58 for his action in killing members of Catiline's group, living in Thessalonica, but was recalled by Pompey in 57. He was proconsul of Cilicia in the period 51–50, and joined Pompey against Caesar in 49. He lived at Brundisium from September, 48, to September, 47, having been pardoned and received by Caesar. After the slaying of Caesar in 44, Cicero pronounced the Philippics in 44 and 43 against Antony, whom he detested, for which he was proscribed by the Second Triumvirate (Octavian, Antony, Lepidus) and slain in 43. Of his orations 57 are extant (with fragments of 20 more), including *Against Verres* (*In Verrem;* six speeches, 70 B.C., five of which were never delivered), *Against Catiline* (*In Catilinam;* four speeches, 63 B.C.), *For Archias* (*Pro Archia;* 62 B.C.), *Against Piso* (*In Pisonem;* 55 B.C.), *For Milo* (*Pro Milone;* 52 B.C.), *For Marcellus* (*Pro Marcello;* 46 B.C.), and the *Philippics* (*Philippicae;* 14 speeches, 44–43 B.C.). His other works include books on rhetoric and oratory, *On the Republic*

(*De republica;* 51 B.C.), *On Law* (*De legibus;* c52 B.C.), *On the Ends of Good and Evil* (*De finibus bonorum et malorum*), *Tusculan Disputations* (*Tusculanae disputationes*), *On the Nature of the Gods* (*De natura deorum*), *Cato major* (also known as *De senectute,* On Old Age), *On Divination* (*De divinatione*), *Laelius* (also known as *De amicitia,* On Friendship), and *On Duty* (*De officiis*). There are, besides, four collections of his letters. He also wrote poetry, including an epic on Marius. Cicero is known as a supreme master of Latin, and imitation of his work and emulation of his style have been the aim of Latin scholars since the Renaissance.

Ciceronian (sis.e.rō'ni.ạn). Pertaining to or characteristic of Cicero (Marcus Tullius Cicero), the Roman orator, or his orations and writings.

> As for his [Maimbourg's] style, it is rather Ciceronian—copious, florid, and figurative—than succinct.   (Dryden, *Post. to Hist. of League.*)

> His delivery of the commonest matters of fact was Ciceronian.   (Lamb, *My First Play.*)

Cid (sid; Spanish, thēᴛн), **the.** [Called **El Cid Campeador,** meaning "The Lord Champion"; original name, **Rodrigo** (or **Ruy**) **Díaz de Bivar;** Arabic, **Seyyid.**] b. at the castle of Bivar, near Burgos, Spain, c1040; d. at Valencia, Spain, July, 1099. The principal national hero of Spain, famous for his exploits in the wars with the Moors. He first achieved renown while fighting on the side of Sancho II of Castile in the battles against Sancho IV of Navarre; siding with Sancho also in the conflict with Alfonso VI (Alfonso el Bravo), he was exiled by the latter and became a soldier of fortune, serving often on the side of the Moors. He conquered Valencia in 1094 and ruled the city for the rest of his life. His death occurred as the result of a successful attack by the Moslem dynasty of the Almoravides. He had married Ximena, daughter of the count of Oviedo, and she attempted to carry on his rule. His glamorous life became a source of many legends almost at once and the 12th-century epic poems *Cantar de mío Cid* (*Song of the Cid*) and the *Crónica Rimada* (*Rhymed Chronicle of the Cid*) attribute to him deeds and actions of purely legendary origin. These works remained such great sources of literary and popular inspiration that they served as a basis not only for countless historical ballads, but for further Spanish poems, popular translations such as John Gibson Lockhart's "The Young Cid" in his *Ancient Spanish Ballads, Historical and Romantic* (1823), also for Corneille's tragedy *Le Cid* (1637) and an opera (1885) by Jules Massenet.

Cid Hamet Benengeli (sid hä.met' ben.en.gä'lē; Spanish, thēᴛн ä.mät' bä.nen.нä'lē). An imaginary chronicler from whom Miguel de Cervantes said he received his account of Don Quixote.

Cimabue (chē.mä.bö'ä), **Giovanni.** [Original name, **Cenni di Pepo.**] b. at Florence, c1240; d. there, c1302. A noted Italian painter, sometimes called the "Father of Modern Painting." He is mentioned as a forerunner of Giotto by Dante, who thereby gives occasion to his own anonymous commentator, writing in 1334, to make some remarks upon Cimabue's fame and ambition, which remarks were later quoted by Giorgio Vasari. Cimabue practiced painting on wall-panels and mosaics. The works accredited to him by Vasari consist of: (*a*) Several large Madonnas on panels with gold grounds. The most celebrated is that in the chapel of the Rucellai family in Santa Maria Novella at Florence. There is another in the Louvre, and another in the Accademia delle Belle Arti at Florence. They are effective in their mild solemnity and simple color, which is lively and clear in the flesh-tints. (*b*) Frescoes in the Church of San Francesco d'Assisi, quite similar to the panels, but slighter and more decorative. (*c*) Mosaics in the apse of the cathedral of Pisa, the only work well authenticated as his by original documents, and probably his last. Cimabue is generally considered the first modern European painter because in his work for the first time the Byzantine forms take on what are now usually classified as a characteristically European expression. Dante's naming of him as Giotto's teacher probably gave rise to the story, related by Vasari but without any historical foundation, of Cimabue's coming upon the young Giotto drawing a sheep on a rock and, recognizing the boy's talent, taking him as a pupil.

Cimber (sim'bėr), **Metellus.** In Shakespeare's *Julius Caesar*, one of the conspirators. His suit to Caesar (to recall his brother, Publius, from banishment) is the pretext for the gathering of the conspirators around Caesar to assassinate him.

Cimberton (sim'bėr.ton). A pedantic fortune-hunter in Steele's *The Conscious Lovers.*

Cimmerians (si.mir'i.anz, ki-). [Older variant names: **Gimir, Kimmerians.**] Early inhabitants of the N shore of the Black Sea, between the Danube and Don rivers. The Cimmerians were forced into Asia Minor by Scythian pressure during the 8th century B.C. Gradually moving west, they came into conflict with the Vannic kingdom (Urartu), the Assyrians, and the Phrygians. They disappeared from history after defeat by the Lydians in the 7th century B.C. These people are mentioned in Homer. Herodotus speaks of "Cimmerian cities," and says that the strait which unites the Azov Sea and the Black Sea was called the Cimmerian Bosporus. In the Old Testament they are mentioned by the name of Gomer. Gen. x. 2.

Cincinnatus (sin.si.nā'tus, -nat'us), **Lucius Quinctius** or **Titus Quinctius.** b. c519 B.C.; fl. 1st half of the 5th century B.C. A Roman legendary hero. He was consul suffectus in 460, and distinguished himself as an opponent of the plebeians in the struggle between them and the patricians in the period 462–454. In 458 a Roman army under Lucius Minucius having been surrounded by the Aequians in a defile of Mount Algidus, he was named dictator by the senate, whose deputies, dispatched to inform him of his appointment, found him digging in the field on his farm beyond the Tiber. He gained a complete victory over the Aequians, and laid down the dictatorship after the lapse of only 16 days, returning to his farm. In 439, at the age of 80, he was appointed dictator to oppose the traitor Spurius Melius, who was defeated and slain. The details of his story vary; the story of the first dictatorship is probably legendary embellishment on a factual basis; that of the second dictatorship is probably wholly false.

Cinderella (sin.dė.rel'a). The title and heroine of the most famous, and probably most widespread, of all folk tales. Cinderella is the beautiful, mistreated little girl who serves as a household drudge to her ugly stepmother and two ugly stepsisters (whose jealousy of her beauty provides a very usual element of the story). According to the best-known version of the tale, the prince of the country falls in love with her at a ball which she attends dressed by her fairy godmother in magic finery which will vanish at midnight. Fleeing from the palace as the clock strikes midnight, she loses one tiny glass slipper, by means of which, as it would fit no one else, the prince finds and marries her. In some versions she is aided by a kindly animal or her own dead mother, instead of the fairy godmother, and her slipper is caught, as she runs from the palace (usually on the third night) by pitch spread, by order of the prince, on the staircase. The story is of very ancient, probably Eastern, origin; some 500 versions in Europe alone have been examined; and it is known and told from Alaska to Indonesia, South America, and South Africa. There is a 9th-century Chinese version. It was told in Egypt of Rhodopis and Psammetichus. In France, Perrault and Madame d'Aulnoy include it in their *Fairy Tales* as "Cendrillon" and "Finette Cendroi"; the brothers Grimm give it in their *Household Tales* as "Aschenbrödel" or "Aschenputtel." There has been some debate as to whether the famous slipper (in the French versions) was of *verre* (glass) or of *vair* (fur), but the detail is of no actual importance to the story and discussion has now been virtually abandoned. The basic human motif underlying the story is that of sudden and very great success, against odds, and the justification of the lowly, despised, and mistreated central character, with whom the hearer or reader identifies himself. This doubtless not only accounts for its popularity and tenacity throughout the world, but also for the fact that it has been used to provide a theme for countless ostensibly "new" stories and plays by professional writers in virtually every one of the world's literatures.

Cinna (sin'a). In Shakespeare's *Julius Caesar*, the historical Gaius Helvius Cinna, a poet. He is mistaken for the other Cinna and is mobbed and murdered.

Cinna. In Shakespeare's *Julius Caesar*, the historical Lucius Cornelius Cinna (the younger), one of the conspirators against Caesar. He plants tracts so that Brutus will find them and join in the conspiracy.

cinque-pace (singk'pās, -ę.pās). See **galliard.**

Cinque Ports (singk). [Eng. trans., "*Five Ports.*"] A collective name for the five English channel ports: Hastings, New Romney, Hythe, Dover, and Sandwich. Winchelsea and Rye were added later. They furnished the chief naval contingent until the time of Henry VII and in return received certain privileges. For all practical purposes, their special privileges have now been abolished, but they are still governed, technically, by a lord warden, who is admiral of the ports and governor of Dover Castle. Of them all, only Dover still remains a seaport (the English coast has moved far enough E and S to make the others now inland towns).

---

fat, fāte, fär, åsk, fāre; net, mē, hėr; pin, pīne; not, nōte, mȯve, nôr; up, lūte, pull; ᴛʜ, then;

Cinthio or Cintio (chēn'tsyō). See **Giraldi, Giovanni Battista.**

Circassians (sēr.kash'ạnz). [Also: **Adyge, Cherkess.**] A people of the Caucasus region of SE Europe, living now in the region between the Caucasus Mountains, the Kuban River, and the Black Sea in the Russian Soviet Federated Socialist Republic (RSFSR), or in Turkey; their principal city is Maikop. Circassian society, based on a pastoral and agricultural culture, was divided into three classes (princes, nobles, and peasants), but in the councils of the tribe any freeman (prisoners of war were often bond servants or slaves) was entitled to speak and the rulers acted through delegated powers. The blood feud existed and the clan organization of the people permitted open warfare between family groups. Professedly Moslem since the 17th century, the Circassians observed a religion in which earlier Christian observances and a still earlier polytheism were apparent. Circassian women, noted for their beauty, were much in demand for harems. Following the cession of their territory by the Turks to the Russians in the treaty of Adrianople (1829), the Circassians offered severe resistance to Russian conquest and many of them fled to Turkey rather than submit to Russian rule.

Circe (sēr'sē). In Greek mythology, an enchantress, and magician, daughter of Helios, on the island of Aeaea. Circe was the aunt of Medea, with whom she shares the distinction of being one of the two great witches of Greek legend. Odysseus and his crew came in their wanderings to her home. She metamorphosed some of the hero's companions into swine. Odysseus resisted her magic but was induced to remain a year with her. Before she would let him depart she sent him to the lower world to consult the seer Tiresias about his voyage home.

Circumlocution Office. The name by which Charles Dickens in *Little Dorrit* (1857) satirizes the red tape of the public-office system in England. The expression has become almost proverbial.

Cirrha (sir'ạ). In ancient geography, the seaport of Crisa (with which it is often confused) in Phocis, Greece. It was destroyed (c575 B.C.) in the first Sacred War, on account of sacrilege in interfering with pilgrims to Delphi.

Cistercians (sis.tēr'shạnz). A monastic order in the Roman Catholic Church.

Citadel, The. A novel by A. J. Cronin, published in 1937.

Citizen, The. A farce (1761) by Arthur Murphy.

Citizen of the World, The. [Full original title, **Letters from a Chinese Philosopher Residing in London to his Friends in the East.**] A series of essays by Oliver Goldsmith, published in 1762 (under the full title shown above; the title now generally used, *The Citizen of the World*, was in this first edition simply the signature over which Goldsmith chose to write). A Chinese philosopher who resides in London writes home describing the life and manners of the English. The author presents the idea that man should have interest in and allegiance to the world, but should not deny a national allegiance.

City, the. See **London, City of.**

City Heiress, The. [Full title, **The City Heiress: or, Sir Timothy Treat-all.**] A play by Aphra Behn, adapted from Middleton's *A Mad World, My Masters*, and produced in 1682.

City Madam, The. A comedy attributed to Philip Massinger, licensed in 1632 and printed in 1658. A 19th-century version of the play was entitled *Riches*.

City Match, The. A comedy by Jasper Mayne, produced in 1639.

City Nightcap, The. A play by Robert Davenport, licensed in 1624. It was adapted by Aphra Behn as *The Amorous Prince* in 1671, and itself is an adaptation of the plot of Robert Greene's novel *Philomela*.

City of Destruction. In John Bunyan's *Pilgrim's Progress*, the starting point of Christian in his journey. It typifies worldliness.

City of Dreadful Night, The. A poem by James Thomson, published first in the *National Reformer* in 1874. It is a long and gloomy work expressive of deep melancholy. The title also belongs to a volume of stories (1891) by Rudyard Kipling, one of which gives its name to the book.

City of the Plague. A poem by John Wilson, published in 1816, taking its theme and material from Daniel Defoe's *Journal of the Plague Year*.

City Politiques (pol.i.tēks'). A comedy by John Crowne (1683) in which the Whigs are ridiculed, and Shaftesbury, Oates, and Sir William Jones are parodied, the last in the character of Bartoline.

City Ramble, The. [Full title, **The City Ramble: or, A Play-House Wedding.**] A play adapted from Beaumont and Fletcher's *The Knight of the Burning Pestle* by Elkanah Settle. It was produced at the Drury Lane Theatre in 1711.

City Wit, or the Woman Wears the Breeches, The. A comedy by Richard Brome, published in 1653.

Civil War. [Also: the **War Between the States,** the **War for Southern Independence,** the **War of Secession,** the **War of the Rebellion.**] In U.S. history, a war from 1861 to 1865, between the North (the Union: 23 states) and the South (the Confederacy: 11 states). Its chief causes were the antislavery agitation of the more radical groups in the newly formed Republican Party, the Abolitionists, and the congressmen representing these groups, and the development of the doctrine of state sovereignty.

Civil War, English. [Also, **The Great Rebellion.**] A civil war (1642–46) between adherents of Charles I of England and the party of Parliament. It found its roots in the dissatisfaction of certain classes (merchants, artisans, nobility) with the Stuart theory of an absolute monarch not answerable to his subjects for his acts. Charles found his chief support in the landed class and the peasantry and in the Anglican clergy. When Charles called Parliament into session (Nov. 30, 1640; it sat until March 16, 1660) he wanted money to pay his Scottish army. Instead of voting the disbursement, Parliament presented to him on Dec. 1, 1641, a Grand Remonstrance, stating the many grievances they held to his account. The king retaliated by ordering (Jan. 3, 1642) the arrest of five leaders of the

ḍ, d or j; ṣ, s or sh; ṭ, t or ch; ẓ, z or zh; o, F. cloche; ü, F. menu; ċh, Sc. loch; ṅ, F. bonbon.

House of Commons; when they hid from his personal search, he left London and thereafter rejected all Parliamentary proposals at compromise of his stand.

Military. The Royalists threw back (Oct. 23, 1642) the Parliamentarians at Edgehill, but Charles did not advance on London. Several lesser engagements occurred: capture of Reading (April 27, 1643) by the Parliamentarians under their commander, Robert Devereux, 3rd Earl of Essex; the fall of Bristol (Aug. 25) to the Royalists under Prince Rupert; the relief of Gloucester by Essex in September; the battle of Newbury (Sept. 20) between Charles and Essex; the battle of Nantwich (Jan. 25, 1644), where Sir Thomas Fairfax defeated the Royalists. On July 2, 1644, Oliver Cromwell, Thomas and Ferdinando Fairfax, and Scots troops under Alexander Leslie met Prince Rupert at Marston Moor in Yorkshire. Cromwell's Ironsides (his own troops) saved the day and put the Royalists to flight. As a result of the battle York (July 16) and Newcastle (Oct. 16) were taken. On June 29, Parliamentary forces under Sir William Waller were defeated at Cropredy Bridge. Essex engaged in a campaign in Cornwall but met defeat and lost his army. Again at Newbury a battle was fought (Oct. 27), but the Parliamentary victory was inconclusive. In Scotland, James Graham, 5th Earl of Montrose, gained one victory after another over Scots adherents to the Parliamentary cause: at Tippermuir (Sept. 1), Inverlochy (Feb. 2, 1645), Auldearn (May 1), Alford (July 2), and Kilsyth (Aug. 16). He took Aberdeen and Dundee and was appointed captain-general of Scotland by Charles. However, the decisive battle of the war was fought at Naseby in Northamptonshire on June 14, 1645, when Cromwell's cavalry turned the tide of battle and routed the Royalists. Soon after this, Montrose, on his way to support Charles, was met by Parliamentarians under David Leslie at Philiphaugh and defeated (Sept. 13). Royalist resistance now crumbled and at Stowe-on-the-Wold the last battle of the war was fought (March 26, 1646), Sir Jacob Astley being defeated and captured.

Political. Before hostilities broke out, Parliament had abolished some of the sore spots of English absolutism, including the Court of Star Chamber, which often had acted arbitrarily and without reference to its stated authority. Several offers of conciliation were fought by Charles; he refused to sign bills or recognize protests. On the other hand, he made attempts to reach a peaceful settlement, even signing the bill of attainder that resulted in the death of the Earl of Strafford, who had been his chief adviser. When Parliament submitted (June 2, 1642) a series of propositions limiting the king's military and political powers, he refused to have anything to do with it. Parliament thereafter placed the military power in the hands of a committee and appointed its own commander, Essex, to lead the army. In September, 1643, by signing the Solemn League and Covenant, it attracted to its cause the Scots, who had fought the episcopacy of England in favor of their own Presbyterianism. Charles surrendered (May 5, 1646) to the Scots, and was turned over (Jan. 30, 1647) to Parliament. Shrewdly he widened a breach between Parliament and the army, but his intransigence when it came

to Parliamentary proposals and bills led Parliament to renounce their allegiance to him on Jan. 15, 1648. When the army resolved to try Charles, Parliament tried once more to make peace with the king, but the army, forcibly excluding (Dec. 6, 7, 1648) more than half the membership of Parliament through the action of Colonel Thomas Pride, made certain that Parliament would accede to the trial. Charles was tried (Jan. 20–27, 1649) and beheaded (Jan. 30). The Commonwealth, with its basic power in the army led by Cromwell, was established and ruled England from 1649 to 1660 (in its later stages, 1653–1659, being known as the Protectorate).

Civil Wars between the Two Houses of York and Lancaster, The. A poem by Samuel Daniel (books I–IV, 1595; books V–VIII, 1609), cast in octava rima. It deals with the period between and including the reigns of Richard II to Henry VI.

Clack (klak), **Drusilla.** A cousin of Rachel Verinder in *The Moonstone* by Wilkie Collins, a "poor relation" with a passion for interfering in the affairs of her relatives to save their souls (one character in the book calls her "that rampant Spinster"). She is the narrator of part of the story.

Clairmont (klär'mont, -mont), **Clara Mary Jane.** [Called **Claire Clairmont.**] b. April 27, 1798; d. 1879. The stepdaughter of William Godwin and mother of Byron's daughter Allegra. From Godwin's house she accompanied (1814) Mary Godwin in the latter's elopement with the poet Shelley. Upon her return she resided with the Shelleys at London and afterwards went to Lynmouth, eventually returning to the Godwin home. She met Byron in 1816, having supposedly introduced herself to him with a view toward getting an acting engagement at the Drury Lane Theatre. She was then only 18. The summer of 1816 was passed by the Shelleys, Claire, and Byron together in Switzerland. Upon the birth of her daughter Allegra in 1817, Byron offered to bring up the child. After Byron's death she served in various European countries as a governess.

Clancy Name (klan'si), **The.** A one-act tragedy by Lennox Robinson, produced in 1908 and published in 1910. It is a study of Irish pride in the family name and honor.

Clandestine Marriage, The. A comedy by Garrick and the elder Colman, produced on Feb. 20, 1766. The plot draws heavily from parts of Fielding's *Tom Jones,* and also from Congreve's *Love for Love* and Shadwell's *The Squire of Alsatia.*

Clara (klar'a̶). In Thomas Otway's *Cheats of Scapin,* a character corresponding to Hyacinthe in Molière's *Fourberies de Scapin.*

Clara. A girl in love with Ferdinand, in Richard Brinsley Sheridan's *The Duenna.*

Clara Barley (bär'li). See **Barley, Clara.**

Clara Groatsettar (grōt'set.a̶r). See **Groatsettar, Clara and Maddie.**

Clara Middleton (mid'l.ton). See **Middleton, Clara.**

Clara Peggotty (peg'o̶.ti). See **Peggotty, Clara.**

Clare (klār), **Ada.** The friend and charge of Esther Summerson in Charles Dickens's *Bleak House.* She marries Richard Carstone.

Clare, John. b. at Helpstone, near Peterborough, England, July 13, 1793; d. at Northampton, England, May 20, 1864. An English nature poet, known as the "Northamptonshire Peasant Poet." The son of a laborer, he was a gardener, a shepherd, an unsuccessful farmer, and, frequently, a vagrant. He enlisted in the militia in 1812. He became insane in 1837 and died so, 27 years later. His works are *Poems Descriptive of Rural Life and Scenery* (1820), *The Village Minstrel* (1821), *The Shepherd's Calendar* (1827), and *The Rural Muse* (1835). His pathetic poem, *Written in Northampton County Asylum* ("I am! yet what I am who cares, or knows?") has been praised by many critics.

Clare, Lady Clare de. An English heiress in Sir Walter Scott's poem *Marmion*, to obtain whose hand Marmion ruins her lover, Ralph de Wilton.

Clare College. One of the colleges of the University of Cambridge. The second oldest of the Cambridge colleges, it was founded in 1326, as University Hall, by Richard de Badew, then chancellor of the university, and was refounded in 1338 by Elizabeth de Clare, daughter of Gilbert de Clare, Earl of Gloucester and Hertford, and granddaughter of Edward I.

Clarence (klar′ens), **George, Duke of.** In Shakespeare's *3 Henry VI*, the historical George Plantagenet, brother of Edward IV, who creates him Duke of Clarence. He deserts the King in anger at his marriage with Lady Grey, but rejoins him later. In *Richard III*, he is imprisoned by Edward IV and ordered to his death. The reprieve which the Queen has persuaded Edward to give him is intercepted by Gloucester (Richard) and he is murdered.

Clarence, Thomas of. In Shakespeare's *2 Henry IV*, the Duke of Clarence, second son of the King and brother of Prince Hal. The King asks Clarence to advise Hal and keep him from his wild companions when he becomes king. In *Henry V*, he is asked by Henry to help arrange the peace terms with the French King (V.ii).

Clarence Barnacle (bär′na.kl). See under **Barnacle, Lord Decimus Tite.**

Clarendon (klar′en.don), **1st Earl of.** Title of **Hyde, Edward.**

Clarendon, Constitutions of. Ordinances adopted at the Council of Clarendon (held at a hunting lodge of that name near Salisbury, England) in 1164, with a view to limiting the jurisdiction of the ecclesiastical courts. There were 16 ordinances in all, including decrees that a member of the clergy accused of a crime should be tried by a royal court (instead of an ecclesiastical one as had previously been the practice) and that papal excommunication of a noble should be subject to the king's approval. Established by Henry II of England, these ordinances were most unwillingly agreed to by Saint Thomas à Becket. He subsequently won the Pope's support in his opposition to them, and after Becket's death popular feeling ran so high in his favor that Henry was forced to modify his position with reference to them.

Clarendon Press. A printing establishment at Oxford, England, in which the University of Oxford long had the preponderant influence, and which is now an adjunct of the Oxford University Press. It was founded partly with profits from the copyright of *History of the Rebellion*, by Edward Hyde, 1st Earl of Clarendon.

Claribel (klar′i.bel). In Edmund Spenser's *Faerie Queene*, the chosen bride of Phaon. She is slandered by Philemon. Phaon slays her, and, finding how he has been deceived, poisons Philemon.

"Claribel". Pseudonym of **Barnard, Charlotte Alington.**

Claribel, Sir. In Edmund Spenser's *Faerie Queene*, one of four knights who had a fray about the false Florimel. Britomart fights with them, and the combat is "stinted" by Prince Arthur.

Clarin (klar′in) or **Clarinda** (kla.rin′da). The trusted handmaid of Queen Radigund in Edmund Spenser's *Faerie Queene*. She betrays her mistress, seeking to alienate her from Artegall.

Clarinda (kla.rin′da). A waiting-woman to Carniola in Philip Massinger's play *The Maid of Honour*.

Clarinda. In Fletcher's *The Lover's Progress*, the adroit and unscrupulous waiting-woman of Calista.

Clarinda. In Thomas Shadwell's comedy *The Virtuoso*, a niece of the Virtuoso, in love with Longvil.

Clarinda. The principal female character in Susannah Centlivre's play *The Beau's Duel*, in love with Colonel Manly.

Clarinda. The niece of Sir Solomon Sadlife in Colley Cibber's comedy *The Double Gallant*. She "blows cold and hot" upon the passion of Clerimont.

Clarinda. The name used by Agnes Maclehose (1759–1841), a Glasgow lady, in writing to Robert Burns, who was "Sylvander."

Clarington (klar′ing.ton), **Sir Arthur.** A profligate, heartless, and avaricious scoundrel in *The Witch of Edmonton* by Dekker, Ford, and others.

Clarissa (kla.ris′a). The wife of Gripe, a rich but stingy husband, and stepmother of Corinna, in Sir John Vanbrugh's comedy *The Confederacy*, first acted at the London Haymarket, Oct. 30, 1705. In the *dramatis personae* of the play, Clarissa, performed by the famous Mrs. Barry, is described as "an expensive luxurious woman, a great admirer of quality."

Clarissa Harlowe (här′lō). [Original title, **Clarissa, or the History of a Young Lady.**] An epistolary novel (his second; *Pamela* was his first) by Samuel Richardson. It was published in 1747 (vols. 1–2) and 1748 (vols. 3–7). The story, which comprises the longest English novel, is told by means of 537 letters written by Clarissa, the heroine, to her "most intimate friend," Miss Howe, and by Robert Lovelace, Esq., to his "principal intimate and confidant," John Belford. The moral aim of the author was to show, as the title page indicates, "the Distresses that May Attend Misconduct both of Parents and Children in Relation to Marriage." Clarissa is courted by the profligate Lovelace, but her parents, anxious to have her marry Mr. Solmes, oppose the match and lock their daughter in her room. She finally turns to Lovelace, to whom she is greatly attracted, for protection. He carries her off but refuses to marry her. Overcome by shame, she pines away and dies. Her lover is killed in a duel with her cousin, Colonel Morden.

Clark (klärk), **William George.** b. in March, 1821; d. at York, England, Nov. 6, 1878. An English scholar, editor, lecturer, poet, and travel writer. He was educated at the grammar school at Sedbergh, at Shrewsbury, and (1840–44) at Trinity College, Cambridge, of which he later became a fellow. He wrote poetry, essays, travel works, and delivered lectures (which were published) on *The Middle Ages* and the *Revival of Learning* (1872), but he is best known for his work in connection with the *Cambridge Shakespeare* (1863–66), and the *Globe Shakespeare* (1864). The Clark lectureship in English literature, at Trinity, named after him, was founded by funds he left the college.

Clarke (klärk), **Austin.** b. 1896—. An Irish novelist and poet. He was educated at Dublin University College, and won the 1932 prize for national poetry at the Tailtean Games. His works are *The Bright Temptation* (1932), *The Singing-Men at Cashel* (1936), novels; *The Vengeance of Fionn* (1917), *The Fires of Baal* (1920), *The Sword of the West* (1921), *The Cattledrive in Connaught* (1925), *Pilgrimage* (1929), *Night and Morning* (1938), poetry; and *The Flame* (1930) and *Sister Eucharia* (1939), poetic plays.

Clarke, Charles Cowden-. b. at Enfield, near London, Dec. 15, 1787; d. at Genoa, Italy, March 13, 1877. An English Shakespeare scholar, editor, lecturer, teacher, and friend of many great literary figures of the 19th century. He began his remarkable lecturing career in 1834, with a lecture on Chaucer, at the Mechanics' Institute at Royston, and he ended it in 1856, with a lecture on Molière, at the Mechanics' Institute at Northampton. During those years, he lectured before thousands of people at London and throughout the provinces, on *Shakespeare*, *British Poets*, *Poets from Charles II to Queen Anne*, *Poetry by Prose Writers*, *Four Great European Novelists* (Boccaccio, Cervantes, Lesage, Richardson), *Schools of Painting in Italy*, *Ancient Ballads*, and *Sonnet Writers*. Many of these were later published. Other works were *Carmina Minima* (1859), poetry, and a series of essays on *The English Comic Poets* (1871, originally published in the *Gentleman's Magazine*). With his wife he wrote *The Shakespeare Key: Unlocking the Treasures of his Style, Elucidating the Peculiarities of his Construction, and Displaying the Beauties of his Expression* (1879), and *Recollections of Writers* (1878), the latter a work they were well qualified for, knowing, as they did, most of the leading authors and artists of their day. Clarke taught Keats his letters and introduced him to Vergil, Homer, and Spenser, and he was a friend of Leigh Hunt, Charles and Mary Lamb, Hazlitt, Dickens, Douglas Jerrold, Macready, and Mendelssohn.

Clarke, Marcus Andrew Hislop. b. at London, April 24, 1846; d. at Melbourne, Australia, Aug. 2, 1881. An Australian novelist and miscellaneous writer. He went (1863) to Australia, where he became a prolific free-lance writer of news stories, plays, pantomimes, light verse, and full-length novels. He is remembered for his classic novel *For the Term of His Natural Life*, a classic reconstruction of convict days in Tasmania, serialized in the period 1870–72, abbreviated, and slightly rewritten for book publication in 1874; the serial version was published as a book in 1929 and again in 1952 with an introduction by L. H. Allen. Clarke was described by a fellow student, Gerard Manley Hopkins, as a "kaleidoscopic, particoloured, harlequinesque, thaumatropic being."

Clarke, Mary Victoria Cowden-. [Maiden name, Novello.] b. at London, June 22, 1809; d. at Genoa, Italy, Jan. 12, 1898. An English Shakespeare scholar and author; wife of Charles Cowden-Clarke. She published *The Complete Concordance to Shakespeare* (1846), which was compiled during the assiduous labor of 16 years (it does not contain the words of the sonnets and poems), *The Girlhood of Shakespeare's Heroines* (1850), *The Iron Cousin*, a novel (1854), *Memorial Sonnets* (1888), and other works. She also collaborated with her husband on several works.

Clarke, Samuel. b. at Norwich, England, Oct. 11, 1675; d. at London, May 17, 1729. An English divine and metaphysical writer; son of an alderman of Norwich. He was a graduate of Cambridge (Caius College), and was successively rector of Drayton, near Norwich, of St. Bennet's at London (1706), and of St. James's at Westminster, London (1709). He was also one of the chaplains of Queen Anne. His metaphysical argument for the existence of God is especially famous, and he also holds a high place in the history of the science of ethics. He upheld the views of Newton against those of Leibnitz, and based his ethic on the principle of the "fitness of things." His most celebrated work is his series of Boyle Lectures (1704–05), published as *A Discourse concerning the Being and Attributes of God, the Obligations of Natural Religion, and the Truth and Certainty of the Christian Revelation, in answer to Mr. Hobbes, Spinoza, . . . and Other Deniers of Natural and Revealed Religion.*

classic. 1. Belonging to or associated with the first or highest class, especially in literature; accepted as of the highest rank; serving as a standard, model, or guide.

> O Sheridan! if aught can move thy pen,
> Let comedy assume her throne again; . . .
> Give as thy last memorial to the age
> One classic drama, and reform the stage.
> (Byron, *Eng. Bards and Scotch Reviewers.*)

2. Pertaining to or having the characteristics of ancient Greece or Rome, especially of their literature and art; specifically, relating to places associated with the ancient Greek and Latin writers.

> With them the genius of classick learning dwelleth, and from them it is derived.
> (Felton, *Reading the Classicks.*)

> Poetic fields encompass me around,
> And still I seem to tread on classic ground.
> (Addison, *Letter from Italy.*)

3. Relating to localities associated with great modern authors, or with great historical events: as, *classic* Stratford; *classic* Hastings.
4. In accordance with the canons of Greek and Roman art: as, a *classic* profile.

classicism. 1. An idiom or the style of the classics.
2. The adoption or imitation of what is classical or classic in style.

The first [kind of verse] was that of an art-school,

taking its models from old English poetry, and from the delicate classicism of Landor and Keats.
(Stedman, *Victorian Poets*.)

Claude Lorrain (klōd lo.raṅ). [Original name, **Claude Gelée** or **Gellée**.] b. in Lorraine, France, 1600; d. at Rome, Nov. 21, 1682. A French painter, notably of landscapes.

Claude Melnotte (mel.not′). See **Melnotte, Claude.**

Claud Halcro (klôd hal′krō). See **Halcro, Claud.**

Claudian (klô′di.an). [Full Latin name, **Claudius Claudianus**.] b. probably at Alexandria, Egypt; d. c408 A.D. A Latin poet, known as the last great poet of the pagan classical world. He was the panegyrist of Stilicho, Theodosius, Honorius, and others. He also wrote epithalamia, idylls, epigrams, *De raptu Proserpinae* (an unfinished work on the rape of Proserpina), and others.

Claudio (klô′di.ō). In Shakespeare's *Measure for Measure*, the brother of Isabella, condemned to death for seducing Juliet. Angelo offers him his life, through Isabella, in exchange for Isabella as his mistress. In a dramatic scene Claudio begs Isabella to yield, but is refused. Later his death is ordered by Angelo, but the Provost of the prison prevents the execution.

Claudio. In Shakespeare's *Much Ado About Nothing*, a young Florentine in love with Hero. He falls too easily into belief in Hero's dishonor, but becomes convinced of her virtue and is finally married to her.

Claudius (klô′di.us). In Shakespeare's *Hamlet*, the King of Denmark and uncle of Hamlet. (He is mentioned by this name only in the Dramatis Personae and in the stage directions for Act I, Scene 2; elsewhere he is referred to simply as the "King.") He has killed his brother (Hamlet's father), married Gertrude, and is ruling as king when Hamlet reaches Denmark at the beginning of the play. After the presentation of the dumbshow, during which he realizes that he has revealed his guilt to Hamlet, he sends Hamlet to England, arranging that he shall there be killed. When this fails, he contrives to have Ophelia's brother, Laertes, duel with Hamlet, and to insure his death he poisons Laertes's foil and also prepares a poisoned goblet. Hamlet, stabbed and dying, kills him in the final scene.

Claudius. In Shakespeare's *Julius Caesar*, a servant of Brutus.

Claus (klôz), **Santa.** See **Santa Claus.**

Clause (klous). In Massinger and Fletcher's *Beggar's Bush*, the assumed name of Gerrard.

Claverhouse (klav′ėrz, klä′vėrz, klav′ėr.hous), **John Graham of.** See **Graham, John.**

Clavering (klav′ėr.ing), **Sir Francis.** In Thackeray's novel *Pendennis*, a baronet who marries the vulgar Mrs. Amory to recoup his losses, and is blackmailed by her first husband, Altamont.

Claverings (klav′ėr.ingz), **The.** A novel by Anthony Trollope, published in 1867. The hero of this work is Harry Clavering, a rector's son who falls in love with Julia Brabazon, a young lady with very expensive tastes. She turns from Harry to marry a wealthy old villain, Lord Ongar, who leads her a terrible life for a year, then dies. She

returns to Harry to find him engaged to Florence Burton, a mild and gentle character. Harry is briefly involved in an affair with Julia, but eventually goes back to Florence and marries her.

Clavijo (klä.ßē′нō), **Don.** An accomplished cavalier in Cervantes's *Don Quixote*, who was metamorphosed into a crocodile and was disenchanted by Don Quixote.

Clavileño (klä.ßē.lä′nyō), **El Alígero.** In Cervantes's *Don Quixote*, the wooden horse used by Don Quixote. It was managed by a wooden pin in its forehead. The magic horse is a folklore subject known throughout Europe and the Near East.

Clay (klā), **Bertha M.** An English writer, whose real name was Charlotte Monica Braeme (1836–84), author of a long series of sensational romantic novels, many of them believed to have been written, under the name Bertha M. Clay, by Frederick Van Rensselaer Day (1861–1922), and Thomas Chalmers Harbaugh (1849–1924).

Clayhanger Trilogy (klā′hang″ėr). [Also, the **Five Towns Trilogy**.] A series of three realistic novels by Arnold Bennett, dealing with the "Five Towns" of the potters' region. It includes *Clayhanger* (1910), *Hilda Lessways* (1911), and *These Twain* (1916). Edwin Clayhanger has his artistic talent repressed by a stern and unimaginative father, and is forced to remain in the small town of his birth, depressed and discouraged by the narrowness and poverty he encounters there. When he is 23 he meets Hilda Lessways, an aggressive and self-confident woman. He is impressed by her strength and mastery and they become secretly engaged, but later he hears of her sudden marriage to George Cannon and begins to hate her. Ten years later, after the death of his father, he discovers her in Brighton, living in destitution, her husband jailed for bigamy, and her son branded with bastardy. In spite of the past, Edwin still loves Hilda and they get married. In *Hilda Lessways*, the story of Hilda's life is told, from her boring life with a widowed mother to the growth of her intimacy with Cannon, the only man who ever mastered her. *These Twain* continues in the depressing and gloomy vein of the other two works. The conflicts between Hilda and Edwin are described, and although Edwin becomes a successful politician he finally yields to the dominance of his neurotic wife. His only real happiness is his interest in his stepson, George.

Claypole (klā′pōl), **Noah.** Mr. Sowerberry's apprentice, a charity boy and afterward a thief, a character in Charles Dickens's *Oliver Twist*. He marries Charlotte, Mrs. Sowerberry's servant.

Cleanness. [Also, **Purity**.] A Middle English alliterative poem (13th century) supposed to have been written by the author of *The Pearl* and *Patience*. It paraphrases the Biblical incidents of the Flood, the destruction of Sodom and Gomorrah, and Belshazzar's feast in order to point up its moral of the sorrow of the Lord over the uncleanliness of man. It contains digressions on various ethical subjects and ends with a prayer to God for grace and forgiveness.

Cleanthe (klē.an′thē). The sister of Siphax in John Fletcher's *The Mad Lover*.

d, d or j; ṣ, s or sh; ṭ, t or ch; ẓ, z or zh; o, F. cloche; ü, F. menu; ċh, Sc. loch; ṅ, F. bonbon.

Cleanthes (klē̇.an'thēz). An Egyptian warrior who is the hero of George Chapman's *Blind Beggar of Alexandria*.

Cleanthes. The son of Leonides in *The Old Law*, a play attributed to Philip Massinger, Thomas Middleton, and William Rowley. He is a model of filial piety and tenderness.

Cleanthes. A friend of Cleomenes, and captain of Ptolemy's guard, in John Dryden's tragedy *Cleomenes*.

Clear (klir), **Claudius.** Pseudonym of **Nicoll**, Sir **William Robertson.**

Clear Horizon. A novel by Dorothy M. Richardson, published in 1935. It is the 11th section of *Pilgrimage* (1915–38), a novel sequence in 12 parts employing the stream-of-consciousness technique.

Cleaver (klē'vēr), **Fanny.** [Called "Jenny Wren."] A deformed little dressmaker of dolls' clothes, in Charles Dickens's *Our Mutual Friend.* "My back's bad and my legs are queer," is her frequent excuse, and she always describes herself with dignity as "the person of the house."

Cleges (klē'jĕs), **Sir.** See **Sir Cleges.**

Clegg (kleg), **Henry.** The husband of the heroine in St. John Ervine's play of middle-class English life and character, *Jane Clegg* (1911). After being saved from a prison sentence by his wife, who is glad to get rid of him, he leaves home to live with his "fancy woman," Kitty, who is about to bear his child.

Cleishbotham (klēsh'boŦH.ạm), **Jedediah.** The assumed compiler of *Tales of My Landlord*, by Sir Walter Scott. Cleishbotham is a schoolmaster at Gandercleugh, and the stories are written by his assistant, one Peter Pattieson, who in turn has collected the tales from the landlord of the Wallace Inn, Gandercleugh.

Cleiveland (klēv'lạnd), **John.** See **Cleveland, John.**

Cleland (klē'lạnd), **John.** b. 1709; d. Jan. 23, 1789. An English writer. He was the author of the novel (notorious in its day) *Fanny Hill, or the Memoirs of a Woman of Pleasure* (1748–50) and of *Memoirs of a Coxcomb* (1751). He was consul at Smyrna, and in 1736 was in the service of the East India Company at Bombay. In the latter part of his life he wrote for the stage and also dabbled in philology.

Cleland, William. b. at or near Douglas, Lanarkshire, Scotland, c1661; d. Aug. 26, 1689. A Scottish Covenanter, soldier, and poet. He was educated at St. Andrews and Utrecht universities. He took part in the battles of Drumclog and Bothwell Bridge (both in 1679), and in the battle of Dunkeld. After receiving a fatal wound at Dunkeld, he is said to have attempted vainly to drag himself off the field so that his men, pitted against the Highland Jacobites, would not lose heart at seeing his dead body. *Hallo, My Fancy*, written during his student days in Scotland, and *A Mock Poem upon the Expedition of the Highland Host who Came to Destroy the Western Shires in Winter 1678*, a satire in the style of *Hudibras*, are considered among his best works. Cleland's collected poetry was not published until 1697.

Clélie (klā.lē). [English, **Clelia** (klē'li.ạ).] A romance by Mademoiselle de Scudéry, published in 1656, named after its heroine. The long novel, based on a theme from Roman history, is written in the precious, romantic style and introduces many of Mademoiselle de Scudéry's contemporaries, in fictional disguise, as characters.

Clement (klem'ent), **Justice.** A city magistrate in Ben Jonson's *Every Man in His Humour.*

Clement Cleveland (klēv'lạnd), **Captain.** See **Cleveland, Captain Clement.**

Clement Flint (flint), **Sir.** See **Flint, Sir Clement.**

Clementina (klem.ẹn.tē'nạ). An Italian beauty passionately in love with Sir Charles Grandison, in Samuel Richardson's epistolary novel *Sir Charles Grandison.*

Clennam (klen'ạm), **Arthur.** In Charles Dickens's *Little Dorrit*, the adopted (although reputed to be the actual) son of Mrs. Clennam, employer of Amy Dorrit (called "Little Dorrit"). After a harsh childhood and 20 years in the Far East, Arthur returns home to a chilly welcome by the woman supposed to be his mother, and meets Amy in her house. A bond grows between the two and, after serving a sentence in prison for debts incurred by a failure in business, Arthur marries her.

Cleofas (klē'ọ.fạs), **Don.** A high-spirited Spanish student in Alain René Le Sage's novel *Le Diable boiteux.* Asmodeus exhibits to him, in a very dramatic manner indeed, the fortunes of the inmates of the houses of Madrid by actually unroofing the houses so that he may look into them.

Cleomenes (klē.om'ẹ.nēz). In Shakespeare's *Winter's Tale*, a Sicilian noble who, with Dion, is sent by Leontes to the oracle at Delphi to ask if Hermione is chaste. They return with an affirmative answer.

Cleomenes, the Spartan Heroe. A play (1692) by John Dryden, modeled on the lines of French tragedy. Part of the fifth act is by Thomas Southerne. The story is taken from Plutarch's account of the life of Cleomenes III of Sparta.

Cleon (klē'on). Killed at Amphipolis, Macedon, 422 B.C. An Athenian demagogue. He was the son of a tanner. Coming forward shortly after the death of Pericles as leader of the democratic party, he violently opposed Nicias, the head of the aristocratic party, who advocated peace with Sparta and the conclusion of the Peloponnesian War. He led a successful expedition against the Spartans at Pylos in 425, capturing a force on the island of Sphacteria and bringing them captive to Athens. Since he had promised to do so despite the Spartans' reputation for never being taken alive, his reputation swelled. Cleon was in 422 entrusted with the command of an expedition destined to act against Brasidas in Chalcidice. He was defeated by the latter at Amphipolis, and fell in the flight. He was satirized by Aristophanes, especially in the *Knights* (424) in which Aristophanes himself was forced to play Cleon, none of the players daring to take the role of the popular hero. Thucydides too, the historian of the Peloponnesian War, expressed a dislike for Cleon.

Cleon. In Shakespeare's *Pericles*, the governor of Tharsus (Tarsus), burned to death to avenge the supposed murder of Marina.

Cleon. A poem (1855) by Robert Browning, concerned with the problem of the artist and intellectual in a time of transition. Browning makes Cleon one of the poets referred to by St. Paul in Acts xvii. 28: "As certain also of your own poets have said." It is similar in theme to Matthew Arnold's *Empedocles on Etna.*

Cleopatra (klē̇.ọ̄.pā′trạ, -pat′rạ, -pä′trạ). [In the chronology of Egyptian queens, **Cleopatra VII.**] b. at Alexandria, Egypt, 69 B.C.; d. there, 30 B.C. The last Macedonian queen of Egypt; daughter of Ptolemy XI (sometimes XIII), called Ptolemy Auletes. In accordance with Egyptian tradition, she was wife of and joint ruler with her brother Ptolemy XII (or XIV) from 51 to 49, when she was expelled by him. Her reinstatement in 48 by Caesar gave rise to war between Caesar and Ptolemy. The latter was defeated and killed, and his younger brother, Ptolemy XIII (or XV), was elevated to the throne in his stead and married to her. Cleopatra lived with Caesar at Rome from 46 to 44, and had by him a son, Ptolemy XIV (or XVI), usually known as Caesarion because of his father; the child was afterward put to death by Augustus. She returned to Egypt after the murder of Caesar, and in the civil war which ensued sided with the Triumvirate (Augustus, Antony, and Lepidus). Mark Antony having been appointed ruler of Asia and the East, she visited him at Tarsus, Cilicia, in 41, making a voyage of extraordinary splendor and magnificence up the Cydnus. She gained by her charms a complete ascendancy over him. On her account he divorced his wife Octavia, the sister of Augustus, in 32. Augustus declared war against her in 31. The fleet of Antony and Cleopatra was defeated in the same year at the battle of Actium, which was decided by the flight of Cleopatra's ships, Antony being forced to follow. After the death of Antony, who killed himself on hearing a false report of her death (according to some, a report deliberately spread by her in an attempt to win Augustus's favor by causing his death), she poisoned herself to avoid being exhibited at Rome at the triumph of Augustus, but not until she had made an attempt to charm Augustus as she had Caesar and Antony. According to the popular belief, she applied to her bosom an asp that had been secretly conveyed to her in a basket of figs. She had three children by Antony. Besides extraordinary charms of person, she possessed an active and cultivated mind, and is said to have been able to converse in seven languages. Her reputed personality and the events of the latter part of her reign, as described by Plutarch, form the basis of Shakespeare's *Antony and Cleopatra;* this play was later adapted by John Dryden as *All for Love.* George Bernard Shaw's *Caesar and Cleopatra* tells the story (considerably modified by Shaw) of Julius Caesar and the young Cleopatra.

Cleopatra. A Senecan tragedy, published 1594, by Samuel Daniel, whose source was North's *Plutarch.* Unlike the heroine of Shakespeare's *Antony and Cleopatra,* Cleopatra does not kill herself immediately after Antony's death, but first leads Octavius Caesar to believe she will yield to him. The play had been reprinted seven times by 1607.

Cleopatra. In Shakespeare's *Antony and Cleopatra,* the heroine, a woman of extraordinary beauty and intelligence: "Age cannot wither her, nor custom stale her infinite variety." Her love for Antony becomes a pervasive thing, larger than death or time, almost (as she herself comes to think) the burning synthesis of an elemental force spreading throughout the entire universe.

Cleopatra's Needles. A pair of Egyptian obelisks of red granite, made c1500 B.C., which were transported from Heliopolis to Alexandria in the 18th year (c14 B.C.) of Augustus. One of them was taken to London and set up on the Thames embankment in 1878, and the other was soon after brought to New York and erected in Central Park. There is no known connection between these obelisks and Cleopatra.

Cleopolis (klē̇.op′ọ̄.lis). A name given by Edmund Spenser in *The Faerie Queene* to the city of London.

Clergyman's Daughter, A. A novel by George Orwell, published in 1935.

Clerimont (kler′i.mont). A gay friend of Sir Dauphine in Ben Jonson's *Epicoene, or the Silent Woman.*

Clerimont. The lover of Clarinda in Colley Cibber's comedy *The Double Gallant.* He assists Atall and Careless in their schemes.

Clerk of Penicuik (klärk; pen′i.kwik), Sir **John.** b. 1684; d. 1755. A Scottish antiquary and patron of Allan Ramsay (1686–1758), Scottish poet. He was a member of the Scottish Parliament (1702–07) and a commissioner (1707) for the union with England. While judge of the court of exchequer in Scotland (1708–55), he collected antiquities and wrote antiquarian tracts.

Clerkenwell (klär′ḳẹn.wẹl, -wel). A former civil parish in E central London, in the County of London, in Finsbury metropolitan borough. It formerly bore an evil reputation. Clerkenwell Green was in the 17th century surrounded by fine mansions, and, among many other noted men, Izaak Walton lived there. Its name derives from the well beside which the clerks of London parish formerly enacted the old miracle plays.

Clerk-Maxwell (klärk′maks′wẹl), **James.** See **Maxwell, James Clerk.**

Clerk of Chatham (chat′ạm). In Shakespeare's *2 Henry VI,* a clerk, assaulted by the mob led by Jack Cade because he can read and write.

Clerk's Tale, The. The tale told by the Oxford student ("the Clerk of Oxenford") in Chaucer's *Canterbury Tales.* It is founded upon Boccaccio's story of the patient Griselda (the tenth novel of the tenth day in the *Decameron*), which the Clerk states he read in Petrarch's version. Its theme, the wife's complete submission to her husband, is in direct contrast to that of the prologue and tale of the Wife of Bath. Chaucer's description of the sober Clerk and his surpassing devotion to knowledge is one of his best-known characterizations:

> As lene was his hors as is a rake,
> And he nas not right fat, I undertake;
> But loked holwe, and ther-to soberly.
> Full thredbar was his overest courtepy. . . .
> For him was lever have at his beddes heed
> Twenty bokes, clad in blak or reed,
> Of Aristotle and his philosophye,

Than robes riche, or fithele, or gay sautrye. . . .
Souninge in moral vertu was his speche,
And gladly wolde he lerne, and gladly teche.

Cleveland (klēv'l̯and), **Captain Clement.** The pirate of the title, in Sir Walter Scott's novel *The Pirate.* He falls in love with Minna Troil but eventually is captured and parted from her.

Cleveland, John. [Also, **Cleiveland.**] b. at Loughborough, Leicestershire, England, in June, 1613; d. April 29, 1658. An English poet, an active Royalist during the English Civil War, and a satirist of the Parliamentary party. He was graduated (B.A., 1631) from Christ's College, Cambridge, and was elected a fellow of St. John's College in 1634. He joined the Royalist army at Oxford, and was made judge-advocate, remaining with the garrison of Newark, in Nottinghamshire, until its surrender. In 1655 he was arrested and imprisoned at Yarmouth, but was soon released by order of Cromwell. One of the Cavalier poets, he wrote satires, including *Scots Apostasie, Hue and Cry after Sir John Presbyter, The Mixt Assembly,* and *Smectymnuus, or the Club Divine.*

cliché (klē.shā'). A stereotype or electrotype plate; figuratively, a stereotyped expression, idea, practice, or the like.

Clifford (klif'o̯rd), **Lady.** [First married name, **de la Pasture;** maiden name, **Elizabeth Lydia Rosabelle Bonham.**] b. at Naples, Italy, 1866; d. 1945. An English novelist and dramatist; married (1887) Count Henry Philip Ducarel de la Pasture (d. 1908); married (1910) Sir Hugh Charles Clifford (1866–1941); mother of Elizabeth Monica Dashwood (1890–1943), known as E. M. Delafield. Among her novels are *The Little Squire* (1893; dramatized 1894), *A Toy Tragedy* (1894), *Deborah of Tod's* (1897; dramatized 1909), *Adam Grigson* (1899), *Catherine of Calais* (1901), *Cornelius* (1903), *Peter's Mother* (1905; dramatized 1906), *The Man from America* (1905), *The Lonely Lady of Grosvenor Square* (1907), *The Grey Knight* (1907), *Catherine's Child* (1909), *The Tyrant* (1909), *Master Christopher* (1911), *Erica* (1912), and *Michael Ferrys* (1913). She also wrote the plays *The Lonely Millionaires* (1906) and *Her Grace the Reformer* (1906).

Clifford, Henry de. [Titles: 14th Baron **Clifford,** 10th Baron of **Westmorland,** 1st Baron **Vesci;** called the **"Shepherd Lord."**] b. c1455; d. 1523. An English nobleman. Because his father, Sir John de Clifford, had been attainted (1461) by the Yorkists, Clifford lived disguised as a shepherd until his estates were restored (1485) by Henry VII of England. In 1513 he fought at Flodden Field. Episodes from his early life were later used by William Wordsworth in *Song at the Feast of Brougham Castle* and *The White Doe of Rylstone.*

Clifford, Lord. In Shakespeare's *2 Henry VI,* a Lancastrian and supporter of the King's party. With Buckingham, he persuades the rebellious mob to desert their leader Cade. He is killed by York at the battle at St. Albans.

Clifford, Lord. In Shakespeare's *2 Henry VI,* Young Clifford, the son of the elder Lord Clifford. In *3 Henry VI,* he is a member of the Lancastrian faction and stabs York at the battle of Wakefield,

after first killing York's son, Rutland, both deeds having been done to avenge his father's death (I.iii, iv). He himself is wounded in battle at Towton and dies despairing of the Lancastrian cause (II.vi.).

Clifford, Lucy. [Maiden name, **Lane.**] b. in Barbados, British West Indies; d. April 21, 1929. An English novelist, dramatist, and writer of books for children. Her works of fiction include *Anyhow Stories* (1882), *Mrs. Keith's Crime* (1885), *Love Letters of a Worldly Woman* (1891), *A Woman Alone* (1891; produced as a play, 1914), *Aunt Anne* (1893), *A Flash of Summer* (1895), *A Long Duel* (1901), *Sir George's Objection* (1910), *The House in Marylebone* (1917), *Miss Fingal* (1919), and *Eve's Lover* (1927). She also wrote the plays *The Likeness of the Night* (1901), *The Searchlight* (1913), and *Two's Company* (1915).

Clifford, Paul. See **Paul Clifford.**

Clifford, Rosamond. [Called **"the Fair Rosamond."**] d. c1176. Daughter of Walter de Clifford (son of Richard Fitz Ponce, ancestor of the great Clifford family), and mistress of Henry II of England. She appears to have been publicly acknowledged by Henry as his mistress c1175, after he had imprisoned his queen, Eleanor of Aquitaine, for her part in his sons' revolt against him. On her death Rosamond was interred in Godstow nunnery. It is said that Hugh, bishop of Lincoln, who visited Godstow in 1191, was offended at the sight of her richly adorned tomb in the middle of the church choir before the altar, and caused its removal, probably to the chapter house. According to a popular legend, which has no foundation in fact, Henry built a labyrinth or maze to conceal her from Queen Eleanor, who nevertheless discovered her and put her to death. Rosamond is commonly, though erroneously, stated to have been the mother of William Longsword and of Geoffrey, archbishop of York.

Clifford, Sir Thomas. The lover of Julia in James Sheridan Knowles's play *The Hunchback.*

Clifford's Inn. One of the inns of chancery at London, named for Robert de Clifford (1273–1314), of the time of Edward II, whose town residence it originally was. It was first used as a law school in the 18th year of Edward III (1345). The building is N of Fleet Street, between Chancery Lane and Fetter Lane.

climax. In rhetoric, originally, such an arrangement of successive clauses that the last important word of one is repeated as the first important word of the next; hence (since this arrangement is usually adopted for the sake of graduated increase in force or emphasis), a figure by which a series of clauses or phrases is so arranged that each in turn surpasses the preceding one in intensity of expression or importance of meaning. An example of climax in both its earlier and its established meaning is found in the following passage: "We glory in *tribulations* also: knowing that *tribulation* worketh *patience;* and *patience, experience;* and *experience, hope;* and *hope* maketh not ashamed." (*Rom.* 5:3,4.)

It may as well be called the clyming figure, for Clymax is as much to say as a ladder.
(Puttenham, *Arte of English Poesie.*)

---

fat, fāte, fär, àsk, fāre; net, mē, hér; pin, pīne; not, nōte, möve, nôr; up, lūte, pull; ᴛʜ, then;

Clim of the Clough (klim; kluf). See **Clym of the Clough.**

Clincher (klin′chẽr). A character in George Farquhar's comedy *The Constant Couple*, also in *Sir Harry Wildair*, its sequel. He is a pert London apprentice turned beau, and affecting to have traveled widely.

Clink (klingk). A prison which was situated at one end of Bankside, at Southwark, London. It belonged to the "Liberty of the Clink," a part of the manor of Southwark not included in the grant to the city of London and under the jurisdiction of the bishop of Winchester. The prison was for the delinquents of this manor. It was burned down in the Gordon riots of June, 1780. Its name is the origin of the slang word "clink," meaning prison.

Clinker (klingk′ẽr), **Humphry.** A poor waif in Tobias Smollett's novel *Humphry Clinker*. He is discovered to be a natural son of Mr. Bramble, into whose service he has entered as coach boy. Humphry is unjustly imprisoned but shortly released, and in the end marries Mrs. Winifred Jenkins, Tabitha Bramble's maid.

Clio (klī′ō). In Greek mythology, the Muse, usually of history, sometimes of lyre-playing. She is most commonly represented in a sitting attitude, holding an open roll of papyrus.

Clio. Pseudonym of Addison, formed from his signatures "C.," "L.," "I.," and "O.," used at various times in *The Spectator;* perhaps the initials of Chelsea, London, Islington, and the "Office."

Clitus (klī′tus). In Shakespeare's *Julius Caesar*, a servant of Brutus.

Clive (klīv), **Caroline.** [Maiden name, **Meysey-Wigley.**] b. at London, June 24, 1801; d. at Whitfield, Herefordshire, England, July 13, 1873. An English writer. She was the author of the novels *Paul Ferroll* (1855) and *Why Paul Ferroll Killed his Wife* (1860), and also wrote *Poems by "V."* (1840, and other editions).

Clive, Catherine. [Called **Kitty Clive**; maiden name, **Raftor.**] b. 1711; d. at London, Dec. 6, 1785. An English actress; the daughter of an Irish gentleman, William Raftor. After a childhood of obscurity and poverty she came to the notice of Colley Cibber, who was manager of Drury Lane Theatre, London. He gave her a position when she was 17, and by 1731 she had established a reputation as a comic actress. She retired from the stage on April 24, 1769. She was in Garrick's company at the Drury Lane from 1746. She early married George Clive, a barrister, but they separated by mutual consent. Her forte was rattling comedy and operatic farce, and she was especially known in Charles Coffey's *The Devil To Pay.* She and Garrick were often at odds, although appreciating each other's talent. He tried in vain to dissuade her from tragedy, especially the role of Ophelia (which she particularly coveted). After her retirement from the stage she lived for many years in a house which Horace Walpole gave her, near Strawberry Hill. She wrote some small dramatic sketches, only one of which, *The Rehearsal, or Boys in Petticoats,* was printed (1753).

Clive, Robert. [Title, Baron **Clive of Plassey.**] b. at Styche, Shropshire, England, Sept. 29, 1725; d. at London, Nov. 22, 1774. A British soldier and empire builder. The son of an impoverished country squire, he became in 1743 a minor employee of the East India Company at Madras. War having broken out between the British and the French in India, he applied for and obtained an ensign's commission in the company's armed forces in 1747, and in the following year served under Admiral Boscawen at the unsuccessful siege of Pondicherry. During a second war in India with the French (1751–54), he manifested his military abilities by capturing Arcot and defending it successfully against a greatly superior force of French and natives. He returned to England in 1753, but in 1755 was sent back to India with the rank of lieutenant governor of Fort St. David. In 1756 he commanded an expedition against Suráj ud Dowlah, nawab of Bengal, ostensibly to avenge the sufferings and deaths of English prisoners in the Black Hole of Calcutta. He defeated the nawab near that city, and after a short interval of peace, won a sweeping victory at Plassey, on June 23, 1757. Practicing the familiar strategy of playing one claimant to a throne against another, Clive had made an alliance with Mir Jaffier, whom he now made nawab of Bengal in place of Suráj ud Dowlah. Following the capture of Murshidabad, the capital city, Mir Jaffier conducted Clive through the treasury, inviting him to help himself, which Clive did to the value of 160,000 pounds sterling. Large sums were also distributed to other British soldiers and officials, and Clive subsequently defended his own course by saying that he marveled at his moderation. In 1758 he was appointed governor of Bengal, in 1759 he defeated the Dutch near Chinsura, and in 1760, his health impaired, he returned to England and was created Baron Clive of Plassey. In 1765, affairs in Bengal having fallen into disorder, he was again made governor of that province, but in 1767 he again resigned for reasons of health. Back in England, his official conduct was made the subject of a parliamentary inquiry, which resulted, in 1773, in his acquittal on the charges brought, and in commendation of his conduct. Nevertheless in the following year he died by his own hand. He had been instrumental in fastening British control on India, and as an administrator he was just and exceedingly able.

Clive Newcome (nū′kum). See **Newcome, Clive.**

Cloaca Maxima (klō.ā′ka̱ mak′si.ma̱). The chief drain of ancient Rome, built about 600 B.C., and still used.

Clockmaker, The. See **Sayings and Doings of Samuel Slick of Slickville, The.**

Clodd (klod), **Edward.** b. at Margate, Kent, England, July 1, 1840; d. 1930. An English banker and writer on science and folklore. He was a clerk (1862–72) and secretary (1872–1915) of the London Joint Stock Bank. Interested in folklore, religion, and science, he was the author of *The Childhood of the World* (1872), *Myths and Dreams* (1885), *Story of Creation* (1888), *Primitive Man* (1895), *Pioneers of Evolution* (1897), *Story of the Alphabet* (1900), *Animism, the Seed of Religion* (1905), and *Magic in Names* (1920). He also wrote lives (1900) of Grant Allen and T. H. Huxley. His *Memories* appeared in 1916.

Clodpate (klod'pāt), **Justice.** A coarse rustic justice in Thomas Shadwell's comedy *Epsom Wells.*

Cloe (klō'ē). A variant spelling of **Chloe,** found in some printings of the works of John Fletcher and other English poets of the 16th and 17th centuries.

Cloister and the Hearth, The. A historical novel by Charles Reade, published in 1861. The story is set in Holland and Italy during the 15th century. Gerard, the son of a Dutch merchant, renounces his plans to study for the priesthood in order that he may marry Margaret Brandt, the daughter of a poor scholar. His angry father and two wicked brothers imprison him, with the help of the burgomaster, and thus prevent the marriage. Gerard escapes and goes to Margaret, but is pursued and forced to leave the country, traveling to Italy through Germany and Burgundy. There his enemies falsely report to him that his beloved Margaret is dead. Despairing, he leads a life of dissipation until he is persuaded to enter the Dominican order. As a Dominican preacher he now returns to Holland, to find Margaret living in poverty and having borne him a son. Gerard will not forsake his vows by living with Margaret, and they live apart but near enough to see each other. Margaret dies of the plague and Gerard follows soon after, dying of a broken heart. Their son is revealed to be the future humanist, Erasmus. One of the most vivid characters in the book is the Burgundian crossbowman, Denys, who befriends and protects Gerard.

Clootie (klō'ti). A Scottish and north of England euphemism for the devil, from "cloot," a dialect word for one half of a cleft hoof.

Clorin (klō'rin). A shepherdess whose lover is dead in John Fletcher's *Faithful Shepherdess.*

Clorinda (klō.rēn'dä). Amazonian leader in *Gerusalemme Liberata* (*Jerusalem Delivered*) of Torquato Tasso. She is of acknowledged prowess in the infidel army, and is loved by Tancred, but cares only for the glories of war. Tancred kills her unwittingly in a night attack, and gives her Christian baptism before she expires.

Cloten (klō'ten). In Shakespeare's *Cymbeline,* the queen's son by a former husband. He is rejected by Imogen. In the first part of the play (written later) he is a foolish and malicious braggart; but in the fourth act, which belongs to an earlier version, he is not deficient in manliness.

Clotho (klō'thō). In Greek mythology, that one of the three Moirae or Fates who spins the thread of life.

Cloud Cuckoo Land. A novel by Naomi Mitchison, published in 1925.

Cloud of Unknowing. A prose religious treatise of the Middle English period by an anonymous author who seems to have written it about 1350. His theme is the love of God and the knowledge of His presence through mysticism and spirituality. The work is intended for a serious young man of 24 who is contemplative by nature and who looks forward to a life of quiet devotion. The author attacks those who take their religion violently and show it by means of physical manifestation which he regards as hypocrisy. The "cloud" of the title, which stands between God and the Soul, is man's ignorance and God's incomprehensibility. The work has been issued in modern versions by Evelyn Underhill (1912), and Dom Justin McCann (1924). The suggestion that the *Cloud* is by Walter Hilton, a Nottinghamshire Augustinian (who died in 1396) does not seem to have met with general acceptance.

Clough (kluf), **Arthur Hugh.** b. at Liverpool, England, Jan. 1, 1819; d. at Florence, Italy, Nov. 13, 1861. English poet. He was educated at Rugby, where he came under the spell of its great master, Thomas Arnold, and at Balliol College, Oxford, where he formed his lifelong friendship with Arnold's son Matthew Arnold. He was made a fellow of Oriel College in 1841, but resigned in 1848 because of religious doubts. He was in America in 1852, writing and teaching, and when he returned to England he became an examiner in the Education Office, and acted as secretary to Florence Nightingale. In 1859 he went to Greece, Constantinople, the Pyrenees, and Italy, in a vain attempt to recover his shattered health. He died of paralysis in 1861, as his mother had done the year before. No one reads the long poems of Clough today, and only a few of his short ones are found in anthologies: *Qua Cursum Ventus* (a title taken from Vergil), *Qui Laborat, Orat* (He who labors, prays), and *Say Not the Struggle Naught Availeth* (a favorite of Winston Churchill and Franklin Delano Roosevelt). In his short life Clough made many friends: Carlyle, who called him "a diamond sifted out of the general rubbish heap," Thackeray, Emerson, Lowell, Charles Eliot Norton, and (the one who has done most for his memory) Arnold, who was inspired by Clough's death to write his great elegy *Thyrsis* (1867). It is interesting to note that Clough died in the same city, and in the same year, as another English poet, Elizabeth Barrett Browning.

Clout (klout), **Colin.** A pastoral name assumed by Spenser, from Skelton's *Colyn Cloute.*

Clove and Orange. An inseparable pair of coxcombs in Ben Jonson's *Every Man Out of His Humour.*

Clown. In Shakespeare's *Winter's Tale,* a rustic countryman, the son of the Old Shepherd. He reports the death of Antigonus (III.iii) and later is forced to go to Sicilia, where he gives himself the airs of a gentleman.

Clowns. In Shakespeare's *Hamlet,* the two Gravediggers who are jesting and singing when Hamlet comes upon them as they dig Ophelia's grave (V.i). Their rough comedy provides a sharp contrast to the sensitive Hamlet's remarks about life and death. There are also unnamed clowns making brief appearances in *Othello, Titus Andronicus,* and *Antony and Cleopatra.* Other characters, such as Touchstone, Feste, and Lavatch, are identified in the Dramatis Personae as clowns, but display a superior, more sophisticated type of humor, quite unlike the buffoonery of most of the clowns. See also under **Fool.**

Clowns' Houses. A collection of poems by Edith Sitwell, published in 1918.

Clumsy (klum'zi), **Sir Tunbelly.** A country gentleman in John Vanbrugh's play *The Relapse;* a coarse, unwieldy boor, the father of Miss Hoyden. The character is retained in Sheridan's *A Trip to Scarborough,* an adaptation of *The Relapse.*

---

fat, fāte, fär, åsk, fāre; net, mē, hėr; pin, pīne; not, nōte, mōve, nôr; up, lūte, púll; ᵺн, then;

Clutterbuck (klut'ẽr.buk), **Captain Cuthbert.** The name which Sir Walter Scott assumed to publish *The Monastery*, *The Abbot*, and *The Fortunes of Nigel*. This, and various other pseudonyms adopted by Scott, were made necessary by the fact that the novelist was also a member of the Scottish bar and believed that the writing of fiction was too undignified an occupation for open acknowledgment by a scholar of the law. He therefore long disavowed the bulk of the work upon which his reputation now rests, and admitted only during his latter years that he had written it (although many people in English letters, including Jane Austen, had long since guessed the truth of the matter).

Clutton-Brock (klut'ọn.brok'), **Arthur.** b. at Weybridge, Surrey, England, March 23, 1868; d. at Godalming, Surrey, England, Jan. 8, 1924. An English editor, essayist, and art and literary critic. Educated at Eton and New College, Oxford, and called to the bar in 1895, he practiced law for several years. In 1904 he began writing with contributions to the *Times Literary Supplement* and as literary editor for the London *Speaker*. Subsequently he was art critic for the London papers *Tribune*, *Morning Post*, and *Times*, and a member (1909 *et seq.*) of the Fabian Society. The author of books on French and English cathedrals, he also wrote *Shelley—The Man and the Poet* (1909), *William Morris—His Work and Influence* (1914), *Thoughts on the War* (2 vols., 1914–15), *Studies in Christianity* (1918), *Essays on Art* (1918), *Essays on Books* (1920), *More Essays* (1921), and *The Necessity of Art* (1924).

Clymene (klim'ẹ.nē). In Greek mythology, a daughter of Oceanus and Tethys, beloved of Apollo, and mother of Atalanta. She was also the mother of Atlas, Prometheus, and Epimetheus by Iapetus.

Clymene. In Greek mythology, a nymph, and mother of Phaëthon, whose father was the sun god Helios.

Clym of the Clough (klim; kluf). [Also, **Clim.**] In the Robin Hood legends, a celebrated archer.

Clym Yeobright (yō'brīt). See **Yeobright, Clym.**

Clytemnestra or **Clytaemnestra** (klī.tẹm.nes'trạ, klit.ẹm-). In Greek legend, the daughter of Tyndareus and Leda, wife of Agamemnon, king of Argos, or Mycenae, and mother of Orestes, Electra, and Iphigenia. She took Aegisthus as paramour during the absence of her husband as leader of the expedition against Troy. The most common version of the legend is that she slew her husband in the bath on his return from Troy, partly to avoid the consequences of her adultery and partly from jealousy of Cassandra, daughter of Priam, whom at the taking of Troy Agamemnon had received as his prize, and by whom he had two sons. She and Aegisthus were in turn put to death by her son Orestes.

Clytie (klī'tē) or **Clytia** (klish'i.ạ). In Greek mythology, a water nymph so enamored of the sun god, Apollo, that every day she watched his course across the sky. The gods took pity on her unrequited love and metamorphosed her into a heliotrope, a flower whose face follows the course of the sun. Hence, the heliotrope has come to symbolize unwavering love.

Cnut (knöt). See **Canute.**

Cnut's Song. See **Song of Canute, The.**

"Coal Hole." A tavern on the Strand, in London, from his knowledge of which Thackeray derived some details for his description of the "Cave of Harmony," in *The Newcomes* and various other works.

Coavinses (kō'vin.ziz). In Dickens's novel *Bleak House*, the office of the sheriff on Cursitor Street.

Cob (kob), **Oliver.** An illiterate water-carrier in Ben Jonson's play *Every Man in His Humour*. Before water from the New River was brought into London the city was chiefly supplied from conduits, generally erected by rich citizens. Water was carried from these by men called "tankard-bearers," and sold. Cob was one of these, and gave a sort of notoriety to his class from his position in Jonson's play.

Cobb (kob), **James.** b. 1756; d. 1818. An English playwright. He was the author of numerous comedies, operas, and other works.

Cobbe (kob), **Frances Power.** b. at Dublin, Ireland, Dec. 4, 1822; d. in Wales, April 5, 1904. A British philanthropist, feminist, editor, and philosophical and religious writer. Largely self-educated, except for a brief period in a Brighton school, she traveled in Greece and Italy, meeting Mazzini, the Italian revolutionist, and becoming Italian correspondent for the London *Daily News*. She aided Mary Carpenter in the latter's work on behalf of neglected children, agitated in favor of votes and college degrees for women and against vivisection, wrote (1868–75) for the *Echo*, and edited the works (14 vols., 1863–71) of Theodore Parker. She was the author of *The Theory of Intuitive Morals* (1855; published anonymously), *Broken Lights* (1864), *Studies of Ethical and Social Subjects* (1865), *Dawning Lights* (1868), *The Final Cause of Women* (1869), *Darwinism in Morals* (1872), *Doomed to be Saved* (1874), *The Duties of Women* (1881), *The Scientific Spirit* (1888), and her *Autobiography* (2 vols., 1904).

Cobbett (kob'ẹt), **William.** [Pseudonym, **Peter Porcupine.**] b. at Farnham, Surrey, England, March 9, 1762; d. at Normandy Farm, near Guildford, England, June 18, 1835. An English journalist, pamphleteer, and politician. After seeing military service in Nova Scotia, he began his journalistic career at Philadelphia, where he was three times sued for libel. Back in England in 1800, he began in 1802 to publish *Cobbett's Weekly Political Register*, which he edited until his death. He spent two years in prison (1810–12) and was fined 1,000 pounds for an article attacking flogging in the army. During the years 1817–19 he was again in America. He was elected a member of Parliament for Oldham in 1832, a vital year in English history. His works are *Observations on the Emigration of Dr. Joseph Priestley* (1794), an anonymous pamphlet, *A Bone to Gnaw for the Democrats, A Kick for a Bite*, and *A Little Plain English Addressed to the People of the United States* (all 1795), political pamphlets, *A New Year's Gift for the Democrats* (1796), *Grammar of the English Language* (1818), *A Journal of a Year's Residence in the United States* (1818–19), *History of the Protestant Reforma-*

d, d or j; ṣ, s or sh; ṭ, t or ch; ẓ, z or zh; o, F. cloche; ü, F. menu; ċh, Sc. loch; ṅ, F. bonbor.

tion (1824–27), *Advice to Young Men* (1829), and *Rural Rides* (1830), dealing with political and agricultural conditions in the English countryside. Cobbett did much of his writing under the name of "Peter Porcupine," which was appropriate enough in view of the invective in which he indulged. Students of style regard his English as clear, vigorous, and idiomatic.

Cobbler of Preston (pres'ton), **The.** A musical farce by Charles Johnson, founded on the adventures of Christopher Sly in Shakespeare's *Taming of the Shrew*, but using incidents also from *The Merry Wives of Windsor*. It was first acted in 1716, and altered and produced with music in 1817. Another, more popular version was produced by Christopher Bullock at about the same time.

Cobbold (kob'ọld), **Richard.** b. at Ipswich, Suffolk, England, 1797; d. Jan. 5, 1877. An English novelist and divine. His chief work is *History of Margaret Catchpole, a Suffolk Girl* (1845), a fictional life of an actual Margaret Catchpole (1773–1841), a servant girl and adventuress who twice escaped a death sentence and was transported to Australia, where she died, a respected woman, 40 years later. Cobbold told the story with her full knowledge and permission, omitting only (at her request) her married name. Other novels by him are *Freston Tower* (1850) and *Courtland* (1852).

Cobden (kob'dẹn), **Richard.** b. at Heyshott, near Midhurst, Sussex, England, June 3, 1804; d. at London, April 2, 1865. An English statesman and publicist, especially noted as an advocate of free trade and of peace. He entered business as a salesman and in 1831 moved to Manchester to start, with partners, a calico-printing firm. In the boom period of the following years it flourished and he was soon able to indulge a strong bent for travel and for public affairs. He visited the U. S. in 1835 and 1859 (his impressions were recorded, and only recently became available, in *The American Diaries of Richard Cobden* (1953), edited by Elizabeth Hoon Cawley), traveled extensively in Europe, and spoke French fluently. From 1838 to 1846 he was the leading figure in the Anti-Corn Law League, which conducted a momentous campaign against protective duties for agriculture. Cobden was a member of Parliament most of the time from 1841 to his death, but declined party affiliation and opportunities to become a cabinet minister. In 1859–60 he negotiated a commercial treaty with France which seemed at the time to be an important step toward universal free trade. All his life Cobden was an "agitator" and reformer whose peculiar mark was persuasiveness, in Parliament, in pamphlets, and at public meetings. His faith in free trade and the power of education had a strong moralistic tinge and led him to strong advocacy of nonintervention in foreign affairs, peace by arbitration, and the freeing of colonies which could govern themselves. He was the most effective voice of the English middle class in the struggle against the monopoly of the old aristocracy and other vested interests, and did much to fix in English thought the principle that free enterprise would lead to universal prosperity and peace. He supported the cause of the North during the Civil War in the U. S. He failed, however, to carry his own Man-

chester with him in opposition to the Crimean War and died somewhat disillusioned with the selfishness and short-sightedness of the middle class. His *Political Writings* were published in 1867; his *Speeches on Questions of Public Policy* (ed. by Bright and Rogers) in 1870.

Cobham (kob'am), **Eleanor.** See under **Gloucester, Eleanor, Duchess of.**

Cobweb (kob'web). A fairy in Shakespeare's *Midsummer Night's Dream*.

Cock, The. A tavern in Fleet Street, London, opposite the Temple. Tennyson immortalized it in his *Will Waterproof's Lyrical Monologue*.

Cockaigne or **Cocagne** (ko.kān'). A fabled land of luxury and idleness, perhaps in part intended to ridicule the stories of the mythical Avalon: called Lubberland by 16th-century English poets.

Cock and the Fox, The. A version of Chaucer's *Nun's Priest's Tale*, by John Dryden.

Cockburn (kok'bẻrn), **Alicia** (or **Alison**). b. at Fairnalee, Selkirkshire, Scotland, c1710; d. at Edinburgh, Nov. 22, 1794. A Scottish lyric poet remembered for her ballad *The Flowers of the Forest* (1765), opening with the line, "I've seen the smiling of Fortune beguiling." She knew Burns, who admired her lyric so much that he imitated it, and she was a friend of Hume. According to Scott, "in person and features, she somewhat resembled Queen Elizabeth . . . she was proud of her auburn hair, which remained unbleached by time even when she was upwards of eighty years old." In her will, she left her emerald ring to Scott's mother.

Cockburn, Catherine. [Maiden name, **Trotter.**] b. at London, Aug. 16, 1679; d. May 11, 1749. An English dramatist and philosophical writer; wife (married in 1708) of Patrick Cockburn, a clergyman. She wrote *Agnes de Castro* (acted 1696), *Fatal Friendship* (acted 1698), *Love at a Loss* (a comedy, 1701), *The Unhappy Penitent* (acted 1701), and *The Revolution of Sweden* (acted 1706).

Cocke Lorell's Bote (kok lôr'ẹlz bōt, lor'ẹlz). A satirical ballad (c1515), written in imitation of Sebastian Brant's *Ship of Fools*. It tells the story of Cocke Lorell, a sea captain, who fills his ship with all kinds of renegades and thieving tradesmen, and sails from port to port in England. The name "Cocke Lorell" means "Chief Rascal," and he was the prototype of the Knave in English Renaissance literature.

Cockeram (kok'ram), **Henry.** fl. about the middle of the 17th century. An English scholar (of whose life virtually nothing is known), author of what is considered the first published dictionary of the English language. The book is entitled *The English Dictionarie, or a New Interpreter of Hard English Words* (c1623; 2nd ed., 1626; 12th ed., revised and enlarged by another editor, 1670). It had been preceded, however, by several books, notably Robert Cawdrey's *The Table Alphabeticall of Hard Words* (1604), which gave definitions and derivations of selected English words.

Cock Lane Ghost. The ghost of a Mrs. Kent who appeared as a "luminous lady" and to whom knockings and other mysterious noises were attributed: exposed as a fraud perpetrated in 1762

---

fat, fāte, fär, ȧsk, fãre; net, mē, hẻr; pin, pīne; not, nōte, mŏve, nôr; up, lūte, pŭll; ᴛʜ, then;

in Cock Lane, Smithfield, London, by a man named Parsons and his 11-year-old daughter Elizabeth. Samuel Johnson, among others, visited the house, and took an interest in exposing the fraud. However, he was attacked for his supposed credulity by Charles Churchill in his long poem *The Ghost* (1763). Parsons was pilloried.

Cockledemoy (kok'l.dę.moi). An adroit and amusing trickster in John Marston's play *The Dutch Courtezan*. His duping of a London tradesman, Mulligrub, forms the subplot of the play, and his name was used as the title in another version.

Cockney School (kok'ni). A name derisively given by some English 19th-century Tory critics to a set of writers including Hazlitt, Shelley, Keats, Leigh Hunt, and others. Leigh Hunt was considered the representative member of this coterie.

Cockpit, The. A London theater (originally a very simple roofed structure used for cockfighting, converted into a theater in 1616) which stood in a narrow court, called Pitt Place, formerly Cockpit Alley, running out of Drury Lane. The theater was owned by Christopher Beeston. It was renamed The Phoenix, and Worcester's Men, an acting company also known as Queen Anne's Men, made it their home until 1619. It was badly damaged in a riot on Shrove Tuesday, in 1617.

Cocktail Party, The. A play in poetry (1950) by T. S. Eliot. The theme, the broken marriage of Edward and Lavinia Chamberlayne, is symbolically treated so as to make it clear that modern society is broken and spiritually sick. The action of the play, in two acts and five scenes, takes place in the Chamberlayne's London flat, and in a consulting room in Harley Street. One of the leading characters, "An Unidentified Guest," turns out to be a psychiatrist who gets at the truth and tries to make his patients see it.

Cockton (kok'ton), **Henry.** b. at London, Dec. 7, 1807; d. at Bury Saint Edmunds, Suffolk, England, June 26, 1853. An English comic novelist. He was the author of *Valentine Vox the Ventriloquist* (1840), *Sylvester Sound the Somnambulist* (1843–44), *Lady Felicia* (1852), *Percy Effingham* (1852), and other novels illustrated by such artists as Cruikshank, Leech, and Thomas Onwhyn.

Cockwood (kok'wùd), **Lady.** In George Etherege's comedy *She Would if She Could*, a female Tartuffe who hides a disgraceful intrigue under a great pretense of religious devotion.

Cockwood, Sir Oliver. In George Etherege's *She Would if She Could*, the lecherous husband of Lady Cockwood. He mistakenly solicits his own wife (thinking her a whore) during a drunken spree.

Cocles (kok'lēz, kō'klēz), **Publius Horatius.** See **Horatius.**

Cocoa-tree Club. A London club, which was the Tory Cocoa-tree Chocolate-house of Queen Anne's reign, at 64 St. James Street. It was converted into a gaming house and a club, probably before 1746, when the house was the headquarters of the Jacobite party, and the resort of the wits of the time. It still exists as a club.

Cocytus (kō.sī'tus). In Greek mythology, one of the five rivers surrounding Hades. Cocytus was the so-called Wailing River. The other four were: the Styx (Hateful), Acheron (Woeful), Pyriphlegethon (Fiery), and Lethe (Forgetful).

Codex Exoniensis (kō'deks ek.sō.ni.en'sis). See **Exeter Book.**

Codlin (kod'lin), **Tom.** A cynical exhibitor of a Punch-and-Judy show, in Charles Dickens's *Old Curiosity Shop.* He is a partner in the show with "Short Trotters" Harris, who is a bright little person in contrast with Codlin's somberness.

Cœlebs (sē'lebz). Any bachelor desirous of marrying: from the hero of Hannah More's novel *Cœlebs in Search of a Wife* (1809).

Cœlebs in Search of a Wife. A novel by Hannah More, published in 1809. It is a tract of social criticism, the episodes tied to the search of the hero for a wife having certain qualities.

Coelica (sē'li.ka). [Also, **Caelica.**] A collection of short poems of different lengths, by Fulke Greville, 1st Baron Brooke. It appeared in a folio volume containing plays and other poems in 1633. The latter are love poems or philosophical poems, for the most part written before 1590.

Coffee Club, the. See **Rota Club.**

Coffee-House Politician, The. The title of Fielding's *Rape upon Rape,* in the edition of 1730.

coherence. Suitable connection or dependence, proceeding from the natural relation of parts or things to each other, as in the parts of a discourse or of any system; consistency.

Little needed the Princes and potentates of the earth, which way soever the Gospel was spread, to study ways how to make a coherence between the Churches politie and theirs.

(Milton, *Reformation in England.*)

Cokayne (kō.kān'), Sir **Aston.** b. at Elvaston, Derbyshire, England, in December, 1608; d. at Derby, England, in February, 1684. An English Royalist poet and dramatist. His works include the comedies *The Obstinate Lady* (1657) and *Trappolin Suppos'd a Prince* (1659), *Tragedy of Ovid* (1662), *Small Poems of Divers Sorts* (1658; reissued, 1652, 1659), and *Choice Poems of Several Sorts, with three new Plays* (1669).

Coke (kùk, kōk), Sir **Edward.** [Called Lord **Coke** (or **Cooke**).] b. at Mileham, Norfolk, England, Feb. 1, 1552; d. at Stoke Poges, England, Sept. 3, 1634. An English jurist. He was speaker of the House of Commons (1592–93), attorney general (1593–94), chief justice of the Common Pleas (1606), and chief justice of the King's Bench (1613). He came into conflict with James I and Francis Bacon on matters touching the royal prerogative, and was removed from the bench on Nov. 15, 1616. Among the noted cases which he conducted as prosecutor are those of Essex and Southampton in 1601, of Sir Walter Raleigh in 1603 (in which he disgraced himself by the brutality of his language), and of the gunpowder plotters in 1605. In the later part of his life he rendered notable service, in Parliament, to the cause of English freedom, his last important speech being a direct attack on Buckingham. His chief works are his *Reports* (1600–15) and his *Institutes,* which consist of a reprint and translation of Littleton's *Tenures* with

ḍ, d or j; ş, s or sh; ţ, t or ch; z̧, z or zh; o, F. cloche; ü, F. menu; ċh, Sc. loch; ṅ, F. bonbon.

a commentary (popularly known as "Coke upon Littleton"); the text of various statutes from Magna Charta to the time of James I, with a commentary; a treatise on criminal law; and a treatise on the jurisdiction of the different law courts.

Cokes (kōks), **Bartholomew.** Foolish young squire in Ben Jonson's comedy *Bartholomew Fair*.

Colbrand (kŏl'brand). [Also, **Coldbrand**.] A legendary Danish giant, slain by Guy of Warwick, as told in the 14th-century metrical romance *Guy of Warwick* and repeated in Michael Drayton's *Polyolbion*.

Colchester (kōl'ches̟.tẽr, -ches″tẽr). [Latin, **Camulodunum**; Old English, **Colneceaster**.] A municipal borough, market town, and industrial center in SE England, in Essex, situated on the river Colne ab. 22 mi. NE of Chelmsford, ab. 52 mi. NE of London by rail. It has long been famous for its oyster fishery. Other industries include printing and bookbinding, manufacture of clothing, and the manufacture of agricultural machinery and gasoline engines. Dairy cattle are kept in the vicinity of Colchester to supply milk to the London market. It was an important textile center in the Middle Ages, and was formerly a seaport, but became a market for agricultural produce when the silting of the estuary of the river Colne destroyed its maritime position. It contains many Roman antiquities, including Roman walls which remain almost entire. It has a castle and the ruins of Saint Botolph's Priory and of a Benedictine monastery. The castle is the most powerful Norman military structure in England. The dimensions of the keep are 168 by 126 ft., and its walls vary in thickness from 11 to 30 ft. In one portion of the walls appears Roman herringbone work in brick. The chapel is now a museum, containing one of the finest collections of Romano-British antiquities in N Europe. Camulodunum was the earliest Roman colony in Britain, and was destroyed by the Iceni, but rebuilt. Later it became a stronghold, and was taken by Fairfax in 1648. Camulodunum (called Camalodunum in the *Itinerary*), was the capital of the British princes after they had submitted to the Romans, and was the first Roman city in the island honored with the rank of a colonia. The Roman walls which have endured leave no doubt that Colchester is the site of the ancient Camulodunum.

Colchis (kol'kis). The legendary land of Medea and the Golden Fleece.

Coldbath Fields (kōld'bàth). Part of Middlesex, England, from which the great Coldbath Fields prison took its name. The original house of correction here was built in the reign of James I. It was long overcrowded and was closed in 1886.

Cold Harbor. A novel by Francis Brett Young, published in 1924. It is a modern example of the 18th-century novel of terror.

Cold Harbour. [Also, **Cole-Harbour**; corrupted, **Coal Harbour**.] Formerly a building in the parish of Allhallows the Less, near the Thames, London. Stow gives a long account of the various merchant princes and great men through whose hands it passed till it came to the Earl of Shrewsbury, who in 1553 changed its name to Shrewsbury House; the next earl "took it down, and in place thereof

builded a number of small tenements, now letten out for great rents to people of all sorts." It was at this time a sanctuary for debtors, gamesters, and such; hence the phrase "To take sanctuary in Cold Harbour."

Coldstream (kōld'strēm), **Lady Catharine.** A Scottish woman of quality in Samuel Foote's play *The Maid of Bath*. She is a shrewd old woman who tries her hand at matchmaking.

Coldstream, Sir Charles. A languid man of fashion in Mathew's farce *Used Up*.

Coldstream Guards. A regiment of British footguards, first enrolled by General Monck at Coldstream, Scotland, 1659–60.

Cole (kōl), **G. D. H.** [Full name, **George Douglas Howard Cole**.] b. at Cambridge, England, Sept. 25, 1889—. An English economist, sociologist, professor, historian, biographer, and (with his wife, Margaret Isabel Cole) author of crime fiction. He was educated at St. Paul's School, London, and at Balliol College, Oxford (of which he is a B.A. 1912 and an M.A. 1915). He has taught philosophy at Durham University, and economics at London and Oxford universities. He is a Fabian Socialist and a member of the Labour Party. On Aug. 18, 1918, he married Margaret Isabel Postgate (b. 1893), who is also his literary partner. He is the author of *The World of Labour* (1913), *Labour in War Time* (1915), *Principles of Socialism* (1917), *Democracy in Industry* (1920), *Out of Work: A Study of Unemployment* (1923), *A Short History of the British Working-Class Movement* (1927), *A Guide to Modern Politics* (1934, with his wife), *What Marx Really Meant* (1934), *Europe, Russia, and the Future* (1941), *Fabian Socialism* (1943), and many other political, economic, and sociological studies. He has written lives of William Cobbett (1924, rev. 1925) and Robert Owen (1925, rev. 1930), and two volumes of poetry, *New Beginnings* (1914) and *The Crooked World* (1933). To a wider and more general reading public, Cole (with his wife) is not merely known but is popular as the author of *The Brooklyn Murders* (1923), *The Death of a Millionaire* (1925), *The Murder at Crome House* (1927), *The Man from the River*, a Wilson Story and *Superintendent Wilson's Holiday* (both 1928), *The Corpse in the Constable's Garden, Dead Man's Watch, The Great Southern Mystery* (the last called *The Walking Corpse* in the American ed.; all 1931), *Death of a Star* (1932), *End of an Ancient Mariner* (1933), *Death in the Quarry* and *Murder in Four Parts* (both 1934), *The Big Business Murder, Dr. Tancred Begins*, and *Scandal at School* (all 1935), *Disgrace to the College* and *The Missing Aunt* (both 1938), *Mrs. Warrender's Profession* and *Off With Her Head!* (both 1938), *Double Blackmail* and *Greek Tragedy* (both 1939), *Murder in the Munitions Works* (1940), *The Counterpoint Murder* (1941), *Knife in the Dark* and *Toper's End* (both 1942), *Death of a Bride* (1945), and many others.

Cole, John William. [Pseudonym, **John William Calcraft**.] fl. in the second half of the 19th century. An English miscellaneous writer. He was the author of *Russia and the Russians* (1854), *Life and Theatrical Times of Charles Kean* (1860), and *The Bride of Lammermoor*, a drama.

Cole, King. See King Cole.

Cole, Margaret Isabel. [Maiden name, **Postgate.**] b. at Cambridge, England, 1893—. English lecturer and writer; wife (married 1918) and literary partner of G. D. H. Cole, and sister of R. W. Postgate, with whom her husband also collaborated in his works on economics. Daughter of a Cambridge professor, she was educated at Rodean School and at the Cambridge college for women, Girton. She taught classical subjects at St. Paul's Girls' School, and has been a London University lecturer. From 1916 to 1925 she was an assistant secretary in the labor research department. Like her husband she is a Socialist and belongs to and has held office in Fabian groups. On her own, she is the author of pamphlets on labor subjects. As individuals or as a literary team, the Coles are considered the English equivalent of "S.S. Van Dine" (Willard Huntington Wright). Her works include *Margaret Postgate's Poems* (1918), *Twelve Studies in Soviet Russia* (1932), *Marriage Past and Present* (1938), and *Makers of the Labour Party* (1947). In collaboration with her husband she wrote the detective stories *The Brooklyn Murders* (1923), *A Lesson in Crime* (1933), *Last Will and Testament* (1936), *Greek Tragedy* (1939), and many others.

Cole, Mrs. A character played by Samuel Foote in his comedy *The Minor*, a procuress whose pretended reformation was intended as a slur on the Methodists. Her reference to her friend Dr. Squintum gave very great offense, as he was at once identified with George Whitefield. She was based on a real person, a "Mother Douglass."

Colepepper (kul′pep″ėr), **Captain John.** [Also called **Peppercul.**] A bully and murderer in Sir Walter Scott's *The Fortunes of Nigel*.

Coleridge (kōl′rij), **Hartley.** [Full name, **David Hartley Coleridge.**] b. at Clevedon, Somersetshire, England, Sept. 17, 1796; d. at Rydal, Westmorland, England, Jan. 6, 1849. An English poet, essayist, and editor; eldest son of Samuel Taylor Coleridge. He was educated at Ambleside, and at Merton College, Oxford. He tried teaching, in which he failed as he did in everything that he attempted. He had great possibilities but he did not know how to make the best of them. He wrote for the *London Magazine* and *Blackwood's*, and he published *Biographia Borealis* (1833), which came out three years later as *The Worthies of Yorkshire and Lancaster*, and edited the plays of Massinger and Ford in 1840. His *Poems* appeared in 1833, and his *Literary Remains* was edited in 1851 by his brother, Derwent. A few sonnets, *On Prayer, To Homer, To Shakespeare*, and the autobiographical *When I Review the Course that I Have Run*, have been praised by critics and lovers of poetry.

Coleridge, Henry Nelson. b. at Ottery St. Mary, Devonshire, England, Oct. 25, 1798; d. Jan. 26, 1843. An English lawyer and man of letters; nephew of Samuel Taylor Coleridge and husband of Sara Coleridge. He became his uncle's literary executor, and edited several of his works, besides publishing his *Table Talk*.

Coleridge, Mary Elizabeth. b. at London, Sept. 23, 1861; d. at Harrogate, Yorkshire, England, Aug. 25, 1907. An English poet, novelist, critic, biographer, and teacher; great-grandniece of Samuel Taylor Coleridge. Educated privately, she began writing and drawing at an early age; two of her literary favorites were Browning and Tolstoy. Influenced by the latter, she taught English literature to poor girls in her own home, and also taught (1895–1907) at the Working Women's College. She was the author of *Fancy's Following* (1896), *Fancy's Guerdon* (1897), *Last Poems* (1905), and *Poems Old and New* (1907), of the novels *The Seven Sleepers of Ephesus* (1893), *The King With Two Faces* (1897), *The Fiery Dawn* (1901), *The Shadow on the Wall* (1904), and *The Lady on the Drawing-Room Floor* (1906), and of *Holman Hunt* (1908), a biography.

Coleridge, Samuel Taylor. b. at Ottery St. Mary, Devonshire, England, Oct. 21, 1772; d. at Highgate, London, July 25, 1834. An English poet, literary critic, lecturer, political journalist, philosopher, and theologian. After the death of his father, a poor clergyman with a large family, Coleridge received a presentation (1782) to the school Christ's Hospital, and from there passed to Jesus College, Cambridge (1791–93, 1794) by means of scholarships. He did not take his degree, but formed with Southey a plan called pantisocracy, of establishing a small communistic society in America. The plan fell through, because of lack of money. In 1795 Coleridge married Sarah Fricker, the sister of Southey's wife, and in 1796 published his first volume of poems. In the same year he began the publication of *The Watchman*, a liberal political periodical which failed after ten issues. After continued money troubles, he was considering entering the Unitarian ministry, but received in 1798 an annuity of 150 pounds from the brothers Josiah and Thomas Wedgwood, which permitted him to continue his literary life.

Peak of Poetic Power. During the year following June, 1797, Coleridge was stimulated by his companionship with Wordsworth to his greatest achievements in poetry, including *The Ancient Mariner, Kubla Khan*, and the first part of *Christabel*. After the joint publication by Wordsworth and Coleridge of *Lyrical Ballads* (1798), both poets went to Germany, where Coleridge learned the language and studied for some months at the University of Göttingen. After his return to England in 1799 he translated Schiller's *Wallenstein*, and wrote political leading articles for the antiministerial newspaper, *The Morning Post*. In 1800 he settled in the Lake District to be near Wordsworth again, but his health suffered in the damp climate, and he became a slave to opium, which he had used as a remedy. Though he wrote the second part of *Christabel* in 1800 and *Dejection* in 1802, he was henceforth to write little poetry. In 1804 he sailed for Malta in search of health and became acting secretary to the governor; but he returned in 1806 without improvement. He gave seven series of disorderly but brilliant lectures on Shakespeare and other literary subjects from 1808 to 1819, published another political and philosophical periodical called *The Friend* in 1809–10, and revised his tragedy *Osorio* (1797) for successful performance at Drury Lane in 1813, but he was often intellectually submerged by opium until in 1816 he became the guest of Mr. Gillman, a physician at Highgate, with whom he lived until his death in 1834. He was re-

ḍ, d or j; ṣ, s or sh; ṭ, t or ch; ẓ, z or zh; o, F. cloche; ü, F. menu; ċh, Sc. loch; ṅ, F. bonbon.

deemed from his slavery to opium by Mr. Gillman, and published several religious or political works, but the collection of his poems in 1817 at the same time as his autobiography was the result of earlier labors. The autobiography *Biographia Literaria* contains his greatest literary criticism, chiefly concerned with Wordsworth.

Evaluation and Bibliography. Though his actual achievement in poetry was small in quantity, Coleridge was the intellectual center of the Romantic Movement, perhaps the greatest of English literary critics, influential in conservative politics and religion, and the first important spokesman of German idealistic metaphysics in England in the early 19th century. The standard edition of his poems is by E. H. Coleridge, and the standard biographies are by J. D. Campbell and E. K. Chambers. *The Road to Xanadu* by J. L. Lowes is the most influential criticism of his poetry. The *Cambridge Bibliography of English Literature* (vol. III) includes a conveniently accessible bibliography. See also *The Letters of Samuel Taylor Coleridge* (1952), selected by Kathleen Raine, and *The Indifferent Horseman* (1954), by Maurice Carpenter.

Coleridge, Sara. b. at Greta Hall, near Keswick, England, Dec. 22, 1802; d. at London, May 3, 1852. An English writer; daughter of Samuel Taylor Coleridge and wife (married in 1829) of Henry Nelson Coleridge. She is best known as the editor, after her husband's death, of her father's writings, and for *Phantasmion* (1837), a fairy tale.

Colet (kol'ĕt), **John.** b. at London, c1467; d. there, Sept. 16, 1519. An English theologian and classical scholar. He became dean of Saint Paul's in 1505, and refounded (1512) Saint Paul's School. He was the intimate friend of Erasmus and More, and one of the chief promoters of the "new learning" of the Renaissance and indirectly of the Reformation. Although not directly advocating the Reformation (he never relinquished his Catholicism), Colet promoted various reforms in clerical procedure. In 1514 he accompanied Erasmus on a pilgrimage to Canterbury. He preached (1515) at the installation of Wolsey as cardinal.

Colevile (kōl'vil), **Sir John.** In Shakespeare's *2 Henry IV*, a "famous rebel" who yields to Falstaff in Gaultree Forest and is sent to his execution at York.

Colin Clout (kol'in klout'). See under **Colin Clout's Come Home Again.**

Colin Clout's Come Home Again. A poem by Edmund Spenser, written after visiting London (1589–91). Spenser took the name from Skelton's *Colyn Cloute*, and called himself Colin Clout in all his poems. Colin Clout is also a character in Gay's pastoral *The Shepherd's Week.*

Coliseum (kol.i.sē'um). See **Colosseum.**

Colkitto (kol.kit'ō). In the first of the two *Tetrachordon* sonnets by John Milton, the chief military commander under the Marquis of Montrose. Scott used him in the *Legend of Montrose.*

collaboration. The act of working together; united labor, especially in literary or scientific work.

Collar, The. A poem (1633) by George Herbert, a religious lyric, the title of which has the dual task of suggesting an ox-yoke and the article of dress

worn by the clergy. The poet expresses religious doubts and fears, but he settles them through his realization of the need for submission to the authority of God. The conflict is resolved in the famous concluding lines:

> Methought I heard one calling, "Child!"
> And I replied, "My Lord!"

Colleen Bawn, or, The Brides of Garry-Owen (kol'ĕn bôn'; gar'i.ō'ĕn), **The.** A play by Dion Boucicault, founded on Gerald Griffin's novel *The Collegians.* It was first performed on Sept. 10, 1860.

College of Arms. See **Heralds' College.**

Collegians, The. A novel by Gerald Griffin, issued anonymously in 1829. In 1861 an edition was produced, illustrated by Phiz, and called *The Colleen Bawn; or, The Collegian's Wife.*

Collier (kol'yėr, kol'i.ėr), **Constance.** [Original surname, **Hardie.**] b. Jan. 22, 1878; d. at New York, April 25, 1955. An English actress. Having made her debut in childhood as a fairy in *A Midsummer Night's Dream*, she first appeared (1893) at London in Shaw's *Don Juan.* Later (1901–08) she was with Sir Beerbohm Tree's company at His Majesty's Theatre, London. She made her first appearance at New York in 1908 and afterward played in the U. S. many times, notably in *Dinner at Eight* (1932–33). Among her other outstanding parts were Gertrude in *Hamlet* (opposite John Barrymore), Nancy in *Oliver Twist*, Mrs. Cheveley in Wilde's *An Ideal Husband*, and the Duchess of Towers in Ibsen's *Peter Ibbetson.* She also played parts in such motion pictures as *Stage Door* and *Shadow of a Doubt.*

Collier, Jeremy. b. at Stow-cum-Qui, Cambridgeshire, England, Sept. 23, 1650; d. at London, April 26, 1726. An English nonjuring clergyman, noted as a controversialist. He was graduated from Cambridge in 1673, was rector (1679–85) of Ampton in Suffolk, and moved (1685) to London, where he was for some time lecturer at Grey's Inn. A political pamphlet, in which he maintained that the withdrawal of the king was not an abdication and that the throne was not vacant, caused his imprisonment for a short time in Newgate prison in 1688, and in 1692 he was again imprisoned for political reasons. In 1696, with two other nonjuring clergymen, he attended Sir John Friend and Sir William Parkyns (who were condemned to death as conspirators against the life of William III) to the scaffold and absolved them. Having concealed himself to avoid arrest, he was outlawed on July 2, 1696. He was consecrated (1713) a bishop. He wrote a large number of controversial pamphlets, *Historical, Geographical, Genealogical, and Poetical Dictionary* (1701–21), the learned *Ecclesiastical History of Great Britain . . . to the End of the Reign of Charles II* (1708–14), and the famous *Short View of the Immorality and Profaneness of the English Stage* (1698). The last work was a vigorous attack upon the coarseness of the contemporary theater, and produced a great impression. It brought from John Dryden a confession of fault and a declaration of repentance, won unwilling recognition from other dramatists, and initiated a reformation.

Collier, John. b. at London, May 3, 1901—. An English novelist, short-story writer, and poet. He was educated at home, and is not a university man.

fat, fāte, fär. àsk, fāre; net, mē, hėr; pin, pīne; not, nōte, mōve, nôr; up, lūte, pùll; ᴛʜ, then;

He began writing poetry in 1920, had a volume out in 1921, and won a prize for four of his poems in 1922. He has been poetry editor of *Time and Tide*, and he showed his scholarly interests by editing John Aubrey, the 17th-century biographer. His works are *His Monkey Wife, or Married to a Chimp* (1930), a satirical novel, *Tom's A-Cold* (1933; American title, *Full Circle*), a gloomy picture of England as it will be in 1995, a war-broken, shattered, primitive country; *Defy the Foul Fiend, or The Misadventures of a Heart* (1934), and *Gemini* (1931), poetry; and *No Traveler Returns* (1931), *Green Thoughts* (1932), *The Devil and All* (1934), and *Variations on a Theme* (1935), collections of short stories. He has been in the U. S. frequently, living in different parts of the country, and in Hollywood he met his wife, Shirley Lee Palmer, whom he married in 1936.

Collier, John Payne. b. at London, Jan. 11, 1789; d. at Maidenhead, England, Sept. 17, 1883. An English journalist, lawyer, and Shakespeare critic. He was a reporter (1809–21) for the London *Times*, and parliamentary reporter, drama and literary critic, and editorial writer (1821–47) for the *Morning Chronicle*. In 1847 he was appointed secretary of the royal commission on the British Museum, and continued in that office until 1850, when he returned to Maidenhead. He published a new edition of Dodsley's *Old Plays* (1825–27), *History of English Dramatic Poetry and Annals of the Stage* (1831), two editions of Shakespeare (1842–44, 1875–78), *Shakespeare's Library* (1844), *A Booke of Roxburghe Ballads* (1847), *Extracts from the Registers of the Stationers' Company* (1848–49), *The Dramatic Works of Thomas Heywood* (1850–51), *The Works of Edmund Spenser* (1862), a *Biographical and Critical Account of the Rarest Books in the English Language* (1865), and *An Old Man's Diary—Forty Years Ago* (1871–72). His able and useful work on the older English literature is marred and brought under general suspicion by a series of literary frauds which he committed, of which the most notable is his use and defense of spurious annotations "by a seventeenth century hand" which he professed to have found on the margin of a copy of the second folio Shakespeare originally belonging to one "Thomas Perkins," and since known as the *Perkins Folio*.

Collins (kol′inz), **John.** b. at Bath, England, c1742; d. at Birmingham, England, May 2, 1808. An English actor and poet.

Collins, John Churton. b. at Burton-on-the-Water, Gloucestershire, England, March 26, 1848; d. at Oulton Broad, Lowestoft, Suffolk, England, in September, 1908. An English literary critic, essayist, biographer, and teacher. Educated at King Edward's School, Birmingham, and at Balliol College, Oxford, he wrote for the *Globe* and the *Quarterly*, was lecturer (1880–1907) in English for the London University Extension Society, and served as professor of English literature (1904–08) at the University of Birmingham. He edited *Plays and Poems of Cyril Tourneur* (1878), *Poems of Lord Herbert of Cherbury* (1881), *Plays and Poems of Robert Greene* (1899, 1905), Dryden's *Satires* (1901), and More's *Utopia* (1904). He was the author of *Sir Joshua Reynolds* (1874), *Bolingbroke and Voltaire in Eng-*

land (1886), *Study of English Literature* (1891), *Dean Swift* (1893), *Essays and Studies* (1895), *Ephemera Critica* (1901), *Studies in Shakespeare* (1904), *Studies in Poetry and Criticism* (1905), *Memories* (1908), *Greek Influence* (1910), and *Posthumous Essays* (1912).

Collins, Mortimer. b. at Plymouth, England, June 29, 1827; d. at Knowl Hill, Berkshire, England, July 28, 1876. An English novelist and poet. Until 1856 he was mathematical master of Queen Elizabeth's College, on the island of Guernsey, and after 1862 was occupied with literary work at his residence at Knowl Hill. He published *Idyls and Rhymes* (1865), *Sweet Anne Page* (1868), *The Inn of Strange Meetings, and Other Poems* (1871), and *The Secret of Long Life* (1871).

Collins, Norman Richard. b. at Beaconsfield, Buckinghamshire, England, Oct. 3, 1907—. An English writer. After serving as assistant literary editor (1929–33) on the *News-Chronicle* and deputy chairman (1934–41) of Victor Gollancz, Ltd., publishers, he was head of the light program (1946–47), until becoming (1947) head of television, for the British Broadcasting Corporation. He is the author of *The Facts of Fiction* (1932), *Penang Appointment* (1934), *The Three Friends* (1935), *Trinity Town* (1936), *Love in Our Time* (1938), *"I Shall Not Want"* (1940), *Anna* (1942), *London Belongs to Me* (1945), and *Black Ivory* (1947).

Collins, Wilkie. [Full name, **William Wilkie Collins.**] b. at London, Jan. 8, 1824; d. there, Sept. 23, 1889. An English novelist, recognized as a master of the involved plot. He knew how to construct a highly complicated plot, and, what is still more difficult, how to keep the mystery unrevealed until the last page. Among his best novels of this type are *The Dead Secret* (1857), *The Woman in White* (1860), *No Name* (1862), and *The Moonstone* (1868). His *Antonina* (1850), a historical novel, dealing with Rome in the 6th century, is considered an inferior work. *The Woman in White* uses the technique, now familiar, of having several characters tell the same story, each one dealing with those phases that he knows best. *The Moonstone*, the story of a huge diamond, is memorable for the character of Sergeant Cuff, first detective in English literature. Swinburne praised it highly, and T. S. Eliot regards it as "the first and the greatest of English detective novels." A master of intriguing titles, Collins also wrote *Mrs. Wray's Cash Box* (1852), *Hide and Seek* (1854), *After Dark* (1856), *The Queen of Hearts* (1859), *Poor Miss Finch* (1872), *Miss or Mrs.?* (1873), *The Law and the Lady* (1875), *The Black Robe* (1881), *I Say No* (1884), *The Evil Genius* (1886), and *The Guilty River* (1886). On the basis of these stories and others, and on the ranking given to him by students of crime and mystery in fiction, Collins deserves his title, "the Father of the English detective novel." Ten stories, including the well-known "A Terribly Strange Bed" and "A Stolen Letter" are included in *Tales of Suspense* (1954), edited by Robert Ashley and Herbert van Thal.

Collins, William. b. at Chichester, Sussex, England, Dec. 25, 1721; d. there, June 12, 1759. An English poet. The son of a hatter who was twice mayor of Chichester, he studied at Winchester and at Oxford, where he was graduated (B.A., 1743). About the year 1745 he went to London to follow literature as a profession. The later years of his life were obscured by insanity. He published *Persian Eclogues* (1742; republished as *Oriental Eclogues*, 1757), and *Odes* (1747). Among his best-known poems are *Ode to Simplicity, Ode to Evening, The Passions, On the Poetical Character, Dirge in Cymbeline* and *On the Popular Superstitions of the Highlands.*

Collins, William. A clergyman in Jane Austen's novel *Pride and Prejudice.* He is a conceited toady, overly impressed by rank and determined to marry at all costs.

colloquialism. A word or phrase peculiar to the language of common or familiar conversation.

colloquy (kol'ọ.kwi). A conversation; especially, a conversation which is of the nature of a discussion or conference.

Colman (kōl'man), **George.** [Called **Colman the Elder.**] b. at Florence, Italy, April 18, 1732; d. at Paddington, London, Aug. 14, 1794. An English dramatist, essayist, poet, and manager of the Covent Garden and Haymarket theaters at London. He was educated at Westminster, and at Christ's Church, Oxford. His chief stage works are *Polly Honeycombe* (1760), a farce satirizing the sentimental novel; *The Jealous Wife* (1761), based partly on Fielding's *Tom Jones*, successfully produced by Garrick; and *The Clandestine Marriage* (1766), with some assistance from Garrick. It was suggested by Hogarth's caricatures. He also wrote one-act comedies and farces of a satirical nature. His poems and his periodical essays are of slight value. His prologues and epilogues, to his own plays and to those of his fellow-dramatists, are of some value as illustrations of the standards of the time. After a breach with Garrick over his last play, he became manager of Covent Garden, where he produced Goldsmith's comedies, *The Good-Natured Man* and *She Stoops to Conquer.* He retired from Covent Garden in 1774, after reviving *Cymbeline* and *King Lear* (with his own alterations). In 1776 he took over the Haymarket Theater from Samuel Foote. He translated Terence (1765), and edited the plays of Jonson and of Beaumont and Fletcher. He was a friend of Jonson, the Wartons, Garrick, Malone, and Walpole, and he was a member of The Club, in itself a high honor in his day. That he was willing to tamper with Shakespeare and to attempt to "improve" him, that he gave *Lear* a "happy ending," leaving the poor old king alive, simply shows that Colman was of his time, not ahead of it.

Colman, George. [Called **Colman the Younger.**] b. Oct. 21, 1762; d. at Brompton Square, London, Oct. 17, 1836. An English dramatist, theater manager, censor of plays, song writer, and humorist. He was educated at Westminster, and at Christ's Church, Oxford (as was his father), and at King's College, in Aberdeen. From 1789 to 1820 he managed the London Haymarket theater, a post in which he succeeded the elder Colman, and in 1824 he was appointed examiner and censor of plays. As his own dramatic work was marked by vulgarity, it is interesting to note that he was exceedingly strict with the plays that came under his eye. His

chief works are *Inkle and Yarico* (1787), a romantic comedy dealing with the situation Inkle, a London citizen, has to face when he must decide between Yarico, a lovely savage who has saved his life, and Narcissa, daughter of the wealthy governor of Barbados, and *The Iron Chest* (1796), a dramatization of Godwin's famous novel *Caleb Williams.* Two other comedies, *The Heir-at-Law* (1797) and *John Bull* (1803) are remembered mainly for two portraits that are important additions to the gallery of English characters, the pompous pedant Dr. Pangloss in the former, and rough-and-ready Job Thornberry, who stands for John Bull, in the latter. His humorous verse, *Broad Grins, My Nightgown and Slippers*, and *Poetical Vagaries*, is as good as work of that type usually is, and his *Random Records* (1830), although autobiographically interesting, is of no great value.

Colmekill (kōm'kil). See **Iona.**

Cologne (kọ.lōn'), **Three Kings of.** In medieval Christian legend, the three Magi, or Wise Men of the East, who followed the star of Bethlehem from the East to lay gifts before the infant Jesus. Their names were Gaspar, or Caspar, Melchior, and Balthazar. They are so called (Three Kings of Cologne) because their bones are said to have been deposited by Barbarossa in Cologne Cathedral.

Colombe's Birthday (kol'ọmz). A play by Robert Browning, published in 1844. It is part of *Bells and Pomegranates.*

Colonel Jack. [Full title, **The History and Remarkable Life of Colonel Jacque, commonly call'd Colonel Jack.**] A tale by Daniel Defoe, published in 1722. The hero is abandoned in youth by his parents and becomes a pickpocket. He enlists in the army, soon deserts, and is kidnapped. He is sent to Virginia and sold to a planter, who makes him an overseer and later gives him his liberty. He winds up his career as a wealthy planter, and returns home repentant and virtuous.

Colonel Stow (stō). A historical novel by Henry Christopher Bailey, published in 1908. Its setting is England during the period of the English Civil War (1642 *et seq.*).

Colonna (kọ.lōn'nä), **Vittoria.** b. at Marino, near Rome, 1490; d. at Rome, Feb. 25, 1547. Italian poet. She was betrothed when four years old to a boy of the same age, the only son of the Marchese di Pescara. In their 19th year they were married at Ischia. Pescara died in November, 1525. His wife survived him by 22 years, spent partly at Ischia, in convents at Orvieto and Viterbo, and, finally, in semi-monastic seclusion at Rome. She was the center of a group of celebrated men of letters and artists, of whom the foremost was Michelangelo. Her poems consisted mainly of sonnets to the memory of her husband, or on sacred and moral subjects. Michelangelo preserved a large number of them and composed several madrigals and sonnets to her.

colophon (kol'ọ.fọn). **1.** An emblematic device, or a note, especially one relating to the circumstances of production, as the printer's or scribe's name, place, and date, put at the conclusion of a book or manuscript.

---

fat, fāte, fär, ȧsk, fāre; net, mē, hėr; pin, pīne; not, nōte, mōve, nôr; up, lūte, pùll; ᴛʜ, then;

2. The end of a book; the word "finis" or "the end," marking the conclusion of any printed work.

Colosseum (kol.ǫ.sē'um). [Also, **Coliseum, Flavian Amphitheater.**] An amphitheater at Rome, just SE of the Forum. It was begun by Vespasian (T. Flavius Sabinus) in 72 A.D. and completed in 80 A.D. For 400 years it was the seat of gladiatorial shows, and was the traditional scene of the martyrdom of early Christians. The axes of this chief of amphitheaters are ab. 617 and 512 ft.; of the arena, ab. 282 and 177 ft. The exterior was ornamented with four tiers of engaged columns with their entablatures, the lowest three enclosing arches, and the highest walled up, with square windows in every second intercolumniation. The material of the interior is stone, of the inner passages and vaults largely brick and concrete. The marble seats accommodated between 40,000 and 50,000 people. The interior was faced with marble. In the substructions there is a most elaborate system of chambers, passages, dens, and drains. Despite the enormous mass of the existing ruin, it is estimated that a large part (perhaps as much as two thirds) has been carried away in the Middle Ages and later, as building material.

Colossus of Rhodes (rōdz). A large bronze statue of the sun god Helios, which anciently stood adjacent to the harbor of Rhodes on the Greek island of that name. Known in ancient and medieval times as one of the Seven Wonders of the World, it was designed by Chares of Lindus, a city on Rhodes, and under his supervision erected between 292 and 280 B.C. It is reputed to have been 70 cubits high, or more than 100 ft., and is said to have been built from the abandoned bronze weapons and armor left by the soldiers of Demetrius I, king of Macedon, when they retired in defeat from their siege of Rhodes. It is a tradition that ships could sail between the colossal legs, which would have been possible especially if it rose above pedestals proportionate to its size. It is not known exactly at what point of the harbor it stood, for it did not stand much more than half a century; in 224 B.C. it was toppled by an earthquake. For many centuries great bronze fragments of the statue lay where they fell; eventually (8th century A.D.) they were sold to the Saracens.

Coloured Dome, The. A novel by Francis Stuart, published in 1932.

Colton (kōl'tǫn), **Charles Caleb.** b. at Salisbury, England, c1780; d. at Fontainebleau, France, April 28, 1832. English clergyman and writer. He was a graduate of Cambridge (King's College), and rector of Kew and Petersham. He led an eccentric life, and committed suicide in preference to undergoing a surgical operation. He published *Lacon, or many things in a few words, addressed to those who think* (1820–22) and others.

Colum (kol'um), **Mary.** [Maiden name, **Maguire.**] b. in Ireland—. A critic and short-story writer; wife of Padraic Colum, whom she married in 1912. She was graduated from the National University of Ireland, arrived (1914) in the U. S., and served as literary critic of the magazines *The Century* and *The Forum.* She is the author of *From These Roots* (1937) and *Life and the Dream* (1947).

Colum, Padraic. b. in County Longford, Ireland, Dec. 8, 1881—. An Irish poet, novelist, dramatist, lecturer, anthologist, and author of juveniles. He was one of the founders, with James Stephens and Thomas MacDonagh, of the *Irish Review*, and, with Yeats and Lady Gregory, a founder of the famous Irish National Theatre (later known as the Abbey), where his first play, *Broken Soil* (1903), was produced. Other dramatic works are *The Land* (1905), *The Fiddler's House* (1907), *Thomas Muskerry* (1910), *Mogu the Wanderer* (1917), *The Miracle of the Corn* (1917), and *The Betrayal* (1920). As a poet he has written *Wild Earth* (1907), *Dramatic Legends* (1922), *Creatures* (1927), which shows his fondness for animals, *Poems* (1932), and *The Story of Lowry Maen* (1937). His works for young readers are *The Boy Who Knew What the Birds Said* (1918), *The Girl Who Sat by the Ashes* (1919), *The Children Who Followed the Piper* (1922), and others. *Castle Conquer* (1923) is a novel, and *The Big Tree of Bunlahy* (1933) and *The Frenzied Prince* (1943) are collected short stories. His *Anthology of Irish Poetry* (1921) is of value for students. He himself is represented in anthologies by *The Plower, An Old Woman of the Roads, Interior, A Drover, The Wild Ass, Polonius and the Ballad-Singers,* and *The Sea Bird to the Wave.* In 1912 he married Mary Maguire, critic and author; in 1914 he came (with his wife) to the U. S., where he has lived since. In 1954 Colum was awarded the medal of the Irish Academy of Letters, which is presented every three years for outstanding work in Irish literature. William Butler Yeats, Lady Augusta Gregory, and George Bernard Shaw were among the many former recipients of this award.

Columba (kǫ.lum'bą), Saint. [Irish: **Colum** (kol'um), meaning "Dove"; **Columcille** (kol.um.kil'ę), meaning "Dove of the Church"; called the **"Apostle of Caledonia."**] b. at Gartan, Donegal, Ireland, Dec. 7, 521; d. at Iona, off the coast of what is now Scotland, June 9, 597. An Irish missionary to the Picts and Scots, the founder of the monastery on the island of Iona (c565). He is one of the three patron saints of the Irish and related peoples in the N of Scotland, on the Isle of Man, and elsewhere (with Patrick and Brigid). His feast day is June 9.

Columban (kǫ.lum'bąn) or **Columbanus** (kol.um.bā'nus), Saint. b. in Leinster, Ireland, c543; d. at Bobbio, Italy, Nov. 21, 615. An Irish missionary in France, Switzerland, and Italy, noted for his scholarship. He founded the monastery of Luxeuil (Vosges) c590–595, and that of Bobbio in the Appenines (Italy), where he is buried. Both were important centers of learning. His feast days are Nov. 21 and (in Ireland) Nov. 24.

Columbine (kol'um.bīn). A traditional stock character in old Italian comedy, the *commedia dell'arte.* She is generally, but not always, the daughter of Pantaloon, and is usually the mistress, sometimes the wife, of Harlequin, whose power of being invisible to mortal eyes she shares. Historically, she goes back to the saucy waiting women of Plautus's comedies, and she anticipates the gay soubrette type. From Italian comedy she goes into French comedy and comic opera, and then into English pantomime. The name derives from the Latin *columbinus,* Italian *columbina,* meaning dovelike, and is used affectionately as a pet name.

Columbus, Christopher. [Italian, **Cristoforo Colombo**; Spanish, **Cristóbal Colón**; Latin, **Christophorus Columbus.**] b. probably at or near Genoa, Italy, c1446; d. at Valladolid, Spain, May 20 or 21, 1506. The most famous discoverer of America. There has been much dispute concerning the place of his nativity and even his nationality, but it is generally accepted that he was the son of Genoese wool combers. He received a fairly good education, and certainly, like a true Genoese, took to the sea at an early age. In 1473 or thereabouts he was in Portugal, where he married and had a son, Diego; he also lived for a time on the island of Porto Santo, near Madeira. It is probable that he sailed with some of the Portuguese expeditions to the African coast; he is known to have visited Ireland, and there is some doubtful testimony that he voyaged as far as Iceland. Being among those who understood that the earth is round, he had already formed the conviction that Asia might be reached by sailing westward, and he tried to get the backing of the king of Portugal for an expedition in that direction. Failing in this, he went to Spain (c1484) and offered the enterprise to its monarchs, Ferdinand and Isabella, but the advisers whom they deputed to examine the project reported adversely. Columbus sent his brother Bartholomew to England in 1488 in a vain effort to interest Henry VII. Oppressed by poverty, he was about to go to France when he obtained a personal interview with the Spanish royal couple at Granada, but the rewards he demanded in case of success of the projected voyage were so excessive that they declined to aid. Columbus was about to leave Granada when some of his friends induced the queen to reconsider; and on April 17, 1492, Ferdinand and Isabella agreed over their signatures that Columbus should be admiral in all regions which he might discover, and viceroy in all countries which he might acquire for Spain, with full powers and a generous share of the revenues, and that these honors and powers should pass to his heirs. Partly with royal aid, partly with the help of the Pinzóns, merchants of Palos, three small ships were fitted out: the *Santa María*, the *Niña*, and the *Pinta*, with the first named as flagship. With crews totaling either 90 or 120 men (accounts differ), the little vessels left Palos on August 3. After touching at the Canaries they continued westward into the unknown, and on Oct. 12, 1492, came to a small island called by its natives Guanahani, but christened by Columbus San Salvador; it was one of the islands now called the Bahamas, but exactly which one is not known with certainty (some believe it to have been Watling Island). After landing and claiming the island for Spain, he sailed on, discovering and claiming other islands, obtaining small quantities of gold and other products. He coasted the northern side of Cuba and of Hispaniola, and at a point on the shore of the latter island, which he called Española, the *Santa María* was wrecked. At this point he built a fort which he called La Navidad and, leaving 40 men there, he returned to Spain in the *Niña*. After pausing to visit the king of Portugal he reached Palos on March 15, 1493, was summoned to the Spanish court, where he was received with great honor, confirmed in his privileges, and given ample means for a new expedition. On Sept. 25,

1493, he sailed from Palos again with 17 vessels and 1,500 men. On November 3 he discovered the island of Dominica, and thereafter touched at several of the Caribbees before making his way to La Navidad, where he found that his colony had been wiped out by the Indians. On a new site he founded Isabella, the first European town in the New World, and continued his explorations. Ill conduct by the Spaniards turned the original friendliness of the Indians into hostility; there were many bloody clashes, and Columbus proposed to enslave all hostile natives. The Spanish colonists also were restive under Columbus' rule, and conveyed their complaints to Spain, from which a commission was sent to investigate the state of affairs in Española. Columbus sailed to Spain, leaving his brothers in charge, and was well received by the king and queen, who dismissed the charges against him. He sailed westward again in 1498, and for the first time came to the mainland of South America, making a landfall near the mouth of the Orinoco. When he came to Española he found that a new town, Santo Domingo, had been founded by Bartholomew in his absence and was in the hands of rebels with whom he had to make humiliating terms. When word of these troubles reached Spain, Francisco de Bobadilla was sent to Española as royal commissioner, and presently the great admiral and his brothers were sent to Spain in chains. Arriving there in October, 1500, they were promptly released, but Columbus could not obtain a reinstatement of his dignities. He did obtain four caravels in which he sailed westward again, intent on circumnavigating the globe. In 1502 he sailed down the coast of Central America from Honduras to Panama, vainly seeking a westward passage. Defeated, he turned eastward, and at Jamaica his ships, worm-eaten, became unnavigable. By means of a canoe his plight was after awhile made known in Española, but not until June, 1504, were he and his men rescued. Once more the weary admiral returned to Spain (Nov. 7, 1504), but before the year was out Isabella died, his petitions for reinstatement were ineffective, and he passed his remaining days in poverty and neglect. Columbus was of course acquainted with the legends of Saint Brendan's Isle and of Hy-Brasil, and with other Irish accounts of a land beyond the western ocean, and similar legends were probably current in other countries, though there was by no means so extensive a knowledge of pre-Columbian transatlantic voyages then as modern scholarship has developed. His great merit was that having a scientific mind at the moment of history when the scientific approach became both possible and imperative, and having indomitable courage as well, he established once and for all the existence of lands westward across the Atlantic from Europe. But the Admiral of the Ocean Sea died believing that he had reached India, quite unaware that he had opened a New World to the peoples of Europe.

column. 1. In printing, one of the typographical divisions of printed matter in two or more vertical rows of lines. The separation of columns is made by a narrow blank space in which is often placed a vertical line or rule. Division into columns economizes space, and saves the fatigue of the eye arising from attempts to trace the connection of an over-long line with the following line.

2. The contents of or the matter printed in such a column, especially in a newspaper.

Colvin (kol′vin), Sir **Sidney.** b. at Norwood, England, June 18, 1845; d. at Kensington, London, May 11, 1927. An English art and literary critic, professor, biographer, editor, and friend of Robert Louis Stevenson. He was educated at Trinity College, Cambridge, of which he was made a fellow in 1868. From 1873 to 1885 he was Slade professor of fine arts at Cambridge, and director of the Cambridge Fitzwilliam Museum from 1876 to 1884. From 1884 to 1912 he was keeper of prints and drawings at the British Museum. He was knighted on Jan. 1, 1911. His works are *Children in Italian and English Design* (1872), *A Florentine Picture Chronicle* (1898), and *Drawings by Old Oxford Masters* (1902–08). For the well-known *English Men of Letters Series*, he wrote lives of Landor (1881) and Keats (1887). He also edited *Selections from Landor* (1882), and wrote *John Keats: His Life and Poetry* (1917), a much more ambitious work than the slight life written 30 years earlier. Colvin knew Stevenson from 1873 until the latter died in 1894. He edited his letters in 1899 and again in 1911, and he published Stevenson's letters to him from Samoa, the *Vailima Letters*, in 1895. During the years 1894–97 he brought out the famous *Edinburgh Edition* of Stevenson's works, in 27 volumes. A student and critic of both art and literature, Colvin tended to be conservative in the former and liberal in the latter.

Colyn Cloute (kol′in klout′). A poem (c1520) by John Skelton, a satire against the clergy of his time.

Combe (köm, kōm), **William.** b. at Bristol, England, 1741; d. at Lambeth, London, June 19, 1823. An English writer, creator of "Dr. Syntax." Educated at Eton and Oxford (where, however, he did not take a degree), he entered the law; thereafter he led for some time the life of an adventurer, being successively a soldier, a waiter, a lieutenant, and a cook, and for the last 43 years of his life resided within the rules of the King's Bench debtors' prison. He published a large number of works, including *The Diaboliad, a poem dedicated to the worst man (Simon, Lord Irnham) in His Majesty's Dominions* (1776), *The Devil upon Two Sticks in England* (1790), *The Tour of Dr. Syntax in Search of the Picturesque* (a poem first published in the *Poetical Magazine*, and republished in 1812), *The Second Tour of Dr. Syntax in Search of Consolation* (1820), and *The Third Tour of Dr. Syntax in Search of a Wife* (1821). Thomas Rowlandson illustrated the "Dr. Syntax" books, and Combe also wrote the text for Rowlandson's *Dance of Death* (1815–16) and *Dance of Life* (1816).

Comberback (kom′ber.bak), **Silas Tomkyn.** The name assumed by Samuel Taylor Coleridge during the brief (and far from enjoyable) period of his youthful service with the British army, as an enlisted man in the Dragoons.

Combined Maze, The. A novel by May Sinclair, published in 1913.

comedy. 1. That branch of the drama which addresses itself primarily to the sense of the humorous or the ridiculous: opposed to *tragedy*, which appeals to the more serious and profound emotions.

Comedy [according to Aristotle], on the other hand, imitates actions of inferior interest ("neither painful nor destructive"), and carried on by characters whose vices are of a ridiculous kind.

(A. W. Ward, *Eng. Dram. Lit.*, I. 89.)

2. In a restricted sense, a form of the drama which is humorous without being broadly or grossly comical: distinguished from *farce*.

Comedy presents us with the imperfections of human nature; farce entertains us with what is monstrous and chimerical; the one causes laughter in those who can judge of men and manners, by the lively representation of their folly and corruption; the other produces the same effect in those who can judge of neither; and that only by its extravagancies.

(Dryden, Pref. to *Mock Astrologer.*)

3. A dramatic composition written in the style of comedy; a comic play or drama.

Comedy Concerning Three Laws. A religious interlude by John Bale, written c1538.

Comedy of Errors, The. A play by Shakespeare, first acted at Gray's Inn, in London, on Dec. 28, 1594. It is known certainly to have been one of the playwright's earliest works (most modern scholars believe 1592 or 1593 to be the years which may most probably be assigned to it, although neither 1591 nor 1594 can definitely be ruled out); some older reference works have suggested that its title was at one time simply *Errors*. It may be the play listed by Francis Meres in his *Palladis Tamia* as *Love's Labour's Won*. Its plot was derived in great part from the *Menaechmi* of Plautus, with modifications that may be traced to the more serious *Amphitruo* by the same playwright. The Aegeon-Aemilia theme is from a story in John Gower's *Confessio Amantis*. The suggestion that Shakespeare's chief source was actually *The Historie of Error*, acted by the boys of Saint Paul's chapel on Jan. 1, 1577, is now discounted by virtually all scholars of Shakespeare; the derivation from Plautus seems not only likely beyond reasonable doubt, but also casts an interesting light on the actual meaning of Ben Jonson's much-quoted statement that his friend Shakespeare had "small Latin and less Greek." In view of the fact that no English translation of the *Menaechmi* is known to have been published before 1594 (and of the *Amphitruo* for about 100 years after that), it would appear that Shakespeare must have worked from Latin sources available at the time (indeed, there is much internal evidence that Shakespeare was influenced by Latin turns of phrase, although his use of the Latin was at no point close to translation). However, if the play was written in 1593, Shakespeare may have seen Warner's translation of the *Menaechmi* in manuscript.

The Story. Aegeon, a Syracusan merchant, had been shipwrecked with his wife, Aemilia, and their twin sons, both named Antipholus, and twin slaves, both named Dromio. One of each pair of twins remained with Aegeon, but the others disappeared with Aemilia. At 18, one of the twins, Antipholus of Syracuse, had been allowed by his

ḍ, d or j; ş, s or sh; ṭ, t or ch; ẓ, z or zh; *o*, F. cloche; ü, F. menu; c̣h, Sc. loch; ṅ, F. bonbon.

father to search for his lost twin brother. When he did not return in five years, his father set out in search of him. The action of the play commences when Aegeon is arrested at Ephesus and sentenced to death because of the enmity between that city and Syracuse. His story moves Solinus, the Duke of Ephesus, to allow him until nightfall to obtain his ransom money. Meanwhile, Antipholus of Syracuse has arrived in Ephesus where, unknown to him, live his brother and his wife Adriana, and their Dromio. From this situation arise the complications, the comedy of errors, because everyone confuses the two sets of twins, including themselves. Antipholus of Syracuse beats Dromio of Ephesus for insisting he go home to dinner; Antipholus of Syracuse does, however, dine at Adriana's house, from which the Ephesian twin is locked out, Adriana believing her husband to be within; Antipholus of Ephesus is arrested for not paying for a gold chain which was mistakenly given to Antipholus of Syracuse. Everyone is convinced of the insanity of the others. At length, the Syracusans take refuge in an abbey. When Aegeon is led to his execution the Ephesian twins arrive to demand justice from the Duke. They, of course, do not recognize Aegeon; they deny receiving the gold chain; and after considerable more confusion, the abbess arrives with the Syracusans. With the presence of everyone the errors are solved, and the pardoned Aegeon discovers the abbess to be his lost wife.

comedy of humours. See **humour comedy.**

Comely Bank (kum'li). A row of two-storied houses in the NW part of Edinburgh. Carlyle lived there for a time, in the cottage numbered 21.

Comical Gallant: or, The Amours of Sir John Falstaffe, The. An adaptation of Shakespeare's *Merry Wives of Windsor* by John Dennis, played in 1702.

Comical History of Alphonsus, King of Aragon (al.fon'sus; ar'a̶.gon), **The.** See **Alphonsus, King of Aragon.**

Comical Lovers, or Marriage à la Mode, The. A comedy by Colley Cibber, produced and printed in 1707. It is made from the comic scenes of John Dryden's *Secret Love* and *Marriage à la Mode.*

Comical Revenge, or Love in a Tub, The. A comedy by Sir George Etherege, produced in 1664. It was published in the same year. Lord Beaufort and Colonel Bruce are suitors to Graciana, their rivalry leading to a duel from which Bruce emerges as the loser. After trying to kill himself for the shame, he finds a cure for his feelings in Graciana's sister. The comic plot centers about a French valet, Dufoy, who plays the part of a mischievous servant, finally ending up in a large tub. His master, Sir Frederick Frolic, adroitly handles a rich widow so that she provides him not only with money but finally with herself. Sir Frederick's wit may be summed up in the following sentence: "Men are now and then subject to those Infirmities in drink which Women have when they're sober."

comic opera. A light, harmonious opera, usually consisting of detached movements with more or less dialogue.

Coming of Arthur, The. A poem (published 1869) by Alfred Tennyson, the first of the series comprising *The Idylls of the King.* It describes the birth of Arthur and his courtship of Guinevere.

Coming Race, The. A Utopian romance by Bulwer-Lytton, published in 1871. The narrator visits a people living deep under the earth, and discovers that they have reached a high level of civilization through the discovery of a form of energy that embodies a combination of all natural forces. In their society there are no conflicting classes or castes, and war and crime have both disappeared. The women are superior in physical strength to the men and they choose their mates, rather than leaving that privilege to the men. Because of this (to him) unusual situation, the hero becomes involved in a situation which is not only highly embarrassing, but which finally presents a threat to his very life. He is saved through the intervention of his host's daughter, and is then restored to his own land.

Coming Up for Air. A novel by George Orwell, published in 1939.

Cominius (kọ.min'i.us). In Shakespeare's *Coriolanus*, a Roman general. He tries to persuade the people of Rome not to banish Coriolanus, and later, when Coriolanus has joined the Volscian forces, undertakes to persuade him to spare Rome.

Commandment of the Love of God. A prose epistle of the Middle English period by Richard Rolle of Hampole.

Commendation of Our Lady. A poem at one time erroneously attributed to Chaucer. Tyrwhitt believed there was evidence that Lydgate might have written it.

Commissary, The. A comedy by Samuel Foote, produced in 1765.

Committee, The. A comedy by Sir Robert Howard, printed in 1665. John Evelyn saw it played in 1662. It was revised by T. Knight and produced as *The Honest Thieves* in 1797. It displays a Royalist's hatred of the Puritan Commonwealth, the committee being the Sequestration Committee chosen by the Long Parliament to confiscate the property of Charles I's supporters.

Common (kom'ọn), **Dol.** [Also, **Doll Common.**] In Ben Jonson's comedy *The Alchemist*, the mistress of Subtle.

common meter. In psalmody, a form of iambic stanza, primarily of four lines, having alternately eight and six syllables to the line: so called because it was the commonest stanza in early psalmody. *Double common meter* consists of a stanza with eight lines having alternately eight and six syllables.

Common Order, Book of. See **Book of Common Order.**

common particular meter. In psalmody, a stanza with six lines, the third and sixth of which have six and the rest eight syllables.

commonplace-book. A book in which things especially to be remembered or referred to are recorded methodically. "Your commonplace-book—where stray jokes and pilfered witticisms are kept with as much method as the ledger of the lost and stolen office." (Sheridan, *The Critic*, i.1.)

fat, fāte, fär, ȧsk, fãre; net, mē, hėr; pin, pīne; not, nōte, mõve, nôr; up, lūte, pùll; ᴛʜ, then;

Common Prayer, Book of. See **Book of Common Prayer.**

Commonwealth of Oceana (ō.shē̱.ā′na̱), **The.** See **Oceana, The Commonwealth of.**

Communism (kom′ū̱.niz.e̱m). A political philosophy, based on Marxian socialism, and developed most fully by the Third or Communist International, especially as the controlling philosophy of government in Russia after 1917. The basic Communist tenet is that of the dictatorship of the proletariat, the control of government by the workers. That achieved, Communism sees the establishment of a socialism in which the means of production are controlled by the government and in which every man works to his best ability, since he is working for the good of all, and receives according to his needs; the end will be a classless society, all being workers to the same end, and in which finally the actual machinery of government and the state will disappear. The establishment of a Communist government in Russia following World War I led to a modification of the basic plan (theoretically a temporary expedient), whereby the ideal of worldwide Communism was surrendered for the immediate goal of establishing Communism in at least one country. The ideological base was similarly shifted from the proletariat as a whole (considered as insufficiently educated in socialism's ultimate aims) to the indoctrinated group of party members; from these strict adherence to doctrine was demanded, and members who deviated from the official "line" were either purged from the party or tried as enemies of the state.

Comnena (kom.nē′na̱), **Anna.** See **Anna Comnena.**

Comparini (kôm.pä.rē′nē), **Pietro.** In Browning's long narrative poem *The Ring and the Book,* the supposed father of Pompilia. Violante Comparini is his wife.

Compass (kum′pa̱s). A soldier and scholar in Ben Jonson's comedy *The Magnetic Lady,* "a Scholar Mathematic . . . one well read in Men and Manners." He, by playing one character against another, reconciles the various humors they represent, and he marries Placentia, the heiress.

Compeyson (kom′pi.so̱n). A convict and hardened criminal in Charles Dickens's *Great Expectations.* He is a scoundrel whom Magwitch describes as having "no more heart than an iron file." He is finally killed by Magwitch.

complaint. A poem bewailing ill fortune in matters of love; a plaint.

> Of such matiere made he many layes,
> Songes, compleyntes, roundelets, virelayes.
> (Chaucer, *Franklin's Tale.*)

Complaint of a Lover's Life. A poem inserted in the 16th-century editions of Chaucer, and attributed to him. Manuscript authority assigns it to John Lydgate.

Complaint of Buckingham, The. A poem (published 1563 in the *Mirror for Magistrates*) by Thomas Sackville, telling of the Duke of Buckingham's betrayal to Richard III by Humfrey Banastaire, a supposedly loyal follower with whom he had sought refuge.

Complaint of Cresseid (kres′id), **The.** A poem attributed by Stow (1561) to Chaucer, but probably the work of Robert Henryson.

Complaint of Mars. [Also, **Compleynt of Mars.**] A possibly allegorical poem by Chaucer, written perhaps c1379 (and conjectured by some to have had its inspiration in an illicit romance which had evoked comment a few years before at the court). Full of astrological allusions, it expresses the lament of Mars at being separated from Venus by the coming of Phoebus. It is supposed to be sung on Saint Valentine's day by a bird. A *Complaint of Venus* is sometimes linked to it, but is much later, and of a totally different character.

Complaint of Philomene (fil.ō̱.mē′nē), **The.** A poem by George Gascoigne, begun in 1562, but not completed until 1576.

Complaint of Rosamond (roz′a̱.mo̱nd). A narrative poem (1592), by Samuel Daniel.

Complaint of Venus. [Also, **Compleynt of Venus.**] A poem by Chaucer, translated by him late in life from the French. It is made up of three independent ballades. The inappropriate title was given by the copyists as a counterpart to the *Complaint of Mars,* to which it is sometimes appended.

Complaints. [Full title, **Complaints, containing Sundry Small Poems of the World's Vanity.**] A volume of poems by Edmund Spenser, published in 1591. It contains, among others, "Muiopotmos" and "Mother Hubberd's Tale."

Complaint to His Empty Purse. [Also, **Compleynt to His Empty Purse.**] A short poem by Chaucer, sometimes attributed to Thomas Hoccleve. It is believed that it was written sometime before 1399, but in that year Chaucer appended a dedicatory postscript and sent the poem to Henry IV, on that monarch's accession (Sept. 30) to the English throne. Chaucer is known to have received an annuity from the king within four days. It was printed before the 1532 edition.

Complaint Unto Pity. [Also, **Compleynt Unto Pite.**] A short poem by Chaucer, printed before 1532, and perhaps written c1367. The "Complaint" is in rhyme royal and may be the earliest English example of this form.

Compleat Angler, The. [Full original title, **The Compleat Angler, or the Contemplative Man's Recreation.**] A work by Izaak Walton, published in 1653. It is a treatise on the art of fishing, and attempts to prove that sport's superiority over hunting and fowling. It is in the form of a dialogue between Piscator and Venator, the former being an angler and the latter a hunter. Their friend Auceps, a fowler, is silenced early in the work. They meet many pleasant people of the countryside, chat with inn-keepers, and discuss the relative merits of each of their sports.

Composer, The. See under **Another Time.**

Compton (komp′to̱n), **Virginia.** [Maiden name, **Bateman.**] b. Jan. 1, 1853; d. at London, May 4, 1940. An English actress; mother of the novelist Compton Mackenzie. In 1865 she began her stage career in England. She played leading parts in a touring comedy company and opened a repertory theater at Nottingham, England.

---

d̶, d or j; s̶, s or sh; t̶, t or ch; z̶, z or zh; o, F. cloche; ü, F. menu; ċh, Sc. loch; ṅ, F. bonbon.

Comte (kôṅt), **Auguste.** [Full name, **Isidore Auguste Marie François Xavier Comte.**] b. at Montpellier, France, Jan. 19, 1798; d. at Paris, Sept. 5, 1857. A French philosopher, founder of positivism. About 1818 he became a friend and disciple of Saint-Simon, whose doctrines he expounded in a work entitled *Système de politique positive* (1822). This friendship terminated in a complete estrangement in 1824, but the trend of Comte's philosophical thought can be traced to this early association. Comte, who originated the term "sociology," proposed social reforms which would promote harmony and the well-being of individuals and nations. He developed his thought further in *Cours de philosophie positive* (1830–42), *Catéchisme positiviste* (1852), *Le Système de politique positive*, and *Synthèse subjective* (1856). Comte was a tutor at the École Polytechnique from 1832 to 1851.

Comus (kō'mus). A morality play by John Milton, with music by Henry Lawes, performed at Ludlow Castle on Sept. 29, 1634. The occasion was the inauguration of the Earl of Bridgewater as President of the Welsh Marches. The play was performed by his children, Viscount Brackley, Thomas Egerton, and Lady Alice Egerton (ages 11 to 13 years). The title page of the editions of 1637 and 1645 called it simply "A Maske," which is really a misnomer. Although like a masque in some respects (for example, it has allegorical figures), the subject is more serious than in most masques, and such elements as the temptations of Comus and their rejection by the virtuous Lady are not in the masque tradition. Milton probably used Peele's *Old Wives' Tale* and Fletcher's *Faithful Shepherdess* as sources, but his principal inspiration came obviously from the motifs of Spenser's *Faerie Queene*, especially Book III. In the introduction, the Attendant Spirit describes a haunted wood where Comus, a god of sensuality and lust, tempts unwary travelers with a fateful drink that changes them into beasts. In the wood, Comus appears with his companions and makes a brilliant speech about the charms of sensuality. A Lady, who has been separated from her two brothers, meets Comus who is in the innocent dress of a shepherd. He invites her to his cottage, and, when they have departed, the brothers appear. After their long discussion about virtue and temptation, the Attendant Spirit, now disguised as the shepherd, Thyrsis, tells them about the dangers of Comus and gives them haemony, a magic herb that wards off evil spells. Meanwhile, the Lady, seated in an enchanted chair in a banquet hall, is being enticed by Comus to drink his magic potion. Across the back of the hall is an arcade supposedly opening toward the Severn River, whose silvery waters can be seen in the moonlight. The lady firmly defends virtue and resists Comus's temptations. Suddenly, the brothers rush in and drive out Comus and his adherents. The Lady, however, cannot move from the enchanted chair. Thyrsis, the Attendant Spirit, thereupon summons Sabrina, the goddess of the Severn, who, with her nymphs, frees the Lady. The Attendant Spirit speaks of virtue and chastity, both then and after he has led the wanderers home. The masque closes with a dance by shepherds and other country people. Although the poetry and songs are highly praised, some critics have objected that the moral is intrusive to the point of impairing the dramatic value of the work as a whole. The elder George Colman produced an alteration of *Comus* at Covent Garden in 1773.

Conachar (kon'a.chär). [Sometimes called **Eachin MacIan.**] The son of the chief of Clan Quhele in Sir Walter Scott's novel *The Fair Maid of Perth*. After becoming the chief himself, he realizes that he has been a coward, and kills himself in despair.

Conaire Mor (kon'e.ri môr). A high king of Ireland, said by the Old Irish chroniclers to have ruled c113–43 B.C.: hero of *The Destruction of Da Derga's Hostel*, one of the most famous epic stories in Old Irish literature. Conaire met his tragic death fighting off a raid of pirates on Ireland, the tragedy of the story lying in the fact that he was tricked by the *sidhe* (the supernaturals of Ireland) into breaking in one night all nine of the magical injunctions which had been placed upon him, and to break which meant death for him. Sir Samuel Ferguson's long poem *Conary* is based on this story.

conceit. 1. *Obs.* That which is conceived, imagined, or formed in the mind; conception; idea; thought; image.

In laughing there ever precedeth a conceit of somewhat ridiculous, and therefore it is proper to man. (Bacon, *Nat. Hist.*)

I do feel conceits coming upon me, more than I am able to turn tongue to.
(B. Jonson, *Bartholomew Fair*, i. 1.)

2. An exaggerated estimate of one's own mental ability, or of the importance or value of what one has done; an overvaluation of one's own acuteness, wit, learning, etc.; self-conceit: as, a man inflated with *conceit*.

So spake he, clouded with his own conceit.
(Tennyson, *Morte d'Arthur*.)

Our vanities differ as our noses do: all conceit is not the same conceit, but varies in correspondence with the minutiæ of mental make in which one of us differs from another.
(George Eliot, *Middlemarch*, I. 165.)

3. A witty, happy, or ingenious thought or expression; a quaint or humorous fancy; wit; humor; ingenuity; especially, in poetry, an extended metaphor in which an idea or emotion is expressed by a description of its metaphorical analogue, as in courtly poetry when the poet describes the virtues of his lady through the conceit of the rose. The metaphysical conceit extends the metaphor, relating two utterly unrelated things, as in Donne's "Get thee with child a mandrake root."

Others of a more fine and pleasant head . . . in short poemes vttered pretie merry conceits, and these men were called Epigrammatistes.
(Puttenham, *Arte of Eng. Poesie*.)

The eloquence of the bar, the pulpit, and the council-board was deformed by conceits which would have disgraced the rhyming shepherds of an Italian academy. (Macaulay, *Dryden*.)

4. *Obs.* A fanciful or ingenious device or invention.

Neuer carde, for silks or sumpteous cost,
For cloth of gold, or tinsel figurie,
For Baudkin, broydrie, cutworks, nor conceits.
(Gascoigne, *Steele Glas* (ed. Arber), p. 71.)

---

fat, fāte, fär, ȧsk, fāre; net, mē, hėr; pin, pīne; not, nōte, mȯve, nôr; up, lūte, pull; ʈH, then;

Bracelets of thy hair, rings, gawds, conceits,
Knacks, trifles. (Shak., *M. N. D.*)

Conchobar (kon.kō′bär). In the Ulster, or Ultonian, cycle of Old Irish epics and romances, a king of Ulster about the beginning of the Christian era. His surname was macNessa, meaning son of Nessa. At the birth of a certain girl-child, Deirdre, the Druids prophesied that she would bring ruin to Ireland. For this reason Conchobar had her brought up in solitude and confinement, but planned to marry her when she was grown. However, she met and fell in love with Naoise, eldest of the three sons of Usnach, who, with his two brothers, escaped with her to Scotland. Conchobar lured them back to Ireland with false promises, and killed the three sons of Usnach. Conchobar was also the uncle and guardian of the hero Cuchulain. In Christian legend, Conchobar is said to have died the same day Christ was crucified, in a fit of rage and protest at the news.

Conclusions of the Astrolabe (as′trō.lāb), **The.** See **Astrolabe, The Treatise on the.**

Concordat of 1801. An agreement concluded on July 15, 1801, between Napoleon Bonaparte (then first consul) and Pope Pius VII. It reëstablished the Roman Catholic Church in France, and granted to the government the right of appointing archbishops and bishops, who were to be confirmed by the Pope. It went into operation on April 8, 1802, and was abrogated by the passage of the Briand bill, on Dec. 6, 1905, except in Alsace and Lorraine, where it continued operative.

Condell (kun′dẹl), **Henry.** [Also, **Cundell.**] d. at Fulham, England, in December, 1627. An English actor, and editor with Heming of the first folio edition of Shakespeare's plays. He was a member of the Lord Chamberlain's Men, to which Shakespeare was also admitted, probably in 1594. A share of the company was given him in 1604 and in 1608 he, along with Shakespeare, received a share in the Blackfriars Theatre owned by the Burbages. He is mentioned in Shakespeare's will. By 1612 he had acquired a portion also of the Globe theater.

Condorcet (kôn.dôr.se), **Marquis de.** [Title of **Marie Jean Antoine Nicolas Caritat.**] b. at Ribemont, in Picardy, France, Sept. 17, 1743; d. at Bourg-la-Reine, near Paris, April 7, 1794. A French social philosopher.

Confederacy, The. A comedy by Sir John Vanbrugh, produced on Oct. 30, 1705. It is a play of contrivance and intrigue, adapted from Dancourt's *Modish Citizens* (*Les Bourgeoises à la mode*). Gripe and Moneytrap, two usurers, fall in love with each other's wives, much to the satisfaction of the two ladies, who plot to turn the tables upon their stingy husbands. Clarissa, Gripe's wife, has pawned her jewels to Mrs. Amlet, who provides fashionable women with cosmetics and finery. Mrs. Amlet has a roguish son, Dick, who in the guise of a military man is wooing Gripe's daughter, Corinna, assisted by Brass, his would-be footman, and Flippanta, Clarissa's maid. Dick steals the necklace and sends Brass to pawn it, but the goldsmith whom he approaches has been warned by Gripe, he having been told by his wife that it was lost. Brass has been active meanwhile in approaching Gripe for a present to Mrs. Moneytrap (Araminta), and Flippanta has been similarly employed by Clarissa to solicit Gripe. The ladies are enjoying their new freedom from poverty at a tea with their husbands, who are also quite pleased by their thoughtfulness to their loves, when the necklace is brought in by the goldsmith. Corinna is made aware of Dick's character when the truth comes out and the two husbands are also put on the scent of their wives' plot, but are silenced when each wife alludes to their presents to the other. Corinna's possible scruples are overcome when Mrs. Amlet offers to endow her son with 10,000 pounds.

Confederation of the Rhine. A league formed by the majority of the German states, under the protectorate of Napoleon I, in July, 1806. It comprised Bavaria, Württemberg, Saxony, Westphalia, Baden, Hesse-Darmstadt, and all the other minor German sovereignties excepting Brunswick and Electoral Hesse. The member states of the Confederation renounced allegiance to the Holy Roman Empire, and in the same year the ruler of Austria gave up the title of Holy Roman Emperor. After the defeat of Napoleon in Russia (1812–13), members of the Confederation turned against him, and the Confederation dissolved.

Confessio Amantis (kọn.fesh′i.ō ạ.man′tis). A Middle English poem (c1386–90) by John Gower, explaining the problems of courtly love and revealing the sins that the poet has committed against Venus, the goddess of love. It uses as a framework the seven deadly sins, with illustrative stories taken from Biblical and mythological sources (including Gideon, Tobias, Jason, and Narcissus).

Confessions (kôṅ.fe.syôṅ), **Les.** An autobiographical work by Jean Jacques Rousseau. It is in 12 volumes, six of which were written at Wootton, England (1766–67), and six in Dauphiné and at Trye, France (1768–70). It was his intention that they should not be published until 1800, as the persons alluded to in them were living; but those in charge of the manuscript published the first six volumes in 1781–82. In 1788 a new edition appeared, containing the whole.

Confessions—A Study in Pathology. An autobiographical work by Arthur Symons, published in 1930. It includes frank descriptions of his attacks of amnesia and insanity.

Confessions of an English Opium-Eater. A partly autobiographical work by Thomas De Quincey, published in 1821. It tells of the author's early life, and his growing dependence on opium to relieve physical suffering. Gradually he becomes a victim of incredible dreams, and realizes that he is bringing on his own death. The story of his efforts, which were finally largely successful, to stop taking laudanum, is vividly told.

Confessions of Harry Lorrequer (lor′ẹ.kẻr), **The.** See **Harry Lorrequer, The Confessions of.**

Confessions of Saint Augustine (ô′gus.tēn, ô.gus′tin), **The.** The memoirs of Saint Augustine. They are divided into 13 books; the first 10 treat of the bad actions of his life, of his conversion, of the love of pleasure, of glory, and of science. The last three are an interpretation of the beginning of the book of Genesis.

Confessions of Ursula Trent (ėr'su.lạ trent'), **The.** A novel by W. L. George, published in 1921.

Confidential Agent, The. A novel by Graham Greene, published in 1939.

Confucius (kọn.fū'shus). [Latinized form of Chinese **K'ung Fu-tse**; also, **K'ung Ch'iu.**] b. in the principality of Lu (now included in Shantung province), China, 550 or 551 B.C.; d. 478 B.C. A celebrated Chinese philosopher. He was descended from an illustrious but impoverished family, and in his youth was successively keeper of stores and superintendent of parks and herds to the chief of the district in which he lived. In his twenty-second year he became a teacher, and in his fifty-second was made chief magistrate of the city of Chung-tu. He was subsequently appointed minister of crime by the Marquis of Lu, but in his fifty-sixth year retired from office in consequence of the intrigues of a neighboring prince. After 13 years of travel he returned in 483 to Lu, where he spent the rest of his life in completing his literary undertakings and in teaching. Apart from his maxims, which were recorded by his disciples, he wrote *Ch'un-chiu* (Spring and Autumn) and the *Four Books.*

Congress of Vienna (vi.en'ạ). See **Vienna, Congress of.**

Congreve (kon'grēv, kong'-), **Richard.** b. at Leamington, England, Sept. 4, 1818; d. at Hampstead, London, July 5, 1899. An English essayist and philosophical writer.

Congreve, William. b. at Bardsey, near Leeds, England, 1670 (baptized Feb. 10); d. at London, Jan. 19, 1729. English dramatist, one of the greatest writers of comedy. Soon after his birth his parents removed to Ireland, where his father became commander of the garrison at Youghal and also agent of the earl of Cork. He was educated at a school in Killkenny (where Swift was one of his schoolfellows) and at Trinity College, Dublin. After a brief period devoted to the study of law, he applied himself chiefly to literature until about 1700, but after this year wrote little or nothing. He filled several unimportant offices, including that of commissioner for licensing hackney coaches (from July, 1695, to October, 1707), that of commissioner of wine licenses (from December, 1705, to December, 1714), and that of secretary for Jamaica (from 1714). His plays include *The Old Bachelor* (acted in January, 1693), *The Double Dealer* (November, 1693), *Love for Love* (April, 1695), *The Way of the World* (1700), and one tragedy, *The Mourning Bride* (1697). Besides his plays he wrote a novel (his first literary work) entitled *Incognita, or Love and Duty reconciled,* a reply to Jeremy Collier's attack upon him in his work on the immorality of the stage, called *Amendments of Mr. Collier's False and Imperfect Citations,* and a few prologues and unimportant operas. The first collected edition of his works was published by him in 1710. He is celebrated especially for the brilliancy of his style and the wit and vigor of his dialogues.

Coningsby (kon'ingz.bi). [Full title, **Coningsby, or The New Generation.**] A political novel by Benjamin Disraeli, published in 1844. The political events of the period between the Reform Bill of 1832 and the fall of the Melbourne ministry in 1841 form the background for this story. Disraeli takes advantage of the setting and plot to express his own ideas on the evils of the new poor law, the harsh treatment of the peasantry at this time, and on the unfavorable aspects of Utilitarianism. The orphaned Harry Coningsby is sent to Eton by his grandfather, Lord Monmouth, and while there he saves the life of Oswald Millbank, son of a rich manufacturer who is Lord Monmouth's bitter political enemy. At Cambridge Harry develops political views that are in opposition to those of his grandfather, and when Monmouth dies, Harry finds that he has been disinherited. He thereupon determines to make his own way in the world as a barrister, and by his strength of character proves to Millbank, the manufacturer, that he is worthy of marrying Millbank's daughter, Edith. Coningsby is then elected to Parliament for Millbank's constituency. Each character is said to have been modeled on a contemporary figure, and much of the work's popularity in the England of its day probably derived from this. Millbank is said to be Gladstone; Monmouth, the Marquis of Hertford; Coningsby, either Lord Lyttleton, Lord Lincoln, or George Smythe.

Conington (kon'ing.tọn), **John.** b. at Boston, England, Aug. 10, 1825; d. there, Oct. 23, 1869. An English classical scholar, a graduate of Oxford, where he became, in 1854, professor of the Latin language and literature. He published an edition and translation of the *Agamemnon* of Aeschylus (1848), an edition of the *Choephori* of Aeschylus (1857), a translation in verse of the *Odes of Horace* (1863), a translation in ballad meter of Vergil's *Aeneid* (1866), an edition of Vergil, and others.

Connoisseur (kon.i.sėr'), **The.** A periodical begun on Jan. 31, 1754, by the elder George Colman and Bonnell Thornton, and continued weekly for three years. In this periodical in 1756 appeared the first publications of William Cowper. His first paper was on "Keeping a Secret."

Connolly (kon'ọ.li), **Cyril.** [Full name, **Cyril Vernon Connolly.**] b. at Coventry, England, Sept. 10, 1903—. An English author and editor. He is both a novelist and a critic, and as the editor of *Horizon,* a literary magazine which he established in 1939 (and which ceased publication in 1951), he held the door open to writers of various schools and tendencies, and exerted considerable influence in the field of criticism. He was literary editor (1942-43) of the London *Observer* and his writings have appeared with frequency in the *New Statesman and Nation* since 1927. His works are *The Rock Pool* (1935), a novel dealing with expatriate artists on the Riviera, *Enemies of Promise* (1938), a volume of literary essays, with some biographical material, *The Unquiet Grave* (1945), essays, for which the author used the name of Aeneas's pilot, Palinurus, and *The Condemned Playground* (1946), a volume of parodies and satires, many of them written at an earlier period. As an editor he has published an anthology of short stories that originally appeared in his own *Horizon;* he edited another anthology from *Horizon* including some work of Stephen Spender, Dylan Thomas, and Bertrand Russell, *The Golden Horizon* (1954), and he has translated

fat, fāte, fär, ȧsk, fāre; net, mē, hėr; pin, pīne; not, nōte, mȯve, nôr; up, lūte, pŭll; ᴛʜ, then;

Put Out the Light and *The Silence of the Sea*, by Jean Bruller (Vercors), from the French. One of his more recent books is *Ideas and Places* (1954), a collection of his own essays on various subjects.

Connor (kon'or), **Ralph.** Pseudonym of **Gordon, Charles William.**

Conquered, The. A novel by Naomi Mitchison, published in 1923.

Conquest (kong'kwest), **Mrs.** A character in Colley Cibber's comedy *Love's Last Stake.*

Conquest of Granada (grạ.nä'dạ), **The.** [Full title, **Almanzor and Almahide, or The Conquest of Granada by the Spaniards.**] A heroic tragedy in two parts, by John Dryden, produced in 1670. It was partly taken from Calprenède's *Cléopâtre* and the anonymous *Le Grand Cyrus.* It is usually known as *The Conquest of Granada.* The prefatory *Essay of Heroique Plays* is a definition of this genre by Dryden and a well-known critical work. There is also an epilogue which comments on Dryden's contemporaries who wrote poetry. The character of Almanzor and the poetry he uses are remarkable for the mixture of reason and grotesque romanticism. As a knight-errant of superhuman prowess in charge of an army he defeats the quarreling Moors of Granada and wins the lovely Almahide from their ruler Boabdelin. Opposed to Almahide is the seductive and villainous Lyndaraxa, who plots against the hero. Osmyn and Benzayda offer an idyllic love touched by the painful choice of love or duty, as is typical in Dryden's heroic drama. Almanzor, who "Acknowledges no pow'r above his own," is startlingly nimble in changing from side to side in battle and boils into enormous rages. The character provoked a cutting satire in the figure of Drawcansir in the 1671 version of *The Rehearsal.*

Conrad (kon'rad). In Byron's long narrative poem *The Corsair*, the pirate chief who is the hero.

Conrad, Joseph. [Original name, **Józef Teodor Konrad Naęcz Korzeniowski.**] b. at Berdyczew, Poland (then under Russian rule), Dec. 3, 1857; d. near Canterbury, England, Aug. 3, 1924. An English novelist of Polish birth and family, and strong patriotic and nationalist heritage. At the age of five he accompanied his father and mother into political exile in Russia. Left an orphan in 1869, he was educated under tutors and at high school at Kraków, and left Poland for France in 1874. At Marseilles (1874–78) he became involved in the Carlist cause in Spain, helping smuggle arms by sea to the Carlists. He made his first sea voyage on French merchant ships to Martinique (1875) and the West Indies (1876–77). Joining an English ship in 1878, he then first landed in England, joined the English merchant service, and sailed, chiefly on English ships, to all parts of the world (1878–94), rising from third mate (1880), to first mate (1883) and master (1886); he was naturalized a British subject in 1886. He made a journey up the Congo River for Belgian interests in 1890, and left the sea unwillingly in 1894. His first novel, *Almayer's Folly*, was published in 1895. Married (1896) to Jessie George, he was the father of two sons, Borys (b. 1898) and John Alexander (b. 1906). He revisited Poland in the summer of 1914 with his family, and was aided in returning to England after the outbreak of World War I by the American ambassador at Vienna, Frederic C. Penfield. He visited naval stations in the North Sea for the British Admiralty in 1916, and made a triumphal visit to the U. S. in the spring of 1923. He died suddenly on Aug. 3, 1924, and is buried at Canterbury.

Written Works. Conrad's novels and tales are marked by strong originality of style and treatment; by richly realized settings in the Orient and the tropics, on the high seas, or in European cities and countries; by probing moral and psychological analysis; by themes of honor, moral alienation, guilt, expiation, and heroism; and by a remarkable distinction of form. They include *Almayer's Folly* (1895), *An Outcast of the Islands* (1896), *The Nigger of the "Narcissus"* (1897), *Lord Jim* (1900), *The Inheritors* and *Romance* (1901, 1903; these two written in collaboration with Ford Madox Hueffer, later called Ford Madox Ford), *Typhoon* (1902), *Nostromo* (1904), *The Secret Agent* (1907), *Under Western Eyes* (1911), *Chance* (1914), *Victory* (1915), *The Shadow-Line* (1917), *The Arrow of Gold* (1919), *The Rescue* (1920), *The Rover* (1923), *Suspense* (1925, unfinished). Books of shorter tales: *Tales of Unrest* (1899), *Youth* (1902), *Typhoon* (1903), *A Set of Six* (1908), *'Twixt Land and Sea* (1912), *Within the Tides* (1915), *Tales of Hearsay* (1925). Books of reminiscence: *The Mirror of the Sea* (1906), *A Personal Record* (1912). Books of literary and personal essays: *Notes on Life and Letters* (1921), *Last Essays* (1926). He dramatized *The Secret Agent* in 1922 and *Victory* was dramatized by others in 1919. See *Life and Letters*, ed. by G. Jean-Aubry (1927).

Conrade (kon'rad). In Shakespeare's *Much Ado About Nothing*, a follower of Don John, the bastard brother of Don Pedro.

Conrade of Montferrat or **Montserrat** (mont.fẹ.rat'; -sẹ-). In Sir Walter Scott's novel *The Talisman*, the bitter opponent of England who tears down the flag of his enemies.

Conrad in Quest of His Youth (kon'rad). A novel (1903) by Leonard Merrick. Considered his best work, it tells the love story of the hero Conrad, who wanted to be 19 again, and how he found his second youth in Rosalind.

Conscious Lovers, The. A comedy by Steele, produced in 1722. It was taken from Terence's *Andria.* In this play Steele attempted to free the stage from the coarseness (and frequent downright obscenity) which then prevailed.

Conservative Club. A London political club, established in 1840.

Conspiracy and Tragedy of Charles, Duke of Byron, The. [Also, **Byron's Conspiracy** and **Byron's Tragedy.**] A melodramatic tragedy (1608) in two parts, each in five acts, by George Chapman. The "Byron" of the title was Charles de Gontaut, Duke of Biron (1562–1602), a brave French soldier, known as "the Thunderbolt of France." The two plays deal with his plots against his king, and his punishment.

Constable (kun'stạ.bl, kon'-), **Henry.** b. at Newark, Nottinghamshire, England, 1562; d. at Liége, Belgium, Oct. 9, 1613. An English poet. He was

ạ, d or j; ṣ, s or sh; ṭ, t or ch; ẓ, z or zh; o, F. cloche; ü, F. menu; ċh, Sc. loch; ṅ, F. bonbon.

graduated at Cambridge (St. John's College) in 1580, became a Roman Catholic, and for the greater part of his later life resided at Paris, occupied with political affairs and especially with schemes for promoting the interests of Catholicism. In 1603 he went to London, and was for a short time confined in the Tower. He published in 1592 a collection of 23 sonnets entitled *Diana: the Praises of his Mistress in certaine sweete Sonnets by H. C.*

Constable, John. b. at East Bergholt, Suffolk, England, June 11, 1776; d. at London, March 30, 1837. An English landscape painter. His father was a miller. In 1799 he became a student at the Royal Academy, in 1802 exhibited his first picture, in 1819 became an associate of the Royal Academy, and in 1829 became a Royal Academician. He was thoroughly English: no foreign master influenced him, and rustic life furnished his inspiration and material. He obtained little recognition in his own country during his lifetime, but was highly appreciated in France, where his work produced a notable effect.

Constable of France. In Shakespeare's *Henry V*, one of the chief French lords and military leaders. He is killed at Agincourt.

Constance (kon'stạns). In Chaucer's *Man of Law's Tale*, the unjustly accused daughter of the Roman emperor.

Constance. In Shakespeare's *King John*, the mother of Arthur, Duke of Britain (Brittany).

Constance. The "Northern Lass," in Richard Brome's play of that name.

Constance. The daughter of Nonesuch, in love with Loveby, in Dryden's play *The Wild Gallant*.

Constance. The daughter of the provost, in G. W. Lovell's play *The Provost of Bruges*. She goes mad and dies when proved to be legally a serf.

Constance. The daughter of Fondlove in J. Sheridan Knowles's comedy *The Love Chase*. Her love affair with Wildrake is not unlike that of Benedick and Beatrice.

Constance Baines (bānz). See **Baines.**

Constance de Beverley (dẹ bev'ẹr.li). See **Beverley, Constance de.**

Constance Neville (nev'il). See **Neville, Constance.**

Constans (kon'stanz). The grandfather of King Arthur, celebrated in the Arthurian romances.

Constant (kon'stạnt). The lover of Lady Brute in Vanbrugh's comedy *The Provok'd Wife*.

Constant Couple, The. [Full title, **The Constant Couple, or, A Trip to the Jubilee.**] A comedy by George Farquhar, produced in 1699. It is based partly on Scarron's *Le Roman bourgeois*. The part of Sir Harry Wildair is in the style of the Restoration beau and was played by Robert Wilks. A less successful sequel appeared in 1701 as *Sir Harry Wildair*.

Constantia Durham (kon.stan'shạ dur'ạm). See **Durham, Constantia.**

Constantine I (kon'stạn.tin, -tēn). [Called **Constantine the Great**; full Latin name, **Flavius Valerius Aurelius Constantinus.**] b. at Naissus (modern Niš), in Upper Moesia (in what is now Yugoslavia), in February, 274 A.D.; d. at Nicomedia

(modern Izmit), in Bithynia (in what is now Turkey), May 22, 337. A Roman emperor. He was the eldest son of the emperor Constantius I (Constantius Chlorus) by his first wife Helena, and was appointed Caesar (subordinate emperor) at the death of his father in 306. About 308 he was recognized as Augustus (emperor) by the emperor Maximian, whose daughter Fausta he married (his first wife having died). In 310 he put to death Maximian, who was implicated in a plot to excite a rebellion among his subjects. He defeated in 312, near Rome, the emperor Maxentius, who was killed as he fled from the field of battle. Before this battle, according to tradition, the sign of a cross appeared in the heavens, with the inscription *In hoc signo vinces* (meaning, approximately, "under this sign be victorious"), which induced him to adopt the labarum (a purple banner hanging vertically from a horizontal crosspiece on a pike or spear, and bearing the monogram "XP," the initials in Greek of Jesus Christ) as his standard. In 323 he became sole emperor by a decisive victory at Chrysopolis (modern Üsküdar, in Turkey) over his colleague Licinius, who subsequently surrendered and was treacherously murdered (324). He caused Christianity to be recognized by the state, convened the Council of Nicaea in 325, and in 330 announced Constantinople (modern Istanbul) as the capital of the Roman Empire. In 324 he put to death his eldest son, Crispus, for high treason. According to tradition, Crispus was the victim of an intrigue on the part of his stepmother, Fausta, who was suffocated in a bath as soon as Constantine discovered the innocence of Crispus. That these two killings did occur on his orders is now accepted as fact by virtually every authority in the field, but Constantine's actual motivation is less easy to determine. His fits of rage were violent to the point of being uncontrollable, and his rule was absolute within his court and throughout his realm; the most plausible explanation of the "executions" is perhaps therefore simply quick temper abetted by unquestioned authority rather than any devious scheme to eliminate two people whose existence he no longer desired. Constantine was, on the whole, one of the most able rulers in the history of the ancient world. Unlike the petty despots and upstart generals who had so often in the generations just before him briefly held the title of "Augustus," he was a brilliant administrator and military leader who aimed at nothing less than the reëstablishment of a strong, unified, and prosperous Roman empire from Britain to the East. The famous story of the cross that appeared in the sky before the battle against Maxentius in 312 has obscured, to some extent, Constantine's own probable attitude toward Christianity. Unquestionably he was influenced by it, but it is equally unquestionably a moot question as to whether this influence was (until the very end of his life) chiefly religious or the adaptation of what was clearly an important force in the world to serve the immediate, and very practical, end of consolidating the imperial power. He convened the Synod of Arles in 314 and the first Council of Nicaea in 325, and specifically dedicated his own imperial city of Constantinople (at the time of its naming, in 330) to Mary, the mother of Jesus; nevertheless, he was not himself actually baptized as a Christian until the time of his death, in 337, and he long encouraged a degree of paganism within his own court. Another fact about Constantine which may lead to some confusion on the part of the modern reader is that, although he may surely be said to have founded what most historians call the Byzantine Empire, he is himself generally and properly referred to as a Roman emperor. This confusion will be eliminated if the reader will recall that at the time of Constantine it was an accepted fact that the Roman Empire could (and usually did) have two emperors, who were theoretically supposed to rule jointly. This concept of joint rule was accepted by Constantine and by the people throughout the Empire (the fact that from the death of Licinius in 324 Constantine was the only emperor was taken by Constantine himself to be an exceptional circumstance, even though he had brought it about); paralleling (and, in a curious way, actually supporting) this concept of joint rule was the concept of the Roman Empire as being an essentially indivisible political unit (in other words, regardless of the number of emperors, there could be only one Empire). The result of this was that Constantine thought of himself as being the ruler of the Roman Empire in its fullest sense, and not simply of its eastern portion. This concept persisted long after Constantine's death, and it is from it that the later emperors at Constantinople (after the division of the Empire into Eastern and Western portions) traced their claim to be recognized as the only rightful "Roman" emperors (which led to the seeming paradox of Byzantine emperors stubbornly insisting on the title of "Roman emperor").

Constant Maid, The. A play by Shirley, printed in 1640, reprinted in 1667 with the second title *Love will find out the Way.*

Constant Wife, The. A comedy of marital infidelity, in three acts, by W. Somerset Maugham. It was published in 1926, produced in 1927, and has been revived several times since.

Constanza (kon.stan′zạ). A gay and sportive girl, in Thomas Middleton's *Spanish Gipsy*, who follows her father into exile disguised as a gipsy under the name Pretiosa.

Constitutional History of England in its Origin and Development, The. A prose work in three volumes (1873, 1875, 1878), by William Stubbs. The period it covers is from the beginning of English history down to 1485.

Constitutions of Clarendon (klar′ẹn.dọn). See **Clarendon, Constitutions of.**

Consuelo (kôṅ.sü.ā.lō). A novel by George Sand (1842), named from its heroine, a Spanish singer.

Contarini Fleming (kon.tạ.rē′nē flem′ing). A psychological romance by Benjamin Disraeli, published in 1832.

Contemplative Quarry, The. A volume of poetry by Anna Wickham, published in 1920.

Continental System. A plan (1806–12) by which Napoleon I waged economic warfare against Great Britain. Insisting that the British violated international law, as it prevailed among civilized nations, by treating individuals of enemy countries as belligerents even though they did not bear arms, and

by confiscation of merchantmen and of private property and by treatment of merchant mariners as prisoners of war, Napoleon, by the successive decrees of Berlin (1806), Warsaw and Milan (1807), and Fontainebleau (1810), undertook to forbid all trade with Great Britain by France, her allies, and all neutral countries. The British Isles were declared to be in a state of blockade. The British retaliated by Orders in Council which in effect declared a blockade of all of the European Continent and still further extended the policy of search and seizure at sea. For a time it almost seemed as if each of the antagonists was seeking to outdo the other in arrogance, neither side taking into account that other nations would ultimately refuse to see their commerce ruined. Napoleon's hopes were doomed by the rapid rise of extensive smuggling in every Continental country, and by continued British domination of the sea. The refusal of Denmark to obey the British orders led to the bombardment of Copenhagen and the destruction of the Danish fleet; the refusal of the Czar to obey Napoleon's decrees led to the latter's disastrous invasion of Russia. American commerce was much harassed by both sides, which caused a brief period of hostilities with France, while the British search and seizure tactics were a chief contributing cause of the War of 1812. The downfall of Napoleon brought operation of the Continental System to an end.

Conundrum of the Workshops, The. A poem by Rudyard Kipling, in which he mockingly explains how the Devil has since Adam whispered into the ear of every artist the question "But is it art?"

Conversations. A prose work by William Drummond of Hawthornden, in which he gives an account of a visit Ben Jonson paid him in 1618. It is valuable to students of the period for the personal picture it gives of Jonson and because it records his opinions on various literary subjects. In a small way it does for the Elizabethan Johnson what Boswell did for the 18th-century Johnson. The work, left in manuscript form, was not published until 1832. Recent editions are those of R. F. Patterson (1923) and Percy Simpson (1925).

Conversion of Edmund (ed′mund), **The.** See under **Bede.**

Conway (kon′wā), **Hugh.** Pseudonym of **Fargus, Frederick John.**

Cook (kŭk), **Charles Henry.** [Pseudonym, **John Bickerdyke.**] b. at London, in July, 1858; d. Jan. 17, 1933. An English novelist, journalist, and writer on sports. Among his works are *An Irish Midsummer Night's Dream* (1885), *The Curiosities of Ale and Beer* (1886; with J. M. Dixon), *The Book of the All Round Angler* (1889), *Sea Fishing* (1895), *Wild Sports in Ireland* (1897), *Practical Letters to Young Sea Fishers* (1898), and others.

Cook, Edward Dutton. b. at London, Jan. 30, 1829; d. there, Sept. 11, 1883. An English novelist and critic. He was drama critic for the *Pall Mall Gazette* and the *World*, and contributor to the first two volumes of the *Dictionary of National Biography.* He published *Paul Foster's Daughter* (1861), *The Trials of the Tredgolds* (1864), and various other novels and works on the stage.

Cook, Eliza. b. at London, c1818; d. at Thornton Hill, Wimbledon, Surrey, England, Sept. 23, 1889.

ḍ, d or j; ṣ, s or sh; ṭ, t or ch; ẓ, z or zh; o, F. cloche; ü, F. menu; çh, Sc. loch; ṅ, F. bonbon.

An English poet. She wrote for various English periodicals, and in 1840 published *Melaia and other Poems*. In 1849 she began to publish *Eliza Cook's Journal*, which appeared until 1854. Among her books are *Jottings from my Journal* (1860) and *New Echoes* (1864); among her single poems are *The Old Arm-Chair, O why does the white man follow my path?*, *The Old Farm Gate*, and *Old Songs*.

Cook, James. b. at Marton, Yorkshire, Oct. 27, 1728; killed in Hawaii, Feb. 14, 1779. An English navigator, son of a Yorkshire farm-laborer. He entered the navy as an able seaman in 1755, was appointed master of the *Mercury* in 1759, and sailed for America, where he was occupied in surveying the channel of the St. Lawrence River, and became marine surveyor of the coast of Newfoundland and Labrador in 1763. In May, 1768, he was appointed lieutenant and placed in command of the *Endeavor*, which carried a party of scientists to Tahiti to observe the transit of Venus. During this voyage, which lasted from Aug. 25, 1768, to June 12, 1771, New Zealand was explored, and the east coast of Australia. Cook was raised to the rank of commander in August, 1771, and on July 13, 1772, started with two ships, the *Resolution* (which he commanded) and the *Adventure*, on another voyage of exploration in the Pacific, which lasted (for the *Resolution*) until July 29, 1775, and during which an attempt was made to discover the reported great southern continent, and New Caledonia was discovered. On Aug. 9, 1775, he became captain, and on July 12, 1776, began his last voyage with the *Resolution* (which he again commanded), and the *Discovery* under Captain Charles Clerke. The object of the expedition was to discover a passage from the Pacific round the north of America. During his northward voyage the Sandwich Islands (Hawaiian Islands) were rediscovered (1778), and shortly after his return to them (January, 1779) he was murdered by the natives.

Cooke (kùk), **Alexander.** fl. 1603–13. An English actor. He is listed in the First Folio edition of Shakespeare's works (1623) and was a member of the Lord Chamberlain's Men. He presumably appeared in their plays until 1613. It is known that he played the principal tragic role in Jonson's *Sejanus*.

Cooke, Sir Edward (or **Lord**). See **Coke, Sir Edward.**

Cooke, George Frederick. b. at Westminster (now part of London), April 17, 1756; d. at New York, Sept. 26, 1812. An English actor. He first appeared on the stage in 1776 at Brentford. During his ten years at Covent Garden he played a wide range of parts including Shakespeare's Richard III, Iago, and Shylock, Massinger's Sir Giles Overreach, and Macklin's Sir Archy MacSarcasm and Sir Pertinax MacSycophant, where he rivaled Macklin himself.

Cooke, John. fl. 1614. An English dramatist, author of *Greene's Tu Quoque, or The Citie Gallant.*

Cooke, Thomas. b. at Braintree, Essex, England, Dec. 16, 1703; d. at Lambeth (now part of London), Dec. 20, 1756. An English writer, best known as the author of a translation of Hesiod (from which he obtained the nickname of "Hesiod Cooke"). He also published translations of Terence and other

Latin and Greek authors, a poem entitled *The Battle of the Poets* (which, with some criticisms of Pope's Greek, brought down upon him the wrath of that poet, who ridiculed him in the *Dunciad*), and various dramatic works. He succeeded Nicholas Amhurst in the editorship of *The Craftsman.*

Cook's Tale, The. One of Chaucer's *Canterbury Tales*. It is an unfinished poem, and a spurious ending was added to it in the folio of 1687. The Cook, Roger of Ware, starts a fabliau about a London apprentice which promises to be as bawdy as the Miller's and Reeve's tales that have just been told. In some manuscripts *The Tale of Gamelyn* (not by Chaucer) has been inserted at this point, and some scholars suggest that the poet may have intended to substitute a version of this for the unfinished piece. Chaucer depicts Roger as an expert cook but (to judge by his complexion) not a sanitary one:

> He coude rost, and sethe, and broille, and frye,
> Maken mortreux, and wel bake a pye.
> But greet harm was it, as it thoughte me,
> That on his shine a mormal hadde he;
> For blankmanger, that made he with the beste.

Cool as a Cucumber. A farce by William Blanchard Jerrold, first played in 1851.

Cooper (kō'pér, kŭp'ér), **Alfred Duff.** [Title, Viscount **Norwich.**] b. 1890; d. Jan. 1, 1954. An English statesman and diplomat; husband of Lady Diana Duff Cooper. Graduated from Oxford, he served (1914–19) in World War I. A Conservative member of Parliament (1924–29, 1931 *et seq.*), he served in the war office (1928–29, 1931–34) and in the treasury (1934–35), and was secretary of state for war (1935–37), first lord of the admiralty (1937–38), minister of information (1940–41), chancellor of the duchy of Lancaster (1941–43), representative (1943–44) to the French Committee of National Liberation, and ambassador (1944–47) to France. He is the author of *Talleyrand* (1932), the two-volume *Haig* (1935, 1936), *The Second World War* (1939), and *David* (1943). He wrote only one fictional work, *Operation Heartbreak* (1951), and his autobiography, *Old Men Forget* (1953).

Cooper, Anthony Ashley. See **Shaftesbury.**

Cooper, Lady Diana Duff. [Maiden name, **Manners.**] b. 1892—. An English actress; granddaughter of John James Robert Manners, 7th Duke of Rutland, and wife of Alfred Duff Cooper. She appeared on stage in the U. S. as the Madonna in Max Reinhardt's production of *The Miracle.*

Cooper, Edith Emma. [Pseudonym (with Katherine Harris Bradley), **Michael Field.**] b. at Kenilworth, Warwickshire, England, Jan. 12, 1862; d. at Richmond, Surrey, England, Dec. 13, 1913. An English lyric and dramatic poet; niece of Katherine Harris Bradley (1848–1914).

Cooper, John. b. at Bath, England, before 1810; d. at Tunbridge Wells, England, July 13, 1870. An English actor. He appeared at Bath in 1811, making his London debut in the same year, and after some years in the provinces was a favorite with London audiences in the period 1820–58.

Cooper, Thomas. b. at Leicester, England, March 20, 1805; d. at Lincoln, England, July 15, 1892. An English Chartist agitator, poet, and author. Self-taught in Hebrew, Greek, Latin, and French, he became a schoolmaster and, later, a Methodist preacher. He led the Leicester Chartists in 1841, and was imprisoned for two years on a charge of sedition. He was the author of the poem *The Purgatory of Suicides* (1845), a collection of tales, *Wise Saws and Modern Instances* (1845), two novels, *Alderman Ralph* (1853) and *The Family Feud* (1854), and the autobiographical *Thoughts at Fourscore* (1885).

Cooper's Hill. A poem by Sir John Denham, first published in 1642, and published in its final form in 1665. Pope, who imitated Denham, also wrote in praise of *Cooper's Hill* in his poem *Windsor Forest*.

Copernicus (kọ.pėr'ni.kus), **Nicolaus.** [Latin form of Polish **Mikołaj Kopernik.**] b. at Toruń, Poland, Feb. 19, 1473; d. at Frombork, Poland, May 24, 1543. Founder of modern astronomy. He entered the University of Kraków in 1491, studied law at Bologna (1495–1500), was appointed canon of the chapter of Frombork (Frauenburg) in 1497, lectured on astronomy at Rome in 1500, studied medicine at Padua (c1501), and became *doctor decretorum* at Ferrara in 1503. The rest of his life was spent chiefly at Frombork in the performance of his duties as canon and in the practice of medicine. He published in 1543 an exposition of his system of astronomy, which has since received the name of the Copernican, in a treatise entitled *De orbium coelestium revolutionibus*.

Cophetua (kọ.feṭ'ū.ạ). The hero of an English ballad, *Cophetua and the Beggar Maid*, a legendary African king who wooed and married Penelophon, a beggar maid. The ballad is preserved in Percy's *Reliques*. Cophetua is alluded to by Shakespeare (who calls the girl Zenelophon) in *Love's Labour's Lost*, and by Ben Jonson. Tennyson also wrote a short poem on the subject entitled *The Beggar Maid*.

Copleston (kop'l.stọn), **Edward.** b. at Offwell, Devonshire, England, Feb. 2, 1776; d. near Chepstow, England, Oct. 14, 1849. An English prelate and author, appointed professor of poetry at Oxford in 1802, and bishop of Llandaff and dean of Saint Paul's in 1828. He wrote *Praelectiones* (1813), *Enquiry into the Doctrines of Necessity and Predestination* (1821), and others.

Coppard (kop'ạrd), **A. E.** [Full name, **Alfred Edgar Coppard.**] b. at Folkestone, England, Jan. 4, 1878—. An English short-story writer and poet. Among his collections of verse are *Hips and Haws* (1922), *Pelagea and Other Poems* (1926), *Collected Poems* (1928), and *Cherry Ripe* (1935); he is the author also of the volumes of stories *Adam and Eve and Pinch Me* (1921), *The Black Dog* (1923), *Fishmonger's Fiddle* (1925), *The Field of Mustard* (1926), *Pink Furniture* (1930), *Easter Day* (1931), *Rummy* (1932), *Tapster's Tapestry* (1938), *You Never Know, Do You?* (1939), and *Dark-eyed Lady* (1947).

"Copper Captain," the. See **Perez, Michael.**

Copperfield (kop'ėr.fēld), **David.** The central character of Dickens's *David Copperfield*. His story, told in the first person, is the most nearly autobiographical of Dickens's novels.

Coquette. A novel by Frank Swinnerton, published in 1921. The central character is Sally Minto.

Cora (kō'rạ). In Richard Brinsley Sheridan's *Pizarro*, the wife of Alonzo, the commander of Ataliba's troops.

Corambis (kọ.ram'bis). The name of Polonius in the first quarto *Hamlet* (1603).

Corbaccio (kôr.bät'chō). In Ben Jonson's comedy *Volpone*, an avaricious old man who seeks to gain a fortune although he is near death.

Corbenic (kôr'bẹ.nik). In the *Romance of the Grail* the castle built as a shrine for the Holy Grail.

Corbet (kôr'bẹt), **Richard.** b. at Ewell, Surrey, England, 1582; d. at Norwich, England, July 28, 1635. An English prelate and poet, elected bishop of Oxford in 1624, and transferred to the see of Norwich in 1632. He was an intimate friend of Ben Jonson, and was noted for his convivial habits. The first collected edition of his poems was published in 1647; some of them were published separately in 1648, under the title *Poetica Stromata*.

Corcoran (kôr'kọ.rạn), **Captain.** In Gilbert and Sullivan's *Pinafore*, the captain of H.M.S. *Pinafore*. He is the father of Josephine and is revealed in the end to be simply an Able Seaman.

Cordatus (kôr.dā'tus). A character in Ben Jonson's comedy *Every Man Out of His Humour*, who with Mitis performs the part of a critic with explanation and comment, always present on the scene, but standing aside.

Cordelia (kôr.dēl'yạ). In Shakespeare's *King Lear*, the youngest daughter of Lear. She offends him by the seeming coolness of her protestations of love for him, and he disinherits her. When, however, he is ill-treated, maddened, and turned out by his elder daughters, to whom he has given everything, she comes with an army to oust them, but is taken captive, and is killed in prison. Lear in a last outburst kills the slave who hanged her and dies holding her body.

Cordeliers (kôr.dẹ.lyā). A political club during the French Revolution. The actual name of this group, established in 1790, was (in English translation) "The Society of the Friends of the Rights of Man and of the Citizen," but the cumbersomeness of this title led to the club being popularly called by the name of its first headquarters, a former monastery of the Cordeliers or Franciscan Observantists. The principal purpose of the organization as stated in its charter was to bring to public attention and to denounce all offenses against the "Rights of Man" and all abuses of power by public bodies or officials. It was a kind of political watch and ward society, and its badge, an open eye, symbolized alertness in the public interest. This alertness soon took on the nature of suspiciousness, and the club's leaders, largely middle-class demagogues who played upon the miseries and the passions of the masses, used it to promote agitations and disorders and to assail all public figures whom they disliked, especially the moderately revolutionary Girondists. The Cordeliers, in fact, got beyond the control of their original leaders Danton and Desmoulins, and were dominated by Marat until his assassination, and later by Hébert. Infiltrating the army and the various sections of Paris, bully-

---

ḍ, d or j; ṣ, s or sh; ṭ, t or ch; ẓ, z or zh; o, F. cloche; ü, F. menu; ch, Sc. loch; ṅ, F. bonbon.

ing the commune, and even threatening the Jacobins, the Cordeliers were high among the dominant forces of the Revolution until Robespierre turned upon Hébert and caused his execution in March, 1794, after which the club went out of existence.

Corelli (kọ.rel′i), **Marie**. [Pseudonym of **Mary Mackay**.] b. in England, 1864; d. 1924. A British novelist. Of Italian and Scottish parentage, she was adopted in her infancy by Charles Mackay, the poet. She wrote *A Romance of Two Worlds* (1886), *Thelma* (1887), *Ardath* (1889), *Barabbas* (1893), *The Mighty Atom* (1896), *The Master Christian* (1900), *Temporal Power* (1902), *God's Good Man* (1904), *The Treasure of Heaven* (1906), *Holy Orders* (1908), *The Devil's Motor* (1910), *The Young Diana* (1917), and *The Secret Power* (1921). See *Marie Corelli* (1953), by Eileen Bigland.

Corflambo (kôr.flam′bō). In Edmund Spenser's *Faerie Queene*, the symbol of lust. He is the abductor of Amoret and is finally slain by Prince Arthur.

Corin (kō′rin). In Shakespeare's *As You Like It*, a shepherd.

Corinna (kọ.rin′ạ). b. at Tanagra, Boeotia, Greece; fl. in the first part of the 5th century B.C. A Greek lyric poet, sometimes called a Theban from her long residence at Thebes. She was a contemporary and instructor of Pindar, from whom she is said to have won the prize five times at the public games. A few fragments of her poems have been preserved.

Corinna's Going A-Maying. A pastoral poem (published in 1648, but thought to have been written some years earlier) of 70 lines by Robert Herrick. It was first published in *Hesperides*, his volume of secular poetry. Corinna is implored by her lover to rise and greet the first day of May with him. Herrick states here his exhortation to enjoy life: "Come, let us go while we are in our prime, And take the harmless folly of the time," in much the same terms as in his poem *To The Virgins, To Make Much of Time*.

Corinne ou l'Italie (ko.rēn ö lē.tà.lē). [Eng. trans., "*Corinne or Italy*."] A novel by Madame de Staël, published in 1807.

Corinthian (kọ.rin′thi.ạn). A gay fellow, or sport; used in Shakespeare's *1 Henry IV*.

Coriolanus (kôr″i.ọ.lā′nus, kor″i-). [Full title, **The Tragedy of Coriolanus**.] Tragedy by Shakespeare, written 1607–08, and founded on North's *Plutarch*. The fable about the belly and other members of the body which is recited by Menenius is found in Camden's *Remaines* (1605). The play was printed in the 1623 folio, but the date of its first performance is not recorded. In the play the mother of Caius (Cnaeus) Marcius Coriolanus is Volumnia, not Veturia, and his wife is Virgilia, not Volumnia, as in the original. John Dennis produced a play in 1705 founded on *Coriolanus*, which he called *The Invader of His Country, or the Fatal Resentment*, and two decades earlier Nahum Tate had adapted the Shakespeare play for political purposes with the additional title, *The Ingratitude of a Commonwealth* (1682).

The Story. Caius Marcius, having heroically captured the Volscian city, Corioli, returns to Rome and is given the surname Coriolanus, in honor of his great accomplishments. The Senate offers him the consulship, but he must first, according to custom, appear before the people of Rome, show them his wounds, and humbly ask for their support. Despite his contempt, as a Roman soldier of good family, for the rabble, he does this, and the people agree to vote for him. However, two tribunes, Sicinius and Brutus, convince the mob that Coriolanus would rule as a tyrant, and the fickle people of Rome reverse their decision. Coriolanus's outspoken rage at their behavior infuriates the crowd and they attack him. Once more, at the persuasion of his friend Menenius, and particularly his mother, Volumnia, he approaches the people willing to conceal his contempt for them. But because of the accusations of the tribunes, he again loses his temper, and this time is banished from Rome. Bent on revenge, he offers his services as leader of the Volscian army to his old enemy, Tullius Aufidius. Under the leadership of Coriolanus the Volscians successfully advance on Rome. His old friends, Menenius and Cominius, meet him outside the gates and plead with him to spare the city, but he is deaf to all entreaties until his wife Virgilia, his young son, and his mother plead with him. He returns to the Volscians to tell them that he will not capture Rome, but has arranged a treaty favorable to the Volscians. Aufidius, already jealous of Coriolanus's greater military talent and popularity, calls him a traitor, and with the angry support of the commoners of Corioli, Aufidius's followers stab him.

Coriolanus. In Shakespeare's *Coriolanus*, the name given to Caius Marcius. He is a stiff-necked Roman soldier aristocrat, arrogant and contemptuous of the common people, but withal modest and of a Cato-like personal integrity.

Coriolanus. A tragedy by James Thomson, based on Shakespeare's tragedy, and left in manuscript by Thomson at his death. It was produced by Sir George Littleton and published in 1749.

Cork (kôrk), 5th Earl of. A title of **Boyle, John**.

Corkery (kôr′kẻr.i), **Daniel**. b. at Cork, Ireland, 1878—. An Irish playwright, critic, and fiction writer. His works include the plays *The Labour Leader*, *The Yellow Bittern*, *The Onus of Ownership*, and *Fohnam the Sculptor*; the novel *The Threshold of Quiet*; *A Munster Twilight* and *The Hounds of Banba*, short stories; literary criticism in *Study of Irish Literature*, *The Hidden Ireland*, and *Synge and Anglo-Irish Literature* (1931).

Cormac (kôr′mak). b. 836; d. 908. A king of Cashel, Ireland, who reigned from 900 to 908. He perished in a battle in the latter year. A glossary of Irish words is attributed to him.

Corneille (kôr.ney′), **Pierre**. b. at Rouen, France, June 6, 1606; d. at Paris, Oct. 1, 1684. A French dramatist. He is the earliest playwright of his country whose works are still produced at Paris and read by the general public. He graduated from the Jesuit College at Rouen, studied law, was admitted to the bar, but did not practice. From 1629 to 1650, however, he earned about 1,200 francs annually as a magistrate. In 1647 he was elected to the French Academy and in 1662 he moved to Paris, where he lived until his death. He began his dramatic career with a comedy, *Mélite*, produced in 1630 by the great actor Montdory at the Théâtre du Marais in Paris. Then followed at the same theater *Clitandre* (tragicomedy, produced in 1630 or 1631), *La Veuve* (comedy, 1631 or 1632), *La Galerie du Palais* (comedy, 1632), *La Suivante* (comedy, 1632 or 1633), and *La Place Royale* (comedy, 1633). The six plays won for their author recognition as the outstanding contemporary French writer of comedies. Corneille, however, now turned to tragedy, the genre which was to give him lasting fame. He produced *Médée* (tragedy, 1634 or 1635), then returned to comedy with *L'Illusion comique* (1635 or 1636), followed by his four masterpieces: *Le Cid* (tragedy, January, 1637), a struggle between love and duty; *Horace* (tragedy, 1640), a test of patriotism; *Cinna* (tragedy, 1640 or 1641), in praise of clemency; and *Polyeucte* (tragedy, 1641 or 1642), concerning the power of Christianity in early times. In these four were first found the dramatic traits for which the author is famous: strong characters, inner struggles between two passions, conflicts of wills, and eloquent expressions of lofty sentiments. With the success of *Polyeucte* Corneille found himself acknowledged as his country's greatest writer of tragedies, an honor which he held until he was forced to share it with Racine after the appearance of the latter's *Andromaque* (1667). From 1642 to 1651 he produced a variety of plays: *Pompée* (tragedy, 1642 or 1643); *Le Menteur* (comedy, 1643), his most popular comedy; *La Suite du Menteur* (comedy, 1644 or 1645); *Rodogune* (tragedy, 1644 or 1645), a favorite with Corneille, probably because it was nearly all his own invention; *Théodore* (tragedy, 1645), a religious play and a failure; *Héraclius* (tragedy, 1646 or 1647); *Don Sanche d'Aragon* (heroic comedy, 1649); *Andromède* (tragedy, 1650), a spectacular machine play; *Nicomède* (tragedy, 1650 or 1651), a remarkable play depicting the resistance of the East to the growing power of Rome; and *Pertharite* (tragedy, 1651), a failure. Corneille now retired from the stage and devoted himself to his *Imitation de Jésus-Christ*, a financial success. In 1659, however, he returned triumphantly with *Œdipe* (tragedy), followed by *La Toison d'or* (tragedy, 1660), a machine play written for the marriage of Louis XIV; *Sertorious* (tragedy, 1662); *Sophonisbe* (tragedy, 1663), a rewriting of Mairet's play of the same name; and *Othon* (tragedy, 1664). *Agésilas* (tragedy, 1666) was a failure, but *Attila* (tragedy, 1667) a great success. *Tite et Bérénice* (heroic comedy) was bought and produced by Molière in 1670. After producing two more plays, *Pulchérie* (tragedy, 1672) and *Suréna* (tragedy, 1674), both failures, Corneille devoted himself to the revision of his works for the 1682 edition and died two years after its publication. A striking trait of Corneille's tragedies is his rejection of love as a theme and his choice of such passions as magnanimity, patriotism, vengeance, ambition, and religious zeal. Guided by these emotions, the characters make sacrifices which arouse in the spectator a feeling of awe or wonder. Racine, on the other hand, preferred love as the subject of tragedy, and his principal characters approach more closely Aristotle's ideal of arousing pity and fear.

Cornelia (kôr.nēl′yạ). fl. 2nd century B.C. A Roman matron, daughter of the elder Scipio Africanus, wife of Tiberius Sempronius Gracchus, and mother of the Gracchi, the tribunes Tiberius and Caius Gracchus. She was celebrated for her accomplishments and virtues as a mother. After the death of her husband, she refused to marry again but devoted her life to her children. The story is told of her answering the boasts of another Roman matron about her jewels with the simple "These are my jewels," and pointing to her children.

Cornelia. In Thomas Kyd's *Pompey the Great* (1594), which was largely a translation of Robert Garnier's *Cornélie*, the wife of Pompey.

Cornelia. In John Webster's tragedy *The White Devil*, the mother of Marcello, Flamineo, and Vittoria. She sorrowfully buries her one virtuous child, Marcello, after he has been killed by his wicked brother, Flamineo.

Cornelia Blimber (blim′ẽr). See **Blimber, Cornelia.**

Cornelius (kôr.nēl′yus). In Shakespeare's *Cymbeline*, a physician. He recognizes the Queen's evil designs and gives her, not the poison she intends to use, but a sleep drug, and thus saves Imogen's life.

Cornelius. In Shakespeare's *Hamlet*, a courtier. He and Voltimand are sent on an embassy to Norway by Claudius.

Cornelius. In Christopher Marlowe's tragedy *Doctor Faustus*, a friend of Faustus.

Cornelius Barry (bar′i). See **Balibari, Chevalier de.**

Cornelius Cinna (sin′ạ), **Lucius.** See **Cinna.**

Cornford (kôrn′fọrd), **Frances Crofts.** [Maiden name, **Darwin.**] b. at Cambridge, England, 1886—. An English poet; granddaughter of Charles Darwin and daughter of Sir Francis Darwin. She is the author of *Poems* (1910), *Spring Morning* (1915), *Autumn Midnight* (1923), *Different Days* (1928), and *Mountains and Molehills* (1935). Some of her best-known poems are *Country Bedroom, The Watch, A Wasted Day, The Old Nurse, The Hills, Autumn Morning at Cambridge, The Unbeseechable,* and the triolet *To a Fat Lady Seen from the Train.*

Cornhill (kôrn′hil). One of the principal London streets, once a grain market.

Cornhill Magazine, The. A monthly periodical (founded 1860). It was first edited by Thackeray, but he soon resigned, as the nature of the work did not appeal to him. However, his last novels, *The Adventures of Philip, Lovel the Widower,* and the unfinished *Denis Duval,* first appeared in its pages, as did *Cousin Phillis* and *Wives and Daughters,* by Mrs. Gaskell. Others who contributed were Ruskin, Matthew Arnold, and Trollope. Among those who followed Thackeray as editor are Sir Leslie Stephen (from 1871 to 1882), James Payn (1883–96), John St. Loe Strachey, and Reginald John Smith. The name of the magazine derived from its place of publication, "our storehouse being in Cornhill," as Thackeray told his readers in the first issue.

Corn King and the Spring Queen, The. A novel by Naomi Mitchison, published in 1931.

"Corn-Law Rhymer," the. See **Elliott, Ebenezer.**

Corn Laws. In English history, a series of laws, extending from 1436 to 1842, regulating the domestic and foreign grain trade of England. Until the repeal of the Corn Laws, the grain trade, both export and import, was the subject of elaborate and varying legislation, which consisted in levying protective or prohibitory duties, or in imposing restrictive conditions, or in granting government bounties for the encouragement of exportation. The passage of the Corn Law of 1815, enacted in an attempt to counteract the post-Napoleonic depression era, caused riots and led to widespread demands for reform. After a prolonged agitation, led by such men as Richard Cobden and John Bright, for the repeal of the Corn Laws by the Anti-Corn Law League (organized in 1839 as a consolidation of several such associations), Parliament in 1846, under the ministry of Sir Robert Peel, passed an act for a large immediate reduction of the duty on imported grain, and providing for a merely nominal duty after 1849, which was subsequently entirely removed.

Corn of Wheat, A. A novel by E. H. Young, published in 1910.

Cornwall (kôrn'wôl, -wạl), **Earl of.** Title of **Gaveston, Piers.**

Cornwall, Barry. Pseudonym of **Procter, Bryan Waller.**

Cornwall, Duke of. In Shakespeare's *King Lear*, the husband of Regan; a "gloomy, laconic, and powerful" man, inflexible in his decisions. He puts out Gloucester's eyes.

Corombona (kō.rom.bō'nạ), **Vittoria.** The "white devil" in John Webster's tragedy of that name. Having fascinated the Duke of Brachiano, she renounces everything for pleasure. At her instigation he procures the deaths of her husband and the duchess. She is brought before the tribunal and arraigned for these murders; her guilt is not proved, but she is confined in a house of convertites (penitent prostitutes) from which Brachiano secretly takes her and marries her. He is shortly poisoned and then strangled by the emissaries of the Great Duke (Francesco de' Medici), and she is stabbed by her brother Flamineo in revenge for Brachiano's failure to advance him, he having instigated his sister to her course of conduct to that end. The trial scene is one of great power. The play is based, rather inaccurately as to detail, on a real occurrence in 16th-century Italy.

coronach, coranach (kor'ọ.nạch). A dirge; a lamentation for the dead. The custom of singing dirges at funerals was formerly prevalent in Scotland and Ireland, especially in the Highlands of Scotland.

He [Pennant] tells us in the same Place "that the Coranich, or singing at Funerals, is still in Use in some Places. The Songs are generally in Praise of the Deceased; or a Recital of the valiant Deeds of him or Ancestors."
(Bourne's *Pop. Antiq.* (1777), p. 27, note.)

The village maids and matrons round
The dismal coronach resound.
(Scott, *L. of the L.* iii.15.)

Coronation, The. A play, licensed (1635) as by James Shirley, and claimed by him as his own in a list of his plays published in 1652. On the title page of its first edition, printed in 1640, it was attributed to John Fletcher, and is included in the

earlier editions of Beaumont and Fletcher's works. There is no reason for supposing that Fletcher had any hand in it.

Coronation Stone. See **Stone of Scone.**

Coronis (kọ.rō'nis). In ancient Greek mythology, the mother of Aesculapius by Apollo. She was false to the god and Apollo's ubiquitous messenger, the raven, told him. Apollo in anger cursed the raven and turned its feathers, until then white, black, but he (or Artemis) killed Coronis and saved the unborn Aesculapius from the funeral pyre.

Corot (ko.rō; Anglicized, kọ.rō'), **Jean Baptiste Camille.** b. at Paris, July 28, 1796; d. there, Feb. 22, 1875. A French painter. Although the immense popularity of Corot's shimmering trees and sunsets dwindled after his death, in part probably because so many poor reproductions of them were circulated, critics have in recent years been finding great strength in the earlier paintings, especially of architectural subjects, which Corot made in Italy, and in his portraits.

Corporate (kôr'pọ.rạt), **Christopher.** In Thomas Love Peacock's *Melincourt*, the sole voter in the "pocket borough" of Onevote.

Corpus Christi (kôr'pus kris'ti), **Feast of.** A Roman Catholic feast day in honor of the Holy Eucharist, celebrated on the first Thursday after Trinity Sunday. Originating in France in the 13th century, Corpus Christi was made a general festival by a bull of Pope Urban IV in 1264, Thomas Aquinas writing the office. By the 15th century it had become the most colorful of all feasts, its procession full of pageantry and followed by performances of miracle plays.

Corpus Christi College. A college of Cambridge University. It was founded in 1352 by two religious societies, the Guild of Corpus Christi and the Guild of the Blessed Virgin Mary. It is the college of Sir Nicholas Bacon, father of the famous Francis (who was a Trinity man), Marlowe, Richard Cavendish, translator of Euclid, John Fletcher, the dramatist, Richard Boyle, 1st Earl of Cork, Archbishop Tenison, Samuel Wesley, father of John and Charles, General Braddock, who was killed trying to drive the French out of America, Stephen Hales, Richard Gough, who translated Camden's *Britannia*, and Peter Sandiford, Gresham professor of astronomy. Its library contains manuscripts of Matthew Paris's *History* and Chaucer's *Troilus and Criseyde*.

Corpus Christi College. A college of Oxford University, England, founded in 1516 by Richard Fox, Bishop of Winchester. Its statutes were issued in 1517.

Correggio (kọ.rej'i.ō, -rej'ō; Italian, kôr.red'jō), **Antonio Allegri da.** b. at Correggio, Italy, 1494; d. there, March 5, 1534. An Italian painter of the Lombard school.

Corsair, The. A poem in three cantos by Byron, published in 1814. It relates the adventures of the pirate Conrad, especially at the court of Sultan Seyd. *Lara* (1814) continues the story. Both poems are supposedly based on Jean Lafitte's career.

Corsairs. As a proper name, the group of sea robbers, chiefly from the Barbary Coast, who infested the Mediterranean for many centuries. In the form "corsairs" it has come to be a general word for "pirates."

Corsica (kôr′si.kạ),. **Account of.** See **Account of Corsica.**

"Corsican" (kôr′si.kạn), **the.** See **Napoleon I.**

Corsican Brothers, The. A translation by Dion Boucicault of a popular French play, *Les Frères corses.* The plot turns on the mysterious sympathy between Louis and Fabian dei Franchi, who are twin brothers.

Cortegiano (kôr.tā.jä′nō), **Il.** [English, **The Courtier;** full Italian title, **Il Libro del Cortegiano.**] A famous Italian book of manners, written by Baldassare Castiglione. It was translated (c1554; not printed until 1561) into English by Sir Thomas Hoby.

Cortes (kôr′tĕsh). The former parliament of Portugal. It consisted of an upper house of hereditary and nominated princes, peers, and bishops, and a lower house elected by the people. The constitution of 1911 substituted two elected chambers.

Cortes (kôr′tās). The national assembly or legislature of Spain, consisting of a senate and chamber of deputies. The senate was formerly composed of not over 360 members, one half princes of the blood, grandees, and certain ex-officio and nominated members, and one half elected. The chamber of deputies was formerly composed of members in the proportion of one for every 50,000 inhabitants, elected for five years. Under the law of July, 1942, the Franco regime reorganized the Cortes. It had, in 1949, 438 members.

Cortés or **Cortez** (kôr.tez′), **Hernando** or **Fernando.** [Title, Marquis of the **Valley of Oaxaca** (Marqués del Valle).] b. at Medellín, Estremadura, Spain, 1485; d. at Castillejo de la Cuesta, an estate near Seville, Spain, Dec. 2, 1547. A Spanish soldier, the conqueror (1519) of Mexico. He was mistakenly credited by John Keats with being the first European to see the Pacific Ocean; actually, the Pacific was discovered by Balboa.

Corvino (kôr.vē′nō). A merchant, the husband of Celia, in Ben Jonson's comedy *Volpone:* a mixture "of wittol, fool, and knave." Out of pure covetousness he falls into Mosca's plot to give his wife up to Volpone.

Corvo (kôr′vō), **Baron.** A name used by Frederick William (Serafino Austin Lewis Mary) Rolfe (1860–1913), English novelist, short-story writer, historian, and contributor to the *Yellow Book.*

Cory (kō′ri), **William Johnson.** [Original name, **William Johnson.**] b. Jan. 9, 1823; d. June 11, 1892. An English educator and poet. In 1872, when he retired as assistant master at Eton after 26 years, he assumed the name of Cory. He wrote *Ionica* (1858; enlarged ed., 1891), *Lucretilis* (1871), *Iophon* (1873), and *Guide to Modern History from 1815 to 1835* (1882). His lyrics are in the polished style of later Greek poetry. *Extracts from the Letters and Journals of William Cory* (1897, ed. by F. W. Cornish) was published after his death.

Coryate or **Coryat** (kôr′yạt, -i.ạt), **Thomas.** b. at Odcombe, Somersetshire, England, c1577; d. at Surat, India, in December, 1617. An English traveler. After a period at court as a jester, he made a journey through France, Savoy, Italy, Switzerland, and other countries of the Continent in 1608, an account of which was published in 1611 under the title *Coryat's Crudities, hastily gobled up in Five Months Travells in France, Savoy, Italy, Rhetia, Helvetia, High Germania and the Netherlands.* He is credited, as the result of seeing them used in Italy, with the introduction of forks into England. In 1612 he started on a tour of the East, and visited Palestine, Persia, and India, in which last-named country he fell a victim to disease.

Corybantes (kor.i.ban′tēz). Priests of the Great Mother goddess in Phrygia, whose worship they celebrated by orgiastic dances. From the identification of Rhea with the Asiatic Great Mother, they are often equated with the Curetes, Rhea's satellite deities, since the priests were themselves representatives of these minor fertility gods.

Corydon (kor′i.dọn). A shepherd in Vergil's seventh eclogue, and in the *Idyls* of Theocritus; hence, a conventional name in pastoral poetry for a shepherd or a rustic swain.

Corydon. A shepherd in Spenser's *Colin Clout's Come Home Again.*

Corydon. A shepherd in Spenser's *Faerie Queene,* in love with Pastorella.

Corydon. A shoemaker of Constantinople, in Sir Walter Scott's novel *Count Robert of Paris.*

Corymbaeus (kor.im.bē′us). Pseudonym of **Brathwaite** or **Brathwait** or **Brathwayte, Richard.**

Costard (kos′tạrd). In Shakespeare's *Love's Labour's Lost,* a clownish peasant who tries to be a learned wit. Into his mouth Shakespeare puts such manifest idiocies as the word "honorificabilitudinitatibus" or has him speak of the "contempts" of a letter. He acts as messenger from Berowne to Rosaline and from Armado to Jaquenetta, confusing the two letters.

Costello (kos.tel′ō), **Louisa Stuart.** b. in Ireland, 1799; d. at Boulogne, France, April 24, 1870. A British writer and miniature painter. She wrote *Songs of a Stranger* (1825), *A Summer among the Bocages and Vines* (1840), *Gabrielle, or Pictures of a Reign* (1843), and *The Rose Garden of Persia* (1845).

Costigan (kos′ti.gạn), **Captain.** In W. M. Thackeray's novel *Pendennis,* a rakish, shabby-genteel old ex-army officer.

Costigan, Emily or **Milly.** In W. M. Thackeray's novel *Pendennis,* the daughter of Captain Costigan, a commonplace but beautiful and industrious actress in the provincial theater, with whom Arthur Pendennis falls in love. She is 26, he 18. Her stage name is Fotheringay.

Cotes (kōts), **Sara Jeanette.** [Maiden name, **Duncan.**] b. at Brantford, Ontario, 1862; d. July 22, 1922. A British journalist and novelist. Her first volume, *A Social Departure* (1890), included letters written from Japan and the East to the Montreal *Star,* of which she had been correspondent. She also wrote *An American Girl in London* (1891), *His Honour and a Lady* (1896), *Those Delightful Americans* (1902), *The Pool in the Desert* (1903), *The Imperialist* (1904), *Set in Authority* (1906), *Cousin Cinderella* (1908), *The Burnt Offering* (1909), and others.

ḑ, d or j; ṣ, s or sh; ṭ, t or ch; ẓ, z or zh; o, F. cloche; ü, F. menu; ċh, Sc. loch; ṅ, F. bonbon.

Cotgrave (kot'grāv), **Randle.** b. in Cheshire, England; d. c1634. An English lexicographer. He was the author of a French-English dictionary, still important in the study of English and French philology, first published in 1611 (2nd ed., 1632, with an English-French dictionary by Robert Sherwood; other eds., revised and enlarged by James Howell, in 1650, 1660, and 1673). He studied at Cambridge (St. John's College), and later became secretary to William Cecil, Lord Burghley.

Cotman (kot'man), **John Sell.** b. at Norwich, England, May 16, 1782; d. at London, July 24, 1842. An English landscape painter and etcher, best known for his architectural drawings. He published *Specimens of Norman and Gothic Architecture in the County of Norfolk* (1817; 50 plates), *A Series of Etchings illustrative of the Architectural Antiquities of Norfolk* (1818; 60 plates), and others. He also executed the plates for Dawson Turner's *Architectural Antiquities of Normandy* (1822). His water colors and oil paintings hang in several museums.

Cotswold Hills (kots'wōld, -wǫld). [Also: **Cotswolds, Cotteswolds, Coteswold Hills.**] A range of hills in W England, in Gloucestershire, extending approximately SW and NE. The district is famous for its breed of sheep. Its highest point is Cleeve Cloud, or Cleeve Hill (1,031 ft.), near Cheltenham. Length, ab. 54 mi.

Cotter's Saturday Night. A poem by Robert Burns, first published in a volume of poems in 1786.

Cottle (kot'l), **Amos Simon.** b. in Gloucestershire, England, c1768; d. at London, Sept. 28, 1800. An English writer; elder brother of Joseph Cottle (1770–1853). He published *Icelandic Poetry, or the Edda of Saemund translated into English Verse* (1797), and several original poems.

Cottle, Joseph. b. 1770; d. at Bristol, England, June 7, 1853. An English bookseller and poet; brother of Amos Simon Cottle. He was a friend of Coleridge, Southey, and Wordsworth, and the publisher of several of their works, including the *Lyrical Ballads* (1798) of Wordsworth and Coleridge. His poetry, *Malvern Hills* (1798), *John the Baptist* (1801), *Alfred* (1801), *The Fall of Cambria* (1809), and *Messiah* (1815), which was of inferior quality, is now known chiefly as an object of Byron's sarcasm. He also wrote *Early Recollections, chiefly relating to Samuel Taylor Coleridge* (1837).

Cotton (kot'ǫn), **Bartholomew de.** d. c1298. An English historian, a monk of Norwich. He was the author of the *Historia Anglicana* in three books, of which the first is taken literally from Geoffrey of Monmouth, the second (taken in part from Henry of Huntingdon) comprises the history of England from 449 to 1298, while the third is an abstract and continuation of the *De gestis pontificum* of William of Malmesbury.

Cotton, Charles. b. at Beresford, Staffordshire, England, April 28, 1630; d. at Westminster (now part of London), in February, 1687. An English poet, best known as the translator of Montaigne's *Essays* (1685). He published anonymously *The Scarronides, or: The First Book of Virgil Travestie* (1664; reprinted with the fourth book in 1670), a translation of Corneille's *Horace* (1671), *A Voyage to Ireland in Burlesque*, a poem (1670), translations

of Gerard's *Life of the Duke of Espernon* (1670) and of the *Commentaries of De Montluc, Marshal of France* (1674), a second part (on fly-fishing) to the fifth edition of Izaak Walton's *Compleat Angler* (1676), and other works. A collection of his poems was published in 1689. His poetry was much admired by Lamb, Wordsworth, and Coleridge.

Cotton, Nathaniel. b. at London, 1705; d. at St. Albans, Hertfordshire, England, Aug. 2, 1788. An English poet and physician. He studied (1729) medicine in the Netherlands under Hermann Boerhaave, and practiced his profession and operated (1740–88) a lunatic asylum at St. Albans in which the poet William Cowper was a patient from 1763 to 1765. Cotton was the author of the anonymously published *Visions in Verse for the Entertainment and Instruction of Younger Minds* (1751), moral essays, sermons, and a medical paper, *Observations on a Particular Kind of Scarlet Fever* (1749). His *Various Pieces in Prose and Verse* (2 vols., 1791) was edited by his son, Nathaniel. Among his poems are "To a Child of Five Years Old," "The Fireside," and "Content," "Slander," and "Pleasure," from the *Visions.*

Cotton, Sir Robert Bruce. b. at Denton, Huntingtonshire, England, Jan. 22, 1571; d. May 6, 1631. An English antiquary, a graduate of Cambridge (Jesus College) in 1585, famous as the founder of the Cottonian Library, now in the British Museum. He was an ardent collector of manuscripts in many languages, coins and antiquities of all kinds, and his library was consulted and his aid obtained by Francis Bacon, Ben Jonson, John Speed, William Camden, and many other men of learning of that day. His collection of original documents became so great as to be regarded as a source of danger to the government, and after he had fallen into disfavor at court, on political grounds, an opportunity was found of placing his library under seal (1629), and he never regained possession of it. His son, Sir Thomas Cotton, succeeded in obtaining it, and it remained in the family (though open to the use of scholars and, in 1700, of the public) until 1707, when it was purchased by the nation. It was kept at various places, suffering considerable damage by fire, Oct. 23, 1731, until the founding of the British Museum (1753), when it was transferred to that institution. Cotton was knighted in 1603, and created a baronet in 1611.

Cottonian Library (kǫ.tō'ni.an). A famous library, especially rich in manuscripts, founded by Sir Robert Bruce Cotton (1571–1631), now in the British Museum.

Cotton Vitellius Manuscript (vi.tel'i.us). See **Manuscript Cotton Vitellius A XV.**

Cotys (kō'tis) or **Cotytto** (kǫ.tit'ō). In ancient Greek mythology, a Thracian goddess, resembling the Phrygian Cybele. Her festival, the Cotyttia, was riotous and, later, licentious.

Coué (kwä; Anglicized, kö'i), **Émile.** b. at Troyes, France, Feb. 26, 1857; d. at Nancy, France, July 2, 1926. The originator of the psychotherapeutic system called Couéism. Until past middle life he was an obscure pharmacist at Troyes, but soon after the turn of the century he began a study of hypnotism and of the therapeutic efficacy of auto-suggestion, and in 1910 set up a clinic at Nancy for the practice of his system. His famous formula, "Day by day, in every way, I am getting better and better," which his patients were instructed frequently to repeat, attracted wide attention (indeed, he had for a time such a vogue that he is often alluded to in the literature of the early 1920's, as in one of the novels of John Galsworthy).

Coulin (kō'lin). A giant in Spenser's *Faerie Queene*. He was killed when, after jumping across a pit, he slipped back and fell.

Coulton (kōl'tọn), **George Gordon.** b. at King's Lynn, England, Oct. 15, 1858—. An English historian, noted expert on medieval history. He studied at Cambridge and Heidelberg, was lecturer (1910 *et seq.*) in history at Cambridge, and professor (1919 *et seq.*) at St. John's College. His works include *St. Francis to Dante* (1906), *Five Centuries of Religion* (1923), *The Medieval Village* (1925), *Art and the Reformation* (1928), *Life in the Middle Ages* (4 vols., 1928–29), and *Medieval Thought* (1939).

Council of Whitby (hwit'bi). See **Whitby, Synod of.**

Counter, the. A name anciently given to two prisons under the rule of the sheriffs of London, one in the Poultry and one in Wood Street. There was another in Southwark which had the same name. This name was formerly a frequent subject of jokes and puns. Baret, in the *Alvearie* (1573), speaks of one who had been imprisoned as singing "his counter-tenor," and there are various similar allusions in the works of 17th-century dramatists.

Counter-Attack. A collection of poems (1918) by Siegfried Sassoon, concerned with the brutality of war (Sassoon was a British infantry officer in World War I). It includes "The Rear Guard," "To Any Dead Officer," and "Does it Matter?"

Countercheck Quarrelsome. See under **Retort Courteous.**

Countess Kathleen (kath'lēn, kath.lēn'), **The.** A poetic tragedy (1892) written by William Butler Yeats for the Irish Literary (which was later to become the famous Abbey) Theatre, which produced it in 1899. The action takes place "in Ireland in old times." Suffering from hunger, the people of the village sell their souls for food to the evil spirits. Kathleen uses her wealth to help them, until the spirits rob her. Unable to stand the misery of her people, she sells her own soul in order to relieve them, well knowing that her act will mean the loss of her own salvation. She is forgiven at the end of the play because her motive was a humane one. The play created a disturbance when it was first produced, and police had to restrain members of the audience who thought that it was an insult to the country and to religion to show an Irishwoman bargaining with the devil and not being punished for it.

Countess of Pembroke's Arcadia (pem'brŭks; är-kā'di.ạ), **The.** See (Sidney's) **Arcadia.**

Count Julian (jōl'yạn). A tragedy by Walter Savage Landor, published in 1812. The subject is the story of Roderick, last of the Goths, also treated in Sir Walter Scott's poem *Roderick.* It tells how Count Julian's daughter is dishonored by the lustful King Roderigo, and how Julian takes revenge. The same story was treated by Rowley in *All's Lost by Lust.*

Count Robert of Paris. A novel by Sir Walter Scott, published in 1831, the 25th of the Waverley novels, in the fourth series of *Tales of My Landlord.* The scene is laid in the 11th century, during the first Crusade, when Godfrey of Bouillon was before Constantinople at the head of the Crusaders. Count Robert was a French Crusader, one of the most famous and reckless of the period.

Country Girl, The. A comedy attributed to Antony Brewer, produced in 1647. John Leanerd reprinted it in 1677, under the title of *Country Innocence,* as his own.

Country Girl, The. An alteration of William Wycherley's comedy *The Country Wife* by David Garrick, who produced it in 1766.

Country House, The. A comedy by Sir John Vanbrugh, produced in 1698. It was translated from the French of Florent Carton Dancourt.

Country House, The. A novel by John Galsworthy, published in 1907. It is a study of country life and customs and a severe condemnation of the complacent attitude towards life.

Country Lasses, or The Custom of the Manor. A play by Charles Johnson, produced in 1715. It was partly taken from John Fletcher and Philip Massinger's *Custom of the Country,* and Thomas Middleton's *A Mad World, My Masters.* John Philip Kemble used it in his *Farm House* (1789), and William Kenrick in *The Lady of the Manor.*

Country-Mouse and the City-Mouse, The. See **Story of the Country-Mouse and the City-Mouse.**

Country of the Blind, The. A collection of short stories by H. G. Wells, published in 1911.

Country Party. An English political party in the reign of Charles II, which opposed the court and sympathized with the nonconformists. It developed into the Whig party.

Country Sentiment. A collection of poems (1919) by Robert Graves.

Country Walk. A poem by John Dyer, published (1726) in Savage's *Miscellaneous Poems and Translations.* It is important as one of the first 18th-century English poems to introduce realistic details into a description of country life.

Country Wife, The. A comedy by William Wycherley, produced in 1675. It was taken from Molière's *L'École des maris* and *L'École des femmes,* and later adapted by Garrick in his play *The Country Girl.* It is a lively farce, later criticized (especially in the 18th century) for its suggestive double-entendres. Mr. Pinchwife brings his young wife, Margery, to London for the marriage of his sophisticated sister, Alithea, to Sparkish, a credulous gallant. He suspects her of infidelity with Horner, a gay young roué whose friends have supposed to be impotent. After Horner cuckolds Pinchwife, Margery politely acquiesces in the fiction that he is what he has pretended, thus curing her husband of his jealousy. Sparkish, meanwhile, goes to the opposite extreme of being so objectionably confident of his powers as a lover that he loses the clever Alithea to Harcourt.

ḍ, d or j; ş, s or sh; ṭ, t or ch; ẓ, z or zh; *o*, F. cloche; ü, F. menu; ċh, Sc. loch; ṅ, F. bonbon.

Country Wit, The. A comedy by John Crowne, produced in 1676. The plot was partly from Molière's *Le Sicilien*. It provides a realistic picture of the world of London fashion in 1675.

Coupler (kup'lėr), **Mrs.** A matchmaker or go-between in Sir John Vanbrugh's play *The Relapse*, and in Richard Brinsley Sheridan's adaptation of it, *A Trip to Scarborough.*

couplet (kup'let). **1.** In prosody, two lines in immediate succession, usually but not necessarily of the same length, forming a pair, and generally marked as such by rhyming with each other. A pair of lines joined by rhyme is considered a couplet, whether it forms part of a stanza or constitutes a metrical group by itself.

> Thoughtless of ill, and to the future blind,
> A sudden couplet rushes on your mind,
> Here you may nameless print your idle rhymes.
> (Crabbe.)

2. In music, two equal notes inserted in the midst of triple rhythm to occupy the time of three; a temporary displacement of triple by duple rhythm.

3. *Obs.* one of a pair, as of twins; a twin.

> Anon, as patient as the female dove,
> When that her golden couplets are disclos'd,
> His silence will sit drooping.
> (Shak., *Hamlet.*)

Course of Time, The. A religious poem by Robert Pollok, published in 1827.

Court (kōrt), **Alexander.** In Shakespeare's *Henry V*, a soldier in the King's army.

Courtain (kėr.tān'). See **Curtana.**

Courtal (kōrt'ôl). In George Etherege's *She Would If She Could*, a gay young rake who invites the attentions of Lady Cockwood to cloak an affair he is having with one of her young charges.

Courtall (kōrt'ôl). A rake in Hannah Cowley's comedy *The Belle's Stratagem*. At a masquerade, he costumes himself like Lady Frances Touchwood's husband, tries to seduce her, and is foiled by Saville.

Court and City. A comedy adapted from Richard Steele's *Tender Husband* and Frances Sheridan's *Discovery*, produced by Richard Brinsley Peake.

Court Beggar, The. A play by Richard Brome, produced in 1632, printed in 1653.

Courthope (kōrt'ōp), **William John.** b. at South Malling, near Lewes, England, July 17, 1842; d. at Sussex, near Whiligh, England, April 10, 1917. An English poet, historian of poetry, critic, editor, and biographer. He was educated at Harrow, and at Corpus Christi College and New College, Oxford. He won the Newdigate prize for poetry in 1864, and the Chancellor's Prize for English prose in 1868, with an essay on *The Genius of Spenser.* From 1895 to 1900 he was professor of poetry at Oxford, delivering a series of lectures published (1901) as *Life in Poetry, Law in Taste.* He wrote a life (1882) of Addison for the *English Men of Letters* series, and edited five (of the ten) volumes of the standard Elwin-Courthope edition of Pope's *Works.* As a poet he wrote *Ludibria Lunae* (1869), an allegorical and political satire, *The Paradise of Birds* (1870), especially attractive to young readers, *The Country Town and Other Poems* (1920), the "town" being

his native Lewes, *The Hop Garden* (1905), suggestive of passages in Vergil, and other verse contributed to the *National Review* and *Blackwood's Magazine.* His chief work, the one by which he is remembered, is *The History of English Poetry,* in six volumes (1895–1910). A worthy example of English scholarship, it completes a work planned by Pope, contemplated by Gray, and begun, but not finished, by Thomas Warton. It begins with Chaucer (although there are chapters on poets and poetry before him) and ends with Scott.

Courtier, The. See **Cortegiano, Il.**

Courtly (kōrt'li, kôrt'li), **Sir James.** In Susannah Centlivre's comedy *The Basset-Table,* a gay, airy, witty, and inconstant gentleman, devoted to gaming.

courtly love. A medieval literary convention that first developed in the lyric poetry of the troubadours of southern France. Its principal exponent among the nobility was William, Count of Anjou and Duke of Aquitaine. It may be summarized as a formal literary expression of utter idealization of the qualities of the lady. In northern France the emphasis was more on the reciprocity of love, and further emphasized the attributes of the knight in his role of a courtly lover. The two courts most noted for its expression were those of Eleanor of Aquitaine (in the south) and her sister, Marie, Countess of Champagne (in the north). In the court of the latter both Andreas Capellanus and Chrétien de Troyes were active as literary figures. Capellanus wrote *De Amore,* based largely on the current interpretation of Ovid, while Chrétien de Troyes did an actual translation of Ovid's *Ars Amatoria. Cligès* by Chrétien de Troyes has been considered the most perfect specimen of the literature of courtly love, from the standpoint of formal adherence to all the prevalent doctrines. By the end of the 12th century these doctrines had become popular literary themes. The aspects most emphasized in the knight were his love for the lady, the chivalric virtues of prowess and loyalty, military reputation, handsome appearance, possession of the social graces, his desire to serve his lady, to demonstrate his affections, to be careful of her honor, and above all to keep the love a secret. Its summation has generally been considered to be the *Roman de la Rose.* In England this literary genre did not have as widespread an effect as on the Continent, although as early as the 12th century it had entered religious literature through its influence on the so-called Cult of the Virgin. It is noted in the 14th century in the works of Chaucer. One of the conventions of this sort of literature was the court of love, in which the defendant could plead his guilt or innocence to the God of Love, depending on how closely he adhered to his doctrines.

Court of Love, The. A poem attributed to Chaucer by Stow, although scholars doubt its authenticity because of linguistic forms that seem to indicate a later date. The poet speaks of going to the Court of Venus, conversing with its frequenters, reading its statutes, and watching scenes that depict various aspects of love. It contains 1,400 lines and is written in rhyme royal.

Court Secret, The. A play by James Shirley, printed in 1653, not acted till after the Restoration.

Covenanters. In Scottish history, the name of the group which, in the 16th and 17th centuries, banded together in solemn covenants to defend and support Presbyterianism. The first of these religious covenants was that of 1557, by which certain Scottish adherents of the Reformation united to promote the evangelical movement. The fear of a revival of Roman Catholicism led to a second covenant in 1581. In 1638 the efforts of Archbishop Laud, supported by King Charles I, to impose an episcopal organization and the Book of Common Prayer on the Church of Scotland, was met by the National Covenant, which denounced all ecclesiastical measures inconsistent with the principles of the Reformation, demanding that such proposals be submitted to an uncoerced Parliament and Assembly. In November of that year the General Assembly declared against the episcopal and for the presbyterian system in Scotland. Charles thought to exact obedience by force, but faced by a determined army of Covenanters, agreed to abide by the decisions of the General Assembly. Again the Assembly, and the Scottish Parliament as well, declared for the presbyterian system, and in addition decreed certain limitations on royal authority, and in 1640 a Scottish army advanced into England with the purpose of compelling the king's compliance. This made it necessary for Charles to summon the English Parliament which is known in history as the Long Parliament and which was to become the source of Charles's downfall. In the ensuing English Civil War the Scots joined forces with the English Parliament when the latter accepted the Solemn League and Covenant, which called for changes in English church government in the direction of stricter Protestant concepts. Charles in May, 1646, surrendered to the Scottish army which, when he continued to reject the Solemn League and Covenant, turned him over to the English Parliamentary army. Following the ascendancy of the Independents in the English army and Parliament, war broke out between the Scots and the English, the former being defeated by Cromwell at Preston in 1648, and after the beheading of Charles I, the Scots espoused the cause of Charles II upon his acceptance of the Solemn League and Covenant. But, defeated by Cromwell in 1651, Charles II had to flee Britain, and when in 1660 he was finally restored to his father's throne, he agreed to the restoration of episcopacy and the suppression of Presbyterianism, measures which were only effectuated after many Presbyterians had been put to death.

Covent Garden (kuv′ent). A space in London, between the Strand and Longacre, which as early as 1222 was the convent garden belonging to the monks of Saint Peter, Westminster. It was originally called Frère Pye Garden. During the period of dissolution when church properties were being taken by the crown it was granted with neighboring properties, by Edward VI, to the protector Edward Seymour, Duke of Somerset. After his attainder in 1552 it went to John Russell, 1st Earl of Bedford. The square was laid out for Francis Russell, 4th Earl of Bedford, and partly built (c1631) by Inigo Jones, whose church, Saint Paul's, Covent Garden, still remains, although rebuilt. The holdings of the Bedfords in this neighborhood were enormous. At one time Covent Garden's coffee houses and taverns were the fashionable lounging places for the authors, wits, and noted men of the kingdom. Dryden, Otway, Steele, Fielding, Peg Woffington, Kitty Clive, Samuel Foote, Barton Booth, David Garrick, and others were among its frequenters. It is now chiefly known as the site of a famous public market, where fruits, flowers, and vegetables have been sold since the 17th century.

Covent Garden Journal. A biweekly periodical first issued in January, 1752, by Henry Fielding, under the name of "Sir Alexander Drawcansir, Knight, Censor of Great Britain." It was discontinued before the end of the year.

Covent Garden Theatre. [Also, **Covent Garden Opera House.**] A theater in Bow Street, Covent Garden, London, built by John Rich, the famous harlequin of Lincoln's Inn Fields Theatre, in 1731. It was opened, under the dormant patent granted by Charles II to Sir William Davenant, with Congreve's comedy *The Way of the World*, on Dec. 7, 1732. There was no first appearance at this house of any importance until that of Peg Woffington in *The Recruiting Officer*, on Nov. 8, 1740. In 1746 Garrick played here. During Rich's management pantomime reigned supreme. Rich died in 1761, leaving the theater to his son-in-law John Beard, the vocalist. In 1767 it was sold to George Colman the elder, Harris, Rutherford, and Powell for 60,000 pounds. On March 15, 1773, Goldsmith's play *She Stoops to Conquer* was brought out here. In 1774 Harris undertook the management alone. In 1803 John Kemble bought a one-sixth share in the patent-right from Harris for 22,000 pounds, and became manager. In September, 1808, the house was burned. Eight months later it was rebuilt, according to the design of Robert Smirke the architect, in imitation of the Parthenon (the pediment by John Flaxman), at a cost of 300,000 pounds. John Philip Kemble was still manager. On account of the great expense of the undertaking Kemble raised the price of admission and built an extra row of boxes. This brought about the famous O.P. (old price) riots, which lasted 61 days and resulted in a general reduction. On June 29, 1817, John Kemble was followed as manager by Charles Kemble. In 1822 the theater was thrown into chancery. In 1847, after a number of managers had tried to succeed with it, it commenced a new career as The Royal Italian Opera House, but on March 4, 1856, it was burned down. It was rebuilt and the present house opened May 15, 1858.

Coventry (kuv′ẹn.tri, kov′-), Countess of. Title of Gunning, Maria.

Coventry, Francis. d. c1759. An English man of letters. He was educated at Cambridge University and wrote poetry and satires, among them *Pompey the Little* (1751), the hero of which is a lap dog.

Coventry Plays. See Hegge Plays.

Coverdale (kuv′ẹr.dāl), Miles. b. in the North Riding of Yorkshire, England, 1488; d. in February, 1568. The first translator of the whole Bible into English. He studied at Cambridge, was ordained priest in 1514 at Norwich, and joined the Austin friars at Cambridge, where he was influenced by Robert Barnes, the prior, who was burned as a Lutheran heretic in 1540. About 1526 he assumed the habit of a secular priest, and, leaving the convent, devoted himself to evangelical preaching. In 1531 he took his degree as bachelor of canon law at Cambridge. He was probably on the Continent the greater part of the time from then until 1535. In this year his translation of the Bible from Dutch and Latin into English appeared at Zurich with a dedication to Henry VIII. This translation was based on William Tyndale's translations of the Old and New Testaments, the Vulgate, and Luther's German translation, among others. In 1538 he was sent by Thomas Cromwell to Paris to superintend a new English edition of the Bible. This was known as the "Great Bible." A second "Great Bible," known as "Cranmer's Bible" (1540), was also edited by him. He returned from Paris in 1539, but in 1540, on the execution of Cromwell, he was obliged to leave England. Shortly afterward he married Elizabeth Macheson. This repudiation of the celibacy of the priesthood identified him with the Reformers. He lived at Tübingen for a short time, and was made doctor of divinity. From 1543 to 1547 he lived at Bergzabern (Deux-Ponts, now Zweibrücken) in the Palatinate, Germany, as Lutheran minister and schoolmaster. In 1548 he returned to England, and was appointed chaplain to the king (Edward VI) through Cranmer's influence. In 1551 he was appointed bishop of Exeter, but was deprived of this office in 1553 when Mary I came to the throne, and went again to Bergzabern. It has been said that he assisted in preparing the Geneva Bible. In 1559 he again came to England, where Elizabeth now was queen. In 1563 he received from Cambridge the degree of doctor of divinity, and obtained the living of Saint Magnus, near London Bridge. In 1566 he resigned this office on account of his objection to the enforced strict observance of the liturgy. He continued preaching, however, and was listened to by great numbers of people.

Coverley (kuv'ẽr.li), **Sir Roger de.** The chief character in the club that supposedly wrote *The Spectator;* an English country gentleman. He was sketched by Steele and developed by Addison. The name is taken from that of a country dance, similar to the American Virginia reel, which, according to Addison's fiction, was invented by Sir Roger's great-grandfather.

Coward (kou'ạrd), **Noel.** b. at Teddington, England, Dec. 16, 1899—. An English playwright, actor, and composer. He first appeared on the stage in 1910. His stage works include the plays *I'll Leave It to You, The Vortex* (1923), *Easy Virtue* (1925), *Fallen Angels* (1925), *Hay Fever* (1925), *The Queen Was in the Parlour* (1927), *The Marquise* (1927), *Sirocco* (1927), *Private Lives* (1930), *Cavalcade* (1931, made into a successful motion picture in 1932), *Design for Living* (1932), *Conversation Piece* (1934), *Point Valaine* (1934), *Operette* (1938), *Blithe Spirit* (1941), and *Peace in Our Time* (1947); the one-act group of plays *To-Night at Eight-Thirty* (1935); the revues *This Year of Grace* (1928), *On with the Dance, Words and Music* (1932),

Present Laughter (1942), and *Sigh No More* (1945); the operettas *Bitter Sweet* (1929) and *Pacific 1860* (1946); the cinemas *In Which We Serve* (1942), *This Happy Breed* (1945), and *Brief Encounter* (1946). He has published *Collected Sketches and Lyrics* (1931), and *To Step Aside* (1939). His autobiographical books include *Present Indicative* (1937), which covers his life from 1899 to 1931, *Middle East Diary* (1945), and *Future Indefinite* (1954), which covers the war years from June, 1939 to V-E Day. Coward's virtuosity of style, his sophistication, and his laconic wit have exerted some influence on other playwrights.

Cowden-Clarke (kou'dẹn.klärk'), **Charles** and **Mary Victoria.** See **Clarke.**

Cowell (kou'ẹl), **Joseph Leathley.** [Original name, **Hawkins Witchett.**] b. near Torquay, England, Aug. 7, 1792; d. near London, Nov. 13, 1863. An English actor. He painted portraits, and was a clever and popular actor, particularly in the U. S., where he played (1821–44 and later) especially as Crack in *The Turnpike Gate.* He published an amusing autobiography in 1844. His daughter Sydney Frances (Mrs. H. L. Bateman) was the mother of Kate Bateman, the American actress.

Cowgate, The. A once fashionable street in Edinburgh Old Town.

Cowley (kou'li), **Abraham.** b. at London, 1618; d. at Chertsey, Surrey, England, July 28, 1667. An English metaphysical poet and essayist. The son of a stationer, he studied at Westminster and at Cambridge (B.A., 1639; M.A., 1642), and retired to Oxford (St. John's College) in 1644. He identified himself with the Royalists, and followed the queen, Henrietta Maria, to France in 1646. He carried messages from the exiles back to the British Isles several times, and coded the letters from the queen to Charles I. He remained in the service of the exiled court until 1656, when he returned to England, and finally settled (1665) at Chertsey. He was buried in Westminster Abbey. He was the author of *Poetical Blossoms* (1633) published while he was still at school, *Love's Riddle* (1638), a pastoral play, *The Mistress* (1647), and *Miscellanies* (1656). The last includes "Davideis," an unfinished epic poem in four books on the Biblical subject of David, his "Pindarique Odes," and several elegies. The first collected edition of his works appeared in 1668.

Cowley, Hannah. [Pseudonym, **Anna Matilda;** maiden name, **Parkhouse.**] b. at Tiverton, Devonshire, England, 1743; d. there, March 11, 1809. English poet and dramatist, daughter of a bookseller of Tiverton, and wife of a captain in the service of the East India Company. She was the author of *The Runaway* (acted February, 1776), *The Belle's Stratagem* (acted February, 1780), and *A Bold Stroke for a Husband* (acted February, 1783). Under the pseudonym "Anna Matilda," which has become a synonym for sentimentality, she carried on a poetical correspondence in the *World* with Robert Merry, who adopted the signature "Della Crusca."

Cowper (kö'pẽr, kou'pẽr), **William.** b. at Great Berkhamstead Rectory, Hertfordshire, England, Nov. 26, 1731; d. at Dereham, Norfolk, England, April 25, 1800. An English poet. Motherless at six, he entered Westminster School, London, at an early age, receiving there an excellent classical education. Later he studied law and entered the Middle Temple. He was called to the bar in June, 1754. A few years later, when a contemplated marriage with his cousin Theodora was forbidden by her father, Cowper returned to the law, verse writing, and the Nonsense Club in London. His funds eked out by his remuneration as a commissioner of bankrupts (1759), Cowper struggled against loneliness, insecurity, and religious doubt until 1763. It was at that time that anxiety over a public examination designed to secure him a clerical post in the House of Lords precipitated the first violent attack of that recurrent emotional insanity which was at last to destroy him. Taken to Dr. Nathaniel Cotton's asylum at St. Albans in December, 1763, Cowper finally recovered and experienced religious conversion. In June, 1765, he went to Huntingdon, shortly entering the household of Morley Unwin. After Unwin's death (1767), Cowper removed with the family to Olney, where he collaborated with John Newton, a Calvinist preacher, in producing the *Olney Hymns* (1779). The strain of religious duties, aggravated, perhaps, by a convention-impelled betrothal to the widowed Mary Unwin, induced another acute depression in January, 1773. In February of that year Cowper experienced the dream of God's explicit reprobation, which was to be thereafter a lurking obsession in his mind. Upon recovering he renounced marriage but shared the home of Mary Unwin until her death in 1796. Although Cowper attributed the fancied abandonment to his failure to commit suicide, a supposed divine command, biographers have equated the fatal dream with a belief in predestination, implicitly and explicitly rejected in various letters and poems. Far from doctrinaire, Cowper discounted scriptural "circumstantials" and considered metaphysics "a serious trifle." Notwithstanding depressions, the poet spent many fruitful years at Olney and (after 1786) at Weston, producing volumes of letters, translations from French, Italian, Latin, and Greek (Homer in 1791), and much felicitous verse inspired by the "slow-winding" Ouse region. The satires (*Poems*, 1782), were surpassed by *Tirocinium, John Gilpin,* and especially *The Task* (1785), which reflects the poet's patriotism, social concern, and fervid joy in nature. Lord David Cecil and other distinguished biographers have related the story of Cowper. According to John C. Bailey, who edited some letters and the *Poems* (1905), "to read him is to feel one's self in the presence of one of the most delightful of human beings." See *The Selected Letters of William Cowper* (1951), edited with an introduction by Mark Van Doren.

"Cowper of the Highlands." See **Buchanan, Dugald.**

Cox and Box. An operetta in one act by Arthur Sullivan, with a libretto by F. C. Burnand, first publicly performed at the London Adelphi Theatre, May 11, 1867.

Coxcomb, The. A play by Beaumont and Fletcher, produced in 1612 and published in 1679.

Coyle (koil), **Kathleen.** d. March 25, 1952. An Irish novelist. Her books include *Piccadilly* (1923), *Liv* (1929), *There Is a Door* (1931), *The Skeleton* (1933), *Immortal Ease,* and *Flock of Birds* (1939), and the autobiography *The Magical Realm* (1943).

Coyne (koin), **Joseph Stirling.** b. at Birr, King's County (now County Offaly), Ireland, 1803; d. at London, July 18, 1868. An Irish humorist and playwright, author of a number of successful farces and other works.

Cozeners (kuz'ẹn.ėrz), **The.** A comedy by Samuel Foote, produced in 1774.

Crab (krab). In Shakespeare's *Two Gentlemen of Verona,* the dog of Launce.

Crab. The crusty guardian of the fortune of Buck in Samuel Foote's comedy *The Englishman Returned from Paris.*

Crabbe (krab), **George.** b. at Aldeburgh, Suffolk, England, Dec. 24, 1754; d. at Trowbridge, Wiltshire, England, Feb. 3, 1832. An English poet. After having failed as a surgeon in his native town, he went (1780) to London, where, through the patronage of Burke, he was rescued from extreme poverty and enabled to publish *The Library* and other works, which gave him an established position in literature. He was for a number of years chaplain to the duke of Rutland, and in 1789 became rector of Muston and Allington. His chief works are *The Library* (1781), *The Village* (1783), *The Newspaper* (1785), *The Parish Register* (1807), and *Tales of the Hall* (1819). An autobiographical sketch, *Biographical Account of the Rev. George Crabbe, LL.B.* appeared in the *New Monthly Magazine* for January, 1816. His biography was published (1834) by his son.

Crabbed Youth and Age. A play by Lennox Robinson, produced in 1922 and published in 1924.

Crabshaw (krab'shô), **Timothy.** In Tobias Smollett's novel *Sir Launcelot Greaves,* a whipper-in, plowman, and carter, selected as a squire by Sir Launcelot when on his knight-errant expedition. He rides a vicious cart horse named Gilbert.

Crabtree (krab'trē). A mischief-maker in Richard Brinsley Sheridan's comedy *The School for Scandal.*

Crabtree, Cadwallader. A cynical deaf old man, a friend of Peregrine Pickle, in Tobias Smollett's novel *Peregrine Pickle.*

Cradock or **Craddocke** (krad'ọk). See **Caradoc.**

Craft of Lovers, The. A poem attributed to Chaucer by Stow, but now generally conceded to have been the work of another writer, who is as yet unidentified.

Craftsman, The. A political periodical, originated 1726 by Nicholas Amhurst: a powerful organ of the opposition to Sir Robert Walpole.

Craigdallie (krāg.dal'i), **Adam.** In Sir Walter Scott's novel *The Fair Maid of Perth,* the good-humored (but extremely efficient) Senior Bailie of Perth.

Craigengelt (krā.gẹn.gelt'), **Captain.** An adventurer in Sir Walter Scott's novel *The Bride of Lammermoor.* He is the friend of Frank Hayston, and the enemy of the Master of Ravenswood.

Craigenputtock (krā.gẹn.put'ọk). A farm ab. 15 mi. from Dumfries, Scotland, which for some years was the home of Thomas Carlyle. It belonged to Mrs. Carlyle before her marriage, and in May, 1828, they

ḍ, d or j; ş, s or sh; ṭ, t or ch; ẓ, z or zh; o, F. cloche; ü, F. menu; ċh, Sc. loch; ṅ, F. bonbon.

first went there to live, leaving it and returning from time to time. Here much of Carlyle's most brilliant work was done.

Craik (krāk), **Dinah Maria.** [Also, **Dinah Maria Mulock.**] b. at Stoke-on-Trent, Staffordshire, England, 1826; d. at Shortlands, Kent, England, Oct. 12, 1887. An English novelist and poet. She was the author of *The Ogilvies* (1849), *The Head of the Family* (1851), *Agatha's Husband* (1853), *John Halifax, Gentleman* (1857), *A Life for a Life* (1859), *A Noble Life* (1866), *A Brave Lady* (1870), *Hannah* (1871), and other novels. She published a volume of poems in 1859 and *Thirty Years' Poems* in 1881, besides many children's books and fairy tales.

Craik, Georgiana Marian. [Mrs. **A. W. May.**] b. at London, in April, 1831; d. at St. Leonards, Sussex, England, Nov. 1, 1895. An English novelist. Her works include *Riverstone* (1857), *Lost and Won* (1859), *Winifred's Wooing* (1862), *Mildred* (1868), *Sylvia's Choice* (1874), *Hilary's Love-Story* (1880), *Godfrey Helstone* (1884), and *Patience Holt* (1891).

Crane (krān), **Walter.** b. at Liverpool, England, August 15, 1845; d. at Horsham, England, 1915. An English painter, illustrator, and artisan who was associated first with the Pre-Raphaelites and later with the arts and crafts movement of William Morris. He was a pupil of W. J. Linton. In 1862 his first painting, *The Lady of Shalot*, was accepted by the Royal Academy; thereafter he exhibited frequently at London. Among his principal works are: *Plato's Garden*, *Diana and the Shepherd*, and *Bridge of Life*. He is equally well known for his illustrations for such children's books as *Beauty and the Beast*, *Cinderella*, and *Goody Two Shoes*.

Cranford (kran'fọrd). A story (1853) of English village life in the second quarter of the 19th century, by Elizabeth Cleghorn Gaskell.

Cranmer (kran'mẽr). In Shakespeare's *Henry VIII*, the historical Thomas Cranmer, Archbishop of Canterbury. He obtains the divorce of Henry from Katherine, and remains a favorite of the King, although nobles try to convict him of heresy. The King names him godfather of Princess Elizabeth, and at her christening Cranmer predicts the glory she will bring England as Queen.

Cranmer, Thomas. b. at Aslacton, Nottinghamshire, England, July 2, 1489; burned at the stake, March 21, 1556. An English ecclesiastic and reformer, one of the most notable of the archbishops of Canterbury. He is remembered as one of the engineers of Henry VIII's divorce from Catherine of Aragon, as a leading figure in the movement for moderation within the then newly founded Anglican Church, and a staunch advocate of royal supremacy in ecclesiastical affairs. Born of an old Lincolnshire family, Cranmer went through a rigorous education, physical and mental, at an early age. As a public examiner in theology (1529) at Cambridge, he met with Henry VIII's advisers on the king's proceedings against Catherine. Largely through Cranmer's efforts, the divorce question was submitted to a disputation at the English universities, which gave Henry a favorable verdict. He served on diplomatic missions on the Continent (1530–33), but was recalled in 1533 and made archbishop of Canterbury. As such, Cranmer made possible Henry's divorce

from Catherine and marriage with Ann Boleyn. Indeed, he succeeded in gaining so much of Henry's confidence that the king used to refer accusations against Cranmer back to the archbishop himself, and was selected (1540) by the Privy Council to inform Henry of the infidelity of the king's fifth wife, Catherine Howard. Cranmer was the English ecclesiastic who most strongly proclaimed independence from Rome, but had little to do with the dissolution of the monasteries. Upon the death of Henry (1547) Cranmer receded into the background of politics. In the convocation of that year he obtained a vote in favor of the marriage of the clergy. During the reign of Edward VI (1547–53), Cranmer supported many of the measures in reforming the Church and doctrine. As the young sovereign was about to die, he was persuaded to approve of the royal will which sought to modify the royal succession. After the collapse of the movement to enthrone Lady Jane Grey and the accession of Mary, Cranmer was one of the first to be investigated for his past actions. Charged with treason because of his aid to Lady Jane Grey, Cranmer pleaded guilty and was sentenced to death but pardoned. In the next year (1554) he was examined by Sir John Williams for heresy. Although his defense of himself won the admiration of his examiners, his case was transferred to a papal court. Maintaining his belief in judicial independence from papal authority, Cranmer refused to plead and was therefore condemned for heresy. He was degraded in 1556. Then followed a series of seven recantations by which he repudiated one after another of his past works as archbishop. In one of these he even acknowledged his submission to the Pope (using, not without a degree of casuistry, the justification that, both king and queen now being Roman Catholic, his belief in royal supremacy in ecclesiastical matters left him no choice but to accept their position, which, obviously, entailed a reversal of his actual former position). Two days before his execution it was arranged that he should make a final recantation in which he would declare his belief in every article of the Catholic faith and confess by repudiating his writings, particularly those against the sacrament of the altar. On the day of execution Cranmer made use of his final opportunity to confess his sin in having signed the previous recantations, and offered to have that hand of his which made the signature to be first burned. During his life Cranmer was married twice, before clerical marriage was allowed. It is said that during that time he used to carry his second wife about in a chest, perforated with air holes to let her breathe; and on one occasion, she and the chest were removed by an unknowing porter and deposited wrong side up, and thereupon she was compelled to disclose her situation by a scream. Of Cranmer's writings, the principal ones include *A Book on Henry VIII's Divorce, against marriage with a Brother's Widow*; *Preface to the Bible* (1540); *A Short Instruction into Christian Religion* (commonly called his *Catechism*); *Answer to the Devonshire Rebels*; *A Defense of the True and Catholic Doctrine of the Sacrament* (1550); *A Confutation of Unwritten Verities*.

Cranmer-Byng (kran'mẽr.bing'), **L.** [Full name, **Launcelot Alfred Cranmer-Byng.**] b. Nov. 23, 1872;

d. 1945. An English editor, author, lecturer, translator, and specialist on Chinese poetry. Educated at Wellington College and at Trinity College, Cambridge, he became a justice of the peace and county alderman for Essex. Some of his works are *A Feast of Lanterns* (1916), *Salma* (1923), *Vision of Asia* (1932), *A Lute of Jade* (1934), selections from Chinese classical poets, *Odes of Confucius*, *The Rose Garden of Sa'di*, and *To-morrow's Star;* as editor of the *Wisdom of the East* series, he played an important part in introducing Chinese literature to Western readers.

Cranstoun (kranz'ton), **Henry.** A character in Sir Walter Scott's poem *The Lay of the Last Minstrel.* He assumes the character of William of Deloraine in the trial by combat, and winning, reconciles the Lady of Banksome, his hereditary foe, to his marriage with her daughter Margaret.

Crapaud (krà·pō'), **Jean.** [Also, **Johnny Crapaud.**] In a use which is historically vulgar, and to some extent offensive, a nickname for a Frenchman.

Crashaw (krash'ô), **Richard.** b. at London, c1613; d. at Loretto, Italy, before Aug. 25, 1649. An English secular and religious poet. He was the only child of the Puritan poet and clergyman William Crashaw (1572–1626), and of a mother whose name has not come down to us. He was educated at Charterhouse, the school of Addison, Steele, and Thackeray, and at Pembroke College, Cambridge, transferring in 1636 to Peterhouse, of which he was a fellow from 1637 to 1643, and from which he was expelled for religious reasons. Always unsympathetic to Puritanism, he became a Catholic in 1644. Between 1646 and 1649 he was at Paris (where his friend Abraham Cowley introduced him to Henrietta Maria, wife of England's Charles I) and at Rome. In 1649 he was appointed sub-canon of the Basilica Church of Our Lady of Loretto, but he died shortly after reaching Loretto (where he is buried), probably as a result of fever caused by traveling in the summer heat. There seems to be no evidence for the suggestion that he was poisoned. Crashaw wrote Greek and Latin poetry, as well as English, and was familiar with the classical languages, and Spanish and Italian. His chief works are *Steps to the Temple*, religious verse which, as the title suggests, was inspired by *The Temple* of George Herbert, and *The Delights of the Muses*, secular poetry, both published in one volume in 1646 (as Herrick did with his *Hesperides* and *Noble Numbers*, in 1648). Some of his best poems, contained in anthologies, are *In the Holy Nativity*, which was good enough to inspire Milton, *The Flaming Heart*, a hymn to Saint Teresa, *Description of a Religious House, Song of Divine Love, An Epitaph upon Husband and Wife Which Died and were Buried Together*, and the still popular *Wishes to his Supposed Mistress.* Less well known, but typical of a kind of poetry common in his day, are his poems on the birth of Princess Elizabeth (1635), Princess Anne (1637), and Prince Charles (1640). He is the subject of Cowley's poem *On the Death of Mr. Crashaw.* Faults have been found in his poetry, and critics have attacked them, but he influenced Milton, Pope, Coleridge, and Shelley.

Crashaw, William. b. at Handsworth, near Sheffield, Yorkshire, England, 1572; d. 1626. A Puritan scholar, preacher, and poet; father, by his first wife, of Richard Crashaw (c1613–49). Educated at St. John's College, Cambridge, he held (1594) the bishop of Ely's fellowship, to which he was nominated by Queen Elizabeth, received his divinity degree in 1603, and subsequently held various church posts. He was the author of *Romish Forgeries and Falsifications* (1606), *The Complaint, or Dialogue betwixt the Soule and the Bodie of a Damned Man* (1616), poetry, *Milke for Babes or a North Countrie Catechisme* (1618), sermons, and other religious works in Latin and English.

Cratchit (krach'it), **Bob.** Scrooge's poor clerk in Charles Dickens's *Christmas Carol;* a cheerful, unselfish fellow, the father of Tim Cratchit ("Tiny Tim").

Cratchit, Tim. [Known as **"Tiny Tim."**] A little cripple in Charles Dickens's *Christmas Carol.*

Crawford (krô'ford), **27th Earl of.** A title of **Lindsay, David Alexander Edward.**

Crawford, Henry and **Mary.** In Jane Austen's novel *Mansfield Park*, a worldly brother and sister who become involved with the Bertram family.

Crawford, Isabella Valancy. b. at Dublin, Dec. 25, 1850; d. at Toronto, Canada, Feb. 12, 1887. A Canadian poet. She wrote *Malcolm's Katie*, a long pastoral poem describing Paisley, in Upper Canada, and *Old Spookses' Pass*, both of which were published in one volume in 1884. She has been praised for her pictures of cowboy life in western Canada.

Crawford, Lord. In Sir Walter Scott's novel *Quentin Durward*, the commander of the Scottish Archers of the Guard.

Crawley (krô'li). The name of a family important in Thackeray's novel *Vanity Fair.* Sir Pitt Crawley, the head of the family, is a rich but sordid old man, fond of low society; to his house Becky Sharp goes as governess. She makes herself so attractive that he offers to marry her, and she is thereby forced to acknowledge her secret marriage with Rawdon Crawley, his youngest son. The latter is a blackleg and a gambler, but is fond of his wife and has a certain honor of his own. His brother, Mr. Pitt Crawley, is a prig with "hay-colored whiskers and straw-colored hair. . . . He was called Miss Crawley at Eton, where his younger brother Rawdon used to lick him violently." The second Lady Crawley, a pale and apathetic woman, is a contrast to her sister-in-law, the little, eager, active, black-eyed Mrs. Bute Crawley. The Reverend Bute Crawley is a "tall, stately, jolly, shovel-hatted man," a horse-racing parson whose wife writes his sermons for him. Miss Crawley, the sister of Sir Pitt and the Reverend Bute, is a kind and yet undeniably selfish, worldly and yet often generous old woman, "who had a balance at her banker's which would have made her beloved anywhere."

Crazy Castle. A nickname of Skelton Castle, the house in Yorkshire of John Hall Stevenson, who wrote a series of broad stories which he called *Crazy Tales.* Stevenson was a kinsman of Laurence Sterne, and is now generally recognized as having been the original in real life of the character Eugenius in *Tristram Shandy.*

Creakle (krē'kl), **Mr.** In Charles Dickens's *David Copperfield*, the principal of the school at Salem

House where David Copperfield was sent; a man of fiery temper who could speak only in a whisper.

Creation, The. A poem by Sir Richard Blackmore, published in 1712.

Credulous (krĕd'ū.lus), **Justice** and **Mrs. Bridget.** An ignorant, good-natured pair in Richard Brinsley Sheridan's farce *St. Patrick's Day.* They are fooled by the scheming lieutenant who marries their daughter Lauretta. Mrs. Bridget is a kind of Mrs. Malaprop.

Creech (krēch), **Thomas.** b. at Blandford, Dorsetshire, England, 1659; committed suicide, in June, 1700. An English writer, translator of *Lucretius* (1682) and other classical authors.

Creech, William. [Pseudonym, **Theophrastus.**] b. at Newbattle, Midlothian, Scotland, April 21, 1745; d. at Edinburgh, Jan. 14, 1815. A Scottish essayist and letter writer, publisher of Burns. Educated at Edinburgh University, he went into business with a Scottish printer, Alexander Kincaid, becoming after Kincaid's retirement (1773) the head of the firm, which is noted as the first publisher of the works of Beattie, Blair, Cullen and Gregory, Dugald Stewart, Mackenzie, and of Burns, with whom he later quarreled. Creech was lord provost of Edinburgh (October, 1811–October, 1813), and a fellow of the Royal Society and the Antiquarian Society. He is the subject of Burns's *Burlesque Lament for the Absence of William Creech, Publisher* (1787). His essays, contributed under his pseudonym to the Edinburgh *Courant*, were published (1791, 1815) as *Fugitive Pieces.*

Creevey (krē'vi), **Thomas.** b. at Liverpool, England, in March, 1768; d. at London, in February, 1838. An English diarist and lawyer. He was on friendly terms with Fox, Sheridan, Grey, and other leading Whigs, and in 1806 was made secretary of the board of control in the "All-the-Talents" Fox-Grenville ministry. For 36 years he kept a diary and various papers that he sent to and received from important political and public characters of his day. This material, much of which was destroyed, is the basis of the *Creevey Papers*, and was not published until 1903, when it was edited by Sir Herbert Maxwell. It is of value for the picture it gives, from the Whig viewpoint, of life and conditions in the late Georgian era.

Creighton (krī'ton), **Mandell.** b. at Carlisle, Cumberland, England, July 5, 1843; d. at Fulham Palace, London, Jan. 14, 1901. An English biographer, bishop, historian, and teacher. Educated at Durham grammar school and at Merton College, Oxford, of which he was a fellow, he was also a fellow of Emmanuel College, Cambridge, and first Dixie professor (1884) of ecclesiastical history at Cambridge. He was founder and first editor (1886–91) of the *English Historical Review.* He served as canon of Worcester and Windsor, bishop of Peterborough, and bishop (1897 *et seq.*) of London. Among his works are *Roman History* (1875), *The Age of Elizabeth* and *Simon de Montfort* (both 1876), *History of England* (1879), *History of the Papacy During the Reformation* (5 vols., 1882–94), *Cardinal Wolsey* (1888), *The Early Renaissance in England* and *Persecution and Tolerance* (both 1895), *Queen Elizabeth* and *The English National Character* (both

1896), *History of the Papacy from the Great Schism to the Sack of Rome* (6 vols., 1897), many sermons, lectures, and essays, and biographical articles in the *Dictionary of National Biography.* His wife edited his *Historical Lectures and Addresses* (1903) and published his *Life and Letters* (2 vols., 1904).

Cremorne Gardens (krem'orn). A former place of amusement at London, situated near Battersea Bridge N of the Thames. It was closed in 1877.

Creon (krē'on). In Greek legend, a king of Thebes, contemporary with Oedipus.

Creon. In Greek legend, a king of Corinth, father of Creusa, or Glauce, the intended wife of Jason.

Crescent Moon. A novel by Francis Brett Young, published in 1918. It is based on the author's experience as a Royal Army Medical Corps officer in Africa during World War I.

Cresphontes (kres.fon'tēz). In Greek mythology, a descendant of Hercules. He was conqueror of the Peloponnesus, king of Messenia, and husband of Merope.

Cresseid (kres'id), **The Testament of.** A poem (1593) by the Scottish poet Henryson, continuing Chaucer's poem *Troilus and Criseyde* with the addition of the incidents of Diomede's fickleness and Cressida's leprosy. The poem ends with Troilus passing Cressida on the roadside and giving her alms. When she learns his identity, she returns his gift and dies.

Cressida (kres'i.da) or **Cressid** (kres'id). Daughter of the Trojan priest Calchas, whose supposed infidelities have made her name a byword for female faithlessness. Her story is not of classical origin, although laid against the background of the Homeric age; it is believed to have originated with Benoît de Sainte-Maure, a 12th-century *trouvère*, who called his character Briseida (she was thus identified with Homer's Briseis). Guido delle Colonne later reproduced the story in a popular Latin work, the *Historia Trojana.* The story was later taken up by Boccaccio, Chaucer, and Shakespeare. A modern version may be found in Christopher Morley's *The Trojan Horse* (1937). Shakespeare's *Troilus and Cressida* is probably the best-known version of the tale.

Cressingham (kres'ing.am), **Lady.** In Thomas Middleton's play *Anything for a Quiet Life*, a whimsical and attractive woman whose caprices are accounted for by her desire to reconcile her husband and stepson and to benefit them both.

Creusa (krē.ō'sa). In Homeric legend, the daughter of Priam, and wife of Aeneas.

Creusa. [Also, **Glauce.**] In Greek legend, the daughter of Creon, king of Corinth. Jason the Argonaut, tiring of his wife Medea, fell in love with Creusa and planned to marry her. Medea sent Creusa as a wedding gown a magic robe which, when she put it on, burned her flesh and caused her to die in terrible convulsions.

Crewler (krö'lėr). The name of a family in Charles Dickens's *David Copperfield.* Horace Crewler is a poor clergyman with a large family, and a wife who has lost the use of her legs; when anything annoys her or excites her it goes "to her legs directly." Sophy, the fourth daughter, is an unselfish girl who finally marries Tommy Traddles.

Cricca (krik'ạ). In Thomas Tomkis's comedy *Albumazar* (1615), the honest servant of Pandolfo.

Crichton (krī'tọn), **James**. [Called "the Admirable Crichton."] b. in Scotland, Aug. 19, 1560; killed at Mantua, Italy, July 3, c1582. A Scottish scholar and adventurer, celebrated for his extraordinary accomplishments and attainments in the languages, sciences, and arts. At the age of 17 he started upon his travels on the Continent. He was then the reputed master of 12 languages. He enlisted (c1577) in the French army, but in 1579 he resigned and went to Italy. Here many debates both public and private were arranged for him, in all of which he was victorious except with Mazzoni. He wrote Latin odes and verses with ease, and his skill as a swordsman was highly lauded. In 1581 he disputed with the professors of the university at Padua on their interpretation of Aristotle. A misadventure led to his being denounced as a charlatan, whereupon he challenged the university, offering to confute their Aristotelian interpretations and to expose their errors in mathematics. The disputation lasted four days, and Crichton was completely successful. He won his first laurels in Mantua by killing in a duel a famous swordsman. His death took place there in a midnight street attack. Crichton is said to have recognized the leader of the brawlers as his pupil, the son of the duke of Mantua, and having drawn his sword upon him to have offered it to him by the handle; whereupon the prince seized it and stabbed him to the heart.

Crichton, The. A London artistic, scientific, and literary club, established in 1872.

Crichton, The Admirable (Barrie's play). See **Admirable Crichton, The.**

Crichton-Stuart (krī'tọn.stū'ạrt), **John Patrick.** See **Stuart, John Patrick Crichton-.**

Cricket on the Hearth, The. A Christmas book by Charles Dickens, published in 1845. The singing match between a teakettle and a cricket on a carrier's hearthstone, in which the latter comes out ahead, gives its name to the book: "To have a cricket on the hearth is the luckiest thing in the world."

crime story. See under **mystery story.**

Cripplegate (krip'l.gāt). [Also, **Crepel-gate.**] Originally, one of the gates of London, and in modern times the name of a section of London. The gate was the fourth from the western end of the wall of the City of London. The original gate was probably built by King Alfred when he restored the walls in 886 A.D. Stow says that in 1010, when the body of Edmund the Martyr, king of the East Angles, was borne through this gate, many lame persons who were congregated there to beg rose upright and were cured by the miraculous influence of the body. The chambers connected to and under the gate were later a prison for debtors and common trespassers. It was rebuilt in 1244 and in 1491, and in the 15th year of the reign of Charles II it was repaired and an opening for pedestrians was made. The rooms over the gate were used by the city water-bailiff. Cripplegate was pulled down in 1760.

Cripple of Fenchurch (fen'chẻrch), **the.** See **Fenchurch.**

crisis (krī'sis). [Plural, **crises** (-sēz).] A vitally important or decisive state of things; the point of culmination; a turning-point; the point at which a change must come, either for the better or the worse, or from one state of things to another.

> This hour's the very crisis of your fate.
> (Dryden, *Spanish Friar*, iv.2.)

> Nor is it unlikely that the very occasions on which such defects are shown may be the most important of all—the very times of crisis for the fate of the country.
> (Brougham.)

Crisparkle (kris'pär.kl), **Septimus.** A clergyman and "true Christian gentleman" in Charles Dickens's *Mystery of Edwin Drood*. A minor canon of Cloisterham Cathedral, it is said of him that he has traveled "upon the chief Pagan high-roads, but [has been] since promoted by a patron (grateful for a well-taught son) to his present Christian beat."

Crispin and **Crispinian** (kris.pin'i.ạn), **Saints.** d. Oct. 25, 285 or 286. Two martyrs of the early Church, believed (although not positively known) to have been brothers. According to legend, they were members of a noble Roman family, and fled to what is now Soissons, France, where they endeavored to spread the Christian faith and supported themselves by mending and making shoes. They were beheaded during the reign of Diocletian at the order of the co-emperor, Maximianus Herculius. They are the patron saints of shoemakers, tanners, and saddlers.

Crispinella (kris.pi.nel'ạ). In John Marston's play *The Dutch Courtezan*, a sparkling, lively girl, the opposite of her sister Beatrice.

Crispinus (kris.pī'nus). In Ben Jonson's *Poetaster*, a bad poet who gives the play its title. He is intended for Marston, with whom Jonson had a quarrel at the time.

Crites (krī'tēz). A man of "straight judgment and a strong mind," in Jonson's play *Cynthia's Revels*. He is supposed to have been designed by Jonson as a picture of himself.

critic. 1. A person skilled in judging of merit in some particular class of things, especially in literary or artistic works; one who is qualified to discern and distinguish excellences and faults, especially in literature and art; one who writes upon the qualities of such works.

> Josephus Scaliger, a great Critick, and reputed one of the greatest Linguists in the world.
> (Purchas, *Pilgrimage*.)

> It will be a question among critiques in the ages to come.
> (Bp. of Lincoln, *Sermon at Funeral of James I.*)

> "To-morrow," he said, "the critics will commence. You know who the critics are? The men who have failed in literature and art."
> (Disraeli, *Lothair*, xxxv.)

2. One who judges captiously or with severity; one who censures or finds fault; a carper.

> When an author has many beauties consistent with virtue, piety, and truth, let not little *critics*

exalt themselves, and shower down their ill-nature.
(Watts, *Improvement of Mind*, v.)

Critic, The. [Full title, **The Critic: or, A Tragedy Rehearsed.**] A farce by Richard Brinsley Sheridan, produced on Oct. 30, 1779. It is an imitation of Buckingham's *Rehearsal*, but is more caricature than parody, resting mainly on impersonation. Sir Fretful Plagiary, a burlesque of Richard Cumberland, is a kind of general satire as well.

criticism. 1. The art of judging of and defining the qualities or merits of a thing, especially of a literary or artistic work.

In the first place, I must take leave to tell them that they wholly mistake the nature of criticism who think its business is principally to find fault. Criticism, as it was first instituted by Aristotle, was meant a standard of judging well; the chiefest part of which is, to observe those excellencies which should delight a reasonable reader.
(Dryden, *State of Innocence*, Pref.)

2. The act of criticizing; discrimination or discussion of merit, character, or quality; the exercise or application of critical judgment.

Criticism without accurate science of the thing criticised can indeed have no other value than may belong to the genuine record of a spontaneous impression.   (Swinburne, *Shakespeare*.)

He has to point out that Spinoza omits altogether criticism of the notion of mutual determination—that is to say, omits to examine the nature and validity of the notion for our thinking.
(Adamson, *Fichte*.)

The habit of unrestrained discussion on one class of subjects begets a similar habit of discussion on others, and hence one indispensable condition of attaining any high excellence in art is satisfied, namely, free criticism.
(Fowler, *Shaftesbury and Hutcheson*.)

3. In a restricted sense, inquiry into the origin, history, authenticity, character, etc., of literary documents. *Higher criticism* concerns writings as a whole; *lower criticism* concerns the integrity or character of particular parts or passages.

One branch of this comprehensive inquiry [the relation of science to the Bible] is Criticism—the investigation of the origin, authorship, and meaning of the several books of the Bible, and of the credibility of the history which it contains.
(G. P. Fisher, *Begin. of Christianity*.)

4. A critical judgment; especially, a detailed critical examination or disquisition; a critique.

There is not a Greek or Latin critic who has not shewn, even in the style of his criticisms, that he was a master . . . of his native tongue.
(Addison, *Spectator*, No. 291.)

Croaker (krō′kėr), **Mr.** and **Mrs.** A strongly contrasted pair in Oliver Goldsmith's *The Good-Natured Man*. He is gifted in saying sadly the most cutting things; she is both merry and spiteful.

Croce (krō′chā), **Benedetto.** b. at Pescasseroli, L'Aquila, Italy, Feb. 25, 1866; d. at Naples, Nov. 20, 1952. An Italian philosopher, historian, and editor. Most authorities agree in attributing to him a truly encyclopedic mind, and in pointing out that,

in America, the full meaning and extent of his philosophical, literary, and political activity has never been adequately investigated. Specifically, Croce was considered a first-rate scholar of esthetics and was famous for his resistance to Fascism, but he left his mark also in the fields of Marxism, of history (especially the history of Italy, of the southern provinces of Italy, of the relations between Spain and Italy, and of Europe in the 19th century), of logic, of political economy, and of ethics. He was the author of several volumes of literary essays on Italian, European, Latin, and Greek authors and of two important works on Shakespeare and Goethe (he is considered to have been especially successful in his rendition into Italian of the poems of the latter). For 27 years he was editor in chief of a famous bimonthly magazine, *La Critica*, and he was the editor of collections of Italian classics and of standard philosophical works. His books are too numerous to list, but a few will indicate the breadth of his intellectual interests: *Materialismo storico ed economia marxista* (1900; Eng. trans., *Historical Materialism and the Economics of Marx*, 1914), *Filosofia della pratica: economia ed etica* (1908; Eng. trans., *Philosophy of the Practical: Economics and Ethics*, 1913), *Frammenti di etica* (1922; Eng. trans., *The Conduct of Life*, 1924), *L'Intuizione pura e il carattere lirico dell'arte* (1908), *La Filosofia di Vico* (1911; Eng. trans., *The Philosophy of Vico*, 1913), *Ciò che è vivo e ciò che è morto della filosofia di Hegel* (1907; Eng. trans., *What Is Living and What Is Dead of the Philosophy of Hegel*, 1915), *Ariosto, Shakespeare e Corneille* (1920; Eng. trans., *Ariosto, Shakespeare and Corneille*, 1920), *La Letteratura della nuova Italia* (4 vols., 1914–15; vol. 5, 1939; vol. 6, 1940), *Storia d'Italia dal 1871 al 1915* (1927; Eng. trans., *A History of Italy 1871–1915*, 1929), *Storia d'Europa nel secolo decimonono* (1932; Eng. trans., *History of Europe in the Nineteenth Century*, 1933).

Crockett (krok′ĕt), **Samuel Rutherford.** b. at Little Duchrae, near New Galloway, Scotland, Sept. 24, 1860; d. April 21, 1914. A Scottish minister and novelist. He was educated at Edinburgh University and at the New Theological College, Edinburgh, and was minister of the Free Church at Penicuik, Midlothian, from 1886 until he resigned his charge (1895) to devote himself to authorship. His first book was published as *Dulce Cor: the Poems of Ford Bereton*. His principal works are *The Stickit Minister* (1893), *The Raiders* (1894), *The Lilac Sunbonnet* (1894), *Mad Sir Uchtred of the Hills* (1894), *Play-Actress* (1894), *The Men of the Moss-Hags* (1895), *Bog-Myrtle and Peat* (1895), *The Gray Man* (1896), *Sweetheart Travellers* (1896), *Cleg Kelly* (1896), *A Galloway Herd* (1896), *Lad's Love* (1897), *Joan of the Sword Hand* (1900), *The Dark of the Moon* (1902), *An Adventurer in Spain* (1903), *Strong Mac* (1904), *Maid Margaret* (1905), *Cherry Ribband* (1905), *Deep Moat Grange* (1908), and *The Men of the Mountain* (1909).

Crockford's (krok′fŏrdz). A gaming clubhouse at London, famous in the first half of the 19th century. It was built by William Crockford, originally a fishmonger, in 1827. He is said to have made a large fortune by gambling. He died May 24, 1844, but the house was reopened in 1849 for the Military, Naval, and Country Service Club. It was closed again in 1851. It was for several years a dining house, "The Wellington," and later became the Devonshire Club.

Crock of Gold, The. A novel by James Stephens, published in 1912. It won the 1913 Polignac Prize. Told in the manner of a fairy tale, it concerns two philosophers and their families, who live in the Irish forest of Coilla Doraca. The two children are kidnapped by leprechauns, but make much trouble for the little people by stealing their crock of gold, always kept on hand for emergency ransoms. The children, Seumas and Brigid, are finally released and the gold is restored. Meanwhile, one philosopher is accused of murder and taken to the city. Certain friendly divinities gain his release, and he returns to the forest. Among the characters are Pan, the Beast in Man; Angus Og, an early Irish god; and Meehawl MacMurrachu, the man who first stole the crock of gold. Many Irish legends are to be found here, and the author holds out an optimistic hope that when the old Irish gods are able to leave their caves and forest haunts, and come out once more into the open country, peace and laughter will be restored to the land.

Crocodile (krok'ọ.dil), **Lady Kitty.** In Samuel Foote's *Trip to Calais*, a hypocritical, intriguing woman of quality, intended to satirize the notorious Duchess of Kingston, whose trial for bigamy was just coming on. The influence of the duchess was sufficient to stop the production of the play.

Croesus (krē'sus). fl. 6th century B.C. A king of Lydia; son of Alyattes, whom he succeeded in 560 B.C. He subjugated the Ionian, Aeolian, and other neighboring peoples, and at the close of his reign ruled over the region extending from the N and W coasts of Asia Minor to the Halys River (modern Kizil Irmak) on the E and the Taurus Mountains on the S. According to Herodotus, he was visited at the height of his power by Solon, to whom he exhibited his innumerable treasures, and who, when pressed to acknowledge him as the happiest of mortals, answered, "Account no man happy before his death." Deceived by a response of the oracle at Delphi to the effect that, if he marched against the Persians, he would overthrow a great empire, he made war in 546 upon Cyrus, by whom he was defeated in the same year near Sardis and taken prisoner. He was, according to Herodotus, doomed to be burned alive, but as he stood upon the pyre he recalled the words of Solon, and exclaimed "Solon! Solon! Solon!" Desired by Cyrus to state upon whom he was calling, he related the story of Solon, which moved Cyrus to countermand the order for his execution, and to bestow upon him distinguished marks of favor.

Croft (krôft), **Admiral.** In Jane Austen's novel *Persuasion*, a wealthy naval officer who, with his wife, rents the home of the heroine's father, Sir Walter Elliot.

Croft, Sir Herbert. b. at Dunster Park, Berkshire. England, Nov. 1, 1751; d. at Paris, April 26, 1816. An English author and lexicographer, known for his life of the English poet Edward Young, published in Johnson's *Lives of the Poets*. Educated at Oxford, he took holy orders (1785) and began

collecting material for a new edition of Johnson's *Dictionary*, which failed, however, to gain enough subscribers and was abandoned in 1793. He was imprisoned for debt in 1795; later he visited Hamburg, Germany, returning to England in 1800, and went to France in 1802, where he spent the remainder of his life. In addition to his life of Young, written in imitation of Johnson, he was the author of *Love and Madness* (1780), *The Abbey of Kilkhampton* (1780), *Sunday Evenings* (1784), *The Will of King Alfred* (1788), *Horace éclairci par la ponctuation* (1810), and *Commentaires sur les meilleurs ouvrages de la langue française* (1815).

Croftangry (krôf'tang.gri), **Chrystal.** The imaginary author of Sir Walter Scott's *Chronicles of the Canongate.* He gives his autobiography in some of the introductory chapters. See also **Clutterbuck, Captain Cuthbert.**

Croft-Cooke (krôft'kŭk'), **Rupert.** b. at Edenbridge, Kent, England, June 20, 1904—. An English poet, playwright, and novelist. He is the author of the plays *Banquo's Chair* (1930), *Tap Three Times* (1931), and *Deliberate Accident* (1934), the volume of poetry entitled *Some Poems* (1929), and of *Night Out* (1932), *Shoulder the Sky* (1934), *Crusade* (1936), *Same Way Home* (1939), *Glorious* (1940), *Octopus* (1946), and *Ladies Gay* (1946).

Crofts (krôfts), **Freeman Wills.** b. at Dublin, 1879—. An Irish civil engineer and detective-story writer. He created the fictional character of Inspector French, who appears as the central figure in such detective novels as *Inspector French's Greatest Case, Inspector French and the Cheyne Mystery,* and *Golden Ashes.* Among his other stories are *The Box Office Murders* and *Fatal Venture.*

Croker (krō'kėr), **John Wilson.** b. in County Galway, Ireland, Dec. 20, 1780; d. at Hampton, near London, Aug. 10, 1857. A British politician and general writer. He was a leading contributor to the *Quarterly Review* after 1809, and editor of Boswell's *Life of Johnson* (1831).

Croker, Thomas Crofton. b. at Cork, Ireland, Jan. 15, 1798; d. at London, Aug. 8, 1854. An Irish antiquary. He wrote *Researches in the South of Ireland* (1824), *The Fairy Legends and Traditions of the South of Ireland* (1825), *The Adventures of Barney Mahoney* (1852), and others.

Crole (krōl) or **Croleus** (krō'lẹ.us), **Robert.** See **Crowley, Robert.**

Croly (krō'li), **George.** b. at Dublin, Aug. 17, 1780; d. at London, Nov. 24, 1860. An Irish clergyman, poet, and novelist. His chief novel is *Salathiel* (1829); he also wrote the poem *Paris in 1815* (1817), the tragedy *Catiline* (1822), *Marston,* a romance (1846), and *Life and Times of George IV* (1830).

Crome (krōm), **John.** [Called **"Old Crome."**] b. at Norwich, England, Dec. 22, 1768; d. there, April 22, 1821. An English landscape painter. He was the son of a poor weaver, and began life as a doctor's assistant and as apprentice to a coach-and-sign painter. He early began to study painting directly from nature in the environs of his native town, later found an opporunity to study drawing, and obtained entrance to a neighboring collection of paintings, where he found some good Flemish pic-

ḍ, d or i̯; ṣ, s or sh; ṭ, t or ch; ẓ, z or zh; *o,* F. cloche; ü, F. menu; ċh, Sc. loch; ṅ, F. bonbon.

tures. In 1803 he created the Norwich Society of Arts. At the annual exhibitions of this society he exhibited many of his works, rarely sending them to the Royal Academy at London. His pupils and associates, among whom were James Stark and John Sell Cotman, acquired distinction, and formed with him the so-called school of Norwich.

Crome Yellow. A novel by Aldous Huxley, published in 1921. The characters include Priscilla and Henry Wimbush, who own the country house from which the novel derives its name; Denis, a poet in love with Henry's niece Anne; Jenny Mullion, a deaf old maid; Gombauld, an artist who paints Anne and makes love to her; and Mary Bracegirdle, a young girl who realizes that she is very repressed and worries about her Freudian dreams.

Crompton (krump′tọn, kromp′-), **Richmal.** Pseudonym of **Lamburn, Richmal Crompton.**

Cromwell (krom′wel, -wẹl, krum′-). In Shakespeare's *Henry VIII*, one of Wolsey's servants. He is the audience for Wolsey's speech bidding farewell to his greatness and as secretary of the Council defends Cranmer against Gardiner's attack.

Cromwell, Oliver. b. at Huntingdon, England, April 25, 1599; d. at Whitehall, London, Sept. 3, 1658. An English revolutionary leader and Lord Protector of the Realm. Not a great deal is known of the early years of this son of a landed proprietor and grazier, who first appeared in public life as a member of Parliament in 1628. From the first he was active among the Puritans, rising slowly to some prominence by virtue of effective work on committees, and by force of sound sense and determination of character rather than by oratory or other more brilliant qualities. As civil war between the forces of Charles I of England and the adherents of Parliament became inevitable, Cromwell was among the first to organize a regiment, which gave a good account of itself in a number of engagements, including those at Edgehill (1642) and Marston Moor (1644), and under his firm leadership won the designation of Ironsides. When the tension between Parliament, which was at that time effectively under Presbyterian control, and the army, dominated by Puritans and Independents, reached a point of danger, Cromwell proposed the reorganization which resulted in the New Model Army, of which (as a result of considerable intrigue, it is supposed) he shared command with Sir Thomas Fairfax. The victories over Charles I at Naseby and over the Scotch at Preston made the army the dominant force in England. Cromwell disavowed responsibility for "Pride's Purge," which eliminated the Presbyterian Parliamentary leadership, but he unquestionably approved of the action, which opened the way for the trial of the king. Cromwell, having sided with the army in its controversy with Parliament over proposals to disband it in part without guarantees of payment of arrears, and having at the same time restrained the extremists among the soldiery, was already the dominant figure in England. The army having seized Charles, Cromwell, who for a long while had apparently sincerely hoped for a compromise, negotiated with the monarch, proposing lenient terms in most respects, but insisting upon religious freedom in the sense that neither an episcopal nor a

presbyterian order should be established. Charles's rejection of these terms sealed his fate, and at his trial, Cromwell was foremost in demanding his death. After the execution of the king, Cromwell led an army to Ireland, acting toward the Royalists and the Irish people so ruthlessly, as in the massacres at Drogheda and Wexford, that to this day "the curse of Cromwell" is the most terrible recollection of English rule among the Irish people. With the Irish helpless, he carried out the most extensive expropriation of Irish lands ever attempted, in the first place as an easy way to pay his soldiers, and with the purpose moreover of ensuring English domination once for all. In 1650 he defeated the Royalist Scots and turned back the first attempt of Charles II to recover the throne. The victorious Parliamentary revolutionaries were long involved in controversies and difficulties in fixing the form of the new government, and in 1653 a monarchy in all but name was established with the naming of Cromwell first as Captain-General, then as Lord Protector. He was offered the title of king on this occasion and subsequently, but refused it. One parliament after another proving intractable, Cromwell dismissed them and eventually ruled as a virtual dictator. He suppressed the Levellers, the real revolutionists, with great severity. A good administrator himself, he brought about efficiency in the government, but never won much popular affection, and could not unify the nation. In foreign affairs his policy was directed to the aggrandizement of his country, but, although ruthless on occasion, it was wavering and not, in the long view, very effective. After his death his son Richard was not long able to rule effectively, and the Cromwellian generals themselves arranged for the restoration of the Stuart heir to the throne, whereupon the remains of Oliver Cromwell were dug up, beheaded, drawn and quartered, and displayed in public ignominy.

Cromwell, The Life and Death of Thomas Lord. See **Thomas Lord Cromwell.**

Cromwell, Thomas. [Title, Earl of **Essex.**] b. probably c1485; d. at London, July 28, 1540. An English statesman. The son of a blacksmith, he served in his youth in the French army in Italy, and after his return to England became a lawyer. He was appointed collector of the revenues of the see of York by Wolsey in 1514, became a member of Parliament in 1523, was appointed privy councilor by Henry VIII in 1531, and was made chancellor of the exchequer in 1533. In 1535 he was appointed vicar-general of the king to carry into effect the Act of Supremacy, in which capacity he began in 1536 the suppression of the monasteries and the confiscation of their property. He became lord privy seal in 1536 and lord high chamberlain of England in 1539, and was created Earl of Essex in 1540. In 1539 he negotiated the marriage of Henry VIII with Anne of Cleves, which took place in January, 1540. Having fallen under the king's displeasure, partly on account of his advocacy of this marriage, he was attainted by Parliament and beheaded on the charge of treason.

Cronica Tripartita (kron′i.kạ trī.pär.tī′tạ). [English, **Tripartite Chronicle.**] A historical poem by John Gower (*q.v.*).

---

fat, fāte, fär, ȧsk, fāre; net, mē, hẽr; pin, pīne; not, nōte, mȯve, nôr; up, lūte, pṳll; ᴛʜ, then;

Cronin (krō′nin), **A. J.** [Full name, **Archibald Joseph Cronin.**] b. at Cardross, Scotland, July 19, 1896—. A British novelist and physician. Graduated from Glasgow University, he served as a surgeon sublieutenant in World War I, and was engaged in general practice in South Wales (1921–24) and at London (1926–30), giving up medicine in the latter year to devote himself to writing. He is the author of the novels *Hatter's Castle* (1931), *Three Loves* (1932), *Grand Canary* (1933), *The Stars Look Down* (1935), *The Citadel* (1937), *The Keys of the Kingdom* (1941), *The Green Years* (1944), *Shannon's Way* (1948), and *The Spanish Gardener* (1950), of the play *Jupiter Laughs* (1940), of the autobiographical *Adventures in Two Worlds* (1952), the two worlds being medicine and literature, and *Beyond This Place* (1953), a melodramatic tale of suspense.

Cronus (krō′nus) or **Cronos** (-nos). In Greek mythology, a Titan, son of Uranus and Ge. At the instigation of his mother, he emasculated his father for having thrown the Cyclopes (who were likewise the children of Uranus and Ge) into Tartarus. He thereupon usurped the government of the world, which had hitherto belonged to his father, but was in turn dethroned by Zeus. He was the husband of Rhea, by whom he became the father of Hestia, Demeter, Hera, Hades, Poseidon, and Zeus. He was identified with Saturnus by the Romans.

Croppies (krop′iz). A name given to the republican party in Ireland in 1798, who wore their hair cropped in imitation of the French revolutionists. The name was applied earlier, in 1642, to the Parliamentary soldiers during the English Civil War.

Crosby Hall (kroz′bi). [Also, **Crosby Place.**] An ancient house in Bishopsgate Street, London. The site was leased from Alice Ashfield, prioress of St. Helen's, in 1466 by Sir John Crosby, a grocer and lord mayor. He built the beautiful Gothic palace. The mansion covered a large part of what later became Crosby Place or Square. Richard of Gloucester lived here at the death of Edward IV, and here held his levees before his usurpation of the crown. It was afterward bought by Sir Thomas More, who wrote here the *Utopia* and the *Life of Richard III*. Crosby Hall was the central feature of Shakespeare's London. Shakespeare himself had a residence in the neighborhood.

Crossing the Bar. A religious poem by Alfred Tennyson. It was written in October, 1889, when the poet was suffering fits of depression, and was first published, in the same year, as the last poem in the volume *Demeter and Other Poems*. It has since always been published at the end of every volume of his works in accordance with his frequently repeated request. It was composed at the suggestion of a nurse Emma Durham, who nursed him during his illness of 1888–89 and said to him, "instead of giving way to depression, you ought to write a hymn."

Crossjay Patterne (krôs′jā pat′ėrn). See **Patterne, Crossjay.**

Cross-Roads, The. A play of Irish middle-class life by Lennox Robinson, published in 1909.

Crotchet Castle (kroch′et). A novel by Thomas Love Peacock, published in 1831. The book has little plot, being composed of bits of prose, dialogue, and poetry from the conversations of a group of people at a country castle owned by Ebenezer MacCrotchet. He is a widower who buys a coat-of-arms along with the castle, and he lives there with his two children, the young Crotchet and Lemma. They entertain a diverse group of characters, including Rev. Dr. Folliott, Susannah Touchandgo, Mr. Chainmail, and Mr. Firedamp.

"Crouchback." See **Richard III** (king of England).

Crowdero (krou.dir′ō). A character in Butler's *Hudibras;* a fiddler, and the leader of the mob.

Crowe (krō), **Captain.** A whimsical, impatient merchant captain in Tobias Smollett's novel *Sir Launcelot Greaves*. He insists upon being a knight-errant with the latter.

Crowe, Catherine. [Maiden name, **Stevens.**] b. at Borough Green, Kent, England, c1800; d. in 1876. An English writer, principally known by her writings on the supernatural. She was the author of *Night Side of Nature* (1848) and *Spiritualism and the Age We Live In* (1859), and also wrote the novels *Susan Hopley* (1841) and *Lily Dawson* (1847).

Crowe, Eyre Evans. b. at Redbridge, Southampton, England, March 20, 1799; d. at London, Feb. 25, 1868. An English journalist, historian, and novelist. He was the author of *History of France* (5 vols., 1858–68).

Crowe, William. b. at Midgeham, Berkshire, England, 1745; d. at Bath, England, Feb. 9, 1829. An English clergyman and poet. He was considered eccentric, but a popular preacher. He wrote *Lewesdon Hill* (1788), *A Treatise on English Versification* (1827), and published several volumes of sermons and orations, and others.

Crowland (krō′land). [Also, **Croyland.**] A parish, market town, and former rural district in E England, in Lincolnshire, in the Parts of Holland, situated on the river Welland ab. 8 mi. NE of Peterborough. It contains the ruins of a famous abbey founded by Ethelbald of Mercia in the 8th century.

Crowley (krō′li), **Robert.** [Also: **Crole, Croleus.**] b. in Gloucestershire, England, c1518; d. at London, June 18, 1588. An English author, printer, and divine. He was educated at Oxford, embraced the doctrines of the Reformation, and set up (c1549) a printing press at Ely Rents, in Holborn (now part of London), which he conducted for three years. He was archdeacon of Hereford (1559–67) and vicar of Saint Lawrence Jewry, London (1576–78). His typographical fame rests chiefly on three impressions which he made in 1550 of the *Vision of Piers Plowman*. His most notable works are *An Informacion and Peticion agaynst the Oppressours of the Pore Commons of this Realme* (1548), *The Voyce of the Laste Trumpet* (1549), *The Way to Wealth* (1550), *One and Thyrtye Epigrammes* (1550), and *Pleasure and Payne, Heaven and Hell: Remember these Foure, and all shall be Well* (1551).

Crowne (kroun), **John.** b. c1640; d. c1703. A British dramatist. Among other plays he wrote *The Country Wit* (1675), *City Politiques* (played c1683), *Sir Courtly Nice, or It Cannot Be* (1685), and *The Married Beau* (1694).

Crown of Wild Olive, The. A series of four lectures (given in 1866) by John Ruskin. The lectures were *War* (delivered before the Royal Military Academy), *The Future of England* (before the Royal Artillery Institute), *Work* (before a labor club, or workingmen's institute), and *Traffic* (at the Bradford Town Hall), by which he meant commercial activity in buying and selling. The "crown" he had in mind was the one awarded as a prize to the victor in the ancient Greek Olympic Games, and Ruskin's idea is that one should work for the sake of the work itself, for the spiritual satisfaction it affords, and not for material reward in the shape of a prize or medal.

Crowquill (krō′kwil), **Alfred.** Joint pseudonym of **Forrester, Alfred Henry** and **Charles Robert.**

Croye (kroi), **Hameline, Countess de.** The voluble and shrill-voiced aunt of Isabelle de Croye in Sir Walter Scott's novel *Quentin Durward*, with whom she becomes infatuated. She is overwhelmed with chagrin when she learns that his affections are centered on her niece. She afterwards becomes the wife of the brutal Baron De la Marck.

Croyland (kroi′land). See **Crowland.**

Croysado (kroi.sä′dō), **the Great.** In Butler's *Hudibras*, a character intended for Lord Fairfax.

Cruden (krö′den), **Alexander.** b. at Aberdeen, Scotland, May 31, 1701; d. at London, Nov. 1, 1770. A London bookseller, author of a famous *Concordance of the Holy Scriptures* (1737). An eccentric, he believed himself to have been specially appointed by God to correct the morals of the British nation, and accordingly assumed the title of "Alexander the Corrector" (probably suggested to him by his work as corrector of the press).

Crudor (krö′dôr), **Sir.** In Edmund Spenser's *Faerie Queene*, a knight who insists that Briana shall supply him with enough hair, consisting of ladies' curls and knights' beards, to purfle his cloak before he will marry her. Sir Calidore overthrows him, and Briana's raid on the passers-by is stopped.

Cruel Brother, The. A tragedy by Sir William D'Avenant, printed in 1627.

Cruel Gift, The. A tragedy by Susannah Centlivre, produced in 1716.

Cruel Mistress, A. A poem by the Cavalier poet Thomas Carew, telling of a woman so cruel in love that even the purest sacrifices and the humblest oblations would not satisfy her:

> Of such a goddess no times leave record,
> That burnt the temple where she was adored.

Cruelty of the Spaniards in Peru, The. An operatic play by Sir William D'Avenant, produced in 1658. It deals with the contrast between bloodthirsty Christians and simple, virtuous natives.

Cruikshank (krŭk′shank), **George.** b. at London, Sept. 27, 1792; d. Feb. 1, 1878. An English artist, best known as a caricaturist. He was the son of a caricaturist, and his brother, Robert Cruikshank, was also a caricaturist. He began his career as an illustrator of children's books, and his satirical genius first found expression in *The Scourge*, a periodical published between 1811 and 1816. At this time his caricatures were in the style of Gillray, but c1819 he began to illustrate books and de-

veloped a style that was uniquely his own. Among the most noted of his caricatures were those of Napoleon, the impostures of Joanna Southcott, the Corn Laws, and the domestic infelicities (and alleged infidelities) of the Prince Regent (later to be George IV) and his wife. In 1827 William Hone issued a collection of Cruikshank's caricatures in connection with the latter scandal, which he called *Facetiae and Miscellanies*. Some of Cruikshank's best illustrations were for Sir Walter Scott and for a translation of German fairy tales. In 1823 he issued his designs for Chamisso's *Peter Schlemihl*. His arrangement with Dickens began with *Sketches by Boz* in 1836. He designed also for Richard Bentley (1837–43) and Harrison Ainsworth (1836–44). *The Bottle* (8 plates, 1847) and *The Drunkard's Children* (8 plates, 1848) were the first products of his satirical crusade against drunkenness. He continued to produce etchings and other works in rapid and brilliant succession until his eighty-third year; three years after this he died. He wrote various pamphlets and squibs and started several magazines of his own, and in his later years undertook to paint in oils. His most celebrated effort in this line is a large picture called *The Worship of Bacchus, or the Drinking Customs of Society* (1862), in the National Gallery at London.

Crummles (krum′lz), **Vincent.** In Charles Dickens's *Nicholas Nickleby*, an eccentric actor and manager associated with a cheap theatrical company. He is the father of two boys and a girl, also in the profession; the last is the "Infant Phenomenon."

Cruncher (krun′chêr), **Jerry.** In Charles Dickens's *Tale of Two Cities*, a man of all work at Tellson's banking house, who spent his nights as a "resurrection man" (a euphemism of the day for a man who dug up freshly buried corpses for sale to medical schools).

Crupp (krup), **Mrs.** In Charles Dickens's *David Copperfield*, David's landlady. She is afflicted with "spazzums."

Crusoe (krö′sō), **Robinson.** See **Robinson Crusoe.**

Cry of the Children, The. A poem by Elizabeth Barrett Browning. It was published in 1843 in *Blackwood's Magazine*.

Crystal Palace. A structure of iron and glass, erected in Hyde Park, London, for the great exhibition of 1851, reërected (1852–53) at Sydenham (now part of London), and there opened in 1854. It was designed by Sir Joseph Paxton, and was used for popular concerts and other entertainments, as well as for a permanent exhibition of the art and culture of various nations. The nave was 1,608 ft. long, the central transept 390 by 120 ft., and 175 ft. high, and the south transept 312 ft. long. A corresponding north transept was burned in 1866. After World War I it housed the Imperial War Museum. The structure was swept by fire, and utterly destroyed, on Nov. 30, 1936.

Cry, the Beloved Country. A novel (1950) by Alan Paton.

Cuchulain (kö.ċhö′lin). [Also: **Cuculain, Cuchullin, Cu Chullin, Cu Cullin;** original name, **Setanta.**] d. c2 A.D. An Irish warrior of pagan times, hero of legendary exploits, sometimes called "the Achilles of the Gael." Scholars now generally agree that he was a historical person, about whose history the poets wove ancient legends, some perhaps going back to the first home of the Gael in Scythia, with later scribes during many centuries adding ever more marvels. Ostensibly of mortal paternity, Cuchulain (as Setanta) is represented to have been in fact the son of Lugh, the sun god. From childhood he was fabulously brave, skilled, and warlike. Having as a mere child killed a ferocious hound which attacked him, and noted the grief of the hound's owner, Culain, he voluntarily assumed the role of watchdog until one as good as his victim could be found, and thereafter he was known as Cuchulain, meaning "the Hound of Culain." To complete his training in arms he became a pupil of the woman warrior Scathach on the island named for her, now called Skye. When another militant female, Aoife, attacked Scathach, Cuchulain overcame her and made love to her, and when leaving the isle, instructed Aoife to send their son, Conlaoch, to Ireland when he came of age to bear arms, under a vow to let no man stop him or compel him to give his name. Years later Conlaoch came to Ireland and slew so many warriors that at last Cuchulain confronted and killed him, learning his identity too late. One version of the legend represents them as killing each other; a variant has Cuchulain in his grief fighting with the sea and sinking exhausted into it. In the most widely known version, however, Cuchulain, while still a stripling, single-handed retards the invading army of Queen Maeve until the Red Branch warriors of Ulster wake from a spell put upon them for a cruelty they committed, as told in the epic of the Tain Bo Cuailgne, in which the most poignant episode is the duel between Cuchulain and his dearest friend, Ferdiad. Some years later, the men of Ulster being again entranced, Medb marshals an army expressly to kill Cuchulain (who as a son of the sun god is immune from the spell) and with the aid of magicians who create an illusory host with which he fights to exhaustion, accomplishes her purpose. Sorely wounded, Cuchulain binds himself to a pillar-stone and dies standing and facing the enemy. His widow Emer, to whom he had returned after being seduced by Fand, the wife of the sea god Mananaan, throws herself into his grave and dies.

Cuckoo and the Nightingale, The. A poem of 290 lines which appeared in the printed editions of Chaucer of the 16th century. The weight of evidence is against Chaucer's authorship of the poem, which has been attributed by some scholars to Sir Thomas Clanvowe, a contemporary of the poet. In the Bodleian manuscript it is called *The Boke of Cupide God of Love;* another manuscript is headed *Liber Cupidinis.* It is based on a popular superstition that he will be happy in love during the year who hears the nightingale before he hears the cuckoo.

Cuckoo Song. See **Sumer is icumen in.**

Cuddie Headrigg (cud'i hed'rig). See **Headrigg, Cuddie.**

Cuddy (kud'i). The shepherd with whom Colin Clout conducts his arguments in Spenser's *Shepherd's Calendar.*

Cuddy. A shepherd in love with Buxoma in John Gay's *Shepherd's Week.*

Cudworth (kud'wėrth), **Ralph.** b. at Aller, Somersetshire, England, 1617; d. at Cambridge, England, June 26, 1688. An English philosopher and divine. He became in 1645 regius professor of Hebrew at Cambridge, a position which he retained until his death. His chief works are *True Intellectual System of the Universe* (1678) and *Treatise concerning Eternal and Immutable Morality* (1731).

Cuff (kuf), **Sergeant.** In Wilkie Collins's novel *The Moonstone*, the merciless, and very effective, detective sent from London to take charge of solving the mystery. He is one of the first detectives to play a major role in English fiction.

Cuffe (kuf), **Lady Sybil Marjorie.** b. Oct. 3, 1879; d. 1943. An English novelist. She married (Dec. 8, 1926) Percy Lubbock. She was the author of *A Book of the Sea* (1918), *Four Tales by Zélide* (1925), and *Child in the Crystal* (1939) and editor of *A Page from the Past* (1936).

Culdee (kul'dē). A member of a fraternity of priests, constituting an irregular monastic order, existing in Scotland, and in smaller numbers in Ireland and Wales, from the 9th or 10th century to the 14th or 15th century.

Culloden Moor (ku.lod'ẹn, -lō'dẹn). [Also, **Drummossie Moor.**] A moor ab. 5 mi. E of Inverness, Scotland. Here, on April 27, 1746, the forces of the English crown (ab. 10,000) under the Duke of Cumberland defeated the Highlanders (ab. 6,000) under Charles Edward Stuart, the Young Pretender.

Cully (kul'i), **Sir Nicholas.** A foolish, gullible knight in Etherege's comedy *The Comical Revenge, or Love in a Tub.*

Cumberland (kum'bėr.lạnd), **Duke of.** Title of William Augustus, son of George II (of England). He commanded the English against the Scots at Culloden Moor in 1746, and was for nearly 100 years thereafter a hated figure in Scotland, as evidenced by his role in Sir Walter Scott's *Waverley* novels and elsewhere.

Cumberland, Prince of. A title formerly bestowed on the successor to the crown of Scotland when succession was declared in the king's lifetime (the crown was originally not hereditary). In Shakespeare's *Macbeth* the title is given to Malcolm by his father Duncan.

Cumberland, Richard. b. at Cambridge, England, Feb. 19, 1732; d. at Tunbridge Wells, England, May 7, 1811. An English dramatist and statesman; grandson of the scholar Richard Bentley. He was in politics before becoming a playwright in 1761. He did a number of indifferent tragedies, including a reworking of *Timon of Athens*, before turning to comedies with *The Brothers* (1769). He also wrote *The West Indian* (1771), considered his best comedy in the sentimental vein, produced by Garrick; *The Fashionable Lover* (1772); and *The Jew* (1794), a study in tolerance. He was satirized in Sheridan's *The Critic* as Sir Fretful Plagiary.

Cumnor Hall (kum'nọr). An old manor house in the environs of Oxford, England, now destroyed. Scott made it famous as Cumnor Place, the house where

Amy Robsart is kept and where she meets her death, in *Kenilworth*. W. J. Meickle wrote a ballad called *Cumnor Hall*, which was a lament for Amy Robsart.

Cundell (kun'del), **Henry.** See **Condell, Henry.**

Cunningham (kun'ing.am, -ham), **Allan.** b. at Keir, Dumfriesshire, Scotland, Dec. 7, 1784; d. at London, Oct. 30, 1842. A Scottish poet and man of letters. He was apprenticed to a stone mason, but went to London in 1810, and became a reporter and writer on the *Literary Gazette*. He became (1814) secretary to the sculptor Francis Legatt Chantrey, a position which he retained until his death. He wrote *Traditional Tales of the Peasantry* (1822), *The Songs of Scotland, Ancient and Modern* (1825), *Lives of the Most Eminent British Painters, Sculptors, and Architects* (1829–33), and several romances.

Cunninghame-Graham (kun'ing.am.grā'am), **Robert.** See **Graham, Robert.**

Cunninghame Graham (kun'ing.am grā'am), **Robert Bontine.** b. at London, May 24, 1852; d. at Buenos Aires, March 20, 1936. A Scottish essayist, short-story writer, biographer, socialist, politician, and traveler. In 1886 he won a seat as Liberal member of Parliament, but he lost the elections of 1892 and 1918. He was suspended from the House of Commons for using the word "damn" in the House, the first member, it is believed, to be so distinguished.

Cunobeline (kū'nō.be̯.lin") or **Cunobelinus** (kū"nō-be̯.li'nus). A semilegendary king of the Silures, the father of Caractacus. He is often confused with Cymbeline. A historical king (d. c43 A.D.) of the name was an ally of the Roman emperor Augustus.

Cup, The. A poetical drama by Alfred Tennyson, produced at the Lyceum Theatre, London, in 1881.

Cupid (kū'pid). [Also: **Amor**; Greek, **Eros.**] In ancient Roman mythology, the god of love, the son of Mercury and Venus. The parallel Greek Eros is similarly son of Hermes and Aphrodite. He is generally represented as a beautiful boy with wings, carrying a bow and a quiver of arrows, and is often spoken of as blind or blindfolded. The bow is used to shoot the arrows, which are invisible and which cause the one shot to fall irrevocably in love. Cupid originally was depicted as a young man, as he is in the story of Cupid and Psyche, but with time developed into the cherubic little scamp of later myth.

Cupid. In Shakespeare's *Timon of Athens*, a participator in the masque presented to Timon in his home.

Cupid, Adam. See **Adam Cupid.**

Cupid and Psyche (sī'kē). An episode in the *Golden Ass* of Apuleius. The beauty of Psyche, the youngest of three daughters of a certain king, and the homage paid to it, arouse the wrath of Venus, who commands Cupid to avenge her. In the attempt he falls in love with Psyche; she is borne to a lovely valley where every night Cupid, always invisible, visits her and commands her not to attempt to see him. Urged by her sisters and by her own curiosity, she violates this command, and is abandoned by the god. After toilsome wanderings in search of her lover, and many sufferings, she is endowed with immortality by Jupiter and united to Cupid forever. The tale, utilizing themes and motifs familiar in folk tales from all over the world, for example the taboo against looking at the supernatural husband and the search for the lost husband, is the clearest example of unadorned folk tale in classical literature. The story has served as a basis for many later accounts, such as the one by La Fontaine, and for paintings, one of the most familiar by Raphael.

Cupid in Waiting. A comedy by William Blanchard Jerrold, produced on July 17, 1871.

Cupid's Revenge. A play by Francis Beaumont and John Fletcher. It was acted in 1612, and published in 1615, and long attributed, incorrectly, to Fletcher alone, though probably he wrote the major part of it. It is based on two of the stories in Sidney's *Arcadia*.

Cupid's Whirligig. A comedy (1607) by Edward Sharpham.

Curan (kur'an). In Shakespeare's *King Lear*, a courtier. He may possibly be the "Gentleman" appearing in Act III, Scene 1.

Curan. See also **Argentile and Curan.**

Cure for a Cuckold, A. A tragicomedy written by John Webster and William Rowley, and possibly Thomas Heywood. It was published in 1661. The play treats somewhat the same theme as *The Dutch Courtezan* by John Marston.

Cure of Souls, A. A novel (1924) by May Sinclair. It is a study of a self-indulgent clergyman.

Curio (kū'ri.ō). In Shakespeare's *Twelfth Night*, a gentleman in attendance on Orsino, Duke of Illyria.

Curiosities of Literature, The. A work by Isaac D'Israeli, containing anecdotes, criticism, and general information in all fields. It was issued anonymously, the first volume in 1791, a second in 1793, a third in 1817, a fourth and fifth in 1823, and a sixth and last in 1834.

Curious Impertinent, The. An episode in Cervantes's *Don Quixote*. John Crowne (c1640–1712) wrote a play, *The Married Beau, or The Curious Impertinent* (1694), the plot of which is taken from this. The story is that of two friends, one of whom induces the other, after much argument, to test the faithfulness of the former's wife. She proves to be not as virtuous as she should be and all ends tragically.

Curll (kėrl), **Edmund.** b. 1675; d. at London, Dec. 11, 1747. An English bookseller. He achieved a reputation for issuing obscene literature, which led to the use in his day of the word "Curlicism" as meaning indecency in literature. In 1716 he had a quarrel with Pope over his ascription of the anonymous *Court Poems* to Pope. The poet thereupon pilloried Curll in the *Dunciad*. He published a number of standard works; of his biographies Arbuthnot said they had added a new terror to death.

Currie (kur'i), **Lady Mary Montgomerie.** [Pseudonym, **Violet Fane**; maiden name, **Lamb.**] b. at Beauport, Littlehampton, Sussex, England, Feb. 24, 1843; d. at Harrogate, Yorkshire, England, Oct. 13, 1905. An English poet, essayist, short-story writer, novelist, and translator. She contributed many essays and poems to *Nineteenth Century*,

Blackwood's Magazine, Littel's Living Age, and other periodicals. She took her pseudonym from a character in Disraeli's novel *Vivian Gray,* adopting it because her parents did not approve of a literary career. She appears as Mrs. Sinclair in William H. Mallock's satirical novel *The New Republic* (1876), which is dedicated to her. She was the author of *Laura Dibalzo* (1880), *Sophy* (1882), *Through Love and War* (1886), and *The Story of Helen Davenant* (1889), novels; *Edwin and Angelina Papers* (1878), *Two Moods of Man* (1901), *Collected Essays* (1902), *Are Remarkable People Remarkable Looking?, Enfants Trouvés of Literature, Feast of Kebobs,* and *Way of Dreams* (all 1904), essays; *From Dawn to Noon* (1872), *Great Peace-Maker* (1872), *Denzil Place: A Story in Verse* (1875), *Queen of the Fairies* (1876), *Collected Verses* (1880), *Autumn Songs* (1889), *Under Cross and Crescent* (1895), *Betwixt Two Seas* (1900), and *In Winter* (1904), poetry.

Curse of Kehama (kē.hä′ma̧), **The.** A poem by Robert Southey, first published in 1810. The theme is the curse of a charmed life, but without food or water, pronounced by Kehama on Ladurlad. Hindu mythology and folklore form the background.

Cursor Mundi (kėr′so̧r mun′dī). A Middle English poem (c1300) in the northern dialect, founded on a paraphrase of Genesis. It relates, in some 24,000 lines, the course of the world from the creation to doomsday. The whole poem was printed by the Early English Text Society (ed. by Richard Morris).

Curtain, The. A London playhouse established (c1576) in Shoreditch, near Bishopsgate. It is thought that Shakespeare acted here in his own plays as a member of the Lord Chamberlain's Men. It remained open until the accession (1625) of Charles I, after which the drama gave way to exhibitions of athletic feats. It was associated, under James Burbage's management, with The Theatre, which stood nearby. Henry Laneman had an agreement to pool profits from the two theaters with Burbage. It took its name not from any theatrical apparatus but because the land upon which it was built was called Curtain Close.

Curtana (kėr.tā′na̧). [Also: **Courtain, Curtein** (kėr-tān′).] Name originally given to the sword of Roland (later Durandal), of which, according to the tradition, the point was broken off in testing it. The name is also given to the pointless sword (also called the sword of Edward the Confessor) carried before the kings of England at their coronation, and emblematically considered as the sword of mercy.

Curtis (kėr′tis). In Shakespeare's *Taming of the Shrew,* a servant. This part was originally described in the Dramatis Personae as that of a serving-man (possibly played by Curtis Greville, a Jacobean actor), but it is now played as an old woman, the housekeeper of Petruchio.

Curvet′o (kėr.vet′ō). An old libertine, affecting youth, in Thomas Middleton's play *Blurt, Master Constable.* He is the butt of many practical jokes.

Curzon (kėr′zo̧n), **George Nathaniel.** [Titles: 1st Baron **Curzon of Kedleston,** 1st Marquess **Curzon of Kedleston.**] b. at Kedleston, Derbyshire, England, Jan. 11, 1859; d. at London, March 20, 1925. An English statesman and publicist. He was undersecretary of state for India (1891–92) and under-

secretary for foreign affairs (1895–98). From 1898 to 1905 he was viceroy of India, pacifying the Northwest Frontier and reforming the administration, but he resigned as the result of a disagreement with the army commander, H. H. Kitchener. He was created Baron Curzon of Kedleston (1898), earl (1911), and marquess (1921). He was a member of the war cabinet and afterwards secretary of state (1919–24) in charge of foreign affairs. He was a proponent of the idea of easing the reparations burden on Germany. From 1916 to 1924 he headed the House of Lords. He wrote *Russia in Central Asia* (1889), *Persia and the Persian Question* (1892), *Problems of the Far East* (1894), *Lord Curzon in India* (1906), *Frontiers* (1908), and *Principles and Methods of University Reform* (1909). In 1908 he was elected a member of the British Academy.

Cusis (kū′sis). A fabulous country in Sir John Mandeville's *Voiage and Travaile.* The people of this country have but one foot, so large that it casts a shadow over the whole body, and with this one foot they make wonderful speed.

Cust (kust), **Henry John Cockayne.** b. at London, Oct. 10, 1861; d. there, March 2, 1917. An English editor, politician, and poet. Educated at Eton and at Trinity College, Cambridge, he was Conservative member of Parliament for Stamford (1890–95) and for Bermondsey (1900–06). He was also editor (1892–96) of the *Pall Mall Gazette,* and cofounder (August, 1914) with George W. Prothero of the Central Committee for National Patriotic Organizations, of which he was chairman; he is honored at Nottingham University by an annual Cust lectureship. His volume *Occasional Poems* was published at Jerusalem in 1918.

Custance (kus′ta̧ns), **Dame Christian.** A rich and beautiful widow in Nicholas Udall's play *Ralph Roister Doister.*

Custom of the Country, The. A play by Fletcher and Massinger, written in 1620 and printed in 1647. It is partly from a story by Cervantes, *Persiles y Sigismunda,* and partly from a story in Cinthio's *Hecatommithi. Love makes a Man,* by Cibber, and *Country Lasses,* by Charles Johnson, were partly taken from it.

Custom of the Country, The. A farce by Susannah Centlivre, produced in 1716. It was originally produced (1710) at the Drury Lane, as *A Bickerstaff's Burying: or, Work for the Upholders,* and said, doubtfully, to be founded on the story of one of Sindbad's voyages.

Cute (kūt), **Alderman.** In Dickens's story *The Chimes,* a magistrate who avows his intention to "put down" every form of what he considered nonsense on the part of the poor (the sick, small children, and suicide all came under the heading of items which he proposed to forbid). He was based on the historical figure of Sir Peter Laurie, Lord Mayor of London in the period 1832–33.

Cuthbert (kuth′bėrt), **Saint.** d. at Farne, in Northumbria, March 20, 687. An English monk. He was prior of Melrose from 661 to 664, and in 664 of Lindisfarne, and bishop of Lindisfarne from 685 to 687.

Cuthbert Clutterbuck (klut′ẽr.buk), **Captain.** See **Clutterbuck, Captain Cuthbert.**

ḍ, d or j; ş, s or sh; ṭ, t or ch; z̧, z or zh; *o,* F. cloche; ü, F. menu; çh, Sc. loch; ṅ, F. bonbon.

Cutpurse (kut′pèrs), **Moll.** A kind-hearted pick-pocket and friend of thieves in Thomas Middleton and Thomas Dekker's *The Roaring Girl.* Histor-ically she was Mary Frith, notorious for her thiev-ing tricks and madcap pranks.

Cutter of Coleman Street, The. See **Guardian, The.**

Cutting of an Agate, The. A volume of essays by William Butler Yeats, published in 1912.

Cuttle (kut′l), **Captain Edward.** In Charles Dick-ens's *Dombey and Son,* "a kind-hearted, salt-looking" old retired sailor with a hook in place of his right hand. He is a friend of Sol Gills, the ships' instrument-maker. One of his favorite expressions is "When found, make a note on."

Cuyp or **Kuyp** (koip), **Albert.** b. at Dordrecht, Netherlands, 1620; d. there, 1691. A Dutch painter. He was a skillful painter of genre scenes, archi-tectural views, and country landscapes and also of animals, all of which he especially liked to place against backgrounds of diffused golden light. Some of his best-known works are *Promenade, Dapple-grey Horses, View of Dordrecht,* and *Piper with Cows.*

Cybele (sib′e̯.lē). [Also, **Rhea.**] In Greek mythol-ogy, the wife of Cronos (Saturnus), and mother of the Olympian gods: hence called the "Great Mother of the Gods." The original home of her worship was Phrygia, in Asia Minor. Her priests were called Corybantes, and her festivals were celebrated with wild dances and orgiastic excesses amid the re-sounding music of drums and cymbals. She was conceived as traversing the mountains in a chariot drawn by lions. From Asia her worship came to Greece, and during the second Punic War in 264 B.C. it was introduced into Rome, where the Mega-lesia, later also the Taurobolia and Criobolia, were celebrated in her honor. The oak, pine, and lion were sacred to her. She is usually represented enthroned between lions, with a diadem on her head and a small drum or cymbal, the instrument used in her rites, in her hand.

Cyclades (sik′lạ.dēz). [Also: **Kikladhes, Kyklades, Kykladon Nesoi.**] A group of islands belonging to Greece, situated in the Aegean Sea. The name, from the Greek word for "circle," derived from the belief that they formed a ring about Delos. Among the major islands are Andros, Tenos, Keos, Syros, Naxos, Melos, and Paros. They now form, with neighboring islands, the *nomos* (department) of Cyclades, which includes the provinces of Andros, Thera, Kea, Milo, Naxos, Syra, and Tenos. Cap-ital, Hermopolis; area, 1,023 sq. mi.

cycle. In literature, the aggregate of legendary or traditional matter accumulated round some mythi-cal or heroic event or character, as the siege of Troy and the Argonautic expedition of antiquity, or the Round Table, the Cid, and the Nibelungs of me-dieval times, and embodied in epic or narrative poetry or in romantic prose narrative.

Their superstition has more of interior belief and less of ornamental machinery than those to which Amadis de Gaul and other heroes of the later cycles of romance furnished a model.

(Hallam, *Introd. Lit. of Europe,* I.ii. § 57.)

It is a well-known fact that many of the most popular traditional ballads, such as those of the Arthurian cycle, "Hynd Horn," and others, were simply abridgments of older metrical romances.

(*N. and Q.,* 7th ser., II. 421.)

Cyclic Poets (sī′klik). The authors of Greek epic poems, composed between 800 B.C. and 550 B.C., relating to the Trojan War and the war against Thebes. Among these poems are *Cypria* (The Cyprian Lays), *Aethiopis* (The Lay of Aethiopia), *The Sack of Troy, The Little Iliad, Nostoi* (The Homeward Voyages), *Telegonia* (The Lay of Teleg-onus), all belonging to the Trojan cycle, and the *Thebais* and the *Epigoni,* belonging to the Theban cycle. A few fragments of these poems are extant.

Cyclops (sī′klops) or **Cyclopes** (sī.klō′pēz). In Greek mythology, a race of one-eyed giants, represented in the Homeric cycle of legends as Sicilian can-nibalistic shepherds, whose leader was Polyphemus. Hesiod names them as the three sons of Uranus and Gaea who helped Zeus in his struggle against Cro-nus, and who gave Zeus his thunderbolts. They were slain by Apollo. In later mythology they were assistant forgers to Hephaestus.

Cymbeline (sim′be̯.lēn). A drama by Shakespeare, produced probably c1610. Part of the play was no doubt derived from Holinshed, who mentions Cym-beline; the part relating to Iachimo may be traced to Boccaccio's *Decameron,* and the Belarius theme is possibly from *The Rare Triumphs of Love and Fortune,* a play produced in 1589. The play (which is now generally considered one of Shakespeare's less successful works) resembles Beaumont and Fletcher's *Philaster,* but it is not known which was first. It was first published in the folio of 1623. Thomas D'Urfey in 1682 added to it material de-signed to please the Restoration taste, and Garrick produced the original again in 1762. Shaw wrote a new fifth act in 1937, and the play as thus amended was produced in that same year.

The Story. Imogen, the daughter of Cymbeline, King of Britain, has secretly married Posthumus Leonatus, a gentleman at court, who is banished when Imogen's step-mother, the Queen (angry that Imogen did not marry her son Cloten) tells the King about the marriage. In Rome, Posthumus brags of the virtue of his wife and makes a wager with Iachimo, a crafty Roman, that he (Iachimo) cannot seduce her; by the terms of the wager, if Iachimo wins Posthumus will give him a diamond ring, which he has as a gift from Imogen. In Britain, Iachimo is scorned by Imogen, but by hiding in a chest in Imogen's room one night he is enabled to describe a fictitious seduction with such a back-ground of detail, backed up by a bracelet which he has stolen, as to convince Posthumus that Imogen has been unfaithful. Posthumus thereupon writes his servant Pisanio instructing him to kill Imogen, but Pisanio instead disguises Imogen as a page and suggests she flee the court and join the in-vading Roman forces under Lucius. However, she loses her way and joins, instead of the Romans, Belarius, a banished nobleman, who twenty years before had kidnapped Cymbeline's two sons, Guiderius and Arviragus. The Queen's son, Cloten, dressed in the clothes of Posthumus and in pursuit of Imogen, is killed by Guiderius. The two sons find Imogen, apparently dead, and lay her beside the beheaded Cloten, whom Imogen mistakes for

fat, fāte, fär, ȧsk, fāre; net, mē, hèr; pin, pīne; not, nōte, mȯve, nôr; up, lūte, pṳll; ᴛʜ, then;

her husband when she revives. Lucius finds her and accepts her in his entourage as a page, but the Romans, with Iachimo, are defeated and taken prisoners as a result of the heroic fighting of Belarius, Cymbeline's two sons, and Posthumus (who has meanwhile returned to Britain). Imogen (still in the guise of a page) is granted a favor by the King, and demands to know how Iachimo obtained the diamond ring. When he explains, and her identity is revealed, the couple are happily reunited. The King now also discovers his sons and makes peace with the Romans.

Cymbeline. In Shakespeare's *Cymbeline*, the King of Britain, dominated by his crafty Queen. After her death he is, according to the prophecy, a "lofty cedar." He treats the defeated Roman forces with clemency and proclaims a generous peace.

Cymochles (sim′o̜.klēz). In Edmund Spenser's *Faerie Queene*, the brother of Pyrochles, a son of Acrates and Despite, and husband of Acrasia. He is a man of great strength who seeks to slay Sir Guyon, but is turned from his purpose by the gentle Phaedria. He is killed by Prince Arthur.

Cymodoce (si.mod′o̜.sē). In Edmund Spenser's *Faerie Queene*, the mother of Marinell. Her name figures in Swinburne's poem *The Garden of Cymodoce*.

Cymry (kim′ri). [Also: **Cymri, Cwmry, Kymry.**] A name given to themselves by the Welsh. In its wider application the term is often applied to that division of the Celtic peoples embracing the Welsh, and including also the Cornishmen and the Bretons or Armoricans.

Cynara (sin′a̜.ra̜). The woman addressed by Ernest Dowson in his poem *Non sum Qualis Eram Bonae Sub Regno Cynarae* (with its well-known refrain "I have been faithful to thee, Cynara! in my fashion"). The actual Cynara was the daughter of a French café owner in London, who later married a waiter.

Cynewulf (kin′e̜.wu̇lf) or **Cynwulf** (kin′wu̇lf). [Also, **Kynewulf.**] fl. in the latter part of the 8th century. An early English poet, probably Northumbrian; sometimes identified with a Cynewulf who was bishop of Lindisfarne from 737 to 780. The discovery of his putative identity was based upon runes spelling out his name inserted at intervals in the epilogues of four poems attributed to him, *The Ascension* (or *Christ*), *Juliana*, *Elene*, and *The Fates of the Apostles*. The first two of these are preserved in the collections of Old English poems known as the *Exeter Book*, as is also *The Phoenix*, which is attributed to but not "signed" by Cynewulf; the latter two are preserved in the *Vercelli Book*. Other works ascribed to Cynewulf include *The Dream of the Rood* and *Andreas* (both in the *Vercelli Book*).

Cynics (sin′iks). A school of Greek philosophers founded by Antisthenes of Athens (b. c444 B.C.), who sought to develop the ethical teachings of Socrates, whose pupil he was. The chief doctrines of the Cynics were that virtue is the only good, that the essence of virtue is self-control, and that pleasure is an evil if sought for its own sake. They were accordingly characterized by an ostentatious contempt of riches, art, science, and amusements. The most famous Cynic was Diogenes of Sinope, a pupil

of Antisthenes, who carried the doctrines of the school to an extreme and ridiculous asceticism, and is improbably said to have slept in a tub which he carried about with him.

Cynosura (sī.nō.shö′ra̜). The constellation of Ursa Minor ("Little Bear") or Little Dipper, containing the polestar (which forms the tip of the tail), and thus often the object to which the eyes of mariners are directed.

Cynthia (sin′thi.a̜). In John Lyly's *Endimion*, a maid, presumably representing Queen Elizabeth, in love with the shepherd Endimion.

Cynthia. In Edmund Spenser's *Colin Clout's Come Home Again*, a gentle and beauteous character intended to represent Queen Elizabeth.

Cynthia. In Congreve's *Double Dealer*, a flippant fine lady, the daughter of Lord and Lady Pliant, in love with Mellefont.

Cynthia's Revels. [Full title, **Cynthia's Revels, or The Fountain of Self-Love.**] A "comicall satyre" by Ben Jonson, acted by the Children of the Royal Chapel in 1600. It was printed in quarto in 1601 and with large additions in a folio of 1616. It is a medley of allegory, satire, and mythology. The allegory of Cupid and Mercury clearly refers to Elizabeth and Essex under the guise of Cynthia and Actaeon. Act V introduces the Revels themselves with a lovely song to Cynthia: "Queen and huntress, chaste and fair." Two masques are presented before her, and then Cupid and Mercury are discovered. The various foolish courtiers are ordered to purge themselves of their folly before attending Cynthia again. Of Crites, her scholar, who pronounces their punishment, it is said that "he hath a most ingenuous and sweet spirit, a sharp and season'd wit, a straight judgment and a strong mind." This is assumed to be Jonson characterizing himself, wherefore the two gallants, Hedon and Anaides, whom he treats with contempt, are taken to be aimed at Marston and Dekker, although they are generalized satirical portraits of fops.

Cynthia, the Lady of the Sea. An elegy by Sir Walter Raleigh, in which he expresses his loyalty and devotion to Queen Elizabeth (who is called "Cynthia" in accordance with a custom common among Elizabethan poets) and his unhappiness at having lost her favor. The poem is mentioned in print for the first time by Spenser, in his *Colin Clout's Come Home Again* (1595), but Raleigh had already read it, or some part of it, to Spenser in or about 1589, when they were in Ireland. Exactly when it was composed is not known. It was long thought to be lost, but a portion of it was discovered, and printed for the first time in 1870, by John Hannah the younger, archdeacon of Lewes, in his volume *The Courtly Poets from Raleigh to Montrose* (later published as *Poems of Sir Walter Raleigh and Other Courtly Poets*, 1875 and 1892). Hannah thought that it was composed when Raleigh was a prisoner in the Tower of London under James I, but evidence indicates that the discovered fragment goes back to the earlier poem. It was Spenser's habit to call Raleigh "the Ocean" or "the Shepherd of the Ocean," a manner of address that Raleigh himself adopted, so that an-

d̜, d or j; s̜, s or sh; t̜, t or ch; z̜, z or zh; o, F. cloche; ü, F. menu; ch̟, Sc. loch; n̟, F. bonbon.

other name by which this poem is called, *The Ocean to Cynthia*, simply means Raleigh to Queen Elizabeth.

Cynwulf (kin'wŭlf). See **Cynewulf.**

Cypria (sip'ri.ạ). [Also, **Cyprian Lays.**] One of the poems of the Trojan cycle, anciently attributed to Homer, and later to Stasinus, or Hegesias, or Hegesinus. It was so named either in reference to the home of the author (Cyprus), or because it celebrated the Cyprian Aphrodite. It served as an introduction to the *Iliad*, relating the first nine years of the siege of Troy.

Cyprian (sip'ri.ạn), Saint. [Full Latin name, **Thascius Caecilius Cyprianus.**] b. c200; beheaded at Carthage, Sept. 14, 258. A Christian church father, bishop, and martyr. Nothing is known of his early life, but he was a man of education and of considerable wealth when in middle age (according to tradition, in 246) he was converted to Christianity, became a priest, and in 248 was made bishop of Carthage. During the persecutions begun by Decius in 250, many Christians apostatized; subsequently some bishops took an unforgiving attitude toward the backsliders, but Cyprian, like Pope Calixtus I, urged a more compassionate course. He gave most of his income to the poor, worked ardently for church unity, and wrote much on theological matters in an elegant style (his works were edited at Rome in 1471, and several times since). He was greatly influenced by Tertullian, and in turn he influenced later theologians, including Saint Augustine. He suffered martyrdom, being beheaded during the persecution begun by Valerian.

Cyrano de Bergerac (sē.rȧ.nō dẹ ber.zhẹ.rȧk; Anglicized, sir'ạ.nō dẹ bėr'zhẹ.räk). A play by Edmond Rostand, first produced in 1897. The character of the hero is modeled upon that of a historic original, but is sketched by the dramatist in superlative. He is depicted as extraordinarily brave, extravagantly lavish, superbly indifferent to patronage, extremely ugly (owing to his very large nose), and loyally self-sacrificing in his love for his cousin Roxane. The events of the play are, however, substantially those which are reported to have befallen the original Cyrano. The elder Coquelin (supported by Sarah Bernhardt as Roxane) originally played the part of Cyrano in French. Richard Mansfield, Walter Hampden, and (most recently) José Ferrer are among the well-known actors who have played it in English.

Cyrenaics (sī.rẹ.nā'iks). A school of Greek hedonistic philosophers, founded by Aristippus of Cyrene, a disciple of Socrates.

Cyrus (sī'rus). [Called **Cyrus the Great**; name in the Old Testament, **Koresh**; in the cuneiform inscriptions, **Kurush, Kurshu**; Old Persian, **Kurush.**] d. 529 B.C. Founder of the Persian Empire. All accounts of his birth and early youth are heavily encrusted by various legends.

Cyrus Choke (chōk), **General.** See **Choke, General Cyrus.**

Cytherea (sith.ẹ.rē'ạ) or **Cythera** (si.thir'ạ). In classical mythology, surnames of Aphrodite, from the island of Cythera, or from a place of the same name which once existed in Crete.

Cythna (sith'nạ). A character in Shelley's poem *The Revolt of Islam.*

Cyveiliog (ku.vä'lyog), **Owain.** See **Owain Cyveiliog.**

D

Dacier (dȧ'si.ėr), **the Honourable Percy.** In George Meredith's novel *Diana of the Crossways*, an ambitious young politician who loves Diana until he finds that she has betrayed a government secret to the editor of a newspaper.

dactyl or **dactyle** (dak'til). 1. A unit of linear measure; a finger-breadth; a digit: used in reference to Greek, Egyptian, and Babylonian measures. The Egyptian dactyl was precisely one fourth of a palm, and was equal to 0.74 inch, or 18.7 millimeters. The Babylonian and Assyrian dactyls are by some authors considered as the fifth part, by others as the sixth part, of the corresponding palms. The ordinary Greek dactyl was one fourth of a palm, and its value in Athens is variously calculated to be from 1.85 to 1.93 centimeters. 2. In prosody, a foot of three syllables, the first long, the second and third short. The dactyl appears to have been so called because, like a finger (from a Greek word meaning which it is derived), it consists of one long and two short members. The dactyl of modern or accentual versification is simply an accented syllable followed by two which are unaccented, and is accounted a dactyl without regard to the relative time taken in pronouncing the several syllables. Thus, the words *cheerily, verily, violate,* and *edify,* which on the principles of ancient metrics would be called respectively a dactyl (– ◡ ◡), a tribrach (◡ ◡ ◡), a Cretic (– ◡ –), and an anapest (◡ ◡ –), are all alike regarded as dactyls. The quantitative dactyl of Greek and Latin poetry is tetrasemic—that is, has a magnitude of four morae; and as two of these constitute the thesis (in the Greek sense) and two the arsis, the dactyl, like its inverse, the anapest (◡ ◡ –́), belongs to the equal (isorrhythmic) class of feet. The true or normal dactyl has the ictus or metrical stress on the first syllable (–́ ◡ ◡). Its most frequent equivalent or substitute is the dactylic spondee (–́ –), in which the two short times are contracted into one long. Resolution of the long syllable (◡́ ◡ ◡ ◡) is rare.

If ye vse too many dactils together ye make your musike too light and of no solemne grauitie, such as the amorous Elegies in court naturally require. (Puttenham, *Arte of Eng. Poesie.*)

From long to long in solemn sort
Slōw spōndēē stālks; strōng fŏŏt! yet ill able
Ēvĕr tŏ cōme ŭp wĭth Dăctyl trĭsў̆llăblĕ.
(Coleridge, *Metrical Feet.*)

Daedalus (dĕd′ạ.lus, dē′dạ.lus). In Greek legend, an Athenian regarded as the personification of all handicrafts and of art, and as such worshiped by artists' guilds in various places, especially in Attica, and becoming a central figure in various myths. He was said to have made various improvements in the fine arts, including architecture, and to have invented many mechanical appliances, as the ax, the awl, and the bevel. For the murder of his nephew Talus, of whose inventive skill he was jealous, he was driven to Crete, where he constructed, to contain the monster Minotaur, the famous labyrinth, in which he, with his son Icarus, was confined for furnishing the clue of it to Ariadne. (In another legend a different account of his imprisonment is given: he built a cow disguise for Pasiphaë in order that the bull sent by Poseidon might mount her.) Escaping, he and Icarus fled over the sea on wings of wax which they had made. Icarus soared too near the sun, his wings melted, and he fell into the sea (which has since been called, from him, the Icarian Sea). Many archaic wooden images were, in ancient times, believed to be the work of Daedalus (and figures of the type are still called Daedalian).

Daffodil Fields, The. A narrative poem (1913) by John Masefield.

Dagon (dā′gon). In the Old Testament, a deity mentioned as the national god of the Philistines, and as worshiped especially in Gaza and Ashdod (Judges, xvi. 23, and 1 Sam. v.). The name is usually derived from Hebrew *dag* (fish), and it is assumed that Dagon was depicted as half man and half fish, and had his female counterpart in Derketo, who was worshiped in Ashkelon (Ascalon). 1 Sam. v. 4 would seem to favor this view. On the other hand, Assyro-Babylonian mythology also includes a divinity Dagan, but there he is, etymologically at least, not connected with the fish, as the Assyrian word for fish is not *dag* but *nun;* the meaning of the name Dagan has not as yet been determined, but may be connected with the word for grain. At the same time the Babylonian historian Berossus gives an account of such a being, half man and half fish, under the name Oannes, who in the beginning of history emerged at intervals from the sea and taught the Babylonians the arts of civilization. This Oannes of Berossus is identified by some scholars with Ea of the Assyro-Babylonian pantheon, the god of the ocean, and is conceived as a human figure with the skin of a fish on his shoulders as a garment, a representation of which is often met on the early monuments. In Phoenicia the name of the god was connected with *dagan* (corn) and is accordingly rendered into Greek in the fragments of Philo Byblius as *sitos* (grain). Dagon was then considered as the god of agriculture, a function which is also emphasized in the Oannes of Berossus.

Dagonet (dag′ọ.net). Pseudonym of **Sims, George Robert.**

Dagonet, Sir. [Also, **Sir Daguenet** (dag′ẹ.net).] In Arthurian romances, the fool of King Arthur, who "loved him passing well and made him knight with his own hands." He was buffeted and knocked about a good deal, and is frequently alluded to by the dramatists of Shakespeare's time and later.

Daguerre (dà.ger), **Louis Jacques Mandé.** b. at Cormeilles, Seine-et-Oise, France, Nov. 18, 1789; d. at Petit-Brie-sur-Marne, France, July 12, 1851. A French painter, and inventor (with Joseph Nicéphore Niepce) of the daguerreotype process of photography. He was at first in the internal revenue service, then devoted himself to scene painting, in which he attained celebrity, and in 1822, with Charles Marie Bouton, opened the Diorama (a theater containing painted scenes viewed through openings and so arranged that the light shone through them, giving the illusion of reality) at Paris (burned 1839). In the successful study of the problem of obtaining permanent pictures by the action of sunlight he was anticipated by Nicéphore Niepce, who began his investigations in 1814, and communicated some of his results to Daguerre, who was then occupied with the subject, in 1826; the two worked together from 1829 until Niepce's death in 1833. Daguerre's perfected process was communicated to the Academy of Sciences by Dominique François Arago, Jan. 9, 1839. The daguerreotype was made by exposure to light of a silver plate coated with silver iodide, development in mercury vapor, and fixation with sodium thiosulfate (hypo). In return for pensions granted to Daguerre and Niepce's heir, the process was detailed to the Academy and a description published by the French government.

Daily Courant (ku.rant′), **The.** The first successful British daily paper. It was begun on March 11, 1702, and ceased publication in 1735.

Dain (dān), **Oliver le.** See Oliver le Dain.

Dainty (dān′ti), **Lady.** A fashionable, frivolous, fine lady in Colley Cibber's comedy *The Double Gallant:* "Dogs, doctors, and monkeys are her favorites." She is courted by Careless.

Dairyman's Daughter. A religious tract by Legh Richmond included in *Annals of the Poor* (1814).

Daisy (dā′zi), **Solomon.** A bell ringer of Chigwell, near London, in Charles Dickens's *Barnaby Rudge,* a rusty little fellow who seems all eyes.

Daisy Miller (dā′zi mil′ẽr). [Full title, **Daisy Miller: A Study.**] A novel by Henry James, published in 1878. Daisy Miller is a frank and innocent American girl who, by her unconventional conduct, alienates the American colony in Rome. The only person in the story sympathetic to her is the young American, Winterbourne, who has lived in Europe for many years, and who understands its customs and prejudices. He falls in love with her in a very quiet way, never declaring himself, but trying to warn her that her conduct is considered scandalous in Rome. He comes to the positive realization that she is completely innocent only after she dies of a fever caught when viewing the Colosseum at midnight.

Dakers (dā′kẽrz), **Jonathan.** An idealistic physician, the hero of Francis Brett Young's novel *My Brother Jonathan* (1928).

Dalai Lama (dä.lī′ lä′mạ). The title of the temporal and spiritual ruler of Tibet, whose seat is at Lhasa. He is supposed to be a reincarnation of the Mahayana Buddhist deity Avalokiteshvara. The manner of his selection in each new physical incarnation is, by Western standards, extremely

---

ḍ, d or j; ṣ, s or sh; ṭ, t or ch; ẓ, z or zh; o, F. cloche; ü, F. menu; c̓h, Sc. loch; ṅ, F. bonbon.

curious: he is born, in a manner of speaking (a Tibetan would say that he becomes incarnate), at the precise moment of the death of his predecessor. This means that after the death of a reigning Dalai Lama a considerable search is instituted to determine the whereabouts of a child who can be ascertained to have been born at exactly the moment the former ceased to live. The search is oftentimes lengthy, during which period Tibet is governed by a priestly junta (which also ordinarily serves as a regency during the minority of each new Dalai Lama). Moreover, from the standpoint of a Tibetan, the child thus found cannot properly be called a "new" Dalai Lama; this will be obvious when the reader recalls that the Dalai Lama is, by definition, a reincarnation of Avalokiteshvara, who may therefore be said to have had an uninterrupted existence in various incarnations (14, to date). From this point of view, there is never a "new" Dalai Lama, but only a new incarnation; as one incarnation "dies" the new one instantly begins to "live" (whence the importance of determining the exact moment of birth).

Dalberg-Acton (dôl'bèrg.ak't͝on), **John Emerich Edward.** See **Acton,** Lord.

Dale (dāl), **Laetitia.** In George Meredith's novel *The Egoist*, one of the principal female characters. She eventually marries Sir Willoughby.

Dale, Lily. The heroine of Anthony Trollope's novel *The Small House at Allington*.

Dalgarno (dal.gär'nō), **Lord.** A malevolent young man in Sir Walter Scott's *Fortunes of Nigel*. He is the secret enemy of Nigel and the favorite of Prince Charles. Having heartlessly betrayed the Lady Hermione, he is compelled by the king to do her justice. After leaving court in disguise, he is murdered.

Dalgetty (dal.get'i), **Captain Dugald.** A soldier of fortune in Sir Walter Scott's *Legend of Montrose*. He had been a divinity student in his youth, and became a mercenary. He was courageous, and not untrustworthy if well paid. The original is said to have been a man named Munro who belonged to a band of Scotch and English auxiliaries in Swinemünde (1630).

Dalida (dal'i.d͝a). The Delilah of the Book of Judges is found as Dalila in the Vulgate, but is Dalida in Chaucer, and Dalida is the form used in Wycliffe's Bible. Chaucer speaks of her in *The Monk's Tale* and in *The Book of the Duchess*.

Dallas (dal'͝as), **Robert Charles.** b. at Kingston, Jamaica, British West Indies, 1754; d. at Ste.-Adresse, in Normandy, France, Nov. 20, 1824. A British author. He was educated in England, returned, on coming of age, to Jamaica in the West Indies to take possession of the estates left him by his father, and eventually settled in England. He is noted chiefly for his intimacy with Byron, to whom he gave literary advice, and for whom he acted as agent in dealings with publishers. He wrote *Recollections of the Life of Lord Byron from the year 1808 to the end of 1814*, which was edited by his son, A. R. C. Dallas.

Dalton (dôl't͝on), **John.** b. probably at Dean, Cumberland, England, 1709; d. at Worcester, England, July 22, 1763. An English poet and divine.

He was graduated (B.A., 1730; M.A., 1734) from Oxford, appointed a canon of Worcester cathedral in 1748, and about the same time obtained the rectory of Saint Mary-at-Hill, London. His most notable work is an adaptation of Milton's *Comus* for the stage, published in 1738 under the title *Comus, a Mask, now adopted to the Stage, as altered from Milton's Mask*.

D'Alvarez (dal'v͝a.rez). In James Shirley's *The Cardinal*, a nobleman in love with the Duchess Rosaura.

Dame du Lac (dàm dü làk). See **Lady of the Lake**.

Dame Durden (dām dèr'd͝en). See **Durden, Dame**.

Dame Partlet (pärt'l͝et). See **Pertelote**.

Dame Sirith (sir'ith). [Also, **Dame Sirth** (sèrth).] A Middle English fabliau, written c1275, and notable as the only true fabliau in English before Chaucer. Dame Sirith is an old bawd who is importuned by a clerk, Wilekin, who has been disappointed in his love for Margeri, a young wife. Sirith takes her dog, rubs something in its eyes to make it cry, and then tells Margeri that the dog is actually her daughter, who has been turned into a bitch because she (the daughter) refused the advances of a clerk. Margeri is terrified, and accepts the clerk as her lover.

Damian (dā'mi.͝an). A young squire in Sir Walter Scott's novel *Ivanhoe*, an aspirant for the holy Order of Templars.

Damian. A young nobleman who falls in love with the heroine in Sir Walter Scott's novel *The Betrothal*.

Damian. See also under **Merchant's Tale, The**.

Damien (d͝a.myaṅ; Anglicized, dā'mi.͝en), **Father.** [Original name, **Joseph de Veuster.**] b. at Tremeloo, Belgium, Jan. 3, 1840; d. on the island of Molokai, Hawaii, April 15, 1888. A Roman Catholic missionary who devoted his life (from 1873) to the welfare of the lepers in the leper colony on the island of Molokai, Hawaii. He himself contracted leprosy in 1885. Certain allegations against Father Damien by a minister evoked Robert Louis Stevenson's *An Open Letter to the Rev. Dr. Hyde* (1890).

Damiens (d͝a.myaṅ), **Robert François.** b. near Arras, France, 1715; executed at Paris, March 28, 1757. A French assassin who made an unsuccessful attempt upon the life of Louis XV, on Jan. 5, 1757. Damiens approached the king at Versailles, as he was entering his carriage, and succeeded in stabbing him. In punishment for this deed, his right hand was burned in a slow fire; his flesh was torn with pincers and burned with melted lead, the while he was chained to a steel frame over a hot fire (whence the allusion by Goldsmith to "Damiens' bed"); resin, wax, and oil were poured upon the wounds; and he was torn to pieces by four horses.

Damiotti (dam.i.ot'i; Italian, dä.myôt't͝e), **Dr.** An Italian charlatan who exhibits the magic mirror in Sir Walter Scott's short novel *Aunt Margaret's Mirror*.

Damocles (dam'͝ō.klēz). fl. in the first half of the 4th century B.C. A Syracusan, a courtier of Dionysius the elder. Cicero relates that Damocles, having extolled the good fortune of Dionysius, was invited by the tyrant to taste this royal felicity, and that, in the midst of a splendid banquet and all the luxury of the court, on looking up he beheld above his head a sword suspended by a single horse-hair.

Damoetas (da.mē'tas). A herdsman in Theocritus and Vergil; hence, in pastoral poetry, a rustic. Sir Philip Sidney introduces in his *Arcadia* a foolish country clown by that name, which afterward seems to have become proverbial for folly.

Damon (dā.mon). A goatherd in Vergil's *Eclogues;* hence, in pastoral poetry, a rustic.

Damon and Musidora (mū.si.dō'ra). Two lovers in James Thomson's *Summer* (1727), a section of *Seasons.*

Damon and Phillida (fil'i.da). A pastoral ballad opera by Colley Cibber, produced and published in 1729. Another edition in 1730 has the subtitle *The Rover Reclaim'd,* and differs widely in text.

Damon and Pythias (pith'i.as). fl. in the first half of the 4th century B.C. Two Pythagorean philosophers of Syracuse, celebrated for their friendship. Pythias (or Phintias) plotted against the life of Dionysius I of Syracuse, and was condemned to die. As Pythias wished to arrange his affairs, Damon offered to place himself in the tyrant's hands as his substitute, and to die in his stead should he not return on the appointed day. At the last moment Pythias came back, and Dionysius was so struck by the fidelity of the friends that he pardoned the offender, and begged to be admitted into their fellowship.

Damon and Pythias (or **Pithias**) (pith'i.as). A play in verse by Richard Edwards, printed in 1571, but earlier (1564) performed before Queen Elizabeth. It celebrates the famous friendship. Its main subject is tragic, but it was nominally a comedy.

Damon and Pythias. A tragedy by John Banim and Richard Lalor Sheil, produced in 1821.

Dampier (dam'pir), **William.** b. at East Coker, Somersetshire, England, probably in June, 1652; d. at London, in March, 1715. An English freebooter, explorer, and author. His seafaring life began in 1668, and until 1691 he led a life of the wildest adventure, as manager of a Jamaica plantation, as a logwood cutter in Mexico, but generally as a sailor on various piratical cruises, especially against the Spanish colonies on the western coast of America and elsewhere.

Damply (dam'pli), **Widow.** A character in David Garrick's play *The Male Coquette.*

D'Amville (dam'vil). The villain of Cyril Tourneur's *The Atheist's Tragedy.* He believes that Nature alone rules the universe, that there is no supreme judgment of God, and that one's own descendants comprise the extent of human immortality. In seeking to endow and secure his issue, however, he finds his plots frustrated by the sickness and lust of his two sons and the return of the noble Charlemont, who patiently waits until judgment is rendered against D'Amville. At the end D'Amville is forced to recognize that there is a power above nature and that he has consigned himself to his own doom by denying it.

Dan (dan). [Older name, **Laish.**] In Biblical geography, a city situated on the slopes of Mount Hermon, not far from the modern Baniyas (still called Tel-el-Kadi, "hill of the Judge"), and often mentioned in the Old Testament as the most northern landmark of Palestine, in the formula "from Dan to Beersheba." It was named Dan after its capture by the Danites. It contained a sanctuary with an image the exact nature of which is not known. At the division of the kingdom Jeroboam put up there one of the golden calves worshiped at that time. It is first mentioned in Gen. xiv. 14 as the place at which Chedorlaomer, king of Elam, and his four allies were overthrown and defeated by Abraham. The occurrence in this account of the name which was given to the place many centuries later is variously explained. If the Dan of Gen. xiv. is identical with that of Judges, xviii., and if the account of Gen. xiv. is authentic, the name Dan may have been later inserted in the manuscripts for Laish, when the latter was superseded by the former.

Danaë (dan'a.ē). In Greek mythology, the daughter of Acrisius of Argos and mother of Perseus by Zeus, who visited her, while she was shut up in a brazen tower by her father, in the form of a shower of gold. She was shut up with her child in a chest, thrown into the sea, and carried by the waves to the island of Seriphos. From various difficulties she was in the end rescued by Perseus and brought back to Greece.

Danaïdes (da.nā'i.dēz). In Greek legend, the 50 daughters of Danaus, by whose command they slew their husbands. According to later writers, they were condemned in Hades to pour water into sieves.

Dance of Death. [Also, **Dance of Macaber;** French, **Danse Macabre;** Latin, **Chorea Machabaeorum.**] Originally, a kind of morality or allegorical representation intended to remind the living of the power of death. It originated in the 14th century in Germany, and consisted of dialogues between Death and a number of typical followers, which were acted in or near churches by the religious orders. Soon after, it was repeated in France. It became extraordinarily popular, and was treated in every possible way, in pictures, bas-reliefs, tapestry, and other forms. Death is made grotesque and a sort of "horrid Harlequin," a skeleton dancer or musician playing for dancing, leading all mankind. A dramatic poem which grew out of this was imitated in Spain in 1400 as *La Danza general de los muertos.* In 1425 the French, having illustrated each verse, had the whole series painted on the wall of the churchyard of the Monastery of the Innocents, where they acted the drama. In 1430 the poem and pictures were produced at London, and not long after at Salisbury (1460), Wortley Hall in Gloucestershire, and other places. In Germany it attained its greatest popularity. The drama was acted until about the middle of the 15th century, when the pictures became the main point of interest. A picture of this kind was painted in the Marienkirche at Lübeck, Germany, and one was on the cloister wall of Klingenthal, a convent at Basel, Switzerland, both of the 14th century; the latter disappeared in 1805. One in the Campo Santo at Pisa has been ascribed to Orcagna. In the reign of Henry VII a processional Dance of Death was painted around the cloisters of old Saint Paul's at London. The younger Hans Holbein left 53 sketches for engraving; these he called *Imagines Mortis;* they are, however, independent, and do not represent a dance. Lydgate wrote a metrical translation of the poem for the chapter of Saint Paul's, to be placed under the pictures in the cloister. Various explanations of the name Macaber or Macabre have been given.

Dance of Death, The. A satirical drama in verse (1933) by Wystan Hugh Auden. The theme of the play, as stated by an announcer at the opening, is the decline and the final death of the British middle class. The unusual nature of the work may be suggested by the fact that it closes with an announcement, made by Karl Marx, that the death has taken place.

Dance of Life, The. A philosophical prose work (1923) by Havelock Ellis. The highly original theme of the work, regarded as his most popular one, is that life and art are identical, and that life, when it reaches its highest development, comes closest to resembling the art of dancing. Dancing, thinking, writing, religion, and morals, all parts of the "dance," are taken up in separate chapters. The idealistic conclusion is the author's belief, or hope, that the world will be saved when man, through his aesthetic impulse, discovers the secret of finding pleasure and enjoyment in things without actually owning or possessing them.

Dance of Macabre. A short didactic poem by John Lydgate. It is in 24 quatrains and was written to accompany illustrations. It was printed in 1554, at the end of Tottell's edition of Lydgate's *Falls of Princes,* in 1658 in Dugdale's *St. Paul's,* and in 1794 in the Douce edition of the younger Hans Holbein's *Dance of Death* woodcuts. It was also published in 1846 in Holbein's *Alphabet of Death,* edited by the French scholar Montaiglon. One of his minor works, it has suffered the fate of virtually all Lydgate's poetry, long or short: it is no longer read.

"Dancing Chancellor," the. See **Hatton, Sir Christopher.**

Dandelion Days. An autobiographical novel by Henry Williamson, published in 1922. It is the second volume of a tetralogy under the general title *The Flax of Dream.*

Dandie Dinmont (dan'di din'mont, -mǫnt). See **Dinmont, Dandie.**

Dane (dān), **Clemence.** [Pseudonym of **Winifred Ashton.**] An English novelist and playwright. Her novels include *Regiment of Women* (1917), *Legend* (1919), *Wandering Stars* (1924), *The Babyons* (1928), *Broome Stages* (1931), *The Moon Is Feminine* (1938), *The Arrogant History of White Ben* (1939), and *He Brings Great News* (1946); her plays, *A Bill of Divorcement* (1921), *Will Shakespeare* (1921), *The Way Things Happen* (1923), *Naboth's Vineyard* (1925), *Granite* (1926), *Mariners* (1926), *Moonlight Is Silver* (1934), *Cousin Muriel* (1940), and *Call Home the Heart* (1947); her essays, *The Women's Side* (1927) and *Tradition and Hugh Walpole* (1930). She edited the anthologies *The Shelter Book* (1939) and *The Nelson Touch* (1942).

Dane, Mrs. The wayward heroine of Henry Arthur Jones's problem play *Mrs. Dane's Defence* (1900). Mrs. Dane, a woman with a past, wishes to marry young Carteret, but under a merciless cross-examination by her foster father, Sir Daniel, she is forced to confess to an affair she had on the Continent. Like another unfortunate heroine of modern drama, Pinero's Paula Tanqueray, she finds out, too late, that a woman cannot live down her past.

Danegeld (dān'geld). An English land tax during the late 10th and until the middle 12th century, originally levied to appease Danish raiders. Unable effectively to protect England against the plundering and ravaging Danes, Norwegians, and Swedes, King Ethelred II bought them off by paying tribute money, raised by taxation on land, in 991 and on four other occasions up to 1012. With the accession (1016) of the Danish King Canute to the English throne, the tax was no longer needed for its original purpose, but the name continued to be applied to taxes levied from time to time for purposes of defense. In the reign of Edward the Confessor the Danegeld fell into disuse, but William the Conqueror seized upon it as a means of raising revenue, and it was partly to facilitate this levy that the Domesday Book came into existence. Under the Norman regime taxes continued to be raised under the name of Danegeld until 1163, after which the designation disappears from the records. Even before the first English payment of Danegeld, similar means were sometimes used to buy off Danish raiders in France.

Danelaw (dān'lô). [Also: **Danelage, Danelagh;** Old English, **Dena lagu.**] That part of England where the Danish influence was paramount during the 9th and 10th centuries. It corresponded to the modern counties of Yorkshire, Lincolnshire, Nottinghamshire, Derbyshire, Leicestershire, Rutlandshire, Norfolk, Suffolk, Essex, Cambridgeshire, Huntingdonshire, Northamptonshire, Buckinghamshire, Bedfordshire, and Hertfordshire.

Dangerfield (dān'jėr.fēld), **Captain.** A bewhiskered, swaggering bully in Sir Walter Scott's novel *Peveril of the Peak.* He is one of Titus Oates's spying agents on behalf of the Popish Plot.

Dangle (dang'gl). An amateur critic, in Richard Brinsley Sheridan's farce *The Critic,* whose peculiarities are agreeably described by his wife in the first scene; supposed to be a satire on Thomas Vaughan, a playwright.

Daniel (dan'yẹl). The last of a series of three Old English poems attributed to the "school of Caedmon" (*Genesis, Exodus,* and *Daniel*), found in the Junius Manuscript. It is a versified version of some of the sections of the Biblical book of Daniel. The present manuscript consists of two separate poems joined together. Lines 1–278 and 362–764 are from an earlier poem, and the intervening lines (279–361) from a later work.

Daniel, Samuel. b. near Taunton, Somersetshire, England, 1562; d. at Beckington, Wiltshire, England, Oct. 14, 1619. An English poet and dramatist. He was educated at Oxford and was for a time tutor to William Herbert, a nephew of Sir Philip Sidney. In 1592 he issued a volume containing *Delia,* one of the first of the Elizabethan sonnet sequences and his best-known work, and *The Complaint of Rosamond,* a narrative poem. *Cleopatra* (1594) was an attempt at Senecan tragedy, as was

Philotas (1605). His poem *Musophilis, or A General Defence of Learning* (1599) upholds poetry as part of the background of the courtier or the warrior. He wrote a *Defense of Rime* (1603) in answer to Thomas Campion's attack on English rhyme in *Observations on the Art of English Poesie* (1602). In 1595 he issued *The Civil Warres between the Two Houses of Lancaster and York* in four books, a verse history expanded in 1609 to eight books but left even then still incomplete. Between 1612 and 1617 he wrote a prose history of England. For a short period in 1599 he is said to have been poet laureate, but to have resigned the post in Ben Jonson's favor. He was appointed (1603) master of the revels and between 1604 and 1615, when he seems to have retired to his Wiltshire farm, he worked at turning out court masques. His complete works, edited by A. B. Grosart, were published in five volumes (1885–96).

Daniel come to judgment. In Shakespeare's *Merchant of Venice* (IV.i), a reference to Portia (as a lawyer) by Shylock, which is later echoed sarcastically by Gratiano when the trial is going against Shylock.

Daniel Deronda (dĕ.ron'dȧ). A novel by George Eliot. It appeared in eight monthly parts, beginning in February, 1876, and as a whole in 1877. The book unfolds the author's conceptions of social growth, the strength of tradition, and the impelling force of nationality. The force of Daniel's noble character guides the unfortunate and self-centered Gwendolen Harleth away from immediate disaster when she is driven to the contemplation of the murder of her selfish and brutal husband, Grandcourt. However, when Grandcourt meets his death through accident (by drowning), Gwendolen is unable not to feel partly guilty (completely innocent though she is, she cannot forget that she once had wished him dead), and she now relies on Daniel more than ever. Meanwhile Daniel, whose parentage had always been a mystery to him, finds that he is of Jewish origin and decides to devote his life to the establishment of a national center for the Jewish people. He also now determines to marry Mirah, the sister of a great-hearted Jewish friend, Mordecai. This decision at first causes Gwendolen to despair (for she has hoped, now she is free, that Daniel may marry her), but she gradually grows resigned to the situation.

Daniel Dravot (drav'ŏt). See **Dravot, Daniel.**

Dannisburgh (dan'iz.bur.ọ, -brọ; danz'-), **Lord.** In George Meredith's novel *Diana of the Crossways,* a great and powerful statesman, supposedly based on the historical figure of Lord Melbourne.

Danny; The Story of a Dandie Dinmont (dan'i). A long and sentimental tale about a dog, by Alfred Ollivant, published in 1902.

Dan Peggotty (dan peg'ọ.ti). See **Peggotty, Dan.**

Dan Russel (dan rus'ẹl). The Fox in Chaucer's *Nuns's Priest's Tale.*

Dante (dan'tē; Italian, dän'tä). [Full name, **Dante Alighieri**; original prename, **Durante.**] b. at Florence, in May, 1265; d. at Ravenna, Italy, Sept. 14, 1321. An Italian poet, generally considered to be the supreme example of integral Christian humanism. In his Latin letters he gives his name variously

as Dantes Alagherius and Dantes Alagherii. His family can be traced back to Adamo of Florence, the father of Cacciaguida who is mentioned in *Paradiso* (xv., 139–144) as having been killed during the second Crusade in 1147. Dante's first meeting with Beatrice Portinari, who was to become the object of his "courtly," artistic, ideal, moral, spiritual, and symbolic love and the source of his poetic inspiration, can be dated as May 1, 1274. His elementary education was entrusted to a professional teacher named Romano; but Dante attributes his higher intellectual inspiration to Brunetto Latini. Dante tells us in the *Convivio* that he spent three years in the "schools of the friars (*religiosi*) and the disputations of the philosophers." It was, however, to his lifelong habit of insatiable reading in the ancient classics, patristic writings, contemporary poets and chroniclers, and scholastic philosophers and theologians that he owed the extraordinarily wide knowledge that is revealed in his works. His first extant sonnet in honor of Beatrice was written in 1283, and published in his first work, the *Vita Nuova,* c1292. Shortly after the death of Beatrice in 1290, Dante married Gemma Donati, to whom he had been betrothed as a boy in 1277. Gemma was the mother of Dante's four children, Peter, James, John, and Antonia, the first two of whom wrote commentaries on the *Divina Commedia;* the last became a nun in Ravenna with the name Sister Beatrice. As a young man Dante was trained as a soldier and took part in the battle of Campaldino in 1289. In 1295 he began to play an active role in Florentine political life. The documents show that he took a firm stand against any outside, including papal, interference in the city government. His patriotism was rewarded in 1300 by his election to the highest political office in Florence. It was in this office, as *Priore,* that he was called upon to banish one of his dearest friends, Guido Cavalcanti, in an effort to curb the factious political rivalry of the Neri (the Blacks, the Guelph faction of the ancient nobility) and Bianchi (the Whites, the Guelph faction of the newly rich banking and commercial bourgeoisie). Shortly after his tenure of office he went to Rome to make the pilgrimage of the Holy Year of Jubilee proclaimed by Pope Boniface VIII. It seems to have been this experience of visiting the center of Christendom and the "capital of the world" that filled Dante with the vision of humanity in history and in eternal life which is the subject matter of the *Divina Commedia* (*The Divine Comedy*). During Dante's absence from Florence on an embassy to Pope Boniface VIII in 1301, the party of the Neri, aided by Charles de Valois, destroyed the property of the Bianchi, and Dante himself was condemned to exile in 1302. His resentment at this betrayal by his beloved but stony-hearted city is reflected in the passionate mood of the Pietra sonnets. Having failed, even with Ghibelline help, to change the situation in Florence, Dante decided to become a "party all by himself." His travels throughout Italy, where he found no less than 14 dialects, suggested to him a philosophico-philological work on "courtly" vernacular diction, *De vulgari eloquentia.* His philosophical reading and reflection prompted him to write the Banquet (*Convivio*) of ethical essays in which he hoped to discuss in detail the Aristotelian-Thomistic description of the 14 moral virtues. In 1307 he left both works unfinished, and appears to have gone for a period of study in the University of Paris. The crowning of Henry VII (Henry of Luxembourg) as emperor of the Romans in 1312 kindled once more Dante's hope of seeing realized a world society under the triple universal authority of law, truth, and grace, organized by the efforts of the emperor (*imperium*), the university (*studium*), and the Pope (*Sacerdotium*), and renewing the highest traditions of Rome, Athens, and Jerusalem in the spheres of civilization, culture, and religion. Dante hastily returned to Italy; but when Henry died in 1313, all Dante could do was to set forth a theory of proper Church-State relationships in his *Monarchia*, just as he had already given his theory of the relationship of imperial power to philosophical authority in Book IV of the *Convivio*. The years after 1314 were filled with the completion of the *Divina Commedia*. He interrupted the work in 1319 to conduct a correspondence in the form of *Eclogae* in Latin verses which are as classical in form as they are poetical in inspiration. On Jan. 20, 1320, in the presence of the lord of Verona Can Francesco della Scala (the Can Grande who patronized the arts and was, especially, Dante's protector) and of high ecclesiastical authorities, in the Chapel of Saint Helen, he formally defended, in Scholastic Latin, a *Quaestio de Aqua et Terra* in order to establish his position as an authorized teacher. An embassy to Venice undermined his health and he died on Sept. 14, 1321. The most authentic painting of Dante is that by his friend Giotto, still to be seen on a wall in the Bargello museum at Florence. However, the bust by Vincenzo Vela, based on the scientific examination of Dante's skull by Fabio Frassetto in 1921, is a trustworthy indication of the poet's appearance. The so-called "death-masks" have no authentic value. The bibliography on Dante's period, life, and works is immense.

Dante's Influence on English Literature. In Chaucer's *House of Fame, Parliament of Fowls,* and *Legend of Good Women* there are many echoes of Dante and some passages directly translated. Similar fragments are embedded in the works of Milton and other English poets. But of greater importance was Dante's example of the use of the vernacular tongue with the dignity and elevation of the ancient, learned languages; it is thought that Dante was Chaucer's chief inspiration to tell the story of Troilus and Cressida in English. The first translation of the *Inferno* into English was by Rogers in 1782. In 1802, Henry Boyd translated the entire *Commedia* into six-line stanzas, but the first adequate rendering was in blank verse by H. F. Cary in 1814. This was followed by translations by Pollock, Plumptre, Hazelfoot, J. A. Carlyle, C. E. Norton, and H. F. Tozer. Maria Rossetti wrote one of many English studies of Dante, "Shadow of Dante," and Dante Gabriel Rossetti translated the *Vita Nuova*.

Dante. A prose criticism (1929) by T. S. Eliot. It is an essay in appreciation and is intended to serve as an introduction to the work of the Italian poet. It was well received and did much to strengthen Eliot's already strong position as a critic. Eliot had discussed Dante, and other authors, in an earlier volume, *The Sacred Wood* (1921).

Danton (dän.tôn), **Georges Jacques.** b. at Arcis-sur-Aube, France, Oct. 28, 1759; guillotined at Paris, April 5, 1794. A French politician, one of the foremost leaders of the French Revolution. He was a lawyer and president of the Cordeliers (a political club which called for drastic reform of the French government). He took part, perhaps as organizer, in the attack (Aug. 10, 1792) on the Tuileries, when the king and queen, Louis XVI and Marie Antoinette, were captured and imprisoned. Soon after, the monarchy was abolished and Danton became minister of justice in the republican government. He was implicated in the "September massacres" of prisoners of the Revolution at a time when it seemed that foreign enemies would march into Paris. In September, 1792, he became a member of the National Convention, where he sat on the "Mountain," the high seats where the Jacobins, the Cordeliers, and the Hébertists sat, near such men as Marat and Robespierre. He was one of those voting (January, 1793) for the death of the king. In March, he was made president of the Jacobins, and he moved the formation of the Revolutionary tribunal. He was one of the nine members, from April to September, 1793, of the Committee of Public Safety. Recognizing that the struggle between the Girondists (the moderates who were slowly swinging towards royalism) and the Jacobins might cause the Revolution to fail, and in view of military reverses, he joined in the purge (June 2, 1793) of the Girondists from the Convention. In March, 1794, he overthrew Jacques René Hébert and his extreme radical party of the Paris commune with the aid of Robespierre, and in turn was overthrown (March 30, 1794) by Robespierre, given a quick semblance of a trial, and executed. Danton was an orator of great power who recognized the need both of eliminating the oppressive monarchy and of preventing the Revolution from deteriorating into a formless anarchy of blood baths, but his lack of resolution in crises doomed him.

Daphnaida (daf.na̱.ē′da̱). An elegy (1590) by Edmund Spenser, on the death of Lady Douglas Gorges, whose husband, Sir Arthur Gorges, poet and translator, was Spenser's friend.

Daphne (daf′nē). In Greek mythology, a nymph, daughter of the river-god Peneius, or, in other accounts of Ladon, an Arcadian. Her lover Leucippus pursued her in woman's clothing, and was killed by the nymphs at the instigation of Apollo. When the god in turn pursued her, she entreated that she might be transformed into the bay tree, and he granted her petition.

Daphnis (daf′nis). In Greek mythology, a shepherd, son of Hermes and a Sicilian nymph. Pan taught him to sing and play the flute, and the Muses endowed him with a love of poetry, and he is said to have originated bucolic poetry. He was turned into a stone according to one legend; according to another his eyes were torn out by a nymph for his infidelity to her, and he threw himself in despair into the sea. In ancient pastoral poetry his name was frequently given to shepherds.

fat, fāte, fär, ȧsk, fāre; net, mē, hėr; pin, pīne; not, nōte, mȯve, nôr; up, lūte, pu̇ll; ᴛн, then;

Daphnis. A gentle shepherd in John Fletcher's play *The Faithful Shepherdess.*

Daphnis and Chloe (klō'ē). A Greek pastoral romance attributed to Longus (4th or 5th century A.D.), a Greek sophist. It recounts the loves and pastoral life of Daphnis, foster son of Lamon, a goatherd, and Chloe, foster daughter of Dryas, a shepherd. The manuscript of Mont-Cassin, taken to Florence, does not name the author. It is known principally through the French version of Amyot (1559), revised by Courier. It has been translated and imitated in all European languages. Tasso's *Aminta*, Montemayor's *Diana*, d'Urfé's *Sireine*, Saint-Pierre's *Paul and Virginia*, and Allan Ramsay's *Gentle Shepherd* are founded on it.

Dapper (dap'ēr). In Ben Jonson's comedy *The Alchemist*, a greedy and credulous lawyer's clerk who desires a "fly" (a spirit or familiar) of the Alchemist to enable him to cheat at horse races by giving him prior information.

Dapperwit (dap'ēr.wit). A vain, foolish, and boastful rake in Wycherley's *Love in a Wood.*

d'Arblay (där.blā'), **Madame.** Married name of **Burney, Fanny.**

Darby and Joan (där'bi; jōn). A married pair who are said to have lived in the 18th century in the West Riding of Yorkshire, noted traditionally for their long and happy married life. There is a ballad on the subject called *The Happy Old Couple*, supposed to have been written by Henry Woodfall, though it has been attributed to Matthew Prior. A poem *Dobson and Joan*, by "Mr. B.," is published with Prior's poems.

Darbyites (där'bi.īts). See **Plymouth Brethren.**

Darcy (där'si), **Mr.** The extremely proud lover of Elizabeth Bennet, in Jane Austen's novel *Pride and Prejudice.*

Dardanius (där.dā'ni.us). In Shakespeare's *Julius Caesar*, one of the servants of Brutus. He refuses his master's request to kill him.

Daredevil (där'dev.il). The atheist in Thomas Otway's comedy of *The Atheist*. He is a cowardly, boasting fellow, who when in danger forgets his principles and says "two dozen paternosters within a half hour."

Dares Phrygius (dār'ēz frij'i.us, dā'rēz). [English, **Dares the Phrygian.**] A priest of Hephaestus in Troy mentioned in the *Iliad*. The authorship of a lost work on the fall of Troy, a pretended Latin translation of which was written about the 5th century A.D., was attributed to him in antiquity.

Darien (där.i.en', där'i.ęn), **Colony of.** [Also, **Darien Scheme.**] A Scottish colony on the Isthmus of Panama, founded by William Paterson. It was chartered by the Scottish Parliament in 1695; the enterprise was begun in 1698 and the settlement was abandoned in 1700.

Darius I (da.rī'us). [Called **Darius the Great;** also known as **Darius Hystaspis.**] b. c550 B.C.; d. c485 B.C. A king of Persia; son of Hystaspes, and fifth in the descent from Achaemenes. He succeeded (521) Cambyses on the Persian throne, after defeating the Magian Gaumata, who claimed to be Bardiya (the Greek Smerdis), brother of Cambyses and son of Cyrus. A record of his reign is given by himself in the long trilingual (Old Persian, Elamite, and Babylonian) inscriptions of Behistun. Besides the revolt in Persia itself, caused by the impostor Gaumata, he had to suppress two uprisings in Babylonia, led by Nidintu-Bel and Arachu, who made claim to be Nebuchadnezzar, son of Nabonidus; in consequence of these uprisings he caused the fortifications of Babylon to be torn down. The other countries under Persian dominion also revolted in turn, but at last were brought to submission. After restoring order in the empire Darius turned his attention to reorganization and reforms of the administration. He divided the whole land into 20 satrapies, introduced regular taxation and uniformity of coinage, constructed roads, and founded a kind of postal system by placing stations and relays with saddled horses at regular intervals on the road between Susa and Sardis.

Dark Ages. A period of European history beginning with or shortly before the fall of the Roman Empire of the West (476 A.D.), marked by a general decline of learning and civilization. It was introduced by the great influx of barbarians into western Europe in the 4th and 5th centuries known as the wandering of the nations, and is reckoned by Hallam as extending to the 11th century, when a general revival of wealth, manners, taste, and learning began, and by others to the time of Dante in the 13th century, or later.

Dark Fire, The. A volume of poetry by W. J. Turner, published in 1918.

Dark Flower, The. A novel by John Galsworthy, published in 1913. Divided into three parts, "Spring," "Summer," and "Autumn," it presents the amorous adventures of Mark Lennan. It is unlike most of Galsworthy's work in that the interest is in personal passion rather than in the social order.

Dark Forest, The. A novel by Hugh Walpole, published in 1916. It is based on the author's experiences (1914–16) with the Red Cross in Russia during World War I. *The Secret City* (1919) is a sequel.

Dark Island, The. A novel by V. M. Sackville-West, published in 1934.

Dark Lady. A woman mentioned in Shakespeare's later sonnets (numbers 127 *et seq.*), who has been thought by some scholars to have been Mary Fitton, a maid of honor to Queen Elizabeth in 1595. She was the mistress of William Herbert, Earl of Pembroke, who has been suggested as the person celebrated in the earlier sonnets. Others have suggested Penelope Devereux, Lady Rich, or any of a number of other women of the court or of London. The speculation concerning her has produced a considerable body of carefully reasoned hypotheses, but as yet no absolute proof of her identity.

Dark Lady of the Sonnets, The. A comedy in one act (1910) by George Bernard Shaw, who calls it "this little pièce d'occasion" in his 28-page preface to the 14-page play. It was first produced at the London Haymarket, on Nov. 24, 1910, with Mona Limerick as the Dark Lady, Suzanne Sheldon as Queen Elizabeth, and Granville Barker as Shakespeare. The occasion for which the play was written and performed was the raising of funds for a national theater to be erected as a tribute to Shakespeare.

Darkling Thrush, The. A poem by Thomas Hardy, describing the poet's feelings as he stands in a desolate spot and hears the joyous sound of a thrush. Unable to perceive anything in surroundings so bleak that will easily explain such an expression of joy, he is nevertheless heartened by it, and says:

> That I could think there trembles through
> His happy good-night air
> Some blessed hope, whereof he knew
> And I was unaware.

Darkness. A three-act tragedy (1926) by Liam O'Flaherty.

Darkness at Noon. A novel by Arthur Koestler, published in 1941.

Dark Night, The. A narrative poem by May Sinclair, published in 1924.

Dark Tower, The. A novel (1915) by Francis Brett Young.

Dark Wind, The. A volume of poems by W. J. Turner, published in 1920.

Darley (där'li), **George.** b. in Ireland, 1795; d. 1846. A British poet, critic, and mathematician, long a member of the staff of the *London Magazine*. He was the author of *Sylvia* (1827), a pastoral drama, and of prose romances collected in *Labours of Idleness* (1826). In his poetry he often used specific symbols to suggest abstract ideas, and thus to some extent anticipated the symbolist school of poetry. Collected volumes of his verse are *Nepenthe* (posthumously, in 1876), *The Errors of Ecstacie* (1822), *Thomas à Becket* (1840), and *Ethelstan* (1841).

Darling (där'ling), **Charles John.** [Title, 1st Baron Darling of Langham.] b. Dec. 6, 1849; d. at Lymington, Hampshire, England, May 29, 1936. English judge, legal writer, and poet. Called to the bar in 1873, he was made queen's counsel in 1885, was Conservative member of Parliament (1888–97) for Deptford, and judge of the king's bench division from 1897 until his retirement in 1923. He was the author of *Scintillae Juris* (1877), *Meditations in the Tea Room* (1879), *Seria Ludo* (1903), *On the Oxford Circuit and Other Verses* (1909), *Musings on Murder* (1925), *A Pensioner's Garden* (1926), *Reconsidered Rimes* (1930), and *Autumnal Leaves* (1933). Knighted in 1897, he was made a peer in 1924. He tried Sir Roger Casement, who was hanged by the British during World War I.

Darling, Grace Horsley. b. at Bamborough, Northumberland, England, Nov. 24, 1815; d. Oct. 20, 1842. An English heroine, who aided in rescuing (Sept. 7, 1838) five persons from the wreck of the steamer *Forfarshire* near Longstone lighthouse, Farne Islands, where her father was lighthouse keeper.

Darling, Mr. and Mrs. The parents of Wendy, Michael, and John, in Sir James M. Barrie's fairy play, *Peter Pan* (1904).

Darling, Wendy. The young girl in Sir J. M. Barrie's *Peter Pan* (1904). Wendy and her brothers, after Peter teaches them how to fly, accompany

him to his home in the Never-Never Land to take care of him; Wendy's home calls her back but she makes Peter happy by her promise that she will return every spring.

Darmesteter (dár.mes.te.ter; Anglicized, därm'stet.ẽr), **Mary.** [Full name, **Agnes Mary Frances Darmesteter;** maiden name, **Robinson.**] b. at Leamington, England, Feb. 27, 1857—. A poet and expert on English literature. She is the author of *Poésies* (1888), *Ernest Renan* (1898), *Grands Écrivains d'outre-Manche* (1901), and others. Her works in English include *A Handful of Honeysuckles* (1878), *The Crowned Hippolytus* (1880), a translation of Euripides (1881), and *The End of the Middle Ages* (1889; a historical work).

Darnay (där.nā'), **Charles.** [Original surname, **St. Evrémonde.**] In Charles Dickens's *Tale of Two Cities*, a young French nobleman who flees France in disgust with the excesses of the aristocracy, including his own family. He changes his name and marries Lucie Manette, but is condemned to death (partly on evidence obtained through a paper written in prison against his family by Doctor Manette, Lucie's father) and is saved only through the self-sacrifice of Sydney Carton.

Darnley (därn'li), **Lord.** [Title of **Henry Stuart** or **Stewart.**] b. at Temple Newsam, Yorkshire, England, Dec. 7, 1545; killed near Edinburgh, Feb. 9 or 10, 1567. The second husband of Mary, Queen of Scots; father of James I of England. He was the son of Matthew Stuart, 4th Earl of Lennox, and Margaret Douglas, granddaughter of Henry VII of England, and was cousin-german to Mary, whom he married July 29, 1565. He was treated at first with much kindness by the queen, who promised to induce the Scottish Parliament to grant him a crown matrimonial, but eventually alienated her affections by his stupidity, insolence, and profligacy, and especially by his participation in the murder (March 9, 1566) of her favorite, the Italian secretary David Rizzio. He attempted to reëstablish himself with her by turning over to her his associates in the murder; but then he refused (December, 1566) to attend the baptism of his son James. While convalescent from an attack of illness, smallpox according to some, poisoning according to others, he was removed to a solitary house called the Kirk o' Field, near Edinburgh, which was blown up with gunpowder under the direction of the Earl of Bothwell, apparently with the queen's knowledge, if not her connivance, on the night of Feb. 9–10, 1567. Darnley's body was found in a garden some distance from the house, leading to the hypothesis that he was strangled and the house blown up to cover the crime.

Darsie Latimer (där'si lat'i.mẽr). See **Latimer, Darsie.**

D'Artagnan (dár.tà.nyän; Anglicized, där.tan'yạn). One of the principal characters in *The Three Musketeers* by the elder Alexandre Dumas, and also in its sequels.

Dartle (där'tl), **Rosa.** In Charles Dickens's *David Copperfield*, Mrs. Steerforth's excitable companion, in love with Steerforth. She has a scar on her face, caused by Steerforth in his youth. She constantly says: "I want to know."

---

fat, fāte, fär, ȧsk, fãre; net, mē, hẽr; pin, pīne; not, nōte, mŏve, nôr; up, lūte, pull; ᴛн, then;

Darwin (där'win), **Charles Robert.** b. at Shrewsbury, England, Feb. 12, 1809; d. at Down, Kent, England, April 19, 1882. An English naturalist, original expounder of the theory of evolution by natural selection since known as Darwinism; grandson of Erasmus Darwin (1731–1802). Though he studied medicine at Edinburgh and began to prepare for the ministry at Cambridge, his absorbing interest in natural history brought him in touch with the botanist John Stevens Henslow, who secured Darwin's appointment as naturalist with the around-the-world expedition which sailed on H.M.S. *Beagle* in 1831. The *Beagle*, on a surveying cruise, stopped at various points along the South American coast and at such neighboring islands as the Galapagos; then it headed across the Pacific to Tahiti, New Zealand, Australia, Tasmania, the Maldives, St. Helena, Brazil, and the Cape Verde and Azores islands, returning to England in 1836. Darwin was much struck by the variations in species in adjacent areas at which the ship stopped, by the close resemblance of the island species to similar species on the mainland, by the differences between fossils and living species in the same area; and he began to attempt to formulate his ideas of the succession of the species. He became friendly with Sir Charles Lyell, the noted geologist, in the period 1838–41, when he was secretary of the Royal Geological Society. In 1842 he took up residence in the secluded village of Down, in Kent, where he devoted himself to a life of study and scientific research. Taking his inspiration from Thomas Malthus's *Essay on Population* (1798), which investigates the rigorous economic laws that limit the number of people capable of maintaining life in view of the available food supply, Darwin began to see illustrated in his materials a natural tendency towards selection of the individuals that survived. In 1857 he wrote to Asa Gray, the American botanist, outlining his theories. In 1858 he was the recipient of a manuscript from Alfred Russel Wallace that explained Darwin's own theory, independently arrived at by Wallace, then in the Molucca Islands. On the advice of Lyell and Sir Joseph Hooker, Darwin included Wallace's paper with a sketch of his own work in a communication to the Linnean Society (1858) and in 1859 he published his work, *On the Origin of Species by Means of Natural Selection, or the Preservation of Favoured Races in the Struggle for Life*, in which he propounded his theory of biological evolution, which came to be known as the Darwinian theory. This book, Darwin's most important and most noted work, discusses his theory of selection and variation of species and marshals the evidence from which the theory developed. The book is said to have sold its first edition in one day; factions sprang up for and against the theory, and within the year the book was beginning to bring to bear that influence that it still maintains as perhaps the leading work in natural philosophy in man's history. Darwin also wrote reports on the biological and geological findings of the *Beagle* expedition, and other books and monographs. The more important of his later works are *The Movements and Habits of Climbing Plants* (1865), *The Variation of Animals and Plants under Domestication* (1868), and *The Descent of Man, and Selection in Relation to Sex* (1871). Few men in-

deed have so greatly influenced human concepts of life and the universe as has Charles Robert Darwin.

Darwin, Erasmus. b. at Elston, Nottinghamshire, England, Dec. 12, 1731; d. of heart disease, at Derby, England, April 18, 1802. An English physician, scientist, poet, and political and religious radical; grandfather, by his first wife, of Charles Robert Darwin, some of whose ideas on evolution he anticipated, and, by his second wife, of Francis Galton. He was educated at Chesterfield Grammar School, at Edinburgh University, where he studied medicine, and at St. John's College, Cambridge. As a prose author, he contributed to the *Philosophical Transactions*, and wrote *Zoonomia, or the Laws of Organic Life* (1794–96), *A Plan for the Conduct of Female Education in Boarding Schools* (1797), expressing views then considered liberal, if not radical, and *Phytologia, or the Philosophy of Agriculture and Gardening* (1799), which expresses many of his scientific speculations. His works in verse (they are hardly considered poetry today) are of the didactic type so popular in the 18th century. They are *The Botanic Garden* (1781), in two parts; the first part, *The Economy of Vegetation*, was published in 1792, the second part, *The Loves of the Plants*, having come out in 1789. Strangely enough, in view of its later, and present, reputation, it was successful at first, and was praised by Walpole, Cowper, and William Hayley. If the poem is not completely forgotten today it is because of Canning's parody of it, "The Loves of the Triangles," which appeared in his periodical, *The Anti-Jacobin*. Darwin had enough of a sense of humor (not apparent in his own verse) to laugh at the satire, and was honest enough to admit that it was a good one. His poetry also includes *On the Death of Frederick, Prince of Wales* (1795) and *The Temple of Nature, or the Origin of Society* (published 1803, a year after his death), a title that speaks for itself. Darwin knew Rousseau, Watt, Josiah Wedgwood, and Maria Edgeworth's father. Johnson he knew and disliked intensely, a feeling that Johnson fully returned, which was natural enough in view of the radicalism of the one and the conservatism of the other.

Dasent (dā'sent), Sir **George Webbe.** b. on the island of St. Vincent, British West Indies, May 22, 1817; d. near Ascot, Berkshire, England, June 11, 1896. An English lawyer and author, best known as a student of Scandinavian literature. While on diplomatic service at Stockholm in 1840, he was interested by Jacob Grimm in Scandinavian literature and began his investigations into Icelandic. He published a translation of *The Prose or Younger Edda* (1842), *Popular Tales from the Norse* (1859), *Saga of Burnt Njal* (1861), *The Vikings of the Baltic* (1875). From 1845–70 he was one of the assistant editors of the London *Times*. He was professor (1853) of English literature and modern history at King's College, London.

Dashwood (dash'wŭd), **Elinor** and **Marianne.** Two sisters in Jane Austen's novel *Sense and Sensibility*. Elinor represents "sense," as opposed to Marianne's "sensibility" or exaggerated sentiment.

Dashwood, Elizabeth Monica. [Pseudonym, **E. M. Delafield**; maiden name, **de la Pasture**; full name,

---

Edmée Elizabeth Monica Dashwood.] b. in Sussex, England, 1890; d. at Cullompton, Devonshire, England, Dec. 2, 1943. An English novelist, short-story writer, and dramatist; daughter of Lady Clifford, Mrs. Henry de la Pasture (a surname of which her pseudonym is an Anglicized version). She was author of the novels *Zella Sees Herself* (1917), *The Pelicans* and *The War-Workers* (both 1918), *Consequences* (1919), *Tension* (1920), *Heel of Achilles* and *Humbug* (both 1921), *The Optimist* (1922), *Mrs. Harter* (1924), *The Chip and the Block* (1925), *Jill* (1926), *The Way Things Are* (1927), *What is Love?* (1928; American title, *First Love*), *Diary of a Provincial Lady* (1931), *Challenge to Clarissa* (1931; American title, *House Party*), *The Provincial Lady Goes Further* (1932; American title, *The Provincial Lady in London*), *Thank Heaven Fasting* (1932; American title, *A Good Man's Love*), and *Gay Life* (1933). Her short stories were published in *Messalina of the Suburbs* (1924), *The Entertainment* (1927), and *Women Are Like That* (1929). She also wrote *To See Ourselves* (1932), *The Glass Wall* (1933), and *The Mulberry Bush* (1935), plays; *General Impressions* (1933), notebooks of sketches, *The Provincial Lady in America* (1934) and *The Provincial Lady in Wartime* (1940), travel books, and *Straw Without Bricks* (1937; American title, *I Visit the Soviet*).

Datchery (dach'ẽr.i), **Dick.** A mysterious person with white hair and a military air who appears inexplicably at Cloisterham, in Charles Dickens's *Mystery of Edwin Drood.*

Dauber (dôb'ẽr). A narrative poem of the sea (1913) by John Masefield. The poem, named after its sailor hero, who is also an artist, is partly autobiographical in that it is based on the author's memories and experiences after he left his Shropshire home and ran away to sea. Dauber, who wants to paint the water he sails on, rather than clean the decks of the ship, is not understood by his rough comrades, and he finally dies in a storm.

Daudet (dō.de), **Alphonse.** b. at Nîmes, France, May 13, 1840; d. at Paris, Dec. 16, 1897. A French humorist and novelist. He went to school at Lyons, and then worked as a tutor for two years. In 1857 he settled at Paris, and published shortly afterward a collection of poems, *Les Amoureuses.* The *Figaro* published his account of a tutor's hardships, *Les Gueux de province.* A series of papers contributed to the same journal came out in book form as *Le Chaperon rouge* (1861). A second collection of poems, *La Double Conversion*, was published in 1859. Daudet wrote his *Lettres sur Paris* to *Le Petit Moniteur* under the nom de plume of Jehan de l'Isle in 1865. His first real success, *Lettres de mon moulin*, signed with the name Gaston-Marie, were addressed to *L'Événement* in 1866. Daudet's early publications include *Le Petit Chose* (1868), *Lettres à un absent* (1871), *Les Aventures prodigieuses de Tartarin de Tarascon* (1872), *Les Petits Robinsons des caves* (1872), *Contes du lundi* (1873), *Contes et récits* (1873), *Robert Helmont* (1874), *Les Femmes d'artistes* (1874), and *Fromont jeune et Risler aîné* (1874), a great success. There followed *Jack* (1876), *Le Nabab* (1877), *Les Rois en exil* (1879), *Contes choisis, la fantaisie et l'histoire* (1879), *Numa Roumestan* (1881), *Les Cigognes* (1883), *L'Evan-*

géliste (1883), *Sapho* (1884), *Tartarin sur les Alpes* (1885), *La Belle Nivernaise* (1886), *Trente ans de Paris* (1887), *Souvenirs d'un homme de lettres* (1888), *L'Immortel* (1888), and *Port Tarascon* (1890).

Daudet, Léon. b. at Paris, Nov. 16, 1867; d. at St.-Rémy-de-Provence, France, July 1, 1942. A French journalist and writer; son of Alphonse Daudet (1840–97). He served as editorial writer (1908 *et seq.*) for the Royalist *Action Française.* Author of *Le Stupide 19 Siècle* (1922) and more than 80 other works, including novels, memoirs, and polemic essays, he is remembered less for his writing than as a public figure.

Daughter, The. A play in verse by J. Sheridan Knowles, produced in 1836.

Daughters of the Late Colonel, The. A psychological short story by Katherine Mansfield. It is included in her volume of 15 stories, *The Garden Party* (1922).

Daughter To Philip. A novel by Beatrice Kean Seymour, published in 1933.

Daulis (dô'lis). In ancient geography, a city of Phocis, Greece: the scene of the myth of Tereus, Philomela, and Procne.

Dauphin (dō.faṅ; Anglicized, dô'fin). A title borne (1364 *et seq.*) by any of several male heirs (there were no female claimants) to the French throne. It originated as the title of the rulers of the old county of Vienne, perhaps as a personal name, and was borne by the Dauphins of the Viennois on their coats of arms as a dolphin. In 1285 the name Dauphiné was first applied to the county ruled by Humbert, Dauphin of Vienne. When Philip VI of Valois, king of France, took possession of the lands, the title was given to his grandson, who was to become Charles V of France, the first to bear the title of Dauphin of France. The eldest sons of the French kings were inheritors of the title; most famous was Monseigneur, Louis de Bourbon, son of Louis XIV and grandfather of Louis XV; the last to bear the title was the eldest son of Charles X, Louis Antoine de Bourbon, Duke of Angoulême, who renounced the throne in 1830. The title was also used by the rulers of the dauphinate of Auvergne from 1155 to 1693.

Dauphin, Charles the. See **Charles, the Dauphin.**

Dauphin, Lewis (or Louis) the. See **Lewis, the Dauphin.**

Dauphine (dô'fin), **Sir.** In Ben Jonson's comedy *Epicoene, or the Silent Woman*, the lively and ingenious nephew of Morose. He concocts the plot by which a portion of his uncle's money is given to him and his debts are paid.

"Dauphins." See **Delphin Classics.**

Davenant (dav'ẹ.nạnt), **Charles.** [Original name, **D'Avenant.**] b. at London, 1656; d. Nov. 6, 1714. An English writer on political economy; son of Sir William D'Avenant. His collected works were published in 1771.

D'Avenant or **Davenant** (dav'ẹ.nạnt), **Sir William.** b. at Oxford, England, in February, 1606; d. at London, April 7, 1668. An English poet and dramatist. William Oldys is chiefly responsible for the story that D'Avenant was the son of Shakespeare, which seems to rest mainly on the fact that the latter used the inn of one John Davenant (the father of William), at Oxford on his journeys to and from Warwickshire. D'Avenant became (c1620) page to the Duchess of Richmond, and then to Fulke Greville, Lord Brooke. In 1628, after the murder of Greville, he began to write plays. In 1638 he was made poet laureate, and about this time had a severe illness which resulted in the loss of his nose, a fact frequently adverted to by the witty writers of the time. He was manager of Drury Lane Theatre for a time, but, becoming implicated in the various intrigues of the English Civil War, fled to France. Returning in 1643, he was knighted by the king, Charles I, at the siege of Gloucester. While on an expedition (1650) to colonize Virginia, he was captured in the English Channel by a Parliamentary ship. He was imprisoned for two years in the Tower of London for political offenses and expected to be hanged. According to one of John Milton's biographers, Milton was instrumental in saving D'Avenant's life, and after the Restoration (1660) he in turn saved Milton from punishment. Right after his release, he published *Gondibert* (1651), an epic poem consisting of 1,500 four-line stanzas. After the Restoration (1660) he was in favor at court, and continued to write till his death. Among his plays are *Albovine* (1629), *The Cruel Brother* (1630), *The Just Italian* (1630), *The Platonic Lovers* (1636), *The Wits* (1636), *The Unfortunate Lovers* (1643), *Love and Honor* (1649), *Law against Lovers* (played in 1662), and *The Rivals* (played in 1664). He produced alterations of *The Tempest* (with Dryden, 1667), of *Macbeth* (printed 1674), and of *Julius Caesar*. D'Avenant was the founder of English opera, his *Siege of Rhodes* (1656) being produced in the period when plays were banned. It was in this opera that a woman first appeared on the English stage.

David (dā′vid). d. c960 B.C. The second king of Israel, c1000–c960 B.C. He was born at Bethlehem, the seventh and youngest son of Jesse of the tribe of Judah. At about the age of 18, while still shepherd of his father's flocks, he was secretly anointed king of Israel by the prophet Samuel. Later he came into a close personal relationship with Saul the king, perhaps through his friendship with the king's son Jonathan, but incurred his bitter enmity. David played music before the king and was his armor bearer. The Philistine giant Goliath was slain by David in single combat. His successes and the praises accorded to him by the people aroused the suspicion and jealousy of Saul (whose daughter Michal David married), which subsequently turned into deadly hatred, so that David was often in jeopardy of his life. He first sought refuge with Samuel, then with the priests in Nob, which resulted in their massacre by Saul, and was finally driven to seek safety with the enemies of his people, the Philistines. But the slayer of Goliath was recognized, and David fled to the wilderness of Judah, where he built a fort at Adullam. There rallied around him "men who were in distress, in debt, and discontented." At the head of these freebooters or outlaws he undertook many expeditions and fought many skirmishes, which made him increasingly popular with the people. All this time he was pursued by Saul, whose mind became more and

more darkened; twice the king came into his power, but because of this awe of the "anointed of the Lord" David did not avail himself of these opportunities (1 Sam. xxiv. 4ff., xxvi. 7ff.). He was compelled to become the vassal of the Philistine king Achish of Gath, who gave him for his support Ziklag on the frontier of Philistia. From here he undertook expeditions against the nomadic tribes of the border, while Achish believed that they were directed against Israel (1 Sam. xxvii.). The Philistines gathered a large army against Israel. In the battle of Gilboa Saul and his host lost their lives. David, who was then about 30 years old, succeeded to the throne. For seven and a half years his reign was limited to Judah, the southern kingdom, with his seat at Hebron, while the other tribes were under the scepter of Ishbosheth, son of Saul, residing at Mahanaim, E of the Jordan. Ishbosheth, however, was murdered, and all the tribes recognized David as king; he reigned over the whole of Israel for 33 years. He removed his residence from Hebron to Jerusalem, which he took from the Jebusites, and there established himself in the "city of David," the oldest quarter of Jerusalem, on Mount Zion. Here also the temporary sanctuary was put up (2 Sam. vi.), which made the city the political and religious center of the nation, and gave to David's reign a genuinely royal character. Through a series of successful wars against the Philistines, Ammonites, Moabites, Edomites, Syrians, Amalekites, and others, and by the introduction of a regular administration and organization of court and army, he became the real founder of the monarchical government of Israel. The constitution of the tribes remained intact, but the military organization was a national one. Each tribe sent a contingent of men (over 20 years of age) to the national army, which stood under one commander in chief, Joab, David's nephew. The bodyguard was formed, it seems, of foreigners, the Cherethites and Pelethites (supposed to be Philistines). The nucleus of the army consisted of the band of heroes (*gibborim*) who rallied about David while he was still an exile. The king presided over judicial cases, and was surrounded by a regular staff of military and administrative counselors and officers. David was also the actual founder of a sanctifying, divine worship, refining and enriching it by the influence of music and psalmody. The last period of his reign was much darkened by national misfortunes and domestic rebellions, the rebellion of his son Absalom, the uprising of Sheba ben Bishri, a drought and famine lasting three years, and a pestilence induced by the counting of the people. Even in his last days when he was prostrated with the infirmities of age, his son Adonijah attempted to secure the succession to which David had appointed Solomon. Solomon was in the eyes of David's other sons, not the rightful heir; Bathsheba, David's wife, had been acquired sinfully and only her hold on the king pushed Solomon to the fore as David's successor. This rebellion, however, like all the others, was successfully repressed, and David died peacefully at the age of 70. He became in tradition the ideal king of Israel, the pattern and standard by which all succeeding rulers were measured, the prototype of the last perfect ruler, the Messiah, who would be descended from David and is sometimes simply called David. As regards the Psalms, modern criticism denies him the authorship of many psalms bearing in the Biblical Book of Psalms the superscription "of David," but there is no reason for entirely disconnecting David from this kind of Hebrew poetry.

David or **Dewi** (dā'wi), Saint. b. c495; d. c589. The patron saint of Wales. He was bishop of Menevia (afterward called St. David's), where he founded a monastery. According to an account which has no historical foundation, he was appointed metropolitan archbishop of Wales at a synod held at Brefi. The wearing of a leek by the Welsh on St. David's day (March 1) is said to stem back to a suggestion by this saint just before a battle with the Saxons that the Welsh should wear leeks and thus be able to distinguish friend from foe in the heat of battle.

David. [Welsh, **Dafydd ap Gwilym** or **Gwillum** (dä'viᴛн äp gwi'lim; gwi'lum).] b. probably at Bro Gynin, Cardiganshire, Wales, c1340; d. c1400. A Welsh 14th-century poet and anticlerical songwriter, contemporary with Edward III. His dates and the places of his birth and death are uncertain. According to some, his life span is the same as that of Chaucer; other sources indicate that he was born in 1300, near Llandaff, Glamorganshire, and that he died in 1368, at the Abbey of Talley, in Carmarthenshire. He knew Latin and Italian and is believed to have lived and studied in Italy. He wrote some 147 poems to Morvid (also variously Morvydd or Morfudd or Morfid) of Anglesey, who loved him and with whom he eloped after she had, against her will, married another; the husband, a wealthy old man, is satirized in David's poetry as "Little Hunchback." Fined and imprisoned for his romantic adventure, David was saved by the men of Glamorgan who paid the fine for him, a favor he returned by celebrating the county in his verse. His collected work, consisting of 262 poems, was published (1789) at London, and English translations were brought out in 1791 and 1834. Much of his poetry, in manuscript form, is in the British Museum.

David. In Dryden's *Absalom and Achitophel*, the character who represents Charles II.

David. A novel in three parts by Naomi Royde-Smith, published in 1934.

David and Bethsabe (beth.sä'be). A tragedy (c1593) by George Peele, printed in 1599 in a corrupt text. The play, whose plot is taken from the Old Testament, is almost entirely in blank verse.

David Balfour (bal'för). See **Balfour, David.**

David Copperfield (dā'vid kop'ėr.fēld). Novel (1850) by Charles Dickens. It was originally published in serial form in monthly parts from May, 1849 to November, 1850. It does not have one plot, but, like Shakespeare's plays, many, and it has a staggering number of characters, both major and minor, which is typical of Dickens. In general it tells the story of the life, adventures, hardships, failures, and the final success and happiness of its hero. It shows us David as a child ("I Am Born" is the title of chapter one), growing up and going to school, struggling to make a living, as a young man

trying to become an author, and, in the end, as a man, still young, who is a happy husband and a successful writer. Some of the characters in the huge portrait gallery are Clara Copperfield, a widow and David's mother; Edward Murdstone, his brutal stepfather; the members of the Peggotty family: Clara Peggotty (usually called by her last name), David's nurse, Dan'l Peggotty, a Yarmouth fisherman, Ham Peggotty, Dan'l's nephew, and Little Em'ly, Ham's cousin and engaged to him; Barkis (remembered for his message "Barkis is willin'"), Peggotty's husband; James Steerforth, David's schoolfellow, a handsome villain who seduces Em'ly and later dies in a shipwreck, although Ham tries to save him: Uriah Heep, an odious villain, a thief and a forger whose name has become a synonym for disgusting hypocrisy; Miss Betsy Trotwood, David's aunt and later his guardian; Mr. Dick, a harmless lunatic who is obsessed by the head of Charles I; Dora Spenlow, a silly creature, David's "child-wife," as he calls her; Agnes Wickfield, as lovely as Dora but more mature, his second wife; Mrs. Gummidge, a complaining widow; Miss Mowcher, a midget; Creakle, a tyrannical teacher; Tommy Traddles, David's friend, a good-natured plodder who finally becomes a barrister; and the immortal Wilkins Micawber, an incurable optimist who is always waiting for "something to turn up." The full title of the novel is *The Personal History, Experience and Observation of David Copperfield the Younger, of Blunderstone Rookery, Which He Never Meant to be Published On Any Account.* It is in 64 chapters, was illustrated by the famous "Phiz," and was Dickens's seventh novel. Of all his works, it was his favorite. "I like this the best," he tells us in his preface. "It will be easily believed that I am a fond parent to every child of my fancy, and that no one can ever love that family as dearly as I love them. But, like many fond parents, I have in my heart of hearts a favorite child. And his name is DAVID COPPERFIELD." An artist's estimate of his own work rarely coincides with general or popular opinion, but *David Copperfield* has long been considered one of his best works and one of the great triumphs of English fiction. Dickens's partiality may stem from the fact that the novel is largely autobiographical.

David Daw (dô), Sir. See **Daw, Sir David.**

Davideis (da.vid'ē.is). An epic poem by Abraham Cowley, on the subject of David, king of the Hebrews, published in 1656. The poem is incomplete.

David Elginbrod (dā'vid el'gin.brod). A novel by George Macdonald, published in 1863.

David Garrick (gar'ik). A play translated by T. W. Robertson from a French play, *Sullivan*, in 1864.

David Gellatley (gel'at.li). See **Gellatley, David.**

David Grieve (grēv). [Full title, **The History of David Grieve.**] A novel by Mrs. Humphry Ward, published in 1892.

David Simple (sim'pl). [Full title, **The Adventures of David Simple in Search of a Real Friend.**] A romance by Sarah Fielding, published in 1744, a picaresque novel of a hero disillusioned by a treacherous brother, whose search for a faithful friend is eventually successful.

Davidson (dā'vid.son), **John.** b. at Barrhead, Scotland, April 11, 1857; d. by suicide at Penzance, Cornwall, England, March 23, 1909. An English poet, dramatist, novelist, and essayist. He was educated at Greenock Academy, and attended (1876–77) Edinburgh University. He engaged in teaching (1877–89) before going (1890) to London, where he made a living as a ghost writer and by translating French novels. He enjoyed a brief period (1906 et seq.) of improved personal circumstances as a result of a government pension of 100 pounds a year. He was the author of books of verse, including *The North Wall* (1885), *In a Music Hall* (1891), *Fleet Street Eclogues* (1893; 2nd series, 1896), *Ballads and Songs* (1894), *St. George's Day* (1895), *New Ballads* (1897), *The Last Ballad* (1899), *Holiday* (1906), and *Fleet Street and Other Poems* (1909). He also wrote the plays *Bruce* (1886), *Smith* (1888), *An Unhistorical Pastoral, A Romantic Farce,* and *Scaramouch in Naxos* (all 1889), *Godfrida* (1898), and *The Knight of the Maypole* (1903); the novels *Perfervid* (1890), *Laura Ruthven's Widowhood* (1892), *Baptist Lake* (1894), *Wonderful Mission of Earl Lavender* (1895), and *Miss Armstrong's and Other Circumstances* (1896); *The Triumph of Mammon* (1907) and *Mammon and His Message* (1909), philosophical works; and a series of five *Testaments* in which he expounded his philosophy of life, *The Testament of a Vivisector* and *The Testament of a Man Forbid* (both 1901), *The Testament of an Empire-Builder* (1902), *The Testament of a Prime Minister* (1904), and *The Testament of John Davidson* (1908). He translated François Coppée's *For the Crown* (1890). Among his poems are *A Ballad of Hell, Ballad of a Nun, Imagination, The Outcast,* and *The Unknown.*

Davies of Hereford (dā'vēz, -vis; her'e.ford), **John.** b. at Hereford, England, c1565; d. at London, 1618. An English writing-master and poet. He was said to be an accomplished penman, and some specimens of his work are preserved in *The Writing Schoolemaster or the Anatomy of Faire Writing* (published c1631 after his death). Among his works are *Mirum in Modum* (1602), *Microcosmos* (1603), *The Wittes Pilgrimage* (1605), *The Scourge of Folly* (1610 or 1611), and *Wit's Bedlam* (1617).

Davies, Sir **John.** b. at Tisbury, Wiltshire, England, in April, 1569; d. Dec. 8, 1626. An English jurist and poet. He was called to the bar in 1595, disbarred in 1598, and readmitted in 1601. In that year he was returned to Parliament for Corfe Castle. In 1603 he was made solicitor general for Ireland, and in 1606 succeeded to the position of attorney general for Ireland. In 1614, and again in 1621, he was member of Parliament for Newcastle-under-Lyme. For the last ten years of his life he was a sergeant-at-law in England. He was made chief justice in 1626, but died before taking possession of the office. Among his works are *Orchestra* (on dancing, 1596), and *Hymns to Astraea* (1599), acrostics to Queen Elizabeth. A number of his epigrams, printed in the same volume as Christopher Marlowe's translation of Ovid's *Elegies,* were ordered burned in 1599 during the censorship campaign of John Whitgift, archbishop of Canterbury. *Nosce Teipsum* (1599), a series of rhyming decasyllabic quatrains, on the soul and its immortal nature,

was a great success and remains one of the best didactic poetical works in English.

Davies, Peter. A young clerk in a second-hand London bookshop, in Gilbert Cannan's autobiographical novel *Peter Homunculus* (1909).

Davies, Thomas. b. c1712; d. at London, May 5, 1785. An English bookseller. He tried acting from time to time, but without success. In 1763 he introduced Boswell to Samuel Johnson. He republished a number of old authors, including William Browne, Sir John Davies, Lillo, and Massinger. In 1785 he published his *Dramatic Miscellanies.*

Davies, William Henry. b. at Newport, Monmouthshire, England, April 20, 1871; d. at Nailsworth, Gloucestershire, England, Sept. 26, 1940. An English tramp, peddler, poet, novelist, dramatist, and anthologist. After losing his right leg while stealing a ride on a train in Canada, he decided to return to England and to take up literature as an occupation. He was the author of a considerable body of work in both prose and poetry; among his writings are *The Soul's Destroyer* (1907), *Nature Poems* (1908), *Songs of Joy* (1911), *Foliage* (1913), *Raptures* (1918), *Song of Life* (1920), *Hour of Magic* (1922), *Secrets* (1924), *Poet's Alphabet* (1925), *Song of Love* (1926), *Poet's Calendar* (1927), and *49 Poems* (1928), books of poetry; *A Weak Woman* (1911), *Adventures of Johnny Walker, Tramp* (1926), and *Dancing Mad* (1927), prose fiction; *Autobiography of a Supertramp* (1908), *Beggars* (1909), *Nature* (1913), *Later Days* (1925), *My Birds* and *My Garden* (both 1933), autobiography and essays; and *A Tramp's Opera in Three Acts* (1923). In 1922 and 1930 he edited two poetry anthologies, *Shorter Lyrics of the 20th Century* and *Jewels of Song.* Some of his best poems are *Days Too Short, The Moon, The Two Stars, Jenny Wren, The Hermit, When Yon Full Moon,* and *Sheep.*

Davie Wilson (dā'vi wil'son). See **Snuffy Davie.**

Davis (dā'vis), **John.** See **Davys, John.**

Davis, Thomas Osborne. b. at Mallow, County Cork, Ireland, Oct. 14, 1814; d. at Dublin, Sept. 16, 1845. An Irish poet and politician. He graduated at Trinity College in 1836, was admitted to the bar in 1838, became joint editor with John Blake Dillon of the *Dublin Morning Register* in 1841, and founded, with Charles Gavan Duffy and Dillon, the *Nation* in 1842. He joined in 1839 the Repeal Association, within which organization he founded the party of Young Ireland in opposition to O'Connell's leadership. His poems, collected after his death, form a volume of Duffy's *Library of Ireland* for 1846.

D'Avolos (dav'o.los). In John Ford's *Love's Sacrifice,* the duke's secretary (modeled on Shakespeare's Iago), a spy and "pander to the bad passions of others."

Davus sum (dā'vus sum). An allusion to a line in *Andria* by the Latin dramatist Terence: *Davus sum, non Oedipus* ("I am Davus, not Oedipus"). The line is spoken by the simple, rustic Davus (a conventional name for a slave in Latin comedies), who is unable (and thus tersely explains why he is unable) to understand the secret of the Sphinx, which was clear enough to Oedipus. Byron employs the allusion in *Don Juan* (Canto XIII).

d, d or j; ş, s or sh; ţ, t or ch; z̧, z or zh; o, F. cloche; ü, F. menu; ch, Sc. loch; ṅ, F. bonbon

Davy (dā′vi). In Shakespeare's *2 Henry IV*, a servant of Shallow. He asks his master to judge his friend leniently because "an honest man is able to speak for himself when a knave is not" (V.i).

Davy, Sir Humphry. b. at Penzance, Cornwall, England, Dec. 17, 1778; d. at Geneva, Switzerland, May 29, 1829. An English scientist. The son of a woodcarver, he grew up in Cornwall, receiving his elementary education at Truro, and becoming in 1795 an apprentice to an apothecary at Penzance. This was a fortunate beginning of his career, in that it confirmed his interest in chemistry, and as early as 1799 he discovered the effects of inhaling nitrous oxide (laughing gas) and experimented with inhalation of other gases. In 1801 he became a lecturer in, and from 1802 to 1813 was a professor of, chemistry at the Royal Institute, London. During this period he first isolated several of the elements by electrolysis. He is noted for his demonstration that the diamond is a carbon, and even more as the inventor of a safety lamp for use in mines, which was of importance in the extension of coal mining in Great Britain and other countries. He was also an early student of agricultural chemistry. He was knighted in 1812 and made a baronet in 1818. In 1820 he was elected president of the Royal Society. Among his important books were *On Some Chemical Agencies of Electricity* (1807) and *Elements of Agricultural Chemistry* (1813). His collected works were published (1839–40) in nine volumes.

Davy Jones (jōnz). In nautical folklore, a personification of the sea, whence "Davy Jones's Locker" means the bottom of the sea, especially as the grave of the drowned. These terms, first current among sailors, are now parts of common speech, and universally understood among English-speaking peoples, but their origin is unknown. There is no legend of a real or mythical Davy Jones. A connection has been surmised between the name Jones and the prophet Jonah who is reported in the Bible to have been swallowed by a whale. The two names ("Davy" and "Jones") together strongly suggest that this modern mythological immortal may have been born in the imagination of Welsh mariners.

Davys (dā′vis), **John.** [Also, **Davis.**] b. at Sandridge, Devonshire, England, c1550; killed in the Strait of Malacca, Dec. 29, 1605. An English navigator. He commanded expeditions in search of the Northwest Passage in 1585, 1586, and 1587, on the first of which he discovered Davis Strait. He discovered the Falkland Islands in 1592. He sailed with Raleigh on the raiding voyage to Cádiz and the Azores in 1596. He took service in 1604 as pilot in the *Tiger*, under Captain Sir Edward Michelborne, destined for a voyage to the East Indies, on which he was killed by Japanese pirates.

Daw (dô), **Sir David.** A foolish baronet in Richard Cumberland's *Wheel of Fortune.*

Daw, Sir John. In Ben Jonson's comedy *Epicoene, or The Silent Woman*, a cowardly, foolish coxcomb.

Dawkins (dô′kinz), **John.** A young pickpocket in the employ of Fagin, in Charles Dickens's *Oliver Twist;* called the "Artful Dodger" from his expertness at his trade.

Dawn's Left Hand. A novel by Dorothy M. Richardson, published in 1931. It is the tenth section of *Pilgrimage* (1938), a novel sequence in 12 parts employing the stream-of-consciousness technique

Dawson (dô′son), **A. J.** [Full name, **Alec John Dawson.**] b. at London, Aug. 25, 1872—. An English novelist. He served (1914–19) in World War I as a major. His books include *Middle Greyness, God's Foundling, Bismillah, Hidden Manna, The Message, Finn the Wolfhound, Jan: Son of Finn, A Temporary Gentleman in France, Peter of Monkslease: his Mortal Tenement* (1924), *The Emergence of Marie* (1926), and *The Case Books of X 37* (1930).

Dawson, Bully. fl. in the 17th century. A notorious London sharper, a contemporary of the dramatist Sir George Etherege, who is supposed to have been not unfriendly to him.

Dawson, James. b. c1717; d. at Kensington Green, London, 1746. A young volunteer officer, of good family, in the service of Charles Edward Stuart, the Young Pretender. He was hanged, drawn, and quartered, and his heart burned, on July 30, 1746, for treason. His betrothed was present, and, when all was over, she died in the arms of a friend. William Shenstone made this the subject of a ballad, *Jemmy Dawson.*

Day (dā), **Fancy.** The heroine of Thomas Hardy's *Under the Greenwood Tree.* She is a young schoolmistress, who finally marries the man she loves.

Day, John. b. c1574; d. c1640. An English dramatist and poet. He was described as the son of Walter Dey, a farmer of Cawston, in Norfolk, when he became a bursary student at Gonville and Caius College, Cambridge, on Oct. 24, 1592. He was expelled on May 4, 1593 for stealing a book. From 1599 to 1603 he wrote for the Admiral's Men, following this by a short stint for the Earl of Worcester's Men. Most of this work was in collaboration, sometimes with Dekker but more often with the hack writers kept by Henslowe to fill his continual need for new plays. The only surviving play of this period is *The Blind Beggar of Bednal Green.* He was the author also of *The Isle of Gulls* (printed in 1606), *Law Tricks, or Who Would Have Thought It?* (printed in 1608, produced c1604), *The Travels of Three English Brothers* (printed in 1607), and *Humour Out of Breath* (printed in 1608). His plays written independently (1604–08) and *The Parliament of Bees* (written probably between 1608 and 1616, but not published until 1641) are better than would have been expected from his earlier work, but Jonson still classed him among the rogues and "base fellows" who were "not . . . of the faithful," that is, not poets. He was mentioned as still living in 1640, but nothing is known of his later years.

Day, Mr. In Sir Robert Howard's play *The Committee*, the chairman of the committee, a kind of Tartuffe, under the thumb of his wife.

Day, Thomas. b. at London, June 22, 1748; d. at Wargrave, Berkshire, England, Sept. 28, 1789. An English follower of Rousseau's theories, educator, essayist, poet, and philanthropist. He was educated at the famous Charterhouse School (where Thackeray spent six years) and at Corpus Christi College, Oxford. He was a friend of Sir William Jones, of R. L. Edgeworth, Maria's father, and of

Erasmus Darwin. As a child, he was in the habit of giving his pocket money to poor people, and was noted for his kindness to animals. In later life, he refused to obey Jones's request, "kill that spider," remarking that he had no more right to do so than he would have to kill Jones if some powerful person said "kill that lawyer." When he married a lady of means, in 1778, he made her take all necessary steps to make it impossible for him to touch her fortune. His theory that animals will always respond to kindness he carried to such an extreme that it caused his death. On a visit to his wife and mother he was thrown on his head by an unbroken colt, the animal becoming frightened and shying as they neared Wargrave. Day died within an hour, and his wife, who never recovered from the shock, died of a broken heart two years later. Day wrote *The Dying Negro* (1773), a poem, *The Desolation of America* (1777), *Reflections on the Present State of England and the Independence of America* (1782), *Letters of Marius, or Reflections upon the Peace, the East India Bill, and the Present Crisis*, and *Fragments of Original Letters on the Slavery of the Negroes* (both 1784), *Dialogue between a Justice of the Peace and a Farmer* (1785), and the *History of Little Jack* (which was published in the *Children's Miscellany*, and separately in 1788), some pamphlets and a few poems. He is remembered, however, as the author of a moral and didactic romance, *The History of Sanford and Merton* (3 vols., 1783, 1787, 1789), in which he sets forth his ideals of right character and conduct.

Day Lewis (lŏ'is), **Cecil.** See **Lewis, Cecil Day.**

Day of the Rabblement (rab'l.ment), **The.** An essay in pamphlet form by James Joyce, published in 1901, bitterly attacking the Irish National Theatre movement.

Days and Nights. An early volume of verse (1889) by Arthur Symons.

Dead, The. A short story (1914) in a collection, *Dubliners*, by James Joyce. The main characters are a middle-aged Irish schoolteacher and book reviewer, Gabriel Conroy, his wife, Gretta, and Michael Furey, who is dead before the story opens, who loved her. Gretta, who has not been thinking of him, tells her husband that a song they have just heard at a party has brought Michael back to her mind. The confession makes Conroy unhappy as he feels that his wife has closed a door on him and that the dead lover has an advantage over him. The story has been praised for its descriptive as well as its narrative power, and was discussed, 20 years later, by T. S. Eliot in his book of criticism *After Strange Gods.* Dublin is the setting of all the stories, and *The Dead* is the fifteenth, and last, story.

Dead, The. Two sonnets, out of the 1914 group of five, by Rupert Brooke. The same title is given to the third sonnet ("Blow out, you bugles, over the rich Dead!") and to the fourth ("These hearts were woven of human joys and cares"). The fifth one in the group is the famous one with which the poet's name is perhaps chiefly associated, *The Soldier* ("If I should die, think only this of me").

Dead Heart, The. A play (1859) by Watts Phillips. It was revised (1889) by W. H. Pollock for Sir Henry Irving.

Deadlock. A novel by Dorothy M. Richardson, published in 1921. It is the sixth section of *Pilgrimage* (1938), a novel sequence in 12 parts employing the stream-of-consciousness technique.

Dead Souls. A novel by Nikolai V. Gogol, which appeared in 1842. He began to write it in 1837, and left it unfinished, destroying the concluding portions in a fit of religious mania. An English translation, entitled *Tchitchikoff's Journeys, or Dead Souls*, by Isabel F. Hapgood, was published (1886) at New York. At the time of serfdom a Russian proprietor's fortune was not valued according to the extent of his lands, but according to the number of male serfs who were held upon them. These serfs were called "souls." Chichikov, or Tchitchikoff, the hero of the book, an ambitious rascal, attempts to gain wealth by traveling about buying "dead souls" (serfs who had died but had not yet been listed as dead by the census), and using them to obtain possession of certain lands the government was offering to those who could prove they had the manpower to develop them. The importance of the book is in its realistic pictures of Russia before the liberation of the serfs, and in the stimulation it gave in the development of the Russian realistic novel of the 19th century. The book is a humorous satire based on a very serious attack on the principle of serfdom and on the idiocies of Russian officialdom.

Deane (dēn), **Lucy.** In George Eliot's novel *The Mill on the Floss*, a pretty, amiable girl, the cousin and rival of Maggie Tulliver.

Dean of Saint Patrick's. The post held by Jonathan Swift from 1713, at Dublin, whence the references very commonly made to "Dean Swift."

Deans (dēnz), **Douce Davie.** A cow-feeder in Sir Walter Scott's novel *The Heart of Midlothian*. He is the father of Jeanie and Effie, and is distracted between his religious principles as an ardent Cameronian and his desire to save his daughter Effie's life.

Deans, Effie. [Formally, **Euphemia Deans.**] In Sir Walter Scott's novel *The Heart of Midlothian*, a beautiful and erring girl, the younger half-sister of Jeanie Deans.

Deans, Jeanie. The heroine of Sir Walter Scott's novel *The Heart of Midlothian*, the half-sister of Effie Deans. In her devotion to her sister she walks all the way to London to obtain pardon for Effie from the queen. Her good sense, calm heroism, and disinterestedness move the Duke of Argyll to procure her the desired interview, which is successful.

Dear Brutus. A comedy (1917) by James M. Barrie. The philosophy of the play is expressed in the lines by Shakespeare from which its title is derived: "The fault, dear Brutus, is not in our stars, But we ourselves" (*Julius Caesar*).

Death and Dr. Hornbook (hôrn'bŭk). A poem by Robert Burns.

Death by Water. The fourth section of T. S. Eliot's *The Wasteland.* This is actually the culminating section of the poem, referring back to the first section ("The Burial of the Dead"), containing the admonition: "fear death by water."

Death of a Hero. A satirical novel, a product of experiences in World War I, by Richard Aldington, published in 1929. This bitter first novel concerns the psychological impact of war on the mind of a young man, George Winterbourne, who was just approaching emotional maturity when the war disrupted his life and consigned him to the trenches in France.

Death of Blanche the Duchess, The. See **Book of the Duchess, The.**

Death of Cuchulain (kŏ.chŏŏ'lin), **The.** A poem (1893) by William Butler Yeats. It tells the story of the great Irish hero, Cuchulain, who unknowingly kills his own son in battle (just as Rustum kills his son, Sohrab, in Arnold's poem). The story has been told in many forms by many Irish authors, and Yeats himself told it later (1904) in his play *On Baile's Strand.*

Death of Marlowe (mär'lō), **The.** A tragedy by R. H. Horne, published in 1837.

Death of Society, The. A novel by Romer Wilson (Mrs. Edward J. O'Brien), published in 1921. It was awarded the Hawthornden Prize.

Death of the Heart, The. A novel by Elizabeth Bowen, published in 1938.

Death of the Moth, and Other Essays, The. A volume of critical essays (1942) by Virginia Woolf. It expresses her views on various phases of the culture of her time, and was published a year after her death.

Death's Head Corps. See **Black Brunswickers.**

Death's Jest Book, or The Fool's Tragedy. A tragedy by T. L. Beddoes, published in 1850. It is the true story of the stabbing of a duke in the 13th century by his court fool.

Death Song. [Also, **Bede's Death Song.**] An Old English poem of five lines by Bede. It is the only poem by Bede that has survived, and that only because it is quoted in a letter by Saint Cuthbert. Like *Beowulf,* it shows the great store that men set by an honorable name after death, and shows an ideal of conduct in transition from non-Christian to Christian times; Bede wrote as a Christian, and obviously had Doomsday in mind, but a very slight alteration would cause the verse to state an attitude characteristic also of Bede's pagan forebears.

De Augmentis (dē ôg.men'tis). [Full title, **De Augmentis Scientiarum.**] A philosophical treatise by Francis Bacon, published (1605) in English under the title *Advancement of Learning.*

Debatable Ground. American title of **Children of No Man's Land.**

Debatable Land. A region on the border of England and Scotland, between the Esk and Sark, formerly claimed by both kingdoms.

Debbitch (deb'ich), **Deborah.** In Sir Walter Scott's novel *Peveril of the Peak,* the governess of Alice Bridgenorth. She was coquettish and deceitful.

De Beringhen (dẹ ber'ing.gẹn). See **Beringhen, De.**

Debonair. A novel by G. B. Stern, published in 1928 and dramatized in 1930.

De Bourgh (dẹ bėrg), **Lady Catherine.** In Jane Austen's novel *Pride and Prejudice,* the bullying aunt of Darcy.

Debrett (dẹ.bret'), **John.** b. c1752; d. at London, Nov. 15, 1822. An English publisher. In 1781 he purchased the Piccadilly business of John Almon, bookseller and political journalist. He compiled and published *Peerage of England, Scotland, and Ireland, Containing an Account of all the Peers* (2 vols., May, 1802), which ran through 14 editions during his lifetime, and *Baronetage of England, Containing their Descent and Present State* (1808). Both works, bearing Debrett's name, are still published annually. He retired from business in 1814.

Decadents. A literary term used to refer to a group of writers of the 19th century, chiefly French, although poets, novelists, dramatists, and artists of other countries (including Great Britain) may exhibit in their work or express sympathy with the tendencies associated with the French originators and leaders of the movement. In England, those influenced by the movement are Arthur Symons, who translated Baudelaire and Louys, Ernest Dowson, who wrote the poem *Cynara,* Aubrey Beardsley, of the *Yellow Book,* and Frank Harris, biographer of Wilde and author of *My Life and Loves,* which no one has yet criticized for its reticence. In France, the outstanding names are Verlaine, Rimbaud, Baudelaire, Mallarmé, Francis Jammes, J. K. Huysmans, Villiers de l'Isle Adam, Régnier, and Pierre Louys, author of *Aphrodite.* The decadents rejected the ordinary and conventional modes of thought and conduct, and violated, both publicly and privately, the accepted rules of social, moral, and sexual behavior. They tend to show a preference for the morbid and the abnormal, as those terms are ordinarily used and understood, and they were either oversensitive to a degree, or they cultivated oversensitiveness. The pomp and pageantry of the medieval period appealed to many of them artistically and emotionally. The terms "vice," "virtue," "evil," "morality," and "immorality," which mean so much and play so large a part in ordinary life and work and play, either mean little to them, or carry a meaning that is radically different from the one generally accepted. With them, content, what the artist says, is inferior to form, which emphasizes how it is said. A Spanish follower of decadence is Rubén Darío. In America, with some modifications, Poe was translated by Baudelaire and Mallarmé, and Whitman may be included as members of the group. Another American, of a later period, Edgar Saltus, wrote two works whose titles express decadent tendencies, *The Philosophy of Disenchantment* and *The Anatomy of Negation.* The term, which signifies decaying, dying, in Latin, probably refers to the disintegration of the old Roman Empire. It is used generally, if not always, in a derogatory sense, although, as frequently happens in such cases, the term is taken up by those against whom it is hurled as a mark or sign of distinction and honor. The French Decadents, certainly, did not object to the term or regard it as a handicap.

Decameron (dẹ.kam'ẹ.ron). [Italian, **Il Decamerone; Principe Galeotto.**] A collection of 100 tales, by Giovanni Boccaccio, written probably not long after 1348. The tales are enclosed by a framework device giving a fictional account of how they came to be told: in the year 1348, in order to escape from the plague-ridden city of Florence, a gay company of seven young ladies and three young gentlemen retire to villas and pleasant gardens above the city where through the hot afternoon hours of ten summer days they pass the time by telling stories, one each on each day, under some general heading or subject matter proclaimed by the one who is elected king or queen for the day. The *Decameron* is a masterpiece of prose style and narrative art. It became a model for Italian prose for centuries after, and enjoyed great popularity throughout Europe. Not even the major part of the stories contained in it were invented by Boccaccio, but all are cast in a manner quite his own. Included are the tales of the day from the French *fabliaux*, from incidents of actual life, or from whatever source was open to the author. The collection has had, through the years, the reputation of being overly licentious, but the tales reflect the mid-14th century in its moral as well as its immoral aspects They present a kind of "human comedy," rich in the variety of characters that people it, a "natural" world quite untouched by any sense of otherworldliness as might be expected in a work written less than half a century after Dante's *Divine Comedy*. Both the proem of the work with its dedication to the "idle ladies" (as its ideal public), and the framework where the author speaks out in his own person in defense of a serene and objective art free from allegory, moralism, and didacticism, give ample evidence that Boccaccio was aware that this "new" art might well be attacked by those who demand that literature should do more than entertain, a fear which history has shown to be not without some ground. The collection of tales is also entitled *Principe Galeotto*, an appellation which the deputies appointed for correction of the *Decameron* considered as derived from the 5th canto of Dante's *Inferno*, Galeotto being the name of the book which was read by Paolo and Francesca. Few works have had an equal influence on literature. From it Chaucer adopted the idea of the framework of his tales, and the general manner of his stories, while in some instances, he merely versified the novels of the Italian. In 1566, William Paynter printed many of Boccaccio's stories in English, in his work called *The Palace of Pleasure*. This first translation, containing 60 novels, was soon followed by another volume, comprising 34 additional tales. Shakespeare made considerable use of the tales as he found them in Paynter.

Decimus Tite Barnacle (bär'na.kl), **Lord.** See **Barnacle, Lord Decimus Tite.**

Decius Brutus (dē'shus brö'tus, desh'us). See **Brutus, Decius.**

De Civili Dominio (dē si.vī'lī dō.min'i.ō). A Latin treatise (c1375) by John Wycliffe, in which he argues that the Church has no power over temporal affairs and that the clergy should not hold property.

Decker (dek'ėr), **Thomas.** See **Dekker, Thomas.**

Declaration of Indulgence. See **Indulgence, Declaration of.**

Declaration of Right, The. An affirmation (1689) of the ancient constitutional rights of the English nation: confirmed by Parliament as the Bill of Rights.

Decline and Fall. A novel by Evelyn Waugh, published in 1928.

Decline and Fall of the Roman Empire, The. A celebrated history by Edward Gibbon, published in six volumes (1776–88). It is regarded as one of the classical works of historical literature in the English language. Gibbon's panoramic sweep embraces three periods covering a total of some 13 centuries: from the rule of Trajan and the Antonines to the decay of the Western Empire; from the era of Justinian in the East to the founding of the German Empire of the West under Charlemagne; and from the restoration of the Western Empire to the capture (1453) of Constantinople by the Turks. Gibbon's point of view is suggested by his observation that history is a record of "little more than the crimes, follies, and misfortunes of mankind." He relies on fact and incident to carry his story, but he expresses a love for the classical and a dislike for Christianity despite his attempted "outside view."

De consolatione philosophiae (dē kon.sọ.lā.shi.ọ'nē fil.ọ.sō'fi.ē). [Eng. trans., *"On the Consolation of Philosophy."*] A Latin work in prose and verse, written by Boethius c525 A.D., while he was imprisoned and awaiting execution. It was translated into Old English by Alfred the Great. Chaucer translated it into English prose before 1382. Caxton published it in 1480.

Decretals of the Pseudo-Isidore (sü'dọ.iz'i.dôr). See **False Decretals.**

de Croye (de kroi'), **Hameline, Countess.** See **Croye, Hameline, Countess de.**

Dedalus (ded'a.lus, dē'da-), **May.** The wife of Simon, and mother of Stephen and Dilly, in James Joyce's autobiographical novel *Portrait of the Artist as a Young Man* (1916). A devout Roman Catholic who is stunned when her son leaves the Church, she is believed to be a portrait of the author's own mother. In *Ulysses*, part of Stephen's day-long thought complex is concerned with her death.

Dedalus, Simon. Stephen's father and May's husband in James Joyce's autobiographical novel *Portrait of the Artist as a Young Man* (1916). A careless, happy-go-lucky character, more interested in pleasure than responsibility, he is regarded as a partial portrait of the author's father. He appears in several scenes in *Ulysses*.

Dedalus, Stephen. The protagonist of *A Portrait of the Artist as a Young Man* (1916) and one of the chief characters in *Ulysses* (1922), two novels by James Joyce. Believed to be a portrait of the author, Stephen is a sensitive artist type whose rich imagination helps him rise above his drab background. In the *Portrait* he is shown in revolt against his Roman Catholic and national cultural heritage as he strives toward an articulated esthetic; in *Ulysses* he is employed as a counterpart of Telemachus in the *Odyssey* in his quest for a father symbol.

Dedlock (ded'lok), **Lady.** The wife of Sir Leicester Dedlock in Charles Dickens's novel *Bleak House:* a haughty woman of fashion, secretly consumed with terror, shame, and remorse. She has an illegitimate child, Esther Summerson, but marries Sir

---

ḍ, d or j; ṣ, s or sh; ṭ, t or ch; ẓ, z or zh; o, F. cloche; ü, F. menu; ċh, Sc. loch; ṅ, F. bonbon.

Leicester, who is ignorant of her history. Her secret becomes known to Mr. Tulkinghorn, her husband's legal adviser, who tells her of his design to reveal it to her husband. She leaves home and dies from exposure and remorse at the gate of the graveyard where Captain Hawdon, the father of her child, is buried.

Dedlock, Sir Leicester. An extremely ceremonious and stately old baronet in Charles Dickens's novel *Bleak House*. He is perfectly honorable, but prejudiced to the most unreasonable degree, with a genuine affection and admiration for Lady Dedlock.

De Dominio Divino (dē dọ.min'i.ō di.vī'nō). A Latin treatise (c1375) by John Wycliffe, in which he argues that the Church has no power over temporal matters.

Dee (dē). [Latin, **Deva**.] A river in N Wales and W England, rising in Lake Bala, in Merionethshire, Wales, flowing through Denbighshire, Wales, and Cheshire, England, through Chester to its estuary on the Irish Sea. Length, ab. 70 mi. (including the estuary).

Dee, John. b. at London, July 13, 1527; d. at Mortlake, Surrey, England, in December, 1608. An English mathematician and astrologer. He took the degree of B.A. at Cambridge in 1545, was appointed one of the foundation fellows of Trinity College, Cambridge, in 1546, and lectured (c1550) on the *Elements* of Euclid at Paris. He returned to England in 1551 and became astrologer to the queen, Mary Tudor, was prosecuted before the Star Chamber on the charge of magic but was released c1555, practiced the various arts of astrology and horoscopy at the court of Elizabeth, gave exhibitions of magic at the courts of various princes in Poland and Bohemia (1583–88), and was appointed warden of Christ's College, Manchester, in 1595. He was patronized by Queen Elizabeth, who received instruction from him in astrology in 1564. According to the *Athenae Cantabrigienses* he wrote 79 works, most of which have never been printed. His most notable work is *Monas Hieroglyphica* (1564). Dee's reputation was primarily that of a magician, and his experiments in crystal-gazing and the evocation of spirits show his interest in magic, but he was also a sober mathematician who advocated the adoption of the Gregorian calendar and who did geographical descriptions of the new lands in America.

Deeping (dēp'ing), **Warwick.** [Full name, **George Warwick Deeping.**] b. at Southend, Essex, England, May 28, 1877; d. at Weybridge, England, April 20, 1950. An English novelist. He studied medicine but abandoned it, after a year of practice, in favor of writing. During World War I he was on active service in Gallipoli, Egypt, and France. His books include *Uther and Igraine* (1903; rev. ed., 1927), *Bess of the Woods* (1906), *Bertrand of Brittany* (1908), *The Red Saint* (1909), *The Lame Englishman* (1910), *Joan of the Tower* (1911), *The House of Spies* (1913), *The King Behind the King* (1914), *Unrest* (1916), *Martin Valliant* (1917), *Valour* (1918), *Lantern Lane* (1921), *Orchards* (1922), *Apples of Gold* (1923), *Sorrell and Son* (1925), *Doomsday* (1926), *Kitty* (1927), *Old Pybus* (1928), *Roper's Row* (1929), *Exile* (1930), *Old Wine and New* (1932), *Blind Man's Year*

(1937), *The Man Who Went Back* (1940), *Mr. Gurney and Mr. Slade* (1944), *Reprieve* (1945), and *The Impudence of Youth* (1946).

Deerbrook. A novel (1839) by Harriet Martineau.

Defarge (dẹ.färzh'), **Thérèse.** In Charles Dickens's *Tale of Two Cities*, the wife of the keeper of a wineshop. A type of the remorseless women of the St. Antoine quarter of Paris during the French Revolution, she takes her seat daily in front of the guillotine and knits while the executions take place.

Defence of Cony-Catching, The. A pamphlet (1592) by an unknown author, written as an answer to two pamphlets by Robert Greene, one of which was entitled *A Notable Discovery of Cozenage Now Daily Practised by Sundry Lewd Persons, Called Cony-Catchers and Crossbiters* (1591). In Elizabethan English, a "cony-catcher" was a thief, a cheat, sharper, trickster, swindler, a criminal of any kind, male or female, and "cony-catching" was stealing, cheating, or swindling in the manner of a cony-catcher. The author of the *Defence* signed himself "Cuthbert Cony-Catcher" and offered his work as "a confutation of those two injurious pamphlets published by R.G."

Defence of Cosmetics, A. An essay (1922) by Sir Max Beerbohm, English novelist, parodist, and humorist. It was written at Oxford, where he was a student at Merton College, and was later called *The Pervasion of Rouge*. It justifies, with a blending of humor and seriousness, the place of artificiality and some forms of trickery or craftiness in modern civilization.

Defence of Guinevere, and Other Poems, The. A volume (1858) by William Morris. As the title suggests, it gives a more favorable view and a more sympathetic and subtle portrait of Arthur's wife than is found in the older Arthurian romances. Several of the poems in this volume, which has been called "that extraordinary book of verse," were originally published in *The Oxford and Cambridge Magazine*. Critics have pointed out that it shows both the defects and the qualities of his age (Morris was 24 at the time) but they have praised the title poem and "King Arthur's Tomb" for their passion and fire and energy.

Defence of Poesie, The. A title given to Sir Philip Sidney's essay on poetry, written c1579 and printed by Ponsonby in 1595; another version of the essay, printed by Olney the same year, is called *An Apologie for Poetrie*. It is a reply to the *School of Abuse* (1579) by the Puritan Stephen Gosson, in which all secular literature is attacked.

Defence of Poetry. A volume in verse by Isaac D'Israeli (the father of Benjamin Disraeli), published in 1790. It was his first work.

Defence of Poetry, The. A literary essay (1821) by Percy Bysshe Shelley, probably his best-known prose work. Published the year before his death, it is an answer to *The Four Ages of Poetry*, by his friend Thomas Love Peacock, and a strong plea for imagination and love in poetry. Its thesis (that the poet is a social and moral force, and that the poet must be a teacher, as well as a singer) is expressed poetically in Shelley's *Ode to the West Wind* and *To a Skylark*. The essay naturally invites a comparison with Sidney's piece of literary criticism (written over 200 years earlier) *An Apologie for Poetrie*, or, as it was called in another edition, *The Defence of Poesie*.

Defence of Rime, A. A critical essay (1603) by Samuel Daniel, "the well-languaged" Daniel, in which he makes a plea for the use of English verse forms. It was written in reply to Campion's *Observations* (1602), advocating the use of Latin meters in English poetry.

Defender of the Faith. A title (in Latin, *Fidei Defensor*) conferred (Oct. 11, 1521) by Pope Leo X upon Henry VIII of England, in recognition of the latter's treatise *Assertio septem sacramentorum* (1521) against Luther. Pope Paul III retracted the title after Henry's break with the Roman Catholic Church, but in 1544 it was granted the king by Parliament and has been retained by succeeding English sovereigns.

Deffand (de.fän), Marquise **du.** [Title of **Marie de Vichy-Chamrond.**] b. at the Château de Chamrond, France, 1697; d. at Paris, Sept. 24, 1780. A French leader in Parisian literary and philosophical circles, noted for her wit and cynicism. She was married to the Marquis du Deffand in 1718, but soon separated from him. In 1753, she became blind. She is noted for her correspondence with Voltaire, Hénault, Montesquieu, Horace Walpole, and other great men of her time.

De Flores (dē flō'rēz). In *The Changeling* by Thomas Middleton and William Rowley, an ill-favored, broken gentleman in the service of Vermandero, the father of Beatrice-Joanna. He loves Beatrice, who loathes him. Trusting in his devotion and poverty, she induces him to murder Alonzo de Pivacquo, to whom her father has betrothed her though she loves Alsemero. In a powerful scene he declares to her that she shall never marry Alsemero unless she first yields to him. He never relents, and after killing Beatrice dies triumphant, by his own hand, when the double discovery of the liaison and murder is made.

Defoe (dẹ.fō'), **Daniel.** [Also, **De Foe.**] b. at London, 1660; d. there, April 26, 1731. An English novelist and political journalist; son of a chandler and butcher who became a Dissenter after the Act of Uniformity (1662). Daniel's surname (originally Foe or De Foe, variously spelled) was usually written De Foe after 1703 (modern editors, however, universally spell it Defoe). He studied for the Presbyterian ministry at Morton's academy at Stoke Newington, and his first poems (in manuscript, 1681) were religious meditations; but he became a merchant. He traveled widely in Great Britain and on the Continent, and was once captured and held by Algerian pirates between Harwich and Holland. In 1684 he married Mary Tuffley, by whom he had seven children. After going into bankruptcy for 17,000 pounds through rashness and wartime difficulties (1692) he satisfied his creditors, but debts were often revived for political persecution and he died in hiding because of an old claim. He joined the rising under the Duke of Monmouth in 1685, entered London in triumph with William of Orange (William III) in 1688, and with few intervals from 1689 to 1731 served four sovereigns as a pamphleteer. He held minor offices under William III and became his trusted confidant, suggesting plans for peace and war. He defended the Dutch in *The True-Born Englishman* (1701), a poem ridiculing racial superiority. After William's death his ironical tract *The Shortest Way with the Dissenters* (1702) gave an excuse for his prosecution by Tories before alderman judges (partly Whigs) whom he had satirized. He was sentenced (July, 1703) to stand three times in the pillory, pay a heavy fine, give sureties for seven years, and remain in prison till all was performed. His business as a tile manufacturer failed before Robert Harley procured his release (November, 1703) from Newgate Prison to serve the government. His *Review* (1704–13) was best known of many journalistic undertakings. He promoted the union with Scotland (1707), urged peace with France (1713), and supported the Hanoverian succession (1714). In 1713 he was imprisoned for a short time when Whigs professed that his ironical tracts against the Old Pretender were treasonable. Although a Whig and a Dissenter, he put national interests first, writing to make the government's policies intelligible and acceptable to the public, and his opponents usually welcomed his services when they got into office; but he never supported the Stuarts or intolerance. In 1719 he began the works of fiction for which he is best known: *The Life and Strange Surprizing Adventures of Robinson Crusoe, of York, Mariner* (1719), *The Memoirs of a Cavalier* (1720), *The Life, Adventures, and Piracies of the Famous Captain Singleton* (1720), *The Fortunes and Misfortunes of the Famous Moll Flanders* (1722), *A Journal of the Plague Year* (1722), *The History and Remarkable Life of Colonel Jacque, Commonly call'd Colonel Jack* (1722), and *Roxana, or The Fortunate Mistress* (1724). Among his later writings are *A Tour thro' the whole Island of Great Britain* (1724–27), *A General History of the Pirates* (1724–28), *The Compleat English Tradesman* (1725–27), *The Memoirs of Captain Carleton* (1728), and *Robert Drury's Journal* (1729). He wrote considerably more than 400 books and tracts, on most subjects of public interest, nearly all issued without his name. He developed a prose style remarkable for simplicity and directness. As a journalist and novelist he had an extraordinary ability to capture details of speech and incident, and in Robinson Crusoe and Moll Flanders he created two memorable characters. As a historical writer he was notable for visualizing and interpreting events; all historians who deal with his period stand (often unconsciously) in his debt. Benjamin Franklin acknowledged his obligation to *An Essay upon Projects* (1697). In his writings on public affairs Defoe expressed many of the best ideas of his age; his own proposals often anticipated the thought of today.

Deformed Transformed, The. A fragment of a Biblical play by Byron, published in 1824. It was partly founded on Goethe's *Faust*. An earlier portion was entitled *Heaven and Earth*, and published in 1823.

Degare (deg'ạ.rẹ) or **Degore** (deg'ọ.rẹ), **Sir.** See **Sir Degare.**

Degas (dẹ.gä), **Hilaire Germain Edgar.** b. at Paris, July 19, 1834; d. 1917. A French painter. He belonged to the group of Impressionists and was early associated with Manet, Monet, Renoir, and Fantin-Latour. His first successes were made with pictures representing race-courses, but his subjects were later usually taken from the theater, and he depicted life behind the scenes, especially of ballet dancers, with great appreciation; remarkable are also his studies of women in everyday poses. He visited America and painted a noted picture of Negroes loading cotton at New Orleans.

Degrevant (deg′rẹ.vạnt), **Sir.** See **Sir Degrevant**.

Dehan (dē′han), **Richard.** Pseudonym of **Graves, Clotilde Inez Mary.**

Deianira (dē.yạ.nī′rạ) or **Dejaneira** (dej.ạ.nī′rạ). In Greek mythology, a daughter of Oeneus and Althaea, sister of Meleager, and wife of Hercules. She inadvertently caused Hercules's death by giving him the blood-steeped shirt of the centaur Nessus to wear, after the latter, dying and seeking revenge on Hercules, who had shot him, had told her that she could compel the love of any one wearing it. It burned him mortally, and she killed herself for sorrow.

Deil (dēl), **Address to the.** See **Address to the Deil.**

De imitatione Christi (dē im.i.tā.shi.ō′nē kris′tī). [Eng. trans., *"Imitation of Christ."*] A religious treatise commonly ascribed to Thomas a Kempis, but about which there has been much controversy. It places the rule of life in seclusion and renunciation. Other candidates have been put forward as its author, among them John Gerson, the famous chancellor of the University of Paris, and an unidentified John Gersen, abbot of Vercelli (supported by the Benedictines), whose name appears as that of the author in one manuscript. For Gerson are brought forward a number of early manuscripts and editions in France and Italy. The name of Thomas a Kempis appears on many early editions, including one c1471 which appears to be the first. A general tradition from his own times, extending over most of Europe, has led a great majority (including the Sorbonne itself) to determine the cause in his favor. It is also said that a manuscript of the treatise *De imitatione* bears these words at the conclusion: *"Finitus et completus per manum Thomae de Kempis, 1441"* and that many erasures and alterations in this manuscript give it the appearance of his original autograph.

Deiphobus (dẹ.if′ọ.bus). In Shakespeare's *Troilus and Cressida*, a son of King Priam of Troy.

Deira (dē′i.rạ). See under **Northumbria.**

Deirdre (dir′drẹ, der′drā). The heroine of the greatest love story of old Irish legendry. She was the daughter of Felim, in some versions of the story called a harper, in others a story-teller to Conchobar, king of Ulster about the beginning of the Christian era. By some accounts it was while Conchobar was feasting at Felim's house that a girl-baby was born to Felim's wife, of whom the druid Cathbad prophesied that she would be the most beautiful of the women of Eire but would cause bloodshed and death. Conchobar said that he would avert that doom by marrying Deirdre when she should be of age for it, and she was entrusted to the nurse Lavarcham who brought her up in a house in a secluded woods, where she saw no one but a few servants. One day when she was in her

fifteenth year she saw a raven drinking the blood of a calf that had been slain on the snow, and she told Lavarcham that the man she would love would not be an old man like Conchobar, but one who had skin like the snow, cheeks like the blood, and hair like the raven. The nurse said there was such a man, Naoise, son of Usnach, and she yielded to Deirdre's pleas to bring him to her. Others tell the story differently to this point, but all agree that in the end Naoise and his brothers Ainle and Ardan took Deirdre to Alba, or Scotland, where they lived for some years, until Conchobar persuaded the famous warrior Fergus to go to Alba and invite the fugitives to return, with a promise of the king's friendship. Deirdre foresaw tragedy, but the three brothers trusted Fergus and the king. When they came to Eire, Fergus was detained by a ruse of Conchobar's while the three sons of Usnach, with Deirdre, went to the Ulster capital. There Conchobar set his minions upon the three brothers, who after an epic battle were slain. Some say that Deirdre died at that time after lamenting the deaths of Naoise, Ainle, and Ardan; another story is that she had to live with Conchobar for a year but then killed herself. Fergus and many others deserted Conchobar because of his treachery, and by joining Queen Medb of Connacht in the war of the Tain Bo Cuailgne, ensured the fulfillment of the druid Cathbad's prophecy that because of this crime, Emain Macha (the capital of Ulster) would be destroyed and no son of Conchobar would ever rule in Ulster.

Deirdre. A tragic drama (1907) by William Butler Yeats, based on the theme of ideal love and using materials from Irish legends.

Deirdre. An adaptation by James Stephens of the tragic story of Deirdre, published in 1923.

Deirdre of the Sorrows. A tragedy by John Millington Synge, published in 1910, a year after his death. It is one of the many retellings by other authors, both Irish and non-Irish, of the story of the beautiful but tragic maid of Irish legend. Although left in an unfinished state, the play is regarded as Synge's greatest work.

deism (dē′izm). **1.** The doctrine that God is distinct and separated from the world.
2. Belief in the existence of a personal God, accompanied with the denial of revelation and of the authority of the Christian church. Deism is opposed to atheism, or the denial of any God; to pantheism, which believes not only in a God, but in his living relations with his creatures; and to Christianity, which adds a belief in a historical manifestation of God, as recorded in the Bible.

deism, "Bible" of. See under **Tindal, Matthew.**

Dejaneira (dej.ạ.nī′rạ). See **Deianira.**

Dejection: An Ode. A poem (1802) by Samuel Taylor Coleridge. It was published in *The Morning Post* on Wordsworth's wedding day (Oct. 4, 1802) and was, for some strange reason which is still unknown, written for and given to Wordsworth as a wedding present. In its original version, the poet is several times addressed by name, "William." Later, after the two poets had a misunderstanding, Coleridge changed "William" to "Edmund," to "Otway," and to "Lady" and "Dear Lady." Al-

---

fat, fāte, fär, åsk, fãre; net, mē, hėr; pin, pīne; not, nōte, mōve, nôr; up, lūte, pull; ᴛʜ, then;

though the poem is regarded as one of his two "noble odes" (*France* being the other), critics also regard it as the beginning of the end of his supreme poetic mastery. Coleridge himself, at the end of the second stanza, expresses regret that now he can merely "see" beauty, but not "feel" it.

Dekker (dek'ẽr), **Thomas.** [Also, **Decker.**] b. at London, c1572; d. at Clerkenwell (now part of London), Aug. 25, 1632. An English dramatist, at various times a collaborator of Middleton, Webster, Massinger, Rowley, and others. Little is definitely known of his life. He is first noticed in Henslowe's diary in 1598 as a playwright for the Admiral's Men; in February of that year he was imprisoned in the Counter. Between 1598 and 1602 he wrote eight plays alone and many others in collaboration (the total, according to Chambers, being 44 plays). In 1601 he wrote *Satiromastix, or the Untrussing of the Humorous Poet* (published 1602), a satirical dramatic attack on Ben Jonson, with whom a quarrel had broken out before 1600 when Jonson reflected upon him in *Every Man Out of His Humour* and *Cynthia's Revels*. In 1601 Jonson attacked Dekker and Marston vigorously in *The Poetaster*. Dekker appears as Demetrius Fannius, the "dresser of plays about the town here," and is made to accuse the poet Horace of being a plagiarist, although he himself knows little about classical literature. *Satiromastix* (1602) was Dekker's retort, parodying and ridiculing Jonson's style. However, he shared with Jonson the pageant produced (1604) at James I's entry into London for his coronation. From 1613 to 1619 he seems to have been imprisoned in the King's Bench prison because of debt. He had always been close to poverty and was saved by Henslowe on two previous occasions from arrest. He wrote many pamphlets ridiculing the follies of the times, and in the plays written with others he excelled in good shop scenes and those laid in inns, taverns, and suburban pleasure-houses. He also had a poetical and luxuriant fancy. He wrote alone *The Gentle Craft* (produced in 1599; published anonymously in 1600 as *The Shoemaker's Holiday, or the Gentle Craft*), *Old Fortunatus* (1600); and with Chettle, *Troilus and Cressida, Agamemnon,* and *The Stepmother's Tragedy* (1599); with Chettle and Haughton, *Patient Grissel* (1603); with Day and Haughton, *The Spanish Moor's Tragedy* (1600), an unfinished lost play. With Webster and others he joined in 1602 in a play in two parts on Lady Jane Grey, which probably appeared as *The Famous History of Sir Thomas Wyat* in 1607. In 1603 he published an account of the plague at London, *The Wonderful Year.* The first part of *The Honest Whore* he wrote about 1604, with Middleton. The earliest edition known of the second part is dated 1630, and there is nothing to show that Middleton was concerned in it. *The Seven Deadly Sins of London,* a pamphlet, he published in 1606, and *News from Hell,* a moralizing tract, in the same year. Between 1605 and 1607 he wrote *The Whore of Babylon.* He also wrote *Westward Ho!* (produced 1604) and *Northward Ho!* (1605), both with Webster, *The Belman of London* (1608, a pamphlet on crimes and criminals), *Lanthorne and Candlelight* (the second part of *The Belman,* 1608), *The Gull's Hornbook* (1609, a pamphlet on how not to behave), *The*

Roaring Girl, with Middleton (published 1611), *If it be not Good the Devil is in it* (published 1612), *The Virgin Martyr,* with Massinger (published 1622), and *Match Me in London* (published 1631, but possibly written during his imprisonment). *The Sun's Darling,* possibly revised by John Ford, was published in 1656 (the lyrical portions are thought to be Dekker's); *The Witch of Edmonton,* with Ford and Rowley, probably written c1621, published in 1658; and in 1637 *Lanthorne and Candlelight* was republished as *English Villainies,* the last of his numerous works.

De Lacy (dẹ lā'si), **Hugo.** The noble constable betrothed to the heroine in Sir Walter Scott's novel *The Betrothed.*

Delafield (del'ạ.fēld), **E. M.** Pseudonym of **Dashwood, Elizabeth Monica.**

De la Mare (dẹ lä mãr', del'ạ.mãr), **Walter (John).** b. at Charlton, Kent, England, April 25, 1873; d. at Twickenham, England, June 22, 1956. An English poet, novelist, short-story writer, and dramatist. Through his mother, Lucy Sophia Browning, he was related to the poet Robert Browning. He was educated at Saint Paul's Cathedral Choir School, at London (founded by John Colet), but he did not go to college. From 1890 to 1908 he was a bookkeeper in the London office of an oil company, dealing with facts and figures, a strange occupation for one with his poetic fancy. In the latter year, at the suggestion of Sir Henry Newbolt, he was awarded a small grant and an annual pension by the Asquith ministry of a hundred pounds on the Civil List. He began his writing career with contributions to the *Sketch* and the *Cornhill Magazine,*" in his early days he used "Walter Ramal," an inversion of his own name, as a pseudonym. His works are *Songs of Childhood* (1902), *The Return* (1910), *The Listeners* and *A Child's Day* (both 1912), *Peacock Pie* (1913), *Motley* (1918), *Flora* (1919), *The Veil* (1921), *Downadown-Derry* (1922), *Ding Dong Bell* (1924), *Stuff and Nonsense* (1927), *The Fleeting* (1933), *A Forward Child* (1934), *Early One Morning* (1935), *The Wind Blows Over* (1936), *This Year, Next Year* (1937), all poetry, and various volumes called *Poems* (1906) and *Collected Poems* (1920, 1935, 1941). He has also edited two anthologies of English poetry, *Come Hither* (1923) and *Behold, This Dreamer!* (1939). His prose includes *Henry Brocken* (1904), a novel, *Memoirs of a Midget* (1921), also a novel, which won the highly-valued James Tait Black memorial prize, several collections of short stories, *The Riddle* (1923), *Broomsticks* (1925), *The Connoisseur* (1926), *On the Edge* (1930), and *The Lord Fish* (1933). For children, he has written *Told Again* (1927), new versions of old fairy tales, and *Stories from the Bible. Desert Islands and Robinson Crusoe* (1930) is an essay in symbolism, and *Crossings* (1921) is a play. His own poetry is represented in anthologies by *The Listeners, An Epitaph, The Truants, Old Susan, The Old Men, Some One* ("Some one came knocking"), *At the Keyhole, The Mocking Fairy, Sam, Berries, All But Blind, Summer Evening, There Blooms No Bud in May, The Scarecrow, The Ghost, Silver, Nod, Shadow, Unregarding, Remembrance, The Three Cherry Trees, Miss Loo, Sam's Three Wishes,* or *Life's Little*

ḍ d or j; ṣ, s or sh; ṭ, t or ch; ẓ, z or zh; o, F. cloche; ü, F. menu; ch, Sc. loch; ṅ, F. bonbon.

Whirligig, The Song of Shadows, The Dreamer, The Scribe ("What lovely things Thy hand hath made"), *The Veil, The Quiet Enemy, The Holly,* and *Lucy,* and by many other selections.

Delane (dẹ.lān'), **John Thadeus.** b. at London, Oct. 11, 1817; d. Nov. 22, 1879. An English journalist. He was editor (1841–77) of the London *Times.*

Delany (dẹ.lā'ni), **Mary.** [Maiden name, **Granville.**] b. at Coulston, Wiltshire, England, May 14, 1700; d. at Windsor, England, April 15, 1788. An English author, friend and correspondent of Swift and patron of Fanny Burney; wife of Patrick Delany. She was the friend of the duchess of Portland, and was called his "dearest Mrs. Delany" by George III. He gave her a house in Windsor, and a pension of 300 pounds a year. She presented to the queen some of the "paper mosaic" for which she was famous, and became a great favorite with the royal family. She left six volumes of autobiography and letters, which contain much interesting gossip of the society of the time.

Delany, Patrick. b. in Ireland, c1685; d. at Bath, England, May 6, 1768. An Irish preacher, dean of Down, in Ireland; husband of Mary Delany. He is noted as having been the intimate friend of Swift. In 1757 he began to publish a paper called the *Humanist,* advocating the prevention of cruelty to animals. He wrote *Reflections on Polygamy* (1738), *The Life and Reign of David, King of Israel* (1740–42), *A Humble Apology for Christian Orthodoxy* (1761), and others.

Delectable History of Forbonius and Prisceria (fôr.bō'ni.us; pri.sē'ri.ạ). See **Forbonius and Prisceria, Delectable History of.**

Delectable Mountains. A range of mountains in Bunyan's *Pilgrim's Progress,* from which a view of the Celestial City is to be had. They are "Emmanuel's Land," and the sheep that feed on them are those for whom Christ died. Isa. xxxiii. 16, 17.

Delia (dē'li.ạ). A name given in ancient Greek myth and religion to Artemis, from the island of Delos, her birthplace. Similarly Apollo, the sun god, was called Delius.

Delia. A sonnet sequence (1592) by "the well-languaged" Samuel Daniel. A collection of 50 sonnets, they are addressed to his patroness, the Countess of Pembroke, whose household he called "my best school." Twenty-eight of the sonnets had been published in 1591. Some of those that are considered the best and that appear most frequently in anthologies are numbers 11 ("Tears, vows, and prayers win the hardest heart"), 18 ("Restore thy tresses to the golden ore"), 25 ("False Hope prolongs my ever certain grief"), 30 ("My cares draw on mine everlasting night"), 31, or 39 in some editions ("Look, Delia, how we esteem the half-blown rose"), 41 ("When men shall find thy flower, thy glory pass"), 42 ("Beauty, sweet love, is like the morning dew"), 45, or sometimes 49 or 54 ("Care-charmer Sleep, son of the sable Night"), perhaps the best known, and 46, or 55 ("Let others sing of knights and paladins"). Daniel has been charged with not knowing when to stop, and the last line of his last sonnet, "I say no more; I fear I said too much," has been used against him, half-humorously, half-seriously, as a

good piece of self-criticism that he should have accepted long before. His work, however, is usually regarded as being worthy to rank among the five outstanding Elizabethan amatory sequences, with Sidney's *Astrophel and Stella,* Drayton's *Idea,* Spenser's *Amoretti,* and Shakespeare's *Sonnets.*

Delicate Situation, The. A novel by Naomi Royde-Smith, published in 1931.

Delilah (dẹ.lī'lạ). In the Bible, a Philistine woman of the valley of Sorek, mistress of Samson. She discovered that Samson's long hair represented the secret of his strength; she cut it off and betrayed him to the Philistines, who were then able to capture him. Judges, xvi.

Deliro (de.lē'rō). A character in Ben Jonson's comedy *Every Man Out of His Humour:* a good, doting citizen, a fellow sincerely in love with his own wife, and so taken by an idealization of her perfections that he simply holds himself unworthy of her.

Dell (del), **Ethel M.** [Full name, **Ethel May Dell;** married name, **Savage.**] d. at London, Sept. 17, 1939. An English novelist and short-story writer. A prolific writer, she published at least one book a year between 1911 and 1939. She was the author of novels including *The Way of an Eagle* (1912), *Knave of Diamonds* (1915), *Keeper of the Door* (1915), *Bars of Iron* (1916), *Greatheart* (1918), *Lamp in the Desert* (1919), *Top of the World* and *The Hundredth Chance* (both 1920), *The Obstacle Race* (1921), *Charles Rex* (1922), *Unknown Quantity* (1924), *A Man Under Authority* (1926), *The Black Knight* (1927), *The Gate Marked "Private"* (1928), *The Prison Wall* and *The Silver Bride* (both 1932), *Dona Celestis* (1933), *The Electric Torch* (1934), *Desire of His Life* and *Where Three Roads Meet* (both 1935), *Juice of the Pomegranate* and *Serpent in the Garden* (both 1938), and *Sown Among Stars* (1939). Among her collections of stories are *The Swindler* (1914), *The Safety Curtain* (1917), *The Tidal Wave* (1920), *The Odds* (1922), and *The Passer-By* (1925).

Della Crusca (del'ạ krus'kạ). Pseudonym of **Merry, Robert.**

Della Cruscans (del'ạ krus'kạnz). A small clique of English poets of both sexes who originally met (c1785) at Florence. Their productions, which were affected and sentimental, were published in England in the *World* and the *Oracle.* They were attacked by William Gifford (1791–96) in *The Baviad* and *The Maeviad.* Robert Merry adopted the pseudonym "Della Crusca," Mrs. Hannah Cowley "Anna Matilda," and Edward Jerningham "The Bard." These, with Edward Topham, Charles Este, James Boswell, Mrs. Piozzi, and others, formed the group. They took their name from the Florentine Accademia della Crusca, of which Merry was a member.

Deloney or **Delone** (dẹ.lō'ni), **Thomas.** b. probably at London, c1543; d. c1607. An English weaver, balladist, pamphleteer, and realistic prose fictionist. Author of more than 50 ballads, all written before 1596, he is best known for his contribution to English fiction in the form of three very popular narratives written after 1596 and before 1600, *Thomas of Reading, or The Six Worthy Yeomen* *of the West, Jack of Newbury,* and *The Gentle Craft,* glorifying, respectively, weavers, clothiers, and shoemakers. The importance of the last, apart from its own merits, is that Deloney's story of Simon Eyre, a shoemaker who became lord mayor of London, served as the basis of Thomas Dekker's *The Shoemaker's Holiday* (1599). The secondary title of Dekker's work is the same one used by Deloney.

Deloraine (del.ọ.rān'), **William of.** In Sir Walter Scott's poem *Lay of the Last Minstrel,* a borderer and trusty vassal of the Buccleuch family. He is sent by the Ladye of Branksome to fetch the magic book from the tomb of Michael Scott, the wizard.

Delos (dē'los). [Also: **Mikra Dilos;** ancient names, **Asteria, Ortygia.**] The smallest island of the Cyclades, in the *nomos* (department) of Cyclades, Greece, situated in the narrow passage between the islands of Mykonos and Rhenea. According to Greek myth it was originally a floating island, and was the birthplace of Apollo and Artemis. It was the seat of a great sanctuary in honor of Apollo, one of the most famous religious foundations of antiquity. From the time of Solon, Athens sent an annual embassy to the Delian festival. Delos was the center of the Delian League, formed to resist Persian aggression in 478 B.C. In 454 B.C. the sacred treasure of Delos was removed to the Athenian Acropolis. The island was an Athenian dependency down to the Macedonian period, when it became semi-independent, and in the 2nd century B.C. it again became subject to Athens. The city of Delos was made a free port by the Romans and developed into a great commercial mart. It was raided in 87 B.C by the forces of Mithridates VI and soon fell to the status of an almost uninhabited place. The sanctuary of Apollo was excavated by the French School at Athens, beginning in 1873. The work ranks as one of the chief achievements of its kind. The buildings disclosed lie for the most part within the enclosure or temenos of Apollo, which is of trapeziform shape, and ab. 650 ft. to a side. In addition to the interesting finds of architecture and sculpture, epigraphical discoveries of the highest importance were made, bearing upon history and particularly upon the ceremonial and administration of the sanctuary. Area of the island, 2 sq. mi.

Delphi (del'fī). [Also, **Delphoi** (Ħel.fē').] In ancient geography, a town in Phocis, Greece, situated ab. 6 mi. from the Corinthian Gulf, at the foot of Mount Parnassus: the seat of the world-renowned oracle of Pythian Apollo, the most famous oracle of antiquity. The temple had been won by Apollo from an earth spirit, presumably a snake, who inhabited the spot. Within the sacred precinct was a stone, the Omphalos, believed to mark the center of the earth, and a chasm leading to the center of the earth from which vapors emerged (this chasm has not been found by excavators). The oracle, known as the Pythia or Pythoness, putting herself in a trancelike state, would answer the question asked and this answer, explained or interpreted by the priests of the temple, was returned as being given from Apollo. Myth and legend emphasize the importance of the oracle. In later times the cult of Dionysus obtained a foot-

hold here and Dionysus was believed to be the oracular god at certain times of the year. The oracle dated from prehistoric times, and was still respected when silenced by the Christian emperor Theodosius at the end of the 4th century A.D. Through the gifts of states and individuals who sought or had obtained the aid of the oracle, the Delphic sanctuary became enormously rich, not only in architecture and works of art, but in the precious metals. Its treasures of metals were plundered in antiquity, and Nero and other emperors robbed it of an astonishing number of statues and other art works.

Delphin Classics (del'fin). An edition of the Latin classics prepared by order of Louis XIV for the use of the Dauphin, Louis de Bourbon ("*In usum Delphini,*" meaning "for the use of the Dauphin"). The first works were published in 1674 under the direction of Bossuet and Huet. They are sometimes called "Dauphins."

Delta (Δ). Pseudonym of **Moir, David Macbeth.**

Delvile (del'vil), **Mortimer.** The hero of Fanny Burney's novel *Cecilia.* He so loves Cecilia that he is prepared to marry her even if it means changing his own name. In the end, however, he is able to marry without giving it up.

Demas (dē'mas). See **Dismas.**

Demeter (dẹ.mē'tèr). In ancient Greek mythology, the daughter of Cronus and Rhea; the goddess of vegetation and of useful fruits, protectress of social order and of marriage; one of the great Olympian deities. She is usually associated, and even confounded, in legend and in cult, with her daughter Persephone (Proserpine) or Kore the Maiden, whose rape by Hades (Pluto) symbolizes some of the most profound phases of Hellenic mysticism. She was a principal character at the celebration of the Thesmophoria, a women's festival memorializing Demeter's establishment of the laws of civilization, and in the Eleusinian mysteries, where her withdrawal from the earth, the consequent failure of crops, the rebirth of the grain, and the whole cycle of the yearly change as symbolized in the Persephone myth, were enacted, presumably, since nothing definite is known of the Eleusinian ritual. The Romans of the end of the republic and of the empire assimilated to the Hellenic conception of Demeter the primitive Italic chthonian divinity Ceres.

Demeter. A poetic play (1905) by Robert Bridges. The nature of the work and its method are indicated by the subtitle, *A Masque.* Like his *Prometheus, Bacchus, Ulysses,* and *Achilles,* it illustrates the author's classical tastes and interests.

Demeter and Other Poems. A volume of 28 poems (1889) by Tennyson. It includes "On the Jubilee of Queen Victoria," "To Professor Jebb," "Vastness," "The Ring," dedicated to James Russell Lowell, "To Ulysses," "Merlin and the Gleam," "Romney's Remorse," a poem about the English painter, "By an Evolutionist," "The Snowdrop," "The Throstle," and "The Oak." The thin volume (of 175 pages) opens with "To the Marquis of Dufferin and Ava" and closes (in accordance with Tennyson's frequently expressed wish) with "Crossing the Bar." The title poem is the fourth one in the collection.

Demetrius (dẹ.mē′tri.us). In Shakespeare's *Antony and Cleopatra*, a friend of Antony.

Demetrius. In Shakespeare's *Midsummer Night's Dream*, a Grecian gentleman in love with Hermia.

Demetrius. In Shakespeare's *Titus Andronicus*, a son of Tamora, Queen of the Goths, and brother of Chiron.

Demetrius. The son of the king in John Fletcher's *Humorous Lieutenant*, in love with Celia.

Demetrius Fannius (fan′i.us). In Ben Jonson's play *The Poetaster*, a shifty "dresser of plays about the town here." The character was intended to humiliate Thomas Dekker, with whom Jonson had had a quarrel; Dekker answered with his burlesque of Jonson's style in *Satiromastix*.

Democrat Dies, A. A novel by Pamela Frankau, published in 1940.

Democritus (dẹ.mok′ri.tus). [Called **"the Abderite"** and **"the Laughing Philosopher."**] b. at Abdera, in Thrace, c460 B.C.; d. c357 B.C. A Greek philosopher. He inherited an ample fortune, which enabled him to visit the chief countries of Asia and Africa in pursuit of knowledge. He adopted and expanded the atomistic theory of Leucippus, which he expounded in a number of works, fragments only of which are extant. He is said to have been of a cheerful disposition, which prompted him to laugh at the follies of men (hence the epithet "the Laughing Philosopher"). According to tradition he put out his eyes in order to be less disturbed by outward things in his philosophical speculations. He distinguished between the things belonging to a substance by convention (heat, hardness) and in reality (atoms). Even the soul was a manifestation of the real existence of the body and it perished with the body. His mechanistic philosophy extended to the gods, mortal to Democritus, though composed of finer atomic stuff than man was. His ethical system was based on pleasure as an end; pleasure was, however, to be tempered by avoidance of excess.

Democritus Junior. Pseudonym of **Burton, Robert.**

Demodocus (dẹ.mod′ọ.kus). In the *Odyssey*, a famous blind bard who, during the stay of Ulysses at the court of Alcinous, delighted the guests by recounting the feats of the Greeks at Troy and singing the amours of Ares and Aphrodite.

Demogorgon (dē.mọ.gôr′gọn). An ancient deity of mysterious powers, first mentioned by a commentator on Statius's *Thebaid*. So evil and so powerful was he thought to be that the mere utterance of his name was long held to be perilous. Milton refers to "the dreaded name of Demogorgon," and Shelley in *Prometheus Unbound* identifies Demogorgon with the eternal principle.

De Monfort (dẹ mont′fọrt). A tragedy by Joanna Baillie, produced in 1800.

De Morgan (dẹ môr′gạn), **William (Frend).** b. at London, Nov. 16, 1839; d. there, Jan. 13, 1917. An English novelist, potter, stained-glass designer, and inventor. He was the son of the mathematician Augustus De Morgan, "the wisest and best man I have ever known," and he derived his middle name from his grandfather, William Frend, scientist and economic reformer. He was educated in

London at the University College School and at the College, where his father had been a professor. At the Royal Academy school, which he entered in 1859, he met, and came to know as lifelong friends, Burne-Jones, D. G. Rossetti, and William Morris. Until 1905, when he retired, he was engaged in the manufacture of pottery and stained glass, both in his own factories and with partners. This phase of his life, of much longer duration than his writing activity, produced a paper on pottery which he read in 1892 before the Society of Arts (published in the 40th volume of its *Journal*), and a *Report on the Feasibility of a Manufacture of Glazed Pottery in Egypt* (1894), written in 1893 when he visited Egypt by special invitation. Always of a scientific turn of mind, an inheritance from his father and grandfather, he invented a mill for grinding clay, several tools and articles connected with pottery, and was working on various mechanisms associated with national defense, both air and submarine, at the time of his death. His first novel, generally considered his best, *Joseph Vance: An Ill-Written Autobiography* (1906), was published in his sixty-seventh year. It created a sensation and was enthusiastically praised by readers and critics. It is a story of low life in London, centering around the adventures of a gutter boy, and Lossie Thorpe, a lovable heroine, who finally marries him after both have had previous mates. His second novel was *Alice-for-Short* (1907), the story of Alicia Kavanagh, a London girl, and Charles Heath, an artist in whom, says De Morgan, "I put much of myself." It was followed in 1908 by *Somehow Good*, dealing with the problem of loss of memory as a result of shock. *It Never Can Happen Again* (1909) and *When Ghost Meets Ghost* (1914) are regarded as examples of Victorian fiction. *An Affair of Dishonor* (1910), a historical romance, and *A Likely Story* (1911), which is something less than a full-length novel, are considered inferior efforts. *The Old Madhouse* (1919) and *The Old Man's Youth* (1921), both left unfinished at his death, were completed by his wife, Evelyn Mary Pickering, 18 years his junior, whom he married in 1887. De Morgan has been compared to Dickens, whom he resembles in many respects, and he is regarded as a belated example of the Victorian type of novelist.

Demosthenes (dẹ.mos′thẹ.nēz). b. at Paeania, in Attica, 384 or 383 B.C.; d. on the island of Calauria, in the Saronic Gulf, 322 B.C. The greatest of Greek orators. He is said to have been the pupil of the orator Isaeus, and entered public life as a speaker in the popular assembly in 355. In 351 he delivered the first of a splendid series of orations directed against the encroachment of Philip II of Macedon, three of which are specifically denominated *Philippics*. In 346 he served as a member of the embassy which concluded with Philip the so-called peace of Philocrates. As Philip immediately after broke this treaty, Demosthenes came forward as the leader of the patriotic party, in opposition to the Macedonian party which was headed by Aeschines. In 340 he caused a fleet to be sent to the relief of Byzantium, which was besieged by Philip. On the outbreak of the Amphictyonic War, he persuaded the Athenians to form an alliance with Thebes against Philip, who defeated the allies at Chaeronea in 338, and usurped the hegemony of Greece. He was one of the leaders of the unsuccessful rising which took place on the death of Philip in 336, was exiled by the Macedonian party in 324, was recalled by the patriotic party on the outbreak of a fresh rising at the death of Alexander in 323, and on the capture of Athens by Antipater and Craterus in 322 fled to Calauria, near Argolis, where he took poison in the temple of Poseidon to avoid capture. His chief orations are three *Philippics* (351, 344, 341), three *Olynthiacs* (349, 349, 348), *On the Peace* (346), *On the Embassy* (343), *On the Affairs of the Chersonese* (341), *On the Crown* (330). This last-named speech, the most famous of Demosthenes's orations, was in answer to Aeschines, who objected when Ctesiphon moved that a crown be given to Demosthenes for his services to the state. Demosthenes was the great opponent of the Macedonian conquest of Greece, holding that Athens, traditionally and actually, was the heart of any Greek nation, and that it was necessary that the spark be rekindled that had died during the Peloponnesian War. Many legendary stories are told of how he obtained his oratorical power: a stammerer, he taught himself to speak slowly by putting pebbles in his mouth; he went to the seashore and declaimed to the waves so that the noise of an audience would not disturb him; he would run uphill while orating in order to strengthen his weak voice; he shut himself in a cave and copied Thucydides's history eight times in order to attain to a fine style. He seems actually to have had a speech defect; his style in oratory is not complex, but simple and pithy, and effective. The first printed collective edition of his orations is that published by Aldus Manutius at Venice in 1504.

Dempster (demp′stẻr), **Janet**. A woman in George Eliot's novel *Janet's Repentance* who is rescued from a passion for drink by her friend and pastor.

Dena lagu (den′ä läg′ủ). See **Danelaw**.

De Naturis Rerum (dē nạ.tū′ris rē′rum). A treatise on natural science written in Latin by the 12th-century English scholar Alexander Neckam.

Denham (den′ạm), Sir **John**. b. at Dublin, 1615; d. at London, in March, 1669. An English poet. He took up arms for the king when the English Civil War began, and was made governor of Farnham Castle, from which he was driven and sent a prisoner to London. His fortunes varied, but revived at the Restoration. He was falsely accused in 1667 of murdering his wife by a poisoned cup of chocolate. He was the author of a tragedy, *The Sophy* (1642), a descriptive poem, *Cooper's Hill* (1642), *Cato Major* (1648), adapted from Cicero, and occasional poems.

Denis Duval (den′is dụ̈.val′). An unfinished novel by Thackeray, published in 1864, after his death. Denis lives in Rye, a colony of French refugees, in the late 18th century. Here he is brought up by his smuggler grandfather, and he tells of his early love for Agnes, daughter of Mme. de Saverne, a lady who fled to England to escape from a cruel husband. The killer of her husband, the Chevalier De la Motte, is an evil person who presently settles in Rye and engages in smuggling. Denis discovers his plots, and the other smugglers' confederacy, and is forced to leave Rye. The fragment stops just as Denis takes to the sea, but Thackeray's

notes reveal that he meant the young man to have many adventures in the naval service, and that De la Motte would have evil designs on Agnes, but would be hanged at the end.

Dennis (den′is). In Shakespeare's *As You Like It*, a servant to Oliver.

Dennis. A hangman in Charles Dickens's novel *Barnaby Rudge*.

Dennis, Geoffrey Pomeroy. b. at Barnstaple, Devonshire, England, Jan. 20, 1892—. An English writer. He served (1920–37) on the League of Nations staff, becoming chief editor and head of the document services, and as chief of the Italian section of the European service of the British Broadcasting Corporation. He is the author of *Mary Lee* (1922), *Harvest in Poland* (1925), *The End of the World* (1930; awarded the Hawthornden prize), *Sale by Auction* (1932), *Bloody Mary's* (1934), and *Coronation Commentary* (1937).

Dennis, John. b. at London, 1657; d. Jan. 6, 1734. An English critic. His writings annoyed Pope, who ridiculed him in the *Dunciad*. He also wrote indifferently successful plays.

Dennis Brulgruddery (brul.grud′ẻr.i). See **Brulgruddery, Dennis**.

Denny (den′i), Sir **Anthony**. In Shakespeare's *Henry VIII*, a gentleman of the court who appears once (V.i) to present Cranmer to the King.

dénouement (dā.nö.môǹ). The solution of a mystery; the winding up of a plot, as of a novel, drama, etc.; the issue, as of any course of conduct; the event.

Denry the Audacious (den′ri). The American title of a novel (1911) by Arnold Bennett, published in England as *The Card*. It is one of the so-called "Five Towns" novels and is concerned more with character than with plot. It is a humorous, but sympathetic, portrait of a young man whose chief quality is suggested by the title, a quality which, rather than real ability, enables him to achieve what he considers to be success in his career.

Dent (dent), **J. M.** [Full name, **Joseph Malaby Dent**.] b. at Darlington, Durham, England, Aug. 30, 1849; d. at Croydon, Surrey, England, May 9, 1926. An English publisher and author, founder of the publishing house of J. M. Dent and Sons. After having served his apprenticeship, he began (1872) his own bookbinding business at Hoxton, a North London suburb. In 1888 he published Lamb's *Essays of Elia*, *Last Essays*, and Goldsmith's *Essays, Poems and Plays* as the first volumes in the Temple Library, so named because both authors had lived in the Temple; in 1890 he began the Medieval Towns series, following it with the Temple Shakespeare (40 vols., 1893–96) edited by Israel Gollancz, distinguished Shakespearian scholar; in 1896 he brought out the first volumes of the Temple Classics. He also published (1898) the Haddon Hall Library and, in 1899, the Waverley novels (40 vols.). In 1904 he began his most ambitious project, the Everyman's Library, securing as general editor Ernest Rhys, who had suggested the name. He also published a series of English novelists from Henry Fielding to Jane Austen, and translations of Balzac with introductions by George Saintsbury. He was the author of

---

ḍ, d or j; ṣ, s or sh; ṭ, t or ch; ẓ, z or zh; o, F. cloche; ü, F. menu; ċh, Sc. loch; ǹ, F. bonbon.

essays on various phases of making and printing books, introductions to several Everyman's Library volumes, and *Memoirs* (1928).

De Nugis Curialium (dē nū'jis kū.ri.ā'li.um). [Eng. trans., *Courtiers' Trifles.*] A collection of legends, anecdotes, witty remarks, gossip about doings at the courts of Henry II and Richard I, and the like by Walter Map, probably written between 1180 and 1193. It is the one extant work known certainly to have been written by Map.

Denzil (den'zil), **Guy.** In Sir Walter Scott's poem *Rokeby*, the chief of a marauding band made up from both Cavaliers and Roundheads.

Deor's Lament (dā'ôrz). [Also, **Deor.**] An Old English poem (9th or 10th century) in the *Exeter Book*, named after its reputed author, a scop who in the last section of the poem tells of his own misfortune. Most commentators believe that this scop is only a fiction, used by the true author as a mouthpiece. The poem falls into seven sections of varying length. All but the sixth conform to one pattern: the scop cites a story, taken from Germanic legend, in which a victim or victims of misfortune outlive their trouble. Each of these sections ends with the same consolatory line: "That now is gone; this too will go." The sixth section deals with earthly misfortune in general, and adds words of consolation correspondingly generalized. The standard edition is that of Kemp Malone (1933).

Departmental Ditties. A volume of poetry (1886) by Rudyard Kipling. The poems, which originally appeared singly in various issues of the Lahore *Gazette*, gave a picture of Anglo-Indian life, something new in literature at the time, and were welcomed accordingly. In *Plain Tales from the Hills* (1888) Kipling accomplished somewhat the same in prose.

Depazzi (dā.pät'sē). A character in Shirley's play *The Humorous Courtier.*

De Prie (dẹ prē'), **Jaques.** A supposed beggar in Ben Jonson's comedy *The Case is Altered.* He is a miser, and is in reality Melun, steward to the old Chamont. He somewhat resembles Shylock, loving both his ducats and his daughter.

De Profundis (dē prō.fun'dis). [Eng. trans., *Out of the Depths.*] The 130th Psalm, so called from the first two words in the Latin version. It forms a part of the Roman Catholic liturgy, and is used in the burial services.

De Profundis. A prose work by Oscar Wilde written while he was in prison, published in part in 1905; the remainder (still in manuscript) is at the British Museum, where it is to be opened on Jan. 1, 1960.

De Proprietatibus Rerum (dē prọ.prī.ẹ.tā'ti.bus rē'rum). A compilation (c1230–50) in Latin, by Bartholomaeus Anglicus, of information about the physical and natural sciences.

Deputy Was King, A. A novel by G. B. Stern, published in 1926. It is the second panel in her trilogy of Jewish life, *The Rakonitz Chronicles* (1932).

De Quincey (dẹ kwin'si, -zi), **Thomas.** b. at Manchester, England, Aug. 15, 1785; d. at Edinburgh, Dec. 8, 1859. An English essayist and miscellaneous writer, famous for his *Confessions of an English Opium-Eater* (in book form, 1822). He was the son of Thomas Quincey, a wealthy wholesale merchant who died in 1793. His guardians entered him in the Manchester Grammar School in 1800, from which he ran away in 1802. After a tour on foot of Wales, Thomas lived for some months in direst poverty at London. Becoming reconciled with his guardians, he entered Oxford late in 1803. Here, a year later, he first began his use of opium, which he continued, in widely varying amounts, for the rest of his life. He left Oxford without taking a degree in 1808. Making the acquaintance of Lamb, Coleridge, and Wordsworth, he moved to Grasmere, where he married Margaret Simpson in 1817. By this time his use of opium had increased to the amount of 8,000 drops of laudanum (about seven wineglasses) a day. Financial difficulties forced him to go to London in 1821 in search of literary work. His *Confessions of an English Opium-Eater*, published anonymously that fall in *The London Magazine* and in book form the following year, established his reputation. His only other books were *Klosterheim* (1832), an unduly neglected Gothic novel, and *The Logic of Political Economy* (1844). He wrote for the *Westmoreland Gazette*, *Hogg's Weekly Instructor*, *Blackwood's*, *Tait's Edinburgh*, and other magazines nearly 200 articles on biographical, literary, philosophical, historical, classical, and miscellaneous subjects. Like Coleridge, De Quincey was extraordinarily well read, had an amazingly retentive memory, and was a brilliant conversationalist. At its worst, his work is prolix, wandering, pedantic, poorly organized, and often grossly inaccurate, even as to easily checked quotations and factual details. At its frequent best, for example in *The Revolt of the Tartars*, *On Murder Considered as One of the Fine Arts*, *The English Mail-Coach*, *On the Knocking at the Gate in Macbeth*, *The Spanish Military Nun*, and *Joan of Arc*, his style is highly polished, stately, musical, and imaginative, often humorous. His autobiographic writings rank with Rousseau's and Cellini's. His essays on his contemporaries, Lamb, Coleridge, Wordsworth, Hazlitt, and others, are honest, charming, and intimate. He is placed by most critics among the great masters of English prose. His works were first collected and published by Ticknor and Fields (Boston, 1850–59, 24 vols.), with De Quincey's consent and remuneration, followed by Hogg's *Selections Grave and Gay* (Edinburgh, 1853–60, 14 vols.), and David Masson's definitive *Collected Writings* (Edinburgh, 1889–90, 14 vols.). The best biographical and critical works on De Quincey are by Horace Ainsworth Eaton (New York, 1936), and Edward Sackville-West (New Haven, 1936).

Derby (där'bi; in the U. S. often dėr'bi). An annual English horse-racing event. It is named for one of the earls of Derby, who instituted it in 1780, and is run at Epsom Downs, a racecourse in the municipal borough of Epsom and Ewell, within the area of Greater London, on the Wednesday of the week after Trinity Sunday, which is variously the last Wednesday in May or the first Wednesday in June. The course measures 29 yards more than a mile-and-a-half, and the race is open to three-year-old colts and fillies, colts being required to carry a minimum of 126 pounds, and fillies not less than

---

fat, fāte, fär, àsk, fāre; net, mē, hėr; pin, pīne; not, nōte, mŏve, nôr; up, lūte, pŭll; ᴛн, then;

121 pounds. The prize money is not great by modern standards, but the race has acquired great prestige and horses, carefully trained for it, are entered not only by English breeders but by Eastern potentates and American politicians and industrial magnates. The British Parliament adjourns for Derby Day, and hundreds of thousands of people crowd Epsom Downs to see the race if possible, to gaze on royalty and the aristocracy, and to admire the latest women's fashions. The name Derby has come to be applied to other sporting events of real or asserted superior character or importance. Thus a race held annually since 1875 at Churchill Downs near Lexington, Ky., is known as the Kentucky Derby, and roller-skating "Derbies" are featured in various American cities.

Derby, Earl of. See under **Stanley, Lord.**

Derby's Men. See **Lord Chamberlain's Men.**

Dercetas (dèr′sẹ.tạs). In Shakespeare's *Antony and Cleopatra*, a friend of Antony who, bearing the sword on which Antony died, informs Octavius of his death.

Derceto (dèr′sẹ.tō). [Also, **Derketo**.] The principal Philistine female deity, worshiped especially in Ashkelon (Ascalon). She was represented in the form of a woman terminating in a fish, and is considered the female counterpart of Dagon. She was a nature goddess, the principle of generation and fertility, and corresponds in her attributes and the mode of her worship to Ashtoreth (Astarte) of the Canaanites and Syrians (the Assyro-Babylonian Ishtar), and to Atargatis of the Hittites. She was the mother of Semiramis, who, though human, was the counterpart of the goddess.

De rerum natura (dē rē′rum nạ.tū′rạ). [Eng. trans., *"Of the Nature of Things."*] A didactic poem by Lucretius. Written just before Lucretius's death in 55 B.C., the poem is one of the monuments of Roman literature, an exposition of things as they are in the world as viewed by an Epicurean. Lucretius discusses superstition, the nature of matter and of the universe, atoms, the mind, mortality, the senses, dreams, sex, the earth, man and society, and the phenomena of nature in the sky and on earth. It is in six books.

Dermody (dèr′mọ.di), **Thomas**. b. at Ennis, County Clare, Ireland, in January, 1775; d. at Sydenham (now part of London), July 15, 1802. An Irish poet. He published *Poems* (1792), *Poems, Moral and Descriptive* (1800), and *Poems on Various Subjects* (1802). His works were published as *The Harp of Erin* in 1807.

Deronda (dẹ.ron′dạ), **Daniel**. The hero of George Eliot's novel *Daniel Deronda*. He is Jewish, and when he discovers his parentage he resolves to devote his whole life to restoring the Jewish nation to its lost political position.

Derrick or **Derick** (der′ik). A hangman employed at Tyburn, London, at the beginning of the 17th century, often mentioned in contemporary plays. The name was applied to a gallows and then to a sort of crane.

He rides circuit with the devil, and Derrick must be his host, and Tyborne the inn at which he will light.   (*Belman of London* (1616).)

Desborough (dez′bėr.ọ̈), **Colonel**. The "brutally ignorant" brother-in-law of Cromwell in Sir Walter Scott's novel *Woodstock*.

Descartes (dā.kärt′; French, dā.kärt), **René**. b. at La Haye, France, March 31, 1596; d. at Stockholm, Feb. 11, 1650. A French philosopher and mathematician. He graduated at the age of 17 from the Jesuit college of La Flèche and later studied at the University of Poitiers, saw some brief military service, lived for a time at Paris, and spent several years in travel, visiting Germany, Italy, Holland, and Poland, studying and seeking knowledge. In 1628 he was at the siege of La Rochelle as a volunteer, but the following year he took up residence in Holland, where he lived a retired life, busily engaged, however, in elaborating and defending his philosophy and formulating his mathematical system, until 1649 when upon the invitation of Queen Christina of Sweden he went to Stockholm, only to die there of pneumonia five months later. He had been marked as a modern philosopher to be reckoned with since the publication in 1637 of his brief treatise entitled *Discours de la méthode*. The theories there set forth he supported in three essays, *La Dioptrique*, *Les Météores*, and *La Géométrie*. Others of his works published during his lifetime were *Meditationes de prima philosophia* (1641), *Principia philosophiae* (1644), *Traité des passions de l'âme* (1649), as well as a polemical pamphlet (1643) entitled *Epistola Renati Descartes ad Gisbertum Voëtium*. After his death his friends published his *De l'homme*, *Traité de la formation du fœtus*, *Le Monde ou traité de la lumière de Descartes* (all of the foregoing appearing in 1664), and a collection of his letters, issued between 1657 and 1667. In 1701 appeared, finally, *Opuscula posthuma, physica et mathematica*. Descartes was one of the great mathematicians of all times, adding much to the theories of algebra and geometry. His philosophical methodology was an attempt to extend the mathematical approach to all fields of human thought and investigation. His name still looms large in the history of philosophy, and his influence remains great. Rejecting scholasticism, he based his speculations upon pure reason, his point of basic approach being derived from his famous axiom, *Cogito, ergo sum* ("I think, therefore I am.") Willing to take nothing for granted (the point of the axiom cited above is, of course, that it enabled Descartes safely to assume his own existence), he proceeds to proof of the existence of God, and from that to a demonstration of the reality of the material world. Between the material world and the mind or soul he posits a complete gulf, which can be bridged only by the direct intervention of God. Writing at a time when speculation could take its stand upon pure reason (still within the framework of Roman Catholic theology) his system inevitably diminished in authority with the rise, beginning a century or so after his death, of the natural sciences as they have since come to be understood.

Descent of Man, The. A scientific work (1871) by Charles Darwin. It is a further exposition of the theory of evolution, previously presented and explained by Darwin in his *Origin of Species* (1859), which caused a scientific and intellectual revolution when it appeared. The *Descent* is as important, as scientific, and as careful a work as the earlier one, but a dozen years makes a difference, and the work aroused nothing like the anger and excitement and resentment that greeted the *Origin of Species*.

Deschamps (dā.shäṅ), **Eustache.** [Called **Morel Deschamps.**] b. at Vertus, in Champagne (now in Marne department), France, in the first part of the 14th century; d. early in the 15th century. A French poet and author of ballades (1,175 in number), rondeaux (171), virelais (80), a long poem, the *Miroir de mariage*, and *L'Art de dictier et de fere chancons, balades, virelais et rondeaulx* (a treatise on French rhetoric and prosody).

Description of Wales. A prose work in Latin by Giraldus Cambrensis, written (c1187) after he had visited Wales, on a preaching mission in support of the Third Crusade.

Desdemona (dez.dẹ.mō′nạ). In Shakespeare's *Othello*, the wife of Othello the Moor, and the daughter of Brabantio, a Venetian senator. Othello smothers her in an outburst of rage produced by a belief in her unfaithfulness, carefully instilled by Iago. In Cinthio's *Hecatommithi*, from which Shakespeare took his plot, she is Disdemona. Shakespeare has carefully heightened the tragedy attendant upon Othello's mistaken feeling by making her a chaste, modest, and wholly devoted wife, who even at the moment of her death is willing to submit to Othello in her love for him. Shakespeare introduces the theme of witchcraft to symbolize the disapproval in the Venetian world of the marriage between the Moor and Desdemona, but Desdemona herself thinks of the marriage in terms of a bond of honor. She cannot even conceive fully of what Othello has imaginatively dwelt upon, under the goading of Iago, and her innocence is the cause of her downfall.

Desdichado (des.di.chä′dō). In Sir Walter Scott's novel *Ivanhoe*, the device, meaning "The Disinherited," assumed by Ivanhoe in the tournament at Ashby.

Deserted Village, The. A poem by Oliver Goldsmith, begun in 1768 and published in 1770. It is a version in rhymed couplets of the popular declamation of the time against luxury and the depopulation of the countryside as the result of the siren call of industrial wages. Goldsmith names his village Auburn, and in his description of it he includes many passages recounting the charm of unspoiled village life. Crabbe's poem *The Village* was written partly in response to what Crabbe considered to be Goldsmith's over-sentimentalization of village life. The last four lines of the poem are attributed by Boswell to Samuel Johnson.

Design for Living. A comedy (1933) by Noel Coward. The main characters are three Bohemians (in spirit, not in nationality), and the three acts take place in Otto's Paris studio, in Leo's London flat, a year and a half later, and in Ernest's New York apartment, two years later. The feminine interest is supplied by Gilda, who finds that she cannot live without Otto and Leo, just as they in their turn find that they cannot live without her, or each other.

Desmas (dez′mạs). See **Dismas.**

Desmond (dez′mọnd), **Shaw.** b. in County Waterford, Ireland, Jan. 19, 1877—. An Irish novelist and poet, founder (1934) of the International Institute for Psychical Research. He is the author of *The Soul of Denmark* (1918), *Democracy* (1919), *Passion* (1920), *The Drama of Sinn Fein* (1923), *The Isle of Ghosts* (1925), *Ragnarok* (1926), *Windjammer: the Book of the Horn* (1932), *We Do Not Die* (1934), *World Birth* (1937), *Reincarnation for Everyman* (1939), *How you live when you Die* (1942), *The Story of Adam Verity* (1947), and *The Edwardian Story* (1950).

Despair, Giant. A giant in Bunyan's *Pilgrim's Progress* who takes Christian and his companion Hopeful while they are asleep and imprisons them in his dungeons in Doubting Castle. Christian, after three days without food or drink and after being cudgeled regularly, opens the dungeon lock with the key "Promise," and he and Hopeful escape.

Desperate Lovers, The. A three-act comedy (1926) by Alfred Sutro.

Desperate Remedies. Thomas Hardy's first novel published (1871) anonymously.

Destiny. A novel by Susan E. Ferrier, dedicated to Sir Walter Scott, and published anonymously in 1831.

Destructive Element, The. A critical work by Stephen Spender, published in 1935.

De Sublimitate (dē su.blī.mi.tā′tē). The Latin title of *On the Sublime*, an essay on literary style, traditionally credited to Longinus. However, modern criticism has demonstrated the improbability of his having written it.

detective story. See under **mystery story.**

Deucalion (dụ.kā′li.ọn). In Greek legend, a king of Phthia in Thessaly; son of **Prome**theus and Clymene, who with his wife Pyrrha was saved from a deluge sent by Zeus. On the advice, according to one story, of Prometheus, he built a wooden chest in which he and his wife were saved. After floating for nine days he landed on Mount Parnassus and sacrificed to Zeus. To renew the human race, destroyed by the deluge, he and Pyrrha were directed to veil their faces and throw behind them the bones of their mother. Understanding this to mean their mother the earth they threw stones, and those thrown by Deucalion became men and those thrown by Pyrrha women; and with these Deucalion founded a kingdom in Locris.

Deuceace (dūs′ās), **The Honourable Algernon Percy.** In W. M. Thackeray's *Memoirs of Mr. C. J. Yellowplush*, a dissolute blackguard (but possessing a certain charm) who pursues both a young widow and her crook-backed stepdaughter in order to gain a large fortune. The widow discovers his objective and lures him into marrying her stepdaughter. He then discovers that his wife is penniless. The widow thereupon marries Deuceace's father, the Earl of Crabs, who gets the fortune. Deuceace also appears in *Vanity Fair* and *Pendennis*.

deus ex machina. 1. In the ancient theater, one of a number of contrivances in use for indicating a change of scene, as a rotating prism with different conventional scenery painted on its three sides, or a device for expressing a descent to the infernal regions, as the "Charonian steps," for representing the passage of a god through the air across the stage (whence the dictum *deus ex machina*, applied to the mock supernatural or providential), etc. Such machines were very numerous in the fully developed Greek theater, and were copied in the Roman.

2. A literary contrivance for the working out of a plot; a supernatural agency, or artificial action, introduced into a poem or tale.

Deuteronomy (dū.tėr.on′ọ̇.mi). The fifth and last book of the Pentateuch, containing the last discourses of Moses, delivered in the plain of Moab. It begins with a recapitulation of the events of the last month of the 40 years' wandering of the Israelites in the desert (i.-iv. 40); then follows the main body of the book, setting forth the laws which were to regulate the Israelites when they should become settled in the promised land; while chapters xxvi-xxxiii contain the farewell speeches of Moses. Deuteronomy is a manual of religion and social ethics. Compared with the other books of the Pentateuch it is distinguished by a warm, oratorical tone. The laws of the preceding books are modified, and their presentation is more spiritual and ethical. On account of these differences Deuteronomy is now assigned by many critics to a different author and date from the rest of the Pentateuch. Owing to the fact that the so-called reformation of King Josiah appears to carry out the principles of Deuteronomy, it is concluded that "the book of the law" discovered by the priest Hilkiah in the temple in 621 B.C., which began the reformation of Josiah, was Deuteronomy. But its composition must certainly have originated at an earlier date. This is put by many critics in the reign of Manasseh, c698–c643 B.C.

Deva (dā′vạ). In Hindu and Buddhist belief, a deity. The Hindu Devas are reckoned as 33; this number includes 12 Adityas, eight Vasus, 11 Rudras, and two Ashvins. In Zoroastrian belief, the Devas are evil spirits, created by Ahriman, lord of darkness.

Deva (dē′vạ). The Latin name of the river Dee, in N Wales.

De Vere (dẹ vir′), **Arthur.** In Sir Walter Scott's novel *Anne of Geierstein*, the young Englishman who wins the heroine's hand.

de Vere, **Sir Aubrey.** b. at Curragh Chase, County Limerick, Ireland, Aug. 28, 1788; d. there, July 5, 1846. An Irish poet. He published *Julian the Apostate* (1822), *The Duke of Mercia*, *The Song of Faith* (1842), *Mary Tudor* (1847: posthumously published), and others.

de Vere, **Aubrey Thomas.** b. at Curragh Chase, County Limerick, Ireland, Jan. 10, 1814; d. there, Jan. 20, 1902. An Irish poet, critic, and essayist; friend of Cardinal Newman, Wordsworth, Tennyson, and Carlyle; son of Sir Aubrey de Vere. He was educated by tutors and at Trinity College, Dublin, and traveled frequently in England and Italy. He entered (1851) the Roman Catholic Church. Among his works are volumes of verse including *Waldenses* (1842), *The Search After Proserpine* (1844), *A Year of Sorrow* (1847),

Poems: Sacred and Miscellaneous (1854), *May Carols* (1857), *Legends of St. Patrick* (1872), *Alexander the Great* (1874), *St. Thomas of Canterbury* (1876), *Antar and Zara* and *The Fall of Rora* (both 1877), *Poetical Works* (3 vols., 1884–89), *Legends and Records of the Church and Empire* (1887), *St. Peter's Chains* (1888), and *Medieval Records and Sonnets* (1893). He also wrote *English Misrule and Irish Misdeeds* (1848), *Picturesque Sketches of Greece and Turkey* (1850), *The Church Settlement of Ireland* (1866), *Ireland's Church Property* and *Pleas for Secularization* (both 1867), *Legends of the Saxon Saints* (1879), *Constitutional and Unconstitutional Political Action* (1882), *Ireland and Representation* (1885), *Critical Essays* (3 vols., 1887–89), and *Recollections* (1897).

Devereux (dev′ėr.ö, -öks). A novel by Edward Bulwer-Lytton, published in 1829.

Devereux, Penelope. [Married name, **Rich**; called **Stella** by Sidney.] A lady loved by Sir Philip Sidney, and celebrated by him in his group of sonnets entitled *Astrophel and Stella*. She was the daughter of Walter Devereux (1541–76), whose plan it was for her to marry Sidney. However, she actually married Robert Rich, 3rd Baron Rich, but did not therefore repudiate Sidney's devoted attentions (literary and otherwise).

Devereux, Robert. [Title, 2nd Earl of **Essex**.] b. at Netherwood, Herefordshire, England, Nov. 19, 1566; beheaded at London, Feb. 25, 1601. An English nobleman; son of Walter Devereux, 1st Earl of Essex of the Devereux line; a favorite of Queen Elizabeth. He was appointed in 1585 general of the horse to the expedition sent under Robert Dudley, 1st Earl of Leicester, his stepfather, to the aid of the States-General in the Netherlands. In 1587 he attended the court of Queen Elizabeth, who at this time began to show him unmistakable signs of attention, emphatically so after the death (1588) of Leicester. He secretly married (1590) the widow of Sir Philip Sidney, Frances Walsingham, daughter of Elizabeth's secretary of state. Despite Elizabeth's great anger when she heard of the marriage, he made his peace with her and became a privy councilor in 1593. He commanded the land forces in the successful raiding expedition against Cádiz in 1596 but failed to win a complete victory or to capture the Spanish treasure ships and was reprimanded by the queen. In 1597 he led an expedition against the Azores, again failing to accomplish a real victory, permitting the Argentine ships to escape and almost falling into a trap. But Elizabeth made peace with him and he was appointed earl marshal of England in 1597. He became chancellor of Cambridge University in 1598. In 1599 he was appointed lord lieutenant of Ireland, in which post he aroused the queen's anger by the failure of his operations against the Irish rebels, and by his inability to follow orders from the queen. He made a truce with Hugh O'Neill, the Earl of Tyrone, leader of the Ulster rebels, and, leaving his post without authorization, returned (September, 1599) to England to lay his defense before the queen in person. Failing to regain his standing at court, and after a trial as the result of which he was stripped of his offices, he formed a conspiracy with Charles Blount, Baron Mountjoy, and Henry

Wriothesley, 3rd Earl of Southampton, to compel her by force of arms to dismiss his enemies in the council, who were and had been the Cecil faction. On Feb. 8, 1601, he led a group of his retainers through the streets of London, trying to arouse the citizenry to join him; but this half-formed uprising was met with apathy and he returned to his palace, Essex House, where he was captured. He was tried for treason; Francis Bacon, who had consistently attempted to mediate between Essex and Elizabeth, prosecuted the charge virulently; and Essex was found guilty and executed on the charge of treason.

Devil, The. A tavern in Fleet street, London, near Temple Bar. The Apollo Club was held here. It was presided over by Ben Jonson, Shakespeare, Beaumont, and Fletcher.

Devil Is an Ass, The. A comedy by Ben Jonson, first acted in 1616. Jonson evidently had in mind the title of Dekker's play (published 1612) *If it be not Good the Devil is in it*. Pug, "the less devil," obtains the privilege from Satan of coming to earth in the guise of a pickpocket. He soon finds, however, that "Hell is A grammar-school to this." The principal fool whom Pug encounters is Fitzdottrel, who takes up with a "projector" named Meercraft, the principal scoundrel (this is a satire on 17th-century science). Fitzdottrel is nearly cuckolded when a pseudo-Spanish "lady," actually Wittipol, the young lover of his wife, pretends to instruct her in the proper decorum for her expected position as Duchess of Drownland, a dependency to be raised out of the English marshes by Meercraft. Fitzdottrel, acting in accordance with a ruling of the Court of Dependencies (another of Meercraft's inventions), makes over his property to the "lady." Wittipol refuses to take advantage of the husband's folly, but it is still necessary for Fitzdottrel to pretend to be bewitched in order to convince the credulous Justice Eitherside that he was not sane when willing his property. Pug, outwitted and surpassed at every turn by human "deviltry," ends up in prison.

Devil's Disciple, The. A comedy (1897) of the American Revolution by George Bernard Shaw, who called it a melodrama. It is one of his *Three Plays for Puritans*, the others being *Caesar and Cleopatra*, a history, and *Captain Brassbound's Conversion*, an adventure. The time of the play is the winter of 1777, and the scene of action is New Hampshire, in the Dudgeon and Anderson homes, and in the town hall, council chamber, and market place. The main characters are Dick Dudgeon, the "disciple," a radical; his mother, a thoroughly disagreeable woman, whose husband has just died; his brother, Christie; Anthony Anderson, a Presbyterian minister; his lovely wife, Judith; Essie, a frightened 17-year-old girl who is never allowed to forget her irregular birth; other characters who are brought in for satirical and comic purposes; and the historical personages, General ("Gentleman Johnny") Burgoyne, and Brudenell, a chaplain. The play, with its satire on British slowness and stupidity, its sly digs at Puritanism, religion, respectability, and conventional morality, and its cynical treatment of love and romance, has always been popular on the stage and has had many re-

vivals, in both England and America. In the attractive role of dashing Dick Dudgeon, Richard Mansfield and Maurice Evans scored great successes.

Devil's Dyke, The. A prehistoric earthwork for defense, in Cambridgeshire, England.

Devil's Island. [French, *Île du Diable*.] An island in the Atlantic Ocean, off the coast of French Guiana, formerly used as a penal colony by France. Alfred Dreyfus was imprisoned (1895–99) here.

Devil's Law-Case, The. A tragicomedy by John Webster, printed in 1623.

Devil's Thoughts, The. A short poem by Coleridge and Southey, sometimes known as *The Devil's Walk*.

Devil upon Two Sticks, The. A comedy by Samuel Foote, first played on May 30, 1768, and printed in 1778. Foote took it from Alain René Le Sage's *Le Diable boiteux*, and himself played the part of the devil.

Devil Upon Two Sticks in England, The. A satirical tale (1790) by William Combe, patterned after Le Sage's *Diable boiteux*.

Devil We Know, The. A novel by Pamela Frankau, published in 1939.

Devious Ways. A novel by Gilbert Cannan, published in 1910.

Devonshire Club (dev'ọn.shėr). A London Liberal club, established in 1875.

Devonshire House. The residence of the Dukes of Devonshire, in Piccadilly, London. It was razed in 1925.

Dewer Rides (dū'ẽr). A novel by L. A. G. Strong, published in 1929.

Dewi (dā'wi), **Saint.** See Saint **David.**

Dewy (dū'i), **Dick.** The rustic hero of Thomas Hardy's novel of village life *Under the Greenwood Tree*.

Diable boiteux (dyȧbl bwȧ.tė), **Le.** [Eng. trans., "*The Lame Devil*."] A satirical romance by Alain René Le Sage, published in 1707. It was an imitation of a Spanish work entitled *El Diablo cojuelo*, written by Luis Vélez de Guevara, and first printed in 1641, and of other satires (by Cervantes and others) long current. The whole work is in dialogue form. Samuel Foote took from it his play *The Devil upon Two Sticks*. The title *Le Diable boiteux* has been given to a number of other publications.

Diafoirus (dē.ȧ.fwȧ.rüs). The physician in Molière's *Malade imaginaire* to whose son Thomas Argan wishes to betroth his daughter Angélique. The father is very comical, and the son, full of folly and erudition, no less so.

Dialogue against the Fever Pestilence, A. [Also, **Dialogue of Death.**] A collection of tales by William Bullein, published in 1564–65. The tales are framed in the narrative of a London man who takes his wife with him when he flees the city to escape the plague of 1564. Many folk tales and fables are told on the journey, some of them not without a degree of light-heartedness, but the stories end on a grim note when death finally catches up with the two travelers.

---

fat, fāte, fär, ȧsk, fāre; net, mē, hẽr; pin, pīne; not, nōte, mȯve, nôr; up, lūte, pu̇ll; ᴛʜ, then;

Dialogues of the Dead. A satirical prose work by Lucian, which various authors, including François de La Mothe-Fénelon, Matthew Prior, and George Lyttelton, used as a model for similar pieces.

Dialogues of the Dead. A prose work (1760) by George Lyttelton.

Dialogus de Scaccario (dĭ.ạ.lō′gus dē ska.kăr′i.ō). A Latin prose work by Richard Fitzneale.

Diamond or **Dyamond** (dī′ạ.mǫnd). One of three brothers, sons of the fairy Agape, in Spenser's *Faerie Queene.* When he is slain by Cambell, his strength passes into his surviving brothers.

Diamond Necklace Affair, The. In French history, a celebrated episode which discredited the court on the eve of the French Revolution. A necklace (valued at about 300,000 dollars), originally ordered for Madame du Barry, was negotiated for (1783–84) by Cardinal de Rohan through an intermediary, the adventuress Countess de Lamotte. The cardinal had probably been duped by forged notes into thinking that Marie Antoinette, with whom he was infatuated, wanted him to get the necklace for her. Despite the charges of her contemporaries, the queen was probably innocent of complicity.

Diana (dĭ.an′ạ). An ancient Italian divinity, goddess of the moon, protectress of the female sex, later identified with the Greek Artemis. Like Artemis she was goddess of the hunt and the woods, protectress of chastity, and patroness of childbirth. Her famous shrine in the grove at Aricia was the scene of the custom investigated by Sir J. G. Frazer in the *Golden Bough.* Her companion, Virbius or Hippolytus, was worshiped there with her. Her priest, who came to his office by killing his predecessor in single combat, likewise might be killed by one in similar straits (specifically, a runaway slave).

Diana. In George Peele's pastoral comedy *The Arraignment of Paris,* the goddess who arbitrates the quarrel between the other goddesses over the golden ball. She finally awards it to Queen Elizabeth as fairer even than the four most beauteous figures of classical mythology.

Diana. A sonnet sequence (1592) by Henry Constable. The first edition contained 23 poems, which was increased to 76 in the second edition of 1594. Eight of these are known to be by Sidney, but it has not been proved that Constable is not the author of the remaining sonnets. Some of those included in anthologies are those whose first lines are "Mine eye with all the deadly sins is fraught," "Dear to my soul, then leave me not forsaken!" "To live in hell and heaven to behold," "Fair grace of graces, muse of muses all," and one called *To Sir Philip Sidney's Soul* ("Give pardon, blessed soul, to my bold cries"). The full title of the sequence is *Certaine sweete sonnets in the praise of his mistress, Diana.*

Diana. In Shakespeare's *All's Well That Ends Well,* the daughter of the Florentine widow with whom Helena lodges. She makes possible the reconciliation of Bertram to Helena by her willingness to permit Helena to take her (Diana's) place in an assignation with Bertram.

Diana. In Shakespeare's *Pericles,* the goddess who appears in a dream to Pericles and sends him to the Temple of Diana to find his wife, Thaisa.

Diana. A character in Honoré d'Urfé's *Astrée,* taken from the *Diana Enamorada* of Jorge de Montemayor.

Diana of the Crossways. A novel by George Meredith, published in 1885. It deals with the romantic complications in the life of Diana Merion. She leaves her husband, Warwick, has an affair with the young politician Percy Dacier, and finally marries Thomas Redworth after Warwick's death. The character of Diana was popularly connected with Caroline Norton, Richard Brinsley Sheridan's granddaughter.

Diana Vernon (vẽr′nǫn). See **Vernon, Diana.**

Diaphanta (dī.ạ.fan′tạ). In Thomas Middleton and William Rowley's play *The Changeling,* the maid to Beatrice. On the night of Beatrice's wedding to Alsemero, Diaphanta substitutes herself for her mistress in the marriage bed.

Diaphanous Silkworm, Sir. See **Silkworm, Sir Diaphanous.**

diary (dī′ạ.ri). An account of daily events or transactions; a journal; specifically, a daily record kept by a person of any or all matters within his experience or observation: as, a diary of the weather; a traveler's diary. "In sea-voyages, where there is nothing to be seen but sky and sea, men . . . make diaries; but in land-travel, wherein so much is to be observed, . . . they omit it."

                            (Bacon, *Travel.*)

Diary of C. Jeames de la Pluche (jēmz dẹ lạ plüsh). A short story by Thackeray. It was originally published in the humorous weekly *Punch* (November, 1845–February, 1846) and was reprinted in Thackeray's *Miscellanies* (1856). The story tells the adventures of James Plush, a footman who becomes wealthy through buying railway shares, changes his ordinary name to a more aristocratic form, and takes a bachelor apartment in the aristocratic London *Albany* (where Byron, Macaulay, "Monk" Lewis, and Bulwer-Lytton once lived). He becomes engaged to the daughter of Lord Bareacres, Lady Angelina (who runs away with another suitor), loses his fortune, as quickly as he made it, in a market crash, settles down as a public-house keeper, and marries Mary Ann Hoggins.

Dibdin (dib′din), **Charles.** b. at Southampton, England, March 4, 1745; d. at London, July 25, 1814. An English song writer and composer, especially noted for his songs of the sea. He went on the stage as a "singing actor" when about 15 years old, and soon began to write operas and other dramatic pieces, for which he sometimes wrote the words as well as the music, and in which he also played. In 1789 he began his series of "table entertainments," which he wrote, acted, sang, and accompanied. Nearly all his best songs (*The Flowing Can, Ben Backstay, Tom Bowling,* and others) were written by him for these entertainments, which were called *The Whim of the Moment, Oddities, The Wags,* and *The Quizzes,* among others. He wrote several novels and *The History of the Stage* (c1800), his own *Professional Life* (1803), poems, and about 70 operas and musical dramas.

ḍ, d or j; ṣ, s or sh; ṭ, t or ch; ẓ, z or zh; *o,* F. cloche; ü, F. menu; ċh, Sc. loch; ṅ, F. bonbon.

Dibdin, Charles Isaac Mungo. b. 1768; d. 1833. An English dramatist and song writer; son of Charles Dibdin. He managed and wrote plays and spectacles for the Sadler's Wells Theatre, including *Speed the Plough: or, The Return of Peace* (1802) and *Edward and Susan: or, The Beauty of Battermere* (1803).

Dibdin, Thomas Frognall. b. at Calcutta, India, 1776; d. at Kensington, London, Nov. 18, 1847. An English bibliographer; nephew of Charles Dibdin (1745–1814). He published *Bibliomania* (1809–11), *Typographical Antiquities of Great Britain* (1810–19), and others.

Dibdin, Thomas John. b. at London, March 21, 1771; d. there, Sept. 16, 1841. An English song writer and dramatist; son of Charles Dibdin (1745–1814). He was the composer of some 2,000 songs, many of which are sometimes attributed to his father, whose style they resemble. His most successful work was the pantomime *Mother Goose* (1806), in which Grimaldi appeared as Clown. His interludes, *The Mouth of the Nile* (1798) and *Nelson's Glory* (1805), were quite popular.

Dicey (dī′si), **Albert Venn.** b. 1835; d. April 7, 1922. An English jurist; brother of Edward Dicey. He was graduated at Balliol College, Oxford, in 1858, was called to the bar in 1863, and was professor of English law at Oxford from 1882 to 1909. He published *Lectures Introductory to the Study of the Law of the Constitution* (1886).

Dicey, Edward. b. at Claybrook Hall, Leicestershire, England, in May, 1832; d. at London, July 7, 1911. An English journalist and historian; brother of Albert Venn Dicey. He was graduated at Trinity College, Cambridge, in 1854, was called to the bar at Gray's Inn in 1875, and was editor (1870–89) of the London *Observer*. He wrote *Rome in 1860* (1861), *Cavour: a Memoir* (1861), *Six Months in the Federal States* (1863), *The Schleswig-Holstein War* (1864), *The Battle-Fields of 1866* (1866), *England and Egypt* (1881), and *The Egypt of the Future* (1907).

Dick (dik). Entries on literary characters having this prename will be found under the surnames Amlet, Bultitude, Datchery, Dewy, Distich, Dudgeon, Swiveller, Tinto, and Turpin.

Dick, Mr. A mildly demented gentleman, whose real name is Richard Babley, in Charles Dickens's *David Copperfield*. Aunt Betsey Trotwood thinks he is a genius, but he has trouble constantly with an intrusive vision of King Charles's head.

Dickens (dik′enz), **Charles.** [Pseudonym, **Boz;** full name, **Charles John Huffam Dickens.**] b. at Landport, near Portsmouth, England, Feb. 7, 1812; d. at Gadshill, near Rochester, England, June 9, 1870. English novelist, after Scott undoubtedly the most influential of all British fiction writers. He was the son of John Dickens, who served as a clerk in the navy pay office and afterward became a newspaper reporter. Young Charles received an elementary education in private schools, served for a time as an attorney's clerk, and in 1835 through his shorthand skill became a reporter for the London *Morning Chronicle*, having already been employed as a reporter in the House of Commons by the *True Sun* and the *Mir-*

ror of Parliament. In 1833 he published in the *Monthly Magazine* his first story, entitled "A Dinner at Poplar Walk," which proved to be the beginning of a series of papers printed collectively as *Sketches by Boz* in 1836. He married Catherine, daughter of George Hogarth, one of the leading figures on the *Morning Chronicle*, in 1836. They separated in 1858. In 1836 and 1837 he published the *Pickwick Papers*, by which his literary reputation was established. He was the first editor (January-February, 1846) of the London *Daily News*, but he did much more important editorial work upon his own family-magazines, *Household Words* (established 1850) and its successor *All the Year Round* (established 1859), in which he published not only his own work but that of Wilkie Collins, Mrs. Gaskell, and many lesser writers who shared his literary ideals. He visited America in 1842 and again in 1867–68, when he read from his own works with overwhelming success. His chief works are *Pickwick Papers* (1836–37), *Oliver Twist* (1837–39), *Nicholas Nickleby* (1836–39), *Master Humphrey's Clock* (including *The Old Curiosity Shop* and *Barnaby Rudge*, 1840–41), *American Notes* (1842), *A Christmas Carol* (1843), *Martin Chuzzlewit* (1843–44), *The Chimes* (1844), *The Cricket on the Hearth* (1845), *Dombey and Son* (1846–48), *David Copperfield* (1849–50), *Bleak House* (1852–53), *Hard Times* (1854), *Little Dorrit* (1855–57), *A Tale of Two Cities* (1859), *The Uncommercial Traveler* (1860), *Great Expectations* (1860–61), *Our Mutual Friend* (1864–65), and *Mystery of Edwin Drood* (1870, unfinished). His *Life of Our Lord*, which he had conceived of originally as a tale for his children, was published during the 1930's in Great Britain and the U. S. He is buried in Westminster Abbey. Most of his novels were first published in monthly parts. His writing was matched by a very able group of illustrators: George Cruikshank, Phiz (Hablot Knight Browne), Marcus Stone, John Leech, and Robert Seymour, illustrator of the first sections of *Pickwick Papers*. Dickens was importantly influenced by the picaresque novels of Tobias Smollett, with their eccentric character-types. His characteristic note is a romantic treatment of realistic materials. Though essentially a humorist, he was often led toward didacticism by his idealism and moral earnestness. As he grew older, he worked away from both the high spirits and the semi-fantastic method of *The Pickwick Papers;* and some of his later novels, such as *Hard Times* (which attacks political economy of the Manchester school) and *Little Dorrit* (which involves imprisonment for debt), are very sombre and sociological. His friend Wilkie Collins was simultaneously exercising an influence in the direction of a more highly organized plot: see *Bleak House*, where the Chancery suit is all-pervasive, *A Tale of Two Cities*, and *The Mystery of Edwin Drood*. Like Scott, Dickens had the power to create scores of characters who talk themselves alive. Many of these have been called "caricatures," but they were not created under the inspiration of modern naturalistic ideals, and there is no denying their tremendous vitality. Even the inanimate often comes alive in Dickens; there survives in his pages much of the folklore quality known to primitive man. At the same time, his technique is often astonishingly forward-looking: see, for example, the short story "George Silverman's Explanation," where he makes use of what would now be called "stream-of-consciousness." Though Dickens's death-bed scenes, and the like, often seem very sentimental to 20th-century readers, he was, judged by Victorian standards, a daring crusader against prudery and hypocrisy. He was always the most passionately loved of Victorian novelists, and his critical reputation now seems to have recovered completely from the attacks made upon him, as a part of the anti-Victorian reaction of about a generation ago. The authorized *Life* by John Forster (1872–74) was brought up to date by J. W. T. Ley (1928). Dickens's *Letters* (first collected, 1880–82) have now been greatly enlarged in volumes 21–23 of "The Nonesuch Dickens" (1937–38). Una Pope-Hennessy's *Charles Dickens* (1945) is an excellent modern biography, except for its uncritical acceptance of the unverified legend of Dickens's liaison with Ellen Ternan, for which see Edward Wagenknecht, "Dickens and the Scandal-Mongers," *College English*, April, 1950. The latter author's *The Man Charles Dickens* (1929) is an elaborate study of Dickens's personality. There is excellent criticism in George Gissing, *Charles Dickens* (1898); G. K. Chesterton, *Charles Dickens* (1906); Walter C. Phillips, *Dickens, Reade, and Collins, Sensation Novelists* (1919); George Santayana, *Soliloquies in England* (1922); J. B. Van Amerongen, *The Actor in Dickens* (1927); George Orwell, *Dickens, Dali, and Others* (1946).

Dickens, Monica Enid. b. at London, May 10, 1915—. An English writer; great-granddaughter of Charles Dickens. Her books *One Pair of Hands* (1939) and *One Pair of Feet* (1942) are both autobiographical; she is the author also of *Mariana* (1940), *The Fancy* (1943), *Thursday Afternoons* (1945), and *The Happy Prisoner* (1946).

Dickinson (dik′in.son), **Goldsworthy Lowes.** b. Aug. 6, 1862; d. Aug. 3, 1932. An English author. He was educated at the Charterhouse and at King's College, Cambridge, was a fellow and lecturer of King's College, Cambridge, and a lecturer at the London School of Economics and Political Science. He delivered the Ingersoll lecture at Harvard in 1909. He published *The Development of Parliament in the Nineteenth Century* (1895), *The Greek View of Life* (1896), *Letters from a Chinese Official* (1903), *Justice and Liberty* (1908), *Religion and Immortality* (1911), *The European Anarchy* (1916), *War: its Nature, Cause, and Cure* (1923), and *After Two Thousand Years* (1930).

Dickon Sludge (dik′on sluj). See **Sludge, Dickon;** see also **Flibbertigibbet.**

Dick's Coffee House. An old coffee house, originally "Richard's," in Fleet Street, London.

Dick the Butcher (dik). In Shakespeare's *2 Henry VI*, a butcher of Ashford, follower of the rebel Jack Cade.

dictionary. A book containing either all or the principal words of a language, or words of one or more specified classes, arranged in a stated order, usually alphabetical, with definitions or explanations of their meanings and other information concerning them, expressed either in the same or in another language; a word-book; a lexicon; a vocabulary: as, an English dictionary; a Greek and Latin dictionary; a French-English or an English-French dictionary. In the original and most usual sense a dictionary is chiefly linguistic and literary, containing all the common words of the language with information as to their meanings and uses. In addition to definitions, the larger dictionaries include etymologies, pronunciations, and variations of spelling, together with illustrative citations, more or less explanatory information, etc. Special or technical dictionaries supply information on a single subject or branch of a subject: as, a dictionary of medicine or of mechanics; a biographical dictionary. A dictionary of geography is usually called a gazetteer.

What speech esteem you most? The king's, said I.
But the best words? O, Sir, the dictionary.
    (Pope, *Donne Versified*, iv.)

The multiplication and improvement of dictionaries is a matter especially important to the general comprehension of English.
    (G. P. Marsh, *Lects. on Eng. Lang.* xxi.)

Dictionary of National Biography. A reference work in 63 volumes and three supplementary volumes, listing and giving brief to rather extensive memoirs of persons prominent in English life since the beginning of English history. The series was founded in 1882 by George Smith, London publisher, and the volumes, edited by Leslie Stephen and subsequently by Sidney Lee, appeared quarterly from 1885 to 1900. The supplementary volumes were published under Lee's editorship in 1901, covering mainly biographies of those who had died since publication had been begun in 1885. In 1912 appeared the first volume of a series supplementary to the main work and intended to include one volume for each decade of the century. Additional volumes have appeared at intervals since. The editors of this series have been Lee, H. W. C. Davis and J. R. H. Warren, and L. G. Wickham Legg.

Dicts or Sayings of the Philosophers, The. A fifteenth-century prose work translated from the French by Anthony Woodville, Lord Rivers. Printed in November, 1477, on Caxton's famous Westminster press, established the year before, it is historically important as the first book printed on English soil, and the first book printed in English with a date. A passage on women, by Socrates, was added by Caxton. The French title of the work is *Les Ditz moraulx des philosophes*.

Dictys Cretensis (dik′tis krē.ten′sis). The reputed author, a native of Cnossus, Crete, of a narrative of the Trojan War, entitled (in the pretended Latin translation of Q. Septimius) *Ephemeris Belli Trojani*, the introduction to which represents him as a follower of Idomeneus in the Trojan War. This narrative, with *De excido Trojae* of Dares Phrygius, was one of the chief sources from which the heroic legends of Greece passed into the literature of the Middle Ages. It was probably composed by Septimius c300 A.D.

Didapper (dī′dap.ėr), **Beau.** In Henry Fielding's novel *Joseph Andrews*, a rich, weak-minded fop.

Diderot (dē.drō), **Denis.** b. at Langres, Haute-Marne, France, Oct. 5, 1713; d. at Paris, July 31,

1784. A French philosopher, encyclopedist, and man of letters. After his formal schooling at Paris he spurned the professions, pursued against his father's wishes the study of Latin, mathematics, science, Italian, and English, and married secretly in 1743. His first literary labors were as a publishers' aid. He translated into French Temple Stanyan's *Histoire de la Grèce* (1743), Shaftesbury's *Essai sur le mérite et la vertu* (1745), and, with three collaborators, Robert James's *Dictionnaire universel de médecine, de chimie, de botanique* (6 vols., 1746–48). The publishers of this work, impressed with his knowledge and skill, soon associated him with Jean le Rond d'Alembert and made him general editor of *L'Encyclopédie*, the greatest publishing venture of the 18th century. In the face of severe censorship and repeated suppressions, Diderot was responsible for the publication of the first 28 volumes (17 of text, 11 of plates) over a period of more than 20 years (1751–72). Five volumes of addenda and two of tables brought the total to 35 by 1780. Diderot's interest in medical and biological sciences led him to write *Lettre sur les aveugles* (1749), *Lettre sur les sourds et muets* (1751), *Pensées sur l'interprétation de la nature* (1753), and *Le Rêve de d'Alembert* (1769, published in 1830). These works show a thorough understanding of the physiological arguments for evolutionary transformism and a naturalistic philosophy of science applied to problems of ethics and esthetics. His *Salons*, written for the foreign subscribers to the *Correspondance Littéraire*, reveal Diderot's superior talents and prophetic insight as critic of literature and the fine arts. Two plays, *Le Fils naturel* (1757) and *Le Père de famille* (1758), were produced, without great success, and published during his lifetime, accompanied by interesting and revolutionary essays on dramatic art. The third and best, *Est-il bon, est-il méchant?*, and the justly praised *Paradoxe sur le comédien* (1830) were left in manuscript for posterity. The same destiny attended his narrative fiction, except for the only occasionally interesting *Bijoux indiscrets* (1748) and two short stories. Posthumously published were *La Religieuse* (1796), *Le Neveu de Rameau* (1823), believed by many to be his masterpiece, *Jacques le fataliste* (1796), and a number of short stories, among the best of which is *Ceci n'est pas un conte*. His *Supplément au voyage de Bougainville*, written in 1772, first printed in 1796, shows (even by 20th-century standards) ultra-modern views concerning religion, sex, and politics. Diderot received financial support from Catherine II of Russia, who bought his valuable library, but left him the use of it during his lifetime. He went to St. Petersburg in 1773–74 to express his gratitude, wrote a *Projet d'une université pour la Russie*, and left in manuscript very frank and critical *Observations* on Catherine's *Instructions* to her legists for a code of laws based on the principles of Montesquieu and other writers of the French enlightenment. Diderot's *Lettres à Sophie Volland* reveal the extraordinary character of the writer and the man, and justify his growing reputation as the great seminal mind of his century. A noteworthy collection of Diderot manuscripts has recently been rescued from oblivion by Herbert Dieckmann, author of "Bibliographical Data on

Diderot" (in *Studies in Honor of Frederick W. Shipley*, 1942). Available works on Diderot in English are scarce, but include *Diderot and the Encyclopaedists*, by John Morley (1878), *The Censoring of Diderot's Encyclopédie*, by Douglas H. Gordon and Norman L. Torrey (1947), and *Diderot, Interpreter of Nature* (with translations of *Le Rêve de d'Alembert*, *Le Neveu de Rameau*, and others), by Jonathan Kemp and Jean Stewart (1938). In French, see *L'Humanisme de Diderot*, by Jean Thomas (1936), and *Diderot*, by A. Billy (1932).

Dido (dī'dō). A surname of the Phoenician goddess of the moon (Astarte), who was worshiped as the protecting deity of the citadel of Carthage. Her name was in later time appropriated by the Tyrian Elissa, founder of Carthage, who was the mistress of Aeneas in Vergil's *Aeneid* and killed herself when he left her.

Dido, Queen of Carthage, The Tragedy of. A tragedy by Christopher Marlowe, published in 1594. Nash is said to have finished it after Marlowe's death, for he added his name to Marlowe's when he published it. Whether he wrote any of the play is uncertain. It is a version of the story of Dido's love for Aeneas and her mourning and death after his departure, a story told in Vergil's *Aeneid*.

Didymus (did'i.mus). See Saint **Thomas**.

Diego (dẹ.ä'gō). A waggish sexton in Fletcher and Massinger's *Spanish Curate*. He longs for a less healthy parish and more funerals.

Diego, Don. See Formal, James.

Dies Irae (dē'ās ē'rā, dī'ēz ī'rē). [Eng. trans., "*Day of Wrath*."] A sequence appointed in the Roman missal to be sung between the Epistle and the Gospel in masses for the dead; named from its first words. The text was written probably by Thomas de Celano, the friend of Saint Francis of Assisi, and is a hymn in triple-rhymed stanzas. Its subject is the day of judgment. The transition from the terror of the day of wrath (*dies irae*) to hope in salvation is used as a natural preparation to the concluding prayer for eternal rest. Sir Walter Scott's translation in *The Lay of the Last Minstrel*, beginning "O day of wrath, O dreadful day," is well known. There have been numerous versions and translations. The author of the old ecclesiastical melody to which it is sung is not known, but it was adapted to the words at the time they were written. It has been a popular subject with many modern composers, notably Colonna, Bassani, Cherubini, Berlioz, Verdi, and Gounod in *Mors et Vita*. It is also introduced with magnificent effect in Mozart's *Requiem*.

Dietrich von Bern (dē'trich fon bern'). In medieval Germanic legend, a figure corresponding to Theodoric the Great, historical king (474–526) of the Ostrogoths (East Goths), whose residence was at Verona. His life and adventures are the subject of the Icelandic *Thidrekssaga* (*Saga Thidhreks konungs af Bern*), also called the *Wilkina Saga*, whose material is from German sources, and is an element in various Middle High German poems, among them the *Nibelungenlied*, *Biterolf*, the *Rosengarten*, and *Ermenrichs Tod*. The South German cycle of Dietrich songs includes *Dietrichs Flucht*, *Alpharts Tod*, and the *Rabenschlacht*, all from the latter part of the 13th century. The *Hildebrandslied* treats a related theme. The figure of Dietrich appears also in the otherwise unrelated *Nibelungenlied*. There is no unified German Dietrich epic. His birth and death are mysterious; he is descended from a spirit, and disappears, ultimately, on a black horse. His name is still preserved in popular legends. In the Lausitz, the Wild Huntsman, the being who rides in furious haste across the heavens in violent storms, is called Dietrich von Bern. The name is also given to Knecht Ruprecht, the bringer of gifts or punishment at Christmas. Many large buildings in different parts of Italy, among them the amphitheater at Verona and the Castle of Sant' Angelo at Rome, have been popularly ascribed to him.

Difficulty, The Hill. A hill, in Bunyan's *Pilgrim's Progress*, encountered by Christian in his journey to the Celestial Country.

Digby (dig'bi), Sir **Kenelm.** b. at Gothurst, Buckinghamshire, England, June (or July) 11, 1603; d. at London, June 11, 1665. An English philosopher, naval commander, diplomat, and Royalist; son of Sir Everard Digby, who was executed for his participation in the Gunpowder Plot. He was educated at Gloucester Hall (later Worcester College), Oxford. In 1641 he fought a duel at Paris in defense of his royal master, Charles I; in 1644 he was made chancellor to Charles's queen, Henrietta Maria, and in 1645 at Rome (he was a Roman Catholic) he pleaded for Charles with Pope Innocent X. He was twice banished from England, in 1643 and again in 1649. He was visited during his exile by Evelyn, and he came to know Descartes. Some of his many works are *A Conference with a Lady about Choice of Religion* (Paris, 1638; London, 1654), *Observations upon Religio Medici* (1643), a criticism of Sir Thomas Browne's work, and often reprinted with it, *Observations on the 22nd Stanza in the Ninth Canto of the Second Book of Spenser's "Faery Queene"* (1644), *A Treatise of the Nature of Bodies* (Paris, 1644; London, 1658, 1665, 1669), *A Treatise declaring the Operations and Nature of Man's Soul, out of which the Immortality of reasonable Souls is evinced* (Paris, 1644; London, 1645, 1657, 1669), *Letters Concerning Religion* (1651), *A Discourse Concerning Infallibility in Religion* (1652), *A Discourse concerning the Vegetation of Plants* (1661), a lecture delivered at Gresham College, Jan. 23, 1661, in which he announced his discovery of the necessity of oxygen for the life of plants. As a philosopher, Digby was a follower of Aristotle and the Schoolmen. As a scientist he is not thought of too highly today, despite the fact that he unquestionably had much genuine scientific curiosity. Evelyn called him "an errant mountebank," after seeing his Paris laboratory, and Lady Fanshawe described him as "a person of excellent parts and a very fine-bred gentleman," apart from his tendency to lie about his experiments. His "sympathetic powder" or "powder of sympathy," for curing wounds, has long since been dismissed as being a quack preparation of no medical value.

Digby, Kenelm Henry. b. at Clonfert, Ireland, 1800; d. at London, March 22, 1880. An English antiquary. He graduated, with the degree of B.A., at Cambridge in 1819, and spent most of his sub-sequent life in literary pursuits at London. His chief works are *The Broadstone of Honour, or Rules for the Gentlemen of England* (1822, anonymous; enlarged edition, with second title omitted, 1826–27), and *Mores Catholici, or Ages of Faith* (1831–40).

Digby Grant (grant). See **Grant, Digby.**

Digby Plays. A collection of three late 15th-century mystery plays, which exist in a manuscript (the Digby Manuscript) in the Bodleian Library at Oxford. The first play deals with *The Massacre of the Innocents and the Flight into Egypt* (also known as *The Killing of the Children*); the second with the *Conversion of Saul* (or Saint Paul), in which the unknown author quotes the "byble" as his authority; the third, regarded as the most important, is *Mary Magdalene*, with the Seven Deadly Sins, Tiberius Caesar, and the king of Marseilles as characters.

Digest, The. See **Pandects of Justinian.**

Diggon (dig'on). A shepherd in Spenser's *Shepherd's Calendar*. He has traveled far and lost all his flock to sharp strangers.

Diggory (dig'o.ri). A loutish servant in Oliver Goldsmith's comedy *She Stoops to Conquer*.

Diggory Venn (ven). See **Venn, Diggory.**

Dighton (dī'ton). In Shakespeare's *Richard III*, a murderer appointed by Tyrrel to kill the Princes in the Tower. He is mentioned (IV.iii) but does not appear.

Dilettanti Society. A London society devoted to the encouragement of a taste for the fine arts, founded in 1734.

Dilke (dilk), **Charles Wentworth.** b. Dec. 8, 1789; d. Aug. 10, 1864. An English journalist, editor (1830–46) of the London *Athenaeum* and (1846–49) of the *Daily News*. He was the author of essays on the *Letters of Junius*. He did valuable research on Alexander Pope's life and continued the series of *Old Plays* begun by Robert Dodsley.

Dilke, Sir Charles Wentworth. b. at Chelsea, London, Sept. 4, 1843; d. at London, Jan. 26, 1911. An English Radical Liberal politician and author; grandson of Charles Wentworth Dilke (1789–1864). He graduated at Cambridge in 1866 and was called to the bar in 1866, elected member of Parliament for Chelsea in 1868, appointed undersecretary of state for foreign affairs in 1880, and became president of the Local Government Board with a seat in the cabinet in 1882. He lost his seat in Parliament in 1886 after he had been corespondent in a divorce case, but again became a member in 1892. He published *Greater Britain* (1868), *Parliamentary Reform* (1879), *Present Condition of European Politics* (1887), *The British Army* (1888), *Problems of Greater Britain* (1890), *Imperial Defense* (with Spenser Wilkinson, 1892), *The British Empire* (1898), and others. He married twice, his second wife being Emilia Frances Strong, Lady Dilke, noted art critic.

Dilke, Lady Emilia. [Maiden name, **Emilia Frances Strong.**] b. at Ilfracombe, Devonshire, England, Sept. 2, 1840; d. at Woking, Surrey, England, Oct. 24, 1904. An English critic and historian of French art; wife (married 1861) of Mark Pattison (1813–84) and (married 1885) of Sir Charles Wentworth

Dilke (1843–1911). Educated at the South Kensington Art School; interested in social questions, labor unions, and votes for women; one of the founders of the Women's Trades Union League, the annual congresses of which she attended from 1884 to 1904. Contributed writings on art to the *Academy*, *Magazine of Art*, and other periodicals. Author of *The Renaissance of Art in France* (1879), *Art in the Modern State* (1884), *French Painters* (1889), *French Architects and Sculptors* (1900), *French Engravers and Draughtsmen* (1902), the last three dealing with the 18th century; she also wrote two collections of mystical stories, *The Shrine of Death* (1886), and *The Shrine of Love* (1891), and *The Book of the Spiritual Life* (1905).

Dillon (dil'ọn), **Charles.** b. in England in 1819; d. there, June 27, 1881. An English actor. He excelled in romantic drama, in such parts as Belphegor.

Dillon, Wentworth. See **Roscommon**, 4th Earl of.

Dilly (dil'i), **Charles.** b. at Southill, Belfordshire, England, May 22, 1739; d. at Ramsgate, Kent, England, May 4, 1807. An English bookseller, publisher of Boswell's *Life of Johnson*. In partnership with his older brother, Edward Dilly (1732–79), he published Boswell's *Corsica*, Lord Chesterfield's *Works*, and many other outstanding 18th-century works; alone, he published Boswell's *Journal of a Tour to the Hebrides* (1780) and the *Life of Samuel Johnson, LL.D.* (1791; 2nd ed., 1793; 3rd ed., 1799). Both brothers were known for the famous dinners they gave to literary lights, and Charles was noted for the liberal terms he extended to his authors. Boswell's *Life* is full of references to "my worthy booksellers and friends," with Boswell more than once paying tribute to their "hospitable and well-covered table."

Diminuendo. A prose sketch (1896) by Max Beerbohm. Something of its whimsical, facetious nature may be gathered from the fact that it appeared in his first book, *The Works of Max Beerbohm*, which the author pretends is to be his last, and in which it is the closing selection. "I feel myself a trifle outmoded. I belong to the Beardsley period," and "I stand aside with no regret," Beerbohm tells his reader, in apparent sincerity. The meaning of the title in music (diminishing in loudness) is appropriate to the title of the sketch.

dimeter (dim'ẹ.tẻr). In prosody, a verse or period consisting of two feet or dipodies: as, an Ionic *dimeter; iambic *dimeters*.

Dimoch or **Dymoke** (dim'ọk). The name of a Lincolnshire family holding since 1377 the feudal office of "champion of England."

Dimple Hill. A novel by Dorothy M. Richardson, published in 1938. It is the twelfth section of *Pilgrimage* (1938), a novel sequence in 12 parts employing the stream-of-consciousness technique.

Dinadan (din'ạ.dan), **Sir.** In Malory's *Morte d'Arthur*, a knight of King Arthur.

Dinah (dī'nạ), **Aunt.** In Laurence Sterne's *Tristram Shandy*, the aunt of Walter Shandy, who occupies himself with schemes for spending the money she leaves him.

Dinah Morris (mor'is). See **Morris, Dinah.**

Dinant (di.nänt'). In John Fletcher and Philip Massinger's *Little French Lawyer*, a gentleman who formerly loved and still pretends to love Lamira.

Dinarzade (dē.när.zä'dẹ). The sister of Scheherazade in *The Arabian Nights' Entertainments*. She passes the night in the bridal chamber, and daily asks her sister, who is condemned to die each morning unless she can win a stay by telling another story, to relate for the last time one of her "agreeable tales."

Dingley Dell (ding'li). The location of Manor Farm, the home of Mr. Wardle, in Dickens's *Pickwick Papers*.

Dinmont (din'mont, -mọnt), **Dandie** (or **Andrew**). A border farmer in Sir Walter Scott's novel *Guy Mannering*. He is the grateful friend of Brown, who had saved his life. Sent by Meg Merrilies, he protects Brown in the Portanferry jail and, after their escape helps him, under the guidance of Meg, to capture Hatteraick. He is the owner of Mustard and Pepper, the progenitors of the Dandie Dinmont terriers.

Diocletian (dī.ọ.klē'shạn). [Full Latin name, **Gaius** (or **Caius**) **Aurelius Valerius Diocletianus**; surnamed **Jovius**.] b. at Dioclea (whence his name), near Salona, in Dalmatia, 245 A.D.; d. near Salona, in Dalmatia, 313 A.D. An emperor of Rome. He entered the army at an early age, and, although of obscure origin, rose to important commands under Probus, Aurelian, and Carus. On the death of Numerianus, joint emperor with Carinus, he was proclaimed emperor by the army at Chalcedon in 284, and advanced against Carinus who was killed by one of his own officers. In 286 he adopted Maximian as his colleague in the government, dividing the empire into eastern and western parts for greater efficiency in government. In 292 the joint emperors appointed Galerius and Constantius Chlorus as their associates, and intending them as their successors. Diocletian and Maximian retained the title of Augusti, while Galerius and Constantius were denominated Caesars. Each of the rulers was independent in the local administration of his province, but the three junior rulers acknowledged Diocletian as the head of the empire. The empire was divided among them as follows: Diocletian received Thrace, Egypt, Syria, and Asia, with Nicomedia (modern Izmit, Turkey) as his capital; Maximian, Italy, Africa, Sicily, and the islands of the Tyrrhenian Sea, with Mediolanum (modern Milan) as his capital; Galerius, Illyricum and the countries of the Danube with Sirmium (near modern Sremska Mitrovica, Yugoslavia) as his capital; and Constantius, Britain, Gaul, and Spain, with Augusta Trevirorum (modern Trier or Treves, Germany) as his capital. Diocletian subdued a revolt in Egypt in 296, Constantius restored the allegiance of Britain in the same year, and Galerius forced the Persians to sue for peace in 297. Under Diocletian, the Roman Empire became more tranquil and prospered greatly. Republican forms of government finally disappeared during his reign; the monarchy became absolute. His economic measures were generally sound, but his attempt in 301 to fix prices and wages, during an economic crisis caused by speculation and bad crops, was a disastrous failure, causing an upheaval in food distribution and ruining many commercial enterprises. In 303 Diocletian, persuaded, it is said, by the false accusations of Galerius, ordered a general persecution of the Christians throughout the empire. He abdicated in 305, compelling Maximian to do the same, and retired to Salona in Dalmatia (near modern Split, Yugoslavia), where he spent his remaining years in the cultivation of his gardens. Diocletian and Maximian were succeeded as Augusti by Galerius and Constantius, who in turn appointed Severus and Maximinus Caesars.

Diodati (dē̱.ō̱.dä′tē̱), **Charles.** b. c1608; d. 1638. An English physician and scholar of the classics, famous for being a close friend of Milton. He came friend to Milton at St. Paul's School. He received an M.A. from Oxford (1628) and an M.A. from Cambridge (1629), and practiced medicine near Chester. To him Milton addressed his first and sixth Latin elegies and an Italian sonnet. His death while Milton was abroad was lamented in *Epitaphium Damonis* (1640), considered by many to be the greatest of Milton's Latin poems.

Diodorus (dī.ō̱.dō′rus). [Surnamed **Siculus,** meaning "of Sicily."] b. at Agyrium, Sicily; fl. in the second half of the 1st century B.C. A Greek historian, author of an unreliable history in 40 books entitled *Historical Library.* The first five (dealing with the legendary histories of Egypt, Assyria, Ethiopia, and Greece) and the 11th to 20th books (beginning with the Persian War and ending with the events following Alexander's death) are all that have survived.

Diogenes (dī.oj′ē̱.nēz). b. at Sinope, in Asia Minor, c412 B.C.; d. at Corinth, 323 B.C. A Greek Cynic philosopher, famous for his eccentricities. He emigrated to Athens in his youth, became the pupil of Antisthenes, and lived, according to Seneca, in a tub. While on a voyage from Athens to Aegina, he was captured by pirates who exposed him for sale on the slave market in Crete. When asked what business he understood, he replied, "How to command men," and requested to be sold to some one in need of a master. He was purchased by Xeniades, a wealthy citizen of Corinth, who restored him to liberty, and in whose house he passed his old age. At Corinth he was, according to tradition, visited by Alexander the Great. Alexander inquired whether he could oblige him in any way. "Yes," replied Diogenes, "stand from between me and the sun." Diogenes taught and believed in an extreme of asceticism as a means of attaining truth and good. As a result he was looked down upon and in turn rejected his contemporaries. The story of his search with a lighted lamp in broad daylight (as he said, "for an honest man"), true or not, vividly illustrates this.

Diogenes Laërtius (lā̱.ėr′shi.us). fl. probably in the early 3rd century A.D. A historian and biographer, author of lives of the Greek philosophers in 10 books, from the early schools to the Epicureans. His work is chiefly valued as containing information preserved nowhere else.

Diomedes (dī.ō̱.mē′dēz). In Greek legend, a king of Argos, and a leader of the Greek warriors at the siege of Troy. He was the son of Tydeus, who fell in the expedition against Thebes. He went with Sthenelus and Euryalus to Troy as the commander of a fleet of 80 ships carrying warriors from Argos, Tiryns, Hermione, Asine, Troezen, Eionae, Epidaurus, Aegina, and Mases. He was, next to Achilles, the most valiant of the Greeks before Troy, and fought against the most distinguished among the Trojans, including Hector and Aeneas. He and Odysseus carried off the Palladium, without which Troy must fall, in a night expedition.

Diomedes. In Greek legend, a Thracian king, son of Ares, and owner of the horses captured by Hercules as one of his labors. The horses were flesh-eaters and Hercules killed Diomedes and fed him to his own horses.

Diomedes. In Shakespeare's *Antony and Cleopatra,* an attendant of Cleopatra.

Diomedes. In Shakespeare's *Troilus and Cressida,* a Greek commander who is sent to Troy to conduct Cressida to the Greek camp. She accepts his advances and gives him the love token which Troilus had given her.

Dion (dī′on). In Shakespeare's *Winter's Tale,* a Sicilian lord who is sent with Cleomenes to the oracle at Delphi.

Dion. The father of Euphrasia in Beaumont and Fletcher's *Philaster.*

Dione (dī.ō′nē). In very early Greek mythology, the consort of Zeus; his feminine counterpart as sky deity. In later mythological genealogy, she is a female Titan, daughter of Oceanus and Tethys, and mother by Zeus of Aphrodite.

Dione. A pastoral tragedy by John Gay, published in 1720.

Dionysius (dī.ō̱.nish′i.us, -nish′us). [Surnamed **"the Elder."**] b. c430 B.C.; d. at Syracuse, 367 B.C. A tyrant of Syracuse. He contrived in 405 to have himself appointed sole general of the forces of the republic in the war against Carthage, whereupon he surrounded himself with a strong bodyguard of mercenaries and usurped the government. He strengthened his position by marrying the daughter of the deceased party leader Hermocrates, and concluded peace with Carthage in 404. He declared war against Carthage in 398, and was besieged in 396 at Syracuse by the Carthaginians, who were compelled by pestilence and a successful sally of the Syracusans to raise the siege after an investment of 11 months. He concluded an advantageous peace in 392. He captured Rhegium in 387 and Croton in 379 (Reggio di Calabria and Crotone, in Italy), which gave him a commanding influence among the Italian Greeks. He fought two further wars with Carthage. His power and influence are said to have exceeded those of any other Greek before Alexander the Great. He encouraged letters, invited Plato to his court, and himself gained the chief prize at the Lenaea with a play entitled *The Ransom of Hector.* His reputation was, despite his literary and scholarly pretensions, one of a despot and an arbitrary ruler.

Dionysius. [Surnamed **"the Younger."**] b. c395 B.C.; d. probably at Corinth, after 343 B.C. A tyrant of Syracuse; a relative of Dion, and son of Dionysius the Elder, whom he succeeded in 367. He was under the influence of Dion for several years, but then drove Dion from Syracuse and, despite Plato's desire to set up under Dionysius an ideal state,

---

ḑ, d or j; ş, s or sh; ţ, t or ch; ẓ, z or zh; o, F. cloche; ü, F. menu; čh, Sc. loch; ń, F. bonbon.

ruled with a profligate hand. He was expelled by Dion in 356, became tyrant of Locri, where he exhibited such cruelty that his wife and daughters were slaughtered when he left to take possession again of Syracuse in 346. He was finally expelled from Syracuse in 343 by Timoleon.

Dionysius of Halicarnassus (hal''i.kär.nas'us). b. at Halicarnassus, in Caria; d. at Rome c7 B.C. A Greek rhetorician and historian, author of a history of Rome (*Archaeologia*). In this work, as the Scottish classicist Richard Jebb has pointed out, Dionysius "aimed at writing an *Introduction* to Polybius. He maintains, on fanciful grounds, that the Romans, who deserve to rule the world, are no 'barbarians,' but of Greek descent. We have Books I.-X., going down to 450 B.C., and fragments of Book XI. He did a better work in his rhetorical writings, and above all in his excellent essays on the Greek orators."

Dionysius the Areopagite (ar.ē.op'ạ.jīt). fl. 1st century A.D. An Athenian scholar, a member of the Areopagus, converted to Christianity by Saint Paul A.D. He was long regarded as the author of several Greek treatises (*The Celestial Hierarchy, The Ecclesiastical Hierarchy, Concerning the Names of God, Of Mystical Theology, Epistles* and a Liturgy) which appeared in the 6th century and were probably written in the 5th. They have been the subject of much theological and critical discussion.

Dionysus (dī.ō.nī'sus). In Greek mythology, a fertility god; often limited to his specific gift of the vine and called the god of wine. He was, according to the common tradition, the son of Zeus and Semele, the daughter of Cadmus of Thebes. Hera, jealous of the attention which Zeus bestowed on Semele, came to her in the guise of a friendly old woman and persuaded her to request him to approach her in the same majesty in which he approached his wife. Zeus appeared in thunder and lightning, with the result that Semele was burned to ashes and in her agony gave birth to Dionysus, whom Zeus rescued from the flames and sewed up in his thigh until he came to maturity. He was brought up by Ino and Athamas at Orchomenus, spent many years in wandering about the earth, introducing the cultivation of the vine, and eventually rose to Olympus. He was also called, both by the Greeks and the Romans, Bacchus, i.e., the riotous god, originally a surname of Dionysus. Dionysus was one of the principal cult gods of Greece. He was the central figure of the Orphic mysteries and appeared in a minor role in the Eleusinian mysteries. He was identified with Zagreus, murdered by the Titans, whose heart Zeus swallowed to bring forth the god again: an explanation of his epithet Dithyrambus, said to mean "twice-born." Violence was attendant on the Dionysian myth, despite his role as culture-bringer. He was attended by Bacchantes, Maenads, Bassarides, and other groups of frenzied women; lustful satyrs and drunken sileni also form part of his train. The cult had its phallic aspects as well. Dionysus is pictured as a mild god, but terrible in anger. Pentheus, king of Thebes, refused to permit the introduction of the Dionysian cult. He was induced to watch the secret rites of the women in Dionysus's cult, was seen by them, and was torn

to bits by the frenzied devotees, who included his mother. See also **Bacchus.**

Dionyza (dī.ō.nī'zạ). In Shakespeare's *Pericles*, the wife of Cleon. She attempts the murder of Marina, and with her husband is finally punished by being burned to death.

Dioscuri (dī.os.kū'rī). Castor and Pollux (Polydeuces), according to Greek legend the sons of Leda and Zeus, or of Leda and Tyndareus (whence their patronymic *Tyndaridae*), and brothers of Helen.

Diotima (dī.ō.tī'mạ). A priestess of Mantinea, the reputed teacher of Socrates, mentioned in Plato's *Symposium*. She is probably fictitious.

Diplomacy. A play adapted by Bolton and Savile Rowe from Sardou's *Dora*, produced in 1878.

Dipsodes (dip'sōdz). A people in François Rabelais's *Gargantua and Pantagruel*. They were ruled by King Anarche, and many of them were giants. Pantagruel subdued them.

Dirae (dī'rē). The Furies.

Dirce (dẽr'sē). In Greek mythology, the second wife of Lycus, put to death by Amphion and Zethus, sons of Antiope, in revenge for her ill treatment of their mother. She was bound to the horns of a bull and dragged to death. (Her execution is represented in the famous sculpture group *The Farnese Bull*.) Her body was thrown into a well on Mount Cithaeron thereafter known as the fountain of Dirce.

dirge (dẽrj). A funeral hymn; the funeral service as sung, so called from an antiphon therein sung beginning "*Dirige*, Domine, Deus meus, in conspectu tuo viam meam" (Direct, O Lord my God, my way in thy sight), the words being taken from the Psalms ("Domine . . . dirige in conspectu tuo viam meam"; Vulgate, Ps. v. 8). From this it has come to mean a song or tune expressing grief, lamentation, and mourning.

> Resort, I pray you, vnto my sepulture,
> To sing my dirige with great deuocion.
> (*Lamentation of Mary Magdalene*, l. 641.)

And ouer yᵗ he ordeyned ther, to be contynued for euer, one day in yᵉ weke, a solempne dirige to be songe, and vpon yᵉ morowe a masse.
(Fabyan, *Chron.*, an. 1422.)

> With mirth in funeral, and with dirge in marriage,
> In equal scale weighing delight and dole.
> (Shak., *Hamlet*, I.ii.)

> First will I sing thy dirge,
> Then kiss thy pale lips, and then die myself.
> (Beau and Fl., *Knight of Burning Pestle*, IV.iv.)

Dirk Hatteraick (dẽrk hat'ẽr.āk). See **Hatteraick, Dirk.**

Discourse of English Poetrie, A. A critical essay (1586) by William Webbe. The subtitle of the work is *Together with the Author's judgment touching the reformation of our English verse*. The author gives an enthusiastic account of the works of Spenser.

Discoveries. A volume of essays by William Butler Yeats, published in 1907.

Discoveries Made Upon Men and Matters. A prose work (1641) by Ben Jonson. It is not a systematic, organized work, but a collection of miscellaneous material on a variety of subjects. It is a result of Jonson's reading, scholarship, observation, and experience. Some of the pieces are as long as a Bacon essay, and some no longer than a sentence.

Dishart (dish′ạrt), **Gavin.**　The hero of *The Little Minister*, a novel (1891) and play (1897) by James M. Barrie.

Dismas (diz′mạs).　[Also: **Demas, Desmas, Dysmas.**] The legendary name of the penitent thief crucified with Christ.

Disobedient Child.　An interlude by Thomas Ingelend, written in the mid-16th century and based on the story of the Prodigal Son.

Disowned, The.　A novel by Edward Bulwer-Lytton, published in 1829.

Disraeli (diz.rä′li), **Benjamin.**　[Title, 1st Earl of **Beaconsfield**; nicknamed **Dizzy**; pseudonym, **Runnymede.**] b. at London, Dec. 21, 1804; d. there, April 19, 1881. An English statesman and novelist; son of Isaac D'Israeli. He was descended from an aristocratic Sephardic family, but joined the Anglican Church in 1817. He was educated at home, and did not go to Oxford or Cambridge. He entered politics in 1832, and for the next three years made several unsuccessful attempts to gain a seat in Parliament. Finally, in 1837, he was elected Conservative member of Parliament for Maidstone. In 1839 he married Mary Ann Evans (Mrs. Wyndham Lewis), a widow 15 years his senior. She was "a perfect wife" for him, and her death, on Dec. 15, 1872, was a tragedy which made him feel that he "no longer had a home." His first speech in Parliament, in 1837, was a complete failure, giving no indication of the great man that he was to become or the great career that was to be his. In 1841 he represented Shrewsbury, and from 1847 to 1876 he was a member of Parliament from Buckinghamshire. In 1847, also, he was made the leader of the opposition in the House of Commons, a post that he held for a quarter of a century. He was three times Chancellor of the Exchequer, in 1853, 1857-58, and again in 1867, and he was twice Queen Victoria's prime minister, an office which since his childhood days he had hoped to hold. He became the queen's first minister in February, 1868, but resigned after the general election at the end of the year; he headed the government again from 1874 to 1880, resigning again after the Tory defeat in April, 1880. He was made Earl of Beaconsfield in 1876, the year in which he had Victoria proclaimed Empress of India, and he entered the House of Lords. He attacked Peel for his repeal of the Corn Laws in 1846, Gladstone's financial policy in 1860 and 1862, and his Irish and foreign policies during the period 1868-73. At the Congress of Berlin, which he forced on Russia in 1878, he accomplished his last great act of political genius, his "Peace with Honor," which brought his popularity to its highest point and won him the honor of being made a Knight of the Garter, on July 22, 1878. When he died, three years later, he was honored as no Englishman had been since Wellington. Had he wished it, he could have been buried in Westminster Abbey, but he was buried at Hughenden, in accordance with his expressed wishes, beside his wife. Victoria expressed her own feeling and that of the nation when she called "the death of my dear Lord Beaconsfield a national calamity." April 19, the day of his death, was, and is, called Primrose Day in his honor, because the primrose was his favorite flower, and a Conservative political organization, the Primrose League, was founded to carry on his principles and to keep his memory alive. As a novelist, Disraeli wrote *Vivian Grey* (1826), of autobiographical interest, *The Young Duke* (1831), *Contarini Fleming* (1832) and *The Wondrous Tale of Alroy* (1833), both of Jewish interest, revealing his pride in the Jewish people, a pride that he always maintained despite the fact that he had departed from the faith of his fathers. He also wrote *Henrietta Temple*, remembered for its Roman Catholic priest, *Glastonbury*, and *Venetia* (both 1837), *Coningsby* (1844), dealing with the English peasantry, *Sybil* (1845), which was instrumental in factory reform, and *Tancred* (1847). Two of his political novels, *Lothair* (1870) and *Endymion* (1880), which he wrote as the leader of "Young England," are regarded as inferior. Most of these works are in three volumes, except *Contarini Fleming*, which is in four, and *Vivian Grey*, in five. His nonfictional works, which now have only historical interest, are *An Enquiry into Plans of American Mining Companies, Lawyers and Legislators*, and *The Present State of Mexico* (both 1825), *England and France* (1832), *Vindication of the English Constitution* (1835), *The Spirit of Whiggism* (1836), and *Lord George Bentinck* (1852), a biography. His *Home Letters*, written in 1830–31, *Correspondence*, written 1852–53, *Selected Speeches*, in 2 volumes, and his *Letters* to Lady Bradford and to Lady Chesterfield, all published after his death, reveal facets of both his personal and his political lives.

D'Israeli (diz.rä′li) or **Disraeli, Isaac.**　b. at Enfield, England, May, 1766; d. at Bradenham House, Buckinghamshire, England, Jan. 19, 1848. An English miscellaneous writer; father of Benjamin Disraeli, 1st Earl of Beaconsfield. His chief works are *Curiosities of Literature* (6 vols., 1791–1834), a miscellaneous collection of anecdotes, quotations, and odd information, *Essay on the Literary Character* (1795), *Miscellanies, or Literary Recreations* (1796), *Calamities of Authors* (1812), *Quarrels of Authors* (1814), *Commentary on the Life and Reign of King Charles I* (1828–31), and *Amenities of Literature* (1841).

dissertation.　A written essay, treatise, or disquisition: as, Newton's *dissertations* on the prophecies.

You would laugh at me, says Philander, should I make you a learned dissertation on the nature of rusts. I shall only tell you there are two or three sorts of them, which are extremely beautiful in the eye of an antiquary, and preserve a coin better than the best artificial varnish.

(Addison, *Ancient Medals*, i.)

Distaffina (dis.tạ.fē′nạ).　The beloved of Bombastes Furioso in Rhodes's burlesque opera of the latter name. She jilted Bombastes for the king.

Distaff's Day, Saint.　January 7, so called because according to tradition on that day the women who have kept the Christmas festival till Twelfth Day (Jan. 6) return to their distaffs, or ordinary work. As a distaff is also called a rock, the day is sometimes called Rock Day.

Distant Lamp, The. A historical novel by Harold Begbie, published in 1912. It is a story of the Children's Crusade of 1212, and is laid in France, Egypt, and the Holy Land.

Distant Prospect of Eton College (ē'tǫn), **Ode on a.** A poem by Thomas Gray, written in 1742 and published anonymously by Robert Dodsley in 1747.

distich (dis'tik). In prosody, a group or system of two lines or verses. A familiar example is the elegiac distich. A distich in modern and rhyming poetry is more generally called a couplet. "The first distance for the most part goeth all by distick, or couples of verses agreeing in one cadence." (Puttenham, *Arte of Eng. Poesie.*)

Distich, Dick. A poet and satirist met in a madhouse by Sir Launcelot Greaves, in Tobias Smollett's novel *Sir Launcelot Greaves.* Alexander Pope used this signature in *The Guardian.*

Distresses, The. A play by Sir William D'Avenant, thought to have been the same as *The Spanish Lovers,* licensed in 1639.

Distrest (or **Distressed**) **Mother, The.** A tragedy by Ambrose Philips, produced in 1712. It was adapted from Racine's *Andromaque,* which it resembles in style. Addison supposedly wrote the epilogue and Steele the prologue.

dithyramb (dith'i.ramb, -ram) or **dithyrambus** (dith.i.ram'bus). A form of Greek lyric composition, originally a choral song in honor of Dionysus, afterward of other gods, heroes, etc. First given artistic form by Arion (c625 B.C.) and rendered by cyclic choruses, it was perfected, about a century later, by Lasos of Hermione, and at about the same time tragedy was developed from it in Attica. Its simpler and more majestic form, as composed by Lasos, Simonides, Bacchylides, and Pindar, assumed in the latter part of the 5th century B.C. a complexity of rhythmical and musical form and of verbal expression which degenerated in the 4th century into a mimetic performance rendered by a single artist. From these different stages in its history the word dithyramb has been used in later ages both for a nobly enthusiastic and elevated and for a wild or inflated composition. In its distinctive form the dithyramb consists of a number of strophes no two of which are metrically identical. "I will not dwell on Naumann's . . . dithyrambs about Dorothea's charm." (George Eliot, *Middlemarch.*)

ditty. A song, or poem intended to be sung, usually short and simple in form, and set to a simple melody; any short simple song. Originally applied to any short poetical composition (lyric or ballad) intended to be sung, the word came to be restricted chiefly to songs of simple rustic character, being often used of the songs of birds.

This litel short dyte
Rudely compyled.   (Lydgate, *Minor Poems.*)

Meanwhile the rural ditties were not mute,
Tempered to the oaten flute.
(Milton, *Lycidas,* l. 32.)

The shortest staffe conteineth not vnder foure verses, nor the longest aboue ten; if it passe that number it is rather a whole ditty then properly a staffe.   (Puttenham, *Arte of Eng. Poesie.*)

Those little nimble musicians of the air, that warble forth their curious ditties.
(I. Walton, *Compleat Angler.*)

The blackbird has fled to another retreat,
Where the hazel affords him a screen from the heat,
And the scene, where his melody charmed me before,
Resounds with his sweet-flowing ditty no more.
(Cowper, *Poplar Field.*)

Dive Bouteille (dēv bö.tāy'), **La.** An oracle to which Panurge makes a long journey. The Order of the Dive Bouteille was instituted in France in the 16th century in honor of Rabelais.

Diversions of Purley (pur'li), **The.** [Full title, **Epea Pteroenta, or The Diversions of Purley.**] A philological work (2 parts; 1786, 1805) by Horne Tooke.

Diverting History of John Gilpin (jon gil'pin), **The.** A humorous poem (1782) of the ballad type, by William Cowper, better known for his poems of melancholy and intense religious devotion. It is frequently called *Gilpin's Ride, John Gilpin's Famous Ride,* and by other inaccurate names, but its full and correct title, which is a good summary of the action, is *The Diverting History of John Gilpin, Showing How He Went Further than He Intended and Came Safe Home Again.*

Dives (dī'vēz). The name given to the "rich man" in the parable of Jesus about Lazarus. Luke, xvi. 19, etc.

Divina Commedia (dē.vē'nä kôm.mä'dyä). [Eng. title, **The Divine Comedy;** original Italian title, **Commedia.**] A celebrated epic poem by Dante, in three parts: *Inferno* (Hell), *Purgatorio* (Purgatory), and *Paradiso* (Paradise). It seems probable that the *Inferno* was begun after Dante's return from a pilgrimage to Rome in the jubilee year 1300, that the *Purgatorio* was finished about 1314, and that the composition of the *Paradiso* occupied the next five or six years of his life. The poem consists of 14,233 eleven-syllable lines arranged in tercets with the rhyming scheme known as *terza rima,* a b a, b c b, c d c, and so forth. After an introductory canto, the remaining 99 cantos are equally divided between the three parts. Read simply as a myth for the imagination, the poem describes a journey to the abodes of the dead. Thus in canto IV of the *Inferno,* Dante guided by Vergil visits the spirits of the heroes, heroines, and philosophers of antiquity who are enjoying a high but purely human happiness in the Noble Castle of Limbo. In the next canto he meets the sinners suffering for illicit love (Semiramis, Cleopatra, Paris, Tristram, and the rest) and sings the immortal tragedy of Paolo and Francesca. In canto X he meets the Epicurean aristocrat, Farinata degli Uberti, suffering for denying the immortality of the soul. Following a carefully worked out system of sins based on Aristotelian and Ciceronian ethics, with subdivisions borrowed from patristic and scholastic ideas and with elements taken from the Roman law and the "code of chivalry," the pilgrim sees the torments of every type of sinner until, at the center of the earth, in the mouths of the three heads of Satan, he finds Judas, the traitor to the Founder of a universal faith, and Brutus and Cassius who betrayed Caesar's efforts to establish a rule of universal law.

fat, fāte, fär, àsk, fāre; net, mē, hėr; pin, pīne; not, nōte, möve, nôr; up, lūte, pùll; ᴛʜ, then;

What, however, gives passion to the poetic vision is the meaning which is addressed to the reader's mind. The great inverted cone of Dante's Hell is, allegorically, the human heart, and the poet's pilgrimage is a vision of human nature in the utmost depths of its possible degradations. In the same way, the seven-story mountain of Dante's *Purgatorio* is a vision of the human will struggling upwards in humanity's historical efforts to reach, by culture and civilization, the highest happiness and peace that men can hope for in a reign of light and law. So, too, the *Paradiso* can be enjoyed as a myth in which Dante meets the lovely Piccarda, the emperor Justinian, Saint Thomas Aquinas, and many others, but what accounts for the passionate poetry and inimitable music in this part is the poet's all-but-mystical vision of the efficacy of supernatural religion in elevating humanity to consummation in the perfect peace and possession of ultimate goodness, truth, and beauty. Thus the poem is about redemption in the widest sense. The six guides who lead "Dante" (that is "fallen" humanity) from the "dark wood" of sin, through the "divine forest" of innocence and upwards to "the light which in itself is true" and "the love which binds in a single volume the scattered leaves of all the universe," are Vergil, Cato, Statius, Matelda, Beatrice, and Bernard. Vergil is a symbol of reason in the form of Hellenic philosophy and Roman law (*ordinatio rationis*); Cato (a combination of Cato the Censor and Cato the Stoic, who preferred liberty with death to tyranny) is a symbol of reason in the form of conscience (*dictamen rationis*). Beatrice represents the role of grace, that is, of divine revelation and redemption and, hence, the ministry of the Church (*Sacerdotium*) as Vergil represents the authority of the State (*Imperium*). Bernard stands to Beatrice somewhat as Cato stands to Vergil. He is a symbol of mystical intuition or the religious light and force of holiness that come from direct communion with God. Statius (a combination of the historical figures of the pagan poet, author of the *Thebaid* and *Achilleid*, and of Statius, the converted rhetorician and teacher of Toulouse) stands for the Christian school (*Studium*) as the *bella donna* Matelda stands for the Christian home, for the role of love in the "age of innocence," for parental guidance in the period of childhood. The root idea of the whole poem is, as Dante tells us in a Latin letter to Can Grande, Can Francesco della Scala, that of human responsibility in the face of divine justice, *homo justitiae obnoxius*. The individual is responsible for his personality, for his inner freedom from the tyranny of ignorance and passion; the parent is responsible for the ministry of love, the teacher for the ministry of truth, the ruler for the ministry of justice, the priest for the ministry of grace, the saint for that holiness which is the nearest image we can know in history of the very life of God. Dante's sinners and saints suffer or rejoice because of the failure or fulfilment of their commission to reach and reveal some image of the divine, whether this be freedom, truth, goodness, beauty, justice, love, or holiness. It is this profound sense of the meaning of man and of history set to incomparable music and illumined and lifted up by "anagogic" intimations of the mystery of man's immortal destiny that has put the *Commedia* in the very forefront of the world's supreme works of art. The poem has been translated into all the great languages of the world, including Japanese and Arabic. Of the many translations into English by Cary, Longfellow, Norton, Fletcher, Wheeler, Binyon, Cummins, Lawrence White, and others, not one conveys the subtle and varied music of the original. The Carlyle-Wicksteed prose version, with its excellent introductions and notes to each canto may, however, serve as a good introduction to the poem. The poem was illustrated (1826–27) by William Blake, and his engravings have been hailed for their "breath-taking grandeur."

Divine Fire, The. A novel by May Sinclair, published in 1904. It tells the story of the beautiful Lucia Harden; Keith Rickman, a Cockney poet who has the "divine fire" in him; and Horace Jewdwine, an Oxford man. Keith is believed to be a fictional portrait of Ernest Dowson.

Divine Lady, The. A historical novel by Lily Adams Beck under the pseudonym E. Barrington. published in 1924. It is set in Naples and London in the years 1782–1803. The "divine lady" is Emma Lyon-Hart, Lady Hamilton (c1761–1815), mistress of Sir Charles Greville, of his uncle, Sir William Hamilton (who later married her), and of Lord Nelson (to whom she bore a daughter, Horatia).

Divine Legation of Moses. A prose work by William Warburton which excited much controversy. The first part was published 1738–41 and the last part posthumously in 1788.

"Divine Sarah" (sâr′ạ). See **Bernhardt, Sarah.**

Divine Vision, The. A book of poems by "Æ" (George William Russell), published in 1904.

"Divino Lodovico" (dē.vē′nō lō.dō.vē′kō). See **Ariosto, Lodovico.**

Dixon (dik′sọn), **Henry Hall.** [Pseudonyms: **General Chassé, The Druid.**] b. at Warwick Bridge, Cumberland, England, May 16, 1822; d. at Kensington, London, March 16, 1870. An English novelist and writer on sport, agriculture, and law. Educated at Rugby and at Trinity College, Cambridge, he wrote (1853 *et seq.*) articles on sport for the *Daily News, Illustrated London News, Sporting Magazine*, and others. He was the author of the novels *Post and Paddock* (1856), *Silk and Scarlet* (1859), and *Scott and Sebright* (1862), first published as serials in the *Sporting Magazine;* also wrote *The Law of the Farm* (1858; many editions), a legal treatise; *The Breeding of Shorthorns* (1865), and *Field and Fern* (1865) and *Saddle and Sirloin* (1870), dealing, respectively, with Scottish and English cattle.

Dixon, Richard Watson. b. at Islington, London, May 5, 1833; d. at Warkworth, Northumberland, Jan. 23, 1900. An English poet, church historian, and friend of Burne-Jones and William Morris; son of James Dixon (1788–1871), a Wesleyan minister whose *Life* (1874) he wrote. He was educated at King Edward's School, Birmingham, and Pembroke College, Oxford. Ordained in 1859, he was master (1863–68) and canon (1868–75) of Carlisle Cathedral, vicar at Cumberland (1875–83), and at Warkworth from 1883 until he died. He was the author of the prize-winning works *The Close of the*

Tenth Century of the Christian Era (1857), an historical essay, *St. John in Patmos* (1863), a religious poem, and *Christ's Company* (1861); also of *Historical Odes* (1864), *Mano* (1883), a long poem, *Odes and Eclogues* (1884), *Lyrical Poems* (1887), *The Story of Eudocia and Her Brothers* (1888), and *Last Poems* (pub. 1905, edited by Mary Elizabeth Coleridge). His prose works are *History of the Church of England From the Abolition of the Roman Jurisdiction* (5 vols., 1878–1902, the last being published after his death), *Seven Sermons* (1888), *A Sermon Preached on the Occasion of the Diamond Jubilee of Queen Victoria* (1897), and other religious works. *Fallen Rain, The Feathers of the Willow, On Conflicting Claims, On Advancing Age,* and *The Spirit Wooed* are among his best poems.

Dixon, William Hepworth. b. at Newton-Heath, England, June 30, 1821; d. at London, Dec. 27, 1879. An English author and journalist. He was editor (1853–69) of the *Athenaeum,* and author of *New America* (1867), *Spiritual Wives* (1868), *Free Russia* (1870), and *Her Majesty's Tower* (1869–71).

Dizzy (diz'i). A character in David Garrick's play *The Male Coquette.*

Dizzy. Nickname of **Disraeli, Benjamin.**

Dobbin (dob'in), **Major William.** In Thackeray's novel *Vanity Fair,* a modest young officer, the devoted friend of George Osborne, the weak husband of Amelia Sedley. He marries Amelia after Osborne's death.

Dobbins (dob'inz), **Humphrey.** A rough but grateful servant in Colman's comedy *The Poor Gentleman.*

Dobell (dō.bel'), **Sydney Thompson.** [Pseudonym, **Sydney Yendys.**] b. at Cranbrook, Kent, England, April 5, 1824; d. at Nailsworth, Gloucestershire, England, Aug. 22, 1874. An English poet. He was a wine merchant at Cheltenham from 1848 until his death. His works (a complete edition of which appeared in 1875–76) include *The Roman* (1850), *Balder* (1854), and *England in Time of War* (1856).

Dobrée (dō'brē), **Valentine.** [Full name, **Gladys May Mabel Dobrée;** maiden name, **Brooke-Pechell.**] b. 1894—. An English author; wife (married 1913) of Bonamy Dobrée. Her works of fiction include *Your Cuckoo Sings by Kind* (1927), *Emperor's Tigers* (1929), and *To Blush Unseen* (1935).

Dobson (dob'son), **Austin.** [Full name, **Henry Austin Dobson.**] b. at Plymouth, England, Jan. 18, 1840; d. at Ealing, London, Sept. 2, 1921. An English poet, critic, essayist, and biographer. Son of a civil engineer, he was educated in French and English schools. Returning to England in 1856, he was until his retirement in 1901 a clerk in the Board of Trade. Beginning in 1904 he received a government pension of 250 pounds a year and devoted himself entirely to research. He was the author of *The Civil Service Handbook of English Literature* (1874), *Four Frenchwomen* (1890), *Eighteenth Century Vignettes* (1892; 2nd series, 1894; 3rd series, 1896), *Miscellanies* (1898), *A Paladin of Philanthropy* (1899), *Side-Walk Studies* (1902), *Old Kensington Palace* (1910), *At Prior Park* (1912), *Rosalba's Journal* (1915), and other collections of essays and papers; also wrote *Hogarth* (1879; final revision, 1907), *Fielding* (1883), *Thomas*

Bewick and His Pupils (1884), *Steele* (1886), *Goldsmith* (1888), *Horace Walpole* (1890), *Samuel Richardson* (1902), and *Fanny Burney* (1903); *Vignettes in Rhyme* (1873), *Proverbs in Porcelain* (1877), *Old-World Idylls* (1883), *At the Sign of the Lyre* (1885), *The Sun Dial* (1890), *The Ballad of Beau Brocade* (1892), *The Story of Rosina* (1895), and *Complete Poetical Works* (1923). Among his poems are *Farewell, Renown, Before Sedan, Rose-Leaves, Ballade of Prose and Rhyme, In After Days, The Sick Man and the Birds,* and *Prayer of the Swine to Circe.* Dobson was one of the group (c1875) who introduced into English poetry such forms as the ballade, the rondel, the triolet, and the villanelle from French.

Doctor, The. A romance (7 vols., 1834) by Robert Southey. It was at first published anonymously, and he explicitly denied his authorship. In it he exhibits his vast store of learning in a rambling manner. The children's tale of *The Three Bears* first appeared here, invented by Southey from incidents in German and Norwegian folk tales.

Doctor and the Devils, The. A dramatic story (1953), written in the form of a film scenario, by Dylan Thomas. It is based on a famous 19th-century criminal case in Edinburgh, involving a Dr. Knox, lecturer in anatomy, and Burke and Hare, who supplied him with his corpses (not only by robbing graves, but also by murder). Thomas changes the names to Rock, for the doctor, and Fallon and Broom for the two body snatchers, and changes the locale from Scotland to Ireland.

Doctor Dodipoll (dod'i.pōl). A comedy (1600) the author of which is unknown. Dr. Dodipoll is a foolish, doddering creature.

Doctor Faustus (fôs'tus, fous'-). [Original full title (on the quarto edition of 1604), **The Tragicall History of D. Faustus.**] A tragedy in blank verse and prose by Christopher Marlowe. It was written, and probably first produced, in 1588, and published in 1604, although it was listed for publication as early as 1601. It is one of the first, if not the first, treatments in English of the old German Faust legend, of a man who enters into a bargain with the devil and sells his soul to him. Marlowe, it is presumed, knew, either in the original German, or in an English translation that appeared in 1588, a *Faustbuch* (Frankfort, 1587), translated as *The History of the Damnable Life and Deserved Death of Dr. John Faustus,* dealing with the magic deeds of a 16th-century German quack, Dr. Johann Faust. The play opens with a short summary of the plot, delivered by the Chorus (regarded and listed as a character), and then shows us Faustus, a great scholar who has mastered law, medicine, theology, and philosophy, in his study, alone, not satisfied with his vast knowledge but thirsting for more. In response to his request, made, of course, in Latin (that being the language of the devil and of evil spirits, whence Marcellus's cry in *Hamlet,* "speak to it, Horatio"), Mephistophilis appears. An agreement is reached and Faustus sells himself to the devil, who swears to serve him in all things for a period of 24 years, at the end of which period Faustus is to give him his soul. The period, although it seems long, at the time, to the young and eager Renaissance scholar, passes all too quickly and

Faustus is called upon to meet the terms of the contract that he signed with his own blood. The play ends with his being dragged down, in horror and agony, to hell. He appeals in vain to God and Christ but the life he has led makes his prayers worthless. The tragedy contains many examples of what is known as Marlowe's "mighty line," the most famous one being his apostrophe to Helen:

Was this the face that launched a thousand ships
And burnt the topless towers of Ilium?

The play ends with Faustus's agonized cries, "See, see where Christ's blood streams in the firmament! One drop would save my soul—half a drop," "My God! my God! look not so fierce on me!" and his final terrible, beautiful, pathetic, terrifyingly human cry, "I'll burn my books!"

Doctor Invincibilis (dok'tôr in.vin.sib'i.lis). See **Ockham, William of.**

Doctor Jekyll and Mr. Hyde (jek'il; hīd). See **Dr. Jekyll and Mr. Hyde.**

Doctor Marigold (mar'i.gōld). A story by Charles Dickens, published in 1865 in a collection called *Doctor Marigold's Prescriptions.* Its narrator and chief character is Doctor Marigold himself, a wandering auctioneer (called, in England, a "Cheap Jack"), with whose life the story is chiefly concerned.

Doctor Mirabilis (dok'tôr mi.rab'i.lis). See **Bacon, Roger.**

Doctor's Dilemma, The. A play (1906) by George Bernard Shaw, in which he satirizes doctors and the medical profession.

Doctor Serocold (ser'ō.kōld). A novel by Helen Ashton, published in 1930.

Doctor's Tale, The. See **Physician's Tale, The.**

Doctor Subtilis (dok'tôr sub.tī'lis). See **Duns Scotus, John.**

Doctor Thorne (thôrn). A novel by Anthony Trollope, published in 1858. It is the third of the Barsetshire series.

Doctrine and Discipline of Divorce, The. A prose pamphlet (1643) by John Milton. It is the first of a series of four so-called divorce tracts. His first wife, Mary Powell, a Royalist, left him in 1642, a few weeks after their marriage, and did not return at the time agreed on, although she did so later. To what extent the pamphlets represent personal anger and to what extent abstract theory, are questions that have been widely discussed. The first edition was anonymous, but the second carried Milton's name. The pamphlet was dedicated to Parliament.

Dodd (dod), **James William.** b. at London, 1734; d. 1796. An English actor. After serving an acting apprenticeship in the provinces, he came to the Drury Lane in 1765 as a member of Garrick's company, and was especially successful as Sir Andrew Aguecheek in *Twelfth Night* and Abel Drugger in Jonson's *Alchemist.* He also played Backbite in Sheridan's *School for Scandal* and Lord Foppington in Vanbrugh's *The Relapse.* He was characterized as being "the soul of empty eminence," since he so often played vacuous fops and young fools.

Dodd, William. b. at Bourne, Lincolnshire, England, May 29, 1729; d. June 27, 1777. An English clergyman and author. He studied at Cambridge, was ordained deacon in 1751, and was appointed chaplain to the king in 1763. In 1777 he forged the name of Lord Chesterfield, his former pupil, to a bond for 4,200 pounds, and in spite of the efforts of Dr. Johnson and other influential persons was executed at London. He wrote *Beauties of Shakespeare* (1752) and *Thoughts in Prison* (1777).

Doddridge (dod'rij), **Philip.** b. at London, June 26, 1702; d. at Lisbon, Oct. 26, 1751. An English dissenting clergyman. He was pastor of an Independent congregation at Northampton from 1729 until his death. He is known chiefly as the author of *Rise and Progress of Religion in the Soul* (1745), and *The Family Expositor* (6 vols., 1739–56), and for his hymns.

Dodgson (doj'son), **Charles Lutwidge.** [Pseudonym, **Lewis Carroll.**] b. at Daresbury, Cheshire, England, Jan. 27, 1832; d. at Guildford, Surrey, England, Jan. 14, 1898. An English mathematician, now best remembered as the author of the two immortal Alice books. He was educated at home by his father, a clergyman, at Rugby, and at Christ Church College, Oxford, where he later taught mathematics. He became a "member of the College" (as English students are called) and he remained that for almost half a century until his death. From 1855 to 1881 he was at Christ Church as a lecturer, a position corresponding to a professor in an American college. He wrote *Euclid and His Modern Rivals* (1879), *Curiosa Mathematica* (1888), and other technical works in his field, but he lives by his authorship of *Alice's Adventures in Wonderland* (1865), which was first called *Alice's Adventures Underground* and *Alice's Hours in Elfland,* and its sequel, *Through the Looking-Glass and What Alice Found There* (1871). His other juvenile books are *The Hunting of the Snark* (1876), *A Tangled Tale* (1885), and *Sylvie and Bruno* (1889). He wrote the works that made him famous under the name of "Lewis Carroll" and he made the name famous. (Neither the works nor the name can be said at first to have claimed Dodgson's serious attention. He thought of *Alice's Adventures in Wonderland* as no more than a fanciful tale contrived for the entertainment of a little girl named Alice Liddell, the daughter of Henry George Liddell, a leading 19th-century classicist and one of Dodgson's friends. It almost certainly never entered Dodgson's head that his name would not be remembered primarily for his achievements as a mathematician.) In 1867 he broke the routine of his Oxford life by visiting Russia, and *A Russian Journal,* a diary, was the result.

Dodington (dod'ing.ton), **George Bubb.** [Title, Baron **Melcombe.**] b. in Dorsetshire, England, 1691; d. at Hammersmith (now part of London), July 28, 1762. An English politician. He was created Baron Melcombe of Melcombe Regis, Dorsetshire, in 1761. He patronized men of letters, and was complimented by Edward Young, Henry Fielding, and Richard Bentley. He left a diary covering the period from 1749 to 1761, which was published in 1784. He was one of the group calling itself the "mad monks of Medmenham Abbey," along with Francis Dashwood, John Wilkes, and others.

ḏ, d or j; ş, s or sh; ţ, t or ch; ẓ, z or zh; o, F. cloche; ü, F. menu; ċh, Sc. loch; ṅ, F. bonbon.

Dodo (dō'dō). A novel (1893) by E. F. Benson, the heroine of which is supposed to be a portrait of Margot Tennant (Lady Asquith).

Dodona (dō.dō'na). In ancient geography, a city in Epirus, probably situated on or near Mount Tomarus, SW of Ioannina. It was the seat of the oldest Greek oracle, dedicated to Zeus, in an oak grove hung with vessels of brass, by which the god's voice was thought to be made audible.

Dods (dodz), **Meg.** The landlady of the inn, in Sir Walter Scott's *St. Ronan's Well.*

Dodsley (dodz'li), **Robert.** b. probably at Mansfield, on the border of Sherwood Forest, Nottinghamshire, England; d. at Durham, England, Sept. 23, 1764. An English dramatist, poet, editor, anthologist, and bookseller, and founder of the *Annual Register.* He was a prolific author, as well as a publisher of the works of others, and he wrote in a variety of forms, including plays, poems, songs, and satires. As a publisher, with a shop in Pall Mall, Dodsley published Pope's *First Epistle of the Second Book of Horace,* poems by Young and Akenside, Goldsmith's *Polite Learning,* and Johnson's *Rasselas, The Vanity of Human Wishes,* and *Irene.* In 1758 he founded a work that is still published, the *Annual Register,* a record, as the title indicates, of the significant events of the past year. He paid Burke, whom he engaged as editor, a hundred pounds a year. Johnson thought well of him and said, "Doddy, you know, is my patron, and I would not desert him." Nichols, of the *Literary Anecdotes,* praises him as "that admirable patron and encourager of learning," and Walpole, in a letter to George Montagu, touches a vital point in his character: "You know how decent, humble, inoffensive a creature Dodsley is; how little apt to forget or disguise his having been a footman."

Dodson (dod'son). The family name of the three aunts in George Eliot's *The Mill on the Floss,* Aunt Pullet, Aunt Glegg, and Aunt Tulliver. Their inherited customs and peculiarities are amusing, and are always referred to with respect by the phrase "No Dodson ever did" so and so.

Dodson and Fogg (fog). In Charles Dickens's *Pickwick Papers,* the legal advisers of Mrs. Bardell in the celebrated breach-of-promise case.

Doe (dō), **John.** Originally, the name of the fictitious plaintiff in actions of ejectment; the use of the name is now extended to include other actions or proceedings to which a person whose name is not known must be a party.

Doeg (dō'eg). In the second part of John Dryden and Nahum Tate's *Absalom and Achitophel,* a character intended to represent Elkanah Settle.

Dog Beneath the Skin. A satirical comedy (1935) by W. H. Auden and Christopher Isherwood.

Dogberry (dog'ber"i). In Shakespeare's *Much Ado About Nothing,* an absurd constable. Dogberry catches Borachio and Conrade after Borachio has staged a pretended assignation with Hero, and forces the truth from him. But because of Dogberry's inability to speak plainly Leonato fails to understand what has happened, and the result is near tragedy for Hero.

doggerel (dog'ér.el). **1.** Burlesque poetry, generally in irregular measure. "Doggerel like that of Hudibras." (Addison, *Spectator.*)
2. Mean, paltry verses, defective in sense and in rhythm.

The rhyming puffs of blacking, cosmetics, and quack medicines are well-known specimens of doggerel, which only the ignorant class style poetry.
(W. Chambers.)

The author of the Dialogus de Scaccario and the Latin biographer of Richard I. both run into what would be doggerel if it were not Latin, apparently out of the very glee of their hearts and devotion to their subject-matter.
(Stubbs, *Medieval and Modern Hist.*)

Doggett (dog'et), **Thomas.** b. at Dublin, Ireland; d. Oct. (or Sept.) 21 or 22, 1721. An English actor. He was before the public from 1691 to 1713. He appeared first at the Drury Lane, and then moved in 1694 with Betterton's group of rebels to Lincoln's Inn Fields. About 1697, however, he had entered into an agreement to return to the Drury Lane and got into some difficulty over it, although he did appear there again. He established in 1716 a prize in the Thames rowing match, given every year on the first of August. It was an orange-colored livery and a badge, and was given in honor of George I. The custom is still kept up.

Doggrell (dog'rel). A foolish poet in Abraham Cowley's play *The Guardian.* He was omitted in *The Cutter of Coleman Street,* a revision.

Dogsditch. See under **Houndsditch.**

Dog Star. See **Sirius.**

Dolabella (dol.a.bel'a). In Shakespeare's *Antony and Cleopatra,* a friend of Octavius who informs Cleopatra that she is to be taken to Rome in triumph.

Dol Common (dol kom'on). See **Common, Dol.**

Dollallolla (dol.a.lol'a), **Queen.** The wife of King Arthur and mother of Huncamunca in Henry Fielding's burlesque *The Tragedy of Tragedies, or the Life and Death of Tom Thumb the Great.* She is "entirely faultless, except that she is a little given to drink, a little too much a virago towards her husband, and in love with Tom Thumb."

Doll Common (dol kom'on). See **Common, Dol.**

Doll Tearsheet (tār'shēt). See **Tearsheet, Doll.**

Dolly Dialogues (dol'i), **The.** A prose work (1894) by Sir Anthony Hope Hawkins.

Dolly Reforming Herself. A comedy (1908) by Henry Arthur Jones. It involves a spendthrift wife and her close friend (married to a psychologist, whom Jones uses as a means of satirizing Herbert Spencer). There is also a clergyman who believes he is reforming people, Dolly, the squabbling wife, in particular.

Dolly's (dol'iz). A well-known tavern in Paternoster Row, London, dating from the time of Queen Anne.

Dolly Varden (vär'den). See **Varden, Dolly.**

Dolly Winthrop (win'throp). See **Winthrop, Dolly.**

Dolores. A poem by Algernon Charles Swinburne in his first *Poems and Ballads* (1866).

Dolorous Garde (dol′or.us, dō′lor-, gärd). In the Arthurian romances, an earlier name of Joyeuse Garde.

Dolorous Valley. In the Arthurian romances, a name for Edinburgh.

Dombey and Son (dom′bi). A novel by Dickens, issued originally in numbers, the first of which appeared in October, 1846. It was brought out in one volume in 1848. The original title was *Dealings with the Firm of Dombey and Son, Wholesale, Retail, and for Exportation*. Mr. Dombey, the father of little Paul and Florence, is a cold, unbending, pompous merchant. His chief ambition is to perpetuate the firm-name. However, after the death of his only son, little Paul, and the loss of his money, his obstinacy and pride are softened. Little Paul, the "son" in the title of the firm, is a delicate child who dies young. Florence, his devoted sister, marries Walter Gay, a clerk in her father's bank. Edith Dombey, the beautiful and scornful second wife of Mr. Dombey, elopes with Carker, his manager.

Domdaniel (dom.dan′yel). In the continuation of the *Arabian Nights' Entertainments* of Chavis and Cazotte, a seminary for evil magicians founded by the great magician Hal-il-Maugraby. It was an immense cavern "under the roots of the ocean" off the coast of Tunis, the resort of evil spirits and enchanters. It was finally destroyed. Southey makes its destruction the theme of his *Thalaba*.

Domesday Book (dömz′dā). [Also, **Doomsday Book.**] A book containing a digest, in Latin, of the results of a census or survey of England undertaken by order of William I (William the Conqueror), and completed in 1086. It consists of two volumes in vellum, a large folio containing 382 pages and a quarto containing 450. They form a valuable record of the ownership, extent, and value of the lands of England (1) at the time of the survey, (2) at the dates of their bestowal (that is, at the time when they had been granted by the king), and (3) at the time of Edward the Confessor. The numbers of tenants and dependents, amount of livestock, and the like, were also recorded. The book was long kept under three different locks in the exchequer, along with the king's seal, but is now kept in the Record Office at London. In 1783 an edition, printed from types made for the purpose, was issued by the British government. The counties of Northumberland, Cumberland, Westmorland, and Durham were not included in the survey. There existed also local domesday books.

Domett (dom′et), **Alfred.** b. at Camberwell Grove, Surrey, England, May 20, 1811; d. in England, Nov. 2, 1887. An English poet and colonial statesman. He was educated at Cambridge and was called to the bar in 1841. In 1842 he went to New Zealand, where he filled many of the chief offices of the colony; he returned to England in 1871. He was the intimate friend of Robert Browning, who writes of him in *Waring* and *The Guardian Angel*. Among his works are volumes of poems published in 1833 and 1839. His "Christmas Hymn" appeared in *Blackwood's Magazine* about that time. He published *Ranolf and Amohia* (1872) and *Flotsam and Jetsam* (1877). He also wrote several official publications relating to New Zealand.

Dominicans (dō.min′i.kanz). [Also, **Order of Preachers.**] A Roman Catholic religious order, founded by Saint Dominic (c1170–1221). It was his observation of the prevalence of the Albigensian heresy in Languedoc which fired him with a purpose to institute an order to defend and propagate the Catholic faith by active, evangelistic preaching of the Gospel in all lands. Sent to Languedoc with one companion by Pope Innocent III in 1204, he established his first house for religious women at Prouille near Toulouse in 1206, and gradually gathered a small company of followers which numbered 16 when in 1215 the Bishop of Toulouse granted them a church and recognized them as a congregation of his diocese. An ecumenical council at Rome in that year having declared against the establishment of new religious orders, Dominic and his followers adopted the Augustinian rule; but in 1216 Pope Honorius III confirmed them as an order and authorized their mission. In 1217, though only 17 in number, they dispersed throughout much of Europe, winning recruits, rapidly growing in numbers, and establishing communities at Rome (where the Pope gave them the church of Saint Sixtus), Bologna, Toulouse, Lyons, Paris, Madrid, Segovia, and other cities, especially at centers of learning. In 1219 the first general chapter of the order came into being at Bologna, and by the year of Saint Dominic's death it numbered eight national provinces. Dominicans, who wore a white habit, to which they added a black mantle when preaching (from this acquiring the name of Black Friars), were dedicated to the propagation of Catholic doctrine, the promotion of good morals, and the uprooting of heresy, by means of learning and teaching (their particular method of teaching being by way of preaching). The authority they acquired by their diligent theological studies resulted among other things in their close association with the Inquisition. The glory of the Dominican order is Saint Thomas Aquinas, but their roster includes many other notable names, as diverse as Albertus Magnus and Savonarola. In modern times the Dominicans continue to be the great evangelistic order of the Roman Catholic Church; in the U. S. they commonly conduct the missions held periodically in Catholic parishes for the instruction of the faithful and the revival of religious zeal. The Dominicans are governed by the decisions of annual general chapters, composed chiefly of elected delegates, and the priors of houses and provinces are chosen by election for limited terms. Because of the tradition that the Blessed Virgin Mary gave the rosary to Saint Dominic in a vision, that form of prayer is especially used and inculcated by Dominicans. Associated with them are sub-orders of Dominican Sisters (contemplative nuns) and of Brothers of Penitence of Saint Dominic (third order, or tertiaries).

Dominie Sampson (dom′i.ni samp′son). See **Sampson, Dominie.**

Domitian (dō.mish′an). In Philip Massinger's play *The Roman Actor*, the emperor of Rome, taken from the historical figure of the same name.

Domitilla (dom.i.til′a). In James Shirley's play *The Royal Master*, a girl of 15 years who, in an innocent delusion, fixes her love upon the king, mistaking his promise to provide her with a husband for a proof of personal affection.

Don Adriano de Armado (don ä.dri.ä′nō dä är-mä′dō). See **Armado, Don Adriano de.**

Doña Emilia (dō′nyä ā.mē′lyä). Charles Gould's wife in Joseph Conrad's novel *Nostromo* (1904).

Donalbain (don′ạl.bān). In Shakespeare's *Macbeth*, a son of Duncan, king of Scotland. He goes to Ireland after Duncan's murder and does not appear after Act II, Scene 3.

Donald Bean Lean (don′ạld bēn′ lēn). See **Bean Lean, Donald.**

Donar (dō′när). See **Thor.**

Donation of Constantine (kon′stạn.tīn, -tēn), **The.** A medieval forgery, of unknown date and origin, which pretends to be an imperial edict issued by Constantine I (Constantine the Great) in 324 conferring the temporal and spiritual sovereignty of Italy and the West on the papal see. It was probably composed about the middle of the 8th century; in 1444 Lorenzo Valla demonstrated that it was a forgery.

Donatists (don′ạ.tists). An early Christian sect in Africa which originated in a dispute over the election (311 A.D.) of Caecilian to the see of Carthage, occasioned by his opposition to the extreme reverence paid to relics of martyrs and to the sufferers for the Christian faith called confessors.

Donatus (dō.nā′tus), **Aelius.** fl. in the middle of the 4th century A.D. Roman grammarian and rhetorician; teacher of Saint Jerome. Of his works we possess a Latin grammar, *Ars grammatica*, a commentary on Terence, and the preface and introduction (with other fragments) of a commentary on Vergil. The grammatical work was extremely popular and was translated into Greek; its reputation was such that it became the common name for an elementary grammar (donet, donat) and was thus used in English as late as the 16th century.

Don Caesar (sē′zạr). See **Caesar, Don.**

Don Carlos (don kär′lọs). [Full title, **Don Carlos, Prince of Spain.**] A tragedy in rhymed verse by Thomas Otway, produced in 1676. The story is taken from the Abbé de St. Real, and the plot is simpler than in Schiller's play on the same subject.

Don Carlos. See also **Carlos, Don.**

Don Clavijo (klä.bē′Hō). See **Clavijo, Don.**

Don Cleofas (klē′ọ.fạs). See **Cleofas, Don.**

Don Felix (fē′liks). See **Felix, Don.**

Don John (jon). See **John, Don.**

Don José (hō.zā′; Spanish, Hō.sā′). See **José, Don.**

Don Juan (don′ wän′; also, especially in Byron, don jō′ạn; Spanish dōn Hwän′). A legendary character of European tradition whose name is of Spanish origin. In the principal form of the legend, Don Juan Tenorio, who lived in the 14th century, the son of an illustrious family of Seville, killed the commandant Ulloa after having seduced his daughter. The Franciscan monks, wishing to put an end to the debaucheries of Don Juan, enticed him to their monastery and killed him, giving out that the statue of his victim (which had been erected there), incensed at an insult offered him (in the plays the statue of Ulloa is jeeringly invited to supper, and

does come to the meal), had come down and dragged him to hell. Spanish and Italian plays were written on the subject, and Nicholas Drovin Dorimond introduced him to the French stage. Don Juan is the symbol of skeptical libertinism, and as such has been made the subject of the 17th-century drama *El Burlador de Sevilla y Convidado de Piedra* (The Deceiver of Seville and the Guest of Stone), by Gabriel Téllez (Tirso de Molina); of Molière's comedy *Don Juan, ou le festin de Pierre* (1665); of Mozart's opera *Don Giovanni* to Lorenzo da Ponte's libretto; of Christian Dietrich Grabbe's German drama *Don Juan und Faust* (1828); and of works by Thomas Corneille, Thomas Shadwell, Antonio de Zamora, Carlo Goldoni, Christoph Willibald Gluck, Alexandre Dumas the elder, José Zorilla y Moral, G. B. Shaw, and others. His name has become a synonym for libertine or rake. Byron's Don Juan takes only his name from the legend, the youthful introspective Byronic hero having no other connection with the cynical gallant of legend.

Don Juan. An incomplete satirical poem by Byron, written in 1818 and published 1819–24, consisting of 16 cantos cast in ottava rima. It tells of the amatory adventures of Don Juan in different places (Greece, Russia, and England) after he was sent away from Seville by his mother for his intrigues with Donna Julia.

Don Juan. The legendary lover who appears in the dream fantasy of Tanner in Shaw's *Man and Superman*. He insists that his reputation as a libertine has no basis in fact; indeed, it is he who is being pursued mercilessly by women determined to marry him rather than he who pursues them. While thus underscoring his distaste for the conventional bond of marriage, he wanders into a discourse on the true nature of heaven and hell, man's possibilities of moral improvement, and the true role of women in their biological and social struggle with men.

Donna Isabella (don′ạ iz.ạ.bel′ạ). A beautiful woman in love with Don Juan in Shaw's *Man and Superman*.

Donna Julia (jöl′yạ). See **Julia, Donna.**

Donn-Byrne (don′bẽrn′), **Brian Oswald.** [Known as **Donn Byrne.**] b. at New York, Nov. 20, 1889; d. in County Cork, Ireland, June 18, 1928. An Irish-American novelist and short-story writer. He was a staff member of the *New Catholic Encyclopedia*, the *New Standard Dictionary*, the *Century Dictionary*, the New York Sun, and the Brooklyn Eagle, and contributed stories to *The Smart Set* and *Harper's*. He was the author of *The Stranger's Banquet* (1919), *The Foolish Matrons* (1920), *Messer Marco Polo* (1921), his great success; *The Wind That Bloweth* (1922), *The Changeling* (1923), *Blind Raftery* (1924), *Hangman's House* (1926), *Brother Saul* (1927), *Crusade* (1928), *Destiny Bay* (1928), and *Field of Honor* (1929).

Donne (dun, don), **John.** b. at London, in 1571 or 1572 (1573 according to his friend and biographer Izaak Walton); d. there, March 31, 1631. An English poet and divine, the first and greatest of the so-called metaphysical poets. On his mother's side he was connected with Sir Thomas More and John Heywood. He was brought up as a Roman Catholic, and was educated at Oxford (1584), Cambridge

(1587), and Lincoln's Inn (1592). In 1596 and 1597 he took part in the expeditions led by the earl of Essex against Cádiz and the Azores. In 1597 he was appointed secretary to Sir Thomas Egerton, Lord Keeper of the Great Seal, but lost his post in 1601 by his clandestine marriage to Egerton's niece, and was imprisoned (1602) for a time, the marriage being a violation of both common and canon law. After several years spent in fruitless attempts to obtain a position through court favor, his *Pseudo-Martyr* (1610) won him the notice of King James I. James, however, refused to promote him except in the Anglican Church, and at last, in 1615, Donne received Anglican orders. He was appointed successively royal chaplain, reader in divinity at Lincoln's Inn, and finally, in 1621, dean of Saint Paul's. In his later years he was widely regarded as the foremost preacher of his day.

Writings. Most of Donne's poems circulated in manuscript during his lifetime, and his collected poems were not published until 1633, after his death. His prose works include over 150 sermons, *Ignatius his Conclave* (a satirical attack on the Jesuits), and a small book of *Devotions* (written during a serious illness in 1623), from which Ernest Hemingway took the title *For Whom the Bell Tolls.* Donne's reputation stood very high during the 17th century, but during the 18th and 19th centuries, though never completely forgotten, he was little read. His modern reputation owes much to the edition of the *Poems* by H. J. C. Grierson (1912) and to the influence of the criticism of T. S. Eliot. Donne is best known for his love poems, his sonnet to Death (*Death, be not Proud*), and his *Anniversaries,* two elegies in memory of the 16-year-old Elizabeth Drury. His poetry is contrary to the courtly Petrarchan tradition established in English by Wyatt and Surrey; his approach is more natural, his attitude towards woman cynical, his writing more abrupt and witty.

Donne, John. [Called **the Younger.**] b. in May, 1604; d. at London, 1662. An English writer; son of John Donne (c1573–1631). He was educated at Westminster School and at Oxford, where he was known for his dissipations. After an acquittal on a charge of manslaughter for the death of a young boy, he left for Padua, where he became a doctor of laws; upon his return to England he took holy orders (c1638). Some of his father's papers he gave to Izaak Walton the younger. He was the author of *Donnes Satyr* (1661–62), an indecent volume.

Donnithorne (don'i.thôrn), **Arthur.** In George Eliot's novel *Adam Bede,* a vain, weak, good-natured young man, whose remorse for Hetty Sorrel's ruin lies chiefly in his chagrin at being found out and losing the approbation of his acquaintances.

Donnybrook (don'i.brŭk). A town and parish in Leinster province, Irish Republic, in County Dublin. Donnybrook is now a part of the city of Dublin, located ab. 3 mi. SE of the city center. The town was formerly famous for its fair (held in August), proverbial for its good-humored rioting, established under King John and suppressed in 1855. It is now the center of an expensive residential district.

Do Not Go Gentle into That Good Night. A poem by Dylan Thomas, written upon the death of his father, maintaining for five three-line stanzas the rhyme *aba,* and in the last stanza of four lines, *abaa.* He exhorts his father not to accept death passively but to "Rage, rage against the dying of the light."

Donovan (don'ọ.van), **Dick.** Pseudonym of **Muddock, Joyce Emerson Preston.**

Don Pedro (pē'drō, pā'-). See **Pedro, Don.**

Don Quixote (don kẹ.hō'tẹ, kwik'sọt; Spanish, dōn kē.ᴎō'tä). [Full Spanish title, **Don Quijote de la Mancha.**] A Spanish satirical romance by Cervantes, printed at Madrid in two parts, the first in 1605, the second in 1615. When the second part was nearly completed (1614), an impudent attempt to malign the character of Cervantes was made by Alonso Fernandes de Avellaneda of Tordesillas (thought to be a pseudonym of Luis de Aliaga), who produced a pretended continuation of the first part. Translations of *Don Quixote* have appeared in every European language, including Turkish. The principal English translations are those of Shelton (1612–20), Motteux (1719), Jarvis (1742), Ormsby (1885), and Putnam (1949). The book is named after its hero, a Spanish country gentleman, who is so imbued with tales of chivalry that he saddles up his nag Rosinante and sets forth with his squire Sancho Panza in search of knightly adventure to honor his lady Dulcinea del Toboso, really an ordinary country girl. At the beginning of the work Cervantes announces it to be his sole purpose to break down the vogue and authority of books of chivalry, and at the end he declares anew that he had "had no other desire than to render abhorred of men the false and absurd stories contained in books of chivalry," exulting in his success as an achievement of no small moment. The work was considered at first to be no more than hilarious satire (the Spanish themselves were notoriously slow to value the book properly), but in time perceptive readers of all countries saw beyond the surface laughter to the thoughtful and skillfully handled treatment of the idealist in a materialistic world, so that its comedy becomes the comedy of irony, not too far removed from something akin to tragedy.

Don Quixote in England. A comedy by Henry Fielding, produced in 1734. Inspired by Cervantes's novel, it is a satire of English life with just a touch of sentiment. There is a certain libertarian sting in the reference to jails as "only habitations for the poor, not for men of quality. If a poor fellow robs a man of fashion of five shillings, to gaol with him: but the man of fashion may plunder a thousand poor, and stay in his own house."

Don Saltero's Coffee House (don sôl.tär'ōz). A house formerly standing in Cheyne Walk, Chelsea, London. It contained not only an eating house but a museum of natural curiosities. It was founded by John Salter c1690. It was torn down in 1866.

Don Sebastian, King of Portugal (sẹ.bas'chạn). A tragedy by John Dryden, printed in 1690, produced in 1689. In the preface Dryden announces that the theme of love opposed to honor has been worn out, and that he has deliberately made the verse rough, used some comic portions, and disregarded classic unity in order to meet the taste of the age. The play marks a turning away from the artificial, tendentious heroic drama which had prevailed during earlier decades. The characters are set against a background of Portugal under the Moors.

Doolin de Mayence (do.o.laǹ dẹ mȧ.yäṅs). [Also, **Doon de Mayence**.] A French *chanson de geste* of the 14th century, adapted as a prose romance in the 15th century. It was first published in 1501. Alxinger, a German poet, made (1787) a translation in the form of an epic poem. Doolin, or Doon, was the son of Guy of Mayence, and the ancestor of Ogier the Dane. His name is attached to a whole cycle of the Charlemagne *chansons de geste*, those dealing with the false knights, the family of Ganelon; included here are such chansons as *The Four Sons of Aymon*.

Doolittle (döʹlit.l), **Liza**. The Cockney girl in Shaw's *Pygmalion* who is turned into a lady by Henry Higgins, a professor of phonetics.

Doom Is Dark and Deeper than Any Sea-Dingle. An early poem by W. H. Auden, first appearing in the 1934 edition of *Poems*. It is entitled "Something Is Bound to Happen" in *Collected Poetry* (1945). It reflects Auden's study of Old English poetry in its meter and general mood, although not nearly so consistently as *The Age of Anxiety* (1946).

Doomsday. The Day of Judgment, a favorite subject of medieval religious literature. Among the earliest works in English on the theme are several Old English poems, the best known of which is in the *Exeter Book*.

Doomsday. A novel by Warwick Deeping, published in 1926. The title derives from the Sussex farm where the action of the story takes place.

Doomsday Book. See **Domesday Book**.

Doon de Mayence (do.ôṅ dẹ mȧ.yäṅs). See **Doolin de Mayence**.

Dora (dōʹrạ). A poem (1842) by Alfred Tennyson.

Dora. A play (1877) by Sardou: in English, *Diplomacy*.

Doralice (dorʹạ.lis). The wife of Rhodophil in John Dryden's comedy *Marriage à la Mode*, remarkable for her brilliant statement of a philosophy of flirtation in the last act.

Doran (dōʹrạn), **John**. b. at London, March 11, 1807; d. there, Jan. 25, 1878. An English journalist and miscellaneous writer. He was editor of *Notes and Queries* from 1869 until his death. His works include *Lives of the Queens of England of the House of Hanover* (1855), *Their Majesties' Servants* (1860), and many works on stage history.

Dora Spenlow (dōʹrạ spenʹlō). See **Spenlow, Dora**.

Dorastus and Fawnia (dọ.rasʹtus; fôʹni.ạ). See **Pandosto**.

Dorax (dōʹraks). A renegade in Dryden's tragedy *Don Sebastian*: a noble Portuguese, formerly Don Alonzo de Sylvera, governor of Alcazar. He has been thought to be the best of Dryden's tragic characters.

Dorcas (dôrʹkạs). [Also, **Tabitha**.] In the New Testament (Acts, ix. 36), a woman who was full of good deeds, and made coats and garments for the poor; hence, a Dorcas society is a society of the women of a church who supply garments to the needy.

Dorcas. In Shakespeare's *Winter's Tale*, a shepherdess.

Dorcas Zeal (zēl). See **Zeal, Arabella** and **Dorcas**.

Doria (dōʹri.ạ), **Lampatho**. In John Marston's play *What You Will*, a cynical observer said to be a caricature of Ben Jonson.

Doric dialect. The language of the Dorians, a dialect of the Greek or Hellenic, characterized by its broadness and hardness: hence applied to any dialect with similar characteristics, especially to the Scotch.

Doricha (dōʹri.kạ). See **Rhodopis**.

Doricles (dôrʹi.klēz). In Shakespeare's *Winter's Tale*, the name assumed by Florizel.

Doricourt (dorʹi.kōrt). A brilliant man of the world in Hannah Cowley's comedy *The Belle's Stratagem*. His wit, humor, and courtliness make him the fashion, while his taste for French piquancy renders him impervious to the charm of English beauty.

Dorigen (dorʹi.jẹn). See under **Franklin's Tale, The**.

Dorimant (dorʹi.mant). In Etherege's comedy *The Man of Mode, or Sir Fopling Flutter*, a witty and fashionable libertine, intended as a portrait of the Earl of Rochester.

Dorinda (dọ.rinʹdạ). The sister of Miranda in Dryden and D'Avenant's version of *The Tempest*. Like Miranda, she has seen no man but her father.

Dorinda. In Farquhar's comedy *The Beaux' Stratagem*, the daughter of Lady Bountiful. She falls in love with and marries Aimwell, whose stratagem to win a rich wife thus succeeds.

Dorking (dôrʹking), **Battle of**. An occurrence in an imaginary narrative of an invasion and conquest of England by a foreign army, written by General Sir George T. Chesney in 1871 and published under the title *The Battle of Dorking, or Reminiscences of a Volunteer*. It called attention to the need of an improved system of national defense, and attracted much notice.

Dornton (dôrnʹtọn), **Harry**. The son of Old Dornton in Holcroft's *Road to Ruin*. His exploits give the name to the play. He is saved from ruin by Sulky, his father's friend.

Dornton, Old. The fond, confiding, but justly offended father of Harry Dornton in Holcroft's *Road to Ruin*.

Dorothea (dor.ọ.thēʹạ), **Saint**. d. c311. A virgin martyr. She was tortured and decapitated in the persecution of Diocletian. She was said to have sent roses and apples miraculously from paradise to a doubting spectator of her martyrdom, Theophilus, who jestingly asked her to do so. He was converted by this miracle, and later tortured and then decapitated. Dorothea is introduced as a character of much resolution and piety by Massinger and Dekker in *The Virgin Martyr*. In their play she refuses the love of Antoninus, the son of the Governor of Caesarea because of her devotion to Christ, and is responsible for converting Theophilus's daughters from idolatry to Christianity.

Dorothea. The "peerless Queen of Scots" in Greene's play *James IV*.

---

fat, fāte, fär, ȧsk, fāre; net, mē, hėr; pin, pīne; not, nōte, mȯve, nôr; up, lūte, pṳll; ꜩʜ, then;

Dorothea. In Fletcher's comedy *Monsieur Thomas*, a bright, affectionate English girl, the sister of Monsieur Thomas.

Dorothea. A beautiful unfortunate woman in an episode of Cervantes's *Don Quixote*.

Dorothea Brooke (brŭk). See **Brooke, Dorothea.**

Dorothy's Wedding (dor'ọ.thiz). A novel by Ethel Sidgwick, published in 1931.

Dorriforth (dor'i.fôrth). In Mrs. Inchbald's *Simple Story*, a Roman Catholic priest. He is the guardian of Miss Milner, who falls in love with him. He becomes the Earl of Elmwood, is released from his vows, and marries her.

Dorrit (dor'it), **Amy.** [Called **"Little Dorrit."**] In Charles Dickens's *Little Dorrit*, the unselfish daughter of the debtor William Dorrit, born in prison.

Dorrit, William. The father of Amy Dorrit, in Charles Dickens's *Little Dorrit*. He is a weak, selfish, good-looking man confined in the Marshalsea prison for a long time for debt, and hence called "the Father of the Marshalsea."

Dorset (dôr'sẹt), 1st Earl of. A title of **Sackville, Thomas.**

Dorset, 6th Earl of. A title of **Sackville, Charles.**

Dorset, Marquess of. In Shakespeare's *Richard III*, the historical Thomas Grey, eldest son of Lady Grey (Elizabeth Woodville), who later became Edward's Queen. When Dorset's brother, Lord Grey, and his uncle, Rivers, are executed by Richard, he joins Richmond in Brittany.

Dorset Garden Theatre. [Also, **Duke's Theatre.**] A theater in London, just south of Salisbury Court, from 1671 to 1706. The Duke of York was its patron, and Christopher Wren the architect. *Sir Martin Mar-all* by Dryden opened it (1671), and ballad opera began to appear in it with D'Avenant's version of *The Tempest*. The theater was the only one open in London from 1672 to 1674. A number of Dryden's comedies were produced there, and Etherege, as well as D'Urfey, Settle, Behn, and Ravenscroft, wrote for it.

Dorus (dō'rus). In Sir Philip Sidney's romance *Arcadia*, the name under which Musidorus, in the disguise of a shepherd, pretends to love Mopsa.

Dory (dō'ri). The vociferous and faithful servant of Sir George Thunder, in O'Keefe's *Wild Oats*.

Dostoevski (dos.to.yef'ski), **Feodor** (also **Fëdor, Fiodor,** or **Fyodor) Mikhailovich.** b. at Moscow, Nov. 11 (or, by the old style calendar then still used in Russia, Oct. 30), 1821; d. at St. Petersburg, Feb. 9 (old style, Jan. 28), 1881. A Russian novelist, short-story writer, and journalist. His father, of Ukrainian origin, was an army surgeon; his mother came from a well-to-do Moscow business family. He was educated at Moscow, and at the St. Petersburg School of Military Engineering, where he made a fine record. From 1841 to 1844 he served in the army, resigning in the latter year because he felt that he wanted to make literature his life work. In the late 1840's he was a member of the radical Petrashevski group, and, as one of them, he was arrested on April 23, 1849, and spent the next eight months in prison. He was tried as a conspirator, found guilty, sentenced to death by shooting, and then deported to Siberia. The death

sentence was recalled, but Dostoevski and his comrades were not allowed to know it until they had been tortured by being made to believe that the original decree was to be carried out. He listened to the formal reading of the death sentence, 20 times witnessed the long and detailed preparations for the execution, and waited blindfolded for the fatal shot to be fired before being informed, when the "joke" could not be further prolonged, that he was not to be killed. This experience, which took place on Dec. 21, 1849, did nothing to help his epilepsy, of which he was a victim from early childhood, and which figures prominently in his novels, as does his passionate fondness for gambling. In 1854 he was released from the Omsk penal colony, and sent to another part of Siberia as a private in the army. He was restored to his former rank in 1855, pardoned in 1859, and allowed to return to St. Petersburg. With his brother, Michael (d. 1864), he edited a review, *Vremya* (the *Times*), which although attacked by both the left and the right and suppressed by the government in 1863, was a success, and its successor, *Epokha* (the *Epoch*), which failed and was discontinued. He began his literary career as a novelist, with a work that immediately brought him recognition as a major force in Russian literature and was praised by the influential critic Belinsky. *Poor Folk* (also *Poor People*, finished 1845, published 1846) is an epistolary novel, telling the story of Makar, a poor government clerk, and Varvara, a poor orphan seamstress, whom he loves but cannot afford to marry, although he goes without food in order to buy her luxuries. He sinks lower and lower in the social scale, falls into debt, sells his clothing, is evicted from his room because he cannot pay his rent, becomes a drunkard, and is forced to accept charity from his superior. Varvara, who blames Makar for his extravagance, without realizing that she is the cause of it, meets Bykov, a wealthy man, and accepts his offer of marriage, without loving him, because she knows that it will mean the end of drudgery and drabness. Makar is left alone with a bitter heart and memories and the prospect of a dull and lonely future. *The Double* (1846) shows that sympathy for the underdog and deep interest in abnormal psychology which are characteristic of Dostoevski. His *Netochka Nezvanova* (1849) is a study in feminine psychology dealing with a "proud woman" type suggestive of the women he married. *The Manor of Stephanchikovo* (1859, also called *The Family Friend*), written in Siberia, is famous for the character of the repulsive Foma Opiskin, regarded as one of the greatest portraits in Russian fiction. *The House of Death* (also *The House of the Dead*, 1861) is a record of his prison impressions and experiences, both of which he never forgot. The sadistic brutality and savagery of the guards, the beatings and floggings, the deadly prison routine (and the pathetic ways in which the convicts sought to break it), their quarrels (frequently brought on by a need for varying the monotony), the psychology of men in chains, all these details of the prison life he saw are realistically described. *The Insulted and the Injured* (1861–62, also known as *The Downtrodden and the Oppressed*) is Dickenslike in its sympathy with the poor, and in its sentimentality. His *Letters from the Underworld* (1864, also called *Memoirs from the Under-*

ground and *Notes from Underground*) is a cross between philosophy and fiction. A short work, in two parts, it deals with a man who takes pleasure in torturing himself and others. The narrative part which deals with Lisa, a prostitute, a familiar Dostoevski type, is almost overshadowed by psychological analysis of and philosophical comments on the nature of evil, and the evil man. It is told in the first person by the hero, who represents spite or malice. In the opinion of most modern critics it may usefully serve the beginning reader of Russian literature as a general introduction to all of Dostoevski. Other short works, long short-stories or novelettes rather than novels, are *The Gentle Maiden* and *The Landlady*. *Crime and Punishment* (1866), one of his greatest works, is generally regarded also as one of the greatest psychological novels in world literature. The main characters (there are many, Dostoevski being not unlike Dickens in this respect) are Raskolnikov, a poor, sick student, his mother and sister, Pulcheria and Eudoxia, Sonia, a high-minded prostitute, whom he loves and who becomes the means of his regeneration, Luzhin, to whom Eudoxia is engaged, and Petrovitch, a shrewd lawyer and police inspector. The crime is Raskolnikov's hatchet-murder of an old, repulsive, selfish, woman money-lender, and her sister, an act that turns out to be senseless as he does not benefit from it in any way. The punishment is not the seven-year sentence he receives, but the torture of his conscience. Dramatized versions have been successful on English, American, and European stages. His *Letters* (c1867) deal with his frequent financial distress, his battle with poverty, his study of literature, his life in Siberia, his travels in France, Germany, Italy, and Switzerland, his passionate feeling for Russia (which was so great that he could not be happy or productive anywhere else), his gambling excesses at Baden-Baden, which led him to lose his wife's wedding ring, his quarrel with Turgenev, and his deep conviction, born during his prison days, that Christ belonged to Russia and the Russian people. *The Idiot* (1868–69) is autobiographical in the sense that its Christlike hero, Prince Myshkin, is an epileptic. He is loved by two women, Aglaia, whom he refuses to marry because he feels that he will not be able to make her happy, and Nastasia, whom he is willing to marry in a spirit of self-sacrifice because she has been thrown over by a former lover. His creator represents him as an "idiot" in a double sense, as a pure, gentle, childlike, honest, unambitious character, laughed at by St. Petersburg fashionable society, and as insane, a real idiot, at the end of the story, as a result of spending the night with the jealous Rogozhin, who has murdered Nastasia, and her dead body. Another short novel, *The Eternal Husband* (1871), tells the story of a wife who fools her husband and of what happens, to him, the wife, and the lover, when he finds out. It has been called "a Russian *Madame Bovary*." *The Demons* (1871, also *The Possessed*) is an anti-Nihilistic novel. Its characters are Nikolay Stavrogin, son of a wealthy widow, Peter Verhovensky, a cold, ruthless Nihilist, Shatov, a peasant and servant, the only decent person in the story, Lebyadkin, army captain and blackmailer, his sister Marya, a half-wit, and Kirillov, an engineer. As in *Hamlet*, most of the

characters kill themselves or are killed at the end. *A Raw Youth* (1875), generally considered an inferior work, is the story of a father and his illegitimate son, who is obsessed by a desire to become a millionaire. Both are in love with the same woman and both do not hesitate to use blackmail when it serves their ends. His third masterpiece is *The Brothers Karamazov* (1880). The brothers are Dmitri, a soldier, Ivan, an intellectual and atheist, and Aloysha, a religious mystic, the sons of a drunken, depraved sot. When he is murdered, suspicion falls on Dmitri, whose hatred for his father was well known, but the act was committed by an illegitimate son of the old man, Smerdyakov, an epileptic, whose mother was an imbecile. The cause of the crime is the conflict between Dmitri and his father over Grushenka, the son wanting her as his wife, the father as his mistress. Different shadings of guilt are finely illustrated: actual or technical guilt by Smerdyakov, who kills himself, moral guilt by Ivan, who planted the seed of the crime in Smerdyakov's mind, and subconscious guilt by Dmitri, who wanted the crime committed, and who pays the legal penalty for it. Dostoevski is recognized as one of the great figures in world literature, and his works have been translated into the chief European languages. To English readers he is known through the translations of Constance Garnett, C. J. Hogarth, S. S. Koteliansky, J. Middleton Murry, and Ethel C. Mayne. He was influenced by Gogol, Balzac, and Dickens, but much of his style and technique was uniquely his own, coming from his experience and observation rather than from reading. So little was Dostoevski known in England during his lifetime that the British press did not even mention his death, although his funeral was an occasion of great public grief in Russia. His *Crime and Punishment* was not translated into English until 1885, nearly 20 years after its Russian publication. In 1894, George Moore, the English novelist, wrote the introduction to an English edition of *Poor Folk;* Moore, known for his deliberate realism, was probably influenced by Dostoevski. Certainly the course of English fiction has been profoundly affected by the conventions of the realistic novel, as established by Dostoevski, Zola, and Flaubert: acute observation of life, especially in its more sordid or dreary aspects; analysis of character through emotion; exploration of the dark places of the human spirit.

Dotheboys Hall (dŏ′тнҽ.boiz). A Yorkshire school in Charles Dickens's *Nicholas Nickleby*, kept by Mr. Wackford Squeers, who starves and beats his pupils, and teaches them very little. Nicholas served there for a short time as an under-master.

Dotterel (dŏt′ėr.ẹl), **Mrs.** A character in David Garrick's play *The Male Coquette*.

Double Dealer, The. A comedy by Congreve, produced in 1693. It has scenes imitated from Molière's *Tartuffe* and occasional suggestions of his *Les Femmes Savantes*. It verges on tragicomedy when Mellefont is deprived of his inheritance and Cynthia, his fiancée, is nearly given over to Maskwell, the villain of the piece, but all is set right at the end. Mellefont is engaged to marry Cynthia, daughter of Sir Paul Pliant; their love is an honest one, somewhat in the vein of Shakespeare's romantic

---

fat, fāte, fär, àsk, fāre; net, mē, hėr; pin, pīne; not, nōte, mŏve, nôr; up, lūte, pùll; тн, then;

lovers. Lady Touchwood, the dissolute wife of Mellefont's uncle, also loves Mellefont, but he rejects her advances. She thereupon enlists the aid of Maskwell, the double-dealer, who wants Cynthia for himself. They succeed in making Pliant and Lord Touchwood suspicious of Mellefont, and by a pretended friendship of Maskwell for Mellefont the latter is lured to Lady Touchwood's room, where Lord Touchwood finds him. But the victory of Lady Touchwood and Maskwell is ruined when the former discovers the true object of Maskwell's desire. As she is upbraiding him, Lord Touchwood overhears her, and Cynthia is soon restored to Mellefont's arms.

Double Falsehood, The. A play published by Theobald in 1728 as by Shakespeare. It is based on the story of Cardenio in *Don Quixote*, and is thought to have been very probably written by Shirley.

Double Gallant, or The Sick Lady's Cure, The. A comedy produced in 1707, compiled by Colley Cibber from Susannah Centlivre's *Love at a Venture* (which owed something to Thomas Corneille's *Le Galant double*) and Burnaby's *The Lady's Visiting-Day* and *The Reformed Wife*.

Double Heart, The. A biographical study by Naomi Royde-Smith, published in 1931. It deals with Julie de Lespinasse, who was in love with d'Alembert, the Marquis de Mora, and Count Jacques Antoine Guibert.

Double Marriage, The. A tragedy by John Fletcher, assisted by Philip Massinger, apparently produced after Burbage's death. It was printed in 1647.

double rhyme. See **feminine rhyme.**

Double Vision of Michael Robartes (mī′kel rob′-arts). A poem by W. B. Yeats, published (1919) in *The Wild Swans at Coole*. In notes written in 1922 Yeats says of the character Robartes (who figures also in two other poems) and of Aherne, who is usually paired with him: "They take their place in a phantasmagoria in which I endeavor to explain my philosophy of life and death." The symbolism of the poem may be understood through the keys Yeats provided in the *Autobiographies* and *Essays*. The Sphinx, half animal and half woman, is a static symbol representing intellect; Buddha is also static and represents love. The dancing girl moves between them, a symbol of bodily perfection and therefore representing art, which is, according to this scheme, halfway between intellect and love.

Doubtful Heir, The. A romantic comedy by James Shirley, originally produced at Dublin under the title of *Rosania, or Love's Victory*, and licensed in 1640 under that name.

Doubting Castle. The abode of Giant Despair, in Bunyan's *Pilgrim's Progress*, in which he locks up Christian and his companion Hopeful.

Douce Davie Deans (dōs′ dā′vi dēnz′). See **Deans, Douce Davie.**

Doudney (dōd′ni), **Sarah.** b. at Portsmouth, Hampshire, England, Jan. 15, 1843; d. Dec. 15, 1926. An English novelist, poet, and author of books for juveniles. Her novels include *The Strength of Her Youth* (1880), *The Family Difficulty* and *A Woman's Glory* (both 1885), *The Missing Rubies* and *Where Two Ways Meet* (both 1886), *When We Two Parted*

(1887), *Under False Colours* (1889), *Through Pain to Peace* (1892), *Violets for Faithfulness* (1893), *A Romance of Lincoln's Inn* (1894), *Katherine's Keys* (1895), *Pilgrims of the Night* (1896), *Silent Strings* (1900), *One of the Few* (1904), *Shadow and Shine* (1906), and *Lady Dye's Reparation* (1907); she also wrote *Miss Irving's Bible* (1875), and other works for children.

Dougal (dö′gal). A wild, shock-headed follower of Rob Roy, in Sir Walter Scott's novel *Rob Roy*.

Doughty (dou′ti), **Charles Montagu.** b. in Suffolk, England, Aug. 19, 1843; d. at Sissinghurst, Kent, England, Jan. 30, 1926. An English poet, scientist, explorer, and traveler. He was educated at the universities of London, Cambridge, Oxford, Leiden, and Louvain, and traveled in Norway, France, Spain, Italy, Greece, Tunis, Algeria, Damascus, Palestine, and Egypt. He was the author of the classic *Travels in Arabia Deserta* (1888), a work notable for its style, of which *Wanderings in Arabia* (1908) is a condensation; he also wrote scientific essays and reports of his exploring trips. Among his other works are *Under Arms* (1890), *The Dawn in Britain* (1906), an epic poem in 30,000 lines, *Adam Cast Forth* (1908), a verse drama dealing with the expulsion, separation, and reunion of Adam and Eve, *The Cliffs* (1909), *The Clouds* (1912), *The Titans* (1916), and *Mansoul, or the Riddle of the World* (1920).

Douglas (dug′las). A tragedy by John Home, first produced at Edinburgh on Dec. 14, 1756. It is partly founded on a Scottish ballad, *Childe Maurice*.

Douglas, Lord **Alfred Bruce.** b. 1870; d. March 20, 1945. An English poet, editor of *The Academy* from 1907 to 1910 and a friend of Oscar Wilde. His volumes of verse include *The City of the Soul* (1899) and *Sonnets* (1900).

Douglas, Archibald. [Title: 3rd Earl of **Douglas;** called **"the Grim"** and **"the Black Douglas."**] b. c1328; d. c1400. A Scottish soldier and lawmaker; natural son of Sir James Douglas, "the Good" (c1286–1330). His wife was Joanna Moray (or Murray), heiress of Bothwell. He was constable of Edinburgh (1361), and warden of the western marches (1364, 1368). He was the ambassador from David Bruce (David II of Scotland) to the French court in the matter of divorce against David's wife (1369), and again on an embassy announcing Robert II's succession and renewing the French alliance (1371). With Robert, Earl of Fife, he invaded England (1389). The inclusion of Scotland in the peace between England and France was partly due to his efforts (1389, 1391).

Douglas, Archibald. [Title, 5th Earl of **Angus;** called **"the Great Earl"**; nicknamed **"Bell-the-Cat."**] b. c1449; d. 1514. A Scottish nobleman. He was one of the disaffected nobles who overthrew and murdered James III's favorite, the Earl of Mar, Robert Cochrane, in 1482. At a meeting of the nobles to concert a plan of attack on the favorite, Lord Gray compared the meeting to that of the mice in the fable who proposed to string a bell round the cat's neck, and asked, with reference to the favorite, "Who will bell the cat?" Douglas answered, "I will bell the cat" (whence his epithet). He plotted with Edward IV of England and Alex-

d, d or j; s, s or sh; t, t or ch; z, z or zh; o, F. cloche; ü, F. menu; ch, Sc. loch; n, F. bonbon.

ander Stuart, Duke of Albany, against James III, but got out of the conspiracy. In the reign of James IV he was chancellor (1493–98) of the kingdom. In Scott's poem *Marmion* he is represented as entertaining Marmion and Lady Clare at his castle by command of the king.

Douglas, Archibald, (4th) **Earl of.** In Shakespeare's *1 Henry IV*, the historical Archibald Douglas, 4th Earl of Douglas, an ally of Hotspur at Shrewsbury; he almost kills King Henry, and is later captured when the rebels flee.

Douglas, Ellen. The daughter of the outlawed James Douglas, in Sir Walter Scott's poem *The Lady of the Lake*. Going to Stirling with the signet ring given her by the Knight of Snowdon (James Fitz-James, the King in disguise), she obtains a pardon for her father.

Douglas, Gawin (or **Gavin**). [Also, **Gawain Douglas.**] b. c1474; d. at London, in September, 1522. A Scottish poet and bishop; younger son of Archibald (Bell-the-Cat) Douglas, 5th Earl of Angus. He prepared a translation of the *Aeneid* into Scottish verse (1513; printed 1553), the first translation, after Caxton's feeble rendering of the *Aeneid*, of a classical work into any form of the English language. He also wrote the allegory *The Palice of Honour; King Hart*, an allegory of the heart, the senses, and the like; and *Conscience*, a conceit.

Douglas, George. Pseudonym of **Brown, George Douglas.**

Douglas, George. In Sir Walter Scott's novel *The Abbot*, the seneschal of Lochleven Castle during his father's absence. Falling in love with his prisoner, Mary, Queen of Scots, he aids her escape and dies at the battle of Langside.

Douglas, Sir James. [Title, Lord of **Douglas**; called **"the Good Sir James"** and **"the Black Douglas."**] b. c1286; killed in Spain, probably on Aug. 25, 1330. A Scottish nobleman. He was the terror of the English in his border raids. His name of "the Black Douglas" is either from this reputation or from his dark skin. He had no hesitation, twice, in destroying his own castle when it was occupied by the British. His exploits on the border were many and romantic, being climaxed in 1327 by his almost capturing Edward III of England in a night raid on the English camp. He joined the standard of Robert Bruce (Robert I of Scotland) in 1306, and commanded the left wing of the Scottish army at the battle of Bannockburn, on June 24, 1314. In accordance with the dying request of Bruce, he set out on a journey to the Holy Land, carrying with him Bruce's heart incased in a casket of gold. Arrived in Spain, he offered his services to Alfonso, king of Castile and León, against the Saracens of Granada, and fell in battle.

Douglas, John Sholto. See **Queensberry,** 8th Marquis of.

Douglas, Norman. [Full name, **George Norman Douglas.**] b. 1868; d. on Capri (the scene of *South Wind*), Feb. 9, 1952. An English novelist. He was the author of *Unprofessional Tales* (1901), *Siren Land* (1911), *South Wind* (1917), *They Went* (1921), *Old Calabria* (1928), *Three of Them* (1930), *Goodbye to Western Culture* (1930), *Paneros* (1931), *Looking Back* (2 vols., 1933), and *Late Harvest* (1946).

Douglas of Kirkcudbright (kêr.kö′bri), **William.** b. at Fingland, Kirkcudbrightshire, Scotland, c1672; d. 1748. A Scottish poet, author of *Annie Laurie*. The daughter of Sir Robert Laurie, of Maxwellton House, Dumfriesshire, Annie Laurie (1682–1764) broke her engagement with Douglas in order to marry (1709) James Fergusson, of Craigdarroch. Douglas later eloped with Betty Clark, of Glenboig, Galloway, but he made his earlier love famous with his song which is known and sung all over the world. *Annie Laurie* was first published as a poem in 1824, and the music was composed (1835) by Lady John Douglas Scott.

Douglas, William. [Titles: 3rd Earl of **March,** 4th Duke of **Queensberry**; latterly known as **"Old Q."**] b. 1724; d. at London, Dec. 23, 1810. A Scottish politician, notorious for his dissolute life and extravagances. He attempted to develop horse racing as a science; Knight of the Thistle, 1761; representative peer for Scotland in the same year; vice-admiral (1767–76) of Scotland; created (1786) Baron Douglas of Amesbury in British peerage; satirized by Burns, called "degenerate Douglas" by Wordsworth, and basis of a character in Thackeray's *Virginians*.

Douglas Larder. In Sir Walter Scott's *Tales of a Grandfather*, an allusion to Douglas Castle, which had been stored with provisions for the British army in the time of Edward I. Sir James Douglas ("the Black Douglas") twice took possession of the castle by surprise, and set fire to it after killing its occupants.

Douglas Tragedy, The. A ballad included in Scott's *Border Minstrelsy*, telling of the flight of the two lovers Lady Margaret and Lord William, the pursuit by her father and brothers, the ensuing fight, and the resultant death of the pair.

Dousabel (dö′sa.bel). [Also, **Dowsabel.**] A common name for a rustic sweetheart in old pastoral poems.

Dousterswivel (dös′tėr.swiv.el), **Herman.** In Sir Walter Scott's novel *The Antiquary*, a German adventurer who tricks Sir Arthur Wardour by a pretended magical discovery of treasure, and is himself similarly tricked by Ochiltree.

Dove (duv), **Doctor.** The chief character in Southey's *The Doctor*.

Dove, Lady. In Cumberland's play *The Brothers*, a termagant, the mother of the principal female character.

Dover Wilson (dō′vėr wil′son), **John.** See **Wilson, John Dover.**

Dove's Nest, The. The title story of a collection of short stories by Katherine Mansfield, published in 1923.

Doves Press (duvz). An English publishing venture (1900–1916) concerned with the making of beautiful books. The press was set up in the Hammersmith borough of London by T. J. Cobden-Sanderson and Emery Walker, both of whom had worked with William Morris at the Kelmscott Press. The Doves type, designed by Walker, was a variant of the famous 15th-century Jenson type. The books printed at the Doves Press, including the renowned Doves Bible, had a great influence on the arts of typography and printing in the early part of the 20th century. When the venture came to an end in 1916, all fonts of Doves type were put beyond possibility of further use by being thrown into the Thames River.

Dowden (dou′dĕn), **Edward.** b. at Cork, Ireland, May 3, 1843; d. at Dublin, April 4, 1913. An Irish Shakespeare editor, critic, biographer, poet, and teacher. Educated at Queen's College (Cork) and Trinity College (Dublin), he was graduated (1863) from Trinity, where he was professor of English literature from 1867 until his death, except for short periods as Taylorian lecturer (1889) at Oxford, Clark lecturer (1893–96) at Cambridge, and special lecturer (1896) at Princeton in celebration of the 150th anniversary of the university. He was (1896–1901) commissioner of national education of Ireland. He was the author of the biographies *Southey* (1880), *Life of Shelley* (1886), *Robert Browning* (1904), and *Montaigne* (1905); of the critical and historical works *Shakespeare: A Critical Study of His Mind and Art* (1875), *Shakespeare: Scenes and Characters* (1876), *A Shakespeare Primer* (1877), *Studies in Literature: 1789–1877* (1878), *Introduction to Shakespeare* (1893), *The French Revolution and English Literature* (1897), *History of French Literature* (1897), *Puritan and Anglican* (1900), *Milton in the 18th Century* (1908), and *Essays: Modern and Elizabethan* (1910); and also of *Poems* (1876, 1914) and *A Woman's Reliquary* (1913). He edited Southey's *Correspondence* (1881), Shakespeare's *Sonnets* (1881), *The Passionate Pilgrim* (1883), *Hamlet* (1899), *Romeo and Juliet* (1900), *Cymbeline* (1903), and Browning's *The Ring and the Book* (1912).

Do-wel (dō.wel′), **Do-bet** (dō.bet′), and **Do-best** (dō.best′). See under **Piers Plowman.**

Dowgate (dou′gāt). The original water-gate of London.

Dowland (dou′land), **John.** b. 1563; d. 1626. An English lutanist at various European courts, remembered chiefly as one of the earliest writers of the art song.

Dowler (dou′lĕr), **Captain.** A retired military man in Charles Dickens's *Pickwick Papers*, noted for his bluster and brag, and his extraordinarily fierce and disjointed manner of talking.

Downfall of Robert, Earl of Huntington, The. A play (1598) by Anthony Munday and Henry Chettle. It is based upon the legends of Robin Hood and recalls certain 15th-century English ballads.

Downing (dou′ning), **Sir George.** b. probably in August, 1623; d. 1684. An English soldier and politician. He emigrated with his parents in 1638 to New England (where he was the second graduate of Harvard College), but subsequently returned to England, and in 1650 was scoutmaster-general of Cromwell's army in Scotland. He was appointed resident at The Hague in 1657, and there is said to have arranged a secret meeting with Charles II, warned him of Cromwell's intention to seize him in Holland, and thereby to have saved Charles's life. He was retained in office by Charles II on the Restoration in 1660, and was created a baronet in 1663. He was given a grant of land in what is now

Downing Street, in Whitehall, London, which derives its name from him.

Downing, Sir George. b. c1684; d. in Cambridgeshire, England, June 10, 1749. An English philanthropist, the founder of Downing College; grandson of Sir George Downing (d. 1684). He was a member of the Parliaments of 1710 and 1713, and kept his seat from 1722 until his death.

Downing College. One of the colleges of Cambridge University. It was founded in 1800 by a bequest of Sir George Downing, of Gamlingay Park in Cambridgeshire, who died in 1749, but did not open until 1807, when its first buildings were erected. It is the college of Sir Busick Harwood, famous physician and medical professor, William Frere, who later became its master, and of Thomas Starkie and Andrew Amos, both Downing professors of law. Its founder was the grandson of the 17th-century Sir George Downing who built the famous London street named after him.

Downing Street. A short street in the West End of London, leading from Whitehall. It contains the building (No. 10) in which the prime minister generally resides, the treasury building, and the foreign office; hence the name Downing Street has come to be used to symbolize the prime minister and his cabinet. It was built by Sir George Downing (1623–84) on a grant of land from Charles II.

Downright (doun′rīt). A rude but manly and consistent squire in Ben Jonson's comedy *Every Man in His Humour*. He is courageous, of plain words and plain actions.

Dowsabel (dou′sa.bel). See **Dousabel.**

Dowsecer (dou′se.kèr), **Lord.** In George Chapman's *An Humorous Day's Mirth*, the contemplative son of Count Labervele. He is concerned with the wickedness of the world and his melancholy eloquence upon this point so charms the King of France that he surrenders the young Martia to him. He falls in love with her somewhat unexpectedly, claiming in Platonic fashion: "I desire thy pure society, But even as angels do to angels fly."

Dowson (dou′sŏn), **Ernest.** [Full name, **Ernest Christopher Dowson.**] b. in Kent, England, Aug. 2, 1867; d. at London, Feb. 23, 1900. An English poet, short-story writer, and translator, often grouped with the so-called Decadents in late 19th-century English literature. His short life was sickly; he was tubercular and his latter years were spent in poverty. He was the author of *Dilemmas* (1895), *Verses* (1896), *The Pierrot of the Minute* (1897), a poetic drama, and *Poems* (1905); and he translated works by Voltaire, Balzac, Zola and other French authors. He is best remembered for his lyric *Non Sum Qualis Eram Bonae Sub Regno Cynarae*, with its repeated "I have been faithful to thee, Cynara! in my fashion" (the work is commonly referred to simply as *Cynara*). The actual Cynara was the daughter of a French café-keeper in London, who later married a waiter. Among other short poems by Dowson are *Extreme Unction, You Would Have Understood Me, A Last Word, Spleen,* and *To One in Bedlam.*

Dowton (dou′tŏn), **William.** b. at Exeter, England, 1764; d. at Brixton, Surrey, England, 1851. English actor. He made his first appearance in 1781, and came to New York in 1836. He had two sons, William and Henry, both of whom became actors. The former afterward became a brother of the Charter House, and died there at the age of nearly 90.

Doyle (doil), Sir **Arthur Conan.** b. at Edinburgh, May 22, 1859; d. at Crowborough, England, July 7, 1930. An English writer of fiction, creator of Sherlock Holmes. A medical doctor, he practiced from 1882 to 1890, but meanwhile began his career in literature with the publication of *A Study in Scarlet* (1887), a crime-and-mystery story in which he introduced the character destined to make his fame and fortune, the detective Sherlock Holmes. He did not immediately concentrate upon Holmes, but during the next four years, besides publishing the historical novels *Micah Clarke* (1889), and *The White Company* (1891), he contributed further stories of Holmes's exploits to the *Strand Magazine*, and when these appeared in book form as *The Adventures of Sherlock Holmes* (1891), their success was sensational. Doyle continued to work the rich vein he had opened, but in the last story of *The Memoirs of Sherlock Holmes* (1893), either tiring of the game or fearful of his invention flagging, he killed off the hero—or so he thought. But the Sherlock Holmes cult continued to recruit avid readers who demanded more adventures, and were glad to accept the implausible explanation that the great detective had disappeared but had not died, since this made possible *The Return of Sherlock Holmes* (1905), and *The Last Bow* (1917). A final collection of stories, *The Case Book of Sherlock Holmes* (1927), completed the portrait and the history of a fictitious character who, more than any other in modern literature, seemed to millions of readers almost more real even than his creator. The name Sherlock Holmes, or merely Sherlock, in English-speaking countries have come to be synonymous with "detective." Certain illustrations of the early stories depicted Holmes as a thin-faced man wearing a peculiar checked cap, smoking an underslung pipe and carrying a magnifying glass; this visualization of his appearance was brought to life by the American actor William Gillette in his play *Sherlock Holmes*, and has become a part of the conventional symbolism of American cartoonists. Doyle also wrote a number of plays, one of which, *The Story of Waterloo*, successfully provided a starring vehicle for Sir Henry Irving. During the Boer War he spiritedly defended the British cause in a book, *The War in South Africa; its Causes and Conduct*, which led to his being knighted, and during World War I his pamphlet, *Cause and Conduct of the World War*, was circulated in millions of copies in a dozen languages. The loss of a son in that war led to the interest in psychic phenomena which made Sir Arthur in his last years a firm believer in spiritualism.

Doyle, Sir **Francis Hastings Charles.** b. at Nunappleton, near Tadcaster, Yorkshire, England, Aug. 21, 1810; d. at Berkeley Square, London, June 8, 1888. An English balladist, poet, and teacher. Educated at Eton and at Christ Church, Oxford, he studied at the Inner Temple, being called to the bar in 1837 and elevated (1839) to the baronetcy on the

death of his father. He gave up law practice to accept positions in the customs office, holding (1846–69) the receiver-generalship of customs and serving (1869–93) as commissioner. He was professor of poetry (1867–77) at Oxford. Among his works are *Miscellaneous Verses* (1834, 1840), *Oedipus, King of Thebes* (1849), a translation of Sophocles, *The Return of the Guards and Other Poems* (1866), *Lectures* (1869, 1877), and several ballads.

Doyle, John Andrew. b. at London, May 14, 1844; d. at Oxford, Aug. 4 or 5, 1907. An English essayist, historian, and librarian. He was educated at Eton and at Balliol College, Oxford, graduating in 1867, was a fellow (1867–1907) of All Souls College, Oxford librarian (1881–88), and author of a prize essay (1869) on *The English Colonies in America Before 1776.* He also wrote *A Summary History of America* (1875), *A History of the American Colonies Down to the War of Independence* (5 vols., 1882–1907), *The Puritan Colonies* (1887), *The Middle Colonies* (1907), and *The Colonies Under the House of Hanover* (1907). Doyle also contributed articles to the *Dictionary of National Biography* and the *Cambridge Modern History.*

Doyle, Lynn. [Pseudonym of **Leslie Alexander Montgomery.**] b. at Downpatrick, County Down, Ireland, 1873—. An Irish writer. He is the author of collections of short stories such as *Ballygullion* (1908), *Lobster Salad—Irish Short Stories* (1922), *Dear Ducks* (1925), and *Me and Mrs. Murphy* (1930). His plays include *Love and Land* (1913; produced 1925 as *Perseverance*), *The Lilac Ribbon* (1919), and *Turncoats* (1922). Among his novels are *Mr. Wildridge of the Bank—a novel* (1916) and *Fiddling Farmer* (1937). He has also published a book of verse entitled *Ballygullion Ballads* (1936).

Doyle, Richard. b. at London, 1824; d. there, Dec. 11, 1883. An English artist. He was a member of the staff of *Punch* (1843–50). Among his best-known works are the illustrations to Thackeray's *Newcomes* (1853–55) and a series of elfin scenes entitled *In Fairy-Land* (1870).

Draco (drā'kō) or **Dracon** (drā'kon). fl. in the last half of the 7th century B.C. An Athenian legislator. According to tradition, he formulated the first written code of laws for Athens in 624 or c621 B.C., at which, there having been no written code previously, the people were so overjoyed that they smothered Draco accidentally under a deluge of cloaks. On account of the number of offenses to which it affixed the penalty of death, his code was said to have been written in blood (whence the phrase "draconian measures" to describe a harsh or ruthless course of action). His code was superseded for the most part by that of Solon (594).

Dragon in Shallow Waters, The. A novel by V. Sackville-West, published in 1921.

Dragonnades (drag.ọ.nädz'). A form of persecution inflicted by the government of Louis XIV upon the French Protestants in the period preceding the revocation of the edict of Nantes. It consisted in billeting troops upon the inhabitants as a means of converting them, license being given to the soldiery to commit all manner of misdeeds.

Dragon of Wantley (wont'li), **The.** An old satirical ballad, preserved in Percy's *Reliques*, which describes the victory over a dragon (who devoured damsels, houses, and trees) by More of More-Hall, the local hero, who provides himself with armor covered with spikes, but who kills the beast with a kick on its rear.

Dragon of Wantley, The. A burlesque opera (1737) by Henry Carey and J. F. Lampe.

Dragon's Blood. A novel by Romer Wilson (Mrs. Edward J. O'Brien), published in 1926.

Drake (drāk). An epic poem (1908) by Alfred Noyes, written in blank verse, concerning the great sea conquests of Elizabethan England.

Drake, Sir **Francis.** b. probably at Tavistock, Devonshire, England, c1540; d. off Portobelo, Panama, Jan. 28, 1596. An English naval hero. In 1567–68 he commanded a small vessel, the *Judith*, one of two which escaped from the destruction of Sir John Hawkins's fleet by the Spanish in the Gulf of Mexico. Under Elizabeth's commission as a privateer, he visited the West Indies and the Spanish Main in 1570 and 1571, and became convinced that the towns there would fall an easy prey to a small armed force. Accordingly, in 1572, he fitted out what was properly a freebooting expedition, England being then at peace with Spain. With only three vessels and 100 men he took the town of Nombre de Dios on the Isthmus of Panama and an immense treasure; but he was badly wounded in the attack, and his men abandoned both town and treasure. Soon after, he burned a Spanish vessel at Cartagena, in what is now Colombia, captured many ships, and intercepted a train loaded with silver on the isthmus. He also crossed to Panama, and was the first English commander to see the Pacific. From his return, in August, 1573, to September, 1576, Drake served under Walter Devereux, 1st Earl of Essex, in Ireland. In December, 1577, with the express purpose of penetrating to the Pacific through the Straits of Magellan, he started on another freebooting expedition with five ships and 166 men. Two ships were abandoned on the west coast of South America, and after the passage of the Straits of Magellan, which took 16 days, his ship became separated from the other two, which returned to England. Drake continued in the *Golden Hind*, obtained an immense booty on the Pacific coast of Spanish America, crossed the Pacific, and returned to England by way of the Cape of Good Hope, arriving in September, 1580, with a vast treasure. This was the first English circumnavigation of the globe. Queen Elizabeth knighted Drake on his own ship, and ordered that the *Golden Hind* be preserved as a monument. (It rotted and was broken up some hundred years later.) Drake was mayor (1581) of Plymouth. In 1584–85 he was a member of Parliament. From 1585 to 1586 he commanded a powerful expedition to the West Indies and the Spanish Main, in which he took and ransomed Santo Domingo and Cartagena, ravaged the coasts of Florida, and on his way back brought off the remnant of the English Virginia colony founded by Sir Walter Raleigh in 1585. In 1587 he made a descent on the coast of Spain, and in the Bay of Cádiz destroyed numerous unfinished vessels intended for the Spanish Armada, besides capturing a rich Portuguese East Indiaman. In July, 1588, as a vice-admiral, he commanded under Lord Charles Howard in the combat with the Spanish Armada, capturing a large Spanish galleon; and next year he was one of the commanders in a descent on the Spanish and Portuguese coasts, which proved unsuccessful. For several years thereafter he was engaged in peaceful pursuits, and in 1593 he was again elected to Parliament. In 1595 he commanded another West India expedition, which met with little success, and in which both he and Sir John Hawkins died.

drama. **1.** A story put into action, or a story of human life told by actual representation of persons by persons, with imitation of language, voice, gesture, dress, and accessories or surrounding conditions, the whole produced with reference to truth or probability, and with or without the aid of music, dancing, painting, and decoration; a play.

> The church was usually the theatre wherein these pious dramas were performed, and the actors were the ecclesiastics or their scholars.
>
> (Strutt, *Sports and Pastimes.*)

> Westward the course of empire takes its way;
>   The four first acts already past,
> A fifth shall close the drama with the day;
>   Time's noblest offspring is the last.
>
> (Bp. Berkeley, *Arts and Learning in America.*)

> A drama is the imitation (in a particular way) of an action regarded as one, and treated as complete. In the observation of the process of a complete action, and in the attempt to imitate it in accordance with such observation, must therefore be sought the beginnings of the drama.
>
> (A. W. Ward, *Eng. Dram. Lit.*, Int.)

2. A composition in verse or prose, or in both, presenting in dialogue a course of human action, designed, or seemingly designed, to be spoken in character and represented on the stage; a form of imitated and represented action regulated by literary canons; the description of a story converted into the action of a play, and thereby constituting a department of literary art: as, the classic *drama;* the Hindu *drama;* the Elizabethan *drama.* The construction of such a composition is, as a general rule, marked by three stages: first, the opening of the movement; second, the growth or development of the action; third, the close or catastrophe, which must in all cases be the consequence of the action itself, as unfolded in acts, scenes, and situations. The drama, whether in actual life or mimic representation, assumes two principal forms, namely, tragedy and comedy; and from modifications or combinations of these result the mixed or minor forms, known as tragicomedy, melodrama, lyric drama or grand opera, opera bouffe, farce, and burletta. Other forms, suggested by the subject and the manner of presenting it, are the nautical drama, the pastoral drama, the society drama, etc. Both tragedy and comedy attained a high degree of development in the ancient Greek drama, which originated in the worship of Bacchus.

> Sophocles made the Greek drama as dramatic as was consistent with its original form.
>
> (Macaulay, *Milton.*)

It is sometimes supposed that the drama consists of incident. It consists of passion, which gives the actor his opportunity; and that passion must progressively increase, or the actor, as the piece proceeded, would be unable to carry the audience from a lower to a higher pitch of interest and emotion.

(R. L. Stevenson, *A Humble Remonstrance*.)

In the epic poem there is only one speaker—the poet himself. The action is bygone. The scene is described. The persons are spoken of as third persons. There are only two concerned in it, the poet and the reader. In the drama the action is present, the scene is visible, the persons are speakers, the sentiments and passions are theirs.

(Dion Boucicault, in New York *Herald*, July 6, 1888.)

3. Dramatic representation with its adjuncts; theatrical entertainment: as, he has a strong taste for the *drama*.

It was on the support of these parts of the town that the playhouses depended. The character of the drama became conformed to the character of its patrons. (Macaulay, *Comic Dramatists*.)

Drama of Exile, A. A poem by Elizabeth Barrett Browning, published in 1844.

Dramatic Poesy, An Essay of. A work by Dryden (1668), written in the form of a dialogue between four friends: Neander (Dryden), Lisideius (Charles Sedley), Crites (Sir Robert Howard), and Eugenius (Charles, Lord Buckhurst, afterward 6th Earl of Dorset). It takes place in a boat on the Thames, and the discussion centers around the use of rhyme in drama, the relative merits of French and English drama, and a comparison of old and contemporary drama.

dramatis personae (dram′a.tis pėr.sō′nē). The persons of the drama; the characters in a play. Abbreviated *dram.pers.*

Dramatis Personae. A volume of poems (1864) by Robert Browning, containing *Abt Vogler, Rabbi Ben Ezra, Caliban Upon Setebos,* and *Prospice.*

Draper (drā′pėr), **Eliza.** See **Eliza.**

Drapier's Letters (drā′pi.ėrz). A series of letters published in 1724 by Jonathan Swift, under the pseudonym M. B. Drapier. They were directed against the acceptance in Ireland of a copper coinage the patent for supplying which had been accorded to William Wood, who with the duchess of Kendal, the king's mistress (who obtained him the privilege), was to divide the profit arising from the difference between the real and the nominal value of the halfpenny (about 40 percent). Owing to the public excitement raised by these letters the patent was canceled. Wood was compensated with a pension, and Swift gained a popularity which he never lost till his death. A large reward was offered at the time for the discovery of the author.

Dravot (drav′ot), **Daniel.** One of the two chief characters in Kipling's story *The Man Who Would Be King*. See also **Carnahan, Peachey.**

Drawcansir (drô′kan.sėr). In *The Rehearsal*, by the Duke of Buckingham and others, a boasting and vainglorious bully. Almanzor in *The Conquest of Granada*, Dryden's favorite hero, was parodied in this character. The name became a synonym for a braggart.

Drayton (drā′ton), **Michael.** b. at Hartshill, Warwickshire, England, 1563; d. at London, Dec. 23, 1631. An English poet. He is buried in Westminster Abbey, and his epitaph is said to be by Ben Jonson. His chief works are *Idea; the Shepherd's Garland* (1593), a pastoral sequence; *Idea's Mirror* (1594), a sonnet sequence; *Mortimeriados* (1596; this afterward appeared with many alterations as *The Barons' Wars*, 1603); *England's Heroical Epistles* (1597); *Poems, Lyric and Pastoral* (c1606, containing "The Ballad of Agincourt" and "To the Virginian Voyage"); *Poly-Olbion* (1613–22), a description of England both topographical and legendary; *Nimphidia, the Court of Faery* (1627), a light-touched fairy poem; and *The Muses' Elysium* (1630).

Dream, The. A short poem by Byron, composed in 1816.

Dreamers, The. A three-act play about Robert Emmet, by Lennox Robinson, published in 1913.

Dream of Eugene Aram (ū.jēn′ ār′am), **The.** A poem by Thomas Hood, published in 1829.

Dream of Fair Women, A. A poem by Alfred Tennyson.

Dream of Fair Women, The. An autobiographical novel by Henry Williamson, published in 1924. It is the third volume of a tetralogy under the general title *The Flax of Dream*.

Dream of Gerontius (jē.ron′ti.us), **The.** An oratorio (Opus 38) by Sir Edward Elgar, based upon Cardinal Newman's poem of that title, first performed at the Birmingham Festival on Oct. 3, 1900.

Dream of Scipio (sip′i.ō), **The.** [Latin, **Somnium Scipionis.**] A work widely read in the Middle Ages, in origin part of Cicero's *De Re Publica* (Book vi), preserved by Macrobius, who added (c400 A.D.) a long commentary. It relates that the younger Scipio Africanus visited Masinissa, King of Numidia, with whom he talked all day of his father. That night he dreamed of his father, who exhorted him to lead a good and noble life in order to attain immortality. The work is summarized by Chaucer at the beginning of *The Parliament of Fowls.*

Dream of the Rood, The. An Old English poem, parts of which closely resemble verses carved in runes (early 8th century) on a stone cross at Ruthwell, in Dumfriesshire, Scotland. The only extant complete version comes from a 156-line manuscript (9th century), written in the West Saxon dialect of Old English and included in the *Vercelli Book*. It is attributed by some scholars to Cynewulf, although there is no definite evidence on which to base this judgment. The poem is divided into three parts: in the first the poet tells of having a vision of the cross, in the second the cross addresses the poet telling him of its history and urging him to follow its cult, and in the third the poet shows how the dream has altered his life. He touches on the subjects of Christ's passion, death, and ascension in his conclusion. The poem, tender and lyrical, possesses an intimate subjectivity rare in Old English literature.

Dreyfus (drā′fus, drī′-; French, drā.füs), **Alfred.** b. at Mulhouse, in Alsace, Oct. 9, 1859; d. at Paris, July 12, 1935. A French army officer of Jewish descent, central figure in the celebrated Dreyfus

---

fat, fāte, fär, àsk, fāre; net, mē, hėr; pin, pīne; not, nōte, mŏve, nôr; up, lūte, pŭll; ᴛʜ, then;

affair. He was convicted (1894) by a secret military tribunal of having divulged state secrets to a foreign power, and was sentenced to penal servitude for life. He was imprisoned on Devil's Island, French Guiana. The so-called *bordereau* (a list of papers supposedly to be turned over by Dreyfus to the Germans), the principal piece of evidence in Dreyfus's conviction, was sufficient evidence to sway the anti-Semitic military court. However, in 1896 Colonel Picquart, of army intelligence, discovered, and in 1897 Dreyfus's brother Mathieu made public, evidence indicating that not Dreyfus but Major Marie Charles Ferdinand Walsin Esterhazy was the writer of the bordereau. The case rapidly became a public scandal and liberals and republicans sided against militarists and royalists in an attempt to reopen the case and obtain justice for Dreyfus. Such men as Émile Zola (convicted in 1898 for printing his pro-Dreyfus series of articles *J'accuse*, which summed up the evidence against the army), Jaurès, Anatole France, and Clemenceau attacked the rightists, who included Déroulède and Barrès. To support their case, the anti-Dreyfus forces made use of manufactured evidence, building a house of cards that tumbled with the suicide in prison of Lieutenant Colonel Henry, of army intelligence, who with Esterhazy was actually responsible for the bordereau. Dreyfus was accorded a second trial at Rennes (Aug. 7–Sept. 9, 1899), and was recondemned and sentenced to ten years' imprisonment, but was pardoned by President Loubet for by this time it was obvious that the case was not being tried on its merits. The decision of the court of cassation, the supreme appeals court of France, announced on July 12, 1906, quashed the verdict of the Rennes tribunal and completely vindicated Dreyfus. Restored (1906) to military rank as a major, he was decorated with the Legion of Honor, served in the French army in World War I, and retired as a lieutenant colonel after holding the temporary rank of brigadier general. Subsequent revelations (1930) indicated the absolute guilt of Major Esterhazy in forging the documents originally ascribed to Dreyfus. The Dreyfus case was used by the anticlerical party in France to further their aim of complete separation of church and state; on the other hand, the antirepublicans made every attempt, including armed resistance to the government, to use the affair to discredit the republic.

Dr. Faustus (fôs′tus, fous′-). See **Doctor Faustus.**

Drift. A novel by James Hanley, published in 1930.

Drinkwater (dringk′wô.tėr, -wot.ėr), **John.** b. at Leytonstone, Essex, England, June 1, 1882; d. at London, March 25, 1937. An English dramatist and poet. He worked in the insurance business at Manchester, Birmingham, and elsewhere, and before turning to full-time writing took part in founding (1907) the Pilgrim Players, an amateur dramatic group which later became the Birmingham Repertory Theatre. Among his historical plays are *Abraham Lincoln, a Play* (produced 1918), *Mary Stuart* (published 1921, produced 1922), *Oliver Cromwell, a Play* (published 1921, produced 1922), and *Robert E. Lee, a Play* (published and produced 1923). Among his other plays are *Rebellion: a Three Act Play in Verse* (1914), *Bird in Hand* (1927), *Mid-*

summer Eve (1932), and *A Man's House* (1934). His biographical and critical works include *William Morris, a Study* (1912), *Swinburne, a Study* (1913), *The Pilgrim of Eternity—Byron* (1925), *Charles James Fox* (1928), *Pepys* (1930), and *Shakespeare* (1933). Among his works of poetry are *Poems* (1903), *Poems of Men and Hours* (1911), *Cromwell and Other Poems* (1913), *Poems 1908–14* (1917), *Seeds of Time* (1921), *From an Unknown Isle* (1924), *Christmas Poems* (1931), and *Summer Harvest* (1933). He wrote two autobiographical volumes, *Inheritance, the First Volume of an Autobiography* (1931) and *Discovery, the Second Volume* (1932).

Dr. Jekyll and Mr. Hyde (jek′il, jē′kil; hīd). [Full title, **The Strange Case of Dr. Jekyll and Mr. Hyde.**] A tale (1886) by R. L. Stevenson about a strange case of dual personality.

Dromina (drom′i.na̤). A novel (1909) by Monsignor Count Francis Browning Drew Bickerstaffe-Drew under the pseudonym John Ayscough. Based on a religious theme, it is set against the historical background of the 1820's. The Dauphin, son of Louis XVI, is a leading character.

Dromio of Ephesus (drom′i.ō; ef′ę.sus) and **Dromio of Syracuse** (sir′a̤.kūs). In Shakespeare's *Comedy of Errors*, twin brothers, servants respectively of the twins Antipholus of Ephesus and Antipholus of Syracuse. The Dromio of Ephesus is a stupid servant, the Dromio of Syracuse a witty one. In Plautus's *Menaechmi*, from which this play is derived, there is only one servant.

Dr. Primrose (prim′rōz). The principal character in Oliver Goldsmith's *The Vicar of Wakefield.*

Dr. Syntax in Search of the Picturesque (sin′taks), **The Tour of.** A descriptive and didactic poem (1809–11) by William Combe. Similar Tours "in Search of Consolation" and "in Search of a Wife" followed.

Dr. Thorne (thôrn). See **Doctor Thorne.**

Drugger (drug′ėr), **Abel.** In Jonson's *The Alchemist*, a tobacco dealer who wishes to marry Dame Pliant, but is cheated by the spurious alchemist and his confederates.

Druid (drö′id), **Dr.** The Welsh tutor of Lord Abberville, in Cumberland's play *The Fashionable Lover.*

Druid, The. A pseudonym of **Dixon, Henry Hall.**

Druids (drö′idz). Ancient Celtic priests, ministers of religion, poets, teachers, and judges of Gaul, Britain, and Ireland. The chief seats of the Druids were in Wales, Brittany, and the regions around what are now the communities of Dreux and Chartres in France, although probably the Druids existed as a class among all the Celtic peoples of Europe and the British Isles. They are believed to have possessed some knowledge of geometry, the physical sciences, and the like. They superintended the affairs of religion and morality and performed the office of judges. They were not a hereditary class; their knowledge was transmitted orally; as a result, all direct knowledge of the Druids died out with them, and our principal sources of information are such writers as Caesar. They are said to have had a common superior, who was elected by a majority of votes from their own members, and who enjoyed his dignity for life. A yearly general meeting supposedly was held in Gaul, perhaps near the present Chartres. The oak and the mistletoe were held by them in the highest veneration; their places of worship were in oak groves; the cutting of the mistletoe, according to Pliny, was performed by a priest clad in white using a golden knife, and was signalized by the sacrifice of two white bulls at the spot. The Continental Druids, who opposed Roman conquest of Gaul, were wiped out as a result of Rome's victory, but they remained longer in the British Isles, succumbing eventually to Christianity's advance. As a result, they appear in the literature that has come down to us as sorcerers and magicians, surrounded by an aura of evil power. They probably performed human sacrifice, and one of their duties was divining the future, but the mystery of their belief and practice has attached to them strange rites at Stonehenge, England, and Carnac, Brittany, which, so far as is now known, are Stone Age relics with no connection to Druidism. The Druids were succeeded by the bards and *fili* (poets); some remnants of Druid powers are seen in the legendary attributes of the poets Merlin and Taliesin; much of the Druid glamour is attached to the Celtic saints. Cathbad, the Druid teacher of Cuchulain, is prominent in the Ulster cycle of Irish legend, in such tales as *The Cattle-Raid of Cooley.*

Drummer, or the Haunted House, The. A comedy by Addison. It was first played in March, 1716, and not known to be Addison's till Steele published the fact, after the author's death.

Drummond (drum'ǫnd), **Henry.** b. at Stirling, Scotland, 1851; d. at Tunbridge Wells, England, March 11, 1897. A Scottish clergyman and author. He was appointed lecturer on natural history and science at the Free Church College, Glasgow, in 1877. He was the author of *Natural Law in the Spiritual World* (1883), *Tropical Africa* (1888), and others.

Drummond of Hawthornden (hô'thôrn.dẹn), **William.** b. at Hawthornden, near Edinburgh, Dec. 13, 1585; d. there, Dec. 4, 1649. A Scottish poet. He took the degree of M.A. at the University of Edinburgh in 1605, and studied law (1607–08) at Bourges and Paris. On succeeding his father, John Drummond, as laird of Hawthornden in 1610, he retired to his estate, and devoted himself to literature and mechanical experiments. He published *Tears on the Death of Meliades* (1613), *Poems* (1616), *Notes of Ben Jonson's Conversations, Flowers of Zion,* and *Cypress Grove* (1623).

Drummond, William Henry. b. near Mohill, County Antrim, Ireland, April 13, 1854; d. at Cobalt, Ontario, Canada, April 6, 1907. A Canadian physician and poet, known as "the poet of the habitant." He moved to Canada in his youth and was educated there. He began the practice of medicine in the province of Quebec, where he came in close contact with the French-Canadian voyageurs and habitants, about whom most of his poems were written. Later he removed to Montreal, and for some years was professor of medical jurisprudence at Bishop University. His works include *The Habitant, and Other French-Canadian Poems* (1897), *Phil-o-rum's Canoe and Madeleine Vercheres* (1898),

Johnnie Courteau (1901), *The Voyageur, and Other Poems* (1905), and *The Great Fight* (1908).

Drummossie Moor (dru.mos'i). See **Culloden Moor.**

Drum's Entertainment. See **Jack Drum's Entertainment.**

Drury (drö'ri), **Robert.** The hero of Daniel Defoe's *Madagascar: or, Robert Drury's Journal, during Fifteen Years Captivity on that Island,* published in 1729. Most of the story is clearly fictitious, and the real Robert Drury could not have been the narrator, but Defoe, using every available oral or printed account of Madagascar, produced a book so accurate in many details that it is often cited as an authority on the island.

Drury Lane. A street in London, near the Strand, with which it communicates through Aldwych. It was one of the great arteries of the parish of Saint Clement Danes, an aristocratic part of London in the time of the Stuarts. It takes its name from Drury House, built by Sir William Drury in the time of Henry VIII, and is probably best known for the Drury Lane Theatre.

Drury Lane Theatre. One of the principal theaters of London, situated on Russell Street near Drury Lane. It was opened under Killigrew's patent in 1663, rebuilt by Sir Christopher Wren and reopened in 1674, and reopened in 1794 and 1812. It was most recently rebuilt in 1921.

Druses (drö'zẹz). [Also, **Druzes.**] A people and religious sect of Syria and Lebanon, living chiefly in the mountain regions of Lebanon and the Anti-Liban and the district of Hauran, including the formerly autonomous region of Jebel ed Druz. The only name they themselves acknowledge is Unitarians (*Muahidin*); the name by which they are commonly known to others comes probably from Ismail Darazi, their first apostle in Syria. Their religion, a monotheistic and messianic form of Mohammedanism, is based on the belief that al-Hakim, sixth of the Fatimid caliphs of Egypt and North Africa, who reigned from 996 to 1021 and declared his own divine nature, was the last appearance to man of the Deity. In his next incarnation, Hakim or the Deity will lead the believers to the establishment of their faith over the world. Darazi, who accepted al-Hakim's divinity, fled from Egypt to Syria, where he converted the hillmen to this belief. The Druse religion is separate and different from the orthodox Mohammedan belief and their customs are separate from those of their neighbors, whether Moslem or Christian. They have been in conflict with these neighbors since the formation of the sect, most notably with the Maronites, a Christian group, whom the Druses several times in the 19th century raided and massacred.

Drusilla Clack (drö.sil'ạ klak'). See **Clack, Drusilla.**

Dr. Wortle's School (wėrt'lz, wôrt'lz). See **Wortle's School, Dr.**

Dryasdust (drī'ạz.dust), **Rev. Dr.** A prosy parson who is supposed to write the introductory letters to several of Sir Walter Scott's novels. He also writes the conclusion to *Redgauntlet.* The name was used by Carlyle as a synonym for dreary platitude (especially in historical writing).

Drybob (drī′bob). In Thomas Shadwell's comedy *The Humorists*, a fantastic coxcomb and would-be wit.

Dryburgh Abbey (drī′bur.ọ). A highly picturesque ruin ab. 4 mi. SE of Melrose, Scotland, whose fragments exhibit excellent Norman and Early English architectural details. It contains the tomb of Sir Walter Scott.

Dryden (drī′dẹn), **John.** b. at the vicarage of Aldwinkle All Saints, Northamptonshire, England, probably on Aug. 9, 1631; d. at London, May 1, 1700. An English poet, critic, and dramatist. He was graduated from Trinity College, Cambridge, in 1654. In 1663 he married Lady Elizabeth Howard, the sister of his friend Sir Robert Howard, and in 1664 he achieved his first independent stage success with *The Rival Ladies*. Originally a Parliamentarian (he mourned Cromwell's death in 1658 with his *Heroic Stanzas*), he went over to the Royalist side, writing (1660) his *Panegyric on the Coronation* to celebrate the coronation of Charles II. He was poet laureate and historiographer royal from 1670 to 1688. In 1679 he had a quarrel with John Wilmot, 2nd Earl of Rochester, who is believed thereupon to have caused him to be cudgeled in the street by masked bravoes. The unsettled state of public feeling created by allegations of "popish plots" (which induced him to write the series of satires of which *Absalom and Achitophel* was the first) brought down upon him a storm of libels. He was converted to Roman Catholicism in 1685, but his sincerity has been impugned. His critical writings, among the most distinguished in English, were numerous and on various subjects. The most famous of these are *An Essay of Dramatic Poesy* (1668) and the prefaces to the *Virgil* (1697), and the *Fables* (1700). He was the first to recognize fully the greatness of Shakespeare and Chaucer. He wrote many prologues, epilogues, epistles, and dedications, and after his conversion to Roman Catholicism employed his pen in defense of his faith. His chief poems are *Heroic Stanzas* (1659), *Astraea Redux*, celebrating the Restoration (1660), *Annus Mirabilis* (1667), *Absalom and Achitophel*, considered by some the greatest satire in English verse (1681; the second part with Tate, 1682), *Mac Flecknoe, or a Satyr upon the True-Blew-Protestant Poet, T.S.* (1682), an attack on Thomas Shadwell, *Religio Laici*, in defense of Anglicanism (1682), *The Hind and the Panther*, in defense of Roman Catholicism (1687), *The Works of Virgil* (1697), *Alexander's Feast; or the Power of Music* (1697), *Fables Ancient and Modern* (1700); also translations of Juvenal, Ovid, and others. His chief plays include *The Indian Emperor, or, The Conquest of Mexico by the Spaniards* (1665), *Almanzor and Almahide, or the Conquest of Granada* (1670), *Aurengzebe* (1675), and *All for Love: or, the World well Lost* (1678). Other notable plays were *Marriage à la Mode* (1673), *Amboyna* (1673), and *The Spanish Friar* (1681). His complete works were edited by Scott in 18 volumes (1808), and revised (1882–93) by George Saintsbury. See his biography by George Saintsbury in the "English Men of Letters" series (1881).

Dryfesdale (drīfs′dāl), **Jasper.** In Sir Walter Scott's novel *The Abbot*, the revengeful old steward at Lochleven Castle, who endeavors to poison Mary, Queen of Scots, and her attendants.

Dry Salvages (sal.vä′jẹz). The third of *The Four Quartets* by T. S. Eliot, published in 1941. The title is explained by Eliot thus: "The Dry Salvages—presumably les trois sauvages—is a small group of rocks with a beacon, off the N.E. coast of Cape Ann, Massachusetts. Salvages is pronounced to rhyme with assuages. Groaner: a whistling buoy." Eliot uses the metaphor of the river as the rhythmic and constant force within us, and by extension of the metaphor, the sea "is all about us." Our perceptions of nature can not be complete; they can only be hints and guesses: "The hint half guessed, the gift half understood, is Incarnation."

Duarte (dū.är′te). A brave but vainglorious man in John Fletcher and Philip Massinger's *Custom of the Country*. Colley Cibber introduces him in a somewhat modified form in his *Love Makes a Man*, taken from the former play.

du Barry (dū bar′i; French, dü bȧ.rē), Comtesse. [Original name, **Marie Jeanne Bécu**; sometimes (but incorrectly), **Marie Jeanne Gomard de Vaubernier**.] b. in Champagne, France, Aug. 19, 1746; guillotined at Paris, Dec. 7, 1793. The mistress of Louis XV after 1769. The illegitimate daughter of a seamstress, she went c1762 to Paris, worked in a milliner's shop, and under the name Mlle. Lange became a prostitute and mistress of Jean, Comte du Barry, a professional gambler. They soon schemed to have her placed at court and, through the king's valet de chambre, had her introduced to Louis. She became the king's mistress (her beauty and wit were remarked upon by the many famous persons who came to know her), was married to du Barry's brother Guillaume, and with this front of respectability was presented at court as the Comtesse du Barry. She exercised great influence over the king, slowly overcame his attachment to his family and advisers, and placed her own friends in power. She, through the triumvirate of the duc d'Aiguillon (reputedly her lover), René Nicolas de Maupeou, and the abbé Joseph Marie Terray, ruled the king and kingdom; the duke Étienne François de Choiseul, the leading French diplomat of the day, was dismissed through her influence; a mansion was built for her near Versailles. When the king died (1774) she was ordered to an abbey by Louis XVI, but instead she took up residence at her mansion with her lover, the count de Cossé-Brissac, after the queen interceded for her. In 1792 she made a trip to England to pawn some jewelry, and in 1793 was arrested as having conspired against the Republic, was tried before the Revolutionary Tribunal, and, still arguing her innocence of any crime, was carried off to the guillotine.

du Bartas (dü bȧr.tȧs), **Guillaume de Salluste, Seigneur du.** See **Bartas.**

Dublin (dub′lin), **University of.** See **Trinity College.**

Dubliners (dub′lin.ẹrz). A collection of sketches and short stories dealing with Dublin life and character, by James Joyce, published in 1914. Among the stories are "Counterparts," "The Dead," and "Ivy-Day in the Committee Room."

Dubric (dö′brik), Saint. [Also, **Dubricus**.] A British ecclesiastic, said to have been the founder of the bishopric of Llandaff in Wales. Geoffrey of Monmouth asserts that he crowned King Arthur, and Tennyson mentions him in "The Coming of Arthur," the first of the *Idylls of the King*.

Du Cange (dü känzh) or **Ducange**, Sieur. [Title of **Charles du Fresne** or **Dufresne**.] b. at Amiens, France, Dec. 18, 1610; d. at Paris, Oct. 23, 1688. A French philologist and historian. He was the author of *Histoire de l'empire de Constantinople sous les empereurs français* (1657), *Glossarium ad scriptores mediae et infimae latinitatis* (1678), *Historia Byzantina* (1680), and *Glossarium ad scriptores mediae et infimae graecitatis* (1688).

ducdame (dŏk'da̧.mē). Jargon; used by Amiens in Shakespeare's *As You Like It* (II.v).

Duchess, The. Pseudonym of **Hungerford, Margaret Wolfe.**

Duchess of Malfi (mal'fi), **The.** A tragedy by John Webster, played c1613, and printed in 1623. There is a dramatic version of the story among Lope de Vega's works, and it forms the subject of one of Bandello's *Novelle;* Webster's direct source was the 23rd tale in William Painter's *Palace of Pleasure* (1566). It is Webster's most popular play, the one oftenest read, and the most original. The crime for which the duchess is reduced by her family to insanity and death is her secret marriage with her steward, whom she loved.

Duchess of Wrexe (reks), **The.** A novel by Hugh Walpole, published in 1914. The first volume of a trilogy, it is noted as an example of Walpole's skill in characterization; it was followed by *The Green Mirror* (1917) and *The Captives* (1920).

Dudeney (dōd'ni), **Mrs. Henry.** [Maiden name, **Alice Whiffin.**] b. Oct. 21, 1866; d. 1945. An English popular novelist. Some of her many novels are *A Man with a Maid* (1897), *The Maternity of Harriott Wicken* and *Folly Corner* (both 1899), *Spindle and Plough* (1903), *The Story of Susan* (1903), *The Wise Woods* (1905), *The Orchard Thief* (1907), *Married When Suited* (1911), *Set to Partners* (1913), *The Secret Son* (1915), *Traveller's Samples* (1916), and *The Head of the Family* (1917).

Dudgeon (duj'o̧n), **Dick.** The "devil's disciple" in George Bernard Shaw's play of that name.

Dudgeon, Mrs. A shrewish New England widow in George Bernard Shaw's *Devil's Disciple.*

Dudley (dud'li), **Robert.** [Title, Earl of **Leicester.**] b. June 24, 1532; d. at Cornbury, England, Sept. 4, 1588. An English courtier, politician, and general. He participated in the attempt of his father and brother to place Lady Jane Grey on the throne at the death of Edward VI in 1553, and was in consequence sentenced to death on the charge of treason in 1554, but was pardoned later in the same year. On the accession in 1558 of Elizabeth, whose affections he had gained during the ascendancy of his father at the court of Edward VI, he became her chief favorite, and intrigued, though unsuccessfully, to obtain the consent of the great nobles to a marriage, in the interest of which project he was said to have procured the murder of his wife Lady Amy (Amy Robsart) in 1560. He was created Earl of Leicester in 1564, presumably in order to facilitate his marriage to Mary, Queen of Scots, but she

married Lord Darnley in 1565 and the projected scheme came to nothing. In 1575 he entertained Queen Elizabeth with great magnificence at Kenilworth, which had been given to him by Elizabeth some years earlier. In 1576 Walter Devereux, 1st Earl of Essex, died in Ireland, according to rumor poisoned at Leicester's instigation, and in 1578 Leicester married Lettice (born Lettice Knollys), Essex's widow. This marriage, unlike an earlier liaison with Lady Douglas Sheffield, came to Elizabeth's notice; her displeasure almost resulted in his going to the Tower. In 1585 he was appointed to the command of the English army sent to the aid of the States-General against the Spaniards. He was made governor of the provinces in revolt; this, however, exceeded the authority granted him by Elizabeth and he was forced to apologize to her. After a defeat at Sluys and as a result of disagreements with the States-General, he was recalled in 1587. He was, however, restored to favor on his return, and in 1588 was appointed lieutenant and captain general of the queen's armies and companies to resist the expected Spanish invasion. He died suddenly soon after the routing of the Spanish Armada. Leicester was a patron of the arts and especially of the drama; the Earl of Leicester's company of players were licensed by the queen to play at London in 1574; this was the company that later included the Burbages and Shakespeare and for which the first London theater, the Theatre, was built in 1576.

Dudone (dö.dō'nā). [English, **Dudon.**] A knight in Ariosto's *Orlando Furioso.*

Dudu (dö.dö'). In Byron's *Don Juan*, a pensive beauty of 17.

Duellist, The. A comedy by William Kenrick, produced in 1773. Three editions were printed in the same year.

Duellists, The. A play by Douglas Jerrold, written in 1818. It was rechristened *More Frightened than Hurt*, was played at the Sadler's Wells Theatre (April 30, 1821), was afterward translated into French, played in Paris, retranslated by Kenney, and played at the Olympic as *Fighting by Proxy.*

Duenna (dū.en'a̧), **The.** A comedy interspersed with songs, a musical mélange, though sometimes called an opera, by Richard Brinsley Sheridan, produced in 1775. Various sources seem to have been used for the plot, including Wycherley's comedy *The Country Wife*, Molière's *Le Sicilien*, and Susannah Centlivre's *A Wonder*. Linley, Sheridan's father-in-law, wrote the music for the songs. It was acted 75 times in one season.

Duessa (dū.es'a̧). A loathsome old woman, in Spenser's *Faerie Queene*, who under the guise of Fidessa, a young and beautiful woman, typifies the falsehood and treachery of the Church of Rome. She also represents Mary, Queen of Scots, as the type of Catholic hostility to Elizabeth. She deceives and nearly ruins the Red Cross Knight; but all her ignominy and loathsomeness are laid bare by Arthur, who is sent by Una to the rescue. She is taken from Ariosto's *Alcina*, and the scene where the "false Duessa" is stripped of her disguise is literally translated from the *Orlando Furioso.*

Duff (duf). See **Blathers and Duff.**

---

fat, fāte, fär, àsk, fâre; net, mē, hér; pin, pīne; not, nōte, mȯve, nôr; up, lūte, pu̇ll; ₮ʜ, then;

Dufferin (duf'ẽr.in), Countess of. A title of **Sheridan, Lady Helen Selina.**

Duffy (duf'i), Sir **Charles Gavan.** b. at Monaghan, Ireland, April 12, 1816; d. at Nice, France, Feb. 9, 1903. An Irish journalist, historian, editor, and poet, political leader in Ireland and Australia. He began his career as a journalist at 17, writing for the *Northern Herald* and the *Vindicator,* Belfast papers, and for the Dublin *Morning Register,* and later was one of the founders (1842), with John Dillon and Thomas Davis, of the *Nation,* a Dublin weekly which became the organ of the Young Ireland party. He was one of the leaders of the movement to popularize Irish letters; he published the series "The Library of Ireland," shilling books of Irish poetry and the like; in 1891 he was chosen first president of the Irish Literary Society. He was associated politically with Daniel O'Connell but broke with O'Connell over the latter's moderation. After serving in Parliament (1852–55) for New Ross and failing in his aim to gain some unity on the land problem, he left Ireland for Australia, where he was elected to the Victoria parliament. He was minister of land and works (1857, 1862), prime minister of Victoria (1871–73), and speaker of the house (1877–80). He returned to Europe in 1880, spending the rest of his life in southern France. He was the author of *Young Ireland* (1880–83), *A Bird's-Eye View of Irish History* (1882), *The League of North and South: An Episode in Irish History* (1886), *Thomas Davis: An Irish Patriot* (1890), *A Fair Constitution for Ireland* and *Conversations With Carlyle* (both 1892), *Revival of Irish Literature* (1894), and *Short Life of Thomas Davis* (1895), *My Life in Two Hemispheres* (1898), autobiography, and *Lays of the Red Branch* (1901). He edited the anthology *The Ballad Poetry of Ireland* (1845).

Dufoy (dū.foi'). An impertinent French servant in Etherege's comedy *The Comical Revenge, or Love in a Tub.* He is the subject of the comical revenge, being fastened in a wooden tub with holes for the head and arms by some women, as a punishment for his boasting and railing against their sex.

du Fresne or **Dufresne** (dü.fren), **Charles.** See **Du Cange** or **Ducange,** Sieur.

Dugald Dalgetty (dū'gạld dal.get'i), **Captain.** See **Dalgetty, Captain Dugald.**

Dugdale (dug'dāl), Sir **William.** b. at Shustoke, Warwickshire, England, Sept. 12, 1605; d. there, Feb. 10, 1686. An English antiquary. He wrote *Monasticon Anglicanum* (1655–73), *Antiquities of Warwickshire* (1656), *History of St. Paul's Cathedral* (1658), *Baronage of England* (1675–76), and others.

Dujardin (dü.zhȧr.dan), **Édouard Émile Louis.** b. at St.-Gervais, France, Nov. 10, 1861—. A French poet, dramatist, and critic. He is the author of various studies of Mallarmé, Laforgue, James Joyce, and others. His novel *Les Lauriers sont coupés* (1887) is sometimes regarded as the earliest example of the stream-of-consciousness technique in fiction.

Dujon (dü.zhôn), **François.** See **Junius, Franziskus.**

Duke, the Iron. Epithet of the 1st Duke of **Wellington.**

Duke Humphrey's Walk (hum'friz). See **Paul's Walk.**

Duke Jones (jōnz). A novel by Ethel Sidgwick, published in 1914. It is a sequel to her novel *A Lady of Leisure* (1914).

Duke of Brachiano (brä.chẹ.ä'nō). See **Brachiano, Duke of.**

Duke of Exeter's Daughter (ek'sẹ.tẽrz). A name given to the rack which the Duke of Exeter introduced as an engine of torture in the Tower of London in 1447.

Duke of Guise (gēz), **The.** A tragedy by John Dryden and Nathaniel Lee, published in 1682. It was an attack on court corruption and raised some political controversy, since it was taken to be directed particularly at Shaftesbury and Monmouth. In *The Vindication,* by Dryden alone, he did what he could to excuse himself.

Duke of Milan (mi.lan'), **The.** A tragedy by Philip Massinger, produced in 1623. It is a variation of the theme of Shakespeare's *Othello.* The duke is a passionate, weak man, without Othello's noble traits.

Dukes (dūks), **Ashley.** b. at Bridgewater, Somersetshire, England, May 29, 1885—. An English dramatist and theater manager. He has been drama critic (1900–14, 1919–25) on various publications, director (1933 *et seq.*) of the Mercury Theatre, and supervisor (1945 *et seq.*) of theatrical productions in the British zone of Germany. His plays include *The Man with a Load of Mischief* (1924), *One More River* (1927), and *Matchmaker's Arms* (1930), and he has translated or adapted *Jew Süss* (1929), *The Dumb Wife of Cheapside* (1929) from Rabelais, and *Mandragola* (1939) from Macchiavelli; author also of *Modern Dramatists* (1911), *The Youngest Drama* (1923), and *Drama* (1926).

Duke Sebastian (sẹ.bas'chạn). The central character in *The Edwardians* (1930), a novel of English life and character in the period of Edward VII, by V. Sackville-West.

Duke Senior. In Shakespeare's *As You Like It,* the father of Rosalind. As his name suggests, he was "the elder duke," and he has no more specific name in the play. He is driven into exile by his brother, Frederick, but is eventually restored when Frederick repents.

Duke's Mistress, The. A play by James Shirley, produced in 1636.

Duke's Theatre. See **Dorset Garden Theatre.**

Dulcinea del Toboso (dul.sin'ẹ.ạ del tō.bō'zō; Spanish, döl.thē.nä'ä del tō.ßō'sō). A lady beloved by Don Quixote in Cervantes's romance. Her real name was Aldonza Lorenzo, but Don Quixote was of the opinion that Dulcinea was more uncommon and romantic (from the Spanish *dulce,* meaning "sweet"); and, as she was born at Toboso, he made her a great lady on the spot with the *del.*

Dull (dul). In Shakespeare's *Love's Labour's Lost,* a constable who (at Armado's suit) arrests Costard for breaking the King's decree and wooing Jaquenetta.

Dumain (dū.mān'). In Shakespeare's *Love's Labour's Lost,* one of the three French lords attending the King of Navarre at his rural academy. He falls in love with Katherine. His song to her, "On a day—alack the day!' appears also in *The Passionate Pilgrim.*

Dumas (dü.mà; Anglicized, dö′mä, dö.mä′), **Alexandre.** [Called **Dumas père** (per).] b. at Villers-Cotterets, Aisne, France, July 24, 1802; d. in his son's home, at Puys, near Dieppe, France, Dec. 5, 1870. A French novelist and dramatist. His full name, now never used, is Alexandre Dumas-Davy de la Pailleterie. He is generally called Dumas père in order to distinguish him from his son, Dumas fils. Dumas was educated by a priest and became a clerk in the office of a local lawyer, later working as a law clerk at Crépy. In 1822 or 1823 he went to Paris, where he met the great French actor Talma, and where, through the aid of General Foy, he was taken into the service of the duke of Orléans. At about this time he began to write dramatic pieces with his Swedish friend Adolphe de Leuven. In 1823 he began an affair with Marie Catherine Labay, a French dressmaker, by whom he had a son, Alexandre, who was to become almost as famous as himself. In 1825 he wrote an *Elegy on the Death of General Foy.* He made his first success as a romantic dramatist with *Henry III and His Court,* which was produced at the Comédie Française on Feb. 11, 1829. It won him the friendship of Hugo, whose *Hernani* was hailed as a triumph of romanticism a year later, of de Vigny, and a promotion from the duke of Orléans, who made him librarian of the Palais Royal. At the Odéon in March, 1830, he duplicated the success of *Henry III* with *Christine,* a poetic play in five acts, with a prologue and an epilogue. The year 1831 saw the production of three more plays, *Napoleon Bonaparte* (at the Odéon on Jan. 10), *Antony* (at the Porte St.-Martin, May 3), a psychological drama whose Byronic hero is largely a self-portrait, and, at the same theater, *Richard Darlington* (Dec. 10), suggested by Scott's *Chronicles of the Canongate.* It is also the year in which Dumas admitted his paternity and acknowledged his son. In 1832 Dumas left Paris for political reasons. In 1840 he married Ida Ferrier, an actress; however, they did not live long together, the wife going to Italy shortly after the marriage. In February, 1847, he opened his own theater, the Historique, which he had founded for the production of his own plays, with a dramatization of his novel *Queen Margot.* In 1851 he was at Brussels, and in 1853, back at Paris, he was publishing *Le Mousquetaire,* a daily newspaper devoted to art and literature. Written almost entirely by Dumas, it contained his *Memoirs,* and lasted until 1857, when it became a weekly, the *Monte-Cristo,* that lived for three years. In 1858 he was in Russia, and in 1860 in Sicily with Garibaldi. He lived at Naples for four years and then returned to Paris. In 1868 his daughter, Madame Petel, came to live with and take care of him. Dumas was a terrific worker and he turned out a staggering amount of work, so much that it was not physically possible for all of it to be the product of one man working alone. He was aided by a group of authors, who gathered material for him under his direction, wrote it up according to his own plans, given to them in outline form, and he then supervised their work, revised it, and largely rewrote it in its final form. It is also be-

lieved that some novels bearing his name on the title page are the work of other hands. Dumas's novels are: *The Chevalier d'Harmenthal* and its sequel, *The Regent's Daughter* (1843, 1845), dealing with France in 1718–19, and Louis XV, Cardinal d'Alberoni, the duke of Orléans (the regent), and his daughter, Mademoiselle de Chartres, among the leading characters; *Ascanio* (1844), dealing with Paris and Fontainebleau in 1540, with Cellini and Francis I dominating the story. One of his best-known and most popular works is *The Count of Monte Cristo* (1844–45), the story of a brave sailor, Edmond Dantes, and of his friends and enemies. A period of 40 years (1625–65) is covered in the trilogy *The Three Musketeers, Twenty Years After,* and *The Vicomte de Bragelonne* (1844, 1845, 1848–50, the last in 26 vols.); 18th-century France, in the period 1770–93, is covered in a series of five romances, *Memoirs of a Physician* (1846–48), *The Queen's Necklace* dealing with one of the most famous affairs in French history, *The Taking of the Bastille* (1852, *Ange Pitou* in French), *The Countess of Charny* (1853–55, in 19 vols.), and *Le Chevalier de Maison Rouge* (1846). Some of the characters who walk through the pages of this quintet are Louis XV, du Barry, Swedenborg, John Paul Jones, Voltaire, Rousseau, Diderot, Louis XVI, Marie Antoinette, Lafayette, Mesmer, Robespierre, Marat, Madame de Staël, Rouget de Lisle, Thomas Paine, Guillotin (of the beheading machine), Napoleon, as a second lieutenant, Necker, Cagliostro, and Danton. *Marguerite de Valois* (1845) begins with the Saint Bartholomew Massacre and ends with the death of Charles IX and the crowning of Henry III. *Agénor de Mauleon* (1846) is a picture of Spain and France in the second half of the 14th century, with Don Pedro (called "the Cruel," king of Castile and León), Queen Blanche, Charles V of France, Edward, the Black Prince, and Pope Urban V as characters. *Chicot the Jester* (1846, *La Dame de Monsoreau*) and *The Forty Five Guardsmen* (1848, also *The Forty Five, Les Quarante-cinq* in French) are connected stories dealing with Henry III, Catherine de Médicis, Henry of Navarre, and Cardinal de Lorraine. *The Black Tulip* (1850), set in 17th-century Holland, tells the story of the horrible murder of the de Witt brothers, John and Cornelius. *Olympe de Clèves* (1852) is a picture of court life in the 18th century and the story of a beautiful actress. *The Companions of Jehu* (1857) shows us Napoleon as first consul, Josephine, his brothers Lucien and Joseph, Fouché, and the Chouan leader Georges Cadoudal. *The She-Wolves of Machecoul* (1859) has a 19th-century setting, the time being the period 1832–43, the theme the attempted Vendean rebellion of the duchess of Berry, and some of the characters Louis XVIII, Louis Philippe, and La Rochejacquelein. *The Neapolitan Lovers* and *Love and Liberty* (both 1864) deal with Naples and Sicily in 1798–99, and center around the career of Luisa San Felice, heroine of the Neapolitan Revolution. Nelson, King Ferdinand, Cardinal Ruffo, Sir William Hamilton, and his wife and Nelson's mistress Emma Hamilton are some of the historical characters. *The Whites and the Blues* (1868), with France at the end of the 18th century, shows us Napoleon, Madame de Staël, Madame Recamier, Constant, Talleyrand, Fouché, Murat, and Junot.

The Two Dianas (1846–47) deals with France in the reigns of Henry II and Francis II, whose death-bed scene is described. Other characters are Diane de Poitiers, Catherine de Médicis, Mary Stuart (Mary, Queen of Scots), Marguerite de Valois, Queen Mary of England, Charles IX, and Philip II of Spain. Its sequel is *The Page of the Duke of Savoy* (1855), in which many of the same characters appear, as well as the duke of Guise, Coligny, Cardinal de Lorraine, and Cardinal Pole. Among those who are known to have helped Dumas, in lesser or greater degree, are Auguste Maquet, Paul Lacroix (who had many pseudonyms), Paul Bocage, J. P. Mallefille, and Pier Angelo Fiorentino, who, with Maquet, assisted him in writing *Monte Cristo*. All of *The Two Dianas* is believed to be the work of François Paul Meurice, although his name is not on the title page. In addition to his novelistic output, huge even with all allowances made for as much aid as he may have received, Dumas wrote *Louis XIV and his Century* (4 vols., 1845) and his interesting *Memoirs* (20 vols., 1852–54). His complete works were published at Paris (1860–64) in 277 volumes. Two English authors who knew how to tell a story, Thackeray and Stevenson, were Dumas enthusiasts and found reading his romances a pleasure that was not spoiled by repetition.

Dumas, Alexandre. [Called **Dumas fils** (fēs).] b. at Paris, July 27, 1824; d. there, Nov. 27, 1895. A French dramatist, novelist, social reformer, and member of the French Academy, to which he was elected on Jan. 30, 1874; son of Alexandre Dumas (1802–70). He is usually referred to as Dumas fils to distinguish him from his father. The little formal schooling he had was made unhappy by the cruel insults and the callous jokes of his school fellows about his illegitimate birth, and, as his later writings show, it left wounds that never healed. As a poet he wrote *La Chronique* (1842) and *Péchés de jeunesse* (1847), and as an essayist, *Tue-la, Monsieur Alphonse* (1874), *La Question du divorce* (1880), and *La Recherche de la paternité* (1883), but it is not as a poet or a writer of essays on moral topics that he is remembered. Like his father, he wrote plays and novels, but, unlike his father, he is remembered chiefly for one play, *La Dame aux camélias*, whereas the name of the elder Dumas calls to mind half a dozen novels. His dramas include *Le Demi-Monde* (1855), a comedy of manners, *La Question d'argent* (1857), a "stock exchange" play, as its title suggests, *Le Fils naturel* (1858), and *Le Pére prodigue* (1859), the very names of which are suggestive, one referring to his own condition, and the other to his father's mode of life. *L'Ami des femmes* (1864), *Une Visite de noces*, and *La Princesse Georges* (both 1871) are problem plays. He again uses the stage as a platform for the discussion of social and moral issues in *Les Idées de Madame Aubray* (1867), in which he develops the thesis that the seducer is morally bound to marry his victim, in *La Femme de Claude* (1873), which defends the right of the husband to slay a wife who has violated her marriage vows, and in *L'Étrangère* (1876), in which the husband is the wrongdoer. With six of the leading French actors (Coquelin, Got, and Mounet-Sully, Sarah Bernhardt, Sophie Croizette, and Madeleine Brohan) in the latter

play, its success was assured. Other plays that came from his pen are *La Princesse de Bagdad* (1881), *Denise* (1885), and *Francillon* (1887). As a patriotic Frenchman, alive to the suffering and the weakness of his country, he wrote *Nouvelle lettre de Junius* (1870) and two *Lettres sur les choses du jour* (1872). His novels are *Césarine* (1848), *Le Docteur Servan, Antonine,* and *Tristan le Roux* (all 1849), *Henri de Navarre* and *Trois hommes forts* (both 1850), *L'Affaire Clémenceau, mémoire de l'accusé* (1866), in which he anticipates the thesis of *La Femme de Claude* and also that of a prose pamphlet, *L'Homme-Femme* (1872). His most famous work, *La Dame aux camélias,* is both a novel (1848) and a play (1849, but not produced, because of censorship regulations, until 1852). It is a sentimental but moving portrait of a Paris courtesan, Marguerite Gautier, who has had many love affairs but has never known love until she meets Armand Duval. At his father's request she gives him up, in order to "save" him and his career. When the father realizes his mistake, it is too late. Marguerite dies, happy in the knowledge that Armand is at her side and happy in his love. Camille, as the heroine is called from her extreme fondness for the flower (the play is usually called *Camille* in English translation), is one of a long line, if not the first, of long-suffering ladies who are victims of consumption, a condition that has romantic possibilities that the romantic writer has not neglected. Marguerite was based on a well-known Parisian woman, known to Dumas, and it is believed that she was his mistress. The Italian actress Eleonora Duse was the first to play the role, which has since been played by many English, American, and European artists, on the stage, the screen, and the air. The appeal of the play, of the heroine's story as Dumas tells it (in both forms), and of her character, has been discussed by critics and students of art and human nature in an attempt to discover the secret of the success of what is, after all, a rather conventional story. Dumas's interest in and extreme preoccupation with questions of morality and ethics has been considered strange in view of his own background and that of his father, but, from the psychological viewpoint, it is probably that very background, a personal matter with him, that accounts for and explains the interest.

Du Maurier (dụ môr′i.ạ), **Daphne.** [Title, Lady Browning.] b. at London, May 13, 1907—. An English novelist and biographer; second daughter of Sir Gerald Du Maurier. She married (1932) Lieutenant General Sir F. A. M. Browning of the Grenadier Guards. She is the author of a biography of her father, *Gerald, a Portrait* (1934), and of *The Du Mauriers* (1937). Her novels include *The Loving Spirit* (1931), *Jamaica Inn* (1936), *Rebecca* (1938), *Frenchman's Creek* (1941), *Hungry Hill* (1943), *The King's General* (1946), *The Parasites* (1950), *My Cousin Rachel* (1952), and *Kiss Me Again, Stranger* (1953).

Du Maurier, George Louis Palmella Busson. b. at Paris, March 6, 1834; d. at London, Oct. 8, 1896. An English artist and novelist. He was educated at Paris, and went to England at the age of 17, studying later at Paris with Gleyre. He was noted for his illustrations in *Punch* and other periodicals. He wrote and illustrated *Peter Ibbetsen* (1892), *Trilby* (1894), and *The Martian* (1897). The hypnotist Svengali in *Trilby* is his most famous character.

Du Maurier, Sir **Gerald.** b. March 26, 1873; d. at London, April 11, 1934. An English actor-manager; son of George Louis Palmella Busson Du Maurier, and father of Daphne Du Maurier. He made his debut (1894) in *An Old Jew*, and toured with Forbes-Robertson and later with Beerbohm Tree. He was well known as a philanthropist. He performed in *Trilby, The Seats of the Mighty,* and *Escape*, and was particularly noted for his roles as a gentleman crook, playing Raffles in the mystery of that name (1906), and later in *Arsène Lupin* and *Alias Jimmy Valentine*.

Dumbarton Castle (dum.bär′tọn). A celebrated fortress overhanging the river Clyde in Scotland.

Dumbiedikes (dum′bi.dīks). An awkward Scottish laird in Sir Walter Scott's novel *The Heart of Midlothian.* He wants to marry Jeanie Deans, but on being refused promptly marries another.

"Dumb Ox." A nickname of fellow students for **Aquinas,** Saint **Thomas.**

dumb show. A part of a dramatic representation shown pantomimically, chiefly for the sake of exhibiting more of the story than could be otherwise included, but sometimes merely emblematical. Dumb shows were very common in the earlier English dramas.

Groundlings who, for the most part, are capable of nothing but inexplicable dumb shows and noise.
(Shak., *Hamlet,* III.ii.)

The Julian feast is to-day, the country expects me; I speak all the dum-shows: my sister chosen for a nymph.
(Fletcher and Rowley, *Maid in the Mill,* II.i.)

Dunbar (dun.bär′), **Agnes.** [Title: Countess of **Dunbar and March;** called **"Black Agnes."**] b. c1312; d. 1369. Scottish heroine, noted for her successful defense of Dunbar Castle in 1337–38. She was given the epithet "Black Agnes" because of her dark skin.

Dunbar, William. b. probably in East Lothian, Scotland, c1460; d. c1525. A Scottish poet. He was a Franciscan who did diplomatic service in France for James IV of Scotland and was afterward attached to the court as laureate. He is one of the Scottish Chaucerian school. His works include *The Thrissil and the Rois* (The Thistle and the Rose, 1503), a prothalamium in honor of James IV and Margaret Tudor; *The Golden Targe,* a dream allegory on beauty and love; *Dance of the Seven Deadly Sins, Merle and Nightingale, The Two Mariit Wemen and the Wedo,* a lusty discourse that outdoes Chaucer's wife of Bath; and *Lament for the Makaris,* an elegy on the poets (makers) who preceded him.

Duncan (dung′kạn). A king of Scotland. He succeeded to the throne c1034 on the death of his grandfather Malcolm II, and was assassinated near Elgin in 1040 or 1039. In Shakespeare's *Macbeth,* he is a gracious, kindly old man, murdered by Macbeth, who looks in horror at the "silver skin laced with golden blood" of the corpse, and likens the result of his monstrous deed to "a breach in nature."

Duncan Gray (grā′). A poem (1792) by Robert Burns, telling of the wooing of Maggie by Duncan, of her stand-offishness, and finally of the happy uniting of the two.

Dunciad (dun′si.ad), **The.** A satirical poem (1728–42; published in four books, 1743) by Alexander Pope, directed against various contemporary writers. The goddess of dullness elects Lewis Theobald poet laureate of that realm. Owing to a quarrel between Colley Cibber and Pope, the latter substituted Cibber for Theobald in the fourth part, published in 1742. The bestowal of the laureateship on Cibber may have added to Pope's venom. The version published in 1728 is considered by some critics to have been greatly influenced by Swift. The 1742 publication saw the addition of the fourth book, and the entire work was then published as *The New Dunciad.*

Dundee (dun.dē′), 1st Viscount. See **Graham, John.**

Dundreary (dun.drir′i), **Lord.** An indolent, foolish, and amusing Englishman in Tom Taylor's comedy *Our American Cousin.* To this part originally only 47 lines were given; but E. A. Sothern, to whom it was assigned, introduced various extravagances to suit himself. He became famous in it, and the whole play hinged on it. The side-whiskers called Dundrearies are named for the character.

Dundrennan Abbey (dun.dren′ạn). A ruined monastery (built 1140) near Kirkcudbright, Scotland.

Dunkerley (dung′kėr.li), **William Arthur.** See **Oxenham, John.**

Dunkerque (dun′kėrk; French, dėṅ.kerk). [Former French spelling, **Dunquerque;** English, **Dunkirk;** German, **Dünkirchen;** Eng. trans., *"Church on the Dunes."*] A town in N France, in the department of Nord, situated on the Strait of Dover, at the junction of a number of canals, near the border of Belgium. It is the fourth largest port in France. Dunkerque belonged originally to the counts of Flanders, and the population still retains a Flemish dialect along with French. The town was often besieged, belonging successively to England, Burgundy, Spain, and France. It fell again to England in 1658, but was sold to France by Charles II in 1662. It was fortified by Vauban. Among its naval heroes was Jean Bart. The British besieged it unsuccessfully in 1793. It suffered bombardment in World War I. At the beginning of World War II, it saw the spectacular evacuation (May 28–June 4, 1940) of more than 330,000 British, Belgian, and French soldiers. Later in World War II it was subjected to damaging air bombardments, in the course of which a large part of the town, including the Church of Saint Eloi, was destroyed.

Dunlop (dun′lop, dun.lop′), **John Colin.** b. in Scotland, 1785; d. there, 1842. A Scottish author and critic. He published *History of Fiction* (1814), adversely criticized by Hazlitt in the *Edinburgh Review; History of Roman Literature, from the Earliest Period to the Augustan Age* (1823–28), *Memoirs of Spain during the Reigns of Philip IV and Charles II* (1834), and *Selections from the Latin Anthology. Translated into English Verse* (1838).

Dunmow Flitch (dun′mō). A flitch of bacon awarded to any married pair who could take oath at the end of the first year and a day of their married life that there had not only been no jar or quarrel, but that neither had ever wished the knot untied. The custom, it is said, was originated in the priory of Little Dunmow, England, by Robert Fitzwalter, in 1244. The first recorded presentation of the bacon is dated 1445 (Chartulary of Dunmow Priory). Similar customs exist elsewhere, in England, Brittany, and other parts of Europe.

Dunnottar Castle (du.not′ạr). A ruined castle, dating from 1392, in Kincardineshire, Scotland.

Dunois (dü.nwà), **Jean.** See under **Bastard of Orleans.**

Dunrobin Castle (dun.rob′in). The seat of the Duke of Sutherland, near Golspie, Scotland, incorporating remains of an 11th-century stronghold.

Dunsany (dun.sā′ni), Lord. [Full name, **Edward John Moreton Drax Plunkett**; title, 18th Baron Dunsany.] b. July 24, 1878—. An Irish poet and dramatist; nephew of Sir Horace Curzon Plunkett (1854–1932). As a member of the Coldstream Guards, he served in the Boer War and in World War I. He was Byron professor of English literature at Athens University, Greece. His many poems and tales include *The Gods of Pegana* (1905), *Evil Kettle* (1926), *Fifty Poems* (1929), *Travel Tales of Mr. Jorkens* (1931), *My Talks With Dean Spanley* (1936), *Patches of Sunlight* (1938), *Mirage Water* (1938), and *Rory and Bran.* He achieved early acclaim as a dramatist with *Glittering Gates* (produced 1909 by W. B. Yeats at the Abbey Theatre, Dublin); among his other plays are *The Gods of the Mountain* (1911), *A Night at an Inn* (1916), *If* (1921), *Cheezo, The Laughter of the Gods,* and *Lord Adrian* (1933). Dunsany's stories and plays are fantasies dealing with the supernatural and supernatural beings; his style is simple yet deals in the paradoxes of human existence.

Duns Scotus (dunz skō′tus), **John.** [Called **Doctor Subtilis.**] b. at Duns, Scotland, c1265; d. at Cologne, Germany, Nov. 8, 1308. A scholastic theologian, one of the most influential in the history of medieval Europe. He was the founder of the scholastic system called Scotism, which long contended for supremacy among the schoolmen with the system called Thomism, founded by Thomas Aquinas. Nothing is known with certainty concerning his personal history. According to the commonly accepted tradition, he was born c1265 at Duns (or Dunse), Berwickshire, Scotland (hence his surname Scotus, or Scot), was a fellow of Merton College, Oxford, became a Franciscan friar, was chosen professor of theology at Oxford in 1301, removed in 1304 to Paris, where, in a disputation on the Immaculate Conception of Jesus Christ by the Virgin Mary he displayed so much ingenuity and resource as to win the title of Doctor Subtilis, and where he rose to the position of regent of the university. He died at Cologne, Germany, on Nov. 8, 1308, while on a mission in the interest of his order. His name, Duns, Dunse, or Dunce, came to be used as a common appellative, meaning "a very learned man," and, being applied satirically to ignorant and stupid persons as being as sensible as the extreme scholastics, gave rise to "dunce" in its present sense. Scotism, the movement he founded, was an extreme form of realism and anti-intellec-

tualism. Instead of the middle of the road between faith and reason sought by Saint Thomas Aquinas, Duns Scotus restricted the sphere of rational thought, thus eventually driving the wedge between philosophy and religion that emancipated the philosophers from strict adherence to religious subjects, an effect opposite to the one Scotus attempted to achieve. The argument concerning the Immaculate Conception found the Thomists on one side and the Scotist Dominicans on the other; the latter were joined by the Franciscans, the Jesuits, and the Sorbonne theologians; the feud was dissolved with the publication (in 1854, after five and one half centuries of argument) of the papal bull *Ineffabilis Deus* of Pope Pius IX. Scotus held that true knowledge could be reached only through revelation from God. As a corollary to this, he held that the existence of God was essentially unprovable (it must be presupposed) and that God's nature was incomprehensible to man.

Dunstan (dun′stạn), Saint. b. near Glastonbury, England, 924 or 925 A.D.; d. at Canterbury, England, May 19, 988 A.D. An archbishop of Canterbury. He was the son of Heorstan, a West Saxon noble, and was brought up at the abbey of Glastonbury and at the court of Ethelstan, but was accused of an interest in black magic, fell from royal favor, and fled to Winchester. In large part, responsibility for persuading him to take monastic vows is considered to have rested with the bishop at that church and scholarly center. He is most directly linked to the body of English literature not by any writings of his own, but by a folk legend that came into existence long after his death and is alluded to by various Elizabethan and later writers. The story, which every schoolboy has heard, is that Dunstan, confronted by the Devil in the guise of a beautiful and amorous woman, grabbed his tempter's nose with a pair of glowing fire-tongs and thus put him to rout. He was appointed abbot of Glastonbury by Edmund not later than 945. He became the chief adviser of Edred (reigned 946–955), but was banished by Edred's successor, the young king Edwig (955–959), whose ill will he incurred by refusing to consent to a marriage upon which the young king had set his heart, and by rudely bringing him back to the banqueting hall when, at his coronation, he left it for the society of the lady of his choice. Dunstan went to Flanders. He was recalled by Edwig's successor, Edgar (reigned 959–975), by whom he was created archbishop of Canterbury in 959 and restored to political power. He retained his influence at court during the reign of Edward (975–978), but appears to have lost it on the accession of Ethelred II (Ethelred the Unready) in 978. He fostered the strict Benedictine rule and the revival of learning in England early in the 10th century. His feast day is May 19.

Dunton (dun′tọn), **John.** b. at Graffham, Huntingdonshire, England, May 4, 1659; d. 1733. An English bookseller and author. In 1694 Dunton printed *The Ladies Dictionary* described as "a *Compleat Directory* to the *Female-Sex* in all *Relations, Companies, Conditions,* and *States* of Life." He wrote *Life and Errors of John Dunton* (1705), and *Letters from New England* (published in 1867).

ḍ, d or j; ṣ, s or sh; ṭ, t or ch; ẓ, z or zh; o, F. cloche; ü, F. menu; ċh, Sc. loch; ṅ, F. bonbon.

Dunwoody (dun′wŭd.i), **Robert.** The central character in *The Wayward Man* (1927), a novel by St. John Ervine.

Dupe (dūp), **Lady.** An old lady in Dryden's comedy *Sir Martin Mar-all.*

Durandarte (dö.rän.där′tä). A legendary Spanish hero whose exploits are related in old Spanish ballads and in *Don Quixote.* He was the cousin of Montesinos, and was killed at the battle of Roncesvalles. One of the ballads, a fragment, can be traced to the *Cancionero* of 1511, and one, *Durandarte, Durandarte,* to the old *Cancioneros Generales.*

Durazzo (dö.rät′sō). A facetious and lively old man in Philip Massinger's play *The Guardian.* He is the guardian of Caldoro.

Durden (dėr′den), **Dame.** A notable housewife in a famous English song; hence the nickname given by Mr. Jarndyce to the careful and conscientious Esther Summerson in Charles Dickens's *Bleak House.*

Durdles (dėr′dlz), **Stony.** "A stone-mason, chiefly in the gravestone, tomb, and monument way, and wholly of their color from head to foot," in Charles Dickens's *Mystery of Edwin Drood.* He is usually drunk, and has wonderful adventures in the crypt of the cathedral.

Dürer (dü′rėr), **Albrecht.** b. at Nuremberg, Germany, May 21, 1471; d. there, April 6, 1528. A German painter, draftsman, and engraver, of Hungarian descent. The son of an able goldsmith, he learned that craft before entering the studio of the painter Michel Wohlgemut in 1486. Later he studied with Martin Schongauer at Colmar, and visited Venice, studying with most interest the works of Mantegna and Bellini, before setting up his own studio at Nuremberg in 1497. His principal achievements at this time were in the field of portraiture. In 1505 he went to Venice again, and stayed two years. Back at Nuremberg, his period (1505–20) of greatest activity ensued, during which especially he brought to superbly powerful perfection his drawings, copper engravings, and woodcuts. Nuremberg at that time was a center of intellectual activity; Humanism and Protestantism were in the air. Dürer, though he was patronized by, and painted the portraits of, the emperors Maximilian I and Charles V, was also a friend of Luther and Melancthon. It is believed, however, that he remained a Catholic, and the Christian tradition certainly gave him by far the greater number of his subjects, as shown by his numerous paintings, engravings, and woodcuts deriving from the stories of the Fall, the Nativity, the Flight into Egypt, the Passion, and the lives of the early Christian saints and martyrs. Although it was said by some Italian painters that if he had been an Italian, Dürer would have been the greatest of Italian artists, his work in all media is almost wholly Gothic in derivation, markedly different from the pictures of the Italian High Renaissance. His portraits of this period are solid, shrewd, uncompromisingly realistic; his copperplates and woodcuts are full of energy, crowded with invention, often grim, sometimes grotesque. Contrasting with all this vehemence and exuberance are many painted landscapes and drawings of small animals or patches of grass and flowers, of a calm and touching beauty. In 1521 he visited the Netherlands; he was received with enthusiasm and respect, and he improved the opportunity to learn from the works of the Van Eycks, whose influence is evident in some of the work of his own last years, especially in the *Four Evangelists,* which some consider his masterpiece. Others give that title to his *Adoration of the Magi* at Florence. But it is perhaps a futile critical exercise to try to name as a masterpiece any particular creation of one whose work was all masterly. Dürer was not, certainly, one of the great colorists, but as a draftsman, as a portraitist, and as a designer, he is among the very greatest in the history of art. That his accomplishments were the reflection of a keen intelligence is shown by his writings on perspective and other aspects of graphic technique, and by his autobiographical writings. The most notable Dürer paintings known today are *Virgin and Child with Saints Anthony and Sebastian* and a *Crucifixion,* at Dresden; *Martyrdom of the Ten Thousand* and a *Madonna,* at Venice; *Virgin Crowned by Two Angels* and a portrait of Hieronymus Holzschuher, at Berlin; *Adoration of the Magi,* in the Uffizi at Florence; *A Young Man,* and portraits of Oswald Krell and Michel Wohlgemut, at Munich; and self-portraits at Leipzig, Madrid, and Munich. There are extensive collections of his drawings and engravings at Vienna, Berlin, London, Florence, Milan, and the Louvre at Paris.

D'Urfey (dėr′fi), **Thomas.** [Called **Tom D'Urfey.**] b. in Devonshire, England, 1653; d. at London, Feb. 26, 1723. An English dramatist and humorous poet. His songs, which appeared for the most part in his successful and (at the time) greatly admired plays, were published as *Wit and Mirth; or Pills to Purge Melancholy* (1719–20).

Durga (dör′gä). In Hindu mythology, one of the malignant forms of Devi, the wife of Shiva.

Durham (dur′am), **Constantia.** In George Meredith's novel *The Egoist,* the first fiancée of Sir Willoughby.

Durham Poem. An Old English poem, dating probably from the 12th century and preserved (in fragmentary form) in a manuscript in the Cambridge University Library. It is an example of the form called *encomium urbis* (praise of a city), used in both classical and medieval periods.

Durovernum (dū.rọ.vėr′num). Latin name of **Canterbury.**

Durward (dėr′ward), **Quentin.** A young archer of the Scottish Guard in Sir Walter Scott's novel *Quentin Durward.* After many adventures he marries Isabelle de Croye.

Duster, A Gentleman With a. Pseudonym of **Begbie, Harold.**

Dusty Answer. A novel by Rosamond Lehmann, published in 1927.

Dutch Courtezan, The. A comedy by John Marston, printed in 1605 and acted c1604 at the Blackfriars Theatre. It was revived in 1613 at Court under the name *Cockle de Moye.* Marston claimed that the play dealt with "the difference betwixt the love of a courtezan and a wife."

---

fat, fāte, fär, ȧsk, fāre; net, mē, hėr; pin, pīne; not, nōte, mȯve, nôr; up, lūte, pull; ŦH, then;

Duval (dö.val'), **Claude.** b. at Domfront, in Normandy, France, 1643; executed at Tyburn, London, Jan. 21, 1670. A French highwayman in England. His adventures as a highwayman and as a gallant form the subject of a number of novels and ballads.

Dweller of the Threshold, The. In Edward Bulwer-Lytton's novel *Zanoni*, a powerful and malignant being:

> Whose form of giant mould
> No mortal eye can fixed behold.

Dyamond (dī'a.mọnd). See **Diamond.**

Dyce (dīs), **Alexander.** b. at Edinburgh, June 30, 1798; d. at London, May 15, 1869. A British literary critic and Shakespeare scholar. He received a B.A. at Oxford in 1819, entered the ministry c1822, abandoned the clerical profession in 1825, and devoted himself to literature. He edited a number of English classics, including the works of William Collins (1827), George Peele (1828–39), John Webster (1830), Robert Greene (1831), James Shirley (1833), Thomas Middleton (1840), Beaumont and Fletcher (1843–46), and Christopher Marlowe (1850), but is chiefly known for his edition of Shakespeare (1857; revised 1866). He was one of those exposing John Payne Collier's inventions in Elizabethan literature. Dyce was a founder of the Percy Society, dedicated to publishing old poetry in English.

Dyer (dī'ẽr), Sir **Edward.** d. 1607. An English poet and courtier. He was employed in several embassies by Queen Elizabeth, by whom he was knighted in 1596. He was a friend of Raleigh and Sidney, and wrote a number of pastoral odes and madrigals. He is known chiefly as the author of a poem descriptive of contentment, beginning "My mind to me a kingdom is" (set to music in William Byrd's *Psalmes, Sonets, and Songs,* 1588).

Dyer, George. b. at London, March 15, 1755; d. there, March 2, 1841. An English scholar. He graduated at Cambridge University in 1778, and subsequently became pastor of a dissenting congregation at Cambridge. Having abandoned the clerical profession, he settled in 1792 at London, where he devoted himself to literature. His chief works are *History of the University and Colleges of Cambridge* (1814) and *Privileges of the University of Cambridge* (1824).

Dyer, John. b. at Aberglasney, Carmarthenshire, Wales, c1700; d. July 24, 1758. An English poet. He became vicar of Calthorp, Leicestershire, in 1741, and subsequently held several church posts in Lincolnshire. He published *Grongar Hill* (1726), which with James Thomson's *The Seasons* is generally recognized as the first of the romantic pastoral poems, *Ruins of Rome* (1740), and *The Fleece* (1757).

Dymoke (dim'ọk). See **Dimoch.**

Dymond (dī'mọnd), **Jonathan.** b. at Exeter, England, Dec. 19, 1796; d. May 6, 1828. An English author. He followed the occupation of a linen-draper at Essex, where in 1825 he founded an auxiliary society of the Peace Society. His chief work is *Essays on the Principles of Morality* (1829).

Dynasts, The. A poem by Thomas Hardy, published in three parts, in 1903, 1905, and 1908. This is a gigantic epic drama (130 scenes in 19 acts) dealing with the Napoleonic wars, with interspersed lyrics and philosophical comments by supernatural spirits and choruses. In spite of its formal and stylistic defects, *The Dynasts* has been acclaimed as the greatest work, at least in its conception, produced by any English poet since Milton's *Paradise Lost.*

Dysmas (diz'mas). See **Dismas.**

E

Eachard (ēch'ard), **John.** b. in Suffolk, England, c1636; d. at Cambridge, England, July 7, 1697. An English divine and satirical writer. He was chosen master of Catharine Hall, Cambridge University, in 1675, and vice-chancellor of the University in 1679 and 1695. He wrote *The Grounds and Occasions of the Contempt of the Clergy and Religion* (1670, published anonymously), and others.

Eadmer (ā'ad.mār, modernized as ed'mẽr) or **Edmer** (ed'mẽr). b. c1060; d. c1124. An English monk and historian, of Canterbury. He was elected (1120) archbishop of St. Andrews through recommendation of Alexander I, king of Scotland, but the king would not allow him to be consecrated by English primates. Eadmer wrote a chronicle of contemporary events, *Historia novorum,* covering the period c1066–1122, and a *Life of Saint Anselm,* Anselm being one of his close friends.

Eadmund (ā'ad.mùnd, modernized as ed'mund). See **Edmund.**

Eadred (ā'ad.rād, modernized as ed'rẹd). See **Edred.**

Eadwacer (ā'ad.wäk"ẽr). [Also, **Wulf and Eadwacer.**] An Old English love poem, preserved in the *Exeter Book.* A short work (19 lines) of unknown authorship, it expresses with remarkable lyric and emotional power the longing of a woman for her lover (Wulf) and, paralleling this, her rejection of her husband (Eadwacer).

Eadward (ā'ad.wärd) or **Eadweard** (ā'ad.wa.ard; both modernized as ed'ward). See **Edward.**

Eadwig (ā'ad.wē). See **Edwy.**

Eagle (ē'gl), **Solomon.** Pseudonym of **Squire, J. C.**

Eagle, Solomon. A religious fanatic in William Harrison Ainsworth's novel *Old St. Paul's.*

"eagle soars in the summit of Heaven, The." The first chorus of T. S. Eliot's long verse drama *The Rock* (1934).

Eahfrith (ā'ach.frith) or **Ealdfrith** (ā'ald-). See **Aldfrith.**

Ealdhelm (a'ald.helm). See **Aldhelm.**

Ealhwine (a'alch.wi.ne). See **Alcuin.**

ḍ, d or j; g̣, s or sh; ṭ, t or ch; z̧, z or zh; *o,* F. cloche; ü, F. menu; ċh, Sc. loch; ṅ, F. bonbon.

Earine (ē.ar′i.nē). In Ben Jonson's *The Sad Shepherd*, a beautiful shepherdess.

Earle (ėrl), **John.** b. at York, England, c1601; d. at Oxford, England, Nov. 17, 1665. An English divine, appointed bishop of Worcester in 1662, and translated to the see of Salisbury in 1663. He wrote various poems (*On the Death of Beaumont*, 1616, *Hortus Mertonensis*, written while a fellow of Merton College) and *Microcosmographie, or a Peece of the World Discovered in Essayes and Characters* (1628, published anonymously), a humorous work which enjoyed great popularity.

Earle, John. b. at Churchstow, Devonshire, England, Jan. 29, 1824; d. at Oxford, England, Jan. 31, 1903. An English scholar. He graduated at Oxford in 1845, became a fellow of Oriel College in 1848, was appointed professor of Anglo-Saxon in 1849 for five years, and was college tutor in 1852. He was presented to the rectory of Swanswick, near Bath, in 1857, and was prebend of Wanstow in Wells Cathedral in 1871 and rural dean of Bath from 1873 to 1877. He was reëlected professor of Anglo-Saxon at Oxford in 1876, the professorship having been made permanent. Among his works are *Two of the Saxon Chronicles Parallel* (1865), *The Philology of the English Tongue* (1866), *Book for the Beginner in Anglo-Saxon* (1866), *English Plant Names . . .* (1880), *Anglo-Saxon Literature* (1884), *A Hand Book to the Land Charters . . .* (1888), *English Prose . . .* (1890), and others.

Earl of Dudley's Company (dud′liz). See **Leicester's Men.**

Earl of Leicester's Men (les′tėrz). See **Leicester's Men.**

Earl of Nottingham's Company (not′ing.ạmz). See **Lord Admiral's Men.**

Earl of Toulouse (tö.löz′), **The.** A Middle English romance based on the Breton lays. It is the story of a man persecuted by the emperor of Rome, but who finally wins both justice and the hand of the emperor's widow.

Earlston (ėrlz′tọn), **Thomas of.** See **Thomas the Rhymer.**

Early English Text Society. A society founded in 1864 by F. J. Furnivall (1825–1910) and directed by him. Its object was the promotion of the study of early English. It rendered valuable service to literature in the publication of specially prepared editions of early English works.

Early History of Jacob Stahl (jā′kọb stäl′), **The.** See **History of Jacob Stahl, The Early.**

Early Hours, The. A novel by Marmaduke Pickthall, published in 1921.

Earnscliff (ėrnz′klif), **Patrick.** A Border laird in Sir Walter Scott's *The Black Dwarf*. He was Isabella Vere's lover.

Earth Breath and Other Poems, The. A volume of verse (1897) by Æ (George William Russell).

Earth Compels, The. A volume of verse (1938) by Louis MacNeice.

Earthly Paradise, The. A collection of narrative poems (1868–71) by William Morris.

Earwicker (ir′wik.ėr), **Maggie.** See under **Anna Livia Plurabelle.**

East Anglia (ang′gli.ạ). One of the Anglian kingdoms in England during the Heptarchy, corresponding to the modern counties of Norfolk and Suffolk. It formed later a part of the Danelaw, and was one of the four earldoms of Canute.

Eastcheap (ēst′chēp). Originally, the eastern market-place of London: now a small street near the northern end of London Bridge.

East Coker (kō′kėr). The second of the *Four Quartets*, by T. S. Eliot, published in 1940, in which the poet expresses the notion that the cycle of life is reduced to one action, for "in my beginning is my end." True wisdom is the wisdom of humility, and the path to salvation is the path of faith. Contemporary civilization has created a life of transiency in which we barely acquire our materials when they become outmoded:

> In order to arrive there
> To arrive where you are, to get from where
>   you are not,
> You must go by a way wherein there is
>   no ecstasy.
> In order to arrive at what you do not know
>   You must go by a way which is the way
>   of ignorance.

East End, The. A large, thickly settled part of London, generally taken to include that part lying east of the Bank of England.

Easter (ēs′tėr). A Christian festival, commemorating the resurrection of Jesus Christ: probably adapted from the Jewish Passover or Pesach (from which the common European name, Pascua or one of its variants, is derived) and taking its English name from a pagan Teutonic goddess of springtime who was celebrated in a spring festival. Easter falls on the first Sunday following the first full moon after the vernal equinox (about March 21), but many disputes about the date existed in the early days of the Church. The date of Easter affects the dates of all other movable feasts in the Christian calendar. Easter is preceded by the 40 days of Lent; the paschal season lasts 50 days, until Whitsunday. Popularly, the custom of distributing colored eggs is a feature of the festival.

Easter 1916. A poem (September, 1916) by William Butler Yeats, concerned with the Irish uprising of 1916 usually known as the Easter Rebellion. It poses the question: "Was it needless death after all?" Yeats's method of pressing this consists of asking a question, giving an answer, and quickly revealing the other side, and then beginning again. The recurring phrase "a terrible beauty is born" seems to give some resolution to the matter, because it simultaneously suggests the good and the bad, the necessary and the unnecessary.

Easter Island. [Spanish, **Isla de Pascua.**] An island in the E Pacific, ab. 2,000 mi. W of Chile: noted for its gigantic prehistoric statues. It belongs to Chile, and is administered as part of Valparaíso province.

Eastern Empire or **Eastern Roman Empire** (rō′mạn). See **Byzantine Empire.**

East India Company. The name of various mercantile associations formed in different countries in the 17th and 18th centuries for the purpose of conducting under the auspices of their governments a monopoly of the trade of their respective countries with the East Indies: **1.** The **Danish East India Company** was organized in 1618. It was dissolved in 1634, reorganized in 1670, and finally dissolved in 1729, when its possessions, the chief of which was Tranquebar on the Coromandel coast of India, were ceded to the government. **2.** The **Dutch East India Company** was formed by the union of several smaller trading companies on March 20, 1602. It received from the state a monopoly of the trade on the further side of the Strait of Magellan and of the Cape of Good Hope, including the right to make treaties and alliances in the name of the States General, to establish factories and forts, and to employ soldiers. It founded Batavia in Java on the site of a native city in 1619, and in the middle of the 17th century held the principal seats of commerce throughout the Indian archipelago, including Ceylon, Sumatra, Java, and Borneo, and had flourishing colonies in South Africa. It was dissolved and its territories transferred to the state on Sept. 12, 1795. **3.** The **British (English) East India Company**, composed originally of London merchants, was incorporated by Queen Elizabeth on Dec. 31, 1600, under the full title of "The Governor and Company of Merchants of London trading with the East Indies." It obtained from the court of Delhi, India, in 1612 the privilege of establishing a factory at Surat, which continued to be the chief British station in India until the organization of Bombay. In 1645 it received permission of the natives to erect Fort St. George at Madras. In 1661 it was invested by Charles II with authority to make peace and war with infidel powers, erect forts, acquire territory, and exercise civil and criminal jurisdiction in its settlements. In 1668 it obtained a grant of the island of Bombay, which formed part of the dower of Catharine of Portugal. In 1675 it established a factory on the Hooghly River in Bengal, which led to the foundation of Calcutta. In 1749 it inaugurated, by the expulsion of the rajah of Tanjore, a series of territorial conquests which resulted in the acquisition and organization of British India. As the result of Robert Clive's military exploits (1751 *et seq.*) the English company ousted the French almost completely in India. Clive's administration (1764–67) in Bengal helped establish British control in the peninsula on a solid basis. A government board of control was established by Parliament in 1784, the company's trade monopoly was ended in 1813, and in 1858 the company relinquished altogether its functions of government to the crown. **4.** The **French East India Company** was founded by Colbert in 1664. It established a factory at Surat, India, in August, 1675, and acquired Pondichéry, which became the capital of the French possessions on the Coromandel coast. It was dissolved on Aug. 13, 1769, when its territories were ceded to the crown. **5.** The **Swedish East India Company** was formed at Göteborg, Sweden, in 1741, and was reorganized in 1806.

Eastlake (ēst′lāk), Sir **Charles Lock.** b. at Plymouth, England, Nov. 17, 1793; d. at Pisa, Italy, Dec. 24, 1865. An English painter, critic, and designer. He lived at Rome (1817–30) and at London (1830–55), was keeper of the National Gallery (1843–47), was president of the Royal Academy

from 1850 until his death, and was knighted in 1850. Though popular in his day for paintings of religious and historical subjects, such as *Pilgrims in Sight of Rome* (1828), and of "banditti" and other Mediterranean types sketched on his travels, he was more influential in his selection of works for the National Gallery, as a critic (with several works on art, including a translation of Goethe's *Theory of Colors*, 1840), and as a designer, especially of stained glass. His emphasis, in his books and designs, was on the intrinsic decorative possibilities of the materials themselves and on the spirit rather than the exact forms of former great periods of art, especially the Gothic, which in his time was being slavishly and sentimentally copied by many architects and designers. His style, often called Eastlake Gothic, is associated with that of William Morris as part of a wholesome trend away from earlier 19th-century eclecticism.

East Lynne (lin). A novel by Ellen Wood (Mrs. Henry Wood), published in 1861. Lady Isabel Vane runs off with another man, leaving her husband and children. She later returns disguised as a nurse and cares for the children, and in the end she and her husband are reconciled. The work is now probably familiar to more people as a play than as a novel.

Eastward Ho! A comedy written chiefly by George Chapman and John Marston, with contributions by Ben Jonson. It was written and acted during the winter of 1604–05, and was entered upon the Stationers' Register on Sept. 4, 1605. The authors were imprisoned for satirizing the Scots in this play, and supposedly sentenced to have their ears and noses split, feeling at the time about the Scots being especially sensitive because the new king, James I, was a Scot. Jonson, though not responsible for the obnoxious passages, gave himself up with his friends. The play was revived in 1751 as *The Prentices*, and in 1775 as *Old City Manners*.

Easy (ē′zi), **Midshipman.** The hero of *Mr. Midshipman Easy* (1836), a sea story by Marryat.

Easy, Sir Charles. The "careless husband" in Colley Cibber's comedy of that name.

Eatanswill (ēt′an.swil). In Dickens's *Pickwick Papers*, a borough where Mr. Pickwick witnesses a parliamentary election.

Ebb and Flood. A novel by James Hanley, published in 1932.

Ebenezer Scrooge (skrö̈j). See **Scrooge, Ebenezer.**

Ebionites (ē′bi.on.īts). A party of Judaizing Christians which appeared in the Church as early as the 2nd century A.D., and disappeared about the 4th century. They agreed in the recognition of Jesus as the Messiah, the denial of his divinity, belief in the universal obligation of the Mosaic law, and rejection of Paul and his writings. The two great divisions of Ebionites were the Pharisaic Ebionites, who emphasized the obligation of the Mosaic law, and the Essenic Ebionites, who were more speculative and leaned toward Gnosticism.

Eblana (eb′la.na). An ancient name of Dublin.

Eblis (eb′lis). [Also, **Iblis.**] In Arabian mythology, the chief of the evil spirits; the devil; a fallen prince of the angels. Beckford introduces him in *Vathek*.

d, d or j; ş, s or sh; ṭ, t or ch; z̧, z or zh; o, F. cloche; ü, F. menu; ćh, Sc. loch; ṅ, F. bonbon.

Eboracum (eb.ọ̄.rā′kum). A Latin name of York, England.

Ecbatana (ek.bat′ạ.nạ). An ancient name of Hamadan, in what is now Iran. It was once the capital of Media.

Ecce Homo (ek′sē hō′mō, ek′e). A name given (from the words of Pilate) to representations of Christ with the crown of thorns. Among the best-known paintings of this subject is one by Titian (1543), in the art museum at Vienna. Christ, bleeding and crowned with thorns, is led out from the palace above a flight of steps by soldiers. Below are a mocking company of soldiers and people, in which a portrait of the sultan Suleiman is conspicuous.

Ecce Homo: A Survey of the Life and Work of Jesus Christ. A work by John Robert Seeley of Cambridge, England. It was first published anonymously in 1865. It created much excitement among various Protestant denominations, and elicited a number of replies.

Ecce Puer (ek′sẹ pū′ėr). A poem (1936) by James Joyce, expressing his conception of the cycle of life and of the parallel between birth and death. At the close of the poem he voices his summary of the theme:

> A child is sleeping:
> An old man gone.
> O, father forsaken,
> Forgive your son!

Eccles (ek′lz). The sponging loafer and drunkard in T. W. Robertson's *Caste*.

Eccles, Robert. In George Meredith's novel *Rhoda Fleming*, a young man who loves Rhoda and tries to see that her sister's hurt is mended after her seduction by a banker's son.

Ecclesiastes (ẹ.klē.zi.as′tēz). [Also, **The Preacher.**] A book of the Old Testament, traditionally ascribed to Solomon, but probably of later date (perhaps as late as 200 B.C.). It is one of the so-called wisdom books of the Bible, expanding on the themes "all is vanity" and the impermanence of man and man's works. The text seems to have been confused by an editor, but the general lightly cynical pessimism has led some modern critics to assume Greek influence. Ecclesiastes is included in both the Jewish and the Christian canon.

Ecclesiastical History. [Latin, **Historia Ecclesiastica.**] A Latin chronicle by an Anglo-Norman Benedictine, Ordericus Vitalis, which covers the time from the creation until the 12th century and is particularly interesting for its account of England after the Norman Conquest.

Ecclesiastical History of the English People, The. See under **Bede.**

Ecclesiastical Polity, Law of. A prose work (1st edition, four books, c1592; fifth book, 1597; the remaining three books were published posthumously) by Richard Hooker.

Ecclesiastical Sketches. A volume of sonnets (1822) by William Wordsworth.

Ecclesiasticus (ẹ.klē.zi.as′ti.kus). The Latin name of a book of the Greek Bible (Septuagint), apocryphal in the Authorized Version, but declared canonical by the Council of Trent (1545–64); it is entitled *Wisdom of Jesus the Son of Sirach*, and was probably written in the first third of the 2nd century. The Hebrew original, which had been lost, was rediscovered as separate fragments (published 1896–1900) but is in mutilated form. The book, part of the Biblical wisdom literature, is mainly proverbial and extols the value of wisdom.

Ecgberht (ej′berçht). See **Egbert.**

Echidna (ẹ.kid′nạ). In Greek mythology, a monster half maiden, half serpent; daughter of Chrysaor and Callirrhoe (or of Phorcys and Ceto), and by Typhon mother of the Chimaera, the Hydra of Lernea, and Cerberus, and by Orthus, of the Sphinx and other monsters. She was slain while asleep by the many-eyed Argus.

Echo (ek′ō). In Greek mythology, a nymph who by her prattling prevented Hera from surprising her husband Zeus in the company of the nymphs. The goddess punished her by condemning her never to speak first and never to be silent when any one else spoke. She pined away to a bodiless voice (echo) for love of Narcissus. According to another explanation, she repulsed Pan's advances and he caused her to be torn to pieces by maddened shepherds. Ge (the earth mother) hid the pieces, which still respond to sounds.

Eckermann (ek′ėr.män), **Johann Peter.** b. at Winsen, Germany, Sept. 21, 1792; d. at Weimar, Germany, Dec. 3, 1854. A German writer, a friend and literary executor of Goethe. He is known chiefly for his *Gespräche mit Goethe* (1836–48).

Eckhardt (ek′härt) or **Eckart** (ek′ärt), **the Trusty.** [Also: **Eckehart** (ek′ẹ-); German, **der getreue Eckart.**] An old man in German traditional lore, in the legend of Frau Holle or Holda (Venus). He appears in the Mansfeld country on the evening of Maundy Thursday with a white staff to save the people from the Wild Hunt, the furious host which travels in Holle's train. His duties differ in different traditions. Sometimes he is the companion of Tannhäuser, and has even been considered to be the same person. He is also said to be in the service of Holle, and to sit outside the Venusberg to warn passing knights of the dangers therein, to which the enamored Tannhäuser has abandoned himself. He is also a knight captured by the Wild Hunt and doomed to abide at the Venusberg till the judgment. He appears as a knight in the *Harlungen Saga* and the *Nibelungenlied*.

Eckhart (ek′härt) or **Eckart** or **Eckardt** (ek′ärt), **Johannes.** [Called **Meister Eckhart.**] b. at Hochheim, near Gotha, in Thuringia, c1260; d. probably at Cologne, c1328. A German Dominican, founder of German mysticism. He was prior (1314) at Strasbourg and then at Cologne. He was accused of heresy in 1326, but denied the charge and appealed to Pope John XXII, who declared in 1329 (in the bull *In Coena Domini*, March 27) that Eckhart's doctrines were partly heretical. His philosophy, very influential on later thinkers, holds that all existence is in God, that creation is eternal because God has neither past nor future, but only the present. This apparently pantheistic philosophy is related, though no direct linkage or borrowing is known, with Plotinus and Neoplatonism, with Mahayana Buddhism, and with Vedanta.

---

fat, fāte, fär, àsk, fâre; net, mē, hėr; pin, pīne; not, nōte, mȯve, nôr; up, lūte, pùll; ᴛʜ, then;

eclectic (ek.lek'tik). One who, in whatever department of knowledge, not being convinced of the fundamental principles of any existing system, culls from the teachings of different schools such doctrines as seem to him probably true, conformable to good sense, wholesome in practice, or recommended by other secondary considerations; one who holds that opposing schools are right in their distinctive doctrines, wrong only in their opposition to one another. In philosophy the chief groups of eclectics have been—(1) those ancient writers, from the first century before Christ, who, like Cicero, influenced by Platonic skepticism, held a composite doctrine of ethics, logic, etc., aggregated of Platonist, Peripatetic, Stoic, and even Epicurean elements; (2) writers in the seventeenth century who, like Leibniz, mingled Aristotelian and Cartesian principles; (3) writers in the eighteenth century who adopted in part the views of Leibniz, in part those of Locke; (4) Schelling and others, who held beliefs derived from various idealistic, pantheistic, and mystical philosophers; (5) the school of Cousin, who took a mean position between a philosophy of experience and one of absolute reason.

> Even the eclectics, who arose about the age of Augustus, . . . were . . . as slavish and dependent as any of their brethren, since they sought for truth not in nature, but in the several schools.
> (Hume, *Rise of Arts and Sciences*.)

> My notion of an eclectic is a man who, without foregone conclusions of any sort, deliberately surveys all accessible modes of thought, and chooses from each his own "hortus siccus" of definitive convictions. (J. Owen, *Evenings with Skeptics*.)

eclogue (ek'log). In poetry, a pastoral composition, in which shepherds are introduced conversing with one another; a bucolic: as, the *eclogues* of Vergil. The term came to be applied especially to a collection of pastoral poems (with special reference to Vergil's pastoral poems (*Bucolica*), which were published under the title of *Eclogae*, 'selections'), whence the false spellings *eglogue*, *aeglogue* (F. *églogue*, etc.), in an endeavor to bring in the pastoral associations of Gr. αἴξ (αἴγ-), a goat.

> Some be of opinion, and the chiefe of those who haue written in this Art among the Latines, that the pastorall Poesie which we commonly call by the name of Eglogue and Bucolick, should be the first of any other. (Puttenham, *Arte of Eng. Poesie*.)

Eclogues. [Full title, **The Eclogues of A. Barclay.**] A collection of pastoral poems (c1515) by Alexander Barclay, the first of their sort to be written in English, cast in rhyming couplets (except for the use of the eight-line stanza in the fourth Eclogue).

Eclympasteyre (e.klim.päs.tā'rę). The name given by Chaucer in *The Book of the Duchess* to the heir of Morpheus, the god of sleep:

> Morpheus, and Eclympasteyre
> That was the god of slepes heyre.

Ector (ek'tor), **Sir.** [Also, **Sir Hector.**] In the Arthurian romances, a faithful knight who with his wife was entrusted with the upbringing of the infant Arthur. He was the father of Sir Kay.

Ector de Maris (de mar'is), **Sir.** [Also: **Sir Hector de Maris** or **Mares.**] In Arthurian romance, the brother of Sir Lancelot. He mourned Lancelot's death with a bitter lament, and afterward went with eight other knights to the Holy Land, where they died on a Good Friday.

Edda (ed'ą). A work written (in prose and verse) by Snorri Sturluson (1178–1241), containing the old mythology of Scandinavia and the old rules for verse-making; also, another work, a collection of ancient Icelandic poems. The name Edda (whether given by Snorri himself is not known) occurs in the inscription of one of the manuscripts of the work. Snorri's *Edda* as it was originally written consisted of three parts: the *Gylfaginning* (delusion of Gylfi), an epitome of the old mythology; *Skaldskaparmal* (art of poetry), an explanation of poetical expressions and periphrases; and *Hattatal* (list of meters), a laudatory poem on the Norwegian king Hakon Hakonsson, and Jarl Skuli, in which all forms of verse used in the old poetry are exemplified. To this was ultimately added a *Formali* (preface), and the *Bragaroedhur* (sayings of Bragi), describing the origin of poetry, and in some manuscripts *Thulur*, or a rhymed glossary of synonyms, list of poets, and similar material. The work was intended as a handbook of poets. In the year 1643 the Icelandic bishop Brynjulf Sveinsson discovered a collection of old mythological poems which was erroneously ascribed to Sæmund Sigfusson (1056–1133), and hence called from him *Sæmundar Edda hins Frodha* (The Edda of Sæmund the Learned). The poems that compose this *Edda* are of unknown origin and authorship. They are supposed to have been collected about the middle of the 13th century, but were composed at widely different periods down from the 9th century, to the first half of which the oldest is to be assigned; hence the name now given to this collection, the *Elder* or *Poetic Edda*, in distinction from the *Younger* or *Prose Edda* of Snorri, to which alone the name *Edda* legitimately belonged. The *Elder Edda* is usually considered to include 32 poems (some of them fragmentary).

Eddington (ed'ing.ton), **Sir Arthur Stanley.** b. at Kendal, England, Dec. 28, 1882; d. at Cambridge, England, Nov. 22, 1944. An English mathematician, astronomer, and astrophysicist, noted for his association of mathematical concepts with the structure of the universe. He calculated the "Eddington number" which he supposed to represent the total number of particles in the universe. He studied at the universities of Manchester and Cambridge, did research at the Cavendish Laboratory, became chief assistant at the Royal Observatory, and in 1913 succeeded Sir George Darwin at Cambridge. He was elected to the Royal Society in 1914, and was president of the Royal Astronomical Society (1921–23), president of the Physical Society (1930–32), and president of the International Astronomical Union (1938 *et seq.*). He was knighted in 1930. His works include *Stellar Movements and the Structure of the Universe* (1914), *Space, Time and Gravitation* (1920), *The Mathematical Theory of Relativity* (1923), *Internal Constitution of the Stars* (1926), *Stars and Atoms* (1927), *The Nature of the Physical World* (1928), *New Pathways in Science* (1935), *Relativity Theory of Protons and Electrons* (1936),

The Philosophy of Physical Science (1939), and *The Combination of Relativity Theory and Quantum Theory* (1943).

Eden (ē'dẹn). In Biblical history, the name of the first abode of man, in the midst of which a garden, the garden of Eden (the "paradise"), was planted. The position of Eden is described in Gen. ii. 8ff. by four rivers that go out from it, and by the countries they surround or pass in their course. Of these two, the Euphrates and Tigris (Hebrew, Perath and Hiddekel), are the well-known rivers of Mesopotamia; the other two, Pishon and Gihon, have been identified with various streams. The hypothesis of Friedrich Delitzsch assumed that the narrator in Genesis thought Eden located near the city of Babylon and meant by the rivers Pishon and Gihon two canals; Delitzsch also attempted to identify the countries mentioned in this passage with territories in that region. Adam and Eve were banished from Eden for eating of the forbidden fruit. An enclosed garden of paradise appears in Persian myth; a tree of life in a gardenlike park is mentioned in Babylonian myth.

Eden. In Dickens's *Martin Chuzzlewit*, a dismal, swampy area in the "American West," containing a small settlement (the members of which all wish they could leave). It is pictured to poor innocents in the East as a veritable heaven on earth by the unscrupulous promoters who own it. It has been identified as Cairo, Ill., which is at the confluence of the Ohio and Mississippi rivers.

Eden, Emily. b. at Westminster, London, March 3, 1797; d. at Richmond, Surrey, England, Aug. 5, 1869. An English novelist, traveler, and travel writer. She was the seventh daughter of the 1st Baron Auckland (William Eden), and the sister of the 1st Earl of Auckland (George Eden). When her brother went to India as governor general, she accompanied him and, with a sister, Frances, stayed with him during his entire term (1835–42). This period of residence resulted in two books, *Portraits of the People and Princes of India* (1844, when she was back in England) and *Up the Country: Letters Written to her Sister from the Upper Provinces of India by the Hon. Emily Eden* (1866; other eds., 1867, 1872). She translated Hugo's tragedy *Marion Delorme* into English blank verse, and she wrote two gently satirical novels, *The Semi-detached House* (1859) and *The Semi-attached Couple* (1860), which have been paid the high compliment of being compared to Jane Austen. Successful in their day, they were reprinted in 1928 after being long forgotten.

Eden, Richard. b. c1521; d. 1576. An English translator. He studied at Cambridge, held a position in the treasury (1544–46), and was appointed to a place in the English treasury of Prince Philip of Spain in 1554, a position which he soon lost, owing to an accusation of heresy. In 1562 he entered the service of a French nobleman, with whom he traveled extensively. Eden's name as a translator is appended to many books on geography, travels, navigation, and the like. Among these are *A Treatyse of the Newe India* (1553, a translation of part of Munster's *Cosmographia*), which is the first intelligible description in English of America, and *Decades of the Newe World* (1555, mainly a translation of Peter Martyr's work).

Eden Bower. A poem by Dante Gabriel Rossetti, published in *Poems* (1870), concerning the jealousy of Lilith (the mythical first wife of Adam) toward Eve.

Edgar (ed'gạr). In Shakespeare's *King Lear*, the legitimate son of the Earl of Gloucester. He is banished by Gloucester as the result of a plot contrived by the bastard son, Edmund, and, pretending to be the mad Tom o'Bedlam, wanders upon the moors, where he meets Lear, cast out by his ungrateful daughters. After Gloucester is blinded by Cornwall for aiding Lear, Edgar leads his father to Dover to meet Cordelia's army and in the ensuing battle kills Edmund. He describes to Albany the breaking of Gloucester's heart at the joy of finding him again. At the end, Edgar is left with Kent and Albany to set about restoring the kingdom. In Edgar, Shakespeare has created a figure of rejected goodness, sanity driven out to live with insanity, and his humility is contrasted with the disloyalty of Goneril and Regan and the cruel ambition of Edmund. In the famous scene "on the cliff," he leads the blind Gloucester almost to destruction (as Gloucester believes) so that he may be "saved" from the fiend who has led him there, and thus brings Gloucester to an acceptance of his affliction. Edgar is derived from a character in the episode of the king of Paphlagonia in Sidney's *Arcadia*.

Edgar. See also **Ravenswood, Edgar, Master of.**

Edgar, Sir John. A pseudonym of Sir Richard Steele, under which he conducted the theatrical journal *The Theatre* from January, 1720, until April, 1720.

Edgar Tryan (trī'ạn), **Reverend.** See **Tryan, Reverend Edgar.**

Edge of Being, The. A volume of verse (1949) by Stephen Spender.

Edgeworth (ej'wẻrth), **Maria.** b. at Black Bourton, Oxfordshire, England, Jan. 1, 1767; d. at Edgeworthstown, County Longford, Ireland, May 22, 1849. An English novelist, known especially for her Gothic tales; aunt of Thomas Lovell Beddoes. She wrote, in conjunction with her father, *Essays on Practical Education* (1798) and *Essay on Irish Bulls* (1802). Her chief independent works are *Castle Rackrent* (1800), *Belinda* (1801), *Moral Tales for Young People* (1801), *Popular Tales* (1804), *Tales of Fashionable Life* (1809–12), *Leonora* (1806), *The Absentee* (1812), *Patronage* (1814), *Ormond* (1817), and *Helen* (1834). She was a friend of Sir Walter Scott, who acknowledged in the preface to *Waverley* his debt to Miss Edgeworth's novels of Irish life.

Edict of Nantes (nants, nänt). See **Nantes, Edict of.**

Edie Ochiltree (ē'di ō'chil.trē, och'il-). See **Ochiltree, Edie.**

Edinburgh (ed'in.bur.ọ). [Older spellings: **Edinborow, Edinbro**; Middle English, **Edenborow**; earlier **Edwinesburch, Edwinesburg**; popularly called **"Auld Reekie."**] A city, royal burgh, seaport, and commercial, industrial, administrative, and cultural center of Scotland, in S Scotland, in Midlothian, situated on the S bank of the Firth of Forth ab. 42 mi. E of Glasgow, ab. 393 mi. N of London by rail. It is the capital of Scotland and of various departments of government, the military headquarters of Scotland, and the county seat of Midlothian. Edinburgh is an important publishing and literary center, having many trades associated with the industry. The city is noted for its picturesque situation on ridges near Calton Hill and Arthur's Seat. It grew up around Edinburgh Castle, dating from the 7th century, built in the middle of the city on a rock which falls 270 ft. on three sides. Edinburgh Castle was captured by Edward I in 1296 and remained in English hands until it was recaptured (1314) in the name of Robert I of Scotland (Robert Bruce) by Thomas Randolph, 1st Earl of Moray, and 30 men who surprised the English garrison. The exterior of the castle has been greatly modified, but much of the interior remains as of old, including some of the royal apartments and the Romanesque chapel. James VI of Scotland (later James I of England) was born in the castle in 1566. Here, in the castle, are preserved the royal regalia of Scotland. Adjoining the castle is the Scottish National War Memorial, containing a shrine and a gallery of honor which has a barrel-vaulted roof supported by octagonal columns, forming 12 bays, one for each of the Scottish regiments. The Parliament House is now occupied by the Supreme Law Courts. It is a large Renaissance building, with porticoes of Ionic columns over an arcaded and rusticated basement. The Parliament House includes the Advocate's Library. The great hall has a handsome roof of oak, and contains interesting portraits and statues. Edinburgh is the seat of a university, founded in 1582 by James VI. Also of note are the ruins of Holyrood Abbey, founded in 1128 by David I, and the adjoining Holyroodhouse, or Holyrood Palace, still used as a royal residence. Holyroodhouse has many associations with Mary, Queen of Scots. It was here that David Rizzio was murdered by the Scottish lords at the instigation of Henry Stuart, Lord Darnley. Rizzio and Darnley are buried at Holyrood Abbey. The palace contains a picture gallery notable for its collection of 110 portraits of Scottish kings, painted in the 17th century by a Dutch artist. It was in this picture gallery that Prince Charlie (Charles Edward Stuart, the "Young Pretender" to the English throne) gave a ball, in 1745, while Edinburgh Castle held out against him. The National Gallery of Scotland, in Edinburgh, contains a valuable art collection, one of its best-known paintings being *Christ in the House of Mary and Martha* by Jan Vermeer. Saint Giles's Church (the cathedral) was founded in the 12th century, but the present structure is of the 15th. The interior has high nave-pillars and Gothic pointed arches. The transept is Norman, with massive piers supporting the tower. The fine recessed and sculptured west doorway is modern. Saint Mary's Episcopal Cathedral, the work of Sir George Gilbert Scott, was completed in 1879. It is a spacious structure in the Early English style, with an imposing central spire 295 ft. high. Other interesting structures in Edinburgh are the Scott monument, the Royal Institution, John Knox's house, Moray House (twice occupied by Cromwell) in the summer house of which the Treaty of Union between England and Scotland was signed, and various charitable and educational institutions. Edinburgh is famous for its colleges and schools. The city was fortified by the Northumbrian king Edwin (whence its name Edwinesburg) c617, succeeded Perth as the Scottish capital in 1437, was taken and sacked by the English in 1544 and again (by Cromwell) in 1650, and was occupied by the Young Pretender in 1745. Fragments of the old town wall still remain. Edinburgh is famous in the literary history of the last half of the 18th and first half of the 19th century, through its connection with Hume, Robertson, Dugald Stewart, Adam Smith, Burns, Scott, John Wilson (Christopher North), the *Edinburgh Review*, and others. It is often called the "modern Athens" or "Athens of the North," both from its topography and as a seat of learning, also "Queen of the North."

Edinburgh, University of. A famous seat of learning, founded (1582) by James VI of Scotland.

Edinburgh Review. A literary and political review, founded at Edinburgh in 1802 by Francis Jeffrey, Sydney Smith, Henry Peter Brougham, and others.

Edinburgh Tolbooth (tōl′bŏth). See **Tolbooth.**

Edith (ē′dith). One of the principal characters in Francis Beaumont and John Fletcher's *The Bloody Brother.*

Edith. The maid of Lorn in Sir Walter Scott's poem *The Lord of the Isles.*

Edith Bellenden (bel′ẹn.dẹn). See **Bellenden, Edith.**

Edith Granger (grān′jėr). See **Granger, Edith.**

Edith Plantagenet (plan.taj′ẹ.nẹt). See **Plantagenet, Edith.**

Edith Swan-neck (swon′nek). fl. 11th century. A mistress of Harold II, king of the English, and mother, probably, of some of his children. By her aid the mutilated body of Harold was identified after the battle of Hastings (1066). She appears as a greatly idealized character in romance and poetry.

edition. **1.** An edited copy or issue of a book or other work; a recension, revision, or annotated reproduction: as, Milman's *edition* of Gibbon's "Rome"; the Globe *edition* of Shakespeare. **2.** A concurrent issue or publication of copies of a book or some similar production; the number of books, etc., of the same kind published together, or without change of form or of contents; a multiplication or reproduction of the same work or series of works: as, a large *edition* of a book, map, or newspaper; the work has reached a tenth *edition;* the folio *editions* of Shakespeare's plays.

The which I also have more at large set oute in the seconde edition of my booke.
(Whitgift, *Defence.*)

As to the larger additions and alterations, . . . he has promised me to print them by themselves, so that the former edition may not be wholly lost to those who have it.
(Locke, *Human Understanding*, "To the Reader.")

editorial (ed.i.tō′ri.ạl). An article, as in a newspaper, written by the editor or one of his assistants, and in form setting forth the position or opinion of the paper upon some subject; a leading article: as, an *editorial* on the war.

ḍ, d or j; ṣ, s or sh; ṭ, t or ch; ẓ, z or zh; o, F. cloche; ü, F. menu; ċh, Sc. loch; ṅ, F. bonbon.

The opening article on the first page [of "Figaro"] is what we should call the chief editorial, and what the English term a "leader." In Paris it is known as a "chronique."   (*The Century*, XXXV.2.)

Edmer (ed'mẽr). See **Eadmer**.

Edmund (ed'mund), Saint. [Also: **Eadmund**; called **Edmund the Martyr**.] b. c840; killed by the Danes, 870. King (855–870) of East Anglia. Details of his life are legendary. He is supposed to have been a Saxon, born at Nuremberg, son of King Alkmund, and to have been adopted by Offa, whom he succeeded as king. In 870 he met the Danes at Hoxne and was defeated by them, dying on the field or, according to one story, being bound to a tree and beheaded, or shot with arrows, when he refused to forswear Christianity or acknowledge Danish overlordship.

Edmund. In Shakespeare's *King Lear*, the bastard son of the Earl of Gloucester. He is considered by the Shakespeare scholar G. B. Harrison the greatest villain in Shakespeare's plays. Like many other villains in Shakespeare his conduct has no real motivation in any wrong done him; there is only an ambition to "top the legitimate," meaning his legitimate brother, Edgar, and to reach ruthlessly for the summit of power. Although the story of the two brothers, Edgar and Edmund, is suggested by an episode related in Sidney's *Arcadia*, the implicating of Edmund in the action attendant upon Lear's dismissal from his daughters' homes is Shakespeare's own invention. Edmund callously toys with both Goneril and Regan, knowing that both love him and determined finally to choose the one who offers him the greater advantage. Already he has betrayed his father so that he may become Earl of Gloucester, and now he orders the death of Lear and Cordelia so that only Lear's two daughters remain between him and the throne, but his ambition is defeated at last by Edgar.

Edmund. Entries on literary characters having this prename will also be found under the surnames Mortimer, Sparkler, and Tressilian, and (for a character from Marlowe and two from Shakespeare, respectively) under the titles Kent, Rutland, and York.

Edmund I. [Also: **Eadmund**; called **Edmund the Magnificent** and **the Deed-doer**.] b. c922; killed at Pucklechurch, Gloucestershire, England, May 26, 946. King of the West Saxons and Mercians. He was the son of Edward the Elder, and half-brother of Athelstan, whom he succeeded in 940. He had fought at Brunanburh for Athelstan, but after he became king he lost a large part of his kingdom to invaders from Ireland, but won it back in 944 or 945. He subdued Cumbria (945), which he bestowed on Malcolm I of Scotland. He was killed by a robber named Liofa while keeping the feast of Saint Augustine of Canterbury at Pucklechurch, Gloucestershire. The robber having entered the hall unbidden, the king ordered a cup-bearer to remove him, and when the robber resisted came to the cup-bearer's relief. In the struggle that ensued he was stabbed to death with a dagger. Edmund was married twice, to Ælfgifu, the mother of Edwy and Edgar, and to Ethelflæd.

Edmunds (ed'mundz), **John.** A felon, the principal character of the tale "The Convict's Return," in Charles Dickens's *Pickwick Papers*.

Edom (ē'dọm). See **Esau**.

Edna Bunthorne (ed'nạ bun'thôrn). See **Bunthorne, Edna**.

Edred (ed'rẹd) or **Eadred** (ã'ạd.rād, ed'rẹd). d. at Frome, England, Nov. 23, 955. A king of England; youngest son of Edward the Elder and Eadgifu, and brother of Edmund I, whom he succeeded in 946. His government was controlled by his mother and Saint Dunstan; his reign was marked by revolts in Northumbria.

Edred Fitzpiers (fits.pirs'). See **Fitzpiers, Edred**.

Edward (ed'wạrd). [Also: **Eadward, Eadweard**; called **Edward the Elder**.] d. at what is now Farndon, Northamptonshire, England, 924. A king of the West Saxons; son of Alfred the Great, whom he succeeded in 901. He defeated his cousin Ethelwold, who disputed his title to the throne. On the death of his sister Ethelfleda (Elfleda), the widow of Ethelred, ealdorman of Mercia, he incorporated Mercia (which had long acknowledged the overlordship of the West Saxon kings) with Wessex. He completed the conquest of the Danelaw, begun by him with Ethelfleda's aid earlier, conquered East Anglia and Essex, and received the submission of Strathclyde and all the Scots. On this Scottish submission (denied later by the Scots) was based the claim of later English kings to Scotland. At his death he ruled Wessex, Kent, and Sussex by inheritance; Mercia, Essex, and East Anglia by conquest; and Northumberland, Wales, Scotland, and Strathclyde as overlord. He was succeeded by Athelstan, his son by Ecgwyn; two sons by Eadgifu, his third wife, Edmund I and Edred, later reigned.

Edward. [Also: **Eadward**; called **Edward the Martyr**.] b. probably in 963; murdered March 18, 978. A king of the West Saxons; son of Edgar, whom he succeeded in 975, and Ethelflæd. He was elected by the witan through the influence of Saint Dunstan, primate of England, in spite of the measures taken by his stepmother, Elfrida, to secure the crown for her son Ethelred. He was murdered by her order, according to tradition, and was succeeded by his stepbrother, Ethelred II (Ethelred the Unready). His youth and popularity led to his recognition as a martyr as early as 1001.

Edward. [Also: **Eadward**; called **Edward the Confessor**.] b. at what is now Islip, Oxfordshire, England, c1004; d. Jan. 5, 1066. A king of the West Saxons; son of Ethelred II (Ethelred the Unready) and Emma of Normandy. He lived chiefly in Normandy during the Danish supremacy, and was elected to the throne of his father through the influence of Godwin, Earl of Wessex, on the death of Harthacnut, in 1042. He married Edith (Edgitha), daughter of Godwin, in 1045. Edward chose as chief advisers a number of Frenchmen and thus came into conflict with Godwin's power. His appointment of Robert of Jumièges as Archbishop of Canterbury, after the regular election of Godwin's relative Ælfric, caused a break with Godwin, and when, soon after, Dover offered resistance to Edward's brother-in-law Eustace II of Boulogne,

Edward ordered Godwin to punish the town. This Godwin refused to do and, Edward threatening to try him for an old alleged crime, Godwin and his sons fled to France and Ireland. The next year (1052) Godwin raised a force and invaded England; Edward lacked support and restored Godwin to favor. He and his son Harold after him became the king's ministers while Edward applied himself to religious study. When his favorite, Tostig, Godwin's son, was faced with revolt in Northumbria in 1065, Edward was forced to submit to Tostig's removal. This and the realization that a struggle over the succession to the English throne among Harold, Harold III (Harold Haardraade) of Norway, Edgar Ætheling, and William of Normandy was due to break probably hastened his death. He died without issue, and was succeeded by his wife's brother Harold, whose title was disputed by William, Duke of Normandy. The so-called Laws of Edward the Confessor, compiled in 1070, were made from sworn statements of 12 men of each shire. He was canonized in 1161.

Edward. A Scottish folk ballad, included in Percy's *Reliques*, written in the form of a dialogue between a mother and her son, and concerning the son's murder of his father, instigated by his mother, whom he now curses. It opens with the line: "Why does your brand sae drop wi' blude, Edward, Edward?"

Edward. Entries on literary characters having this prename will be found under the surnames Casaubon, Christian, Cuttle, Ferrars, Glendinning, Mortimer, Murdstone, Ponderevo, Rochester, Scrope, and Strong.

Edward I. [Called **Edward Longshanks.**] b. at Westminster (now part of London), June 17 or 18, 1239; d. at Burgh-on-the-Sands, near Carlisle, England, July 7, 1307. King of England from 1272 to 1307. He was the son of Henry III and Eleanor of Provence. In 1254 he married Eleanor of Castile, half sister of Alfonso X of Castile. He took an active part in the struggle between his father and the barons, inflicting a decisive defeat on their leader, Simon de Montfort, at Evesham in 1265. He engaged (1270-72) in the seventh Crusade, and was returning from the Holy Land when he heard of his accession to the throne. He returned slowly, visiting his lands in Gascony, and reaching England in 1274, in which year he was crowned. In 1277 he began the conquest of Wales, which had become practically independent during the barons' wars, and in 1284, after defeating Llewelyn, annexed that country to England. He expelled the Jews from England in 1290. On the death (1290) of Margaret, the Maid of Norway, granddaughter and heiress of Alexander III of Scotland, the Scottish estates were unable to decide between the two chief claimants to the throne, John de Baliol and Robert Bruce, with the result that Edward was appointed arbitrator. He decided in favor of Baliol, whose homage he received. In 1294 he became involved in a war with France, Philip IV of France forming an alliance with Scotland. In 1296 he defeated the Scots at Dunbar, compelled Baliol to resign the crown, carried the Scotch coronation stone (the Stone of Scone) to London, and placed Scotland under an English regent, who was, however, defeated by the patriot Sir William Wallace at Stirling in 1297. Edward defeated the Scots under Wallace in the battle of Falkirk, on July 22, 1298. In 1303 he concluded the peace of Amiens with France, having married in 1299 Philip IV's sister, Margaret. Invading Scotland in 1303, he received the submission of Bruce, and in 1305 he ordered the execution of Wallace, who had been betrayed to the English. He died on the way to Scotland, where a new insurrection had placed Robert Bruce, grandson of the claimant against whom Edward had earlier decided, on the throne in 1306. Edward's reign is of great importance in the internal history of England. The statutes of Westminster (1275, 1285, 1290) revised the landholding system and limited the feudal political power; although the aim was to break altogether the barons' power, Edward was forced, through need of money to finance his foreign struggles, to grant exemptions from the rules and to confirm the charters granted by John and Henry III. The old King's Court was separated into three tribunals: the Court of Exchequer, the Court of King's Bench, and the Court of Common Pleas. The jurisdiction of the Royal Council (later the Star Chamber) was established. In 1279, the statute of mortmain was promulgated, forbidding the extension of clerical landholding without the king's consent. This was opposed by the clergy and they received backing from Pope Boniface VIII, whose bull *Clericos Laicos* (1296), though intended to stop Philip IV of France from taxing the clergy, was applied in 1297 in England when the English clergy refused to contribute to Edward's campaign against France. Edward then announced that he could no longer protect the church holdings against the possible inroads of the barons. But when the barons allied themselves with the clergy, Edward gave way, reaffirmed the charters, and signed further articles against arbitrary taxation without parliamentary consent. In 1295 Edward convened the so-called Model Parliament, with representation from all three estates (clergy, nobility, commons), the type after which later Parliaments were formed. Edward established the royal power over the clergy when Pope Clement V, an Englishman, permitted him to suspend (1306) Robert de Winchelsea, archbishop of Canterbury, one of the leading ecclesiastical opponents of the king. Edward's reign is marked by his victory over the barons and the clergy, his conquest of Wales, his victory over Philip IV of France, and his firm establishment of the royal power under law in England.

Edward I. [Full title, **The Famous Chronicle of King Edward I.**] A play by George Peele, printed in 1593.

Edward II. [Called **Edward of Caernarvon** (or **Carnarvon**).] b. at Caernarvon, Wales, April 25, 1284; murdered at Berkeley Castle, near Gloucester, England, Sept. 21, 1327. King of England from 1307 to 1327. He was the fourth son of Edward I by his first wife, Eleanor of Castile. He was created (1301) the first Prince of Wales. On his accession to the throne he recalled his favorite, Piers Gaveston, who had been banished as being a bad influence on Edward by Edward I. He married Isabella of France in 1308. The insolence of Gaveston having aroused the anger of the barons, the favorite was banished through their influence in 1308, only to be shortly recalled by the king. In 1310, in consequence of the incompetence of Edward, who was completely under the ascendancy of Gaveston, the government was entrusted by the barons to 21 ordainers, who procured the passage of the ordinances of the Parliament of 1311, in accordance with which Gaveston was exiled, and provisions were made for annual Parliaments and for the reform of administrative abuses. In 1312 the barons brought about the execution of Gaveston, who had been again recalled by the king. In 1314 Edward was defeated by the Scots under Robert I (Robert the Bruce) at the battle of Bannockburn (June 24). The exile of his new favorites, the two Despensers, by Parliament in 1321 involved him in a war with the barons, who were defeated at the battle of Boroughbridge in 1322. In 1323, after an unsuccessful invasion of Scotland, he concluded a peace for 13 years with Bruce, whose assumption of the royal title of Scotland was passed over in silence. His queen, Isabella, having in 1325 been sent to France, accompanied by the prince Edward, heir to the throne, to negotiate with her brother Charles IV concerning the English fiefs in France, intrigued with Roger de Mortimer, her lover, and other disaffected barons, landed in England in 1326, captured Bristol, executed the Despensers, and imprisoned Edward. Edward, the prince, refused to become king as long as his father claimed the throne, so Edward II was deposed by Parliament, forced to resign his claim, and brutally murdered in Berkeley Castle.

Edward II. A tragedy by Christopher Marlowe, entered on the Stationers' Register on July 6, 1593. It was probably written c1591–93, but was not published till 1598, after Marlowe's death. As its title implies, the play is about the reign of King Edward and it deals with the events leading up to his deposition and death. The scenes are quite brief; the dialogue has none of the luxuriance found in *Tamburlaine* or even *The Jew of Malta*. The play gave Shakespeare suggestions for his *Richard II*, in which the same theme is treated. Edward as a ruler is capable of courage, humanity, and loyalty, but he is also the victim of his emotions and confused and weakened by an inefficient government. When he transfers much of his power to his favorite, Piers Gaveston, he makes a grave mistake. Kent, Edward's brother, who opposes the powerful barons when Edward is acting prudently, reverses his stand when Gaveston gets into power. Mortimer, the opponent of the King, is first presented sympathetically when he is being rescued from the Tower by Kent, but his intellectual ambition (forming a kind of foil to the enlightened intellectual power of Edward) becomes arrogance. Mortimer cruelly turns the Queen against her husband and incites the barons to rebel against the King and Gaveston. Once again Kent changes back to the King's side, and dies vainly trying to rescue Edward from Mortimer's power. Around these chief figures others are arranged as studies in political morality. Marlowe does not pass overt judgment upon any of these people, but one can sense an implicit comment on their morality.

Edward III. [Called **Edward of Windsor**.] b. at Windsor, England, Nov. 13, 1312; d. at Shene (Richmond), England, June 21, 1377. King of England from 1327 to 1377. He was the son of Edward II and Isabella of France. On the deposition of his father, he was proclaimed king under a council of regency, the actual government being exercised by the queen and her favorite, Roger de Mortimer. He married (1328) Philippa of Hainaut, and in the same year concluded the treaty of Northampton with the Scots, in which Robert I (Robert Bruce) was recognized as king. In 1330 he took the government into his own hands, securing the execution of Mortimer and removing the queen-mother from any further influence. On the death of Robert I in 1329, Edward Baliol seized the Scottish crown, to the exclusion of Robert's young son David (1324–71), who, despite his years, was already Edward's brother-in-law. Baliol did homage to Edward, and a revolt of the nobles drove him across the border. Edward defeated the national party at Halidon Hill in 1333, and restored Baliol, who was soon driven out by the Scots. In 1337 he became involved in a war with France (the Hundred Years' War), whose throne he claimed in right of his mother. His claim brought him as allies the Flemings, who were subject to the French king; he made alliances with the emperor Louis IV and with other German princes. The naval victory at Sluys (1340) gave England control of the Channel. In 1346, at the battle of Neville's Cross, his army defeated the invading Scots under David II (Bruce), who had recovered the Scottish throne in 1342; the Scots, however, succeeded in maintaining their independence. He gained with his son, Edward the Black Prince, the victory of Crécy over the French in 1346, and reduced Calais in 1347, while the Black Prince gained the battle of Poitiers in 1356. In 1360 he concluded with the French the peace of Brétigny, by which he renounced the French crown and Normandy, Anjou, Maine, and Touraine, in return for the cession in full sovereignty to England of Aquitaine, Ponthieu, Guisnes, and Calais. He subsequently, in a war with Charles V, lost all his possessions in France, with the exception of Bordeaux, Calais, and Bayonne, due principally to the incompetence of John of Gaunt, who replaced the Black Prince, Edward, as steward of the English possessions in France. During his reign occurred several visitations of the Black Death (1348–49, 1361, and 1369). This plague, by halving the population of England, caused a social revolution that was stopped neither by an ordinance (1349) fixing wages and prices nor by the Statute of Laborers (1351) to force the unemployed to work at the fixed wages. This emancipation of labor from the feudal system was accompanied by a growth of class-consciousness reflected in such literary works as *Piers Plowman* and in the rapid spread of Lollardy. The reign of Edward III was also marked by a revolt against the papal authority and the establishment of national strictures on the power of the papacy, then resident at Avignon and under the influence of the French. This was only one aspect of the growth of national feeling: among other such manifestations was the establishment of the English language on an official basis in the courts, the schools, and Parliament, where until then French had held sway. The business class grew in importance and asserted its right to be heard. Parliament, obtaining the whip hand because of Edward's need of money for his wars, consolidated its position as a check on monarchal power. In his later years Edward turned over actual rule of the kingdom to Edward the Black Prince and then, in the latter's illness, to John of Gaunt. The latter, with the support of the king's mistress Alice Perrers, rallied to himself the forces of the court, and was opposed by the parliamentary and clerical factions. After the Black Prince's death, John of Gaunt was actual ruler of England until the accession of Richard II. Edward III had 12 children; of his seven sons, five grew to manhood and were of importance to history: Edward of Woodstock, the Black Prince; Lionel of Antwerp (the place names indicate where the princes were born), Duke of Clarence; John of Gaunt (i.e., Ghent), Duke of Lancaster, whose descendants formed the Lancastrian party in the later Wars of the Roses; Edmund of Langley, later 1st Duke of York, from whom the Yorkists took their name; and Thomas of Woodstock, later Duke of Gloucester.

Edward III. [Full title, **The Raigne of King Edward the Third**.] An anonymous play printed c1595, based on the version of history found in Holinshed's *Chronicles*. It has been attributed to Shakespeare and to Marlowe. It has similarities to Shakespeare's history plays in its theme of the acquisition of wisdom and maturity in a ruler: the Black Prince, Edward's son, and Edward both learn lessons, the first about valor and self-reliance, the second about controlling his passion for the Countess of Salisbury.

Edward IV. b. at Rouen, France, probably April 28, 1442; d. April 9, 1483. King of England from 1461 to 1483. He was the son of Richard Plantagenet, 3rd Duke of York, and Cecily Neville, daughter of the Earl of Westmorland. He was known as the Earl of March previous to his accession, and played a prominent part in the struggle of his house (the house of York) with that of Lancaster for the possession of the throne. In conjunction with the earls of Salisbury and Warwick, his uncle and his cousin, both named Richard Neville, he defeated the Lancastrians under Henry VI at Northampton in 1460, and took the king prisoner. His father, the duke of York, was defeated and killed at the battle of Wakefield later in the same year, whereupon Edward succeeded to the title, defeated the Lancastrians at the battle of Mortimer's Cross in 1461, and was proclaimed king at London on March 4, 1461. The early part of his reign was disturbed by constant attempts of the Lancastrians to regain the throne. In 1464 he secretly married Elizabeth Grey, daughter of Richard Woodville, Baron Rivers, and widow of Sir John Grey, a Lancastrian. This caused a revolution under the earl of Warwick, who joined forces with the Lancastrians and proclaimed the deposed and captive Henry VI king. Edward fled to France, but returned and suppressed the rising in the battles of Barnet (April 14, 1471) and Tewkesbury (May 4, 1471); in the former Warwick was slain and following the latter Henry VI died, probably murdered, in the Tower of London. Edward's reign thereafter was more or less peaceful, only the rivalry of his brothers, the dukes of Clarence and Gloucester, marring the domestic scene (this was ended with Clarence's murder in 1478) and a war with France in 1475 disturbing the peace. From the French war came a subsidy which enabled Edward to avoid going to Parliament for money. As a result Edward reverted to autocracy and attempted to live the life of a Renaissance despot. His profligacy was well known; Jane Shore is the most famous of his several mistresses.

Edward IV. A play in two parts, possibly by Chettle and Day, printed in 1600. It was apparently known also as *Jane Shore*.

Edward IV. See also under **Edward, Earl of March.**

Edward V. b. at Westminster, London, Nov. 2 or 3, 1470; murdered in the Tower of London, 1483. King of England from April to June, 1483. He was the son of Edward IV by Elizabeth Woodville. He succeeded to the throne under the regency of his uncle Richard, Duke of Gloucester, who secretly put him and his brother to death and usurped the government as Richard III. The mystery surrounding the deaths of Edward and his younger brother Richard, Duke of York, has never successfully been solved, but there is little doubt that Richard III procured their deaths through Sir James Tyrell after the Tower's constable, Sir Robert Brackenbury, refused to kill them.

Edward V. See also under **Edward, Prince of Wales.**

Edward VI. b. at Hampton Court, England, Oct. 12, 1537; d. at Greenwich, near London, July 6, 1553. King of England from 1547 to 1553. He was the son of Henry VIII by his third queen, Jane Seymour, and succeeded to the throne under the regency of his uncle, Edward Seymour, Duke of Somerset, who was supplanted c1550 by John Dudley, Duke of Northumberland. During his reign occurred the publication of the 42 articles of religion (1553) and the introduction of the Book of Common Prayer (1549), compiled by Thomas Cranmer. Before his death he was induced by the duke of Northumberland to assign the crown to Northumberland's daughter-in-law, Lady Jane Grey, to the exclusion of Henry VIII's children Mary and Elizabeth.

Edward VII. [Full name, **Albert Edward;** called **the Peacemaker.**] b. at London, Nov. 9, 1841; d. there, May 6, 1910. King of Great Britain and Ireland and emperor of India from 1901 to 1910; eldest son of Victoria. He married Princess Alexandria, daughter of Christian IX of Denmark, on March 10, 1863. In 1860 he made a tour of the U. S. and Canada, in 1862 of Egypt and Palestine, and in 1875–76 of British India, the latter visit laying the groundwork for Victoria's assumption (1877) of the title Empress of India. As king he fostered international agreements with France, Germany, Italy, Portugal, and Spain. He ascended the throne as Edward VII on Jan. 22, 1901. He died during the parliamentary crisis of 1910–11 over the veto power of the House of Lords, in which dispute he preserved a neutral stand. Edward was a popular king, and his genial taste for good food, wine, and other attributes of a gay life (including love affairs; he appeared as a witness not only in a divorce suit but in a libel suit in connection with an alleged instance of cheating in gambling) probably actually added to the affection in which he was held

ḏ, d or j; ş, s or sh; ṭ, t or ch; ẕ, z or zh; o, F. cloche; ü, F. menu; c̀h, Sc. loch; ṅ, F. bonbon.

by most of his subjects (after the austerity of Victoria, his escapades had the effect of reminding the world that an English ruler could be, so to speak, more human without thereby becoming less royal). His horses won the Derby several times and his racing yacht was one of the best of the times. As Albert Edward, Prince of Wales, he was an ambassador of good will both internationally and domestically, making it evident that the king would participate in national life without necessarily attempting to direct political matters.

Edward VIII. [Full name, **Edward Albert Christian George Andrew Patrick David**; known after his abdication as Duke of **Windsor.**] b. at White Lodge, Richmond, England, June 23, 1894—. King of England from Jan. 20 to Dec. 10, 1936 (324 days). The eldest son of King George V and Mary (Victoria Mary of Teck), he became Prince of Wales in 1911, making his investiture speech at Caernarvon Castle in Welsh. During World War I he served with the British Expeditionary Forces in France, Flanders, and Italy. Following the war, his travels in Canada, the U. S., Australia, the West Indies, South Africa, and Latin America made him a familiar figure in the British Empire and the world at large. On the death of George V in 1936 he succeeded to the throne, still unmarried. Later that year it became known that he was planning to marry Mrs. Wallis Warfield Simpson, an American divorcee who was about to divorce her second husband. The proposed marriage was met with opposition from the cabinet, led by the Conservative Stanley Baldwin. The king insisting on his right to choose a wife and the king's ministers insisting that the king must accede to his subjects' wishes, a constitutional crisis developed that was resolved only with Edward's abdication. In a speech that has since become famous he declared that he could not "carry on the heavy burden of responsibility and discharge the duties of King as I would wish to do without the help and support of the woman I love." The abdication speech, delivered over the air on Dec. 11, has been many times reprinted in full, or quoted in part. He was succeeded by his brother, the duke of York, as George VI. On June 3, 1937 Edward, now known as Duke of Windsor, married Mrs. Simpson in France. He served for a short time in France in World War II and then was appointed governor of the Bahama Islands, a post he held from 1940 to 1945. Students of his character have called attention to apparent contradictions in his acts and utterances. His sympathies with miners and with other workers, and with the unemployed, are well known, but one of his best friends is Charles Bedaux, associated with a "speed-up" system that is highly unpopular with labor groups in England and elsewhere. When he left England in 1937 he found a welcome in the home of his friend, Baron Rothschild, but when he went to Germany, "to study labor conditions," he called on, and posed with, Hitler, Goebbels, and Goering. His story, told by himself, has been serialized and published in book form in *A King's Story* (1951).

Edward, Earl of March (märch). In Shakespeare's *2 Henry VI*, the eldest son of Richard Plantagenet, Duke of York. In *3 Henry VI*, he shows his father his sword, bloody from the wounds of the Duke of

Buckingham (I.i). On the death of his father he becomes Duke of York. He defeats the Lancastrians, is proclaimed king, as Edward IV, and marries Lady Grey. In *Richard III*, sick, he learns that the order for Clarence's death was executed despite his reversal of it (II.i). In the following scene word comes of his death.

Edward, Earl of Warwick (wôr′ik, wor′ik). See **Warwick, Edward, Earl of.**

Edwardes (ed′wardz), Sir **Herbert Benjamin.** b. at Frodesley, Shropshire, England, Nov. 12, 1819; d. at London, Dec. 23, 1868. An English general and author, distinguished in the Sikh wars in India (1845–49). He published *A Year on the Punjab Frontier* (1851) and other works.

Edwardian. Pertaining to or denoting the fashions, literature, etc. of the period immediately following the reign of Victoria and roughly corresponding to the reign of Edward VII. After the death of Victoria, a reaction from the rigidity of Victorian propriety and conservatism produced a period of brilliance and elegance (not utterly free, however, from superficiality and exhibitionism). Among writers, the reaction against late 19th-century standards resulted in a deep distrust of authority in religion, morality, and literature, and in an increasing awareness of the need to examine critically and to reevaluate existing institutions. Arnold Bennett, who wrote of the pathetic, drab lives of commonplace people in an industrial society; H. G. Wells, a reformer at heart, who used fiction to advance his criticisms of society, his plans for improving the methods of politics, business, and education, and his visions of a future world; and G. B. Shaw, who in his witty, entertaining, and sometimes shocking dramas conveyed the frequently revolutionary theories by which he hoped to force his public to reconsider their standards, all reflect different manifestations of the critical, questioning temper of the Edwardian age.

Edwardians, The. A novel of English life in the time of Edward VII, by V. Sackville-West, published in 1930.

Edward, Prince of Wales. In Shakespeare's *3 Henry VI*, the only son of Henry VI. He is disinherited when the Yorkists persuade the King to leave the crown to the heir of York, and is captured at Tewkesbury and killed.

Edward, Prince of Wales. In Shakespeare's *3 Henry VI*, the son of Edward IV. In *Richard III*, he becomes King, as Edward V, on the death of his father, but he and his brother are put in the Tower and murdered by Richard, Duke of Gloucester.

Edwards (ed′wardz), **Amelia Ann Blandford.** b. at London, 1831; d. at Weston-super-Mare, Somersetshire, England, April 15, 1892. An English novelist and Egyptologist; cousin of Matilda Barbara Betham-Edwards (1836–1919). She showed talent for drawing and music, and in 1853 began to write for periodicals. After 1880 she devoted herself to archaeological studies. In 1883 she became the honorary secretary of the Egyptian exploration fund. *A Thousand Miles up the Nile* (1877) was illustrated from her own sketches. She also wrote *A Summary of English History* (1856), *An Abridg-*

fat, fāte, fär, ȧsk, fāre; net, mē, hėr; pin, pīne; not, nōte, mȯve, nôr; up, lūte, pull; ŦH, then;

ment of French History (1858), and *Pharaohs, Fellahs, and Explorers* (1891).

Edwards, Jonathan. b. at East Windsor, Conn., Oct. 5, 1703; d. of smallpox, at Princeton, N. J., March 22, 1758. An American theologian, philosopher, metaphysician, and college president. He was the fifth child and the only son of his parents. He was educated at home before he entered Yale at the age of 13, graduating (at the age of 17) at the top of his class. He read Latin at 6, wrote a pamphlet (*The Nature of the Soul*) at 10, a scientific essay (*The Habits of Spiders*) at 12, and at 14 read Locke's *Essay Concerning Human Understanding,* which is ordinarily regarded as a difficult book. After his graduation he spent two additional years at Yale studying theology. In 1722–23, he was pastor of a Presbyterian church at New York. In 1726 he was assistant minister to his grandfather, whose death, two years later, enabled him to become minister of one of the largest and richest churches in all Massachusetts. In July, 1727, he married Sarah Pierrepont, a girl of 17, who became the mother of their 12 children. He had loved her since meeting her four years previously, and his description of her, in a beautiful prose-poem, is one of his best-known and most popular pieces of writing. Its opening lines have been many times quoted: "They say there is a young lady [in New Haven] who is beloved of that Great Being who made and rules the world, and that there are certain seasons in which this Great Being, in some way or other invisible, comes to her and fills her mind with exceeding sweet delight, and that she hardly cares for anything except to meditate on Him. . . . She has a strange sweetness in her mind, and singular purity in her affections; is most just and conscientious in all her conduct; and you could not persuade her to do anything wrong or sinful, if you would give her all the world, lest she should offend this Great Being. . . . She will sometimes go about from place to place, singing sweetly, and seems to be always full of joy and pleasure, and no one knows for what. She loves to be alone, walking in the fields and groves, and seems to have some one invisible always conversing with her." From 1750 until his death he was a missionary to the Indians at Stockbridge, Mass. In the last year of his life, he was elected president of the College of New Jersey (now Princeton University). Appointed on Sept. 26, 1757, he served for less than three months, coming to Princeton early in January, 1758. He wrote *Resolutions* (1722–23), outlining a drastic spiritual program, *A Narrative of Surprising Conversions* (1735), *A Personal Narrative* (1739), describing his own conversion in 1719, *A Treatise Concerning the Religious Affections* (1742–43, 1746), collected sermons, *Qualifications for Full Communion in the Visible Church* (1749), *Of Insects* (1751), *The Great Christian Doctrine of Original Sin Defended* (1758), which claims that man is naturally bad, *History of the Work of Redemption* (1765), an unfinished work, a philosophical discussion of life, heaven, hell, and earth, that its author intended to be a masterpiece, and *The Nature of True Virtue* (1772). *Sinners in the Hands of an Angry God* (1741), a sermon preached at Enfield during "the Great Awakening," is famous for its vivid picture of man

hanging over hell. His great work, the one by which he is remembered, is *A Careful and Strict Enquiry into the Modern Prevailing Notions of that Freedom of the Will which is Supposed to be Essential to Moral Agency, Virtue and Vice, Reward and Punishment, Praise and Blame* (1754), regarded as one of the greatest philosophical works written in America, as a masterpiece of logical reasoning, as the product of a tremendous intellect, and as one of the first American works to attract European attention. Edwards has been called "the greatest single figure produced by Puritanism and Calvinism," "the greatest American mind of the Colonial Period," "the most saintly American that ever lived," "the intellectual flower of New England Puritanism," and "one of the finest minds ever developed on the American continent." He has been compared to Saint Francis of Assisi, and as a mystic he has been contrasted with the practical Franklin.

Edwards, Richard. b. in Somersetshire, England, c1523; d. Oct. 31, 1566. An English dramatist. In 1561 he was appointed master of the Children of the Chapel. He wrote a drama, *Damon and Pythias* (1571; reprinted by Dodsley), and a number of poems, some of which appeared in *The Paradyse of Daynty Devises* (1576). There is also a lost *Palamon and Arcite*, acted in 1566, and written originally in Latin.

Edwin and Angelina (ed'win; an.jẹ.lī'nạ). A ballad by Oliver Goldsmith, privately printed originally for the Countess of Northumberland. The ballad was first published in *The Vicar of Wakefield*, and is also called "The Hermit."

Edwin and Emma (em'ạ). A ballad by David Mallet, written in 1760.

Edwin Cheeryble (chir'i.bl). One of the **Cheeryble Brothers.**

Edwin Drood (dröd), **The Mystery of.** See **Mystery of Edwin Drood, The.**

Edwin Shalford (shal'fọrd). See **Shalford, Edwin.**

Edwy (ed'wi). [Also: **Eadwig;** called **Edwy the Fair.**] b. c940; d. 959. Son of Edmund I and Ælfgifu. He became king of Wessex in 955, succeeding his uncle Edred. When at his coronation feast he retired to the company of his intended wife and her mother, his nobles grew angry and an open fight was prevented only when Saint Dunstan convinced Edwy that he must return to the table. In 957 he exiled Dunstan for his part in the affair. That year Mercia and Northumbria rebelled and chose Edgar as king, but Edwy died in 959 before fighting took place.

Effie Deans (ef'i dēnz). See **Deans, Effie.**

Effie Rink (ringk). See **Rink, Effie.**

Égalité (ā.gȧ.lē.tā), **Philippe.** A name given during the French Revolution to Louis Philippe Joseph, Duc d'Orléans.

Egan (ē'gạn), **Pierce.** b. at London, 1772; d. there, Aug. 3, 1849. An English writer on sports; father of Pierce Egan (1814–80). He was the author of a monthly serial, *Boxiana; or Sketches of modern Pugilism* (1818–24), and of *Life in London* (1821), a serial illustrated by George and Isaac R. Cruikshank.

ḍ, d or j; ş, s or sh; ţ, t or ch; ẓ, z or zh; *o,* F. cloche; ü, F. menu; ċh, Sc. loch; ṅ, F. bonbon.

Egan, Pierce. b. at London, 1814; d. July 6, 1880. An English novelist and artist; son of Pierce Egan (1772–1849). He wrote *Wat Tyler* (1851), *Paul Jones* (1842), *The Snake in the Grass* (1858), and other novels.

Egbert (eg′bĕrt). [Old English, **Ecgberht.**] b. c775; d. 839. A king of Wessex (802–839); grandfather of King Alfred. It was with Egbert that the consolidation of the kingdoms of the Heptarchy into one English realm began, and that the way was first opened for the flowering of literature and scholarship which we associate with the reign of Alfred. He was probably the son of a Kentish underking who was exiled from England to the court of Charlemagne by King Offa of Mercia and King Beorhtric of Kent. In 802 he returned and ascended the throne of Wessex. In 815 he attacked the West Welsh in Cornwall, and in 825 defeated Beornwulf of Mercia at Ellandun, thus obtaining the submission of Kent, Surrey, Sussex, and Essex. Soon after the East Anglians acknowledged him, and in 829 Mercia and Northumbria submitted, thus making him overlord of all the English. He engaged in battles with the Danes, and in 838 beat them and the West Welsh, their British allies, in Cornwall.

Egdon Heath (eg′dọn). The scene of Hardy's *The Return of the Native*, which dominates the story.

Eger and Grime (ē′jĕr; grīm). A Middle English romance, probably based on materials from the late Old English period, but modified by the tone and point of view of the *chansons de geste*. In this tale the lady will marry only a knight who has never been conquered.

Egeria (ẹ.jir′i.ạ). [Also, **Aegeria.**] In Roman mythology, one of the Camenae, or nymphs of springs, by whom Numa was instructed with regard to the forms of worship he was to introduce.

Egerton (ej′ẽr.tọn), Sir **Thomas.** [Titles: Baron **Ellesmere,** Viscount **Brackley.**] b. in Cheshire, England, c1540; d. at London, March 15, 1617. An English jurist, lord chancellor of England from 1603 to 1617.

Egeus (ẹ.jē′us). In Shakespeare's *Midsummer Night's Dream*, the father of Hermia.

Eginhard (ā′gin.härt). See **Einhard.**

Eglamore (eg′lạ.mōr) or **Eglamour** (-mör), Sir. A valiant knight and heroic champion of the Round Table, in the Arthurian cycle of romances. There is a ballad which recounts how he "slew a terrible huge great monstrous dragon."

Eglamour (eg′lạ.mör). In Shakespeare's *Two Gentlemen of Verona*, a courtly knight who helps Silvia escape from Milan and from Thurio, whom her father wishes her to marry. Eglamour deserts her when she is captured by a band of outlaws.

Eglamour, Sir. See **Sir Eglamour.**

Eglantine (eg′lạn.tīn) or **Eglentyne** (-lẹn-), **Madame.** The prioress of Chaucer's "The Prioress's Tale," in *The Canterbury Tales*.

Eglinton (eg′lin.tọn), **John.** Pseudonym of **Magee, William Kirkpatrick.**

Ego Dominus Tuus (ē′gō dom′i.nus tū′us). A poem by William Butler Yeats, published in *The Wild Swans at Coole* (1919).

Ego Dormio (ē′gō dôr′mi.ō). A Middle English prose epistle by Richard Rolle of Hampole, written to advise three holy women. He urges that they love God and lead a contemplative life.

Egoist, The. [Full title: **The Egoist: a Comedy in Narrative.**] A novel by George Meredith, published in 1879. The central character is the vain and selfish Sir Willoughby Patterne, whose cunning exploitation of others to further his purposes finally leads to his own humiliation.

Egremont (eg′rẹ.mont), **Charles.** The hero of Benjamin Disraeli's novel *Sybil*. He is a "Tory Democrat" who falls in love with the daughter of a Chartist.

Egyptian Thief. Thyamis, the lover of Chariclea, referred to in Shakespeare's *Twelfth Night*. Their story is found in "Theagenes and Chariclea" in Heliodorus's *Ethiopica*.

Eikon Basilike (ī′kon ba.sil′i.kē). A book describing the sufferings of Charles I of England, published in 1649. It is usually attributed to Bishop John Gauden.

Eikonoclastes (ī.kon.ọ.klas′tēz). A pamphlet written by John Milton in answer to Gauden's *Eikon Basilike*.

Einhard (īn′härt). [Sometimes called **Eginhard.**] b. in Austrasia, c770; d. at Seligenstadt on the Main, Germany, probably on March 14, 840. A Frankish scholar and biographer of Charlemagne. He was of noble birth, and was educated at the monastery of Fulda. He removed not later than 796 to the court of Charlemagne, who appointed him minister of public works and sent him in 806 as imperial legate to Rome. He was retained in office by Louis le Débonnaire, to whose son Lothaire he became tutor in 817. He retired in 830 to Mulinheim (which he named Seligenstadt), where he erected a monastery. He was married to Imma, who was the sister of Bernhard, bishop of Worms, but who was supposed by later tradition to be a daughter of Charlemagne. He wrote a life of Charlemagne, *Vita Caroli Magni*. He may have been the architect of the cathedral at Aachen.

Eisteddfod (ā.steᴛʜ′vōd). An annual musical and literary festival and competition which originated in the triennial assembly of Welsh bards; the latter dates back to an early period. An Eisteddfod is mentioned as having been held in the 7th century. They are now held every year at various places in Wales. Concerts and competitions for prizes are still held; but, except that they take place in Wales and retain some ancient forms, they are no longer particularly national in character.

Eitherside (ē′ᴛʜĕr.sīd, ī′-), **Sergeant.** A character in Mackenzie's *Man of the World*.

Eitherside, Sir Paul. In Ben Jonson's comedy *The Devil is an Ass*, a hard, unfeeling justice and superstitious wiseacre.

Elagabalus (ē.lạ.gab′ạ.lus). [Also: **Heliogabalus;** as emperor called **Marcus Aurelius Antoninus;** original name, **Varius Avitus Bassianus.**] b. at Emesa (modern Homs), Syria, 205 A.D.; d. 222. Emperor of Rome. He was the son of Sextus Varius Marcellus and Julia Soaemias, and first cousin of Caracalla. He became while very young a priest in the temple of the sun god Elagabalus at Emesa. Being put forward as the son of Caracalla, he was proclaimed emperor by the soldiers in 218, in opposition to Macrinus who was defeated on the borders of Syria and Phoenicia in the same year. He gave himself up to the most infamous debauchery, and abandoned the government to his mother and grandmother. He adopted his cousin, Bassianus Alexianus, who succeeded to the throne as Severus Alexander. He was put to death at Rome by the praetorians.

Elaine (ẹ.lān'). In the Arthurian legends: **1.** A half sister of King Arthur. In some versions she bore Arthur a son, Modred (elsewhere identified as his nephew and the daughter of Margawse).
2. The daughter of King Pelles. She was the mother of Sir Lancelot's son Sir Galahad.
3. The "lily maid of Astolat" who pined and died for Lancelot, usually considered the same character as the preceding. Tennyson makes her story the subject of his *Elaine*.
4. The wife of Ban of Brittany, mother of Sir Lancelot. She was also called Elein.

Elbow (el'bō). In Shakespeare's *Measure for Measure*, a constable, comparable but inferior to Dogberry in *Much Ado About Nothing*.

Elder Brother, The. A comedy by Fletcher and Massinger, published first in 1637 and produced at the Blackfriars Theatre. Although it was ascribed to Beaumont and Fletcher in 1651, the 1661 quarto mentioned Fletcher only, and it is now generally agreed that Massinger had a hand in it. Its plot concerns two brothers, dissimilar in nature: one a bookish scholar, the other a foppish courtier. In their concern over the same girl the younger brother, Eustace, tries to carry her off so that the elder, Charles, whose interest has been whetted by her beauty, will not be able to marry her. Charles prevents this attempt and Eustace challenges him to a duel, which results in his proving his manhood and in Charles's showing his love for the lady.

Elder Loveless (luv'lẹs). See **Loveless, Elder.**

Elder Sister, The. A novel by Frank Swinnerton, published in 1925. It is a study of jealousy and the eternal triangle.

Eldest Son, The. A drama (1909) by John Galsworthy.

El Dorado (el dō.rä'ᴛʜō). [Also, **Manoa.**] A legendary city of great wealth which, during the 16th and 17th centuries and part of the 18th, was supposed to exist somewhere in the N part of South America. Beginning c1532, a number of expeditions were made by the Spaniards in search of this phantom; the explorers suffered terrible hardships, and hundreds died. The conquest and settlement of New Granada resulted from the quest; the mountain regions of Venezuela, the Orinoco and Amazon rivers, and the great forests E of the Andes were made known to the world; and later in the 16th century the English, led or sent by Sir Walter Raleigh, penetrated into Guiana, obtaining a claim on that country which resulted in their modern colony. The story of El Dorado arose from a yearly ceremony of an Indian tribe near what is now Bogotá, Colombia. According to the story, the chief of the Guatavitá in the highlands of Bogotá (Colombia) was periodically smeared with oil or balsam, and then covered with gold dust until his whole body had a gilded appearance, after which he threw gold, emeralds, and other precious stones into a sacred lake and then bathed there. This ceremony ceased upon the conquest of the tribe of Guatavitá by the Chibchans, but the tradition of this extraordinary rite remained and gradually spread very far, though in a more or less distorted form. In common and poetical language the name El Dorado, originally applied to the ruler, has now been transferred to the city or country which was the object of the quest.

Eleanor, Duchess of Gloucester (el'ạ.nọr; glos'tẻr). See **Gloucester, Eleanor, Duchess of.**

Eleanor of Aquitaine (ak.wi.tān'). [Also: **Eleanor of Guienne**; French, **Aliénor.**] b. c1122; d. at Fontevrault, Maine-et-Loire, France, April 1, 1204. Queen of France and England. She was the daughter of William X, Duke of Aquitaine, and came into her inheritance on his death in 1137. She married the same year Louis of France, who within a month of the marriage became Louis VII of France. She accompanied him on the second Crusade and there, it is said (but without foundation) was improperly intimate with her uncle, Raymond of Antioch. In 1152, despite the fact that she had borne him two daughters, Louis divorced her (or had the marriage annulled) on the grounds of consanguinity. That same year she was married to the English prince, Henry of Anjou, bringing to him the possessions in Aquitaine. When he became king as Henry II in 1154, the stage was set for the long series of wars between England and France over the French territories of the English crown. Eleanor soon discovered that her husband was unfaithful and, though his affair with Rosamond Clifford occurred later, she soon grew to dislike him. In 1173 she backed her sons in their revolt against Henry and was kept under surveillance until Henry's death in 1189. She became a chief adviser to both Richard I and John. When John attempted to usurp the throne during Richard's absence on the third Crusade, she broke up the conspiracy and later reconciled the brothers. She was instrumental in ransoming Richard from his captivity in France. She saw to it that the succession passed to John and supported him against the claims of her grandson Arthur of Brittany. She was a patron of literature and maintained a brilliant court at Poitiers.

Eleanor of Aquitaine. See also under **Elinor, Queen.**

Eleatics (el.ẹ.at'iks). A school of Greek philosophy founded by Xenophanes of Colophon, who resided in Elea, or Velia, in Magna Graecia. The most distinguished philosophers of this school were Parmenides and Zeno. The main Eleatic doctrines are developments of the conception that the One, or Absolute, alone is real.

Eleazar (el.ẹ.ā'zạr). In *Lust's Dominion*, all or parts of which have been attributed to Christopher Marlowe, a lustful and revengeful Moor, passionately loved by the sensual Queen of Spain. In his villainies he resembles Barabas in Marlowe's *Jew of Malta*.

Elector Palatine's Company. See **Lord Admiral's Men.**

Electra (ẹ.lek′trạ). In Greek legend, the daughter of Agamemnon and Clytemnestra, and sister of Orestes. The events of her life have been dramatized by Aeschylus, by Sophocles in his *Electra*, by Euripides in his *Electra*, and by various modern poets.

elegiac (e.lē′ji.ak, el.ẹ.jī′ak), *a.* and *n.* *a.* **1.** In ancient prosody, an epithet noting a distich the first line of which is a dactylic hexameter and the second a pentameter, or verse differing from the hexameter by suppression of the arsis or metrically unaccented part of the third and the sixth foot, thus:

$$\dot{\smile} \smile \smile \mid \dot{\smile} \smile \smile \mid \dot{\smile} \smile \smile \mid \dot{\smile} \smile \smile \mid \dot{\smile} \smile \smile \mid \dot{\smile} \smile$$
$$\dot{\smile} \smile \smile \mid \dot{\smile} \smile \smile \mid \dot{\smile} \mid\mid \dot{\smile} \smile \smile \mid \dot{\smile} \smile \smile \mid \dot{\smile}$$

Verses or poems consisting of elegiac distichs are called *elegiac verses* or *poems* (*elegiacs*); poetry composed in this meter, *elegiac verse* or *poetry* (*the elegy*); and the writers who employed this verse, especially those who employed it exclusively or by preference, are known as the *elegiac poets*. Elegiac verse seems to have been used primarily in threnetic pieces (poems lamenting or commemorating the dead), or to have been associated with music of a kind regarded by the Greeks as mournful. Almost from its first appearance in literature, however, it is found used for compositions of various kinds. The principal Roman elegiac poets are Catullus, Tibullus, Propertius, and Ovid. In modern German literature the elegiac meter has been frequently used, especially by Goethe and Schiller. Coleridge's translation from the latter poet may serve as an example in English.

Ĭn thĕ hĕx | āmĕtĕr | rīsĕs thĕ | fōuntāin's | sīlvĕrў | cōlŭmn,
Ĭn thĕ pĕn | tāmĕtĕr | āyĕ || fāllĭng ĭn | mĕlŏdў | bāck.
(Coleridge, *The Ovidian Elegiac Meter.*)

    You should crave his rule
For pauses in the elegiac couplet, chasms
Permissible only to Catullus!
(Browning, *Ring and Book*, I. 276.)

2. Belonging to an elegy, or to elegy; having to do with elegies. "Arnold is a great elegiac poet, but there is a buoyancy in his elegy which we rarely find in the best elegy, and which certainly adds greatly to its charm."
(*Contemporary Rev.*, XLIX. 528.)

3. Expressing sorrow or lamentation: as, *elegiac* strains.

    Let elegiack lay the woe relate,
Soft as the breath of distant flutes.
(Gay, *Trivia*.)

    Mr. Lyttleton is a gentle elegiac person.
(Gray, *Letters*, I. 220.)

n. In prosody: (*a*) A pentameter, or verse consisting of two dactylic penthemims or written in elegiac meter. (*b*) *pl.* A succession of distichs consisting each of a dactylic hexameter and a dipenthemim; a poem or poems in such distichs: as, the Heroides and Tristia of Ovid are written in *elegiacs*.

elegy (el′ẹ.ji). **1.** In classical poetry, a poem written in elegiac verse.

    The third sorrowing was of loues, by long lamentation in Elegie: so was their song called, and it was in a pitious maner of meetre, placing a limping

Pentameter after a lusty Exameter, which made it go dolourously more then any other meeter.
(Puttenham, *Arte of Eng. Poesie.*)

2. A mournful or plaintive poem; a poem or song expressive of sorrow and lamentation; a dirge; a funeral song.

    And there is such a solemn melody,
'Tween doleful songs, tears and sad elegies.
(Webster, *White Devil*, V.i.)

Let Swans from their forsaken Rivers fly,
And sick'ning at her Tomb, make haste to dye,
That they may help to sing her Elegy.
(Congreve, *Death of Queen Mary*.)

3. Any serious poem pervaded by a tone of melancholy, whether grief is actually expressed or not: as, Gray's "*Elegy* in a Country Churchyard."

Elegy is the form of poetry natural to the reflective mind. It may treat of any subject, but it must treat of no subject for itself, but always and exclusively with reference to the poet himself.
(Coleridge.)

4. In music, a sad or funereal composition, vocal or instrumental, whether actually commemorative or not; a dirge.

Elegy on Ben Jonson, An. A poem by John Cleveland on the death of Ben Jonson.

Elegy Upon the Death of the Dean of St. Paul's, Dr. John Donne. A poem by Thomas Carew on the death of John Donne. It ends with an epitaph:

    Here lies a king, that ruled as he thought fit
The universal monarchy of wit;
Here lie two flamens, and both those the best:
Apollo's first, at last the true God's priest.

Elegy Written in a Country Churchyard. An elegiac poem by Thomas Gray, published in 1751. It went through 11 editions in a short time, and has been many times pirated, imitated, and parodied. (In the course of the several generations since it was written it has also been so often misquoted, in print, that few scholars now have the temerity to insist that anyone can be sure of exactly what all the original words and spellings may have been.) It has also been translated into Hebrew, Greek, Latin, Italian, Portuguese, French, Russian, and German.

Elene (el′ẹ.nẹ). An Old English poem by Cynewulf, one of the four works signed by the poet, preserved in the *Vercelli Book*. It relates, in some 1300 lines, the story of Constantine's vision of the cross, his conversion, and the finding of the true cross in the Holy Land by Saint Helena, his mother. One passage, which tells of the poet's former sinfulness and of his happiness since devoting his art to God, has been considered as possibly autobiographical.

Eleonora (el″ẹ.ọ.nō′rạ). A poem written by Dryden, in 1692, in memory of the Countess of Abingdon.

Eleusinian Mysteries (el.ū.sin′i.ạn). Religious ceremonies performed in ancient Greece in honor of Demeter, the Greek equivalent of the Roman Ceres, and her daughter, Persephone (the Roman Proserpine). They were held at Eleusis, in Attica, about 10 miles from Athens, and were the chief cause of its fame. At first initiation into the mysteries was limited to residents of Attica; later it was extended to all Greek citizens, and still later, Romans were admitted to the privileges of membership. Barbarians (which initially, of course, included the Romans), murderers, and all who were guilty of serious crimes were barred. A candidate for initiation was proposed by an Athenian citizen who already belonged. The candidates were called *mystae* before full initiation, and *epoptae*, or seers, after. The mysteries were divided into two parts, the Lesser, held in Antestherion, corresponding more or less to February, and the Greater, in Boedromion, equivalent to part of the end of September and the beginning of October. The mysteries were regarded by the ancients themselves as having moral and ethical values in that they promised, or seemed to promise, life after death as a reward for goodness. Hadrian and Marcus Aurelius did not think it beneath them to accept initiation. Valentinian, the Christian emperor, allowed the Eleusinian mysteries after he had abolished all others, but Theodosius did away with them at the end of the 4th century.

Elfrida (el.frē′dạ). [Also, **Ælfthryth**.] b. c945; d. c1000. An Anglo-Saxon queen, daughter of Ordgar, ealdorman of Devon, wife first of Aethelwald, ealdorman of the East Anglians, and, after his death, of King Edgar, by whom she was the mother of Ethelred II (Ethelred the Unready). She is said to have caused the murder of her stepson Edward, at Corfe, in order to secure the election of Ethelred.

Elgin Marbles (el′gin). A collection of Greek sculptures comprising the bulk of the surviving plastic decoration of the Parthenon, and a caryatid and column from the Erechtheum, and recognized as containing the finest existing productions of Greek sculpture. The marbles, now in the British Museum, were brought from Athens between 1801 and 1803 by Thomas Bruce, the 7th Earl of Elgin. The Parthenon sculptures were executed under the direction of Phidias, c440 B.C. The collection includes remains of the pediment statues in the round, a great part of the frieze, in low relief, ab. 525 ft. long, which surrounded the exterior of the cella, and 15 of the metopes of the exterior frieze, carved in very high relief with episodes of the contest between the Centaurs and the Lapiths. Among the chief of the pediment figures are the reclining figure of Theseus, Iris with wind-blown drapery, and the group of one reclining and two seated female figures popularly called the "Three Fates."

El Greco (grek′ō). See **Greco, El.**

Elia (ē′li.ạ). The pseudonym of Charles Lamb in his essays contributed (1820 *et seq.*) to the *London Magazine*. They were collected as *Essays of Elia* in 1823, and *Last Essays of Elia* in 1833. The name was that of a clerk in the South Sea House, which Lamb remembered having heard there as a boy, and was at first used as a jest at the end of *Recollections of South Sea House*, the first of his essays. The Briget and James Elia of the essays are Mary and John Lamb, the brother and sister of the author.

Eliab (ẹ.lī′ab). In Dryden and Tate's *Absalom and Achitophel*, Henry Bennet, Earl of Arlington.

Elidure (el′i.dör). A legendary king of Britain, mentioned as the brother of Artegal in Geoffrey of Monmouth's *Historia regum Britanniae.*

Elijah (ẹ.lī′jạ). [Greek, **Elias** (ẹ.lī′ạs).] A Hebrew prophet of the 9th century B.C. An account of him is given in 1 Kings, xvii.–xxi., 2 Kings, i.–xi., and 2 Chron. xxi. 12–15. He appears before Ahab, king of Israel (who had given himself up to the idolatry of his Phoenician wife Jezebel), and predicts a great drought. Compelled to seek refuge in flight and concealment, he is miraculously fed by ravens in the torrent bed of the stream Cherith, and by the widow of Zarephath, whose dead son he restores to life. In the extremity of the famine he reappears before Ahab, before whom he calls down fire from heaven to consume a sacrifice to Jehovah, with the result that the king orders the extermination of the prophets of Baal, who are unable to call down fire to consume the offerings to Baal. Elijah then puts an end to the drought by prayers to Jehovah. Later he denounces Ahab and Jezebel for having despoiled and murdered Naboth, and is eventually carried to heaven in a chariot of fire. In the New Testament he is called Elias.

Elijah Pogram (pō′grạm). See **Pogram, Elijah.**

Elinor (el′i.nọr), **Queen.** In Shakespeare's *King John*, the mother of John. She follows him to France and he learns she has died there (IV.ii). She is the historical Eleanor of Aquitaine, first married to Louis VII of France and then to Henry II of England.

Elinor Barley (bär′li). A novelette by Sylvia Townsend Warner, published in 1930.

Elinor Dashwood (dash′wụd). See **Dashwood, Elinor.**

Eliot (el′i.ọt, el′yọt), **George.** [Pseudonym of **Mary Ann** (or **Marian**) **Evans**.] b. at Arbury Farm, near Nuneaton, Warwickshire, England, Nov. 22, 1819; d. at Chelsea, London, Dec. 22, 1880. An English psychological novelist, poet, and essayist. She is considered by some authorities the greatest of English women novelists and the equal of Dickens and Thackeray. She began her literary career by translating (1844–46) into English a life of Jesus written by the German theologian David Friedrich Strauss and as a contributor to and assistant editor of the *Westminster Review* (1850–53). Her career as a novelist opened (1857) with *The Sad Fortunes of the Reverend Amos Barton*, the beginning of *Scenes from Clerical Life* (1858). Her other major works include *Adam Bede* (1859), the story of an idealistic carpenter, *The Mill on the Floss* (1860), in which Tom and Maggie Tulliver represent the author and her brother Isaac, *Silas Marner* (1861), a long short-story rather than a novel, *Romola* (1863), an historical novel dealing with Florence in the days of Savonarola, and *Middlemarch* (1871–72), a psychological study of provincial life. Her lesser works, in the opinion of most modern critics, are *Felix Holt, the Radical* (1866), a political novel which has Gerald Massey, the English poet and radical, as its hero, *Daniel Deronda* (1876), her last fiction, a study of spiritual conflict and development, her poems *How Lisa Loved the King* (1867), *The Spanish Gypsy* (1868), and *The Legend of Jubal* (1870), and her satirical essays, *Impressions of Theo-*

ḍ, d or j; ṣ, s or sh; ṭ, t or ch; ẓ, z or zh; o, F. cloche; ü, F. menu; ċh, Sc. loch; ṅ, F. bonbon.

phrastus Such (1879). In 1854 she entered into a union (that lasted until his death) with the philosopher George Henry Lewes, who was unable to marry her because of the refusal of his wife to grant him a divorce. On May 6, 1880, she married an old friend, John Walter Cross, who later (1885–86) published *George Eliot's Life as Related in Her Letters and Journals.*

Eliot, T. S. [Full name, **Thomas Stearns Eliot.**] b. at St. Louis, Mo., 1888–. An American-born poet and critic who became (1927) a naturalized British subject. His poetic commentaries on the civilization and spirit of his day (notably *The Waste Land*, 1922, which was awarded the Dial poetry prize), with their distinctive technique of ironic juxtaposition of ideal and reality, subtle allusions to direct or disguised quotations from a great variety of earlier literary works, and a poetic logic which eliminated the conventional transitions between images and episodes, profoundly influenced younger writers on both sides of the Atlantic. He was awarded the 1948 Nobel prize for literature. Educated at Harvard, the Sorbonne, and Oxford, he lived (1914 *et seq.*) in England, where he worked first as a bank clerk and then with the publishing firm of Faber and Gwyer (later Faber and Faber), and until 1939 edited *The Criterion*, a literary review. His earlier poetry, characterized by pessimism, includes *Prufrock and Other Observations* (1917), *Poems* (1919), which includes "Portrait of a Lady," "Sweeney Among the Nightingales," "Gerontion," and 21 other poems, *The Hollow Men* (1925), and *Journey of the Magi* (1927). He then developed a more limpid and meditative style, as in *A Song for Simeon* (1928), *Animula* (1929), and *Marina* (1930). After turning to Anglo-Catholicism he struck a note of quietist religious acceptance in *Ash Wednesday* (1930), *The Rock* (1934), and *Four Quartets* (1944), in all of which works he made use of the Anglican liturgy and such mystical writers as Saint John of the Cross in order to present a mood of restrained penitential hope and faith. He is the author also of the poetic dramas *Murder in the Cathedral* (1935), *Family Reunion* (1939), *The Cocktail Party* (1949), and *The Confidential Clerk* (1954). His critical essays appeared in *The Sacred Wood* (1920), *An Essay of Poetic Drama* (1928), *Dante* (1929), *Selected Essays* (1932), *The Use of Poetry and the Use of Criticism* (1933), *After Strange Gods* (1934), *Elizabethan Essays* (1934), *Essays Ancient and Modern* (1936), *The Idea of a Christian Society* (1939), *What is a Classic?* (1945), and *Notes toward the Definition of Culture* (1949).

Eliphaz (el'i.faz). In the Bible, the chief of the three friends of Job, surnamed the "Temanite." Job, ii. 11, etc.

Elisha (ē.lī'sha). [Also, **Eliseus** (el.i.sē'us).] fl. in the 9th century B.C. A Hebrew prophet, the attendant and successor of Elijah. 1 Kings, xix. 15–21.

elision (ē.lizh'on). A striking or cutting off; specifically, in grammar, the cutting off or suppression of a vowel or syllable, naturally or for the sake of euphony or meter, especially at the end of a word when the next word begins with a vowel; more generally, the suppression of any part of a word in speech or writing: as, in "th' embattled plain"

there is an elision of *e*; in "I'll not do it" there is an elision of *wi*.

The Italian is so full of Vowels, that it must euer be cumbred with Elisions.
(Sir P. Sidney, *Apol. for Poetrie.*)

He has made use of several Elisions that are not customary among other English Poets.
(Addison, *Spectator*, No. 285.)

Nor praise I less that circumcision
By modern poets call'd elision,
With which, in proper station plac'd,
Thy polish'd lines are firmly brac'd.
(Swift, *The Dean's Answer to Sheridan.*)

Elissa (ē.lis'a). [Also, **Elisa.**] Under the name Dido, the heroine of the fourth book of Vergil's *Aeneid*. According to the tradition she was the daughter of King Matgen (or Belus), grandson of Eth-Baal of Phoenicia. She was married to her uncle Sicharbaal or Sicharbas (the Greek Acerbas and the Sychaeus of Vergil). After her husband was murdered by her brother Pygmalion, she set out at the head of Tyrian colonists to Africa. In Africa she bought as much land as could be enclosed in the hide of a bull, but by cutting the hide into thin strips managed to obtain a fairly large area on which she built the citadel around which Carthage grew up. To escape wedding the barbarian king Iarbas (Hiarbas) she erected a funeral pyre and stabbed herself upon it. According to Vergil her death was due to her despair at her desertion by Aeneas. In the popular mind she became confounded with Dido, a surname of Astarte as goddess of the moon, who was also the goddess of the citadel of Carthage.

Elissa. In the second book of Spenser's *Faerie Queene*, the eldest of three sisters who were always at odds. She is the sister of Medina and Perissa, and mistress of the rash Hudibras.

Eliza (ē.lī'za). In *Letters of Yorick to Eliza* by Laurence Sterne, the name used for Mrs. Eliza Draper, the young wife of an official of the East India Company. Sterne had known her in London and wrote to her after she had gone to Bombay. He also kept a journal for her, called *The Bramine's Journal.*

Elizabeth (ē.liz'a.beth). [Also, **Elizabeth I, Elizabeth Tudor**; sometimes called the "Virgin Queen."] b. at Greenwich Palace, London, Sept. 7, 1533; d. at Richmond, Surrey, March 24, 1603. Queen of England (1558–1603). She was the daughter of Henry VIII and his second wife, Anne Boleyn. Henry's marriage to Catherine of Aragon had been declared invalid by a court headed by Thomas Cranmer in 1533, and Henry married Anne Boleyn, one of the court ladies and a sister of one of Henry's former mistresses, Mary Boleyn. This marriage, secretly performed in January, 1533, was followed by Anne's coronation on Whitsunday, 1533; but while recognition of the marriage was official in England, Catherine and her adherents, including Pope Clement VII, refused to sanction the annulment of the previous marriage or the legitimacy of the issue of the new marriage. Thus, the right of Elizabeth to the throne was a live question throughout her reign and the many conspirators based their plots on what they considered a usurpation. In 1534, after the birth of Elizabeth, a parliamentary act of succession recognized the rights of Anne's issue as heirs to the throne; Elizabeth, who was to be Anne's only surviving child, became heir presumptive of England, taking place ahead of Mary, Catherine's child. In 1536, when Anne was tried and executed on a charge of adultery, Henry's second marriage was invalidated too; since this annulment constituted more than a divorce in that the offspring of the marriage were disowned, Elizabeth's claim to the English throne was afterwards called by many illegitimate, for the invalid marriage (the excuse for the annulment was that Anne Boleyn had been betrothed by contract to Henry Percy, Earl of Northumberland) was regarded as never having taken place legally and no heirs from the marriage could legally be recognized. Soon after the execution of Anne and the immediately following marriage of Henry to Jane Seymour, a new act of succession established the issue of the Seymour marriage in line of title. Later, after Jane's death in 1537 as the result of the birth of a male heir (who became Edward VI), Parliament passed an act (following Henry's will) that put the order of succession as it actually later occurred: Edward, son of Jane Seymour; Mary, daughter of Catherine of Aragon; and Elizabeth, daughter of Anne Boleyn. Since none of these rulers had children and since Henry had no further issue from his three remaining marriages, the line of succession of the Tudors was not complicated further, and after Elizabeth's death the crown passed to James VI of Scotland, who as great-great-grandson of Henry VII, had next claim to the throne of England through his mother, Mary Queen of Scots. The Tudor line died with Elizabeth and the Stuarts came to the English throne.

Early Years. Elizabeth's education as a child and young girl was by teachers who followed the new Humanism of Erasmus, Colet, and More. She and her half-brother Edward were taught together and both were brought up as Protestants, since Henry had broken with the Roman Catholic Church over the question of the divorce from Catherine of Aragon. But whereas Edward was a deeply religious youth, Elizabeth's religious persuasion was never very strong; during Mary's reign she did not antagonize the Roman Catholics; during her own reign she did not persecute them. Among her tutors were Roger Ascham (who later wrote *The Scholemaster* and who became Elizabeth's secretary) and William Grindal. She became expert in languages, learning not only Greek and Latin, but French, German, and Italian as well. She was an accomplished writer and an eloquent speaker; tradition is quite specific about her command both of the courtly and flowery language and of the vigorous and vulgar tongue of her times. Elizabeth seems to have been rather handsome and, after Edward's accession as Edward VI, she was courted by Thomas Seymour, brother of the Protector, Edward Seymour, Duke of Somerset. Seymour, plotting to take his brother's place as the king's guardian, had married Catherine Parr, widow of Henry VIII, with whom Elizabeth lived after Edward became king. After Catherine Parr's death in 1548, Seymour openly tried to marry Elizabeth, but though it is possible that certain intimacies occurred, nothing came of the match. Seymour was implicated in the plot that attempted to supersede the order of succession and place Lady Jane Grey on the throne and Elizabeth was severely questioned about the matter, but she was cleared of complicity; Seymour was executed. Elizabeth supported Mary Tudor's claim to the throne and when Mary came to London as queen after the suppression of the plot Elizabeth was at her side. Although she was not tied to the insurrection (1554) of Sir Thomas Wyatt to unseat Mary, who was about to make her unpopular marriage with Philip II of Spain, Elizabeth was nevertheless, as a danger to Mary's continuance on the throne, imprisoned in the Tower and later at Woodstock. She was afterwards received at court but spent most of her time until the end of Mary's reign in seclusion at Hatfield.

Accession and Consolidation. Mary died on Nov. 17, 1558, and Elizabeth, though opposed by Roman Catholics on the grounds of illegitimacy, came to the throne of England. The persecutions of Mary were fresh in the minds of the English and thus Roman Catholic objections to Elizabeth probably served only to strengthen her popular position. After a brief struggle with the English bishops over her position in the English church, Elizabeth saw to it that a bill of uniformity was passed in 1559 making her "Supreme Governor" (a compromise title in place of "Supreme Head") of the kingdom in religious matters. This compromise bill both placated the group that did not want to see a woman as head of the church and forestalled immediate action by the Roman Catholics and the Calvinists against her. Her coronation in 1559, however, was performed by the bishop of Carlisle, since the majority of the bishops refused to act. In choosing her privy council Elizabeth retained a number of people who had served under Mary, but she also appointed seven of her own people as advisers, including William Cecil (who was created Baron Burghley in 1571) as her secretary of state and Nicholas Bacon as lord privy seal and later as lord chancellor. There were no clerics on her privy council. Her principal subsequent appointment was of Francis Walsingham as Burghley's successor as secretary of state.

Foreign Policy. Elizabeth's reign was marked by the avoidance of war openly while at the same time it followed a policy of aggressive resistance to the spread of Spanish power and necessarily encouraged an atmosphere of extreme nationalism. The policy of the Tudors led them towards absolutism and Elizabeth early recognized that wars would mean expenditures heavier than the normal budget would allow, and that these expenditures would require the convening of Parliament with its limiting power on the monarchy. Therefore, while her privateers waged unofficial war on Spain, returning huge fortunes to the royal coffers, officially England remained at peace for almost 30 years. Her armies and navies were only partly royal levies; a large proportion of her troops and ships were supplied by the great noblemen. Not until 1588 did open warfare really break out, and then nature and chance came to her defense by virtually destroying the Spanish Armada after it met (and was crippled by) the English. The later years of her reign were marked, however, by increasing taxes to support the war against Spain. Elizabeth came to the throne in the year that Calais was lost (January, 1558) to the French; English spirit and fortunes were at a low ebb. Her appointment of Cecil to handle her foreign affairs was a wise one. By the treaty of Cateau-Cambrésis (1559), France was to return Calais to England in eight years. England and Spain temporarily sided with one another; negotiations were going on for a marriage between Elizabeth and Philip II of Spain. Trouble now began over Scotland. Mary Stuart had married Francis of Valois, who came to the French throne in 1559 as Francis II. Mary claimed to be queen of both Scotland and England and issued orders to obtain Scottish conformity with the Roman Catholic Church. Elizabeth made an alliance with the Scottish reformers and, by July, 1560 (Treaty of Edinburgh), forced the withdrawal of the French from Scotland. Francis died in 1560 and Mary, returning to Scotland, became embroiled with the followers of John Knox. She married Lord Darnley and then, after his death, the earl of Bothwell, but eventually fled (1568) to England before the fury of the Scots and appealed to Elizabeth for sanctuary. Elizabeth, recognizing that she had her hands on a strong claimant to the English throne, kept Mary in custody for almost 20 years. Eventually, because of the many plots to free the Scots queen and to revive her claims to both thrones, Elizabeth permitted her execution in 1587. Before this, however, English alliance had swung from Spain to France. The marriage with Philip of Spain had fallen through and the activities of the Roman Catholics in England, supported by Philip, grew stronger and culminated in the rebellion in 1569 of the earls of Westmorland and Northumberland. The piratical activities of Drake and Hawkins on the Spanish Main were a constant cause of friction, but Spain, faced with revolt in the Netherlands, could not afford an open break. Instead, Philip entered into further intrigue: the Ridolfi plot of 1571 was aimed at deposing Elizabeth (a papal bull had already deposed and excommunicated her) and placing Mary Queen of Scots on the throne along with Thomas Howard, the duke of Norfolk. The plot was exposed, Norfolk was executed, and Mary fell further into the queen's displeasure. The new reorientation of policy toward France was accompanied by marriage negotiations with the duke of Anjou (later Henry III of France) and François d'Alençon, but yet again the attempts to get the queen married came to nothing. When the Dutch revolted against Spain, Elizabeth supported them (treaty of alliance, 1577) and, therefore (after Elizabeth had returned the Spanish ambassador in 1586 for organizing plots against her), and also to put a halt to the increasingly serious raids of English mariners on his shipping, Philip determined to attack England. To this end he began gathering a fleet to carry soldiers to Britain. Francis Drake's daring raid on Cadiz in 1587 sank a sufficient number of ships to put off the invasion for a year, but in July, 1588, the Spanish Armada (the Invincible Armada) sailed with 25,000 troops and 30,000 seamen against England. It was supposed to pick up 25,000 more troops in the Netherlands before the invasion actually took place, but the English fleet under Charles Howard caught up with the Armada in the English Channel and for a week the 130 ships of the Armada were harried until on July 29 they were caught off Calais and scattered. The Spanish admiral, the duke of Medina-Sidonia, abandoned the plan to invade England and tried to get his ships back to Spain. The Channel was blocked and he sailed north around the British Isles. But the gale that had aided the English off Calais increased and the Armada was torn to bits off the Hebrides; fewer than half the ships ever got back to Spain. Now, after 30 years, Elizabeth found herself at war. In 1585, the earl of Leicester, Robert Dudley, had been sent to the Netherlands to aid the Dutch in their rebellion. In 1589 Drake raided Portugal (at the time a part of the Spanish king's domain) and raids were carried out against Cadiz (1596) and the Azores (1597). The Spanish war continued until the end of Elizabeth's reign. In 1597, the Irish rebelled; Robert Devereux, the earl of Essex, was sent to put down the revolt but he failed; not until 1603, after Charles Blount was appointed to the command there, was the rebellion suppressed.

Religion. Elizabeth's accession in 1558 followed a period of active suppression of Protestantism under Mary Tudor. The new queen was welcomed by the English who, with the rising feeling of nationalism, were turning against the rule of Rome in spiritual affairs. In 1559 two bills passed Parliament establishing the Church of England: the act of uniformity called for the use of the second Prayer Book (1552, by Thomas Cranmer) that made of the Roman Catholic Mass the Anglican Communion; the act of supremacy established Elizabeth as supreme governor in spiritual matters. Matthew Parker, who had been Anne Boleyn's chaplain, was appointed (1559) archbishop of Canterbury. Parker rewrote the 42 articles of convocation of Edward VI into the 39 articles (proclaimed by Elizabeth, 1563) and supervised the edition of the Bible known as the Bishop's Bible (1572). Elizabeth's policy, once the church had been cleared of ecclesiastics who refused to accept the acts of uniformity and supremacy, was one of toleration. Only the extreme Puritans (Brownists) and the Roman Catholics were not included in the new Anglican Church. Elizabeth supported the Calvinists in Scotland against the claims of the Roman Catholic Mary Queen of Scots, and under Elizabeth Protestantism was carried into Ireland. In 1570 Pope Pius V excommunicated her; she was faced, both before and after that, with several Roman Catholic plots to depose her and to bring Mary to the throne. The English Roman Catholics had set up a college at Douai in 1561 (located at Reims after 1571) from which missionary priests were sent to England to convert the English to Roman Catholicism and, incidentally, to support the plots against the queen. Among the famous priests who so acted were Edmund Campion (executed for conspiracy in 1581) and Robert Parsons (who later headed the English College at Rome). The controversy within the Anglican Church over Puritanism was carried even into Parliament, where members (like Peter and Paul Wentworth) agitated for reform. John Whitgift (later archbishop of Canterbury) and Thomas Cartwright (Cambridge professor of divinity, removed for his part in the argument) carried on a heated debate over conformity. The Martin Marprelate pamphlets of 1588–89 began a controversy concerning Whitgift's authority that ended with vigorous suppression of the pamphleteering.

Internal Policy. Elizabeth avoided, as long as she could, excess taxation, in the well-founded belief that thus she would avoid domestic unrest and would foster financial soundness within the country. Her avoidance of war was a result of this policy; when it was necessary to raise money, she sold royal lands rather than raise the tax burden. Her popularity, in fact, began to wane only after the beginning of the Spanish war in the late 1580's. Her shares of such matters as Drake's raiding voyage (1577–80) on Spanish shipping off South America were far from negligible. In 1560 and 1561 the coinage was standardized on a silver basis and in 1563 the Statute of Artificers set up a labor code that attempted to establish employment standards on a national basis, whereby unemployment would cease and wages would be regulated. This domestic policy culminated in the Elizabethan Poor Laws of 1597 and 1601 which made the parishes responsible for the care of the needy and imposed very heavy penalties for vagabondage. Elizabeth, true to the Tudor tradition, called few parliaments; in her more than 44 years on the throne only 13 parliaments were assembled. But even then Parliament made advances in these years; it grew from 308 to 372 members; it established its right to debate and legislate on matters only barely approaching those for which it was specifically called. Monopolies were granted by the crown in everything from foreign trade to domestic commodities, and while this helped in England's commercial and industrial expansion, it resulted in rising costs (as much as 400 percent) and the tyranny of arbitrary search and seizure. Elizabeth's later parliaments (1592, 1597, 1601) attempted to deal with the problems raised by these monopolies. In 1600 the East India Company, which in later years was to bring its richest empire to England, was chartered. A recurrent and a constant problem was Elizabeth's spinsterhood. Diplomatic marriages with Philip II of Spain or the French dukes of Anjou and Alençon were projected, but Elizabeth would not risk her hold on the throne by a foreign marriage. Despite certain rumored physical incapabilities (the legend that Elizabeth was really a man still has some currency), her liaisons with court favorites resulted in extreme jealousy on her part; perhaps her one real love was Robert Dudley, Earl of Leicester, but rumor made of him a wife-killer (Amy Robsart, his wife, had been killed in 1560, probably accidentally, when Leicester's marriage to Elizabeth was a strong possibility) and Elizabeth could not risk the scandal. Her affair with Robert Devereux, earl of Essex, towards the end of her life, ended unhappily with his rebellion and execution (1601). Elizabeth died, in 1603, the only English ruler of adult years since the Norman Conquest in 1066 who had not married. She recognized clearly the problem that would face the kingdom at her death and part of her reluctance to order the execution of Mary Queen of Scots is traceable to the fact that Mary's son, James VI of Scotland, was the logical successor to the English throne. On Elizabeth's death, he became James I of England.

The Elizabethan Age. The four and a half decades of Elizabeth's reign mark probably the most brilliant period in English history, and one of the top half dozen in world history. The long period of official peace with other nations built up about Elizabeth a colorful court whose energies were turned to other matters than war, although freebooting and soldiering expeditions by her military captains gave glamour to their names. Literature reached a golden age in this time, a period marked with Elizabeth's name, although much of the so-called Elizabethan literature (for example much of the body of dramatic literature) dates from the period of the first Stuart kings (1603–1642). Such poets as Spenser, Drayton, and Gascoigne, playwrights like Marlowe, Greene, Lyly, and Shakespeare, essayists, romancers, and critics of the stamp of Raleigh, Bacon, and Sidney make the period incomparable in its brilliance. Elizabeth's captains and advisers, the Cecils, Dudley, the Walsinghams, Raleigh, Hawkins, Drake, the Bacons, while not uniformly successful, were nevertheless instrumental in carrying out her policies. England became in Elizabeth's time a world power, not yet as strong as Spain but soon to surpass her; the English navy grew to be second to none; commerce expanded and colonies were established where such explorers as Frobisher and Drake had gone.

Elizabeth. In Shakespeare's *Henry VIII*, the future Queen Elizabeth. She is not often referred to by Shakespeare, but in this play her christening forms a kind of climax, as a sign that a better time is in the offing for the English nation:

> This royal infant . . .
> Though in her cradle, yet now promises
> Upon this land a thousand thousand blessings,
> Which time shall bring to ripeness   (V.v).

Elizabeth. A novel by Frank Swinnerton, published in 1934.

Elizabeth. Pseudonym of **Russell, Elizabeth Mary.**

Elizabeth, Queen. See under **Grey, Lady.**

Elizabethan Age (ē.liz.ạ.bē′thạn, -beth′ạn). In literature, a term used generally, and somewhat loosely, for that period of the late 16th century and early 17th century during which English drama reached a peak of eloquence, power, and virtuosity which has no rival in any other period of English letters (if not, indeed, as many think, without a rival in world literature, even including the great period of the Greek drama), and during which also English poetry attained a brilliance which has perhaps been equaled but seldom, if ever, surpassed. Although lesser, by comparison, in both quantity and quality, Elizabethan prose also reflected an abundance of talent and technical competence which sets it apart from anything that had preceded it. From the standpoint of chronology, the Elizabethan Age is taken by some to cover the entire period from the accession of Elizabeth in 1558 to the closing of the theaters in 1642, but it is perhaps most often thought of as comprising the four decades between 1580 and 1620; this span includes the last 23 years of Elizabeth's reign and the first 17 of that of James I (whence the designation Jacobean Age preferred by some authorities for the period after 1603). During this brief period of 40 years England underwent and was altered by a variety of historical and cultural experiences of a significance that cannot be too heavily emphasized (for the history, the reader's attention should be drawn to the entry under **Elizabeth**; for the cultural change, useful information will be found in the entry under **English**). In a sense, England may be said to have begun the Elizabethan Age with a great portion of its attention directed to the past, and a limited sense of national identity; by the end of the first decade of the Elizabethan Age this had been sharply altered: the point of view of the Renaissance, and especially of the humanists, had prevailed overwhelmingly with a number of eloquent spokesmen (for example, Christopher Marlowe in his characterization of Doctor Faustus) and there were few Englishmen who had not been awakened to a proud nationalism (the defeat of the Spanish Armada in 1588 was perhaps the climactic event contributing to this). With respect to their language, the Elizabethans borrowed heavily from Latin, and to a lesser extent from French, Spanish, and Italian (this process was not new, but the amount of the borrowing was enormously greater than it had been; so much so, indeed, as to arouse a considerable amount of criticism), while at the same time the language had dispensed with the "weak inflections" which had survived in verse as late as the third or fourth decades of the 16th century. What emerged was a linguistic tool considered polyglot or "barbaric" by some, but which became in the hands of such writers as Shakespeare, Jonson, and Marlowe, to name only three, a medium for the expression of literary masterpieces as yet unsurpassed in the English-speaking world. But preceding these, and utilized by them to a greater or lesser degree, were various prose writers: the collectors of tales, beginning with William Painter and *The Palace of Pleasure* (1566); the chroniclers, including Holinshed, North (who translated Plutarch's *Lives*), and Hakluyt; and the enormously style-conscious men of letters led by John Lyly, remembered as the founder of the ornate, artificial, but technically very important fashion of writing known as "Euphuism." Apart from these, but tremendously influential as a critic and scholar, was Francis Bacon, remembered for his *Advancement of Learning* and various other works. Perhaps the greatest of the poets (if one considers Shakespeare and Marlowe to be more properly classified as dramatists) was Edmund Spenser, whose *Shepherd's Calendar* and *Faerie Queene* continue to rank high on any list of major English poems. Sir Philip Sidney (important also as a writer of Euphuistic prose), George Chapman (now perhaps best remembered for his translation of Homer), Michael Drayton, Samuel Daniel, Thomas Campion, and Sir Walter Raleigh must also be included in the list of poets, and taking full rank with them would be several of the great dramatists (Shakespeare, for his *Sonnets* alone, as well as Marlowe and Jonson). Indeed, the explicitly poetic output of many of the dramatists would alone be sufficient to win them enduring fame, and if the Elizabethan Age is sometimes thought of as being chiefly an age of great drama it is rather because of the towering stature of the best Elizabethan plays than because of any important qualitative deficiencies in the best short verse of the period. In a

very real sense, Elizabethan drama was intertwined with both Elizabethan poetry and prose, and had its roots, to some extent, in earlier drama. The rigidly formal Senecan tragedy *Gorboduc* (1562), by Thomas Norton and Thomas Sackville, and the plays of John Lyly, were among the most important of these. However, it is with Christopher Marlowe that true Elizabethan drama is usually thought to have begun, and Marlowe's output, although limited in quantity, includes at least two tragedies (*Doctor Faustus* and *Edward II*) that are usually included with the greatest of the Elizabethan plays. But even as Marlowe's brief career came to an end (*Tamburlaine*, his first play, was staged in 1587, and its writer was killed in a tavern brawl only six years later), a greater figure was coming onto the stage; by the close of 1593, Shakespeare was far along in his early period of trial and experiment, and was about to enter the period of his mature greatness as a dramatist. In the span 1594–1611 Shakespeare produced, to name only a few of the greatest, such tragedies as *Macbeth, Hamlet, King Lear,* and *Othello;* such light-hearted comedies as *Much Ado About Nothing, As You Like It,* and *Twelfth Night* (all written between 1598 and 1601); such biting comedies as *Measure for Measure;* and finally works that may perhaps be said to stand apart from all of these, as *Romeo and Juliet* (for its sheer lyric beauty) and *The Tempest* (for its consummate technical mastery). Shakespeare, however, was far from the only great dramatist of this period. In comedy he may certainly be said to have had a rival in Ben Jonson, whose bitterly satirical *Volpone* is a classic. Thomas Dekker, with *The Shoemaker's Holiday*, was another whose work entitles him to high rank. In tragedy, the Elizabethan Age saw the writing also of Beaumont and Fletcher's *The Maid's Tragedy*, of John Webster's *The White Devil* and *The Duchess of Malfi*, and of John Ford's *'Tis Pity She's a Whore.*

Elizabeth and Essex (es′iks). A biographical study by Lytton Strachey, published in 1928.

Elizabeth Bennet (ben′et). See **Bennet, Elizabeth.**

Ella (el′a), **King.** See under **Man of Law's Tale, The.**

Ellen (el′en). See under **Childe Waters.**

Ellen Douglas (dug′las). See **Douglas, Ellen.**

Ellen's Isle (el′enz). [Also, **Eilean Molach** (ā′lin mō̇.läch′).] A wooded island in Loch Katrine, in C Scotland, in Perthshire ab. 8 mi. W of Callander. It is famous in early romance, and Scott makes it the favorite haunt of the *Lady of the Lake.*

Ellesmere (elz′mir), **Baron.** A title of **Egerton, Sir Thomas.**

Elliot (el′i.ot, el′yot), **Anne.** The heroine of Jane Austen's novel *Persuasion.*

Elliot, Halbert or **Hobbie.** A character in Sir Walter Scott's *The Black Dwarf*, who gained the friendship of the cynical Dwarf.

Elliot, Jane or **Jean.** b. at Minto, Teviotdale, Scotland, 1727; d. March 29, 1805. The author of a single poem, *The Flowers of the Forest* (1756), at first believed, because of its genuine flavor, to be a true popular ballad. Apart from her one poem, Jane Elliot is remembered for her charming cleverness at the age of 18 in saving her father, Sir Gilbert Andrew Elliot (1693–1766), from capture by a band of Jacobites; she was also the last lady in Edinburgh to use a sedan chair.

Elliot, Sir Walter. The father of the heroine in Jane Austen's novel *Persuasion*.

Elliott (el'i.ọt, el'yọt), **Charlotte.** b. at Clapham, London, March 17, 1789; d. at Brighton, Sussex, England, Sept. 22, 1871. An English hymnist, best known for her *Just as I Am*. For 50 years an invalid, she came under the influence of Caesar H. A. Malan (1787–1864), a Swiss Protestant divine, and devoted her life to writing religious songs and poems. She was the author of *Hymns for a Week*, which had a sale of 40,000 copies, *Hours of Sorrow* (1840; many editions), and the *Invalid's Hymn Book* (1834; published privately), containing "Just as I am, without one plea," the most popular of her 150 hymns.

Elliott, Ebenezer. [Called the **"Corn-Law Rhymer."**] b. at Masborough, Yorkshire, England, March 17, 1781; d. near Barnsley, England, Dec. 1, 1849. An English poet. He was the author of *Corn-Law Rhymes* (1831), *The Village Patriarch* (1829), *The Ranter, The Splendid Village*, and many other poems opposing the English corn laws as a "bread tax."

ellipsis. 1. In grammar, omission; a figure of syntax by which a part of a sentence or phrase is used for the whole, by the omission of one or more words, leaving the full form to be understood or completed by the reader or hearer: as, "the heroic virtues I admire," for "the heroic virtues which I admire"; "prythee, peace," for "I pray thee, hold thy peace."
2. In printing, a mark or marks, as --, ***, . . . , denoting the omission or suppression of letters (as in *k--g* for *king*) or of words.

Ellis (el'is), **George.** b. at London, 1753; d. April 10, 1815. An English author. He published *Specimens of the Early English Poets* (1790; 6th ed., 1851), *Specimens of Early English Romances in Metre* (1805; ed. by Halliwell, 1848), and others.

Ellis, Havelock. [Full name, **Henry Havelock Ellis.**] b. at Croydon, Surrey, England, Feb. 2, 1859; d. at Hintlesham, England, July 8, 1939. An English man of letters and anthropologist. For a short time he practiced medicine in England, but left the medical profession to write. He edited the works of John Ford and of Christopher Marlowe in, and was over-all editor of, the Mermaid Series of old English dramatists, and wrote *The New Spirit* (1890), *The Criminal* (1890), *Man and Woman* (1894), *Affirmations* (1897), *The Evolution of Modesty* (1899), *Analysis of Sexual Impulse* (1903), *Sexual Selection in Man* (1905), *The Soul of Spain* (1908), *The Task of Social Hygiene* (1912), and *The Dance of Life* (1923); his seven separate volumes on the manifestations of sex form *Studies in the Psychology of Sex* (1897–1928). The latter work was of the greatest importance in changing the general attitude towards sex and the problems caused by it. Ellis's anthropo-sociological approach to the psychology of sexual abnormality has influenced almost all writers since on the subject.

Ellis, Sarah Stickney. b. at London, 1812; d. at Hoddesdon, Hertfordshire, England, June 16, 1872. An English authoress. She wrote *Women of England* (1838), *Daughters of England* (1842), and others.

Ellis-Fermor (-fèr'môr), **Una Mary.** b. Dec. 20, 1894—. An English lecturer and literary critic. She was a lecturer (1918–30) and reader (1930–47) in English literature at Bedford College, University of London. Her books include *Christopher Marlowe* (1926), *Jacobean Drama* (1936), *Some Recent Research in Shakespeare's Imagery* (1937), *The Irish Dramatic Movement* (1939), and *Frontiers of Drama* (1945).

Ellison (el'i.sọn), **Mrs.** A landlady in Henry Fielding's novel *Amelia*.

Ellwood (el'wůd), **Thomas.** b. at Crowell, Oxfordshire, England, 1639; d. at Amersham, Buckinghamshire, England, March 1, 1714. An English Quaker, a friend of Milton. He wrote *Sacred History of the Old Testament and New Testament* (1705–09), his autobiography (1714), and others.

Elohim (el'ọ.him). One of the names of God, of frequent occurrence in the Hebrew text of the Old Testament. Biblical critics are not agreed as to the reason for the use of the plural form: some regard it as a covert suggestion of the Trinity; others as a plural of excellence; others as an indication of an earlier polytheistic belief; still others as an embodiment of the Hebrew faith that the powers represented by the gods of the heathen were all included in one Divine Person.

Eloi (ẹ.loi'). One of the races of future man encountered by the Time Traveller in H. G. Wells's *The Time Machine*.

Eloïsa to Abelard (el.ọ.ē'zạ; ab'ẹ.lärd). A poem (1717) by Alexander Pope, based on John Hughes's translation of the letters written by Héloïse to Abelard. Pope casts the story in the form of a monologue on the subject of the tragic separation of the two lovers.

Elphege (el'fej), **Saint.** See Saint Ælfheah.

Elphinstone (el'fin.stộn, -stọn), **Mountstuart.** b. Oct. 6, 1779; d. at Limpsfield, Surrey, England, Nov. 20, 1859. An English statesman and historian, one of the chief founders of the Anglo-Indian empire. He entered the civil service of the East India Company in 1796, was appointed ambassador to the court of Kabul in 1808, was resident at the court of Poona (1810–17), and was governor of Bombay (1819–27). Author of *Account of the Kingdom of Cabul* (1815) and *History of India* (1841).

Elsevier (el'zẹ.vēr). See **Elzevir.**

Elshender (el'shẹn.dèr). [Also called **Canny Elshie** (el'shi).] In Sir Walter Scott's novel *The Black Dwarf*, the name used by Sir Edward Mauley, the Black Dwarf.

Elsinore (el'si.nôr). English name of Helsingør, a city in Denmark, in which is situated Kronborg Castle, the traditional scene of Shakespeare's *Hamlet*.

Elspeth (el'spẹth). In Sir Walter Scott's novel *The Antiquary*, an apathetic old woman burdened with the guilt of a crime in which she had assisted her mistress.

ḍ, d or j; ş, s or sh; ṭ, t or ch; ẓ, z or zh; o, F. cloche; ü, F. menu; ċh, Sc. loch; ṅ, F. bonbon.

Elton (el'tọn), **Mr.** In Jane Austen's novel *Emma*, a conceited young clergyman whom Emma considers a possible suitor for her protégée, Harriet Smith.

Elton, Oliver. b. at Holt, Norfolk, England, June 3, 1861—. An English literary historian. Lecturer (1890–1900) at Owens College at Manchester; professor (1900–25) of English literature at Liverpool University. Author of *The Augustan Ages* (1899), *Modern Studies* (1907), a series entitled *Survey of English Literature: 1780–1830* (1912), *1830–80* (1920), and *1730–1780* (1928); *The English Muse* (1930), and *Essays and Addresses* (1939).

Elvira (el.vī'rạ). In Dryden's *Spanish Friar*, a young wife who by the aid of the Spanish friar attempts to intrigue with Lorenzo, who turns out to be her brother.

Elvira. The sister of Don Duarte in Colley Cibber's *Love Makes the Man.*

Elvira. The mistress of Pizarro in Richard Brinsley Sheridan's *Pizarro*, adapted from Kotzebue.

Elwin (el'win), **Whitwell.** b. at Thurning, Norfolk, England, Feb. 26, 1816; d. at Booton, Norfolk, England, Jan. 1, 1900. An English divine, critic, and editor. For many years (1849–1900) rector at Booton, he was also associated with the *Quarterly Review*, as a contributor (1843–85) and as an editor (1853–60). He edited (1871–72) five volumes of a ten-volume edition of Pope, the work later being completed by W. J. Courthope. A specialist in the 18th century, he wrote for the *Quarterly Review* papers on Johnson, Fielding, Goldsmith, Sterne, Gray, and Cowper; with others, they were published in *Some Eighteenth Century Men of Letters* (1902).

Ely (ē'li), **Bishop of.** In Shakespeare's *Henry V*, a counsellor who supports the Archbishop of Canterbury on the legality of the King's proposed war with France.

Ely, Bishop of. See also under **Morton, John.**

Elyot (el'i.ọt, el'yọt), **Sir Thomas.** b. probably in Wiltshire, England, before 1490; d. at Carlton, Cambridgeshire, England, March 20, 1546. An English scholar and diplomat. He was educated at home. In 1511 he was clerk of assize on the western circuit, and in 1523 Cardinal Wolsey gave him the position of clerk of the privy council. He was sheriff of Oxfordshire and Berkshire in 1527. In 1531 he published *The Boke named the Governour*, which related to the education of statesmen and was dedicated to Henry VIII. This secured royal patronage, and he was appointed ambassador to the emperor Charles V. In 1535 he was again sent to the emperor, following him to Naples. He was member of Parliament for Cambridge in 1542. He also wrote *Of the Knowledge which maketh a Wise Man* (1533), *Pasquil the Playne* (1533), *The Castel of Helth* (a lay medical guide, 1534), *Bibliotheca* (a Latin and English dictionary, 1538), *The Defence of Good Women* (1545), and others.

Ely Chapel. The chapel of the former palace of the bishops of Ely, in London.

Ely Place. A place on Holborn Hill, London, the entrance to which is almost opposite Saint Andrew's Church. The town house of the bishops of Ely stood here, and the place was entered by a great gateway built (1388) by Bishop Arundel.

Elysium (ē.liz'i.um, -lizh'um). [Also, **Elysian Fields** (ē.lizh'ạn).] The abode of the souls of the good and of heroes exempt from death, in ancient classical mythology. It is described, particularly by later poets, as a place of exceeding bliss, and contrasted with Tartarus, an afterworld of torment. Some have thought it to be in the center of the earth, some in the Islands of the Blest, and some in the sun or mid air. In the *Odyssey* it is a plain at the end of the earth "where life is easiest to man. No snow is there, nor yet great storm nor any rain."

Elzevir or **Elsevier** or **Elzevier** (el'zē.vēr). A family of Dutch printers, celebrated especially for their editions of classical authors, and of French authors on historical and political subjects. Louis, the founder of the family, was born (c1540) at Louvain, near Brussels, and died at Leiden, Feb. 4, 1617. The first book he printed was *J. Drusii Ebraicarum quaestionum, sive quaestionum ac responsionum libri duo* (1583), but the first book he published at his own risk was a Eutropius by P. Merula (1592). He had seven sons, five of whom followed his profession: Matthieu (1564 or 1565–1640), Louis (1566 or 1567–c1621), Gilles (d. 1651), Joost (1575 or 1576–c1617), and Bonaventure (1583–1652). The last was the most celebrated.

Emanuel (ē.man'ū.ẹl), **Paul.** In Charlotte Brontë's novel *Villette*, a lecturer in Madame Beck's school.

Emaré (em'ạ.rē). A Middle English romance (14th century), called a "Breton lay" by its author (whose identity is unknown). It tells of the beautiful and patient Emaré who is cast out by her father, the Emperor, and set adrift clothed in a beautifully embroidered robe. She is found by King Cador and they are married, but Emaré is again cast out, this time through the intrigues of the King's mother. She and her son are cared for in Rome by a kindly merchant, and the husband and wife are happily reunited seven years later, when they meet, through accident, in Rome. A similar story is told in Chaucer's *Man of Law's Tale.*

Embankment, the. See **Thames Embankment.**

ember days. Days in each of the four seasons of the year set apart by the Roman Catholic and other western liturgical churches for prayer and fasting. They are the Wednesday, Friday, and Saturday after the first Sunday in Lent, after Whit-Sunday, after September 14th, and after December 13th. The weeks in which ember days fall are called *ember weeks.* The Sundays immediately following these seasons are still appointed by the canons of the Anglican Church for the ordination of priests and deacons.

emblem. A symbolical design or figure with explanatory writing; a design or an image suggesting some truth or fact; the expression of a thought or idea both in design and in words: as, Quarles's *Emblems* (a collection of such representations). "Emblem reduceth conceits intellectual to images sensible." (Bacon, *Advancement of Learning*, ii.232.)

emblem-book. A type of book particularly popular in the Elizabethan period. It consisted of a series of pictures (usually woodcuts) underlined by a motto and/or an explanatory verse. It originated in Milan with Alciati's *Emblematum Libellus* (1552).

Emblems. A series of religious poems (1635) by Francis Quarles, written in the style of the emblem-book. The verse shows the influence of Phineas Fletcher and others.

Emblems of Love. A volume of poems (1912) by Lascelles Abercrombie, consisting of blank-verse dialogues.

Emelye (em'e̞.li). [Also: **Emely, Emelya, Emelie, Emilia.**] The heroine of Chaucer's "Knight's Tale," in *The Canterbury Tales*. She appears in many versions of the tale of Palamon and Arcite and is the Emilia of *The Two Noble Kinsmen*.

Emendatio Vitae (e̞.men.dā'shi.ō vī'tē). A Latin prose work of the Middle English period by Richard Rolle of Hampole. It offers advice on the means to grace and discusses the joys of the contemplative life.

"Emerald Isle." A nickname of Ireland.

Émile (ā.mēl). [Full title, **Émile, ou De l'Education** (ö dĕ lā.dü.kȧ.syôṅ).] A treatise (1762) on education, ostensibly a romance, by Rousseau.

Emilia (e̞.mil'i.ȧ, -mil'yȧ). In Shakespeare's *Othello*, the wife of Iago. She reveals his perfidy, and he kills her. Previously she has helped Iago in his scheme to persuade Othello of Desdemona's guilt by unwittingly keeping a handkerchief which Desdemona drops and also by arranging for Cassio to talk with Desdemona alone.

Emilia. In *The Two Noble Kinsmen*, the heroine, sister of Hippolyta. Palamon and Arcite both fall in love with her, and although Arcite wins her in a tournament, he relinquishes her to Palamon as he dies, fatally injured in a fall from his horse.

Emilia. In Shakespeare's *Winter's Tale*, a lady attendant on Hermione.

Emilia. In Dryden's *Palamon and Arcite*, a very beautiful woman, loved by both Palamon and Arcite, and won by the former.

Emilia. See also **Emelye.**

Emilia (ā.mē'lyä), **Doña.** See **Doña Emilia.**

Emilia in England (e̞.mil'i.ȧ, -mil'yȧ). The title under which George Meredith's novel *Sandra Belloni* originally appeared (1864) in England.

Emily (em'i.li). The heroine of Ann Radcliffe's *Mysteries of Udolpho*.

Emily. See also **Em'ly, Little.**

Emily Costigan (kos'ti.gȧn). See **Costigan, Emily.**

Emily Wardle (wôr'dl). See under **Wardle, Mr.**

Éminence Rouge (ā.mē.näṅs rözh). See **Richelieu, Cardinal.**

Eminent Victorians (vik.tōr'i.ȧnz). A volume of biographical studies of Cardinal Manning, Florence Nightingale, Dr. Thomas Arnold, and General Charles Gordon, by Lytton Strachey, published in 1918. Strachey's satirical and intimate analyses of character helped usher in a new era in biographical writing.

Em'ly (em'li), **Little.** In Charles Dickens's *David Copperfield*, Mr. Peggotty's niece. She is affianced to Ham Peggotty, but is seduced and later abandoned by Steerforth.

Emma (em'ȧ). A novel by Jane Austen, published in 1816. It is the story of Emma Woodhouse, a clever, wealthy, and beautiful young lady who is left alone with her father when her companion and former governess, Miss Taylor, marries a widowed neighbor, Mr. Weston. Emma sets about plotting the advancement of a young protégée, Harriet Smith, a pretty, very foolish girl of 17, who is the illegitimate daughter of some unknown person. Emma, convinced that Harriet may be of noble birth, advises her not to marry Robert Martin, a young farmer, because, she says, he is beneath Harriet's station. In doing this Emma upsets Mr. Knightley, Robert's landlord and a friend of the Woodhouses, who believes that her friendship with Harriet is ill-advised. Emma has hopes that Mr. Elton, the vicar, will marry Harriet but is shocked to have him propose to her (Emma) when he finds her alone. Emma realizes that he has misinterpreted her attempts to encourage his attentions to Harriet and has thought that Emma herself was attracted to him. Emma makes her third mistake when she advises Harriet to aspire to a marriage with Frank Churchill, Mr. Weston's son by his first marriage. Harriet begins to fall out of love with Mr. Elton when he returns to the village with a pretentious and ill-mannered bride, and, impressed by Mr. Knightley's kindness to her at a ball, proceeds to fall in love with him. Emma, believing that Harriet is talking about Frank Churchill, encourages her when she is really praising Mr. Knightley. It is now disclosed that Frank Churchill is secretly engaged to Jane Fairfax, the niece of the talkative Miss Bates, a girl so clever and beautiful, Mr. Knightley hints, that Emma is unable to bring herself to be very friendly with her. Eventually Emma, sobered by the realization of how close she has come to wrecking Harriet's chances for happiness not once but several times, is made completely happy when Mr. Knightley proposes to her and at the same time makes clear that he has been pleading Robert's suit with Harriet. When Robert again proposes to Harriet, she accepts him.

Emma Haredale (hȧr'dāl). See **Haredale, Emma.**

Emmanuel Burden (e̞.man'ū.e̞l bėr'de̞n). A novel (1904) by Hilaire Belloc.

Emmanuel College. One of the colleges of Cambridge University, England. It was founded in 1584, on the site of a convent of the Black Friars, by Sir Walter Mildmay, chancellor of the exchequer and privy councilor under Queen Elizabeth. It is the college of John Harvard, Richard Knight (Gresham professor of music), Samuel Foster (Gresham professor of astronomy), the poet William Basse, Edward Hulse, William Staine, William Croone, William Barrowby, Anthony Askew (all distinguished physicians), John Wallis (Oxford professor of geometry), William Law (author of the *Serious Call*), Richard Farmer (author of the famous *Essay on the Learning of Shakespeare*), Robert Potter (translator of Aeschylus, Euripides, and Sophocles), Richard Hurd (of the *Letters on Chivalry and Romance*), Bishop Percy (of the Ballads), and Thomas Young (who first described astigmatism). Its chapel was designed by Christopher Wren. The college was long regarded as a stronghold of Puritanism. Soon after he founded Emmanuel, Mildmay came

---

d̦, d or j; ș, s or sh; ț, t or ch; z̦, z or zh; o, F. cloche; ü, F. menu; ċh, Sc. loch; ṅ, F. bonbon.

to court to visit Queen Elizabeth, who greeted him with "Sir Walter, I hear you have erected a Puritan foundation." "No, Madam," he replied, "far be it from me to countenance anything contrary to your established laws, but I have set an acorn, which, when it becomes an oak, God alone knows what will be the fruit thereof." The first head of the college was Laurence Chaderton, one of the translators of the King James Version of the Bible. The library contains manuscripts of the Old Testament in Hebrew, the New Testament in Greek, Herodotus, two 14th-century English translations of the New Testament, and, among its rare books, a 1498 Aristophanes, printed by Aldus, and a 1465 Cicero.

Emmanuel's Land. In Bunyan's *Pilgrim's Progress*, the Delectable Mountains.

Emmaus (em′ą.us, e.mā′us). In Biblical geography, a village in Palestine not far from Jerusalem. Its exact position is unknown. It was long identified with another city (Emmaus, later Nicopolis, modern 'Amwas) ab. 20 mi. from Jerusalem.

Emmy Lou (em′i lö′). A story (1902) by George Madden Martin, telling a timid child's experiences, especially at school.

Empedocles (em.ped′ọ.klēz). b. at Agrigentum (modern Agrigento), Sicily; fl. c490–430 B.C. A Greek philosopher, poet, and statesman. He was a supporter of the democratic party in his native city against the aristocracy, and possessed great influence through his wealth, eloquence, and knowledge. He followed Pythagoras and Parmenides in his teachings. He professed magic powers, prophecy, and a miraculous power of healing, and came to have, in popular belief, a superhuman character. He was said to have thrown himself into the crater of Etna in order that, from his sudden disappearance, the people might believe him to be a god. Matthew Arnold used this story in his *Empedocles on Etna*.

Empedocles on Etna (et′nạ). A dramatic dialogue by Matthew Arnold, published in 1853 and in a revised version in 1867.

Empire Day. May 24, the anniversary of the day of birth of Queen Victoria (1819–1901), observed throughout most of the British Commonwealth.

Empusa (em.pū′sạ). In Greek legend, a cannibal monster sent under various forms by Hecate to frighten travelers.

empyrean (em.pi.rē′ạn, em.pir′ẹ.ạn). The region of pure light and fire; the highest heaven, where the pure element of fire was supposed by the ancients to exist: the same as the ether, the ninth heaven according to ancient astronomy.

> The deep-domed empyrean
> Rings to the roar of an angel onset.
> (Tennyson, *Experiments in Quantity*.)

Enanthe (ē.nan′thē). In Fletcher's *Humorous Lieutenant*, the name under which Celia disguises herself.

Enarchus (e.när′kus). In Sir Philip Sidney's *Arcadia*, the king of Macedon. He is the father of Pyrocles and uncle of Musidorus.

Enceladus (en.sel′ą.dus). In Greek mythology, one of the giants who waged war against the gods; a son of Uranus and Ge. He was killed by Athena, and buried with the other giants beneath Mount Etna

in Sicily. When Enceladus stirs his 100 arms the mountain shakes, and when he breathes there is an eruption.

Enchanted Horse, The. A fabulous horse in *The Arabian Nights' Entertainments*.

Enchanted Island, The. Dryden's alteration (1667) of Shakespeare's *Tempest*.

Encyclopædia Britannica (bri.tan′i.kạ). An English "dictionary of arts, sciences, and general literature," first published in parts (1768–71) at Edinburgh. The 10th edition comprised 11 supplementary volumes to the 24 of the 9th edition (1875–89), including an atlas and an index to the whole work (35 vols., 1902–03). The 11th edition (29 vols., 1910–11) was sponsored by Cambridge University. The 14th edition, edited by J. L. Garwin and Franklin Hooper, was published (24 vols., 1929) at London and New York.

Encyclopédie (äṅ.sē.klo.pā.dē). [Full title, **Dictionnaire raisonné des sciences, des arts et des métiers,** meaning in English, "*Methodical Dictionary of the Sciences, Arts, and Trades.*"] A French encyclopedia which had as its basis a French translation (1743–45), by John Mills, of Ephraim Chambers's *Cyclopaedia* (1728). As developed by D'Alembert and Diderot, it became the organ of the most advanced and revolutionary opinions of the time, was the object of the most violent persecution by the conservative party in church and state, and was subjected to considerable editing not only by hostile censors but by fearful printers. So thoroughly was it identified with the philosophic movement of the time that the term Encyclopedist (in French, *Encyclopédiste*) became the recognized designation of all attached to a certain form of skeptical, rationalist philosophy. It appeared at Paris in 28 volumes between 1751 and 1772; it was followed by a supplement in five volumes (Amsterdam, 1776–77), and an analytical index in two volumes (Paris, 1780). Voltaire's *Questions sur l' Encyclopédie* (1770) formed a kind of critical appendix. La Porte's *Esprit de l' Encyclopédie* (Paris, 1768) gave a résumé of the more important articles. Hennequin compiled (Paris, 1822–23) a similar epitome under the same title.

Encyclopedists (en.sī.klọ.pē′dists). [Also, **Encyclopaedists.**] The collaborators in the *Encyclopédie* of Diderot and D'Alembert (1751–72). The Encyclopedists as a body were among the most influential exponents of the French rationalist philosophy of the 18th century.

Endeavour (en.dev′ọr). A British ship commanded by Captain James Cook, then lieutenant. It was sent out in 1768 by the Royal Society to the Pacific to observe the transit of Venus. Captain Cook returned in 1771, having made important explorations and discoveries.

Endimion (en.dim′i.ọn). A prose play (c1588) by John Lyly. It has been thought to be an allegory of Queen Elizabeth's court and her reputed love for the Earl of Leicester. Most authorities are now inclined to doubt this, however, believing that Lyly would hardly have risked his career by presenting at Court something which might so easily bring down Elizabeth's wrath on his head.

End of the Affair, The. A novel by Graham Greene, published in 1951.

Endor (en'dôr). In scriptural geography, a village in Palestine, near Tabor, where Saul consulted the "witch of Endor." I Sam. xxviii. 7–25.

end-rhyme or **caudate rhyme.** [Also, **tailed rhyme.**] Rhyme at the end of successive lines; opposed to leonine or other rhyme between the ends of sections of the same line.

Endymion (en.dim'i.ọn). In Greek legend, a beautiful youth loved by Selene (the moon). The legends about him vary greatly. He is described as a king, as a shepherd on Mount Latmos, and as a hunter, and various accounts of his parentage are given. According to one, he had asked Zeus for immortality, eternal slumber, and undying youth, and had fallen asleep on Latmus, never to awake. The best-known story says that Selene herself put him to sleep so that her visits to him might be untroubled.

Endymion. An early poem by John Keats, published in 1818, and divided into four parts. It tells the story of a youth, Endymion, who is seeking to unite "fellowship with essence." His search leads him to the realization of the beauty of nature, art, friendship, and poetry. Within the framework of the poem, Keats tells the stories of Venus and Adonis, Glaucus and Scylla, and Alpheus and Arethusa. The poem (with which Keats himself was far from satisfied) was badly received (the reviews in *Blackwood's Magazine* and the *Quarterly Review*, two of the most powerful literary journals of the day, were particularly scathing).

Endymion. A novel by Benjamin Disraeli, Lord Beaconsfield, published in 1880. William Pitt Ferrars, a successful politician, is ruined by a series of political reverses and financial disasters, and dies penniless, leaving two children. Endymion, the son, withdraws from Eton and obtains the position of clerk at Somerset House (the office in London containing the records of births and deaths for all of England), while Myra, his sister, becomes companion to Adriana, daughter of a rich banker, Adrian Neuchatel. Myra's beauty and driving ambition help her to achieve social prominence. She marries first the foreign secretary, Lord Roehampton, and later the monarch himself, King Florestan. Endymion wins political success, largely as a result of the support given him by his brother-in-law, Lord Roehampton. The author gives a good picture of social and political life during the administrations of Lord Melbourne and Sir Robert Peel.

Enfield (en'fēld), **William.** b. at Sudbury, England, March 29, 1741; d. at Norwich, England, Nov. 3, 1797. An English dissenting divine. He published *Preacher's Directory* (1771), *The Speaker* (1774), and other compilations.

Engagement, The. In English history, an agreement (1647) between Charles I and representatives of the Scottish Covenanters, by which the Scottish army was to restore Charles, who consented to an establishment of Presbyterianism in England.

England (ing'glạnd). [Middle English, **Englond** (eng'glônd), **Inglond;** Old English, **Engla-land** (eng'glä.länd); Danish, **Engeland;** French, **Angle-** terre; German, **England** (eng'länt); Italian, **Inghilterra;** Spanish and Portuguese, **Inglaterra;** Latin, **Anglia.**] A constitutional hereditary monarchy, forming part of the United Kingdom of Great Britain and Northern Ireland. It forms (with Wales) the S portion of the island of Great Britain. England is bounded on the N by Scotland, on the E by the North Sea, on the S by the Strait of Dover and the English Channel, and on the W by the Atlantic Ocean, Bristol Channel, Wales, and the Irish Sea. England includes the Isle of Wight and a few smaller islands. The surface is generally level or undulating in the E, S, and center, and mountainous in the NW (the English Lake District), near the Welsh border, and in the SW. The highest mountain is Scafell Pike (3,210 ft.). The chief river systems are those of the Thames, Humber, and Severn. England has important agriculture, but its chief interests are commercial, manufacturing, and mining. It is a very important maritime nation. The largest commercial cities are London, Liverpool, Manchester, Birmingham, Leeds, Sheffield, Bristol, and Bradford. The chief manufactures are cotton and woolen goods, iron and steel, hardware, and leather. Its mineral products include iron and coal, tin (now greatly declined in output), and copper. England has 40 geographical counties divided into 50 administrative counties. The administrative counties are: Bedfordshire, Berkshire, Buckinghamshire, Cambridgeshire, Cheshire, Cornwall, Cumberland, Derbyshire, Devonshire, Dorsetshire, Durham, East Suffolk, East Sussex, Essex, Gloucestershire, Herefordshire, Hertfordshire, Huntingdonshire, Isle of Ely, Isle of Wight, Kent, Lancashire, Leicestershire, Lincolnshire (Parts of Holland), Lincolnshire (Parts of Kesteven), Lincolnshire (Parts of Lindsey), County of London, Middlesex, Monmouthshire, Norfolk, Northamptonshire, Northumberland, Nottinghamshire, Oxfordshire, Rutlandshire, Shropshire, Soke of Peterborough, Somersetshire, Southampton, Staffordshire, Surrey, Warwickshire, Westmorland, West Suffolk, West Sussex, Wiltshire, Worcestershire, Yorkshire (East Riding), Yorkshire (North Riding), and Yorkshire (West Riding). The geographical counties are for the most part identical with the above, with the following exceptions: the County of London is not a geographical county; the Isle of Ely is a part of Cambridgeshire; the Isle of Wight and Southampton together form Hampshire; Lincolnshire is made up of the Parts of Holland, Parts of Kesteven, and Parts of Lindsey; the Soke of Peterborough is a part of Northamptonshire; East Suffolk and West Suffolk together form Suffolk; East Sussex and West Sussex together form Sussex; and Yorkshire consists of the East, North, and West Ridings. There are monuments of its primeval inhabitants before the Celts, of whom, however, but little is known. England was invaded by Julius Caesar, 55 and 54 B.C., and the Celtic Britons were subjugated by the Romans, 43 A.D. and succeeding years (Agricola's campaigns, 78–84). The Romans abandoned England in 410. The invasions by the Jutes, Angles, and Saxons, traditionally, began in 449 and extended through the 6th century. Christianity was introduced from Rome in 597, and from Scotland soon after. The early English kingdoms of Kent, Northumbria, Mercia,

ḍ, d or j; ṣ, s or sh; ṭ, t or ch; ẓ, z or zh; ọ, F. cloche; ü, F. menu; ċh, Sc. loch; ṅ, F. bonbon.

Wessex, East Anglia, Essex, and Sussex (the Heptarchy) merged under Egbert of Wessex as "king of the English" in 829. The division of England between Alfred and the Danes was accomplished by the treaty of Wedmore, 878. In the 10th century consolidation of the country occurred under Edward (the Elder), Athelstan, and others. The second Danish invasion under Sweyn took place c1000, and was followed by the rule of Canute the Dane and his sons, 1016–42. The Norman conquest was begun by William I, 1066. The commencement of the Plantagenet line under Henry II occurred in 1154. Normandy and other French provinces were separated c1204. King John granted the Magna Charta, 1215, and parliamentary government began, c1264–65. The Hundred Years' War raged, c1337–1453, during which reigned kings of the house of Lancaster (1399–1461). The kings of the house of York (1461–85) took the crown during the Wars of the Roses, 1455–85. The Tudor dynasty (beginning with Henry VII in 1485) united in one house the York and Lancaster claims. The introduction of the Reformation occurred under Henry VIII and Edward VI, but Roman Catholic worship was restored by Mary, and the Church of England was restored by Elizabeth (1558–1603). The Elizabethan period saw the culmination of English (and Tudor) power in the Renaissance. The accession of the Stuart line and personal union with Scotland under James I took place in 1603. The beginnings of the colonial empire, 17th century, followed the growth of English power during the Tudor period. The civil war between Charles I and Parliament was waged from 1642–48, and was followed by the period of the Commonwealth and Protectorate, 1649–59. The monarchy under Charles II was restored in 1660, but in the revolution of 1688 the Stuarts were ejected, and William of Orange and Mary acceded in 1689. The Act of Settlement was put in force, 1700–01; union with Scotland occurred in 1707. Accession of the Hanoverian dynasty (with George I) came in 1714. Large territorial acquisitions in America and India resulted (1763) from the French and Indian Wars. The U. S. was lost to the crown 1783. Union with Ireland was accomplished, 1801. Wars with France under the republic and Napoleon's empire, were waged, 1793–1802, 1803–14, and 1815. The Catholic Emancipation Act was passed in 1829, the Electoral Reform Acts in 1832, 1867–68, and 1884–85. Slavery was abolished, 1833. The accession of Victoria, and the separation of Hanover opened a new era in 1837. The Afghan war (1838–42), the Chinese war (1840–42), the Crimean War (1854–56), Chinese wars (1856–58 and 1860), the Indian Mutiny (1857–58), the Ashanti War (1873–74), the Afghan War (1878–80), the Zulu War (1879), the Transvaal War (1881), wars in Egypt and the Sudan (1882–85), and the Boer War (1899–1902) kept the English military power active all over the world. Chartist agitation, Irish agitation (c1845), the repeal of the English Corn Laws (1846) were elements of internal politics. The act for disestablishment of the Irish Church was passed in 1869, and in 1870 the Irish Land Act, and the Elementary Education Act. The Irish Land Act of 1881 attempted a revision of the act of 1870. In World War I (1914–18) and World War II (1939–45) English and Commonwealth troops fought the German challenge to European hegemony.

England, Church of. See **Church of England.**

England's Helicon (hel'i.kon, -kọn). An anthology of poetry published in 1600. It contains about 150 poems from other similar anthologies, written by such poets as Spenser, Sidney, Greene, Lodge, and Shakespeare. Critical appraisal often maintains it as the best of the period.

England's Parnassus (pär.nas'us). An anthology of verse extracts and fragments (published 1600), compiled by Robert Allot. It contains more than 2,000 items, divided into such categories as "angels," "temperance," and "sorrow."

English. A member of the West Germanic subgroup of the Indo-European linguistic stock and hence genetically related in varying degrees of closeness to Dutch, Low German, and High German; to the languages of Scandinavia and Iceland; and to other Indo-European languages outside the Germanic group, like Spanish, Latin, Greek, Russian, and Hindustani. Despite alterations which have occurred over many centuries this relationship is still visible in such correspondences of form and meaning as are exhibited in English *mother*, German *Mutter*, Swedish *moder*, Latin *mater*, Greek *meter*, and Sanskrit *matar-*, or in English *three*, German *drei*, Swedish *tre*, Latin *tres*, Greek *treis*, and Sanskrit *tri*. English has not always been spoken in the British Isles, which at the beginning of the Christian era were inhabited by tribes speaking various Celtic languages, of which Welsh, Scotch Gaelic, and Irish are modern descendants. Furthermore, for more than 300 years almost all of what is today England was a Roman province, where Latin was regularly employed not only by the Romans themselves, but by a certain number of Romanized Celts. In the 5th century, however, the withdrawal of the legions laid the islands open to attack by Germanic invaders, Jutes and later Angles and Saxons according to the traditional account, who came from the Danish peninsula and the regions to the southwest of it on the North Sea coast. Within a few generations they had seized and occupied all of the largest island except for the highlands of the west and north. The somewhat divergent dialects which they spoke are the basis of all forms of modern English. It is customary to divide the history of the language into three main periods: *Old English* (or *Anglo-Saxon*) from the time of the settlement until about 1100, *Middle English* from 1100 to 1450, and *Modern English* from 1450 to the present day. It should of course be realized that the development of the language has been an uninterrupted one and that these divisions are in a sense merely convenient and quite arbitrary.

Old English. The grammatical structure of Old English was very different from that of the modern language. Nouns were inflected for four cases in the singular and in the plural and there were furthermore a number of noun-classes, each of which had a fairly distinct set of endings. Every noun also fell into one of three gender categories (masculine, feminine, and neuter), which determined the inflectional form of accompanying articles and adjectives. As in the other Germanic languages, there were two patterns for the declension of adjectives, "strong" and "weak," both having different endings to indicate gender, number, and case. The verb, although its inflectional system had already undergone a considerable simplification, was also much more elaborately inflected than it is today. In a general way, in respect to these matters Old English resembled Modern German far more than it does Modern English. The regional dialects of Old English referred to above are Northumbrian, in what are today the North of England and the Lowlands of Scotland; Mercian, in the territory between the Thames and the Humber; West Saxon, in most of the region south of the Thames; and Kentish. Northumbrian and Mercian, taken together, are spoken of as the Anglian dialects. In the 7th and early 8th centuries Northumbria became a center of learning and culture and the Northumbrian dialect the vehicle of the first important literature in English. The Scandinavian invasions, however, put an end to this cultural flowering and surviving monuments of Northumbrian Old English are not numerous. Toward the end of the 9th century Wessex rose to power and importance and it is in the West Saxon dialect that most extant Old English literature has come down to us. In its store of words, English in this early period was still almost entirely Germanic: the markedly hybrid character of the modern vocabulary did not develop until long afterwards. Whereas in later centuries speakers and writers of English would have recourse to French and the classical languages to express new concepts, particularly in the realm of abstract ideas, Old English made much greater use of the process of compounding native elements. The introduction of Roman Christianity as a consequence of missionary activities beginning at the end of the 6th century did in time add an appreciable new element to the vocabulary, Latin words relating to the service of the church and theology, to the sciences and the domestic arts. But viewed against the whole body of the language, these additions do not really bulk very large.

Scandinavian Influence. A further foreign addition to the vocabulary was not reflected in written records until somewhat later, but was nevertheless the result of historical events which occurred during Old English times. Before 800 A.D. raiders out of Scandinavia had begun descending upon the British Isles and in the 9th and 10th centuries invaded and established themselves in large numbers, particularly in the north and east. After a long period of conflict and turmoil, the Norse newcomers and the English settled down peaceably side by side. The long-continued and intimate contact which ensued and the eventual fusion of the two peoples had the linguistic result of adding thousands of Norse words to the dialects of certain parts of England, for example the county of Lincoln. In the course of time quite a number of these words made their way into London English and hence into the later standard language. This Norse element in the English vocabulary has the distinctive character of having no distinctive character. The earlier loanwords from Latin and the later ones from French in large part reflect cultural borrowing by a relatively primitive society from other societies of a more elaborated sort. Consequently a large pro-

portion of such loans fall into clearly marked cultural realms. But the Norse loans, for example, *awkward, birth, egg, fellow, leg, low, raise, steak, thrive,* and *window,* are everyday words that might be taken over whenever languages spoken by two peoples very similar in culture are thoroughly mixed and mingled.

The Norman Conquest. Middle English. The conquest of Anglo-Saxon England by the Norman French in the 11th century had a very considerable effect on the later development of the English language, although it did not in any major respect alter its fundamentally Germanic structure. Within a short time the French-speaking conquerors had taken over all positions of power in church and state, and England had become a country in which linguistic divisions corresponded closely to those of class. The upper classes (landed nobles, officers of the royal government, the clergy, particularly on the higher levels) and many members of the developing middle class of merchants spoke French, the common people English. From the very beginning a certain amount of bilingualism must have existed, but it is nevertheless true that many upper-class Englishmen in the 12th century could not have framed a single English sentence. In the next century, as a result of a whole complex of historical causes, the situation changed and by 1300 English had again become the mother tongue of all classes. Because of the weight of tradition, however, and because of the cultural preeminence of France in the western world, French continued in many uses for a long time. As a literary language it was frequently employed throughout the 14th century; English did not supplant it as the language of the law courts until after 1362; and for many documentary purposes (town and guild records, wills, records of Parliamentary petitions and enactments) French continued to be used well into the 15th century. But much of this is highly artificial, some of it, indeed, on a par with a modern physician's use of Latin in writing prescriptions. It is quite clear that even before the birth of Chaucer everyone born and reared in England, if he spoke French at all, spoke it as a second tongue, often imperfectly mastered. When English reëmerged as the language of all classes in society, it had undergone a sea-change. The complicated system of inflections that characterized the old English noun and adjective, while not entirely swept away, was vastly simplified. The -s plural suffix of nouns, for example, was already firmly established in most of England as the regular type and there were not many more exceptions to this pattern than are to be found at the present time. Grammatical gender, according to which in old English *bough, moon,* and *stone* were masculine, *book, soul,* and *sun* feminine, and *head, word,* and *wife* neuter, was completely gone. A certain simplification in the verbal inflections had occurred and in addition many verbs once "strong" had already become "weak" (that is, vocalic alternation of the *sing-sang-sung* type had been replaced by the employment of a suffix as in *flow-flowed*). In respect to all of these features, Chaucer's English is far closer to our own than it is to the English of the 11th century. It would be quite wrong to suppose that the Norman Conquest and the influence of French were in any real sense

---

ḍ, d or j; ṣ, s or sh; ṭ, t or ch; ẓ, z or zh; *o,* F. cloche; ü, F. menu; ċh, Sc. loch; ṅ, F. bonbon.

the major causes of these extensive grammatical alterations. There is abundant evidence that the old English inflectional system was already beginning to break down some time before William of Normandy ever set foot on English soil. What the Normans did do was to eliminate, within a short space of years and quite thoroughly, the Anglo-Saxon upper classes. In so doing, they also destroyed many of the forces which make for conservatism in the use of language and which tend to slow down the rate of linguistic change. For more than 250 years English was a language spoken almost exclusively by an unlettered peasantry, and so free to develop unchecked. Briefly, the chief effect of the Conquest was not to initiate changes, but to accelerate changes that would presumably have occurred in any case. On the vocabulary, however, the influence of French was all-pervading. (One should not make the mistake of equating the lexical "content" of a language with the language itself, which is a complicated set of grammatical and phonetic patterns.) The Normans possessed a culture which was in many ways far more elaborated than that of the English and which largely replaced the latter. As an inevitable consequence French words were adopted in every field: in law and government, theology and ecclesiastical affairs, art and literature, medicine and the sciences, cooking and gardening, dress and deportment, architecture and domestic arrangements, to name only some. Nor was the borrowing confined by any means to those words for which the English had not possessed equivalents and which therefore met a real need. In many cases the French word merely supplanted an English one of similar meaning; in others both the French and the English word survived as a pair of synonyms. In any event, the number of borrowed words was tremendous and was the chief factor in giving to the vocabulary of the later language that mixed character which distinguishes it so sharply from the vocabularies of other Germanic languages. During the whole of the Middle English period nothing like a standard form of the language existed, no one way of speaking and writing, that is, which was recognized throughout the whole land as possessing superior prestige. There were only the local dialects, which varied so much from place to place as to be, in the case of the extremes, mutually unintelligible. The major Middle English dialects customarily treated as more or less distinct larger entities are the Northern (in general continuing Northumbrian Old English), the East and West Midland (continuing Mercian), the Southern (continuing West Saxon), and the Kentish (continuing Kentish Old English).

Emergence of Modern English. At the beginning of the 15th century, however, the English of London began to rise rapidly to a position of ascendancy over the other dialects. In earlier centuries it had had a markedly southern cast but in the course of time had been assimilated more and more to the East Midland dialects of the counties lying just to the north. The English of the East Midlands possessed the inherent advantage of being in a sense a compromise between the extremes of north and south. But more important in the rise of London English was a combination of social forces. London

was the seat of the king's court and of the royal government, it was already becoming an important cultural center, and it was the chief commercial and trading city in the land. Not unnaturally the English of the capital came increasingly to be imitated by the privileged and more educated classes in other parts of England. The standard form which thus began to spread was essentially a written one: in Tudor England it was no longer possible to tell where an educated man came from from the way he wrote, but the cultivated pronunciation of the spoken language still varied strikingly from place to place. Indeed, even today there is far more uniformity in cultivated written English than in the corresponding spoken form. The transition from Middle to Early Modern English was marked by a series of extensive phonetic changes. For one thing, all the long vowels began to shift in a regular and systematic fashion, long "ee" and "oo," for instance, moving towards long "i" and "ou," so that what had been pronounced "meen" and "hoos" have become modern *mine* and *house*. The weak final vowel of such words as *name* and *ride*, pronounced like the *a* of *sofa*, was lost and as a consequence thousands of words which once had had two syllables now became monosyllabic. The consonants in general were more stable, but were not untouched. To illustrate with an example, Middle English, like Old English, had possessed a consonant like the *ch* of German, which appeared in many words such as *right* and *through*. Early in the Modern period this sound was either lost entirely, as in these words, or shifted to *f*, as in *rough*. Many other changes would still occur in later centuries but by 1500 English pronunciation had already moved appreciably closer to its present state. In the 16th century the vocabulary of English was again enriched by wholesale borrowing from other languages. This time it was the classical tongues, and especially Latin, which furnished the bulk of the new words. Renaissance scholars, thoroughly at home in these languages, often had recourse to them to eke out what they considered to be the poverty of their own. In extreme cases, this tendency ran riot and provoked a very natural reaction. Critics charged that these words were not English words at all, but "ink-horn terms" which constituted a barbarous, outlandish jargon. But the net result was to add thousands of words to the learned and literary vocabulary of English, words which soon lost their look of strangeness and which today we could ill do without. Other languages also contributed their share: French continued to be drawn upon, and many words were borrowed from Spanish and from Italian. The modern student of Elizabethan England is likely to be a little bit surprised when he finds that the Elizabethans, although they wrote books on almost every conceivable subject, did not write English grammars and did not compile English dictionaries. Their linguistic interests were largely confined to two problems: the borrowing of foreign words, referred to above, and the spelling of English, which was still rather haphazard and in addition almost as unphonetic as it is today. Grammar they left to custom to determine and made no attempts to regulate. And custom was in many respects unsettled. So it is that by the standards of a later

fat, fāte, fär, ȧsk, fāre; net, mē, hėr; pin, pīne; not, nōte, mȯve, nôr; up, lūte, pull; ᴛʜ, then;

day (which do not of course apply) the language of Shakespeare and his contemporaries is often very "ungrammatical" indeed. The double negative was still in common cultivated use, the case forms of pronouns were often confused, and the agreement between sentence elements was much less rigorous than it later became. It was not until the next century that attitudes characteristic of a later time really made their appearance. The first English dictionary, a very faint foreshadowing of the massive volumes of our century, was issued in 1604. (Actually this little work was written with no normative, regulatory purpose, but merely to explain a certain number of difficult words.) Grammars began to appear and when the works of Elizabethan writers were reissued they had often been subjected to extensive grammatical amendment. Cultivated English was already moving in the direction of that well-pruned orderliness which was the ideal of the 18th century. This ideal was part and parcel of a more general climate of opinion. "Reason and orderliness": in these words a great deal of the 18th century may be summed up, whether we look at literature and philosophy, art and music, or architecture and landscape gardening. So also, when the men of this century approached the problems of language, they believed it possible, under the rule of reason, to legislate usage, to rid the language of all "corruptions" and irrationalities, and then to fix it once and for all. To this great end they devoted themselves with enthusiasm, proposing academies on the model of France and Italy to regulate the language, producing dictionaries which culminated in Johnson's great work of 1755, and writing prescriptive grammars by the score. They were very deficient in historical knowledge, they often took a rather cavalier attitude towards the actual facts of cultivated usage, and they had a fatal tendency to reason from "universal grammar," which they imagined to lie behind the several forms of different languages. The net result of all their labors was consequently less than they had hoped and a surprising number of the usages which they condemned have continued to flourish, even though the condemnations have been reiterated in later grammars written in the same tradition. Only in relatively recent years has this tradition begun to give way, as grammarians have come to realize that, so far as the standard language is concerned, their proper task is to describe cultivated usage as it actually is and not to make arbitrary statements about what it should be.

Late Modern English Developments. In the past two centuries, even though the language has continued to evolve, there have been no major alterations in the English grammatical system. Minor changes have occurred, for example the development of the progressive passive (*the book is being written*) which established itself in the course of the 19th century, but there has been nothing comparable to the grammatical refashioning that was going on in the 12th and 13th centuries. On the phonetic side there is more to record, of both disuse and innovation. Many common 18th-century pronunciations, such as are reflected in rhymes like *seat-state, join-line, warm-harm,* and *sermon-arming,* have either disappeared entirely or survive only in rather isolated dialects. As an instance of innovation we may cite the loss of *r* before consonants and at the end of the word in some varieties of English, making rhymes of *short* and *caught* and *fear* and *idea.* The English vocabulary has grown enormously in this period as a reflection of the growth of knowledge in many fields. The development of technology and of the physical sciences alone has produced such a vast number of new technical terms that even the largest of our general dictionaries record no more than a selection of them. At the same time, the contacts of men of English speech with other peoples in every corner of the earth have continued to enrich the vocabulary from the most diverse sources. The Indian languages of the Americas, the languages of Asia and Africa, have all contributed so generously to Modern English that no other form of human speech has so varied a store of words.

Development Outside the British Isles. American English. So far, for the sake of clarity, this sketch has proceeded as though English were exclusively the language of the British Isles. Actually, in the 20th century the inhabitants of these islands form only a relatively small minority among those for whom English is the mother tongue. It is spoken in the U. S., in Canada, Australia, New Zealand, and the Union of South Africa, and in a number of British colonies. In all of these countries, a longer or shorter period of independent existence has caused the language to diverge somewhat from the English of England. This differentiation has occurred everywhere in roughly similar fashion, but has gone farthest in the U. S. Since this is so, a brief account of American developments will suffice to indicate the nature of the changes which have also occurred in the Dominions. When British settlers in the 17th and early 18th centuries came to the eastern coast of North America, they brought with them various forms of contemporary British English. Many spoke dialects of the different counties of England; a small but important number of educated men, some of them graduates of the universities, spoke and wrote the standard English of their day. In the colonies none of the provincial dialects were able to maintain themselves intact and an accommodation among them occurred, resulting in new mixtures which varied somewhat from colony to colony. Hence it is that no local form of American speech resembles in all or most of its characteristic details any particular dialect of the British Isles. At the same time that these new dialects were being shaped, some of the port cities were developing as centers of wealth and a certain refinement. Between them and the mother country trade was lively and through them the influence of the developing British standard continued for some generations to be exercised on American English. From the very beginning the colonists found that the resources of their inherited vocabulary were not fully adequate for the conditions of life in a new world. Here they looked out upon a very different landscape, filled with different birds and animals and plants. Domestic arrangements (the building of houses, the tilling of land, the preparation of foods) were not the same as those of England. Social and political institutions similarly came to differ from those of the land they

d̦, d or j; ṣ, s or sh; ṭ, t or ch; ẓ, z or zh; *o,* F. cloche; ü, F. menu; c̄h, Sc. loch; n̄, F. bonbon.

had left. In response to the needs thus created, the vocabulary was expanded in various ways. Old words were extended in meaning: the name *robin*, for example, was applied to a bird which was not the same as the English robin, and *lot*, because of the device of castings lots in the partitioning of new townships, came to mean a parcel of land. Furthermore, new terms like *bullfrog*, *live oak*, and *backwoods* were created by the combination of old elements. And a few hundred words (for instance, *hickory*, *squash*, *skunk*, and *wampum*) were borrowed, often in very garbled form, from the Indians, along with thousands of place names. Other causes also operated to give the vocabulary of American English a distinctive quality. For one thing, the colonists continued to use a number of older British words which now went out of use in England or were altered in meaning there. Some usages which strike the modern Englishman as very definitely American, for instance certain meanings of *sick* and *bug* and *guess*, are actually survivals of this sort. Second, the vocabulary of British English was itself developing and not all of these new words and meanings were exported to the colonies. Third, in the new land, men of English speech mingled with settlers from other European countries, who made their contributions to the colonial vocabulary. From the New York Dutch, for example, words like *cookie*, *cruller*, *scow*, *sleigh*, and *waffle* were borrowed, only some of which passed over into British English. By the time of the Revolutionary War, the differences in vocabulary that thus resulted were already considerable enough to command attention. And since then the process has continued. American English has borrowed words from French as the result of contacts on the old Northwest Frontier and in the valleys of the Mississippi and Missouri, from Spanish in the Southwest, and, in much smaller numbers, from the languages of the 19th-century immigrants. The westward expansion of the country and the conditions of frontier life caused further additions, often rather gaudy. The political conflicts of the 19th century gave rise to many new words, some of which soon died out again along with the movements which produced them, while others survive in use today. Industrial expansion and the growth of cities also played a part in causing differentiation between the vocabularies of British and American English. For example, many modern trades, like those of the auto mechanic and the radio repairman, which have developed in recent generations, use very different technical terms in the two countries. So far, indeed, has the process of differentiation gone that a recent dictionary of Americanisms filled two large volumes. More than 300 years of largely independent existence have caused American and British English to differ noticeably in pronunciation and to some extent in grammar, as well as in vocabulary. In certain cases, the American pronunciation represents an innovation, or at least the general adoption of some features which occurred only in a small area in England. The very common tendency to pronounce *t* more or less like *d* in certain positions (*better*, *petal*) is an example of this sort. On the other hand, when we Americans pronounce *ask* and *dance* with the "flat *a*," while many Englishmen say "ahsk" and "dahnce," we

are merely preserving the fashion of an older time. In this instance, it is the English who have made the innovation. So far as grammar is concerned, while the popular dialects of the U. S. have often developed features which probably cannot be found in any form of British speech, the educated usage of the two countries is identical, except for minor details. When an Englishman writes "the Cabinet have not yet been named," we are struck by the plural verb, which we would hardly use. But a list of all such instances would not be very long and would include nothing of any great importance. Impressed particularly by the many differences in the vocabulary of everyday life, some have argued that the divergent development of the language in the two countries has now gone so far that two separate languages have resulted. It is unreasonable, they say, to speak of "British English" and "American English"; "English" and "American" would be more accurate terms. Such views as these have found little support among competent scholars in either country. In basic matters of grammatical structure (the plural formation of nouns, the conjugational system of verbs, the comparison of adjectives) differences either do not exist at all or are very slight. Differences in pronunciation, though instantly apparent, are for the most part more a matter of "shading" and nuance than of anything very fundamental. And even the differences in vocabulary need to be viewed in true perspective, that is, against the much larger body of words which are our common possession. What the future will bring, we cannot say: if that future is one of chaos and disorder, marked by a widespread breakdown of communication, American and British English may drift so far apart as to be mutually unintelligible, like English and Dutch, or Italian and Rumanian. But that state of affairs has not yet been reached.

English Bards and Scotch Reviewers. A satirical poem by Byron, directed against those who had put him, as he imagined, on the defensive after reviews in the *Edinburgh Review* of his *Hours of Idleness* (1807). It was published in 1809, and was said by himself, in the edition of 1816, to be a "miserable record of misplaced anger and indiscriminate acrimony."

English Civil War. See Civil War, English.

English Dramatick Poets, An Account of the. See Account of the English Dramatick Poets, An.

Englishman in Paris, The. A comedy by Samuel Foote, produced in 1753 and printed in 1756. Both Macklin and Foote played Buck in this play.

Englishman Returned from Paris, The. A comedy by Samuel Foote, produced in 1756. It was a sequel to *The Englishman in Paris*.

English-men for My Money, or A Woman Will Have Her Will. A comedy (c1598) by William Haughton.

English Merchant, The. A comedy by George Colman the elder. It was founded on Voltaire's *L'Écossaise*, and was produced at the Drury Lane Theatre, London, on Feb. 21, 1767.

English Monsieur (mę.syė′), **The.** A play by James Howard, produced in 1666 and printed in 1674. The principal character, Frenchlove, admires everything

fat, fāte, fär, àsk, fāre; net, mē, hèr; pin, pīne; not, nōte, mȯve, nôr; up, lūte, pùll; ᴛʜ, then;

French, even to the "French step" with which a French lady scornfully walks away after rejecting him.

English Traits. Lectures delivered by Ralph Waldo Emerson in 1848. They were published in 1856. A discerning analysis of the English mind and national character, the series praises England for its contributions to government, literature, and commerce, but criticizes the nation for its lack of social vitality and spiritual fervor.

English Traveller, The. A tragedy by Thomas Heywood, probably acted c1624 and published in 1633. The subplot was borrowed from Plautus's *Mostellaria* but the main plot is Heywood's own.

Enid (ē'nid). A character originally appearing in the romance of *Erec et Énide* by Chrétien de Troyes. This was probably his first poem. She reappears in the *Geraint* of the *Mabinogion*, and Tennyson has used her story in *Geraint and Enid*, one of his *Idylls of the King*.

Enid. A novel by Marmaduke Pickthall, published in 1904.

Enitharmon (ē.ni.thär'mọn). In Blake's mystical poems, a character usually intended to represent the female counterpart of Los, and to be the minister of Urizen's moral laws for man.

Enlightenment. As a proper name, the term used in literature and history to indicate a period of intense artistic and intellectual productivity in 18th-century Europe. It was a phase of rationalism and, as such, emphasized man as a rational being who could be appealed to and made to do the right thing, and desire to do it, when he was called upon to use his reasoning power. In Germany it is associated with Lessing, Moses Mendelssohn, and Reimarus, a rational theologian who examined Gospel history critically. In France the term, or movement, includes Voltaire, Diderot (whose *Encyclopédie* was a powerful impetus to the Enlightenment), Rousseau, Condillac, and Montesquieu. In England it applies to Locke and Newton, and to Johnson.

Enna (en'ạ; Italian, en'nä). A city and commune in SW Italy, on the island of Sicily. In ancient times, Enna was the seat of the cult of the goddess Demeter, whose temple was here; Enna, more specifically the nearby Lake of Pergusa, was supposed to be the location at which the rape of Persephone, Demeter's daughter, occurred. The city has been called the navel of Sicily, because of its position in the center of the island.

Ennever (en'ẹ.vėr), **William Joseph.** b. at London, 1869; d. there, 1947. An English journalist, who originated the mnemonic training system known as Pelmanism. He founded (1896) the first Pelman Institute at London, and opened branches in India, South Africa, Canada, France, and the U. S. He published a pamphlet series entitled *Your Mind and How to Use It.*

Ennius (en'i.us), **Quintus.** b. at Rudiae, in Calabria, 239 B.C.; d. probably at Rome, 169 B.C. A Roman epic poet, one of the founders of Latin literature. He served in the Roman army in Sardinia (204 B.C.), and there met Marcus Porcius Cato (Cato the Censor), who brought him to Rome, where he taught Greek and translated Greek plays.

He gained Roman citizenship in 184. He was the author of *Annales* (in 18 books, only fragments of which survive), an epic poem on the early history of Rome, designed as a pendant to the Homeric poems; of tragedies; and of miscellaneous poems in various meters.

Enobarbus (ē.nọ.bär'bus, en.ọ̄-). In Shakespeare's *Antony and Cleopatra*, a friend of Antony. He is a blunt, rough-spoken man, but possesses a degree of humorous sagacity. It is he who gives the famous description of Cleopatra in her barge coming down the Cydnus (II.ii), and the fact that Cleopatra's beauty should so deeply move a practical, unromantic man like Enobarbus emphasizes her tremendous power to stir men. Enobarbus deserts Antony, but dies of a heart broken by remorse at his betrayal of his friend when Antony sends his treasure after him.

Enoch (ē'nok, -nọk). In the Bible, the eldest son of Cain. A city which Cain built was named for him. Gen. iv. 17, 18.

Enoch Arden (ē'nọk är'dẹn). A poem by Alfred Tennyson, published in 1864, named from its hero, a sailor who returns from an enforced absence of years to find that his wife, thinking him dead, has married his friend. For her sake he does not reveal himself, and dies broken-hearted.

Entail, The. A novel (1823) by John Galt.

Enthusiast, or The Lover of Nature, The. A poem (1744) by Joseph Warton, in the pastoral style, expressing his conviction that unspoiled nature is preferable to the contrivings of art ("Lead me from gardens deck'd with art's vain pomps"), and his delight in the serene pleasure of quiet happiness.

envoy (en.voi'). Formerly, and sometimes still archaically, a postscript to a composition, particularly a ballade or other sentimental poem, to enforce or recommend it. It sometimes served as a dedication. As a title it was often, and is still occasionally, written with the French article, *l'envoy* or *l'envoi* (len.voi'). "The Blind Minstrel is a vigorous versifier . . . As a specimen of his graver style we may give his envoy or concluding lines." (Craik, *Eng. Lit.*)

Enyo (e.nī'ō). In Greek mythology, a goddess of war, associated with Ares.

Éon de Beaumont (dā.ôṅ dẹ bō.môṅ), **Charles Geneviève Louis Auguste André Timothée d'.** [Called the Chevalier **d'Éon.**] b. at Tonnerre, Yonne, France, Oct. 5, 1728; d. at London, May 21, 1810. A French diplomat, a famous secret agent of Louis XV. He served (1755–60) the king at the court of the empress Elizabeth of Russia, and later at London. He was particularly noted for his success in assuming a female disguise. When in 1763 the intrigues of Madame Pompadour caused his recall from England, he refused either to leave England or to surrender certain state papers. Not until 1774, after the death of Louis XV, would he give in, and on his return to France was forced by the agreement he had reached to wear women's clothes. He fled to England in 1784 and lived out his life there, giving fencing exhibitions. The mystery of his sex continued, for he persisted in wearing women's clothes, and only by a post-mortem examination was it possible finally to prove that he was a man and not a woman.

Eos (ē'os). [Latin, **Aurora.**] In Greek mythology, the goddess of the dawn; daughter of Hyperion, and sister of Helios and Selene. Her husband was Astraeus, but among her lovers were Orion, Cephalus, and Tithonus. She is identified with the Latin Aurora.

Eothen (ē.ō'then). A book of travels in the East, by Alexander William Kinglake, published 1844.

Ephesians (e.fē'zhạnz). Boon companions; used in Shakespeare's 2 *Henry IV* and *Merry Wives of Windsor.*

Ephesus (ef'ẹ.sus), **Duke of.** See **Solinus.**

Ephialtes (ef.i.al'tēz). In ancient Greek mythology, a blind giant who was deprived of his left eye by Apollo, and of his right by Hercules. He and his brother Otus, called the Aloidae, piled Ossa on Olympus, and Pelion on Ossa, to attack the gods. Luckily they were only nine years old at the time and the gods were able to defeat them. Ephialtes was also the name of the nightmare demon of ancient Greece, and the name is given as that of the traitorous guide who led the Persians to the Spartan rear at Thermopylae.

Ephraim Jenkinson (ē'frạ.im, ē'frạm, jeng'kin.sọn). See **Jenkinson, Ephraim.**

epic. A long poem which relates the story of an event, or of a series of events, whether historical or imaginary, concerning heroic action by one or more individuals, usually over a relatively long period of time. Vergil's *Aeneid,* Homer's *Iliad,* and Milton's *Paradise Lost* are examples of epics.

epicedium (ep.i.sē'di.um). A funeral song or dirge.

> Funerall songs were called *Epicedia* if they were sung by many. (Puttenham, *Arte of Eng. Poesie.*)

> A more moving quill
> Than Spenser used when he gave Astrophil
> A living epicedium.
> (Massinger, *Sero sed Serio.*)

Epicoene, or The Silent Woman (ep'i.sēn). A comedy by Ben Jonson, produced in 1609.

Epictetus (ep.ik.tē'tus). [Also, **Epictetus of Hierapolis** (hī.ẹr.ap'ọ.lis).] fl. c100 A.D. A Greek Stoic philosopher. He was a native of Hierapolis in Phrygia, was a freedman of Epaphroditus (the freedman and favorite of Nero), was a pupil of Musonius Rufus, and taught philosophy at Rome until c94 A.D., when he removed to Nicopolis in Epirus, in consequence of an edict of Domitian banishing the philosophers from Rome. Although he left no written works, his essential doctrines are preserved in a manual compiled by his pupil Arrian. He taught that the sum of wisdom is to desire nothing but freedom and contentment, and to bear and forbear; that all unavoidable evil in the world is only apparent and external; and that our happiness depends upon our own will, which even Zeus cannot break.

Epicure Mammon (ep'i.kūr mam'ọn), **Sir.** See **Mammon, Sir Epicure.**

Epicurus (ep.i.kū'rus). b. on the island of Samos, 342 or 341 B.C.; d. at Athens, 271 or 270 B.C. A Greek philosopher, the founder of the Epicurean school of philosophy. He was the son of Neocles, an Athenian cleruch (colonist) settled on Samos, and belonged to the Attic *deme* of Gargettus (whence he is sometimes called the Gargettian). He revealed an early aptitude for philosophy, which he studied as a youth at Athens and subsequently taught as a young man at Mytilene and Lampsacus. In 306 B.C. he returned to Athens, where he established a school in a garden outside the city walls. There, in an atmosphere of quiet withdrawal, he devoted the rest of his life to teaching. We owe most of our information about him to a biography by Diogenes Laërtius. Of the approximately 300 volumes which he is said to have written only fragments remain. Fortunately, however, his biographer gives us the texts of three of his rather lengthy epistles, a transcript of his will, and some 40 propositions known as "Principal Doctrines," all of which contain the substance of his views on "physics" and ethics. As Epicurus developed his system of hedonism, he was influenced by Plato's views on pleasure as well as by the Cyrenaic doctrine of Aristippus. With the ethical principle of pleasure as the highest good, Epicurus blended the physics of Democritus and the other atomists of the 5th century B.C. This materialistic physics asserted such principles as "nothing can come from nothing," and "all that exists is atoms and void." As such it could be supported by empirical evidence, and was easily made to integrate on rational grounds with a hedonistic ethic. Adhering to an enlightened view of pleasure, Epicurus primarily desired that his system should free mankind from religious superstition and fear of death. He argued that the view of the universe as consisting only of atoms and void would rid man of his besetting anxieties and hence would enable him to achieve that best of pleasures, inner calm and security. He advocated the principle of moderation, and urged men to seek the pleasures of friendship, of simple living, even to the extent of recommending withdrawal from active life. Only by these and like means, Epicurus insisted, could real freedom and its attendant peace be attained. So carefully articulated was his philosophy that it endured without any significant change for centuries after his death.

Epidaurus (ep.i.dô'rus). An ancient town on the E coast of the Peloponnesus, in the district called Argolis under the Romans. Throughout the flourishing period of Greek history it was an independent state, possessing a small territory, bounded on the W by the Argeia, on the N by Corinthia, on the S by Troezenia, and on the E by the Saronic Gulf. It was the most celebrated seat of the ancient cult of Aesculapius, and Milton uses it in a reference to this ancient god of medicine ("the God in Epidaurus") in *Paradise Lost.* The sanctuary occupied a valley among hills, at some distance from the city. An inner enclosure contained a temple to Aesculapius, the architecturally important *tholos* (round building) of Polycletus, extensive porticoes which served as hospitals to the sick who came to seek the aid of the god and his priests, and many votive offerings. Outside of this enclosure were the stadium, one of the most important of ancient theaters, a gymnasium, propylaea, and other buildings, the arrangements for the collection and distribution of water being especially noteworthy. Almost all our

---

fat, fāte, fär, àsk, fāre; net, mē, hèr; pin, pīne; not, nōte, mȯve, nôr; up, lūte, pùll; ŦH, then;

knowledge of this sanctuary comes from the extensive excavations conducted by the Archaeological Society of Athens (1881 *et seq.*).

Epigoni (ẹ.pig′ọ̄.nī). In Greek mythology, the seven sons of the seven Argive chiefs who had unsuccessfully attacked Thebes. The Epigoni, ten years after the first attempt, defeated the Thebans and avenged their fathers. This victory was supposed to have occurred shortly before the Trojan War.

epigram (ep′i.gram). **1.** In Greek literature, a poetical inscription placed upon a tomb or public monument, as upon the face of a temple or public arch. The term was afterward extended to any little piece of verse expressing with precision a delicate or ingenious thought, as the pieces in the Greek Anthology. In Roman classical poetry the term was somewhat indiscriminately used to designate a short piece in verse; but the works of Catullus, and especially the epigrams of Martial, contain a great number with the modern epigrammatic character.

> This Epigramme is but an inscription or writting made as it were vpon a table, or in a windowe, or vpon the wall or mantell of a chimney in some place of common resort.
> > (Puttenham, *Arte of Eng. Poesie.*)

Probably the first application of the newly adapted art [engraving words on stone or metal] was in dedicatory inscriptions or epigrams, to use this word in its original sense.
> > (C. T. Newton, *Art and Archæol.*)

2. In a restricted sense, a short poem or piece in verse, which has only one subject, and finishes by a witty or ingenious turn of thought; hence, in a general sense, an interesting thought represented happily in a few words, whether verse or prose; a pointed or antithetical saying.

> The qualities rare in a bee that we meet
> In an epigram never should fail;
> The body should always be little and sweet,
> And a sting should be left in its tail.
> > *Trans. from Latin* (author unknown).

From the time of Martial, indeed, the epigram came to be characterized generally by that peculiar point or sting which is now looked for in a French or English epigram; and the want of this in the old Greek compositions doubtless led some minds to think them tame and tasteless. The true or the best form of the early Greek epigram does not aim at wit or seek to produce surprise. (Lord Neaves.)

epilogue (ep′i.log). **1.** In rhetoric, the conclusion or closing part of a discourse or oration; the peroration. The office of the epilogue is not merely to avoid an abrupt close and provide a formal termination, but to confirm and increase the effect of what has been said, and leave the hearer as favorably disposed as possible to the speaker's cause and unfavorably to that of his opponents. Accordingly, an epilogue in its more complete form consists of two divisions: (a) a repetition of the principal points previously treated, and (b) an appeal to the feelings. **2.** In dramatic or narrative writing, a concluding address or a winding up of the subject. Specifically, in spoken dramas, it is a closing piece or speech, usually in verse, addressed by one or more of the

performers to the audience. Dramatic epilogues were in vogue during the Elizabethan period, became increasingly more popular during the late 17th century and throughout the 18th century, and gradually waned during the 19th century almost to the point of never being used. Their occurrence in contemporary English drama usually reflects an effort by the dramatist to achieve some special effect through the use of what modern stagecraft considers an archaic device. In Shakespeare's *Henry V* a characteristic type of epilogue is recited by a chorus, depreciating the play, praising the accomplishments of King Henry, and deploring the later loss of his conquests. Frequently, epilogues pleaded for the good will of the audience and for kindness from critics. The decline in the use of epilogues may be attributed to the effort to achieve a realistic effect on the stage, an effect which would be destroyed by actors who step from their roles, directly address the audience, and comment on the play.

> A good play needs no epilogue.
> > (Shak., *As You Like It*, Epil.)

> Why there should be an epilogue to a play,
> I know no cause, the old and usual way
> For which they were made, was to entreat
>   the grace
> Of such as were spectators in this place.
> > (Beaumont, *Custom of the Country*, Epil.)

Epimenides (ep.i.men′i.dēz). fl. in the 7th and 6th centuries B.C. A Cretan poet and prophet. He was said to have gone into a cave to rest while looking for a lost sheep, to have fallen asleep, and to have awakened 57 years later. He came home to find his younger brother now an old man. He became a well-known sage and was called (596 B.C.) to Athens to determine the reason and cure for a plague. This was due to the murder of Cylon (640 B.C.) who had been killed by Megacles despite a promise of safeconduct. He performed the proper rites and freed the city of its impurity.

Epimetheus (ep.i.mē′thūs, -thẹ.us). In Greek mythology, the brother of Prometheus and husband of Pandora. Although warned by his brother, he accepted Pandora as a gift from Zeus, with the result that through her curiosity she liberated the evils peculiar to man, which the gods had concealed in a box she had been forbidden to open.

Epiphany (ẹ.pif′ạ.ni). [Also, **Twelfth Day.**] A Christian religious and secular holiday falling on January 6. It commemorates the revelation of Jesus as divine on the occasions of his baptism, the visit of the Magi, and the marriage feast at Cana.

Epipsychidion (ep″i.psi.kid′i.ọn). A poem by Shelley, published in 1821.

episode (ep′i.sōd). **1.** A separate incident, story, or action introduced in a poem, narrative, or other writing for the purpose of giving greater variety; an incidental narrative or digression separable from the main subject, but naturally arising from it.

> But since we have no present Need
> Of Venus for an Episode,
> With Cupid let us e'en proceed.
> > (Prior, *The Dove.*)

Faithfully adhering to the truth, which he does

ḍ, d or j; ṣ, s or sh; ṭ, t or ch; ẓ, z or zh; o, F. cloche; ü, F. menu; ċh, Sc. loch; ṅ, F. bonbon.

not suffer so much as an ornamental episode to interrupt.   (Hallam, *Introd. Lit. of Europe*.)

The tale [the history of Zara] is a strange episode in a greater episode.   (E. A. Freeman, *Venice*.)

2. An incident or action standing out by itself, but more or less connected with a complete series of events: as, an episode of the war; an episode in one's life.

Then thou think that Episode between Susan, the Dairy-Maid, and our Coach-Man is not amiss.   (Congreve, *Double-Dealer*, III.x.)

epistle (ẹ.pis′l). **1.** A written communication directed or sent to a person at a distance; a letter; a letter missive: used particularly in dignified discourse or in speaking of ancient writings: as, the *epistles* of Paul, of Pliny, or of Cicero.

Called nowe Corona, in Morea, to whome seynt Poule wrote sondry epystolles.
(Sir R. Guylforde, *Pylgrymage*.)

I Tertius, who wrote this epistle, salute you in the Lord.   (Rom. xvi. 22.)

He has here writ a letter to you; I should have given it you to-day morning, but as a madman's epistles are no gospels, so it skills not much when they are delivered.   (Shak., *Twelfth Night*, V.i.)

2. [*cap.*] In liturgics, one of the eucharistic lessons, taken, with some exceptions, from an epistolary book of the New Testament and read before the gospel. In the early church a lection from the Old Testament, called the *prophecy*, preceded it, and such a lection is still sometimes used instead of it. In the Greek Church the epistle (called the *apostle*, as also in the early church) is preceded by the prokeimenon and followed by "Peace to thee" and "Alleluia"; in the Western Church it is preceded by the collects and followed by the Deo gratias, the gradual, tract, or alleluia, with the verse or sequence. It is read in the Greek Church by the anagnost or lector at the holy doors, and in the Western Church by the subdeacon or epistler (in the Roman Catholic Church the celebrant also reciting it in a low voice) at the south side of the altar, that is, at a part of the front of the altar on the celebrant's right as he faces it. Formerly it was read from the ambo (sometimes from a separate or epistle ambo) or pulpit, or from the step of the choir. Sometimes called the *lection* simply.

Epistle of Privy Counsel. A Middle English prose work of the 14th century by the author (whose identity is unknown) of *Cloud of Unknowing*.

Epistle to Dr. Arbuthnot (är.buth′nọt, är′buth.not). A poem (1735) by Alexander Pope addressed to his friend, the physician Dr. John Arbuthnot. It is a summary of Pope's estimation of his own work and his attitudes toward his contemporaries. Two of his most noted objects of satire are included here, Atticus (Addison) and Sporus (Lord Hervey).

Epistolae Ho-Elianae: Familiar Letters (e.pis′tọ.lē hō.e.lī′ạ.nē). A collection (1650) of letters by James Howell, said to be the earliest epistolary publication in the English language.

Epistolae Obscurorum Virorum (ob.skū.rō′rum vi-rō′rum). [Eng. trans., "*Letters of Obscure Men.*"] A collection of 41 anonymous letters, first published in 1515, satirizing the ignorance, hypocrisy,

and licentiousness of the Roman Catholic monastics at the time of the Reformation, and addressed to Johann von Reuchlin, the German humanist. It was occasioned by the controversy between Reuchlin and Johannes Pfefferkorn, a converted Jew, who advocated the destruction, as heretical, of the whole Jewish literature, except the Bible, and who was supported by the Dominicans of Cologne. The authorship of the letters is attributed by some to Ulrich von Hutten, Crotus Rubianus, and Buschius.

epitaph (ep′i.tàf). **1.** An inscription on a tomb or monument in honor or memory of the dead.

After your death you were better have a bad epitaph than their [the players'] ill report while you lived.   (Shak., *Hamlet*, II.ii.)

2. A brief enunciation or sentiment relating to a deceased person, in prose or verse, composed as if to be inscribed on a monument.

An Epitaph . . . is an inscription such as a man may commodiously write or engraue vpon a tombe in few verses, pithie, quicke, and sententious, for the passer by to peruse and iudge vpon without any long tariaunce. (Puttenham, *Arte of Eng. Poesie*.)

One of the most pleasing epitaphs in general literature is that by Pope on Gay:

Of manner gentle, of affection mild,
In wit a man, simplicity a child.
(W. Chambers.)

Epithalamion (ep″i.thạ.lā′mi.ọn). A poem by W. H. Auden, included in *Another Time* (1940). It pleads for the idea of the unity of marriage as a symbol for all unifying forces needed in a world of disintegrating values and standards.

epithalamium (ep″i.thạ.lā′mi.um) or **epithalamion** (-on). A nuptial song or poem; a poem in honor of a newly married person or pair, in praise of and invoking blessings upon its subject or subjects.

I made it both in form and matter to emulate the kind of poem which was called epithalamium, and (by the ancients) used to be sung when the bride was led into her chamber.
(B. Jonson, *Masque of Hymen*.)

The book of the Canticles is a representation of God in Christ, as a bridegroom in a marriage-song, in an epithalamion.   (Donne, *Sermons*, vii.)

Epithalamium. [Also, **Epithalamion**.] A poem by Spenser, published in 1595. It is thought that the song celebrates Spenser's marriage (1594) with Elizabeth Boyle.

epithet (ep′i.thet). **1.** An adjective, or a word or phrase used as an adjective, expressing some real quality of the person or thing to which it is applied, or attributing some quality or character to the person or thing: as, a *benevolent* or a *hard-hearted* man; a *scandalous* exhibition; *sphinx-like* mystery; a *Fabian* policy.

When ye see all these improper or harde Epithets vsed, ye may put them in the number of vncouths, as one that said, the flouds of graces.
(Puttenham, *Arte of Eng. Poesie*.)

By the judicious employment of epithets we may bring distinctly to view, with the greatest brevity, an object with its characteristic features.
(A. D. Hepburn, *Rhetoric*, § 60.)

In no matter of detail are the genius and art of the poet more perceptible and nicely balanced than in the use of epithets.

(*Amer. Jour. Philol.*, IV. 455.)

2. In rhetoric, a term added to impart strength or ornament to diction, and differing from an adjective in that it designates as well as qualifies, and may take the form of a surname: as, Dionysius *the Tyrant;* Alexander *the Great.*

The character of Bajazet . . . is strongly expressed in his surname of Ilderim, or the lightning; and he might glory in an epithet which was drawn from the fiery energy of his soul and the rapidity of his destructive march.

(Gibbon, *Decline and Fall,* lxiv.)

epitome (ẹ.pit′ọ.mē). **1.** An abridgment; a brief summary or abstract of a subject, or of a more extended exposition of it; a compendium containing the substance or principal matters of a book or other writing.

He that shall out of his own reading gather for the use of another must (I think) do it by epitome or abridgment, or under heads and commonplaces. Epitomes also may be of two sorts; of any one art or part of knowledge out of many books, or of one book by itself.

(Essex, *Advice to Sir Fulke Greville,* 1596, in Bacon's *Letters,* II.22.)

As for the corruptions and moths of history, which are Epitomes, the use of them deserveth to be banished.

(Bacon, *Advancement of Learning,* ii.127.)

Epitomes are helpful to the memory.

(Sir H. Wotton.)

2. Anything which represents another or others in a condensed or comprehensive form.

Thus God beholds all things, who contemplates as fully his works in their epitome as in their full volume. (Sir T. Browne, *Religio Medici,* i.50.)

A man so various that he seem'd to be
Not one, but all mankind's epitome.

(Dryden, *Abs. and Achit.,* i.546.)

The Church of St. Mark's itself, harmonious as its structure may at first sight appear, is an epitome of the changes of Venetian architecture from the tenth to the nineteenth century. (Ruskin.)

epode (ep′ōd). In ancient prosody: **1.** A third and metrically different system subjoined to two systems (the strophe and antistrophe) which are metrically identical or corresponsive, and forming with them one pericope or group of systems.

The Third Stanza was called the Epode (it may be as being the After-song), which they sung in the middle, neither turning to one Hand nor the other. (Congreve, *The Pindaric Ode.*)

2. A shorter colon, subjoined to a longer colon, and constituting one period with it; especially, such a colon, as a separate line or verse, forming either the second line of a distich or the final line of a system or stanza. As the closing verse of a system, sometimes called *ephymnium.*

3. A poem consisting of such distichs. Archilochus (c700 B.C.) first introduced these. The Epodes of Horace are a collection of poems so called because mostly composed in epodic distichs.

Horace seems to have purged himself from those splenetic reflections in those odes and epodes, before he undertook the noble work of satires.

(Dryden, *Ded. of Juvenal.*)

I shall still be very ready to write a satire upon the clergy, and an epode against historiographers, whenever you are hard pressed.

(Gray, *Letters,* I.262.)

eponymous (e.pon′i.mus). Giving one's name to a tribe, people, city, year, or period; regarded as the founder or originator. "Will Summer—the name of Henry VIII.'s court-fool, whose celebrity probably made him eponymous of the members of his profession in general." (A. W. Ward, *Eng. Dram. Lit.*)

"Lydus and Asies are . . . eponymous heroes; Meles is an ideal founder of the capital." (G. Rawlinson, *Origin of Nations.*)

epopee (ep.ọ.pē′). **1.** An epic poem. "The Kalevala, or heroic epopee of the Finns." (*Encyc. Brit.*) **2.** The history, action, or fable which makes or is suitable for the subject of an epic. "The stories were an endless epopee of suffering." (G. Kennan, *The Century,* XXXV. 760.)

Eppie (ep′i). In George Eliot's novel *Silas Marner,* the daughter of Cass, eventually adopted by Silas.

Epsom (ep′sọm). A former urban district (until 1933), parish, and market town in SE England, in Surrey, situated at the foot of Banstead Downs, ab. 14 mi. SW of London by rail. Epsom is famous for its horse racing, at the race course on Epsom Downs.

Epsom Wells. A comedy by Thomas Shadwell, produced in 1672 and printed in 1673. It imitates some scenes from Molière's *Le Médecin malgré lui.* The play depicts middle-class Londoners on a holiday in the country; Bevil is typically the Restoration hero who finds that "it's impossible to be a man of honour" unless he cuckolds "this honest fellow" (one of the men on holiday).

Er (ẽr). A Pamphylian, the son of Armenius, a character introduced by Plato into the tenth book of *The Republic.* He was slain in battle, and on the 12th day after his death, as he was lying on the funeral pile, returned to life and told what he had seen in the other world.

Erasmus (ẹ.raz′mus), **Desiderius.** [Original name, **Gerhard Gerhards** ("Gerhard's son"), Dutch, **Geert Geerts.**] b. at Rotterdam, Netherlands, probably Oct. 28, 1465; d. at Basel, Switzerland, July 12, 1536. A Dutch classical and theological scholar and satirist. He was the illegitimate son of Gerhard de Praet, was left an orphan at the age of 13, and was defrauded of his inheritance by his guardians, who compelled him to enter the monastery of Stein. He was ordained as a priest in 1492. He entered in 1494 the service of the bishop of Cambrai, under whose patronage he was enabled to study at the University of Paris. He subsequently visited the chief European countries, including England (1498–99, 1505–06, 1510–14), where he met John Colet, Thomas More, and other English humanists. His *Moriae encomium* (*Praise of Folly*) was written in England. His travels and writing brought him into contact with most of the scholars of Europe. In 1521 he settled at Basel, whence he removed to

ḍ, d or j; ṣ, s or sh; ṭ, t or ch; ẓ, z or zh; o, F. cloche; ü, F. menu; ċh, Sc. loch; ṅ, F. bonbon.

Freiburg im Breisgau in 1529. At Basel he was editor of the press of Johann Froben, which under Erasmus's lead became the first press of the Continent. But Froben died in 1527 and Erasmus moved on. In this period were published a number of Erasmus's series on the Church Fathers. Refusing all offers of ecclesiastical preferment, he devoted himself wholly to study and literary composition. He aimed to reform without dismembering the Roman Catholic Church, and at first favored, but subsequently opposed, the Reformation, and engaged in a controversy with Luther. A well-known saying is that Erasmus laid the egg that Luther hatched, but where Luther's reform spread to a fanatical evangelism, Erasmus's desired reform was within the Church, an attempt to bring his high intellectualism to bear to wipe out the superstition he found fostered by the clerics, to limit their power. His method, however, appealed only to his own level of humanistic learning; his satirical and humorous pen never reached the lower clergy with its message, and his friendship with the Pope or Henry VIII of England was of no avail in such a struggle. His chief performance was an edition of the New Testament in Greek with a Latin translation, published in 1516. Besides this edition of the New Testament his most notable publications are *Colloquies*, the *Moriae encomium*, the *Adagia*, and the *Institutio principis christiani*. A collective edition of his works was published (1703–06) by Le Clerc.

Erato (er'a.tō). In Greek mythology, the Muse of erotic poetry. In art she is often represented with the lyre.

Erceldoune (ėr'sel.dön), **Thomas of.** See **Thomas the Rhymer.**

Erckmann-Chatrian (erk.màn.shà.trē.äṅ). The signature of the literary collaborators Émile Erckmann (b. at Phalsbourg, Meurthe-et-Moselle, France, May 20, 1822; d. March 14, 1899) and Louis Gratien Charles Alexandre Chatrian (b. at Soldatenthal, Meurthe-et-Moselle, France, Dec. 18, 1826; d. at Raincy, Seine, France, Sept. 3, 1890). In 1847 these two men became associated in literary labors, the former writing chiefly and the latter editing and adapting for the stage. Among their first publications were *Science et génie* and *Schinderhannes* (1850), and many short stories. The series of novels to which Erckmann-Chatrian owe, in great part, their reputation includes *Le Fou Yégof* (1862), *Madame Thérèse, ou les volontaires de 1792* (1863), *Histoire d'un conscrit de 1813* and *L'Ami Fritz* (1864), *Waterloo* and *Histoire d'un homme du peuple* (1865), *La Guerre* and *La Maison forestière* (1866), and many others. Their dramatic compositions and adaptations are *Georges, ou le chasseur des ruines* (1848), *L'Alsace en 1814* (1850), *Le Juif polonais* (1869), *L'Ami Fritz* (1876), *Madame Thérèse* (1882), *Les Rantzau* (1882), and others. Erckmann claimed sole authorship of the novel *Les Brigands des Vosges il y a soixante ans* (1850), a totally different version of which was published by him in *La Revue de Paris* under the title "L'Illustre docteur Mathéus" (1857). After Chatrian's death, Erckmann contributed to *Le Temps* two publications, "Kaleb et Khora" and "La Première Campagne du grand-père Jacques,"

the latter being the first in a series of stories dealing with the wars of the empire.

Ercles (ėr'klēz). A variant of Hercules. The term is used by Bottom in Shakespeare's *Midsummer Night's Dream.*

Erebus (er'ẹ.bus). [Also, **Erebos** (-bos).] In Greek mythology, a place or region, and a state or condition. As the first, it is that part or section of the underworld through which the souls of the dead must pass in order to reach Hades. As the second, it is "darkness" itself, and, in particular, the darkness of the west.

Erechtheum (er.ek.thē'um). An Ionic temple in Athens, of the 5th century B.C., remarkable for its architectural variety.

Erechtheus (ẹ.rek'thūs, -thẹ.us). In Greek legend, a king of Athens, protégé of Athena. He is remembered for his three daughters, one of whom he sacrificed to save Attica from invaders. The other two killed themselves. He is sometimes confused with Erichthonius.

Erechtheus. A tragedy by Algernon Swinburne, printed in 1876. It utilizes a classical theme to show the author's sympathy with the revolutionary ardor of Mazzini.

Erewhon (er'ẹ.hwon). A satirical romance by Samuel Butler (1835–1902), published in 1872. From it Butler is sometimes referred to as "Erewhon" Butler, to distinguish him from the 17th-century Samuel ("Hudibras") Butler. Strong, the narrator, crosses an unexplored chain of mountains (Butler was thinking of New Zealand in his geography, but the satire was aimed at 19th-century England) and comes upon the fabulous land of Erewhon (an anagram of "nowhere"). The book is a satire on the social and political institutions of a land ruled by compromise and hypocrisy. The author derides the ecclesiastical system, parental tyranny, the system of punishment for crime, and the growing encroachment of the factory system on men's lives. The narrator escapes in a balloon he has made, and carries off with him Arowhena, an Erewhonian lady with whom he is in love.

Erewhon Revisited. A sequel to *Erewhon* by Samuel Butler (1835–1902), published in 1901. Strong is overwhelmed by the desire to revisit Erewhon after an absence of 20 years. He arrives there to find that his departure in the balloon appeared to the people to be a miracle, and that he himself is now worshiped as the child of the sun. A great temple is being built in his honor, and is being dedicated by the professors Hanky and Panky. Dismayed by the new religion, Strong reveals himself at the dedication, but is hurried away by friends before he can be harmed, and is smuggled out of the country.

Erichthonius (er.ik.thō'ni.us). In Greek legend, a king of Athens; son of Hephaestus and grandfather of Erechtheus.

Ericson or **Ericsson** (er'ik.sọn), **Leif.** A Norse adventurer. According to the Icelandic sagas, he sailed (c1000 A.D.) from Greenland with 35 companions in quest of a strange land to the west which had been sighted in 986 by an earlier Norse seafarer. He discovered the country which he named Vinland from the grape vines he found growing in it, and spent a winter there. Historians think more likely, however, the story told in another Icelandic saga. Leif Ericson had visited Norway after spending his youth in Greenland, and in Norway became a Christian. He set out again for Greenland as a missionary but was blown off his course and landed on the North American continent. He explored the area casually and then resumed his voyage to Greenland. The coast on which he landed has been identified by some as that of Labrador, Nova Scotia, or Newfoundland, and by others as that of New England.

Eridanus (ē.rid′a̱.nus). In Greek legend, the name of a large river in Europe, later identified with the Rhone, or, usually, with the Po. It was connected with the myth of Phaethon, the youth supposedly having fallen here when Zeus killed him with a thunderbolt. The Eridanus was famous as a source of amber, hence its identification with the Po, at whose mouth amber used to be gathered.

Erigena (e.rij′e̯.na̱), **Johannes Scotus.** [Original name, **Johannes Scotus.**] b. probably in Ireland, between 800 and 815; d. probably c891. A scholar of the Carolingian period. He came to the court of Charles the Bald before 847, and became director of the palatial school; it was while he held this office that his chief literary work was done. He is said by William of Malmesbury and others to have been invited to England by Alfred the Great (c883), to have been appointed teacher at the school of Oxford and abbot of Malmesbury, and to have been killed by his own pupils: the story seems baseless. His chief work was the translation of Dionysius the Areopagite, and the consequent introduction of Neo-platonism into western Europe. His orthodoxy was several times called in question. He identified philosophy and religion and maintained the freedom of the will over the officially accepted doctrine of predestination. His systematic picture of the universe making a unity of all, identifying God with intellect, was condemned by Pope Honorius III. Erigena is a precursor of the later scholastics but maintains strong ties with the earlier Platonism. The most notable of his original productions is *De Divisione Naturae* (edited by Gale 1681, Schlüter 1838, and Floss 1853).

Erigone (ē.rig′o̱.nē). In Greek mythology, the daughter of Icarius. Icarius was taught the cultivation of the vine by Dionysus, but when his wine made people drunk they suspected him of poisoning them and killed him. Erigone, perhaps the mistress of Dionysus, searched for and found her father's body and, grief-stricken, hanged herself. She was changed to a constellation (the Latin Virgo). She and her father were probably minor fertility deities absorbed into the Dionysian myth; they were celebrated in a country festival in Attica.

Erin (er′in, ir′-). A literary name of Ireland.

Erinyes (ē.rin′i.ēz). In Greek mythology, female divinities, avengers of iniquity. According to Hesiod, they are daughters of Ge (earth), sprung from the blood of the mutilated Uranus; according to others, they are the children of night and darkness. They hunted down offenders, made them mad. and punished them in the afterworld. They were also called the Eumenides (a euphemism meaning "the kind ones") and, by the Romans, Furiae or Dirae. In later times their number was limited to three, Alecto ("the unresting"), Megaera ("the jealous"), and Tisiphone ("the avenger"). The Erinyes are not vindictive; their punishments are impartial and impersonal. Orestes, who slew his mother Clytemnestra because she killed his father Agamemnon, is hounded by the Erinyes even though his act was fully in consonance with what he was required to do: he had killed his mother and the Erinyes demanded payment for the crime.

Eriphyle (er.i.fī′lē). The sister of Adrastus, slain by her son Alcmaeon for inciting her husband Amphiaraus to join the fatal expedition against Thebes.

Eris (ē′ris, er′is). In Greek mythology, the goddess of discord, sister of Ares.

Erl-King (èrl′king). [German, **Erl-König** (erl′-kė″niċh).] In German legend, a goblin who haunts the forests and lures people to destruction. He is particularly addicted to destroying children. The creation of the figure of a giant wearing a crown who carries children off to his kingdom is recent and is due to a mistranslation by Johann Gottfried van Herder of the Danish *ellerkonge*, "elf king." The older German myth and legend has no such being among its characters. The Erl-King is the subject of a well-known poem by Goethe, which was set to music by Franz Schubert.

Ermine Street (èr′min). [Also, **Ermyn Street.**] A Roman road from London N to Lincoln and York. It left London at Bishopsgate, where a branch, the Vicinal Way, was thrown off to Essex; or (according to some historians) it started at Pevensey, in East Sussex. The first stopping place on the N road was Adfines, in what is now Hertfordshire; thence it went to Durolipons, now Godmanchester, in Huntingdonshire on the Ouse; thence to Durobrivae, near what is now the village of Castor, in Northamptonshire; thence due N to Causennae, now Ancaster, in Lincolnshire; thence to Lindum, now Lincoln; thence to Segelocum, now Littleborough; thence to Danum, now Doncaster; thence to Calcaria, the modern Tadcaster, in Yorkshire; and thence to Eboracum, now York. From York there was a branch which went N to the wall of Hadrian.

Erminia Pauletti (er.mē′nyä pô.let′i), **Lady.** See **Hermione, Lady.**

Ernani (er.nä′nē). An opera in four acts by Verdi, first produced at Venice in March, 1844. It was founded on Victor Hugo's *Hernani.* When it was produced in France in 1846, the title was altered to *Il Proscritto* and the characters were made Italian at Victor Hugo's request.

Ernest Maltravers (èr′ne̯st mal.trav′e̯rz). A novel by Edward Bulwer-Lytton, published in 1837. The sequel to this novel is *Alice, or the Mysteries.* The books tell the story of Ernest Maltravers, who has position and wealth, and who is rescued from robbery and murder by Alice, daughter of a cutthroat. Ernest constitutes himself the protector of this helpless, beautiful, and uneducated girl, but be-

d̤, d or j; ṣ, s or sh; ṭ, t or ch; z̤, z or zh; o, F. cloche; ü, F. menu; ċh, Sc. loch; ṅ, F. bonbon.

trays his trust when he falls victim to his passion for her. She swears to remain faithful to him, and keeps her word in spite of the fact that circumstances separate the two lovers for many years. Ernest has many adventures before his eventual reunion with and marriage to Alice.

Ernest Pontifex (pon'ti.feks). See **Pontifex, Ernest.**

Ernle (ern'l), 1st Baron. Title of **Prothero, Rowland Edmund.**

Ernulf (er'nulf) or **Arnulf** (är'nulf). b. in France, 1040; d. March 15, 1124. An English prelate, abbot of Peterborough (1107–14) and bishop of Rochester (1114–24). He was educated at the famous monastery of Bec, and was a close friend of Lanfranc and Anselm. He was an authority on canon law, and left a large number of documents bearing on English ecclesiastical and legal history (*Textus Roffensis*, preserved in Rochester cathedral).

Eros (ē'ros, er'os). In Shakespeare's *Antony and Cleopatra*, the freed slave of Antony. He is devoted to Antony, and kills himself with his own sword when ordered by Antony to slay him.

Eros. See also **Cupid.**

Erpingham (èr'ping.ham), **Sir Thomas.** In Shakespeare's *Henry V*, one of Henry's officers.

Erse (èrs). See **Irish.**

Erskine (èr'skin), **Henry.** b. at Edinburgh, Nov. 1, 1746; d. in Linlithgowshire, Scotland, Oct. 8, 1817. A Scottish lawyer, wit, orator, poet, and classical translator. He was lord advocate (1783, 1806–07) and dean of the faculty of advocates (1785–95); his opposition (Nov. 28, 1795) to the government's "Seditious Writings Bill" cost him reëlection to that post in 1796. He was the author of *Love Elegies dedicated to Amanda* (1770), *The Emigrant, an Eclogue Occasioned by the Late Numerous Emigrations from the Highlands of Scotland* (1773), verse fables, and metrical versions and imitations of classical authors. *The Nettle and the Sensitive Plant* is considered one of his best poems.

Erskine, Ralph. b. March 15, 1685; d. at Dunfermline, Scotland, Nov. 6, 1752. A Scottish clergyman. He was the author of *Gospel Sonnets*, which reached the 25th edition in 1795.

Erskine of Linlathen (lin.laᴛʜ'en), **Thomas.** b. at Edinburgh, Oct. 13, 1788; d. there, March 20, 1870. A Scottish theological writer. He wrote *Internal Evidence for the Truth of Revealed Religion* (1820).

Ertz (èrts), **Susan.** b. in England, c1894—. An English novelist, of American parentage. Her books include *Madame Claire* (1922), *Nina* (1924), *Afternoon* (1926), *The Galaxy* (1929), *Woman Alive* (1935), *Black, White, and Caroline* (1938), *One Fight More* (1940), and *Two Names Upon the Shore* (1947); author of *Face to Face* and other collections of stories.

Ervine (èr'vin), **St. John.** [Full name, **St. John Greer Ervine.**] b. at Belfast, Ireland, 1883—. An Irish novelist and playwright. He was named (1915) manager of the Abbey Theatre at Dublin, and was professor of dramatic literature (1933–36) for the Royal Society of Literature. He has taken up various social themes in his plays: *The Mag-*

nanimous Lover (1907), *Mixed Marriage* (1911), *Jane Clegg* (1913), *John Ferguson* (1915), *The Lady of Belmont* (1925), *Anthony and Anna* (1926), *The First Mrs. Fraser* (1929), *People of Our Class* (1934), *Boyd's Shop* (1936; American production, 1940, as *Boyd's Daughter*), *Robert's Wife* (1937), *The Christies* (1939), *Friends and Relations* (1940), and *Private Enterprise* (1947). His novels include *Mrs. Martin's Man* (1914), *Alice and a Family* (1915), *Changing Winds* (1917), and *The Wayward Man* (1927). His other prose writings include *The Theatre in My Time* (1934), *A Journey to Jerusalem* (1936), *Some Impressions of My Elders* (1923), and *If I Were Dictator.*

Erysichthon (er.i.sik'thon). In Greek mythology, a prince who cut down trees in a sacred grove and was punished by a hunger which caused him to devour his own flesh.

Esau (ē'sô). [Also, **Edom.**] The eldest son of Isaac and Rebekah, and twin brother of Jacob. He was the ancestor of the Edomites. Two stories in Genesis tell how he sold his birthright to Jacob for a mess of pottage; the better-known story is that Jacob put on a hairy animal-skin so that his blind father might think that it was Esau he was blessing. Traditional stories, based on the conflict between the Israelites and the Edomites, relate of the conflict of the twins in the womb and fall within the world-wide folk-tale type of the enemy twins, one good and one bad. Gen. xxv. 21–34, etc.

Escalibor (es.kal'i.bor). See **Excalibur.**

Escalus (es'ka.lus). In Shakespeare's *Measure for Measure*, an old lord who urges Angelo to deal more leniently with offenders.

Escalus. In Shakespeare's *Romeo and Juliet*, the Prince of Verona. The real Romeo and Juliet supposedly lived during the reign (1301–04) of Bartolomeo della Scala. "Escalus" is a corruption of della Scala.

Escanes (es'ka.nēz). In Shakespeare's *Pericles*, a lord of Tyre who appears with Helicanus, another lord.

Eschenburg (esh'en.burk), **Johann Joachim.** b. at Hamburg, Germany, Dec. 7, 1743; d. at Brunswick, Germany, Feb. 29, 1820. A German literary historian, professor at the Carolinum at Brunswick; a friend of Lessing. His translation of Shakespeare's plays (1775–82, 1798–1806) was a reworking and completion of the earlier translation by Wieland.

Escorial (es.kōr'i.al; Spanish, es.kō.ryäl'). [Also, **Escurial.**] A group of buildings in Spain, situated at the town of El Escorial, ab. 27 mi. NW of Madrid, containing the monastery of San Lorenzo del Escorial, and a palace, church, and mausoleum of the Spanish sovereigns. The edifice originated in a vow to Saint Lawrence made by Philip II at the battle of St.-Quentin (1557), and was erected in the period 1563–84. Its general form is that of a gridiron (in memory of Saint Lawrence's martyrdom), the length being ab. 780 ft. and the breadth ab. 620 ft. It is celebrated for its paintings and library.

Esdraelon (es.dra.ē'lon, es.drā'ē.lon). A valley in Palestine, the scene of Gideon's victory over the Midianites. Judges. vii.

Esdras (ez′dras), **Books of.** The first two books of the Apocrypha. The first book consists, to a large extent, of matter compiled or transcribed from the books of Chronicles, Ezra, and Nehemiah. The second is mainly of an apocalyptic character.

Esdras Barnivelt, Apothecary (bär′ni.velt). See **Barnivelt.**

Esher (ē′shėr), 2nd Viscount. [Title of **Reginald Baliol Brett.**] b. at London, June 30, 1852; d. there, Jan. 22, 1930. An English statesman, government official, historian, and friend of Victoria and Edward VII.

Esmond (ez′mond), **Beatrix.** In Thackeray's novel *Henry Esmond,* a capricious, heartless, and brilliant beauty. She appears in *The Virginians* as Mrs. Tusher and the Baroness Bernstein.

Esmond, Francis. See **Castlewood, Colonel Francis Esmond, Lord.**

Esmond, Henry. In Thackeray's novel *Henry Esmond,* a brave and chivalrous youth, in love with his cousin Beatrix, a heartless, ambitious beauty.

Esop (ē′sop). See **Aesop.**

Esplandián (es.plän.dē.än′). Son of Amadis of Gaul and Oriana, in the old romances. He is called the Black Knight, because of the color of his armor. The story of his exploits, by Montalvo, is the first sequel to the four books of *Amadis of Gaul,* or the fifth book.

Espousals, The. See under **Angel in the House, The.**

Espriella's Letters (es.pri.el′äz). See **Letters of Espriella.**

essay. A discursive composition concerned with a particular subject, usually shorter and less methodical and finished than a treatise; a short disquisition: as, an *essay* on the life and writings of Homer; an *essay* on fossils; an *essay* on commerce.

To write just treatises requireth leisure in the writer and leisure in the reader, . . . which is the cause that hath made me choose to write certain brief notes, set down rather significantly than curiously, which I have called *Essays.* The word is late, but the thing is ancient.

(Bacon, *To Prince Henry.*)

Seneca's Epistles to Lucilius, if one mark them well, are but Essays, that is dispersed meditations, though conveyed in the form of epistles.

(Bacon, quoted in Abbott, p. 438.)

The essay is properly a collection of notes, indicating certain aspects of a subject, or suggesting thought concerning it, rather than the orderly or exhaustive treatment of it. It is not a formal siege, but a series of assaults, essays, or attempts upon it. It does not pursue its theme like a pointer, but goes hither and thither like a bird to find material for its nest, or a bee to get honey for its comb.

(*New Princeton Rev.,* IV. 228.)

Essay of Dramatic Poesy, An. See **Dramatic Poesy, An Essay of.**

Essay on Criticism, An. A poetical essay by Alexander Pope, published in 1711, written in heroic couplets. It concerns the principles and rules on which criticism of literature should rest,

and touches on various deviations from these rules. It was originally published anonymously when Pope was only 21 years old.

Essay on Man, An. A didactic poem by Alexander Pope, published anonymously in 1732–34, but soon acknowledged by Pope. It discusses the platonic concept of the "Great Chain of Being," the relation of man to God, the relationship between reason and passion, man's role in society, and the question of man's happiness.

Essays. [Full title, **Essays, or Counsels, Civill and Morall.**] Collections of essays by Francis Bacon, published in three editions in 1597, 1612, and 1625, instructing the citizen on how best to serve the public interests through education and understanding. The first edition contains ten essays; the second, 38; and the last, 59. Bacon gives practical advice on many matters that pertain to the individual's importance as an efficient part of the state, and each of these works is a short and unified discussion of one theme, largely depending on imagery and aphorism for structure and style. Some of his best-known are "Of Truth," "Of Friendship," "Of Death," "Of Marriage and Single Life," "Of Great Place," and "Of Atheism."

Essays and Reviews. A collection of seven articles, relating to religious and theological subjects by Frederick Temple, Rowland Williams, Robert Baden-Powell, Henry Bristow Wilson, Charles Wycliffe Goodwin, Mark Pattison, and Benjamin Jowett, published in 1860.

Essay upon Projects, An. A book by Daniel Defoe, published in 1697, offering proposals for public improvements. Benjamin Franklin said that it influenced his own thought and life.

Essenes (es′ēnz, e.sēnz′). A Jewish sect appearing in and after the 2nd century B.C., supposed to have sprung from the Hasidim (Chasidim), the zealous religio-political party that originated during the struggles of the Maccabean period against Hellenistic invasions. The Essenes, however, stood aloof from political and public affairs, forming a kind of monastic order. Their ideal was to attain the highest sanctity of priestly consecration. To this end they separated themselves from the world, and lived in settlements in the desert west of the Dead Sea. Most of them lived there in celibacy and practicing a community of goods. Other peculiarities were disapproval of oaths and war, strict observance of the Sabbath, and, especially, scrupulous attention to the Levitical laws of cleanliness. Their name is said to be derived from their frequent bathing. Their asceticism evolved a theoretical mysticism, and miraculous cures and exorcisms were ascribed to them. Their external symbols were the white garment, apron, and shovel. They never gained any hold on Judaism, and their number never exceeded 4,000. Their relation to Christianity, and their influence on it, are much discussed points, as is the source of the sect.

Essex (es′iks). One of the Saxon kingdoms in England during the Heptarchy, including the area of present-day Essex, London, Middlesex, and most of Hertfordshire. It was settled in the 6th century, though first mentioned in 604. During the 8th century Essex was under the influence of

Mercia, but in 825 it joined Wessex, under King Egbert, and became an earldom. In 870 the Danes conquered Essex, but it was reconquered in the early 10th century.

Essex, Earl of. Title of **Cromwell, Thomas.**

Essex, 2nd Earl of. Title of **Devereux, Robert.**

Essex, Earl of. In Shakespeare's *King John*, a lord in attendance on the King.

Este (es'tā). One of the oldest and most celebrated of the princely houses of Italy; according to modern genealogists, a branch of the house of the Guelphs. It traces its origin to Alberto II, margrave of Casalmaggiore, the youngest son of the margrave Alberto I, imperial count palatine in Italy under the emperor Otto I. Alberto's grandson, Alberto Azzo II (996–1097), was invested by the emperor Henry III, with Este and other Italian fiefs, was created Duke of Milan, and adopted the name of Este. His two sons Guelph IV (d. 1101) and Folco I (1060–1135) became the founders, respectively, of a German and an Italian branch of the house of Este, the German branch being in modern times represented by the houses of Brunswick and Hanover. The Italian branch continued with Obizzo I (d. 1194), son of Folco I, who became powerful in Italian politics. His successor and grandson, Azzo VI (1170–1212) became overlord of Ferrara and head of the Guelph party. Under Aldobrandino (d. 1215) and Azzo VII (1205–64) the family lost its power in Ferrara to the Torellis, but with the help of Pope Gregory IX Azzo and the Guelphs regained the rule of the city. Obizzo II (1240–93) proved to be a tyrant and after his death his sons and grandsons fought for control of Ferrara and finally were forced to accept papal direction. Niccolo III (1384–1441) was a soldier in the papal army and ruled over Ferrara, Parma, Modena, and Reggio. His sons, Lionello (1407–50) and Borso (1413–71) were able rulers who established courts where the arts and literature were patronized and who aided the prosperity of Ferrara. Borso received the title of Duke of Modena and Reggio from the emperor Frederick III, and that of Duke of Ferrara from Pope Paul II. Ercole I (1431–1505), another brother, succeeded Borso and continued the patronage of letters, Boiardo being one of his ministers and Ariosto receiving his aid. Ercole's daughter, Beatrice (1475–97), was a noted noblewoman whose diplomatic talents served the cause of her husband, Lodovico Sforza, Duke of Milan, but who died in childbirth. Her sister Isabella (1474–1539) was the wife of Francesco Gonzaga, Marquis of Mantua, and one of the great Renaissance diplomats and patrons of art; Raphael and Andrea Mantegna were among those residing at her court and Baldassare Castiglione was one of her advisers. The heir of Ercole was his son Alfonso I (1486–1534), a famous commander of artillery. He at first sided with the Pope against the Venetians, but after the treaty between Venice and the Pope found himself fighting against the papal forces. He lost and regained Modena and Reggio and received the aid of the emperor Charles V in retaining them against papal wishes. His brother Ippolito I, Cardinal d'Este, was Ariosto's patron. Ercole II (1508–59) succeeded to the dukedom; his wife was Renée, daughter of Louis XII of France;

his brother, Ippolito II, Cardinal d'Este, was archbishop of Milan and built the Tivoli palace known as the Villa d'Este. Alfonso II (1533–97), patron of Tasso, attempted reforms in the Ferraran army and in agriculture, but when he named as his successor his cousin Cesare (1533–1628), Pope Clement VIII effectively achieved the elimination of the house of Este as an Italian power by declaring Cesare illegitimate and obtaining cession of the Este possessions to the papal dominions through treaty with Alfonso's sister Lucrezia. Mary Beatrice, wife of James II of England, was a member of the family, her father being Alfonso IV (1634–62), but the family was in eclipse and the male line died out with Ercole III Rinaldo (1727–1803). Ercole's only daughter, Maria Beatrice, married Archduke Ferdinand of Austria, third son of the emperor Francis I, who became the founder of the Austrian branch of the house of Este, the male line of which became extinct in 1875.

Estella (es.tel'ȧ). The heroine of Charles Dickens's *Great Expectations;* adopted daughter of Miss Havisham and actual daughter of Magwitch.

Esther Summerson (es'tėr sum'ėr.sọn). See **Summerson, Esther.**

Esther Waters (wô'tėrz, wot'ėrz). A naturalistic novel by George Moore, published in 1894. Esther, a devoutly religious girl of 17, leaves the home of her drunken father in order to take a situation as a servant in the house of Mrs. Barfield. The Barfield establishment is characterized by ostentatious wealth (a racing stable is only one of its adjuncts), and Esther finds herself in a world for which she is completely unprepared. She is seduced by a fellow servant, who deserts her, and is forced to leave (although Mrs. Barfield makes various kindly efforts to help her). Her trials, and the poverty and misery she faces as she tries to bring up her child, are fully described. Her seducer returns and marries her, proving to be a good husband, but his death leaves her penniless once more. She returns to the Barfield house and is able finally to find happiness in living with the widowed and now impoverished Mrs. Barfield.

Estienne (es.tyen), **Charles.** [Also: **Étienne**; Latinized, **Stephanus.**] b. at Paris, c1504; d. 1564. A French printer, bookseller, physician, and scholar. He was the third son of Henri Estienne (c1460–1520), and the brother of François and Robert. He studied medicine at Paris, where he took his degree, and he taught Jean Antoine de Baïf, who later became a distinguished poet and a member of the Pleiade. In 1551, Robert having left Paris for Geneva, he took full charge of the printing business, and was made king's printer. Ten years later he was bankrupt, and it is believed that he died in a debtor's prison. His works have been praised as models of typography and correctness. He published *De dissectione partium corporis humani libri tres* (1548), an important work on anatomy with valuable woodcuts, *Dictionarium historicum ac poëticum* (1533), the first French encyclopedia, *Praedium rusticum* (1554), a volume of pamphlets on agriculture by ancient authors, and an edition of Cicero (1557). In 1543 he translated an Italian comedy, *Gli ingannati* (under the title *Le Sacrifice*), important for its influence on French comedy, and ten years later he brought out *Paradoxes*, an imitation of the "scandalous" *Paradossi*, by the Italian wit Ortensio Landi.

Estmere (est'mir), **King.** See **King Estmere.**

Estotiland (es.tot'il.and). A legendary region supposed, several centuries ago, to lie in the N part of North America, near the Arctic Circle.

Estrildis (es.tril'dis). [Also, **Estrild** (es'trild).] The daughter of a legendary German king. She was loved by King Locrine, and was the mother by him of Sabrina. The story is narrated by Geoffrey of Monmouth.

Eteocles (ę.tē'ọ.klēz). In Greek legend, a king of Thebes, son of Oedipus and Jocasta, and brother of Polynices and Antigone. He had agreed to surrender the throne to his brother in alternate years, but broke his promise. This led to the expedition of the Seven against Thebes to seat Polynices on the throne. The brothers fought and killed each other.

Eternal City, The. A novel (1901) by Hall Caine.

Ethelburga (eth.ęl.bėr'ga), **Saint.** [Also, **Saint Æthelburh.**] d. c676. Abbess of Barking, Essex. She is commemorated on Oct. 11.

Ethelfleda (eth.ęl.flē'da). [Also: **Ælfled, Æthelflaed;** known as **Lady of the Mercians.**] d. c918. The eldest daughter of King Alfred and wife of Ethelred of Mercia, with whom she shared the rule until his death (c911); she was sole ruler from that time to her own death (c918). She built fortifications against the Norwegians and Danes (912–915), fought the Welsh at Brecknock (916), and took Derby from the Danes (917). She extended her rule to Leicester and York (918).

Ethel Newcome (eth'ęl nū'kum). See **Newcome, Ethel.**

Ethelred (eth'ęl.red), **Saint.** [Also: **Æthelred, Ailred, Aelred.**] b. 1109; d. June 12, 1166. An English ecclesiastical writer. He was educated at the Scottish court, entered the Cistercian order, and became abbot of Revesby in Lincolnshire, and afterward of Rievaulx in Yorkshire. His works include *Historia de Vita et Miraculis S. Edwardi, Genealogia Regum Anglorum, De Bello Standardi,* and *Historia de Sanctimoniali de Watton,* which have been published in Sir Roger Twysden's *Historiae Anglicanae Scriptores decem* (1652). His theological works were collected by Richard Gibbons. The *Margaritae Vita* attributed to him is not his work.

Ethelred I. [Also, **Æthelred I.**] d. 871. King of the West Saxons (866–871). He was aided by his brother, Alfred, against the Danes (868) and in the victory over them at Aescesdun or Ashdown (871). Alfred succeeded him.

Ethelred II. [Also: **Æthelred II;** called **"Ethelred the Unready."**] b. c968; d. at London, 1016. King of England; son of Edgar and Elfrida. He succeeded to the throne upon the murder (978) of his half-brother, Edward the Martyr. He instituted (991) payment of the "danegeld," a tax to pay tribute to the invading Danes. He ordered a general massacre of the Danes (c1002), and made strenuous but futile efforts to raise the weak English power to match the strength of the Danes. He was deposed (1013) when the Danish king Sweyn virtually

subjugated England. Ethelred fled to Normandy and was restored after Sweyn's death (1014).

Ethelwerd (eth'ęl.wėrd). [Also, **Æthelweard.**] d. c998. An English chronicler, said to be a descendant of King Alfred. His chronicle extends from the creation to 973 and was first edited by Savile (1596).

Ethelwold (eth'ęl.wōld), **Saint.** See **Æthelwold, Saint.**

Etherege (eth'ėr.ęj), **George.** b. in Oxfordshire, England; fl. c1588. An English classical scholar. He studied at Corpus Christi College, Oxford, and was licensed to practice medicine in 1545. He was regius professor of Greek at Christ Church, Oxford (1547–50 and 1554–59). His health was seriously impaired by frequent imprisonments during a period of 30 years on account of his adherence to the Roman Catholic faith. He was living in 1588, but his death is not recorded. His works include a Latin translation of Justin Martyr, various poems in Greek and Latin, the Psalms of David in Hebrew verse set to music, and a manuscript copy of musical compositions.

Etherege, Sir George. [Also, **Etheredge.**] b. c1635; d. 1691. An English dramatist. The facts of his early life are obscure. In 1676 he was obliged to leave the country with John Wilmot, Earl of Rochester, on account of a disgraceful brawl, but before 1685 had obtained diplomatic employment. He was sent to The Hague by Charles II, and in 1685 to Ratisbon (Regensburg) by James II. He disgusted the Germans by his habits of debauchery and breaches of etiquette. In 1688 he retired hastily to Paris, where Luttrell reports that he died. He wrote *The Comical Revenge or Love in a Tub* (1664), *She Would if She Could* (1668), and *The Man of Mode, or Sir Fopling Flutter* (1676). He was the inventor of the witty comedy of intrigue.

Etherington (eᴛʜ'ėr.ing.tọn), **Earl of.** The handsome and courtly lion of the hour at St. Ronan's Well in Sir Walter Scott's *St. Ronan's Well.*

"Ethiop queen" (ē'thi.op). An allusion made by Milton in *Il Penseroso* to Cassiopeia (in full "the Starr'ed Ethiop queen"), legendary wife of the king of Ethiopia, whose vain boasting incurred the wrath of Poseidon and caused her to be changed into the northern constellation that bears her name.

Ethwald (eth'wôld). A tragedy (published 1802) in two parts by Joanna Baillie. It is written on the theme of ambition, being one of her *Plays on the Passions.*

Étienne (ā.tyen), **Charles.** See **Estienne, Charles.**

Eton (ē'tọn). An urban district in S central England, in Buckinghamshire, on the left bank of the river Thames, opposite Windsor, ab. 22 mi. W of London by rail. It is known chiefly for Eton College, a famous English public school, founded in 1440 by Henry VI. The low and picturesque battlemented and towered brick buildings enclose two courts, which communicate by a vaulted passage. The large chapel, in Perpendicular style, forms the S side of the outer quadrangle. The new quadrangle was finished in 1889.

Eton College. One of the most famed of English public schools, founded (1440) by Henry VI. It is situated at Eton, in Buckinghamshire.

---

d̦, d or j; ş, s or sh; ț, t or ch; z̦, z or zh; *o*, F. cloche; ü, F. menu; ċh, Sc. loch; ṅ, F. bonbon.

Ettarre (e.tär'). A character in *The Idylls of the King* by Tennyson.

Etruria (ẹ.trö'ri.ạ). An ecclesiastical district and village in C England, in Staffordshire, ab. 147 mi. NW of London by rail. It was amalgamated (1910) in Stoke-on-Trent county borough. Etruria is noted as the seat of the Wedgwood potteries, founded by Josiah Wedgwood.

Etruscans (ẹ.trus'kạnz). [Also, **Etrurians** (ẹ.trö'ri-ạnz).] The people of ancient Etruria, a region in Italy corresponding to what is now Tuscany and part of Umbria. Exactly who or what these people were has never been satisfactorily determined. Their inscriptions have never been completely deciphered; only the proper names emerge with certainty; and their language still defies sure classification. It was entirely different from the language of their predecessors in the region. That it is not Indo-European is the consensus to date; the alphabet resembles the Greek and Phoenician. Several theories as to the origin of the Etruscans have been advanced: (1) the Greek historian Dionysius of Halicarnassus thought that they were the original inhabitants of Italy; (2) Herodotus said that during a famine in Lydia the current king divided his people into two groups, one group to remain in Lydia, the other to emigrate under the leadership of his son Tyrsenus. The emigrants went first to Smyrna to build ships, and from there to the land of the Umbrians, where they settled, built towns, and called themselves Tyrrhenians; (3) Livy proposed that they came from invading Alpine peoples, probably the Rhaetians. The most recent specialists in Etruscan ethnology and archeology corroborate Herodotus, insofar as it is now believed that the Etruscans entered Italy in the 9th century B.C. from the sea, were probably from Asia Minor, subdued the Umbrians, and built a number of fortified towns which were eventually unified into a powerful state. That they came from the north is now a discredited theory, because archeologists are satisfied that they entered Italy from the sea and that the northernmost of their settlements were the latest to be founded. Flinders Petrie believed in their Asiatic origin because their weights were unlike those throughout the Mediterranean region, but seemed related to those of India.

Culture. A new era of culture began with them, the most advanced in Italy before Roman arms overwhelmed it. The Etruscans were skilled ironworkers and bronzeworkers, active traders, and their products were sought and bought not only by the Greeks, but even trickled into the area of what is now Germany, France, and Spain through the trade routes and passes. The Etruscans imported as assiduously as they exported, and many an "Etruscan" objet d'art has since been proved to be an imported piece of Greek workmanship. The greatest similarity between Etruscan and Greek art, however, lies in the fact that both arts derived from the same Eastern sources. The Etruscan peculiarity of style, reflecting both Asiatic and Egyptian influence, distinguishes their early productions; later, Greek influence predominates and finally supersedes their own. The Etruscans are especially noted for their characteristic polygonal town walls (sometimes called Cyclopean) and their cupolaed sepulchers (also called tower-tombs). The sepulcher paintings depict a high level of life: banquets, dancers, musicians, races, wrestling matches, hunting scenes. Silver and gold objects and carved gems were found in the tombs, where the findings also reveal that these people were advanced in dentistry (artificial teeth, gold crowns, etc., bear testimony to this). They are much noted also for their black *bochero* pottery and terra cotta vases and figurines. Of their twelve cities Tarquinii (modern Tarquinia) is noted for its tombs and tomb paintings. Caere (modern Cervetri) is noted for its necropolis; Veii (modern Veio) for its sculptures. Vetulonia is famous as one of the oldest Etruscan settlements. Clusium (modern Chiusi) was the stronghold of the king Lars Porsena, and is noted for its tombs. Cosa, Volteria, Perugia were among the other cities. By the 6th century B.C. the Etruscans had crossed the Apennines and founded Felsina (now Bologna). By the 5th century B.C. their expansion, power, and civilization was at its height. The Greeks repeatedly tried to curb Etruscan expansion and power, but it was the Romans who finally first halted them in the 5th century B.C. They became weakened by Gallic invasions, and after the Romans captured Veii (396 B.C.) the rest of the cities succumbed. Etruscan culture made its mark on Roman culture during the first two centuries of the Roman hold, throughout Latium especially. But as the Roman powers strengthened, Etruscan civilization weakened, and by the 1st century B.C. had disappeared.

"Ettrick Shepherd" (et'rik). See **Hogg, James.**

Etzel (et'sẹl). In German heroic legend, the name of Attila, king of the Huns; he is the Atli of Icelandic saga.

Euclid (ū'klid). fl. at Alexandria, c323–285 B.C. A Greek mathematician and physicist, whose systematization of the mathematical knowledge of his time remains to this day a basis for the teaching of elementary geometry. Despite the tremendous importance of this contribution, very little is definitely known about the man himself. He was probably trained in the Academy, at Athens, after the time of Plato, but several decades before the time of Archimedes. An Alexandrian scholar of the period has written that he was unassuming and of a notably mild temper, although by no means servile (according to one account, when he was asked by the reigning Egyptian king if there was not some easier way than his to learn geometry, he replied: "There is no royal road to geometry"). The type of man suggested by this fragmentary information is surely no humble slave, but a true scientist, and this conjecture is supported by the fact that much of the material in the 13 books of *The Elements* was probably original with him, and that the work as a whole is a synthesis of the highest order in the elaboration of which there is clear evidence of a considerable genius. The formulation of the postulates (and more particularly, of the fifth postulate) was due to Euclid alone (and the many attempts since to prove the fifth postulate is an indirect tribute, surely, to his wisdom). In addition to this, Euclid discovered the earliest theorems of the theory of numbers (leaving aside some undatable Pythagorean knowledge) and fundamental principles of geometrical optics (including laws of reflection and propagation of light in straight lines).

Works. Euclid's best-known work is, of course, *The Elements*, in 13 books (of which the first six are the ones chiefly used in introductory geometry). The translation of this, with commentary, by Thomas L. Heath (3 vols., 1908) is generally considered by historians of science to be not only the best one now existing in English, but one of the best ever to be made in any language. Among Euclid's other works are *The Pseudaria* (which are now lost, but are known to have been exercises in elementary geometry), *The Data* (also exercises, but in its modern form showing some deviation from that with which Euclid's contemporaries were familiar), *The Porisms* (three books which are now, and very unfortunately, no longer extant, but are known to have dealt with higher geometry), *The Phaenomena* (a treatise on astronomy or, more precisely, on spherical geometry), *The Optics* (although attribution of this to Euclid has been disputed by some authorities), and probably also various writings on musical theory.

Eugene Aram (ār′ạm). A novel by Edward Bulwer-Lytton, published in 1832. Hood's poem on the same subject is called *The Dream of Eugene Aram*. Both authors based their works on the story of Eugene Aram, a schoolmaster of Knaresborough, who was tried and executed for murder in 1759. In the novel, Eugene is persuaded by dire poverty to consent to a murder, which is committed by an accomplice, Houseman. Aram is never able to escape from his feeling of guilt and remorse. He settles in a small village, and there falls in love with Madeline Lester, a woman of high character and standards. They are about to be married when Houseman appears and reveals the entire story. Aram is tried and sentenced to death, and Madeline herself dies soon afterward, her health shattered by the shock of discovering her lover's involvement in crime.

Eugene Wrayburn (rā′bẽrn). See **Wrayburn, Eugene.**

Eugenius (ū.jē′ni.us, ū.jēn′yus). In Laurence Sterne's *Tristram Shandy*, the friend and mentor of Yorick.

Euhemerus (ū.hē′mẽr.us, ū.hem′ẽr.us). [Also: **Euemerus, Evemerus.**] fl. in the second half of the 4th century B.C. A Greek mythographer. He wrote a *Sacred History*, in which he gave an anthropomorphic explanation of current mythology. Euhemerus claimed that mythology was simply human history distorted, that the gods were originally men whose exploits had been twisted and magnified with time, and that the events of mythology could be explained as historical occurrences. Euhemerism, as this approach to mythology is still called, still finds its occasional supporters; at the time Euhemerus propounded his theory he was simply extending the then current skeptical-scientific approach to matters until then accepted without question.

Eulenspiegel (oi′lẹn.shpē.gẹl), **Till** (or **Tyll**). [Also: **Ulenspiegel; English, Owlglass.**] The name of a German of the 14th century who was probably born at Kneitlingen, near Brunswick, and buried at Mölln (according to a history of his life written

in North Germany in 1515 and translated into High German and printed c1550). Only a small part of the deeds attributed to him are possibly his own. The name is merely the center about which have been grouped popular tales describing the mischievous, rascally pranks of a vagabond of peasant origin, just as tall tales have been attracted to the name of Baron Munchausen. The stories have been widely translated; in English Howleglass is mentioned by Ben Jonson and in French *espièglerie* has come to mean a sharp prank. In the Leipzig edition (1854), by J. M. Lappenberg, the editor erroneously assumed Thomas Murner (1475–1537) to have been the author of the book. Among the several treatments Eulenspiegel has received is that of the musical tone-poem (1895) of Richard Strauss.

eulogy (ū′lọ.ji). High commendation of a person or thing, especially when expressed in a formal manner or to an undue degree; specifically, a speech or writing delivered or composed for the express purpose of lauding its subject.

Many brave young minds have oftentimes, through hearing the praises and famous eulogies of worthy men, been stirred up to affect the like commendations. (Spenser, *State of Ireland*.)

Yet are there many worthy personages that deserve better than dispersed report or barren eulogies. (Bacon, *Advancement of Learning*, ii.132.)

Eumaeus (ū.mē′us). The faithful swineherd of Ulysses, a character in the *Odyssey*. He helps his master slay the suitors of Penelope.

Eumenides (ū.men′i.dēz). A euphemistic name, meaning "the gracious or kindly ones," for the Erinyes in Greek mythology.

Eumolpus (ū.mol′pus). In Greek mythology, a priestly bard, reputed founder of the Eleusinian mysteries.

Eunomia (ū.nō′mi.ạ). In Greek mythology, one of the Horae.

Euphemia Deans (dēnz). See **Deans, Effie.**

euphemism (ū′fẹ.mizm). **1.** In rhetoric, the use of a mild, delicate, or indirect word or expression in place of a plainer and more accurate one, which by reason of its meaning or its associations or suggestions might be offensive, unpleasant, or embarrassing.

This instinct of politeness in speech—euphemism, as it is called—which seeks to hint at an unpleasant or an indelicate thing rather than name it directly, has had much to do in making words acquire new meanings and lose old ones: thus 'plain' has usurped the sense of 'ugly'; 'fast,' of 'dissipated'; 'gallantry,' of 'licentiousness.' (Chambers, *Inf. for the People*.)

2. A word or expression thus substituted: as, to employ a *euphemism*.

When it was said of the martyr St. Stephen that "he fell asleep," instead of "he died," the euphemism partakes of the nature of a metaphor, intimating a resemblance between sleep and the death of such a person. (Beattie, *Moral Science*, par.866.)

euphony (ū′fọ.ni). **1.** Easy enunciation of sounds; a pronunciation which is pleasing to the sense; agreeable utterance. As a principle active in the historical changes of language, euphony is a misnomer, since it is ease of utterance, economy of effort on the part of the organs of speech, and not agreeableness to the ear, that leads to and governs such changes.

Euphony, which used to be appealed to as explanation [of phonetic change], is a false principle, except so far as the term may be made an idealized synonym of economy [in utterance].

(Whitney, *Encyc. Brit.*)

2. Harmonious arrangement of sounds in composition; a smooth and agreeable combination of articulate elements in any piece of writing.

Euphony consists, also, in a well-proportioned variety of structure in successive sentences. A monotonous repetition of any construction can not be made euphonious, except by singing it.

(A. Phelps, *Eng. Style*, p.327.)

Euphorbus (ū.fôr′bus). In Greek mythology, a brave Trojan, slain by Menelaus. Pythagoras professed to be animated by his soul.

Euphormionis Satyricon (ū.fôr.mi.ō′nis sạ.tir′i.kon). [Also: **Satyricon, Euphormio.**] A volume of satirical Latin verse (1603; second part, 1607) by John Barclay.

Euphorion (ū.fō′ri.ọn). b. at Chalcis, in Euboea, 274 B.C.; d. in Syria, probably c200 B.C. A Greek grammarian and poet. Fragments of his work were edited (1823) by Meineke.

Euphrasia (ū.frā′zhạ). In Beaumont and Fletcher's play *Philaster*, a girl in love with Philaster who disguises herself as the page Bellario.

Euphronius (ū.frō′ni.us). In Shakespeare's *Antony and Cleopatra*, an ambassador from Antony to Octavius.

Euphrosyne (ū.fros′i.nē). In Greek mythology, one of the three Charities or Graces.

Euphues (ū′fū.ēz). [Full title, **Euphues, or the Anatomy of Wit.**] A work by John Lyly, published in 1578–79. This book and its successor, *Euphues and his England* (1580–81), brought into prominence and into further use the affected jargon, full of conceits and extravagances, used by the gallants of Elizabeth's court. Euphues is an Athenian youth who embodies the qualities implied in his name. He is elegant, handsome, amorous, and roving. He goes to Naples, where he proceeds to steal the affections of Lucilla away from his friend, Philautus. Curio then comes along to supplant Euphues in Lucilla's graces, and the two friends, Euphues and Philautus, join in denouncing Lucilla. Euphues returns to Greece, leaving a letter concerning love for his friend, Philautus. In the second part of the work, *Euphues in England*, Philautus and Euphues are in London, where they again have many adventures of love and romance, but are just as sadly disillusioned as in Italy. This time Euphues writes a letter to the ladies of Naples, describing England and his experiences there. The affected style of the work was so distinctive that it came to be known as "Euphuism," and was much admired and imitated in its own day.

Euphues, his Censure to Philautus (fi.lô′tus). A pamphlet by Robert Greene, published in 1587, and intended as a continuation of Lyly's *Euphues*.

Euphues Shadow, the Battaile of the Senses. A pamphlet by Thomas Lodge, edited by Robert Greene and published in 1592.

euphuism (ū′fū.izm). In English literature, an affected literary style, originating in the 15th century, characterized by a wide vocabulary, alliteration, consonance, verbal antithesis, and odd combinations of words. The style, although bombastic and extreme originally, contributed to the flexibility and verbal resources of later English. It assumed its most extreme form in the works of John Lyly, called the Euphuist.

All our Ladies were then his [Lyly's] Scholars; and that Beauty in Court which could not Parley Eupheisme was as little regarded as She which now there speaks not French.

(Edward Blount, in Lyly's *Euphues*, "Epist. to Reader.")

The discourse of Sir Piercie Shafton, in "The Monastery," is rather a caricature than a fair sample of euphuism. . . . Perhaps, indeed, our language is, after all, indebted to this writer [Lyly] and his euphuism for not a little of its present euphony. (Craik, *Hist. Eng. Lang.*)

So far, then, there is in the father of euphuism [Lyly] nothing but an exaggerated developement of tastes and tendencies which he shared not only with a generation of writers, but with the literary currents of a century, indeed of more centuries than one. (A. W. Ward, *Eng. Dram. Lit.*)

Eurione (ū.rī′ọ.nē). In George Chapman's *Monsieur D'Olive*, the sister of Countess Marcellina.

Euripides (ū.rip′i.dēz). b. on the Greek island of Salamis, probably Sept. 23, 480 B.C.; d. 406 B.C. An Athenian dramatic poet; with Aeschylus and Sophocles one of the great triad of Greek tragic writers. He was the son of Mnesarchus and Cleito, who appear to have fled from Athens to Salamis on the invasion of Xerxes, and was, according to popular tradition, born on that island on the day of the battle of Salamis. He studied physics under Anaxagoras and rhetoric under Prodicus, and at about the age of 25 produced the *Peliades*, the first of his plays which was acted. He is said to have gained the first prize in five dramatic contests, the first of which occurred in 441. He left Athens (c408) for the court of Archelaus, king of Macedonia, owing, it is said, to the ridicule thrown upon him by the populace in consequence of the attacks of Sophocles and Aristophanes. He died at the Macedonian court (according to doubtful tradition being torn to pieces by a pack of hounds set upon him by two rival poets, Arrhidaeus and Crateuas), and was buried with great pomp by Archelaus, who refused a request of the Athenians for his remains. He wrote 75 plays, of which the following 18 are extant: *Alcestis, Electra, Medea, Hippolytus, Hecuba, Andromache, Ion, Suppliants, Orestes, Heracleidae, Heracles Mainomenos, Iphigenia among the Tauri, Iphigenia in Aulis, Troades, Helena, Phoenissae, Bacchae,* and *Cyclops; Rhesus* is probably not his. His style is realistic and he tends to be more experimental and less traditional than Sophocles, his great rival in competitions. His dramas, based though they are on myth and having gods and heroes as characters, are appealing because the personages come alive. The *Cyclops* is the only complete satyr play surviving. He was one of the skeptics of his day and his presentation of problems and his ridiculing of popular religion marked him as the recipient of popular obloquy and the satirical or broad humor of Aristophanes.

Europa (ū.rō′pạ) or **Europe** (-pē). In Greek mythology, a daughter of Phoenix or of Agenor; sister of Cadmus, and mother by Zeus of Minos and Rhadamanthus. She was borne over the sea to Crete by Zeus, who assumed the form of a white bull and induced her to mount his back.

Europeans, The. [Full title: **The Europeans: A Sketch**.] A novel by Henry James, published in 1878. Eugenia and Felix decide to visit their cousins in America and, if possible, to find a husband for Eugenia, who is about to be abandoned by her German husband. Felix marries his cousin, Gertrude, and Eugenia, after unsuccessfully trying her wiles on a young man recently expelled from Harvard and on the sophisticated Mr. Acton, returns to Europe feeling that Americans are immune to her charms. The theme of the novel is the contrast between the dreary, complacent New England family and the casual European relatives.

European Settlements in America, An Account of the. See **Account of the European Settlements in America, An.**

Eurus (ū′rus). In classical mythology, the east wind personified.

Euryclea (ū.ri.klē′ạ). In Homeric legend, the nurse of Odysseus, who after twenty years identified him by a scar.

Eurydice (ū.rid′i.sē). In Greek mythology, the wife of Orpheus. She died from the bite of a serpent, whereupon Orpheus descended into Hades, and by the charms of his lyre persuaded Pluto to restore her to life. He did this on condition that she should walk behind her husband, who should not look back until both had arrived in the upper world. Orpheus, overcome by anxiety, looked round only to behold her carried back into the infernal regions. The Japanese myth of Izanami and Izanagi is only one example of many found all over the world using this same theme of the narrow missing of victory over death.

Eurynome (ū.rin′ọ.mē). In Greek mythology, a daughter of Oceanus and mother by Zeus of the Graces.

Eurystheus (ū.ris′thūs). In Greek mythology, a king of Mycenae, who imposed upon Hercules the twelve labors.

Eusden (ūz′dẹn), **Laurence**. b. at Spofforth, Yorkshire, England, 1688; d. at Coningsby, Lincolnshire, England, Sept. 27, 1730. An English poet. Appointed (1718) poet laureate by the duke of Newcastle as a reward for having celebrated (1717) the duke's marriage in a flattering poem, Eusden is remembered because of the satire and ridicule of which Pope and Swift made him the victim.

Eusebius of Caesarea (ū.sē′bi.us; sē.zạ.rē′ạ, ses.ạ-, sez.ạ-). [Surnamed *Pamphili*.] b. probably at Caesarea, Palestine, c264 A.D.; d. there, c340. A theologian and historian, sometimes called the "Father of Church History." He was consecrated

bishop of Caesarea c315, and in 325 attended the Council of Nicaea, where he was appointed to receive the emperor Constantine with a panegyrical oration, and to sit at his right hand. His best-known work is the *Historia Ecclesiastica*.

Eustace (ūs′tạs). See **Wace.**

Eustace, Father. The Sub-Prior, then Abbot, of the Monastery of St. Mary's in Sir Walter Scott's novel *The Monastery* and its sequel *The Abbot*.

Eustace Diamonds, The. A novel by Anthony Trollope, published in 1873. Lizzie Greystock, who is as greedy as she is beautiful, marries the wealthy Sir Florian Eustace, who presents her as a wedding present with a diamond necklace worth 10,000 pounds. Upon the death of Sir Florian, the Eustace family lawyer seeks to recover the necklace (it is an heirloom in the family), but Lizzie is determined to keep it. She wants to marry Lord Fawn, who insists on the surrender of the necklace, and thus Lizzie's schemes are finally revealed. Lizzie is forced to marry Mr. Emilius, a preacher, after her other attempts to catch an admirer fail.

Eustacia Vye (ū.stā′shạ vī′). See **Vye, Eustacia.**

Euterpe (ū.tėr′pē). In classical mythology, one of the Muses, a divinity of joy and pleasure, the patroness of flute-players. She invented the double flute, and favored rather the wild and simple melodies of primitive peoples than the more finished art of music, and was thus associated more with Bacchus than with Apollo. She is usually represented as a maiden crowned with flowers, having a flute in her hand, or with various musical instruments about her.

Euxine Sea (ūk′sin). An old name of the Black Sea.

Evadne (ẹ.vad′nē). In Beaumont and Fletcher's *Maid's Tragedy*, the sister of Melantius and wife of Amintor. She has been married at the order of the King, who thus conceals the fact that he has forced her to become his mistress. When her brother, Melantius, makes clear to her the disgusting aspects of this relationship, she swears to kill the King. However, her husband, instead of delighting in her release from sin, spurns her for having taken justice into her own hands in killing a king.

Evadne. A tragedy (1819) by Richard Lalor Sheil, based upon Shirley's *The Traitor* and Massinger and Field's *The Fatal Dowry*.

Evandale (ev′ạn.dāl), **Lord.** An officer in the Life Guards in Sir Walter Scott's *Old Mortality*, protector of Edith Bellenden and friend of his rival, Henry Morton.

Evander (ẹ.van′dėr). In classical legend, a son of Hermes, and founder of an Arcadian colony before the Trojan War.

Evan Harrington (ev′ạn har′ing.tọn). A novel by George Meredith, published in 1860.

Evans (ev′ạnz), **Arthur Benoni.** b. at Compton-Beauchamp, England, March 25, 1781; d. at Market Bosworth, England, Nov. 8, 1854. An English teacher and writer; father of Sir John Evans (1823–1908). Educated at Oxford, he was professor of classics and history at the Royal Military College (1805–22) and headmaster of the grammar school at Market Bosworth (1829–54). Among his published works are many sermons and *Leicester Words, Phrases, and Proverbs* (1848) which was reprinted (1881) by the English Dialect Society.

Evans, Sir **Arthur John.** b. at Nash Mills, Hertfordshire, England, 1851; d. 1941. An English archaeologist, keeper of the Ashmolean Museum 1884–1908 (honorary), and fellow of Brasenose College, Oxford. He was especially known for his explorations in Crete, which were begun in 1893 and resulted in the important discovery of a pre-Phoenician script and the excavating (1900–08) of a prehistoric palace at Cnossus (palace of Minos) containing many remains of Minoan civilization. He published *Cretan Pictographs* (1896), *Further Discoveries of Cretan and Ægean Script* (1898), *The Mycenaean Tree* (1901), reports on the excavations at Cnossus, and others. He was knighted in 1911.

Evans, Caradoc. b. at Pantycroy, Llanandyssul, Wales, 1883; d. at Aberystwyth, Wales, Jan. 11, 1945. A Welsh editor, novelist, dramatist, and short-story writer. Educated at a Welsh school, he knew no English until he reached his early teens. He wrote stories for the *English Review*, and was on the editorial staff of the *Daily Mirror, T. P.'s Weekly*, and *Everybody's Weekly*. He was the author of *My People, Stories of the Peasantry of West Wales* (1915), *Capel Sion* (1916), and *My Neighbors* (1919), short stories; *Nothing to Pay* (1930), *Wasps* (1933), and *This Way to Heaven* (1934), novels: and *Taffy* (1924), a three-act play of Welsh village life. Because of their savage treatment of Welsh life, his works and lectures caused riots and demonstrations, and he was himself stoned, and burned in effigy.

Evans, Sir **John.** b. at Britwell Court, Berkhamstead, Buckinghamshire, England, Nov. 17, 1823; d. there, May 31, 1908. An English archaeologist; son of Arthur Benoni Evans. His works include *The Coins of the Ancient Britons* (1864; supplement, 1890), *The Ancient Stone Implements of Great Britain* (1872), *The Ancient Bronze Implements of Great Britain and Ireland* (1881), and others.

Evans, Marguerite Florence Hélène. See **Sandys, Oliver.**

Evans, Mary Ann (or **Marian**). See **Eliot, George.**

Evans, Sebastian. b. in Leicestershire, England, March 2, 1830; d. Dec. 19, 1909. An English poet, editor, translator, and artist. Educated at the Market Bosworth Free Grammar School and at Emmanuel College, Cambridge, he designed (1857–67) stained-glass windows for churches, served (1867–70) as editor of the Birmingham *Daily Gazette*, a Conservative newspaper, and was elected (1868) a member of Parliament. He was founder and first editor (1878–81) of *The People*, a Conservative weekly. His oil paintings and sketches were exhibited at the Royal Academy. He was the author of *Brother Fabian's Manuscripts and Other Poems* (1865), *Songs and Etchings* (1871), *In the Studio* (1875), and *In Quest of the Holy Grail* (1898), and also published a translation from the Old French of *The High History of the Holy Grail* (1898–1903, 1910).

Evans, Sir **Hugh.** In Shakespeare's *Merry Wives of Windsor*, a ludicrous, officious, and simple-minded Welsh parson. On the evening when Falstaff is be-

ing baited, Evans leads the children's revels as Fairy Queen.

Evans, William. d. 1632. An English giant, a porter of Charles I. He was nearly 8 feet tall, and is introduced in Fuller's *Worthies* and in Scott's *Peveril of the Peak*.

Eve (ēv). In the Bible, the first woman, the mother of the human race. According to the account of the creation in Gen. iii, she was created from one of Adam's ribs. After being lured by the serpent into eating forbidden fruit from the tree of knowledge of good and evil, she tempted Adam to eat the fruit also, and as a result, the Lord sent them out of the Garden of Eden. Eve was the mother of Cain and Abel. According to certain legendary additions to this story, based on the earlier statement in the Bible that God created male and female, Eve is said to be Adam's second wife, being preceded by Lilith, who would not accept man's mastery of woman.

Eve. A poem (1913) by Ralph Hodgson, retelling the story of the temptation of Eve by the serpent, but set against a rustic English background.

Evelina (ev.ẹ.lī′nạ). A novel by Fanny Burney, published in 1778, named from its principal character. Sir John Belmont deserts his wife and child, Evelina, when he finds that he is not to receive the fortune that he expected from his wife. Evelina is brought up by a guardian, Mr. Villars, after the death of her mother, and goes to visit a friend, Mrs. Mirvan, in London. There she is introduced to society, and falls in love with the dignified Lord Orville, but is humiliated by the actions of her ill-bred relatives. Sir John is asked to make it known that Evelina is his daughter, but he insists that he already has his daughter (he points out that she was brought to him in infancy by the woman who attended Lady Belmont in her last illness). He finds, however, that the nurse had passed off her own child as his, and finally recognizes his own daughter, Evelina, making her his heir. She then marries Orville.

Eveline Berenger (ev′ẹ.lin ber′ẹn.jèr). See **Berenger, Eveline.**

Evelyn (ev′ẹ.lin, ēv′lin, ev′lin), **John.** b. at Wotton, Surrey, England, Oct. 31, 1620; d. there, Feb. 27, 1706. An English author and Royalist. He was admitted to study at the Middle Temple in 1637 and received the honorary degree of D.C.L. in 1669. He passed the years from 1641 to 1647 principally in travel, with occasional returns to England. For a short time he joined the king's army. A strong Royalist, he published (1649) a translation of La Mothe le Vayer's *Of Liberty and Servitude*, with a Royalist preface. In 1652, thinking the cause of the Royalists hopeless, he settled at Sayes Court, Deptford, the estate of his wife's father, Sir Richard Browne, ambassador at Paris. He lived here till 1694, when he went to Wotton to live with his elder brother; upon the death (1699) of the latter, the estate became his, and he passed the rest of his life here. At both places he devoted himself to gardening. He was in favor at court after the Restoration, and held some minor offices. He was deeply interested in the Royal Society, of which he was a fellow in 1661, one of the council in 1662,

---

fat, fāte, fär, àsk, fāre; net, mē, her; pin, pīne; not, nōte, mȯve, nôr; up, lūte, pùll; ᴛʜ, then;

and in 1672 secretary. He obtained for it the Arundelian library in 1678, and for the University of Oxford the Arundelian marbles in 1667, both from the duke of Norfolk. He was treasurer (1695–1703) of Greenwich Hospital. Among his works are *The State of France* (1652), *A Character of England* (1659), *Apology for the Royal Party* (1659), *Fumifugium* (1661), *Sculptura* (1662), *Sylva* (1664), *Kalendarium Hortense* (1664), *Numismata* (1697), and *The Complete Gardener* (translated from the French of Quintinie, 1698). His memoirs, first published in 1818–19 and edited by William Bray, contain his letters and diary. The latter covers the years from 1620 to 1706 and, along with the diary of Samuel Pepys, is an important source of information about the period.

Evelyn Innes (in′ẹs). A novel by George Moore, published in 1898. It depicts the career of an opera singer and the development of her spiritual life. Its sequel is *Sister Teresa* (1901).

Evening's Love, or The Mock-Astrologer, An. A comedy by Dryden, acted in 1668. It was taken in part from Thomas Corneille's *Le Feint Astrologue*, a version of *El Astrólogo fingido* (by Calderón), and from Molière's *Le Dépit amoureux*.

Eve of Saint Agnes (ag′nẹs), **The.** A poem by John Keats, written in 1818. Madeline's lover, Porphyro, comes to her on the night (Saint Agnes's Eve) when, according to legend, young maidens are permitted to have a glimpse of their future husbands. Once met, the lovers depart together into the timeless world of love. Keats used here a rich imagery of antique settings and dreams to create the atmosphere.

Everard (ev′ẽr.ärd), **Colonel Markham.** The hero of Sir Walter Scott's *Woodstock*, who was the nephew of Sir Henry Lee and Alice Lee's lover.

Everard Webley (ev′ẽr.ạrd web′li). See **Webley, Everard.**

Everdene (ev′ẽr.dēn), **Bathsheba.** In Thomas Hardy's novel *Far From the Madding Crowd*, the passionate and fascinating young woman who is the heroine of the story.

Everlasting Mercy, The. A narrative poem by John Masefield, published in 1911. It portrays the reformation of a drunkard, Saul Kane.

Ever the Twain. A three-act comedy (1930) by Lennox Robinson.

Everyman (ev′ri.man). An English morality play of the late 15th century, one of the best-known of all morality plays. It is a sermon in dramatic form, dealing with a favorite theme of the medieval period: the struggle between the forces of good and evil for the possession of man's soul. The dramatic action is concentrated upon the hour of Everyman's death rather than depicting his earlier follies. When he is told that he must go on a journey, he pleads fruitlessly for a delay and finally asks his intimate friends to go with him, only to find that Kindred, Cousin, and Worldly Goods are not able or willing to do so. Good Deeds, with whom he has had little contact, offers to go with him and be his guide into the grave. Everyman concludes:

Methinketh, alas, that I must be gone,
To make my reckoning, and my debts pay;
For I see my time is nye spent away.
Take example . . .
How they that I loved best do forsake me
Except my Good Deeds. . . .

The popularity of the play is attested by four editions after 1500 and numerous revivals in succeeding centuries. It can be found in Clarence G. Child's *The Second Shepherd's Play, Everyman, and Other Early Plays* (1910).

Every Man in His Humour. A comedy by Ben Jonson, first acted in 1598, and published in quarto in 1601 and in folio in 1616. In its earlier form, its scene was Italy and the characters had Italian names, but Jonson soon changed both locale and names to English, and he also altered the more rhetorical style for a colloquial one in various places. Using the Roman theme of the Philistine father and his sprightly young heir, Jonson involves his plot with various "humour" characters. The elder Knowell is angered at rumors of his son's behavior and word of this is communicated by Brainworm (an intriguing servant similar to those in the comedies of Plautus) to young Edward Knowell. Although this serves as an excuse for the antics of Brainworm, who disguises himself as a needy soldier and later a justice's clerk, Knowell does not entirely motivate the plot, and his love affair with Bridget, the sister of a jealous merchant, Kitely, is rather unobtrusive. Of greater interest, perhaps, is Wellbred, Kitely's brother-in-law (and also a friend of Edward), whom Kitely suspects of attempts to cuckold him. Kitely is a "humour" character who, in characteristic Jonsonian fashion, must be brought by his suffering to acknowledge the error of his suspicions. This is done when Cob, a water-carrier, informs him that several gentlemen have been at his house during his absence. Upon his rushing home, his wife's remarks about Edward Knowell are construed as proof of her infidelity, and he dashes off to the place where she is supposedly going to meet still another lover. With the assistance of Justice Clement, the elder Knowell realizes his errors concerning his son's behavior, and Kitely realizes that he has erred in his suspicions of his wife. An amusing minor character is Captain Bobadill, a braggart warrior who affects the fashionable Jacobean graces of smoking, swearing, fencing, and melancholy. His glorious career as a man of honor is brought to an end when he is beaten ignominiously in a duel with a plain country squire, Downright.

Every Man Out of His Humour. A comedy by Ben Jonson, first produced in 1599, and published in quarto in 1600 and in folio in 1606. He called it "a comical satire." It is in a different style than Jonson's other comedies, having a very loose construction, actually consisting of little more than a series of episodes involving characters who are forced out of their "humours." This is done with the scorn of the satirist; as Asper says at the outset: "I'll strip the ragged follies of the time Naked as at their birth." Sordido is an avaricious farmer whose hatred of taxation causes him to hang himself, only to be cut down before he dies by his neighbors, whose cursing of him for his greed acts as a catharsis for his "humour." Sogliardo, a country bumpkin, is the familiar Jonsonian character of an underbred man trying to become a fashionable gallant. Introduced by Carlo Buffone (another "humour" character, whose inclination is to gourmandizing and cynicism) to a gallant, Fastidious Brisk (who is what his name implies, being industriously engaged in pursuing high fashion and gentlemanly decorum), he goes off to the country house of Puntarvolo, an eccentric knight, and is soon put in his place.

Evoe (ē′vē). Pseudonym of **Knox, Edmund George Valpy.**

Ewart (ū′ạrt), **Nanty.** The captain of the smuggling brig *Jumping Jenny* in Sir Walter Scott's novel *Redgauntlet.*

Ewing (ū′ing), **Juliana Horatia.** [Maiden name, **Gatty.**] b. at Ecclesfield, Yorkshire, England, 1841; d. at Bath, England, May 13, 1885. An English writer of stories for juveniles. Her works include *Melchior's Dream* (1862), *The Brownies* (1870), *A Flat-iron for a Farthing* (1872), *Lob-lie-by-the-Fire* (1873), *We and the World* (1873), *Six to Sixteen* (1875), *Jan of the Windmill* (1876), *Jackanapes* (1883), and *The Story of a Short Life* (1885).

Example, The. A comedy by James Shirley, published in 1637.

Excalibur (eks.kal′i.bėr). [Also: **Caliburn, Escalibor, Excalibar** (eks.kal′i.bạr).] The sword of King Arthur. Arthur received it from the hands of the Lady of the Lake, to whom it was returned after Arthur was mortally wounded in the last battle against Modred. It had a scabbard whose wearer could lose no blood. Some versions of the romance call it "Mirandoise." There seems, however, to have been also another sword called Excalibur in the early part of the story. This was the sword, plunged deep into a stone, which could be drawn forth only by the man who was to be king. After 200 knights had failed, Arthur drew it out without difficulty.

Excelente Balade of Charitie, An. A poem by Thomas Chatterton, considered by some critics to be his best work. In it he incorporated both the medieval atmosphere of his famous Rowley poems, and a Renaissance imagery reminiscent of Spenser.

Excursion, The. A long didactic poem in nine books by William Wordsworth, forming the middle part of the projected but never finished *Recluse*, published in 1814.

Exeter (ek′sẹ.tẹr), **Duke of.** In Shakespeare's *Henry V*, the historical Sir Thomas Beaufort, an uncle of the King. He arrests Cambridge, Scroop, and Grey for treason, acts as ambassador to France, and goes with Henry on the French campaign, where he reports the deaths of Suffolk and York after the battle. In *1 Henry VI*, he mourns the death of Henry V, but looks forward to defeating the French under the young King, whose special governor he is (I.i). He plays the part of a peacemaker, but foresees the Wars of the Roses.

Exeter, Duke of. In Shakespeare's *3 Henry VI*, the historical Henry Holland, a supporter of King Henry during the Wars of the Roses.

Exeter Book. [Latin, **Codex Exoniensis.**] A collection of Old English poems given by Bishop Leofric to the library of the cathedral at **Exeter,** England, between 1046 and 1072. The manuscript, which most authorities believe to have been copied c975, includes *Juliana, The Phoenix, The Ascension,* and other poems thought to have been written by Cynewulf, *Widsith, Deor's Lament, The Seafarer, Doomsday, The Harrowing of Hell, Azariah, The Husband's Message, The Rhyming Poem, The Wanderer, The Wife's Lament, Guthlac, Eadwacer, Ruin,* three gnomic poems, about a hundred riddles, and one version of *Soul and Body* (the other is in the *Vercelli Book*). A facsimile edition was published at London in 1933.

Exeter College. One of the colleges of Oxford University. It was founded in 1314 by Walter de Stapledon, Bishop of Exeter, and was first known as Stapledon Hall, and later as Exeter Hall. It was considerably enlarged in 1565 by gifts of Sir William Petre. It is the college of Archbishop Temple, of Blackmore (author of *Lorna Doone*), and of William Morris and Burne-Jones, both of whom made decorations for its 19th-century chapel. In the 17th century, Exeter was known as a great home of Puritanism.

Exeter Hall. A building on the Strand, London, used for charitable, religious, and musical assemblies.

Exiles. A three-act play (1918) by James Joyce. The characters are Richard Rowan, an Irish author; his wife, Bertha; Robert Hand, a journalist, in love with Bertha; and Beatrice Justice, a teacher of music, loved by Richard in his younger days. The play, which shows the influence of Ibsen, has a special interest in the character of Richard, believed to be a self-portrait.

Exmoor (eks′mür, -mör, -mōr). A hilly moorland and marshy region in SW England, in W Somersetshire and N Devonshire. It is noted for its breed of ponies and for wild red deer. The scene of Blackmore's novel *Lorna Doone* is laid in it. Highest point, Dunkery Beacon (1,707 ft.). Area, ab. 30 sq. mi.

Exodus (ek′sọ.dus). An Old English poem of 591 lines in the *Junius Manuscript*, generally attributed to an unknown Northumbrian poet of the late 7th or early 8th century, though some authorities, on the evidence of Bede, have credited it to Caedmon. It is characteristic of the epic poetry of the period in its treatment of Moses and his followers, reminiscent of the heroes and their thanes in the old Germanic tradition.

Experiences of an Irish R. M., The. Tales of Irish life by E. E. Somerville and Martin Ross, published in 1890.

Exton (eks′tọn), **Sir Pierce of.** In Shakespeare's *Richard II*, the nobleman who overhears Henry IV's wish for Richard's death and murders him in Pontefract Castle. Holinshed reports this, possibly confusing him with Sir Nicholas Exton, who violently opposed Richard in Parliament.

Extreme Unction. A poem by Ernest Dowson. In it he speculates as to how he will feel and behave when the time comes for him to receive extreme unction (that is to say, when he is dying).

Eyck (īk), **Hubert van.** b. at Maaseyck, near Liége, in Flanders, 1366; d. at Ghent, in Flanders, Sept. 18, 1426. A Flemish painter; brother of Jan van Eyck.

Eyck, Jan van. b. at Maaseyck, near Liége, in Flanders, c1386; d. at Bruges, in Flanders, July 9, 1440. A Flemish painter, court painter of Philip the Good, Duke of Burgundy; brother of Hubert van Eyck.

Eyeless in Gaza (gā′zạ). A novel by Aldous Huxley, published in 1936.

Eyre (ār), **Jane.** The poor and plain, but ardent, governess in Charlotte Brontë's *Jane Eyre*. She marries Rochester, her employer.

Eyre, Simon. See **Simon Eyre.**

Ezra Jennings (ez′rạ jen′ingz). See **Jennings, Ezra.**

F

Fabel (fā′bẹl), **Peter.** An Englishman buried at Edmonton in the reign of Henry VII, around whom the tradition grew that he had sold his soul to the devil and then cheated him out of it. He was made the hero of the anonymous play *The Merry Devil of Edmonton* (c1603).

Faber (fā′bẽr), **Frederick William.** b. at Calverley, Yorkshire, England, June 28, 1814; d. Sept. 26, 1863. An English hymn-writer. He was a clergyman of the Church of England until 1845, and afterward became a priest (1847) of the Roman Catholic Church. He was a friend and follower of John Henry Newman and was an intimate of many well-known people of his day; a book of his in 1842 was dedicated to his friend Wordsworth. A complete edition of his hymns was published in 1861.

Faber, Geoffrey Cust. b. at Great Malvern, England, Aug. 23, 1889—. An English publisher and writer. He has been chairman (1924 *et seq.*) of Faber and Faber, Ltd. He is the author of *Interflow* (1915), *The Valley of Vision* (1917), *Oxford Apostles* (1933), *A Publisher Speaking* (1934), and *The Buried Stream* (1941), a volume of verse.

Fabian (fā′bi.ạn). In Shakespeare's *Twelfth Night*, a servant to Olivia. He joins Maria's plot against Malvolio because the latter has brought him into disfavor with Olivia.

Fabian dei Franchi (fā′byän dā′ē fräng′kē). See **Franchi.**

Fabian Society (fā′bi.ạn). An organization for the advancement of socialism, formed by Edward R. Pease and Frank Podmore as a result of informal conferences for the discussion of social questions held by Thomas Davidson in London in 1883. The society (named for the Roman Quintus Fabius Maximus Verrucosus, named Cunctator because of his cautious waiting tactics) held its first public meetings in 1888 and supported the establishment of socialism by evolutionary rather than revolutionary means. The society, joined by George Bernard Shaw in 1884 and by Sidney Webb in 1885, also attracted Graham Wallas and Annie Besant. Their contributions appeared in *Fabian Essays* (1889). The society also issued a noted series of *Tracts*. In 1900 the members of the group became identified with the British Labour Party.

Fabiola, or the Church of the Catabombs (fab.i.ō′lạ). A historical novel (1854) by Nicholas Wiseman.

Fabius Maximus Verrucosus (fā′bi.us mak′si.mus ver.ū.kō′sus, ver.ö-), **Quintus.** [Surnamed **Cunc-** tator,** meaning "the Delayer."] d. 203 B.C. A Roman general. He was consul for the first time in 233, when by a victory over the Ligurians he obtained the honor of a triumph. In 218 he was at the head of the legation sent by the Roman senate to demand reparation from Carthage for the attack on Saguntum. After the defeat of the consul Flaminius by Hannibal at Trasimenus, he was, in 217, appointed dictator. Avoiding pitched battles (whence his surname Cunctator, "delayer"), he weakened the Carthaginians by numerous skirmishes which hit at stragglers and scouts, while at the same time keeping clear of the main body of Hannibal's troops (whence the term "Fabian tactics" in English). Dissatisfaction having arisen at Rome with this method of carrying on the war, a bill was passed in the senate dividing the command between the dictator and his master of the horse, Minucius, who engaged with Hannibal, and would have been destroyed if Fabius had not hastened to his assistance. Fabius was succeeded in command by the consuls Paulus Aemilius and Terentius Varro, who, adopting a more aggressive policy, were totally defeated at the battle of Cannae in 216. He was consul for the fifth time in 209, when he inflicted a severe loss on Hannibal by the recapture of Tarentum in southern Italy.

fable. A brief narrative, usually comic or satiric, with its roots deep in the cultures of man. In England in the Middle Ages, two types of fable were current: the fabliau, a comic story about men and women; and the beast fable, a story in which animals were used to symbolize various types of human characters. Both forms were popular from about 1200 in the written literature of the vernacular. Chaucer made use of both in his *Canterbury Tales* (1475).

"Among all the different ways of giving counsel, I think the finest and that which pleases the most universally is fable, in whatsoever shape it appears. . . . Upon the reading of a fable we are made to believe we advise ourselves."

(Addison, *Spectator*, No. 512.)

Fable of the Bees, or Private Vices, Public Benefits, The. A prose work (1714) by Bernard Mandeville, a revision of *The Grumbling Hive, or Knaves Turn'd Honest* (1705).

Fables, Ancient and Modern. A series of poems (1699) by John Dryden, paraphrasing some of the tales of Boccaccio, Chaucer, and Ovid. Included in the collection are *Palamon and Arcite, The*

ḏ, d or j; ṣ, s or sh; ṭ, t or ch; ẓ, z or zh; o, F. cloche; ü, F. menu; c̀h, Sc. loch; ṅ, F. bonbon.

Cock and the Fox, and *The Wife of Bath's Tale* from Chaucer, *Sigismonda and Guiscardo* from Boccaccio, and some of Ovid's *Metamorphoses.*

Fables of Pilpay (pil'pī). See **Kalilah and Dimnah.**

fabliau (fab.li.ō'). [Plural, **fabliaux.**] A short, pithy, often bawdy tale, classified as a type of fable, originally cast in a simple verse form (usually octosyllabic couplets), that was popular in the Middle Ages in England and on the Continent. A fabliau is always about human beings (as opposed to the beast fable, which tells its story through animals), and was one of the first literary forms to be written in the vernacular language of the common people of England. The fabliau writer always tacked a moral to the end of his story, which may have flattered the reader's pretense that he was improving himself, while what he was really doing was enjoying a rollicking tale of cuckoldry or roguery. This would appear, at least, to have been the opinion of the English clergy who condemned them in a *caveat* from Oxford in 1292. In form, the fabliau consists of a rapid succession of events in a single episode. Its humor is humor of situation, based on the frailties of human nature. Women and the clergy are favorite victims: wives trick their husbands and take lovers; clergyman are venal, lustful, grasping, and hypocritical. Rogues come off best in the fabliaux, by cleverness duping the greedy and gullible, but at the end of the mirth-provoking episode comes the moral or *significatio,* affecting to teach a moral lesson. Since the subject matter of the fabliau is universal, and as old as mankind, it is difficult to point with any exactitude to the origins of particular stories. Often the plot of a tale will seem to derive from some known Oriental parallel, but quite possibly both the Eastern and Western versions come from some common source, very ancient, and now lost. We do know that the fabliaux of Middle English came into the language through a number of literatures, including French, Flemish, Dutch, and German. As with other medieval forms such as the romance, early examples are in verse and later ones in prose. They formed an important part of French poetry in the 12th and 13th centuries, and they featured largely in Boccaccio's *Decameron* in the 14th century. In 1450, the Latin *Gesta Romanorum* appeared, a miscellaneous collection of fabliaux, beast fables, and other popular short forms. Chaucer put this old form to excellent use in *The Canterbury Tales.* His tales of the Miller, Reeve, Friar, Summoner, Merchant, Shipman, and Man-ciple are actually fabliaux retold with great art. Before Chaucer the only true Middle English fabliau that survives is *Dame Sirith,* concerning a bawd who terrifies a young wife into taking a clerk for a' lover. It is a typical fabliau plot, told realistically, with natural dialogue. After Chaucer there were some pieces like *The Wright's Chaste Wife* and *The Prioress and Her Three Suitors.* William Dunbar, at the end of the 15th century, comes close to Chaucer with his vigorous satire, broad comedy, and realistic characterizations in *Twa Mariit Wemen and the Wedo, The Devil's Inquest,* and others of the genre, proving that he was capable of common writing for commoners despite the larger body of courtly and moral work

he produced. In 1566 William Painter brought forth his *Palace of Pleasure,* a collection in which were translations of both classical stories and the more modern tales, many of them fabliaux, of Boccaccio, Bandello, and Margaret of Navarre. *Middle English Humorous Tales in Verse,* by George H. McKnight (1913), and *Sources and Analogues of Chaucer's Canterbury Tales,* by Bryan and Dempster (1941), provide samples of the fabliaux.

Fabricius Luscinus (fa.brish'us lu.sī'nus), **Gaius.** d. c250 B.C. A Roman consul and general, noted for his incorruptibility. He was ambassador to Pyrrhus in 280.

Fabyan (fā'bi.an), **Robert.** d. probably Feb. 28, 1513. An English chronicler. He appears to have followed the trade of a clothier at London, where he became a member of the Drapers' Company and alderman of the ward of Farringdon Without, besides holding in 1493 the office of sheriff. He wrote a chronicle of England from the arrival of Brutus to his own day, entitled *The Concordance of Histories,* which was first printed by Richard Pynson in 1516 under the title *The New Chronicles of England and France,* but ending with Richard III. Subsequent editions, with additions and alter-ations, were published by John Rastell (1533), John Reynes (1542), and Kingston (1559).

Façade. A collection of poems (1922) by Edith Sitwell, set to music by William Walton. It con-tains, among others, the *Black Mrs. Behemoth* and *En Famille.*

Face (fās). In Ben Jonson's play *The Alchemist,* a servant of Lovewit. He is left in charge of his house, where all the deviltries of the play take place. He becomes the confederate of Subtle, the pretended alchemist, and of Dol Common, his mistress.

Faddle (fad'l). In Edward Moore's play *The Foundling,* a knavish fop, intended to satirize Russell, a well-known social favorite of the day.

Fadladeen (fad.la.dēn'). In Thomas Moore's met-rical romance *Lalla Rookh,* the grand chamberlain of the harem. He is an infallible judge of every-thing, from the penciling of a Circassian's eyelids to the deepest questions of science and literature.

Fadladinida (fad.la.din'i.da). In Henry Carey's burlesque *Chrononhotonthologos,* the Queen of Queerummania and wife of King Chrononhoton-thologos. Her conduct is easy in the extreme.

Faerie Queene (fār'i kwēn'), **The.** An allegorical poem of chivalry by Edmund Spenser. The original plan comprised 12 books, each representing a moral virtue, but only six books (each containing 12 cantos) and fragments of a seventh were completed. Each canto has from 50 to 60 stanzas, and the en-tire poem consists of some 4,000 stanzas. The work is based in part upon the Arthurian romance and Ariosto's *Orlando Furioso.* Books I to III were published in 1590, IV to VI in 1596, and the frag-ments in 1611. The six finished books, containing an intricate double allegory, portray the legends of the knights at the court of Gloriana, the Faerie Queene, who typifies Glory and frequently repre-sents Queen Elizabeth. The legends include those of the knights of Holiness (the Red Cross Knight),

Temperance (Sir Guyon), Chastity (Britomartis and Belphoebe), Fidelity (Triamond and Cambel), Justice (Sir Artegal), and Courtesy (Sir Calidore). The fragments depict the virtue of Mutability (Constance).

Fafnir (făf'nir). [Also: **Fafner**; Old Norse, **Fáfnir**.] In Old Norse mythology, the giant son of Hreidmar, a king of the dwarfs. Fafnir killed his father to obtain the famous gold which was originally owned by the dwarf Andvari, and from his perpetual lying and brooding upon it, became transformed into a venomous dragon. The hero Sigurd killed Fafnir by digging a pit and hiding in it until the monster crawled across it, when he thrust his sword into the dragon's heart from below. Thus Sigurd became owner of the fatal gold, cursed by Andvari, and victim of the curse that ill would befall every unlawful taker of it. Fafnir figures in the *Eddas*, the *Volsunga Saga*, and in the medieval German *Nibelungenlied*, and is slain by Sigurd (German, Siegfried) in all versions. In the Old Norse versions, Sigurd eats Fafnir's heart, and thus receives the gift of understanding bird and animal speech; in the *Nibelungenlied*, Siegfried bathes in the dragon's blood, and thus becomes invulnerable, except in the one spot where a leaf fell on his shoulder.

Fag (fag). In Richard Brinsley Sheridan's comedy *The Rivals*, the lying and ingenious servant of Captain Absolute.

Fagin (fā'gin). In Charles Dickens's *Oliver Twist*, a villainous old man, an employer of thieves and pickpockets, a receiver of stolen goods, and the abductor of Oliver Twist. He is finally sentenced to death for complicity in a murder.

Fainall (făn'ôl). In Congreve's comedy *The Way of the World*, a scoundrel in love with Mrs. Marwood.

Fainall, Mrs. In Congreve's comedy *The Way of the World*, the daughter of Lady Wishfort, now the wife of Fainall but formerly in love with Mirabell.

Fainéant (fā.nā.äṅ'), **Le Noir**. In Scott's *Ivanhoe*, the name given to the Black Knight (Richard Cœur de Lion) on account of his behavior during a tournament, in which, however, he finally conquers.

Fainwell (făn'wel), **Colonel**. [Also, **Colonel Feignwell**.] In Susannah Centlivre's comedy *A Bold Stroke for a Wife*, an ingenious gallant who is in love with Mrs. Lovely's person and fortune. By means of various disguises he wins her from her several guardians, among them Simon Pure.

Fairclough (făr'kluf), **Daniel**. See Featley or **Fairclough, Daniel**.

Fair Em (fār' em'). A play printed in 1631. It was formerly ascribed to Shakespeare for the single reason that in Garrick's collection was a volume, which once belonged to Charles II, containing this and other doubtful plays, and marked on the back "Shakespeare, Vol. I."

Fair Example, or The Modish Citizens, The. A play by Estcourt, taken from the same source as Vanbrugh's *Confederacy*. It was performed at the Drury Lane Theatre, London, in 1703.

Fairfax (făr'faks), **Edward**. b. at Denton, Yorkshire, England; d. in January, 1635. An English

poet. He wrote a translation of Tasso's *Gerusalemme Liberata* (1600), and 12 eclogues.

Fairfax, Thomas. [Title, 3rd Baron **Fairfax of Cameron**.] b. at Denton, Yorkshire, England, Jan. 17, 1612; d. at Nunappleton, Yorkshire, England, Nov. 12, 1671. A Parliamentary leader in the English Civil War. He was educated at St. John's College, Cambridge, and learned the art of war under Sir Horace Vere in the Low Countries. At the outbreak of the Civil War he was appointed second in command, under his father, of the Parliamentary forces in Yorkshire, captured Wakefield, May 21, 1643, and commanded the horse of the right wing at the battle of Marston Moor. He was appointed commander in chief of the Parliamentary army, Jan. 21, 1645, succeeding Robert Devereux, 3rd Earl of Essex, and in April of the same year organized the "New Model," as the Parliamentary force, reorganized after the wholesale resignations because of the Self-Denying Ordinance, was called. He defeated Charles I at Naseby on June 14, 1645, defeated George, Baron Goring, at Langport, Somersetshire, on July 10, 1645, reduced Bristol, Sept. 10, 1645, and took Oxford, June 20, 1646. He disapproved of the seizure of the king by George Joyce, but was forced by the attitude of the army to acquiesce in this measure as well as in "Pride's Purge" and in the execution of the king. On the establishment of the Commonwealth, he was reappointed commander in chief of all the forces in England and Ireland (March 30, 1649), but resigned (June 25, 1650) on account of conscientious scruples about invading Scotland. During the rest of the Commonwealth period, and during the Protectorate, he lived in retirement at Nunappleton, Yorkshire. He represented Yorkshire in Richard Cromwell's Parliament, in which he acted with the opposition. Having in November, 1659, entered into negotiations with Monk for the restoration of Charles II, he placed himself at the head of an army, and took possession (Jan. 1, 1660) of York, and later in the same year was chosen to head the commissioners of the two houses sent to the king at the Hague. He left two autobiographical works, *A Short Memorial of the Northern Actions during the War there, from the Year 1642 till 1644* and *Short Memorials of some Things to be cleared during my Command in the Army*. His only daughter, Mary, married (1657) George Villiers, 2nd Duke of Buckingham.

Fairfield (făr'fēld), **Cicily Isabel**. See **West, Rebecca**.

Fairford (făr'fôrd, -fôrd), **Alan**. In Sir Walter Scott's novel *Redgauntlet*, a young barrister, the devoted friend and correspondent of Darsie Latimer.

Fair Helen of Kirkconnell (hel'en; kèrk.con'el). A Scottish ballad. It is founded on the story that a lady, Helen Bell or Helen Irving (the name is variously shown), the daughter of the Laird of Kirkconnell in Dumfriesshire, while meeting her lover clandestinely in the churchyard of Kirkconnell, saw another and rejected lover taking aim at him. She threw herself before him, was shot, and died in his arms. A mortal combat between the two lovers followed, and the murderer was killed. The ballad is in two parts: an address by the lover to his lady, and the lament of the lover over her grave. There are several versions. Sir Walter Scott included this ballad in his *Minstrelsy of the Scottish Border* (1802). It occurs also in Francis James Child's *English and Scottish Ballads* (1st ed., 1856–58); but Child dropped it from later editions on the grounds that it was more lyrical than narrative in type, and therefore not a true traditional ballad.

Fairies, The. An operatic adaptation by David Garrick of Shakespeare's *Midsummer Night's Dream*, produced in 1755. The songs were taken from Milton, Dryden, Shakespeare, and various minor 18th-century poets.

Fairies and Fusiliers. A volume of verse (1917), by Robert Graves.

Fairleigh (fār'li), **Frank.** The psuedonym used by F. E. Smedley in the publication of *Frank Fairleigh* and *Lewis Arundel*, two novels which appeared originally in *Sharpe's London Magazine*, of which Smedley was the editor (1848–49).

Fairlie (fār'li), **Laura.** The heroine of Wilkie Collins's *Woman in White*. She marries the evil Sir Percival Glyde.

Fair Maid of Perth (perth), **The.** [Full title, **St. Valentine's Day, or The Fair Maid of Perth.**] A historical novel by Sir Walter Scott, published in 1828. The story takes place at the end of the 14th century. The Duke of Rothsay, son of King Robert III of Scotland, is aided by the villainous Sir John Ramorny in an attempt to carry off Catherine, the "fair maid of Perth," daughter of the burgher Simon Glover. Catherine is rescued by the armorer Henry Smith, who cuts off Ramorny's hand. Henry is in love with Catherine, but she will not accept him until he gives up his addiction to fighting. Meanwhile, Ramorny is eager for vengeance, and he lures Rothsay, who he believes betrayed him, to the tower of Falkland, where he (Rothsay) is murdered. Ramorny does not succeed, however, in avenging himself on Henry. Catherine is also pursued by another man, the hot-headed young Conachar, who has become head of the clan Quhele. Conachar and Henry quarrel over Catherine, and the dispute is settled by a battle between 30 members of the Quhele and Chattan clans. The two young men find themselves face to face in the course of the combat, but Conachar's cowardice leads him to flee from the field. Shamed by his weakness, he commits suicide. Henry realizes for the first time the tragedy of the bloodshed resulting from combats, gives up fighting, and marries Catherine.

Fair Maid of the Exchange, The. A play printed in 1607 and attributed to Thomas Heywood on the basis of an ascription of authorship in 1671, but denied in 1687. Charles Lamb thought it was Heywood's, but the matter remains still very much in doubt. The second title is *The Pleasant Humours of the Cripple of Fenchurch.*

Fair Maid of the Inn, The. A comedy begun by John Fletcher, finished after his death by Philip Massinger and perhaps William Rowley, licensed in 1626, and printed in 1647.

Fair Maid of the West, The. [Full title, **The Fair Maid of the West, or A Girl Worth Gold.**] A two-part play by Thomas Heywood, acted at least in the first part as early as 1617, and printed (both parts) in 1631. It was played at Court. It concerns Captain Spencer, in love with Bess Bridges, a tavern girl ("the fair maid of the west"), whom he defends (by killing a man) from insult.

Fair Penitent, The. A tragedy by Rowe, produced in 1703. It was founded on Massinger's *Fatal Dowry* and was a "wholesale felony." Mrs. Barry was the original representative of Calista, the "fair penitent," a part which she created in her 45th year, and which was one of her greatest tragic triumphs.

Fair Quaker of Deal, or The Humours of the Navy, The. A comedy by Charles Shadwell, produced at Drury Lane in 1710 and also published in that year.

Fair Quarrel, A. A play by Middleton and Rowley, published in 1617 and acted shortly before. It concerns the dilemma confronting Captain Ager, who finds that he must either be branded a coward for not fighting a duel with his Colonel, who has slurred his mother, or perjure himself, since his mother informs him that she has committed adultery (although in fact, she hasn't).

"Fair Rosamond" (rō'za̯.mond), **the.** Epithet of Clifford, Rosamond.

Fairscribe (fār'skrĭb). An imaginary legal friend who with his daughter Kate was of assistance to Chrystal Croftangry in writing *Chronicles of the Canongate* (the actual author, of course, was Sir Walter Scott). Chrystal Croftangry, Fairscribe, and various others were invented by Scott as the "real" people who had recounted the "true" tales which he recorded.

Fairservice (fār'sẽr''vis), **Andrew.** In Sir Walter Scott's novel *Rob Roy*, a pious and meddlesome gardener. He is shrewd but cowardly, and, though discharged as a nuisance, will not go.

Fair Virtue, or the Mistress of Philarete (fil'a̯ rēt). A poem by George Wither.

Faithful (fāth'fụl). One of Christian's companions in the first part of Bunyan's *Pilgrim's Progress*. He is burned to death at Vanity Fair.

Faithful, Jacob. See **Jacob Faithful.**

Faithful Forever. See under **Angel in the House, The.**

Faithful Shepherdess, The. A pastoral drama by John Fletcher, published probably in 1609 and probably acted also in that year. It was somewhat influenced by the Italian pastorals, especially by Guarini's *Pastor Fido.* Milton obtained some hints for *Comus* from it. Designed for a courtly audience, the play did not fulfil Fletcher's claim that it represented shepherds in their true actions and passions (i.e., that it was realistic); Fletcher's characters remain stock creatures out of fantasy. Amoret, the faithful shepherdess, is impersonated by a spirit under the name of Amaryllis, and wounded by her lover, Perigot, who, seeing Amaryllis making love to another, believes that she (Amoret) has betrayed him. When Perigot learns about the deception he wounds her a second time, believing now that she is the false Amaryllis when she claims to be constant to him.

Falcon, The. A ship commanded by Raleigh in Sir Humphrey Gilbert's expedition of 1578.

Falcon, The. A London tavern, on the Bankside. It is said to have been patronized by Shakespeare and his company. It was taken down in 1808.

Falconer (fôk′nẽr, fô′kǫn.ẽr, fôl′-), **Lance.** Pseudonym of Hawker, Mary Elizabeth.

Falconer, William. b. Feb. 11, 1732; d. at sea, 1769. A Scottish poet. He was the son of a barber at Edinburgh, became a servant to Archibald Campbell, who discovered and encouraged his literary tastes, and was lost at sea in the frigate *Aurora*, of which he was purser. His chief poem is the *Shipwreck*, published in 1762. He also published *The Universal Marine Dictionary* (1769; revised and enlarged by William Burney).

Falconer, William. b. at Chester, England, Feb. 23, 1744; d. at Bath, England, Aug. 23, 1824. An English physician and miscellaneous writer. In 1770 he began to practice medicine at Bath, where he was physician to the Bath General Hospital (1784–1819). He published *Remarks on the Influence of Climate, . . . Nature of Food, and Way of Life on . . . Mankind* (1781), *A Dissertation on the Influence of Passions upon Disorders of the Body* (1788), and others.

Falconer of Balmawhapple (bal.mǫ.hwap′l). See **Balmawhapple.**

Falder (fôl′dẽr), **William.** A junior clerk in the office of James and Walter How, lawyers, in John Galsworthy's four-act tragedy *Justice* (1910). After serving a sentence for forgery, committed to help the woman he loved, he jumps to his death rather than return to prison for having violated a technicality.

Falk (fôk, fôlk). A story (1903) by Joseph Conrad.

Falkland (fôk′lǫnd, fôlk′-), 2nd Viscount. [Title of **Lucius Cary.**] b. at Burford, Oxfordshire, England, c1610; killed at the battle of Newbury, Sept. 20, 1643. An English poet, scholar, soldier, and secretary of state. Educated at Trinity College, Dublin, and successor (1633) to his father's title, he was a member of Parliament for Newport, on the Isle of Wight, in the Short Parliament (April, 1640) and in the Long Parliament (November, 1640). Appointed (January, 1642) secretary of state by Charles I, he was with him at the battles of Edgehill (Oct. 23, 1642) and Gloucester (August, 1643). An idealist, disgusted with civil war, seeing the faults of both sides, and pessimistic about the possibilities of peace, he is thought to have virtually committed suicide at Newbury. He was the author of poems, parliamentary speeches, philosophical essays, *A Discourse on the Infallibility of the Church of Rome*, and other works, most of them published after his death.

Falkland. The hero-villain of William Godwin's novel *Caleb Williams.* He stabs his enemy in a moment of passion, allows innocent persons to hang for the murder, and is thenceforth dominated by a desire for concealment.

Falkland. A romance by Edward Bulwer-Lytton, published anonymously in 1827.

Falkland. See also **Faulkland.**

Falkland Islands. [Spanish, **Islas Malvinas**; French, **Îles Malouines.**] A group of islands in the South Atlantic, administered by Great Britain, off the coast of SE Argentina, comprising East and West Falkland and about 100 smaller islands. The islands were discovered by John Davis in 1592, were settled by the French in 1763, and were seized by the English in 1765, and later by the Spanish. The British claim, disputed by Argentina, dates from 1833. Dependencies of the colony are South Georgia, South Shetlands, the South Orkneys, Graham's Land, and the Sandwich group. Capital, Stanley; area, 4,618 sq. mi.

Fallen Yew, A. A poem by Francis Thompson, considered by some critics to rank with his *Hound of Heaven.*

Fall of Mortimer (môr′ti.mẽr), **The.** [Also, **Mortimer his Fall.**] A fragment of a tragedy by Ben Jonson.

Fall of Princes. A narrative poem by John Lydgate, consisting of nine books of "Tragedies," as he entitles them, translated from a Latin work of Boccaccio's written between 1430 and 1438.

Fall of Robespierre (rōbz′pi.ãr, -pir), **The.** A tragedy by Coleridge and Southey, produced in 1794. Act I was by Coleridge, Acts II and II by Southey.

False Decretals. [Also: **Decretals of the Pseudo-Isidore,** and **Pseudo-Isidorian Decretals.**] Certain spurious papal letters, published in France between 847 and 852, included in a compilation of canon laws by an ecclesiastic whose identity remains unknown, but who used the name Isidore Mercator. The term is sometimes applied to the entire compilation, but this in fact contains much authentic material, including a dissertation by the Pseudo-Isidore on early church history and the Council of Nicaea, the canons of 54 church councils, and a number of verified letters of popes from the 1st to the 8th centuries. The false material consists of 58 letters or decrees supposedly written by popes from Clement I (88–97 A.D.) to Melchiades (311–314), one purported canon of an early council, and a number of forged letters attributed to various popes between the reigns of Silvester (314–335) and Gregory II (715–731). The apocryphal character of these documents is now universally acknowledged. The Pseudo-Isidore's method was simple: in old records he found references to papal letters and decrees, the texts of which had disappeared, and he proceeded to write his own versions of these lost documents. The compilation as a whole had great authority in the Middle Ages, being much quoted in textbooks and much cited by teachers of canon law. However, during the Renaissance, when scholarly study of medieval writings became increasingly possible, anachronisms began to be noted in the Pseudo-Isidorian text. Time and again the forged letters quote from or cite documents which were not written until long after the dates assigned to these letters. Cunning as was the scholarship that went to the making of this great forgery, it gradually fell apart under the examination of later scholars, Catholic and Protestant, beginning in the mid-15th century. By the early 19th century the False Decretals had been definitely distinguished from the genuine com-

---

ḍ, d or j; ṣ, s or sh; ṭ, t or ch; ẓ, z or zh; o, F. cloche; ü, F. menu; c̣h, Sc. loch; ṅ, F. bonbon.

ponents of the compilation, and the approximate date of their publication had been established, together with the strong probability that they were written in northern France, most likely either at Reims or at Le Mans. The purpose behind the work, moreover, became clear. In the early centuries the Church in Western Europe, and nowhere more than in France, was constantly harassed by the secular power, which intervened in ecclesiastical appointments, convened and dominated councils, subjected churchmen to the secular courts, and occasionally seized coveted church property. The Pseudo-Isidore wrote at a time when the empire of Charlemagne was falling apart, and resistance which would have been futile while he lived could now be attempted against the lesser kings and dukes who followed him. The true purpose of the compilation of which the False Decretals were a part was thus simply to support, by the authority of ancient papal writings, the bishops in their struggle against secular interference.

False Delicacy. A comedy (1768) by Hugh Kelly, written in rivalry to Goldsmith's *The Good-natured Man*. It was acted 20 times the first year and 10,000 copies were sold.

False Friend, The. A comedy by Vanbrugh, printed in 1702. It was adapted from a novel of Le Sage. The prologue was directed against Jeremy Collier for his censure of the Restoration stage as being immoral.

False One, The. A play by Fletcher and Massinger, written c1620, and printed in 1647. It is an indirect imitation of Shakespeare's *Antony and Cleopatra*, dealing with the fortunes of Julius Caesar in Egypt. With a plot based upon Lucan's *De Bello Civili*, the play presents Pompey's flight to Egypt, his murder by Septimius, and Caesar's appearance at the court of Ptolemy to mourn his rival and censure those who have ordered his death. Cleopatra, chafing at the restraints of Ptolemy's court, and particularly of Photinus, his chief minister, arranges to be conveyed into Caesar's presence and arouses his passion. However, Ptolemy diverts him by showing a masque about the Nile in which the wealth of Egypt is displayed, and Cleopatra now sees Caesar as a kind of mean bargainer, seeking only riches; she therefore deals scornfully with him when he seeks to command her charms. This arouses him once more and he valiantly suppresses an uprising instigated by Photinus. Her brother loses his life, leaving the kingdom to Cleopatra, who now recognizes Caesar's honor.

Falstaff (fôl′stȧf), **Sir John.** A celebrated character in Shakespeare's historical plays *1* and *2 Henry IV*, and also in his comedy *The Merry Wives of Windsor*. In the *Henry IV* plays he is a very fat, sensual, and witty old knight; a swindler, drunkard, and good-tempered liar; and something of a coward. Morgann in his *Essay on the Dramatic Character of Sir John Falstaff* (1777) argued that Falstaff was not a coward, and proponents of this view have sought to see the "wholeness" of his character, looking upon his flight from Henry and Poins at Gadshill as merely carrying a joke along. He characteristically gets out of this scrape by his quick wit: "Was it for me to kill the heir apparent?

But beware instinct, the lion will not touch the true prince. I was a coward upon instinct." It might better be argued that he believed, as he says: "The better part of valour is discretion." He provides a kind of mock contrast to the heroic, poetic Hotspur, whom Prince Hal parodies (*1 Henry IV*, II.iii), and pretends to have killed Hotspur at Shrewsbury, although actually he played dead until Hal defeated Hotspur. A change in character can be noted in *2 Henry IV*, where the incidents assume almost a burlesque quality: he deftly insults the Lord Chief Justice with a play on words and ideas, defrauds Mistress Quickly, who is nearly bankrupt with debt, captures Colevile only because Colevile gives himself up, then assumes the airs of a hero, and comments satirically on Justice Shallow's administration of justice and his feeble reminiscences of younger days. His character becomes more coarse, and he oversteps the bounds when Hal becomes King (whereupon he is dismissed). Many critics have found it difficult to approve Hal's action in sending his favorite away, and at least one has seen in Falstaff a kind of private conscience for Hal, which he must put away on assuming the burden of royal politics. Falstaff was originally called Sir John Oldcastle, the name of a well-known Lollard (member of a religious sect of the 14th century). Oldcastle was a friend of Henry V, who tried vainly to dissuade him from the Wycliffite heresy. He entered a conspiracy against Henry and was captured in 1417. As a boon companion of Prince Henry he appears in *The Famous Victories of Henry V*, which Shakespeare used as a source for the plays. However, one of Oldcastle's descendants was moved to protest and the name was changed. The new name chosen for him is associated with Sir John Fastolfe, whom Talbot strips of his honor after the siege of Rouen in *1 Henry VI*. He is represented by a messenger as having fled the field of battle, deserting Talbot. The real Fastolf, governor of Maine and Anjou, did leave Talbot at Patay but only when the situation seemed hopeless. He was deprived of his Order of the Garter, although reinstated in that honor later on. He owned a Boar's Head Tavern in Southwark. This name also caused some complaints from those who revered Fastolf's memory. In *Henry V* Falstaff does not appear, but his death is reported by Mistress Quickly. Although Falstaff may have been thinking of his past sins and green youth (the present reading of Mistress Quickly's speech in II.iii is the result of one of the famous Shakespearian emendations by the 18th-century scholar, Theobald), Pistol comments "his heart is fracted and corroborate," giving the impression that Falstaff has died broken-hearted from Henry's illtreatment. The Epilogue to *2 Henry IV* promises more of Falstaff "unless a' be killed with your hard opinions, for Oldcastle died a martyr, and this is not the man," thus seeking to mollify the relatives of Oldcastle. This promise, as noted, does not materialize, but Sir John does appear again, according to legend at the request of Queen Elizabeth herself, in *The Merry Wives of Windsor*. It is not the same Sir John, but a debased version of him, a mere buffoon serving as butt for the tricks of others. The first actor of the part is said to have been John Heming.

Falstaffian (fôl.staf'i.an). Pertaining to, characteristic of, or resembling Sir John Falstaff.

Family History. A novel by V. Sackville-West, published in 1932.

Family of Love, The. A comedy by Thomas Middleton, licensed in 1607 and produced in 1608. It was a satire on the religious sect of the same name, better known now under their other name of Familists.

Family Reunion, The. A verse play by T. S. Eliot, produced and published in 1939. Harry, returning to his English estate on the occasion of his mother's birthday, is obsessed by fears stemming from the murder of his young wife. In his search for peace he confesses the crime and learns from his aunt that his father suppressed the inclination to kill Harry's domineering mother. Harry leaves to continue the agony of his atonement; the shock of his departure causes the death of his mother.

Famous History of Friar Bacon (bā'kon), **The.** See **Friar Bacon.**

Famous History of Sir Thomas Wyatt (wī'at), **The.** See **Sir Thomas Wyatt.**

Famous History of the Life of King Henry the Eighth, The. See **Henry VIII.**

Famous Victories of Henry V, The. See **Henry V** (1588).

Fanciful (fan'si.ful), **Lady.** A vain and malicious fine lady in Vanbrugh's comedy *The Provoked Wife.* She is impertinent, capricious, and open to flattery, and is the villain of the plot.

fancy. The result or product of an exercise of the fancy; a fanciful image or conception of the mind; a representation in thought, speech, or art of anything ideal or imaginary: as, a pleasing *fancy* or conceit.

> How now, my lord? why do you keep alone,
> Of sorriest fancies your companions making?
> (Shak., *Macbeth*, III.ii.)

Fancy Day (fan'si dā'). See **Day, Fancy.**

Fane (fān), **Violet.** Pseudonym of **Currie,** Lady **Mary Montgomerie.**

Fang (fang). In Shakespeare's *2 Henry IV*, a sheriff's officer who with Snare tries to arrest Falstaff.

Fang, Mr. A police magistrate in Charles Dickens's *Oliver Twist*. He is an outrageous and brutal man, so fair a likeness to Justice Laing, a London police magistrate in office at the time of publication, that the latter was removed from his position by the Home Office.

Fannius (fan'i.us), **Demetrius.** See **Demetrius Fannius.**

Fanny (fan'i). The heroine of Henry Fielding's novel *Joseph Andrews.*

"Fanny," Lord. See **Hervey, John.**

Fanny Bolton (bōl'ton). See **Bolton, Fanny.**

Fanny Cleaver (klē'vėr). See **Cleaver, Fanny.**

Fanny Price (prīs). See **Price, Fanny.**

Fanny Robarts (rō'bärts), **Mrs.** See **Robarts, Mrs. Fanny.**

Fanny's First Play. A comedy (1911) by George Bernard Shaw, aimed at the hypocrisies of the middle-class point of view which are revealed when a son and a daughter of two respectable families serve short sentences in jail. Each marries one of the thoroughly unconventional people he or she thus meets, to the utter dismay of their parents.

Fanny Squeers (fan'i skwirz). See **Squeers, Fanny.**

Fanny Sterling (stėr'ling). See **Sterling, Fanny.**

Fanshawe (fan'shô), **Catherine Maria.** b. at Shabden, England, July 6, 1765; d. at Putney Heath, England, April 17, 1834. An English poet. Her home was much frequented by the literary men of the day. Limited editions of her *Memorials* (which contained most of her poems) and of her *Literary Remains* appeared in 1865 and 1876, respectively.

Fanshawe, Sir Richard. b. at Ware Park, Hertfordshire, England, in June, 1608; d. at Madrid, June 26, 1666. An English diplomat and author. He was appointed (1635) secretary to Lord Aston, ambassador to Spain; joined Charles I in Oxford at the beginning of the English Civil War; was made (c1644) secretary of war to Prince Charles; was captured at the battle of Worcester, Sept. 3, 1651; was made master of requests and secretary of the Latin tongue to Charles II at the Restoration; was appointed ambassador to Portugal in 1661; was made a privy councilor in 1663; and was sent as ambassador to Spain in 1664. His chief work is *The Lusiad, or Portugal's Historical Poem, written in the Portugall Language by Luis de Camoens and now newly put into English by Richard Fanshawe, Esq.* (1655).

Faraday (far'a.dā), **Michael.** b. at Newington, Surrey, England, Sept. 22, 1791; d. at Hampton court, near London, Aug. 25, 1867. An English physicist and chemist. He began adult life as a journeyman bookbinder, but was persuaded, through hearing some of Sir Humphry Davy's lectures, to devote himself to the study of chemistry, and in 1813 was appointed Davy's assistant in the laboratory of the Royal Institution. He was made director of the laboratory in 1825, and professor of chemistry for life in the institution in 1833. His researches and discoveries in chemistry are noteworthy, but the great additions made by him to the range of human knowledge were mostly in the related sciences of electricity and magnetism. Especially notable are his discoveries of electromagnetic induction in 1831 and the magnetization of light in 1845. In 1846 he discovered diamagnetism. Faraday is also responsible for advances in the study of electrolysis, liquefaction of gases, catalysis, the vacuum tube, and in other areas of physics and chemistry. However, his successful demonstration of electromagnetic induction (which he described to a meeting of fellow scientists on Nov. 24, 1831) has come to be the achievement most often associated with his name, and with good reason: it established the principle which made possible both the modern dynamo and electric motor, and hence may surely be considered one of the principles basic to the industrial development of our day. Working first with magnets, which he passed through coils of wire, and then by passing a current of electricity through another coil of wire (which had been insulated from and arranged spirally next to still another coil of wire), he was able clearly to establish the momentary existence of an induced current of electricity (the method of this experiment is now, of course, familiar to virtually every schoolboy). Even Faraday did not fully understand the enormous implications of electromagnetic induction, and it was not until some 30 years later, when his ideas were given mathematical expression by Clerk Maxwell, that their true importance began to be understood. He published *Chemical Manipulation* (1827), *Experimental Researches in Electricity* (1844–55), *Experimental Researches in Chemistry and Physics* (1859), *Lectures on the Chemical History of a Candle* (1861, edited by W. Crookes), *Various Forces in Nature* (also edited by W. Crookes), and others.

Farange (far′ạnj), **Maisie.** The heroine of Henry James's novel *What Maisie Knew.*

Farebrother (fâr′brуTH.ẻr), **Rev. Camden.** In George Eliot's novel *Middlemarch,* an unpopular rector.

Far Away and Long Ago. An autobiographical account (1918) of childhood in South America by W. H. Hudson.

farce. 1. A secular dramatic composition of a ludicrous or satirical character; low comedy. Originally the name (*farsia*) was applied to a canticle in a mixture of Latin and French, sung in many churches at the principal festivals, especially on Christmas. The modern farce is: (a) A dramatic composition of a broadly comic character, differing from other comedy chiefly in the grotesqueness and exaggeration of its characters and incidents. (b) An opera in one act, of an absurd, extravagant, or ludicrous character.

Farce is that in poetry which grotesque is in a picture; the persons and actions of a farce are all unnatural, and the manners false.
(Dryden, *Parallel of Poetry and Painting.*)

Fardorougha the Miser (fär.dôr′ŏ.ạ). A novel (1839) by William Carleton.

Far from the Madding Crowd. A novel by Thomas Hardy, published in 1874. The title, taken from a line in Thomas Gray's *Elegy Written in a Country Churchyard,* is an appropriate designation of the group of rustics in "Wessex," Hardy's fictional English county, who provide an amusing background for the lively pursuit of a fascinating heroine, Bathsheba Everdene, by three men: Farmer Boldwood, Sergeant Troy, and Gabriel Oak, a shepherd.

Fargus (fär′gus), **Frederick John.** [Pseudonym, **Hugh Conway.**] b. at Bristol, England, Dec. 26, 1847; d. at Monte Carlo, May 15, 1885. A British novelist. He was for a time a student on board the school frigate *Conway.* He studied subsequently in a private school at Bristol, and in 1868, on the death of his father, succeeded to the latter's business as an auctioneer at Bristol. He wrote *Called Back* (1883), *Dark Days* (1884), and others.

Farjeon (fär′jọn), **Benjamin Leopold.** b. at London, May 12, 1838; d. at Hampstead, London, July 23, 1903. An English editor, novelist, and dramatist; husband (married 1877) of Margaret Jefferson, daughter of the American actor Joseph Jefferson (1829–1905). He lived (1855 *et seq.*) in Australia and New Zealand, was editor, at Dune-

din, New Zealand, of the *Otago Daily Times,* then the only daily newspaper in New Zealand, and author of many novels in the style of his two favorites, Charles Dickens and Wilkie Collins. His novels include *Grif* (1866; also a play, *London's Heart,* 1873), *Blade o' Grass* (1874), *The Duchess of Rosemary Lane* (1876), *House of White Shadows* and *Great Porter Square* (both 1884), *Toilers of Babylon* (1888), *Aaron the Jew* (1894), and *The Mesmerists* (1903); he also wrote the drama, *Home, Sweet Home* (1876).

Farjeon, Eleanor. b. at London, 1881—. An English novelist, poet, dramatist, and author of works for juveniles; daughter of Benjamin Leopold Farjeon. She is the author of *Martin Pippin in the Apple Orchard* (1922), *Mighty Men* (1925), *Faithful Jenny Dove and Other Tales* (1929), *The King's Daughter Cries for the Moon* (1929), *Katy Kruse at the Seaside* (1932), *Jim at the Corner and Other Stories* (1934), *Jim and the Pirates* (1936), and *Martin Pippin in the Daisy Field* (1938); and also wrote *Poems* (1929) and *Over the Garden Wall* (1933), poetry; *Granny Gray* (1939), a play for children; *A Nursery in the '90's* (1935; American title, *Portrait of a Family*), autobiography; and *Love Affair* (1949), a novel of life at Paris in the 1870's.

Farjeon, Herbert. d. at London, May 3, 1945. An English journalist and playwright; son of Benjamin Leopold Farjeon. Staff member of London *Daily Mail* and *Answers;* drama critic for *World.* Author of such plays and revues as *Friends* (1917), *Picnic, Diversion No. 1, Diversion No. 2,* and *Light and Shade;* collaborated with his sister Eleanor Farjeon on *Kings and Queens* (1932), *An Elephant in Arcady* (1938), *The Two Bouquets* (1938), and other productions.

Farjeon, Joseph Jefferson. b. at London, June 4, 1883—. An English playwright; son of Benjamin Leopold Farjeon. He is the author of *No. 17* (1925), *After Dark* (1926), *The Green Dragon* (1929), and *Philomel* (1932), as well as some 60 novels, including *The Master Criminal* (1924).

Farley (fär′li), **Charles.** b. at London, 1771; d. there, Jan. 28, 1859. An English actor and dramatist. He made his appearance as a page at Covent Garden Theatre, London, in 1782, and subsequently played with much success the characters of Sanguinback in *Cherry and Fair Star,* Grindoff in *The Miller and his Men,* Jeremy in *Love for Love,* and Lord Trinket in *The Jealous Wife.* He is said to have been without a rival in his day as a theatrical machinist. He retired from the stage in 1834. He wrote *The Magic Oak: or, Harlequin Woodcutter* (1799), *The Battle of Bothwell Brigg* (1820), and others.

Farley, James Lewis. b. at Dublin, Ireland, Sept. 9, 1823; d. at London, Nov. 12, 1885. An Irish author. He was for a time chief accountant of the Beirut branch of the Ottoman Bank, and in 1860 was appointed accountant-general of the state bank of Turkey at Constantinople (Istanbul), which subsequently became merged in the Imperial Ottoman Bank. He wrote *Banking in Turkey* (1863), *Turkey: a Sketch of its Rise, Progress, and Present Position* (1866), *Modern Turkey* (1872), *Turks and Christians: a Solution of the Eastern*

Question (1876), *Egypt, Cyprus, and Asiatic Turkey* (1878), and others.

Farmer (fär′mẽr), **Hugh.** b. near Shrewsbury, England, 1714; d. at London, in February, 1787. An English dissenting clergyman and scholar. He published *Christ's Temptation in the Wilderness* (1761), *Dissertation on Miracles* (1771), *Demoniacs of the New Testament* (1775), and others.

Farmer, John. fl. 1591–1601. An English composer of madrigals whose works are preserved in the third volume of the *English Madrigal School.*

Farmer, Richard. b. at Leicester, England, Aug. 28, 1735; d. at Cambridge, England, Sept. 8, 1797. An English scholar. He was educated at Emmanuel College, Cambridge, of which college he was appointed master in 1775. In 1778 he became chief librarian at the university. His only published work is a scholarly paper entitled *Essay on the Learning of Shakespeare* (Cambridge, 1767), showing that Shakespeare's knowledge of foreign literature, including the classical, came from translations and not from originals.

"Farmer George" (jôrj). A nickname of George III of England.

Farmer's Boy, The. A poem by Robert Bloomfield, published in 1800.

Farnborough (färn′bur.ọ̈), 1st Baron. Title of **May, Sir Thomas Erskine.**

Farnese Bull (fär.nā′zä). A large group of Greek sculpture of the Trallian school (3rd century B.C.), in the Museo Nazionale at Naples. It represents the chastisement of Dirce by her stepsons for her treatment of their mother, Antiope, by binding her to the horns of a bull. It is much restored, but is considered very remarkable for its composition and execution. It was discovered in the Baths of Caracalla in 1546.

Farnese Hercules (hẽr′kụ̈.lēz). A Greek statue in the Museo Nazionale at Naples. The demigod is represented undraped, leaning on his club. The bearded head is somewhat small, and the muscular development prodigious. It dates from the early empire (1st century B.C.).

Farnol (fär′nọl), **Jeffery.** [Full name, **John Jeffery Farnol.**] b. Feb. 10, 1878; d. at Eastbourne, Sussex, England, Aug. 9, 1952. An English novelist, noted as a writer of popular historical romances. His books include *The Broad Highway* (1910), *The Amateur Gentleman, Beltane the Smith* (1915), *Peregrine's Progress* (1922), *The Quest of Youth* (1927), *The Way Beyond* (1933), *The Lonely Road* (1938), *Murder by Nail* (1942), *The King Liveth* (1944), and *Heritage Perilous* (1947).

Far-Off Hills, The. A three-act comedy (1928) by Lennox Robinson.

Farquhar (fär′kwạr, -kạr), **George.** b. at Londonderry, Ireland, 1678; d. April, 1707. An Irish dramatist. He studied at Trinity College, Dublin (1694–95), became a corrector of the press, or proofreader, and appeared on the stage at Dublin, apparently without success. He removed to London in 1697 or 1698, and in 1699 his first play, *Love in a Bottle*, was successfully produced at the Drury Lane Theatre. He obtained a lieutenant's commission from the earl of Orrery, possibly in 1702, and saw

some service, which enabled him to write the *Recruiting Officer*, produced in 1706, one of his most successful plays. He married in 1703, and died in great poverty, leaving a widow and two daughters. Besides the plays already mentioned, he wrote *A Constant Couple* (1699), *Sir Harry Wildair* (1701), *The Inconstant, or the Way to Win Him* (1702), *The Twin Rivals* (1702), *The Stage Coach* (1704), and *The Beaux' Stratagem* (1707).

Farrar (far′ạr), **Frederic William.** b. at Bombay, India, Aug. 7, 1831; d. at Canterbury, England, March 22, 1903. An English clergyman, educator, theologian, and philological writer. He was educated at the University of London and at Cambridge, was ordained in 1854, and served as headmaster (1871–76) of Marlborough College and select preacher (1868, 1874–75) to Cambridge University. He was appointed a canon of Westminster Abbey and rector of Saint Margaret's in 1876 and became archdeacon of Westminster in 1883 and dean of Canterbury in 1895. He published the works of fiction *Eric* (1858), *Julian Home* (1859), and *St. Winifred's* (1863). His theological works include *Witness of History to Christ* (1871), *Life of Christ* (1874), *Life and Work of St. Paul* (1879), *Early Days of Christianity* (1882), and others.

Farren (far′ẹn), **Elizabeth.** b. 1759; d. at Knowlsey Park, England, 1829. An English actress. She first appeared in 1777 at the Haymarket Theatre, then went to the Drury Lane. She was noted for her comic roles, appearing in 1797 as Lady Teazle, her last role.

Farren, William. b. May 13, 1786; d. at London, Sept. 24, 1861. An English actor. He appeared at Covent Garden in 1818 as Sir Peter Teazle in Sheridan's *School for Scandal*, one of his best parts, in which he was noted for his "animation, ease, naturalness of manner." He also played Shakespearian roles such as Shallow in *Henry IV*, Malvolio in *Twelfth Night*, and Polonius in *Hamlet*. He retired in 1853.

Farrer (far′ẽr), **Thomas Henry.** [Title, 1st Baron **Farrer.**] b. at London, June 24, 1819; d. at Dorking, England, Oct. 12, 1899. An English lawyer and government official, author of works on economics. Educated at Eton and Oxford; called to bar (1844) but did little practice; joined Board of Trade (1850) and served as permanent secretary (1865–86); helped frame Merchant Shipping Law Consolidation Bill and Merchant Shipping Code (1870); member of the London County Council (1889–98). Published *Free Trade versus Fair Trade* (1886), *Studies in Currency* (1898), and other works on economics.

Fascinating Mr. Vanderveldt (van′dẽr.velt), **The.** A four-act comedy (1907) by Alfred Sutro.

Fascination Fledgeby (fas.i.nā′shọn flej′bi). See **Fledgeby, Mr.**

Fashion (fash′ọn), **Sir Novelty.** In Colley Cibber's *Love's Last Shift*, "a coxcomb that loves to be the first in all foppery." Vanbrugh adapted him as Lord Foppington in *The Relapse.*

Fashion, Young. [Also, **Tom Fashion.**] In Vanbrugh's comedy *The Relapse*, the young brother of Lord Foppington (formerly Sir Novelty Fashion). He impersonates his brother to get possession of Miss Hoyden and her fortune.

Fashionable Lover, The. A play by Richard Cumberland, produced in 1772.

Fashionable Tales, or Tales of Fashionable Life. Tales by Maria Edgeworth. The first installment appeared in 1809, and the last in 1812. They comprise "Ennui," "The Dun," "Manœuvring," "Almeria," "Vivian," "The Absentee," "Madame de Fleury," and "Émilie de Coulanges."

Fastidious Brisk (brisk). See **Brisk, Fastidious.**

Fastolf (fas'tolf), Sir **John.** b. c1378; d. at Caister, England, Nov. 5, 1459. An English soldier and benefactor of Magdalen College, Oxford. He was a page of Thomas Mowbray, Duke of Norfolk, and afterward entered the service of Thomas of Lancaster (Duke of Clarence), Henry IV's second son, who became lord deputy of Ireland in 1401. He was appointed by Henry V custodian of the castle of Veires in Gascony in 1413, became lieutenant of Normandy and governor of Maine and Anjou in 1423, took John II, Duke of Alençon, prisoner at the battle of Verneuil in 1424, and was created a Knight of the Garter in 1426. On Feb. 12, 1429, during Lent, while convoying provisions, consisting chiefly of herrings, to the English before Orléans, he repulsed an attack of a largely superior French force under the Comte de Clermont at Rouvray ("the Battle of the Herrings"), and on June 18, 1429, was defeated with Talbot at Patay. He retired from military service in 1440. He left a legacy for the founding of a college at Caister, which was diverted by papal authority to Magdalen College, Oxford. He is supposed by some to be the original of Shakespeare's Sir John Falstaff (q.v.), the evidence being slight but definite: Fastolf was accused of cowardice for his flight (although this did not take place until after Talbot had lost the battle) at Patay; Fastolf was connected with Lollardry; also, he served under Mowbray.

Fatal Curiosity. A tragedy by Lillo, produced in 1736 and published in 1737. It has a domestic setting, based on a Cornish story, and is in three acts (rather than the five still conventional at that time). Wilmot, a poor man, murders a stranger at the urging of his wife, only to discover that the man is his long-lost son. The play was sometimes acted under the title of *Guilt its own Punishment, or Fatal Curiosity.*

Fatal Discovery, The. A tragedy by John Home, produced by Garrick in 1769.

Fatal Dowry, The. A tragedy by Philip Massinger and Nathaniel Field. It was written sometime in the period 1616–19 and published in 1632. It served later as a principal source for Rowe in his *Fair Penitent* (1703).

Fatal Marriage, or The Innocent Adultery, The. A tragedy by Southerne, acted in 1694. On its revival in 1757 the comic subplot was omitted, and the play was afterward renamed *Isabella, or The Fatal Marriage.*

Fata Morgana (fä'tạ môr.gä'nạ). The sister of King Arthur, in the medieval romances, better known as Morgan le Fay (q.v.). The name *fata morgana* is given to mirages seen in the Strait of Messina, said to be magically caused by her.

Fat Boy, the. [Prename, **Joe.**] In Charles Dickens's *Pickwick Papers*, a servant of Mr. Wardle. He is able to fall asleep in almost any position or place, and does so constantly. His constant thought, when awake, is of food.

Fat Contributor, The. One of the many pseudonyms of **Thackeray, William Makepeace.**

Fates (fāts). In Roman mythology, the three goddesses of destiny who preordained the course and outcome of every human life. Their Latin name, Fata, is the plural of *fatum*, meaning an unalterable decree of the gods, hence, fate. Because they functioned at every human birth, they became identified with the Moirae, the three birth goddesses of Greek religion, who are also called Fates. This identification gave rise to the development of the three Roman Parcae, or Fates, from the original Roman birth goddess, Parca. The Fates of Teutonic mythology are the three Norns.

Fates of the Apostles, The. An Old English poem by Cynewulf, preserved in the *Vercelli Book.* It is one of the four works signed by the poet.

Father Brown (broun). A character in many stories by G. K. Chesterton.

Father Eustace (ū'stạs). See **Eustace, Father.**

Father Hubberd's Tales, or The Ant and the Nightingale (hub'ẽrdz). A coarse but humorous attack on the vices and follies of the times, partly in prose and partly in verse, by Thomas Middleton. It was suggested by Spenser's *Prosopopoia, or Mother Hubberd's Tale.* It was published in 1604.

"Father of Angling," the. See **Walton, Izaak.**

"Father of History," the. See **Herodotus.**

Father O'Flynn (ọ.flin'). An Irish song by Alfred Percival Graves, published in the *Spectator* in 1875.

"Father of Medicine." See **Hippocrates.**

"Father of Moral Philosophy." See **Aquinas,** Saint **Thomas.**

"Father of the English detective novel." See **Collins, Wilkie.**

"Father of the Marshalsea" (mär'shạl.sē), **the.** See **Dorrit, William.**

Fathers, The. [Full title, **The Fathers, or The Good-natured Man.**] A comedy by Henry Fielding, posthumously published in 1778.

Fathers of the Church. fl. c100–750. Those Christian ecclesiastical writers of the early centuries whose authority is especially recognized in matters of Christian doctrine and Scriptural interpretation. Foremost among them are six who were during some part of their lives contemporary with the Apostles, and are styled Apostolic Fathers: these are Barnabas (fl. c70–100 A.D.), Clement of Rome (d. c100), Hermes (fl. c100), Ignatius (d. c107), Papias (fl. c130), and Polycarp (d. 155). The further list of Church Fathers is not so definitely fixed, but is generally considered to include, from the Greek church, Saints Athanasius, Basil the Great, Gregory Nazianzen, and John Chrysostom; and from the Latin church, Saints Jerome, Ambrose, Augustine, and Gregory the Great.

Fathom (faтн'ọm), **Ferdinand, Count.** See **Ferdinand, Count Fathom.**

Fatima (fä'ti.mạ, fat'i.mạ, fạ.tē'mạ). b. at Mecca, Arabia, c606; d. at Medina, Arabia, 632. The daughter of Mohammed by his first wife, Kadijah; wife of Ali.

Fatima. In "Aladdin and the Wonderful Lamp," in the *Arabian Nights' Entertainments*, an enchantress who is killed by a magician, and disguised in whose garments the evil magician thereupon enters the house of Aladdin to destroy him and steal the wonderful lamp. Aladdin, however, sees through the disguise and kills the magician.

Fatima (fạ.tē'mạ). In the folk tale *Bluebeard*, the last and seventh wife of Bluebeard. Her curiosity and disobedience in opening the forbidden door reveals the murder of the six previous wives; and her cleverness results in the death of Bluebeard and her own escape.

"fat woman of Brentford" (brent'fọrd). See under **Merry Wives of Windsor, The.**

Faucit (fô'sit), **Helen.** [Title, Lady **Martin.**] b. 1817; d. Oct. 31, 1898. An English actress. She made her first appearance at London, in 1836, as Julia in *The Hunchback*. She afterward gained success as Juliet, Portia, Desdemona, and in other Shakespearian roles, and created the leading female characters in *The Lady of Lyons*, *Money*, *Richelieu*, and many other plays. Her last appearance was in 1879, at the opening of the Memorial Theatre at Stratford-on-Avon. She wrote a work *On Some of the Female Characters of Shakspere* (1885).

Faulconbridge (fô'kọn.brij, fôl'-), **Lady.** In Shakespeare's *King John*, the widow of Sir Robert Faulconbridge and mother of Robert and Philip Faulconbridge. She confesses to Philip that his father was the late King Richard I (the Lion-Hearted) (I. i).

Faulconbridge, Philip. [Called **Philip the Bastard.**] In Shakespeare's *King John*, the illegitimate son of Richard I (the Lion-Hearted), and the half-brother of Robert Faulconbridge. He follows John in his French wars and is recognized by Queen Elinor as her grandson. He comments with bitter wit upon the politics involved in making peace with France, preferring instead a good open fight (which eventually occurs).

Faulconbridge, Robert. In Shakespeare's *King John*, the legitimate, younger son of Lady Faulconbridge.

Faulkland (fôk'lạnd, fôlk'-). [Also, **Falkland.**] In Richard Brinsley Sheridan's comedy *The Rivals*, the wilfully obstinate lover of Julia.

Faultless Painter, the. A name sometimes given to Andrea del Sarto, as in the poem (1855) by Robert Browning.

Faunus (fôn'us). An ancient Italian god of forests and wild life, an agricultural and pastoral fertility deity who later became identified with the Greek Pan. He had two annual festivals, in December and February, called Faunalia, accompanied by libations of milk and wine, sacrifice of goats, and the performance of games. In Roman mythology, he figures as the brother, father, or consort of Bona Dea. In ancient legend, Faunas was a Latin king, father of Latinus, and taught the Latin peoples their agriculture and religion.

Fausset (fô'set), **Hugh I'Anson.** b. at Sedbergh, Yorkshire, England, June 16, 1895—. An English poet and literary critic. He has been a reviewer (1919 *et seq.*) for the *Times Literary Supplement* and the Manchester *Guardian*. His works include *The Spirit of Love: a Sonnet Sequence* (1921), *Keats* (1922), *Tennyson: A Modern Portrait* (1923), *Before the Dawn: Poems* (1924), *John Donne: A Study in Discord* (1924), *Samuel Taylor Coleridge* (1926), *The Modern Dilemma* (1930), *A Modern Prelude* (1933), *Whitman, A Study* (1942), and *Poets and Pundits* (1947).

Faust (foust). A tragedy by Goethe, commenced in 1772, and first published as *Faust, ein Fragment* in 1790. Part I, complete, was published as *Faust, eine Tragödie* in 1808; Part II, finished in 1831, was published in 1833. It has been translated into English by Bayard Taylor, Blackie, Anster, Hayward, Martin, and others (nearly 40 in all).

Faust, Johann. See **Fust** or **Faust, Johann.**

Faustus (fôs'tus, fous'-), **Doctor.** See **Doctor Faustus.**

Favonius (fạ.vō'ni.us). In Roman mythology, the gentle west wind, bringer of spring and the rebirth of vegetation, hence regarded as auspicious; identified with Zephyr.

Fawcett (fô'set), **John.** b. Aug. 29, 1768; d. 1837. An English actor and dramatist. He appeared at Covent Garden, London, in 1791, and maintained his connection with that theater until his retirement from the stage in 1830. A number of plays were written especially for him by Colman the younger, the most notable of which was the *Heir-at-Law*, in which he appeared as Dr. Pangloss. He wrote *Obi, or Three-fingered Jack* (produced at the Haymarket in 1800), *Pérouse* (1801), *Fairies' Revels* (produced at the Haymarket in 1802), *The Enchanted Island* (produced at the Haymarket in 1804), and others.

Fawcett, Millicent. [Maiden name, **Garrett.**] b. at Aldeburgh, Suffolk, England, June 11, 1847; d. at London, Aug. 5, 1929. An English feminist. She is remembered chiefly as a leader of the woman suffrage movement (as distinct from the militant suffragettes led by members of the Pankhurst family). She was president of the National Union of Women's Suffrage Societies (1897–1918) and a founder of Newnham College at Cambridge University. Author of *Political Economy for Beginners* (1870), *Some Eminent Women of Our Time* (1889), *Women's Suffrage* (1912), *Women's Victory* (1919), and *What I Remembered* (1924).

Fawkes (fôks), **Francis.** b. at Warmsworth, England, 1720; d. Aug. 26, 1777. An English clergyman, poet, and translator. Educated at Cambridge, he gained the post of vicar of Orpington (1755) by flattering Archbishop Herring with an ode; later he was curate of Downe (1774–77). Among his works are *Works of Anacreon, Sappho, Bion, Moschus, and Musaeus Translated into English by a Gentleman of Cambridge* (1760), *Original Poems and Translations* (1761), *The Poetical Calendar* (1763), and a song, *The Brown Jug*.

Fawkes (fôks), **Guy.** See under **Gunpowder Plot.**

Fawnia (fô'ni.ạ). In Greene's *Dorastus and Fawnia* (afterward called *Pandosto*), the lady loved by

ḏ, d or j; ṣ, s or sh; ṭ, t or ch; ẓ, z or zh; o, F. cloche; ü, F. menu; ċh, Sc. loch; ṅ, F. bonbon.

Dorastus. She is the original of Shakespeare's *Perdita*.

Fazio (fät'si.ō). A tragedy by Henry Hart Milman, first produced, without his knowledge, as *The Italian Wife*. In 1818 it was brought out with great success at Covent Garden Theatre, London. The plot is from a story in the *Annual Register* for 1795.

Feast of Fools. [Also, **Fools' Festival.**] A medieval European festival, celebrated usually on Jan. 1, the Roman Catholic Feast of the Circumcision. It was a day of burlesqued ritual, mummery and masked processions, and bawdy songs. Gambling took place inside the church, hearty food was eaten at the altar, rags and old shoes were burned as incense, and a bishop of fools was elected and ordained, who took charge of the revelries. The Feast of Fools was a complete reversal and mockery of all that was regarded as holy every other day of the year. Its observance was abandoned in the 16th century, after many earlier attempts to prohibit it. It has sometimes been confused with April Fools' Day, with the Feast of the Ass (Jan. 14), and other European burlesque observances.

Feast of the Holy Innocents. See **Childermas Day.**

Featherstone (feᴛн'ér.stọn, -stŏn), **Peter.** In George Eliot's novel *Middlemarch*, an old miser who delights in tormenting his expectant relatives.

Featley (fēt'li) or **Fairclough** (fār'kluf), **Daniel.** b. at Charlton-upon-Otmoor, Oxfordshire, England, March 15, 1582; d. at Chelsea College, in England, April 17, 1645. An English controversialist and devotional writer. He was chaplain (1610–13) to Sir Thomas Edmondes, English ambassador at Paris, and acted subsequently as domestic chaplain to Abbot, archbishop of Canterbury, by whom he was appointed rector of Lambeth in 1619. He became rector of Acton, Middlesex, in 1627. During the English Civil War he was suspected of acting as a spy for Charles I.

Fedele and Fortunio (fā.dā'lā; fôr.tö'nyō). [Full title, **Fedele and Fortunio, the Deceits in Love, or A Pleasant Comedy of two Italian Gentlemen.**] A comedy (c1585) by Anthony Munday, adapted from *Il Fedele* by Luigi Pasqualigo.

Feeble (fē'bl), **Francis.** In Shakespeare's *2 Henry IV*, one of Falstaff's recruits, characterized by Falstaff as "most forcible feeble."

Feenix (fē'niks), **Cousin.** In Charles Dickens's *Dombey and Son*, a well-preserved society man, very youthful in appearance; a bachelor, and the cousin of Edith Granger.

Feignwell (fān'wel), **Colonel.** See **Fainwell, Colonel.**

Feiling (fī'ling, fā'-), **Keith Grahame.** b. 1884—. An English historian and biographer. His books include *History of the Tory Party, 1640–1714* (1924), *British Foreign Policy, 1660–1672*, (1930), *The Second Tory Party, 1714–1832* (1938), *The Life of Neville Chamberlain* (1946), *A History of England* (1950), and *Warren Hastings* (1955).

Felice Charmond (fe.lēs' shär'mọnd). See **Charmond, Felice.**

Feliche (fā.lē'kā). A young courtier to the Doge of Venice in John Marston's tragedy *Antonio's Revenge*.

Felisbravo (fē.lis.brä'vō). The Prince of Persia in Sir Richard Fanshawe's translation of *Querer Por Solo Querer* (*To Love for Love's Sake*), a romantic drama written in Spanish by Mendoza in 1649.

Felix (fē'liks), **Don.** In Susannah Centlivre's comedy *The Wonder! A Woman Keeps a Secret*, a Portuguese gentleman in love with Violante. His lively jealousy is roused by Violante's unusual accomplishment of keeping another's secret. Garrick played this part on his last appearance.

Felix Holt, the Radical (hōlt). A novel by George Eliot, published in 1866. Felix Holt is a young man of high standards and noble character who adopts the life of a humble artisan in order to prove to the workers that their hopes of betterment can only be realized through education and reason, and not through various legislative programs. In contrast with Felix is the rich politician, Harold Transome, essentially a good man, but one whose political stands can easily be changed and compromised. Esther, the heroine, must choose between the lives that these men can offer her, and she eventually chooses the life of poverty with Felix.

Felkin (fel'kin), **Ellen Thorneycroft.** [Maiden name, **Fowler.**] b. at Wolverhampton, Staffordshire, England, April 9, 1860; d. at Bournemouth, Hampshire, England, June 22, 1929. An English novelist and poet. She was the author of *Songs and Sonnets* (1888), *Verses, Grave and Gay* (1891), *Verses, Wise or Otherwise* (1895), and of once-popular moral, religious, and didactic novels such as *Concerning Isabel Carnaby* (1898), *A Double Thread* (1899), *The Farringdons* (1900), *Fuel of Fire* (1902), *Place and Power* (1903), *Kate of Kate Hall* (1904), *In Subjection* (1906), *Miss Fallowfield's Fortune* (1908), *The Wisdom of Folly* (1910), *The Lower Pool* (1923), and *Signs and Wonders* (1926).

Fell (fel), **John.** b. probably at Longworth, Berkshire, England, June 23, 1625; d. July 10, 1686. An English scholar and prelate. He was educated at Oxford, served under the standard of Charles I in the English Civil War, and was made dean of Christ Church, Oxford, in 1660, and bishop of Oxford in 1675. His chief work is *The Interest of England Stated* . . . (1659). He is said to have edited *A Paraphrase and Annotations upon the Epistles of St. Paul* (1675), often quoted as Fell's Paraphrase. He was satirized by Tom Brown in the epigram beginning "I do not like thee, Dr. Fell," said to have been paraphrased extempore from Martial's "Non amo te, Sabidi," on penalty of expulsion from Oxford if he failed.

Fellowes (fel'ōz), **Edmund Horace.** b. at London, Nov. 11, 1870—. An English musicologist, noted for his research in the field of English madrigals. He is the editor of *English Madrigal School* (1913–24) and *English School of Lutenist Song-Writers*, and author of *The English Madrigal Composers* (1921) and *English Madrigal Verse*.

Felltham or **Feltham** (fel'thạm), **Owen.** b. at Mutford, Suffolk, England, c1602; d. at Great Billing, Northamptonshire, England, 1668. An English author. He was either secretary or chaplain in the family of the earl of Thomond, in Northamptonshire. He was an ardent Royalist, and in a poem

---

fat, fāte, fär, ȧsk, fāre; net, mē, hėr; pin, pīne; not, nōte, mŏve, nôr; up, lūte, pùll; ᴛн, then;

entitled *Epitaph to the Eternal Memory of Charles the First . . . Inhumanly murthered by a perfidious Party of His prevalent Subjects*, refers to Charles as "Christ the Second."

Felton (fel'tọn), **John.** b. c1595; hanged at Tyburn, London, Nov. 28, 1628. An English assassin. He entered the army at an early age, and served as a lieutenant under Sir Edward Cecil at Cádiz in 1625. Made reckless by poverty, and inflamed by the reading of the remonstrance of Parliament against the collection of tonnage and poundage (a tax on wine, wool, etc., imported and exported) by Charles I, he assassinated (Aug. 23, 1628) George Villiers, 1st Duke of Buckingham, who had refused him the command of a company.

Female Patriotism. A tragedy by John D. Burk, published in 1798.

Female Quixote (kē.hō'tẹ), **The.** A novel by Charlotte Lennox, published in 1752. It was intended to ridicule the novels of the romantic school of Gomberville and Scudéry.

Female Quixotism: Exhibited in the Romantic Opinions and Extravagant Adventures of Dorcasina Sheldon (dôr.ka.sī'nạ shel'dọn). A satirical novel by Tabitha Tenney, published in 1801.

feminine rhyme. [Also, **double rhyme.**] A rhyme between words each of which terminates in an unaccented syllable or syllables, as between *very* and *merry*, or between *verily* and *merrily*.

Fenchurch (fen'cḣerch), **the Cripple of.** A cripple, in Thomas Heywood's *Fair Maid of the Exchange*, who performs feats of valor, and with whom the "fair maid" is in love. She is persuaded by him to transfer her affections to a younger and uncrippled man.

Fenella (fe.nel'ạ). [Original name, **Zarah.**] In Scott's novel *Peveril of the Peak*, an elflike creature, attendant on the Countess of Derby. She pretends to be a deaf-mute, and is the illegitimate daughter of Edward Christian.

Fénelon (fän.lôṅ, fā.nẹ-), **François de Salignac de La Mothe-.** b. at Château de Fénelon, Dordogne, France, Aug. 6, 1651; d. at Cambrai, France, Jan. 7, 1715. A French prelate, orator, and author. He studied at the college of Saint Sulpice after 1669, and in 1679 was put in charge of a convent for converted Huguenot women. Probably from this experience he wrote *Traité de l'éducation des filles* (1688), which brought him to the attention of the court through Madame de Maintenon. He was appointed (1689) tutor to the duke of Burgundy, son of the Dauphin, and who later was to be heir apparent to the throne. For the duke he wrote a series of *Fables*, *Dialogues des morts* (imaginary conversations between the shades of heroes of bygone days), and his most famous work, *Télémaque* (published in 1699; a utopian novel, outlining the ideal state, framed on the search of Telemachus for his father, Ulysses).

Fenian Cycle (fē'ni.ạn). [Also, **Finn Cycle.**] A group of heroic and romantic Irish legends of which the 3rd-century Fionn mac Cumhail (Finn MacCool) is the central figure. The exploits of Fionn and his famous warriors, the Fenians or Fianna, are told in detail along with stories of Oisin, his son, and Oscar, his grandson. Among the most famous stories included in the cycle are *The Boy-*

hood Deeds of Fionn, Oisin in the Land of Youth, *The Pursuit of Diarmuid and Grainne*, and the *Colloquy of the Old Men*, which in itself is a collection of tales about Fionn, presented as being told by Oisin to Saint Patrick. Middle and Modern Irish manuscripts dating from the 11th to the 17th century contain the material.

Fenians (fē'ni.ạnz). [Irish, **Fianna** or **Fianna Éireann.**] A modern English form of the Irish name applied to the bands of professional warriors who formed a militia around the high kings of Ireland up to and during the time of Fionn mac Cumhail. They are frequently called Fianna Éireann, meaning "the champions of Ireland." The central figure in the Fenian legends is Fionn mac Cumhail, who figures as Fingal in the spurious Ossianic poems of James Macpherson. The Fenians, while based on historical organized warrior bands of the 2nd and 3rd centuries, have become, with their hero Fionn, the center of a great mass of legends known as the Fenian Cycle.

Fenians (fē'ni.ạnz). [Full name, **Fenian Brotherhood.**] An association of Irish nationalists, founded in New York in 1857 with a view to securing the independence of Ireland. The movement soon spread over the U. S. and Ireland (where it absorbed the previously existing Phoenix Society), and among the Irish population of Great Britain, and several attempts were made at insurrection in Ireland, and at invasion of Canada from the U. S. The association was organized in district clubs called "circles," presided over by "centers," with a "head center" as chief president, and a general "senate": an organization afterward modified in some respects. Between 1863 and 1872 eleven "national congresses" were held by the Fenian Brotherhood in the U. S. after which it continued in existence as a secret society. It was forerunner of the Irish Republican Brotherhood.

Fenn (fen), **George Manville.** b. at Westminster, London, Jan. 3, 1831; d. Aug. 26, 1909. An English author. He contributed numerous sketches and short stories to various magazines, published more than 100 books for boys, and many novels, was editor of *Cassell's Magazine*, and editor and proprietor of *Once a Week*. Among his books are *The Parson o' Dumford* (1879), *Double Cunning* (1886), *This Man's Wife* (1887), *A Crimson Crime* (1899), and *The Cankerworm* (1901).

Fennell (fen'ẹl), **James.** b. Dec. 11, 1766; d. June 14, 1816. An English actor and dramatist. He studied at Trinity College, Cambridge, and at Lincoln's Inn, London, and in 1787 appeared at the Theatre Royal, Edinburgh. He subsequently played at London, and about 1793 emigrated to America. He published *Linda and Clara, or the British Officer* (1791), and an *Apology* for his life (1814).

Fenris (fen'ris). [Also: **Fenrir** (fen'rir), **Fenriswolf**; Old Norse, **Fenrisūlfr.**] In Old Norse mythology, a gigantic wolf, offspring of Loki and the giantess Angurboda (Old Norse, *Angrbodha*), and the brother of the Midgard serpent and the goddess Hel. He was fettered by the gods with a magic cord, but freed himself at Ragnarök and swallowed Odin. He was, in his turn, slain by Vidar, Odin's son.

Fenton (fen'tǫn). In Shakespeare's *Merry Wives of Windsor*, a gentleman in love with Anne Page. He intends to marry her for her money alone, but is won over to true love by her charms.

Fenton, Elijah. b. at Shelton, Staffordshire, England, May 20, 1683; d. in August, 1730. An English poet. He graduated with the degree of B.A. at Jesus College, Cambridge, in 1704, and subsequently was for a time headmaster of the grammar school at Sevenoaks. He assisted Pope in the translation of the *Odyssey*. He wrote a tragedy, *Mariamne* (acted in 1723), in which he was assisted by Southerne.

Fenton, Sir Geoffrey. d. at Dublin, Ireland, Oct. 19, 1608. An English translator and politician. He was for many years principal secretary of state in Ireland, being knighted for his services in this capacity by Queen Elizabeth in 1589. His chief work is a translation of a number of novels from Boaisteau and Belleforest's *Histoires tragiques, extraictes des œuvres italiennes de Bandel* [*Bandello*], published under the title of *Certaine Tragicall Discourses written oute of French and Latine by Geffraie Fenton* (1567).

Feramorz (fer'ạ.mōrz). In Thomas Moore's long poem *Lalla Rookh*, a young poet. He is Aliris, the sultan of Lower Bucharia, who is betrothed to Lalla Rookh. He wins her heart in his disguise, and reveals himself only when she is led into his presence as a bride.

Ferdinand (fėr'di.nand). In Shakespeare's *Tempest*, the son of the King of Naples, and lover of Miranda.

Ferdinand. In John Webster's *Duchess of Malfi*, the count of Calabria and brother of the duchess. He is a cynical villain, who murders his sister after she has injured his family pride.

Ferdinand. In Richard Brinsley Sheridan's *Duenna*, the lover of Clara.

Ferdinand Barnacle (bär'nạ.kl). See under **Barnacle, Lord Decimus Tite.**

Ferdinand, Count Fathom (faᴛʜ'ǫm). [Full title, **The Adventures of Ferdinand, Count Fathom.**] A novel by Tobias Smollett, published in 1753; so called from the name of its hero, who is a repulsive scoundrel. He is the son of a thieving camp follower but is brought up by a count, whom he later betrays, as he does all of his benefactors. He deserts from the army when faced with the probability of actually having to fight in a war. He is entrusted with the care of Monimia, beloved of Renaldo, son of the count, and proceeds to attempt to seduce her. She pretends death to escape him. His repentance at the conclusion of the book is quite unconvincing. At least one episode in the novel (Ferdinand's night lost in a forest) anticipates the later Gothic novel.

Ferdinand, King of Navarre (nạ.vär'). In Shakespeare's *Love's Labour's Lost*, the King of Navarre who wishes to make his court a "little Academe." He, as well as each of his lords, soon breaks his vow to avoid women for three years (he falls in love with the Princess of France shortly after she appears in the play).

Fergus mac Erc (fėr'gus mak ärk'). [Also, **Fergus I.**] A legendary king of Scotland; brother of a king of Ireland in the 5th century. Fergus is said to be the first Irish king of Scotland. His legend is that early in the 6th century he begged the loan of the coronation stone of Ireland (the Lia Fail, a stone which in pagan times always cried out under every lawful king of Ireland who was crowned upon it, but has not cried out since the birth of Christ), His brother sent the stone, and Fergus was crowned. It is said that he never returned it, but that it is the very Stone of Scone which was taken to England by Edward I in 1297, the coronation stone which is now in Westminster Abbey.

Fergus MacIvor (mạk.ē'vǫr). See **MacIvor, Fergus.**

Ferguson (fėr'gu.sǫn), **Adam.** b. at Logierait, Perthshire, Scotland, June 20, 1723; d. at St. Andrews, Scotland, Feb. 22, 1816. A Scottish philosopher and historian. He graduated with the degree of M.A. from the University of St. Andrews in 1742, served as a military chaplain (1745–54), became professor of natural philosophy at Edinburgh University in 1759, and was professor of mental and moral philosophy at the same university (1764–85). In the latter year he became professor of mathematics. He published *Essay on Civil Government* (1766), *Institutes of Moral Philosophy* (1772), *History of the Progress and Termination of the Roman Republic* (1782), and *Principles of Moral and Political Science* (1792).

Ferguson, Robert. [Called "the Plotter."] d. 1714. A Scottish conspirator and political pamphleteer. He removed to England c1655, and was appointed to the living of Godmersham, Kent, from which he was expelled by the Act of Uniformity in 1662. He was concerned in the Rye House plot to assassinate Charles II in 1683, and in 1696 was implicated in a similar conspiracy against William III. He wrote *History of the Revolution* (1706), *Qualifications requisite in a Minister of State* (1710), and others.

Ferguson, Sir Samuel. b. at Belfast, Ireland, March 10, 1810; d. at Howth, County Dublin, Ireland, Aug. 9, 1886. An Irish poet and antiquary. He graduated (B.A., 1826) from Trinity College, Dublin, was admitted to the Irish bar in 1838, served as queen's counsel (1859–67), and was appointed (1867) deputy keeper of public records of Ireland. He was knighted in 1878. He collected all the known Ogham inscriptions of Ireland, and wrote *Lays of the Western Gael* (1865), *Congal, an Epic Poem in Five Books* (1872), *Poems* (1880), and others.

Fergusson (fėr'gu.sǫn), **James.** b. at Ayr, Scotland, Jan. 22, 1808; d. Jan. 9, 1886. A Scottish writer on architecture. He acquired a fortune as a manufacturer of indigo in India, and retired from business to devote himself to archaeological studies. He was general manager of the Crystal Palace Company (1856–58). His chief works are *The Illustrated Handbook of Architecture* . . . (1855), *A History of the Modern Styles of Architecture* (1862), and *Fire- and Serpent-Worship, or Illustrations of Mythology and Art in India in the First and Fourth Centuries after Christ* . . . (1868).

Fergusson, Robert. b. at Edinburgh, Sept. 5, 1750; d. Oct. 16, 1774. A Scottish poet. He studied at St. Andrews University, and became an extracting clerk in the commissary clerk's office at Edinburgh. He published *Poems by R. Fergusson* (1773).

Fermor (fẽr'mọr), **Arabella.** d. 1738. The lady the theft of whose curl was the subject of Pope's *Rape of the Lock.* She was the daughter of James Fermor of Tusmore, and married Francis Perkins of Ufton Court, near Reading. The adventurous nobleman who stole the lock was Lord Petre.

Fermor, Henrietta Louisa. [Title, Countess of Pomfret.] d. Dec. 15, 1761. An English letter writer. She was the daughter of John, 2nd Baron Jeffreys of Wem, Shropshire, and married Thomas Fermor, 2nd Baron Leominster (later Earl of Pomfret), in 1720. Her letters were published in *Correspondence between Frances, Countess of Hartford (afterward Duchess of Somerset), and Henrietta Louisa, Countess of Pomfret, between . . . 1738 and 1741* (1805).

Fernando (fẽr.nan'dō). In Massinger and Fletcher's comedy *The Laws of Candy,* the lover of Annophel.

Fernando. In Southerne's *Fatal Marriage,* a character who for his own good is made to believe he has been dead and buried and in purgatory.

Fernando. In J. Sheridan Knowles's *John of Procida,* the son of John of Procida. He is killed in the bloody uprising known as the Sicilian Vespers.

Fernandyne (fẽr'nan.dēn). In Thomas Lodge's *Rosalynde,* the character from which Jaques de Boys in Shakespeare's *As You Like It* is taken.

Ferneze (fär.nād'zā). A debauched courtier in John Marston's *The Malcontent.* He is the lover of Aurelia, the wife of the usurping duke, Pietro.

Fern Hill. A poem (1943) by Dylan Thomas, inspired by the poet's memories of his youth in the country, and representing an effort to recapture the feeling he then often had of joyful identity with all that was around him. He is able to see a parallel between the newness of the look of the farm and the country in the early morning and the newness of the world on the day of creation:

And then to awaken and the farm, like a wanderer
  white
With the dew, come back, the cock on his shoulder:
  it was all
Shining, it was Adam and maiden,
    The sky gathered again
And the sun grew round that very day.

Ferolo Whiskerandos (fẹ.rō'lō hwis.kẽr.an'dōz), **Don.** See **Whiskerandos, Don Ferolo.**

Feronia (fẹ.rō'ni.ạ). An Etrurian goddess of Sabine origin: patroness of freedmen. Her chief shrine is at the foot of Mount Soracte.

Ferracute (fer'ạ.kūt) or **Ferragus** (fer'ạ.gus). A giant in medieval romance, famous for his possession of a bronze head which answers every question put to it.

Ferragus (fe.rà.güs). An extraordinary beggar in a novel of the same name in Honoré de Balzac's *Scènes de la vie parisienne.* He is the captain of a mysterious association called "Les Treize," appears in society as a diplomat, and murders a young gentleman, who is obnoxious to the Treize, by causing a slow poison to be put on his hair.

Ferrar (fer'ạr), **Nicholas.** d. at Little Gidding, Huntingdonshire, England, Dec. 4, 1637. An English theologian.

Ferrars (fer'ạrz), **Edward.** A young man who loves Elinor Dashwood, although he is engaged to the selfish Lucy Steele, in Jane Austen's novel *Sense and Sensibility.*

Ferrers (fer'ẽrz), **George.** b. at St. Albans, Hertfordshire, England, c1500; d. in January, 1579. An English poet and politician. He was educated at Cambridge, was a member of Lincoln's Inn, and represented (1542 *et seq.*) Plymouth in Parliament. Upon his arrest (1542) as surety for a debt, the House of Commons demanded his release by virtue of the constitutional right of its members to freedom from arrest (except for treason, felony, or breach of the peace). When the sheriffs and jailers resisted the demand, the House of Commons sent them to the Tower, this being the first occasion on which the house acted independently in vindication of its privilege. Ferrers took part with W. Baldwin in the production of the series of historical poems entitled *Mirrour for Magistrates.*

Ferret (fer'ẹt). In Ben Jonson's comedy *The New Inn,* the servant of Lovel: a quick, nimble, and insinuating fellow, with a perceptive knowledge of human nature.

Ferret. In Tobias Smollett's novel *Sir Launcelot Greaves,* a character who never smiles, never speaks in praise of anyone, and never gives a direct answer.

Ferrex and Porrex (fer'iks; por'iks). See under **Gorboduc.**

Ferrier (fer'i.ẽr), **James Frederick.** b. at Edinburgh, June 16, 1808; d. at St. Andrews, Scotland, June 11, 1864. A Scottish metaphysician. He studied at Edinburgh and Oxford, and was professor of civil history at Edinburgh (1842 *et seq.*) and of moral philosophy and political economy at St. Andrews (1845 *et seq.*). He wrote *Institutes of Metaphysic* (1854) and others. His *Lectures on Greek Philosophy* were published posthumously (1866).

Ferrier, Susan Edmonstone. b. at Edinburgh, Sept. 7, 1782; d. there, Nov. 5, 1854. A Scottish novelist. She was a friend of Sir Walter Scott, whom she visited in 1811, 1829, and 1831. Her chief works are *Marriage* (1818), to which Miss Clavering, niece of the duke of Argyll, contributed a few pages, *The Inheritance* (1824), and *Destiny* (1831).

Ferrovius (fẹ.rō'vi.us). In Shaw's *Androcles and the Lion,* the great brute of a man who unsuccessfully tries to practice Christian forbearance.

Ferumbras (fẽr.um'brạs). [French, **Fierabras.**] The hero of a group of Middle English verse romances in the Charlemagne cycle, all based on French *chansons de geste.* He is portrayed as a formidable Saracen knight (20 feet high, in one account) who aids his father, the sultan of Babylon, in the sacking of Rome and the subsequent transfer of various holy relics from Rome to Spain. Charlemagne leads his army into Spain to recover the relics, and Ferumbras is defeated in single combat by the French knight Oliver, friend of Roland. Ferumbras thereupon becomes a Christian, and fights from that time forward under the banner of Charlemagne. Oliver is captured by the Saracens and, with various companions, befriended by Floripas, beautiful sister of Ferumbras, who is disposed kindly toward the Christian cause because of her love for one of Charlemagne's knights. With the help of Floripas, in the Saracen camp, and of Ferumbras, now one of Charlemagne's most stalwart knights, the Saracens are finally routed and the relics recovered. A version of the complete story may be found in *The Sowdone of Babylone;* the best account of the portion of the story that starts with the arrival of Ferumbras in Spain is generally considered to be that in *Sir Ferumbras.*

Ferumbras, Sir. See **Sir Ferumbras.**

Fescennine Verses or **Songs** (fes′e̩.nīn, -nin). Ancient Roman popular verses or songs: so named from Fescennia in southern Etruria. They were recited or sung at rustic merrymakings, and especially at popular harvest festivals.

Fesole (fā′zō̩.lä). The spelling under which Milton refers in *Paradise Lost* to the Italian town of Fiesole, near Florence.

Feste (fes′te̩). In Shakespeare's *Twelfth Night,* Olivia's clown. He takes part in the baiting of Malvolio, pretending to be Sir Topas, who treats Malvolio as a lunatic. He sings the well-known songs "O mistress mine," "Come away, come away, death," and "When that I was and a little tiny boy."

Festial (fes′ti.a̩l). A prose collection of sermons from the Middle English period by John Mirk.

Festus (fes′tus). A poem by Philip James Bailey, published in 1839.

Festus, Porcius. fl. 1st century A.D. A Roman procurator in Palestine c60–62 A.D. He refused to put the apostle Paul in the power of the Jews, and, after a hearing in which Paul in the presence of Herod Agrippa II stood on his rights as a Roman citizen, sent him to Caesar at Rome.

Fetter Lane (fet′ėr). A street in London running from Fleet Street to Holborn. It became known as the spot where Edmund Waller's plot (1643) to seize London for Charles I terminated disastrously. Dryden and Otway, it is said, lived opposite each other in Fetter Lane.

feudal system. A system of political organization with reference to the tenure of land and to military service and allegiance prevalent in Europe in the Middle Ages. Its main peculiarity was that the bulk of the land was divided into feuds or fiefs, held by their owners on condition of the performance of certain duties, especially military services, to a superior lord, who, on default of such performance, could reclaim the land. This superior might be either the sovereign, or some subject who thus held of the sovereign, and in turn had created the fief by subinfeudation. According to the pure feudal system, the lord was entitled to the fealty of his tenants, but not to that of their subtenants, every man looking only to his immediate lord. On the continent of Europe, while the system was in full operation, this principle made the great lords practically independent of their nominal sovereigns, who could command their allegiance only through their self-interest or by superior force; and therefore kings were often powerless against their vassals. In England, however, the sovereign was always entitled to the fealty of all his subjects. Feudal tenures were abolished in England by act

of Parliament in 1660, in Scotland in 1747, and in France at the revolution of 1789.

Feverel (fev′e̩.rel), **Richard.** The hero of Meredith's novel *The Ordeal of Richard Feverel.* He is the victim of a dogmatic father's attempt to rear him by a "system."

Fez (fez), **King of.** A noble savage in Thomas Heywood's two-part play *The Fair Maid of the West.* He helps Bess Bridges to be reunited with her long-lost lover, Captain Spencer, although he is charmed by her himself. In the second part of the play his nobility is somewhat tarnished when, lustfulness awakened, he attempts to separate her from her husband, first on her wedding night and then by threatening to execute Spencer unless she is yielded to him. However, when Bess, Goodlack, and another friend of Spencer's come from their ship, in which they had planned to escape, to offer their heads for Spencer's life, the King is so touched that he allows all to go free and adds a dowry for Bess.

Fezziwig (fez′i.wig). The name of a family in Charles Dickens's *Christmas Carol.* It comprises a jolly old father, a mother ("one vast substantial smile"), and three fair daughters.

Fiacre (fyåkr), **Saint.** d. c670. An Irish monk who lived for years in France. He is the patron saint of gardeners.

Fiammeta (fyäm.mät′tä). A fictitious name given by Giovanni Boccaccio in some of his works (*Elegy of Madonna Fiammetta,* and others) to Maria d'Aquino, natural daughter of King Robert of Naples, a lady courted by the Italian novelist in early years (c1335–40) spent in that city.

Fichte (fich′te̩), **Johann Gottlieb.** b. at Rammenau, near Kamenz, Germany, May 19, 1762; d. at Berlin, Jan. 27, 1814. A German metaphysical philosopher. The son of a poor weaver, he nevertheless secured a good education at the universities of Jena and Leipzig. Supporting himself by tutoring, he continued his studies in philosophy, especially the works and theories of Immanuel Kant. His first published philosophical work, *Kritik aller Offenbarung* (Critique of All Revelation, 1792), which was at first thought by some readers to be from the pen of Kant himself, and which was praised by Kant, established his reputation and led to his taking the chair of philosophy at Jena in 1793. In the following year appeared his principal work, *Grundlage der gesammten Wissenschaftslehre* (Fundamental Principles of the Whole Theory of Science). Under charges of atheism he left Jena in 1799, going to Berlin where he remained, except for two short periods, the rest of his days, being in his last years (1810–12) rector of the University of Berlin. The turmoils, divisions, and hardships of the German people at that time turned his thoughts chiefly to political and patriotic issues, and his celebrated *Reden an die deutsche Nation* (Addresses to the German Nation), delivered in the winter of 1807–08, made him a leader of the nationalist and liberal causes and one of the great voices of their hopes and purposes. Later generations indeed have tended to think of Fichte more as a patriot and a political liberal than as a philosopher. Fichte, rejecting Kant's concept of things-in-themselves, beyond human cognition, made the conscious ego the starting point of knowledge of the nature of the universe, and by idealistic dialectic arrived at the concept of God as an absolute ego originating and embracing all knowledge. His works, edited by his son, Immanuel Hermann von Fichte, were published in eight volumes (1845–46).

fiction. Novels, short stories, and other writings that tell about imaginary people and events, and whose primary purpose is to entertain, in contrast to biography and history which tell of real people and events and whose primary purpose is to inform. Borderline forms are the historical novel and the fictional biography, in which there is a mingling of fact and invention, and in which the writer's object is both to inform and to entertain. Prose fiction is a comparatively new form in literature, requiring a literate public as the spoken forms of drama and poetry originally did not. Partly for this reason, it was not until about 1600 that prose fiction became popular in England, although by that date drama and poetry had come into full flower. In the words of Joseph Conrad, one of the greatest fiction writers in the English language, the purpose of fiction should be "to arrest, for the space of a breath, the hands busy about the work of the earth, and compel men entranced by the sight of distant goals to glance for a moment at the surrounding vision of form and color, of sunshine and shadows; to make them pause for a look, for a sigh, for a smile. . . ."

Fidele (fi.dē′lē, fi.dāl′). In Shakespeare's *Cymbeline*, the name assumed by Imogen, when disguised as a boy.

Fidelia (fi.dē′li.ạ). In Wycherley's *Plain Dealer*, a young girl disguised as a boy, Fidelio, who follows Manly. She is similar to Viola in Shakespeare's *Twelfth Night*.

Fidelia. The foundling in Edward Moore's play *The Foundling*.

Fidelio (fē.dā′lē.ō, fi.dā′li.ō). [Full title, **Fidelio oder die eheliche Liebe;** Eng. trans., "*Fidelio, or Conjugal Love.*"] An opera in two acts by Beethoven, with a libretto by Sonnleithner and Treitschke, first produced at Vienna on Nov. 20, 1805. It was Beethoven's only opera, and was several times altered by him. The words were adapted from Jean Nicolas Bouilly's comic opera *Léonore, ou l'amour conjugal.*

Field (fēld), **Inspector.** A shrewd detective officer in Charles Dickens's *On Duty with Inspector Field*, taken from life.

Field, Michael. The joint pseudonym of **Bradley, Katherine Harris,** and **Cooper, Edith Emma.**

Field, Nathaniel (or **Nathan**). b. in the parish of St. Giles, Cripplegate, London, 1587; date of death unknown. An English actor and occasional playwright. He is chiefly remembered as the author of *A Woman is a Weathercock* (acted c1609 and printed in 1612) and *Amends for Ladies* (acted c1615 and printed in 1618), probably intended with its character of Moll Cutpurse to challenge Dekker and Middleton's very successful *Roaring Girl*, and as the joint author with Massinger of *The Fatal Dowry* (1632). He was the son of John Field, a preacher (and, curiously enough, one of those who censured the stage). It was his brother

who was apprenticed to a stationer (printer) in 1596, and published on his own between 1624 and 1627. He has been widely confused with this brother. He was impressed by Nathaniel Giles, master of the Children of the Chapel, to serve this company while he was still at St. Paul's Grammar School (c1600). Ben Jonson must have continued his education, since he recorded that he had read Latin classics with him. Jonson complimented him in *Bartholomew Fair* as an actor, but his work apparently did not spare him financial embarrassment because Henslowe occasionally had to save him from arrest for debt. In 1615 he joined the King's Men, appearing in *The Loyal Subject* (by Fletcher) and *Bussy D'Ambois* (by Chapman), as well as various other popular plays. In 1619 he apparently left this company, since his name disappears from the livery lists after that year. Nothing is known about his later life and the entry of the death of a Nathaniel Field on Feb. 20, 1633, in the register of Blackfriars Parish is probably that of his brother. It has been conjectured that he collaborated on some of the Beaumont and Fletcher plays.

Fielding (fēl′ding), **A. E.** The name used by a popular writer of detective fiction since 1924. The real name of this person is unknown, but is now supposed to be Dorothy Feilding, of Kensington, London. The best-known character created by Fielding is Inspector Pointer of Scotland Yard.

Fielding, Henry. b. at Sharpham Park, Glastonbury, Somersetshire, England, April 22, 1707; d. at Lisbon, Portugal, Oct. 8, 1754. An English novelist, dramatist, essayist, and barrister. He was educated at Eton, at the University of Leiden, and at the Middle Temple, in London. He was called to the bar in 1740, and was appointed justice of the peace for Westminster in 1748. In 1734, on November 28, he married Charlotte Cradock, who appears as Sophia in *Tom Jones* and as Amelia in the novel of that name, a story that Johnson "read through without stopping." Her death in 1743 was such a shock to him that his friends were afraid he might lose his mind, but on Nov. 27, 1747, he married Mary Daniel (or MacDaniel or MacDonald), who had been his wife's maid. She bore him two sons and three daughters, and died at Canterbury, on March 11, 1802. In March, 1753, if not earlier, it was clear that he was a sick man and that he could not live long. In 1749 he was attacked by gout and fever, both of which troubled him intermittently for the rest of his life. The keenness he showed as a novelist in portraying character and on the bench in punishing wrongdoers seems to have deserted him when he came to consider his own physical condition, which was caused, partially, by the careless living not uncommon among members of the English upper middle class in his day. He was constantly taking pills, powders, drops, and waters for his illnesses, and he seems to have had a weakness for consulting men who were quacks rather than reliable, scientific physicians. In March, 1754, he was dangerously ill, suffering from the cold of winter, and it was thought that a warmer climate might help, if not save, him. A few months later he left England for Lisbon on the *Queen of Portugal*. He arrived in August, but it was too late. His spirit

ḍ, d or j; ṣ, s or sh; ṭ, t or ch; ẓ, z or zh; o, F. cloche; ü, F. menu; ċh, Sc. loch; ṅ, F. bonbon.

was strong, and he kept until the end the humor he shows in his works, but his body was weak, and he died after a stay of two months. Fielding is regarded as one of the great novelists of the 18th century, and would rank as a master of narrative in any century. With Richardson, Smollett, and Sterne, he is one of "the Big Four" in the history of the 18th-century English novel. His four main works, on which his reputation chiefly rests, are *The History of the Adventures of Joseph Andrews and his Friend, Mr. Abraham Adams* (Feb. 22, 1742), generally called by the short title of *Joseph Andrews*, which began as a parody on Richardson's *Pamela; The Life of Mr. Jonathan Wild the Great* (1743), a satirical treatment of the life and character of a criminal; *The History of Tom Jones, a Foundling* (February, 1749, and two other editions in the same year on April 13, one in six, the other in four volumes), considered by some to be the greatest novel ever written; and *Amelia* (Dec. 18, 1751), in which the character of Captain Booth is a portrait of the author. Fielding is rarely thought of as a dramatist, and his work in that field is usually disregarded, not being included in collections that are called his "Complete Works," but three large volumes are needed for his plays. They include *Love in Several Masques* (1728), *The Temple Beau* (1730), *Rape Upon Rape, or the Justice Caught in His Own Trap* (1730), and *The Tragedy of Tragedies, or the Life and Death of Tom Thumb the Great* (1730), with such characters as King Arthur, a passionate sort of king, Lord Grizzle, Noodle, Doodle, and Foodle, courtiers, Queen Dollallolla, Arthur's wife, in love with Tom, her daughter Princess Huncamunca, in love with Tom and Grizzle and anxious to marry both, Glumdalca, a captive queen, loved by King Arthur but in love with Tom, and the title character, Tom Thumb, a little hero with a great soul. This burlesque of the dramatists of his day is remembered chiefly, if not solely, for its famous line, "O Huncamunca, Huncamunca O!," a parody of James Thomson's "O Sophonisba, Sophonisba O!" in the tragedy *Sophonisba*. Other plays are *The Letter Writers, or a New Way to Keep a Wife at Home* (1731), a three-act farce, *The Lottery* (1731), *The Grub Street Opera*, *The Modern Husband* (1731), *The Covent Garden Tragedy* (1731), which is not a tragedy, *The Debauchees, or the Jesuit Caught* (1732), *The Mock Doctor, or the Dumb Lady Cured* (1732), derived from Molière, *The Miser* (1732), derived from Plautus and Molière, *The Intriguing Chambermaid* (1733), in two acts, *Don Quixote in England* (1733), dedicated to Chesterfield, *An Old Man Taught Wisdom, or the Virgin Unmasked* (1734), *Pasquin* (1736), a dramatic satire on the times, being the Rehearsal of Two Plays, a Comedy, called *The Election*, and a Tragedy, called *The Life and Death of Common-Sense* (1736), *The Historical Register for the Year 1736* (acted at the London Haymarket in May, 1737), *Eurydice*, a farce, *Eurydice Hissed, or a Word to the Wise, Miss Lucy in Town*, a sequel to *An Old Man Taught Wisdom*, *The Wedding-Day*, and *The Fathers, or the Good-Natured Man*. As a prose essayist he wrote *The Covent-Garden Journal* (Jan. 4–Nov. 11, 1752), 70 periodical essays, *The True Patriot* (Nov. 5, 1745–April 15, 1746), 24 essays, *Of the Remedy of Afflic-*

tion for the Loss of Our Friends, A Dialogue between Alexander the Great and Diogenes the Cynic, On Conversation, An Essay on the Knowledge of the Characters of Men, An Essay on Nothing, A Clear State of the Case of Elizabeth Canning* (1753), one of his best-known pieces in this field, dealing with a sensational mystery of the day, in which all London was divided into two camps, those for and those against Elizabeth Canning, and another paper on a controversial affair, *A True State of the Case of Bosavern Penlez, Who Suffered on Account of the Late Riot in the Strand, in which the Law Regarding these Offences and the Statute of George I, commonly called the Riot Act, are Fully Considered* (1749). *The Journal of a Voyage to Lisbon* (published 1755) is an autobiographical record. *A Charge Delivered to the Grand Jury at the Sessions of the Peace Held for the City and Liberty of Westminster* (June 29, 1749) and *An Inquiry into the Causes of the Late Increase of Robbers, &c. with Some Proposals for Remedying this Growing Evil* (1751), in 11 sections, are legal papers. *A Fragment of a Comment on Lord Bolingbroke's Essays* (published 1755) is an unfinished work as the title indicates. His prefaces to his novels are of value to students of this type of fiction, revealing as they do the critical principles and standards he followed. His verse is not now generally regarded as worthy of serious critical study. Some of his poems are *Of True Greatness* (to George Dodington), *Of Good-Nature* (to the duke of Richmond), *Liberty* (to Lyttelton), *To a Friend on the Choice of a Wife, The Beggar*, a song, epigrams, epitaphs, and several short pieces to a Celia. He also translated part of Juvenal's *Sixth Satire* into burlesque verse. His novels are known all over the world, *Tom Jones* having been translated into French, German, Russian, Spanish, Swedish, and Dutch, and having been made into a motion picture, a play, and a comic opera. As *Sophia* it was dramatized in 1886 by Robert Buchanan, and *Joseph Andrews* appeared on the stage as *Joseph's Sweetheart* (1888).

Fielding, May. A character in Charles Dickens's tale *The Cricket on the Hearth*, who is a friend of Mrs. Peerybingle.

Fielding, Mrs. In Charles Dickens's tale *The Cricket on the Hearth*, May Fielding's mother.

Fielding, Sarah. b. at East Stour, Dorsetshire, England, Nov. 8, 1710; d. at Bath, England, 1768. An English author; sister of Henry Fielding. Among her works are a romance, *The Adventures of David Simple in Search of a Real Friend* (1744) and a translation of Xenophon's *Memoirs of Socrates: with the Defense of Socrates before his Judges* (1772).

Field of the Cloth of Gold. A plain near Ardres, in the department of Pas-de-Calais, N France, the scene of an inconclusive diplomatic meeting between Francis I of France and Henry VIII of England, in June, 1520. It was so called from the magnificence of the display.

Field of the Forty Footsteps. Fields which formerly lay behind Montagu House, London. From c1680 until toward the end of the 18th century they were the scenes of robbery, murder, and every species of depravity. In one portion there was an area where, according to tradition, grass would not grow, supposedly on the spots trodden by two brothers who killed each other in a duel.

Field of Waterloo, The. A romance in verse (1815) by Scott.

Fierabras (fye.rà.brà). [English, Sir **Ferumbras.**] One of the paladins of Charlemagne. He gave his name to the most popular of the French Charlemagne romances.

Fife (fīf), **Thane of.** See **Macduff.**

Fifine at the Fair (fē.fēn'). A poem by Robert Browning, published in 1872.

Fifth Monarchy Men. A sect of millenarians of the time of Cromwell, differing from other Second-Adventists in believing not only in a literal second coming of Christ, but also that it was their duty to inaugurate this kingdom by force. This kingdom was to be the fifth and last in the series of which those of Assyria, Persia, Greece, and Rome were the preceding four; hence their self-assumed title. They unsuccessfully attempted risings against the government in 1657 and 1661.

Figaro (fē'gạ.rō). A character introduced by Beaumarchais in his plays *Le Barbier de Seville, Le Mariage de Figaro,* and *La Mère coupable;* used later by Mozart, Paisiello, and Rossini in operas. In the *Barbier* he is a barber; in the *Mariage* he is a valet. In both he is gay, lively, and courageous; his stratagems are always original, his lies witty, and his shrewdness proverbial. He typifies intrigue, adroitness, and versatility. In the *Mère coupable* he has become virtuous and has lost his verve. He also appears in Holcroft's *Follies of a Day,* taken from Beaumarchais's *Mariage de Figaro.*

Fig for Momus (mō'mus), **A.** A collection of satires by Thomas Lodge, printed in 1595.

Figgis (fig'is), **Darrell.** [Pseudonym, **Michael Ireland.**] b. 1882; d. 1925. An Irish poet and novelist, a follower of George Russell (Æ). His writings include *A Vision of Life* (1909) and *Æ, a Study* (1916).

Fight at Finnsburg (finz'bėrg), **The.** See **Finnsburg.**

Fighting by Proxy. See under **Duellists, The.**

Figure in the Carpet, The. A tale by Henry James, published in the collection *Embarrassments* (1896).

Filer (fī'lėr), **Mr.** A middle-aged gentleman in Charles Dickens's tale *The Chimes.* He is a friend of Alderman Cute.

Filmer (fil'mėr), **Sir Robert.** d. May 26, 1653. An English Royalist political writer. He was knighted by Charles I. His *Patriarcha, or the Natural Power of Kings Asserted* (1680) was criticized sharply by Locke, as were Filmer's writings on witchcraft and usury.

Filostrato (fē.lôs'trä.tō), **Il.** A narrative poem by Boccaccio. It was written in 1344, and is the chief source of Chaucer's *Troilus and Criseyde,* some of which is a literal translation.

"Finality John." Nickname of **Russell,** Lord **John.**

Finch (finch), **Anne.** [Title, Countess of **Winchilsea.**] d. Aug. 5, 1720. An English poet. She was celebrated by Pope under the name of Ardelia. She wrote a poem, *Spleen* (1701, republished, 1709, as *The Spleen, a Pindarique Ode*), and *Miscellany Poems* (1713).

Finch, Sir **Henry.** b. 1558; d. 1625. An English legal writer. Author of important treatise in French on common law (1613), published (1627) in English as *Law, or a Discourse thereof in Four Books;* treatment of common law superseded only by Blackstone, jurisprudence only by Austin. With Bacon, Noy, and others, sought unsuccessfully to codify statute laws. *The World's Great Restauration* (1621) brought him the charge of libel and subsequent arrest by King James I; to obtain liberty, Finch disavowed much of the work.

Finching (fin'ching), **Flora.** [Maiden name, **Casby.**] In Dickens's novel *Little Dorrit,* a woman loved during her youth by Arthur Clennam. When Arthur returns to England from China he finds her "very broad . . . and short of breath; but that was not much. Flora, who had seemed enchanting in all she said and thought, was diffuse and silly. That was much." It is now generally agreed that this characterization is based on that of Maria Beadnell, Dickens's first love, in later life; as various of the novelist's biographers have pointed out, the Maria Beadnell whom Dickens met as a married woman in early middle age shocked him deeply by the change he saw in the person of his romantic memory.

fin de siècle (fań dė syekl). The end of the century: used attributively of anything that exhibits certain characteristics supposed to mark the closing years of the 19th century, regarded as a period of emancipation from the traditional social and moral order.

Findlater (fin'lạ.tėr), **Andrew.** b. at Aberdour, Aberdeenshire, Scotland, in December, 1810; d. at Edinburgh, Jan. 1, 1885. A Scottish literary writer. He was the editor of the earlier editions of *Chambers's Encyclopaedia.*

Findlater, Jane Helen. b. at Edinburgh, 1866—. A Scottish novelist and short-story writer. She is the author of *The Green Graves of Balgowrie* (1896), *A Daughter of Strife* (1897), *Rachel* (1899), *The Story of a Mother* (1902), *Stones from a Glass House* (1904), and *The Ladder to the Stars* (1904). With her sister, Mary (1865—), also a novelist of Scottish life, she wrote *Tales that are Told* (1901), short stories, *Crossriggs* (1908), and *Penny Moneypenny* (1911).

Findlay (find'li, fin'li), **John Ritchie.** b. at Arbroath, Scotland, Oct. 21, 1824; d. at Aberlour, Banffshire, Scotland, Oct. 16, 1898. A Scottish newspaper publisher and philanthropist. Educated at Edinburgh University, he was associated (1842 et seq.) with *The Scotsman,* a newspaper, as employee, editor, partner, and owner. He is remembered chiefly for his gift of 70 thousand pounds establishing the Scottish National Portrait Gallery, which was opened at Edinburgh on July 15, 1889. Interested in health, education, and social and economic problems, Findlay helped many worthy causes.

Fine-Ear (fīn'ir''). In the fairy tale of Fortunio, an attendant with so acute an ear that he could hear the grass grow.

Fingal (fing'gạl). The hero of the poems "Fingal" and "Temora" in the spurious *Poems of Ossian,* in six books, by James Macpherson, published in

1760 and 1762. Fingal is based on the legendary Irish hero, Fionn mac Cumhail. Macpherson claimed the poems to be authentic translations of poems by Ossian, Fingal's son, who in turn was based on Oisin, the son of Fionn mac Cumhail, but they are not translations of any text.

Fingal's Cave (fing'gạlz). A basaltic grotto in the island of Staffa, in the Inner Hebrides, W Scotland, in Argyllshire ab. 33 mi. W of Oban, and ab. 8 mi. W of the island of Mull. It figures in Sir Walter Scott's *Lord of the Isles*. The cave may be entered at low tide by an arch 65 ft. in height. Length of the cave, ab. 200 ft.

Finlay (fin'lạ), **George.** b. at Faversham, Kent, England, Dec. 21, 1799; d. at Athens, Greece, Jan. 26, 1875. An English historian. He joined Byron in Cephalonia, and for a time devoted himself to the Greek cause. He resided long in Greece, and his life was spent in the study of Greek history. He published *Greece under the Romans* (1844), *Greece to its Conquest by the Turks* (1851), *Greece under Ottoman and Venetian Domination* (1856), and *The Greek Revolution* (1861), which were combined (1877) under the title *A History of Greece from its Conquest by the Romans to the Present Time* (edited by H. F. Tozer).

Finlay, John. b. at Glasgow, in December, 1782; d. at Moffat, Dumfriesshire, Scotland, Dec. 8, 1810. A Scottish poet and prose writer. He published *Scottish Historical and Romantic Ballads* (1808), a life of Cervantes, and an edition of Adam Smith's *Wealth of Nations*.

Finn (fin). See **Fionn.**

Finn Cycle. See **Fenian Cycle.**

Finnegans Wake (fin'ẹ.gạnz). A novel by James Joyce, published in 1939. This is Joyce's last work, and it took him 17 years to complete. It deals with the subconscious life of H. C. Earwicker, a keeper of a public house in Dublin, during one Saturday night's dream. Tim Finnegan is a symbol used many times through the book; he was the central figure in an old ballad, who was killed while working in the fields, but he is miraculously resurrected at his own wake. Joyce draws from many fields of knowledge to illustrate his ideas of cyclical history (Giambattista Vico), the universal conflict of opposites (Bruno), theories of sex desires and dreams (Freud), and religious life (Saint Patrick, Adam, Lucifer). Using the dreams of Earwicker as the basic structure, Joyce portrays the entire history of civilization, of philosophical thought, and of religious feeling. He employs the use of much allegory, many foreign languages and unknown dialects, and portmanteau words; this was a great source of confusion to many readers before scholars began serious study of the work. The dreamer takes on the form of many famous men of history in order to show their ideas. These include Tristan, Jonathan Swift, Oliver Cromwell, and Adam. His wife is Maggie, who appears as Anna Livia Plurabelle in one of the most famous sequences. The first section takes place in Phoenix Park at Dublin, where Earwicker goes through a trial scene and the female symbol is introduced in the form of the rhythm of rivers. The second section takes place in Chapelizod, and the romance of Tristan and

Isolde plays a major part. Section three is on the hill of Howth, the male symbol, and a sermon is preached on chastity. The family of Earwicker begins to awaken, and each member is described. Section four is a soliloquy by Maggie (Anna Livia Plurabelle), whose last sentence is cut off, but is found at the beginning of the work. This sentence represents the cyclical theory of the development of civilization, propounded by Vico.

Finnsburg (finz'bẻrg). [Also: **Finsburh** (fins'bủrch), **Finnsburgh, Finn's Borough;** full title, **The Fight at Finnsburg.**] An Old English poem of uncertain but early date, surviving in fragmentary form: 47 lines (including two half lines) out of a presumed 300 or thereabouts. It is the only surviving example of a genre which flourished in English courtly circles from the 6th to the 11th century: short narrative poems dealing with events of the Germanic heroic age, the great migration period which came to an end in the 6th century. The extant fragment tells of a fight between the Danes, under the leadership of Hnaef, and the Frisians, under the leadership of Finn, and later of his wife Hildeburh (sister of Hnaef), the death of Hnaef, the temporary treaty, and the final siege in which the Danes under Hengist are victorious, and Hildeburh and the Frisian treasure are carried back to the land of the Danes. This story is mentioned in *Beowulf* as being the subject of a "gleeman's song" and is partly recounted there.

Finsbury (finz'bẻr.i). A metropolitan borough in C London, in the County of London, situated immediately N of the City of London, ab. 3 mi. N of King's Cross station. The areas of the borough on the S boundary adjoining the City of London suffered severely from aerial bombardment during World War II. The district was once the great prebendal manor of Holywell, and was leased by its incumbent in 1315 to the mayor and commonalty of the city for an annual rent of 20 shillings; this lease ran out in 1867. It became a shooting field in 1498. In Jonson's time it had become a resort of the common people and was avoided by people of fashion. Both Jonson and Shakespeare made reference to it in their writings.

Finsbury Park. A London park of 120 acres, on the old grounds of Hornsey Wood House.

Fiona Macleod (fī.ō'nạ mạ.kloud'). Pseudonym of **Sharp, William.**

Fionnauala (fē'ạ.nạ.wä''lạ). A character in Irish legend, the daughter of Lir. She was transformed into a swan and doomed to wander over Ireland until Christianity should arrive. Thomas Moore made her the subject of one of his *Irish Melodies.*

Fionn mac Cumhail (fin mạ.kōl'). [Also: **Finn mac Cumhail, Finn MacCool.**] A legendary hero of Ireland, hero of the Fenian Cycle, chief of the Fenians, and now believed to have an actual historical 3rd-century basis. Both Fionn and his warriors were famous for their great stature, prodigious strength, fearlessness, generosity, and remarkable deeds. The boy Fionn was educated in the forest by a learned poet. His great wisdom came from his unwittingly tasting the salmon of knowledge which fed on the hazelnuts of wisdom. His story consists of a series of adventures with giants and hags as well as exploits in the service of the high king at Tara, for whom he organized the Fenians or Fianna. Fionn had two great love stories: his first wife was Sadb, mother of his son Oisin, who was born in the forest while Sadb was under enchantment as a deer; his second wife was Grainne, who seduced and eloped with Fionn's kinsman, Diarmuid. *The Pursuit of Diarmuid and Grainne* is the longest and most famous of all the stories about Fionn mac Cumhail.

Firbank (fèr′bangk), **Ronald.** [Full name, **Arthur Annesley Ronald Firbank.**] b. at London, 1886; d. at Rome, May 21, 1926. An English novelist, dramatist, and essayist. He studied at Trinity Hall, Cambridge, and traveled in Cuba, France, Spain, Egypt, and Italy. His works include *Odette D'Antreverues* and *A Study in Temperament* (both 1905), *Odette, a Fairy Tale for Weary People* (1916), *Valmouth* (1919), *The Princess Zoubaroff* (1920), *The Flower Beneath the Foot* (1923), and *Prancing Nigger* (1924; published in England as *Sorrow in Sunlight*).

Firbolgs (fir′bōlgz). A mythical prehistoric people of Ireland. One story is that they were defeated and expelled by the Fomorians, but the more common story is that they were driven out by the Tuatha De Danann (the gods or divine race of Ireland), who were the fourth of the five invading hosts of Ireland. After their defeat the Firbolgs took refuge with the Fomorians in the Isle of Man, Islay, and Rathlin. The short, dark people of these islands are thought to be their descendants.

Firdausi (fir.dou′sē). [Also: **Ferdus, Firdousi, Firdusi;** pseudonym of **Abul Kasim** (or **Qasim**) **Mansur** (or **Hasan**).] b. near Tus, Kurasan (now in Iran), c941 A.D.; d. at Tus, 1020 A.D. A Persian poet; author of the *Shahnamah* (*Book of Kings*), the Persian national epic, narrating the history and legends of Persia down to the fall (641) of the Sassanids. According to the usual version of his life story (much of it probably legendary), he was born to a family settled on the land for many years and early dedicated himself to compose a historical poem on his country's great past. He obtained a copy of such a work begun under the Sassanids before 650 and rendered some of it into verse. His historical and poetical knowledge brought him to the attention of the sultan of Ghazi, who assigned the work of compiling and writing the history to the poet, to whom he gave the name Firdausi (from Firdus, "paradise," in honor of his metrical skill). Jealousy, especially that of the court treasurer, made life miserable for Firdausi, despite the sultan's offer of one thousand gold pieces for every one thousand verses; the poet preferred to let the money accumulate so that he might eventually use it for irrigation work near his home city. Only gifts from other princes in honor of his work saved him from living in absolute penury. In 1011, after 35 years of composition, he completed his epic, in 60,000 couplets. He sent it to the sultan and received (thanks to the treasurer's machinations) only 60,000 silver pieces. Firdausi, in anger and scorn, gave one third to the messenger, one third to the keeper of the bath he was enjoying when the reward arrived, and spent the other third on a glass of beer. When the sultan heard of this he was en-

raged and threatened to have the poet's life, but Firdausi calmed him next morning. Then he quit the court, leaving for the sultan's perusal a bitter satirical poem (which still appears at the front of copies of the *Shahnamah*). During his remaining years, Firdausi constantly fled before the anger of the sultan; at Baghdad, he wrote a 9,000-couplet version of the Joseph and Zuleika story from the Koran (the story of Joseph and Potiphar's wife) to show that his interests were orthodox as well as secular. Eventually, through the mediation of a friendly prince, peace was made between the sultan and Firdausi and the poet returned home to die. It is said that the 60,000 gold pieces were sent to Firdausi, but the messenger carrying them met the poet's funeral train; his daughter, at first inclined to refuse the much belated reward, at last accepted them to carry out the poet's wishes in the matter of irrigation at Tus. The *Shahnamah* is unique in Persian literature, large sections having been taken over as popular folklore and transmitted orally by the tribesmen.

Fire Sermon, The. The third section of Eliot's long poem *The Wasteland*. In it the central influencing character, Tiresias, is introduced. He unites the images of the Phoenician sailor, the one-eyed merchant, and Shakespeare's Ferdinand, in *The Tempest*. His is the role of the seer; though blind, he can foretell the future.

Firmilian (fèr.mil′i.an). A mock tragedy by W. E. Aytoun, parodying the poets of the "Spasmodic School."

Firouz Schah (fē′röz shä′). [Also, **Firuz Shah.**] In "The Enchanted Horse" in *The Arabian Nights' Entertainments*, the son of the king of Persia. He wins his bride by means of the enchanted horse, which could carry its rider in a second to any desired spot.

First Hundred Thousand, The. A volume of sketches (1915) of the early days of World War I, by Ian Hay (Major John Hay Beith).

First Love. A comedy by Richard Cumberland, produced in 1795.

First Love. The American title of Charles Morgan's novel *Portrait in a Mirror* (1929), winner of the Femina-Vie Heureuse Prize.

First Part of Hieronimo (hī.ę.ron′i.mō) or **Jeronimo** (ję.ron′i.mō). See **Hieronimo.**

First Part of King Henry the Fourth, The. See **Henry IV** (*Part One*).

First Part of King Henry the Sixth, The. See **Henry VI** (*Part One*).

First Part of the Contention betwixt the two Famous Houses of York and Lancaster . . . (yôrk; lang′-kas.tèr), **The.** See under **Henry VI** (*Part Two*).

Firth (fèrth), **Charles Harding.** b. at Sheffield, England, March 16, 1857; d. Feb. 19, 1936. An English historian. He was the author of *Scotland and the Protectorate* (1899), *Oliver Cromwell and the Rule of the Puritans in England* (1900), *Cromwell's Army* (1902), *The House of Lords during the Civil War* (1910), and others, and edited numerous biographical and historical volumes.

Firuz Shah (fē′röz shä′). See **Firouz Schah.**

ḍ, d or j; ṣ, s or sh; ṭ, t or ch; ẓ, z or zh; *o*, F. cloche; ü, F. menu; ċh, Sc. loch; ṅ, F. bonbon.

Fisher (fish′ẽr), **Herbert Albert Laurens.** b. at London, 1865; d. there, April 17, 1940. An English historian. He served (1916–26) as a member of Parliament; author of the Fisher Act (1918), which reorganized the public education system in England; delegate (1920–22) to League of Nations Assembly; appointed (1925) warden of New College, Oxford; a governor (1935–39) of British Broadcasting Corporation. His works include *The Mediaeval Empire* (1898), *Bonapartism* (1908), *Napoleon Bonaparte* (1913), *Life of Lord Bryce* (1926), *A History of Europe* (3 vols., 1935), *England and Europe* (1936), *O. M.* (1937), *A Political History of England*, *Pages From the Past* (1940), and *An Unfinished Autobiography* (1941).

Fitch (fich), **Ralph.** fl. in the second half of the 16th century. An English traveler in India and the East (1583–91). He made an overland journey down the Euphrates valley toward India. An account of his travels was published by Hakluyt.

Fitzalan (fits.al′ạn), **Thomas.** See under **Surrey, Earl of.**

Fitz-Boodle (fits.bödl), **George Savage.** One of the many pseudonyms of **Thackeray, William Makepeace.**

Fitzdottrel (fits.dot′rẹl). In Ben Jonson's *The Devil is an Ass*, a simple but conceited Norfolk squire.

FitzGerald (fits′jer′ạld), **Edward.** b. at Bredfield House, near Woodbridge, Suffolk, England, March 31, 1809; d. at Merton, Norfolk, England, June 14, 1883. An English poet and translator. His father's name was Purcell, but he adopted his wife's family name and arms in 1818. He published *Euphranor: a Dialogue on Youth* (1851), *Polonius: a Collection of Wise Saws and Modern Instances* (1852), a translation of six dramas of Calderon (1853), a translation (actually a free adaptation) of the quatrains of the *Rubáiyát of Omar Khayyám* (1859; revised ed., 1868), and other translations. FitzGerald's work, admired publicly by Rossetti and Swinburne, became popular and extremely influential with the poets of the latter part of the 19th century.

Fitzgerald (fits.jer′ạld), Lady **Elizabeth.** [Called "the Fair Geraldine."] b. at Maynooth, Ireland, c1528; d. 1589. Youngest daughter of the 9th Earl of Kildare. To her Henry Howard, Earl of Surrey, addressed a series of songs and sonnets, first published in Tottel's *Miscellany* in 1557.

Fitz Marshall (fits mär′shạl), **Charles.** See **Jingle, Alfred.**

Fitzneale (fits.nēl′) or **Fitznigel** (fits.nī′jẹl), **Richard.** [Also, **Richard of Ely.**] d. Sept. 10, 1198. An English cleric, statesman, and author; son of Nigel, bishop of Ely. He was treasurer (1169) of England, dean (1184) of Lincoln, bishop (1189) of London. Author of *Dialogus de Scaccario* and *The Acts of King Henry and King Richard.*

Fitzpatrick, Mr. and Mrs. Characters in Henry Fielding's novel *Tom Jones.*

Fitzpiers (fits.pirs′), **Edred.** The young doctor in Thomas Hardy's *The Woodlanders.*

Fitzroy (fits.roi′, fits′roi), **Robert.** b. at Ampton Hall, Suffolk, England, July 5, 1805; d. at London, April 30, 1865. A British naval officer. From 1828 to 1830, and again from 1831 to 1836, he commanded the *Beagle* in extended surveys to the South American coast and in the circumnavigation of the globe. During the second trip Charles Robert Darwin accompanied him as naturalist. The Geographical Society awarded its gold medal to Fitzroy in 1837. In 1839 he published *Narrative of the Surveying Voyages of H. M. ships Adventure and Beagle*, in three volumes (the third by Darwin). He was governor of New Zealand (1843–45) and superintendent of the Woolwich dockyard (1848–49) and held other important posts. Several well-known works on navigation and meteorology were published by him, and he is regarded as the founder of the modern meteorological service. Pressure of work connected with his duties as chief of the meteorological service of the Board of Trade caused his mind to give way, and he committed suicide.

Fitzroy Timmins (tim′inz). See **Timmins, Fitzroy.**

Fitzstephen (fits.stē′vẹn), **William.** d. c1190. An English clerk, friend, and biographer of Thomas à Becket. His *Vita Sancti Thomae* was first printed in 1723 (in Sparkes's *Historiae Anglicanae Scriptores*).

Fitzurse (fits.ẽrs′), **Waldemar.** In Sir Walter Scott's novel *Ivanhoe*, a follower of Prince John.

Fitzwater (fits′wô″tẽr, -wot″ẽr), **Lord.** In Shakespeare's *Richard II*, a nobleman who accuses Aumerle of causing the Duke of Gloucester's death and challenges him to a duel.

Fitzwilliam House (fits.wil′yạm). One of the colleges of Cambridge University. It was established in 1887 as a center for non-collegiate students, who are not members of any of the recognized colleges, or societies of students. It was known as Fitzwilliam Hall until 1924, when the word House was substituted. It is generally referred to as Fitz, or Fitzwilliam.

Fitzwilliam Museum. A museum of illuminated manuscripts, engravings, ancient prints, etc., at Cambridge University. The collection, bequeathed 1816, was that of the 7th Viscount Fitzwilliam, who also provided for the building (begun 1837).

Five Gallants, The. [Also, **Five Witty Gallants.**] A comedy by Thomas Middleton, entered on the Stationers' Register in 1608, and printed without date, but probably written in 1607.

Five Towns. The towns of Burslem, Hanley, Longton, Stoke-on-Trent, and Tunstall in the industrial area in northern Staffordshire, England, which appear, respectively, as Bursley, Hambridge, Longshaw, Knype, and Turnhill in many of the realistic novels and stories by Arnold Bennett. Among them are *The Old Wives' Tale* (1908) and the first "Five Towns" trilogy, including *Anna of the Five Towns* (1902), *Leonora* (1903), and *Sacred and Profane Love* (1905; revised ed., 1911, *The Book of Carlotta*). The Five Towns, situated in the area known as the Potteries, now comprise the borough of Stoke-on-Trent.

Five Towns Trilogy (second). See **Clayhanger Trilogy.**

Five Variations on a Theme. A volume of poems by Edith Sitwell, published in 1933.

---

fat, fāte, fär, ȧsk, fāre; net, mē, hẽr; pin, pīne; not, nōte, mȯve, nôr; up, lūte, pŭll; ᴛʜ, then;

Fizkin (fiz′kin), **Horatio.** The candidate of the Buffs in the Parliamentary election at Eatanswill, in Dickens's *Pickwick Papers*.

Flaccus (flak′us), **Gaius Valerius.** A Roman poet of the time of Vespasian, author of a heroic poem, *Argonautica* (8 books), a free imitation of Apollonius of Rhodes.

Flaherty (fla′ĕr.ti), **Margaret.** A romantic Irish girl, called "Pegeen Mike," daughter of a publichouse keeper, in *The Playboy of the Western World* (1907), a one-act play by John Millington Synge.

Flaherty, Michael James. A keeper of a public house, Margaret's father, in *The Playboy of the Western World*.

Flamborough (flam′bur″ọ̄). In Oliver Goldsmith's *Vicar of Wakefield*, the name of a farmer and his family.

Flamineo (flạ.min′ẹ̄.ō). The cynical and self-calculating brother of Vittoria Corombona in John Webster's tragedy *The White Devil*. His actions to forward the love of his sister and the proud Brachiano, in defiance of their marriages to Camillo and Isabella, result eventually in his own death at the hands of Lodovico and an accomplice, instigated by Francisco and Cardinal Monticelso.

Flaming Heart, The. A poem (1646) by Richard Crashaw, dedicated to Saint Teresa (the Spanish mystic, who had been canonized in 1622).

Flaming Tinman, The. In George Borrow's novel *Lavengro*, a character who engages in a duel with Lavengro, on which occasion Belle Berners acts as Lavengro's second.

Flaminian Way (flạ.min′i.ạn). [Latin, **Via Flaminia.**] One of the oldest and most famous highways of ancient Rome. It extended in a direct line from Rome to Ariminum (Rimini), and was built by the censor Gaius Flaminius in 220 B.C. Its superintendence was held to be so honorable an office that Augustus himself assumed it in 27 B.C., as Julius Caesar had been curator of the Appian Way. Augustus restored it through its entire extent, in commemoration of which triumphal arches were erected to him over the road at Ariminum and at Rome; the arch at the former place still exists. Much of the old pavement survives, together with many tombs by the roadside.

Flaminius (flạ.min′i.us). In Shakespeare's *Timon of Athens*, a servant to Timon.

Flaminius. A cruel Roman ambassador in Philip Massinger's *Believe as You List*.

Flanders (flan′dĕrz), **Moll.** See **Moll Flanders.**

Flash (flash), **Captain.** In David Garrick's play *Miss in her Teens*, a cowardly braggart.

Flash, Sir Petronel. In George Chapman, John Marston, and Ben Jonson's comedy *Eastward Ho!*, a knight adventurer. He is eager to escape from London to the untried land of Virginia.

Flashing Stream, The. A play (1938) by Charles Morgan.

Flatman (flat′mạn), **Thomas.** b. at London, 1637; d. there, Dec. 8, 1688. An English painter, poet, and lawyer, remembered chiefly as a miniaturist. He was educated at Oxford and Cambridge. Of his portraits, two of himself and one of Charles II are considered among his best.

Flaubert (flō.ber), **Gustave.** b. at Rouen, France, Dec. 12, 1821; d. at Croisset, near Rouen, May 8, 1880. A French writer and novelist, often regarded as the master of naturalism. He traveled in Brittany, Greece, Syria, Egypt, and elsewhere, and undertook to relate his travels, but went no further than an opening paper entitled *À bord de la Cange*. In 1857 he published in *La Revue de Paris* the novel *Madame Bovary*, and in *L'Artiste* published parts of *La Tentation de Saint Antoine*, though the work was not completed until 1874. The former gave rise to considerable litigation, Flaubert being ultimately cleared of a charge of immorality in literature. In 1858 he visited the site of ancient Carthage, and in 1862 published *Salammbô*. This was followed in 1869 by *L'Éducation sentimentale, roman d'un jeune homme*, and in 1877 by *Trois contes*, containing "Un Cœur simple," "La Légende de Saint-Julien-l'Hospitalier," and "Hérodias." Flaubert's plays, *Le Candidat* and *Le Château des cœurs*, were failures; they were published after his death in *La Vie moderne* (1885). His other posthumous publications are the satirical novel *Bouvard et Pécuchet* (in *La Revue Politique et Littéraire*), *Lettres à George Sand* (1884), *Par les champs et par les grèves*, reminiscences of Brittany in *Le Gaulois*, an essay on Rabelais, and a voluminous correspondence. Flaubert's influence on the history of the novel can hardly be overestimated. Writing for him was very difficult and he strove unceasingly for the exact phrasing (*le mot juste*) of what he wanted to say; he took four years and seven months to write *Madame Bovary*, seven to write *L'Éducation sentimentale; Bouvard et Pécuchet* he never finished. His influence over his friends, among them Zola, Daudet, the Goncourts, and Turgeniev, was great; his naturalistic approach to the novel, analyzing fact, describing it in terms of forces, maintaining the neutral attitude as author, was systematized by Zola. Essentially a romantic, Flaubert treated the exotic with great detail (*Salammbô*); when he turned nearer home, he permitted his scorn for bourgeois pretension to become apparent, but despite his essential misanthropy his psychological portraits are true.

Flavian Amphitheater (flā′vi.ạn). See **Colosseum.**

Flavius (flā′vi.us). In Shakespeare's *Julius Caesar*, a tribune of the people. With Marullus, his fellow tribune, he is opposed to the growth of Caesar's power.

Flavius. In Shakespeare's *Timon of Athens*, Timon's steward. Timon ignores his warning of the dangers of reckless spending, and after Timon's ruin, he visits him in his cave. Here Timon first curses him, then calls him "thou singly honest man" (IV.iii) and offers him gold if he will promise to "show charity to none."

Flaw (flô). In Samuel Foote's comedy *The Cozeners*, one of the cozeners or cheats.

Flaw in the Crystal, The. A novel by May Sinclair, published in 1912.

Flax of Dream, The. A collective title given to four autobiographical novels by Henry Williamson: *The Beautiful Years* (1921), *Dandelion Days*

(1922), *The Dream of Fair Women* (1924), and *The Pathway* (1928).

Fleance (flē'ạns). In Shakespeare's *Macbeth*, the son of Banquo. He escapes when his father is murdered. Like his father, he has no basis in history (although he has been mentioned in Scottish tradition as an ancestor of the Stuart Kings).

Fleay (flā), **Frederick Gard.** b. 1831; d. at Upper Tooting, London, March 10, 1909. A British Shakespeare scholar. He graduated from King's College, London, in 1849, and from Trinity College, Cambridge, in 1853. Among his well-known works are *A Chronicle History of the Life and Work of William Shakespeare* (1886), *Chronicle History of the London Stage, 1559–1642* (1890), and *Biographical Chronicle of the English Drama, 1559–1642* (1891).

Flecker (flek'ẽr), **James Elroy.** [Full name, **Herman James Elroy Flecker.**] b. at Lewisham, London, Nov. 5, 1884; d. at Davos, Switzerland, Jan. 3, 1915. An English poet, dramatist, and translator. He was educated at Uppingham School at Rutland, at Trinity College, Oxford, and at Caius College, Cambridge, studying languages at the latter in preparation for a diplomatic career. After serving (1910 *et seq.*) in the consular service, he was compelled to leave because of tuberculosis and spent his remaining years at Paris, Beirut, and Athens, and in Switzerland. He was author of *The Bridge of Fire* (1908), *The Last Generation* (1908), *36 Poems* (1910), *42 Poems* (1911), *The Golden Journey to Samarkand* (1913), *The Old Ships* (1915), *God Save the King* (1915), *Collected Poems* (1916), and *Selected Poems* (1918). He also wrote two dramas, *Hassan* (1922) and *Don Juan* (1925), *The Grecians a Dialog on Education* (1910), *The Scholar's Italian Book* (1911), and a novel, *The King of Alsander* (1913). His *Collected Prose* appeared in 1920 and *Some Letters from Abroad* was published in 1930. Some of his best poems are *The Old Ships*, *Stillness*, *War Song of the Saracens*, *The Town Without a Market*, and *To a Poet a Thousand Years Hence*. Flecker's work shows the influence of his models, the French Parnassian school.

Flecknoe (flek'nō), **Richard.** b. apparently in Ireland, c1600; d. c1678. A British poet and playwright. He furnished Dryden with the name "MacFlecknoe," under which he satirized Shadwell.

Fledgeby (flej'bi), **Mr.** [Called **Fascination Fledgeby.**] A dandified young man in Charles Dickens's novel *Our Mutual Friend*, who is sharp in affairs of money.

Fleece, The. A poem (1757) by John Dyer, written in the pastoral style, describing the activities of sheep raising and the wool trade.

Fleece'em (flēs'ẹm), **Mrs.** In Samuel Foote's play *The Cozeners*, a cheat and confederate of Flaw.

Flee from the Press. A short poem by Chaucer, printed before the folio of 1532. It is sometimes known as *Truth*, *Balade de bon Conseyl*, *Good Counsel of Chaucer* (Shirley), or *Balade that Chaucer made on his Deeth-bedde* ("probably a mere bad guess," according to Skeat).

Fleet Prison. [Called "the Fleet."] An old London prison, formerly standing on the east side of the Fleet brook (now a covered sewer, flowing into the Thames at Blackfriars Bridge). It was nearly 800 years old when it was destroyed in 1846. It was called the "gaol of the Fleet" in the time of Richard I, and was a debtors' prison as early as 1290. It was used also as a state prison for religious and political offenders till 1641, when it was reserved entirely for debtors. It was burned by Wat Tyler's men in 1381. In 1666 it was burned in the Great Fire, and again in 1780 by the rioters. In the 17th and early part of the 18th century persons wishing to be married secretly came within the rules of the Fleet, where degraded clergyman were easily found, among the debtors, to perform the ceremony. This custom was stopped by act of Parliament in 1754. Attention was called to the outrageous treatment of the prisoners in 1726, when the warden was tried for murder.

Fleet Street. A London street running from Ludgate Circus to the Strand and the West End. It is named from the Fleet brook. In the early chronicles of London many allusions are made to the deeds of violence done in this street. The London apprentices waged war against young students in the Inns of Court, and elsewhere. By the time of Elizabeth the street had become a favorite spot for shows of all descriptions; "puppet-shows and monsters" are frequently alluded to. It is now one of the busiest streets of London, being the site of many newspaper offices.

Fleming (flem'ing), **Agnes.** The mother of Oliver in Charles Dickens's novel *Oliver Twist*, and sister of Rose Fleming.

Fleming, Archdeacon. A character in Sir Walter Scott's novel *The Heart of Midlothian*, to whom Meg Murdockson makes her dying confession.

Fleming, Lady May. In Sir Walter Scott's novel *The Abbot*, a maid of honor to Mary, Queen of Scots, imprisoned with her at Lochleven.

Fleming, Margaret (or **Marjorie**). b. Jan. 15, 1803; d. Dec. 19, 1811. A daughter of James Fleming of Kirkcaldy, Scotland. A precocious child, she was the pet of Sir Walter Scott. Her life was written by John Brown, *Pet Marjorie: a Story of Child Life Fifty Years Ago* (1858).

Fleming, Oliver. A pseudonym of MacDonald, Philip.

Fleming, Peter. b. May 31, 1907—. An English writer. He has been a special correspondent for the London *Times* in eastern and central Asia. His books include *Brazilian Adventure* (1933), *News From Tartary* (1936), and *The Flying Visit* (1940).

Fleming, Rhoda. See **Rhoda Fleming.**

Fleming, Rose. In Charles Dickens's *Oliver Twist*, a gentle girl who marries Henry Maylie.

Fleming, Sir Malcolm. A character in Sir Walter Scott's *Castle Dangerous*, who is a follower of Bruce and a friend to Douglas.

Fleshly School. The name given to a number of English poets (Swinburne, Morris, Rossetti, and others) by R. W. Buchanan, writing under the pseudonym of Robert Maitland, in the *Contemporary Review*, October, 1871.

Flestrin (fles'trin), **Quinbus.** The Man-Mountain; the name which the Lilliputians gave to Lemuel Gulliver in Swift's *Gulliver's Travels*.

Fleta (flē′tạ). An anonymous Latin book on English law, written c1290. From a statement in the one extant manuscript, that "this book may well be called Fleta because it is written in Fleta," is inferred that it was written by a prisoner in the Fleet Prison.

Fletcher (flech′ẽr), **Giles.** [Called "**Fletcher the Elder.**"] b. at Watford, Hertfordshire, England, c1549; d. at London, in March, 1611. An English diplomat and poet; uncle of John Fletcher and father of Giles ("Fletcher the Younger") and Phineas Fletcher. He was graduated from King's College, Cambridge, of which he became a fellow in 1568. In 1588 he was sent as ambassador to Russia, and published an account of that country in 1591, which was suppressed because the Russia Company feared some of it would offend the Russians and injure trade. It was called *Of the Russe Common Wealth*. It was abridged, and passages were suppressed by Hakluyt and Purchas, and reprinted as *The History of Russia* (1643), and also, with the original title, for the Hakluyt Society (1856). He also wrote *Licia: Poems of Love* (1593) and others.

Fletcher, Giles. [Called "**Fletcher the Younger.**"] b. c1588; d. 1623. An English poet; younger son of Giles Fletcher (c1549–1611). He is particularly noted for his religious allegory *Christ's Victorie and Triumph in Heaven and Earth* (1610).

Fletcher, John. b. at Rye, Sussex, England, in December, 1579; d. at London, in August, 1625. An English dramatist. He was the son of Richard Fletcher, afterwards bishop of London, a nephew of Giles Fletcher (c1549–1611), and a cousin of Phineas and Giles Fletcher (c1588–1623). He is best known as the collaborator in several plays with Francis Beaumont, with whom he wrote from c1606 to 1616. The two playwrights were friends and lived together for part of the time. After Shakespeare's retirement, Fletcher seems to have been the principal writer for the King's Men; his collaboration with Beaumont was succeeded by a similar partnership with Philip Massinger, and he wrote a number of plays with various other playwrights of the day. His name is linked with those of Ben Jonson, Nathan Field, Cyril Tourneur, William Rowley, and others. Fletcher is thought to have had a hand in two plays in the Shakespearian canon: *The Two Noble Kinsmen* (printed 1634) and *Henry VIII* (1613); some critics assign the latter to Fletcher and Massinger, with Shakespeare writing only a few scenes or speeches. The solution to the problem of Fletcher's part in plays assigned to him in whole or in part is mainly conjectural; scholars disagree not only about who wrote given parts of plays but also about whose hand actually appears in the writing.

Fletcher Alone. The following plays are usually assigned to Fletcher alone, without collaborators: *The Faithful Shepherdess* (printed c1609), *Wit Without Money* (c1614, printed 1639), *Bonduca* (written before 1619, printed 1647), *Valentinian* (c1614, printed 1647), *The Loyal Subject* (1618, printed 1647), *The Mad Lover* (c1616, printed 1647), *The Humorous Lieutenant* (1619, printed 1647), *Women Pleased* (c1620, printed 1647), *The Pilgrim* (1621, printed 1647), *The Wild-Goose*

Chase (1621, printed 1652), *The Island Princess* (c1622, printed 1647), *Monsieur Thomas* (printed 1639), *The Woman's Prize, or The Tamer Tamed* (a reversal of *The Taming of the Shrew*, which may be very early; played before 1633, printed 1647), *A Wife for a Month* (1624, printed 1647), *Rule a Wife and Have a Wife* (1624, printed 1640), *The Chances* (c1620–25, printed 1647).

With Beaumont. Although his collaboration with Beaumont was not the first such teaming (*Gorboduc*, the first English blank-verse tragedy, was written, c1561, by Thomas Norton and Thomas Sackville), Fletcher's partnership with the younger poet was by far the most successful. The earliest result of the combination of talents, *The Knight of the Burning Pestle* (1607–08, printed 1613), is often assigned to Beaumont alone. Usually assigned to both are *A King and No King* (1611, printed 1619), *The Maid's Tragedy* (c1611, printed 1619), *Philaster, or Love Lies a-Bleeding* (c1608–11, printed 1620), *The Scornful Lady* (c1616, printed 1619), *The Coxcomb* (c1609, printed 1647; perhaps by Fletcher alone).

With Others. After Beaumont's death in 1616, Massinger became Fletcher's principal partner. To them are ascribed *Sir John Van Olden Barnavelt* (1619, printed by Bullen in his *Collection of Old English Plays* in 1882), *The Little French Lawyer* (c1620, printed 1647), *The Custom of the Country* (c1622, printed 1647), *The Spanish Curate* (1622, printed 1647), *The Beggar's Bush* (c1622, printed 1647), *The Elder Brother* (printed 1637), *The Honest Man's Fortune* (1613, printed 1647; Field may have had a hand in this), *A Very Woman* (c1621, licensed 1634, printed 1655), *Cupid's Revenge* (printed 1615; probably by Beaumont and Fletcher, though a third writer is suspected, perhaps Field), *Four Plays in One* (perhaps as early as 1608; printed in 1647; the first two plays are probably by Field), *Love's Cure* (c1623, printed 1647; perhaps by Massinger and Middleton, or by Beaumont and Fletcher revised by Massinger), *Love's Pilgrimage* (printed 1647; with Massinger, but it may be entirely by Fletcher), *The Lover's Progress* (printed 1647; with Massinger), *The Double Marriage* (c1620, printed 1647; with Massinger), *The Prophetess* (licensed 1622, printed 1647; with Massinger), *Thierry and Theodoret* (c1616; probably with Massinger and Field), *The False One* (c1620, printed 1647; with Massinger), *The Sea-Voyage* (licensed 1622, printed 1647), *The Queen of Corinth* (c1616, printed 1647; with Massinger and Field or Middleton and Rowley), *The Nice Valour, or The Passionate Mad-Man* (c1624, printed 1647; with Massinger, but Fleay thinks Middleton rewrote much of it), *The Maid in the Mill* (1623; with Rowley or Massinger), *The Laws of Candy* (printed 1647; largely by Massinger), *The Night-Walker, or The Little Thief* (1634, printed 1640 as by Fletcher; probably a revision by Shirley of a Fletcher play). *The Bloody Brother, or Rollo, Duke of Normandy* (c1616, printed probably 1639) was probably written in collaboration with Jonson and revised by Massinger; it is sometimes assigned entirely to Massinger. This play is one of an extremely difficult group: *The Knight of Malta* (c1616, printed before 1647; perhaps by Fletcher, Massinger, and Field), *The Fair Maid of the Inn*

ḍ, d or j; ṣ, s or sh; ṭ, t or ch; z̧, z or zh; o, F. cloche; ü, F. menu; ċh, Sc. loch; ṅ, F. bonbon.

(licensed 1626, printed 1647; perhaps with Rowley), *The Captain* (c1613, printed 1647; with either Jonson or Middleton). Both *The Noble Gentleman* (licensed 1626, printed 1647) and *Faithful Friends* are sometimes assigned to Fletcher, but he apparently had no hand in them. *The Coronation* was printed in 1640 as being Fletcher's, but it was written by Shirley, who licensed it in 1635. *The Widow* was printed in 1652 as the joint work of Middleton, Jonson, and Fletcher, but it seems to be an early (c1616) play by Middleton alone.

Fletcher, Joseph Smith. [Pseudonym, **A Son of the Soil.**] b. at Halifax, Yorkshire, England, Feb. 7, 1863; d. at Dorking, Surrey, England, Jan. 31, 1935. An English essayist, historian, journalist, and novelist, an early writer of detective fiction. His work enjoyed great popularity during the author's lifetime, and helped to bring the detective story into fashion, but few of his books are read today. His most famous character is Ronald Camberwell.

Fletcher, Phineas. b. at Cranbrook, Kent, England, in April, 1582; d. c1650. An English poet; son of Giles Fletcher (c1549–1611). His chief works are *Sicelides*, a pastoral play (1614, printed 1631), *The Purple Island, or the Isle of Man, together with Piscatory Eclogs and other Poetical Miscellanies* (1633), and *The Apollyonists* (1627).

Fleur et Blanchefleur (flër ä blänsh.flër). See **Flore et Blanchefleur.**

Flibbertigibbet (flib″ĕr.ti.jib′et). A fiend ("of mopping and mowing") named by Edgar in Shakespeare's *King Lear* (IV.i). Latimer, in a sermon, used the name "flibbergib" to stand for a chattering or gossiping individual. However, Shakespeare probably derived it from Samuel Harsnett's *Popish Impostures* (1606).

Flibbertigibbet. A name given to Dickon Sludge, a character in Sir Walter Scott's novel *Kenilworth*.

Flimnap (flim′nap). The Lilliputian premier in Swift's *Gulliver's Travels*. He was designed as a satire on Sir Robert Walpole.

Flint (flint), **Francis Stewart.** b. at London, Dec. 19, 1885—. An English poet, essayist, translator, and civil servant. Although he possessed only an elementary education, he mastered ten languages and translated works on Lenin, Gandhi, Beethoven, Madame de Pompadour, and Rasputin, and French and Latin poetry. He served in the British army in World War I, and after 1919 was employed in the labor ministry, where he became head of the statistics division. He is an advocate of what he calls "unrhymed cadence," and claims that rhyme and meter are "artificial and external additions to poetry." His poetical works include *In the Net of the Stars* (1909), *Cadences* (1915), and *Otherworld* (1915, 1920). He has contributed to issues of *Poetry* (1913, 1916, 1918) and to *Some Imagist Poets* (1915, 1916, 1917). *London, The Swan, In the Garden, Plane-Tree, Sadness, Beggar,* and *Chrysanthemums* are typical poems.

Flint, Robert. b. at Dumfries, Scotland, March 14, 1838; d. at Edinburgh, Nov. 25, 1910. A Scottish philosophical and religious writer. Educated at Glasgow University, he served as minister (1858–64) in Aberdeen and Fife churches, traveled ex-

tensively in Germany, was professor of moral philosophy (1864–76) at St. Andrews University and of divinity (1876–80) at Glasgow, and lectured at Princeton University in 1880. Author of *The Philosophy of History in France and Germany* (1874), *Theism* (1877), *Antitheistic Theories* (1879), *Vico* (1883), *Socialism* (1894), *Hindu Pantheism* (1897), *Agnosticism* (1903), and *Philosophy as Scientia Scientarum* (1904).

Flint, Sir Clement. A cynical but kind-hearted old bachelor in Burgoyne's play *The Heiress.*

Flint, Solomon. In Samuel Foote's play *The Maid of Bath,* a rich, miserly old man. He is described as an "old, fusty, shabby, shuffling, money-loving, water-drinking, mirth-marring, amorous old hunks." He is intended to satirize Walter Long for his ungallant treatment of Miss Linley (Mrs. R. B. Sheridan).

Flintwinch (flint′winch), **Jeremiah.** In Charles Dickens's *Little Dorrit,* the sinister and intriguing servant of Mrs. Clennam.

Flip (flip). In Charles Shadwell's comedy *The Fair Quaker of Deal,* an illiterate commodore. He is a drunken "sea-brute," contrasted with Mizen the "sea-fop."

Flippant (flip′ant), **Lady.** In Wycherley's comedy *Love in a Wood,* an affected widow. She is on the lookout for a husband, but declaims against marriage.

Flippanta (fli.pan′ta). In Vanbrugh's *Confederacy,* a shameless and witty lady's-maid.

Flite (flīt), **Miss.** In Charles Dickens's *Bleak House,* "a curious little old woman," deranged by long waiting for the settlement of her suit in chancery.

Flodden (flod′en). A hill in Northumberland, England, ab. 12 mi. SW of Berwick. At its base on Sept. 9, 1513, the English (32,000) under Thomas Howard, Earl of Surrey, defeated the Scots (30,000) under James IV. The loss of the English was from 3,000 to 4,000; that of the Scots is variously given as from 5,000 to 12,000. The king and many of the nobles were among the slain.

Flodoard (flo.do.àr). [Also, **Frodoard.**] b. at Épernay, France, 894; d. March 28, 966. A French chronicler who was for a time keeper of the episcopal archives at Reims. He wrote a history of the church of Reims, and a chronicle of France from 919 to 966.

Flora (flōr′a). The ancient Italian goddess of flowers and spring, and perhaps of love. Her cult in later Roman religion was definitely a vegetation cult; her festival, the Floralia, was celebrated from April 28 to May 1 with mummery and games and the type of license associated with all fertility festivals.

Florac (flo.ràk), **Vicomte De.** In Thackeray's *The Virginians,* a young French officer who rescues George Warrington from the Indians. In *The Newcomes* he is an émigré from France, whose mother was Colonel Newcome's first love.

Flora Finching (flōr′a fin′ching). See **Finching, Flora.**

Flora MacIvor (mak.ē′vor). See **MacIvor, Flora.**

Flore et Blanchefleur (flôr ä blänsh.flêr). [Also, **Fleur et Blanchefleur.**] An early French metrical romance of which the theme is the love of a young Christian prince for a Saracen slavegirl who has been brought up with him.

Florence (flor'ens), **Duke of.** In Shakespeare's *All's Well That Ends Well*, a minor character.

Florence of Worcester (wûs'tẽr). d. July 7, 1118. An English chronicler, a monk of Worcester. His (Latin) *Chronicon ex Chronicis* (first printed in 1592) is founded on a chronicle of Marianus, an Irish monk, and ends with the year 1117.

Florent (flor'ent). In one of the tales told in Gower's *Confessio Amantis*, a knight who is compelled to marry an ugly old hag in order to learn a secret and thus save his life. When he is finally reconciled to his lot, his wife is suddenly transformed into a beautiful young woman. The story is also told by Chaucer as *The Wife of Bath's Tale.*

Florent et Lyon (flo.rän ä lyôn). See under **Octavian.**

Flores (flor'es, -ēz; Portuguese, flŏ'rẽsh). The westernmost of the Azores Islands, belonging to Portugal. Its port is Santa Cruz.

Florestan (flor'es.tan), **King.** In Disraeli's *Endymion*, the ruler of the mythical country used by the author as the geographical locale of his work.

Florez (flor'ēz). In *The Beggar's Bush*, by John Fletcher and others, the son of the King of the Beggars. He becomes a rich merchant at Bruges. He appears also in *The Merchant of Bruges*, an adaptation of *The Beggar's Bush*. Eventually he is restored to the throne of Flanders after the King of the Beggars is revealed not only to be his father, but also the consort of the Countess of Flanders.

Florilla (flŏ.ril'a). The young and beautiful wife of Count Labervele in George Chapman's comedy *An Humorous Day's Mirth.*

Florimel (flor'i.mel). In Edmund Spenser's *Faerie Queene*, a chaste and "goodly" lady, representing the complete charm of womanhood. A counterfeit Florimel was made of snow, mixed with "fine mercury and virgin wax," by a witch. It was impossible to tell the real from the false Florimel. The latter created much mischief till the enchantment was dissolved and she melted into nothingness.

Florimel. The heroine of Fletcher and Rowley's *Maid in the Mill.*

Florimel. In John Dryden's play *Secret Love, or The Maiden Queen*, a maid of honor and a saucy flirt. This was one of Nell Gwyn's most famous roles.

Florinda (flŏ.rēn'dä). In Spanish tradition, the daughter of Count Julián, the governor of Ceuta. Southey used the story of her violation in his *Roderick, the Last of the Goths;* as the result of the crime, her father called on the Moors, who drove Roderick from the throne and established themselves in Spain.

Florinda (flŏ.rin'da). The principal female character in Richard Lalor Sheil's tragedy *The Apostate.*

Florio (flō'ri.ō, flôr'i.ō), **John.** b. at London, c1553; d. at Fulham (now part of London), 1625. An English lexicographer and author; son of an Italian Protestant refugee who settled in England. He published *First Fruits, which yield Familiar Speech, Merry Proverbs, Witty Sentences, and Golden Sayings* (dialogues in English and Italian, 1578), *Second Fruits, to be gathered of Twelve Trees, of divers but delightsome Tastes to the Tongues of Italian and English men* (mainly dialogues, 1591), and an Italian-English dictionary called *A Worlde of Wordes* (1598), which was issued again, revised and enlarged, under the title *Queen Anna's New World of Words* (1611). Florio translated Montaigne's *Essays* (1603) in three books, still considered the standard translation. He had several patrons, among them Henry Wriothesley, Earl of Southampton, who was also Shakespeare's patron. Florio was tutor to James I's son, Prince Henry, and reader in Italian to Queen Anne. He married a sister of Samuel Daniel.

Florismart (flor'is.märt). One of Charlemagne's peers, the friend of Roland.

Floriz and Blanchfleur (flôr'iz; blänch.flêr'). A Middle English verse romance (c1250), based on a French version of an Oriental tale, telling the story of the love of Floriz, son of the Saracen queen, for Blanchfleur, daughter of a widow whose husband was killed by the Saracens at the time of her capture. The family of Floriz try to thwart his love: Blanchfleur is sold as a harem girl during one of his absences, and he is told she is dead. When he tries to kill himself at her supposed grave his family relents and promises to help him find Blanchfleur. He eventually finds her in the harem of the emir of Babylon and after various complications with the emir, they are reunited and Blanchfleur and Floriz are married.

Florizel (flor'i.zel). In Shakespeare's *Winter's Tale*, the Prince of Bohemia, in love with Perdita. The name was taken by the Prince of Wales, who became George IV, in his affair with Mary Robinson, who played Perdita in Garrick's version (1779) of the play.

Florizel and Perdita (pẽr.dē'ta). A pastoral drama by Garrick, adapted from Shakespeare's *Winter's Tale*. It was produced on Jan. 21, 1756. Garrick played Leontes.

Flos Regum Arthurus (flos rē'gum är.thū'rus) or **Flower of Kings.** A name applied to King Arthur by Joseph of Exeter (c1200).

Flower and the Leaf, The. A poem added by Speght to his edition of Chaucer (1598). It professes to be written by a gentlewoman who pays homage to the "worth that wears the laurel." It is believed from internal evidence not to be Chaucer's.

Flower of Courtesy, The. A poem attributed to Chaucer by Thynne, assigned by Stow to Lydgate.

Flower of Old Japan, The. A whimsical poem (1903) by Alfred Noyes.

"Flower of Strathearn" (strath.ẽrn'), **the.** See **Nairne, Carolina.**

Fludd or **Flud** (flud), **Robert.** b. at Bearsted, Kent, England, 1574; d. at London, Sept. 8, 1637. An English physician and mystical philosopher. He wrote several treatises in defense of the fraternity of the Rosy Cross (Rosicrucians).

Fluellen (flö.el'en). In Shakespeare's *Henry V*, a pedantic but courageous Welsh captain. He expounds the virtues of Roman military life much as one faction of Shakespeare's contemporaries argued the advantages of war according to the mode of the ancients. Shakespeare also uses the incident of Fluellen and the leek (symbol of Wales) to show the tolerance which must be practiced as the price of unity among the English allies.

Flush—A Biography (flush). A work by Virginia Woolf, published in 1933, dealing with the life at London and Florence of "Flush," the pet cocker spaniel of Elizabeth Barrett Browning.

Flute (flōt), **Francis.** In Shakespeare's *Midsummer Night's Dream*, a bellows-mender. He plays the part of Thisby (Thisbe) in the interpolated play.

Flutter (flut'ėr). In Hannah Cowley's comedy *The Belle's Stratagem*, a good-natured, irresponsible beau, devoted to telling gossiping stories about which he remembers correctly everything except the facts.

Flutter, Sir Fopling. In Etherege's comedy *The Man of Mode, or Sir Fopling Flutter*, an affected and fashionable fop. He is intended to imitate Hewit, the reigning exquisite of the hour. According to his own account, a complete gentleman "ought to dress well, dance well, fence well, have a genius for love-letters, an agreeable voice for a chamber, be very amorous, something discreet, but not over-constant."

Flying Dutchman. A phantom full-rigged ship said to appear to mariners trying to round the Cape of Good Hope in a storm. The story is known to seamen in various versions. In all tellings the spectral ship is doomed never to enter port, but the reasons differ: the captain is doomed to sail forever because he said he would round the Cape or be damned, because he was cruel, or because of a pact with the Devil. Sight of the ship is still occasionally reported, and she is usually seen as the typical phantom ship: she sails full-rigged against the wind, and captain and crew remain silent when hailed or else they seem to perform their duties as if dead. Wagner's opera *Der Fliegende Holländer* is based on the story.

Foedera (fed'ėr.ą). A work, edited by Thomas Rymer, intended to contain all the existing documents relating to alliances and state transactions between England and other countries from 1101 to the time of publication. He died after having issued 15 volumes (1704–13), but left material down to the end of the reign of James I. This was edited by his assistant, Robert Sanderson, who issued two volumes in 1715–17, and the last three in 1726–35. This brought it down to 1654.

Foible (foi'bl). In Congreve's comedy *The Way of the World*, the intriguing waiting-woman of Lady Wishfort.

Foigard (fwä.gär'). In Farquhar's *The Beaux' Stratagem*, a vulgar Irishman who pretends to be a French priest to further his villainies. He is discovered by his brogue.

Foker (fō'kėr), **Harry.** In Thackeray's novel *Pendennis*, a school friend of Arthur Pendennis. He is a somewhat loud youth, infatuated with Blanche Amory.

Folengo (fō.leng'gō), **Teofilo.** [Pseudonym, **Merlino Coccaio.**] b. at Cipada, a former village near Mantua, Italy, Nov. 8, 1491; d. at Santa Croce di Campese, near Bassano, Italy, Dec. 9, 1544. An Italian poet, especially noted as an early and successful cultivator of macaronic verse. He became a Benedictine at 16 years of age, but abandoned the order for a wandering and licentious life in 1515, returning to it later.

folio (fō'li.ō). 1. A sheet of paper folded once, usually through the shorter diameter, so as to consist of two equal leaves.
2. A book or other publication, or a blank book, etc., consisting of sheets or of a single sheet folded once.

> This folio of four pages, happy work!
> (Cowper, *Task*, iv. 50.)

3. The size of such a book, etc.: as, an edition of a work in folio. Abbreviated *fol.*: as, 3 vols. fol.
4. One of several sizes of paper adapted for folding once into well-proportional leaves, whether intended for such use or not, distinguished by specific names. The untrimmed leaf of a pot folio is about 7½ x 12½ inches; foolscap folio, about 8 x 12½; flat-cap folio, 8½ x 14; crown folio or post folio, 9½ x 15; demy folio, 10½ x 16; medium folio, 12 x 19; royal folio, 12½ x 20; superroyal folio, 14 x 22; imperial folio, 16 x 22; elephant folio, 14 x 23; atlas folio, 16½ x 26; columbier folio, 17½ x 24; double-elephant folio, 20 x 27; antiquarian folio, 26½ x 31.

Folio, Tom. The name in *The Tatler*, No. 158, under which Addison is said to have introduced Thomas Rawlinson.

folklore (fōk'lōr). The lore of the common people; the traditional beliefs and customs of the people, especially such as are obsolete or archaic; traditional knowledge; popular superstitions, tales, traditions, or legends.

> Among the proofs of his [William John Thomas's] happiness of hitting on names may be cited his . . . invention of the word folk-lore.
> (*N. and Q.*, 6th ser., XII. 141.)

> Mr. Gomme offers as a definition of the science of folk-lore the following: it is "the comparison and identification of the survivals, archaic beliefs, customs, and traditions in modern ages."
> (*Science*, IX. 479.)

Folliott (fol'i.ǫt), **Dr.** One of the principal characters in Thomas Peacock's *Crotchet Castle*.

Follywit (fol'i.wit). A gay young prodigal whose tricks upon his grandfather, Sir Bounteous Progress, form the plot of Thomas Middleton's comedy *A Mad World, My Masters*.

Fomorians (fō.môr'i.ąnz). [Also: **Fomors** (fō'-môrz); incorrectly, **Formorians.**] In Old Irish mythology and legend, a prehistoric people who raided the coasts of Ireland from the sea. They were so named from the Irish word *fomor*, meaning giant or pirate. They were defeated and driven away by the Tuatha De Danann (the gods or divine race of ancient Ireland).

Fonblanque (fon.blangk'), **Albany.** b. at London, 1793; d. there, Oct. 13, 1872. An English journalist. He was editor of the London *Examiner*, and his *England under Seven Administrations* (1837) is a collection of the best of his articles published originally in that newspaper.

Fondlewife (fon'dl.wĭf). In Congreve's comedy *The Old Bachelor*, a doting old man, deceived by his outwardly quiet and submissive wife.

Fondlove (fond'lŭv), **Sir William.** An amorous, garrulous old gentleman in J. Sheridan Knowles's comedy *The Love Chase*. He is pursued by the widow Green.

Fontarabie (fôṅ.tȧ.rȧ.bē). French name of **Fuenterrabia.**

Fonthill Abbey (font'hĭl). A magnificent residence built (1790) on Lansdowne Hill, near Bath, England, by William Beckford, the author of *Vathek*. Its designer was James Wyatt.

Fool. In Shakespeare's *King Lear*, a companion of Lear in his wanderings on the heath. He acts as the conscience of the King, reminding him continually of his folly in giving away his kingdom, and sits as a judge with Edgar (disguised as Tom o'Bedlam) in the mock trial of Lear's daughters (III.vi).

Fool. In Shakespeare's *Timon of Athens*, a servant who arrives with Apemantus and jests with the servants of Timon's creditors (II.ii).

Fool, The. A historical novel by Henry Christopher Bailey, published in 1921. It is set in France and England during the period 1140–89.

Fool Errant: Memoirs of Francis-Anthony Strelley, Esq., Citizen of Luca (strel'i; lö'kạ), **The.** A historical novel by Maurice Hewlett, published in 1905. It deals with the adventures of an English gentleman traveling in Italy in the third and fourth decades of the 18th century.

Foolish Virgins. A play (1904) by Alfred Sutro.

Fool of Quality, The. A novel published by Henry Brooke in 1766. It was republished by Charles Kingsley in 1859. The "fool" is Henry, the second son of the Earl of Moreland, and so called because his parents thought his intelligence inferior to that of his brother.

Fool of the World, The. A volume of poetry by Arthur Symons, published in 1906.

Fools' Festival. See **Feast of Fools.**

foot. In prosody, a group of syllables, of which one is distinguished above the others, which are relatively less marked in enunciation; a section of a rhythmical series consisting of a thesis and an arsis. The Greeks first gave the name foot (πούς) to the group of times marked by and coincident with one rise and one fall of the human foot in dancing or in beating time. The time or syllable marked alike by the ictus or stress of voice, and by the beat of foot or hand in marking time, they accordingly called the thesis (θέσις) or "setting down" (of the foot), and the remaining interval before or after this the arsis (ἄρσις) or "raising" (of the foot). Many Latin and modern writers have introduced great confusion into metrical nomenclature by directly interchanging the meaning of the words arsis and thesis. An uninterrupted succession of feet constitutes a colon or series, and the name line or verse is given to a colon, cola, or period, if written in one line. In accentual poetry, as in English, and other modern languages in which the syllabic accent is chiefly a stress of the voice, the rhythmical ictus regularly coincides with the syllabic accent, and the relative length of time taken in pronouncing a syllable is almost entirely disregarded. In the poetry of the Greeks, Romans, Hindus, and other nations in whose languages the syllabic accent was chiefly a matter of tone or pitch, quantity (that is, the length of time taken in pronouncing each syllable) determined the ryhthm. In Greek and Roman rhythmics and metrics a unit of time is assumed, called a *primary* or *fundamental time* or *mora*, or specifically a *time*, and this is regarded as the ordinary or normal short (marked ⌣), and expressed in verbal composition by a short syllable. The ordinary or normal long (marked –) is equal to two times or more, and is expressed by a long syllable. Metrical classification of such feet is based either on metrical *magnitude* (that is, on the length of the foot as measured in morae or times, each long being reckoned as two shorts) or on the *pedal ratio* (that is, the proportion of the number of times in the thesis to that in the arsis).

> From long to long in solemn sort
> Slow Spondee stalks; strong foot! yet ill able
> Ever to come up with Dactyl trisyllable.
> (Coleridge, *Metrical Feet*.)

Foote (fût), **Samuel.** b. at Truro, England, 1720; d. at Dover, England, Oct. 21, 1777. An English dramatist and actor. He first appeared on the stage in 1744. In 1747 he opened the Haymarket Theatre with a mixed entertainment, in which he played Fondlewife in *The Careless Husband* (a farce taken from Congreve's *Old Bachelor*), and other parts, principally in *Diversions of the Morning*, which he wrote and acted himself. He bought the Haymarket Theatre, pulled it down, and reopened (1767) in a new building with Barry as the star. His talent for mimicry was his chief gift, and he employed it upon prominent personages of the day in his satirical entertainments *Tea at 6:30*, *Chocolate in Ireland*, *An Auction of Pictures*, and others. In 1776 he caricatured the notorious Duchess of Kingston in the *Trip to Calais*, an act which subjected him to much criticism and to an indictment. Among his plays are *The Knights* (1749), *Taste* (1752), *The Englishman in Paris* (1753), *The Englishman Returned from Paris* (1756), *The Author* (1757), *The Minor* (1760), a satire on Whitfield and Methodism, *The Orators* (1762), *The Mayor of Garratt* (1763), *The Patron* (1764), *The Commissary* (1765), *The Devil upon Two Sticks* (1768), *The Lame Lover* (1770), *The Maid of Bath* (1771), *The Nabob* (1772), *The Bankrupt* (1773), *The Cozeners* (1774), *The Capuchin* (1776; an alteration of the *Trip to Calais*). He also wrote a number of witty prose tracts. From his scathing wit he was known as "the English Aristophanes."

Fopling Flutter (fop'ling flut'ẽr), **Sir.** See **Flutter, Sir Fopling.**

Foppington (fop'ing.tọn), **Lord.** In Vanbrugh's comedy *The Relapse*, a foolish fine gentleman, a further development of Colley Cibber's Sir Novelty Fashion in *Love's Last Shift*. He also appears (as Lord Foppington) in Cibber's *Careless Husband*, and in Sheridan's *Trip to Scarborough*, an alteration of *The Relapse*.

Forbes (fôrbz), **Rosita.** [Full name, **Joan Rosita Forbes**; maiden name, **Torr.**] b. in Lincolnshire,

England, Jan. 16, 1901—. An English writer, traveler, and lecturer. She accompanied expeditions to Kufara (or Cufra), in Libya (1920), and Asir, in Arabia (1922–23); author of *Quest* (1922), *Conflict* (1931), *India of the Princes* (1939), *A Unicorn in the Bahamas* (1939), and *Appointment with Destiny* (1946).

Forbes-Robertson (fôrbz′.rob′ėrt.sọn), **Diana.** An English journalist and writer; wife (married 1935) of Vincent Sheean. She collaborated with Robert Capa on *The Battle of Waterloo Road* (1941). Author of *A Cat and A King* (1949).

Forbonius and Priscera (fôr.bō′ni.us; pri.sē′ri.ạ), **Delectable History of.** A romance in prose and verse by Thomas Lodge (1584).

Forced Marriage, The. A tragicomedy (1670) by Aphra Behn.

Forced Marriage, The. A tragedy (1754) by John Armstrong.

Forcellini (fôr.chel.lē′nē), **Egidio.** b. near Feltre, Belluno, Italy, Aug. 26, 1688; d. at Padua, Italy, April 4, 1768. An Italian lexicographer, a pupil and collaborator of Facciolati. He began the *Totius latinitatis lexicon* in 1718, and completed it with Facciolati's aid in 1753. It was published at Padua in 1771.

Ford (fôrd), **Ford Madox.** [Original name, **Ford Madox Hueffer.**] b. at Merton, England, 1873; d. at Deauville, France, June 26, 1939. An English novelist, poet, critic, and editor; grandson of Ford Madox Brown (1821–93) and son of Francis Hueffer (1845–89). He changed his name to Ford in 1919. He was educated at London, and in France and Germany. He founded and edited (1908 *et seq.*) the *English Review*, and established the *Transatlantic Review* at Paris after World War I. He was author of *The Fifth Queen* (1906), *The Half Moon* (1909), *The Good Soldier* (1915), and many other novels, including a cycle of four, published (1950) as *Parade's End* and including *Some Do Not* (1924), *No More Parades* (1925), *A Man Could Stand Up* (1926), and *The Last Post* (1928). He also wrote *Collected Poems* (1913), *On Heaven and Poems Written in Active Service* (1918), and *New Poems* (1927); *Ford Madox Brown* (1896), *Rossetti* (1902), *Hans Holbein, the Younger* (1905), *Henry James* (1913), *Joseph Conrad* (1924), and *The English Novel* (1929), critical studies; *Memories and Impressions* (1911), *Thus to Revisit* (1921), *It Was the Nightingale* (1933), and *Mightier than the Sword* (1938), autobiographical works. With Joseph Conrad he was coauthor of *The Inheritors* (1901) and *Romance* (1903). *Gray Matter, There Shall Be More Joy, Winter-Night Song, On Heaven,* and the dialogue *A House* are some of his best poems.

Ford, John. b. at Ilsington, Devonshire, England, 1586 (baptized April 17); d. after 1639. An English dramatist. Little is known of his life except that he was a member of the Middle Temple and not dependent on his pen for his living, and that he was popular with playgoers. He apparently retired to Ilsington to end his days. His principal plays are *The Lovers' Melancholy* (1628, printed 1629), '*Tis Pity She's a Whore* (c1626, printed 1633), *The Broken Heart* (1632–33, printed 1633), *Love's Sacrifice* (c1630, printed 1633), *The Chronicle*

Historie of Perkin Warbeck (printed 1634), *The Fancies Chaste and Noble* (printed 1638), *The Lady's Trial* (1638, printed 1639), *The Sun's Darling* (1624, with Dekker; printed 1657), *The Witch of Edmonton* (c1621 with Dekker and Rowley; printed 1658). A number of other works, either never printed or now lost, are licensed in Ford's name. Attributed to him on internal evidence is *The Queen, or the Excellency of the Sea* (privately printed 1653). Some of the lost plays are believed to have been destroyed by John Warburton's cook in the 18th century, when she used what she considered worthless old paper for various kitchen chores. His works were collected by Weber in 1811, by Gifford in 1827, and by Gifford with Dyce's notes in 1869.

Ford, Master. In Shakespeare's *Merry Wives of Windsor*, a well-to-do gentleman. He assumes the name of Master Brook, and induces Falstaff to confide to him his passion for Mistress Ford and his success in duping Ford, her husband.

Ford, Mistress. In Shakespeare's *Merry Wives of Windsor*, the wife of Ford. Falstaff writes identical love notes to her and Mistress Page, the "merry wives," and they set about making a fool of him.

Ford, Richard. b. at London, 1796; d. at Heavitree, near Exeter, England, 1858. An English traveler and author. He wrote *Handbook for Travelers in Spain* (1845), one of the first and best (and in its original form the fullest) of Murray's Handbooks.

Foresight (fōr′sīt). In Congreve's comedy *Love for Love*, an old man with a fondness for judicial astrology. He is made up of dramas, nativities, and superstitions of all kinds, and is always searching for omens. He has a hypocritical, vicious wife.

Forester (for′ẹs.tėr), **C. S.** [Full name, **Cecil Scott Forester.**] b. at Cairo, Egypt, Aug. 27, 1899—. An English writer. He is the author of biographies of *Napoleon* (1924), *Josephine* (1925), *Victor Emmanuel* (1927), *Louis XIV* (1928), *Nelson* (1929), and others. His novels include *The Gun* (1933), *The General* (1936), *To the Indies* (1940), *The Captain from Connecticut* (1941), *The Ship* (1943), and *The Sky and the Forest* (1948). He dramatized and scenarized *Payment Deferred* (1924), his first novel, a study of murder. Forester is known especially for his Horatio Hornblower stories, including *Beat to Quarters* (1927), *Ship of the Line* (1938; awarded James Tait Black memorial prize), and *Flying Colours* (1939), comprising the *Captain Horatio Hornblower* trilogy (1939). His later Hornblower stories include *Commodore Hornblower* (1945), *Lord Hornblower* (1946), and *Lieutenant Hornblower* (1952). In 1954 he issued a statement that after having written more than half a million words about Hornblower, he would cease using the indomitable naval officer as a subject, saying "There simply is no more Hornblower . . . I've used him up." His most recent works are *The Nightmare* (1954), a collection of short stories based on the trials at Nuremberg and Belsen, and *The Good Shepherd* (1955), a novel about an American destroyer during World War II.

Forester, Frank. Pseudonym of **Herbert, Henry William.**

Forest Lovers, The. A romance (1898) by Maurice Hewlett.

---

fat, fāte, fär, ȧsk, fāre; net, mē, hėr; pin, pīne; not, nōte, mȯve, nôr; up, lūte, pull; ᵺH, then;

Forest of Arden (är'dẹn). See **Arden, Forest of.**

Forest of Wild Thyme, The. A poem (1905) by Alfred Noyes.

For Lancelot Andrews (lan'sẹ.lọt an'dröz). A volume of critical essays by T. S. Eliot, published in 1928. The author asserts the need for a central core of belief under recognized religious authority. The work is in part a criticism of the New Humanism.

Formal (fôr'mạl), **James.** In Wycherley's comedy *The Gentleman Dancing Master,* an old, rich merchant, also known as Don Diego.

Forman (fôr'mạn), **H. Buxton.** [Full name, **Harry Buxton Forman.**] b. at Camberwell, South London, July 11, 1842; d. at St. John's Wood, London, June 15, 1917. An English scholar, critic, and editor. From 1860 to 1907 he was in the civil service, as clerk, secretary, and controller of the packet services in the post office. He contributed articles (1869 *et seq.*) to *Tinsley's Magazine* and the London *Quarterly Review.* His works include *Our Living Poets* (1871), *Elizabeth Barrett Browning and Her Scarcer Books* (1896), *The Books of William Morris* (1907), *George Meredith* (1909), biography and criticism; he also edited the poetical works of Shelley (1876), the letters (1878) of Keats to Fanny Brawne, Shelley's *Note Books* (1911), and *Hitherto Unpublished Poems and Stories of Elizabeth Barrett Browning* (1914); for the Temple Classics he edited Browning's *Sordello* and Mrs. Browning's *Aurora Leigh.*

Former Age, The. A poem by Chaucer on the happy Golden Age of myth and legend, discovered by Bradshaw and first printed by Morris in 1870.

Form of Living. [Also, **The Form of Perfect Living.**] A Middle English prose epistle by Richard Rolle of Hampole, written for Margaret Kirkby, a recluse. It is an exposition of Rolle's religious mysticism.

Fornarina (fôr.nä.rē'nä), **La.** A picture by Raphael, painted c1509, now in the Palazzo Barberini at Rome. It represents a half-nude woman seated in a wood. On her bracelet is written "Raphael Urbinas." It is commonly called "Raphael's Mistress," the name "Fornarina" having been given to it c1750.

Forobosco (fō.rọ.bos'kō). A cheating mountebank in *The Fair Maid of the Inn,* by John Fletcher and others.

Forrest (for'ẹst). In Shakespeare's *Richard III,* a murderer (mentioned in IV.iii) hired by Tyrrel to kill the Princes imprisoned in the Tower.

Forrest, The. A collection of poems (published 1616) by Ben Jonson, including the very well-known ones containing the lines "Drink to me only with thine eyes" and "Come, my Celia, let us prove."

Forrester (for'ẹs.tèr), **Alfred Henly.** [Pseudonym (with Charles Robert Forrester), **Alfred Crowquill.**] b. at London, Sept. 10, 1804; d. there, May 26, 1872. An English author and artist; younger brother of Charles Robert Forrester. He contributed sketches to Volumes II, III, and IV of *Punch,* and illustrated numerous works.

Forrester, Charles Robert. [Pseudonyms: **Hal Willis,** (with Alfred Henry Forrester) **Alfred Crowquill.**] b. at London, 1803; d. there, Jan. 15, 1850. An English author; elder brother of Alfred Henry Forrester. Among his works are *Absurdities in Prose and Verse, written and illustrated by Alfred Crowquill* (1827) and *Phantasmagoria of Fun* (1843), both of which were illustrated by his brother.

Forsaken Merman, The. A poem (1849) by Matthew Arnold.

Fors Clavigera (fôrz klav.i.gē'rạ). [Full title, **Fors Clavigera: Letters to the Workmen and Laborers of Great Britain.**] A social and economic study (1871–74) by John Ruskin.

Forseti (for.set'ē). In Norse mythology, the god of justice, son of Balder.

Forster (fôr'stèr), **Edward Morgan.** b. at London, Jan. 1, 1879—. An English novelist. His works include *Where Angels Fear to Tread* (1905), *The Longest Journey* (1907), *A Room with a View* (1908), *Howards End* (1910), *The Celestial Omnibus and Other Stories* (1911), *A Passage to India* (1924; Prix Femina Vie Heureuse and James Tait Black prize, 1925), *Aspects of the Novel* (Clark lecture, 1927), *Abinger Harvest* (1936), *What I Believe* (1939), *Virginia Woolf* (Rede lecture, 1942), *The Development of English Prose between 1918 and 1939,* and *Two Cheers for Democracy* (1951). He served as Rede lecturer at Cambridge (1941), and W. P. Ker lecturer at Glasgow (1944), and was a member of the committee appointed (1947) by the lord chancellor to examine the law of defamatory libel.

Forster, John. b. at Newcastle, England, April 2, 1812; d. Feb. 2, 1876. An English historian and biographer. He studied at University College, London, was called to the bar at the Inner Temple in 1843, became editor of the *Examiner* in 1847, was appointed secretary to the commissioners of lunacy in 1855, and was made a commissioner of lunacy in 1861, a position which he resigned in 1872. He bequeathed "the Forster Collection" to the nation. It is now at South Kensington. It consists of 18,000 books, many manuscripts (including nearly all the original manuscripts of Dickens's novels), 48 oil paintings, and a large number of drawings, engravings, and other items. His works include *Historical and Biographical Essays* (collected in 1858), *Life of Sir John Eliot* (expanded 1864), *Life of Landor* (1869), and *Life of Dickens* (1872–74). He wrote a number of other biographies, and contributed masterly articles to the leading periodicals.

Forsyte Saga (fôr'sīt), **The.** A trilogy by John Galsworthy, including the novels *The Man of Property* (1906), *In Chancery* (1920), and *To Let* (1921). With the addition of two "interludes," *The Indian Summer of a Forsyte* (1920) and *The Awakening* (1921), the entire work was published under the collective title *The Forsyte Saga* (1922). It depicts the development of an English upper-middle-class family in the later Victorian era. The main character is Soames Forsyte, the "man of property" who represents the chief theme of the work, the proprietary instinct. Another collective volume dealing with the Forsytes is *A Modern*

ḍ, d or j; ṣ, s or sh; ṭ, t or ch; ẓ, z or zh; o, F. cloche; ü, F. menu; ċh, Sc. loch; ṅ, F. bonbon.

Comedy (1929), consisting of *The White Monkey* (1924), *The Silver Spoon* (1926), and *Swan Song* (1928), and two "interludes," *The Silent Wooing* (1925) and *Passerby* (1927).

Fortescue (fôr′tĕs.kū), **George.** b. at London, c1578; d. 1659. An English essayist and poet. He was the son of Roman Catholic parents, and was educated at the English College at Douai and at the English College at Rome. His chief work is *Feriae Academicae, auctore Georgio de Forti Scuto Nobili Anglo* (1630). He is also credited with the authorship of the anonymous poem *The Sovles Pilgrimage to Heavenly Hierusalem* (1650).

Fortescue, Sir **John.** b. c1394; d. c1476. An English jurist. He was made chief justice of the King's Bench in 1442. As a Lancastrian he followed Queen Margaret to Flanders in 1463, returned to England in 1471, was captured at the battle of Tewkesbury, and accepted a pardon from Edward IV. His most notable works are *De laudibus legum Angliae*, first printed in 1537, and *On the Governance of the Kingdom of England* (also entitled *The Difference between an Absolute and Limited Monarchy* and *De dominio regali et politico*), first printed in 1714.

For the Time Being. The formal title of "A Christmas Oratorio" by W. H. Auden, and of the volume in which both it and *The Sea and the Mirror* were published in 1944. Many critics consider it his outstanding work. It is divided into nine parts corresponding to the traditional elements in the Christmas story, and contains long prose passages (for example, "The Meditation of Simeon") and light verse (for example, "When the Sex War Ended with the Slaughter of the Grandmothers").

Fortinbras (fôr′tin.bras). In Shakespeare's *Hamlet*, the Prince of Norway. He aspires to recover the lands and power lost by his father. On the way to attack Poland, he marches through Denmark, where Hamlet encounters him (IV.iv), Hamlet's reaction being the Soliloquy "How all occasions do inform against me."

Fortitude. A novel by Hugh Walpole, published in 1913.

Fortuna (fôr.tū′na̱). In Roman mythology, the counterpart of Tyche, the Greek goddess of fortune.

Fortunate Islands. [Also, **Isles of the Blest.**] The happy otherworld of Greek and Roman mythology where the souls of the blessed dead live in pleasure and rejoicing. They were regarded as situated in the Western Ocean. In later Greek mythology, Elysium was said to be located in the Fortunate Islands. With the discovery of the Canary and Madeira Islands the name became attached to them. All Celtic mythologies have their Isles of the Blest, a paradise of feasts, music, and generous women, where there is no age and no death. Saint Brendan's Island, which he found in the western Atlantic in the 6th century, is called the Isle of the Blest, and was believed by him to be the Christian paradise. Later Irish seekers of it said Brendan had found America.

Fortunate Mistress, The. A title often applied to *Roxana*, a novel (1724) by Daniel Defoe. It was Defoe's own name for the book.

Fortune. A short poem, attributed to Chaucer by Shirley. Its subtitle is *Balades de Visage* [some-times written *village*] *sanz Peinture* ("The Face of the World as it Really Is, not Painted"). It is based chiefly on Boethius, partly on a portion of the *Roman de la Rose.*

Fortune (fôr′chun), **Reggie.** In Henry Christopher Bailey's "Mr. Fortune" series of detective stories, the central character.

Fortune, the. A public playhouse built at London in 1600. Edward Alleyn had the lease of the site, on Golders Lane; Philip Henslowe, his father-in-law, became his partner in 1601. In 1621 it was burned down but another round building of brick was put up in 1623. This was dismantled in 1649.

Fortune by Land and Sea. A comedy by John Heywood and William Rowley, printed in 1655. Its heroine, Anne Harding, has been called by C. F. Tucker Brooke "among the most charming women of minor Elizabethan drama."

Fortune's Fool. A novel by Rafael Sabatini, published in 1923.

Fortunes of Nigel (nī′jĕl), **The.** A historical novel by Sir Walter Scott, published in 1822. The scene is laid at London during the reign of James I.

Fortunes of Richard Mahony (rich′a̱rd ma̱.hō′ni), **The.** Trilogy by Henry Handel Richardson (Mrs. Henrietta Robertson), published in 1930. It consists of *Australia Felix* (1917), *The Way Home* (1925), and *Ultima Thule* (1929).

Fortunio (fôr.tū′ni.ō). A folk tale of ancient but unknown origin. Fortunio is the daughter of an aged nobleman, in whose stead she offers her services to the king, disguised as a cavalier. A magic horse named Comrade, and seven servants, Strongback, Lightfoot, Marksman, Fine-ear, Boisterer, Gormand, and Tippler, aid her to slay a dragon and regain the treasures for the king.

Fortunio. A young man in love with Valerio's sister in George Chapman's comedy *All Fools, or All Fools but the Fool.*

Forty, The. The 40 members of the French Academy.

Forty Footsteps, Field of the. See **Field of the Forty Footsteps.**

Forty Thieves, The. One of the tales of *The Arabian Nights' Entertainments.* It is often called *Ali Baba and the Forty Thieves.*

Forty Thieves, The. A play by the younger George Colman, produced in 1805.

Foscari (fōs′kä.rē), **Francesco.** d. 1457. Doge of Venice (1423–57). He began in 1426 a war against Filippo Maria Visconti, Duke of Milan, which resulted in the acquisition of Brescia, Bergamo, and Cremona in 1427. A second war, which lasted from 1431 to 1433, fixed the Adda River as the boundary of the Venetian dominion. A war against Bologna, Milan, and Mantua, in which he was supported by Francisco Sforza and Cosimo de' Medici, resulted in 1441 in the conquest of Lonato, Velaggio, and Peschiera. He was with his son the subject of Byron's tragedy *The Two Foscari.*

Fosco (fos′kō), **Count.** In Wilkie Collins's novel *The Woman in White*, a fat, insidious, and agreeable villain.

Foss (fos), **Corporal.** In *The Poor Gentleman*, by George Colman the younger, the faithful servant and former soldier of Worthington. He is modeled on Sterne's Corporal Trim.

Fosse Way (fos′ wā). [Also: **Foss Way, the Fosse.**] An ancient British and Roman road in England, running from the English Channel coast of Devonshire NE through Bath, Cirencester, Leicester, and Lincoln to the river Humber, in the vicinity of Grimsby, in N Lincolnshire.

Foster (fos′tẽr), **Anthony.** In Sir Walter Scott's novel *Kenilworth*, a sullen hypocrite, the warder of Amy Robsart at Cumnor Place. Overcome by his love for gold, he assists in her murder. He accidentally shuts himself in a cell with a springlock, and perishes with his ill-gotten gold.

Foster, John. b. Sept. 17, 1770; d. Oct. 15, 1843. An English essayist.

Fothergill (foᴛʜ′ẽr.gil), **Jessie.** b. at Manchester, England, 1856; d. at London, July 30, 1891. An English novelist. She wrote *The First Violin* (1878) and other works.

Fothergill, John. b. at Carr End, Wensleydale, Yorkshire, England, March 8, 1712; d. at London, Dec. 26, 1780. An English physician, philanthropist, and author. From 1736 to 1738 he was on the staff of St. Thomas's Hospital, at London, working under the supervision of Sir Edward Wilmot, physician to George II and George III. In 1740 he began his own practice at London, and in 1744, on October 1, he was admitted as a licentiate of the London Royal College of Physicians, an honor which he was the first Edinburgh graduate to receive. In 1754, on August 6, the Edinburgh College of Physicians made him a fellow; he became a fellow of the London Royal Society in 1763, and a fellow of the Paris Royal Society of Medicine in 1776. He was also interested in general science, botany, and in philanthropic activity. He collected and cultivated rare plants and set up a large botanical garden at Upton, near Stratford. He corresponded with botanists and collectors in all parts of the world who sent him rare plants and flowers for his garden. He also employed a group of artists to make drawings of the various specimens (the value of these drawings, 1,200 of them, may be gathered from the fact that they were purchased, after his death, by Catherine II of Russia). His collection of shells and insects later became a part of William Hunter's London Museum. As a philanthropist, Fothergill helped the Society of Friends and supported a Quaker school at Ackworth but he did not limit his charities to his own group. He did not concern himself with politics, but when there was bad feeling between the American colonies and the mother country, he did what he could in his public and private capacities to encourage a peaceful and friendly approach to the problem. In 1765 he published *Considerations Relative to the North American Colonies*, in which he urged that the Stamp Act be repealed, and in 1774 he was working with Benjamin Franklin on plans aimed at settling the dispute without resorting to arms. His medical works are *An Account of the Sore Throat Attended with Ulcers* (1748; 6th ed., 1777, and several European translations), historically important as being the first description in English of diphtheria, dealing with the 1747-48 London epidemic and giving a description of the disease throughout Europe; *Of a Painful Affection of the Face* (1773), describing what is now known as tic-douloureux, or facial neuralgia; and *On the Epidemic Disease of 1775*, an account of influenza. *Rules for the Preservation of Health*, a work not by him, seeking to trade on his high reputation, carried his name (wrongly spelled) on the title-page and ran through 14 editions, in spite of his repeated protests. There is no reason to dispute Franklin's opinion of him: "I can hardly conceive that a better man has ever existed."

Fotheringay (foᴛʜ′ẽr.ing.gā′′), **Miss.** In Thackeray's novel *Pendennis*, the stage name of Emily Costigan.

Foulis (foulz), **Robert.** b. at Glasgow, April 20, 1707; d. at Edinburgh, June 2, 1776. Scottish printer, noted for his editions of Horace, Homer, Herodotus, and other classics.

Foul Play. A novel (1869) by Charles Reade, dramatized with Dion Boucicault in 1879.

"Foul-weather Jack." See **Byron, John.**

Foundling, The. A sentimental comedy by Edward Moore, produced in 1748.

Fountain, The. A novel by Charles Morgan, published in 1932 and awarded the Hawthornden Prize in 1933. It is a love story dealing with the conflict between the passionate and the spiritual elements in character.

Fountain of Youth. [Also, **Fountain of Life.**] A fabulous fountain or spring whose waters would restore or preserve youth, heal the sick, and resuscitate the dead. The concept and the universal human hope reflected in it are very ancient and almost worldwide. The Fountain of Youth is one of the well-known and frequent quests of European folk tale. The Koran tells the story of Alexander the Great's search for the Fountain of Life, for instance. Certain Central American Indians located it on one of the Bimini islands of the Bahamas. Spaniards under Ponce de Leon, Narvaez, De Soto, and others penetrated far into the interior of America, seeking it. Tales of a youth- and life-giving fountain are found also among the peoples of the Pacific and among various North American Indians; the story is also told in French Canada.

Fountains Abbey. A Cistercian monastery of the 14th century, near Ripon, England. It is considered by many to be the most picturesque of ecclesiastical ruins in England.

Fouqué (fö.kā′), **Baron Friedrich Heinrich Karl de la Motte-.** [Pseudonym, **Pellegrin.**] b. at Brandenburg, Germany, Feb. 12, 1777; d. at Berlin, Jan. 23, 1843. A German writer of the romantic period. He served in the War of Liberation (1813), and later lived at Paris, Halle (where he lectured on modern history and poetry), and Berlin. In 1808 appeared the drama *Sigurd der Schlangentötter*. His *Der Zauberring* is a romance of the age of chivalry. His principal work is the romantic story *Undine*, which appeared in 1811. He was the author of numerous lyrics, among them the patriotic song beginning "Frisch auf zum fröhlichen Jagen" (1813).

Four Days' Wonder. A novel by A. A. Milne, published in 1933.

d̞, d or j; ṣ, s or sh; ṭ, t or ch; ẓ, z or zh; o, F. cloche; ü, F. menu; ċh, Sc. loch; ṅ, F. bonbon.

Foure Sonnes of Aymon (ā'mọn). A Middle English prose translation from the French of a work in the Ferumbras group of the Charlemagne cycle, printed by Caxton c1489.

Four Georges (jôr'jiz), **The.** A series of lectures (1855) by Thackeray, presented both in England and the United States.

Four Horsemen of the Apocalypse. Allegorical figures in the Bible (Rev. vi. 1–8), four horses, each of a different color and each with a rider. There are many interpretations of their significance, one of the most familiar being that the white horse represents Christ, who is its rider, the red horse War or Slaughter, the black horse Famine, and the pale horse Death, who rides it, or Pestilence. Another interpretation is that the white horse symbolizes Conquest. *The Four Horsemen of the Apocalypse* is also a highly successful novel (1916) and motion picture by the Spanish author Blasco-Ibáñez.

Fourier (fö.ryā), **François Marie Charles.** b. at Besançon, France, April 7, 1772; d. at Paris, Oct. 10, 1837. A French socialist and writer. He entered the army as a chasseur in 1793, but was discharged because of ill health after two years of service. He was subsequently connected, in subordinate positions, with various commercial houses at Marseilles, Lyons, and elsewhere. He resided at Paris after 1826. He published (1808) *Théorie des quatre mouvements et des destinées générales*, in which he propounded the coöperative social system subsequently known as Fourierism. This system contemplated the organization of society into phalanxes or associations, each large enough for all industrial and social requirements, arranged in groups according to occupation, capacities, and attractions, living in phalansteries or common dwellings. He also wrote *Traité de l'association domestique et agricole* (1822; published later as *Théorie de l'unité universelle*) and *Le Nouveau Monde* (1829–30).

Four Just Men, The. A novel by Edgar Wallace, published in 1906. It tells the story of four men who start a crusade for the destruction of wicked members of society.

Four Plays for Dancers. A collection of short plays by William Butler Yeats, suggested by the Japanese Noh plays, and making use of masks, music, and dancing.

Four Plays in One. A collection of four pageants by Beaumont and Fletcher, printed in 1647; *Honour* and *Love* being by Beaumont, and *Death* and *Time* usually being assigned to Fletcher. They are founded on stories in *The Decameron* of Boccaccio.

Four Prentices of London. [Full title, **Four Prentices of London: With the Conquest of Jerusalem.**] A comedy by Thomas Heywood, printed in 1615 and possibly produced as early as the 1590's, since he calls it an early effort "as plays were then some fifteen or sixteen years ago" (actually he may have revised it around 1610, so that the printed version would differ from the original).

Four P's, The. A "merry interlude" by John Heywood. The four P's were a "Palmer, a Pardoner, a Poticary, and a Pedlar." It was probably written c1522, and was printed c1533.

Four Quartets. A sequence of four poems by T. S. Eliot, published in 1943, comprising *Burnt Norton* (1939), *East Coker* (1940), *Dry Salvages* (1941), and *Little Gidding* (1942).

Four Sons of Aymon (ā'mọn). An old play relicensed by Herbert in 1624. Balfe wrote an opera with the same title in 1843.

Fourteen Revelations of Divine Love. A Middle English prose discourse of the early 15th century by Juliana Lampit. She discloses Christ's teachings as they were revealed to her.

Fowler (fou'lėr). In James Shirley's *Witty Fair One*, a brilliant libertine, reformed by being persuaded that he is dead, and suffering for his vices as a disembodied spirit.

Fowler, Edward. b. at Westerleigh, Gloucestershire, England, 1632; d. at Chelsea, London, Aug. 26, 1714. An English prelate and theological writer, bishop of Gloucester in 1691. He wrote *Design of Christianity* (1671), which was attacked by Bunyan and Baxter, *Dirt wip'd off: or a manifest discovery of the wicked spirit of one John Bunyan* (1672), and others.

Fowler, Ellen Thorneycroft. Maiden name of **Felkin, Ellen Thorneycroft.**

Fowler, Henry Watson. b. 1858; d. at London, Dec. 27, 1933. An English lexicographer and author. Educated at Oxford, he was a schoolmaster for 17 years at Sedbergh School, Yorkshire. He produced two abridgments of the *Oxford English Dictionary: The Concise Oxford Dictionary* (1911) and *The Pocket Oxford Dictionary* (1924); coauthor with his brother of *The King's English* (1906); compiled *A Dictionary of Modern English Usage* (1926), considered one of the standard works of reference on the English language; his other books include *On Grammatical Inversions* (1922), *Some Comparative Values* (1929), *Between Boy and Man, If Wishes Were Horses* (1929), *Rhymes of Darby to Joan* (1931), and a translation of Lucian.

Fox (foks), **Caroline.** b. at Falmouth, England, May 24, 1819; d. there, Jan. 12, 1871. An English diarist. She was the daughter of Robert Were Fox (a physicist and mineralogist), and the friend of John Sterling, J. S. Mill, Carlyle, and other noted persons. Extracts from her diary covering the period 1835–71 were published in 1881 (3rd ed., 1882).

Fox, Charles James. b. at Westminster, London, Jan. 24, 1749; d. at Chiswick, Middlesex, England, Sept. 13, 1806. An English politician and orator. He was the third son of Henry Fox, later 1st Baron Holland. He was educated (entirely by his own choice, his father carrying to the extreme limit the idea of allowing his children complete freedom) at Wandsworth (a school run by a French refugee, Monsieur Pampellone), at Eton (1758–64), and at Hertford College, Oxford, where, unlike most of his fellows, he studied so hard that his father took him away before he could secure a degree. In 1763 and later, during vacation periods, he went with his father to Paris and to Spa, famous as a health resort since the 16th century, enjoying himself to the full (with his father's approval) in wild living and gambling. In 1768 he was elected member of Parliament for Midhurst, Sussex, and he made a name for himself in the following year by attacking Wilkes, for which he was rewarded by being made lord of the admiralty in 1770, in North's administration. He resigned two years later in order to oppose the Royal Marriage Bill, an act for which George III, who considered him "as contemptible as he is odious," never forgave him. In 1774 and later, he was a vigorous opponent of North's policy in dealing with the American Colonies. He believed in the justice of the American cause, predicted that it would triumph, and voted for the repeal of the tea tax. From 1780 until his death he represented Westminster in Parliament. In 1782 he was secretary of state in Lord Rockingham's government; in February, 1783, he joined North's short-lived coalition ministry, which was unpopular and which George dismissed before the year was out. In the general election of 1784 his party suffered a crushing defeat and from then until his death Fox was a member of the opposition. He was against Hastings and for his impeachment, for Canadian self-government, for parliamentary reform, for helping the Irish people, and for repealing the Test Acts. He hated slavery and the slave trade, advocated abolition, and defended the French Revolution to such an extent that he lost the friendship of Burke, which he had enjoyed since 1775. During the decade of 1790–1800 his personal popularity and his political power reached their lowest point. He hailed the fall of the Bastille as "the greatest event that ever happened in the world and the best." For this, for his insistence that the Revolution must be judged by its principles and theories rather than by its excesses, and for his attack on what he considered the despotism of Pitt's foreign policy, he was openly called an enemy of his country. In 1792 his own party deserted him, and in 1797 he withdrew from Parliament and stopped attending its sessions. He retired to St. Anne's Hill, near Chertsey in Surrey, and made no appearance in public life until 1800 (February 3), when he cast a vote of censure against the ministers who had refused to consider Napoleon's peace proposals. In May, 1798, he shocked many people by giving the toast "Our sovereign, the people," a toast that in January of the same year had cost the Duke of Norfolk his post as lord lieutenant. In 1802 he made a grand tour of the Netherlands and France, where he had several meetings with Napoleon, whom he described as "a young man considerably intoxicated with success." The next year (on May 24) after a declaration of war had been passed, he spoke for three hours in favor of peace in a speech that was praised by all sides. In 1806, as foreign secretary in Grenville's "All-the-Talents" cabinet, he informed Talleyrand of a plot to assassinate Napoleon, and in the same year he voted against the motion to accord public honors to Pitt (by whose side he was to be buried in Westminster Abbey less than eight months later). His last public act, a few days before his health forced him to end his political career, was to call for the abolition of the slave trade. Fox had a complex, many-sided character: he loved his friends and hated his enemies, and he has been praised and blamed, without restraint, by both. He was a good student, in spite of his father, and he was thoroughly familiar with the classics, as well as French, Italian, and Spanish. His knowledge of these languages and of their literatures gave

him pleasure until the end of his life. He read Homer, both the *Iliad* and the *Odyssey*, every year of his adult life; he preferred Euripides to Sophocles, declaring that "I should never finish, if I let myself go upon Euripides," and he read the *Aeneid* over and over again. As a critic of his own century, he thought that the four masterpieces were the *Isacco* of the Italian Metastasio, Pope's *Eloisa*, Voltaire's *Zaïre*, and Gray's *Elegy*. He enjoyed Burnet the historian, but he could not stand Milton as a prose writer. He loved Dryden and played with the idea of editing his works, but Wordsworth's poetry meant nothing to him. His own venture in authorship, the unfinished *History of the Early Part of the Reign of James II*, was published two years after his death.

Fox, George. b. at Fenny Drayton (Drayton-in-the-Clay), Leicestershire, England, in July, 1624; d. Jan. 13, 1691. The founder of the Society of Friends (Quakers). He was the son of Christopher Fox, a Puritan weaver, and in his youth was apprenticed to a shoemaker at Nottingham. About the age of 25 he began to disseminate as an itinerant lay preacher the doctrines peculiar to the Society of Friends, the organization of which he completed c1669. He made missionary journeys to Scotland in 1657, to Ireland in 1669, to the West Indies and North America in the years 1671–72, and to Holland in 1677 and 1684, and was frequently imprisoned for infraction of the laws against conventicles, as at Lancaster and Scarborough (1663–66) and at Worcester (1673–74). He married in 1669 Margaret Fell, a widow, who was a woman of superior intellect and gave him much assistance in the founding of his sect.

Fox, The. A novelette by D. H. Lawrence, published in 1923.

Foxe (foks), **John.** b. at Boston, Lincolnshire, England, 1516; d. at London, April 18, 1587. An English martyrologist. He studied at Magdalen College, Oxford, where he took a B.A. in 1537, became a full fellow in 1539, and obtained an M.A. in 1543. He resigned his fellowship in 1545, became in 1548 tutor to the orphan children of Henry Howard, Earl of Surrey (a post which he retained five years), and in 1550 was ordained a deacon. At the accession of Queen Mary he fled to the Continent to avoid persecution as a Protestant, and lived during her reign chiefly at Frankfort on the Main and at Basel, where he was employed as a reader of the press (proofreader) in the printing office of Johann Herbst (Oporinus). He returned to England in 1559, was ordained a priest in 1560, and in 1563 was made a prebendary in Salisbury Cathedral and given the lease of the vicarage of Shipton. His chief work is *Actes and Monuments*, of which four editions appeared during his lifetime (1563, 1570, 1576, and 1583), and which is popularly known as Foxe's *Book of Martyrs;* a Latin version preceded (1559) the English edition. The book was attacked by the Roman Catholics almost immediately, among them Robert Parsons, but despite its many inaccuracies remains a monument to Foxe's energy.

Foyes (foiz), **Count.** In George Chapman's *An Humorous Day's Mirth*, an aged gentleman who

ḍ, d or j; ş, s or sh; ṭ, t or ch; ẓ, z or zh; o, F. cloche; ü, F. menu; ċh, Sc. loch; ṅ, F. bonbon.

tries to force his daughter, Martia, into a marriage with the wealthy simpleton La Bestia.

Frail (frāl), **Mrs.** In Congreve's *Love for Love*, a woman whose nature is as her name. It was one of Mrs. Bracegirdle's best-known roles.

Fra Lippo Lippi (frä lip′ō lip′i). A poem by Robert Browning, published in *Men and Women* (1855), written in the form of a dramatic monologue in which the Italian painter narrates the events of his life (his boyhood of poverty, admission into a Carmelite convent, his conflicts with the prior over his art, and his sly breaking of the rules) as he wanders through the streets at night.

Fram (främ). A specially constructed steam schooner in which Fridtjof Nansen attempted to reach the North Pole. She was 113 ft. long on the water-line, and was built at Raekvik, near Laurvig, Norway. She sailed from Christiania (now Oslo) on June 24, 1893. Nansen left her to continue his journey on sledges on March 14, 1895 (at lat. 84°4′ N., long. 102° E.). Under command of Captain Otto Neumann Sverdrup she reached lat. 85°55.5′ N., long. 66°31′ E. on Nov. 15, 1895, and, returning, passed Spitsbergen in August, 1896, having circumnavigated Novaya Zemlya and the Franz Josef and Spitsbergen archipelagoes. Amundsen sailed in her for the Antarctic trip of 1910–12.

Framley Parsonage (fram′li). A novel by Anthony Trollope, published in 1861, the fourth of the Barsetshire series.

France (fräns), **Anatole.** [Pseudonym of **Jacques Anatole Thibault**.] b. at Paris, April 16, 1844; d. at La Bechellerie, near Tours, France, Oct. 12, 1924. A French novelist, short-fiction writer, critic, historian, essayist, and poet. He won the Nobel prize for literature in 1921. Among his works are *Les Poèmes dorés* (1872), *Le Crime de Silvestre Bonnard* (1881), *Le Livre de mon ami* (1885), *Thaïs* (1890), *L'Étui de nacre* (1892), *Les Opinions de Jérôme Coignard* (1893), *La Rôtisserie de la Reine Pédauque* (1893), *Le Jardin d'Epicure* (1894), *Histoire contemporaine* (4 vols., 1896–1901), *L'Orme du mail* (1897), *M. Bergeret à Paris* (1901), *L'Île des Pinguoins* (1908), *La Vie de Jeanne d'Arc* (1908), *Les Dieux ont soif* (1912), and *La Révolte des Anges* (1914). Many of his works have been translated. Son of a Parisian bookseller, he grew up on books, and failed ingloriously in school; he entered literature as a critic with a study of Alfred de Vigny (1868). His marriage (1877) ended in divorce (1892), but was followed by his long liaison with Mme. Arman de Caillavet, who was responsible for much of his later success. He was literary critic for *Le Temps* (1888–92) and a member of the French Academy (1896). He joined Émile Zola and others in defense of Alfred Dreyfus (1898–99), and from that time on developed a new social seriousness in his work, although no party ever gained his complete support. His funeral was the first "national" funeral given a writer since that of Victor Hugo. His limpid, easy prose combined the traditional French virtues of precision and smoothness, with a skeptical sensuousness learned from such masters as Renan.

France (frans), **King of.** See **King of France.**

Francesca da Rimini (frän.chäs′kä dä rē′mē.nē). fl. 13th century. An Italian lady; daughter of Guido da Polenta, lord of Rimini, and wife of Giovanni Malatesta. The story of her love for Paolo, the young brother of her husband, and their subsequent death (c1288) at the hand of the latter, has been told by Dante in a famous episode in the *Inferno*. Silvio Pellico wrote a tragedy on the subject, and Leigh Hunt a poem. George Henry Boker, Gabriele d'Annunzio, and Francis Marion Crawford wrote tragedies with the same title. Pictures illustrating the story have been painted by Ingres, Cabanel, Ary Scheffer, George Frederic Watts, and others, and it is the subject of a tone poem by Tchaikovsky and an opera by Roccardo Zandonai.

Franceschina (frän.ches.kē′nä). The principal character in John Marston's *Dutch Courtezan.* Her beauty succeeds in overcoming the austerity of Malheureux, after her lover, Freevill, has given her over to Malheureux in order to marry the modest Beatrice. However, with a vindictiveness equal to her beauty, she decides that Malheureux shall only enjoy her at the price of murdering Freevill, but this price Malheureux will not pay.

Franceschini (frän.ches.kē′nē), **Count Guido.** In Browning's *Ring and the Book*, the cold, utterly cruel husband of Pompilia, whose actions are the cause of her flight to Rome.

Franchi (fräng′kē), **Fabian** and **Louis dei.** Twin brothers, characters in Boucicault's play *The Corsican Brothers.*

Francis (fran′sis), **Saint.** See **Francis of Assisi.**

Francis. In Shakespeare's *1 Henry IV*, a drawer (bartender) in a tavern, made fun of by Poins and Prince Hal.

Francis. Entries on literary characters having this prename will be found also under the surnames Acton, Arabin, Archer, Clavering, Feeble, Flute, Gripe, Osbaldistone, Spenlow, and Tyrrel.

Francis, Friar. In Shakespeare's *Much Ado About Nothing*, a friar who suggests to Leonato that he pretend Hero has died of grief, in order to revive Claudio's lost love.

Francis, John. b. at London, July 18, 1811; d. there, April 6, 1882. An English publisher. He was prominently connected with the agitation for the repeal of the duty on newspaper advertisements (1853), of the stamp duty on newspapers (1855), and of the paper duty (1861).

Francis, Mary E. Pseudonym of **Blundell, Mrs. Francis.**

Francis, Philip. b. c1708; d. at Bath, England, March 5, 1773. An Irish author. He took the degree of B.A. at Trinity College, Dublin, in 1728, and after having been for a time curate of St. Peter's, Dublin, went to England, where he obtained the rectory of Skeyton in Norfolk in 1744. He was afterward tutor to Charles James Fox, whom he accompanied to Eton in 1757, and was rector of Barrow in Suffolk from 1762 until his death.

Francis, Sir Philip. b. at Dublin, Oct. 22, 1740; d. Dec. 23, 1818. A British administrator and writer; son of Philip Francis (c1708–73). He was educated at St. Paul's school, became a junior clerk in the secretary of state's office in 1756, was amanuensis (1761–62) to Pitt; was first clerk (1762–72) at the War Office; went to India in 1774 as one of the council of four appointed to advise the governor general of India; returned to England in 1781 (having left India in 1780); entered Parliament in 1784; and was made (c1806) Knight Commander of the Bath. He wrote numerous papers, under various pseudonyms, in support of the Whig Party, and has been credited with the authorship of the *Letters of Junius,* chiefly on the evidence adduced by Charles Chabot, who compared the handwriting of Junius with that of Francis.

Francisca (fran.sis′kạ). In Shakespeare's *Measure for Measure,* a nun.

Franciscans (fran.sis′kạnz). An order of mendicant friars founded (1209) by Saint Francis of Assisi, Italy, confirmed by Pope Innocent III in 1210, and more formally approved in 1223 by Honorius III. In addition to the usual vows of poverty, chastity, and obedience, special stress is laid upon preaching and ministry to the body and soul. Under various names, such as Minorites, Barefooted Friars, and Grey Friars, the order spread rapidly throughout Europe. Among its members were Alexander of Hales, Duns Scotus, Roger Bacon, Occam, Popes Sixtus V and Clement XIV, and other eminent men; the order was long noted for its rivalry with the Dominicans. Differences early arose in regard to the severity of the rule, culminating in the 16th century in the division of the order into two great classes, the Observantines or Observants and the Conventuals; the former follow a more rigorous, the latter a milder rule. The order has been noted for missionary zeal, but suffered considerably in the Reformation and the French Revolution. The usual distinguishing features of the garb are a gray or dark-brown cowl, a girdle, and sandals.

Francisco (fran.sis′kō). In Shakespeare's *Hamlet,* a soldier who, at the beginning of the play, is relieved from watch by Bernardo.

Francisco. In Shakespeare's *Tempest,* a lord shipwrecked with Alonso.

Francisco. In John Webster's tragedy *The White Devil,* the unscrupulous, coldly ruthless Duke of Florence, brother of the kindly Isabella.

Francisco. In Philip Massinger's play *The Duke of Milan,* the duke's favorite, a cold, vindictive hypocrite.

Francis Esmond (fran′sis ez′mọnd). See **Castlewood, Colonel Francis Esmond, Lord.**

Francis of Assisi (ạ.sē′zē), Saint. [Original name, **Giovanni Francesco Bernardone.**] b. at Assisi, Umbria, Italy, c1182; d. there, Oct. 3, 1226. An Italian monk and preacher; founder of the Roman Catholic order of Franciscans. He was the son of a well-to-do merchant who, at the time of his son's birth, was traveling in France; the name Francesco (Francis), attached to the son as a memento of this absence, was then a rare one and its popularity since is due to the growth of the Franciscan order. After a serious illness in his youth, Francis turned, at the age of 26, to a life of ascetic devotion. He gathered about him a small group of disciples, drew up a set of rules for a new monastic order (Friars Minor) which would renounce the acquisition of worldly goods and devote itself to extolling the glory of God, and traveled (1210) to Rome to obtain the sanction of the pope. Though he might easily have denounced the pantheism of Francis's religious approach (Francis preached to the birds as his little brethren, he composed a canticle to the sun, and he would not put out fire lest he injure it), Innocent III saw in Francis and his doctrine a great religious force and recognized the order (in 1226 the rule, modified, was confirmed by Honorius III).

Francis Stuart (stū′ạrt). See **Bothwell, Sergeant.**

Francis Xavier (zā′vi.ėr, zav′i.ėr), Saint. See **Xavier, Saint Francis.**

Frank (frangk). Entries on literary characters having this prename will be found under the surnames Cheeryble, Churchill, Gresham, Hayston, Illidge, and Innes.

Frankau (frang′kou), **Gilbert.** b. at London, April 21, 1884; d. Nov. 4, 1952. An English writer. He was the author of *One of Us* (1912), *Tid'apa* (1914), *The City of Fear* (1917), *Peter Jackson, Cigar Merchant* (1919), *The Love-Story of Aliette Brunton* (1922), *Men, Maids, and Mustard-Pots* (1923), *Life—and Erica* (1925), *Wine, Women, and Waiters* (1932), *Farewell Romance* (1936), *The Dangerous Years* (1937), *Self-Portrait* (1939), *World Without End* (1943), *Selected Verses* (1943), and *This Side of God* (1947).

Frankau, Pamela. b. 1908—. An English novelist and short-story writer. Her books have been published in America and England. She began writing when she was 18, and her most popular works are *A Democrat Dies* (1940), *The Devil We Know* (1939), and *A Wreath for the Enemy* (1954).

Frankenstein (frangk′en.stīn). A romance by Mary W. Shelley (the wife of Percy Bysshe Shelley), published in 1818. Frankenstein, a young student of natural philosophy, is obsessed with the desire to learn how to impart life to inanimate matter. He creates a being from bones collected from charnel houses, and finds the creature endowed with great strength as well as enormous size, but so hideous that everyone who sees it is revolted and terrified. It is lonely because no one can stand the sight of it, and demands that Frankenstein create a female in the same fashion and mold as itself to serve as its wife. The student starts to do this, but is horrified at the idea of an entire race of these monsters, and so refuses to complete the woman. In revenge, the monster kills Frankenstein's brother and his bride. Frankenstein starts out to find the monster and kill it, and trails it as far as the North Pole, where he dies of exposure. The monster then appears to the crew and passengers of the ship on which Frankenstein had taken refuge, and reveals that Frankenstein's crime was greater than the monster's: he had created something in the image of man, but without heart or soul, and therefore deserved his punishment.

Frankford (frangk′fọrd). The forgiving husband of Alice Frankford in Thomas Heywood's tragedy *A Woman Killed with Kindness.* Upon discovering that his wife has been unfaithful, he determines not to punish her in any usual fashion, but merely to lavish kindness upon her. When she dies repentant he forgives her, admitting that everyone has sins to repent and that he is not qualified to pass judgment on her, wronged though he has been.

ḍ, d or j; ṣ, s or sh; ṭ, t or ch; ẓ, z or zh; o, F. cloche; ü, F. menu; ćh, Sc. loch; ṅ, F. bonbon.

Frankford, Alice. The erring wife in Thomas Heywood's tragedy *A Woman Killed with Kindness.*

Frankland (frangk'lạnd), **Edward Percy.** b. at London, Jan. 5, 1884—. An English writer. His novels, set in the dales of Westmorland, include *Swarthmoor Tragedy* (1922), *Retreat* (1926), *Power* (1927), *Huge as Sin* (1932), *The Bear of Britain* (1944), *England Growing* (1946), and *The Half Brothers* (1947).

Franklin (frangk'lin), **Benjamin.** [Pseudonyms: **The Busybody** and **Richard Saunders.**] b. at Boston, Jan. 17, 1706; d. at Philadelphia, April 17, 1790. American printer, author, inventor, scientist, statesman, philanthropist, and diplomat, signer of the Declaration of Independence and America's first world citizen. Given some education by his father, he worked in the latter's Boston tallow and soap business until apprenticed to his half brother James, publisher of the *New England Courant.* In this paper appeared Franklin's first writings, anonymously submitted. He edited the paper briefly when his brother was jailed after attacking local authorities. A quarrel with James saw him leave for Philadelphia and, later, London, where he worked as a master craftsman in the printing trade. Throughout his life he continued a careful plan of self-education. In 1730 he headed his own Philadelphia print shop, publishing the *Pennsylvania Gazette* and *Poor Richard's Almanack* (1732–57). The latter, a colonial best seller, made his name known also abroad (a part of it was translated into many languages). Witty and packed with homely wisdom, it reflects Franklin's characteristic skeptical pragmatism and, with some of the writings of Roger Williams, shares the distinction of being the first American literary production to attain international renown. Franklin's other writings reflect his doctrines of civic betterment and self-improvement. These he translated into reality by initiating or participating in the establishment at Philadelphia of the first Anglo-American colonial circulating library (1731), the founding of the American Philosophical Society (1741), an early hospital (1751), and in this same year the Academy for the Education of Youth (later the University of Pennsylvania), as well as inaugurating city police and a fire company. His earnest interest in science was first displayed at meetings of the "Junto," a club for mutual improvement made up of his friends and organized in 1727. His interests and researches extended through a very wide range of natural phenomena, bringing him international recognition and the friendship of the greatest scientists of his day. He invented (c1744) the "Pennsylvania Fireplace," a form of stove (as the "Franklin Stove," still being manufactured and used), and devised a timepiece later known as Ferguson's clock. By 1748 his business was so successful that a partnership arrangement permitted him to devote much of his time to scientific investigation. During these years he made his famous experiments with electricity, including the kite experiment with lightning in 1752.

Entry into Politics. Political activity ended this more leisurely period, however. He had already served (1736–51) as clerk of the Pennsylvania Assembly, of which he was a member (1751–64), had been deputy postmaster (1737–53) at Philadelphia, a position offering particular advantages to the editor of a newspaper, and in 1753 had become deputy postmaster general for the colonies, a position held jointly with William Hunter and retained until 1774. In 1754 he represented Pennsylvania at the Albany Congress, to which conclave he submitted his "Plan of Union" which, although not adopted by the colonial assemblies, was later to play a significant part in the drafting of the Articles of Confederation and the federal Constitution. In 1757 he was sent to England as political agent of the Pennsylvania Assembly in a quarrel with the Penn family, proprietors of the colony. He returned to America in 1762, but subsequently went back to England, becoming also the agent of Georgia (1768), New Jersey (1769), and Massachusetts (1770). He was accepted by the English as "unofficial ambassador" of the American colonies, and became the respected consultant of many English leaders, including William Pitt. His "Examination before the House of Commons" (in the matter of the Stamp Act) made him a world figure.

Activity for American Independence. On the eve of the Revolution he returned to America, becoming (1775) a member of the second Continental Congress, first colonial postmaster general, a commissioner to arrange a union with Canada, and a member of the committee to draft the Declaration of Independence, which he signed. In 1776 he was sent to France to arrange a treaty and later became American plenipotentiary. He became the focal point of a "Franklin cult" which swept all France, and was taken to be the exemplification of the "natural man" of Rousseau. As commissioner, he helped negotiate the final peace treaty with England in 1783, his old friendships there contributing to the smoothness of proceedings. He left France in 1785, becoming president of the executive council of Pennsylvania, and was later a member of the Constitutional Convention (1787). He took as his common-law wife Deborah Read in 1730, having two children by her, Francis Folger and Sarah (who became the wife of Richard Bache). He had one illegitimate son William Franklin, who became royal governor of New Jersey and was a Loyalist during the Revolution. See *The Writings of Benjamin Franklin, Collected and Edited with a Life and Introduction,* by Albert Henry Smyth (10 vols., 1905–07); for the best edition of Franklin's *Autobiography,* see *Benjamin Franklin's Memoirs,* parallel text edition, edited by Max Farrand (1949).

Franklin, Eleanor Ann. [Maiden name, **Porden.**] b. in July, 1795; d. Feb. 22, 1825. An English poet; the first wife of Sir John Franklin, whom she married in 1823.

Franklin, Sir John. b. April 16, 1786; d. June 11, 1847. An English arctic explorer. He entered the Royal Navy in his youth and served at the battle of Trafalgar in 1805, and in the expedition against New Orleans in 1814. He commanded the brig *Trent* in the arctic expedition under Captain Buchan in 1818, commanded an exploring expedition to the northern coast of North America 1819–22;

commanded a similar expedition 1825–27; was knighted in 1829; and was lieutenant governor of Van Diemen's Land 1836–43. In 1845 he was appointed to the command of an expedition, consisting of the *Erebus* and the *Terror*, sent out by the British admiralty in search of the Northwest Passage. The expedition sailed from Greenhithe, Kent, on May 18, 1845, and was last spoken off the entrance of Lancaster Sound, between Baffin and Devon islands in the Arctic Archipelago, on July 26, 1845. Thirty-nine relief expeditions, public and private, were sent out from England and America in search of the missing explorers between 1847 and 1857. In the last-mentioned year the yacht *Fox*, under Captain Leopold McClintock, was sent by Lady Franklin. McClintock found traces of the missing expedition in 1859, which confirmed previous rumors of its total destruction. From a paper containing an entry by Captain Fitzjames of the missing expedition, it was learned that Franklin died on June 11, 1847, having in the previous year penetrated to within 12 miles of the northern extremity of King William Island.

Franklin Blake (blăk). See **Blake, Franklin.**

Franklin's Tale, The. One of Chaucer's *Canterbury Tales*. It is said in the prologue to be from a Breton lay. The story is that of Boccaccio's fifth tale of the tenth day in the *Decameron*, and is introduced also in the fifth book of his *Il Filocolo*, which is generally believed to have been Chaucer's source. Dorigen is the faithful wife of Arviragus (or Arveragus). She is beloved by Aurelius, "a lusty squire," to escape whose importunity she says she will never listen to him till all the rocks on the seashore are removed. He having by magic removed them, Arviragus sacrifices her to her promise. When Aurelius beholds her gentle obedience to her husband's overstrained sense of honor, he releases her from the bargain. This tale is often characterized as the closing section of the "marriage group," the cynical views of married love that have been propounded, especially by the Wife of Bath and the Merchant, being refuted by the kindly Franklin. This "worthy vavasour" is described by Chaucer as follows:

Whyt was his berd, as is the dayesye.
Of his complexioun he was sangwyn.
Wel loved he by the morwe a sop in wyn.
To liven in delyt was ever his wone,
For he was Epicurus owne sone,
That heeld opinioun that pleyn delyt
Was verraily felicitee parfyt.

Frankly (frangk′li). A character in Colley Cibber's comedy *The Refusal, or The Ladies' Philosophy.*

Franks (frangks), Sir **Oliver** (**Shewell**). b. at Birmingham, England, Feb. 16, 1905—. An English statesman. He was educated at the Bristol grammar school (his father then being principal of the Bristol Western College) and at Queen's College, Oxford, where from 1927 to 1937 he taught philosophy, as fellow, tutor, and university lecturer. In 1935 he was a professor at the University of Chicago. From 1937 to 1945 he taught moral philosophy at Glasgow University, interrupting his academic duties during World War II to work at London for the Ministry of Supply. In 1942 he was appointed second secretary to the Ministry of Supply, and

two years later he was made secretary of the combined ministries of Supply and Aircraft Production, resigning in April, 1946, to accept the provostship of Queen's College. He was knighted in 1945, and in 1947 his country selected him to head its delegation at Paris, when the Committee on European Economic Coöperation met there on July 12. He served (1948–52) as ambassador of Great Britain to the U. S. He is the author of *The Experience of a University Teacher in the Civil Service*, originally delivered at Oxford (May 9, 1947), and *Central Planning and Control in War and Peace* (1947).

Fra Rupert (frä rö′pèrt). See under **Andrea of Hungary.**

Fraser (frā′zèr), **Alexander Campbell.** b. at Ardchattan, Argyllshire, Scotland, Sept. 3, 1819; d. at Edinburgh, Dec. 2, 1914. A Scottish professor, philosopher, and editor. He was editor (1850–57) of the *North British Review*, and edited Berkeley's philosophical works. He was the author of *Essays in Philosophy* (1856), *Life and Letters of Berkeley* (1871, 1901), *Locke* (1890), *Philosophy of Theism* (1895–96), *Biographica Philosophica* (1904), and *Berkeley and Spiritual Realism* (1908).

Fraser, James Baillie. b. at Reelick, Invernessshire, Scotland, June 11, 1783; d. there, in January, 1856. A Scottish traveler and author. He wrote travels and tales of Eastern life, many of them dealing with Persia.

Frateretto (frat.èr.et′ō). In Shakespeare's *King Lear*, a fiend mentioned by Edgar. The name comes from Samuel Harsnett's *Popish Impostures.*

Fraternity. A novel (1908) by John Galsworthy.

Fraunce (frôns, fräns), **Abraham.** b. at Shrewsbury, Shropshire, England, c1558; d. 1633. An English Elizabethan poet, scholar, and lawyer. He wrote translations from Latin and Italian, *The Lawiers Logike, Exemplifying the Praecepts of Logike by the Practice of the Common Lawe* (1588), *Victoria*, a Latin comedy, and a considerable amount of poetry in English hexameter verse. Fraunce is the "Corydon" of Spenser's *Colin Clout's Come Home Again*, and Peele called him "a peerless sweet translator of our time," while Nashe termed him "Sweete Master Fraunce."

Frazer (frā′zèr), Sir **James George.** b. at Glasgow, Jan. 1, 1854; d. at Cambridge, England, May 7, 1941. A Scottish anthropologist, probably now best known as the author of *The Golden Bough* (1890). Educated at Glasgow and Cambridge; professor (1907–19) of social anthropology at University of Liverpool. His work *The Golden Bough* was revised (1900) and expanded into a series of 12 volumes including bibliography and index (1915); there is also an abridgment (1922) and a supplementary volume, *Aftermath* (1936). The work leads from a study of the priesthood of Diana at Lake Nemi to a comparison of primitive cults, rites, myths, and customs, in terms of their origin and significance in the history of the world's religions. His other books include *Questions on the Customs, Beliefs, and Languages of Savages* (1907), *The Belief in Immortality and the Worship of the Dead* (3 vols., 1913, 1922, 1924), *Folklore in the Old Testament* (1918; abridged ed., 1923), *Man, God, and Immortality* (1927), *Myths of the Origin of Fire*

(1930), *The Fear of the Dead in Primitive Religion* (3 vols., 1933, 1934, 1936), *Creation and Evolution in Primitive Cosmogonies* (1935), *Anthologia Anthropologica* (vol. I, 1938; vols. II-IV, 1939); his *Totemism and Exogamy* (1910) was reissued (1935) and supplemented by *Totemica* (1937); his other books include *Garnered Sheaves, The Worship of Nature,* and an edition of Ovid's *Fasti.*

Frea (frā′ạ). See **Freya.**

Frederick (fred′rik, -ẽr.ik). Entries on literary characters having this prename will be found under the surnames Bayham, Bramble, Frolic, Verisopht, and Wentworth.

Frederick I. [Also: **Frederick I** (of *Germany*); called **Frederick Barbarossa,** meaning "Frederick Redbeard."] b. c1123; d. in Cilicia, Asia Minor, June 10, 1190. Emperor of the Holy Roman Empire, the most noted of the Hohenstaufen line; son of Frederick II, Duke of Swabia, and nephew of Conrad III, whom he succeeded as king of Germany in 1152. He was crowned emperor at Rome by Pope Adrian IV in 1155. His reign was chiefly occupied by wars against the turbulent German nobility and by six expeditions to Italy for the purpose of restoring the imperial authority in the republican cities of Lombardy (1154–55, 1158–62, 1163, 1166–68, 1174–77, and 1184–86). In 1176 he was, in consequence of the defection of the powerful feudatory Henry the Lion, Duke of Saxony, defeated by the Lombards at the battle of Legnano, and was compelled to accept the definitive peace of Constance in 1183, by which he renounced all regalian rights in the cities. In 1180 he punished Henry the Lion by putting him under the ban of the empire and depriving him of his fiefs. In 1189 he joined the third Crusade; in the course of it he was drowned in the Calycadnus (modern Göksu) River in Asia Minor.

Frederick II. [Called **Frederick the Great;** also familiarly, by his soldiers, **Der Alte Fritz.**] b. at Berlin, Jan. 24, 1712; d. at Sans Souci, near Potsdam, Germany, Aug. 17, 1786. King of Prussia (1740–86); son of Frederick William I of Prussia and Sophia Dorothea, daughter of George I of England. As a young boy, he rebelled against his father's authority, and planned to escape (1730) from the country; the plan was discovered, however, and Frederick was severely disciplined. A friend who was helping him, Lieutenant Katte, was, on the king's orders, beheaded just outside Frederick's prison window, and the king threatened a similar punishment for the crown prince (stripped of that title for his disobedience) unless he reformed. In the year in which Frederick ascended the throne, the emperor Charles VI died without male issue. He was succeeded by his daughter Maria Theresa by virtue of the pragmatic sanction of 1713, the validity of which was disputed by the elector of Bavaria (who was after 1742 the emperor Charles VII) and other claimants. Frederick embraced the opportunity presented by the insecurity of Maria Theresa's title to invade (1740) Silesia, to part of which he laid claim as a Hohenzollern inheritance. He defeated the Austrians at Mollwitz (Malujowice) in 1741, and at Chotusitz (Chotusice) in 1742, and in 1742 concluded the treaty of Breslau and Berlin, by which in return for the cession

of Silesia he withdrew from the alliance which he had in the meantime entered into with France and Bavaria against Austria. In 1744, alarmed by the successes of Austria against France and Bavaria, he entered into a second alliance with those powers, defeated the Austrians and Saxons at Hohenfriedberg in 1745, defeated the Austrians at Soor in 1745, and, after the victory at Kesseldorf by Leopold of Dessau, in 1745 concluded the peace of Dresden, which confirmed the treaty of Breslau and Berlin. To regain Silesia, Maria Theresa formed an alliance with France (1756), joined by Russia, Sweden, and Saxony. Frederick, anticipating the allies, invaded Saxony in 1756. In the ensuing war, called the Seven Years' War, he was supported by England, chiefly in the form of subsidies. He made himself master of Saxony by the defeat of the Austrians at Lobositz (Lovosice) in 1756. In 1757 he invaded Bohemia and defeated the Austrians at Prague, but was defeated at Kolín by Marshal Daun, who drove him out of Bohemia. He defeated the French and Austrians at Rossbach and the Austrians alone at Leuthen (Lutynia) in the same year. In 1758 he defeated the Russians at Zorndorf. In 1759 he was defeated by the Austrians and Russians at Kunersdorf (Kunowice). After Prussian victories at Liegnitz (Legnica) and Torgau, Berlin was taken by the Russians in 1760, England withdrew her subsidies in 1761, and Frederick was reduced to desperation. In 1762, however, Elizabeth of Russia died, and Frederick's fortunes changed. Peter III, Elizabeth's successor, concluded peace in 1762, and the defection of France in that year caused Maria Theresa to sign in 1763 the treaty of Hubertusburg, which confirmed the treaty of Breslau and Berlin, including that of Dresden. In 1772 Frederick joined with Russia and Austria in the partition of Poland, by which he added Polish Prussia to his dominions. In 1778–79 he took part in the War of the Bavarian Succession. He was the organizer of the *Fürstenbund,* or league of princes, to resist what he considered the dangerous ambitions of the emperor Joseph II. Through his military genius and administrative abilities, he raised Prussia to the rank of a powerful state. He had, before he became king, written *Considérations sur l'état présent du corps politique de l'Europe,* in which he showed the need for a third power in Europe to balance the growing power of France and Austria; this gap he filled with the Prussian state. He left a well-trained army of 200,000 men backed by a country much larger than that he had inherited and a treasury enriched by strict economy and even stricter tax collection. His own military talents were supplemented by his generals, among them Friedrich Wilhelm von Seydlitz, Ferdinand of Brunswick, Leopold of Dessau, James Keith, and Hans Joachim von Zieten. He sponsored internal improvements, extending the canal system, sponsoring the planting of orchards, encouraging such manufactures as silk. His heroic efforts to rehabilitate the Prussian economy after the Seven Years' War (remittance of taxes, distribution of seed, rebuilding of destroyed houses, and the like) brought an amazingly quick return to prosperity. From the beginning of his reign he acted for codification of the Prussian laws; the compilations

---

fat, fāte, fär, ȧsk, fãre; net, mē, hẽr; pin, pīne; not, nōte, mōve, nôr; up, lūte, púll; ᴛʜ, then;

made by Samuel von Cocceji and Johann von Carmer were made effective in 1794, after Frederick's death. He promoted educational activity, especially on the elementary level. Despite the rigidity in which he approached matters in the name of efficiency, Frederick's reign was a tolerant one; he permitted men to worship as they pleased, though he himself was a confirmed atheist. Frederick disliked the German language. He had learned French in his early schooling and, even before he became king, corresponded with Voltaire. The latter came to Frederick's court in 1750; the two eventually quarreled, and Voltaire left the court in 1753, though later the friendship was resumed, by correspondence. Frederick's writing was in French, his poetry inconsequential, his prose of forceful style. Many anecdotes survive of his wit; in them the figure of Frederick becomes almost a folk hero, short, wiry, dressed in an old blue and red uniform with crumbs of snuff visible on it, a spry and sparkling old man. He left a number of written works, published in 30 volumes (1846–57), among them *Mémoires pour servir à l'histoire de Brandebourg* and *Anti-Macchiavel*, the latter, written in 1740, containing Frederick's credo, that the prince is the first servant, not the master, of his people.

Frederick, Duke. In Shakespeare's *As You Like It*, the usurping brother of the exiled duke.

Frederick the Great. See **Frederick II.**

Fred Trent (trent). See **Trent, Fred.**

Freelands (frē'landz), **The.** A novel by John Galsworthy, published in 1915.

Freelove (frē'luv), **Lady.** A character in Colman's *Jealous Wife.*

Freeman (frē'man). A fashionable gentleman about town and friend to Courtal in Etherege's *She Would if she Could.*

Freeman. In Wycherley's comedy *The Plain Dealer*, Manly's lieutenant and friend.

Freeman. In Farquhar's *The Beaux' Stratagem*, the friend of Aimwell.

Freeman, Edward Augustus. b. at Harborne, Staffordshire, England, 1823; d. at Alicante, Spain, March 16, 1892. An English historian.

Freeman, John. b. at Dalston, East London, Jan. 29, 1880; d. at Anerley, Kent, England, Sept. 23, 1929. An English poet, critic, essayist, and novelist.

Freeman, Mrs. The name under which Sarah Jennings, Duchess of Marlborough, carried on a correspondence with her friend Queen Anne (who signed herself Mrs. Morley).

Freeman, Richard Austin. b. at London, 1862; d. at Gravesend, Kent, England, Sept. 30, 1943. An English surgeon and health official, author of detective stories; creator of the detective novel character Dr. John Thorndyke. After pursuing private medical practice and serving as medical superintendent for Holloway prison and the port of London, he took up writing and produced several volumes of detective novels and tales of which Dr. John Thorndyke is the hero. (Thorndyke was based on Alfred Swaine Taylor (1806–80), medical jurist and authority on poisons.)

Freeman-Mitford (-mit'fǫrd), **Algernon Bertram.** [Title, 1st Baron **Redesdale** (of the 2nd creation).] b. at London, Feb. 24, 1837; d. at Batsford, England, Aug. 17, 1916. An English diplomat and author; great-grandson of William Mitford (1744–1827). An embassy attaché at St. Petersburg (1863) and in Japan (1866–70), Mitford's travels included visits to Garibaldi, and to Brigham Young at Salt Lake City. As heir to a cousin's estates, he assumed the surname Freeman in 1866. His writings include *Tales of Old Japan* (1871) and *Memoirs* (1915).

Freeport (frē'pōrt), **Sir Andrew.** A London merchant, one of the members of the fictitious club which issued *The Spectator.*

Freevill (frē'vil). The hero of John Marston's comedy *The Dutch Courtezan.*

Freia (frā'yä). See **Freya.**

Freischütz (frī'shüts), **Der.** In German folklore, a marksman celebrated for his compact with the Devil, from whom he obtained seven *Freikugeln* (free bullets), six of which always hit the mark. The agreement was, however, that the Devil might direct the seventh at his pleasure.

French Academy. [French, **Académie française.**] An association originating about 1629 in the informal weekly meetings of a few (eight) men of letters in Paris, and formally established Jan. 2, 1635, by Cardinal Richelieu, for the purpose of controlling the French language and regulating literary taste. It consisted of forty members, the "forty immortals," the officers being a director and a chancellor, both chosen by lot, and a permanent secretary, chosen by votes. Among the objects provided for in the constitution was the preparation of a dictionary, a grammar, a treatise on rhetoric and one on poetry. In 1694 the first edition of the celebrated "Dictionnaire de l'Académie" appeared, while the seventh appeared in 1878. The Academy was suppressed by the Convention in 1793, but was reconstructed in 1795, under the name of the "Class of French Language and Literature," as part of the National Institute. Its original organization was restored by Louis XVIII in 1816.

Frenchman's Creek. A novel by Daphne Du Maurier, published in 1942.

French Revolution. The name specifically given to the revolution which occurred in France at the close of the 18th century. The meeting of the States-General on May 5, 1789, marks the beginning; the end is variously taken either as 1795 (the end of the Convention), 1799 (the end of the Directory), or 1804 (the end of the Consulate), and sometimes the whole Napoleonic period (through 1815) is included in the treatment of the French Revolution. However, the beginning of the Napoleonic era is most often said to mark the end of the Revolution, and Napoleon's assumption of the Consulate (Nov. 9, 1799), though preserving the Republic outwardly, was symptomatic of reversion to one-man rule.

The Background. The France of 1789 was not poverty-stricken, nor was its peasant class very badly off. The great majority, perhaps as many as 90 percent, were free and many were landowners; such certainly was not true elsewhere on the Continent. But some attempt was being made by the nobility to reëstablish its rights to certain feudal dues, and this, combined with the desire of the agrarian class to better its lot, caused unrest throughout the country. The bourgeoisie had grown enormously, due to the spread of French trade, yet this middle class of merchants and city-dwellers, versed in the writings of the French 18th-century philosophers, found itself unable to obtain a voice in politics. The States-General, in which at least they had an equal voice with the clergy and nobility, had not met for 175 years, and whereas their wealth was taxed to the limit, that of the other classes was for the greater part tax-exempt. The spirit of critical inquiry found in the writings of Rousseau, and Voltaire and Montesquieu before him, affected not only the bourgeoisie but made converts from the privileged classes of nobility and clergy as well. Moreover, despite the country's wealth, which made it the most prosperous on the Continent at the time, the government was in serious financial difficulties. Taxes fell most heavily on the unrepresented class, and the taxes were used most ostentatiously to build the glorious court of Louis XVI and his queen, Marie Antoinette (called Madame Deficit by her critics). A growing tide of complaint was met by rigid government censorship. French participation in the American Revolutionary War, while it saw England's defeat and France's triumph, was financially disastrous. With clergy and nobility still exempt from most taxes, loans had to be resorted to more than ever, and eventually the borrowing power of the French government was strained to the limit. In this crisis, Louis XVI gave in to popular demand and called for the first meeting of the States-General since 1614.

The Constituent Assembly. The States-General, which met on May 5, 1789, was composed of 300 representatives each of the nobility and clergy, and 600 representatives of the third estate, the commons, two thirds of them lawyers. Sitting with the latter group were several noblemen and members of the clergy, among them the Abbé Siéyès, author of the pamphlet *What Is the Third Estate?* When a dispute arose over voting procedure, the question being whether the estates were to vote separately and cast their votes as units, thus giving the two upper estates the voting majority, or whether the entire group was to be polled, Siéyès moved that the third estate meet separately. On June 17 its members did so, setting up a Constituent Assembly (National Assembly) and inviting the other estates to join them. When on June 20, their meeting place was closed to them by troops under the orders of the king, the members adjourned to a nearby tennis court (a building housing a court for the old game of *jeu de paume*, not the modern lawn tennis) and took an oath not to separate before a constitution for France had been written. They were joined by many members of the lesser clergy and by some of the nobility, including Lafayette. The king then deferred to them and ordered the National Assembly to meet as a group. But almost at once rumors began to circulate: the Assembly was to be dissolved, troops were being concentrated near the city. On July 11, Jacques Necker, the minister of finance and a proponent of government economy, was dismissed; this set off a series of riots in Paris,

which had their culmination on July 14, a day still commemorated as the French national holiday. The Bastille, the great fortress prison that symbolized the arbitrary powers of arrest of the king and the nobility, was stormed and captured by the rioting crowd. Only seven prisoners were in the Bastille at the time, but the enraged mob killed de Launay, governor of the prison. Paris was in control of the rioters; soon similar uprisings were occurring in the provinces; local prisons, and local record offices, were assaulted and destroyed. The nobility began its exodus from France. The establishment of a National Guard in Paris was matched by the setting up of provincial bodies of defense. All France was aflame with the spirit of revolt against the *ancien régime.* The National Assembly set up a provisional government at the Hôtel de Ville and adopted the tricolor as the national flag. On August 4 the nobility announced acceptance of a *fait accompli:* they renounced all feudal rights and privileges, accepted equality of representation, and gave up their titles. On August 27, the basic document of the Revolution, the Declaration of the Rights of Man, later prefixed to the Constitution of 1791, was adopted. This declaration was a bill of rights, modeled after the English Declaration of Rights (1689) and the American Declaration of Independence (1776) as molded by and modified by the doctrines of the French philosophers. But a general instability was felt; on October 5–6 a mob of women marched from Paris to Versailles to demand food from the king. Only with difficulty was the royal family extricated from the clutches of the mob by Lafayette, but henceforth they were to stay at the Tuileries in Paris. Thither the National Assembly followed, and during the next two years worked out a system of limited monarchy. The constitution they wrote set up a one-chamber legislature, but the Assembly, dominated by the upper middle class, restricted the voting to taxpayers and office-holding to landowners. France was reorganized into 83 departments of approximately equal population, instead of the ancient provinces; the church lands were nationalized, the clergy were to be salaried and appointed by the government. But the émigrés, the nobility that had fled the country, were gathering on the northeast borders and the lower clergy, which had supported the government until now, refused to accept the constitution and carried the support of their parishes with them. Things looked propitious for the royal cause and on June 20, 1791, the king fled from Paris to join his friends. He was quickly recaptured and returned to Paris, but now he was forced to accept the constitution, and in September it was officially adopted.

The Legislative Assembly. The new Assembly, elected under the Constitution, met on Oct. 1, 1791. Here the political parties which were to be so active in the course of the Revolution first made themselves felt as major national forces. During the period of the Constituent Assembly certain political clubs had become powerful in Paris: the Jacobins (with many branch organizations throughout the country) led by Robespierre; the Cordeliers led by Danton, Marat, Hébert, Desmoulins; the Feuillants led by Lafayette and Bailly. The latter was a royalist group, seeking a moderate, limited monarchy, and sat as the right in the new Assembly. Opposing them on the left was a group led at different times by the Girondists, a bloc led by politicians from the department of Gironde who were interested in preserving some provincial autonomy and desired to see a federal republic established, and the Mountain (a group taking its strength from the Jacobins and the Cordeliers and getting its name from the seats of its leaders high in the legislative chamber) desirous of seeing a strongly centralized republic. The struggle between the right and the left was decided early; even before the Assembly met in October the king of Prussia and the emperor Leopold II had issued (Aug. 27, 1791) the declaration of Pillnitz, asserting their interest in France's internal affairs. Pressure from the émigrés pushed Austria close to the point of war; the Girondist ministry of Roland, which succeeded the moderate ministry that fell immediately after the Pillnitz declaration, saw in that rather neutral statement a threat to France. On April 20, 1792, France declared war on Austria. Immediate defeats in the field led to the rise of an extreme radical sentiment in Paris, and the flame was fanned by the manifesto of the commander of the Prussian-Austrian forces, the duke of Brunswick, that Paris would pay if the royal family was harmed. On August 10 the Tuileries was stormed, the Swiss Guard was massacred, and the king, arrested and imprisoned, was suspended from his duties. The Paris coalition of clubs and commune now took over the actual government from the Assembly. A call went out for elections to a national convention to write a new constitution. In the early part of September, with Danton's outspoken encouragement (also suspected in the march on the Tuileries), mobs at Paris, and in various other parts of France, gave summary trials to as many royalists as they could find, and executed them.

The National Convention and the Reign of Terror. On Sept. 21, 1792, the Convention, elected by universal manhood suffrage, met at Paris. On the preceding day the French army had won a victory over the Prussians at Valmy and the convention convened in an atmosphere of optimism. Now the right was composed of the Girondists, while the left was led by the Mountain. The Convention immediately declared the monarchy abolished and proclaimed the republic (September 21). A new calendar was established; the year I began on Sept. 22, 1792 (1st Vendémiaire); the old polite forms of address were dropped for the more familiar *tu* and *toi;* people addressed each other as Citizen (*citoyen*) and Citizeness (*citoyenne*). Everywhere French arms were triumphant; Belgium was occupied after the victory at Jemappes (November 6); Nice and Savoy were annexed (November 27). In December, Louis XVI went on trial before the Convention for treason and on January 15 was found guilty. On January 16, by a one-vote majority in the 721 votes cast, he was condemned to death, and on Jan. 21, 1793, he was executed. England, Holland, Spain, Austria, Prussia, and Sardinia now joined in a coalition to defeat the regicide government, and on February 1 France declared war against them. In March, royalists in the Vendée revolted and on the 18th of that month the Aus-

trians won a victory over General Dumouriez at Neerwinden (for which defeat the Convention severely criticized the general, one of the early bulwarks of the republic, who thereupon deserted to the Austrians. The execution of General Custine for negligence in 1793, although he had won brilliant victories the year before, makes Dumouriez's action understandable). Uneasy, the Convention now found itself torn between the Girondists and the Mountain. To concentrate effective power it established (April 6, 1793) the Committee of Public Safety, which at first was led by Danton. The committee soon made itself an extreme revolutionary power under the control of the Mountain. On June 2 the Girondists were effectively suppressed when 31 of their representatives were arrested. In July Robespierre became a member of the Committee of Public Safety. On July 13, Marat, one of the Jacobin leaders, who had helped in the overthrow of the Girondists, was assassinated by Charlotte Corday. Robespierre forced himself upward and now became the great power in the government. Under him, partly as the result of the frightening military successes of the anti-French coalition, the Reign of Terror flourished; the defeats of the republican armies aroused the hopes of the Girondists and the royalists and their resulting agitation led to revolts which in turn were cruelly suppressed. All former aristocrats, all officials of the monarchy, anyone tainted by contact with the government under the Bourbons was suspect; trials were hurried, farcical; sentences of death were the rule for anyone who might even remotely be a danger to the republic; the guillotines were busy all over France. Paris's Terror was matched by those at Lyons, Nantes, Bordeaux, and Arras; it is said that over 17,000 executions were legally decreed in the little over a year that the Reign of Terror lasted, but many more were killed without even the semblance of a trial. At its height the Terror was responsible for as many as 354 executions in a single month in Paris. Marie Antoinette was executed (October 20); the Girondist leaders (October 31), the Hebertists (March 24, 1794), Danton himself (April 6), and finally Robespierre (July 28) all found their way to the guillotine in the Place de la Révolution. A universal military draft (beginning Aug. 23, 1793) raised a republican army that by December had driven the coalition's armies across the Rhine. Toulon was captured in that month; in April Pichegru won a victory at Turcoing; on June 26 the French took Belgium with a victory at Fleurus. With the fall of Robespierre (9–10 Thermidor) the motive force of the Terror began to fail; the conspiracy of the radicals of the Mountain and the more moderate elements was directed principally against Robespierre's personal power, and the grouping did not last long. Slowly the moderate bourgeois group eliminated the Jacobins, and the Reign of Terror died away. By the beginning of December, 1794, Girondists were filtering back into the Convention. Now economic difficulties in the form of inflation began to cause trouble. The issue of *assignats*, paper money originally backed by the value of the confiscated church lands, got out of hand, and in April and May, 1795, bread riots, directed against the Convention and backed by the Jacobins, occurred and were suppressed only with difficulty. The war against the coalition was going well for the republicans. Holland was invaded and in 1795 the Batavian Republic was established there under French protection. Prussia quit the war on March 5, signing a treaty at Basel, and in June Spain also withdrew. An attempted invasion of Brittany by émigrés from England was defeated in July, large numbers of prisoners on both sides being killed without mercy. On August 22 the Convention promulgated a new constitution. The Convention was to go out of existence; in its place were to be two houses, a Council of Ancients, of 250 members, and a Council of Five Hundred. The executive body was to be a Directory of five members. However, provision was made that two thirds of the membership of the new Chambers would be chosen from the roster of the Convention. The Parisians objected to this and, spurred on by royalist elements, revolted on Oct. 5, 1795. The army of the republic, led by the 26-year-old Napoleon Bonaparte, did not hesitate to use cannon against the rioters (Napoleon's "whiff of grapeshot" was most effective) and the revolt was quickly put down.

The Directory. The new government, which lasted for a little more than four years, ruled in a period of reaction to the excesses of the Reign of Terror. The natural lessening of the revolutionary ardor was reflected in the corruption of some of the Directory's own members (one of the five was replaced each year, the new member to serve five years before being replaced) and in the internal struggle between the republicans and the reactionaries, resolved eventually on Sept. 4, 1797 (18th Fructidor), when the republican group threw out of the Directory the rightist members (Carnot and Barthélemy) and purged the two Councils of their followers. The long-lived revolt in the Vendée was ended in 1796 and a determined campaign was undertaken to end the war with the coalition. Moreau and Jourdan were not successful in Germany, but Napoleon entered Italy and won a series of brilliant victories (Lodi, May 10, 1796; Arcola, November 15–19; Rivoli, Jan. 14, 1797). Then he crossed the Alps to meet the Austrians but instead of fighting them (under the handicap of having his supply lines stretched too long) he signed a peace treaty at Leoben (April 18). The war against the first coalition ended with the treaty of Campo Formio (Oct. 17, 1797), by the terms of which France lost nothing she really desired. These campaigns and Napoleon's further campaigns during the struggle with the second coalition (1798–1802) were accompanied by the announced French aim of establishing republican governments wherever the people of Europe desired them. The Batavian Republic of 1795 was followed by the Lombard Republic (May, 1796), the Cisalpine Republic (July, 1797), the Ligurian Republic (July, 1797), the Roman Republic (February, 1798), the Helvetian Republic (April, 1798), and the Parthenopean Republic (January, 1799). Napoleon's campaigns in Egypt (1798–99) and Syria (1799) were failures; the Egyptian campaign, despite successes on land, was ruined by Nelson's victory on the Nile (Aug. 1, 1798). However, Napoleon stood out, in the period of the Directory's venality and the second coalition's successes against the republic's Euro-

pean armies, as a man of great executive ability. On Nov. 9, 1799 (18 Brumaire), Napoleon, aided by Siéyès, now a member of the Directory, overthrew the rule of the Directory and, the following day, by using military force, prevented the meeting of the Council of Five Hundred. The revolution was ended and France again was to be ruled by one man, in practice if not in theory. The Consulate, with Napoleon as first consul, lasted less than five years; on May 18, 1804, he was proclaimed emperor.

French Revolution, Reflections on the. [Full title, **Reflections on the Revolution in France, and on the proceedings in certain societies in London relative to that event.**] A political treatise (November, 1790) by Edmund Burke, to which Thomas Paine replied in *The Rights of Man* (in two parts, 1791–92).

Frend (frend), **William.** b. at Canterbury, England, Nov. 22, 1757; d. at London, Feb. 21, 1841. An English author. He graduated (1780) from Christ's College, Cambridge, and in 1781 became a fellow and tutor in Jesus College at the same university. In 1793 he published *Peace and Union recommended to the Associated Bodies of Republicans and Anti-Republicans*, a tract in which, among other things, he attacked the liturgy of the Church of England, and was in consequence deprived of his residence at the college.

Frere (frir), **John Hookham.** [Pseudonym, **William and Robert Whistlecraft.**] b. at London, May 21, 1769; d. at the Pietà Valetta, Malta, Jan. 7, 1846. An English diplomat and author. He was named envoy extraordinary and plenipotentiary at Lisbon in 1800; held the same position at Madrid 1802–04; was sworn on the privy council in 1805; and was plenipotentiary to the central junta of Spain 1808–09. He published *Aristophanes*, a metrical version of the *Acharnians*, the *Knights*, and the *Birds*. He wrote a *Prospectus and Specimen of an intended National Work, by William and Robert Whistlecraft, of Stowmarket, in Suffolk, Harness and Collar Makers, intended to comprise the most interesting Particulars relating to King Arthur and his Round Table*. In this work he introduced the bernesque style into the English language. Byron, when sending *Beppo* to his publisher, writes: "I have written a poem humorous, in or after the excellent manner of Mr. Whistlecraft, and founded on a Venetian anecdote which amused me . . . Whistlecraft is my immediate model, but Berni is the father of that kind of writing; which, I think, suits our language, too, very well."

Fretful Plagiary (fret′ful plā′ji.ạ.ri), **Sir.** See **Plagiary, Sir Fretful.**

Freud (froid; German, froit), **Sigmund.** b. at Freiberg, in Moravia, May 6, 1856; d. at London, Sept. 9, 1939. An Austrian physician and psychoanalyst, founder of psychoanalysis. He studied neuroanatomy and neuropathology, and became (1885) a lecturer in neuropathology at the University of Vienna, where he was named professor in 1902. He studied under Josef Breuer, who introduced him to hypnosis; and worked with J. M. Charcot at Paris (1885), where he was introduced to the problems of hysteria. Unsatisfied with the results of hypnotic treatment of hysterical patients, Freud noticed that while he was attempting hypnosis patients occasionally fell into a reverie, talked their problems out, and seemed greatly improved afterwards. He developed this to the method of free association, and was able to get the coöperation of the patients in attempting to cure themselves. From this he developed the psychoanalytic method: the recall of emotional episodes that precipitated conflicts, and the recognition and release of pent-up emotion (catharsis). Freud fostered the concepts of unconscious motives and the importance of sex in our life. He postulated three governing forces of mental life: (1) the id, the instinctual force of life, the original libidinal or love force; (2) the ego, the executive force that has commerce with the external world of reality; and (3) the super-ego, the disciplinary force, the conscience, that is superior to, and capable of coercing, the ego. A principal key to the unconscious is the dream; analysis of the dream material in depth by the patient with the aid of the analyst tends to bring to the conscious area of the mind things which have been repressed because they do not fit the personality picture of the ego; the dream is analyzed by free association, one idea leading to another, the psychoanalyst directing rather than controlling the associations. Another method found useful was that of analyzing certain symbolic material in the dream; it was found that certain occurrences, artifacts, animals, and the like had an underlying symbolic common meaning for almost everyone brought up in a given cultural milieu (in Freud's practice, principally the Viennese environment). Freud's theories, under attack as being unscientific since they were first propounded, have nevertheless been of tremendous influence in other fields than medicine. In the arts and literature the exposition of the unconscious, as for example in surrealist painting or stream-of-consciousness writing, has added new dimensions to expression. In anthropology customs and beliefs have been interpreted in the light of Freud's theories and seemingly basic human drives have been uncovered. In 1906 Freud became associated with Eugen Bleuler, C. G. Jung, and Alfred Adler and in 1908, with the former two, founded the *Jahrbuch für psychoanalytische und psychopathologische Forschungen*. The International Psychoanalytical Association was founded but Jung and Adler soon resigned in protest against Freud's insistence on the universal influence of sexuality. Among Freud's books are *Klinische Studie über die halbseitige Cerebrallähmung der Kinder* (1891), *Zur Affassung der Aphasien* (1891), *Studien über Hysterie* (with Breuer, 1895), *Die Traumdeutung* (1900; Eng. trans., *The Interpretation of Dreams*), *Zur Psychopathologie des Alltagslebens* (1904; Eng. trans., *The Psychopathology of Everyday Life*), *Drei Abhandlungen zur Sexualtheorie* (1905; Eng. trans., *Three Contributions to the Theory of Sex*), *Der Witz und seine Beziehung zum Unbewussten* (1905; Eng. trans., *Wit and Its Relation to the Unconscious*), *Totem und Tabu* (1913), *Vorlesungen zur Einfuhrung in die Psychoanalyse* (1916–18; Eng. trans., *A General Introduction to Psychoanalysis*, 1920), *Massenpsychologie und Ich-Analyse* (1921), *Das Ich und das Es* (1923; Eng. trans., *The Ego and the*

Id, 1927), *Neue Folge der Vorlesungen zur Einfuhrung* (1932; Eng. trans., *New Introductory Lectures in Psychoanalysis*, 1933), *Der Mann Moses und die monotheistische Religion* (1939; Eng. trans., *Moses and Monotheism*). Freud went into exile in England in 1938 and died there a year later after completing his last book, *An Outline of Psychoanalysis* (1949).

Frey (frā). [Old Norse, **Freyr** (frār).] In Old Norse mythology, the god of love, marriage, and fruitfulness, presiding over rain, sunshine, and all the fruits of the earth, and dispensing wealth among men; the son of Njord and Nerthus. He was especially worshiped in the temple at Uppsala in Sweden. In ancient Danish legend he was believed to be reborn incarnate in the Danish kings.

Freya (frā′ạ). [Also: **Frea, Freia, Fria** (frī′ạ); Old Norse, **Freyja** (frā′yä).] In Old Norse mythology, the goddess of love and fertility; the daughter of Njord, and sister (and sometimes wife) of Frey. Her dwelling was Folkvang (Old Norse, *Folkvangr*). Her chariot was drawn by two cats. To her, with Odin (whose wife she is in late German mythology), belonged those slain in battle.

Frey and His Wife. (frā). A historical novel by Maurice Hewlett, published in 1916.

Friar (frī′ạr). Entries on friars from literature and folklore will be found at Francis, John, Laurence, Lodowick, Rush, and Tuck.

Friar Bacon (bā′kọn), **The Famous History of.** A popular legend concerning Roger Bacon. It was published in a prose tract at London in 1627 (reprinted in Thom's *Early Prose Romances*). No earlier edition is known, but that it is much older is evident from the fact that Robert Greene's play *Friar Bacon and Friar Bungay*, which was founded on it, was played, at Devonshire House c1589.

Friar Bacon and Friar Bungay (bung′gä). [Full title, **The Honorable History of Friar Bacon and Friar Bungay.**] A comedy by Robert Greene, produced c1589. It is based on legends about the scholar Roger Bacon and the monk Bungay, a 13th-century Franciscan who was supposedly a skilled magician. The plot hinges on the construction of a marvelous head by Bacon and Bungay to which the Devil gives the power of speech. It speaks, however, while Bacon is sleeping, and the great moment of magic comes and goes leaving Bacon no wiser than before. The comedy of the subplot is based on the love of Lord Lacy for a country lass, Margaret, and their misunderstandings.

Friar Bungay (bung′gä). See **Bungay, Thomas.**

Friar's Tale, The. One of Chaucer's *Canterbury Tales*. It is the story of a summoner who, as he is riding to extort some money from a poor widow, meets a foul fiend and enters into a compact with him. The fiend finally carries him off. Huberd, the Friar who tells the tale, is a "limitour," that is, one licensed to beg alms within a certain district. He has also received from his order the privilege of hearing confession and granting absolution. He is "wanton and merry," a handsome hypocrite who makes a good thing of religion and can wheedle a farthing out of a widow who hasn't so much as a shoe:

ḍ, d or j; ṣ, s or sh; ṭ, t or ch; ẓ, z or zh; o, F. cloche; ü, F. menu; čh, Sc. loch; ṅ, F. bonbon.

In alle the ordres foure is noon that can
So moche of daliaunce and fair langage. . . .
His tipet was ay farsed full of knyves
And pinnes, for to yeven faire wyves. . . .
His nekke whyt was as the flour-de-lys;
Ther to he strong was as a champioun,
He knew the tavernes well in every toun. . . .

Fribble (frib′l). A haberdasher in Thomas Shadwell's comedy *Epsom Wells*.

Fribble. In David Garrick's play *Miss in her Teens*, a weak-minded fop. Garrick played the character himself. In the reign of George II any one who affected the extreme of fashionable folly was called a "fribble."

Friday (fri′dạ). A young savage who becomes the servant of Robinson Crusoe, in Daniel Defoe's novel of that name. He was so named by his master because the latter had saved him from death on that day.

Friday Club. A club instituted at Edinburgh by Sir Walter Scott in June, 1803.

Friendly (frend′li), **Sir John.** In Vanbrugh's play *The Relapse*, a country gentleman. Sheridan metamorphosed him into his Colonel Townly in the *Trip to Scarborough*.

Friends and Relations. A novel by Elizabeth Bowen, published in 1931.

Friendship in Fashion. A comedy by Thomas Otway, produced in 1678.

Frigg (frig). [Also, **Frigga** (frig′ạ).] In Old Norse mythology, the principal wife of Odin, and the queen of the gods. She is a sky goddess, the goddess of married love, and patroness of housewives. She was the mother of Balder, Hermod, Hoder, and in some legends of Tyr. In later German mythology, Frigg became confused with Freya, but they are originally two distinct goddesses.

Friscobaldo (fris.kọ.bal′dō), **Orlando.** In Dekker and Middleton's *Honest Whore*, the father of Bellafront.

Frisians (frizh′ạnz). An ancient Germanic people, settled on the coast of the North Sea between the Weser and the Rhine and on the adjacent islands. The extent to which they participated in the Anglo-Saxon invasion of the British Isles cannot be determined. They are presumably the *Frissones* mentioned by Procopius about the middle of the 6th century in his *De Bello Gotthico* as one of the peoples of Britain. Bede does not speak of them in his later account of the settlement. It is probable that some among the Frisians took part in the migration, but in insufficient numbers to be distinctly remembered in the 8th century.

Frith (frith), **Mary.** [Known as **Moll Cutpurse**.] b. at London, c1585; d. c1660. A notorious "thief, pickpocket, bully, prostitute, procuress, fortune-teller, receiver of stolen goods, and forger of writings," who nearly always wore a man's dress. She is said to have been the first woman who used tobacco. She was introduced by Middleton and Dekker as the chief personage (but in reformed character) in their play *The Roaring Girle*. Field also introduces her in his play *Amends for Ladies*. Her life was published anonymously at London in 1662.

Frithjof's Saga (frēt′yôfs). [Also, **Fridthiof's Saga.**] An Icelandic saga, assigned to the 14th century, relating the adventures of the 8th-century hero Frithjof (or Fridthiof). He is also the hero of a poem by Tegner, *Frithiof's Saga*, published in 1825. The saga recounts the pirate adventures of Frithjof, and his eventual finding and winning of his beloved after she was married off to an aging king by her two brothers.

Frobisher (frō′bi.shẻr), **Sir Martin.** b. c1535; d. at Plymouth, England, Nov. 22, 1594. An English navigator. He was of a family of Welsh origin settled at Altofts in the West Riding of Yorkshire. He commanded an expedition, consisting of two ships of less than 25 tones each, a pinnace of 10 tons, and a total crew of 35, in search of the Northwest Passage in 1576, on which he discovered, in the *Gabriel*, the only ship remaining, the bay since known as Frobisher Bay. One of his sailors having brought home a piece of ore supposed to contain gold, he was sent out again in command of two expeditions in search of gold, in 1577 and 1578. These were larger and better equipped expeditions, the queen herself taking an interest and lending a ship of the royal navy. On both occasions, however, the ore which he brought home proved to be worthless. He fought with distinction with Drake in the West Indies in 1585 and against the Spanish Armada in 1588. He was in Raleigh's expedition to raid Spain in 1592 and received a mortal wound at the relief of Brest in 1594.

Frodoard (fro.do.àr). See **Flodoard.**

Frog (frog), **Nicholas** or **Nic.** A nickname for the Dutch in John Arbuthnot's "Law is a Bottomless Pit," in *The History of John Bull*.

Frogmore Lodge (frog′mōr). A mansion near Windsor Castle. It was once the residence of Queen Victoria's mother, the Duchess of Kent.

Froissart (froi′särt; French, frwå.sàr), **Jean.** b. at Valenciennes, France, 1338; d. at Chimay, Belgium, c1410. A French chronicler. Nothing is known of his family or early life beyond the few facts to be gleaned from his own writings. In 1360 he was welcomed to England by his countrywoman Queen Philippa of Hainaut, wife of Edward III. In 1365 he visited Scotland, and in May, 1368, he was at Milan in the company of Petrarch and Chaucer. After several years spent in travel, Froissart decided to enter the church (c1372). The period of his activity as a chronicler extends from 1367 to 1400. His great work is the *Chronique de France, d' Angleterre, d' Écosse et d' Éspagne*, relating the events of history from 1325 till 1400. It was published before the close of the 15th century, and was thus among the first books to be printed. One of the six editions of the 16th century was by Denis Sauvaye, historian to Henry II of France. The best editions in modern times are by Kervyn de Lettenhove (25 vols., 1867–77) and by Siméon Luce (incomplete; 8 vols., 1869–88). The standard English translations are those by John Bourchier, 2nd Baron Berners (1523–25) and by Thomas Johnes (1803–05).

Frolic (frol′ik), **Sir Frederick.** A witty suitor in Etherege's comedy *The Comical Revenge*.

Frollo (frol'ō). In Arthurian legend and romance of the first half of the 15th century, a French knight. Arthur kills him in single combat.

Fronde (frônd). In French history, a civil war (1648–53) during the minority of Louis XIV, waged against the royal power as exemplified in the king's chief minister Mazarin, by the Parliament of Paris and the high nobility. The movement began (1648) with the resistance of the Parliament of Paris (the administrative court of justice) to several financial measures resuscitated by Mazarin to obtain more money, which was not otherwise available to the royal treasury. Ignoring a direct command from the queen mother, Anne of Austria, the Parliament took the entire court group about Mazarin and its extravagance to task and demanded that certain rights remain to it and not be usurped by the crown. This resistance to arbitrary rule had its echoes elsewhere (for example, in the arrest that year in England of Charles I), and the queen bowed to the Parliamentary will. But with the victory of the Prince of Condé over the Spaniards at Lens, she attempted to suppress the revolt and arrested (Aug. 26, 1648) several leading members of the Parliament. The Parisians rioted in the streets, and from the smashing of the windows of Mazarin's adherents the revolt took its name, *fronde* meaning "sling," a toy weapon then highly popular with boys. Anne once more gave way but when Condé appeared before Paris the court fled to Saint Germain (Jan. 15, 1649). From there Mazarin ordered Condé to crush the Parliamentary group and their allies, the nobility and the mob, led by the vehement Paul de Gondi (later Cardinal de Retz). The fighting was inconclusive and light and ended with the agreement of Rueil (March 11, 1649). But by January, 1650, Condé had become obnoxiously overbearing and was arrested on Mazarin's orders. A group of the nobility, led by Condé's sister, Madame de Longueville, demanded his release. This New Fronde or Fronde of the Nobility (or Princes) met an initial setback when Turenne was defeated (Dec. 15, 1650), but when Mazarin forgot his promises to Gondi for the latter's neutrality in the struggle, the Parliamentary group joined forces with the nobles. Mazarin fled to Germany in February, 1651. However, Condé and Gondi soon fell out, and in December Mazarin returned. Condé allied himself with Spain, but Turenne now was on the side of the king, who had attained his majority, and Turenne met and defeated (July 2, 1651) Condé just outside Paris. Condé escaped into the city through the intervention of Mlle. de Montpensier and was saved from capture, but he set up a government in the city that soon alienated the Parisian populace. Mazarin having diplomatically withdrawn from France, Louis XIV entered Paris in October and was accepted without protest. Mazarin followed in February. Condé fled to Spain, where he continued fighting in an extension of the Fronde until he was defeated in 1658 in the battle of the Dunes. The result of the Fronde rebellion was a further weakening of the French financial structure and a strengthening of the absolute power of the king at the expense of both nobility and commons.

Front de Boeuf (frôn' dẹ bêf'), **Sir Reginald.** In Sir Walter Scott's novel *Ivanhoe*, a brutal and fierce Norman baron who uses his castle of Torquilstone to imprison and torture his enemies, and finally perishes in its flames.

Frost (frôst), **Jack.** In English nursery folklore, a personification of frost or cold.

Froth (frôth). In Shakespeare's *Measure for Measure*, a tapster and "foolish gentleman" who is arrested by Elbow (II.i).

Froth, Lord. A solemn, foolish fop with a coquettish wife, in Congreve's comedy *The Double Dealer*.

Froude (frōd), **James Anthony.** b. at Dartington, Devonshire, England, April 23, 1818; d. Oct. 20, 1894. An English historian. He was educated at Westminster School, London, and at Oriel College, Oxford. There he came under the influence of the Tractarian movement, his brother Richard Hurrell Froude being one of its leaders. He became a fellow of Exeter in 1842, and took deacon's orders in 1844. For some time he was connected with the High-Church party under Newman. A change in his views caused him to abandon his fellowship and his profession, and he devoted himself entirely to literature, formally resigning his deacon's orders in 1872. In the same year he lectured in the U. S. on the relations between England and Ireland. In 1874 he was sent on a mission to the Cape of Good Hope. He afterward went to Australia and the West Indies. In 1892 he was elected regius professor of modern history at Oriel College, Oxford, as successor to Freeman. He wrote *History of England from the Fall of Wolsey to the Defeat of the Spanish Armada* (1856–70), *Short Studies on Great Subjects* (1867–77), *The English in Ireland in the Eighteenth Century* (1872–74), *Caesar* (1879), *Oceana* (1886), *The Two Chiefs of Dunboy*, a romance (1889), *Life of Lord Beaconsfield* (1890), and others. As executor of Carlyle he published *Reminiscences of Carlyle* (1881) and *Life of Thomas Carlyle* (1882).

Frugal (frō'gạl), **Lady.** The "city madam" in Massinger's comedy of that name.

Frugal, Luke. The principal character in Philip Massinger's *City Madam:* a vindictive, hypocritical villain. He is the brother of the charitable Sir John.

Frugal, Sir John. In Massinger's *City Madam,* the kind-hearted brother of Luke Frugal.

Fry (frī), **Christopher.** b. 1907—. An English playwright. His plays include *The Boy with a Cart* (1939), *The Firstborn* (1946), *A Phoenix Too Frequent* (1946), *The Lady's Not for Burning* (1949), *Thor, with Angels* (1949), *Venus Observed* (1950), *A Sleep of Prisoners* (1951), and *The Dark Is Light Enough* (1954). He translated into English and adapted Jean Anouilh's play *Ring Round the Moon* in 1950.

Fry, Elizabeth. [Maiden name, **Gurney.**] b. at Earlham, Norfolk, England, May 21, 1780; d. at Ramsgate, England, Oct. 12, 1845. An English philanthropist, a minister of the Society of Friends. She was especially noted as a promoter of prison reform.

Fry, Francis. b. at Westbury-on-Trym, near Bristol, England, Oct. 28, 1803; d. at Bristol, England, Nov. 12, 1886. An English bibliographer. He was a partner in the firm of J. S. Fry and Sons, cocoa and chocolate manufacturers at Bristol. He published *The First New Testament printed in the English Language (1525 or 1526), translated from the Greek by William Tyndale, reproduced in facsimile, with an Introduction* (1862), *The Souldiers Pocket Bible, printed at London by G. B. and R. W. for G. C. 1643, reproduced in facsimile, with an Introduction* (1862), *The Christian Soldiers Penny Bible: London, printed by R. Smith for Sam. Wade, 1693, reproduced in facsimile, with an Introductory Note* (1862), and others.

Fry, Roger Eliot. b. at Highgate, North London, Dec. 14, 1866; d. at London, Sept. 9, 1934. An English artist and art critic. He studied art under Francis Bate, and at Paris at the Julian Academy. From 1905 to 1910 he was at New York, as director of the Metropolitan Museum of Art, a position he was invited to fill by J. P. Morgan, whom he had previously advised as a collector and whom he frequently helped to buy pictures in Europe. He had hoped for the directorship of the London National Gallery, but when a vacancy occurred early in 1905 and he was offered the position he did not feel free to take it after having accepted Morgan's invitation. His works on art and criticism are *Giovanni Bellini* (1899), his edition of *Sir Joshua Reynold's Discourses* (1905), considered by authorities one of his most valuable contributions to the study of art, *Vision and Design* (1920), a collection of essays originally published in the *Burlington Magazine* (of which he was a founder), *A Sampler of Castile* (1923), *Transformations* (1926), *Cézanne and Flemish Art* (both 1927), *Henri Matisse* (1930), *Characteristics of French Art* (1932), and *Reflections on British Painting* (1934), both, with *Flemish Art*, the lectures he delivered in London at Queen's Hall. He created a sensation in November, 1910, when he arranged an exhibition in London's Grafton Galleries of modern French painting, for which he was attacked verbally as a charlatan, a fraud, and a maniac, and was informed by Sir William Blake Richmond, who represented the "correct" view, that he must expect to be "boycotted by decent society."

Fudge Family in Paris (fuj; pär'is), **The.** A satire by Thomas Moore, published in 1818. Its sequel is *The Fudge Family in England.*

Fuenterrabia (fwen.ter.rä'вyä). [Basque, **Ondarrabia;** French, **Fontarabie.**] A city in N Spain, in the province of Guipúzcoa, situated near the Bay of Biscay and the French frontier, at the mouth of the Bidassoa River. The old town has a fishing harbor, a castle, and a Gothic church; the new town is a popular summer resort; there are a number of hotels and villas. Because of its strategic importance, Fuenterrabia in the past was frequently contested between France and Spain; it was sacked in 1794 by the French. In 1813 the Duke of Wellington forced a passage here into France. Fighting took place here in the Carlist war of 1837 and in the civil war of 1936–39.

Fugger (fûg'ẻr). A Swabian family of ennobled merchants, famous in the 16th century. It traces its decent from Johann Fugger, a weaver who lived at Graben, near Augsburg, in the first half of the 14th century. His son Johann became a citizen of Augsburg. After his death in 1408, his sons Andreas (d. 1457) and Jakob (d. 1469) carried on the family

business. Lukas, Andreas's son, was a well-known Augsburg politician and moneylender, rich enough to be ruined by the default of Louvain on a note held by him. His brother Jakob obtained the right to display family arms. Ulrich (1441–1510), Georg (1453–1506), and Jakob (1459–1525), sons of Jakob (d. 1469), widened the scope of the family's business. Ulrich became banker to the Hapsburgs and obtained control of several lands in Germany through his mortgage holdings; Jakob obtained mines in the Tirol and in Hungary and traded in spices and textiles with India and Europe. The Fuggers reached their greatest influence and wealth under Raymund (1489–1535) and Anton (1493–1560), sons of Georg. Before his death Jakob had backed with his great wealth the successful candidacy (1519) of Charles V as Holy Roman emperor. To Jakob's heirs and nephews, Charles granted many concessions in mining and in rents; he raised them to the nobility in 1530 and in 1534 they obtained the right to coin money. They further expanded the family's business horizon to the New World and extended the family's land holdings. Both brothers were patrons of the arts and supporters of the charities and other works of the Roman Catholic Church. Among later descendants of the Fuggers were several scholars and writers, art patrons, and soldiers, but the wealth of the three surviving branches of the family has shrunk in the 20th century to small land holdings.

Fugitive, The. A drama (1913) by John Galsworthy, dealing with the problem of an unhappy marriage.

Fulgens and Lucres (ful'jẹns; lö.krēs'). A 15th-century play by Henry Medwall, English author and chaplain to Archbishop John Morton, of whom little else is known. The importance of the play in literary history is that it is the first secular play in English. It was produced sometime between 1490 and 1501, probably in 1497.

Fulke (fûlk), **William.** b. at London, 1538; d. Aug. 28, 1589. An English Puritan divine. He studied at Cambridge, where he subsequently lectured on the Hebrew language. He became master of Pembroke Hall, Cambridge, in 1578. His most notable publication is *A Defense of the sincere and true Translations of the Holie Scriptures into the English Tong* (1583).

Fuller (fûl'ẻr), **Andrew.** b. at Wicken, Cambridgeshire, England, Feb. 6, 1754; d. at Kettering, Northamptonshire, England, May 7, 1815. An English Baptist preacher and theologian. He wrote *The Calvinistic and Socinian Systems Compared* (1794), *The Gospels its own Witness* (1799–1800), and others.

Fuller, John Frederick Charles. b. 1878—. A British soldier and military analyst. He served in the Boer War (1899–1902) and in World War I. His books include *Tanks in the Great War, 1914–1918* (1920), *War and Western Civilization 1832–1932* (1932), *The Last of the Gentlemen's Wars* (1937), *Decisive Battles: Their Influence Upon History and Civilization* (1940), and *Decisive Battles of the U.S.A.* (1942).

Fuller, Thomas. b. in June, 1608; d. at London, Aug. 16, 1661. An English divine. He was educated at Cambridge, and was curate of the Savoy at

London at the beginning of the English Civil War. In 1643 he joined the king at Oxford, and after the Restoration was appointed chaplain to Charles II. Among his works are *The History of the Holy Warre* (1639), *The Holy State and the Profane State* (1642), *A Pisgah-sight of Palestine* (1650), *History of the University of Cambridge* (1655), and *History of the Worthies of England* (1662).

Fuller-Maitland (-māt′land), **John Alexander.** b. at London, April 7, 1856; d. at Carnforth, Lancashire, England, March 30, 1936. An English music critic and writer. He was music critic for the *Pall Mall Gazette* (1882–84), the *Guardian* (1884–89), and the London *Times* (1889–1911); author of *Schumann* (1884), *English Music of the Nineteenth Century* (1902), *Brahms* (1911), and *The Suites of Bach* (1924).

Fullerton (fŭl′ėr.tọn), **Georgiana Charlotte.** See **Leveson-Gower,** Lady **Georgiana Charlotte.**

Fulvia (ful′vi.ạ). In Ben Jonson's *Catiline*, a voluptuous wanton: a satire on the causes of Rome's degeneration.

Funeral, or Grief à-la-mode, The. A comedy by Steele, produced c1701 and printed in 1702.

Fungoso (fung.gō′sō). In Ben Jonson's *Every Man Out of His Humour*, the extravagant son of Sordido. He spends all he can wring out of his avaricious father in imitating the foppish Brisk.

Fungus (fung′gus), **Zachary.** The principal character in Samuel Foote's *Commissary.* Foote played it himself.

Furiae (fū′ri.ē). In Roman mythology, goddesses adopted from the Erinyes of Greek mythology.

Furness (fėr′nẹs), **Horace Howard.** b. at Philadelphia, Nov. 2, 1833; d. at Wallingford, Pa., Aug. 13, 1912. An American Shakespeare scholar and legal writer. He edited a Variorum of Shakespeare's plays, which includes *Romeo and Juliet* (1871), *Macbeth* (1873), *Hamlet* (1877), *King Lear* (1880), *Othello* (1886), *The Merchant of Venice* (1888), *As You Like It* (1890), *The Tempest* (1892), *Midsummer-Night's Dream* (1895), *The Winter's Tale* (1898), *Much Ado About Nothing* (1899), *Twelfth Night* (1901), *Love's Labour's Lost* (1904), *Antony and Cleopatra* (1907), *Richard III* (1908), and others.

Furnivall (fėr′ni.val), **Frederick James.** b. at Egham, Surrey, England, Feb. 4, 1825; d. July 2, 1910. An English scholar and editor. He was educated at University College, London, and Trinity College, Cambridge; called to the bar in 1849, he soon gave up law for his literary and linguistic

interests. He was one of the founders (1854) of the London Workingmen's College. A member (1847 *et seq.*) and secretary (1862–1910) of the Philological Society, he was an editor of its contemplated dictionary, which was to emerge in published form as the *New English Dictionary* (*Oxford English Dictionary*). He founded, between 1864 and 1886, the Chaucer, Ballad, New Shakespeare, Browning, Shelley, Wycliffe, and Early English Text societies, and edited during his lifetime over a hundred works in English literature, including the *Canterbury Tales* (1868–77), the *Leopold Shakespeare*, the *Century Shakespeare*, the *Percy Ballads, Political, Religious, and Love Poems*, works on the Holy Grail, Thomas Hoccleve's works, *The English Conquest of Ireland: A.D. 1165–85* of Giraldus Cambrensis, William Harrison's *Description of England*, and Philip Stubb's *Anatomie of Abuses.*

Furor (fū′rôr). In Spenser's *Faerie Queene*, a madman, typifying wrath. He is the son of a wretched hag, Occasion. To tame the son the mother had to be subdued.

Fusbos (fus′bos). In Rhodes's burlesque opera *Bombastes Furioso*, the minister of state. He kills Bombastes, who has killed all the other characters.

Fuseli (fū′zẹ.li), (**John**) **Henry.** [Original name, **Johann Heinrich Füssli** (füs′lē).] b. at Zurich, Switzerland, Feb. 7, 1741; d. at Putney, near London, April 16, 1825. A Swiss-English painter and art critic.

Fust (fŏst) or **Faust** (foust), **Johann.** d. probably at Paris, 1466 or 1467. A German printer. He was the partner of Gutenberg from c1450 to 1455. In the latter year the partnership was dissolved, and Fust obtained possession of the printing press constructed by Gutenberg. He continued the business with his son-in-law Peter Schöffer.

Fyfe (fīf), **H. Hamilton.** [Full name, **Henry Hamilton Fyfe.**] b. at London, Sept. 28, 1869; d. June 19, 1951. An English writer and editor. Editor (1902–03) of the *Morning Advertiser*, of the *Daily Mirror* from 1903 to 1907, and of the London *Daily Herald* from 1922 to 1926. Author of *A Player's Tragedy* (1894), *A Trick of Fame* (1897), *Prague* (1910), *The Widow's Cruise* (1920), *And Have Not Love* (1922), *Religion of an Optimist* (1927), *Revolt of Women* (1933), *What Communism Means To-day* (1937), *The Illusion of National Character* (1940), and *Britain's War-time Revolution* (1944); wrote the plays *A Modern Aspasia* (1909), *The Borstal Boy* (1913), and *The Kingdom, The Power, and the Glory* (1920).

G

Gaberlunzie Man (gab.ėr.lun′zi), **The.** A Scottish ballad traditionally ascribed, though without evidence, to James V. The gaberlunzie (or gaberlunyie) was a wallet or bag, and the gaberlunzie man was a wandering beggar or tinker who carried the wallet.

Gabhra (gä′vrạ), **Battle of.** In Irish legend, the battle between the Fenians under Fionn Mac-Cumhail (Finn MacCool) and the forces of the high king of Ireland, who had turned against him. At this battle Oscar, the grandson of Fionn, was killed and Fionn and the Fenians overcome. It is

d, d or j; ṣ, s or sh; ṭ, t or ch; ẓ, z or zh; o, F. cloche; ü, F. menu; ċh, Sc. loch; ṅ, F. bonbon.

conjectured to have taken place in the 3rd century.

Gaboriau (gȧ.bo.ryō), **Émile.** b. at Saujon, Charente-Maritime, France, Nov. 9, 1835; d. at Paris, Sept. 28, 1873. A French novelist, creator of the fictional detectives M. Lecoq and Père Tabaret, and author of *L'Affaire Lerouge* (1866), *Le Dossier No. 113* (1867), *Le Crime d'Orcival* (1867), *M. Lecoq* (1869), *La Dégringolade* (1871), *La Corde au cou* (1873), and other detective stories.

Gabriel (gā'bri.el). In Jewish and Christian tradition, one of the seven archangels. He usually appears as God's messenger or interpreter (as in Milton's *Paradise Lost*). He interprets to Daniel his visions (Dan. viii. 16, ix. 21), announces the birth of John the Baptist and Jesus (Luke, i. 19, 26), and is the angel who appears to Mary at the Annunciation. In the Koran he is represented as the medium of revelation to Mohammed. In Christian tradition, Gabriel is the angel of mercy. He will blow the trumpet announcing the arrival of the judgment day.

Gabriel Betteredge (bet'rij). See **Betteredge, Gabriel.**

Gabriel Hounds. [Also: **Gabblerachet, Gabrielrache** (gā'bri.el.rach''), **Gabriel's Hounds.**] In English folklore, a cry heard in the upper air at night, called also the Wild Hunt. It is said to be the lost souls of unbaptized infants wandering through space in the form of spectral hounds (the noise is actually attributed to the gabble of migrating wild geese). To hear the Gabriel Hounds is popularly regarded as an omen of evil or death.

Gabriel Oak (ōk). See **Oak, Gabriel.**

Gabriel Varden (vär'den). See **Varden, Gabriel.**

Gadabout (gad'ȧ.bout), **Mrs.** A character in David Garrick's play *The Lying Valet.*

Gadshill (gadz'hil). A hill ab. 3 mi. NW of Rochester, England, on the road to Gravesend. It commands a fine view, and is noted as the place, in Shakespeare's *1 Henry IV*, where Falstaff had his encounter with the "men in buckram." Gadshill, one of the thieves, is a character in the play. There is an inn there called the Falstaff Inn. Opposite stands Gadshill Place, the residence of Charles Dickens, who died there.

Gadshill. In Shakespeare's *1 Henry IV*, a rascally companion of Falstaff. With Falstaff and others he robs travelers and is in turn robbed by Prince Hal and Poins. He supports Falstaff's lies when Prince Hal questions him about the episode.

Gaea (jē'ȧ). [Also: **Gaia, Ge.**] In Greek mythology, the earth goddess; first-born of Chaos, and mother of Uranus (the sky god) and Pontus (a sea god). As consort of Uranus she was the mother of the Cyclopes, the Hecatoncheires, and the Titans; as consort of Pontus she was the mother of five sea gods. As earth goddess, and thus as mother goddess, she was also regarded as an underworld deity. Her cults were very numerous. The earliest oracle at Olympia was hers, as was also the first oracle at Delphi. The Romans identified Gaea with their Tellus.

Gaelic (gā'lik). [Irish, **Gaedealac.**] A language spoken by the people of Ireland, of the Scottish Highlands, and of the Isle of Man. It belongs, with

Old Irish and Middle Irish, to the Goidelic branch of the Celtic languages.

Gaels (gālz). [Irish, **Gaedeal.**] A Celtic people of Ireland, of the Scottish Highlands, and of the Isle of Man.

Gage (gāj), **Thomas.** b. probably in Surrey, England, c1596; d. in Jamaica, 1656. An English missionary and author. He joined the Dominicans in Spain, and from 1625 to 1637 was a missionary in Mexico and Guatemala. Returning, he renounced Roman Catholicism in 1640, and became a Protestant preacher in England. In 1648 he published his *English American, or New Survey of the West Indies,* describing his travels in America. He pointed out that the rich Spanish colonies were nearly defenseless, and his account soon led to privateering expeditions against them. Gage was appointed chaplain to the squadron sent under Venables and Penn to the West Indies, where he died.

Gahagan (gȧ.hā'gan), Major **Goliah.** One of the many pseudonyms of **Thackeray, William Makepeace.**

Gaheris (gā'her.is). In Arthurian romance, the son of King Lot and Margawse, Queen of Orkney (sister of King Arthur); nephew of Arthur, and brother of Gawain and Gareth. He killed his mother for adultery.

Gaiety Theatre. A London theater situated on the north side of the Strand. It was opened in 1868, and in it *opéra bouffe* was given its first regular performances in England.

Gaillard (gȧ.yàr), **Château.** See **Château Gaillard.**

Gainsborough (gānz'bur.ọ). An urban district, market town, and river port in E England, in Lincolnshire, in the Parts of Lindsey, situated on the river Trent, ab. 15 mi. NW of Lincoln, ab. 146 mi. N of London by rail. It is popularly supposed that the wedding of Alfred the Great (871–901) was celebrated here. Gainsborough is the town called St. Ogg's in George Eliot's novel *The Mill on the Floss.*

Gainsborough, Thomas. b. at Sudbury, Suffolk, England, 1727; d. at London, Aug. 2, 1788. An English painter, best known for his portraits but also one of the foremost English landscape painters. The son of a wool manufacturer, he went to London in his fifteenth year, and studied with Gravelot, a French engraver and teacher of drawing, and also at St. Martin's Lane Academy with Francis Hayman. In 1745 he returned to Sudbury, where he set up a studio as portrait painter. He soon removed to Ipswich, remaining there till 1760, when he went to Bath. At the foundation of the Royal Academy in 1768 Gainsborough was one of the original 36 members. In 1774 he left Bath for London. In 1779 he was at the height of his fame. From 1769 to 1783 (except 1772–76) he was a constant exhibitor at the Royal Academy. He sent nothing to the exhibitions after that year, owing to a disagreement with the council. He painted over 300 pictures, more than 220 being portraits. In the National Gallery at London are his *Musidora, The Market Cart, The Watering Place, Gainsborough's Forest,* and five portraits, one of them being Mrs. Siddons. There are five of his portraits in the Dulwich Gallery, and others also in the National Portrait Gallery, at Hampton Court, at Buckingham Palace, and at Grosvenor House. The Huntington Art Gallery at San Marino, Calif., has the *Blue Boy*, a portrait of Master Buttall, probably the most famous of several to which the same title has been given. He painted George III eight times. The famous portrait of the Duchess of Devonshire was painted in 1783. The *Girl with Pigs* (1782) was purchased by Sir Joshua Reynolds. There are also pictures of his in galleries at Dublin, Glasgow, and Edinburgh, in the Metropolitan Museum of Art and the Frick Art Gallery at New York, and elsewhere.

Gairdner (gärd'nėr, gärd'-), **James.** b. at Edinburgh, March 22, 1828; d. at Pinner, Middlesex, England, Nov. 4, 1912. A Scottish historian, biographer, and editor. From 1846 until March, 1893, when he retired, he was in the Public Records Office, after 1859 as assistant keeper of the records. He wrote *Life of Richard III* (1878), *Henry VII* (1889), *The Early Tudors* (1902), *Lollardry and the Reformation in England* (4 vols., 1908–13), and many essays for historical reviews; he edited *Calendar of Letters and Papers of the Reign of Henry VIII* (21 vols.), a digest of 100,000 documents; for the Rolls Series of Chronicles and Memorials and the Camden Society, he edited *Memorials of King Henry VII* (1858), *Letters and Papers of Richard III and Henry VII* (1861–63), *Historical Collections of a Citizen of London in the 15th Century* (1876), *Three Fifteenth-Century Chronicles* (1880), *The Spousells of Princess Mary* (1893); his final edition of *The Paston Letters* (6 vols.) appeared in 1904.

Gaius (gā'us, gī'us). [Also, **Caius.**] b. c110 A.D.; d. c180. A Roman jurist, a native, probably, of the eastern part of the empire. He was, for the greater part of his life, a teacher and writer in Rome. He wrote numerous works on the civil law, the most noted being seven books of *Aurea* (*Rerum Quotidianarum Libri VII*) and four books of *Institutiones*, a favorite manual and the foundation of Justinian's *Institutes*. A manuscript (palimpsest on which the *Letters* of Saint Jerome had been written; in some parts the parchment had been twice used, after the original writing had been erased) of the *Institutiones* was found by Niebuhr at Verona in 1816. It was edited (1820) by Göschen.

Gaius Cassius Longinus (kash'us lon.jī'nus). See under **Cassius.**

Gaius Helvius Cinna (hel'vi.us sin'a). See under **Cinna.**

Galahad (gal'a.had), **Sir.** In Arthurian romance, the noblest and purest knight of the Round Table; son of Sir Lancelot and Elaine. In some versions of the Grail story, as a result of his purity he is the only knight completely successful in the quest of the Holy Grail.

Galahalt or **Galahault** (gal'a.hôlt), **Sir.** In Malory's *Morte d'Arthur*, a knight described as the "haut prince" of Suluse and the Long Isles. He figures in an early French version of the Lancelot and Guinevere story.

Galaor (gal'a.ôr). The brother of Amadis de Gaul.

Galapas (gal'a.pas). In Arthurian romance, a

giant slain by King Arthur. Arthur first cut his legs off in order to reach his head, and then smote that off too.

Galatea (gal.a.tē'a). In Greek mythology, a sea nymph, the daughter of Nereus and Doris, loved by the one-eyed Cyclops, Polyphemus. However, she loved Acis and Polyphemus, in a fit of jealousy, crushed Acis under a huge rock, whereupon Galatea wept until she was transformed into a fountain.

Galathea or **Gallathea** (gal.a.tē'a). A comedy by John Lyly, printed in 1592 and written between 1584 and 1588.

Gale (gāl), **Norman.** [Full name, **Norman Rowland Gale.**] b. at Kew, Surrey, England, 1862; d. 1942. An English nature poet and short-story writer. He was the author of prose works including *A June Romance* (1894), *All Expenses Paid* (1895), *Barty's Star* (1902), and *Solitude* (1913); his books of poetry include *A Country Muse* (1892; 2nd series, 1895), *Orchard Songs* (1893), *Cricket Songs* (1894), *Songs for Little People* (1896), *More Cricket Songs* (1905), *A Book of Quatrains* (1909), *Song in September* (1912), *The Candid Cuckoo* (1918), *Merry-Go-Round of Song* (1919), *Verse in Bloom* (1925), *Flight of Fancies* (1927), *Messrs. Bat and Ball* (1930), and *Love-in-a-Mist* (1939).

Gale, Theophilus. b. at Kingsteignton, Devonshire, England, 1628; d. at Newington, London, in February or March, 1678. An English nonconformist divine. He was appointed preacher in Winchester cathedral in 1657, was deprived of this preferment on the Restoration in 1660, and in 1677 became pastor of an Independent congregation at Holborn. His chief work is *The Court of the Gentiles, or a Discourse teaching the Original of Humane Literature* (1669–77).

Galen (gā'len). [Latin, **Claudius Galenus.**] b. at Pergamum, in Mysia, Asia Minor, c130 A.D.; d. c200 A.D. A Greek physician and philosophical writer. Her father, Nicon, was a mathematician and an architect, who saw to it that his son was well educated. Galen began studying medicine at about the age of 16, traveling and furthering his studies at Smyrna, Corinth, and Alexandria. He returned (c158) to Pergamum and took the post of surgeon to the gladiators there. He went (c164) to Rome, where he became a much-sought-after physician, but after four years returned to Pergamum. From there he was summoned by the emperor Marcus Aurelius. The emperor wanted Galen to accompany him on his expedition against the Germans, but Galen did not go, remaining in Rome as the attending physician to the emperor's son Commodus. He worked at Rome for some time, and apparently eventually returned to Pergamum. Galen was a prolific writer and is credited with some 500 works, on medicine, logic, grammar, ethics, philosophy, and literature; he wrote on comedy and prepared commentaries on Plato and Aristotle. So extensive were his writings, and so widely imitated, or rather so often were works falsely attributed to him, that Galen himself wrote a descriptive catalogue of his writings, *De propriis libris*. Some 100 treatises known to be, or considered, genuine are extant; the edition of Kuhn (1821–33) is the only complete modern one. Galen's work in medicine and physiology remained the standard for more than 1,000 years until it was upset, in the 16th century and after, by the work of such men as Harvey. The reason for its long life was Galen's method of accurate observation; his facts, derived from experimental data, were accurate, but since his experiments were not performed on human beings, somè inaccuracies were present. The facts as he found them, however, and as he fitted them into a system of natural philosophy seemed so precisely what was to be expected that only the skeptical mind of the Renaissance could upset them.

Galeotti Martivalle (gal.ẹ.ot'ẹ mär.tẹ.val'ẹ). See **Martivalle, Galeotti.**

Galignani (gä.lē.nyä'nē). A publishing family in France and England, including John Anthony Galignani (b. at London, Oct. 13, 1796; d. at Paris, Dec. 31, 1873) and William Galignani (b. at London, March 10, 1798; d. at Paris, Dec. 12, 1882). Their father, Giovanni Antonio Galignani, settled at Paris shortly after 1798, and in 1801 he started a monthly which soon became a weekly paper. In 1814 he began to issue guidebooks and started *Galignani's Messenger*, which circulated widely among English residents on the Continent. The sons carried on the publishing business after their father's death in 1821, and issued reprints of many English books. In 1832 William was naturalized, Anthony remaining a British subject. In 1852 their reprints were stopped by the copyright treaty. They were liberal contributors to British charities, and built a hospital at Neuilly for indigent English. William left money and a site at Neuilly to build the Retraite Galignani Frères for a hundred printers, booksellers, or their families.

Galileo (gal.i.lē'ō; Italian, gä.lē.lä'ō). [Full name, **Galileo Galilei.**] b. at Pisa, Italy, in February, 1564; d. at Arcetri, near Florence, Jan. 8, 1642. An Italian physicist and astronomer. He was descended from a noble but impoverished Florentine family. After studying (1581–86) at the University of Pisa without taking a degree, he became professor of mathematics there (1589–91), later serving at Padua (1592–1610) and Florence. He discovered (1583), while watching a lamp swing in the cathedral of Pisa, that its oscillations could be used to time his pulse; from this he deduced the isochronic nature of the swing of the pendulum, which he later demonstrated might be used to measure time. In 1586 he invented the hydrostatic balance, an instrument for determining the specific gravities of substances by comparing their weights in and out of water. He also developed an experiment to determine the speed of light; a flash was to be timed from two points, but the timing mechanisms then in use were too inaccurate to measure the extremely small time intervals involved, and the experiment came to nothing. According to a famous story, he dropped bodies of various weights from the Leaning Tower of Pisa and thus showed that all bodies would fall with equal velocities in a vacuum. He continued his experiments with falling bodies with the use of the inclined plane, from which experiments he developed theories relative to motion that were later to be demonstrated as laws by Isaac Newton. He showed also that the parabola of a projectile's flight was made up of a

horizontal and a vertical component, and that the latter was ruled by the same forces that governed falling bodies. He invented the first thermometer in 1597, and the first telescope in 1609. With this instrument, magnifying to about 30 diameters, Galileo discovered (1610) that Jupiter had satellites (he saw four of them), that Saturn was surrounded by rings, that the Moon's surface was mountainous and not smooth, that Venus went through phases like the Moon's (due to its position between Earth and Sun). He noted (c1610) the existence of sunspots and developed thence the idea that the sun rotated on its axis; and he stated that given a better telescope, an observer might resolve the Milky Way into individual stars. His publication of *Letters on the Solar Spots* (1613) embodied his acceptance of the Copernican system of the universe, which made of the earth a mere planet circling about the sun instead of the fixed center of the universe (which it was according to the Ptolemaic theory). He was summoned to Rome where, in 1616, his doctrines, which he had attempted to justify by Biblical quotation, were condemned as heretical by the Pope. An essay on comets, *Saggiatore*, which he published in 1623, was well received, however, despite several oblique defenses of the Copernican system. But his publication of *Dialogo dei due massimi sistemi del mondo* (*Dialogue on the two chief systems of the universe,* 1632) caused a storm. It was acclaimed all over Europe, but its advocacy of Copernicanism, despite the papal injunction of 1616, brought down the wrath of the Church on his head. The book was banned by Rome and Galileo was called (1633) before the Inquisition. There, under the threat of torture, he was forced to abjure his belief in the Copernican theory; the familiar legend states that as he arose after his recantation he murmured: "Eppur si muove" (And yet it does move). As a result of his quarrel with the Church, he was removed from his academic posts and retired to his home at Arcetri. There, despite almost total blindness, he discovered (1637) the moon's libration (presentation of more than half its surface to the view of observers on Earth). Galileo's *Dialoghi delle nuove scienzi* (1638) summed up his experiments and theories on mechanics. Galileo established the method of modern science, a deductive-inductive method that verifies theory by practical experiment and surrenders the rationalized, universal "proofs" of scholasticism for the amassing of data, later to be systematized by theory, in limited fields.

Gall (gäl), **Franz Joseph.** b. at Tiefenbrunn, near Pforzheim, Baden, Germany, March 9, 1758; d. at Montrouge, near Paris, Aug. 22, 1828. A German physician, the founder of phrenology. He studied and practiced (1785 *et seq.*) medicine at Vienna and in 1796, following studies in the relationship between cranial forms and personal abilities, began lecturing on phrenology. In 1802 the government banned the lectures and publications on the subject as atheistic, thereby arousing interest in the study. He embarked on a lecture tour (1805–07), creating a sensation. In 1807 he settled at Paris, where he continued his work as physician, lecturer, and writer, often with the assistance of his disciple Johann Kaspar Spurzheim. Gall's theories, based on the idea that certain regions of the brain are responsible for certain recognizable faculties, that the activity or lack of activity of these regions may be inferred from an examination of the skull by a trained observer, have been attacked from the very beginning and are given little credence today. His chief work is *Anatomie et physiologie du système nerveux* (1810–20).

Gallathea (gal.a̱.tē′a̱). See **Galathea**.

galliard (gal′yard). [Sometimes called **cinque-pace** or **sink-a-pace**.] Italian dance of five steps and six beats, which is found in many Elizabethan plays. It was also the name of a musical form.

Gallio (gal′i.ō). [Full name, **Lucius Junius Gallio**; original name, **Marcus Annaeus Novatus**.] d. c65 A.D. A Roman proconsul of Achaea (53); brother of Seneca. When he had dismissed the Jews' complaint against Paul at Corinth, and the synagogue ruler was beaten, we read (Acts, xviii. 17) that he "cared for none of these things," not from indifference about religion, but because such matters did not concern him.

Gallions Reach (gal′i.o̱nz). A novel of the London docks, by H. M. Tomlinson, published in 1927. It won the Femina-Vie Heureuse Prize.

Gallus (gal′us). In Shakespeare's *Antony and Cleopatra*, a friend of Octavius.

Galoshio (ga̱.lō′shi.ō). In *The Nice Valour*, by John Fletcher and another, a clown.

Galsworthy (gôls′wėr″ᴛʜi), **John**. [Pseudonym, **John Sinjohn**.] b. at Kingston, Surrey, England, Aug. 14, 1867; d. Jan. 31, 1933. An English novelist, short-story writer, and playwright. His first novels, which appeared under the pseudonym John Sinjohn, were *From the Four Winds* (1897), *Jocelyn* (1898), *Villa Rubein* (1900), and *A Man of Devon* (1901). He wrote *The Island Pharisees* (1904), *The Country House* (1907), *Fraternity* (1909), *A Motley* (1910), *The Patrician* (1911), *The Inn of Tranquillity* (1912), *The Dark Flower* (1913), *The Freelands* (1915), *Beyond* (1917; revised ed., 1923), *Saint's Progress* (1919), *The Burning Spear* (1921), and *One More River* (1933); and the plays *The Silver Box* (1906), *Joy* (1907), *Strife* (1909), *Justice* (1910), *The Pigeon* (1912), *The Eldest Son* (1912), and *The Fugitive* (1913). In 1922 he published his trilogy, *The Forsyte Saga;* the work, which embraces *The Man of Property* (1906), *In Chancery* (1920), and *To Let* (1921), delineates the lives of the members of one family centering about Soames Forsyte. This collective work also includes two "interludes," *The Indian Summer of a Forsyte* (1920) and *The Awakening* (1921). In *A Modern Comedy* (1929), another trilogy, he carried the family history into the 20th century and to the death of Soames. This group includes *The White Monkey* (1924), *The Silver Spoon* (1926), and *Swan Song* (1928), and two "interludes," *The Silent Wooing* (1925) and *Passersby* (1927). Among his later plays are *The Skin Game* (1920), *Loyalties* (1922), and *Escape* (1926). He became (1929) a member of the Order of Merit and was awarded (1932) the Nobel prize for literature.

Galt (gôlt), **John**. b. at Irvine, Ayrshire, Scotland, May 2, 1779; d. at Greenock, Scotland, April 11, 1839. A Scottish novelist. His writings are noted for their delineations of Scottish life and character. His best novels are *The Ayrshire Legatees* (1820–21), *Annals of the Parish* (1821), *Sir Andrew Wylie* (1822), *The Provost* (1822), *The Entail* (1823), and *Lawrie Todd* (1830).

Galton (gôl′to̱n), Sir **Francis**. b. near Birmingham, England, Feb. 16, 1822; d. at Haslemere, Surrey, England, Jan. 17, 1911. An English scientist, founder of the science of eugenics; grandson of Erasmus Darwin. He was educated at the Birmingham General Hospital, where he secured his first scientific training, at King's College, London, and at Trinity College, Cambridge, and traveled in Germany, Egypt, and Africa. He founded (1904) a eugenics laboratory at London University, endowing it with 45,000 pounds, and was knighted in 1909. After 1860 he did much work in meteorology, and was a member of the Meteorological Council for more than 30 years. He first described the theory of anticyclones and his investigations led to the modern weather map. His work in anthropometry is no less important. He published several volumes on fingerprints and their use as a means of identification, methods of making them clear, and a demonstration of their invariability. He invented the method of composite portraiture. A man of many interests, he exerted a great influence on British and American psychology. He pioneered the field of individual differences. In 1869, in his *Hereditary Genius* (2nd ed., 1892), he advanced the theory that genius tended to run in families. Investigations begun here led him into the fields of mental testing and statistics. To accomplish investigations he developed the questionnaire method of collecting data, many tests of mental capacities, and the apparatus (now standard laboratory equipment) with which to make the tests (e.g., the Galton whistle with which to measure the range of audibility, and the Galton bar with which to measure a person's ability to judge visual distances). He was the first person to work out the method of statistical correlation which, with the aid of J. D. H. Dickson, he developed as the "index of co-relation." This came about when he noticed that the intelligence of the sons tended to be nearer the average intelligence (regressed toward the mean) than the intelligence of their fathers, but that there still seemed to be some relation between the intelligence of father and son. Galton also made many anthropological contributions, principally in the field of measurement. He was the author of *Narrative of an Explorer in Tropical South Africa* (1853), *The Art of Travel* (1855), *Meteorigraphica, or Methods of Mapping the Weather* (1863), *Experiments in Pangenesis* (1871), *The Life-History Album* (1884), *Natural Inheritance* (1889), *Noteworthy Families* (1906), and *Memories of My Life* (1908). He is best known for his *Hereditary Genius* (1869), *English Men of Science, Their Nature and Nurture* (1874), and *Inquiries into Human Faculty and Its Development* (1883).

Galvani (gäl.vä′nē), **Luigi** (or **Aloisio**). b. at Bologna, Italy, Sept. 9, 1737; d. there, Dec. 4, 1798. An Italian physician and physicist, professor of anatomy at Bologna. His investigations of the contractions produced in the muscles of frogs by contact with metals marked the beginning of the discovery of galvanic or voltaic electricity. He published *De viribus electricitatis in motu musculari commentarius* (1791) and others.

Gama (gu'mạ), **Vasco da.** b. at Sines, Alentejo, Portugal, c1469; d. in Cochin-India, Dec. 24, 1524. A Portuguese navigator; the first European explorer to make a sea voyage to India and the founder of the Portuguese empire in the East. Having been appointed to the command of an expedition fitted out by Emanuel of Portugal with a view to discovering an ocean route to the East Indies, he sailed from Lisbon, probably on July 8, 1497, doubled the Cape of Good Hope on Nov. 20 or 22, 1497, arrived at Calicut, on the Malabar coast of India, on May 20, 1498, and returned to Lisbon in September, 1499. He commanded a second expedition to India in 1502–03, primarily to punish the Indians for wiping out a factory at Calicut established by Cabral. Da Gama was named admiral of India and, after bombarding Calicut, he raided shipping along the coast and collected much booty. During this voyage he established a factory in Mozambique. He was made viceroy of India in 1524. His voyage is celebrated in the *Lusiads* of Camões.

Gamaliel (gạ.mā'li.ẹl). There are several Gamaliels mentioned in the Talmud as descendants of Hillel, who held the dignity of president of the Sanhedrim and of patriarch (*nasi*) of the Jewish community in Palestine after the fall of Jerusalem. **1.** Gamaliel "the elder" was the grandson of Hillel. The laws emanating from him breathe a mild and liberal spirit. He dissuaded the Jews from taking strict measures against the apostles (Acts, v. 34), and is described as "a doctor of the law, had in honor of all the people." He was a teacher of the apostle Paul. **2.** Another Gamaliel (called Gamaliel of Jabneh), grandson of the preceding, president of the Sanhedrim from 80 to 118 A.D., was the first to assume the title of patriarch. He maintained his authority with great energy and even severity, was a good mathematician, and was favorable to the study of Greek.

Game at Chess, A. A comedy or satirical drama by Thomas Middleton and William Rowley, licensed for staging in 1624, and printed in 1625. The play is a political allegory, dealing with the visit of Prince Charles and the Duke of Buckingham to the Spanish court in 1623 to arrange a marriage between Charles (later to rule as Charles I) and the Infanta. The visit was planned by Gondomar, the Spanish ambassador who had considerable influence over James I but was hated by the English populace as being a tool of Spanish intrigue and the Papacy. Under the guise of chessmen, Gondomar, as the Black Knight, is seen in league with Marco Antonio de Dominis, as the Fat Bishop, who had received preferment in the Anglican Church upon coming to England. The Black Knight wishes to bribe the Fat Bishop into returning to an allegiance with Rome, so that he will make no trouble for the Black Kingdom (Spain). After pointed references to the visit to Madrid, the White Knight (Prince Charles) is able to checkmate the Black King (Philip IV of Spain). The produc-

tion in 1624 was an immediate success but resulted in a protest by Gondomar, which caused the temporary closing of the Globe theater.

Gamelyn (gam'ẹ.lin), **The Tale of.** A poem found in a number of manuscripts of *The Canterbury Tales*. It is supposed that Chaucer had it in hand to use as material for some poem of his own, possibly for "The Cook's Tale," and that it was reproduced as his by scribes who found it among his papers. A similar story was used by Lodge in *Rosalynde*, and by Shakespeare in *As You Like It*.

Game of Chess, A. The second section of T. S. Eliot's long poem *The Waste Land*, portraying two people completely submerged in the most luxurious surroundings, but unable to think of anything to do or say and resorting finally to idle activity and a game of chess:

> What shall I do now? What shall I do?
> I shall rush out as I am, and walk the street
> With my hair down, so. What shall we do
>   tomorrow?
> What shall we ever do?

Gamester, The. A play by James Shirley, licensed in 1633, and acted at Court in 1634. Garrick brought out an alteration of this play in 1757, called *The Gamesters*, in which he played Wilding, the chief role.

Gamester, The. A comedy by Susannah Centlivre, printed first in 1705. It was adapted from Regnard's *Le Joueur. Le Dissipateur*, by Destouches, was partly taken from Mrs. Centlivre's play.

Gamester, The. A tragedy by Edward Moore, produced in 1753. One scene is attributed to David Garrick.

Gammer Gurton's Needle (gam'ėr gėr'tọnz). A comedy composed by Master S, who is usually taken to be William Stevenson, an eminent scholar and educator. It was acted (c1553) at Christ's College, Cambridge, and printed in 1575. Owing to Warton's mistake in supposing that it was printed in 1551, it was for some time thought to be the first English comedy. *Ralph Roister Doister* preceded it. *Gammer Gurton's Needle* is a rustic play whose plot revolves about the loss of a needle, the confusion caused by the search for it, and the eventual recovery when Gammer Gurton's servant Hodge puts on the breeches she had been mending (his howls of pain immediately revealing that the needle has been left in them). The play includes the drinking song "Back and side go bare."

Gamp (gamp), **Mrs. Sairey.** In Charles Dickens's *Martin Chuzzlewit*, a fat old woman "with a husky voice and a moist eye," engaged in the profession of nursing. She is always quoting her mythical friend Mrs. Harris, and her affection for the bottle is proverbial. She is often called Dickens's greatest piece of characterization, in the tradition which includes Falstaff and the Wife of Bath. From a part of her varied belongings, a very stumpy umbrella is called a "gamp."

Gan (gan). See **Ganelon.**

Gandercleugh (gan'dėr.klūch). The residence of Jedediah Cleishbotham, whom Sir Walter Scott named as the editor of his *Tales of My Landlord.*

Ganelon (gan'ẹ.lọn; French, gȧn.lôṅ). [Also: **Gan, Gano.**] Paladin in the Charlemagne cycle of romances. By his treachery as an officer of Charlemagne he caused the death of Roland and the loss of the battle of Roncesvalles. He was torn in pieces by wild horses, and his name became a synonym of treason. Chaucer introduces him in his *Nun's Priest's Tale*, and Dante places him in the *Inferno*.

Ganesh (gạ.nesh'). [Also: **Ganapati** (gä.nä.pä'tē), **Ganesha** (gạ.nä'shạ).] An important god of the Hindu pantheon, the god of wisdom and remover of obstacles. He is propitiated at the beginning of any important undertaking, and is invoked at the beginning of orthodox Hindu books. Ganesh is variously said to be the son of Siva and Parvati or of Parvati only. He is represented as a short fat man having an elephant head with only one tusk. He has four hands which hold a shell, a discus, a club, and a water lily. He is the lord of the Ganas (troops of inferior deities who are servants of the gods), especially those attendant on Siva. He is depicted as accompanied by a rat, sometimes riding on one. The elephant head symbolizes his power in the jungle; the rat symbolizes his power to enter anywhere.

Ganlesse (gan'les), **Richard.** In Sir Walter Scott's *Peveril of the Peak*, the name that Edward Christian used when incognito.

Gann (gan), **Caroline.** See **Brandon, Mrs.**

Gano (gan'ō). See **Ganelon**

Ganore (gạ.nōr'). See **Guinevere.**

Ganymede (gan'i.mēd). In Greek mythology, the cupbearer of Zeus or of the Olympian gods; originally a beautiful Trojan youth, transferred to Olympus (according to Homer, by the gods; according to others, by the eagle of Zeus, or by Zeus himself in the form of an eagle) and made immortal. He supplanted Hebe in her function as cupbearer. Later he was regarded as the genius of water, especially of the Nile, and is represented by the constellation Aquarius in the zodiac.

Ganymede. In Shakespeare's *As You Like It*, the name assumed by Rosalind when disguised as a boy.

Gaol Gate, The. A tragedy (1906) by Augusta Gregory (Lady Gregory) about an Irish peasant family and the struggle against the English.

Gap in the Curtain, The. A novel by John Buchan, published in 1932.

Garamantes (gar.ạ.man'tēz). In ancient history, a nomadic people dwelling in the Sahara, east of the Gaetuli.

Garamond (gar'ạ.mọnd; French, gȧ.rȧ.môṅ), **Claude.** b. at Paris; d. 1561. A French engraver and type designer. He was commissioned by King Francis I to design and cut the Greek characters for the great Estienne editions of the Greek classical authors. These types, and others made by him, were used also by Colines, Christophe Plantin, and the Italian Giambattista Bodoni. He was responsible for bringing roman type into general use, to replace Gothic (or black-letter) type. His name is still used to describe several popular type faces.

Garbett (gär'bẹt), **Cyril Forster.** b. at Tongham, Surrey, England, Feb. 6, 1875; d. at York, England, Dec. 31, 1955. An English clergyman, archbishop of York (1942–55). He was educated at Oxford.

Following his ordination, he became vicar of Portsea, and was later bishop of Southwark (1919–32) and bishop of Winchester (1932–42). He was author of *A Call to Christians* (1935), *The Church and Social Problems* (1939), *Physician, Heal Thyself* (1945), *The Claims of the Church of England* (1947), and others.

Garcias (gär.thē'äs), **Pedro.** A licentiate, referred to in the preface to Alain René Le Sage's *Gil Blas*, whose soul was buried in a leathern purse which held his ducats.

Garcilaso de la Vega (gär.sē.lä'sō dä lä Bā'gä). [Called "el Inca," meaning "the Inca."] b. at Cusco, Peru, c1539; d. at Córdoba, Spain, 1616. A Peruvian soldier, historian, and translator. He was the son of Sebastián Garcilaso de la Vega y Vargas, who served under Córtes and Pizarro, and an Inca princess (whence his epithet "el Inca"). He went (c1560) to Spain, was given a pension by Philip II, and was a captain in the Spanish army fighting the Moors. He later settled at Córdoba and devoted himself to literature. His works are *La Florida del Inca: historia del adelantado Hernando de Soto* (1605) and his history of Peru, *Commentarios reales que tratan del origen de los Incas* (part 1, 1609; part 2, 1617, both parts being translated into English, 1688 and 1869–71, and into French, German and Italian). In 1590 he translated the *Dialoghi di amore* of Leon Hebro. His account of De Soto's conquest of Florida was for a long time regarded as more fiction than fact, but it was used to advantage by historians such as Robertson and Prescott, by Marmontel for his historical novel *Les Incas*, and by Sheridan for his *Pizarro*. He has been called "the first South American in Spanish Literature." His birth date is variously given as about 1530, 1536, 1539, and 1540 the same uncertainty existing about his death, which is placed as early as 1568, and as late as 1620, with 1616 being given some preference.

Garde Joyeuse (gȧrd zhwȧ.yèz), **La.** See **Joyeuse Garde, La.**

Garden, The. A novel by L. A. G. Strong, published in 1931.

Garden, Thoughts in a. See **Thoughts in a Garden.**

Garden of Allah (al'ạ), **The.** A novel (1905) by Robert Hichens. A popular play was adapted from the novel.

Garden of Cyrus (sī'rus), **The.** [Full title, **The Garden of Cyrus: or the Quincuncial Lozenge.**] A fanciful treatise (1658) by Sir Thomas Browne.

Garden Party, The. The title story of a collection of short stories by Katherine Mansfield, published in 1922.

Gardiner (gärd'nẹr, gär'dẹn.ẹr). In Shakespeare's *Henry VIII*, the historical Stephen Gardiner. He is secretary to the King, and later Bishop of Winchester and leader of the attack on Cranmer as a heretic.

Gardiner, Alfred George. [Pseudonym, **Alpha of the Plough.**] b. at Chelmsford, Essex, England, 1865; d. 1946. An English journalist, essayist, and biographer. On the staff of the *Essex County Chronicle* and the *Northern Daily Telegraph* for 15 years, he later edited (1902–19) the London

ḍ, d or j; ṣ, s or sh; ṭ, t or ch; z̧, z or zh; o, F. cloche; ü, F. menu; ċh, Sc. loch; ṅ, F. bonbon.

Daily News, and was president (1915–16) of the Institute of Journalists; he contributed essays to the London *Star* under the pseudonym Alpha of the Plough. He was the author of *Prophets, Priests, and Kings* (1908), *Pillars of Society* (1913), *The War Lords* (1915), *Pebbles on the Shore* (1917), *Leaves in the Wind* (1918), and *Windfalls* (1920), the last three being volumes of essays and character sketches.

Gardiner, James. b. at Carriden, near Linlithgow, Scotland, Jan. 11, 1688; killed at the battle of Prestonpans, Sept. 21, 1745. A Scottish colonel of dragoons, now remembered chiefly for his services (1719 *et seq.*) to the English against their enemies on the Continent and in his native Scotland.

Gardiner, Samuel Rawson. b. at Ropley, Hampshire, England, March 4, 1829; d. at Sevenoaks, Kent, England, Feb. 23, 1902. An English historian, teacher, and editor. Educated at Winchester School and at Christ Church, Oxford; lecturer (1872–77) and professor of modern history (1877–85) at King's College, London; taught (1863–81) at Bedford College for Women, and at Toynbee Hall, both in London; in 1894 was offered, but declined, history professorship at Oxford. He edited *Constitutional Documents of the Puritan Revolution* (1899), a dozen volumes for the Camden Society, of which he was director (1869–97), and was editor (1891–1901) of the *English Historical Review.* Author of *History of England from the Accession of James I to the Outbreak of the Civil War: 1603–42* (10 vols., 1863–84), *Prince Charles and the Spanish Marriage* (1869), *History of the Great Civil War: 1642–49* (4 vols., 1886), *Student's History of England* (2 vols., 1890–91), *History of the Commonwealth and Protectorate: 1649–60* (3 vols., 1894–1903), *What the Gunpowder Plot Was* (1897), *Oliver Cromwell* (1901), and other works.

Gareth (gar'ĕth). In Arthurian romance, the nephew of King Arthur. He was introduced to Arthur's court as a scullion, and concealed his name for a year at his mother's request. He was nicknamed "Beaumains" by Sir Kay on account of the size of his hands. He is engaged by Linet to rescue her sister Lionês from Castle Perilous, and marries Lionês. Tennyson used his story, with some alterations, in *Gareth and Lynette.* See also **Persant of India,** and **Pertolepe.**

Gareth and Lynette (li.net'). One of Tennyson's *Idylls of the King.*

Gargamelle (gàr.gà.mel). The mother of Gargantua, in François Rabelais's romance *Gargantua.*

Gargantua and Pantagruel (gär.gan'tū.ạ; French, gàr.gäṅ.tü.à; pan.tag'rŏ.el; French, päṅ.tà.grü.el), **The Life of.** A satirical work in prose and verse by François Rabelais. Rabelais edited and perhaps in part rewrote a prose romance, *Les Grandes et Inestimables Chronicques du Grant et Énorme Géant Gargantua.* This work, the author of which is unknown, and no earlier copies of which exist, probably gave him the idea of his own famous book. The next year (1532) followed the first instalment of this, *Pantagruel Roi des Dipsodes Restitué en Son naturel avec ses Faicts et Prouesses Espouvantables.* Three years afterwards came *Gargantua* proper, the first book of the entire work as we now have it.

Eleven years, however, passed before the work was continued, the second book of *Pantagruel* not being published until 1546, and the third six years later, in 1552, just before the author's death. The fourth or last book did not appear as a whole until 1564, although the first 16 chapters had been given to the world two years before. This fourth book, the fifth of the entire work, has, from the length of time which elapsed before its publication and from certain variations which exist in the manuscript and the first printed editions, been suspected of spuriousness. Gargantua is a giant with an enormous appetite, and his name has become proverbial for an insatiable eater. The misspelling *Garagantua,* originated by Pope in his edition of Shakespeare's plays (*As You Like It,* iii. 2), has been followed by some other editors. There was a chapbook, popular in England in the 16th century, giving the history of the giant Gargantua, who accidentally swallows five pilgrims, staves and all, in his salad.

Gargery (gar'jẽr.i), **Joe.** In Charles Dickens's *Great Expectations,* a good-natured blacksmith with a shrewish wife; Pip's brother-in-law.

Gargrave (gär'grāv), **Sir Thomas.** In Shakespeare's *1 Henry VI,* an English officer.

Garibaldi (gar.i.bôl'di; Italian, gä.rē.bäl'dē), **Giuseppe.** b. at Nice, France, July 4, 1807; d. on the island of Caprera, near Sardinia, June 2, 1882. An Italian patriot and soldier. Exiled from Italy for political reasons in 1834, he went to South America, where he was employed in the service of the republic of Rio Grande do Sul and afterward in that of Uruguay (1836–48). In 1849 he entered the service of the Roman Republic, which was abolished in the same year. In 1850 he went as an exile to the U. S., where he was naturalized as a citizen, and where for a time he followed the occupation of a candlemaker on Staten Island. He returned to Italy in 1854 and settled as a farmer on the island of Caprera. He commanded an independent corps, known as the "Hunters of the Alps," in the Sardinian service during the war of Sardinia and France against Austria in 1859. Secretly encouraged by the Sardinian government, he organized, after the conclusion of peace, an expedition against the Two Sicilies for the purpose of bringing about the union of Italy. He descended upon Sicily with 1,000 volunteers in May, 1860, and after having made himself dictator of Sicily crossed to the mainland, where he expelled Francis II from Naples and entered the capital on Sept. 7, 1860. He retired to Caprera on the union of the Two Sicilies with Sardinia and the proclamation (March 17, 1861) of Victor Emmanuel of Sardinia as king of Italy. Striving for the complete unification of Italy, he organized an expedition against Rome in 1862, but was defeated and captured by the Sardinians at Aspromonte in August. He was again in arms against the Pope in 1867, and was defeated by the French and papal forces at Mentana in November. In 1870–71 he commanded a French force in the Franco-Prussian War.

Garland (gär'land), **Mr.** and **Mrs.** Characters in Charles Dickens's novel *The Old Curiosity Shop,* who are a placid couple with whom Kit Nubbles lives after he leaves Little Nell.

Garm (gärm). [Old Norse, **Garmr.**] In Old Norse mythology, the monstrous watchdog of Hel. Only those who had given bread to the poor could get past him. At Ragnarök he and the god Tyr slew each other.

"garmombles" (gär'mom.blz). See under **Merry Wives of Windsor, The.**

Garnett (gär'net), **Constance.** [Maiden name, **Black.**] b. 1862; d. at Edenbridge, England, Dec. 17, 1946. An English translator of Russian literature; wife of Edward Garnett and mother of David Garnett. Her translations of Chekhov, Gogol, Dostoievsky, Turgenev, and Tolstoy were influential in spreading a knowledge of Russian literature throughout England and America.

Garnett, David. b. 1892—. An English writer; son of Edward and Constance Garnett. His works include *Lady into Fox* (1923), which won the Hawthornden and James Tait Black memorial prizes, *The Old Dovecote* (1928), *No Love* (1929), *The Grass-hoppers Come* (1931), *A Rabbit in the Air* (1932), *Pocahontas* (1933), *Beany-Eye* (1935), and *War in the Air* (1941); edited *The Letters of T. E. Lawrence* (1938). His most recent work is *The Golden Echo* (1954), the first volume of his autobiography.

Garnett, Edward. [Full name, **Edward William Garnett.**] b. at London, 1868; d. there, Feb. 21, 1937. An English essayist, dramatist, critic, biographer, editor, and student of Russian literature; son of Richard Garnett and father of David Garnett. Author of *The Breaking Point* (1907), *The Feud* (1909), and *The Trial of Jeanne d'Arc* (1931), plays; *Hogarth* (1910), *Tolstoy* (1914), and *Turgenev* (1917), biographical and critical studies; *An Imaged World* (1894) and *Friday Nights: Literary Criticisms and Appreciations* (1922), essays; also wrote *Papa's War and Other Satires* (1919). He edited Doughty's *Arabia Deserta* (1888) as *Wanderings in Arabia* (1908). As a publisher's reader for various London houses he was instrumental in introducing Conrad, Doughty, Galsworthy, and D. H. Lawrence to the reading public.

Garnett, Richard. b. at Litchfield, Staffordshire, England, Feb. 27, 1835; d. at Hampstead, London, April 13, 1906. An English librarian, literary historian, poet, critic, and biographer; father of Edward Garnett. He was with the British Museum as clerk (1851–75), assistant keeper of printed books (1875–90), and chief keeper (1890–99). He edited *Relics of Shelley* (1862) and contributed to the *Encyclopædia Britannica* and the *Dictionary of National Biography*. Author of *Primula* (1858), *Io in Egypt* (1859), *Iphigenia in Delphi* (1891), *The Queen and other Poems* and *W. Shakespeare: Pedagog and Poacher* (both 1904), poetry; *The Twilight of the Gods* (1888), prose fables; *Milton, Carlyle* (1887), *Emerson* (1888), *Edward Gibbon Wakefield* (1898), and other biographies; *Poems from the German* (1862), *Idylls and Epigrams* (1869), *Sonnets from Dante, Petrarch, and Camoens* (1896), translations; *Shelley and Lord Beaconsfield* (1887), *Age of Dryden* and *William Blake* (both 1895), *History of Italian Literature* (1897), *Essays in Librarianship and Bibliography* (1898), and *Essays of an Ex-Librarian* (1901).

Garnier (gär.nyä), **Robert.** b. at La Ferté-Bernard, France, 1534; d. at Le Mans, France, Aug. 15, 1590. A French dramatist, considered the most important French writer of tragedy before Corneille. He was a member of the Paris bar, became lieutenant criminel at Le Mans, and was finally appointed councilor of state. He was a disciple of Ronsard and a member of the group of poets known as the Pléiade. His works, which were composed between the years 1568 and 1580, consist of eight plays: *Porcié, Cornélie, Marc Antoine, Hippolyte, La Troade, Antigone, Les Juives,* and *Bradamante.*

Garratt (gar'at). A village situated between Tooting and Wandsworth, Surrey, England. The practice of electing a mayor (really a chairman appointed to defend the rights of the commons) at every general election, adopted (c1780) by the inhabitants, gave rise to a series of satirical *Addresses by the Mayors of Garratt.* Foote wrote a play on the subject, *The Mayor of Garratt.*

Garraway's Coffee House (gar'a.wāz). A London coffee house which stood for two centuries in Exchange Alley, Cornhill. Tea was first sold here; the promoters of the South Sea Bubble met here; and sales of drugs, mahogany, and timber were held here periodically.

Garrick (gar'ik), **David.** b. at Hereford, England, Feb. 19, 1717; d. at London, Jan. 20, 1779. An English actor, manager, and author. Educated at Lichfield Grammar School under Samuel Johnson, he accompanied Johnson to London in 1737. He entered for law at Lincoln's Inn, but soon undertook partnership in the wine trade with his brother; however, the stage overcame his interest in retailing wine. After playing minor parts in amateur performances and with Giffard's company at Ipswich, he made stage history on Oct. 19, 1741 at Goodman's Fields Theatre (after both the Drury Lane and Covent Garden had rejected him) as Richard III, wherein he introduced a new style of natural, vivacious acting opposed to the prevailing statuesque, declamatory style. Twice (1742, 1745) he appeared for profitable sessions in Dublin. In 1747 he became joint manager of the Drury Lane Theatre with Lacy. Upon the death of Lacy he became sole manager of Drury Lane, leaving his share to Sheridan, Linley, and Ford upon his death. Ruling that partnership for the next 29 years he made the Drury Lane renowned as a theater. His temper got him the malicious enmity of Samuel Foote, and also involved him in a disagreement with Johnson, over the latter's unsuccessful *Irene* (1749), and the elder Colman when he refused to play Lord Ogleby in their joint play, *The Clandestine Marriage,* causing Colman to go to Covent Garden, where he became manager in opposition to Garrick (at the Drury Lane). In his 35 years on stage he acted 98 different roles, including 18 from Shakespeare in which he considerably influenced a change in Shakespearian criticism. His versatility extended from the aged Lear to youthful Romeo; from sophisticate Archer in Farquhar's *The Beaux' Stratagem* to simpleton Abel Drugger in Jonson's *Alchemist;* from rake Lothario in Rowe's *Fair Penitent* to sentimentalist Aboan in Southerne's *Oroonoko.* His mad Lear was particularly noted: "He presented a sight of woe

---

ḍ, d or j; ṣ, s or sh; ṭ, t or ch; ẓ, z or zh; o, F. cloche; ü, F. menu; ċh, Sc. loch; ṅ, F. bonbon.

and misery, and a total alienation of mind from every idea, but that of his unkind daughters." He brought out 27 Shakespearian plays, adapting some, but restoring quantities of the original text to the stage. He both helped and hindered Shakespearian production in the original versions: *Lear* was given without the Fool, and *Romeo and Juliet* had a tomb scene in which the lovers were together before dying. On the positive side he restored the texts from 17th-century corruptions (such as that of *Lear* which has Cordelia happily married to Edgar). In 1769 he held at Stratford the Shakespeare Jubilee, which some critics considered to contain more of the work of Garrick than of Shakespeare. He wrote or adapted, individually or in collaboration, 29 other comedies, tragedies, farces, interludes, musicals, and pantomimes. *The Clandestine Marriage*, with the elder Colman, is outstanding. He wrote over 450 items of verse (prologues, epilogues, occasional pieces, songs, and satires). Some 1,300 letters record his association with prominent contemporaries. On his death his large dramatic library went to the British Museum for the use of scholars. Twice (1751, 1763) he journeyed abroad and was feted by literary circles in France and Italy. He retired (June 10, 1776) from the stage at the height of his powers, his last role being Don Feliz in Susannah Centlivre's *The Wonder*, having helped found a theatrical fund for decayed actors. Intimate acquaintance with nobility and politicians enabled him to help deserving friends to government positions, and in one instance to save a fellow actor's son from hanging. He died with a fortune of 100,000 pounds and was the last actor to be buried in Westminster Abbey. Burke proposed as an epitaph: "He raised the character of his profession to a liberal art," and Johnson said his "death eclipsed the gaiety of nations." Garrick married (1749) a Viennese dancer, Eva Maria Veigel (Mlle. Violette); his earlier infatuation with Peg Woffington is notorious. Among Garrick's supporting players were Mrs. Cibber and Kitty Clive.

Garrick Club. A London club instituted in 1831 for the patronage of the drama, and as a rendezvous for men of letters. After 1864 it occupied a house in Garrick Street.

Garrod (gar'ọd), **Heathcote William.** b. at Wells, Somersetshire, England, Jan. 21, 1878—. An English poetry scholar and essayist. Professor of poetry at Oxford (1923–28) and Harvard (1929). Author of *Religion of all Good Men* (1905), *A Book of Latin Verse* (1915), *The Profession of Poetry* (1923), *Poetry and Life* (1930), and *Epigrams* (1946).

Garter, Order of the. [Full name, **Most Noble Order of the Garter.**] A British order of knighthood. It was founded (c1344) by Edward III. A popular legend of its origin is that it is connected with the Countess of Salisbury whose garter slipped from her leg while she was dancing with the king, who restored it to her with the famous remark, *Honi Soit Qui Mal Y Pense* (variously translated as "Evil be to him who thinks evil," "May he be shamed who thinks ill of it," or "Dishonored be he who evil thinks"). The remark became the motto of the order, and is inscribed in gold on the dark-blue garter. It is worn on the left leg, below

the knee. Original membership was limited to 26, the king himself, the prince of Wales, and 24 knights companions, but both George III and William IV expanded the list by not limiting membership to British princes and by admitting princes and nobles of foreign countries. The officials of the order are the prelate (who is the bishop of Winchester), the chancellor (originally the bishop of Salisbury, but now of Oxford), the registrar (the dean of Windsor), the garter king of arms, the gentleman usher of the black rod,.and the secretary. The habits and insignia of the order consist of the garter (originally light blue silk), the mantle, the surcoat, the hood, the star, the gold collar of 26 Tudor roses, alternately red and white, the George, representing Saint George and the dragon, which is suspended from the collar, and the lesser George, with the same device, which is passed over the left shoulder and under the right arm. The Order is dedicated to Saint George, and the original regulations provided for a special service to be held on his day, April 23, at Saint George's Chapel in Windsor. The insignia of the order belong to the knight during his life, but when he dies they are returned to the king (or queen). When the ruler is a queen, she wears the garter on her left arm below the elbow. Members sign K.G. after their name.

Garth (gärth), **Caleb.** A character in George Eliot's novel *Middlemarch.*

Garth, Sir **Samuel.** b. in Bowland Forest, Yorkshire, England, 1661; d. at London, Jan. 18, 1719. An English physician and poet. He studied at Cambridge (Peterhouse) and Leiden, and established himself at London in the practice of medicine. Among his works is *The Dispensary* (1699), a poem which ridicules apothecaries, and records the first attempt to establish dispensaries for outdoor patients. It passed through many editions.

Garvice (gär'vis), **Charles.** b. 1833; d. at Richmond, Surrey, England, March 1, 1920. An English poet, novelist, and dramatist. His works include *Eve*, a volume of poetry, *Maurice Durant* (3 vols., 1875), *Just a Girl* (1899), *Nance* (1900), *Her Heart's Desire* (1900), *The Outcast of the Family* (1901), *In Cupid's Chains* (1903), *Love Decides* (1904), *Love the Tyrant* (1905), *Diana and Destiny* (1906), *Gold in the Gutter* (1907), *Kyra's Fate* (1908), *Barriers Between* and *The Heart of a Maid* (both 1910), *Lady of Darcourt* (1911), *Adrian Leroy* and *Two Maids and a Man* (both 1912), and *The One Girl in the World* (1916). The author of more than 100 novels and plays, he was exceedingly popular in the U. S. before he achieved literary success in his own country.

Garvin (gär'vin), **J. L.** [Full name, **James Louis Garvin.**] b. 1868; d. 1947. An English journalist, editor, and lecturer. He received degrees from Edinburgh and Durham universities, and in 1941 was made a Companion of Honor. He was on the staff of the Hull *Eastern Morning News*, correspondent (1890) for *United Ireland*, editorial writer (1891–99) for the *Newcastle Chronicle* and a staff-member (1899–1905) of the *Daily Telegraph;* editor of *The Outlook* (1905–06), *Observer* (1908–42), and *Pall Mall Gazette* (1912–15); president (1917–18) of the Institute of Journalists. He contributed to the *Encyclopædia Britannica, Fortnightly Review,*

fat, fāte, fär, ȧsk, fãre; net, mē, hėr; pin, pīne; not, nōte, mõve, nôr; up, lūte, pull; ᴛʜ, then;

National Review, Quarterly Review, and wrote *Economic Foundations of Peace* and *Life of Joseph Chamberlain* (3 vols., 1932–34).

Gascoigne (gas'koin), **George.** b. probably in Bedfordshire, England, c1535; d. at Stamford, England, Oct. 7, 1577. An English poet. He was educated at Trinity College, Cambridge, studied law at Gray's Inn, and was member of Parliament (1557–59) for Bedford. His *Posies of G. Gascoigne* (1575) included *Jocasta,* a tragedy in blank verse which is supposedly the second of its kind in English, and *Certayne Notes of Instruction concerning the making of verse or ryme in English,* held by some to be the first English critical essay. Other works by him include *The Steele Glas* (1576) and *The Droomme of Doomesday* (1576).

Gascoigne, Sir **William.** b. c1350; d. 1419. An English judge. He was made chief justice of the King's Bench by Henry IV c1400. According to a tradition, followed by Shakespeare in *2 Henry IV,* he committed Prince Henry to prison when the latter struck him for venturing to punish one of the prince's riotous companions. The incident is described by the Lord Chief Justice in the play.

Gashford (gash'ford). In Dickens's *Barnaby Rudge,* the villainous secretary to Lord George Gordon. He plays a leading part in the plotting against Catholics which culminates in the terrifying Gordon Riots.

Gaskell (gas'kel, -kel), **Elizabeth Cleghorn.** [Maiden name, **Stevenson.**] b. at Chelsea, London, Sept. 29, 1810; d. at Alton, Hampshire, England, Nov. 12, 1865. An English novelist. She moved (1832) to Manchester, where she obtained material for those of her novels which describe the life of the industrial population. Her best novels include *Mary Barton* (1848), *Ruth* and *Cranford* (1853), *North and South* (1855), *Cousin Phillis* (1865), and *Wives and Daughters* (1866). She also published *Life of Charlotte Brontë* (1857).

Gaspar (gas'par). [Also: **Caspar, Kaspar.**] The legendary name of one of the three Magi, or Wise Men of the East, who came from the East to Bethlehem to worship the infant Jesus.

Gasquet (gas.kā'), **Francis Aiden.** b. at London, Oct. 5, 1846; d. at Rome, April 5, 1929. An English Roman Catholic prelate, a leading authority on the ecclesiastical history of England during the later Middle Ages and the Tudor period. He was created a cardinal in 1914. His works include *Henry VIII and the English Monasteries* (1888–89), *Eve of the Reformation* (1900), *English Monastic Life* (1903), *Henry III and the Church* (1905), *Parish Life in Medieval England* (1906), and *Monastic Life in the Middle Ages* (1922).

Gassendi (gà.san.dē) or **Gassend** (gà.sän), **Pierre.** b. at Champtercier, Basses-Alpes, France, Jan. 22, 1592; d. at Paris, Oct. 24, 1655. A French philosopher, physicist, and astronomer. He studied theology, and became professor of theology at Digne in 1613, and of philosophy at Aix in 1616. In 1645 he became professor of mathematics at the Collège Royal at Paris. He sought to link the philosophy of Epicurus with Christian theology and modern science. Among his works are *Disquisitiones anticartesianae* (1643), *De vita, moribus,*

et placitis Epicuri (1647), and *Syntagma philosophicum.*

Gatty (gat'i), **Juliana Horatia.** Maiden name of **Ewing, Juliana Horatia.**

Gatty, Margaret Scott. b. at Burnham, Essex, England, June 3, 1809; d. at Ecclesfield, Yorkshire, England, Oct. 4, 1873. An English writer. Her best-known works are stories for children, such as *Aunt Judy's Tales* (1859). She edited (1866–73) *Aunt Judy's Magazine.*

Gatty, Nicholas Comyn. b. at Bradfield, England, Sept. 13, 1874—. An English composer. He was graduated (1896) from Downing College, Cambridge, and studied at the Royal College of Music. He served as music critic (1907–14) for the *Pall Mall Gazette* and as assistant editor of Grove's *Dictionary of Music and Musicians.* His compositions include the operas *Greysteel* (1906), *Prince Ferelon* (1919), and *The Tempest* (1920); he also wrote choral and orchestral works and piano pieces.

Gauden (gô'den), **John.** b. at Mayland, Essex, England, 1605; d. Sept. 20, 1662. An English prelate, appointed bishop of Exeter in 1660, and translated to the see of Worcester in May, 1662. He studied at Cambridge, became vicar of Chippenham in 1640, was chaplain to the Earl of Warwick, was appointed dean of Bocking, Essex, in 1641, and was chosen a member of the Assembly of Divines in 1643, but was not allowed to take his seat. He wrote *Cromwell's Bloody Slaughter House . . .* (1660), *Tears of the Church* (1659), *Ecclesiae Anglicanae Suspiria, or the Tears, Sighs, Complaints, and Prayers of the Church of England,* and others.

Gauguin (gō.gan), **Paul.** [Full name, **Eugène Henri Paul Gauguin.**] b. at Paris, June 7, 1848; d. in the Marquesas islands, May 6, 1903. A French post-impressionist landscape and figure painter and sculptor, who exerted a profound influence on 20th-century art. He spent his early years in Peru, but returned to France to be educated in a Jesuit school at Orléans. At 17 he left school to join the merchant marine and the navy, and in 1871 he became a bank clerk. He married in 1873, after he had started a successful banking career; soon after his marriage he started to draw, and in 1875 exhibited his first painting. Shortly afterwards he bought a large collection of impressionist paintings. He exhibited his works with the impressionists, and in 1883 gave up banking for painting. Two years later he deserted his family, and the following year met Vincent Van Gogh. He had spent time in Normandy, Denmark, and Martinique, and in 1891 went to Tahiti to paint. He returned to Paris in 1893, and two years later went back to the South Pacific, where he died embittered and alone. His brilliant use of color, and distortion for the sake of design, were revolutionary achievements. Among his best-known works are *Landscape in Brittany, The Three Dogs, Riders by the Sea, Ta Matete, An Interior in Tahiti, Arii Matamoe, Portrait of a Breton Woman, Self-Portrait, Tehamana's Farewell, Bust of Clovis Gauguin, The Seine in Paris, Winter, Tahitian Landscape, Hina Tefatu,* and many others.

Gaunt (gônt), **John of.** See **John of Gaunt.**

Gautama (gô'ta.ma) or **Gautama Buddha** (bud'a, bö'da). See **Buddha.**

---

d̦, d or j; ṣ, s or sh; ṭ, t or ch; ẓ, z or zh; o, F. cloche; ü, F. menu; c̵h, Sc. loch; ṅ, F. bonbon.

Gautier (gō.tyā), **Marguerite.** The principal character in *La Dame aux camélias*, by Alexandre Dumas fils.

Gautier, Théophile. b. at Tarbes, France, Aug. 31, 1811; d. at Neuilly, France, Oct. 23, 1872. A French poet, critic, and novelist. He graduated from the Lycée Charlemagne at Paris, studied painting for a time, and then entered into the Romantic Movement in French literature. His first book, *Poésies* (1830), was followed by *Albertus* (1833), *Jeune France* (1833), and *Mademoiselle de Maupin* (1835). From 1837 to 1845 he was art and dramatic critic for *La Presse*. A series of 12 papers, *Exhumations littéraires*, appeared in *La France Littéraire* (1834–35) and in the *Revue des Deux Mondes* (1844). This work and the *Rapport sur les progrès de la poésie française depuis 1830*, published in *L'Histoire du romantisme* (1854), show Gautier at his best as a critic. His papers on Lamartine and Charles Baudelaire were considered masterpieces of literary criticism. In 1845 he joined the editorial staff of the *Moniteur Universel* (later the *Journal Officiel*) and was identified with that paper until his death. As a result of his travels in Spain (1840), Belgium, Holland, Algeria (1845), Italy 1850), Constantinople and Athens (1852), and Russia (1858), he wrote his *Voyage en Espagne* (1843), *Zigzags* (1845), *Italia* (1852), *Constantinople* (1854), *L'Orient, Trésors d'art de la Russie ancienne et moderne* (1860–63), *Loin de Paris* (1864), *Quand on voyage* (1865), and *Voyage en Russie* (1866). During his travels he found materials for such novels as *Militona* (1847), *Arria Marcella* (1852), and *Le Roman de la momie* (1856). He wrote *Fortunio* for the *Figaro* (1837), and *Le Capitaine Fracasse* for *La Revue Nationale* (December, 1861–June, 1863). Other stories of his are *La Toison d'or*, *Omphale*, *Le Petit Chien de la marquise*, *Le Nid de rossignols* (1833), *La Morte amoureuse* (1836), *La Chaine d'or*, *Une Nuit de Cléopâtre* (1845), *Jean et Jeannette* (1846), *Les Roués innocents*, *Le Roi Candaule* (1847), *La Belle Jenny*, *La Peau de tigre* (1864–65), *Spirite* (1866), *Ménagerie intime* (1869), *Partie carée*, *Mademoiselle Dafné*, *Tableaux de siège*, and others. For the stage Gautier wrote *Le Tricorne enchanté*, *Pierrot posthume* (1845), *La Juive de Constantine* (1846), *Regardez mais n'y touchez pas* (1847), *L'Amour souffle où il veut*, and others. His works of pure fantasy are *Une Larme du diable* (1839), and themes for ballets including those for *Giselle* (1841), *Lapéri* (1843), *Gemma* (1854), and *Sakountala* (1858). Gautier's poems from 1833 to 1838 were gathered under the title *La Comédie de la mort*. His later poetry appeared as *Émaux et camées* (1852). Besides collaborating on *L'Histoire des peintres* (1847), Gautier wrote independently *Le Salon de peinture de 1847*, *L'Art moderne* (1852), *Les Beaux-arts en Europe* (1852), and *Histoire de l'art théâtral en France depuis vingt-cinq ans* (1860). Scattered sketches by Gautier appeared after the author's death, under the collective titles *Fusains et eauxfortes*, *Tableaux à la plume*, and *Portraits contemporains*.

Gaveston (gav'ẹs.tọn), **Piers.** [Title, Earl of **Cornwall**.] Executed June 19, 1312. A favorite of Edward II of England. He was the son of a Gascon knight in the service of Edward I, and was brought up in the royal household as the foster brother and playmate of Prince Edward, over whom he acquired a complete ascendancy. He incurred the enmity of the barons by his insolent and supercilious bearing, and, under their pressure, was banished by Edward I in 1307, but was recalled on the accession of Edward II in the same year. He was created Earl of Cornwall in 1307, and in 1308 acted as regent of the kingdom during the king's absence in France. His conduct, however, so irritated the barons that, in spite of the protection of Edward, he was again forced into exile in 1308–09 and 1311–12. His recall in 1312 provoked a rising of the barons, in the course of which he was captured and executed.

Gaveston, Piers. In Christopher Marlowe's tragedy *Edward II*, a favorite of the King. He is a scholarly man, but the power Edward gives him goes to his head and his dissolute and irresponsible behavior finally brings Edward and the kingdom to ruin.

Gavin Dishart (dish'ạrt). See **Dishart, Gavin.**

Gavroche (gȧ.vrosh′). In Victor Hugo's *Les Misérables*, a street Arab. He has become a type.

Gawain or **Gawayne** (gä′win, -wän), **Sir.** One of the principal knights of the Round Table, in the Arthurian cycle of legend and romance; nephew of King Arthur; brother of Gaheris and Gareth. He appears first in Geoffrey of Monmouth's *Historia Regum Britanniae* as Walwain or Walwanius, and then in nearly every one of the romances. He is known as "the courteous," also as "the perfect knight." Chrétien de Troyes gives him the first place among the knights. There was another of this name who served under Amadis of Gaul and achieved great deeds.

Gawain and the Green Knight, Sir. The title of a 14th-century (Middle English) Arthurian romance, a long alliterative narrative poem ascribed to the author of *The Pearl* (possibly Huchoun or Ralph Strode, or an unknown, although some scholars doubt the connection). It is the best-known of the stories about Gawain, presenting the famous beheading bargain between Gawain and the mysterious Green Knight. A Green Knight arrived at Arthur's court and challenged the knights: who would behead him tonight on condition that he give the beheader a like blow one year from tonight? Only Gawain took the challenge and beheaded the Green Knight. The Green Knight then picked up his head, told Gawain to meet him at his castle in a year, and departed. Gawain in due time arrived at the Green Knight's castle, was warmly entertained, but did not realize that his host was the Green Knight himself. The lady of the castle tried to seduce him, but Gawain was loyal to his host, except for one kiss from the lady (which he delivered to his host) and a magic protecting girdle which he accepted from her (but concealed from her lord). When the beheading time came, Gawain did not flinch. The Green Knight, however, gave Gawain only a slight wound, and this only because he had concealed the girdle. The entire affair was merely a plot to test the honor and courage of Arthur's knights.

Gay (gā), **John.** b. at Barnstaple, England (baptized Sept. 16, 1685); d. at London, Dec. 4, 1732. An English poet. He was educated at the Barnstaple Grammar School, in Devon, and apprenticed

---

at 17 to a silk mercer. He abandoned his trade in 1706, and began writing. He served as secretary to the Duchess of Monmouth, and also held various minor official posts. Among his chief works are *The Fan* and *The Shepherd's Week*, a series of eclogues depicting rustic life "with the gilt off" (1714), *The What-d'ye-call-it*, a farce (1715), *Trivia, or the art of Walking the Streets of London* (1716), *Poems* (1720; including "Black-ey'd Susan"), *The Captives*, a tragedy (1724), *Fables* (1727), *Acis and Galatea* (1731), *Achilles* (1733), and *The Beggar's Opera* (1728). This last "Newgate pastoral" made his reputation. However, Sir Robert Walpole was clearly satirized in it and the representation of *Polly*, a sequel, was forbidden by the lord chamberlain. The sale of the book (printed 1729) was great. With Pope and Arbuthnot he wrote *Three Hours after Marriage* (1717). *The Shepherd's Week* is partly aimed at Ambrose Philips, whose *Pastorals* seemed to Gay to have various glaring faults. His *Fables* (of which more were published in 1738) are filled with sophisticated wisdom, tinged with a sardonic humor. He probably contributed to *The Memoirs of Martinus Scriblerus* (published by Pope in 1741), a satire upon pedantry and contemporary poetry.

Gay, Joseph. Pseudonym of **Breval, John Durant.**

Gay, Walter. A character in Charles Dickens's *Dombey and Son*, who is the young nephew of Sol Gills and in the employ of Mr. Dombey.

Gay-Dombeys (gā'dom'biz), **The.** A novel by Sir Harry Hamilton Johnston, published in 1919. It continues the story of Dickens's *Dombey and Son* (1846).

Gayless (gā'les), **Charles.** The impecunious master of the "lying valet," in David Garrick's play of that name.

Gay Lord Quex (kweks), **The.** A comedy of manners (1899) by Arthur Wing Pinero.

Gaymar (gā'mär), **Geoffrey.** An English chronicler who translated Geoffrey of Monmouth's history into Anglo-Norman verse c1146. He continued it by adding a metrical *History of Anglo-Saxon Kings*.

Gazette (ga.zet'), **Sir Gregory.** In Samuel Foote's comedy *The Knights*, a gullible provincial politician. He has an inordinate appetite for news, but is incapable of making sense out of the most ordinary paragraph of a newspaper.

Ge (jē). See **Gaea.**

Geatland (gēt'land). See under **Beowulf.**

Geber (jē'bėr, gä'bėr). [Also: **Jabir;** probable original name, **Abu Musa Jabir ben Haijan.**] d. c776. An Arab alchemist. He occupies a position in the history of chemistry analogous to that held by Hippocrates in that of medicine. The theory that the metals are composed of the same elements, and that by proper treatment the base metals can be developed into the noble, which was the leading theory in chemistry down to the 16th century, is clearly defined in his writings. Roger Bacon was greatly influenced by his theories. The titles of 500 works reputed to be from his pen are known; of these, the following have appeared in print: *Summa perfectionis, Liber investigationis,* or *De investigatione perfectionis, De inventione veritatis, Liber Fornacum,* and *Testamentum.*

Gebir (jē'bėr, gä'bir). A poem by Walter Savage Landor, published in 1798.

Geddes (ged'es), **Janet** (or **Jenny**). fl. 17th century. The reputed originator of a riot in Saint Giles's Church, Edinburgh, July 23, 1637. She is said to have emphasized her protest against the introduction of the English liturgy into Scotland by throwing her folding stool at the head of the officiating bishop.

Gehenna (gē.hen'a). [Hebrew, **Gehinnom, Ge Hinnom** (gē.hin'om).] The valley of Hinnom, situated S of Jerusalem. The name of the valley occurs first in the description of the boundaries of Judah and Benjamin (Josh. xviii. 16). Traditionally certain Israelites sacrificed children to Moloch in this place, for which reason it was called *Topheth,* or abomination. Hence it became a refuse dump, where fires were kept constantly burning to prevent pestilence. Later it was regarded as the prototype of the place of punishment, hell, and hell fire, and was so referred to in the New Testament.

Geierstein (gī'ėr.stīn; German, -shtīn), **Anne of.** The principal character in Sir Walter Scott's novel of that name. She is the daughter of Count Albert, and inherits the title of Baroness of Arnheim.

Geierstein, Count of. See **Albert.**

Geikie (gē'ki), **Sir Archibald.** b. at Edinburgh, Dec. 28, 1835; d. at Haslemere, Surrey, England, Nov. 10, 1924. A Scottish geologist. He was appointed director of the geological survey of Scotland in 1867, professor of geology at Edinburgh University in 1871, and was director-general of the geological survey of the United Kingdom (1881–1901). He was knighted in 1891. He wrote numerous works on geology and related subjects, including a *Students' Manual* (1871), a *Text-book* (1882), a *Class-book* (1886), *Memoir of Sir Roderick I. Murchison* (1874), *Field Geology* (5th ed., 1900), *Memoir of Sir Andrew Crombie Ramsay* (1895), *The Ancient Volcanoes of Britain* (1897), *The Founders of Geology* (1897), *Geological Map of England and Wales* (1897), *Types of Scenery, and their Influence on Literature* (1898), *The Geology of Central and Western Fife and Kinross* (1901), *The Geology of Eastern Fife* (1902), *Scottish Reminiscences* (1904), *Landscape in History* (1905), and *Charles Darwin as Geologist* (1909). He was made secretary to the Royal Society in 1903, and president in 1908.

Gellatley (gel'at.li), **David.** A half-witted servant in the novel *Waverley* by Sir Walter Scott.

Gellert (gel'ėrt). In Welsh legend, the faithful hound of Llewelyn. He was killed by his master, who, seeing him come toward him covered with blood, thought that the dog had killed the child he was set to guard. The child was found sleeping safely under the overturned cradle, and a huge wolf beside it, slain by the dog. Llewelyn was overcome with remorse, buried Gellert honorably, and erected a monument to his memory. The place, Bethgelert in North Wales, is still shown. This story, with variations, has been current from ancient times in Persia, India, China, and all over Europe. The misjudged loyal animal differs according to the locality. In Greece it is a huge snake which saves the child from a wolf; in India it is often a pet mongoose that saves the child from a snake.

Gellius (jel′i.us), **Aulus.** b. perhaps c130 A.D.; fl. in the 2nd century. A Roman grammarian, author of *Noctes Atticae*, in 20 books (first printed 1469). Of the eighth book only the table of contents survives. His work is valuable as a conscientious account of all that he could learn about archaic literature and language, laws, philosophy, and natural science.

Gemara (ge.mä′rạ). Part of the Talmud, the complement or commentary to the Mishnah, being its dialectical analysis, discussion, and explanation. Its relation to the Mishnah is that of exposition to thesis. The two together constitute the Talmud.

Gemini (jem′i.nī). A zodiacal constellation, giving its name to a sign of the zodiac, lying E of Taurus, on the other side of the Milky Way. It represents the two youths Castor and Pollux sitting side by side. In the heads of the twins respectively are situated the two bright stars which go by their names. The sun is in Gemini from about May 21 till about June 21 (the longest day).

General, Mrs. A character in Charles Dickens's novel *Little Dorrit*, a widow of 45. Mr. Dorrit engages her to "form the mind" and manners of his daughters.

Generall Historie of Virginia, New-England, and the Summer Isles. A narrative by Captain John Smith (1580–1631) and others, published in 1624.

Generides (jẹ.ner′i.dēz). A Middle English romance existing in two manuscripts, one in couplets and the other in rhyme royal. The hero, Generides, is nursed to health by Clarionas, and the two are finally united in marriage.

Genesis (jen′ẹ.sis). [Hebrew, **Breshith, Bereshith.**] The first book of the Old Testament. It records the creation of the world, the Flood, and the ensuing dispersion of races, and gives a detailed history of the patriarchs Abraham, Isaac, and Jacob. The traditional view ascribes the authorship to Moses. Most modern scholars, however, find in it various periods of authorship, and particularly two chief sources, the so-called Jehovistic and Elohistic, named for their different use of the name of the Deity, Yahweh in the first, Elohim in the second. According to the latter (modern) view, the dates of composition fall chiefly within the periods of Judah and Israel (about the 8th century B.C.), the last redaction occurring perhaps after the return from Babylon. In Hebrew the book is designated by its first word, *Breshith*, "In the beginning"; the title *Genesis* was supplied in the early Greek translation.

Genesis. An Old English poem of nearly 3,000 lines in the *Junius Manuscript*, now considered by most scholars to consist actually of two works, commonly designated *Genesis A*, which is dated at the beginning of the 8th century and attributed to an unknown follower of Caedmon, and *Genesis B*, which is known to be a translation (probably of the 9th century) of an early German poem, interpolated in *Genesis A*. The later work contains an account of the fall of the angels considered by

some to be comparable in its power to that in Milton's *Paradise Lost*.

Genesis and Exodus (ek′sọ.dus). A Middle English poem (c1250) by a Norfolk poet, paraphrasing Biblical material. The Genesis story uses much legendary material (the idea that Adam's wife was called Issa until the time of the Fall, when Adam named her Eve, and the idea that Abel was 100 years old when Cain slew him), while that of Exodus follows the Biblical story of Moses more accurately. The source is usually given as Petrus Comestor's *Historia Scholastica*. It is noted as the first example of the iambic dimeter in English literature. (Coleridge uses this meter in *Christabel*).

Genetyllis (jen.ẹ.til′is). In Greek mythology, a goddess, protectress of births.

Geneura (gẹ.nev′rạ). See **Guinevere.**

Geneva (jẹ.nē′vạ). [French, **Genève** (zhẹ.nev′); German, **Genf** (genf); Italian **Ginevra** (jē.ne′vrä).] A city in W Switzerland, the capital of the canton of Geneva, situated at the SW end of the Lake of Geneva (Lac Léman), where the Rhone River issues from the lake. The Rhone divides the city in two parts; on the left bank lies the old town, the seat of government and of commerce, on the right bank are the suburbs of Quartier St. Gervais and Les Plaquis. Geneva is an important commercial and financial center. Watchmaking, introduced by Cusin in 1587, is the principal industry, but there are also manufactures of jewelry, gold and silver ware, and motors and electrical locomotives (Sécheron). It is the site of the palace used by the League of Nations, which was created in Geneva on Jan. 10, 1920. Geneva is the seat of the International Red Cross and of the International Labor Office. It has a university which developed out of Calvin's academy, famous for the teaching of natural science, with an important library, the Institute Jean-Jacques Rousseau (educational science), the Institute of International Studies (Institut des Hautes Études Internationales), theater and conservatory of music, numerous training schools, and other educational institutions. Museum of art and history; Ariana Museum; natural history museum; the *hotel de ville* (town hall) is a Renaissance building from the 16th century; the Cathedral of Saint Pierre is from the 12–14th centuries. Various monuments, beautiful parks and botanic gardens. Geneva was a Helvetian and Roman town, part of the Burgundian and Frankish kingdoms, later under the influence of the bishops of Geneva and the dukes of Savoy. It became a center of the Reformation under the leadership of Calvin, was incorporated into France in 1798, and entered the Swiss Confederation in 1815. It was the birthplace of Jean-Jacques Rousseau.

Geneva. A play (1938) by George Bernard Shaw. It satirizes the helplessness and futility of the League of Nations in the face of aggressive nationalism as epitomized by the Hitler movement in Germany and the racist theories which were a part of that movement.

Geneva Bible. [Also, **Breeches Bible.**] An English translation of the Bible issued from Geneva in 1560 by several English divines who had fled thither to escape the persecution of the reign of

---

fat, fāte, fär, àsk, fāre; net, mē, hėr; pin, pīne; not, nōte, möve, nôr; up, lūte, pùll; тн, then;

Mary. It was the first complete Bible to appear in Roman type, the first to omit the Apocrypha, and the first to recognize the division into verses. This translation was in common use in England till the version made by order of King James was introduced in 1611. The Geneva Bible has also been called the *Breeches Bible*, because Gen. iii. 7 is translated, "Then the eyes of them both were opened, and they knew that they were naked, and they sewed fig leaves together and made themselves *breeches.*" "Breeches" occurs in previous translations, though the name is given especially to this one.

Geneviève (jen'ẹ.vēv, jen.ẹ.vēv'; French, zhẹn-vyev), Saint. [Latinized, **Genovefa.**] b. at Nanterre, near Paris, c422; d. at Paris, Jan. 3, 512. The patron saint of Paris, reputed to have saved the city from the Huns under Attila by her prayers in 451.

Genevieve (jen'ẹ.vēv, jen.ẹ.vēv'). The heroine of a poem by Coleridge, entitled *Love.* The poem is sometimes called by her name.

Genghis Khan (jen'gis kän"). [Also: **Jenghiz Khan, Jinghis Khan,** original name, **Temuchin.**] b. near the river Onon, in Mongolia, 1162; d. in Mongolia, 1227. A Mongol conqueror; son of Yesukai, a petty tribal chieftain; grandfather of Kublai Khan. He proclaimed himself khan of the Mongol nation in 1206, completed the conquest of northern China with the capture of Peking (Peiping) in 1215, and conquered central Asia (1218–21), ruling from northern China to Azerbaijan and Georgia. In 1223 the Mongols defeated the Russians at the Kalka River (modern Kalmius), and swept on to Bulgaria, which they sacked before returning to Asia. Genghiz was a hard ruler; when Herat deposed its governor, he sent a force against the city, besieged it for six months, took it, and for a week permitted his Mongols to kill and burn; it is said that more than a million and a half people died in the city.

genre. In literature, a distinct type or category, into which works are grouped according to form, technique, or purpose.

Gentili (jen.tē'lē), **Alberico.** b. at Sanginesio, Ancona, Italy, Jan. 14, 1552; d. at London, June 19, 1608. An Italian jurist, one of the earliest authorities on international law. He lived in England from 1580, and taught law at Oxford, settling (c1590) at London. Among his works are *De legationibus, De jure belli,* and *Advocatio Hispanica.*

Gentilness and Nobility. A morality play, probably by John Rastell, printed c1526–29. Its theme is stated by the line "where honor or nobility shall rest." A Merchant, a Gentleman, and a Ploughman argue over the matter, and the work concludes with a plea that those who govern should be just, limited in term of office, and punishable for wrongdoing.

Gentle Geordie (jôr'di). See **Staunton, Sir George.**

Gentleman (jen'tl.man), **Francis.** b. at Dublin, Oct. 13, 1728; d. there, in December, 1784. An Irish actor and dramatist. He acted Othello in Edinburgh and appeared in his own comedies, *The Modish Wife* (1761) and *The Tobacconist* (c1760), the latter based upon Jonson's *Alchemist.* He also

wrote several tragedies. In 1770 he published a series of criticisms called *The Dramatic Censor,* which dealt with Shakespeare and contemporary dramatists as well as contemporary actors, and he afterward edited Bell's acting edition of Shakespeare.

Gentleman Adventurer, The. A historical novel by Henry Christopher Bailey, published in 1914. Set in England and the West Indies during the period of William III and Queen Anne, the story concerns Jacobite plots and adventures on both land and sea.

Gentleman: A Romance of the Sea, The. A novel by Alfred Ollivant, published in 1908. A historical novel of England at the opening of the 19th century, it tells the story of a plan by agents of Napoleon to kidnap Nelson, just a few weeks before Trafalgar.

Gentleman Dancing-Master, The. A comedy (1672) by Wycherley, suggested in part by Calderón's *El Maestro de danzar.*

Gentleman Usher, The. A comedy by George Chapman, printed in 1606. It was probably produced around 1601, although there is no printed record of performances. Chapman made some use of Plautus, and also of Sidney's *Arcadia,* for the rivalry of a father and son and the episode involving a heroine's disfigurement.

Gentleman With a Duster, A. Pseudonym of **Begbie, Harold.**

Gentle Shepherd, The. A pastoral drama by Allan Ramsay, published in 1725. It was acted privately in 1729 at the Haddington Grammar School, and publicly at Edinburgh, in 1747.

Geoffrey of Monmouth (jef'ri; mon'muth). b. probably at Monmouth, England, c1100; d. at Llandaff, Wales, 1152 or 1154. An English chronicler. He may have been a monk at the Benedictine monastery at Monmouth. He was in Oxford in 1129, where he met Archdeacon Walter (not Walter Map), from whom he professed to have obtained the foundation of his *Historia Regum Britanniae* (History of the Kings of Britain). In 1152 he was consecrated bishop of St. Asaph, having been ordained priest in the same year. It does not appear that he visited his see. Geoffrey also wrote a Latin translation of the prophecies of Merlin. A life of Merlin has also been ascribed to him, perhaps incorrectly.

George (jôrj), Saint. d. c303. A Christian martyr, a native of Cappadocia and military tribune under Diocletian, said to have been put to death at Nicomedia in 303. The details of his life and death are unknown, and even his existence has been doubted. He was honored in the Oriental churches, and in the 14th century, under Edward III, was adopted as the patron saint of England, where he had been popular from the time of the early Crusades (he was said to have come to the aid of the Crusaders against the Saracens under the walls of Antioch in 1089, and was then chosen by many Normans under Robert, son of William the Conqueror, as their patron). Many legends were connected with his name during the Middle Ages, the most notable of which is the legend of his conquest of the dragon (the Devil) and the delivery from

---

ḍ, d or j; ṣ, s or sh; ṭ, t or ch; ẓ, z or zh; o, F. cloche; ü, F. menu; ċh, Sc. loch; ṅ, F. bonbon.

it of the king's daughter Sabra (the Church). He was the "Christian hero" of the Middle Ages. April 23 is Saint George's day.

George. Entries on literary characters having this prename will be found under the surnames Airy, Barnwell, Bevis, Carleton, Douglas, Osborne, Ponderevo, Staunton, Swidger, and Warrington.

George I. [Full name, **George Louis.**] b. at Hanover, Germany, March 28, 1660; d. at Osnabrück, Germany, June 11, 1727. King of Great Britain and Ireland (1714–27); son of Ernest Augustus, elector of Hanover, and Sophia, granddaughter of James I of England through Elizabeth Stuart, queen of Bohemia. He married his cousin Sophia Dorothea, daughter of the Duke of Zelle, in 1682; they were divorced in 1694 after her lover, Count Königsmark, had been killed. George succeeded his father as elector of Hanover in 1698. His mother died on May 28, 1714. On the death (Aug. 1, 1714) of Queen Anne, he succeeded to the English throne by virtue of the Act of Settlement, passed by Parliament in 1701, which, in default of issue from Anne and William, entailed the crown on the electress Sophia and her heirs, they being Protestant. Crowned at Westminster on Oct. 20, 1714, he was the first of the Hanoverian kings. George spoke no English and was not interested in English politics; the result was a strengthening of the cabinet's power in English administration. He nominated at his accession a Whig ministry, with Townshend as prime minister, to the exclusion of the Tory Party, which he regarded with suspicion as the stronghold of the Jacobites and of the Roman Catholics. In January, 1715, he dissolved the Tory Parliament left by Queen Anne, and by a liberal use of the crown patronage secured a large Whig majority in the new Parliament, which convened in March following. In September, 1715, a Jacobite rising took place in Scotland under the Earl of Mar, who was subsequently joined by the Pretender. The rebellion was speedily put down by the Duke of Argyll, but the excitement which it produced was taken advantage of to pass the Septennial Act, providing for septennial instead of triennial parliaments, thus enabling the new dynasty to become firmly settled on the throne before a new election of Parliament. In 1717 he further strengthened his position by concluding the Triple Alliance with France and Holland, which guaranteed the Hanoverian succession, and which was joined by the emperor in the following year. In 1717 Stanhope was appointed prime minister; he was succeeded in 1721 by Walpole, who held office during the remainder of the reign.

George II. [Full name, **George Augustus.**] b. at Hanover, Germany, Nov. 10, 1683; d. at London, Oct. 25, 1760. King of Great Britain and Ireland (1727–60); son of George I and Sophia Dorothea. He married Wilhelmina Charlotte Caroline of Ansbach on Sept. 2, 1705, was declared Prince of Wales on Sept. 27, 1714, and succeeded to the throne of Great Britain and Ireland and to the electorate of Hanover on the death of his father, on June 11, 1727. He continued his father's domestic policy of favoring the Whigs, and retained Walpole as prime minister until 1742. His foreign policy was chiefly dictated by his anxiety for the safety of Hanover amid the contending powers on the Continent. He maintained an alliance with Maria Theresa of Austria in the first and second Silesian wars (1740–42 and 1744–45), and commanded the Pragmatic army in person at the victory of Dettingen over the French, on June 27, 1743. In 1745 a Jacobite rising took place in Scotland under Charles Edward Stuart, the Young Pretender, who was totally defeated by William Augustus, Duke of Cumberland, second son of George II, at the battle of Culloden (April 27, 1746). In June, 1754, hostilities (French and Indian Wars) broke out between England and France in America. The probability of a French attack on Hanover induced George II to conclude a treaty for the mutual guarantee of the integrity of Germany with Frederick II of Prussia at Westminster, on Jan. 17, 1756. In the same year Frederick commenced the third Silesian or Seven Years' War, in which England sided with Prussia. The Duke of Cumberland was defeated by the French at Hastenbeck (July 26, 1757) and driven out of Hanover. The accession to power of the coalition ministry under Pitt and Newcastle (June 29, 1757) gave, however, a new aspect to the war. The Duke of Cumberland was replaced by Prince Ferdinand of Brunswick, who regained Hanover in 1758; and the last years of the king's reign saw the British armies victorious in India and in Canada, and the British fleet in control of the seas.

George III. [Full name, **George William Frederick;** nickname, **Farmer George.**] b. at London, June 4, 1738; d. at Windsor, England, Jan. 29, 1820. King of Great Britain and Ireland (1760–1820); son of Frederick Louis, Prince of Wales, and Augusta, daughter of Duke Frederick II of Saxe-Gotha. His father having died in 1751, he succeeded to the throne of Great Britain and Ireland and to the electorate of Hanover on the death of his grandfather, George II, on Oct. 25, 1760, and married Charlotte Sophia of Mecklenburg-Strelitz on Sept. 8, 1761. His domestic policy was characterized by a prolonged and partly successful effort to break the power of the Whig Party, which had maintained control of the government under his two predecessors, and to restore the royal prerogative to the position which it had occupied under the Stuarts. He was involved in the war of the American Revolution and the Napoleonic wars. His most notable prime ministers were Lord North (1770–82) and the younger Pitt (1783–1801 and 1804–06), both of whom consented to shape their policy in the main in accordance with the demands of the king. At his accession he found the Seven Years' War in progress, of which the French and Indian Wars in America formed a part. He concluded (Feb. 10, 1763) the peace of Paris with France, Spain, and Portugal, by which England acquired Canada from France and Florida from Spain. The arbitrary and oppressive financial policy which he adopted toward the American colonies after the return of peace caused the outbreak of the American Revolutionary War in 1775. The war which ensued was practically ended by the capitulation at Yorktown of Cornwallis on Oct. 19, 1781; and the independence of the colonies was acknowledged by the peace of Versailles, Sept. 3, 1783. The legislative union of

fat, fāte, fär, ȧsk, fāre; net, mē, hėr; pin, pīne; not, nōte, mȯve, nôr; up, lūte, pū́ll; ᴛʜ, then;

Great Britain and Ireland was effected on Jan. 1, 1801. In 1793 war broke out between England and the revolutionary government in France, which, with a short interruption (1802–03), was continued until the downfall of Napoleon and the restoration of the Bourbons. During the period 1812–15 a war was also carried on against the U. S. After several temporary attacks of mental derangement, the king became hopelessly insane in 1811, and during the rest of his reign the government was conducted under the regency of the Prince of Wales (afterward George IV).

George IV. [Full name, **George Augustus Frederick.**] b. at London, Aug. 12, 1762; d. at Windsor, England, June 26, 1830. King of Great Britain and Ireland (1820–30); son of George III and Charlotte Sophia of Mecklenburg-Strelitz. He contracted an illegal (because made without the king's consent) marriage with Mrs. Maria Anne Fitzherbert on Dec. 21, 1785, and on April 8, 1795, married his cousin Caroline Amelia Elizabeth of Brunswick. While Prince of Wales he cultivated the friendship of the opposition leaders, including Fox and Sheridan, and gained the ill will of his father by his extravagance and dissolute habits. He was appointed regent when his father became insane in 1811, and succeeded him on the throne of Great Britain and in the kingdom of Hanover on Jan. 29, 1820. On his appointment to the regency he abandoned his former Whig associates and allied himself with the Tories. He refused (1821) to permit his queen to be present at the coronation and on June 6, 1820, he instituted proceedings in the House of Lords for a divorce on the ground of infidelity. The proceedings were subsequently abandoned for want of evidence. The queen died in August, 1821. The chief event of his reign was the passage of the Catholic Emancipation Act during the ministry of the Duke of Wellington, on April 13, 1829.

George V. [Full name, **George Frederick Ernest Albert.**] b. at Marlborough House, London, June 3, 1865; d. at Sandringham, Norfolk, England, Jan. 20, 1936. King of Great Britain and Ireland and emperor of India (1910–36); second son of Edward VII. In 1892 by the death of his elder brother, the Duke of Clarence, he became the heir to the throne of Great Britain and Ireland. He was created Duke of York in 1892, married Princess Victoria Mary (May) of Teck, daughter of Queen Victoria's first cousin, on July 6, 1893, succeeded his father as Duke of Cornwall in 1901, and on Nov. 9, 1901, was given the title of Prince of Wales. He was crowned in Westminster Abbey on June 22, 1911. During World War I he changed (1916) the name of the ruling house from the German Saxe-Coburg-Gotha to that of Windsor. He was succeeded by his son, the Prince of Wales, as Edward VIII. His second son also reigned, as George VI.

George VI. [Full name, **Albert Frederick Arthur George.**] b. Dec. 14, 1895; d. at Sandringham, Norfolk, England, Feb. 6, 1952. King of Great Britain and Northern Ireland (1936–52); second son of George V, and brother of Edward VIII, whom he succeeded on Dec. 11, 1936. He married (1923) Elizabeth Bowes-Lyon. The beginning of his reign was marked by the parliamentary crisis resulting from his brother's abdication. During World War II he worked closely with Winston Churchill. He was succeeded by his daughter Elizabeth II.

George, Henry. b. at Philadelphia, Sept. 2, 1839; d. at New York, Oct. 29, 1897. An American economist and reformer, noted as the founder of the single-tax movement and the author of *Progress and Poverty* (author's ed., 1879; regular ed., 1880). He left school at the age of 14, later making a voyage to Australia and India as foremast boy in the *Hindoo.* Upon his return in 1856, he became a typesetter, returned to the sea, and in 1857 went to San Francisco, where he prospected for gold, was a store clerk, and finally a typesetter. After his marriage in 1861, he struggled against privation at Sacramento and San Francisco, finally entering newspaper work with the San Francisco *Times,* with which he served from 1866 to 1868, finally becoming managing editor. He became (c1869) editor of the Oakland *Transcript,* meanwhile developing his economic philosophy centered around land values. His ideas appeared in *Our Land and Land Policy* (1871). The single-tax theory is based on land values; since the land belongs to all, according to this theory, the benefit of the land should accrue to all. Therefore, a tax on land (otherwise paid as rent), if intelligently applied, should supply all needed revenue and result in the abolition of all other taxes. He was (1871 *et seq.*) editor and part proprietor of the *Daily Evening Post* and in 1876 became state inspector of gas meters. His memorable work, *Progress and Poverty,* expounding his ideas on social wealth, was begun in 1877 and brought out in a trade edition by the Appleton firm in 1880. Afterwards he became a lecturer and newspaper correspondent and wrote magazine articles. He appeared on the platform in Ireland and Great Britain. Among his other writings are *The Irish Land Question* (1881), *Social Problems* (1883), *Protection or Free Trade* (1886), *An Open Letter to the Pope* (1891), *A Perplexed Philosopher* (1892), and *The Science of Political Economy* (1897). See *The Life of Henry George,* by Henry George, Jr. (1900).

George, W. L. [Full name, **Walter Lionel George.**] b. at Paris, March 20, 1882; d. at London, Jan. 30, 1926. An English novelist, short-story writer, journalist, and critic. Educated in France (where he lived until 1905) and in Germany, he later served in the French army; he subsequently lived in England and America, writing for the press and lecturing. Among his novels are *A Bed of Roses* (1911), *The Second Blooming* (1914), *Blind Alley* (1919), *Caliban* (1920), a novel of newspaper life, *The Confessions of Ursula Trent* (1921), *One of the Guilty* and *The Triumph of Gallio* (both 1923), *Gifts of Sheba* and *Children of the Morning* (both 1927). He also wrote *Olga Nazimov* (1915), short stories, and *Engines of Social Progress* (1907), *France in the 20th Century* (1908), *Dramatic Actualities* (1914), *Anatole France* (1915), and *A Novelist on Novels* (1915), literary and social criticism. A confirmed feminist, he wrote *Woman and Tomorrow* (1913), *The Intelligence of Woman* (1917), and *The Story of Woman* (1925).

д, d or j; ş, s or sh; ţ, t or ch; z̧, z or zh; o, F. cloche; ü, F. menu; ch, Sc. loch; ṅ, F. bonbon.

George-a-Greene, the Pinner of Wakefield (jôrj.ạ-grēn'; wāk'fēld). A "pleasant conceyted comedie" attributed to Robert Greene, licensed in 1595 and printed in 1599. It is thought to be founded on an early prose romance, "The History of George-a-Green," preserved in Thom's *Early Prose Romances*. It also owes something to the ballad *The Jolly Pinder of Wakefield with Robin Hood Scarlet and John*. George a Green, a "Huisher of the Bower," is introduced by Jonson in *The Sad Shepherd*.

George Barnwell (bärn'wel). See **London Merchant**.

George, Duke of Clarence (klar'ęns). See **Clarence, George, Duke of**.

George Silverman's Explanation (sil'vẻr.mạnz). A story by Charles Dickens, written especially for the *Atlantic Monthly*, and published serially in that magazine during the months of January, February, and March, 1868. In it Dickens used a technique very close to what is now called "stream-of-consciousness" writing.

Georgian. A term applied loosely to many of the English writers, especially the poets, of the second decade of the 20th century. More specifically it refers to the poets Rupert Brooke, William H. Davies, John Drinkwater, Walter de la Mare, James Elroy Flecker, Harold Monro, and John Masefield, who appeared in one or more of the five volumes that were published between 1912–22 of the anthology *Georgian Poetry*, edited by Edward Marsh. Pieces by Robert Graves and D. H. Lawrence were also included. Because the aims of these poets were various, the movement does not have distinct characteristics; it may, however, be said that as a whole the group turned from the ornamental and stylistically somewhat weak verse of the late 19th century, that they wrote mildly sentimental poetry that was more likely to be set in rural areas than in urban, and that their general tone is one of restraint.

Georgian House, The. A novel by Frank Swinnerton, published in 1932.

Georgian Poetry. An anthology of verse edited by Edward Marsh, in five volumes which appeared in 1912, 1915, 1917, 1919, and 1922.

Georgics (jôr'jiks). A poem by Vergil, in four books, dealing with agriculture, the cultivation of trees, domestic animals, and bees.

Geraint (ge.rānt'). One of the knights of the Round Table. Tennyson used his story in "The Marriage of Geraint" and "Geraint and Enid," in the *Idylls of the King*.

Geraint and Enid (ē'nid). One of the *Idylls of the King*, by Tennyson.

Gerald (jer'ạld). See **Gerrold**.

Gerald de Barri (or **de Barry**) (dę bar'i). See **Giraldus Cambrensis**.

Geraldine (jer'ạl.dēn, -din). In Thomas Heywood's tragedy *The English Traveller*, a young man who is in love with the wife of his old friend.

Geraldine, the Fair. A lady celebrated in the sonnets of Henry Howard, Earl of Surrey, identified as the historical Lady Elizabeth Fitzgerald, daughter of Gerald Fitzgerald (1487–1534), 9th Earl of Kildare. She was nine years old when the poet met her, but Thomas Nash (in *Jack Wilton, or The Unfortunate Traveller*) and some other later writers invented a love affair between the two.

Gerald Scales (jer'ạld skālz'). See **Scales, Gerald**.

Gerard (ję.rärd'). The hero of Charles Reade's novel *The Cloister and the Hearth*.

Gerard (ję.rärd'; British, jer'ärd), **John**. b. at Nantwich, Cheshire, England, 1545; d. at London, in February, 1612. An English surgeon and botanist. He published in 1597 his *Herball*, based on Rembert Dodoens's *Pemptades*, of which it is nearly a translation. The genus *Gerardia* was named for him by Linnaeus.

Gerardine (ję.rär'dēn). In Thomas Middleton's *Family of Love*, the passionate lover of Maria.

Gerhardi (jer.här'di), **William Alexander**. b. at St. Petersburg, Nov. 21, 1895—. An English fiction writer. He served as military attaché (1917–18) at the British embassy at Petrograd, and was a member (1918–20) of the British military mission to Siberia. His novels include *Futility* (1922), *The Polyglots* (1925), *My Sinful Earth* (1928), *Resurrection* (1934), *Of Mortal Love* (1936), and *My Wife's the Least of It* (1938). He is the author also of *Anton Chekhov: A Critical Study* (1923), *Pretty Creatures* (1927), *Memoirs of a Polyglot* (1931), *The Romanoffs* (1940), and *Highlights of Russian History* (1947).

German Prisoner, The. A collection of short stories by James Hanley, published in 1931.

German-Roman Empire. See **Holy Roman Empire**.

Géronte (zhā.rônt). In French comedy, a common name for a credulous and ridiculous old man. Originally, as in Corneille's *Le Menteur*, he was old and not ridiculous, but the Gérontes in Molière's *Le Médecin malgré lui* and *Les Fourberies de Scapin* became a type. Regnard introduces a Géronte in *Le Joueur*, *Le Retour imprévu*, and *Le Légataire universel*.

Gerontius (ję.ron'shus). A British general in the army of the usurper Constantine. He rebelled against his master in 409, and proclaimed Maximus emperor. He drove Constantine's son, Constans, out of Spain, and, when Constans was captured by the insurgents at Vienne, ordered him to be put to death. He was eventually abandoned by his troops, and, being surrounded by a superior enemy, put himself to death.

Gerrard (ję.rärd'). The real name of the King of Beggars in Massinger and Fletcher's *Beggar's Bush*. He goes under the name of Clause. He is actually a nobleman, the consort of the Countess of Flanders, but ousted and exiled by a usurper after her death. His son eventually is restored to the Flemish throne and takes one of the company of beggars, Bertha, as his bride after it is discovered that his love for her, disapproved by his father because of her seemingly low estate, may be honorably celebrated since she is actually the daughter of the Duke of Brabant.

Gerrard. The "gentleman dancing-master" in Wycherley's comedy of that name. He is a perfumed coxcomb who, to conduct an intrigue with Hippolita under the nose of her father and aunt, is induced to assume the role of a dancing-master.

Gerridge (ger'ij). The plumber in T. W. Robertson's *Caste:* a type of the humorous Cockney workman.

Gerrold (jer'ọld). [Also, **Gerald.**] In *The Two Noble Kinsmen,* a schoolmaster.

Gertrude (gėr'trŏd). In Shakespeare's *Hamlet,* the mother of Hamlet, and Queen of Denmark. She dies accidentally of the poison prepared by Claudius, her husband, for Hamlet.

Gertrude. The ambitious, extravagant daughter of the goldsmith in Marston, Chapman, and Jonson's *Eastward Ho!* Her father describes her as being "of a proud ambition and nice wantonness," a person who "must be ladyfied—and be attired just to the court-cut and long tail."

Gertrude. The heroine of Campbell's poem *Gertrude of Wyoming* (1809).

Gertrude. See also **Bertha.**

Gertrude of Wyoming (wī.ō'ming). A work in verse by the Scottish poet Thomas Campbell, published in 1809.

Gervase of Tilbury (jėr'vạs; til'ber.i, -bėr.i). [Also, **Gervaise.**] b. probably at Tilbury, Essex, England; d. probably c1235. An English historical writer. He was called, without foundation, a grandson of Henry II. He became a favorite of the emperor Otho IV, and wrote for his amusement *Otia Imperialia* (c1211), a valuable medley of the tales and folklore of the Middle Ages.

Geryon (jē'ri.ọn, ger'i.ọn) or **Geryones** (jē.rī'ọ.nēz). In Greek mythology, a monster with three heads or three bodies and powerful wings dwelling in the island of Erytheia in the far west; son of Chrysaor and Callirrhoe. He possessed a large herd of red cattle guarded by Eurytion (his shepherd) and the two-headed dog Orthros. To carry away these cattle was the tenth labor of Hercules, which he successfully performed, after killing the shepherd, the dog, and Geryon himself.

Geryoneo (jē.ri.on'ẹ.ō, ger.i-). In Spenser's *Faerie Queene,* a great giant with three bodies, representing respectively Philip II of Spain, the portion of the Netherlands ruled by Spain, and the Inquisition.

Gesner (ges'nėr), **Johann Matthias.** b. at Roth, near Nuremberg, Germany, April 9, 1691; d. at Göttingen, Germany, Aug. 3, 1761. A German classical scholar. He became professor of rhetoric at the University of Göttingen in 1734. He edited a number of Latin classics, including Quintilian (1738), Pliny the Younger (1739), Horace (1752), and Claudian (1759).

Gessler (ges'lėr), **Hermann.** In Swiss legend and ballad, an imperial magistrate in Uri and Schwyz, shot by William Tell in 1307, according to the *Chronicon Helveticum.* It was Gessler who sentenced Tell to shoot an apple from the head of his own son, and it was for Gessler that Tell intended the second arrow in his belt, in case he had killed the child.

Gestapo (gẹ.stä'pō; German, -shtä'-). [Acronym of **Geheime Staatspolizei.**] The Nazi state police of Germany, organized by Hermann Goering in March, 1933.

Gesta Regis Henrici Secundi (jes'tạ rē'jis hen.rī'sī sẹ.kun'dī). [Eng. trans., *Events (of the Reign) of King Henry II.*] A prose chronicle in Latin of the 12th century, sometimes ascribed, probably erroneously, to Benedict, abbot of Peterborough.

Gesta Regum Anglorum (jes'tạ rē'gum ang.glō'rum). [Eng. trans., *Chronicle of the Kings of England.*] A chronicle by William of Malmesbury covering the kings of England and English history from the 5th century until c1125; its continuation, the *Historia Novella,* dealt with events down to 1142.

Gesta Romanorum (jes'tạ rō.ma.nō'rum). [Eng. trans., *Deeds of the Romans.*] A popular collection of stories in Latin, compiled, perhaps in England, at the end of the 13th or the beginning of the 14th century. Many of the stories are Eastern in origin. This compilation long retained its popularity; it was printed as early as 1473, reprinted at Louvain a few months later and again in 1480, translated into Dutch in 1484, printed again in 1488, and went through six or seven editions in England during the succeeding century. The earliest printed Latin texts contained 150 or 151 sections. In the next following editions the number quickly rose to 181, and these 181 tales form the commonly received text. There was a German edition at Augsburg in 1489 containing only 95 tales, of which some are not in the accepted Latin version. In like manner, including tales not in the Latin anonymous text, there is an English series of 43 or 44 sections. The name of the work, *Gesta Romanorum,* commonly applied to any records of the history of Rome, is justified by little more than the arbitrary, but not invariable, reference of tale after tale to the life or reign of Roman emperors, ancient or then modern, as Conrad, or Frederick, or Henry II. Some scholars have thought that a first collection of these tales was in accordance with the title, and gave only illustrations out of Roman history, each with its ready-made moral or "application" added for the use of preachers, but that by the addition of more striking marvels and much livelier matter, with omission of familiar bits of ancient history, the work itself was developed to its later shape. Chaucer, Shakespeare, and other English poets have used material from it as a basis for various of their own works.

Gest Historiale of the Destruction of Troy (jest his.tō'ri.ạl). A historical poem of 14,000 lines in alliterative verse, written in northern English in the late 14th century. It covers the story from Jason's quest for the Golden Fleece to the wanderings of Ulysses and Telemachus.

Gethsemane (geth.sem'ạ.nē). A garden east of Jerusalem, near the brook Kedron: the scene of Christ's agony and betrayal. Mat. xxvi. 36, etc.

getreue Eckart (gẹ.troi'ẹ ek'art), **der.** see **Eckhardt.**

Getting Married. A one-act comedy (1908) by George Bernard Shaw. It is aimed at what Shaw considers to be a lack of realism in the Victorian attitude toward the marriage contract.

Getting of Wisdom, The. A novel by Henry Handel Richardson (Mrs. Henrietta Robertson), published in 1910.

ḍ, d or j; ṣ, s or sh; ṭ, t or ch; ẓ, z or zh; o, F. cloche; ü, F. menu; ċh, Sc. loch; ṅ, F. bonbon.

Ghibellines (gib′ẹ.linz, -lēnz, -līnz). The imperial and aristocratic party of Italy in the Middle Ages, opposed to the Guelphs, the papal and popular party. The name was derived from the German *Waiblingen*, the name of an estate in the part of the ancient *Kreis* (district or circle) of Franconia (later included in Württemberg) belonging to the house of Hohenstaufen (to which the then reigning emperor Conrad III belonged), when war broke out (c1140) between this house and the Welfs or Guelphs. It is said to have been first employed as the rallying cry of the emperor's party at the battle of Weinsberg.

Ghost. In Shakespeare's *Hamlet*, the ghost of Hamlet's father, who appears to tell how Claudius poisoned him in his sleep and later to warn Hamlet against killing his mother. It is claimed that Shakespeare himself once acted the part. Ghosts also appear in *Richard III, Julius Caesar,* and *Macbeth* and are found in many other Elizabethan plays, usually with the purpose of prodding the consciences of various characters. According to tradition they could, if they chose, appear only to a single individual, they must return to the grave at daybreak, and (if they were messengers of the devil) could not abide light, holy objects, or seasons (like Christmas) which were sacred in character. Although some modern scholars have interpreted these appearances of ghosts as being the Elizabethan equivalent of mental delusions, others maintain that the Elizabethans found them more than a useful dramatic convention (possibly derived from Senecan revenge tragedy) and also believed in their actual existence.

Giafar (jä′fär). In the *Arabian Nights' Entertainments*, the grand vizier of Harun-al-Rashid, who accompanies his master in his nightly wanderings.

Giaffir (jaf′ir). In Byron's poem *The Bride of Abydos*, the ruler of Abydos and father of Zuleika.

Giant Despair. See **Despair, Giant.**

Giant Grim. See **Grim, Giant.**

Giant's Causeway, The. A group of basaltic columns on the coast of Antrim, northern Ireland.

Giant Slay-Good (slā′gụd). See **Slay-Good, Giant.**

Giaour (jour), **The.** A narrative poem by Byron, published in 1813.

Gibbet (jib′ẹt). In Farquhar's comedy *The Beaux' Stratagem*, a highwayman and convict. He remarks that it is "for the good of my country that I should be abroad," and prides himself on being the "best behaved man on the road."

Gibbie (gib′i), **Goose.** A half-witted lad in *Old Mortality*, by Sir Walter Scott.

Gibbon (gib′ọn), **Edward.** b. at Putney, Surrey, England, April 27, 1737; d. at London, Jan. 16, 1794. An English historian. His health in childhood was poor, and his instruction was notably irregular. He entered Oxford (Magdalen College) in April, 1752, but left the university after a residence of 14 months. At this time he became a Roman Catholic, a creed which he soon afterward renounced. In June, 1753, he was placed under the care and instruction of Pavilliard, a Calvinist minister, at Lausanne, in Switzerland, where he remained until August, 1758, when he returned to England. At

Lausanne he fell in love with Susanne Curchod (afterward Madame Necker and mother of Madame de Staël), but on his return to England the affair was broken off by his father. He served (1759–70) in the militia, attaining the rank of colonel. From January, 1763, to June, 1765, he traveled in France, Switzerland, and Italy. In 1774 he was elected to Parliament. In September, 1783, he established himself at Lausanne, where he resided for the remainder of his life. His great work is *The History of the Decline and Fall of the Roman Empire* (1776–88), still the chief authority for the period which it covers, and acclaimed as one of the greatest histories ever written. The first volume appeared in 1776 and the last in 1788. He also wrote *Memoirs of My Life and Writings.*

Gibbon, John Murray. b. in Ceylon, April 12, 1875; d. July 2, 1952. A Canadian writer. Author of *Canadian Folksongs Old and New* (1927), *A Canadian Chapbook* (1929), and *Canadian Mosaic* (1938).

Gibbon, Perceval. b. at Trelech, Carmarthenshire, Wales, Nov. 4, 1879; d. 1926. An English novelist, short-story writer, poet, and war correspondent. He was the author of *African Items* (1904), poetry, and of the novels *Souls in Bondage* (1905), *Vrouw Grobelaar's Leading Cases* (1906), *Adventures of Miss Gregory* (1911), *Margaret Harding* (1912), and *Those Who Smiled* (1920).

Gibbons (gib′ọnz), **Grinling.** b. at Rotterdam, Netherlands, April 4, 1648; d. at London, Aug. 3, 1720. An English wood carver and sculptor. Among his notable works in wood were a copy of Tintoretto's *Crucifixion* (Venice), containing over 100 figures, and *The Stoning of Stephen.* He excelled especially in carving flowers, fruit, and game, and in decorative work. He did bronze statues of Charles II, who was his patron, and James II.

Gibbons, Orlando. [Called **the English Palestrina.**] b. in England, 1583; d. at Canterbury, England, June 5, 1625. An English composer and organist, best known by his church music. His works have been mostly printed in Barnard's *Church Music* (1641), and in 1873 in a volume edited by Sir F. A. Gore Ouseley. His madrigals are considered among the best of the English school.

Gibbons, Stella (Dorothea). b. at London, Jan. 5, 1902—. An English poet and novelist. She is the author of the volumes of verse *The Mountain Beast* (1930), *The Priestess* (1934), and *The Lowland Venus* (1938). Her novels include *Cold Comfort Farm* (1932), *Bassett* (1934), *Enbury Heath* (1935), *Miss Linsey and Pa* (1936), *Nightingale Wood* (1938), *The Rich House* (1941), *The Bachelor* (1944), and *Westwood* (1946). She is author also of the collected short stories *Roaring Tower* (1937) and *Christmas at Cold Comfort Farm* (1940).

Gibbs (gibz), **Arthur Hamilton.** b. at London, March 9, 1888—. An English author, resident in the U. S.; brother of Sir Philip Gibbs. He arrived in the U. S. in 1912, served with the British forces in World War I, and returned to the U. S. in 1919. Among his works are *The Complete Oxford Man* (1910), *The Persistent Lovers* (1914), *Gunfodder* (1919), *Chances* (1930), *Undertow* (1932), and *Way of Life* (1947).

Gibbs, Sir Philip. b. at London, May 1, 1877—. An English novelist, journalist, and editor; brother of Arthur Hamilton Gibbs. War correspondent (1912) with the Bulgarian army, French and Belgian troops (1914), and with British forces in the field (1915–18); editor (1921–22) of the *Review of Reviews.* Author of *The Individualist, Back to Life* (1920), *Venetian Lovers* (1922), *The Unchanging Quest* (1925), *The Golden Years* (1931), *The Cross of Peace* (1933), *Cities of Refuge* (1936), *The Battle Within* (1944), *Through the Storm* (1945), and *The Hopeful Heart* (1947); his historical works include *The Battles of the Somme* (1916), *Now It Can Be Told* (1920), *Ordeal in England* (1937), *Across the Frontiers* (1938), *The Pageant of the Years* (1946); author also of the essays *Ten Years After* (1924) and *The Day After To-morrow* (1938).

Gibby (gib'i). In Susannah Centlivre's comedy *The Wonder! A Woman Keeps a Secret,* the Highland servant of Colonel Briton. He is an undaunted and incorrigible blunderer.

Gibraltar (ji.brôl'tạr; Spanish, нē.bräl.tär'). A town and fortified promontory (often called the Rock of Gibraltar) on the S coast of Spain, a crown colony of Great Britain. It is an important coaling station. The rock was the classical Calpe, and one of the Pillars of Hercules, was the landing-place of the Saracen leader Tarik (hence called in Arabic *Jebel-al-Tarik,* meaning "Hill of Tarik"), was taken finally from the Moors by the Spaniards in 1462, was fortified by Charles V, was taken by an English and Dutch force under Rooke in 1704, and was unsuccessfully besieged by the Spaniards and French in 1704–05, by the Spaniards in 1726, and by the Spaniards and French (1779–83). In the last siege, commencing on June 21, 1779, the defenders were commanded by Lord Heathfield. The chief attack was made on Sept. 13, 1782, when the floating batteries devised by the Chevalier d'Arcon were used. Greatest height of the rock, ab. 1,400 ft.; area, 2¼ sq. mi.

Gibson (gib'sọn), **Wilfrid (Wilson).** b. at Hexham, Northumberland, England, Oct. 2, 1878—. An English poet. He is the author of *Stonefolds* (1907), *Daily Bread* (1910), *Fires* (1912), *Thoroughfares* (1914), *Borderlands* (1914), *Battle* (1915), *Friends* (1916), *Whin* (1918), *Home* (1920), *Neighbours* (1920), *I Heard a Sailor* (1925), *The Golden Room* (1928), *Hazards* (1930), *Islands* (1932), *Fuel* (1934), *The Alert* (1941), *Challenge* (1942), *The Outpost* (1944), *Cold-knuckles* (1947), and *The Island Stag* (1947).

Gide (zhēd), **André.** [Full name, **André Paul Guillaume Gide.**] b. at Paris, Nov. 22, 1869; d. at Paris, Feb. 19, 1951. A French poet, essayist, novelist, and critic. He was awarded (1947) the Nobel prize for literature. He was the author of *Les Cahiers d'André Walter* (1891), *Les Poésies d'André Walter* (1892), *Traité du Narcisse* (1892), *Voyage d'Urien* (1893), all of which are symbolist in inspiration; of *Paludes* (1895), in which he renounces his earlier life and works; of *Les Nourritures terrestres* (1897; Eng. trans., *Fruits of the Earth*, 1948), in which he advocates departure from traditional morality in the name of freedom; of two verse dramas, *Le Roi Candaule* (1901) and *Saul* (1903); a short novel, *L'Immoraliste* (1902; Eng. trans.,

1930), in which departure from tradition brings on tragedy; of *La Porte étroite* (1909; Eng. trans., *Strait is the Gate*, 1924), which illustrates the dangers of the opposite moral attitude; of *Les Caves du Vatican* (1914; Eng. trans., *The Vatican Swindle*, 1925), *Les Faux-Monnayeurs* (1926; Eng. trans., *The Counterfeiters*, 1927), and others. His critical writings are collected in *Prétextes* (1903), *Nouveaux prétextes* (1911), *Dostoievski* (1923), *Incidences* (1924), and in his *Journal* (1939 and later supplements; Eng. trans., 3 vols., 1946–49). Other works of special significance are his *Voyage au Congo* (1927) and *Retour du Tchad* (1928), in which he reopened the vexed French colonial question; *Corydon* (1924), a dialogue on the subject of homosexuality; *Si le grain ne meurt* (1926; Eng. trans., *Lest it Die*, 1935); and *Retour de l'U.R.S.S.* (1936; Eng. trans., *Return from The U.S.S.R.*, 1937), in which he announced the termination of his short-lived sympathy for Communism. After a delicate childhood and an education at the École Alsatienne at Paris, interrupted by much travel, he began writing as a follower of Mallarmé, succeeded Léon Blum as literary critic of the *Revue Blanche,* and founded (1909) the important *Nouvelle Revue Française.* Relatively obscure before 1914, he emerged as a leader of the postwar generation. Critics disagree about the value of his work but not about the extent of his great influence, which has been hardly less great in the English-speaking world than in France. A Protestant preoccupied by moral problems, his ethical libertarianism precluded his receiving many of the honors which French writers of his stature generally receive.

Gideon (gid'ẹ.ọn). [Surnamed **Jerubbaal** (je.rub'-ạ.ạl, jer.u.bā'ạl).] A Hebrew liberator and religious reformer, conqueror of the Midianites, and judge in Israel for 40 years. Judges, vi. 11, etc.

Gideon Gray, Dr. See **Gray, Dr. Gideon.**

Gifford (gif'ọrd), Countess of. A title of **Sheridan, Lady Helen Selina.**

Gifford, William. b. at Ashburton, Devonshire, England, in April, 1756; d. at London, Dec. 31, 1826. An English critic and satirical poet. He first became known by his satires *The Baviad* (1794) and *The Maeviad* (1795), published together in 1797. He was the first editor (1809–24) of the *Quarterly Review.*

Gigadibs (gig'ạ.dibz), **Mr.** In Robert Browning's *Bishop Blougram's Apology,* a young poet through whom, ostensibly, the story is unfolded.

Giglio (jē'lyō), **Prince.** In Thackeray's tale *The Rose and the Ring,* the deposed ruler of Paflagonia.

Gilbert (gil'bẽrt), Sir **Humphrey.** b. at Compton, near Dartmouth, England, c1539; drowned off the Azores, Sept. 9, 1583. An English soldier and navigator; a half brother of Sir Walter Raleigh. He served (1566–70) in Ireland, where he defeated McCarthy More in 1569, and was made governor of the province of Munster, and in the Netherlands in 1572, where he unsuccessfully besieged Goes. In 1578, in accordance with designs which he had long entertained to discover the Northwest Passage to the Far East, he obtained the royal permission to set out on a voyage of discovery and colonization; but the expedition, which started in September of that year, was a failure. On June 11, 1583, he again set out with five ships (*Delight, Golden Hind, Ark Raleigh*, which soon returned, *Swallow*, and *Squirrel*), and on July 30 sighted the northern shore of Newfoundland. On August 5 he landed at the site of the present city of St. John's, where he established the first English colony in North America. On the return voyage the *Squirrel*, in which he sailed, foundered in a storm. His last words were the famous "We are as near to heaven by sea as by land." He wrote a *Discourse of a Discovery for a New Passage to Cataia*, and sponsored a scheme for the founding of an academy and library at London (published by Furnivall, 1869, as *Queen Elizabethes Achademy*).

Gilbert, William. b. at Colchester, England, 1540; d. Nov. 30, 1603. An English physician and natural philosopher. He studied at Cambridge, took up the practice of medicine at London in 1573, became president of the College of Physicians in 1600, and was physician in ordinary to Queen Elizabeth and James I. His chief work is *De magnete, magneticisque corporibus, et de magno magnete tellure, physiologia nova* (1600).

Gilbert, Sir **William Schwenck.** b. at London, Nov. 18, 1836; d. at Harrow, England, May 29, 1911. An English dramatist, writer of the texts of the Gilbert and Sullivan comic operas. He wrote *Dulcamara* (1866), *The Palace of Truth* (1870), *Pygmalion and Galatea* (1871), *Engaged* (1877), *The Mountebanks* (music by Cellier, 1891), and other dramatic pieces. He collaborated with Sir Arthur Sullivan, who wrote the music, in *Thespis; or The Gods Grown Old* (1871), *Trial By Jury* (1875), *The Sorcerer* (1877), *H.M.S. Pinafore* (1878), *The Pirates of Penzance; or The Slave of Duty* (1880), *Patience; or Bunthorne's Bride* (1881), *Iolanthe; or The Peer and the Peri* (1882), *Princess Ida; or Castle Adamant* (1884), *The Mikado; or The Town of Titipu* (1885), *Ruddigore* (1887), *The Yeomen of the Guard* (1888), *The Gondoliers* (1889), *Utopia, Limited* (1893), and *The Grand Duke* (1896). He also published *The Fairy's Dilemma*, the *Bab Ballads* (1869), and other works. He was knighted in 1907. The Gilbert and Sullivan operas, produced after 1881 by Richard D'Oyly Carte at the Savoy Theatre in London, a theater built especially for the popular productions, are considered by many the outstanding achievement of musical collaboration. Gilbert's lyrics are often highly satirical; he pokes fun at his Victorian contemporaries and their foibles. It is said that his character of Admiral Sir Joseph Porter, K.C.B., in *Pinafore* so angered the queen that she refused to have him knighted. The Gilbert and Sullivan following, called Savoyards after the name of the theater, is still numerous. The first of their operas, and the last two, written after a serious quarrel between the partners in 1896, are seldom performed.

Gilbert Glossin (glos'in). See **Glossin, Gilbert.**

Gilbertines (gil'bėr.tins). A religious order founded in England in the first half of the 12th century by Saint Gilbert of Sempringham. The monks of this order observed the rule of Saint Augustine, and the nuns that of Saint Benedict. The Gilbertines were confined to England, and their houses were suppressed by Henry VIII.

Gilbert Markham (gil'bėrt mär'kạm). See **Markham, Gilbert.**

Gilbert of Sempringham (sem'pring.ạm), Saint. b. at Sempringham, Lincolnshire, England, c1083; d. in February, 1189. An English priest, founder of an order known (from him) as the Gilbertines.

Gil Blas (zhēl blås). [Full title, **Histoire de Gil Blas de Santillane.**] A romance by Alaine René Le Sage, published in 1715, but not entirely completed until 1735. It is named after its hero, who tells the story of his life. Many of the incidents are modeled on Espinel's picaresque romance *Marcos de Obregón*. Smollett translated it in 1761, and in 1809 another translation was brought out in his name.

Gildas (gil'dạs). [Called **"Saint Gildas the Wise."**] b. probably in 516; d. probably in 570. A British historian. He appears to have been born in the North Welsh valley of the Clwyd, to have been a monk, to have left Britain for Armorica in 546, and to have founded the monastery of Saint Gildas at Ruys. He was the author of *De Excidio Britanniae*, which has been suggested as one of the sources used by Bede.

Gilderoy (gil'dẹ.roi). Hanged in July, 1638. A notorious Scottish freebooter, a native of Perthshire. His execution, with five of his gang, terminated a career of barbarous harrying and outrage. Many stories of his crimes were current among the common people. Among other performances he is said to have "picked the pocket of Cardinal Richelieu in the king's presence, robbed Oliver Cromwell, and hanged a judge." The ballad concerning him has been preserved by Ritson and Percy.

Giles (jīlz), Saint. [Also, **Aegydius.**] fl. 7th century. An anchorite, believed to have been a Greek who emigrated to France, and fabled to have been nourished by a hind. Gradually a monastic establishment grew around him, of which he became the head. The better to mortify the flesh, he is said to have refused to be cured of lameness, and hence became the patron saint of cripples. Saint Giles's Church, Cripplegate, London, is a memorial of him. His festival is celebrated in the Roman and Anglican churches on Sept. 1.

Giles, Blessed. See **Aegidius of Assisi.**

Giles Amaury (ạ.mô'ri). See **Amaury, Giles.**

Giles Overreach (ō'vėr.rēch), Sir **Giles.** See **Overreach, Sir Giles.**

Gilfil (gil'fil), Maynard. The somewhat unspiritual but conscientious clergyman in George Eliot's *Mr. Gilfil's Love-Story.*

Gilfillan (gil.fil'ạn), George. b. at Comrie, Perthshire, Scotland, Jan. 30, 1813; d. at Dundee, Scotland, Aug. 13, 1878. A Scottish Presbyterian clergyman and writer. Among his works are *Gallery of Literary Portraits* (three series, 1845–55), *Bards of the Bible* (1851), and *Night: a Poem* (1867).

Gilfillan, Robert. b. at Dunfermline, Scotland, July 7, 1798; d. at Leith, Scotland, Dec. 4, 1850. A Scottish poet. He was the son of a weaver, and was a merchant's clerk and collector at Leith for

Gillespie (gi.les'pi), **George.** b. at Kirkcaldy, Scotland, Jan. 21, 1613; d. there, Dec. 17, 1648. A Scottish Presbyterian clergyman, member of the Westminster Assembly. He wrote *Aaron's Rod Blossoming* (1646) and other works considered controversial in their day.

Gillray (gil'rā), **James.** b. at Chelsea, London, 1757; d. at London, June 1, 1815. An English caricaturist and painter, known for his satirical drawings of George III of England. Two plates engraved by him for Goldsmith's *Deserted Village* were published in 1784; they were in the style of Ryland. *The Burning of the Duke of Athole*, an East Indiaman, and two portraits of William Pitt slightly caricatured, a portrait of Dr. Arne, and several others belong to the same period. He occasionally signed his plates with fictitious names. The earliest caricature to which he signed his name is entitled *Paddy on Horseback* (1779). Between 1,200 and 1,500 are ascribed to him, most of them reflecting on the king ("Farmer George"), and his wife, the court, and the government. He died insane.

Gills (gilz), **Solomon.** In Charles Dickens's *Dombey and Son*, an old nautical-instrument maker.

Gil Morrice (gil mor'is). [Also, **Childe Morrice** or **Maurice** (chīld mor'is).] The title and hero of a Scottish ballad, included in Percy's *Reliques*, telling of a letter sent by Gil Morrice to his mother, Lady Barnard, but construed by her husband, Lord Barnard (not his father), to be a love letter and thus leading the husband to slay the son. In another version the husband is called James (or John) Steward.

Gilpin (gil'pin), **William.** b. at Carlisle, England, June 4, 1724; d. at Boldre, Hampshire, England, April 5, 1804. English biographer, and writer on the natural scenery of Great Britain.

Gilpin's Ride. See **Diverting History of John Gilpin, The.**

Gimcrack (jim'krak), **Sir Nicholas.** The virtuoso in Thomas Shadwell's comedy *The Virtuoso*, remarkable for his "scientific" vagaries.

Gines de Passamonte (hē'näs dä pä.sä.mōn'tä). In Cervantes's *Don Quixote*, a galley slave who was freed with others by that knight. The freed slaves set upon Don Quixote and despoiled him, and broke Mambrino's helmet.

Ginevra (gē.nev'ra). A poem by Samuel Rogers, named from its heroine. She is an Italian bride who hides herself, for a jest, in an old chest which has a springlock. It closes tightly, and her body is not found for many years. The story is told as connected with several old houses in England. T. Haynes Bayly's ballad *The Mistletoe Bough* embodies the same story.

Ginnungagap (gin'nöng.ä.gäp). In the Old Norse cosmogony, chaos; the "gaping abyss" between Niflheim and Muspellheim. Icy winds from Niflheim, the realm of cold and fog in the north, came into contact with sparks from Muspellheim, the realm of fire in the south, and through the working of heat and cold there arose in Ginnungagap a mass of hoarfrost, which received life and from which arose the giant Ymir. His dead body, afterward hurled by Odin and his brothers Vili and Ve (Old Norse *Vē*), back into the abyss, became the world.

Gioconda (jō.kōn'dä), **La.** See **Mona Lisa.**

Giotto (jôt'tō). [Full name, **Giotto di Bondone** (dē bōn.dō'nä).] b. at Vespignano, near Florence, 1276 (or c1266); d. at Florence, Jan. 8, 1337. An Italian painter, architect, and sculptor, generally considered the leader of the early Renaissance in Italy. He was the son of a peasant. He became the pupil of Cimabue, and was the head at Florence of a celebrated school of painters. In 1334 Giotto was appointed chief master of the works on the *Duomo* (cathedral) at Florence, the city fortifications, and all public architectural undertakings. He designed the façade of the Duomo, which was not finished, and furnished part or all of the design for the famous Campanile. The works usually ascribed to him include 28 frescoes in the aisle of the upper church of San Francesco at Assisi, under those by Cimabue; the frescoes on the ceilings of the lower church of San Francesco at Assisi, and an altarpiece (according to Vasari the most completely executed of all his works); 38 frescoes in the Capella dell'Arena at Padua; the frescoes of four chapels in the Church of Santa Croce, two of which have been destroyed; a very small number of genuine panel pictures in Saint Peter's, in Santa Croce, in the Academy at Florence, in the Louvre, at Munich, and in the Berlin Museum; a *Madonna with Angels* (Academy, Florence); *Two Apostles* (National Gallery, London); and *Saint Francis Receiving the Stigmata* (in the Louvre). In the frescoes of the Bargello at Florence, are the well-known portraits of Dante.

Giovanna of Naples (jō.vän'nä; nä'plz). See under **Andrea of Hungary.**

Giovanni (jō.vän'nē). In John Ford's *'Tis Pity She's A Whore*, the brother of Annabella, and her partner in the incestuous love affair which is a chief motivating factor in the drama.

Gipsies (jip'siz). See **Gypsies.**

Gipsy's Warning, The. An opera by Sir Julius Benedict, with text by Linley and Peake. It was produced at the Drury Lane Theatre, London, on April 19, 1838.

Giralda (hē.räl'dä). The bell tower of the cathedral at Seville, Spain: so called from the figure of Faith which forms the weather vane upon its summit. To the height of 250 ft. the tower is Moorish, with rich windows and surface decoration; the ornate belfry, 100 ft. high, in recessed stages above this, was built in 1568. The tower is 50 ft. square at the base. The tower of the old Madison Square Garden at New York was, in general, a copy of it.

Giraldi (jē.räl'dē), **Giovanni Battista.** [Called **Cynthius, Cinthio,** or **Cintio.**] b. at Ferrara, Italy, in November, 1504; d. there, Dec. 30, 1573. An Italian novelist and tragic poet, professor (1525) of medicine and philosophy and later (1537) of belles-lettres at the University of Ferrara. For several years after 1560 he taught at Mondovì. He published *Orbecche*, a tragedy (1541), *Gli Hecatommithi* (A Hundred Tales, 1565), and others. Two of

Shakespeare's plays (*Othello* and *Measure for Measure*), as well as a number of Beaumont and Fletcher's, are indebted to him for their plots.

Giraldus Cambrensis (ji.ral'dis kam.bren'sis). [Also **Giraldus** (or **Gerald**) **de Barri** (or **de Barry**).] b. near Pembroke, Wales, probably in 1146; d. probably in 1220. A British historian and ecclesiastic. He was appointed chaplain to Henry II in 1184, and accompanied Prince John in his expedition to Ireland. In 1198 he was elected bishop of St. David's, but failed to receive the papal confirmation. His chief work is *Itinerarium Cambriae* (Itinerary of Wales), which he wrote after traveling through Wales. He also wrote *Topographia Hibernica* (Topography of Ireland) and *Expugnatio Hibernica* (Conquest of Ireland), accounts of the geography and history of Ireland, and another work on Wales (*Description of Wales*). The best edition of his works is that by Brewer and Dimock in the Rolls Series (1861–77).

Giraudoux (zhē.rō.dö), **Jean.** [Full name, **Hippolyte Jean Giraudoux.**] b. at Bellac, France, Oct. 29, 1882; d. 1944. A French novelist and dramatist. He was the author of two books about World War I, *Lectures pour une ombre* (1918) and *Adorable Clio* (1920); of a travel book, *Amica America* (1919); several novels, including *Suzanne et le Pacifique* (1920; Eng. trans., 1923) and *Juliette aux pays des hommes* (1924); and of plays, such as *Siegfried* (1928; Eng. trans., 1930), *Amphitryon 38* (1929; Eng. trans., 1938), *La Guerre de Troie n'aura pas lieu* (1935), *Electre* (1937), and *La Folle de Chaillot* (1946; Eng. trans., *The Mad Woman of Chaillot*, 1949). His plays, with the exception of the last, are fantasies based on the Greek myths and laden with implications for the present.

Girling (gèr'ling), **Zoë.** [Married name, Mrs. **Aleksandre Piotr Zajdler;** pseudonym, **Martin Hare.**] b. in County Cork, Ireland, c1907—. An Irish writer and journalist, author of *Describe A Circle* (1933), *The Enchanted Winter* (1933; English title, *Butler's Gift*), *If This Be Error* (1934), *Mirror for Skylarks* (1935; English title, *Irene*), *Diary of a Pensionnaire* (1935), *English Rue* (1938), and *Polonaise* (1940).

Girondists (ji.ron'dists). [French, **Girondins** (zhē-rôṅ.daṅ).] An important political party during the French Revolution. The original leaders of the party came from the Gironde department of France. From Jacques Pierre Brissot, one of their leaders, they were sometimes called Brissotins. They were moderate republicans, were the ruling party in 1792, and were overthrown by their opponents in the Convention, the Montagnards (the Mountain), in 1793; many of their chiefs were executed during the night of Oct. 30–31 of that year, including Brissot, Gensonné, Vergniaud, Ducos, and Sillery. Other executions followed both at Paris and in the provinces.

Girton College (gèr'ton). A college for women at Cambridge, England, but not formally connected with the University of Cambridge. It was founded at a small house at Hitchin, on Oct. 16, 1869, by Emily Davies, Barbara (Smith) Bodichon, and a few others, some men among them, who favored higher education for women. It moved to Cambridge in 1873, and derives its name from that of a small village just outside of Cambridge. It has, in addition to classrooms, laboratories and libraries, a dining hall, a chapel, and a hospital, as well as orchards, gardens, and courts for tennis, hockey, lacrosse, and similar activities. It is staffed entirely by women.

Gismond of Salerne in Love (jiz'mond; sạ.lėrn'). [Later title, **The Tragedy of Tancred and Gismund.**] A tragedy written in rhyme by five members of the Inner Temple. It was acted there (1567–68) and later recast in blank verse by Robert Wilmot, Sir Christopher Hatton (who wrote the fourth act), and others, who published it under the title of *The Tragedy of Tancred and Gismund* in 1591. It is based on Boccaccio and is remarkable as the oldest English play extant with a plot known to be taken from an Italian novel.

Gissing (gis'ing), **George.** [Full name, **George Robert Gissing.**] b. at Wakefield, Yorkshire, England, Nov. 22, 1857; d. at St.-Jean-Pied-de-Port, France, Dec. 28, 1903. An English critic, essayist, and novelist. He was educated at a Quaker academy and at Owens College, Manchester, worked at Liverpool, then came to the U. S. to settle (working chiefly at Boston and Chicago), but soon returned to England (autumn of 1877). His distinction as a critic is best evidenced by his *Charles Dickens, A Critical Study* (1898); his charm and thoughtfulness as an essayist from *The Private Papers of Henry Ryecroft* (1903); and his achievement as a novelist from *Thyrza* (1887), *New Grub Street* (1891), and *Born in Exile* (1892). His first master was Dickens, but his novels broke new ground in English fiction in their naturalistic treatment of lower middle-class poverty and its brutalizing effects. Some of his other novels are *Workers in the Dawn* (1880), *The Unclassed* (1884), *Isabel Clarendon* (1886), *Demos* (1886), *A Life's Morning* (1888), *The Nether World* (1889), *The Emancipated* (1890), *The Odd Women* (1893), *In the Year of Jubilee* (1894), *The Whirlpool* (1897), which may almost be called an English *Madame Bovary*, *Our Friend the Charlatan* (1901), and *Will Warburton* (1905). *Veranilda* (1904), his historical romance of the time of the collapse of the Roman Empire, was almost completed when he died.

Giuseppe Caponsacchi (jö.zep'ē käp.ọn.säk'ē). See **Caponsacchi, Giuseppe.**

Give Me My Sin Again. American title of **Summer Holiday, or Gibraltar.**

Gjallarhorn yäl'lär.hôrn). [Also, **Gjallar.**] In Old Norse mythology, the horn of Heimdal. He blows it to warn the gods when anyone approaches the bridge Bifröst, and will blow it to announce Ragnarok, the final battle of the gods.

Gladsheim (gläds'hīm). [Also: **Glathsheim;** Eng. trans., "*Home of Gladness.*"] In Old Norse mythology, one of the realms of Asgard; the home of Odin and the 12 chief gods. It contains Valhalla, the assembling place of the gods and heroes.

Gladstone (glad'ston, -stŏn), **John Hall.** b. at London, March 7, 1827; d. there, Oct. 6, 1902. An English chemist and champion of spelling reform, professor of chemistry (1874–77) at the Royal Institute. He published the *Life of Michael Faraday* (1872), *Spelling Reform from an Educational Point*

---

fat, fāte, fär, ȧsk, fāre; net, mē, hėr; pin, pīne; not, nōte, mȯve, nôr; up, lūte, pŭll; ᵺн, then;

of View (1878), and numerous technical papers.

Gladstone, William Ewart. [Called the **"Grand Old Man."**] b. at Liverpool, England, Dec. 29, 1809; d. at Hawarden Castle, England, May 19, 1898. An English statesman, financier, and orator. Both his parents were natives of Scotland, his father, Sir John Gladstone, Bart., a Liverpool merchant, being descended from an old Scottish family named Gledstanes (i.e., "hawkstones"). He was educated at Eton and at Christ Church, Oxford, graduating in 1831 with highest honors both in classics and mathematics (a double first-class). He was returned to Parliament in 1832, in the first election after the passing of the Reform Bill, as Tory member for Newark, a pocket borough of the Duke of Newcastle. His exceptional political abilities were at once recognized by his party, and in the short-lived administration of Sir Robert Peel (December, 1834–April, 1835) he was made first a junior lord of the treasury, and then undersecretary for the colonies. On the return of Peel to office in September, 1841, he was appointed vice-president of the Board of Trade, and had the principal share in working out and expounding the elaborate scheme of tariff revision that was then adopted. In June, 1843, he became president of the Board of Trade, with a seat in the cabinet. In January, 1845, he left the ministry on account of the proposed grant to the Roman Catholic College of Maynooth; he felt that he could not support this officially because it was at variance with opinions he had published, although he now could and subsequently did support it as a private member. The Peel ministry was reorganized in December, 1845, and he was secretary of state for the colonies till the ministry's fall in June, 1846. Six and a half years then elapsed before he again held office, and during that period (especially in the earlier years of it) he was gradually borne along, in spite of his native Conservative instincts, toward that political Liberalism of which he was to become the most conspicuous exponent. In December, 1852, a coalition ministry of Whigs and Peelites was formed under the Earl of Aberdeen, Gladstone taking what appears to have been his strongest role, that of chancellor of the exchequer. He held the same office at first in the Liberal ministry of Lord Palmerston, formed in February, 1855, but retired with the other Peelites in a few weeks. During the years 1858–59 he was sent by the Conservative ministry on a special mission as lord high commissioner extraordinary to the Ionian Islands. From June, 1859, to July, 1866, he was again chancellor of the exchequer under Lord Palmerston and Earl Russell, and after Palmerston's death he was leader of the House of Commons. The defeat of a reform bill which he introduced brought the Tories back to power, themselves to pass an important reform measure. On Dec. 9, 1868, he became prime minister. This distinguished position he occupied no less than four times: December, 1868, to February, 1874; April, 1880, to June, 1885; February to July, 1886; and August, 1892, to March, 1894, when the "Grand Old Man" retired from office on account of his advanced age and failing physical powers. Besides being prime minister and first lord of the treasury, he was also chancellor of the exchequer during his first administration and part of his sec-

ond, and lord privy seal during his third and fourth. The history of his various ministries is the history of the British Empire for the time. One of the first measures which he carried as premier was the disestablishment of the Irish Church, and the condition of Ireland was throughout his leadership of a quarter of a century in office or in opposition the object of his peculiar concern. He prepared and introduced (1886 and 1893) two bills for providing that country with a separate legislature, but both Home Rule bills were defeated. With the exception of about a year and a half, he sat continuously in the House of Commons from 1832 to 1895. He retired as member from Newark in January, 1846, because his views had diverged from those of its patron, and subsequently represented the University of Oxford (1847–65), South Lancashire (1865–68), Greenwich (1868–80), and Midlothian, or Edinburghshire (1880–94). He is understood to have been offered a peerage on more than one occasion, but declined that honor, remaining "the Great Commoner." Although the most prominent man in the politics of his time, his preëminence being rivaled only by his perennial Tory opponent, Benjamin Disraeli, he found leisure for considerable contributions to literature. His publications include *The State in its Relations to the Church* (1838), *Letters on the State Persecutions of the Neapolitan Government* (1851), *Studies on Homer and the Homeric Age* (1858), *Juventus Mundi* (1869), pamphlets on *The Vatican Decrees* (1874, 1875) and *Bulgarian Horrors* (1876, 1877), *Homeric Synchronism* (1876), and *Gleanings of Past Years* (1879), besides various articles in magazines and reviews. Two significant biographies of Gladstone are *William Ewart Gladstone* (3 vols., 1903), by John Morley, and *Gladstone* (1954), by Sir Philip Magnus.

Glamis (in Scottish use, glämz; in Shakespeare, glä′mis), **Thane of.** In Shakespeare's *Macbeth*, the title that Macbeth holds at the beginning of the play. The Witches show their recognition of him by hailing him "Thane of Glamis." There is in S Scotland an actual village of Glamis (or Glammis), with a castle associated by tradition with Macbeth.

Glansdale (glanz′dāl, -dḁl), **Sir William.** In Shakespeare's *1 Henry VI*, an English officer.

Glanvill (glan′vil), **Joseph.** b. at Plymouth, England, 1636; d. at Bath, England, in November, 1680. An English divine. He was a voluminous author. His best-known work is *The Vanity of Dogmatizing* (1661; enlarged, as *Scepsis scientifica*, 1665). In this he is thought to have anticipated the electric telegraph and Hume's theory of causation.

Glanville (glan′vil), **Ranulf de.** d. 1190. A chief justiciar of England. He was sheriff of Yorkshire (1163–70), became sheriff of Lancashire in 1173, with Robert Stuteville defeated the Scots at Alnwick on July 13, 1174, and was one of the most important persons in the kingdom during the remainder of the reign of Henry II. He is credited with the authorship of a historical prose work in Latin, *De Legibus et Consuetudinibus Regni Angliae.*

Glapthorne (glap′thôrn), **Henry.** Known to have written between 1635 and 1642. An English dramatist. Among his plays are *Argalus and Parthenia*, *Albertus Wallenstein*, and *The Ladies Privilege*. *The Paraside, or Revenge for Honer* was licensed in 1653 as by Glapthorne. It was printed later with Chapman's name; the latter had nothing to do with it, but it may have been revised by Glapthorne.

Glasgerion (glas.jir'i.ọn). An English ballad, included in Percy's *Reliques*, telling of the love of a prince for the daughter of the King of Normandy. The prince's page impersonates his master and compromises the honor of the princess, who kills herself. The prince then cuts off the page's head and dies by his own hand.

Glasse (glås), **Hannah.** fl. 1747. The English author of a popular book called *The Art of Cookery*. It was published in 1747, and at one time its authorship was attributed to Dr. John Hill. Mrs. Glasse wrote other books on similar subjects. The ironical proverb "First catch your hare," attributed to her, is not in *The Art of Cookery*, but was probably suggested by the words "Take your hare when it is cased," i.e., skinned.

Glastonbury (glas'tọn.ber.i). A municipal borough in SW England, in C Somersetshire, ab. 21 mi. S of Bristol, ab. 133 mi. SW of London by rail. Its abbey, founded in Roman times, was refounded in the 9th century. The great early Gothic church, of which the picturesque ruins exist, was begun by Henry II and desecrated by Henry VIII. Glastonbury is associated in Arthurian legend with Joseph of Arimathea, who is said to have visited it and, in sign of possession, planted his staff, which took root and became the famous Glastonbury thorn that bursts into bloom on Christmas Eve. Local legend has it that both Arthur and Guinevere are buried at Glastonbury.

Glatisant (glat'i.zạnt). In Malory's *Morte d'Arthur*, the "questing beast" whom the Saracen knight Palamedes seeks to slay.

Glauce (glô'sē). See **Creusa.**

Glaucus (glô'kus). fl. c6th century B.C. A Greek sculptor in metals, living at Chios but belonging to the Samian school of art. He is said to have been the inventor of the art of soldering metals.

Glaucus. In Greek mythology, the steersman of the ship *Argo*, afterward transformed into a sea divinity. He loved the sea nymph Scylla, who was changed into a monster by Circe, who also loved Glaucus.

Glaucus. In Greek legend, a charioteer; the son of Sisyphus and father of Bellerophon. He was torn to pieces by his own horses.

Glaucus. In Greek legend, a son of Minos and Pasiphaë. He was smothered in a jar of honey.

Glaucus. In Greek legend, a Lycian prince, ally of Priam in the Trojan War. The story of his exchange of his golden armor for the brass armor of his friend Diomedes is proverbial for getting the worst of a bargain.

Glaucus. The hero of Bulwer-Lytton's *Last Days of Pompeii*, an aristocrat who struggles against his love for the blind flower-girl, Nydia.

gleeman (glē'mạn). See **scop.**

Glegg (gleg), **Mrs.** [Also, **Aunt Glegg.**] In George Eliot's novel *The Mill on the Floss*, a precise, narrow-minded woman, the aunt of Maggie Tulliver. See also under **Dodson.**

Gleire (glär), **The.** A comedy (c1607) by Edward Sharpham.

Glenallan (glen.al'ạn), **Countess of.** The mother of the Earl of Glenallan in Sir Walter Scott's novel *The Antiquary*. She is a selfish, imperious, and cruel woman.

Glenallan, Earl of. In Sir Walter Scott's novel *The Antiquary*, the son of the Countess of Glenallan and father of Lovel.

Glenarvon (glen.är'vọn). A novel by Lady Caroline Lamb. Almost all the characters are portraits. Lord Glenarvon is Lord Byron.

Glencoe or **Glen Coe** (glen.kō'). A deep valley in W Scotland, in Argyllshire, ab. 25 mi. NE of Oban. It is the valley of the river Coe, and was the scene of the "massacre of Glencoe" (February, 1692), in which some 40 Macdonalds were killed by royal troops at the instigation of the Master of Stair.

Glendinning (glen.din'ing), **Edward.** In Sir Walter Scott's novels *The Monastery* and *The Abbot*, the younger of the Glendinning brothers. He is the abbot, Father Ambrose, for whom the second novel is named.

Glendinning, Halbert. In Sir Walter Scott's novel *The Monastery*, the elder of the Glendinning brothers; the Knight of Avenel in *The Abbot*.

Glendower (glen'dȯr, glen'dou''ẽr), **Owen.** [Welsh, **Owain ab Gruffydd.**] b. in Wales, probably in 1359; d. probably in 1415. A Welsh rebel, lord of Glyndyvrdwy or Glyndwr. He proclaimed himself Prince of Wales in 1402, and in 1403 joined the rising under Harry Percy (Hotspur), together with whom he was defeated at Shrewsbury on June 21, 1403. He subsequently allied himself with the French, but was defeated by Henry V (then Henry, Prince of Wales), in 1405. Shakespeare introduces him in *1 Henry IV.*

Glendower, Owen. In Shakespeare's *1 Henry IV*, a Welsh ally of the Percys. His claim to supernatural powers antagonizes Hotspur and the two men exchange heated words (III.i.). Glendower is not present at the battle of Shrewsbury.

Glenlivet or **Glenlivat** (glen.liv'ẹt). A valley in C Scotland, in Banffshire, ab. 23 mi. S of Elgin. It is the valley of Livet Water. Here, in 1594, the Catholic insurgents under the Earl of Huntly, defeated the Protestants under the Earl of Argyll.

Glenvarloch (glen.vär'lọch), **Lord.** See **Olifaunt, Nigel.**

Glister (glis'tẽr). In Thomas Middleton's play *The Family of Love*, a doctor of physic.

Globe, the. A celebrated London theater, built by Richard and Cuthbert Burbage, William Shakespeare, John Heming, Augustine Phillipps, Thomas Pope, and Will Kempe in 1599. When The Theatre in Shoreditch was taken down, the materials were carried to Bankside and used in the erection of the Globe. The Globe was octagonal in shape and open to the sky in the middle, the state and galleries only being originally covered with a thatched roof, and later, when rebuilt after the fire of 1613, with a tile roof. The interior was arranged on the plan of the innyards where entertainments had formerly been given. It had three galleries. It served as a model for the Fortune, built in 1600, although that theater was square. The Globe was a public theater. Shakespeare may occasionally have played here, and he with Heming, Condell, and others shared in the profits. As the result of a misfiring of a small cannon during the pageantry of *Henry VIII*, the Globe was burned down in 1613, but it was rebuilt in the following year, at a cost of 1,400 pounds. It was pulled down during the Puritan regime in 1644. Shakespeare wrote his plays for the Blackfriars and Globe theaters.

"Gloomy Dean," the. See **Inge, William Ralph.**

Gloria in Excelsis Deo (glō'ri.ạ in ek.sel'sis dā'ō). A doxology, or Christian hymn of praise (from the Greek *doxologia*, "a praising"). It is called the Angelic Hymn, or the Greater Doxology, in order to distinguish it from the Lesser Doxology (*Gloria Patri*). It is used in the Roman Catholic Church and the Church of England. Like the Lesser Doxology it goes back to the 4th century. It begins "Gloria in excelsis Deo, et in terra pax hominibus bonae voluntatis" (Glory be to God in the highest, and on earth peace to men of good will). Its basis is Luke, ii. 14.

Gloriana (glō.ri.an'ạ). The "Faerie Queene" in Spenser's poem of that name. She typifies glory and also represents Queen Elizabeth in her royal aspect.

Glorious Apollo (ạ.pol'ō). A historical novel by Lily Adams Beck under the pseudonym E. Barrington, published in 1925. It deals with political and romantic phases in the life of Byron, and closes with his death in Greece.

Glorvina O'Dowd (glôr.vī'nạ ọ.doud'). See **O'Dowd, Glorvina.**

Glossin (glos'in), **Gilbert.** In Sir Walter Scott's novel *Guy Mannering*, a wicked, scheming lawyer.

Gloster (glos'tèr), **Earl of.** See **Gloucester, Earl of.**

Gloucester (glos'tèr), **Duke of.** A title of **Humphrey** (1391–1447).

Gloucester, Duchess of. In Shakespeare's *Richard II*, the historical Eleanor de Bohun, widow of Thomas of Woodstock, Duke of Gloucester, whose murder (by Mowbray at the command of Richard II) she recalls to Gaunt with a demand for vengeance.

Gloucester, Earl of. [Also, **Gloster.**] In Shakespeare's *King Lear*, the father of Edgar and Edmund. His story is taken from that of the Prince of Paphlagonia in Sidney's *Arcadia*. His desertion by his son, Edmund, and his willful cruelty to another son, Edgar, correspond on a lower plane to Lear's desertion by his daughters and his harshness to Cordelia. Like Lear, he realizes the burden of life ("As flies to wanton boys are we to the gods"), mutely accepting his fate as they wander in the storm and briefly echoing Lear's words. When his son is restored to him, he dies of joy and grief.

Gloucester, Eleanor, Duchess of. In Shakespeare's *2 Henry VI*, the historical Eleanor Cobham, wife of Humphrey of Gloucester, who, desiring to be Queen, engages in sorcery and is betrayed by

Richard, Duke of York. She is banished, after doing penance by walking three days about the streets with a taper in her hand. Meeting Gloucester in the street, she chides him for permitting her shame and warns him against Suffolk, York, and Cardinal Beaufort.

Gloucester, Humphrey of. In Shakespeare's *2 Henry IV* and *Henry V*, the youngest son of Henry IV, who plays a minor part as Prince Humphrey of Gloucester and the Duke of Gloucester. In *1 Henry VI*, he is the King's uncle and quarrels with Henry Beaufort, Bishop of Winchester, because he suspects the Beaufort family of seeking to rule England. As the faithful protector of the King and a patiently suffering man, he is seen in Shakespeare's *2 Henry VI*, where he is deprived of the Protectorship by the influence of various enemies banded together. Later he is falsely arrested on the charge of torturing prisoners and purloining army payrolls and is executed.

Gloucester, Richard, Duke of. In Shakespeare's *2 and 3 Henry VI* and *Richard III*, the fourth son of Richard Plantagenet, Duke of York, and later Richard III. In *3 Henry VI*, Margaret refers to him as "that valiant crookback prodigy—that with his grumbling voice was wont to cheer his dad in mutinies," and he himself has already looked beyond those who are in succession to the throne to the throne itself, which he will get by hewing his way with a bloody axe. After the battle of Tewkesbury he kills the Prince of Wales, murders Henry VI in the Tower, and goes on in *Richard III* to execute all those who stand between him and the throne. Even when he realizes his wickedness Richard plays the sophist, inverting the harsh terms by which his conscience judges him to serve his own will, just as he has done when the chorus of women dwelt on his perfidy (IV.iv). Palmer considers Richard a gay villain, whose frank admission of hypocrisy and verbal skill illustrate the cynical politician at his finest. Van Doren compares him to a serpent winding its way along a gray wall of voices, the voices of the women who come like avenging furies throughout the play. Richard's villainy is imaginative, and may seem unreal in its intensity, yet he is an astonishing poet whose thoughts almost deliberately affront all conventions. There may be repentance when the ghosts come, but Richard is still ready to dare Richmond.

Glove, The. An old French story told by Ronsard and retold in many forms by Schiller, Leigh Hunt, Browning, and others.

Glover (gluv'èr), **Catherine.** The "fair maid of Perth" in Sir Walter Scott's novel of that name. She is the daughter of Simon Glover.

Glover, Richard. b. at London, 1712; d. there, Nov. 25, 1785. An English poet and amateur Greek scholar, chiefly remembered for his popular ballad, *Admiral Hosier's Ghost* (1739). He was the son of a Hamburg merchant, and entered into business with his father. His most ambitious work, an epic poem, *Leonidas*, appeared in 1737. He enlarged it and republished it in 1770, and it was translated into French and German. Its success was partly due to its usefulness to the opponents of Walpole. He also published the epic poem *London* (1739) and two tragedies: *Boadicea* (1753) and *Medea* (1761). After his death, a third tragedy, *Jason* (1799), and another epic, *The Athenaid* (1787, in 30 books) were published.

Glover, Simon. The father of the heroine in Sir Walter Scott's novel *The Fair Maid of Perth.*

Glub-dub-drib (glub'dub''drib'). A land filled with magicians, visited by Gulliver, in Swift's *Gulliver's Travels.*

Gluck (glŭk), **Christoph Willibald.** b. at Weidenwang, near Neumarkt, Bavaria, July 2, 1714; d. at Vienna, Nov. 15, 1787. A German composer. He studied music at Prague, Vienna (1736), and Milan (1738–45), producing (1741–45) a number of successful operas. In 1745 he went to England as composer of operas for the Haymarket Theatre, returning to Vienna in 1746, where he acted for a time as singing master to Marie Antoinette, who later rendered him important aid in the production of his works at Paris. He introduced important changes in the art of the opera. His most celebrated works are *Orfeo ed Euridice* (1762), *Alceste* (Vienna, Dec. 16, 1767), *Paride ed Elene* (1769), *Iphigénie en Aulide* (1774), *Armide* (1777), and *Iphigénie en Tauride* (1779).

Glumdalca (glum.dal'kạ). In Henry Fielding's burlesque *Tom Thumb the Great*, a captive quᴗen of the giants, beloved by the King, but in love with Tom Thumb. She is intended as a satire on the exotic and highly dramatic royal ladies then popular in heroic drama.

Glumdalclitch (glum.dal'klich). In Swift's *Gulliver's Travels*, a giantess of Brobdingnag. She is Gulliver's nurse, and, though only nine years old, is nearly 40 feet high. Her attentions are extremely humiliating to him.

Glyn (glin), **Elinor.** [Maiden name, **Sutherland**.] b. on the island of Jersey, Channel Islands, c1864; d. at London, Sept. 23, 1943. An English novelist. She lived (1922–27) in the U. S., at Hollywood, writing scenarios, and at New York, writing syndicated newspaper articles and short stories for popular magazines. *Three Weeks* (1907), her best-known novel, was translated into all the European languages, was a best seller for years and a favorite with small stock companies, and was made into a motion picture starring Theda Bara. Among her works are *The Visits of Elizabeth* (1900), *Reflections of Ambrosine* (1902), *Vicissitudes of Evangeline* (1905), *Beyond the Rocks* (1906), *Elizabeth Visits America* (1909), *His Hour* (1910), *The Contrast and other Stories* (1913), *Three Things* (1915), *The Career of Katherine Brush* (1917), *Man and Maid* (1922), *Great Moment* (1923), *Six Days* (1924), *This Passion Called Love* (1926), *Love's Blindness* (1926), *It* (1927; made into a movie with Clara Bow as the "It" girl), *The Flirt and the Flapper* (1930), *Love's Hour* (1932), *Sooner or Later* (1933), *Did She?* (1934), and *The Third Eye* (1940). In 1936 she published her autobiography, *Romantic Adventure.*

gnomic verses (nō'mik). [Also, **gnomics**.] The aphorisms, maxims, or moral sayings in the form of verses or poems which formed a considerable portion of both popular and classical literature in the Old English period, though they are now valued chiefly for the light they throw on the customs and beliefs of the time. Best known are three long gnomic poems (over 200 lines) in the *Exeter Book;* passages of the same nature are also to be found in *Beowulf*, among others.

Gnostics (nos'tiks). Certain rationalistic sects which arose in the Christian church in the 1st century A.D., flourished in the 2nd, and had almost entirely disappeared by the 6th. The Gnostics held that knowledge rather than faith is the road to heaven, and professed to have a peculiar knowledge of religious mysteries. They rejected the literal interpretation of the Scriptures, and attempted to combine their teachings with those of the Greek and Oriental philosophies and religions. They held that God was the unknowable and the unapproachable; that from him proceeded, by emanation, subordinate deities termed *eons*, from whom again proceeded other still inferior spirits. The Gnostics were in general agreed in believing in the principles of dualism (the existence of principles of good and of evil) and Docetism (the existence of Christ as celestial emanation only) and in the existence of a demiurge or world-creator. Christ they regarded as a superior eon who had descended from the infinite God in order to subdue the god or eon of this world. Their chief seats were in Syria and Egypt, but their doctrines were taught everywhere, and at an early date they separated into a variety of sects.

Gnotho (nō'thō). A clownish old fellow anxious to put away his old wife and take a younger one, according to the provisions of *The Old Law*, in Philip Massinger, Thomas Middleton, and William Rowley's play of that name.

Gobble (gob'l), **Justice.** An insolent magistrate in Tobias Smollett's novel *Sir Launcelot Greaves*, a satirical romance.

Gobbo (gob'ō), **Launcelot.** In Shakespeare's *Merchant of Venice*, a whimsical, conceited servant. In an involved bit of rationalization (II.ii), he persuades himself that to stay with Shylock, as his conscience bids him, would be to serve the devil; and to run away, as the fiend, who is the devil, bids him, is to obey more friendly counsel. He leaves Shylock and helps Lorenzo escape with Jessica. He is one of Shakespeare's best clowns.

Gobbo, Old. In Shakespeare's *Merchant of Venice*, the "sand-blind" father of Launcelot Gobbo. Appearing in Act II, Scene 2 with a present for Shylock, he is persuaded by Launcelot to give it to Bassanio, thus aiding Launcelot to enter Bassanio's service.

Gobelins (gob.lan; Anglicized, gob'e.linz). A family of dyers, descended from Jean Gobelin (d. 1476), and established at Paris. They introduced the manufacture of tapestries in the 15th century. Their factory was changed to a royal establishment under Louis XIV, c1667.

Goblin Market. A poem (1862) by Christina Rossetti. It tells the story of Laura, who is tempted by goblins and nearly dies, and of her sister Lizzy, who refuses to be tempted and is thus able to save Laura.

Goblins, The. A comedy by Sir John Suckling, staged in 1638 and printed in 1646. The Goblins are noblemen and gentlemen disguised as a band of robbers.

fat, fāte, fär, ȧsk, fâre; net, mē, hėr; pin, pīne; not, nōte, mŏve, nôr; up, lūte, pu̇ll; ᴛʜ, then;

Godden (god'ẹn), **Rumer.** [Pseudonym of Mrs. Laurence Foster.] b. Dec. 10, 1907—. An English novelist. Her books include *Chinese Puzzle* (1935), *Black Narcissus* (1939), *Gypsy, Gypsy* (1940), *Breakfast with the Nikolides* (1941), *Take Three Tenses—A Fugue in Time* (1945), *Thus Far and No Further* (1946), *A Candle for St. Jude* (1948), *A Breath of Air* (1951), and *Kingfishers Catch Fire* (1953). *In Noah's Ark* (1949) is an allegory in verse. She collaborated with Jean Renoir in writing *The River* (1951), a motion picture filmed in India.

Godeffroy of Boloyne (god'fri; bọ.loin'). A prose translation by Caxton, printed in 1481, which tells the story of the siege of Jerusalem in the first Crusade.

Godeman (gōd'man). fl. 10th century. Chaplain of the bishop of Winchester when abbot of Thornby (963–984). He illuminated the *Benedictionel of Godeman*, now the property of the Duke of Devonshire. In the Bibliothèque at Rouen is a manuscript apparently by his hand.

Godfrey Bertram (god'fri bèr'tram). See **Bertram, Godfrey.**

Godfrey of Bouillon (bö.yôñ'). [French, **Godefroy de Bouillon.**] b. at Baisy, in Brabant, c1061; d. at Jerusalem, July 18, 1100. Leader of the first Crusade. He was made duke of Lower Lorraine (having Bouillon for its capital) by Henry IV of Germany in 1088, and in 1096 joined the Crusade for the recovery of the Holy Sepulcher. He fought with distinction at the storming of Jerusalem (July 15, 1099), and, after the crown had been declined by Raymond IV, Count of Toulouse, was elected king of Jerusalem, on July 22, 1099. He exchanged the title of king, however, for that of Protector of the Holy Sepulcher. He completed the conquest of the Holy Land by defeating the sultan of Egypt on the plain of Ascalon, Aug. 12, 1099. In later legend, reflected in the chansons de geste, Godfrey became a great hero, the principal leader of the Crusades, the wise and noble king, though actually his choice as king was dictated by his adherence to no particular party in the complex political struggle going on in Palestine, and until his choice as king he was simply a competent soldier. He is connected in legend with the story of the Swan Knight, and appears in Sir Walter Scott's novel *Count Robert of Paris.*

Godiva (gọ.dī'vạ) or **Godgifu** (gôd'yi.vö). [Also, Lady **Godiva.**] fl. middle of 11th century. The wife of Leofric, earl of Mercia, celebrated in the annals of Coventry, Warwickshire, England. She was a woman of great beauty and piety, the benefactress of numerous churches and monasteries. According to the legend, she begged her husband to relieve Coventry of its burdensome taxes, and he consented on the condition that she ride naked through the marketplace. This she did, covered only by her hair, and won relief for the people. In some versions of the story, the people were commanded to keep within their houses, and not look upon her. One fellow ("Peeping Tom") disobeyed, and was miraculously struck with blindness. Her festival is still occasionally celebrated at Coventry.

Godley (god'li), **Alfred Denis.** b. at Ashfield, County Cavan, Ireland, Jan. 22, 1856; d. at Oxford, England, June 27, 1925. An English poet, classical scholar, editor, and teacher. He was educated at Harrow and at Balliol College, Oxford, winning many prizes for excellence in Greek and Latin, and served as assistant classical master (1879–83) at Bradfield College, a boys' school, and tutor and fellow (1883–1912) at Magdalen College, Oxford. From 1910 until his death he was public orator for the university. He translated Herodotus, Tacitus, and Horace, and was editor (1910–20) of the *Classical Review.* Author of *Verses to Order* (1892), *Lyra Frivola* (1899), *The Casual Ward* (1912), *Reliquiae* (1926), and *Fifty Poems* (1927); *Aspects of Modern Oxford* (1894), *Socrates and Athenian Society in His Age* (1896), and *Oxford in the 18th Century* (1908). He edited (1909) the poetical works of Winthrop Mackworth Praed and in 1910 the poetry of Thomas Moore.

Godly Queen Hester (hes'tèr). An interlude written (c1561) by an unknown author, and based on the Biblical story of Queen Esther.

Godmer (god'mèr). In Spenser's *Faerie Queene,* the son of the giant Albion.

God of Clay, The. A historical novel by Henry Christopher Bailey, published in 1908.

Gods and Mr. Perrin (per'in), **The.** A novel (1911) by Hugh Walpole, showing the effect of a school atmosphere upon the masters. Published in England as *Mr. Perrin and Mr. Traill.*

God Save the King (or **Queen**). The English national anthem, which had its first recorded performance as "God Save the King" (in direct reference to George II who was then being challenged by the Young Pretender) at the Drury Lane, on September 28, 1745. The words and tune had been found by T. A. Arne in the collection *Thesaurus Musicus* (1744), and the manuscript copy, with some slight changes by Arne, is now in the British Museum. The tune was adopted in France in 1776, and was afterward used as the Danish, Prussian, and German national airs, as well as inspiring some 15 other European countries to use the tune and provide their own words. Beethoven introduced it in his *Battle Symphony,* Weber used it in three or four compositions, Brahms, Liszt, Paganini, and Gounod also further developed the theme in their own compositions. The American hymn *My Country 'tis of Thee,* written by Samuel Francis Smith and published in 1843, is set to the same music.

Gods of the Mountain, The. A romantic drama (1911) by Lord Dunsany.

Gods of War. A book of poems by George William Russell (Æ), published in 1915.

Godwin (god'win), **Francis.** b. at Hannington, Northamptonshire, England, 1561; d. 1633. An English bishop and author. He was appointed bishop of Llandaff in 1601, and was translated to the see of Hereford in 1617. His chief work is *A Catalogue of the Bishops of England* (1601).

Godwin, Mary. [Maiden name, **Wollstonecraft.**] b. at London, April 27, 1759; d. there, Sept. 10, 1797. An English author. She was employed by Samuel Johnson as a reader and translator, and for five years in this way assisted her parents, who were very poor. In 1791 she first met William Godwin, and after one or two other connections, especially

---

ḍ, d or j; ṣ, s or sh; ṭ, t or ch; ẓ, z or zh; o, F. cloche; ü, F. menu; ćh, Sc. loch; ṅ, F. bonbon.

with Gilbert Imlay, who deserted her after the birth of their daughter, Fanny Imlay, she went to live with Godwin in 1796. The expectation of a child induced them to marry in 1797. The birth of the child (a daughter, Mary, who became the second wife of the poet Shelley) proved fatal to her. Her chief work was *Vindication of the Rights of Woman* (1792).

Godwin, William. b. at Wisbeach, England, March 3, 1756; d. at London, April 7, 1836. An English political philosopher, novelist, biographer, historian, and miscellaneous writer. He was educated at a dissenting academy and began life as a dissenting minister, but after five years he turned to radical political and religious speculation under the influence of the philosophers of the French Revolution and their English disciples. The rest of his life was devoted primarily to writing. He became a notable figure in London among the radical thinkers during the decade following the French Revolution and the source of inspiration for many brilliant youths, among them Wordsworth, Coleridge, and Southey. But by the beginning of the 19th century he had attracted the special abhorrence of most political and religious leaders, who were caught in the backwash of thought that followed the degeneration of the Revolution into violence and Napoleonic tyranny. However, the years brought little fundamental change in his philosophy, to which he continued to give expression in a copious stream of novels and miscellaneous essays. In 1797 Godwin married Mary Wollstonecraft, the leading woman radical of her time and the pioneer vindicator of the rights of women. Mary Godwin, their daughter, became the second wife of the poet Shelley, who had been early attracted to Godwin's philosophic utopia, who based his first great revolutionary poem, *Queen Mab*, very largely on Godwin's ideas, and who never appreciably modified his adherence to Godwin's belief in the power of reason to regenerate the world and to perfect mankind. After his first wife's death, Godwin married (1801) Mary Jane Clairmont, a widow with two children. One of these children, Clara Mary Jane, became Byron's mistress. The marriage was not a happy one, and the new Mrs. Godwin was unkind to Godwin's daughter Mary and his step-daughter Fanny Imlay.

Written Works and Philosophy. The only one of his many books by which he is now remembered is *The Inquiry concerning Political Justice and its Influence on General Virtue and Happiness*, published in 1793. It is perhaps the greatest monument of strictly philosophic radicalism in English political literature. It became the principal medium through which French revolutionary ideas were brought into England. It is not, then, a treatment of political justice in the narrow sense. His two fundamental theses about the nature of man are that character is shaped by environment and that men are capable of directing all their voluntary actions by reason, if they are let alone by authority. The first involves the denial of the existence of innate principles and, therefore, the denial of any innate tendency to evil. The second involves the displacement of authority by reason in the pursuit of truth and the determination of conduct. With reason as the only guide to virtue, his uncompromising logic

led him to argue gravely against any special claims of affection, against gratitude to benefactors, against all corporal punishment, against private property rights, against marriage as an institution established by law, against pardon, against patriotism, and against all established religion. With the enthronement of reason in the individual through universal education, he looked forward to the simplification and eventual elimination of government without violence through the mental and moral competence of the average man. The best-known of his revolutionary novels is *The Adventures of Caleb Williams, or Things as they are* (1794). He also published, among other works, *St. Leon, a Tale of the Sixteenth Century* (1799); *Of Population* (1820), a reply to Malthus's essay; and the able *History of the Commonwealth* (1824–28).

Goëmot (gō'e̜.mot) or **Goëmagot** (gō'e̜.ma̜.got). See *Gogmagog*.

Goethe (ge̜'te̜), **Johann Wolfgang von.** b. at Frankfort on the Main, Germany, Aug. 28, 1749; d. at Weimar, Germany, March 22, 1832. A German poet, dramatist, novelist, philosopher, statesman, and scientist. He was the son of Johann Caspar Goethe (1710–82), imperial councilor, and Katharina Elizabeth Textor (1731–1808). His grandfather was Johann Wolfgang Textor, chief magistrate of Frankfort. He was taught at home by his father (from whom, he tells us, he caught his earnestness of purpose) and by tutors. He studied law at the University of Leipzig (which he entered in 1765), and at Strasbourg, where he had a love affair with Friderike Brion, and where he met Herder. Friderike inspired some of his most beautiful lyrics (*Kleine Blumen, kleine Blätter* and *Wie herrlich leuchtet mir die Natur!*), and Herder taught him to love and understand Gothic architecture, German folk songs, and Shakespeare. In 1771 he was licensed to practice law and in August of that year he returned to Frankfort, to begin what was to be a very short career in law. In 1772 he was, for some months, at Wetzlar, where the German imperial law courts were in session. Here he supplemented his academic knowledge of law by gaining practical experience which, at the time, he evidently intended to put to use. At the end of 1774 he met Karl August, the young hereditary prince of Weimar, who invited him to pay a visit to his court. When the invitation was repeated less than a year later, Goethe accepted it, and on Nov. 7, 1775, he arrived at Weimar, where he spent the rest of his life, except for periods of travel in the Harz Mountains (1777), Switzerland (1779), and Italy (Verona, Venice, Naples, Sicily, Rome; September, 1786–April, 1788). The Italian phase of his life had an importance for Goethe as man, thinker, and artist that is out of all proportion to its length, and made him see himself, as a literary creator, in a new light. In 1776 Karl August (who died in 1828) made him a privy councilor, entrusted him with the care and management of the most important affairs, and made him his minister of state. In 1791 he went with Karl August to Breslau, and he was with him in 1792 in the campaign against France when the Germans were defeated (September 20) at Valmy. This campaign and the one at Mainz (1793) produced as literary results *Campagne in Frankreich* and *Belagerung von Mainz*. From 1791 to 1813

---

fat, fāte, fär, ȧsk, fāre; net, mē, hėr; pin, pīne; not, nōte, möve, nôr; up, lūte, púll; ᴛʜ, then;

he was director of the ducal theater at Weimar. In 1794 he began his close friendship with Schiller, whom he had previously (1789) helped to obtain a history professorship at Jena, and he contributed to *Die Horen*, a periodical edited by Schiller, and with him wrote *Die Xenien* (1796), a collection of 600 satirical epigrams on current literary and philosophical movements. In 1797 he translated Cellini's *Autobiography*, and a year later he undertook the editorship of *Die Propylaen*, an art magazine. It is customary to divide Goethe's literary life into four periods: I. early youth to 1775, when he came to Weimar; II. 1775–94, residence at Weimar to meeting Schiller; III. 1794–1805, friendship and literary activity with Schiller, lasting until the latter's death; and IV. 1805–32, old age, last works, and death. He wrote in many fields including prose, poetry, drama, opera, satire, philosophy, criticism, and science. Some of his works are *Götz von Berlichingen* (1773), which ushered in the Romantic school and the Storm and Stress (*Sturm und Drang*) movement, *The Sorrows of Young Werther* (1774), *Egmont* (1778), a psychological tragedy, *Iphegenie in Tauris*, which he wrote in prose (1779) and in verse (1787), *Torquato Tasso* (1790), considered one of his best plays (also written in prose form in 1781), dealing with the poet in conflict with the world, *Reynard the Fox* (1793), a verse treatment of the medieval beast epic, *Wilhelm Meister's Apprenticeship* (1795–96), its sequel *Wilhelm Meister's Travels* (vol. 1, 1821; vol. 2, 1829), and *Hermann and Dorothea* (1797), which is regarded by many as the most perfect idyll in German literature. Other works are *The Caprices of the Lovers*, *The Accomplices*, poetic dramas, *Clavigo* and *Stella*, tragedies, *Erwin and Elmire* and *Claudine of Villa Bella*, operas, *Gods, Heroes, and Wieland* (1774), a satire, *Roman Elegies* (1795), published in *Die Horen*, and *Italian Journeys* (vol. 1, 1816; vol. 2, 1817; vol. 3, 1829). As a scientist, he wrote a *History of the Theory of Colors* (1805; revised 1810), a work on optics in which he disagreed with Newton, and *On Natural History*, a series of scientific essays (1817–24), discovered the rudimentary intermaxillary bone in man, and put forth theories of the common origin of all forms of animal life and of plant development that paved the way for Darwinism and evolution. *From My Life: Truth and Poetry* is his autobiography in four volumes (1, 1811; 2, 1812; 3, 1814; and 4, finished shortly before his death, published in 1833). *Faust* (part 1, 1808; part 2, 1832) is one of his great works, if indeed not his masterpiece. It has been translated into the principal languages of Europe, and into English many times. It has had such an influence on art and artists the world over and has been treated in such a variety of forms that one thinks of it, as one does of its author, in world terms rather than as a work written in the German language by a German writer. Love, or passion, of varying degrees of intensity and lasting for a longer or shorter period, played an important part in Goethe's life, both artistic and personal. Among those who were involved with him emotionally and who left some mark on his character are Gretchen (she is mentioned by no other name), the heroine of his first love affair, Anna Katharina Schonkopf (Leipzig), the "Annette" of some of his lyrics, Friderike Brion

(Strasbourg), Charlotte Buff (Wetzlar), who appears in *Werther*, Maximiliane von Larchom (the Rhine), Lili Schönemann (Frankfurt), to whom he was actually engaged and whom he almost married, Charlotte von Stein, wife of a Weimar official, seven years his senior and the mother of seven children, who held him emotionally from the time he came to Weimar until he went to Italy, Bettina von Arnim, who wrote her own account of the episode, Christiane Vulpius (1765–1816), whom he finally married in 1806 after she had been his mistress for years and had given him a son in 1789, Minna Herzlieb, who inspired some of his sonnets, Marianne von Willemer, whom he met in 1814–15, and Ulrike von Levetzow.

Goffe (gof), **Matthew.** In Shakespeare's *2 Henry VI*, a follower of Jack Cade.

Gog (gog). In Biblical history, according to Ezek. xxxviii, xxxix, a ruler in the land of Magog, mentioned as the prince of Meshech and Tubal. In Rev. xx. 8, Gog and Magog appear as two allied warring tribes. They were formerly regarded as connected with the invasion of the Scythians in W Asia, but of late Gog has been identified with Gagu, referred to in the annals of the Assyrian king Assurbanipal (c669–626 B.C.) as the mighty ruler of a warlike tribe in the territory of Sahi, N of Assyria.

Gog and Magog (mā'gog). Names given to two 14-foot statues in the Guildhall at London. They are now thought to have been intended for Gogmagog and Corineus. The original statues stood there in the days of Henry V. They were burned in the Great Fire of 1666, and new ones were put up in 1708. During World War II they were again destroyed. The older ones were made of wickerwork, pasteboard, and other materials, and were carried in procession at the lord mayor's show. Stone figures, ab. 9 ft. tall, were constructed in 1953 to stand in the restored Guildhall.

Gogarty (gō'gạr.ti), **Oliver St. John.** b. at Dublin, Aug. 17, 1878—. An Irish novelist, poet, politician, physician, surgeon, and wit. He is a fellow of the Royal College of Surgeons of Ireland, and his medical specialty is throat surgery. From 1922 to 1936 he was a senator in the Irish Free State parliament. Politically, he is against Eamon de Valera and the extreme Irish Home Rule party. He was a friend of Yeats, George Moore, George William Russell (Æ), and James Joyce, in whose *Ulysses* he appears as the Irish medical student, Malachi ("Buck") Mulligan. His works are *Poems and Plays* (1920), *An Offering of Swans and Other Poems* (1924), *Hyperthuliana* and *Wild Apples* (both 1930), *Selected Poems* (1933), *Others to Adorn* (1938), *Elbow Room* (1939), poems, *Tumbling in the Hay* (1939), an autobiographical novel, *As I was Going Down Sackville Street* (1937) and *I Follow St. Patrick* (1938), memoirs, *Going Native* (1940), *Mad Grandeur* (1941), and *It Isn't This Time of Year At All!* (1954), a book the author himself alternatively calls "An Unpremeditated Autobiography." Horace Reynolds, who wrote a foreword to *Others to Adorn*, describes his poems as "cool and fresh as a fountain," and Russell called him "the wildest wit in Ireland." In 1954 Gogarty was awarded a Fellowship of the Academy of

ḍ, d or j; ṣ, s or sh; ṭ, t or ch; ẓ, z or zh; o, F. cloche; ü, F. menu; ċh, Sc. loch; ṅ, F. bonbon.

American Poets (the grant is $5,000, the largest award for poets in the United States).

Gogmagog (gog′mạ.gog). [Also: **Goëmot, Goëmagot.**] According to Geoffrey of Monmouth, a giant king who, with his brother, held the western part of England in subjection. He was killed by Corineus, one of Brut's warriors.

Gogmagog Hills. A spur of the range of chalk hills known as the East Anglian Heights, in E central England, in Cambridgeshire ab. 3 mi. SE of Cambridge. There are remains of Roman earthworks here.

Gogol (gô′gọl), **Nikolai Vasilyevich.** [Original name, **Gogol-Yanovsky.**] b. near Mirgorod, in the government of Poltava, in the Ukraine, March 21, 1809; d. at Moscow, March 4, 1852. A Russian novelist, short-story writer, and dramatist; sometimes called the father of Russian realism. He was educated in a public *Gymnasium* (advanced secondary school) at Poltava and subsequently in the lyceum, then newly established, at Nezhinsk. He attempted several pieces while yet in school; one, which he published in 1829, was so severely criticized that he burned all the copies he could obtain. In 1829 he went to St. Petersburg and tried in vain to get on the stage; instead he became a government clerk in 1830. In 1831 he was appointed teacher of history at the Patriotic Institution, a post which he exchanged in 1834 for the professorship of history at the University of St. Petersburg. This he resigned at the end of a year and devoted himself entirely to literature. In 1829 he published *Italy*, a poem, and in 1830, in a periodical, the first of his Cossack stories, which in 1831 were collected and published as *Evenings on a Farm Near Dikanka: by Rudy Panko.* These tales, and those in *Mirgorod* (1835), including *Taras Bulba* (enlarged in 1842), *The King of the Gnomes, The Story of a Madman,* and *Family Life in Olden Times,* were well received. In 1836 his play *Revizor* (*The Inspector General*) was staged. It is a satirical story of the bribery of a supposed investigator (really a down-and-out traveler); it struck a chord with the public and (of a very different type) with the corrupt Russian officialdom it pictured. Probably as a direct result of the interference of this official class with his activities, Gogol left Russia in 1836, and thereafter spent much of his time at Rome. There he worked on his novel, *Dead Souls*, the first part of which was published in 1842, Gogol having returned to Russia for a short period in 1840 to superintend its publication. The novel is a humorous but sarcastic series of pictures of life in Russia, strung on a plot concerning an enterprising land speculator who buys up serfs ("souls") who have died since the taking of the last census in order to use their names to obtain land grants which he in turn mortgages for cash. *Taras Bulba, a Tale of the Cossacks,* published in an expanded version in the same year, is a historical novel of 15th-century Cossack life, full of adventure and gory cruelty, vividly told. At this period Gogol began to slip into a state of fanatical mysticism the effects of which were heightened by his acquaintanceship with a priest who played on the tendency. Gogol went on a pilgrimage to Jerusalem in 1848, returning to Moscow in a heightened state of religious feeling. He now turned against his former approach to the evils of Russian life and destroyed the concluding portion of *Dead Souls*, which he considered harmful in its attacks on the institution of serfdom. A shortened version of Part II was published in 1852, the year of his death.

Goibniu (goiv′nyö). In Old Irish mythology, the divine smith who made the marvelous swords, shields, and spears for the Tuatha De Danann (the old gods or divine race of Ireland). Like all supernatural smiths, he was also a magician. He brewed the ale which kept the gods forever young. His Brythonic counterpart is Govannon.

Goidels (goi′delz). [Also: **Gadhels, Gaedheals, Gaidheal.**] One of two large groups of Celtic speakers who invaded Britain in the Bronze Age. The other group was the Brython.

Golagros and Gawain (gō′lạ.grōs; gä′win, -wān). A Middle English alliterative poem, important for its development of the figure of Gawain, concerning a journey of Arthur and his knights to the Holy Land and the vanquishing of Golagros, lord of a castle on the Rhone, by Gawain.

Golconda (gol.kon′dạ). A village and ruined city in Hyderabad, Union of India, ab. 7 mi. NW of the city of Hyderabad: noted for its fort, for the mausoleums of the ancient kings, and for the diamonds which were cut and polished here. It was the capital of a kingdom from 1512 until its overthrow by Aurangzeb in 1687.

Gold Coast Customs. A book of poems by Edith Sitwell, published in 1929.

Golden Age, The. The perfect age, when everyone was happy and there was no evil or sorrow or sickness in the world: in classical mythology, the age of Saturn.

Golden Age, The. A story of children (1895) by Kenneth Grahame.

Golden Arrow, The. A novel by Mary Webb, published in 1916.

Golden Ass, The. [Alternative and original title, **Metamorphoses.**] A romance of a fantastic and satirical character, by Apuleius, written in the 2nd century A.D.; probably his earliest work. It was said to have imitated a portion of the dialogue, *Lucius or the Ass,* of Lucian. The best-known episode in it is that of Cupid and Psyche, which was taken from a popular legend or myth. Some of the adventures of Don Quixote and of Gil Blas are drawn from this source, and Boccaccio used many of the comic episodes. The author relates the story in his own person. His dabbling in magic results in his transformation into an ass, a form in which, however, he retains his human intelligence.

Golden Bough, The. The title of a series of books by Sir James George Frazer. It was originally published in two volumes (1890) but the title eventually embraced 12 volumes (1911–15) which comprise a comparative study of world religions, magic, vegetation and fertility beliefs and rites, kingship, taboos, totemism, and the like. The title alludes to the mistletoe, that "golden bough" which gave Aeneas access to the underworld, and which is associated also with Balder, and with the priest-king ritual anciently performed in Diana's

---

fat, fāte, fär, ȧsk, fāre; net, mē, hėr; pin, pīne; not, nōte, mȯve, nôr; up, lūte, pŭll; ᴛʜ, then;

sacred grove at Nemi. *The Golden Bough* includes the following titles: *The Magic Art and Evolution of Kings* (2 vols.), *Taboo and the Perils of the Soul, The Dying God, Adonis, Attis, Osiris: Studies in Oriental Religion* (2 vols.), *Spirits of the Corn and of the Wild* (2 vols.), *The Scapegoat, Balder the Beautiful* (2 vols.), and *The Golden Bough: Bibliography and General Index.* In 1936 *Aftermath, a Supplement to the Golden Bough* appeared.

Golden Bowl, The. A novel by Henry James, published in 1904. To please his daughter Maggie, the millionaire Adam Verver marries Charlotte, a school friend of his daughter. Maggie and her husband, Prince Amerigo, live near the newly wedded couple until it becomes known to both Mr. Verver and his daughter that Charlotte and the Prince are renewing an old liaison. With admirable restraint Adam removes Charlotte, sacrificing proximity to his daughter, and Maggie tactfully maneuvers the Prince into falling in love with her. The golden bowl is a symbol of the Prince's supposedly flawless character; it becomes cracked at the time Maggie finds out about her husband's early liaison and more recent dalliance with Charlotte.

Golden Bull. A bull published at the Diet of Nuremberg by the emperor Charles IV in 1356. It was so named from its golden seal. It was the electoral code of the Holy Roman Empire, determining the prerogatives and powers of the electors, and the manner of the election of the emperor.

Golden Dog, The. A romance by William Kirby, published in 1877.

Golden Doom, The. A drama (1914) by Lord Dunsany.

"Golden Dustman," the. See **Boffin, Nicodemus.**

Golden Fleece. In Greek mythology, the fleece of the winged ram Chrysomallus, the recovery of which was the object of the expedition of the Argonauts.

Golden Hind. [Original name, **Pelican.**] The ship in which Sir Francis Drake sailed around the world. He left Plymouth with five ships on Nov. 15, 1577, but the other four either were lost or deserted him. He completed his famous voyage on Sept. 26, 1580. His vessel, renamed during the voyage *The Golden Hind*, was carefully preserved by order of Queen Elizabeth, but was finally broken up about 100 years later; a chair made from her timbers at the order of John Davis, the arctic navigator, is now in the Bodleian Library.

Golden Horde. [Also, **Khanate of Kipchak** (or **Kapchak**).] A Mongol government organized in 1243 by Batu, grandson of Genghis Khan and conqueror of Russia: the name also applied to his followers. He established a capital at Sarai, on the Volga River, near what is now Astrakhan; from his gorgeous tent the settlement, and thence the government, took the name "Golden." The territory ruled by the Golden Horde stretched from the Danube to the western Siberian steppes, south to the Caucasus and the Aral Sea. The rulers of Kiev, Moscow, and Novgorod were its vassals. Within its territory the Golden Horde built up cities of slave artisans, while nomadic horsemen remained the rulers. Lively trade was carried on with western Europe. In the 15th century, the Golden Horde broke up into separate khanates in the Crimea, at Kazan and Astrakhan, and in Siberia. It was destroyed in 1503 by Ivan III, Grand Duke of Moscow, and his ally the Crimean khan.

Golden Horn. An inlet of the Bosporus, in European Turkey, forming the harbor of Istanbul, and separating Pera and Galata from the main part of Istanbul. Length, ab. 5 mi.

Golden Journey to Samarkand (sam.ạr.kand'), **The.** The title poem of a volume of poems (1913) by James Elroy Flecker.

Golden Legend. A collection of biographies of saints, compiled by Jacobus of Voragine (or Varagine) in the 13th century. The book, arranged as a calendar of the Christian year, was one of the most popular works of the Middle Ages and held its audience until the critical eye of the Renaissance examined its improbabilities and pedestrian style and brought it into disrepute as real biographical history. It remains, however, a storehouse of folklore, though its reputation as a devotional inspiration is somewhat impaired. It was translated from the original Latin into the several vernacular tongues of Europe before the 16th century. An English translation was printed (1483) by Caxton.

Golden Legend, The. A cantata (1886) by Sir Arthur Sullivan, who used the words from a poem (1851) by Longfellow.

Golden Spurs, Battle of the. See **Battle of the Spurs.**

Golden Terge or **Targe** (tärj). An allegorical poem by William Dunbar, published in 1508.

Golden Vanity, The. One of three historical narratives in *The Ladies!* (1922), written by Lily Adams Beck under the pseudonym E. Barrington.

Goldilocks (gōl'di.loks). See under **Three Bears.**

Golding (gōl'ding), **Arthur.** b. probably at London, c1536; d. c1605. An English writer. He finished a translation of Philippe de Mornay's treatise *Sur la vérité du Christianisme*, commenced by Sir Philip Sidney, which he published under the title *A Worke concerning the Trewenesse of the Christian Religion* (1589). He translated Caesar's *Gallic War* (1565), and other works. His translation of Ovid's *Metamorphoses* (1565–67) was a principal source of Elizabethan knowledge of the Roman poet.

Golding, Louis. b. at Manchester, England, Nov. 19, 1895—. An English novelist and poet. His verse includes *Sorrow of War* (1919), *Shepherd Singing Ragtime* (1921), and *Prophet and Fool* (1923). Among his novels are *Forward from Babylon* (1920), *Day of Atonement* (1925), *Store of Ladies* (1927), *Give up Your Lovers* (1930), *Magnolia Street* (1932; adapted for the stage, 1934), *The Camberwell Beauty* (1935), *Mr. Emmanuel* (1939), *The Glory of Elsie Silver* (1945), and *Three Jolly Gentlemen* (1947). He is the author also of *Sicilian Noon* (1925), *James Joyce* (1933), *Letter to Adolph Hitler* (1933), and *The Jewish Problem* (1938).

Goldoni (gōl.dō'nē), **Carlo.** b. at Venice, Feb. 25, 1707; d. at Paris, Jan. 6, 1793. An Italian dramatist. He created the modern Italian comedy character, somewhat in the style of Molière, superseding the old conventional comedy (*commedia dell'arte*) which was played by Harlequin, Pantalone, and the like. His first attempts, however, were tragedies, *Belisario* (1732) being among the earliest. He wrote more than 120 comedies, among which are *Zelinda e Londoro*, *La Locandiera*, *Ventaglio*, *Le Baruffe Chiozzotte*, *La Bottega di caffè*, and others.

Goldring (gōl'dring), **Douglas.** b. at Greenwich (now part of London), Jan. 7, 1887—. An English editor and writer. He has been an editorial staff member of *Country Life* and the *English Review*. His works include *Ways of Escape*, *Dream Cities*, *A Book of London Verses*, *Margot's Progress*, *Cuckoo*, *The Façade*, *The Coast of Illusion*, *Pot Luck in England*, *Marching with the Times*, and *The Last Pre-Raphaelite*.

Goldsmith (gōld'smith), **Oliver.** b. near Bally-mahon, County Longford, Ireland, Nov. 10, 1728; d. at London, April 4, 1774. An Irish poet, novelist, dramatist, essayist, physician, and traveler. He was the second son and the fifth child of an idealistic clergyman, Charles Goldsmith, and Anne Jones. He was educated at various local schools, at one kept by Mrs. Elizabeth Delap, who thought him "impenetrably stupid," at a village school run by an old soldier, Thomas Byrne (who appears in *The Deserted Village*), at a school at Elphin operated by a Mr. Griffin, at one at Athlone (c1739), and finally (1741) at a school at Edgeworthstown, County Longford, run by Patrick Hughes. On June 11, 1744, he entered Trinity College, Dublin, and on Feb. 27, 1749, he was awarded the B.A. degree. Goldsmith's life thereafter is a record of almost unbroken failure in everything that he tried to reach by study or effort: he tried law, medicine, the church, and teaching, and failed in all of them; the only thing he succeeded in was literature, which he did not study and for which he had no technical preparation. In 1752 he went to Edinburgh to study "physic," as medicine was called in his day, and there he remained for about two years, studying little but playing a great deal. From 1754 to 1756 he made a tour of Europe, largely on foot, wandering through Flanders, France, Switzerland, Italy, and Germany. He went from one place to another, attending university lectures at which he was welcomed as a foreign traveling student, playing the flute and telling stories in return for food and lodging. He returned to England in 1756 with a few pennies in his pocket, and tried without success to make a living in a dozen different ways, including acting, teaching, clerking in an apothecary's shop, reading proof (for Richardson), practicing medicine at Southwark, and hack writing. Milner, at whose Classical Academy at Peckham he had taught, tried to secure him a post as surgeon but nothing came of the project, and when Goldsmith took an examination (in borrowed clothing) for surgeon's mate in the navy he did not pass. As a hack writer, he produced a large number of works on subjects of which he knew nothing, but he wrote of them, as he always did on any topic, with a delightful charm and ease. Facts meant little to him, and they mean nothing to the reader who enjoys his works for their style. He began a periodical, *The Bee*, in 1759, which lasted for eight weeks, from October 6 to November 24, and he contributed

to *The Busy-Body* and *The Lady's Magazine*. He wrote essays for Smollett's *British Magazine* and the "Chinese Letters" (1760–61) for Newbery's *Public Ledger*, later (1762) published in book form as *The Citizen of the World*, in which he delightfully assumes the character of a Chinese philosopher visiting England and expressing his opinions on English life and manners in a series of letters to his friends at home. Some of his hack works are *A History of the Seven Years' War* (1761), *A History of England in a Series of Letters from a Nobleman to His Son* (1764), *A History of England from the Earliest Times to the Death of George II* (4 vols., 1771), *A History of Rome from the Foundation of the City to the Destruction of the Roman Empire* (1769), *A History of the Earth and Animated Nature* (8 vols., 1774), *A History of Greece from the Earliest State to the Death of Alexander the Great* (1774), and *A Survey of Experimental Philosophy Considered in its Present State of Improvement* (1776). Many of these works were later published, or are referred to, under different titles, in abridged form. He translated from the French *The Memoirs of a Protestant Condemned to the Galleys of France for his Religion* (February, 1758), Formey's *Concise History of Philosophy* (1766), and Scarron's *Comic Romance* (1776). However, his first work of great importance was his *Enquiry into the Present State of Polite Learning in Europe* (1759). As a literary critic he reviewed Home's *Douglas*, Burke's *On the Sublime and Beautiful*, Smollett's *History of England*, Wilkie's *Epigoniad*, and Gray's *Odes*. Other works by him are *The Traveler* (1764), a didactic poem, and *The Good-natured Man*, a comedy, with a prologue by Samuel Johnson, first produced at Covent Garden Theatre at London, on Friday, Jan. 29, 1768. But he chiefly owes his place in English literature to *The Vicar of Wakefield* (1766), *The Deserted Village* (1770), and one of the greatest comedies in the history of the English theater, *She Stoops to Conquer, or the Mistakes of a Night*, first produced at Covent Garden on Monday, March 15, 1773. The latter was dedicated to Johnson, and its prologue was written by Garrick. Goldsmith first met Johnson on May 31, 1761, and the two men, totally different in manners, personality, and genius, became and remained firm friends. In 1764 he was, with Johnson, Garrick, Burke, Boswell, Sir Joshua Reynolds, and Gibbon, one of the original members of "The Club," the famous dinner-and-discussion group that met in London at the Turk's Head in Gerrard Street. Much has been written about the defects of Goldsmith's character, but the worst that can be said of him is that he was careless with money, allowing it to run through his fingers when he had it, that he was not practical, that he liked fine clothing, was fond of entertaining on a lavish scale, was usually in debt (he owed two thousand pounds when he died), and that he had a passion for gambling. It must also be noted that he was kindhearted and perhaps foolishly generous (he gave away as much money, to unfortunates even poorer than himself, as he lost at the gaming table). He has been charged with being vain and conceited and with strutting about in fancy clothes that he had no right to buy, but in his "Advertisement" to *The Vicar of Wakefield* he found "a hundred faults in this thing" (being the only one to do so), and he called *She Stoops to Conquer* "this slight performance" in his dedication. Horace Walpole called him "an Inspired Idiot" and "a poor soul," and Garrick wrote "Here lies Poet Goldsmith, for shortness called Noll, Who wrote like an angel, but talked like Poor Poll." Superior to these estimates are those of Johnson: "He touched nothing which he did not adorn" was the epitaph he wrote for Goldsmith, and his summary was "Let not his frailties be remembered: he was a very great man." When they learned of Goldsmith's death, Burke burst into tears and Reynolds threw down his brush and was unable to paint for the rest of the day, which had never happened to him before even in his closest personal bereavements. A public funeral was planned, but the idea was given up when it was found that he had died in debt.

Golgotha (gol′gọ.tha̧). A place of interment; a graveyard; a charnel. See also under **Calvary.**

Goliardic verse (gō.li.är′dik). A type of loose or satirical Latin verse of the 12th and 13th centuries in Germany, France, and England. Produced by university students and wandering scholars, it is defiant of authority, civil and ecclesiastical, and extols the Bohemian life and the delights of love and wine. It drew its name from the fact that a poet named Golias, dignified with the titles of *episcopus* and *archipoeta*, is supposed to have written some of the poems, as is Walter Map, who, however, cannot have written all the Goliardic verse attributed to him. Much of the Goliardic verse has been translated by various hands into modern English. See also **Primas.**

Goliath (gō.lī′a̧th). In Biblical history, a giant of Gath, the champion of the Philistines, killed in single combat by David, who slew the Philistine with a pebble from his sling. 1 Sam. xvii. 4.

Go, lovely Rose! A poem by Edmund Waller, considered to be one of the most delightful of his lyrics. It is an exhortation to a rose to bring the poet's loved one to him:

> Go, lovely Rose!
> Tell her that wastes her time and me,
> That now she knows
> When I resemble her to thee
> How sweet and fair she seems to be.

Gomorrah or **Gomorrha** (gọ.mor′a̧). An ancient city which was destroyed (together with Sodom) for the wickedness of its inhabitants (Gen. xviii–xix); hence, any extremely wicked place.

Goncourt (gôṅ.kör), **Edmond Louis Antoine Huot de.** b. at Nancy, France, May 26, 1822; d. at Champrosay, France, July 16, 1896. A French novelist. He and his brother Jules were collaborators until Jules's death in 1870; until that time they were always together, only once being separated for more than a day; neither ever married. Their approach to both history and fiction was impressionistic; small details were piled up, with no attempt at emphasis and in apparent confusion, to give an overall picture of a fluid world in which time only gives significance to events. The result was a series of novels and histories in which the daily incidents of life were detailed as they had not been before. The Goncourts, to the horror of certain critics,

combined with this fragmentary method of storytelling a fresh approach to the French language: they invented words, emphasized certain rhythms of the language, were inclined to have favorite word-endings, used alliteration, and the like; this *style artiste*, as they called it, caused their critics to complain that the Goncourts no longer wrote in French. Their historical works, reflecting their interest in the 18th century (they were collectors of *objets d'art* and other souvenirs of 18th-century France and Japan), include *Histoire de la société française pendant la Révolution* (1854), *Portraits intimes du XVIIIe siècle* (2 vols., 1857–58), *L'Art du XVIIIe siècle* (3 vols., 1859–75), and *La Femme au XVIIIe siècle* (1862). Among their novels are *Charles Demailly* (1860), *Soeur Philomène* (1861), *Renée Mauperin* (1864), *Germinie Lacerteux* (1865), *Manette Salomon* (1865), and *Madame Gervaisais* (1869). After Jules died in 1870, Edmond published several novels of his own, including *La Fille Elisa* (1878), *Les Frères Zemgganno* (1879), *La Faustin* (1882), and *Chérie* (1884). His monographs on Japanese art, *Outamaro* (1891) and *Hokusaï* (1896), were among the first appreciations of an art style and vogue (*japonisme*) that gained popularity through Edmond's decoration of his house, where he received members of the literary world on Sundays. Nine volumes of *Le Journal des Goncourt*, a diary kept by the brothers from 1851, have been published (1887–96); it is one of the most famous journals in the world, containing their plans, the sayings of such friends and acquaintances as Flaubert, Sainte-Beuve, and Renan, and the gossip of their times. Edmond willed the bulk of his fortune for the establishment of the Académie des Goncourt (10 members, established 1900), which awards an annual prize (Prix Goncourt) to the writer of a meritorious prose work, generally a novel.

Gondibert (gon′di.bẹrt). An unfinished epic poem by Sir William D'Avenant, published in 1651.

Gondomar (gōn.dō.mär′), **Diego Sarmiento de Acuña,** Count of. b. at Gondomar, in Galicia, Spain, Nov. 1, 1567; d. near Haro, in La Rioja, Spain, Oct. 2, 1626. A Spanish diplomat. He was ambassador to England during the periods 1613–18 and 1619–22. He managed the negotiations for the proposed match between Charles I (then Prince of Wales) and the Spanish infanta Maria, and he was notorious for his influence over James I, whom he prevented from helping his son-in-law Frederick V of Bohemia in the Thirty Years' War. His large share of responsibility for the execution of Sir Walter Raleigh made him an object of intense hatred in England. The Elizabethan dramatist Thomas Middleton attacked him in his political play *A Game of Chesse* (1625), in which Gondomar is the Black Knight.

Goneril (gon′ẹr.il). In Shakespeare's *King Lear*, the eldest daughter of Lear. She despises her honorable husband Albany for his kindness toward Lear, whom she has driven from her house. Planning to put Edmund, whom she loves, in Albany's place by killing the latter, she jealously poisons her sister Regan when she discovers that she too loves Edmund. When Edgar finds her love letter to Edmund, he gives it to Albany. Refusing to explain, she

---

ḍ, d or j; ş, s or sh; ṭ, t or ch; z̧, z or zh; o, F. cloche: ü, F. menu; c̆h, Sc. loch; ṅ, F. bonbon.

says, "The laws are mine, not thine. Who can arraign me for it?" Shortly after, word comes of her suicide.

Gone To Earth. A novel by Mary Webb, published in 1917.

gongorism (gong'gō.rizm). [Also, **Gongorism**.] A kind of affected elegance of style introduced into Spanish literature in imitation of that of the Spanish poet Góngora y Argote (1561–1627).

A folio volume, with numerous plates, . . . not withstanding the Gongorism of its style, is a book to be read for the history of Spanish art.
(Ticknor, *Span. Lit.*)

Tales . . . told in that euphuistic language which more or less corresponded in date or character with gongorism in Spain. (*Quarterly Rev.*, CLXIII.)

Gonne (gon), **Maud.** b. at London, 1866—. An Irish patriot and philanthropist. She married (1903) the Irish patriot Major MacBride, who was executed (1916) by British authorities after the Easter Rebellion. She was later (1921) the first diplomatic emissary of the Irish Free State at Paris. Known as an actress, painter, and linguist, and famous for her beauty, she was a heroine of poems and plays by William Butler Yeats. She published the autobiography *A Servant of the Queen* (1940).

Gonville and Caius College (gon'vil; kēz). [Commonly called **Caius**.] One of the colleges of Cambridge University. It was founded in 1348 as Gonville Hall by Edmund de Gonville, rector of Torrington, Norfolk, and was refounded in 1557 by the physician John Caius. The official name of the college is Gonville and Caius, but it is always in speaking, and almost always in writing, referred to as Caius, partly because the shorter name is easier, and partly because of the greater fame of its second founder. There are three gates to the college which Caius named Humility, Virtue (or Wisdom), and Honor, the last designed by Caius himself.

Gonzago (gon.zä'gō). In Shakespeare's *Hamlet*, the king who is murdered in the interpolated play (and, therefore, in Claudius's eyes, the character standing for Hamlet's father). The name of the character is not mentioned in the Dramatis Personae for *Hamlet*.

Gonzalo (gon.zä'lō). In Shakespeare's *Tempest*, an "honest old counsellor" who gave supplies and books to Prospero and Miranda when they were set adrift. He is shipwrecked with Alonso on Prospero's magic isle. He is also introduced as a "Savoy nobleman" in Dryden's version.

Goodbye, Mr. Chips. A novel by James Hilton, published in 1934. It opens with the old schoolmaster, Mr. Chipping (affectionately dubbed "Mr. Chips" by his students), sitting in his room on a gray November day and thinking back over his teaching career, starting with the day in 1870 when he came to Brookfield School. Although he soon established a reputation with the boys in the school for kindliness and good humor, he also early decided that he was not the type to assume leadership as the headmaster, and so concentrated all his energies on becoming a good and well-liked teacher. He had married Kathy Bridges, and had loved her deeply, but she had died two years after their marriage, on April Fool's day. He recalls that on that very day

the boys had played pranks on him, not knowing of the tragic loss which had befallen him. When World War I came, Chips was asked to serve, however reluctantly, as headmaster of Brookfield, and he still recalls the names he read to the assembled students in chapel, when the casualty lists were published, of the Brookfield boys who had died in battle. After the war Chips had given up his position, and now had lived at Mrs. Wickett's boarding house, across from the school, for 15 years. Distinguished visitors, who were once his students, still come to call on Chips, and his association with Brookfield has, if anything, been strengthened over the years. On this day a young boy cautiously rings the doorbell, enters, and says that he has been told that Chips wanted to see him. Chips recognizes the old trick played on new boys, and invites the lad for tea. The next day the boy is able to say that he was the last Brookfield boy ever to see the old man alive; Chips died quietly in his sleep that very night.

Good Companions, The. A novel by J. B. Priestley, published in 1929. Three people leave their homes to join a troupe of traveling performers, the Good Companions. Their experiences are described in the letters they write home. The principal characters include Jesiah Oakroyd, a Yorkshire laborer who becomes a handyman; Elizabeth Trant, a maiden lady who becomes the manager; and Inigo Jollifant, a school teacher who becomes the piano player.

Goodfellow (gûd'fel.ō), **Robin.** See **Puck**.

Good Friday. A dramatic poem (1916) by John Masefield.

Goodlack (gûd'lak). The friend of Captain Spencer in Thomas Heywood's *Fair Maid of the West*.

Good Morrow, The. A poem (1633) by John Donne, telling how love has made the poet's life full and why, therefore, he hails love as the awakener of his soul:

And now good-morrow to our waking souls,
Which watch not one another out of fear;
For love all love of other sights controls,
And makes one little room an everywhere.

Good-natured Man, The. A comedy by Oliver Goldsmith, produced on Jan. 29, 1768. Honeywood, a likeable but somewhat extravagant young man, is arrested for debt upon the order of his uncle, who wishes him to see how his "friends" will treat him when he is without money. Honeywood loves Miss Richland, a wealthy and beautiful young woman, but he has never proposed. When he is released from arrest he assumes his freedom is owed to Lofty, a government official whom he has known, but actually she is responsible. In the end, Honeywood's uncle intervenes, and a match with Miss Richland is arranged.

Good Short Debate Between Winner and Waster. [Also, **Winner and Waster**.] A Middle English poem of the 14th century, cast in alliterative verse, dealing with current social problems.

"Good Sir James," the. See **Douglas, Sir James**.

Goodstock (gûd'stok). The host in Ben Jonson's play *The New Inn*. He is Lord Frampul in disguise.

Goody Two Shoes. A nursery tale relating the story of Little Goody Two Shoes, who, owning but one shoe, is so pleased to have a pair that she shows them to every one, exclaiming "Two shoes!" The story was first published in 1765 by Newbery, and is supposed to have been written by Oliver Goldsmith.

Googe (gōj), **Barnabe.** b. at Alvingham, Lincolnshire, England, 1540; d. 1594. An English poet. His most important work is a set of eight eclogues published in 1563 in *Eglogs, Epytaphes, and Sonnetes* which are thought to have had some influence on Spenser's *Shepherd's Calendar.* He translated a number of works, and wrote also a long poem, *Cupido Conquered.*

Goose (gōs), **Mother.** See **Mother Goose.**

Goose Gibbie (gib'i). See **Gibbie, Goose.**

Gorboduc (gôr′bọ.duk). A legendary king of Britain. His story, with that of his sons Ferrex and Porrex, is told in the early chronicles. He succeeded to the crown soon after the death of Lear, but profited so little by the example of his predecessor that he divided his realm during his life between his two sons, Ferrex and Porrex. The two boys fought and the younger killed the elder. The mother then killed the younger son, with the result that a horrified populace killed both Gorboduc and his wife. This bloody history is the subject of the first regular English tragedy. This drama was written by Thomas Norton and Thomas Sackville (Lord Buckhurst), was acted in 1561, and was afterwards printed in 1565, under the name of *Gorboduc.* Sir Philip Sidney stated that this drama climbed to the height of Seneca, and Pope declared that it possessed "an unaffected perspicuity of style."

Gordian (gôr′di.ạn). Pertaining to Gordius, an ancient king of Phrygia, who tied a knot (the "Gordian knot") which was to be undone only by one who should rule Asia, and which was summarily cut by Alexander the Great; hence, resembling this knot; intricate.

Gordius (gôr′di.us). In Greek legend, a king of Phrygia (originally a peasant); father of Midas. An oracle had declared to the people of Phrygia that a king would come to them riding in a cart, and, as Gordius thus appeared to them, the popular assembly which was then discussing the disposition of the government accepted him as their sovereign. His car and the yoke of his oxen he dedicated to Zeus at Gordium; and an oracle declared that whoever should untie the knot of the yoke would rule over Asia. Alexander the Great cut the famous Gordian knot with his sword.

Gordon (gôr′don), **Adam Lindsay.** b. on the island of Fayal, Azores, Oct. 19, 1833; d. at Brighton, Victoria, Australia, June 24, 1870. An Australian poet. He lived "wildly" as a youth and was sent to Australia in 1853 to begin life anew; he became identified with horses as a horsebreaker, hurdle racer, steeplechaser, and livery-stable keeper. He began writing florid lyrical poetry (1857), publishing some of his verse in 1864. He was the author of about 20 first-rate poems. He committed suicide in a fit of depression over money. He is the only Australian poet whose bust is in Westminster Abbey.

Gordon, Charles George. [Called **Chinese Gordon** and **Gordon Pasha.**] b. at Woolwich, London, Jan.

28, 1833; d. at Khartoum, in Nubia, Jan. 26, 1885. An English soldier. He served (1854–56) in the Crimea. In 1860 he was attached to the British force under Sir James Hope Grant operating with the French against China, and in 1863 took command of a Chinese force, called the Ever Victorious Army, against the Taiping rebels. He put down the rebellion in 33 engagements, and resigned his command in 1864, receiving from the emperor the yellow jacket and peacock's feather of a mandarin of the first class. He was governor (1874–76) of the equatorial provinces of central Africa in the service of the khedive of Egypt, was created pasha by the khedive in 1877, and in the same year was promoted lieutenant colonel in the British army. He was governor general (1877–79) of the Sudan, Darfur, the equatorial provinces, and the Red Sea littoral, in which capacity he stamped out the slave trade in his district. He acted as adviser of the Chinese government in its relations with Russia in 1880, went as commanding royal engineer (1881–82) to Mauritius, and was commandant of the colonial forces of the Cape of Good Hope in 1882. In 1884 he was sent by the British government to the Sudan to assist the khedive in withdrawing the garrisons of the country, which could not be held any longer against the Mahdi. He was besieged by the Mahdi at Khartoum on March 12, 1884, and was killed in the storming of the city on Jan. 26, 1885. Significant studies about Gordon include a biographical sketch in the *Eminent Victorians* (1918), by Lytton Strachey, and two full-length biographies, *Chinese Gordon: The Story of a Hero* (1954), by Lawrence and Elisabeth Hanson, and *Gordon of Khartoum* (1955), by Lord Elton.

Gordon, Charles William. [Pseudonym, **Ralph Connor.**] b. at Indian Lands, Ontario, Canada, 1860; d. Oct. 31, 1917. A Canadian clergyman, missionary, and author. From 1890 to 1894 he was engaged in missionary work among the miners and lumbermen in the Canadian Rocky Mountains; he represented the Canadian Western Missions of the Presbyterian Church in Great Britain (1893–94), and from 1894 was minister of Saint Stephen's Church at Winnipeg. During World War I he was chaplain (1916), with the 9th brigade and member (1917) of the British mission in the U. S. He was the author of *Black Rock* (1898), *The Sky Pilot* (1899), *Beyond the Marshes* (1901), *The Man from Glengarry* (1901), *Glengarry School Days* (1902), *The Prospector* (1904), *The Doctor* (1906), *Life of James Robertson* (1908), *The Recall of Love* (1910), *Corporal Cameron* (1912), and *The Girl from Glengarry* (1933).

Gordon Riots. [Also called **No Popery Riots.**] A rising of the London populace in June 1780, the culmination of an anti-Roman Catholic agitation instigated and abetted by Lord George Gordon. The House of Commons was attacked, Newgate Prison was burned and all other London prisons were forced open, the Bank of England, as well as other public buildings, was stormed unsuccessfully; Roman Catholic churches and dwellings were burned. There were 450 casualties before troops ended the rioting.

Gore (gōr), **Catherine Grace Frances.** [Maiden name, **Moody.**] b. at East Retford, Nottingham-

ḍ, d or j; ṣ, s or sh; ṭ, t or ch; ẓ, z or zh; o, F. cloche; ü, F. menu; ċh, Sc. loch; ṅ, F. bonbon.

shire, England, 1799; d. at Lyndhurst, Hampshire, England, Jan. 29, 1861. An English novelist and playwright. Among her works are *Theresa March-mont*, a novel (1824), *The Lettre de Cachet* (1827), *School for Coquettes*, a comedy (1831), *Mrs. Army-tage* (1836), *Cecil, or the Adventures of a Coxcomb* (1841), *The Banker's Wife* (1843), and some 60 other works, some of them translations from the French.

Gore, Charles. b. at Wimbledon, Surrey, England, Jan. 22, 1853; d. at London, Jan. 17, 1932. An English ecclesiastic, a bishop of the Church of England. He was a leader of the "Modernist" group in the High Church party, Oxford librarian, and editor.

Gore, John Francis. b. at Wimbledon, Surrey, England, May 15, 1885—. An English biographer and journalist. Author of *The Trial Stone* (1919), *Creevey's Life and Times* (1934), *A Londoner's Calendar* (1925), and *Nelson's Hardy and his wife* (1935); commissioned by King George VI and Queen Mary to write *King George V* (1941).

Gore-Booth (gōr′bŏoth′), **Eva.** b. in County Sligo, Ireland, 1871; d. at Hampstead, London, 1926. An Irish poet, a figure in the Irish literary revival which included George Russell (Æ) and W. B. Yeats. Her volumes of poetry include *Poems* (1898), *The One and the Many* (1904), *Unseen Kings* (1904), *The Three Resurrections* (1905), *The Sor-rowful Princess* (1907), *The Egyptian Pillar* (1907), *The Perilous Light* (1915), *The Agate Lamp* (1912), and *The Sword of Justice* (1918). She is com-memorated in a poem by Yeats, *In Memory of Eva Gore-Booth and Con Marcievicz*.

Gorges (gôr′jez), Sir **Arthur.** d. 1625. An English poet. He was formerly known chiefly as the hus-band of the woman (Daphne, whom he married in 1584) mentioned in two of Spenser's poems, *Colin Clout's Come Home Again* and *Daphnaïda*, an elegy on Daphne's death. A translation of Lucan's *Pharsalia* (1614) is also credited to him. However, in 1940, a manuscript (now catalogued as Egerton 3165) by Gorges was discovered and acquired by the British Museum. This manuscript, entitled in the poet's own hand, *The Vanytyes of Sir Arthur Gorges Youthe*, or *Sir Arthur Gorges his vannetyes and toyes of yowth*, contains in large part a collection of 100 poems (two of which are dupli-cates), some possibly written as early as 1584. The poet sometimes employs the technique of incor-porating an adaptation of borrowed material into his own work (Stanza 5 of Poem 100 is modeled on lines in Spenser's *Fairie Queene*). Another part of the *Vanytes* was possibly written as late as 1614, and still another part contains poems written chiefly for the Stuarts. Gorges also wrote an elegy of almost 2,000 lines, *The Olympian Catastrophe* (published in 1925), which strongly indicates Spen-ser's influence. A recent study of the poet's work is *The Poems of Sir Arthur Gorges* (1954) edited by Helen Estabrook Sandison.

Gorgons (gôr′gonz). In Greek mythology, three horrible sisters with serpent hair, brazen claws, and staring eyes. According to Hesiod they were daugh-ters of Phorcys (whence also called Phorcydes) and Ceto, dwelling in the Western Ocean near Night and the Hesperides (in later mythology, in Libya). Their names were Stheno, Euryale, and Medusa.

Medusa, who was slain by Perseus, is the most famous of the three.

Gorlois (gôr′lois). See under **Igerna.**

Gospel of the Brothers Barnabas (bär′na.bas). See under **Back to Methusaleh.**

Gosse (gos), Sir **Edmund William.** b. at London, Sept. 21, 1849; d. 1928. An English poet and literary critic. He was a librarian (1867–75) at the British Museum, and in 1875 became translator for the Board of Trade. He was Clark lecturer (1884–90) in English literature at Trinity College, Cambridge; his early lectures there were published in 1885 as *From Shakespeare to Pope*. He served as librarian (1904–14) of the House of Lords. Gosse is credited with bringing modern Scandinavian literature, es-pecially the dramas of Henrik Ibsen, before the English public. His papers on Ibsen, who became a controversial figure among English critics and with the public, were written beginning in 1871; some of them are reprinted in *Northern Studies* (1890). He wrote a biography, *Henrik Ibsen*, in 1907. His translations of Ibsen include *Emperor and Galilean* (1876), *Hedda Gabler* (1891), and *The Master-Builder* (1893, with William Archer). Gosse's critical work was centered in 17th-century English literature, and he is sometimes credited with be-ginning the revival of interest in John Donne; he wrote *Life and Letters of John Donne, Dean of St. Paul's* (1899). In this field he also wrote *Seventeenth Century Studies* (1883), *Life of William Congreve* (1888), *The Jacobean Poets* (1894), *Jeremy Taylor* (1904, in the *English Men of Letters* series), and *Life of Sir Thomas Browne* (1905). He wrote a *Life of Thomas Gray* (1882) and published the *Works of Thomas Gray* (1884); his biography *Raleigh* was published in 1886, and *The Life of Algernon Charles Swinburne* in 1917. His critical writings also include *Studies in the Literatures of Northern Europe* (1879), *History of Eighteenth Century Literature, 1660–1780* (1889), *Critical Kit-Kats* (1896), *Short History of Modern English Literature* (1897), *Illustrated Record of English Literature* (in collaboration with Richard Garnett, 1903–04), *French Profiles* (1905), *Books on the Table* (1921), *More Books on the Table* (1923), and *Leaves and Fruit* (1927). He published an anonymous autobiographical study, *Father and Son*, in 1907, in which some critics profess to see the pen of George Moore. His *Collected Essays* were printed in 12 volumes (1912–27). Gosse as a poet practiced the forms adopted from the French, especially ac-knowledging his debt to Theodore de Banville. His volumes of verse include *On Viol and Flute* (1873), *New Poems* (1879), *Firdausi in Exile and Other Poems* (1885), *In Russet and Silver* (1894), *Collected Poems* (1896, 1911), and *The Autumn Garden* (1908). He wrote a verse play, *King Erik* (1876), and a prose fantasy (with some blank verse), *Hy-polympia, or the Gods on the Island* (1901); the latter takes place on an island in the 20th century, but the characters are the ancient Greek gods.

Gosson (gos′on), **Stephen.** b. at Canterbury, Eng-land, 1554; d. Feb. 13, 1624. An English author. He became rector of Great Wigborough, in Essex, in 1591, a post which he exchanged for that of St. Botolph's, Bishopsgate, London, in 1600. Gosson seems to have been a playwright, though none of his plays survive, and became upset at what he

fat, fāte, fär, ȧsk, fāre; net, mē, hėr; pin, pīne; not, nōte, mõve, nôr; up, lūte, pŭll; ᴛʜ, then;

thought were the immoral tendencies of the writers and poets of the day. In 1579 he wrote, and dedicated without permission to Sir Philip Sidney, *Schoole of Abuse, containing a pleasant invective against Poets, Pipers, Plaiers, Jesters, and such like Caterpillars of the Commonwealth*. He followed this in the same year with *The Ephemerides of Phialo* and in 1582 with *Playes Confuted in Five Actions*. The latter was a defense of his position, for the *Schoole of Abuse* had drawn a series of answers, including a vigorous pamphlet from Thomas Lodge. Sidney's *Apologie for Poetry*, written c1581, seems to have been written in answer to Gosson's attack on the poets.

Gostanzo (go.stän′tsō, gos.tan′zō). The father of Valerio in George Chapman's *All Fools, or All Fools but the Fool*. He is misled by Rinaldo into believing that Fortunio, rather than his son, Valerio, has been secretly married and is persuaded to take the couple into his home, supposedly to avoid the wrath of Fortunio's father.

Gotha (go.tà), **Almanach de**. An annual register published (1764 *et seq.*) in French and German at Gotha, Germany. It comprises a genealogical detail of the principal royal and aristocratic families of Europe, and a diplomatic and statistical record for the time of the different states of the world.

Gotham (goth′am, gō′tham; locally, got′am). A civil parish and village in N central England, in Nottinghamshire, ab. 7 mi. SW of Nottingham. The foolishness and stupidity of its inhabitants, which has passed into tradition and story, is said to have been simulated in the 13th century to avoid losing good land for public roads. When King John's men came to punish the villagers for refusing their lands, they averted the king's anger by behaving like fools. The "foles of Gotyam" are mentioned as early as the 15th century in the *Towneley Mysteries*. *Merie Tales of the Mad Men of Gotam* was published in 1630. But the famous nursery rhyme:

> Three wise men of Gotham
> Went to sea in a bowl:
> And if the bowl had been stronger
> My song would have been longer.

did not appear until c1765 in Newbery's *Mother Goose's Melody*. It has been reprinted in numerous compilations.

Gotham Election, A. A farce by Susannah Centlivre, published in 1737, but never acted.

Gothic (goth′ik). The language of the Goths. The Goths spoke various forms of a Germanic tongue, belonging to the eastern group of the Germanic subfamily of languages. All forms of Gothic have perished without record, except that spoken by some of the western Goths (Visigoths), who at the beginning of the 4th century occupied Dacia (approximately what is now Rumania), and who before the end of that century passed over in great numbers into Moesia (now Serbia and part of Bulgaria). Revolting against the Roman Empire, they extended their conquests even into Gaul and Spain. Their language, Gothic, also called Moeso-Gothic, is preserved in the fragmentary remains of a nearly complete translation of the Bible made by their bishop, Ulfilas (a name also used in the forms

Ulfila, Ulphila, Wulfila), who lived in the 4th century A.D., and in some other fragments. These remains are of a high philological importance, preceding by several centuries the next earliest Germanic records (Anglo-Saxon and Old High German). The part of Ulfilas's Bible still extant consists of a considerable portion of each of the Gospels, and of each of Saint Paul's Epistles; also small fragments of the books of Ezra and Nehemiah. Of the six different manuscripts found, the most important was that discovered in the 16th century in a monastery at Werden, Germany; it changed ownership repeatedly before being housed at the University of Uppsala, Sweden. The language has been extinct since the 9th century.

Gothic novel. A type of story, usually in a pseudomedieval setting, full of mysterious, occult, and violent incident, in a pervading atmosphere of gloom and terror. It is usually considered to have had its origin, in a formal sense, with Horace Walpole, who settled at Strawberry Hill in Twickenham in 1747, and made his home into "a little Gothic castle," a form of architecture which he and the newly founded Society of Antiquaries greatly favored. In 1765, a decade after Smollett's *Ferdinand Count Fathom* with its horrors appeared, Walpole wrote *The Castle of Otranto*, which established the form and the name of Gothic novel, and pointed the way to a flood of prolific followers. Walpole's first edition purported to be a translation "by William Marshall, Esq. From the original Italian of Onuphrio Muralto, Canon of the Church of St. Nicholas, at Otranto"; but when the novel became (to Walpole's considerable surprise) almost immediately a tremendous success, he claimed authorship. Walpole's castle is crammed with giant swords, enormous, black-plumed helmets, bleeding statues, walking portraits, gloomy cloisters, strange and other-worldly noises, which gruesome properties became the stock in trade of later writers of novels in the Gothic vein. The fragile Isabella cries, "Oh transport! here is the trap-door!" or, elsewhere, "Oh heavens, it is the voice of Manfred?" More stilted and artificial dialogue would be hard to find, but everything about Otranto was admired and copied.

Historical Gothic. As the Gothic form crystallized, two main types emerged: the historical Gothic and the horror Gothic. In the historical variety some attempt at reconstruction of a period was made. Chief among the writers in this field were two women, Sophia Lee, author of *The Recess* (1785), and Jane Porter, who wrote *Thaddeus of Warsaw* (1803) and *Scottish Chiefs* (1810).

Horror Gothic. Ann Radcliffe produced a number of English horror stories, although for the most part she relied on terrifying her public by suggestion rather than gore. Her gloomy landscapes are excellently painted, although her dialogue is stiff and unnatural. Rarely does Mrs. Radcliffe permit herself a truly ghostly ghost, preferring mysteries that have some rational explanation. Her best-known works are *A Sicilian Romance* (1790), *Romance of the Forest* (1791), and *The Mysteries of Udolpho* (1794, at which Jane Austen poked fun 25 years later in her *Northanger Abbey*). A new source of the macabre was opened to English readers when William Taylor of Norwich, Matthew

---

ḍ, d or j; ṣ, s or sh; ṭ, t or ch; ẓ, z or zh; o, F. cloche; ü, F. menu; ćh, Sc. loch; ṅ, F. bonbon.

Gregory ("Monk") Lewis, and others, began about 1790 to bring home from travels in Germany the works of Tieck, Spiess, Musäus, and others who specialized in the grotesque, the horrible, and the criminal. Translations of these German stories soon appeared, including Earl Grosse's *Horrid Mysteries* (1796). In 1797 Lewis wrote *The Monk*, under the influence of this German material, a novel so popular and admired that he was thereafter known as "Monk" Lewis. This book far outdistanced predecessors in fiendish wickedness, supernatural ghastliness, and sadistic sensuality. Lewis had many followers including Edmund Montague, Charlotte Dacre, and H. J. Sarratt. There were hundreds of imitations of his works and those of Mrs. Radcliffe, of which perhaps the only one whose fame survived the age of the Gothic novel is *Frankenstein* by Mary Wollstonecraft (1817). In a different category is Charlotte Smith, who wrote gloomy-sentimental stories featuring deep woods, ruined mansions, moonlight and moaning wind, in which the long-lost heir is a favorite theme; her novels *Emmeline, The Orphan of the Castle, The Old Manor House*, were perhaps more influenced by Goethe's *Sorrows of Werther* (which her sentimental lovers have read) than by the macabre German school that "Monk" Lewis followed. Maria Edgeworth, although popularly known for her Gothic tales, actually wrote very few, and it was her friend Sir Walter Scott who, at last, turned the popular taste to something other than the Gothic novel.

Goths (goths). An ancient Germanic-speaking people which was established in the regions between the Elbe and Vistula rivers in the 3rd century. They made many inroads into different parts of the Roman Empire in the 3rd and 4th centuries, and gradually accepted the Arian form of Christianity. The two great historical divisions were the Visigoths (West Goths) and the Ostrogoths (East Goths). A body of Visigoths settled in the province of Moesia (the present Serbia and part of Bulgaria), and were hence called Moeso-Goths; and their apostle Ulfilas (Wulfila) translated the Scriptures into Gothic. The Visigoths formed a monarchy c418, which existed in southern France until 507, and in Spain until 711. An Ostrogothic kingdom existed in Italy and neighboring regions from 493 to 553. The so-called Tetraxitic Goths are mentioned in the Crimea as late as the 18th century. By extension the name was applied to various other tribes which invaded the Roman Empire.

Götz (or **Goetz**) **von Berlichingen** (gẹts'fon ber'liching.ẹn). A play by Goethe. It is the story of the attempt of the hero to escape from the corrupting influences of the civilized court of the late medieval period, and his ultimate defeat by these influences. The first sketch was finished in 1771. In 1773 Goethe rewrote and published it. In 1804 he prepared another edition for the stage. It is treated in the manner of a Shakespearian historical drama.

Goudge (gŏj), **Elizabeth.** b. in Somersetshire, England, April 24, 1900—. An English novelist. Author of *Island Magic* (1932), *A City of Bells* (1934), *Towers in the Mist* (1936), *The Bird in the Tree* (1939), *Green Dolphin Country* (1944; American title, *Green Dolphin Street*), *Gentian Hill* (1950),

and the short-story collections *Pedlar's Pack* (1935) and *The Icon on the Wall* (1943).

Gould (gōld), **Charles.** An English capitalist in Costaguana, in Joseph Conrad's novel *Nostromo* (1904).

Gould, Sir **Francis Carruthers.** b. at Barnstaple, England, Dec. 2, 1844; d. Jan. 1, 1925. An English caricaturist and politician, noted particularly for his drawings of important financial events, done while he was a member of the London Stock Exchange. Many of these drawings were lithographed and circulated privately. In 1879 he began to illustrate the Christmas editions of *Truth;* in 1887 he began to contribute to the *Pall Mall Gazette;* later he was assistant editor of the *Westminster Gazette.* Among his independent publications are: *Who Killed Cock Robin?* (1897), *Tales Told in the Zoo* (1900), *Froissart's Modern Chronicles* (1902–03), and the serialized *Picture Politics*. He was knighted in 1906.

Gould, Gerald. b. at Scarborough, Yorkshire, England, 1885; d. Nov. 2, 1936. An English critic, essayist, and poet. Educated at University College, London, and Magdalen College, Oxford; writer (1915–19) for the *Daily Herald*, of which he was associate editor (1919–22); literary editor (1922–26) for the *Saturday Review;* fiction critic for *New Statesman* and London *Observer;* interested in liberal causes and a member of the Labour Party. Author of *Lyrics* (1906), *Poems* (1911), *My Lady's Book* (1913), *Monogamy* (1918), *The Happy Tree and Other Poems* (1919), *The Journey* (1920), *Beauty, the Pilgrim* (1927), and *Collected Poems* (1929); *Isabel* (1932), a novel; *Lady Adela* (1920), prose sketches; *Essay on the Nature of the Lyric* (1909), *The English Novel of To-Day* (1924), *Democritus, or the Future of Laughter* (1929), *The Musical Glasses* (1929), and *Refuge from Nightmare* (1933), essays; *The Way to Peace* (1915), *The Coming Revolution in Great Britain* (1920), and *Lesson of Black Friday—A Note on Trade Union Structure* (1921), social studies. *Song, Mortality, Twilight, Wander Thirst*, and *The Happy Tree* are characteristic poems.

Gounod (gö.nō), **Charles François.** b. at Paris, June 17, 1818; d. at St.-Cloud, France, Oct. 18, 1893. A French composer. He entered the Paris Conservatory in 1836, took the second prix de Rome for his cantata *Marie Stuart et Rizzio* in 1837, and in 1839 took the grand prix for his cantata *Fernando*. He thought at one time of entering the church. After some years of study he produced his *Messe Solennelle in G*, some numbers of which were brought out by Hullah at London in 1851. From 1852 to 1860 he was conductor of the Orphéon at Paris. *Faust* was produced at the Théâtre Lyrique, March 19, 1859, and placed him at once in the first rank of his profession. Among his other operas are *Sapho* (1851), *Le Médecin malgré lui* (1858), from Molière's comedy, *Philémon et Baucis* (1860), *La Reine de Saba* (1862), *Mireille* (1864), *Roméo et Juliette* (1867), *Cinq-Mars* (1877), and *Polyeucte* (1878). He also wrote much church music, an oratorio (*La Rédemption*, 1882), the religious work *Mors et vita* (1885), and many single songs and pieces, besides a great deal of music for the Orphéonistes. His *Ave Maria* (properly *Meditation on the*

First Prelude of Bach) is one of the most popular numbers in the vocal repertoire.

Governor of Harfleur (French, àr.flèr; in Shakespeare, här'flö). In Shakespeare's *Henry V*, the governor who surrenders his town to Henry (IV.iv).

Governour, The. [Full title, **The Boke named the Governour.**] An educational and political treatise (1531) by Thomas Elyot, dedicated to Henry VIII.

Gow (gou), **Henry.** See **Smith, Henry.**

Gower (gou'èr). In Shakespeare's *2 Henry IV*, an officer in the royal army. In *Henry V*, he tells Fluellen that the King has ordered all the prisoners killed (IV.vii).

Gower (gō'èr, gou'èr). In Shakespeare's *Pericles*, a character who appears as chorus. He is the poet Gower, speaking octosyllabic couplets or sometimes decasyllabics, in couplets or alternating quatrains. In view of this style, Shakespeare is thought not to have written his part.

Gower, John. b. c1325; d. in Southwark (now part of London), 1408. An English poet. Little is known of his early life, but he appears to have lived in Kent and to have been a man of wide reading. He was well known at court in his later years. His principal work, the *Confessio Amantis* (written in English, probably in 1386), was originally dedicated to Richard II, but in 1394 he changed the dedication to Henry of Lancaster (afterward Henry IV). Caxton printed it in 1483. Among his other works are *Speculum Meditantis* (found 1895, under the title *Mirour de l'omme*) and *Vox Clamantis* (written in Latin, begun in 1381). After the accession of Henry IV, Gower wrote the *Cronica Tripartita*. It treats of occurrences of the time, and the strength of its aspirations and teaching caused Chaucer to call him "the moral Gower." Gower's ballads and other poems (mostly in French) were printed in 1818.

Gowers (gou'èrz), Sir **Ernest Arthur.** b. 1880—. An English government official and linguist. His book *The Complete Plain Words* (1954) is a revised, enlarged edition combining two pamphlets concerning the use of the written word, *Plain Words* (1948), and the *ABC of Plain Words* (1951).

Gowkthrapple (gouk'thrap.l). In Sir Walter Scott's novel *Waverley*, an uncompromisingly devout Puritan preacher.

Gowther (gou'thèr), **Sir.** See **Sir Gowther.**

Goya y Lucientes (gō'yä ē lö.thyen'täs), **Francisco José de.** b. at Fuendetodos, near Saragossa, Spain, March 30, 1746; d. at Bordeaux, France, April 16, 1828. A Spanish painter and etcher. He first studied with Luzán at Saragossa; at 18 he moved to Madrid, and despite poverty, managed to spend several years painting at Rome. Returning to Spain, he designed for the royal tapestry manufactories tapestry cartoons which present a stimulating panorama of the lighter side of Spanish life. Appointed "Painter to the King" in 1786, he recorded with a rapid brush the greatest figures of Spain. His chief interest, however, remained with the plain people, of whom he had intimate knowledge and of whom he painted many pictures. His matchless canvases of a reclining nude young woman, *Maja Nude*, and of the same model in the same pose but dressed, *Maja Clothed*, rank as his most celebrated work. Bold and headstrong, Goya worked and lived in audacious and arrogant independence. His life reflected the disorders of his time. His friendship with the Duchess of Alba is famous. He painted some seven portraits of her and, when she was banished from court, accompanied her into exile; whatever their relations, their lives are inseparably linked. At the age of 50 he produced the etchings known as *Los Caprichos* (Caprices), satires on the superstition and corruption of the time, varied by fantasies involving witches and nightmare figures. Another series of etchings, *La Tauromaquia*, depicted incidents of bullfighting, while in *The Disasters of War* he etched hideous scenes of the French invasion. When over 80 he still painted vigorously at Bordeaux, where he passed his last years amid Spanish refugees.

Evaluation and Technique. Goya's fame rests on his portraits, easel paintings, and etchings. His ecclesiastical decorations lack religious feeling. The main characteristic of Goya's art is its intense realism: his witches, his goblins, even his ghosts are solid. His realism, however, was not concerned only with exteriors; although too much of a painter not to make use of an accident of the moment, he penetrated beyond superficialities and, through generalization and simplification, reached the essence of his subject matter. He was a brilliant though uneven painter. He painted as a whole with considerable impasto, rarely using glazes, and frequently varied his technique to accord with his subject or the personality of his sitter. As he aged, he painted in general more thinly. His work fascinates through its verve, originality, and strangeness. In his imagination and emotionalism he had more kinship to El Greco than to Velázquez. He wrote that he had three masters, Nature, Velázquez, and Rembrandt. He founded no school, as his art was too personal, but he greatly influenced many painters who followed him. Manet, Courbet, and Regnault are among those who felt his spell.

Graal (gräl). See **Grail.**

Grace (grās), **William Gilbert.** b. at Downend, Gloucestershire, England, July 18, 1848; d. at Eltham, Kent, England, Oct. 23, 1915. An English cricket player. He was especially distinguished as a batsman, and had the reputation of being the best all-round player known up to his time. In his 35 years of play (1865–1900) in top-rank cricket, he is said to have held every record worth holding, whether in bowling, batting, or fielding. By profession he was a surgeon.

Grace Abounding. [Full title, **Grace Abounding to the Chief of Sinners.**] An autobiographical work by John Bunyan, published in 1666. This remarkably fervent and sincere narrative describes Bunyan's limited education, youth in company with "all manner of vice and ungodliness," and marriage to a poor but devout wife. The two religious books which constituted her dowry he felt were responsible for his conversion. After much spiritual struggle he joined a Nonconformist community at Bedford and a few years later received from God the call to the ministry.

ḍ, d or j; ṣ, s or sh; ṭ, t or ch; ẓ, z or zh; o, F. cloche; ü, F. menu; ċh, Sc. loch; ṅ, F. bonbon.

Grace-be-here Humgudgeon (grās'bē.hir' hum'-guj.ọn). See **Humgudgeon, Grace-be-here.**

Grace Harkaway (grās härk'ạ.wā). See **Harkaway, Grace.**

Graces, the Three. In Roman mythology, the Gratiae, personifications of grace and beauty. In Greek mythology, they are the Charites, daughters of Zeus by Hera (or Eurynome). The names generally given to the Charites are Euphrosyne, Aglaia, and Thalia. In Sparta and in Athens only two were recognized. They were worshiped at Athens, Messene, and elsewhere in Greece, but they had no cult in Rome.

Gracioso (grä.thyō'sō). A popular addition made by Lope de Vega to the stock characters of Spanish comedy. He was a comic character, sometimes half buffoon, like the "fantastical person" of the contemporary English stage.

Gradgrind (grad'grīnd), **Louisa** and **Tom.** In Dickens's *Hard Times*, the daughter and son of Thomas Gradgrind. Louisa marries the wicked Bounderby.

Gradgrind, Thomas. A retired merchant in Dickens's *Hard Times*. He is "a man of facts and calculations," in his own words, and is so practical that he is hardly human: "Now, what I want is facts. Teach these boys and girls nothing but facts. Facts alone are wanted in life. Plant nothing else, and root out everything else. You can only form the minds of reasoning animals upon facts; nothing else will ever be of any service to them. This is the principle on which I bring up my own children, and this is the principle on which I bring up these children. Stick to facts, sir!"

Graeme (grām), **Malcolm.** In Sir Walter Scott's poem *The Lady of the Lake*, a ward of the king. He rebels to aid the outlawed James Douglas, but is pardoned at the intercession of Ellen Douglas.

Graeme, Roland. In Sir Walter Scott's novel *The Abbot*, the lawful heir of the castle of Avenel, educated as her page by the Lady of Avenel, who believes him to be of mean birth.

Graevius (grä'vẹ.ús), **Johann Georg.** [German surname: **Gräve, Greffe.**] b. at Naumburg-on-the-Saale, Germany, Jan. 29, 1623; d. at Utrecht, Netherlands, Jan. 11, 1703. A German classical scholar, for many years professor at Utrecht. He wrote *Thesaurus antiquitatum Romanarum* (1694–99), *Thesaurus antiquitatum et historiarum Italiae* (1704–25), and others.

Graham (grā'ạm), **Dougal.** b. 1724; d. July 20, 1779. A Scottish chapbook writer and bellman, who, although badly deformed, followed the army of Prince Charles Edward Stuart in 1745 and described his military exploits in rough but humorous doggerel. His other chapbooks, descriptive of his townsmen, are valuable to students of folklore for their references to local superstitions.

Graham, Ennis. Pseudonym of **Molesworth, Mary Louisa.**

Graham, Harry Jocelyn Clive. b. 1874; d. Oct. 30, 1936. An English dramatist, poet, and journalist. Coauthor of some 20 plays, he is the author also of *Ruthless Rhymes for Heartless Homes* (1899), *Ballads of the Boer War* (1902), *Misrepresentative Men* (1904), *Fiscal Ballads* and *Verse and Worse* (both 1905), *Misrepresentative Women* (1906), *Familiar Faces* (1907), *A Group of Scottish Women* (1908), *The Mother of Parliaments* (1910), *Lord Bellinger* and *Canned Classics* (both 1911), *Perfect Gentleman* (1912), *The Motley Muse* and *Splendid Failures* (both 1913), *The Complete Sportsman* (1914), *Rhymes for Riper Years* (1916), *Biffin and His Circle* (1919), *The World We Laugh In* (1924), *The Last of the Biffins* (1925), *Strained Relations* (1926), *More Ruthless Rhymes* (1930), *The Biffin Papers* (1933), and *Private Life of Gregory Gorm* (1936).

Graham, James. [Titles: 5th Earl and 1st Marquis of **Montrose.**] b. 1612; hanged at Edinburgh, May 21, 1650. A Scottish nobleman and soldier. He served in the army of the Scottish Covenanters at the beginning of the English Civil War, but afterward joined the king, by whom he was made lieutenant general of Scotland, in 1644. He defeated the Covenanters at Tippermuir on September 1 and at Aberdeen on Sept. 13, 1644, and at Inverlochy on February 2, Auldearn on May 9, Alford on July 2, and Kilsyth on Aug. 15, 1645. He was defeated by David Leslie at Philiphaugh on Sept. 13, 1645, and expelled from Scotland. He afterward entered the service of the emperor Ferdinand III, by whom he was made a field marshal. In 1650 he conducted an abortive Royalist descent on Scotland, and was captured and executed.

Graham, John. [Called **Graham of Claverhouse** (klav'ẽrz, klā'vẽrz, klav'ẽr.hous); title, 1st Viscount **Dundee;** known as **Bloody Claverse** and **Bonny Dundee.**] b. c1649; d. July 27 or 28, 1689. A Scottish soldier. He served in the Dutch army under the Prince of Orange, returning to Scotland in 1677. In 1678 he was appointed captain of a troop of dragoons, and was ordered to enforce certain stringent laws that had been enacted against the Scottish Covenanters. The severity with which he executed his orders provoked a rising, and the Covenanters defeated him at Drumclog on June 1, 1679. He spent the next ten years systematically searching out and punishing severely the leaders of the Covenanters. In 1689 Claverhouse raised a body of Highlanders to fight for James II, who remained in France, against William III, and on July 27, 1689, gained the battle of Killiecrankie, but fell mortally wounded. With his death, the Jacobite rebellion collapsed. His epithets indicate the position he holds in Scottish legend: to the Covenanters he was a hated tyrant; to the Jacobites, Bonny Dundee was the invincible hero, invulnerable to lead, killed by one of his own silver buttons. He is a character in Sir Walter Scott's novel *Old Mortality.*

Graham, Mary. In Dickens's *Martin Chuzzlewit*, the young woman whom Martin finally marries, after his adventures in America and after his reconciliation with his father.

Graham, Robert. [Also, **Cunninghame-Graham.**] b. at Gartmore, near Perthshire and Stirlingshire, Scotland, c1735; d. c1797. A Scottish poet. He added Cunninghame (his mother's maiden name) to his surname in 1796. Politically radical and in active sympathy with French revolutionary principles, he was member of Parliament (1794–96) for Stirlingshire, presenting without success a bill that anticipated the reform bill of 1832. Author of many songs and poems, he is remembered for his charming lyric *If doughty deeds my lady please.*

Graham, Stephen. b. 1884—. An English traveler and writer. Many of his books are concerned with Russian customs, history, and literature, and include *Russia and the World* (1915), *Through Russian Central Asia* (1916), *Russia in Division* (1925), *Stalin—An Impartial Study* (1931), *Boris Godunof* (1933), and *A Life of Alexander II, Tsar of Russia* (1935); among his other works are *The Moving Tent* (1939), and *From War to War* (1940).

Grahame (grā'ạm), **James.** b. at Glasgow, April 22, 1765; d. near Glasgow, Sept. 14, 1811. A Scottish poet. His chief work is *The Sabbath* (1804). He also wrote *Wallace: a Tragedy* (1799), *British Georgics*, and others.

Grahame, Kenneth. b. at Edinburgh, March 8, 1859; d. July 6, 1932. An English author. He was secretary (1898–1908) of the Bank of England. His books include *Pagan Papers* (1893), *The Golden Age* (1895), *Dream Days* (1898), *The Headswoman* (1898), and *The Wind in the Willows* (1908), a story for children.

Graham of Claverhouse (klav'ẽrz, klä'vẽrz, klav'ẽrhous). See **Graham, John.**

Grail (grāl). [Also: **Graal, Holy Grail, Sangreal** (sang'grẹ.ạl).] In Arthurian romance and legend, a cup or chalice, used by Christ at the Last Supper. In this vessel Joseph of Arimathea caught the last drops of Christ's blood as He was taken from the Cross. By Joseph, according to one account, it was carried to Britain. Other accounts affirm that it was brought by angels from heaven and entrusted to a body of knights, who guarded it on the top of a mountain; when approached by any one not perfectly pure, it vanished from sight. The Grail having been lost, it became the great object of search or quest to knights errant of all nations, none being qualified to discover it but a knight perfectly chaste in thought and act. Perceval, Gawain, and Galahad are the knights who usually achieve the quest of the Grail. The best-known version is that of Thomas Malory in his *Morte d'Arthur*. In the *Parsifal* of Wolfram of Eschenbach the Grail is a precious stone confided by angels to the care of a religious brotherhood, "the Chevaliers of the Grail." The earliest extant version of the story is Chrétien de Troyes's *Perceval* (c1180).

Grainger (grān'jẽr), **James.** b. probably at Duns, Berwickshire, Scotland, c1721; d. on the island of St. Christopher (St. Kitts), West Indies, Dec. 16, 1766. A Scottish physician and poet. After 1753 he settled at London, where he became intimate with Johnson and other famous men. In 1759 he went to the West Indies. He published a number of works, including essays on medicine. Among his poems are an *Ode on Solitude* (in Dodsley's collection, 1755) and *The Sugar Cane* (1764). He translated part of Ovid's *Epistles* (1758), and the *Elegies of Tibullus* and the poems of Sulpicia (1759). He assisted, with others, Charlotte Lenox in her translation of Brumoy's *Théâtre des Grecs* (1759).

Grainne (grän'yẹ). In the Fenian cycle of Irish legend, the second wife of Fionn mac Cumhail (Finn MacCool), who eloped with Diarmuid,

Fionn's kinsman. In *The Pursuit of Diarmuid and Grainne*, the longest and most famous story in the Fenian cycle, Fionn follows the lovers across Ireland and finally kills Diarmuid. After a number of years, Grainne forgets her resentment and hatred of Fionn; and finally marries him.

Grammarian's Funeral, A. A poem (1855) by Robert Browning.

Granby (gran'bi), Marquis of. See **Manners, John.**

Granby, The Marquis of. See **Marquis of Granby, The.**

Grand (grand), **Sarah.** [Pseudonym of **Frances Elizabeth McFall**; maiden name, **Clark.**] b. at Donaghadee, Ireland, 1862; d. at Calne, Wiltshire, England, May 12, 1943. English novelist, essayist, and feminist. She served (1923, 1925–29) as mayoress of Bath. Author of *Ideala* (1888), *The Heavenly Twins* (3 vols., 1893), *Our Manifold Nature* (1894), *The Beth Book* (1897), *The Modern Man and Maid* (1898), *Babs the Impossible* (1900), *Emotional Moments* (1908), *Adnam's Orchard* (1912), *The Winged Victory* (1916), and *Variety* (1922).

"Grand Corrupter," the. A nickname of **Walpole, Sir Robert.**

Grandcourt (grand'kōrt), **Henleigh Mallinger.** One of the principal characters in George Eliot's novel *Daniel Deronda*.

Grand Duke, The. [Full title, **The Grand Duke, or the Statutory Duel.**] An operetta in two acts by Sir Arthur Sullivan, with a libretto by W. S. Gilbert, first performed at the London Savoy Theatre on March 7, 1896.

Grandfather, Little Nell's. In Charles Dickens's *Old Curiosity Shop*, a good and honest man who has established the shop from which the book takes its name in order to support himself and his granddaughter, in whom he sees his own beloved wife and daughter. Unable to provide security for Little Nell from the shop alone, he takes to gambling, and presently loses everything he possesses. His younger brother learns of his hardships, and returns from abroad with money enough to support both Little Nell and her grandfather, but Nell has died by the time he arrives, and her grandfather dies shortly thereafter.

Grandfather Smallweed (smôl'wẽd). See **Smallweed, Grandfather.**

Grand Guignol (grän gē.nyol). See under **Guignol.**

Grandison (gran'di.sọn), **Cardinal.** A character in Benjamin Disraeli's novel *Lothair*.

Grandison, Sir Charles. The central figure of Richardson's novel *Sir Charles Grandison*, supposed to be the ideal embodiment of masculine character and sentiment, as Clarissa Harlowe is of feminine.

Grand Monarque (grän mo.nårk), **le.** See **Louis XIV.**

"Grand Old Man," the. See **Gladstone, William Ewart.**

Grandpré (French, grän.prā; in Shakespeare, gran'prā). In Shakespeare's *Henry V,* a French lord who vividly describes the worn and desperate appearance of the English army on the morning of Agincourt (IV.ii).

ḍ, d or j; ṣ, s or sh; ṭ, t or ch; ẓ, z or zh; o, F. cloche; ü, F. menu; čh, Sc. loch; ń, F. bonbon.

Grand Remonstrance. See **Remonstrance, Grand.**

Granger (grān'jẻr). A character in Southerne's comedy *The Maid's Last Prayer.*

Granger. A character in Colley Cibber's comedy *The Refusal.*

Granger, Edith. Dombey's second wife in Dickens's *Dombey and Son.*

Granger, James. b. at Shaston, Dorsetshire, England, 1723; d. at Shiplake, Oxfordshire, England, April 4, 1776. An English writer and print collector. He matriculated at Christ Church, Oxford, in 1743, but took no degree. He took holy orders, and was presented to the vicarage of Shiplake. About 1773 he made a tour through Holland. He wrote *A Biographical History of England . . . with a preface showing the utility of a collection of engraved portraits . . .* (1769). This was continued with additions at different times till in 1824 the work had increased to 6 volumes. In 1806 another continuation appeared from materials left by Granger and the collections of the Rev. Mark Noble, who edited it. The wholesale destruction of illustrated biographical works necessary to accomplish this gave rise to the term "grangerize."

Grangousier (grän.gö.zyā). [Eng. trans., *"Great Gullet."*] The father of Gargantua in François Rabelais's romance *Gargantua.* He is supposed by some to represent Jean d'Albret.

Grant (grant), **Anne.** [Maiden name, **Macvicar;** called Mrs. **Grant of Laggan** (lag'an).] b. at Glasgow, Feb. 21, 1755; d. at Edinburgh, Nov. 7, 1838. A Scottish author. She wrote *Original Poems, with some Translations from the Gaelic* (1802), *Letters from the Mountains* (1803), *Memoirs of an American Lady* (1808), *Essays on the Superstitions of the Highlands* (1811), and others. Among her poems is "Oh, Where, Tell Me, Where Has My Highland Laddie Gone?"

Grant, Digby. In James Albery's *The Two Roses,* a typical blackguard of society. Henry Irving was successful in the role.

Grant, James. b. at Edinburgh, Aug. 1, 1822; d. there, May 5, 1887. A Scottish novelist. He served (1840–43) in the English army. He wrote nearly 50 historical romances on Scottish subjects and edited *Old and New Edinburgh* (3 vols., 1880–83). Among his novels are *The Romance of War* (1845) and *The Adventures of an Aide-de-Camp* (1848).

Granta (gran'ta). See **Cam.**

Grant Duff (grant' duf'), **Douglas Ainslie.** Original full name of **Ainslie, Douglas.**

Grantly (grant'li), **Archdeacon.** A principal character in Anthony Trollope's novels of the Barsetshire series, including *The Warden* and *Barchester Towers.* He represents the opposition to Mrs. Proudie.

Grantorto (gran.tôr'tō). In Spenser's *Faerie Queene,* the giant who held Irena (Ireland) captive, eventually slain by Sir Artegal. He is intended to represent rebellion.

Granuffo (gra.nuf'ō). In John Marston's play *The Parasitaster,* a character who makes a reputation for wisdom by saying nothing.

Granville (gran'vil), **George.** See **Grenville, George.**

Granville-Barker (gran'vil.bär'kẻr), **Harley Granville.** b. at London, Nov. 25, 1877; d. at Paris, Aug. 31, 1946. An English playwright, actor, and manager. He first appeared on the stage with the Ben Greet Company, and subsequently acted with the Elizabethan Stage Society and opposite Mrs. Patrick Campbell. He was manager (1904 *et seq.*) with J. E. Vedrenne of the Court Theatre, presenting plays of the "new drama" of Shaw, Ibsen, Sudermann, and other dramatists. This venture was of much value in establishing modern British drama and in bringing before the public the Scandinavian drama which had furnished such an impetus to it. He was visiting professor at Yale (1940–41) and Harvard (1941–43). Author of *A National Theatre* (1907) with William Archer, *The Exemplary Theatre* (1922), *Prefaces to Shakespeare* (1923 *et seq.*), *On Dramatic Method* (1931), *The Study of Drama* (1934), *On Poetry in Drama* (1937), and *The Perennial Shakespeare* (1937). With his wife, Helen Huntington Granville-Barker, he translated plays from the Spanish of G. Martínez Sierra and the brothers Quintero and by himself from the German of Schnitzler and the French of Guitry and Romains. His own plays include *The Marrying of Ann Leete* (1901), *Brunella* (1904), *The Voysey Inheritance* (1905), *Waste* (1907), *The Madras House* (1910), and *Vote By Ballot* (1907).

Grass of Parnassus (pär.nas'us), **The.** A volume of poetry (1888) by Andrew Lang.

Grateful Servant, The. A play by James Shirley, licensed in 1629 under the title of *The Faithful Servant,* but printed in 1630 under the former name, by which it is known.

Gratiano (grash.i.ä'nō, grä.shi-, grā-). In Shakespeare's *Merchant of Venice,* one of Bassanio's companions. He marries Nerissa.

Gratiano. In Shakespeare's *Othello,* the brother of Brabantio. As the uncle of Desdemona, he succeeds to Othello's fortunes after the latter has killed both her and himself.

Grattan (grat'an), **Thomas Colley.** b. at Dublin, 1792; d. at London, July 4, 1864. An Irish novelist, poet, and general writer. He became British consul at Boston in 1839. He assisted in the negotiations which resulted in the Webster-Ashburton treaty (1842). In 1846 he returned to England, and thereafter resided chiefly at London. He was a friend of Washington Irving. His works include *Highways and Byways, or Tales of the Roadside picked up in the French Provinces by a Walking Gentleman* (1823; dedicated to Washington Irving), *Ben Nazir, the Saracen: a Tragedy* (1827), and many others.

Grave, The. A Middle English fragment of 25 lines of alliterative verse, written probably in the early 12th century and retaining the form of the Old English elegy. The fragment is of some importance in the history of English literature as one of the few existing transitional pieces between the Old English and Middle English periods, but it has also considerable poetic merit (as Longfellow perceived when he paraphrased it eight centuries later).

Grave, The. A didactic poem by Robert Blair, of about 800 lines, published in 1743. It was illustrated by designs by William Blake.

Graveairs (grāv'ärz), **Lady.** A character in Colley Cibber's comedy *The Careless Husband.*

Gravediggers. See under **Clowns.**

Graves (grāvz), **Alfred Perceval. b.** at Dublin, July 22, 1846; d. at Harlech, Wales, Dec. 27, 1931. An Irish poet, editor, and anthologist, leader of the Irish literary and musical renascence and of the Pan-Celtic movement; father of Robert Graves. He contributed to *John Bull, Punch,* the *Athenaeum* and the *Spectator,* and was president (twice) and secretary of the Irish Literary Society. He edited *Songs of Irish Wit and Humour* (1894), *Irish Song Book* (1894), *Welsh Poetry, Old and New in English Verse* (1912), *Book of Irish Poetry,* a complete anthology of Irish Verse (1915), *Treasury of Irish Prose and Verse* (1915), and was editor in chief of *Every Irishman's Library.* He was the author of *The Elementary School Manager* (1875), *Songs of Killarney* (1872), *Irish Songs and Ballads* (1879; several editions), and *Father O'Flynn and Other Lyrics* (1889). He also rendered into English the verse works of Cieriog Huges, the "Welsh Burns." He is best known as a poet for his ballad "Father O'Flynn," which first appeared (1872) in the *Spectator;* he is represented in anthologies by "The Girl with the Cows," "The Limerick Lasses," "The Irish Spinning-Wheel," "Irish Lullaby," "Fan Fitzgerl," "Herring is King," and "The Beautiful Bay."

Graves, Clotilde Inez Mary. [Pseudonym, **Richard Dehan.**] b. June 3, 1863; d. Dec. 3, 1932. An Irish novelist and playwright.

Graves, Ida. b. in India, 1902——. An English poet and sculptress.

Graves, Richard. b. at Mickleton, Gloucestershire, England, May 4, 1715; d. at Claverton, near Bath, England, Nov. 23, 1804. An English poet and novelist. He served (1748 *et seq.*) as rector of Claverton. He was the author of a large number of works, some of which were popular; one only, a novel, *The Spiritual Quixote* (1772), is now remembered.

Graves, Robert. [Full name, **Robert Ranke Graves.**] b. at London, July 24, 1895——. An English poet, novelist, and critic; son of Alfred Perceval Graves. He is the author of *Poems 1914–1926, Poems 1926–30, Poems 1930–1933, Goodbye to All That, An Autobiography* (1929), *But It Still Goes On, a Miscellany* (1930), *The Real David Copperfield* (1933), *I, Claudius* (1934), *Claudius the God* (1934), *T. E. Lawrence to his Biographer* (1937), *Count Belisarius* (1938), *Wife to Mr. Milton* (1943), *Hercules, My Shipmate* (1945), *The White Goddess* (1947), *Watch the North Wind Rise* (1949; published in Great Britain as *Seven Days in New Crete*), *Occupation: Writer* (1950), *Poems and Satires* (1951), and *Poems,* 1953 (1953). *Sergeant Lamb's America* (1940) and *Proceed, Sergeant Lamb* (1941) are both based on a British soldier's memoirs of the Revolutionary War. He has translated Apuleius's *The Golden Ass* (1950). His most recent novel, *Homer's Daughter* (1955), discusses the author's contention (agreeing with Samuel "Erewhon" Butler) that the *Odyssey* was written by a woman, Nausicaa, the Princess of the Phaeacians.

Graveyard School. A name applied to the group of mid-18th-century English poets who were the literary followers of Robert Blair and Edward Young. Their poetry was of a predominantly melancholy nature.

Gray (grā), **David. b.** at Merkland, Scotland, Jan. 29, 1838; d. there, Dec. 3, 1861. A Scottish poet. He was the author of *The Luggie and Other Poems* (1862).

Gray, Dr. Gideon. The surgeon of Middlemas in Sir Walter Scott's *The Surgeon's Daughter.*

Gray, Ellington. Pseudonym of **Jacob, Naomi Ellington.**

Gray, Menie. The heroine of Sir Walter Scott's short novel *The Surgeon's Daughter.*

Gray, Thomas. b. at London, Dec. 26, 1716; d. at Cambridge, England, July 30, 1771. An English poet. He was sent to Eton c1725, forming an intimacy there with Horace Walpole, Richard West, and Thomas Ashton ("the Quadruple Alliance"). In 1734 he was admitted as a pensioner at Peterhouse, Cambridge, and in 1739 went abroad with Walpole on the grand tour. They quarreled in May, 1741, but several years later (1745) resumed their friendship. Gray returned alone from Europe in 1741 and settled at Cambridge, where he resided, except for summer visits to his mother, for the rest of his life. In 1757 he refused the laureateship. He became (1768) professor of modern history at Cambridge. His best-known work is *An Elegy Written in a Country Churchyard* (1751), one of the most-quoted works in English literature. His other principal works are *Ode on a Distant Prospect of Eton College* (1747), *The Progress of Poesy* (1754), and *The Bard* (1757). He was an able literary critic and an accomplished scholar in many fields, among them natural history, philosophy, history (modern, classical, and Oriental), and classical, French, Italian, and English literature. He also made several translations from medieval Welsh and Scandinavian poetry. He is ranked among the finest of the 18th-century letter-writers and (largely because of his interest in the Middle Ages and his appreciation of the scenery of the Alps and the English Lake District) is regarded as a forerunner of the 19th-century Romantic poets. His poems and letters were edited by W. Mason in 1775, and the works, including the letters, by Mitford (5 vols., 1835–43) and E. W. Gosse (4 vols., 1884). The poems have also been edited by A. L. Poole and L. Whibley (1937) and the letters by P. Toynbee and L. Whibley (3 vols., 1935). Biographies of him have been written by Gosse (1882), R. W. Ketton-Cremer (1935), and David Cecil (1947).

Gray Friars. See **Grey Friars.**

Gray's Inn. One of the London Inns of Court. It is situated on the N side of Holborn and to the W of Gray's Inn Lane. It is the fourth inn of court in importance and size. It derives its name from the noble family of Gray of Wilton, whose residence it originally was. It still contains a handsome hall dating from 1560.

Great Adventure, The. A drama (1913) by Arnold Bennett, based on his novel *Buried Alive.*

Great Catherine. A play (1913) by George Bernard Shaw, included by most critics among his lesser works.

Great Cham of Literature (kam). A nickname given to Samuel Johnson by Smollett in a letter to Wilkes.

"Great Commoner," the. See **Pitt, William** (1708–78).

Great Duke of Florence (flor'ens), **The.** A play by Philip Massinger, licensed in 1627 and printed in 1636. It was one of Charles Lamb's favorite plays.

"Great Earl," the. See **Douglas, Archibald** (c1449–1514).

Great Eastern. A steamship, the largest built prior to 1899, when the *Oceanic* was launched. It was designed by I. K. Brunel, and was launched at Millwall on the Thames in 1858; made its first voyage across the Atlantic in June, 1860; was frequently employed from 1865 in cable laying; and in 1886 was sold to be broken up for scrap. Length over all, 692 ft.; width, 83 ft.; depth, 58 ft.; displacement, 27,000 tons.

Great Expectations. A novel by Charles Dickens, which appeared serially (1860–61) in his own magazine, *All the Year Round*. It was first published in book form in 1861. It is, like *David Copperfield*, an autobiographical novel, but it is less spontaneous and more finely wrought. Technically, it is probably Dickens's most successful first-person narrative, and contains his best portrayal (in Pip) of a developing character. The original unhappy ending of Pip's love affair with Estella was scrapped at the suggestion of Bulwer-Lytton.

Great Harry (har'i). The first warship of the British navy. She was built in 1488, in the reign of Henry VII, was a three-master, and is said to have cost 14,000 pounds. She is supposed to have been burned accidentally at Woolwich in 1553.

Greatheart (grāt'härt). In the second part of Bunyan's *Pilgrim's Progress*, the guide and valiant protector of Christiana and her children.

Great Hoggarty Diamond (hog'ạr.ti), **The.** A novel by Thackeray, published in 1841. The Hoggarty diamond has been given to Mr. Samuel Titmarsh by an old aunt, and brings him temporary prosperity. Soon, however, he comes under the power of a swindler, Mr. Brough, and the West Diddlesex Association. He is sent to prison, but is rescued through the efforts of his young wife.

Great Rebellion, The. See **Civil War, English.**

Greats. [Also: **greats**; formerly, **Great-Go**.] In the great English universities, a colloquial term for the main body of examinations required before the granting of a degree. See also **Smalls.**

Great Schism. See **Schism, Great.**

Great Well, The. A four-act play (1923) by Alfred Sutro.

Great White Army, The. A historical novel by Sir Max Pemberton, published in 1915. It deals with Napoleon and his Grand Army at Moscow in 1812.

Grecian Coffee House (grē'shạn). A London coffee house in Devereux Court, on the left of Essex Street. It was one of the earliest establishments of its kind, opened in 1652. It was named for the nationality of its proprietor, was frequented by Addison and Steele, and did not close until 1843.

Grecian Daughter, The. A tragedy by Arthur Murphy, produced in 1772. It is a story of filial

piety; the stage success of the play was greatly due to Spranger Barry and his wife.

Grecian Urn, Ode on a. See **Ode on a Grecian Urn.**

Greco (grek'ō), **El.** b. at Candia, Crete, c1548; d. at Toledo, Spain, April 7, 1614. A Greek-Spanish religious and portrait painter, sculptor, architect, philosopher, and scholar. He studied at Venice under Titian, and was influenced by Bassano and Tintoretto. During his residence at Rome he studied the work of Michelangelo, and painted for Cardinal Farnese, before going to live in Spain, some time before 1577. Some of his famous paintings are *The Stripping of Christ before the Crucifixion*, *Dead Christ in the Arms of God*, *Pentecost*, *Baptism of Christ*, *Crucifixion*, and *Resurrection* (all in the Prado, Madrid), *The Healing of the Blind* (at the Parma and Dresden museums), *Ascension of Christ*, *Saint Maurice and His Legion*, *Coronation of the Virgin*, *Saint Joseph*, (the last two in the San José Chapel, Toledo), *Saint Martin* and *Virgin with Saints* (Widener Collection, Philadelphia), *Dream of Philip II*, *Saint John the Evangelist*, *Saint Francis*, *Saint Peter* (Phillips Memorial Gallery, Washington, D. C.), *Saint Eugene*, *Laocoön* (Munich), *The Holy Family*, *Saint Dominic*, *Saint Ildefonso* (Hospital of the Caridad, Castile), *Christ Driving the Money Changers from the Temple* (Minneapolis Institute of Art), *Christ and the Money Changers*, another strikingly different treatment of the same theme, *Boy Lighting a Coal*, and *Toledo in a Storm*. Many of his portraits are in the Prado, but except in a few cases the names of the sitters have not come down to us. His *Lady with the Flower* (J. Stirling Maxwell Collection) and *Lady with the Mantilla* (Johnson Collection, Philadelphia) are two of his best paintings of women. His *Assumption of the Virgin* (1578) is in the Art Institute of Chicago. His *Burial of Count Orgaz* (1578), which he did for the Church of Saint Thomas at Toledo, is regarded as his masterpiece. He is represented in the Metropolitan Museum of Art at New York by *View of Toledo*, in which he aimed at painting the spirit of the city rather than the city itself, *Cardinal Don Fernando Niño de Guevara*, in which he caught the cruelty of the Grand Inquisitor, *The Adoration of the Shepherds*, one of his favorite subjects and one to which he returned many times, and *Portrait of a Man*, which has erroneously been regarded as a portrait of himself. El Greco is first mentioned in a letter (Rome, Nov. 16, 1570) by Julio Clovio, the miniaturist, to Cardinal Farnese: "There has arrived in Rome a young man from Candia, a pupil of Titian, who, I think, is a painter of rare talent. . . . He has painted a portrait of himself which is admired by all the painters in Rome. I should like him to be under the patronage of your reverend lordship without any other contribution towards his living than a room in the Farnese Palace." He made portraits of Clovio (Naples Museum), who also appears, along with Titian and Michelangelo, in the lower right-hand corner of the (Minneapolis) *Christ Driving the Money Changers from the Temple*, and of Hortensio Félix Paravicino, the preacher, who wrote a sonnet to his memory. The *Self-Portrait*, mentioned by Clovio as having aroused the admiration of his fellow artists, has been lost, unless one regards it as identical with the *Portrait of a Man*, which authoritative art critics are inclined to doubt. His attention-compelling elongated *Saint Jerome* is in the Frick Collection at New York. His last work was *The Baptism*. At his death he left 150 drawings (none of which have come down to us), 115 paintings in a finished state, 15 sketches, and 4 grisailles. He had a fine library of works on architecture and the works of Homer, Aristotle, Plutarch, Petrarch, Tasso, and Ariosto, and he lived and worked in 24 rooms of the palace of the Marquis of Villena. According to Pacheco, the teacher and father-in-law of Velázquez, who visited him in 1611, he was a great philosopher and a wit as well as a painter. Ortensio, the orator, and Luis de Gongona, the poet, remembered him in sonnets. Maino and Tristan studied under him, but not with any great degree of success, students finding it difficult to catch or imitate, and El Greco to teach, his style. His Greek name was Kyriakos Theotokopoulos, his Spanish name, Domingo Teotocopuli (or Theotocopuli), and his Italian name, Domenico Teotocopulo (or Teoscopoli or Teoscopuli). His son, Jorge Manuel (1578–after 1619), also a painter, sculptor, and architect, worked with him, carried out his instructions, and finished those paintings that his father put aside unfinished. The mother of Jorge was Doña Jeronima de las Cuevas, but it is not definitely known that she was El Greco's wife. The dates of his birth and death are uncertain, every year between 1541–48, both inclusive, being given for his birth, with a certain preference on the part of students for the earlier, rather than the later, dates. There seems to be more agreement on 1614 for his death, but some authorities give 1625. El Greco was recognized as an amazing genius in his day, was forgotten and neglected for a long time after, was rediscovered in the 20th century, and now ranks as one of the great masters. Like Van Gogh he has inspired a large and growing bibliography. He is the subject of studies by Cossio (1908), Calvert and Hartley (1909), Barrè (1911), August L. Mayer (1911 and 1926), E. du Cue Trapier (1925), J. F. Willumsen (1927), Virginia Hersch (1929), and Frank Rutter (1930). Some of the best El Greco criticism in print is to be found in W. Somerset Maugham's novel of art and artists, *Of Human Bondage*, in the remarks made by Thorpe Athelny to the club-footed hero, Philip Carey.

Green (grēn). In Shakespeare's *Richard II*, a servant of the King.

Green, Henry. [Pseudonym of **Henry Yorke**.] b. 1905—. An English novelist. Educated at Oxford, he is the managing director of an industrial firm at Birmingham, but his identity was for long carefully concealed from the reading public. Author of the novels *Blindness* (1926), *Living* (1929), *Party Going* (1939), *Pack My Bag* (1940), *Caught* (1943), *Loving* (1945), *Back* (1946), *Concluding* (1948), and *Doting* (1952).

Green, John Richard. b. at Oxford, England, Dec. 12, 1837; d. at Menton, France, March 7, 1883. An English historian. He was graduated from Oxford in 1859, became a curate at London in 1860, and in 1866 was appointed incumbent of St. Philip's, Stepney. He became librarian at Lambeth in 1869. He published a *Short History of the English People* (1874), *A History of the English People* (1877–80),

The Making of England (1882), and *The Conquest of England* (1883). His *Short History*, written with an eye to color and to the social history of the people, has been extremely popular.

Green, Matthew. b. at London, 1696; d. there, 1737. An English poet. A minor 18th-century poet and wit, he was author of *The Grotto* (1732) and *The Spleen* (1737), admired by both Pope and Gray. Gray admitted that he had unconsciously borrowed from *The Grotto* the expression "Father Thames," used in his Eton College ode.

Green, Thomas Hill. b. at Birkin, Yorkshire, England, April 7, 1836; d. at Oxford, England, March 26, 1882. An English philosopher. He was educated at Rugby and at Balliol College, Oxford, and taught at Oxford, first as tutor and later as professor (1878–82) of moral philosophy. He was the leading British exponent of the doctrines of Hegel, and exerted a powerful influence on the philosophical thought of his time. Of his published works the most important, the *Prolegomena to Ethics*, appeared in 1883.

Green, Verdant. See **Adventures of Mr. Verdant Green, An Oxford Freshman.**

Green, Widow. In J. Sheridan Knowles's *The Love Chase*, "the pleasant widow whose fortieth year, instead of autumn, brings a second summer in."

Greenaway (grēn'a̤.wā), **Kate.** b. at London, March 17, 1846; d. at Hampstead, London, Nov. 6, 1901. An English water-color painter and illustrator. She enjoyed great popularity as an illustrator of children's stories. Her figures were dressed in a peculiar fashion, based on the Empire style in France, which became known as the "Kate Greenaway style."

Green Branches. A volume of poems (1916) by James Stephens.

Greene (grēn), **Graham.** b. Oct. 2, 1904—. An English novelist and journalist. He was a staff member (1926–30) of the London *Times*, and motion-picture critic (1935–39) and literary editor (1940–41) for *The Spectator*. He is the author of travel books, detective fiction, short stories, and novels, some of which he describes as "entertainments," to distinguish them from novels of deeper purpose. Among his works are *The Man Within* (1929), *Stamboul Train* (1932), *England Made Me* (1935; published in the United States as *The Shipwrecked* in 1953), *Journey Without Maps* (1936), *The Basement Room* (1936), *Brighton Rock* (1938), *The Lawless Roads—A Mexican Journey* (1939), *The Confidential Agent* (1939), *The Labyrinthine Ways* (1940), *The Ministry of Fear* (1943), *The Heart of the Matter* (1948), *Nineteen Stories* (1949), *The Third Man* (1950), *The End of the Affair* (1952), *The Lost Childhood* (1952), and *Loser Takes All* (1955). His novel *The Power and the Glory* (1940) received the Hawthornden prize. Many of his books have been scenarized. He is a Roman Catholic; both his fiction and his travel writing reveal a deep interest in the problem of evil.

Greene, Maurice. b. at London, c1695; d. there, Dec. 1, 1755. An English organist and composer, principally of church music. His chief work is *Forty Select Anthems* (1743).

Greene, Robert. b. at Norwich, England, c1560; d. at London, Sept. 3, 1592. An English dramatist, novelist, and poet. He was educated at St. John's College and at Clare Hall, Cambridge, where he took his master's degree in 1583, and was incorporated at Oxford in 1588. After leaving the university he seems to have led a dissolute life abroad for some time. In 1592, after ten years of reckless living and hasty literary production, he died from an excess of pickled herrings and Rhenish wine, deserted by all his friends. Gabriel Harvey attacked him shortly after his death in *Four Letters and Certain Sonnets*, Meres, Chettle, Nashe, and others defended him, and Nashe, who had also been attacked, published his *Strange News*, directed more against Harvey than in defense of Greene. The quarrel was prolonged. Greene's fame rests mostly on the songs and eclogues which are interspersed through his prose works. Among his works are the tracts and pamphlets *Mamilia* (entered on the Stationers' Register, 1580 and 1583), *Gwydonius, the Carde of Fancie* (1584), *Arbasto, the Anatomie of Fortune* (1584), *Planetomachia* (1585), *Euphues his Censure to Philautus* (1587), *Perimedes the Blacke-Smith* (1588), *Pandosto, the Triumph of Time* (1588; called in later editions *Dorastus and Fawnia*), *Alcida* or *Greene's Metamorphosis* (licensed 1588), *Menaphon: Camilla's Alarum to Slumbering Euphues* (1589; this appeared as *Greene's Arcadia* in 1599), *Greene's Mourning Garment* (1590), *Greene's Never too Late* (1590) and its sequel *Francesco's Fortunes* (1590), *Greene's Farewell to Folly* (1591), *A Notable Discovery of Coosnage* (1591), *The Second and last part of conny-catching* (1592), *The Thirde and last part of conny-catching* (1592), *A Disputation, betweene a Hee conny-catcher and a Shee conny-catcher* (1592), *The Blacke Bookes Messenger* (1592), *Greene's Groatsworth of Wit Bought with a Million of Repentance* (published at his dying request; licensed 1592). In the latter Greene exhorts other playwrights (Marlowe and probably Peele and Nashe) to repent from their evil ways; it is in this pamphlet that Greene made his famous attack on the young Shakespeare, the countryman trying to write plays, the actor attempting to enter the circle of university men, the "upstart crow . . . an absolute Iohannesfac-totum . . . the only shake-scene in a countrey." Greene's plays include *The Comicall History of Alphonsus, King of Arragon* (c1588), *A Looking Glass for London and England* (c1590; with Lodge), *The Historie of Orlando Furioso, one of the Twelve Peeres of France* (c1591), *The Honourable History of Friar Bacon and Friar Bungay* (c1591; acted 1594), *The Scottish Historie of James IV* (c1591), and, ascribed to Greene but without much evidence, *George-a-Greene, the Pinner of Wakefield*. It is thought by some that he took part in writing the original Henry VI plays, later revised or rewritten by Shakespeare. Dyce collected and edited his works (1831–58).

Greene's Groatsworth of Wit. See **Groatsworth of Wit.**

Greene's Mourning Garment. See **Mourning Garment.**

Greene's Tu Quoque, or The Citie Gallant (grēnz tö′ kwō′kwe; sit′i). A play by John Cooke, published in 1614.

Green Helmet, The. A volume of verse (1910) by W. B. Yeats, including "The Coming of Wisdom with Time" and "Upon a House Shaken by the Land Agitation."

"Green Isle," the. An epithet of Ireland.

Green Mansions. A novel by W. H. Hudson, published in 1904. Mr. Abel, the narrator, lost in the jungles of Guiana, discovers the "Bird Girl," Rima. She has never known civilization, and has acquired supernatural powers over the animals in the jungle, especially the birds (with whom she is able to converse freely). Abel falls passionately in love with her, but it is clear that she will never leave her home in the jungle. In the end she is burned to death in a blazing tree by hostile and ignorant Indians.

Greenmantle. A novel by John Buchan, published in 1916.

Green Mirror, The. A novel by Hugh Walpole, published in 1917. The second volume of a trilogy, it is the story of Katherine Trenchard, a heroine in revolt against family traditions. The trilogy begins with *The Duchess of Wrexe* (1914) and ends with *The Captives* (1920).

Greensleeves. A ballad (1580) included in the Roxburghe collection, and referred to by Shakespeare in *The Merry Wives of Windsor*. It is about a young man who bewails the inconstancy and cold-heartedness of his lady Greensleeves:

> Alas, my love, you do me wrong
> To treat me so discourteously.

Greenwell (grēn′wel, -wẹl), **Dora.** b. at Greenwell Ford, Durham, England, Dec. 6, 1821; d. March 29, 1882. An English poet and prose writer. Her poetical works are chiefly of a religious character. Among her prose works is *The Patience of Hope* (1860).

Greenwich Hospital (gren′ij, -ich; grin′-). A hospital for seamen, formerly situated at Greenwich (now a borough of London). It occupied the site of a royal palace which was removed during the Commonwealth. It was rebuilt in the reigns of Charles II and William III and in 1694 was converted into a sailors' hospital. Beginning in 1865 a considerable proportion of the pensioners were nonresident, and in 1873 part of the building was taken over by the Royal Naval College.

Greenwood (grēn′wụd), **Frederick.** b. at London, March 25, 1830; d. at Sydenham (now part of London), Dec. 14, 1909. An English journalist, editor, novelist, and essayist. He was first editor (1861–63) of *The Queen*, a joint editor (1862–64) and editor (1864–68) of the *Cornhill Magazine*, first editor (1865–80) of the *Pall Mall Gazette*, founder and editor (1880–88) of *St. James' Gazette*; he also founded and edited (1891–92) the *Anti-Jacobin*. He was the author of *Margaret Denzil's History* (1864) and other novels, and also wrote *The Lover's Lexicon* (1893) and *Imagination in Dreams* (1894).

Greenwood, Walter. b. at Salford, Lancashire, England, Dec. 17, 1903—. An English novelist and playwright. He was variously employed as delivery boy, pawnbroker's clerk, sign writer, car driver, factory worker, and salesman. He is the author of the novels *Love on the Dole* (1933), *Standing Room Only* (1936), *Only Mugs Work* (1938), *How the Other Man Lives* (1939), and *Something in My*

Heart (1944). He also published the collection of short stories *The Cleft Stick* (1937). He dramatized, in collaboration, *Love on the Dole* (1934) and *Only Mugs Work* (1938), and is author also of the plays *My Son's My Son* (1935), *Give Us This Day* (1936), *The Cure for Love* (1945), and *So Brief the Spring* (1945).

Greg (greg), **William Rathbone.** b. at Manchester, England, 1809; d. at Wimbledon, England, Nov. 15, 1881. An English essayist.

Gregorian Calendar (grē.gō′ri.an). [Also, **New Style Calendar.**] The calendar used in the Western Hemisphere today. It is a reformation of the Julian Calendar (Old Style Calendar), and was instituted by Pope Gregory XIII. It became effective on Oct. 5, 1582, which then became Oct. 15; the intervening dates do not exist according to the Gregorian Calendar. According to this calendar the year consists of 365 days and a leap year of 366 days. Leap years are those years into which 4 can be divided exactly; centenary years, however, which are not precisely divisible by 400 are not taken as leap years. When the Gregorian Calendar was adopted (1752) in Great Britain and her colonies in America, there was a difference of 11 days between the two calendars. By the Calendar Act of 1750, the day after Sept. 2, 1752, was to be Sept. 14. Reckoning by the Julian Calendar is now called Old Style (abbreviated O.S.); reckoning by the Gregorian is called New Style (abbreviated N.S.).

Gregory (greg′ō.ri). In Shakespeare's *Romeo and Juliet*, a servant to Capulet. He and Sampson fight with the servants of Montague in the first scene.

Gregory. In Henry Fielding's *Mock Doctor*, the name given to the character called Sganarelle in Molière's *Le Médecin malgré lui*, from which it is taken. He is a fagot-maker who pretends to be a doctor.

Gregory I, Saint. [Surnamed **the Great.**] b. at Rome c540; d. there, March 12, 604. Pope from 590 to 604. He was descended from an illustrious Roman family, probably the Anicians, studied dialectics, rhetoric, and law, entered the civil service, and c574 was appointed prefect of the city of Rome by the emperor Justin II. Retiring from this office in order to consecrate himself to an ecclesiastical life, he employed the wealth left him at his father's death to establish six monasteries in Sicily and one at Rome, and in the last-named foundation (the monastery of Saint Andrew) he himself became a monk. About 579 he was sent as papal legate to Constantinople by Pelagius II. He returned to Rome in 585, and in 590 was elected Pope. He restored the monastic discipline, enforced the rule of celibacy of the clergy, arranged the Gregorian modes or chant, and displayed great zeal in propagating Christianity. It is said that while still a monk he saw some heathen Anglo-Saxon youths exposed for sale in the slave market at Rome, and that on ascertaining their nationality he exclaimed, "They would be indeed not *Angli*, but *angeli* [angels], if they were Christians!" He would have gone himself as a missionary to Britain, but was restrained by the Pope. In 597 he sent Augustine, accompanied by 40 monks, to Ethelbert, king of Kent, who was baptized with 10,000 of his subjects in the space of a year. He wrote an unfortunate adulatory letter of congratulation to the usurper and murderer Phocas on his accession to the imperial throne, written with a view of gaining his support in a dispute with the patriarch of Constantinople. He was the author of numerous homilies on Ezekiel and the Gospels, *Moralia*, *Regula* (or *Cura*) *pastoralis*, *Dialogues*, *Letters*, *Liber sacramentorum*, *Liber antiphonarius*, and others.

Gregory VII, Saint. [Original name, **Hildebrand.**] b. at Soana (or Soano), Tuscany, Italy, c1020; d. at Salerno, Italy, May 25, 1085. Pope from 1073 to 1085. He was of obscure origin, assumed the Benedictine habit at Rome, and became chaplain of Gregory VI, whom he accompanied in his exile. He entered the monastery of Cluny in 1048, and in 1049 was invited to Rome by Pope Leo IX. He was created (c1050) cardinal archdeacon, from which time he almost uninterruptedly conducted the temporal policy of the curia until his own elevation. He procured the election of Nicholas II and of Alexander II, whom he succeeded in 1073. The grand object of his policy was to establish the supremacy of the papacy within the church, and to safeguard the church against the state. He issued a decree against lay investitures (i.e., the investiture of the clergy with the secular estates and rights of their spiritual benefices by the temporal power) in 1075, and in 1076 cited Henry IV of Germany to Rome to answer to the charge of simony, sacrilege, and oppression. Henry, enraged at this assertion of authority, declared the deposition of Gregory, who retorted by excommunicating Henry. Henry was suspended from the royal office by the disaffected German princes in alliance with the Pope at the Diet of Tribur in October, 1076, but did penance before the Pope at Canossa (Jan. 25–27, 1077), and received a conditional absolution. The excommunication was, however, renewed in 1078, and war ensued. Henry defeated (1080) Rudolf of Swabia, put forward as king by the papal party in Germany, appointed Clement III antipope (1080), captured Rome (1084), and besieged Gregory in the castle of Sant' Angelo. Gregory was rescued by Robert Guiscard (1084), but died in exile.

Gregory, Lady **Augusta.** [Maiden name, **Isabella Augusta Persse.**] b. March 5, 1852; d. May 22, 1932. An Irish poet and dramatist. She married (1881) Sir William Henry Gregory (d. 1892). She was identified with the revival of Irish national literature and was a founder of the Irish National Theatre Society (she long directed the Abbey Theatre at Dublin). Her interest in the folklore and legends of the Irish was reflected in her books, many of which retell the ancient myths and legends. Among her publications are *Poets and Dreamers* (1903), *Cuchulain of Muirthemne* (1902), *Gods and Fighting Men* (1904), *A Book of Saints and Wonders* (1907), *Seven Short Plays* (1909, including *Spreading the News*, *The Workhouse Ward*), *New Comedies* (1912), *Irish Folk History Plays* (1912), *Our Irish Theatre* (1914), *Visions and Beliefs in the West of Ireland* (1920), and *Coole* (1931).

Gregory Gazette (ga.zet′), Sir. See **Gazette, Sir Gregory.**

Gregory of Tours (tör), Saint. [Original name, **Georgius Florentius.**] b. at Clermont, in Auvergne, France, 538; d. at Tours, France, Nov. 17, 594. A

Frankish historian. He became bishop of Tours in 573. His chief work is a *Historia Francorum* in 10 books, the chief authority for the history of the Merovingians to 591.

Gremio (grē′mi.ō). In Shakespeare's *Taming of the Shrew*, a rich but old suitor of Bianca. In Act III, Scene 2, he brilliantly describes the marriage of Petruchio and Katherina. He is found in Ariosto's comedy *I Suppositi*, from which Gascoigne probably took his *Supposes*.

Grendel (gren′dẹl). In *Beowulf*, the monster who comes to attack and destroy the people of Hrothgar, king of the Danes. He is slain by Beowulf.

Grenfell (gren′fel), Sir **Wilfred Thomason.** b. at Parkgate, Cheshire, England, Feb. 28, 1865; d. at Charlotte, Vt., Oct. 9, 1940. An English physician and missionary, superintendent of the Labrador medical mission of the Royal National Mission to Deep Sea Fishermen. He fitted out the first hospital ship for North Sea fisheries and began his work on the Labrador coast in 1892. He wrote *Vikings of To-day, The Harvest of the Sea, Off the Rocks* (1906), *Forty Years for Labrador* (1932), his autobiography, and others.

Grenville (gren′vil), **George.** [Also: **Granville;** title, Baron **Lansdowne.**] b. 1667; d. at London, Jan. 30, 1735. An English statesman, poet, and dramatist. He succeeded Walpole as secretary of war (1710); suspected of being a Jacobite, he was imprisoned (1715–17) in the Tower of London. Author of *She Gallants* (1696), a comedy, *Heroick Love* (1698), a tragedy, *The Jew of Venice* (1701), a version of Shakespeare's *Merchant of Venice, The British Enchanters* (1706), an opera, and *Poems upon Several Occasions* (1712; many editions); also wrote *Vindications* of General Monck and Sir Richard Grenville, both published in 1732.

Grenville, Sir **Richard.** [Also (from his own signature), **Greynvile.**] b. c1541; d. in September, 1591. A British naval hero. He was a cousin of Sir Walter Raleigh. In 1585 he commanded a fleet of seven vessels which took part in the colonization of Virginia. In 1591 he was vice-admiral aboard the *Revenge* in the fleet of 16 ships under Thomas Howard which sailed to the Azores to intercept the Spanish treasure ships. While the English were at anchor off Flores, a Spanish fleet of 53 sail appeared, and Howard put to sea to avoid it. Grenville, however, refused to follow, and when, later, he rashly attempted to pass through the Spanish fleet, was becalmed and was attacked by about 15 of the largest vessels. He maintained a hand-to-hand fight for 15 hours, and surrendered only when all but 20 of his 150 men were slain. He died aboard the Spanish flagship *San Pablo* a few days after the battle.

Gresham (gresh′ạm), **Frank.** A principal character in Anthony Trollope's *Doctor Thorne.*

Gresham, Sir **Thomas.** b. c1520; d. at London, Nov. 21, 1579. An English financier. He was employed to negotiate loans for the government both at home and abroad, and was knighted by Queen Elizabeth in 1559. He founded the Royal Exchange in 1565, and in 1575 made provision in his will for the founding of Gresham College, which was opened in 1596. He observed and commented on the tend-

ency of the inferior of two forms of currency in circulation to circulate more freely than the superior, an economic phenomenon which has been named from him Gresham's Law.

Gresham College. An educational foundation (1597) in London.

Gresham's Law. See under **Gresham,** Sir **Thomas.**

Gresley (gres′li), **William.** b. at Kenilworth, Warwickshire, England, March 16, 1801; d. at Boyne Hill, near Maidenhead, Berkshire, England, Nov. 19, 1876. An English clergyman and writer. He published a number of tales and many religious works. Among the latter are *Ordinance of Confession* (1851), *Sophron and Neologos* (1861), *Priests and Philosophers* (1873), and *Thoughts on Religion and Philosophy* (1875). *Bernard Leslie*, written in 1842, was intended to show the influence of the Oxford Movement.

Greta Hall (grē′tạ). The residence of Southey in the vale of Keswick, Cumberland, England.

Gretchen (grech′ẹn; German, grāt′shẹn). The principal female character of Goethe's *Faust*. She is a simple girl of the lower ranks of life, charming in her innocence and confiding love for Faust. The name is a German diminutive of Margaret.

Gretna Green (gret′nạ). A farm near the village of Springfield, Dumfriesshire, Scotland, ab. 9 mi. NW of Carlisle. The name was afterward applied to the village, which became notorious for the celebration of irregular marriages contracted by runaway parties from England (in 1754 an English law had finished the lively runaway marriage racket which centered around London's Fleet Prison). These marriages were rendered invalid (unless one of the parties had resided for some weeks in Scotland) by an act passed in 1856. The present rule requires the residence for 15 full days, plus another delay of seven days. However, the marriage business here is still active, even though it is not what it was before the tightening of the laws.

Greuze (grèz), **Jean Baptiste.** b. at Tournus, France, Aug. 21, 1725; d. at Paris, March 21, 1805. A French genre and portrait painter, pupil at Lyons of Grondon and at Paris (1755) of the Academy of Fine Arts. In 1755 he went to Italy. In 1767 he retired to Anjou, whence he returned to exhibit pictures in his studio. He amassed a large fortune, which was lost in the Revolution. Neglected by the public, which admired only the new school of David, he passed his last years in misery and neglect.

Greville (grev′il). The conceited and obstinate lover of Harriet Byron in Samuel Richardson's epistolary novel *Sir Charles Grandison.*

Greville, Charles Cavendish Fulke. b. April 2, 1794; d. at London, Jan. 18, 1865. An English diarist; great-great-grandson of Robert Rich (1620–75), 5th Earl of Warwick, and, on his mother's side, grandson of William Henry Cavendish Bentinck, 3rd Duke of Portland. He was secretary of Jamaica and clerk of the privy council. For 40 years he recorded in his diary his impressions and intimate knowledge of contemporary English politics and politicians. These *Greville Memoirs* were published after his death by Henry Reeve:

first series, 1817–37 (3 vols., 1875), second and third series, 1837–60 (3 vols., 1885; 2 vols., 1887).

Greville, Sir Fulke. [Title, 1st Baron **Brooke.**] b. at Beauchamp Court, Warwickshire, England, 1554; d. Sept. 30, 1628. An English poet and statesman. He studied at Jesus College, Cambridge, became a favorite of Queen Elizabeth, and was an intimate friend and the biographer of his kinsman Sir Philip Sidney. He became secretary for Wales in 1583, treasurer "of the wars" in March, 1598, and of the navy in September, 1598, chancellor of the exchequer in 1614, and commissioner of the treasury in 1618. He was murdered by a servant, Ralph Haywood, one of the witnesses to his will, to whom he failed to leave a legacy. His epitaph, composed by himself, was: "Fulke Greville, servant to Queen Elizabeth, councillor to King James, and friend to Sir Philip Sidney." His works, containing tragedies, sonnets, and didactic poems, were edited by Grosart (1870) and in part by Bullough (1939).

Grewgious (grö'ji.us), **Mr.** In Dickens's unfinished novel *The Mystery of Edwin Drood*, the guardian of Rosa Bud.

Grey (grā), Sir **Edward.** [Title, 1st Viscount **Grey of Fallodon** (fal'ọ.dọn).] b. April 25, 1862; d. Sept. 7, 1933. An English Liberal statesman. He was educated at Winchester and at Balliol College, Oxford, and succeeded to the baronetcy in 1882. He represented Berwick-upon-Tweed in the House of Commons (1885 *et seq.*), and was undersecretary for foreign affairs (1892–95), and secretary for foreign affairs from December, 1905, until 1916. Grey, as foreign minister in the period preceding World War I, exerted his efforts to preserve peace: he strengthened the entente with France, negotiated (1907) an agreement with Russia over Persia and Afghanistan, attempted pacification in the Balkans, and tried at various times to reach agreement with the Germans, though maintaining a strong stand for England's course of action, as during the Agadir crisis (1911) when he quarreled with the German ambassador. He resigned because of ill health in December, 1916, when the Asquith ministry was superseded by that of Lloyd George. He came to the U. S. in 1919 to discuss matters concerned in the peace, and was a strong supporter of the League of Nations.

Grey, Lady. In Shakespeare's *3 Henry VI*, the historical Elizabeth Woodville, now the widow of Sir John Grey, who pleads for her husband's confiscated property, getting instead a gross proposal from Edward IV, which results in marriage. This causes Warwick to desert him. In *Richard III*, as Queen Elizabeth, she attempts to make peace between Richard and her relations. When Edward dies, she takes the Princes off to sanctuary, from which Richard fetches them. With the Duchess of York and Margaret she learns to curse Richard, who despoils her of her brothers and children much as Margaret has been despoiled of hers. Yet in the midst of her cursing, she listens as he solicits her interest in wooing her daughter. Her answer is ambiguous and later it is learned that her daughter, Elizabeth, has married Richmond.

Grey, Lord. In Shakespeare's *Richard III*, a son of Queen Elizabeth (Lady Grey) by her former

husband. Grey and Rivers are executed by order of Richard at Pomfret.

Grey, Sir Thomas. In Shakespeare's *Henry V*, a conspirator with Scroop and Cambridge against the King. When he is discovered he claims joy that he is "prevented from a damn enterprise" (II.ii).

Grey, Thomas. See under **Dorset, Marquess of.**

Grey, Vivian. See **Vivian Grey.**

Grey Friars. [Also, **Gray Friars.**] In the Roman Catholic Church, a name often applied to the Franciscans. At London the Grey Friars were located in Ludgate Street, where Christ's Hospital (Bluecoat School) afterward stood. The monastery was founded by John Ewin, a mercer, in 1225. The choir of Grey Friars Church was built by Joyner, lord mayor in 1239, and the nave was added by Henry Walings. The church was rebuilt in 1306 by Margaret, queen of Edward I. In 1421 Sir Richard Whittington gave the monks a large library. It was a favorite place of burial for members of the royal family for many years. Grey Friars was surrendered in 1588, and (except for a few traces of the monastic residence) was swept away in the great fire of 1666.

Grey Wethers. A romantic novel by V. Sackville-West, published in 1923.

Grey World, The. A novel by Evelyn Underhill, published in 1904.

Gride (grīd), **Arthur.** An old miser in Charles Dickens's novel *Nicholas Nickleby*.

Grierson (grir'sọn), Sir **Herbert John Clifford.** b. at Lerwick, Shetland Islands, Scotland, Jan. 16, 1866—. A Scottish literary historian, an authority on 17th-century English literature. He was a professor at Aberdeen (1894–1915) and Edinburgh (1915–35), and rector (1936–39) of Edinburgh University. Author of *The First Half of the Seventeenth Century* (1906), *Metaphysical Poets, Donne to Butler* (1921), *The Background of English Literature, and other Collected Essays* (1925), *Cross-Currents in the Literature of the Seventeenth Century* (1929), *Carlyle and Hitler* (1933), *Prophets and Poets* (1937), and *Rhetoric and English Composition* (1945).

Grieve (grēv), **Christopher Murray.** See **McDiarmid, Hugh.**

Griffin (grif'in), **Gerald.** b. at Limerick, Ireland, Dec. 12, 1803; d. at Cork, Ireland, June 12, 1840. An Irish novelist, dramatist, and poet. His principal novel, *The Collegians* (1828), has been dramatized as *Colleen Bawn.* Among his other works are *The Invasion* and *The Rivals.*

Griffith (grif'ith). In Shakespeare's *Henry VIII*, a gentleman usher to Queen Katherine.

Griffith Gaunt (gônt, gänt). A novel by Charles Reade, published in 1866.

Griffiths (grif'iths), **Evan.** b. at Gellibeblig, Glamorganshire, Wales, 1795; d. Aug. 31, 1873. A Welsh clergyman. He published a *Welsh-English Dictionary* (1847).

Grildrig (gril'drig). The name given to Gulliver by the people of Brobdingnag, in Swift's *Gulliver's Travels.* It meant a very little man.

Grim (grim). In medieval legend, a fisherman. According to the traditional accounts, he gave his name to the fishing port of Grimsby. He saved the life of Havelok the Dane.

Grim, Giant. A giant, in Bunyan's *Pilgrim's Progress*, who is killed by Greatheart.

Grimald (grim′ạld) or **Grimalde** (grim′ôld) or **Grimoald** (grim′wold), **Nicholas.** b. in Huntingdonshire, England (at "Brownshold," according to his own statement), 1519; d. 1562. An English writer. He studied at Cambridge and Oxford, and was chaplain to Bishop Ridley. He was the contributor of 40 poems to the first edition of *Tottel's Miscellany* (of which he was, perhaps, the editor), many of which were omitted from the second edition. He also published a translation of Cicero's *De Officiis*.

Grimaldi (gri.môl′di), **Joseph.** b. at London, Dec. 18, 1778; d. there, May 31, 1837. An English pantomimist and actor. He came of a well-known family of clowns, and first appeared as a child dancer in 1782. He obtained his greatest success at the Covent Garden Theatre, London, in 1806 in the pantomime of *Mother Goose*, in which he appeared as Squire Bugle, producing the type of clown known (from him) as "the Joey." He made his last appearance on June 27, 1828, as Harlequin Hoax. He was a polished dancer and a good acrobat, and had the ability to portray a mixture of innocence and mischief at the same time. He performed elaborate clown jokes in pantomimes, such as trying to construct a carriage out of a basket and cheeses, or a soldier's uniform from coal-buckets, a cape, and a muff. One of his songs, "Hot Codlins," about an old woman who drank too much gin, was sung regularly in pantomimes for 30 years after his death.

Grimes (grīmz), **Peter.** In George Crabbe's poem (in 24 parts) *The Borough*, the subject of one of the parts, a mean, ill-natured man who killed his apprentices by overwork and finally died insane. Benjamin Britten made him the subject of an opera produced at London in 1945.

Grimes, Thomas. In Charles Kingsley's *Water-Babies*, the chimney sweep whose blackened visage peering into the water provides one of the most striking scenes in the book.

Grimm (grim), Baron **Friedrich Melchior von.** b. at Regensburg, Germany, Dec. 26, 1723; d. at Gotha, Germany, Dec. 19, 1807. A German diplomatic and literary figure. He spent more than 40 years at Paris, and counted among his friends Rousseau, d'Alembert, and Diderot. He was secretary to the Count of Friesen, and then to the Duke of Orléans; he represented the Duke of Gotha at the French court as minister plenipotentiary. When the French Revolution compelled him to leave France he accepted ministerial duties for Catherine the Great at Hamburg. Grimm's lasting monument is his *Correspondance littéraire, philosophique et critique*, which contains brilliantly written periodic reports on the intellectual life of the French capital sent to various German princes in the period 1753–89.

Grimm, Jakob Ludwig Karl. b. at Hanau, in Hesse-Cassel, Germany, Jan. 4, 1785; d. at Berlin, Sept. 20, 1863. A German philologist and writer. He studied jurisprudence at Marburg. In 1805 he went to Paris to assist Savigny, whose pupil he had been. The following year he was at the military school at Kassel. In 1808 he became librarian to Jérôme Bonaparte, king of Westphalia. After 1814 he lived and worked with his brother Wilhelm in the closest association. They were together librarians at Kassel and professors (1830–37) at Göttingen, where Jakob was one of the seven professors dismissed for signing the protest against the king of Hanover's abrogation of the 1833 constitution. Subsequently they were again at Kassel and in 1841, on the invitation of the king, settled at Berlin. In 1812 and 1815 they published jointly the well-known book of fairy tales *Kinder- und Hausmärchen* (Children's and Domestic Tales), in 1816 *Deutsche Sagen* (German Legends), and after 1852 worked together on the great *Deutsches Wörterbuch* (German Dictionary). Jakob's independent work consists of an essay, *Poesie im Recht* (1816), expanded (1828) into *Deutsche Rechtsalterthümer*. Beginning in 1819, his *Deutsche Grammatik* (German Grammar) appeared. This last is the fundamental work in comparative German philology, of which specific branch he may be called the founder. Its principal terminology originated with him, and one of its most characteristic phases, that of the relative correspondence of consonants in the Germanic languages, though first formulated by Rask, bears the name of Grimm's law. In 1835 appeared another great work, the *Deutsche Mythologie*, tracing the origins of Teutonic myth and showing how its remnants remain in popular beliefs, folk tales, and language. Among his other works are *Über den altdeutschen Meistergesang* (1811) and *Die Geschichte der deutschen Sprache* (2 vols., 1848). His minor works, *Kleinere Schriften* (6 vols.), appeared at Berlin in the period 1864–82.

Grimmelshausen (grim′ẹls.hou.zẹn), **Christoffel von.** b. at Gelnhausen, in Prussia, Germany, 1625; d. at Renchen, Baden, Germany, Aug. 17, 1676. A German writer. Until the peace of Westphalia, in 1648, he was a soldier, but subsequently is supposed to have traveled in the Netherlands, France, and Switzerland. He was afterward in the service of the bishop of Strasbourg, and finally magistrate at Renchen. His principal work, and the most important of its class in German literature, is the novel *Der abenteuerliche Simplicissimus Teutsch, d.h.: Beschreibung des Lebens eines Seltzamen Vagantens genannt Melchior Sternfels von Fuchsheim* (1669). This realistic account of the adventures and the development of a participant in the Thirty Years' War is one of the monuments of German literature.

Grimm's Law. A phonetic law covering the consonant changes from Indo-European to the Germanic languages and from Low German to High German, formulated by Jakob Grimm (1820–22) and in outline independently by Rask (1819).

Grim, the Collier of Croydon (grim; kroi′dọn). A play first printed in 1662 as by "I. T." Haughton wrote a play called *The Devil and his Dam*, which has been indiscriminately identified with this. Richard Crowley wrote *The Collier of Croyden* (1550), and there is an interlude in Richard Edwards's *Damon and Pythias* (1565) called "Grim the Collier."

Grimwig (grim'wig), **Mr.** In Charles Dickens's *Oliver Twist*, an old friend of Mr. Brownlow, rough and irascible in conduct but kindly at heart, ready to "eat his head" if he is mistaken on any point.

Gringolet (gring'gō.let). The horse of Sir Gawain in the Middle English romance *Sir Gawain and the Green Knight*.

Grip (grip). In Dickens's *Barnaby Rudge*, a talkative raven who is Barnaby's constant companion. He is taken from a raven owned by the author.

Gripe (grīp). A hypocritical old Puritan usurer in Wycherley's comedy *Love in a Wood*.

Gripe. The miserly father of Leander, cheated by Scapin, in Thomas Otway's *Cheats of Scapin*. He is the Géronte of Molière's play.

Gripe. A miserly usurer or moneylender in Vanbrugh's comedy *The Confederacy*.

Gripe, Charles. The son of Sir Francis Gripe, in love with Isabinda, daughter of the jealous Traffick, in Susannah Centlivre's comedy *The Busybody*.

Gripe, Sir Francis. In Susannah Centlivre's comedy *The Busybody*, an old man, the guardian of Miranda. He wishes to marry his ward for the sake of her money, but is duped by her and Sir George Airy.

Griselda (gri.zel'da). [Also, **Griseldis** (gri.zel'dis), **Grissel** (gri.sel').] A character noted for the patience with which she submitted to the most cruel ordeals as a wife and mother. Her story, whose elements have their ultimate source in various widespread folk tales, was given literary form by Boccaccio in the *Decameron* and also treated by Petrarch, Chaucer (in *The Clerk's Tale*), Dekker, and other writers. The song of *Patient Grissel* appeared about 1565, and a prose history shortly after.

Grizzle (griz'l), **Aunt.** Peregrine Pickle's aunt in Tobias Smollett's novel *Peregrine Pickle*. She marries Commodore Trunnion, and henpecks him. "She goes a little crank and humorsome by being often overstowed with Nantz and religion."

Grizzle, Lord. In Henry Fielding's burlesque *Tom Thumb the Great*, a peer of the realm: "a flighty, flaunting, and fantastical" personage.

Groatsettar (grōt'set.ar), **Clara** and **Maddie.** Two young heiresses in Sir Walter Scott's novel *The Pirate*.

Groatsworth of Wit. [Full title, **Greene's Groatsworth of Wit, bought with a Million of Repentance.**] A posthumous tract by Robert Greene. It was licensed in 1592; the earliest existing edition known is 1596. It was edited by Henry Chettle. Roberto, the young man whose conversion and adventures are related, corresponds in some, though not in all, respects to Robert Greene himself. Marlowe, Peele, and probably Nashe are warned to repent of their wild ways. The exhortation to Peele contains a passage obviously attacking Shakespeare, towards whom the university-bred, established dramatists were very often resentful.

Grocyn (grō'sin), **William.** b. at Colerne, Wiltshire, England, c1446; d. at Maidstone, Kent, England, 1519. An English humanist, first teacher of Greek at Oxford. He was a friend of Linacre, More, Colet,

and Erasmus, and an ardent promoter of the "new learning," though an adherent of the old religious faith. With the exception of a letter to Aldus and an epigram (on a lady who threw a snowball at him), no writings of his are known.

Grongar Hill (grong'gar). A descriptive poem by John Dyer, published in 1727; named from a hill in South Wales.

Groome (gröm), **Francis Hindes.** b. at Earl Soham, Suffolk, England, Aug. 30, 1851; d. at Edinburgh, Jan. 24, 1902. An English author, best known for his works on the gypsies. During his early manhood, he traveled in Europe, living with gypsies and studying their life, and in 1876 he married a gypsy. Author of *In Gypsy Tents* (1880), *A Short Border History* (1887), *Two Suffolk Friends* (1895), *Kriegspiel* (1896), a novel, and *Gypsy Folk Tales* (1899); edited the *Journal of the Gypsy Folk-Lore Society*.

Grose (grōs), **Francis.** b. at Greenford, Middlesex, England, c1731; d. at Dublin, May 12, 1791. An English antiquary. He studied art, and exhibited at the Royal Academy for a number of years, chiefly architectural drawings. He was Richmond herald (1755–63), and afterward held offices in several corps of militia. In 1789 he made an antiquarian tour in Scotland, where he met Robert Burns, who wrote two poems about Captain Grose; and in 1791 started on a similar tour in Ireland, but died of apoplexy about a month after. He wrote *The Antiquities of England and Wales* (6 vols., 1773–87), *A Classical Dictionary of the Vulgar Tongue* (1785), *Military Antiquities* (1786–88), *A Provincial Glossary* (1787), *The Antiquities of Scotland* (1789–91), *The Antiquities of Ireland* (1791–95), finished by Ledwich, and other works.

Grosseteste (grōs'test), **Robert.** b. at Stradbrook, Suffolk, England, c1175; d. Oct. 9, 1253. English divine and scholar. He studied law and medicine at Oxford and theology on the Continent, returning to England to become chancellor at Oxford and first rector (1224) of the influential Franciscan school there. He was archdeacon of Wiltshire (1214, 1220), of Northampton (1221), and of Leicester (1231). In 1232 he resigned all his posts except that of prebendary at Lincoln and his chancellorship. He was elected (1235) bishop of Lincoln and set about energetically to reform abuses in his diocese. He found himself in conflict with the several establishments in the diocese and also with the secular power, Grosseteste claiming in the one case his rights as bishop and in the other his authority as stemming from the papal chair. These struggles, which were to occupy the rest of his life, saw him striving to maintain clerical rights against the encroachments of the secular power and the rights of the English church against the inroads of papal preferment. In 1239 he entered into a protracted quarrel with the chapter of Lincoln over his right of visitation, which was finally settled by the pope in his favor after he had traveled (1245) to Lyons to the papal court. When the papal legate was assaulted by Oxford students, Grosseteste demanded their release, finding himself in conflict with both king and Holy See. His resistance to the collection of one fifth of the English clerical revenues for papal purposes was joined by

Edmund Rich; again the king and the pope were on the same side, and Rich, archbishop of Canterbury, left England never to return. When the pope nominated (1253) his nephew Federico di Lavanga to a canonry at Lincoln, Grosseteste wrote a letter refusing him on the ground of unfitness; he had previously (1251) been suspended for a similar refusal. Grosseteste was an early leader in the struggle of the barons against Henry III. In 1244 he refused to permit the clergy to be split from the barons in a council from which Henry was demanding money; the meeting demanded reforms in the administration of the kingdom before any funds would be granted. Neither side would give in and the incipient struggle remained as part of the English political atmosphere until after Grosseteste's death. While he lived, he did block the claim of the king to make ecclesiastical appointments. He was noted as a student of the sciences, as a mathematician and physicist. Among his students was Roger Bacon, who carried on the scientific studies he began under his master. Grosseteste wrote voluminously. His French poetry includes the religious allegory *Le Chasteau d'Amour;* he wrote on philosophy and theology, and translated from the Greek and wrote commentaries on Aristotle and Boethius. A recent critical study of his life and work is *Robert Grosseteste: Scholar and Bishop* (1955) edited by Daniel Callus.

Grosvenor Gallery (grŏv'nẽr). A gallery for the exhibition of paintings of the contemporary "aesthetic school" (the works of Burne-Jones, Rossetti, and others), established in New Bond Street in 1876. The exhibitions have been discontinued. It was satirically alluded to by Gilbert and Sullivan in *Patience* with the line: "A greenery-yallery, Grosvenor Gallery . . . young man."

Grosvenor Square. A fashionable square in London, east of Hyde Park.

Grote (grōt), **George.** b. at Clay Hill, near Beckenham, Kent, England, Nov. 17, 1794; d. at London, June 18, 1871. An English historical writer. He studied at the Charterhouse, and in 1810 entered his father's bank, devoting himself thereafter to that business, his father having refused to give him a university education. He was a "philosophic radical," following the school of Mill and Bentham for electoral reform. He was a member of Parliament (1833–41); with J. S. Mill and Henry Brougham, he was one of the founders of University College, London. His great work is a *History of Greece* (12 vols., 1846–56), much of which is today obsolete because of later scholarship and discovery, but which by its emphasis on the democratic growth of the Greek city-state helped overcome the conservative approach of earlier histories of the era. He also published *Plato and the Other Companions of Socrates* (3 vols., 1865). His *Minor Works* were collected by Bain (1873).

Grote, Harriet. [Maiden name, **Lewin.**] b. near Southampton, England, July 1, 1792; d. at Shiere, near Guildford, Surrey, England, Dec. 29, 1878. An English author; wife of George Grote (married 1820), whose biography she wrote (1873).

Grotius (grō'shi.us), **Hugo.** [Latinized form of his original Dutch name, **Huig de** (or **van**) **Groot.**] b.

at Delft, Netherlands, April 10, 1583; d. at Rostock, Germany, Aug. 28 or 29, 1645. A Dutch jurist, theologian, statesman, and poet, the founder of the science of international law. He was one of the most precocious children in history, entering the university at the age of 12 and taking his degree in law at 15. In 1598 he served in the mission of Count Justin of Nassau and Jan van Olden Barnevelt to France; in that year too he edited the encyclopedic work of Martianus Capella. During his early youth he was responsible also for some Latin verse and three Latin plays on religious themes: *Adamus exul* (a formative influence on the final plan of Milton's *Paradise Lost*), *Christus patiens*, and *Sophomphaneas* (on Joseph and his brothers). Grotius began practice at the bar at Delft in 1599; one of his cases, dealing with the right of a private company, the Dutch East India Company, to seize a prize on the high seas, led to his interest in the principles of international law. He seems to have written a draft in 1604 that was later useful to him in the composition of his masterpiece; in 1609 he published *Mare liberum*, maintaining that the seas are free to all nations. Although he did not seek the post, he was chosen (1603) historiographer of the States-General, and became (1607) fiscal advocate of the provinces of Holland and Zeeland. In 1608, he married Marie Reigersberg. In the service of the States-General, he wrote (1610) *De antiquitate reipublicae Batavae*, a reasoned historical account of the antiquity of Dutch independence. In 1613 he became pensionary of Rotterdam and soon after was part of a deputation to England. About 1615 he became involved in the religious dispute between the Remonstrants and the Antiremonstrants, at first attempting to pacify both sides with a plea for religious toleration. But he himself was a Remonstrant and when Maurice of Nassau, in a coup d'état to destroy van Olden Barneveldt's power, seized the governments of Utrecht and Holland, he was arrested. He was imprisoned (1619) in Louvestein, near Gorinchem, where he settled down to his books, expecting to spend the rest of his life in captivity. His wife, however, planned an escape carefully; gradually she accustomed the jailers to pass without examination cases of books that Grotius had finished with, and in 1621 he escaped from his prison by hiding in one of the cases. He fled to France, where his reputation gained him the support of powerful Frenchmen. He was established on an estate near Senlis where he wrote his *De jure belli et pacis*, a treatise on natural and international law, still considered one of the great books of all time and the foundation-stone of international law. The book, published in 1625, brought Grotius tremendous international prestige; it has been translated into every European language. In 1631, because of the enmity of Richelieu, he left France for the Netherlands, but his enemies there were in power and in 1632 he left for Hamburg. There he was recruited for the foreign service of Queen Christina of Sweden, serving (1635–45) as ambassador to France. But Richelieu and Mazarin were not friendly and he accomplished little. In 1645 he asked to be recalled. Among Grotius's other works are *De veritate religionis Christianae* (1627), a legalistic approach to the proof of the identity of all of Christianity and an attempt to mediate sectary differences; annotations on the Old Testament (1644) and on the New Testament (1641–46), and *Via et votum ad pacem ecclesiasticam* (1642).

Grove (grōv), Sir **George.** b. at Clapham, Surrey, England, Aug. 13, 1820; d. at Sydenham, London, May 28, 1900. An English engineer and writer, now best known for his *Dictionary of Music and Musicians*. He built (1841) at Jamaica the first iron lighthouse, and was employed on the Britannia Bridge. As secretary to the Crystal Palace, he became interested in the concerts being given there; for many years he wrote annotations for the programs. He was director (1882–94) of the Royal College of Music, Kensington. He edited *Macmillan's Magazine* for several years, and the *Dictionary of Music and Musicians* (1878–89; new ed., 1904–07; 3rd ed., 1927 *et seq.*). This dictionary, containing articles by Grove and other principal music critics, has become the standard work in the field.

Grub Street (grub). A London street, still existing, but for many years known as Milton Street. It is in the parish of St. Giles Cripplegate, and runs from Fore Street to Chiswell Street. As Grub Street it was noted as the abode of indigent writers (whence Gissing's *New Grub Street*).

Grub Street Opera, The. A burlesque by Henry Fielding, produced in 1731. It was produced earlier in the year, before being revised, as *The Welsh Opera: or, The Grey Mare the Better Horse.* It is in ballad opera form, centering on the love affair of Robin and Sweetissa, whose amour runs afoul of forged letters left by Squire Owen.

Grueby (grö′bi), **John.** A servant to Lord George Gordon in Charles Dickens's novel *Barnaby Rudge.* He is self-possessed, hard-headed, and imperturbable.

Gruffydd (grif′iᴛʜ), **Owain ab.** See **Glendower, Owen;** see also **Owain Cyveiliog.**

Grumbler, The. A comedy by Sir Charles Sedley, printed in 1702. It is a translation of Brueys's *Le Grondeur* (1691), and was adapted as a farce by Goldsmith in 1773.

Grumbletonians (grum.bl.tō′ni.ạnz). In Great Britain in the late 17th century, a nickname for members of the Country Party.

Grumbo (grum′bō). A giant in the English Tom Thumb stories.

Grumio (grö′mi.ō). In Shakespeare's *Taming of the Shrew,* a servant of Petruchio.

Grundy (grun′di), **Mr.** In Charles Dickens's *Pickwick Papers,* a friend of Mr. Lowten.

Grundy, Mrs. In Thomas Morton's comedy *Speed the Plough* (1798), one of two rival farmers' wives. She is constantly alluded to by Mrs. Ashfield, the other farmer's wife, in the phrase "What will Mrs. Grundy say?" but never appears on the scene. Her name has become proverbial for conventional propriety and morality.

Grundy, Sydney. b. at Manchester, England, March 23, 1848; d. there, July 4, 1914. An English dramatist. He began his literary career with *A Little Change* (1872), produced at the London Haymarket, and a novel, *The Days of His Vanity.* He published *The Snowball* (1879), *In Honor Bound*

(1880), *The Bells of Haslemere* (1887, with Henry Pettitt), *A Fool's Paradise* (1889), *A Pair of Spectacles* (1890), one of his greatest successes, *Sowing the Wind* (1893), *A Bunch of Violets* and *Slaves of the Ring* (both 1894), *The Late Mr. Castello* (1895), *A Marriage of Convenience* (1897), *The Musketeers* (1899), *The Garden of Lies* (1904), *Business is Business* and *The Diplomatists* (both 1905), *A Fearful Joy* (1908), and many others.

Gryll Grange (gril grānj). A novel (1860) by Thomas Love Peacock. It was his last novel and like his others has a simple plot on which philosophical discourses are hung. Dr. Opimian reflects the author's opinions; Lord Brougham is characterized in Lord Facing-both-ways, and Shelley, the author's friend, is Falconer.

Guanhamara (gwän′hạ.mä.rạ). See **Guinevere.**

Guard (gärd), **Theodore de la.** Pseudonym of **Ward, Nathaniel.**

Guardian, The. A play by Philip Massinger, licensed in 1633, played in 1634, and published in 1655, when Moseley issued it in octavo as *Three New Plays.*

Guardian, The. A comedy by Abraham Cowley, acted at Cambridge in 1641 for Prince Charles. It was printed in 1650, and rewritten as *The Cutter of Coleman Street* in 1658.

Guardian, The. A daily periodical published at London in 1713, and edited by Steele. It comprised 176 numbers (51 of them by Addison). It followed the suspension of publication of *The Spectator,* and was somewhat inferior to its predecessor, though of high rank among English periodicals of the time.

Guarini (gwä.rē′nē), **Giovanni Battista.** b. at Ferrara, Italy, Dec. 10, 1537; d. at Venice, Oct. 4, 1612. An Italian poet and diplomat, professor of belleslettres at Ferrara. He was in the service of the Duke of Ferrara (1567–82), and later in that of Tuscany and that of Urbino. His chief work is the pastoral drama *Il Pastor fido* (1585; published 1590), the summation in drama of the polished decadence of 16th-century Italian court life.

Gudrun (gûd′rún). [Also: **Guthrun, Kudrun.**] The heroine of a 13th-century German epic, the *Gudrun Lied,* after the *Nibelungenlied* the most important in the medieval literature of Germany. Gudrun is the daughter of King Hetel of Hegelingen. The scene of action is principally the coast region of the North Sea and Normandy. She is kidnaped by an unwanted lover, and rescued after 13 years by her brother and a faithful suitor.

Guedalla (gwẹ.dal′ạ), **Philip.** b. March 12, 1889; d. at London, Dec. 16, 1944. An English historian, biographer, and essayist. He was educated at Rugby and at Balliol College, Oxford, where he was president of the Oxford Union. He was called to the bar in 1913. Author of *Palmerston* (1926), *Bonnet and Shawl—An Album* (1928), *The Duke* (1931; American title, *Wellington*), biographies; *Conquistador* (1927), *Argentine Tango* (1932), travel books; *The Partition of Europe, 1715–1815* (1914), *Supers and Supermen* (1920), *The Second Empire* (1922), *Masters and Men* (1923), *Napoleon and Palestine* (1925), *Independence Day—A Sketchbook* (1926; American title, *Fathers of the Revolution*), *Gladstone and Palmerston* (1928), *The Queen* *and Mr. Gladstone* (1933), *The Hundred Days* (1934), *The Hundred Years* (1936), and *Mr. Churchill* (1941), historical and literary essays and studies; *Ignes Fatui* (1911), a collection of parodies; and *Metri Gratia—Prose and Verse* (1911), the last two products of his Oxford days. His scattered writings appeared in the London *Times, Vanity Fair,* the *New Statesman,* and the *Daily News.*

Guelphs or **Guelfs** (gwelfs). The papal and popular party of Italy in the Middle Ages: opposed to the Ghibellines, the imperial and aristocratic party. The Welfs (Guelfs) were a powerful family of Germany, so called from Welf I in the time of Charlemagne. His descendants, several of whom bore the same name, held great possessions in Italy. Through intermarriage they were at different times dukes of Bavaria, Saxony, and Carinthia, and founded the princely house of Brunswick and Hanover, to which the present royal family of England belongs. The names Welf and Waiblingen (German names for which Guelf and Ghibelline are the Italian equivalents) are alleged to have been first used as war cries at the battle of Weinsberg in 1140, which Welf VI lost to the Hohenstaufen emperor Conrad III. The contest soon ceased in Germany, but was taken up on other grounds in Italy, over which the emperors claimed supreme power; the names continued to designate bitterly antagonistic parties there till the end of the 15th century.

Guenever (gwen′ẹ.vėr). See **Guinevere.**

Guest (gest), **Stephen.** In George Eliot's novel *The Mill on the Floss,* the pleasant young man who is engaged to Lucy Deane but powerfully drawn to Maggie Tulliver.

Gueux (gė), **Les.** A term applied, originally in contempt but later adopted as a title of honor, to Netherlanders who rose in revolt against Spain and Philip II in the 16th century. The term, which means beggars or scoundrels in French, originated in 1566 when a group of burghers and noblemen approached Margaret, Duchess and regent of Parma, with a list of their grievances. According to the story, one of her advisers, noticing her hesitation to meet them, sneeringly referred to them as "ces gueux" (these beggars), in order to stimulate her courage. The petitioners adopted the epithet as a term of honor, at the same time adopting also the traditional emblems of beggary, the wallet and the bowl.

Guicciardini (gwēt.chär.dē′nē), **Francesco.** b. at Florence, March 6, 1483; d. near there, in May, 1540. An Italian historian and statesman in the pontifical and Medicean service. His chief work is *Storia d'Italia* (History of Italy, 1561–64; edited by Rosini, 1819). His *Opere inedite* were published in 1857.

Guiderius (gwi.dir′i.us). In Shakespeare's *Cymbeline,* the son of Cymbeline. He is disguised under the name of Polydore, and brought up as the son of Morgan.

Guido Franceschini (gwē′dō frän.ches.kē′nē), **Count.** See **Franceschini, Count Guido.**

Guignol (gē.nyol). One of the chief characters of the traditional French puppet shows, and thence the puppet shows themselves. From the customary bloody, violent character of the puppet and marionette plays, the Grand Guignol, a theater in Mont-martre, Paris, devoted to the production of horror plays, takes its name.

Guilbert (gēl.ber′). See **Bois-Guilbert, Brian de.**

Guildenstern (gil′dẹn.stėrn). In Shakespeare's *Hamlet,* a former school friend of the Prince. With Rosencrantz, he spies on Hamlet, under Claudius's orders, and is killed when Hamlet substitutes his and Rosencrantz's names for his own in instructions sent by Claudius.

Guildford (gil′fọrd), **Nicholas de.** See under **Owl and the Nightingale, The.**

Guildford, Sir Henry. In Shakespeare's *Henry VIII,* a gentleman of the court.

Guildhall (gild′hôl). The council hall of the City of London, rebuilt in 1411, and restored after the fire of 1666. The most recent great hall, which was again burned out in World War II, measured 153 by 48 ft., and was 55 ft. high; it had a handsome open-framed roof, Victorian stained-glass windows, and the two colossal wooden figures of Gog and Magog (which were totally destroyed in World War II, and were afterward replaced by stone figures). Along the walls were placed statues of famous men.

Guillaume de Champeaux (gē.yōm dẹ shäň.pō). [Also: **William of Champeaux;** Latinized surname, **Campellensis.**] b. at Champeaux, near Melun, France, toward the end of the 11th century; d. 1121. A French scholastic philosopher, an opponent of Peter Abelard, who was his pupil.

Guillaume de Machault (or **Machaut**) (mà.shō). b. c1284; d. after 1370. A French poet and musician. Chaucer's indebtedness to him is marked. Author of *La Prise d'Alexandre, Voir Dit,* and numerous ballades and long poems.

Guillim (gwil′im), **John.** b. at Hereford, England, c1565; d. at London, May 7, 1621. An English writer on heraldry. He published *A Display of Heraldrie* (1610; sometimes ascribed to John Barkham).

Guillotin (gē.yo.taň), **Joseph Ignace.** b. at Saintes, France, May 28, 1738; d. at Paris, March 26, 1814. A French physician, incorrectly regarded as the inventor of the guillotine. As deputy to the Constituent Assembly in 1789, he proposed that all capital punishment should be by decapitation, a privilege till then reserved for the nobility. He suggested that decapitation could be most quickly and humanely performed by a machine. The device actually adopted as a result of this suggestion was prepared by a German mechanic named Schmidt under the direction of Dr. Antoine Louis, life secretary of the Academy of Surgery, and was first used on April 25, 1792, for the execution of a highwayman named Pelletier. The machine was first named *louison* or *louisette,* but later Guillotin's name was attached to it. Guillotin was not, as has been asserted, guillotined, but died a natural death.

Guinea, Adventures of a. See **Chrysal, or the Adventures of a Guinea.**

Guinevere (gwin′ẹ.vir). [Also: **Guenever, Guinever** (gwin′ẹ.vėr), **Geneura, Guanhamara, Ganore.**] The wife of King Arthur in the Arthurian cycle of legend and romance. She was the daughter of Leodegrance, king of Cameliard, beloved and lover of Sir Lancelot, with whom she was unfaithful to Arthur. She was sentenced to be burned, was rescued by Lancelot, became a nun, and was buried with Arthur at Glastonbury.

Guinevere. One of the *Idylls of the King* by Alfred Tennyson, published in 1859. It recounts the episodes of Lancelot's and Guinevere's last tryst, the spying of Modred, Guinevere's entrance into the nunnery at Almesbury, her visit from Arthur (who finally forgives her for the evil that her sin has wrought), and her death.

Guise (gēz, gwēz), **Duchy of.** Former duchy in NE France, which took its name from the town of Guise and corresponded to the N part of the modern department of Aisne. It was situated in the government of Picardy. Formerly it was a county. It was famous in the 16th and 17th centuries as a duchy in the hands of the Guise family, a branch of the house of Lorraine.

Guise, The. A nobleman at the Court of France in George Chapman's *Bussy D'Ambois* and *The Revenge of Bussy D'Ambois.*

Guizot (gē.zō), **François Pierre Guillaume.** b. at Nîmes, France, Oct. 4, 1787; d. at Val-Richer, in Normandy, France, Sept. 12, 1874. A French historian and statesman. At the age of 12 he left his native city for Geneva, Switzerland, and in 1805 he took up the study of law at Paris. In 1812 he became assistant professor of literature at the Sorbonne, and later was called to the new chair of modern history, resigning (1825) from this post after writing a number of controversial pamphlets. He was restored to his post in 1828. His courses of lectures at the Sorbonne (delivered 1828–30) appeared under the titles *Histoire de la civilisation en Europe* (1828) and *Histoire de la civilisation en France* (1830). In 1830 he was elected to the Chamber of Deputies. After the revolution of July, 1830, he became minister of the interior, and, with the exception of a few months in 1840 spent as French ambassador to England, remained almost continuously in some ministerial capacity until he fell from power (Feb. 23, 1848) on the eve of Louis Philippe's abdication. He had been prime minister for the eight years preceding his downfall, but had made himself so unpopular that he failed to be elected to the National Assembly of 1848. Guizot's policies, which he believed to the end of his life to be liberal, became more and more conservative as he struggled to maintain the constitutional monarchy of the Bourbon-Orléans line. His program of peace with England (which was seen by many Frenchmen as a "peace-at-any-price" policy), his reliance on corrupt aides, his refusal to countenance electoral reforms (despite the existence of an electorate of only 200,000), his more or less cynical playing of political venality against his desired ends, were all contributory to a growing unpopularity, which he met with a practiced disdain. The latter part of his life was spent in retirement. His many other works include *Histoire de la révolution d'Angleterre depuis Charles I à Charles II* (2 vols., 1826–27), *Washington* (1840), *De la démocratie en France* (1849), *Discours sur l'histoire de la révolution d'Angleterre* (1850), *Mémoires pour servir à l'histoire de mon temps* (9 vols., 1858–68), *Trois générations* (1861), *Histoire parlementaire de France* (1863), *Mélanges biographiques*

et littéraires (1868), *Mélanges politiques et historiques* (1869), and *Le Duc de Broglie* (1872).

Gula (gö'lạ). In Assyro-Babylonian mythology, a goddess presiding over life and death.

Gulbeyaz (gŭl.bā'yaz). In Byron's long satirical poem *Don Juan*, the sultana who brings Don Juan into the harem for herself, but ousts him peremptorily when she finds him giving his attentions to another member of the harem.

Gulistan (gö.li.stän'). [Eng. trans., "*The Rose-Garden.*"] The most celebrated work of the Persian poet Sadi. It is a kind of moral work in verse and prose, consisting of eight chapters on kings, dervishes, contentment, taciturnity, love and youth, decrepitude and old age, education, and the duties of society, the whole intermixed with stories, maxims, and puns.

Gulliver (gul'i.vėr), **Lemuel.** The ostensible narrator of Swift's *Gulliver's Travels.*

Gulliver's Travels. [Full title, **Travels into Several Remote Nations of the World. . . by Lemuel Gulliver.**] A social and political prose satire, in the form of a book of travels, written by Jonathan Swift and published in 1726. It consists of four voyages by Lemuel Gulliver, an honest, blunt English ship's captain. Gulliver's first voyage ends in his shipwreck on the island of Lilliput, where the people are six inches high and everything else on the island is in proportion to their size. Although the book seems to begin merely as entertainment, it soon becomes a biting satire of English institutions and political parties as seen through a microscope. The Lilliputians' earnestness over their problems of war and peace, fame and glory, and the like, so ridiculous in a race of pygmies, is an obvious caricature of the disputes and worries of Hanoverian England. The greatest controversy of the Lilliputian political parties, whose members are identified according to the height of their heels, is over which end of an egg ought to be broken. Gulliver's second voyage is to Brobdingnag, a land of giants as much taller than Gulliver as he is taller than the Lilliputians. England and humanity are again ridiculed, this time from the viewpoint of a people large of mind as well as body. The king of the country cannot understand how such small people as the English can have such large pretensions and observes "how contemptible a thing was human grandeur, which could be mimicked by such diminutive insects" as Gulliver. The third voyage is to the flying island of Laputa and the nearby city of Lagado, capital of the country of Balnibarbi, inhabited by scientists, philosophers, and inventors occupying themselves with how to obtain sunbeams from cucumbers and problems of similar importance. On the Island of Sorcerers, Gulliver is able to question famous men of old and discovers how often history has credited cowards with courageous deeds, the wicked with virtue, the foolish with wisdom. He meets here the Struldbrugs, a race of immortals, who prove to be the most unhappy people in the land. The last voyage gives Swift an opportunity for the most bitter and vigorous satire of all. Gulliver comes to the land of the Houyhnhnms, a race of supremely intelligent horses. They are served by the Yahoos, reasonless and conscienceless beasts in the shape of men. Gulliver attempts to show the Houyhnhnms how unlike the Yahoos he is, but his accounts of human life only reveal, to himself as well as them, how little distance separates the Englishman from the Yahoo. Gulliver returns to his home in England after this voyage, but finds that his family fills him with disgust after the life of the wise and happy Houyhnhnms.

Gull's Hornbook, The. A book by Thomas Dekker, published in 1609. It gives a graphic description of the manners of Jacobean gallants. The tract is to some extent modeled on Dedekind's *Grobianus*.

Gulnare (gŭl.nä′rē). In Byron's long poem *The Corsair*, the queen of the harem, who flees with Conrad after murdering Seyd.

Gummidge (gum′ij), **Mrs.** In Dickens's *David Copperfield*, "a lone, lorn creetur" who keeps house for Mr. Peggotty.

Gun For Sale, A. A novel by Graham Greene, published in 1936.

Gunga Din (gung′ga dēn). A poem by Rudyard Kipling, in ballad style, written in 1890 and printed in *The National Observer*. It appeared in *Barrack-Room Ballads, and Other Verses* (1892). Gunga Din is a regimental *bhisti* (water carrier), despised as a colored native, and killed as he rescues the soldier who recites the story:

> Tho' I've belted you an' flayed you,
> By the livin' Gawd that made you,
> You're a better man than I am, Gunga Din!

Gunn (gun), **Neil M.** b. Nov. 8, 1891—. A Scottish novelist. His books include *Grey Coast* (1926), *Morning Tide* (1931), *Highland Night* (1935), *Highland River* (1937), *Wild Geese Overhead* (1939), *The Silver Darlings* (1941), *Young Art and Old Hector* (1945), *The Drinking Well* (1947), and *The Shadow* (1948).

Gunnar (gŭn′när, gun′ar). In the *Volsunga Saga*, the king of the Nibelungs and the husband of Brynhild. William Morris uses him in his poem *Sigurd the Volsung*.

Gunning (gun′ing), **Elizabeth.** [Titles: Duchess of **Hamilton** and of **Argyll**.] b. 1734; d. May 20, 1790. An Irishwoman celebrated for her beauty; sister of Maria Gunning. She married James, 6th Duke of Hamilton, in 1752, and in 1759 she married John Campbell, Marquis of Lorne, afterward 5th Duke of Argyll.

Gunning, Maria. [Title, Countess of **Coventry**.] b. 1733; d. Oct. 1, 1760. An Irishwoman celebrated for her beauty; daughter of John Gunning of Castle Coote, County Roscommon, Ireland. She and her sister Elizabeth went to London in 1751, and were at once pronounced to be "the handsomest women alive." They were followed by crowds wherever they went, and Maria, who was the better-looking, was mobbed one evening in Hyde Park. The king gave her a guard to protect her, and she once walked in the park for two hours with two sergeants of the guard before her and 12 soldiers following her. "The beautiful Misses Gunning" were painted a number of times, and there are many engravings from these portraits.

Gunning, Susannah. [Maiden name, **Minifie**.] b. c1740; d. at London, Aug. 28, 1800. An English novelist. She married John Gunning, the brother

of the beautiful Gunning sisters, Elizabeth and Maria. He had one daughter, Elizabeth; owing to her flirtations (in which her mother took her part), she and her mother left his house. Many squibs and satires were written on the ensuing complication, which Walpole called "the Gunningiad."

Gunpowder Plot. In English history, a conspiracy of certain Roman Catholics having for its object the destruction of James I and the lords and commoners in the Parliament House, London. The leaders were Robert Catesby, Thomas Percy, Everard Digby, Robert Winter, Guy Fawkes, and others. It was foiled by the arrest of Fawkes on Nov. 4, 1605, in the cellar under the House of Lords. The other conspirators were trapped in Staffordshire on November 8; four were killed in the fight with the sheriff and the rest captured. Eight of the plotters were executed. Guy Fawkes' Day, November 5, is still a popular holiday in England, celebrating the failure of the plot.

Gunroom, The. A novel by Charles Morgan, published in 1919, dealing with conditions in the Royal Navy. Its exposé of harsh conditions caused it to be withdrawn shortly after publication.

Gunther (gŭn′tėr). In the *Nibelungenlied*, a Burgundian king; brother of Kriemhild and husband of Brunhild.

Guppy (gup′i), **William.** In Dickens's *Bleak House*, a young articled clerk, hopelessly in love with Esther Summerson.

Gurnall (gėr′nal), **William.** b. near Lynn, Norfolk, England, 1617; d. at Lavenham, Suffolk, England, Oct. 12, 1679. An English clergyman, author of *The Christian in Complete Armour* (1655–62).

Gurney (gėr′ni), **James.** In Shakespeare's *King John*, a servant of Lady Faulconbridge.

Gurth (gėrth). In Sir Walter Scott's novel *Ivanhoe*, a swineherd and bondsman of Cedric.

Gushington (gush′ing.ton), **Impulsia.** Pseudonym of **Sheridan**, Lady **Helen Selina**.

Gustavus Adolphus (gus.tā′vus, -tä′-; a.dol′fus). [Called the **Lion of the North** and the **Snow King**; also, **Gustaf Adolf II**, **Gustavus II Adolphus**.] b. at Stockholm, Dec. 9, 1594; d. at Lutzen, Germany, Nov. 16, 1632. King of Sweden (1611–32); son of Charles IX of Sweden. He was reared as a militant Lutheran and was trained, while still a boy, to the duties he would inherit. As the better alternative to a period of regency, on the death of Charles IX he was declared, almost immediately on his accession, of age. He inherited three wars from his father: with Denmark, Poland, and Russia. The war of Kalmar against Denmark he ended by treaty in 1613 at Knäred: neither side actually gained but peace was restored. In 1617 he ended the Russian war with the treaty of Stolbova, gaining Karelia and Ingria and thus cutting off Russian access to the Baltic. Meanwhile, his internal policy, controlled by the chancellor Axel Oxenstierna, was calculated to obtain the support of all parties in the country. The king granted (1611) a charter establishing a parliament based on what was for the period advanced political thought. Under it, nobility and commons joined in the legislative process, giving advisory opinions on the king's initiative in legislation, and they obtained some control over questions of foreign policy. Various reforms were instituted in administration and the judicial system and the industrial and commerical development of the country was fostered. In 1621 he began vigorously to prosecute the Polish war. After capturing Riga and Mitau, Gustavus was forced to stop by winter and illness in his army. After a three-year hiatus, he again undertook hostilities in 1625 and soon had conquered all of Livonia. But despite limited successes in the next few years, he could make no headway against the Poles, who were aided in 1629 by troops sent by Wallenstein, and after a decisive defeat at Stuhm in June, 1629, Gustavus Adolphus agreed to the truce of Altmark, by which Sigismund III of Poland, who had been king of Sweden until 1604, gave up his claim to the Swedish throne; Sweden was confirmed in possession of Livonia, and peace was settled for six years. Gustavus now recognized in the Thirty Years' War, then raging on the Continent, a threat to Sweden's sea power. He had met with some of the power of the Imperial forces in Wallenstein's forces, and this, combined with a feeling that his fellow Protestants were being oppressed, led him to enter the war. He embarked for the mainland on June 7, 1630, leaving Oxenstierna as regent in his absence and indicating that the succession was to go to his daughter Christina if he failed to return. He captured Stettin and Frankfort-on-the-Oder, driving the forces of the emperor from Pomerania. On Jan. 13, 1631, he concluded a treaty of alliance with France, but the vacillation of the elector of Brandenburg and of the neutral John George of Saxony delayed his advance to occupy Madgeburg until it was too late. The city was stormed and burned by the Imperialists on May 20. On September 12, the Saxon elector joined with Gustavus Adolphus, and on September 17, at Breitenfeld, near Leipzig, the Swedish army defeated Tilly. The Saxon and Swedish forces went on to take Mainz and Prague, but Wallenstein recaptured Prague and cleared the Saxons out of Bohemia. Gustavus, faced with Tilly's advance from the Danube, came out of his winter quarters at Mainz to meet the Imperialists, crossed the Danube at Donauwörth, and met Tilly at Rain (April 15, 1632) on the Lech near the Danube. Tilly was mortally wounded and his army was chased to Ingolstadt, where Gustavus besieged the emperor in vain. He took Munich, but found that Wallenstein had come up to prevent his advance into Bohemia to aid the Saxons. At Nuremberg both armies encamped and faced each other from trenches on either side of the Regnitz. For eleven weeks, until the end of August, the impasse held; then Gustavus, after a futile attempt to break through, began a general retirement southward. Wallenstein turned to punish Saxony and had completed his work of ravaging the countryside and was heading for winter quarters when he was confronted at Lützen by the Swedish force. The numercial superiority hitherto held by the Imperialists had been reduced by the expedition of a force to the Rhine and the two armies were of approximately equal strength. After a preliminary fight on November 1, the final battle was fought on Nov. 16, 1632. The victory went to the Swedish army, but Gustavus Adolphus fell in the battle.

Gustavus Vasa (vä′să). [Also: **Gustavus Eriksson, Gustavus I.**] b. at Lindholmen, in Uppland, Sweden, May 12, 1496; d. at Stockholm, Sept. 29, 1560. King of Sweden (1523–60). He was the son of Erik Johansson (hence called Gustavus Eriksson) of the house of Vasa, and was descended on the mother's side from the house of Sture, two of the most influential noble families in Sweden. He received a careful education, chiefly at the court of his kinsman, the regent Sten Sture the younger, under whom he served (1518) against the Danes at the battle of Brännkyrka. In the negotiations which followed this Swedish victory, he was sent as a hostage to Christian II of Denmark, by whom he was treacherously carried off to Denmark. He escaped (1519), and on the massacre of Stockholm, in which 90 of the leading men of Sweden, including the father of Gustavus, were executed by Christian II, headed (1520) a revolt of the Dalecarlians. He captured Stockholm in 1523, the year in which a diet at Strengnäs chose (June 6) him king, and repudiated the Kalmar union with Denmark. He favored the Reformation in opposition to the Roman Catholic clergy, who had supported the Danes during the war for freedom; and at the Diet of Vesterås, procured (1527) the passage of measures placing the lands of the bishops at his disposal, and granting the liberty of preaching the new doctrine. During the reign of Gustavus Vasa the New Testament was translated (1526) into Swedish by Olaus Petri. The power of the Hanseatic League, crippling to the new Swedish state, was broken (1537) with a victory over Lübeck. Royal power was consolidated; several revolts were suppressed, and in 1544 the line of Vasa was declared hereditary in the rule of Sweden.

Guster (gus′tėr). [Supposedly christened **Augusta.**] A maidservant of the Snagsbys in Charles Dickens's novel *Bleak House*, a lean young woman, subject to fits.

Gutenberg (gö′ten.bėrg; German, gö′ten.berk), **Johannes** (or **Henne**). [Original surname, **Gensfleisch.**] b. at Mainz, Germany, c1400; d. probably at Mainz, c1468. A German printer; usually considered to have been the inventor of printing. His claim to the invention has been much disputed, especially by proponents of the priority of Laurens Janszoon Coster. Gutenberg was the son of Friela Gensfleisch and Else Gutenberg (or Wyrich, Gutenberg being an adopted place name), and took his mother's name. In 1420 his father was exiled, and various legal proceedings growing out of this show that Gutenberg was at Strasbourg in 1434. The claim that he was the inventor of printing rests in large part on a legal decision handed down at Strasbourg on Dec. 12, 1439, from which it would appear that he entered into partnership with certain persons to carry on various secret operations, one of which involved the use of a press with an attachment conjectured to have been a type mold. In 1450 he formed a partnership with Johann Fust, a moneylender, which terminated in 1455. Fust demanded payment of money loaned; in default of this, he seized all of Gutenberg's types and stock, and carried on the business himself, with Peter Schöffer (later his son-in-law) as manager. Gutenberg continued his work with inferior types. None of the work ascribed to Gutenberg bears his name and much of the ascription of books to him is conjectural. It is generally agreed that he printed the Mazarin Bible (so called because the first copy described was in the library of Cardinal Mazarin), which is also known as the 42-Line Bible; some claim, however, that Schöffer and Fust are responsible for the book.

Guthlac (göth′läk), Saint. b. c673; d. at Crowland, Lincolnshire, England, April 11, 714. An English hermit who for about 15 years lived with a few companions at Crowland. The church reared by Ethelbald over his relics grew into Crowland Abbey.

Guthlac (göth′läk). Either of two Old English poems, both in the *Exeter Book*, based on the life of Saint Guthlac (c673–714), an English Christian hermit. The second has sometimes been attributed to Cynewulf.

Guthrie (guth′ri), **Thomas Anstey.** [Pseudonym, **F. Anstey.**] b. at Kensington, London, Aug. 8, 1856; d. March 10, 1934. English novelist. He wrote *Vice Versa* (1882), *The Giant's Robe* (1883), *The Tinted Venus* (1885), *The Pariah* (1889), *The Brass Bottle* (1900), and others, as well as several stage adaptations from Molière.

Guy (gī), **Thomas.** b. c1645; d. at London, Dec. 27, 1724. An English bookseller and philanthropist. He founded Guy's Hospital, London, in 1722, and endowed other charitable institutions.

Guy and Pauline (gī; pô.lēn′). [American title, **Plasher's Mead.**] A novel by Compton Mackenzie, published in 1915. The experiences at Oxford of Michael Fane, whose story begins in *Sinister Street* (1913), form the basis of the plot.

Guy Denzil (den′zil). See **Denzil, Guy.**

Guy Fawkes' Day (gī′ fôks′). The anniversary of the day, Nov. 5, 1605, on which the Gunpowder Plot was discovered and Fawkes, the agent of the conspirators, seized.

Guy Livingstone (liv′ing.stọn). An adventure novel (1857) by George Alfred Lawrence.

Guy Mannering (gī′ man′ėr.ing). A novel by Sir Walter Scott, published in 1815. The story takes place in Scotland during the middle of the 18th century. Mannering, traveling through the country, stops at the home of the Laird of Ellangowan. There he makes a forecast for the future of the newborn son of the Laird. He says that there will be two crises in the boy's life, one at the age of five and another at the age of twenty-one. Mannering goes his way, and when Harry Bertram, the son, is five he is kidnapped and carried to Holland at the instigation of the wicked lawyer, Glossin. Bertram, knowing nothing of his real parents, later serves in India as a soldier under Guy Mannering. He uses the name of Brown. Mannering suspects the young man of paying attentions to his wife, although Brown is really in love with Mannering's daughter, Julia. They fight a duel, and Mannering leaves Brown for dead; he returns shortly to England, not knowing that Brown actually survived. Brown follows Julia to England, where he is recognized by Meg Merrilies, an old gypsy who is devoted to the Laird's family. Meg and a farmer, Dandie Dinmont, foil the plans of the lawyer, Glossin, in his

attempt to kidnap Bertram again; Bertram is restored to his own property, and marries Julia.

Guy of Gisborne (gī; giz′bọrn). See under **Robin Hood and Guy of Grisborne.**

Guy of Warwick (gī; wor′ik). A Middle English verse romance, written probably c1300. The four extant versions vary in length from 7,000 to 12,000 lines. The hero, the son of the Earl of Warwick's steward, falls in love with Felice, the Earl's daughter. In many trials he proves his worth and marries her. He then decides to go to the Holy Land and fight for God against the Saracens. When he returns to England, he aids King Athelstan against the Danes and defeats the Danish giant Colbrand (a part of the story accepted and recorded by many of the chroniclers of the time as history). He eventually becomes a hermit, receiving his food from his wife, who does not recognize him. He reveals his identity on his deathbed. This romance was very popular with writers up to the 17th century, particularly in Elizabethan times, and was treated in poetry, drama, and ballads.

Guyon (gī′ọn), **Sir.** A knight personifying temperance in Spenser's *Faerie Queene*. He overcomes Acrasia.

Guzmán de Alfarache (göth.män′ dä äl.fä.rä′chä). A Spanish picaresque romance by Mateo Aleman, named after its hero. It is a series of unusual, unconnected adventures, accompanied by sarcastic commentary. It is divided into two parts, the first of which was published at Madrid in 1599, the second part in 1605. Its hero, who supposes himself to be the son of a decayed and not very reputable Genoese merchant established at Seville, escapes, as a boy, from his mother, after his father's ruin and death, and begins a life of adventure. He undergoes various experiences at Madrid, Toledo, Genoa, and Rome, serving in turn as a scullion, errand boy, thief, soldier, beggar, page to a cardinal, and servant of a French ambassador.

Gwendolen Harleth (gwen′dọ.lẹn här′lẹth). See **Harleth, Gwendolen.**

Gwilym (gwi′lim) or **Gwillum** (-lum), **Dafydd ap.** See **David.**

Gwyn (gwin), **Nell.** b. perhaps at Hereford, England, Feb. 2, 1650; d. Nov. 13, 1687. An English actress; mistress of Charles II. There is little information as to her early life; tradition says that she was born in an alley near Drury Lane, London. She is supposed to have sold oranges outside Drury Lane Theatre, and thus to have come to the notice of the actors. Her first known appearance on the stage was in 1665, as Cydaria in Dryden's *Indian Emperor.* The romantic pairs of young lovers in a number of Dryden's comedies were probably created for her and Charles Hart. She was a great favorite with the public, as she was gay and sprightly and played piquant, bustling parts. Her dancing was much admired. After various adventures with other lovers besides the king, whose mistress she became in 1669, she left the stage in 1682. The king retained his affection for her till his death; his dying request to his brother and successor was "Let not poor Nelly starve." She had two children by him: Charles Beauclerk (1670– 1726; afterward Duke of St. Albans), and James

(1671–80). Large sums of money, and Bestwood Park (Nottingham), Burford House (Windsor), and other gifts were bestowed on her.

Gwynn (gwin), **Stephen Lucius.** b. Feb. 13, 1864—. An Irish novelist and poet. His numerous writings include *The Decay of Sensibility* (1900), *The Queen's Chronicler* (1901), *The Fair Hills of Ireland* (1906), *Duffer's Luck* (1924), *Irish Literature and Drama* (1936), *Fond Opinions* (1938), *Student's History of Ireland, Claude Monet and his Garden, Thomas Moore,* and *Dublin Old and New.*

Gyges (gī'jēz, jī'-). fl. 7th century B.C. A king of Lydia (c716–678 B.C.), founder of a new dynasty. Pressed by the Cimmerians, he invoked the help of Asurbanipal, and submitted to his supremacy. Afterward he allied himself with Psammetichus, king of Egypt, against Assyria, and seems to have fallen (c653) in one of the repeated attacks of the Cimmerians, who were no longer checked by the Assyrian power. Plato's story is that Gyges, a shepherd of the king of Lydia, after a storm came upon a hollow brazen horse in a chasm. Within the horse lay a corpse from which he took a magic ring which had the property of making the wearer invisible. Wearing the ring, Gyges killed the king, and thus became king himself. Herodotus tells still another story: Gyges spies on the queen in her bedchamber, is discovered, and given the choice between the crown and death.

Gyges. In Greek mythology, a brother of Briareus.

Gymnosophists (jim.nos'ọ.fists). A sect of ancient Hindu philosophers who lived solitarily in the woods, wore little clothing, ate no meat, renounced all bodily pleasures, and devoted themselves to mystical contemplation; so called by Greek writers. By some they are regarded as Brahman penitents;

others include among them a sect of Buddhist ascetics, the Shamans.

Gypsies (jip'siz). [Also: **Gipsies, Romany.**] A swarthy, black-haired people of Indian origin who first appeared in eastern Germany in the 15th century, and have since spread all over the world. They have become famous as metalworkers and animal handlers, and especially as musicians. Traditionally they are known as fortunetellers, especially the women, and as sharp horse-traders. "Romany" is the name by which they designate themselves. Conjecturally this name is associated either with their anciently having dwelt in the Byzantine Empire, called *Roum,* or with their long concentration in Rumania. The origin of these people was long a matter of dispute. They were thought to have originated in Egypt, India, Turkey, or Hungary. Groups of them who migrated into Germany in the 15th century spread the legend that they had come from Egypt on a pilgrimage of penance because their ancestors had renounced Christianity. The true clue to their origin, however, lies in their language (called Romany), which philologists classify as belonging to the Indic group of Indo-European languages. In spite of migration and local assimilations from the countries of their sojourn, it remains fundamentally unchanged. Irish Gypsies could understand Turkish Gypsies, for instance. Thus their origin is indicated as being somewhere in C or SE Asia, from whence they spread northward and westward. They were reported in Persia c900 A.D. They appeared in Germany in the 15th century, and in spite of persecution and purge they have since spread and rooted themselves in every country in the world.

Gypsies Metamorphosed, The. A masque (produced in 1621; published in 1640) by Ben Jonson.

H

Habakkuk (hạ.bak'uk, hab'ạ.kuk). [Also: **Habacuc, Habbacuc.**] A Hebrew prophet. Nothing authentic of his life is known, and he therefore has become the subject of many legends. Thus, in the apocryphal book *Bel and the Dragon,* he is carried through the air by an angel from Judea to Babylon to feed Daniel. The book of his prophecies, consisting of three chapters, holds the eighth place among the minor prophets in the Biblical canon. The first two chapters bear on the wickedness reigning in the country and the growing power of the Chaldeans; the third chapter is a lyric ode representing God as appearing in judgment. Habakkuk exhibits poetical genius of high order. His prophecy is constructed dramatically in the form of a dialogue between himself and Jehovah. The lyric ode ranks, for sublimity of poetic conception, picturesqueness of imagery, and splendor of diction, with the highest which Hebrew poetry has produced. He prophesied most probably in the reign of Jehoiakim (c609–c597 B.C.).

Habakkuk Mucklewrath (muk'l.ràth). See **Mucklewrath, Habakkuk.**

Habington (hab'ing.tọn), **William.** b. at Hindlip, Worcestershire, England, Nov. 4, 1605; d. there, Nov. 30, 1654. An English poet. He published the lyrical collection *Castara* (1634).

Habsburg (haps'bėrg, häps'bürk). See **Hapsburg.**

Hackney (hak'ni). A metropolitan borough in E London, in the County of London, ab. 3 mi. NE of Liverpool Street station.

Hackum (hak'um), **Captain.** A bully in Shadwell's *Squire of Alsatia.*

Haddock (had'ọk), **Albert.** Pseudonym of **Herbert, A.P.**

Haddon, Hall (had'ọn). A mansion of the Dukes of Turland, near Bakewell, Derbyshire, England.

Haddon Hall. An opera in three acts by Arthur Sullivan, with a libretto by Sidney Grundy, first performed at the London Savoy Theatre on Sept. 24, 1892.

Hades (hā'dēz). In Greek mythology: **1.** The lord of the lower world; a brother of Zeus, and the husband of Persephone. He reigned in a splendid

palace, and, besides his function of governing the shades of the dead, he was the giver to mortals of all treasures derived from the earth. In art he was represented in a form kindred to that of Zeus and that of Poseidon, and bearing the staff or scepter of authority, usually in company with Persephone. As the god of wealth he was also called by the Greeks Pluto; he is identified with the Roman Dis or Orcus.
2. The lower or subterranean world in which dwelt the spirits of the dead. Sometimes it was said to be situated in the west. The souls in Hades were believed to carry on there a counterpart of their material existence: those of the righteous without discomfort, amid the pale sweet blooms of asphodel, or even in pleasure, in the Elysian Fields, and those of the wicked amid various torments in Tartarus. Hades was surrounded by five rivers, of which the Styx (across which Charon ferried the souls of the buried dead) and Lethe (the river of forgetfulness) are the best known. The gates were guarded by the monstrous three-headed (sometimes 50-headed) dog Cerberus to prevent the shades from escaping to the upper world.

Hadrian (hā′dri.ạn). [Also: **Adrian;** full Latin name, **Publius Aelius Hadrianus.**] b. at Rome or at Italica, in Hispania Baetica (near modern Seville, Spain), Jan. 24, 76 A.D.; d. at Baiae, Italy, July 10, 138. A Roman emperor (117–138); nephew and ward of Trajan, whom he succeeded. He held several positions in various parts of the empire under Trajan, accompanying him in his campaigns. On the death of Trajan, it is said, he succeeded to the emperor's place through the slyness of Plotina, Trajan's wife, who announced Trajan's adoption of his nephew and then withheld news of Trajan's death until Hadrian could consolidate his position. Renouncing the policy of conquest, he abandoned the new provinces of Armenia, Mesopotamia, and Assyria, and established the Euphrates as the eastern boundary of the empire. In 119 he began a progress through the provinces, in the course of which he began the construction of the wall that bears his name, designed to keep the Picts and the Scots out of Britain. He returned finally about 131, having visited Gaul, Germany, Britain, Spain, Mauretania, Parthia, Asia Minor, Athens, Sicily, Rome (for a year), Syria, Palestine, Arabia, and Egypt. He promulgated the *Edictum perpetuum*, a collection of the edicts of the praetors by Salvius Julianus, in 132; this formed the groundwork for the *Corpus juris* of Justinian. In 132 a revolt was occasioned among the Jews by the planting of the Roman colony of Aelia Capitolina on the site of Jerusalem, and the building of a temple to Jupiter Capitolinus on the site of the Temple; the revolt, led by Bar Kochba, was suppressed in 135. Hadrian devoted himself to building and strengthening the position of the emperor. Through the *Edictum* of 132, lawmaking by the praetors was ended; thereafter laws became a matter of senatorial confirmation of the suggestions of the emperor. He reduced taxes, provided for less arbitrary treatment of slaves, and fostered regulations to reduce immorality. His public works include the wall in Britain, similar structures in Germany, the Pantheons of Rome and Athens, and the temple of the Olym-

pian Zeus at Athens, as well as many other buildings in Rome and in the provinces. He was a patron of the arts and himself a poet; perhaps his most famous composition is the address to his soul, supposed to have been said on his deathbed, beginning: "Animula, vagula, blandula." Hadrian's first choice as his successor, Lucius Ceionius Commodus, died Jan. 1, 138, and Hadrian then chose Antoninus (Antoninus Pius) on condition that Antoninus would adopt Commodus's son (later the emperor Commodus) and Antoninus's own nephew (later the emperor Marcus Aurelius).

Hadrian's Wall. A wall of defense for the Roman province of Britain, constructed by Hadrian between the Solway Firth and the mouth of the Tyne. The work has been ascribed to Severus and others, but was probably constructed under Hadrian alone.

haemony (hē.mọ.ni). A medicinal herb mentioned by Milton in *Comus*, used to ward off evil spirits or enchantments.

Haemus (hē′mus). Latin name of the Balkans, a mountain system in SE Europe, chiefly in Bulgaria.

Hafed (hä′fed). In "The Fire-Worshippers," a tale included in Thomas Moore's *Lalla Rookh*, the principal male character. He falls in love with the beautiful daughter of the leader of his people's Mohammedan enemies.

Hafen Slawkenbergius (hä′fẹn slô.kẹn.bẻr′ji.us). See **Slawkenbergius, Hafen.**

Hafiz (hä′fēz′). [Pseudonym of **Shams ud-din Mohammed.**] b. at Shiraz, Persia, in the beginning of the 14th century; d. between 1388 and 1394. A Persian divine, philosopher, and grammarian, one of the greatest poets of all time. His pseudonym means "The Memorizer" (that is, one who recalls the Koran by heart). He was not only appointed teacher in the royal family, but a special college was founded for him. Although nominally a member of an order of dervishes, he celebrated nonascetic activities and often satirized the dervishes. He was a member of the Sufi sect and, accordingly as the editor of his works is a Sufite, a Sunnite, or a non-Moslem, his works are interpreted as being philosophically religious or hedonistic and profane. He sings of wine, love, nightingales, and flowers, and sometimes of Allah and the Prophet and the instability of life. His tomb, about two miles northeast of Shiraz, is sumptuously adorned, and is still the resort of pilgrims.

Hafnia (haf′ni.ạ). A medieval name of Copenhagen, Denmark.

Hagar (hā′gär). An Egyptian concubine of Abraham, mother of Ishmael. Gen. xvi.

Hagenbach (hä′gẹn.bäch), **Archibald of.** See **Archibald of Hagenbach.**

Haggadah (hạ.gä′dạ). See **Agada.**

Haggard (hag′ạrd), Sir **Henry Rider.** b. in Norfolk, England, June 22, 1856; d. at London, May 14, 1925. An English author. He was in the colonial service in the Transvaal (1875–79), and published in 1882 *Cetywayo and his White Neighbours.* Among his novels, popular for their romantic settings and strange adventure, and his books on land problems, are *King Solomon's Mines* (1885), *She; A History of Adventure* (1887), *Allan Quatermain* (1887),

Cleopatra (1889), *Montezuma's Daughter* (1893), *Black Heart and White Heart and Other Stories* (1900), *Lysbeth, A Tale of the Dutch* (1901), *A Winter Pilgrimage* (1901), *Stella Fregelius* (1904), *The Brethren* (1904), *Ayesha, or the Return of She* (1905), *A Gardener's Year* (1905), *The Poor and the Land* (1905), *Fair Margaret* (1907), *The Yellow God* (1909), *Regeneration* (1910), *Rural Denmark and its Lessons* (1911), *The Mahatma and the Hare* (1911), *Red Eve* (1911), *Marie* (1912), *The Holy Flower* (1915), *When the World Shook* (1919), *The Ancient Allan* (1920), and *Wisdom's Daughter* (1923). His books, especially *She* and *King Solomon's Mines*, have been dramatized and made into motion pictures. The style and content are often burlesqued, as in the anonymous parodies *He* and *King Solomon's Wives*.

Haidee (hī'dē). The beautiful Greek girl in Byron's *Don Juan*.

Hail and Farewell. An autobiography in three parts (*Ave*, 1911; *Salve*, 1912; *Vale*, 1914) by George Moore.

Hail Mary. See **Ave Maria.**

Haimon (hī'mon). See **Aymon.**

Hajji Baba (häj'i bä'bạ). [Full title, **The Adventures of Hajji Baba of Ispahan** (is.pạ.hän').] A novel by James J. Morier, published in 1824 (second part, 1828). The hero gives an accurate picture of life in Persia, and is then (in the second part) transported to England, and the manners and customs of that country are described as seen through his eyes.

Hajji Baba. See also **Baba, Hajji.**

Hakim (hä'kim). [Also, **Hakem.**] b. 985; d. c1021. A Fatimite caliph (996–c1021) in Egypt, regarded as the founder of the Druses. His reign was one of terror: the Holy Sepulcher at Jerusalem was destroyed (1009) and the non-Islamic peoples were placed under strict regulation. His claim to be an incarnation of Allah was carried by Darazi to Arabia and Syria, where the Druse sect was established.

Hakim (hak'ēm), **Adonbeck al.** See **Adonbeck al Hakim.**

Hakluyt (hak'löt), **Richard.** b. c1552; d. at London, Nov. 23, 1616. An English geographer. He studied at Oxford, took holy orders, and was attached (1583–86) to the suite of the English ambassador, Sir Edward Stafford, in France. In 1603 he was made archdeacon of Westminster. While in France he published an annotated edition of Peter Martyr's *De orbe novo*, and an account of Laudonnière's expedition to Florida. His great collection of travels, *The Principall Navigations, Voiages, and Discoveries of the English Nation*, first appeared in 1589, and was republished in a greatly enlarged form, in three volumes, 1598 to 1600. There are several modern editions. The work is a collection of the accounts of the voyages of exploration of Englishmen and of their exploits on the seas; perhaps its most famous paper is the story of the last fight of the *Revenge*, but stories of Frobisher's voyages and Harriot's account of Raleigh's Virginia colony and other similar papers make Hakluyt's book an invaluable source of knowledge. His trans-

lations, including one of De Soto's description of Florida, and his own original writings were intended as an impetus to English colonization and discovery. He was a member of the South Virginia Company and at one time was granted the living of James Town, in the proposed colony.

Hakluyt Society. A society established (1846) in London to print annotated English editions of rare works on early geography, travels, and history.

Hal (hal), **Prince.** In Shakespeare's *1* and *2 Henry IV*, the historical Henry, Prince of Wales, a gay and roistering young man who is one of Falstaff's boon companions. See also under **Henry V.**

Halbert Elliot. See **Elliot, Halbert** or **Hobbie.**

Halbert Glendinning (hal'bẹrt glen.din'ing). See **Glendinning, Halbert.**

Halcombe (hal'kọm), **Marian.** In Wilkie Collins's *Woman in White*, the half sister of the heroine.

Halcro (hal'krō), **Claud.** A whimsical old bard in Sir Walter Scott's novel *The Pirate*, whose minstrelsy and improvisations delighted the Zetlanders.

Haldane (hôl'dān), **Charlotte.** [Maiden name, Franken.] An English novelist and essayist; wife (married 1926) of J. B. S. Haldane. Author of *Brother to Bert* (1930), *I Bring Not Peace* (1932), *Russian Newsreel, an Eye-Witness Account of the Soviet Union at War* (1942). She also wrote *Man's World* (1927), *Motherhood and Its Enemies* (1928), *Melusine, or Devil Take Her* (1936), and the autobiographical *Music, My Love!* (1936) and *Truth Will Out* (1951).

Haldane, John Burdon Sanderson. b. at Oxford, England, Nov. 5, 1892—. An English geneticist and writer. He was professor (1933–37) of genetics at London University, and has been professor of biometrics (1937 *et seq.*) at University College at London. His publications include *Daedalus* (1924), *Callinicus* (1925), *Possible Worlds* (1927), *Science and Ethics* (1928), *The Causes of Evolution* (1933), *Fact and Faith* (1934), *My Friend Mr. Leakey* (1937), for children, *Heredity and Politics* (1938), *A.R.P.* (1938), *The Marxist Philosophy and the Sciences* (1938), *Science and Everyday Life* (1939), *Keeping Cool* (1939), *Science in Peace and War* (1940), and *New Paths in Genetics* (1949). He collaborated with Julian S. Huxley on *Animal Biology* (1927).

Haldane, Richard Burdon. [Title, 1st Viscount **Haldane of Cloan**.] b. in Scotland, 1856; d. Aug. 19, 1928. A British author and Liberal and Labour statesman; grandson of James Alexander Haldane. He was educated in the universities of Edinburgh and Göttingen, was called to the bar in 1879, and was appointed queen's counsel in 1890. He sat (1885–1911) for Haddingtonshire in the House of Commons, was vice-president of the Liberal Imperialist League in 1901, was appointed secretary of state for war in December, 1905, and became lord high chancellor in June, 1912. He did much to prepare the army for the threatened war during his tenure as secretary; the general staff and the integration of the imperial forces were created through his efforts. He served as lord chancellor (1912–15, 1924) and led (1925–28) the Labour opposition in the upper house. He was created a viscount in March, 1911. He published *Essays in Philosophical Criticism* (1883; with Andrew Seth), *Education and Empire* (1902), *The Pathway to Reality* (1903), *Army Reform, and other Addresses* (1907), and others.

Hale (hāl), Sir **Matthew.** b. at Alderley, Gloucestershire, England, Nov. 1, 1609; d. there, Dec. 25, 1676. An English jurist. He was judge of the Common Pleas (1653–58), and was made chief baron of the exchequer in 1660, and lord chief justice in 1671. His chief works are *Historia placitorum coronae* (published 1736), *History of the Common Law of England*, and *Contemplations, Moral and Divine*.

Halfway House. A novel by Maurice Hewlett, published in 1908. Its vagabond hero is Maxwell Senhouse.

Haliburton (hal'i.bėr.tọn), **Thomas Chandler.** [Pseudonym, **Sam Slick.**] b. at Windsor, Nova Scotia, December, 1796; d. at Isleworth, near London, Aug. 27, 1865. A Canadian humorist. He practiced law at Annapolis Royal, and became (1828) chief justice of the court of common pleas of Nova Scotia. On the abolition of this court in 1840, he became judge of the supreme court. He resigned (1842) and went to England in 1856. He was a Conservative member of Parliament from 1859 to 1865. He wrote *The Clockmaker, or Sayings and Doings of Samuel Slick of Slickville* (1837; 2nd series, 1838; 3rd series, 1840), histories of Nova Scotia, *The Attaché, or Sam Slick in England* (1843), *The Bubbles of Canada* (1839), *The Old Judge, or Life in a Colony* (1843), and others.

Halifax (hal'i.faks), 1st Earl of. [Title of **Edward Frederick Lindley Wood.**] b. near Exeter, Devonshire, England, April 16, 1881—. An English statesman. He was elected to the British House of Commons in 1910, and remained a member of that body until 1925. During World War I he served as a major of the Yorkshire Dragoons. He was undersecretary of state for colonies (1921), president of the board of education (1922–24), and minister of agriculture and fisheries (1924–25) before accepting the post of governor general of India (1925–31). He was successful in strengthening British relations with the Indian princes, but despite many conferences with Mohandas Gandhi, made little progress in his efforts to curb the Swaraj, or Freedom, movement among Indian nationalists. Returning to Great Britain, he served as president of the Board of Education (1932–35), succeeded, upon his father's death, to the title of Viscount Halifax (1934), and was Conservative leader in the House of Lords (1935–38), holding the portfolios of secretary of state for war (1935), lord privy seal (1935–37), and lord president of the council (1937–38), before becoming foreign secretary (1938–40). In the last-named post he was active in the negotiations leading to the Munich agreement (September, 1938), and accordingly was widely criticized by opponents of the policy of appeasing the Hitler regime in Germany. Having been succeeded in the foreign office by Anthony Eden, Lord Halifax in 1941 was named ambassador to the U. S., and continued to serve his government at Washington until 1946. During this time he

was, in 1944, created 1st Earl of Halifax. Collections of his public addresses were published under the titles *Indian Problems* (1932), *Speeches on Foreign Policy* (1940), and *American Speeches* (1947).

Halifax, 1st Earl of. Title of **Montagu, Charles.**

Halifax, Marquis of. Title of **Savile,** Sir **George.**

Hali Meidenhad (hō'li mäd'ẹn.hȯd; *modern* hō'li mä'dn.húd). See under **Katherine Group.**

Hall (hôl), **Anna Maria.** [Maiden name, **Fielding.**] b. at Dublin, Jan. 6, 1800; d. at East Moulsey, Surrey, England, Jan. 30, 1881. A British author; wife of Samuel Carter Hall. She wrote *Sketches of Irish Character* (1829), *Lights and Shadows of Irish Life* (1838), and other novels and tales of Irish life.

Hall, Edward. b. c1498; d. 1547. An English historian, author of *The Union of the Noble and Illustre Famelies of Lancastre and York* (1542; generally called *Hall's Chronicle*), a history of England from Henry IV to Henry VII, written so as to glorify the Tudors. Grafton, Holinshed, and Stow borrowed from him, and Shakespeare followed him in some of his historical plays. The chronicle, based on the Latin work (1534) of Polydore Vergil, was reprinted in 1809 by Ellis.

Hall, John Vine. b. at Diss, Norfolk, England, March 14, 1774; d. at London, Sept. 22, 1860. An English bookseller and temperance advocate. He was in the book business from 1786 to 1801 and from 1801 to 1804 was a traveling wine salesman; in book business (1814–50) for himself at Maidstone, as owner of the store that had employed him in 1786. Addicted to drink from 1801 to 1818, he was afterwards a total abstainer and temperance worker. His volume *The Sinner's Friend* (1821; many editions) immediately became popular in religious circles, was translated into 30 languages, and sold three million copies.

Hall, Joseph. b. near Ashby-de-la-Zouch, England, July 1, 1574; d. at Higham, near Norwich, England, Sept. 8, 1656. An English bishop and author. He was educated at Emmanuel College, Cambridge, of which he became a fellow, held the living of Halsted and a canonry at Wolverhampton, and became bishop successively of Exeter and Norwich; he was deprived of the latter See by Parliament. He published satires under the title *Virgidemiarum: First three books of toothless Satires* (1597) and a second volume, *Last three books of byting Satires* (1598), *Epistles* (1608–11), *Contemplations* (1612–26), *Paraphrase of Hard Texts* (1633), and controversial works.

Hall, Radclyffe. [Full name, **Marguerite Radclyffe Hall.**] b. at Bournemouth, Hampshire, England, c1886; d. at London, Oct. 7, 1943. An English novelist and poet, noted as the author of the controversial novel *The Well of Loneliness*. Educated at King's College, London, and in Germany. Author of the books of poetry *'Twixt Earth and Stars* (1906), *Poems of the Past and Present* (1910), *Songs of Three Counties* (1913), and *The Forgotten Island* (1915); of novels including *The Forge* and *The Unlit Lamp* (both 1924), *A Saturday Life* (1925), *Adam's Breed* (1926; awarded the James Tait Black and the Femina-Vie Heureuse prizes, and,

fat, fāte, fär, ȧsk, fãre; net, mē, hėr; pin, pīne; not, nōte, mȯve, nȯr; up, lūte, pu̇ll; ŦH, then;

in 1930, a Humane Award gold medal), *The Well of Loneliness* (1928), *The Master of the House* (1932), and *The Sixth Beatitude* (1936); and of *Miss Ogilvy Finds Herself* (1934), short stories. *The Well of Loneliness*, a sympathetic study of female homosexuality, created a controversy, was the subject of court action, and was banned in London and New York before an American judge finally decided that the theme and its treatment were not immoral. The author was supported in England by Shaw, Wells, Bennett, Julian Huxley, Hugh Walpole, John Middleton Murry, Virginia Woolf, Storm Jameson, and V. Sackville-West, and in the U. S. by Sherwood Anderson, Sinclair Lewis, H. L. Mencken, and Theodore Dreiser.

Hall, Samuel Carter. b. at Waterford, Ireland, May 9, 1800; d. at Kensington, London, March 16, 1889. A British author and editor; husband of Anna Maria Hall. He edited or subedited *The Literary Observer, The Amulet, New Monthly Magazine, The Town, Art Union Journal,* and *Social Notes.* He wrote *Baronial Halls of England* (1848), and, with his wife, *Ireland, its Scenery* (1841–43), and numerous other works.

Hallam (hal'ạm), **Arthur Henry.** b. at London, Feb. 1, 1811; d. at Vienna, Sept. 15, 1833. An English essayist; son of Henry Hallam. He formed an intimacy with Tennyson, to whose sister he was betrothed, and by whom he has been commemorated in the long elegiac poem *In Memoriam.* His literary remains were published in 1834.

Hallam, Henry. b. at Windsor, England, July 9, 1777; d. at Penshurst, Kent, England, Jan. 21, 1859. An English historian. He graduated with the degree of B.A. at Oxford (Christ Church) in 1799, was afterward called to the bar, and was for many years a commissioner of stamps. In 1812 he inherited a competent fortune from his father, which enabled him to withdraw from the practice of law and devote himself to historical studies. His chief works are *A View of the State of Europe during the Middle Ages* (1818), *The Constitutional History of England from the Accession of Henry VII. to the Death of George II.* (1827), and *Introduction to the Literature of Europe in the 15th, 16th, and 17th Centuries* (1837–39).

Halley (hal'i), **Edmund.** b. at Haggerston, Shoreditch, London, Nov. 8, 1656; d. at Greenwich, London, Jan. 14, 1742. An English astronomer. His father was engaged in the business of soap boiling at London. He studied at St. Paul's School, and in 1673 entered Queen's College, Oxford, but left the university in 1676 without taking a degree. His astronomical studies were begun in his boyhood (his first communication to the Royal Society was sent before he was 20), and in 1676 he sailed for St. Helena for the purpose of observing the positions of the fixed stars in the Southern Hemisphere in order to make astronomical calculation more accurate, others then being at work on the northern stars. The importance of observations made during this trip led Flamsteed to name him "the Southern Tycho." On Nov. 7, 1677, he made at St. Helena "the first complete observation of a transit of Mercury." In 1678 he was elected a fellow of the Royal Society. He was a friend of Sir Isaac Newton, and printed (1686–87) the *Principia* at

his own cost. He was assistant secretary of the Royal Society and editor (1685–93) of the *Philosophical Transactions,* was appointed Savilian professor of geometry at Oxford in 1703, became secretary of the Royal Society in 1713, and was appointed successor to Flamsteed as astronomer royal in 1721. From November, 1698, to September, 1700, he explored the South Atlantic in the *Paramour Pink* (returning once to England) for the purpose of studying the variation of the compass and discovering southern lands, and reached lat. 52° S. In 1701, in the same vessel, he surveyed the tides and coasts of the English Channel. He is best known for his studies of comets. He inferred from his computations that the comets of 1531, 1607, and 1682 were in reality the same body, and predicted its return in 1758, a prediction which was verified by its appearance on Christmas day of that year. This comet has since been known by his name.

Halliwell-Phillipps (hal'i.wel.fil'ips, -wẹl-), **James Orchard.** b. at Chelsea, London, June 21, 1820; d. at Hollingbury Copse, near Brighton, England, Jan. 3, 1889. An English antiquary and Shakespeare scholar. He became connected with the Shakespeare Society in 1841. In March, 1872, he bought the theater at Stratford-on-Avon; he was also the means of buying Shakespeare's house, New Place, at Stratford-on-Avon, and conveying it to the corporation of Stratford. Among his works are *Early History of Free-Masonry in England* (1843), *Nursery Rhymes of England* (1845), *Dictionary of Archaic and Provincial Words* (1847), and *Outlines of the Life of Shakspere* (1848). In the period 1853–65 he published a folio edition of Shakespeare in 16 volumes, and in 1862–71 *Lithographed Facsimiles of the Shaksperian Quartos.* He edited many Middle English and early modern English works.

Halloween or **Hallowe'en** (hal.ọ.wēn'). A popular celebration in the British Isles and America, falling on the evening of October 31. Traditionally, it is an occasion for children to play harmless pranks. Although associated with the eve of All Saints or All-Hallows Day, the festival has its origins in pre-Christian rites, as testified by the prevalence of ghost and witch stories associated with it. People in the British Isles still bob for apples, tell fortunes, and light bonfires on this night. In America masquerading and pumpkin-head jack-o'-lanterns are featured. The use of pumpkins and ears of corn as typical decorations associate it with old harvest celebrations.

Hall's Chronicle. See under **Hall, Edward.**

Hall-Stevenson (hôl'stē'vẹn.sọn), **John.** See Stevenson, **John Hall-**.

Hal o' the Wynd (hal; wīnd). See **Smith, Henry.**

Hamadryad (ham.ạ.drī'ad), **The.** A poem (1846) by Walter Savage Landor.

Hamblet (ham'blet). [Full title, **Hystorie of Hamblet, Prince of Denmarke.**] A translation made in 1608 from one of Belleforest's *Histoires tragiques* (published in 1576), which was a French translation from the Latin of Saxo Grammaticus, a 12th-century Danish chronicler. The story concerns Amleth, Prince of Denmark, and the incidents in

ḍ, d or j; ṣ, s or sh; ṭ, t or ch; ẓ, z or zh; o, F. cloche; ü, F. menu; ċh, Sc. loch; ṅ, F. bonbon.

Shakespeare's *Hamlet* are similar, up to the point where Amleth returns from England (Amleth has adventures in England, which the Shakespearian Hamlet does not mention, except to tell of his capture by pirates). Amleth makes the courtiers at Feng's palace drunk, sets fire to the palace and kills Feng with his sword. He then seizes the throne and is later killed in battle. Despite the later date of this work, some authorities have assumed that *Hamlet* was derived from *Hamblet*, but certain echoes in this work of the Shakespeare play would seem to indicate that the relationship was probably the other way around.

Hamelin (ham′ę.lin) or **Hameln** (hä′męln), **the Pied Piper of.** See **Pied Piper of Hamelin.**

Hameline de Croye (ham′ę.lĭn dē kroi′). See **Croye, Hameline, Countess de.**

Hamerton (ham′ẽr.tọn), **Philip Gilbert.** b. near Oldham, Lancashire, England, Sept. 10, 1834; d. near Paris, Nov. 4, 1894. An English writer on art, landscape painter, and etcher. His books include *Thoughts about Art* (1862), *Etching and Etchers* (1866), *Contemporary French Painters* (1867), *Painting in France* (1868), *The Intellectual Life* (1873), *The Graphic Arts* (1882), and *Human Intercourse* (1884). He also wrote several romances, and reprinted (1888) his articles written for *The Portfolio*, an art periodical which he planned in 1869. In 1889 he published *French and English: a Comparison*, founded on his contributions to the *Atlantic Monthly*.

Hamilton (ham′il.tọn), **Duchess of.** A title of **Gunning, Elizabeth.**

Hamilton, Count Anthony. b. probably at Roscrea, County Tipperary, Ireland, 1646; d. at St.-Germain-en-Laye, France, April 21, 1720. French author; brother-in-law of the Comte de Gramont, whose *Mémoires* he wrote (1713). Hamilton was appointed (1685) governor of Limerick by James II, but after the battle of the Boyne (1690) returned to France. He wrote a series of satirical tales modeled after the *Arabian Nights* translation by Galland. His complete works were published in 1812.

Hamilton, Clive. Pseudonym of **Lewis, C. S.**

Hamilton, Cosmo. [Original surname, **Gibbs.**] b. 1872; d. at Shanley Green, Surrey, England, Oct. 14, 1942. An English novelist and dramatist; brother of Sir Philip Hamilton Gibbs and Arthur Hamilton Gibbs; he dropped his last name in 1898 and legally assumed his mother's maiden name. He edited the *Sovereign* and the *World* (1905–06), and was for a time on the staff of the *Pall Mall Gazette*. Author of *Through a Keyhole* (1899), *Impertinent Dialogues* (1901), *The Duke's Son* (1905), *Adam's Clay* and *Brummell* (both 1907), *Keepers of the House* (1908), *The Blindness of Virtue* (1908; also a play), *The Princess of New York* (1911), *Outpost of Eternity* (1912), *The Miracle of Love* (1915), *The Sins of the Children* (1916), *His Friend and His Wife* (1920), *The Rustle of Silk* (1922), *The Laughing Mask* (1924), and *Caste* (1927), all novels and stories. Among his plays are *The Wisdom of Folly* (1902), *The Mountain Climber* (1905), *Mrs. Skeffington* (1910), *Danger* (1921), *The New Poor* (1924), *Parasites* (1924), *Society* (1924), *Women and Ladies* (1925), *The Girl in the Garden* (1926),

Mr. Pickwick (1927), and *Two Women* (1929). His autobiography, *Unwritten History*, appeared in 1924.

Hamilton, Elizabeth. b. at Belfast, Ireland, July 21, 1758; d. at Harrogate, England, July 23, 1816. A British writer.

Hamilton, Emma. [Commonly known as **Lady Hamilton;** maiden name, **Lyon.**] b. c1765; d. at Calais, France, Jan. 15, 1815. The wife of Sir William Hamilton (ambassador at Naples), best known as the mistress of Lord Nelson. She was of humble birth, virtually illiterate, and the mistress of several persons before Nelson. She attained considerable social success, became an intimate friend of Queen Maria Carolina of Naples, and is thought to have played a considerable part in the political intrigues of that court in relation to England. Nelson first met her in 1793 at Naples, and after her husband's death in 1803 she lived with Nelson at Merton. He acknowledged their daughter, Horatia, born in 1801. She was arrested and imprisoned for debt in 1813, but was released in the following year.

Hamilton, George Rostrevor. b. at London, April 11, 1888—. An English poet. Author of *Escape and Fantasy* (1918), *Pieces of Eight* (1923), *The Making* (1926), *Epigrams* (1928), *Light in Six Moods* (1930). *Unknown Lovers* (1935), *The Sober War* (1940), *Apollyon* (1941), *Crazy Gaunt* (1946), and *The Inner Room* (1947). His prose writings include *Bergson and Future Philosophy* (1921), *Poetry and Contemplation* (1937), *The World to Come* (1939), and *Hero or Fool?* (1944).

Hamilton, John. b. 1761; d. probably at Edinburgh, Sept. 23, 1814. A Scottish music teacher and song writer. His best pieces are *Miss Forbes' Farewell to Banff*, *The Ploughman*, *Up in the Mornin' Early*, and *The Rantin' Highlandman*. He contributed songs to James Johnson's *Scots Musical Museum* (1787–1803) and helped Sir Walter Scott with his ballad collection, *Border Minstrelsy* (1802–03).

Hamilton, Thomas. b. at Glasgow, 1789; d. at Pisa, Italy, Dec. 7, 1842. A Scottish author; brother of Sir William Hamilton (1788–1856). He wrote *Cyril Thornton* (1827), *Annals of the Peninsular Campaign* (1829), and *Men and Manners in America* (1833).

Hamilton, William. b. at Bangour, Linlithgowshire, Scotland, 1704; d. at Lyons, France, March 25, 1754. A Scottish poet, author of the ballad *Braes of Yarrow*, of *Ode to the Battle of Gladsmuir*, and other works in verse. He was the first to translate Homer into English blank verse.

Hamilton, Sir William. b. at Glasgow, March 8, 1788; d. at Edinburgh, May 6, 1856. A Scottish philosopher. He was professor of logic and metaphysics (1836–56) at Edinburgh. He published *Philosophy of the Unconditioned* (1829), and other contributions to the *Edinburgh Review*, collected as *Discussions in Philosophy, Literature and Education* (1852–53), and edited Thomas Reid's (1846) and Dugald Stewart's (1854–55) works. His lectures on *Metaphysics and Logic* were edited by Mansel and Veitch (1858–60).

Hamilton, William Gerard. [Called "Single-speech Hamilton."] b. at London, Jan. 28, 1729; d. there, July 16, 1796. An English politician. He was elected to Parliament in 1754, and on Nov. 13, 1755, during the debate on the king's address, delivered his maiden speech, which, as it remained his most notable effort, procured for him the nickname "Single-speech Hamilton." He was chancellor of the exchequer in Ireland from 1763 to 1784.

Hamilton, Sir William Rowan. b. at Dublin, Aug. 4, 1805; d. Sept. 2, 1865. A British mathematician, the inventor of quaternions. He was remarkably precocious, especially in the study of languages, knowing, it is said, at least 13 at the age of 12. He entered Trinity College, Dublin, in 1823. In 1824 he discovered, by theoretical reasoning, conical refraction. He was appointed in 1827, before graduation, professor of astronomy at Dublin and superintendent of the observatory. He became president of the Royal Irish Academy in 1837. He wrote *Lectures on Quaternions* (1852), *The Elements of Quaternions* (1866), and others.

Hamilton Veneering (ve.nir′ing). See **Veneering, Hamilton.**

Hamlet (ham′let). [Full title, **The Tragedy of Hamlet, Prince of Denmark.**] A tragedy by Shakespeare, considered by many to be the greatest in the history of English letters. Shakespeare's work was probably derived from Belleforest's *Histoires tragiques* (see also *Hamblet*) and another play which Henslowe mentions as represented at Newington Butts on June 11, 1594; the latter was an "old play" and is now lost, but is referred to as the *Ur-Hamlet* ("Ur" meaning "source") by scholars. Possibly Kyd wrote this play; at any rate Greene mentions "whole Hamlets" in a passage apparently referring to Kyd. Thomas Lodge refers to a ghost crying "like an oister wife, Hamlet, revenge," but the ghost in *Hamlet* has no such words or such lack of dignity. Dekker in *Satiromastix* (1601) has a character say "My name's Hamlet revenge" and refer to Paris Garden, where the Chamberlain's Company probably acted it in 1596. Shakespeare's *Hamlet* was played in 1600 or 1601, and printed first in 1603. It was entered on the Stationers' Register on July 26, 1602, "A booke called the Revenge of Hamlett Prince Denmarke as yt was latelie Acted by the Lord Chamberleyne his Servantes." This was a very imperfect text, known as the first quarto, possibly based on the *Ur-Hamlet*, and less than half the length of the second quarto. The second quarto, published in 1604, was a good text, thought to be as Shakespeare left it. The third quarto, a reprint of the second, and the fourth appeared in 1611. There is a fifth quarto, undated. No others appeared during Shakespeare's lifetime. The four folios are essentially the same text, which differs from the quartos by 200 lines, these being omitted (probably by acting cuts). The German play *Der Bestrafte Brudermord, oder Prinz Hamlet aus Dænnemark* (Fratricide Punished, or Prince Hamlet of Denmark) is now thought to be a corrupt version of the *Hamlet* produced at Dresden in 1626, with resemblances to the "bad" first quarto and also to the "good" second quarto and the first folio. It is suggested that it was constructed from a player's memory of the first quarto, second quarto, and the *Ur-Hamlet*.

The Story. Hamlet, Prince of Denmark, returns to the royal castle of Elsinore to find that his father has recently died and his mother, Gertrude, has married his father's brother, Claudius, now ruling as King. Hamlet's initial dismay at the unseemly haste of the marriage turns to horror and disgust when he learns from his father's Ghost that he was murdered by Claudius, and he determines to avenge his father by killing the murderer. At this point in the play Hamlet's fatal tendency toward hesitation and the urge to justify too meticulously every action before he takes it are not yet apparent; his wrath is great, and seemingly vengeance will not be too long delayed. To conceal his designs from Claudius, Hamlet feigns madness and spurns Ophelia, the daughter of the Lord Chamberlain Polonius, whom he had previously courted. To test the truth of the Ghost's information he stages a play before the King which re-enacts the circumstances of the murder. Utterly convinced of the King's guilt by his reaction to this, Hamlet nevertheless hesitates to kill Claudius when he comes upon him at prayer, and instead violently reproaches his mother for her "incestuous" marriage. Hearing a noise behind the arras, and thinking it is Claudius, he kills the eavesdropping Polonius. Claudius, now keenly aware of Hamlet's purpose, sends Hamlet to England with instructions that he be killed, but Hamlet escapes when his vessel is intercepted by pirates, and returns to Denmark to discover that in his absence Ophelia has gone mad and drowned herself. Laertes, son of Polonius, and a former close friend of Hamlet, has meanwhile returned to avenge his father's death, and is now persuaded by Claudius that he should participate with him (Claudius) in a seemingly foolproof scheme to kill Hamlet. A fencing match is arranged between the two young men, and Laertes's foil is poisoned. Laertes wounds Hamlet, and thus ensures his death, but Hamlet seizes the poisoned foil and kills Laertes, who, dying, reveals the treachery. Gertrude also dies, having drunk unwittingly from a poisoned chalice prepared by Claudius for Hamlet; and Hamlet now stabs the King with the poisoned sword, and compels him to drain the chalice left unfinished by Gertrude.

Hamlet. In Shakespeare's *Hamlet*, the central character. He derives in name from a legendary Danish prince first mentioned by Saxo Grammaticus, but Shakespeare has made of this bare skeleton a human figure of unique and tantalizing complexity. Superficially, he is the model of a young prince reared in the customs of Shakespeare's day, and Shakespeare's contemporaries had much to say about the molding of such a person, from Ascham's *Scholemaster* to Hoby's translation of *The Courtier.* Hamlet, as is reported by various characters in the play, has had all the proper training. Shakespeare, however, is interested in finding out what happens when such a man encounters a situation requiring action, but offering little honor in the performance. The courtier was expected to be a gallant commander of troops, an orator before the populace, an inspiring teacher of younger men, and the idol of courtly love, but not a skulker in dark corners plotting to kill a king, even a usurping king who is guilty of murder and beyond that incest (for in the eyes of an Elizabethan Englishman

Claudius's relation to Gertrude was incestuous). The Romantic critics led by Coleridge tended to see Hamlet in psychological terms, as an individual torn by doubt and seeking to form a course of action. However, it has been suggested that the Coleridge Hamlet tends to personify in an auto-biographical sense Coleridge himself. Nevertheless, it has been difficult to get away from this external criticism to one based upon the play itself. T. S. Eliot has asserted that the play, in a technical sense, is not successful because there is no "objective correlative" to the emotions which Hamlet expresses; that is, the actual circumstances of Claudius's assumption of the throne and Gertrude's marriage would not account in themselves for the terrific disgust which Hamlet feels toward life, and he is therefore unmotivated. So far as the average playgoer or reader of Shakespeare is concerned, however, neither these nor the many other criticisms and analyses which have been made of Hamlet can be said to have crucial importance: he is to them a difficult but nevertheless deeply moving figure in one of the greatest tragic dramas ever written.

Hammon (ham'ọn). A rich citizen of London in Dekker's comedy *The Shoemaker's Holiday*. He woos Jane, the young bride of Ralph, after deluding her with a false report that Ralph has been killed in the wars abroad, but Jane is rescued at the church door by Ralph and his fellow shoemakers.

Hammon. See also **Amen.**

Hampden (hamp'dẹn, ham'-), **John.** b. at London, 1594; d. at Thame, Oxfordshire, England, June 24, 1643. An English statesman; first cousin of Oliver Cromwell. He entered Parliament in 1621, was one of the leaders of the patriotic party in the Short and Long Parliaments, and was one of the five members (with Pym, Strode, Lenthall, and Holles) impeached (1642) by Charles I. He commanded a regiment for the Parliament (1642–43), and was mortally wounded at Chalgrove Field on June 18, 1643. He was the defendant in the case of the King vs. John Hampden before the Court of the Exchequer (1637–38) for resisting the collection of the obsolete tax of ship-money, which Charles I attempted to revive without the authority of Parliament. The case was decided against him, but in 1641 the House of Lords ordered the judgment to be canceled. This case, which established him as a leader of the resistance to royal tyranny, brought Hampden to the forefront in the popular mind as the great Parliamentary champion.

Hampdenshire Wonder (hamp'dẹn.shir, ham'-), **The.** A novel (1911) by J. D. Beresford.

Ham Peggotty (ham peg'ọti). See **Peggotty, Ham.**

Hampton Court (hamp'tọn). An English royal palace on the Thames, ab. 12 mi. from Charing Cross, London, built by Cardinal Wolsey. Much of the battlemented, red brick, Tudor construction, surrounding three courts, still remains. The total property originally consisted of about 1,000 acres of more or less barren land belonging to the Knight Hospitallers of Saint John of Jerusalem. It was leased from the Priory of Saint John in 1515 by Thomas Wolsey, archbishop of York and primate of England, who erected the original Gothic palace.

In 1526 he surrendered the estate to Henry VIII, who added the chapel and great hall in the period 1531–35. In the reign of William III, the great façade, modern state apartments, and a gallery for the cartoons of Raphael (since moved to the South Kensington Museum) were added by Sir Christopher Wren. The front of the French gardens is later, in the Renaissance style. The great hall is 106 by 40 ft. and 60 ft. high. The state apartments are filled with paintings. Hampton Court is most intimately associated with James I and William III, and was a place of imprisonment of Charles I.

Hampton Court Conference. A conference appointed by James I at Hampton Court in 1604, to settle the disputes between the Puritan party and the High Church party in the Church of England. It was conducted on three days (January 14, 16, and 18), and resulted in a few alterations of the liturgy, but entirely failed to secure the objectives sought by the Puritans. An important indirect result of it was the revision of the Bible called the King James or Authorized Version, which was suggested at that time by John Reynolds, president of Corpus Christi, Oxford.

Hanaud (à.nō'). The name of the detective in the stories of A. E. W. Mason.

Hand (hand), **Robert.** In James Joyce's play *Exiles*, a journalist who falls in love with Bertha, the wife of Richard Rowan.

Handel, George Frederick. [Original German name, **Georg Friedrich** (or **Frideric**) **Händel** (hen'dẹl).] b. at Halle, Germany, Feb. 23, 1685; d. at London, April 14, 1759. A German-born English composer, noted for his mastery of vocal composition as illustrated in his oratorios and operas, for both of which he won great popularity in England. His father was a barber who wanted his son to study law and who objected to a possible musical career. He studied under Zachau, organist of the cathedral at Halle, for three years. He then went to Berlin, where his powers of improvisation caused him to be regarded as a prodigy; he subsequently returned to Halle, where his father died (1697). Though he now followed his father's wishes and entered the University of Halle as a law student, it became necessary for him to support his mother, and he took the opportunity to drop law for music and went to Hamburg, where he entered the orchestra of the Opera House as *violino di ripieno*. He soon became known, and was made conductor. In 1705 his first opera, *Almira*, was produced there. In 1706 he went to Italy, where, despite his becoming the lion of Roman, Venetian, and Neapolitan society, he could not get a real musical opportunity. Returning to Germany in 1709, he accepted the position of *Kapellmeister* (choir leader) from the Elector of Hanover (later George I of England), on condition that he should be allowed to visit England, having already received pressing invitations to do so. He first went to London in 1710. His opera *Rinaldo* was produced there in 1711, and was a sensational success. He returned to Hanover, but soon was back in England, where he remained, except for short visits to the Continent, from 1712 to his death. He undertook the direction of the Italian opera at the Haymarket Theatre in 1720. Buononcini and Ariosti, both of whom he had known at Halle, also went to London about this time and formed an opposition to him, which gave rise to much feeling and to John Byrom's epigram ending: "Strange all this difference should be 'twixt Tweedledum and Tweedledee!" In 1726 Handel became a naturalized British subject. He was in partnership (1729–34) with Heidegger at the King's Theatre, in 1737 became bankrupt, and in 1739, when he was about 54, began to compose the oratorios which made him famous. In 1752 he was attacked by cataract, and was nearly if not entirely blind for the rest of his life, but continued to preside at the organ during his own oratorios. His fame increased, and the animosity which had pursued him during his earlier years died away. He was buried in Westminster Abbey. Outstanding among his works are the oratorios *Esther* (1720), *Saul* (1739), *Israel in Egypt* (1739), *Messiah* (1742), *Samson* (1743), *Judas Maccabaeus* (1747), *Joshua* (1748), and *Jephthah* (1752). He composed also more than 40 operas, from which arias are still popular, like "Ombra mai fu" (Handel's Largo) from *Serse* (1738), and the cantatas *Acis and Galatea* and *Alexander's Feast.* He composed several anthems and the *Dettingen Te Deum* (1743), celebrating George II's victory over the French at Dettingen, Bavaria. His instrumental works include the *Water Music* (c1715), the *Firework Music* (1749), 12 concerti grossi (1740), organ concertos, chamber sonatas, fugues, and suites.

Handford (hand′fọrd), **Julius.** A name assumed by John Harmon in Dickens's *Our Mutual Friend.*

Handley Cross (hand′li). A novel by R. S. Surtees, published in 1843.

Handlyng Synne (han′dling sin). A Middle English religious treatise in verse, a translation (c1303) by Robert Mannyng (or Robert of Brunne) of the Anglo-Norman *Manuel des Pechiez* of William of Wadington. It describes in 12,630 lines the seven deadly sins, the seven sacraments, the requisites of confession, and the twelve graces by means of tales and anecdotes which are very revealing of the details of medieval life.

Hand of Ethelberta (eth′ẹl.bẻr.tạ), **The.** A novel by Thomas Hardy, published in 1876. It deals with Ethelberta, one of the many children of Chickerel, a butler. She is an ambitious woman, who marries the son of the wealthy people by whom she is employed as a governess, but is widowed at the age of twenty-one. She wants to maintain her social position and to conceal her background, but at the same time help her brothers and sisters. She finally marries (and proceeds to dominate in every way) an old peer, leaving Christopher Julian, an adoring musician, to marry her sister, Picotee.

Handy Andy (an′di). A novel by Samuel Lover, published in 1842. It contains humorous sketches of Irish life. The hero is Andy Rooney, who finally wins the hand of Oonah and inherits Lord Scatterbrain's wealth.

Hanging Gardens. See under **Babylon.**

Hankin (hang′kin), **St. John.** b. 1860; d. 1909. A British dramatist. He wrote *The Two Mr. Weathbys* (1903), *The Return of the Prodigal* (1904), *The Cassilis Engagement* (1907), and *The Last of the De Mullins* (1908).

Hanley (han′li), **James.** b. 1901—. An English journalist and novelist. His novels and collections of short stories include *A Passion Before Death* (1930), *Drift* (1930), *The German Prisoner* (1931), *The Last Voyage* (1931), *Men in Darkness* (1931), *Boy* (1931), *Stoker Haslett* (1932), *Ebbard Flood* (1932), *Captain Bottell* (1933), *The Furys* (1935), *Stoker Bush* (1935), *The Secret Journey* (1936), *What Farrar Saw* (1945), and *Don Quixote Drowned* (1953).

Hannay (han′ā), **James.** b. at Dumfries, Scotland, Feb. 17, 1827; d. at Barcelona, Spain, Jan. 9, 1873. A British critic and novelist. He served (1868–73) as consul at Barcelona. Among his works are *Satire and Satirists* (1854), *Studies on Thackeray* (1869), the novels *Singleton Fontenoy* (1850) and *Eustace Conyers* (1855), and critical essays.

Hannay, James Owen. [Pseudonym, **George A. Birmingham.**] b. at Belfast, Ireland, July 16, 1865; d. Feb. 2, 1950. An Irish novelist. Ordained a deacon in 1888 and a priest in 1889, he was a rector in County Mayo until 1912, when he became canon of Saint Patrick's Cathedral, Dublin, holding that post until 1921. He was rector (1924–34) of Wells, and rector (1934 *et seq.*) of Holy Trinity Church, Kensington, London. Among his writings are *The Spirit and Origin of Christian Monasticism* (1903) and *The Wisdom of the Desert* (1904). Under his pseudonym he wrote novels including *The Seething Pot* (1905), *The Northern Iron* (1907), *The Bad Times* (1908), *Spanish Gold* (1908), *Doctor Whitty* (1913), *Up the Revels* (1919), *Lady Bountiful* (1921), *The Runaways* (1928), *Two Fools* (1934), and *The Search for Susie* (1941). Among his plays are *General John Regan* (1913) and *Send for Dr. O'Grady* (1923).

Hannay, Sir Richard. A fictional detective in John Buchan's novels *The Thirty-Nine Steps* (1915), *Greenmantle* (1916), and *The Three Hostages* (1924).

Hannibal Chollup (han′i.bạl chol′up), **Major.** See **Chollup, Major Hannibal.**

Hanover Square (han′ō.vẻr). A famous square in the West End of London.

Hansard (han′sạrd), **Luke.** b. at Norwich, England, July 5, 1752; d. at London, Oct. 29, 1828. An English printer, best known for his publication of parliamentary reports. He printed (1774 *et seq.*) the *Journal of the House of Commons.* The official report of the proceedings of the House of Commons (which serves the same purpose in Great Britain as the Congressional Record in the U. S.) is still called *Hansard.*

Hansard, Thomas Curson. b. at London, Nov. 6, 1776; d. at Chatham Place, Blackfriars, London, May 14, 1833. An English publisher. He patented improvements on the hand press, and printed (1803 *et seq.*) the *Parliamentary Debates.* Author of *Typographia, an Historical Sketch of the Origin and the Progress of the Art of Printing; with Practical Directions for Conducting every Department in an Office, with a Description of Stereotype and Lithography* (1825).

Hanseatic League (han.sẹ.at′ik). [Also: **Baltic Hanse** (hans), **German Hanse, Hansa** (han′sạ), **Hanse Towns.**] A medieval confederation of cities

ḍ, d or j; ṣ, s or sh; ṭ, t or ch; ẓ, z or zh; o, F. cloche; ü, F. menu; ċh, Sc. loch; ṅ, F. bonbon.

of N Germany and adjacent countries, called the Hanse towns, at one time numbering about 90, with affiliated cities in nearly all parts of Europe excepting the Mediterranean area, for the promotion of commerce by sea and land, and for its protection against pirates, robbers, and hostile governments. At the height of its prosperity it exercised sovereign powers, made treaties, and often enforced its claims by arms in Scandinavia, England, Portugal, and elsewhere. Its origin is commonly dated from a compact between Hamburg and Lübeck in 1241, although commercial unions of German towns had existed previously. At its height (c1350–c1450) the league traded all over northern Europe, with Bergen in Norway, London in England, Visby in the Baltic, Novgorod in Russia, Bruges in Flanders, and the cities along the Baltic (Hamburg, Lübeck, Rostock, and others) and their markets inland. Through Novgorod it maintained contact with the East until Ivan III destroyed the Hansa depot there in 1494; in London, the Hansa currency, called "Easterling" money, became a standard of currency (later the name was modified to "sterling"), and its great depot, the Steelyard, was the center of London trading. At Bergen, its agents traded for timber, fish, and furs from as far west as Iceland and from an area covering the Atlantic north of Scotland; at Bruges, they obtained the textiles of Flanders; at London, wool. The trade was not strictly a monopoly, for the competition of the cities of the Low Countries and even of the Venetian galleys had to be met, but in its period of ascendancy the Hanseatic League controlled the trade of the Baltic and North Sea regions. Its political power extended through the free imperial cities of the Empire and to the countries of Scandinavia; the victory over the Danes that led to the Treaty of Stralsund (1370) gave it not only commercial privileges but also a voice in the selection of Danish kings; in 1285 the league forced Norway under Eric Magnusson (Eric II) to become a member. The league held triennial general assemblies (usually at Lübeck, its chief seat); and, after a long period of decline and attempts at resuscitation, the last general assembly, representing six cities, was held in 1669. The name was retained, however, by the union of the free cities of Lübeck, Hamburg, and Bremen. No one cause can be given for the decline of the Hanseatic League. The consolidation of national power in Russia, England, Sweden, and elsewhere cut off its great depots and eliminated all its special privileges, since the monarchs invariably desired these privileges for themselves. The internal troubles of the league, the struggles between the cities which were its members, led to a breaking away of some of its strength. Perhaps the principal cause was the shift of commercial emphasis from trading along the internal seas (Baltic, Mediterranean) to an oceanic, intercontinental trade, but the decline had set in before the great era of discovery opened, and the failure of the league, like its very beginnings, is somewhat obscure.

Hans Frost (hans' frôst'). A novel by Hugh Walpole, published in 1929. The central figure is a famous, aging novelist, longing for a freedom a young wife has never allowed him.

Hans Meyrick (mī'rik). See **Meyrick, Hans.**

Hansom (han'sǫm), **Joseph Aloysius.** b. at York, England, Oct. 26, 1803; d. at London, June 29, 1882. An English architect, inventor of a patent safety cab which was named for him the "Hansom." The principal feature of the original vehicle was the "suspended" axle.

Happer (hap'ér), **Mysie.** The miller's daughter in Sir Walter Scott's novel *The Monastery.*

Happy Family, The. A novel of autobiographical interest by Frank Swinnerton, published in 1912.

Happy Fool, The. A novel by John Palmer, published in 1922.

Happy Meddler, The. A novel by G. B. Stern in collaboration with Geoffrey Lisle Holdsworth, published in 1926.

Happy Valley, The. In Samuel Johnson's *Rasselas,* a garden of peace where the Prince of Abyssinia lived. It was almost impossible to get into or out of it.

Hapsburg (haps'bérg; German, häps'bŭrk), **House of.** [Also: **Habsburg;** original name, **Habichtsburg,** meaning "Hawk's Castle."] A German princely family which derived its name from the castle of Habsburg, in Switzerland, and which furnished sovereigns to the Holy Roman Empire, Austria, and Spain. The title Count of Hapsburg was assumed by Werner I, who died in 1096. Count Rudolf was elected emperor as Rudolf I in 1273 and acquired Austria, and founded the imperial line which reigned during the periods 1273–91, 1298–1308, and 1438–1740. The title Archduke of Austria was revived in 1453. In 1477 the emperor Maximilian I acquired the domain (except the duchy) of the ducal house of Burgundy by marriage with the heiress Mary, and in 1490 had all the Hapsburg possessions united in his hands by the abdication of Count Sigismund. His son, Philip I of Spain, married Joanna (Juana) the Insane, queen of Aragon and Castile. Their eldest son became king of Spain as Charles I in 1516, and emperor as Charles V in 1519; their second son, Ferdinand I, received the Austrian crown, to which he added, by election, the kingdoms of Bohemia and Hungary. The Spanish line was continued by Charles's son Philip II, and reigned from 1516 to 1700. On the abdication (1556) of the imperial crown by Charles V, he was succeeded by his brother Ferdinand, who continued the imperial line, the last male representative of which was Charles VI. On the death of Charles VI (1740), his daughter Maria Theresa succeeded to the Austrian inheritance by virtue of the pragmatic sanction. She married Francis I, Grand Duke of Tuscany, of the house of Lorraine, who became emperor in 1745, and founded the Hapsburg-Lorraine line, members of which ruled as emperors of the Holy Roman Empire until its abolition in 1806, and until 1918 ruled as emperors of Austria.

Harbours of Memory. Sketches by William McFee, published in 1921.

Harcourt (här'kŏrt, -kôrt, -kǫrt). In Shakespeare's *2 Henry IV,* a member of the King's party who announces to Henry the victory of the sheriff of Yorkshire (IV.iv).

---

fat, fāte, fär, ȧsk, fāre; net, mē, hėr; pin, pīne; not, nōte, mōve, nôr; up, lūte, půll; ᴛʜ, then;

Harcourt. A young gentleman in love with the witty Alithea in Wycherley's farce *The Country Wife.*

Hard Cash. [Full title, **Hard Cash, or Very Hard Cash.**] A novel by Charles Reade, published in 1863. It was intended to arouse public indignation about the shocking and brutal conditions prevailing in the lunatic asylums, and thus to compel some degree of reform. Captain David Dodd returns from a sea voyage with money for the support of his family. He entrusts his fortune to a banker, Richard Hardie, not knowing that he is a bankrupt scoundrel. Dodd loses his sanity when he finds his money gone, and is confined in an asylum. Alfred Hardie, the banker's son, who is engaged to Dodd's daughter, now discovers that his father has misappropriated the money, but Hardie has his own son committed to the asylum for fear that he will otherwise make public the fact of his father's guilt. The horrors encountered by Captain Dodd and Alfred in the asylum are described in some of the most powerful scenes in the book. Finally, however, Dodd (who has recovered his sanity) escapes and returns to the sea. Hardie is revealed as a criminal, Alfred is released, and Dodd's fortune is recovered.

Hardcastle (härd'käs''l), **Kate.** In Oliver Goldsmith's play *She Stoops to Conquer*, the daughter of Squire Hardcastle. She takes the part of a barmaid to win Marlowe, who is afraid of ladies; thus she "stoops to conquer."

Hardcastle, Squire and **Mrs.** Characters in Oliver Goldsmith's play *She Stoops to Conquer.* The squire is an English country gentleman of the old school, fond of everything old. Mrs. Hardcastle, his second wife, is an extremely "genteel" lady who devotes herself to the spoiling of her ungrateful hobbledehoy of a son, Tony Lumpkin.

Hardicanute (här''di.ka.nūt'). [Also: **Hardecanute, Harthacnut;** known as **Canute II** (of *Denmark*).] b. c1019; d. at Lambeth (now part of London), June 8, 1042. A king of England (1040–42); son of Canute and Emma of Normandy. He became king of Denmark in 1035 and nominal king of the West Saxons in the same year, his half brother Harold I (Harold Harefoot) being king of the north. Harold rallied many of Hardicanute's adherents to his side while the latter was in Denmark and thereby attained rule of the whole kingdom. Hardicanute raised a large force to invade England, but Harold died, and Hardicanute was unopposed. His rule was marked by cruelties, such as the burning of Worcester in 1040 for refusal to pay a tax to support his Danish fleet.

Hardie (här'di), **Keir.** [Full name, **James Keir Hardie.**] b. in Scotland, Aug. 15, 1856; d. at Glasgow, Sept. 26, 1915. A British labor leader and member of Parliament. He worked in the mines from his seventh to his twenty-fourth year, and was editor of the *Cumnock News* (1882–86) and of the *Miner* and *Labour Leader* (1887–1903). He was a Labour member of Parliament (1892–95, 1900–05, and 1906–15). He was the founder of the Independent Labour Party, and was chairman (February, 1906–1908) of the Labour Party in the House of Commons. He wrote *India, Impressions and Suggestions* (1909).

Harding (här'ding), **Septimus.** The principal character in Anthony Trollope's novel *The Warden*, a clergyman who is warden of a small hospital for aged men. He also appears in *Barchester Towers* and *The Last Chronicle of Barset.*

Hard Times. A novel by Charles Dickens, published serially in *Household Words* in 1854. It was published in book form in 1854. It is an attack on industrial conditions in the Midlands. Thomas Gradgrind has tried to teach his children, Louisa and Tom, to care for nothing but material values, suppressing utterly the creative and spiritual sides of their nature. He arranges to marry Louisa to a grasping and wealthy factory-owner, Bounderby, who is not only many years older than she, but personally offensive to her. However, Louisa consents to the marriage because she wants to help her brother, who is employed by Bounderby. James Harthouse, an unprincipled young politician now comes to Coketown, and tries to seduce Louisa. She flees to her father for protection (she has already left Bounderby), and when it is discovered that Tom has robbed the bank of his employer, Gradgrind finally realizes, through the tragedy of his children's shattered lives, the perilous inadequacy and fundamental error of his utterly materialistic point of view. Tom flees the country, and Louisa remains separated from her husband, under her father's protection. Other characters are Stephen Blackpool, a weaver; Sleary, owner of a circus; and Sissy Jupe, daughter of a circus performer.

Hardwicke (härd'wik), **2nd Earl of.** Title of **Yorke, Philip.**

Hardy (här'di), **Laetitia.** In Hannah Cowley's comedy *The Belle's Stratagem*, a young girl betrothed to Doricourt. His indifference causes her to get him to hate her, in order that she may turn his hatred into love.

Hardy, Thomas. b. at Higher Bockhampton, near Dorchester, Dorsetshire, England, June 2, 1840; d. at Dorchester, Jan. 11, 1928. An English novelist and poet. He was twice married: in 1874 to Emma Lavinia Gifford (1840–1912) and in 1914 to Florence Emily Dugdale (1879–1937); he had no children. After failing to obtain publication of his youthful poems (1862–67), Hardy turned to novel writing, and in the 26-year period between 1871 (when his first novel, *Desperate Remedies*, appeared anonymously) and 1897 (when his last, *The Well-Beloved*, was published) he produced 14 novels. These deal vividly and sympathetically with country life in "Wessex," an imaginary southwestern English county. Among these novels are *Far from the Madding Crowd* (1874), *The Return of the Native* (1878), *The Mayor of Casterbridge* (1886), *The Woodlanders* (1887), *Tess of the D'Urbervilles* (1891), and *Jude the Obscure* (1895). Of these, all but the first are tragedies. Hardy's novels, carefully and often artificially plotted, are the principal English reflection of the school of naturalism; his characters are admirably drawn against a background of irresistible nature, which contains a force almost malevolent in its defeats of man's efforts. This natural force, expressing itself as Egdon Heath or as the sex impulse, is too strong for even the strongest of Hardy's people.

In 1898 Hardy returned to the production of poetry and in the next 30 years published eight volumes of verse (later in one volume as *Collected Poems*, 1931) and a gigantic dramatic epic of the Napoleonic wars, *The Dynasts* (3 parts, 1903–08). Of the poems, "The Darkling Thrush," "The Oxen," and "Afterwards" are deservedly among the best known. In 1910 Hardy was awarded the royal Order of Merit, and upon his death at 87 his ashes were buried in Poets' Corner, Westminster Abbey, though his heart, in obedience to his wishes to be buried at his home, was interred at Dorchester. He died at Max Gate, a house which he built for himself in 1884 on the outskirts of Dorchester. In 1952 a long-lost story by Hardy, *Our Exploits at West Poley* (6 installments; published in 1892–93), was discovered by Richard L. Purdy. It had originally been written by Hardy for an American journal in 1883. See *Thomas Hardy, Poet and Novelist* (1928), by Samuel C. Chew, *Hardy of Wessex* (1940) and *Hardy in America* (1946), by Carl J. Weber, *On a Darkling Plain* (1948), by Harvey C. Webster, *The Letters of Thomas Hardy* (1954), edited by Carl J. Weber, and *Thomas Hardy* (1954) by Douglas Brown.

Hare (hâr), **Augustus J. C.** [Full name, **Augustus John Cuthbert Hare.**] b. at Rome, March 13, 1834; d. at Holmhurst, St. Leonards-on-Sea, England, Jan. 22, 1903. An English writer and artist. He was author of many travel books with illustrations by himself; *Memorials of a Quiet Life* (3 vols., 1872–76) is a biography of his aunt Maria Hare. He also wrote *Life and Letters of Frances, Baroness Bunsen* (1878), *Story of Two Noble Lives: Charlotte, Countess Canning, and Louisa, Marchioness of Waterford* (1893). Hare's autobiography, *The Story of My Life* (6 vols., 1896–1900), was edited and abridged into two volumes by Malcolm Barnes, the original first three volumes appearing as *The Years with Mother* (1952) and the last three as *In my Solitary Life* (1953).

Hare, Julius Charles. b. at Valdagno, Italy, Sept. 13, 1795; d. at Hurstmonceaux, Sussex, England, Jan. 23, 1855. An English divine and theological writer, archdeacon of Lewes (1840 *et seq.*). Among his works are *Mission of the Comforter* (1846), *The Contest with Rome* (1852), *Vindication of Luther* (1854), and, conjointly with A. W. Hare, *Guesses at Truth* (1827).

Hare, Martin. Pseudonym of **Girling, Zoë.**

Haredale (hâr′dāl), **Emma.** In Dickens's novel *Barnaby Rudge*, the principal female character, in love with Edward Chester. Her uncle (and guardian), Mr. (Geoffrey) Haredale, opposes a marriage until the end of the book, when he is finally reconciled to it by Edward's heroism, because Edward is a Protestant and the son of his most bitter enemy.

Haredale, Mr. In Dickens's novel *Barnaby Rudge*, a country gentleman and devout Roman Catholic, the uncle of Emma Haredale.

Hargrave Pollexfen (här′grāv pol′iks.fen), **Sir.** See **Pollexfen, Sir Hargrave.**

Harington (har′ing.tọn), **James.** See **Harrington, James.**

Harington, Sir John. [Also, **Harrington.**] b. at Kelston, near Bath, England, 1561; d. there, Nov.

20, 1612. An English poet. His chief work was a translation of the *Orlando Furioso* (1591), which was prefaced by an *Apologie for Poetrie*. He also wrote *A Short View of the State of Ireland written in 1605*, and many pamphlets and epigrams. Harington was master of a witty style and in 1596 was banished from court (he was Elizabeth's godson) for some of his satires, including the ribald but serious *Metamorphosis of Ajax* (Ajax being then pronounced "a jakes," i.e., a close stool or privy). This was followed by *An Anatomie of the Metamorphosed Ajax* and *Ulysses upon Ajax*, but the latter seems wrongly attributed to Harington, being a criticism of the *Metamorphosis*. He was one of Essex's men and, after the latter's disgrace, acted as his ambassador to the queen, but she would not see Harington. He wrote a *Tract on the Succession to the Crown* (1602) and an account of Elizabeth's last days.

Harkaway (härk′a.wā), **Grace.** In Dion Boucicault's comedy *London Assurance*, a young woman of fortune.

Harleian Library (här′lē.ạn). A collection of manuscripts and documents included in the British Museum. The eminent Whig statesman and patron of men of letters, Robert Harley, 1st Earl of Oxford, and his son Edward Harley, 2nd Earl of Oxford, accumulated thousands of manuscripts and of ancient legal documents, which in 1754 were purchased by the British government and, with some other collections, formed the nucleus of the British Museum library.

Harlequin (här′lē.kwin, -kin). [Italian, **Arlecchino;** French, **Harlequin** (är.lē.kàn′).] A conventional clown in the improvised Italian comedy, or *commedia dell' arte*. He was the servant of Pantalone, or Pantaloon, lover of Columbine, and was noted for his agility and gluttony, and carried a sword of lath. He was the descendant of the old Roman *sannio* (zany); the German Hanswurst was borrowed from him. In English pantomime Harlequin was dignified and made popular by the acting of Rich, Woodward, O'Brien, and Grimaldi. He scarcely exists today except in Christmas pantomimes, improvised Italian plays, and puppet shows.

harlequinade (här′lē.kwin.ād′). A kind of pantomime; that part of a pantomime which follows the transformation of characters, and in which the harlequin and clown play the principal parts; hence, buffoonery; a fantastic procedure.

No unity of plan, no decent propriety of character and costume, could be found in that wild and monstrous harlequinade [the reign of Charles II].
(Macaulay, *Hallam's Const. Hist.*)

Harleth (här′lẹth), **Gwendolen.** The principal female character in George Eliot's novel *Daniel Deronda*.

Harley (här′li). The "man of feeling" in Henry Mackenzie's novel of that name; a sensitive, irresolute person, too gentle to battle with life.

Harley, Adrian. The tutor of Richard in George Meredith's novel *The Ordeal of Richard Feverel*. He is patterned on the figure of Meredith's close friend, Maurice Fitz-Gerald.

Harley, Robert. [Title, 1st Earl of **Oxford.**] b. at London, Dec. 5, 1661; d. May 21, 1724. An English

Tory (originally Whig) statesman. He entered Parliament in 1689, was speaker of the House of Commons (1701–05), secretary of state (1704–08), chancellor of the exchequer in 1710, and was raised to the peerage in 1711. He was lord treasurer and premier (1711–14). He dismissed Marlborough and forced, by the creation of new peers, the acceptance of the treaty of Utrecht (1713). When George I, who favored the Whigs, succeeded Anne in 1714, Harley was impeached for high treason on the ground that the treaty favored the Stuart pretender, but he was acquitted in 1717. He left a valuable collection of manuscripts, which was increased by his son Edward Harley, and eventually acquired by the government for the British Museum. A selection of rare pamphlets and other documents from his library was published under the title of *The Harleian Miscellany* (1744–46).

Harley Street. A fashionable street in London, running from Cavendish Square to Marylebone Road. It has long been known as the site of the offices of many prominent doctors.

Harlowe (här′lō), **Clarissa.** The heroine of *Clarissa Harlowe*, and Richardson's ideal embodiment of feminine character and sentiment.

Harmodius (här.mō′di.us) and **Aristogiton** (a̱.ris.tō̱-ji′tǫn, ar″is.tō̱-). Killed 514 B.C. Two Athenian youths who killed Hipparchus, tyrant of Athens, in 514. They are represented as entertaining a strong affection for each other, which remained unaltered despite the endeavors of Hipparchus to draw that of the young and beautiful Harmodius toward himself. Enraged at the indifference of Harmodius, Hipparchus put a public insult upon him by declaring his sister unworthy of carrying the sacred baskets at the religious procession of the Panathenaea, in revenge for which the youths organized a conspiracy to overthrow both Hipparchus and his brother Hippias. Harmodius and Aristogiton slew the former on the festival of the great Panathenaea, but their precipitancy prevented the coöperation of the other conspirators. Harmodius was cut down by the guard. Aristogiton was captured, and, when put to the torture to reveal his accomplices, named the principal friends of Hippias, who were executed. When pressed for further revelations, he answered that there remained no one whose death he desired, except the tyrant. After the expulsion of the tyrant in 510, they became popular heroes, the subject of ballads and songs. A statue of them was placed on the approach to the Acropolis; a copy of this is in the Museo Nazionale at Naples.

Harmon (här′mǫn), **John.** [Also: **John Rokesmith, Julius Handford.**] In Dickens's *Our Mutual Friend*, the heir to the Harmon property.

Harmonia (här.mō′ni.a̱). In Greek mythology, the daughter of Ares and Aphrodite, or of Zeus and Electra. She was given by Zeus in marriage to Cadmus of Thebes. All the gods of Olympus were present at her wedding, and she received either from Cadmus or from Hephaestus as a wedding gift a robe and an unlucky necklace which proved fatal to every person who successively possessed them. Harmonia is sometimes construed as an aspect of Aphrodite.

Harmonius Blacksmith, The. A set of variations in E major (published 1720) by George Frederick Handel, based on an anonymous air of that name.

Harmon's Jail (här′mǫnz). See under **Boffin's Bower.**

Harmsworth (härmz′wẻrth), **Alfred Charles William.** [Title, Viscount **Northcliffe.**] b. at Chapelizod, County Dublin, Ireland, July 15, 1865; d. at London, Aug. 14, 1922. An English journalist and newspaper publisher; brother of Harold Sidney Harmsworth, Sir Hildebrand Aubrey Harmsworth, Sir Robert Leicester Harmsworth, and Cecil Bisshopp Harmsworth. At 15 he was on the staff of the *Hampstead and Highgate Express*; at 17 he was assistant editor of *Youth* and a writer for the *St. James' Gazette* and the *Morning Post.* He founded his own publishing business (1887) and *Answers* (1888), a weekly journal that became the basis of the Amalgamated Press, long the largest publishing business in the world. He traveled (1889–94, and during World War I) in Europe, India, Africa, Russia, Canada, and America. In 1894, with his brother Harold, he purchased the bankrupt London *Evening News* and financed the Harmsworth Arctic Expedition. On May 4, 1896, he founded the London *Daily Mail*, a morning paper, also publishing it at Manchester (1900 *et seq.*) and at Paris (1905 *et seq.*). He founded (1903) the London *Daily Mirror.* He was made a baron in 1904 and a peer in 1905, organized the Anglo-Newfoundland Development Company in 1906, became owner of the London *Times* in 1908, and was made viscount in 1917. During World War I he was hated intensely by the Germans, being the sole target of attack in a paper issued by them, *The Anti-Northcliffe Mail*, and was represented on a bronze "hate medal." He was offered, but declined, positions of air minister and British ambassador to Washington. He was author of *At the War* (1916), collected articles, and *My Journey Round the World* (1923). Northcliffe's policy of conciseness in news reporting helped revolutionize journalism and his position at the head of a newspaper empire with vast circulation made him one of the most powerful men in the world. The fall of the Asquith cabinet in 1916 has been considered the result of his criticism of its conduct of the war.

Harmsworth, Cecil Bisshopp. [Title, 1st Baron **Harmsworth.**] b. at London, Sept. 28, 1869—. An English politician; brother of A. C. W. Harmsworth, Viscount Northcliffe. He was undersecretary of state for the Home Office (1915), undersecretary of state for foreign affairs (1919–22), and acting minister of blockade (1919). He served as a member of the Supreme Economic Council and of the Council of the League of Nations (1922). He was the author of *Pleasure and Problem in South Africa* (1908) and *Immortals at First Hand* (1933).

Harmsworth, Harold Sidney. [Title, 1st Viscount **Rothermere.**] b. at Hampstead, London, April 26, 1868; d. in Bermuda, Nov. 26, 1940. An English newspaper publisher; brother of A. C. W. Harmsworth, Viscount Northcliffe. He joined his brother's publishing house as a partner in 1889, and with him founded the Amalgamated Press, reorganized the London *Evening News*, and established the *Daily Mail* in 1896, the *Daily Mirror* in 1903, and the Anglo-Newfoundland Development Company in 1906. Independently, he owned the Glasgow *Daily Record*, the Leeds *Mercury*, and founded (1915) the *Sunday Pictorial*. He endowed (1910) a professorship of English literature at Cambridge University in memory of Edward VII, and founded chairs of American history at Oxford and naval history at Cambridge in honor of his sons, both killed in World War I. Author of *Solvency or Downfall* (1921), *My Fight to Rearm Britain* (1939).

Harmsworth, Sir Hildebrand Aubrey. b. 1872; d. April 18, 1929. An English journalist and statesman. He joined (1888) the newspaper publishing firm of his brothers, A. C. W. Harmsworth, Viscount Northcliffe, and Harold Sidney Harmsworth, Viscount Rothermere. He founded the *New Liberal Review* in February, 1901, joined Joseph Chamberlain's Fiscal Reform Party in 1904, and was sole proprietor (1908–11) of the *Globe*.

Harmsworth, Sir Robert Leicester. b. 1870; d. at Bexhill, England, Jan. 19, 1937. An English politician and publisher; brother of A. C. W. Harmsworth, Viscount Northcliffe. He purchased (1920) the *Western Morning News*, was a director of the Amalgamated Press, and was chairman of Consolidated Press and the Field Press.

Harold (har'ǫld). An extended drama in verse by Alfred Tennyson, published in 1877. It was part of his series of dramatizations of the "making of England" and deals with the life of Harold II, last of the Anglo-Saxon kings of England.

Harold I. [Called **Harold Harefoot.**] d. at Oxford, England, March 17, 1040. A king of the English (1035–40); illegitimate son of Canute by Aelfgifu of Northampton. At the death of his father in 1035, he became a candidate for the English crown before the witan in opposition to Canute's legitimate son Hardicanute, king of Denmark (as Canute II). He obtained by a compromise the region north of the Thames, while Hardicanute obtained that to the south. The absence of Hardicanute in Denmark, however, enabled him to gain many of the latter's adherents, including Godwin, earl of Wessex, and in 1037 he was chosen king over all England. He died during the preparations of Hardicanute for an invasion of England.

Harold II. b. c1022; d. Oct. 14, 1066. A king of the English (Jan. 6–Oct. 14, 1066); son of Godwin, earl of Wessex, and Gytha. He became earl of East Anglia c1045, was banished with his father and brothers by Edward the Confessor in 1051, and was restored with them in 1052. He succeeded his father as earl of Wessex in 1053 (giving up his earldom of East Anglia), and was the chief minister of Edward from 1053 to 1066, becoming virtual king after obtaining ascendancy over Edward's French followers. He led the English against uprisings of the Welsh, especially the rebellion (1063) under Gruffydd, who was slain by the Welsh after Harold and his brother Tostig defeated him. Probably in 1064 he was shipwrecked on the coast of Normandy and fell into the hands of William, duke of Normandy, who compelled him to take an oath whereby he promised to marry William's daughter and to assist him in securing the succession in England. This agreement, and William's claim that Edward had willed him the crown, led

to the later invasion from Normandy and William's accession as William I. He married about this time, probably on his return to England, Ealdgyth or Aldgyth, widow of Gruffydd, and sister of Edwin, earl of the Mercians; and on the death of Edward procured his own election as king, on Jan. 6, 1066. Expecting the invasion of William or of his brother Tostig, Harold kept a force under arms on the coast all summer, finally dispersing it in September. The attempt in the north came first; Tostig landed and took York. Harold marched north from London and defeated Tostig (who had been deposed from his earldom of Northumbria and outlawed in the previous reign) and Harold III (Harald Haardraade), king of Norway, at Stamford Bridge, on Sept. 25, 1066. On the 27th word came that the Norman had landed and Harold rushed south into Sussex. He was defeated by William, duke of Normandy, and killed at the battle of Hastings (or Senlac), Oct. 14, 1066. His mutilated body is said to have been recognized among the slain by his former mistress Edith Swanneck, and to have been buried by William's order on the coast which he sought to defend, the grave being marked by a cairn of stones.

Harold in Italy (it'ǎ.li). [French title, **Harold en Italie** (à.rold aṅ nē.tà.lē).] A symphonic poem composed by Hector Berlioz in 1834. The theme is derived from Byron's *Childe Harold*.

Harold, or The Last of the Saxon Kings (sak'sǫn). A historical romance by Edward Bulwer-Lytton, published in 1848. The scene is laid in the time of Harold II.

Harold Skimpole (skim'pōl). See **Skimpole, Harold.**

Harold the Dauntless. A romance in verse (1817) by Sir Walter Scott.

Harold Transome (tran'sǫm). See **Transome, Harold.**

Haroun al-Raschid (hä.rön' äl.rä.shēd', al.rash'id). See **Harun al-Rashid.**

Harpagon (àr.pà.gôṅ). A character in Molière's comedy *L'Avare* (taken from Plautus's *Euclio*); a miser.

Harpier (här'pir). In Shakespeare's *Macbeth* (IV.i), a demon or (possibly) harpy.

Harpocrates (här.pok'rǎ.tēz). The Egyptian sun god, Horus, as personification of the young sun; son of Osiris. He is depicted as a little boy with his finger on his lips, and was thus later interpreted as a god of silence. His cult was adopted by both the Greeks and Romans.

Harpocration (här.pǫ.krā'shi.ǫn), **Valerius.** fl. probably in the 2nd century A.D. A Greek rhetorician of Alexandria, author of a lexicon of the works of the Attic orators.

Harraden (har'ǎ.dẹn), **Beatrice.** b. at Hampstead, London, Jan. 24, 1864; d. May 5, 1936. An English novelist. Author of *Ships that Pass in the Night* (1893), *In Varying Moods* (1894), *Hilda Strafford* (1897), *Interplay* (1908), *Rachel* (1926), and *Search Will Find it Out* (1928).

Harriet (har'i.ẹt). A young lady in love with the rake, Dorimant, in Etherege's *Man of Mode*. At the end of the play she lures him into marriage and presumably intends to reform him.

Harriet Beadle (bē'dl). See **Tattycoram**.

Harriet Byron (bī'ron). See **Byron, Harriet**.

Harriet Hume: A London Fantasy (hūm). A psychological novel by Rebecca West, published in 1929.

Harriet Smith (smith). See **Smith, Harriet**.

Harriett Frean (har'i.et frēn). See **Life and Death of Harriett Frean, The**.

Harrington (har'ing.ton), **Evan**. See **Evan Harrington**.

Harrington, James. [Also, **Harington**.] b. at Upton, Northamptonshire, England, Jan. 7, 1611; d. at London, Sept. 11, 1677. An English political writer. His chief work was a treatise on civil government, *The Commonwealth of Oceana* (1656).

Harrington, Sir John. See **Harington, Sir John**.

Harriot (har'i.ot). The gentle heroine of the elder George Colman's comedy *The Jealous Wife*. She somewhat resembles Sophia Western in Fielding's novel *Tom Jones*.

Harris (har'is), **Benjamin**. fl. 1673–1716. An English publisher, author, and bookseller. He printed (1690) *Publick Occurrences Both Forreign and Domestick*, the first newspaper in America, and earlier (c1683), the influential *New England Primer*. Returning (1694) to England at the end of eight years, he published (1695) *Intelligence Domestick and Foreign* and (1699) the *London Post*. Charles Blount's *Appeal from the Country to the City*, which he published (1679), brought his imprisonment; he commemorated his release with his own pamphlet, *Triumphs of Justice over Unjust Judges*. His quarrels with Dr. John Partridge concerning plagiarism of the latter's almanacs are said to have inspired Swift's Bickerstaff papers.

Harris, Frank. b. at Galway, Ireland, 1854; d. Aug. 26, 1931. A novelist, biographer, and dramatist. At London, he was editor of the London *Evening News* and the *Fortnightly Review*, and obtained control of the *Saturday Review*. At New York he was for a time editor of *Vanity Fair* and also edited (1916–23) *Pearson's*. His biographical studies include *The Man Shakespeare* (1909), four volumes of *Contemporary Portraits* (1915–23), and *Latest Contemporary Portraits* (1927). In fiction, he published the collections of short stories *Elder Conklin* (1894), *Montes the Matador* (1900), *The Veils of Isis* (1915), and *A Mad Love* (1920), and the novels *The Bomb —A Story of the Chicago Anarchists of 1886* (1908), *Great Days* (1914), and *Love in Youth* (1915). His plays include *Mr. and Mrs. Daventry* (1900), *Shakespeare and His Love* (1910), and *Joan La Ramée* (1926). His *Oscar Wilde* (2 vols., 1916) and the three-volume *My Life and Loves* (1923–27) were widely criticized for their outspokenness, the autobiography being banned in England and America.

Harris, John. b. c1667; d. Sept. 7, 1719. English divine and scientific writer. He published *Lexicon technicum, or an Universal English Dictionary of Arts and Sciences* (1704), the first of its kind in English.

Harris, Mrs. In Charles Dickens's *Martin Chuzzlewit*, an entirely imaginary person, constantly named by Sairey Gamp as one for whose opinions she has great respect, in order to lend greater weight to her own.

Harrison (har'i.son), **Doctor**. In Henry Fielding's novel *Amelia*, a generous clergyman who endeavors to protect Booth against his own weakness.

Harrison, Frederic. b. at London, Oct. 18, 1831; d. at Bath, England, Jan. 14, 1923. An English positivist philosopher, biographer, and critic. He was professor of jurisprudence and international law (1877–89) at the London Inns of Court. One of the founders of the English Positivist Society and its president (1880–1905), he wrote many works on positivism and lectured on it at Oxford and Cambridge. Author of *The Meaning of History* (1862), *Order and Progress* (1875), *The Choice of Books* (1886), *Cromwell* (1888), *Dickens' Place in Literature* (1894), *Victorian Literature* (1895), *Kingsley's Place in Literature* (1895), *Charlotte Brontë's Place in Literature* (1895), *William the Silent* (1897), *Tennyson, Ruskin, Mill, and Others* (1899), *American Addresses* (1901), *Ruskin* (1902), *Theophano* (1904), *Chatham* (1905), *Nicephorus* (1906), *Philosophy of Common Sense* (1907), *National and Social Problems* and *Realities and Ideals* (both 1908), *Autobiographical Memoirs* (1911), *Among My Books* (1912), *Positive Evolution of Religion* (1912), *The German Peril* (1915), *On Society* (1918), and many other works. In 1892 and again in 1920 he edited *The New Calendar of Great Men*, an expansion of the original *Positivist Calendar* (1849), by Auguste Comte, founder of Positivism, a work containing short biographies of the 559 "worthies of all ages and nations" selected by Comte to illustrate his theories.

Harrison, Jane Ellen. b. at Cottenham, Yorkshire, England, Sept. 9, 1850; d. at London, April 16, 1928. An English classical scholar. Among her influential books are *Myths of the Odyssey in Art and Literature* (1882), *Prolegomena to the Study of Greek Religion* (1903), *Ancient Art and Ritual* (1913), and *Epilegomena to the Study of Greek Religion* (1921). Her autobiography, *Reminiscences of a Student's Life*, appeared in 1925.

Harrison, William. b. at London, April 18, 1534; d. at Windsor, England, in April, 1593. An English topographer and historian. His *Description of England* (1577), containing accounts of English institutions, people, and the country, was printed, along with his translation of Bellenden's *Description of Scotland*, in Holinshed's *Chronicle* (1577, 1586–87) and is a reliable source for Elizabethan life.

Harrow (har'ō). [Also, **Harrow-on-the-Hill**.] An urban district in SE England, in Middlesex, ab. 9 mi. NW of Marylebone station, London. Formerly a detached suburb, it is now part of London's metropolitan area. Its school for boys (founded by John Lyon in 1571, opened in 1611) is one of the great public schools of England.

Harrowing of Hell, The. An Old English poem, of unknown authorship and date, preserved (incomplete) in the *Exeter Book*. It is an account of the visit of Christ to the souls in hell, a favorite theme of medieval literature.

Harrowing of Hell, The. A Middle English poem (c1250) based on the apocryphal *Gospel of Nicodemus*. The opening 40 lines are a narrative introduction, followed by dialogue spoken by Satan, the doorkeeper of Hell, Adam, Eve, Abraham, David, John the Baptist, and Moses. Christ descends to Hell, binds Satan, and frees his servants.

Harry (har′i). Entries on literary characters having this prename will be found under the surnames Bailey, Beagle, Bertram, Blount, Bumper, Dornton, Foker, Lorrequer, Wakefield, and Wildair.

Harry Lorrequer (lor′e̩.ke̩r), **The Confessions of.** A novel (1839) by Charles Lever, first published in the *Dublin Magazine* in 1837.

Harry Percy (pėr′si). See under **Hotspur.**

Harry Richmond (rich′mo̩nd). [Full title, **The Adventures of Harry Richmond.**] A novel by George Meredith, published in 1871.

Harsnett (härs′ne̩t), **Samuel.** b. 1561; d. 1631. An English ecclesiastic, writer of *Popish Impostures*, entitled in full *A declaration of egregious popish impostures to withdraw the hearts of her Majesty's subjects from their allegiance, and from the truth of the Christian religion, professed in England, under the pretense of casting out devils* (1606), attacking the Jesuit exorcists. He was chaplain to the Bishop of London, was appointed bishop of Chichester (1609) and archbishop of York (1629), and took part in the religious controversy over John Darrell, a supposedly fraudulent Puritan exorcist. The scene between the clown (as Sir Topas) and Malvolio in *Twelfth Night* probably owes much of its contemporary interest to this argument. The names of the fiends Frateretto, Flibbertigibbet, Hoppedance, Modo, and Mahu, in *King Lear*, also come from Harsnett's work.

Harthacnut (här.ᴛʜa̩.knöt′). See **Hardicanute.**

Harthouse (härt′hous), **James.** In Dickens's novel *Hard Times*, a cruel and unscrupulous politician.

Hartley (härt′li), **David.** b. Aug. 30, 1705; d. at Bath, England, Aug. 28, 1757. An English materialistic philosopher. His chief work is *Observations on Man, his Frame, his Duty, and his Expectations* (1749). He explained all mental processes as founded upon minute nervous vibrations which he called "Vibratiuncles." He was the founder of the English school of associational psychology.

Hartley, Dr. Adam. A frank, honorable, young Englishman in Sir Walter Scott's *The Surgeon's Daughter.*

Hartley, L. P. [Full name, **Leslie Poles Hartley.**] b. 1895—. An English writer of novels, short stories, and literary criticism. His works include two collections of short stories, *Night Fears* (1924), and *The Killing Bottle* (1932), and the novels *Simonetta Perkins* (1925), *The Shrimp and the Anemone* (1944), *The Sixth Heaven* (1946), *Eustace and Hilda* (1947; awarded the James Tait Black Memorial Prize), *The Boat* (1950), *My Fellow Devils* (1951), and *The Go-Between* (1954).

Harun al-Rashid (hä.rön′ äl.rä.shĕd′, al.rash′id). [Also, **Harun ar-Rashid** (är.rä.shēd′), **Haroun al-Raschid.**] b. at what is now Rhages, a ruin near Tehran, Iran, either 763 or 766 A.D.; d. at Tus, in Khurasan, March, 809 A.D. A caliph of Baghdad (786–809 A.D.), the fifth and most renowned of the Abbassides. Under him the Eastern caliphate

attained the height of its splendor and power. All the lands from the Jaxartes (modern Syr Darya) and the Indus through northern Africa to Gibraltar acknowledged his rule; Baghdad became a center of learning and civilization. Harun made successful expeditions against the Khazars in southern Russia and into the Byzantine empire, forcing the emperor Nicephorus I to pay him tribute, and he entertained friendly relations with Charlemagne and the Chinese emperors. In 803 Harun eliminated the power of the Barmecides, a family that had risen to power under his father and had aided him to the throne. Harun had his vizier Yahya the Barmecide and his sons executed for some now-unknown palace intrigue, and it is said that only one of the family escaped death. As one result of his removal of this able group of advisers, he was faced with insurrections in several parts of his widespread realm. It was while proceeding in person against rebels in Khurasan that he died. Harun is best known in the West from the tales of *The Arabian Nights' Entertainments*, in which much that is curious, romantic, and wonderful is connected with his name, or is supposed to have happened in his reign. The period is looked back on as being a golden age. Harun typically meets his strange adventures while strolling in the evening through Baghdad with his vizier, both incognito.

Harvest. A play by Lennox Robinson, published in 1910. It attacks the practice of educating children of poor families above their natural social position.

Harvey (här′vi). In Shakespeare's *1 Henry IV*, apparently the original name of Bardolph. The change was made, it is assumed, because of protest by someone of that name at the royal court.

Harvey, F. W. b. in Gloucestershire, England, 1888—. An English poet, noted particularly for *The Bugler*, a poem written while he was in a German prison camp in 1916. His volumes of verse include *Gloucestershire Friends* (1917) and *Farewell* (1921).

Harvey, Gabriel. b. at Saffron Walden, Essex, England, 1545; d. there, 1630. An English author. He matriculated at Christ's College, Cambridge, in 1566, and in 1570 was elected a fellow of Pembroke. While there he became intimate with Edmund Spenser, who introduces him in *The Shepherd's Calendar* as Hobbinol. Harvey was an advocate of the use of hexameters in English and the adoption of quantity rather than stress in scansion. His theories were to some extent experimented with by Sidney and for some years Harvey exercised an influence over Spenser, from which the latter, who admired him, freed himself with difficulty. He was of an arrogant nature, and engaged in bitter disputes with those who surrounded him. This finally culminated in a scurrilous paper warfare with Nash and Greene, which began with Greene's *Quip for an Upstart Courtier*, written in retaliation for contemptuous references to himself in the writings, during the Martin Marprelate pamphlet controversy, of Harvey's brother Richard, to which Harvey replied in his *Four Letters* (1592), vituperating Greene unmercifully. Even the death of Greene, which had occurred shortly before publication of the pamphlet, did not prevent Harvey's attempts to blacken his character. Nash now began, with great powers of invective and sarcasm, to defend his friend's memory. In his *Strange Newes* (1593), he proclaimed "open warres" against Harvey and his brother. Harvey replied with *Pierce's Supererogation*. The warfare continued till 1596, when Nash, hearing that Harvey boasted of having silenced him, published his satire *Have with you to Saffron Walden*, which he dedicated by way of farce to "Richard Lichfield, barber of Trinity College, Cambridge"; to this Harvey once more rejoined in his *Trimming of Thomas Nashe* (1597). The scandal had, however, now reached a climax, and in 1599 the authorities, proceeding against all such controversial satires, ordered the suppression of all works by Nash and Harvey. Among his works, besides those mentioned, are *Rhetor, sive 2 dierum oratio de natura, arte et exercitatione rhetorica* (1577), *Ciceronianus, sive oratio post reditum habita Cantabrigiæ ad suos auditores* (1577), *The Story of Mercy Harvey* (1574–75), *Letters to and from Edmund Spenser* (1579–80), and *A Letter of Notable Contents* (1593).

Harvey, William. b. at Folkestone, Kent, England, April 1, 1578; d. at London, June 3, 1657. An English physician, anatomist, and physiologist. He was the eldest of seven sons of Thomas Harvey, a merchant, and was educated at the King's School, Canterbury, and Gonville, and Caius College, Cambridge. He took the degree of B.A. in 1597, studied at Padua, where he attained a distinguished place among the students, and became the friend of Fabricius, the great anatomist, and took the degree of M.D. (Padua) and M.D. (Cambridge) in 1602. Elected a fellow of the College of Physicians in 1607, he was appointed physician to St. Bartholomew's Hospital, London, in 1609, and held this office until 1643, when his attendance on the king made it impossible for him to continue with the duties of this post. He was appointed Lumleian Lecturer at the College of Physicians in 1616; some of his lecture notes from this period are extant, and these show that at this time he began to put forward his then novel views about the circulation of the blood. It was Harvey who demonstrated, after actually viewing the action in animals, the function of the heart, the circulation of the blood through arteries and veins, the identity of venous and arterial blood; these had been either theoretical or unthought-of until then. Nevertheless, he did not publish his epoch-making treatise, *Exercitatio anatomica de motu cordis et sanguinis in animalibus*, until 1628 (translated and published in English, *Essay on the Motion of the Heart and the Blood*, 1653). The book was published at Frankfort on the Main, and so was readily circulated all over Europe. It aroused enormous interest everywhere, but Harvey was reluctant to enter into controversy, and published only one brief reply to his critics, *Exercitationes duae anatomicae de circulatione sanguinis* (Cambridge, 1649). Meanwhile he conducted a successful practice as physician and surgeon at London, attending the lord chancellor, Francis Bacon, and other famous men. He was appointed physician extraordinary to King James I in 1618 at the age of 40 and physician to King Charles I in 1631. He traveled in Europe on the king's behalf, and attended him throughout the

English Civil War; he was appointed warden of Wadham College while with the king at Oxford. He was present at the battle of Edgehill, and is said to have been in charge of the two young princes. He held high offices in the College of Physicians, but, owing to his age and infirmities, refused the presidency when it was offered to him in 1654. Throughout his life he carried on investigations in natural history and comparative anatomy. His important work on insects was destroyed during the Civil War. He published an important, though inconclusive, work on generation, *Exercitationes de generatione animalium* (London, 1651; translated and published in English, 1653). Harvey was small, dark, choleric, and energetic. Portraits made at about the age of 45 and in old age hang in the Royal College of Physicians, London, and another done at the age of 80 is in the Hunterian Collection, Glasgow. Harvey holds a preëminent position as an anatomist and physiologist, the publication of *De motu cordis* in 1628 marking the beginning of experimental science and laying the foundation of modern medicine. The book had profound influence on the development of every department of human thought. He is buried in the parish church at Hempstead, Essex, where there is a monument with a lifelike bust in marble by Edward Marshall.

Harwood (här'wŭd), **Harold Marsh.** b. at Eccles, Lancashire, England, Nov. 29, 1874—. An English playwright; husband (married 1918) of Fryniwyd Tennyson Jesse, with whom he wrote *The Mask*, *Billeted* (1917), *The Pelican* (1924), and *While London Burns* (1942). He was author also of *Interlopers* (1913), *A Social Convenience* (1921), *The Golden Calf* (1927), *So Far and No Farther* (1932), *These Mortals* (1935), and *London Front* (1940), and collaborated with Laurence Kirk on *The Innocent Party* (1938).

Hassall (has'ạl), **Christopher Vernon.** b. March 24, 1912—. An English poet and playwright. He is the author of the plays *Devil's Dyke* (1936) and *Christ's Comet* (1937). His verse includes *Poems of Two Years* (1935), *Penthesperon* (1938), which won the Hawthornden Prize, and *Crisis* (1939), a sonnet sequence.

Hassan (has'ạn), **Bedreddin.** See **Bedreddin Hassan.**

Hastings (hãs'tingz), **Lord.** In Shakespeare's *2 Henry IV*, a rebel leader who is arrested after making peace with Prince John.

Hastings, Lord. In Shakespeare's *3 Henry VI* and *Richard III*, a loyal supporter of Edward IV, whom he helps to escape from prison. Although Edward's Queen is his enemy, he refuses to help Richard to the throne after Edward's death, is accused by Richard of treachery, and is executed.

Hastings, Sir Patrick. b. 1880; d. Feb. 26, 1952. An English lawyer and playwright. He wrote only as an avocation, and his plays include *The River* (1925), *Scotch Mist* (1926), *Escort* (1942), and *The Blind Goddess* (1947). He also wrote his autobiography, *Autobiography* (1948) and two legal studies, *Cases in Court* (1949), and *Famous and Infamous Cases* (1950).

Hastings, Warren. b. at Churchill, Oxfordshire, England, Dec. 6, 1732; d. Aug. 22, 1818. An Eng-

ḍ, d or j; ṣ, s or sh; ṭ, t or ch; ẓ, z or zh; o, F. cloche; ü, F. menu; ċh, Sc. loch; ṅ, F. bonbon.

lish statesman. He went out to Calcutta as a writer (the lowest grade of clerk) in the East India service in 1750 and, because of his services to Clive in the recapture of Calcutta in 1756, was made resident at Murshidabad, where he served from 1758 to 1761. In the latter year he became a member of the council at Calcutta, but as a result of the corruption he found among the council members he resigned and returned to England in 1764. In 1769 he went out again as a member of the council at Madras and in 1772 became governor of Bengal. He set about instituting reforms in the revenue system, in the suppression of banditry, and in establishing a more satisfactory judicial code. He was made (1774) first governor general of India when the British government established its influence in India by appointing a council of four to rule with a governor general. Hastings immediately found himself in a struggle with the councilors, who considered that they had not been treated with sufficient pomp and circumstance. They insisted on reviewing (and when they could, reversing) all of Hastings's acts. One of his old native enemies brought charges against him before the council and they were considering the allegations seriously when the native was tried and executed (1775) for forgery. So serious did the fight with the council become that Hastings submitted his resignation through an agent in England, but the death of one of the council members gave him control again and he decided to remain as governor general. In 1780, as the result of an argument over patronage, he fought a duel with Philip Francis, one of the council; Francis was wounded and returned to England. Between 1778 and 1782, Hastings found himself embroiled in a struggle with the Mahratta confederacy, the French, and Haidar Ali and other native rulers. He seized (1778) the French possessions in India, caused the Mahrattas and then the French to withdraw from the struggle, and in 1782 signed a treaty with the Mahrattas. But the war was expensive, and in 1781 Hastings expelled Chait Singh, *zemindar* (landholder under lease) of Benares, who refused a demand for a war contribution; in 1782 he confiscated a portion (over a million pounds sterling) of the lands and treasure of the begum of Oudh (the mother of the nawab of Oudh), whom he accused of aiding Chait Singh. After the passage of Pitt's India Act of 1784, which established a new constitution in which both crown and company shared the rule, Hastings resigned, considering that he could not work with such divided authority; the dual regime was not ended until 1858. He returned to England in 1785 to find himself caught in the midst of the struggle of the government to share in the rich plum of India and to obtain some of the patronage in offices there for itself. In 1787 Hastings was impeached on the charge of high crimes and misdemeanors, based chiefly on his conduct in reference to Chait Singh and the begum of Oudh, the accusation being pressed by Philip Francis, his dueling opponent in India. Among the opposition to Hastings the Whigs were prominent, and Edmund Burke, Charles John Fox, and Richard Brinsley Sheridan spoke against him. The trial opened before the House of Lords in 1788 and resulted in an acquittal on all charges in 1795. The seven-year trial used up all

of Hastings's money, about 70,000 pounds, and he found himself destitute. An appeal to the East India Company brought him an annuity and an immediate cash settlement. In the years that followed he gained a place in public favor and respect, serving for a time on the privy council.

Hatch (hach), **Edwin.** b. at Derby, England, Sept. 14, 1835; d. Nov. 10, 1889. An English theologian and educator. He gave the Bampton lectures in 1880, and the Hibbert lectures in 1888; the former were published as *The Organization of the Early Christian Churches* (1881), and the latter as *The Influence of Greek Ideas and Usages on the Christian Church* (1890).

Hatchway (hach′wā), **Lieutenant Jack.** In Tobias Smollett's novel *Peregrine Pickle*, a retired naval officer, the friend and companion of Commodore Trunnion.

Hatchways (hach′wāz). A novel (1916) by Ethel Sidgwick.

Hathaway (hath′ạ.wā), **Anne.** b. c1556; d. 1623. The maiden name of the wife of William Shakespeare. According to the records of the diocese of Worcester, England, a license was issued on Nov. 27, 1582, for the marriage of William Shakespeare and Anne Whately of Temple Grafton. On November 28, certain friends of the deceased father of Anne Hathway or Hathaway of Stratford posted a bond as security in the matter of the marriage of this Anne to William Shakespeare. It is generally supposed that the name Whately in the first entry was a clerical error. The license in question was a special one permitting the marriage after only one publication of the banns; the normal triple publication would have made it impossible, for various reasons, to proceed with the ceremony in less than two months; this evidently was judged inadvisable, in view of the fact that Anne was already pregnant. Her first child, Susanna, presumably Shakespeare's child, was christened on May 26, 1583. Subsequently she bore twins, who were christened Hamnet and Judith on Feb. 2, 1585, and these three, so far as the records show, were her only children. Anne lived to the year 1623, and the inscription on her tombstone says she was 67 years of age at her death, which indicates that she was eight years older than her husband.

Hatteraick (hat′ér.āk), **Dirk.** A Dutch smuggler in Sir Walter Scott's novel *Guy Mannering.*

Hatter's Castle. A novel by A. J. Cronin, published in 1931.

Hatto I (hat′ō, hät′ō). Archbishop of Mainz (891–913). He became regent of Germany on the accession of Louis III (Louis the Child) in 900, and continued to exercise a predominant influence in German politics until his death. He sought to strengthen the royal authority at the expense of an unruly nobility, a policy which caused him to be feared and hated by a considerable part of the people. According to a medieval legend, he was carried away by the devil and thrown into the crater of Etna.

Hatto II. [Called **Bishop Hatto.**] b. 969 or 970. Archbishop of Mainz. He became abbot of Fulda in 942 or 943, and in 968 was appointed by the emperor Otto I to succeed William of Saxony in the archbishopric of Mainz. According to a medieval legend, which was incorporated with the Magdeburg Centuries, to stop the grumbling of the people during a famine, he announced that he would open his barn to them the next day. Once the crowd was inside, he set fire to the building and burned up the grain and the people together. Their dying shrieks he likened to the piping of mice. At once hordes of mice appeared and attacked the bishop, who fled to a tower on an island in the Rhine, which has been called the Mouse Tower in local legend ever since. Hatto did not escape, however; the mice swarmed after him and devoured him. Robert Southey uses the legend in a poem, and it is also told in *Croyat's Crudities*.

Hatton (hat′ǫn), Sir **Christopher.** [Called the "**Dancing Chancellor.**"] b. at Holdenby, Northamptonshire, England, 1540; d. at Ely House, London, Nov. 20, 1591. A lord chancellor of England. His relations with the queen were intimate; Mary, Queen of Scots, accused them of being lovers. He was one of the commission who declared Mary guilty of plotting Elizabeth's death. Elizabeth appointed him lord chancellor on April 25, 1587. He was called the "dancing chancellor" in allusion to the fact that he first attracted the attention of Queen Elizabeth by his graceful dancing at a masque at court. Hatton was a patron of literature, Edmund Spenser being one of those he befriended, and himself essayed part of a play, the fourth act of *Tancred and Gismund*, a 1591 revision of an earlier play.

Hatton, G. Noel. Pseudonym of **Caird, Alice Mona.**

Hatton, Joseph. b. at Andover, Hampshire, England, Feb. 3, 1841; d. at London, July 31, 1907. An English journalist, dramatist, and novelist. He edited (1863–68) the Bristol *Mirror*, *Gentlemen's Magazine* (1868–74), the *Sunday Times*, and *The People*. Author of *Clytie* (1874; later dramatized), *John Needham's Double* (1885), *By Order of the Czar* (1890), and *When Rogues Fall Out* (1899), novels; *Today in America* (1881), *The New Ceylon* and *Journalistic London* (both 1882), *Henry Irving's Impressions of America* (1884), *Old Lamps and New* (1889), and *Cigarette Papers for After-Dinner Smoking* (1892).

Haughton (hô′tǫn), **William.** fl. in the last half of the 16th century. An English dramatist. He wrote a number of plays, principally in collaboration with Dekker, Day, Chettle, and others. *English-men for My Money, or A Woman will have her Will* (printed 1616) is the only play he is known to have written alone.

Hauksbee (hôks′bē), **Mrs.** A character in many of Kipling's stories of Anglo-Indian life.

Haunted Man, The. A story by Charles Dickens, published in 1848.

Hauptmann (houpt′män), **Gerhart.** b. at Obersalzbrunn, Germany, Nov. 15, 1862; d. June 6, 1946. German dramatist, novelist, and poet; brother of Carl Hauptmann. He studied sculpture for a time at Breslau and Rome, at which time also his first larger work, the epic *Promethidenlos* (1885), was written. When he gave up sculpture for literature he went to Berlin, where he associated with the naturalist group, dominated at that

time by Arno Holz. In this atmosphere he wrote several realistic plays, *Vor Sonnenaufgang* (1889), *Das Friedensfest* (1890), *Einsame Menschen* (1891), and *Die Weber* (1892). The last-named is remarkable for making the whole working class, rather than any one person, the hero of the action. In all these plays Hauptmann shows himself a master of natural dialogue. *Hanneles Himmelfahrt* (1893) marks a turn to romanticism, and *Die versunkene Glocke* (1897) is a fairy drama. The dramatization of Hartmann von Aue's epic *Der arme Heinrich* in 1902 was still in the romantic vein, but this was balanced in the following year by one of his most realistic tragedies, *Rosa Bernd*. Of his comedies, *Der Biberpelz* (1893) is generally considered to be the best. His control of the shorter prose narrative is well demonstrated by the realistic sketch *Bahnwärter Thiel* (1892) and by *Der Ketzer von Soana* (1918), a story of lyric beauty and sensuality. *Der Narr in Christo, Emanuel Quint* (1910) is a mystical novel. *Till Eulenspiegel* (1928) is an epic dealing with postwar conditions. During the Nazi regime Hauptmann remained in Germany. *Das Abenteuer meiner Jugend* (1937) is an account of his earlier years. He received the Nobel prize for literature in 1912. A number of Hauptmann's plays have been translated into English, including *The Weavers*, *Beaver Coat*, *The Sunken Bell*, and *Rose Bernd*.

Hautlein (ōt.laṅ′), **Marquis de.** A gentleman of the *ancien régime* at whose house Scott professed to have gathered the materials for *Quentin Durward*.

Haut-ton (ō′tôṅ′), Sir **Oran.** In Thomas Love Peacock's satirical novel *Melincourt*, the name given an educated orang-outang.

Havelok (hav′ẹ.lok). [Full title, **The Lay of Havelok the Dane.**] An Anglo-Danish story, composed in Lincolnshire, England, before 1300, and containing the legend of the founding of the town of Grimsby in Lincolnshire. It is an adaptation of an Anglo-Norman romance called *Le Lai d'Aveloc*, written in the first half of the 12th century, and probably founded on an Old English original, and of a story found in Geoffrey Gaimar's *L'Estorie des Engles* (c1150). It was edited by Sir F. Madden for the Roxburghe Club (1828) and reëdited for the Early English Text Society by W. W. Skeat (1868; revised by K. Sisam, 1915). The story is a popular one and appears in earlier and later literature. It contains many elements of folklore and folk tale that possess even greater antiquity, among them the motifs of the abandoned child, the scullion prince, the light of kingship issuing from the mouth, and others of wide occurrence. Havelok was the son of the Danish king Birkabeen. He was doomed by his guardian to be put to sea, but was saved by Grim, a fisherman, who brought him up as his son. Grim fled to England and settled at the site of Grimsby, or Grim's town. Havelok grew up and entered the Earl of Lincoln's service as a cook. When he performed certain feats of strength, the earl, regent for Princess Goldborough (or Argentille), married her to the kitchen menial. She recognized in Havelok (who went by the name of Cuaran) a royal personage by virtue of a luminous mark on his shoulder and by his luminous breath.

ḏ, d or j; ṣ, s or sh; ṯ, t or ch; ẕ, z or zh; o, F. cloche; ü, F. menu; ċh, Sc. loch; ṅ, F. bonbon.

He conquered Denmark and then returned to conquer England. Havelok has been identified by some with Anlaf (or Olaf) Cuaran, Danish son-in-law of Constantine II of Scotland, who was defeated at the battle of Brunanburh in 937 A.D.

Havisham (hav′i.shạm), **Miss.** In Dickens's *Great Expectations*, the mother (through adoption) of Estella. Her life has been embittered by an engagement broken many years before, by Compeyson, on the very day of the wedding; since that time her house has been entirely shuttered from the light of day, and every clock in it has been stopped at 20 minutes to nine, which was the hour when she received the note from Compeyson. She adopts Estella, at first thinking only to make her happy, but as the years go by she seeks to make Estella utterly heartless, so that she may be able to break the hearts of the young men who love her, and thus serve as Miss Havisham's weapon of vengeance for the suffering caused her by Compeyson.

Haweis (hô′is, hois), **Hugh Reginald.** b. at Egham, Surrey, England, April 3, 1838; d. Jan. 29, 1901. An English clergyman and author. He published *Music and Morals* (1871) and *Travel and Talk* (1896).

Hawes (hôz), **Stephen.** b. c1476; d. c1523. An English poet and courtier of Henry VII. He wrote (c1506) an allegorical poem, *The Passetyme of Pleasure, or the History of Graunde Amour and la Bel Pucel, conteining the knowledge of the Seven Sciences and the Course of Man's Life in this Worlde,* printed by Wynkyn de Worde in 1509.

Hawk (hôk), **Sir Mulberry.** In Dickens's novel *Nicholas Nickleby,* a dissolute old rake, whose insulting behavior toward Kate Nickleby is punished by a sound thrashing from Nicholas.

Hawker (hô′kẹr). [Pseudonym, **Lance Falconer.**] b. at Inverary, Aberdeenshire, Scotland, Jan. 29, 1848; d. at Broxwood Court, Herefordshire, England, June 16, 1908. A Scottish author of short stories. She wrote *Mademoiselle Ixe* (1890), a short mystery story that was translated into several European languages, and *Cecelia de Noel* (1891), *Hampshire Vignettes* (1907), and other collections of short stories.

Hawker, Robert Stephen. b. at Stoke Damerel, Devonshire, England, Dec. 3, 1803; d. at Plymouth, England, Aug. 15, 1875. An English writer, vicar (1834 *et seq.*) of Morwenstow. Author of *Records of the Western Shore* (1832–36), *Quest of the Sangraal* (1864), and *Footprints of Former Men in Cornwall* (1870).

Hawkesworth (hôks′wẹrth), **John.** b. c1715; d. at London, Nov. 16, 1773. An English essayist and translator. With Samuel Johnson and others he founded and edited *The Adventurer,* a periodical which ran for 140 issues (Nov. 7, 1752–March 9, 1754), of which he wrote more than half. Author of some unimportant dramatic works, and adapter of others, he is remembered chiefly for editing (1754–55) the works of Swift. He translated (1768) Fénelon's *Adventures of Telemachus.*

Hawkins (hô′kinz), **Sir Anthony Hope.** [Pseudonym, **Anthony Hope.**] b. at London, Feb. 9, 1863; d. July 8, 1933. An English novelist and playwright. He wrote *Father Stafford, The Prisoner of Zenda*

(1894), *The Dolly Dialogues* (1894), *Comedies of Courtship* (1896), *Phroso* (1897), *Rupert of Hentzau* (1898), *Simon Dale* (1898), *The King's Mirror* (1899), *Tristram of Blent* (1901), *The Intrusions of Peggy* (1902), *Double Harness* (1904), *A Servant of the Public* (1905), *Sophy of Kravonia* (1906), *Helena's Path* (1907), *The Great Miss Driver* (1908), *Love's Logic* (1908), *Second String* (1910), *Mrs. Maxton Protests* (1911), and *Little Tiger* (1925). Among his plays are *Simon Dale, Pilkerton's Peerage,* and *The Adventure of Lady Ursula. The Prisoner of Zenda,* while by no means the first novel of high political adventure of the period, began a trend that for a decade was to keep such novels on the best-seller lists. Set in the Balkanlike imaginary country of Ruritania it mixed romantic love, political intrigue, and dashing adventure in a formula that was soon extended to the historical novel.

Hawkins, Jim. In Robert Louis Stevenson's *Treasure Island,* the youthful hero, whose adventures with Blind Pew, Long John Silver, Ben Gunn, and other veterans of Captain Flint's piratical crew lead eventually to the recovery of the buried treasure.

Hawkins or **Hawkyns** (hô′kinz), **Sir John.** b. at Plymouth, England, 1532; d. at sea off Puerto Rico, Nov. 12, 1595. An English naval hero. In 1562, 1564, and 1567 he carried cargoes of slaves from Africa to the West Indies and the Spanish Main. Several English noblemen, and, it is said, Queen Elizabeth, had a financial interest in these voyages. The trade was a violation of Spanish law, and ultimately Hawkins was attacked (Sept. 24, 1568) by a Spanish fleet in the harbor of Veracruz, and escaped with difficulty, after losing all his ships except the *Minion* (under him) and the *Judith* (owned and commanded by his cousin Francis Drake). In apparent disgrace, Hawkins, with the connivance of Lord Burleigh (William Cecil), the secretary of state, undertook negotiations with the Spanish to enable them to invade England and overthrow Elizabeth; for these supposed services he was granted a Spanish title and a large sum of money. In 1573 he was made treasurer of the English navy, and shortly thereafter comptroller. As rear admiral he took a prominent part in the defeat of the Spanish Armada (August, 1588), and was knighted. He was with Frobisher on the Portuguese coast in 1590 in an attempt to meet the Spanish silver fleet, but the expedition failed in its purpose. He died while second in command in Drake's unsuccessful expedition to the West Indies.

Hawkins, Sir John. b. at London, March 30, 1719; d. at Westminster, London, May 21, 1789. An English author. He was one of Samuel Johnson's legal executors, and wrote his life, which he published with an edition of Johnson's works in 1787. His chief work is *A General History of the Science and Practice of Music* (5 vols., 1776). See *The Life and Activities of Sir John Hawkins* (1953), by Percy A. Scholes.

Hawkshaw (hôk′shô). In Tom Taylor's play *The Ticket-of-Leave Man* (1863), a detective who relentlessly tracks down the evildoer Tiger Dalton. Hawkshaw's implacability, his disguises, his memory for faces and facts made a great impression on audiences and made of his name a synonym for "detective."

Hawkwood (hôk′wŭd), Sir **John de.** b. in Essex, England, c1320; d. at Florence, Italy, 1394. An English leader of condottieri. He served under Edward the Black Prince in France, and after the peace of Bretigny (1360) organized his famous White Company, whose services he sold to various Italian city-states. He finally became the permanent military adviser and captain general of Florence.

Hawser Trunnion (hô′zẽr trun′yọn), **Commodore.** See **Trunnion, Commodore Hawser.**

Hay (hā), **Ian.** Pseudonym of **Beith, John Hay.**

Hay Cliff. See **Shakespeare's Cliff.**

Haydn (hī′dn), **Joseph.** [Full name, **Franz Joseph Haydn.**] b. at Rohrau, Lower Austria, March 31, 1732; d. at Vienna, May 31, 1809. An Austrian composer, the first of the great masters of the classical period in music. He set and established the sonata form, brought the symphony to an advanced stage of structural and artistic development, and crystallized string-quartet writing. The modern age of instrumental music can be said to have been born with him. In 1791–92, and again in 1794–95, he visited London, on an invitation by the impresario Johann Peter Salomon, to conduct concerts of his own works and to introduce his celebrated 12 "Salomon symphonies" written expressly for these visits. In 1793 he had as his pupil the 22-year-old Beethoven. His works include approximately 125 symphonies, 83 string quartets, the oratorios *The Creation* (1798) and *The Seasons* (1801), concertos, operas, sonatas, cantatas, and the Austrian national hymn. Haydn is sometimes called "Papa" Haydn, partly in the belief that he is the father of the modern symphony, and partly in recognition of the genial quality of his music. Certain of his symphonies have had nicknames attached to them, because of actual occurrences or because of apocryphal incidents connected with them or because of some suspected programmatic content: *La Poule, La Passione, L'Ours, La Chasse, Le Soir* (1761), *Le Midi* (1761), *Farewell* (1772), *Maria Theresa* (1773), *The Queen of France* (1784), *Toy* (1788), *Oxford* (1788), *Surprise* (1791), *Military* (1794), *Clock* (1794), *Drum Roll* (1794), *London* (1795), and the like.

Haydon (hā′dọn), **Benjamin Robert.** b. at Plymouth, England, Jan. 26, 1786; committed suicide at London, June 22, 1846. An English historical painter. Among his works are *Christ's Entry into Jerusalem, The Raising of Lazarus,* and *The Judgment of Solomon.* He published *Lectures on Painting and Design* (1844–46).

Hayley (hā′li), **William.** b. at Chichester, England, Oct. 29, 1745; d. at Felpham, near Chichester, Nov. 12, 1820. An English poet and prose writer, a friend of Southey, Blake, Romney, and Cowper. He wrote *Triumph of Temper* (1781), *Philosophical Essay on Old Maids* (1785), *Life of Milton* (1794), *Life of Cowper* (1803), and *Memoirs* (1823). His poems were published in a single volume in 1785.

Haymarket (hā′mär″kẹt). A former London market, established in 1644 on the site now partly covered by Lower Regent Street, near Piccadilly

Circus. It was abolished in 1830, but the site is still called the Haymarket.

Haymarket Theatre. A London theater standing in the Haymarket opposite Charles Street. During the patent monopoly it was a kind of chapel of ease or training house to Drury Lane and Covent Garden theaters. In 1720 John Potter purchased the site of an old inn, the King's Head, in the Haymarket, and erected there a small theater. The house was leased to a company of French actors, and opened with *La Fille à la mode, ou le Badeau de Paris,* under the patronage of the Duke of Montague. Fielding's is the first great name connected with this theater. In 1730 he produced *The Tragedy of Tragedies, or Tom Thumb the Great,* and became manager in 1734. In February, 1744, Charles Macklin opened the Haymarket with a company largely composed of his own pupils. On April 22, 1747, Samuel Foote assumed the management. In 1776 Foote sold the theater to George Colman the elder, who managed it till 1794. When Harris became manager in 1820, he demolished the old house, and erected a new one a little farther north. It was opened on July 4, 1821, with *The Rivals.* The present theater was built in 1880.

Haymon (hā′mọn). See **Aymon.**

Hayraddin Maugrabin (hā′rad.n mô′grạ.bin). See **Maugrabin, Hayraddin.**

Hayston (hās′tọn), **Frank.** See **Bucklaw, Laird of.**

Hayward (hā′wạrd), **Abraham.** b. at Lyme Regis, England, Nov. 22, 1801; d. at London, Feb. 2, 1884. An English essayist and general writer. Among his works is a translation of *Faust* (1833).

Hayward, Sir **John.** b. in Suffolk, England, c1564; d. at London, June 27, 1627. An English historian. He published *First Part of the Life and Raigne of King Henrie the IV* (1599), and other historical works. Parts of his history (which was issued under the patronage of Essex) appeared to Elizabeth to contain treasonable suggestions, and he was brought before the Star Chamber and imprisoned.

Haywood (hā′wŭd), **Eliza.** [Maiden name, **Fowler.**] b. c1693; d. at London, Feb. 25, 1756. An English actress, novelist, dramatist, and poet. Among her many works are *The Rash Resolve* (1724), *The Fatal Secret* (1725), *The Female Spectator* (a periodical, 1744–46), *The Fortunate Foundlings* (1744), *The History of Miss Betsy Thoughtless* (1751), and *History of Jemmy and Jenny Jessamy* (1753). Pope, Walpole, and Swift attacked her violently, Swift calling her "a stupid, infamous, scribbling woman" in a letter (Oct. 26, 1731) to the Countess of Suffolk.

Hazard (haz′ạrd), **Will.** The "gamester" in James Shirley's play of that name.

Hazlitt (haz′lit), **William.** b. at Maidstone, Kent, England, April 10, 1778; d. at London, Sept. 18, 1830. An English critic and essayist; father of William Hazlitt (1811–93) and grandfather of William Carew Hazlitt (1834–1913). He studied to be a painter, but perceiving that his talent was insufficient, turned to writing. How at an early age he became a friend of Wordsworth, Coleridge, and Southey, he related in an essay, *My First Acquaintance with Poets.* However, before long, being one of those who thought the three Lake Poets had betrayed the liberalism of their early years, he quar-

ḍ, d or j; ṣ, s or sh; ṭ, t or ch; ẓ, z or zh; o, F. cloche; ü, F. menu; ċh, Sc. loch; ṅ, F. bonbon.

reled with them vehemently, for he was a man ardent in his convictions, little inclined to compromise, and quick of temper. Going to London about 1808, he became a contributor to newspapers and periodicals including the *Edinburgh Review* and the *Examiner*, edited by Leigh Hunt and his brother John. He became an intimate friend of Leigh Hunt, Charles Lamb, and Thomas Moore, but subsequently quarreled with the last two of these (though he and Lamb were never really estranged, and Lamb was with him at his death). The bulk of Hazlitt's work may be classified in three categories: intimate and graceful essays, such as *On Going a Journey;* pen portraits and critical evaluations of contemporary writers, as in *Table-Talk* (1821–22) and *The Spirit of the Age* (1825); and penetrating studies of Shakespeare and other Elizabethan and later English dramatists. Hazlitt was no less influential than Coleridge in broadening appreciation of Shakespeare as an artist, and to him may be traced a revived appreciation of Dekker and other minor playwrights. His principal works in this field were *Characters of Shakespeare's Plays* (1817), *Views of the English Stage* (1818), *Lectures on the English Comic Writers* (1819), and *Dramatic Literature of the Age of Elizabeth* (1821). The miscellany of his other writings includes a *Life of Napoleon* (1828), which, though he set much store by it, was perhaps his least impressive work; the unhappy record of a love affair entitled *Liber Amoris, or the New Pygmalion* (1823); and the interesting collections posthumously published under the titles *Winterslow* and *Sketches and Essays*. Hazlitt continues to be generally considered one of the most perceptive critics, one of the most generous spirits, and one of the greatest masters of prose among English writers.

Hazlitt, William. b. in Wiltshire, England, Sept. 26, 1811; d. at Addlestone, Surrey, England, Feb. 22, 1893. An English writer; son of William Hazlitt (1778–1830) and father of William Carew Hazlitt (1834–1913). He edited Johnson's *Lives of the Poets,* and wrote on legal subjects.

Hazlitt, William Carew. b. Aug. 22, 1834; d. at Richmond, Surrey, England, Sept. 8, 1913. An English author and lawyer; son of William Hazlitt (1811–93) and grandson of William Hazlitt (1778–1830).

Head (hed), **Richard.** b. in Ireland, c1637; d. by drowning, c1686. An English hack writer and gambler. He was responsible for the first part of *The English Rogue, described in the Life of Meriton Latroon, a Witty Extravagant, being a Compleat History of the most Eminent Cheats of both Sexes* (1665), a vulgar but entertaining narrative that was, or pretended to be, the life of its author. The remaining three parts were written by Francis Kirkman. Among Head's other works are *Proteus Redivivus, or the Art of Wheedling or Insinuation* (1675) and *Life and Death of Mother Shipton* (1677), a 16th-century seer who was supposed to be a daughter of the devil and whose prophecies were still subjects for investigation as late as 1881.

Headlong Hall (hed'lông). A novel by Thomas Love Peacock, published in 1816. It has almost no plot, but contains much discussion between Mr. Foster, the optimist, and Mr. Escot, the pessimist.

Headrigg (hed'rig), **Cuddie.** The plowman on the estate of Lady Margaret Bellenden in Sir Walter Scott's novel *Old Mortality.* He is arrested, with Henry Morton, by Bothwell, who is in the service of the king.

Headrigg, Mause. The mother of Cuddie, the plowman, in Sir Walter Scott's novel *Old Mortality.*

Headstone (hed'stōn), **Bradley.** In Dickens's *Our Mutual Friend,* an ungainly and stiff but excitable schoolmaster, madly in love with Lizzie Hexam, and the deadly enemy and would-be murderer of Eugene Wrayburn.

Heard (hèrd), **Gerald.** [Full name, **Henry Fitz Gerald Heard.**] b. Oct. 6, 1889—. An English essayist and writer of fiction. A popularizer of science and philosophy, he has also done a great deal of radio broadcasting. He visited the U. S. in 1937. The better-known books of this very prolific writer include *Narcissus, The Social Substance of Religion, The Ascent of Humanity, The Emergence of Man, This Surprising World, These Hurrying Years, The Source of Civilization, The Creed of Christ, The Code of Christ, Science in the Making, Man the Master, Pain, Sex, and Time,* and *A New Hypothesis of Evolution.*

Hearn (hèrn), **Lafcadio.** [Japanese name, **Yakumo Koizumi.**] b. in Santa Maura, Ionian Islands, June 27, 1850; d. at Okubo, near Tokyo, Sept. 26, 1904. A writer, notable for his works on Japan. He was of Irish and Greek parentage and went to America in 1869, working on several Cincinnati and New Orleans newspapers. He spent some time as a correspondent in the West Indies, and in 1890 went to Japan, where he became a lecturer on English literature at the Imperial University at Tokyo. He married a Japanese woman, and was naturalized as a Japanese subject under the name of Yakumo Koizumi. He published *Stray Leaves from Strange Literature* (1884), *Some Chinese Ghosts* (1887), *Chita* (1889), *Two Years in the French West Indies* (1890), *Youma* (1890), *Glimpses of Unfamiliar Japan* (1894), *Out of the East* (1895), *Kokoro* (1896), *Gleanings in Buddha-Fields* (1897), *Exotics and Retrospectives* (1898), *In Ghostly Japan* (1899), *Shadowings* (1900), *A Japanese Miscellany* (1901), *Kotto* (1902), *Japan: an Attempt at Interpretation* (1904), *Kwaidan* (1904), and *The Romance of the Milky Way* (1905). Hearn's writing, notable for its exquisite stylistic approach, was an attempt to explain in its own terms the culture, ethics, and psychology of the Japanese to the Western world. *The Life and Letters* (1906) and *The Japanese Letters of Lafcadio Hearn* (1910) were edited by Elizabeth Bisland.

Hearne (hèrn), **Thomas.** b. at White Waltham, Berkshire, England, 1678; d. June 10, 1735. An English antiquary.

Heartbreak House. A play by George Bernard Shaw, published in 1917. Set against the background of World War I, it deals with the fears and frustrations of 20th-century civilization in time of crisis (it draws largely upon Chekov's *The Cherry Orchard*).

Heartfree (härt'frē). A supposedly cynical young man, claiming immunity to any woman, in Vanbrugh's *The Provok'd Wife.* He succumbs, however, to Belinda.

fat, fāte, fär, àsk, fāre; net, mē, hèr; pin, pīne; not, nōte, mõve, nôr; up, lūte, pùll; ᴛн, then;

Heart of Midlothian (mid.lō'ᴛʜi.an), **The.** A novel by Sir Walter Scott, published in 1818, taking its title from the popular name of the Tolbooth, an Edinburgh prison, demolished in 1817. It is one of the *Tales of My Landlord*. The scene is laid in the time of the Porteous riot during the reign of George II. Porteous, captain of the City Guard, causes the death of several people when he orders his men to fire on a crowd gathered to protest (but only by their presence) the hanging of a reprieved convict. Various citizens, headed by a man called Robertson, thereupon break into the prison, carry out Porteous, and hang him. Robertson, whose real name is Staunton, is the lover of Effie Deans, who is imprisoned on a charge of murdering her child, the son of Staunton, and Staunton's action in leading the riot is attributable in part to his desire to free her. However, Effie refuses to leave, is tried for murder, and is convicted because her sister, Jeanie, will not tell the lie that would save her. Jeanie then goes to London to obtain a pardon for Effie from Queen Caroline, and wins it. Jeanie now marries her true love, the minister Reuben Butler, and Effie marries Staunton, who is the son of a nobleman, and leaves the country with him. Later she returns, and it is revealed that her child has been living all the while. He had been stolen by the crazy Madge Wildfire, daughter of the midwife Meg Murdockson, and had been given to bandits. But tragedy closes the story: Staunton, in his efforts to find the boy, unexpectedly comes across the bandits, and is attacked and killed by his own child.

Hearts Insurgent. The title under which the novel *Jude the Obscure*, by Thomas Hardy, was published in *Harper's Magazine* in 1895.

Heart's Journey, The. A volume of poems (1928) by Siegfried Sassoon.

Heartwell (härt'wel). The woman-hating "Old Bachelor" in Congreve's comedy of that name.

Heath (hēth), **Charles.** A London artist, in William De Morgan's novel *Alice-for-Short* (1907). He marries Alicia Kavanagh.

Heath, Peggy. The sister of Charles Heath, in *Alice-for-Short*, by William De Morgan. She falls in love with, and marries, Rupert Johnson, a doctor, who takes care of Alicia and who saves her life.

Heath, Pierre. The young son of Charles Heath, by his first marriage, in William De Morgan's *Alice-for-Short*. When he contracts smallpox he is cared for by Alicia Kavanagh, the heroine of the story.

Heathcliff (hēth'klif). The hero of Emily Brontë's novel *Wuthering Heights*.

Heather-Field, The. A tragedy by Edward Martyn (1899), produced by the Irish Literary Theatre (forerunner of the Abbey Theatre). It is a symbolic drama showing a trace of influence by Ibsen in its depiction of Carden Tyrrell's unsuccessful struggle to reclaim a heather field with money gained by mortgaging his property.

Heat of the Day, The. A novel by Elizabeth Bowen, published in 1949.

Heaton (hē'tọn), Sir **John Henniker.** b. at Rochester, Kent, England, 1848; d. Sept. 8, 1914. An English politician. He promoted the imperial penny postage scheme in 1898, the Anglo-American penny postage in 1907 (in operation 1908), and other postal improvements. He wrote *Australian Dictionary of Dates and Men of the Time.*

Heaven and Earth: A Mystery. A verse drama by Byron, written in 1821 and published in *The Liberal* in 1823 (and again in 1824). It is far indeed from a mystery play in the medieval sense, being actually a blistering challenge of religious orthodoxy, which Byron emphasizes by showing his contempt for the Omnipotent. He deals with the love of the angels for the daughters of men, but breaks off abruptly at the Flood. A fragment of later events exists in *The Deformed Transformed*, written in 1822.

Heavenfield (hev'ẹn.fēld), **Battle of.** A battle (c634) in the north of England, in which Oswald of Northumbria defeated (according to legend, by a miraculous intervention of heaven) the Britons under Cadwallon.

Heaven Haven. [Full title, **Heaven Haven: A Nun Takes the Veil.**] A poem (1866) by Gerard Manley Hopkins, expressing the quiet joy of a religious person who is leaving the cares of the world and going to a place of beauty, symbolizing both the actual convent and the state of the soul, where all is in harmony with God:

> And I have asked to be
>   Where no storms come,
> Where the green swell is in the haven dumb
>   And out of the swing of the sea.

Heavenly Ladder, The. A novel by Compton Mackenzie, published in 1924, the concluding volume of a trilogy of which the other panels are *The Altar Steps* (1922) and *The Parson's Progress* (1923). The collective work traces the spiritual development of Mark Lidderdale, an Anglican minister who finally enters the Roman Catholic Church.

Heavenly Twins, The. A story (1893) by Sarah Grand.

Hebe (hē'bẹ). In Greek mythology, the goddess of youth and spring; the personification of eternal and exuberant youth, and, until supplanted in this office by Ganymede, the cupbearer of Olympus. She was a daughter of Zeus and Hera, who gave her as wife to Hercules after his death and deification, as a reward for his achievements. She bore him two sons. Hebe was worshiped as Dia in certain localities, and in this aspect she is associated with Aphrodite. Powers of rejuvenation were ascribed to her. The Romans called her Juventas.

Heber (hē'bẹr), **Reginald.** b. at Malpas, Cheshire, England, April 21, 1783; d. at Trichinopoly, Madras, India, April 3, 1826. An English prelate and hymn-writer, made bishop of Calcutta in 1823; half brother of Richard Heber. In *Hymns written and adapted to the Weekly Church Service of the Year*, 58 are by Bishop Heber, including *From Greenland's Icy Mountains, Brightest and Best, Holy, holy, holy, Lord God Almighty, By Cool Siloam's Shady Rill*, and others.

Heber, Richard. b. at Westminster, London, Jan. 5, 1773; d. at London, Oct. 4, 1833. An English book collector; half brother of Reginald Heber. He originated the statement "No gentleman can be

---

ḍ, d or j; ṣ, s or sh; ṭ, t or ch; ẓ, z or zh; o, F. cloche; ü, F. menu; ċh, Sc. loch; ṅ, F. bonbon.

without three copies of a book, one for show, one for use, and one for borrowers."

Heberden (heb'ĕr.dẹn), **William.** b. at London, March 23, 1767; d. there, Feb. 19, 1845. An English physician and scholar. He was appointed physician in ordinary to Queen Charlotte (1806) and to King George III (1809). In addition to medical papers his works include *On Education: A Dialogue after the Manner of Cicero's Philosophical Disquisitions* (1818) and *Letters of Cicero to Atticus*, a translation (1825).

Hebrew Melodies. A collection of poems by Lord Byron, published in 1815.

Hebrides (heb'ri.dēz). [Also: **Western Islands, Western Isles;** ancient names, **Ebudae** (Ptolemy), **Hebudes** (Pliny).] A group of islands lying W of N Scotland. It comprises the Outer Hebrides (also called Long Island), which consist of Lewis with Harris, North Uist, Benbecula, South Uist, Barra, and smaller islands; and the Inner Hebrides, which consist of Skye, Raasay, Mull, Iona, Eigg, Rum, Coll, Tiree, Colonsay, Jura, Islay, and smaller islands. Bute and Arran are also sometimes included in the Hebrides. The islands are noted for picturesque scenery. The early Celtic inhabitants were Christianized by Columba. The islands were colonized from Norway in the 9th century, were ceded by Norway to Scotland in 1266, and were ruled by the "Lords of the Isles" in the 14th, 15th, and 16th centuries.

Hecate (hek'ạ.tē). [Also, **Hekate.**] In Greek mythology, a triple goddess combining the concepts of moon goddess, earth goddess, and underworld goddess. She had powers over the sky, earth, and sea, and was also a giver of riches and good fortune. As moon goddess, she was identified with Artemis. As underworld goddess she was an attendant of Persephone; and as leader of souls of the dead she was associated with ghosts, magic, and witchcraft. She was invisible to mortals, but dogs could see her pass; and she was often conceived of as tearing through the night followed by a pack of spectral hounds. Hounds were sacred to her. Hecate was also a crossroads goddess, and as such was represented with triple bodies back to back. In this aspect the Romans named her Trivia. She was also identified variously with Demeter, Rhea, and Persephone.

Hecate. In Shakespeare's *Macbeth*, a superior of the Witches, borrowed from lore already old in Shakespeare's day (actually, she stems from Greek mythology, where she has threefold powers involving the moon and night, the earth, and the lower world, whence her later association with demons and witchcraft). In *Macbeth* (III.v), she scolds the Witches for acting without her advice. Some authorities have attributed her speeches to Thomas Middleton, who later (about 1612) wrote a play called *The Witch*.

Hecate. The "witch" in Thomas Middleton's play of that name.

Hector (hek'tọr). In Greek legend, the son of Priam and Hecuba; brother of Paris and husband of Andromache. He was the greatest warrior of the Trojans, and the principal character of the *Iliad* on the Trojan side. He killed Patroclus, the friend

of Achilles, and in turn was slain by Achilles, who, in his chariot, dragged Hector's body thrice around the walls of Troy.

Hector. In Shakespeare's *Troilus and Cressida*, a son of Priam, King of Troy, and husband of Andromache. He challenges the Greeks to single combat, fights with Ajax, and is later murdered by the jealous Achilles.

Hector, Annie. [Pseudonym; Mrs. **Alexander;** maiden name, **French.**] b. at Dublin, 1825; d. at London, July 10, 1902. A British novelist. Author of *The Wooing O't* (1873), *Ralph Wilton's Weird* (1875), *Her Dearest Foe* (1876), *The Frères* (1882), and others.

Hector, Sir. See **Ector, Sir.**

Hector de Maris (dẹ mar'is) or **Mares** (mar'ẹs), **Sir.** See **Ector de Maris, Sir.**

Hecuba (hek'ụ.bạ). In Greek legend, queen of Troy; second wife of Priam, daughter of Dymas of Phrygia (according to others, of Cisseus). She was the mother of Hector, Cassandra, Paris, Troilus, Helenus, Polyxena, and Polydorus. She was enslaved after the fall of Troy by Odysseus, witnessed the sacrifice of her daughter Polyxena by the Greeks to the shade of Achilles, and saw the body of her last son, Polydorus, who was murdered by Polymestor, washed to her feet by the waves. On the murderer she took vengeance by slaying his children and tearing out his eyes.

Hecuba. A tragedy by Euripides, exhibited in 425 B.C. It portrays the misfortunes of Hecuba, widow of Priam, king of Troy, including the sacrifice of her daughter Polyxena at the grave of Achilles, the murder of her son Polydorus by Polymestor, and the vengeance executed by her upon Polymestor.

Hedon (hē'dọn). In Ben Jonson's play *Cynthia's Revels*, a voluptuous coxcomb and polished courtier. He is believed to have been intended as a satirical portrait of John Marston.

Heep (hēp), **Uriah.** In Dickens's *David Copperfield*, Mr. Wickfield's swindling clerk and partner. He is a cadaverous, red-haired, ostentatiously humble hypocrite. His name has come to have general use in describing a hypocrite of his type.

Heever (hā'vér), **C. M. van den.** b. in an English concentration camp, 1902—. A South African author. His *Collected Poetry* was published in 1945. His pessimistic novels include *Droogte* (Drought, 1930), *Kromburg* (1937), *Laat Vrugte* (Late Fruits, 1939), and *Anderkant die Berge* (Over the Mountains, 1944). Among his other works are a group of essays, *Die Afrikaanse Gedagte* (The African Idea, 1935).

Hegel (hā'gẹl), **Georg Wilhelm Friedrich.** b. at Stuttgart, Germany, Aug. 27, 1770; d. at Berlin, Nov. 14, 1831. A German philosopher. Educated in theology, he was for several years a private tutor before becoming professor of philosophy at Jena in 1805, editor of a political newspaper at Bamberg (1806–08), rector of the *Gymnasium* (advanced secondary school) at Nuremberg, and professor of philosophy at Heidelberg (1816–18). Already famous, having published *Phänomenologie des Geistes* (Phenomenology of Mind, 1807), *Wissenschaft der Logik* (Science of Logic, 1812–16), and *Encyclopädie der philosophischen Wissen-*

schaften (Encyclopedia of Philosophical Sciences, 1817), in 1818 he was appointed to the chair of philosophy, in succession to Fichte, at the University of Berlin. From that time to his death he dominated the field of German philosophy, as his system continued to do throughout the second quarter of the 19th century. His *Grundlinien de Philosophie des Rechts* (Philosophy of Right, 1821) and various comparatively minor works were published during his Berlin period, and after his death his complete works, including the notes from which he lectured on the philosophy of religion, of aesthetics, and of history, and on the history of philosophy, were published in 18 volumes (1832–41). A man of wide learning, subtle mind, and great confidence, Hegel formulated a complete philosophy which undertook to explain the universe and being, in the largest abstract concepts and in the minutest concrete details. The core of his system was the concept of a complete and perfect design, existing timelessly, to which all things tend to conform, by force of the dialectical logic which he revealed. Hegelian dialectic, as it came to be called, is asserted to be the real law of the movement of thought, the scheme of which is thesis, antithesis, and synthesis; or, otherwise stated, the original tendency, the opposing tendency to which it inevitably gives rise, and the unification of the two tendencies in a new movement. By the operations of this law, an illimitable series of logical developments is envisioned, and this is the law of the development not only of thought but of being also, for thought and being are identical. Hegelianism is sometimes considered the most complete and powerful formulation of pure philosophical idealism, radically hostile to natural science, and especially to the Newtonian philosophy with its scientific methods and conclusions.

Hegge Plays (hej). [Also: **Coventry Plays, Ludus Coventriae.**] A cycle of 42 mystery plays once thought to be associated with Coventry, England. They received their present name from one of the owners of the manuscript in which they were found, which dates from 1468.

Hegira (hẹ.jï′rạ, hej′i.rạ). See **Hejira.**

Heidelberg (hï′dẹl.berk; Anglicized, -bèrg). A city in S Germany, in the *Land* (state) of Württemberg-Baden, formerly in the free state of Baden, on the Neckar River ab. 12 mi. SE of Mannheim. Picturesquely situated at the point where the narrow valley of the Neckar River opens into the plain of the Upper Rhine, it is a center for tourists. It is the seat of a famous university, founded in 1386, with numerous scientific institutes and scholarly societies; the university library contains over a million books, manuscripts, papyri, and documents, some of them of great value. The university has been of far-reaching influence at various times. In the period of the Reformation Agricola and Reuchlin were teachers here; from 1559 to 1619 it was the center of Calvinism. At the turn of the 18th and 19th centuries it had ties to the Romantic Movement; the collection of songs called *Des Knaben Wunderhorn* was published here; in the 19th century it was the seat of the Rickert-Windelband philosophical school; in the 20th century the sociologist Max Weber, the literary his-

torian Gundolf, and the philosopher Jaspers have been among the members of the faculty.

Heidelberg, Mrs. A domineering old lady in *The Clandestine Marriage*, by the elder George Colman and Garrick.

Heimdall (hām′däl). [Old Norse, **Heimdallr.**] In Old Norse mythology, a god of sun and light. Because he could see all and hear all, he was made guardian of the bridge of the gods, Bifröst, at the end of which he dwelt in Himinbjörg. He possessed the trumpet Gjallarhorn, with which the gods were finally summoned together at Ragnarök, when he and Loki slew each other.

Heimskringla (hāms′kring.lä). A history of the Norse kings, from the earliest mythical times down to the battle of Re in 1177, written by the Icelander Snorri Sturluson. It receives its name from its first words, "*Kringla heimsins*," the circle of the world. In subject matter and literary style it is the most important prose work in Old Norse literature.

Heine (hï′nẹ), **Heinrich.** b. at Düsseldorf, Germany, Dec. 13, 1797; d. at Paris, Feb. 17, 1856. A German lyric poet and critic, originally grouped with Junges Deutschland. Destined for a business career, he was sent, against his own desire, to his uncle Solomon Heine, a banker at Hamburg, but through the latter's assistance he was enabled to study jurisprudence at Bonn, Berlin, and Göttingen. In 1825 he renounced the Jewish faith and embraced Christianity. He lived alternately at Hamburg, Berlin, and Munich. After 1831 until his death he lived for the most part at Paris, during the last years of his life a great sufferer from an incurable spinal malady. From 1837 to 1848 he received an annuity from the French government. The first collection of his poems, *Gedichte*, appeared in 1822, his *Buch der Lieder* in 1827, *Neue Gedichte* in 1844, and *Romanzero* in 1851. Among his songs are some of the best-known lyrics of Germany: for instance, *Die Lorlei, Du bist wie eine Blume*, and *Nach Frankreich zogen zwei Grenadier*. He also left a number of characteristic prose works, the most celebrated of which, the *Reisebilder*, had appeared in four parts from 1826 to 1831. The *Romantische Schule* appeared in 1836. His complete works were published at Hamburg (1861–66) in 21 volumes.

Heinemann (hï′nẹ.man), **William.** b. at Surbiton, England, May 18, 1863; d. at London, Oct. 5, 1920. An English publisher. He founded his own firm in January, 1890, bringing out as his first book Hall Caine's successful novel *The Bondman* (1890). He published translations of outstanding Russian, French, and Scandinavian writers. Among his English authors were Stevenson, Pinero, Conrad, Zangwill, Kipling, Wells, Galsworthy, and Somerset Maugham. Scholars and lovers of classical literature are indebted to him for the Loeb Classical Library, a series of authoritative translations of Greek and Latin works containing the original text and a parallel translation.

Heir, The. A collection of short stories by V. Sackville-West, published in 1922.

Heir-at-Law, The. A comedy by the younger George Colman, produced in 1797 and printed in 1800.

Heiress, The. See under **Stolen Heiress.**

ḍ, d or j; ṣ, s or sh; ṭ, t or ch; ẓ, z or zh; *o*, F. cloche; ü, F. menu; ċh, Sc. loch; ṅ, F. bonbon.

Heir of Linne (lin), **The.** An old ballad (probably Scottish) preserved in Percy's *Reliques.* It deals with the story of the spendthrift son of the Laird of Linne, who loses his money and land to his father's steward but finally regains his heritage.

Heir of Redclyffe (red'klif), **The.** A story for the young, with a moral purpose, by Charlotte M. Yonge. It was published in 1853.

Hejira (hḗ.jī'rạ, hej'i.rạ). [Also, **Hegira.**] The starting point of the Mohammedan calendar, July 16, 622, commemorative of the flight of Mohammed from Mecca to Yathrib (modern Medina). The actual date of the flight was June 20. The fixing of the calendar was accomplished under the second caliph, Omar I, in 639 A.D.

Hekate (hek'ạ.tē). See **Hecate.**

Hel (hel). In Old Norse mythology, the daughter of Loki and the giantess Angurboda (Old Norse, *Angrbodha*), and goddess of Niflheim, or Niflhel, the realm of the dead below the earth, which is also called Hel. Originally all the dead went to her. In later mythology she is horrible in appearance, half blue-black and half flesh-color, and her abode becomes the abode of the damned and a place of misery.

Hélas (ā.lä'). A poem by Oscar Wilde in which he attempts an analysis of his life, trying to determine just what it was that caused him to "lose a soul's inheritance."

Helen (hel'ẹn). [Also, **Helen of Troy.**] In Greek legend, the wife of Menelaus, king of Sparta. According to the usual tradition, she was the daughter of Zeus and Leda; according to another, of Zeus and Nemesis. She was celebrated for her beauty. Before her marriage to Menelaus, Theseus took her by force to Athens, from where Castor and Pollux, her brothers, rescued her. Her flight to Troy with Paris was the cause of the Trojan War. After the fall of Troy she returned to Sparta with Menelaus. Goethe introduces her in the second part of *Faust,* and Marlowe's Faustus addresses her thus:

> Oh! thou art fairer than the evening air
> Clad in the beauty of a thousand stars!

Helen. In Shakespeare's *Cymbeline,* an attendant of Imogen.

Helen. In Shakespeare's *Troilus and Cressida,* the beautiful wife of Menelaus. Her elopement with Paris caused the Trojan War.

Helen. In Christopher Marlowe's tragedy *Doctor Faustus,* the legendary beauty whose abduction by Paris caused the Trojan War. To Faustus, she represents ideal beauty and symbolizes the summit of intellectual power to which he aspires. She causes him to voice the famous apostrophe:

> Was this the face that launched a thousand ships
> And burnt the topless towers of Ilium?

Helena (hel'ẹ.nạ). A Greek painter; daughter of the Egyptian Timon. She is said to have lived in the time of the battle of Issus, and to have painted a picture of that subject. This picture was hung by Vespasian in the Temple of Peace at Rome. The great Pompeian mosaic of the battle of Issus must have been made about this time, and is perhaps a copy of the picture.

Helena, Saint. b. c250; d. c330. The mother of Constantine the Great. She was, reputedly, the daughter of an innkeeper at Drepanum, in Bithynia, Asia Minor. She became the wife of Constantius Chlorus, who, on his elevation to the dignity of Caesar in 292, divorced her in order to marry Theodora, the stepdaughter of the Augustus (emperor) Maximianus Hercules. Subsequently, on the elevation to the purple of Constantine, her son, by Constantius, she received the title of Augusta and was treated with marked distinction. About 325 she made a pilgrimage to Jerusalem, where she built the Church of the Holy Sepulcher and that of the Nativity.

Helena. A tragedy (exhibited 412 B.C.) by Euripides.

Helena. In Shakespeare's *All's Well That Ends Well,* the heroine, who pursues the unwilling Bertram until she fulfills the conditions he has set for acknowledging her as his wife.

Helena. In Shakespeare's *Midsummer Night's Dream,* an Athenian maiden in love with Demetrius, who is himself in love with Hermia when the play opens. Puck accidentally contrives that both Demetrius and Lysander should fall in love with her, but at Oberon's instruction restores both lovers to their senses, and in the end Helena obtains Demetrius.

Helen, a Tale (hel'ẹn). The last novel by Maria Edgeworth, published in 1834.

Helena Landless (hel'ẹ.nạ land'lẹs). See **Landless, Helena.**

Helen Huntingdon (hel'ẹn hun'ting.dọn). See **Huntingdon, Helen.**

Helen of Kirkconnell (kėr.kon'ẹl). In Sir Walter Scott's *Border Minstrelsy,* a ballad telling the story of a courageous woman, loved by Adam Flemming, who died in shielding him from the bullets fired at him by a rival suitor. Wordsworth made this story the subject of his poem *Ellen Irwin.*

Helen Scrymgeour (skrim'jėr). See **Scrymgeour, (Mrs.) Helen.**

Helenus (hel'ẹ.nus). In Greek legend, a son of Priam and Hecuba, celebrated as a prophet. He, with his sister Cassandra, acquired the gift of prophecy as small children when, unbeknownst to them, serpents came and licked their ears. After the Trojan War Helenus became king of Epirus.

Helenus. In Shakespeare's *Troilus and Cressida,* a Trojan prophet, son of Priam. He favors giving Helen back to the Greeks.

Heliand (hā'lē.änd). An Old Saxon epic poem on the Saviour, written in alliterative verse by an unknown author between the years 822 and 840. It is a Christian poem with old Germanic heathen elements, and one of the important works of early Germanic literature.

Helias (hē'li.as). The Brabantine counterpart of Lohengrin, the Knight of the Swan.

Helicanus (hel.i.kā'nus). In Shakespeare's *Pericles,* the faithful minister of Pericles.

Helicon (hel'i.kon, -kọn). [Also: **Elikon, Helikon, Zagora.**] A mountain range in S central Greece, on the N shore of the Gulf of Corinth, ab. 50 mi. NW of Athens, celebrated in Greek mythology as the abode of Apollo and the Muses. It contained the fountains of Aganippe and Hippocrene. Peak elevation, ab. 5,738 ft.

Heliodorus (hē″li.ọ.dō′rus). b. at Emesa (modern Homs), Syria; fl. end of the 4th century. A Greek romance writer, later a Christian bishop of Tricca in Thessaly. He was the author of the earliest extant Greek romance, the *Aethiopica*.

Heliogabalus (hē″li.ō.gab′a.lus). See **Elagabalus**.

Helios (hē′li.os). In Greek mythology, the sun god (called Hyperion by Homer); son of the Titan Hyperion and the Titaness Theia; husband of Clymene; father of Aeetes and Circe. He was worshiped also as a god of herds and flocks. He is represented as a strong and beautiful youth, with heavy, waving locks and a crown of rays, driving a four-horse chariot, rising in the morning from the ocean on the east, driving across the heavens in his glowing car, and descending at evening into the western sea. At night, while asleep, he is borne along the northern edge of the earth in a golden boat or cup made by Hephaestus to his rising-place in the east. His son was Phaethon. In later times he was confused with Apollo because of his association with the sun. At Rhodes, the principal seat of his worship, stood his famous statue, the Colossus of Rhodes. The Romans identified him with their Sol.

Hellas (hel′as). A lyrical drama by Shelley, written in 1822 and published in 1824. It expresses the poet's sympathy with the Greek revolutionists in their struggle against the Turks.

Helle (hel′ē). In Greek legend, the daughter of Athamas and Nephele, drowned in the Hellespont (whence its name).

Hellen (hel′en). In Greek legend, the eponymous ancestor of the Hellenes, or Greeks. He was the son of Deucalion and Pyrrha, and father of Aeolus (founder of the Aeolians), and of Dorus (founder of the Dorians).

Hell Fire Clubs. Clubs consisting of reckless and unscrupulous men and women. Three such associations were suppressed at London in 1721. See also **Medmenham Abbey**.

Héloïse and Abélard (ā.lō.ēz′; à.bā.làr′). A novel by George Moore, published in 1921. This version of the famous story opens when Héloïse is ten years old and is put under the guardianship of Canon Fulbert of Notre Dame, her uncle. When she returns from school at a convent at the age of sixteen, she falls in love with Abélard, her tutor. They leave Paris with Madelon, a serving woman, and when their son is born, they return to Paris to be married. Later, mistakenly convinced that Abélard has been unfaithful to Héloïse, Fulbert hires a band of ruffians to seize and castrate him. The lovers then part forever, each turning to the life of the church.

Help (help). A character in Bunyan's *Pilgrim's Progress* who pulls Christian out of the Slough of Despond.

Helps (helps), Sir **Arthur.** b. at Streatham, Surrey, England, July 10, 1813; d. at London, March 7, 1875. An English historian. From June, 1860, he was clerk of the privy council, enjoying the special confidence of Queen Victoria. He is best known for his three series of social essays, *Friends in*

Council (1847–59), and for his various works on the early history of Spanish America, especially *The Spanish Conquest in America* (1855–61).

Helstone (hel′stōn), **Doctor Matthewson.** The rector of Briarfield in Charlotte Brontë's *Shirley*, an uncompromising and brusque, but upright and conscientious man.

Helvetia (hel.vē′sha). The Latin name of Switzerland, from the Helvetii, a Celtic people which in the time of Caesar occupied a district east of the Jura, north of the Lake of Geneva, and west and south of the Rhine. They were defeated by Caesar in 58 B.C., and thoroughly subjugated by Augustus in 15 B.C.

Helvétius (el.vā.syüs), **Claude Adrien.** b. at Paris, in January, 1715; d. Dec. 26, 1771. A French philosopher and littérateur. He published in 1758 a metaphysical work entitled *De l'esprit*, in which he derived all virtue from self-interest, and which was burned by the public hangman in 1759 by order of the Sorbonne. He made a journey to England in 1764, and in the following year was entertained by Frederick the Great (Frederick II of Prussia) at Potsdam. According to an apocryphal story it was on the occasion of the storm aroused by the publication of *De l'esprit* that Voltaire wrote to Helvétius the letter in which is supposed to appear the sentence: "I do not agree with a word that you say, but I will defend to the death your right to say it"; the letter, however, was the invention of one of Voltaire's biographers. His *Œuvres complètes* were published at Liége in 1774, since which time numerous other editions have appeared.

Helvius Cinna (hel′vi.us sin′a), **Gaius.** See under **Cinna.**

Hemans (hem′anz), **Felicia Dorothea.** [Maiden name, **Browne.**] b. at Liverpool, England, Sept. 25, 1793; d. near Dublin, May 16, 1835. An English poet, best known for her lyrics, including *Casabianca* (beginning "The boy stood on the burning deck"), *England's Dead*, *The Better Land*, *The Treasures of the Deep*, and *The Landing of the Pilgrim Fathers*. Among her other works are *The Vespers of Palermo* (1823) and *The Forest Sanctuary* (1826). Her *Poetical Works* were edited by W. M. Rossetti in 1873.

Heming (hem′ing), **John.** [Also, **Hemminge.**] b. at Shottery, England, c1556; d. at Aldermanbury, England, Oct. 10, 1630. An English actor. In 1593 he belonged to Strange's Men, a company of Elizabethan actors, and toured with Edward Alleyn. He probably joined the Lord Chamberlain's Men in 1594 and he seems to have been treasurer of the King's Men, later formed from the Lord Chamberlain's company. He played in the first part of *Henry IV*, and in Jonson's *Volpone, The Alchemist*, and several other of his plays. With Henry Condell he edited the first folio of Shakespeare in 1623. He was a quarter owner, apparently, of the Globe and Blackfriars theaters, and closely associated with Shakespeare, who mentions him in his will. This intimacy has been one of the reasons for accepting the 36 plays in the first folio as actually Shakespeare's.

Henchard (hench′ard), **Michael.** A principal character in Thomas Hardy's novel *The Mayor of Casterbridge*.

ḍ, d or j; ṣ, s or sh; ṭ, t or ch; ẓ, z or zh; o, F. cloche; ü, F. menu; čh, Sc. loch; ṅ, F. bonbon.

hendecasyllabic (hen″dek.ạ.si.lab′ik). In prosody, a term designating a line of 11 syllables, used originally by Catullus and in modern English literature by Tennyson.

Henderson (hen′dèr.sọn), **James.** b. in the north of England, c1783; d. at Madrid, Sept. 18, 1848. An English author. His principal work is *History of Brazil* (1821).

Henderson, Sir Nevile Meyrick. b. 1882; d. at London, Dec. 30, 1942. A British diplomat, known for his services in trying to maintain peace with Germany while serving (1937–39) as British ambassador to Berlin. A career diplomat, he had served at St. Petersburg (1905–08), Tokyo (1909–11), Rome (1914), Paris (1916), Constantinople (1921–24), and Belgrade (1929–35), and as ambassador to Argentina and minister to Paraguay (1935–37). Author of *Failure of a Mission* (1940), which seeks to explain the origin of World War II.

Henderson, Robert. See **Henryson, Robert.**

Hengist (heng′gist). [Also, **Hengest.**] d. 488. Chief of the Jutes, joint founder with Horsa of the kingdom of Kent. They landed (c449) at Ebbsfleet, and are accounted the first Germanic invaders of Britain. Some authorities have questioned their existence as historical personages.

Hengist, King of Kent. See **Mayor of Quinborough, The.**

Henleigh Mallinger Grandcourt (hen′li mal′in.jèr grand′kŏrt). See **Grandcourt, Henleigh Mallinger.**

Henley (hen′li), **John.** [Called **"Orator Henley."**] b. at Melton-Mowbray, England, Aug. 3, 1692; d. 1756. An English preacher, celebrated for his eccentricities. Pope, in the *Dunciad*, called him the "zany of his age."

Henley, William Ernest. b. at Gloucester, England, Aug. 23, 1849; d. at Woking, Surrey, England, July 11, 1903. An English poet, dramatist, and critic. He was educated at the Crypt Grammar School, in Gloucester, where he came under the influence of Thomas Edward Browne, the Manx poet. He passed examinations for Oxford, but was unable to attend. He was a close friend of R. L. Stevenson, who modeled Long John Silver in *Treasure Island* after Henley. He contributed to the *Encyclopaedia Britannica, Cornhill Magazine, Athenaeum, St. James's Gazette, Vanity Fair,* and the *Saturday Review;* edited *London,* a weekly, *Magazine of Art,* the *Scots* (later, the *National) Observer,* and the *New Review.* Author of *A Book of Verses* (1888), *Song of the Sword* (1892), *London Voluntaries* (1893), *For England's Sake* (1900), *Hawthorn and Lavender* (1901), and other volumes of poetry; and co-author, with Robert Louis Stevenson, of the plays *Deacon Brodie* (1892), *Beau Austin* (1892), *Admiral Guinea* (1892), and *Macaire* (1892). He wrote *Views and Reviews* (1890), critical essays, and edited *Lyra Heroica* (1892), an anthology of verse for boys, a *Book of English Prose* (1894), and, with John S. Farmer, the *Dictionary of Slang and Colloquial English* (17 vols., 1894–1904). As a poet he is popularly associated mainly with his famous *Invictus;* other characteristic poems are *The Blackbird, A Bowl of Roses, We'll Go No More A-Roving, Madam Life, Out of Tune,*

England, My England, and a series of poems *In Hospital* (1888), written during the 20 months he was a patient (1874) in an Edinburgh infirmary.

Henriade (äṅ.ryȧd). An epic poem (printed 1723) by Voltaire, in ten cantos. It is a picture of war undertaken in the name of religion, and was intended to inspire a hatred of intolerance and persecution.

Henrietta Petowker (hen.ri.et′ạ pẹ.tou′kèr). See **Petowker, Henrietta.**

Henriques (hen.rē′kẹs), **Robert (David Quixano).** b. at London, Dec. 11, 1905—. An English novelist. Author of *Death by Moonlight* (1938), *No Arms No Armour* (1939), *Captain Smith and Company* (1943; American title, *The Voice of the Trumpet), The Journey Home* (1944), and *Too Little Love* (1950).

Henry (hen′ri). Entries on literary characters having this prename will be found under the surnames Amundeville, Bailey, Bolingbroke, Clegg, Cranstoun, Crawford, Guildford, Higgins, Morton, Ryecroft, Smith, Warden, and Warrington.

Henry I. [Called **Henry Beauclerc** (bō′klȧr).] b. in England, probably in Yorkshire, 1068; d. in France, Dec. 1, 1135. King of England (1100–35); youngest son of William I (William the Conqueror) and Matilda of Flanders. He was well educated (hence his surname), perhaps because he was intended for the church. He became embroiled with his brothers, William II and Robert Curthose, Duke of Normandy, over his possessions in France, and made his peace with William but kept up a sporadic struggle with Robert until the latter left on the first Crusade in 1097. Henry was with William when the latter was mysteriously killed by an arrow while hunting. Henry immediately set out for Winchester, seized the royal treasure, and proclaimed himself king. He was accepted by the witan and crowned three days after William's death, the claims of Robert Curthose being overlooked entirely. Henry set about consolidating his position before Robert could act. In addition to the regular oath he took at his coronation, he issued a coronation charter, promising to recognize the baron's feudal rights and the privileges of the church; though he ignored this charter during his reign, it was later to be the basis of the claims of the barons during their struggle with John that led to the Magna Charta in 1215. He married (1100) Edith (renamed Matilda), daughter of Malcolm III of Scotland and a descendant of the Saxon kings of England, thus uniting the Normans with the older rulers of the country. He recalled Anselm, archbishop of Canterbury, who had been in exile since 1097 after a quarrel with William II over the investiture of the clergy. Anselm, during his stay on the Continent, had become even stronger in his opinions and refused to consecrate the bishops invested by Henry. In 1103 Anselm again left England, but, both sides desiring some solution to the problem, Henry met the archbishop in Normandy in 1105 and the two made their peace: the bishops would henceforth be invested with staff and ring by the clerical power but they would pay homage, as landholders and as feudal lords, to the crown. Since Henry continued to nominate the bishops, this solution, the first in a series that established clerical investiture in Europe, was a victory for him. Robert Curthose, who had been in Italy at the time of William's death, invaded England in 1101, but was bought off by Henry and returned to Normandy. Henry then invaded Normandy and at Tinchebrai in 1106 defeated the Normans. Robert gave up all claim to Normandy and for the rest of his life was a prisoner, though nominally free, in England. Robert's son, William Clito, disputed the right of Henry to Normandy and allied himself with Louis VI (Louis the Fat) of France. Two wars were fought over Normandy, in 1109–12 and 1116–20. These resulted, however, only in a better definition of the French boundary with Normandy. Henry chose his principal councilors well, creating nobles when he could. His principal adviser, Roger, bishop of Salisbury, who became chancellor and justiciar, was of humble birth. Under Henry the court of the exchequer was established as a separate unit to decide questions that arose during the collections of taxes; the circuit of justices about the kingdom (justices in eyre) became a regular event; the royal council became differentiated into more or less separate bodies with distinct duties. Henry was twice married: Matilda, his first wife, was the mother of William, who was lost at sea off France in 1120, and of another Matilda, who was married to both the Emperor Henry V (d. 1125) and to Geoffrey of Anjou, by whom she became the mother of Henry II of England. Henry expected that Matilda would succeed him, but the crown was usurped by Stephen. Henry's second marriage (1121) was to Adela, daughter of Godfrey VII, Count of Louvain, in hopes of male offspring after the death of William, but the marriage was childless.

Henry II. [Also **Henry of Anjou** (an'jö), **Henry Curtmantle** (kèrt'man''tl), **Henry Plantagenet** (plan.taj'e.net).] b. at Le Mans, Maine, France, March 25, 1133; d. at Chinon, Touraine, France, July 6, 1189. King of England (1154–89); son of Matilda, daughter of Henry I of England, and Geoffrey IV, Count of Anjou, her second husband. Henry was the founder of the Angevin (Plantagenet) line of English kings and ruled over an area that stretched from the Pyrenees to the Scottish border; his mother ceded to him in 1150 her claim to the English throne and her possessions in Normandy, his father's death in 1151 brought him Anjou, his marriage (1152) to Eleanor of Aquitaine (divorced wife of Louis VII of France) made him ruler of Aquitaine, Poitou, Guienne, and Gascony. In 1153, pursuing his mother's claim to the English throne, he invaded England and fought against Stephen. The death of Stephen's only son made the fighting unnecessary and at Wallingford in that year it was agreed that Stephen was to rule in England until his death and that Henry would be recognized as his heir. Stephen died the next year and Henry was crowned on Dec. 19, 1154. Henry made further attempts to extend his realm: he forced Scotland to acknowledge him as overlord; Brittany too became a vassal state, but he failed to conquer Toulouse in 1159 when Louis VII intervened. In 1170 he divided his domains among his sons: Henry became king of England and was given Normandy, Maine, and Anjou; Richard (Richard the Lionhearted) was given possession of

Aquitaine and his mother's other lands; Geoffrey was made overlord of Brittany; only John (hence called John Lackland) remained without a grant. These proved to be only nominal gifts, however; Henry retained actual control of his lands and their revenues. As a result, he faced, for the remainder of his reign, a series of revolts by his sons, who fought him and also battled among themselves; Eleanor, his queen, was a moving spirit behind the trouble, perhaps because of Henry's open infidelity with such mistresses as Rosamond Clifford (Fair Rosamond). John, who despite his lack of possessions was his father's favorite, was to be married in 1173 and Henry demanded certain castles of his son Henry as a wedding gift. Henry, Richard, and Geoffrey, aided by Scotland, France, and several of the discontented English barons, rose in revolt, but Henry subdued them; at Falaise in 1174 the sons were confirmed in their possessions, but John got the castles and the king of Scotland agreed to do homage to Henry. In 1183 the young Henry died and Richard was asked to give Aquitaine to John since he was to come into possession of England. Richard refused and had to fight John and Geoffrey. Geoffrey died in 1186 and the reshuffling of lands led to Richard's open warfare against his father. In 1189 Richard and Philip II of France defeated Henry; Henry signed the agreement at Colombières whereby he was to do homage to Philip and to agree that Richard was his heir. In addition, the names of those who had been treating traitorously with the other side were to be exchanged between the kings; Henry's discovery that John was one of those secretly in league with his enemies undoubtedly killed him.

Internal Affairs. Henry has been called by some historians the greatest of the English kings, and this reputation is due in part to his selection of his lieutenants. Richard de Lucy was chosen as his justiciar early in his reign, and among his other appointments was his choice of Thomas à Becket as chancellor in 1155. Thomas was an ardent supporter of the king and helped him to extend his power within and outside the realm. When in 1162 the archbishopric of Canterbury fell vacant, Henry, over Thomas's objections, appointed him to the post. Thomas immediately made it clear that he would not serve two masters and that, as an ecclesiastic, he would fight extensions of the royal power over clerical privileges. He resigned the chancellorship and, by various actions, brought the matter of church rights to a head. Henry convened a council at Clarendon which issued (1164) the Constitutions of Clarendon, limiting clerical power (for example, they eliminated appeal to Rome from royal decisions and placed in the civil courts the sentencing of those found guilty in clerical courts). Thomas's actions soon brought him fines for contempt and, further, led to a demand for an accounting of his chancellorship. He appealed to Rome, thus violating the Clarendon provision, and was adjudged guilty by a secular court. Thomas fled to France; his lands were confiscated, but he constantly held the threat of an interdict over Henry's head. After several meetings in France between the two, Thomas returned to England in 1170. There he suspended those who had taken part in the coronation of young Henry as king of England and excommunicated those who had taken over his property. Henry, then in France, flew into a rage when he heard of this and his remarks were taken as orders by four of his knights, who came to England and murdered Thomas on Dec. 29, 1170, at Canterbury. Becket, as symbol of resistance to a greedy monarchy, became a popular hero and martyr; Henry found it expedient to make a pilgrimage to the tomb of his former friend and to revoke most of the anticlerical provisions that had been adopted (though he later reinstated them); in particular, jurisdiction over ecclesiastical clerks went to the church's courts (benefit of clergy). One of Henry's discoveries as king was that much revenue could be obtained from the courts through the issuance of writs and the assignment of cases in which the crown had an interest (principally land cases) to the correct courts. He established (1178) the court of common pleas to take care of other cases. The jury system, whereby crimes were noted and tried by men rather than by ordeal, finds its roots in his reign. The power of the sheriffs was reduced. The teaching of Roman law, then undergoing a revival of interest on the Continent, was forbidden in England; instead, Henry established the common law as the English system. He regularized the circuits of the justices in eyre and increased their number. The power of the barons was reduced; the Inquest of Service (1166) instituted a check on the scutage (financial payment in place of actual military service) collected by the underlords and made certain that the barons withheld none of it from the king. Also, the barons were limited in the forces they could raise to those required by the king; excessive levies, made into private armies, were stopped. By the Assize of Arms (1181) all freedmen in the kingdom were required to maintain themselves as a militia according to their station in life. Henry also instituted (Saladin Tithe, 1188) the first tax on personal property in an effort to raise money for the third Crusade. Richard I (Richard the Lionhearted) succeeded him.

Henry III. b. at Winchester, England, Oct. 1, 1207; d. at Westminster, London, Nov. 16, 1272. King of England (1216–72); son of John and Isabella of Angoulême. He succeeded at the age of 9 years, under the regency of William Marshal, Earl of Pembroke. He pacified the barons by an immediate reissue of Magna Charta (again the next year), but his title was disputed by Louis, son of Philip of France, who had been chosen king by the barons opposed to John. The regent defeated Louis's army at Lincoln May 20, 1217, and compelled him to abandon his claim to the crown after having suffered the loss of his reinforcements in a naval battle off Dover, Aug. 24, 1217. After the death of Pembroke in 1219, the government was carried on by the justiciar Hubert de Burgh, supported by Stephen Langton, archbishop of Canterbury, until 1227, when Henry personally assumed the direction of affairs. After the failure of his invasion (1230) of Provence and Gascony, he dismissed (1232) de Burgh and came under the sway of Peter des Roches, bishop of Winchester, but the baronial party, when de Burgh was imprisoned for witchcraft (1233), rose and forced des Roches' dismissal and de Burgh's reinstatement to his lands. Henry's marriage (Jan. 14, 1236) to Eleanor of Provence

brought a still further influx of Frenchmen to the court and to high position. The feeling of the English nobility that they were being imposed on was further strengthened by Henry's subservience to the papal power, both in the collection of money and in the appointment of Italians to vacant English church positions. The opposition to Roman domination was led by Edmund Rich (exiled c1234) and Robert Grosseteste; the leaders of the baronial party were Simon de Montfort (originally one of the French nobles who came over in the train of Eleanor) and Roger Bigod. The dissatisfaction came to a head in 1257 when Henry demanded money to repay the pope for an unsuccessful war to capture the kingdom of Sicily; the throne was to go to Edmund, Henry's son, but the war failed; the king nevertheless asked for the money. The barons forced on the king the Provisions of Oxford (1258), whereby a permanent governing council was to be established to control the king's actions, the foreigners were to be dismissed, and money powers were to be in the hands of a committee. Under this government the Treaty of Paris (1260) was agreed to with France: England gave up claim to Normandy and Anjou; for such lands as the king still held in France he would do homage to the French king. Henry fought against the Provisions of Oxford; he and the barons agreed to permit the dispute to be arbitrated by Louis IX of France, and that monarch decreed in Henry's favor. He repudiated the Provisions, whereupon the barons rose in arms under Simon de Montfort and defeated the king at the battle of Lewes May 14, 1264. Henry was kept a virtual prisoner by Simon, who became actual ruler of the kingdom. But soon Simon's supporters among the barons began to suspect him of building his personal power at their expense and, when he turned to the Welsh for support in the face of coalitions against him, they rose against him. Led by Prince Edward (later Edward I) they crushed Simon's power, first at Kenilworth Aug. 1, 1265, then at Evesham Aug. 4, 1265, where de Montfort was killed. Henry was freed, but Edward now became virtual ruler; he reaffirmed Magna Charta and issued the Statute of Marlborough (1267) which embodied most of the barons' program. So secure was he that he went on a crusade, and he was absent from England when Henry died.

Henry III. See also under **Henry, Prince.**

Henry IV (of *England*). [Called **Henry of Bolingbroke, Henry of Lancaster.**] b. at the castle of Bolingbroke, near Spilsby, Lincolnshire, England, April 3, 1367; d. at Westminster, London, March 20, 1413. First king (1399–1413) of England of the house of Lancaster; son of John of Gaunt (fourth son of Edward III) and Blanche, heiress of Lancaster. His marriage (1380) to Mary de Bohun brought him the dukedom of Hereford in 1397, but it was as Earl of Derby that he was known in his early career. From 1390 to 1393 he was absent on a pilgrimage in the East, making a name for himself as a soldier and an accomplished knight. He fell victim to Richard II's struggle for supremacy over the nobility and was banished for ten years in 1398. John of Gaunt died in 1399 and Richard confiscated all the lands of Lancaster, contradicting a promise he had made to retain them for Henry. While the king was absent in Ireland, Henry landed in England in July, 1399, gathered to him many of the nobility, who hated Richard's usurpations, and took possession of the kingdom. Richard rushed back from Ireland but, deserted by his forces, fled to Wales, where he was captured. On Sept. 29, 1399, Richard resigned the throne, but Parliament gratuitously insulted him the next day by voting his abdication and proclaiming Henry king. An uprising by Richard's supporters early in 1400 was put down; the ex-king died, under mysterious circumstances, in prison on Feb. 14, 1400. Troubles with the Scots and the Welsh occupied much of Henry's time for the next years; the constant watch on the Percies of Northumberland took most of the rest of it. He had the support of the Percys against the Scots at Homildon Hill (September, 1402) but they felt that their services were poorly repaid and joined the forces of Owen Glendower, in revolt in Wales since 1400. They and other disaffected nobles gathered a great force and marched against the king. He met them at Shrewsbury (July 21, 1403) and routed them; Harry Percy (Hotspur) was killed, Thomas Percy, Earl of Worcester, was captured and executed, and Northumberland was forced to submit. In 1405 Henry put down two revolts; the second, as the result of which he executed Archbishop Scrope of York, was the more serious. In 1409 Prince Henry (later Henry V) ended the Glendower rebellion, soon after Northumberland was finally eliminated as a threat at Bramham Moor (February, 1408). Henry was now in failing health, attributed popularly to his execution of the cleric Scrope, and was too feeble to fight off the strong bid for power of Prince Henry and Thomas and Henry Beaufort. He summoned enough strength, however, in November, 1411, to dismiss Henry and reinstate his faithful chancellor, Thomas Arundel, archbishop of Canterbury. Henry's reign was marked by a scrupulous adherence to constitutional government and by a severe persecution of the Lollards (1401 *et seq.*). He married twice: by Mary de Bohun he had four sons (Henry V; Thomas, Duke of Clarence; John, Duke of Bedford; Humphrey, Duke of Gloucester) and two daughters (Blanche, wife of Louis III, elector palatine; Philippa, wife of Eric XIII of Sweden); by Joan, widow of the Duke of Brittany, whom he married in 1402, he had no children.

Henry IV (of *France*). [Also: **Henry of Navarre, Henry the Great;** French, **Henri.**] b. at Pau, France, Dec. 14, 1553; d. at Paris, May 14, 1610. King of France (1589–1610), first Bourbon king of France; son of Antoine de Bourbon, king of Navarre, and Jeanne d'Albret. Reared as a strict Calvinist, he became the head of the Huguenot party on the death of Louis, Prince de Condé, at the battle of Jarnac in 1569. He succeeded to the throne of Navarre as Henry III in 1572, and married Margaret of Valois, sister of Charles IX of France, at Paris, Aug. 18, 1572. Only by an abjuration of Calvinism did he escape the general massacre of his partisans inaugurated on the 24th (St. Bartholomew's Day), during the nuptial festivities. He was nevertheless kept prisoner until his escape (1575) after the death of Charles IX; he retracted his abjuration and put himself once more at the head of the Huguenots. The death of Francis,

Duc d'Anjou, in 1584 left him heir presumptive to the throne of France, but the Holy League refused to recognize his title, and proclaimed the cardinal Charles de Bourbon heir presumptive. War (known as the War of the Three Henrys: Henry III of France, Henry III of Navarre, Henry, Duke of Guise) broke out in consequence in 1585. His victory at Coutras (1587) ended the fighting. The cardinal was proclaimed king under the title of Charles X by the League on the assassination of Henry III in 1589 during the siege of Paris. Henry was forced to raise the siege, but after defeating the Leaguers under the Duke of Mayenne at Ivry on March 14, 1590, and taking Paris and Chartres, he permitted the League to destroy itself. Spain's ambitions in France became clear and when Henry embraced the Roman Catholic religion at St. Denis, July 25, 1593, he secured the general recognition of the Roman Catholics, and was crowned at Chartres, Feb. 27, 1594, although the war was still continued by the League in alliance with Spain. He published the Edict of Nantes on April 13, 1598, giving religious and some degree of civil liberty to the Protestants, and concluded the peace of Vervins with Spain and the League on May 2, 1598, which ended the so-called Wars of the Huguenots. He divorced the childless Margaret of Valois in 1599, and married Marie de' Medici in 1600. Henry's program was intended to speed recovery from the religious wars and to reëstablish the power of the monarchy; he reorganized the administration and its financial structure, encouraged agriculture, commerce, and industry, and set about creating a navy. His principal minister was the Duc de Sully. Expansion overseas, marked by trade agreements and attempts to colonize Canada under Champlain, were the highlights of his foreign policy. He was in constant rivalry with the Hapsburgs and was about to embark on a war with Austria over the succession in Cleves, Jülich, and Berg when he was assassinated by the Roman Catholic fanatic, François Ravaillac. Of his children, Louis XIII succeeded him, Gaston d'Orléans became an important military figure in the mid-century, Elizabeth married Philip IV of Spain, Christine married Victor Amadeus I of Savoy, and Henrietta married Charles I of England. He had several illegitimate children, notably by Gabrielle d'Estrées.

Henry IV (*Part One*). [Full title, **The First Part of King Henry the Fourth.**] A historical play by Shakespeare, first acted c1597 and printed in 1598. With *Henry IV* (*Part Two*) and *Henry V* it comprises a trilogy on the youth and young manhood of the victor at Agincourt, conceived of as the ideal of kingship by the ardently nationalistic English population of the Elizabethan period. However, the plays are usually taught, and always staged, as separate works; for purposes of quick identification the two parts of *Henry IV* are often referred to by Shakespeare scholars as "*1 Henry IV*" and "*2 Henry IV*," and the reader will find that this system of reference has been used throughout this book. Shakespeare's sources for both parts of *Henry IV*, and also for *Henry V*, were Holinshed's *Chronicles* and an older Elizabethan play entitled *The Famous Victories of Henry V.* In *1 Henry IV* we receive no inkling of the heights which Henry (here called Prince Hal) is eventually to reach; he is here overshadowed as a character by both Sir John Falstaff (one of Shakespeare's most richly human portraits, in the vein of broad comedy) and Hotspur (Harry Percy).

The Story. When Henry IV refuses to ransom Lady Percy's brother, Edmund Mortimer, rightful claimant to the throne, from his captor Owen Glendower, the Percys refuse to give their Scottish prisoners to Henry. Moreover, Henry Percy (nicknamed Hotspur), with his father, Northumberland, and his uncle, Worcester, determine to raise a rebellion against Henry with York, Glendower, Mortimer, and Douglas. Meanwhile Prince Hal, the young Prince of Wales, is amusing himself with carefree deviltry as the boon companion of Sir John Falstaff and his carousing friends; when the play opens they are laying their plans to rob a group of travelers. But Prince Hal and Poins arrange not to be present at the robbery so that they may be able to attack and put to flight Falstaff and his companions; this they are able to do easily, and without being recognized. The prank is revealed at the Boar's Head Tavern after Falstaff has given his exaggerated version of the adventure (from which Sir John emerges, by his own account, as a valiant warrior, afraid of no man), and much merriment ensues. Hal is now strongly rebuked by his father for his irresponsibility and is given part of the royal forces to lead against the rebels, who have, meanwhile, been arguing about how to divide the kingdom when they have captured it. At Shrewsbury, Hotspur and Douglas learn that they have been deserted by Northumberland and Glendower, but prepare nevertheless to meet the advancing royal army. Worcester does not deliver to his rebel allies the King's offer of peace terms, and in the following battle the rebels are severely defeated. Hal's conduct in the battle does not lack for valor (indeed, he is able to slay Hotspur), but one is not yet convinced that he has, or will ever have, the capacity for greatness (although a hint of his largeness of heart is revealed by his willingness to let Falstaff take the credit for killing Hotspur). In this play, taken by itself, Hotspur rather than Hal emerges as the personification of manly honor.

Henry IV (*Part Two*). [Full title, **The Second Part of King Henry the Fourth.**] A historical play by Shakespeare, first acted c1598 and printed in 1600. Shakespeare's sources for it were Holinshed's *Chronicles* and the earlier play *The Famous Victories of Henry V*, the same sources used for *1 Henry IV* and *Henry V* (with which this play may be taken to form a trilogy on the youth and young manhood of the victor at Agincourt). Most authorities now believe that Shakespeare wrote this play largely because of the tremendous welcome given by audiences to the character of Sir John Falstaff in *1 Henry IV* (most of the characters, and many of the situations, are carried over from that work), but Prince Hal has drawn away at the end from Falstaff and his cronies to assume the mantle of kingly responsibility, thus providing an explicit bridge in characterization between the carousing youth of *1 Henry IV* and the great king of *Henry V*. However, the popularity of Falstaff was too great for him to be utterly eliminated from future consideration, and the Epilogue to this play

promises another one which will include both Falstaff and Henry (thus creating a situation which troubles many people in their reading of the three plays about Henry V: as Henry attains greatness he must sacrifice his close friendship with Falstaff, and because Falstaff is one of the most irresistibly human of all of Shakespeare's characters this process is impossible without causing some people to feel Henry's kingly greatness was obtained at the expense of a true friendship, and that Henry was therefore perhaps more the king, but also less the man).

The Story. As the play opens, Westmoreland and Lancaster are preparing to lead an army against the remaining rebels. In London the King has commissioned Falstaff to go on the expedition to enlist soldiers en route. Prince Hal and Falstaff finally leave their friends at the Boar's Head Tavern and set out for the north. In Gloucester, at the home of Justice Shallow, Falstaff allows recruits to buy themselves off and enlists only a few poor and ragged men. Northumberland again deserts the rebels, and York, Mowbray, Hastings, and the others face the royal forces with a low morale. Lancaster tricks them into disbanding by promising to redress their wrongs, and then has them executed. The King is too sick and weary of his duties to rejoice over the defeat of the rebels, but he indicates before he dies that he now has confidence in his son (a confidence which Hal demonstrates not to have been misplaced by the tone of his speeches in the last scene of the play). Hearing that Hal is now Henry V, Falstaff hurries to London, but is there coldly rejected by the new King.

Henry IV. See also under **Bolingbroke, Henry.**

Henry V. b. at Monmouth (at that time in Wales), probably Aug. 9, 1387; d. at Vincennes, France, Aug. 31, 1422. King of England (1413–22); son of Henry IV and Mary, daughter of Humphrey de Bohun, Earl of Hereford. He came to responsibility early and when not yet 16 was commander of the royal forces at Shrewsbury against the Percies; an unfounded legend says that he personally killed Harry Percy (Hotspur) at that battle. In the later years of the reign of his father he was prominent in the council, but his insistence on a rapprochement with Burgundy led to his dismissal in 1411. He succeeded to the throne on March 20, 1413, and immediately set about arranging matters to secure domestic peace, among other things restoring those who had lost their titles or lands. In 1415, a plot by Richard, Earl of Cambridge, to make the Earl of March king was discovered; Cambridge was executed. The rebellious Lollards were a more difficult matter, but he firmly enforced the anti-Lollard statute *De Heretico Comburendo* of 1401, Sir John Oldcastle being one of those burned (1417) for his part in the revolt of 20,000 Lollards in 1414. Under Henry's rule constitutional government made further advances: the consent of Parliament to a law was made necessary for its validity and Parliament obtained the right to draft bills without amendment; the privy council became a permanent body. Henry now decided to embark on a career of reconquest in France, principally because of French support of the Welsh during Glendower's rebellion during his father's reign, but also, according to some historians, to divert attention from domestic complaints. He crossed to France in 1415, besieged and took Harfleur, and marched on Calais. At Agincourt, his army of 13,000, thinned by disease, was faced by 50,000 French; on Oct. 25, 1415, St. Crispin's Day, the battle was fought; the French were routed with great loss, and Henry continued on to Calais. He returned almost at once to England. In 1416 he made alliances with Burgundy and with the Emperor Sigismund; the latter treaty led to the ending of the Western Schism in the church with the election in 1417 of Martin V as pope. In 1417, having completed preparations, Henry again crossed the Channel. He took Caen and besieged Rouen; most of Normandy fell into his hands, and after the fall of Rouen in 1419 his army approached Paris. The French diplomatic picture was quite complex, but with the murder of the Duke of Burgundy by the Dauphin's men in September, 1419, the way was clear for Henry's success. He played one party against the other, made himself master of the situation, and, by the Treaty of Troyes (May 21, 1420), attained his principal aims. He was to marry Catherine of Valois, daughter of Charles VI of France; he would serve as regent for the insane king; and he was to be the king's heir, the Dauphin being specifically excluded. On June 2, he married Catherine; in December he made a triumphal entry into Paris. He returned with his queen to England to have her crowned and to have the treaty ratified, but in his absence a revolt occurred in Normandy and the Duke of Clarence was defeated by the Dauphin's forces at Baugé in Anjou. Henry returned to France and, while besieging Meaux (1421–22), weakened his health and died the following summer. He was succeeded by his nine-months-old son Henry VI. Henry is often considered the ideal knightly king, and he modeled himself deliberately in the image of King Arthur and Godfrey of Bouillon. He is said on doubtful authority to have been wild and dissolute in his youth (probably a story spread by prejudiced religious controversialists who disliked his friendship with the Lollard Oldcastle), and is so represented by Shakespeare; but Shakespeare took him as the model king and as the culmination of English greatness before Elizabeth.

Henry V. [Full title, **The Famous Victories of Henry V.**] An anonymous historical play (1588) acted by Queen Elizabeth's Company. Apparently Shakespeare took the names of Sir John Oldcastle and Gadshill and the character of Prince Henry from this play for his *Henry IV* and *Henry V.* (Oldcastle was later changed to Falstaff upon a protest from a descendant.) It has been argued also that this play is really a cut version of Shakespeare's plays.

Henry V. [Full title, **The Life of King Henry the Fifth.**] A historical play by Shakespeare, first acted before 1600 (it may have been the first play in the new Globe theater), printed in 1600 in an incomplete pirated edition, and included in the folio of 1623, where there is a fair text (which Dover Wilson believes to be from Shakespeare's manuscript). The material for the wooing scenes was taken from *The Famous Victories of Henry V;* it is based on Holinshed's *Chronicles* for historical events. The play is one of the few that can be dated exactly as to its composition, this being between March and September, 1599, from a reference to the Earl of Essex's expedition to Ireland in the Chorus to Act V. With *1 Henry IV* and *2 Henry IV* it comprises a trilogy on the youth and young manhood of the victor at Agincourt. Here we see Hal grown into the mighty king, having cast off completely the carousing companions and devil-may-care manners of his youth. Falstaff appears not at all; his death is announced briefly at an early point in the development of the plot.

The Story. Henry V, supported in his claim to the throne of France by the arguments of the Archbishop of Canterbury, and angered by the insulting gift of tennis balls from the French Dauphin (a gift meant to underline the fact of Henry's youthful follies), sets forth to invade France. Before he leaves he discovers the conspiracy of Grey, Scroop, and Cambridge, and orders their execution. At the Boar's Head Tavern, Mistress Quickly describes the death of Falstaff, and his old cronies (Pistol, Nym, and Bardolph) thereupon enlist in the army. Henry captures Harfleur and proceeds to face a much larger French army at Agincourt. The evening before the battle, the King, disguised as a common soldier, mingles in the ranks. The English are victorious on the following day, and in the Treaty of Troyes, Henry wins the hand of the Princess Katherine and the promise of the French throne upon the death of the French king then reigning.

Henry VI. b. at Windsor, England, Dec. 6, 1421; d. at London, May 21, 1471. King of England (1422–61 and 1470–71); son of Henry V and Catherine of Valois. By the Treaty of Troyes (1420), Henry V became heir to the French throne; when he and his father-in-law, Charles VI of France, died within a few months of each other, the infant Henry VI inherited both kingdoms under the treaty. He was opposed by Charles's son, the Dauphin (later Charles VII), in France. He succeeded to the English throne at the age of not quite nine months, under the protectorship of his uncle John, Duke of Bedford, the protectorship being exercised in England by Bedford's brother Humphrey, Duke of Gloucester, during Bedford's absence as regent in France. There Bedford continued the prosecution of the Hundred Years' War, moving as far as the Loire, where in 1428 Orléans was besieged. But in 1429 Joan of Arc came to the aid of the French king, drove the English from their positions around the city, and began the long retreat of the English from France. Charles continued on to Reims, where he was crowned king in 1429. Henry's holdings in France (despite his coronation as king of France at Paris in 1431) slowly shrank until, in 1453, the English retained nothing but Calais. Bedford died in 1435, but even before that Gloucester's rule at home was complicated by the control of the council by the Beauforts, opposed to his policies. When Henry was declared of age in 1437, control of the government passed into the hands of the Beauforts, especially Henry Beaufort (Cardinal Beaufort), and of William de la Pole, Duke of Suffolk. Gloucester was aided by Richard, Duke of York, the king's cousin and nearest kinsman, but Henry's preference lay in the Beaufort party. Suffolk arranged the king's marriage (April 22, 1445) with Margaret of Anjou, daughter of the titular king of Naples and Jerusalem and duke of Lorraine; their only son, Edward, was born in 1453. When both Gloucester and Beaufort died in 1447, Suffolk became leader of the king's party and York, leader of the opposition to Suffolk, was sent to Ireland as governor. The steady collapse of the French war (in which the English were now under the leadership of Edmund Beaufort) led to Suffolk's removal in 1450; he was banished by the king, but his ship was stopped off Dover and he was executed (probably by York's orders). Popular discontent reached a climax in 1450 in Cade's rebellion; London was taken by the rebels but they were persuaded to return to their homes. York now returned from Ireland and demanded that he be named heir presumptive, but Parliament refused his claim. In 1453 Henry became insane, the first of a series of attacks of insanity that may be traceable to his grandfather Charles VI of France. A contest for the regency ensued between Queen Margaret (supported by Edmund Beaufort, Duke of Somerset) and the Duke of York. The council named York regent and in 1454 protector of the infant Prince Edward. Henry regained his sanity in 1455 and dismissed York. The latter then laid claim to the throne: Henry's claim was as a descendant of John of Gaunt, fourth son of Edward III; York's mother, however, was descended from Lionel, Duke of Clarence, Edward III's third son. Though York's claim was strong, Henry's father, and his father before him, had reigned and received homage, as had Henry. The factions resorted to arms; York obtained the aid of Richard Neville, Earl of Warwick; the king's party (called Lancastrian because of his descent from John of Gaunt, Duke of Lancaster) was led by Margaret and Somerset. Somerset was killed in the battle of St. Albans (May 22, 1455) and for four years a truce was maintained, York again being regent during another of Henry's spells of insanity (from 1455). Sane again, Henry dismissed York, who was defeated at Ludlow in 1459; York escaped to Ireland, Warwick to France. They returned in 1460 and captured the king at Northampton (July 10, 1460). York was declared heir to the throne, but Margaret, fighting for her son's rights, struck back. York was killed at Wakefield (Dec. 29, 1460) and Warwick was defeated at the second battle of St. Albans (Feb. 17, 1461). York's son Edward, Earl of March, took the field against the Lancastrians and, after defeating them at Mortimer's Cross, had himself crowned king (February, 1461) at London as Edward IV. The decisive battle of the Wars of the Roses was fought at Towton on March 29, 1461; the Lancastrians were routed, Margaret fled to France, and Henry took refuge in Scotland. He made an attempt to invade England in 1464 and was captured in 1465 and imprisoned. Warwick, who had turned against the Yorkists, allied himself with Margaret in France and in 1470 returned to England. Henry was restored, but Warwick was slain at the battle of Barnet and Margaret's army was defeated at Tewkesbury (May 4, 1471), where Edward, Henry's son, was killed. Henry died in the Tower soon afterwards, probably murdered.

Henry VI (*Part One*). [Full title, **The First Part of King Henry the Sixth.**] A historical play attributed to Shakespeare, written between 1589 and 1591, and first acted on March 3, 1592 (if Henslowe's reference in his diary entry of that date to a performance of "Harry the VI" is taken to apply to this play). The greatest part of the work (which appears in the folio of 1623) is almost certainly Shakespeare's, but it is now generally conceded that some portions (perhaps most notably the French scenes) were written by another. For purposes of quick identification, this and the other two parts of *Henry VI* are often referred to by Shakespeare scholars as "*1 Henry VI*," "*2 Henry VI*," and "*3 Henry VI*," and the reader will find that this system of reference has been used throughout this book. The three plays can hardly be viewed as a trilogy (and are thus contrasted to *1 Henry IV*, *2 Henry IV*, and *Henry V*), but there is a consistent theme: that punishment is being visited upon Henry VI as the heir in the third generation of the usurper, Henry IV, and this punishment is climaxed when Henry VI is overthrown in favor of Edward IV. Shakespeare's sources were probably the chroniclers Holinshed, Fabyan, and Hall.

The Story. The play begins with the death of Henry V and the accession of the boy king Henry VI to the throne. With the strong hand of Henry V no longer controlling the realm, dissension immediately breaks out between the great nobles, particularly between Gloucester and Winchester, and between the factions of York and Lancaster (thus portending the Wars of the Roses). The English domain in France fares worst of all: Orleans is relieved and the English are driven steadily back toward the coast by the French under Joan of Arc (here portrayed, not unnaturally from the English point of view, as a whore and a witch) Talbot, who meets his death during the course of the play, is the only really powerful figure on the English side, and the play comes to an end as Henry prepares to enter upon marriage with Margaret of Anjou in an effort to bolster the crumbling fortunes of his realm.

Henry VI (*Part Two*). [Full title, **The Second Part of King Henry the Sixth.**] A historical play attributed to Shakespeare, written between 1589 and 1591 and published in 1594. The date of first performance is not known, but the play appears in the folio of 1623. Its original title was *The First Part of the Contention betwixt the two Famous Houses of York and Lancaster. . . .* As with *1 Henry VI* and *3 Henry VI*, controversy has existed as to the matter of Shakespeare's authorship, Marlowe, Greene, Kyd, Lodge, and even Nash being mentioned as the authors of greater or lesser portions of the work. The sources were the same as for *1 Henry VI* (Holinshed, Fabyan, and Hall), with the addition somewhat conjecturally of Stow and Grafton.

The Story. The marriage of Henry to Margaret of Anjou has worsened rather than helped Henry's position in England; it has added Gloucester's resentment at the cession of Maine and Anjou as the price of the marriage to Henry's other troubles, and added no equivalent stabilizing factor to his rule. Margaret, supported by York and Suffolk, intrigues against Gloucester, contriving first to have the Duchess of Gloucester arrested as a sorceress, and finally securing the murder of Gloucester himself. Various other historical events, including the uprising under Jack Cade and the banishment of Suffolk, Margaret's lover, are also brought into the action of the play. At the end, the York-Lancaster dissension culminates in the initial struggle of the Wars of the Roses; the play ends with the death of Somerset in 1455 at the Battle of St. Albans.

Henry VI (*Part Three*). [Full title, **The Third Part of King Henry the Sixth.**] A historical play attributed to Shakespeare, written between 1589 and 1591 and published in 1595. It was first performed sometime before September, 1592, and appears in the folio of 1623. Its original title was *The true Tragedie of Richard Duke of York, and the Death of Good King Henry the Sixt* . . . (it was reprinted, under this title, with *2 Henry VI* under its original title, in 1619 as the second half of a two-part work entitled *The Whole Contention betweene . . . Lancaster and Yorke . . .*), and the amount of Shakespeare's contribution to it is as conjectural as it is with *1 Henry VI* and *2 Henry VI*. Indeed, it was long thought, on a basis of Greene's sharp remark in *A Groatsworth of Wit* about an "upstart Crow beautified with our feathers," that Shakespeare had stolen all or most of *2 Henry VI* and *3 Henry VI*, but most authorities now believe that Greene was here simply venting his spleen at Shakespeare as an upstart, without intending a charge of plagiarism in addition. Whoever may have shared in the work with Shakespeare, however, the sources used were the same as for *2 Henry VI* (Holinshed, Fabyan, Hall, and possibly also Stow and Grafton).

The Story. Henry yields the succession to the throne to York, whereupon Queen Margaret, furious that her son should be disinherited, seeks (with the help of Clifford) to resolve the matter on the field of battle. At Wakefield, she is victorious; York himself is captured, and subsequently killed. But York's sons Edward (who is to rule England as Edward IV) and Richard (who is also to rule England, as Richard III) vanquish Margaret and the Lancastrians at Towton, capturing Henry himself (now only a figurehead in the affairs of the kingdom) and enabling the crowning of Edward as king. But the matter is not yet settled; dissension within the Yorkist ranks makes further fighting inevitable, and the throne remains in dispute until the Lancastrian faction is finally defeated at Tewkesbury, Margaret's son is slain, and Richard ruthlessly murders Edward VI.

Henry VII. [Frequently called **Henry Tudor** (tū′dọr); before his accession known as the Earl of **Richmond** (rich′mọnd).] b. Jan. 28, 1457; d. at Richmond, near London, April 21, 1509. King of England (1485–1509), the first of the Tudor line. He became head of the house of Lancaster on the death of Henry VI in the Tower of London in 1471, and, as an object of jealousy as the principal Lancastrian to the kings of the house of York (Edward IV and Richard III), spent the years from 1471 to 1485 in exile, chiefly in Brittany. He was to have joined in Buckingham's rebellion of 1483, but storms prevented his landing in England and

Buckingham was defeated. Encouraged by desertions, especially those of Yorkists, from Richard III's tyranny, in 1485 he effected a landing in England, and having gained the victory at Bosworth Field, Aug. 22, 1485, in which King Richard was killed, was crowned king Oct. 30, 1485. Henry VII traced his descent on his mother's side back to John of Gaunt, Duke of Lancaster, fourth son of Edward III; his father, Edmund Tudor, Earl of Richmond, was the son of Owen Tudor and Catherine of Valois, widow of Henry V of England. When Henry married (Jan. 18, 1486) Elizabeth, eldest daughter of Edward IV, he united in his own person the titles of the houses of Lancaster and York. Edward's brothers being dead (George, Duke of Clarence, murdered in 1478, and Richard III dying at Bosworth) and his sons (Edward V and Richard, Duke of York) being slain in the Tower, Henry Tudor stood as undeniably having the best claim to the throne. He immediately arrested Edward, Earl of Warwick, son of the Duke of Clarence, and imprisoned him in the Tower. But in 1487 an impostor, Lambert Simnel, claiming to be Warwick, landed in England, backed by John de la Pole, Earl of Lincoln, who had been chosen heir presumptive by Richard III. Henry exposed the imposture by bringing Warwick from the Tower to show that he was still a prisoner, and then marched against Simnel and Lincoln. At Stoke-upon-Trent (June 16, 1487) Lincoln was killed and Simnel defeated. Simnel was later pardoned and ended his career as a scullion in the king's kitchen. In 1488 another impostor, a Fleming named Perkin Warbeck, began visiting European courts, pretending to be Richard, Duke of York, the son of Edward IV who had been murdered in the Tower on Richard III's orders. Warbeck was turned out of several countries, either because his claim was patently foolish or because Henry made strong diplomatic protests. He finally obtained the aid of James IV of Scotland and landed in Cornwall in 1497, proclaiming himself Richard IV. He was soon captured and put in the Tower. There his active mind conceived a plan of escape that included Warwick but, the plot being discovered soon after another attempt to impersonate Warwick had been made in London, Henry had both Warbeck and Warwick executed in 1499. In the early years of his reign Henry faced almost continual revolts, but no really serious rebellion occurred until 1497. Then, in protest against taxation for a war against Scotland, the men of Cornwall, led by Thomas Flammock (or Flamank), who was subsequently joined by James Touchet, Baron Audley, marched across England to Blackheath, near London. The king's forces easily defeated them there on June 17; the leaders were executed and their followers were sent home. Henry's policy was to avoid war and to build up the internal economy and the royal treasury. He invaded France briefly in 1492 to protest forcibly against the destruction of Brittany's independence by Charles VIII, who had married Anne, Duchess of Brittany, but accepted the Peace of Étaples (Nov. 9, 1492) which gave him 750,000 crowns as an indemnity. The incipient trouble with Scotland, due to Scotland's adherence to France and to James IV's support of Perkin Warbeck, was calmed by the suppression of Warbeck's rebellion, and in 1502 by the marriage of Margaret, Henry's eldest daughter, to James. His eldest son, Arthur, married Catherine of Aragon on Nov. 15, 1501; Arthur died on April 2, 1502, and Henry, wishing to preserve the Spanish connection, made several attempts to match Catherine again, including himself as a suitor after the death of Elizabeth of York in 1503; Catherine eventually married Arthur's younger brother Henry, after the latter ascended the throne as Henry VIII, the marriage being perhaps the most fateful in English history. Another of Henry's daughters, Mary, married Louis XII of France in 1514. Henry established his monarchy as an absolute rule, though outwardly maintaining the limitations on his powers established in the preceding 270 years. He put his trust in able men, regardless of their status, raising them to the nobility where necessary, and, by making them dependent on him, controlled them absolutely. His council, sitting in the Star Chamber, became the supreme court of the land (and a lucrative one in fees), and its powers were strengthened by statutes passed by subservient parliaments giving it great scope. Laws were passed controlling the economic life of the nation; exports of unfinished cloth were forbidden, for example, and wages and prices were made subject to law. In 1496 the Intercursus Magnus, a commercial treaty fixing duties and providing for reciprocal privileges, was negotiated with the Flemish. Henry reëstablished ancient taxes and fees where he could, and saw to it that they were collected. He himself checked the accounts of the treasury (to which he diverted much of the business of the exchequer) and obtained the reputation of being extremely tight-fisted. Typical of his financial maneuvers was the call for a war subsidy against France and the retention of the subsidies when no war developed. "Morton's fork," named for John Morton, his chancellor, was a typical tax scheme: those who lived well paid a tax because they obviously could afford one; those who lived less sumptuously also paid because they obviously saved money through their economies. But Henry's taxation caused great hatred for his tax collectors, and early in his son's reign the principal collectors, Richard Empson and Edmund Dudley, were executed on a trumped-up charge of treason. Henry's reign also saw the passage of Poynings' Law (the Statute of Drogheda, 1495) which made Ireland a vassal state under the English crown. Henry's enforcement of the Statute of Liveries eventually broke down the private armies of retainers maintained by the nobility; the severe fines and other punishments made the royal military force paramount in the nation and permitted economies in the military budget. Henry's reign is notable as the period when English overseas exploration began (Cabot's voyages of 1496 and later) and when the New Learning came to England (John Colet's lectures at Oxford, 1496–1504).

Henry VII. See also under **Richmond, Henry Tudor, Earl of.**

Henry VIII. b. at Greenwich (now part of London), June 28, 1491; d. at Westminster, London, Jan. 28, 1547. King of England (1509–47); second and only surviving son of Henry VII and Elizabeth of York.

Well educated in the New Learning by such teachers as poet laureate John Skelton, he had great respect for scholarship and was himself an accomplished linguist, a poet, and a musician on lute, organ, and harpsichord; he was also a fine horseman, swordsman, runner, and wrestler, all accomplishments that led to his early popularity. After the death of his older brother Arthur, he became (1503) Prince of Wales. He succeeded his father on April 22, 1509, and on June 3 married his betrothed, Catherine of Aragon, widow of his brother, for which marriage negotiations had been proceeding, principally concerned with her dowry, for some five years.

Foreign Policy. Where Henry VII had avoided foreign adventures, Henry VIII entered freely into European politics, at first through the interests of Thomas Wolsey, who by 1511 had become his principal adviser, and later through his own desires and ambitions. In 1515 Francis I became king of France; in 1516 Charles I attained the Spanish throne and in 1519, as Charles V, became Holy Roman Emperor. European politics of the next 40 years revolved about the struggles for power of these kings, and Henry sought to keep the balance of power in his hand. In 1511 he joined the Holy League, with Ferdinand of Aragon, the Republic of Venice, and the Pope, against the French. The English navy under the Howards won several victories in 1511, and when in 1513 the emperor Maximilian I joined the League Henry crossed to France to join him and to take personal charge of his army. With Maximilian he won the victory of Guinegate (called the Battle of the Spurs) on Aug. 16, 1513. During his absence in France, James IV of Scotland, an ally of France, invaded England and was defeated and killed by the English under Thomas Howard, Earl of Surrey, at Flodden, on Sept. 9, 1513. France made peace in 1514, giving up Touraine to the English; in 1518 the French bought it back for 600,000 crowns. The election of Charles V as emperor in 1519 led to a series of negotiations by both France and Spain with Henry: Charles came to Kent in 1520 to confer and on June 7, 1520, Henry met Francis outside Calais at the Field of the Cloth of Gold, a magnificent but futile parley with all the trappings of a departed feudalism. The result of the conferences, after a further interview with Charles, was an alliance with the emperor (according to some because Wolsey desired the emperor's support in his candidacy for the papacy, but neither in 1522 nor in 1523 was his election forthcoming). The tremendous sum left to Henry by his father had been used up in the French war and in the subsequent diplomatic maneuvers; Parliament refused to give more money to Wolsey and a forced loan brought practically nothing into the treasury. Henry was shackled by lack of funds and was unable to participate in the events that brought matters in Europe to a climax. Francis was captured by the emperor at Pavia in 1525 and after the subsequent sack of Rome (1527) by the emperor's troops Henry was excluded even from the making of the Treaty of Cambrai in 1529. Henry did make an attempt to ally himself with France, signing (Aug. 30, 1525) a treaty of alliance, but he could not support the alliance. Charles V was now master of Italy (therefore also of Rome), and, although opposed by Francis, still the most powerful ruler in Europe. The tremendous upset resulting when Henry attempted to divorce Catherine led to Wolsey's downfall. Thomas Cromwell now became the king's chief adviser and, following Henry's break with the Roman Catholic Church, saw quite clearly the danger of a coalition against, and an invasion of, England. He therefore suggested and arranged a marriage with Anne of Cleves, daughter of the principal Protestant prince of Europe. The marriage took place in January, 1540, but the king now had a two-year-old son and did not care at all for his German bride. They were divorced in June, and Cromwell, caught in a court cabal, was executed almost immediately. In 1542 Henry proclaimed Ireland a kingdom and reasserted England's old claim to Scottish submission. War between Scotland and England resulted and at Solway Moss (Nov. 25, 1542) James V of Scotland was defeated. James died on December 14, and Mary Queen of Scots, then a week old, succeeded. Henry thereupon proposed that the new Scottish queen and his son Edward be married; the Scots refused the proposition and Henry turned to Charles V for an alliance. He sent (1544) troops into Scotland to punish the regent for his refusal of the suit, and in 1545 took Boulogne, but he received no support from the emperor and was forced to make peace with Francis. Henry's foreign policy, apart from its resulting in a strong English navy, was a failure. He had dissipated his father's fortune in fruitless adventures and England, instead of becoming the power on the Continent he had wished it to be, was of little consequence in the Continental struggle for power. Calais alone still remained in English hands, but so weak was England that in ten years Calais would be lost.

The Reformation. Henry's marriage to Catherine of Aragon had required a papal dispensation, one about which both the pope and the archbishop of Canterbury had had doubts at the time. When, in the course of years, Catherine had a long series of miscarriages, there was talk, in 1514, of a dissolution of the marriage; but the accession of Francis I in France brought closer ties with Spain and the matter was dropped. Catherine bore a daughter in 1516, the future queen Mary I, but again the miscarriages began. Henry, knowing he was not at fault, earnestly desired a son; were he to die leaving only a daughter, the civil strife that had plagued England in the Wars of the Roses in his father's time might again break out. He had a son, Henry Fitzroy, born illegitimately in 1519 to Elizabeth Blount, but he wanted an heir, and as time passed he became determined to have one. He was a firm adherent of the Church of Rome; his book *Assertio septem sacramentorum contra M. Lutherum* (1521) a vigorous defense of the sacraments against Luther's doctrines, had won for him the title of Defender of the Faith (Fidei Defensor) from Pope Leo X. But his position as head of the English nation was paramount in his thoughts and in 1527 he began proceedings for a divorce from the 42-year-old Catherine, alleging the invalidity of the marriage with a deceased brother's wife, despite the papal dispensation. How large a part Henry's desire for Anne Boleyn played in his decision to divorce Catherine is conjectural; it is certain that unless they married their children could not inherit and that she conducted the affair very cleverly. Pope Clement VII, well aware of the immediate power of the emperor, whose niece Mary would become illegitimate if the marriage with Catherine were annulled, and of the distance separating him from England, temporized. He appointed (1528) a commission to sit in England, composed of Wolsey, appointed papal legate for the purpose, and Lorenzo Campeggio, bishop of Salisbury, the regular papal legate, to hear and decide on the case; but in 1529, Campeggio having delayed a decision on papal orders, the case was called to Rome for hearing. Wolsey was very shortly dismissed and Cranmer was put in charge of the negotiations. Cranmer traveled in Europe, parleying with Charles V and obtaining opinions from scholars on the question. Henry gathered opinions from various English and foreign universities, and with these opinions to back him, Cranmer held that the marriage was invalid and that the pope had been incompetent to grant a dispensation. Anne Boleyn was carrying Henry's child, and the marriage had to be arranged quickly. Cranmer secretly performed the ceremony on Jan. 25, 1533, and on May 23, as archbishop of Canterbury since March, declared the marriage with Catherine void and that with Anne Boleyn valid (May 28, 1533). Elizabeth, the future queen, born on Sept. 7, 1533, was thus legitimatized. Meanwhile Henry had been carrying on a war of nerves with the pope. He convoked Parliament in November, 1529, and with his new chancellor, Thomas More, as speaker, worked on the anticlerical feelings of the assembly. Acts limiting the power of the clergy were passed, including one, in 1532, reducing the annates paid to Rome to five percent. At the same time he fined (1531) the convocations of the clergy at Canterbury and York 119,000 pounds under the same statute of praemunire (acting on papal authority without the king's consent) under which he had ruined Wolsey. This submission of the English clergy was anything but acceptable to the pope; in September, 1533, he excommunicated Henry. Earlier in 1533 the king had had passed an act whereby spiritual appeals had to be made to Canterbury or to the king; in 1534 a group of 32 religious bills were passed by Parliament, which among other things cut Rome off from English revenue, declared that episcopal and archiepiscopal offices were to be filled by royal nomination and election by chapters, authorized an oath to the crown before consecration, established dispensations in the hands of the archbishop of Canterbury, and gave the king control of canons. The Act of Supremacy, at the end of the same year, appointed the king (and his successors) protector and only supreme head of the church and clergy of England. In addition to the clerical acts, Parliament passed an act of succession, declaring the children of Henry's second marriage heirs to the throne and requiring an oath to uphold the succession, on pain of conviction of treason, from all subjects. Both Thomas More, the chancellor, and John Fisher, bishop of Rochester, refused to take the oath, and in 1535 both were beheaded. At the instance of his new adviser, Thomas Cromwell, who was made vicar general or vicegerent of the king in matters ecclesiastical in 1535, Henry first

d̦, d or j; ş, s or sh; ţ, t or ch; z̧, z or zh; o, F. cloche; ü, F. menu; c̆h, Sc. loch; ń, F. bonbon.

suppressed the smaller (1536) and afterward the larger (1539) monasteries, whose property was confiscated. Most of the land was later sold for revenue; the precious metal and jewelry were kept by the crown; the buildings and libraries were in many instances destroyed. This revolution in the religious life of the country was not to pass without protest; in 1536 occurred the Pilgrimage of Grace, an uprising of Roman Catholics in the north of England. They forced Cromwell's men to stop their depredations, but, after they dispersed, their leaders were tried and executed. In 1535 Coverdale's Bible and in 1539 the Great Bible, its successor, were printed, in English. The Ten Articles of Faith, put forth in convocation in 1536, contained far too much of Protestantism for Henry, and in 1539 he procured the enactment of the Statute of Six Articles, a definition of heresy that adhered closely to Roman Catholic doctrine. But this could not hold back the flood he had released, and the Reformation flowed on to its full tide under his successors.

Internal Events. Henry's marriage to Anne Boleyn ended on May 19, 1536, when she was executed for adultery. The next day he was married for the third time, to Jane Seymour. Elizabeth, daughter of Anne Boleyn, was declared illegitimate; Henry had earlier possessed as one of his mistresses Mary, Anne's sister, and this was believed to attaint Elizabeth. Jane Seymour gave birth to the future Edward VI and then died on Oct. 24, 1537. Henry's fourth wife (Jan. 6, 1540) was Anne of Cleves; their divorce took place on June 24, 1540. On August 8, 1540, Henry married Catherine Howard, the day Cromwell was executed for being too zealous a Protestant. Catherine Howard was beheaded in less than two years (Feb. 12, 1542) for adultery, apparently a more justifiable charge than the one against Anne Boleyn. Henry's sixth wife was Catherine Parr; they were married on July 12, 1543, and she survived him. By these six marriages, Henry had three children: Mary, daughter of Catherine of Aragon, who reigned as Mary I; Elizabeth, who was the daughter of Anne Boleyn; Edward VI, the son of Jane Seymour, who was Henry's immediate successor. Henry's advisers, besides the great Wolsey, More, Cranmer, and Cromwell, included his early mentors William Warham, archbishop of Canterbury, who crowned Henry king, Richard Foxe, bishop of Winchester, and Thomas Howard, Earl of Surrey. A few pretenders were dealt with in the early years of the reign; Richard de la Pole, a descendant of the Yorkist family, was declared king of England by Louis XII of France in 1511, and in 1513 his brother Edmund, Earl of Suffolk, a prisoner in the Tower, was executed as a danger to the crown. Edward Stafford, 3rd Duke of Buckingham, was executed for disloyalty in 1521. Wolsey, deprived of his magnificence, died in disgrace in 1530 while on his way to answer charges of high treason. More was beheaded for his adherence to the original succession and Cromwell for treason. Cranmer alone of the king's principal aides outlived him, to die at the stake in 1556. Henry's reliance on Parliament, especially during his struggle with Rome, resulted in a widening of that body's powers and of its membership to include Wales and other regions.

Its refusal to grant funds in 1523 resulted in Cromwell's so-called amicable loan, everyone being asked to give according to his means; the attempt to raise money failed, but Cromwell became heartily disliked as a result. Under Henry the power of the crown was further centralized and that of the feudal nobility was reduced in proportion. The councils of the North and of Wales, similar to the Star Chamber court (and like it established under Henry VII), became powerful weapons against feudal barons who resisted the royal authority. The great distribution of church lands led to further close adherence to the crown by recipients of the royal favor. Henry's intention throughout his reign was to strengthen his country and to strengthen the position of the monarch; it was his boast that he did nothing unconstitutional, but often the constitutionality of his acts depended on laws enacted after the acts they legitimized.

Henry VIII. [Full title, **The Famous History of the Life of King Henry the Eighth.**] A historical play, partly by Shakespeare, who appears to have left it unfinished, the rest being probably by Fletcher. It was first acted on June 29, 1613 (an exact date is possible, because we know that cannon fired during the performance started the fire that burned the Globe theater to the ground on that day), and published in the folio of 1623. It is founded on Holinshed's *Chronicles*, Foxe's *Christian Martyrs*, and possibly Samuel Rowley's *When You See Me, You Know Me* (1605). An actor, John Lowin, was supposed to have been instructed by Shakespeare himself in the role of King Henry. Betterton acted it in 1664 and it was produced thereafter with much attention to the pageant element. It is unlike any of the other Shakespeare historical plays, being more like the medieval morality tales about the falls of famous men. The alternative name "All Is True" (first mentioned in 1613, from the repeated insistence in the Prologue on the truth of the events to be recounted) was unquestionably applied to the play at an early date, and has been accepted by the late George L. Kittredge and other eminent Shakespearians as historically authentic; however, neither Kittredge nor any other scholar now uses it as a variant name for the play.

The Story. Buckingham, about to expose the ambitious Cardinal Wolsey to the King, is arrested for high treason at the instigation of Wolsey. Queen Katherine (in history, Catherine of Aragon, mother of Queen Mary) pleads with Henry to remove certain oppressive taxes and to pardon Buckingham. The first request the King grants, but the trial and execution of Buckingham are carried out. Meanwhile, the King has met Anne Bullen (in history, Anne Boleyn, mother of Queen Elizabeth) at a party given by Wolsey, and has fallen in love with her. He hopes to get a divorce from Katherine on the grounds that his marriage was not permissible for reasons of near relationship, Katherine being his brother's widow (in the eyes of the Elizabethans, this made the match almost incestuous). Wolsey halts proceedings on the divorce because he realizes that if they are completed Henry will marry Anne, and he opposes her on religious grounds. The King discovers the duplicity of Wolsey and the Cardinal retires. Cranmer, Archbishop of Canterbury, annuls the marriage to Katherine, who shortly dies of a broken heart. Henry now secretly marries Anne, but Cranmer, accused of heresy, is brought to trial; however, the King gives him a ring for protection, and later honors him by asking him to be the godfather of Elizabeth. The christening is the final scene of the play.

Henry, Prince. In Shakespeare's *King John*, the son of John. After John's death the lords swear loyalty to him (as Henry III).

Henry and Emma (em'ạ). A poem by Matthew Prior upon the model of the old ballad *The Nut Brown Maid.*

Henry Amundeville (ạ.mun'dẹ.vil), **Lord.** See **Amundeville, Lord Henry.**

Henry Bailif (bā'lif). See **Bailey, Harry.**

Henry Bolingbroke (bol'ing.brŭk). See **Bolingbroke, Henry.**

Henry Clegg (kleg). See **Clegg, Henry.**

Henry Cranstoun (kranz'tọn). See **Cranstoun, Henry.**

Henry Crawford (krô'fọrd). See **Crawford, Henry.**

Henry Esmond (ez'mọnd). A novel by William Makepeace Thackeray, published in 1852. The book is a reproduction of the manners, thoughts, and literary style which prevailed in England in the time of Queen Anne. Henry Esmond, the principal character, is a brave, polished, true, and loyal gentleman, almost too self-sacrificing. He is supposed to be the illegitimate son of the 3rd Viscount Castlewood, and enters the household of the 4th Viscount as a page. He wins the affection of both Lord and Lady Castlewood, but unfortunately he brings smallpox into the house, and Lady Castlewood thereby loses some of her beauty and most of her husband's love. The wicked Lord Mohun tries to take advantage of this situation to seduce her, whereupon Lord Castlewood challenges him to a duel, and is mortally wounded. He reveals to Henry as he dies that the young man is the legitimate and rightful heir to the title and property of Castlewood. Henry decides not to claim his rights, but to let Lady Castlewood and her son and daughter stay there; however, Lady Castlewood cannot forgive him for allowing the duel to take place, and tells him to leave the house. Henry then takes service in the army, but later hears a rumor that Lady Castlewood is going to marry her chaplain, Tom Tusher, and rushes home, where he is lovingly greeted by Lady Castlewood (who has long since recovered from her hostility toward him). Esmond now realizes that he is in love with Beatrix, the daughter, but she is vain and ambitious, and will have nothing to do with him. He does not despair, however, until she betrays a plot supported by Henry for the proclamation of the Stuart Pretender. Henry is then utterly disgusted and disillusioned, and marries her mother, who by now has learned of his sacrifice of title and fortune for her. As the book closes, Lady Castlewood and Henry are about to migrate to Virginia, there to begin a new life together.

Henry Esmond Warrington (wôr'ing.tọn, wor'-). See under **Warrington, George.**

Henry Gow (gou). See **Smith, Henry.**

Henry Guildford (gil'fọrd), **Sir.** See **Guildford, Sir Henry.**

Henry Higgins (hig'inz). See **Higgins, Henry.**

Henry Morton (môr'tọn). See **Morton, Henry.**

Henry of Huntingdon (hun'ting.dọn). b. c1084; d. 1155. An English historian. He became archdeacon of Huntingdon in 1110. He wrote *Historia Anglorum*, bringing it up to 1154.

Henry Percy (pėr'si), **Sir.** See under **Hotspur.**

Henry, Prince of Wales. See under **Hal, Prince.**

Henry Ryecroft (rī'krôft). See **Ryecroft, Henry.**

Henry Smith (smith). See **Smith, Henry.**

Henryson (hen'ri.sọn), **Robert.** [Also, **Henderson.**] b. c1430; d. c1506. A Scottish poet. He wrote *Testament of Cressid* (a sort of tragic sequel to Chaucer's *Troilus and Criseyde*), *Robin and Makyne* (said to be the earliest English pastoral poem), *Morall Fabillis of Esope the Phrygian* (probably written between 1470 and 1480), and other works. The fables include "The Taill of the Uponlandis Mous and the Burges Mous" (The Country Mouse and the City Mouse). His collected works were edited by D. Laing (1865).

Henry the Minstrel (hen'ri). See **Blind Harry.**

Henry Warden (wôr'dẹn). See **Warden, Henry.**

Henslowe (henz'lō), **Philip.** d. 1616. An English theater manager. He was a servant of the bailiff of Viscount Montague, whose town house was in Southwark (now part of London). Henslowe took care of the property there, and gradually made money and bought property. He owned the Boar's Head and other inns. In 1585 he bought land on the Bankside, and in 1591 built the Rose theater there. In 1592 he began to keep the accounts of his theatrical ventures in his *Diary*. In it he gives the dates of new plays, the amounts he paid for them or advanced to the usually impecunious playwrights, and similar material of great value to students of the drama. In 1600 he built, with Edward Alleyn, his son-in-law, the Fortune theater. The *Diary* and other papers were lost in a mass of printed material at Dulwich College until 1790, when Edmund Malone recovered them for his variorum edition of Shakespeare. The *Diary*, as edited by W. W. Greg, is a record of the years 1592–1603, in two sections: one, companies performing at the Rose, names of plays, and Henslowe's receipts as theater owner for performances; and two, after 1597, a listing of his advances to the Lord Admiral's Men for plays, costumes, properties, and licensing fees, and to the actors themselves.

Henslowe's Diary. See under **Henslowe, Philip.**

Henty (hen'ti), **George Alfred.** b. at Trumpington, near Cambridge, England, Dec. 8, 1832; d. aboard his yacht in Weymouth harbor, Dorsetshire, England, Nov. 16, 1902. An English war correspondent and novelist. He was educated at Westminster School, London, and at Caius College, Cambridge, leaving without a degree when the Crimean War broke out. He served as correspondent (1855) for the *Morning Advertiser*, and was correspondent (1865–66) for the *Standard*, covering the Austro-Italian War. He was in Ethi-

---

ḍ, d or j; ṣ, s or sh; ṭ, t or ch; ẓ, z or zh; o, F. cloche; ü, F. menu; ċh, Sc. loch; ṅ, F. bonbon.

opia (1867–68), Paris (1871), Spain (1874), India (1875), and Serbia (1876) during the fighting in these places. A facile writer, he produced, in addition to articles and stories for the *Union Jack* (of which he was editor) and other magazines, more than 80 very popular historical novels for juvenile readers. Author of *Out on the Pampas* (1868), *The Young Franc-Tireurs* (1872), *The Young Buglers* (1880), *Facing Death* (1883), *With Clive in India* (1884), *Bravest of the Brave* (1887), *Orange and Green* (1888), *The Cat of Bubastes* (1889), *By Pike and Dyke* (1890), *By Right of Conquest* (1891), *Redskin and Cowboy* (1892), *With Frederick the Great* (1898), *With Roberts to Pretoria* (1902), *With Kitchener to the Sudan* (1903), and *With the Allies to Pekin* (1904).

Heorot (he′o.rot). The great hall of Hrothgar in *Beowulf*.

Hepburn (hep′l.bèrn), **James.** See **Bothwell,** 4th Earl of.

Hephaestus (hē.fes′tus). In Greek mythology, the god of fire and metallic arts; son of Zeus and Hera, and one of the great Olympians; husband of Charis, sometimes of Aphrodite; father of Erectheus. He was identified by the Romans with their Vulcan, who became assimilated to him. He was the creator of all that was beautiful and mechanically wonderful in Olympus, especially arms and armor for the gods. Volcanoes, especially those of Lemnos and Sicily, were held to be his smithies and the Cyclopes were his forgers. In art he was represented as a bearded man, usually with the short sleeveless or one-sleeved tunic (*exomis*) and the conical cap, and holding the smith's hammer and tongs. He was lame, either from birth, or from having been hurled out of heaven by Zeus in a quarrel.

Heppelwhite (hep′l.hwīt), **George.** d. 1786. An English cabinetmaker and designer. Several plates representing pieces from his shop appear in *The Cabinet-maker's London Book of Prices*, dated 1788, and the only other source of information concerning his work is his own book, *The Cabinet-Maker and Upholsterer's Guide*, published in the same year. Undoubtedly George Heppelwhite and his shop in Cripplegate greatly influenced furniture design, but in a sense "Heppelwhite" should be understood as meaning a style and a mode rather than an individual and his work. He seems to have devised the winged easy chair, and may have been the first to use the shield chair back, which with the oval back and the interlaced back is characteristic of the period, as are certain decorative motifs, such as wheat-ears and the ostrich feathers taken from the arms of the Prince of Wales.

Heptameron (hep.tam′e̱.ron). A collection of stories by Margaret of Angoulême, queen of Navarre (1492–1549), supposed to have been related during seven days, modeled on the *Decameron* of Boccaccio.

heptameter (hep.tam′e.tèr). In prosody, a verse consisting of seven measures.

Heptarchy (hep′tär.ki). The early English kingdoms, prior to their consolidation under the royal house of Wessex a few decades before the ascent to the throne of King Alfred; also, the period of English history when these kingdoms had independent status, within a loose and constantly shifting confederation, between c449 and c828. The number of kingdoms was seldom exactly seven, however. The chief kingdoms were Kent, Wessex, Mercia, East Anglia, Deira and Bernicia (united as Northumbria), Essex, and Sussex.

Hera (hir′a̱). [Also, **Here.**] In Greek mythology, the greatest feminine divinity of Olympus, queen of heaven; daughter of Cronus and Rhea; wife and sister of Zeus, and inferior in power to him alone. She was the mother of Hephaestus and Ares. She was the goddess of women and childbirth, the type of virtuous womanhood, and of the wife and mother. She also typifies the jealous wife, and many myths deal with her punishment of Zeus's paramours. In art she is represented as a majestic woman, fully clad in flowing draperies, characteristically with a crown on her brow, and bearing a scepter. By the Romans Hera was early identified with their Juno, originally a distinct divinity; and the Latin name is often incorrectly given to the Greek goddess.

Heracles (her′a̱.klēz). See **Hercules.**

Heraclitus (her.a̱.klī′tus). b. at Ephesus, Asia Minor, probably c535 B.C.; d. there, probably c475 B.C. A Greek philosopher. He is one of the earliest of the metaphysical school, and was known as the "Dark" or "Weeping" philosopher (the latter in contrast to Democritus's epithet the "Laughing" philosopher) because of his depth of concept and his misanthropy. He held a theory of the relativity of things: nothing was absolute, all was subject to change and constantly changing; the individual is part of a general harmony in the world and virtue consists of becoming part of that harmony by denial of individuality.

Heralds' College. [Also, **College of Arms.**] A corporation (established in 1484) charged and entrusted, in England, with the granting of coats of arms and with deciding questions of lineage and heraldic rights. Heralds and their assistants, known as pursuivants, were during the early Middle Ages functionaries whose characteristic duties were to proclaim decrees of monarchs and higher nobles, and to act as intermediaries between hostile armies. The institution of the College of Heralds by Richard III was a measure in line with the increasing ascendancy of the English crown over the feudal nobles. The appointment of heralds and pursuivants by the nobles fell into desuetude, and eventually it became the chief function of the royal appointees to determine who were entitled to bear coats of arms, and to devise arms and crests for claimants determined to be entitled to them. Kings of arms, heralds, and pursuivants participate in such ceremonies as proclamations of the accession of a new sovereign, coronations, royal marriages, and royal funerals, and in court observances of Christmas, Easter, Whitsunday, All Saints' Day, and Saint George's Day.

Herbert (hèr′bèrt), **A. P.** [Full name, Sir **Alan Patrick Herbert;** pseudonym, **Albert Haddock.**] b. Sept. 24, 1890—. An English writer. He started writing (1910) for *Punch*, becoming (1924) a staff member. A member of Parliament since 1935, he secured passage (1937) of the Matrimonial Causes Bill revising out-of-date English divorce laws. Author of *Poor Poems and Rotton Rhymes* (1910), *The Secret Battle* (1919), *The House by the River* (1920), *Light Articles Only* (1921; American title, *Little Rays of Moonshine*), *The Man About Town* (1923), *The Old Flame* (1925), *Laughing Ann* (1925), *The Trials of Topsy* (1928), *Honeybubble and Co.* (1928), *Topsy, M.P.* (1929), *The Water Gipsies* (1930), *No Boats on the River* (1932), *Holy Deadlock* (1934), *The Ayes Have It* (1937), *Siren Song* (1940), *Light the Lights* (1945), *The Point of Parliament* (1946), *Independent Member* (1951), *Full Enjoyment* (1952), and the comic operas *The Blue Peter, Tantivy Towers,* and *Mother of Pearl*.

Herbert, Edward. [Title, 1st Baron **Herbert of Cherbury** (chär′bėr.i.).] b. at Eyton-on-Severn, England, March 3, 1583; d. at London, Aug. 20, 1648. An English philosopher, soldier, diplomat, and historian; brother of George Herbert (1593–1633) and Thomas Herbert (1597–c1642). He studied at Oxford and afterwards traveled on the Continent, making many influential friends in France, the Low Countries, and Italy. After military service as a volunteer in the Low Countries, he returned (c1616) to England, where he became acquainted with such leading literary figures of the day as John Donne, Ben Jonson, and Thomas Carew, among others. In 1619 he went to France as English ambassador but, after a quarrel with the Duc de Luynes, was recalled. De Luynes died in 1621 and Herbert returned to France. His mission was twofold: to arrange a marriage between Prince Charles (later Charles I) and Princess Henrietta Maria, sister of the French king Louis XIII, and to obtain aid for Frederick V, the elector palatine, King James's son-in-law. Neither plan coming to quick fruition, he was recalled in 1624. He was with Charles in Scotland in 1639–40, but when the trouble erupted between king and Parliament he attempted to take a middle course. He was forced to turn over Montgomery Castle, where he had taken refuge, to Parliamentary troops in 1644, and in 1645 submitted to the Parliamentarians and was granted a pension. Herbert's poetry is well-written metaphysical verse, but his fame rests on his other works. His autobiography (discovered by Horace Walpole and printed by him in 1764) is a flamboyant account of his career to 1624; it is anecdotal and does not go very deeply into the background of Herbert's embassies, but it is a very readable work. *De Veritate* (1624) is a metaphysical approach to truth and *De religione gentilium* (c1645), a study in comparative religion, is an early argument for deism in that it discovers certain universal bases in man's religious beliefs. He also wrote a biography of Henry VIII and other philosophical and historical works.

Herbert, George. b. at Montgomery Castle, Wales, April 3, 1593; d. at Bemerton, near Salisbury, England, in February, 1633. An English metaphysical poet; brother of Edward Herbert, 1st Baron Herbert of Cherbury, and of Thomas Herbert (1597–c1642). He graduated B.A. at Trinity College, Cambridge, in 1613, and M.A. in 1616, when he was elected fellow. In 1618 he was prelector in the rhetoric school at Cambridge, and in 1619 he was made public orator. He was much in favor at court, and in his position as orator it was

his duty to write all official letters to the government. In 1627 he resigned the post on the excuse of ill health. In 1630 Charles I presented him to the rectory of Fugglestone with Bemerton, Wiltshire. Here he wrote the religious poems for which he is principally remembered, and which were published after his death in a volume called *The Temple; Sacred Poems and Private Ejaculations* (1633), said to have sold more than 20,000 copies by 1670. He also wrote *A Priest to the Temple, or the Country Parson,* in prose (1652), and other works. Herbert's poetry, marked by conceits and symbols but intensely personal and religious, is associated with the body of work produced by the English metaphysical school, which includes Richard Crashaw, Andrew Marvell, John Donne, Thomas Traherne, and others. His short poems include *The Pulley, The Collar,* and *The Quip.* See *A Reading of George Herbert* (1952), by Rosemond Tuve, *George Herbert* (1954), by Margaret Bottrall, and *George Herbert* (1954) by Joseph H. Summers.

Herbert, George Robert Charles. [Titles: 13th Earl of **Pembroke,** 9th Earl of **Montgomery.**] b. at London, July 6, 1850; d. at Frankfort on the Main, Germany, May 3, 1895. An English author and traveler. He traveled in Italy, Spain, Egypt, Palestine, and elsewhere, always accompanied by his physician, George Henry Kingsley. His two journeys to the South Pacific with Kingsley produced an entertaining narrative of joint authorship, *South Sea Bubbles, by the Earl and the Doctor* (1872; other editions). Named (1874) undersecretary of war in Disraeli's second cabinet, he was compelled by his health to resign in 1875. His other works include *Roots, a Plea for Tolerance* (1873) and *Letters and Speeches* (1896).

Herbert, Henry William. [Pseudonym, **Frank Forester.**] b. at London, April 7, 1807; committed suicide at New York, May 17, 1858. An Anglo-American author of historical works, novels, and translations. He edited (1833–35) *The American Monthly Magazine.* He is best known by his works on sports: *My Shooting Box* (1846), *Field Sports of the United States* (1849), *Frank Forester and his Friends* (1849), and *The Horse and Horsemanship in the United States* (1857). He also wrote *The Brothers: A Tale of the Fronde* (1835), *The Deerstalkers* (1849), and *The Quorndon Hounds* (1852).

Herbert, Mary. See **Pembroke,** Countess of.

Herbert, Philip. [Titles: 4th Earl of **Pembroke,** 1st Earl of **Montgomery.**] b. Oct. 10, 1584; d. at Whitehall, London, Jan. 23, 1650. An English Parliamentarian. A favorite of James I, he served (1626–41) as lord chamberlain under Charles I. He was sent (1640) as commissioner to negotiate peace with the Scots. Dismissed (1641) from his post as lord chamberlain, Herbert deserted Charles I for the Parliamentary side, and became Parliamentary governor (1642) of the Isle of Wight. As vice-chancellor (1641–50) of Oxford, he was bitterly satirized for compliancy in ejecting Royalists and for his crude language. Heming and Condell dedicated the famous first folio (1623) of Shakespeare's plays to him and his brother, William Herbert, 3rd Earl of Pembroke. The folio edition of Beaumont and Fletcher was also dedicated to him by the King's Men in 1647.

Herbert, Sir Walter. In Shakespeare's *Richard III,* a supporter of Richmond.

Herbert, Thomas. b. at Montgomery, Wales, May 15, 1597; d. at London, c1642. An English sailor and author; brother of George Herbert (1593–1633), and of Edward Herbert, 1st Baron Herbert of Cherbury. He was in command (1616) of the *Globe,* an East Indiaman, after his captain, Benjamin Joseph, was killed in an attack, and in command (October, 1623) of the vessel returning Prince Charles (later Charles I) from Spain to England following his unsuccessful wooing of the Spanish princess. Reputed author of *An Elegie upon the Death of Thomas, Earle of Strafford* (1641), *Newes out of Islington* (1641), and various satirical pieces, all dated 1641 except *Stripping, Whipping, and Pumping* (1638).

Herbert, Sir Thomas. b. at York, England, c1606; d. there, March 1, 1682. An English traveler and author. He made an extensive tour (1628–29) of the Persian dominions. Among his works are *A Description of the Persian Monarchy* (1634; reprinted with additions as *Some Yeares Travels into Africa and Asia the Great* in 1638), and *Threnodia Carolina* (1678; reprinted with additions as *Memoirs of the last two years of the reign of that Unparallell'd Prince of very blessed memory, King Charles I,* in 1702).

Herbert, William. [Title, 3rd Earl of **Pembroke.**] b. at Wilton, Wiltshire, England, April 8, 1580; d. at London, April 10, 1630. An English statesman and patron of poets. He was educated privately by Samuel Daniel, author of the *Delia* sonnets, and later at New College, Oxford. Soon after he became (1601) Lord Herbert of Pembroke, he was disgraced, imprisoned, and exiled from court because of his affair with Mary Fitton, maid of honor to Elizabeth. He was the patron of Jonson, Massinger, Inigo Jones the architect, and William Browne, author of *Britannia's Pastorals.* He was chancellor (1617–30) of Oxford University, Pembroke College (formerly Broadgates Hall) being renamed (1624) in his honor. He has been suggested by several scholars as the "Mr. W.H." celebrated by Shakespeare in the earlier sonnets. To him and his brother Philip, Heming and Condell dedicated one of the most famous books in English literature, the first folio (1623) of Shakespeare; it is this dedication and his patronage of poets and dramatists that are his chief claims to fame. He was the author of *Poems* (1660).

Herbert, William. See also under **Pembroke, Earl of.**

Herbert Pocket (pok'ẹt). See **Pocket, Herbert.**

Hercule Poirot (er.kül pwà.rō). See **Poirot, Hercule.**

Hercules (hėr'kū.lēz). [Also, **Heracles.**] In Greek and Roman legend, a mighty hero of extraordinary strength and courage, originating in Greek legend, but adopted by the Romans, and deified and worshiped after his death as the god of physical strength, courage, and related qualities. He was the son of Zeus and Alcmene (wife of Amphitryon). Hera, jealous of the child of a rival, put two ser-

pents in his cradle, which the infant strangled easily. Later she sent a cloud of madness on him, and in that madness Hercules killed his wife and sons. Upon recovery he went into voluntary exile and sought the Delphic oracle for guidance. There he was told he might purify himself and expiate his crimes by serving Eurystheus (king of Mycena) for 12 years. Eurystheus set for him 12 perilous tasks, which, if accomplished, would bring the hero immortality. These 12 labors of Hercules were already famous in legend in the 5th century B.C. They were as follows: (1) the strangling of the Nemean lion; (2) the killing of the Lernean hydra; (3) the capture of the Arcadian hind; (4) the capture of the Erymanthian boar; (5) the cleaning of the Augean stables; (6) the slaughter of the Stymphalian birds; (7) the capture of the Cretan bull; (8) the capture of the man-eating mares of Diomedes; (9) the securing of the girdle of Hippolyte, queen of the Amazons; (10) the fetching of the red oxen of Geryon; (11) the procuring of the golden apples of the Hesperides; (12) the bringing to the upper world the dog Cerberus, guardian of Hades. The hero of this most famous of the Herculean legends (of comparatively late date) is distinguished as the Tirynthian Hercules from other personifications of Hercules worshiped in different places and countries (as the Cretan or the Egyptian Hercules) under the same or other names, the attributes of these various personifications being essentially the same, but their legendary history being different. After the 12 labors, Hercules married Deianira. When they came to a river to be crossed, the centaur Nessus offered to carry Deianira across. In midstream he tried to abduct her, whereupon Hercules killed the centaur with poisoned arrows. Later, again for a murder committed in madness, Hercules served at the court of Omphale, queen of Lydia, for one year, donning women's clothes and doing women's work. Here Deianira sent him the poisoned shirt given her by Nessus, which she thought was a love charm to bring him home to her. The shirt caused the hero's death; he built his own funeral pyre and died upon it. After his death he was taken to Olympus, where after his deification he married Hebe. Among other famous exploits, Hercules took part in the Calydonian boar hunt and the expedition of the Argonauts. His struggle with Death in person at the tomb to win back the dead Alcestis for her husband Admetus is among the most famous stories about Hercules. He is represented as brawny and muscular, with broad shoulders, generally naked or draped merely in the skin of the Nemean lion, the head of the lion being often drawn over that of the hero as a helmet. He is usually armed with a club, sometimes with a bow and arrows.

Hercules, Pillars of. See **Pillars of Hercules.**

Hercynian Forest (hėr.sin'i.ạn). [Latin, **Hercynia Silva;** Greek, **Herkynia Hule.**] In ancient geography, a mountain range forming the N boundary of what was then known as Europe, and seemingly identified by Aristotle with the Alpine mass. It has been variously represented as in C Germany, and as identical with the Böhmerwald, the Thüringerwald, and others. In modern times it has usually been regarded as comprising the mountains of C Germany (Wesergebirge, the Harz, the Thuringian and Saxon highlands, Riesengebirge, and others).

Herder (her'dĕr), **Johann Gottfried von.** b. at Mohrungen, in East Prussia, Aug. 25, 1744; d. at Weimar, Germany, Dec. 18, 1803. A German critic and poet of the so-called classical period of German literature. He was the son of a poor schoolteacher. He supported himself by giving private instruction while attending the University of Königsberg. From 1764 to 1769 he was a teacher at Riga. In the latter year he went to Paris, where he accepted the position of companion to the young Prince of Holstein on a journey to Italy. He accompanied the latter, however, only as far as Strasbourg, where he remained the succeeding half year. In 1771 he received a call as pastor to Bückeburg, where he lived until 1776. At the recommendation of Goethe, whom he had known at Strasbourg, he was called that year to Weimar as court chaplain and superintendent of the church district, and here, with the exception of a journey to Italy in 1788, he lived until his death. In 1802 he was ennobled by the Elector of Bavaria. His first important works, both of which were published at Riga, were *Fragmente über die neuere deutsche Literatur* (1767) and *Kritische Wälder* (1769). In 1772 appeared the treatise *Über den Ursprung der Sprache.* In 1773 he published, in collaboration with Goethe, *Von deutscher Art und Kunst einige fliegende Blätter.* In 1774 appeared *Die älteste Urkunde des Menschengeschlechts.* With these earlier writings Herder did more than any other person to bring in the period of the Sturm und Drang. The most important of his later works are *Volkslieder* (1778 and 1779; called in later editions *Stimmen der Völker in Liedern*), *Ideen zur Philosophie der Geschichte der Menschheit* (1784–91), and *Briefe zur Beförderung der Humanität* (1793–97). The poem *Der Cid,* written in 1802–03, appeared posthumously in 1805. A complete edition of his works was published at Stuttgart (1827–30) in 60 volumes.

Here Are Ladies. Stories (1913) by James Stephens.

Hereford (her'ę.fǫrd), Duke of. See under **Bolingbroke, Henry.**

Here Lies a Most Beautiful Lady. A novel by Richard Blaker, published in 1935.

Here Prophecy (hir), **The.** A bit of old English rhyme, which was preserved by the Abbot Benedict. It is connected with the image of a hart set up in 1289 by Ralph Fitzstephen over his house. The date of setting up the hart was that of the death of Henry II and the accession of Richard I, and the verse was considered to be a prophecy concerning the future of Richard and his brother John.

Hereward (her'ę.wạrd). [Called **Hereward the Wake.**] fl. c1070. An English outlaw and patriot who defended Ely against the Normans under William the Conqueror. He was a Lincolnshire man, incorrectly said to have been a son of Leofric, Earl of Mercia. In 1070 he joined the Danes, who had appeared in the Humber, and attacked Peterborough and sacked the abbey. He took refuge with his band in the Isle of Ely, from which he was finally driven by William I. According to John of Peterborough (c1380), he was surnamed "the Wake." Many legends sprang up about his name

as they have with other outlaws who resist despised authority. He may have been the center of a cycle of ballads and poems now lost.

Hereward the Wake. A historical novel by Charles Kingsley, published in 1866. Kingsley makes this legendary English hero the son of Lady Godiva and Leofric of Mercia. He is outlawed for robbing a monastery, has many adventures in England, and then marries the faithful Torfrida. The Norman Conquest begins, and Hereward tries valiantly to save England from William the Conqueror, but is finally defeated. Hereward is conquered also by the wiles of another woman, and he and Torfrida end their lives in sorrow.

Herford (her'fǫrd), **Oliver (Brooke).** b. at Sheffield, England, Dec. 12, 1863; d. 1935. An English writer who illustrated his own whimsical works. He lived chiefly in the U. S., where he published work in *Life, Harper's Weekly,* and other journals. Author of *Pen and Inklings* (1893), *Artful Anticks* (1894), *A Child's Primer of Natural History* (1899), *The Fairy Godmother-in-Law* (1905), *The Peter Pan Alphabet* (1907), *The Simple Jography* (1908), *The Jingle-Jungle Book* (1913), *Confessions of a Caricaturist* (1917), *The Laughing Willow* (1918), *Excuse it Please* (1929), and *Sea Legs* (1931).

Heritage. A novel by V. Sackville-West, published in 1919.

Herman Dousterswivel (her'man dös'tėr.swiv.ęl). See **Dousterswivel, Herman.**

Hermaphroditus (her.maf.rǫ.dī'tus). In Greek mythology, the son of Hermes and Aphrodite; a deity combining both male and female attributes. The nymph of the fountain Salmacis, in Caria, loved him so greatly that she prayed they might be united into one person.

Hermengyld (her'men.gild). See under **Man of Law's Tale, The.**

Hermes (her'mēz). In Greek mythology, the herald and messenger of the gods, protector of herdsmen, god of science, commerce, invention, and the arts. As herald of the gods, he became god of roads and patron of travelers. As an ancient fertility god, he became also a god of wealth, hence of luck, hence of thieves. He was the son of Zeus and Maia, born on Mount Cyllene in Arcadia. He was the guide (psychopompus) of the souls of the dead to their final abode. In art he is represented as a vigorous youth, beardless after the archaic period, usually but slightly draped, with caduceus, petasus, and talaria as attributes. The Roman Mercury, their god of commerce, became identified with Hermes. The name has also been given to quicksilver.

Hermes, Count. One of the roles played by the disguised "blind beggar," Irus, in George Chapman's *Blind Beggar of Alexandria.*

Hermes Trismegistus (tris.mę.jis'tus). Hermes as identified with the Egyptian god Thoth, the reputed author of 42 encyclopedic works on the ancient wisdom of Egypt, especially magic, astrology, and alchemy, called the *Hermetic Books.* A partial collection of Hermetic writings was translated into French by Ménard in 1866.

Hermia (her'mi.ạ). In Shakespeare's *Midsummer Night's Dream,* an Athenian lady, the daughter of Egeus, in love with Lysander.

ḍ, d or j; ṣ, s or sh; ṭ, t or ch; ẓ, z or zh; o, F. cloche; ü, F. menu; ċh, Sc. loch; ṅ, F. bonbon.

Hermione (hẽr.mī′ọ.nē). In Greek legend, the daughter of Menelaus and Helen, and wife of Neoptolemus and later of Orestes.

Hermione. In Shakespeare's *Winter's Tale*, the Queen of Sicilia, wife of the jealous Leontes. She is the Bellaria of Greene's *Pandosto*, the story from which *The Winter's Tale* was taken.

Hermione. The wife of Damon in the tragedy *Damon and Pythias* by Banim and Sheil.

Hermione, Lady. [Also, **Lady Erminia Pauletti**.] A rich Genoese lady in Sir Walter Scott's novel *The Fortunes of Nigel*.

Hermod (hẽr′mọd). [Also, **Hermodr**.] In Old Norse mythology, son of Odin, messenger of the gods. It was Hermod whom Odin sent to Hel to bring back Balder (who had been accidentally killed with the mistletoe shaft by his blind brother Hoder). Hermod won entrance to Hel by leaping over the walls. The message he brought back was that Balder might return if all things on earth wept for him.

Hernani (er.nà.nē). [Full title, **Hernani, ou l'Honneur Castillan**.] A tragedy by Victor Hugo, first acted on Feb. 25, 1830. The appearance of the play, an outstanding example of Hugo's romantic tendencies, and a work which was to have a tremendous influence on writing in English as well as French, caused rioting and conflict between the Romanticists and classicists.

Herne the Hunter (hẽrn). A phantom hunter said to range near an old oak, known as Herne's Oak, in Windsor Forest. The tree was blown down in 1863, and was supposed to be about 650 years old. Queen Victoria planted a young oak on the spot. Herne the Hunter figures in Shakespeare's *Merry Wives of Windsor*, when Falstaff is persuaded to impersonate him and go through Windsor Forest at night.

hero. The principal male personage in a poem, play, or story, or the person who has the chief place and share in the transactions related, as Achilles in the *Iliad*, Odysseus (Ulysses) in the *Odyssey*, Aeneas in the *Aeneid*.

> The shining quality of an epic hero, his magnanimity, his constancy, his patience, his piety, ... raises first our admiration.
> (Dryden, Æneid, Ded.)

> Why not a summer's as a winter's tale? . . .
> Heroic if you will, or what you will,
> Or be yourself your hero.
> (Tennyson, Princess, Prol.)

Hero (hir′ō). In Greek legend, a priestess of Aphrodite at Sestos, on the Hellespont, beloved by Leander, who swam across the Hellespont every night from Abydos to see her. One night Leander was drowned and Hero, heartbroken, drowned herself also.

Hero. In Shakespeare's *Much Ado About Nothing*, the daughter of Leonato, and friend and cousin of Beatrice. When denounced by Claudio at the church as unchaste, she faints, and on Friar Francis's advice it is announced she is dead, supposedly to awaken Claudio's pity.

Hero and Leander (lē.an′dẽr). A poem in 340 verses, ascribed to Musaeus (c5th century A.D.),

dealing with the classic love story already known to earlier writers but here treated more fully. It is the story of Hero and her love for Leander, who swam the Hellespont nightly to visit her. Marlowe, Hood, and Nash are only a few among the many English writers who have used this story.

Herod I (her′ọd). [Called **Herod the Great**.] b. c73 B.C.; d. at Jericho, 4 B.C. A king of Judea (40–4 B.C.). He came of an Idumean family which was converted to Judaism. His father, Antipater, succeeded, during the conflict between Hyrcanus II and his brother Aristobulus II, in obtaining a hold in Judean politics and befriending the Romans. Accordingly when Antipater was appointed (47 B.C.) by Caesar procurator of Judea, Herod, though only 15 years old, was made governor of Galilee, and shortly afterward of Coele-Syria (El Bika). In 40 he had to flee from Judea to Rome, and was appointed by the senate king of Judea. In 37 he took possession of Jerusalem with the aid of the Romans. During the civil war he was on the side of Mark Antony, but after the battle of Actium (31 B.C.) he secured the favor of the victorious Augustus (Octavian), who not only confirmed him in his kingdom but also considerably increased his territory, so that it extended from the sea to Syria and from Damascus to Egypt. His policy toward Rome was that of servility, though his secret aim may have been the founding of an independent monarchy. His attitude toward the people over whom he ruled was characterized by entire want of understanding of or sympathy with its nature, ideals, and aspirations. His rule was marked by unscrupulous selfishness and bloody despotism. In his family relations he showed himself passionate, jealous, and cruel. He was married ten times and his family connections with the Judean nobility led to much of the political intrigue of his reign. At the same time he was bold, prudent, understanding his opportunities, and knowing how to avail himself of them, liberal, and fond of pomp and display. To these qualities may be ascribed his success, and what popularity he obtained. Thus, to strengthen his position he had his benefactor Hyrcanus II executed, and it was assumed that his brother-in-law Aristobulus, appointed by him high priest, was drowned at his instigation for fear of his great popularity with the people. The people he held in abeyance by bloody terror. Even the magnificent temple, begun 20 B.C. and finished in eight years, could not gain him the hearts of the outraged people. At the same time as the temple, he had erected everywhere theaters, gymnasia, and heathen temples. Even some cities owe their origin to his love of building, notably Caesarea. Samaria was turned by him into a fortress, and named Sebaste. In a fit of jealousy he executed his beautiful wife Mariamne, granddaughter of Hyrcanus II, and later his two sons by her, Alexander and Aristobulus, and five days before his death, his eldest son by Doris, Antipater. His last order, according to a story in Josephus, was for the massacre of the leaders of the Jews immediately after his decease, so that at least his death might cause mourning. He died in great agony from a loathsome disease, which drove him to a suicidal attempt, in 4 B.C. In Mat. ii. 1 ff. he is represented as having ordered the massacre of the infants of

Bethlehem, in order to exterminate the child Jesus, an act which would have been quite in harmony with his character as a superstitious despot and tyrant, but the historicity of which causes chronological difficulties.

Herod Agrippa I (ạ.grip′ạ). [Also known as **Agrippa I, Julius Agrippa I,** or simply **Agrippa**.] b. c11 B.C.; d. at Caesarea, Palestine, 44 A.D. Grandson of Herod I (Herod the Great), appointed king over the tetrarchies of NE Palestine in 37 A.D., and in 41 A.D. over Judea also. He persecuted the Christians in 44 (Acts, xii), and is said to have died in a horrible manner (Acts, xii. 23).

Herodas (hẹ.rō′dạs), or **Herondas** (-ron′-). fl. c3rd century B.C. A Greek satirical poet. He seems to have lived on Kos, one of the Dodecanese Islands, but little is known of him beyond a few lines quoted by other writers, and the seven poems of his preserved in a manuscript in the British Museum.

Herodias (hẹ.rō′di.ạs). fl. in the first half of the 1st century. Sister of Herod Agrippa I, and mother of Salome.

Herodotus (hẹ.rod′ọ.tus). b. at Halicarnassus, Asia Minor, probably c484 B.C.; d. at Thurii, Italy, probably c424 B.C. A Greek historian, often called "the Father of History." According to the commonly accepted account of his life, gleaned chiefly from his own works, he was the son of Lyxes and Dryo, persons of means and station at Halicarnassus; he assisted in the expulsion of the tyrant Lygdamus from his native city, traveled in the Persian empire, Egypt, Asia Minor, and Greece, lived in Samos and later at Athens, and settled as a colonist at Thurii (probably in 444). He wrote a history in nine books (named after the nine Muses) of the Persian invasion of Greece down to 479 B.C. The history, which is discursive, has been criticized as being too inclusive; Herodotus's credulity, his inclusion of material taken without an absolute regard for its truth, has led some to rank him below Thucydides. But Herodotus is primarily a stylist and in his wealth of anecdote and incident he remains readable. There is little of the subtle in his history, the discussion of motives and movements is lacking in depth, but he draws a picture of what was happening as colorful event and his depiction of the peoples involved in the war is graphically vivid. It was first printed in the original by Aldus Manutius in 1502, a Latin version by Valla having appeared as early as 1474.

heroine. The principal female character in a poem, play, story, or romance, or the woman who plays the most important part.

"Take Lilia, then, for heroine," clamour'd he,
"And make her some great princess, six feet high."
(Tennyson, *Princess*, Prol.)

Heron (her′ọn), **Irene.** An important character in Galsworthy's *Forsyte Saga*, first married to Soames Forsyte and later to his cousin, Young Jolyon.

Herostratus (hẹ.ros′trạ.tus). An Ephesian who set fire to the temple of Diana (Artemis), one of the seven wonders of the world, at Ephesus (as it happened, on the night of the birth of Alexander the Great) in order to immortalize himself.

Herrick (her′ik), **Robert.** b. at London, in August, 1591; d. at Dean Prior, Devonshire, England, in October, 1674. An English lyric poet. The son of a prosperous goldsmith, Herrick was a fellow-commoner of St. John's, Cambridge, in 1613, and in 1616 entered Trinity Hall to study law. After taking his B.A. in 1617, he probably returned to London and joined the literary group centered around the poet-dramatist Ben Jonson. Herrick accepted the benefice of Dean Prior in 1629 and continued as vicar until 1647, when he was ejected for his royalist principles. Thereafter he lived in London until restored to his parish by Charles II in 1662. Herrick is thought to surpass all other Cavalier lyrists, among whom are the graceful poets Carew, Lovelace, and Suckling. Metrical diversity, adroitness of rhyme, and tonal variety throughout a wide range of poetic forms principally account for his supremacy. As an admirer of Ben Jonson and a follower of his in his admiration of the classical writers, Herrick was strongly influenced by Horace and other Roman poets of the Augustan Age. Herrick's collected poems were published (1648) in London as *Hesperides, or the Works both Human and Divine of Robert Herrick, Esq.* The "human" works (*Hesperides*) are a versatile miscellany of more than a thousand secular poems and are in general superior to the less numerous "divine" poems (*Noble Numbers*). Representative of the *Hesperides* are "Corinna's going a-Maying," "To Daffodils," "To Meadows," "To the Virgins, to make much of Time," and "Upon Julia's Clothes." Enduring poems from *Noble Numbers* include "His Litany to the Holy Spirit" and "His Thanksgiving to God, for his House." Among the several editions of Herrick's complete poems are those by Grosart (1876) and F. W. Moorman (1915).

Herries Chronicles (her′is), **The.** Series of four novels, by Hugh Walpole, consisting of *Rogue Herries* (1930), *Judith Paris* (1931), *The Fortress* (1932), and *Vanessa* (1933).

Herr Teufelsdröckh (her toi′fẹls.drẹk). See **Teufelsdröckh, Herr.**

Herschel (hẹr′shẹl), **Sir John Frederick William.** b. at Slough, near Windsor, England, March 7, 1792; d. at Collingwood, near Hawkhurst, Kent, England, May 11, 1871. An English astronomer and physicist; son of Sir William Herschel. He continued his father's researches on double stars and nebulae, and conducted (1834–38) observations at the Cape of Good Hope. His own personal interest, however, lay in chemistry and the physics of light, and led to several important developments in the new science of photography. He used (1819) sodium hyposulfite (hypo) as a solvent for silver salts, invented (simultaneously and independently with W. H. F. Talbot in 1839) a sensitized photographic paper, and was the first to use the terms "positive" and "negative" in relation to photographic prints. He also did pioneering work in spectroscopic analysis and in crystallography. His chief work is *Results of Astronomical Observations made 1834–38 at the Cape of Good Hope* (1847). Among his other works are *Study of Natural Philosophy* (1830), *Outlines of Astronomy* (1849), and *Familiar Letters on Scientific Subjects* (1866).

Herschel, Sir William. [Original name, **Friedrich Wilhelm Herschel.**] b. at Hanover, Germany, Nov. 15, 1738; d. at Slough, near Windsor, England,

---

ḍ, d or j; ṣ, s or sh; ṭ, t or ch; ẓ, z or zh; o, F. cloche; ü, F. menu; ċh, Sc. loch; ṅ, F. bonbon.

Aug. 25, 1822. An English astronomer. He joined the band of the Hanoverian Guards as oboist at the age of 14, but deserted and went to England in 1757. There he was engaged in the teaching of music, and attained considerable success as a violinist and organist. He instructed himself in mathematics and astronomy, and in 1773 constructed a telescope with which he observed the Orion nebula. In 1775 he erected his first large reflecting telescope. On March 13, 1781, he discovered the planet Uranus, naming it, in honor of George III, "Georgium Sidus," a name which was not accepted by astronomers. He was made court astronomer in 1782. On Jan. 11, 1787, he discovered two satellites of Uranus (Oberon and Titania), on Aug. 28, 1789, a sixth satellite of Saturn (Enceladus), and on Sept. 17, 1789, a seventh (Mimas). His great reflecting telescope (tube 39 ft. 4 in. long) was erected in 1789. He investigated the problem of binary stars and indicated their revolution about each other in concordance with the laws of gravitation. He forwarded the hypothesis that stars evolve from the condensation of nebulae and showed Earth's position as a member of the stellar system of the Milky Way, whose construction he demonstrated as a comparatively flat, but extensive, system. His discovery of Saturn's rotational period and of the snow caps on Mars and his discussion, to no definite conclusion, of the effects of sunspots on terrestrial phenomena (like the growth of crops) mark him as one of the great astronomers; his discoveries and hypotheses concerning the stars outside the solar system give him his place as the founder of modern stellar astronomy. See *William Herschel* (1953), by J. B. Sidgwick.

Hertford College (här′fọrd, härt′fọrd). A college of Oxford University, founded c1282 by Elias de Hertford.

Hertha (hėr′thạ). See **Nerthus.**

Hertha. A poem (1871) by Swinburne.

Hervé Riel (er.vä ryel). A poem (1871) by Robert Browning.

Hervé Riel. See also **Riel, Hervé.**

Hervey (här′vi, hėr′-), **James.** b. at Hardingstone, near Northampton, England, Feb. 26, 1714; d. at Weston Favell, near Northampton, England, Dec. 25, 1758. An English Episcopal clergyman and devotional writer.

Hervey, John. [Title: Baron **Hervey of Ickworth;** nicknamed **"Lord Fanny."**] b. in October, 1696; d. in August, 1743. An English politician. He was lord privy seal (1740–42). He wrote a very frank exposé of the court in the period 1727–37 in *Memoirs of the Court of George II*, which was withheld from publication until after the death of George III.

Hervey, Thomas Kibble. b. at Paisley, Scotland, Feb. 4, 1799; d. at London, Feb. 27, 1859. A Scottish poet, critic, and editor. He was editor (1846–53) of the *Athenaeum*, resigning because of poor health. Author of the poems *Australia* (2nd ed., 1824) and *The Convict Ship* (1825).

Herzog (er.zog), **Émile Salomon Wilhelm.** See **Maurois, André.**

Hesiod (hē′si.ọd, hes′i-). b. at Ascra, Boeotia; fl. c735 B.C. A Greek poet. His youth was, according to a poem attributed to him, spent in rural pur-

suits at his native village. He appears to have lived during the latter part of his life at Orchomenus, where he is said to have been buried. The obscurity in which his life is involved has led some critics to adopt the opinion that the name does not represent an actual person, but is a mere personification of the Boeotian or Hesiodic school of poetry, as opposed to the Homeric or Ionic. Of the numerous works commonly ascribed to him the most important are *Works and Days* and *Theogony*. The former is chiefly composed of precepts on rural economy and maxims of morality; the latter is an account of the origin of the world and the birth of gods, and is one of the principal sources of our knowledge of the mythology of the early Greeks.

Hesione (hẹ.sī′ọ.nē). In Greek legend, a daughter of Laomedon, king of Troy, and Leucippe. She was exposed, as a propitiatory sacrifice, to be killed by a sea monster sent by Poseidon to devastate the land because Laomedon had refused to pay Poseidon and Apollo for their help in building the walls of Troy. Hercules slew the monster and set her free, and, when the promised reward (Laomedon's horses) was refused him, took Troy, slew Laomedon and his sons, and gave Hesione to his companion, Telamon, by whom she became the mother of Teucer.

Hesperia (hes.pir′i.ạ). According to the ancient Greeks, the region of the west, especially Italy, and sometimes, according to the poets, the Iberian peninsula.

Hesperides (hes.per′i.dēz). In Greek mythology, the maidens who guarded the tree with the golden apples which Gaea (Earth) caused to grow as a marriage gift for Hera. They dwelt in the gardens of the west, or, according to one account, among the Hyperboreans. A dragon helped them guard the tree. According to Hesiod they were daughters of Nox (Night); in later accounts, they are given as daughters of Atlas.

Hesperides. A collection (1648) of lyrical poems by Herrick.

Hesperus (hes′pẹ.rus). The personification of the evening star, in Greek mythology; son of Astraeus and Eos (according to Hesiod): identified with the planet Venus. The Latin name for it was Vesper.

Hesperus. See also **Pertolepe.**

Hestia (hes′ti.ạ). In Greek mythology, the virgin goddess of the hearth and the hearth fire; eldest daughter of Cronos and Rhea. She was tutelary especially of domestic living, but patroness also of public hearths. The Romans identified her with their Vesta.

Hetherington (heTH′ėr.ing.tọn), **Earl of.** See **Bulmer, Valentine.**

Hetty Sorrel (het′i sor′ẹl). See **Sorrel, Hetty.**

Hewlett (hū′lẹt), **Maurice (Henry).** b. at London, Jan. 22, 1861; d. near Salisbury, England, June 15, 1923. An English writer of historical romances and sketches. His works include *Earthwork out of Tuscany* (1895), *A Masque of Dead Florentines* (1895), *The Forest Lovers* (1898), *Little Novels of Italy* (1899), *Life and Death of Richard Yea-and-Nay* (1900), *New Canterbury Tales* (1901), *The Queen's Quair* (1904), *The Road in Tuscany* (1904), *Fond Adventures*, including *The Love Chase* (1905), and *The Heart's Key* (1905), *The Fool Errant* (1905),

---

fat, fāte, fär, ȧsk, fãre; net, mē, hėr; pin, pīne; not, nōte, mŏve, nôr; up, lūte, pull; ᴛн, then;

The Stooping Lady (1907), *Halfway House* (1908), *Spanish Jade* (1908), *Artemision* (1909), *Open Country* (1909), *Rest Harrow* (1910), *The Agonists* (1911), *Brazenhead the Great* (1911), *Song of Renny* (1911), *Mrs. Lancelot* (1912), *Bendish* (1913), *A Lovers' Tale* (1915), *Song of the Plow* (1916), *Frey and His Wife* (1916), *Love and Lucy* (1916), *Mainwaring* (1920), and *Wiltshire Essays* (1922).

Hexam (hek'sạm), **Lizzie.** The object of the rivalry between Wrayburn and Headstone in Dickens's *Our Mutual Friend.*

hexameter (hek.sam'ẹ.tẻr). In prosody, a period, line, or verse consisting of six measures. In books on modern versification, the "measure" and "foot" being ordinarily assumed to be identical, the word *hexameter* is used as precisely equivalent to *hexapody;* but according to the nomenclature of classical metrics, a hexameter is a group of six feet only in those classes of feet which are measured by single feet (monopodies). Since iambi, trochees, and anapests are measured by dipodies, an iambic, trochaic, or anapestic hexameter would be a group of twelve feet, a group of six such feet being a *trimeter.* The name *hexameter* is given by preëminence to the *dactylic hexameter,* also called the *heroic* or *epic hexameter,* or *heroic* or *epic verse,* from its use in Greek and Roman epic poetry from the earliest to the latest period. It is a compound verse consisting of two cola or members, either both of three feet or one of two feet and one of four feet. The heroic hexameter never consists of six dactyls, the last foot being always a spondee (– –), or, as the last syllable of a period may always be either long or short, a trochee (– ◡) as a substitute for a spondee. Some authorities have regarded this meter as catalectic, so that the last foot would be a trochee by omission of the last syllable of the dactyl, or a spondee for the trochee. The fifth foot is rarely a spondee, but a spondee can always be used instead of a dactyl in any of the first four places. The ordinary form of the hexameter is accordingly – ◡◡ | – ◡◡ | – ◡◡ | – ◡◡ | – ◡ ◡ | – ◡. A verse with a spondee as fifth foot is said to be *spondaic,* one consisting entirely of spondees *holospondaic,* and one entirely (except the last foot) of dactyls *holodactylic.* The principal caesuras are the trochaic of the third foot, the penthemimeral, and the hephthemimeral; besides which the bucolic caesura or dieresis and the trithemimeral caesura are to be noted.

> They ben versifyed comounly
> Of six feet, which men clepe exametron.
> (Chaucer, Prol. to *Monk's Tale.*)

The English verse which we call heroick consists of no more than ten syllables; the Latin hexameter sometimes rises to seventeen.
(Dryden, *Orig. and Prog. of Satire.*)

> In the hexameter rises the fountain's silvery column,
> In the pentameter aye falling in melody back.
> (Coleridge, tr. of Schiller's *Ovidian Elegiac Meter.*)

> Fancy, borne perhaps upon the rise
> And long roll of the Hexameter.
> (Tennyson, *Lucretius.*)

Hexapla (hek'sạ.plạ). An edition of the Bible in six versions. The name is especially given to a collection of texts of the Old Testament collated by Origen. It contained in six parallel columns the Hebrew text in Hebrew characters and in Greek characters, the Septuagint with critical emendations, and versions by Symmachus, Aquila, and Theodotion. There were also fragments of several other versions.

Hext (hekst), **Harrington.** Pseudonym of **Phillpotts, Eden.**

Heylin or **Heylyn** (hā'lin, hī'-), **Peter.** b. at Burford, Oxfordshire, England, Nov. 29, 1600; d. at London, May 8, 1662. An English church historian and controversialist. Among his works are *Cosmography* (1662) and *Ecclesia Restaurata: the History of the Reformation of the Church of England* (1661).

Heyst (hīst), **Axel.** The hero of Joseph Conrad's *Victory.*

Heywood (hā'wŭd), **John.** b. c1497; d. at Mechelen (Malines), Belgium, c1580. An English epigrammatist and dramatist. He was a sort of court jester, though of good social position, and known for his powers of repartee. He was a favorite with Queen Mary but when Elizabeth ascended the throne he retired to Mechelen, where he is supposed to have died. He wrote three interludes in which for the first time characters were personal and not mere abstractions; he thus paved the way for English comedy. The best-known of the interludes is *The Playe called the foure PP: a newe and a very mery interlude of a palmer, a pardoner, a potycary, a pedler,* printed between 1543 and 1547. His *Epigrams and Proverbs* (1562) show both wit and humor, and were very popular. He wrote also *The Play of Love, The Play of the Wether,* and *Witty and Witless;* probably also by him are the plays *The Pardoner and the Friar* and *A mery play Betwene Johan Johan the husbande, Tyb his wyfe, and Syr Jhan the preest.*

Heywood, Thomas. b. in Lincolnshire, England, c1575; d. 1641. An English dramatist and miscellaneous writer. He speaks of his residence at Cambridge in his *Apology for Actors,* but there is no record of him there. He was an actor, a member of the Lord Admiral's, Earl of Southampton's, Earl of Derby's, Earl of Worcester's, and the Queen's companies. After the death of the queen (1603) he went back to the Earl of Worcester's company. He was a prolific writer. Among his plays are *The Four Prentices of London* (produced c1600; printed 1615), *Edward IV* (c1599; in 2 parts), *If You Know not Me, You Know Nobody; or, The Troubles of Queene Elizabeth* (1605–06; in 2 parts), *The Royal King and the Loyall Subject* (printed 1637; acted much earlier), *A Woman Killed with Kindness* (acted 1603; printed 1607), *The Golden Age* (1611), *The Silver Age* (1612–13), *The Brazen Age* (1612–13), *The Iron Age* (1632; in 2 parts), *A Fair Maid of the West, or A Girl Worth Gold* (acted 1617; printed 1631), *The English Traveller* (printed 1633), *Love's Mistress, or The Queen's Masque* (1636), *The Wise Woman of Hogsden* (c1604; printed 1638), *Fortune by Land and Sea* (with William Rowley, c1607; printed 1655), *The Rape of Lucrece* (c1607), *A Challenge for Beauty* (c1635), and *A Maidenhead Well Lost* (c1633). He wrote the lord mayor's pageants for many years. Among his miscellaneous works are selections from

Lucian, Ovid, and others; *Troia Britannica*, a long heroic poem (1609); *An Apology for Actors* (1612; reprinted with alterations by William Cartwright in 1658, with the title *The Actors' Vindication*); *England's Elizabeth* (1631); and *The Hierarchy of the Blessed Angels*, a long didactic poem (1635).

Hibernia (hī.bér'ni.ạ). Latin name of Ireland.

Hichens (hich'ẹnz); **Robert Smythe.** b. in England, Nov. 14, 1864; d. July 20, 1950. An English novelist. His works include *The Green Carnation* (1894), *New Love* (1895), *An Imaginative Man* (1895), *Flames* (1897), *Byways* (1898), *The Londoners* (1898), *Felix* (1902), *The Woman with the Fan* (1904), *The Garden of Allah* (1904; dramatized), *The Call of the Blood* (1906), *Barbary Sheep* (1907), *Egypt and its Monuments* (1908), *Bella Donna* (1909; dramatized), *The Holy Land* (1910), *The Dweller on the Threshold* (1911), *The Fruitful Vine* (1911), *Mrs. Marden* (1919), *Doctor Artz* (1929), *The Paradine Case* (1933), *The Journey Up* (1938), *The Million* (1940), and *A New Way of Life* (1942).

Hickathrift (hik'ạ.thrift), **Tom.** In English legend, a laboring man of the time of William the Conqueror, who had prodigious strength. He was knighted for his wonderful exploits, and became a byword in folklore for the fabulous strong-man hero. His story may allude to some of the insurrections in the Isle of Ely.

Hicks (hiks), Sir **Seymour.** [Full name, **Edward Seymour Hicks.**] b. at St. Heliers, Island of Jersey, Jan. 30, 1871; d. in Hampshire, England, April 6, 1949. An English actor, playwright, and manager. He originated theatrical and concert performances for soldiers during World War I. He was known especially as dancer and singer in musical comedies. Author of *The Earl and the Girl, The Gay Gordons, The Price of Silence*, and other plays.

Hick Scorner (hik' skōr'nér). [Also, **Hycke Scorner.**] A moral interlude printed by Wynkyn de Worde, and written probably soon after 1500 by an unknown author.

Hierocles (hī.er'ọ.klēz). fl. in late 3rd and early 4th century A.D. A native of Caria, Roman proconsul in Bithynia, and later Alexandria, during the reign of Diocletian; said to have incited that emperor to his persecution of the Christians.

Hieronimo (hī.ẹ.ron'i.mō). [Also, **Jeronimo.**] In Thomas Kyd's *Spanish Tragedy*, a marshal of Spain who is seeking revenge for the murder of his son Horatio.

Hieronimo, The first part of. [Also, **The first part of Jeronimo.**] A play included in editions of the works of Thomas Kyd. The only version extant was printed in 1605. The second part was *The Spanish Tragedy*, which is definitely known to be by Kyd. Hieronimo (or Jeronimo), the hero of both, is an old man, the marshal of Spain, who goes mad with grief over the murder of his son. His ravings were ridiculed by contemporary and later dramatists, and became regular expletives in the slang of the period. Shakespeare alludes to this in his "Go by Jeronymy" in *The Taming of the Shrew*. There is also a reference to it in the Introduction to Marston's *Malcontent*.

Hieronimo (hī.ẹ.ron'i.mō). See also **Jeronimo.**

Higden (hig'dẹn), **Mrs. Betty.** In Dickens's *Our Mutual Friend*, an aged but still very active woman, who lives in dread of being sent to the poorhouse.

Higden (hig'dẹn) or **Higdon** (-dọn), **Ranulf.** b. c1299; d. at Chester, England, c1363. An English chronicler. He was the author of a general history entitled *Polychronicon*.

Higgins (hig'inz), **Frederick Robert.** b. at Foxford, County Mayo, Ireland, April 24, 1896; d. at Dublin, Jan. 8, 1941. An Irish poet and theater director, managing director (1935–41) of the Abbey Theatre at Dublin. He was author of the poetic works *Salt Air* (1924), *Island Blood* (1925), *The Dark Breed* (1927), *Arable Holdings* (1933), and *The Gap of Brightness*, and of the play *A Deuce of Jacks* (1935).

Higgins, Henry. In Shaw's *Pygmalion*, the teacher of phonetics whose experiment in changing a Cockney flower-girl into someone who has the bearing and speech of a fine lady finally brings about his own change from a cold person into a man of emotion, passionately in love with the girl who is the object of his experiment.

High-Heels and Low-Heels. The two political parties in Lilliput, in Swift's *Gulliver's Travels*, intended to satirize the Tories and Whigs.

Highland Mary. The name given by Burns, in a poem (1792), to his dead sweetheart Mary Campbell.

Highlands, the. [Also, **Scottish Highlands.**] A largely mountainous region in N and C Scotland, lying generally NW of a line from the Firth of Clyde to Aberdeen. It includes the counties of Argyllshire, Inverness-shire, Ross and Cromarty, Sutherland, and parts of Caithness-shire, Nairnshire, Moray, Banffshire, Aberdeenshire, Kincardineshire, Angus, Perthshire, Stirlingshire, Dunbartonshire, and Buteshire. The Highlands are an area of old eroded mountains, broken by many deep valleys; the great valley of Glen More breaks the region into two separate mountain groups, the Grampians and the Western Highlands (also called the Northern Highlands). The Highlands include Ben Nevis (4,406 ft.), the highest summit in the British Isles; the climate is extremely raw and most of the upland is either barren or poor heath and moorland used for extensive sheep grazing. There are extensive areas of timber on the lower slopes. As a major area, the Highlands are the least densely populated and the most isolated part of the British Isles; the inhabitants are mainly of Celtic stock and their Gaelic speech has survived down to the present day, although most of the population is now bilingual. Because of their magnificent scenery and romantic historical associations, the Highlands attract many tourists. The Highland clans took an active part on the Royalist side in the civil wars of 1642–50, for James II in 1689, and in the Jacobite risings of 1715 and 1745.

Highland Widow, The. A story by Sir Walter Scott, published in 1827.

High Life Below Stairs. A farce (1759) by James Townley. Lovel, recently returned from the West Indies, obtains a position as servant in his own household. He thus secures first-hand knowledge of the servants' world "below stairs," and is enabled finally to dismiss those who have been robbing him.

Highwayman, The. A historical novel by Henry Christopher Bailey, published in 1915. It is set in the period of Queen Anne.

Hild (hild), **Saint.** [Also, **Hilda** (hil′dạ).] b. in the West Riding of Yorkshire, England, 614; d. at Whitby, England, Nov. 17, 680. An English abbess, founder of the monastery at Whitby, remembered for her aid to Caedmon, who entered the monastery under her aegis and was encouraged by her in the composition of religious verse. She was a descendant of the royal Northumbrian line.

Hilda Lessways (hil′dạ les′wāz). A novel by Arnold Bennett, published in 1911. It is the second volume in the "Clayhanger" trilogy (also known as the second "Five Towns" trilogy). Its companion volumes are *Clayhanger* (1910) and *These Twain* (1916).

Hildebrandslied (hil′dẹ.bränts.lēt). An Old High German poem in alliterative verse, of unknown authorship, preserved in a fragmentary form in a single manuscript which dates from the end of the 8th century. It is important as the only extant example of Old High German heroic poetry. The surviving fragment relates how Hadubrand, the son of Hildebrand, not knowing his father, compels the latter to do battle, in which the son is killed. It is thus a variant of the widespread legend which in Persian literature is the story of Sohrab and Rustum, and in the old Irish tales is the episode of Conlaoch and Cuchulain.

Hill (hil), **Aaron.** b. at London, Feb. 10, 1685; d. Feb. 8, 1750. An English poet, dramatist, and general writer. He published the *Plain Dealer* (1724–25) and the *Prompter* (1734–36), both periodicals, the former with William Bond. He wrote the tragedy *Elfrid* (1710; revised as *Athelwold*, 1731), and *Zara* (1736) and *Merope* (1749), adaptations from Voltaire. *The Walking Statue* (1710), a farce, was a success.

Hill, George Birbeck Norman. b. at Tottenham, Middlesex, England, June 7, 1835; d. at Hampstead, London, Feb. 27, 1903. An English author and educator. He wrote *Dr. Johnson, his Friends and his Critics* (1878), a biography (1880) of his uncle, Sir Rowland Hill, *Footsteps of Dr. Johnson in Scotland* (1890), *Writers and Readers* (1891), *Harvard College by an Oxonian* (1894), and *Talks About Autographs* (1896). His editorial work, of the highest value to students and teachers, includes Boswell's *Correspondence* (1879) and *Journal* (1879), Boswell's *Johnson* (6 vols., 1887), Johnson's *Rasselas* (1887), Goldsmith's *Traveler* (1888), *Wit and Wisdom of Samuel Johnson* (1888), *Lord Chesterfield's Worldly Wisdom* (1890), *Johnsonian Miscellanies* (1897), *Memoirs of the Life of Edward Gibbon* (1900), Johnson's *Lives of the English Poets* (3 vols., 1905), and editions of the letters of Charles G. Gordon (1881), David Hume (1888), Johnson (2 vols., 1892), Rossetti (1897), and Swift (1899).

Hill, Sir Rowland. b. at Kidderminster, England, Dec. 3, 1795; d. at Hampstead, near London, Aug. 27, 1879. The originator of the English penny postal system. He published in 1837 a pamphlet entitled *Post Office Reform: its Importance and Practicability,* in which he recommended the adoption throughout the United Kingdom of a uniform rate of one penny for letters not exceeding half an ounce. An act embodying this proposition was passed by Parliament in 1839, and the penny rate was introduced on Jan. 10, 1840. He was appointed secretary to the postmaster general in 1846, was secretary to the post office (1854–64), and was knighted in 1860.

Hill Difficulty, The. See **Difficulty, The Hill.**

Hilliad (hil′i.ạd), **The.** A satirical poem (c1758) by Christopher Smart, attacking Sir John Hill, a notorious quack doctor of the day.

Hilton (hil′tọn), **James.** b. at Leigh, Lancashire, England, Sept. 9, 1900; d. at Long Beach, California, Dec. 20, 1954. An English novelist. Author of *Catherine Herself* (1920), *And Now Goodbye* (1931), *Contango* (1932), *Lost Horizon* (1933; awarded the 1934 Hawthornden prize), *Goodbye, Mr. Chips* (1934; dramatized, 1938), *We Are Not Alone* (1937), *To You, Mr. Chips* (1938), *Random Harvest* (1941), *So Well Remembered* (1946), *Nothing so Strange* (1947), and *Morning Journey* (1951).

Hilton, Walter. d. at Newark, Nottinghamshire, England, 1396. An Augustinian canon of Thurgarton and author of the *Scale of Perfection.*

Hind and the Panther, The. A satirical poem by Dryden, published in 1687; a defense of Roman Catholicism. The hind typified the Church of Rome; the panther, the Church of England.

Hindi (hin′dē). An Indo-European language of N and C India, spoken by over 121 million people. It is written in characters like those of the standard Sanskrit alphabet and began to be used as a literary language in the 16th century. It is the most widely spoken language in India; many speakers of other languages in India have adopted it as a second language out of nationalist sentiment. Urdu is essentially the same language, but it is written in the Arabic, rather than the Sanskritic script. In its literary form, Urdu usually contains somewhat more Persian words than does ordinary Hindi. Urdu also has important symbolic meanings for the Moslem nationalists of Pakistan. Hindustani is a term which is loosely used for the spoken forms of both Hindi and Urdu. There are many dialects of Hindi; these are grouped into two main divisions, Eastern Hindi and Western Hindi.

Hindle Wakes (hin′dl). A comedy (1912) by Stanley Houghton.

Hindley (hind′li), **Charles.** d. at Brighton, England, in May, 1893. An English bookseller. He wrote a good deal for the press, but is best known as the author of *Mother Shipton's Prophecy* (1862), purported to have been published in 1448.

Hindustani (hin.dọ.stän′ē). [Also: **Hindostani, Hindoostani.**] A term applied to the standard vernacular forms of both Hindi and Urdu. It belongs to West Hindi, one of the languages of the Indic group of Indo-Iranian languages.

Hinkson (hingk′sọn), **Katharine Tynan.** b. at Dublin, Ireland, Jan. 23, 1861; d. at Wimbledon, England, April 2, 1931. An Irish poet and novelist, particularly noted for her reminiscences of William Butler Yeats. Her books of poetry include *New Poems* (1911), *Flower of Youth* (1914), *Late Songs*

(1917), and *Collected Poems* (1930). Her prose works include *Twenty-five Years* (1913), *The Middle Years* (1917), *The Years of the Shadow* (1919), *The Wandering Years* (1922), and *Memories* (1924).

Hippo (hip′ō). [Also, **Hippo Regius** (rē′ji.us).] In ancient geography, a city in Numidia, near what is now Bône, Algeria. It was burned (430) by the Vandals. Saint Augustine was bishop of Hippo.

Hippocrates (hi.pok′ra.tēz). [Called the **"Father of Medicine."**] b. on the island of Kos, c460 B.C.; d. at Larissa, Thessaly, c377. A Greek physician. Nothing definite is known of his life: he is said to have been a descendant (17th or 19th in direct line) of Aesculapius, to have traveled widely, and to have practiced in various places. Of the 72 (or 87) medical works attributed to him, it is not known which, if any, he wrote; there is, however, general recognition of a Hippocratic school of medicine and a corpus of Hippocratic treatises that were preserved in the Alexandrian library. The Hippocratic physician discarded the philosophic approach and also the ancient customs and beliefs in his insistence that the effect must have a cause; moreover, the effect was the result of ascertainable causes and was not of supernatural origin. Climate, food, even the kind of government under which the patient lived had to be considered. Observation was the keynote of the teaching of Hippocrates; of necessity his knowledge of anatomy was weak, since current religious beliefs did not sanction vivisection, and his theories of essences or humors were incorrect. But his observation was sharp enough to make the *facies Hippocratica*, described in his *Prognostics*, a still recognizable symptom in the dying patient. His *Aphorisms* contains the famous "Life is short, but the art is long." The Hippocratic Oath, taken by doctors today, is perfectly in harmony with Hippocrates's reported medical practice, even though it was not written by him.

Hippocrene (hip′ō.krēn, hip.ō.krē′nē). A fountain on Mount Helicon, in Boeotia, sacred to the Muses. Traditionally it sprang up from a hoof mark of Pegasus, and is alluded to as a source of poetic inspiration (as in Keats's *Ode to a Nightingale*).

Hippodamia or **Hippodameia** (hi.pod.a.mī′a). In Greek legend: **1.** The daughter of Oenomaus. She was won in marriage by Pelops in a race against her father's horses.
2. A daughter of Atrax, one of the Lapithae. At her marriage with Perithous (king of the Lapithae) the battle of the Centaurs and Lapithae took place. One of the Centaurs attempted to abduct her; but the Centaurs were defeated.

Hippolita (hi.pol′i.ta). The principal female character in Wycherley's comedy *The Gentleman Dancing-Master*.

Hippolito (hi.pol′i.tō). The uncle of Isabella, guilty of an incestuous passion for his niece, in Thomas Middleton's *Women Beware Women*.

Hippolito, Count. One of the chief characters in Middleton and Dekker's *The Honest Whore*.

Hippolyta (hi.pol′i.ta). In Shakespeare's *Midsummer Night's Dream*, the Queen of the Amazons, betrothed to Theseus.

Hippolyta. In *The Two Noble Kinsmen*, the wife of Theseus and sister of the heroine, Emilia. She begs Theseus to spare Palamon and Arcite.

Hippolyte (hi.pol′i.tē). In classical mythology, a queen of the Amazons. She was the daughter of Ares and Otrera, and wore as an emblem of her dignity a girdle received from her father. This girdle was coveted by Eurystheus (king of Mycena) who ordered Hercules to fetch it, as one of the famous 12 labors. Hercules was kindly received at her court, and was promised the girdle; but Hera roused the Amazons by spreading the report that their queen was being robbed, and Hercules, believing that Hippolyte was plotting against his life, killed her, and carried away the girdle.

Hippolytus (hi.pol′i.tus). In Greek legend, the son of Theseus and either the Amazon queen, Hippolyte, or her sister, Antiope. He was stepson of Phaedra, whom Theseus later married. Phaedra fell in love with him, but was repulsed, and in revenge falsely accused him to Theseus of making advances to her. Theseus called upon Poseidon to avenge him, and, accordingly, as Hippolytus was riding along the shore, the god sent a bull out of the sea against him. His horses were frightened, and he was thrown out of his chariot and dragged until he died. When Theseus discovered the innocence of his son, Phaedra killed herself in despair. Hippolytus is one of the people whom Aesculapius is said to have restored to life.

Hippopotamus, The. A poem by T. S. Eliot, published in 1920, comparing the mortal life of the hippopotamus to that of the "True Church," whose foundations are built upon everlasting rock. He extends the analogy to sharpen his point about the enduring (although earthbound) qualities of the church in contrast to the transitory life of the "'potamus."

Hiren (hī′ren). A form of the name "Irene," used for a character in the play *The Turkish Mahomet and Hiren the Fair Greek*, attributed to George Peele. It came to be synonymous with "strumpet" as in the phrase "Have we not Hiren here?" which appears in Dekker's *Satiromastix* and a number of 17th-century works.

Hirlas Horn (hėr′läs), **The.** A Welsh poem, written by Owain Cyveiliog, prince of Powys, in the 12th century. The Hirlas horn is "a drinking-horn, long, blue, and silver-rimmed," which Owain fills and drinks to each of his chiefs, with a song.

Hirst (hėrst), **Francis W.** b. at Huddersfield, Yorkshire, England, 1873—. An English editor and author. In 1907 he became editor of the London *Economist*. Among his published works are *Adam Smith* (1904), *Trusts and Cartels* (1905), *The Arbiter in Council* (1906), *The Stock Exchange* (1911), *Liberty and Tyranny* (1935), and *Armaments* (1937).

His House in Order. A drama (1906) by A. W. Pinero.

His Litany to the Holy Spirit. A poem by Robert Herrick, notable for the refrain "Sweet Spirit, comfort me!" (which is repeated as the poet thinks of a time of torment to his soul, of his last illness and death, and his final judgment before the Lord).

fat, fāte, fär, åsk, fāre; net, mē, hėr; pin, pīne; not, nōte, möve, nôr; up, lūte, pùll; ᴛʜ, then;

Hispalis (his′pạ.lis). A Latin name of Seville, Spain.

Hispania (his′pā′ni.ạ). See **Iberia.**

Historia Brittonum (his.tō′ri.ạ brit′ọ.num). A chronicle of the early history and geography of Britain, written by the Welshman Nennius in the late 8th or early 9th century. Whether Nennius was a compiler of earlier works or a reviser of a still earlier history of the Britons is a matter of dispute, as is his actual text, since none of the extant manuscripts are earlier than c1000 and may be corrupt. The story of King Arthur (here simply a war leader said to have won twelve great battles in the last of which, the battle of Mount Badon, he killed 960 of the enemy singlehanded) first appears in this chronicle. The *Historia Brittonum* is thought to have been one of the sources for Geoffrey of Monmouth's *Historia Regum Britanniae.*

Historia Ecclesiastica (e.klē.zi.as′ti.kạ). See **Ecclesiastical History**; See also under **Bede.**

Historia Regum Britanniae (rē′gum bri.tan′i.ē). An imaginative account (the title means "History of the Kings of Britain") of the early history of Britain, by Geoffrey of Monmouth. The publication of this book marks an epoch in the literary history of Europe; in less than 50 years the Arthurian and Round Table romances based upon it were naturalized in Germany and Italy, as well as in France and England. It is thought that Geoffrey compiled it from the Latin *Historia Brittonum* of Nennius and a book of Breton legends now perished. It was abridged by Alfred of Beverley, and Geoffrey Gaimar and Wace translated it into Anglo-Norman about the middle of the 12th century. Layamon and Robert of Gloucester translated Wace into the English of their day, and later chroniclers used it as sober history. Shakespeare knew the legends through Holinshed. As history, the book is impossible; as a source of legend and tradition it is justly famous. It was issued in some form in Latin from the British or Cymric manuscript by 1139. The final edition, as we now possess it, was finished in 1147. The first critical printed edition is *Galfredi Monemutensis Historia Britonum, nunc primum in Anglia novem codd. MSS. collatis,* ed. J. A. Giles (1844).

Historia Rerum Anglicarum (rē′rum ang.gli.kā′rum). A Latin prose history (the title means "History of English Affairs"), by William of Newburgh, particularly interesting for its account of the reign of Henry II.

historical novel. The reconstruction in a prose work of relatively great length of a historical event, character, or period in a blend of fact and fiction. At its best, the historical novel gives an interpretation of the essential truth of some past era, illuminating the dark places by introducing fictional characters and incidents that are plausible and consistent with known fact. Often the choice of a fictional character as the protagonist gives the writer greater scope than if he chooses a historical personage, whose career is a matter of record. Among the chief English writers of historical novels who have invented their heroes, putting historical characters in minor parts, are

Sir Walter Scott and Thackeray; some of the greatest novelists of other countries, such as Tolstoy, Hugo, and Dumas, use the same device. Other writers prefer to rest their stories on some colorful, important historical personage, the advantage of this method being that the intrinsic literary value of such a character gives the story weight, color, and drama. Many good novels have been woven around real historical personages, such as Maurice Hewlett's *The Queen's Quair*, concerning Mary, Queen of Scots, H. C. Bailey's *The Lonely Queen*, about Queen Elizabeth, Bulwer-Lytton's *Rienzi*, and Charles Reade's *The Cloister and the Hearth*, with Erasmus as a focal character.

Development of the Historical Novel. The doings of historical persons of importance have long had a place in English literature. The romance of the Middle Ages was often concocted of a number of stories of doubtful authenticity about some great hero like Charlemagne or King Arthur. With the full development of the drama in the 16th century, the chronicle (or history) play became a favorite. In the late 16th century a number of short novels, or novelettes, of a historical nature appeared. These were mostly picaresque stories, with a meager background of some past era. Thomas Nash's *Unfortunate Traveller* (1594), one of the best of these short novels, is set in the time of Henry VIII and makes use of such well-known figures of the time as the Earl of Surrey, Sir Thomas More, and Erasmus. The picaresque mode has often been used since Nash's time by writers of historical fiction, as an excellent way of moving their heroes from place to place; Hervey Allen's massive *Anthony Adverse* is a recent example of how much wordage can be squeezed from the traveling hero. Another early historical novel, Thomas Deloney's *Jack of Newbury* (1597), a story of adventure rather than purely picaresque, also has a very sketchy background of the time of Henry VIII, but relies for its appeal on the charm of its hero, Jack, who is described as being attractive, resourceful, a good fellow and a dapper dresser, free with his money, always ready to stand a drink but never drunk, "wondrous wel-beloved of Rich and Poore." In the 18th century another mode was adopted by the historical novel, that of the Gothic novel, its favorite period being the medieval. Soon after, in the beginning of the 19th century, Sir Walter Scott developed the historical novel to more or less its present form. From 1814 to 1831, Scott turned out his novels at the rate of about one and one half each year. In his *Waverley* series, people from real history figure in *Waverley, The Black Dwarf, Rob Roy,* and *Redgauntlet. Ivanhoe* has an English setting, with tournaments and sieges, and involves such characters as Richard the Lion-Hearted and Robin Hood. *Kenilworth* introduces the Earl of Leicester and the pageantry of the court of Elizabeth. *Quentin Durward* is about the court of Louis XI of France; *The Talisman* and *Count Robert of Paris* are concerned with crusaders in Palestine in the 12th century and in Constantinople in the 11th. Scott's early novels emphasize the chivalry of the Scottish clan, and later he passes to the chivalry of kingdoms, empires, and of Christendom itself. He stresses such virtues as loyalty to friend and lord, generosity

ḍ, d or j; ṣ, s or sh; ṭ, t or ch; ẓ, z or zh; *o*, F. cloche; ü, F. menu; c̆h, Sc. loch; ṅ, F. bonbon.

to foe, tenderness to the weak and oppressed. Sometimes there is a confusion of values, as when faithfulness within the clan is coupled with the worst sort of banditry outside it. A favorite theme is that of the heir cheated of his rights, but finally regaining them. Bulwer-Lytton, whose popularity has not lasted so well as Scott's, wrote his *Last Days of Pompeii* in 1834, two years after Scott's death. *Rienzi*, about the medieval Roman "tribune"; *Leila*, about the conquest of Granada; *The Last of the Barons*, about the Wars of the Roses; *Harold*, about the Norman Conquest, followed within the next 15 years. Following Scott and Bulwer, historical novels were voluminous and popular. William Harrison Ainsworth turned out 40; G. P. R. James, 70. Among the best of that period were Charles Kingsley's *Hypatia*, and *Westward Ho!* A few years later, in 1861, Charles Reade published his *Cloister and the Hearth*, drawing on contemporary documents to create a rich background of 15th-century Europe. While neither Dickens nor Thackeray was primarily a historical novelist, both at times touched the historical form. Dickens's *Tale of Two Cities* suggests the horrors and inhumanities of the time of the French Revolution in an unforgettable way; and in Thackeray's *Henry Esmond* are reconstructed the atmosphere of plotting Papists and the brilliant literary London of Queen Anne. In the 19th and the 20th centuries, other forms of fiction were developed, such as the novels of social comment and reform, and the realistic novel, but the historical novel kept turning up among the newer fiction. Thomas Hardy wrote *The Dynasts*, and George Moore, after his early naturalistic novels, wrote long, dreamy stories about historical and legendary characters, including *Héloïse and Abélard*. One has only to think of the popularity of *Anthony Adverse*, or of C. S. Forester's "Hornblower" series, to see that the historical novel remains a favorite with the reading public.

Historie of Virginia. See **Generall Historie of Virginia, New-England, and the Summer Isles.**

History and Fall of Caius Marius (kā'us mār'i.us), **The.** See **Caius Marius, The History and Fall of.**

History and Remarkable Life of Colonel Jacque . . . (jak). See **Colonel Jack.**

History of Cardenio (kär.dā'ni.ō), **The.** See **Cardenio, The History of.**

History of Anthony Waring (an'thọ.ni wār'ing), **The.** A novel by May Sinclair, published in 1927.

History of Beryn (ber'in). See **Beryn, History of.**

History of Jacob Stahl (jā'kọb stäl'), **The Early.** A novel by John Davys Beresford, published in 1911. It is the first volume of a trilogy, dealing with the adventures of an architect hero. Its companion volumes are *A Candidate for Truth* (1912) and *The Invisible Event* (1915).

History of Mr. Polly (pol'i), **The.** A novel by H. G. Wells, published in 1910. It is the story of Alfred Polly, a small shopkeeper who runs away from home and responsibility, and establishes his own "death." Returning after five years of freedom, he finds that his wife, Miriam, is getting along satisfactorily. Polly then goes back to the Potwell

Inn and the "plump woman" with whom he has a happy understanding.

History of Richard III. See under **Morton, John.**

History of the Holy Grail, The. A Middle English romance by Henry Lovelich, a London skinner, written c1450, and dealing with the early history of the Grail. In comparison with the treatments of the theme found in Malory and various French sources, it is a clumsy piece of work.

History of the Kings of Britain. See **Historia Regum Britanniae.**

Histriomastix (his"tri.ọ.mas'tiks). A play by John Marston, produced before 1599, in which year Jonson satirized it in his *Every Man Out of His Humour.* It was printed in 1610. Chrisoganus is a distinct caricature of Jonson.

Histrio-Mastix. [Also: **Histriomastix;** full title, **Histrio-Mastix, the Player's Scourge, or Actor's Tragaedie.**] A treatise by William Prynne, published in 1632, though dated 1633. The book was designed to promote (on the ground of immorality) the total suppression of stage plays. In 1649 a mock retraction, entitled *Mr. William Prynne, his Defence of Stage-Plays, or a Retraction of a former Book of his called Histrio-Mastix,* was published.

H. M. S. Pinafore (pin'ạ.fōr). See **Pinafore.**

Hoadly or **Hoadley** (hōd'li), **Benjamin.** b. at Westerham, Kent, England, Nov. 14, 1676; d. at Chelsea, London, April 17, 1761. An English divine and controversialist.

Hoadly, Benjamin. b. at London, Feb. 10, 1706; d. at Chelsea, London, Aug. 10, 1757. An English physician and author; son of Benjamin Hoadly (1676–1761). He assisted Hogarth in his *Analysis of Beauty.* He was the author of *The Suspicious Husband* (produced in 1747) and, with the help of his brother, of *The Contrast* (produced in 1731).

Hobbema (hôb'ẹ.mä), **Meindert** (or **Meyndert** or **Minderhout**). b. at Amsterdam, or Koeverdam, Netherlands, c1638; d. at Amsterdam, in December, 1709. A Dutch landscape painter.

Hobbes (hobz), **Thomas.** b. at Westport (now in Malmesbury), Wiltshire, England, April 5, 1588; d. at Hardwick Hall, Dec. 4, 1679. An English philosopher. His father, Thomas Hobbes, was vicar of Charlton and Westport. In 1603 Hobbes entered Magdalen Hall, Oxford, where he graduated in 1608. He soon entered the service of William Cavendish (later 1st Earl of Devonshire) as tutor and companion to his eldest son (later 2nd Earl of Devonshire), and retained this position until the death of his pupil in 1628. They made a continental tour in 1610. In 1629 he became traveling tutor to the son of Sir Gervase Clifton, and visited Paris and, probably, Italy. He returned to the service of the Cavendishes in 1631 as tutor to the 3rd Earl of Devonshire, with whom he made (1634–37) an extended tour on the Continent, during which he established friendly relations with many distinguished men, including Galileo, Gassendi, Mersenne, and Descartes. Previous to this time (probably before 1625) he had served Francis Bacon as amanuensis, and in translating some of his essays into Latin. He lived with Devonshire until 1640, when fear of persecution by Parliament for his political opinions drove him to Paris, where he remained until 1651, when, in the belief that his life was in danger from those who accused him of heterodoxy and even atheism, he fled back to England and became reconciled to the Cromwellian government. For a time in 1646 he instructed the Prince of Wales (later Charles II) in mathematics. After the Restoration he lived with the Earl of Devonshire. Hobbes was a pronounced nominalist in philosophy, an antagonist of scholasticism, one of the suggesters of the associational psychology, and a leader of modern rationalism. He insisted especially upon the complete separation of theology and philosophy, and the subordination of the church to the state. He is best known for his doctrine that the power of the state is absolute as against the individual, that it is the "Leviathan" that swallows all, a mortal god who, like the Deity, governs according to his pleasure, and gives peace and security to his subjects. His chief works are a translation of Thucydides's *De cive* (1642), *Human Nature, or the Fundamental Elements of Policy* (1650), *De corpore politico* (1650), *Leviathan, or the Matter, Form, and Power of a Commonwealth, Ecclesiastical and Civil* (1651), and *Of Liberty and Necessity* (1654). His collected works (five in Latin) were edited (1839–45) by Sir W. Molesworth in 16 volumes.

Hobbididence (hob″i.di.dens′, hob.i.did′ens). In Shakespeare's *King Lear*, a fiend ("prince of dumbness") mentioned by Edgar (IV.i).

Hobbie Elliot (hob′i el′yǫt). See **Elliot, Halbert** or **Hobbie.**

Hobbinol (hob′i.nol). The name used by Edmund Spenser to designate his friend Gabriel Harvey in his writings.

Hobhouse (hob′hous), **John Cam.** [Title, Baron Broughton de Gyfford.] b. at Redland, near Bristol, England, June 27, 1786; d. at London, June 3, 1869. An English politician and writer. He entered Parliament in 1820, became secretary at war in 1832, and was appointed chief secretary for Ireland in March, 1833, but soon resigned his office and his seat. He reëntered Parliament in 1834, and was president of the board of control (1835–41, 1846–52). In 1819 he was arrested and committed to Newgate Prison for an anonymous pamphlet (*A Trifling Mistake in Thomas, Lord Erskine's recent Preface*), the publication of which was held to be a breach of privilege by the House of Commons. He was one of the intimate friends of Lord Byron, a connection which was formed at Cambridge. They traveled together (1809–10) on the Continent. Hobhouse was one of Byron's executors. He was created Lord Broughton in 1851. He wrote *Historical Illustrations of the Fourth Canto of "Childe Harold"* (2nd ed., 1818), *A Journey through Albania* (1813), and others. His *Diaries, Correspondence, and Memoranda* could not be opened until the year 1900. His *Recollections of a Long Life* (1909–12) were edited by his daughter.

Hobson (hob′sǫn), **John Atkinson.** b. at Derby, England, July 6, 1858; d. at Hampstead, London, April 1, 1940. An English economist. Known as a pioneer of the welfare school of economic thought, he advanced the oversaving theory of the business cycle. His works include *Problems of Poverty* (1891), *The Problem of the Unemployed* (1896), *Imperialism*

(1902; revised, 1938), *Problems of a New World* (1921), *Wealth and Life—A Human Evaluation* (1929), *God and Mammon* (1931), *Democracy* (1934), and *Confessions of an Economic Heretic* (1938).

Hobson, Thomas. b. c1544; d. Jan. 1, 1630. An English carrier and keeper of a livery stable at Cambridge, whose habit of obliging his customers to take the horse that happened to be nearest the door gave rise to the expression "Hobson's choice," that is, "this or none." Milton wrote two kindly poems about him and Steele wrote (*Spectator*, Oct. 14, 1712) an essay on his life.

Hoccleve (hok′lēv), **Thomas.** See **Occleve, Thomas.**

Hocking (hok′ing), **Joseph.** b. at St. Stephens, Cornwall, England, Nov. 7, 1860; d. at St. Ives, Cornwall, England, March 4, 1937. An English Nonconformist minister, traveler, and novelist; brother of Silas Kitto Hocking. Author of *Jabez Easterbrook* (1891), *Zillah* (1892), *All Men Are Liars* (1895), *Fields of Fair Renown* (1896), *The Scarlet Woman* (1899), *O'er Moor and Fen* (1901), *Follow the Gleam* (1903), *Esau* (1904), *A Strong Man's Vow* (1907), *The Soul of Dominic Wildthorne* (1908), *God and Mammon* (1912), *All for a Scrap of Paper* (1914), *The Path of Glory* and *Tommy and the Maid of Athens* (both 1917), *The Pomp of Yesterday* (1918), *In the Sweat of Thy Brow* (1920), *Prodigal Daughters* (1922), *Prodigal Parents* (1923), *Out of the Depths* (1930), *Caleb's Conquest* (1932), and *Deep Calleth Deep* (1936). *The Birthright* (1897) and *Felecity Treverbyn* (1927) are Cornwall novels; *The Trampled Cross* (1907), *The Jesuit* (1911), and *The Eternal Challenge* (1929) reflect his career as a clergyman; *A Flame of Fire* (1903), set in the period of Martin Luther, is an example of his work as a historical novelist.

Hocking, Silas Kitto. b. at St. Stephens, Cornwall, England, March 24, 1850; d. Sept. 15, 1935. An English Free Church (Methodist) minister and novelist; brother of Joseph Hocking. Author of *Alec Green* (1878), *Her Benny* (1879), *His Father* and *Reedyford* (both 1880), *Ivy* (1881), *Sea Waif* (1882), *Dick's Fairy* (1883), *Caleb Carthew* (1884), *Cricket* (1885), *Real Grit* (1887), *For Abigail* (1889), *For Light and Liberty* (1890), *Where Duty Lies* (1891), *One in Charity* (1893), *A Son of Reuben* (1894). *The Heart of Man* (1895), *For Such is Life* (1896), *In Spite of Fate* (1897), *God's Outcast* (1898), *Day of Recompense* and *Strange Adventures of Israel Pendray* (both 1899), *Gripped* (1902), *Pioneers* (1905), *Flaming Sword* and *The Silent Man* (both 1906), *Who Shall Judge?* (1910), *The Third Man* (1911), *The Wrath of Man* (1913), *Beautiful Alien* (1916), *His Own Accuser* (1917), *Watchers in the Dawn* (1920), *The Greater Good* (1922), and *The Mystery Man* (1930).

Hoder (hō′der). [Also: **Hödur, Hoth** (hoth); Old Norse, **Höðr, Hothr** (hō′тнеr).] In Old Norse mythology, a blind son of Odin and Frigg, who, at the instigation of Loki, unwittingly killed his brother Balder by means of a shaft of mistletoe. He was regarded as a god of darkness. He was in turn slain by Vale, another son of Odin. The prophecy is that after the battle of Ragnarok at the end of the world Hoder and Balder will be reconciled.

ḍ, d or j; ṣ, s or sh; ṭ, t or ch; ẓ, z or zh; o, F. cloche; ü, F. menu; ċh, Sc. loch; ṅ, F. bonbon.

Hodge (hoj). The typical English farm-laborer or rustic; (*l.c.*) a rustic; a countryman.

Hodge. In *Gammer Gurton's Needle*, the servant of Gammer Gurton (in whose breeches, just mended by Gammer Gurton, the lost needle is finally found).

Hodgson (hoj'sọn), **Ralph.** b. in Yorkshire, England, 1872—. An English poet. Among his works are *The Beggar* (1913), *Poems* (1917), and *Silver Wedding and Other Poems* (1941). His better-known poems include *Eve, The Gypsy Girl, The Bull, The Bride, The Last Blackbird,* and *Time, You Old Gypsy Man.*

Hodgson, Shadworth Hollway. b. at Boston, Lincolnshire, England, Dec. 25, 1832; d. at London, June 13, 1912. An English philosophical writer. Author of *Time and Space* (1865), *The Theory of Practice* (1870), *The Philosophy of Reflection* (1878), *The Metaphysic of Experience* (1898), and of many philosophical papers.

Hödur (hĕ'dŭr). See **Hoder.**

Hoenir (hĕ'nir). In Old Norse mythology, one of the three gods who created the first man and woman: the giver of sense.

Hofer (hō'fẽr), **Andreas.** b. at St. Leonhard, Passeyr valley, Tyrol, Nov. 22, 1767; executed at Mantua, Italy, Feb. 20, 1810. A Tyrolese patriot, the head of the Tyrolese insurrection (1809) against the transfer of the Tyrol from Austria to Bavaria under the treaty of Pressburg (1805). He won victories at Sterzing (now Vipiteno), Innsbruck, and elsewhere, and was the head of the government in 1809. Twice he ceased fighting after defeating the Bavarians and attaining his objectives, having the Austrian emperor's word that he would not again cede the Tyrol, but both times Francis I gave the area up. Hofer was executed after his defeat by Bavarian and French forces and his betrayal to the enemy by a neighbor.

Hoffman (hof'mạn), **Tragedy of.** [Full title, **Tragedy of Hoffman, or a Revenge for a Father.**] A tragedy by Henry Chettle, produced in 1602. It is the one extant play attributed to Chettle alone.

Hoffmann (hof'män), **Ernst Theodor Amadeus.** [Original name, **Ernst Theodor Wilhelm Hoffmann.**] b. at Königsberg, in East Prussia, Jan. 24, 1776; d. at Berlin, July 24, 1822. A German story writer and musician, the most popular of all the German romanticists. The substitution of Amadeus for Wilhelm in his name was made in honor of Mozart. He studied law at Königsberg, was in state service (1796–1806), then became music conductor at Bamberg (1808–13) and at Leipzig and Dresden (1813–15). In 1816 he was made a member of the supreme court at Berlin, a post which he held until his death. He inherited from his musician father a passionate love of music; his opera *Undine* had a long run at Berlin (1816). He began his literary career with a story about Gluck, and his Kapellmeister Johannes Kreisler, a character modeled on his father, was of all his figures the one nearest his heart. Such musicians as Offenbach and Wagner used his stories for material. His literary fame rests on stories in such collections as *Phantasiestücke in Callots Manier* (4 vols., 1814–15), *Nachtstücke* (2 vols., 1817), *Serapionsbrüder*

(4 vols., 1819–21), and on the novels *Die Elixiere des Teufels* (1815–16) and *Lebensansichten des Katers Murr* (1820–21).

Hofmannsthal (hōf'mäns.täl, hof'-), **Hugo von.** b. at Vienna, Feb. 1, 1874; d. at Rodaun, near Vienna, July 15, 1929. An Austrian dramatist, lyric poet, and prose writer. One of the foremost members of the *Jung-Wien* (Young Vienna) group of writers, he has come to be generally acclaimed as one of the very great Austrian authors. Among his plays are *Der Tor und der Tod* (1893; Eng. trans., *Death and the Fool,* 1913), *Die Hochzeit der Sobeide* (1899; Eng. trans., *The Marriage of Sobeide,* 1913–15), *Jedermann* (1911; a translation of the old morality *Everyman,* retranslated as *The Play of Everyman,* 1917), *Das grosse Salzburger Welttheater* (The Salzburg Great Theater of the World, 1922), and *Der Turm* (The Tower, 1925; revised, 1927). He also wrote librettos for the operas by Richard Strauss *Elektra* (1903; Eng. trans., *Electra,* 1908), *Der Rosenkavalier* (1911, Eng. trans., *The Knight of the Rose,* 1912), and *Ariadne auf Naxos* (1912; Eng. trans., *Ariadne on Naxos,* 1913). His prose includes *Loris, die Prosa des jungen Hugo von Hofmannsthal* (1930). See *Hugo von Hofmannsthal—Rudolf Borchardt* (1955), an exchange of letters edited in German by Marie Luise Borchardt and Herbert Steiner.

Hogarth (hō'gärth), **William.** b. at London, Nov. 10, 1697; d. there, Oct. 26, 1764. An English painter and engraver. In 1712 he was apprenticed to Ellis Gamble, a silversmith, in 1718 he turned his attention to engraving, and in 1726 he first became known by his plates for *Hudibras.* In 1729 he ran away with Sir James Thornhill's only daughter, Jane, and was married at Paddington church. He published in 1733 *The Harlot's Progress,* which was soon followed by *The Rake's Progress.* In 1735 Hogarth obtained the passage of an act securing the rights of artists to their own designs. In 1736 he painted on the stairway of St. Bartholomew's Hospital *The Good Samaritan* and *The Pool of Bethesda.* Among his other pictures are the *Distressed Poet* (1736), the *Enraged Musician* (1741), *Marriage à la Mode* (1745), *Industry and Idleness* (1747). He made a famous journey to France in 1748. In his later years he indulged in literary compositions, and wrote *The Analysis of Beauty.* He painted a number of portraits of himself, the best of which is in the National Gallery, London. His pictorial series are noted for their social satire.

Hogarth Club. A London club (established 1870) for artists.

Hogben (hog'bẹn), **Lancelot.** b. 1895—. An English scientist and writer; husband (married 1918) of Enid Charles. His books include *Nature and Nurture* (1933), *Mathematics for the Million* (1936), *Science for the Citizen* (1938), *Retreat from Reason* (1938), *Dangerous Thoughts* (1940), and *Author in Transit* (1940).

Hogg (hog), **James.** [Called the **Ettrick Shepherd.**] b. at Ettrick, Selkirkshire, Scotland, 1770; d. at Eltrive Lake, Scotland, Nov. 21, 1835. A Scottish poet. In 1790 he began to be known as a songmaker, and in 1796 his education had advanced so far that he began to write his verses. He made the acquaintance of Scott in 1802, and in 1810 he settled in Edinburgh with a view to devoting himself to literature, but went (c1816) to Eltrive Lake in Yarrow. Among his poems are *The Queen's Wake* (1813), *The Pilgrims of the Sun* (1815), *Madoc of the Moor* (1816), *The Poetic Mirror, or the Living Bards of Great Britain* (1816; parodies), and *Queen Hynde* (1826). Among his prose works are *The Brownie o' Bodsbeck* (1817), *Winter Evening Tales* (1820), and *The Private Memoirs and Confessions of a Justified Sinner* (1824). His *Jacobite Relics of Scotland* (1819–20) are both prose and verse.

Hogg, Thomas Jefferson. b. at Norton, Durham, England, 1792. An English friend and biographer of Percy Bysshe Shelley. Hogg and Shelley became friends while both were students at University College, Oxford, and when Shelley was expelled upon discovery of his authorship of the pamphlet *The Necessity of Atheism*, Hogg, who had influenced Shelley's thought, notified the university authorities that he was equally responsible, and was visited with the same punishment. Soon after his first marriage in 1811, Shelley left his young wife Harriet in Hogg's protection at York for a week, and learned upon his return that his friend had made love to his wife. Shelley forgave Hogg, but saw no more of him for two years. The friendship, when resumed in 1813, continued until Shelley's death, and Hogg was one of the beneficiaries of his will. Hogg undertook the writing of Shelley's life at the request of the poet's widow and family, but being dissatisfied with the two volumes issued in 1858, they refused him further access to material necessary to complete the work. Though it has been commented that there is too much Hogg and too little Shelley in these pages, yet it is conceded that Hogg's account of the earlier life of his famous friend is loyal in spirit and factually valuable.

Hoggarty Diamond (hog′ạr.ti), **The Great.** See **Great Hoggarty Diamond, The.**

Hogmanay (hog′mạ.nā̤). In the north of England and in Scotland, the day or evening of December 31, New Year's Eve, when troops of children go from house to house singing and soliciting pennies or cakes. In Scotland it is sometimes called Cake Day. The term is also applied to the gift given for the entertainment.

Hohenlinden (hō.ẹn.lin′dẹn). A village in S Germany, in the *Land* (state) of Bavaria, in Upper Bavaria ab. 19 mi. E of Munich. Here on Dec. 3, 1800, the French under Moreau defeated the Austrian army under the Archduke John. The Austrians lost 8,000 killed and wounded and 12,000 prisoners, and the battle virtually ended the war of the second coalition. The poet Thomas Campbell wrote a lyric on the battle.

Holbach (dol.bȧk), **Paul Henri Thiry, Baron d'.** b. at Heidelsheim, Baden, Germany, 1723; d. at Paris, Jan. 21, 1789. A French skeptic and materialistic philosopher. He wrote *Le Christianisme dévoilé* (1767), *Le Système de la nature* (1770, published in popular form as *Le Bon Sens*, 1772), and numerous articles in the *Encyclopédie*. He resided at Paris from his youth, and his home became a rendezvous for the free thinkers of his time. His dinners were exceptionally celebrated, and earned for him, from the Abbé Galiani, the title of the "premier maître d'hôtel de la philosophie."

Holbeach (hōl′bēch), **Henry.** A pseudonym of **Rands, William Brighty.**

Holbein (hōl′bīn; German, hȯl′bīn), **Hans.** [Called **Holbein the Younger.**] b. probably at Augsburg, Bavaria, Germany, c1497; d. at London, 1543. A German historical and portrait painter and wood engraver. In 1523 he painted the portrait of Erasmus at Longford Castle. About 1526 he visited Antwerp to see Quentin Massys, and afterward went to England, where he was lodged at Sir Thomas More's house, near London. In 1528 he went to Basel, and returned to England in 1532, where he remained for the rest of his life. He became court painter to Henry VIII c1536. Among his works are a series of 89 sketches in red chalk and India ink, belonging to this period, now in the Windsor collection; a series of designs for wood engraving, *The Dance of Death*, engraved by Hans Lützelburger and published in 1538 and 1547; a portrait of Sir Thomas More (1527); a portrait of Anne of Cleves (1539); a number of portraits of German merchant goldsmiths of the Steelyard, some of which are in Germany; *The Ambassadors* (in the National Gallery, 1533); and portraits of Henry VIII and of the principal personages of the time. He also designed the title pages to Coverdale's and Cranmer's Bibles.

Holborn (hō′born, hōl′-). A metropolitan borough in C London, immediately NW of the City of London. Holborn is the smallest metropolitan borough (405 acres) in London. It contains Covent Garden, Hatton Garden (the diamond market), London University, the British Museum, Bloomsbury, and parts of Soho.

Holcroft (hōl′kroft), **Thomas.** b. at London, Dec. 10, 1745; d. there, March 23, 1809. An English dramatist, miscellaneous writer, and actor. In 1794, having embraced the principles of the French Revolution, he was indicted for high treason, but after remaining for about two months in Newgate Prison he was discharged without a trial. Among his plays are *The Follies of a Day*, a translation of Beaumarchais's *Mariage de Figaro* (produced in 1784, Holcroft appearing as Figaro), *The Road to Ruin* (1792; revived in 1873, and translated into Danish and German), and *The Deserted Daughter*, founded on Cumberland's *Fashionable Lover* (1795). He also wrote *Tales of the Castle* from the French of Madame de Genlis (1785), *Life of Baron Frederic Trenck* (1788), *A Tale of Mystery* (the first melodrama, 1802), with several novels and translations.

Holda (hol′dä). [Also: **Frau** (or **Mother**) **Holde, Holle, Hulde.**] In ancient Germanic religion, a sky goddess conceived as riding the wind and followed by a host of spirits of the dead or unborn. In this aspect she has become associated with the Wild Hunt and her south German counterpart, Perchta. Very anciently she was an earth and fertility goddess. As a domestic hearth deity she is a tutelary of spinning and weaving. In modern German folklore, Holda has become a sort of witchlike bogey with whom mothers frighten naughty children. In Grimm's tale *Mother Holle* she lives, typically, at the bottom of a well and is a benefactor of good, kind children, and punisher of bad, unkind ones.

Holger Danske (hȯl′gẹr dän′skẹ). See **Ogier the Dane.**

Holiday Romance. A story in four parts by Charles Dickens, written especially for the American juvenile magazine *Our Young Folks* and there published during the months of January, March, April, and May 1868.

Holinshed (hol'inz.hed, -in.shed), **Raphael.** [Also, **Hollingshead.**] b. probably at Sutton Downes, Cheshire, England; d. c1580. An English chronicler. He is said to have been educated at one of the universities, possibly Cambridge. He began as a translator for Reginald Wolfe, a London printer, who was preparing a history of the world. Wolfe died in 1573, and the work came out in 1577 as the *Chronicles of England, Scotland, and Ireland*. Holinshed did the history of England, while the Scotch and Irish histories were adaptations or translations. A second and enlarged edition, edited by John Hooker, was published (1587) after Holinshed's death. The work furnished Shakespeare with plots for Macbeth, part of *Cymbeline*, perhaps *King Lear*, and most of the material in the historical plays.

Holinshed's Chronicles. See **Chronicles of England, Scotland, and Ireland, The.**

Holland (hol'and), **Henry.** See under **Exeter, Duke of.**

Holland, John. In Shakespeare's *2 Henry VI*, a follower of Jack Cade.

Holland, Philemon. b. at Chelmsford, Essex, England, 1552; d. at Coventry, England, Feb. 9, 1637. An English writer, noted as a translator. He graduated from Cambridge (Trinity College) in 1571, and after 1595 lived at Coventry. His translations include Livy (1600), the *Natural History* of Pliny (1601), the *Morals* of Plutarch (1603), the *History of the Caesars* of Suetonius (1606), Camden's *Brittania* (1610), and the *Cyropaedia* of Xenophon (1632).

Holland, Thomas. See under **Surrey, (1st) Duke of.**

Holland House. A mansion (built 1607) in Kensington, London, once noted as a social center.

Holle (hol'e). See **Holda.**

Hollingshead (hol'ingz.hed), **Raphael.** See **Holinshed, Raphael.**

Hollow Men, The. A poem (1925) by T. S. Eliot, bitterly depicting modern men as having "dried voices," and a "headpiece stuffed with straw."

Holly-Tree, The. A story by Charles Dickens, published in *Household Words* in December, 1855.

Holmes (hōmz, hōlmz), **Sherlock.** A remarkable detective whose powers of ratiocination solve the most baffling mysteries, in many stories by Sir Arthur Conan Doyle.

Holofernes (hol.ọ.fėr'nēz). In Biblical history, a general of Nebuchadnezzar; the leading character in the book of Judith (Apocrypha). He was killed by Judith.

Holofernes or **Holophernes** (hol.ọ.fėr'nēz). A conventional character of Italin comedy, a pedant or pompous schoolmaster.

Holofernes. In Shakespeare's *Love's Labour's Lost*, a pedantic schoolmaster who takes the part of Judas Maccabaeus in the masque of the Nine Worthies.

Holofernes or **Holophernes** (hol.ọ.fėr'nēz). A pedant in François Rabelais' *Gargantua* and *Pantagruel*. He teaches Gargantua to say the alphabet backward in five years and three months.

Holt (hōlt), **Father.** In W. M. Thackeray's novel *Henry Esmond*, a Jesuit priest, involved in the conspiracy to restore the throne of England to the Stuarts.

Holtby (hōlt'bi), **Winifred.** b. at Rudstone, Yorkshire, England, 1898; d. at London, Sept. 25, 1935. An English novelist, essayist, and critic. Author of *Eutychus, or the Future of the Pulpit* (1928), *Virginia Woolf—A Critical Study* (1932), *Mandoa! Mandoa!* (1933), a satire, *Women and a Changing Civilization* (1934), essays and criticism, and *Truth Is Not Sober* (1934), stories. Her masterpiece, *South Riding*, a Yorkshire novel completed three weeks before she died, was published in 1936; *Pavements at Anderby*, a volume of short stories, and *Letters to a Friend* appeared in 1937.

Holy Alliance. A league formed by the sovereigns of Russia, Austria, and Prussia in person after the fall of Napoleon, signed at Paris, on Sept. 26, 1815, and afterward joined by all the other European sovereigns except the Pope and those of England and Turkey. Its professed object was to unite the respective governments in a Christian brotherhood, but its real one, as seen by Metternich of Austria, was to perpetuate existing dynasties by joint opposition to all attempts at change. The Holy Alliance was paralleled by (and is often confused with) the Quadruple Alliance, entered into by England, Austria, Prussia, and Russia (later joined by France); however, unlike the Holy Alliance, which existed for all practical purposes only as a statement of principles, the Quadruple Alliance provided for regular consultations. This latter broke up when England repudiated the extension of European power in the Western Hemisphere (the Monroe Doctrine, which was evoked in answer to this same threat, was actually made effective at the time largely by this English action). The Holy Alliance continued rather feebly after the French and Belgian revolutions of 1830 and collapsed after the revolutions of 1848, to be replaced by the informal Concert of Europe that lasted until World War I.

Holy Deadlock. A satirical novel by A. P. Herbert, published in 1934. It is an attack upon the out-of-date English divorce laws, which were to some extent revised as a result of the novel.

Holy Dying and **Holy Living.** Two tracts (1650–51) by Jeremy Taylor.

Holy Grail (grāl). See **Grail.**

Holy Grail, The. One of the four "idylls" in Tennyson's *Idylls of the King* to appear in 1869. In it, Sir Percivale tells a fellow monk (he has left the Court to enter a monastery) the story of the quest for the Grail, and how only Galahad was successful (although Sir Percivale nearly attained it).

Holy Island. [Also, **Lindisfarne.**] An island (at low water a peninsula), in the North Sea, ab. 1 mi. off the Northumberland coast, NE England, ab. 10 mi. SE of Berwick-upon-Tweed. It is celebrated for the ruins of its monastery, founded by Saint

Aidan in 635, and famous under Saint Cuthbert. Length, ab. 3 mi.

Holy Living. See **Holy Dying.**

Holyoake (hōl'i.ōk), **George Jacob.** b. at Birmingham, England, April 13, 1817; d. Jan. 22, 1906. An English reformer. He took a prominent part in promoting schemes for the education of the working classes and for the advancement among them of various forms of coöperation. He was an advocate of secularism. Among his works are *The History of Co-operation in England: its Literature and Advocates* (1875–78) and *The Rochdale Pioneers: Thirty-Three Years of Co-operation in Rochdale* (1858), of which a ninth edition appeared in 1883 under the title of *Self-Help by the People.* He wrote also *Life of Joseph Rayner Stephens* (1881), *The Co-operative Movement of Today* (1891), *Sixty Years of an Agitator's Life* (1892), *Public Speaking and Debate* (1894), *Nature and Origin of Secularism* (1896), *Bygones Worth Remembering* (1905), and others.

Holy Roman Empire (rō.man). [Also: **German-Roman Empire;** often called the **German Empire;** German, **Römisches Reich deutscher Nation,** or **Deutsches Reich.**] A realm ruled by various emperors who claimed to be the representatives of the ancient Roman emperors, and who asserted (in theory) authority over the states and countries of W central Europe: called "holy" from the theoretical interdependence of the empire and the church (it has been a classroom witticism for generations that the Holy Roman Empire "was neither Holy, nor Roman, nor an Empire"; and, indeed, it was for most of its history more nearly a concept than a political entity). It comprised in general the German-speaking peoples in C Europe, and it had for a long time a close connection with Italy. Various regions outside of Germany proper were at different times nominally under the empire. It began with Charlemagne, king of the Franks, who was crowned emperor of the West (800), and was succeeded by various Carolingian emperors. By the treaty of Verdun (843) the Carolingian dynasty continued in the E part of Charlemagne's empire (i.e., Germany). The German nation grew from the union of Thuringians, Franks, Saxons, Bavarians, Swabians, Lorrainers, and others. The Saxon line of German kings began with Henry the Fowler in 919. The lasting union of Germany with the empire began in 962, when Otto I, king of Germany, became Roman emperor. The Saxon line of emperors continued until 1024. The Franconian line (Conrad IV, Henry III, Henry IV, Henry V) reigned from 1024 to 1125; the Hohenstaufen or Swabian line (Conrad III, Frederick I, Frederick II, Conrad IV) from 1138 to 1208 and from 1215 to 1254. There was an interregnum from 1254 to 1273. Emperors from the Hapsburg, Luxemburg, and other houses reigned from 1273 and 1437. The continuous line of Hapsburg emperors, who were powerful Austrian rulers, began in 1438. After Maximilian I and Charles V the empire degenerated through the 17th and 18th centuries, and Francis II (Francis I of Austria) abdicated as the last emperor in 1806.

Holyrood Palace (hol'i.röd). A large ancient royal palace of Scotland, situated at Edinburgh.

Holy Sonnets. A series of 28 sonnets (including two dedicatory ones) by John Donne, written in the Petrarchan form before and after his ordination in 1615, describing the varieties of religious experience which he has undergone, and his final affirmation of truth in God. Included in this series are the well-known "Death, be not proud . . . " "At the round earth's imagined corners," "This is my play's last scene . . . ," and "Batter my heart, three-personed God . . . ."

Holy War, The. A work by Thomas Fuller, published in 1639.

Holy War, The. A work by John Bunyan, published in 1682. It is an allegorical treatment of the salvation of the soul of man. The city, Mansoul (representing both the soul of man and the capital of the world), is besieged and captured by Diabolus (the figure of Evil). The legions of Emmanuel (the figure of Christ Himself) come to recapture the city, but in spite of their efforts Mansoul again falls under the influence of Diabolus. However, the evil besieger is never again able to recapture the central fortress of the town. Bunyan uses more political and military allegory in this work than in any of his others.

Holywell Street (hol'i.wel, -wel). A former London street parallel to the Strand: once a street of small bookshops.

Holy Willie's Prayer. A poem by Robert Burns, from which comes the use of the term "Holy Willie" to mean a religious hypocrite.

Homage to Catalonia (kat.a.lō'ni.a). A novel by George Orwell, published in 1938.

Home (hūm), **Daniel Dunglas.** b. near Edinburgh, March 20, 1833; d. at Auteuil, France, June 21, 1886. A spiritualist and medium, brought to the U. S. in childhood. In 1855 he went to England, and later to the Continent, giving many demonstrations of his alleged powers before people of prominence, including French, Dutch, and Prussian royalty, convincing many, and by others being denounced as a charlatan. Robert Browning satirized him in the poem *Sludge the Medium,* but the scientist Sir William Crookes, after Home had achieved his usual effects not, as was customary, in a darkened room but in full light, accepted these phenomena as the work of spirits. That they were the work of the devil was evidently the opinion of the authorities at Rome who, although Home had become a Roman Catholic, expelled him from that city as a sorcerer. Home never charged admission to, nor accepted fees for, his séances, but gifts from admirers made him moderately wealthy. He wrote and published two books, *Incidents of My Life* and *Lights and Shadows of Spiritualism.*

Home, Henry. [Title, Lord **Kames.**] b. at Kames, Berwickshire, Scotland, 1696; d. at Edinburgh, Dec. 27, 1782. A Scottish judge and philosophical writer. He published *Essays on the Principles of Morality and Natural Religion* (1751), *Elements of Criticism* (1762), and various legal works.

Home, John. b. at Leith, Scotland, Sept. 21, 1722; d. near Edinburgh, Sept. 5, 1808. A Scottish clergyman and dramatist, the author of *Douglas* (produced in 1756 at Edinburgh). This play was long a favorite with young elocutionists. He was settled as minister at Athelstaneford in East Lothian in 1747. His connection with the stage aroused clerical hostility, and a number of heated pamphlets were written on *Douglas*. Proceedings against him were begun in the presbytery, but he resigned in 1757. He also wrote the unsuccessful *Agis* (acted 1758), *The Fatal Discovery* (1769), *Alonzo* (1773), and *Alfred* (1778).

Home Counties. Middlesex, Surrey, Kent, Essex, and Hertfordshire, in England.

Homer (hō'mėr). fl. before 700 B.C. The poet to whom is assigned by very ancient tradition the authorship of the *Iliad* and the *Odyssey*, and of certain hymns to the gods (*Homeric Hymns*). Other poems also, as the *Batrachomyomachia* (Battle of the Frogs and Mice), were with less certainty attributed to him. Seven cities (Smyrna, Rhodes, Colophon, Salamis in Cyprus, Chios, Argos, and Athens) contended for the honor of being his birthplace; of these, the best evidence connects him with Smyrna. He was said to have died on the island of Ios. The tradition that he lived on the island of Chios, and in his old age was blind, is supported by the *Hymn to the Delian Apollo*. Modern criticism, especially that stemming from the great scholarly debate of the 19th century, when the Homeric works were the focus of classical study, has led to doubt whether such a person as Homer existed at all, the great epics which bear that name being supposed to be, in their existing form, of composite character, the product of various persons and ages. It is possible, however, that the nucleus of the *Iliad*, at least, was the work of a single poet of commanding genius; debate still continues, the only agreement being that in the *Iliad* and the *Odyssey* we have the prototype of epic poetry. According to Herodotus, Homer lived c850 B.C.; others give a later date, and some a date as early as 1200 B.C. His poems were sung by professional reciters (rhapsodists), who went from city to city. They were given substantially their present form under Pisistratus or his sons Hipparchus and Hippias, who ordered the rhapsodists to recite them at the Panathenaic festival in their order and completeness. The present text of the poems, with their division into books, is based upon the work of the Alexandrine critics.

Homespun (hōm'spun), **Zekiel** and **Cicely.** Brother and sister in the younger George Colman's *The Heir-at-Law*. Their names have become almost a synonym for rustic worth and simplicity.

Homeward Songs By the Way. A volume of verse (1894) by George Russell (Æ).

Homilies, Book of. A collection of sermons of the Church of England. The first volume is supposed to have been composed by Archbishop Cranmer and Bishops Ridley and Latimer, but in neither volume can the several homilies be assigned with any certainty to their respective authors.

Hone (hōn), **William.** b. at Bath, England, June 3, 1780; d. at Tottenham, near London, in November, 1842. An English political satirist, miscellaneous writer, and publisher. His best-known works are *Every-day Book* (1826), *Table-book* (1827–28), and *Year-book* (1829).

Honest Man's Fortune, The. A play by Fletcher, Massinger (he wrote Act III), and others, acted in 1613. It was first printed in the 1647 folio.

Fletcher wrote a poem *Upon an Honest Man's Fortune*, printed with the play.

Honest Thieves, The. See under **Committee, The.**

Honest Whore, The. A play by Dekker and Middleton, in two parts. Part 1 was printed in 1604; the earliest copy extant of part 2 was printed in 1630.

Honeybubble & Co. (hun'i.bub.l). A collection of short stories by A. P. Herbert, published in 1928.

Honeycomb. A novel by Dorothy M. Richardson, published in 1917. It is the third section of *Pilgrimage* (1938), a novel sequence in 12 parts employing the stream-of-consciousness technique.

Honeycomb (hun'i.kōm), **Will.** A member of the fictitious club that purported to publish *The Spectator*.

Honeyman (hun'i.man), **Charles.** In W. M. Thackeray's novel *The Newcomes*, the brother-in-law of Colonel Newcome. He is a hypocritical clergyman, who for a time is very popular with the ladies.

Honeyman, Martha. In W. M. Thackeray's novel *The Newcomes*, a kindly spinster, sister of Charles Honeyman and staunch friend of Colonel Newcome. She keeps a modest rooming house at Brighton.

Honeymoon, The. A comedy by John Tobin, produced in 1805. It is to some extent based on Shakespeare's *Taming of the Shrew*, with ideas from Fletcher and Shirley.

Honeywill (hun'i.wil), **Ruth.** A young woman married to a brutal husband, in John Galsworthy's social tragedy in four acts, *Justice* (1910). It is for her sake that William Falder, a lawyer's clerk, commits forgery.

Honeywood (hun'i.wùd). The "good-natured man" in Oliver Goldsmith's play of that name. He suffers from a foolish eagerness to be philanthropic with everyone, even wishing to give up the woman he loves to a friend who also loves her. He is cured by his uncle.

Honorable History of Friar Bacon and Friar Bungay (bā'kon; bung'gā), **The.** See **Friar Bacon and Friar Bungay.**

honorificabilitudinitatibus (on''o.rif''i.ka̤.bil''i.tū''di‧ni.tat'i.bus). A word in Shakespeare's *Love's Labour's Lost* thought by some to be an anagram referring to Francis Bacon. See also under **Baconian Theory.**

Hood (hùd), **Robin.** A legendary English outlaw and popular hero, celebrated especially in a cycle of ballads. He is said to have been born at Locksley, Nottingham, c1160. He lived in the woods with his band, either for reasons of his own or because he was really outlawed, his haunts being chiefly Sherwood Forest and Barnsdale in Yorkshire. He is also said to have been the outlawed Earl of Huntingdon. He was extravagant and adventurous, and traditionally robbed the rich to give to the poor. According to one tradition the prioress of Kirkley, to whose care he had entrusted himself to be bled when he was a very old man, treacherously allowed him to bleed to death. His companions were Friar Tuck, Maid Marian, Little John, Will Scarlett, Allan-a-Dale, and George-a-Greene. He is a favorite subject in ballad tradition, and in fact the ballads are to all appearance the original source of the legends concerning him. He has become also a stock character of popular May Day plays and festivities.

Hood, Thomas. b. at London, May 23, 1799; d. there, May 3, 1845. An English poet and humorist. He began the study of engraving, but soon abandoned it and in 1821 became an undereditor of the *London Magazine.* In 1830 he began the *Comic Annual,* and in 1843 *Hood's Magazine.* From 1835 to 1837 he lived at Koblenz, and from 1837 to 1840 at Ostend. Hood's humorous style is well adapted to caricature, but he placed too much reliance on the pun, especially in the rhyme, and the reader is often distracted. He wrote *Whims and Oddities* (1826–27), *Plea of the Midsummer Fairies* (1827), *Lamia* (published 1852), *Dream of Eugene Aram* (1829), *Tylney Hall,* a novel. (1834), *Up the Rhine* (1840), and others. Some of his best-known lyrics are *The Song of the Shirt, The Bridge of Sighs,* and *Eugene Aram.*

Hood, Thomas. [Called **Tom Hood.**] b. at Wanstead, near London, Jan. 19, 1835; d. Nov. 20, 1874. An English author; son of Thomas Hood (1799–1845). He was editor (1865 *et seq.*) of *Fun.*

Hook (hŭk), **Captain.** A vicious pirate captain with one hand (having lost the other to a hungry crocodile) and a cruel iron hook, in Sir James M. Barrie's fairy play *Peter Pan* (1904). Hook is Peter's sworn enemy. The crocodile, which liked the taste of the first morsel of Hook, and which follows the pirate faithfully in hope of another, has swallowed a loudly ticking clock and warning of Hook's approach is thus always audible.

Hook, Theodore Edward. b. at London, Sept. 22, 1788; d. there, Aug. 24, 1841. An English humorist and novelist. He became the editor of *John Bull* in 1820. Among his novels are *Maxwell* (1830), *Gilbert Gurney* (1835), and *Jack Brag* (1837). He was the original of Mr. Wagg in Thackeray's *Vanity Fair.*

Hook, Walter Farquhar. b. at London, March 13, 1798; d. at Chichester, England, Oct. 20, 1875. An English divine (dean of Chichester) and writer. He published *A Dictionary of Ecclesiastical Biography* (1845–52), *Church Dictionary* (8th ed., 1859), and *Lives of the Archbishops of Canterbury* (1860–76).

Hooker (hŭk′ẽr), **Richard.** b. at Heavitree, Exeter, England, c1553; d. at Bishopsbourne, near Canterbury, England, Nov. 2, 1600. An English divine and theological writer. His great work is *Of the Laws of Ecclesiastical Polity* (1st ed., 4 books, c1592; 5th book, 1597; the remaining 3 books were published after his death). The work is a defense of the Anglican Church against the attacks of a narrower Presbyterianism and is important as a document in the religious struggle of the period, but its greater importance lies in its being the first really independent, full-fledged English prose work, adorned with all the richness of Elizabethan prose but not stooping to Euphuism or the fads of the time.

Hooker, Thomas. b. at Markfield, Leicestershire, England, c1586; d. at Hartford, Conn., July 7, 1647. An English clergyman. He emigrated to Massachusetts in 1633, and was one of the founders of the Connecticut colony. He was the author (with

John Cotton) of the *Survey of the Summe of Church Discipline* (1648).

Hooker, Sir William Jackson. b. at Norwich, England, July 6, 1785; d. at Kew, near London, Aug. 12, 1865. An English botanist, appointed director of the Royal Botanical Gardens at Kew in 1841. He published numerous botanical works, including *British Jungermanniae* (1816), *Flora Scotica* (1821), *Icones Plantarum* (1837–54), and *Species Filicum* (1846–64).

Hoole (hōl), **John.** b. at London, in December, 1727; d. near Dorking, England, 1803. An English poet and dramatist. He translated Tasso's *Jerusalem Delivered* (1763), the *Orlando Furioso* of Ariosto (1773–83), and other Italian poems. He wrote three plays, *Cyrus* (1768), *Timanthes* (1770), and *Cleonice* (1775).

Hope (hōp), **Alexander James Beresford.** [Also, **Beresford-Hope.**] b. Jan. 25, 1820; d. near Cranbrook, Kent, England, Oct. 20, 1887. An English politician and writer; adopted (1854) additional surname upon inheriting the English estates of his stepfather, William Carr Beresford (1768–1854), Viscount Beresford. In partnership with John Douglas Cook he founded the *Saturday Review* in 1855. He devoted himself especially to the promotion of the interests of the Church of England. He wrote *A Popular View of the American Civil War* (1861), *The Results of the American Disruption* (1862), and others.

Hope, Anthony. Pseudonym of **Hawkins,** Sir **Anthony Hope.**

Hope, the. A playhouse built for Philip Henslowe on the Bankside, Southwark, London, in 1613. Ben Jonson's *Bartholomew Fair* was produced on the occasion of its opening in October, 1614. It also doubled as a pit for the baiting of bears and bulls. From this it acquired a stench which persisted even during playtime, a fact which Jonson noted in his play. It was a cylindrical building near the Globe and was demolished in 1656.

Hope, Thomas. b. at London, c1770; d. there, Feb. 3, 1831. An English novelist and antiquary. His works include the novel *Anastasius, or Memoirs of a Greek: written at the Close of the Eighteenth Century* (1819), *Costume of the Ancients* (1809), *Modern Costumes* (1812), and *Historical Essay on Architecture* (1835).

Hopeful (hōp′fùl). A companion of Christian in Bunyan's *Pilgrim's Progress.*

Hopeful Journey, The. A novel by Beatrice Kean Seymour, published in 1923.

Hope of the World, The. A poem (1897) by William Watson, thought by some critics to be his most characteristic work.

Hope-on-High Bomby (hōp′on′hī′ bom′bi). See **Bomby, Hope-on-High.**

Hopkins (hop′kinz), **Gerard Manley.** b. at Stratford, Essex, England, June 11, 1844; d. at Dublin, June 8, 1899. An English poet, painter, priest, and teacher. He was educated at Sir Robert Cholmondeley's Grammar School, Highgate, North London, winning (1859, 1862) two poetry prizes, and at Balliol College, Oxford. He became (1865) a Roman Catholic, and began studies for the priesthood the

---

d̦, d or j; ṣ, s or sh; ṭ, t or ch; ẓ, z or zh; *o,* F. cloche; ü, F. menu; ċh, Sc. loch; ṅ, F. bonbon.

next year (being sponsored by John Henry Newman), studied philosophy and theology at Roman Catholic colleges in Lancashire and North Wales, was ordained in 1874, and served in London, Chesterfield, Oxford, and Liverpool churches. He was classical professor (1882–84) at St. Mary's Hall, and professor of Greek (1884–89) at the Royal University, Dublin. Most of his poetry was not published until after his death. His collected *Poems*, appearing in 1918, were edited with notes and an introduction by his friend, Robert Bridges; an enlarged edition was published in 1934. Influenced by the 17th-century metaphysical poets, Hopkins in turn exerted an influence over several poets of a later generation, among them W. H. Auden and Cecil Day Lewis. Hopkins's poetry is distinguished by several technical devices, among them sprung rhythm (using stress and not syllable count to determine the line), revealing his skill and importance as an innovator. Two volumes of critical value, his letters to Bridges and to Richard Watson Dixon, were published in 1935. Among his notable individual poems are *The Wreck of the Deutschland, The Windhover, Pied Beauty, The Habit of Perfection, The Golden Echo, The Leaden Echo, God's Grandeur, The Starlight Night, Spring, The Caged Skylark, Felix Randal, A Nun Takes the Veil,* and *Peace.* See *Gerard Manley Hopkins* (1953), a selection of his poems and prose by W. H. Gardner.

Hopwood (hop'wŭd), **Ronald Arthur.** b. 1868—. A British admiral, poet, and writer, especially on naval gunnery. His poems include *The Laws of The Navy* and *Secret Orders.*

Hor (hōr). See **Horus.**

Horace (hor'ăs). [Full Latin name, **Quintus Horatius Flaccus.**] b. at Venusia (modern Venosa), in Apulia, Dec. 8, 65 B.C.; d. at Rome, Nov. 27, 8 B.C. A Roman poet. The son of a freedman, he was educated at Rome and Athens and served in the republican army under Brutus at Philippi in 42 B.C. as a *tribunus militum,* so becoming a knight. Later he was reconciled to the rule of Augustus and lauded his work for peace. His literary patron was Maecenas, who in 33 B.C. gave him a farm in the Sabine Hills. His works (all dates are approximate) are *Satires,* conversation pieces in hexameters (first book 35 B.C., second 30 B.C.), *Epodes* (29 B.C.), often in iambics, with a refrain, *Odes* (first three books 23 B.C., fourth 13 B.C.), lyrics in various meters of great originality, beauty, and melody, *Epistles* (first book 20 B.C., second 13–8 B.C.), personal letters in hexameters addressed to friends, *Carmen Seculare* (17 B.C.), and *Ars Poetica* (13–8 B.C.), a treatise on the art of poetry, especially dramatic poetry. Many complete editions have been published. Probably no other Roman poet has had so great an influence on modern poetry, both in English and in the romance languages.

Horace. In Ben Jonson's satiric comedy *The Poetaster,* the great Latin poet, but here intended actually to represent Jonson himself.

Horace Crewler (krö'lẽr). See under **Crewler.**

Horae (hō'rē). In classical mythology, the hours.

Horatio (họ.rā'shō, -shi.ō). In Thomas Kyd's *Spanish Tragedy,* the son of Hieronimo, Marshal of Spain, for whose murder Hieronimo seeks revenge.

Horatio. In Shakespeare's *Hamlet,* a close friend of Hamlet.

Horatio. In Rowe's tragedy *The Fair Penitent,* the friend of Altamont who discovers his wife's previous indiscretion with Lothario.

Horatio Fizkin (fiz'kin). See **Fizkin, Horatio.**

Horatius (họ.rā'shus, -shi.us). [Full name, **Publius Horatius Cocles.**] A Roman legendary hero who with Spurius Lartius and Titus Herminius prevented the entire Etruscan army under Lars Porsena (c508 B.C.) from approaching the wooden Sublician bridge at Rome until it could be destroyed. Horatius then swam across the Tiber to the Roman shore. The story is the subject of one of Macaulay's *Lays of Ancient Rome.* The Greek historian Polybius states that Horatius, weakened by his wounds, was drowned in the Tiber.

Horn (hôrn), **Cape.** [Original name, **Cape Hoorn;** Spanish, **Cabo de Hornos.**] The southern end of a rocky island in extreme S Chile: the southernmost point of South America. It was first rounded by Le Maire and Schouten in 1616, and named by them from Hoorn in North Holland. Peak elevation, ab. 1,391 ft.

Horn, Charles Edward. b. in England, 1786; d. at Boston, 1849. An English singer and composer of operettas and songs.

Horn, King. See **King Horn.**

hornbook. 1. A leaf or page, usually one containing the alphabet, the nine digits, and the Lord's Prayer, covered with transparent horn and fixed in a frame with a handle: formerly used in teaching children to read.

> He teaches boys the horn-book.
> (Shak., *L. L. L.,* V.i.)

> To Master John the English Maid
> A horn-book gives of Ginger-bread;
> And that the Child may learn the better,
> As he can name, he eats the Letter.
> (Prior, *Alma,* ii.)

Hence—**2.** A book containing the first principles of any science or branch of knowledge; a primer.

Horn Childe and Maiden Rimnild (hôrn chĭld; rim'nild). A Middle English verse romance (early 14th century) of the King Horn group, dealing with the same material as *The Geste of Kyng Horne* but with the addition of different details. The romance, found in the Auchinleck manuscript, relates the love story of Horn, son of Hatheolf, and Rimnild, daughter of King Hornlac, the betrayal of their love to the king, Horn's subsequent banishment, his adventures in Ireland, his return to Rimnild, his slaying of the rival suitors, and the marriage of the pair.

Horne (hôrn), **John.** Original name of **Tooke, Horne.**

Horne, Richard Henry (or **Hengist**). b. at London, Jan. 1, 1803; d. at Margate, England, March 13, 1884. An English poet and miscellaneous writer. He served (1852–69) as commissioner for crown lands in Australia. Author of the epic *Orion* (1843), the dramas *Cosmo de Medici* (1837), *Death of Marlowe* (1837), *Gregory the Seventh* (1840), and others; with Elizabeth Barrett (later Mrs. Browning) he wrote the essays *A New Spirit of the Age* (1844).

Horner (hôr'nẽr). A gay young libertine in Wycherley's *Country Wife* who cynically cuckolds Pinchwife.

Horner, Jack. See **Jack Horner.**

Horner, Thomas. In Shakespeare's *2 Henry VI*, an armorer accused of treasonous sayings by his apprentice. In a combat with the apprentice, Peter Thump, he is mortally wounded and confesses his treason.

Horniman (hôr.ni.mạn), **Annie Elizabeth Fredericka.** b. at Forest Hill, London, Oct. 3, 1860; d. at Shere, Surrey, England, Aug. 6, 1937. An English theater manager. She managed (1904 *et seq.*) the Abbey Theatre at Dublin for the Irish National Theatre Society, and bought (1908) and managed (1908–21) the Gaiety Theatre at Manchester. See *Miss Horniman and the Gaiety Theatre, Manchester* (1952), by Rex Pogson.

Hornung (hôr'nung), **Ernest William.** b. at Middlesborough, Yorkshire, England, June 7, 1866; d. at St.-Jean-de-Luz, France, March 22, 1921. An English novelist, creator of the fictional gentleman-burglar "Raffles." Author of *A Bride from the Bush* (1890), *The Boss of Taroomba* (1894), *At Large* and *The Shadow of the Rope* (both 1902), *No Hero* and *Stingaree* (both 1903), *The Camera Fiend* (1911), *The Crime Doctor* (1914), novels; *The Young Guard*, war poetry; *Notes of a Camp Follower on the Western Front* (1919), a record of his war impressions; several stories of "Raffles," the gentleman thief, including *The Amateur Cracksman* (1899), *Raffles—Further Adventures of the Amateur Cracksman* (1901), *A Thief in the Night—Further Adventures of A. J. Raffles* (1905), and *Mr. Justice Raffles* (1909).

Horrabin (hor'ạ.bin), **James Francis.** b. at Peterborough, England, Nov. 1, 1884—. An English illustrator and writer. Author and illustrator of *An Outline of Economic Geography* (1923), *The Plebs Atlas* (1926), *An Atlas of Current Affairs* (1934), *Atlas of Empire* (1937), and the ten-volume *Horrabin's Atlas-History of the Second Great War* (1940–47).

Horrocks (hor'ọks), **Sam.** A character in *Lonesome-Like* (1911), a one-act play of Lancashire life by Harold Brighouse.

Hortensio (hôr.ten'shi.ō). In Shakespeare's *Taming of the Shrew*, a suitor of Bianca. He persuades Petruchio to marry Katherina, Bianca's older sister, so that he may marry Bianca, but she marries Lucentio, and he marries a widow instead.

Hortensius (hôr.ten'shi.us, -shus). In Shakespeare's *Timon of Athens*, a servant of one of Timon's creditors.

Horus (hō'rus). [Also, **Hor.**] In Egyptian mythology, a solar deity of dual personality; brother of Osiris, Isis, and Set, and also son of Osiris and Isis, and the avenger of his father's death upon Set. As the brother of Osiris, Isis, and Set, he was generally represented as falcon-headed, and is hardly distinguishable from Ra, like whom he was the lord of Upper Egypt. As a sun deity he was identical with the Elder Horus, ancient sun god of the Delta.

Hosier's Ghost (hō'zhẽrz). See **Admiral Hosier's Ghost.**

Hospitalers of Saint John of Jerusalem (hos'pi.tạl-ẽrz; jon; jẹ.rö'sạ.lẹm), **Order of the.** [Also: **Knights of Malta, Knights of Rhodes.**] A body of military monks, which took its origin from an earlier community, not military in character, under whose auspices a hospital and a church had been founded at Jerusalem. Its military organization was perfected in the 12th century. After the retaking of Jerusalem by the Moslems, these knights defended Acre in vain, took shelter in Cyprus, and in the 14th century occupied the island of Rhodes. In 1522 the island of Rhodes was seized by the Turks, and the knights, after some wanderings, had possession given them of Malta, the government of which island they administered until it was occupied by Napoleon in 1798. The badge of the order was the cross of eight points, without any central disk, and consisting in fact of four barbed arrow-heads meeting at their points: the well-known Maltese cross. This is modified in modern times, with slight differences for the different nations in which branches of the order have survived. At different times the order has been called officially Knights of Rhodes and Knights of Malta. It maintains to the present day a certain independent existence. The most famous grand master of the order was Jean Parisot de La Valette, who successfully defended Malta against the Turks in 1565; Valletta is named for him.

Host. In Shakespeare's *Two Gentlemen of Verona*, the hospitable character who takes Julia in search of Proteus (IV.ii).

Host (of the Garter Inn). In Shakespeare's *Merry Wives of Windsor*, an innkeeper who participates in the schemes of his guests. He urges Dr. Caius to fight with Evans, and when the two realize that they have been fooled they steal his horses. He helps Fenton court Ann Page.

Host (of the Tabard). See **Bailey, Harry.**

Hostess. In Shakespeare's *Taming of the Shrew*, a woman in charge of an alehouse, who appears only in the Induction. She goes for the "thirdborough" (a local official) to arrest the drunken Sly, who will not pay for glasses he has broken.

Hostess (of the Boar's Head). See **Quickly, Mistress.**

Hotel, The. A novel by Elizabeth Bowen, published in 1927.

Hôtel des Invalides (ō.tel dā zaṅ.vȧ.lēd). An establishment founded in 1670 at Paris for disabled and infirm soldiers. The monumental façade, ab. 650 ft. long, has three stories, and is adorned with military trophies and an equestrian statue of Louis XIV. The interior possesses halls adorned with military paintings, and contains the Musée d'Artillerie, which includes a remarkable collection of medieval and Renaissance armor. The Church of the Invalides consists of two parts, the Église St. Louis and the Dôme, since 1840 the mausoleum of Napoleon I. The nave of the former is adorned with captured battle flags. The Dôme was built by J. H. Mansart in 1706. In plan it is a square of 198 ft., surmounted by a gilded dome on a circular drum which is 86 ft. in diameter, and with its cross and lantern 344 ft. high. The entrance is adorned with two tiers of classical columns and a pediment. The tomb of Napoleon is a large monolithic sarcophagus of red granite, placed beneath the dome in an open circular crypt 20 ft. deep and 36 in diameter. The walls of the crypt bear allegorical reliefs, and against its 12 piers stand collosal Victories. In alternate intercolumniations are placed six trophies, each of ten flags taken in battle.

Hotspur (hot′spêr). In Shakespeare's *Richard II* and *1 Henry IV*, Sir Henry (or Harry) Percy, son of Northumberland. He leads the northern rebellion against Henry IV and is killed at Shrewsbury. Shakespeare makes him the same age as Prince Hal (the historical Hotspur was 20 years Hal's senior) to sharpen the contrast between the man who thinks "it were an easy leap, To pluck bright honor from the pale-faced moon" and Prince Hal, who has not yet shown his mettle.

Houghton (hô′tọn, hou′-), 1st Baron. Title of **Milnes, Richard Monckton.**

Houghton, (William) Stanley. b. at Ashton-on-Mersey, Cheshire, England, Feb. 22, 1881; d. at Manchester, England, Dec. 11, 1913. An English dramatist, chiefly remembered for his *Hindle Wakes* (1912), a play about a young middle-class woman who scandalizes her family by spending a weekend alone with a young man, and then refuses to marry him.

Hound of Heaven, The. A poem (1893) by Francis Thompson, the best known of all his poems. It portrays the poet's soul inexorably pursued by God "down the labyrinthine ways of my own mind."

Houndsditch (hounz′dich). A district in the E part of London, near Whitechapel. It was called "Dogs-ditch" contemptuously by Beaumont and Fletcher. Its name is a relic of the old fosse (formerly a receptacle for dead dogs) which encircled the city.

Hounds of Spring, The. A novel by Sylvia Thompson, published in 1925.

Hounslow Heath (hounz′lō). A heath formerly situated near London. It was long notorious as a resort of highwaymen.

Hour-Glass, The. A morality play (1903) by William Butler Yeats.

Hour of Magic, The. A volume of verse (1923) by William H. Davies.

House by the River, The. A novel by A. P. Herbert, published in 1920.

Household (hous′hōld), **Geoffrey.** b. 1903—. An English novelist and short-story writer. His best-known work is *Rogue Male* (1939).

Household Words. A periodical conducted by Charles Dickens. It first appeared on March 30, 1850.

House in Demetrius Road (dẹ.mē′tri.us), **The.** A novel (1914) by J. D. Beresford.

House in Dormer Forest (dôr′mêr), **The.** A novel by Mary Webb, published in 1920.

House in Paris, The. A novel by Elizabeth Bowen, published in 1935.

House-Mates. A novel (1917) by J. D. Beresford.

House of Commons. In English history and politics, one of the two parts of the British Parliament, the other being the House of Lords. It is the popular branch of Parliament and is actually the chief legislative body of the country. In earlier days its members were servants in fact as well as in name, of the monarch, but they have for a long time been, and now are, servants of the sovereign in name only. Its membership (since 1948) has been 625 divided as follows: England, 506 seats, Scotland, 71, Wales, 36, and Northern Ireland, 12. Members must be at least 21 years old.

House of Fame, The. An unfinished poem by Chaucer in three books, totaling 2,158 lines, written sometime between 1374 and 1385 and probably closer to the earlier date. Probably the first work of Chaucer's so-called Italian period, it shows the marked influence of Dante, but is also indebted to Vergil, Ovid, and various medieval Latin writers. The form of the dream-vision is provided by the French works which were Chaucer's first models, but he adds many elements foreign to that body of love poetry. At the beginning, the poet falls asleep and in his dream visits the temple of Venus, where he sees depicted the story of Aeneas up to the betrayal of Dido. He then is seized and borne aloft by a friendly and talkative eagle, who carries him to the House of Fame. Here the Goddess of Fame, to various companies of suppliants, haphazardly apportions fame, disgrace, or oblivion. The poet then moves to the nearby House of Rumor and is just about to hear something from "a man of gret auctorite," when the poem breaks off.

House of Gold, The. A novel by Liam O'Flaherty, published in 1929.

House of Islam (is′lạm, is.läm′), **The.** A novel by Marmaduke Pickthall, published in 1906.

House of Life, The. A series of sonnets by Dante Gabriel Rossetti, written between 1848 and 1881. It comprises, in large part, an autobiographical account of the poet's deeply spiritual love for his wife and his sorrow at her death. The title refers to the astrological "house of life," which is considered the most important of all the astrological houses.

House of Lords. In English history and politics, one of the two parts of the British Parliament, the other being the House of Commons. Its members hold their office by hereditary right, by royal appointment, by right of their office (law lords and archbishops), and by election ("representative peers") for a single Parliamentary term, which is not more than five years, and may be less. The members of the House of Lords include the Lord Chancellor of England (who is the speaker, and who technically sits outside the House), the royal dukes, the archbishops, the dukes, the marquesses, the earls, the viscounts, 24 bishops, the barons, and 16 Scottish peers elected for the life of the Parliament. Their number varies slightly from year to year, but is usually between 850 and 860. As members they have certain privileges, such as freedom of speech in the House and freedom from arrest in civil cases (they may be arrested for crime) while Parliament is in session and for 40 days before and after the opening and closing of Parliament. Until the Parliament Act of 1911 restricted its power, the House of Lords was technically an equal legislative branch with the House of Commons, although its actual power had been whittled down during the 19th century and it made itself felt only from the fact that no law could be passed without its consent. However, this gave it what was essentially a power of absolute veto in the legislative realm, and it was this last legislative power that was stripped from it in 1911. It remains, however, the highest court of appeal in the United Kingdom, and thus now serves almost as the British equivalent of a supreme court; its legislative powers are, for all practical purposes, nonexistent.

House of Spies, The. A historical novel by Warwick Deeping, published in 1913.

House of the Titans, The. A volume of poems by George William Russell (Æ) published in 1934.

House of the Wolfings (wŭl'fingz), **The.** A prose romance (1889) by William Morris.

House of War, The. A novel of Marmaduke Pickthall, published in 1916.

House that Jack Built, The. An English tale, probably the most famous of the cumulative tales, and now a favorite nursery chant.

House with the Echo, The. A volume of 26 stories by Theodore Francis Powys, published in 1928.

House With the Green Shutters, The. A novel by George Douglas Brown, published in 1903. His sole work in this field, it appeared under the pseudonym George Douglas.

Housman (hous'mạn), **Alfred Edward.** b. March 26, 1859; d. April 30, 1936. An English poet, essayist, and scholar; brother of Laurence Housman. He was graduated at Oxford, was professor of Latin (1892–1911) at University College, London, and was professor of Latin (1911–36) at Cambridge University. His verse, characterized by a degree of *fin de siècle* pessimism, published in *A Shropshire Lad* (1896), *Last Poems* (1922), and the posthumous *More Poems* (1936), includes the widely anthologized "When I Was One and Twenty," "To an Athlete Dying Young," "Be Still, My Soul, Be Still," and "Epilogue." He also edited the works of Juvenal, Lucan, and Manilius, and wrote an essay on *The Name and Nature of Poetry* (1933). See *Housman the Poet* (1953), by Robert Hamilton, and *The Manuscript Poems of A. E. Housman: Eight Hundred Lines of Hitherto Uncollected Verse from the Author's Notebooks* (1955), edited by Tom Burns Haber.

Housman, Laurence. b. July 18, 1865—. An English illustrator and author; brother of Alfred Edward Housman. He first came to public notice with his illustrations of such works as Meredith's *Jump to Glory Jane*, Christina Rossetti's *Goblin Market*, and Shelley's *Sensitive Plant*. His works include *Gods and their Makers* (1897), *Spikenard* (1898), *Rue* (1899), *An Englishwoman's Love Letters* (1900, a sensation, published anonymously), *A Modern Antaeus* (1901), *Bethlehem*, a nativity play (1902), *Sabrina Wareham* (1904), *The Blue Moon* (1904), *Prunella* (1904, with Granville Barker), *The Cloak of Friendship* (1905), *The Chinese Lantern* (1908), *The Sheepfold* (1918), *Angels and Ministers* (1921), *Trimblerigg* (1924), *Nunc Dimittis* (1933), the play *Victoria Regina* (1934), the biographical *A. E. H.* (1937), dealing with his poet brother, and his autobiographical *The Unexpected Years* (1936).

Houyhnhnms (hö.in'ẹmz, hwin'ẹmz). A community of horses endowed with reason and intelligence, in the fourth part of *Gulliver's Travels*, by Jonathan Swift. Their inferiors, their beasts of burden, are the Yahoos, a degraded race embodying all that is worst in mankind.

Hoveden or **Hovedon** (hov'dẹn, huv'-), **Roger of.** See **Roger of Hoveden.**

Howard (hou'ạrd), **Frederick.** [Title, 5th Earl of Carlisle.] b. May 28, 1748; d. at Castle Howard, Yorkshire, England, Sept. 4, 1825. English politician, viceroy of Ireland (1780–82). He was chief of the commissioners sent to America by Lord North in 1778.

Howard, Henry. [Title (by courtesy), Earl of Surrey.] b. c1517; beheaded on Tower Hill, London, Jan. 21, 1547. An English poet; son of Thomas Howard (1473–1554). He was known in youth as "Henry Howard of Kenninghall," from an estate owned by his grandfather in Norfolk. He received an unusually good education, and from 1530 to 1532 lived at Windsor with the young Henry Fitzroy, Duke of Richmond, the natural son of Henry VIII, accompanying the king to France in 1532. He remained at the French court for about a year, returning for the marriage of Surrey's sister Mary to Richmond. In 1541 he was installed Knight of the Garter, and in 1543 joined the English forces at Landrecies with special recommendations from Henry VIII to the emperor Charles V, and a little later was appointed cupbearer to the king. He was present at the surrender of Boulogne, of which he was made governor in 1545, but was recalled to England the next year. Henry VIII was ill, and, when his death was near, Surrey's father, Thomas, 3rd Duke of Norfolk, who was premier duke, was suspected of aiming at the throne. A month before the king's death both Norfolk and Surrey were arrested, and the former, as a peer of the realm, was tried by his peers. The latter, however, who had only a courtesy title, was tried by a jury picked for the occasion, who found that he "falsely, maliciously, and treacherously set up and bore the arms of Edward the Confessor, then used by the Prince of Wales, mixed up and joined with his own proper arms." He had borne these arms without question in the presence of the king, as the Howards before him had done since their grant by Richard II. He was tried for high treason and beheaded. His poems were first printed as "Songes and Sonettes" in *Tottel's Miscellany* in 1557, with those of Sir Thomas Wyatt. He was the first English writer of blank verse (unrhymed iambic pentameter), translating the second and fourth books of the *Aeneid* into this form, and with Wyatt he introduced the sonnet into English literature.

Howard, H. L. Pseudonym of **Wells, Charles Jeremiah.**

Howard, John. See under **Norfolk, (1st) Duke of.**

Howard, Thomas. See under **Norfolk, (2nd) Duke of;** see also under **Surrey, Earl of.**

Howard's End. A novel (1911) by E. M. Forster.

Howden (hou'dẹn), **Roger.** See **Roger of Hoveden.**

Howe (hou), **John.** b. at Loughborough, Leicestershire, England, May 17, 1630; d. at London, April 2, 1705. An English Puritan clergyman. He became domestic chaplain to Cromwell, and settled at London in 1676. His complete works were pub-

ḍ, d or j; ṣ, s or sh; ṭ, t or ch; ẓ, z or zh; o, F. cloche; ü, F. menu; ċh, Sc. loch; ṅ, F. bonbon.

lished in 1724, including the *Living Temple of God* (1676–1702).

Howe, Miss. The friend with whom Clarissa corresponds in Samuel Richardson's novel *Clarissa Harlowe*.

Howell (hou'ĕl), **James.** b. in Wales, c1594; d. 1666. An English author, best known for his *Epistolae Ho-elianae: Familiar Letters* (collected in 1650). He edited the third and fourth editions of Cotgrave's *French and English Dictionary* (1650 and 1660), and compiled a polyglot dictionary, *Lexicon Tetraglotton* (1660), with a classified glossary and list of proverbs.

How Green Was My Valley. A realistic novel by Richard Llewellyn, published in 1940. It is the story of a young Welsh boy, Huw Morgan, whose family works in the mines. It is set against a background of the coal-mining district in the south of Wales during the early 1930's.

How He Lied to Her Husband. A farce (1905) by George Bernard Shaw, included by most critics among his lesser works.

Howitt (hou'it), **Mary.** [Maiden name, **Botham**.] b. at Coleford, Gloucestershire, England, March 12, 1799; d. at Rome, Jan. 30, 1888. An English author; wife (married 1821) and collaborator of William Howitt. Among her separate works are translations from Frederika Bremer and Hans Andersen, and juvenile works.

Howitt, William. b. at Heanor, Derbyshire, England, 1792; d. at Rome, March 3, 1879. An English poet and miscellaneous author; husband (married 1821) of Mary Howitt. He wrote *Book of the Seasons* (1831), *Rural Life of England* (1838), *Visits to Remarkable Places* (1840–42), *Rural and Domestic Life of Germany* (1842), *History of the Supernatural* (1863), and *Northern Heights of London* (1869); jointly with his wife, *Literature and Romance of Northern Europe* (1852), *Ruined Abbeys and Castles of Great Britain* (1862–64), *. . . of the Wye* (1863), *. . . of Yorkshire* (1865), and *. . . of the Border* (1865).

How They Brought the Good News from Ghent to Aix (gent; āks, eks). A poem (1845) by Robert Browning, published in the *Bells and Pomegranates* series, telling of three horsemen (Dirk, Joris, and the narrator) who carry the word, as fast as their horses can gallop, to beleaguered Aix that desperately needed succor is now on the way. The horses of Dirk and Joris drop by the way, and the news is delivered by the narrator, whose own good mount, Roland, barely survives the cruel punishment of the ride.

Hoxton (hoks'tọn). A district, noted for the number of its charitable institutions, in Shoreditch and Hackney, London.

Hoyden (hoi'dẹn), **Miss.** The daughter of Sir Tunbelly Clumsy in Vanbrugh's comedy *The Relapse*, a pert and amorous country girl.

Hoyle (hoil), **Edmund.** b. 1672; d. at London, Aug. 29, 1769. An English writer on games. He published a short treatise on whist (1742), which came to be regarded as authoritative, giving rise to the expression "according to Hoyle." In subsequent printings of his book, he added sections on other card games and on backgammon, and later

editors have added many other games, almost universally using Hoyle's name in their title pages.

Hrothgar (hrōth'gär). The King of the Danes in *Beowulf*.

Hubbard (hub'ạrd), **Mother.** See **Mother Hubbard.**

Huberd (hū'bẹrd). The Friar who relates Chaucer's *Friar's Tale*.

Hubert (hū'bẹrt; French, ü.ber), **Saint.** b. c656; d. 727. Bishop of Liége and Maastricht, the patron saint of hunters. On the death of his wife he became a hermit, and was elected bishop of Liége in 722.

Hubert de Burgh (dẹ bėrg). In Shakespeare's *King John*, the King's chamberlain. Ordered to kill John's young nephew, Hubert is softened by Arthur's entreaties, lets him live unharmed, and reports to the King that Arthur is dead. When Arthur is discovered dead (he is accidentally killed while trying to escape), Hubert is suspected of responsibility.

Hubert Stanley (stan'li), **Sir.** See **Stanley, Sir Hubert.**

Huchoun (huch'ọn). fl. probably in the 14th century. A Scottish poet, sometimes identified with Sir Hugh of Eglintoun. No specific work can be assigned to him with any confidence, although he has been credited with the authorship of *The Pearl*, *Patience*, *Cleanness* (or *Purity*), *Sir Gawain and the Green Knight*, *The Pistyl of Susan*, and a variety of others. Recent scholarship tends to avoid assigning a single author to this group of poems, despite the reference that Andrew of Wyntoun makes to Huchoun in his *Orygynale Cronykil*, which would indicate his authorship.

Huddleston (hud'l.stọn), **Sisley.** b. at Barrow in Furness, England, May 28, 1883; d. 1952. An English writer and journalist. He was Paris correspondent of the London *Times* and subsequently European correspondent of the *Christian Science Monitor*. Author of *Peace-Making in Paris* (1919), *France and the French* (1925), *In and About Paris* (1927), *Europe in Zigzags* (1929), *Le Livre de St. Pierre* (1941), and *Le Mythe de la Liberté* (1943).

Hudibras (hū'di.bras). A satirical poem in nine cantos by Samuel Butler (1612–80), directed against the Puritans, published in three parts (1663–78); so called from the name of its hero, who is a Presbyterian country justice. Accompanied by a clerk, Ralpho, one of the Independents, he ranges the country after the manner of Don Quixote, with zealous ignorance endeavoring to correct abuses and repress superstition. From this poem Butler has come to be referred to occasionally as "Hudibras" Butler, as distinguished from Samuel ("Erewhon") Butler (1835–1902).

Hudibras, Sir. A rash and melancholy man, the lover of Elissa, in Spenser's *Faerie Queene*.

Hudibrastic (hū.di.bras'tik). A term originating from Samuel Butler's poem *Hudibras*, referring to the mock-heroic meter employed there:

> Beside he was a shrewd Philosopher;
> And had read every text and gloss over.

Hudson (hud'sọn), **Jeffery.** b. at Oakham, Rutlandshire, England, 1619; d. 1682. An English dwarf. He was but 18 or 20 inches high till he was about 30 years of age, when he grew to the height of 3 feet 9 inches. He made his first appearance served up in a pie at the table of the Duke of Buckingham. After the marriage of Charles I he was a page in the service of the queen. He was a captain in the royal army at the beginning of the English Civil War. Sir Walter Scott introduces him in *Peveril of the Peak*. He was finally arrested in 1682 upon some suspicion connected with the Popish Plot, and confined in the Gatehouse prison. He was released, and did not die there as Scott and others state.

Hudson, Roderick. See **Roderick Hudson.**

Hudson, Stephen. [Pseudonym of **Sydney Schiff.**] d. 1944. An English novelist, friend of Marcel Proust. His works include *Concessions* (1913), *Richard Kurt* (1919), *Elinor Colhouse* (1921), *Prince Hempseed* (1923), dedicated to Marcel Proust, *Tony* (1924), *Myrtle* (1925), *Richard, Myrtle, and I* (1926), *A True Story* (1930), and *The Other Side* (1937), psychological novels; and of *War-Time Silhouettes* (1916) and *Celeste and Other Sketches* (1930), short stories and character sketches. He also translated *In Sight of Chaos* (1923) from the German of Hermann Hesse. He was a friend of Katherine Mansfield, whose many letters to him are in her *Letters* (1928).

Hudson, W. H. [Full name, **William Henry Hudson.**] b. at Quilmes, near Buenos Aires, Aug. 4, 1841; d. at London, Aug. 18, 1922. An English naturalist and author. Born of American parents, he lived in Argentina until 1870 and then went to England, where he was naturalized in 1900. He is remembered for *Green Mansions* (1904), a combination of nature-essay, novel, and fantasy. Author of *The Purple Land that England Lost* (1885), *A Crystal Age* (1887), *Argentine Ornithology* (1888–89, with P. L. Schlater), *The Naturalist in La Plata* (1892), *Birds in a Village* (1893), *British Birds* (1895), *Birds in London* (1898), *Nature in Downland* (1901), *Birds and Man* (1901), *Hampshire Days* (1903), *A Little Boy Lost* (1905), *Land's End* (1908), *South American Sketches* and *Afoot in England* (both 1909), *A Shepherd's Life* (1910), *Adventures Among Birds* (1913), *Far Away and Long Ago—A Story of My Early Life* (1918), *Birds in Town and Village* (1919), *A Hind in Richmond Park* (1922), and many others. He wrote many essays and papers for the London Society for the Protection of Birds. A bird sanctuary, designed by the sculptor Jacob Epstein, was erected (1925) in his honor in Kensington Gardens, a part of Hyde Park, London.

Hudson, William Henry. b. at London, May 2, 1862; d. Aug. 12, 1918. An English author, critic, and educator. Among his works are *Introduction to the Philosophy of Herbert Spencer* (1894), *Studies in Interpretation* (1896), *The Study of English Literature* (1898), *Rousseau and Naturalism in Life and Thought* (1903), and *The Story of the Renaissance* (1912).

Hudson's Bay Company. A British joint stock company chartered in 1670 for the purpose of purchasing furs and skins from the Indians of British North America. Its original possessions, called Hudson Bay Territory, came under control of the Canadian government in 1869.

Hue and Cry after Cupid, The. A masque (1608) by Ben Jonson.

Hugh (hū). The ostler of the Maypole Inn in Dickens's novel *Barnaby Rudge*. He is aroused by the wicked Gashford to a frenzy of anti-Catholicism, and plays a leading part in the Gordon Riots which result from this.

Hughes (hūz), **John.** b. at Marlborough, Wiltshire, England, Jan. 29, 1677; d. at London, Feb. 17, 1720. An English dramatist, essayist, and translator. Among his works are *Calypso and Telemachus* (1712), an opera; *The Siege of Damascus* (1720), a tragedy produced at Drury Lane; *Poems on Several Occasions with Some Select Essays in Prose* (1735); translations from Molière and Fontenelle; cantatas and operas set to music by Handel, Galliard, and Pepusch; and contributions to the *Tatler*, *Spectator*, and *Guardian*.

Hughes, John Ceiriog. [Pseudonym, **Ceiriog.**] b. in Denbighshire, Wales, Sept. 25, 1832; d. 1887. A Welsh poet. One of the leading Welsh poets of the 19th century, he is the author of some 600 songs, published in *Evening Hours* (1860), *Morning Hours* (1862), *A Hundred Songs* (1863), *Other Hours* (1868), *Summer Hours* (1870), and *Last Hours* (1888). His *Owain Wyn* (1856), considered the best pastoral poem in the Welsh language, is only one of his many prize-winning works.

Hughes, Richard (**Arthur Warren**). b. in England, April 19, 1900—. An English novelist, short-story writer, and dramatist. Author of *Gypsy-Night and Other Poems* (1922), *The Sisters' Tragedy and Other Plays* (1924), the collected short stories *A Moment of Time* (1926), verse collected in *Confessio Juvenis* (1926), *A High Wind in Jamaica* (1929; American title, *The Innocent Voyage*), *In Hazard* (1938), and two volumes of children's stories, *The Spider's Palace* (1931) and *Don't Blame Me* (1940).

Hughes, Thomas. b. at Uppington, Berkshire, England, Oct. 20, 1822; d. at Brighton, England, March 22, 1896. An English author, reformer, and politician. He was educated at Rugby under Thomas Arnold and at Oxford. He was later associated with Charles Kingsley and Frederick Denison Maurice in the movement for improving the condition of the poor known as Christian Socialism. In 1854 he helped found the Working Men's College in London, and was later (1872–83) its principal. He lectured in the U. S. in 1870 and in 1880 founded the "Rugby Colony" in Tennessee. He wrote *Tom Brown's School-Days* (1857), the most famous depiction of English public-school life and the author's tribute to Rugby and Dr. Arnold. His other books include *The Scouring of the White Horse* (1859), *Tom Brown at Oxford* (1861), *The Manliness of Christ* (1879), and *Rugby, Tennessee* (1881).

Hugh Evans (hū ev'anz), **Sir.** See **Evans, Sir Hugh.**

Hugh Mortimer (môr'ti.mėr), **Sir.** See **Mortimer, Sir John** and **Sir Hugh.**

Hugh of Lincoln (ling'kọn) or **Hugh of Avalon** (av'a.lon), **Saint.** b. at Avalon, France, c1135; d. at London, in November, 1200. An English prelate. His organizing abilities at La Grande Chartreuse caused Henry II of England to invite him to found a Carthusian monastery in England; he did so at Witham in Somersetshire. Henry made him bishop of Lincoln in 1186. He consistently resisted royal encroachment on his prerogatives but maintained the respect of Henry and his sons, Richard I and John; he excommunicated John in 1194 because of his actions while Richard was a prisoner of the emperor, but John later went out of his way to keep in the good graces of the bishop.

Hugh of Lincoln. An English boy alleged to have been put to death by Jews at Lincoln, England, 1255. The story is told in an English ballad of the Child collection entitled *Sir Hugh*, of which there are 21 versions. *Hugh of Lincoln, or The Jew's Daughter* is the title in Percy's *Reliques*. He is referred to by the Lady Prioress in Chaucer's *Canterbury Tales*, who tells a similar story.

Hugh Rebeck (rĕ′bek). See under **rebec.**

Hugh Strap (strap). See **Strap.**

Hugh The Drover. An opera in two acts by Ralph Vaughan Williams, with a libretto by Harold Child, first performed at the Royal College of Music on July 4, 1924.

Hugh Tyrold (tir′ọld), **Sir.** See **Tyrold, Sir Hugh.**

Hugo (hū′gō; French, ü.gō), **Victor Marie.** b. at Besançon, France, Feb. 26, 1802; d. at Paris, May 22, 1885. A French poet, novelist, and dramatist, the recognized leader of the French romantic school of the 19th century, and as such (especially through *Hernani*), influential on many English writers of the 19th century. His childhood was spent partly with his mother at Paris, and partly in Corsica, Elba, Italy, and Spain, wherever his father, an officer in the French army, could gather his family about him. He received his early education from his mother, a royalist, and also from an old priest, Larivière. In 1815 he went to school, and thence to the Lycée Louis-le-Grand at Paris. In 1816 he wrote his first tragedy, *Irtamène*. While still at school he began another tragedy, *Athélie*, and composed a melodrama, *Inez de Castro*, and several poems. He also competed for a prize of the French Academy with a poem, *Sur les avantages de l'étude* (1817). Again, in 1818, he competed with his poems *Sur l'institution du jury* and *Sur les avantages de l'enseignement mutuel*. His success encouraged him to send to the Academy of Floral Games at Toulouse *Les Derniers Bardes*, *Les Vierges de Verdun*, and *Le Rétablissement de la statue de Henri IV* (1819), for which he was awarded the principal prize. In 1820 he took another prize with his poem *Moïse sur le Nil*, and was made *Maître ès jeuz-floraux*. In 1819 he had founded a fortnightly review, *Le Conservateur Littéraire;* he wrote also for *La Muse Française*. His poetical works include *Odes et poésies diverses* (1822), *Nouvelles odes* (1824), *Odes et ballades* (1826; revised and enlarged ed., 1828), *Les Orientales* (1829), *Les Feuilles d'automne* (1831), *Les Chants du crépuscule* (1835), *Les Voix intérieures* (1837), *Les Rayons et les ombres* (1840), *Les Châtiments* (1853), *Les Contemplations* (1856-57), first series of *La Légende des siècles* (1859), *Les Chansons des rues et des bois* (1865), *L'Année terrible* (1872), *L'Art d'être grandpère* (1877), second series of *La Légende des siècles* (1877), *Le Pape* (1878), *La Pitié suprême* (1879), *L'Ane* (1880), *Religion et religions* (1880), *Les Quatre Vents de l'esprit* (1881), third series of *La Légende des siècles* (1883), *La Fin de Satan* (1886), *Toute la lyre* (1889-

93), and *Dieu* (1891). As a dramatist Hugo adapted *Amy Robsart* (1828) from Scott's *Kenilworth*, and also wrote *Cromwell* (1827), *Marion Delorme* (1829), *Hernani* (1830), *Le Roi s'amuse* (1832), *Lucrèce Borgia* (1833), *Marie Tudor* (1833), *Angelo* (1835), *Esmeralda* (1836), *Ruy Blas* (1838), and *Les Burgraves* (1843). This last play was a failure on the stage. Hugo wrote no more plays for theatrical production, although near the end of his life he wrote another great tragic poem, *Torquemada* (1882). A sequence of seven dramatic poems, *Le Théâtre en liberté*, was published posthumously (1885), as was an unfinished tragedy, *Les Jumeaux* (1889). Hugo's plays mark the entry of melodrama into the serious theater. His poetry, which cast off the rigid conventions of classical French verse, influenced many of the English romantic poets, especially the Pre-Raphaelite Swinburne (who wrote a *Study of Hugo* in 1886). Hugo's prose writings are *Han d'Island* (1823), *Bug-Jargal* (1826), *Le Dernier Jour d'un condamné* (1829), *Notre Dame de Paris* (1831), *Littérature et philosophie mêlées* and *Claude Gueux* (1834), *Napoléon le petit* (1852), *Les Misérables* (1862), *William Shakespeare* (1864), *Les Travailleurs de la mer* (1866), *L'Homme qui rit* (1869), *Actes et paroles* (1872-76), *Quatrevingt-treize* (1874), *Histoire d'un crime* (1877-78), *Choses vues* (1887), and *En voyage: Alpes et Pyrénées* (1890). Henri Guillemin, a well-known authority on Hugo, reconstructed some fragmentary material Hugo wrote as a political diary of a revolutionary period in France, and included the notes in one volume, *Souvenirs personnels, 1848-1851* (1954). Guillemin also published for the first time, *Carnets intimes, 1870-1871* (1954), a frank diary of Hugo's sexual life in his old age, and formerly used by the poet's biographers as a sourcebook. He was elected to the French Academy, Jan. 7, 1841. His interest in politics and journalism led him to found a newspaper, *L'Événement*, in 1848. After the revolution of that year he was exiled (1851) from France, and did not return till the fall of the empire in 1870. He went first to Belgium, in 1852 to Jersey, and in 1855 to Guernsey. Hugo was elected a life member of the French senate in 1876.

Hugo De Lacy (dẹ lā′si). See **De Lacy, Hugo.**

Huguenots (hū′gẹ.nots). The Reformed or Calvinistic communion of France in the 16th and 17th centuries. The name as applied to the Protestants of France was apparently imported from Geneva, Switzerland, where it appears to have been for some time in use as a political nickname. The Huguenots were persecuted in the reign (1515-47) of Francis I and his immediate successors, and after 1562 under the leadership of such men as Admiral Gaspard de Coligny and Henry of Navarre (afterward Henry IV of France), were frequently at war with the Catholics. In spite of these wars and the Massacre of Saint Bartholomew (Aug. 24, 1572), they continued numerous and powerful, and the Edict of Nantes, issued by Henry IV (1598), secured to them full political and civil rights. Their political power was broken with the surrender of La Rochelle in 1628; the revocation (1685) of the Edict of Nantes by Louis XIV, and the subsequent persecutions, forced hundreds of thousands into exile in Prussia, the Netherlands, Switzerland, England, and elsewhere. Many settled in New York, Virginia,

---

fat, fāte, fär, àsk, fãre; net, mē, hèr; pin, pīne; not, nōte, mȯve, nôr; up, lūte, pùll; ᴛʜ, then;

and other American colonies, but especially in South Carolina. It was not until 1787 that they received civil equality; the Declaration of the Rights of Man (1789) gave them religious equality. The name is sometimes applied at the present day to the descendants of the original Huguenots.

Huitzilipochtli (wēt″sē.lē.pōch′tlē). In Aztec mythology, the god of war and principal deity, who was also believed to be the sun, reborn daily. The Aztecs offered immense numbers of human sacrifices at the temple dedicated to him.

Hulde (hŭl′dē). See **Holda**.

Hull (hul), **Edith Maude.** An English novelist. She is best known for *The Sheik* (1921), as popular a success in book form as it was on the silent screen in the motion picture starring Rudolph Valentino. Author also of *The Shadow of the East* (1921), *The Desert Healer* (1923), *Sons of the Sheik* (1925), *The Lion Tamer* (1928), *Captive of the Sahara* (1931), *The Forest of Terrible Things* (1939), and *Jungle Captive* (1939). *Camping in the Sahara* (1927) is a travel book.

Hulse (huls), **John.** b. at Middlewich, Cheshire, England, March 15, 1708; d. there, Dec. 14, 1790. An English clergyman. He bequeathed estates to the University of Cambridge, which form an endowment for the Hulsean professorship of divinity, for the Hulsean lectures (on the Christian evidences, or in explanation of difficult or obscure parts of Scripture), and for certain Hulsean prizes.

Hulton (hul′ton), Sir **Edward.** b. at Ashton-on-Mersey, Lancashire, England, 1869; d. May 23, 1925. An English newspaper owner. He began (1884) his career as a journalist at Manchester, under his father, Edward, founder of the *Sporting Chronicle, Evening Chronicle, Sunday Chronicle,* and other papers. In 1897 he purchased the Manchester *Evening Chronicle,* in 1900 the *Daily Dispatch,* and in 1921 founded the *Daily Sketch* and the *Illustrated Sunday Herald,* later purchasing the *Evening Standard.* Retiring in 1923, he disposed of his chain of newspapers to Harold Sidney Harmsworth (Lord Rothermere) and William Maxwell Aitkin (Lord Beaverbrook) for the sum of six million pounds.

Hulton, Edward George Warris. b. at Harrowgate, Yorkshire, England, Nov. 29, 1906—. An English newspaper owner; son of Sir Edward Hulton. Proprietor of the *Picture Post, Farmers Weekly, Lilliput, Housewife,* and *The Leader;* editor and owner of *World Review.*

humanism. A system or mode of thought in which human interests predominate, or any purely human element is made prominent.

The Hegelian idealism first bred the more sensualistic system of humanism, and then humanism bred socialism. (Rae, *Contemporary Socialism.*)

Here we have the stern Puritanism of old Birmingham passing into modern nonconformity, . . . and this milder form of the old spirit mellowing at last into nineteenth-century humanism.
(*Nineteenth Century, XX.*)

I neither admit the moral influence of theism in the past, nor look forward to the moral influence of humanism in the future.
(W. K. Clifford, *Lectures,* II.)

Humber (hum′bėr). [Latin, **Abus.**] An estuary in E England, lying between Yorkshire on the N and Lincolnshire on the S. It is formed by the junction of the rivers Trent and Ouse and, with these rivers and their tributaries, drains about one sixth of the area of England. The chief ports are Hull and Grimsby. It was part of the boundary between ancient Northumbria (Deira) and Mercia. Length, ab. 38 mi.

Humble Fisherman, A. A book of essays by Morley Roberts, published in 1932.

Humboldt (hum′bōlt; German, hŭm′bolt), Baron **Alexander von.** [Full name, **Friedrich Heinrich Alexander von Humboldt.**] b. at Berlin, Sept. 14, 1769; d. there, May 6, 1859. A German scientist and author. He studied at the universities of Frankfort on the Oder and Göttingen, and, after traveling in Holland, Belgium, and England, continued his studies at the Mining School at Freiberg. From 1792 he was for several years assessor of mines at Berlin, but resigned the position in 1797 to travel in Switzerland, Italy, and France. In Paris he became acquainted with Aimé Bonpland, with whom he undertook from 1799 to 1804 a scientific journey to South America and Mexico. From 1809 to 1827 he lived for the most part at Paris, engaged in scientific work. After 1827 he took up his permanent residence at Berlin. In 1829, at the instance of the emperor of Russia, he undertook another scientific expedition, to Siberia and the Caspian Sea. Subsequently, until his death, he lived at Berlin. The results of the American journey were published in a large series of works with the general title *Voyage aux régions équinoxiales du nouveau continent.* They include *Relation historique* (1814–25, covering only the first part of the trip), *Essai politique sur la Nouvelle Espagne* (1811), *Essai politique sur l'île de Cuba* (1826–27), scientific monographs, atlases, and other material. *Asie Centrale* (1843) and other works describe the Asiatic journey. *Kosmos* (1845–62), perhaps the greatest of Humboldt's books, first published in German, is an attempt to describe the physical universe as a functioning unity.

Hume (hūm), **David.** b. at Edinburgh, April 26 (O.S.), 1711; d. there, Aug. 25, 1776. A Scottish philosopher and historian. He studied at Edinburgh, and went to France in 1734, where he remained until 1737, chiefly at La Flèche in Anjou. He retired to Ninewells, Berwickshire, in 1740, became companion to the Marquis of Annandale in 1745, and was dismissed in 1746; and became secretary to General James Sinclair or St. Clair, by whom he was appointed judge advocate, and whom he accompanied on an embassy to Vienna and Turin. He was appointed keeper of the library of the Faculty of Advocates at Edinburgh in 1752. He again visited France (1763–66), and was undersecretary of state (1767–68). He is chiefly celebrated as the expounder of skeptical views in philosophy, which have produced an effect upon metaphysical thinking since his day. Hume based his system on a strict empiricism, only sensation forming the mind and causation being, like facts themselves, a matter impossible of demonstration. He wrote *A Treatise of Human Nature, being an Attempt to Introduce the Experimental Method of*

d, d or j; ş, s or sh; ţ, t or ch; z, z or zh; o, F. cloche; ü, F. menu; ch, Sc. loch; n, F. bonbon.

Reasoning into Moral Subjects (1739–40), *Essays, Moral and Political* (1741–42), *Philosophical Essays concerning Human Understanding* (1748, afterward called *An Enquiry concerning Human Understanding*), *Political Discourses* (1751), *An Enquiry concerning the Principles of Morals* (1751), *History of England* (1754–61), *Four Dissertations* (1757), *Natural History of Religion* (1757), *Two Essays* (1777), and *Dialogues concerning Natural Religion* (1779). His collected works were edited by Green and Crose (4 vols., 1874); his life was written by J. H. Burton (1846).

Hume, Fergus. [Full name, **Ferguson Wright Hume.**] b. in England, July 8, 1859; d. near Thundersley, Essex, England, July 13, 1932. An English writer of detective novels and stories. Author of *The Mystery of a Hansom Cab* (1886), *The Piccadilly Puzzle* (1889), *The Black Carnation* (1892), *The Lone Inn* (1894), *The Bishop's Secret* and *The Lady From Nowhere* (both 1900), *Jonah's Luck* (1906), *The Other Person* (1920), *The Caravan Mystery* (1926), and more than 100 other detective and mystery stories.

Hume, John. In Shakespeare's *2 Henry VI*, a priest bribed to undertake witchcraft on behalf of the Duchess of Gloucester.

Hume, Martin Andrew Sharp. [Original name, **Martin Sharp.**] b. at London, Dec. 8, 1843; d. at Forest Gate, Essex, England, July 1, 1910. An English historian. Editor (1892–1912) of *Spanish State Papers Relating to Negotiations Between England and Spain.* Author of *The Courtships of Queen Elizabeth* and *The Year After the Armada and Other Studies* (both 1896), *Sir Walter Raleigh* and *Philip II of Spain* (both 1897), *Spain—Its Greatness and Decay* (1898), *Modern Spain* (1899), *The Spanish People: Their Origin, Growth, and Influence* (1901), *The Love Affairs of Mary Queen of Scots* (1903), *Spanish Influence on English Literature* (1905), *The Wives of Henry VIII* (1905), and *The Court of Philip IV* (1907).

Humfrey Banastaire (hum'fri, um'-; ban'ạs.tẻr). See **Banastaire, Humfrey.**

Humgudgeon (hum'guj.ọn), **Grace-be-here.** A fanatical corporal in Sir Walter Scott's novel *Woodstock,* of Cromwell's army, who was hurled by Albert Lee from a high tower at Woodstock, where he had been placed as a sentinel.

Humorous Day's Mirth, An. A comedy by George Chapman, performed in 1597 and printed in 1599.

Humorists, The. A comedy by Thomas Shadwell, produced in 1670. It is in the style of Jonsonian humour comedy, and ridicules the vices of the period.

Humorous Lieutenant, The. A play by John Fletcher, probably produced in 1618 and printed in 1647.

humour comedy. [Also, **comedy of humours.**] A type of comedy popular in Elizabethan England, perhaps chiefly through Ben Jonson, in which character is considered to be determined by a predominance of one of the four "humours" believed to exist in the human body. Hippocrates originated the theory in the 5th century B.C. that these substances were blood, phlegm, yellow bile, and black bile, and that they produced good health in the

right proportions and bad health when unbalanced. Galen brought forth the idea in the 2nd century A.D. of humours mixing in different proportions so as to produce differences of temperament. The humours were later equated with the four medieval elements of earth (black bile), water (phlegm), air (blood), and fire (yellow bile). A preponderance of earth produced a melancholy temperament; of fire, a choleric temperament; of air, a sanguine temperament; and of water, a phlegmatic temperament. Thomas Elyot popularized this notion in his *Castel of Health* (1539), which by 1618 had reached 15 editions. Ben Jonson was familiar probably with Seneca's *De Ira,* which discusses the effect of a humour on anger, and with Aristotle's *Rhetoric* (Book II), which also takes up the theory. Chapman's comedy *An Humorous Day's Mirth* actually made use of the theory before Jonson, and Shirley uses it much more fully as a "scientific" theory in his *Lover's Melancholy.* However, this type of comedy is now usually associated with Jonson, from the two plays *Every Man in His Humour* and *Every Man Out of His Humour.*

Humour Out of Breath. A play (1608) by John Day.

Humphrey (hum'fri). [Titles: Duke of Gloucester and Earl of **Pembroke;** called **"the Good Duke Humphrey."**] b. 1391; d. at Bury St. Edmunds, England, Feb. 23, 1447. An English soldier and statesman; youngest son of Henry IV by his first wife, Mary Bohun. He studied at Balliol College, Oxford, and was noted as a patron of learning and a collector of books. He was the founder, by his gifts of books, of the library of that university. In 1420 he was appointed lieutenant of England, and held that office until the return of Henry V in 1421. On Henry's death Gloucester, though only deputy for Bedford, became, in effect, protector of the young king Henry VI, through Bedford's occupation with affairs in France. In 1422 he married Jacqueline, only daughter of William VI, Count of Hainaut, to whose estates she had succeeded, but of which she had been deprived; and in 1424 conquered Hainaut and was proclaimed its count. In 1428 his marriage with Jacqueline was annulled, and he soon married his mistress, Eleanor Cobham. His protectorate, which was throughout unfortunate, was terminated by the coronation (Nov. 6, 1429) of Henry VI. In 1441 he was disgraced through the dealings of his wife with the astrologer Bolingbroke. In 1447 he was arrested by order of the king, and in a few days died.

Humphrey. In Shakespeare's *3 Henry VI,* one of the keepers. Sinklo is the other.

Humphrey Dobbins (dob'inz). See **Dobbins, Humphrey.**

Humphrey of Gloucester (glos'tẻr). See **Gloucester, Humphrey of.**

Humphrey Stafford (staf'ọrd), **Sir.** See **Stafford, Sir Humphrey** and **William.**

Humphrey's Walk, Duke. See **Paul's Walk.**

Humphry Clinker (hum'fri kling'kẻr). [Full title, **The Expedition of Humphry Clinker.**] A novel, in epistolary form, by Tobias Smollett, published in 1771. It tells the adventures of the Bramble family during their travels through England and Scotland. Matthew Bramble is an eccentric but essentially kind-hearted old bachelor. With him is his sister, the spinster Tabitha; his nephew and niece, Jery and Lydia; Tabitha's maid, Mrs. Winifred Jenkins; and Humphry Clinker, a ragged waif who is picked up along the road to act as coachman. Lydia's uncle is anxious to have her forget her fondness for a handsome young actor, Wilson, who continually turns up during their travels, but when it is discovered that he is really a gentleman of property and title, he is allowed to marry her. Humphry turns out to be the natural son of Matthew Bramble, and he marries the maid, Winifred, who is thus "removed to a higher spear." Tabitha finally finds a husband in Obadiah Lismahago, an argumentative Scottish soldier whose tales of his sufferings when captured by Indians promise to make him a valuable addition to Matthew Bramble's home.

Huncamunca (hung′ka̱.mung′ka̱). A character in Henry Fielding's burlesque tragedy *Tom Thumb the Great*. She is the daughter of King Arthur and Queen Dollallolla, and is sweet, gentle, and amorous. (Indeed, she is all of these to the point of absurdity, and not by accident: Fielding intended her as a satire on the genteel heroines then popular in sentimental comedy.)

Hunchback, The. A comedy by J. Sheridan Knowles, produced in 1832.

Hundred and One Harlequins, The. A volume of verse (1922) by Sacheverell Sitwell.

Hundred Days. The period of about 100 days, from the middle of March to June 28, 1815, during which Napoleon I, after his escape from Elba, made his final effort to reëstablish his empire. It ended in the crushing defeat at Waterloo, his abdication, and the accession once more of Louis XVIII.

Hundred Days, The. A historical novel by Sir Max Pemberton, published in 1905. It deals with the period between Napoleon's return from Elba and his defeat at Waterloo.

Hungarian Brothers, The. A novel by Anna Maria Porter.

Hungerford (hung′gẽr.fọrd), **Margaret Wolfe.** [Maiden name, **Hamilton;** pseudonym, **The Duchess.**] b. c1855; d. at Bandon, Ireland, Jan. 24, 1897. An Irish novelist.

Huns (hunz). An Asiatic people of undetermined origin first mentioned in Chinese chronicles, dating from at least 400 B.C., in NW China and the Gobi. Gradually they extended their power west into Central Asia, a part of the people moving into India. After defeat by the Chinese in 36 B.C., they moved north of the Caspian Sea, and established a kingdom between the Don River and the Carpathians in the 4th century A.D. Under Attila (445–453), the Huns penetrated to Constantinople and Rome. Soon after Attila's death, his kingdom disintegrated. The Huns, although notorious for their barbarity, acted as intermediaries in the trade between China and Europe. The Hungarians are not their descendants.

Hunt (hunt), **Leigh.** [Full name, **James Henry Leigh Hunt.**] b. at Southgate, near London, Oct. 19, 1784; d. at Putney, near London, Aug. 28, 1859. An English essayist, poet, and miscellaneous author. He edited (1808 *et seq.*) the *Examiner* and was editor (1810) of the *Reflector*. Some of his *Examiner* papers casting reflections on the prince regent resulted in Hunt's being sentenced (1813) to two years' imprisonment. From 1819 to 1821 he wrote in the *Indicator*. He was the friend of Lamb, Bentham, Moore, and Byron, and with the last edited *The Liberal* (1822–23), a magazine. His frank criticism of his friend Byron in *Lord Byron and some of his Contemporaries* (1828) shocked the English sense of propriety and lost him many friends. His chief works are essays, the poem *Story of Rimini* (1816), *Autobiography* (1850), and several books of poetry, dramas, and translations. He is best remembered for his influence on Keats (giving rise to criticism of the "Cockney School" of poetry) and for the two poems *Abou Ben Adhem* and *Jenny Kissed Me.*

Hunt, Violet. b. at Durham, England, 1866; d. 1942. An English novelist and writer of biographical works. Her chief works are *Unkist, Unkind* (1897), *The Wife of Altamont* (1910), *The House of Many Mirrors* (1915), *Their Lives* (1916), and *The Wife of Rossetti* (1932).

Hunted Down. A story by Charles Dickens, written especially for the New York *Ledger* and there published serially during August and September, 1859.

Hunter (hun′tẽr), **John.** b. at Long Calderwood, Lanarkshire, Scotland, Feb. 13, 1728; d. at London, Oct. 16, 1793. A British surgeon, anatomist, and physiologist. He collected at London a museum of anatomical, physiological, and pathological specimens. He wrote *Natural History of the Human Teeth* (1771–78), *Treatise on the Blood, Inflammation and Gunshot Wounds* (1794), and others.

Hunter, Mrs. Leo. The author of an ode to "an expiring frog"; a character devoted to celebrities, in Dickens's *Pickwick Papers.*

Hunter, William. b. at Long Calderwood, Lanarkshire, Scotland, May 23, 1718; d. at London, March 30, 1783. A British physician, anatomist, and physiologist; brother of John Hunter. He was noted as a lecturer on anatomy, and as the collector of a museum (now in the University of Glasgow). He wrote *Anatomy of the Gravid Uterus* (1774) and others.

Hunter, Sir William Wilson. b. at Glasgow, July 15, 1840; d. at Oxford, England, Feb. 6, 1900. A British civil servant and author. He entered the Bengal civil service in 1862, holding various government posts until he retired in 1887 and returned to England. As director general of statistics, he edited (1869–81) a statistical survey of India in 128 volumes, later issuing a nine-volume condensation in the *Imperial Gazetteer of India* (1881). Among his many works are *A Comparative Dictionary of Non-Aryan Languages of India and High Asia* (1868), *The Indian Empire—Its People, History, and Products* and *History of the Indian Peoples* (both 1882), *The Thackerays in India* (1897), *A History of British India* (2 vols., 1899, 1900), and *The India of the Queen and Other Essays* (1903).

Hunter and Other Poems, The. A volume of verse (1916) by W. J. Turner, containing the much-quoted lyric poem "Romance," which opens with the verse:

When I was but thirteen or so
I went into a golden land,
Cimborazo, Cotopaxi
Took me by the hand.

Huntingdon (hun'ting.dọn), **Arthur** and **Helen.**
Two of the principal characters, husband and wife,
in Anne Brontë's *Tenant of Wildfell Hall.*

Huntingdonians (hun.ting.dō'ni.ạnz). A denomination of Calvinistic Methodists in England and
Wales.

Hunting of the Snark, The. A poem (1876) by
Charles L. Dodgson (Lewis Carroll), written in the
mock-heroic style, telling of a journey planned to
capture a snark, and of the actual involvement
with the Boojum, a particularly terrible and dangerous species of snark.

Huntly (hunt'li), **Frances E.** Pseudonym used
prior to 1898 by **Mayne, Ethel Colburn.**

Hunyadi or **Hunyady** (hö'nyô.dě), **János.** [English,
John Hunyadi.] b. at Hunyad, in Transylvania,
c1387; d. at Zemun, in what is now Yugoslavia,
Aug. 11, 1456. A Hungarian general. In 1443 he
embarked on an expedition that drove the Turks
from the Adriatic and in 1444 began a campaign
aimed at supporting Constantinople. In 1446 Hunyadi was elected regent of Hungary for Ladislas V,
who was being held against his will by Frederick
III of Germany. Hunyadi marched against Frederick but was forced to return to battle the Turks.
At Kossovo (October, 1448) he was defeated
through the machinations of men he had counted
as allies. Constantinople fell to the Turks in 1453
and Hunyadi began, unsupported by his own nobles,
to rally an army for the defense of Hungary. The
result was his most celebrated exploit, the successful defense of Belgrade against Mohammed II in
1456. The Turks broke off the siege and retired,
but Hunyadi died of plague three weeks afterward.
His life, and legends accreting to it, became a
national legend and Hunyadi the national hero.

Huon de Bordeaux (ü.ôṅ dẹ bôr.dō). A French
chanson de geste. Probably through the translation
(c1540) into English by John Bourchier, Lord
Berners, it supplied Shakespeare with some of the
dramatis personae of *A Midsummer Night's Dream*
(for example, Oberon), though there were earlier
dramatic versions of the Huon story on the English
stage. It is believed to have been written in the
13th century, although no manuscripts of the
original are extant.

Hurd (hėrd), Sir **Archibald.** b. at Berkeley, Gloucestershire, England, Aug. 13, 1869—. An English
journalist and naval expert. He served on the editorial staff (1899–1928) of the *Daily Telegraph,* and
was joint editor (1922–28) of Brassey's *Naval and
Shipping Annual.*

Hurd, Sir **Percy Angier.** b. at Berkeley, England,
May 18, 1864; d. June 5, 1950. An English editor
and current-events specialist; brother of Sir Archi-
bald Hurd. He was instrumental in founding (1898)
The Outlook, which he edited (1898–1904), was
London editor of the Montreal *Star,* editor of the
Canadian Gazette, and subsequently of *Canada's
Weekly.*

Hurdcott (hėrd'kot, -kọt). A novel (1911) of 19th-
century English country life, by Monsignor Count

Francis Browning Drew Bickerstaffe-Drew under
the pseudonym John Ayscough.

Hurlothrumbo (hėr.lō.thrum'bō). [Full title, **Hurlothrumbo, or, The Super-Natural.**] A burlesque
opera written and brought out by Samuel Johnson
of Cheshire (not the famous critic and lexicographer) in 1729. He played the part of Lord Flame.
The piece was successful and a Hurlothrumbo
Society was formed, the word becoming proverbial
for absurdity and nonsense.

Hus (hus; Czech, hös), **John.** [Also: **Huss;** Czech,
Jan Hus.] b. at Husinec, in Bohemia, c1369; burned
at Konstanz (Constance), Baden, Germany, July
6, 1415. A Czech preacher, the most important of
the native Czech religious reformers of his time.
He was educated at the University of Prague, where
he studied liberal arts and divinity. He began to
lecture there in 1398. Three years later he was
appointed dean of the philosophical faculty, and
was rector of the university (1402–03). Having
been ordained priest, he became in 1402 preacher
of the Bethlehem Chapel at Prague, the recognized
center of the native reform movement; he thus
became the leader of that movement. He preached
in Czech. At first, he was supported in his endeavors
to reform the clergy and the religious life generally
by the young archbishop of Prague, Zbyněk. But
when he joined the king's side in the current conciliar
struggle which had for its aim the termination of
the papal schism, Zbyněk turned against him. King
Wenceslaus IV of Bohemia supported Alexander V,
who was elected to the papacy by the Council of
Pisa in 1409 in an attempt to heal the schism that
found both Gregory XII and Benedict XIII claiming the papacy; the archbishop, however, remained
faithful to Gregory XII. As a result of this disagreement, Zbyněk excommunicated Hus (1409) when
the latter protested against the indiscriminate
burning of Wycliffe's writings. But since Hus had
the support of the king, he was able to defy the
archbishop, and to continue preaching. Nevertheless, in 1411 the whole city of Prague was placed
under an interdict on account of Hus; thereupon,
he left, and sought refuge in hiding. This step was
particularly necessary when he lost the protection
of the king after he had denounced the bull of Pope
John XXIII decreeing a crusade against King
Ladislas of Naples and granting indulgence to those
joining the crusade. Hus objected to the use of
ecclesiastical power of this sort in a struggle over a
purely temporal matter; the whole question of indulgences was brought to the fore. The papal indulgences were sold at Prague in a manner which,
a hundred years hence, was to arouse the protest
of Luther, and thus become an occasion of the outbreak of the Protestant Reformation. During his
voluntary seclusion, Hus wrote some of his most
important works, particularly the tract on *Simony*
and *De ecclesia.* But when the Council of Constance
met in 1414, and Hus was offered a safe-conduct
by the emperor Sigismund, he accepted the invitation to appear before the Council, hoping thus to
be able to answer charges of heresy. Nevertheless,
shortly after his arrival, he was arrested on orders
of Pope John XXIII and imprisoned. The charges
against him were prepared by his avowed enemies,
both Czech and German. The chief of these was a
charge of Wycliffism, although Hus himself never

fat, fāte, fär, ȧsk, fāre; net, mē, hėr; pin, pīne; not, nōte, mȯve, nôr; up, lūte, pu̇ll; ᴛʜ, then;

held many of Wycliffe's radical doctrines (for instance, that of the denial of transubstantiation), while others he held in a greatly modified form. The Council ordered him to recant unconditionally, which his conscience would not permit him to do, especially since he did not hold many of the doctrines imputed to him and recantation would imply that he had held to those doctrines. He was, accordingly, burned at the stake as a heretic. A year later, Jerome of Prague, one of Hus's defenders at the trial, suffered the same fate. Hus was primarily a representative of the native Czech reform which comprised among his predecessors such men as Milič of Kroměříž and Matthew of Janov. He did not derive his doctrine from Wycliffe, although he accepted in a modified form many of Wycliffe's formulations of doctrines common to both the English and the Czech reform movements and probably carried from England to Bohemia by churchmen attendant on Anne of Bohemia, queen (1382–94) of Richard II of England. His condemnation for Wycliffism by the Council of Constance, therefore, does not rest on essentially factual grounds.

Husband's Message, The. [Also, **The Lover's Message.**] An Old English poem (c950) included in the *Exeter Book*, divided into four sections, of which the first has been considered by some scholars to be a separate poem. The entire poem is now more generally regarded as a single work, in which the lover inscribes a speech to his lady on a piece of wood, which in turn speaks to her on his behalf. It tells of the lover, forced to leave the country because of a feud, who now requests that his lady come over the seas to join him.

Huss (hus), **John.** See Hus, John.

Hutcheson (huch′e.sọn), **Francis.** b. in County Down, Ireland, Aug. 8, 1694; d. at Glasgow, 1746. A Scottish philosopher, professor of moral philosophy (1729–46) at Glasgow.

Hutchinson (huch′in.sọn), **John.** b. in Nottinghamshire, England, 1615; d. at Sandown Castle, Kent, England, Sept. 11, 1664. An English revolutionist and regicide, one of the members of Parliament who signed the death warrant of Charles I.

Hutchinson, R. C. [Full name, **Ray Coryton Hutchinson.**] b. at London, Jan. 23, 1907–. An English novelist. Author of *Thou Hast A Devil* (1930), *The Answering Glory* (1932), *The Unforgotten Prisoner* (1933), *One Light Burning* (1935), *Shining Scabbard* (1936), *Testament* (1938), *The Fire and the Wood* (1940), *Interim* (1945), *Elephant and Castle* (1949), *Journey With Strangers* (1952), and the play *Last Train South* (1938).

Hutten (hut′ẹn), **Ulrich von.** b. at Castle Steckelberg, near Fulda, Germany, April 21, 1488; d. on the island of Ufenau, on the Lake of Zurich, Switzerland, Aug. 23, 1523. A German humanist. Intended for the church, he was placed (1498) in the monastery of Fulda, whence he fled in 1505. He subsequently studied the humanities at various German and Italian universities, including those of Frankfort on the Oder and Pavia. He served in the imperial army in 1513, was crowned poet by the emperor Maximilian I at Augsburg in 1517, entered the service of the archbishop of Mainz in 1518, joined the Swabian League against Ulrich,

Duke of Württemberg, in 1519, and in 1522 fought unsuccessfully in association with Franz von Sickingen at the head of the nobility of the Upper Rhine against the spiritual principalities. He was a friend and supporter of Luther, one of the authors of the *Epistolae obscurorum virorum*, and one of the principal satirical writers of his time. His works were edited by Eduard Böcking (1859–62); life by Strauss (1857).

Hutton (hut′ọn), **Richard Holt.** b. at Leeds, England, June 2, 1826; d. at Twickenham, England, Sept. 9, 1897. An English journalist and essayist. He was editor (1861–97) of the *Spectator*.

Huxley (huks′li), **Aldous Leonard.** b. at Godalming, Surrey, England, July 26, 1894–. English novelist, short-story writer, dramatist, essayist, poet, and biographer; son of Leonard Huxley, grandson of Thomas Henry Huxley, and nephew of Matthew Arnold. Mrs. Humphry Ward was his aunt and Julian Sorell Huxley is his brother. From 1919 to 1924 he was on the staff of the London *Athenaeum* and the *Westminster Gazette*. During the years 1923–30 he lived in Italy, and in 1925–26 he traveled in India and the West Indies. In 1934–35 he visited Central America and the U. S., and he was again in America in 1938. An early intention to study medicine (he majored in biology at Eton) had to be given up because of defective vision, so serious that at times it became almost complete blindness, making it necessary for him to learn the Braille system so that he could read books and music. During his late teens, when he was practically blind, he wrote a full-length novel on a Braille typewriter. As he tells us, he never read the novel, because he could not see, and when his vision later returned, so that he could manage to read with a large magnifying glass, the manuscript was lost. His works include *Limbo* (1920), *Crome Yellow* (1921), *Mortal Coils* (1922), *Antic Hay* (1923), *Those Barren Leaves* (1925), *Two or Three Graces* (1926), *Point Counter Point* (1928), which contains portraits of his friends J. Middleton Murry and D. H. Lawrence, *Brave New World* (1932), a futuristic satire, and *Eyeless in Gaza* (1936), all prose fiction; *Little Mexican and Other Stories* (1924; American title, *Young Archimedes and Other Stories*) and *Rotunda* (1932), stories and essays; *The Burning Wheel* (1916), *Jonah* (1917), *The Defeat of Youth* (1918), *Leda* (1920), and *The Cicadas* (1931), poetry. His collected essays are *On the Margin* (1923), *Along the Road* (1925), *Jesting Pilate* (1926), *Proper Studies* (1927), *Do What You Will* (1929), *Brief Candles* and *Vulgarity in Literature* (both 1930), *Music at Night* (1931), *Texts and Pretexts* (1932), *The Olive Tree* (1936), and *Ends and Means* (1937). *The World of Light* (1931) is a play, and *Grey Eminence* (1941) is a life of Father Joseph, known as "Éminence Grise" because of the gray habit he wore. Other works are *After Many a Summer Dies the Swan* (1939) and *Ape and Essence* (1948), fiction, *The Art of Seeing* (1942), a subject in which Huxley has a vital interest, "the onset of eye trouble," being "unquestionably the most important single event in my life," *Time Must Have a Stop* (1944), and *The Perennial Philosophy* (1945). For the screen, while at Hollywood, he wrote scripts for *Madame Curie* and *Pride and Prejudice*. His recent work includes the play *The Gioconda Smile*

ḍ, d or j; ṣ, s or sh; ṭ, t or ch; ẓ, z or zh; o, F. cloche; ü, F. menu; ch, Sc. loch; ṅ, F. bonbon.

(1950), *The Devils of Loudun* (1952), a study of witchcraft and mass hysteria, *The Doors of Perception* (1954), a narrative of the author's experience with using the drug mescalin, and *The Genius and the Goddess* (1955).

Huxley, Julian Sorell. b. at London, June 22, 1887—. An English biologist, essayist, and poet; son of Leonard Huxley, grandson of Thomas Henry Huxley, and brother of Aldous Leonard Huxley. Educated at Eton and at Balliol College, Oxford, he served as research associate (1912–13) and assistant professor (1913–16) at the Rice Institute at Houston, Tex. Following service in Italy during World War I, he became a fellow and senior demonstrator (1919–25) in zoölogy at New College, Oxford, and professor (1925–27) of zoölogy and honorary lecturer (1927–35) at King's College, London. He was Fullerian professor (1926–29) of physiology at the Royal Institution. He is director general (1946 *et seq.*) of the United Nations Education, Scientific, and Cultural Organization. Author of *The Individual in the Animal Kingdom* (1911), *Essays of a Biologist* (1923), *The Stream of Life* (1926), *Essays in Popular Science* (1926), *Ants* (1926), *Africa View* (1931), *What Dare I Think?* (1931), *Problems of Relative Growth* (1932), *The Captive Shrew and Other Poems* (1932), *If I Were Dictator* (1934), *At the Zoo* (1936), *Evolution Restated* (1940), *Evolution: the Modern Synthesis* (1942), *Man in the Modern World* (1947), and *From An Antique Land* (1954). He collaborated with H. G. and G. P. Wells on *The Science of Life* (1929).

Huxley, Leonard. b. Dec. 11, 1860; d. at Hampstead, London, May 3, 1933. An English biographer, teacher, and editor; son of Thomas Henry Huxley and father of Julian Sorell Huxley and Aldous Leonard Huxley. He was educated at University College School, St. Andrews University, and at Balliol College, Oxford, and became master (1884–1901) at the Charterhouse School, Godalming, Surrey. He was later assistant professor of Greek at St. Andrews. Author of *Life of Huxley* (1900), *Scott's Last Expedition* (1913), *Life of Sir Joseph Hooker* (1918), *Thomas Henry Huxley: A Character Sketch* (1920), *Charles Darwin* (1921), *The House of Smith, Elder* (1923), and *Progress and the Unfit* (1926). He translated the *New Testament Times* of Adolf Hausrath, edited *Jane Welsh Carlyle: Letters to Her Family* (1924) and *Letters to Her Sister from Elizabeth Barrett Browning* (1929), and contributed to the *Cornhill Magazine*, of which he was editor.

Huxley, Thomas Henry. b. at Ealing, near London, May 4, 1825; d. at Eastbourne, Sussex, England, June 29, 1895. An English biologist. He was educated at Ealing School and at Charing Cross Hospital, London. He served (1846–50) as assistant surgeon on board H.M.S. *Rattlesnake*, collecting a mass of information on the biological phenomena of the south Pacific. He became lecturer in natural history (1854) at the Royal School of Mines, where he taught for 31 years. He was installed lord rector of Aberdeen University for a term of three years in 1874, was Rede lecturer at Cambridge in 1883, and was president of the Royal Society (1881–85). Among his works are *Oceanic Hydrozoa* (1859), *Evidence as to Man's Place in Nature* (1863), *Lec-*

tures on the Elements of Comparative Anatomy (1863), *Lessons in Elementary Physiology* (1866), *An Introduction to the Classification of Animals* (1869), *Lay Sermons* (1870), *A Manual of the Anatomy of Vertebrated Animals* (1871), *Critiques and Addresses* (1873), *Physiography* (1877), *A Manual of the Anatomy of Invertebrated Animals* (1877), *The Crayfish* (1880), *Science and Culture* (1881), *A Course of Practical Instruction in Elementary Biology* (with H. M. Martin, 1875), *Essays upon some Controverted Questions* (1892), and *Evolution and Ethics* (1893).

Hyacinth Halvey (hī′a̤.sinth hal′vi). A comedy (1906) by Augusta Gregory (Lady Gregory) about the virtuous reputation which a young man tries desperately (and unsuccessfully) to get rid of. He finds that it brings him all kinds of dull social obligations, and to destroy it he first tries stealing a sheep from a butcher, only to earn his gratitude because the inspectors would otherwise have arrested the butcher for selling diseased meat. Trying next to ruin his reputation by robbing a poor box, Hyacinth finds that no one will believe his confession because they attribute it to a noble desire to shield another.

Hyacinthus (hī.a̤.sin′thus). [Also, **Hyacinth.**] In Greek mythology, a beautiful youth; son of Amyclas, king of Amyclae in Laconia. He was killed through jealousy by Zephynes or accidentally by Apollo by a discus throw. From his blood the god caused the hyacinth to spring, and upon the petals of the plant was thought to be marked the exclamation *AI* ("woe!"). His festival, the Hyacinthia, was observed at Amyclae during three days in July.

Hyades (hī′a̤.dēz). [Also, **Hyads** (hī′adz).] In Greek mythology, a group of nymphs; daughters of Atlas and Aethra, and sisters of the Pleiades. They nursed the infant Dionysus, and as a reward were transferred to the heavens as a part of the constellation Taurus. Their rising with the sun was associated with the beginning of the rainy season. The Romans, through a mistaken etymology, called the constellation "the little pigs" (Succulae).

Hybla (hī′blä). A town in ancient Sicily celebrated for its honey; hence, honeyed; mellifluous (Hyblaean).

Hycke Scorner (hik′ skôr′nėr). See **Hick Scorner.**

Hyde (hīd), **Douglas.** [Known in Ireland as **An Craoibhín Aoibhinn,** meaning "the Fair Branch."] b. in County Roscommon, Ireland, 1860; d. at Dublin, July 12, 1949. An Irish nationalist and writer, associated from its inception with the movement toward Irish independence. He was the first president (1893–1915) of the Gaelic League, became a member (1909–19) of the senate, and was the first president (1938–45) of Ireland (Eire). Author of *Beside the Fire* (1890), *Love Songs of Connacht* (1894), *Story of Early Irish Literature* (1897), *Literary History of Ireland* (1899), *Ubhla den Chraoibh* (1900), a volume of Irish poems, the Irish play *Casadh an tsugáin* (1901), *Raftery's Poems* (1904), five collected Irish plays (1905), *The Religious Songs of Connacht* (1906), *Maistin an Bheurla* (1913), a play, *Legends of Saints and Sinners from the Irish* (1915), *An Leath-rann* (1922), *Mise Agus an Connradh* (1938), and *Sgéalta Thomáis Uí Chathasaigh* (1939).

Hyde, Edward. [Title, 1st Earl of **Clarendon.**] b. at Dinton, Wiltshire, England, Feb. 18, 1609; d. at Rouen, France, Dec. 9, 1674. An English statesman and historian. He entered Parliament in 1640, became chancellor of the exchequer in 1643, was the chief adviser of Charles I during the English Civil War and of Prince Charles during his exile, and was lord chancellor of England from 1660 to 1667, when he was impeached and banished by Parliament. His chief works are a *True Historical Narrative of the Rebellion and Civil Wars in England* (generally termed *History of the Rebellion*, 1702–04) and *The Life of Edward, Earl of Clarendon, . . . Written by Himself* (1759).

Hyde Park. A park in Westminster, London, situated ab. 2¼ mi. W of Saint Paul's. It is one of the largest of the London parks, extending from Westminster to Kensington. It originally belonged to the manor of Hyde, the property of the monks of Saint Peter, Westminster, which fell into the hands of Henry VIII at the dissolution of the monasteries. During the Commonwealth and for ten years after the Restoration, a large part was leased to private holders. In 1670 it was enclosed with a wall and restocked with deer. It is now a principal recreation ground of London, and is noted as the scene of much outdoor oratory. Area, ab. 364 acres.

Hyde Park. A comedy by James Shirley, acted in 1632 and published in 1637. It concerns three pairs of lovers: Julietta, whose love for Trier surmounts the trial of her virtue by Lord Bonvile; her brother Fairfield, in love with Mistress Carol, who is won perversely when he swears he does not love her; and Lacy, whose long wooing of a supposed widow, Bonavent, is undone by the return of a husband supposedly lost at sea.

Hydra (hī′drạ). In Greek mythology, a monstrous dragon of Lake Lerna in Argolis, represented as having nine heads, each of which, being cut off, was immediately succeeded by two new ones unless the wound was cauterized. The destruction of this monster (by searing each neck as he cut off the head) was one of the 12 labors of Hercules.

Hydriotaphia, or Urn-Burial (hī″dri.ọ.taf′i.ạ). A work by Sir Thomas Browne, published in 1658. It is ostensibly, at the outset, simply a report on certain Roman burial urns found in England, but develops into a broad discussion of death and immortality. Succeeding generations of critics have continued to commend it as an example of nearly flawless English prose. The last chapter is a prose poem on the subject of death.

Hygeia (hī.jē′ạ). [Also, **Hygieia.**] In Greek mythology, the goddess of health. She was the daughter of Aesculapius, and in later myth, his wife. In later myth also, she became the goddess of mental health.

Hyksos (hik′sōs, -sos). [Wrongly called (from an incorrect etymology) the **"Shepherd Kings."**] A name given to the kings of Egypt, of a foreign (probably Semitic) race, whose rule (c1675–c1575 B.C.) fell between the XIIIth and XVIIIth dynasties. They introduced the horse into Egypt.

Hylas (hī′lạs). In Greek legend, a boy who was a favorite of Hercules, and accompanied him on the Argonauts' expedition. Hylas was carried off by the Naiads, who fell in love with him when he went ashore to draw water from a fountain in Mysia.

Hymen (hī′men) or **Hymenaeus** (hī.me̤.nē′us). Originally, the marriage song among the Greeks. The names were gradually personified, and Hymen, the marriage song personified, was invoked as the god of marriage. He is represented as a beautiful youth, more serious than Eros, carrying a bridal torch.

Hymen. The classical god of marriage. He appears as a character in Shakespeare's *As You Like It* and in *The Two Noble Kinsmen.*

Hymettus (hī.met′us). [Also, **Trelo Vouni.**] A mountain in Attica, Greece, SE of Athens. It was celebrated in ancient times for its honey, and also for its marble. Elevation, ab. 3,368 ft.

Hymir (hī′mir, hü′-). In Old Norse mythology, a giant, personification of the winter sea. He dwelt far in the east, at the end of the heavens, by the sea. The glaciers resounded when he returned home from the chase, and his beard was covered with ice. He was the original owner of the kettle in which the gods brewed ale.

Hymn on Solitude. A poem by James Thomson, first published in James Ralph's *Miscellaneous Poems by Several Hands* (1729). It is a contemplative poem, primarily concerned with nature.

Hymn to God, My God, in My Sickness, A. A poem by John Donne, written during the period (1623) of his great illness and asserting the idea that death and resurrection are simultaneous. Through the bold metaphysical conceits of the map of his body and the cosmographer-physicians, Donne reveals both an anatomy of his physical illness and his apprehension of the ways of the Lord: "Therefore that He may raise, the Lord throws down."

Hymn to God the Father, A. A poem by John Donne, written as a result of the same illness that prompted *A Hymn to God, My God, in My Sickness.* He asks God for forgiveness for his sins, which he has recognized and which he now fears will bar him from salvation:

But Swear by Thyself, that at my death Thy Son
  Shall shine as He shines now, and heretofore;
    And, having done that, Thou hast done.
      I fear no more.

Hymn to the Name and Honor of the Admirable Saint Teresa, A. A poem (1646) by Richard Crashaw, dealing with the life of Saint Teresa, her mystical experiences, her life of service, and her martyrdom.

Hyne (hīn), **Charles John Cutcliffe Wright.** b. at Bibury, Gloucestershire, England, May 11, 1865; d. March 10, 1944. An English novelist and traveler. Much of his fictional material was based on his travel in the Shetland Islands, the Arctic, the Spanish Main, Mexico, Brazil, Lapland, and the Belgian Congo. Author of *People and Places* (1930), *Ivory Valley* (1938), and *Wishing Smith* (1940). He is best known, however, as the creator of a plucky, quick-witted Welsh shipmaster, Captain Kettle, who appears in *Honor of Thieves* (1895), *Adventures of Captain Kettle* (1898), *Further Adventures* (1899), *The Little Red Captain* (1902), *Captain Kettle, K.C.B.* (1903), *The Marriage of Captain*

ḍ, d or j; ṣ, s or sh; ṭ, t or ch; ẓ, z or zh; o, F. cloche; ü, F. menu; ch, Sc. loch; ṅ, F. bonbon.

Kettle (1912), *Captain Kettle on the Warpath* (1916), *Captain Kettle's Bit* (1918), *Reverend Captain Kettle* (1925), *President Kettle* (1928), *Mr. Kettle, Third Mate* (1931), and *Captain Kettle, Ambassador* (1932). *My Joyful Life* (1935) is his autobiography.

Hypatia (hī.pā′sha̧, -shi̧.a̧). fl. at Alexandria, Egypt, at the end of the 4th and beginning of the 5th century. A neoplatonic philosopher, celebrated for her beauty and her unhappy fate. In her day, the principal teacher of philosophy (which she derived from Plotinus) at the Greek city of Alexandria, she became the object of the fanatic zeal of Cyril, newly appointed bishop of Alexandria. Her teachings in the pagan philosophy and her liaison with Orestes, prefect of the city and a pagan, caused a riot (March, 415 A.D.) against her by a band of monks, led by an ecclesiastic named Peter. Knowing that they would be protected by Cyril, and perhaps at his instigation, the rioters seized her, stripped her naked in one of the Christian churches, threw her into the street, and pelted her to death with shells or potsherds. Her body was torn to pieces and burned. Her tragic fate provides the theme of the novel *Hypatia*, by Charles Kingsley.

Hypatia. [Full title, **Hypatia, or New Foes with an Old Face.**] A novel by Charles Kingsley, published in 1853.

hyperbole (hī.pėr′bọ.lē). In rhetoric, an obvious exaggeration; an extravagant statement or assertion not intended to be understood literally.

> When we speake in the superlatiue and beyond the limites of credit, that is by the figure which the Greeks call Hiperbole.
> (Puttenham, *Arte of Eng. Poesie.*)

> Three-pil'd hyperboles, spruce affectation.
> Figures pedantical. (Shak., *L. L. L.*, V.ii.)

> No city brings better home to us than Ragusa the Eastern hyperbole of cities great and fenced up to heaven. (E. A. Freeman, *Venice.*)

Hyperboreans (hī.pėr.bō′rē.a̧nz). In early Greek legend, a people who were believed to live beyond the north wind, and were not exposed to its blasts, but enjoyed a land of perpetual sunshine and abundant fruits. They were free from disease, violence, and war. Their natural life lasted a thousand years, and was spent in the worship of Apollo. In later times the Greeks gave the name to inhabitants of northern countries generally.

Hyperion (hī.pir′i.o̧n). In Greek mythology, a Titan; a son of Uranus and Gaea. By his sister Theia he was the father of Helios, Selene, and Eos. In late mythology, he became identified with Apollo. The story of the Titans, and particularly of Hyperion, served as a thematic source for works (both named *Hyperion*) by Longfellow and Keats.

Hyperion. A poetical fragment by Keats, published in 1820, written during 1818 and 1819. It is in two parts, *Hyperion* and *The Fall of Hyperion*. The first part is a narrative in which Saturn and the Titans (except Hyperion) try to find a way to regain their lost realm. Hyperion's aid is sought, but he refuses it. With the introduction of Apollo, the first fragment ends. Both fragments show the influence of the Miltonic epic in diction, epic devices, and other stylistic features, although most scholars find the influence of Wordsworth strongest in the first. The second fragment is in the form of a vision in which the poet hears the fate of Hyperion, the last of the Titans, from Moneta, goddess of the Titans, at the shrine where none "but those to whom the miseries of the world are misery" may come.

Hypermnestra (hī.pėrm.nes′tra̧). In Greek mythology, one of the 50 daughters of Danaüs (king of Egypt) who married the 50 sons of Aegyptus (twin brother of Danaüs). Danaüs gave each of the girls a knife on their bridal night with orders to kill their husbands. Hypermnestra was the only one who disobeyed and spared the life of her bridegroom, Lynceus. Lynceus then killed Danaüs and the other 49 daughters and became king of Argos.

Hypnos (hip′nos). In Greek mythology, the personification and god of sleep, a brother of Death (Thanatos) and son of Night.

Hypocrite, The. A play by Isaac Bickerstaffe, in which Colley Cibber's *Non-Juror*, an adaptation of Molière's *Tartuffe*, survives. It was produced in 1768.

Hyrcania (hėr.kā′ni.a̧). In ancient geography, a region in W Asia, around the S end of the Caspian Sea; now part of N Iran.

Hysteron Proteron (his′tėr.on prō′tėr.on), **Cousin.** See under **Poggio.**

Hystorie of Hamblet, Prince of Denmarke (ham′-blet). See **Hamblet.**

I

Iacchus (ī.ak′us). In Greek mythology, an Athenian divinity connected with the Eleusinian mysteries; son of Demeter and Zeus.

Iachimo (yä′ki.mō). In Shakespeare's *Cymbeline*, a worldly and affected Roman courtier who deceives Posthumus in order to win a wager that the latter's wife, Imogen, is unchaste.

Iago (ȩ̄.ä′gō). In Shakespeare's *Othello*, a malign villain, filled with jealousy of Othello's rank and power. His cool and calculating villainy, his

speciousness, and his bitter sarcasm form an artistic contrast to the noble and large-natured Othello. He dupes Othello into believing in the unfaithfulness of Desdemona, whom Othello thereupon kills in a rage of jealousy. There has been much critical concern over the apparent lack of motivation for Iago's villainy (his intimated fear that Othello has dishonored Emilia and his resentment that he should be passed over for promotion in favor of Cassio cannot really be taken as adequate justifications). In fact, Iago is a fully developed dramatic form of the evil tempter who appears in the morality plays, hoping to overcome the forces of good and win the soul of Everyman. Indeed, in the last scene, when Othello finally perceives Iago's consummate villainy, he hurls himself on him with the words: "If that thou be'st a devil, I cannot kill thee."

iambic (ī.am'bik), *a.* and *n.* **I.** *a.* **1.** Pertaining to the iambus; employing iambics: as, *iambic* meter; an *iambic* poet. **2.** Consisting of an iambus, or of iambics: as, an *iambic* foot; an *iambic* verse or poem. **II.** *n.* In prosody: (*a*) Same as iambus. (*b*) A verse or metrical period consisting of iambi. Iambics have been a favorite form of verse in the poetry of many nations. They were used among the Greeks from early times in popular poetry, especially of a festive or a vituperative character. English heroic verse is the iambic pentapody or trimeter brachycatalectic ($\smile\!-\!/\!\smile\!-\!/\!\smile\!-$). Iambics of various lengths form the great bulk of all English poetry, other meters being comparatively rare.

Iamblichus (ī.am'bli.kus). b. at Chalcis, in Coele-Syria (modern El Bika); d. c330 A.D. A Syrian Neoplatonic philosopher. His main work was an encyclopedia of Pythagorean doctrine, in nine books, of which four or five remain. In his mathematical books, Pythagorean mysticism is carried to the extreme. He mentions the first pair of amicable numbers (220 and 284), but the interest of the Pythagoreans in the properties of numbers makes it virtually certain that they were not his own discovery but were already known by the time he wrote.

iambus (ī.am'bus). [Plural, **iambi** (-bī); also, rarely, **iamb**, plural **iambs**.] In prosody, a foot of two syllables, the first short or unaccented and the second long or accented. The iambus of modern or accentual versification consists of an unaccented syllable followed by an accented one, without regard to the relative time taken in pronouncing the two syllables. Thus in English verse the words *ălīght'*, *dīlāte'*, *ēmĭt'*, *ăbĕt'* would all be treated as iambi, while on the principles of ancient prosody the first of these words would be an iambus, but the second a spondee (an anapestic spondee, $-$ ⊿), the third a trochee, and the last a pyrrhic. The iambus of Greek and Latin poetry ($\smile$⊿) is quantitative, and as the first syllable is short, and the second being long is equal to two shorts, the whole foot has a magnitude of three shorts (is trisemic).

Ianthe (ī.an'thē). The name given by Byron to Lady Charlotte Mary Harley in his dedication to her of his *Childe Harold's Pilgrimage* (she was 11 years old at the time).

Ianthe. The name of Shelley's daughter, used as the name of the maiden in *Queen Mab*.

Iapetus (ī.ap'ę.tus). In Greek mythology, a Titan; son of Uranus (the sky) and Gaea (the earth); father of Prometheus (and therefore ancestor of the human race), Epimetheus, Atlas, and Menoetius. He was thrown by Zeus into Tartarus after the Titans were overthrown.

Iberia (ī.bir'i.ą). [Latin, **Hispania.**] In ancient geography, the peninsula of SW Europe, including the area of modern Spain and Portugal.

Iberians (ī.bir'i.ąnz). The ancient inhabitants and eponymous settlers of Iberia, thought to have entered the region from Africa as far back as the New Stone Age. Various theories have been advanced in regard to them: (1) that they preceded the Celts in Spain and merged with them to the extent of interabsorption; (2) that they were identical with the Basques (a supposition now discredited). They were a short, dark people to whom are attributed various characteristic neolithic cairns and dolmens which survive in sections of North Africa, Spain, Portugal, and Great Britain. They were eventually conquered by the Romans, whose culture absorbed them.

Ibernia (ī.bėr'ni.ą). A Latin name of Ireland.

Iblis (ib'lis). See **Eblis.**

ibn-Batuta (ib"n.bä.tö'tä). [Prenames, **Abu Abdallah Mohammed.**] b. at Tangier, Morocco, c1304; d. at Fez, Morocco, c1377. An Arab traveler. He visited N and C Africa, W and C Asia, Russia, India, China, and elsewhere. His *Travels* were first translated into English in 1829; other translations have been made since (most recently during the 1920's).

Ibsen (ib'sęn; Norwegian, ip'sęn), **Henrik.** b. at Skien, Norway, March 20, 1828; d. at Christiania (Oslo), May 23, 1906. A Norwegian dramatic poet. He studied medicine, but soon devoted himself entirely to literature. His first dramatic attempt, the three-act tragedy *Katilina*, was published at Christiania in 1850, under the pseudonym Brynjolf Bjarme. In the same year he went to Christiania University. With A. O. Vinje and Botten-Hansen the bibliographer, young men of his own age, he edited the short-lived weekly *Andhrimner*, to which he contributed lyrics and satirical pieces. A short saga piece *Kæmpehøjen* (The Warrior's Mound), written at this time, was produced upon the stage. When the weekly closed down, in the following year, he obtained from the violinist Ole Bull the position of manager in the newly opened National Theater at Bergen, a post which he held until 1857. In 1852 he undertook a short journey to Denmark and Germany to study scenic art. From this period is the historical drama *Gildet paa Solhaug* (The Banquet of Solhaug). In 1857 he was made director of the Norwegian Theater at Christiania, and finished the historical drama *Fru Inger til Østraat* (Mistress Inger at Østraat), which subsequently, however, was almost wholly rewritten. In 1858 he wrote the historical drama *Hermændene paa Helgeland* (The Warriors at Helgeland). *Kjærlighedens Komedie* (Love's Comedy), the first of the satirical social plays that have particularly made his name famous, was the next important work to appear (in 1862). In 1863 appeared the historic drama *Kongs-Emnerne* (The Pretenders). In 1864, after writing the poem *En Broder i Nød* (A Brother in Need), a demand to the people to take up the cause of Denmark, which, however, fell unheeded, he left Norway in a sort of voluntary exile. At Rome in 1866 he completed one of the greatest of his works, the drama *Brand*. This was followed the succeeding year (1867) by the dramatic poem *Peer Gynt*, also written in Italy. His next work was the satiric comedy *De Unges Forbund* (The Young Men's Union, 1867), like all his

---

ḍ, d or j; ṣ, s or sh; ṭ, t or ch; ẓ, z or zh; o, F. cloche; ü, F. menu; ċh, Sc. loch; ṅ, F. bonbon.

later works written in prose. This was followed in 1871 by the long historic drama *Kejser og Galilæer* (Emperor and Galilean), which consists of two parts, *Julian's Apostasy* and *Julian the Emperor*. In the meantime he had changed his place of residence, first to Dresden and later to Munich, where he lived until 1891, when he returned to Christiania. In 1877 appeared, further, *Samfundets Støtter* (*The Pillars of Society*), another satiric comedy. This was followed in 1879 by *Et Dukkehjem* (*A Doll's House*) in the same vein. His later plays are *Gjengangere* (*Ghosts*, 1881), *En Folkefiende* (*An Enemy of the People*, 1882), *Vildanden* (*The Wild Duck*, 1884), *Rosmersholm* (1886), *Fruen fra Havet* (*The Lady from the Sea*, 1888), *Hedda Gabler* (1890), *Bygmester Solness* (Architect Solness, 1892, usually called in English *The Master Builder*), *Lille Eyolf* (*Little Eyolf*, 1894), *John Gabriel Borkman* (1896), and *Nar vi Döde vågner* (*When We Dead Awaken*, 1899). Among his minor writings are the epic *Terje Vigen* and the long poem *Paa Vidderne* (1860). Ibsen's plays, especially the later ones, realistic in dialogue but with the inevitability of Greek tragedy in their situations, have been translated into all the major European languages. A large body of critical writing has grown up about them; in English, Ibsen's principal publicizers have been Edmund Gosse and George Bernard Shaw. Ibsen's pioneering efforts in the drama of the conflict between society and the individual caused a breakdown of the Victorian taboos about what might not be seen on the stage (*Ghosts*, describing the blighting effects of syphilis, was abused in Norway and banned in England); discussion of similar problems in novels and plays by other authors marked the rise of a new drama of society.

Icarian (ĭ.kăr′i.ạn). Pertaining to or characteristic of Icarus; hence, presumptuously ambitious, venturesome, or foolhardy (as, an Icarian undertaking).

Icarius (ĭ.kăr′i.us). In Greek mythology, an Athenian who entertained the god Dionysus, not knowing he was a god. As a reward for his hospitality, Dionysus taught Icarius the cultivation of the vine and the art of wine-making.

Icarus (ik′ạ.rus, ī′kạ-). In Greek legend, the son of Daedalus, drowned in the Icarian Sea (named for him), near Samos, in his flight from Crete. Although warned not to do so by his father, he flew so near the sun that the wax binding of his wings, made by Daedalus, melted and he fell into the sea.

Icknield Way (ik′nēld). An ancient Roman road in S England, extending SW from Venta Icenorum (Norwich) along the ridges of the Chilterns and S of the Berkshire Downs, into SW England.

Icolmkill (ik′ọlm.kil). See **Iona.**

I Crown Thee King. A historical novel by Sir Max Pemberton, published in 1902. The scenes of action are London and Sherwood Forest in 1554.

ictus (ik′tus). In prosody and music, rhythmical or metrical stress; additional intensity of utterance or delivery distinguishing one time or syllable in a foot or series from the others. Metrical ictus in poetry is analogous to syllabic stress or accent in ordinary speech. In modern or accentual poetry an ictus regularly coincides with the syllabic stress or accent, primary or secondary. In classical or quantitative poetry the ictus was also a stress accent, but was independent of the syllabic accent, which was a difference in tone or pitch. It regularly attached itself to a long time or syllable as contrasted with one or more shorts, but a long or longs could be metrically unaccented. The conflict between ictus and accent in ancient poetry may be exemplified by the line:

Connúbio júng*am* stábi*li* própriám*que* dicábo
(Vergil, *Aeneid*, i.73),

in which the accent is marked and the syllables bearing the ictus are italicized. The part of a foot on which the ictus falls is called the thesis. In a dipody one ictus is stronger than the other. In a colon the ictus of one measure dominates all others. A subordinate ictus can also accompany the principal ictus within the same foot.

Ida (ī′dạ). The name of the heroine of Tennyson's poem *The Princess.*

Ida. See also **Ida Mountains.**

Ida (ī′dạ), **Mount.** [Modern name, **Psiloriti** (psē-lô.rē′tē); Latin, **Ida Mons.**] A mountain in C Crete, the highest peak of the island. According to Greek mythology, the infant Zeus was raised on Mount Ida by Amalthea. Elevation, ab. 8,195 ft.

Idalium (ī.dā′li.um). [Also: **Idalia** (ī.dā′li.ạ); modern village name, **Dali.**] In ancient geography, a town and promontory on the coast of Cyprus, with a temple to Aphrodite, who was therefore sometimes called Idalia.

Ida Mountains (ī′dạ). [Modern Turkish, **Kaz Dagh, Kazdaği.**] In ancient geography, a mountain range in Phrygia and Mysia, Asia Minor. At the base of it was the Troad (the ancient district whose capital was Troy). It was famous as a seat of the worship of Cybele (Phrygian mother goddess). Highest summit, Gargaron (5,749 ft.).

Idea. A series of nine pastoral poems (subtitled "The Shepherd's Garland") by Michael Drayton. The first edition was published in 1593, with a revised edition following in 1619.

Ideal Husband, An. A comedy (1895) by Oscar Wilde, dealing with the "ideal husband," Sir Robert Chiltern. He is coerced by Mrs. Cheveley into supporting a government scheme for an utterly useless Argentine canal, which will, however, be profitable to her, through her knowledge that he (a Cabinet member) has sold a state secret. He finally denounces the scheme before Parliament, and is saved from the vengeance of Mrs. Cheveley through the discovery that she has stolen a bracelet. It thus becomes possible to force her to destroy the evidence against him in return for silence about her own crime.

Ideas of Good and Evil. A volume of essays by William Butler Yeats, published in 1903.

Iden (ī′den), **Alexander.** In Shakespeare's *2 Henry VI*, the slayer of Jack Cade.

Ides of March. In Shakespeare's *Julius Caesar*, the 15th of March, the day on which Caesar is murdered. According to the Roman calendar the Ides occurred on the 15th of March, May, July, and October, and on the 13th of the other months.

---

fat, fāte, fär, ȧsk, fāre; net, mē, hėr; pin, pīne; not, nōte, mȯve, nôr; up, lūte, pull; ᴛʜ, then;

idiom (id′i.ǫm). **1.** A mode of expression peculiar to a language; a peculiarity of phraseology; a phrase or form of words approved by the usage of a language, whether written or spoken, and often having a signification other than its grammatical or logical one.

> There are certain idioms, certain forms of speech, certain propositions, which the Holy Ghost repeats several times, upon several occasions in the Scriptures.   (Donne, *Sermons*, vi.)

> Some that with Care true Eloquence shall teach,
> And to just Idioms fix our doubtful Speech.
>   (Prior, *Carmen Seculare* (1700), st. 34.)

2. The genius or peculiar cast of a language; hence, a peculiar form or variation of language; a dialect.

> The beautiful Provençal, . . . more rich and melodious than any other idiom in the Peninsula.
>   (Prescott, *Ferd. and Isa.*, Int.)

Idler, The. A series of essays by Samuel Johnson, published (1758–60) in a newspaper called *The Universal Chronicle.*

Idle Thoughts of an Idle Fellow. Sketches (1889) by Jerome K. Jerome.

Idomeneus (ī.dom′ę.nūs). In Greek legend, a king of Crete, one of the leading heroes of the Greek army in the Trojan War. His ship was beset by storm on his way home. He prayed to Poseidon to abate it, promising to sacrifice the first thing he met upon landing. This, to his sorrow, was his son. He was true to the vow, however, and in consequence Crete was swept by pestilence. The story of Idomeneus is one of many featuring the motif of the hasty vow, like that of Jephthah.

Idun (ē′dŏn). [Also: **Ithunn** (ē′ᚦŭn); Old Norse, **Idhunn**.] In Old Norse mythology, the goddess of spring, who had in her keeping, in Asgard, the apples eaten by the gods to preserve eternal youth. Because of these she was kidnaped by the giants with the aid of Loki, but Loki was compelled by the gods to get her back. Later myths make her the wife of Bragi.

idyll (ī′dil). [Also, **idyl**.] **1.** Primarily, a poem descriptive of rural scenes and events; a pastoral or rural poem, like the idylls of Theocritus, Goldsmith's *Deserted Village*, or Burns's *Cottar's Saturday Night;* applied also to longer poems of a descriptive and narrative character, as Tennyson's *Idylls of the King*, and to prose compositions of similar purport treated in a poetic style.

> I heard her turn the page; she found a small
> Sweet Idyl, and once more, as low, she read.
>   (Tennyson, *Princess*, vii.)

[Tennyson spells the word in both ways, as here given.]
2. An episode, or a series of events or circumstances of pastoral or rural simplicity, fit for an idyll.

Idylls of the King. A series of poems by Alfred Tennyson based on the Arthurian romances. Published between 1859 and 1885, they comprise "The Coming of Arthur," "Gareth and Lynette," "Geraint and Enid," "Merlin and Vivien," "Lancelot and Elaine," "The Holy Grail," "Pelleas and Etarre," "The Last Tournament," "Guinevere," and "The Passing of Arthur." The theme that dominates and colors Tennyson's interpretation of the Arthurian legend is that of sin by Lancelot in his adulterous love for Guinevere, through which evil is introduced into the originally unblemished Camelot. Some critics have criticized Tennyson's conception of Arthur, objecting that he lacks the substance of the warrior king and becomes instead little more than a symbolic foil for the actions of Lancelot and Guinevere.

Ierne (ī.ėr′nē). A Latin name of Ireland.

If All These Young Men. A novel by Romer Wilson (Mrs. Edward J. O'Brien), published in 1919.

If It Be Not Good, the Devil Is in It. A kind of tragicomic morality play by Thomas Dekker, published in 1612 and written c1610.

If You Know Not Me, You Know Nobody. A two-part play by Thomas Heywood, published in 1605 and 1606 in unauthorized versions. Queen Elizabeth is the central figure of the play and is portrayed as a strong defender of right and of Protestantism. At the end of the first part she opens the Bible and in ringing tones extends its message to all her people.

Igdrasil or **Iggdrasil** (ig′drą.sil). See **Yggdrasil.**

Igerna (i.gėr′ną). [Also: **Igerne** (i.gėrn′), **Igraine, Yguerne.**] In the Arthurian cycle of romance, the wife of Gorlois, Duke of Cornwall, and the mother, by Uther Pendragon, of Arthur. Uther either killed Gorlois in battle and then married Igerna, or by magic assumed the appearance of Gorlois in order to enter her bed.

Ignatius (ig.nā′shus), Saint. [Surnamed **Theophorus.**] b. in Syria, c50 A.D.; d. at Rome, 107. A bishop of Antioch who suffered martyrdom under Trajan. He was the reputed author of epistles to the Ephesians, Romans, Polycarp, and others.

Ignatius of Loyola (loi.ō′lä), Saint. [Also: **Ignatius Loyola;** original name, **Íñigo López de Recalde** or **Íñigo de Oñez y Loyola.**] b. at the Castle of Loyola, in the Spanish province of Guipúzcoa, Dec. 24, 1491; d. at Rome, July 31, 1556. A Spanish Roman Catholic ecclesiastic, soldier, and mystic, founder of the Society of Jesus (Jesuit order) and one of the leaders in the Counter Reformation. As a boy he was sent to the court of Ferdinand I and Isabella, where he was a page and learned the ways and customs of knighthood. From 1517 to 1521 he was in military service, rising to the rank of captain and being so seriously wounded (May 19, 1521) at the battle of Pampeluna (modern Pamplona) that he was crippled for life. During his long recovery he read the only books that he was able to obtain, a *Life of Christ*, by Ludolphus of Saxony, and a popular devotional book, the *Flowers of the Saints*. The result was a complete change in his life, character, and outlook. He gave himself up to mysticism, renounced the material world and all its pleasures, gave up his army career, and, as soon as he was strong enough to do so, made a pilgrimage, barefoot, to the shrine of the Virgin at the Benedictine monastery of Montserrat. There, on March 21, 1522, he put away his arms, gave away his clothing and possessions, and swore himself a knight to the Virgin. He went thence to Rome and to Jerusalem, and from 1524 to 1527 he studied at the universities of Barcelona, Alcalá de Henares, and Salamanca. At the end of this period he went to Paris, where he studied (1528–34), begging for a living during

---

ḍ, d or j; ṣ, s or sh; ṭ, t or ch; ẓ, z or zh; o, F. cloche; ü, F. menu; ċh, Sc. loch; ñ, F. bonbon.

the term, and where he organized, in 1535, when he received his Master's degree, what was to become the Society (or Company) of Jesus five years later. During his stay at Paris he met six men, Pierre Lefèvre (Faber), with whom he roomed, Francis Xavier, professor of philosophy at St. Barbara, Diego Lainez, a Castilian who came to Paris after hearing about Ignatius at Alcalá, Alfonso Salmeron, from Toledo, Simon Rodriguez, a Portuguese, and Nicholas Bobadilla, who had already finished his studies. These men were to become the first fathers of the society he founded. On the day of the Feast of the Assumption (Aug. 15) in 1534, this group of seven gathered in the chapel of the Church of Saint Mary of Montmartre, dedicated themselves to the great work of converting sinners and heathens, took vows of chastity and poverty, and solemnly agreed to go to the Holy Land as missionaries or to take care of the sick, or to go to Rome to undertake any task that might be pleasing to the Pope. In 1536 they met at Venice, where Loyola had been for a year, and went on to Rome. While waiting at Venice for his comrades to join him, Loyola had been ordained as a priest in June, 1537, but he said his first mass on Christmas, 1538, at Rome in the Church of Santa Maria Maggiore. On Sept. 27, 1540, Pope Paul III officially recognized the Company of Jesus. Loyola was the first general, or superior, of the Order, a post to which he was unanimously elected in April, 1541, and which he held until his death, although he tried to resign in 1547 and 1550, his offer being rejected both times. He died of fever, unexpectedly, without being able to receive the last sacraments. He was beatified in 1609 by Pope Paul V, and canonized by Pope Gregory XV in 1628. He was the author of the *Constitutions of the Order*, which was issued in final form after his death, and of *The Book of the Spiritual Exercises* (1548), the title coming from a work written in 1500 by Abbot Garcias de Cisneros, which had influenced and interested him. It has been called a world-moving book, and has been translated, from its original Spanish, into Latin, English, and other languages, two Latin versions of it appearing while Loyola was alive. A great believer in unquestioning obedience, possibly as a result of his military experience, he wrote an important *Letter on Obedience* (1553) to the Portuguese Jesuits. There are many lives of him in English, French, German, and Spanish, and there are many editions of his works. The official life is by Daniello Bartoli, a 17th-century Italian Jesuit.

Ignoge (ig.nō′jē). A character recorded by Geoffrey of Monmouth, a Greek princess who was the wife of Brut. Spenser refers to her in *The Faerie Queene* as Ignogene of Italy.

Ignoramus (ig.nō.rā′mus). An academic comedy written (1615) by George Ruggle, as a personal satire. It is in Latin and English, and based upon della Porta's *Trappolaria*. It lampoons the deputy-recorder at Cambridge, who had led an attack on the privileges of the university students (this is also meant to be understood, however, as an attack on the royal prerogative). Ignoramus, the chief character, is mocked for spouting common-law terms and for his bad Latin. He is in love with the fair heroine, but is tricked into taking an elderly shrew. When

she attacks him, his outcries make others believe that he is bewitched and that he must be exorcised. By 1737 there were nine editions of the play and it was supplemented in 1787 by notes and a glossary. An English translation was made (1662) and a version by Edward Ravenscroft, *The English Lawyer*, was performed at the Drury Lane (1678).

Igraine (i.grān′). See **Igerna.**

I Hear an Army. A poem by James Joyce, published in his volume *Chamber Music* (1918).

Ikhnaton (ik.nä′ton). [Also: **Akhenaten, Amenhotep IV.**] fl. 14th century B.C. Egyptian king (1375–1358 B.C.), the tenth of the XVIIIth dynasty; son of Amenhotep III. He took as his queen Nefertiti, probably a Hittite princess and perhaps influential in shaping Ikhnaton's revolutionary policies. His father had been an extremely able ruler of a great empire, but Ikhnaton, concentrating on internal reforms and ignoring revolts in the provinces, permitted his empire to dwindle away almost completely. He established a new form of worship in Egypt, that of the all-giving sun disk Aten, and, while recognizing the other gods, made them all subordinate to the principal god. Ikhnaton wrote new hymns for the new religion, which in its insistence on the sun disk as the source of all life approached monotheism. He likewise fostered new forms of art, emphasizing sun-derived nature, freed like religion from the empty, millennia-old traditions, symbols, and conventions; apart from many wonderful pictures of persons and animals, the period has left us the most famous Egyptian work of art, the reversed-pyramid bust of the beautiful Nefertiti. The reforms were, however, too thoroughgoing for the Egyptians, and soon after the king's death the resurgent priesthood of Amen began expunging the name of Aten from Ikhnaton's works. Even his son-in-law (or younger brother) Tut-ankh-amen, who ruled after him, returned to an Amen-name. Tell el-Amarna, Ikhnaton's capital, has proved to be one of the great archaeological sites; diplomatic correspondence and other material dating from Ikhnaton's reign found there have given a name to the period (Amarna period) and furnish an exceptionally good picture of Egypt and her neighbors in a period of international unrest.

Ilia (il′i.ạ). See **Rhea Silvia.**

Iliad (il′i.ạd). A Greek epic poem, composed, according to tradition, by the poet Homer sometime during or before the 9th century B.C. With its companion poem, the *Odyssey*, it is one of the greatest of epics of world literature and one of the earliest examples of literary invention. The subject of the Iliad is the ten years' siege of Ilium or Troy, by the confederated states of Greece under Agamemnon, king of Mycenae, to redress the injury done to Menelaus, king of Sparta, in the carrying off of his wife, Helen, by the Trojan prince Paris. Helen had been given to Paris by Aphrodite as a reward for his decision in favor of Aphrodite in the contest of beauty between her, Athene, and Hera. The direct narrative relates only to a part of the last year, leaving the fall of the city untold. The mighty deeds of the Greek Achilles and of the Trojan Hector, son of King Priam, supply some of the chief episodes of the poem, which reaches its climax in the battle between Achilles and Hector, in which Hector is slain.

Ilissus (i.lis'us). [Modern Greek name, **Ilissos** or **Eilissos**.] In ancient geography, a small river in Attica, Greece, flowing just S of Athens.

Ilithyia (il.i.thī'yạ). In Greek mythology, the goddess who presides over childbirth.

Ilium (il'i.um). See **Troy**.

Illidge (il'ij), **Frank**. In Aldous Huxley's *Point Counter Point* (1928), a scientist and Communist, employed in Lord Tantamount's biological laboratory.

I'll Never Be Young Again. A novel by Daphne Du Maurier, published in 1932.

Illuminati (i.lö.mi.nā'tī). A name given to various religious societies or sects because of their claim to perfection or enlightenment in religious matters. The most noted among them were the Alumbrados ("the Enlightened") of Spain in the 16th century; an ephemeral society of Belgium and N France (also called Guérinets) in the 17th century; and an association of mystics in S France in the 18th century, combining the doctrines of Swedenborg with the methods of the Freemasons.

Illyria (i.lir'i.ạ), **Duke of.** See **Orsino**.

Ilmarinen (ēl'mä.rē.nen). In the Finnish epic, the *Kalevala*, the divine smith who made the sky, sun, and moon; brother of Väinämöinen. He also forged the mysterious Sampo, a device which produced good luck and wealth for the owner.

Il Penseroso (il pen.sẹ.rō'sō). See **Penseroso, Il.**

Ilse (il'zẹ). In German folklore, a princess who was changed into the river Ilse.

Ilus (ī'lus). In Greek legend, the son of Tros and mythical founder of Ilium.

Image, The. A comedy (1909) by Augusta Gregory (Lady Gregory), satirizing Irish impracticality. She depicts a group of villagers on the west coast of Ireland who find two whales washed up on their beach, and promptly become so involved in an argument over the use to be made of the whale oil that they lose both carcasses.

imagery. Descriptive representation; exhibition of ideal images to the mind; figurative illustration. "I wish there may be in this poem any instance of good imagery." (Dryden.)

Images Old and New. A volume of poetry (1915) by Richard Aldington.

Imaginary Conversations. Five volumes of conversations (1824–29) between people of note, by Walter Savage Landor.

Imagists. A group of 20th-century poets, among whom Hilda Doolittle ("H.D."), F. S. Flint, and J. G. Fletcher are prominent.

Imaus (im'ạ.us). An ancient name of the Himalayas, the great mountain system of S central Asia.

Imhotep (ēm.hō'tep). In Egyptian mythology, the god of knowledge, first-born of Ptah and Sekhmet.

Imitation of Christ. See **De imitatione Christi**.

Imlac (im'lak). In Samuel Johnson's *Rasselas*, a man of learning who accompanies Rasselas from the monotonous "happy valley."

Immaturity. A novel by G. B. Shaw, published in 1930.

Immortal Hour, The. An opera in two acts by Rutland Boughton with a libretto by William Sharp (Fiona Macleod), first performed at the Glastonbury Festival in August, 1914.

Immortal Moment, The. American title of **Kitty Tailleur**.

Immortal Youth. A novel by Morley Roberts, published in 1902.

Imogen (im'ọ.jen). In Shakespeare's *Cymbeline*, the daughter of Cymbeline and wife of Posthumus. Swinburne called her "the woman best beloved in all the world of song and all the tide of time."

Imoinda (im.ọ.in'dạ). The beautiful young Indian girl loved by Oroonoko in Aphra Behn's novel of that name, and in Southey's stage adaptation of it.

Imperial Palace. A novel by Arnold Bennett, published in 1930. It is a cross-section study of life in a modern luxury hotel.

Importance of Being Earnest, The. A comedy (1895) by Oscar Wilde. Earnest attempts to shelter a young girl under his care from the gallantries of one of his young friends, while at the same time himself making love to the romantic Gwendolyn. Eventually the flirtatious young ward and Gwendolyn find themselves both apparently pursuing the same young man, who uses the name Earnest, only to discover that Earnest's friend has been wooing the ward under that name. Gwendolyn is piqued by the knowledge that Earnest apparently has no family, only an old handbag in which he was left as a child, and Lady Bracknell (in the plot as guardian of Gwendolyn) presently unravels the mystery: Earnest is the son of dear friends of hers, absent-mindedly left in a railway checkroom as an infant. When the knowledge of Earnest's parenthood is thus discovered, he rushes off to find what his real name is and is agreeably pleased to find that it is, indeed, Earnest.

impression. 1. In printing, a copy taken by pressure from type, or from an engraved or stereotyped plate or block, or from an assemblage of them.

He can also print wonderful counterproofs from the original impressions.
(*Harper's Mag.*, LXXVI. 335.)
2. The aggregate of copies of a printed work made at one time.

He did, upon my declaring my value of it, give me one of Lilly's grammars of a very old impression, as it was in the Catholique times, at which I shall much set by. (Pepys, *Diary*.)

impressionism. In art and literature, the doctrine that natural objects should be painted or described as they first strike the eye in their immediate and momentary effects (that is, without selection, or artificial combination or elaboration).

That aim at tone and effect, and nothing more, which is merely the rebound from photographic detail into the opposite extreme of fleeting and shadowy Impressionism.
(F. T. Palgrave, *Nineteenth Century*, XXIII. 88.)

Impressionism implies, first of all, impatience of detail. (*The Century*, XVIII. 482.)

ḍ, d or j; ş, s or sh; ṭ, t or ch; ẓ, z or zh; o, F. cloche; ü, F. menu; čh, Sc. loch; ň, F. bonbon.

Impressions of Theophrastus Such (thē.ọ̄.fras'tus such'), **The.** See **Theophrastus Such.**

In a German Pension. Stories (1911) by Katherine Mansfield.

In Black and White. A collection of eight short stories (Calcutta, 1888) of native Indian life by Rudyard Kipling. Its contents were included with "Soldiers Three" and "The Story of the Gadsbys" in *Soldiers Three and other Stories* (London, 1895).

Inca of Perusalem (ing'kạ; pẹ̄.rö'sạ.lem), **The.** A drama (1915) by George Bernard Shaw.

Incendium Amoris (in.sen'di.um ạ.mō'ris). A Latin prose work of the Middle English period by Richard Rolle of Hampole, describing the author's mystical experiences.

In Chancery. A novel by John Galsworthy, published in 1920. It was later included as one of the novels in *The Forsyte Saga* (1922).

Inchbald (inch'bôld), **Elizabeth.** [Maiden name, Simpson.] b. at Stanningfield, near Bury St. Edmunds, England, Oct. 15, 1753; d. at London, Aug. 1, 1821. An English novelist, dramatist, and actress. Among her novels are *A Simple Story* (1791) and *Nature and Art* (1796). She ran away from home and had a number of adventures before she married, and appeared at the Drury Lane as an actress before turning to writing. Her plays include *Wives as They Were and Maids as They Are* (1797) and *To Marry or Not to Marry* (1805). She was also a contributor to the Edinburgh *Journal.*

Inchcape Rock or **Inch Cape** (inch'kāp). See **Bell Rock.**

Inchcape Rock, The. A ballad by Robert Southey. The story is that of the shipwreck of Sir Ralph the Rover upon the Inchcape or Bell Rock, from which he had maliciously cut loose the warning bell placed there for the safety of mariners by the abbot of Aberbrothock (Arbroath).

incident. That which falls out or takes place; an occurrence; something which takes place in connection with an event or a series of events of greater importance.

> A writer of lives may descend, with propriety, to minute circumstances and familiar incidents.
> (H. Blair, *Rhetoric*, xxxvi.)

> The incident had occurred and was gone for me; it was an incident of no moment, no romance, no interest in a sense; yet it marked with change one single hour of a monotonous life.
> (Charlotte Brontë, *Jane Eyre.*)

Inconstant, or the Way to Win Him, The. A comedy by George Farquhar, produced in 1702. It is an adaptation of Fletcher's *Wild-Goose Chase.*

Incredible Tale. A novel by Naomi Royde-Smith, published in 1932.

increment (in'krẹ.mẹnt). In rhetoric, a species of amplification which consists in magnifying the importance of a subject (person or thing) by stating or implying that it has no superior, or that the greatest of all others is inferior to it.

incunabula (in.kụ.nab'ụ.lạ). In bibliography, books printed in the infancy of the art; generally, books printed before the year 1500: in this sense rarely with a singular *incunabulum.*

Indamora (in.dạ.mō'rạ). The captive queen loved by Aureng-Zebe in Dryden's heroic play of that name.

In Darkest England, and the Way Out. A book by William Booth, of the Salvation Army, published in 1890.

Indiana (in.di.an'ạ). A poor but beautiful orphan girl in Richard Steele's *Conscious Lovers*, befriended by Bevil.

Indian Emperor, or the Conquest of Mexico by the Spaniards, The. A play by Dryden, produced in 1665, a sequel to *The Indian Queen.*

Indian Queen, The. A tragedy by Sir Robert Howard and John Dryden, produced in 1664.

Indo-European (in'dō.ū.rọ.pē'ạn). A large family of languages comprising most of the languages of Europe together with the Indo-Iranian subfamily, and the now extinct Anatolian and Tokharian subfamilies. All the Germanic, Celtic, Italic, and Greek languages are of the Indo-European linguistic family, as are also all the Slavic languages, and the Lithuanian and Lettish Baltic tongues. The prehistoric language from which all these have evolved, reconstructed by scholars, is also called Indo-European.

Indra (in'drạ). A principal deity of the Vedas, the early scriptures of the Hindus; the greatest god of the *Rig-Veda*, in which one fourth of all the hymns are addressed to him. He is the great god of the firmament and the weather. His great gift to the gods and mankind was his killing of Vritra, the dragon of drought. Thus he is regarded as a dispenser of rain, fertility god, and benefactor. In later Hindu mythology he became identified with Parjana, an ancient Vedic rain-fertility god. He is described as riding in a golden chariot, drawn by two (sometimes 10,000) tawny horses. His weapon is the thunderbolt, and he also uses arrows, a hook, a spear, and a net, in which he entangled his foes. He is also often depicted riding on his elephant, named Airavata, the first of the divine elephants from whom all elephants are descended. Indra is the great type of Aryan hero, heavily bearded, a great eater and drinker, strong in battle and a terror to enemies. In later Hindu mythology, Indra is of lesser rank, inferior to the triad of Brahma, Siva, and Vishnu, but he still is a chief among gods.

induction. In a literary work, an introduction or preface; a preamble; a prologue; a preliminary sketch or scene; a prelude, independent of the main performance, but exhibiting more or less directly its purpose or character.

> Gentlemen, Inductions are out of date, and a prologue in verse is as stale as a black velvet cloak and a bay garland.
> (Beau. and Fl., *Woman-Hater*, Prol.)

> The opening or induction to these tales contains perhaps the most poetical passages in Berceo's works. (Ticknor, *Span. Lit.*)

Indulgence, Declaration of. In English history, one of several royal proclamations promising greater religious freedom to nonconformists. The principal ones were: **1.** A proclamation by Charles II in 1671 or 1672, promising the suspension of penal laws relating to ecclesiastical matters which were di-

---

fat, fāte, fär, ȧsk, fāre; net, mē, hėr; pin, pīne; not, nōte, mȯve, nôr; up, lūte, pŭll; ᴛʜ, then;

rected against nonconformists. It was rejected by Parliament.

2. A proclamation by James II in 1687, annulling penal laws against Roman Catholics and nonconformists, and abolishing religious tests for office. The refusal to read this declaration by several prelates led to their trial, and was one of the causes of the revolution of 1688.

"Infant Phenomenon," the. In Dickens's *Nicholas Nickleby*, a child actress, the youngest of Vincent Crummles's children.

Infelice (ēn.fä.lē´chä). The daughter of the Duke of Milan in Dekker and Middleton's play *The Honest Whore*.

Inferno (in.fêr´nō; Italian, ēn.fer´nō). The first part of Dante's *Divina Commedia* (*Divine Comedy*). It consists of a general introductory canto to the whole poem followed by 33 cantos in terza rima. Under the allegory of an imaginary journey to the center of the earth, the poet gives us a passionate vision of the wilfulness of the human heart from the less culpable sins of sensuality, through the graver irrationality of the rejection of revelation, to the injustice of deliberate violence and the malice of calculated fraud and infidelity. In certain episodes, as that of the death of Conte Ugolino and his sons (canto XXXIII), the poetry and music are directly related to the tragedy in its literal sense. For the most part, however, as in the journey of Ulysses (canto XXVI), it is the deeper meaning symbolized by the myth which is the center of the poet's vision, the source of his feeling, and the stimulus to creative fancy.

In Flanders Fields. A poem by John McCrae, published posthumously in 1919, one of the best-known poems to come out of World War I. It follows very closely the French rondeau form.

Informer, The. A novel by Liam O'Flaherty, published in 1925. The story of a man who betrays his comrade to the police, it won the James Tait Black memorial prize and was later made into a screen play which won (1935) the Motion Picture Academy award.

Inge (ing), **William Ralph.** [Sometimes called the "Gloomy Dean."] b. at Craike, Yorkshire, England, June 6, 1860—. An English Anglican clergyman and theologian. He studied at Cambridge, where he was professor (1907–11) of divinity, after serving as fellow and tutor (1889–1904) at Hertford College at Oxford. He was dean (1911–34) of Saint Paul's at London. Noted for his philosophical pessimism, he was the author of *Christian Mysticism* (1899), *Faith and Knowledge* (1904), two series of *Outspoken Essays* (1919, 1922), *The Ideas of Progress* (1920), *The Platonic Tradition* (1926), *Lay Thoughts of a Dean* (1926), *The Church in the World* (1927), *Christian Ethics and Modern Problems* (1930), *Things New and Old* (1933), *Vale* (1934), *The Gate of Life* (1935), *Our Present Discontents* (1938), *The Fall of the Idols* (1940), *Talks in a Free Country* (1943), and *Diary of a Dean* (1949).

Ingelow (in´jẹ.lō), **Jean.** b. at Boston, Lincolnshire, England, March 17, 1820; d. at London, July 20, 1897. An English poet and novelist. Her works include poems (1863, 1876, 1885), *Studies for*

Stories (1864), *Mopsa the Fairy* (1869), *Off the Skelligs* (a novel, 1872), *Fated to be Free* (1875), *Sarah de Berenger* (1879), *Don John* (1881), *John Jerome* (1886), *A Motto Changed* (1893), and a number of children's books.

Ingoldsby (ing´goldz.bi), **Thomas.** Pseudonym of Barham, Richard Harris.

Ingoldsby Legends, The. A series of satirical stories in prose and verse by Richard Harris Barham. The best known is probably *The Jackdaw of Rheims*. The earlier numbers were published in *Bentley's Miscellany*, and afterward in *The New Monthly Magazine*. In 1840 the first series was published collectively; a second and third series appeared in 1847.

Ingomar the Barbarian (ing´gọ.mär). A play by Maria Anne Lovell, produced at the Drury Lane Theatre, London, in 1851.

In Good King Charles's Golden Days. A play (1939) by George Bernard Shaw, included by most critics among his lesser works.

Ingram (ing´gram), **Arthur Foley Winnington.** b. in Worcestershire, England, Jan. 26, 1858; d. at London, May 26, 1946. An English clergyman, bishop of London (1901–39). In 1888 he founded the Oxford House in the East End of London, and he was the leader of the Oxford settlement movement. His works include *Work in Great Cities* (1896), *Under the Dome* (1902), *The Gospel in Action* (1906), *Early English Colonies in America* (1908), and *Joy in God* (1909).

Ingram, John Kells. b. in County Donegal, Ireland, July 7, 1823; d. at Dublin, May 1, 1907. An Irish philosopher, economist, pacifist, and poet. He was educated at Trinity College, Dublin, where he later served as professor of English (1852–66) and of Greek (1866–77). One of the founders (1842) of the Dublin Philosophical Society, he contributed papers on geometry to its *Transactions* and sonnets to the *Dublin University Magazine*, and wrote for the *Positivist Review*. Author of *History of Political Economy* (1888), *History of Slavery* (1895), *Outlines of the History of Religion* (1900), *Practical Morals* (1904), and *The Final Transition* (1905). He also wrote *Sonnets* (1900) and other volumes of poetry, and is best known for the poem *Memory of the Dead*, which was adopted as their own by the Irish Nationalists.

Ingres (aṅgr), **Jean Auguste Dominique.** b. at Montauban, France, Aug. 29, 1780; d. at Paris, Jan. 13, 1867. A French historical painter. At the age of 16 he went to Paris and entered the atelier of David. He won the Grand Prix de Rome in 1801, studied for five years at Paris, and went in 1806 to Italy, where he remained about 15 years. In 1824 the *Vow of Louis XIII* was exhibited in the Louvre, and the artist returned to Paris in great favor. He was made a member of the Institute in 1825. Among his works are *Oedipus and the Sphinx* (1808), *Odalisque* (1814), *Apotheosis of Homer* (1826), *Martyrdom of Saint Symphorian* (1834), *Stratonice* (1839), *The Golden Age* (unfinished, 1848), *Joan of Arc* (1854), and *La Source, or The Spring* (1856).

Inheritance, The. A novel by Susan E. Ferrier, published in 1824.

ḍ, d or j; ş, s or sh; ţ, t or ch; z̧, z or zh; o, F. cloche; ü, F. menu; ċh, Sc. loch; ṅ, F. bonbon.

In Hospital. A volume of poems (1903) by William Ernest Henley.

inkhorn. A portable case for ink and writing instruments, made of a horn, or (usually) of wood or metal, formerly in common úse in Europe, and still in some parts of the East.

> One man among them was clothed with linen, with a writer's inkhorn by his side. (Ezek. ix. 2.)

> Hang him with his pen and inkhorn about his neck.   (Shak., *2 Hen. VI*, IV. ii.)

inkhornism (ingk'hôrn.izm). A bookish, pedantic, or bombastic expression.

> Singing his love, the holy Spouse of Christ,
> Like as she were some light-skirts of the rest,
> In mightiest inkhornisms he can thither wrest.
>   (Bp. Hall, *Satires*, II. viii. 12.)

Inkle and Yarico (ing'kl; yar'i.kō). A comedy, with musical interpolations, by the younger George Colman, based on a story by Addison in *The Spectator* (No. 11). It was produced at the Haymarket Theatre, London, on Aug. 4, 1787.

In Memoriam (in mẹ.mō'ri.ạm). An elegiac poem, in stanzas of four octosyllabic lines, by Alfred Tennyson, published in 1850. It is a philosophic lament for the poet's friend Arthur Henry Hallam, written during the period 1833–50. The poem, although motivated originally by deep personal grief, is in its final form an expression of much more than Tennyson's sorrow at the loss of a friend. It covers a considerable span of attitudes toward life and death; indeed, the poet is finally able to transcend his own sense of loss and realize a spiritual justification for Hallam's death, and a new sense of the love of God. The work concludes with a marriage song for his sister Cecilia and Edward Lushington. Some of Tennyson's most noted lyrics are found in it, including "The path by which we twain did go," "Be near me when my light is low," "The Time draws near the birth of Christ," and "Ring out, wild bells, to the wild sky."

In Memory of W. B. Yeats (yāts). A commemorative poem by W. H. Auden in the volume *Another Time* (1940).

In My Craft or Sullen Art. A poem by Dylan Thomas in which he expresses the idea that he does not write his poetry to satisfy ambition or for financial gain, but "for the common wages of their [Ed: lovers'] most secret heart," because only they can fully understand the "griefs of the ages" of which he writes.

Inn Album, The. A poem (1875) by Robert Browning, telling of a young girl's seduction, her marriage to an old and bigoted clergyman, her true love, and her final resort to suicide. It is said to be based on actual events.

Inner Temple. One of the Inns of Court.

Inner Temple and Gray's Inn Mask. A masque by Francis Beaumont, performed Feb. 20, 1613 and published c1613. It was given by the Inns of Court for King James and his Queen at Whitehall. The masquers included 15 knights of Olympia, 12 musicians as priests of Jove, and the presenters of the masque were Mercury and Iris.

Innes (in'ẹs), **Frank.** In Robert Louis Stevenson's unfinished novel *Weir of Hermiston*, the false friend who betrays Archie Weir.

Innes, Michael. Pseudonym of **Stewart, John Innes.**

Innisfail (in'is.fāl). [Also, **Inisfail**.] An old poetical name for Ireland, meaning the Island of Fal (from *inis*, "island," and *Fail*, the genitive of *Fal*). Ireland was called the Island of Fal from the wonderful stone brought by the Tuatha De Danann (the ancient divine race of Ireland) from the mythical city of Falias. This stone was once in Tara and became the coronation stone of the kings of Ireland, and legend has it that it was taken to Scotland for the crowning of Fergus mac Erc, and after that was taken to England, where it is today in Westminster Abbey, the Stone of Scone, which is the coronation stone for the kings and queens of England.

Innocent Birds. A novel by Theodore Francis Powys, published in 1926.

Inns of Chancery. Inns subordinate to the Inns of Court, at London. Clifford's Inn, Clement's Inn, and Lyon's Inn (pulled down in 1868), were attached to the Inner Temple; New Inn and Strand Inn (which have disappeared), to the Middle Temple; Barnard's Inn and Staple's Inn, to Gray's Inn; Thavies' Inn and Furnival's Inn (both demolished), to Lincoln's Inn. Serjeant's Inn, in Chancery Lane, was formerly used by the Society of Serjeants-at-law.

Inns of Court. Legal societies at London which have the exclusive privilege of calling candidates to the bar, and maintain instruction and examination for that purpose; also, the precincts or premises occupied by these societies respectively. They are the Inner Temple, Middle Temple, Lincoln's Inn, and Gray's Inn. The first two originally belonged to Knights Templars (whence the name Temple). These inns had their origin about the end of the 13th century.

innuendo (in.ụ.en'dō). An oblique hint; an indirect intimation about a person or thing; an allusive or inferential suggestion: commonly used in a bad sense, but sometimes in an innocent one.

> Pursue your trade of scandal picking, . . .
> Your innuendoes, when you tell us
> That Stella loves to talk with fellows.
>   (Swift, *Stella's Birthday*.)

> Solomon's Proverbs, I think, have omitted to say, that as the sore palate findeth grit, so an uneasy consciousness heareth innuendoes.
>   (George Eliot, *Middlemarch*.)

Inquisition. The name given to a tribunal of the Roman Catholic Church established in 1229 at the Synod of Toulouse, by Pope Gregory IX. It began to function in 1233, its purpose being to discover and to punish heretics and heresy. Acts that paved the way for the Inquisition were the third Lateran Council (March 5–19, 1179), held under Pope Alexander III, which excommunicated groups of heretics in southern France, the Council of Verona (1184), which endorsed it, and the fourth Lateran Council (Nov. 11–30, 1215), one of the most important in church history, which, under Pope Innocent III, ordered the bishops to be active in finding out heretics and seeing that they were brought to a

---

fat, fāte, fär, ȧsk, fâre; net, mē, hêr; pin, pīne; not, nōte, mȯve, nôr; up, lūte, pull; ᴛʜ, then;

speedy trial. In the 12th and 13th centuries the Inquisition was directed chiefly against the Cathari, the Waldenses, and the Albigenses; in the 14th century its activity was directed against Franciscan heretics.

Insatiate Countess, The. A tragedy acted in 1610, printed in 1613, and attributed to John Marston, though altered by William Barksted. It was sometimes mentioned as *Barksted's Tragedy.*

In Single Strictness. See under **Celibates.**

Inspector Calls, An. A tragedy (1946) by J. B. Priestley about a lower-class girl who becomes involved with various members of an upper-class family, none of whom know that the others have had anything to do with her. However, her appeals for help are ignored by all of them, and she eventually commits suicide. Priestley's moral is that everyone has a responsibility toward his fellow humans; in the play the calling of a police inspector after the girl's suicide awakens the members of the "guilty" family to an awareness of this.

Instauratio Magna (in.stô.rā′shi.ō mag′na̧). A comprehensive philosophical work planned and partially carried out by Francis Bacon, comprising the *Advancement of Learning, Novum Organum,* and other works.

Institute of France, The. An association of the members of the five French academies, for the advancement of science, the publication of discoveries, etc.

Insurrections. A volume of verse (1909) by James Stephens.

In Temptation. A famous hymn by Charles Wesley. It opens with the line "Jesu, Lover of my Soul."

Interim (in′tėr.im). The name given to a provisional arrangement for the settlement of religious differences between Protestants and Roman Catholics in Germany during the Reformation, pending definite settlement by a church council. There were three interims: the Ratisbon (Regensburg) Interim, promulgated by the emperor Charles V, July 29, 1541, but ineffective; the Augsburg Interim, proclaimed also by Charles V, May 15, 1548, but not carried out by many Protestants; and the Leipzig Interim, carried through the Diet of Saxony, Dec. 22, 1548, by the efforts of the elector Maurice, and enlarged and published as the Greater Interim in March, 1549; it met with strenuous opposition. Religious toleration was secured for the Lutherans by the peace of Passau in 1552.

Interim. A novel by Dorothy M. Richardson, published in 1919. It is the fifth section of *Pilgrimage* (1938), a novel sequence in 12 parts employing the stream-of-consciousness technique.

interlude. A type of dramatic entertainment popular in England in the 15th and 16th centuries and usually presented at Court, at the colleges, or at the Inns of Court. The term, as it is used now, generally refers to those plays which were a development from the earlier miracle and morality plays and are significant in the history of the drama as a transition to the Elizabethan plays. Both the interlude and the morality play present a human hero and forces of good and evil which contend for his soul, and this matter of didactic intent is apt to obscure a distinction between the morality plays and the interludes. However, the interludes, intended for entertainment in addition to edification, made more use of the realistic, comic, and homely detail; they were generally shorter, though not always; and, although allegorical, they were less concerned with religious abstraction and usually presented a hero somewhat individualized. The growth away from the abstract to the human and particular, as well as the gradual disappearance of anonymous plays and the emergence of a definite person as author, reflect the humanistic spirit of the times, mainly in the plays of Heywood and Rastell, who were closely connected with Thomas More. The origin of the term "interlude" is obscure. Whether the plays were merely insertions in a larger entertainment, were presented during banquets and state occasions, or were equivalent to the secular miracle plays so often mentioned in Middle English literature, has not been definitely established.

Interlude for Sally (sal′i). A novel by Beatrice Kean Seymour, with the secondary title, *Being Some Further Chapters in the Life of Sally Dunn,* published in 1934. It is a sequel to *Maids and Mistresses* (1932).

Interlude of Vice Containing the History of Horestes (hǫ.res′tēz). An interlude written in 1567 by John Pickering (or Pikering).

Interlude of Youth. An interlude of unknown authorship, written in the early 16th century, preaching Catholic doctrine.

Interludes and Poems. A volume of verse (1909) by Lascelles Abercrombie, the first of his published works to attract wide attention from critics and the reading public.

International Episode, An. A novel by Henry James, published in 1879. The plot is based on a conflict between an American girl and an English duchess.

Interpreter, the. A character in Bunyan's *Pilgrim's Progress.* He is intended as an allegorical representation of the Holy Ghost. The house of the Interpreter was just beyond the Wicket Gate, the entrance to the road to the Celestial City.

In the Beginning. See under **Back to Methuselah.**

In the Days of the Comet. A novel by H. G. Wells, published in 1906.

In the Holy Nativity of Our Lord God. A poem by Richard Crashaw, subtitled "A Hymn Sung As By Shepherds." Tityrus and Thyrsis are the two shepherds who sing, in alternate stanzas, the story of Christ's birth.

In the Seven Woods. A volume of verse (1904) by William Butler Yeats. Included in it are "Never Give All the Heart," "Adam's Curse," and "The Old Men Admiring Themselves in the Water."

In the Shadow of the Glen. A drama (1903) by J. M. Synge.

In the Wood. American title of **Children in the Wood.**

In Time Like Glass. A volume of poetry by W. J. Turner, published in 1921.

---

ḑ, d or j; ş, s or sh; ţ, t or ch; z̧, z or zh; o, F. cloche; ü, F. menu; c̈h, Sc. loch; ṅ, F. bonbon.

In Time of War. "A Sonnet Sequence with a verse commentary" by W. H. Auden from *Journey to a War* (1939) by Isherwood and Auden. The 27 sonnets exhibit a great deal of variety, and the verse "commentary" exceeds the sonnets in length.

Intrigo (in.tre′gō). A man of business in Sir Francis Fane's comedy *Love in the Dark.*

intrigue (in.trēg′). The plot of a play, poem, or romance; the series of complications in which a writer involves his imaginary characters.

As these causes are the beginning of the action, the opposite designs against that of the hero are the middle of it, and form that difficulty or intrigue which make up the greatest part of the poem.
(Le Bossu, tr. in pref. to Pope's *Odyssey.*)

Intriguing Chambermaid, The. A farce by Henry Fielding (produced 1734), based on Regnard's *Le Retour imprévu.*

introduction. **1.** Something that leads to or opens the way for the understanding of something else; specifically, a preliminary explanation or statement; the part of a book or discourse which precedes the main work, and in which the author or speaker gives some general account of his design and subject; an elaborate preface, or a preliminary discourse.

Thou soon shalt . . . see before thine eyes
The monarchies of the earth, their pomp and state;
Sufficient introduction to inform
Thee, of thyself so apt, in regal arts.
(Milton, *Paradise Regained.*)

Were it not that the study of Etruscan art is a necessary introduction to that of Roman, it would hardly be worth while trying to gather together and illustrate the few fragments and notices of it that remain. (J. Ferguson, *Hist. Arch.*)

2. A more or less elementary treatise on any branch of study; a treatise leading the way to more elaborate works on the same subject.

Intrusion. A novel by Beatrice Kean Seymour, published in 1921.

Invader of His Country, or the Fatal Resentment, The. See under **Coriolanus.**

Invaders, The. A novel by William Plomer, published in 1934.

Invalides (dā zaṅ.vȧ.lēd), **Hôtel des.** See **Hôtel des Invalides.**

invention. The faculty or power of inventing; skill or ingenuity in original contrivance; the gift of finding out or producing new forms, methods, processes, effects, etc.; in art and literature, the exercise of imagination in production; the creative faculty.

I will prove these verses to be very unlearned, neither savouring of poetry, wit, nor invention.
(Shak., *Love's Labour's Lost.*)

I had not the assistance of any good book whereby to promote my invention, or relieve my memory.
(Sir T. Browne, *Religio Medici*, Pref.)

My own invention . . . can furnish me with nothing so dull as what is there.
(Dryden, *Mock Astrologer*, Pref.)

inversion. **1.** In grammar, a change of the natural or recognized order of words.

2. In rhetoric, a mode of arguing by which the speaker tries to show that the arguments adduced by an opponent tell against his cause and are favorable to the speaker's.

Invictus (in.vik′tus). A poem by William Ernest Henley (1849–1903), written in an Edinburgh infirmary where the author was hospitalized for 20 months (1873–74) while undergoing treatment for a tuberculous disease of his remaining leg. Originally published (1875) in the *Cornhill Magazine*, it contains the well-known lines:

I am the master of my fate,
I am the captain of my soul.

Invincible Armada. See **Armada, Spanish.**

Invisible Event, The. A novel (1915) by John Davys Beresford, the last volume in the Jacob Stahl trilogy. Its companion volumes are *The Early History of Jacob Stahl* (1911) and *A Candidate for Truth* (1912).

Invisible Man, The. A novel by H. G. Wells, published in 1897. It is a "scientific" romance, but founded solely upon the invention of Wells's imagination. A stranger comes to the lodging house of Mrs. Hall and demands a room. His face is entirely bandaged and his eyes are hidden by dark glasses. He arouses her curiosity when he refuses to allow anyone in his room, and her active suspicion when she discovers that his baggage consists solely of boxes packed with small bottles. When he does not pay his bill she gets officers from town to serve a warrant for his arrest; when he resists, they seize him and force him to unmask. It is then revealed that he is completely invisible. He escapes in the confusion that ensues, but later appears in the home of Dr. Kemp in need of medical attention (he has been shot while robbing a bar). He explains to Kemp that he is Griffin, a student of science who has found how to make the cells of his body transparent (whence the pills which he carries in his baggage), and in this way to become invisible. He has terrorized many villages, stealing money and frightening people. He thereupon states that he has decided to use the doctor's home as a base for his future activities. The doctor calls in the police while his strange visitor is asleep, and they answer the call but lose the prisoner in a fight. He not only swears vengeance on the doctor, but says that he will, in addition, kill one person every day. The doctor runs to a nearby house, but the invisible man catches him. They fight, and other men join in the struggle. The invisible man is at last killed, and he takes on his visible form as he lies dead on the ground.

Invisible Tides. A novel by Beatrice Kean Seymour, published in 1919.

Invitation to the Waltz. A novel by Rosamond Lehmann, published in 1932.

invocation. The act of invoking or calling in prayer; the form or act of summoning or inviting presence or aid.

'Tis a Greek invocation to call fools into a circle.
(Shak., *As You Like It.*)

There is in religion no acceptable duty which

devout invocation of the name of God doth not either presuppose or infer.   (*The Puritan.*)

Invoice (in'vois). One of the principal characters in Samuel Foote's *Devil upon Two Sticks*.

Io (ī'ō). In Greek mythology, the beautiful daughter of Inachus, king of Argos, Greece, beloved by Zeus. She was changed by Hera in a fit of jealousy into a white heifer, and placed under the watch of Argus of the hundred eyes. When Argus was killed by Hermes at the command of Zeus, the heifer was tormented and maddened by a terrible gadfly sent by Hera. She wandered about and finally jumped into the sea and swam until she arrived in Egypt. This was the Ionian Sea, named for her. In Egypt she recovered her own shape, and bore Epaphus to Zeus. Epaphus became the ancestor of Aegyptus, Danaus, Cepheus, and Phineus. According to another story, Io was carried off by Phoenician traders who landed in Argos. Later the Greeks identified Io with Isis, the Egyptian moon goddess. The starry skies symbolized the hundred-eyed Argus; her transformation into a horned heifer was represented by the crescent moon.

Iolaus (ī.ō.lā'us). In late Greek mythology, the charioteer and companion of Hercules. Originally he was a hero of Boeotia, whose legend and cult rivaled that of Hercules.

Iolcus (ī.ol'kus). The point of embarkation of the Argonauts, in Thessaly, on the site of the modern Volos.

Ion (ī'on). In Greek mythology, the son, by Apollo, of Erechtheus's daughter Creusa: the eponymous ancestor of the Ionians.

Ion (ī'on, ī'ọn). A tragedy in blank verse by Thomas Noon Talfourd, privately printed in 1835, and produced the next year at Covent Garden Theatre, London.

Iona (ī.ō'na). [Also: **Icolmkill, Colmekill**; original Irish name, **Hii, I,** or **Ioua**, meaning "island."] An island of the Inner Hebrides, in C Scotland, in Argyllshire, ab. 1 mi. W of SW Mull, from which it is separated by the Sound of Iona. It was an ancient seat of the Druids. Saint Columba (with about 12 missionaries) founded a monastery here in 563, which became a leading center for the spread of Celtic missions. The Culdees were replaced by Benedictines in 1203. A new monastery as well as a nunnery were built by the Benedictines, the old monastery having been demolished in 1151. The burial ground attached to the chapel of Saint Oran is the burial place of many Scottish kings, among them King Duncan, victim of Macbeth. The cathedral is a small but very interesting building, now roofless, though the masonry is complete. It was founded in the 13th century, but exhibits some details as late as the 16th. Saint Martin's and Maclean's crosses nearby are interesting examples of the many sculptured Runic crosses with which Iona formerly abounded. The inhabitants of the island engage in subsistence agriculture and fishing. Area, ab. 3½ sq. mi.

Ione (ī.ō'nē). The heroine of Bulwer-Lytton's novel *The Last Days of Pompeii.*

Iphigenia (if″i.jẹ.nī'ạ). In Greek legend, the daughter of Agamemnon and Clytemnestra (or of Theseus and Helen, but adopted by Clytemnestra); sister of Orestes and Electra. According to one legend, the fleet which was to sail against Troy was becalmed at Aulis because of the anger of Artemis with Agamemnon (who had killed one of her stags). The seer Calchas (or the Delphic oracle) declared that the sacrifice of Iphigenia was the only means of propitiating the goddess. Agamemnon sent for his daughter, but when she arrived Artemis carried her away in a cloud to Tauris, and a stag (or other animal, or another person) was substituted for her in the sacrifice. While she was at Tauris as a priestess of Artemis, her brother Orestes, accompanied by his friend Pylades, came intending to carry off the celebrated image of the goddess. Iphigenia saved him from being put to death as a stranger, and fled with him and the image. Her story has frequently been made the subject of dramatic poetry. Euripides wrote two plays on the theme, as did Goethe; Racine was the author of another drama based on the legend and his play served as the basis for Gluck's opera.

Iphigenia. A tragedy by John Dennis, acted at Lincoln's Inn Fields in 1699. The story is taken from Euripides's *Iphigenia in Tauris.*

Ipomedon (i.pom'ẹ.dọn). A Middle English verse romance (c1185), a variation of the romance *Guy of Warwick.* It tells of the prince Ipomedon, who gains the favor of the Queen of Calabria through a series of daring exploits.

ipse dixit (ip'sē dik'sit). An assertion without proof; a dogmatic expression of opinion; a dictum.

> It requires something more than Brougham's flippant ipse dixit to convince me that the office of chancellor is such a sinecure and bagatelle.
>   (Greville, *Memoirs,* Mar. 15, 1831.)

> To acquiesce in an ipse dixit.   (Whately.)

> That day of ipsedixits, I trust, is over.
>   (J. H. Newman, *Letters* (1875).)

Iras (ī'rạs). In Shakespeare's *Antony and Cleopatra,* one of the two female attendants (the other being Charmian) who die with Cleopatra.

Ireland (īr'land). [Irish, **Éire**; French, **Irlande**; German, **Irland**; called the "**Emerald Isle**," the "**Green Isle**"; in literature, **Erin, Innisfail**; Latin, **Hibernia, Ibernia, Ierne, Ivernia.**] The western of the two principal islands in the British Isles. It is bounded on the NE by the North Channel, on the E by the Irish Sea, on the SE by St. George's Channel, and on the S, W, and N by the Atlantic Ocean. The coastline is irregular and deeply indented in many places. The surface consists of a central plain, mostly flat or undulating, poorly drained, and covered with much bogland, many large and small lakes (called loughs), and meandering streams. The largest lake is Lough Neagh in Northern Ireland. The plain is generally ringed with hilly uplands or mountains, the best access to it being by the coastal lowland extending N from the vicinity of Dublin to the vicinity of Dundalk. Carrantuohill (3,414 ft.), in County Kerry, in the SW part, is the highest mountain in Ireland. Numerous small islands lie offshore, most of them off the W coast. Agriculture and livestock raising are the chief pursuits of the population. Fishing is locally important at various points along the coasts. Much of the industry is associated with the processing of agricultural products. Ireland is divided politically into Northern Ireland (occupying about one sixth of the area, in the NE part of the island), part of the United Kingdom of Great Britain and Northern Ireland; and the Irish Republic, now a sovereign, independent republic (occupying about five sixths of the area of the island). The two states have been separated since 1921. Belfast is the capital of Northern Ireland; Dublin, the capital of the Irish Republic. Ireland is divided for many purposes into the four ancient, historical provinces: Ulster, in the N; Leinster, in the E; Munster, in the S; and Connacht, in the W. Northern Ireland consists of six counties, and lies wholly within Ulster province. The Irish Republic consists of 26 counties, and includes Leinster, Munster, Connacht, and a portion of Ulster. Linen, for which Ireland is famous, is made almost entirely in Ulster province. The early inhabitants were Celts; the colonizations of Ireland by Firbolgs, Milesians, and other races are legendary. The following are the leading events and incidents of Irish history: Christianity introduced by Saint Patrick, 5th century; settlements on the E coasts by the Northmen, 9th and 10th centuries; Danish invasions, ended in 1014 by the victory at Clontarf of the Irish chieftain Brian Boru; conquest of the English Pale made in the reign of Henry II by Strongbow, beginning in 1169; expedition of Poynings sent by Henry VII, leading to Poynings's Act, 1494; revolt of the Irish under the Geraldines suppressed by Henry VIII, who took the title of King of Ireland; rebellions during the reign of Elizabeth, under the leadership of Shane O'Neill, later of Desmond, and later of Hugh O'Neill (Earl of Tyrone), who was defeated by Mountjoy in 1601; English and Scottish settlement made in Ulster by James I; the lieutenancy of Strafford, followed by the "massacre of 1641"; rising put down (1649–50) by Cromwell, who made additional settlements of English and Scots; adherence of Ireland to James II, 1689; battle of the Boyne, July 1, 1690; the Irish Parliament declared independent, 1782; unsuccessful rebellion, 1798; Act of Union, ending the separate Irish Parliament and uniting Ireland with Great Britain, carried through under the lieutenancy of Cornwallis (came into force Jan. 1, 1801); unsuccessful rebellion under Emmet, 1803; Catholic Emancipation passed, 1829; repeal agitation under O'Connell, 1842–44; potato famine of 1846–47, followed by great emigration to America; "Young Ireland" rebellion, 1848; Fenian outbreaks, 1865 and 1867; Land Act, 1870; disestablishment of the Irish Church, 1871; Land Act, 1881; Land League suppressed, 1881; National League organized, 1882; Phoenix Park murders, 1882; Home Rule agitation under the lead of Parnell; introduction by Gladstone of a Home Rule Bill which failed to pass the House of Commons, 1886; Home Rule Bill passed by the House of Commons, but rejected by the House of Lords, 1893; Land Act, 1896; Agricultural and Technical Instruction Act, 1899; Land Purchase Act, 1903; Irish Universities Act, 1908; and the establishment of the United Irish League (under William O'Brien), 1898. In 1908 an act of Parliament was passed providing for the dissolution of the Royal University of Ireland and for the establishment of

two new universities, the National University of Ireland, at Dublin, and the Queen's University, at Belfast, both nonsectarian. University College, Dublin; University College, Cork; and University College, Galway City, are constituent colleges of the National University. The University of Dublin is a separate organization. Area, ab. 31,838 sq. mi.

Ireland, John. b. near Wem, Shropshire, England; d. at Birmingham, England, in November, 1808. An English author. In 1793 he edited for Boydell *Hogarth Illustrated* (1791). In 1798, as a supplementary volume of this work, he published his *Life of Hogarth*, with engravings of some hitherto unpublished drawings, which became the standard biography of Hogarth.

Ireland, Michael. Pseudonym of **Figgis, Darrell.**

Ireland, William Henry. b. probably at London, 1777; d. there, April 17, 1835. An English forger of Shakespeare manuscripts. He is supposed to have been an illegitimate son of Samuel Ireland. He visited (c1794) Stratford-on-Avon with his father, who was an admirer of Shakespeare and who fully believed a story of the recent destruction of Shakespeare's own manuscripts. On his return to London the son began a series of forgeries of Shakespeare manuscripts. Among these are a mortgage deed copied on old parchment from a genuine deed of 1612, which had been copied in facsimile by George Steevens, Shakespeare's signature on the flyleaves of old books, a transcript of *Lear*, and extracts from *Hamlet* (the orthography copied from Chatterton's Rowley poems). In February, 1795, these documents were exhibited by the elder Ireland at his house in Norfolk Street. On Feb. 25, 1795, Dr. Samuel Parr, Sir Isaac Heard, Herbert Croft, Henry James Pye, the poet laureate, and 16 others signed a paper testifying to their belief in the authenticity of the documents. To these Ireland added a new blank-verse play, *Vortigern and Rowena*, in Shakespeare's autograph, and a tragedy, *Henry II.* On April 2, 1796, *Vortigern* was produced by Kemble at Drury Lane. Its complete failure led to the exposure of the entire fraud, and before the end of the year Ireland published *An Authentic Account of the Shakespearian MSS.* He also published a number of ballads, poems, novels, memoirs, and translations.

Ireland and Other Poems. A volume of verse (1897) by Lionel Johnson.

Irena (ī.rē′na̠). The personification of Ireland in Spenser's *Faerie Queene*, saved from a tyrant by Sir Artegal.

Irene (ī.rē′nē). A tragedy by Samuel Johnson, played under the title *Mahomet and Irene*, under Garrick's management, on Feb. 6, 1749.

Irene Heron (her′o̠n). See **Heron, Irene.**

Iris (ī′ris). In Greek mythology, goddess of the rainbow and (in the *Iliad*) messenger of the gods. As Hera's messenger she carried a jug of water which put perjurers to sleep.

Iris. In Shakespeare's *Tempest*, a character in the masque celebrating the betrothal of Ferdinand and Miranda.

Iris. A tragedy (1901) by Arthur Wing Pinero.

Irish (ī′rish). [Sometimes also, **Erse**.] A language of the people of Ireland, belonging to the Goidelic group of the Celtic subfamily of the Indo-European family of languages. It includes Old Irish, Middle Irish, and modern Irish, which is commonly referred to as Gaelic. It is in age and philological value the most important language of the Celtic subfamily. The alphabet is an adaptation of the Latin. The letters are usually made to resemble a conventionalized form of the Latin alphabet which was in use in Britain in the early Middle Ages. Gaelic as spoken in the Scottish Highlands and on the Isle of Man differs but slightly from Irish. Modern Irish is greatly changed in pronunciation, as compared with the Old Irish; but it retains in great part the old orthography. Though almost moribund at the end of the last century, Irish as a living language is making its return, with the official support of the Irish Republic. English as spoken in Ireland, showing traits of Irish idiom and brogue, is also called Irish. Erse is more properly applied to the Gaelic of the Scottish Highlands but is also sometimes loosely applied to Irish Gaelic.

Irish Land League. See **Land League, Irish.**

Irish Literary Theatre. See under **Abbey Theatre.**

Irish Widow, The. A comedy by David Garrick, taken in part from Molière's *Le Mariage forcé*. It appeared on Oct. 23, 1772.

Irminsul (ėr′min.söl). Pillars, either carved tree trunks or stone, found in ancient Germanic territory, and especially associated with the old continental Saxons. They were sacred to the ancient Germanic god Irmin, god of roads and ways and guide of souls of the dead.

Iron (ī′ėrn), **Ralph.** Pseudonym of **Schreiner, Olive.**

Iron Age, The. A play by Thomas Heywood, published in two parts in 1632. This play, together with *The Golden Age* (1611), *The Silver Age* (1612), and *The Brazen Age* (1613), is a dramatization of mythological events from Saturn's assumption of power in heaven until the fall of Troy.

"Iron Chancellor," the. See **Bismarck.**

Iron Chest, The. A play by the younger George Colman, with music by Storace, taken from Godwin's *Caleb Williams* and produced on March 12, 1796.

"Iron Duke," the. See **Wellington, 1st Duke of.**

Ironmaster, The. A play translated from Georges Ohnet's *Maître de forges* (1882), by Arthur Wing Pinero, produced in 1884.

Ironside (ī′ėrn.sīd), **Nestor.** A pseudonym of **Steele, Sir Richard.**

Ironsides (ī′ėrn.sīdz). A famous cavalry regiment led by Cromwell in the English Civil War. The name was afterward applied to the entire army under his control.

irony. 1. Simulated ignorance in discussion; a method of exposing an antagonist's ignorance by pretending to desire information or instruction from him. This method of discussion, the Socratic irony, was characteristic of Socrates, with reference to whom the term was first used.

Socrates at Athens undertook with many sharp and cutting Ironies to reprove the vices of his Age.
(Stillingfleet, *Sermons*.)

The Athenian's [Socrates's] modest irony was of another taste, and better suited to the decorum of conversation, than the Syrian's [Lucan's] frontless buffoonry.
(Bp. Hurd, *Manner of Writing Dialogues*, Pref.)

Hence—2. Covert sarcasm; such a use of agreeable or commendatory forms of expression as to convey a meaning opposite to that literally expressed; sarcastic laudation, compliment, or the like.

And call her Ida, tho' I knew her not,
And call her sweet, as if in irony.
(Tennyson, *Princess*.)

A drayman in a passion calls out "You are a pretty fellow," without suspecting that he is uttering irony. (Macaulay, *Lord Bacon*.)

Irrational Knot, The. A novel by George Bernard Shaw, published in 1884.

"Irrepressible," the. See **Wilfer, Lavinia.**

Irus (ī′rus). In Homeric legend, a beggar of gigantic stature who kept watch over the suitors of Penelope, and was employed by them as a messenger. He was celebrated for his voracity.

Irus. The Blind Beggar of Alexandria in George Chapman's play of that name. He disguises himself as Count Hermes, as a usurer, and as Cleanthes, an Egyptian general.

Irving (ėr′ving), **Edward.** b. at Annan, Dumfriesshire, Scotland, Aug. 4, 1792; d. at Glasgow, Dec. 7, 1834. A Scottish preacher and divine. As a boy he was much influenced by the services of the extreme Presbyterians, seceders from the Church of Scotland. In 1812 he obtained the mastership of the academy at Kirkcaldy, where he formed a warm friendship for Thomas Carlyle. In 1818 he went to Edinburgh to obtain a permanent position, and in October, 1819, became assistant to Dr. Chalmers at Glasgow. He removed to the little chapel in Hatton Garden, London, in July, 1822, when he immediately won extraordinary popularity. At this time began the peculiar mental and religious aberrations which are associated with his career. In May, 1828, he made a tour of Scotland with the object of proclaiming the imminence of the second advent. Another expedition to Scotland followed, and in 1830 his tract on *The Orthodoxy and Catholic Doctrine of Our Lord's Human Nature* exposed him to direct charges of heresy. The "unknown tongues," a pentecostal phenomenon, were first heard in March, 1830, from the mouth of Mary Campbell. They were at first heard only in private assemblies, but on Oct. 16, 1831, the services of his new Regent Square church were disturbed by a woman who gave utterance to an outbreak of unintelligible discourse. An attempted prosecution for heresy failed in December, 1830; but on April 26, 1832, he was removed from his church. On March 13, 1833, he was condemned by the Presbytery of Annan on a charge of heresy concerning the sinlessness of Christ. This practically terminated his career. The Irvingite or Catholic Apostolic Church still survives.

Irving, Sir Henry. [Original name, **John Henry Brodribb.**] b. at Keinton, near Glastonbury, England, Feb. 6, 1838; d. at Bradford, England, Oct. 13, 1905. An English actor. He made his first appearance at the Sunderland Theatre in 1856 in Bulwer-

Lytton's *Richelieu*. After playing at Edinburgh for some time he made his first London appearance at the Princess's Theatre in 1859. He made no distinct mark till 1870, when he played Digby Grant in James Albery's *Two Roses*. He played with success until 1874, when his performance of Hamlet created genuine interest. In 1878 he undertook the management of the Lyceum Theatre, where his success was great. He produced a large number of new plays and Shakespearian revivals. He came frequently to the U.S. with his company, including Ellen Terry. He was especially distinguished in *Hamlet*, *Othello*, *Merchant of Venice*, *Richard III*, *Richelieu*, *The Bells*, *Louis XI*, *Henry VIII*, and Tennyson's *Becket*, considered his greatest role. He was knighted in 1895, the first actor so honored, and was buried in Westminster Abbey.

Irvingites (ẽr'ving.īts). [Official name, **Catholic Apostolic Church.**] Religious denomination named after Edward Irving. Irving was not the founder of the sect popularly called after him, but accepted and promoted the spread of the principles úpon which, after his death, the sect was formed.

Irwine (ẽr'win), **Mr.** In George Eliot's novel *Adam Bede*, a wise and patient clergyman. He proves a stalwart friend to Adam in his time of sorrow for Hetty Sorrel.

Isaac Bickerstaff, Astrologer (ī'zạk bik'ẽr.stȧf). See **Bickerstaff.**

Isaac of York (yôrk). In Sir Walter Scott's novel *Ivanhoe*, the father of Rebecca. He is a Jewish moneylender, based in part on the historical Isaac of York, a good and patient man who was in his day the chief figure in the Jewish community in England.

Isabel (iz'ạ.bel). In Shakespeare's *Henry V*, the Queen of Charles VI of France. She is present at the meeting of the two kings (V.ii).

Isabel Archer (är'chẽr). See **Archer, Isabel.**

Isabella (ē.zä.bel'lä). A character in Ludovico Ariosto's *Orlando Furioso*, loved by Zerbino, and killed by Rodomont.

Isabella (iz.ạ.bel'ạ). In Shakespeare's *Measure for Measure*, the sister of Claudio, and object of the passion of Angelo, but married by Vincentio, the Duke. She is the innocent object of the only two really evil proposals in the play: that of Angelo, who wishes to violate her chastity; and that of Claudio, who begs for his life at the expense of her honor.

Isabella. The gentle, sweɛt wife of the Duke of Brachiano in John Webster's tragedy *The White Devil*.

Isabella. The "insatiate countess" in John Marston's play of that name. She alternately attracts men to be her lovers and induces their successors to kill them.

Isabella (iz.ạ.bel'ạ) or **Isabelle** (iz'ạ.bel). An amusing and mischievous girl in Dryden's *Wild Gallant*.

Isabella. In Susannah Centlivre's comedy *The Wonder*, a young lady in love with Colonel Britton, but intended by her father for another.

Isabella. The wife of Biron in Thomas Southerne's *Fatal Marriage*. She marries Villeroy, being de-

ceived into a belief in Biron's death; after his return and actual death she dies distracted.

Isabella, Donna. See **Donna Isabella.**

Isabella, or the Pot of Basil. A poem (1820) by John Keats, a retelling of one of the tales from Boccaccio's *Decameron*, concerning the murder of Isabella's lover by her brothers.

Isabella Thorpe (thôrp). See **Thorpe, Isabella.**

Isabella Vere (vir). See **Vere, Isabella.**

Isabella Wardle (wôr'dl). See under **Wardle, Mr.**

Isabella Wardour (wôr'dẽr). See **Wardour, Isabella.**

Isabel of France (iz'ạ.bel). See under **Queen.**

Isabinda (is.ạ.bin'dạ). One of the principal characters in Susannah Centlivre's comedy *The Busybody;* the daughter of Sir Jealous Traffick, who keeps her from the sight of all men.

Isaiah (ī.zā'ạ). [Also: **Esaias, Isaias.**] A Hebrew prophet who prophesied from 740 B.C. till 701 B.C. Usually considered to have been the greatest of the Old Testament prophets and orators, he was a consistent opponent of the policy of the Hebrew kings to enter into entangling alliances with foreign powers. Once, however, the alliance with Assyria had been formed, he counseled the keeping of faith, continually asserting that no dependence could be placed on Egypt. Chapters xl–lxvi of Isaiah, which relate to the captivity and return, are considered by some scholars the work of a post-exilic prophet called by them Deutero-Isaiah. An ancient scroll of the Book of Isaiah was found in 1947 in a cave overlooking the Dead Sea, the oldest complete Biblical work ever to have been discovered.

Iscanus (is.kā'nus), **Josephus.** See **Joseph of Exeter.**

Isenbras (ī'zẹn.bras), **Sir.** [Also, **Sir Isumbras.**] A proud hero of medieval romance, who was humbled.

Isengrim (ī'zẹn.grim), **Sir.** The wolf in *Reynard the Fox*.

Iseult (i.sölt'). See **Isolt.**

Iseult of Brittany (brit'ạ.ni). A play (1920) by Arthur Symons.

Isherwood (ish'ẽr.wud), **Christopher.** [Full name, **Christopher William Bradshaw-Isherwood.**] b. at Disley, Cheshire, England, Aug. 26, 1904—. An English novelist and playwright. Author of *All the Conspirators* (1928), *The Memorial* (1932), *Mr. Norris Changes Trains* (1935), *Goodbye to Berlin* (1939), *Prater Violet* (1945), *Condor and the Cows* (1949), and the autobiographical *Lions and Shadows* (1938). He edited *Vedanta and the West* (1943), and was coauthor with Wystan Hugh Auden of the plays *The Dog Beneath the Skin* (1935), *The Ascent of F. 6* (1937), and *On the Frontier* (1938), and the travel account *Journey to a War* (1939). *I Am a Camera*, a play based on his Berlin stories and written by John Van Druten, opened at New York in 1951.

Ishmael (ish'mā.ẹl). [Also, **Ismael** (is'-).] In the Bible, the son of Abraham and Hagar, cast out with his mother because of Sarah's fears for the rights of her son, Isaac. After nearly perishing in the desert, Ishmael and Hagar settled at Paran where he married an Egyptian. From his 12 sons were descended the Arabs. Esau married his daughter. The Biblical story has resulted in the name becoming an epithet for the social outcast, the misfit; this is, understandably, not true among the Moslems, since Mohammed traced his ancestry to Ishmael. Gen. xvi. 11, 12; xxi. 14.

Ishtar (ish′tär). [Also, **Istar** (is′-).] The principal goddess of Assyrian and Babylonian mythology, great mother goddess or earth mother, goddess of love, fertility, sex, and war. As mother goddess she was identified with the Sumerian Nana or Inanna, Phoenician Astarte or Ashtoreth, Greek Aphrodite, Roman Venus. She was also associated with the planet Venus. In her warlike character she was conceived of by the Babylonians as ruling the morning star; as goddess of love she ruled the evening star. The Assyrians distinguished between the Ishtar whose shrine was at Arbela, who presided over battles, and Ishtar of Nineveh, in whom the voluptuous aspect predominated. Ishtar also occurs as an appellation, or generic name, for a goddess in general. The story of Ishtar and her lover Tammuz, his death, her mourning for him, and her descent to the underworld to bring him back, the parching of the earth in her absence, and the return of vegetation with her return is the great vegetation myth of Asia Minor and the Mediterranean region.

Isidore of Seville (iz′i.dōr, se.vil′), Saint. [Latin, **Isidorus Hispalensis**.] b. at Cartagena, Spain, c560; d. April 4, 636. A Spanish encyclopedist and ecclesiastic. He was bishop of Seville from about 600. His works, which were held in high esteem during the Middle Ages, include the encyclopedic work *Originum sive etymologiarum libri xx*, usually shortened to *Origines* or *Etymologiae*. Written probably between the years 622 and 633, this work had a great influence upon medieval thought. In it Isidore sought to cover all available knowledge concerning not only the liberal arts but also the sciences. His sources were, for the most part, classical authors (particularly the grammarians) and the writers of patristic literature. The result is that the *Origines* seems, to the modern mind, to be a work so entirely derivative (and oblivious to the advantages of what we now call the scientific method) as to have little value; nevertheless, in its own day, it performed a great service if only because it made available to scholars much of the substance of classical thought within a single comprehensive framework. For historians of science, Isidore's *De natura rerum* is a work of some significance, covering cosmography, astronomy, and meteorology. His other works include *De ecclesiasticis officiis libri duo*, and *Sententiarum sive de summo bono libri tres*. He has been erroneously accredited with the compilation of the so-called Isidorian Decretals.

Isidorian Decretals (iz.i.dō′ri.an). [Also, **Spanish Decretals**.] A code of native and foreign canons which circulated in Spain in the 6th century, and was afterward accepted through the Roman Catholic Church: so called from Saint Isidore of Seville (Isidorus Hispalensis), who was erroneously supposed to have compiled it.

Isis (ī′sis). In Egyptian mythology, the chief female deity; the sister, wife, and female counterpart of Osiris, and the mother of Horus. The most famous of all Egyptian goddesses, she was distinguished by the solar disk and cow's horns on her head, and in this aspect was often identified with Hathor. She was identified by the Greeks with Athena and Demeter. Her worship in a modified form, as a nature goddess, was introduced subsequently to the Alexandrine epoch into Greece, and was very popular at Rome from the end of the republic. The Greek and Roman priests and priestesses of Isis wore a special costume, and had as an attribute a form of dance rattle, the sistrum, which traveled with the cult of Isis through the Roman Empire as far as Gaul. On her statue was an inscription mentioned by Proclus: "I am that which is, has been, and shall be. My veil no one has lifted. The fruit I bore was the Sun"; hence the well-known allusion to a mystery as covered with "the veil of Isis." In Egypt she was also identified with Sothis, the Dog Star, and in later days with the planet Venus. As Neith she was the divine originator and patroness of weaving and other womanly arts. Her cult persisted in Europe until the latter half of the 6th century A.D.

Isis. A name sometimes given to the river Thames, in England. Specifically the name applies only to the upper course of the river to its confluence with the river Thame.

Islam (is′lam, is.läm′). See **Mohammedanism**.

Island, The. A love story by Naomi Royde-Smith, published in 1930.

Island of Saints. [Latin, **Insula Sanctorum**.] A medieval name given to Ireland as an early stronghold of Christianity.

Island of the Seven Cities. See **Seven Cities, Island of the.**

Island of Youth, and Other Poems. A volume of poems by Edward Shanks, published in 1921.

Island Pharisees (far′i.sēz), **The.** A novel by John Galsworthy, published in 1904.

Island Princess, The. A play by John Fletcher, produced at court in 1621, and printed in 1647. The play was converted into an opera by Motteux in 1699, the music being by Daniel Purcell and others. It is based on a story appended to the French translation of Cervantes' *Novelas Exemplares*.

Isle (lēl), **Claude Joseph Rouget de l'.** See **Rouget de Lisle.**

Isle of Dogs, The. A comedy (1597), now lost, by Ben Jonson and Thomas Nash. It contained matter offensive to the Privy Council, which in punishment for its presentation briefly closed all theaters in and around London.

Isle of Gulls, The. A play (1606) by John Day, based on Sir Philip Sidney's *Arcadia*.

Isles, Lord of the. See **Lord of the Isles.**

Isles of the Blest. See **Fortunate Islands.**

Is Life Worth Living? A three-act comedy (1933), called "an exaggeration" by its author, Lennox Robinson. It shows what happens to a small Irish town after its happy, healthy citizens see some of the social and intellectual dramas of Ibsen.

Isocrates (ī.sok′ra.tēz). b. at Athens, 436 B.C.; d. 338 B.C. An Athenian orator and rhetorician, a pupil of both Socrates and Gorgios. He was distinguished (c392 *et seq.*) as a teacher of eloquence, his school being responsible for nearly all the noted orators of the middle 4th century. He did not speak himself but wrote his speeches for others. Of his

d, d or j; s, s or sh; t, t or ch; z, z or zh; o, F. cloche; ü, F. menu; ch, Sc. loch; ṅ, F. bonbon.

orations 21 are extant. According to tradition, he starved himself to death after Philip II of Macedon's victory at Chaeronea over the Athenians and Boeotians ended the hope of Greek freedom and independence.

Isolt (i.sōlt', is'ōlt). [Also: **Iseult, Isolde** (i.sōld'; *German*, ē.zol'dẹ).] In Arthurian romance, the daughter of the king of Ireland, known as Isolt the Fair, or Isolt of Ireland. She was the wife of Mark, king of Cornwall, but loved Sir Tristram (or Tristan). Mark had sent his nephew Tristram in a ship to Ireland to bring his bride to Cornwall. En route they unwittingly drank the magic love potion intended for Isolt and Mark. Their consequent tragic love for each other constitutes one of the greatest love stories of the world. Tristram, finally unable to endure the situation, went to Brittany, and there married another Isolt, Isolt of the White Hands, daughter of the king of Brittany. Later he was mortally wounded and sent for Isolt of Ireland to come to him. The ship bringing her was to fly white sails if she were on board, black if she were not. The sails were white, but Isolt of the White Hands, in jealousy, told him they were black, and Tristram died of grief before the ship landed. When Isolt of Ireland came ashore and was told that he was dead, she died of grief beside him, and the ship took the bodies of the two lovers back to Cornwall for burial.

Isopel Berners (iz'ọ.pel bẽr'nẽrz). See **Berners, Belle.**

Israfeel or **Israfil** (ĕs.rä.fēl'). In the Koran, one of the four archangels; the angel of music. His voice is more melodious than that of any other creature. He is to sound the resurrection trumpet on the last day.

Isumbras (iz'um.bras), **Sir.** See **Isenbras, Sir.**

Italian, The. A mystery novel (1797) by Ann Radcliffe.

Italian Visit, An. A volume of verse (1953) by Cecil Day Lewis.

Italy. A descriptive poem by Samuel Rogers, published 1822–28.

Ithaca (ith'ạ.kạ). [Modern Greek, **Ithake** (ē.thä'kē), **Thiaki** (thyä'kē).] One of the Ionian Islands, Greece, in the *nomos* (department) of Cephalonia, ab. 2 mi. NE of Cephalonia. The chief place is Ithaca (or Vathy). It is famous as the reputed home of Ulysses, which, however, was identified by Dörpfeld with the island of Leukas. Length, 14 mi.; area, ab. 37 sq. mi.

Ithamore (ith'ạ.mōr). In Christopher Marlowe's play *The Jew of Malta*, a Turkish slave.

Ithocles (ith'ọ.klēz). A general of Sparta and brother to Penthea in John Ford's tragedy *The Broken Heart.*

Ithuriel (i.thū'ri.ẹl). An angel, a character in Milton's *Paradise Lost*. He was sent by Gabriel to find out Satan. The slightest touch of his spear exposed deceit.

Itinerary, The. An account by John Leland (1506–52) of his journeys through England, with descriptions of routes and matters of antiquarian interest.

It Is Never too Late to Mend. A novel by Charles Reade, published in 1856. The author uses two separate themes in this book. The first is the story of a young farmer who leaves England for Australia in order to earn the 1,000 pounds that will enable him to marry the girl of his choice. The villainous Meadows tries to ruin his plans, but he obtains the money in spite of this by taking part in the gold rush. The second story concerns a thief who is transported to Australia, and the author uses this as an opportunity to expose the evils of the English prison system.

It Never Can Happen Again. A novel (1909) by William De Morgan, commenting on the English church ban on marriage with a deceased wife's sister.

It's a Battlefield. A novel by Graham Greene, published in 1934.

Itys (ī'tis). In Greek legend, the son of Tereus and Procne, killed and served as a meal to his father by Procne and her sister Philomela. Tereus had seduced Philomela and torn out her tongue. After the revenge of the sisters, they fled, with Tereus in pursuit.

Ivanhoe (ī'van.hō). A historical novel by Sir Walter Scott, published in 1820; named from its hero, Wilfred, knight of Ivanhoe. The scene is laid in England during the reign of Richard I (1189–99).

Ivanhoe. An opera in three acts by Arthur Sullivan, with a libretto by Julian Sturgis adapted from Sir Walter Scott's novel of the same name, first performed at the opening of the Royal English Opera House on Jan. 31, 1891.

Ivernia (ī.vẽr'ni.ạ). A Latin name of Ireland.

Ivory Gate. In Greek mythology, the gate of sleep by which false dreams are sent from the lower world.

Ivory Tower, The. An unfinished novel by Henry James, published in 1917.

Ivy-Day in the Committee Room. One of the short stories in James Joyce's *Dubliners* (1914). A story of Irish politicians who assemble on the birthday of Charles Stewart Parnell, it tells of the disputes that arise among his sympathizers and opponents.

Ixion (ik.sī'ọn, ik'si.ọn). In Greek mythology, a king of the Lapithae; father of Pirithous, and father by a cloud (which was caused by Zeus to take the form of Hera) of the Centaurs. For boasting of the favors of Hera, which he supposed he had had, he was punished in the lower world by being fastened to an ever-revolving wheel.

Ixion in Heaven. A burlesque by Benjamin Disraeli, in the style of Lucian, published in 1833.

Izdubar (iz.dö.bär'). The principal hero of ancient Babylonian legends: a prototype of Nimrod.

---

fat, fāte, fär, ȧsk, fãre; net, mē, hẽr; pin, pīne; not, nōte, mŏve, nôr; up, lūte, p͓ull; ŦH, then;

J

Jabberwocky (jab'ẽr.wok.i). A nonsense poem in *Through the Looking Glass*, by Charles Dodgson (Lewis Carroll). It tells the story of the killing of the Jabberwock (presumably a type of dragon, even more dangerous than the "Jubjub bird" or the "frumious Bandersnatch"). The invented vocabulary of the poem is undeniably brilliant; indeed, several words from it ("burble," "galumphing," and "frabjous") have entered the English vocabulary on the level of informal speech.

Jachin (jā'kin). A column set up in the court of Solomon's temple. Its companion was named Boaz. 1 Kings, vii. 21.

Jack Absolute (jak ab'sọ.löt), **Captain.** See **Absolute, Captain Jack.**

Jack Altamont (al'tạ.mont), **Colonel.** See **Altamont, Colonel Jack.**

Jack and Jill (jil). An English nursery rhyme, probably the most popular of them all. In the 19th century it was a common chapbook title with the story strung along sometimes up to 15 verses. Several attempts have been made to root this old rhyme in antiquity. Probably the best-known of these analogies is that of Baring-Gould, who saw Jack and Jill in the Icelandic myth of Hjuki and Bil, two children who were kidnaped by the moon while drawing water, which is carried on their shoulders in a bucket suspended from a pole. Scandinavian folklore still accounts for the moon spots in this way; but any direct connection between the Eddaic myth and the rhyme is not substantiated. A play with this title was popular at the English court between 1567 and 1578. But this too probably had nothing to do with the children's rhyme. Early English quotations (Shakespearian included) about Jack and Jill patently use the names in the generic sense of "lad" and "lass."

Jack and the Beanstalk. The title of an English folk tale, now classed as a nursery tale in the British Isles and America. It belongs to what is called the Jack tale cycle, which is common all over Europe and America, the story itself being practically the same everywhere except for details determined by local culture. The beanstalk, for instance, which is familiar in England and America, is some other plant or tree, even a cabbage, which grows to the sky, in other localities. The objects which Jack steals from the giant's (or ogre's) castle in the sky also differ according to the values of the people among whom it is told. British and European children are told that Jack stole from the giant a little hen that laid a golden egg, a bag of gold, and a wonderful harp. In one U.S. Southern mountain version he steals a rifle, a "skinnin' knife," and a wonderful quilt decorated with bells. In most instances the story begins with the foolish bargain (i.e., Jack's stupid exchange of the cow for a handful of beans), but quite often the plant that grows to the sky grows from seeds swept out of the house with some trash.

Jack Brag (brag). A novel by Theodore Hook, published in 1837. Jack Brag is a vulgar braggart who contrives to get into good society.

Jack Cade (kād). See **Cade, Jack,** and **Cade, John.**

Jack Dawkins (dô'kinz). See **Dawkins, John.**

Jackdaw of Rheims (rēmz), **The.** The best-known work in the collection entitled *The Ingoldsby Legends.*

Jack Drum's Entertainment. A play written c1600, presumably by John Marston, although it was printed anonymously. Jonson was caricatured in the character of Brabant Senior.

Jack Frost (frôst). See **Frost, Jack.**

Jack Hatchway (hach'wā), **Lieutenant.** See **Hatchway, Lieutenant Jack.**

Jack Horner (hôr'nẽr). The subject of an English nursery rhyme, who "sat in a corner eating his Christmas pie." It is one of the oldest of this class of rhymes. A copy of his "pleasant history" is to be found in the Bodleian Library, and is taken from *The Fryer and the Boy,* a story extant c1520 and published in London in 1617. Halliwell says both are from the more ancient *Jak and his Stepdame* (c1340).

Jack-in-the-Green. A mummer in the English May Day pageants and plays. Jack-in-the-Green is a boy or youth wearing a light lattice frame covered so completely with green leaves and boughs (usually holly and ivy) as to hide him, and topped with colored ribbons.

Jack Maldon (môl'dọn). See **Maldon, Jack.**

Jack of Dover (dō'vẽr). A variety of pie, referred to by Chaucer in the prologue to *The Cook's Tale:* "And many a Jakke of Dover hastow sold."

Jack Pudding (pŭd'ing). See **Pudding, Jack.**

Jack Rattlin (rat'lin). See **Rattlin, Jack.**

Jack Sheppard (shep'ạrd). **1.** Defoe's account (1724) of the notorious criminal of that name.
2. A novel (1839) by Ainsworth on the same subject.

Jacks (jaks), **Lawrence Pearsall.** b. at Nottingham, England, Oct. 9, 1860—. An English Unitarian clergyman and writer. He was professor (1903–31) and principal (1915–31) of Manchester College at Oxford, and first editor (1902–47) of the *Hibbert Journal.* His works include *Education through Recreation* (1932), *The Revolt Against Mechanism* (1934), *The Last Legend of Smokeover* (1939), *Construction Now* (1940), and *The Confession of an Octogenarian* (1942).

Jackson (jak'sọn), **Frederick George.** b. 1860; d. at London, March 13, 1938. An English explorer. He commanded the Alfred Harmsworth polar expedition (1894–97) which proved Franz Josef Land to be an archipelago and not a continent. He explored the Congo forest, the Australian deserts, Lapland, and the Arctic tundra, and descended the

ḍ, d or j; ṣ, s or sh; ṭ, t or ch; ẓ, z or zh; o, F. cloche; ü, F. menu; ċh, Sc. loch; ṅ, F. bonbon.

Congo River to the sea. Author of *The Great Frozen Land*, *A Thousand Days in the Arctic*, and *The Lure of Unknown Lands*.

Jackson, Holbrook. b. at Liverpool, England, Dec. 31, 1874; d. at Bournemouth, England, June 15, 1948. An English writer and editor. He edited *The Beau* (1910), *T.P.'s Magazine* (1911–12), *T.P.'s Weekly* (1911–16), and *Today* (1917–23). Author of *The Eternal Now* (1900), poetry; *Bernard Shaw: A Study* (1907), *William Morris* (1908), *Platitudes in the Making* (1911), *Romance and Reality* (1911), *All Manner of Folk* (1912), *Occasions* (1922), *Anatomy of Bibliomania* (2 vols., 1930, 1931), *William Caxton* (1933), *The Printing of Books* (1937), *The Reading of Books* (1946), and *Dreamers of Dreams* (1948).

Jack Sprat (sprat). An English nursery rhyme ("Jack Sprat could eat no fat, his wife could eat no lean"), already well enough known in 1639 to be included in John Clarke's *Paroemiologia Anglo-Latina*. When Howell published his *Proverbs or Old Sayed Sawes & Adages* in 1659, it contained a rhyme concerning an Archdeacon Pratt who would "eat no Fatt." This reference is thought to be an archdeacon of very small stature, probably from the fact that the term Jack Sprat was a proverbial term in the 16th and 17th centuries for a dwarfed person. Jack Sprat was also the hero of a series of chapbook stories featuring Jack Sprat and his one-eared cat.

Jack the Giant-killer. The title and hero of an English folk tale, perhaps the most widespread of all stories in the Jack tale cycle. It is known all over Europe as *The Boy Who Steals the Giant's Treasure*, and is thought to be of northern origin. The plot consists of a series of adventures in which Jack beheads giant after giant, or tricks stupid ogres into killing themselves, either making off with their treasures, being rewarded by grateful newly released victims, or by the stupid monsters themselves. The story even appears as an accretion to the Arthur cycle: King Arthur and his son encounter Jack and join company with him. Arthur needs money, so Jack proposes to visit a three-headed giant and trick him out of some gold. This he does; Arthur gets the money and Jack gets for himself a cloak of invisibility, shoes of swiftness, and the like.

Jack Upland (up'land). An attack on friars, in prose, added by Speght to Chaucer's works in his 1602 edition, but evidently not Chaucer's.

Jacob (jā'kob), **Naomi Ellington.** [Pseudonym, **Ellington Gray.**] b. July 1, 1889—. An English novelist. Author of *The Wild Lie* (1930), *The Loaded Stick* (1935), *Barren Metal* (1937), *Time Piece* (1937), *Straws in Amber* (1938), *Sally Scarth* (1940), *The Cap of Youth* (1941), and *Me and the Mediterranean* (1945).

Jacob, Violet. [Maiden name, **Violet Mary Augusta Frederica Kennedy-Erskine.**] b. in Angus, Scotland, 1863—. A Scottish poet and novelist. Among her works are *The Sheep-Stealers* (1902), *The Interloper* (1904), *The History of Aythan Waring* (1908), *Flemington* (1911), *Songs of Angus* (1916), *More Songs of Angus and Others* (1918), and *The Lairds of Dun* (1931).

Jacob and Josep (jō'zep). A Middle English verse paraphrase of Biblical material, written during the second half of the 13th century. It is completely medieval in setting, action, and description, the characters concerned being depicted as lords, knights, and hunters with bent bows.

Jacob Caxon (kak'son). See **Caxon, Jacob.**

Jacobean Age (jak.ọ.bē'an). See under **Elizabethan Age.**

Jacob Faithful (fāth'ful). A novel of seafaring life by Frederick Marryat, published in 1834. Its title is taken from the name of its hero.

Jacobins (jak'ọ.binz). In France, a name applied to the Dominican order; so called from the Church of Saint Jacques (Jacobus), in which they were first established at Paris.

Jacobins. Members of a club or society of French revolutionists organized in 1789 under the name of Society of Friends of the Constitution, and called Jacobins from the Dominican convent at Paris in which they met. The club originally included many of the moderate leaders of the Revolution, but the more violent members speedily gained control. It had branches in all parts of France, and was for a time all-powerful in determining the course of government, especially after Robespierre became its leader. Many of its members were executed with Robespierre in July, 1794, and the club was suppressed in November.

Jacobites (jak'ọ.bīts). In English history, the partisans or adherents of James II (whose name in Latinized form was Jacobus) after he abdicated the throne, or of his descendants. The Jacobites engaged in fruitless rebellions in 1715 and 1745, in behalf of James Francis Edward Stuart and of Charles Edward Stuart, the son and grandson of James II, called the Old and Young Pretender respectively. Jacobite sentiment was concentrated among the Scottish clans, and tended to exist throughout Great Britain among the families which remained Roman Catholic. It is important in the plots of several of Scott's novels, and also in Thackeray's *Henry Esmond*.

Jacob Marley (jā'kob mär'li). See **Marley, Jacob.**

Jacob Stahl (stäl), **The Early History of.** See **History of Jacob Stahl, The Early.**

Jacobs (jā'kobz), **W. W.** [Full name, **William Wymark Jacobs.**] b. at London, Sept. 8, 1863; d. there, Sept. 1, 1943. An English novelist and dramatist. His first publication was *Many Cargoes* (1896), a volume of short stories. He was the author of sea stories including *The Skipper's Wooing* (1897), *Sea Urchins* (1898), *A Master of Craft* (1900), *Light Freights* (1901), *At Sunwich Port* (1902), *Odd Craft* (1903), *Dialstone Lane* (1904), *Captains All* (1905), *Short Cruises* (1907), *Salthaven* (1908), *Sailors' Knots* (1909), *Ship's Company* (1911), *Night Watches* (1914), *The Castaways* (1916), *Deep Waters* (1919), *Sea Whispers* (1926), and *Snug Harbor* (1931), an omnibus volume. With Louis Napoleon Parker he wrote *The Lady of the Barge and Other Stories*; the title story was dramatized as *Beauty and the Barge* (1913). His best-known work is a short story of the occult, *The Monkey's Paw*, made into a one-act play by Parker and first produced (Oct. 6, 1903) at the London Haymarket. Other plays by Jacobs are *Establishing Relations* (1925), *The Warming-Pan* (1929), *A Distant Relative* (1930), and *Dixon's Return* (1932).

Jacob's Room. A novel by Virginia Woolf, published in 1922. It tells the story of the life of Jacob Flanders, from his boyhood, through his college years, to his death in World War I. It describes his early love affairs and his travels through France, Italy, and Greece. Many of the characters are described in word portraits, and the personality of Jacob is emphasized through the reactions of the other characters to his thoughts and actions.

Jacob's Well. A Middle English collection of 95 prose sermons, written c1425. It compares man to a well which must be cleansed and purified.

Jacobus de Voragine (jạ.kō′bus dē vọ.raj′i.nē). [Also: **Jacobus de Varagine** (vạ.raj′i.nē); Italian, **Jacopo de Voragine** (yä′kō.pō dā vō.rä′jē.nä).] b. at Viraggio, near Genoa, Italy, 1230; d. 1298. An Italian ecclesiastic, archbishop of Genoa (1292 *et seq.*). He was the compiler of the *Legenda aurea* (Eng. trans., *The Golden Legend*), a collection of saints' lives.

Jacquard (zhạ.kàr), **Joseph Marie.** b. at Lyons, France, July 7, 1752; d. at Oullins, near Lyons, Aug. 7, 1834. A French mechanic, inventor of the Jacquard loom (c1801), the first loom to weave figured patterns.

Jacquerie (zhäk.rē). In French history, a revolt of the peasants against the nobles in northern France (Île-de-France, Beauvaisis, Picardy, Champagne) in 1358. The peasants objected to the depredations of the free companies and to the paying of taxes levied to ransom captured soldiers. They burned castles and harried the nobles. The rebels were quickly scattered and a campaign of extermination was instituted against them, led by Charles II of Navarre; some 20,000 peasants are said to have been killed.

Jaffeir (jaf′yẻr). A conspirator in Thomas Otway's *Venice Preserv'd.* He is the husband of Belvidera. He is torn in his loyalties between love of his wife and friendship for Pierre, who has involved him in a political revolt.

Jaggard (jag′ạrd), **William.** b. c1568; d. 1623. An English printer and publisher. He is chiefly famous for bringing out the First Folio (1623) of the plays of Shakespeare. The Colophon on page 399 (which is misnumbered 993) informs the reader that it was "Printed at the Charges of W. Jaggard, Ed. Blount, I. Smithweeke, and W. Aspley, 1623."

Jaggers (jag′ẻrz), **Mr.** The lawyer in Dickens's novel *Great Expectations.*

Jahangir (jạ.hän″gēr′). [Also, **Jehangir.**] fl. in the 17th century A.D. A Mogul emperor (1605–27); son of Akbar. His name, while he was a prince, was Selim, and he adopted his ruling name, meaning "World Conqueror," on his accession. His reign was marked by a series of fruitless wars and by the influence of his queen, Nur Jahan or Nur Mahal, whose favoritism to her own family led to a revolt. The English first came to India in Jahangir's reign: William Hawkins in 1609 and Thomas Roe, ambassador of James I, in 1615.

Jailer. [Also, **Keeper.**] In *The Two Noble Kinsmen*, the keeper of the jail where Palamon and Arcite are confined.

Jailer's Daughter. In *The Two Noble Kinsmen*, the daughter of the Jailer. She loves Palamon, whom she frees.

Jakin (jā′kin), **Bob.** In George Eliot's novel *The Mill on the Floss*, a peddler. He is a minor, but both amusing and touching, character, stubbornly loyal to his friends Tom and Maggie.

Jamaica Inn (jạ.mā′kạ). A novel by Daphne Du Maurier, published in 1936.

James (jāmz). Entries on literary characters having this prename will be found under the surnames Blunt, Carker, Courtly, Elia, Gurney, Harthouse, Morell, Steerforth, Tyrrel, and Wait.

James I (of *England*). [Also, **James VI** (of *Scotland*).] b. in Edinburgh Castle, June 19, 1566; d. March 27, 1625. King of England, Scotland, and Ireland (1603–25); son of Lord Darnley and Mary, Queen of Scots. He became, on the abdication of his mother, king of Scotland as James VI on July 24, 1567; and by virtue of his descent, both through his father and his mother, from Margaret Tudor, daughter of Henry VII, succeeded to the English throne on the death of Elizabeth without issue, on March 24, 1603. He was crowned king of England (and Ireland) on July 25, 1603. He was a learned but pedantic, weak, and incapable monarch, whence he was aptly characterized by the Duc de Sully as the "wisest fool in Europe." In domestic politics he sought to assert the theory of the divine right of kingship and of episcopacy; in his foreign relations he strove to maintain peace at all hazards, even to the prejudices of his natural allies, the Protestant powers on the Continent. He presided, in 1604, over the Hampton Court Conference between the bishops and the Puritans, at which the latter sought but failed to obtain a relaxation of the laws directed against nonconformists. In the same year he concluded peace with Spain (he had inherited a Spanish war from Elizabeth) and appointed a commission to revise the English translation of the Bible, which commission completed the so-called King James Version (Authorized Version) in 1611. He sanctioned in 1606 penal laws of increased severity against Roman Catholics in consequence of the discovery of the Gunpowder Plot in the preceding year, and granted a patent organizing the London and Plymouth companies, the former of which founded the settlement of Jamestown in 1607, while a band of English separatists from Holland founded, without authority, the settlement of Plymouth in the territory of the latter in 1620. Another important event which took place in 1606 was the restoration of episcopacy in Scotland. He began in 1611 negotiations for the marriage of his eldest son Charles (later to become Charles I) with a Spanish princess, and in the same year entered into a defensive alliance with the Protestant Union in Germany, which was followed in 1613 by the marriage of his daughter Elizabeth to the elector palatine Frederick V, head of the union. He refused to assist his son-in-law in the struggle with the emperor Ferdinand II for the crown of Bohemia; and after the defeat of Frederick by the Imperialists on the White Mountain,

---

ḍ, d or j; ṣ, s or sh; ṭ, t or ch; ẓ, z or zh; o, F. cloche; ü, F. menu; ċh, Sc. loch; ṅ, F. bonbon,

and the invasion of the Palatinate by the Spanish troops in 1620, sought by futile negotiations to induce Philip III of Spain to reinstate Frederick in the electorate and to assist in restoring peace. In answer to a rebuke from the king for meddling in affairs of state by sending in a petition against popery and the proposed Spanish marriage, Parliament passed (Dec. 18, 1621) the Great Protestation, declaring that affairs which concerned the king and the realm were proper subjects for debate in Parliament. The king tore the page containing the protestation from the journal of the Commons. In 1623 he reluctantly permitted his son Charles and George Villiers, 1st Duke of Buckingham, to depart for Spain to conclude the negotiations for a marriage treaty which had been kept up, with interruptions, since 1611; but as Philip was unwilling to procure the restoration of the Palatinate, Charles and the duke returned in the same year, and the negotiations were finally abandoned.

James I (of *Scotland*). b. at Dunfermline, Scotland, 1394; d. at Perth, Scotland, Feb. 20, 1437. King of Scotland (1406–37); son of Robert III and Annabella Drummond. He was captured (c1406) by the English while on his way to France, and was detained by Henry IV and Henry V in captivity until 1423. He repressed the great feudal lords of Scotland, with the assistance of the clergy and the burghs, and maintained peaceful relations both with England and with France. He was murdered at Perth by Walter Stuart, Earl of Atholl, and Robert Graham. He was the author of *The Kingis Quair*, an allegorical poem on his courtship while in England of his future wife, Jane Beaufort.

James II (of *England*). b. at St. James's Palace, London, Oct. 14, 1633; d. at St.-Germain, France, Sept. 6, 1701. King of England, Scotland, and Ireland (1685–88); son of Charles I and Henrietta Maria. Before his accession he was known as the Duke of York. He became lord high admiral of England on the restoration of his brother Charles II in 1660, received a grant of the New Netherlands in 1664, embraced the Roman Catholic faith probably before 1672, and was forced by the Test Act to resign the admiralty in 1673. Under the guidance of Father Petre, his confessor and chief adviser, he aimed on his accession to make himself an absolute monarch and to restore the Roman Catholic Church. He increased the standing army from 6,000 to about 30,000 men by keeping up the military force raised to suppress the Scottish rebellion under the Duke of Monmouth in 1685, and granted commissions in the new regiments to Roman Catholics. He published a declaration of liberty of conscience for all denominations in England and Scotland early in 1687, and on April 25, 1688, ordered the declaration to be read in all the churches. A petition from the primate and six bishops against the order was pronounced a seditious libel by the king, who sent the seven bishops to the Tower and brought them to trial before the Court of King's Bench. The trial resulted in acquittal on June 30, 1688, and the same day an invitation, signed by the earls of Danby, Devonshire, and Shrewsbury, the bishop of London, and others, was dispatched to William of Orange (later to become William III of England) to save the country from a

Roman Catholic tyranny. William landed at Torbay on Nov. 5, 1688, and on December 22 James escaped to France, where he was assigned the chateau of St.-Germain by Louis XIV, as a place of refuge. In 1689 he made a descent on Ireland, but was totally defeated by William at the battle of the Boyne, July 1, 1690.

James IV. [Full title, **The Scottish History of James IV.**] A comedy (c1591) by Robert Greene, based on a story by Cinthio.

James, George Payne Rainsford. b. at London, Aug. 9, 1799; d. at Venice, May 9, 1860. An English novelist and historical writer. *Richelieu*, his first novel, was published in 1829, and was followed by many others. He was appointed historiographer royal by William IV. James is parodied by Thackeray in *Barbazure, by G. P. R. Jeames, Esq.*

James, Henry. b. at New York, April 15, 1843; d. in England, Feb. 28, 1916. An American novelist, playwright, and critic; brother of William James (1842–1910). He was naturalized a British subject in 1915. He was educated largely in Europe, studied law briefly at Harvard, and began to contribute to periodicals in 1866. From first to last a vigorous experimenter and innovator in the craft of fiction, following more closely the methods of Flaubert and Turgenev than those of his English and American contemporaries, he made a profound contribution to the development of the novel as an art form. His influence and reputation increased to great proportions after his death; he was the acknowledged master of Edith Wharton, Joseph Conrad, and many others. Although his own attempts to write for the theater met with failure during his lifetime, later dramatic versions of his works, such as *Washington Square* and the tale *The Turn of the Screw* (under the titles *The Heiress* and *The Innocents* respectively) enjoyed great popular success. His *Complete Plays* were edited in 1949 by Leon Edel. The informative and highly personal *Notebooks* were published in 1947. Between 1907 and 1909 James revised many of his novels and tales, providing them with explanatory prefaces, which were collected in 1934 in a single volume entitled *The Art of Fiction*.

Evaluation and Works. Although the background of so many of James's novels is Europe, and the situations in them the conflict between the European and the American character, they remain essentially American in spirit. The vast body of his fiction is usually subdivided into three periods. The first includes *The American* (1877), *The Europeans* (1878), *Daisy Miller* (1879), *The Portrait of a Lady* (1881), *The Bostonians* (1886), *The Princess Casamassima* (1888), and *The Tragic Muse* (1890). The second period includes his story *The Figure in the Carpet* (1896), *The Other House* (1896), *The Spoils of Poynton* (1897), *What Maisie Knew* (1897), the tale *The Turn of the Screw* (1898), and *The Awkward Age* (1899). The final period includes *The Wings of the Dove* (1902), *The Ambassadors* (1903), *The Golden Bowl* (1904), *The Altar of the Dead* (1909), and two uncompleted novels, *The Ivory Tower* (1917) and *The Sense of the Past* (1917). Other writings include *Hawthorne* (1879), *Partial Portraits* (1888), *Notes of a Son and*

Brother (1914), *Notes on Novelists* (1914), and *The Middle Years* (1917).

James, Montague Rhodes. b. 1862; d. at Eton, England, June 12, 1936. A British medievalist, writer of ghost stories, and authority on Christian religious art. He was provost of King's College, Cambridge (1905–18), and of Eton (1918–36), and discovered a number of medieval psalters, pseudepigrapha, and other writings. Author of commentaries on Biblical texts, catalogues of library manuscripts, investigations of antiquarian subjects, treatises on stained glass, bibliographies, and such popular works as *Ghost Stories of an Antiquary* (1910), *More Ghost Stories* (1912), and *A Thin Ghost and Others* (1919).

James, William. b. at New York, Jan. 11, 1842; d. at Chocorua, N.H., Aug. 26, 1910. An American psychologist and philosopher; brother of Henry James (1843–1916).

Jameson (jăm′sọn), **Anna Brownell.** [Maiden name, **Murphy.**] b. at Dublin, May 17, 1794; d. at Ealing, Middlesex, England, March 17, 1860. A British author; eldest daughter of D. Brownell Murphy, Irish miniature painter. Her journal was published anonymously as *A Lady's Diary*, and then as *The Diary of an Ennuyée* in 1826. She traveled extensively in Europe and America, and in 1847 revisited Italy to write her *chef-d'oeuvre, Sacred and Legendary Art*. This appeared in four parts: *Legends of the Saints* (1848), *Legends of the Monastic Orders* (1850), *Legends of the Madonna* (1852), and *The History of our Lord*. The last was left unfinished, and was completed by Lady Eastlake after Mrs. Jameson's death. Among her other works are *Loves of the Poets* (1829), *Celebrated Female Sovereigns* (1831), *Visits and Sketches* (1834), *Winter Studies and Summer Rambles in Canada* (1838), *Social Life in Germany*, a translation of the dramas of Princess Amelia of Saxony (1840), *Memories of the Early Italian Painters* (1845), and *Miscellaneous Essays* (1846).

Jameson, Sir **Leander Starr.** [Known as **Dr. Jameson.**] b. at Edinburgh, 1853; d. Nov. 20, 1917. A Scottish physician. He practiced medicine at Kimberley, Cape Colony, and was appointed (c1890) administrator of the British South Africa Company. In this capacity he organized an attack upon the Matabele in 1893. In 1895, at the instigation of Cecil Rhodes and others, he prepared to lead an armed force to Johannesburg. He started (Dec. 29) from Pitsani, Bechuanaland, with about 600 men (chiefly drawn from the Bechuanaland and Matabele mounted police), before the preparations were complete, and was obliged to surrender to the South African Republic at Doornkop, Jan. 2, 1896. The attempt, which evoked a storm of controversy, has gone down in history as the Jameson Raid. President Kruger sent him to Great Britain for trial. In July, 1896, he was condemned to serve a term of imprisonment for having infringed the foreign enlistment act, but was released on Dec. 3, 1896, on account of ill health. He returned to South Africa, was elected a member of the Cape legislative assembly for Kimberley in 1900, was appointed a director of the De Beers Consolidated Company in 1900, and of the British South Africa Company in 1902, and was premier of Cape Colony (1904–08).

Jameson, Storm. [Full name, **Margaret Storm Jameson.**] b. at Whitby, Yorkshire, England, 1897–. An English novelist. Her books include *Happy Highways* (1920), *Farewell to Youth* (1928), *A Richer Dust* (1931), *Here Comes a Candle* (1938), *The Moon is Making* (1938), *Farewell Night, Welcome Day* (1939; American title, *The Captain's Wife*), *Europe to Let* (1940), *The Fort* (1941), *The Journal of Mary Hervey Russell* (1945), *Black Laurel* (1948), and *The Moment of Truth* (1949).

Jameson Raid. See under **Jameson,** Sir **Leander Starr.**

James Steerforth (stir′fôrth, -fọrth). See **Steerforth, James.**

James Stewart of the Glens (stū′ạrt). See **Stewart of the Glens.**

James Tyrrel (tir′ẹl), Sir. See **Tyrrel,** Sir **James.**

James Wait (wāt). See **Wait, James.**

Jamieson (jă′mi.sọn), **John.** b. at Glasgow, March 3, 1759; d. at Edinburgh, July 12, 1838. A Scottish clergyman, antiquary, and philologist. His chief work is *An Etymological Dictionary of the Scottish Language* (1808, supplement 1825).

Jammes (zhăm), **Francis.** b. at Tournay, in the Pyrenees, France, Dec. 2, 1868; d. at Orthez, France, 1938. A French poet and novelist. He was the author of much verse of rural and religious inspiration, of which the best-known collections are *De l'angélus de l'aube à l'angélus du soir* (1898) and *Géorgiques chrétiennes* (3 vols., 1912). His novels include *M. le Curé d'Ozeron* (1918) and *Le Poète rustique* (1920). Recognized as a unique talent from the publication of *De l'angélus*, he became renowned, after his conversion (1905) to Roman Catholicism, as a "Christian Vergil." Closely associated with Gide for a time, he later broke with him under the influence of a fellow Roman Catholic, Paul Claudel. His later works are considered less successful than those written before World War I.

Jamshid (jam′shid; Persian, jam.shēd′). [Also, **Jem.**] In the *Shahnamah*, by the poet Firdausi, the fourth king of the Pishdadian or earliest dynasty, and culture hero of Persia. He is said to have reigned 700 years, the first 300 of which were happy and beneficent. According to tradition, he smelted iron and taught its use in the arts, taught weaving, distinguished castes, subdued the demons or demons, discovered precious stones and minerals, invented medicine, and first practiced navigation. In his homage men first celebrated the New Year. However, Jamshid became proud and boasted of being immortal. For this he was punished and forced to flee before Dahak (the three-headed dragon who devoured the faithful) and remained concealed 100 years. When he appeared on the shore of the China Sea he was seized and sawed asunder by Dahak. Jamshid is the Avestan Yima, the first man of Iranian mythology.

Jamy (jā′mi). In Shakespeare's *Henry V*, a Scottish captain. He does not appear in the quarto of 1600, possibly because of fear of offending the feelings of James VI of Scotland.

ḑ, d or j; ş, s or sh; ţ, t or ch; ẓ, z or zh; o, F. cloche; ü, F. menu; čh, Sc. loch; ñ, F. bonbon.

Jane (jān). The innocent young bride of Ralph, Simon Eyre's journeyman shoemaker in Dekker's *Shoemaker's Holiday.*

Jane Bennet (ben'ęt). See **Bennet, Jane.**

Jane Clegg (kleg). A drama (1913) of middle-class Irish life and character, by St. John Ervine. Jane Clegg, the key figure, must bear the burden of a weak and cringing husband, who is involved in an affair with Kitty. Jane finally realizes his utter inability to be loyal to her, and firmly but quietly sends him off to Kitty despite his protest that it is indecent to do so.

Jane Eyre (ār). A novel by Charlotte Brontë, published in 1847 under the pseudonym Currer Bell. Its title is the name of its principal character, a woman who is made interesting in spite of a lack of beauty, birth, money, and all the conventional attributes of a heroine. The book is partly autobiographical, and caused much comment, bringing its writer prominently before the public. An orphan, Jane lives with her harsh and unsympathetic aunt, Mrs. Reed. At the age of ten she is sent away to the Lowood Asylum, a charitable institution. After much unhappiness there she finds a position as a governess to the young ward of Mr. Rochester, at Thornfield Hall. The grim Rochester is softened by the wit and spirit he finds in Jane, and they fall in love. Their marriage is prevented by the announcement that Rochester already has a wife. Jane finds that she is insane and is kept in a small room in the Hall; unable, knowing this, to endure her situation at the Hall, she flees into the moors, where she is found by the clergyman, St. John Rivers, and his sisters. She is almost persuaded to marry Rivers, but senses intuitively that Rochester is in trouble and needs her. She returns to Thornfield Hall to find that the mad wife has set fire to it, has perished in the flames, and that Rochester is blinded as a result of his efforts to rescue his wife. Jane marries him, and helps him escape from the despair into which he has fallen as a result of these catastrophes.

Jane Fairfax (fār'faks). A novel by Naomi Royde-Smith, published in 1940.

Jane Murdstone (mėrd'stōn, -stǫn). See **Murdstone, Jane.**

Jane Shore (shōr). A tragedy by Henry Chettle and John Day, entered in Henslowe's diary in May, 1603, thought to be a revision of an older play.

Jane Shore. [Full title, **The Tragedy of Jane Shore.**] A tragedy (1714) by Rowe. According to Rowe, the play was "written in imitation of Shakespeare's style," but various critics have pointed out that it is more akin to the plays of the Restoration playwright John Banks. The heroine is a self-sacrificing woman who gives up everything for her lover, the Marquess of Dorset, Thomas Grey. She is accused by King Richard of sorcery, made to do penance, and then turned out in poverty, from which she is finally rescued by her husband.

Janet Dempster (jan'ęt, jạ.net', demp'stėr). See **Dempster, Janet.**

Janet's Repentance. One of the tales in George Eliot's *Scenes of Clerical Life.*

Jane Wackles (jān wak'lz). See **Wackles, Jane.**

Janiculum (ja.nik'ụ.lum). A ridge on the right bank of the Tiber, in Rome, opposite the Capitoline and the Aventine.

Janizaries (jan'i.zär.iz). [Also, **Janissaries** (jan'i-sär.iz).] A former body of Turkish infantry, constituting the sultan's guard and the main standing army, first organized in the 14th century, and until the latter part of the 17th century largely recruited from compulsory conscripts and converts taken from the Rayas or Christian subjects. In later times Turks and other Mohammedans joined the corps on account of the various privileges attached to it. The body became large and very powerful and turbulent, often controlling the destiny of the government; and, after a revolt purposely provoked by the sultan Mahmud II in 1826, many thousands of Janizaries were massacred, and the organization was abolished.

Januarius (jan.ụ.ār'i.us), Saint. d. c305. A Christian martyr, beheaded during the reign of Diocletian. He was bishop of Beneventum and is the patron saint of Naples, where relics, which are said to be his head and some of his blood, are preserved. The blood is supposed to have the miraculous power of becoming fluid when it is brought near the head. Some skeptics have doubted the authenticity of the miracle, and it has been suggested that the liquefaction of the substance within the vial is actually induced by a rise in temperature or by the chemistry of the substance itself, quite independent of the temperature. However, no critic has yet succeeded in explaining satisfactorily by any known scientific law the fact that the substance not only undergoes periodic liquefaction but also changes in volume and weight. The festival of this saint is celebrated on September 19.

January (jan'ụ.ār.i). See under **Merchant's Tale, The.**

Janus (jā'nus). In Roman mythology, the two-faced god of doorways and the special patron of the beginning of all undertakings. As god of beginnings his blessing was sought for the beginning of each day, month, and year, and at births, the beginning of life. Janus was undoubtedly an ancient pre-Italian deity; he and his female counterpart, Jana, were sun and moon gods. The primitive Janus, as god of light and sky, was rapidly obscured by Roman concepts. As a Roman deity, he was credited with having given man the knowledge of agriculture, civil law, and coinage. As the protector of doors and gateways, he was represented as holding a staff or scepter in the right hand and a key in the left; and as the god of the sun's rising and setting he had two faces, one looking to the east, and the other to the west. His temple at Rome was kept open in time of war, and was closed only in the rare event of universal peace. His festival, the Agonia, was celebrated on January 9.

Japhetic (jạ.fet'ik). A disputed linguistic grouping developed especially by the Russian philologist Marr. This was an attempt to link the early, unknown languages of Europe and W Asia (the mysterious Basque and Etruscan tongues, for instance, and sometimes Sumerian and Elamite) into one family with the Caucasian languages. This grouping is now generally considered to be quite without foundation.

fat, fāte, fär, ȧsk, fāre; net, mē, hėr; pin, pīne; not, nōte, möve, nôr; up, lūte, pùll; ᴛн, then;

Jaquenetta (jak.ẹ.net′ạ). In Shakespeare's *Love's Labour's Lost*, a country maid with whom Costard and Armado are in love.

Jaques (jā′kwēz). In Shakespeare's *As You Like It*, a philosophical companion of the exiled duke. He is usually spoken of as "the melancholy Jaques," and serves as a kind of commentator upon the others. It is he who makes the famous speech about man's seven ages beginning "All the world's a stage" (II.vii). He does not appear in Lodge's *Rosalynde*, from which Shakespeare derived his story.

Jaques. [Also, **Jaques de Boys** (or **de Bois**).] In Shakespeare's *As You Like It*, an elder brother of Orlando and second son of Sir Rowland de Boys.

Jaques De Prie (dẹ prē′). See **De Prie, Jaques.**

jargon. **1.** Confused, unintelligible talk; irregular, formless speech or language; gabble; gibberish; babble.

> He was al coltissh, ful of ragerye,
> And ful of jargon as a flekked pye.
> (Chaucer, *Merchant's Tale*.)

What more exquisite jargon could the wit of man invent than this definition?—"The act of a being in power, as far forth as in power."
(Locke, *Human Understanding*.)

Specifically—**2.** A barbarous mixed speech, without literary monuments; a rude language resulting from the mixture of two or more discordant languages, especially of a cultivated language with a barbarous one.

> For my own part, besides the jargon and patois of several provinces, I understand no less than six languages. (Sir T. Browne, *Religio Medici*.)

3. Any phraseology peculiar to a sect, profession, trade, art, or science; professional slang or cant.

> This society has a peculiar cant and jargon of their own. (Swift, *Gulliver's Travels*.)

Jarley (jär′li), **Mrs.** In Dickens's *Old Curiosity Shop*, the merry, kind-hearted owner and exhibitor of Jarley's wax-works, "the delight of the nobility and gentry, and the peculiar pet of the royal family." She befriends Little Nell.

Jarndyce (järn′dis), **John.** In Dickens's *Bleak House*, the owner of Bleak House, and the benevolent guardian of Richard Carstone, Ada Clare, and Esther Summerson. It is his habit, when he is disappointed in human nature, to feel a severe east wind.

Jarvie (jär′vi), **Nicol.** A magistrate of Glasgow, a character in Sir Walter Scott's novel *Rob Roy*.

Jarvis Lorry (jär′vis lor′i), **Mr.** See **Lorry, Mr. Jarvis.**

Jason (jā′sọn). [Also, **Iason**.] In Greek legend, the leader of the Argonautic expedition. He was born at Iolcus, in Thessaly, was a son of Aeson and Polymede, and was brought up under the instruction of Chiron, the centaur. The legends concerning him are numerous and varied. His greatest exploit was the expedition to Colchis with the other Argonauts to obtain the Golden Fleece. This was a quest imposed by Pelias, Jason's uncle, who had usurped the kingdom of Iolcus. He secured the Golden Fleece with the aid of the sorceress Medea, daughter of Aeetes, king of Colchis, who fell in love with him. She protected him from the bulls breathing fire and hoofed with brass, which he was obliged, in order to obtain the fleece, to yoke to the plow, and from the armed men who sprang up from the dragon's teeth which he was required to sow in the fields. From other perils, also, she saved him, and fled with him and the fleece. Jason finally deserted Medea for Glauce, daughter of Creon, king of Corinth. But Medea, in revenge, killed both Glauce and Creon. Jason died alone, while sitting in the shade of his famous old ship, the *Argo*.

Jason. [Full title, **The Life and Death of Jason.**] A long poem (1867) by William Morris, based on the Jason legend. The style is deliberately medieval rather than classical, infused with a spirit of melancholy and romance.

Jasper Dryfesdale (jas′pẹr drĭfs′dāl). See **Dryfesdale, Jasper.**

Jasper Packlemerton (pak′ẹl.mẻr.tọn). See **Packlemerton, Jasper.**

Jasper Petulengro (peṭ.ụ.leng′grō). See **Petulengro, Jasper.**

Javan (jā′vạn). In the Bible, according to Genesis, son of Japheth and ancestor of Elisha, Tarshish, and Kittim. In Ezek. xxvii. 13 he is mentioned as carrying on trade with the Tyrians (compare also Isa. lxvi. 19).

Javier (Hä.Byer′), Saint **Francisco.** See **Xavier, Saint Francis.**

Jeaffreson (jef′ẻr.sọn), **John Cordy.** b. at Framlingham, Suffolk, England, Jan. 14, 1831; d. Feb. 2, 1901. An English novelist and miscellaneous writer. Among his works are *A Book about Doctors* (1860), *Olive Blake's Good Work* (1862), *Live it Down* (1863), *Not Dead Yet* (1864), *Life of Robert Stephenson* (1864), *A Book about Lawyers* (1866), *A Book about the Clergy* (1870), *Annals of Oxford* (1870), *The Real Lord Byron* (1883), *The Real Shelley* (1885), and *Lady Hamilton and Lord Nelson* (1887).

Jealous Ghost, The. A novel by L. A. G. Strong, published in 1930.

Jealous Lovers, The. An academic play by Thomas Randolph, presented at Cambridge in 1632 before Charles I and his Queen.

Jealous Wife, The. A comedy (1761) by the elder George Colman, presumably founded on various episodes involving Sophia Western in Fielding's *Tom Jones*. The play was very successful in its time and continued to be produced well into the next century.

Jeames (jēmz). A conventional name for a footman or flunkey. Thackeray's story *The Diary of C. Jeames de la Pluche*, which appeared in *Punch*, is the diary of a footman; Thackeray himself occasionally used the full name as a pseudonym.

Jeames's Diary. See **Diary of C. Jeames de la Pluche.**

Jean Crapaud (zhäṅ krȧ.pō′). See **Crapaud, Jean.**

Jean de Meung (or **Meun**) (dẹ mẻṅ′). [Pseudonym of **Jean Clopinel**.] b. at Meun-sur-Loire, Orléanais, France, c1250; d. at Paris, c1305. A French poet. He is known chiefly as having continued, after a lapse of 40 years, *Le Roman de la rose*, a poem undertaken c1237 by a young poet, Guillaume de Lorris, and left incomplete at the time of his death. To the 4,000 lines of Guillaume, Jean de Meung added almost 19,000; his satirical, critical verses on clergy, nobility, and especially women and their wiles contrast with the courtly approach of the earlier part. His translations into French include the *De re militari* of Vegetius (1284), the correspondence of Héloïse and Abélard, and the *Topographia Hiberniae* of Giraldus Cambrensis (Giraldus de Barri). *L'Amitié spirituelle*, translated from the English of the monk Aelred, and the French translation of Boethius's *De consolatione philosophica* have both been lost. Between 1291 and 1296 Jean de Meung wrote his *Testament*, a curious piece of work replete with sarcasm and criticism, especially of the women and of the mendicant orders of his day.

Jeanie Deans (jē'ni dēnz). See **Deans, Jeanie.**

Jeans (jēnz), Sir **James Hopwood.** b. at Southport, England, Sept. 11, 1877; d. at Dorking, England, Sept. 16, 1946. An English astronomer, physicist, mathematician, and philosopher, noted especially for his investigations on the dynamical theory of gases as applied to cosmogony, thus giving an explanation of the formation of spiral nebulae, and author of numerous works, both technical and popular, on the relationships between mathematical concepts and the natural world. He was educated at Cambridge, taught at Princeton (1905–09) and Cambridge (1910–12), and was professor at the Royal Institution (1935–46). He was elected to the Royal Society in 1906, to the Royal Astronomical Society in 1913, and he was knighted in 1928. His works include *Theoretical Mechanics* (1906), *The Mathematical Theory of Electricity and Magnetism* (1908), *Radiation and the Quantum Theory* (1914), *Problems of Cosmogony* (1919), *Atomicity and Quanta* (1926), *Astronomy and Cosmogony* (1928), *The Universe Around Us* (1929), *The Mysterious Universe* (1930), *Through Space and Time* (1930), *The Stars in Their Courses* (1931), *Physics and Philosophy* (1942), and *The Growth of Physical Science* (1948).

Jean Valjean (zhäṅ vȧl.zhäṅ). See **Valjean, Jean.**

Jebb (jeb), Sir **Richard Claverhouse.** b. at Dundee, Scotland, Aug. 27, 1841; d. at Cambridge, England, Dec. 9, 1905. A British professor, scholar, and translator. He founded the Cambridge Philological Society, the Society for the Promotion of Hellenic Studies, and the British School of Archaeology at Athens. He served as professor of Greek (1875–89) at Glasgow, and at Cambridge from 1889 until his death, and was professor of ancient history (1898 *et seq.*) at the Royal Academy. His works include *Translations from Greek and Latin* (1873), *The Attic Orators* (1876–80), *Primer of Greek Literature* (1877), *Modern Greece* (1880), *Bentley* (1882), *Homer: An Introduction to the Iliad and the Odyssey* (1887), and *The Growth and Influence of Greek Poetry* (1893). He translated the *Characters* of Theophrastus (1870), the *Rhetoric* of Aristotle (1873), and the *Tragedies* of Sophocles (8 vols., 1880–96). His *Essays and Letters* were published in 1907.

Jebusites (jeb'ū̇.sīts). A Canaanitish nation which long withstood the Israelites. The stronghold of the Jebusites was Jebus on Mount Zion, a part of the site of Jerusalem, of which they were dispossessed by David. 2 Sam. v. 6–9.

Jedburgh (jed'bur.ọ). [Locally called **Jeddart**.] A royal burgh and manufacturing town in SE Scotland, in Roxburghshire, ab. 12 mi. SE of Selkirk, ab. 370 mi. N of London by rail. Its abbey is one of the chief Scottish ecclesiastical ruins. It was founded in 1118 by David I, but the existing nave, well-proportioned and excellent in details, is in Early English style. What remains of the choir is massive Norman. The town has associations with Mary, Queen of Scots, who was once taken ill here, and with Prince Charlie, Burns, and Wordsworth.

Jeddart justice (jed'ȧrt). [Also: **Jedwood** (jed'wụ̇d) or **Jedburgh justice**.] The practice of hanging the culprit first and finding him guilty afterwards, originating in a summary practice of this sort associated with the Scottish town of Jedburgh during the period of warfare in the border country between England and Scotland. It may be compared with "Abingdon Law" in the south of England, and "lynch law" in the United States.

Jedediah Cleishbotham (jed.ẹ.dī'ạ klēsh'boᴛʜ.ạm). See **Cleishbotham, Jedediah.**

Jeeves (jēvz). The valet or "gentleman's personal gentleman" of Bertie Wooster, in the stories of P. G. Wodehouse. Skillful at extricating his young master from ridiculous difficulties, he has become the type of the obsequious but intelligent manservant.

Jefferies (jef'riz), **Richard.** b. near Swindon, Wiltshire, England, Nov. 6, 1848; d. at Goring, Sussex, England, Aug. 14, 1887. An English writer, noted principally for his descriptions of nature. Author of *The Game-Keeper at Home* (1878), *Wild Life in a Southern Country* (1879), *Nature near London* (1883), *Story of My Heart* (1883), *Life of the Fields* (1884), *Red-Deer* (1884), *Amaryllis at the Fair* (1887), and others.

Jefferson Brick (jef'ėr.sọn brik'). See **Brick, Jefferson.**

Jeffrey (jef'ri), **Francis.** [Title, Lord **Jeffrey**.] b. at Edinburgh, Oct. 23, 1773; d. there, Jan. 26, 1850. A Scottish critic, essayist, and jurist. He studied at Queen's College, Oxford, for a part of one year (1791–92), and was admitted to the Scottish bar on Dec. 16, 1794. He succeeded Sydney Smith as responsible editor of the *Edinburgh Review*, of which, with Smith, H. P. Brougham, and Francis Horner, he had been a founder. The review was a success from its first number (Oct. 10, 1802). Jeffrey's legal practice continued to increase until July 2, 1829, when he was unanimously chosen dean of the Faculty of Advocates, and resigned his editorship of the *Review* to Macvey Napier. In 1830 he was appointed lord advocate. After the passage of the Reform Bill he was returned to Parliament for Edinburgh, Dec. 19, 1832. In May, 1834, he accepted a seat in the Court of Session, and became Lord Jeffrey. Jeffrey's criticisms of the writings of Wordsworth, Shelley, Keats, and the other poets of the romantic school were entirely unsympathetic, though later in life he admitted the excellence of their work. He visited America in 1813 for six months.

Jeffreys (jef′riz), **George.** [Title, 1st Baron **Jeffreys of Wem.**] b. at Acton, Denbighshire, Wales, 1648; d. at London, April 18, 1689. A British judge. He was called to the bar in 1668, and was appointed common sergeant of the city of London in 1671. Seeing no hope of further advancement from the popular party, with which he had hitherto been associated, he ingratiated himself with the Duke of York (later James II), with the result that he was appointed solicitor general to the duke, and was knighted in 1677. In 1678 he was made recorder of London, a position which he was compelled by Parliament to resign in 1680. He became chief justice of Chester in 1680 and of England in 1683, and was elevated to the post of lord chancellor of England in 1685. He used his position as chief justice and as chancellor to make the judiciary, which had been a stronghold of the opposition, the chief agent in furthering the attempt of James II to make himself an absolute monarch. He rendered himself notorious by the flagrant injustice and brutality which he displayed in the trials (called "the Bloody Assizes") of the participants in Monmouth's Rebellion (1685). At least 320 were executed, after trials in which often no defense was heard; hundreds more were transported. He was imprisoned on the overthrow of James II and died in the Tower of London.

Jehane Saint-Pol (zhän sänt.pôl′; French, saṅ.pol). See **Saint-Pol, Jehane.**

Jehangir (jẹ.hän″gēr′). See **Jahangir.**

Jehu (jē′hū). A common name for a coachman, especially a reckless one. 2 Kings, ix. 20: "the driving is like the driving of Jehu the son of Nimshi; for he driveth furiously."

Jekyll (jek′il, jē′kil), **Dr.** A physician who, by a miraculous drug, can transform himself into a vicious being known as Mr. Hyde, in R. L. Stevenson's *Dr. Jekyll and Mr. Hyde.*

Jellyby (jel′i.bi), **Mrs.** In Dickens's *Bleak House,* a strong-minded woman, so completely occupied with missionary and charitable work, and particularly with emigration to the fictitious African settlement of Borrioboola-Gha, that she has no time to attend to her household duties.

Jemmy Dawson (jem′i dô′sọn). See under **Dawson, James.**

Jemmy Twitcher (twich′ẽr). See **Twitcher, Jemmy.**

Jenghiz Khan (jeng′giz kän′). See **Genghis Khan.**

Jenkins (jeng′kinz), **Herbert.** b. at Norwich, Norfolk, England, 1876; d. June 8, 1923. An English publisher and detective writer. After managing the publishing firm of John Lane, the Bodley Head, for 11 years, he founded his own London firm. In addition to his business activities, he wrote many articles and stories, including those dealing with Bindle, a London Cockney. Author of *Bindle* (1916), *The Night Club* (1917), *Adventures of Bindle* (1918), *John Dene of Toronto* (1919), *Malcolm Sage, Detective* (1920), and *Mrs. Bindle* (1921). His chief work is *Life of George Borrow* (1911).

Jenkins, Mrs. Winifred. Tabitha Bramble's maid in Tobias Smollett's novel *Humphry Clinker.*

Jenkins' Ear, War of. A name popularly given to the war between Great Britain and Spain which broke out in 1739 and became merged in the War of the Austrian Succession. Its immediate cause was the grievance of an English mariner, Robert Jenkins, who alleged that he had been tortured by the Spaniards, with the loss of his ear. Activity in the war was primarily in the Caribbean area, Puerto Bello being captured and Cartagena bombarded, but some fighting also occurred in Georgia and in Florida, which was attacked twice (1740, 1743) by Oglethorpe.

Jenkinson (jeng′kin.sọn), **Ephraim.** A venerable-looking swindler in Oliver Goldsmith's *Vicar of Wakefield.* He swindles the vicar out of his horse.

Jenkinson, Mrs. Mountstuart. In Meredith's *Egoist,* an epigrammatic lady who says always "the remembered if not the right thing."

Jenner (jen′ẽr), **Edward.** b. at Berkeley, Gloucestershire, England, May 17, 1749; d. there, Jan. 26, 1823. An English physician, famous as the discoverer of vaccination. His investigation of cowpox began very early, and was suggested by the local rustic tradition that dairymaids who contracted the disease were exempt from smallpox. On May 14, 1796, he vaccinated James Phipps, a boy of eight, with lymph from the hand of a dairymaid, and on July 1 inoculated the same boy with smallpox. The experiment was successful; an account of it (*Inquiry into the Cause and Effects of the Variolae Vaccinae*) was published in June, 1798.

Jenner, Thomas. fl. 1631–56. An English author, engraver, and publisher. In the reigns of Charles I and Charles II he kept a print shop at the Royal Exchange which was frequented by Pepys and Evelyn.

Jennifer (jen′i.fẽr). A novel by John Palmer, published in 1926.

Jennings (jen′ingz), **Ezra.** In Wilkie Collins's novel *The Moonstone,* a doctor's assistant, a man of haunting demeanor, with "piebald hair." He is instrumental in solving the mystery.

Jennings, Mrs. A vulgar friend of Elinor and Marianne Dashwood in Jane Austen's novel *Sense and Sensibility.*

Jenny Balchristie (jen′i bal.kris′ti). See **Balchristie, Jenny.**

Jenny Rintherout (rin′thẽr.out). See **Rintherout, Jenny.**

"Jenny Wren" (ren). See **Cleaver, Fanny.**

Jenyns (jen′inz), **Soame.** b. at London, Jan. 1, 1704; d. there, Dec. 18, 1787. An English writer and politician. In 1757 he published *Free Enquiry into the Nature and Origin of Evil,* and in 1765 *The Objections to the Taxation of our American Colonies by the Legislature of Great Britain briefly considered.* His *View of the Internal Evidences of the Christian Religion* was published in 1776.

Jephthes (jef′thēz) or **Jephtha** (jef′thạ). A play by George Buchanan, written between 1539 and 1542.

Jepson (jep′sọn), **Edgar.** b. at Kenilworth, Warwickshire, England, Nov. 28, 1863; d. at Hampstead, London, April 11, 1938. An English novelist. Author of *Sibyl Falcon* (1895), *The Passion for Romance* (1896), *The Keepers of the People* (1898), *On the Edge of the Empire* (1899), *The Admirable Tinker* (1904), *Tangled Wedlock* (1908), *The Girl's*

ḍ, d or j; ṣ, s or sh; ṭ, t or ch; ẓ, z or zh; o, F. cloche; ü, F. menu; ċh, Sc. loch; ṅ, F. bonbon.

Head (1910), *Pollyooly* (1911), *The Gillingham Rubies* (1915), *The Night Hawk* (1916), *The Professional Prince* (1917), *The Loudwater Mystery* (1919), *A Prince in Petrograd* (1921), *The Smuggled Masterpiece* (1923), *Buried Rubies* (1925), *The Tragedies of Mr. Pip* (1926), *The Splendid Adventure of Hannibal Tod* (1927), *The Murder in Romney Marsh* (1929), *The Moon Gods* (1930), *A Hundred Thousand Guineas* (1931), *The Secret Square* (1933), *The Grinning Avenger* (1934), *An Accidental Don Juan* (1935), and *Lucy and the Dark Gods* (1936). His *Memories of a Victorian* (1933) and *Memories of an Edwardian* are autobiographical.

Jeremiah (jer.ẹ.mī′ạ). The second of the major prophets of Israel. His history is given in the Old Testament book which bears his name.

Jeremiah Flintwinch (flint′winch). See **Flintwinch, Jeremiah.**

Jeremy (jer′ẹ.mi). A witty valet in Congreve's *Love for Love.*

Jeremy. A story of school life, from a small boy's point of view, by Hugh Walpole, published in 1919. It was followed by *Jeremy and Hamlet* (1923) and *Jeremy at Crale* (1927). Hamlet is the boy's dog.

Jerome (jẹ.rōm′; British also jer′ọm), Saint. [Original name, **Eusebius Hieronymus.**] b. at Stridon, Pannonia (in what is now Yugoslavia), c340; d. at Bethlehem, in Palestine, Sept. 30, 420. A Father and Doctor of the Roman Catholic Church. He studied at Rome under Donatus the grammarian and Victorinus the rhetorician. In 373, during a journey through the Orient, he was attacked with a severe illness. During his convalescence he studied Greek and scriptural exegesis. From 374 he led an eremetical life in the desert, leaving it to be ordained at Antioch in 379. After two years at Constantinople with Saint Gregory Nazianzus, he removed to Rome in 382, where he advised Pope Damasus I. While there he taught a school of Roman ladies and expounded to them the doctrine of monasticism. He also undertook, at the Pope's request, a revision of the Latin Bible in the light of his scholarly knowledge of Eastern languages. After the death of Damasus he entered a monastery at Bethlehem, where he continued his work on the Bible and on his other writings. He published the Latin version of the Bible known as the Vulgate, which was established (1546) by the Council of Trent as the official version of the Bible for the Roman Catholic Church. Jerome by his knowledge of Greek and Hebrew introduced the treasures of the Eastern Church into the West.

Jerome, Jerome K. [Full name, **Jerome Klapka Jerome.**] b. at Walsall, England, May 2, 1859; d. June 14, 1927. An English novelist and dramatist, known chiefly as a humorist. He was at various times clerk, teacher, actor, and journalist. His stage experiences are embodied in *On the Stage—and Off* (1885) and *Stage Land* (1889); and he wrote a number of plays, among them *Barbara* (1886), *When Greek Meets Greek* (1888), *Sunset* (1888), *New Lamps for Old* (1890), *MacHaggis* (1897), *Miss Hobbs* (1900), *Susan in Search of a Husband* (1906), *The Passing of the Third Floor Back* (1908), and *The Master of Mrs. Chilvers* (1911). In 1892 he founded the *Idler* with Robert Barr, retiring in

1897; he was editor (1893–97) of *To-day*. His other publications include *Idle Thoughts of an Idle Fellow* (1886), *Three Men in a Boat* (1889), *Novel Notes* (1893), *Sketches in Lavender, Blue, and Green* (1897), *Three Men on Wheels* (1900), *Tea Table Talk* (1903), *Tommy and Co.* (1904), *American Wives and Others* (1904), and *Idle Ideas in 1905* (1905).

Jeronimo (je.ron′i.mō). See **Hieronimo.**

Jerrold (jer′ọld), **Douglas William.** b. at London, Jan. 3, 1803; d. there, June 8, 1857. An English dramatist, satirist, and humorist. From 1813 to 1815 he served as midshipman in the Royal Navy, which was engaged in operations against Napoleon. Returning to London in 1816, he supported himself by working as a printer's apprentice, and by contributions to periodical literature. A farce, *More Frightened than Hurt*, was produced at London on April 30, 1821, and later at Paris. *Black-eyed Susan, or All in the Downs*, a melodrama, produced June 8, 1829, at the Surrey Theatre, was his first important success. In 1836 he undertook the management of the Strand Theatre, but without success. He now turned his attention to the reviews and magazines, contributing to the *Athenæum, Blackwood's*, and others. He attached himself to *Punch* at its appearance in 1841, and was a constant contributor until his death. His articles were signed Q. His greatest success was *Mrs. Caudle's Curtain Lectures* (1846). From 1852 until his death he edited *Lloyd's Weekly Newspaper*. In all, he wrote about 40 plays.

Jerrold, William Blanchard. b. at London, Dec. 23, 1826; d. at Westminster, London, March 10, 1884. An English journalist and author; eldest son of Douglas William Jerrold. On the death of his father he succeeded to the editorship of *Lloyd's Weekly Newspaper*. A Liberal in politics, he argued for the North during the Civil War. His chief work is *Life of Napoleon III* (1875–82). He also wrote a number of plays, including *Cool as a Cucumber* (1851).

Jerry Blackacre (jer′i blak′ā″kėr). See **Blackacre, Jerry.**

Jerry Cruncher (krun′chėr). See **Cruncher, Jerry.**

Jerry Sneak (snēk). See **Sneak, Jerry.**

"Jersey Lily," the. See **Langtry, Lily.**

Jerusalem (jẹ.rö′sạ.lẹm). A symbolic and mystical work by William Blake, published in 1804, in which the world of the imagination is defined as the world of eternity, "the real and eternal world of which the Vegetable Universe is but a faint shadow."

Jerusalem Chamber. A room at the SW side of Westminster Abbey, London, dating from 1376 or 1386. Henry IV died in this room (thus fulfilling a prophecy that he would die in "Jerusalem"). The Upper House of Convocation of the Province of Canterbury meets in it. It probably derives its name from tapestries with the history of Jerusalem on them, which hung on the walls.

Jerusalem Delivered. [Italian, **Gerusalemme Liberata.**] An epic poem by Torquato Tasso, relating to the deliverance of Jerusalem from the unbelievers by the Crusaders under Godfrey of Bouillon (published 1581; Eng. trans. by Fairfax, 1600, and James, 1865).

Jervis (jär′vis, jẽr′-), **Mrs.** The housekeeper of Mr. B. in Samuel Richardson's novel *Pamela*. She tries to protect Pamela from Mr. B.'s advances.

Jessamy Bride, the. A name given by Goldsmith in certain of his writings to Miss Mary Horneck, with whom he is supposed to have been in love.

Jessamy Bride, The. A novel (1897) by F. Frankfort Moore.

Jesse (jes′ē). [Also, **Isai**.] In the Bible, the father of David, king of Israel. As the ancestor of the royal family, he also figured as the progenitor of the Messiah, and he appears in genealogies, as in the medieval "trees of Jesse," as the base of the line from which Jesus sprang. 1 Sam. xvi.

Jesse, Fryniwyd Tennyson. An English novelist and playwright; grandniece of Alfred Tennyson, and wife (married 1918) of Harold March Harwood. She collaborated with her husband on the plays *The Mask, Billeted, The Pelican,* and *How to Be Healthy Though Married,* and is author also of the dramas *Quarantine* and *Anyhouse.* Her novels include *The Milky Way, Secret Bread, Beggars on Horseback, Tom Fool, Moonraker, Act of God,* and *London Front.*

Jessel (jes′el), **Miss.** A character in "The Turn of the Screw," published in *The Two Magics* (1898) by Henry James.

Jessica (jes′i.ka). In Shakespeare's *Merchant of Venice,* the daughter of Shylock. She elopes with Lorenzo, taking her father's jewels and money.

jestbook. A book containing a collection of jests, jokes, or funny stories or sayings.

Jesuits (jez′ū.its). Members of the Society of Jesus (or Company of Jesus), founded by Saint Ignatius of Loyola in 1534. They were so called (first, according to one tradition, by Calvin, c1550) from the name given to the order by its founder, *Societas Jesu,* "the Company (or Society) of Jesus." Membership includes two general classes (non-priests and priests) and six grades, namely, novices, formed temporal coadjutors, approved scholastics, formed spiritual coadjutors, the professed of three vows, and the professed of four vows. The professed of the four vows are the most influential class; they form the general congregation and fill the highest offices and the leading missions. The general is elected for life by the general congregation.

Jew of Malta (môl′ta), **The.** A tragedy by Christopher Marlowe. It was written c1589, and was frequently acted between 1591 and 1596 by the Lord Admiral's and possibly the Lord Chamberlain's companies. It was revived in 1601 and 1633. The earliest English edition extant is dated 1633, and was edited, somewhat altered, by Thomas Heywood. Its success may have influenced Shakespeare in his writing of *The Merchant of Venice.* Marlowe may have got the germ of his plot from contemporary gossip about a Jew, David Passi, who lived in Constantinople, and the part played by him in a Turkish attack upon Malta. The ghost of Machiavelli (or Machiavel, in one of the spellings of the day), who scorns religion and "holds there is no sin but ignorance," introduces the play. At the beginning some sympathy is aroused for Barabas because, as a Jew, a large portion of his wealth is to be taken for the defense of Malta. When Barabas protests, his whole estate is confiscated and his house made into a nunnery. He thereupon bids his daughter, Abigail, to pretend to be converted to Christianity so that she may become a nun and recover a portion of the wealth which he has hidden beneath the floor of the house. In preparation for revenge he also educates Ithamore, a vicious slave, in the ways of a Machiavellian villain. Abigail is in love with Don Mathias and both he and Don Lodowick are in love with her. Barabas turns this to account by making each so jealous of the other that they kill each other in a duel. When Abigail, in despair at losing her lover, actually does become a Christian nun, her enraged father sends poisoned porridge to the nunnery and kills everyone. Two friars now determine to proclaim the fact of Barabas's dreadful deeds, but he has Ithamore strangle one and the other is accused of the murder. Fearing now that Ithamore may blackmail him, Barabas poisons him, his mistress, and her servant. The Governor of Malta imprisons Barabas, but he escapes by feigning death and betrays the island to the Turks. After being made governor himself by the Turks, he decides to betray them to the Christians. The Christian governor, however, has now learned the game, and traps Barabas in his own contrivance, a collapsible banquet floor laid over a cauldron. In the third and fourth acts the sensational trickery makes the play almost a parody of villainy.

Jewsbury (jöz′bẽr.i), **Geraldine Endsor.** b. at Measham, Derbyshire, England, 1812; d. Sept. 23, 1880. An English novelist; sister of Maria Jane Jewsbury. In 1841 she became associated with Thomas Carlyle and his wife; moved to Chelsea to be near them in 1854. Among her novels are *Zoe* (1845), *The Half-Sisters* (1848), and *Sorrows of Gentility* (1856). She was also the author of several children's stories and short tales.

Jewsbury, Maria Jane. b. at Measham, Derbyshire, England, Oct. 25, 1800; d. at Poona, India, Oct. 4, 1833. An English author; sister of Geraldine Endsor Jewsbury. She wrote *Phantasmagoria, Letters to the Young,* and *Lays of Leisure Hours.* Her best work appeared in the *Athenæum.*

Jezebel (jez′e.bel). [Also, **Jezabel**.] In the Bible, the wife of Ahab, king of Israel, whom she married before his accession, and by whom she became the mother of Athaliah, queen of Judah, and of Ahaziah and Jehoram, kings of Israel. She was a Phoenician princess, daughter of Ethbaal, king of the Sidonians, and established the Phoenician worship at the court of Ahab. She was put to death by order of Jehu. 1 Kings, xvi. 31, xxi. 25; 2 Kings, ix. 30–37.

Jezebel. From the wicked Jezebel of the Bible, any shameless, abandoned woman, especially one who paints her face or uses meretricious adornments: as, "Mrs. Jenkins was . . . insulted with the opprobrious name of painted Jezebel" (Smollett's *Humphry Clinker*).

Jim Hawkins (jim hô′kinz). See **Hawkins, Jim.**

Jim Lingard (ling′gärd). See **Lingard, Jim.**

Jingle (jing′gl), **Alfred.** [Also, **Charles Fitz Marshall**.] A swindler with an airy temperament and a glib tongue, in Dickens's *Pickwick Papers.* He

---

ḍ, d or j; ṣ, s or sh; ṭ, t or ch; ẓ, z or zh; o, F. cloche; ü, F. menu; ch, Sc. loch; ṅ, F. bonbon.

speaks in headlines, with the verbs left mostly to the imagination.

Jiniwin (jin′i.win), **Mrs.** In Dickens's *Old Curiosity Shop*, the mother-in-law of the monstrous Quilp, whom he takes great delight in tormenting.

J. K. S. See **Stephen, James Kenneth.**

Jo (jō). In Dickens's *Bleak House*, a youthful crossing sweeper. The episode of his death is one of the most touching in the book.

Joan (jōn). The name of a supposed female pope, said (without documentary proof) to have reigned c855–858. She is represented as of English descent, although born at Ingelheim or Mainz, Germany, and as having fallen in love with a young Benedictine monk, with whom she fled in male attire to Athens. After his death, according to the traditional account, she removed to Rome, where (still posing as a man) she rose to the rank of cardinal. According to this tale she was elected Pope as John VIII on the death of Leo IV, and died in childbirth during a public procession. However, the real Pope between 855 and 858 was Benedict III, and the story of "Pope Joan" has long since been known to have no basis in historical fact.

Joan and Peter. A novel (1918) by H. G. Wells, dealing with the faults of the English educational system.

Joan of Arc (ärk). [French, **Jeanne** (or **Jehanne**) **d'Arc** (or **Darc**); called by the English the **Maid of Orleans**, by the French **La Pucelle.**] b. at Domremy (now Domremy-la-Pucelle), France, c1412; d. at Rouen, France, May 30, 1431. French national heroine. She was the fourth child of a peasant proprietor, Jacques d'Arc, who occupied a position comparable to that of mayor of a present-day French village. In her time the English and their allies, the Burgundians, were masters of the whole of France north of the Loire, and the queen mother, Isabella, supported the claim of Henry VI of England to the throne of France, in opposition to her son the Dauphin of France (later Charles VII). There was a prophecy made by Marie d'Avignon to Charles VI that "France ruined by a woman would be restored by a maid from the border of Lorraine." The young girl was undoubtedly familiar with this saying, as well as a similar prophecy attributed to Merlin, regarding a "Bois Chênu" or "Chesnu," though this latter was not as well known, and did not specify any particular oak forest in France. She believed she heard supernatural voices commanding her to liberate France, and eventually gained access to the court of the Dauphin at Chinon in 1429. She raised the siege of Orléans on May 8, 1429, and by gaining the victory of Patay on June 18, 1429, enabled the Dauphin triumphantly to enter Reims, the city where the kings of France were crowned and consecrated with the holy oil, and where he was crowned Charles VII of France on July 17, 1429. On May 24, 1430, while making a sally against the Burgundians at Compiègne unassisted by Charles's armies, she was captured by one of John of Luxemburg's men. John of Luxemburg sold her to the Duke of Burgundy, who turned her over to his close friend and ally, John of Lancaster, Duke of Bedford, and consented to let him and the cardinal of Winchester

have her tried under the jurisdiction of the University of Paris, which was at that time under the domination of the English. She was burned at the stake as a heretic on May 30, 1431. The rehabilitation trial which reversed the verdict of the earlier court was ordered by Charles VII in 1450, but owing to political and ecclesiastical intrigues the actual hearings did not take place until 1455. Hearings begun at Rome in 1869 led to her beatification (April 11, 1909) by Pope Pius X and her canonization (1920) by Pope Benedict XV. She was made patroness of France in 1922. She has been the subject of works by many literary figures, among them Schiller, Mark Twain, Anatole France, and G. B. Shaw; biographies by Michelet, Lang, and others are more reliable treatments of her life.

Joan of Arc. [In the Dramatis Personae, **Joan la Pucelle**; also, **La Pucelle.**] In Shakespeare's *1 Henry VI*, a leading character. She convinces the Dauphin of her marvelous powers, raises the siege of Orléans, persuades Burgundy to desert the English cause, and finally conjures up fiends to whom she offers herself in exchange for French victory. When captured by the English, she claims to be royal in blood and a virgin, but later states that she is with child, when she is sentenced to burning. Unlike the heroic conception of her which Schiller popularized, Shakespeare, following the Elizabethan viewpoint, sees her as a coarse instrument of the devil and makes even the French somewhat dubious of her divine attributes.

Joan of the Tower. A historical novel by Warwick Deeping, published in 1911.

Job (jōb). The hero of the book of the Old Testament named after him. He is a man of great wealth and prosperity, who is suddenly overtaken by dire misfortunes. These give rise to a series of discussions between Job and a number of friends who come to visit him. The problem discussed is whether suffering is always the punishment for sin, and, conversely, whether sin is always followed by punishment. Job asserts his righteousness, but his friends assume that his suffering must be a punishment for sin. A righteous man named Job is mentioned in Ezek. xiv. 14, but it is generally assumed that the book itself is not historical in character. This assumption is found as far back as the Talmud. The authorship has been ascribed to Moses, Jeremiah, Ezra, and other Biblical writers. Some modern critics consider it an Israelitish production and place it directly after the fall of Samaria (722 B.C.); others hold that it is a Judaic production dating from the period of the Babylonian captivity; others see in it the direct influence of the Greek tragic dramatists and place its composition in the period 500–300 B.C. The work is poetic in form, with a prose prologue and epilogue. Some writers call it a drama, others a didactic lyric. It is held by some that the book in its present form is not the original poem. The prologue and epilogue are considered later additions. The speeches of Elihu (one of the friends) are held to be interpolations made in the interest of orthodox beliefs, and some writers consider still other passages interpolations made from the same point of view. The great literary merit of the book is recognized by all modern students; the poetic imagery is perhaps the most vivid in all the Bible; the section (xxxviii–xlii) in which the Lord speaks from the whirlwind is considered to be probably the best Biblical statement of man's presumptuous position in the universe.

Job Trotter (trot′ėr). See **Trotter, Job.**

Jocasta (jō.kas′tạ) or **Jocaste** (-tē). [Called in Homer **Epicaste.**] In Greek legend, the wife of Laius, and mother of Oedipus, whom she afterward married. Their children were Eteocles, Polynices, Antigone, and Ismene. Upon discovery of their unwitting incest, Oedipus blinded himself and Jocasta committed suicide.

Jocasta (jō.kas′tạ). A play by George Gascoigne and Francis Kinwelmarsh, acted in 1566 and published in 1575. It has been supposed to be the only early English play derived from the Greek, but is really a translation from the Italian of Lodovico Dolce. It is one of the earliest English tragedies in blank verse.

Jocelin de Brakelonde (jos′e.lin dẹ brāk′lọnd). [Also, **Brakelond.**] fl. 1200. A native of Bury St. Edmunds, and chronicler of Saint Edmund's Abbey, which he entered in 1173. His chronicle of the abbey covers the period from 1173 to 1202. The graphic account of the abbot Samson suggested Carlyle's *Past and Present* (1843).

Jocelyn (jos′e.lin), **Rose.** The heroine of George Meredith's novel *Evan Harrington.*

Jockey of Norfolk (nôr′fọk). In Shakespeare's *Richard III,* the name by which the Duke of Norfolk is addressed in a warning note he receives before Bosworth:

Jockey of Norfolk, be not so bold,
For Dickon thy master is bought and sold (V. iii).

Jock O' Hazeldean (jok′ ọ.hā′zẹl.dēn). A ballad by Sir Walter Scott (but including one stanza taken directly from an older, anonymous work), telling of a lady, the intended bride of a nobleman, who elopes with Jock on her wedding day.

Joe (jō). See **Fat Boy, the.**

Joe Bagstock (bag′stok), **Major.** See **Bagstock, Major Joe.**

Joe Gargery (gar′jėr.i). See **Gargery, Joe.**

Joel (jō′ẹl). The second of the minor prophets of Israel, and author of the Old Testament book bearing his name.

Joe Miller (mil′ėr). A joke, especially an old joke; also a book of jokes. The term derives from Joseph Miller (1684–1738), English comic actor, whose name was attached to a jestbook published in 1739. Since then the word has become synonymous not only with any joke book, but with any old joke.

Joe Willet (jō wil′ẹt). See **Willet, Joe.**

"Joey," the. See under **Grimaldi, Joseph.**

John (jon). [Frequently called **John Lackland.**] b. probably at Oxford, England, Dec. 24, 1167; d. at Newark, Nottinghamshire, England, Oct. 19, 1216. King of England (1199–1216); youngest son of Henry II and Eleanor of Aquitaine. Undoubtedly his father's favorite son, he nevertheless received no grant when Henry assigned his lands to his sons. Henry, though nominally he had turned the kingships of these territories to the older sons,

retained his power and the sons were in constant revolt against their father. That John too was party to their schemes was a discovery that probably killed Henry. During Richard I's absence on crusade in the East John plotted with Philip II of France to take the throne and divide Richard's lands but Richard returned in 1194 and scotched the plan. John was forgiven. He ascended the English throne on the death of Richard, who died without issue. His succession was recognized also in the duchy of Normandy, but the lords of Anjou, Maine, and Touraine declared, according to their custom of inheritance, in favor of Prince Arthur, son of Geoffrey, John's deceased older brother. He procured Arthur's death in 1203, and as a result his French fiefs were declared forfeited by Philip II of France, nominal overlord in his French possessions, who took Château Gaillard, on the Seine in Normandy, the last of John's strongholds in France, March 6, 1204. On the death of Hubert Walter, archbishop of Canterbury, in 1205, a disputed election for the archbishopric was followed by a reference to Rome, which resulted in the election of Stephen Langton by the command of Pope Innocent III in 1206. John refused to recognize the new archbishop, and England was laid under an interdict in 1208. In 1212 the Pope issued a bull deposing John and entrusting the execution of the deposition to Philip II of France. John made his peace with the Pope by consenting to hold his kingdom in fief from the Pope and to pay an annual tribute of 1,000 marks (May 15, 1213). He thereupon invaded France in alliance with the emperor Otto IV, the Flemings, and others, but was defeated with his allies at Bouvines in 1214. In the meantime the barons, with whom he had been embroiled ever since his accession by his exactions and misgovernment, and faced once again with a tax to pay the expenses of the French adventure, had combined to secure a reform in the government, and on his return from France John was compelled to sign the Magna Charta at Runnymede, June 15, 1215. He appealed to the Pope, from whom he now held the land in fief, and the Pope, Innocent III, declared the charter void. The barons retorted by declaring the crown forfeited and bestowing it upon Louis (later Louis VIII), son of Philip II of France, who landed in England in 1216. John died during the ensuing war and his opportune death preserved the crown for his son Henry III.

John. The carpenter in Chaucer's *Miller's Tale.*

John. One of the Cambridge students (clerks of Cantebregge) in Chaucer's *Reeve's Tale.*

John. Entries on literary characters having this prename will be found also under the surnames Balfour of Burley, Bates, Blifil, Bold, Bretton, Brough, Browdie, Brute, Bunce, Buncle, Bunsby, Chester, Chivery, Colepepper, Colevile, Daw, Dawkins, Edmunds, Falstaff, Friendly, Frugal, Grueby, Harmon, Holland, Hume, Jarndyce, Jorrocks, Learoyd, Littlewit, Melvil, Montgomery, Mortimer, Morton, Nailor, Osborne, Ramorny, Ridd, Rugby, Sedley, Somervile, Southwell, Stanley, Talbot, Thorndyke, Thorpe, Walton, Watson, Wemmick, Westlock, Willet, and Willoughby.

John, Don. In Shakespeare's *Much Ado About*

ḍ, d or j; ş, s or sh; ṭ, t or ch; ẓ, z or zh; o, F. cloche; ü, F. menu; ċh, Sc. loch; ṅ, F. bonbon.

Nothing, the bastard brother of Don Pedro. It is he who causes Claudio to suspect Hero's chastity.

John, Don. In Beaumont and Fletcher's comedy *The Chances*, a harebrained but honorable Spanish gentleman.

John, Evan. Pseudonym of **Simpson, Evan John.**

John, Friar. In Shakespeare's *Romeo and Juliet*, a Franciscan friar sent by Friar Laurence to tell Romeo about Juliet's feigned death. He is prevented from going by constables who think he may be infected with the plague. Romeo does not find out, therefore, that Juliet is merely sleeping and, upon arriving at the Capulets' tomb, believes her to be dead.

John, King. The chief character of Shakespeare's *King John*. Historically he was the youngest son of Henry II and seized the throne on the death of Richard I. It is clear that Shakespeare does not regard his title as certain, but he does represent him as a champion of English unity against the Papacy and the French.

John, Little. See **Little John.**

John, Prester. See **Prester John.**

John, The Gospel of. The fourth gospel, attributed to John, "the disciple whom Jesus loved."

John a Kent and John a Cumber (kent; kum'bèr). A play (c1594) by Anthony Munday, about the rivalry between two magicians.

John Anderson, My Jo. A well-known poem by Robert Burns, based on an old ballad.

John Baptist (bap'tist). [Full title, **John Baptistes Preaching in the Wilderness.**] A religious interlude by John Bale, written c1538.

John Barleycorn (bär'li.kôrn). See **Barleycorn, John.**

John Barsad (bär'sad). See **Pross, Solomon.**

John Bull (bùl). The English nation personified; used also of the typical Englishman: from the *History of John Bull* by John Arbuthnot. He is usually depicted as short and stout, wearing the traditional 18th-century English dress.

John Bull, The History of. A satirical work by John Arbuthnot, issued originally as *Law is a Bottomless Pit* in 1712. The objective was to oppose the war between France and England (and thus also to attack the Whigs, who supported the war). John Bull and Nicholas Frog (representing Holland) are shown as opposing Louis Baboon (representing France) in a lawsuit which Bull wins. John Bull is pictured as a fat, blunt little man with a hot temper.

John Bull, or The Englishman's Fireside. A comedy by the younger George Colman, produced in 1803.

John Bull's Other Island. A play by George Bernard Shaw, produced in 1904, published in 1907. His first popular success, it deals with the problem of Irish home rule.

John Buncle (bung'kl). [Full title, **The Life of John Buncle, Esq.**] A novel by Thomas Amory, published 1756–66. The hero, John Buncle, marries seven wives after extremely short intervals. He is "a prodigious hand at matrimony, divinity, a song, and a peck." He usually finds his wives

when, after a series of hairbreadth escapes, he approaches a handsome country house in the middle of a wilderness in the north of England and there is introduced to a strikingly beautiful and learned young lady. Shortly after they marry, the young lady inevitably dies, whereupon the entire process is repeated with minor variations. The author interlards these accounts of John Buncle's marriages with passages on the joys of eating and drinking, discussions of theology and science, descriptions of the countryside, and various other digressions.

John Campbell, (2nd) **Duke of Argyll** (kam'bel, kam'el; är.gīl'). See **Argyll.**

John Company (kum'pa.ni). An old colloquial designation, in use in India and England, for the East India Company.

John Doe (dō). See **Doe, John.**

John Dory (dō'ri). A ballad frequently referred to in the 16th and 17th centuries.

John Fanning's Legacy (fan'ingz). A novel by Naomi Royde-Smith, published in 1927.

John Ferguson (fèr'gu.son). A realistic drama (1915) by St. John Ervine.

John Gilpin's Famous Ride (gil'pinz). See **Diverting History of John Gilpin, The.**

John Glayde's Honor (glādz). A four-act play (1906) by Alfred Sutro.

John Halifax, Gentleman (hal'i.faks). A story by Dinah Maria Craik, published in 1857. The author tries to show that true gentlemanly character is not determined by position or wealth, but by honesty and integrity. John is a poor but hard-working orphan who wins an education, a good position, and the hand of the heroine, Ursula March, through his own efforts.

Johnie Armstrong (jon'i ärm'strông). See under **Armstrong, John.**

John Inglesant (jon ing'gl.sant). A romance by J. H. Shorthouse, published in 1880.

Johnny Crapaud (jon'i krà.pō'). See **Crapaud, Jean.**

John of Gaunt (jon; gänt, gônt). [Title, Duke of **Lancaster.**] b. at G*l*.ent, Belgium, March, 1340; d. at London, Feb. 3, 1399. An English statesman; fourth son of Edward III. His name comes from an English version of Ghent. In 1342 he was created earl of Richmond, and in 1359 married his cousin Blanche, second daughter of Henry, Duke of Lancaster. On the death of Henry (May, 1361) and his eldest daughter Maud, Duchess of Bavaria, he succeeded by right of his wife to the rank and possessions of the dukes of Lancaster. In 1367 he accompanied his brother, Edward, the Black Prince, on the Spanish expedition against Henry of Trastamara; he fought at Nájera in 1367. Blanche died in 1369, and in 1371 he married Constance, eldest daughter of Pedro the Cruel, the deposed king of Castile. Returning to England in 1372, he styled himself King of Castile by right of his wife. Lancaster was constantly engaged in the struggle with France, but although a brave knight he was never a competent general, and his repeated failures contributed much to his increasing unpopularity. The Black Prince died June 8, 1376, and the Good Parliament, which under his patronage had undertaken to reform abuses, was dissolved. On July 6 the supreme power passed into the hands of Lancaster, Edward III being more or less incompetent to rule because of his early aging. His most powerful opponent, William of Wykeham, bishop of Winchester, was disgraced. In the struggle with the clerical party Lancaster was drawn into an alliance with the Reformers, especially with Wycliffe, whom he defended before the convocation at Saint Paul's, Feb. 19, 1377. His brutal behavior excited a riot in London; his palace, the Savoy, was attacked, and he was forced to take refuge with Prince Richard and his mother, the widow of the Black Prince, at Kennington. Edward III died June 21, 1377, and Richard II became king, and Lancaster's political power declined. He was engaged in futile expeditions to France and Scotland. While absent in the north his extreme unpopularity was shown by the destruction of his palace of the Savoy in Wat Tyler's insurrection, June 13, 1381. He made a futile attempt (1386–89) to take the Spanish throne but his separation from English politics brought him back into Richard's favor. Richard II created him Duke of Aquitaine on March 2, 1390, and he assisted in negotiating the French truce on May 24, 1394. He never recovered from the shock of the exile of his son Henry (later Henry IV). From John of Gaunt sprang the house of Lancaster, whose struggles with the Yorkists (descendants of John's younger brother) for the throne are known as the Wars of the Roses. From John of Gaunt and Blanche were descended Henry IV, Henry V, and Henry VI; his children by Catherine Swynford, legitimatized after their marriage in 1396, were the ancestors of Henry VII.

John of Gaunt, Duke of Lancaster (lang'kas.tèr). In Shakespeare's *Richard II*, the father of Bolingbroke and uncle of the King. On his deathbed he utters the well-known speech beginning "This royal throne of kings, this sceptr'd isle" and warns Richard of the result of his careless practices.

John of Lancaster, Prince. See **Lancaster, Prince John of.**

John of Salisbury (sôlz'bèr.i). [Called **Parvus.**] b. at Salisbury, Wiltshire, England, c1115; d. at Chartres, France, Oct. 25, 1180. An English ecclesiastic, scholar, and author, bishop of Chartres (1176–80). In 1136 he went to Paris to attend the lectures of Abelard. He also studied with Alberic of Reims, Robert of Melun, and William of Conches. At Chartres he laid the foundation of his classical scholarship. In 1141 he returned to Paris to study theology under Master Gilbert de la Porrée, Robert Pullus, and Simon de Poissy. In 1148 he attended the council held by Eugenius III at Reims, and followed the Pope to Rome. Returning to England c1150, he lived until 1164 at the court of Canterbury with Archbishop Theobald. He was repeatedly entrusted with delicate affairs of state, and frequently visited the papal court in Italy. His close alliance with the bishops brought him into such disfavor with Henry II that he had to abandon England in 1164 and find shelter at Reims. He later returned to Canterbury, and was present at the murder of Saint Thomas à Becket. His works consist of his letters, *Policraticus, Metalogicon, Entheticus, Vita Sancti Anselmi, Vita Sancti Thomae Cantuar.*, and *Historia Pontificalis.*

John of the Cross, Saint. [Spanish, San **Juan de la Cruz;** original name, **Juan de Yepis** (or **Yepes**) y **Álvarez.**] b. at Fontiveros, Avila, Spain, June 24, 1542; d. at Úbeda, in Andalusia, Spain, Dec. 14, 1591. A Spanish mystic. He attended the poor school at Medina del Campo, studied under the Jesuits, and in 1563 entered the Carmelite order at Medina. He studied at Salamanca and was ordained in 1567. He followed the primitive rule of Carmel, and after meeting Saint Teresa embarked on a reform of the order. For nine months (1577–78) he was imprisoned by the Carmelites at Toledo. Escaping, he founded convents of Discalced Carmelites and finally suffered accusations from the Zelanti faction of Nicholas Doria, who wrested control of the order from the moderates. After additional persecution he died at the convent of Úbeda. His chief works are *Ascent of Mount Carmel, Dark Night of the Soul, Spiritual Canticle,* and *Living Flame of Love.*

John o' Groat's House (ọ.grōts'). A locality in N Scotland, in Caithness-shire, near the N extremity of the island of Great Britain. It was named after a Dutchman, Johan de Groot, whose house formerly occupied the site. The house was a curious structure, of octagonal shape, whose site is now outlined by a mound.

John Osborne (oz'bọrn). See **Osborne, John.**

John Rugby (rug'bi). See **Rugby, John.**

John Silence (sī'lẹns). A novel by Algernon Blackwood, published in 1908.

John Silver (sil'vèr). See **Long John Silver.**

John Somervile (sum'èr.vil), Sir. See **Somervile, Sir John.**

Johnson (jon'sọn), **Captain Charles.** The pseudonym under which Defoe wrote *A General History of the Robberies and Murders of the most notorious Pyrates* (2 vols., 1724–28). This is an important source for later historical writings and for many works of fiction, among them *The Pirate* by Scott and *Treasure Island* by Stevenson. After Defoe's death the name "Captain Charles Johnson" was attached to inferior compilations based on Defoe's *History* and on *A History of the Highwaymen* (1714–20) by "Captain Alexander Smith," a pseudonym for an unidentified author or authors.

Johnson, Charles. b. 1679; d. at London, March 11, 1748. An English dramatist. Among his plays are *Force of Friendship*, played together with *Love in a Chest* (1710); *The Wife's Relief, or the Husband's Cure* (1711), *Country Lasses* (1715), *The Tragedy of Medaea* (1730), *Caelia, or The Perjured Lover* (1733), and *The Cobbler of Preston* (1716), based on *The Taming of the Shrew.*

Johnson, Dorothy. b. at York, England. An English novelist and short-story writer. Author of *Doris* (1925), *To Meet Mr. Stanley* (1926), *The Death of a Spinster* (1931), and *Private Inquiries* (1932).

Johnson, Esther. b. at Sheen, Surrey, England, March 13, 1681; d. at Dublin, Jan. 28, 1728. A pupil and friend of Jonathan Swift, and the "Stella" of his *Journal to Stella.* Her relations with Swift are not clear; she met him when both were

ḍ, d or j; ṣ, s or sh; ṭ, t or ch; ẓ, z or zh; o, F. cloche; ü, F. menu; ċh, Sc. loch; ṅ, F. bonbon.

staying (1689) with Sir William Temple, at Moor Park, Surrey; in 1696, when they met again, she was a beautiful girl of 15, and he a young man of 29. Whatever the nature of their relationship, Esther Johnson is immortalized by the famous *Journal to Stella* (1710–13), a series of letters and a diary. It is possible, but not at all likely, that they were secretly married, in 1706 or 1715. The shock of her death made Swift so ill that he was unable to attend the funeral. He preserved a lock of her hair in an envelope on which he wrote four words: "Only a woman's hair."

Johnson, Hewlett. [Called the **"Red Dean."**] b. at Manchester, England, Jan. 25, 1874—. An English clergyman, dean of Manchester (1924–31) and Canterbury (1931 *et seq.*). He was founder (1905) and editor (1905–24) of *The Interpreter.* Author of *The Socialist Sixth of the World* (1940), which was published in America as *The Soviet Power*, and of *The Soviet Strength.*

Johnson, Lionel (Pigot). b. at Broadstairs, Kent, England, March 15, 1867; d. at London, Oct. 4, 1902. An English poet, critic, essayist, and journalist. Author of *The Fools of Shakespeare* (1887), *The Art of Thomas Hardy* (1894), *Poems* (1895), *Ireland and Other Poems* (1897), and *Post Liminium* (1911). He contributed reviews to the *Academy*, *National Observer*, *Daily Chronicle*, and *Pall Mall Gazette*, and poetry to the *Yellow Book.*

Johnson, Richard. b. at London, 1573; d. c1659. An English poet and prose writer. His best-known work is the *Famous Historie of the Seaven Champions of Christendom: St. George of England, St. Denis of France, St. James of Spain, St. Anthony of Italy, St. Andrew of Scotland, St. Patrick of Ireland, and St. David of Wales*, which was printed as early as 1597.

Johnson, Rupert. A London physician, in William De Morgan's novel *Alice-for-Short* (1907).

Johnson, Samuel. b. 1640; d. 1703. An English clergyman, a member of the Whig party, severely punished under James II for his ardently Protestant pamphlets. He figures as Ben Jochanan in Dryden's *Absalom and Achitophel.*

Johnson, Samuel. [Commonly known as **Dr. Johnson**; also called the **Great Cham of Literature.**] b. at Lichfield, England, Sept. 18, 1709; d. at London, Dec. 13, 1784. An English lexicographer, essayist, and poet; son of Michael Johnson, a bookseller at Lichfield, a High Churchman and Jacobite. He lost the use of one eye from scrofula, and was "touched" by Queen Anne. His uncouth appearance and manner were against him through life. In 1728 he entered Pembroke College, Oxford, and resided there continuously until Dec. 12, 1729, and afterward at intervals until Oct. 8, 1731. A Latin translation of Pope's *Messiah* (much admired by Pope) was written at this time. He began to suffer from violent attacks of the hypochondria which followed him through life. In 1732 he became usher at Market Bosworth school, but soon abandoned the place and returned to Lichfield and Birmingham, in which latter town he married the recently (1734) widowed Mrs. Henry Porter, on July 9, 1735. She was some 20 years his senior, but he remained devoted to her until her death in 1752.

He established a school at Edial, near Lichfield, in 1736, which soon failed. Among his pupils was David Garrick, with whom he started for London in March, 1737. In March, 1738, his Latin ode to Sylvanus Urban appeared in Cave's *Gentleman's Magazine*, to which he became a regular contributor. In May, 1738, *London*, an imitation of Juvenal, was published by Dodsley. The *Life of Savage* appeared in February, 1744. In January, 1749, he published the *Vanity of Human Wishes*, the finest of his poems. His tragedy *Irene* (begun at Edial) was produced Feb. 6, 1749, with indifferent success, by Garrick at Drury Lane. The *Rambler* appeared every Tuesday and Saturday from March 20, 1750, until March 14, 1752, and, with the exception of Nos. 10, 30, 44, 97, and 100, was entirely his work (No. 97 was written by Richardson). His wife died on March 17, 1752. On Feb. 20, 1755, he received the degree of M.A. from Oxford. His work *Rasselas* was written in the evenings of one week in 1759. Among his political tracts is *Taxation no Tyranny* (1775), in answer to the address of the American Congress. After the accession of George III, Johnson received a pension of 300 pounds. During his last years he devoted himself almost exclusively to society and conversation, and his sayings and doings were carefully reported by James Boswell and Mrs. Thrale (Hester Lynch Piozzi). In 1773 he took his well-known journey with Boswell, an account of which was published in 1775 as *A Journey to the Western Isles of Scotland*. He also wrote nearly all the numbers of *The Idler* (1758–60), and published an edition of Shakespeare in eight volumes, with notes, in 1765. His critical and biographical *Lives of the Poets* appeared in ten volumes from 1779 to 1781. For his dictionary, see immediately below.

Johnson's Dictionary. [Full title, **A Dictionary of the English Language.**] The first great English dictionary, edited by Samuel Johnson. The plan, inscribed to Lord Chesterfield, was issued in 1747. Chesterfield's offer of help soon proved empty and his offer, made again when it was apparent that the work would appear and be a success, was turned down vigorously by Johnson in a famous letter (1755). A group of booksellers agreed to pay 1,575 pounds for the copyright, including the entire work of preparation for the press. He employed six amanuenses, five of whom were Scotsmen. The book was based on an interleaved copy of Nathan Bailey's dictionary, and appeared in two volumes, folio, April 15, 1755. The dictionary, though not the first in the language, was the most thorough and despite its faults (weak etymology and personally prejudiced definitions among them) remains one of the monuments of English scholarship.

Johnston (jon'stọn), **Denis William.** b. at Dublin, June 18, 1901—. An Irish playwright, producer, and director, associated with the Dublin Gate Theatre as director (1931–36) and with the Abbey Theatre, Dublin Gate Theatre, and the Earl of Longford's company as actor and producer (intermittently, 1927 *et seq.*). Author of *The Old Lady Says 'No'!* (1929), *The Moon in the Yellow River* (1931), *A Bride for the Unicorn* (1933), *Storm Song* (1934), *The Golden Cuckoo* (1939), *Weep for the Cyclops* (1940), and an adaptation of Ernest Toller's

Die Blinde Göttin under the title *Blind Man's Buff* (1936).

Johnston, Sir Harry Hamilton. b. at Kennington, London, June 12, 1858; d. July 31, 1927. An English explorer and official in Africa. He was educated at King's College, London, made various journeys in Africa during the years 1879–84 (Portuguese West Africa, Congo River, Mount Kilimanjaro), led the expedition which founded the British Central Africa Protectorate in 1889, was consul general at Tunis (1897–99), and was consul general and commander in chief for the Uganda Protectorate (1899–1901). He published a number of works on Africa, in-including *The River Congo* (1884), *Kilimanjaro* (1885), *British Central Africa* (1897), *A History of the Colonization of Africa by Alien Races* (1899), *The Uganda Protectorate* (1902), *The Nile Quest* (1903), *Liberia* (1906), *George Grenfell and the Congo* (1908), and *British Empire in Africa* (1910). His novels include *The Gay Dombeys* (1919) and *Mrs. Warren's Daughter* (1920).

Johnstone (jon'stọn), **Charles.** b. c1719; d. at Calcutta, c1800. An English writer. He was the author of *Chrysal, or The Adventures of a Guinea* (1760–65), a short satirical novel, and *Arsaces* (1774), a short novel with an Oriental background.

Johnstone, Christian Isobel. b. in Fifeshire, Scotland, 1781; d. at Edinburgh, Aug. 26, 1857. A Scottish novelist and journalist.

John Southwell (south'wel, -wẹl). See **Southwell, John.**

John Stanley (stan'li), **Sir.** See **Stanley, Sir John.**

John Talbot (tôl'bọt, tal'-). See **Talbot, John.**

John the Baptist (jon; bap'tist). The forerunner of Jesus. Mat. iii.

John the Evangelist. An interlude of unknown authorship, written in the early 16th century.

John Thorndyke (thôrn'dīk), **Dr.** See **Thorndyke, Dr. John.**

John Thorpe (thôrp). See **Thorpe, John.**

John Walton (wôl'tọn), **Sir.** See **Walton, Sir John.**

John Watson (wot'sọn), **Dr.** See **Watson, Dr.**

John Wemmick (wem'ik). See **Wemmick, John.**

John Westlock (west'lok). See **Westlock, John.**

John Willet (wil'ẹt). See **Willet, John.**

John Willoughby (wil'ọ.bi). See **Willoughby, John.**

Joinville (zhwaṅ.vēl), **Jean de.** b. at Joinville, in Champagne, France, c1224; d. on his ancestral estates, July 16, 1317. A French chronicler. His family was noble and wealthy, and held for four generations the office of seneschal of Champagne. By virtue of his birth he had access to the court circles of Champagne and France. He followed Louis IX on the seventh Crusade (1248–54) with a retinue of 700 men, and spent six years in Egypt and Syria. In 1250, at St.-Jean-d'Acre (now Acre), he drew up the articles of his religious belief, his *Credo*, which he subsequently revised in 1287. The great work, however, to which he has left his name is the *Histoire de Saint Louis*, a personal appreciation of the writer's hero, Louis IX, that remains the best source on the period, its customs and events, and its people. The original copy, presented in 1309 by the author in person to Louis X, great-grandson of Louis IX, is lost. A second copy, belonging to Joinville, shared a like fate; this was presumably used, however, in preparing the first printed edition in 1547. A good modern edition was made by Natalis de Wailly for the Société de l'Histoire de France in 1868.

Jolley (jol'i), **Sir Joslin.** In Sir George Etherege's comedy *She Would If She Could*, a convivial country gentleman.

Jolly Beggars, The. A humorous cantata by Robert Burns, written c1785 and published in 1799, in which the beggars sing of the sorrows and miseries of their lives. There is also included some indirect satire of the church and the nobility.

Jolyon (jol'yọn). A name borne by three members of the Forsyte family, in Galsworthy's *Forsyte Saga:* the grandfather, Old Jolyon; the father, Young Jolyon or Jo (the artist); and the son, called Jon.

Jonah (jō'nạ). [Also, **Jonas** (jō'nạs).] In the Bible, a Hebrew prophet who flourished in or before the reign of Jeroboam II. His story is given in the Book of Jonah, the date and authorship of which are unknown. The incident in which Jonah was swallowed by a whale, lived in its belly for three days, and emerged safe has parallels in Babylonian, Egyptian, Indian, and Greek mythology.

Jonas Chuzzlewit (jō'nạs chuz'l.wit). See **Chuzzlewit, Jonas.**

Jonathan (jon'ạ.thạn). In the Bible, a Hebrew commander; son of Saul and the bosom friend of David. 1 Sam. xiii., etc.

Jonathan Dakers (dā'kẹrz). See **Dakers, Jonathan.**

Jonathan Oldbuck (ōld'buk). See **Oldbuck, Jonathan.**

Jonathan Wild (wīld). [Full title, **The Life of Mr. Jonathan Wild the Great.**] A satirical novel by Henry Fielding, published in 1743. Fielding here attacks the confusion of "greatness" with goodness. Jonathan Wild, a scoundrel and rogue, presented by the author as though he were as great a man as Alexander, Caesar, or Napoleon, shows his true character early in life. His career as a thief begins early, under Mr. Snap, the keeper of a sponging-house (place where debtors were confined), and he soon shows a remarkable and precocious talent as a pickpocket. He then becomes the leader of a gang of robbers and marries Snap's daughter, Laetitia, who is as worthless as he is. Heartfree, the honest jeweler whom Jonathan robs and then has imprisoned for bankruptcy, is treated by Fielding as a foolish, easily victimized dupe. Jonathan induces Heartfree's wife to leave the country, after which he tries to have Heartfree convicted for her murder. His schemes are finally brought to light, and he dies on the gallows, rewarded with "a death as glorious as his life had been."

Jones (jōnz), **Davy.** See **Davy Jones.**

Jones, Ebenezer. b. at Islington, London, Jan. 20, 1820; d. at Brentwood, Essex, England, Sept. 14, 1860. An English poet and economic theorist. He was the author of *Studies of Sensation and Event* (1843), a volume of poetry, and *Land Monopoly* (1849), a work advocating the nationalization of land and anticipating the single-tax doctrine of the American reformer Henry George.

Jones, Ernest Charles. b. at Berlin, Jan. 25, 1819; d. at Manchester, England, Jan. 26, 1869. An English Chartist, poet, and novelist. He joined the Chartist movement in 1846, siding with the extremist wing of the party, and was imprisoned (1848–50) for sedition. Author of *The Wood Spirit* (1841) and *The Lass and the Lady* (1855), novels; *The Battle Day and Other Poems* (1855) and *Evenings with the People* (1856), political speeches and revolutionary poems.

Jones, Henry. b. near Drogheda, Ireland, 1721; d. at London, in April, 1770. An Irish poet and dramatist.

Jones, Henry Arthur. b. at Grandborough, Buckinghamshire, England, Sept. 28, 1851; d. Jan. 7, 1929. An English dramatist. A theorist and active proponent of realism in the drama, Jones was one of the leading dramatists of his day. Among his plays are *The Silver King* (1882, with Henry Herman), *Saints and Sinners* (1884), *The Middleman* (1889), *Judah* (1890), *The Crusaders* (1891), *The Case of Rebellious Susan* (1894), *Michael and his Lost Angel* (1896), *The Liars* (1897), *Mrs. Dane's Defence* (1900), *Joseph Entangled* (1904), *The Chevalier* (1904), *The Heroic Stubbs* (1906), *The Hypocrites* (1906), *The Evangelist* (1907), *We Can't be as Bad as All That* (1910), *The Lie* (1915), and *The Pacifists* (1917). He also published a volume of essays, *The Renascence of the English Drama* (1895).

Jones, Inigo. b. at London, July 15, 1573; d. there, June 21, 1652. An English architect. He went to Italy to study painting and architecture and resided there many years, especially at Venice, whence he was called (1604) to Denmark by King Christian IV. He returned to England in 1605. As court architect to the queen, and after her death to James I and Charles I, he designed the sets and staging for the court masques, by Jonson, Shirley, Carew, and other writers of the time. In 1620 he was appointed commissioner of repairs of Saint Paul's, which, however, were not commenced before 1631. In 1643 he was thrown out of his office, and in 1646 fined 345 pounds for being a royal favorite and a Roman Catholic, having been taken in arms at the capture of Basing House. He is supposed to have died of grief, misfortune, and old age at old Somerset House on the Strand. He sat twice to Vandyck, and a portrait by this master was sent with the Houghton collection to St. Petersburg. Among his works are the banqueting hall, Whitehall (1619–22), Covent Garden Piazza, the famous gateway of St. Mary's, Oxford (1632), the equally famous portico of old Saint Paul's and the reconstruction of that church (1631–41), and other architectural works. He introduced the classical style of Palladio to England which, superseding the Jacobean, developed into the Georgian style of the next century.

Jones, Richard. b. at Birmingham, England, 1779; d. at London, Aug. 30, 1851. An English actor and dramatist.

Jones, Sidney. b. at Leeds, England, 1869; d. 1946. An English composer. His light operas include *The Geisha*, a work reminiscent of *The Mikado* of Gilbert and Sullivan.

Jones, Tom. In Henry Fielding's novel *Tom Jones*, the title character, an impulsive and manly, but easygoing youth. It transpires that he is the (illegitimate) nephew of his foster-father, Allworthy, whose heir he becomes. He marries Sophia Western.

Jones, William. b. at Lowick, Northamptonshire, England, July 30, 1726; d. at Nayland, Suffolk, England, Jan. 6, 1800. An English clergyman and theological and miscellaneous writer. Among his works are *Catholic Doctrine of the Trinity* (1756), and *Figurative Language of the Holy Scripture* (1786).

Jones, Sir William. b. at Westminster, London, Sept. 28, 1746; d. at Calcutta, India, April 27, 1794. An English Orientalist and linguist. He entered University College, Oxford, in 1764, and became a fellow of that college in 1766. In 1770 he published a translation into French of the Persian life of Nadir Shah, brought to England on his visit in 1768 by Christian VII of Denmark. It was followed (1770) by the *Traité sur la poésie orientale*. In 1771 he issued his grammar of the Persian language, followed by *Poems, consisting chiefly of translations from the Asiatick languages* (1772) and *Poeseos Asiaticae commentatorium libri sex* (1774). He was called to the bar at the Middle Temple in 1774. In 1778 he published a translation of the *Speeches of Isaeus in Causes concerning the Law of Succession to Property at Athens*. His essay on the *Law of Bailments* appeared in 1781, and in the same year was issued the translation of the Arabic *Moallakat*. In 1784 he founded the Bengal Asiatic Society. He was the first English scholar to master Sanskrit, and to recognize its importance for comparative philology. In 1789 he finished his translation of *Sakuntala;* he also translated the *Hitopadesa* and other Sanskrit works. In 1794 he began a complete digest of Hindu law with the *Institutes of Hindu Law*, followed by *Mohammedan Law of Succession* and *Mohammedan Law of Inheritance.*

jongleur (zhôṅ.glėr′). In medieval France, and in England under the Norman kings, a minstrel who went from place to place singing songs, generally of his own composition and to his own accompaniment; later, a mountebank.

> The jongleurs or jogelors (joculatores) were originally minstrels who could perform feats of sleight of hand, etc., but they soon became mere mountebanks, and the name became . . . a term of contempt.
> (Piers Plowman's Crede (*E.E.T.S.*), Notes.)

Jonson (jon′sọn), **Ben.** b. at Westminster (now part of London), c1573; d. Aug. 6, 1637. An English actor, poet, dramatist, and essayist. His father, whom he never knew, was a minister, and his stepfather, whose trade he followed for a short time (thoroughly detesting it), was a bricklayer. He studied at Westminster School, and attended Cambridge University, but did not take a degree, although both Cambridge and Oxford were later happy to award him an honorary M.A. He fought in Flanders under Sir Francis Vere and Prince Maurice of Nassau. He seems to have been back at London c1592 and to have begun his connection with the theater c1595. Various entries in Henslowe's *Diary* indicate that Jonson worked for him in 1597. The next year was one of the most important in his career. In 1598 he wrote one of his best comedies, *Every Man in His Humour*, in which Shakespeare acted; he was cited in the famous *Palladis Tamia: Wits Treasury* of Francis Meres as "one of the best for tragedy" (a viewpoint that is no longer held); and he fought a duel with, and killed, a fellow actor, Gabriel Spenser, for which he was imprisoned and was saved from hanging only by pleading benefit of clergy. Some of his best plays are *Every Man Out of His Humour* (1599), *Volpone, or the Fox* (1606), *Epicoene, or the Silent Woman* (1609), *The Alchemist* (1610), by many considered to be his masterpiece, and *Bartholomew Fair* (1614). Other plays, all comedies, are *Cynthia's Revels* (1600), *The Poetaster* (1601), in both of which he attacks rival dramatists, *The Devil is an Ass* (1616), *The Staple of News* (1625), *The New Inn* (1629), a failure, *The Magnetic Lady* (1632), and *A Tale of a Tub* (1633), a title later used by Swift. *Sejanus* (1603) and *Catiline* (1611) are Roman tragedies, superior in scholarship and historical accuracy, but in no other respect, to the Roman plays of Shakespeare. *The Hue and Cry After Cupid* (1608), unfinished, *The Masque of Queens* (1609), and *Oberon* (1611) are court masques, entertainments combining music, dancing, singing, with a thin plot, of which he wrote at least 30. *Timber, or Discoveries Made upon Men and Matter* (published 1640) is an example of his prose. As a poet he is best remembered for the lovely "Drink to me only with thine eyes" (*To Celia*), for his tribute to Shakespeare, written for and published in the 1623 Folio, *To the Memory of My Beloved Master, Mr. William Shakespeare, and What He Hath Left Us*, for the lines *To the Reader*, also in the First Folio, *Hymn to Diana*, *The Triumph of Charis*, the pathetic *Epitaph on Salathiel Pavy*, and for some short pieces taken from his comedies. His classical knowledge is evidenced not only through his observance of the Unities in his plays, but by his verse translation of Horace's *Art of Poetry*. As a literary dictator, in the manner of Dryden, Pope, and Samuel Johnson, his word was law at the Mermaid, the Dog, the Sun, the Triple Tun, the Devil, and other inns, where his disciples, "the sons o' Ben," gathered. With Marlowe and Shakespeare he ranks as one of the three great Elizabethan dramatists. His powers as a conversationalist have been recorded in the *Conversations* of William Drummond of Hawthornden, whose work (published 1832) does in a small way for him what Boswell did for Samuel Johnson. Some of his comedies are still occasionally produced, but he does not hold the modern stage as well as does Shakespeare. He himself best summed up the difference between himself and his rival in his famous line, "He was not of an age, but for all time!" Jonson is buried in Westminster Abbey, where his grave is marked by the inscription, "O Rare Ben Jonson."

Jordan (jôr'dạn), **Mrs. Dorothea** or **Dorothy.** [Assumed name of **Dorothy Bland.**] b. near Waterford, Ireland, c1762; d. at St.-Cloud, France, 1816. An Irish actress. She became the mistress of the Duke of Clarence (later William IV) in 1790, having ten children by him; the children were known by the family name of Fitz Clarence and were ennobled.

Jordan, Thomas. b. at London, c1612; d. c1685. An English actor, dramatist, and poet.

Jörmungand (yẽr'mŭng.änd). [Old Norse, **Jörmungandr** (-än.dẽr).] In Old Norse mythology, the name of the huge Midgard Serpent which encircles the earth with his tail in his mouth. When he stirs or struggles the earth has tempests.

Jorrocks (jor'ọks), **John.** A cockney grocer in the stories of R. S. Surtees, such as *Jorrocks' Jaunts and Jollities* and *Handley Cross*. Surtees introduced him in his *New Sporting Magazine*.

Joscelyn or **Josselin** (jos'ẹ.lin), **John.** b. 1529; d. at High Roding, Essex, England, Dec. 28, 1603. One of the earliest students of Old English. He was Latin secretary to Matthew Parker, archbishop of Canterbury, and at his suggestion made collections of Old English documents, which he annotated.

José (hō.zä'; Spanish, hō.sä'), **Don.** Don Juan's father in Byron's poem of that name.

Joseph (jō'zẹf). In the Bible: **1.** A son of Jacob and Rachel, sold by his brethren into Egypt. Gen. xxx.22–24, xxxvii.1.
2. The husband of Mary, the mother of Jesus. Mat. i.16–25.

Joseph Andrews (an'drōz). [Full title, **The History of the Adventures of Joseph Andrews, and of His Friend Mr. Abram Adams Written in Imitation of the Manner of Cervantes.**] A novel by Henry Fielding, published in 1742, and named for its hero. The book was intended at first simply as a satire on Samuel Richardson's *Pamela*, but after the first few chapters has grown to be much more than a mere burlesque. Joseph, the supposed brother of Pamela (and a Fielding invention), is a young footman in the service of Lady Booby. He is dismissed from her house for refusing her amorous advances and trudges to the next village, where his sweetheart Fanny lives. On the way he is set upon and robbed, but is met and cared for by Parson Adams, the forgetful, kindly clergyman who is the real hero of the book. Parson Adams also saves Fanny, who, on her way to London to help Joseph, is attacked by a ruffian. After a series of adventures Joseph, Fanny, and Parson Adams reach the parson's home, which happens to be in the parish where Lady Booby has her summer home. Lady Booby vengefully tries to have Joseph and Fanny put in prison for robbery in order to prevent them from marrying, but the arrival of Squire Booby, Pamela's husband, saves the two young people. It is then discovered that Fanny is Pamela's sister, and that Joseph is the son of a fine gentleman, Mr. Wilson. The novel ends with their marriage.

Joseph Bagnet (bag'net), **Mr.** and **Mrs.** See **Bagnet, Mr.** and **Mrs. Joseph.**

Joseph Bowley (bou'li), **Sir.** See **Bowley, Sir Joseph.**

Josephine (jō'zẹ.fēn). In Gilbert and Sullivan's *Pinafore*, the daughter of Captain Corcoran. She is loved by the First Lord of the Admiralty, but gives her heart to Ralph Rackstraw.

Joseph of Arimathea (jō'zẹf; ar"i.mạ.thē'ạ). In the Bible, a rich Israelite who apparently was a member of the Sanhedrin at the time of the Crucifixion. He was afraid to confess his belief in Jesus. After the

Crucifixion, however, he went and begged the body of Jesus, and buried it in his own tomb. There is a legend that he was imprisoned for 42 years, which seemed but three to him on account of the Grail which he kept with him in prison. This was the vessel in which he received the blood of Christ from the cross, and which he carried, after his release by Vespasian, to Glastonbury in Britain. That he founded a church at Glastonbury, and that he planted the hawthorn there which blooms at Christmas, are probably local Glastonbury legends. There is an alliterative English romance *Joseph of Arimathea*, written c1350 (edited by W. W. Skeat in 1871). Robert de Boron is said to have composed two versions of the legend of Joseph.

Joseph of Exeter (ek'se.tèr). [Latin, **Josephus Iscanus** (jō.sē'fus is.kā'nus).] fl. c1200. A medieval Latin poet in England. A native of Exeter, he resided much in France, and in 1188 went with Archbishop Baldwin on a crusade to the Holy Land, returning to England in 1190. His chief works are *De Bello Trojano* in six books (modeled on Vergil), *Antiocheis*, a poem on the third Crusade, and *Panegyricus ad Henricum*.

Joseph Sedley (sed'li). See **Sedley, Joseph**.

Joseph Surface (sèr'fas). See **Surface, Joseph**.

Josephus (jō.sē'fus), **Flavius**. [Usually shortened to **Josephus**.] b. at Jerusalem, 37; d. at Rome, sometime between 95 and 100. A Jewish priest, soldier, statesman, and historian. The son of a priest and descendant of royalty, he studied Hebrew law and Greek and Hebrew literature. After spending three years in the desert with Banus, a hermit, he was chosen to serve as a delegate to Nero in 64. Upon his return from Rome, he was appointed governor of Galilee by the Sanhedrin, the great council of the Jews, at Jerusalem. In 66 he was active in the Jewish revolt against Rome, and led in the defense of Jotapata for 47 days before he surrendered to Vespasian, whose favor he won (as he had previously won that of Nero's mistress, Poppaea Sabina) by making predictions calculated to please their hearers (he told Vespasian that he would become emperor). He went with Vespasian to Alexandria, was later freed, adopted the family name of Vespasian (Flavius), became a Roman citizen, and was given a pension and a considerable estate in Judea. He continued to enjoy the protection of Vespasian, and later of Titus and Domitian (he was at the fall (70) of Jerusalem with Titus). His works are a *History of the Jewish War*, in seven books, first written in Aramaic and then translated into Greek, *Antiquities of the Jews*, in 20 books, dealing with the history of the Jewish people from the beginning of time to the year 66, *Vita* (his autobiography), in which he denies the charges made by his enemy, Justus of Tiberias, that he was responsible for the Jewish rebellion, and *Contra Apionem*, two essays in which he defends the Jews against the attacks of Apion, an anti-Semitic Alexandrian.

Joseph Vance (jō'zef vans). [Full title, **Joseph Vance: An Ill-Written Autobiography**.] A novel by William De Morgan, published in 1906. His first novel, it was a sensational success from its appearance. The novel is of autobiographical interest, the author drawing freely on the events and impressions of his own childhood.

Joseph Wittol (wit'ōl), **Sir**. See **Wittol, Sir Joseph**.

Joshua (josh'ū.a). In the Bible, the successor of Moses as leader of the Israelites. Ex. xvii. 9–14; Book of Joshua.

Josiah (jō.sī'a). A king of Judah, son of Amon: slain at the battle of Megiddo. 2 Kings, xxii., etc.

Josiah Bounderby (boun'dèr.bi). See **Bounderby, Josiah**.

Joslin Jolley (jos'lin jol'i), **Sir**. See **Jolley, Sir Joslin**.

Jötunheim (yē'tön.hām). In Old Norse mythology, the outer world, or realm of giants; Utgard.

Joueur (zhö.èr), **Le**. A comedy by Jean François Regnard, produced in 1696. Susannah Centlivre's *Gamester* was adapted from it.

Jourdain (jör.dān'), **Margery**. In Shakespeare's *2 Henry VI*, a witch who summons a spirit for the Duchess of Gloucester (I. iv).

Jourdain (zhör.dan), **Monsieur**. In Molière's *Le Bourgeois Gentilhomme*, a good, plain citizen, who is consumed with a desire to pass for a perfect gentleman. To this end he endeavors to educate not only himself but all his family. His astonishment at learning that he had been talking prose all his life has become proverbial in English as well as in French.

Journal of a Voyage to Lisbon (liz'bon), **A**. A record kept by Henry Fielding on a voyage which he took in a vain effort to recover his health. It was published in 1755.

Journal of the Plague Year, A. A fictional narrative by Daniel Defoe, published in 1722. Ostensibly a diary, it tells of the plague of 1665–66 as seen by a citizen who remained in London. Written at least partly to support Walpole's Quarantine Act, it has enjoyed great popularity as a work of religion, of history, and of fiction. Defoe, who was only five at the time his narrative takes place, has nevertheless managed to reproduce so realistically such grim and horrifying details as the nightly circulation of the dead-carts, with the mournful cry "Bring out your dead," that his reader believes in him as an eyewitness.

Journal to Stella (stel'a). A private personal record kept (1710–13) by Swift for Esther Johnson (Stella).

Journey of the Magi. A poem by T. S. Eliot. It is simultaneously a realistic description of the actual hardships and events involved in the journey of the Magi and a metaphysical questioning of the full implications of the birth of Christ:

> . . . were we led all that way for
> Birth or Death? . . . .

Journey's End. A play about World War I by Robert Cedric Sherriff, published in 1929.

Journey to London, A. The name given by Vanbrugh to the unfinished comedy afterward completed by Cibber and called *The Provoked Husband* (produced in 1728).

Jove (jōv). The Roman god Jupiter (as, "Keep in mind What Jove decrees," Dryden's tr. Vergil's *Aeneid*, iii.328; the bird of Jove, the eagle; by

Jove!); also, the planet Jupiter (poetic: as, "the moons of Jove," Cowper's *Tirocinium*).

Jovial Crew, A. [Full title, **A Jovial Crew, or the Merry Beggars.**] A comedy by Richard Brome, produced in 1641 and printed in 1641.

Jowett (jou′et), **Benjamin.** b. at Camberwell, London, 1817; d. Oct. 1, 1893. An English classical scholar, professor of Greek (1855 *et seq.*) at Oxford, and master of Balliol College (1870 *et seq.*). In 1882 he was appointed vice-chancellor of the university. His works include *The Dialogues of Plato translated into English, with Analyses and Introductions* (1871), a translation of Thucydides (1881), and a translation of the *Politics* of Aristotle (1885). These form a monumental tribute to Jowett's scholarship, his Plato still ranking among the best translations of the work. In 1860 he was tried and acquitted before the chancellor's court of the University of Oxford on a charge of heresy.

Joyce (jois), **James (Augustine Aloysius).** b. at Dublin, Feb. 2, 1882; d. at Zurich, Switzerland, Jan. 13, 1941. An Irish novelist, short-story writer, essayist, poet, and dramatist. He was educated, toward the end of becoming a priest, at Clongowes Wood College at Clane, Belvedere College at Dublin, and at the Dublin Royal University, receiving his bachelor's degree from the latter in 1902. He studied philosophy and theology, Latin, French, Italian, and Norwegian (the last so that he might be able to read in the original the plays of Ibsen, whom he admired intensely, and by whom he was influenced to some extent). In his early teens, while at Belvedere, he wrote a prize-winning essay, *My Favorite Hero*, which has some significance in view of his later work (the "favorite hero" being Ulysses). In 1900 he wrote a critical essay, *Ibsen's New Drama*, which appeared in the April issue of the *Fortnightly Review*. He married in 1904 and spent the next ten years teaching languages in Switzerland and Trieste, in addition to writing. His works include *The Day of the Rabblement* (1901), an essay attacking nationalism in art and literature in general and the Irish National Theatre in particular, *Chamber Music* (1907), *Pomes Penyeach* (1927), *Collected Poems* (1927), *Dubliners* (1914), collected short stories and sketches originally intended for publication in 1907 but delayed because it contained references offensive to Edward VII, *Exiles* (1918), a three-act play, *A Portrait of the Artist as a Young Man* (1916), an autobiographical novel in which the hero, Stephen Dedalus, is Joyce himself, its sequel, *Ulysses* (1922), the work for which he is best known, and *Finnegans Wake* (1939), a novel on which he worked for 17 years and which appeared in parts during the years 1927–38. It is in four parts and 17 episodes. Joyce's *Ulysses* has been called both the "greatest fiction of the 20th century," by the Irish Æ, and "the foulest book that ever found its way into print," by the English Alfred Noyes. Regardless of which view may finally prevail, the fact remains that Joyce himself is now generally conceded to have been one of the greatest literary geniuses in modern world literature. He has exerted a strong influence on many American and English writers, including Hemingway, Dos Passos, Thomas Wolfe, James T. Farrell, William Faulkner, and Virginia Woolf.

Joyce, Patrick Weston. b. at Limerick, Ireland, 1827; d. at Dublin, Jan. 7, 1914. An Irish teacher and historian. Author of *Origin and History of Irish Place Names* (2 vols., 1869), *Irish Local Names Explained* (1870), *Irish Grammar* (1879), *A Short History of Ireland to 1608* (1895), *Social History of Ancient Ireland* (2 vols., 1903), and *Story of Ancient Irish Civilization* (1907). He is best known to students for his *Ancient Irish Music*, containing previously unpublished songs, and *Old Celtic Romances*.

Joyeuse (zhwȧ.yèz). The sword of Charlemagne.

Joyeuse Garde (zhwȧ.yèz gȧrd; joi′e̥s gärd), **La.** [Also, **La Garde Joyeuse.**] In Arthurian romance, the castle of Lancelot of the Lake, and the place of his burial. It was given to him by Arthur for his defense of the queen's honor in a conflict with Sir Mador, who had accused her of poisoning his brother. It is thought to have stood on the site of what is now Berwick-upon-Tweed.

Joyous Adventures of Aristide Pujol (ar.is.tēd′ pü.zhôl′), **The.** A picaresque novel by William John Locke, published in 1912.

Juan (wän, jö′an̳; Spanish, ʜwän), **Don.** See **Don Juan.**

Juan Fernández (fẽr.nan′dez; Spanish, ʜwän′fer.nän′des). A group of three volcanic islands in the Pacific Ocean ab. 500 mi. SW of Valparaíso, Chile, belonging to Chile; part of Valparaíso province. It includes the islands of Más a Tierra, Más Afuera, and Santa Clara. Site of a wireless station; lobster fisheries. Alexander Selkirk, on whose adventures Defoe probably based *Robinson Crusoe*, lived on Más a Tierra for about five years in the first decade of the 18th century. Total area, ab. 72 sq. mi.; pop. ab. 300.

Juba (jö′ba̳). In Addison's *Cato*, a supporter of Cato and the republican cause.

Jubal (jö′bal). In the Bible, according to Genesis, a son of Lamech by Adah, called the inventor of stringed and wind instruments, from the words "father of all who play the lyre and the pipe." Gen. iv. 21.

Judah (jö′da̳). In the Bible, the fourth son of Jacob and Leah (Gen. xxix. 35, etc.); also, the powerful tribe of his descendants.

Judas Iscariot (jö′da̳s is.kar′i.ọt). In the Bible, one of the 12 apostles, the betrayer of Jesus. He was the only non-Galilean among the apostles, his name probably signifying "man of Kerioth." He betrayed Jesus to the Romans for 30 pieces of silver and afterwards killed himself. He is the most ignoble traitor of Christian tradition; during the Middle Ages, his biography was filled out by Jacobus de Voragine and others, who attached the Oedipus myth and other motifs of legend and folklore to his name. Mat. xxvi. 14–16, 47–49.

Judas Maccabaeus (mak.a̳.bē′us). d. c160 B.C. A Jewish patriot. He succeeded his father in 166 as commander and leader in the struggle against Antiochus IV (Antiochus Epiphanes). In the battles at Beth-horon and Bethzur (S of Jerusalem) he gained a decisive victory over the Syrians, and in Chisleu (December), 165, he entered Jerusalem and reconsecrated the Temple; in memory of this event the feast of dedication (Hanukkah) was instituted. Later he fought many battles, and at last fell in an encounter with the Syrians under Bacchides.

Jude (jōd) or **Judas** (jō'dạs), Saint. One of the 12 apostles, probably identical with Thaddaeus and Lebbaeus. Mat. x. 3.

Jude the Obscure. A novel by Thomas Hardy, published serially in 1895 as *Hearts Insurgent* in *Harper's Magazine* and in book form in 1896. It deals with the tragic career of a humble stonecutter whose ambition for an education is frustrated by a cold reception at Oxford, and whose personal life is shipwrecked by the selfishness of two women. This was the last novel written by Hardy. According to Edwin Arlington Robinson, *"Jude the Obscure* will live, because it is the truest thing that Hardy ever wrote." However, the outcry that greeted its publication led to Hardy's renunciation of prose fiction.

Judge (juj), **Jack.** b. 1878; d. at Birmingham, England, July 28, 1938. An English vaudeville performer, and composer (1912) with Harry Williams of the song *It's a Long, Long Way to Tipperary*. He introduced the song at the Stalybridge Grand Theatre, and more than five million copies were sold by 1915.

Judgment House, The. A novel by Sir Gilbert Parker, published in 1913, dealing with industrial life in England and South Africa during the period 1895–1902.

Judgment of Eve (ēv), **The.** A collection of short stories by May Sinclair, published in 1908.

Judges, Book of. A book of the Old Testament, containing the history of Israel under the leaders ("judges") from Deborah and Barak to Samuel.

Judith (jō'dith). The name of the heroine of the Book of Judith in the Old Testament Apocrypha.

Judith. An Old English poem, probably of the 7th century, first printed in 1698. It is found in the manuscript (Manuscript Cotton Vitellius A xv) which also contains the only known copy of *Beowulf*. The poem was formerly ascribed to Caedmon. The extant fragment consists of 350 lines, containing episodes from the apocryphal tale of Judith.

Judith, Book of. An apocryphal book of the Old Testament. Judith, a native of Bethulia, delivers her people by entering the camp of Holofernes and slaying him in his sleep.

Judith Anderson (an'dẽr.sọn). See **Anderson, Judith.**

Judy (jō'di). See under **Punch.**

Juggernaut (jug'ẽr.nôt). [Also: **Jagannath, Jagannatha.**] In Hindu religion, a form of Krishna, and also of Rama and Dattatreya, all incarnations of Vishnu. Juggernaut is Krishna as lord of the world. He is worshiped elsewhere in India, but his two festivals at Puri, near Cuttack in Orissa, are especially famous. These are the Snanayatra, during which the image of the god is bathed, and Rathayatra, when the image is placed on a huge car and drawn in procession. Such cars are attached to every large Vishnu pagoda in the south of India, and typify the moving active world over which the god presides. The car is 45 ft. high, 35 ft. square, and supported on 16 wheels 7 ft. in diameter. Balarama, the brother, and Subhadra, the sister of Juggernaut, have separate cars a little smaller. When the images are placed on the cars, the worshipers kneel, bow their foreheads in the dust, and, rushing forward, draw the cars down the broad street toward Juggernaut's country house. The distance is less than a mile, but the journey takes several days. It has been said that pilgrims overcome by religious frenzy have thrown themselves under the wheels of the great car, and possibly, in the press of thousands, some worshipers may sometimes have been crushed under the wheels. The possibility of deliberate suicide is extremely unlikely, however, since all devotees know that such shedding of blood could defile the sacred event.

Julia (jōl'yạ). In Shakespeare's *Two Gentlemen of Verona*, the young woman who loves Proteus.

Julia. [Full name, **Julia Melville** (mel'vil).] In Richard Brinsley Sheridan's comedy *The Rivals*, the long-suffering object of the jealousy of Falkland.

Julia. In J. Sheridan Knowles's play *The Hunchback*, a type of commonplace sentiment.

Julia, Donna. In Byron's *Don Juan*, a lady of Seville. She provides the hero with his first amorous adventure (the first, that is, about which Byron tells us).

Julia Mannering (man'ẽr.ing). See **Mannering, Julia.**

Julián (нŏ.lyän'), **Count.** In Spanish legend, a governor of Andalusia in the 8th century. According to the story, his daughter Florinda was seduced by Roderic, and in revenge he betrayed Ceuta to the Moors.

Juliana (jō.li.an'ạ). An Old English poem by Cynewulf, one of the four works signed by the poet, preserved (except for two passages) in the *Exeter Book*. An account of the persecution and martyrdom of a young Christian virgin in the 4th century A.D., it is a conventional work of this genre in most respects, but contains one noteworthy sequence in which a devil, upon being seized by the saint, is forced to reveal the secrets and techniques of deviltry.

Julian Avenel (jōl'yạn āv'nẹl). See **Avenel, Julian.**

Julie (zhü.lē). In Rousseau's *La Nouvelle Héloïse*, the wife of Wolmar, and former mistress of Saint-Preux.

Juliet (jōl'yẹt, jōl'i.ẹt, jō.li.et'). In Shakespeare's *Measure for Measure*, Claudio's betrothed. Claudio is sentenced to death when, through her pregnancy, it becomes known that he has seduced her. Later, Claudio and she are married.

Juliet. The heroine of Shakespeare's tragedy *Romeo and Juliet*. She is the daughter of Capulet, and loves Romeo, the heir of the hostile family of Montague. Beginning as a demure young girl who listens to the advice of her mother, she becomes a woman of courage and action, even willing to die for her husband. In the famous balcony scene she carefully questions the circumstances of Romeo's love and wittily refuses his vows. When she next appears the girlish reserve has gone, as she impetuously asks for news of Romeo. Very simply she says that her wealth of love is so great, she cannot sum up half. Her love is seen in a continual play upon words or terms associated with Romeo: "I," "Tybalt's dead," "banished," "faith," and "heart." As her forebodings of Romeo's doom are borne out by events, her mind dwells on the terrors of the grave, questioning the action she must take, just as she questioned Romeo's love. Yet when Romeo enters her mind, she acts quickly in taking the sleeping potion, and even more quickly when she finds Romeo dead beside her. The poison, which she feared, becomes the kiss of Romeo's poisoned lips and symbolically death is turned into an act of love.

Julius (jŏl'yus), **Charles.** Pseudonym of **Bertram, Charles.**

Julius Caesar (sē'zạr). [Full title, **The Tragedy of Julius Caesar.**] A historical tragedy by Shakespeare, written and produced c1599 (a performance date of Sept. 21, 1599, at the Globe theater has been tentatively accepted). It was printed in the folio of 1623. As his principal sources, Shakespeare used Plutarch's *Lives* (those of Brutus, Caesar, and Antony) in the 1579 translation by Sir Thomas North from the French of Jacques Amyot. All of the events in the play which have a basis in history occurred in 44 B.C., but over a greater span of time than the two days assigned to them by Shakespeare.

The Story. Caesar's triumphal return to Rome (of which he has already been made dictator), after a series of military victories in Spain, brings to a climax the fear held by a faction of Roman leaders that the traditional freedoms of the republic may perish through Caesar's overweening ambition, and the plot to assassinate him quickly begins to take shape. Cassius (the chief conspirator, and motivated by jealousy fully as much as by a love of freedom), Casca, Cinna, and others persuade Caesar's close friend Marcus Brutus (a somewhat ambiguous figure; initially a very strong character, motivated by lofty idealism, he later succumbs almost to petulance) to join their faction, and that night at Brutus's house they complete their plans. The night is disturbed, stormy, and full of portents of disaster. Caesar, despite a warning from a soothsayer that he should beware the Ides of March, and the ominous dream of his wife Calphurnia, goes to the Senate where, as planned by the conspirators, he is stabbed to death. Mark Antony, in a clever and unscrupulous speech at Caesar's funeral, arouses the crowd to fury at the assassination. He then joins Octavius and Lepidus to form a governing triumvirate. The conspirators leave Rome and take refuge at Sardis. There, as Antony's army approaches, Cassius and Brutus quarrel, but they are reconciled when Brutus tells Cassius of the suicide of his (Brutus's) wife Portia (in this very moving scene Cassius reveals a depth of sympathetic understanding hardly consistent with the stereotype of cold villainy which tradition has attached to him). In an unwise military move, the conspirators meet Antony's army on the plains of Philippi and are there defeated. Cassius and Brutus both die honorably.

Julius Caesar. A tragedy published in 1607 by Sir William Alexander. It is in the Senecan tradition,

and was intended for private performance only. It was one of his *Monarchicke Tragedies.*

Julius Caesar. See also **Caesar, Julius.**

Julius Handford (hand'fọrd). See **Handford, Julius.**

Jungle Books, The. Two collections of stories for children by Kipling, published in 1894 (*The Jungle Book*) and 1895 (*The Second Jungle Book*) respectively. They include the stories of Mowgli, a boy found and reared by the beasts of the jungle. The wolves who are his original "foster parents" are aided in the task of his upbringing by Baloo, the bear, Bagheera, the panther, and Kaa, the rock python.

Junius (jŏn'yus). The pseudonym of the unknown author of a series of letters directed against the British ministry, Sir William Draper, the Duke of Grafton, and others. The letters appeared in the London *Public Advertiser* from Nov. 21, 1768, to Jan. 21, 1772. Their authorship has been attributed to Edmund Burke, Earl Temple, and others, but they probably were written by Sir Philip Francis.

Junius (jŏn'yus; German, yö'nẹ̇.u̇s), **Franziskus.** [Also, **François Dujon.**] b. at Heidelberg, Germany, 1589; d. at Windsor, England, Nov. 19, 1677. A German student of the Teutonic languages. He served (1621–51) as librarian and tutor in the family of Thomas Howard, 2nd Earl of Arundel. His collection of manuscripts, edited by him and including the group of Old English works comprising what is now called the *Junius Manuscript,* was willed to Oxford University. Among his works is *Etymologicum Anglicanum* (edited by Lye, 1743).

Junius Brutus (jŏn'yus brō'tus). See **Brutus, Junius.**

Junius Manuscript. A manuscript in the Bodleian Library at Oxford, dating from the late 10th or early 11th century and containing Old English poems on Biblical subjects formerly attributed to Caedmon. These comprise two main divisions: the first, dealing with Old Testament subjects, contains three parts usually designated *Genesis, Exodus,* and *Daniel;* the second, based on the New Testament, is called as a whole *Christ and Satan.* The manuscript is named for Franziskus Junius (also known as François Dujon), who had it printed in the 17th century.

Juno (jö'nō). In Roman mythology, the queen of heaven, the highest deity in the Roman pantheon next to Jupiter, of whom she was the sister and the wife. She was identified with the Greek Hera. She was the special protectress of marriage, and the month of June (named for her) is still the popular marriage month. She was also guardian of woman from birth to death. The Matronalia was her festival, celebrated on March 1. And every woman had her own tutelary *juno,* conceived of as a kind of guardian spirit. As Juno Lucina she was invoked during childbirth, and a table was spread for her in the house where a child was born. In Rome as Juno Moneta she was also the patron of the national finances, and a temple which contained the mint was erected to her on the Capitoline Hill. As Juno Regina she headed the state cult along with Jupiter. As Juno Curitis she was regarded as a war goddess. As Juno Lanuvina she had a special cult and priesthood at Lanuvina, where her sacred serpents ate

---

ḍ, d or j; ṣ, s or sh; ṭ, t or ch; ẓ, z or zh; *o,* F. cloche; ü, F. menu; ċh, Sc. loch; ṅ, F. bonbon.

the cakes offered by pure virgins and refused all others.

Juno. In Shakespeare's *Tempest*, a character appearing in the masque celebrating the betrothal of Ferdinand and Miranda.

Juno and the Paycock. A tragicomedy (1924) by Sean O'Casey.

Junto (jun'tō). A group of English Whigs, influential under William III and Anne.

Jupe (jöp). In Dickens's novel *Hard Times*, a circus performer.

Jupiter (jö'pi.tėr). [Also, **Jove.**] In Roman mythology, the supreme deity, predominantly a sky god; brother and husband of Juno. He was identified with the Greek Zeus, and was the embodiment of the might and national dignity of the Romans. The central seat of his cult was the Capitoline Hill at Rome, where as god of the state he had the title of Optimus Maximus (Best and Greatest). As god of the sky, he was the originator of all atmospheric changes. His weapon was the thunderbolt, and all places struck by lightning were sacred to him. He controlled and directed the future, and sacrifices were offered to secure his favor (with Janus's) at the beginning of every undertaking. He was also the guardian of property, whether of the state or of individuals, and also guardian of honor, the keeping of oaths, treaties, and vows. White, the color of the light of day, was sacred to him: hence white animals were offered to him in sacrifice, his priests wore white caps, his chariot was drawn by four white horses, and the consuls were dressed in white when they sacrificed to him upon assuming office. The eagle was especially consecrated to him. The surviving artistic representations of Jupiter are comparatively late, and betray Greek influence, imitating the type of the Greek Zeus.

Jupiter. In Shakespeare's *Cymbeline*, an apparition that appears to Posthumus while he is asleep. Jupiter descends amid thunder and lightning, seated upon an eagle (V. iv).

Jupiter Stator (stā'tôr). Jupiter the stayer-of-flight, or giver of victory.

Justice. A social tragedy (1910) in four acts by John Galsworthy.

Justice (jus'tis), **Beatrice.** In James Joyce's three-act play *Exiles* (1918), a music teacher.

Justice. Entries on justices in literature will be found under their surnames, including Balance, Buzzard, Clement, Clodpate, Credulous, Gobble, and Stareleigh.

Justinian I (jus.tin'i.an). [Full name, **Flavius Anicius Justinianus;** called **Justinian the Great.**] b. at Tauresium, Dardania, Illyricum, probably May 11, 483; d. Nov. 14, 565. A Byzantine emperor (527–565); nephew of Justin I, whom he succeeded. He married (525) Theodora, an actress who exercised great influence during his reign, chiefly in ecclesiastical affairs. In 532 a fight broke out in the hippodrome between the Green and the Blue factions, the latter of which favored the emperor and the orthodox church. The fight spread

from the hippodrome to the city, and the Green proclaimed as emperor Hypatius, nephew of Anastasius I. The revolt was put down by the general Belisarius with the assistance of the Blue, but not before 30,000 of the insurgents had been slain and a large part of the city destroyed, including the Church of Santa Sophia, which was rebuilt (532–537) with great splendor according to plans furnished by the architect Anthemius. In the East, Justinian purchased (531) peace from the Persians, but in the West the victories of his generals Belisarius and Narses destroyed the Vandal and the Ostrogothic kingdoms in Africa and Italy respectively, and restored those countries to the Byzantine empire. An important event of his reign was the publication of a code of law now called the Justinian Code. This law compilation, prepared under Tribonian, includes the *Pandects* (previous judicial decisions), a *Code*, the *Institutes* (a textbook), and the *Novellae* (laws issued under Justinian). This, the *Corpus Juris Civilis*, is the basic Roman law used by many European countries.

Just So Stories. [Full title, **Just So Stories for Little Children.**] A collection of twelve stories (1902) by Rudyard Kipling. The tales range from what might be called "fictitious" folklore ("How the First Letter Was Written") to fanciful tales of animal origins ("How the Camel Got His Hump"). The work was the only one to be illustrated by the author.

Jutes (jöts). A Germanic people who, with the Angles and Saxons, invaded Britain from c449. According to tradition they were invited by the Britons to aid them against the Picts, and landed at Ebbsfleet, under Hengist and Horsa. They founded the kingdom of Kent, and settled along the south bank of the Thames almost as far as the site of London, and also on the Isle of Wight. Their connection with Jutland has been a matter of dispute; some scholars believe their place of origin was the region around the mouth of the Rhine. From a literary and cultural standpoint, they played a minor role in the early history of England; it was the two Anglian dialects (of Northumbria and Mercia) and the Saxon dialect (of Wessex) which became dominant, and from which came standard Old English (whence the term "Anglo-Saxon" sometimes applied to Old English).

Jutland (jut'land), **Battle of.** The greatest naval battle of World War I. It was fought (May 31–June 1, 1916) in the arm of the North Sea called the Skagerrak, off the Jutland peninsula (the continental portion of Denmark), and involved British vessels under Admirals Beatty and Jellicoe and a German fleet under Admirals von Hipper and Scheer. In the action the British lost three battle cruisers, three light cruisers, eight destroyers, and 6,800 killed and wounded, while the Germans lost one battleship, one battle cruiser, three light cruisers, five destroyers, and 3,000 men. The battle was not decisive for either side. Though it can be considered a German tactical success, it brought no strategic advantages to Germany. The Allied blockade was not broken and was not challenged again except by German submarine warfare.

fat, fāte, fär, ȧsk, fāre; net, mē, hėr; pin, pīne; not, nōte, mōve, nôr; up, lūte, půll; ᴛʜ, then;

Juvenal (jö'vẹ.nạl). [Full Latin name, **Decimus Junius Juvenalis**.] fl. c60–140 A.D. A Roman rhetorician and satirical poet of the age of Trajan. Little is known of his life. Sixteen of his satires (in five books) are extant; they display an epigrammatic style that is used to expose the vices of the Roman society of his day.

Juventas (jö.ven'tạs). In Roman mythology, the goddess of youth; Hebe.

K

Ka (kä). In Rudyard Kipling's Mowgli stories, the great rock python who is Mowgli's friend and occasional adviser.

Kaaba (kä'bạ, kä'ạ.bạ). [Also, **Caaba**.] A cube-shaped, flat-roofed building in the center of the Great Mosque at Mecca: the most sacred shrine of the Mohammedans, believed to have been built first by Adam, and rebuilt by Abraham and Ishmael. In its southeast corner it contains the sacred black stone called *hajar al aswad*, said to have been given to Ishmael by the angel Gabriel. It was originally shining white, but is now blackened from being touched by pilgrims seeking forgiveness for their sins. The stone is an irregular oval about seven inches in diameter, and is thought to be a meteorite. It is the point toward which all Mohammedans face during their devotions. The Kaaba is opened to worshipers twice or three times a year, but only the faithful are permitted to approach it. Devout Mohammedans believe that on the Judgment Day the black stone will praise Allah, and recognize all the pilgrims who have kissed it.

Kabir (kạ.bēr'). fl. 1488–1512. A Hindu religious reformer. He was a weaver, and probably a Moslem by birth, who lived at Benares, and also at Magar near Gorakhpur. His teachings exercised an important influence in upper India in the 15th and 16th centuries, and formed the basis of the Sikh movement in the Punjab. He became a pupil of Ramananda and a Vaishnava with much of the democracy and tolerance of Buddhism; but he denounced all idol worship, and taught Vaishnavism as a form of strict monotheism. True religion, he said, ultimately could mean nothing but devotion to one God, whether called Vishnu, Rama, or Hari, or by Mohammedan names. Basically, he rejected every distinction of caste, religion, and sect. By his view, all authority in faith and morals belongs to the guru, or spiritual guide, though the rights of conscience of the believer are reserved. Kabir's aim was evidently to found a religion that should unite the Hindus and Mohammedans.

Kaf (käf). [Also: **Caf, Qaf**.] In Mohammedan legend, a range of emerald mountains encircling the earth, the chief abode of the jinn. The term is also generic for "mountain."

Kaikhusrau (kī.kus.rou'). In the Persian epic, the *Shahnamah*, the 13th and greatest of the Iranian kings. He reigned 60 years. He was the son of Syawaush (son of Iraj) and Farangis daughter of Afrasyab (Turanian enemy of Iran). After the murder of Syawaush, Afrasyab was about to slay Farangis that none of the offspring of Iraj might live; but she was sent away instead and her child was brought up by shepherds. Afrasyab, frightened by a dream in which the son of Syawaush destroyed him, sought to destroy the child, but his fears were again allayed when he was told that the boy was an idiot. When he warred with Kaikawus, Afrasyab sent Farangis and her young son to a remote place, but they were found and brought to Kaikawus, who appointed Kaikhusrau his successor. Kaikhusrau continued the war, and slew Afrasyab. The name Kaikhusrau has been identified with that of the elder Cyrus, chiefly on a basis of similarities between Greek and Iranian legend.

Kailyal (kāl'yạl, kīl'yäl). In Robert Southey's *The Curse of Kehama*, the daughter of the humble Ladurlad. She is, second only to him, a principal object of the wrath of Kehàma.

Kain (kān), **Saul**. A pseudonym of **Sassoon, Siegfried**.

Kaiser (kī'zėr), **Georg**. b. at Magdeburg, Germany, 1878; d. at Ascona, Switzerland, June 5, 1945. A German author, leading dramatist of the expressionist school. Like Hans Grimm, Kaiser tried business abroad (Buenos Aires) before settling down to literature. With the exception of two novels late in life, *Es ist genug* (1932) and *Villa Aurea* (1940; Eng. trans., *A Villa in Sicily*, 1939), he wrote entirely for the stage. His first plays were satirical treatments of old themes: *Rektor Kleist* (1905) flays school tyranny, *Die jüdische Witwe* (1911) gives the Judith theme a sardonic twist, *König Hahnrei* (1913) makes mock of King Mark. *Von Morgens bis Mitternachts* (1916) has, however, more social significance, and the trilogy *Koralle* (1917), *Gas I* (1918), and *Gas II* (1920) argue for class leveling. Kaiser, with Thomas Mann and Franz Werfel, was expelled from the Prussian Academy in 1933 when Hitler rose to power; his works were among those included in the Nazi book-burning.

Kalevala (kä'le.vä.lä). [Also, **Kalewala**.] A national epic of Finland. The elements of the poem are ancient folk and heroic songs collected in parts of Finnish and adjacent territory, for the most part within the 19th century. A number of folk songs, runes, tales, riddles, and the like had been collected by scholars in the 18th century, but the first considerable collection of folk songs was published in five parts by Zacharias Topelius in the period 1822–31. The most important collector, however, was Elias Lönnrott (1802–44). Lönnrott was both author and editor of the *Kalevala* (first edition, 1835). This was a collection of 16 hero poems, amounting to some 5,000 lines. In 1849 appeared a second edition, containing 50 songs in some 22,800 lines, which is the present form of the poem. The *Kalevala* is written in eight-syllabled trochaic verse,

ḍ, d or j; ṣ, s or sh; ṭ, t or ch; ẓ, z or zh; o, F. cloche; ü, F. menu; ċh, Sc. loch; ṅ, F. bonbon.

with alliteration, but without rhyme. Although the unity and actual writing of the *Kalevala* are the work of one man, Lönnrott, 95 percent of the lines come direct from the people. *Kalevala* means "the land of Kaleva," ancient Finnish culture hero; but its main characters are his descendants, the central hero being Väinämöinen, the god of poetry and music. It is the prototype, in form, of Longfellow's *Hiawatha*.

Kali (kä′lē). In Hindu mythology, the Black One, consort of Shiva; a destructive form of Parvati (the name Calcutta probably represents *Kalighat*, the ghat or landing-place of Kali). In her images the body is black, or dark-blue, the insides of the hands red. She wears a necklace of human heads and a cincture of blood-stained hands, while she stands on the body of Shiva. Her tongue protrudes from her mouth, which is marked with blood. Bloody sacrifices are made to her. She has a celebrated temple called the Kalighat, near Calcutta. She personifies the mother goddess as devouring, i.e., taking back, the life she has produced.

Kalidasa (kä.lē̇.dä′sä). fl. probably in the 5th century A.D. A Hindu poet and dramatist. Accounts of his life tell us only that he lived at Ujjain, and that he was one of the "Nine Gems" of the court of one of the kings named Vikramaditya. Kalidasa is the undisputed author of the two dramas *Sakuntala* and *Vikramorvasi*, and some have credited to him also the *Malavikagnimitra*. The *Raghuvansa*, *Kumarasambhava*, *Meghaduta*, *Ritusanhara*, *Nalodava*, and *Srutabogha* have also all been ascribed to him with varying degrees of improbability. He is known to Europeans especially through the drama of *Sakuntala*, which, when first translated by Sir William Jones in 1789, produced such a sensation that the early success of Sanskrit studies in England and Germany may be ascribed to this masterpiece.

Kalilah and Dimnah (kä.lē′lä; dim′nä). [Also: **Calila and Dimna, Bidpai, Pilpay, Fables of Pilpay.**] An Arabic translation (made during the 8th century) of the Pahlavi translation of the Sanskrit original of the *Panchatantra*. *Kalilah and Dimnah* is also the name of the later Syriac version made in the 10th or 11th century. English translations of both were published in the 19th century.

Kalmucks (kal′muks). [Also: **Calmucks, Kalmyks** (kal′miks, käl.miks′).] Western Mongols, of the Buddhist religion, who migrated from Dzungaria (in what is now Sinkiang, China) and settled the region of the Lower Volga in the early 17th century. Although they willingly served the Russian government as mercenary soldiers, their tribal privileges and customs were nevertheless interfered with to such an extent that the bulk of the tribe fled back toward China in 1771. It is said that only 15,000 out of 300,000 survived this famous flight. The survivors settled in the Ili valley in Sinkiang. A group west of the Volga did not join this exodus, but remained to follow their own brand of Lamaism. Descendants of this group constituted the ethnic basis of the Kalmuck Autonomous Republic, SW of the Volga River in the U.S.S.R., which was liquidated in 1943 for collaboration with the Germans during World War II. There are a few thousand Kalmucks today surviving as "displaced

persons" in C and W Europe, or as resettled persons in the U.S.S.R.

Kalpa (käl′pä). In Hindu cosmogony, a day and night of Brahma, consisting of 1,000 yugas, or 432 million years.

Kama (kä′mä). The Hindu god of love. In the *Rig-Veda*, desire is the first movement that arose in the One after it had come into life through the power of fervor or abstraction. It is the bond which connects entity with nonentity. He is armed with a bow and arrows, the bow being of sugar cane, the bowstring a line of bees; each of the five arrows, tipped with a distinct flower, conquers one of the five senses. He rides on a parrot attended by nymphs, one of whom bears his banner. His wife is Rati, or Delight.

Kames (kāmz), **Lord.** Title of **Home, Henry.**

Kane (kān), **Saul.** A reformed drunkard, the hero of John Masefield's narrative poem *The Everlasting Mercy* (1911).

Kant (kant; German, känt), **Immanuel.** b. at Königsberg, in East Prussia, April 22, 1724; d. there, Feb. 12, 1804. A German philosopher, one of the most influential thinkers of modern times, founder of the "critical philosophy." He was the son of a saddler in very moderate circumstances. His early education was obtained in his native city, where he entered the university in 1740 and began the study of theology. Subsequently he was tutor in several families, but took his degree in 1755 and settled as docent at the university. In 1766 he received a small salaried position in the Royal Library. Finally in 1770 he was made professor of logic and metaphysics, a position which he held until his death. Although he had advantageous calls to other universities, he preferred to remain at Königsberg, and during his whole life is said never to have been further away than Pillau, some 30 English miles distant. During his university career he lectured not only on logic and the various branches of metaphysics, but also, at various times, on anthropology, physical geography, and mathematics.

Written Works. His first treatise, *Gedanken von der wahren Schätzung der lebendigen Kräfte*, appeared in 1747. His real literary activity began in 1755 with the treatise on cosmic physics, *Allgemeine Naturgeschichte und Theorie des Himmels* (General History of Nature and Theory of the Heavens), in which he suggested for the first time the "nebular hypothesis" later developed by Laplace. In 1764 appeared *Beobachtungen über das Gefühl des Schönen und Erhabenen* (Observations on the Sense of the Beautiful and the Sublime). In 1766 he published *Träume eines Geistersehers* (Dreams of a Ghost-seer). The first of his great philosophical works, the most important in modern philosophy, appeared in 1781. This is the *Kritik der reinen Vernunft* (Critique of Pure Reason). The best German edition is that of Raymund Schmidt, published in 1926; the best English version is by Norman Kemp Smith (1929). His second great work, the *Kritik der praktischen Vernunft* (Critique of Practical Reason), appeared in 1788. This deals with morals; according to it the ideas of God, human liberty, and immortality are postulates of practical reason. Finally, the third *Critique*, an inquiry into the faculty of judgment, appeared in 1790 under the title *Kritik der Urteilskraft* (Critique of the Power of Judgment). In addition to the works mentioned, he published a number of smaller treatises and essays. To 1784 belongs the short essay *Was ist Aufklärung?* (What is Enlightenment?), which pronounces the century of Frederick the Great the age of German enlightenment. *Grundlegung der Metaphysik der Sitten* (Foundation of the Metaphysics of Ethics) appeared in 1785, *Religion innerhalb der Grenzen der blossen Vernunft* (Religion within the Limits of Mere Reason) in 1793, *Metaphysische Anfangsgründe der Rechtslehre* (Metaphysical Elements of Legal Science) in 1797. A late edition of his collected works is that of E. Cassirer (1912–22), in 10 volumes.

Position and Contribution as Philosopher. Kant's *Critique of Pure Reason* was the turning point of modern thought. His problem arose from the conflict between the opposed conceptions of knowledge that had dominated modern philosophy. The rationalists held that all genuine knowledge is the work of thought as distinguished from sense-perception. But if this is true then it would seem that knowledge can contain nothing not already implicit in its premises, and so must be analytical. Kant had been educated in the rationalist philosophy but happened to become acquainted with some of the writings of David Hume, the great Scottish empiricist and critic of reason. Hume, Kant tells us, awakened him from his "dogmatic slumber" and forced him to reconsider the whole problem of the nature and limits of knowledge. Although Kant's conviction that mathematics and physics provide us with genuine and certain knowledge independently of experience was unshaken by the skeptical conclusions at which Hume had arrived, yet Hume did convince him that the basic principles of our knowledge of nature are not analytical but synthetical. So Kant found himself agreeing with the rationalists that some of our knowledge is a priori and agreeing with Hume that these same principles are synthetical. The insight from which Kant's critical philosophy developed is his discovery that the rationalists and empiricists were making an identical unexamined assumption. They both assumed that if knowledge is a priori it must also be analytical and if, on the other hand, it involves the addition of anything new it cannot be a priori. Convinced that this assumption is false Kant asks how it is possible for knowledge to be both a priori and synthetical, and with this he opens a new line of development for European thought. He answers his own question by using the traditional distinction between the form and material of knowledge. He accounts for its synthetical character in terms of the material which it obtains from sensation, and for the a priori factor in terms of the processes of the mind which organize the material of sensation into an awareness of objects. The heart of Kant's argument is his attempt to show that in order to constitute an awareness of objects our sensations must be organized into certain definite patterns such as space, time, quality, quantity, substance, causality, and the like, and consequently we know before we experience an object that it must exhibit these forms. From the characteristics of these forms Kant thinks he can account for the basic principles

of our knowledge of the physical world, especially those of Euclidean geometry and Newtonian physics. This justification, as against skepticism, of the use of reason with respect to the objects of sense-perception has two consequences. First, the world of space and time objects is a world of phenomena, of things which do not exist in themselves but which depend for their form upon the processes by which they come to be known. Second, the existence of another world of things-in-themselves must be postulated, but pure reason is unable to discover anything about the nature of this other world. Consequently such objects as God, the world as a whole, and the soul cannot be known by reason even though reason inevitably speculates about them.

Karmathians (kär.mạ'thi.ạnz). [Also, **Carmathians.**] A Mohammedan sect which arose in Turkey about the end of the 9th century, so named from Karmat, the principal apostle of the sect, a poor laborer, who professed to be a prophet. The Karmathians regarded the Koran as an allegorical book, rejected all revelation, fasting, and prayer, and were communistic, even in the matter of wives. They carried on wars against the caliphate, particularly in the 10th century, but disappeared soon after. According to some accounts the Druses developed from them.

Karttikeya (kärt.ti.kā'yạ). See **Skanda.**

Kaspar (käs'pär). See **Gaspar.**

Kastril (kas'tril). In Ben Jonson's *Alchemist, a* young country fellow, brother of Dame Pliant, and anxious to learn the art of quarreling.

Kate Hardcastle (kāt härd'kȧs''l). See **Hardcastle, Kate.**

Kate Nickleby (kāt nik'l.bi). See **Nickleby, Kate.**

Katherina (kath.ẹ.rē'nạ). In Shakespeare's *Taming of the Shrew,* the "Shrew." The daughter of Baptista, she is married to Petruchio and is tamed by his rough treatment.

Katherine (kath'rin, -ẹ.rin). In Shakespeare's *Henry V,* "fair Kate," daughter of Charles VI of France, whom Henry woos (V. ii). Henry insists on her hand as part of the peace treaty with France. The historical Catherine of Valois (1401–37) was the mother of Henry VI and after the death of Henry V married Owen Tudor; her grandson became Henry VII.

Katherine. In Shakespeare's *Henry VIII,* the historical Catherine of Aragon, first wife of King Henry, and one of those whose fall from power is depicted. When she receives the news of Henry's divorce, she regrets the downfall of Wolsey, whom she has previously taken to be the source of her troubles.

Katherine. In Shakespeare's *Love's Labour's Lost,* a lady in attendance on the Princess of France. She is wooed by Dumain.

Katherine Group. Five closely related prose pieces from the Middle English period, probably written in the late 12th or early 13th century. *Saint Katherine, Saint Margaret,* and *Saint Juliana* are the lives of three saints, each of whom endures torture rather than lose her virginity. *Hali Meidenhad* and *Sawles Warde* are religious treatises, the first of

---

which is another acclamation of virginity. *Sawles Warde* (The Safeguarding of the Soul) is an allegory of a house, symbolizing the body, ruled by Wit and Will, and containing a treasure (the soul). Two visitors to the house describe at length the horrors of Hell and the joys of Heaven.

Kathleen Mavourneen (kath.lēn' mav.ör.nēn'). A song by Louisa Macartney Crawford (1790–1858). The music was written by Frederick N. Crouch (1808–96).

Katinka (ka̤.ting'ka̤). In Byron's *Don Juan*, one of the women in the harem of which Don Juan is also briefly, in one of the episodes, a resident.

Katisha (kat'i.shä). In Gilbert and Sullivan's *The Mikado*, a lady of somewhat advanced years at the court of the Mikado. She loves Nanki-Poo, but is eventually married by Ko-Ko (who is thus able to save himself from execution).

Kavanagh (kav'a̤.nä, -nô, -na̤), **Alicia.** "Alice-for-Short" in William De Morgan's novel (1907) of that name.

Kavanagh, Julia. b. at Thurles, County Tipperary, Ireland, Jan. 7, 1824; d. at Nice, France, Oct. 28, 1877. A British novelist. Among her works are *Madeleine* (1848), *Nathalie* (1850), *Daisy Burns* (1853), *Grace Lee* (1855), *Adèle* (1857), *Queen Mab* (1863), and *John Dorrien* (1875). She also wrote *French Women of Letters* and *English Women of Letters* (1862).

Kay (kā), **Sir.** [Called "the Rude" and "the Boastful."] In Arthurian legend and romance, a knight of the Round Table, son of Sir Ector and the foster brother of Arthur, who made him his seneschal. He was treacherous and malicious.

Kaye (kā), **Sir John William.** b. at Acton, Middlesex, England, 1814; d. at London, July 24, 1876. An English historical and biographical writer. His works include *History of the War in Afghanistan* (1851), *Administration of the East India Company* (1853), and *The History of the Sepoy War in India 1857–58* (1864–76).

Kaye-Smith (kā'smith'), **Sheila.** b. c1889—. An English novelist, author notably of stories with a Sussex background. Her novels include *The Tramping Methodist* (1908), *Three Against the World* (1914), *Sussex Gorse* (1916), *Joanna Godden* (1921), *The End of the House of Alard* (1923), *The Village Doctor* (1929), *Susan Spray* (1931), *Superstition Corner* (1934), *Rose Deeprose* (1936), *The Valiant Woman* (1938), *Ember Lane* (1940), *Kitchen Fugue* (1945), *The Lardners and the Laurelwoods* (1948), and *The Treasures of the Snow* (1949). With G. B. Stern, she has published two studies of Jane Austen, *Talking of Jane Austen* (1943) and *More Talk of Jane Austen* (1949).

Keable (kē'bl), **Robert.** b. in Bedfordshire, England, March 6, 1887; d. in Tahiti, Dec. 23, 1927. An English clergyman, freethinker, poet, essayist, and novelist. After being ordained (1911), he took up missionary work in Africa, and served in France (1917–18) as chaplain to the South African forces. He left the church, and in his later years, when he produced his literary works, was a radical freethinker. Author of *Simon Called Peter* (1921), *Mother of All Living* (1922), a novel of Africa, *Per-*

adventure, or the Silence of God (1923), *Numerous Treasure* (1925), *Recognition* (1926), *Lighten Our Darkness* (1927; American title, *Ann Decides*), *The Madness of Monty* (1929; American title, *Though This Be Madness*), and *The Great Galilean* (1929). Other works are *A City of the Dawn* (1915), *Standing By—War Time Reflections in France and Flanders* (1919), *Pilgrim Places* (1920), and *Tahiti—Isle of Dreams* (1926).

Kean (kēn), **Charles John.** b. at Waterford, Ireland, Jan. 18, 1811; d. at Chelsea, London, Jan. 22, 1868. An English actor; son of Edmund Kean. His first appearance was in 1827, after which he played with his father till 1833, appearing as Iago to the elder Kean's Othello in the latter's last performance. In 1842 he married Ellen Tree. In 1850 he leased the Princess's Theatre, at first with Robert Keeley, where in 1851 he began his notable series of spectacular revivals, notably of Shakespeare's plays, done with historical accuracy. He was a careful but not a great actor. His last appearance was as Louis XI at Liverpool in 1867.

Kean, Edmund. b. at London, March 17, 1787; d. at Richmond, Surrey, England, May 15, 1833. English actor. His father was of Irish descent; his mother was an itinerant actress named Anne Carey, who deserted him. He played children's parts c1790, and in 1795 he ran away to sea. Under his mother's name (Carey) he led the life of a roving actor until 1806, when he first appeared at the Haymarket, London, as Ganem in the *Mountaineers*. In 1807 he played opposite Mrs. Siddons. On Jan. 26, 1814, he appeared at Drury Lane, where, as Shylock, he made one of the most sensational debuts in the history of the theater. This was followed by Hamlet, Othello, Iago, and Luke in *Riches*. One of his greatest successes was in Lear at the Drury Lane, in April, 1820. His first appearance at New York was on Nov. 29, 1820. He returned to Drury Lane in 1821 as Richard III, and played there at intervals until 1825 when (November 14) he appeared at the Park Theater, New York. Early in 1825 he had been found guilty of adultery in the case of Cox vs. Kean; his wife left him and he thereafter almost continually faced vociferously hostile audiences in England and America. He continued to act at Drury Lane, Covent Garden, and elsewhere; but the strain of working before unpredictable audiences and his own personal tragedy had caused him to turn excessively to drink and this contributed to such irregularity of life as finally to destroy his career. From 1829 his health continued to decline, and he acted only occasionally from that time until March 25, 1833, when he collapsed on the stage during a performance of *Othello*. He was probably unequaled as Richard III, Othello, Lear, and Sir Giles Overreach.

Keats (kēts), **John.** b. at Finsbury Pavement, Moorfields, London, Oct. 31 (or Oct. 29), 1795; d. at Rome, Feb. 23, 1821. An English poet. He was the eldest child of Thomas Keats, a head ostler, who died in 1804. In 1803 John was put into the Clarke School at Enfield, where he remained until the summer of 1811, when, with a surgeon's certificate in view, he became an apothecary's assistant to Mr. John Hammond at Edmonton. Four years later, in October, 1815, in further preparation for the surgeon's profession, he left Hammond's to enroll in Guy's and St. Thomas's Hospitals at London. Having completed the prescribed lecture and clinical courses, he passed his examinations in July, 1816, and emerged a full-fledged surgeon. Poetry rather than surgery was his destined profession, however. As early as 1812 he had begun to write verse (*Imitation of Spenser*), and before he left the hospitals he had produced a number of promising poems, among them his first-published piece, the sonnet "O Solitude" (in Leigh Hunt's *Examiner*, May 5, 1816), and the sonnet on Chapman's Homer (July 25, 1816). By the end of 1816, he had virtually abandoned the idea of ever practicing surgery.

Written Works. The volume *Poems of John Keats*, containing many short pieces and the longer "I Stood Tiptoe" and "Sleep and Poetry," was published in 1817. This was followed a little over a year later (April, 1818) by the long poetic romance *Endymion*, uneven, in ways immature, but full of beautiful passages. Then, in July, 1820, came his third and greatest volume, *Lamia, Isabella, the Eve of St. Agnes, and Other Poems.* Had Keats written nothing else, the contents of this book would have insured him a permanent place in world literature. For here were the matchless, brilliantly colorful *Eve of St. Agnes*, aflame with the imaginative exuberance inspired by the poet's own ripening love affair with the petite Fanny Brawne; the grand *Hyperion*, nearer to *Paradise Lost* than any other work since Milton; the lustrous and vibrantly dramatic *Lamia*; and those richly mature, gemlike works of artistic perfection, the great odes on melancholy, on a Grecian urn, to Psyche, and to a nightingale. In February, 1820, Keats discovered that he was a victim of tuberculosis, a disease which had already claimed his mother (1810) and his brother Tom (1818). Accompanied by his friend Joseph Severn, he sought relief in Italy, first going to Naples (September, 1820), then to Rome (Nov. 12) where a few weeks later he died.

Contemporary Neglect and Later Recognition. Keats numbered among his friends Leigh Hunt, Benjamin Haydon, Charles Cowden Clarke, Charles Armitage Brown, Benjamin Bailey, Charles Wentworth Dilke, John Hamilton Reynolds, William Hazlitt, and Percy Bysshe Shelley. His letters to these and others and to his family constitute one of the finest bodies of literary correspondence in existence. In spite of the support of his friends, Keats's poetry was largely neglected while he was alive, and was savagely attacked in such high places as *Blackwood's Magazine* (August, 1818) and *The Quarterly Review* (September, 1818). Heartsick with such knowledge and with thoughts of the great works he would never live to write, and borne down with grief over his great unfulfilled love for Fanny Brawne, he one day asked Severn, as he lay dying, to have inscribed on his tomb the words "Here lies one who writ in water." The words are there, as Keats requested, on the small stone above the grave in the Protestant cemetery in Rome where Keats was buried. But today this bitter, ironic epitaph reads strangely. For Keats has become one of the most highly honored of all English poets, whose fame promises to surpass, possibly even to outlive, that of some of his once more popular contemporaries.

Keble (kē'bl), **John.** b. at Fairford, Gloucestershire, England, April 25, 1792; d. at Bournemouth, Hampshire, England, March 27, 1866. An English clergyman and religious poet, one of the chief promoters of the Oxford movement. He graduated from Oxford (Corpus Christi College), and from 1831 to 1841 was professor of poetry there. His sermon "National Apostasy," delivered at Oxford July 14, 1833, was said by Newman to have marked the beginning of the Oxford movement. He became vicar of Hursley (March 9, 1836), and remained there 30 years. His influence was due especially to his hymns, which were published in the *Christian Year* (1827), one of the most popular books of 19th-century England. He published a new edition of Hooker (1836), the *Library of the Fathers* (in conjunction with Newman and Pusey, begun 1838), several numbers of the *Tracts of the Times*, and others.

Keble College. One of the colleges of Oxford University. It was founded in 1870 in honor of John Keble. The college owes its origin partly to the religious movement in which Keble himself played so large a part, and partly to a conviction that Oxford badly needed a college for students who could not afford to go to the other colleges then in existence. Lord Shaftesbury and Gladstone were among those who signed a widely circulated petition urging the foundation of such a college.

Kedar (kē'dạr). In the Bible, the second son of Ishmael (Gen. xxv. 13). His descendants, called Kedar or Kedarenes, were nomadic tent-dwellers, and next to the Nabataeans the most important tribe of the ancient Arabs. They are often mentioned in the Old Testament. In Pliny (*Histor. Natur.*, V. 12) they are called Cedrei. Assurbanipal, king of Assyria (668–626 B.C.), mentions in his annals a son of Hazilu (Hazael) as king of the country of the Kadri or Kidri. Their settlements are thought to have been in N Arabia.

Kedron (kē'drọn) or **Kidron** (kid'rọn). A brook to the north and east of Jerusalem, emptying into the Dead Sea. 2 Sam. xv. 23.

Keeper. See **Jailer.**

Kehama (kē.hä'mạ). An Indian rajah, a principal character in the poem *The Curse of Kehama*, by Robert Southey.

Keightley (kēt'li, kīt'li), **Thomas.** b. in Ireland, in October, 1789; d. at Erith, Kent, England, Nov. 4, 1872. An Irish writer. He settled at London in 1824, and was mainly occupied with the preparation of university textbooks on historical and literary subjects. He wrote *Fairy Mythology* (1828).

Keith (kēth), **Arthur Berriedale.** b. at Dunbar, Scotland, April 5, 1879; d. Oct. 6, 1944. A Scottish Sanskrit scholar and constitutional historian of the British Commonwealth and Empire. He was professor of Sanskrit and comparative philology at Edinburgh University (1914–44), and lecturer on the constitution of the British Empire (1927–44). Author of *Responsible Government in the Dominions* (1907), *The Sankhya System* (1918), *Selected Speeches and Documents on British Colonial Policy, 1763–1917* (1918), *War Government of the British Dominions* (1921), *Treatise on the Conflict of Laws* (with A. V. Dicey, 1922), *Buddhist Philosophy*

d, d or j; ṣ, s or sh; ṭ, t or ch; ẓ, z or zh; o, F. cloche; ü, F. menu; ch, Sc. loch; ṅ, F. bonbon.

(1923), *Classical Sanskrit Literature* (1923), *Constitutional History of the First British Empire* (1930), *The Dominions as Sovereign States: Their Constitutions and Governments* (1938), and *The British Commonwealth* (1941).

Keith Rickman (rik′man). See **Rickman, Keith.**

Kells (kelz). [Irish, **Ceannanus** (or **Ceannannus**) **Mór.**] An urban district and market town in the Irish Republic, in County Meath, on the river Blackwater ab. 10 mi. NW of Navan. The town is noted for its antiquities, especially for the *Book of Kells,* a 9th-century manuscript, now in the Trinity College Library, Dublin. It had an ancient monastery, founded by Saint Columba c555 and dissolved in the 16th century.

Kelly (kel′i), **Hugh.** b. in Ireland, 1739; d. 1777. A British dramatist and journalist. He arrived in London in 1760, and thereafter edited at various times in his career *The Court Magazine, The Ladies' Museum,* and a newspaper, *The Public Ledger.* His sentimental comedy *False Delicacy* (1768) was produced by Garrick to rival Goldsmith's *Good-Natured Man* at Covent Garden. The comedy of manners is represented in his *School for Wives* (1773), and he also wrote *A Word for the Wise* (1770).

Kelts (kelts). See **Celts.**

Kelvin (kel′vin), 1st Baron. [Title of **William Thomson;** full title (created 1892), 1st Baron **Kelvin of Largs** (lärgz).] b. at Belfast, Ireland, June 26, 1824; d. Dec. 17, 1907. An English mathematical physicist and inventor, noted for his formulation (1851–54) of two great laws of thermodynamics, inventor of 56 telegraphic, navigational, mechanical, electric, and other instruments, and described by the noted Continental scientist Helmholtz as "one of the first mathematical physicists of Europe."

Kemble (kem′bl), **Charles.** b. at Brecknock, Wales, Nov. 25, 1775; d. at London, Nov. 12, 1854. An English actor; brother of John Philip Kemble and Sarah Siddons. He went on the stage in the winter of 1792–93, and played Malcolm in *Macbeth* at the Drury Lane Theatre, London, in 1794. He excelled in such roles as Mercutio in *Romeo and Juliet,* Mirabell in Congreve's *Way of the World,* Charles Surface in Sheridan's *School for Scandal,* and Benedick in *Much Ado About Nothing.* He was frequently associated with his brother and sister in the production of new plays. On July 2, 1806, he married Marie Thérèse de Camp, who acted afterward as Mrs. Charles Kemble. In August, 1832, he sailed with his daughter, Fanny Kemble, to America, where he appeared as Hamlet at New York, Sept. 17, 1832. In 1835 he returned to the Haymarket Theatre at London. His last appearance was on April 10, 1840.

Kemble, Frances Anne. [Generally known as **Fanny Kemble.**] b. at London, Nov. 27, 1809; d. there, Jan. 15, 1893. An Anglo-American actress, Shakespearian reader, and author; daughter of Charles Kemble. She made her first public appearance in 1829, with the intention of retrieving the fortunes of her family (which aim she achieved in three years). She visited America in 1832, and there married Pierce Butler in 1834, from whom she afterward

(1848) obtained a divorce. She resumed her maiden name, and lived at Lenox, Mass., returning to Europe at intervals. In 1848–49 she gave her first series of Shakespearian readings at Boston, followed by readings in other cities. In these she was very successful. In 1851 she again went upon the stage in England. From 1869 to 1873 she was also in Europe. She wrote *Journal of a Residence in America* (1835), *The Star of Seville* (1837, a play), *Poems* (1844), *A Year of Consolation* (1847), *Records of a Girlhood* (1878), *Notes upon some of Shakespeare's Plays* (1882), *Records of Later Life* (1882), and *Life on a Georgia Plantation* (1863).

Kemble, John Mitchell. b. at London, April 2, 1807; d. at Dublin, March 26, 1857. An English philologist and historian; son of Charles Kemble and nephew of John Philip Kemble and Sarah Siddons. On Feb. 24, 1840, he succeeded his father as examiner of stage plays, and held that office until his death. He edited *Beowulf* (1833–37). His most important works are his unfinished *History of the Saxons in England* (1849) and the *Codex Diplomaticus Ævi Saxonici* (1839 *et seq.*).

Kemble, John Philip. b. at Prescott, near Liverpool, England, Feb. 1, 1757; d. at Lausanne, Switzerland, Feb. 26, 1823. English tragedian; brother of Charles Kemble and Sarah Siddons. On Jan. 8, 1776, he made his debut, at Wolverhampton as Theodosius, and thereafter played on the York circuit, as well as at Dublin and Cork, with growing success till Sept. 30, 1783, when he made his first appearance in London at the Drury Lane Theatre as Hamlet. In November, 1783, his sister, Sarah Siddons, first played with him. In 1788–89 he undertook the management of Drury Lane, and in 1802 of Covent Garden, which burned in 1808. It was on the occasion of his opening the New Covent Garden Theatre, in 1809, with a new scale of higher prices rendered necessary by the expenses incurred, that the famous "old-price riots" occurred. He was a stately actor, with a somewhat stilted and declamatory style. In Coriolanus, Cato, and Brutus he was at his best, and as Macbeth, opposite Mrs. Siddons, he was excellent, but in comedy he was not so successful.

Kempe (kemp), **Anna Eliza.** Maiden name of **Bray, Anna Eliza.**

Kempe, Margery. b. at Lynn (now King's Lynn), England, c1373; d. c1438. An English mystic, author of *The Book of Margery Kempe.*

Kempenfelt (kem′pen.felt), **Richard.** b. at Westminster, London, 1718; went down with the *Royal George* off Spithead, England, Aug. 29, 1782. An English admiral. He served in the West Indies, at the capture of Portobello, and passed through various grades to captain of the *Elizabeth* (1757), and rear admiral of the Blue (1780). When Lord Howe took command of the fleet (April, 1782), Kempenfelt was one of his junior admirals, his flag being on the *Royal George* at Spithead. In the refitting of this ship, the guns were shifted to one side to give her a slight heel; but the strain was too great, and she broke up and sank with her admiral and some 800 persons aboard.

Kempis (kem′pis), **Thomas a.** See **Thomas a Kempis.**

Kemp Owyne (kemp ō'ẹn). [Also, **Kempion** (kemp'-i.ọn).] The title and hero of a Scottish popular ballad in which a beautiful girl is bewitched by her stepmother and turned into a hideous sea monster. Nothing can save her but the kiss of love. Finally Kemp Owyne comes, gives her the required "kisses three," and the girl is retransformed to youth and beauty. The ballad has parallels in many languages, Icelandic and Danish especially.

Ken (ken), **Thomas.** b. at Little Berkhampstead, Hertfordshire, England, in July, 1637; d. at Longleat, Wiltshire, England, March 19, 1711. An English bishop and hymn writer. In 1679 he was chaplain to Mary, sister of the king and wife of William II, prince of Orange. He was created bishop of Bath and Wells in 1684. On Feb. 2, 1685, he attended King Charles II on his deathbed. In May, 1688, he was one of the "seven bishops" to petition the king not to oblige the clergy to read the second Declaration of Indulgence; and in April, 1691, he was deprived of his see as a nonjuror. His most widely known hymns include the morning and evening hymns *Awake, my soul* and *Glory to Thee, my God, this night* (both of which end with the familiar doxology, *Praise God, from whom all blessings flow*).

Kendall (ken'dạl), **Henry Clarence.** b. near Ulladulla, New South Wales, Australia, April 18, 1839; d. at Sydney, Australia, Aug. 1, 1882. An Australian poet, usually considered the first of major significance in Australian history.

Kendon (ken'dọn), **Frank.** b. at Goudhurst, Kent, England, 1893—. An English poet and journalist. He has characterized himself as "a countryman by birth and youth, Londoner by necessity, poet by chance, businessman for one year by fate." He has published *Poems and Sonnets* (1922), and contributed to *Poems by Four Authors* (1920).

Kenelm Chillingly (ken'ẹlm chil'ing.li). A novel by Edward Bulwer-Lytton, published after his death in 1873.

Kenilworth (ken'il.wẻrth). A novel by Sir Walter Scott, published in 1821. The scene is laid in England in the reign of Queen Elizabeth. Amy Robsart, daughter of Sir Hugh Robsart of Devon, secretly marries Leicester, the Queen's favorite, rejecting the suit of a good and worthy gentleman, Edmund Tressilian. Leicester hides Amy away at Cumnor Place so that he will not incur the Queen's jealous anger. In the meantime, Tressilian suspects that Varney, a confederate of Leicester, is keeping Amy as his mistress, and goes to the Queen with a charge of seduction. The Queen demands that Amy should be brought before her at Kenilworth after Varney announces that Amy is his wife. Varney now persuades Leicester to ask Amy to say that she is Varney's wife, in order to protect her true husband from the Queen's displeasure. Amy refuses and manages to gain admittance to Kenilworth, where she convinces Leicester that he should acknowledge her openly. He agrees to do this, and thus brings the wrath of Elizabeth down upon his own head. Varney, however, manages to misrepresent the relations between Amy and Tressilian, and Leicester permits Varney to arrange her murder. Tressilian and the young Walter Raleigh are too late to save the girl, and she perishes. Her husband is later restored to Elizabeth's favor.

Kennedy (ken'ẹ.di), **Margaret.** b. at London, April 23, 1896—. An English novelist and dramatist. Author of *A Century of Revolution* (1922), *The Constant Nymph* (1924), which she dramatized (1926) in collaboration with Basil Dean, *Red Sky at Morning* (1927), *The Fool of the Family* (1930), *Return I Dare Not* (1931), *A Long Time Ago* (1932), *Together and Apart* (1936), *The Midas Touch* (1938), *The Feast* (1950), and *Lucy Carmichael* (1951). Her plays include *Escape Me Never* (1933) and *Autumn* (1937, in collaboration with Gregory Ratoff).

Kennedy, Rann. b. probably in Ayrshire, Scotland, 1772; d. at Birmingham, England, Jan. 2, 1851. An English schoolmaster, divine, and poet. He was educated at St. John's College, Cambridge (B.A., 1795; M.A., 1798), where he met Samuel Taylor Coleridge. He served as master (1807–36) at King Edward's School, Birmingham, and was curate (1797–1817) and incumbent (1817–47) of St. Paul's, Birmingham. In addition to Coleridge, he counted among his many distinguished friends Wordsworth, Charles Kemble, Sarah Siddons, H. F. Cary, James Montgomery, and Washington Irving. Author of *A Poem on the Death of Princess Charlotte* (1817), *Britain's Genius* (1840), a masque celebrating Queen Victoria's marriage, *The Reign of Youth* (1840), a lyrical poem; and translator (1849) of portions of Vergil.

Kennedy, Walter. b. at Carrick, Ayrshire, Scotland, c1460; d. c1508. A Scottish poet and churchman. He engaged (c1504) in a "flyting" (a literary battle, not necessarily serious or indicating real enmity) with his fellow poet William Dunbar. He also wrote *The Passion of Christ*, a long poem.

Kenneth (ken'ẹth), **Sir.** In Sir Walter Scott's novel *The Talisman*, the name used by David, the Prince Royal of Scotland and Earl of Huntingdon, in order to conceal his real identity from his enemies.

Kennett (ken'ẹt), **White.** b. at Dover, England, 1660; d. at London, 1728. An English bishop, antiquary, and theological writer.

Kensal Green (ken'sạl). A cemetery in the northwest of London.

Kensington (ken'zing.tọn, -sing-). A borough of London, west-southwest of Saint Paul's, containing Kensington Gardens and Palace, and also Holland House.

Kensington Gardens. A volume of short poems (1924) by Humbert Wolfe, describing Kensington Gardens.

Kent (kent). [Latin, **Cantium, Cantia**; Old English, **Cent, Caent, Cantii.**] A maritime county in SE England. The closest of all English counties to Europe, Kent was the scene of Caesar's invasions in 55 and 54 B.C., of the earliest Teutonic invasions in the 5th century, and was the seat after c449 of the Jutish kingdoms in the Heptarchy. It was annexed to Wessex in 823.

Kent, 3rd Earl of. See under **Surrey,** (1st) **Duke of.**

Kent, Earl of. In Shakespeare's *King Lear*, an upright and faithful counselor. In the play *King Leir*, from which Shakespeare borrowed, he is the faithful counselor Perillus, but Shakespeare has greatly refined this shadowy character. It is Kent who seeks to excuse Cordelia's answer to Lear, and who suffers banishment by Lear because of it. His vehement defense of her conceals what might otherwise appear to be a fantastically improbable response on Cordelia's part (namely, her curious failure to explain herself and to reveal her sisters' hypocrisy). Kent (in disguise and calling himself Caius) suffers with Lear when he is cast out by Regan and Goneril. It is the ignominy of Kent's being placed in stocks for having resented Oswald's overbearing manner that awakens Lear to a full realization of the disrespect with which he is now being treated by his children. Throughout the play Kent is the factual realist, commenting without passion or conjecture on the action. Yet in the last scene the facts are too much for Kent, who can only murmur "Is this the promised end?" (referring to the Day of Judgment) when Lear comes howling before him with the dead Cordelia in his arms.

Kent, Edmund, Earl of. In Christopher Marlowe's tragedy *Edward II*, the brother of the King. Loyal to his wavering brother at first, he later joins the barons in opposition to Edward's transference of power to Gaveston. After Mortimer, the leader of the barons, deposes the King, he returns to Edward's side even though Edward has banished him. He dies trying to rescue Edward from the Tower, where Mortimer has imprisoned him.

Kentigern (ken'ti.gėrn) or **Mungo** (mung'gō), Saint. b. at Culross, Perthshire, Scotland, probably 518; d. Jan. 13, 603. An apostle of the Strathclyde Britons in Scotland, and patron saint of Glasgow. Forced to flee Scotland, he joined Saint David in Wales, founded Saint Asaph's monastery at Llanelwy, and returned to Scotland in 573 when the Christians overthrew the pagans.

Kent's Cavern (kents). A cave near Torquay, Devonshire, noted for its paleolithic flint tools and animal remains.

Kenwigs (ken'wigz), **Morleena.** In Dickens's novel *Nicholas Nickleby*, a young lady with flaxen pigtails and white-ruffled trousers, who has a habit of fainting at intervals.

Kenwigs, the. In Dickens's novel *Nicholas Nickleby*, the parents of Morleena.

Kenyon (ken'yon), Sir **Frederic George.** b. at London, Jan. 15, 1863—. An English classicist, director and chief librarian (1909–30) of the British Museum. Author of *Aristotle's Constitution of Athens* (1891), *Palaeography of Greek Papyri* (1899); editor of *Centenary Edition of Robert Browning* (1912), *New Poems of Robert and Elizabeth Barrett Browning* (1914), and Greek and Egyptian texts and catalogues.

Kenyon, John. b. in the parish of Trelawney, Jamaica, 1784; d. at Cowes, Isle of Wight, Dec. 3, 1856. An English poet and philanthropist. He published a few poems, but is best known for the financial help he gave to various literary figures of his time (he willed a substantial amount to Robert and Elizabeth Browning, whom he had originally introduced to each other).

Keown (koun), **Anna Gordon.** b. 1897—. An English poet and novelist. Her poetry includes *The Bright of Eye* and *The Winds*, and she is the author of *The Cat Who Saw God, Mr. Theobald's Devil, Mr.*

Thompson in the Attic, Wickham's Fancy, and other novels.

Kephisos (kē.fē.sôs'). See **Cephissus.**

Kepler (kep'lėr), **Johann.** b. at Weil der Stadt, Württemberg, Germany, Dec. 27, 1571; d. at Regensburg, Bavaria, Germany, Nov. 15, 1630. A German astronomer and mathematician, one of the founders of modern astronomy. Kepler obtained Tycho's observations of the planet Mars, from the study of which he discovered the three laws of planetary motion with which his name is associated: (1) that the orbits of the planets are ellipses, the sun being in one focus; (2) that the straight line joining a planet to the sun sweeps out equal areas in equal intervals of time; (3) that the squares of the periodic times of the planets are proportional to the cubes of their mean distances from the sun.

Keppel (kep'el), **George Thomas.** [Title, 6th Earl of **Albemarle.**] b. June 13, 1799; d. at London, Feb. 21, 1891. An English general and writer of travel accounts.

Keppel, Sir **Henry.** b. at Kensington, London, June 14, 1809; d. at London, Jan. 17, 1904. A British naval officer, appointed admiral of the fleet in 1875. He commanded the naval brigade at the reduction of Sevastopol in 1855, and served in the Chinese war in 1857, notably at Fatshan Creek. He wrote *Reminiscences* (1898), *A Sailor's Life under Four Sovereigns* (1899), and other books.

Kept. A novel of life in postwar London, by Alec Waugh, published in 1925.

Kernahan (kėr'na.han), **Coulson.** b. at Ilfracombe, Devonshire, England, Aug. 1, 1858; d. in February, 1943. An English author; husband of Mary Jean Hickling Kernahan. He wrote *A Dead Man's Diary* (1890), *A Book of Strange Sins* (1894), *God and the Ant* (1895), *The Child, the Wise Man, and the Devil* (1896), and *The Man of No Sorrows* (1911); *Captain Shannan* (1897) and *Scoundrels and Co.* (1901), novels; *Wise Men and a Fool* (1901), *In Good Company* (1917), *Swinburne as I Knew Him* (1919), *Six Famous Living Poets* (1926), criticism and recollections; *Begging the Moon's Pardon* (1930), *A Dog and His Master* (1932), and *A World Without the Christ* (1934), imaginative and religious studies. He was coeditor, with Frederick Locker-Lampson, of *Lyra Elegantiarum* (1891), long a standard anthology of light verse.

Kernahan, Mary Jean Hickling. [Maiden name, **Gwynne.**] b. 1857; d. at Fairlight, Sussex, England, Jan. 17, 1941. An English novelist; wife of Coulson Kernahan. Author of *A Laggard in Love* (1890), *The Sinnings of Seraphine* (1906), *The Thirteenth Man* (1910), *The Mystery of Mere Hall* (1913), *A Fair Sinner* (1913), *The Stolen Man* (1916), and *Tales of Our Village* (1928).

Kern-baby (kėrn'bā.bi) or **Kernababy** (kėr'na.bā.bi). A harvest folk-festival of northern England and Scotland. The last gleanings of the fields were made into an image of the harvest goddess and burned.

Kerr (kär, kėr), **Robert.** b. at Bughtridge, Roxburghshire, Scotland, 1755; d. at Edinburgh, Oct. 11, 1813. A Scottish author.

Ketch (kech), **John.** [Called **Jack Ketch.**] d. in November, 1686. An English hangman. On Dec. 2,

1678, his name first appears in a broadside entitled *The Plotter's Ballad, being Jack Ketch's incomparable receipt for the cure of Traitorous Recusants.* . . . About the time of his death *Punchinello* was introduced into England from Italy, and his name passed naturally to the executioner in the English Punch and Judy puppet-shows.

Kettle (ket'l), **Captain.** A Welsh shipmaster, the hero of a series of stories by C. J. C. W. Hyne.

Kettle, T. M. b. at Dublin, 1880; d. in France, 1916. An Irish poet and essayist. His writings include *The Day's Burden* (1915) and *Poems and Parodies* (1916).

Kew (kū). A civil parish and ward of Richmond municipal borough, in SE England, in Surrey, on the S bank of the Thames, ab. 15 mi. W of Broad Street station, London. Part of the village (Kew Bridge) is on the Middlesex side of the Thames, connected by a bridge with the part in Surrey (Kew Green). Kew is celebrated for its botanical gardens (Royal Botanic Gardens and Arboretum). These originated in gardens laid out by Henry Capel, Baron Capel of Tewkesbury, about the middle of the 17th century. They were extended by George III, and since 1840 have been national property. The total area of the gardens is ab. 288 acres.

Kew Observatory. The central meteorological observatory of Great Britain, built in 1769 at the order of George III.

Keynes (kānz), **John Maynard.** [Title, 1st Baron of Tilton.] b. at Cambridge, England, June 5, 1883; d. at Firle, Sussex, England, April 21, 1946. An English economist. He served (1906–08) in the revenue department of the India Office and was editor (1912–46) of the *Economic Journal*. He served as a member (1913–14) of the royal commission on Indian finance and currency, was a staff member (1915–19) of the treasury department, and was the principal representative of the treasury at the Paris Peace Conference (1919). He was elected vice-president of the World Bank and Fund, and was a delegate to the Bretton Woods conference. Although he was to become one of the most influential of modern economists, Keynes encountered very considerable opposition during the 1920's (he had resigned from the Versailles Commission when it adopted policies which he believed must lead to economic disaster. Germany, he maintained, would inevitably collapse, and bring the rest of Europe down with her, under the financial strain placed upon her by the economic clauses of the Versailles Treaty). When the depression virtually halted world economic activity in the 1930's, the Keynesian hypothesis of a type of "controlled capitalism" was influential in the policies of public spending adopted by many governments to overcome the stagnation of unemployment and idle production facilities. His works include *The Economic Consequences of the Peace* (1919), *A Treatise on Probability* (1921), *A Revision of the Treaty* (1922), *A Tract on Monetary Reform* (1923), *A Short View of Russia* (1925), *The End of Laissez-Faire* (1926), *A Treatise on Money* (1930), *The General Theory of Employment, Interest, and Money* (1936), and *How to Pay for the War* (1940).

Key of Life, The. A novel by Francis Brett Young, published in 1928.

Keys of the Kingdom, The. A novel by A. J. Cronin, published in 1941.

Khartoum (kär.töm'). [Also, **Khartum.**] A city in NE Africa, capital of the Anglo-Egyptian Sudan and of Khartoum province, situated at the union of the White Nile and Blue Nile rivers. It was founded by Mehemet Ali in 1823, and was formerly the capital of the Egyptian Sudan. It was occupied (1884–85) by General Charles Gordon, and taken by the troops of the Mahdi after a long siege, Jan. 26, 1885. General Gordon was killed (1885) there by the Mahdists. It was reëntered by the British Sept. 4, 1898, under General Kitchener, who laid out the streets of the city in the pattern of a Union Jack in commemoration of Gordon's death. The Gordon Memorial College, established through the efforts of Kitchener, was opened in 1902.

Khayyám (kī.äm'), **Omar.** See **Omar Khayyám.**

Khios (chē'ôs). See **Chios.**

Kid (kid), **Thomas.** See **Kyd, Thomas.**

Kidd (kid), **William.** [Called **Captain Kidd.**] b. probably at Greenock, Scotland, c1645; hanged at London, May 23, 1701. An English pirate and sea rover. During King William's War (1689–97) he saw service against French privateers in Atlantic and West Indian waters. A shipowner and sea captain at New York, where he held considerable property, he was rewarded by the Provincial Council for helping to suppress the colonial insurrection of Leisler and Milborne. In 1695 he went to London, where he undertook a commission to lead a man-of-war against the pirates infesting the Indian Ocean. Sailing (April 23, 1696) aboard the *Adventure Galley* from Plymouth, England, he stopped at New York, where he completed his crew, and left on Sept. 6, 1696, making his way to the Indian Ocean by way of the Cape of Good Hope. By early 1697 he was in difficulties; one third of his crew had died of cholera, the survivors had not been paid since leaving port, his ship was leaking, and mutiny threatened. These circumstances combined to make Kidd decide to prey upon the ships he had been instructed to protect. Capturing his greatest prize, the Armenian *Quedagh Merchant*, in January, 1698, he abandoned the *Adventure Galley* for the Armenian merchantman and struck up a connection with Culliford and Kelly, two of the pirates he had been sent out to capture. Sailing from Madagascar in September, 1698, Kidd arrived at the West Indies in April, 1699, and there learned that the British authorities had proclaimed him a pirate. Promised a pardon, he went ashore at Boston, was imprisoned, tried at London, and hanged, having been found guilty of murder and piracy. A portion of the *Quedagh Merchant's* treasure was buried on Gardiners Island, New York, and was long popularly supposed never to have been recovered (but was actually removed by the colonial authorities in 1699).

Kidnapped. A historical romance (1886) by R. L. Stevenson. It was followed (1893) by a sequel, *Catriona.*

Kidron (kid'ron). See **Kedron.**

ḍ, d or j; ṣ, s or sh; ṭ, t or ch; ẓ, z or zh; o, F. cloche; ü, F. menu; ch, Sc. loch; ṅ, F. bonbon.

Killigrew (kil′i.grö), **Anne.** b. at London, 1660; d. there, in June, 1685. An English poet, painter, and scholar; niece of Thomas Killigrew (1612–83). She painted portraits of James and Mary, Duke and Duchess of York (later to be James II and Queen Mary). She is now remembered chiefly through John Dryden's *To the Pious Memory of the Accomplished Young Lady Mrs. Anne Killigrew, Excellent in the Two Sister Arts of Poesy and Painting* (1686), a pindaric ode in ten stanzas.

Killigrew, Thomas. [Called **Killigrew the Elder.**] b. in Lothbury, London, Feb. 7, 1612; d. in Whitehall, London, March 19, 1683. An English dramatist; brother of Sir William Killigrew. He was a page of Charles I, and remained loyal to him and his successor. He produced and wrote many new plays and built several theaters. He is, however, best remembered as a wit. Among his plays are *Claracilla* (printed 1641), *The Prisoners, The Princess* (c1635–36) and *The Parson's Wedding* (1644). His style is somewhat like D'Avenant's and imitative of Jonson.

Killigrew, Thomas. [Called **Killigrew the Younger.**] b. in February, 1657; d. July 21, 1719. An English dramatist; son of Thomas Killigrew (1612–83). He wrote *Chit Chat* (1719).

Killigrew, Sir William. Baptized at Haworth, near London, May 28, 1606; d. at London, 1695. An English poet and dramatist; brother of Thomas Killigrew (1612–83). His works include the plays *Selindra, Omasdes, Pandora,* and *The Siege of Urbin.*

Kilmansegg (kil′man.seg), **Miss.** In Thomas Hood's humorous poem so named, an heiress with a golden leg.

Kilmeny (kil.mä′ni). The thirteenth bard's song in James Hogg's *The Queen's Wake.*

Kim (kim). A long story (1901) of native and Anglo-Indian life in India, by Rudyard Kipling.

Kind-Hart's Dreame (kīnd′härts). [Full title, **Kind-Harts Dreame. Conteining fiue Apparitions with their Inuectives against abuses raigning.**] A pamphlet written by Henry Chettle in 1592. In the preface is the first allusion to Shakespeare after that in Robert Greene's *Groatsworth of Wit:* "Because myselfe haue seene his demeanor no lesse ciuill, than he excelent in the qualitie he professes: Besides, diuers of worship haue reported his vprightnes of dealing, which argues his honesty, and his facetious grace in writting, that aprooues his Art."

Kind Keeper, or Mr. Limberham (lim′bėr.am), **The.** A comedy by John Dryden, produced in 1678. The character of Mrs. Saintly was suggested by Molière's *Tartuffe.* It attacked the "crying sin of keeping," for which it was damned by the fashionable audience. Saintsbury considered it one of Dryden's best comedies.

Kindness in a Corner. A novel by Theodore Francis Powys, published in 1930.

King (king), **Edward.** b. in Ireland, 1612; drowned at sea on his way to Ireland, Aug. 10, 1637. An English poet, schoolfellow of John Milton, and the "Lycidas" of Milton's famous elegy of that name. At Christ's College, Cambridge (1630–34), as student, fellow, and tutor, he prepared for a career in

the church. Author of Latin poems on various subjects, he is now remembered chiefly as the subject of a collection of poems published (1638) by the university, including Milton's tribute to "a learned Friend."

King, Edward. b. at Cork, Ireland, Nov. 16, 1795; d. at Dublin, Feb. 27, 1837. An Irish writer on Mexican antiquities.

King, Henry. b. 1592; d. 1669. An English poet. He was educated at Christ Church, Oxford, and was acquainted with both Ben Jonson and Izaak Walton. He was a close friend of John Donne. His poems include the sonnet *Tell me no more how fair she is, Upon the Death of my Ever-desired Friend, Doctor Donne of Saint Paul's,* and *The Exequy.*

King, William. b. at Stepney, Middlesex, England, March 16, 1685; d. at Ealing, Middlesex, Dec. 30, 1763. An English educator and writer. He was author of *The Toast* (books 1–2, 1732; books 3–4, 1736), a mock-heroic poem, praised by Swift before its publication and dedicated to him.

King Alisaunder (al.i.sôn′dėr). A Middle English verse romance (c1300), depicting the life of Alexander the Great from his birth to his death and including descriptions of his conquests. It contains approximately 8,000 lines and is written in octosyllabic couplets. See also **Alexander, Romance of.**

King and No King, A. A play by Francis Beaumont and John Fletcher, licensed in 1611 and printed in 1619. It deals with the delirious intoxication of power suffered by Arbaces, King of Iberia, after his defeat of Tigranes, and his consequent loss of moral scruples as he rushes impetuously toward an incestuous affair with Panthea, whom he believes to be his sister. Eventually he fulfills his desire by marriage, after it is discovered that he is not a king and that she is not his sister.

King and the Lady, The. One of five historical tales in *The Gallants* (1927), by Lily Adams Beck under the pseudonym E. Barrington. The king is Henry II of England and the lady, "Fair Rosamond" (Rosamond de Clifford).

King Argimenes and the Unknown Warrior (är.ji.-mē′nēz). A drama (1914) by Lord Dunsany.

King Arthur (är′thėr). An epic poem by Edward Bulwer-Lytton, published in 1849.

King Arthur, or The British Worthy. A dramatic opera in blank verse by John Dryden, music by Henry Purcell, performed and printed in 1691. It has some well-known lyrics, including "Fairest Isle, all Isles Excelling."

King Behind the King, The. A historical novel by Warwick Deeping, published in 1914. It is a story of the peasants' revolt in 14th-century England.

King Bomba (bōm′bạ). See **Bomba, King.**

King Cole (kōl). The subject of an English nursery rhyme, popular in the 18th century. There has been much conjecture as to who Old King Cole really was. The most popular surmise is that he was a prince, eponymous builder of Colchester, who came to the throne of Britain in the 3rd century; but there is no substantiation for this. He is mentioned by Geoffrey of Monmouth in the 12th century and by the dramatists Thomas Dekker and John Marston in the 17th. Sir Walter Scott was

fat, fāte, fär, ȧsk, fāre; net, mē, hėr; pin, pīne; not, nōte, mŏve, nôr; up, lūte, pŭll; ᴛʜ, then;

fond of the theory that "Auld King Coul" was the father of Finn MacCool. Several others have thought that the rhyme referred to a merchant clothier of Reading named Colebrook.

King Darius (dạ.rī′us). An interlude written in 1565 by an unknown author on the Biblical story of the Tower of Babel.

Kingdom of Theophilus (thẹ.of′i.lus), **The.** A novel by William John Locke, published in 1927.

King Edward the Fourth. A historical play (1599) by Thomas Heywood.

King Henry. Shakespeare's historical plays on the English kings of this name are entered under their short titles. They are *Henry IV (Part One)*, *Henry IV (Part Two)*, *Henry V*, *Henry VI (Part One)*, *Henry VI (Part Two)*, *Henry VI (Part Three)*, and *Henry VIII*.

King Horn (hôrn). The hero of a cycle of medieval romances called the Horn cycle. The English versions are preserved in three manuscripts. *The Geste of Kyng Horne* (ab. 1,550 verses) is the oldest and dates sometime after 1250; the other two date from c1300. There is a shorter version entitled *Horn Childe and Maiden Rimnild* in a later 14th-century manuscript. The French romance, *Horn et Rymenhild* (ab. 5,250 verses) is also of the 14th century. The outstanding feature of the story is the ring which serves both as fidelity and recognition token. Young Horn received from his promised love (the king's daughter) a ring which would "grow pale and wan" if she were untrue or in danger, and then sailed away seeking adventure to prove his worthiness. One day he noticed that the ring no longer glittered and sailed home again as fast as he could. On landing he learned that the king's daughter was being married that very day against her will. In beggar's garb young Horn went to the castle, where, according to custom, the bride offered the beggar a cup of wine. Horn drank the wine and returned the cup with the ring in it, whereupon the lady asked if she got it from a dead man's hand. On being told no, that he got it from hers, she at once declared that she would beg her bread by his side rather than marry the bridegroom. Horn then revealed that the beggar's garb was mere sham, and the pair were reunited. The Horn story is perhaps best known to English readers through the Scottish popular ballad *Hind Horn*, of which there are nine versions.

Kingis Quair (kingz kwär), **The.** A Middle English poem (1423–24) by James I of Scotland, written in the stanza of Chaucer's *Troilus and Criseyde* and since called, from the king's use of it, rhyme royal. It shows the influence of Chaucer in the incident of the young man's instantaneous love for the lady walking in the garden below his prison cell (as in *The Knight's Tale*), and in the idea of the poet being carried aloft to the court of Venus (as in *The House of Fame*). The poem ends with the promise of Venus that the young man will be successful in his love. Rossetti quotes from this poem in *The King's Tragedy*.

King James Version. An English translation of the Bible prepared by a special commission of scholars in England under James I, and published in 1611.

King John (jon). [Also, **Kyng** (or **Kynge**) **Johan**.] A morality play by John Bale, written c1538, amplified c1558, and considered a link with the historical plays of the Elizabethans. The text of the play was not known until it was discovered in the 19th century. It deals with the abused virtue of Widow England, with her blind son, Commonalty, and with the interference of Roman Catholic agents in King John's efforts to reduce their suffering. The play shifts erratically from allegory to historical fact, but there is some possibility that Shakespeare used it as part of the background for his *King John*.

King John. [Full title, **The Troublesome Raigne of King John**.] A play classed as a chronicle history. It is in two parts, partly prose and partly verse, probably acted in 1588 and printed in 1591; reprinted in 1611 as "By W. Sh.," and in 1622, after Shakespeare's death, as "by William Shakespeare." It is probably by Peele, with Lodge, Greene, and perhaps Marlowe. Shakespeare used incidents from it for his *King John*, but rewrote them entirely. Some scholars have argued that Shakespeare actually did write this play, but most consider it rather crude for his work, even in his early period.

King John. [Full title, **The Life and Death of King John**.] A historical play by Shakespeare, founded on the anonymous *Troublesome Raigne of King John* (1591). It was written probably in 1597 or 1598, and first printed in the 1623 folio. The theme of papal tyranny embodied in it fits in with the general Elizabethan antagonism toward the Papacy, and it is noteworthy (but understandable, in view of the Tudor emphasis on the absolute nature of the royal power) that nowhere in the play is there even a passing reference to the Magna Charta.

The Story. John refuses the demand of King Philip of France that he surrender his throne to his youthful nephew, Arthur, and invades France with an army under the leadership of Philip Faulconbridge (Philip the Bastard), the most gallant and wittiest figure in the play. After an indecisive battle at Angiers, a peace is arranged and sealed by the marriage of the Dauphin to John's niece, Blanch. However, the peace proves to be a short one; Pandulph, a papal legate, excommunicates John for not seating his (Pandulph's) choice as Archbishop of Canterbury, and orders Philip and the Dauphin to recommence the war. During the ensuing hostilities, Arthur is captured by the English. John thereupon orders his chamberlain, Hubert, to kill the boy and (although Hubert spares him) the English nobles suspect a murder when Arthur (who actually died escaping) is found dead. The disaffected nobles desert John and join the French army which, at Pandulph's insistence, has invaded England. To regain Pandulph's support, John surrenders his crown to the papal legate and receives it back in fief. During the battle at St. Edmundsbury, Melun, a dying French lord, tells the English deserters that the Dauphin plans to execute them when John is defeated, and the nobles return to John. John, however, dies of poison administered by a monk at Swinstead Abbey. An honorable peace follows and the English are unified under the new King Henry III.

King John and Matilda (mạ.til′dạ). A tragedy (1624) by Robert Davenport.

---

dạ, d or j; ṣ, s or sh; ṭ, t or ch; ẓ, z or zh; o, F. cloche; ü, F. menu; ch, Sc. loch; ṅ, F. bonbon.

Kinglake (king'lăk), **Alexander William**. b. at Taunton, England, Aug. 5, 1809; d. Jan. 2, 1891. An English historian. In 1844, after traveling in the East, he published *Eothen, or Traces of Travel Brought Home from the East*. He went to Algiers in 1845. In 1854 he followed the army to the Crimea, and stayed until the siege of Sevastopol. The *Invasion of the Crimea* appeared in eight volumes between 1863 and 1887. He was a member of Parliament (1857–68).

King Lear (lir). [Full title, **The Tragedy of King Lear**.] A tragedy by Shakespeare, written c1605, performed in 1606, and printed in 1608. The quarto of 1608 and first folio of 1623 differ, the former lacking about 100 lines which the latter has, but the folio having 300 lines of the quarto omitted. The story of Lear was originally told by Geoffrey of Monmouth in his *History of the Kings of Britain* (c1136), and is to be found in Layamon's *Brut*, and the *Gesta Romanorum*. Holinshed repeats it from Geoffrey and Spenser gives it the second book of the *Faerie Queene*. John Higgins's *Mirrour for Magistrates* also tells the story and Shakespeare follows it in the matter of Lear's showing his bounty to the most deserving. All of these versions, and also the anonymous *King Leir* printed in 1605, have an ending where Lear is restored to his kingdom and reunited with Cordelia. The old ballad of "King Leir and his Three Daughters" is preserved by Percy in his *Reliques of Ancient English Poetry*. Sidney's *Arcadia* (Book II, Chapter 10) is the source for the Gloucester story. Finally, Shakespeare's own play suffered somewhat from 1679 on by being altered. Nahum Tate, a dramatist of the Restoration period, gave it a happy ending and his version was acted by Betterton, Garrick, Kemble, and Kean.

The Story. Lear, intending to divide his kingdom between his three daughters, demands, with some arrogance, protestations of love from them. When Cordelia, whose love for him is genuine, declines to affirm it, he disinherits her, banishes her supporter, Kent, and divides the kingdom between his other daughters, Goneril and Regan, and their husbands, Albany and Cornwall. Goneril, with whom he first stays, treats him disrespectfully, and he goes to Regan, who refuses to admit him (and puts Kent, who in disguise has become a servant to Lear, in stocks). Lear, driven to the point of madness by rage and sorrow at the ingratitude of his daughters, rushes into a violent storm with Kent and the Fool. On the heath they meet Edgar, the legitimate son of the Duke of Gloucester (who has banished him because Edmund, the Duke's illegitimate son, has falsely persuaded the Duke that Edgar plans to murder him). Edgar is disguised as the mad Tom o' Bedlam. Lear has by this time utterly lost his mind; Gloucester has been blinded by Cornwall for aiding Lear. Lear with Kent and Gloucester with Edgar separately make their way to the coast to meet Cordelia, who is landing with her husband, the King of France, to rescue Lear. There Edgar saves the life of his father and Cordelia tenderly cares for Lear, although they are taken prisoners by the English forces. Meanwhile, Regan and Goneril have fallen in love with Edmund, and the jealous Goneril poisons Regan and takes her own life when Edmund is killed by Edgar.

Meanwhile, but too late to avert further tragedy, it is revealed that Edmund has ordered Cordelia's execution, and Lear now enters carrying his dead daughter. Lear dies of a broken heart, believing at the last moment before his death that she still lives. Gloucester too has died from "joy and grief" upon learning the identity of Edgar. The kingdom is left to Albany.

King Leir (lir). [Full title, **The True Chronicle History of King Leir, and his three daughters, Gonorill, Ragan, and Cordella**.] An anonymous play, printed in 1605, from which Shakespeare must have obtained incidents in his *King Lear* (but this play has a happy ending and there is no reference to Lear's insanity or the Gloucester subplot). The author has been variously conjectured to be Lodge, Peele, Greene, or Kyd.

King Log (log). In Aesop's fable of the *Frogs Asking For a King*, a big heavy log sent by Zeus to the frogs who prayed for a king. King Log's first splash was so big that the frogs thought him wonderful; later, they sat on his back in the sun; but eventually complained of so inert a monarch. So Zeus sent them a stork who ate them up.

Kingmaker, the. See under **Warwick, Earl of.**

King of Antioch (an'ti.ok). See **Antiochus.**

"King of Bath" (bath). Nickname of **Nash, Richard.**

King of Bohemia (bọ.hē'mi.ạ). See **Polixenes.**

King of Dunces. A name given to Colley Cibber in Alexander Pope's *Dunciad*.

King of Fez (fez). See **Fez, King of.**

King of France (frans). In Shakespeare's *All's Well That Ends Well*, the ailing King whom Helena cures, and who later suspects Bertram of having murdered Helena. He speaks the Epilogue to the play.

King of France. In Shakespeare's *King Lear*, the husband of Cordelia. He arrives with an army to rescue Lear, but he does not appear on stage after the first scene.

King of Naples (nā'plz). See **Alonso.**

King of Navarre (nạ.vär'). See **Ferdinand, King of Navarre.**

King of Pentapolis (pen.tap'ọ.lis). See **Simonides.**

King of Sicilia (si.sil'yạ, -sil'i.ạ). See **Leontes.**

King of Tars (tärz), **The.** A Middle English romance concerning a Christian princess married to a heathen sultan. Her child is so deformed at birth that all the gods are petitioned to help him, but only after his baptism does he become a handsome young boy.

King of the Bean. A holiday king formerly chosen for the Twelfth Night (January 6) celebration in England and northern Europe. He was chosen by lot: whoever got the piece of cake containing a bean was King of the Bean, the cake having been baked for this special purpose. The King of the Bean was in charge of the Twelfth Night festivities for the day, or for the duration of the celebration.

King of the Fairies. See **Oberon.**

King of the Great Clock Tower, The. A volume of verse (1935) by W. B. Yeats.

---

fat, fāte, fär, ȧsk, fāre; net, mē, hėr; pin, pīne; not, nōte, mȯve, nôr; up, lūte, pull; ᴛʜ, then;

King Orfeo (ôr'fē̤.ō). See under **Sir Orfeo.**

King Richard the Second, The Tragedy of. See **Richard II.**

King Richard the Third, The Tragedy of. See **Richard III.**

King's College. One of the colleges of Cambridge University. It was founded in 1441 by King Henry VI.

King's Daughter. A poem by V. Sackville-West, published in 1930.

King's English. The standard language, that form of English regarded as being best and purest and having, as it were, the royal sanction. The term, with a variant **Queen's English,** used during the reign of a female sovereign, has been employed since the 16th century. Although strictly applicable, of course, only to British English, it is sometimes used in the United States by a loose extension to designate cultivated, "correct" English in general, without reference to national differences. Today its employment is often jocular.

Kingsley (kingz'li), **Charles.** b. at Holne, Devonshire, England, June 12, 1819; d. at Eversley, Hampshire, England, Jan. 23, 1875. An English clergyman and author; brother of Henry Kingsley, and father of Mary St. Leger Kingsley. He studied at King's College, London, and then at Magdalene College, Cambridge. He became (1842) curate and later rector of Eversley, Hampshire, and in 1845 was made canon of Middleham. He was appointed professor of English literature at Queen's College, London, and later became professor of modern history at Cambridge (1860), canon of Chester (1869), and canon of Westminster (1873). In 1874 he visited America. As a leader in Christian socialism he published many pamphlets, and wrote two novels, *Yeast* (1848) and *Alton Locke* (1850), relating to the movement. *St. Elizabeth of Hungary,* a drama, appeared in 1848, the historical novel *Hypatia* in 1853, *Westward Ho* in 1855, and *Hereward the Wake* in 1866. In 1859 he was made one of the queen's chaplains in ordinary. His controversy (1864) concerning Roman Catholicism, with John Henry Newman, led to the writing of *Apologia pro vita sua,* usually considered Newman's greatest work. Among his other works are *Glaucus, or the Wonders of the Shore* (1855), *Two Years Ago* (1857), *The Water Babies* (1863), *Prose Idylls* (1873), and *Plays and Puritans* (1873).

Kingsley, Henry. b. at Barnack, Northamptonshire, England, Jan. 2, 1830; d. in Sussex, England, May 24, 1876. An English novelist and journalist; brother of Charles Kingsley. He wrote *Recollections of Geoffry Hamlyn* (1859), *Ravenshoe* (1862), *Austin Elliott* (1863), *The Hillyars and the Burtons* (1865), *Leighton Court* (1866), *Silcote of Silcotes* (1867), and *Stretton* (1869).

Kingsley, Mary Henrietta. b. at Islington, London, Oct. 13, 1862; d. at Simonstown, South Africa, June 3, 1900. An English ethnologist and traveler. She began her travels in 1892, visiting (1893–95) various parts of West Africa, and was in South Africa (1899–1900) during the Boer War, nursing wounded soldiers. Author of *Travels in West Africa* (1897), *African Religion and Law* (1897), *West African Studies* (1899), and *West Africa from an Ethnological Point of View* (1900).

Kingsley, Mary St. Leger. [Pseudonym, **Lucas Malet.**] b. at Eversley, Hampshire, England, 1852; d. Oct. 27, 1931. An English novelist; second daughter of Charles Kingsley. As Lucas Malet she wrote *Mrs. Lorimer* (1882), *Colonel Enderby's Wife* (1885), *Little Peter* (1887), *A Counsel of Perfection* (1888), *The Wages of Sin* (1891), *The Carissima* (1896), *The Gateless Barrier* (1900), *The History of Sir Richard Calmady* (1901), *The Far Horizon* (1906), *Adrian Savage* (1911), *The Golden Galleon* and *Damaris* (both 1916), *The Tall Villa* and *Deadham Hard* (both 1920), *The Survivors* (1923), and *The Dogs of Want* (1924). She also revised and completed her father's unfinished novel, *The Tutor's Story* (1914).

King's Men. See **Lord Chamberlain's Men.**

King's Men, The. A novel by John Palmer, published in 1916.

Kingsmill (kingz'mil), **Hugh.** [Original name, **Hugh Kingsmill Lunn.**] b. Nov. 21, 1889—. A British novelist and biographer. Author of *The Will to Love* (1919), *The Dawn's Delay* (1924), *Blondel* (1927), *Matthew Arnold* (1928), *The Return of William Shakespeare* (1929), *Frank Harris* (1932), *Samuel Johnson* (1933), *The Sentimental Journey* (1934), *D. H. Lawrence* (1938), *This Blessed Plot* (1942), and *Talking of Dick Whittington* (1947).

Kings of Brentford (brent'fọrd), **the Two.** See **Brentford, the Two Kings of.**

King Solomon's Mines. A novel by H. Rider Haggard, published in 1886.

King's Revoke, The. A historical novel by Margaret Louisa Woods, published in 1905.

King Stork. See **Stork, King.**

King's Threshold, The. A poetic play (1903) by William Butler Yeats. The poet Seanchan, who chooses starvation at King Guaire's gate rather than take an inferior place at the King's table, represents Yeats's assertion of pride in the essential dignity of the poet in society.

"Kinmont Willie" (kin'mont wil'i). See **Armstrong, William.**

Kinsayder (kin.sā'dẹr, kin'sā.dẹr), **W.** Pseudonym of **Marston, John.**

Kiomi (kẹ.ō'mẹ). A Gypsy girl in George Meredith's *Harry Richmond.*

Kipling (kip'ling), **John Lockwood.** b. at Pickering, Yorkshire, England, 1837; d. at Tisbury, Wiltshire, England, Jan. 29, 1911. An English artist; father of Rudyard Kipling. By profession an architectural sculptor, he was director of the Bombay (India) school of art (1865–75), and principal of the Mayo School of Art and curator of the Central Museum at Lahore (1875–93). He published *Beast and Man in India* (1891), and also illustrated some of his son's works.

Kipling, (Joseph) Rudyard. b. at Bombay, India, Dec. 30, 1865; d. at London, Jan. 18, 1936. An English poet, short-story writer, and novelist; son of John Lockwood Kipling and Alice Macdonald (sister of Lady Burne-Jones and Lady Poynter and aunt of Stanley Baldwin). In 1871 his parents took

Kipling and his sister Alice ("Trix") to England, where, at Southsea, they spent the six dismal years described in the autobiographical *Baa, Baa, Black Sheep*. In 1878 the boy entered the United Services College at Westward Ho, Devonshire, later celebrated in *Stalky & Co*. Though the stories in that volume are fictional, the chief characters are drawn from life, including the Head (Cormell Price), "King" (Crofts), and the boys "Beetle," "M'Turk" and "Stalky" (who were, respectively, Kipling, Beresford, and Dunsterville). At 17 Kipling returned to India, where his father had secured for him a job on the *Civil and Military Gazette* of Lahore. The verses collected as *Departmental Ditties* (1886) and the stories in *Plain Tales from the Hills* (1888) were written as "fillers" for the *Gazette*. In his last two years in India, as editor of the weekly edition of the Allahabad *Pioneer*, Kipling had more space to work in, and produced such masterly tales as *The Man Who Would Be King* (described by H. G. Wells as one of the finest stories ever written) and *Without Benefit of Clergy*.

Recognition in England and America. In 1889 Kipling returned to England via Japan and America, writing en route the letters collected in *From Sea to Sea* (1899). Once established at London, his rise to fame was meteoric. All his Indian volumes were reissued, followed swiftly by *Life's Handicap* (1890), *Ballads and Barrack-Room Ballads* (1891), *The Light that Failed* (1891), and *The Naulahka* (1892). This last was a collaboration with Charles Wolcott Balestier of Brattleboro, Vt., whose sister, Caroline, Kipling married on Jan. 18, 1892. The Kiplings lived at Brattleboro until 1897, when they were driven out by a quarrel with Caroline's tempestuous brother Beatty. The books written in Vermont include *Many Inventions* (1893), *The Jungle Book* (1894), *The Second Jungle Book* (1895), *The Seven Seas* (1896), and *Captains Courageous* (1897). After 1897 Kipling lived in England, first at Rottingdean and after 1905 at Bateman's, Burwash, Sussex. On a disastrous visit to New York in 1899 he nearly died of pneumonia, and his daughter Josephine, who was the Taffymai of *Just-So Stories* (1902), did die of the same disease. He never again entered the U. S., and his later comments on America were frequently bitter, though during the 1890's no other author except Mark Twain had been so widely loved and esteemed in this country. In the years between 1897 and 1914 he was awarded (1907) the Nobel prize for literature and published *The Day's Work* (1898), *Stalky & Co.* (1899), *Kim* (1901), *The Five Nations* (1903), *Traffics and Discoveries* (1904), *Puck of Pook's Hill* (1906), *Actions and Reactions* (1909), and *Rewards and Fairies* (1909). His only son, John, was killed in World War I; as a memorial, Kipling wrote *The Irish Guards in the Great War* (1923). His last volumes of stories were *A Diversity of Creatures* (1917), *Debits and Credits* (1926), and *Limits and Renewals* (1932). An autobiography, *Something of Myself* (1937), was left unfinished.

Later Years. In his later years Kipling's uncompromising Tory opinions antagonized many critics, but had little more effect on his reader-popularity than had his almost psychopathic avoidance of publicity. Many critics still fail to understand his more poetic side. *Kim*, for instance, is often dismissed as an adventure story, though its real central theme is the gulf between the life of the spirit (the Lama) and the life of action (Kim), a gulf which only love can bridge. Nevertheless, Kipling is widely recognized as one of the greatest masters of the short story. Kipling's poetry, often dismissed as the doggerel verse of imperialism, contains much that is admirable. His *Recessional* is on a higher plane than *Danny Deever*, *Gunga Din*, or *The Ballad of East and West*, but all are, despite their insistent rhythms, basically musical.

Kipps (kips). [Full title, **Kipps: The Story of a Simple Soul.**] A novel (1905) by H. G. Wells. It was adapted as a play in 1912. It tells the story of Arthur Kipps, born a bastard and raised by an aunt and uncle in New Romney until he is old enough to be apprenticed to a trade, whereupon he serves Edwin Shalford, owner of the Folkestone Drapery Bazaar, for seven years. He is retained by Shalford after his apprenticeship ends, but is discharged when he returns to the shop after a night of drinking (Shalford insists that his employees observe a curfew set by him, and Kipps does not return until morning). He is saved from job-hunting, however, by the unexpected inheritance of a legacy, and finds himself thrust suddenly into a society of "gentlefolk." He becomes engaged to the daughter of a family of considerable local prominence (linked, somewhat vaguely, to "the Earl of Beaupres"), but finds himself depressed and confused by the effort to be something called a "gentleman." He elopes with Ann Pornick, whom he has known since childhood (and who has become a maid in Folkestone), but their marriage is not completely happy until all of the legacy except a thousand pounds is lost. With this sum, Ann and Kipps open a small bookstore, and are presently blissfully happy; later, when a play in which Kipps had earlier taken a financial share becomes a tremendous success, they become wealthy again, but they refuse now to change the way of life which has brought them happiness.

Kipps, Arthur. The hero of H. G. Wells's novel *Kipps*.

Kirk (kėrk), **Sir John.** b. at Barry, Angus, Scotland, Dec. 19, 1832; d. Jan. 15, 1922. A Scottish administrator in Africa, and physician and naturalist on David Livingstone's second Zambezi expedition (1858–63). In Zanzibar, he served as vice-consul (1866), assistant political agent (1868), consul general (1873), and political agent (1880–87). He persuaded the sultan to abolish the slave trade (1873) and to concede mainland territories (1887) to the British East Africa Company.

Kirkdale Cave (kėrk'dāl). A cavern in the West Riding of Yorkshire, England, famous for its remains of mammals.

Kirke (kėrk), **Edward.** b. 1553; d. at Risby, Suffolk, England, Nov. 10, 1613. An English clergyman. As "E.K." he wrote a preface (dated from London, April 10, 1579), 12 arguments, and commentary for his friend Edmund Spenser's first major work, *The Shepherd's Calendar*.

Kirke, Percy. b. c1646; d. at Brussels, Oct. 31, 1691. An English soldier, colonel of "Kirke's Lambs," the old Tangier regiment, which had a lamb as its badge. As brigadier general he was present (July 6, 1685) at the battle of Sedgemoor, which ended Monmouth's rebellion, after which he hanged 19 prisoners at Taunton (he is said to have hanged 100 persons without trial within a week of the battle). In 1689 he relieved Londonderry, which had been besieged by James II from April 20 to July 30.

Kirkpatrick (kèrk.pat′rik), **Frederick Alexander.** b. 1861—. An English author of books on Latin-American history, including *Latin America—A Brief History* (1939).

Kirkrapine (kèrk′rap.in). In Spenser's *Faerie Queene*, the robber of the churches, intended to represent the plundering of the clergy.

Kiss on the Lips. A collection of short stories by Katharine Susannah Prichard, published in 1932.

Kit-Cat Club (kit′kat). A London club which flourished, according to the generally accepted account, from 1703 to 1733. Its meetings were held at the "Cat and Fiddle," kept by Christopher Cat, a noted mutton-pieman, near Temple Bar. It was founded by members of the Whig Party, and among its frequenters were Steele, Addison, and Marlborough. Its name is thought to be derived from the name of the landlord of the tavern, though *The Spectator* (No. 9) says it was from the name of the pies, which were called "kit-cats." The club occasionally met in summer at the house of Jacob Tonson at Barn Elms, where a room was built for it, the walls of which were adorned with portraits of its members. As the ceiling was low, Sir Godfrey Kneller, who painted the portraits, used a small canvas (36 by 28 inches), which was later called kit-cat size.

Kite (kīt), **Sergeant.** A mock astrologer in Farquhar's *Recruiting Officer*, who hopes by prophesying to gain recruits for the army.

Kitely (kīt′li). A jealous merchant in Ben Jonson's comedy *Every Man in His Humour*, whose "humour" causes him to suspect his wife's infidelity. He is encouraged in his suspicions by his wife's brother, Wellbred, but finally cured when he overreaches himself by making a public scandal of "the black poison of suspect."

Kit Nubbles (kit nub′lz). See **Nubbles, Kit.**

Kit's Coty House. A noted dolmen near Aylesford, Kent.

Kitto (kit′ō), **John.** b. at Plymouth, England, Dec. 4, 1804; d. at Cannstatt, Germany, Nov. 25, 1854. An English scholar, author of the *Pictorial Bible*. In his youth he fell from a ladder and became entirely deaf. The Church Missionary Society sent him to Malta as a printer in 1827. In 1829 he went with a private mission party to Baghdad, returning in 1832. He published *The Lost Senses* (1845), the *Pictorial Bible* (1835–38), *Pictorial History of Palestine and the Holy Land* (1840), *Cyclopedia of Biblical Literature* (1845), and *Daily Bible Illustrations* (1849–54).

Kittredge (kit′rij), **George Lyman.** b. at Boston, Mass., Feb. 28, 1860; d. at Barnstable, Mass., July 23, 1941. An American educator. He was graduated (1882) from Harvard, where he was instructor (1888–90) and professor (1894–1936) of English. Kittredge was an authority on Shakespeare,

Chaucer, and *Beowulf* and other early English literature; his Shakespeare course, English 2, became a Harvard tradition. He was also a folklorist, serving for a time as editor of the *Journal of American Folklore.* His publications include *The Language of Chaucer's Troilus* (1894), *Words and Their Ways in English Speech* (with J. B. Greenough, 1901), *The Old Farmer and His Almanack* (1904), *English Witchcraft and James I* (1912), *Advanced English Grammar* (with F. E. Farley, 1913), *Chaucer and His Poetry* (1915), *Shakespeare* (1916), *Dr. Robert Child, the Remonstrant* (1919), *Sir Thomas Malory* (1925), and *Witchcraft in Old and New England* (1929). Works which he edited include *Albion Series of Anglo-Saxon and Middle English Poetry* (with J. W. Bright, 5 vols., 1900–07), *English and Scottish Popular Ballads* (with Helen Child Sargent, 1904), *Gawain and the Green Knight* (1916), *Ballads and Songs* (1917), and *Complete Works of Shakespeare* (1936).

Kitty (kit′i). A novel by Warwick Deeping, published in 1927.

Kitty Bennet (ben′ęt). See **Bennet, Kitty.**

Kitty Crocodile (krok′ọ.dĭl), **Lady.** See **Crocodile, Lady Kitty.**

Kitty Linnet (lin′ęt). See **Linnet, Kitty.**

Kitty Tailleur (tä′lėr). A novel by May Sinclair, published in 1908. It was issued in the U. S. under the title *The Immortal Moment.*

Klaus (klôz), **Santa.** See **Santa Claus.**

Klopstock (klop′shtok), **Friedrich Gottlieb.** b. at Quedlinburg, Germany, July 2, 1724; d. at Hamburg, Germany, March 14, 1803. A German poet. Before 1745, when he went to Jena to study theology, he had already conceived the plan of the religious epic later written as *Der Messias* (and comparable, in English literature, to Milton's *Paradise Lost*). At Leipzig in 1748 he published anonymously, in the journal *Bremer Beiträge*, the first three cantos of the poem. In 1750 he accepted the invitation of Bodmer, the translator of *Paradise Lost*, to Zurich, but the succeeding year was summoned by Frederick V of Denmark to Copenhagen, that he might there find the leisure to complete his poem. He remained there until 1771, went then to Hamburg, in 1775 was for a year at Karlsruhe, and then returned to Hamburg, where he subsequently lived. *Der Messias*, a poem consisting of 20 cantos written in hexameters, did not appear in its complete form until 1773. *Geistliche Lieder* appeared in 1758, and *Oden* in 1771. He also wrote three dramas on Biblical subjects: *Der Tod Adams* (1757), *Salomo*, and *David* (1772). Three others were written on subjects from early national history: *Hermannsschlacht* (1769), *Hermann und die Fürsten* (1784), and *Hermanns Tod* (1787). The last three dramas were in prose interspersed with bardic choruses, so called, and were consequently named by him "Bardiete." Their title character Hermann is the German hero Arminius. Minor poems are the ode *An meine Freunde* (1747), later (1767) changed to *Wingolf*, addressed to the poets of the Saxon school; the *Kriegslied*, written in 1749 in honor of Frederick II; and the ode *Hermann und Thusnelda*, written in 1752. His principal prose work is *Die Gelehrtenrepublik.*

Knatchbull-Hugessen (nach′bŭl.hū′je̯.sen), **Edward Hugessen.** [Title, 1st Baron **Brabourne.**] b. at Mersham, Hatch, Kent, England, April 29, 1829; d. at Smeeth, Kent, Feb. 6, 1893. An English politician and author of books for children; grandnephew of Jane Austen. He held various posts under Gladstone but became (1880) a Conservative upon entering the House of Lords. Author of *Crackers for Christmas* (1870), *Higgledy-Piggledy, or Stories for Everybody and Everybody's Children* (1875), and other books for children. For older readers he wrote *Life, Times, and Character of Oliver Cromwell* (1877) and *Facts and Fictions in Irish History* (1886). In 1884 he published two volumes of letters written by Jane Austen to her sister, Cassandra.

Knibbs (nibz), **Harry Herbert.** b. at Clifton, Ontario, Canada, 1874—. A Canadian writer. Author of *Lost Farm Camp* (1912), *Songs of the Outlands* (1914), *Riders of the Stars* (1916), *Songs of the Trail* (1920), *Partners of Chance* (1921), *Saddle Songs and Other Verse* (1922), *Tomescal* (1925), *Songs of the Lost Frontier* (1930), and *The Tonto Kid* (1936).

Knight (nīt), **Charles.** b. at Windsor, England, March 15, 1791; d. at Addlestone, Surrey, England, March 9, 1873. An English publisher and author. His chief work is *Popular History of England* (8 vols., 1856–62). He edited *The Penny Magazine* (1832–45), *The Penny Cyclopaedia* (1833–44), *The Pictorial Shakespeare* (1841), *The English Cyclopaedia* (1853), and others.

Knight, George Wilson. b. at Sutton, Surrey, England, Sept. 19, 1897—. A Canadian professor and literary scholar, chiefly known for studies of Shakespeare such as *The Wheel of Fire* (1930) and *Principles of Shakespearian Production* (1936).

Knight, Joseph. b. at London, May 24, 1829; d. there, June 23, 1907. An English essayist, biographical writer, and editor. He was at London (1860 *et seq.*) as drama critic for the London *Gazette* and for the *Athenaeum* from 1867 to 1907, wrote for the *Gentlemen's Magazine*, and was editor (1883–1907) of *Notes and Queries*. He was cofounder, with the poet Alfred Austin, of the Leeds Mechanics' Institute. He was the author of *Life of Dante Gabriel Rossetti* (1887), *Theatrical Notes* (1893), and *Life of David Garrick* (1894).

Knight, Joseph Philip. b. at Bradford-on-Avon, England, July 26, 1812; d. at Great Yarmouth, England, June 2, 1887. An English composer of songs, including *Rocked in the Cradle of the Deep*, famous for its basso profundo solo.

Knight, William Angus. b. in Scotland, Feb. 22, 1836; d. March 4, 1916. An English philosopher, teacher, and Wordsworth specialist. He served (1871–95) as examiner for St. Andrews, London, Victoria, and New Zealand universities, and for the Civil Service Commission, and played a major part in introducing the L. L. A. (Licentiate in Literature and Arts) degree for women. Author of *The English Lake District as Interpreted in the Poems of Wordsworth* (1878–91), *Studies in Philosophy and Literature* (1879), *Through the Wordsworth Country* (1892), *Aspects of Theism* (1894), and *Some 19th Century Scotsmen* (1902). He edited *Poems from the Dawn of English Literature to the Year 1699* (1863), Wordsworth's *Poetical Works* (11 vols., 1881–89), Wordsworth's *Prose* (1893), *Works of William Wordsworth and Dorothy Wordsworth* (12 vols., 1896–97), *Letters of the Wordsworth Family* (1907), and the *Poetical Works* of Coleridge (1905) and Scott (1907).

Knight At Arms. A historical novel by Henry Christopher Bailey, published in 1924.

Knightley (nīt′li), **Mr.** In Jane Austen's novel *Emma*, Emma's brother-in-law and, eventually, her fiancé.

Knight of Malta (môl′ta̯), **The.** A play by John Fletcher and Philip Massinger, produced before 1619 and printed in 1647.

Knight of Snowdoun (snō′dun). See **Snowdoun, Knight of.**

"Knight of the Burning Lamp." See under **Bardolph.**

Knight of the Burning Pestle, The. A mock-heroic drama by Francis Beaumont, produced c1607 and published anonymously in 1613. It was intended to satirize such plays as Heywood's *Four Prentices of London*, in which extravagantly chivalric and knightly language was put into the mouths of the middle class.

Knight of the Leopard. An epithet of David, the Prince Royal of Scotland, and hero of Sir Walter Scott's novel *The Talisman*.

Knight of the Rueful Countenance. Don Quixote: so called by Sancho Panza.

Knight of the Swan. In 12th-century German legend, a knight who appears in a small boat coming upstream on the Rhine, drawn by a swan. He steps ashore and saves the lady of the story, and marries her; but he can remain with her only on condition that she does not ask his origin or mention in what manner he arrived. The condition is broken, the swan and boat reappear, and he is carried swiftly away. There are romances in French, German, and English on this subject. It was in commemoration of the myth of the Knight of the Swan that Frederick II of Brandenburg instituted the Order of the Swan, in 1440. Scholars think that the swan-knight theme is of Oriental origin, but its fullest development is Teutonic only.

Knights, The. A comedy by Samuel Foote, produced in 1749 and printed in 1754.

Knights of Araby (ar′a̯.bi). A novel by Marmaduke Pickthall, published in 1917.

Knights of Malta (môl′ta̯) or **of Rhodes** (rōdz). See **Hospitalers of Saint John of Jerusalem.**

Knight's Tale, The. One of Chaucer's *Canterbury Tales*. It is a recasting by Chaucer of his version of Boccaccio's *Il Teseida*, which he made before he wrote *The Legend of Good Women*. It tells of Palamon and Arcite, two Theban youths who are prisoners of Theseus, King of Athens, their love for the beautiful Emelye, sister of the Queen, their contest for her hand, the victory of Arcite, his accident and death, and the final uniting of Emelye and Palamon. The final outcome represents also a victory of Venus (to whom Palamon has prayed) over Mars (who sponsored Arcite). The same story was told by Dryden, Fletcher, and others. Chaucer's version is less lively and inventive than many of the other *Canterbury Tales*, though it is the longest of the tales in verse; it emphasizes the ideals of chivalry and of courtly behavior, as does the characterization of the Knight himself in the Prologue:

> And evermore he hadde a sovereyn prys.
> And though that he were worthy, he was wys,
> And of his port as meke as is a mayde.
> He never yet no vileinye ne sayde
> In al his lyf, un-to no maner wight.
> He was a verray parfit gentil knight.

See also **Palamon and Arcite.**

Knights Templars or **Knights of the Temple.** See **Templars.**

Knight without Armour. A novel by James Hilton, published in 1933.

Knoblock (nob′lok), **Edward.** b. at New York, 1874; d. at London, July 19, 1945. An English novelist, playwright, and scenarist. His plays include *The Faun* (1911), *Kismet* (1911), *My Lady's Dress* (1914), *Marie-Odile* (1915), *Tiger, Tiger* (1918), *The Lullaby* (1923), *The Mulberry Bush* (1930), *If a Body* (1935), *Rolling Stone* (1936), *The Henry Irving Centenary Matinee* (1938), and *Bird of Passage* (1943); coauthor with Lawrence Sterner of *The Club Baby* (1895). He collaborated with Arnold Bennett on *Milestones* (1912) and *London Life* (1924), with J. B. Priestley on *The Good Companions* (1931), and with Beverley Nichols on *Evensong* (1932), and adapted *Grand Hotel* (1931) from the novel by Vicki Baum. Author of *The Ant Heap* (1929), *The Man with Two Mirrors* (1931), *The Love Lady* (1933), *Inexperience* (1941), and other novels.

Knole and the Sackvilles (nōl; sak′vilz). An informal history of the Sackville family and of the family seat at Knole, Sevenoaks, by V. Sackville-West, published in 1922. The chronicle begins in the Elizabethan period.

Knolles (nōlz), **Richard.** b. probably at Cold Ashby, Northamptonshire, England, c1550; d. at Sandwich, Kent, England, 1610. An English historian. His chief work is *Generall Historie of the Turkes from the first beginning of that Nation* (1603).

Knott (not), **Herman.** A pseudonym of **Smith, Walter Chalmers.**

Knowell (nō′wel), **The Elder.** In Ben Jonson's comedy *Every Man in His Humour,* a sententious old gentleman. His "humour" is a strained solicitude for his son's morals.

Knowles (nōlz), **James Sheridan.** b. at Cork, Ireland, May 12, 1784; d. at Torquay, England, Nov. 30, 1862. A British playwright. His father and Richard Brinsley Sheridan were first cousins. He served in the militia, studied medicine, went on the stage, and taught school at Glasgow before his first successful play (*Caius Gracchus*) was produced in 1815. In 1830 he left Glasgow and settled near Edinburgh. In 1834 he visited the U. S. Until 1843 he continued to act at intervals both in his own plays and others. He also lectured, and in 1844 became a Baptist and preached at Exeter Hall and in other places sermons against Roman Catholicism. Among his plays are *Caius Gracchus* (1815), *Virginius* (1820), *William Tell* (1825), *Alfred the Great* (1831), *The Hunchback* (1832), *The Wife* (1833), *The Beggar of Bethnal Green* (1834; abridged

from *The Beggar's Daughter of Bethnal Green,* 1828), *The Love-Chase* (1837), *Love* (1839), and *John of Procida* (1840).

Knowles, Sir **James Thomas.** b. Oct. 13, 1831; d. at London, Dec. 13, 1908. An English architect and editor. He edited (1870–77) the *Contemporary Review* and founded and was first editor (1877–1908) of the *Nineteenth Century.* He also founded (1869) the Metaphysical Society.

Knox (noks), **Edmund George Valpy.** [Pseudonym, Evoe.] b. at Oxford, England, May 10, 1881—. An English humorist on the staff (1921 *et seq.*) and editor (1932 *et seq.*) of *Punch.* Author of *The Brazen Lyre, A Little Loot, Parodies Regained, Fiction As She is Wrote, Quaint Specimens, This Other Eden, Things That Annoy Me, Slight Irritations,* and *Folly Calling.*

Knox, John. b. at or near Haddington, East Lothian, Scotland, in 1505, 1513, or 1515; d. at Edinburgh, Nov. 24, 1572. A Scottish reformer, one of the principal figures of the Reformation during the 16th century. He was educated at Glasgow or at St. Andrews University, but he did not take a degree. About 1530 he became a Roman Catholic priest. Nothing definite is known of his early life, but apparently he studied under John Major, whose theory that government derives from the people was later supported by Knox against Mary, Queen of Scots. He read Jerome and Augustine and the Bible, and he absorbed the sermons of Patrick Hamilton, William Tyndale, and George Wishart: these apparently were the principal formative influences on his later thought. Knox became attached to Wishart, espousing Protestantism, and, after Wishart's death at the stake in 1546 and the subsequent murder of his condemner, Cardinal Beaton, at the hands of assassins, preached at St. Andrews Castle to Beaton's murderers, thus making common cause with them. When the castle fell to the French in 1548, Knox was taken prisoner to France and spent 19 months as a galley slave. Released when the English government acted in his behalf, he became a minister of the crown (his repudiation of Rome was by this time complete) and for a time (1551) was a royal chaplain of Edward VI. He had a part in the revision of the Book of Common Prayer. When the Roman Catholic Mary Tudor (Bloody Mary) became queen of England in 1553, Knox fled to the Continent, preaching at Frankfort on the Main, Geneva, and Dieppe. At Geneva he met with Calvin and other leading Protestants and carried on correspondence with Protestants in England and Scotland; his connection with Calvin remained firm through the years and he often approached the Genevan for advice. In 1555–56 Knox was permitted briefly to preach in Scotland by the regent, Mary of Guise, and at this time probably made the influential ties that brought him to preëminence as leader of the Scottish Reformation. In 1557 the Protestant barons of Scotland entered into their first covenant and soon afterwards invited Knox to counsel them. However, Knox delayed his return, sending to the lords an "Appellation" to defend their beliefs. In 1558, he issued, among six of his tracts of this period, a *First Blast of the Trumpet Against the Monstrous Regiment* [government] *of Women,* in-

---

ḍ, d or j; ṣ, s or sh; ṭ, t or ch; ẓ, z or zh; o, F. cloche; ü, F. menu; c̆h, Sc. loch; ṅ, F. bonbon.

tending it as an attack upon Mary Tudor, Catherine de Médicis of France, her daughter-in-law Mary, Queen of Scots, and Mary's mother Mary of Guise, but Elizabeth of England took the attack as directed against her and never thereafter fully trusted Knox, though he opposed Mary, Queen of Scots, and was an advocate of an English-Scottish union. Knox returned to Scotland in 1559 to discover that the regent now adhered closely to her French alliance and its enmity to Protestantism, and he was therefore forced to do his preaching outside Edinburgh. Correspondence between the Scots nobles and Elizabeth occurred during the struggle between the regency and the barons; the fighting for a time went against the Protestant party and in favor of the French army of the young queen, but when English troops came on the scene a peace (Treaty of Edinburgh, July 6, 1560) was signed, the French left, and the Protestants remained in undisputed control of Scotland. In August the Scottish estates adopted the Confession of Faith written by Knox and three others; soon legislation followed abolishing the Pope's authority and providing severe penalties, including death, for celebrating Mass. In December the first General Assembly of the new Church of Scotland met, but the intemperate *Book of Discipline*, drawn up by Knox for the rule of the congregations, was not adopted. In 1561 Mary, Queen of Scots arrived from France, her husband dead, to take possession of her realm. She was a Roman Catholic and insisted on hearing Mass. Knox protested and, through the mediation of James Stuart (later Earl of Moray), obtained several interviews with the queen. Their arguments concerning the duty of subjects to worship as did their sovereigns and of the ultimate religious authority served only to convince each that the problem was insoluble. Mary's charm and diplomacy slowly caused defections in the ranks of Knox's followers, but her actions (planning a Spanish or French marriage, her confidence in David Rizzio, her marriage to Darnley, Darnley's murder with her apparent compliance, her sudden marriage to Bothwell) gave Knox powerful ammunition for his incessant attacks on the modern "Jezebel," as he called her. The capture of Mary by the insurgent nobles and her imprisonment at Lochleven Castle in 1567 gave Knox his chance; he appeared at the assembly that dethroned Mary and placed her infant son on the throne as James VI. Knox preached the coronation sermon in July, 1567. His triumph was complete, and even the disturbances that followed (Mary's escape, the battle of Langside in May, 1568, the assassination of Moray, and the civil war that followed) failed to shake the now solidly established Calvinism of the Scottish Church or to diminish the triumph of the principle of the right of the people to unseat their rulers. His major written work is *The History of the Reformation of Religioun Within the Realme of Scotland*, not published in full until after his death. The standard edition of his complete works is that of David Laing (6 vols., 1864).

Knox, Ronald Arbuthnott. b. Feb. 17, 1888—. An English Roman Catholic priest and author. He was Catholic chaplain (1926–39) at Oxford after entering (1917) the Church, and served as domestic prelate (1936) to the Pope. Author of *Some Loose Stones* (1913), *Reunion All Round* (1914), *A Spiritual Aeneid* (1918), *The Viaduct Murder* (1925), *The Belief of Catholics* (1927), *Caliban in Grub Street* (1930), *The Body in the Silo* (1933), *Let Dons Delight* (1939), *In Soft Garments* (1942), *God and the Atom* (1945), and *A Retreat for Priests* (1946).

Knut (knŏt). See **Canute.**

Koestler (kĕst′lẽr), **Arthur.** b. at Budapest, Hungary, Sept. 5, 1905—. A Hungarian novelist and journalist. He was educated at the Vienna Polytechnic High School and the University of Vienna. In 1927, a year after his graduation, he was Middle East correspondent for the Ullstein chain of German newspapers, and in 1929 he was Paris correspondent for the same organization, and later foreign editor at Berlin. He became a Communist in the early 1930's, and spent a year in the U.S.S.R. According to his own statement, he had repudiated Communism, and particularly Stalinism, by February, 1938. In 1938, at Paris, he edited an anti-Nazi and anti-Communist German weekly, the *Future*. In October, 1939, he was arrested as an anti-Fascist refugee and imprisoned in the detention camp at Le Vernet, from which he was not released until Jan. 17, 1940. He joined (but never served in) the French Foreign Legion, and by the end of 1940 he managed to escape to England, where he was also under arrest for a short time and where he later enlisted in the British army. His works include *The Gladiators* (1939), *Darkness at Noon* (1941), *Scum of the Earth* (1941), *Dialogue with Death* (1942), *Arrival and Departure* (1943), *Thieves in the Night* (1946), *Insight and Outlook* (1949), *Promise and Fulfilment* (a book on Palestine, 1949), *The Age of Longing* (1952), and the autobiographical *Arrow in the Blue* (1952).

Koh-i-noor or **Koh-i-nur** (kō′ē.nŏr′). [Eng. trans., "*Mountain of Light*."] A diamond belonging to the British crown. It was acquired by Nadir Shah in 1739, and by Queen Victoria in 1850. It then weighed 186 1/16 carats, but has been recut, and is now considerably smaller.

Ko-Ko (kō′kō). In Gilbert and Sullivan's *The Mikado*, the Lord High Executioner. He is engaged to Yum-Yum, but eventually marries Katisha.

Koppenberg (kop′ẹn.berk). In the legend of the Pied Piper of Hamelin, the mountain into which the sorcerer and the children disappeared.

Koran (kō̇.rän′, -ran′). [Also, **Quran**; in some older sources, **Alcoran** or **Alkoran**.] The sacred book of the Mohammedans. It is the most important foundation on which the Mohammedan religion rests, and is held in the highest veneration by all sects in the Mohammedan world. When being read it must be kept on a stand elevated above the floor. No one may read it or touch it without first making a legal ablution. It is written in the Arabic language, and its style is considered a model. At first no translations of the Arabic Koran were permitted, but now translations of the Koran, as of the Bible, are available in all the leading languages of the world. The substance of the Koran is held, by the orthodox, to be uncreated and eternal; Mohammed was merely the person to whom the work was revealed. The

Koran, as and when revealed, was committed to memory by Mohammed's friends and followers, a few of whom made private written collections as an aid to memory. But when a great many of the Koran reciters had been killed in battle, Omar suggested to Abu-Bakr (the successor of Mohammed) that it should be written down. Abu-Bakr accordingly commanded Zaid, an amanuensis of the prophet, to commit it to writing. This was the authorized text until 23 years after the death of the prophet. A number of variant readings had, however, crept into use. By order of the caliph Othman in the year 30 of the Hejira, Zaid and three assistants made a careful revision which was adopted as the standard, and all the other copies were ordered to be burned. The Koran consists of 114 *suras* (divisions). These are not numbered, but each one has a separate name. They are not arranged in historical order. Most of these *suras* purport to be the addresses delivered by Mohammed during his career at Mecca and Medina. As a general rule the shorter *suras*, which contain the theology of Islam, belong to the Meccan period, while the longer ones, relating to social duties and relationships, belong to that of Medina. The Koran is indebted to Jewish and Christian sources. Moses and Jesus, with the majority of the patriarchs, are reckoned among the prophets. The Biblical narratives are interwoven with rabbinical legends. The customs of the Jews are made, in fact, to conform to those of the Arabians. Mohammedan theology consists in the study of the Koran and its commentaries. A very fine manuscript collection of Korans, including many in Cufic (the old Arabic character), is to be found in the National Library at Cairo, Egypt. Other collections exist in religious centers in the Near East and in the leading European museums and libraries.

Kotzebue (kŏt′sẹ.bö), **August Friedrich Ferdinand von.** b. at Weimar, Germany, May 3, 1761; d. at Mannheim, Baden, Germany, March 23, 1819. A German dramatist. He was in the Russian service until 1790; after traveling, he settled at Reval (now Tallin), in Estonia. He became dramatist at the Vienna court theater in 1798 but quarreled with the actors and resigned. He went to Weimar but soon found the atmosphere there uncomfortable, since he had previously attacked Goethe and the romantics. On his way back to St. Petersburg he was arrested and exiled (1800) to Siberia. However, Czar Paul I, who admired his work, ordered him returned and made him director of the St. Petersburg German theater. Paul died in 1801 and Kotzebue returned to Germany, living first at Weimar and then at Berlin, where he published (1803–07) *Der Freimütige*, an antiromantic journal. In 1806 he returned to Russia, where he published attacks on Napoleon in his journals *Die Biene* and *Die Grille*. He returned (1818) to Germany as a political spy for Russia and that year founded at Mannheim (and published later at Weimar) the journal *Literarisches Wochenblatt*, in which he gave free rein to his contempt for freedom, liberal aspirations, and popular movements in general. His reactionary sentiments aroused strong feeling against him, especially among students, one of whom, Karl Ludwig Sand, stabbed him to death in 1819. Sand was executed and the authorities took advantage of the

event to suppress the Burschenschaften, the students' political clubs, and to place the universities under close surveillance. Kotzebue's plays, numbering more than 200, are now usually considered vastly too sentimental but, through their facility in situational development, they attained great popularity, even in translation in England, where Kotzebue was at one time the best-liked German dramatist. The plays had a great influence on later dramatists, not for their content, but for their technique. They comprise tragedies, historical dramas, comedies, and farces; among them are *Die deutschen Kleinstädter, Pagenstreiche, Die beiden Klingsberge, Menschenhass und Reue, Der arme Poet,* and *Die Kreuzfahrer*. He also wrote histories, biographies, and miscellaneous pieces, including several autobiographical works.

Kratim (krä.tēm′). [Also, **Kratimer** (krat′i.mẹr).] In Christian legend, the dog of the Seven Sleepers of Ephesus, who slept with the seven youths in the cave. In Mohammedan legend, he is one of the very few animals who will go to Paradise.

Kremlin (krem′lin). The citadel of Moscow, U.S.S.R. It is a triangular enclosure, ab. 1½ mi. in circuit, fortified with battlemented walls from which project cylindrical and square towers, many of them terminating in spires behind which rise the multiform domes and belfries of the churches, brilliant with gold and colors. The present walls date from 1492. The Kremlin contains the imperial palace, the cathedrals of the Assumption, the Archangel Michael, and the Annunciation, the Miracle monastery, the Ascension convent, the arsenal, and the famous Great Bell (virtually all of the buildings here listed have, of course, long since been adapted by the present regime in Russia to purposes other than those originally intended). The Great Palace has been extensively rebuilt since 1920, and actually dated prior to that for the most part only from the middle of the 19th century, its predecessors having repeatedly been burned, most recently by the soldiers of Napoleon. It is an enormous structure which now provides the official chamber of the supreme council of the U.S.S.R. Several of the chapels also are noteworthy, as well as the Red Staircase, used only for grand functions and recalling many historic scenes from Ivan IV (Ivan the Terrible) and Peter I (Peter the Great) to Napoleon.

Kreutzer Sonata (kroit′sẻr). A sonata in A (Opus 47) for piano and violin by Ludwig van Beethoven, dedicated to the violinist Rodolphe Kreutzer. It was first played in May, 1803, and published in 1805. It is said that Kreutzer never played the piece.

Kriemhild (krēm′hilt). [Also **Chriemhild**.] The heroine of the *Nibelungenlied*. She was the daughter of King Gibich (whose seat was at Worms on the lower Rhine), the sister of the Burgundian princes Gunther, Gernot, and Giselher, and the wife of Siegfried, who bestowed upon her the Nibelungen gold. Siegfried was murdered for the gold. Afterward, as the wife of Etzel (Attila), king of the Huns, Kriemhild encompassed the death of her brothers, and avenged Siegfried's murder, but was herself slain. In the Old Norse *Volsunga Saga* her counterpart is Gudrun.

ḍ, d or j; ṣ, s or sh; ṭ, t or ch; ẓ, z or zh; o, F. cloche; ü, F. menu; ċh, Sc. loch; ṅ, F. bonbon.

Krishna (krish′nạ). The Hindu god of joy and voluptuousness, evolved from the earlier god of redemption. He is the eighth avatar of Vishnu, or Vishnu himself. In his physical character mingle myths of fire, lightning, and storm, of heaven and the sun. In the epics he is a hero invincible in war and love, brave, but above all crafty. He was the son of Vasudeva and Devaki, and born at Muttra (Mathura), on the Jumna River between Delhi and Agra, the last of the Yadavas. Like that of many heroes, his birth was beset with peril. On the night when it took place, his parents had to remove him from the reach of King Kansa (cousin to Devaki), who sought his life because he had been warned that a son of Devaki would kill him (Kansa had already managed to kill six male children of Devaki). Conveyed across the Jumna, Krishna was brought up as their son by the shepherd Nanda and his wife Yashoda, together with his brother Balarama, "Rama the strong," who had likewise been smuggled to safety. The two brothers grew up among the shepherds, slaying monsters and demons and sporting with the shepherdesses of Vrindavana. Their birth and infancy, their juvenile exploits, and their erotic gambols with the shepherdesses became in time the essential portion of the legend of Krishna, and their scenes are today the most celebrated centers of his worship. When grown, the brothers put their uncle Kansa to death, and Krishna became king of the Yadavas. He cleared the land of monsters, warred against impious kings, and took part in the war of the sons of Pandu against those of Dhritarashtra, as described in the *Mahabharata*. He transferred his capital to Dvaraka ("the city of gates"), the gates of the West, since localized in Gujarat. There he and his race were overtaken by the final catastrophe. After seeing his brother slain, and the Yadavas kill each other to the last man, he himself perished, wounded in the heel, like Achilles, by the arrow of a hunter. His legend is developed in the *Mahabharata*, the Puranas, and in the Bhagavad-Gita, which Krishna recited to Arjuna (one of the Pandu or Pandava princes) while serving as Arjuna's charioteer.

Krook (krŏŏk), **Mr.** A drunkard, in Dickens's *Bleak House*, who dies by spontaneous combustion.

Kublai Khan (kŏb′lī kän′). [Also, **Kubla Khan** (kŏ′blạ kän′).] b. c1216; d. 1294. A Mongol emperor (c1259–94), founder of the Mongol (Yüan) dynasty of China; grandson of Genghis Khan. Under his brother Mangu he campaigned in western China (to c1259). Mangu died in 1259 and Kublai ascended the throne; his accession was disputed by a brother and a cousin, but he maintained his hold on the khanship. In 1264 he founded a city, his capital, on the site of modern Peiping and after it was finished proceeded with his plan, a continuation of the aims of his predecessors, for the conquest of all of China. By 1279, as the result of the efforts of his general Bayan, Kublai had driven the Sung dynasty from China south of the Yangtse and ruled over an area stretching from the Pacific Ocean to the Volga River and Poland. The major units of this empire were actually ruled, except for its easternmost portions (China and Mongolia), by subchiefs, but they recognized Kublai as their overlord. He made further attempts to extend his ter-

ritories, conquering Burma and Korea, but failing in several expeditions against Japan and in one against Java. Kublai's fame spread throughout the world. To his capital came merchants and diplomats; foreigners, including Europeans, traveled across Asia to enter his service as soldiers, ministers, and court attendants. Perhaps the best-known visitor to Kublai's court was the Venetian Marco Polo, who served the khan in various capacities from 1275 to 1292. Kublai was known as a patron of literature and the arts. He was a tolerant ruler, and (although himself a Buddhist) sent envoys to Rome to get Christian missionaries to come to China. The magnificence of his reign and of his court mark one of the high points of Asiatic civilization.

Kulturkampf (kŭl.tör′kämpf″). In German history, the struggle (literally, "conflict of civilizations," a term first used of it in the Prussian Diet in 1873 by Rudolf Virchow) directed by Bismarck, as chancellor of the newly formed German Empire, against the Roman Catholic Church. The fight began in 1871 and lasted until 1879, though it was not until 1883 that the last of the anti-Catholic laws became inactive. The *Syllabus errorum*, appended to the papal encyclical *Quanta cura* of 1864, proclaimed complete supremacy of the church over temporal matters; in it Pope Pius IX attacked nationalism, secular education, and state control of the church, among other things. When this was followed in 1870 by the declaration of the dogma of papal infallibility by the Vatican Council, Bismarck was one of the national leaders who broke with the church.

Kuyp (koip), **Albert.** See **Cuyp, Albert.**

Kyd (kid), **Thomas.** [Also, **Kid.**] b. at London, 1558; d. 1594. An English dramatist. His play *The Spanish Tragedy*, written probably in 1589 and printed illicitly in 1592 (by proper authorization in 1594), was one of the most sensational and perhaps the most popular of the whole Elizabethan period. Based on Seneca's techniques, it includes, in addition to the ghost and revenge theme, brutal and bloodcurdling action; it became a byword, its characters so well known that passing reference was made to them as to proverbs. The only other play definitely ascribable to Kyd is a translation of Robert Garnier's *Cornélie*. Sometimes attributed to Kyd are *Soliman and Perseda*, and *Arden of Feversham* (also attributed to nearly every other playwright of the early 1590's). A reference to Kyd and "Hamlet" in Nash's epistle to Greene's *Menaphon* (1591) indicates a possible relationship of Kyd to the "Ur-Hamlet," possibly the basis of Shakespeare's play. *The First Part of Jeronimo* (printed in 1605) has been shown not to be Kyd's, though it tells the story forming the background of *The Spanish Tragedy*. Two prose pamphlets of Kyd's are known, and he apparently wrote much that is now lost. As a result of antiforeign propaganda inciting riots at London in 1593, Kyd's rooms were entered during the search for the author of the inflammatory literature. Among his papers was found a blasphemous writing that Kyd, under torture, swore belonged to Christopher Marlowe, who was thereby implicated further in pending charges of atheism and blasphemy. Kyd was released after Marlowe's death, but he failed to find a patron or regular employment and died in poverty.

Kynaston (kin′ạs.tọn), **Sir Francis.** b. at Oteley, Shropshire, England, 1587; d. 1642. An English poet and scholar.

Kynewulf (kin′ẹ.wŭlf). See **Cynewulf.**

Kyng (or **Kynge**) **Johan** (jō′han, jon). See **King John.**

Kyrle (kẽrl), **John.** [Called **"the Man of Ross."**] b. at Dymock, Gloucestershire, England, May 22, 1637; d. at Ross, Hertfordshire, England, Nov. 7, 1724. An English landowner, known as a benevolent and public-spirited man, a general mediator in the neighborhood of the estates he inherited from his father. Pope has immortalized him in his *Moral Essays*, iii. 250.

L

Laar or **Laer** (lär), **Pieter van.** [Called **Il Bamboccio,** meaning "the Cripple."] b. in Netherlands, c1592–95; d. at Haarlem, Netherlands, c1642. A Dutch genre painter. He painted with much humor and naturalness, and his style was so widely imitated that "bambocciade" (from his epithet) became a special artistic term applied to scenes of low life.

Labervele (lā′bẽr.vēl), **Count.** The old and jealous husband of Florilla in George Chapman's *An Humorous Day's Mirth.*

La Bestia (lạ bes′ti.ạ). A wealthy fool in George Chapman's *An Humorous Day's Mirth.*

La Boétie (là bo.ā.sē), **Étienne de.** b. at Sarlat, Dordogne, France, Nov. 1, 1530; d. at Germainac, near Bordeaux, France, Aug. 18, 1563. A French writer, known as a friend of Montaigne.

Labouchère (la.bö.shãr′), **Henry du Pré.** b. 1831; d. at Florence, Italy, Jan. 16, 1912. An English journalist and advanced Liberal politician. He was engaged in the diplomatic service from 1854 to 1864. As member of Parliament he represented Windsor (1865–66), Middlesex (1867–68), and Northampton (1880–1905). He was owner and editor of the London weekly journal *Truth*, notable for its exposures of corruption. His *Diary of a Besieged Resident in Paris* appeared in 1871. He was appointed a privy councilor in 1905.

Laburnum Branch, The. A volume of poems by Naomi Mitchison, published in 1926.

La Calprenède (là kàl.prẹ.ned), **Gautier de Costes de.** b. at the Château de Tolgon, near Sarlat, Dordogne, France, c1610; d. at Le Grand-Andely, Eure, France, in October, 1663. A French novelist and dramatist. He borrowed extensively from his English contemporaries, as did they from him. He wrote the historical romances *Cassandre* (1642–50), *La Cléopatre* (1647–58), and *Faramond, ou l'histoire de France* (1661), and several tragedies, including *La Mort de Mithridate* (1637), *Le Comte d'Essex* (1638), and *Édouard, roi d'Angleterre* (1640).

Lachaise or **La Chaise** (là shez), **François d'Aix de.** b. at Aix, Loire, France, Aug. 25, 1624; d. at Paris, Jan. 20, 1709. A French Jesuit, confessor (1674 *et seq.*) of Louis XIV. Père Lachaise cemetery in E Paris, named for him, was opened in 1806.

Lachesis (lak′ẹ.sis). In Greek mythology, one of the three Moirae or Fates. According to Hesiod,

Lachesis was the one who decided on the length of life for each individual.

Lachmann (läċh′män), **Karl Konrad Friedrich Wilhelm.** b. at Brunswick, Germany, March 4, 1793; d. at Berlin, March 13, 1851. A German philologist and critic. He wrote *Zu den Nibelungen und zur Klage* (1836), *Betrachtungen über die Ilias* (1847), and published editions of the *Nibelungenlied* (1826), Walther von der Vogelweide, Wolfram von Eschenbach, Propertius, Catullus, Tibullus, Lucretius, and others.

Lackland (lak′land), **John.** See **John** (King of England).

La Creevy (lạ krē′vi), **Miss.** In Dickens's *Nicholas Nickleby*, a 50-year-old lady who fancies herself as able to appear very much younger. A painter of miniatures, she becomes a close friend of the Nickleby family and marries Tim Linkinwater.

Lacy (lā′si). The son of the Earl of Lincoln in Dekker's *Shoemaker's Holiday.*

Lacy, Earl. The lover of Margaret in Robert Greene's comedy *Friar Bacon and Friar Bungay.*

Lacy, John. b. near Doncaster, Yorkshire, England; d. at London, Sept. 17, 1681. An English dramatist and actor, noted in his day as a comedian and mimic. His Teague in Howard's *The Committee* was famous; he also played Falstaff and a leading role in his own adaptation of *The Taming of the Shrew.* Among his plays are *The Old Troop, or Monsieur Raggou* (c1665), and *Sir Hercules Buffoon, or the Poetical Squire* (1684).

Ladder of Swords, A. A historical novel by Sir Gilbert Parker, published in 1904.

Ladies!, The. A series of three historical tales by Lily Adams Beck under the pseudonym E. Barrington, published in 1922. The narratives include *My Lady Mary, The Golden Vanity,* and *A Bluestocking at Court,* all with an 18th-century background.

Ladies' Battle, The. A comedy by Robertson, from the French of Scribe and Legouvé. It was produced in 1851.

Ladies' Mile, The. A drive in Hyde Park, London, on the north side of the Serpentine.

Ladislaw (lad′is.lô), **Will.** One of the principal characters in George Eliot's novel *Middlemarch:* a young artist who marries Dorothea Brooke after the death of her first husband, Mr. Casaubon. As an artist, he has cleverness rather than talent; as

---

ḍ, d or j; ṣ, s or sh; ṭ, t or cʰ; ẓ, z or zh; o, F. cloche; ü, F. menu; ċh, Sc. loch; ṅ, F. bonbon.

a husband, he brings Dorothea great happiness.

Ladon (lā'dǫn). In Greek mythology, the dragon who guarded the golden apples of the Hesperides in the wonderful gardens of the west. Ladon never slept, but was killed by Hercules when he came to steal the apples.

Ladurlad (lä'dör.läd). In Robert Southey's *The Curse of Kehama*, the humble peasant who kills Kehama's son and is therefore the principal object of the curse invoked by Kehama.

Lady Bountiful. See **Bountiful, Lady.**

Lady Chatterley's Lover (chat'ẽr.liz). A novel by D. H. Lawrence, published in 1928. Its frank treatment of sexual matters caused the book to be banned for a time in England and the U. S.

Lady Clara Vere de Vere (klär'ạ vir dẹ vir). A poem (1842) by Tennyson, praising simple goodness and condemning aristocratic pride.

Lady Day. One of the various days celebrated in honor of the Virgin Mary, now only the Feast of the Annunciation, March 25.

Lady Elizabeth's Men. A Jacobean theatrical company. It was formed under the patronage of Lady Elizabeth, daughter of James I, in 1611 and performed at Court in 1612. Apparently the group acted at the Rose theater, since Henslowe mentions financing them, and also (1614) at his new Hope theater. After Henslowe died in 1616, there is no mention of them until 1622 when they appear on the rolls of the Cockpit theater.

Lady in Green Gloves, A. A novel by Sylvia Thompson, published in 1924.

Lady Jane Grey. [Full title, **The Tragedy of Lady Jane Grey.**] A drama by Nicholas Rowe, produced in 1715. The heroine is a suffering woman, based upon the historical character but deriving more directly from a Restoration play by John Banks on the same theme.

Lady Macbeth (mak.beth'). See **Macbeth, Lady.**

Lady Margaret Hall (mär'gạ.rẹt). A college for women in Oxford University. It was founded in 1878 by Edward Stuart Talbot, first warden of Keble College, and opened the following year with nine students. It is staffed entirely by women. It is not formally connected with Oxford University, but is one of its "recognized societies" for instruction and residence. An extension, known as the Wordsworth Building, was added in 1896. The college is named after Margaret, Countess of Richmond and Derby, mother of Henry VII, noted for her gifts to the university.

Lady of Belmont (bel'mont), **The.** A five-act play (1925) by St. John Ervine. A continuation of *The Merchant of Venice*, it shows what happens to Shylock after he leaves the courtroom, and also traces the development of the married couples, Bassanio and Portia, Gratiano and Nerissa, and Lorenzo and Jessica.

Lady of Leisure, A. A novel by Ethel Sidgwick, published in 1914.

Lady of Lyons (lī'ǫnz), **The.** [Full title, **The Lady of Lyons; or, Love and Pride.**] A comedy by Edward Bulwer-Lytton, produced in 1838. It was originally written under the title of *The Adventurer*,

which was altered at W. C. Macready's suggestion to *The Lady of Lyons*.

Lady of Pleasure, The. A comedy by James Shirley, licensed in 1635 and printed in 1637.

Lady of Shalott (shạ.lot'), **The.** A poem by Alfred Tennyson, published in the volume *Poems* in 1832. It deals with the Arthurian legend of Elaine and Lancelot of the Lake.

Lady of the Lake. [French, **Dame du Lac** (dȧm dü lȧk).] A name given in Arthurian romance to the mistress of the enchanter Merlin. She lived in a palace in the midst of a magical lake which prevented approach. It was she who gave the sword Excalibur to Arthur and who educated Sir Lancelot. Tennyson and Matthew Arnold named her Vivien or Vivian. She turns up with many names; in Caxton's edition of Malory's *Morte d'Arthur* she is Nimue, Nymue, or Nyneue.

Lady of the Lake, The. A long narrative poem by Sir Walter Scott, published in 1810. It tells the story of Ellen Douglas, daughter of the outlawed Lord James ("the Douglas"), and the three suitors for her hand, Rhoderick Dhu, James Fitz-James, and Malcolm Graeme.

Lady of the Lake, The. A cantata based on Sir Walter Scott's poem, the music by G. A. Macfarren, produced in 1877.

Lady of the Mercians (mẽr'shạnz). See **Ethelfleda.**

Lady's Last Stake, or The Wife's Resentment, The. A comedy by Colley Cibber, produced in 1707.

Lady's Not for Burning, The. A comedy (1949) in blank verse by Christopher Fry.

Lady's Trial, The. A play by John Ford, published in 1639.

Lady Windermere's Fan (win'dẽr.mirz). A comedy (1892) by Oscar Wilde about the rather disreputable Mrs. Erlynne who saves her daughter, Lady Windermere, from a charge of adultery, a sin of which she has herself been many times guilty. Lady Windermere does not know that Mrs. Erlynne is her mother; she suspects her, indeed, of efforts to seduce Lord Windermere into an affair. Believing him to be reciprocating her attentions, Lady Windermere herself visits the apartment of a man with a considerable reputation for his conquests of women, and absent-mindedly leaves her fan behind when she departs. The fan is claimed by Mrs. Erlynne as having been left by her, with the consequent public assumption that she is the female principal in the affair. However, Mrs. Erlynne is presently able to marry an old admirer, Augustus, and goes off leaving Lady Windermere still innocent of any knowledge of their true relationship. The play contains many of Wilde's best-known epigrams, including the one about a cynic ("a man who knows the price of everything and the value of nothing").

"Lady with the Lamp," the. See **Nightingale, Florence.**

Laertes (lā.ẽr'tēz). In Greek legend, king of Ithaca; father of Odysseus. He was one of the Argonauts in the quest for the Golden Fleece. He was still living when Odysseus returned from his wanderings, and helped his son kill Penelope's suitors.

---

fat, fāte, fär, ȧsk, fāre; net, mē, hẽr; pin, pīne; not, nōte, möve, nôr; up, lūte, pull; ᴛʜ, then;

Laertes. In Shakespeare's *Hamlet*, the son of Polonius and brother of Ophelia. It is he who cautions Ophelia against Hamlet's love and receives from her the reply that he should not be one who "the primrose path of dalliance treads And recks not his own rede" (I.iii). Later he seeks a duel with Hamlet (who has killed his father, Polonius, and whom he holds responsible for Ophelia's suicide) and he falls in readily with Claudius's plot to ensure Hamlet's death by using a poisoned foil.

Laestrygones (les.trig'ọ.nēz). [Also, **Laestrygonians** (les.tri.gō'ni.ạnz).] In the *Odyssey*, a race of cannibal giants visited by Odysseus in a northern country, where "the nights are so short that the shepherd driving his flock out meets the shepherd who is driving his flock in." They killed many of the companions of Odysseus. They were placed by later writers in Sicily, south of Etna, and by the Romans near Formiae (modern Formia) in Latium.

Laetitia Dale (lẹ.tish'ạ dāl'). See **Dale, Laetitia.**

Laetitia Hardy (här'di). See **Hardy, Laetitia.**

Lafew (lạ.fū'). [Also, **Lafeu** (là.fė').] In Shakespeare's *All's Well That Ends Well*, a sagacious old lord.

La Fleur (lạ ฏlėr'). The servant of Yorick in Laurence Sterne's *Sentimental Journey*.

La Fontaine (là fon.tān'; French, là fôn.ten), **Jean de.** b. at Château-Thierry in Champagne, France, July 8, 1621; d. at Paris, April 13, 1695. A French writer, best known for his fables. He left the College of Reims at the age of 19 to study for the priesthood, but gave up that pursuit after two years. He is commonly said to have given the first evidence of his literary genius when he was 26 years old. His first six books of fables, published in 1668, were inscribed to the Dauphin of France. The next five books appeared in 1673 and 1679, and were prefaced with a eulogy of Madame de Montespan. The 12th book was dedicated to the young Duc de Bourgogne (1694). They have been popular since their publication and have been translated a great many times. Besides these fables, La Fontaine wrote his *Contes* (1665), *Amours de Psyché et de Cupidon* (1669), *Nouveaux contes* (1671), *La Captivité de Saint Malo* (1673), and *Le Quinquina* (1682). His comedies, *L'Eunuque* (translated from Terence), *Le Florentin*, *La Coupe enchantée*, *Je vous prends sans vert*, and *Ragotin*, were collected as *Pièces de théâtre de J. de La Fontaine* (1702). He had many generous patrons in the highest court circles, but never won favor in the eyes of Louis XVI, undoubtedly because of his attachment to Nicolas Fouquet. La Fontaine was elected to the French Academy in 1683. The king, however, did not sanction his admission till several months after his election. La Fontaine numbered Racine, Boileau, and Molière among his friends.

La Foole (lä föl'), **Sir Amorous.** A "brave heroic coward" in Ben Jonson's comedy *Epicœne*.

Lagado (lạ.gä'dō). In Swift's *Gulliver's Travels*, a city which figures in the voyage to the flying island of Laputa.

Lagnier (là.nyä). See **Rigaud.**

Laidley Worm of Spindlestonheugh (lād'li; spin'delz.ton.hūch), **The.** A ballad by Duncan Frasier of Cheviot, made in 1270. The story is of an enchanted lady who could only be released from the form of a "laidley worm" or "loathly serpent" by a knight brave enough to give her three kisses. There are various ballad versions of the story: *The Worme of Lambton*, *The Lambton Worm of Durham*, *Kemp Owyne* or *Kempion*, and others. The version preserved in Child's *English and Scottish Popular Ballads* as the *Laily Worm and the Machrel of the Sea* is the original traditional ballad.

Laing (lang, lāng), **Samuel.** b. at Kirkwall, Orkney, Scotland, Oct. 4, 1780; d. at Edinburgh, April 23, 1868. A Scottish author and traveler in Norway and Sweden. He published the *Journal of a Residence in Norway during the Years 1834–1835 and 1836* (1836) and *A Tour in Sweden* (London, 1839). In 1844 he published his most important work, the translation of the *Heimskringla or Icelandic Chronicle of the Kings of Norway*, with a *Preliminary Dissertation* (1844; revised by Rasmus B. Anderson, 1889).

Lais (lā'is). [Also, **Laïs.**] The name of two Greek courtesans celebrated for their beauty. The elder, probably a native of Corinth, lived in the 5th century B.C., and was famous for her beauty and for her vices. She died at Corinth, where a monument (a lioness tearing a ram) was erected to her. The younger (born probably in Sicily, and brought to Corinth when a child) lived in the middle of the 4th century B.C. Apelles is said to have induced her to follow the life of a courtesan. She is said to have been slain in Thessaly by women whose jealousy she had aroused.

Lake, The. A novel by George Moore, published in 1905.

Lake Poets. [Also **Lake School.**] In English literature, a name given to a group of poets including Wordsworth, Coleridge, and Southey, from their residence in or connection with the Lake District in England (Cumberland, Westmorland, and Lancashire). The term, first used in derision in the *Edinburgh Review*, has achieved wide currency and long since lost any derogatory meaning.

Laker (lā'kėr). [Also, **Lakist.**] One of the Lake Poets, originally used contemptuously.

And now, my Epic Renegade! what are ye at?
With all the Lakers, in and out of place?
    (Byron, *Don Juan*, Ded., st.1.)

Lakshmi (läksh'mē). [Also, **Shri.**] In Hindu mythology, the Lotus goddess; wife of Vishnu, and symbol of creative force. In some myths she was self-existent and lotus-borne at the beginning of creation; in the *Ramayana* she rose from the churning of the Ocean bearing a lotus, and Vishnu took her for his wife. In the *Rig-Veda* she is referred to as Shri and as Lakshmi. As fertility goddess she is the giver of plentiful crops, cattle, and offspring, and hence came to be regarded as a goddess of wealth, prosperity, and fortune. Her cult is still alive in India.

Lalla Rookh (lal'ạ rủk'). A poem by Thomas Moore, composed c1815 and published in 1817. It is a series of four Eastern stories connected by a slight prose narrative describing how these poems were recited to please Lalla Rookh, an Indian princess, on her journey to meet her betrothed, the Sultan of Bucharia, in the vale of Kashmir. Félicien David produced an opera *Lalla Roukh*, based on this poem, in 1862, with words by Lucas and Carré. Anton Rubinstein also composed one, produced in 1863. A number of other musical compositions have been based on it, such as Robert Schumann's cantata *Das Paradies und die Peri* and William Sterndale Bennett's overture *Paradise and the Peri.*

L'Allegro (lä.lā'grō). A poem by John Milton, written c1632. Its title may be translated to mean "the happy man," and it is dedicated to the goddess Euphrosyne (Mirth) and her right-hand companion "the mountain nymph, sweet Liberty," with whom the poet wishes to live "in unreproved pleasures free." It is the companion poem to *Il Penseroso* ("the brooding, melancholy man").

La Mancha (lä män'chä). A region and former province in S central Spain, corresponding roughly with the modern province of Ciudad Real. In a wider sense it included also parts of Albacete, Cuenca, and Toledo. It is the country celebrated in *Don Quixote,* and is a district composed of monotonous steppes traversed by the Guadiana and other rivers.

Lamb (lam), Lady **Caroline.** b. Nov. 13, 1785; d. at Melbourne House, Whitehall, London, Jan. 26, 1828. An English novelist; daughter of Frederick Ponsonby, 3rd Earl of Bessborough, and wife (married 1805) of William Lamb, later 2nd Viscount Melbourne, from whom she was separated in 1825. She was infatuated with Byron, who left her in 1813. She wrote *Glenarvon* (1816), which contained a caricature of Byron, *A New Canto* (1819), *Graham Hamilton* (1822), and *Ada Reis: a Tale* (1823). She accidentally encountered the procession carrying Byron's remains, fainted on the spot, and never fully recovered her reason.

Lamb, Charles. [Pseudonym, **Elia.**] b. in Crown Office Row, in the Temple, London, Feb. 10, 1775; d. at Edmonton, Middlesex, England, Dec. 27, 1834. English essayist, critic, and humorist. His father, John Lamb, was engaged in his youth in domestic service, and became the clerk of a bencher of the Inner Temple. In 1782 Charles entered Christ's Hospital (Blue-coat School), where he remained until November, 1789. Samuel Taylor Coleridge was a fellow pupil and lifelong friend. In 1789 Lamb became a clerk in the South Sea House, and in 1792 in the India House. The Lambs left the Temple, and in 1796 lodged in Little Queen Street, Holborn. For a short period at the end of 1795, probably as the result of an unhappy love affair, he was confined in an asylum. In 1796 his sister, Mary Ann Lamb, stabbed her mother to death in a fit of temporary insanity, and was placed under the guardianship of her brother Charles (her father being almost imbecile), who cared for her during the rest of his life, working with her and watching for the danger signs that appeared periodically and required her to be sent to an asylum until the fit of insanity had passed. In 1796 Coleridge published in *Poems on Various Subjects* four sonnets by Charles Lamb. To a second edition in 1797 Coleridge added poems by Charles Lamb and Charles Lloyd, a pupil of Coleridge's. In 1798 was published a little volume,

Blank Verse, by Lamb and Lloyd, containing Lamb's best poem, "The Old Familiar Faces." Later that year, Lamb published *Tale of Rosamund Gray* and *Old Blind Margaret.* In 1802 appeared *John Woodvil*, a play, showing the influence of Beaumont and Fletcher and the writers of that period. *Mr. H.*, a two-act farce, was produced at the Drury Lane Theatre on Dec. 10, 1806, and was roundly damned by the critics of the day. His first success was in *Tales from Shakespeare* (1807), in which Charles did the epitomizing of the tragedies and Mary handled the comedies. This was followed by *Specimens of English Dramatic Poets Who Lived About the Time of Shakespeare* (1808), which secured his position as critic. In 1810–11 he contributed several pieces, including essays on Shakespeare's tragedies, to Leigh Hunt's quarterly, *The Reflector.* His contributions to the *London Magazine* began with "Recollections of the South Sea House," August, 1820, signed "Elia." Twenty-five essays thus signed were collected and published in 1823 as *Essays of Elia.* In 1822 Charles and Mary went abroad. In March, 1825, he was retired from the India House with a pension of 441 pounds a year. In 1833 were published *Last Essays of Elia,* his last literary work. He had retired from town life (where he had become acquainted with the leading literary figures of the day) first to Enfield (1827) and then to Edmonton (1833), in order to permit his sister to have better care. His last years were lonely: his adopted daughter, Emma Isola, married in 1833; his friends seldom saw him, and many of them died, including his old friend Coleridge (1834); his sister's attacks grew more and more frequent. He died after a very brief illness.

Lamb, Mary Ann. b. in Crown Office Row, in the Temple, London, 1764; d. probably at St. John's Wood, London, May 20, 1847. An English author; sister of Charles Lamb, whom she assisted in *Tales from Shakespeare* (1807) (Mary epitomized the comedies). While temporarily insane, she stabbed and killed (1796) her mother; she was thereafter for the rest of his life under the care of her brother, her attacks of insanity growing more and more frequent.

Lambeth (lam'beth). A metropolitan borough in SW London, on the S bank of the river Thames, opposite Westminster metropolitan borough. It contains Lambeth Palace, built in 1197 (damaged in World War II). The London County Hall is also in this borough.

Lambeth Palace. The official London residence of the Archbishop of Canterbury.

Lambeth Homilies. A collection (c1200) of religious material, chiefly homilies, three of which are at least partly by Ælfric.

Lamburn (lam'bern), **Richmal Crompton.** [Pseudonym, **Richmal Crompton.**] b. at Bury, Lancashire, England, Nov. 15, 1890—. An English novelist. She is the author of *The Innermost Room, The Hidden Light, Ladies First, Chedsy Place, Quartet* (1935), *Journeying Wave* (1938), *Steffan Green* (1940), *Westover* (1946), and *The Ridleys* (1947).

Lame Englishman, The. A historical novel by Warwick Deeping, published in 1910.

Lame Lover, The. A comedy by Samuel Foote, produced in 1770.

lament. **1.** An expression of grief or sorrow; a sad complaint; a lamentation.

> And these external manners of laments
> Are merely shadows to the unseen grief
> That swells with silence in the tortured soul.
> (Shak., *Rich. II*, IV.i.)

2. A set form of lamentation or mourning; an elegy; a mourning song or ballad.

At Busiris, which was the alleged burial-place of Osiris, there was an annual festival at which the votaries, having fasted and put on mourning dresses, uttered a lament round a burnt-offering: the death of Osiris being the subject of the lament. (H. Spencer, *Prin. of Sociol.*)

3. The music for an elegy, or a tune intended to express or excite sorrowful emotion; a mournful air.

Lamentable Tragedy of Locrine (lō.krīn′, -krēn′), **The.** See **Locrine.**

Lamentation of Mary Magdalen (mār′i mag′da̦.le̦n). A poem erroneously attributed to Chaucer and printed in the early editions of his work. It was inserted under the impression that it was his lost *Origenes upon the Maudeleyne*, which was probably a translation from a piece attributed to Origen. This idea arose from Chaucer's lines in the Prologue to *The Legend of Good Women:*

> He made also, goon sithen a greet whyl,
> Origines upon the Maudeleyne.

Lamia (lā′mi.a̦). fl. in the early 3rd century B.C. An Athenian courtesan who possessed great influence over Demetrius Poliorcetes (Demetrius I of Macedonia).

Lamia. In Greek mythology, a Libyan queen, beloved by Zeus. Hera, out of jealousy, killed all Lamia's children; thereafter, because she could not revenge herself on Hera, Lamia sought to destroy the children of men. She is usually depicted with a serpent's body and beautiful woman's head. In later belief she was regarded as a seducer of young men. Keats's poem *Lamia* treats of this story.

Lammas Day (lam′a̦s). An English harvest holiday, formerly celebrated on August 1. Loaves of bread made from the first grain were taken to the church to be blessed.

Lammle (lam′l), **Alfred.** In Dickens's *Our Mutual Friend*, a mature young man, a swindler and fortune hunter. He marries Sophronia Akershem, each of the pair believing, mistakenly, that the other is wealthy.

Lamoracke or **Lamorake** (lam′o̦.rak), **Sir.** [Also, **Sir Lamerocke** (lam′e̦.rok).] In Arthurian romance, a knight of the Round Table, a Welshman. He was killed by the sons of King Lot for adultery with their mother.

La Mothe-Fénelon (là mot.fān.lôn̄), **François de Salignac de.** See **Fénelon.**

Lampatho Doria (lam.pä′thō dō′ri.a̦). See **Doria, Lampatho.**

Lampit (lam′pit), **Juliana.** b. c1342; d. 1443. An English religious figure, a recluse at Norwich and author of *Fourteen Revelations of Divine Love.*

lampoon (lam.pön′). A sarcastic writing aimed at a person's character, habits, or actions; a personal satire; a sarcastic diatribe; humorous abuse in writing.

Here they still paste up their drolling lampoons and scurrilous papers. (Evelyn, *Diary*, Feb. 20, 1645.)

These personal and scandalous libels, carried to excess in the reign of Charles II., acquired the name of lampoon, from the burden sung to them: "Lampone, lampone, camerada lampone"—"Guzzler, guzzler, my fellow guzzler." (Scott.)

"Lancashire Burns" (lang′ka̦.shir), **the.** See **Waugh, Edwin.**

Lancashire Witches and Tegue O'Divelly the Irish Priest (tēg′ o̦.div′e̦.li), **The.** A comedy (1681) by Thomas Shadwell. He ridiculed both the Roman Catholic and the Anglican clergy, with the result that large portions of the play were excised by the censor.

Lancaster (lang′ka̦s.tėr), **Duke of.** Title of **John of Gaunt;** see also under_**Bolingbroke, Henry.**

Lancaster, G. B. Pseudonym of **Lyttleton, Edith Joan.**

Lancaster, Joseph. b. at London, 1778; d. at New York, Oct. 24, 1838. An English educator. He founded in 1801 a private school in the Borough Road, Southwark, London, in which he employed the monitorial system of instruction (using older students as monitors to drill the younger in fundamentals), which obtained great popularity. He emigrated to the U. S. in 1818. He published *Improvements in Education* (1803) and others.

Lancaster, Prince John of. In Shakespeare's *1* and *2 Henry IV*, the younger brother of Prince Hal, and son of Henry IV. In *1 Henry IV*, he is at the battle of Shrewsbury, where he is commended for his conduct in battle by Hal (V.iv). In *2 Henry IV*, he leads an army against the rebels and in a most dishonorable manner executes them after he has promised them pardon if they disband. He is cold, rather dull, and with none of the virtues of his brother, Hal; according to Falstaff, "a man cannot make him laugh—but that's no marvel, he drinks no wine" (IV.iv). In *Henry V*, he appears as Duke of Bedford, and in *1 Henry VI*, as Regent of France, he captures Orleans and Rouen, where he dies (III.ii).

Lancaster, William. A pseudonym of **Warren, John Byrne Leicester.**

Lancelot (làn′se̦.lot, -lot), **Sir.** [Also: **Lancelot du Lac** (dŏ lak′), **Launcelot of the Lake.**] A knight in Arthurian legend. In the 13th-century French prose version, Sir Lancelot was the son of Ban, king of Brittany, and became one of the most famous knights of the Round Table. He received the name "du Lac" from the fact that he was educated at the castle of Vivian, known as the Dame du Lac or Lady of the Lake. The main features of the legend are his guilty love for Guinevere, the exploits he performed in her service, and the war with Arthur in which his passion involved him. Guinevere retired to a convent, and Lancelot became a monk and a holy man, and died saying masses for the souls of his old companions in arms.

ḏ, d or j; ṣ, s or sh; ṭ, t or ch; ẓ, z or zh; o, F. cloche; ü, F. menu; ċh, Sc. loch; ń, F. bonbon.

He was the father of Sir Galahad by Elaine, the daughter of King Pelles. Malory's *Morte d' Arthur* tells the story of Elaine's hopeless love for Lancelot. Chrétien de Troyes's metrical romance *Lancelot, ou le Chevalier de la Charrette* (c1170) recounts some of Lancelot's adventures.

Lancelot and Elaine (ẹ.lān′). A poem (1859), one of the *Idylls of the King*, by Alfred Tennyson. It tells of Lancelot's guilty love for Queen Guinevere, his arrival at Astolat for the jousts, the love of Elaine ("the lily maid of Astolat") for him, the death of Elaine, and his return to the court and his subsequent remorse.

Lancelot of the Laik (lāk). A Middle English verse romance of the late 15th century, probably written by a Scot. It tells the story of Lancelot's part in the battle between Arthur and Galiot (Galahalt).

Land, The. A play (1905) by Padraic Colum about the conflict between generations in Ireland, the older realizing the intense associations it has with the land, the younger drawn away to urban life.

Land, The. A poem in four parts, "Winter," "Summer," "Spring" and "Autumn," by V. Sackville-West, published in 1926. It won the Hawthornden prize in 1927.

Landau (län′dou). A town in W Germany, in the *Land* (state) of Rhineland-Palatinate, formerly in the Rhenish Palatinate, Bavaria, on the Queich River and the slopes of the Hardt Mountains, ab. 18 mi. SW of Speyer. The type of carriage called a *Landau* was first made here.

Landeval (lan′dẹ.val), **Sir.** See **Sir Landeval.**

Landfall. A novel by Nevil Shute, published in 1940.

Land League, Irish. A league formed in October, 1879, by the Irish Nationalist Party, led by Michael Davitt and C. S. Parnell, under which organized resistance was made to the payment of rent. It was "proclaimed" on Oct. 20, 1881, by Gladstone's Liberal government at London to be "an illegal and criminal association." It was nevertheless viewed by Irish nationalists, then and since, as a justifiable and necessary protest against absentee landlordism.

Landless (land′lẹs), **Helena.** In Dickens's *Mystery of Edwin Drood*, an attractive young girl who becomes the close friend of Rosa Bud at Miss Twinkleton's School for Young Ladies in Cloisterham.

Landless, Neville. In Dickens's *Mystery of Edwin Drood*, a young man who is studying with the Reverend Septimus Crisparkle; twin brother of Helena Landless. He is suspected of the murder of Edwin Drood.

"Land of Cakes." Scotland: so named (in jest) on account of the general use of oatmeal cakes as an article of diet.

Land of Heart's Desire, The. A verse drama (1894) by William Butler Yeats. The Celtic folklore which so deeply interested Yeats provides the background of the story of Maire, a young bride who answers a summons to the world of elfish spirits.

Landon (lan′dọn), **Letitia Elizabeth.** [Pseudonym, **L. E. L.**] b. at Chelsea, London, Aug. 14, 1802; d. at Cape Coast, Gold Coast, Africa, Oct. 15, 1838. An English poet and novelist; married (June, 1838) George Maclean, governor of Cape Coast Castle (now Cape Coast). She was the author of poems (collected 1838; later editions 1850, 1873), and of the novels *Romance and Reality* (1831), *Francesca Carrara* (1834), *Ethel Churchill* (1837), and *Lady Granard* (1842).

Landor (lan′dọr), **Walter Savage.** b. at Warwick, England, Jan. 30, 1775; d. at Florence, Sept. 17, 1864. An English poet and prose writer. He entered Trinity College, Oxford, in 1793, became conspicuous for his advocacy of republican principles, and was rusticated (equivalent to suspension by an American college) in 1794 for firing a gun (without damage to anyone) at the windows of a Tory. He refused to return to college and for some years led an unsettled life, visiting Paris in 1802, and joining the Spaniards at La Coruña against the French in 1808. In 1809 he purchased Llanthony Abbey, in Monmouthshire, and in 1811 married Julia Thuillier, daughter of a banker. A combination of troubles drove him in 1814 to Jersey, then to Tours, and in 1815 to Italy. In 1821 he settled at Florence, where he resided until 1835, when, separating from his wife, he went to England. He returned to Florence in 1858. He published *Poems* (1795), *Gebir* (1798), *Simonidea* (1806; English and Latin poems), *Count Julian* (1812), *Idyllia Heroica* (1814, enlarged 1820), *Imaginary Conversations* (1824–48), *The Citation and Examination of William Shakespeare . . . Touching Deerstealing* (1834), *Pericles and Aspasia* (1836), *The Pentameron* (1837), *Andrea of Hungary* (1839), *Giovanna of Naples* (1839), *Fra Rupert* (1840), *Hellenics* (1847, revised 1859), *Poemata et Inscriptiones* (Latin poems, 1847), *Italics* (1848), *The Last Fruit off an Old Tree* (1853), *Dry Sticks Fagoted by W. S. Landor* (1858), and *Heroic Idylls* (1863).

Land o' the Leal (land′ ọ ᴛнẹ lēl′). In the folk literature of Scotland and the north of England, the land of happiness. Lady Carolina Nairne, in her poem (1798) of that name, used it for heaven, and the usage later became an accepted one.

Landseer (land′sir, -syèr), **Sir Edwin Henry.** b. at London, March 7, 1802; d. there, Oct. 1, 1873. An English animal painter. He is best known as a painter, but his carved lions at the base of the Nelson monument in Trafalgar Square, London, are the Landseer works which have probably been seen in the original by the greatest number of people.

Lane (lān), **Edward William.** b. at Hereford, England, Sept. 17, 1801; d. at Worthing, England, Aug. 10, 1876. An English Orientalist and Egyptologist; brother of Sophia Lane. His works include *An Account of the Manners and Customs of the Modern Egyptians* (1836; fullest ed., 1860), a translation, with valuable notes, of the *Arabian Nights* (1838–40), and *Arabic-English Lexicon* (5 parts, 1863–74; and, under the editorship of S. Lane-Poole and others, 3 additional parts, 1877–92).

Lane, John. b. at West Putford, North Devon, England, 1854; d. Feb. 2, 1925. An English publisher. After some years as a London clerk he founded (1887) with Elkin Mathews (who withdrew in 1894) the Bodley Head publishing firm. He founded (1894) the *Yellow Book*, an illustrated quarterly that featured the work of Aubrey Beardsley and Max Beerbohm among others.

Lane, Margaret. b. June 23, 1907—. An English journalist, biographer, and novelist. Her books include *Faith, Hope, No Charity* (1935), *At Last the Island* (1937), *Walk into My Parlor* (1941), *Where Helen Lies* (1944), and biographies of her father-in-law, Edgar Wallace (1938), and Beatrix Potter (1946).

Lane, Ralph Norman Angell. Original name of Angell, Sir **Norman.**

Lane, Sophia. [Married name, **Poole.**] b. at Hereford, England, Jan. 16, 1804; d. at London, May 6, 1891. An English traveler and author; sister of Edward William Lane. She married (1829) Edward Richard Poole, and was the mother of Edward Stanley Poole and Reginald Stuart Poole. With her sons and her brother she lived and traveled (July, 1842–October, 1849) in Egypt; the product of this period of observation and study was the work by which she is known, *The Englishwoman in Egypt* (3 vols., 1844–46). With her son Reginald she was co-author of the descriptive text of Frith's *Photographic Views of Egypt, Sinai, and Palestine* (1860–61).

Lane-Poole (lān'pōl'), **Stanley.** b. at London, Dec. 18, 1854; d. Dec. 29, 1931. An English numismatist; grandson of Sophia Lane. He wrote the official *Catalogue of the Oriental and Indian Coins* for the British Museum. It appeared in 14 volumes in 1875–92. On the death of his great-uncle Edward William Lane in 1876, he continued the latter's Arabic lexicon (two of three parts, 1877–87). Among his other works are *Egypt* (1881), *Studies in a Mosque* (1883), *The Art of the Saracens in Egypt* (1886), and *Life of the Right Hon. Stratford Canning, Viscount de Redcliffe* (1888).

Lanfranc (lan'frangk). b. at Pavia, Italy, c1005; d. at Canterbury, England, May 24, 1089. A Lombard prelate and scholar, archbishop of Canterbury (1070–89). He emigrated from Italy and established (c1039) a school at Avranches, France, entered the monastery of Bec in 1042, and became (c1045) its prior. He contended against his friend and former teacher Bérenger of Tours on the doctrine of transubstantiation, and succeeded in having his position maintained by Hildebrand and other influential churchmen. He opposed the marriage of William of Normandy (who was later to become William I of England) and Matilda, William's cousin, but regained the friendship of William (c1053) and obtained papal approval of the match. He was installed as abbot of Caen in 1066, and was called to England to become archbishop of Canterbury in 1070, after Archbishop Stigand had been deposed. As the chief counselor of William the Conqueror, he played an important part in English ecclesiastical and civil affairs. He replaced many of the native prelates with Norman churchmen. A controversy with the archbishop of York over the supremacy of the see of Canterbury was settled in Lanfranc's favor, and his use of forgeries to win his victory may be justified, from the stand-

point of contemporary political necessity, in that it preserved the English church from a split in authority. He supported William II as successor to William I and crowned him (1087). He wrote *De corpore et sanguine Domini* and others.

Lang (lang), **Andrew.** b. at Selkirk, Scotland, March 31, 1844; d. at Banchory, Aberdeenshire, Scotland, July 20, 1912. A Scottish poet, biographer, editor, essayist, and folklorist. A prolific writer in a variety of literary forms, he was the author of *Ballads and Lyrics of Old France* (1872), *XXII Ballades in Blue China* (1880), *Helen of Troy* (1882), and *Grass of Parnassus* (1888), poetry; *The Mark of Cain* (1884), *A Monk of Fife* (1896), and *The Valet's Tragedy* (1906), novels; *J. G. Lockhart* (1896), *Prince Charles Edward* (1900), *John Knox and the Reformation* (1906), *Maid of France* (1908), *Sir George Mackenzie* (1909), and *Sir Walter Scott* (1910), biography; *Pickle the Spy* (1897), *The Companion of Pickle* (1898), *Scotland from the Roman Occupation to the Suppression of the Last Jacobite Uprising* (1900), *Mystery of Mary Stuart* (1901), *The Portraits and Jewels of Mary Stuart* (1906), and *History of English Literature* (1912), political and literary history; *Homer and the Epic* (1893), *Homer and His Age* (1908), and *The World of Homer* (1910), criticism. He translated the *Odyssey* (1879, with S. H. Butcher) and the *Iliad* (with E. Myers and W. Leaf, 1883), both conservative prose versions. He edited Poe, the brothers Grimm, Scott, Burns, Dickens, the *Compleat Angler* of Walton, and a series of well-known and still popular fairy books beginning with *The Blue Fairy Book* (1889), followed by others published annually at Christmas between 1890 and 1910. A founder of the Society for Psychical Research, he was also interested in mythology and religion, and wrote authoritative works on *Custom and Myth* (1884), *Myth, Ritual, and Religion* and *Modern Mythology* (both 1887), *The Making of Religion* (1891), *The Book of Dreams and Ghosts* (1897), and *Magic and Religion* (1901). He was an opponent of the school of comparative mythology led by Max Müller and maintained the connection between custom and folklore and literary myth.

Lang, Cosmo Gordon. [Title, 1st Baron **Lang of Lambeth.**] b. at Aberdeen, Scotland, Oct. 31, 1864; d. 1945. A prelate of the Church of England. Ordained to the Anglican priesthood in 1890, he held a curacy at Leeds until 1893, and was subsequently dean of divinity at Magdalen College, Oxford, vicar of the university church of Saint Mary's, and vicar of Portsea, before becoming suffragan bishop of Stepney (London), and a canon of Saint Paul's Cathedral in 1901. In 1908 he was named archbishop of York, and in 1928 became archbishop of Canterbury. He was noted for his efforts toward amelioration of the deplorable living conditions of workers both at London and in other English industrial cities. As a member of the House of Lords he played a large part in securing the approval of that House for the revision of the Book of Common Prayer, a measure which failed in the House of Commons in 1927 and 1928. In the constitutional crisis of 1936, precipitated by the determination of Edward VIII to marry an American divorcée, Lang had much to do with bringing about the monarch's abdication, and in 1937 he officiated at the coronation of George VI. He retired from his archiepiscopal office in 1942, and in the same year was created 1st Baron Lang of Lambeth. He had been a privy councilor since 1910, and lord high almoner for the crown since 1933. In 1918 he visited the U. S. He was the author of *The Miracles of Jesus, as Marks of the Way of Life* (1900), *The Parables of Jesus* (1906), and *The Opportunity of the Church of England* (1906).

Langdon-Davies (lang′dọn.dā′vis, -vēz), **John.** b. 1897—. An English journalist and writer. He was a war correspondent in Spain (1937–38) and during the Russo-Finnish War (1940). Author of *A Short History of Women* (1928), *Man and His Universe* (1930), *Inside the Atom* (1934), *A Short History of the Future* (1936), *Behind the Spanish Barricades* (1937), *British Achievement in the Art of Healing* (1946), and other books.

Langhorne (lang′hôrn), **John.** b. at Winton, Westmorland, England, in March, 1735; d. at Blagdon, Somersetshire, England, April 1, 1779. An English poet and prose writer. He is best known for his translation of Plutarch's *Lives* (1770), in collaboration with his brother. His poetical works were collected and published by his son in 1804.

Langland (lang′lạnd) or **Langley** (lang′li), **William.** b. probably in S Shropshire, England, c1332; d. c1400. An English poet, supposed author of *Piers Plowman*, and possibly of *Mum, Sothsegger*, a poem entitled by Skeat *Richard the Redeless*. Of his life very little is known; the name itself of the author is a conjecture. From passages in his poems it appears that his early years were spent in the western midland counties of England (Worcestershire, Shropshire); that he received a considerable education, and probably took minor orders; that he was married and had a daughter; that he lived as a mendicant singer; and that most of his later life was spent at London, where he lived in Cornhill.

Langley (lang′li), **Edmund de.** See under **York, (1st) Duke of.**

Langtoft (lang′toft), **Peter of.** b. probably at Langtoft, in the East Riding of Yorkshire, England; d. c1307. An English chronicler, author of a history of England to the death of Edward I, in French verse. The latter part of it was translated into English by Robert Mannyng of Brunne.

Langton (lang′tọn), **Bennet.** b. in Lincolnshire, England, 1737; d. at Southampton, England, Dec. 18, 1801. An English Greek scholar, an intimate friend of Samuel Johnson.

Langtry (lang′tri), **Lily.** [Maiden name, **Emily Charlotte Le Breton;** called the **"Jersey Lily."**] b. at St. Helier, Jersey, Channel Islands, 1852; d. at Monte Carlo, Feb. 12, 1929. An English actress. After gaining celebrity in English society as a beauty, she went on the stage in 1881, playing Kate Hardcastle in Goldsmith's *She Stoops to Conquer.* Her company toured in England and America.

Languebeau Snuffe (lang′bō snuf′). See **Snuffe, Languebeau.**

Languish (lang′gwish), **Lydia.** In Richard Brinsley Sheridan's comedy *The Rivals*, a romantic girl,

unwilling to marry unless the affair is conducted on the most sentimental principles.

Lankester (lang′kes.tẽr), **Edwin.** b. at Melton, Suffolk, England, April 23, 1814; d. Oct. 30, 1874. An English physician and man of science. He edited the work on natural history in the *Penny* and *English* encyclopedias, and published a *Natural History of Plants yielding Food* (1845), *Memorials of John Ray* (1845), and others.

Lankester, Sir **Edwin Ray.** b. at London, May 15, 1847; d. Aug. 15, 1929. An English anatomist and zoölogist; eldest son of Edwin Lankester. He wrote *Comparative Longevity* (1871), *Degeneration* (1880), *Spolia Maris* (1889), *The Advancement of Science* (1889), *A Treatise on Zoology* (1900–05), *Extinct Animals* (1905), *The Kingdom of Man* (1907), and many special monographs; and he edited, with M. Foster, the *Scientific Memoirs of Th. H. Huxley* (1898–1902).

Lansbury (lanz′bẽr.i, -ber″i), **George.** b. at Halesworth, Suffolk, England, 1859; d. at London, May 7, 1940. An English politician, editor, and author, a leader (1931–35) of the Labour Party. He joined (1890) the Socialist Party. He was a member (1905–09) of the Royal Commission on the Poor Law, and served (1910–12, 1922 *et seq.*) as a member of Parliament. He was editor (1913–22) of the Manchester *Guardian.* He was one of the leading British advocates of pacifism.

Lansdowne (lanz′doun), **Baron.** Title of **Grenville, George.**

Lantern Lane. A novel by Warwick Deeping, published in 1921.

Lanthorn Leatherhead (lan′thôrn leᴛʜ′ẽr.hed). See **Leatherhead, Lanthorn.**

Laocoön (lā.ok′ọ.on). In Greek legend (post-Homeric), a priest of Apollo at Troy, who, because he had offended the god, was strangled with one of his sons by two serpents while he was offering a sacrifice to Poseidon. In Vergil's version of the story two of his sons are killed with him. Laocoön is the one who tried to prevent the Trojans from hauling the wooden horse inside the walls of Troy. The Trojans, seeing the serpents strangle their priest and his sons, took it as a sign that Laocoön was wrong, and took the wooden horse into the city.

Laodamas (lā.od′ạ.mạs). In Greek legend, a son of Eteocles, and king of Thebes.

Laodamia (lā.od.ạ.mī′ạ). In Greek legend, the daughter of Acastus and wife of Protesilaus, with whom she voluntarily died. Wordsworth published (1815) a poem with this title.

Laodicean (lā.od.i.sē′ạn), **A.** A novel by Thomas Hardy, published in 1881.

Laodogant (lā.od′ọ.gant). [Also, **Leodegrance** or **Leodegran of Carohaise.**] In the 13th-century Arthurian romance *Arthour and Merlin*, the father of Guinevere. Geoffrey of Monmouth does not mention him, but says Guinevere is the ward of one Cador of Cornwall.

Laokoon (lā.ok′ọ.on; German, lä.ō′ko.on). [Full title, **Laokoon, oder über die Grenzen der Malerei und Poesie**, meaning "Laokoon, or on the Limits of Painting and Poetry."] Critical treatise on art by Gotthold Ephraim Lessing, published in 1766.

---

fat, fāte, fär, ȧsk, fãre; net, mē, hẽr; pin, pīne; not, nōte, mõve, nôr; up, lūte, pͧll; ᴛʜ, then;

and deriving its inspiration from the Greek statue of Laocoön and his sons. From this Matthew Arnold derived the theme of his poem *Lessing's Laokoon.*

Laomedon (lạ.om'ẹ.don). In Greek legend, the son of Ilus and Eurydice and father of Priam, founder and king of Troy. For refusing to pay Poseidon for building the walls of Troy, he was forced to offer his daughter Hesione to a sea monster. Hercules found her chained to a rock, and agreed to free her for a pair of magical horses which Zeus had given to Laomedon in exchange for Ganymede. Laomedon again failed to keep his promise, and Hercules captured his city and slew him and all his sons except Priam.

Lao-tse (lou'dzu'). [Also: **Lao-tsze, Lao-tzu.**] b. c604 B.C. A Chinese philosopher, said to have been the founder of the system of Taoism, and the reputed author of the book *Tao-teh Ching,* which embodies Taoist philosophy. Most modern scholars, however, are skeptical of the latter.

Lapithae (lap'i.thē). In Greek legend, a Thessalian people, descendants of a son of Apollo and Stilbe, and brother of Centaurus. They were governed by Pirithous, a half brother of the Centaurs. On the occasion of the marriage of Pirithous to Hippodameia, a fierce struggle took place between the Centaurs (who had been invited to the wedding) and the Lapithae, which ended in the expulsion of the former from Pelion. The cause of the quarrel was the attempt of a drunken Centaur to carry off the bride.

La Pucelle (là pü.sel; Anglicized, la pü.sel'). See **Joan of Arc.**

Laputa (lạ.pü'tạ). A flying island inhabited by scientists, philosophers, and inventors in Swift's *Gulliver's Travels.*

Lara (lä'rạ). A narrative poem by Byron, written in heroic couplets, published in 1814. Its title is taken from the name of its hero, who is the same character as Conrad in Byron's earlier poem *The Corsair.* The pirate chief has, in this poem, returned to his home in Spain, accompanied by his page Kaled (who is actually the beautiful Gulnare, in disguise), and is the object of much speculation as to identity. Eventually he is involved in a feud (after the discovery of his identity), and dies in the arms of Gulnare.

Larbaud (làr.bō), **Valéry.** b. at Vichy, France, 1881—. A French novelist, poet, critic, and translator. He is the author of *Poèmes d'un riche amateur* (1908), *Fermina Marquez* (1911), *Journal d'A. O. Barnabooth* (1913), *Amants, heureux amants* (1924), *Ce vice impuni, la lecture* (1925), and others. His translations have ranged from Coleridge to Joyce. Born wealthy, Larbaud has used his leisure to "naturalize" the work of various European writers in France. Critics have called him the leading cosmopolitan of his generation.

Lardner (lärd'nėr), **Dionysius.** b. at Dublin, April 3, 1793; d. at Naples, Italy, April 29, 1859. An English clergyman and scientific writer. Among his numerous publications are the *Cabinet Cyclopaedia* (1830–44), to which he contributed the articles on hydrostatics, pneumatics, arithmetic, and geometry (and collaborated in others), *The Great Exhibition*

and London in 1851 (1852), and numerous works and papers on natural science and railway economics.

Lardner, Nathaniel. b. at Hawkhurst, Kent, England, June 6, 1684; d. there, July 24, 1768. An English nonconformist divine and Biblical scholar. Author of *The Credibility of the Gospel History* (1727–57, a work that pioneered in the application of the critical method to the literary materials of the early church), sermons, and others.

Lares (lâr'ēz). In Roman religion, a class of benevolent spirits presiding over the house and family. They were looked upon also as protectors of the state and city, and as very powerful for evil if not duly respected and propitiated. The public Lares, originally two in number, were the guardians of the unity of the state, and were honored with temples and an elaborate ceremonial. After the time of Augustus, at least, each division of the city had also its own public Lares (*Lares compitales*). The private Lares differed for each family, and were worshiped daily in the house, being domiciled sometimes on the family hearth but usually in a special niche with the Penates. Food was offered to them at every meal. They received also special recognition upon every occasion of festivity, public or private, and on certain days devoted particularly to them, and claimed tribute alike from the bride upon entering the family and from the youth upon attaining his majority. The chief of the private Lares in each family, the domestic or household Lar (*Lar familiaris*) was the spirit of the founder of the family. To the family spirits were often added in later times, among the household Lares, the shades of heroes, or other personalities who were looked upon with admiration or awe. In their character as malignant divinities, the Lares were commonly classed as *lemures* or *larvae.*

Larkmeadow (lärk'med″ō). A novel by Marmaduke Pickthall, published in 1912.

La Rochefoucauld (là rosh.fö.kō), **François, Duc de.** [Additional title, Prince of **Marcillac.**] b. at Paris, Dec. 15, 1613; d. there, March 17, 1680. A French moralist and writer. He is known for his maxims, his memoirs, and his correspondence. The first edition of the *Maxims* was issued anonymously under the title *Réflexions ou sentences et maximes morales* (1665). The fifth edition (1678), published during the author's lifetime, is considered definitive. A sixth edition appeared posthumously (1693), containing 50 maxims. The best modern edition was made by Gilbert for the series of the *Grands écrivains de la France* (1868). La Rochefoucauld's memoirs were published in 1662 under the title *Mémoires sur la régence d'Anne d'Autriche.* His correspondence was made public in 1818 through Belin's edition. He participated in the court intrigue against Richelieu and Mazarin, fought in the Fronde disorders, and was a friend of Mme. de Sévigné and Mme. de La Fayette.

Larousse (là.rös), **Pierre Athanase.** b. at Toucy, Yonne, France, Oct. 23, 1817; d. at Paris, Jan. 3, 1875. A French grammarian, lexicographer, and author; editor of the *Grand dictionnaire universel du XIXᵉ siècle* (1866–78).

ḍ, d or j̧; ş, s or ş̣h; ṭ, t or ch; z̧, z or zh; o, F. cloche; ü, F. menu; c̦h, Sc. loch; ñ, F. bonbon.

Lars Porsena (lärz pôr'sẹ.nạ). See **Porsena, Lars.**

Lartius (lär'shi.us, -shus), **Titus.** See **Titus Lartius.**

Las Casas (läs kä'säs), **Bartolomé de.** [Called "Apostle of the Indians."] b. at Seville, Spain, 1474; d. at Madrid, in July, 1566. A Spanish Dominican, celebrated as a defender of the Indians against their Spanish conquerors. He went to Hispaniola in 1502, accompanied Diego Velásquez during the conquest of Cuba, and became a curate there. In 1514 he began to preach against the prevailing system of Indian slavery, and in 1515 went to Spain to intercede for the Indians with Ferdinand. By Cardinal Ximenes he was named "Protector of the Indians," with considerable powers, and returned to Hispaniola in 1516. He again visited Spain to urge his views on Charles V, attempted to plant a colony on the coast of Cumaná, in what is now Venezuela, which was destroyed by the Indians (1521), took the Dominican habit at Santo Domingo (1522) and remained in retirement for eight years, and finally returned to Spain. From 1544 to 1547 he was bishop of Chiapas in Mexico. He published *Breuissima relacion de la destruycion de las Indias* ("Destruction of the Indies," Seville, 1552), *Historia de las Indias* (published 1875, but well known before by manuscript copies), and others.

Laski (las'ki), **Harold Joseph.** b. at Manchester, England, June 30, 1893; d. at London, March 24, 1950. An English political scientist. He was a lecturer at McGill (1914–16), Harvard (1916–20), Amherst (1917), and Yale (1919–20, 1931), served as vice-chairman (1921–30) of the British Institute of Adult Education, was a lecturer (1922–25) at Cambridge, and was professor (1926 *et seq.*) at the University of London. He served as a member of the executive committee of the Fabian Society (1922–36) and of the Labour Party (1936 *et seq.*), of which he was chairman (1945–46). Author of *The Problem of Sovereignty* (1917), *Authority in the Modern State* (1919), *Foundations of Sovereignty* (1921), *A Grammar of Politics* (1925), *Communism* (1927), *Liberty in the Modern State* (1930), *Democracy in Crisis* (1933), *Parliamentary Government in England* (1938), *The American Presidency* (1940), *Faith, Reason, Civilization* (1944), and *The American Democracy* (1948).

Last (lȧst), **Doctor.** A shoemaker who passes an amusing examination for the degree of M.D. in Samuel Foote's *Devil upon Two Sticks.*

Last Chronicle of Barset (bär'sẹt), **The.** A novel by Anthony Trollope, published in 1866–67, the last in the Barsetshire series.

Last Days of Pompeii (pom.pā'ē), **The.** A historical novel by Edward Bulwer-Lytton, published in 1834. The novel is set against a background of Pompeii in the first century A.D., a few days before the great eruption of Mount Vesuvius. Ione, a beautiful young Greek girl who is in love with Glaucus, is the ward of the evil and licentious Arbaces, an Egyptian who has much influence in the city and who is determined to have her for his wife. He murders her brother when that unfortunate young man learns of his lewdness and cruelty, and then accuses the brilliant and noble Glaucus of the crime. However, the blind slave girl, Nydia, also deeply in love with Glaucus, saves him from the lions of the arena just as Vesuvius begins to erupt, and leads Ione and Glaucus to safety on a ship in the harbor through the blackness of the doomed city. Nydia, realizing the hopelessness of her love for Glaucus, jumps overboard that night and drowns.

Last Judgment, The. An English version of Ludwig Spohr's oratorio *Die Letzten Dinge*, produced in 1830, prepared by Edward Taylor.

Last of the Barons, The. A historical novel by Edward Bulwer-Lytton, published in 1843. The Baron is the historical Earl of Warwick, called "the Kingmaker." The story takes place in the 15th century, and the historical events in it include the quarrel between Warwick and Edward IV over the marriage of Edward's sister, Margaret, the restoration of Henry VI, and the battle of Tewkesbury. The fictitious story of the poor philosopher Adam Warner, and his daughter Sibyll, is woven with these.

Last Ride Together, The. A poem by Robert Browning, a part of the series entitled *Dramatic Romances*, and published in *Men and Women* (1855).

Last Tournament, The. One of the *Idylls of the King*, by Alfred Tennyson. Published in 1872 with *Gareth and Lynette*, it is concerned with the last tournament held at Arthur's court, "The Tournament of the Dead Innocence," in which the victor is Tristram. His prize of a necklace of rubies he gives to his beloved, Iseult, the wife of Mark of Cornwall, rather than to Iseult of Brittany, his wife. Mark returns, finds the two together, and slays Tristram on the spot.

Late Murder in Whitechapel, or Keep the Widow Waking, The. A lost tragedy by Dekker, Rowley, Ford, and Webster, written in 1624 and played that year at the Red Bull theater. Its plot was based upon two notorious cases at the Old Bailey in the same year, involving the murder of a mother by her son and the plundering of a rich old widow by a young tobacconist who had married her when she was drunk.

Lateran (lat'ẹ.rạn). A palace in the E part of Rome. The present edifice dates from the 16th to 18th centuries. The palace was originally named for the Roman family Lateranus to which, until the time of Nero, it belonged. Nero put the last owner, Plautius Lateranus, to death, and appropriated the palace. It was given by Constantine (who also built a church in its precincts) to the Pope.

Latimer (lat'i.mèr), **Darsie.** In Sir Walter Scott's *Redgauntlet*, the name by which the hero, Sir Arthur, is known through much of the story.

Latimer, Hugh. b. at Thurcaston, Leicestershire, England, c1485; burned at Oxford, England, Oct. 16, 1555. An English prelate and reformer. He was graduated from Cambridge in 1510, became a priest, rose in favor at court, especially with Thomas Cromwell, and obtained the benefice of West Kington (or Kineton), Wiltshire. He was cited to appear before the Bishop of London on a charge of heresy Jan. 29, 1532, but recanted

April 10. He was made a royal chaplain (1534) and bishop of Worcester (1535), and resigned his bishopric July 1, 1539, on account of his opposition to the Act of the Six Articles (by his own account at the request of King Henry VIII). He was ordered into the custody of the Bishop of Chichester, but was soon released. During the reign of Edward VI, he regained his influence at court and identified himself more closely with the Reformation. On the accession of Mary Tudor he was arrested and committed to the Tower of London (September, 1553). He was sent to Oxford with Nicholas Ridley and Thomas Cranmer to defend their doctrines regarding the Mass before the divines of Oxford and Cambridge, in March, 1554. He was excommunicated April 20, and was burned with Ridley "at the ditch over against Balliol College" on Oct. 16, 1555. His words to Ridley as the torch was applied to the faggots have become famous: "Be of good comfort, Master Ridley, and play the man; we shall this day light such a candle, by God's grace, in England, as I trust shall never be put out."

Latinus (lạ.tī′nus). In Roman legend, a king of Latium; father of Lavinia and father-in-law of Aeneas. He is variously said to be the son of Faunus, Odysseus, or Hercules, or an aspect of Jupiter.

Latona (lạ.tō′nạ). See **Leto**.

Latter-Day Symphony. A novel by Romer Wilson (Mrs. Edward J. O'Brien), published in 1927.

Laud (lôd), **William.** b. at Reading, England, Oct. 7, 1573; beheaded at London, Jan. 10, 1645. An English prelate, archbishop of Canterbury (1633–45). In 1594 he graduated at St. John's College, Oxford; he was made vicar of Stamford in Northamptonshire in 1607 and of Caxton in Kent in 1610, and was elected president of St. John's College, May 10, 1611. On Jan. 22, 1621, he became a prebendary of Westminster, and on June 29 bishop of St. David's, resigning the presidency of St. John's in the same year. He was elected bishop of London in 1628, chancellor of the University of Oxford, and archbishop of Canterbury in 1633. Throughout the reign of Charles I he was one of the foremost supporters of the king and most influential men of the state, first as a supporter of George Villiers, 1st Duke of Buckingham, and later as a counselor of the king of equal stature with the Earl of Strafford. His anti-Calvinist, High Church doctrines were backed by the crown's absolute tools, the Court of Star Chamber and Court of High Commission. He was impeached by the Commons (Long Parliament) Dec. 18, 1640, and committed to the Tower of London on March 1, 1641. His trial began March 12, 1644, and he was executed on Tower Hill on Jan. 10, 1645.

Lauder (lô′dẻr), Sir **Harry MacLennan.** b. at Portobello, Scotland, Aug. 14, 1870; d. at Strathaven, Scotland, Feb. 26, 1950. A Scottish singer, song writer, and composer. At the age of 11 he went to work in a mill, and he subsequently became a coal miner; but the possession of a good baritone voice, acting ability, and a sense of humor pointed the way to the music-hall stage. After some years with a traveling troupe, he made his London debut in 1900, achieving immediate success with his broadly comic songs, his kilts of the MacLennan tartan, and his exaggeratedly twisted walking stick. In 1906 he made the first of some 40 tours of the U. S., and in 1908 sang "by command" before King Edward VII. During World War I he became an ardent recruiter for the British armed forces, not the less so after the death of his only son at the front. In 1919 he set up the Harry Lauder Fund for disabled veterans, and in that same year was knighted. During World War II he came out of retirement to sing for British and Allied servicemen, refusing all compensation. He himself wrote the words and the music of most of his songs. They had no relation to ancient Gaelic minstrelsy, and only occasionally referred to the Highlands in a superficial and conventional way, but they gave lyric life for the first time to the simple, courageous humor and the unabashed sentimentality of the Scottish working people, and particularly those of the Clydeside. These were his people, and he was theirs. They listened raptly to *I Love a Lassie* and *Roamin' in the Gloamin'*, and roared with delight when he sang *Stop Yer Ticklin' Jock* or *It's Nice to Get Up in the Mornin'* (*But It's Nicer to Lie in Yer Bed*).

Lauder, William. d. in Barbados, 1771. A Scottish literary impostor, a graduate of Edinburgh University, who became notorious by charging (1747) John Milton with plagiarism in writing *Paradise Lost*. He supported the accusation with forged, garbled, and interpolated quotations from modern Latin authors. The fraud was exposed (1750) by John Douglas, and Samuel Johnson, who had countenanced Lauder's attack, forced him to confess his guilt.

Lauderdale of Thirlestane (lô′dẻr.dāl; thẻrl′stạn), Baron. Title of **Maitland, James.**

Laud Troy Book (lôd troi). A Middle English verse romance (c1400) dealing with the fall of Troy, in 18,000 lines.

"Laughing Philosopher," the. See **Democritus.**

Launce (lôns, läns). In Shakespeare's *Two Gentlemen of Verona*, a servant of Proteus, noted for his remarks to his dog Crab.

Launcelot Gobbo (lôn′sẹ.lọt, län′-; gob′ō). See **Gobbo, Launcelot.**

Launcelot of the Lake. See **Lancelot, Sir.**

Launfal (lôn′fạl), Sir. A knight of the Round Table, in the Arthurian cycle of romance; steward of King Arthur. Thomas Chestre wrote a metrical romance with this title in the reign of Henry VI (15th century). He is, however, best known to most modern readers through Lowell's *Vision of Sir Launfal.*

Launfal, Sir. See also **Sir Launfal.**

Laura (lô′rạ; Italian, lou′rä). [Traditionally identified with **Laure de Noves,** later Madame de Sade.] b. 1308; d. at Avignon, France, April 6, 1348. A French lady beloved by Petrarch, and celebrated in his poems.

Laura Bell (lô′rạ bel′). See **Bell, Laura.**

Laura Fairlie (fãr′li). See **Fairlie, Laura.**

Laura Matilda (mạ.til′dạ). A writer of sentimental verse in Horace and James Smith's *Rejected Addresses.*

ḏ, d or j; ṣ, s or sh; ṭ, t or ch; ẓ, z or zh; o, F. cloche; ü, F. menu; ċh, Sc. loch; ṅ, F. bonbon.

Laura Pendennis (pen.den′is). See **Pendennis, Laura**; see also **Bell, Laura**.

laureate, poet. See **poet laureate.**

"Laureate of the Nursery," the. See **Miller, William**; see also **Rands, William Brighty**.

Laurence (lô′rẹns, lor′ẹns), **Friar.** In Shakespeare's *Romeo and Juliet*, a Franciscan friar, the confidant and adviser of Romeo and Juliet.

Laurentian Library (lô.ren′shi.ạn). A library, in Florence, Italy, named after Lorenzo de' Medici.

Laurie (lou′ri), **Simon Somerville.** b. at Edinburgh, Nov. 13, 1829; d. March 2, 1909. A Scottish philosopher and teacher.

Lavatch (lạ.vach′). A clown in Shakespeare's *All's Well That Ends Well*.

Lavater (lä′vä.tẽr, lä.vä′tẽr), **Johann Kaspar.** b. at Zurich, Switzerland, Nov. 15, 1741; d. there, Jan. 2, 1801. A Swiss poet and theologian, founder of the so-called science of physiognomy. As a poet he is chiefly known by his *Schweizerlieder* (Swiss Songs, 1767). *Aussichten in die Ewigkeit* (Looks into Eternity) appeared the following year. His principal work, in which he gives an account of his science of physiognomy and attempts its justification, is *Physiognomische Fragmente zur Beförderung der Menschenkenntnis und Menschenliebe* (Physiognomical Fragments for the Promotion of a Knowledge of Man and of Love of Man, 1775–78). Goethe contributed to it a chapter on the skulls of animals.

Lavengro (lä.veng′grō). A novel by George Borrow, published in 1851. The work is a mixture of the fictitious and the autobiographical. "Lavengro" in gypsy language means "philologist," and this is the tale of the wanderings of a man interested in the science of languages, and in literatures. He is the son of an army officer, and he travels with him until he (the father) dies. He then starts out on his own, nearly starving as a hack writer in London, then embarking on a life of adventure with a family of gypsies. During his travels he meets many interesting people, including a tinker called the Flaming Tinman, and Belle Berners. Belle is a beautiful blonde wanderer whose past stands between her and Lavengro. She finally goes to America when she realizes that he might want to marry her, and that he would be unhappy if he did. *The Romany Rye* is a sequel to this novel.

Laver (lä′vẽr), **James.** b. at Liverpool, England, March 14, 1899—. An English novelist, dramatist, and poet. He won (1921) the Newdigate prize for the poem *Cervantes*. His plays include *The Heart Was Not Burned* (1938), the musical comedy *Nymph Errant* (1932), and, for children, *The House That Went to Sea* (1936) and *Swiss Family Robinson* (1938), the latter written with Sir Barry Jackson. He is author also of the short stories collected in *Laburnum Tree* (1935), and of *His Last Sebastian* (1922), *The Young Man Dances* (1925), *Whistler* (1930), *Winter Wedding* (1934), *Poems of Baudelaire* (1940), *Ladies of Hampton Court* (1942), and *Titian* (1949).

Lavinia (lạ.vin′i.ạ). In Roman legend, the daughter of Latinus, king of Latium, and wife of Aeneas; eponymous ancestress of the city of Lavinium.

Lavinia. In Shakespeare's *Titus Andronicus*, the daughter of Titus. She is ravished and mutilated by Tamora's sons, Demetrius and Chiron, and finally is killed by Titus.

Lavinia. In Shaw's *Androcles and the Lion*, the beautiful Christian girl.

Lavinia Wilfer (wil′fẽr). See **Wilfer, Lavinia**.

Law (lô), **John.** b. at Edinburgh, in April, 1671; d. at Venice, March 21, 1729. An English financier and projector of commercial schemes. In April, 1694, he killed "Beau" (Edward) Wilson in a duel at London and was condemned to death, but escaped to the Continent where for a time he led a roving life, largely that of a gambler. At the same time he endeavored to secure the adoption by various governments of his banking and other financial schemes, especially of his plans for the issue of paper money, of which he was an earnest advocate. In May, 1716, he, with others, founded the private Banque Générale in France, and succeeded in carrying out with success his views with regard to paper currency, his notes being accepted in payment of taxes, and commanding a premium over specie. Soon after this he acquired from the French government colonization and trade rights over the territory then called Louisiana, the Compagnie d'Occident being incorporated for this purpose in 1717; the enterprise became famous under the name of the Mississippi Scheme or the System. This company soon absorbed the East India and China companies (being thereafter formally known as the Compagnie des Indes), the African Company, the mint, and the power of receivers general, thus becoming supreme both in the American and Asiatic commerce of France and in its internal financial affairs. Meanwhile, in 1718, the Banque Générale had been transformed into the Banque Royale, with Law as director general and its notes guaranteed by the king. On Jan. 5, 1720, Law was made controller general of finance, and on Feb. 23 the company and the bank were combined. For a while the System prospered, fortunes were made in speculation, and Law possessed great power; but the overissue of paper money and the hostile action of the awakened government brought on the inevitable catastrophe, and in May, 1720, the System collapsed (thereupon acquiring the name "Mississippi Bubble," by which it is now remembered). Law was driven from France, and his estates were confiscated. In December, 1720, however, he was invited by Czar Peter I to take charge of the finances of Russia, but declined. Later (1721) he returned to England, remaining there until 1725, when he went to Italy.

Law, Thomas Graves. b. in Somersetshire, England, Dec. 14, 1836; d. at Edinburgh, March 12, 1904. An English essayist, biographer, and historian. He contributed to the *Cambridge Modern History* and the *Dictionary of National Biography*. Author of *The Conflicts Between Jesuits and Seculars in the Reign of Queen Elizabeth* (1889) and *Collected Essays and Reviews* (1904).

Law, William. b. at King's Cliffe, near Stamford, Northamptonshire, England, 1686; d. there, April 9, 1761. An English controversial and devotional writer. He was ordained in 1711 and in the same year became a fellow of Emmanuel College, Cambridge. When George I came to the throne in 1714, Law refused to take the oath of allegiance to the new king or to abjure the Stuarts. He was therefore removed, as a nonjuror, from his fellowship. He supported himself thereafter by acting as a tutor, and in 1727 entered the household of Edward Gibbon, grandfather of the historian, as tutor and private chaplain. There he was adviser not only to the Gibbon family but to such visitors as John and Charles Wesley and John Byrom. After 1740 he lived at King's Cliffe with two woman companions, Hester Gibbon and Mrs. Archibald Hutcheson, the widow of an old friend. In 1734 he became acquainted with the work of Jakob Böhme and afterward wrote several mystical works influenced by Böhme's theosophy. Law's influence on John Wesley and other leaders of the evangelical movement was considerable; especially influential were his *A Treatise of Christian Perfection* (1726) and *A Serious Call to a Devout and Holy Life* (1728). The latter was much praised by Samuel Johnson and remains Law's best-known work. Law's defense of the church in the Bangorian controversy (*Three Letters to the Bishop of Bangor,* 1717) was one of the principal contributions to the argument; his attack on the Deism of Matthew Tindal (*The Case of Reason,* 1732) was the first answer to the Deists; his *Remarks on Mandeville's Fable of the Bees* (1723) and *Letters to a Lady Inclined to Enter the Church of Rome* are excellent examples of his controversial style. He was the author of the tract *Absolute Unlawfulness of the Stage-Entertainment* (1726).

Lawless (lô′lẹs), **Anthony.** A pseudonym of **MacDonald, Philip.**

Lawless, Emily. b. at Dublin, June 17, 1845; d. in Surrey, England, Oct. 19, 1913. An Irish nature poet and novelist. Author of *A Millionaire's Cousin* (1885), *Hurrish* (1886), *With Essex in Ireland* (1890), and *Grania* (1892), novels; *History of Ireland* (1887) and a biography of Maria Edgeworth (1904); *With the Wild Geese* (1902), *Point of View* (1909), and *The Inalienable Heritage* (1914), poetry. Among her poems are *Spain* and *A Drinking Song.*

Lawman (lô′mạn). See **Layamon.**

Law of Ecclesiastical Polity. See **Ecclesiastical Polity, Law of.**

Lawrence (lô′rẹns, lor′ẹns), **Saint.** A prelate of the early English church, successor to Saint Augustine as archbishop of Canterbury.

Lawrence, Charles Edward. b. at Thurlstone, Yorkshire, England, Dec. 24, 1870; d. at London, March 14, 1940. An English novelist, dramatist, and critic. Author of *Pilgrimage* (1907; revised, 1914), *Much Ado About Something* (1909), *Mrs. Bente* and *Youth Went Riding* (both 1918), *Such Stuff As Dreams* (1919), *The God in the Thicket* (1920), *The Iron Bell* (1921), *Week-End at Forthries* (1935), *The Gods Were Sleeping* (1937), novels; *The Year* (1927) and *The Reckoning* (1934), plays. He also wrote *Wisdom of the Apocrypha* (1910), *The Gentle Art of Authorship* (1924), and several one-act plays, including *The Hour of Prospero* (1927), *Swift and Stella* (1928), *Spikenard* (1930), *The Day Before Yesterday* (1931), *Home* (1932),

The Touch of Nature (1934), and *Gloriana* (1939). He was coeditor of the *Quarterly Review,* and on the staff (1904–18) of the *Daily Chronicle.*

Lawrence, D. H. [Full name, **David Herbert Lawrence.**] b. at Eastwood, Nottinghamshire, England, Sept. 11, 1885; d. at Vence, near Nice, France, March 2, 1930. An English novelist, short-story writer, poet, and essayist. Son of a coal miner, he was educated at Nottingham High School and at the Nottingham Day Training College for Teachers, and taught (1908–12) at the Davidson Road Elementary School, at Croydon, near London. He lived and traveled in Australia, Mexico, Sicily, Sardinia, Italy, the U. S., and elsewhere in vain attempts to cure or improve his tubercular lung condition. Author of *The White Peacock* (1911), *The Trespasser* (1912), *Sons and Lovers* (1913), *The Rainbow* (1915), *The Lost Girl* (1920; awarded the James Tait Black memorial prize), *Women in Love* (1920), *Aaron's Rod* (1922), *Kangaroo* (1923), *St. Mawr* (1925), *The Plumed Serpent* (1926), *Lady Chatterley's Lover* (1928; banned in both England and America), *The Virgin and the Gipsy* (1930), novels; *The Prussian Officer* (1914), *England, My England* (1922), *The Fox* (1923), *The Ladybird* (1923; American title, *The Captain's Doll*), *Glad Ghosts* and *Sun* (both 1926), *Rawdon's Roof* and *The Woman Who Rode Away* (both 1928), *The Lovely Lady* and *Love Among the Haystacks* (1933), collected short stories and tales; *The Widowing of Mrs. Holroyd* (1914), *Touch and Go* (1920), *David* (1926), and *A Collier's Friday Night* (1934), plays; *Love Poems* (1913), *Amores* (1916), *Look! We Have Come Through* (1917), *New Poems* (1918), *Tortoises* (1921), *Birds, Beasts and Flowers* (1923), *Pansies* (1929), *Nettles* and *The Triumph of the Machine* (both 1930), and *The Ship of Death* (1933), poetry; *Movements in European History* (1921), *Psychoanalysis of the Unconscious* (1921), *Fantasia of the Unconscious* (1922), *Studies in Classic American Literature* (1923), *Pornography and Obscenity* (1929), volumes of critical essays and studies; *Twilight in Italy* (1916), *Sea and Sardinia* (1921), and *Mornings in Mexico* (1927), travel books. His *Letters* were published in 1932 and 1934. He translated some of the short stories of Ivan Bunin, Russian novelist, and *Little Novels of Sicily* (1925), *Cavelleria Rusticana* (1928), and other works by Giovanni Verga. Among his single poems are *Suspense, A Youth Mowing, A Young Wife, Cherry Robbers, A Winter's Tale, Love on the Farm, Piano, Wedding Morn, Service of All the Dead, Nostalgia, A Baby Asleep After Pain, Moonrise, Tommies in the Train,* and *Resurrection.* Tormented throughout his life by ill-suppressed feelings of inferiority, aggravated by the suppression of his sincere *The Rainbow* in 1915 and by his illness, Lawrence preached a freedom of the "male" principle that was reflected in his preoccupation with the physicomental processes. The message he sought to bring to the world was often obscured by his passionate and sometimes incoherent exposition of the theme, but his powers as a novelist of deep psychological insight and descriptive power are nevertheless apparent.

Lawrence, George Alfred. b. at Braxted, Essex, England, March 25, 1827; d. at Edinburgh, Sept. 23,

---

ḑ, d or j; ṣ, s or sh; ṭ, t or ch; ẓ, z or zh; o, F. cloche; ü, F. menu; ċh, Sc. loch; ṅ, F. bonbon.

1876. An English novelist. He wrote the adventure novel *Guy Livingstone, or Thorough* (1857).

Lawrence, Gertrude. [Original name, **Gertrude Alexandra Dagmar Lawrence Klasen.**] b. at London, July 4, 1902; d. at New York, Sept. 6, 1952. An English actress, noted especially for her roles in musical comedy and revue. She arrived (1924) in America with the cast of *Charlot's Revue,* in which she shared the lead with Beatrice Lillie. Her leading roles were in *Candlelight* (1929), *Susan and God* (1937), *Skylark* (1939), *Lady in the Dark* (1940), *Pygmalion* (1946) and *The King and I* (1951). She appeared opposite Noel Coward in his *Private Lives* (1930) and *To-Night at Eight-Thirty* (1935-37). She taught (1951-52) a course in dramatics at Columbia University. Author of *A Star Danced* (1945).

Lawrence, Sir Thomas. b. at Bristol, England, May 4, 1769; d. at London, Jan. 7, 1830. An English portrait painter. He was knighted April 22, 1815, and elected president of the Royal Academy to succeed Benjamin West, on March 20, 1820. He was patronized by George III, among a large number of other notable persons.

Lawrence, Thomas Edward. [Often shortened to T. E. Lawrence; called **Lawrence of Arabia;** during his later years, **T. E. Shaw.**] b. at Portmadoc, Caernarvonshire, Wales, Aug. 15, 1888; d. at Bovington Camp, Dorsetshire, England, May 19, 1935. An English archaeologist, secret agent, soldier, and writer, who has been called "the most romantic figure of his time." While a student at Oxford he became interested in archaeology, and after some solitary travel in Syria, in 1911 he joined a British Museum expedition engaged in excavating ancient sites in the valley of the Euphrates. On the outbreak of World War I, he became a member of the British secret service and, operating out of Cairo, made an extraordinarily penetrating study not only of the Turkish military forces and leaders, but also of the possibility of a successful Arab revolt against Turkish overlordship. In 1916 he received permission to promote such a revolt, and considering Faisal al-Husain (later to be Faisal I of Iraq), son of the sherif of Arabia (Husein ibn-Ali, who was to be first king of Hejaz), the ablest and most dependable of the insurgent Arabs, he proceeded to Faisal's camp and induced him to undertake a campaign which disrupted the communications of the Turkish forces in Arabia, prevented them from attacking the Suez Canal and Egypt, and brought about the liberation of Arabia from Turkish domination. The high point of his brilliant military career came in 1918 when, with Faisal, he entered Damascus in triumph. Officially a subordinate first of General Wingate and subsequently of Allenby, Lawrence in fact and of necessity operated independently, and in the desert campaign displayed a strategic genius rarely surpassed in military annals. Attending the Paris Peace Conference in 1919 as a member of the British delegation, Lawrence is said to have been embarrassed and dismayed to learn that while he had made certain promises to the Arabs concerning their hopes of independence and their territorial expectations, the British government had made in other directions commitments which conflicted with his pledges. Refusing a peerage and rejecting the Distinguished Service Order and other honors, he consented to serve as adviser to the Middle East division of the Colonial Office in 1921-22, during which time he was instrumental in bringing about the recognition of Iraq as a kingdom and of Faisal as its king. Thereafter Lawrence, shunning fame and public notice, enlisted as an aircraftman (equivalent to private) in the Royal Air Force under the name of Ross. When his identity was discovered, he transferred to the tank corps, adopted the name T. E. Shaw, and later again served in the Royal Air Force under that designation. His death in 1935 resulted from a motorcycle accident. His extraordinary book *The Seven Pillars of Wisdom,* based on his wartime experiences in Arabia, was privately printed in an edition limited to nine copies, in 1926; in 1927 an abridgment of it was published under the title *Revolt in the Desert,* and in 1935 the complete text was published, under the original title. In 1932 Lawrence's translation of the *Odyssey,* considered one of the best in English, appeared. A selection of his letters was published in 1939, and in 1940 a collection of his miscellaneous writings, under the title *Oriental Assembly.*

Lawrence Boythorn (boi'thôrn). See **Boythorn, Lawrence.**

Laws of Candy (kan'di), **The.** A play by John Fletcher, printed in 1647. It was probably written c1619.

Lawson (lô'son), **Harry Lawson Webster.** See **Burnham,** 1st Viscount.

Lawson (lô'son), **Henry.** [Also: **Henry Hertzberg Lawson, Henry Archibald Lawson.**] b. near Grenfell, New South Wales, Australia, June 17, 1867; d. at Sydney, Australia, Sept. 2, 1922. An Australian short-story writer and poet, the greatest writer of fictional sketches in Australian literature. He was the son of a Norwegian father (Larsen, Anglicized as Lawson) and an Australian mother. Meagerly educated, he learned the trade of a carriage painter, but his mother, a working journalist from 1884, encouraged him to write, and he published his first book in 1894. The best single volumes of his work are *While the Billy Boils* (1896) and *Joe Wilson and His Mates* (1902); his poetry is of lesser worth.

Law Tricks, or Who Would Have Thought It? A play (c1608) by John Day.

lay. A type of short lyric poem, originally intended to be sung by a minstrel, and dealing with stories of romance and adventure.

Layamon (lā'a̧.mon, lä'ya̧.mon, lä'mon). [Also, **Lawman.**] fl. 1200. An English priest, author of *Brut,* a Middle English paraphrase of Wace's Norman French *Roman de Brut.* All that is known of his life is contained in a few passages of his work which refer to himself. From these it appears that he was a priest and lived at "Ernley" (identified with Arley Regis in north Worcestershire).

Layard (lā'ård), **Sir Austen Henry.** b. at Paris, March 5, 1817; d. at London, July 5, 1894. An English archaeologist and diplomat, noted for his archaeological discoveries in Asiatic Turkey. In 1845-47 he continued the excavations at Kuyunjik begun by Bolta and dug also at Nimrud. He identified Kuyunjik as the site of ancient Nineveh. He was a member of Parliament for Southwark (1860–70), undersecretary for foreign affairs (1861–66), commissioner of works (1868–69), minister to Spain (1869–77), and ambassador to Constantinople (1877–80). He published *Nineveh and its Remains* (1848), *The Monuments of Nineveh* (1849–53), *Inscriptions in the Cuneiform Character from Assyrian Monuments* (1851), *Fresh Discoveries at Nineveh, and Researches at Babylon* (1853), and others.

Lay Down Your Arms! The title of the English translation by T. Holmes of *Die Waffen nieder* (1889) by the Baroness von Suttner. The author was awarded the Nobel peace prize in 1905. The book is known also as *Ground Arms!*

Lay of Havelok the Dane (hav′ẹ.lok), **The.** See **Havelok.**

Lay of the Last Minstrel. A narrative poem by Sir Walter Scott, published in 1805, written in six cantos in an irregular stanza pattern. It was this poem that brought Scott his first notice of fame. The plot outline is tied together principally by the minstrel who is reciting the lay, and concerns the feud between the Buccleuchs of Branksome Hall and the Cranstoun family.

Lays of Ancient Rome, The. A volume of poems by Thomas Babington Macaulay, published in 1842.

Lazarillo (laz.ạ.ril′ō). A character in Beaumont and Fletcher's *The Woman-Hater*, described in the dramatis personae as a voluptuous "smell-feast." He is a poor and hungry courtier, whose whole soul is given to the subject of delicate eating, with a particular desire for a fish head, which he pursues through the play and finally obtains by marrying its possessor, a courtesan.

Leacock (lē′kok), **Stephen Butler.** b. at Swanmoor, Hampshire, England, 1869; d. at Toronto, Canada, March 28, 1944. A Canadian economist and humorist. He was professor (1901–36) and head of the economics department (1908–36) at McGill University, Montreal. Author of *Elements of Political Science* (1906), *Economic Prosperity in the British Empire* (1930), *Montreal: Seaport and City* (1942), and other serious works. His literary studies include *Humour: Its Theory and Technique* (1935) and biographies of Mark Twain (1932) and Charles Dickens (1933). Among his humorous books are *Literary Lapses* (1910), *Nonsense Novels* (1911), *Arcadian Adventures with the Idle Rich* (1914), *Moonbeams from the Larger Lunacy* (1915), *Frenzied Fiction* (1917), *Afternoons in Utopia* (1932), *Funny Pieces* (1936), *Laugh Parade* (1940), *My Remarkable Uncle* (1942), and *Happy Stories Just to Laugh at* (1944). He published *My Discovery of England* (1922) after a lecture tour in England, and he was the author of *How To Write* (1943).

Leadbeater (led′bē″tėr), **Mary.** [Maiden name, **Shackleton.**] b. at Ballitore, County Kildare, Ireland, in December, 1758; d. there, June 27, 1826. An English writer, friend and correspondent of Burke. She published *Poems* (1808), *Cottage Dialogues among the Irish Peasantry* (1811), *Cottage Biography* (1822), and *Annals of Ballitore*

(published 1862 as *The Leadbeater Papers* by R. D. Webb).

Leaf (lēf), **Walter.** b. at Norwood, London, Nov. 26, 1852; d. March 28, 1927. An English scholar and banker. Entering the firm of Leaf, Sons and Company as a young man, he became chairman of Leaf and Company, Ltd., in 1888, and chairman of the Westminster Bank in 1918. He served as president of the Institute of Bankers (1919–21), and as president of the International Chamber of Commerce in 1925. As a banker, he was the author of an authoritative work entitled *Banking* (1926). As a classical scholar, he made, between 1886 and 1902, a translation of the *Iliad*, and published *Companion to the Iliad* (1892), *Troy, a Study in Homeric Geography* (1912), *Homer and History* (1915), *Little Poems from the Greek* (1922), and *Strabo on the Troad* (1923). He collaborated with Andrew Lang and E. J. Myers in the preparation of the widely used Lang, Leaf, and Myers translation of the *Iliad* into English prose, which was first published in 1882 and has been several times reprinted.

League of Nations. The international organization created after World War I by the treaty of Versailles to act as an international forum and a place to mediate or conciliate international disputes. Its chief bodies were the League of Nations Council, the League of Nations Assembly, the Permanent Court of International Justice, and the League of Nations Secretariat. With headquarters in Geneva, Switzerland, the organization endured until January, 1946, when it was dissolved after the first meeting of the General Assembly of the United Nations.

Lean (lēn), **Donald Bean.** See **Bean Lean, Donald.**

Leander (lẹ.an′dėr). In Greek legend, a youth of Abydos, the lover of Hero. Each night he swam the Hellespont to visit her secretly. Marriage was forbidden them because Hero was a priestess of Aphrodite at Sestos. One stormy night the light in the tower, by which his course was guided, was extinguished, and he perished. His body was washed ashore, and on discovering it Hero threw herself into the sea and was drowned.

Leantio (lẹ.än′shō, -shi.ō). In Thomas Middleton's *Women Beware Women*, the young merchant's agent who loves Bianca.

Lear (lir), **Edward.** b. at London, May 12, 1812; d. at San Remo, Italy, 1888. An English artist and writer, noted for his nonsense verse and limericks. Among his publications are *Illustrations for the Family of the Psittacidœ* (1832), *The Book of Nonsense* (1846), *Journal of a Landscape Painter in Corsica* (1870), the last of a series of journals of his travels in the Mediterranean area, *Nonsense Songs, Stories, Botany, and Alphabets* (1870), *More Nonsense* (1871), and *Laughable Lyrics* (1876). Author of *The Owl and the Pussy-Cat* (1871), *The Pobble Who Had No Toes*, and *The Jumblies.*

Lear, King. A legendary king of Britain.

Lear, King. In Shakespeare's *King Lear*, the King of Britain, the chief figure of the drama. Of all those who have written the story of this king who tested the devotion of his daughters and disinherited the most faithful, Shakespeare is the only

ḍ, d or j; ṣ, s or sh; ṭ, t or ch; ẓ, z or zh; o, F. cloche; ü, F. menu; ch, Sc. loch; ṅ, F. bonbon.

writer who has Lear go mad, and it is part of the greatness of the character that his madness paradoxically helps him finally to obtain sanity. As Edith Sitwell has pointed out, Lear's madness is the doom of Nature upon a man who has called upon her powers to curse his daughters. He denies any parental affinity with Cordelia. He invokes the curse of sterility upon Goneril, desiring that the storm "crack nature's molds, all germanes spill at once." In his attempt to extort the tributes of love from his daughter we see a tyrant indulging in an unrestrained display of egotism, but his pride soon suffers from the cold words of his ungrateful daughters, one of whom, Regan, cruelly tells him that he is old. The irritation grows on seeing Kent in stocks before Gloucester's castle. As his madness begins, he insists vehemently on his proper entourage, but the sisters insist that he needs no one. Unable to weep at the tragic truth that they now deny him even the smallest portion of his need, Lear rushes into the storm. Its violence calls forth the sympathetic comment about "poor naked wretches" caught in it. Lear has begun to understand what other men feel, but he must learn more about the fellowship of pain and does this through the insistent torment of thinking of his daughters' unnatural ways. Edgar perceives this fellowship, as does Gloucester when he says to a beggar "That I am wretched makes thee happier." The lesson is finally learned when Lear can cry and when he identifies himself as old and foolish. He dies, not of madness, but of old age and a broken heart.

Lear, The Tragedy of King. See **King Lear.**

Learmont (lir'mǫnt), **Thomas.** See **Thomas the Rhymer.**

"Learned Printer," the. See **Bowyer, William.**

Learoyd (lē'roid), **John.** One of the "Soldiers Three" in Kipling's series of stories grouped under that title.

Lease-Lend. British term for **Lend-Lease.**

Leatherhead (leᴛʜ'ẻr.hed), **Lanthorn.** In Ben Jonson's comedy *Bartholomew Fair*, a toy-man who is said, though on doubtful authority, to be intended to ridicule Inigo Jones, with whom Jonson had a continual quarrel.

Le Beau (lẹ bō'; in Shakespeare, lẹ bū'). In Shakespeare's *As You Like It*, a courtier in attendance on Frederick, the usurping duke. The first folio (1623) spells his name Le Beu.

Le Bon Florence of Rome (lẹ bon flor'ẹns). A Middle English romance telling the story of a suffering wife.

Lecky (lek'i), **William Edward Hartpole.** b. near Dublin, March 26, 1838; d. at London, Oct. 22, 1903. An Irish historian and essayist. He was educated at Cheltenham and at Trinity College, Dublin, served as a Liberal member of Parliament (1895–1902), and was offered, but declined, an Oxford professorship in history. His widow (who was Elizabeth van Dedem, maid of honor to Sophia, Queen of the Netherlands, when he married her in 1871) published his *Historical and Political Essays* in 1908, and founded the Lecky professorship of history at Trinity College. He was the author of *Religious Tendencies of the Age* (1860), *The*

Leaders of Public Opinion in Ireland (1861), *The Declining Sense of the Miraculous* (1863), *A History of the Rise and Influence of Rationalism in Europe* (2 vols., 1865), *A History of European Morals from Augustus to Charlemagne* (2 vols., 1869), *A History of England in the Eighteenth Century* (8 vols., 1878–90), *Democracy and Liberty* (2 vols., 1896), and *The Map of Life* (1899). He also wrote *Friendship and Other Poems* (1859) and *Poems* (1891).

Leda (lē'dạ). In Greek mythology, the wife of Tyndareus of Sparta, and mother of Helen, Clytemnestra, Castor, and Pollux. According to the later legends, she was approached by Zeus in the form of a swan, and brought forth two eggs; but the paternity of her twins, Castor and Pollux, is disputed. Clytemnestra was the daughter of Leda and Tyndareus, Helen of Leda and Zeus. Homer says that Tyndareus fathered Castor and Pollux also, but other legends make one or both the sons of Zeus.

Leda. A volume of poetry (1920) by Aldous Huxley.

Ledwidge (led'wij), **Francis.** b. at Slane, Ireland, June 19, 1891; d. in Belgium, July 31, 1917. An Irish poet, killed in World War I. He was discovered and helped in his writing career by Lord Dunsany. His volumes of verse are *Songs of the Fields* (1915), *Songs of Peace* (1916), *Last Songs* (1917), and *Complete Poems* (published posthumously in 1919).

Lee (lē), **Alice.** One of the principal characters in Sir Walter Scott's *Woodstock.*

Lee, Harriet. b. at London, 1757; d. at Clifton, near Bristol, England, Aug. 1, 1851. An English author; sister of Sophia Lee, her collaborator in the *Canterbury Tales* (1797–1805). She also published *The Errors of Innocence*, a novel (1786), *The New Peerage, or Our Eyes May Deceive Us*, a comedy (1787), and *Clara Lennox*, a novel (1797). *Kruitzner*, one of her *Canterbury Tales*, was dramatized by Byron as *Werner.*

Lee, Henry. b. in Nottinghamshire, England, Oct. 27, 1765; d. at London, March 30, 1836. An English writer and actor.

Lee, Jennie. b. at Lochgelly, Scotland, Nov. 3, 1904—. A British politician; wife (married 1934) of Aneurin Bevan. A journalist, she served (1929–31, 1945 *et seq.*) as a member of Parliament. Author of *Tomorrow Is a New Day* (1939), *Our Ally Russia* (1941), and others.

Lee, Nathaniel. b. at Hatfield, Hertfordshire, England, c1649; d. at London, 1692. An English dramatist. He wrote *Nero* (1675), *Gloriana* (1676), *Sophonisba, or Hannibal's Overthrow* (1676), *The Rival Queens, or the Death of Alexander the Great* (1677: in which appeared the line "When Greeks joined Greeks then was the tug of war"), *Mithridates, King of Pontus* (1678), *Caesar Borgia* (1680), *Theodosius, or The Force of Love* (1680), and *Lucius Junius Brutus* (1681, published 1685). With Dryden, he wrote *Oedipus, King of Thebes* (1679), *The Duke of Guise* (1682), and *Constantine the Great* (1684). Lee became insane in 1684, and was confined in an asylum for five years. He died in a fit of intoxication.

Lee, Sarah. [Maiden name, **Wallis.**] b. at Colchester, England, Sept. 10, 1791; d. at Erith, Kent, England, Sept. 22, 1856. An English writer and artist.

Lee, Sir **Sidney.** b. at London, Dec. 5, 1859; d. there, March 3, 1926. An English scholar and editor. He was assistant editor of the *Dictionary of National Biography* (1883–90), was joint editor with (Sir) Leslie Stephen (1890–91), and upon the retirement of the latter in 1891 became editor in chief. Among his publications are *Stratford-on-Avon from the Earliest Times to the Death of Shakespeare* (1884), *Life of William Shakespeare* (1898), a biography of Queen Victoria (1902), *Shakespeare First Folio Facsimile* (1902), *Elizabethan Sonnets* (1904), *Great Englishmen of the Sixteenth Century* (1904), *Shakespeare and the Modern Stage* (1906), and *The French Renaissance in England* (1910). He was engaged in writing an official biography of Edward VII when he died.

Lee, Sophia. b. at London, 1750; d. at Clifton, England, March 13, 1824. An English novelist and dramatist; sister of Harriet Lee, with whom she collaborated in writing the *Canterbury Tales.* Author of *The Chapter of Accidents,* a comedy (produced Aug. 5, 1780), *The Recess,* a novel (1785), and *Almeyda, Queen of Grenada,* a tragedy (1796).

Lee, Vernon. Pseudonym of **Paget, Violet.**

Leech (lēch), **John.** b. at London, Aug. 29, 1817; d. there, Oct. 29, 1864. An English caricaturist, especially noted for his contributions to *Punch.* His father was an Irishman, the proprietor of a coffee house, and a man of some culture. John went to Charterhouse school, where he gained the friendship of Thackeray. He left the school at 16, and was apprenticed to one Whittle, a surgeon, at Haxton, an extraordinary character, who furnished him with much material. He continued his medical studies with Dr. John Cockle of the Royal Free Hospital. He finally abandoned medicine, and at 18 published *Etchings and Sketches by A. Pen, Esq.* When Seymour shot himself in 1836, Leech applied to Dickens for the place of illustrator of *Pickwick Papers,* but failed to obtain it. It was only c1840 that Leech matured the style and manner which afterward made him famous. In 1841 he joined the staff of *Punch,* on which he remained 23 years.

Lee-Hamilton (lē′ham′il.ṭọn), **Eugene Jacob.** b. at London, Jan. 6, 1845; d. near Florence, Italy, Sept. 7, 1907. An English poet. His volumes of verse include *Poems and Transcripts* (1878) and *Sonnets of the Wingless Hours* (1894), a series of autobiographical poems from which his reputation chiefly stems.

Le Fanu (lef′ạ.nū), **Joseph Sheridan.** b. at Dublin, Aug. 28, 1814; d. there, Feb. 7, 1873. An Irish journalist and novelist, noted especially for stories set within an atmosphere of dread. As a journalist he was connected with the *Dublin University Magazine, The Evening Mail,* and other journals. He wrote the ballads *Phaudhrig Crohoore* and *Shamus O'Brien* (1837). Among his novels are *The House by the Churchyard* (1863), *Uncle Silas* (1864), *Guy Deverell* (1865), *The Tenants of Malory* (1867), *A Lost Name* (1868), *The Wyvern Mystery* (1869),

Checkmate (1870), *The Rose and the Key* (1871), *Chronicles of Golden Friars* (1871), and *In a Glass Darkly* (1872).

Le Fevre (lẹ fē′vẻr). A poor lieutenant in Laurence Sterne's *Tristram Shandy,* with reference to whose death Uncle Toby swore his famous oath which the recording angel dropped a tear upon "and blotted it out for ever."

Le Gallienne (lẹ.gal′yẹn, -gal.i.en′), **Richard.** b. at Liverpool, England, Jan. 20, 1866; d. at Menton, France, Sept. 14, 1947. An English journalist and author. Among his works are *The Book-bills of Narcissus* (1891), *The Religion of a Literary Man* (1893), *Prose Fancies* (1894, 1896), *The Quest of the Golden Girl* (1896), *Painted Shadows* (1904), *Romances of Old France* (1905), *The Worshiper of the Images* (1906), *Attitudes and Avowals* (1910), *October Vagabonds* (1910), *Loves of the Poets* (1911), *The Magic Seas* (1930), and *From a Paris Garret* (1943).

legend. An entertaining story, especially in early times one relating to wonders or miracles told of a saint; hence, any unauthentic and improbable or nonhistorical narrative handed down from early times; a tradition.

Thou shalt, whyl that thou livest, yere by yere,
The most party of thy tyme spende
In making of a glorious Legende
Of Goode Wommen, maidenes, and wives
That weren trewe in lovinge all her lives.
(Chaucer, *Prol to Good Women.*)

It were infinite, and indeed ridiculous, to speak of all the Miracles reported to be done by this St. Dunstan, which may be fit for a Legend, but not for a Chronicle. (Baker, *Chronicles.*)

This also was furthered by the Legend of Daphne, recorded by the Poets. (Purchas, *Pilgrimage.*)

Legend (lej′end), Sir **Sampson.** In Congreve's *Love for Love,* an overbearing old man with a perverse and ill-natured wit.

Legend of Good Women, The. An unfinished poem by Chaucer. The Prologue, a courtly love-vision influenced by such poets as Deschamps, Machaut, and Froissart, introduces some ten "legends" of martyrs of Cupid, beginning with Cleopatra. These are represented as being offered to the beautiful Queen Alceste, because she has interceded for him with the god of love (who was offended by the poet's portrayal of Criseyde, among others). Chaucer adapted from Ovid and from medieval redactors, especially Boccaccio, most of these stories of classical heroines who suffered or died out of devotion to their lovers. The "legends," which appear to have been written earlier than the Prologue, reveal a considerable advance in narrative skill over the poems of the French period and are important as marking the introduction of the decasyllabic couplet into English versification. The Prologue contains the famous lines which tell of Chaucer's love of the daisy.

Legend of Jubal, and other Poems (jö′bạl). Poems by George Eliot, published in 1874.

Legend of Montrose (mon.trōz′, mon′trōz). A historical novel by Sir Walter Scott, published in 1819.

ḍ, d or j; ș, s or sh; ṭ, t or ch; ẓ, z or zh; o, F. cloche; ü, F. menu; ċh, Sc. loch; ṅ, F. bonbon.

Legion of Honor. [Full French name, **Ordre de la Légion d' Honneur.**] In France, an order of distinction and reward for civil and military services instituted in May, 1802, during the Consulate, by Napoleon Bonaparte, but since modified from time to time in important particulars. Under the First Empire the distinctions conferred invested the person decorated with the rank of legionary, officer, commander, grand officer, or grand cross. The order holds considerable property, the proceeds of which are paid out in pensions, principally to wounded and disabled members.

Legouis (le̞.gwē), **Émile.** b. at Honfleur, Calvados, France, Oct. 31, 1861; d. at Paris, Oct. 16, 1937. A French literary historian, specialist in English literature. He was the author (with Louis Cazamian, who wrote of the period after 1660) of a standard *Histoire de la littérature anglaise* (1925 and subsequent editions) and of numerous studies of English writers. He was professor of English language and literature (1904–32) at the Sorbonne.

Lehmann (lā′man̞), **Rosamond (Nina).** b. c1904–. An English novelist. Her books include *Dusty Answer* (1927), *A Note in Music* (1930), *Invitation to the Waltz* (1932), *The Weather in the Streets* (1936), *No More Music* (1939), *The Ballad and the Source* (1944), and *The Gypsy's Baby* (1946).

Leibniz or **Leibnitz** (līp′nits), Baron **Gottfried Wilhelm von.** b. at Leipzig, Germany, July 1, 1646; d. at Hanover, Germany, Nov. 14, 1716. A German philosopher, mathematician, and courtier. A precocious child, he was learned in Latin and Greek, and a student of philosophy, before he entered the University of Leipzig at the age of 15. Dissatisfied with the teaching at that institution, he continued his studies at the universities of Jena and Altdorf, receiving the degree of doctor of law from the latter in 1666. The brilliance of his dissertation on this occasion led to an offer of a professorship at Altdorf, but he had already determined to play his role on a larger stage. The publication of his *Nova Methodus* in 1667 with a dedication to the archbishop of Mainz led, as expected, to his employment by that imperial elector, chiefly in the writing of political tracts and memoranda. While Louis XIV was making his preparations for the Third Dutch War, Leibniz wrote a memorandum suggesting that Christian princes, instead of fighting each other, should direct their efforts toward non-Christian lands, and proposing Egypt as a suitable scene for Louis's martial activities. This proposal was forwarded to the French monarch, and Leibniz was invited to visit Paris, where, however, Louis neglected to give him an audience. He remained in the French capital from 1672 to 1676 in a diplomatic capacity, and availed himself of the opportunity to discuss philosophy with Descartes's disciple Malebranche, and mathematics with the scientist Huygens. During these years also he visited England, meeting Boyle and Newton, and exhibiting a calculating machine of his invention at the Royal Society, of which he was made a fellow in 1673. At this time mathematics became his real major interest, and it was during the years 1675–76 that he worked out his method of infinitesimal calculus, which when published in 1684 led to some controversy with Newton, who

had developed his calculus in 1665; but of this it appears that Leibniz was ignorant. Meanwhile he had won the favor of the Duke of Brunswick-Lüneburg, who appointed him his librarian and made him a privy councilor, and in 1676 he proceeded (by way of Holland, where he lingered for long discussions with Spinoza) to Hanover, thenceforth his permanent home. Among the tasks set for him by his ducal patron was the writing of a history of the Brunswick-Lüneburg family; this entailed a good deal of travel, including a long stay at Rome, during which he was tempted by the Pope's offer to make him librarian of the Vatican, but as this would have required him to become a Catholic, he declined. During this period he wrote *Systema theologicum* in an effort to reconcile Catholicism and Protestantism; later he worked for the more moderate aim of promoting unity between the Lutheran and Reformed churches, with equal lack of success. Through the electress Sophia of Hanover, Leibniz came to the notice of her daughter, the electress Sophia Charlotte of Brandenburg, who became his most admiring patron. At her invitation he went to Berlin in 1700, and after the Elector of Brandenburg assumed the title of Frederick I of Prussia, at Leibniz's suggestion he founded the Academy of Science at Berlin, installing the philosopher as president for life. Already a privy councilor of Hanover, Leibniz was granted the same honorary rank by the ruler of Brandenburg, by Peter I of Russia, and by the emperor, who moreover made him a baron of the empire. But when the elector George Louis of Hanover became George I of England, he did not take Leibniz with him, but required him to remain at Hanover and to complete the Brunswick-Lüneburg chronicle. Since the death of Sophia Charlotte in 1705 Leibniz's star had in fact been in decline; the last years of the man who had so assiduously courted princes and princesses were solitary and embittered, and when he died, attended only by his secretary, the event went unnoticed except by the French Academy, where he was eulogized. Some others of Leibniz's principal works were *De Arte combinatoria* (1666), *Hypothesis physica nova* (1671), *Codex juris gentium diplomaticum* (1693), *Essais de Théodicée sur la bonté de Dieu, la liberté de l'homme, et l'origine du mal* (1710), *La Monadologie* (1714), *Principes de la nature et de la grace* (1714), and *Nouveaux essais sur l'entendement humain*, written in 1704 but published posthumously. Leibniz was regarded in his day as a kind of universal genius. In the precise field of mathematics, as well as in the science of comparative philology, which was another of his interests, his accomplishments were solid. Like many another system of philosophy, his before long became more a subject of historical study than a vital force, yet he had some influence on Hegel, more on Kant, and still more on Goethe. The core of his thought lay in the concept of the multiplicity of substance, of substance as force, and of monads as the units of substance. The subtleties of his system cannot be briefly summarized, but the grand conclusion was that between the physical and moral realms there is a preëstablished harmony, so that the universe cannot be other, or better, than it is. This was an idea naturally congenial to princes and privileged persons, but it is remembered today chiefly because of Voltaire's satirization of it in *Candide*.

Leicester (les'tẻr), **Earl of.** Title of **Dudley, Robert.**

Leicester Dedlock (ded'lok), **Sir.** See **Dedlock, Sir Leicester.**

Leicester's Men. [Also, **Earl of Leicester's Men.**] An Elizabethan theatrical company, led by James Burbage. It was licensed in 1574 by Queen Elizabeth to act in London and throughout England under the patronage of the Earl of Leicester. Until that time, the company had been known as the Earl of Dudley's Company. There is a possibility that Shakespeare may have joined them in 1586 at Stratford.

Leidenberck (lī'dẹn.berk). An adherent of Sir John Van Olden Barnavelt in Fletcher and Massinger's play of that name.

Leif Ericson or **Ericsson** (lẽf' er'ik.sọn). See **Ericson** or **Ericsson, Leif.**

Leigh (lē), **Amyas.** The adventurous hero of Charles Kingsley's *Westward Ho!*, published in 1855. Leigh accompanies Drake on his voyage around the world and wanders for three years through South America, returning finally, having lost his sight as a result of his adventures, to his home in Devonshire.

Leigh, Augusta. The half-sister of the English poet Byron. Their alleged incestuous relationship was a precipitating factor in the separation of Byron and his wife, Anne Millbanke.

Leigh, Edward. b. at Shawell, Leicestershire, England, March 24, 1602; d. at Rushall Hall, Staffordshire, England, June 2, 1671. An English Puritan theologian.

Leigh, Egerton. b. in Cheshire, England, 1815; d. at London, July 1, 1876. An English soldier and antiquary, author of *A Glossary of Words Used in the Dialect of Cheshire* (1877).

Leighton (lā'tọn), **Alexander.** b. in Scotland, 1568; d. 1649. A Scottish physician and divine, a victim of Archbishop Laud's persecutions. He was a vigorous opponent of Roman Catholicism, and was fined, mutilated, and imprisoned (1630–40) for his attack upon the episcopacy and the queen, and released and recompensed with a gift of 6,000 pounds by the Long Parliament. He wrote *Speculum Belli Sacri, or the Looking Glass of War* (1624), and *An Appeal to the Parliament, or Sion's Plea against the Prelacie* (1628).

Leila (lē'lạ, lā'-). In Byron's long poem *Don Juan*, the Mohammedan girl rescued by Don Juan at the siege of Ismail.

Leila. In Byron's poem *The Giaour*, the slave of the Caliph Hassan who meets an untimely end when she is cast into the sea during her flight from the seraglio.

Leila, or the Siege of Granada (grạ.nä'dạ). A novel by Edward Bulwer-Lytton, published in 1838.

L. E. L. Pseudonym of **Landon, Letitia Elizabeth.**

Leland or **Leyland** (lē'lạnd), **John.** b. at London, Sept. 13, c1506; d. April 18, 1552. An English

antiquary. He was appointed king's antiquary by Henry VIII in 1533, with a commission to search for English antiquities in all libraries and other places where they might be found, and for this purpose journeyed for six years (1536–42), through England, making exhaustive researches and minutely recording his observations. He was adjudged insane in 1550. Most of his work was left in manuscript at his death. His *Itinerary* was published in 1710, and his *Collectanea* in 1715.

Leland, John. b. at Wigan, England, Oct. 18, 1691; d. at Dublin, Jan. 16, 1766. An English Presbyterian clergyman and controversialist. He was the author of *A View of the Principal Deistical Writers that have Appeared in England During the Last and Present Centuries* (1754–56) and others.

Lemnos (lem'nos). [Also: **Limni, Limno, Limnos.**] An island in the Aegean Sea, belonging to Greece, in the *nomos* (department) of Lesbos. The surface is hilly and fertile, and produces grain, wine, olives, tobacco, and fruits. It has hot springs and a harbor on the S coast at Moudros. Sacred to Hephaestus in ancient times, it was conquered by the Persians, and recovered for Athens by Miltiades. In 1912 it was taken by the Greeks from the Turks. In World War I it was the base of the British fleet in the Dardanelles campaign. Chief town, Kastro; length, ab. 20 mi.; area, ab. 180 sq. mi.; pop. 25,477 (1940). According to an ancient myth, the Argonauts touched at Lemnos for supplies soon after they began their voyage. They found the island populated only by women, who had murdered all the men for cohabiting with Thracian female captives. The Argonauts were hospitably greeted and stayed for some time, Jason fathering the twin sons of Hypsipyle, the Lemnian queen, and the other Argonauts leaving an island soon repopulated with males. Students see evidence in the myth of a former gynocracy (rule by women). Both Aeschylus and Sophocles wrote plays, now lost, on the story.

Lemoine (lẹ.moin'), **Henry.** b. at London, Jan. 14, 1756; d. there, April 30, 1812. An English bookseller and writer.

Lemon (lem'ọn), **Mark.** b. at London, Nov. 30, 1809; d. at Crawley, Sussex, England, May 23, 1870. An English journalist, dramatist, and novelist, one of the founders and the first editor (1841–70) of *Punch*. Among his numerous plays are *Hearts Are Trumps, Lost and Won, Self-Accusation,* and *Love and War*. He also wrote a number of Christmas tales, and published a jest-book in 1867.

Lemot (lẹ.mō', lẹ.mot'). The favorite of the French king in, and the originator of the various mischievous tricks which motivate the plot of, George Chapman's *An Humorous Day's Mirth*.

Lemprière (lem.prir'), **John.** b. in Jersey, Channel Islands, c1765; d. at London, Feb. 1, 1824. An English classical scholar. He published *Bibliotheca Classica, or Classical Dictionary* (1788), for many years, and through many editions, one of the standard reference works on mythology and the ancient world.

Lemuel (lem'ū.ẹl). In the Bible, an unknown king, identified with Solomon by rabbinical commentators. Prov. xxxi. 1, 4.

Lemuel Gulliver (gul'i.vėr). See **Gulliver, Lemuel.**

Lemuria (lẹ.mū'ri.ạ). A land supposed formerly to have existed in the Indian Ocean, connecting Madagascar, the peninsula of India, and Sumatra.

Lena (lē'nạ), **Popilius.** In Shakespeare's *Julius Caesar*, a senator. His conversation with Caesar just before the assassination alarms the conspirators, who fear that their plan has been discovered.

Lenaea (lẹ.nē'ạ). The "feast of vats," an ancient Greek festival in honor of Dionysus.

Lenclos or **L'Enclos** (län.klō), **Anne.** [Called **Ninon de Lenclos** (or **L'Enclos**).] b. at Paris, c1620; d. there, 1705 (some sources say 1706). A French courtesan and wit. She retained her beauty and charm to a very old age. Mademoiselle de Scudéry drew her portrait in *Clélie* under the name of Clarisse. She received the highest society in her salon, which has been compared for its tone with the Hôtel Rambouillet. Madame Scarron (afterward de Maintenon), Madame de Lafayette, and Queen Christina of Sweden were her friends. St. Évremond, La Rochefoucauld, D'Estrées, the great Condé, and three generations of the family of Sévigné were among her lovers. Her career of sensuality, stretching over an almost incredible length of time, has made her perhaps the most legendary of the famous French women of fashion.

Lend-Lease. [Called, by the British, **Lease-Lend.**] A term applied to the system devised by the U. S. for providing material aid to the other Allied powers in World War II. Originally designed (and narrowly passed, as such, by Congress in March, 1941) as "aid short of war," it gave the President power to have manufactured, and to sell, lease, or exchange any defense article to or with any nation whose defense he considered vital to U. S. security. In return, the U. S. would receive money, materials, or "any other direct or indirect benefit which the President deems satisfactory." When the U. S. entered World War II, Lend-Lease became a system of inter-Allied aid with provisions made for mutual credits. After having provided just over 50 billion dollars of aid, with Great Britain and the U.S.S.R. as the principal recipients, Lend-Lease was brought to an end by President Truman on Aug. 25, 1945.

Lennox (len'ọks). In Shakespeare's *Macbeth*, a Scottish thane. Convinced of Macbeth's guilt (after the murder of Banquo and as a result of Macbeth's behavior at the banquet), he joins the anti-Macbeth faction headed by Malcolm.

Lennox, Charlotte. [Maiden name, **Ramsay.**] b. at New York, 1720; d. in England, Jan. 4, 1804. An English novelist and poet. She published *The Female Quixote; or the Adventures of Arabella* (1752) and *Shakespear Illustrated* (1753–54), and wrote *The Sister*, a comedy (to which Goldsmith wrote the epilogue), acted Feb. 18, 1769.

Lennox, Lord William Pitt. b. at Winestead Abbey, Yorkshire, England, Sept. 20, 1799; d. at London, Feb. 18, 1881. An English soldier, writer, and journalist; fourth son of Charles Lennox (1764–1819), 4th Duke of Richmond. He wrote several novels, books on sports, and reminiscences.

Le Noir (lẹ nwär), **Elizabeth Anne.** [Maiden name, **Smart.**] b. c1755; d. at Caversham, Berkshire, England, May 6, 1841. An English novelist and poet; daughter of Christopher Smart. Author of *Village Annals* (1803), *Village Anecdotes* (1804), and *Miscellaneous Poems* (1825).

Lenore (lẹ.nōr'). A ballad (1773) by G. A. Bürger: so called from the name of its heroine. It is related to the English ballad *The Suffolk Miracle*, in that both are based on the dead rider motif (the story of the dead lover who returns from his grave on horseback to carry off his inconsolable true love is widespread in Europe).

Lenten Stuffe (len'tẹn stuf). [Full title, **Nash's Lenten Stuffe, or the Praise of the Red Herring.**] A pamphlet by Thomas Nash, published in 1599. It is a lively description of Great Yarmouth, where he had found a safe shelter, with a panegyric on the red herring, its staple commodity.

Leo (lē'ō). An ancient zodiacal constellation, the Lion, containing Regulus, a star of magnitude 1½, and two stars of the second magnitude. It is easily found, for the pointers of the Great Bear point S to its brightest star, distant about 45 degrees. Four stars in the body of Leo form a characteristic trapezium, and those about the neck and mane make a sickle. It is the fifth sign of the zodiac.

Leo X. [Original name, **Giovanni de' Medici.**] b. at Florence, Dec. 11, 1475; d. at Rome, Dec. 1, 1521. Pope from 1513 to 1521; second son of Lorenzo de' Medici (Lorenzo the Magnificent). He expelled the petty tyrants from the ecclesiastical states, added Perugia, Sinigaglia, and Fermo to the domains of the church, and restored Parma and Piacenza to the holy see. During his pontificate the Reformation began with Luther's protest against the sale of indulgences in 1517; he excommunicated Luther in 1521. He honored Henry VIII of England, author of a pamphlet against Luther, with the title *Fidei Defensor* (Defender of the Faith). He was a liberal patron of art and literature.

Leodegrance (lẹ.od'ẹ.grans) or **Leodegran** (-gran) **of Carohaise** (kar'ọ.hāz). See **Laodogant.**

Leo Hunter (lē'ō hun'tėr), **Mrs.** See **Hunter, Mrs. Leo.**

Leoline (lē'ọ.lin), **Sir.** A character in Samuel Taylor Coleridge's *Christabel.*

Leon (lē'ọn). A character in John Fletcher's *Rule a Wife and Have a Wife.*

Leonardo (lē.ọ.när'dō). In Shakespeare's *Merchant of Venice*, the servant of Bassanio.

Leonardo da Vinci (lä.ọ.när'dō dä vēn'chē; Anglicized, le.när'dō dạ vin'chi). See **Vinci, Leonardo da.**

Leonato (lē.ọ.nä'tō). In Shakespeare's *Much Ado About Nothing*, the governor of Messina; the uncle of Beatrice and father of Hero.

Leonatus (lē.ọ.nä'tus), **Posthumus.** See **Posthumus Leonatus.**

Leonidas (lẹ.on'i.dạs). Killed at Thermopylae, Greece, 480 B.C. A Greek hero, king of Sparta (c490–480 B.C.), famous for his defense of the pass of Thermopylae against the Persian army of Xerxes I. He was slain in company with 300 Spartans and 700 Thespians when Ephialtes, a Malian, guided the Persians to the Greek rear.

Leonidas. An epic poem by Richard Glover, published in 1737 in nine books of blank verse. It was expanded in 1770 to twelve books.

Leonine (lē'ọ̄.nīn). In Shakespeare's *Pericles*, the attendant of Dionyza, employed to murder Marina. As he prepares to do so, he is attacked by pirates and runs off. However, he tells Dionyza that Marina is dead, and Dionyza poisons him.

Leonine City. That part of the city of Rome which is W of the Tiber and N of Trastevere. It contains the Vatican, the Castle of Sant'Angelo, and the district between (known as the Borgo), and is enclosed within a separate line of walls. It was first fortified by Pope Leo IV.

Leonine verse. A verse form said to have been originated by Leonius, canon of the Church of Saint Victor at Paris in the 12th century, consisting of hexameters, or alternate hexameters and pentameters, in which the syllable at the end of the line rhymes with the one preceding the caesura. In English verse the term refers to the rhyming of the last syllable of the line with the middle one.

Leonists (lē'ọ̄.nists). See **Waldenses.**

Leonnoys (lē.ọ̄.nois'). See **Lyonesse.**

Leonora, A Story of the Five Towns (lē.ọ̄.nō'rạ). The second volume in the first "Five Towns" trilogy by Arnold Bennett. Published in 1903, it is a study of a middle-aged woman of the nouveau riche. The other novels in the trilogy are *Anna of the Five Towns* (1902) and *Sacred and Profane Love* (1905; revised ed., *The Book of Carlotta*, 1911).

Leontes (lē.on'tēz). In Shakespeare's *Winter's Tale*, the King of Sicilia and husband of Hermione. His jealousy, unlike that of Othello, is willful and tyrannical. He is the Pandosto of Robert Greene's *Pandosto*, from which the play was taken.

Leopardi (lā.ō.pär'dē), Conte **Giacomo.** b. at Recanati, Italy, June 29, 1798; d. at Naples, Italy, June 14, 1837. Italian poet and philologist. From his youth sickly and deformed, he was educated at home, and devoted himself to the study of the Greek and Latin classics. He published in 1818 an ode to Italy, in which he lamented the political and intellectual degeneracy of his country, and which created a profound impression. Other odes in the same vein, notably one occasioned by Cardinal Mai's discovery of part of Cicero's *De republica*, shortly secured for him a place among the first lyric poets of Italy. He went in 1822 to Rome, where he pursued the study of philology. He afterward resided for short periods at Recanati, Bologna, Florence, Rome, and Naples. The first collected edition of his poems was published in 1824. A collection of miscellaneous prose essays was published in 1827 under the title of *Operette morali*.

Leopold Bloom (lē'ọ̄.pōld blöm). See **Bloom, Leopold.**

Lepanto (lẹ.pan'tō). A poem by G. K. Chesterton, published in *Poems* (1915), depending for its effect upon the quick succession of images and the galloping, marching meter:

Dim drums throbbing, in the hills half heard
Where only on a nameless throne a crownless
prince has stirred.

Lepidus (lep'i.dus), **M. Aemilius.** In Shakespeare's *Julius Caesar*, the historical Marcus Aemilius Lepidus, a Roman leader who becomes one of the triumvirate after Caesar's death. He witnesses the assassination and joins Octavius in the civil strife following, but is referred to in slighting fashion by Antony. In *Antony and Cleopatra*, he attempts to serve as a moderator between his fellow triumvirs, Antony and Octavius.

Le Queux (lẹ kū'), **William Tufnell.** b. at London, July 2, 1864; d. Oct. 13, 1927. An English novelist and journalist. He reported the Balkan War (1912–13) for the *Daily Mail*. Author of *Strange Tales of a Nihilist* (1890), *Guilty Bonds* (1890), *The Great White Queen* (1896), *The Day of Temptation* (1897), *The Eye of Istar* (1897), *England's Peril* (1899), *The Tickencote Treasure* (1902), *Secrets of the Foreign Office* (1903), *The Mask* (1904), *The Czar's Spy* (1903), *Confessions of a Ladies' Man* (1905), *Who Giveth This Woman?* (1905), *A Spider's Eye* (1905), *An Observer in the Near East* (1907), *Fatal Fingers* (1912), *The Hand of Allah* (1914), *German Spies in England* (1915), *Rasputin, the Rascal Monk* (1920), *Landru* (1921), *Things I Know* (1923), *Where the Desert Ends* (1923), *Hidden Hands* (1925), *The Fatal Face* (1926), and *Blackmailed* (1927). His two fictional but highly realistic stories *The Great War in England in 1897* (1894) and *The Invasion of 1910* (1906) anticipated World War I.

Ler (lãr). [Also, **Lir.**] In Old Irish mythology, the personification of the sea, and father of the sea god, Manannan mac Lir, or Manannan son of Ler (*Lir* is the genitive of Ler, but in translations is often mistakenly taken as nominative). See also **Llyr.**

Lesbia (lez'bi.ạ). The name by which Clodia, the favorite of Catullus, is referred to in his poems.

Lesbos (lez'bos). [Also: **Mytilene, Mytilini.**] An island in the Aegean Sea, belonging to Greece, W of Asia Minor. Colonized by Aeolians, it was celebrated in ancient times as a seat of literature. Between the 8th and 4th centuries B.C. Lesbos was the home of many notable persons including Sappho, Arion, Alcaeus, Terpander, Theophrastus, Pittacus, and Hellanicus.

Leslie (les'li, lez'li), **Shane.** [Full name, **John Randolph Shane Leslie.**] b. 1885—. Irish writer. Author of *Songs of Oriel* (1908), *The End of a Chapter* (1916), *Verses in Peace and War*, *The Oppidan* (1922), *Doomsland* (1923), *George the Fourth* (1926), *The Skull of Swift* (1928), *The Epic of Jutland* (1930), *Poems and Ballads* (1933), *American Wonderland* (1936), *The Film of Memory* (1938), *The Life of Mrs. Fitzherbert* (1939), and *Letters of Mrs. Fitzherbert* (1940).

Lesly (les'li, lez'li), **Ludovic.** In Sir Walter Scott's *Quentin Durward*, an archer of Louis XI's bodyguard. He is called "le Balafré."

Lessing (les'ing), **Gotthold Ephraim.** b. at Kamenz, Germany, Jan. 22, 1729; d. at Brunswick, Germany, Feb. 15, 1781. A German critic and dramatist. The son of a clergyman, he attended school at Kamenz and Meissen, and in 1746 went to Leipzig to study theology. Instead, however, of pursuing his studies in this direction, he soon gave his principal attention to the theater. His first comedy, *Der junge Gelehrte* (The Young Scholar),

ḍ, d or j; ṣ, s or sh; ṭ, t or ch; ẓ, z or zh; o, F. cloche; ü, F. menu; ċh, Sc. loch; ṅ, F. bonbon.

was produced in 1748, during his third semester at the university. His association with the theater having given offense to his parents, he was summoned home. He soon, however, returned to Leipzig, where he matriculated as a student of medicine. This same year (1748) he went to Berlin, where he supported himself by making translations and writing criticisms and reviews. In 1751 he went to Wittenberg to complete his studies at the university there. After taking a master's degree, he returned to Berlin in 1752 (he had already, in 1751, published a collection of poems under the title *Kleinigkeiten*). In 1753 he began the publication of his collected works, two volumes of which were issued that year, two in 1754, and two more in 1755, in which year he also wrote his first major play, *Miss Sara Sampson*. Several minor comedies fall in this early period, namely, *Der Misogyn*, a bourgeois tragedy on the English model, *Die Juden*, *Der Freigeist*, and *Der Schatz*. He had also written a number of Anacreontic poems, poetic fables, epigrams, and didactic poems. In the autumn of 1755 he returned once more to Leipzig, where with slight interruptions he remained until 1757. In 1758 he went back to Berlin, and began there the following year, in conjunction with Moses Mendelssohn and the bookseller Nicolai, his *Litteraturbriefe* (in full, *Briefe, die neueste Litteratur betreffend*), with which he was connected until 1760. He published too, at this time, a collection of prose fables, a number of odes in prose, the one-act tragedy *Philotas*, and sketched the plan of a *Faust*, which, however, was never to be completed (and he later lost the manuscript for that portion which he had done). In 1760 he went to Breslau as secretary to General von Tauentzien. In 1763 he wrote the comedy *Minna von Barnhelm*, which was not published until 1767. From Breslau he returned in 1765 to Berlin, where he next wrote his great critical work *Laokoön* (1766), which compares plastic art (as a static form) with poetry (as a dynamic form). The succeeding year he went to Hamburg in order to take part as a critic in the foundation of a German national theater. The result of this undertaking was the series of dramatic criticisms published twice a week from 1767 to 1769 under the title *Hamburgische Dramaturgie*. In 1768 appeared *Briefe antiquarischen Inhalts*, directed against Professor Klotz of Halle. In 1769 appeared the archaeological treatise *Wie die Alten den Tod gebildet*. In this year he received a call as librarian to the ducal library at Wolfenbüttel, a position which he held from the spring of 1770 until his death. In 1772 appeared the tragedy *Emilia Galotti*. From 1773 to 1781 were published a series of *Beiträge zur Geschichte und Litteratur aus den Schätzen der Wolfenbütteler Bibliothek*. In this series Lessing published *Fragmente eines Wolfenbüttelschen Ungenannten*, theological criticisms purporting to be extracts from the writings of "an anonymous Wolfenbütteler," but really written by the Hamburg professor and philosopher H. S. Reimarus, whose book criticizing miracles had been left to Lessing, and from which Lessing had published excerpts from 1774 to 1778, thus involving himself in a bitter controversy, most notably with Pastor Johann Melchior Goeze of Hamburg (against whom Lessing wrote the scathing

polemics contained in his *Anti-Goeze*, which appeared also in 1778). This same year was published *Ernst und Falk, Gespräche für Freimaurer*. In 1779 appeared the drama *Nathan der Weise*, and in 1780, finally, the treatise *Die Erziehung des Menschengeschlechts*, which was, like the *Anti-Goeze* papers and *Nathan*, a result of the theological controversies of the last years of his life.

Lesson of the Master, The. A collection of tales by Henry James, published in 1892.

L'Estrange (les.trānj', lẹs-), Sir **Roger.** b. at Hunstanton, Norfolk, England, Dec. 17, 1616; d. at London, Dec. 11, 1704. An English journalist and Royalist pamphleteer, licenser of the press under Charles II and James II. He served in the royal army against the Parliament, and in an attempt to carry out a plot for the capture of Lynn was betrayed, arrested, and condemned to death, but remained at Newgate until 1648, when he escaped to the Netherlands. He returned to England in 1653. In 1663 he was appointed surveyor of printing offices and licenser of the press, and founded *The Public Intelligencer* and *The News*, both of which ceased to exist in 1666. From 1681 to 1687 he issued the *Observator*. He published a great number of political pamphlets, *The Fables of Æsop and other Eminent Mythologists with Moral Reflections* (1692), *The Works of Flavius Josephus compared with the Original Greek* (1702), and a translation of the *Visions of Quevedo*.

Lethe (lē'thē). In Greek mythology: **1.** The personification of oblivion; a daughter of Eris.
2. The river of oblivion, one of the streams of Hades, the waters of which possessed the property of causing those who drank of them to forget their former existence. The dead drank upon their arrival in Hades; and those about to be reborn also drank of it. Ariosto places Lethe in the moon; Dante places it in purgatory.

Lethington (leth'ing.tọn), Lord. See **Maitland, Sir Richard.**

Leto (lē'tō). [Latin, **Latona.**] In Greek mythology, the daughter of the Titan Coeus and Phoebe, and mother by Zeus of Apollo and Artemis. According to an early form of the myth, she was the wife of Zeus before he married Hera; in later myth, she was his mistress after his marriage with Hera. Hera in jealous rage decreed that no place on earth where the sun shone should allow Leto to give birth to her children. So Leto bore her twins, Apollo and Artemis, either on the island of Delos, protected by Poseidon, or, in some versions, in an undersea cave. Leto's name became Latona in Roman mythology.

letterpress. Letters or words impressed on paper or other material from printing types; printed text.

The letterpress with which the illustration is accompanied is no less interesting than the plate, and furnishes much valuable information. (*N. and Q.*, 7th ser., II.360.)

letters. Literature in general; hence, knowledge derived from books; literary culture; erudition: as, the republic of *letters;* a man of *letters*.

Pericles was an able minister of state, an excellent orator, and a man of letters.

(Swift, *Nobles and Commons*, ii.)

But the valuable thing in letters . . . is, as we have often remarked, the judgment which forms itself insensibly in a fair mind along with fresh knowledge. (M. Arnold, *Literature and Dogma*, Int.)

Letters from a Chinese Philosopher . . . . See **Citizen of the World, The.**

Letters of Espriella (es.pri.el'ą). A prose work (1807) by Robert Southey.

Letters of Yorick to Eliza (yor'ik; ę.lī'zą). A volume of witty, often satirical correspondence by Laurence Sterne, published in 1775. "Eliza" was Mrs. Eliza Draper in real life.

Leucothea (lö.koth'ę.ą). In Greek mythology, the name of Ino after her deification as a sea goddess.

Leukas (lö'kąs). [Also: **Leucadia** (lö.kā'di.ą), **Leukados** (lö.kā'dos); Italian, **Santa Maura**; Latin, **Leucas.**] One of the Ionian Islands, Greece, W of Aetolia and Acarnania, from which it is separated by a narrow channel. The surface is hilly and mountainous. In its SW part is a steep cliff, known as Sappho's Leap, from which Sappho is said to have thrown herself into the sea.

Levelers. See **Whiteboys.**

Lever (lē'vėr), **Charles James.** b. at Dublin, Aug. 31, 1806; d. at Trieste, June 1, 1872. An Irish novelist. He graduated from Trinity College, Dublin, having studied medicine, which he practiced first in Ireland and then at Brussels (1840–42). He was editor of the *Dublin University Magazine* (1842–45), settled at Florence in 1847, and was appointed consul at La Spezia in 1857, and at Trieste in 1867. He wrote *Harry Lorrequer* (1837), *Charles O'Malley* (1840), *Tom Burke of Ours* (1844), *Arthur O'Leary* (1844), *Con Cregan* (1849), *Roland Cashel* (1850), *The Daltons* (1852), *The Dodd Family Abroad* (1853–54), *Lord Kilgobbin* (1872), and others. His earlier novels, chiefly about military life and deeds, were episodic, formless artistically, and popular; his later works, more controlled, were not as widely read.

Leveridge (lev'ėr.ij), **Richard.** b. 1670; d. March 22, 1758. An English singer. He had a very deep bass voice, which was unimpaired for many years. He published a collection of songs with music in 1727. To him is credited the song *Roast Beef of Old England.*

Leveson-Gower (lö'sǫn.gōr'), Lady **Georgiana Charlotte.** [Also, Lady **Georgiana Charlotte Fullerton.**] b. Sept. 23, 1812; d. Jan. 19, 1885. An English novelist; daughter of Granville Leveson-Gower, 1st Earl Granville. She wrote *Laurentia* (1861), *Rose Leblanc* (1861), *Too Strange not to be True* (1864), *Constance Sherwood* (1865), *A Stormy Life* (1867), *Mrs. Gerald's Niece* (1869), *A Will and a Way* (1881), *Life of St. Francis of Rome* (1885), and various other lives of saints, and translations, principally from the French.

Levidulcia (lev.i.dul'shą). The wife of Lord Belforest in Cyril Tourneur's *The Atheist's Tragedy.*

Levy (lē'vi), **Amy.** b. at Clapham, London, Nov. 10, 1861; committed suicide Sept. 10, 1889. An English poet and novelist. She wrote several volumes of poems, including *Xantippe and other Poems* (1881), *A Minor Poet* (1884), and *A London Planetree* (1889), and the novel *Reuben Sachs* (1889).

Levy, Benn. [Full name, **Benn Wolfe Levy.**] b. at London, March 7, 1900—. An English playwright and politician. He was a member (1945–50) of Parliament. Author of *This Woman Business, Mud and Treacle, Mrs. Moonlight, Art and Mrs. Bottle, The Devil Passes, Evergreen, Springtime for Henry, The Poet's Heart, The Jealous God,* and *Clutterbuck.* He was the translator of *Topaze* from the French of Marcel Pagnol.

Levy, Joseph Moses. See under **Burnham, 1st Baron.**

Levy-Lawson (lē'vi.lô'sǫn), **Edward.** See **Burnham, 1st Baron.**

Lewes (lö'is), **George Henry.** b. at London, April 18, 1817; d. there, Nov. 28, 1878. An English philosophical and miscellaneous writer, largely influenced by the philosophy of Auguste Comte. Lewes was married in 1840, but in 1854 left his wife, living thereafter with George Eliot (Mary Anne Evans). He wrote a *Biographical History of Philosophy* (1845–46), *The Spanish Drama* (1847), *The Life of Goethe* (1855), *Seaside Studies* (1858), *Physiology of Common Life* (1859–60), *Studies in Animal Life* (1862), *Aristotle* (1864), *Problems of Life and Mind* (1874–79), *Actors and the Art of Acting* (1875), and *Physical Basis of Mind* (1877). He was the first editor (1865–66) of the *Fortnightly Review.*

Lewesdon Hill (lö'is.dǫn). A poem by William Crowe, published in 1788.

Lewin (lö'in), **Thomas.** b. April 19, 1805; d. Jan. 5, 1877. An English lawyer, antiquary, and writer. He wrote *A Practical Treatise on the Law of Trusts and Trustees* (1837), *The Life and Epistles of St. Paul* (1851), *An Essay on the Chronology of the New Testament* (1854), and other works.

Lewis XI (lö'is). In Shakespeare's *3 Henry VI,* the historical Louis XI, King of France. He promises aid to Margaret in her fight against Edward IV, then turns against her when Warwick offers to arrange Edward's marriage to Lewis's sister-in-law, Lady Bona. When Edward marries Lady Grey, Lewis is reconciled to Margaret and pledges arms to help restore Henry to the throne.

Lewis, Cecil Day. [Pseudonym, **Nicholas Blake;** original name, **Cecil Day-Lewis.**] b. at Ballintubber, Ireland, April 27, 1904—. An English poet and critic, with W. H. Auden and Stephen Spender a principal exponent of the "poetic political" school of the 1930's in England. Author of *The Friendly Tree* (1936), *Child of Misfortune* (1939), *Poetry for You* (1944), *The Poetic Image* (1947), a verse translation of Vergil's *Georgics* (1940), the modern morality play *Noah and the Waters,* as well as numerous detective novels under the pseudonym of Nicholas Blake. His verse includes *Transitional Poem* (1929), *From Feathers to Iron* (1931), *The Magnetic Mountain* (1933), *A Time to Dance* (1935), *Overtures to Death* (1938), and *Word Over All* (1943).

Lewis, C. S. [Pseudonym, **Clive Hamilton;** full name, **Clive Staples Lewis.**] b. at Belfast, Ireland, Nov. 29, 1898—. A British medievalist and Christian apologist. Author of *The Pilgrim's Regress* (1933), *The Allegory of Love* (1936), *Out of the Silent Planet* (1938), *The Screwtape Letters* (1942),

---

ḑ, d or j; ṣ, s or sh; ṭ, t or ch; ẓ, z or zh; o, F. cloche; ü, F. menu; čh, Sc. loch; ṅ, F. bonbon.

Perelandra (1943), *Christian Behaviour* (1943), *That Hideous Strength* (1945), *The Great Divorce* (1945), *Miracles* (1947), and *Transposition* (1949).

Lewis, David. b. in Wales, c1683; d. at Low Leyton, Essex, England, in April, 1760. A British poet, author of *Philip of Macedon,* a tragedy (1727).

Lewis, D. B. Wyndham. [Full name, **Dominic Bevan Wyndham Lewis.**] b. 1894—. English journalist and writer, especially of biographies. His books include *On Straw and Other Conceits* (1927), *François Villon* (1928), *King Spider—Louis XI of France* (1930), *Emperor of the West, Charles V* (1932), *Ronsard* (1944), *Take it to Bed* (1944), *The Hooded Hawk—Or, the Case of Mr. Boswell* (1947), and *Four Favourites* (1948).

Lewis, Mrs. Ethelreda. b. in England; d. at Port Alfred, Cape of Good Hope province, South Africa, Aug. 1, 1946. A South African novelist. Author of *The Harp* (1925), *The Flying Emerald,* and *Mantis* (1926), novels of African life, she achieved an international audience with *The Life and Works of Alfred Aloysius Horn, an Old Visitor, Taken Down and Edited by Ethelreda Lewis* (1927; American title, *Trader Horn*) and *Harold the Webbed, or The Young Vykings* (1928). *Trader Horn* was one of the greatest popular successes of its time in the U. S.

Lewis, Sir George Cornewall. b. at London, April 21, 1806; d. at Harpton Court, Radnorshire, Wales, April 13, 1863. An English statesman, scholar, and author. He was poor law commissioner for England and Wales (1839–47), undersecretary for the home department (1848), financial secretary to the treasury (1850–52), chancellor of the exchequer (1855–58), home secretary (1859–61), and secretary for war (1861–63). He was editor of, and a contributor to, the *Edinburgh Review* from 1852 to 1855. His chief work is *Enquiry into the Credibility of the Early Roman History* (1855); among his other works are books on international law, the philosophy of politics, and ancient astronomy.

Lewis, John. b. at Bristol, England, Aug. 29, 1675; d. Jan. 16, 1747. An English biographer, antiquary, and bibliographer.

Lewis, Matthew Gregory. [Called "Monk" Lewis.] b. at London, July 9, 1775; d. at sea, May 14, 1818. An English poet, dramatist, and romance writer, best known as the author of the Gothic novel *Ambrosio, or the Monk* (1795), the most vivid exemplar of the tale of weird horror popular in the late 18th century, from which he was commonly known as "Monk" Lewis. He visited (1792–93) Weimar, became (1794) an attaché of the British legation at The Hague, was a member (1796–1802) of the House of Commons, and went to Jamaica (where he owned property) in November, 1815, and again toward the end of 1817. He also wrote *Village Virtues,* a satire (1796), *The Castle Spectre* (acted at the Drury Lane Theatre, London, Dec. 14, 1797), *Tales of Horror* (1799), *Alphonso, King of Castile,* a tragedy (1801), and *Adelgitha,* a tragedy (acted at Drury Lane, April 30, 1807).

Lewis, Wyndham. [Full name, **Percy Wyndham Lewis.**] b. 1884—. An English painter, draftsman, and writer, founder of vorticism, the first English abstract movement, which drew its subject matter from futurism and its method from the abstrac-

tionists. In 1914 and 1915 he published *Blast,* the official journal of vorticism; in 1921 and 1922 he published *The Tyro.* Meanwhile he abandoned pure abstraction and reintroduced the human figure. His principal paintings include *Plan of War* and *Women;* among his written works are *Tarr* (1918), *The Art of Being Ruled* (1926), *Time and Western Man* (1928), *The Wild Body* (1931), *Hitler* (1931), *Doom of Youth* (1932), *Men Without Art* (1934), *The Revenge for Love* (1937), *The Mysterious Mr. Bull* (1938), *The Hitler Cult* (1939), *The Vulgar Streak* (1941), *Anglosaxony* (1942), and *America and Cosmic Man* (1948).

Lewis Baboon (ba.bön'). See **Baboon, Lewis** and **Philip.**

Lewis Lambert Strether (lam'bèrt strē'thèr, streth'-èr). See **Strether, Lewis Lambert.**

Lewis, the Dauphin. [Also, **Louis.**] In Shakespeare's *Henry V,* the son of Charles VI of France. He sends Henry a present of tennis balls to mock his claim upon the French throne. He later boasts of French prowess when preparations are being made for the battle of Agincourt.

Lewis, the Dauphin. In Shakespeare's *King John,* the historical Louis (VIII), son of Philip II of France. To bring about peace with France a marriage is arranged between him and John's niece Blanch of Spain.

lexicography (lek.si.kog'ra.fi). **1.** The art or science of compiling lexicons or wordbooks; the scientific exposition of the forms, pronunciation, signification, and history of words.
2. The act or process of making a dictionary.

Such is the fate of hapless lexicography, that not only darkness, but light, impedes and distresses it: things may be not only too little but too much known, to be happily illustrated.
(Johnson, *Pref. to Dict.*)

lexicon (lek'si.kon). A wordbook; a vocabulary; a collection of the words of a language, usually arranged alphabetically and defined and explained; a dictionary: now used especially of a dictionary of Greek or Hebrew.

In the lexicon of youth which Fate reserves for a bright manhood, there is no such word as—fail.
(Bulwer, *Richelieu.*)

Leyden (lā'den), **John.** b. at Denholm, Roxburghshire, Scotland, Sept. 8, 1775; d. at Batavia, Java, Aug. 28, 1811. A Scottish poet, physician, and Orientalist. An assistant to Walter Scott, he helped in gathering material for *Minstrelsy of the Scottish Border.* He wrote descriptive and other poetry based on Scottish scenes and traditions and translated material from the Persian and the Arabic. He was appointed (1803) assistant surgeon at Madras, traveled extensively in India, settled at Calcutta in 1806, was made assay-master of the mint there in 1810, and went to Java in 1811. He published *A Historical and Philosophical Sketch of the Discoveries and Settlements of the Europeans in Northern and Western Africa at the Close of the Eighteenth Century* (1799), an "Essay on the Languages and Literature of the Indo-Chinese Nations" (in *Asiatic Researches*), and others.

Leyland (lē′lạnd), **John.** See **Leland** or **Leyland, John.**

L'Hermite (ler.mēt′), **Tristan.** See **Tristan L'Hermite.**

Liar, The. See **Lyar, The.**

Liars, The. A comedy (1897) by Henry Arthur Jones.

Libeaus Desconus (lib′i.us des.kọ.nös′). [From **Li Biaux Desconneus,** meaning "The Fair Unknown."] A Middle English verse romance (14th century), dealing with the exploits of Gingelein, bastard son of Gawain, who frees the Queen of Sinadoun from her captivity after various adventures and then weds her. Chaucer refers to it in *The Rime of Sir Thopas* as the romance of "Sir Lybeux." The source of the poem is a French romance resembling *Le Bel Inconnu.*

Libel of English Policy, The. [Also, **The Libell** (Little Book) **of Englische Policye.**] A Middle English poem (c1436) dealing with England's foreign trade and her commercial policy. The poem was included by Hakluyt.

Libertine, The. A tragedy by Thomas Shadwell, produced in 1675. It is derived from Rosimond's *Nouveau Festin de Pierre.*

Libitina (lib.i.tī′nạ). The ancient Italian goddess of gardens and vineyards. By confusion with the word "libido" she was mistakenly regarded as a goddess of passion. Later Venus became identified with her as Venus Libitina, especially in her aspect as goddess of death and of burials. In this aspect she was later identified with Proserpine. By tradition, a piece of money was deposited in her temple for every one who died in Rome.

Libra (lī′brạ). An ancient zodiacal constellation, representing an ordinary pair of scales. This constellation was not commonly used among the Greeks, its place being occupied by the Chelae, or Scorpion's Claws. It is found, however, in all the Egyptian zodiacs going back to 600 B.C.; but there is reason to believe that it is not so old as the rest of the zodiac (that is, 2,000 years or more B.C.). Its principal stars, Kiffa Borealis and Kiffa Australis, 2.7 and 3.0 magnitudes respectively, are at the base of an isosceles triangle of which Antares forms the vertex.

libretto (li.bret′ō). **1.** a book containing the words of an extended musical composition, like an opera or an oratorio.
2. The words themselves of such a work; the text.

Libya (lib′i.ạ). In ancient geography, a name of varying signification, denoting Africa, or Africa excluding Egypt, or Africa excluding Egypt and Ethiopia.

Lichas (lī′kạs). In Greek legend, the friend of Hercules whom Deianira sent to him bearing (unwittingly) the poisoned shirt which caused the hero's death. Neither Lichas nor Deianira knew the fatal powers of the shirt. Hercules in pain and rage hurled Lichas into the sea.

Liddell (lid′ẹl), **Henry George.** b. at Binchester, Durham, England, Feb. 6, 1811; d. at Ascot, Berkshire, England, Jan. 18, 1898. An English clergyman and classical scholar, dean (1855–91) of Christ Church, Oxford. He published (1843) with Robert Scott a Greek lexicon, based on Franz Passow's German work, and considered the standard Greek-English lexicon. He also wrote *History of Ancient Rome* (1855), and others. Among the many children of his marriage (1846) to Lorina Reeve was Alice, his second daughter, for whom Lewis Carroll (C. L. Dodgson) wrote *Alice's Adventures in Wonderland* and *Through the Looking-Glass.*

Liddell Hart (lid′ẹl härt′), **Basil Henry.** b. Oct. 31, 1895—. An English military authority and writer. He was military correspondent (1925–39) for several newspapers, including the London *Times.* He is also known for his development of the battle drill system (1917), the "expanding torrent" method of attack, and other tactical innovations later officially adopted. He was an early exponent of air power and of mechanization, his theories being highly influential in the development of modern battle strategy. Author of *New Methods of Infantry Training* (1919), *Science of Infantry Tactics* (1921), *The Remaking of Modern Armies* (1927), *The Decisive Wars of History* (1929), *Foch— The Man of Orléans* (1931), *T. E. Lawrence—In Arabia and After* (1934), *A History of the World War, 1914–18* (1934), *The Defence of Britain* (1939), *The Strategy of Indirect Approach* (1941), *The Revolution in Warfare* (1946), *The Other Side of the Hill* (1948), and *Defence of the West* (1950).

Lido (lē′dō). [Also, **Lido di Venezia** (dē vā.ne′tsyä).] An island and resort town in NE Italy, a part of Venice, situated ab. 2 mi. SE of the center of the city and bordering on the open Adriatic Sea. It is one of the most fashionable seashore resorts in Europe, and is much frequented by foreign visitors. The airport of Venice is at the N end of the island. Length of island, ab. 8 mi.

Lie, The. A poem by Sir Walter Raleigh in which the poet tells his soul to go forth into the world "to give the lie" to all the different forms of hypocrisy.

Lie Circumstantial and **Lie Direct.** See under **Retort Courteous.**

Lieutenant. In Shakespeare's *Coriolanus,* an officer in Aufidius's army, whose account of Coriolanus's popularity and superiority on the battlefield arouses Aufidius's jealousy (IV.vii).

Lieutenant. In Shakespeare's *3 Henry VI,* the Lieutenant of the Tower who apologizes to King Henry for having kept him prisoner (IV.vi).

Life and Death of Harriett Frean (har′i.ẹt frēn), **The.** A psychological novel by May Sinclair, published in 1922.

Life and Death of Jason (jā′sọn), **The.** A poem (1867) by William Morris.

Life and Death of King John, The. See **King John.**

Life and Death of Mr. Badman, The. An allegory by John Bunyan, published in 1680, which points out the evil end that comes to all wickedness. Mr. Badman's story is told by Mr. Wiseman to Mr. Attentive; this dialogue form Bunyan took from *The Plain Man's Pathway to Heaven,* one of the two religious books owned by his wife which greatly influenced him. Mr. Badman travels through life making trouble for everyone, especially for his two wives, and lives by swindling and cheating.

He finally dies unrepentant, his sins accompanying him "to gnaw him in his conscience for ever and ever."

Life and Death of Richard Yea-and-Nay (rich'ard yā'and.nā'). A historical novel by Maurice Hewlett, published in 1900.

Life and Death of Thomas, Lord Cromwell (krom'-wel, -wĕl, krum'-), **The.** See **Thomas, Lord Cromwell.**

Life and Death of Tom Thumb the Great, The. See **Tom Thumb the Great.**

Life and Opinions of Tristram Shandy, Gentleman (tris'tram shan'di), **The.** See **Tristram Shandy.**

Life in London. See **Tom and Jerry, or Life in London.**

Life of King Henry the Fifth, The. See **Henry V.**

Life of Mr. Jonathan Wild the Great (jon'a.than wīld), **The.** See **Jonathan Wild.**

Life of Timon of Athens (tī'mon; ath'enz), **The.** See **Timon of Athens.**

Ligarius (li.gār'i.us). In Shakespeare's *Julius Caesar*, one of the conspirators against Caesar. He does not, however, take part in the assassination.

Light (līt), **Christina.** A character in the novels *Roderick Hudson* (1876) and *The Princess Casamassima* (1886) by Henry James.

Light Articles Only. Short stories and sketches by A. P. Herbert, published in 1921. It was issued in America under the title *Little Rays of Moonshine.*

Light Brigade, Charge of the. See **Charge of the Light Brigade.**

Lightfoot (līt'fut), **John.** b. at Stoke-upon-Trent, England, March 29, 1602; d. at Ely, England, Dec. 6, 1675. An English Hebraist and rabbinical scholar. He was vice-chancellor of Cambridge University (1654). He was appointed to a prebend at Ely in 1668. His chief works are *Horae Hebraicae et Talmudicae* (1658–74), and an incomplete *Harmony of the Four Evangelists* (1644 et seq.). He assisted Brian Walton in the preparation of the *Polyglot Bible* (1657).

Lightfoot, Joseph Barber. b. at Liverpool, England, April 13, 1828; d. at Bournemouth, England, Dec. 21, 1889. An English prelate and scholar, made bishop of Durham in 1879. He became a fellow of Trinity College, Cambridge, in 1852, and Hulsean professor of divinity in 1861. In 1871 he was appointed a canon of Saint Paul's. He was an influential member of the committee for the revision of the New Testament. He published commentaries on Saint Paul's Epistles to the Galatians (1865), the Philippians (1868), and the Colossians and Philemon (1875), *A Fresh Revision of the New Testament* (1871), an edition of Ignatius and Polycarp (1885), sermons, addresses, and others.

Light of Asia (ā'zha, ā'sha), **The.** A poem by Sir Edwin Arnold, published in 1878.

Light of the World, The. A poem by Sir Edwin Arnold, published in 1890.

Light That Failed, The. A novel by Rudyard Kipling, published in 1890.

Ligurian Republic (li.gū'ri.an). The name assumed by the republic of Genoa, formed on the model of France, in 1797. It was formally annexed to France in 1805; French control ended with the fall of Napoleon.

Like Bayes's Troops (bāz'iz). See **Bayes's Troops, Like.**

Likely Story, A. A novel by William De Morgan, published in 1911.

Lilburne (lil'bėrn), **John.** b. at Greenwich (now part of London), c1614; d. at Eltham (now part of London), Aug. 29, 1657. An English political agitator and Puritan pamphleteer. He was arrested Dec. 11, 1637, on the charge of printing unlicensed books (William Prynne's and others), whipped and pilloried, and imprisoned until released at the opening of the Long Parliament. At the battle of Brentford he was taken prisoner, and was subsequently tried for treason, but was exchanged in 1643, and became (1644) lieutenant colonel of dragoons. He refused to take the covenant and resigned from the army in 1645, dissatisfied with the Presbyterian dominance and aiming for a more democratic establishment. He was several times imprisoned and fined for attacks on persons of authority, and finally tried for sedition. Notwithstanding his acquittal, he was transferred to the Tower of London, thence to Elizabeth Castle, Guernsey, and from there to Dover Castle (October, 1655). He became a Quaker, and shortly after that Cromwell released him. He wrote a large number of controversial pamphlets.

Lilian (lil'i.an). A novel by Arnold Bennett, published in 1922.

Lilith (lil'ith). In the Bible and in Talmudic tradition, a demon that dwells in deserted places, mentioned in Isa. xxxiv. 14 as a screech owl. She is otherwise depicted as a female roaming in the night, especially dangerous to children and to women in childbirth. Lilith is probably of Babylonian origin: a demon of waste places, whose name occurs frequently in the incantations. In rabbinical tradition Lilith was Adam's first wife, created simultaneously with Adam and therefore his equal. Unwilling to take an inferior role, she left Adam, and was expelled from Eden. One variant of the story says she slept with Adam once more after this and give birth to evil spirits. In Mohammedan legend, she became the consort of the Devil and gave birth to evil spirits. However, for her disobedience and defiance, she was condemned to lose all her offspring forever. In Talmudic legend, she became a night demon who slept with men who slept alone, causing nocturnal emissions. By medieval times the legend was that Lilith envied all mothers their children and would take them unless special precautionary magic was observed.

Lillibullero (lil''i.bu.lē'rō) or **Lilliburlero** (-bėr.lē'rō). A political song satirizing James II of England, who had made an unwelcome nomination to the lord-lieutenancy of Ireland. The words were written (c1686) by Thomas Wharton (1648–1715). It is claimed that the music, originally a quickstep march, was by Henry Purcell, but it is also said to have been known in Ireland in the first quarter of the 17th century. The song is the merest doggerel, but contributed a great impetus to the revolution of 1688. The whole army and the people sang it constantly. The refrain "Lillibullero bullen a la" was specially adapted to the music of the quickstep with which the soldiers were familiar.

Lilliput (lil′i.put). The country on the shore of which Lemuel Gulliver is wrecked, in Swift's *Gulliver's Travels*. The inhabitants (the Lilliputians) are so small that Gulliver is a giant to them.

Lilliput. An interlude (performed between other dramatic performances) taken from Swift's *Gulliver's Travels*, produced by David Garrick in December, 1756. It was played by children whom he trained himself.

Lilliputians (lil.i.pū′shans). The pygmy inhabitants of the imaginary country of Lilliput, described in Swift's *Gulliver's Travels*.

Lillo (lil′ō), **George.** b. near Moorfields, London, Feb. 4, 1693; d. at London, Sept. 3, 1739. An English dramatist. He wrote *Silvia, or the Country Burial*, a ballad-opera (acted 1730); *The Merchant*, renamed *The London Merchant, or the History of George Barnwell*, and often called *George Barnwell* (acted 1731), long a successful play; *Britannia, or the Royal Lovers* (acted 1734); *The Christian Hero* (acted 1735); *Fatal Curiosity* (acted 1736); *Marina* (1738), based on Shakespeare's *Pericles;* and an adaptation of an Elizabethan play, *Arden of Feversham*, completed after Lillo's death by John Hoadly (acted 1759).

Lilly (lil′i), **William.** [Pseudonym, **Zadkiel.**] b. at Diseworth, Leicestershire, England, May 1, 1602; d. at Hersham, Surrey, England, June 9, 1681. An English astrologer. He was the author of a series of almanacs (1644–80, yearly), of many prophetic pamphlets, of *Christian Astrology* (1647), which was long an authority on the subject (reprinted as *Introduction to Astrology*, 1852), of *True History of King James I, and King Charles I* (1651), and of *The History of Lilly's Life and Times* (1715), an autobiography.

Lillyvick (lil′i.vik), **Mr.** In Dickens's *Nicholas Nickleby*, a collector of London water-taxes who marries Henrietta Petowker and is presently forsaken by her for a "half-pay captain, . . . a bottle-nosed captain that any man might have considered himself safe from."

Lily or **Lilye** (lil′i), **William.** b. at Odiham, Hampshire, England, c1468; d. at London, Feb. 25, 1522. An English grammarian, a friend of Colet, Erasmus, and More, and one of the first teachers of Greek in England. He studied the classics in Italy under Sulpicius and Pomponius Laetus, and in 1512 was appointed high master of Colet's school in Saint Paul's Churchyard. He contributed a Latin syntax (*Grammatices rudimenta*) to the *Æditio* of Colet (written probably c1509), and, with the aid of Erasmus, wrote a syntax (*Absolutissimus de octo orationis partium constructione*), published in 1513. The two (*Æditio* and *Absolutissimus*) were revised and combined as a Latin grammar (1540), entitled *Institutio compendiaria totius grammaticae*, which was again issued, in altered form, in 1574, under the title *A Short Introduction of Grammar*. In this form it was used and quoted by Shakespeare. It was the national Latin grammar, and continued in popular use in various editions for many years.

Lily Dale (dāl). See **Dale, Lily.**

Lily Maid of Astolat (as′tō.lat). In Arthurian legend, Elaine of Astolat, who died of love for Sir Lancelot.

Limberham (lim′bėr.am), **Mr.** See **Kind Keeper, or Mr. Limberham, The.**

Limbo (lim′bō). A name given to that region of the afterworld to which go the souls of those who die unsaved through no fault of their own. Medieval cosmography locates it on the edge of hell; Dante numbered it as first of the ten circles of hell. It is inhabited by the souls of unbaptized infants, the souls of the ancients who never heard of Christ, and the souls of fools who knew no better than to live as they did.

limerick. A form of nonsense verse first occurring in *Anecdotes and Adventures of Fifteen Young Ladies* and *The History of Sixteen Wonderful Old Women* (1820). It was later popularized by Edward Lear in his *Book of Nonsense.* It has been asserted that the name is derived from a custom whereby a group of people would extemporize on nonsense themes following each stanza with the line "Will you come up to Limerick?"

Linacre (lin′a.kėr), **Thomas.** b. probably at Canterbury, England, c1460; d. at London, Oct. 20, 1524. An English physician and classical scholar, a pioneer in the New Learning of the Renaissance in England, the projector and one of the founders of the College of Physicians at London, and the founder of lectureships at Oxford and Cambridge. He was elected fellow of All Souls College, Oxford, in 1484, and traveled and studied in Italy, taking the degree of M.D. at Padua. He returned to Oxford, where he had among his pupils in Greek Thomas More and Erasmus. Soon after Henry VIII came to the throne, Linacre was appointed one of his physicians and thereafter lived chiefly at London. He received priest's orders in 1520. He published grammatical works and translations, especially of Galen, from Greek into Latin.

Lincoln (ling′kon), **Bishop of.** In Shakespeare's *Henry VIII*, the historical John Longland. The King asks him to admit that he formerly advocated the divorce (II.iv).

Lincoln College. One of the colleges of Oxford University. It was founded in 1427 by Richard Fleming, bishop of Lincoln, who dedicated it to the Blessed Mary and All Saints. It is the college of John Wesley, and of John Morley, biographer of Voltaire and Rousseau. One of its rectors was Mark Pattison, Milton scholar, and the original of Casaubon in *Middlemarch*.

Lincoln's Inn. One of the London Inns of Court. It takes its name from the Earl of Lincoln who built his town house here in the 14th century, on property originally belonging to the Black Friars.

Lincoln's Inn Fields. The largest square in London, near the junction of High Holborn and Chancery Lane. It was laid out by Inigo Jones.

Lindabrides (lin′da.brīdz). A character in the *Mirror of Knighthood*, belonging to the Amadis cycle of romances. She is often mentioned by old writers. Lindabrides became with them a common name for a mistress or a courtesan.

Lindisfarne (lin′dis.färn). See **Holy Island.**

---

d̦, d or j; s̩, s or sh; t̩, t or ch; z̩, z or zh; o, F. cloche; ü, F. menu; ċh, Sc. loch; ṅ, F. bonbon.

Lindor (lin'dôr). A poetical name for a lover, usually a shepherd lover.

Lindsay (lin'zi), Lady **Anne.** See **Barnard,** Lady **Anne.**

Lindsay, Sir **David.** [Also, **Lyndsay.**] b. 1490; d. before April 18, 1555. A Scottish poet and diplomat. He was appointed (c1529) Lyon king at arms, and an usher in the household of Prince James, who later became James V of Scotland. His poetry, in the Chaucerian tradition, attacked the vices of the church and is considered as one of the factors that aided the Reformation in Scotland. He was the author of *The Complaynt to the King* (1529), *Ane Satyre of the Three Estaits* (1540, a dramatic poem satirizing abuses in church and state, acted again in 1555), *The Monarchie* (1543, his last and longest poem), and *The Register of the Arms of the Scottish Nobility and Gentry* (first published in 1821).

Lindsay, David Alexander Edward. [Titles: 27th Earl of **Crawford,** 10th Earl of **Balcarres.**] b. at Aberdeen, Scotland, Oct. 10, 1871; d. at Wigan, Lancashire, England, March 8, 1940. A Scottish politician. He served (1914–16) as an enlisted man in World War I. He was in Lloyd George's cabinet as lord privy seal (1916–18), was chancellor of the Duchy of Lancaster (1919–20), first commissioner of works (1921–22), minister of transport (1922), and was appointed (1926) presiding officer of the government committee on radio development. Author of books on art, such as *Donatello* (1903) and *The Evolution of Italian Sculpture* (1909).

Lindsay, Philip. b. at Sydney, Australia, May 1, 1906—. An English historian and novelist. Author of *Morgan in Jamaica* (1930), *King Richard III* (1933), *King Henry V* (1934), *Kings of Merry England* (1936), *Crowned King of England* (1937), *Mirror for Ruffians* (1939), and other historical studies. His works of fiction include the novels *Panama is Burning* (1932), *Here Comes the King* (1933), *London Bridge is Falling* (1934), *Gentleman Harry Retires* (1937), *Bride for a Buccaneer* (1938), *The Fall of the Axe* (1940), *Jack Laughs at Locksmiths* (1943), and *He Rides in Triumph* (1945), as well as motion-picture scenarios.

Lindsay, Robert. b. at Pitscottie, Fifeshire, Scotland, c1500; d. c1565. A Scottish writer.

Linet (li.net'). [Also, **Lynette.**] In Arthurian romance, the sister of Lionês of Castle Perilous. In Malory's *Morte d'Arthur* she engages Gareth to rescue Lionês. He does so, and marries her. Tennyson treats the story in his *Gareth and Lynette.*

Lingard (ling'gärd), **Jim.** The hero of Joseph Conrad's novel *Lord Jim* (1900). He appears also in *Almayer's Folly* and *The Rescue.*

Lingard, John. b. at Winchester, England, Feb. 5, 1771; d. at Hornby, Lancashire, England, July 17, 1851. An English Roman Catholic priest and historian. He wrote *A History of England* (8 vols., 1819–30; last edition, revised by the author, 10 vols., 1849–51), *The Antiquities of the Anglo-Saxon Church* (1806, enlarged as *The History and Antiquities of the Anglo-Saxon Church,* 1845), and others.

Lingo (ling'gō). A character in Samuel Foote's *Agreeable Surprise.*

Linkinwater (ling'kin.wô.tèr, -wot.ėr), **Tim.** In Dickens's *Nicholas Nickleby,* the faithful and trustworthy clerk of Cheeryble Brothers.

Linklater (lingk'lä''tèr), **Eric.** b. in the Orkney Islands, 1899—. An English novelist and biographer. Author of *White Man's Saga* (1929), *Poet's Pub* (1929), *A Dragon Laughed* (1930), *Juan in America* (1931), *Ben Jonson and King James* (1931), *The Men of Ness* (1932), *Mary Queen of Scots* (1933), *Robert the Bruce* (1934), *The Devil's in the News* (1934), *The Lion and the Unicorn* (1935), *God Likes Them Plain* (1935), *Juan in China* (1937), *The Impregnable Women* (1938), *Judas* (1939), *The Wind on the Moon* (1944), *Private Angelo* (1946), *The Art of Adventure* (1947), *Sealskin Trousers* (1947), *A Spell for Old Bones* (1949), *Mr. Byculla* (1950), and *Laxdale Hall* (1952).

Linley (lin'li), **George.** b. at Leeds, England, 1798; d. at London, Sept. 10, 1865. English composer and poet, best known as the author of numerous popular songs.

Linley, William. b. at Bath, England, c1771; d. at London, May 6, 1835. An English writer and composer. He was for a time (1790–96, 1800–06) in the service of the East India Company at Madras. He was the author of several operatic pieces, glees, and others, *Shakespeare's Dramatic Lyrics* (1816), and several novels and poems.

Linnet (lin'et), **Kitty.** A poor and pretty actress, the chief character in Samuel Foote's *The Maid of Bath.*

Linskill (lin'skil), **Mary.** [Pseudonym, **Stephen Yorke.**] b. at Whitby, Yorkshire, England, Dec. 13, 1840; d. there, April 9, 1891. An English novelist. Author of *Tales of the North Riding* (1871), *Cleveden* (1876), and *The Haven under the Hill* (1886).

Linton (lin'ton), **Eliza.** [Maiden name, **Lynn.**] b. at Keswick, England, Feb. 10, 1822; d. at London, July 14, 1898. An English novelist and author; wife of William James Linton.

Linton, William. b. at Liverpool, England, April 22, 1791; d. at London, Aug. 18, 1876. An English landscape painter and writer. Author of *The Scenery of Greece and its Islands* (1856), *Colossal Vestiges of the Older Nations* (1862), and others.

Linton, William James. b. at London, Dec. 7, 1812; d. at New Haven, Conn., Dec. 29, 1897. An Anglo-American engraver and author. A republican and a Chartist, he was engaged in journalistic work in England until 1867, when he removed to the U. S., living first at New York, and then at New Haven, Conn., where he had an engraving establishment. His works include *Claribel, and Other Poems* (1865), *A History of Wood-Engraving in America* (1882), *Poems and Translations* (1889), *European Republicans* (1892), *The Life of John Greenleaf Whittier* (1893), and *Threescore and Ten Years* (1894; also published as *Memories,* 1895).

Lintot (lin'tot), **Barnaby Bernard.** b. at Southwater, Sussex, England, Dec. 1, 1675; d. at London, Feb. 3, 1736. An English bookseller, noted as the publisher of the translations of the *Iliad* and *Odyssey,* and other works of Pope. He is a prominent figure in the literary anecdotes of the period.

fat, fāte, fär, ȧsk, fãre; net, mē, hèr; pin, pīne; not, nōte, möve, nôr; up, lūte, pùll; ᴛн, then;

Linus (lī'nus). Song of lamentation for the death of vegetation or for the "killing" (i.e., cutting or reaping) of the vine and grain, anciently sung in Phoenicia and W Asia at the time of vintage and harvest. Sappho identified Linus with Adonis, and the Linus song with the Adonis songs, sung all over W Asia, Asia Minor, and into Greece and the Mediterranean region as the Adonis cult spread. Sir James G. Frazer suggested that the name Linus was a corruption of the words *ai lanu*, meaning "woe to us," expressing grief for the death of Adonis, symbolized in the cutting of the grain. Herodotus mentions a like song of mourning being sung by Egyptian reapers.

Lion. In Shakespeare's *Midsummer Night's Dream*, the part played by the joiner, Snug, in the interpolated play.

Lionel Carteret (lī'ọ.nẹl kär'tẻr.ẹt). See **Carteret, Lionel.**

Lionês (lī.ọ.nes'). [Also, **Lyones**.] In Malory's *Morte d' Arthur*, the sister of Linet. She is imprisoned in the Castle Perilous, and rescued and married by Gareth.

Lion of the North. See **Gustavus Adolphus.**

Lir (lir). See **Ler.**

Lisbeth Bede (liz'bẹth bēd'). See **Bede, Lisbeth.**

Lisle (lēl), **Claude Joseph Rouget de.** See **Rouget de Lisle.**

Lisle or **L'Isle** (līl, lēl), **William.** b. at Tandridge, Surrey, England, c1579; d. in September, 1637. An English scholar and poet.

Lismahago (lis.mạ.hā'gō), **Obadiah.** A proud, disputatious, but honorable Scottish officer, in Tobias Smollett's novel *Humphry Clinker*.

Lissardo (li.sär'dō). A conceited manservant in Susannah Centlivre's comedy *The Wonder.* His voluble love affair with Flora forms the underplot of the play.

Lister (lis'tẻr), **Joseph.** [Title, 1st Baron **Lister of Lyme Regis**.] b. at Upton, Essex, England, April 5, 1827; d. at Walmer, Kent, England, Feb. 10, 1912. An English surgeon, the founder of antiseptic surgery. Though Ignaz Semmelweiss had used antiseptic measures earlier in combating puerperal fever, his method was more or less empirical and Lister is credited with being the first to practice antisepsis as a germ-destroying method. He is also responsible for the use of ligatures which are absorbed by the body and for drainage tubes in wounds and incisions, the practice until his introduction of the latter having been to leave long protruding ends on ligatures to facilitate drainage. Lister's methods, combined with the earlier invention of anesthesia, extended the range of surgical intervention and made possible many operations until then impossible.

Lister, Thomas Henry. b. near Lichfield, England, 1800; d. at Kent House, Knightsbridge, London, June 5, 1842. An English novelist and dramatist.

Listners, The. A volume of verse (1912) by Walter De la Mare, containing the famous poems "An Epitaph" and "The Listners." The latter is a description of a traveler coming to the door of a seemingly deserted house in a forest:

But only a host of phantom listners
    That dwelt in the lone house then
Stood listening in the quiet of the moonlight
    To that voice from the world of men.

Lisuarte (lis'ụ.ärt). In the Amadis romances, the grandson of Amadis.

Lisuarte of England. In *Amadis of Gaul*, the king of England, and the father of Oriana, the wife of Amadis.

Literary Club. A club founded in 1764 by Sir Joshua Reynolds, Samuel Johnson, and others. It met originally at the Turk's Head in Gerrard Street, London, and continued to meet there till 1783. After several removals, in 1799 it settled in the Thatched House in St. James's Street. The name was changed to "the Johnson Club," and on the taking down of the Thatched House the club removed to the Clarendon Hotel in Bond Street, where it celebrated its centennial in 1864.

Literary Lapses. A collection of humorous sketches (1910) by Stephen Leacock.

Lithgow (lith'gō), **William.** b. at Lanark, Scotland, 1582; d. probably at Lanark, c1645. A Scottish traveler in Europe and the Near East, mostly afoot. He was the author of *The Totall Discourse of the Rare Adventures and Painfull Peregrinations of Long Nineteen Years* (1614, 1632).

litotes (lit'ọ.tēz). In rhetoric, a figure in which an affirmative is expressed by the negative of the contrary. Thus, "a citizen of no mean city" means one "of an illustrious city."

litterateur (lit.ẹ.ra.tẻr'). A literary man; one who is engaged in literary work; one who adopts literature as a profession.

Littimer (lit'i.mẻr). In Dickens's novel *David Copperfield*, the valet of Steerforth.

Little (lit'l), **Thomas.** A pseudonym of Thomas Moore. He published a volume of love poems in 1808 under this name. He was also spoken of as "Master Little."

Little Billee (bil'ē). A comic ballad by W. M. Thackeray, based on a story very old in English literature, about three sailors who decide to eat Little Billee, the youngest of the three, when their food runs out. However, Little Billee manages to escape with his life.

Little Britain (brit'ạn). See **Britain, Benjamin.**

Little Dorrit (dor'it). A novel by Charles Dickens. It was first published serially from December, 1855, to June, 1857. It is an elaborated and highly plotted novel involving, among other things, attacks upon imprisonment for debt and upon the inefficiency and red tape of parliamentary and governmental procedure (which are satirized under "the Circumlocution Office"). George Bernard Shaw called this novel "a more seditious book than *Das Kapital*."

Little Dream, The. A drama (1911) by John Galsworthy.

Little Em'ly (em'li). See **Em'ly, Little.**

Little Englander. In English politics until c1920, an opponent of the colonial extension or territorial aggrandizement of the empire.

Little French Lawyer, The. A comedy by John Fletcher and Philip Massinger, written c1620 and printed in 1647. The plot is from *The Spanish Rogue*, a novel which was also used by Mateo Alemán in his *Guzmán de Alfarache*.

Little Gidding. The last of the *Four Quartets* by T. S. Eliot, published in 1942. Eliot again reiterates the notion of the oneness of the beginning and the end: "The end is where we start from . . . We die with the dying . . . We are born with the dead."

Little-Go. See **Smalls.**

Little John (jon). In the English Robin Hood ballad cycle, one of the chief followers of Robin Hood, said to have been one John Nailor. He was enormously tall and strong, a devoted friend and supporter of Robin Hood. He is probably best known through the ballad *Robin Hood and Little John* (Number 125 in Child's *English and Scottish Popular Ballads*) although he figures in most of the other ballads also.

Littlejohn (lit′l.jon), **Hugh.** A name given to John Hugh Lockhart, son of John Gibson Lockhart and grandson of Sir Walter Scott, for whom the latter wrote *Tales of a Grandfather*.

Little Minister, The. A novel by J. M. Barrie, published in 1891.

Little Musgrave and Lady Barnard (muz′grāv; bär′nard). An old ballad, included in Percy's *Reliques*, telling of the treachery of a page in revealing to Lord Barnard the love tryst of Little Musgrave and Lady Barnard. Lord Barnard comes upon them, kills them, and afterwards feels great remorse. Beaumont and Fletcher refer to Musgrave in *The Knight of the Burning Pestle* and D'Avenant refers to him in *The Wits*.

Little Nell (nel). A child character in the novel *Old Curiosity Shop*, by Charles Dickens. The passage describing her death, in which Dickens unconsciously wrote blank verse, is generally considered one of the classics of Victorian sentimentalism.

Little Nell's Grandfather. See **Grandfather, Little Nell's.**

Little Parliament. [Also, **Barebone's Parliament.**] The Parliament convened by Cromwell July 4, 1653, after he had dissolved the Rump Parliament: so called from the small number (about 140) of its members. It constituted Cromwell Lord Protector. It is also called, from Praisegod Barbon or Barebone, one of its members, "Barebone's Parliament."

Little Rays of Moonshine. American title of **Light Articles Only.**

Little Red Horses. A novel by G. B. Stern, published in 1932. It was issued in America under the title *The Rueful Mating*.

Little Red Ridinghood. See **Red Ridinghood, Little.**

"Little Sister," the. See **Brandon, Mrs.**

Littleton (lit′l.ton), **Sir Thomas.** b. at Frankley, Worcestershire, c1407 (some authorities say 1422); d. there, Aug. 23, 1481. An English jurist. He was made justice of the Common Pleas April 27, 1466, and was the author of a famous work (in the French then standard in English law) on tenures, which, with Edward Coke's commentary, was long the authority on the English law of real property.

Littlewit (lit′l.wit), **John.** A foolish proctor in Ben Jonson's *Bartholomew Fair*. He adores his hypocritical wife, Winifred. Possibly he is a satire on Samuel Daniel, the poet and dramatist.

Littré (lē.trā), **Maximilien Paul Émile.** b. at Paris, Feb. 1, 1801; d. there, June 2, 1881. A French philologist and philosopher. He took up the study of medicine, but his decided taste for literary labors induced him to turn his attention to the acquisition of Greek, Arabic, and Sanskrit. He was a fervent advocate of the doctrine of positivism, and greatly admired Auguste Comte. At the death of Comte, Littré was recognized as head of the positivist school. His great work is the *Dictionnaire de la langue française* (1863–72). He made a French translation of the works of Hippocrates (10 vols., 1839–61), and also published translations of David Friedrich Strauss's *Life of Jesus* (1839–40) and Pliny's *Natural History* (1848). He edited the works of Armand Carrel (1857), and a new *Dictionnaire de médecine de Nysten* (1855). Besides a number of books and papers on positivism, he wrote *Le Choléra oriental* (1832), *Histoire de la langue française* (1862), *Études sur les barbares et le moyen-âge* (1867), *Médecine et médecins* (1871), *Restauration de la légitimité et de ses alliés* (1873), *La Science au point de vue philosophique* (1873), *Littérature et histoire* (1875), and *De l'établissement et la troisième république* (1880).

Liutprand (lē′ut.pränd) or **Luitprand** (lö′it.pränd). d. 972. An Italian chronicler. He served under Hugh of Provence and Berengar, kings of Italy, and under the emperor Otto I, who made him (961) bishop of Cremona. He went on several diplomatic missions, notably to Constantinople in 949 and 968, the latter embassy to arrange for the marriage of Theophano to Otto (later Otto II). His writings include *Antapodosis*, a history of the years 887 to 950, *Historia Ottonis*, an account of the years 960 to 964 of Otto I's reign, and *Relatio de legatione Constantinopolitana*, his most famous and most valuable work, describing his second embassy to Constantinople and containing much valuable material on the Eastern and Western empires of his day.

Livelihood. Poems (1917) by W. W. Gibson.

Lives and Characters of the English Drama. See under **Account of the English Dramatick Poets, An.**

Livia (liv′i.a). In Thomas Middleton's play *Women Beware Women*, an artful court lady who betrays Bianca, the young wife of Leantio, to the lust of the Duke.

Livingstone (liv′ing.ston), **David.** b. at Blantyre, near Glasgow, March 19, 1813; d. at Chitambo, in central Africa, April 30, 1873. A British missionary and explorer in Africa. After working in a cotton mill from the age of ten, he entered college in 1837 and received a medical degree in 1840. He left England in 1840 as medical missionary to Bechuanaland, south Africa. He discovered Lake Ngami in 1849, crossing the Kalahari Desert. In

1851 he traveled down the Zambezi River and in the next several years explored the water system of that part of the continent. In 1855 he again traveled down the Zambezi, from what is now Angola, discovering Victoria Falls, and reaching Quelimane in 1856. The result of these years of exploration was a general filling-in of the map of Africa from the Tropic of Capricorn northward. He returned to England in 1856 and published *Missionary Travels and Researches in South Africa* (1857). He resigned from the London Missionary Society and in 1858 left as head of a government expedition to the Zambezi. The party explored the Zambezi and Shire rivers and Lake Nyasa, which they discovered in September, 1859. Further exploration in the area revealed widespread slave trading, which Livingstone renewed his resolve to wipe out. On his return (1864) to England, he published *Narrative of an Expedition to the Zambezi and Its Tributaries* (1865). Appointed British consul in central Africa with the express aims of destroying the slave trade and determining the watershed of the Nyasa-Tanganyika region, he returned to Africa in 1866. He explored the Rovuma valley in 1866, the Chambezi in 1867, and lakes Tanganyika, Moero, and Bangweulu in 1867–68. Worn with fever, he spent some months at Ujiji early in 1869, navigated Lake Tanganyika, but was driven back by the Manyema and by slavers to Ujiji, where he arrived Oct. 13, 1871. On Oct. 18, the expedition headed by H. M. Stanley, sent out expressly to find Livingstone, reached Ujiji; the famous encounter of the two men began with Stanley's anticlimactic "Dr. Livingstone, I presume." Together they explored the northern part of Tanganyika; they parted (1872) in Unyamwezi. Livingstone returned to Lake Bangweulu, where in Chief Chitambo's village on the south shore he died of dysentery. His body was brought to England and he was buried in Westminster Abbey April 18, 1874. His journals covering the years 1866–73 were published as *Last Journals of David Livingstone in Central Africa* (1874). Livingstone's example was followed by many missionary explorers and he may be said to have opened up the African continent. In addition to his exploration, he was influential in reducing the slave trade appreciably.

Livy (liv'i). [Latin name, **Titus Livius**.] b. at Patavium (Padua), 59 B.C.; d. there, 17 A.D. A Roman historian, the most important prose writer of the Augustan age. He wrote a comprehensive history of Rome, from the founding of the city to the death (9 B.C.) of Drusus, in 142 books, of which only 35 are extant (1–10 and 21–45), although the content of the lost books (except for two) is known through epitomes, and also several philosophical dialogues and a work on rhetorical training. He spent the greater part of his life (over 40 years of which were given to his history) at Rome.

Liza Doolittle (li'za dö'lit.l). See **Doolittle, Liza**.

Liza of Lambeth (lam'beth). A novel by W. Somerset Maugham, published in 1897. His first novel, it draws upon the author's early experiences as a medical student (experiences which were to be used again as a background for *Of Human Bondage*)

in London. The work deals with slum life in that city.

Lizzie Hexam (liz'i hek'sam). See **Hexam, Lizzie**.

Llewellyn (lö.el'in), **Richard**. [Pen name of **Richard David Vivian Llewellyn Lloyd**.] An English writer. He served five years in the army, which he left in 1931, and has been employed (1931 *et seq.*) in the production of motion pictures. During World War II, he was an officer in the Welsh Guards. He published the mystery play *Poison Pen* (1938). His novels include *How Green Was My Valley* (1940; scenarized in 1941), *None But the Lonely Heart* (1943), and *A Few Flowers for Shiner* (1947).

Lloyd (loid), **Charles**. b. at Birmingham, England, Feb. 12, 1775; d. at Chaillot, near Versailles, France, Jan. 16, 1839. An English poet, a friend and pupil of Coleridge, with whom he lived for some time, and also a friend of Lamb. He became insane (c1815) and died in a madhouse.

Lloyd, Edward. fl. early 18th century. The keeper of a coffee house in Tower Street, London, and later (1692) of "Lloyd's Coffee House" in Lombard Street. His coffee house became the center of ship brokerage and marine insurance. He published a paper, *Lloyd's News* (September, 1696–February, 1697), which was revived as *Lloyd's List* (1726), containing shipping and commercial news. From him the association and the corporation now known as Lloyd's were named.

Lloyd, Edward. b. at Thornton Heath, Surrey, England, Feb. 16, 1815; d. at Westminster, London, April 8, 1890. A London publisher. He founded (1842) *Lloyd's Illustrated London Newspaper*, and was the proprietor (1876 *et seq.*) of the *Daily Chronicle*.

Lloyd, Robert. b. at Westminster, London, 1733; d. in the Fleet Prison, London, Dec. 15, 1764. A British poet. He wrote *The Actor: a Poetical Epistle* (1760), and others. He was imprisoned for debt in 1763.

Lloyd's (loidz). An association at the Royal Exchange, London, comprising underwriters, merchants, shipowners, and brokers, for the furtherance of commerce, especially for marine insurance and the publication of shipping news. It originated in meetings at Lloyd's Coffee House about 1688. It publishes *Lloyd's List*.

Lludd (lud). See **Lud**.

Llyr (lēr). In Brythonic mythology, the personification of the sea, and father of Bran (who was interpreted as a kind of sea deity) and of Manawydan, the old Brythonic sea god. Llyr is cognate with the genetive (Lir) of Ler, father of the Old Irish sea god, Manannan.

Loadstone (lōd'stōn), **Lady**. The "magnetic lady" in Ben Jonson's play of that name.

Lochiel (loch.ēl'). See **Cameron of Lochiel**.

Lochiel's Warning. A poem by Thomas Campbell; so called from its subject, Donald Cameron of Lochiel.

Lochinvar (loch.in.vär', lok'in.vär). A ballad in the poem *Marmion* by Sir Walter Scott; so called from the name of its hero, the young Lochinvar, who suddenly arrives at the bridal feast of Ellen, his beloved, and a man considered to be "A laggard

d, d or j; s, s or sh; t, t or ch; z, z or zh; o, F. cloche; ü, F. menu; ch, Sc. loch; n, F. bonbon.

in love and a dastard in war," and rides off with Ellen.

Locke (lok), **Alton.** See **Alton Locke, Tailor and Poet.**

Locke, John. b. at Wrington, Somersetshire, England, Aug. 29, 1632; d. at Oates, High Laver, Essex, England, Oct. 28, 1704. An English philosopher. Upon graduating from Christ Church College, Oxford, he continued to live in the university town, where he was intermittently a lecturer on Greek and on rhetoric, and censor of moral philosophy. In December, 1665, he accompanied Sir Walter Vane as secretary of a mission to the elector of Brandenburg, and after his return to Oxford in January, 1666, he studied medicine, and even practiced it for a short while, but did not take a medical degree. In 1667 he became a member of the household of Baron Ashley, at first as a physician, later as a confidential agent. Ashley being one of the proprietors of Carolina, in 1669 Locke drew up his celebrated constitution for that colony. When Ashley, in 1672, was created 1st Earl of Shaftesbury and became Lord Chancellor of the realm, Locke was appointed secretary of presentations, and the following year was made secretary of the Board of Trade. After Shaftesbury's fall from power in 1675, Locke went to France, remaining until 1679 and enjoying the company of that country's philosophers and scientists. After his return to England he fell under the suspicion of the government as a supposed radical, and found it necessary to take refuge in Holland, where he remained until 1689. The accession of William of Orange to the English throne led to Locke's return and to his appointment as a commissioner of appeals, but after 1691 he was a member of the household of Sir Francis Masham at High Laver in Essex. Locke's most famous and influential work, the *Essay Concerning Human Understanding*, published in 1690, was followed by *Some Thoughts Concerning Education* (1693), and *The Reasonableness of Christianity* (1695), while his *Letters on Toleration* appeared on various occasions. Locke engaged in little metaphysical speculation, but his insistence on the senses (or, more precisely, on things, events, or conditions perceived by the senses) as the origin of all knowledge laid the ground for the empiricism which so importantly shaped subsequent British and French thought. In no derogatory sense he has been called a practical philosopher, who thought in terms of human experience and built his system upon observable data, though at the same time he accepted the concepts of Protestant Christianity, including the existence of souls and the belief in personal immortality. He perceived that it is the nature of man to pursue happiness, and he prescribed piety as a check upon the passions. Although he himself wished to bar atheists and Roman Catholics from the area of toleration, he recognized that different men may hold very different views with equal sincerity. However, it is perhaps as a political philosopher that Locke was most important. In the late 17th and in the 18th centuries, when nations were struggling to throw off the surviving dead weight of feudalism, to curb monarchical despotism, and to grapple with new economic problems, his plausible, reasoned, cautiously liberal proposals, with their safeguards for property and their promise of stability and peace, attracted wide attention and approval. Hume and Kant, Voltaire and Rousseau, were among those whom he influenced, as well as the authors of the American Declaration of Independence and of the Constitution of the United States.

Locke, William John. b. March 20, 1863; d. May 15, 1930. An English novelist. He wrote *The Morals of Marcus Ordeyne* (1905), *The Beloved Vagabond* (1906), *Septimus* (1909), *A Christmas Mystery* (1910), *Simon the Jester* (1910), *The Glory of Clementina Wing* (1911), *The Joyous Adventures of Aristide Pujol* (1912), *Stella Maris* (1913), *The Mountebank* (1921), *The Great Pandolfo* (1925), *The Kingdom of Theophilus* (1927), *Ancestor Jorico* (1929), and others.

Locked Chest, The. A drama (1916) by John Masefield.

Locker-Lampson (lok´ėr.lamp´sọn, -lam´-), **Frederick.** [Original name, **Frederick Locker.**] b. at London, May 29, 1821; d. at Rowfant, Sussex, England, May 30, 1895. An English poet. He married (1874) as his second wife the daughter of Sir Curtis Lampson, and assumed (1885) the name of Locker-Lampson. Among his poems are *London Lyrics* (1857, 1893). He edited *Lyra Elegantiarum* (1867) and *Patchwork* (1879), and contributed to various periodicals.

Lockhart (lok´ạrt, -härt), **John Gibson.** b. at Cambusnethan, Lanarkshire, Scotland, July 14, 1794; d. at Abbotsford, Roxburghshire, Scotland, Nov. 25, 1854. A Scottish author; son-in-law and biographer of Sir Walter Scott. He became an advocate in 1816, joined the staff of *Blackwood's Magazine* in 1817, married Sophia, the eldest daughter of Sir Walter Scott, in 1820, and edited (1825–53) the *Quarterly Review*. His principal work is the *Memoirs of the Life of Sir Walter Scott* (7 vols., 1837–38), generally placed among the best biographies in English. Among his other publications are *Peter's Letters to his Kinsfolk* (1819), *Adam Blair* (1822), and other novels, translations of *Ancient Spanish Ballads* (1823), and *The Ballantyne Humbug Handled* (1839), a pamphlet defending his account of Scott's relations with his publishers. Lockhart was also a biographer of Robert Burns and of Napoleon.

Lockhart of Carnwath (kärn.woth´), **George.** b. 1673; killed in a duel, Dec. 17, 1731. A Scottish Jacobite. He was named (1706) a commissioner for the union of Scotland and England, joined the rising of 1715 in favor of the Stuart Pretender, and was imprisoned but later freed without trial. While acting as confidential agent (1718–27) to Prince James Francis Edward Stuart in Scotland, he was detected (1727) but escaped to Holland. Author of *Memoirs of the Affairs of Scotland from Queen Anne's Succession . . . to the Commencement of the Union . . . 1707* (1714) and *Papers on the Affairs of Scotland* (1718), which contain much valuable material on the Jacobites.

Lockit (lok´it). The villainous jailer of Newgate in John Gay's *Beggar's Opera*. He has an agreement with Peachum, a receiver of stolen goods, to divide reward money for informing on highwaymen and pickpockets with whom he (Peachum) deals. In part, Lockit was a satire of Lord Townshend.

Lockit, Lucy. In John Gay's *Beggar's Opera*, the daughter of the jailer and rival of Polly Peachum for the love of Macheath.

Locksley (loks′li). The name assumed (from his reputed birthplace) by Robin Hood at the tournament at Ashby de la Zouche, in Sir Walter Scott's *Ivanhoe.*

Locksley Hall. A poem by Alfred Tennyson, published in 1842, considered one of his first poems of "social protest" and an affirmation of his belief in the progress of modern civilization: "Forward, forward let us range. Let the great world spin forever down the ringing grooves of change." But his essential complacency of attitude, noted by many critics, is revealed in the lines following: "Better fifty years of Europe than a cycle of Cathay." *Locksley Hall, Sixty Years After* was published in 1886, and here the poet expresses some doubts as to the worth of the "progress" he had earlier advocated.

Locrine (lŏ.krīn′, -krēn′). [Also, **Logris.**] A legendary king of Loegres, corresponding to modern England. He was the eldest son of Brut or Brutus, and father of the Sabrina celebrated in Milton's *Comus.* His story is told by Geoffrey of Monmouth in his *History of the Kings of Britain.*

Locrine. [Full title, **The Lamentable Tragedy of Locrine.**] A play published in 1595 and in the second issue of the third Shakespeare folio (1664) and variously attributed to Shakespeare, Peele, Marlowe, and Greene.

Locusta (lŏ.kus′ta). [Also, **Lucusta.**] A professional poisoner living at Rome c54 A.D. Juvenal speaks of her as the agent for ridding many a wife of her husband, and Tacitus as "long reckoned as among the instruments of government." She was employed by Agrippina to prepare a poison for the emperor Claudius. She was executed in the reign of Galba (c68 A.D.).

Lodbrok (lŏd′brŏk), **Ragnar.** See **Ragnar Lodbrok.**

Lodge (loj), **Sir Oliver Joseph.** b. at Penkhull, Staffordshire, England, June 12, 1851; d. at Amesbury, Wiltshire, England, Aug. 22, 1940. An English physicist and spiritualist, principal of the University of Birmingham from 1900, especially noted for his investigations in electricity, light, magnetism, and the nature of the ether. He was professor of physics (1881–1900) in University College, Liverpool. He published *Elementary Mechanics* (1877), *Modern Views of Electricity* (1889), *Pioneers of Science* (1893), *Electrons* (1907), *Science and Mortality* (1908), *The Ether of Space* (1909), *Reason and Belief* (1910), and others. He was president (1901–04) of the Society for Psychical Research.

Lodge, Thomas. b. at West Ham, near London, c1558; d. 1625. An English novelist, lyric poet, and dramatist. He studied at Trinity College, Oxford, and entered (1578) Lincoln's Inn, but soon left the study of law for a career as a writer. In 1579 or 1580 he published a reply, *Honest Excuses* (sometimes called *Defence of Poetry, Music and Stage Plays*), to Stephen Gosson's attack on the morality of the contemporary stage, *The School of Abuse.*

Gosson's rejoinder was answered by Lodge in the *Alarum Against Usurers* (1584), to which he appended a novel, *The Delectable History of Forbonius and Prisceria.* Lodge sailed in the Canaries expedition of 1588 and on a voyage to South America in 1591. He became an M.D. in 1602 and practiced medicine until his death. Among his works are *Rosalind, Euphues Golden Legacy* (1590), a novel written during the Canaries voyage, the source of Shakespeare's *As You Like It; Euphues Shadow: the Battaile of the Sences* (1592), and *A Margarite of America* (1596), novels; *The Wounds of Civil War* (1594) and *A Looking Glasse for London and England* (1594, with Robert Greene), plays; *Scillaes Metamorphosis* (1589) and *Phillis* (1593), poems; *A Fig for Momus* (1595), verse satire; and translations of Josephus and Seneca. Lodge's poetry is considered among the most tuneful and original of the Elizabethan period, despite his reliance on Italian and French originals.

Lodore Falls (lŏ.dōr′). A cascade in NW England, in Cumberland, near the S end of Derwent Water, ab. 4 mi. S of Keswick. Robert Southey, who lived at Keswick, wrote (1820) a poem, *The Cataract of Lodore*, describing the "way the water comes down at Lodore." Height, over 100 ft.

Lodovico (lō.dọ̄.vē′kō). In Shakespeare's *Othello*, a kinsman of Brabantio. He produces the letters (found in Roderigo's pockets) that incriminate Iago and, after Othello's death, vehemently denounces the villain.

Lodovico. The silent lover of Isabella in John Webster's *The White Devil.*

Lodowick (lŏ′dọ̄.wik, lod′ọ̄-), **Friar.** In Shakespeare's *Measure for Measure*, the name assumed by the disguised Duke Vincentio.

Loegres (lō′grēz). [Also: **Loegria** (-gri.a̧), **Logres** (lō′grẹz).] The name by which Geoffrey of Monmouth refers to England in his *Historia Regum Britanniae* (History of the Kings of Britain), from the name (Locrine or Logris) of the son of the legendary King Brut.

Logistilla (lō.jēs.tēl′lä). In *Orlando Furioso*, the sister of Alcina and Morgana. She represents Reason or Virtue.

Logris (lō′gris). See **Locrine.**

Lohengrin (lō′ẹn.grin). In medieval German legend, a knight of the swan, the son of Parzival, and a knight of the Holy Grail. He is carried in a boat drawn by a swan to Antwerp, where he becomes the husband of the Princess of Brabant, on the condition that she shall never ask who he is. She nevertheless breaks the agreement, and the swan comes with the boat and bears him away to the Grail. Allusion is made to his history at the end of the 13th-century poem *Parzival*, ascribed to Wolfram von Eschenbach, in which he is Parzival's son. He is also mentioned in the *Titurel*, written by one Albrecht between 1260 and 1270; and the same legend is the subject of the poem *Schwanritter* (The Swan Knight), by Konrad von Würzburg (d. 1287), who does not, however, connect his hero with the Grail.

Loki (lō′kē). In Old Norse mythology, the god of destruction, fire, mischief, and evil. His father was

---

ḍ, d or j; ş, s or sh; ţ, t or ch; ẓ, z or zh; o, F. cloche; ü, F. menu; ċh, Sc. loch; ṅ, F. bonbon.

the giant Farbauti (Old Norse, *Fárbauti*), his mother Laufey or Nal (Old Norse, *Nál*). By the giantess Angurboda (Old Norse, *Angrbodha*) he had three children: Jormungandr, the Midgard-serpent; the Fenris-wolf; and Hel. Loki had throughout a twofold nature. He was of handsome appearance but of evil disposition, and was at the same time the friend and the enemy of the gods. It was Loki who prompted the blind Hoder to cast the mistle-toe dart at Balder, thus causing his death. For his evil deeds he was finally seized by the gods and bound in a cave. Over him was set a serpent whose poison would have fallen in drops upon his face had not his wife, Signe, caught them in a bowl. Earthquakes are said to be caused by the writhing of Loki from the drops which fall on him while Signe is emptying the bowl. Loki will remain in this cave until Ragnarok, the end of the world, when he will lead the forces of evil against the gods.

Lokman (lok'man; Arabic, luk.män'). [Arabic, **Luqman**; called **"Lokman the Wise."**] The re-puted pre-Islamic compiler of a collection of fables and proverbs in Arabic. *Luqman* is the title of the 31st *surah* of the Koran, in the 11th verse of which are found the words "We gave to Luqman wis-dom." To this shadowy character have been ascribed the circumstances and sayings of a num-ber of men; hence Lokman has been represented as a nephew of Job or Abraham, a councilor of David or Solomon, Balaam, an ugly Ethiopian slave, a king of Yaman, a tailor, a carpenter, a shepherd. The fables are very like those of Aesop, and still more like those of Syntipas. They were first put into their present form by an Egyptian Christian named Barsuma, probably toward the end of the 13th century. They were first edited (with a Latin translation) by Erpenius (Leiden, 1615). Later editions are by Rödiger (2nd ed., 1839) and Deren-bourg (1850).

Lollards (lol'ardz). The English followers of John Wycliffe, adherents of a widespread movement, partly political and socialistic, and in some respects anticipating Protestantism and Puritanism, in the 14th and 15th centuries. They were also called "Bible men," from their reverence for the Bible. They differed on some points both among them-selves and from Wycliffe, but in the main con-demned the use of images in churches, pilgrimages to the tombs of saints, the temporal lordship of the clergy, the hierarchical organization, papal author-ity, religious orders, ecclesiastical decorations, the ceremony of the mass, the doctrine of transub-stantiation, waging of wars, and capital punish-ment. Some of them engaged in seditious proceed-ings, and they were severely persecuted for more than a hundred years, especially after the adoption of a special statute (*De hæretico comburendo*) against them in 1401. Under Henry IV the place of origin and intellectual center of the movement was cut off by close clerical supervision of Oxford Uni-versity; after that its principal followers were found among the landed gentry and the lower classes. Persecution became more severe under Henry V and in 1414 an uprising took place under the leadership of Sir John Oldcastle, formerly one of Henry's companions. Oldcastle was eventually captured and executed (1417) according to the

statute, one of the few who actually were burned. The movement continued, but gradually it lost force, although its doctrines, and its critical spirit towards Roman Catholicism, survived in the Ref-ormation. At the peak of the movement, probably one Englishman in four was a Lollard.

Lollius (lol'i.us). A nonexistent writer from whom Chaucer professed to have taken the story of his *Troilus and Criseyde*. Chaucer and others may have believed that there actually was a historian of Troy bearing that name, but this notion is usually ex-plained as arising from a misreading of Horace, *Epistolae*, I, 2, 1: "Trojani belli scriptorem, maxime Lolli."

Lolly Willowes, or The Loving Huntsman (lol'i wil'ōz). A novel by Sylvia Townsend Warner, published in 1926.

Lombard (lom'bärd, -bard; lum'-), **Peter.** [Also: **Peter the Lombard**; Latin, **Petrus Lombardus.**] b. at Novara, Italy, c1100; d. at Paris, c1160. An Italian theologian, appointed bishop of Paris in 1159. He was called "Master of Sentences," from his work *Sententiarum libri IV* (Four Books of Sentences). This work, one of the principal the-ological books of the Middle Ages, is a collection of opinions on various subjects and was widely used as a textbook in theology and widely commented upon. Of especial importance is its section on the sacraments, which sets forth the doctrine adopted as the official Roman Catholic doctrine at the Council of Trent (1546–47).

Lombard Street. A street in London, where the north Italian merchants (some, but not all, of whom were Lombards) of the Middle Ages established themselves before the reign of Edward II. In their day, with the Germans of the Hanseatic League at the Steelyard, they had a virtual monopoly of the more profitable branches of English trade. The gold-smiths seem to have had the most ready money. On occasion they lent money on interest, and gradually took up the business of banking, as it was then understood. They did not call themselves bankers, but kept "running cashes" or current accounts. In 1677 there were no less than 37 gold-smiths keeping "running cashes" in Lombard Street. The seizure by Charles I of 200,000 pounds stored in the Tower of London forced them to keep their money in circulation, and thus contributed the origin of modern systematic banking. Lombard Street remains to this day one of the world's great banking centers.

London (lun'don). [French, **Londres** (lôńdr); Ital-ian, **Londra** (lôn'drä); Spanish, **Londres** (lōn'drās); Latin, **Augusta, Londinium** (lon.din'i.um).] The capital of England, and the commercial and cul-tural center of the British Commonwealth. It is situated in SE England, and comprises the County of London, on both sides of the river Thames, ab. 50 mi. from its mouth. London was first mentioned as a seaport in a charter given by King Ethelbald, dated 734. The early growth of London was due in large part to its position at the head of tidewater navigation on the Thames, to the fact that it is on a natural routeway from the continent of Europe to England, and to the fact that it was situated at the lowest practical point for crossing the Thames

(Westminster Abbey is built near the ford which was the chief crossing before London Bridge was built). London was probably an ancient British town. One of the early determining factors of the site of London was the presence of hills which were safe from flood. It appears to have been resettled (c43 A.D.) by the Romans, and Londinium (called also Augusta) was the capital of Britannia in the last part of the Roman period. Watling Street, an important Roman road to Chester, had its S terminus here. After the departure of the Romans (c410) and in the early Saxon period its history is obscure, though there were bishops of London from the 7th century. However, London again became a major political center, this time because of its position of relative isolation from the Welsh and Danish menaces to the Saxon kingdom (it was once plundered by the Danes, but rebuilt by Alfred and Athelstan). It received a charter from William I (William the Conqueror), and many privileges from Henry I. Its lord mayor was one of the signatories of the Magna Charta. By the 14th century its commerce had greatly developed, and trade with the Hanseatic merchants continued until the 16th century. With the later growth of foreign trade, London's advantages and previous experience in the North Sea trade quickly brought the city a leading position in world commerce. London sided with the Yorkists in the Wars of the Roses, and with the Parliamentarians in the English Civil War. It was scourged by the plague in 1665, and was almost entirely destroyed by the great fire of 1666. Fifteen wards, 400 streets, 13,400 buildings, and 89 churches are said to have been destroyed. London is very important in the industrial economy of Great Britain. In 1935, Greater London had 24.8 percent of all industries in Great Britain. Heavy industry and textile manufactures are not present to any great extent, but it has a motor-car industry, machinery and engine manufactures, and manufactures of electrical apparatus. Other important industries include tin-plate manufactures, and lead, copper, brass, bronze, gold, and silver refining. London has 10 percent of all the ferrous and nonferrous metal refineries in the country. Food and tobacco processing are important. London has half of all the workers in England and Wales engaged in the printing and bookbinding trades. It is the leading British wool market (two thirds of all the wool imported into the United Kingdom is landed here), and has a large clothing industry. Shipbuilding, formerly important, is now almost nonexistent, only ship repair being carried on. Most of the industrial enterprises in London employ fewer than 100 workers each. The city is well served by a railroad and subway network radiating to the residential suburbs, and bus lines within the metropolitan district. About two thirds of the water supply for London is taken from the river Thames. Because of the many parks and the prevalence of buildings of from two to five stories, London covers a proportionately greater area than many other large European cities. It suffered heavily during World War II from air-raid and flying-bomb damage, mention of which is made under the headings of the separate metropolitan boroughs and districts of London. (For various objects of interest, such as the British Museum, the Guildhall, the Monument, the National Gallery, the Houses of Commons and Lords (of Parliament), Royal Academy, Saint Paul's Cathedral, the Tower of London, and Westminster Abbey, and for very many local details, see the special headings.)

London. A satirical poem (1738) by Samuel Johnson, written in imitation of Juvenal. It attacks the degeneracy of city life, the distasteful mores of the rich, and the emulation of French ideas and fashions.

London, City of. [Called "the City."] The historical "core" of London, including the area (ab. 380 acres) of the Roman Londinium and of the larger medieval walled London. It contained about one sixth of the total population of London as late as 1801, but its population has since declined drastically with the outward movement to the suburbs, and the virtually complete occupation of the City of London by offices. The first expansion took a westward direction toward Westminster, now a metropolitan borough of the County of London. As late as 1878, the City of London was separated from Westminster by Temple Bar, an archway across Fleet Street. In 1908, the 114 "parishes and places" in the City of London were unified and made one "Parish of the City of London." The City of London is under the control of the Corporation of London's Common Council, legally defined as "The Mayor and Commonalty and Citizens of Common Councilmen," consisting of the lord mayor, 25 aldermen, and 206 common councilmen. The Corporation maintains Billingsgate Market (for fish), and the London Central Markets (Smithfield Market; for meat, fish, poultry, provisions, vegetables, and flowers) in the City. In addition, it maintains Spitalfields Market, founded in 1682 (for vegetables, fruit, and flowers) in Stepney metropolitan borough, and the Metropolitan Cattle Market and slaughterhouses, in Islington metropolitan borough, from which meat is sent to Smithfield Market. Spitalfields Market was originally associated with the old fine-silk industry of the area. The City of London is the commercial heart of the British Commonwealth, with the Bank of England situated here. It has its own police force of 700 men, separate from the metropolitan police force of the County of London. The nighttime (resident) population of the City was 5,268 in the 1951 census; the daytime population is over a million. Area of City, ab. 677 acres (slightly over 1 sq. mi.).

London, University of. An educational institution founded 1836 in London.

London Assurance. A comedy by Dion Boucicault, produced in 1841.

London Company. A company of merchants and others, formed to plant colonies in America. It founded (1607) a colony at Jamestown, Va.

London Cuckolds, The. A comedy by Edward Ravenscroft, produced in 1681 and using part of Molière's *L'École des femmes* for its plot.

London Merchant: or, The History of George Barnwell (bärn'wel)**, The.** A tragedy by George Lillo, produced in 1731. It is founded on an old ballad preserved by Ritson and Percy.

London Nights. A volume of verse (1895) by Arthur Symons.

London Please. A collection of four Cockney plays by William Pett Ridge, published in 1925. The volume includes the plays *Some Showers, Early Closing, Damages for Breach,* and *Happy Returns.*

London Prodigal, The. A comedy published in 1605, attributed to Shakespeare at that time, and included by Chetwood in the second issue of the third folio (1664). It is not now considered to have been by Shakespeare.

London Snow. A short poem by Robert Bridges, describing a city snowfall at night and the reactions of the people in the morning.

London Stone. A stone preserved at London from some old monument. In Shakespeare's *2 Henry VI* (IV.vi), Jack Cade uses it as a symbol of the city when he announces that London is taken.

London Visions. A volume of verse (1908) by Lawrence Binyon.

London Wall. A Roman wall built (350–369) around London.

Lonely Queen, The. A historical novel by Henry Christopher Bailey, published in 1911.

Lonely Road. A novel by Nevil Shute, published in 1932.

Lonely Unicorn, The. A novel by Alec Waugh, published in 1922 and issued in America under the title *Roland Whately.*

Long (lông), **Gabrielle Margaret Vere.** [Pseudonyms: **Marjorie Bowen, George Runnell Preedy, Joseph Shearing;** maiden name, **Campbell.**] b. at Hayling, Hampshire, England, 1888; d. at London, Dec. 23, 1952. English writer. She was awarded (1923) the Eve's prize for *Windfall.* Author of the biographies *Mary, Queen of Scots* (1929), *Patriotic Lady,* about Emma Hamilton (1936), *This Shining Woman: a Life of Mary Wollstonecraft Godwin* (1937), *The Cockney's Mirror,* about William Hogarth (1936), and books on William Cobbett, John Wesley (1937), and John Paul Jones (1940); of the novels *General Crack* (1928), *My Tattered Loving* (1937), *Primula* (1940), and *The Abode of Love* (1944); and of the plays *Captain Banner* and *The Rocklitz.* Under the pseudonym Joseph Shearing she wrote *Forget-Me-Not* (1932; American title, *Lucile Cléry*), *Moss Rose* (1934), *Blanche Fury* (1939), and *The Fetch* (1942; American title, *The Spectral Bride*).

Long Acre. A street in London near Covent Garden, running into Drury Lane. It was long the headquarters of carriage builders.

Longaville (lông'ga.vil). In Shakespeare's *Love's Labour's Lost,* one of the three lords attending the King of Navarre at his rural academy. He falls in love with Maria.

Longdon (lông'don). A character in *The Awkward Age* (1899), a novel by Henry James.

Longespée (lông'ā.pā), **William de.** See under **Salisbury,** (3rd) **Earl of.**

Longest Journey, The. A novel by E. M. Forster, published in 1907.

Longinus (lon.jī'nus), **Gaius Cassius.** See under **Cassius.**

Long John Silver (sil'vėr). In Robert Louis Stevenson's *Treasure Island,* a piratical villain, but not without a certain charm.

Longland (lông'land), **John.** See under **Lincoln, Bishop of.**

Longman (lông'man), **Sir Hubert Harry.** b. Nov. 29, 1856; d. at London, March 16, 1940. An English publisher. He was a partner (1880–1933) in Longmans, Green and Company.

Longman, Thomas. b. at Bristol, England, 1699; d. at London, June 18, 1755. An English publisher. He was apprenticed to his uncle, John Osborn, a London bookseller, whose daughter he married (c1723) and with whom he later entered into partnership. He ultimately succeeded (c1734) to control of the business. He was a part owner of *Chambers's Cyclopædia* and of Johnson's *Dictionary.*

Longman, Thomas. b. at London, 1730; d. near London, 1797. An English publisher; nephew, partner, and successor of Thomas Longman (1699–1755).

Longman, Thomas. b. 1804; d. Aug. 30, 1879. An English publisher; son of Thomas Norton Longman (1771–1842). Entering the publishing firm established by Thomas Longman (1699–1755), he became partner (1832 *et seq.*) and head (1842 *et seq.*) of the house. During his management, the company published Macaulay's *Lays of Ancient Rome* and *History of England,* the novels of Benjamin Disraeli, and many works by distinguished 19th-century authors.

Longman, Thomas Norton. b. at London, 1771; d. at Hampstead, London, Aug. 29, 1842. An English publisher; son and successor of Thomas Longman (1730–97). He published, with Owen Rees, Lardner's and Rees's cyclopaedias, Lindley Murray's *English Grammar,* and works of Scott, Moore, Macaulay, Wordsworth, Southey, and others. After 1826 they were sole proprietors of the *Edinburgh Review.*

Longman, Thomas Norton. b. at Farnborough Hill, Hampshire, England, June 15, 1849; d. at King's Langley, Hertfordshire, England, Nov. 1, 1930. An English publisher; son of Thomas Longman (1804–79). He purchased (1890) the publishing business of the Rivington family, and published the Badminton Library, the Silver Library, the *English Historical Review,* the 12-volume *Political History of England,* the *Fairy Books* of Andrew Lang, the *Collected Works* of William Morris, and many other notable works.

Longman, William. b. Feb. 9, 1813; d. Aug. 13, 1877. An English publisher and author; son of Thomas Norton Longman (1771–1842), and brother of Thomas Longman (1804–79). He entered (1829) the Longman publishing house, becoming a partner in 1839. Author of *Journal of Six Weeks' Adventures in Switzerland, Piedmont, and on the Italian Lakes* (1856), *History of England to the Close of the Reign of Edward II* (1869), and *Life and Times of Edward III* (1869), and an essay, *History of the Three Cathedrals Dedicated to St. Paul in London* (1873).

Long Meg of Westminster (meg; west'min"stėr). A name given to a noted scold and procuress in the time of Henry VIII. A play with this name was performed at the Fortune Theatre in 1594. The name of "Long Meg" has since been given to a number of things of unusual length, particularly to a column of red freestone near Penrith, England. It is 15 ft. in circumference and 18 ft. high, and is supposed to be part of a Druidical temple.

Long Parliament. The Parliament which assembled on Nov. 3, 1640, and ruled during the English Civil War. On its showing a disposition to come to terms with the party of Charles I, it was purged (Dec. 6, 1648) by the army-enforced expulsion (Pride's Purge) of a large number of its members. With these members absent, the remaining members then declared the power of the House of Lords void, and appointed the High Court of Justice which tried and condemned the king; later both the House of Lords and the office of king were abolished. The Parliament was forcibly dissolved by Cromwell on April 20, 1653, but was twice restored in 1659, and was finally dissolved March 16, 1660, after providing for the summoning of a free Parliament. In its later history, especially after the 1648 purge, it was known as the Rump Parliament, since less than half of its original members were left.

Longus (long'gus). fl. probably 3rd or 4th century A.D. A Greek romancer and sophist. He is the reputed author of the pastoral romance *Daphnis and Chloe*. Nothing is known of his life.

Lonsdale (lonz'dāl), Earl of. See **Lowther**.

Look at All These Roses. A collection of short stories by Elizabeth Bowen, published in 1941.

Looking After Joan (jōn). A novel by John Palmer, published in 1923.

Looking-Glass for London and England, A. A play by Thomas Lodge and Robert Greene, written c1590 and published in 1594. The plot is the story of Jonah and the Ninevites, with satirical application to London and England. It was very popular with Elizabethan audiences.

Look, Stranger! [American title, **On This Island.**] A volume of poetry (1936) by W. H. Auden, comprised mostly of songs and poems concerned with problems of society. The title poem, "Look, stranger, on this island now," is generally considered one of the best and purest lyrics Auden has written. "Hearing of harvests rotting in the valley" (under the title "Paysage Moralisé") and "Casino" ("Only the hands are living; to the wheel attracted") are also considered noteworthy.

Look! We Have Come Through! A volume of verse (1918) by D. H. Lawrence.

Loom of Youth, The. A novel by Alec Waugh, published in 1917.

Lope de Vega (lō'pä dā Bā'gä). See **Vega, Lope de.**

Lorbrulgrud (lôr'brul.grud). The capital of Brobdingnag in Swift's *Gulliver's Travels.*

Lord Admiral's Men. [Also: **Admiral's Men;** until 1585, **Lord Howard's Company;** after 1596, **Earl of Nottingham's Company;** after 1603, **Prince Henry's Company;** finally, the **Elector Palatine's Company,** or **Palsgrave's Company.**] An Elizabethan and Jacobean theatrical company, led for a time by Edward Alleyn. This company and the Lord Chamberlain's Men were the two most important companies of the many that were performing on the Elizabethan stage. Henslowe's *Diary* gives more information about this company than is available about any other. When their first patron, Charles Howard, became, in 1585, Lord High Admiral, they changed their name from Lord Howard's Company to Lord Admiral's Men. For a time they joined Strange's Men and toured (1593–94) the provinces under the leadership of Edward Alleyn. In London after 1594, Henslowe (whose step-daughter had married Alleyn) was the backer and manager of the company, and received one half of the entrance money. They played at his Rose theater every weekday from October to Lent and from Easter to midsummer, when they left to tour the provinces for three months. After 1600 Alleyn, who had temporarily retired, resumed his acting career, and the company moved to the Fortune theater on the north side of the Thames. In 1596 they took the newest title of their patron as their name, and were called the Earl of Nottingham's Company. In the reign of James I they became known as Prince Henry's Company; later they were under the patronage of the Elector Palatine and were consequently called the Elector Palatine's Company, or, sometimes, the Palsgrave's Company.

Lord Chamberlain. In Shakespeare's *Henry VIII,* an official at Wolsey's feast and at the arraignment of Cranmer. He is in charge of the christening of the infant Elizabeth.

Lord Chamberlain's Men. [Also: **Chamberlain's Men;** until 1594, **Strange's Men** or **Derby's Men;** after 1603, **King's Men.**] An Elizabethan theatrical company. They had formerly been Strange's Men, or Derby's Men (after Lord Strange became the Earl of Derby in 1572). This earlier company, in existence from the 1560's, was a group of traveling actors until they began to perform in the 1580's at Court. In 1591 they played at the Curtain, in 1592 at the Rose. Their members included James and Richard Burbage, William Kempe, Thomas Pope, John Heming, and Augustine Phillips. As the Lord Chamberlain's Men, after 1594, they were under the patronage of Henry Carey, who became Lord Chamberlain in 1585, and his son, George Carey, who became Lord Chamberlain in 1597. About 1594 Shakespeare and Richard Burbage joined the company as shareholders as well as actors. It was this company that principally acted the plays of Shakespeare and Jonson. Probably they performed at the Swan and the Curtain until the Globe was built in 1599. Between 1594 and 1603 they gave 32 performances at Court. By the time they became the King's Men in 1603, they had presumably acted Shakespeare's *Two Gentlemen of Verona, A Comedy of Errors, Love's Labour's Lost, Midsummer Night's Dream, The Merchant of Venice, Richard II, Richard III, Henry IV, King John, Titus Andronicus,* and *Romeo and Juliet.* As the King's Men they continued acting at the Globe, until, in 1609, they moved to Blackfriars theater, which became their winter quarters. Between 1603 and 1616 they gave approximately 12 performances at Court each year. Shakespeare is last mentioned as an actor in their performance of Jonson's *Sejanus,* first acted in 1603. In 1611 they performed *Macbeth, Cymbeline, The Winter's Tale,* and Jonson's *Catiline.* In 1619, when they were issued a new patent, some new actors including Nathan Field joined them. The company dissolved in 1642 when the theaters were closed, but the actors of the company collaborated in publishing (1647) the first folio edition of Beaumont and Fletcher.

Lord Chancellor. In Shakespeare's *Henry VIII*, the historical Sir Thomas Wriothesley. He is president of the Council arraigning Cranmer.

Lord Chief Justice. In Shakespeare's *2 Henry IV*, the historical Sir William Gascoigne, the judge who warns Falstaff and orders him to repay Mistress Quickly. He later fears that Prince Hal as King may hold a grudge against him, because once Hal was imprisoned by his order. The new King, however, confirms his impartial justice and orders him to enforce the penalties against Falstaff and his followers.

"Lord Fanny" (fan'i). See **Hervey, John.**

Lord Howard's Company (hou'ạrdz). See **Lord Admiral's Men.**

Lord Jim (jim). A novel (1900) by Joseph Conrad, dealing with the efforts of an Englishman in the Malay country to atone for a single failure in courage.

Lord Linlithgow (lin.lith'gō). A novel by Morley Roberts, published in 1900.

Lord of Burleigh (bėr'li). A poem by Alfred Tennyson.

Lord of Misrule. See **Abbot of Misrule.**

Lord of the Isles. A title assumed intermittently from the 12th to the 16th century by various Scottish chieftains who maintained a status of virtual independence on the islands west of Scotland.

Lord of the Isles, The. A romance in verse (1815) by Sir Walter Scott.

Lord Ormont and his Aminta (ôr'mont; ạ.min'tạ). A novel by George Meredith, published in 1894.

Lord Raingo (rāng'gō). A novel by Arnold Bennett, published in 1926.

Lord's Cricket Ground. A cricket ground in England, probably the most famous one in the world. It is the contesting field for the most important British and international matches. In 1787 Thomas Lord, a then famous English cricketer, desired to secure a suitable ground for a metropolitan cricket club. He succeeded in obtaining a field now known as Dorset Square, the ground being called "Lord's" and the club the "Marylebone Club." Owing to the expansion of London and the consequent increase of rent, a new ground had to be sought, and the present site, on St. John's Wood Road, a little north of the old field, was purchased. The first recorded match on the original field was played in 1788, and the first contest on the present ground took place June 22, 1814.

Lords' Masque, The. A masque by Thomas Campion, originally produced with sets by Inigo Jones, presented as part of the festivities celebrating the marriage between Princess Elizabeth and the Elector Palatine in 1613.

Lord's Prayer. [Also: **Our Father, Pater Noster, Paternoster.**] The most widely known and used of Christian prayers. Its primacy arises from the fact that it is the one prayer which Jesus taught his disciples and instructed them to use. From the time when the Vulgate came into general use in the 5th century until the Reformation in the 16th century, this prayer was always spoken in Latin, even by uneducated persons, and in consequence was universally known as Pater Noster, from the first two words of the Latin version; as the title of the prayer, these two words are sometimes spelled as one, Paternoster. Since the Reformation, it is generally called by English-speaking Protestants the Lord's Prayer, and by English-speaking Roman Catholics the Our Father, from its first two words in English. The prayer derives from two passages in the New Testament, but principally from Matt. vi. 9–13, which are a part of the Sermon on the Mount. Another version appears in Luke, xi. 2–4, briefer than that in Matthew, and differing in other small respects. Saint Jerome believed that Jesus had explicitly commanded the daily recitation of the prayer; in any case, its inclusion in the Mass at an early date ensured its recitation many millions of times every day.

Lord Ullin's Daughter (ul'inz). A ballad by Thomas Campbell, published in 1809.

Lorel (lō'rẹl, lor'ẹl). In Ben Jonson's *Sad Shepherd*, a swineherd, lover of Earine.

Lorelei (lôr'ẹ.lī; German, lō.rẹ.lī'). [Also: **Loreley, Lurlei.**] A dangerous cliff 430 ft. above the Rhine, between St. Goar and Oberwesel, Germany, the traditional abode of a river nymph. It is the subject of poems by Heine and others, and of operas by Mendelssohn (fragmentary) and Lachner.

Lorenzo (lọ.ren'zō). In Shakespeare's *Merchant of Venice*, a Venetian gentleman in love with Jessica. He elopes with her, taking part of Shylock's treasure.

Lorenzo. The principal character in James Shirley's tragedy *The Traitor*, the kinsman and favorite of the duke; a subtle and traitorous schemer for the duke's death.

Lorna Doone: a Romance of Exmoor (lôr'nạ dōn'; eks'mör). A novel by Richard D. Blackmore, published in 1869.

Lorrain (lo.raṅ), **Claude.** See **Claude Lorrain.**

Lorraine (lo.ren'), **Henri de.** [Surnamed **Le Balafré;** title, 3rd Duke of **Guise.**] b. Dec. 31, 1550; d. at Blois, France, in December, 1588. A French general and politician; son of François de Lorraine, 2nd Duke of Guise. One of the instigators of the Saint Bartholomew Massacre (1572), he became head of the Holy League in 1576. In 1588 he entered Paris with an army, with a view to deposing the king, Henry III, and was popularly acclaimed. The residents of Paris rose against the king, who fled. At the instigation of the king, Guise was assassinated at Blois.

Lorrequer (lor'ẹ.kėr), **Harry.** The hero of *Harry Lorrequer*, a novel of adventure (1837) by Charles Lever.

Lorry (lor'i), **Mr. Jarvis.** In Dickens's *Tale of Two Cities*, a clerk of the London banking firm of Tellson and Company. He is a friend and companion of the Manettes during the period of their tribulations in the French Revolution.

Los (los). A principal character in the mystical poems of William Blake.

Lossie Thorpe (los'i thôrp'). See **Thorpe, Lossie.**

Lost Endeavor. A novel by John Masefield, published in 1910.

Lost Horizon. A novel by James Hilton, published in 1933.

Lost Leader, The. A poem by Robert Browning, referring to William Wordsworth, supposedly inspired by the latter's acceptance of the poet laureateship.

Lost Leader, The. A play about Charles Stewart Parnell, by Lennox Robinson, published in 1918. In it Parnell, the great Irish leader of the 19th century, returns to life during a riot, but is struck dead by a blind man, an ironic allegory of his ruin by his own people.

Lost Silk Hat, The. A short play (1914) of sophisticated humor, by Lord Dunsany.

Lost Tales of Miletus (mī.lē'tus, mi-), **The.** A volume of poems by Edward Bulwer-Lytton, published in 1866.

Lost Word, The. A novel by Evelyn Underhill, published in 1907.

Lot (lot). In the Old Testament, the son of Haran and nephew of Abraham. Gen. xiii. 1–12, etc.

Lot. In the writing of Geoffrey of Monmouth, a king of Norway; in Malory's *Morte d' Arthur*, a king of Orkney. In the first he marries Anne, sister of Arthur; in the second he marries Margawse, the sister of Arthur. Tennyson makes him the husband of Bellicent and king of Orkney.

Lothair (lō.thär'). A Norman knight in Matthew Gregory Lewis's tragedy *Adelgitha.*

Lothair. A novel by Benjamin Disraeli, published in 1870. Lothair is a young orphan of noble birth, left in the joint care of Lord Culloden and of a clergyman, who enters the Roman Catholic church and becomes Cardinal Grandison. The action centers around the attempts of the cardinal to convert Lothair to the Catholic faith in order to obtain his wealth and support for the church. Lothair comes of age at the time when the forces of Garibaldi are threatening the papal government, and he enters the fight on the side of Italian liberty. Those opposed to his becoming a Catholic are Lord Culloden, Lady Corisande, whom Lothair wants to marry, and the brave Theodora, a fighter for Italian freedom. Theodora is killed fighting the papal forces, and on her deathbed she makes Lothair promise never to become a Catholic. Lothair goes through many more adventures in his efforts to keep himself free from the schemes of the wily cardinal, and finally returns to England to marry Lady Corisande.

Lothario (lō.thär'i.ō). The principal male character in Nicholas Rowe's play *The Fair Penitent* (1703). He is a libertine ("that haughty gallant, gay Lothario"), the seducer of Calista, the fair penitent. His name has become the synonym for a fashionable and unscrupulous rake. He was the original of Richardson's Lovelace in *Clarissa Harlowe.*

Lot of Talk, A. A novel by Helen Ashton, published in 1927.

Lotophagi (lō.tof'a.gī). In Greek legend, especially as given in the *Odyssey*, the name of a people who ate the fruit of a plant called the lotus, conjecturally identified with various plants which have borne that name. Those of the followers of Odysseus (or Ulysses) who ate of it are described as being rendered forgetful of their friends, homes, and native land. The Lotophagi lived on the northern coast of Africa in Tripoli, and on the island of Meninx (Lotophagitis, modern Djerba) in Tunisia.

Louis (VIII) (lö'is, lö'i). See under **Lewis, the Dauphin.**

Louis XI. b. at Bourges, France, July 3, 1423; d. at Plessis-les-Tours, near Tours, France, Aug. 30, 1483. King of France (1461–83); son of Charles VII. He was married (1436) to Margaret of Scotland, daughter of James I, but the marriage was unhappy and she died in 1445, before he came to the throne. As dauphin, Louis was several times involved in plots against the king. He was a member of the Praguerie (1440); he quarreled with Agnes Sorel, the king's mistress and adviser, and thereafter plotted actively against the king until the plot was discovered and he was sent (1447) into Dauphiné. There he ruled with an iron hand; he allied himself with the bourgeoisie to break the power of the nobility; he entered into foreign intrigues in Italy, his marriage to Charlotte of Savoy in 1452, despite the refusal of the king to the alliance, being part of his diplomatic maneuvering. In 1456 Louis fled to Burgundy, fearing that the king, until then lenient towards his rebellious acts, might have him killed. His accession to the throne of France was followed by a general purge of the ministers of Charles VII. His own ministers were drawn principally from the middle class, although he did reinstate some of the more able of the ministers he had ousted; the reputation of many of these men was not of the best, but their ability was undeniable. Louis destroyed the power of the great feudatories, and laid the foundation of the absolute monarchy which afterward prevailed in France. The arbitrary measures which he adopted provoked a conspiracy of the nobles under the lead of Charles the Bold of Burgundy. The conspirators organized a "league of the public weal," and fought a drawn battle at Montlhéry in 1465, but succumbed to the diplomacy of the king, who detached by bribery the league's leaders, Charles the Bold and the Duke of Berry. While this temporary alliance was maintained, he proceeded to destroy his less formidable opponents. Then he made war on Charles, who had allied himself with Edward IV of England by marrying the king's sister Margaret; Louis captured Normandy but found himself captured (1468) by Charles during an interview. He bought his way out by treaty but inflicted severe punishment on those he held responsible for the fiasco. He supported the English Lancastrians against the Yorkist allies of Charles the Bold, aiding the expedition of Warwick and Margaret that put Henry VI again on the English throne. But Edward regained the throne, and Charles of Burgundy was successful in the fighting in France. The death (1472) of the king's brother Charles, nominally leader of the coalition of nobles against the king, forced Charles of Burgundy to come to terms and permitted Louis to consolidate his hold on the French throne. In the next few years he firmly established, against the claims and military force of Aragon, the French border at the Pyrenees. He maintained a continuous intrigue against Charles the Bold, supporting and encouraging others to fight against him and buying off (1475) Charles's ally Edward IV of England. On the death of Charles at the battle of Nancy against the Swiss in January, 1477, he united the duchy of Burgundy to the French crown, but the marriage of Charles's daughter Mary to Maximilian of Austria (later Maximilian I of the Holy Roman Empire) left Flanders in Austrian hands. In 1480 he annexed the duchies of Anjou and Bar; in 1481, Maine and Provence; in 1482, Picardy, Artois, and Franche Comté. His influence in Italy was great, especially in the north, but his diplomacy failed in Spain, where the marriage (1469) of Ferdinand and Isabella united Aragon and Castile. The last years of his life were spent in fear of murder and in isolation, surrounded by guards and attended by physicians and astrologers.

Louis XI. See also **Lewis XI.**

Louis XIV. [Called **Le Grand** (lẹ grän), "the Great," and **le Grand Monarque**, meaning "the Great Monarch"; also **Le Roi Soleil**, meaning "the Sun King."] b. at St.-Germain-en-Laye, France, Sept. 5, 1638; d. at Versailles, Sept. 1, 1715. King of France (1643–1715); son of Louis XIII and Anne of Austria. He ascended the throne under the guardianship of his mother, who chose Cardinal Mazarin as her chief minister. The early years of his reign were marked by the end of the Thirty Years' War with the Treaty of Westphalia (1648), the Wars of the Fronde (1648–53), and the cession by Spain of Rousillon in the Peace of the Pyrenees (1659). He was declared of age at 14, but despite popular objection to him retained Mazarin in office until the cardinal's death in 1661, when he assumed personal control of the government. Not once during his 73-year reign did he convene the States-General. He assumed the direction of affairs at a time when the policy inaugurated by Richelieu and continued by Mazarin had made the Bourbons absolute at home and paramount abroad. The reforms of J. B. Colbert, who replaced Nicolas Fouquet as comptroller-general of the finances (1661–83), swelled his treasury while promoting industry and economy; and those of Louvois, his minister of war (1666–91), transformed his army into the most perfect military organization in Europe. His desire of conquest and dreams of a French universal monarchy embroiled him in numerous wars, in which his military forces were led by Turenne, Condé, Luxembourg, Catinat, Villars, Vendôme, and Vauban. His first war, the War of Devolution (1667–68), was fought with Spain on account of the Spanish Netherlands, which he claimed through his wife Maria Theresa, daughter of Philip IV of Spain, whom he had married in 1660. It was ended by the treaty of Aix-la-Chapelle, and resulted in the acquisition of a number of fortified towns on the Belgian frontier. His second war (1672–78) was directed against Holland supported by the Empire, Spain, Brandenburg, and Sweden, and resulted in the acquisition of territory

from Spain and Austria at the peace of Nijmegen. In 1681 he annexed Strasbourg and other cities on the Rhine. His third war, the War of the League of Augsburg (1688–97), was with England, the Netherlands, the Empire, Spain, and Savoy, and concerned the Palatinate, to which he laid claim. It was unsuccessful, and was ended by the peace of Ryswick, by which Alsace and Strasbourg were formally ceded to France. His fourth war (1701–14) concerned the succession in Spain, whose throne he claimed for his grandson, Philip of Anjou. This war, the great War of the Spanish Succession, he fought, after 1703, almost single-handed against the bulk of Europe. Faced by such generals as Marlborough and Eugene, the French suffered the great defeats of Blenheim (1704), Ramillies (1706), Oudenarde (1708), and Malplaquet (1709). The peace of Utrecht (1713) and of Rastatt and Baden (1714) secured Spain for his grandson, Philip V, but left Louis with an exhausted treasury and a broken army. As a result of these wars, of the fiscal policy which he introduced after the death of Colbert, and of his bigoted and intolerant policy, including the revocation (1685) of the Edict of Nantes, toward the Huguenots, which drove 50,000 families from France, the country was prostrated, and the way prepared for the French Revolution. The reign of Louis XIV, the longest in European history, has been styled the Augustan Age of France, and certainly the flowering of the arts and the magnificence of the court are unparalleled. Louis is famous for his dictum, "L'état c'est moi" (I am the state), but, while he did possess absolute power, it was through his capable ministers that he succeeded so well in the middle period of his reign. The king's mistresses, Mademoiselle de la Vallière, Madame de Montespan, and Madame de Maintenon, all influenced him greatly.

Louisa Chick (lö.ē′zạ chik′), **Mrs.** See **Chick, Mrs. Louisa.**

Louisa Gradgrind (grad′grīnd). See **Gradgrind, Louisa.**

Louis Napoleon (lö′i nạ.pō′lē.ọn, -pōl′yọn). See **Napoleon III.**

Louis Philippe Scatcherd (lö′i fi.lēp′ skach′ẽrd), **Sir.** See **Scatcherd, Sir Louis Philippe.**

Louis the Dauphin (lö′is, lö′i). See **Lewis, the Dauphin.**

Louis dei Franchi (lö′i dä′ē fräng′kē). See **Franchi.**

Louka (lö′kạ). A scheming servant-girl in George Bernard Shaw's *Arms and the Man.*

Lourdes (lörd). A town in SW France, in the department of Hautes-Pyrénées, situated at the foot of the Pyrenees ab. 13 mi. SW of Tarbes. It is a tourist center, but has become more famous as a place of pilgrimage since a 14-year-old shepherdess, Bernadette Soubirous (Saint Bernadette), was believed to have had (1858) several miraculous visions of the Holy Virgin here. A huge basilica was consecrated (1876) near the grotto where the vision is said to have appeared. The town is visited by hundreds of thousands of pilgrims annually.

Lousiad (lous′i.ad), **The.** A poem by John Wolcot, published in 1785, written in a mock-heroic style, satirizing George II, in which a louse appeared on a pea served to the king, causing him to order all the kitchen servants to shave their heads.

Louvre (lövr). A castle (at Paris) of the kings of France from or before the 13th century, and the chief royal palace until Louis XIV built Versailles. The existing palace was begun by Francis I, whose chief architect was Pierre Lescot, in 1541, and was extended (additions being designed by Jacques Lemercier, Louis Levau, and others) by his successors down to Louis XIV, who added much, including the imposing east front, designed by Claude Perrault, with its celebrated Corinthian colonnade, 570 ft. long, with 28 pairs of coupled columns. Napoleon I made some additions, to which Napoleon III added very largely; and a large section of the north wing was rebuilt after it had been burned by the Commune. The whole forms one of the most extensive and historically interesting buildings in the world. The façade on the west side of the court ranks as perhaps the most perfect example of the style of the early French Renaissance; the additions of Catherine de Médicis are also architecturally important. Those of Napoleon III, designed by Visconti and Lefuel, are of great richness, with profuse use of sculpture. In the interior the splendid Galerie d'Apollon, rebuilt by Louis XIV, is one of the few apartments which retain their original aspect. A great part of the interior has been occupied since 1793 by the famous museum, and successive governments have employed the best artists at their command for its decoration.

Love. A play by J. Sheridan Knowles, produced in 1839

Love à la Mode. A farce by Charles Macklin, written in 1759 and printed in 1793.

Love Among the Artists. A novel by G. B. Shaw, published in 1884.

Love and a Bottle. A comedy by George Farquhar, produced in 1699.

Love and Business. A miscellany by George Farquhar, printed in 1702.

Love and Honour. A play (1634) by Sir William D'Avenant, written for performance at Court. It emphasizes the theme of Platonic love, which was enjoyed by the Queen of Charles I.

Love and Lucy (lö'si). A novel by Maurice Hewlett, published in 1916.

Love and Mr. Lewisham (lö'i.shạm). A semiautobiographical novel by H. G. Wells, published in 1900.

Love at a Venture. A comedy by Susannah Centlivre, printed in 1706. It is founded on Thomas Corneille's *Le Galant doublé* and may also owe something to Dryden's *Secret Love*.

Loveby (luv'bi). The "wild gallant" in John Dryden's play of that name.

Love Chase, The. A comedy by J. Sheridan Knowles, produced in 1837.

Love Chase, The. A historical novel with a psychological theme by Maurice Hewlett, published in 1905.

Love for Love. A comedy by William Congreve, printed in 1695.

Love in a Forest. A play adapted from Shakespeare's *As You Like It* and *A Midsummer Night's Dream* by Charles Johnson in 1722.

Love in a Maze. A comedy by James Shirley, licensed in 1631. The title was borrowed by Dion Boucicault for a comedy in 1844.

Love in a Riddle. A pastoral ballad opera by Colley Cibber, written in imitation of *The Beggar's Opera*, printed in 1729, and played at the Drury Lane Theatre, London, on Jan. 7, 1729. It was later converted into *Damon and Phillida*, after being hooted down on its opening night by political enemies of Cibber. Theophilus Cibber, son of Colley, later rewrote the alteration as *Damon and Phillida: or, The Rover Reclaim'd*.

Love in a Village. A comic opera with text by Isaac Bickerstaffe, produced in 1762 and printed in 1763 (7 editions). The music is by Arne, Handel, Galuppi, and others.

Love in a Wood, or St. James's Park (sānt jām'zẹz). A play by William Wycherley, produced c1671. It shows a series of love affairs according to social classes, and somewhat in the style of George Etherege. The ridiculous Puritan survives in Alderman Gripe, who is fated to marry a loose woman. His daughter manages to obtain a fashionable fool in Dapperwit, but he is cheated of her fortune.

Love in Several Masques. A comedy (1728) by Henry Fielding, showing the influence of humour comedy in the characters of Sir Positive Trap, Formal, Rattle, and Catchit.

Love in the Dark, or The Man of Bus'ness. A comedy (1675) by Sir Francis Fane, taking its main plot from Pierre Scarron's *The Invisible Mistress*. Thomas Otway also used the plot for *The Souldier's Fortune* (1680).

Love in These Days. A novel by Alec Waugh, published in 1926.

Lovel (luv'ẹl). In Ben Jonson's comedy *The New Inn*, a soldier and scholar, and a chivalric lover.

Lovel. The name under which Charles Lamb describes his father, John Lamb, in his essay *Old Benchers of the Inner Temple*.

Lovel. The name under which the hero follows Isabella to Scotland in Sir Walter Scott's novel *The Antiquary*.

Lovel, Lord. In Shakespeare's *Richard III*, a follower of Richard. He executes Hastings and brings in his head (III.v).

Lovelace (luv'lās), Countess of. [Title of **Augusta Ada Byron**.] b. Dec. 10, 1815; d. Nov. 29, 1852. The daughter of Lord Byron.

Lovelace. The principal male character in Samuel Richardson's novel *Clarissa Harlowe*. He is an unscrupulous libertine whose name became a synonym for characters of that nature. He is an expansion of Nicholas Rowe's Lothario in *The Fair Penitent*. In order to overcome Clarissa's resistance to his advances, he drugs her; he later makes an offer of marriage, but Clarissa dies of mortification and grief.

Lovelace, Richard. b. in Kent, England, 1618; d. at London, 1658. An English Cavalier poet. He was imprisoned by the Parliament in 1642, took part in

---

ḍ, d or j; ṣ, s or sh; ṭ, t or ch; ẓ, z or zh; o, F. cloche; ü, F. menu; ch, Sc. loch; ṅ, F. bonbon.

the siege of Dunkerque in 1646, and was imprisoned on his return to England in 1648. Released after the king's execution, he died in poverty in the vicinity of London, his whole fortune having been spent in the Royalist cause. In 1649 he published *Lucasta* (from Lux Casta, his name for a lady said to have been Lucy Sacheverell), which was revised while he was in prison. After his death his brother collected and published his poems as *Lucasta: Posthume Poems* (1659). His name survives chiefly on account of his lyrics *To Althea from Prison* and *To Lucasta on going to the Wars*, the former containing the lines

> Stone walls do not a prison make
> Nor iron bars a cage,

and the latter the even more famous

> I could not love thee, Dear, so much,
> Loved I not Honour more.

Love Laughs at Locksmiths. An operatic farce (1803) by the younger George Colman.

Loveless (luv′lĕs). A character in Colley Cibber's comedy *Love's Last Shift*, and in its continuation, John Vanbrugh's *The Relapse;* a debauched libertine.

Loveless, Elder. The principal male character in Francis Beaumont and John Fletcher's play *The Scornful Lady.*

Loveless, Young. The brother of the Elder Loveless in Beaumont and Fletcher's *The Scornful Lady;* a heartless, callous prodigal.

Lovelich (luv′lich), **Henry.** fl. at London, c1450. An English skinner, remembered as the author of the Middle English romance *The History of the Holy Grail.*

Lovell (luv′el), **George William.** b. 1804; d. at Hampstead, London, May 13, 1878. An English dramatic writer. Among his plays are *The Provost of Bruges* (1836), *Love's Sacrifice* (1842), *Look before you Leap* (1846), *The Wife's Secret* (1848), and *The Trial of Love* (1852).

Lovell, Lord. A kindly gentleman in Philip Massinger's comedy, *A New Way to Pay Old Debts.* He arranges the marriage of his page, Tom Allworth, to the daughter of Sir Giles Overreach, thereby destroying the latter's hope that she would marry Lovell and thus become a peeress.

Lovell, Sir Thomas. In Shakespeare's *Henry VIII*, a courtier in King Henry's confidence.

Lovel the Widower (luv′el). A novel by W. M. Thackeray, published in 1861.

Lovely (luv′li), **Ann.** A character in Susannah Centlivre's comedy *A Bold Stroke for a Lover;* an heiress.

Love Makes a Man, or The Fop's Fortune. A comedy by Colley Cibber, made from John Fletcher's *The Custom of the Country* and *The Elder Brother.* It was acted 1700.

Lover (luv′ėr), **Samuel.** b. at Dublin, Feb. 24, 1797; d. at St. Helier, Jersey, Channel Islands, July 6, 1868. An Irish novelist, song writer, and painter. His chief novels are *Rory O'More* (1837; it was dramatized and had a run of 108 nights) and *Handy Andy* (1842). His *Songs and Ballads* were published in 1839, including "The Angel's Whis-

per," "The Low-backed Car," "The Four-leaved Shamrock," "Molly Bawn," "Father Molloy," and others.

Lover's Complaint, A. A poem supposedly by Shakespeare, written probably c1594, and published with the sonnets in 1609. No evidence, internal or external, beyond ascription of the poem to him in the 1609 and 1640 editions, connects it to Shakespeare.

Lover's Life, Complaint of a. See **Complaint of a Lover's Life.**

Lovers' Melancholy, The. A play by John Ford, produced in 1628 and printed in 1629.

Lover's Message, The. See **Husband's Message, The.**

Lover's Progress, The. A play by John Fletcher and Philip Massinger, printed in 1647.

Lovers' Quarrels. A play by King, altered from Vanbrugh's *The Mistake* in 1790.

Lover's Vows. A comedy by Elizabeth Inchbald, produced at Covent Garden Theatre, London, on Oct. 11, 1798.

Love Rune. See **Luve Ron.**

Love's Contrivance, or Le Médecin Malgré Lui (lĕ mäd.san̊ mȧl.grā lwē). A comedy by Susannah Centlivre, acted and printed in 1703. It was largely taken from *Le Médecin malgré lui* by Molière, but part of the plot is original. It concerns the attempt of a young lover, Bellmie, to win Lucinda, whose father desires to marry her to another.

Love's Cure, or the Martial Maid. A play by John Fletcher and probably Beaumont. It was produced c1623 and printed in 1647.

Love's Deity. A poem by John Donne, speaking of the god of love whose perverse nature fits opposites together so that "I should love her who loves not me."

Love's Labour's Lost. A comedy by Shakespeare, first acted c1595, printed in quarto in 1598. The full original title (*A Pleasant Conceited Comedie called Love's Labour's Lost as it was presented before her Highness this last Christmas, Newly corrected and augmented by W. Shakespere. Imprinted 1598*) marks the first appearance of Shakespeare's name on a play's title page. The earlier version, which some have thought to be implied by this title, probably does not exist. From 1605 to 1839, when it was staged at Covent Garden, the play had no performances in London, a neglect which can perhaps be attributed to its bewildering array of topical references, plays on contemporary literary and philosophic terms, and satires of personalities unknown to later audiences.

The Story. It is a highly stylized play with a very simple plot, hinging upon the revenge of Cupid upon four men (Ferdinand, King of Navarre, Berowne, Longaville, and Dumain) who have vowed to deny love for three years and devote themselves to study. The ladies (the Princess of France, Rosaline, Maria, and Katherine), having come upon the academic retreat, are forbidden to enter, and thereupon determine to punish the foolish ascetics by causing them to break their vows. This is accomplished (although not without some remorse on the part of each lord, but Berowne argues that forswearing is less dangerous than denying love's power), but when the smitten lovers woo their ladies in Russian costume, the ladies confuse them by wearing masks and then exchanging them. In their own persons the lovers then engage their ladies in a game of wit, and then sit with them to watch a pageant, but their laughter is cut short by news of the death of the father of the Princess. Following this episode, a year's penance is laid on each lover before he may have his lady. It seems clear that this play was written for a courtly audience which would appreciate its obvious allusion to the philandering French monarch Henry IV (Henry of Navarre).

Love's Labour's Won. A play ascribed to Shakespeare by Francis Meres (1598), perhaps the original of *Much Ado about Nothing*.

Love's Last Shift, or the Fool in Fashion. A comedy by Colley Cibber, produced in January, 1696. Vanbrugh's *The Relapse* is a sequel to this. Loveless is a roué separated from his wife, Amanda, whom he has not seen for eight years. He fails to recognize her when they meet again, but upon learning of her faithfulness to him, he is restored once more to constancy and temperate living. The plot also includes a foppish individual, Sir Novelty Fashion, played by Cibber himself.

Love's Metamorphosis. A comedy by John Lyly, published in 1601.

Love's Mistress. See **Queen's Masque, The.**

Loves of the Angels, The. A poem by Thomas Moore, published in 1822.

Loves of the Plants, The. The second part of the *Botanic Garden*, a versified treatise on botany, by Erasmus Darwin, published in 1789. The first part, *The Economy of Vegetation*, did not appear till 1792.

Loves of the Triangles, The. A satirical poem by George Canning and J. H. Frere, published in the *Anti-Jacobin*. It was in ridicule of Erasmus Darwin and his *Loves of the Plants*.

Love Song of J. Alfred Prufrock (prö'frok)**, The.** A poem (1917) by T. S. Eliot. It weaves into the story of a slightly aging man, somewhat bound by convention, quick flashes of the emptiness of modern life, a theme later fully developed in *The Hollow Men, Ash Wednesday,* and *The Waste Land.* This theme is embodied in the chorus-like lines:

> In the room the women come and go
> Talking of Michelangelo.

Love's Pilgrimage. A romantic comedy by John Fletcher and Francis Beaumont, written in 1615 and printed in 1647.

Love's Sacrifice. A tragedy by John Ford, written in 1630 and published 1633.

Lovewell (luv'wel). A young clerk secretly married to Fanny Sterling, daughter of his employer, in *The Clandestine Marriage*, by David Garrick and the elder George Colman.

Lovewit (luv'wit). The owner of the house in or before which the action in Ben Jonson's *The Alchemist* takes place.

Loving Spirit, The. A novel by Daphne Du Maurier, published in 1931.

Low (lō)**, Maurice.** [Full name, **Alfred Maurice Low.**] b. at London, 1860; d. at Washington, D. C., June 17, 1929. An English journalist. In World War I he played a chief part in the Allied propaganda effort in America. Author of *Protection in the United States* (1904), *America at Home* (1908), *The American People* (2 vols., 1909–11), *Great Britain and the War* (1914), *Freedom of the Seas* (1915), *The Law of Blockade* (1916), *Blockade and Contraband* (1916), and *Woodrow Wilson—An Interpretation* (1918).

Low, Sir Sidney. b. at London, Jan. 22, 1857; d. there, Jan. 13, 1932. An English journalist, teacher, and historian. He edited (1888–97) the *St. James' Gazette.* He served in the Ministry of Information as an editorial writer during World War I. Author of *The Governance of England* (1904), *A Vision of India* (1906), *Political History of England: 1837–1901* (1907), *De Quincey* (1911), *Egypt in Transition* (1914), *Italy in the War* (1916), *The Call of the East* (1921), *The British Constitution* (1928), and *Indian States and Princes* (1929).

Lowes (lōz)**, John Livingston.** b. at Decatur, Ind., Dec. 20, 1867—. An American scholar and professor, best known for his critical study of Coleridge, *The Road to Xanadu* (1927). He was professor of English at Washington University, St. Louis, professor of English at Swarthmore College, and professor of English literature (1918–39) at Harvard. He was the first George Eastman visiting professor (1930–31) at Oxford. His works include *Convention and Revolt in Poetry* (1919), *The Art of Geoffrey Chaucer* (1931), *Geoffrey Chaucer and the Development of His Genius* (1934), and *Essays in Appreciation* (1936).

Low-Heels. See **High-Heels and Low-Heels.**

Lowin (lō'in)**, John.** b. 1576; d. 1659. An English actor of the Jacobean period. He is mentioned as one of the "principal actors" in Shakespeare's plays in the first folio edition of 1623. It is recorded that he acted "with mighty applause" Falstaff, Volpone (in Jonson's comedy of that name), and Epicure Mammon (in Jonson's *The Alchemist*). It is supposed that Shakespeare himself instructed him in the part of Henry VIII. He ended his days keeping the Three Pigeons, a tavern at Brentford.

Lowndes (loundz)**, Mrs. Belloc.** [Pen name of Mrs. **Frederic Sawrey Lowndes;** maiden name, **Marie Adelaide Belloc.**] b. 1868; d. at Eversley Cross, Hampshire, England, Nov. 14, 1947. An English novelist; sister of Hilaire Belloc. Author of historical works, novels, plays, and especially murder and mystery tales, including *The Heart of Penelope* (1904), *Barbara Rebell* (1905), *The Chink in the Armour* (1912), *The Lodger* (1913), *Who Rides on a Tiger* (1936), *Lizzie Borden* (1940), and *A Passing World* (1947). She published the autobiography *I, Too, Have Lived in Arcadia* (1941).

Lowth (louth)**, Robert.** b. at Winchester, England, Nov. 27, 1710; d. at Fulham, near London, Nov. 3, 1787. An English divine and scholar, bishop of London (1777–87). He was professor (1741 *et seq.*) of poetry at Oxford, and in his lectures there examined Biblical poetry as poetry, apart from its sacred context; this study was the effective beginning of the examination of the Bible as a literary work. He published *Praelectiones de sacra poesi*

d, d or j; ş, s or sh; ţ, t or ch; z̧, z or zh; o, F. cloche; ü, F. menu; ch, Sc. loch; ṅ, F. bonbon.

Hebraeorum (Lectures on the Sacred Poetry of the Hebrews, 1753), a translation of Isaiah (1778), and others.

Lowther (lou′ℸΗėr), **William.** [Title, 1st Earl of **Lonsdale** (of the 2nd creation).] b. 1757; d. at Twickenham, England, March 19, 1844. An English nobleman and patron of William Wordsworth. Wordsworth dedicated (1814) *The Excursion* to him, and subsequently also a sonnet upon the Lowther motto "Magistratus Indicat Virum."

Lowther, William. [Title, 2nd Earl of **Lonsdale** (of the second creation).] b. at Uffington, near Stamford, Lincolnshire, England, July 21, 1787; d. March 4, 1872. An English government official. He was junior lord (1809) of the admiralty, first commissioner (1828) of woods and forests, president (1834–35) of the Board of Trade, postmaster general (1841) and president (1852) of council. He was the original of Lord Eskdale in Disraeli's novel *Tancred.*

Loyal Subject, The. A play by John Fletcher, written in 1618 and printed in 1647.

Loyalties. A play (1922) by John Galsworthy.

Loyola (loi.ō′lạ; Spanish, lō.yō′lä), Saint **Ignatius (of).** See Saint **Ignatius of Loyola.**

Luath (lö′ath). See **Caesar and Luath.**

Lubbock (lub′ǫk), **Basil.** [Full name, **Alfred Basil Lubbock.**] b. Sept. 9, 1876; d. Sept. 4, 1944. An English soldier, authority on the history of sailing ships; son of Sir John Lubbock (1834–1913), 1st Baron Avebury. Author of *The China Clippers* (1914), *The Colonial Clippers* (1921), *The Log of the Cutty Sark* (1924), *Western Ocean Packets* (1925), *The Down Easters—American Sailing Ships 1869–1929* (1929), *The Nitrate Clippers* (1932), *The Opium Clippers* (1933), and *The Arctic Whalers* (1935).

Lubbock, Sir John. [Title, 1st Baron **Avebury.**] b. at London, April 30, 1834; d. at Kingsgate, Kent, England, May 28, 1913. An English banker, naturalist, educator, and politician. He entered (1848) his father's banking house, becoming head of the firm in 1865. He served as a Liberal member of Parliament for Maidstone (1870–80) and for London University (1880–1900). He entered (1900) the House of Lords. He was vice-chancellor (1872–80) of London University, and principal (1890–92) of the London Workingmen's College. Author of *Prehistoric Times* (1865), *The Origin of Civilization and the Primitive Condition of Man* (1870), *Ants, Bees, and Wasps* (1882), *The Pleasures of Life* (1887), *On the Senses, Instincts, and Intelligence of Animals* (1888), *The Beauties of Nature* (1892), *The Use of Life* (1894), *Peace and Happiness* (1909), *Marriage, Totemism, and Religion* (1911), and other works. In 1891 he compiled a list of *The Hundred Best Books,* a work which has been reprinted many times.

Lubbock, Percy. b. June 4, 1879—. An English literary critic and essayist. His works include *The Craft of Fiction* (1921), *Earlham* (1922), *Roman Pictures* (1923), *The Region Cloud* (1925), *Shades of Eton* (1929), and *Portrait of Edith Wharton* (1947).

Lucan (lö′kạn). [Full Latin name, **Marcus Annaeus Lucanus.**] b. at Córdoba, Spain, 39 A.D.; committed suicide, 65 A.D. A Roman poet and prose writer, author of the *Pharsalia,* in 10 books, an epic poem on the civil war between Caesar and Pompey. He was forbidden by Nero, through jealousy, to recite in public, and in revenge joined the conspiracy of Piso. He was betrayed, and by a promise of pardon was induced to turn informer, but, after denouncing his mother and his other accomplices, he was condemned to death. He anticipated his punishment by causing his veins to be opened.

Lucas (lö′kạs), **E. V.** [Full name, **Edward Verrall Lucas.**] b. at Eltham, Kent, England, June 11, 1868; d. at London, June 26, 1938. English author and critic. He was connected with the London *Globe* (1893–1900), with the *Academy* (1896–1901), and was on the staff of *Punch.* He was the compiler of *The Open Road* (1899), and the author of *Wisdom While You Wait* (1903; with O. L. Graves), *Highways and Byways in Sussex* (1904), *A Wanderer in Holland* (1905), *The Life of Charles Lamb* (1905), *A Wanderer in London* (1906), *Listener's Lure* (1906), *The Hambledon Men* (1907), *The Gentlest Art* (1907), *Her Infinite Variety* (1908), *Over Bemerton's* (1908), *A Wanderer in Paris* (1909), *The Slowcoach* (1910), *Mr. Ingleside* (1910), *The Same Star* (1924), *The More I See of Men* (1927), *Pleasure Trove* (1935), and many other works. He edited (1935) the complete *Letters of Charles and Mary Lamb* after having earlier (1903–05) published *The Works of Charles and Mary Lamb.*

Lucas, Frank Laurence. b. at Hipperholme, Yorkshire, England, Dec. 28, 1894—. An English scholar and novelist. Author of *Cécile* (1930) and *Doctor Dido* (1938). His plays include *The Bear Dances* (1932) and *Land's End* (1938). He is author also of *Poems* (1935), and *A Journal Under the Terror* (1938).

Lucas, St. John Welles. b. at Rugby, Warwickshire, England, Jan. 22, 1879; d. Oct. 23, 1934. An English poet, essayist, and editor. Author of *The Absurd Repentance* (1903), *The Vintage of Dreams* (1904), *Aubrey Ellison* (1904), *The Florentine Chair* (1904), *Poems* (1904), *Quicksilver and Flame* (1906), *The Marble Sphinx* (1906), *Gallio* (1908), *New Poems* (1908), *The Rose-Winged Hours* (1908), *Ronsard* (1908), *The First Round* (1909), *Saints, Sinners, and the Usual People* (1912), *The Lady of the Canaries* (1913), *Heroines and Others* (1914), *April Folly* (1916), *The Plunge* (1921), and *Certain People* (1922). He edited the *Oxford Book of French Verse* (1907; revised and enlarged ed., 1926) and the *Oxford Book of Italian Verse* (1910).

Lucas de Beaumanoir (dẹ bō.ma.nwär′), **Sir.** See **Beaumanoir, Sir Lucas de.**

Luce (lös). In Shakespeare's *Comedy of Errors,* a female servant to Adriana.

Lucentio (lö.sen′shi.ō). In Shakespeare's *Taming of the Shrew,* an accomplished young student from Pisa, whose skillful wooing of Bianca forms the subplot of the play.

Lucetta (lö.set′ạ). In Shakespeare's *Two Gentlemen of Verona,* a waiting-woman to Julia.

Lucia (lö′shạ). In Thomas Southerne's *Sir Anthony Love, or The Rambling Lady,* a young girl who disguises herself as a man (Sir Anthony) and follows her lover to win him.

---

fat, fāte, fär, àsk, fãre; net, mē, hėr; pin, pīne; not, nōte, mōve, nôr; up, lūte, pùll; ℸΗ, then;

Lucia. A young woman loved by Cato's sons, Portius and Marcus, in Addison's *Cato*.

Lucia di Lammermoor (lö.chē′ä dē läm.mer.mör′). An opera (1835) by Donizetti, based on Scott's *Bride of Lammermoor*.

Lucian (lö′shạn). b. at Samosata, Syria, c120 A.D.; d. c200. A Greek satirist. He was a freethinker, attacking with pungent satire the religious beliefs of his time; for this, according to Suidas, he was called "the Blasphemer," and was torn to pieces by dogs (doubtless a pious invention). He wrote rhetorical, critical, and biographical works, romances, dialogues, and poems. Outstanding among his works are *The True History*, a parodied travelogue, and the satirical *Dialogues of the Gods* and *Dialogues of the Dead*. *Auction of Philosophers* is the satiric evaluation of various schools of thought. He was author also of *Peregrine* and *Timon*.

Luciana (lö.shi.an′ạ). In Shakespeare's *Comedy of Errors*, the sister of Adriana.

Luciano (lö.shi.ä′nō). In Shakespeare's *Hamlet*, a character in the play presented before the King. He is the murderer of the sleeping Gonzago.

Lucie Manette (lü.sē′ ma.net′). See **Manette, Lucie.**

Lucifer (lö′si.fėr). The morning star; the planet Venus when it appears in the morning before sunrise; when it appears in the evening, it is called Hesperus, or the evening star. The name "day-star" is applied by Isaiah figuratively to a king of Babylon; this was rendered in the authorized version by "Lucifer." From this passage (Isa. xiv. 12) the name was also given to the leader of the fallen angels, and hence to Satan.

Lucifera (lö.sif′ẹ.rạ). In Spenser's *Faerie Queene*, the personification of pride and worldliness. She lives in a palace built on sand and is attended by the seven deadly sins.

Lucile (lö.sēl′). A romantic novel in verse (1860) by Owen Meredith.

Lucilius (lö.sil′i.us). In Shakespeare's *Julius Caesar*, a friend of Brutus and Cassius. He describes (IV.ii) the coldness with which Cassius received Lucilius as Brutus's emissary.

Lucilius. In Shakespeare's *Timon of Athens*, a servant of Timon. One of Timon's generous acts is to give Lucilius enough money to win the girl he wants to marry.

Lucilius, Gaius (or **Caius**). b. at Suessa Aurunca, Campania, Italy, c180 B.C.; d. at Naples, Italy, 103 B.C. A Latin satirical poet, author of *Saturae*, miscellaneous poems containing a very free criticism of contemporary life. These satires influenced those of Horace, Persius, and Juvenal.

Lucina (lö.sī′nạ). In Roman mythology, the goddess who presided over childbirth, an aspect of Juno, and as such called Juno Lucina. The name was also applied to Diana and to Hecate. She corresponded to the Greek goddess Ilithyia.

Lucinda (lö.sin′dạ). The daughter of Mr. Sealand, a wealthy merchant, in Steele's *The Conscious Lovers*.

Lucio (lö′shi.ō). In Shakespeare's *Measure for Measure*, a "fantastic" (i.e., profligate), but nevertheless sincere, friend of Claudio who urges Isabella

to intercede for Claudio. Not recognizing the Duke in a friar's disguise, he slanders the Duke and then reports that a friar has been maligning the Duke. The Duke finally orders him to marry a woman he has wronged.

Lucius (lö′shus). In Shakespeare's *Julius Caesar*, a boy, servant of Brutus.

Lucius. In Shakespeare's *Timon of Athens*, a flattering lord; also, in the same play, a servant of this lord who is sent to recover a debt from Timon.

Lucius. In Shakespeare's *Titus Andronicus*, a son of Titus. After his brothers are executed, his sister Lavinia raped, and his father mutilated, he joins the invading Goths. The emperor Saturninus is overthrown, Tamora and Aaron are killed, and Lucius becomes the ruler of Rome. He has a son who is also named Lucius.

Lucius, Caius. In Shakespeare's *Cymbeline*, a Roman general who invades Britain. He discovers Imogen, disguised as a boy, and she follows his army. When Lucius and Imogen are captured by the Britons, Cymbeline recognizes his daughter and frees Lucius.

Lucius Cornelius Cinna (kôr.nēl′yus sin′ạ). See under **Cinna.**

Lucius Junius Brutus, Father of his Country (jön′yus brö′tus). A tragedy by Nathaniel Lee, produced in 1680.

Lucius O'Trigger (ọ.trig′ėr), **Sir.** See **O'Trigger, Sir Lucius.**

Luck of Eden Hall (ē′dẹn). A drinking cup long preserved at Eden Hall in Cumberland, England. It is a chalice of enameled glass, of 10th-century workmanship, presumably Venetian. There is a legend that it was left for the Musgrave family by the fairies at Saint Cuthbert's Well, and that the family luck depends on its preservation:

> If this cup either break or fall,
> Farewell the luck of Eden Hall.

Lucrece (lö.krēs′). See **Rape of Lucrece, The.**

Lucretia (lö.krē′shạ). [Also, **Lucrece** (lö.krēs′).] In Roman legend, the wife of Tarquinius Collatinus. She was raped by Sextus Tarquinius and killed herself. This led to the expulsion of the Tarquins and the establishment of the republic.

Lucretia MacTab (mak.tab′), **the Hon. Miss.** See **MacTab, the Hon. Miss Lucretia.**

Lucretia, or the Children of Night. A novel by Edward Bulwer-Lytton, published in 1846.

Lucretia Tox (toks). See **Tox, Miss.**

Lucretius (lö.krē′shus). [Full name, **Titus Lucretius Carus.**] b. at Rome, probably c96 B.C.; d. Oct. 15, 55 B.C. A Roman philosophical poet. He was the author of *De rerum natura* (On the Nature of Things), a didactic and philosophical poem in six books, treating of physics and cosmology, of psychology, and (briefly) of ethics from the Epicurean point of view. He committed suicide probably in a fit of insanity. According to a popular but doubtless erroneous tradition (which was picked up and used by Tennyson in his dramatic monologue *Lucretius*), his madness was due to a love philter administered to him by his wife.

ḍ, d or j; ṣ, s or sh; ṭ, t or ch; ẓ, z or zh; o, F. cloche; ü, F. menu; ch, Sc. loch; ṅ, F. bonbon.

Lucrezia Borgia (lö.krä′tsyä bôr′jä). An opera in two acts by Donizetti, with a libretto by Romani, first produced at La Scala, Milan, in 1833.

Lucullus (lö.kul′us). In Shakespeare's *Timon of Athens*, a flattering lord.

Lucullus, Lucius Licinius. [Surnamed **Ponticus.**] b. probably c110 B.C.; d. c57 B.C. Roman general. He served under Sulla in the East, and was curule edile in 79 and consul in 74. He defeated Mithridates VI of Pontus in Asia Minor 74–71, defeated Tigranes near Tigranocerta in 69, and was recalled to Rome in 66. He was afterward famous for his wealth and his luxury. His villas at Tusculum and near Neapolis (modern Naples) were famous for their splendor, and he is said to have spent fabulous sums on his table (a rich banquet is still called a Lucullan feast). He is said to have been the first to introduce cherries into Italy. He was also a collector of books and a patron of learning.

Lucusta (lŏ.kus′tạ). See **Locusta.**

Lucy (lö′si), Saint. [Italian, **Santa Lucia.**] b. c283; killed in 303. A martyr of the primitive church in Syracuse, who perished during the persecution of Diocletian. According to the legend, she rejected a pagan suitor whom her mother desired her to marry, was denounced as a Christian, and was condemned to be outraged, but escaped this fate and died by the sword in 303. She is the patroness especially of those who suffer from distemper of the eyes (the attribution probably comes from the resemblance of her name to Latin *lux*, light, and has attracted to her the legend that when a nobleman wished to marry her because of her beautiful eyes, she tore them from her head and gave them to him in order to be permitted to live a virgin). She is represented in art with a sword point (thorn) in her neck and sometimes with a salver on which rest her eyes.

Lucy. In Richard Brinsley Sheridan's comedy *The Rivals*, a clever waiting maid of great apparent simplicity.

Lucy. Entries on literary characters having this prename will also be found under the surnames Ashton, Bertram, Deane, Lockit, and Snowe.

Lucy, Sir Henry. [Pseudonym, **Toby, M.P.**] b. at Crosby, Lancashire, England, Dec. 5, 1845; d. Feb. 20, 1924. An English journalist and philanthropist. He was a staff member (1881–1916) of *Punch*, for which he wrote under his pseudonym. In 1903 and again in 1913 he established the Lucy Trust funds to aid parliamentary employees and writers. Author of various parliamentary manuals, a novel, *Gideon Fleyce* (1882), and *Men and Manner in Parliament* (1875), *Peeps at Parliament* (1903), *Memories of Eight Parliaments* (1908), *Sixty Years in the Wilderness* (1909–12), *Nearing Jordan* (1916), and *The Diary of a Journalist* (3 vols., 1921–23).

Lucy, Sir William. In Shakespeare's *1 Henry VI*, a leader who implores York and Somerset to go to Talbot's aid at Bordeaux. He obtains Talbot's body after his defeat.

Lucy Robarts (rō′bärts). See **Robarts, Lucy.**

Lucy Temple (tem′pl). A sequel to *Charlotte Temple* (1791), sentimental novel by Susanna Rowson. The book was issued (1828) under the title *Charlotte's Daughter*.

Lud (lud). [Also: **Lludd, Nudd.**] A legendary king of Britain, mentioned by Geoffrey of Monmouth in his *History of the Kings of Britain* as having built, or rebuilt, the walls of London. Ludgate Hill, London, preserves his name. He is evidently the same character as the Lludd of Brythonic legend, a king of Britain.

Luddites (lud′īts). A name given to the industrial workers who attempted (1811–12, 1816) to destroy machinery at Nottingham and elsewhere in England, so called from Ned Ludd, a Leicestershire "village idiot" who had broken (c1799) some stocking frames.

Ludgate (lud′gāt). A gate in the western part of the old city wall of London. It was destroyed in 1760. Near it stood a debtors' prison of the same name.

Ludovic Lesly (lö′dọ.vik les′li, lez′li). See **Lesly, Ludovic.**

Ludovico Sforza (lö.dō.vē′kō sfôr′tsä). See **Sforza, Ludovico.**

Ludus Coventriae (lü′dus kọ.ven′tri.ē). See **Hegge Plays.**

Lug (lö). [Also, **Lugh.**] In Old Irish mythology, the sun god, god of light, and god of genius. He was sometimes called Lug Lamfada, or Lug of the Long Hand. He was the grandson of Balor, one-eyed king of the giant Fomorians, whom he killed in the great battle between the Fomorians and the Tuatha De Danann by slinging a stone into the one eye. Lug gave the arts to the Tuatha De Danann, and is therefore often called Lug of All the Arts. His great festival was the Lugnasad, celebrated with harvest games on Aug. 1. In the Ulster cycle legends, Lug was the supernatural father of the hero Cuchulain, and at one time helped his son in battle.

Lugard (lö.gärd′), Lady. See **Shaw, Flora Louise.**

Luggnagg (lug′nag). An imaginary island mentioned in Swift's *Gulliver's Travels*. It is the home of the Struldbrugs, the people who are immortal.

Luke (lök), Saint. The author, according to tradition, of the third gospel and also of the Acts of the Apostles. He has been regarded as identical with the Luke several times mentioned in the New Testament as a companion of Saint Paul (called in Colossians "the beloved physician"). Of his life little is known. According to tradition he was a painter as well as a physician, and the only one of the apostles not of Jewish origin. Whether or not he suffered martyrdom is uncertain. His symbol is the ox (often winged), which was given him as an emblem of sacrifice and priesthood because "he devised about the priesthood of Jesus Christ."

Luke Frugal (frö′gạl). See **Frugal, Luke.**

Lully (lü.lē′), Jean Baptiste. [Original name, **Giovanni Battista Lulli.**] b. at Florence, Nov. 29, c1633; d. at Paris, March 22, 1687. A French composer, chiefly of operas. He is credited with being the founder of the French grand opera. He inaugurated and was head (1672–87) of the Académie Royale de Musique, later the Paris Opéra. He is noted for his development of the operatic overture and the recitative with accompaniment. Among his operas are *Cadmus et Hermione* (1673), *Alceste* (1674), *Théese* (1675), *Psyché* (1678), *Proserpine* (1680), *Phaéton*

(1683), *Amadis de Gaule* (1684), *Roland* (1685), and *Acis et Galathée* (1686).

Lully (lul'i), **Raymond.** [Latin, **Raimundus Lullus;** Catalan, **Ramón Lull;** Spanish, **Raimundo Lulio;** French, **Raimond Lulle.**] b. at Palma, Balearic Islands, c1235; d. at Bougie, Africa, June 30, 1315. A Spanish scholastic, missionary to the Mohammedans. His early life as a scion of a rich family was spent, according to him, in dissipation, but in 1266, after several visions of the crucified Christ, he turned to religion and resolved to become a missionary. He studied Arabic for nine years and taught it for ten more. From 1287 to 1289 he taught at Paris, becoming known as an eccentric; at last, in 1291, he traveled to Tunis, where he expounded Christian doctrine. In 1292 he was jailed and then expelled. He attempted to obtain aid for his objectives at Rome, Paris, Cyprus, Genoa, and Lyons, but failed. He returned to Africa and was again imprisoned; he lectured again at Paris and elsewhere in France and Italy and in 1314 again went to Africa. He was stoned to death by Moslems who objected to his proselytizing. His *Ars Magna* is a treatise on symbolic logic, but this and the rest of his serious work are marked by an obscuring mysticism; this mysticism is present also in his purely literary work, which includes a Utopian novel, *Blanquerna*, and such poetry as *El Desconort* and *Lo Cant de Ramon.* Lully's eccentricity resulted in the attribution to him of many works on alchemy and the occult which are not his.

Lumpkin (lump'kin), **Tony.** In Oliver Goldsmith's comedy *She Stoops to Conquer*, an ignorant, but also crafty, noisy, conceited country squire, both loutish and mischievous.

Lun (lun). See under **Rich, John.**

Luna (lö'nạ). The Italian goddess of the moon.

Lunsford (luns'fọrd), Sir **Thomas.** b. c1610; d. c1653. An English jailer, long in charge of the Tower of London, and noted for his mean and vindictive temper. He was finally removed from his position on formal petition by the House of Commons. Samuel Butler refers to him in *Hudibras.*

Lupercal (lö'pėr.kạl). A cave or grotto near the W angle of the Palatine Hill, in ancient Rome, dedicated, according to tradition, by the original Arcadian settlers to Lupercus, a fertility deity. It was said to be the den of the she-wolf that suckled Romulus and Remus. As time went on the Lupercal was adorned architecturally, and its decoration was renewed by Augustus. Near the Lupercal was the Ficus Ruminalis, the fig tree beneath which Romulus and Remus were left by the retiring waters of the Tiber, and above it was the primitive thatched hut preserved to imperial days as a relic of Romulus.

Lupercalia (lö.pėr.kā'li.ạ). One of the most ancient Roman festivals, celebrated every year in February.

Lupercus (lö.pėr'kus). A Roman rural deity, the protector of flocks: identified with Faunus and Pan.

Lupino (lö.pē'nō), **Stanley.** b. at London, May 15, 1894; d. there, June 10, 1942. An English actor, playwright, and producer. He starred (1915–23) on the English stage in pantomime and acrobatic performances, and appeared (1926 *et seq.*) in the U. S. He played in *Sleeping Beauty, Naughty Riquette,*

The Nightingale, The Love Race, and other productions, and wrote and produced musical comedies.

Luqman (lûk.män'). See **Lokman.**

Lurewell (lör'wel), **Mistress.** In Farquhar's comedy *The Constant Couple*, a jilt with a strong desire to wreak vengeance on men for the wrongs done her.

Luria (lö'ri.ạ). A tragic drama in blank verse by Robert Browning, published as part of *Bells and Pomegranates* (1846). It tells about the gallant exploits of Luria, the Moor, in leading a Florentine army to victory over Pisa. However, before news of his success can reach Florence, the distrustful Florentines put him on trial for crimes invented by his enemies (the plot resemblance here to *Othello* will be obvious to every reader). The disappointment causes him to kill himself.

Lurline (lėr.lēn'). An opera in three acts by W. Vincent Wallace, with a libretto by E. Fitzball, first produced at Covent Garden Theatre, London, in 1860.

Lusiads (lö'si.adz), **The.** [Portuguese, **Os Lusíadas.**] The most famous work in Portuguese literature, an epic poem in ten cantos of *oitavas* (ottava rima) by Luiz de Camões; it celebrates the discovery of the sea route to India by Vasco da Gama, the Portuguese navigator, and praises the Portuguese nation for its past accomplishments. First published in 1572, *The Lusiads* has had scores of editions and has been translated into nearly every European language. Sir Richard Fanshawe made the first English translation (1655). Mickle's translation appeared in 1776, Musgrave's in 1826, Quillinan's (five cantos) in 1853, and Sir Thomas Mitchell's in 1854. A recent one, by William C. Atkinson, appeared in 1952.

Lusitania (lö.si.tā'ni.ạ). In ancient geography, the country of the Lusitanians, comprising the modern Portugal N to the river Durius (Douro), and adjoining parts of W Spain. In a later, more extended use, it was one of the Roman provinces into which Hispania was divided by Augustus.

Lusitania. A British passenger vessel (Cunard Line, 40,000 gross tons) which was sunk during World War I (May 7, 1915) by a German submarine, with little or no warning, ab. 10 mi. off the Old Head of Kinsale, on the S coast of Ireland. The sinking aroused intense feeling in the U. S. and did much to destroy the considerable body of pro-German sentiment which existed in America during the early period of World War I. The vessel was carrying a crew of more than 600 and upwards of 1,250 passengers (including 188 Americans), of whom 1,198 (including 128 Americans) are said to have been lost.

Lussurioso (lu.sör.i.ō'sō). The lustful heir of the Duke in Cyril Tourneur's *The Revenger's Tragedy.*

Lust's Dominion, or the Lascivious Queen. A play published in 1657. It was attributed to Christopher Marlowe, and was published as his in 1657; but it is probably the same play as the lost *Spanish Moor's Tragedy*, attributed to Thomas Dekker, William Haughton, and John Day.

Lusty Juventus (jö.ven'tus). An interlude of unknown authorship, written in the early 16th century.

ḍ, d or j; ṣ, s or sh; ṭ, t or ch; ẓ, z or zh; o, F. cloche; ü, F. menu; c̄h, Sc. loch; ṅ, F. bonbon.

Luther (lö'thèr; German, lö'tèr), **Martin.** b. at Eisleben, Germany, Nov. 10, 1483; d. there, Feb. 18, 1546. A German religious reformer and translator of the Bible. His first important action in the direction of ecclesiastical reform was his publication (Oct. 31, 1517), on the church door at Wittenberg, of 95 theses against the sale of indulgences by the Dominican Johann Tetzel. His propositions were immediately condemned as heretical, and violent attacks were made upon him from various quarters, both before and after a summons to Rome (which he did not obey). In 1520 he published three tracts: *Address to the Christian Nobles of the German Nation, On the Babylonian Captivity of the Church of God,* and *Christian Liberty.* These tracts are known as his "Primary Works" and contain the first principles of the Reformation. The material principle of the Reformation was justification by faith. The formal principle was that the Bible is the only rule of faith and practice. Another fundamental principle was the priesthood of all believers. In 1520, with his adherents, he was excommunicated by Pope Leo X, and his writings were burned at Rome, Cologne, and Louvain. He retaliated by publicly burning, at Wittenberg, the bull of excommunication and the decretals of the Pope, to whom he now renounced all allegiance. At the Diet of Worms (April, 1521), whither he was summoned by the emperor Charles V, he made the celebrated speech which ended with: "Here, I stand. I cannot do otherwise. God help me. Amen." The Lutheran translation of the whole Bible, completed in 1532, was finally published in 1534. It was revised in 1541, and the subsequent editions of 1543 and 1545 also received a few amendments. During the whole of his struggles for the Reformation, he wrote numerous polemical pamphlets which exhibited him as a most powerful though passionate controversialist. His *Tischreden* (Table-Talk) contains his opinions on a variety of subjects, the principal source of the material being Lauterbach's *Tagebuch* (Diary) from 1538. In 1530 he began to make a new version, in prose, of Aesop's and other classical fables. Besides prose, he also wrote a number of sacred hymns, whose prototype in construction and melody he found in the folk songs. The *Hymn-Book* of 1524 contains four hymns written by him; that of 1545 thirty-seven. In the edition of 1528 was published for the first time the most celebrated of his hymns, *Ein feste Burg ist unser Gott* (*A Mighty Fortress Is Our God*), written probably in 1527, the melody of which he is also said to have composed. Luther may also be regarded as the founder of the present literary language of Germany, that is, of so-called New High German.

Luve Ron (lúv'ę rön; modern, luv rön). [Also, **Love Rune.**] A Middle English poem (c1216–40) of 210 lines, dealing with the virtues to be derived from a mystic union with Christ, which is interpreted by the poet to mean an eternal love in contrast to the transitory amours of Paris and Helen or Tristram and Isolt.

Lyall (lī'ạl), Sir **Alfred Comyn.** b. in Surrey, England, 1835; d. on the Isle of Wight, England, April 10, 1911. An English administrator (in India) and writer. As lieutenant governor of the United Provinces (1882–87), he carried out land reforms

and a scheme of local self-government. He served as a member of the India Council at London (1887–1902). Author of *Verses Written in India* (1889), *Asiatic Studies,* a study of Indian culture (1882, 1889), *Rise and Expansion of the British Dominion in India* (1893), and biographies of Hastings (1889), Tennyson (1902), and the Marquis of Dufferin (1905).

Lyall, David. Pseudonym of **Reeves, Helen Buckingham.**

Lyall, Edna. Pseudonym of **Bayly, Ada Ellen.**

Lyar, The. [Also, **The Liar.**] A comedy (1762) by Samuel Foote, based on Thomas Corneille's *Le Menteur.*

Lybeux (lę̇.bö'), **Sir.** See under **Libeaus Desconus.**

Lycaon (lī.kā'on). In Greek legend, a king of Arcadia, who was visited by Zeus in disguise, because of either the impiety of his sons or his own impiety. The most common story is that Lycaon (or his sons) suspected the divinity of the guest, and to test it served the god with human flesh. Zeus punished the insult by striking the sons with thunderbolts and changing Lycaon into a wolf. This is thought to be the etiological myth for the cult of Zeus Lycaeus.

Lyceum (lī.sē'um). A gymnasium and exercise ground of ancient Athens, lying on the right bank of the Ilissus, at the place now called Ilissia, a short distance E of the palace garden. It was dedicated to Apollo Lyceius, and was already the chief gymnasium of Athens in the time of Pisistratus. It was noted for its fine groves of plane trees. Aristotle and his disciples formed the habit of discussing their philosophy while following the shady walks of this gymnasium, and hence received the name of Peripatetics.

Lyceum Theatre. A London theater, built originally in 1765, and remodeled twice (in 1794 and in 1815). It was destroyed by fire in 1830 and a new structure built in 1834. Although no longer used as a legitimate theater, this building still stood after World War II (John Gielgud's *Hamlet* in 1939 was its last drama). The Drury Lane company played there for three years (1809–12), during the rebuilding of their theater, destroyed by fire.

Lychorida (lī.kôr'i.dạ). In Shakespeare's *Pericles,* the nurse of Marina.

Lycidas (lis'i.dạs). An elegiac poem by John Milton, one of the most famous elegies in English literature. It was published in 1637, and commemorates the death of Milton's friend Edward King.

Lycophron (lī'kǫ.fron). b. at Chalcis, in Euboea; fl. in the 3rd century B.C. An Alexandrian tragic poet and grammarian. His only extant poem is the *Alexandra* or *Cassandra,* comprising about 1,400 iambic verses, in which Cassandra predicts the results of the voyage of Paris to Sparta.

Lycurgus (lī.kèr'gus). fl., according to tradition, in the 9th century B.C. A Spartan legislator, the traditional author of the laws and institutions of Sparta. The effect of his laws was to make Sparta into a military state in which all the economy and political institutions were aimed at preserving Spartan hegemony in the Peloponnesus. It is thought that the laws may have resulted from the Messenian revolt in the 7th century. Also, the probability that some of the laws attributed to Lycurgus are actually from the 6th century casts doubt on his historicity and leads to the hypothesis, held by some, that he was a legendary personage to whom the reforms were attributed.

Lydgate (lid′gāt), **Doctor.** A physician in George Eliot's *Middlemarch*. He is ambitious, but a selfish wife takes the savor out of his ambition; he dies comparatively young and obscure.

Lydgate (lid′gāt, -git), **John.** b. at Lydgate, near Newmarket, Suffolk, England, c1370; d. c1451. An English poet, one of the most prolific in the history of English letters. He was ordained as a priest in 1387, and gained a position as poet at the court of Henry IV, which he held during the reign of Henry V and after the accession of Henry VI (this position at Court after 1420 was further strengthened by the patronage of the powerful Humphrey, Duke of Gloucester). After 1390 he made the acquaintance of Geoffrey Chaucer, often calling himself "Chaucer's disciple." His numerous works include *The Fall of Princes*, a narrative poem written between 1430 and 1438; *Troy Book*, in heroic couplets, containing a panegyric on Chaucer (1412–20; first printed by Pynson in 1513); *The Story of Thebes*, intended as an additional Canterbury tale (1420); *The Life of Our Lady*, a religious narrative poem, printed by Caxton in 1484; *The Dance of Death*, from the French, printed first in 1554 (also, with Holbein's drawings, in 1794); *The Court of Sapience*, a philosophical work printed by Caxton (c1481); *The Temple of Glass*, printed by Caxton (c1479); and a number of lives of saints, allegories, fables, historical and political poems, and satires. A number of the minor poems which were once attributed to Chaucer are now credited to Lydgate. Most of his longer works, like the *Troy Book*, are translations. Modern readers find them interminable and tedious, but many of his shorter poems may still be read with pleasure.

Lydia (lid′i.ạ). [Early name, **Maeonia**.] An ancient country, later a Roman province, on the W coast of Asia Minor, bordering on the Aegean Sea and on Mysia, Phrygia, and Caria. The earliest known inhabitants were Phrygians. Later it was invaded by Semites, who gave it the name of Lydia (compare the Old Testament Lud, descendants of Shem, Gen. x. 22). The name Maeonia was afterward confined to the E part of the country near the upper Hermus River, and Lydia to the W. About 700 B.C. a revolution overthrew the Semitic reign, and brought the native dynasty of the Mermnadae to the throne, with Gyges as first king. Under them Lydia rose to the position of a mighty kingdom extending from the coast to the river Halys (modern Kizil Irmak), with Sardis as capital. The prosperous Greek cities were brought either to subjection or alliance. But under the fifth and best-known of the dynasty, Croesus, the Lydian empire was brought to a sudden end by the Persian conqueror Cyrus, who in 546 B.C. captured Sardis and the king himself. From the Persians Lydia passed over, through Alexander the Great, to Syria, and later to Eumenes of Pergamum. During the Roman period Lydia formed a separate province, with

Sardis as capital. Sardis was a prominent episcopal see (compare Rev. iii. 1), but was destroyed by Tamerlane in 1402 A.D.

Lydia Bennet (ben′ęt). See **Bennet, Lydia.**

Lydia Languish (lang′gwish). See **Languish, Lydia.**

Lying Lover, or the Ladies' Friendship, The. A comedy by Richard Steele, produced in 1703. It was taken from Thomas Corneille's *Le Menteur*. Steele summarized it: "the hero . . . makes false love, gets drunk, and kills his man; but in the fifth act awakes from his debauch, with . . . compunction and remorse."

Lying Valet, The. A comedy by David Garrick (1741), adapted from P. A. Motteux's *Novelty*. It was apparently intended to be used in a free performance, to lure patrons to Goodman's Fields Theatre (in which Garrick had an interest).

Lyle (līl), **Annot.** The heroine of Sir Walter Scott's *The Legend of Montrose*, a beautiful young girl, kidnapped in her infancy by enemies of her family. She is loved by both the gallant Earl of Monteith and Allan M'Aulaym, the latter of whom rescues her from a band of murderers.

Lyly (lil′i), **John.** b. in the Weald of Kent, England, c1554; d. at London, in November, 1606. An English dramatist and novelist. He graduated at Oxford (Magdalen College) in 1573, went to London, where he entered upon literary work and endeavored to establish himself at court, championed the bishops in the "Martin Marprelate" controversy, and became a member of Parliament in 1589 (reëlected in 1593, 1597, and 1601). His principal work is *Euphues, or the Anatomy of Wit* (1579), and its sequel, *Euphues and his England* (1580), which brought into prominence the affected style named from it Euphuism, consisting of an overuse of figures of speech, and much admired (and burlesqued) and imitated in its own day. In the Marprelate controversy he wrote *Pappe with an Hatchet*. He also wrote a number of plays, including *Alexander and Campaspe*, *Mother Bombie*, *Midas*, *The Woman in the Moon*, *Sapho and Phao*, and *Endimion, the Man in the Moon*. These plays, the first effective high comedy in English, are considered the best of the type before Shakespeare; Lyly's use of prose instead of verse in these comedies was followed by later writers.

Lymoges (lī′mọ.jēz). See **Austria, Duke of.**

Lynceus (lin′sę.us). In Greek mythology, the husband of Hypermnestra, the only one of the 50 daughters of Danaus to spare her husband after Danaus had ordered them all killed. Lynceus was among the heroes of the Argonaut expedition. He had such keen eyesight that he could see through a stone wall or look into the earth and see buried treasure.

Lynd (lind), **Robert.** b. at Belfast, Ireland, April 20, 1879; d. at London, Oct. 6, 1949. An Irish writer and journalist. He was literary editor of the London *News Chronicle* and contributor, as John O'London, to *John O' London's Weekly*, and the author of *Irish and English: Portraits and Impressions* (1908), *Home Life in Ireland* (1909), *Rambles in Ireland* (1912), *Old and New Masters* (1919), *Solomon in All His Glory* (1922), *Dr. Johnson and Company* (1928), *It's a Fine World* (1930), *Search-*

ḍ, d or j; ṣ, s or sh; ṭ, t or ch; ẓ, z or zh; o, F. cloche; ü, F. menu; ċh, Sc. loch; ṅ, F. bonbon.

lights and Nightingales (1939), *Life's Little Oddities* (1941), and *Things One Hears* (1945).

Lynd, Sylvia. [Maiden name, **Dryhurst.**] b. at London, 1888—. An English writer; wife of Robert Lynd (1879–1949). Author of *The Chorus* (1916) and *The Swallow Dive* (1921), novels; *The Mulberry Bush* (1925), short stories; *The Goldfinches* (1920), *The Yellow Placard* (1931), and *The Enemies* (1934), volumes of poetry. She was editor of the anthology *The Children's Omnibus* (1932).

Lyndaraxa (lin.dạ.rak'sạ). A beautiful woman, the sister of Zulema, responsible for villainous plotting against the noble Almanzor in Dryden's *Conquest of Granada*.

Lyndon (lin'dọn), **Barry.** See **Barry Lyndon.**

Lyndsay (lin'zi), Sir **David.** See **Lindsay, Sir David.**

Lynette (li.net'). See **Linet.**

Lyones (lī.ọ.nes'). See **Lionês.**

Lyonesse (lī.ọ.nes'). [Also, **Leonnoys.**] A legendary region west of Cornwall, England. Tradition has it that it is now more than 40 fathoms under water between Land's End and the isles of Scilly, the sea having gradually encroached upon the land. See also under **Tristan.**

Lyre (līr), **Pinchbeck.** A pseudonym of **Sassoon, Siegfried.**

lyric (lir'ik), *a.* and *n.* **I.** *a.* **1.** Pertaining or adapted to the lyre or harp; fit to be sung to an accompaniment; hence, pertaining to or characteristic of song; suggestive of music or song.

> Æolian charms and Dorian lyrick odes.
> (Milton, *P.R.*, iv. 257.)

2. Writing for or as if for the lyre, or with musical effect; composing songs, or poems of a songlike character: as, a lyric poet.
II. *n.* **1.** *Obs.* A composer of lyric poems.

> The greatest conqueror in this nation, after the manner of the old Grecian lyricks, did not only compose the works of his divine odes, but set them to musick himself. (Addison.)

2. A lyric composition or poem.
3. A verse of the kind commonly used in lyric poetry.

Lyrical Ballads. A collection of poems by William Wordsworth and Samuel Taylor Coleridge, including the latter's *Ancient Mariner*, published in 1798. Wordsworth's preface to the second edition (1800) was the manifesto of the new romantic school of poetry. It forms, with the poems, one of the landmarks of English literary history.

lyric poetry. Among the ancients, poetry sung to the lyre; in modern usage, poetry composed for musical recitation, or distinctively that class of poetry which has reference to and delineates the poet's own thoughts and feelings, as opposed to epic or dramatic poetry, which details external circumstances and events.

Lysander (lī.san'dėr). Killed near Haliartus, in Boeotia, Greece, 395 B.C. A Spartan commander. He gained the victory of Notium in 407, and that of Aegospotami in 405 and took Athens and destroyed its walls in 404, thus ending the Peloponnesian War. The rapid extension of oligarchies

throughout Greece made him, the military man of the day, extremely powerful in Greece and caused his recall to Sparta. He avoided attempts to keep him in obscure positions and was plotting to substitute an elective for the hereditary monarchy when war with Thebes broke out. He captured Orchomenus but died in a hopeless attack on strongly fortified Haliartus.

Lysander. In Shakespeare's *Midsummer Night's Dream*, a young Athenian in love with Hermia. He runs off with her and while sleeping in the woods is mistaken by Puck for Demetrius. Puck squeezes in his eyes the juice of a magic herb, making him fall in love with Helena, and recriminations follow between him and Hermia. Oberon orders Puck to restore the lovers to their natural state, and Theseus then sanctions Lysander's marriage with Hermia.

Lysias (lis'i.ạs). d. c380 B.C. One of the ten Attic orators. He lived at Thurii until about 412, and later at Athens, and lived in exile under the rule of the Thirty Tyrants, 404. He returned (403) to make a speech, still extant, against the tyrant Eratosthenes.

Lysimachus (lī.sim'ạ.kus). In Shakespeare's *Pericles*, the governor of Mytilene.

Lyte (līt), **Henry Francis.** b. at Kelso, Scotland, June 1, 1793; d. at Nice, France, Nov. 20, 1847. A British hymn writer, author of *Abide with Me* and others.

Lyttelton (lit'ẹl.tọn), **Edith Joan.** [Pseudonym, **G. B. Lancaster;** maiden name, **Balfour.**] b. in Tasmania, c1865; d. at London, Sept. 2, 1948. An English writer and public official. She was British substitute delegate (1923, 1926, 1927, 1928, 1931) to the League of Nations Assembly. Her books include *Our Superconscious Mind* (1931), *Some Cases of Prediction* (1937), and a book on her travels in Japan, Korea, China, and India. Among her plays are *Warp and Woof*, *The Thumbscrew*, and *Peter's Chance.*

Lyttelton, George. [Title, 1st Baron **Lyttelton of Frankley.**] b. at Hagley, Worcestershire, England, Jan. 17, 1709; d. there, Aug. 22, 1773. An English author and politician. He was chancellor of the exchequer (1755–56). His chief works are *Observations on the Conversion and Apostleship of St. Paul* (1747), *Dialogues of the Dead* (1760), *History of Henry II* (1767–71), and poems. He was a friend of Alexander Pope and Henry Fielding. James Thomson addressed him in his long poem *The Seasons.*

Lytton (lit'ọn), **Edward George Earle Lytton Bulwer-.** See **Bulwer-Lytton.**

Lytton, Edward Robert Lytton Bulwer-. See **Meredith, Owen.**

Lytton, Victor Alexander George Robert. [Title, 2nd Earl of **Lytton.**] b. at Simla, India, Aug. 9, 1876; d. at Knebworth, Hertfordshire, England, Oct. 25, 1947. A British administrator and diplomat; son of Owen Meredith (Edward Robert Lytton Bulwer-Lytton). He was undersecretary for India (1920–22), governor of Bengal (1922–27), and viceroy and acting governor of India (April–August, 1925). He was appointed (1931) British delegate to the League of Nations, and became

(1931) president of the League of Nations commission on Japanese aggression in Manchuria, which published the Lytton Report. Author of a biography of his son (killed in an air crash, 1933)

entitled *Antony Viscount Knebworth: A Record of Youth* (1935). His other books include *Life of Edward Bulwer, First Lord Lytton* (1913), *The Web of Life* (1938), and *Pundits and Elephants* (1942).

M

Mab (mab), **Queen.** In English fairy lore and folk-lore, the queen of the fairies. According to one folklore theory (i.e., that fairies are the ancient gods and heroes in lesser but supernatural role) this Queen Mab is a descendant of the great Queen Medb (pronounced mav) of Old Iris legend. She is first mentioned as Queen Mab in Shakespeare's *Romeo and Juliet.* Drayton introduces her in his *Nymphidia,* written several years later, and Ben Jonson in his *Entertainment of the Queen and Prince at Althrope.* Shakespeare represents her not only as adroit in all kinds of teasing and mischief, but as the hag Nightmare herself. In literary allusion, she is the fairies' midwife, that is, the fairy whose duty it is to deliver the fancies of men and to produce dreams by driving over the sleeper in her chariot. Titania, the fairy queen, is not the same person. In Shelley's *Queen Mab* she has a wider sphere, and is made to rule over men's thoughts.

Mabillon (mȧ.bē.yôṅ), **Jean.** b. at St.-Pierremont, Ardennes, France, Nov. 23, 1632; d. at Paris, Dec. 27, 1707. A French scholar and historian, a member of the Benedictine order. He lived after 1664 in the Abbey of St.-Germain-des-Prés at Paris. His *De re diplomatica* (1681) is still a classic work; in it Mabillon founded the study of diplomatic history and also of paleography and the authentication of documents. His other works include *Acta sanctorum ordinis S.-Benedicti* (1668–1702), *Vetera analecta* (1675–85), and *Musaeum Italicum* (1687–89).

Mabinogion (mab.i.nō′gi.on), **The.** A compilation of English translations of old Welsh tales made (1838–49) by Lady Charlotte Guest. *Mabinogion* is the plural of the Welsh word *mabinogi,* which means "tale of a hero," the word being derived from *mab,* a boy or youth. The great collection of these tales is at Jesus College, Oxford, in a manuscript volume of the 14th century, known as the *Red Book of Hergest.* The *Mabinogion* contains Welsh redactions, made c1200, of three of the French Arthurian prose romances, namely, *The Lady of the Fountain, Peredur, the Son of Evrawc,* and *Geraint, the Son of Erbin.* The Guest collection also contains two British tales, *Kilhwch and Olwen* (written c1100 from a 10th-century text), and the *Dream of Rhonabwy,* probably of the 13th century. The rest are tales in which King Arthur does not appear, or is named only as by interpolation, namely, *Pwyll, Prince of Dyved, Branwen, the Daughter of Llyr,* and *Math, the Son of Mathonwy.* The rest, composed in a later period, include the *Dream of Maxen Wledig* and *Lludd and Llevelys.* The tale of *Taliesin* is as late as the 16th century, although dealing with the story of a 6th-century bard.

Mac (mak). Pseudonym of **MacManus, Seumas.**

Macalister (mạ.kal′is.tẻr), **Robert Alexander Stewart.** b. at Dublin, July 8, 1870; d. April 26, 1950. An Irish archaeologist. Among his published works are *Studies in Irish Epigraphy* (1897–1907), *Bible Side-Lights from the Mound of Gezer* (1906), *Two Irish Arthurian Romances* (1908), *The Crosses of Clonmacnois* (1909), and many papers on archaeological subjects.

macaronic (mak.ạ.ron′ik). In literature, using, or characterized by the use of, many strange, distorted, or foreign words or forms, with little regard to syntax, yet with sufficient analogy to common words and constructions to be or seem intelligible.

　A macaronic stage seems very often to mark the decline of an old literature and language, in countries exposed to powerful foreign influences.
　(G. P. Marsh, *Lectures on English Language.*)

macaronic verse or **poetry.** A kind of burlesque verse in which words of another language are mingled with Latin words, or are made to figure with Latin terminations and in Latin constructions. The term was brought into vogue by the popular satirical works in this style of the Mantuan Teofilo Folengo (d. 1544). It is probable that this use of the word has reference to the varied ingredients which enter into the preparation of a dish of macaroni.

Macaulay (mạ.kô′li), **Rose.** b. at Cambridge, England, c1889—. An English novelist, poet, critic, and essayist. Author of books of poetry, including *The Two Blind Countries* (1914), *Three Days* (1919), and *Poems* (1927); and of *Non-Combatants and Others* (1916), *A Casual Commentary* (1925), *Catchwords and Claptrap* (1926), *Some Religious Elements in English Literature* (1931), *The Minor Pleasures of Life* (1934), *John Milton* (1934), and *The Writings of E. M. Forster* (1938), literary criticism, essays, and biography. She wrote the novels *Abbots Verney* (1906), *The Furnace* (1907), *The Secret River* (1909), *The Valley Captives* (1911), *The Lee Shore* (1912), *Views and Vagabonds* (1912), *The Making of a Bigot* (1914), *What Not* (1919), *Potterism* (1920), *Dangerous Ages* (1921; winner of the 1922 Femina-Vie Heureuse prize), *Mystery at Geneva* (1922), *Told by an Idiot* (1923), *Orphan Island* (1924), *Crewe Train* (1926), *Keeping Up Appearances* (1928; American title, *Daisy and Daphne*), *Staying With Relations* (1930), *They Were Defeated* (1932; American title, *The Shadow Flies*), *Going Abroad* (1934), *And No Man's Wit* (1940), and *The World My Wilderness* (1950).

Macaulay, Thomas Babington. [Title, 1st Baron **Macaulay of Rothley** (rôth′li).] b. at Rothley Temple, Leicestershire, England, Oct. 25, 1800; d. at Kensington, London, Dec. 28, 1859. English historian, essayist, poet, and statesman; son of

---

ḍ, d or j; ṣ, s or sh; ṭ, t or ch; ẓ, z or zh; o, F. cloche; ü, F. menu; ċh, Sc. loch; ṅ, F. bonbon.

Zachary Macaulay. A precocious child, he had made a historical compendium and had written a poem in three cantos before he was eight. He entered Trinity College, Cambridge, in 1818, and was called to the bar in 1826. In 1823–24 he contributed to Knight's *Quarterly Magazine*, but made his first success as a writer with his essay on Milton for the *Edinburgh Review* (August, 1825), to which journal he continued to contribute for many years. A Whig, he was a member of Parliament (1830–34, 1839–47, and 1852–57), being raised to the peerage in 1857. He served (1834–38) as a member of the supreme council in India, and was responsible for the drawing up of an excellent criminal code which was adopted in 1860. He was secretary at war (1839–41) in Melbourne's cabinet and paymaster general (1846–47) under Lord John Russell. His chief work is *The History of England from the Accession of James the Second* (vols. I and II, 1848; vols. III and IV, 1855; vol. V, posthumously 1861; an unfinished work), in which, despite the apparent Whig prejudices of the author, his attempt to apply the techniques of the historical novel through reconstruction of incident and anecdote and the social and cultural background, succeed in making a vivid picture of the period. In addition to his *Lays of Ancient Rome* (1842), he wrote numerous essays and historical sketches, including pieces on Dryden (1828), Byron (1830), Walpole (1834), Bacon (1837), Warren Hastings (1841), Frederick the Great (1842), and Addison (1843). His complete works, including his speeches, were edited in eight volumes by his sister, Lady Trevelyan (Hannah More Macaulay). See life by his nephew, George Otto Trevelyan (2 vols., 1876).

"Macaulay's History of England." The popular title of *The History of England from the Accession of James the Second*. See under **Macaulay, Thomas Babington.**

Macbeth (mak.beth′, mạk-). [Full title, **The Tragedy of Macbeth.**] A tragedy by Shakespeare, probably written in 1605 or 1606. Its first recorded production is April 20, 1610, but it is thought to have been played before. It was printed in the 1623 folio, but it is thought that cuts were made from the stage manuscript. The Hecate scenes are probably Middleton's. In the Restoration period D'Avenant made it into an opera. The plot is from Holinshed's *Chronicles*.

The Story. Macbeth and Banquo, Scottish generals, are returning from a victorious campaign when they meet upon the heath three Witches who hail them, prophesying that Macbeth will be Thane of Cawdor and King hereafter, and that Banquo will beget kings. Part of the prophecy is immediately fulfilled when a messenger announces that Duncan, King of Scotland, has promoted Macbeth to Thane of Cawdor. Lady Macbeth, having learned of the Witches, plays upon her husband, already tempted by dreams of royal power, to kill the King, who falls into their hands when he arrives for a visit at the castle of Macbeth. But when the murder is done, Macbeth is completely unnerved; in his own words:

Will all great Neptune's ocean wash this blood
Clean from my hand? No. This my hand will rather
The multitudinous seas incarnadine. . . .

Lady Macbeth, also nervous, must return to Duncan's room with the daggers that Macbeth has neglected to leave behind. Into this timeless scene of horror comes the sound of knocking at the gate. The murder is discovered, and Macbeth puts the grooms to death to conceal his action. Duncan's sons, Malcolm and Donalbain, flee from Scotland, and Macbeth is crowned. He then hires murderers to kill Banquo and his son, Fleance, but the latter escapes. At a banquet given by Macbeth, the ghost of Banquo appears to him, and Lady Macbeth, vainly trying to make light of her husband's agitation, dismisses the guests. Macbeth returns to consult with the Witches, who show him apparitions which tell him to beware Macduff, that "none of women born shall harm Macbeth," and that he shall be safe until "Birnam Wood to high Dunsinane Hill shall come." However, he is then also shown a procession of future kings, all descendants of Banquo. Macduff, meanwhile, has gone to England to raise an army with Malcolm to defeat Macbeth and there learns that his wife and children have been killed at the order of Macbeth. Macbeth, preparing to meet the invading army, learns of Lady Macbeth's death, and he conceives that her dying is merely part of the timeless flux which is his life: "Life's but a walking shadow . . . a tale told by an idiot, full of sound and fury, signifying nothing." The army advances, bearing branches cut from Birnam Wood for concealment, and Macduff who was "from his mother's womb untimely ripped" kills Macbeth. Malcolm is crowned King of Scotland.

Macbeth. The chief figure of Shakespeare's *Macbeth*. He is a brave and skillful soldier, driven by his misguided ambition to commit the murder of Duncan, the initial and unforgivable crime from which all else in the tragedy stems. Compared to the cold villainy of such characters as Iago, in *Othello*, and Edmund, in *King Lear*, he seems not evil so much as tragically, but humanly, weak, and for this reason he excites the sympathy of an audience when these other Shakespearian villains do not.

Macbeth, Lady. In Shakespeare's *Macbeth*, the wife of Macbeth. Unlike her husband, she is in all matters utterly realistic and intensely practical. She cannot sympathize with Macbeth's fears of damnation. After he returns from Duncan's chamber with blood on his hands, she says calmly that it can be washed off. One must not think on the deed or one will go mad; later she urges that he sleep to forget his cares. But when Macbeth finally does realize that his actions have counted for nothing, he finds that Lady Macbeth has broken down. The sleep which she urged has turned into sleepwalking. In her attempt to escape from the darkness of her memory, she keeps light continually around her. And she reënacts the washing of blood from guilty hands, but the "damned spot" will never come out. Suicide is her only escape.

Maccabaeus (mak.ạ.bē′us), **Judas.** See **Judas Maccabaeus.**

Maccabees (mak′ạ.bēz). A family of Jewish heroes who became the deliverers of Judea and Judaism during the bloody persecutions of the Syrian king

Antiochus I (Antiochus Epiphanes), and established a dynasty of priest-kings which lasted until supplanted by Herod in 40 B.C. The original name of the family was the Hasmoneans. It consisted of the aged Mattathias and his five sons, Jochanan (or John), Simon, Judas, Eleazar, and Jonathan, living at Modin, a small town near Jerusalem. When the sufferings of the Judeans at the hands of the Syrians became unbearable, and the existence of the Jewish religion was at stake, Mattathias and his sons became the leaders of an open rebellion against Antiochus. On Mattathias and his sons being summoned by Apelles, one of the Syrian overseers, to sacrifice to the gods, Mattathias answered, "If all the people in the kingdom obey the order of the monarch to depart from the faith of their fathers, I and my sons will abide by the covenant of our forefathers." When one of the Judeans approached the altar to sacrifice to Zeus, Mattathias rushed upon the apostate and killed him at the altar. His sons then fell upon Apelles and his troops, killed them, and destroyed the altar. Gradually an army of religious patriots rallied around these hero-leaders, and carried on a kind of guerrilla warfare against the oppressing Syrians. Mattathias died in 167, appointing Judas as his successor in the command, and Simon as the man of counsel. Judas bore the name "Maccabi," either made up of the initials from the Hebrew words *mî kamocha baëlim Jehova* ("Who is like thee among the gods, Jehovah?"), or derived from the Hebrew word *makeb*, "a hammer," expressive of his heroism, and gave by his genuinely heroic bearing his name to this whole epoch of Jewish history.

MacCalain More (mạ.kal'ạn mōr'). A name given to the earls, marquises, and dukes of Argyll.

MacCarthy (mạ.kär'thi), **Denis Florence.** b. at Dublin, May 26, 1817; d. at Blackrock, near Dublin, April 7, 1882. An Irish poet, known for his political verses and for his translation of works by the Spanish dramatist Calderón. His contributions to various periodicals were variously signed "Desmond," "Vig," "Trifolium," "Antonio," or "S.E.Y." Author of *Ballads, Poems, and Lyrics* (1850), *An Ode on the Death of the Earl of Belfast* (1856), *The Bell-founder* (1857), *Under-glimpses* (1857), and *The Centenary of More* (1880). His translations include *Justina* (1848), *Dramas* (1853), *Love, the Greatest Enchantment* (1861), and *The Wonder-working Magician* (1873).

MacCarthy, Sir **Desmond.** b. 1877; d. at Cambridge, England, June 7, 1952. An English dramatic and literary critic. He was editor of the *New Quarterly* and the *Eye Witness* (later called the *New Witness*), and was with the *New Statesman* as staff writer, literary editor, and dramatic critic. He was a contributor to the *Sunday Times*, delivered talks on literature for the British Broadcasting Corporation, and was coeditor of *Life and Letters.* Author of *The Court Theater: 1904–1907* (1907), *Remnants* (1918), *Portraits* (1931), *Criticism* (1932), *Experience* (1935), *Leslie Stephen* (1937), *Drama* (1940), critical essays and studies. He edited *Lady John Russell—A Memoir, with Selections from her Diaries and Correspondence* (1910) and *Letters of the Earl of Oxford and Asquith* (1933), and

translated (1914) Jules Romains's *The Death of a Nobody* (*Mort de Quelqu'un*, 1911).

MacCathmhaoil (mak.ka'wil), **Seosamh.** Irish form of **Campbell, Joseph.**

MacCunn (mạ.kun'), **Hamish.** b. at Greenock, Scotland, March 22, 1868; d. at London, Aug. 2, 1916. A Scottish composer. His works include operas such as *Jeanie Deans* (1894) and *Diarmid and Ghrine* (1897), cantatas, orchestral compositions, and songs.

MacDonagh (mạk.dun'ạ), **Thomas.** b. in Ireland, 1878; d. there, 1916. An Irish poet and patriot, executed for his part in the uprising against British rule (the Easter Rebellion) at Dublin in 1916. His writings include *Thomas Campion* (1913) and *Literature in Ireland* (1916). His collected poems were published posthumously, in 1917.

Macdonald (mạk.don'ạld), **Flora.** b. 1722; d. at Kingsburgh, Scotland, March 5, 1790. A Scottish Jacobite heroine. She was the daughter of Ranald Macdonald, a farmer in South Uist, an island of the Hebrides. She assisted Prince Charles Edward Stuart, the Young Pretender, who was a fugitive after the battle of Culloden Moor, to escape, disguised as her female attendant, from the island of Benbecula to Skye, June 27, 1746.

Macdonald, George. b. at Huntley, Aberdeenshire, Scotland, Dec. 10, 1824; d. at Ashstead, Surrey, England, Sept. 18, 1905. A Scottish poet, novelist, and writer of books for juveniles; a friend of Emerson, Carlyle, Tennyson, Ruskin, and Matthew Arnold. Author of *At the Back of the North Wind* (1871), *The Princess and the Goblin* (1872), and *The Princess and Curdie* (1873), for juveniles; *Within and Without* (1855), *Poems* (1857), *Phantastes* (1858), and *The Diary of an Old Soul* (1880), poetry; *David Elginbrod* (1863), *Alec Forbes* (1865), *Robert Falconer* (1868), *Malcolm* (1875), *The Marquis of Lossie* (1877), and *Sir Gibbie* (1879), novels of Scottish life; and *Thomas Wingfold* (1876), *Paul Faber* (1879), and *Lilith* (1895), novels of English life.

Macdonald, Lucy Maud. [Maiden name, **Montgomery.**] b. at Clifton, Prince Edward Island, Canada, 1874; d. at Toronto, April 24, 1942. A Canadian novelist. Author of *Anne of Green Gables* (1908).

MacDonald, Philip. b. c1896—. An English novelist and writer of detective fiction. He is reticent about the details of his own life, and has published works under the names of "Oliver Fleming," "Anthony Lawless," and "Martin Porlock." His best-known character is Colonel Gethryn, a detective.

MacDonald, Ramsay. [Full name, **James Ramsay MacDonald.**] b. at Lossiemouth, Scotland, Oct. 12, 1866; d. at sea, Nov. 9, 1937. A British statesman, first Labour prime minister (1924) of England. An illegitimate child, he spent his childhood in poverty. In 1888 he established himself at London, where as a member (from 1886) of the Fabian Society he spoke often for the moderate Socialist program. MacDonald joined (1894) with Keir Hardie and others in the Independent Labour Party, the basis of the Labour Party, of which he was secretary (1900–12) and treasurer (1912–24). He was elected (1906) a member of Parliament and was leader

ḍ, d or j; ṣ, s or sh; ṭ, t or ch; ẓ, z or zh; o, F. cloche; ü, F. menu; ċh, Sc. loch; ṅ, F. bonbon.

(1911–14) of the Labour Party, resigning from the latter post because of his opposition to the granting of war credits. He was a pacifist and became known as an opponent of the war and a pro-German, although his stand was essentially one of winning the war while preserving social gains. In the "Khaki election" of December, 1918, he lost his seat in Commons. The failure of the Lloyd George government brought him back (1922) to Parliament and to leadership of the Labour Party. The fall of Stanley Baldwin's cabinet in 1923 brought a general election, in which Labour and the Liberals won control of the House of Commons; MacDonald formed (January, 1924) a cabinet in which he was prime minister and secretary for foreign affairs. His emphasis was on foreign policy, attempting the rehabilitation of the German economy and a rapprochement with the U.S.S.R. The Russian commercial treaty was opposed by the Liberals, and the Labour cabinet, the first in English history, fell in November. His defeat in the election was to a large extent the result of the publication of the so-called Zinoviev letter, a document calling for a revolution in England and supposedly signed by the head of the Comintern, but probably a forgery. MacDonald, never a believer in direct action by labor, nevertheless supported the general strike of 1926 and regained the confidence of much of the labor group. In the general election of 1929, Labour for the first time had a clear majority in Parliament and MacDonald formed his second ministry. He carried through a program of improvement of workers' conditions (improved unemployment insurance, public housing, agricultural wages board), but the deepening of the economic depression of the 1930's resulted eventually in a budget calling for a cut in unemployment benefits (the dole). This split the Labour Party and resulted in MacDonald's forming, after an attempt to resign, the National (coalition) government of 1931. He was read out of the Labour Party and for the remainder of his life was attacked as a renegade by the Socialists who formed the core of the party. MacDonald, Philip Snowden, and J. H. Thomas headed a National Labour Party and in the general election of 1931 the coalition government won a tremendous majority. Under MacDonald the National government passed the Statute of Westminster, establishing the dominions of the British Commonwealth as more or less independent members, abandoned the gold standard, and dropped the free-trade principle. The failure of the World Economic Conference (1933) and the necessity to rearm in the face of growing German militarism resulted in MacDonald's retirement (1935) as prime minister. He held (1935–37) the post of lord president of council in the National cabinet now headed by Stanley Baldwin. He wrote *Socialism and Society* (1905), *Socialism* (1907), *Socialism and Government* (1909), *The Awakening of India* (1910), *The Social Unrest* (1913), and others.

Macdonell (mak.dǫ.nel'), **Alastair Ruadh.** [Called **Pickle the Spy.**] b. c1725; d. Dec. 23, 1761. A Scottish chieftain and spy. He joined (1748) Lord Drummond's regiment of Royal Scots Guards and was employed (1745) by Highland leaders on a secret mission to Prince Charles Edward Stuart. After his capture and imprisonment (1745–47) by

the English, he spied (1749–54) on Charles for the English.

Macduff (mak.duf'). In Shakespeare's *Macbeth*, the Thane of Fife. He discovers the murdered Duncan and is probably the first to suspect Macbeth. He goes to England to beg Malcolm to return with him to fight Macbeth, and there hears of the slaughter of his wife and children. He was "from his mother's womb untimely ripped," and thus not naturally "born of woman." Therefore, according to the Witches' prophecy, he is the only agent capable of destroying Macbeth, whom he kills in battle.

Macduff, Lady. In Shakespeare's *Macbeth*, Macduff's wife. She and her son are murdered on Macbeth's orders.

MacDuncan (mak.dung'kạn), **Malcolm.** See **Malcolm III.**

Macfarren (mak.far'ẹn), Sir **George Alexander.** b. at London, March 2, 1813; d. there, Oct. 31, 1887. An English composer and writer on music. Among his works are the operas *The Devil's Opera* (1838), *Don Quixote* (1846), *Robin Hood* (1860), and *Jessy Lea* (1863), and the oratorios *Saint John the Baptist* (1873), *The Resurrection* (1876), and *Joseph* (1877), besides a number of cantatas and numerous cathedral services. He also published *Rudiments of Harmony* (1860) and *Six Lectures on Harmony* (1866), and harmonized Chappell's *Popular Music of the Olden Time.* From about 1860 he was totally blind.

Macfirbis (mak.fėr'bis), **Duald.** b. 1585; d. 1670. The last of the hereditary chroniclers of Ireland. His chief work is a treatise on Irish genealogy, completed in 1650.

MacFlecknoe, or a Satire on the True Blue Protestant Poet T. S. (mak.flek'nō). A satirical poem by John Dryden (1682), directed against Thomas Shadwell. It served as a model for the *Dunciad* of Alexander Pope. Flecknoe was a Roman Catholic priest addicted to scribbling very bad verses. His name has been chiefly preserved by this satire, in which the author has depicted Shadwell as the literary son and heir (albeit a "True Blue Protestant") of this "wretched poetaster."

Macgill (mạ.gil'), **Patrick.** b. in County Donegal, Ireland, 1890–. An Irish poet, novelist, and playwright. His writings include *Gleanings from a Navvy's Scrap Book, Songs of a Navvy, Songs of the Dead End, Children of the Dead End, The Rat-Pit, The Great Push, Soldier Songs, Songs of Donegal,* and *Sid Puddiefoot.* Among his plays are *Moleskin Joe* (1921), *Suspense* (1930), and *So Said the Women* (1938).

Macgreegor (mạ.greg'ọr), **Wee.** See under **Bell, John Joy.**

Macgregor (mạ.greg'ọr), **John.** b. at Gravesend, England, Jan. 24, 1825; d. at Boscombe, near Bournemouth, England, July 16, 1892. An English traveler. He invented (c1865) the "Rob Roy" canoe, in which he made trips in many parts of the world, publicizing it in such books as *A Thousand Miles in the Rob Roy Canoe on Rivers and Lakes in Europe* (1866), *The Rob Roy on the Jordan, Red Sea, and Gennesareth* (1869), and others.

Macgregor, Robert. [Also: **Robert Campbell;** commonly called **Rob Roy.**] b. in Buchanan parish,

Scotland, 1671; d. at Balquhidder, Scotland, Dec. 28, 1734. A Scottish outlaw. He was the younger son of Donald Macgregor, a lieutenant colonel in the army of James II. He got his name Roy from his red hair. After the accession of William III he obtained a commission from James II, and in 1691 made a descent on Stirlingshire. In 1712 he was evicted and outlawed on a charge of embezzlement. He became a Highland freebooter, and was included in the Act of Attainder. Under the protection of the Duke of Argyll, he continued to levy blackmail on the Scottish gentry. He is the subject of a novel by Sir Walter Scott (published in 1818).

Machault or **Machaut** (mȧ.shō), **Guillaume de.** See Guillaume de Machault.

Macheath (mak.hēth'), **Captain.** A principal character in John Gay's *Beggar's Opera:* a gay and dissolute highwayman.

Machen (mak'ẹn), **Arthur.** b. at Caerleon, Monmouthshire, England, 1863; d. at Beaconsfield, England, Dec. 15, 1947. An English novelist and essayist, noted for his stories of fantasy.

Machiavelli or **Macchiavelli** (mak″i.ạ.vel'i; Italian, mä.kyä.vel'lē), **Niccolò.** b. at Florence, Italy, May 3, 1469; d. there, June 22, 1527. A Florentine statesman and author. His father, a lawyer, was the hereditary owner of a small farm south of the city. Niccolò received a good education of the humanist type, of which no precise details have reached us. He came first into public view in June, 1498, on his appointment as secretary both of the Second Chancery and of the Ten in Charge of War. Although these were purely administrative posts, his zeal and marked political acumen gradually won him an important share in shaping policy, especially after Piero Soderini became (1502) *gonfalonier* (chief executive) for life. When the Florentine republic fell (1512) and the Medici returned to power he was dismissed from office and never again employed. As politics were the breath of life to him, he solaced himself by turning to the theoretical study of politics with its focal center in the state. His leading works in this field are *Il Principe* (The Prince), *Arte della Guerra* (Art of War), and *Discorsi sopra le Prima Deca di Tito Livio* (Discourses on the First Ten Books of Livy). With the *Istorie fiorentini* (History of Florence) he ventured with much less success into the field of history, and with a number of comedies, of which *La Mandragola* is the outstanding example, he took rank among the leading dramatists of his time. Of the many editions of his works the handiest to consult is *Tutte le Opere Storiche e Letterarie a cura di Guido Manzoni e Mario Casella* (Florence, 1929). There are English versions of all his works, particularly of *The Prince.* With his story of the functioning of the state, particularly as presented by *The Prince,* Machiavelli stirred up a furore which has not subsided down to our day. The reason is simple: throughout the Middle Ages political writers, theologically inspired, had accepted the state as a divine agency and had concerned themselves with expounding how, in view of its origin, it ought to act, but living in a new and frankly secular age, Machiavelli faced a new kind of state, the absolute monarchy, and with cold, scientific detachment set himself to describe its actual behavior. He had no difficulty in showing that the state which had recently taken over the many small principalities of Italy and, far more strikingly, the great monarchies of France, Spain, and England, practiced an unlimited sovereignty, the goal of which was power. Consequently, he deduced that modern states, no longer checked by considerations of religion and morality, dealt with one another on the level of unadulterated power politics. While this contention, commonly called Machiavellianism or Machiavellism, was and has continued to be heatedly rejected by many political scientists, it has so frequently been found to be in accord with the facts that its author has throughout the ages been alternately vilified and praised. The outstanding biography is *Niccolò Machiavelli e i suoi Tempi,* by P. Villari (3 vols., 1877–82; Eng. trans. by Linda Villari, 2 vols., 1898).

Machin (mā'kin) or **Macham** (-kạm), **Robert.** The legendary discoverer of Madeira. He is represented as an English squire who fled from England with his inamorata, Anna d'Arset or Dorset, daughter of a powerful noble at the court of Edward III. The vessel in which he sailed was driven by stress of weather to the coast of an unknown island, where he landed with part of the crew at a port which they named Machico. During their absence the ship was driven out to sea, and Anna, who had remained on board, died of grief and fatigue, while Machin and his companions made their way to Spain and thence to England. His story incited the Spanish and the Portuguese to search for the island, which was found by Gonsalvez Zarco in 1419. The legend was first printed in the *Descobrimentos* of Antonio Galvano (1503–57), of which Hakluyt published a translation in 1601.

MacIan (mạ.kī'ạn), **Eachin.** See Conachar.

MacIvor (mạk.ē'vọr), **Fergus.** A Highland chief, a character in Sir Walter Scott's novel *Waverley.*

MacIvor, Flora. The sister of Fergus MacIvor, and the principal female character, in Sir Walter Scott's novel *Waverley.*

Mackail (mạ.kāl'), **Denis George.** b. June 3, 1892—. An English novelist; son of John William Mackail. Author of *Romance to the Rescue* (1921), *Bill the Bachelor* (1922), *What Next?* (1923), *The "Majestic" Mystery* (1924), *The Fortunes of Hugo* (1926), *Tales from Greenery Street* (1928), *How Amusing!* (1929), *Having Fun* (1933), *The Wedding* (1935), *London Lovers* (1938), *Tales for a Godchild* (1944), *Huddleston House* (1945), and *We're Here!* (1947).

Mackail, John William. b. at Ascog, Buteshire, Scotland, Aug. 26, 1859; d. 1945. A British scholar; father of Angela Thirkell and of Denis George Mackail. He published *Select Epigrams from the Greek Anthology* (1890), *Biblia Innocentium* (1891–93), *Latin Literature* (1895), *Life of William Morris* (1899), a translation of the *Odyssey* (1903–10), *The Springs of Helicon* (1909), and *Lectures on Greek Poetry* (1910).

Mackay (mạ.kī'), **Charles.** b. at Perth, Scotland, March 27, 1814; d. at London, Dec. 24, 1889. A Scottish poet. He was editor (1844–47) of the Glasgow *Argus,* editor (1852–59) of the *Illustrated London News,* and special New York correspondent of

ḍ, d or j; ṣ, s or sh; ṭ, t or ch; ẓ, z or zh; o, F. cloche; ü, F. menu; ċh, Sc. loch; ṅ, F. bonbon.

the London *Times* during the Civil War. He revealed in the *Times* in 1862 the existence of the Fenian conspiracy in America. Among his works are *The Salamandrine, or Love and Immortality* (1842), *Voices from the Crowd* (1846), *Voices from the Mountains* (1847), and *History of the Mormons* (1851).

Mackay, Mary. See **Corelli, Marie.**

Mackenzie (mạ.ken'zi), Sir **Alexander.** b. c1755; d. at Mulnain, near Dunkeld, Perthshire, Scotland, March 11, 1820. A Scottish explorer. He entered the service of the Northwest Fur Company in 1779, and in 1789 commanded an exploring expedition to the Northwest, during which he discovered the Mackenzie River, June 29, 1789. He published *Voyages on the River St. Lawrence and through the Continent of North America to the Frozen and Pacific Oceans in the years 1789 and 1793* (1801).

Mackenzie, Compton. b. at West Hartlepool, England, Jan. 17, 1883—. An English writer. During World War I, he served (1915) with the Dardanelles expedition, was military control officer (1916) at Athens, and was director (1917) of intelligence service in Syria. He was literary critic (1931–35) of the *Daily Mail.* His plays include *The Gentleman in Grey* (1906), *Carnival* (1912), *Columbine* (1920), and *The Lost Cause* (1931). Author of the novels *The Passionate Elopement* (1911), *Carnival* (1912), *Sinister Street* (1913), *Guy and Pauline* (1915), *Sylvia Scarlett* (1918), *Sylvia and Michael* (1919), *The Altar Steps* (1922), *The Parson's Progress* (1923), *The Heavenly Ladder* (1924), *Vestal Fire* (1927), *Gallipoli Memories* (1929), *The Four Winds of Love* (1937–45), *A Musical Chair* (1939), *The Monarch of the Glen* (1941), *The Vital Flame* (1946), *Whiskey Galore* (1947), and others. He also published *Poems* (1907).

Mackenzie, Henry. [Called the "Addison of the North."] b. at Edinburgh, in August, 1745; d. there, Jan. 14, 1831. A Scottish novelist. He wrote *The Man of Feeling* (anonymous, 1771), *The Man of the World* (1773), and *Julia de Roubigné* (1777). He wrote several plays, of which *The Prince of Tunis* (1773) achieved some success, but is principally known for his first-named novel, a very successful book."

Mackenzie, Robert Shelton. b. at Drews Court, County Limerick, Ireland, June 22, 1809; d. at Philadelphia, Nov. 30, 1880. An Irish author.

Mackenzie, Rose. [Called **Rosey.**] In Thackeray's novel *The Newcomes*, the pretty and amiable first wife of Clive Newcome. She dies after a very brief and not very happy married life.

Mackintosh (mak'in.tosh), Sir **James.** b. at Aldourie, near Inverness, Scotland, Oct. 24, 1765; d. at London, May 30, 1832. A Scottish philosopher. A physician, he came to London in 1788 and in 1791 published a reply to Burke's attack on the French Revolution that was recognized as meritorious even by Burke. He was admitted to the bar at Lincoln's Inn, London, in 1795, accepted the recordership of Bombay in 1803, and was commissioned judge in the court of vice-admiralty at Bombay in 1806. He returned to England in 1811, entered Parliament in 1813, and was professor of law at Haileybury (1818–24). Among his works are *Dissertation on the*

Progress of Ethical Philosophy (1830) and *History of the Revolution in England in 1688* (1834).

Macklin (mak'lin), **Charles.** [Original surname, **McLaughlin.**] b. in Ireland, c1697; d. at London, July 11, 1797. An English actor and dramatist. He rose steadily in public favor till his famous appearance as Shylock in 1741. From this time he played constantly in tragedy, comedy, and farce for nearly 50 years. When about 90 years old he created the part of Sir Pertinax Macsycophant in his own play *The Man of the World*, one of the most arduous roles in his very large repertory. He also wrote plays, taught acting, and kept a coffee-house for some years in Covent Garden. He wrote *King Henry VII* (produced 1746), *Love à la Mode* (1759), and *The Man of the World* (1781; originally *The True-born Scotchman*, 1766).

Maclaren (mạ.klar'ẹn), **Archibald.** b. in the Highlands of Scotland, March 2, 1755; d. at London, 1826. A Scottish playwright.

Maclaren, Charles. b. at Ormiston, Scotland, Oct. 7, 1782; d. at Edinburgh, Sept. 10, 1866. A Scottish editor and author. He founded (1817) *The Scotsman*, an Edinburgh political newspaper which he edited (1820–45). He also edited (1820) the sixth edition of the *Encyclopaedia Britannica.* Author of *Topography of the Plain of Troy* (1822), *Geology of Fife and the Lothians* (1839), and similar works.

Maclaren, Ian. Pseudonym of **Watson, John** (1850–1907).

Maclehose (mak'lẹ.hōz), **Agnes.** [Also: **M'Lehose**; maiden name, **Craig.**] b. at Glasgow, April 17, 1759; d. at Edinburgh, Oct. 22 or 23, 1841. A Scottish beauty, the "Clarinda" of Robert Burns. She is known for the correspondence she carried on with Burns, who was "Sylvander" to her "Clarinda"; she inspired the poet's song *Ae Fond Kiss* (1791), which Scott declared contained the "essence of a thousand love tales." Mrs. Maclehose first met Burns at a party in Edinburgh on Dec. 7, 1787, a meeting that was followed by mutual infatuation and a correspondence that lasted until July 25, 1794, although personal contact had ceased in 1791. Author of a few short poems, enclosed in her letters, such as *When First You Saw Clarinda's Charms, Talk Not of Love!*, and *To a Blackbird Singing on a Tree.*

Macleod (mạ.kloud'), **Fiona.** Pseudonym of **Sharp, William.**

Macleod, Norman. b. at Campbeltown, Argyllshire, Scotland, June 3, 1812; d. at Glasgow, June 16, 1872. A Scottish clergyman. He was parish minister successively of Loudoun, in Ayrshire; Dalkeith, near Edinburgh; and Barony parish, Glasgow; and was editor of the Edinburgh *Christian Instructor* from 1849, and of *Good Words* from 1860. In 1867 he was sent by the General Assembly to visit the mission stations in India. Among his works are *Parish Papers* (1862), *Wee Davie* (1864), *The Starling* (1867), *Reminiscences of a Highland Parish* (1867), *Character Sketches* (1872), and others.

MacManus (mạk.man'us), **Seumas.** [Pseudonym, **Mac.**] b. in County Donegal, Ireland, 1869—. An Irish writer of prose and verse. He is the author of *Through the Turf Smoke* (1899), *In Chimney Corners* (1899), *Donegal Fairy Stories* (1900), *The Be-*

witched Fiddle, and Other Tales (1900), *A Lad of the O'Friels* (1903), *The Red Poocher* (1903), *Dark Patrick* (1939), and many shorter stories.

Macmillan (măk.mil′an), **Daniel.** b. at Upper Corrie, Arran, Scotland, Sept. 13, 1813; d. at Cambridge, England, June 27, 1857. A Scottish bookseller and publisher, founder of the Macmillan firm. After serving (1837–43) his apprenticeship at Cambridge and London, he established (1843) with a brother the firm of Macmillan and Company at London. The firm began to publish books in 1844. Specializing at first in religious, scientific, and technical books, he made publishing history with Charles Kingsley's *Westward Ho!* (1855) and Thomas Hughes's *Tom Brown's Schooldays* (1857).

Macmillan, Sir Frederick Orridge. b. Oct. 5, 1851; d. at London, June 1, 1936. An English publisher; son of Daniel Macmillan. Admitted to partnership in 1874, he became chairman of Macmillan and Company, Ltd., and was a director of the Macmillan Company, a New York branch which had become independent in 1890.

Macmillan, George Augustin. b. at Cambridge, England, Aug. 1, 1855; d. at Danby, Yorkshire, England, March 3, 1936. An English classical scholar and publisher; nephew of Daniel Macmillan. He became (1879) a partner in the Macmillan publishing firm. He was elected (1879) honorary secretary of the Hellenic Society, a post he held for 40 years.

Macmillan, Maurice Crawford. b. at Cambridge, England, April 19, 1853; d. at London, March 30, 1936. An English publisher; son of Daniel Macmillan. For many years, until his death, he was a director of both Macmillan and Company, Ltd., at London, and the Macmillan Company at New York, an independent branch since 1890.

Macmorris (măk.mor′is). In Shakespeare's *Henry V*, an Irish captain.

MacMunn (măk.mun′), **Sir George Fletcher.** b. at London, Aug. 14, 1869; d. at East Grinstead, Sussex, England, Aug. 24, 1952. An English soldier who served (1919–20) as British commander in chief in Mesopotamia. He was quartermaster general (1920–24) in India. He is the author of books on India and on military campaigns and figures.

MacNally (măk.nal′i), **Leonard.** b. at Dublin, 1752; d. Feb. 13, 1820. An Irish playwright and political informer. He worked with the Irish revolutionary leaders, and served at the same time as a secret agent of the British government. He was in London during the Gordon Riots (June, 1780), and rescued at risk of his own life Dr. Thurlow, brother of the lord chancellor, whom the rioters had suspected as being a Catholic agent. He was editor (1782) of the *Public Ledger*, and a contributor (1792) of rebellious verses to the *Northern Star*. He betrayed Irish revolutionary leaders to the government and defended them (notably 1797, 1798, and 1803) as their lawyer. These double dealings were so skillfully handled that they were not discovered until after his death.

MacNeice (măk.nēs′), **Louis.** b. at Belfast, Ireland, Sept. 12, 1907—. An English poet and classical scholar. He was lecturer in classics (1930–36) at Birmingham, lecturer in Greek (1936–40) at Bed-

ford College for Women, and feature writer and producer (1941 *et seq.*) for the British Broadcasting Corporation. His works include *Blind Fireworks* (1929), *Poems* (1935), *Out of the Picture* (1937), *The Earth Compels* (1938), *Zoo* (1938), *Autumn Journal* (1939), *Plant and Phantom* (1941), *Christopher Columbus* (1944), and *Holes in the Sky* (1948). He translated Aeschylus's *Agamemnon* (1936). Coauthor with W. H. Auden of *Letters from Iceland* (1937). His critical studies include *Modern Poetry* (1938) and *The Poetry of W. B. Yeats* (1941).

Macneill (măk.nēl′), **Hector.** b. at Rosebank, Midlothian, Scotland, Oct. 22, 1746; d. at Edinburgh, March 15, 1818. A Scottish poet, pamphleteer, and novelist. Author of *On the Treatment of Negroes in Jamaica*, a pamphlet defending slavery (1788), of *The Harp* (1789), *Scotland's Scaith, or the History of Will and Jean* (1795), and *The Waes o' War, or the Upshot of the History* (1796), poetry, and of *Memoirs of Charles Macpherson* (1800) and *The Scottish Adventurers* (1812), novels. His reputation rests on a few songs, among which are *My Boy Tammy, I Lo'ed Ne'er a Laddie but Ane, Come Under My Plaidie*, and *Mary of Castlecary*.

MacNeill (măk.nēl′), **John Gordon Swift.** b. at Dublin, March 11, 1849; d. there, Aug. 24, 1926. An Irish historian. He was an active parliamentarian (1890–1917), and was responsible for procuring (1906) the abolition of flogging in the Royal Navy and for establishing (1906) the principle that ministers of the Crown should not hold directorships in public companies. He was professor of constitutional law and of the law of public and private wrongs (1909–26), and dean of the faculty of law (1912–26) at the National University of Ireland. Author of *The Irish Parliament, What it was and what it did* (1885), *English Interference with Irish Industries* (1886), *The Constitutional and Parliamentary History of Ireland* (1917), *Studies in the Constitution of the Irish Free State* (1925), and *What I Have Seen and Heard* (1925).

Macnish (măk.nish′), **Robert.** b. at Glasgow, Feb. 15, 1802; d. there, Jan. 16, 1837. A Scottish medical and miscellaneous writer.

MacPhail (măk.fāl′), **Sir Andrew.** b. at Orwell, Prince Edward Island, Canada, Nov. 24, 1864; d. at Montreal, Sept. 23, 1938. A Canadian pathologist and writer. He was professor of the history of medicine (1906–37) at McGill. His books include *Essays in Puritanism* (1905), *The Vine of Sibmah* (1906), *Essays in Politics* (1909), *Essays in Fallacy* (1910), *The Book of Sorrow* (1916), *Three Persons* (1929), and *The Bible in Scotland* (1931). He translated Louis Hémon's *Maria Chapdelaine*.

Macpherson (măk.fèr′sọn), **James.** b. at Ruthven, Inverness-shire, Scotland, Oct. 27, 1736; d. in Inverness-shire, Feb. 17, 1796. A Scottish writer, the alleged translator of the Ossianic poems. In 1759, while a schoolmaster in his native village, he showed to Alexander Carlyle (Jupiter Carlyle) and John Home some fragments of Gaelic verse with translations. They were published (*Fragments of Ancient Poetry collected in the Highlands of Scotland, and translated from the Galic or Erse Language*) in 1760, and excited so much interest that he was sent to the Highlands for the purpose of discovering more of these poems. The result was the *Poems of Ossian*, consisting of *Fingal, an Ancient Epic Poem in six books* (1762), and *Temora, an Ancient Epic Poem in eight books* (1763), purporting to be translations from the Gaelic of the 3rd-century poet Ossian (or Oisin). At once a controversy arose over their genuineness as Gaelic remains; Samuel Johnson, no Scottish enthusiast, declared them to be a fabrication based on fragments of stories and poems, and they were also attacked by Thomas Gray and others. Macpherson was challenged to produce his originals, but he never did so nor did he successfully refute the arguments against the authenticity of his Ossianic works. Regardless of their legitimacy, the poems, written for the most part in rhythmic prose (a reaction to the rhymed couplets of the Augustan age), had tremendous influence on the romantic revival then setting in, especially on the Continent, where the Germans, led by Herder and Goethe, were ardent admirers of the melancholy and descriptive power of the writing. In 1764 Macpherson was sent as governor general to the Floridas; in 1779 he was made agent to Mohammed Ali, Nabob of Arcot; and in 1780 he entered Parliament, where he sat for ten years. His other writings include a translation in prose of the *Iliad* (1773) and *Original Papers, containing the Secret History of Great Britain from the Restoration to the Accession of the House of Hanover* (1775).

Macready (mạ.krē'di), **William Charles.** b. at London, March 3, 1793; d. at Cheltenham, Gloucestershire, England, April 27, 1873. An English tragedian. His father was an actor and manager of the theater at Birmingham where Macready made his first appearance in 1810. In 1816 he appeared at London at Covent Garden. In 1837 he had advanced to the front rank of his profession, having for many years struggled for supremacy with Kean, Young, and Charles Kemble. He then undertook the management of the Covent Garden Theatre, and produced Shakespeare's plays. After two seasons he abandoned it and played in the provinces and in Paris. He managed (1841–43) the Drury Lane Theatre. He made several visits to America, during the last of which occurred the famous Astor Place riot, the cause being the jealousy of Edwin Forrest. In 1851 he left the stage. He was noted for his Macbeth, Cassius, Lear, Henry IV, Iago, Virginius, Richelieu, and other parts.

Macro Plays (mak'rō). Morality plays found in a manuscript that once belonged to an English antiquary, Cox Macro. They include *The Castle of Perseverance* (c1405), *Mind, Will and Understanding* (c1460), and *Mankynd* (c1475).

MacSarcasm (mak.sär'kaz.ẹm), **Sir Archy.** A character in Charles Macklin's *Love à la Mode*.

MacTab (mak.tab'), **the Hon. Miss Lucretia.** One of the principal characters in Colman's *Poor Gentleman.* She is a proud and prudish old maid.

Madame Bovary (mả.dảm bo.vả.rē). A novel by Gustave Flaubert, published in 1857. Notable as an expression of realism, it is the story of Emma Bovary who, unhappy as the wife of a dull small-town doctor, indulges in extramarital affairs and incurs many debts. When her actions place her in

a position from which she can see no escape, she commits suicide.

Madame Tussaud's Waxworks (tu.sōz'). See **Tussaud's Waxworks, Madame.**

Madan (mad'ạn), **Martin.** b. 1726; d. at Epsom, Surrey, England, May 2, 1790. An English Methodist divine. He was called to the bar in 1748, but shortly abandoned law in order to enter the ministry, and was for many years chaplain to the Lock Hospital. He is chiefly known as the author of *Telyphthora, or A Treatise on Female Ruin* (1780), in which he advocated polygamy.

Maddie Groatsettar (mad'i grōt'set.ạr). See **Groatsettar, Clara** and **Maddie.**

Madeline Bray (mad'ẹ.lin brā'). See **Bray, Madeline.**

Madeline Neroni (nẹ.rō'ni) or **Vesey-Neroni** (vē'zi-). See **Neroni, Signora Madeline.**

Madge (maj), **Old.** In George Peele's *The Old Wives' Tale*, an old woman.

Madge Wildfire (wīld'fīr). See **Wildfire, Madge.**

Mad Hatter. A character in *Alice's Adventures in Wonderland*. He helps entertain Alice at a tea party.

Mad Lover, The. A play by John Fletcher, produced before 1616 and printed in 1647. It is founded on Josephus's *Antiquities of the Jews*, xviii.

Madoc (mad'ọk, mä'dọk). [Also, **Madog.**] A legendary Welsh prince, said to have discovered America c1170 (Welsh-speaking American Indians have been "discovered" to support the story, but the "evidence" thus far available has left U. S. scholars unconvinced).

Madoc. A poem (1805) by Robert Southey.

Madonna of the Future, The. A story (1879) by Henry James.

Mador (mad'ọr), **Sir.** In Arthurian romance, a Scottish knight slain by Sir Lancelot because he had accused Guinevere of poisoning his brother.

Mad Parliament, The. A great council held at Oxford in 1258 to deal with evasions by Henry III of the obligations imposed by Magna Charta.

"Mad Priest," the. See **Ball, John.**

Madras House (mạ.dras', -dräs'), **The.** A play (1910) by Harley Granville-Barker. It satirizes a prosperous, self-satisfied draper (seller of dry goods), both in his personal life and in his business. Huxtable, the draper, is contrasted with Constantine Madras, a newly converted Mohammedan who paints the joys of polygamy (an institution which would be particularly helpful to Huxtable, in view of his six unmarried daughters). Philip Madras, Constantine's son, is concerned that neither Huxtable nor his father have any real feeling for human misery, and thinks that one may rescue people from savagery through the wide popularization of letters, music, and art.

madrigal (mad'ri.gạl). **1.** A medieval poem or song, amorous, pastoral, or descriptive. The distinguishing characteristics of the madrigal are now hard to determine.

> By shallow rivers to whose falls
> Melodious birds sing madrigals.
> (Marlowe, *Passionate Shepherd to his Love*.)

---

fat, fāte, fär, ȧsk, fãre; net, mē, hėr; pin, pīne; not, nōte, möve, nôr; up, lūte, pull; TH, then;

2. In music, a musical setting of such a poem. Strict madrigal writing involves the use of a *canto fermo*, adherence to one of the ecclesiastical modes throughout, the abundant use of contrapuntal imitation in all its varieties, and the absence of instrumental accompaniment. This form of composition appeared in the Low Countries in the 15th century, and soon spread to Italy, Germany, France, and England. In Italy and England it attained a notable perfection and beauty, passing over in the latter country into the modern glee. Madrigals were written for from three to eight or more voices. The sentiments embodied varied from grave to gay, with a constant tendency to the latter. The choruses in the earlier operas and oratorios were madrigals.

Mad World, My Masters, A. A dialogue by Nicholas Breton, printed in 1603.

Mad World, My Masters, A. A play by Thomas Middleton, produced c1606 and printed in 1608. Aphra Behn copied it in *The City Heiress* (1682), and it was used by Charles Johnson in *Country Lasses*.

Maeander (mē.an'dėr). [Modern Turkish, **Menderes** (men.de.res').] In ancient geography, a river of W Asia Minor, flowing, with many windings, generally SW and W through Phrygia and Ionia to the Aegean Sea. The name is the origin of the word "meander." Length, ab. 250 mi.

Maecenas (mē.sē'nas). In Shakespeare's *Antony and Cleopatra*, a friend of Octavius who tries to reconcile the triumvirs. He later supports Octavius against Antony.

Maecenas, Gaius (or **Caius**) **Cilnius.** d. 8 B.C. A Roman statesman and patron of literature. He was descended from an ancient Etruscan family, and belonged to the equestrian order. He appears in 40 as the agent of Octavian (afterward emperor under the title of Augustus) in negotiating a marriage with Scribonia, daughter of Libo, the father-in-law of Sextus Pompeius. He was entrusted with the administration of Rome during the absence of Octavian on an expedition against Pompey in 36; and after the battle of Actium in 31, when Octavian made himself master of the Roman world, urged him to establish an empire instead of restoring the republic. He remained, with Agrippa, the chief adviser of Augustus down to 16, when he became estranged from his master and retired to private life. He was the friend and patron of Horace and Vergil, and wrote a number of works, fragments only of which are extant. His name has become a synonym for the generous patron of the arts.

Maelstrom (māl'strom). [Also: **Moskenström** (môs'ken.strem); Norwegian, **Malstrøm** (mäl'strem).] A whirlpool caused by the tidal current off the NW coast of Norway, S of the island of Moskenes, formerly supposed to suck in and destroy anything that approached it at any time, and still considered dangerous to small craft. In ancient Germanic legend the Maelstrom was caused by the two magic millstones which ground out so much salt for the Viking Mylsingr that the load sank his ship. It is said that they are still grinding away under water, grinding out the salt which makes sea water salty, and causing the turbulent whirlpool.

Maenads (mē'nadz). See **Bacchae** or **Bacchantes.**

Maeonia (mē.ō'ni.ạ). An early name of Lydia, in Asia Minor.

Maeonides (mē.on'i.dēz). A surname of Homer, by one account a native of Maeonia (Lydia).

Maeterlinck (mā'tėr.lingk, met'ėr-; French, mä.ter.laṅk; Flemish, mä'tėr.lingk), Count **Maurice.** b. at Ghent, Belgium, Aug. 29, 1862; d. near Nice, France, May 6, 1949. A Belgian dramatist, essayist, and poet. After practicing law at Ghent, he went to Paris in 1886, where he came under the influence of Villiers de l'Isle Adam and became a member of a group of symbolist writers. The pessimism of his earlier works is in contrast to the calm optimism of his mature writings. He was the author of such dramas as *Pelléas et Mélisande* (1892), the basis of the opera (1902) by Claude Debussy, *Monna Vanna* (1902), and *L'Oiseau bleu* (*The Bluebird*, 1909), all concerned with problems of the soul. His interest in nature is represented by *La Vie des abeilles* (1901), generally considered a classic in popular nature-study, *L'Intelligence des fleurs* (1907), *La Vie des termites* (1927), and *La Vie des fourmis* (1930). Among his other works, nearly all of which have been translated into English, are *Serres chaudes* (poems, 1889), *La Princesse Maleine* (1889), *L'Intruse* (1890), *Les Sept Princesses, La Quenouille et la besace, Trois Petites Drames pour marionettes,* dramas; and various critical works. He also wrote *La Mort de Tintagiles* (1894), *Aglavaine et Sélysette* (1896), *Le Trésor des humbles* (1896), *La Sagesse et la destinée* (1898), *Soeur Béatrice* (1899), *Le Temple enseveli* (1902), *Joyzelle* (1903), *Le Double Jardin* (1904), *Le Miracle de Saint Antoine* (1905), *Mary Magdalene* (1910), *La Mort* (1912), *L'Hôte inconnu* (1917), *Le Grand Secret* (1921), and others. He was awarded (1911) the Nobel prize in literature for his contributions to the drama.

Maeve (māv). A drama (1899) by Edward Martyn, about a girl who finds herself being hailed as a heroine of the movement for Irish independence just as she is about to be married to a wealthy Englishman. William Butler Yeats thought of the play as symbolizing the contrast between Irish nationalism and English materialism.

magazine. A pamphlet periodically published, containing miscellaneous papers or compositions. The earliest publication of this kind in England was the *Gentleman's Magazine,* which was first issued in 1731 by Edward Cave, under the pseudonym of "Sylvanus Urban," and is still continued, though now entirely changed in character.

Magda (mag'dạ). The name of the English version of *Heimat,* a drama by Hermann Sudermann, published in 1893. A translation by Charles Edward Amory Winslow was published in 1895.

Magdalen College (môd'lin). [Full name, **St. Mary Magdalen College.**] A college of Oxford University, England, founded in 1457 by Bishop William of Waynflete. The charter was issued in 1458 and the foundation stone was laid May 5, 1474.

Magdalene (mag'dạ.lēn, mag.dạ.lē'nẹ) or **Magdalen** (mag'dạ.len), **Mary.** See **Mary Magdalene.**

Magdalene College (môd'lin). A college of Cambridge University, England, founded in 1519. The

Pepysian Building in the second court contains Samuel Pepys's library, the manuscript of his *Diary*, and many other literary treasures and curiosities.

Magdalen Proudfute (proud′fût). See **Proudfute, Magdalen.**

Magee (mạ.gē′), **William Kirkpatrick.** [Pseudonym, **John Eglinton.**] b. at Dublin, 1868—. An Irish essayist and poet. Author of *Irish Literary Portraits* (1935), *Letters of George Moore* (1942), and others.

Magellan (mạ.jel′ạn), **Ferdinand.** [Portuguese, **Fernão de Magalhães** (fèr.noun′ dẹ mu.gạ.lyïñs′); Spanish, **Fernando de Magallanes** (fer.nän′dō dä mä.gä.yä′näs).] b. at Saborosa, Traz-os-Montes, Portugal, c1480; d. on the island of Mactan, Philippine Islands, April 27, 1521. A Portuguese navigator in the Spanish service, discoverer of the Strait of Magellan and of the Philippine Islands, and the first man to circumnavigate the globe.

Maggie Earwicker (mag′i ir′wik.èr). See under **Anna Livia Plurabelle.**

Maggie Steenson (stēn′sọn). See **Steenson, Maggie.**

Maggie Tulliver (tul′i.vèr). See **Tulliver, Maggie.**

Magi (mā′jī). Members of the learned and priestly caste of Medians in ancient Persia, who had official charge of the sacred rites, practiced interpretation of dreams, professed supernatural arts, and were distinguished by peculiarities of dress and insignia. They are believed to have been originally pre-Zoroastrian; but their beliefs are embodied in Zoroastrianism, and Zoroastrian priests were Magi. The word "magic" is derived from Magi. The first Biblical reference to the Magi occurs in Jer. xxxix. 3, 13, where a Babylonian rab-mag, or chief of the Magi, is mentioned in connection with the siege, capture, and rule of Jerusalem.

Magi. The three "wise men" who came "from the east" to Jerusalem to do homage to the infant Jesus, as narrated in Mat. ii. 1, 2 (later said to be three kings, and still later named as Gaspar (or Kaspar), Melchior, and Balthazar (or Balthasar): the "Adoration of the Magi" being the subject of many famous paintings).

Maginn (mạ.gin′), **William.** b. at Cork, Ireland, July 10, 1793; d. at Walton-on-Thames, England, Aug. 21, 1842. An Irish author. He contributed (1819 *et seq.*) to *Blackwood's Magazine.* He founded, with Hugh Fraser, *Fraser's Magazine* in 1830. He is known chiefly as the author of *The City of Demons* and *Bob Burke's Duel with Ensign Brady.* His *Miscellanies* were edited by Dr. Shelton Mackenzie (1855–57). Maginn was the original of Captain Shandon in Thackeray's *Pendennis.*

Maginot Line (maj′i.nō; French, mȧ.zhē.nō). A system of fortifications along the eastern frontier of France, named for André Maginot. Essentially the system consisted of a series of great fortresses built into hills or otherwise concealed, connected by subterranean galleries. Each fortress contained quarters for troops and storage for supplies against a siege as well as for weapons and ammunition, and emplacements, sometimes in turrets, for heavy artillery, antiaircraft guns, antitank guns, and machine guns. Numerous smaller structures of the nature of blockhouses or bunkers, designed mainly as cover for machine-gun fire, covered the approaches, and the whole length of the fortified zone was further protected by antitank obstacles and by barbed wire. After the military collapse of France in 1940, it was widely alleged that the Maginot Line had been in fact a military liability in that it had bred a false sense of security. But actually the invaders breached the Line at only two points; they were able to overrun northern France by going through Belgium and simply outflanking the Line, which had not been extended along the Franco-Belgian boundary; and military opinion, upon second thought, has tended to reverse the unfavorable opinion formed during the first bitter days of French defeat.

Magliabechi (mä.lyä.bā′kē), **Antonio.** b. at Florence, in October, 1633; d. July 4, 1714. An Italian bibliophile. He was for many years librarian of Cosimo III (Cosimo de′ Medici), Grand Duke of Tuscany, and was famous for his vast and varied knowledge of languages and antiquities. He bequeathed to the Grand Duke a valuable collection of manuscripts and early editions, which now forms part of the Biblioteca Nazionale at Florence.

Magna Charta or **Magna Carta** (mag′nạ kär′tạ). The great charter of England, granted and sealed by King John in a conference between him and his barons at Runnymede, June 19, 1215. Its importance lies not so much in its actual provisions (which scholars in the field of English constitutional law have shown to be actually a reversion to ancient feudal privileges rather than a conscious forward step to freedom) as in the general principle implicit in its acceptance, that the king recognized a higher principle than his own personal will, the principle of law. The charter was based on a series of articles drawn up by the insurgent barons and presented to the king on June 8, 1215. From June 15 to 19 the charter was written, article by article (63 are generally recognized), on the basis of the barons' demands, principally by William Marshal for the king and Stephen Langton, Archbishop of Canterbury, for the barons. The most famous section is article 39, which provides that "No freeman shall be arrested, or detained in prison, or deprived of his freehold, or outlawed, or banished, or in any way molested; and we [the king] will not go forth against him, nor send against him, unless by the lawful judgment of his peers and by the law of the land." Research has demonstrated that the language used is such that the intention was to have it apply only to the upper classes, but traditionally (and in the subsequent development of the English constitution) it was held to grant jury trial to all freemen; similarly the other articles, misread though they were through lack of knowledge of the period, were held to grant freedoms on a wider basis than that originally intended by the barons, who, scholars have pointed out, were interested primarily in protecting against royal encroachment their own right to tyrannize. The charter's weakness lay in its lack of provision for enforcement and in August, 1215, John obtained an annulment of the charter from Pope Innocent III. John died during the ensuing civil war against the barons, but in

November, 1216, the charter was reissued in the name of Henry III, who later confirmed it several times, as did subsequent kings.

Magnetic Lady, or Humours Reconciled, The. A comedy by Ben Jonson. It was licensed and acted in 1632, but not published till 1640. Lady Loadstone, the "magnetic lady," attracts to her house various persons of assorted "humours," who are reconciled to normality by her friend, Compass, a mathematical scholar. Perhaps the most interesting character is Mistress Polish, a gossipy retainer of Lady Loadstone who tries to marry her to an affected courtier. Lady Loadstone's niece, Placentia a rich heiress, is at the center of various romantic complications, and is eventually found to be the daughter of Polish, substituted for the true heiress in infancy.

Magnificence. A political interlude written c1516 by John Skelton.

Magnus Troil (mag'nus troil'). See **Troil, Magnus.**

Magog (mā'gog). In the Old Testament, the land ruled by Gog (Ezek. xxxviii. 2): thought to be identical with Lydia.

Magog. See also **Gog and Magog.**

Maguire (mạ.gwīr'), **John Francis.** b. at Cork, Ireland, 1815; d. there, Nov. 1, 1872. An Irish journalist and author.

Magwitch (mag'wich), **Abel.** [Assumed name, **Provis.**] In Dickens's *Great Expectations*, an escaped convict, Pip's anonymous benefactor.

Mahabharata (mạ.hä'bä'rạ.tạ). One of the two great epics of ancient India, the other being the *Ramayana*. It contains over 100,000 distichs, divided into 18 *parvans* ("knots" or "joints," and then "sections," "chapters"). It is about eight times as large as the *Iliad* and *Odyssey* together. The tales originally composing it were probably first circulated in prose, and put later into metrical form. It was composed between 200 B.C. and 200 A.D.

Mahaffy (mạ.haf'i), Sir **John Pentland.** b. in Switzerland, July 12, 1839; d. April 30, 1919. An Irish classical scholar. He wrote *Social Life in Greece* (1874), *Greek Antiquities* (1876), *A History of Greek Classical Literature* (1880), *The Story of Alexander's Empire* (1890), *The Petrie Papyri Deciphered and Explained* (1891–1905), *Problems in Greek History* (1892), *Empire of the Ptolemies* (1896), *An Epoch in Irish History* (1904), *The Silver Age of the Greek World* (1906), and others.

Mahdi (mä'dē). [Sometimes spelled **Mehdee.**] According to Mohammedan belief, a spiritual and temporal ruler destined to appear on earth at the end of the world and save the faithful. Some sects hold that the Mahdi has appeared, and in concealment awaits the time of his manifestation. There have been a number of professed Mahdis, of whom the latest of importance was Mohammed Ahmed, whose armed followers resisted the advance of the British troops into the Sudan in 1884–85, and overthrew the Egyptian power in that region.

Mahmud of Ghazni (mä.mŏd'; gäz'nē). b. c971; d. at Ghazni, Afghanistan, 1030. Sultan of Ghazni (997–1030); son of Subuktigin. He was appointed (994) governor of Khurasan, and on Subuktigin's death (996) drove out his brother Ismail, who was his father's heir in Ghazni. He was an ardent Moslem and spent his career attempting to carry Islam into neighboring areas, especially into India, which he attacked (1000 *et seq.*) repeatedly. His most famous expedition was that against Somnath (1024–26), where he destroyed the temple of Shiva and smashed the idol of the god there; legend states that when he split the idol with his battle-ax gold and gems spilled out. Certainly his 17 expeditions into India, which eventually brought the Punjab and other sections of India under Afghan suzerainty, gave to Ghazni tremendous riches in the form of plunder and slaves and made it one of the most important centers of the Moslem world. Mahmud fought also in central Asia and won victories from the Tigris to the Ganges and from the Indian Ocean to the Oxus. He was a notable patron of the arts, Firdausi's *Shahnamah* being dedicated to him.

Mahomed (mạ.hom'ẹd) or **Mahomet** (mạ.hom'ẹt). See **Mohammed.**

Mahomet and Irene (ī.rē'nē). The name given to Samuel Johnson's tragedy *Irene* when it was played by Garrick (1749).

Mahomet Boabdelin (bō.ab'dẹ.lin). See **Boabdelin, Mahomet.**

Mahon (mạ.hŏn', -hōn'), Lord. See **Stanhope, Philip Henry.**

Mahon, Christy. A farmer's son, the hero of John Millington Synge's one-act play *The Playboy of the Western World* (1907).

Mahon, Old. A squatter farmer, Christy's father, in John Millington Synge's one-act play *The Playboy of the Western World* (1907).

Mahony (mä'ọ.ni), **Francis.** [Pseudonym, **Father Prout.**] b. at Cork, Ireland, c1804; d. at Paris, May 18, 1866. An Irish journalist and poet. He was educated for the priesthood at Paris and Rome, and was ordained, but gave up (c1834) his calling and began to write on the staff of *Fraser's Magazine.* The articles which he contributed were published as *Reliques of Father Prout* in 1836; a final volume was published in 1876 by Blanchard Jerrold. He contributed to *Bentley's Magazine*, and wrote to the *Daily News* from Rome for some years. These letters were published as *Facts and Figures from Italy, by Don Jeremy Savonarola, Benedictine Monk*, in 1847. He retired to a monastery in 1864, and died there. Among his original poems is *The Bells of Shandon.*

Mahound (mạ.hound'). Formerly in literature, but now archaic, the Arabian prophet Mohammed, supposed by many during the Middle Ages to be worshiped as a deity (as, "Nor fright the reader with the pagan vaunt Of mightie Mahound, and great Termegaunt": J. Hall's *Satires*); hence, a false god, or idol; also, the devil.

Mahrattas (mạ.rä'tạz). [Also: **Marathas, Marhattas.**] A people of W central India. They were the dominant power in India by the end of the 17th century, but were conquered by the British in 1818. Their language is Marathi.

Mahu (mä'hū). In Shakespeare's *King Lear*, a fiend ("of stealing") alluded to by Edgar (IV.i).

ḍ, d or j; ṣ, s or sh; ṭ, t or ch; ẓ, z or zh; o, F. cloche; ü, F. menu; ċh, Sc. loch; ṅ, F. bonbon.

The name is taken from Harsnett's *Popish Impostures.*

Maia (mā′yạ, mī′ạ). In Greek mythology, a daughter of Atlas. She was the eldest of the Pleiades, mother by Zeus of Hermes, and the nurse of Arcus after the death of Callisto. She became identified with a primitive Italian goddess who was associated with fertility and growth. As such the Romans called her Maia Majesta, and because of the fertility association identified her with the Phrygian mother goddess, Cybele, and their own Bona Dea.

Maidenhead Well Lost, A. A tragicomedy by Thomas Heywood, printed in 1633 and acted probably in the same year.

Maiden Lane. A London street between Covent Garden and the Strand.

Maiden Queen, The. [Full title, **Secret Love, or the Maiden Queen.**] A tragicomedy (produced 1667) by John Dryden, derived from *Le Grand Cyrus* and similar 17th-century French romances.

Maid in the Mill, The. A comedy by John Fletcher, written in 1623 and published in 1647.

Maid Marian (mǎr′i.ạn, mar′-). In the English Robin Hood ballad cycle, Robin Hood's sweetheart. She was the daughter of an earl, and loved Robin Hood when he was Earl of Huntingdon. When he was outlawed for debt she dressed herself as a page and followed him, living with his company as a virgin huntress till the marriage rites could be performed. This is a late legend concerning her. The ballad which tells the story is *Robin Hood and Maid Marian*, Number 150 in Child's *English and Scottish Popular Ballads*. Originally she had been the May Queen in the early English May Day dances and games. It was not until Tudor times that she became Robin Hood's sweetheart and supplanted Matilda Fitzwalter as wife of Robert, Earl of Huntingdon.

Maid Marian. A novel by Thomas Love Peacock, published in 1822. It is a parody of medieval romance and is based on the Robin Hood theme (Peacock uses the version in which Robert is the Earl of Huntingdon and Maid Marian is Matilda Fitzwalter).

Maid of Artois (är.twä′), **The.** A comic opera in three acts by Michael William Balfe, with a libretto by Alfred Bunn, produced at London in 1836. It contains the song *The Light of Other Days.*

Maid of Athens (ath′ẹnz). A daughter of Theodore Macri, a consul at Athens. She made Byron's acquaintance, and he is said to have addressed to her the song beginning "Maid of Athens, ere we part."

Maid of Bath (bȧth), **The.** A comedy by Samuel Foote, produced in 1771. The play holds up to ridicule (as Mr. Flint) Walter Long for his ungallant treatment of the Maid of Bath, Elizabeth Ann Linley, who afterward married Richard Brinsley Sheridan.

Maid of Honour, The. A play by Philip Massinger, produced between 1625 and 1632, and printed in the latter year.

Maid of Honour, The. An opera by Michael William Balfe, produced in 1847. The subject is the same as that of Friedrich von Flotow's *Martha.*

"Maid of Kent." See **Barton, Elizabeth.**

Maid of Mariendorp (mạ.rē′ẹn.dôrpt), **The.** A play in verse by James Sheridan Knowles, produced in 1838.

Maid of Norway (nôr′wā). See **Margaret** (of Scotland).

Maid of Orleans (ôr′lẹ.ạnz). Joan of Arc: so named on account of her efforts for the relief of Orléans. Schiller produced a play with the title *Die Jungfrau von Orleans* (1801).

Maid of Sker (skėr), **The.** A novel by Richard D. Blackmore, published in 1872.

Maid of the Mill, The. A comic opera by Isaac Bickerstaffe, printed in 1765. It was founded on Samuel Richardson's *Pamela.*

Maid of the Mist. The name by which Anne is sometimes called in Sir Walter Scott's novel *Anne of Geierstein.*

Maids and Mistresses. A novel by Beatrice Kean Seymour, published in 1932.

Maid's Last Prayer, The. [Full title, **The Maid's Last Prayer; or, Any rather than Fail.**] A comedy (1693) by Thomas Southerne.

Maid's Tragedy, The. A play by Beaumont and Fletcher, first acted not later than 1611 and printed in 1619.

Maimonides (mī.mon′i.dēz). [Full name, **Moses ben Maimun;** also called **Maimuni** (mī.mö′nē), and **RaMbaM** (from the initials of the words Rabbi Moses ben Maimun).] b. at Córdoba, Spain, March 30, 1135; d. at Cairo, Egypt, Dec. 13, 1204. A Jewish rabbi, Talmudic scholar, and philosopher. His greatest work, the *Mishneh Torah* (Repetition of the Law), also known among scholars as "Yad Hahazagah" (The Strong Hand), appeared in 1180, having been ten years in the writing, in Hebrew. This is a masterly systematic exposition in 14 books of the whole of the Jewish law as contained in the Pentateuch and in the vast Talmudic literature. It was preceded by a short introduction in Arabic, entitled *Sefer ha-Micvoth* (Book of the Commandments), being a treatise on the 613 precepts of the law. Almost equally famous, and perhaps even more widely influential, was his philosophical work in Arabic, *Dalalt al Haïrin* (Guide of the Perplexed; Hebrew, *More Nebuchim*). Many of his thoughts, such as those on the nature and origin of evil, on divine providence, and on the communion of man with God, greatly influenced Christian theologians, and it has been said that if there had been no Maimonides, there might have been no Aquinas.

Maine (mān), Sir **Henry James Sumner.** b. Aug. 15, 1822; d. at Cannes, France, Feb. 3, 1888. An English jurist. He studied at Cambridge, where in 1847 he became regius professor of civil law, a position which he held until 1854. He was called to the bar in 1850, became reader on Roman law and jurisprudence at the Inns of Court, London, in 1852, was legal member of council in India (1862–69), was Corpus professor of jurisprudence at Oxford (1869–78), was elected master of Trinity Hall, Cambridge, in 1877, and in 1887 became Whewell professor of international law at Cambridge. Among his works are *Ancient Law* (1861), *Village Communities* (1871), *Early History of Institutions* (1875), *Dissertations on Early Law and Custom*

(1883), *Popular Government* (1885), and *International Law* (1888).

Main Plot. The principal one of two plots (the other was the Bye Plot) in favor (1603) of Arabella Stuart against James I of England.

Maintenon (mant.nôṅ), Madame **de.** [Original name, **Françoise d'Aubigné,** title, Marquise **de Maintenon.**] b. in a prison at Niort, France, Nov. 27, 1635; d. at St.-Cyr, near Versailles, France, April 15, 1719. Mistress and second wife of Louis XIV of France. She was the granddaughter of Théodore Agrippa d'Aubigné, general under Henry IV of France, and the daughter of Constant d'Aubigné, a Huguenot imprisoned as a malcontent. Her mother, a Roman Catholic, had her baptized in that faith. She lived with her father in Martinique from 1639 to 1645, returned to France with her mother, and was brought up by her aunt as a Protestant. She was reconverted to Roman Catholicism within a short time. On the death (1650) of her mother she found herself in poverty, and was married in 1652 to the wit and poet Paul Scarron, who offered either to pay for her entrance to a convent or to make her his wife. She lived nine years with him, and their salon was frequented by the intellectual society of the time. In 1660 he died, and left her again in poverty. Her pension was discontinued in 1666 at the death of Anne of Austria, who had augmented it, and it was not till 1669 that Madame de Montespan gave her the charge of her son by Louis XIV. She was given a large income and a house at Vaugirard in which to bring up this child and another, born later, in secrecy. She was devoted to them, and established an ascendancy over the heart of the king, who advanced her to various positions in the court. In 1674 she purchased the estate of Maintenon, and in 1678 the king made it a marquisate. Soon afterward she replaced Madame de Montespan as the king's mistress. In 1685, two years after the death of the queen, who died in Madame de Maintenon's arms, she married Louis privately. Her influence was almost unbounded in matters both of church and state, and she was a patroness of letters and the fine arts. Her somewhat questionable position induced her to behave with rigid propriety, and her reputation for orthodoxy was extreme. She founded a home for the daughters of poor gentlemen at St.-Cyr, and on the death (1715) of the king she retired there for the rest of her life.

Mainwaring (mān'wär.ing). A novel by Maurice Hewlett, published in 1920.

Mais (māz), **Stuart Petre Brodie.** b. July 4, 1885—. An English lecturer, journalist, and writer. He taught (1909–20) in various schools, and became literary critic on the *Evening News* (1918) and the *Daily Express* (1921–23), literary editor (1923–26) of the *Daily Graphic,* and book reviewer and editorial writer (1926–31) on the *Daily Telegraph.* He is author of *April's Lonely Soldier* (1916), *Eclipse* (1925), *Frolic Lady* (1930), *Raven Among the Rocks* (1939), *Who Dies?* (1948), and others.

Maisie Farange (mā'zi far'anj). See **Farange, Maisie.**

Maitland (māt'land), **Frederic William.** b. May 28, 1850; d. on Grand Canary, Canary Islands, Dec.

21, 1906. An English jurist, professor of English law at Cambridge from 1888; grandson of Samuel Roffey Maitland. His works include *Gloucester Pleas* (1884), *Justice and Police* (1885), *Bracton's Notebook* (1887), *History of English Law Before the Time of Edward I* (with Sir F. Pollock, 1895), *Domesday Book and Beyond* (1897), *Township and Borough* (1898), *Canon Law in England* (1898), *Political Theories of the Middle Ages* (1900), *English Law and the Renaissance* (1901), *Life and Letters of Leslie Stephen* (1907), and *Constitutional History of England* (1908).

Maitland, James. [Titles: 8th Earl of **Lauderdale,** Baron **Lauderdale of Thirlestane.**] b. at Ratho, Midlothian, Scotland, Jan. 26, 1759; d. in Berwickshire, Scotland, Sept. 13, 1839. A Scottish politician and author. He became a Scottish representative peer (1790). An opponent of Pitt's hostile policy toward France, he was created (1806) Baron Lauderdale of Thirlestane when the Whig Party gained power. He served as lord high keeper of the great seal of Scotland, and privy councilor (1806). Author of *Inquiry Into the Nature and Origin of Public Wealth* (1804; enlarged ed., 1819) and numerous tracts on political issues and political economy.

Maitland, Sir Richard. [Title, Lord **Lethington.**] b. 1496; d. March 20, 1586. A Scottish lawyer, poet, and collector of early Scottish poetry. He was blind from October, 1560, until his death but continued to hold important posts and to discharge state duties, serving (1562–67) as keeper of the great seal. He is remembered by his collection of early Scottish verse, in two large volumes, in the Pepysian Library at Magdalene College, Cambridge. His *Satire on Town Ladies* and *The Blind Baron's Comfort* are his best-known poems.

Maitland, Samuel Roffey. b. at London, Jan. 7, 1792; d. at Gloucester, England, Jan. 19, 1866. An English clergyman, and theological and historical writer. He was librarian (1838–48) to the archbishop of Canterbury. Among his works are *The Dark Ages* (1844) and *The Reformation in England* (1849).

Major Barbara (bär'ba.ra). A play (1905) by George Bernard Shaw.

Making of an Englishman, The. A novel (1914) by W. L. George.

Malabari (mä.lä.bä'rē), **Behramji Maharbanji** (or **Merwanji**). b. 1854; d. 1912. A Hindu poet and social reformer, a Parsee (Zoroastrian) by birth. He was instrumental in procuring enactment of the "Age of Consent" Act (which forbade marriages involving child brides), and championed the movement to remove the restrictions on the remarriage of Indian widows. He was editor (c1880–1900) of the *Indian Spectator* and also edited (1901–12) *East and West.* Author of *Origin and Growth of Religion* (1898) and *The Indian Eye on English Life* (1893).

Malagigi (mä.lä.jē'jē). In the Charlemagne cycle of romances, an enchanter and magician, the cousin of Rinaldo.

Malagrowther (mal.a.grou'ŦHėr), **Malachi.** The pseudonym of Sir Walter Scott in "Three Letters by Malachi Malagrowther" on paper money, first

ḍ, d or j; ṣ, s or sh; ṭ, t or ch; ẓ, z or zh; o, F. cloche; ü, F. menu; ċh, Sc. loch; ṅ, F. bonbon.

published in the *Edinburgh Weekly Journal* in 1826. In 1830 a fourth letter was added.

Malagrowther, Sir Mungo. In Sir Walter Scott's *The Fortunes of Nigel*, a malicious old courtier.

Malaprop (mal′a.prop), **Mrs.** A vain, good-natured woman in Richard Brinsley Sheridan's *The Rivals*, remarkable for her misapplication of words. Of feminine education she says that a girl "should be [a] mistress of orthodoxy, that she might not misspell, and mis-pronounce words . . . and likewise that she might reprehend the true meaning of what she is saying."

malapropism (mal′a.prop.izm). **1.** The act or habit of misapplying words through an ambition to use fine language.
2. A word so misapplied.

The Fieldhead estate and the De Walden estate were delightfully contagious—a malapropism which rumour had not failed to repeat to Shirley.
(Charlotte Brontë, *Shirley*.)

Malbecco (mal.bek′ō). In Spenser's *Faerie Queene*, a contentious, ill-tempered person who kills himself when his wife elopes with Sir Paridel. His spirit lives after him as "jealousy."

Malcolm (mal′kom). In Shakespeare's *Macbeth*, a son of Duncan. He flees to England when Duncan is murdered and is there approached by Macduff, who hopes he will return and claim the throne. To test Macduff's loyalty, he represents himself as a man of disgraceful and vile character (IV.iii). At Macbeth's defeat he is crowned King of Scotland.

Malcolm III. [Also: **Malcolm III MacDuncan**; called **Canmore**.] d. near Alnwick, Northumberland, Nov. 13, 1093. King of Scotland (1054–93); son of Duncan I. He ascended the throne on the defeat of the usurper Macbeth by Earl Siward of Northumbria July 27, 1054, which was followed by his own victory at Lumphanan in Aberdeenshire, where Macbeth was slain. Shakespeare introduces him in *Macbeth*.

Malcolm Fleming (flem′ing), **Sir.** See **Fleming, Sir Malcolm.**

Malcolm Graeme (grām). See **Graeme, Malcolm.**

Malcontent, The. A play by John Marston, printed in 1604. Another edition, with an induction by John Webster, appeared the same year.

Maldon (môl′don). [Full title, **The Battle of Maldon.**] An Old English poem (late 10th century) dealing with the Scandinavian invasion of Essex and the battle on the river Blackwater near Maldon in 991 in which Byrhtnoth, leader of the English forces, holds his people firm against the invaders, refuses to end the battle by paying tribute to the Scandinavians, and finally is killed by a poisoned spear. Some of his men flee, but the battle is continued by the English leader Ælfwine, who is losing ground at the end of the extant 325-line poem, the actual conclusion of which is missing. It is notable for its glorification of the hero Byrhtnoth and of the relationship between lord and retainer.

Maldon, Jack. In Dickens's *David Copperfield*, a cousin of Mrs. Strong.

Malebolge (mä.lā.bōl′jā). In Dante's *Inferno*, the eighth circle of Hell. It consisted of ten concentric *bolgie*, or trenches.

Malecasta (mal.e.kas′ta). In Spenser's *Faerie Queene*, the personification of lust.

Maleger (mal′e.gėr). In Spenser's *Faerie Queene*, the leader of the seven deadly sins and of the passions that lead the five senses to evil. He is finally killed when Prince Arthur, after his sword has been used to no avail, lifts him from the ground, thus cutting off the nourishment from earth (his mother) which had sustained him.

Malengin (mal′en.gin). In Spenser's *Faerie Queene*, the personification of guile, finally destroyed by Talus after eluding Sir Arthur and Sir Artegal.

male or **masculine rhymes.** Rhymes in which only the final syllables correspond, as *disdain* and *complain*.

Malet (mal′et), **Lucas.** Pseudonym of **Kingsley, Mary St. Leger.**

Malevole (mä.lā′vō.lā). A name assumed by Giovanni Altofronto, former Duke of Genoa, a character in John Marston's play *The Malcontent*, to which he gives its name. He plays the part of a bitterly cynical observer of the corrupt court of Genoa.

Malfi (mal′fi), **Duchess of.** The tender widow who marries her steward in the play by John Webster bearing her name.

Malheureux (mal′e.rö). A virtuous young man, somewhat of a prig, whose head is turned by the beauty of the "Dutch courtesan," Franceschina, in John Marston's *The Dutch Courtezan*.

Malibran (mà.lē.brän), Madame **Maria Felicia.** [Maiden name, **García.**] b. at Paris, March 24, 1808; d. at Manchester, England, Sept. 23, 1836. A French operatic contralto; daughter and pupil of Manuel del Popolo Vicente García. She made her operatic debut (June 7, 1825) at London, made a great sensation, and was at once engaged for the rest of the season. Shortly after this she went to New York with her father. In the midst of a successful season there he married her to a businessman named Malibran, who soon became bankrupt. In 1827 she left him and returned to France.

Mall (môl, mal), **the.** A broad promenade in St. James's Park, London, planted with rows of trees.

Mallarmé (mà.làr.mā), **Stéphane.** b. at Paris, March 18, 1842; d. at Fontainebleau, France, Sept. 8, 1898. A French poet, one of the most prominent of the group known as the decadents, and the leader of the symbolist movement. In his attempts to free poetry from the limitations of language, he became more and more obscure; his later work is almost incomprehensible without aid, but his influence on other writers, such as Valéry in France and various of the "decadents" in England, was tremendous. He wrote much for *Le Décadent* and *Le Parnasse Contemporain*. Among his works are *L'Après-midi d'un faune* (1876), which inspired Claude Debussy's orchestral work, *Les Dieux antiques* (1880), *Poésies* (1887), *Pages* (1890), *Vers et prose* (1892), *Les Divagations* (1897), and a translation of the poems of Poe (1888).

Mallet (mal′et), **David.** [Original name, **Malloch** (mal′och, -ok).] b. at Crieff, Perthshire, Scotland, c1705; d. in England, April 21, 1765. A Scottish poet and author. He wrote the plays *Eurydice*

(1731), *Mustapha* (1739), and *Elvira* (1763). *Alfred, a Masque* was written with James Thomson (1700–48), with music by Thomas Arne, and "Rule, Britannia," one of the songs contained in it, has been claimed for both. Among his poems were *William and Margaret* (1723), *The Excursion* (1728), *The Hermit* (1747), and several volumes of miscellaneous verse.

Mallet, Rowland. A character in *Roderick Hudson* (1876), a novel by Henry James.

Mallock (mal′ọk), **William Hurrell.** b. in Devonshire, England, 1849; d. April 2, 1923. An English author. Among his works are *The New Republic* (1877), *The New Paul and Virginia* (1878), *Lucretius* (1878), *Is Life Worth Living?* (1879), *Poems* (1880), *A Romance of the Nineteenth Century* (1881), *Social Equality* (1882), *Property and Progress* (1884), *Landlords and the National Income* (1884), *Atheism and the Value of Life* (1884), *The Old Order Changes* (1886), *Labour and the Popular Welfare* (1893), *Classes and Masses* (1896), *Aristocracy and Evolution* (1898), *Tristram Lacy* (1899), *Doctrine and Doctrinal Disruption* (1900), *Religion as a Credible Doctrine* (1902), *The Veil of the Temple* (1904), *The Reconstruction of Belief* (1905), *Critical Examination of Socialism* (1907), *An Immortal Soul* (1908), and *The Nation as a Business Firm* (1910).

Malone (mạ.lōn′), **Edmund** (or **Edmond**). b. at Dublin, Oct. 4, 1741; d. at London, April 25, 1812. An Irish literary critic and Shakespeare scholar. He graduated at Trinity College, Dublin, and in 1763 went to London and became a law student in the Inner Temple. Returning to Ireland, he was called to the Irish bar in 1767. Not long after this his father's death left him in possession of a small estate and sufficient money to live upon. He therefore returned to London to devote himself to literature. He soon entered political and literary society, and counted among his friends Samuel Johnson, Sir Joshua Reynolds, Bishop Percy, Burke, Canning, Horace Walpole, and others. His edition of Shakespeare was published in 1790, but he had previously written *Attempt to ascertain the order in which the plays of Shakespeare were written* (1778), a supplement to Johnson's edition of Shakespeare (1780), containing observations on the Elizabethan stage and the text of five plays wrongly ascribed to Shakespeare. He published an edition of Sir Joshua Reynolds's works in 1797, and an edition of Dryden, four volumes of which appeared in 1800. Malone was an excellent literary detective and was one of the first to decry the spurious antiquity of Thomas Chatterton's poems and the purported Shakespearian works of William Ireland. Besides writing a number of minor works, he found time to devote himself to book-collecting, and accumulated a large library. After his death the greater part of it was sent to Oxford. He left material for another edition of Shakespeare, which was published by James Boswell the younger in 1821, and is known as the "third variorum Shakespeare," sometimes as "Boswell's Malone."

Malory (mal′ọ.ri), **Sir Thomas.** d. March 12, 1471. An English author of the group of medieval prose romances entitled by William Caxton (the printer) *Morte d' Arthur*. Malory is said to have written this in prison. His own original title for the eight ro-

mances included was *The Book of King Arthur and His Knights of the Round Table.* Little is known about his life, but he was probably born c1408. He was a knight of Warwickshire and served in Parliament in 1445. Imprisoned for various offenses in 1451, he remained in confinement until his death.

Malta (môl′tạ), **Knights of.** See **Hospitalers of Saint John of Jerusalem, Order of the.**

Malta Bagnet (bag′net). See under **Bagnet, Mr. and Mrs. Joseph.**

Malthus (mal′thus), **Thomas Robert.** b. near Guildford, Surrey, England, Feb. 17, 1766; d. at St. Catharine's, near Bath, England, Dec. 23, 1834. An English political economist. He graduated from Cambridge in 1788, and became a fellow of Jesus College in 1793. In 1798 he took orders, and was made curate of Albury, Surrey. In 1798 he published the first edition of *An Essay on the Principle of Population as it affects the Future Improvement of Society, with Remarks on the Speculations of Mr. Godwin, M. Condorcet, and other Writers.* This principle he defined to be that population increases in a geometrical ratio and the means of subsistence in an arithmetical ratio, and that vice and crime, war and disease, are necessary checks of this increase in numbers (the so-called Malthusian doctrine). He published in 1803 a revision of the *Essay on Population,* in which he suggested "moral restraint" as another check on population. In 1805 he was made professor of history and political economy at Haileybury. His other works include *The Nature and Progress of Rent* (1815) and *Political Economy* (1820). In politics he was a Whig; he supported the Catholic emancipation, and accepted the Reform Bill.

Malvolio (mal.vō′li.ō). In Shakespeare's *Twelfth Night,* Olivia's steward, a conceited, grave, self-important personage forced into comic situations (in the most ludicrous of which he imagines Olivia to be in love with him). He was probably intended as a satire on the Puritans.

Malynes or **Malines** or **de Malines** (dẹ ma.lēn′), **Gerard.** fl. 1586–1641. An English merchant and economist. In 1586 he was commissioner of trade in the Low Countries, and in 1609 was appointed commissioner of the mint. He was one of the first English economists to recognize the laws on which modern economics are based, and was a strong exponent of mercantilism. Among his works are *A Treatise of the Canker of England's Commonwealth* (1601), *St. George for England* (1601), *The Maintenance of Free Trade* (1622), *Consuetudo vel lex mercatoria* (1622), and *The Center of the Circle of Commerce, or the Balance of Trade* (1623).

Mambrino (mäm.brē′nō). A pagan king in an old romance, *Innamoramento di Rinaldo,* antedating Ariosto's *Orlando Furioso.* He is killed by Rinaldo. No mention is made in this romance of his helmet, but in *Orlando Furioso* Rinaldo is said to have won it. It is the same helmet so frequently mentioned in *Don Quixote,* made of pure gold and rendering its wearer invisible. Don Quixote took possession of a barber's basin which he conceived to be the helmet of King Mambrino.

Mamelukes (mam′ẹ.lŏks). A corps of cavalry formerly existing in Egypt, whose chiefs were long the

d, d or j; ṣ, s or sh; ṭ, t or ch; ẓ, z or zh; o, F. cloche; ü, F. menu; ċh, Sc. loch; ṅ, F. bonbon.

sovereign rulers of the country. They originated with a body of Mingrelians, Turks, and other slaves, who were sold by Genghis Khan to the Egyptian sultan in the 13th century. About 1251 they established their government in Egypt by making one of their own number sultan. Their government was overthrown by Selim I of Turkey in 1517, but they formed part of the Egyptian army until 1811, when Mehemet Ali destroyed most of them by a general massacre.

Mamillius (ma.mil′i.us). In Shakespeare's *Winter's Tale*, the young Prince, son of Leontes and Hermione. He gives the play its title, when he says, "A sad tale's best for winter" (II.i). His death is later reported.

Mammon (mam′on). An Aramaic word used once in the New Testament as a personification of riches and worldliness, or the god of this world; hence, the personification of avarice; cupidity personified.

Mammon, Cave of. The dwelling place of Mammon, who personifies greed, described in the second book of Edmund Spenser's *Faerie Queene.*

Mammon, Sir Epicure. In Ben Jonson's *The Alchemist,* a worldly sensualist finally gulled by the spurious alchemist, Subtle, and his henchman, Face.

Man (man), **Isle of.** [Ancient and medieval Latin, **Monapia, Mona, Eubonia;** Manx, **Mannin or Vannin.**] An island in the Irish Sea, one of the British Isles, ab. 17 mi. S of Scotland, and nearly equidistant from England and Ireland. The Isle of Man forms an independent administrative unit of the British Isles, administered by a governor (appointed by the Crown) and a legislature, under its own laws. The C part is mountainous, the highest point, Snaefell, rising to 2,034 ft. English is generally spoken, and the native Manx (a Gaelic language) has nearly disappeared. The earliest known inhabitants were Celtic tribes. The island was ruled by Norsemen from the 9th to the 13th century, was annexed to Scotland by Alexander III, and was afterward ruled by various kings. It was ruled by the Stanley (Derby) family from the beginning of the 15th century to 1735, when it passed to the Murrays, dukes of Atholl. In 1765 the British government acquired most of the royal rights of the Atholls, the last rights falling to the crown in 1829. Capital, Douglas; length, ab. 32 mi.; area, ab. 221 sq. mi.

Man About Town, The. A collection of short stories by A. P. Herbert, published in 1923.

Man and Superman. A play by George Bernard Shaw, published in 1903. As one critic has pointed out, the play minus its long preface and the Don Juan fantasy of the third act is a simple comedy about Tanner's unsuccessful attempt to escape from the predatory Ann, his ward. However, when the preface is taken into account, the play is revealed in its full Shavian meaning, as a penetrating and satirical examination of the full implications of contemporary attitudes toward marriage and love. Tanner is the rational man, convinced that it is both possible and desirable to be guided by logic alone; Ann represents the principle of woman as mother, and regardless of obstacles she proceeds to her goal, which is simply the creation of another generation. Don Juan, the great lover, is actually

as helpless as Tanner in his efforts to escape the woman he is usually thought of as "pursuing "

Manannan mac Lir (man.a.nan′ mak lēr′). In Old Irish mythology, the god of the sea, son of Ler (the sea itself), and lord of the Isle of Man. He possessed a magic coracle which swept over the sea, wonderful white horses, a cap of invisibility, and an inexhaustible pig forever roasting on the spit, however much was eaten from it. It was he who established the Tuatha De Danann (the divine race of Ireland) safe in the hills and mounds of Ireland and gave them the Feast of Age, which kept them young and immortal. He dwelt on an elysian island in the western ocean called Land Under Wave, Land of Promise, and other names, where there was neither age nor death. His Brythonic counterpart is Manawyddan fab Llyr.

Manasseh (ma.nas′e). [Also, **Manasses** (ma-nas′ēz).] In the Bible, the eldest of the sons of the patriarch Joseph, and eponym of the tribe holding territory north of Ephraim. Gen. xli. 51.

Manawyddan fab Llyr (man.a.wŭ′dan fab lēr). See under **Manannan mac Lir.**

Manchester New College (man′ches.tèr, -ches-). A college at Oxford, originally a Unitarian institution in London.

"Manchester Poet," the. See **Swain, Charles.**

Manciple's Tale (man′si.plz), **The.** One of Chaucer's *Canterbury Tales.* It is partly from Ovid's *Metamorphoses,* being the story of how the Crow, once white, is turned black by its master, Phoebus Apollo, for telling him of the adultery of his wife. Phoebus in his rage has killed his wife; then he turns on the Crow, pulls out all its white feathers, curses it for a mischief-maker, and flings it out of the door. The listeners are warned to guard their tongues. The story is told by the "gentil maunciple" (a steward), whom Chaucer represents as managing so well in buying food for his household (or "temple") of thirty lawyers that he is always ahead of them, clever and shrewd though they are:

> For whether that he payde, or took by taille,
> Algate he wayted so in his achat,
> That he was ay biforn and in good stat.
> Now is nat that of God a ful fair grace,
> That swich a lewed mannes wit shal pace
> The wisdom of an heep of lerned men?

Mandalay (man.da.lā′, man′da.lā). A poem (1890) by Rudyard Kipling telling of the love of a British soldier for a Burma girl. It contains the famous stanza:

> On the road to Mandalay!
> Where the flyin'-fishes play
> An' the dawn comes up like thunder outer
> China 'crost the Bay!

Mandane (man′dan). The mother of Cyrus. According to Herodotus she was the daughter of Astyages, king of Media, and wife of Cambyses, a Persian noble.

Mandeville (man′de.vil), **Bernard.** b. at Dordrecht, Netherlands, c1670; d. at London, Jan. 21, 1733. An English writer. He took his degree in medicine at Leiden in 1691, and settled at London. In 1714 he published his *Enquiry into the Origin of Moral Virtue,* with notes, under the title *The Fable of the*

---

fat, fāte, fär, àsk, fàre; net, mē, hèr; pin, pīne; not, nōte, mŏve, nôr; up, lūte, pŭll; ᴛʜ, then;

Bees, or Private Vices, Public Benefits. This work, a revision of his *The Grumbling Hive, or Knaves Turn'd Honest* (1705), aroused a great storm of controversy because of the thesis of the author that all that is called virtue is a delusion and that actually selfishness is responsible for all human advances. The book was pronounced a nuisance by the grand jury of Middlesex in 1723. His other works are *Treatise of Hypochondriack and Hysteric Passions* (1711), *Free Thoughts on Religion* (1720), and *A Modern Defense of Public News* (1740).

Mandeville, Sir John. See under **Travels of Sir John Mandeville.**

Mandricardo (män.drē.kär′dō). The son of Agrican in Boiardo's and Ariosto's *Orlando* romances. He laid siege to Albracca for the love of Angelica, and was slain by Orlando. He was noted for his pride and cruelty.

Manetho (man′ę.thō). fl. c250 B.C. An Egyptian historian and priest. He was a native of Sebennytus, in Lower Egypt. He wrote a history of Egypt in Greek, fragments only of which are extant. His tables on the dynasties of Egypt have proved extremely useful despite their inaccuracies.

Manette (ma.net′), **Doctor Alexander.** In Dickens's *Tale of Two Cities*, a French physician who is imprisoned for 18 years, and whose mind has crumbled almost to the point of complete blankness when he is finally released.

Manette, Lucie. In Dickens's *Tale of Two Cities*, the gentle daughter of Dr. Manette, later the wife of Charles Darnay, a French émigré.

Man Frail and God Eternal. The famous hymn by Isaac Watts which opens with the line "O God, our help in ages past."

Manfred (man′frẹd). The Prince of Otranto, the principal character in Horace Walpole's *Castle of Otranto*.

Manfred. A dramatic poem by Byron, published in 1817. It was so called from the name of its hero, Manfred, who in Byron's own words is "a kind of magician who suffers from a half-unexplained remorse." He lives in a castle among the Alps, and is substantially alone throughout the piece. Schumann wrote music for this drama and adapted it for the stage himself; it was first produced by Liszt at Weimar in 1852. Manfred lives alone in the Alps, unable to expiate his undefined crime. He is tempted by evil spirits, but resists, and finally has a vision of Astarte, his earthly love, who prophesies his death on the following day and disappears. Tempted at the very last by the evil spirits, he again withstands them, and dies.

Mangan (mang′gạn), **James Clarence.** b. at Dublin, May 1, 1803; d. June 20, 1849. An Irish poet. His chief works are *German Anthology* (1849), *Poets and Poetry of Munster* (1849), and *Romances and Ballads of Ireland* (1850). His best-known poems, such as *Dark Rosaleen* and *O'Hussey's Ode to the Maguire*, are close adaptations of Old Irish originals.

Mania (mā′ni.ạ). An old Italian goddess of the dead (Manes), mother by Mercury of the Lares.

Manichean or **Manichaean** (man.i.kē′ạn). An adherent of the religious system of the Persian teacher Mani or Manichaeus (c216–c276), composed of Gnostic Christian, Buddhistic, Zoroastrian, and various other elements, the principal feature being a dualistic theology which represented a conflict between light and darkness and included belief in the inherent evil of matter.

Man in the Iron Mask. d. Nov. 19, 1703. A French prisoner of state, in the 17th–18th centuries, whose identity remains unknown to this day. He was buried in the St. Paul Cemetery, at Paris, under the name of Marchioly, undoubtedly a false name, and was described in the church register as "aged about 45." When he went from one prison to another, he wore a heavy black velvet mask, and romantic imagination has transformed this into the more exciting and dramatic iron (the touch was originally added by Voltaire). According to the various theories put forth, some wilder than others, he was: (1) Louis, Count of Vermandois, an illegitimate son of Louis XIV, (2) an illegitimate son of Anne of Austria, which would make him Louis's natural elder brother, (3) a twin brother of Louis XIV, (4) the Duke of Beaufort, (5) the Duke of Monmouth, (6) Nicholas Fouquet, agent of Cardinal Mazarin, and embezzler, (7) Count Ercole Mattioli, a Mantuan, (8) Eustache Dauger, a valet, (9) the Duke of Buckingham, (10) a son of Oliver Cromwell, (11) a son of Charles II, (12) Molière himself, and (13) the ringleader, his name being unknown, of a plot to murder Louis XIV. There are three facts in the case and three documents: they are the date on which a prisoner wearing a black mask was brought to the Bastille, the date of his death, and his burial the next day; the papers record his arrival at the prison, his death, and his funeral.

Mankynd (man.kīnd′). [Also: **Mankind, Mankynde.**] An English morality play (c1475) by an unknown author. The work is historically interesting in that it shows the large element of farce which had got into the morality play by the end of the 15th century.

Manley (man′li), **Mary de la Rivière.** b. on Jersey or on Guernsey, Channel Islands, c1663; d. July 11, 1724. An English novelist, dramatist, and political pamphleteer. On May 26, 1709, she published *Secret Memoirs and Manners of Several Persons of Quality of both Sexes, from the New Atalantis*, usually known as *The New Atalantis*, devoted entirely to intrigue and scandal, attacking especially the Whig politicos then under the fire of Swift and others. She was arrested (Oct. 29, 1709), for libel and discharged on Feb. 13, 1710. In 1711 she succeeded Swift as editor of the *Examiner*. She also published *Memoirs of Europe* (1710), *The Power of Love* (1720), a collection of seven novels, and others. She worked as a pamphleteer in the Tory cause. She died at the house of Barber, a printer, with whom she had lived for some years.

Manlius Capitolinus (man′li.us kap″i.tọ.lī′nus), **Marcus.** d. 384 B.C. The deliverer of the Capitol at Rome from the Gauls. He was a patrician by birth, and was consul in 392. According to tradition, he was aroused by the cackling of geese one night when the Gauls, who were besieging the Capitol under Brennus in 390, attempted to surprise the fortress; collecting a handful of men, Manlius repelled the attack. To this circumstance the origin of his surname Capitolinus is commonly ascribed, although it was also borne by his father and had already acquired the force of a family name in his gens. In 385 he began to champion the cause of the plebeians against the patricians, with a view to making himself tyrant of Rome, and in the following year was arrested by the dictator Camillus. He was tried in the Poetelinian grove, instead of on the Campus Martius, which commanded a view of the Capitol which he had saved and which might have stirred emotion in his behalf, and was sentenced to be thrown from the Tarpeian rock.

Manlius Imperiosus Torquatus (im.pir.i.ō'sus tôr-kwā'tus), **Titus.** fl. 4th century B.C. A Roman hero. He was elected military tribune in 362 B.C., and in 361 served under the dictator Titus Quintius Pennus against the Gauls. During this campaign he slew a gigantic Gaul in single combat in the presence of the two armies, and despoiled him of a chain (*torques*), which he placed around his own neck (whence the surname Torquatus). He was appointed dictator in 353 and again in 349, and was consul in 347, 344, and 340. During his third consulship, while engaged with his colleague Publius Decius Mus in a campaign against the Latins, he put to death his own son, who, contrary to orders, had fought and killed in single combat an enemy from the opposing army.

Manly (man'li). In Ben Jonson's *The Devil Is an Ass*, a young gallant, the friend of Wittipol.

Manly. The "plain dealer" in William Wycherley's play of that name, who rails at the fidelity of women and the behavior of honest people in general. He is a rough, pessimistic individual, who is, however, finally forced to change his attitude by the sweetness and loyalty of Fidelia.

Manly. In John Vanbrugh and Colley Cibber's *The Provoked Husband*, a man of worldly good sense.

Manly, John Matthews. b. in Sumter County, Ala., Sept. 2, 1865; d. April 2, 1940. An American educator and Chaucerian scholar. He was professor and head (1898–1933) of the English department at the University of Chicago. Editor of *Macbeth* (1896), *Specimens of the Pre-Shakespearean Drama* (1897), *English Prose and Poetry* (1916), and *Chaucer* (1928); coauthor of *A Manual for Writers* (1914), *The Writer's Index* (1923), and *The Text of the Canterbury Tales* (1940); author of *Some New Light on Chaucer* (1926) and *Chaucer and the Rhetoricians* (1926).

Mann (man), Sir **Horace.** b. 1701; d. at Florence, Italy, Nov. 6, 1786. An English diplomat. In 1740 he became minister to the court of Florence, which post he retained until his death. His principal duty was to watch the Old Pretender (James Edward Stuart). He is chiefly known from his correspondence (1741–86) with Horace Walpole.

Mannering (man'ėr.ing), **Julia.** The daughter of Guy in Sir Walter Scott's *Guy Mannering.*

Manners (man'ėrz), **John.** [Title, Marquis of Granby.] b. Aug. 2, 1721; d. at Scarborough, Yorkshire, England, Oct. 18, 1770. An English general. In 1759 he became a lieutenant general, serving at Minden (Aug. 1, 1759), and was commander in chief of the British contingent in Germany from

Aug. 14, 1759. He fought with great bravery at Warburg (July 31, 1760), at Villingshausen (July 15, 1761), at Gravenstein (June 24, 1762), and at Homburg (Aug. 6, 1762). His portrait was twice painted by Reynolds.

Mannin (man'in), **Ethel (Edith).** b. at London, Oct. 11, 1900—. An English novelist and journalist. Author of *Martha* (1923), *Hunger of the Sea* (1924), *Sounding Brass* (1925), *Crescendo* (1929), *Ragged Banners* (1931), *Men are Unwise* (1934), *The Pure Flame* (1936), *Rose and Silvie* (1938), *Julie* (1940), *The Dark Forest* (1946), *Comrade, O Comrade* (1947), and *Bavarian Story* (1950).

Manning (man'ing), **Anne.** b. at London, Feb. 17, 1807; d. at Tunbridge Wells, Kent, England, Sept. 14, 1879. An English historical novelist. Among her more than 50 volumes are *The Maiden and Married Life of Mistress Mary Powell, afterwards Mistress Milton* (1849) and *The Household of Sir Thomas More* (1860), both originally published as serials. Her first work was *A Sister's Gift* (1826); her last, *An Idyll of the Alps* (1876). *Stories from the History of Italy* (1831) was the only one to appear under her name, all the others being issued as by "the author of *Mary Powell.*"

Manning, Henry Edward. b. at Totteridge, Hertfordshire, England, July 15, 1808; d. at Westminster, London, Jan. 14, 1892. An English cardinal. He was the youngest son of William Manning, a West India merchant. He entered Harrow in 1822, and Balliol College, Oxford, in 1827, where Charles Wordsworth was his tutor and William E. Gladstone an associate. He was made a fellow of Merton, Oxford, in 1832, and was ordained rector of Woollavington-cum-Graffham in 1833. He was married Nov. 7, 1833, and his wife died July 24, 1837. In the succeeding years, Manning became one of the prominent members of the Oxford movement. In 1840 he was created archdeacon of Chichester. He took no part in the secession (1845) of W. G. Ward and John Henry Newman, but continued a leader of the High-Church party until 1848. In May, 1848, he visited Rome, and on his return found himself in opposition to the established church. In April, 1850, he resigned his archdeaconry, and on June 14, 1851, was ordained a priest of the Roman Catholic Church. In 1854 he was made D.D. by Pope Pius IX, and installed as superior of the Congregation of the Oblates of Saint Charles at Bayswater (March 31, 1857). On April 30, 1865, he succeeded Cardinal Nicholas Wiseman as archbishop of Westminster, and was created cardinal March 31, 1875. Manning was a militant Roman Catholic and in the forefront of the struggle to obtain amelioration of the condition of workingmen; he was a principal supporter of the liberal movement that was climaxed by the encyclical *Rerum novarum* (1891) of Pope Leo XIII. He likewise supported to the full the dogma of papal infallibility enunciated in 1870, which many of his colleagues felt to be a premature statement. He was the author of *Unity of the Church* (1842), *Temporal Mission of the Holy Ghost* (1865), *Temporal Power of the Pope* (1866), *England and Christendom* (1867), and others.

Manning, Thomas. b. at Broome, Norfolk, England, Nov. 8, 1772; d. at Bath, England, May 2,

1840. An English traveler and physician, friend of Charles Lamb. He was the first Englishman to enter (December, 1811) Lhasa, the "Forbidden City" and capital of Tibet. After traveling in India, China, Italy, and elsewhere, Manning returned to England in 1829. He figures in Lamb's *Essays of Elia* as "my friend M." from whom Lamb purports to have gotten the manuscript of the story contained in the *Dissertation on Roast Pig.*

Manny (man'i) or **Mauny** (mō'ni), Sir **Walter de.** [Title, Baron **de Manny.**] d. at London, Jan. 15, 1372. A soldier in the English service, founder of the Charterhouse, London. He was a native of Manny, near Valenciennes, in Hainaut (now in France), and a fellow-townsman of Froissart. He probably came to England with Queen Philippa in 1327, and was knighted in 1331. He was one of the ablest of the commanders of Edward III. In 1371 he was licensed to found a house of Carthusian monks to be called La Salutation Mère Dieu. This "Chartreuse" became the London Charterhouse.

Mannyng (man'ing), **Robert.** [Also, **Robert of Brunne.**] fl. in the latter part of the 13th and the first half of the 14th century. An English chronicler and poet. He was a native of Brunne (now Bourne), in Lincolnshire, and in 1288 joined the Gilbertine canons at Sempringham. He wrote *Handlyng Synne* (c1303), a translation, with many additions and omissions, of the *Manuel des Pechiez* of William of Wadington, who wrote in the time of Edward I; *The Chronicle of England* (finished in 1338); and *Medytacyuns of the Soper of our Lorde Ihesus.* His importance is principally literary, rather than historical, but the information about pre-Chaucerian England contained in his illustrative tales and anecdotes is important, as is the author's use of the Midland dialect, which makes his work a milestone in the history of the development of modern English.

Manoa (mä.nō'ä). See **El Dorado.**

Man of Business, The. A comedy by George Colman the elder, produced in 1774.

Man of Destiny, The. A play (1897) by George Bernard Shaw, published in *Plays, Pleasant and Unpleasant* in that same year. In it Napoleon is portrayed as an ordinary man who succeeds chiefly because he has more common sense and greater egotism than those he opposes. The play was written especially for Richard Mansfield, whom Shaw had met in 1894, and who had impressed Shaw as being similar in character and manners to his conception of Napoleon.

Man of Feeling, The. A novel of "sensibility" by Henry Mackenzie, published in 1771.

Man of Law's Tale, The. One of Chaucer's *Canterbury Tales.* John Gower tells the same story in his *Confessio Amantis.* Both poets took it from the Anglo-Norman *Chronicle* of Nicolas Trivet. The prologue contains a list of Chaucer's works. The lawyer tells of the misfortunes of Constance, daughter of the king of Rome, who is to marry the Sultan of Syria on condition that he become a Christian. The Sultan's mother, angry over his conversion, causes Constance to be cast adrift on a raft, on which she is carried to Britain by the sea. Here she is falsely accused of the murder of one Hermengyld,

then miraculously cleared of the charge, marries King Alla (or Ella) of Northumbria, is again cast adrift by his jealous and angry mother, and after many vicissitudes is happily reunited with King Alla. The story is related to the 14th-century metrical romance *Emaré.* Chaucer in the Prologue has described the narrator as a prosy, officious man immersed in his dusty subject, not striking even in appearance, from whom such a dramatic story comes as a surprise:

> Of fees and robes hadde he many oon.
> So greet a purchasour was nowher noon.
> Al was fee simple to him in effect,
> His purchasing mighte nat been infect.
> Nowher so bisy a man as he ther nas,
> And yet he semed bisier than he was.

Man of Mode, or Sir Fopling Flutter (fop'ling flut'ėr), **The.** A comedy (1676) by Sir George Etherege, taken as the prototype of the comedy of manners (however, it earned the scorn of Addison and Steele in the 18th century for its "Contradiction to good Manners, good Sense and common Honesty"). Molière's comedy *Les Précieuses Ridicules* suggested some of its scenes, and it is probably the closest to him in feeling of any of the many Restoration dramas which imitated or took suggestions from his plays.

Man of Property, The. A novel by John Galsworthy, published in 1906, and later included in *The Forsyte Saga* (1922).

"Man of Ross," the. See **Kyrle, John.**

Man of the World, The. A novel by Henry Mackenzie, published in 1773.

Man of the World, The. A comedy by Charles Macklin, played in 1781. It was produced originally (1764) at Crow Street, Dublin, as *The Trueborn Scotsman.* Sir Pertinax MacSycophant is a Scottish politician who wishes to gain control of three boroughs by marrying his eldest son to the daughter of a needy politician. The proposed lovers are averse to the arrangement and manage finally to defeat their parents' scheming.

Manon Lescaut (må.nôṅ les.kō). A romance written by the Abbé Prévost, published in 1733, appended to *Memoirs of a Man of Quality.*

Man's Bewitched, or, The Devil to Do about Her, The. A comedy by Susannah Centlivre, produced in 1709, and based on Thomas Corneille's *Le Deuil.*

Mansel (man'sẹl), **Henry Longueville.** b. at Cosgrove, Northamptonshire, England, Oct. 6, 1820; d. July 30, 1871. An English metaphysician. He was a follower of Sir William Hamilton, and developed the latter's theory of "the conditioned" as limiting knowledge. He maintained the duality of consciousness, including the external world and the inner self. Among his works are *Phrontisterion, or Oxford in the Nineteenth Century,* an imitation of Aristophanes (1850), *The Limits of Demonstrative Science Considered* (1853), *On the Philosophy of Kant* (1856), the article on metaphysics in the eighth edition of the *Encyclopaedia Britannica* (1857), *Bampton Lectures* (1858), and others.

Mansfield (manz'fēld), **Katherine.** [Maiden name, **Beauchamp;** married name, **Murry.**] b. at Wellington, New Zealand, Oct. 14, 1888; d. near Fontainebleau, France, Jan. 9, 1923. English short-story writer, also known as a letter-writer and diarist. Her first story was published when she was nine, and her first collection of stories in 1911 under the title *In a German Pension*. She compiled and edited (1915) with John Middleton Murry (whom she later married, 1918) and D. H. Lawrence a magazine called *The Signature*. During World War I she wrote stories of her childhood, which were published under the titles *Prelude* (1918) and *Je ne parle pas français* (1919). After 1918, when it was definitely established that she was suffering from tuberculosis, she lived chiefly in France, Italy, and Switzerland. Her delicate and penetrating short stories, which show the influence of Chekhov, rank among the finest written in the 20th century. Her reviews of current novels were published (1919–30) in the *Athenaeum*, under the title *Novels and Novelists* (1930). *Bliss* (1920) established her reputation. Other collections of stories include *The Garden Party* (1922), *The Doves' Nest* (1923), *Something Childish* (1924). She also wrote *Poems* (1923), *Journal* (1927), *Letters* (1928), and *Scrapbook* (1940).

Mansfield College. A college founded at Oxford University in 1886, primarily for dissenters.

Mansfield Park. A novel by Jane Austen, written in 1796 and published in 1814. The Bertram family of Mansfield Park consists of Sir Thomas, a kind baronet, his selfish wife, their two sons, Tom and Edmund, and two daughters, Maria and Julia. Lady Bertram has two sisters, the selfish widow Mrs. Norris, and Mrs. Price, wife of a poor marine officer. Mrs. Price has so many children that the Bertrams offer to care for one of them, Fanny. Fanny, a sensitive child when she comes into the household, finds a friend only in Edmund as she grows up. When Sir Thomas is called to the West Indies, the older son, Tom, accompanies him. Once Sir Thomas is away, Maria indulges in a flirtation with Henry Crawford, a new arrival in the village, in spite of the fact that she is engaged to the rather stupid Mr. Rushworth. Edmund is fascinated by Henry's sister Mary, a very shallow young woman, and does not realize that Fanny loves him. Sir Thomas returns unexpectedly to interrupt some amateur theatricals in which all but Fanny are participating, and Henry soon leaves for Bath. Maria finally marries Mr. Rushworth, and Henry becomes interested in Fanny, who rejects his proposal of marriage, to the displeasure of her uncle. Matters reach a crisis when Maria runs away with Henry, and Julia elopes with the fashionable but undesirable Mr. Yates. When Mary Crawford treats her brother's escapade lightly, Edmund at last recognizes her true character and turns to Fanny.

Mansion House, The. The official residence of the Lord Mayor of London.

Mansoul (män.söl′). [Full title, **Mansoul, or the Riddle of the World.**] A long poem (1920) by Charles M. Doughty.

Mant (mant), **Richard.** b. at Southampton, England, Feb. 12, 1776; d. at Ballymoney, Ireland, Nov. 2, 1848. An English author and ecclesiastic in Ireland.

Mantalini (man.ta̯.lē′nē). In Dickens's *Nicholas Nickleby*, a foppish parasite who bankrupts his industrious wife.

Mantalini, Madame. In Dickens's *Nicholas Nickleby*, a dressmaker much sought after by ladies of fashion. Her husband is a feeble-minded, elegant person.

Mantle of Elijah (ē̯.lī′ja̯), **The.** A political novel by Israel Zangwill, published in 1900.

Manton (man′ton), **Joseph.** b. c1766; d. at Maida Hill, England, June 29, 1835. An English gunsmith. He patented many improvements in large and small arms, and was a principal mover in the introduction of the percussion system.

"Mantuan Poet" (man′tū̯.a̯n). An allusion to Vergil, who was born near Mantua.

Manuel (man′ū̯.el). A tragedy by Charles Robert Maturin, produced at Drury Lane Theatre, London, on March 8, 1817, with Edmund Kean in the title role.

manuscript, *a.* and *n.* **I.** *a.* **1.** Written with the hand; in handwriting (not printed).

> In a manuscript account of the building of the palace, it is mentioned that at the entrance were two columns. (E. A. Freeman, *Venice*.)

2. Consisting of writings or written books.

> He expended upwards of £300 in arranging and improving the manuscript library at Lambeth. (Bp. Porteus, *Abp. Secker*.)

II. *n.* **1.** A book, paper, or instrument written by hand with ink or other pigment, or with a pencil or the like; a writing of any kind, as distinguished from anything that is printed. Especially—
2. Such a book, paper, or instrument so written before the introduction and general adoption of printing in the 15th century, or in a style in vogue before the invention of printing. The oldest surviving manuscripts are Egyptian, of which some are at least 3,500 years old. Ancient manuscripts are written on papyrus, parchment, or vellum, and are usually in the form of a long band which was rolled for convenience about a rod. Greek manuscripts are in uncial, cursive, or minuscule characters. The uncials are the oldest form, and resemble modern capitals. The cursive characters are derived from the uncials, though they came to differ much from these in shape, and are used in manuscripts from the second century before Christ. The minuscule writing is that practiced with few or no exceptions since the 9th century; the forms of the earliest printed Greek closely resemble it. Latin manuscripts are in capital, uncial, cursive, or minuscule characters. The capitals are the earliest form, but their use was not entirely discontinued until the Carolingian epoch. The uncials, of which the letters are characterized by their rounded shape, were developed very early, attained their highest perfection in the 4th century, and continued in use until the 9th century. The cursive writing was developed from the uncial; it appears in the graffiti found scratched on the walls of Pompeii, Rome, etc., and is the parent of many old systems of writing, as the Lombard and Merovingian. The minuscule style was developed in the 8th century, in the monastery of Saint Martin at Tours, and reached

its perfection in the 12th century. In this style are written the splendid manuscripts of the Middle Ages, produced for the most part in monasteries, and enriched with superbly illuminated initial letters and elaborately painted miniatures. Upon the introduction of printing, the minuscule writing supplied models to the earliest type-makers. *Palimpsest manuscripts* are manuscripts written in antiquity or in the early Middle Ages upon papyrus or vellum from which earlier writing had been erased. Modern science has been successful in deciphering the imperfectly effaced characters of many such manuscripts, and has recovered in this way some of our most valuable remnants of classic literature. The three most important Biblical manuscripts extant are the Alexandrian Codex, the Vatican Codex, and the Sinaitic Codex. Often abbreviated *MS.*, plural *MSS.*

Manuscript Cotton Vitellius A xv (kot'n vi.tel'i.us). [Often called the "**Beowulf Manuscript.**"] A manuscript in the British Museum, from the late 10th century and containing, besides the earliest known version of *Beowulf*, the religious poem *Judith* and other examples of Old English poetry and prose. The manuscript takes its title from Sir Robert Cotton, 17th-century English antiquary, with whose collection it was acquired by the British Museum.

Manutius (ma.nū'shi.us, -shus), **Aldus.** [Italian, **Aldo** (or **Teobaldo**) **Mannucci** or **Manucci** (mä.nöt'-chē) or **Manuzio** (mä.nö'tsyō).] b. at Bassiano, near Velletri, Italy, c1450; d. at Venice, Feb. 3, 1515. An Italian classical scholar and celebrated printer, the founder (c1490) of the Aldine Press at Venice. He published editions of Aristotle, Aristophanes, Herodotus, Demosthenes, Plato, and other Greek classics, and Latin and Italian works. His professed aim was to produce good editions of good books at a low price. For the Latin and Italian books, he invented a type face, modeled after the Italian manuscript hand, that has since been called "italic." The Aldine firm, which lasted through three generations, used as its colophon the famous dolphin and anchor with the motto *Festina lente.*

Man Who Lost Himself, The. A novel by Sir Osbert Sitwell, published in 1929.

Man Who Pays the Piper, The. A play (1931) in a prologue and three acts by G. B. Stern.

Man Who Saw and Other Poems Arising Out of the War, The. A work by Sir William Watson (1858–1935), published in 1917.

Man Who Understood Women, The. A story which gives its name to a collection (1908) by Leonard Merrick.

Man Who Was Thursday, The. A novel by G. K. Chesterton, published in 1908.

Man Who Would Be King, The. A long tale by Rudyard Kipling, first published in 1889 in *The Phantom Rickshaw.* See also **Carnahan, Peachey.**

Man with a Hammer, The. A volume of poetry by Anna Wickham, published in 1921.

Man with a Heart, A. A four-act play (1924) by Alfred Sutro.

Man Within, The. A novel by Graham Greene, published in 1929.

Man with the Muck-rake. See **Muck-rake, Man with the.**

Manzoni (män.dzō'nē), **Alessandro Francesco Tommaso Antonio.** b. at Milan, Italy, March 7, 1785; d. there, May 22, 1873. An Italian novelist and poet, the chief of the Italian romantic school. He went in his early youth to Paris with his mother, who was a daughter of the Marquis Beccaria, and who introduced him to literary society. He became acquainted with Count de Volney, Madame Condorcet, Claude Fauriel, and others, and became imbued with many of their deistical and other opinions. In 1807 he returned to Italy. He wrote the historical novel *I Promessi Sposi* (1825–27; Eng. trans., *The Betrothed*), considered not only a magnificent example of Italian prose style but also one of the chief novels of 19th-century European romanticism. Among his other works are the tragedies *Il Conte di Carmagnola* (1820) and *Adelchi* (1823), the lyric poem *Il Cinque Maggio* (*The 5th of May*, an ode on Napoleon's death, 1821), *Inni sacri* (1810; sacred lyrics), *Osservazioni sulla morale cattolica* (a vindication of Catholic morality), and *Storia della Colonna infame* (a historical treatise, 1842). Verdi's *Requiem*, first performed a year after Manzoni's death, was dedicated to his memory.

Map (map), **Walter.** [Also, **Mapes** (mā'pēz).] b. probably c1140; d. c1209. An English author and satirist. He was of a Welsh family in Herefordshire, and studied (c1154–60) at Paris. He was present at the court of Henry II, while Thomas à Becket was still chancellor, as one of the clerks of the royal household, and was employed as an itinerant justice. In 1197 he was made archdeacon of Oxford. The only extant work known to be his is the *De nugis curialium* (Courtiers' Trifles), probably composed between 1180 and 1193, a gossipy collection of tales, legends, anecdotes, and the like, told wittily and often sharply. He was also credited with a large share in the composition of the Arthurian romances, and it is barely possible that the prose *Lancelot* is based on an Anglo-French poem by him. A great part of the goliardic verse of the 12th and 13th centuries was attributed to Map in the Middle Ages, and he probably wrote verse of this genre, but certainly not nearly everything which has been attributed to him.

Maradick at Forty (mar'a.dik). A novel (1910) by Hugh Walpole. The character Maradick reappears in *Portrait of a Man with Red Hair* (1925).

Marall (mär'ôl). An agent in the service of Sir Giles Overreach in Philip Massinger's play *A New Way to Pay Old Debts*.

Marathon (mar'a.thon). A plain in Attica, Greece, ab. 18 mi. NE of Athens, between Mount Pentelicus and the sea. It is celebrated as the site of the battle of September, 490 B.C., between the Greeks (10,000 Athenians and 1,000 Plataeans), under Miltiades, and more than 100,000 Persians, under Datis and Artaphernes. The result was a Greek victory, owing to the tactics of Miltiades. The Greek loss was 192; the Persian, 6,400. The victory ended Darius's attempt against Greece, and is classed among the decisive battles of the world. The conical mound, 40 ft. high and 200 in diameter, which covers the Athenian dead, marks the central point of the

ḍ, d or j; ṣ, s or sh; ṭ, t or ch; ẓ, z or zh; *o*, F. cloche; ü, F. menu; ċh, Sc. loch; ṅ, F. bonbon.

famous battle. All doubt as to its identification was set at rest by an excavation made by the Archaeological Society of Athens, which disclosed ashes, charred remnants of the funeral pyre, and fragments of pottery dating from the beginning of the 5th century B.C. The modern marathon race is run over a distance approximating that run by the messenger carrying news of the victory in battle to Athens. At first (1896) 25 miles, the distance has been standardized since 1908 at 26 miles 385 yards.

Marazan (mar′a̱.zan). A novel by Nevil Shute, published in 1926.

Marc (märk). See **Mark**.

Marcade (mär′ka̱.dẹ). In Shakespeare's *Love's Labour's Lost*, the messenger who brings the news of the death of the King of France.

Marcella (mär.sel′a̱). A novel (1894) by Mrs. Humphry Ward: a sequel is *Sir George Tressady* (1896).

Marcellina (mär.sẹ.lē′na̱, -lĭ′-), **Countess.** The misjudged wife of Count Vaumont in George Chapman's *Monsieur D'Olive*.

Marcello (mär.sel′ō). The virtuous and innocent younger brother of the wicked Flamineo and Vittoria Corombona in John Webster's tragedy *The White Devil*.

Marcellus (mär.sel′us). In Shakespeare's *Hamlet*, an officer on watch upon the battlements who has twice seen the Ghost (of Hamlet's father) when the play opens.

March (märch), **3rd Earl of.** A title of **Douglas, William** (1724–1810).

March, (5th) Earl of. See **Mortimer, Edmund, (5th) Earl of March.**

March, Edward, Earl of. See **Edward, Earl of March.**

March Hare. In *Alice's Adventures in Wonderland*, one of the two characters (the Mad Hatter is the other one) who preside over the tea party.

Marchioness, The. A little half-starved servant of Sampson Brass in Dickens's *Old Curiosity Shop*. She is so nicknamed by Dick Swiveller, the devil-may-care fellow who eventually marries her.

Marcia (mär′sha̱, -shi.a̱). The young daughter of Cato in Addison's play of that name, loved by Juba, an ally of her father.

Marcian Codex (mär′shan), **The.** A codex of the *Iliad*, discovered at Venice in the 18th century. Its publication (1778) revolutionized Homeric studies.

Marcionites (mär′shon.īts). A heretical Christian sect comprising the followers of Marcion (fl. 2nd century), son of a bishop of Sinope in Pontus, which remained in existence until the 7th century or later. They held that there were three primal forces: the good God, first revealed by Jesus Christ; the evil matter, ruled by the Devil; and the Demiurge, the finite and imperfect God of the Jews. They rejected the Old Testament, denied the incarnation and resurrection, and admitted only a gospel akin to or altered from that of Saint Luke and ten of Saint Paul's epistles as inspired and authoritative. They repeated baptism thrice, excluded wine from the Eucharist, inculcated an extreme asceticism, and allowed women to minister.

Marcius (mär′shi.us, -shus). [Also, **Young Marcius**.] In Shakespeare's *Coriolanus*, the young son of Coriolanus.

Marcius, Caius. See under **Coriolanus**.

Marck (märk), **William de la.** d. 1485. A historical character in Sir Walter Scott's novel *Quentin Durward*, nicknamed the "Wild Boar of Ardennes" on account of his resemblance to the animal both in looks and in disposition.

Marco Polo (mär′kō pō′lō). See **Polo, Marco**.

Marcus Aemilius Lepidus (mär′kus ẹ.mil′i.us lep′-i.dus). See **Lepidus, M. Aemilius**.

Marcus Andronicus (an.dron′i.kus). In Shakespeare's *Titus Andronicus*, a tribune of the people and the brother of Titus. Unlike most of the other characters in the play, he is not bloodthirsty and vengeful, but gently tries to comfort Titus and to assist Lavinia after her mutilation, showing her how, in order to reveal the wrongdoers, to hold a stick in her mouth and write in the sand.

Marcus Antonius (an.tō′ni.us). See **Mark Antony**.

Marcus Aurelius (ô.rē′li.us, ô.rēl′yus). [Surnamed **Antoninus**; original name, **Marcus Annius Verus**.] b. at Rome, April 20, 121 A.D.; d. in Pannonia, March 17, 180. A Roman emperor (161–180) and Stoic philosopher. He was the son of Annius Verus, and was a nephew of Antoninus Pius, by whom he was adopted in 138, and whom he succeeded as emperor in 161, with Lucius Verus, also an adopted son of Antoninus Pius, as his associate in the government. He was a pupil of the Stoic Cornelius Fronto, and is frequently called "the philosopher" on account of his devotion to philosophy and literature. In 162 Verus undertook an expedition against the Parthians, but soon abandoned himself to dissipation at Antiochia. His generals, however, stormed Artaxata, burned Seleucia and Ctesiphon, reconquered Mesopotamia, and enabled him to dictate terms of peace in 165. In 166 a war broke out with the Marcomanni and Quadi, which was continued with various fortunes during the rest of the reign of Aurelius. Verus died in 169, leaving his colleague sole emperor. In 175 the general Avidius Cassius organized a revolt in Syria, but was killed by his own officers in the same year. In 177, after Marcus Aurelius's return from the East, he instituted a persecution of the Christians, whom he consistently opposed. Aurelius died in Pannonia, either at Vindobona (Vienna) or at Sirmium, March 17, 180. He wrote a work in Greek, entitled *The Meditations of Marcus Antoninus*, one of the finest works of antiquity, expressing through moral precepts based on experience the philosophy of life that seeks moderation and tranquillity in all things. There is a bronze equestrian statue of Marcus Aurelius in the Piazza del Campidoglio, Rome, considered by many to be the finest extant piece of ancient bronze-work.

Marcus Brutus (brö′tus). See **Brutus, Marcus**.

Mardian (mär′di.an). In Shakespeare's *Antony and Cleopatra*, a eunuch in attendance on Cleopatra. He is sent by Cleopatra to tell Antony that she is dead (IV.xiv).

---

fat, fāte, fär, a̱sk, fāre; net, mē, hėr; pin, pīne; not, nōte, mȯve, nôr; up, lūte, pu̇ll; ᴛʜ, then;

Margarelon (mär.gą.rel'on). In Shakespeare's *Troilus and Cressida*, a bastard son of Priam, King of Troy.

Margaret (mär'gą.ret), Saint. [Also, Saint **Marina**.] b. c255 A.D.; d. c275. A Christian martyr. Daughter of a pagan priest, she was disowned by him on embracing Christianity and adopted by a pious woman near Antioch, whose flocks she tended. She had taken a vow of virginity, and resisted the approaches of the Roman prefect Olybrius, even after torture. He finally had her beheaded. She is patroness of pregnant women.

Margaret, Saint. b. between 1038 and 1057; d. at Edinburgh, Nov. 16, 1093. Queen of Scotland; daughter of Edward, son of Edmund Ironside. She married Malcolm III of Scotland about 1067, and used her influence as queen for ecclesiastical reform. She is held responsible for the heightened influence of English customs, as opposed to Celtic, that eventually led to Scottish orientation towards England and to union of the two kingdoms. Her influence was especially felt during the reigns of her sons, Edgar, Alexander I, and David I.

Margaret. [Called the **Maid of Norway**.] b. in Norway, 1283; d. at sea, 1290. Queen of Scotland; daughter of Eric II of Norway, and granddaughter of Alexander III of Scotland whom she succeeded in 1286. Edward I of England arranged the betrothal of his son (afterward Edward II) to the Scottish queen, and she died, somewhat mysteriously, while on her way to meet him. Her death was followed by the contests of the families of Bruce and Baliol for the throne.

Margaret. In Shakespeare's *1, 2,* and *3 Henry VI* and *Richard III*, the historical Margaret of Anjou, a protagonist against the Yorkist party. She is first depicted as a timid young girl, the daughter of Reignier, then after her marriage with Henry VI a determined enemy of York and Gloucester and in love with Suffolk. In *3 Henry VI*, she is characterized as a cruel but politically righteous woman fighting to keep the throne for her son. Her last appearance, in *Richard III*, is as an old woman who leads Queen Elizabeth and the Duchess of York in a chorus of cursing against Richard. This last is unhistorical, but Shakespeare makes her an almost ghostly figure whose suffering is transmuted into a kind of externalized conscience for the villainous Richard.

Margaret. In Shakespeare's *Much Ado About Nothing*, a gentlewoman attending Hero, whom she impersonates in a pretended assignation with Borachio.

Margaret. A country girl in Robert Greene's comedy *Friar Bacon and Friar Bungay*.

Margaret. The beautiful heroine of George Chapman's tragicomedy *The Gentleman Usher*. She falls in love with Prince Vincentio, whose father is also in love with her. Although her father is about to force her into a marriage with Vincentio's father, she solemnly promises Vincentio that she will celebrate her nuptials only with him even though she is legally betrothed to his father. On the false report of Poggio that Vincentio has been murdered, she disfigures her beauty with an oint-

ment, but is able to restore it by "recureful mask" when Vincentio appears.

Margaret Brandt (bränt). See **Brandt, Margaret**.

Margaret Flaherty (fla'ẽr.ti). See **Flaherty, Margaret**.

Margaret of Anjou (an'jö). b. probably at Pont-à-Mousson or Nancy, France, March 23, 1430; d. at Dampierre, near Saumur, France, Aug. 25, 1482. Queen consort of Henry VI of England. She was the daughter of René I of Anjou and Isabella of Lorraine, and was married to Henry VI at Titchfield Abbey, April 22, 1445. The marriage was brought about by William de la Pole, Earl (afterward Duke) of Suffolk, in confirmation of a truce with France, and was extremely unpopular with the nation, which desired a continuance of the war (the Hundred Years' War). Margaret, after her marriage, supported the peace policy of Suffolk and afterward of the Duke of Somerset (Edmund Beaufort). In August, 1453, Henry was seized with his first attack of insanity, and in the following October the queen gave birth to her only son, Edward. A contest for the regency ensued between her and Richard, Duke of York (until the birth of Edward heir presumptive to the throne), who represented the popular party, and who was appointed protector of the realm in March, 1454. The protectorate came to an end with the king's recovery in January, 1455; but the birth of an heir apparent and the hostile attitude of the queen induced the Duke of York to take up arms in 1455, thereby inaugurating the series of wars between the houses of Lancaster and York known as the Wars of the Roses, which ended in the defeat and capture of Margaret and the death of her son at Tewkesbury, May 4, 1471, and in the death of her husband in the Tower of London, May 21, 1471. Margaret was liberated in 1475 on the renunciation of her claim to the throne and on the payment of a ransom by Louis XI of France, and returned to the Continent.

Margaret of Navarre (ną.vär'). [Also, **Margaret** or **Marguerite of Valois** (val'wä) or **of Angoulême** (äng.gö.lem') or **of Alençon** (ą.len'son).] b. at Angoulême, France, April 11, 1492; d. in Bigorre, France, Sept. 21, 1549. Queen of Navarre; daughter of Charles d'Orléans, Duc d'Angoulême, and sister of Francis I of France. She married (1509) Charles d'Orléans, Duc d'Alençon, and later (1527) Henri d'Albret, King of Navarre. Through the second marriage she was grandmother of Henry IV of France (Henry of Navarre). After the death of the king in 1544, she assumed the direction of the government. For a time she was favorably disposed to Protestantism, but subsequently abandoned it. She is especially famous as a patroness of literature and as the author of the *Heptameron*, a collection of tales modeled on the *Decameron* and believed actually to have been written by members of the literary circle she gathered about her at her courts at Pau and Nérac. A number of her poems were published (1547) by Sylvius de la Haye under the title *Marguerites de la marguerite des princesses*. Her letters were published in 1841–42.

Margaret Plantagenet (plan.taj'ę.net), **Lady**. See **Plantagenet, Lady Margaret**.

Margaret Ramsay (ram'zi). See **Ramsay, Margaret.**

Margaret's Ghost. See **William and Margaret.**

Margawse (mär'gôz). [Also, **Morgawse.**] In Malory's *Morte d' Arthur*, a sister of King Arthur, wife of King Lot, and mother of Modred, Gawain, Gaheris, and Gareth. She appears in Geoffrey of Monmouth as Anne.

Margery Jourdain (mär'jẹ.ri jör.dān'). See **Jourdain, Margery.**

Margites (mär.jī'tēz). [Eng. trans., "*The Booby.*"] A Greek comic poem with a fool and dandy for hero, probably written c700 B.C. Aristotle considered it the beginning of true comedy.

Marguerite Gautier (mȧr.gẹ.rēt gō.tyā). See **Gautier, Marguerite.**

Marguerite of Valois (val'wä) or **of Angoulême** (äng.gö.lem') or **of Alençon** (ȧ.len'sọn). See **Margaret of Navarre.**

Marhaus (mär'hôs), **Sir.** See **Morhault, Sir.**

Maria (mạ.rī'ạ, mạ.rē'ạ). In Shakespeare's *Love's Labour's Lost*, a lady attending the Princess of France. She is wooed by Longaville.

Maria. In Shakespeare's *Twelfth Night*, Olivia's witty waiting-woman. She sets up the plot to prove Malvolio mad by writing a love letter in a hand like Olivia's.

Maria. The wife of Andrugio, Duke of Genoa, and later the wife of Piero, Doge of Venice, in John Marston's *Antonio's Revenge*.

Maria. The wife of Altofronto, the banished Duke of Genoa, in John Marston's *The Malcontent*.

Maria. In Francis Beaumont and John Fletcher's comedy *The Woman's Prize, or the Tamer Tamed*, a sequel to Shakespeare's *Taming of the Shrew*, the daughter of Petrovius and second wife of Petruchio, whom she subjugates by a series of witty and well-planned attacks, as completely as his first wife Katharina was tamed by him.

Maria. In Philip Massinger's *Bashful Lover*, the daughter of Octavio.

Maria. In Richard Brinsley Sheridan's *School for Scandal*, a witty young girl who marries Charles Surface.

Mariamne (mär.i.am'nē). fl. c20 B.C. The daughter of the priest Simon, and one of the wives of Herod I, who raised her father to the high-priesthood.

Mariamne. A tragedy (1723) by Elijah Fenton.

Mariam, the Fair Queen of Jewry (mär'i.ạm). A tragedy (printed in 1613) by a certain Elizabeth Cary (about whom virtually nothing else is definitely known). It was possibly the first play written by an Englishwoman.

Marian (mär'i.ạn), **Maid.** See **Maid Marian.**

Mariana (mär.i.an'ạ). In Shakespeare's *All's Well That Ends Well*, a Florentine girl.

Mariana. In Shakespeare's *Measure for Measure*, a lady betrothed to Angelo, but after her loss of her dowry, rejected by him. She takes Isabella's place in an assignation with Angelo, and later the Duke orders him to marry her. It was in allusion to her that Tennyson wrote his *Mariana in the Moated Grange* and *Mariana in the South*.

Mariana. The principal character in J. Sheridan Knowles's play *The Wife*, a faithful and constant wife entangled in a mesh of circumstantial evidence.

Marian Halcombe (mär'i.ạn hal'kọm). See **Halcombe, Marian.**

Marianne Dashwood (mär.i.an' dash'wụd). See **Dashwood, Elinor** and **Marianne.**

Marie de France (mȧ.rē dẹ fräns). fl. probably in the latter part of the 12th century. A French poetess. She was born in France, but lived in England. Her works include narrative poems (*Lais*), drawn to a great extent from Celtic tales, a collection of fables (*Ysopet*), and a poem on the purgatory of Saint Patrick.

Marigold (mar'i.gōld), **Doctor.** See **Doctor Marigold.**

Marina (mạ.rē'nạ, -rī'-). In Shakespeare's *Pericles*, the extraordinarily virtuous and beautiful daughter of Pericles and Thaisa. Rescued by pirates from the murderous jealousy of Dionyza, she is sold to the keeper of a brothel, where nevertheless she keeps her virtue. She is finally reunited with Pericles and marries Lysimachus, Governor of Mytilene. In Gower's *Confessio Amantis*, from which Shakespeare got his plot, she is called Thaise.

Marina. A poem (1930) by T. S. Eliot. It is based on the story of Marina, daughter of Pericles, as told by Shakespeare in *Pericles*.

Marina, Saint. See **Saint Margaret.**

Marinism (ma.rē'nizm). Extreme mannerism in literature, like that of the school of Italian poets of the 17th century founded by G. B. Marini (1569–1625), which was characterized by extravagance in the use of metaphor, antitheses, and forced conceits.

> Achillini of Bologna followed in Marini's steps. . . . In general, we may say that all the poets of the 17th century were more or less infected with Marinism. (*Encyclopaedia Britannica.*)

Marino Faliero (mạ.rē'nō fäl.yär'ō). A tragedy by Byron, published in 1820 and acted in 1821.

Maris (mar'is) or **Mares** (mar'ẹs), **Sir Ector** (or **Hector**) **de.** See **Ector de Maris, Sir.**

Maritana (mar.i.tä'nạ). An opera in three acts by William Vincent Wallace, first produced at London in 1845. The libretto, by Edward Fitzball, was adapted from the drama *Don César de Bazan*.

Marius (mär'i.us), **Gaius** (or **Caius**). b. near Arpinum, Italy, c155 B.C.; d. Jan. 13, 86 B.C. A Roman general. He served in the Numantine War in 134, was tribune in 119 and praetor in 115, was legate under Metellus in the Jugurthine War (109–108), and was consul in 107, 104, 103, 102, 101, 100, and 86. He commanded against Jugurtha (107–106), and against the Cimbri and Teutones (104–101), defeated the Teutones at Aix in 102 and the Cimbri at the Raudian Fields, near Vercellae, in 101, and defeated the Marsi in the Social War in 90. His rivalry with Sulla over the command against Mithridates VI of Pontus caused the first civil war in 88. He was driven from Rome in that year, but returned after Sulla left for the East, and with Cinna captured Rome in 87, and massacred many of the aristocrats.

Marius the Epicurean. A philosophical novel by Walter Pater, published in 1885. It tells the story of a young Roman who lived in the 2nd century A.D., during the reign of Marcus Aurelius. It is set against a background of the life and customs of the time, and deals with the various philosophies then current in the empire. Marius spends his early years on his family's Etruscan farm, is educated at Pisa, and then lives at Rome. He is tempted by many philosophical systems, including Cynicism, Stoicism, Epicureanism, and Platonism. However, he meets Cornelius, a young Christian, at Rome, and finally gives his own life to save his new friend.

Marivaux (mà.rē.vō), **Pierre Carlet de Chamblain de.** b. at Paris, Feb. 4, 1688; d. Feb. 12, 1763. A French dramatist and novelist. His best work was done between 1722 and 1746; in that time he wrote some 25 plays, foremost among which are *Le Jeu de l'amour et du hasard* (1730), *L'École des mœurs* (1732), *Les Fausses Confidences* (1736), *Le Legs* (1736), and *L'Épreuve* (1740). All Marivaux's plays are more or less alike in their subject matter; the various situations are effected not through outside events, but by the expression of inner feelings on the part of the different characters; difficulties arise entirely through the fault of the lovers themselves, either in their curiosity, their timidity, their ignorance, their pride, or their pique. As a novelist Marivaux wrote *La Vie de Marianne* (1731–41), his masterpiece; also *Le Paysan parvenu* (1735) and *Pharamond, ou les folies romanesques* (1737). Marivaux's peculiar style has been named for him *marivaudage*.

Marjory Pinchwife (mär'jọ.ri pinch'wīf). See under **Pinchwife, Mr.**

Mark (märk). [Also, **Marc.**] In Arthurian romance, a king of Cornwall; uncle of Tristram, for whom Tristram went to Ireland to bring Isolt home as Mark's bride.

Mark, Basilica of Saint. [Also, **Saint Mark's.**] A superb basilica founded 830 in Venice, and given its definitive form in 1052.

Mark Antony (an'tọ.ni). [Also: **Antony**; Latin, **Marcus Antonius.**] In Shakespeare's *Julius Caesar*, one of the triumvirs with Octavius and Lepidus after Caesar's death. Although Brutus believes him to be a dissolute young man who will do little about Caesar's assassination, he obtains permission to deliver a funeral oration over Caesar's dead body as it lies in front of the Capitol. The famous speech beginning "Friends, Romans, countrymen, lend me your ears" (III.ii), although at first seeming to praise the conspirators, as he had promised, finally turns the populace against them by insisting upon Caesar's goodness. With Octavius, he later defeats Brutus and Cassius at the Battle of Philippi (after somewhat callously dividing the rule of the Roman empire with Octavius). He appears as the hero of Shakespeare's *Antony and Cleopatra*, which has its setting in the later years of his life. A much weaker, but also more attractive, person than the Mark Antony of *Julius Caesar*, he succumbs to Cleopatra's charms and in his passion degenerates into a fool, whom Octavius sees at his worst and for whom Lepidus tact-

fully apologizes when, upon the threat of further civil war, he returns to Rome. After marrying Octavia as a political expedient to bind Octavius closer to him, Antony hurries off to Egypt again to prepare for war with Octavius. His fleet is defeated at Actium and he stabs himself upon hearing a false report of Cleopatra's death.

Market Bosworth (boz'wẽrth). [Also, **Bosworth.**] A rural district and market town in C England, in Leicestershire, ab. 12 mi. W of Leicester, ab. 100 mi. N of London. It has associations with Samuel Johnson. Bosworth Field is in the rural district.

Markham (mär'kạm), **Gervase** or **Jervis.** b. c1568; d. at London, in February, 1637. An English author. He fought in the Low Countries and in Ireland, and later wrote on military matters. He wrote also on agriculture, forestry, horsemanship, and farriery. He wrote a number of plays in collaboration and was the author of *The Most Honorable Tragedy of Sir Richard Grinville Knight* (1595), a long poem on the hero of the *Revenge*. Jonson listed him as one "not of the number of the faithful" (that is to say, not a true poet) and "a base fellow." Attributed to Markham are *The Tears of the Beloved, or the Lamentations of St. John* (1600) and *The New Metamorphosis* (c1612), the latter a long poetical romance.

Markham, Gilbert. In Anne Brontë's *The Tenant of Wildfell Hall*, the narrator of the story. He is the second husband of Helen Graham.

Markham Everard (ev'ẽr.ärd), **Colonel.** See **Everard, Colonel Markham.**

Markleham (mär'kẹl.ạm), **Mrs.** In Dickens's *David Copperfield*, the mother-in-law of Dr. Strong, David's schoolmaster at Canterbury.

Mark Robarts (rō'bärts). See **Robarts, Mark.**

Mark Tapley (märk tap'li). See **Tapley, Mark.**

Marlborough (märl'bur.ọ, -bẽr.ọ; môl'-), 1st Duke of. [Title of **John Churchill.**] b. in Devonshire, England, May or June, 1650; d. near Windsor, England, June 16, 1722. An English general and statesman, renowned as commander (1702–11) of the allied armies at war with Louis XIV of France. He was educated at St. Paul's School and became (c1665) a page to the Duke of York (later James II). He entered the military service and served under the Duke at Nijmegen (1672) and Maestricht (1673), where he saved the Duke's life. His rise to prominence was further assured by his sister Arabella, maid of honor to the Duchess of York, who became the Duke's mistress. His marriage (1678) to Sarah Jennings, favorite of the future Queen Anne, likewise helped his fortunes, which received great impetus at the accession (1685) of James II. As a military commander under James, he contributed greatly to the suppression of the Monmouth rebellion (1685), he being responsible for the victory at Sedgemoor. When sent to France, however, on a diplomatic mission to Louis XIV, he was already known to have declared against the king if the latter should attempt to change the religion of the nation to Roman Catholicism. Meanwhile he was also in communication with William of Orange, to whom he pledged support. Thus, when William landed (1688) in England, and Churchill was sent at the head of 5,000 men to oppose him, James discovered that his general had gone over into the enemy camp. This flexibility in Churchill's personal loyalties probably prevented him from being employed by William (now William III) for important duties, aside from service in the Netherlands (1689) and in Ireland (1690). Marlborough undoubtedly was in constant communication with the exiled James and actually spent some time (1692) in the Tower, but such was the political atmosphere that William could not afford to alienate him. Upon the accession of Anne in March, 1702, Marlborough (whose wife Sarah was the queen's favorite) attained the height of his power. Having been made Baron Churchill of Sandridge (1685) and Earl of Marlborough (1689), he was made (1702) Duke of Marlborough and captain general of English troops. The almost immediate opening (May, 1702) of the War of the Spanish Succession put Marlborough at the head of the combined English and Dutch armies. During this decade of war, the domestic political scene moved gradually against Marlborough, who first lost the support of the Tories, opponents of the war, and was later opposed by strong elements in Parliament, which advocated peace with France. For the time being, however, Marlborough was virtual ruler of England, his close friend Sidney Godolphin being prime minister and his wife controlling the queen. In the field he swept the French from Gelderland by his victories at Kaiserswerth, Venlo, and Liége, but in 1703, despite the capture of Bonn, failed in his campaign against Antwerp through disagreement with his Dutch allies. With Prince Eugene, Marlborough inflicted (1704) a crushing defeat on the French at Blenheim, thus occupying Bavaria. The disputes between the Allies continued and the French forces regained their strength, but at Ramillies (1706) Marlborough again routed the French, taking Brabant and Flanders. Again in 1708, at Oudenarde, the French were defeated; Lille fell in December and France attempted to arrange a truce, but Marlborough refused. In 1709 Tournai and Mons fell and at the murderous battle of Malplaquet the French, though defeated, retired in order; Malplaquet was the last great battle of the war, which ended with the Treaty of Utrecht in 1712. But Marlborough had meanwhile lost valuable ground at court. Sarah, his wife, who had been the queen's favorite, had now become the object of her hatred and was succeeded in the queen's favor by her cousin Abigail Hill Masham. Every opportunity was used to bring about the fall of the Duke. Godolphin was removed (1710); the Duchess was dismissed (1711); and, in December, 1711, charged with embezzlement of moneys, Marlborough was himself relieved of his offices. Though cleared of the charges, he left for the Continent in 1712. Marlborough returned after the queen's death (1714) and regained his military posts under George I, but his last years were spent quietly.

Marlborough House. A London residence belonging to the British government. It is a large building of brick trimmed with stone, with extensive gardens fronting on the Mall. It was built (1710) for John Churchill, 1st Duke of Marlborough, by Christopher Wren.

Marley (mär'li), **Jacob.** In Dickens's *Christmas Carol*, the partner (now deceased) of Scrooge. His ghost appears, clanking with chains, to aid in reforming the old man.

Marlow (mär'lō). A character in several of Joseph Conrad's novels, *Chance, Lord Jim*, etc.

Marlow, Sir Charles. The father of the "shy" Young Marlow in Goldsmith's *She Stoops to Conquer.*

Marlow, Young. The son of Sir Charles Marlow in Oliver Goldsmith's *She Stoops to Conquer.* He is extremely shy with women of high station and reputation, but bold enough among women of lesser position; hence Miss Hardcastle "stoops" to the disguise of a barmaid "to conquer" him.

Marlowe (mär'lō), **Christopher.** b. at Canterbury, England, Feb. 6, 1564; d. at Deptford, England, May 30, 1593. An English poet and dramatist. Son of a shoemaker, he secured a good education at Cambridge University, taking his B.A. in 1584 and M.A. in 1587. He was forced to appear at the Middlesex Sessions in London in 1588, but the charge is unknown. It appears that by 1587 he was attached to the Lord Admiral's Men as a playwright, enjoying the familiar acquaintance of Sir Walter Raleigh and other writers, adventurers, and men about town, and probably living a gay and roistering life. He was the "gracer of tragedians" reproved for atheism by Greene in his *Groatsworth of Wit* (1592). Chettle is probably referring to him when he speaks of "one he cares not to be acquainted with." Marlowe freely avowed the heretical and even atheistic views for which eventually, in 1593, he was called to account. An information against him was lodged with the authorities, but before he could be brought to trial, he was slain by an Ingram Frisar in a tavern brawl at Deptford. This is the generally accepted circumstance of his death, although many other accounts have been circulated. Some have advanced the theory that Marlowe, secretly involved in politics (perhaps as a French agent), was the victim of a conspiracy. It has been said that if Shakespeare, born in the same year with Marlowe, had like the latter died at the age of 29, Marlowe's name would have come down in literary history as the greatest of the Elizabethan dramatic poets. *Tamburlaine*, in two parts, probably first acted about 1587 and licensed for printing in 1590, is universally ascribed to him on internal evidence alone. *Doctor Faustus* appears to have been first acted in 1588, but it was not entered on the Stationers' Register for publication until 1601. It is known to have been produced by Henslowe 24 times between 1594 and 1597, and subsequently it was performed frequently by English companies in several of the chief German cities. *The Jew of Malta*, another tragedy, was written and first produced probably in 1589, was frequently acted in England between 1591 and 1596, and was also given by English companies on the Continent. In 1818 Edmund Kean revived it at the Drury Lane Theatre in a modernized version. Marlowe's historical play *Edward II* was entered on the Stationers' Register in 1593. About the same time he collaborated with Thomas Nash in writing *The Tragedy of Dido, Queen of Carthage*, and wrote

The Massacre at Paris alone. *Lust's Dominion, or the Lascivious Queen,* published in 1657, has been attributed to him, but without much substantiation. It is generally thought that he had a hand in fashioning some of the earlier plays of the Shakespeare canon. The greatest of his nondramatic works was an unfinished paraphrase of the *Hero and Leander* of Musaeus, which was completed by George Chapman; but he is now most often remembered for one of the most famous of English lyrics, *The Passionate Shepherd to His Love,* which begins with the much-quoted line, "Come live with me and be my love." His advent in the London theater marked the beginning of great drama in England, and there are few who will deny that he was surely a dramatist of authentic genius (there are many readers who will insist, indeed, that no list of the greatest Elizabethan plays is complete which fails to include at least *Doctor Faustus* and *The Jew of Malta* from among Marlowe's works).

Marmion (mär′mi.ọn). A narrative poem (1808) by Sir Walter Scott, subtitled "A Tale of Flodden Field," written in six cantos, concerning the actions of a favorite of King Henry VIII who is unfaithful to Constance, a former nun, and seeks instead the hand of Lady Clare, wife of Sir Ralph de Wilton. By means of a forged letter he is enabled to charge de Wilton with treason; he thereupon meets him on the field of honor, and leaves him for dead. Meanwhile, Constance has been returned to her convent and walled up alive for perjury. Through a series of circumstances the truth is revealed, de Wilton meets Marmion again (having been disguised as a palmer), and rejoins the English forces. At the Battle of Flodden Marmion is killed, and de Wilton and Clare are thereafter reunited. The poem is particularly noted for the two ballads "Where Shall the Lover Rest" and "Lochinvar."

Marmion, Shackerley or **Shakerley.** b. near Brackley, Northamptonshire, England, in January, 1603; d. at London, in January, 1639. An English dramatist and poet. He wrote *Holland's Leaguer* (licensed and printed 1632), *A Fine Companion* (1633), and *The Antiquary* (his best-known play; acted in 1636, printed 1641). He also wrote *Cupid and Psyche,* and other poems.

Marne (märn; French, màrn), **Battles of the.** A name applied to two battles, nearly four years apart, on the Western Front, in World War I. Both represented successful Allied counteractions to German attempts to get to Paris and the broad plains of France. The first battle (Sept. 5–12, 1914) was fought over a wide front from the north of Paris to the west of Verdun. It was initially of uneven outcome, but the Germans, worried about the position of their right wing, ordered the retreat of their five armies to the Aisne on September 9. Thereby they accepted the failure of their attempt to win the war in the West by an offensive in the first six weeks. It was during this battle (September 7–8) that Gen. Galliéni moved the 7th division into battle from Paris in taxicabs. Almost two years later, in the final spring and summer offensives of 1918, German troops crossed the Aisne and Marne again, but a French counterattack forced their retreat. As a consequence the Allies gained the initiative and the offensives begun soon thereafter eventually culminated in Germany's request for an armistice.

Marner (mär′nẻr), **Silas.** The title character of George Eliot's *Silas Marner,* a poor weaver whose life has been wrecked by a false accusation.

Maro (mā′rō). The family name of the Roman poet Vergil (Publius Vergilius Maro).

Marot (mȧ.rō), **Clément.** b. at Cahors, France, 1497; d. at Turin, Italy, 1544. A French poet. His father had been court poet to the Queen of France, Anne de Bretagne, and through him the son obtained access to the court circles, where he won the good will of Margaret of Navarre, sister of Francis I. When Francis I came to the throne of France in 1515, Clément Marot attracted the king's attention by his poem *Le Temple de Cupidon,* and was retained by him at court. The poet followed his royal patron on his expeditions, and led on the whole an eventful life. His tendency was towards humanism and, to some extent, the Reformation, and he was after 1526 always under suspicion of heresy. He was arrested in 1526 but freed the same year, and in 1535 had to flee to Ferrara and later to Rome, where he obtained the aid of Pope Paul III to enable him to return (1539) to France. There he got into a literary quarrel with Sagon, an adherent of the Sorbonne, with the result that he again fled (1543), this time to Geneva and Calvin. But Calvinism was not palatable to the liberal mind of Marot and he left Geneva for Turin, where he died. Besides a great deal of original poetry, light, graceful, satirical, and including *Enfer* (written in prison, 1526), *Adolescence Clémentine* (a collection published 1532), and *Blasons* (c1536), Marot also translated portions of Vergil, Ovid, and Petrarch, and 52 psalms of David. His complete works have been variously edited; the last edition from the author's lifetime is dated 1544.

Marpessa (mär.pes′ạ). A volume of verse (1900) by Stephen Phillips.

Marplot (mär′plot). [Full title, **Marplot; or, The Second Part of the Busybody.**] A comedy by Susannah Centlivre, produced in 1710. Henry Woodward altered it, and called it *Marplot in Lisbon.*

Marplot, Martin. A bumbling busybody in Susannah Centlivre's *The Busybody* and *Marplot,* whose well-meaning attempts to be helpful nearly ruin the plans of various lovers in the plays.

Marprelate (mär′prel″ạt), **Martin.** See **Martin Marprelate.**

Marpriest (mär′prēst″), **Martin.** Pseudonym of **Overton, Richard.**

Marquis of Granby (gran′bi, gram′bi), **The.** In Dickens's *Pickwick Papers,* the inn at Dorking kept by Mrs. Tony Weller.

Marriage. A novel by Susan E. Ferrier, published anonymously in 1818.

Marriage. A novel by H. G. Wells, published in 1912.

Marriage à la Mode. A play by John Dryden, acted in 1672, and considered his best comedy. Rhodophil and Doralice, having tired of marriage after two years, decide to disregard their marriage

---

ḍ, d or j; ṣ, s or sh; ṭ, t or ch; ẓ, z or zh; o, F. cloche; ü, F. menu; ċh, Sc. loch; ṅ, F. bonbon.

vows and proceed to enter into affairs with Melantha and Palamede respectively. Palamede dislikes his intended fiancée Melantha (for her affectation of French ways), and willingly surrenders to Doralice, despite his father's threat to disinherit him if he refuses Melantha. Eventually the couples return to their proper alliances after a series of amusing incidents, culminating in the discovery that each lover is jealous of the other.

Marriage à la Mode, or the Comical Lovers. A comedy by Colley Cibber, a combination of the comic scenes of John Dryden's *Marriage à la Mode* and *Secret Love, or The Maiden Queen*, produced in 1707.

Marriage of Heaven and Hell, The. A prose work by William Blake, published in 1790, in which the author denies eternal punishment for sin and rejects the code of authority.

Marriage of Wit and Science. An anonymous interlude (c1569), imitating John Redford's *Wit and Science.*

Married Man, The. A play by Elizabeth Inchbald, produced in 1789. It is taken from *Le Philosophe marié* of Philippe Destouches.

Marriott (mar'i.ọt), Sir **John Arthur Ransome.** b. 1859; d. in Wales, June 6, 1945. An English historian. Known for his writings on historical, political, and other subjects of current interest, he was the author of *Makers of Modern Italy* (1889), *George Canning and his Times* (1903), *Second Chambers* (1910), *England Since Waterloo* (1913), *The English Land System* (1914), *The Right to Work* (1919), *Economics and Ethics* (1923), *The Crisis of English Liberty* (1930), *25 Years of the Reign of King George V* (1935), *Dictatorship and Democracy* (1935), *The Tragedy of Europe* (1941), *Federalism and the Problem of the Small State* (1943), and others.

Marryat (mar'i.ạt), **Florence.** b. at Brighton, England, 1837; d. at London, Oct. 27, 1899. An English novelist; daughter of Frederick Marryat. She was also known as a dramatic reader. She was editor (1872–76) of *London Society*, published many novels, and wrote a life of her father (1872).

Marryat, Frederick. [Called **Captain Marryat.**] b. at London, July 10, 1792; d. at Langham, Norfolk, England, Aug. 9, 1848. A British naval officer and novelist. In 1806 he entered the navy, and in 1815 was made commander. He was serving on the St. Helena station when Napoleon died (1821). He served (1824–25) in Burma during the Burmese War, and led an expedition to Bassein to seize Burmese stores. He resigned (1830), and devoted himself to literature, using his naval background as the basis of a series of adventure novels. He published *Frank Mildmay, or Adventures of a Naval Officer* (1829), *The King's Own* (1830), *Peter Simple* (1834), *Jacob Faithful* (1834), *Mr. Midshipman Easy* (1836), *Japhet in Search of a Father* (1836), *Snarleyyow, or the Dog Fiend* (1837), *The Phantom Ship* (1839), *Masterman Ready* (1841), *The Children of the New Forest* (1847), and *The Little Savage* (1848). He edited the *Metropolitan Magazine* from 1832 to 1835.

Mars (märz). In Roman mythology, the god of war. Mars was the father of Romulus and Remus,

and thus ancestor of the Roman state. Jupiter, Mars, and Quirinus (who was identified with Romulus) comprised an early triad. Mars was an ancient Italian god of fertility and vegetation before he was a Roman god, and the first month of the year (March) was named for him. His transition from spring and fertility god to war god is not satisfactorily explained, but it has been suggested that wars usually start in the spring. His priests (the Salii) danced in the great March festival dressed in armor. Bellona (Roman war goddess) was his charioteer, and wife, sister, or daughter. In later mythology, Mars became identified with the Greek Ares.

Marseillaise (mär.sẹ.lāz'; French, mår.se.yez), **La.** French national anthem. The words and music are by Claude Joseph Rouget de Lisle, a captain of engineers, and were composed at Strasbourg on the night of April 24, 1792. It was first called *Chant de guerre de l'armée du Rhin;* sung by a group of soldiers from Marseilles who entered Paris late in July and marched on the Tuileries on Aug. 10, it became known as the *Chant des Marseillais.* The tune has often been utilized by composers.

Marsh (märsh), **Anne.** [Maiden name, **Caldwell.**] b. in Staffordshire, England, c1798; d. there, in October, 1874. An English novelist.

Marsh, Sir Edward Howard. b. Nov. 18, 1872—. An English public official and writer. He served as private secretary to Winston Churchill (1905, 1917–22, 1924–29), to V. C. W. Cavendish, 9th Duke of Devonshire (1922–24), to J. H. Thomas (1924, 1929–36), and to Malcolm MacDonald (1936–37). Author of *Memoir of Rupert Brooke* (1915), *A Number of People* (1939), and *Minima* (1947).

Marsh, Ngaio. b. at Christchurch, New Zealand, April 23, 1899—. A New Zealand detective fiction writer. She is the author of *A Man Lay Dead* (1934), *Death in Ecstasy* (1937), *Vintage Murder* (1937), *Overture to Death* (1939), *Colour Scheme* (1943), *Died in the Wool* (1945), *Final Curtain* (1947), *Night at the Vulcan* (1951), and others.

Marshal (mär'shạl), **William.** See under **Pembroke,** (1st) **Earl of.**

Marshall (mär'shạl), **Alfred.** b. at London, July 26, 1842; d. at Cambridge, England, July 13, 1924. An English economist, professor of political economy (1885–1908) in the University of Cambridge. He published *The Economics of Industry* (1879, with Mary Paley), *Principles of Economics* (1890), *Industry and Trade* (1919), *Money, Credit and Commerce* (1923), and others. Through his teaching and his *Principles*, long an authoritative text, he influenced economic thought in its approach to such problems as money and value for many years.

Marshall, Archibald. b. at London, Sept. 6, 1886; d. at Cambridge, England, Sept. 29, 1934. An English journalist, editor, and novelist. He was a correspondent for the London *Daily Mail* and *Daily News*, editor of the *Cambridge Review*, and contributor to *Punch.* Author of *Peter Binney, Undergraduate* (1899), *The House of Merrilees* (1905), which he brought out after every English publisher had rejected it, *Richard Baldock* (1906),

Exton Manor (1907), *Many Junes* (1908), *The Squire's Daughter* (1909), *The Eldest Son* (1911), *The Mystery of Redmarsh Farm* (1912), *The Honor of the Clintons* (1913), *Roding Rectory* (1914; American title, *The Greatest of These*), *Rank and Riches* (1915; American title, *The Old Order Changeth*), *Sir Harry—A Love Story* (1920), *Pippin* (1923), *Anthony Dare* (1923), *The Education of Anthony Dare* (1924), *Anthony Dare's Progress* (1925), *The Allbright Family* (1926), *Simple People* (1928), *Two Families* (1931), and *The Birdikin Family* (1932), novels. He also wrote *The Terrors* (1913), *The Clintons and Others* (1919), *Peggy in Toyland* (1920), *Audacious Anne* (1924), *Joan and Nancy* (1925), *Angel Face* (1933), collected short stories; and *Out and About* (1933), autobiography.

Marshall, Bruce. b. at Edinburgh, June 24, 1899—. A Scottish novelist. Author of *Father Malachy's Miracle* (1931), *Prayer for the Living* (1934), *The Uncertain Glory* (1935), *Luckypenny* (1937), *Yellow Tapers for Paris* (1943), *All Glorious Within* (1944), *George Brown's Schooldays* (1946), *The Red Danube* (1947), and *To Every Man a Penny* (1949).

Marshalsea Prison (mär'shạl.sē). A prison in Southwark, London, used for debtors, and abolished in 1849. Charles Dickens's father was held here. In Dickens's *Little Dorrit*, William Dorrit, also imprisoned here, is called the "Father of the Marshalsea."

Marston (mär'stọn), 1st Baron. A title of **Boyle, Charles.**

Marston, John. [Pseudonym, **W. Kinsayder.**] b. c1575; d. at London, June 25, 1634. An English dramatist, satirist, and divine. He studied at Brasenose College, Oxford, taking his B.A. in 1594. Under his pseudonym, he published *The Metamorphosis of Pigmalions Image, and certaine Satyres* (1598) and *The Scourge of Villanie* (1598), poems so coarsely erotic that they were burned (1599) by order of John Whitgift, Archbishop of Canterbury. Marston's reputation among writers was not harmed by this episode and he soon began writing for the stage. *The History of Antonio and Mellida* (1599) and its sequel, *Antonio's Revenge* (1600), were both published in 1602. Their overdone melodrama, in addition to an attack on the comedy of humors contained in the induction to the first play, caused Ben Jonson to attack Marston in *The Poetaster* (1601), with the result that Marston, collaborating with Thomas Dekker, caricatured Jonson in *Satiromastix* (1602). Jonson and Marston soon became friends, however, and Marston dedicated *The Malcontent* (1604) to Jonson. They collaborated (1605) with George Chapman in *Eastward Ho*, and all three were imprisoned for a time for certain scenes in the play ridiculing the Scots, who had become numerous in London after the accession (1603) of James I. Among Marston's other plays are *What You Will* (1601), *The Dutch Courtezan* (1604), *Parasitaster, or the Fawn* (c1605), *The Wonder of Women, or the Tragedy of Sophonisba* (c1605), and parts of *Histriomastix* (c1599) and *Jack Drum's Entertainment* (c1600). He gave up writing for the stage in 1616 to become rector of Christchurch, Hampshire.

Marston, John Westland. b. at Boston, Lincolnshire, England, Jan. 30, 1819; d. at London, Jan.

5, 1890. An English dramatist. In 1834 he entered the office of his uncle, a London solicitor. He was closely associated with a group of mystics corresponding somewhat to the Transcendentalists of New England. He wrote a number of dramas in verse, including *The Patrician's Daughter* (performed, 1842), *Strathmore* (1849), *Marie de Méranie* (1850), *A Life's Ransom* (1857), *A Hard Struggle* (1858), *Donna Diana*, his best play (1863), and *The Favourite of Fortune* (1866). He contributed much poetical criticism to the *Athenaeum*, including a review of A. C. Swinburne's *Atalanta in Calydon*. In 1888 appeared *Our Recent Actors* and *Recollections of Late Distinguished Performers of both Sexes*. Some of his smaller poems were very successful, especially one on the charge at Balaklava.

Marston, Philip Bourke. b. at London, Aug. 13, 1850; d. Feb. 13, 1887. An English poet; son of John Westland Marston. From his youth he was almost totally blind. He published *Songtide, and Other Poems* (1871), *All in All* (1875), and *Wind Voices* (1883). After his death appeared *For a Song's Sake, and Other Stories* (1887), *Garden Secrets* (1887), and *A Last Harvest* (1891).

Marsyas (mär'si.ạs). In Greek mythology, a Phrygian (in some accounts a peasant, and in others a satyr) defeated by Apollo in a musical contest. Marsyas picked up the aulos (a flutelike instrument) which the goddess Athene, who had invented it, had thrown away on seeing, from the reflection of her face in water, how playing distorted her features. Marsyas found that when he blew it beautiful strains came forth from it. He challenged Apollo to a combat, aulos against lyre. Marsyas played well, but Apollo turned his lyre upside down and continued to play. This Marsyas could not match with the aulos, and Apollo was declared victor. Nevertheless, for his presumption Apollo flayed Marsyas alive. Chaucer, in his *House of Fame*, makes Marsyas a woman, Marcia.

Martano (mär.tä'nō). A character in Ariosto's *Orlando Furioso*, probably the original of Spenser's Braggadocchio.

Martens (mär'tenz), **Paul.** A pseudonym of **Southwold, Stephen.**

Martext (mär'tekst), **Sir Oliver.** In Shakespeare's *As You Like It*, a country curate.

Martha Bardell (mär'thạ bär.del'), **Mrs.** See **Bardell, Mrs. Martha.**

Martha Honeyman (hun'i.mạn). See **Honeyman, Martha.**

Martia (mär'shạ). The heroine of George Chapman's *An Humorous Day's Mirth*.

Martial (mär'shạl). [Full Latin name, **Marcus Valerius Martialis.**] b. at Bilbilis, Spain, 43 A.D.; d. in Spain, c104. A Latin poet. In Rome (64 A.D. et seq.) he was a friend of Juvenal and Quintilian and worked under the patronage of Titus, Domitian, and other influential persons. He returned to Spain in 98 A.D. His fourteen books of epigrams (84–99 A.D) contain many sharp pictures of Roman life of his time and formed the model for later epigrammatists.

ḍ, d or j: ṣ. s or sh; ṭ, t or ch; ẓ, z or zh; o, F. cloche; ü, F. menu; ċh, Sc. loch; ṅ, F. bonbon.

Martianus Capella (mär.shi.ā′nus ka̤.pel′a̤). [Full name, **Martianus Minneus Felix Capella**.] Lived in the 5th century A.D. A Latin writer of northern Africa (Carthage). His chief work is an allegorical encyclopedia of the liberal arts, *De Nuptiis Philologiae et Mercurii et de septem Artibus liberalibus*, in nine books. This work, sometimes also called *Satyricon*, comprises a discussion of contemporary knowledge and was highly regarded in the Middle Ages.

Martin (mär′tin). In John Dryden's *The Hind and The Panther*, the Lutheran party.

Martin, Sir Theodore. b. at Edinburgh, Scotland, Sept. 16, 1816; d. at Llangollen, Wales, Aug. 18, 1909. A Scottish poet, dramatist, biographer, and translator. He practiced law (1846–1907) at Edinburgh and London, and wrote humorous poetry and prose sketches for various periodicals. He married (1851) Helen Faucit, distinguished Shakespearean actress, whose biography he wrote in 1900. He translated Horace, Catullus, and Vergil, Heine's poems, Goethe's *Faust*, and Dante, and contributed dramatic articles to *Fraser's Magazine*, the *Quarterly Review*, and *Blackwood's Magazine*. He was knighted for writing, at Queen Victoria's request, a five-volume *Life of His Royal Highness, The Prince Consort* (1875–80).

Martin Chuzzlewit (chuz′l.wit). A novel by Charles Dickens, originally produced in 20 monthly parts, the first coming out in 1843. It was published in one volume in 1844, and in Dickens's own words was intended "to show how selfishness propagates itself, and to what a grim giant it may grow from small beginnings." Martin's trip to America gave Dickens an opportunity to parody many crude and "spread-eagle" types which he associated with the U.S. at that time, and these caricatures offended many American readers of that day.

Martineau (mär′ti.nō), **Harriet.** b. at Norwich, England, June 12, 1802; d. at Clappersgate, near Ambleside, Westmorland, England, June 27, 1876. An English author; sister of James Martineau. At the age of 16 she became very deaf, and she never possessed the senses of taste and smell. In 1820 she became interested in the writings of David Hartley and Joseph Priestley, who exerted a strong influence upon her philosophical and religious beliefs. Her first literary success was with a series of stories illustrating the political economy of Thomas Malthus, David Ricardo, and James Mill (1832). In 1834 she visited America and assisted the abolitionists. Among her works are *The Essential Faith of the Universal Church, The Faith as Unfolded by Many Prophets, Providence Manifested through Israel* (these were prize essays published by the Unitarian Society); *Society in America* (1836), *Retrospect of Western Travel* (1838), *Deerbrook*, a novel (1839), *Forest and Game-Law Tales* (1845), *History of England during the Thirty Years' Peace, 1816–1846* (written for Charles Knight, 1848), *The Philosophy of Comte, freely translated and condensed* (1853), *British Rule in India* (1857), *The Endowed Schools of Ireland* (1859), and *Health, Husbandry, and Handicraft* (1861). Her autobiography was edited by Maria Weston Chapman in 1877.

Martineau, James. b. at Norwich, England, April 21, 1805; d. at London, Jan. 11, 1900. An English Unitarian clergyman; brother of Harriet Martineau. He was principal of Manchester New College (1868–85). He was the author of *Endeavours after the Christian Life* (1843–47), *Miscellanies* (1852), *Studies of Christianity* (1858), *Essays* (1866), *A Word for Scientific Theology* (1868), *Religion as Affected by Modern Materialism* (1874), *Modern Materialism* (1876), *The Relation between Ethics and Religion* (1881), *A Study of Spinoza* (1882), *Types of Ethical Theory* (1885), *The Study of Religion* (1888), *The Seat of Authority in Religion* (1890), and others.

Martin Hyde (mär′tin hīd′). A historical novel by John Masefield, published in 1910.

Martin Marplot (mär′plot). See **Marplot, Martin**.

Martin Marprelate (mär′prel″ā̆t). The name used by the author of vigorous and vituperative pamphlets in a war of letters waged during the late 1580's and early 1590's by the Puritans against the defenders of discipline as considered necessary by the official group within the Church of England. The pamphlets were written by a number of persons, but were published under the name of Martin Marprelate. The origin of the controversy lay in one of the regular pamphlet arguments between the Anglicans and the Puritans, the first of the pamphlets being issued from the secret press of Robert Waldegrave. The press which printed the tracts was moved from place to place to avoid government suppression, and was once seized, near Manchester, but the publications were continued. John Penry, Henry Barrow, Job Throckmorton, John Field, and others have all been supposed to be the authors of the tracts, but some think Martin Marprelate to have been a layman about the court. The Marprelate tracts were answered by pamphlets by Thomas Nash, John Lyly, Robert Greene, and other professional writers hired to defend the authorities in the same ranting style as the pamphlets. The controversy was suppressed by the death of John Udall in prison, and the execution of Penry and Barrow in 1593, but the identity of the original Martin Marprelate remains a mystery.

Martinists (mär′tin.ists). The controversial supporters of Martin Marprelate.

Martin Poyser (mär′tin poi′zėr). See **Poyser, Martin**.

Martin Schüler (shü′lėr). A novel by Romer Wilson (Mrs. Edward J. O'Brien), published in 1918.

Martinus Scriblerus (mär.tī′nus skrib.lē′rus). [Full title, **Memoirs of Martinus Scriblerus**.] A satire written by the Scriblerus Club, principally by John Arbuthnot, published in 1741, and of which all but the first book is now lost. Pope and Swift were also among the contributors and members of the Scriblerus Club. Cornelius Scriblerus, the pedantic father of Martinus, educates his son in what he conceives to be the manner of the ancients, having, for example, the Greek alphabet printed on the boy's gingerbread. Martinus, who grows up to become a critic and student of the soul and the diseases of the mind, eventually travels to the countries Swift invented in *Gulliver's Travels*.

Sterne drew many of his ideas for the education of Tristram Shandy from this account of Martinus' early life.

Martin Valliant (mär′tin val′yạnt). A historical novel by Warwick Deeping, published in 1917.

Martius (mär′shus). In Shakespeare's *Titus Andronicus*, one of the four sons of Titus.

Martivalle (mär.tẹ.val′ẹ), **Galeotti**. A character in Sir Walter Scott's *Quentin Durward*, who is King Louis's astrologer.

Martyr, The. A novel by Liam O'Flaherty, published in 1933.

Marty South (mär′ti south′). See **South, Marty.**

Marullus (mạ.rul′us). In Shakespeare's *Julius Caesar*, a tribune. He and Flavius fear the growing power of Caesar and attempt to stop a triumphal celebration from being held for him.

Marvell (mär′vẹl), **Andrew.** b. in Holderness, Yorkshire, England, March 31, 1621; d. at London, Aug. 18, 1678. An English poet and satirist. He graduated at Cambridge in 1638. In 1653 he became tutor of Cromwell's ward, William Dutton, and in 1657 was appointed Milton's assistant in the Latin secretaryship. A Parliamentary adherent, he wrote a number of satires on Charles II and the Stuarts, originally circulated in manuscript and collected in *Poems on Affairs of State* (1689). For a time toward the end of his life, Marvell was in danger from the Stuarts and their adherents for his writings. His most notable poem is the *Horatian Ode to Cromwell* (printed 1776). He also wrote *The Rehearsal Transposed* (1672–73), a successful attack on Samuel Parker for his assaults on the nonconformists. Perhaps the most noted of his minor poems is *To His Coy Mistress.*

"Marvellous Boy." A name given to Thomas Chatterton by Wordsworth in his poem *Resolution and Independence.*

Marwood (mär′wửd), **Mrs.** The jealous, revengeful confidante of Lady Wishfort in Congreve's comedy *The Way of the World.* She finally attempts to obtain part of Millamant's fortune and that of Mrs. Fainall as bribery to prevent public disgrace to Lady Wishfort and Mrs. Fainall, her daughter.

Mary I or **Mary Tudor** (mär′i tū′dọr). [Called Bloody Mary.] b. at Greenwich Palace, Feb. 18, 1516; d. Nov. 17, 1558. Queen of England and Ireland (1553–58); only surviving child of Henry VIII and his first wife, Catherine of Aragon. She was affianced first to the Dauphin Francis in 1518, and later to the emperor Charles V in 1522. An attempt was also made to marry her to Francis I in 1526. At the divorce of Catherine in 1533, Mary was adjudged illegitimate, but on Feb. 7, 1544, the crown was entailed upon her after Edward, son of Henry VIII and Jane Seymour, and later Edward VI, or any lawful child of the king. This period of her life was made hideous for her because of her refusal to give up her Roman Catholicism and because of her loyalty to her mother. She was separated from Catherine, and could not visit her even on her deathbed; she was forced to repudiate her religion and acknowledge her illegitimacy; she served as Elizabeth's lady in waiting. Edward VI died July 6, 1553, and on July 13, 1553, Mary was

proclaimed queen at Norwich, and crowned at Westminster Oct. 1, 1553. The council proclaimed Lady Jane Grey queen, but Mary quickly overcame opposition. An insurrection headed by Henry Grey, Duke of Suffolk, in favor of his daughter, Lady Jane Grey, and one of Kentishmen led by Sir Thomas Wyatt were suppressed early in 1554. She married Philip of Spain (later Philip II) at Winchester, July 25, 1554. In 1555 Parliament restored the papal power, and revived the penal laws against heresy. The first martyr was burned at Smithfield, Feb. 4, 1555. After 1556 her principal adviser was Reginald, Cardinal Pole. On Nov. 10, 1558, the last heretics were burned at Canterbury, the total number of martyrs during her reign being 300, the most famous being Ridley, Latimer, and Cranmer. In 1557 England joined Spain in the war against France, with the result that Calais, the last remainder of the once extensive English holdings on the Continent, was lost.

Mary II. b. at St. James's Palace, April 30, 1662; d. at Kensington Palace, Dec. 28, 1694. Queen of England, Scotland, and Ireland (1689–94); eldest child of James II. By the death of her younger brother, Edgar, in 1671, she became heiress presumptive to the crown, and on Nov. 4, 1677, married William, prince of Orange. In the struggle with James II she identified herself with her husband. On Dec. 22, 1688, James II, expelled by the English who feared that he would attempt to reëstablish Roman Catholicism in England, fled to France, and on Feb. 13, 1689, William and Mary assented to the Declaration of Right, and were crowned (April 11, 1689) joint sovereigns. She took little interest in public business, and in the king's absence ruled through the council.

Mary Avenel (āv′nẹl). See **Avenel, Mary.**

Mary Barton (bär′tọn). A novel by Mrs. Gaskell, published in 1848.

Mary Bennet (ben′ẹt). See **Bennet, Mary.**

Mary Crawford (krô′fọrd). See **Crawford, Henry** and **Mary.**

Mary Graham (grā′ạm). See **Graham, Mary.**

Marylebone Gardens (mär″i.lẹ.bōn′, mär′lẹ.bọn). A former place of entertainment in London, on High Street, Marylebone: celebrated for about a century after 1650.

Mary Magdalene (mär′i mag′dạ.lẹn, mag.dạ.lē′nẹ). [Also: **Mary Magdalen** (mag′dạ.lẹn), **Mary of Magdala** (mag′dạ.lạ).] In the Bible, a woman described by Luke, and mentioned elsewhere in the gospels as a demoniac from whom seven devils had been cast out, and who was closely associated with Jesus, especially at the Resurrection. She has commonly been identified, erroneously, with the woman who was "a sinner" mentioned in Luke (vii. 37–50), and also, with even less ground, with Mary of Bethany.

Mary Magdalene. A Middle English religious play, one of the three Digby Plays. Of unknown authorship, the play dates from the very late 15th century. It combines elements of both mystery and morality plays, and is considered important as illustrating the evolution of dramatic representations from the religious to the secular in theme.

Mary, Mary. American title of **Charwoman's Daughter, The.**

Mary Olivier, A Life (ō̤.liv′i.ā). A psychological novel by May Sinclair, published in 1919. The novel is an early example of the stream-of-consciousness technique.

Mary, Queen of Scots. [Also, **Mary Stuart.**] b. in Linlithgow Palace, Dec. 7 or 8, 1542; beheaded at Fotheringay, Feb. 8, 1587. Queen of Scotland; third child and only daughter of James V of Scotland and Mary of Guise. She was thus the granddaughter of Margaret Tudor, wife of James IV and sister of Henry VII, and next in succession to the English throne after Henry VIII and his children. But Henry's complex series of marriages resulted in only one child that the Roman Catholics recognized as legitimate, Mary Tudor (later Mary I of England), the daughter of Catherine of Aragon. The divorce from Catherine and Henry's subsequent marriages and children, Elizabeth and the future Edward VI, were not recognized as legitimate. The death of Mary Tudor could therefore be seen as creating a situation which might precipitate a religious civil war in England over the rights of Mary Stuart and Elizabeth to the throne. Mary's father, James V, died Dec. 14, 1542, and she became queen of Scotland in her first week of life. She was crowned at Stirling Castle Sept. 9, 1543, the regency of the kingdom being exercised by James Hamilton, 2nd Earl of Arran. A projected marriage with Edward VI was frowned upon by the Scots, suspicious of Henry VIII's ambitions, and on July 7, 1548, a marriage with the Dauphin (later Francis II of France) was agreed upon. Mary was sent to Saint Germain in October of that year and was educated with the royal children of France. She was as a consequence brought up in the Roman Catholic faith. The marriage with the French prince took place at Notre Dame on April 24, 1558. At the death of Mary I of England (Mary Tudor) on Nov. 17, 1588, Mary Stuart therefore became a principal claimant to the English throne; the death of Henry II of France and the accession of her husband, Francis II, to the throne of France on July 10, 1559, seemed to make probable the union of the three kingdoms. But Francis died Dec. 5, 1560, and Mary's advisers, her uncles the Guises, duke and cardinal, fell from power. At the same time open fighting broke out between the adherents of John Knox and those of Mary of Guise, who had become regent in Scotland. The Protestants were defeated by the French troops of the royal house, but Mary of Guise died June 10, 1560, leaving Scotland without a government. Mary therefore decided to return to Scotland. She landed in August, 1561, and set about trying to pacify the country. She recognized the rights of the Protestants, while reserving her own right to observe her own religion, a decision that went against the grain of the rigid reformer Knox. A northern rebellion was suppressed with ease. In 1563 Mary pressed her claim to the English succession by an embassy to Elizabeth headed by her principal adviser, William Maitland of Lethington, but Elizabeth gave no reply. Her scheme for a marriage with Don Carlos of Spain having fallen through, she married (July 29, 1565) her cousin Henry Stewart, Lord Darnley, son of Lady Margaret Douglas, daughter of Mary's grandmother Margaret Tudor and thus next heir after Mary to the English throne. This marriage to a Roman Catholic aroused resentment in Scotland and Mary was forced to suppress a rebellion led by James Stewart, Earl of Moray, Mary's half-brother and until then one of her principal supporters. Mary labored assiduously to restore the Roman Catholic faith in her kingdom and to establish an absolute royal authority. She was a completely charming person and well schooled in diplomacy; the only man to resist her successfully was Knox. Her refusal to grant Darnley the crown matrimonial, which would secure to him during his life and to his heirs after him the crown of Scotland, and her growing reliance on her French secretary, David Rizzio, caused her husband to join with other dissidents among the nobles in a plot to murder Rizzio. Convinced that the queen had been unfaithful to him during her private conferences with Rizzio, Darnley influenced others to join the conspiracy, and on March 9, 1566, Rizzio was seized in the Queen's presence and dragged into another room at Holyrood Castle, where he was murdered without even the pretense of a trial. For the moment Darnley acted as if he were king in fact, but within a short time Mary had convinced him that his safety lay with her and she escaped with him to Edinburgh, guarded by troops under the command of James Hepburn, 4th Earl of Bothwell. The murderers of Rizzio were outlawed and fled to England and Mary once again ruled alone. On June 19, Mary bore a son, acknowledged as his own by Darnley, who was to be James VI of Scotland and James I of England. But Darnley's conduct grew worse and he alienated most of the nobles loyal to the queen. A divorce was proposed; the baptism of the infant prince took place without the presence of the father; all signs indicated a final break between the royal couple. Suddenly Darnley fell ill, so suddenly that poison was suspected. It proved to be smallpox and the queen accompanied him (Jan. 31, 1567) to Kirk o' Field, near Edinburgh. On the night of Feb. 9–10, the house was blown up with a roar heard in Edinburgh, and in the morning Darnley's body was found in the garden. He had been strangled, and suspicion pointed directly at Bothwell as the murderer. The queen, known to be close to Bothwell, if not his mistress, was also implicated and the subsequent trial of Bothwell in April was farcical. Whether Mary actually was privy to the assassination remains an unsolved question; some evidence (principally the so-called Casket Letters written later by Mary to Bothwell) exists connecting her with the plot, but its genuineness is not agreed upon. Almost immediately after Bothwell's trial, he intercepted (April 24, 1567) Mary on her way to Edinburgh, probably by arrangement, and carried her off to Dunbar Castle. On May 7, Bothwell's wife secured a divorce, and on May 15, Bothwell and Mary were married. The queen's questionable conduct caused a revolt of the Scottish lords, who, at Carberry Hill, outside Edinburgh, routed (June 15, 1567) a force led by Mary and Bothwell. Bothwell fled from Scotland and Mary was taken prisoner and confined to Lochleven Castle. She was compelled to abdicate (July, 1567) in favor of her son, who became James VI. On May 2, 1568, Mary escaped from Lochleven to the safety of her adherents and sent to Elizabeth for aid. A promise of forthcoming assistance was sent by Elizabeth, but it arrived after Mary's force had been defeated (May 13, 1568) by Moray at Langside, near Glasgow. Mary escaped to England, where she expected asylum from Elizabeth. But Elizabeth recognized the threat that Mary represented to the peace of her kingdom and kept the Scottish queen confined, first at Carlisle, and finally at Sheffield, where she remained from 1569 to 1583. The fourteen-year period was a difficult one for both queens. Mary wanted her freedom, and Elizabeth did not want to have Mary killed; but a long succession of plots, engineered principally by the Roman Catholics, who looked upon Mary as the rightful queen of England and Elizabeth as a usurper, disturbed the peace of the country. A projected divorce from Bothwell and marriage to Thomas Howard, Duke of Norfolk, who had strong claim to the throne by birth, the Ridolfi plot, was discovered, and Norfolk was executed (1572). Communication between Mary, the Pope, and Philip II of Spain (a possible husband for Mary) was constant, and culminated in the Throckmorton plot (1582) for a Spanish invasion of England. Elizabeth's secret service, headed by the able Walsinghams, had full knowledge of the progress of these intrigues; letters were intercepted, decoded, and then forwarded; spies were placed within Mary's own household and some of her own secret agents and messengers were in Elizabeth's pay. The climax was the Babington plot (1586) which envisaged the murder of Elizabeth and the liberation of Mary, though it is difficult to believe that Mary would be party to a conspiracy headed by anyone as inept and foolish as Babington and his friends. Mary was removed to Fotheringay Sept. 25, 1586, and on Oct. 14 and 15 she was tried on the charge of conspiring against the life of Elizabeth. She conducted her own defense and constantly demanded written proof in her own writing of her complicity. She answered every charge brought against her, but evidence was produced that linked her with the already executed conspirators, the open court was adjourned to the Star Chamber, and Mary, in her absence from the court, was found guilty. She was beheaded at Fotheringay on Feb. 8, 1587.

Mary Scatcherd (skach'ĕrd) or **Mary Tomlinson** (tom'lin.sọn). See **Scatcherd, Mary.**

Mascarille (màs.kà.rēy'). An adroit, ingenious, unscrupulous valet who appears in three of Molière's plays, *L'Étourdi, Le Dépit amoureux,* and *Les Précieuses ridicules.* In the last he is at his best, and assumes the role of a marquis to oblige his master. His name has passed into the French language, and has become a synonym for skillful impudence, effrontery, lying, and intrigue.

Masefield (mās'fēld), **John.** b. at Ledbury, Herefordshire, England, 1878–. An English poet, dramatist, and novelist, poet laureate (1930 *et seq.*) succeeding Robert Bridges. He received his education in the common schools and at the age of fourteen ran away to sea. He spent three years

at sea and two years working at odd jobs in the vicinity of New York City before returning to London in 1897. Among his publications are *Salt Water Ballads* (1902), *A Mainsail Haul* (stories, 1905), *Captain Margaret* (novel, 1908), *Multitude and Solitude* (novel, 1909), *The Tragedy of Nan and Other Plays* (1909), *The Tragedy of Pompey the Great* (1909), *William Shakespeare* (criticism, 1911), *The Everlasting Mercy* (narrative poem, 1911), *The Widow in the Bye Street* (narrative poem, 1912), *The Daffodil Fields* (narrative poem, 1913), *Dauber* (narrative poem, 1913), *The Story of the Roundhouse and Other Poems* (1913), *Philip the King* (drama, 1914), *Gallipoli* (war sketches, 1916), *Reynard the Fox* (narrative poem, 1919), *The Dream* (narrative poem, 1922), *Sard Harker* (novel, 1924), *Odtaa* (novel, 1926), *The Coming of Christ* (play, 1928), *The Wanderer of Liverpool* (narrative poem, 1930), *The Bird of Dawning* (novel, 1933), *The Conway* (biographical study of a ship, 1933), *The Taking of the Gry* (novel, 1934), *Dead Ned* (novel, 1938), *Live and Kicking Ned* (novel, 1939), *Basilissa* (fictional biography of the empress Theodora, 1940), *Gautama the Enlightened* (narrative poetry, 1941), *The Nine Days Wonder* (story of the Dunkirk retreat, 1941), *In the Mill* (autobiography, 1941), *Generation Risen* (poetry, 1942), *So Long To Learn* (autobiography, 1952), and others. Best known among his single poems are those dealing with the sea, such as "Sea Fever" and "Cargoes."

mask. See **masque.**

Masks and Faces. A dramatic version (1854) of Charles Reade's novel *Peg Woffington*, by Reade and Tom Taylor.

Maskwell (màsk'wel). The "double dealer" in Congreve's play of that name. He is the epitome of an unmitigated scoundrel.

Mason (mā'sọn), **A. E. W.** [Full name, **Alfred Edward Woodley Mason.**] b. at Dulwich, London, May 7, 1865; d. at London, Nov. 22, 1948. An English novelist. He served in Parliament (1906–10) as a member of the Liberal Party. Among his works are *The Courtship of Morrice Buckler* (1896), *The Philanderers* (1897), *Parson Kelly* (1899, with Andrew Lang), *Miranda of the Balcony* (1899), *The Four Feathers* (1902), *Running Water* (1907), *The Broken Road* (1907), *At the Villa Rose* (1910), *The Witness for the Defense* (1911), *The Turnstile* (1912), *The Winding Stair* (1923), *Fire Over England* (1936), *Königsmark* (1938), and *The Life of Francis Drake* (1941).

Mason, William. b. Feb. 12, 1724; d. at Aston, England, April 7, 1797. An English poet, a friend of the poet Thomas Gray. He was rector (1754 *et seq.*) of Aston, Yorkshire. He published *Life and Letters of Gray* (1774), the dramas *Elfrida* (1752) and *Caractacus* (1759), and a blank-verse poem, *The English Garden* (1772–82).

Masora or **Massorah** (mạ.sō'rạ). [Eng. trans., "*Tradition.*"] A name given to the results of the work of Jewish scholars in establishing the proper pronunciation of the Old Testament writings, which were in the Hebrew alphabet, consisting only of consonants. The vowel sounds had to be supplied, and to this end the Masoretes or Massoretes, as the scholars engaged in this study were called, relied mainly on tradition. Their work went on for centuries, beginning soon after the return from the Babylonian captivity, when the study of the law became the center of Jewish religious life. The Masora as it now survives was mainly written down in the 8th, 9th, and 10th centuries A.D. During that period the principal Masoretes were the family ben Asher and the family ben Naftali. These held respectively to different systems of indicating the vowel sounds. The system of ben Asher in the end prevailed, and the last of that family, Aaron ben Moses ben Asher, brought the Masora to a close.

masque. [Also, **mask.**] A type of dramatic entertainment consisting, in its most usual form in early 17th-century England, of a silent entrance by masked figures into a banquet or gathering of distinguished guests, and completed by a dance between the masquers and those already present. Lyly and Jonson established the French form "masque" in preference to "mask." The players in a masque (the masquers) wear facial masks, this being especially appropriate for Court performances in Jacobean and Caroline times, when although there was no real secrecy, a disguise would be appropriate for a noble amateur who would ordinarily disdain theatrical performances. The form started in Italy, where it received much of its original form and style at the court of Lorenzo de' Medici. Later it appeared in France, and appeared in England in the late 15th century, where there occurred a separation of the masquers and spectators (the early masque in France had its spectacular climax in the masquerade, in which everyone had a part). In the reign of Henry VIII the first masque was performed at Court, no disguises being worn, but the masquers already having rich costumes. By the time of Elizabeth an allegorical element was present (used as a means of flattering her, especially in the course of her various progresses through the country). The greatest development of the masque was under James I, partly because Queen Anne loved to participate in entertainments. Whereas the Elizabethan masque was mimetic, having only a few speeches by a presenter, when Ben Jonson began to write masques (*The Masque of Blackness*, *The Masque of Queens*, *The Hue and Cry After Cupid*) dialogue was used. Earlier masques had comic characters but Jonson was the first to make them a formal part of the masque. Unfortunately, Jonson and Inigo Jones, who did the elaborate scenery and stage devices for Court masques under James I and Charles I, split over the primacy of their contributions: should the scenery be more important or the dialogue itself? Jones won, and the later masques (particularly those of James Shirley) had complicated stage machinery but very little else. The influence of the masque may be noted in Shakespeare's *Love's Labour's Lost*, *Romeo and Juliet*, *The Tempest*, *Timon of Athens*, and his and Fletcher's *Henry VIII*. The masque was important later as the source of scenery and staging for Restoration plays.

Masque of Anarchy, The. A poem (1819) by Percy Bysshe Shelley, prompted by the "Peterloo

Massacre" of August, 1819. The poem, written as a protest, is simple and forceful in its language. It was originally intended for immediate publication in *The Examiner*, but did not actually receive publication until 1832.

Masque of Blackness, The. A masque (1605) by Ben Jonson. It was designed for a Twelfth Night performance, using Queen Anne and eleven of her ladies as Ethiopians.

Masque of Queens, The. A masque (1609) by Ben Jonson, presented at Court. It was an elaborate production making use of the interest of James I in witchcraft.

Masque of the Middle Temple and Lincoln's Inn. A masque performed at Whitehall, printed 1613, by George Chapman and "invented and fashioned" by Inigo Jones.

Massacre at Paris, The. A tragedy (1593) by Christopher Marlowe. Like the other plays of Marlowe it has a villain-hero, Guise, who reveals his ambition in a few good soliloquies, but the play, on the whole, is an inferior work.

Massacre of Saint Bartholomew (bär.thol′ọ.mū). See **Saint Bartholomew, Massacre of.**

Massey (mas′i), **Bartle.** A schoolmaster in the novel *Adam Bede* by George Eliot.

Massey, Gerald. b. near Tring, Hertfordshire, England, May 29, 1828; d. Oct. 29, 1907. An English poet, Christian Socialist, and mystic. The self-educated son of a canal boatman, he began to work in a mill at eight and was a London errand boy at 15. He became a freethinker, a Chartist, a Christian Socialist, and, finally, a spiritualist. Author of *Poems and Chansons* (1848), *Voices of Freedom and Lyrics of Love* (1850), *Ballad of Babe Christabel* (1854), *A Tale of Eternity* (1869), and *My Lyrical Life* (1899), poetry; *Concerning Spiritualism* (1871), *The Book of the Beginnings* (1881), *Natural Genesis* (1883), *Ancient Egypt: Light of the World* (1907), and other books on the spirit world and Egyptology; and *The Secret Drama of Shakespeare's Sonnets* (1866, 1888). His career inspired George Eliot to write her political novel *Felix Holt the Radical* (1866).

Massinger (mas′in.jėr), **Philip.** Baptized at Salisbury, England, Nov. 24, 1583; buried at Southwark, London, March 18, 1640. An English dramatist; son of Arthur Massinger, a "servant" to the Herbert family. He entered St. Alban Hall, Oxford, on May 14, 1602, but left without a degree. Thereafter he spent an apparently impoverished period at London, where he collaborated with the playwrights Thomas Dekker, Nathaniel Field, Robert Daborne, Cyril Tourneur, and John Fletcher. The dominant influence was that of Fletcher, whom he succeeded as chief dramatist for the King's Men when the elder dramatist died in 1625. In 1621 or 1622 he wrote unaided *The Duke of Milan*, a tragedy based on the Herod-Mariamne theme; and in 1623–24 for Princess Elizabeth's Men he composed *The Bondman*, *The Renegado*, and *The Parliament of Love*. He continued to write, both independently and in collaboration, throughout the 1630's. Of the 18 plays in which Massinger's hand has been established as having a total or major part, the most popular has been *A New Way to Pay Old Debts* (c1625–26), the main character of which is Sir Giles Overreach, an avaricious entrepreneur, created in the Jonsonian "humor" pattern. In the same vein, critical of current social decadence and ostentation in London, is *The City Madam* (licensed 1632). Massinger's censure of the soft pacifism, political corruption, and mercenary spirit of Jacobean England was frequently conveyed, however, through plays with ancient and foreign settings, such as *The Bondman* (1623) and *Believe As You List* (1631). His own favorite among his plays was *The Roman Actor* (1626), a tragedy in which he voices his own theory of the didactic potentialities of the stage. Though much of Massinger's vogue may be attributed to the elevated moralistic vein of his tragedies and to the forthright social satire of his comedies, he also proved himself adept at a lighter touch in the "comical histories," *The Great Duke of Florence* (c1624) and *The Guardian* (licensed 1633), and in such tragicomedies as *The Bashful Lover* (licensed 1636), *The Maid of Honor* (c1623–25), and *The Picture* (licensed 1629). He also tried his hand at horror-tragedy in *The Unnatural Combat* (c1624–26). Among his more successful collaborations are *The Virgin Martyr* (licensed 1620) with Dekker, *The Fatal Dowry* (c1618–19) with Field, and *Sir John Van Olden Barnavelt* (1619) with Fletcher. What part he may have had in *Henry VIII* and *The Two Noble Kinsmen* has not been definitely established.

Massingham (mas'ing.ạm), **Henry William.** b. at Norwich, Norfolk, England, May 25, 1860; d. at Tintagel, Cornwall, England, Aug. 28, 1924. An English journalist of advanced Liberal opinion. He was editor of the *Daily Chronicle* (1895–99), a frequent contributor (1899–1905) to the *Manchester Guardian* and the *Daily News*, and editor (1907–23) of the *Nation*. He joined the Labour Party in 1923 and transferred his "Wayfarer's Diary" to the *New Statesman*.

Massingham, H. J. [Full name, **Harold John Massingham.**] b. at London, March 25, 1888; d. Aug. 22, 1952. An English journalist and critic, and writer on ornithology and animal life. Author of *Letters to X* (1919), *People and Things* (1919), *Some Birds of the Countryside* (1921), *Pre-Roman Britain* (1927), *The Heritage of Man* (1929), *The Friend of Shelley* (1930), *Country* (1934), *Genius of England* (1937), *This Plot of Earth* (1944), *The Wisdom of the Fields* (1945), *Where Man Belongs* (1946), and the autobiographical *Remembrance* (1942).

Masson (mas'ọn), **David.** b. at Aberdeen, Scotland, Dec. 2, 1822; d. at Edinburgh, Oct. 6, 1907. A Scottish professor, editor, essayist, and biographer. He edited *The Banner*, an Aberdeen weekly, and then went to London, where he wrote for *Fraser's Magazine*. He wrote (1844–47) for the Edinburgh publishing firm of W. and R. Chambers. He served as professor of English (1853–65) at London University College and held a similar post (1865–95) at Edinburgh University. He was the first editor (1859–67) of *Macmillan's Magazine*. He wrote *Life of Milton, Narrated in Connection with the Political, Ecclesiastical, and Literary His-*

tory of His Own Time (6 vols., 1858–80), which remains the standard biography.

Masson, George Joseph Gustave. b. at London, March 9, 1819; d. at Ewhurst, Surrey, England, Aug. 29, 1888. An English writer, principally of educational compilations and translations.

Massorah (mạ.sō'rạ). See **Masora.**

"Master Betty" (bet'i). See **Betty, William Henry West.**

Master Blifil (blĭ'fil). See **Blifil.**

Master Brook (brŭk). See **Brook, Master.**

Master Ford (fōrd). See **Ford, Master.**

Master Gunner of Orleans (ôr'lẹ.ạnz). In Shakespeare's *1 Henry VI*, a minor character.

Master Humphrey's Clock (hum'friz). A collection of tales by Charles Dickens, published in 1840–41. They included *The Old Curiosity Shop* and *Barnaby Rudge*. When these stories were expanded to their full length, as novels, the machinery of the miscellany was largely scrapped.

Masterman Ready. A juvenile story (1841) of seafaring life, by Frederick Marryat.

Master of Ballantrae (bal'ạn.trā), **The.** A novel by Robert Louis Stevenson, published in 1889. It is the story of a tragic feud between two brothers. James Durie is the Master of Ballantrae, and he leaves home to fight for Charles Edward Stuart ("Bonnie Prince Charlie") in 1745. His brother, the quiet and honest Henry, stays at home. James is reported killed at Culloden, and Henry inherits Ballantrae and marries Alison Graeme, the betrothed of James. It is soon revealed to Henry that his brother is alive, and is having many adventures at sea. Henry drains the estate to supply James's demands for money, but the Master returns when Henry finally refuses to give him any more. James and Henry both finally meet their death in America and are buried side by side.

Master of Gray, The. A historical novel by Henry Christopher Bailey, published in 1903.

Master of the Revels. See under **Revels Office.**

Master Walter (wôl'tẹr). See **Walter, Master.**

"Matchless Orinda" (ọ.rin'dạ), **the.** See **Philips, Katharine.**

Match Me in London. A tragicomedy by Thomas Dekker, published in 1631 and written sometime before 1623 (in which year it was first acted).

Matheo (math'ẹ.ō). A young wastrel who has seduced Bellafront into being the "honest whore" in Middleton and Dekker's play of that name.

Mathers (maᴛн'ẹrz), **Helen.** See **Reeves, Helen Buckingham.**

Mathews (math'ūz), **Charles James.** b. at Liverpool, England, Dec. 26, 1803; d. at Manchester, England, June 24, 1878. An English actor and dramatist. On May 4, 1819, he entered the atelier of Augustus Pugin the architect, and he continued to practice architecture for several years. On April 26, 1822, he appeared for the first time as an amateur, at the Lyceum, London. On July 18, 1838, he married Madame Vestris (Lucia Elizabeth Mathews), his manager. Madame Vestris died Aug. 8, 1856; a year later he visited New York, where he married Mrs. A. H. Davenport, an actress at Burton's Theater. Among his own compositions are *The Black Domino, Dead for a Ducat, Married for Money, The Court Jester, My Awful Dad, Little Toddlekins*, and *Mathews and Co.*

Mathews, Lucia Elizabeth (or **Elizabetta**). [Known as Madame **Vestris**; maiden name, **Bartolozzi**.] b. at London, in January, 1797; d. there, Aug. 8, 1856. An English actress. On Jan. 28, 1813, she married Auguste Armand Vestris, ballet-master at the King's Theatre. She had a fine contralto voice, and first appeared as Proserpina in Peter Winter's opera *Il Ratto di Proserpina* (July 20, 1815). She appeared first in English at Drury Lane Theatre on Feb. 19, 1820, and continued to play until Jan. 3, 1831, when she undertook the management of the Olympic. On Dec. 7, 1835, Charles James Mathews made his debut under her management, and they were married July 18, 1838. She undertook the management of the Lyceum in 1847, and appeared there for the last time July 26, 1854.

Mathias (ma̯.thī′a̯s), **Thomas James.** b. c1754; d. at Naples, Italy, in August, 1835. An English satirist and Italian scholar. His *Pursuits of Literature* was begun in 1794. Other satires are *The Political Dramatist* (1795) and *An Equestrian Epistle in Verse to the Earl of Jersey* (1796). His *Works of Gray* were published in 1814.

Matilda Price (ma̯.til′da̯ prīs). See **Price, Matilda.**

Matisse (ma̯.tēs), **Henri.** b. at Cateau-Cambrésis, France, Dec. 31, 1869—. A French figure and landscape painter, founder of the fauve movement, and one of the most influential artists in France of this century.

Matriarch, The. A novel by G. B. Stern, published in 1925. It was issued in England under the title *Tents of Israel* (1924). The work is the first volume of her trilogy on Jewish life, *The Rakonitz Chronicles* (1932). *The Matriarch* was dramatized in 1931.

Matthew (math′ū). Entries on literary characters having this prename will be found under the surnames Bramble, Goffe, Merygreek, Mite, Mug, and Weyburn.

Matthew, Master. In Ben Jonson's comedy *Every Man in His Humour*, "a town-bred gull," half fool, half coxcomb, vain of his own poetry, his affairs with women, and his association with those above him in rank.

Matthews (math′ūz), **Miss.** In Henry Fielding's novel *Amelia*, a friend of Booth who entices him into an affair while they are both in prison.

Matthew's Bible. A folio Bible, based on the versions of Tyndale and Coverdale, published in 1537, which professed to be translated into English by Thomas Matthew, a pseudonym of John Rogers (a friend of Tyndale).

Matthewson Helstone (math′ū.son hel′stŏn), **Doctor.** See **Helstone, Doctor Matthewson.**

Maturin (mat′ū.rin), **Charles Robert.** b. at Dublin, 1782; d. there, Oct. 30, 1824. An Irish author, especially of Gothic novels. He graduated at Trinity College, Dublin, in 1800, and became curate of Saint Peter's, Dublin. He published *The Fatal Revenge, or the Family of Montorio* (1807), *The Wild Irish Boy* (1808), and *The Milesian Chief* (1812), which attracted the attention of Sir Walter Scott. His tragedy *Bertram* was brought out by Kean at Drury Lane Theatre, London, May 9, 1816. He also wrote the tragedies *Manuel* (1817) and *Fredolfo* (1817). His best novel, *Melmoth the Wanderer*, appeared in 1820 and is said to have influenced the romantic school in France, especially Honoré de Balzac, who wrote a sequel to it.

Maud (môd). A poem by Alfred Tennyson, published in 1855. It is written in the form of a dramatic monologue, wherein the action is revealed through a series of soliloquies. Maud is beloved by a poor poet (the narrator), but she is forced to bow to the demands of her wealthy family and marry the poet's haughty and wealthy rival.

Maude (môd), **Aylmer.** b. March 28, 1858; d. near Chelmsford, England, Aug. 25, 1938. An English author. He was educated at Christ's Hospital, London, and at the Lyceum in Moscow, Russia, where he lived until 1897, being occupied chiefly with business interests. In 1898 he aided in arranging the Doukhobor emigration to Canada. He was a personal friend of Count Leo Tolstoy (1828–1910), several of whose works Maude and his wife Louise translated into English. He published *Tolstoy and His Problems* (1901), *A Peculiar People: the Doukhobors* (1905), *Life of Tolstoy* (1908–10), and others.

Maugham (môm), **W. Somerset.** [Full name, **William Somerset Maugham**.] b. Jan. 25, 1874—. An English novelist, short-story writer, dramatist, and essayist. He was left an orphan at the age of ten and raised by a childless uncle, who was vicar of Whitstable, in Kent. He attended King's School, Canterbury, spent a year at Heidelberg University, and trained as a physician at St. Thomas's Hospital, London, but did not practice medicine. During World War I he served in the Red Cross and later in British Intelligence. He has traveled extensively, particularly in the East. He is famous principally for his novel *Of Human Bondage* (1915), considered by many a classic of the 20th century. Among his other novels are *The Making of a Saint* (1898), *The Merry-Go-Round* (1904), *The Moon and Sixpence* (1919), *Cakes and Ale* (1930), and *The Razor's Edge* (1944). Representative volumes of his short stories (most of which were written after 1920) are *The Trembling of a Leaf* (1921), including "Miss Thompson," later dramatized as *Rain* (1922), *The Casuarina Tree* (1926), and *First Person Singular* (1931). His themes both in novels and short stories are the unpredictability of human behavior and the enslavement of man by his passions. Maugham's plays, entertaining and amusing, but sometimes bitter, are generally of lighter stuff than his narrative fiction. Among them are *A Man of Honour* (1903), *Lady Frederick* (1907), *Penelope* (1909), *Smith* (1909), *Home and Beauty* (1919), *The Circle* (1921), *Our Betters* (1923), *The Letter* (1927), originally a short story, *The Sacred Flame* (1929), and *For Services Rendered* (1932). His most important nonfiction works are probably *The Gentleman in the Parlour* (1930), a travel book, and

The Summing Up (1938), an autobiography. *A Writer's Notebook* (1949) contains excerpts from his journals.

Maugrabin (mô'gra̧.bin), **Hayraddin.** A gypsy in Sir Walter Scott's *Quentin Durward.*

Maul (môl). A giant killed by Greatheart in John Bunyan's *Pilgrim's Progress.*

Maumbury Rings (môm'bȩ.ri). The best-preserved Roman amphitheater in England. It is south of Dorchester.

Maunder (môn'dėr), **Samuel.** b. 1785; d. at Gibson Square, Islington, London, April 30, 1849. An English publisher and compiler of *Treasury of Knowledge* (1830), *Biographical Treasury* (1838), *Scientific and Literary Treasury* (1841), and other works with similar titles for history (1844), natural history (1848), and geography (1849), all exceedingly popular in their day.

Maundevylle (man'dȩ.vil), Sir **John.** See under **Travels of Sir John Mandeville.**

Mauny (mō'ni), Sir **Walter de.** See **Manny.**

Maupassant (mō.pȧ.sän), **Guy de.** [Full name, **Henri René Albert Guy de Maupassant.**] b. at the Château de Miromesnil, Seine-Inférieure, France, Aug. 5, 1850; d. at Passy, Paris, July 6, 1893. A French novelist and short-story writer. He went to school at Yvetot, and graduated from the *collège* at Rouen, while Gustave Flaubert, his godfather, looked after his literary training. He spent about ten years in civil service in the navy department. In February, 1879, his one-act play *Histoire du vieux temps* was performed at Paris, without, however, attracting any special attention. The next year, however, the success of his short story *Boule de suif* stamped him at once as a writer of marked ability. Then he published in rapid succession *La Maison Tellier* (1881), *Mademoiselle Fifi* (1882), *Contes de la bécasse* (1883), *Une Vie* (1883), *Miss Harriet* (1884), *Les Sœurs Rondoli* (1884), *Au soleil* (1884), *Clair de lune* (1884), *Yvette* (1884), *Bel-Ami* (1885), *Contes du jour et de la nuit* (1885), *Contes et nouvelles* (1885), *M. Parent* (1886), *La Petite Roque* (1886), *Toine* (1886), *Contes choisis* (1887), *Mont-Oriol* (1887), *Le Horla* (1887), *Pierre et Jean* (1888), *Sur l'eau* (1888), *Le Rosier de Mme. Husson* (1888), *Fort comme la mort* (1889), *La Main gauche* (1889), *Histoire d'une fille de ferme* (1890), *La Vie Errante* (1890), *L'Inutile Beauté* (1890), and *Notre cœur* (1890). Among his other works are *Trois contes, Enmer, L'Homme de lettres* (1892), and two plays, *Musotte* (1891) and *La Paix du ménage* (1893). The insanity and death of a brother unbalanced him, and he attempted suicide during a fit of depression in December, 1891; general paresis set in, and he had to be confined in a private asylum.

Maurice (mô'ris, mor'is), **Frederick Denison.** b. at Normanston, near Lowestoft, England, Aug. 29, 1805; d. at London, April 1, 1872. English divine. He entered Trinity College, Cambridge, in 1823, and Exeter College, Oxford, in 1830. He was appointed curate of Bubbenhall, near Leamington, in 1834, chaplain of Guy's Hospital in 1836, and in 1840 professor of English literature and history and, in 1846, professor of theology, at King's College, London. From 1839 to 1841 he edited the *Educational Magazine.* In 1848 he assisted in establishing Queen's College, London. During the revolutionary movement of 1848 he became the leader of the "Christian Socialists." His *Theological Essays,* published in 1853, excited so much criticism that he was obliged to resign his professorship at King's College. On Oct. 30, 1854, he became principal of St. Martin's Hall, Queen Square, a workingmen's college. On Oct. 25, 1866, he was elected professor of moral philosophy at Cambridge. He wrote *Eustace Conway, or the Brother and Sister: a novel* (1834), the article "Moral and Metaphysical Philosophy" for the *Encyclopaedia Metropolitana* (subsequently enlarged and published in 3 volumes: *Ancient Philosophy,* 1850, *Philosophy of the First Six Centuries,* 1853, and *Mediaeval Philosophy,* 1857), *Modern Philosophy* (1862), and numerous other works on religious, historical, theological, and philosophical topics.

Maurice de Bracy (dȩ brā'si). See **Bracy, Maurice de.**

Maurice Guest (gest). A novel by Henry Handel Richardson (Mrs. Henrietta Robertson), published in 1908.

Maurois (mō.rwȧ), **André.** [Pseudonym of **Émile Salomon Wilhelm Herzog.**] b. at Elbeuf, France, 1885—. A French novelist, biographer, and historian. Author of *Les Silences du Colonel Bramble* (1918), *Les Discours du Colonel O'Grady* (1922), *Ariel ou la vie de Shelley* (1923), *Climats* (1928), *Le Cercle de famille* (1933), and other works, including biographies of Disraeli, Byron, and Chateaubriand. His early, humorous books are regarded as his most permanent successes; in later life he has been an immensely popular lecturer in England and America.

Maurras (mō.rȧ), **Charles.** [Full name, **Charles Marie Photius Maurras.**] b. at Martigues, Bouches-du-Rhône, France, 1868; d. at Tours, France, Nov. 16, 1952. A French poet, publicist, and critic. Author of poems collected in *La Musique intérieure* (1925), and of thousands of philosophical and political essays, largely polemical in nature, many of which have been collected in such volumes as *L'Avenir de l'intelligence* (1905), *Kiel et Tanger* (1910), and *Enquête sur la monarchie* (1909; definitive edition, 1924). Born in the remote provinces and educated in Roman Catholic schools, he began a journalistic career at Paris in the late 1880's, joined the Action Française at the time of the Dreyfus case, converted its leaders to royalism, and directed its destinies up to World War II. Although he advocated a "Catholic France," he and his group fell under papal interdict in 1926. In 1945 he was condemned to life imprisonment for collaboration with the enemy; but he was released because of illness in 1952 and died soon afterward.

Maurya (môr'ya̧). In John Millington Synge's one-act tragedy *Riders to the Sea* (1904), the central character, an old woman who has lost her husband and four sons to the sea, and who loses her fifth son, Bartley.

Mause Headrigg (môz hed'rig). See **Headrigg, Mause.**

Mausolus (mô.sō′lus). d. c353 B.C. A king or dynast of Caria, who first appears in history in the revolt of the satraps against Artaxerxes II (Artaxerxes Mnemon) in 362 B.C. He married his sister Artemisia, who after his death erected at Halicarnassus in his honor the celebrated monument named from him the Mausoleum. A Greek statue of Mausolus from the Mausoleum (352 B.C.) is in the British Museum.

Mavourneen (mav.ör.nēn′), **Kathleen.** See **Kathleen Mavourneen.**

maxim (mak′sim). **1.** A proposition serving as a rule or guide; a summary statement of an established or accepted principle; a pithy expression of a general rule of conduct or action, whether true or false.

All which points· were obserued by the Greekes and Latines, and allowed for maximes in versifying. (Puttenham, *Arte of English Poesie.*)

In human laws there be many grounds and maxims which are . . . positive upon authority. (Bacon, *Advancement of Learning.*)

2. Rarely, an axiom.

Maximin (mak′si.min). The Emperor of Rome in Dryden's *Tyrannick Love.* His great rages evoked ridicule in *The Rehearsal,* by the Duke of Buckingham and others.

Max Müller (maks mil′ẽr, mul′ẽr; German, mäks mül′ẽr), **Friedrich.** b. at Dessau, Germany, Dec. 6, 1823; d. at Oxford, England, Oct. 28, 1900. A German-English Sanskrit scholar and comparative philologist; son of Wilhelm Müller. He was educated at Leipzig, Berlin, and Paris, went to England in 1846, and in 1850 settled at Oxford. He became professor of modern languages and literature there in 1854, and was professor of comparative philology (1868–1900). In 1856 he became connected with the Bodleian Library, and was curator (1865–67) of Oriental works. He edited and translated the *Hitopadesa* (1844), and edited the Rig-Veda (6 vols., 1849–74). His chief works are *A History of Ancient Sanskrit Literature* (1859), *Lectures on the Science of Language* (1861–64), *Handbooks for the Study of Sanskrit* (1865–70; comprising grammar, dictionary, texts), *Chips from a German Workshop* (1868–75), *Lectures on the Science of Religion* (1870), *On the Origin and Growth of Religion as illustrated by the Religions of India* (1878), and translations of various Oriental works. His major work is the monumental *Sacred Books of the East* (51 vols., 1875 et seq.). He was extremely influential in establishing comparative philology as a study, but his main interest lay in comparative mythology and religion. Here, however, his enthusiasms, exaggerated by his followers, led him into untenable hypotheses and resulted in his being the object of severe criticism from other mythologists and folklorists, among them Andrew Lang.

Maxwell (maks′wel, -wẹl), **James Clerk.** b. at Edinburgh, Nov. 13, 1831; d. at Cambridge, England, Nov. 5, 1879. A Scottish physicist. First professor (1871–79) of experimental physics at Cambridge and chiefly responsible for the building of the Cavendish laboratory there, he is noted for studies in electricity and magnetism which laid the groundwork for a tremendous number of modern developments in physics. His contributions lie mainly in his application of dynamic equations to the problems of electromagnetism and in his proposition that electromagnetic actions resemble waves of light (his successors later proved them to be identical). His other physical studies deal with the application of Faraday's ideas in mathematics, the theory of color in relation to color-blindness, and the kinetic theory of gases. His practical contributions include experiments which made possible a system of standardized electrical measurements and experiments on the velocity of propagation of electromagnetic waves. His first paper was presented to the Royal Society of Edinburgh when he was 15 years of age. He served as professor of natural philosophy (1860–65) at Marischal College, Aberdeen. His writings include the essay *On the Stability of Saturn's Rings* (1859), *Electricity and Magnetism* (1873), *Matter and Motion* (1876), and the textbook *Theory of Heat* (1871).

Maxwell, William Babington. b. at Richmond, Surrey, England, 1866; d. at Kensington, London, Aug. 4, 1938. An English novelist, short-story writer, and dramatist. Author of *The Countess of Maybury* (1901), *The Ragged Messenger* (1904), *Vivien* (1905), *The Guarded Flame* (1906), *Seymour Charlton* (1909), *The Rest Cure* (1910), *Mrs. Thompson* (1911), *General Mallock's Shadow* (1912), *The Devil's Garden* (1913), *The Mirror and the Lamp* (1918), *A Man and His Lesson* (1919), *A Remedy Against Sin* (1920), *Spinster of This Parish* (1922), *The Day's Journey* (1923), *Elaine at the Gates* (1924), *Gabrielle* (1926), *The Case of Bevan Yorke* (1927), *We Forget Because We Must* (1929), *To What Green Altar?* (1930), *The Concave Mirror* (1931), *And Mr. Wyke Bond* (1934), *People of a House* (1934), novels; *Tales of the Thames* (1892), *Fabulous Fancies* (1903), *Odd Lengths* (1907), *Children of the Night* (1925), and *Jacob's Ladder* (1937), collected short stories; *The Last Man In* (1910) and *The Naked Truth* (1921), plays; and *Time Gathered* (1937), autobiography.

Maxwell, William Hamilton. b. at Newry, County Down, Ireland, 1792; d. at Musselburgh, near Edinburgh, Dec. 29, 1850. An Irish novelist. In 1812 he was made captain in an infantry regiment, and served in the Peninsular campaign and at Waterloo. He later took holy orders and was made rector of Ballagh in Connemara. His best-known works are *O'Hara, or 1798,* a novel (1825), *Sports of the West* (1832), *Stories of Waterloo* (1834), and *Life of the Duke of Wellington* (1839–41).

May (mā). See under **Merchant's Tale, The.**

May, Thomas. b. in Sussex, England, 1595; d. Nov. 13, 1650. An English author. In 1620 he produced *The Heir,* a comedy, and in the same period *The Old Couple* (printed 1658). He wrote several tragedies along classical lines and did some translation from the classics, including Lucan's *Pharsalia* (1627). In 1630 he wrote a continuation of Lucan and was soon afterward commissioned by Charles I to write metrical histories of Henry II and Edward III. May became the royal poet and expected to become laureate on Ben Jonson's death (1637). His disappointment was probably the reason for his siding with Parliament against the king, a shift of party that brought him many enemies. He was a secretary to the Long Parliament, and in 1647 published his most important work, *The History of the Long Parliament of England which began Nov. 3, 1640.*

May, Sir **Thomas Erskine.** [Title, 1st Baron **Farnborough.**] b. at London, Feb. 8, 1815; d. at Westminster Palace, London, May 17, 1886. An English jurist. He was appointed (1831) assistant librarian of the House of Commons. He published *A Practical Treatise on the Law, Privileges, Proceedings, and Usage of Parliament* (1844). After 1871 he was clerk of the House of Commons. In 1854 his *Rules, Orders, and Forms of Procedure of the House of Commons* was printed by order of Parliament. His other works include *The Constitutional History of England since the Accession of George III* (1861) and *Democracy in Europe* (1877).

May Day. The first day of May; the day on which spring, the season of flowers and fruit, is celebrated throughout Europe, the U. S., and Canada. The chief traditional features of the celebration in Great Britain (where it is considered the first day of summer) have been the gathering of Mayflowers (hawthorn blossoms) and green branches, the crowning of a May queen, and dancing round a Maypole. In 20th-century Europe, particularly in the case of groups with a socialist or communist tradition or affiliation, the day has become the chief holiday of workers, and on this day parades are held in honor of labor.

May Day. A comedy by George Chapman, acted c1600 and printed in 1611. It is an adaptation of Piccolomini's *Alessandro*, a comedy based upon works by Plautus and Terence. Another comedy of the same name has been ascribed, somewhat dubiously, to Garrick.

May Dedalus (ded′a̯.lus, dē′da̯-). See **Dedalus, May.**

Mayfair (mā′fār). A locality in London, E of Hyde Park. All streets N of Piccadilly now lead into the district of Mayfair, which takes its name from a fair which used to be held in Shepherd's Market and its surrounding streets. It has long been one of London's most fashionable sections.

May Fielding (fēl′ding). See **Fielding, May.**

May Fleming (mā flem′ing), **Lady.** See **Fleming, Lady May.**

Mayhew (mā′hū), **Augustus Septimus.** b. at London, 1826; d. there, Dec. 25, 1875. An English comic author and dramatist; brother of Horace Mayhew. Author of *Paved with Gold, or Romance and Reality of London Streets* (1857), *The Finest Girl in Bloomsbury* (1861), *Faces for Fortunes* (1865), and other stories of London life; and co-author of six farces (1851–71). He was associated with the *Comic Almanac* as contributor (1845–53) and editor (1848–50).

Mayhew, Horace. b. at London, 1816; d. at Kensington, London, April 30, 1872. An English comic author and journalist; brother of Augustus Septimus Mayhew. Author of *Plum Pudding Pantomime* (1847), *Change for a Shilling* (1848), *Model Men* (1848), *Model Women* (1848), *A Plate of Heads* (1849), *The Toothache* (1849), *Guy Faux* (1849), and *Letters Left at the Pastry-Cook's* (1853).

He is best known for his contributions to Cruikshank's *Table Book* (1845), to *Lloyd's Weekly News* (1852), and to *Punch.*

Maynard Gilfil (mā′na̯rd gil′fil). See **Gilfil, Maynard.**

Mayne (mān), **Ethel Colburn.** [Pseudonym, **Frances E. Huntly.**] d. at Torquay, Devonshire, England, April 30, 1941. English journalist, critic, novelist, and biographer. She began writing (1895) for the *Yellow Book* and *Chapman's Magazine* under the pseudonym Frances E. Huntly, a name she dropped in 1898. She contributed articles, essays, and literary criticism to the *Nation, Daily News, Daily Chronicle,* and *Yorkshire Post,* and translated works from Russian, French, and German. Author of *Jessie Vandeleur* (1902), *The Fourth Ship* (1908), *Gold Lace—A Study of Girlhood* (1913), and *One of Our Grandmothers* (1916), novels; *The Clearer Vision* (1898), *Things That No One Tells* (1910), *Come In* (1917), *Blindman* (1919), *Nine of Hearts* (1923), and *Inner Circle* (1925), collected short stories; *Enchanters of Men* (1909), *The Romance of Monaco and Its Rulers* (1910), *Byron* (1912), *Browning's Heroines* (1913), *Life and Letters of Anne Isabella, Lady Noel Byron* (1929), and *Regency Chapter—Lady Bessborough and Her Friendships* (1939), literary and social studies.

Mayor of Casterbridge (kàs′tèr.brij), **The.** A novel by Thomas Hardy, published in 1886. "Casterbridge" is Hardy's name for the old Roman Dorsetshire town of Dorchester, where Michael Henchard, hero of this story, rises to the position of mayor, only to have his own irascible temper, together with some unfortunate accidents, bring him to ruin. The novel opens with a striking incident in which Henchard sells his wife, and ends with his poignant and tragic death.

Mayor of Garratt (gar′a̯t), **The.** A comedy by Samuel Foote, produced in 1763.

Mayor of London. A character in two of Shakespeare's plays: In *1 Henry VI,* he stops the fighting between followers of the Bishop of Winchester and those of the Duke of Gloucester. In *Richard III,* he supports Richard's claim to the throne.

Mayor of Quinborough (kwin′bur.o̱, -bèr.o̱), **The.** [Also, **Hengist, King of Kent.**] A comedy by Thomas Middleton, printed in 1661. It has been suggested that William Rowley had a hand in the play; possibly Middleton and Rowley revised an older one. It was acted at Blackfriars, between 1615 and 1620. The chief source was Holinshed, supplemented by Fabyan.

Mayor of York (yôrk). In Shakespeare's *3 Henry VI,* Thomas Beverly, who reluctantly admits Edward IV into the town.

Maypole Inn. In Dickens's novel *Barnaby Rudge,* the inn which is a gathering place for various of the characters most active in the Gordon Riots.

May Queen, The. A poem by Alfred Tennyson, published in 1832.

May Queen, The. A cantata by W. Sterndale Bennett, produced in 1858. The words are by H. F. Chorley.

Mazarin (maz'ạ.rin; French, mȧ.zȧ.raṅ), **Jules.** [Italian, **Giulio Mazarini** (mä.tsä.rē'nē).] b. at Pescina, Abruzzi e Molise, Italy, July 14, 1602; d. at Vincennes, Seine, France, March 9, 1661. A French statesman. He was descended from a Sicilian family, studied at a Jesuit college at Rome and at the University of Alcalá, Spain, and in 1622 entered the papal military service. He attracted the attention of Richelieu, at whose instance he entered the French service. He became a naturalized Frenchman in 1639, and in 1641 was made a cardinal on the presentation of Louis XIII, although he had never taken anything but minor orders. He was appointed prime minister on the death of Richelieu in 1642, and was retained in office by the queen regent, Anne of Austria, after the death of Louis XIII in 1643. He continued the foreign policy of Richelieu, which looked to the abatement of the power of the house of Austria by interfering in favor of the Protestants in the Thirty Years' War, and which resulted in complete success at the peace of Westphalia in 1648. At home his policy of centralizing all administrative authority in the crown, also a legacy from Richelieu, was opposed by the nobles and the Parliament of Paris, and gave rise to the wars of the Fronde (1648–53), during which he was twice expelled by his opponents from the court (1651–52 and 1652–53). In 1659 he concluded the peace of the Pyrenees, putting an end to the hostilities with Spain which had sprung up during the Thirty Years' War, and securing an increase of French territory. Mazarin's policy of destroying the power of the nobility while strengthening that of the crown established the basis of the great power held by Louis XIV. Mazarin himself built a great fortune, which he used to create the famous Mazarin library and to patronize such figures as Descartes and Pierre Corneille.

Mazarin Bible. An edition of the Bible printed by Johann Gutenberg at Mainz in 1450–55, being the first book ever printed with movable types. It is so named because the first known copy of it was discovered in the Mazarin library at Paris in 1760.

Mazeppa (mạ.zep'ạ). A narrative poem by Byron, published in 1819. It tells the story of Ivan Mazeppa, a page in the Polish court, who later became *hetman* (chieftain) of the Ukraine under Peter the Great. He later deserted to Charles II of Sweden (to whom, supposedly, he is telling his story in the poem).

Mazzini (mät.tsē'nē, mäd.dzē'nē), **Giuseppe.** b. at Genoa, Italy, c1805; d. at Pisa, Italy, March 10, 1872. An Italian patriot and revolutionist. He graduated at the University of Genoa in 1826, became a member of the bar of that city, and joined (1830) the Carbonari, the Italian republican underground. In 1830 he was arrested by the authorities of Piedmont on the charge of conspiring against the government, but after an imprisonment of six months was released for want of sufficient evidence to procure a conviction. He thereupon left Italy and resided successively at Marseilles, Paris, and London, whence he conducted agitations for the liberation of Italy. Among his writings was a widely circulated letter to Charles Albert, King of Sardinia, so inflammatory that Mazzini was put under

perpetual banishment. He founded (c1832) the secret revolutionary society of "Young Italy," whose object was the unification of Italy under a republican government. He returned to Italy at the outbreak of the revolutionary movements of 1848, and in 1849 became a member of the triumvirate in the short-lived republic at Rome, being again driven into exile on the restoration of the papal government (1849). He afterward organized insurrections at Mantua (1852), Milan (1853), and Genoa (1857), but played a subordinate part in the movement which resulted in the unification of Italy (except Venice and the Papal States) under Victor Emmanuel I in 1861. Unwilling to take the oath of allegiance to a monarchy, he remained abroad. In 1870 he took part in an insurrection at Palermo, during which he was captured. He was, however, released by the general amnesty published by the Italian government after the occupation of Rome.

M'Carthy (mạ.kär'thi), **Justin.** b. at Cork, Ireland, Nov. 22, 1830; d. at Folkestone, England, April 24, 1912. An Irish journalist, politician, historian, and novelist. He was a Home Rule member of Parliament (1879–1900), and on the fall (1890) of C. S. Parnell became the chairman of the Irish Parliamentary Party (Anti-Parnellites), resigning in January, 1896. His works include *History of Our Own Times* (5 vols., 1878–1905), *History of the Four Georges* (1884), *Camiola* (1885), *Pope Leo XIII* (1896), *Story of Gladstone's Life* (1897), *Mononia* (1901), *Reign of Queen Anne* (1902), *Portraits of the Sixties* (1903), and *An Irishman's Story* (1904). With Mrs. Campbell-Praed he wrote the novels *The Right Honorable* (1886), *The Rebel Rose* (1887), and others.

McCabe (mạ.kāb'), **Joseph Martin.** b. in England, Nov. 11, 1867—. An English rationalist philosopher. After entering (1883) the Franciscan order, he was ordained (1890) to the priesthood and was professor (1890–94) of scholastic philosophy, but withdrew (1896) from the church in order to lecture and write. Author of *Twelve Years in a Monastery* (1897), *Modern Rationalism* (1897), *St. Augustine and His Age* (1902), *The Decay of the Church of Rome* (1909), *The Evolution of Mind* (1910), *The Story of Evolution* (1912), *Goethe* (1912), *The Principles of Evolution* (1914), *The Soul of Europe* (1915), *The Tyranny of Shams* (1916), *The Bankruptcy of Religion* (1918), *Ice Ages* (1922), *The Twilight of the Gods* (1923), *The Marvels of Modern Physics* (1925), *Key to Love and Sex* (1929), *The Hundred Men Who Moved the World* (1931), *The New Science* (1931), *The Riddle of the Universe Today* (1934), *A History of the Popes* (1939), and *A Rationalist Encyclopedia* (1948).

M'Combich (mạ.kum'bi), **Robin Oig.** [Called **Robin Oig.**] In Sir Walter Scott's tale *The Two Drovers*, the Scottish drover who kills Harry Wakefield, the English drover, and is therefore tried and executed.

McCrae (mạ.krā'), **John.** b. in Canada, 1872; d. 1916. A Canadian poet, now chiefly remembered for his poem of World War I, "In Flanders Fields," first published (1915) in *Punch* and later published as part of *In Flanders Fields and Other Poems* (1919).

---

fat, fāte, fär, àsk, fāre; net, mē, hėr; pin, pīne; not, nōte, mȯve, nôr; up, lūte, pull; ᴛʜ, then;

McDiarmid (mạk.dẽr′mid), **Hugh.** [Pseudonym of **Christopher Murray Grieve.**] b. at Langholm, Dumfriesshire, Scotland, Aug. 11, 1892—. A Scottish poet. His books of poetry include *Sangschaw, Penny Wheep, A Drunk Man Looks at the Thistle, Stony Limits and Other Poems, First Hymn to Lenin and Other Poems, Cornish Heroic Song for Valda Trevlyn,* and *A Kist for Whistles.* His prose works include *Annals of the Five Senses, Albyn, or the Future of Scotland, Scottish Scene, What Lenin Has Meant to Scotland, The Scottish Islands,* and the autobiographical *Lucky Poet.*

McFall (mạk.fôl′), **Frances Elizabeth.** See **Grand, Sarah.**

McGee (mạ.gẽ′), **Thomas D'Arcy.** b. at Carlingford, Ireland, April 13, 1825; killed at Ottawa, Canada, April 7, 1868. An Irish journalist in Great Britain, the U. S. and Canada. At the age of 17 he came to Boston, where he became prominent as a writer and speaker. He returned (1845) to England, where he was a correspondent of the *Freeman's Journal* and the *Nation.* He joined (1846) the Young Ireland movement and fled (1848) to the U. S., where he founded the *New York Nation* and the *American Celt.* His views became more moderate and in 1857 he was forced to go to Canada because of the opposition of the more radical members of the Irish nationalist movement. He became (1858) a member of parliament and was appointed president of the council (1862) and minister of agriculture (1864). He supported confederation and was elected to the first Dominion parliament (1867). He was assassinated by a member of the Fenian brotherhood. He wrote *A History of the Irish Settlers in North America* (1851), *A Popular History of Ireland* (1862), and others.

McHenry (mạk.hen′ri), **James.** [Pseudonym, **Solomon Secondsight.**] b. at Larne, County Antrim, Ireland, Dec. 20, 1785; d. there, July 21, 1845. An Irish author and physician in America. He was the founder (1824) and editor of the *American Monthly Magazine.* As chief poetry reviewer for the *American Quarterly Review,* his conservative theories led him to attack the English romantics to such an extent as to provoke a reply in *Blackwood's Magazine,* at Edinburgh.

McKenna (mạ.ken′ạ), **Stephen.** b. Feb. 27, 1888—. An English novelist. Author of *The Reluctant Lover* (1912), *Sheila Intervenes* (1913), *The Sixth Sense* (1915), *Sonia* (1917), *The Education of Eric Lane* (1921), *Tales of Intrigue and Revenge* (1924), *Due Reckoning* (1927), *Happy Ending* (1929), *Magic Quest* (1933), *Breasted Amazon* (1938), *A Life for a Life* (1939), *Mean, Sensual Man* (1943), and others.

McKerrow (mạ.ker′ọ), **Ronald Brunlees.** b. at Putney, London, Dec. 12, 1872; d. at Wendover, England, Jan. 20, 1940. An English scholar, teacher, bibliographer, and publisher. He was professor of English (1897–1900) in the government school of foreign languages at Tokyo. After his return to England, he specialized in the Elizabethan period, becoming a bibliographer. He entered (1908) the publishing firm of Sidgwick and Jackson, Ltd., of which he became managing director in 1917. He was professor of English literature (1914– 18) and, later, of bibliography, at King's College, London. He founded (1925) and was the first editor of the *Review of English Studies.* Author of *Dictionary of Printers, 1558–1640* (1910), *Introduction to Bibliography for Literary Students* (1927), *Printers' and Publishers' Devices in England and Scotland, 1485–1640* (1933), and *The Treatment of Shakespeare's Text by His Earlier Editors, 1709–1768* (1933). His edition of the works of Thomas Nash (5 vols., 1904–10) remains standard. At his death he was engaged in preparing a revision of the Oxford Shakespeare, for which he had written (1939) *Prolegomena for the Oxford Shakespeare.*

McLaughlin (mạ.klâf′lin), **Charles.** Original name of **Macklin, Charles.**

McLeod (mạ.kloud′), **Irene Rutherford.** b. Aug. 21, 1891—. An English poet. Author of *Swords for Life* and *Songs to Save a Soul* (both 1916), the latter a volume of poems previously published in the *Nation,* the *Smart Set, Votes for Women,* and the *New Weekly.* She also wrote *Before Dawn* (1918) and *Towards Love* (1923).

McNeile (mạk.nẽl′), **Cyril.** [Pseudonym, **Sapper**; full name, **Herman Cyril McNeile.**] b. at Bodmin, Cornwall, England, Sept. 28, 1888; d. at Pulborough, Sussex, England, Aug. 14, 1937. An English soldier and author, creator of the fictional character "Bulldog Drummond." He served (1907–19) with the royal engineers as lieutenant and lieutenant colonel. Under his pseudonym, the military term for a member of the engineers, he wrote *Sergeant Michael Cassidy, The Fatal Second,* and *Men, Women, and Guns* (1916), *No Man's Land* (1917), *Bulldog Drummond: The Adventures of a Demobilized Officer Who Found Peace Dull* (1920), *The Dinner Club* (1923), *Jim Maitland* (1923), *Bulldog Drummond's Third Round* (1924), *The Final Count* (1926), *The Hidden Witness* (1929), *Tiny Carteret* (1930), *Bulldog Drummond Strikes Back* (1933), and *Challenge* (1934).

M'Crie (mạ.krẽ′), **Thomas.** b. at Duns, Scotland, in November, 1772; d. at Edinburgh, Aug. 5, 1835. A Scottish Presbyterian clergyman and author. His works include *Life of John Knox* (1812), *Life of Andrew Melville* (1819), and *The Reformation in Italy* (1827).

Meal-Tub Plot, The. A pretended anti-Protestant conspiracy (1679), trumped up by Dangerfield.

Meaning of Art, The. A critical study by Herbert Read, published in 1931. It was issued in America under the title *The Anatomy of Art* (1932).

Measure for Measure. A comedy by Shakespeare, first acted in 1604 or 1605, printed in the folio of 1623. The play is founded on George Whetstone's *Promos and Cassandra* (1578); the story had previously appeared as the 85th novel in Cinthio's *Hecatommithi.* Often referred to as a "problem play," *Measure for Measure* gives certain indications of having been started as a tragedy and converted, somewhat abruptly, into a comedy during the course of its writing. Certainly, without the Duke as a *deus ex machina,* the play would have proceeded to an unhappy ending; moreover, the characters of Mariana (loyal to the man who has abandoned her), Angelo (rather too quick in his repentance at the end), and Isabella (convent-

ḍ, d or j; ş, s or sh; ṭ, t or ch; ẓ, z or zh; o, F. cloche; ü, F. menu; c̷h, Sc. loch; ṅ, F. bonbon.

bound at the beginning, but conveniently willing to marry the Duke at the end) give the impression of having been forced into molds quite different from those which the beginning of the play would suggest.

The Story. Unwilling to be directly connected with the enforcement of certain long-neglected laws against unchaste behavior, Vincentio, Duke of Vienna, has entrusted to his deputy, Angelo, all governmental powers during his supposed absence (actually, however, he remains in the city, disguised as a friar). Angelo immediately arrests Claudio (who has got with child Juliet, his (Claudio's) betrothed) and sentences him to death. Claudio sends for his sister, Isabella, who is about to enter a nunnery, to try to prevail upon Angelo for mercy. He is at first adamant, but the beauty of Isabella arouses his lust and he offers to pardon Claudio if she will yield herself to him. She refuses indignantly and returns to the prison to tell Claudio, who begs her to sacrifice her chastity for his life. The Duke, still disguised as a friar, overhears the conversation and suggests that Isabella agree to Angelo's request, but that they get Mariana, formerly the fiancée of Angelo, to substitute for Isabella at the assignation. After his meeting with this spurious "Isabella" (by whom he is nevertheless utterly deceived), Angelo breaks his word and orders the execution of Claudio. However, the Provost of the prison prevents this by the dexterous substitution of a prisoner already awaiting execution for another offense. The Duke now lays aside his disguise, hears the complaints, and straightens everything out; judgment is given upon Angelo (who still assumes that Claudio is dead) with the words: " 'An Angelo for Claudio, death for death!' . . . and measure still for measure." Angelo, pardoned upon Mariana's plea, marries her, while the Duke marries Isabella, and Claudio, Juliet.

Mecca (mek′ạ). [Also: **Makka, Makkah, Mekka**.] A city in W Arabia, one of the two capitals of Saudi Arabia, and the capital of Hejaz viceroyalty: most sacred city of the Moslem world; the birthplace of Mohammed and the site of the Kaaba. It is situated in a sandy valley ab. 50 mi. from the Red Sea. Its principal building is the Great Mosque, in the center of which is the Kaaba. Every Moslem is bound to undertake once in his life a pilgrimage to Mecca, and in the rites performed on this occasion are included the circuit around the Kaaba and the kissing of the black stone. As many as 100,000 pilgrims come to the city in a year.

Mechitarists (mek.i.tär′ists). See **Mekhitarists**.

Medal, The. A satire by John Dryden, which appeared in 1682. It attacked the Earl of Shaftesbury and the Whigs who had exonerated him from a charge of high treason for his support of Monmouth (the illegitimate son of Charles II) against James, the Duke of York (later James II). The preface to the poem was in prose, entitled *An Epistle to the Whigs.*

Meddle (med′l). In Dion Boucicault's comedy *London Assurance,* a pettifogging lawyer.

Medea (mẹ.dē′ạ). In Greek legend, a sorceress; daughter of Aetes, king of Colchis, and wife of Jason. When Jason came with the Argonauts to obtain the Golden Fleece, Medea aided him by her magic arts, and escaped with him to Corinth, where, ten years later, she murdered Creusa or Glauce, daughter of King Creon, for whom Jason had determined to abandon her. From Corinth she fled to Athens, and married Aegeus (father of Theseus), by whom she had a son Medeus, regarded by the Greeks as the eponymous ancestor of the Medes. Medea plotted against the life of Theseus several times, but when Aegeus recognized his son, he drove her out of Athens. Hera gave Medea immortality for having repulsed the advances of Zeus. In Elysium she married Achilles.

Medea. A tragedy by Richard Glover, published in 1761 and produced in 1767.

Medes (mēdz). The inhabitants of Media, an ancient country in what is now NW Iran. They first appear in history as Amadai in 836 B.C., when Shalmaneser, the Assyrian conqueror, received tribute from them. In 715 and 713 B.C. Sargon subjected them. In the second half of the 7th century they won their independence and were united under a single dynasty. The Medes were eventually defeated by the Persians under Cyrus, and absorbed into the Persian Empire.

Medina (mẹ.dē′nạ). [Arabic: **al-Medinat al-Munowarrat**, meaning "the City of Light"; **Medinat-Rasul-Allah, Medinat-el-Rabi** (or **-en-Nabi**), meaning "the City of the Prophet"; ancient name, **Yathrib**; called (by Ptolemy) **Lathrippa**.] A city in Hejaz, W Saudi Arabia, the second holy city of the Mohammedans, situated ab. 220 mi. N of Mecca and ab. 100 mi. from the Red Sea. It is celebrated as the place where Mohammed took refuge at the flight (622 A.D.) called the Hegira, and where he died and was buried. From this it is sometimes designated "the city of the Prophet."

Medina (mẹ.dī′nạ). In Edmund Spenser's *Faerie Queene,* the second of the three sisters Elissa, Medina, and Perissa. She far excelled the other two, representing the golden mean, for Elissa was froward and always discontented and Perissa was loose and extravagant and indulgent in all pleasures.

Meditations on the Passion. A short Middle English prose work by Richard Rolle of Hampole.

Medley (med′li). In George Etherege's comedy *The Man of Mode,* the friend of Young Bellair; supposed by some to be a portrait of Sir Charles Sedley, by others a portrait of the author himself.

Medmenham Abbey (med′men.ạm). An abbey at Medmenham, a village in S England, in Buckinghamshire, NW of Maidenhead. The ruined abbey, formerly a Cistercian monastery, acquired notoriety as the scene of the orgies of a convivial association known as the Mad Monks of Medmenham Abbey, including such notables as John Wilkes and George Bubb Dodington, in the latter part of the 18th century.

Medora (mẹ.dō′rạ). In Byron's poem *The Corsair,* the wife of Conrad, "the Corsair." She dies of a broken heart when he does not return from his captivity in the dungeons of the Seyd.

Medusa (mẹ.dū′sạ, -zạ). In Greek mythology, one of the Gorgons, originally a beautiful maiden whose hair was transformed into serpents by

fat, fāte, fär, ȧsk, fãre; net, mē, hẻr; pin, pīne; not, nōte, mōve, nôr; up, lūte, pŭll; ᴛʜ, then;

Athena because with Poseidon (by whom she was the mother of Chrysaor and Pegasus) she had violated one of the temples of that goddess. Her face was so fearful to look upon that whoever saw it was changed into stone. Accordingly when Perseus sought her to cut off her head, he attacked her with averted face, seeing only her reflection in the shield of Athena, who also guided his hand. Perseus gave the head to Athena, who used it on her aegis.

Meercraft (mir'kråft). In Ben Jonson's comedy *The Devil Is an Ass*, a clever rogue, a projector or speculator who carries about with him prospectuses to suit all tastes.

Megaera (mę̇.jir'ą̇). In late Greek mythology, one of the three Eumenides (or Furies). Megaera was called the "jealous one."

Meg Dods (meg dodz). See **Dods, Meg.**

Meg Merrilies (mer'i.lęz). See **Merrilies, Meg.**

Meg Murdockson (mėr'dǫk.sǫn). See **Murdockson, Meg.**

Meg of Westminster (west'min''stėr). See **Long Meg of Westminster.**

Mehdee (me'dē). See **Mahdi.**

Meinhold (mīn'holt), **Johann Wilhelm.** b. on the Baltic island of Usedom, Feb. 27, 1797; d. at Charlottenburg, Germany, Nov. 30, 1851. A German pastor. Author of two novels (both translated into English), *Marie Schweidler, die Bernsteinhexe* (1843) and *Sidonia von Bork, die Klosterhexe* (1847). The former, which he published anonymously under the pretense that it was an old chronicle, attracted much attention. It was dramatized in 1847 by Laube and in 1911 by Max Geissler.

Meissonier (mä.so.nyä), **Jean Louis Ernest.** b. at Lyons, France, Feb. 21, 1815; d. at Paris, Jan. 31, 1891. A French genre and historical painter. He first made himself known as an illustrator of books (*Les Français peints par eux-mêmes* and others), but soon began to paint genre pictures on a small scale, with the microscopic detail and finish for which he became famous. He painted between 450 and 500 of these. His favorite subjects were military, and many of his pictures represent men at arms, guards, cavaliers, or soldiers playing cards, drinking, or the like. The most celebrated of his pictures are the four known as the "Napoleon Cycle."

Meister Eckhart (mī'stėr ek'härt). See **Eckhart.**

Mekhitarists (mek.i.tär'ists). [Also, **Mechitarists.**] An order of Armenian monks in communion with the Roman Catholic Church, under a rule resembling the Benedictine, founded (1701) by Peter Mekhitar at Constantinople, confirmed (1712) by the Pope, and finally settled (1717) on the island of San Lazzaro, near Venice. This is still their chief seat, while they have an independent monastery at Vienna, and branches in Russia, France, Italy, Turkey, and elsewhere. The Mekhitarists are devoted to the religious and literary interests of the Armenian people wherever found, and have published many ancient Armenian manuscripts as well as original works; their society is also organized as a literary academy which confers honorary membership without regard to race or religion.

Melampus (me.lam'pus). In Greek legend, a famous prophet and soothsayer; brother of Bias, the sage, and eponymous ancestor of a family of seers. The legend has it that some serpents which he had saved from death cleansed his ears with their tongues while he was asleep, and on awakening he found that he could understand the speech of birds and beasts, and thus learned many secret things.

Melanchthon (me.langk'thon; German, mä.längch'-ton), **Philipp.** [Also, **Philipp Melanthon**; original name, **Philip Schwarzerd.**] b. at Bretten, Baden, Feb. 16, 1497; d. at Wittenberg, Germany, April 19, 1560. A German reformer, a collaborator of Martin Luther. He was educated at Tübingen, and became (1518) professor of Greek at Wittenberg. He helped Luther in his translation of the Bible and soon became one of his chief followers in the Reformation. Melanchthon in many ways acted as a balance in the movement; his was the calm moderation that curbed and stated in reasoned terms Luther's more drastic reforms, at the same time recognizing completely Luther's leadership. In his *Loci communes rerum theologicarum* (1521), he set forth in scholarly fashion the first systematic exposition of the theology of the reformers. During the next years he served often as a disputant in discussions and conferences with other reformers (for example, at Marburg in 1529, when he was Zwingli's opponent) and with Roman Catholic theologians. He drew up (1530) the Augsburg Confession, the basic 17 articles of the evangelical faith.

Melantha (me.lan'thạ). In John Dryden's comedy *Marriage à la Mode*, an attractive and impertinent fashionable lady, said by Colley Cibber to exhibit the most complete system of female foppery that could possibly be crowded into the tortured form of a fine lady.

Melantius (me.lan'ti.us). In Francis Beaumont and John Fletcher's *The Maid's Tragedy*, a rough, honest soldier, the brother of Evadne.

Melba (mel'bạ), **Dame Nellie.** [Stage name of **Helen Porter Mitchell**; married name, **Armstrong.**] b. at Melbourne, Australia, May 19, 1861; d. at Sydney, Australia, Feb. 23, 1931. An Australian operatic soprano, a leading figure (c1887–c1928) in her field with a repertoire of 25 operas. She first used the name Madame Nellie Melba at a recital at Paris in December, 1886, and subsequently never used any other publicly. She first appeared in grand opera at the Théatre de la Monnaie, Brussels, on Oct. 13, 1887, in *Rigoletto*, and appeared at the Paris Opéra in May, 1889, as Ophelia in *Hamlet*. Her original success was on the Continent, but she later conquered London and New York, where she first appeared in 1893. After 1907 she divided her time between Australia and Europe.

Melchizedek (mel.kiz'ẹ.dek). [Also: **Melchisedec, Melchisedech.**] In Old Testament history, a king and priest of Salem, who entertained and blessed Abraham and received tithes from him. His relation to Christ as a type is discussed in Heb. v-vii.

Melchior (mel'ki.ôr). In medieval Christian legend, one of the three Magi who came from the East to welcome the infant Jesus.

Melcombe (mel'kǫm), **Baron.** Title of **Dodington, George Bubb.**

ḍ, d or j; ṣ, s or sh; ṭ, t or ch; ẓ, z or zh; o, F. cloche; ü, F. menu; ċh, Sc. loch; ṅ, F. bonbon.

Meleager (mel.ē.ā′jer). In Greek legend, a celebrated hero, son of Oeneus of Calydon and Althaea: one of the Argonauts and slayer of the Calydonian boar. At his birth it was prophesied that he would die when a certain brand in the fire was burned out. Althaea pulled it from the fire, quenched it, and hid it. When Meleager killed his uncles (brothers of Althaea) for attempting to rob Atalanta of the boar's hide, Althaea threw the brand back in the fire and let it be consumed. Meleager died, and Althaea in turn put an end to herself.

Melema (me.lā′ma), **Tito.** In George Eliot's novel *Romola*, a likable, handsome Greek youth, who is unfortunately led by selfishness and egotism to the betrayal of those to whom he owes the greatest loyalty.

Meliadus (mē.lī′a.dus). [Also, **Meliodas** (-ō.das).] In Arthurian romance, the father of Tristram, and king of Lyonesse.

Meliagrance (mē.lī′a.grans), **Sir.** A character in Malory's *Morte d'Arthur*, who captures Queen Guinevere and carries her off to his castle. Some scholars identify him with Melwas, the god of darkness in early British mythology.

Melibeus (mel.i.bē′us), **The Tale of.** One of Chaucer's *Canterbury Tales*, represented as being told by the poet himself after the Host has interrupted *The Rime of Sir Thopas*. It is a prose translation of the Latin *Liber consolationis et concilii* of Albertano of Brescia, through a free French version of the latter, the *Livre de Melibée et Dame Prudence*, probably by Jean de Meung. The story is one of the two prose sections of *The Canterbury Tales* (the other being *The Parson's Tale*), and, though it has a plot, is chiefly a didactic discussion of morality, tedious to most modern readers. One critic has said that Chaucer, prevented from continuing *Sir Thopas*, revenged himself by recounting the dull *Tale of Melibeus*. But there is no reason to believe that the 14th century looked upon such treatises with our eyes or that Chaucer would have gone to the trouble of translating the work if he had not thought it valuable. The tale itself concerns the wisdom of the wife of Melibeus, Prudence, who is beaten by his enemies but nevertheless persuades him to forgive them.

Melicertes (mel.i.ser′tēz). In Greek mythology, a son of Athamas and Ino, who was changed, after his death with her by drowning, into a sea divinity with the name of Palaemon. Melicertes is identified with the Phoenician Melkarth, and was worshiped on the coast, especially at Megara and the Isthmus of Corinth. The Isthmian Games were celebrated in honor of Melicertes, whose body was washed ashore there; whenever they were neglected, famine struck the locality. By the Romans he was identified with Portunus, god of harbors. Thus he and his mother both became sea deities.

Melincourt (mel′in.kort). [Full title, **Melincourt, or, Sir Oran Haut-ton.**] A satirical novel by Thomas Love Peacock, published in 1817. This work, like the author's others, has relatively little plot, but contains much discussion by a large group of people. The people in this case are the suitors for the hand of Anthelia Melincourt, and their talk centers around slavery in the West Indies, the Lake poets,

and rotten boroughs. Certain of the characters are caricatures of actual men. Mr. Feathernest represents Southey; Mr. Mystic, Coleridge; and Mr. Paperstamp, Wordsworth. An interesting feature is introduced in the form of an educated orangoutang, named Sir Oran Haut-ton.

Meliodas (mē.lī′ō.das). See **Meliadus.**

Melissa (mē.lis′a). In Greek legend, the wife of Periander of Corinth, who murdered her in a fit of jealousy.

Melissa (Italian, mā.lēs′sä). An enchantress in Ariosto's *Orlando Furioso*. She assists Ruggiero and Bradamante, and restores the lovers of Alcina to their natural shapes.

Melissa Wackles (mē.lis′a wak′lz). See **Wackles, Melissa.**

Mell (mel), **Mr.** A humble, kind-hearted assistant teacher, employed by the bullying Creakle, in Dickens's *David Copperfield*.

Mellefont (mel′e.font). One of the principal characters in William Congreve's comedy *The Double Dealer*. He is in love with Cynthia.

Mellida (mel′i.da). The heroine of John Marston's double play, *Antonio and Mellida* and *Antonio's Revenge*. She loves Antonio, son of the Duke of Genoa.

Melmoth the Wanderer (mel′moth). A novel by Charles Robert Maturin (generally considered to be his best), published in 1820. It is a powerful tale of horror and mystery, and concerns a man who sold his soul to the Devil in return for freedom from death. He made the bargain in the 17th century, and has been trying ever since to get someone to agree to change places with him (which will free him of his pact with the Devil). Melmoth offers relief from distress to many people, but they all refuse to accept his bargain at the expense of their souls. The people he approaches include Stanton, prisoner in a lunatic asylum; Monçada, caught in the Inquisition; Walberg, witness to the starvation of his children; and Isidora, Melmoth's wife.

Melnotte (mel.not′), **Claude.** The hero of Bulwer-Lytton's *Lady of Lyons*.

melodrama (mel′ō.drä.ma, mel.ō.drä′ma) [Also, **melodram.**] **1.** Originally, a dramatic composition in which music was used, or an opera in the broad sense.
2. A drama with incidental music, or an operetta with more or less spoken dialogue; a piece in which speech and song (or instrumental music) alternate.
3. A form of the drama characterized by compositions in which music is either not present or is of but moderate importance or value, and the plot and scenes are of a decidedly romantic and sensational nature.

Melpomene (mel.pom′e.nē). In Greek mythology, the Muse of tragedy, or of lyre-playing.

Melton Mowbray (mel′ton mō′brā). An urban district, market town, and manufacturing center in C England, in Leicestershire, ab. 13 mi. NE of Leicester, ab. 105 mi. NW of London by rail. It is located in a grassland region and specializes in fattening cattle and sheep for market. Melton Mowbray has long been noted (and often mentioned in English writing) for its Stilton cheese (cheese fairs are held here annually) and its pork pies.

Melum Contemplativorum (mē′lum kon.tem.plā.ti-vō′rum). A Latin prose work of the Middle English period by Richard Rolle of Hampole, known as the *Book of the Glory and Perfection of the Saints.* It describes some of his mystical experiences.

Melun (mẹ.lun′). In Shakespeare's *King John,* a French lord who warns the English nobles who have deserted to the French side that the Dauphin intends to kill them when he has defeated John.

Melusina (mel.ụ.sē′nạ). [French, **Mélusine** (mā.lü-zēn).] In French local legend, a water fairy of great power and wealth. She married Raymond, son of a Comte de Lusignan, who found her near a fountain or spring in the forest of Colombiers, in Poitou. The marriage took place in a castle which she built around the fountain. They lived happily until, breaking a promise he had made before marriage that he would never intrude on her seclusion on Saturdays, Raymond discovered her, half serpent and half woman, in a bath. His breach of faith and breaking of the taboo compelled her to leave him. Until the destruction of Lusignan (1574) she was said to appear high on its towers, and to shriek thrice whenever the head of that family or the king of France lay dying. The story of Jean d'Arras, compiled (1387) by the order of his master, the Duc de Berry, differs somewhat from the legend. Stephan, a Dominican of the house of Lusignan, developed the work of Jean d'Arras, and made the story so famous that the families of Luxembourg, Rohan, and Sassenaye altered their pedigrees in order to be able to claim descent from her. She is connected with the legends of both the banshee and the mermaid.

Melusine (mel′ụ.sēn). See **Partenay.**

Melvil (mel′vil), **Sir John.** A young nobleman in love with Fanny Sterling in *The Clandestine Marriage,* by David Garrick and the elder George Colman.

Melville (mel′vil), **Julia.** See **Julia.**

Melville, Lewis. Pseudonym of **Benjamin, Lewis Saul.**

Memling (mem′ling), **Hans.** [Also: **Memlinc,** occasionally (wrongly) **Hemling.**] b. c1430; d. 1494. A Flemish painter of Bruges, one of the leaders of the so-called school of Bruges. He apparently studied under Rogier van der Weyden and came to Bruges c1466 (according to tradition, he fled wounded from the battle of Nancy). Memling is noted for the clarity of his line, the warmth of his color, and his smooth style, rich in detail, as in landscape backgrounds to his portraits. His works include a *Shrine of Saint Ursula* (Bruges), considered his masterpiece, *Seven Griefs of Mary* (Turin), *Seven Joys of Mary* (Munich), *Last Judgment* (Florence), the *Donne Triptych* (Chatsworth), *Last Judgment* (Danzig), Madonnas, and portraits, such as that of *Thomas Portinari and His Wife.*

Memnon (mem′non). In Greek legend, an Ethiopian hero on the side of Priam in the Trojan War, slain by Achilles. He was a solar hero, son of Eos, Dawn, depicted as a youth of marvelous beauty and strength. His original home was said to be at Susa

in Elam, where his temple or monument, the Memnonion, was situated. The Greeks gave his name to one of the colossi of Amenophis III at Thebes in Egypt, "the vocal Memnon," so called because the stone, when reached by the rays of the rising sun, was said to give forth a sound resembling that of a breaking chord.

Memnon. A character in John Fletcher's *The Mad Lover.* He is "the mad lover."

Memoirs of a Cavalier, The. A historical romance by Daniel Defoe, published in 1720. According to Winston S. Churchill, its method has been adopted for his volumes entitled *The Second World War.* The narrator, Colonel Andrew Newport, is a young English gentleman who starts traveling in Europe in 1630. He joins the Catholic forces in the Thirty Years' War at Vienna and is present when Tilly storms Magdeburg. He then enters the service of Gustavus Adolphus, the Swedish king and Protestant leader, in which he remains until the king's death at Lützen in 1632. He returns to England where he participates, on the side of the Royalists, in battles against the Scots and later against the Parliamentarians at Edgehill and Naseby in the English Civil War.

Memoirs of a Fox-Hunting Man. An autobiographical narrative, winner of the James Tait Black memorial prize and the Hawthornden prize, by Siegfried Sassoon. It was published in 1928.

Memoirs of a Midget, The. A novel by Walter De la Mare, published in 1921. It is the story of Miss M., a midget who is left orphaned but wealthy at the age of 18. She had been kept in seclusion all her life, so did not realize how people would treat her after she went out into the world. She takes lodgings with Mrs. Bowater, and her daughter, Fanny, of whom she grows very fond. Fanny is a teacher, and when the local curate falls in love with her she refuses his offer of marriage (whereupon he eliminates himself from any further action in the story by committing suicide). Miss M. now decides to mingle with more people, and meets the wealthy Mrs. Monnerie, who becomes her patroness, and who delights in showing her off to her friends. Miss M. gets Fanny a position with Mrs. Monnerie, and that young lady becomes the dowager's favorite. She forgets about Miss M., who has used all her money, and who decides to get work in a circus. Her old friends quarrel with her when they find what she is doing, and the only loyal person is Mr. Anon, a deformed dwarf who is in love with her. She refuses his advances, and he takes her place in the circus one night, falls from a horse, and is killed. Miss M. again comes into much money, but one night she disappears, and is never heard from again.

Memoirs of an Infantry Officer. An autobiographical narrative by Siegfried Sassoon, published in 1930.

Memoirs of Barry Lyndon (bar′i lin′dọn). See **Barry Lyndon.**

Memoirs of Captain Carleton (kärl′tọn), **The.** A narrative by Daniel Defoe, published in 1728. Attempts have been made to identify Carleton as a real soldier or to establish Jonathan Swift as the author, and historians often cite the work as a

---

ḍ, d or j; ṣ, s or sh; ṭ, t or ch; ẓ, z or zh; o, F. cloche; ü, F. menu; ċh, Sc. loch; ṅ, F. bonbon.

source, but it is now known to be one of Defoe's historical romances. Carleton serves on the *London* during the war with the Dutch in 1672, then enters the service of the Prince of Orange (later William III of England). After his return to England he receives a commission from James II. He accompanies the English general Lord Peterborough to Spain in the latter's attempt to support the claims of Archduke Charles (later the emperor Charles VI) to the Spanish throne and participates in the siege and capture of Barcelona.

Memoirs of Martinus Scriblerus (mär.tī′nus skriblē′rus). See **Martinus Scriblerus.**

Memoirs of Mr. C. J. Yellowplush (yel′ọ.plush). A satire by Thackeray, published in 1838, which deals with a footman and his observations on fashionable life.

Memoirs of P.P. See **P.P., Clerk of this Parish, Memoirs of.**

Menaechmi (mẹ.nek′mī). A comedy by Plautus, the plot of which turns upon the comical mistakes arising from the resemblance of twin brothers. It was translated into English in 1594 by "W.W." (William Warner). Shakespeare used its plot as a basis of his *Comedy of Errors.*

Menander (mẹ.nan′dẻr). b. at Athens, 342 B.C.; said to have been drowned c291 B.C. An Athenian comic poet, the chief of the writers of the "new comedy." He wrote more than 100 plays, each with its love story. The titles of some 80 are known, with numerous fragments available to modern scholars. Papyrus finds in Egypt have brought to light whole scenes and enable us to reconstruct a few plots, notably *Epitrepontes* ("The Arbitration") and *Perikeiromene* ("She Is Shorn of Her Locks"). In the former, a foundling infant, aided by slaves, recovers his rights and finds his parents, who had been estranged because of him. In the latter, a soldier-lover maltreats and loses his mistress, but regains her as wife after repentance. Through Plautus and Terence, Menander's influence passed to modern writers of comedy of manners. Plautus's influence on English literature is apparent in Udall's *Ralph Roister Doister,* Lyly's *Mother Bombie,* Shakespeare's *Comedy of Errors,* many of Ben Jonson's comedies, and Dryden's *Amphitryon.* Terence, whose plays (with only two exceptions) were adapted from Menander's, was a major influence in the writings of Congreve, Steele, and Sheridan. Menander won first prize only eight times, but was later extolled as supreme in depicting lively, natural characters in domestic difficulties. He took from Homer's *Odyssey* and from tragedy the theme of family reunion and recognition of lost relatives, but is original in his treatment of good women sinned against and men reformed by love for them.

Men and Women. A selection of 50 poems by Robert Browning, first published in 1855, but abridged and reëdited in 1868 to include only 13 of the original 50. The original volume included *Fra Lippo Lippi, Bishop Blougram's Apology, A Woman's Last Word,* and *Any Wife to Any Husband.*

Menaphon: Camilla's Alarum to Slumbering Euphues (men′ạ.fon; kạ.mil′ạz; ū′fū.ēz). A love story by Robert Greene. It was published in 1589,

and as *Greene's Arcadia, or Menaphon* in 1599. It contains his best lyrical verses. Princess Sephestia is shipwrecked in Arcadia, where the shepherd Menaphon falls in love with her. She is eventually restored to her husband and son.

Menas (mē′nạs). In Shakespeare's *Antony and Cleopatra,* a pirate who proposes to Pompey that they fall upon the triumvirs as they are feasting.

Mendel—A Story of Youth (men′dẹl). A novel by Gilbert Cannan, published in 1916.

Mendelssohn (men′dẹl.son; German, men′dẹl.sön), **Felix.** [Full name, **Jakob Ludwig Felix Mendelssohn-Bartholdy** (-bär.tol′dē).] b. at Hamburg, Germany, Feb. 3, 1809; d. at Leipzig, Germany, Nov. 4, 1847. A German composer and musician. He began to compose regularly in his 12th year, and the symphonies, quartets, concertos, and other works which he produced after this time were performed at the musical parties which took place at his father's house on alternate Sunday mornings, his brother and two sisters assisting; he, however, always conducted and generally played the pianoforte parts. Many great artists visited the house on these occasions. He visited Paris in 1825, and in 1829 triumphantly conducted J. S. Bach's *Matthew Passion* at Berlin, after much opposition, for the first time after the death of the composer. The same year he went to England, where he was enthusiastically received; and he traveled there and on the Continent till July, 1832. In 1833 he was made musical director at Düsseldorf, in 1834 member of the Berlin Academy of Fine Arts, and in 1835 conductor of the Gewandhaus concerts at Leipzig, where he became the idol of the town. He became engaged to Cécile Charlotte Sophie Jeanrenaud in 1836 and was married in 1837. He went to Berlin in 1841 to assist in founding an academy of arts and paid his ninth visit to England in 1846, for the purpose of producing *Elijah* (revisited England in 1847). On his return he heard of the death of his sister Fanny. This, with the severe work which was beginning to tell on him, produced illness and depression from which he did not recover. He left between one and two hundred works, among which are the opera *The Wedding of Camacho* (1825), songs, chamber and orchestral music, five symphonies, a violin concerto, two piano concertos, the oratorios *Elijah* (1846) and *St. Paul* (1836), overture (1826) and music (1843) for *Midsummer Night's Dream, Märchen von der schönen Melusine* (Story of the Beautiful Melusine, 1833), *Die Hebriden* (*The Hebrides*), *Lieder ohne Worte* (*Songs without Words*), music to Goethe's *Walpurgisnacht, Antigone* (1841), *Œdipus Coloneus,* and *Athalie,* sonatas, and fragments of the opera *Die Lorelei* and of the oratorio *Christus.* His letters from 1830 to 1832 were published in 1861; from 1833 to 1847, in 1863.

Menderes (men.de.res′). A modern Turkish name of the **Scamander.**

Mendesian Goat (men.dē′zhạn). A sacred animal of Egyptian mythology, held to be a manifestation of Osiris, and symbolizing the productive force in nature.

Mendoza (men.dō′zạ). The treacherous villain in John Marston's *The Malcontent.*

fat, fāte, fär, ȧsk, fâre; net, mē, hėr; pin, pīne; not, nōte, mõve, nôr; up, lūte, pull; ᴛн, then;

Mendoza Codex (men.dō'thä), **The.** A historically important European copy, with Spanish translation, of an Aztec manuscript. It was published (1625) by Purchas, and is now in the Bodleian Library.

Menecrates (me̤.nek'ra̤.tēz). In Shakespeare's *Antony and Cleopatra*, a pirate (associated with Pompey).

Menelaus (men.e̤.lā'us). In Greek legend, a king of Sparta; brother of Agamemnon, and husband of Helen. After the abduction of Helen by Paris, Menelaus enlisted the help of the Greeks to regain her. Thus began the Trojan War. After the fall of Troy Menelaus returned with Helen to Sparta.

Menelaus. In Shakespeare's *Troilus and Cressida*, the brother of Agamemnon and husband of Helen.

Menenius Agrippa (me̤.nē'ni.us a̤.grip'a̤). In Shakespeare's *Coriolanus*, the talkative, sometimes witty friend of Coriolanus. To calm the plebeians and tribunes, he tells them the fable of the belly and members; later he urges Coriolanus to control his wrath and to speak less arrogantly to the populace. He is sometimes likened to Polonius in *Hamlet*.

Menie Gray (mē'ni grā'). See **Gray, Menie.**

Men in Darkness. A collection of short stories by James Hanley, published in 1931.

Menschenhass und Reue (men'she̤n.häs ûnt roi'e̤). A drama (1790) by Kotzebue. It was translated into English as *The Stranger*, and somewhat altered, by Sheridan.

Menteith (men.tēth'). In Shakespeare's *Macbeth*, a Scottish thane.

Mephistopheles (mef.i.stof'e̤.lēz). [Also: **Mephostophilis, Mephostophilus;** original form, **Mephostophiles.**] A familiar spirit mentioned in the medieval German legend of Doctor Johannes Faust, and a principal agent in Christopher Marlowe's play *Doctor Faustus* and in Goethe's *Faust*. He represents the spirit of evil, or the Devil. He is the Mephostophilus of Shakespeare and Fletcher, and the Mephostophilis of Marlowe.

Mercator (mer.kā'to̤r; Flemish, mer.kä'tôr), **Gerardus.** [Original name, **Gerhard Kremer.**] b. at Rupelmonde, Belgium, March 5, 1512; d. at Duisburg, Germany, Dec. 2, 1594. A Flemish geographer. He studied philosophy and mathematics at the University of Louvain, and afterward devoted himself to geography. Through the influence of Cardinal Granvella, he received a commission from the emperor Charles V to manufacture a terrestrial globe and a celestial globe, which are said to have been superior to any that had then appeared. He took up his residence at Duisburg in 1559, and eventually became cosmographer to the Duke of Jülich and Cleve. He invented the Mercator system of projection, a projection in which the parallels of latitude and the meridians of longitude intersect at right angles; this, the most famous and widely used of all map projections, is accurate only along the line of the equator, but its greatest distortion occurring in the high and low latitudes makes it less objectionable for ordinary use than projections that distort the areas in the temperate and tropical zones. Mercator is likewise credited with breaking the hold that Ptolemaic maps had on European

geographical study by his accurate execution. His chief works are *Tabulae geographicae* (1578–84) and *Atlas* (1595), the latter being completed after his death by his son.

Mercedonius (mer.se̤.dō'ni.us). In the old Roman calendar, an intercalary month of 22 or 23 days, inserted every second year between the 23rd and 24th of February.

Merchant of Bruges (brözh, brö'jez), **The.** An alteration, by D. J. W. Kinnaird, of *The Beggar's Bush* by John Fletcher and others, produced in 1815, Kean taking the part of Flores.

Merchant of Venice (ven'is), **The.** A comedy by Shakespeare, entered on the Stationers' Register in 1598, published in quarto in 1600, 1619, 1637, and 1652, and in folio in 1623. It was probably written in 1596 or 1597. The theme of the bond for a pound of flesh is from *Il Pecorone* (1558) by Fiorentino and the story of the three caskets is found in Richard Robinson's version of the *Gesta Romanorum*. Marlowe's characters, Abigail and Barabas, in *The Jew of Malta* somewhat resemble Jessica and Shylock. Poor versions and adaptations of *The Merchant of Venice* were made by Dryden, Otway, Shadwell, Lansdowne, and others, which held the stage until 1741, when Macklin restored Shakespeare's version. Two of Shakespeare's most famous characters are in this play: Portia, the woman turned lawyer, and Shylock, an unusually sympathetic characterization of a Jew for the Elizabethan age.

The Story. Antonio, the merchant of Venice, is asked for a loan by his well-born, but impecunious, friend Bassanio in order that the latter may be enabled to pursue his courtship of the heiress Portia. Antonio, whose money is tied up in ships that have not yet returned to port, borrows 3,000 ducats from the Jewish usurer Shylock, who makes Antonio promise to forfeit a pound of flesh if he is unable to pay on the agreed date. Meanwhile, at Belmont, Portia has turned away two suitors, the Prince of Morocco and the Prince of Arragon, both of whom fail to pass the test (set by the terms of Portia's father's will) of selecting from three caskets (one each of gold, silver, and lead) the one containing Portia's portrait. Bassanio chooses the correct casket, the lead one, but as they are rejoicing in the thought of an early marriage, word comes that Antonio has been unable to pay his debt and that Shylock is demanding the pound of flesh. After a hasty wedding, Bassanio returns to Venice and, as soon as he has left, Portia and her maid, Nerissa (who has married Bassanio's friend Gratiano), leave also for Venice, disguised respectively as a lawyer and a clerk. In court, the disguised Portia first pleads with Shylock for mercy; rebuffed in this approach, she concedes the legality of Shylock's claim, but points out that if he exacts more than a pound of flesh, or if one drop of blood is shed, his life and lands are forfeit. Moreover, she points out, death is the penalty for conspiring against the life of a Venetian citizen. The Duke of Venice pardons Shylock from the death sentence, but orders that his fortune be divided between Antonio and the state. Antonio returns his share to Shylock, with the stipulation that he must leave it in his will to his daughter Jessica, disinherited

---

ḍ, d or j; ş, s or sh; ṭ, t or ch; ẓ, z or zh; o, F. cloche; ü, F. menu; ċh, Sc. loch; ṅ, F. bonbon.

when she eloped with Lorenzo, a Christian, and finally that Shylock himself must become a Christian. Portia and Nerissa (whose real identity remains unknown to the others) will accept as payment only the rings Bassanio and Gratiano have received from their wives. Back at Belmont, the wives reproach their husbands for no longer having the rings, but, after much teasing, reveal the fact of their disguise, and with the news that Antonio's ships have also returned, all ends happily.

Merchant Prince, The. A historical novel by Henry Christopher Bailey, published in 1926.

Merchant's Second Tale, The. See under **Beryn, History of.**

Merchant's Tale, The. One of Chaucer's *Canterbury Tales.* It is a cynical story of the deception of an old husband (January) by a young wife (May) and her young lover (Damian). The so-called Pear-Tree episode, which forms the basis of the plot, has been greatly elaborated, particularly in the detailed characterization of January, a classic picture of senility in love. The original is Eastern; an account of the Indo-Persian, Turkish, Arabic, Singhalese, and other versions of it is given in the Chaucer Society's *Originals and Analogues.* The Latin versions are Boccaccio's and Caxton's; the immediate source of Chaucer's version, however, is thought to be the Latin fable of Adolphe (c1315). Chaucer describes the Merchant as having "a forked berd" and wearing "a Flaundrish bever hat," his mind on his profits and on keeping up appearances:

> This worthy man ful wel his wit bisette;
> Ther wiste no wight that he was in dette,
> So estatly was he of his governaunce,
> With his bargaynes, and with his chevisaunce.

The Merchant, himself unhappily married, tells the story to illustrate his bitter condemnation of the married state.

Mercia (mer'sha). One of the Anglian kingdoms in England during the Heptarchy, S of Northumbria and N of Wessex, and reaching W of Wales. It was founded probably in the 6th century, flourished under Penda and his successors in the 7th century, attained the overlordship of England under Ethelbald and Offa in the 8th century, passed under the supremacy of Wessex c827, and later, until the Norman conquest, was one of the great earldoms.

Merciless Parliament. An English Parliament of 1388, noted for its ruthless treatment of the adherents of Richard II.

Mercilla (mer.sil'a). In Spenser's *Faerie Queene,* one of several characters intended to represent Queen Elizabeth.

Mercury (mer'kū.ri). In Roman mythology, the god of commerce, who became identified with the Greek Hermes and took on various other attributes of Hermes, such as being messenger of the gods. His cult came from S Italy into Rome c495 B.C. Mercury was the tutelary deity of thieves and tricksters; he became also the god of science, eloquence, and of the arts, and the patron of travelers and athletes. It was he who guided the shades of the dead to the underworld. He is represented in art as a young man, usually wearing a winged hat and the talaria or winged sandals, and bearing the caduceus, and often a purse.

Mercutio (mer.kū'shi.ō). In Shakespeare's *Romeo and Juliet,* a friend of Romeo, slain in an encounter with Tybalt. He is endowed with courage, an easy mind, wit, fancy, and a light heart. He is remembered particularly for his Queen Mab speech (I.iv).

Mercy (mer'si). In John Bunyan's *Pilgrim's Progress,* the friend and companion of Christiana, who eventually marries the oldest son of Christian and Christiana.

Mercy Pecksniff (pek'snif). See under **Pecksniff.**

Merdle (mer'dl). In Dickens's novel *Little Dorrit,* a banker who commits suicide.

Meredith (mer'ę.dith), **George.** b. at Portsmouth, Hampshire, England, Feb. 12, 1828; d. at Box Hill, Surrey, England, May 18, 1909. An English poet, novelist, and critic. The son and grandson of tailors, he was educated at Portsmouth and Southsea schools and at the Moravian Academy at Neuwied on the Rhine. He married (1849) a widow, Mary Ellen (Peacock) Nicholls (who left him in 1858), daughter of Thomas Love Peacock, and after her death (1861) married (1864) Marie Vulliamy. He made his living until 1894 as a journalist and publisher's reader. He was president (1892–1909) of the Society of Authors, and was awarded (1905) the Order of Merit. His works in verse are *Poems* (1851), *Modern Love,* a brilliant treatment of marital tragedy (1862), *Poems and Lyrics of the Joy of Earth,* a celebration of evolutionary naturalism as contrasted with sentimentalism (1883), *Ballads and Poems of Tragic Life* (1887), *A Reading of Earth* (1888), *A Reading of Life* (1901), and *Last Poems* (1910). Works of fiction are *The Shaving of Shagpat,* an Oriental extravaganza (1855), *Farina,* a rollicking burlesque of German romanticism (1857), *The Ordeal of Richard Feverel,* a tragedy of misapplied educational doctrines (1859), *Evan Harrington* (1860), *Sandra Belloni,* a satire on sentimentalism (1864), *Rhoda Fleming* (1865), *Vittoria* (1866; the sequel to *Sandra Belloni*), *The Adventures of Harry Richmond,* a picaresque romance (1870), *Beauchamp's Career,* a novel of political ideas (1874), *The Tale of Chloe,* a brief and moving tragedy (1879), *The Egoist,* a subtle study of selfishness (1879), *The Tragic Comedians,* a novel centered about the career of Ferdinand Lassalle (1880), four novels on feminism and politics, *Diana of the Crossways* (1885), *One of Our Conquerors* (1890), *Lord Ormont and His Aminta* (1894), and *The Amazing Marriage* (1895), and *Celt and Saxon* (1910), an unfinished novel. He was the author also of the critical work *The Idea of Comedy and the Uses of the Comic Spirit* (1877), an analysis of the corrective powers of laughter. The Memorial Edition of his *Works* (29 vols.) was published from 1909 through 1912; his collected *Poetical Works and Letters* (2 vols.) in 1912. His novels, presenting political and social ideas in advance of their time, are, like Ibsen's plays, now dated. Although overwritten and often obscure, they are notable for vivid metaphors, epigrammatic wit, subtleties of characterization, and philosophic insights. His best poems, such as *Love in the Valley, Modern Love, The Woods of Westermain, Hymn to Color,* and *Lucifer in Starlight,* endure for their startling imaginative and intellectual power. As a thinker, Meredith foreshadowed the emergent evolutionists, Lloyd Morgan and Samuel Alexander.

Meredith, Owen. [Pseudonym of **Edward Robert Lytton Bulwer-Lytton;** title, 1st Earl of **Lytton.**] b. at London, Nov. 8, 1831; d. at Paris, Nov. 24, 1891. An English diplomat, politician, and poet; son of Edward George Earle Lytton Bulwer-Lytton (1803–73). He was minister to Portugal (1874–76), governor general of India (1878–80), and ambassador to France (1887–91). During his tenure in India occurred the crowning of Victoria as Empress of India (1877) and the Afghan War (1878–79) that removed Shere Ali from the amirship of Afghanistan. He wrote *Clytemnestra* (1855), *The Wanderer* (1859), *Lucile* (1860), *Serbski Pesme: National Songs of Servia* (1861), *The Ring of Amasis* (1863), *Chronicles and Characters* (1867), *Poems* (1867), *Orval* (1869), *Julian Fane* (1871), *Fables in Song* (1874), *Poems* (1877), *The Life, Letters, and Literary Remains of Edward Bulwer, Lord Lytton*, Vols. I and II (1883), *Glenaveril, or the Metamorphoses* (1885), and *After Paradise* (1887). *King Poppy* was published posthumously in 1892.

Meres (mirz), **Francis.** b. in Lincolnshire, England, 1565; d. at Wing, Rutlandshire, England, Jan. 29, 1647. An English divine and author. He was a graduate of Cambridge (Pembroke College), became rector of Wing in 1602, and kept a school there. Among his works is *Palladis Tamia, Wits Treasury; being the second part of Wits Commonwealth* (1598), one of a series of volumes of collected apothegms, containing criticisms of 125 English writers, painters, and musicians, a list of Shakespeare's plays, and a distorted account of the death of Christopher Marlowe.

Merigreek (mer'i.grēk). See **Merygreek.**

Mérimée (mā.rē.mā), **Prosper.** b. at Paris, Sept. 28, 1803; d. at Cannes, France, Sept. 23, 1870. A French novelist, archaeologist, historian, and literary critic. After spending some time in the study of law, he entered public life, served as inspector-general of historical monuments, and became (1853) a senator under the empire. He first published *Théâtre de Clara Gazul* (1825) and *La Guzla* (1827), the former purporting to be by a Spanish lady, the second supposedly being a translation from the Illyrian, both successful hoaxes. He gave further evidence of his talent in *La Jacquerie* (1828) and *La Famille Carvajal*. He wrote a novel, *La Chronique du temps de Charles IX* (1829), which testifies to careful historical preparation; and in 1830 he published *Colomba*, his masterpiece, which deals with the Corsican vendettas. From 1835 to 1843 Mérimée published a number of works describing his travels in France. In 1845 his novel *Carmen* appeared, a story from which Georges Bizet took his opera. As a historian he wrote *Essai sur la guerre sociale* (1841), *Histoire de Don Pèdre* (1843), *La Conjuration de Catilina* (1844), and *Le faux Démétrius* (1852). He translated from the Russian stories by Pushkin, Turgenev, and Gogol. In 1855 he edited the works of Brantôme and Agrippa d'Aubigné. He wrote frequently for *La Revue de Paris*, *La Revue des Deux Mondes*, and *Le Moniteur*. These articles and other papers by Mérimée have appeared in book form, as for instance *Mélanges historiques et littéraires* (1855),

Dernières Nouvelles (1873), *Portraits historiques et littéraires* (1874), and *Études sur les arts au moyen âge* (1874). Another posthumous publication is *Lettres à une inconnue* (1873). Mérimée was elected a member of the French Academy in 1844. None of Mérimée's fiction is very long, his stories being novelettes rather than novels.

Merion (mer'i.ọn), **Diana.** The full name (very seldom used) of the title character in George Meredith's *Diana of the Crossways*.

Merivale (mer'i.val), **Charles.** b. at Barton Place, Devonshire, England, 1808; d. Dec. 27, 1893. An English historian and divine; son of John Herman Merivale. He was rector (1848–69) of Lawford, Essex, and became dean of Ely in 1869. His chief work is *History of the Romans under the Empire* (7 vols., 1850–62). He also wrote *A General History of Rome* (1875), *Lectures on Early Church History* (1879), *Contrast between Christian and Pagan Society* (1880), a translation of the *Iliad* in rhymed verse, and others.

Merivale, Herman. b. at Dawlish, Devonshire, England, Nov. 8, 1806; d. at London, Feb. 9, 1874. An English lawyer, author, and politician; son of John Herman Merivale. He was professor of political economy at Oxford (1837–42), assistant undersecretary of state for the colonies in 1847 and undersecretary (1848–59), and undersecretary for India (1859–74). He wrote *Historical Studies* (1865) and others.

Merivale, Herman Charles. b. at London, Jan. 27, 1839; d. Jan. 14, 1906. An English poet, dramatist, novelist, and editor; son of Herman Merivale. He gave up the law for literature in 1874. He edited (1870–80) the *Annual Register*. Author of *All for Her* (1875), *Forget-Me-Not* (1879), *The White Pilgrim* (1883), dramas; *The Butler* (1886) and *The Don* (1888), farces; *Faucit of Balliol*, a three-volume novel of Oxford life (1882), *Binko's Blues*, a fairy tale (1884), and *Bar, Stage, and Platform*, recollections (1902).

Merivale, John Herman. b. at Exeter, England, Aug. 5, 1779; d. April 25, 1844. An English scholar and poet. In 1831 he was appointed commissioner in bankruptcy. In 1814 he published *Orlando in Roncesvalles;* a collection of his *Poems* appeared in 1838. Byron was his friend and admirer.

Merlin (mẻr'lin). [Welsh, **Myrddhin** (mir'ᴛʜin).] A legendary Brythonic poet and prophet of the 6th century. In 12th-century Arthurian romance he became the enchanter Merlin. In the romances he was of miraculous birth, was a powerful magician, and was beguiled by the enchantress Vivian (the Lady of the Lake), who buried him under a rock from which he could not escape; or she left him spellbound in the tangled branches of a thorn bush, where he still sleeps, although sometimes his voice is heard. Tennyson, in his *Idylls of the King*, adopts nearly the latter version. Among other famous deeds Merlin instituted the Round Table. He first appears in Nennius's *History of the Britons* as Ambrosius. Geoffrey of Monmouth's *Vita Merlini* (1139–49) was translated by Wace into French verse (1155). This was probably familiar to Robert de Boron, who compiled a Merlin romance c1200. Robert de Boron's poem was translated into

ḏ, d or j; ṣ, s or sh; ṭ, t or ch; ẓ, z or zh; *o*, F. cloche; ü, F. menu; čh, Sc. loch; ṅ, F. bonbon.

Italian in 1379, into Spanish in 1498, and into German in 1478. An English prose version of the Merlin romance appeared as *Arthour and Merlin* c1300. Two other English versions appeared in the 15th century.

Merlin and Vivien (viv′i.ẹn). A long poem (1859) by Alfred Tennyson, included in *The Idylls of the King*. It tells the story of the wicked Vivien, daughter of King Mark, who goes to Arthur's court to seek revenge for her father's death at Arthur's hand. She wins the favor of Merlin and lures from him a secret charm that enables her to lock him up, forthwith and forever, in an oak tree.

Mermaid Club. A club said to have been established (1603) by Sir Walter Raleigh. It met at the Mermaid Tavern, London.

Mermaid Tavern. In English history, an Elizabethan literary gathering place, at London. Sir Walter Raleigh, Ben Jonson, Francis Beaumont, John Fletcher, John Selden, and probably William Shakespeare were among the notable figures who frequented it.

Merope (mer′ọ.pē). In Greek mythology, one of the Pleiades. In some versions of the myth, Merope became the dim one of the seven stars because she married a mortal.

Merope. A tragedy (1858) by Matthew Arnold.

Merovingians (mer.ọ.vin′ji.ạnz). A dynasty (486–751) of Frankish kings. The name was derived, according to tradition, from Merowig or Merwig (Latinized, Merovaeus), a king of the Salian Franks who flourished in the early 5th century. His grandson Clovis made himself sole ruler of the Franks after defeating the Roman governor of Gaul, Syagrius, in 486. Clovis, who became a Christian in 496, died in 511, and his kingdom was divided among his four sons, one of whom, Clotaire I, reunited the several parts in 558. Further divisions took place, however, and subsequent reunions; at different times the kingdoms of Austrasia, Neustria, Burgundy, Paris, and Aquitaine were separate or united in various combinations, and violent family feuds prevailed.

Merrick (mer′ik), **James.** b. at Reading, England, 1720; d. there, 1769. An English poet.

Merrick, Leonard. [Original surname, **Miller.**] b. at London, Feb. 21, 1864; d. there, Aug. 7, 1939. An English actor, novelist, dramatist, and short-story writer. He worked at diamond mining in South Africa, as a court clerk, and in the office of a Kimberley lawyer before returning to London. He became an actor, using the name Merrick, which later became his legal name. Author of *Violet Moses* (1891), *The Man Who Was Good* (1892), *This Stage of Fools* (1896), *Cynthia* (1897), *One Man's View* (1897), *The Actor-Manager* (1898), *The Worldlings* (1900), *Conrad in Quest of His Youth* (1903), *The Quaint Companions* (1903), *The House of Lynch* (1907), *Lynch's Daughter* (1908), *The Position of Peggy Harper* (1911), *While Paris Laughed* (1918), *A Chair on the Boulevard* (1921), and *The Little Dog Laughed* (1930), novels; *Whispers About Women* (1906) and *The Man Who Understood Women* (1908), short-story collections; *When the Lamps Are Lighted, The Free Pardon, My*

Innocent Boy, The Elixir of Youth, and *A Woman in the Case,* plays.

Merrilies (mer′i.lẹz), **Meg.** In Sir Walter Scott's novel *Guy Mannering,* a weird and masculine gypsy woman.

Merriman (mer′i.mạn), **Henry Seton.** Pseudonym of **Scott, Hugh Stowell.**

Merry, Merry Cuckoo, The. See under **Welsh Honeymoon, The.**

Merry (mer′i), **Robert.** [Pseudonym, **Della Crusca.**] b. at London, in April, 1755; d. at Baltimore, Dec. 14, 1798. An English poet and dilettante. He became a member of the English Della Cruscan group at Florence (indeed, his pseudonym gave its name to this school of poetry). His affected style is exhibited in the correspondence with "Anna Matilda" (Hannah Cowley), which continued in the *World* till 1789.

Merry Conceited Humours of Bottom the Weaver, The. See **Bottom the Weaver, The Merry Conceited Humours of.**

Merry Conceited Jests of George Peele, The. A collection of jokes by George Peele, published (1607) after his death.

Merry Devil of Edmonton (ed′mọn.tọn), **The.** A comedy acted (c1603) by the King's Men, formerly the Lord Chamberlain's Men, at the Globe theater, London. A prose tract, *The Life and Death of the Merry Devil of Edmonton,* was entered on the Stationers' Register in 1608 by "T.B." (sometimes thought to be Antony Brewer). The popularity of the comedy probably suggested this tract, which does not cover quite the same ground. The play has been ascribed without reason to Shakespeare, to Thomas Heywood, and to Michael Drayton, but the authorship has not been established.

Merrygreek (mer′i.grēk). See **Merygreek.**

Merry Pecksniff (mer′i pek′snif). See under **Pecksniff.**

Merrythought (mer′i.thôt), **Master.** The carefree, bibulous father of Jasper in Francis Beaumont's *Knight of the Burning Pestle.*

Merry Wives of Windsor (win′zọr), **The.** A comedy by Shakespeare, produced c1600. It was first printed as we know it in the folio of 1623 from an authoritative manuscript. In 1602 an imperfect and unauthorized version in quarto was printed (reprinted in 1619). This version seems to have been based on an actor's report (probably by one who played the Host) and has passages from other works by Shakespeare (*Henry IV* and *Hamlet*). For the plot Shakespeare was probably but little indebted to other writers. *The Two Lovers of Pisa* from a story by Straparola, and a story from *Il Pecorone* of Fiorentino, which suggests the hiding of Falstaff in the soiled linen, may possibly have suggested some of the incidents. References to "garmombles" in Act IV, Scene 5, and to the Garter in Act V, Scene 5 stem from a visit by the German Count of Mömpelgart to England in 1592, and his election to the Order of the Garter in 1597. An opera, *Die lustigen Weiber von Windsor,* by Otto Nicolai, words from Shakespeare by Mosenthal, was produced at Berlin in 1849. John Dennis, an English critic of the early 18th century, maintained that this comedy was written at the request of Queen Elizabeth, who wanted to see Falstaff in love.

The Story. Sir John Falstaff decides to pay court to Mistress Page and Mistress Ford, the merry wives of Windsor, hoping thereby to obtain some money (the two women are known to have charge of their husbands' purse strings). He sends identical notes to them and they, comparing them, decide to make a fool of the corpulent knight by appearing to encourage him. Meanwhile, Nym and Pistol, the cast-off cronies of Falstaff, inform the husbands of Falstaff's intentions (at this stage Ford himself is not confident of his wife's fidelity, and, in disguise, retains Falstaff to plead with her for him, as still another suitor). Mistress Ford, knowing all this, arranges an assignation with Falstaff, during which Ford returns, and Falstaff is hidden in a basket of dirty laundry and dumped in a muddy stream. At the second assignation, Ford again appears, and Falstaff tries to flee disguised as a woman ("the fat woman of Brentford"), but is beaten by Ford as a witch. Meanwhile, Anne Page, daughter of Mistress Page, has been courted by Slender, who is favored by Page, by Dr. Caius, who is favored by Mistress Page, and by Fenton, whom Anne loves. Mistress Quickly, Dr. Caius's servant, bears messages from all of them to her and encourages them all impartially. In the last act, everyone gathers in Windsor Forest: Falstaff to meet the wives, who leave him to be tormented by mock fairies; Slender to elope with Anne who, as Page tells him, is to be dressed in white; Caius also to elope with her, but thinking her to be dressed in green; and Fenton, who succeeds in carrying her off. Slender and Caius discover that they have eloped with boys disguised as fairies.

Merton College (mẽr′tọn). One of the colleges of Oxford University. It was founded in 1264 by Walter de Merton, bishop of Rochester, at Malden, Surrey, and was transferred to Oxford in 1274. It is the college of Bodley, remembered in the name of a great library, Anthony à Wood, of the *Athenae Oxonienses*, Mandell Creighton, ecclesiastical historian and biographer of Wolsey and Elizabeth, Steele, who left before taking a degree, and Lord Randolph Churchill, father of the 20th-century prime minister.

Merygreek (mer′i.grēk), **Matthew.** [Also: **Merigreek, Merrygreek.**] In Nicholas Udall's play *Ralph Roister Doister*, a parasite and mischievous boon companion of Ralph. He adroitly gets his own way by flattery and abuse.

Mesmer (mes′mẽr; Anglicized, also, mez′mẽr), **Friedrich** (or **Franz**) **Anton.** b. near Konstanz, Baden, Germany, May 23, 1733; d. at Meersburg, Baden, March 5, 1815. A German physician, originator of the theory of mesmerism or animal magnetism. He studied divinity at Dillingen and Ingolstadt, but afterward studied medicine at Vienna, where he took his degree in 1766. He began (c1771) an investigation into the supposed curative powers of the magnet, which led him to adopt the theory of animal magnetism. This he made public in 1775 in a pamphlet entitled *Sendschreiben an einen auswärtigen Arzt über die Magnetkur.* In 1778 he settled at Paris, where he created a sensation as a practitioner of hypnotism or mesmerism. In 1785 the French government appointed a commission of eminent physicians and scientists to investigate his system. An adverse report followed, and he fell into disrepute and spent his last years at Meersburg.

Mesopotamia (mes″ọ.pọ.tã′mi.ạ). [From Greek, meaning *"Between Rivers"*; Hebrew, **Aram Naharaïm.**] A region and former country between the Euphrates and Tigris. It is usually divided into Upper Mesopotamia (ancient Chaldea) and Babylonia. It is a great lowland plain, and was formerly very extensively irrigated and cultivated; in recent decades there has been a considerable extension of the irrigated area. It was invaded and conquered several times by the Egyptians and has belonged at different times to the Median, Persian, Macedonian, Syrian, Parthian, Roman, New Persian, Saracenic, Mongol, and Turkish empires. It became a Turkish province, with Baghdad as capital, and after World War I became part of the kingdom of Iraq.

Messala (mẹ.sã′lạ). In Shakespeare's *Julius Caesar*, a friend of Brutus and Cassius.

Messalina or **Messallina** (mes.ạ.lī′nạ), **Valeria.** Executed 48 A.D. A Roman empress. She became the third wife of Claudius, who afterward ascended the imperial throne. She was a woman of infamous vices, and during a temporary absence of her husband publicly married her favorite, Gaius Silius. Her partner in influence over Claudius, the freedman Narcissus, informed the emperor, and she was put to death by order of Claudius. She was the mother of Claudius Tiberius Germanicus and of Octavia, Nero's wife, by Claudius.

Messer Marco Polo (mes′ẽr mär′kō pō′lō). A romance by Brian O. Donn-Byrne, published in 1921.

Messiah (mẹ.sī′ạ). An oratorio by George Frederick Handel, composed in 1741 (first produced at Dublin in 1742). The words are by Charles Jennens from the Scriptures. Mozart composed additional accompaniments to it in 1789. Few other musical compositions have created such lasting and deep enthusiasm.

Messiah, The. A sacred pastoral by Alexander Pope, published in *The Spectator*, May 14, 1712, containing the words of the prophet Isaiah concerning the coming of the Messiah.

Meston (mes′tọn), **William.** b. in Aberdeenshire, Scotland, c1688; d. at Aberdeen, Scotland, 1745. A Scottish burlesque poet. His poems are mostly imitations of Butler's *Hudibras.* Among them are *The Knight of the Kirk* (1723), *Mob contra Mob* (1731), and *Old Mother Grim's Tales* (1737).

Metalogicon (met.ạ.loj′i.kon). A prose work in Latin on logic by John of Salisbury, finished in 1159.

Metamorphoses (met.ạ.môr′fọ.sēz). A poetical work by Ovid, based on the principal classical legends, much used by English poets as a source in the 16th and 17th centuries.

metaphor (met′ạ.fọr, -fôr). A figure of speech by which, from some supposed resemblance or analogy, a name, an attribute, or an action belonging to or characteristic of one object is assigned to another to which it is not literally applicable; the figurative transfer of a descriptive or affirmative word or phrase from one thing to another; implied comparison by transference of terms, as "the ship spread its *wings* to the breeze"; "Judah is a *lion's whelp*." (Gen. xlix.9.) If Jacob had said "is *like or resembles* a lion's whelp," the expression would have been a simile instead of a metaphor. A simple metaphor is contained in a single word or phrase, like those in italics above; a continued metaphor is one in which the figurative description or characterization is maintained throughout a variety of phrases or applications.

> What els is your Metaphor but an inuersion of sence by transport; your allegorie by a duplicitie of meaning or dissimulation vnder couert and darke intendments?
>
> (Puttenham, Arte of English Poesie.)

> Whatever here seems beauteous, seem'd to be
> But a faint Metaphor of Thee.
> (Cowley, The Mistress, Not Fair.)

metaphysical poetry. A type of English poetry that flourished in the 17th century, partly influenced by the "New Science." Its principal adherents included John Donne, Abraham Cowley, George Herbert, Henry Vaughan, Richard Crashaw, and John Cleveland. Metaphysical poetry was concerned especially with religious themes, and was characterized by an involved method of expression known as the conceit. Its most noticeable qualities are an obscurity of idea and an extravagance and harshness of expression. The term "metaphysical poets" was originally a term of derision, used first by Drummond of Hawthornden and Dryden, and later by Samuel Johnson in his condemnation of them for what seemed to him to be a gratuitous display of excessive learning. However, the 20th century has seen a great revival of interest in these poets, especially under the critical leadership of T. S. Eliot, I. A. Richards, and H. J. C. Grierson.

Metastasio (mä.tä.stä′zyō). [Original name, **Pietro Antonio Domenico Bonaventura Trapassi.**] b. at Rome, Jan. 3, 1698; d. at Vienna, April 12, 1782. An Italian poet, court poet at Vienna (1730–82). He was the author of numerous lyric dramas (various composers supplying the music for each): *Didone abbandonata* (1724), *Catone in Utica, Ezio, Semiramide, Alessandro nell' Indie, Artaserse, Demetrio, Adriano in Siria, Olimpiade, Demofoonte, La Clemenza di Tito* (1734), *Achille in Sciro, Antigone, Il Trionfo di Clelia, Partenope,* and others. He also wrote poems for cantatas, oratorios, and others. Burney wrote his memoirs (1796).

Metellus Cimber (mẹ.tel′us sim′bẻr). See **Cimber, Metellus.**

Metham (mē′thạm), **John.** See under **Amoryus and Cleopes.**

Methuen (meth′ụ.ẹn), Sir **Algernon Methuen Marshall.** [Original surname, **Stedman.**] b. at London, Feb. 23, 1856; d. at Haslemere, Surrey, England, Sept. 20, 1924. An English publisher. For some years (1880 *et seq.*) a teacher, he engaged also (after 1889) in publishing; in 1895 he forsook teaching completely. His authors included Rudyard Kipling, Hilaire Belloc, J. B. Bury, G. K. Chesterton, Joseph Conrad, Anthony Hope Hawkins ("Anthony

Hope"), E. V. Lucas, John Masefield, Sir Charles Oman, Sir Gilbert Parker, R. L. Stevenson, and Oscar Wilde. Methuen entered the publishing field at first in order better to market his own textbooks (in elementary Greek, Latin, and French). He compiled *An Anthology of English Verse* (1921) and *Shakespeare to Hardy* (1923).

Methuselah (mẹ.thū′zẹ.lạ). In the Bible, according to the account in Genesis, the son of Enoch. He is said to have died at the age of 969 years, the oldest man mentioned in the Bible. Gen. v. 27.

Metis (mē′tis). In Greek mythology, the daughter of Oceanus and Tethys and first wife of Zeus: a personification of prudence.

metonymy (me.ton′i.mi). In rhetoric, a change of name; a trope or figure of speech that consists in substituting the name of one thing for that of another to which the former bears a known and close relation. It is a method of increasing the force or comprehensiveness of expression by the employment of figurative names that call up conceptions or associations of ideas not suggested by the literal ones, as *Heaven* for God, the *Sublime Porte* for the old Turkish government, *head and heart* for intellect and affection, *the town* for its inhabitants, the *bottle* for strong drink, etc.

> These and such other speaches, where ye take the name of the Author for the thing it selfe, or the thing conteining for that which is contained, in many other cases do as it were wrong name the person or the thing. So neuerthelesse as it may be vnderstood, it is by the figure metonymia, or misnamer.   (Puttenham, Arte of English Poesie.)

Meung or **Meun** (mėṅ), **Jean de.** See **Jean de Meung.**

Mew (mū), **Charlotte Mary.** b. 1869; d. 1928. An English poet, befriended by Thomas Hardy, Walter De la Mare, and John Masefield (who procured a pension of 70 pounds per year for her). Her writings include *The Farmer's Bride* (1916, published in the U. S. as *Saturday Market* in 1921, with the addition of 11 poems) and *Rambling Sailor* (published posthumously in 1929).

Meyerbeer (mī′ẻr.bār; Anglicized, mī′ẻr.bir), **Giacomo.** [Original name, **Jakob Liebmann Beer.**] b. at Berlin, Sept. 5, 1791; d. at Paris, May 2, 1864. A German composer of opera. He lived chiefly at Paris after 1826. He was a pupil of Lauska, who was a pupil of Clementi, and the latter also gave him lessons. When only 7 years old he played Mozart's D minor concerto in public. He early obtained fame as a pianist, but his compositions were not successful till he went in 1815 to Italy to study vocal composition. There he began to produce operas in the style then recently introduced by Rossini; and *Il Crociato in Egitto*, produced at Venice in 1824, was completely successful, while three or four other operas were well received. From 1831 till 1849 he produced operas in a new style, the result of a study of French art. In 1849 he turned his attention to opéra comique. Among his operas are *Robert le Diable* (1831), *Les Huguenots* (1836), *Ein Feldlager in Schlesien* (1840), overture and entr'actes to *Struensee* (1846), *Le Prophète* (1849), *L'Étoile du Nord* (1854), *Le Pardon de Ploërmel* (in Italian, *Dinorah*, 1859), and *L'Afri-*

caine (1865). Among his other compositions are a number of cantatas and songs, and several *Fackeltänze* (torch dances), marches, and overtures, besides pianoforte music, some of which has never been published.

Meyerstein (mī'ĕr.stīn), **Edward Harry William.** b. at Hampstead, London, in August, 1889; d. at London, Sept. 12, 1952. An English writer. Author of the poetry collections *The Door* (1911), *Selected Poems* (1935), *Odes* (1936), *Sonnets* (1939), *Eclogues* (1940), *The Visionary* (1941), *In Time of War* (1942), *Division* (1946), and a translation of *The Elegies of Propertius* (1935). His novels include *Terence Duke* (1935), *Seraphine* (1936), and *Joshua Slade* (1938). His plays are *Heddon* (1921), and *The Monument* (1923). He was the author also of the short-story collections *The Pageant* (1934) and *Four People* (1939).

Meynell (men'ĕl), **Alice Christiana.** [Maiden name, **Thompson.**] b. at London, 1847; d. there, Nov. 27, 1922. An English poet and essayist; wife of Wilfrid Meynell. Her works include *Preludes* (1875; later published as *Poems*, 1893), *The Rhythm of Life, and Other Essays* (1893), *The Colour of Life, and Other Essays on Things Seen and Heard* (1896), *London Impressions* (1898), *The Spirit of Place, and Other Essays* (1898), *John Ruskin* (1900), *Later Poems* (1901), *The Children of the Old Masters* (1903), *A Seventeenth Century Anthology* (1904), *Ceres' Runaway* (1910), and *Hearts of Controversy* (1917).

Meynell, Francis. b. May 12, 1891—. An English typographer and book designer; son of Wilfrid and Alice Meynell. He founded (1923) the Nonesuch Press. Author of *The Typography of Newspaper Advertisements* (1929) and *English Printed Books* (1946).

Meynell, Viola. An English poet and novelist; daughter of Wilfrid and Alice Meynell. Author of *The Frozen Ocean and Other Poems* (1931) and *Alice Meynell, a Memoir* (1929). Her novels include *Second Marriage* (1918) and *Kissing the Rod* (1937).

Meynell, Wilfrid. b. in Yorkshire, England, 1852; d. at Pulborough, Sussex, England, Oct. 20, 1948. An English journalist, biographer, and essayist; husband (married 1877) of Alice Christiana Meynell. He collaborated with his wife on the publication of the monthly reviews *Pen* and *Merry England* and the Roman Catholic *Weekly Register*, and was the first to publish work by Francis Thompson. He edited the works of Thompson, and wrote biographies of Disraeli (1903) and Johnson (1913). Author of *Verses and Reverses, Rhymes with Reason,* and other collections of verse.

Meyrick (mī'rik), **Hans.** One of the principal male characters in George Eliot's novel *Daniel Deronda.*

Micah Balwhidder (mī'ka̧ bal.hwid'ėr). See **Balwhidder, Micah.**

Micah Clark (klärk). A novel by Arthur Conan Doyle, published in 1888.

Micawber (mi.kô'bėr), **Wilkins.** One of the principal characters in Dickens's *David Copperfield.* He is remarkable for his rapid alternations of depression and elevation of spirits, his "temporary embarrassments of pecuniary nature," and his constant persuasion that "something will turn up." His wife, as far as the elasticity of her spirits

goes, is quite his equal. Her devotion to "the parent of her children and the father of her twins" induces her frequent well-known exclamation, "I never will desert Mr. Micawber!" The couple appear to have been suggested, more or less, by Dickens's father and mother.

Michael (mī'kȩl). One of the seven archangels of Christian legend; one of the four of Mohammedan legend. He is regarded as the leader of the whole host of angels, and, owing to miraculous appearances recorded in church legends, is considered to be the representative of the church triumphant. His feast occurs on Sept. 29 in the Roman Catholic and the Anglican churches. He is mentioned five times in the Bible, always as fighting; John mentions him as fighting at the head of the angels against the dragon and his host.

Michael. In Shakespeare's *2 Henry VI*, a follower of Jack Cade.

Michael. A long poem (1800) by William Wordsworth, in the form of a pastoral narrative describing the hardships of an honest herdsman.

Michael. Entries on literary characters having this prename will be found also under the surnames Cassio, Flaherty, Henchard, O'Dowd, Perez, and Williams.

Michael, Sir. In Shakespeare's *1 Henry IV*, a priest or knight who is in the service of the Archbishop of York and is sent by him with letters to the rebels (IV.iv).

Michael and His Lost Angel. A play (1896) by Henry Arthur Jones. It was noteworthy at the time it appeared in that it treated sex relations outside of marriage with some degree of frankness, even though this is compromised by the ending (as Shaw noted, "Surely not so much an ending as a sopping up of the remains"). It tells the story of Michael Feversham, who has forced a girl in his congregation to confess to an illicit love affair, but soon finds himself involved with the charming Audrie Lesden, and also finds that he does not regard himself as a sinner. By some logic which is far from clear, however, he becomes repentant, publicly confesses his sin, leaves his church, and doesn't see Audrie until she is dying, at which point she again stresses her belief in the righteousness of their position on the grounds that God will pardon them since he is a forgiving God.

Michael Angelo Titmarsh (mī'kȩl an'jȩ.lō tit'märsh). See **Titmarsh, Michael Angelo.**

Michaelmas (mik'ȩl.ma̧s). A Roman Catholic and Anglican festival, which probably originated as a religious commemoration of the founding of a Roman basilica in honor of Saint Michael; later a more secular day on which, in England, quarterly rents were paid, at which time a goose was also usually given for the lord's dinner. It falls on Sept. 29. In the Eastern Church it falls on Nov. 8.

Michaelmas Terme. A play by Thomas Middleton, produced and printed in 1607. It is a lively and effective comedy of city intrigue.

Michal (mī'ka̧l). In Dryden's *Absalom and Achitophel,* a character representing the historical Catherine of Braganza, wife of Charles II of England. She was one of the many innocent people accused by Titus Oates of plotting against the life of the king.

Michelangelo (mī.kĕl.an'je.lō; Italian, mē.kel.än'-je.lō). [Full name, **Michelangelo Buonarroti** (bwô-när.rôt'tē).] b. at Caprese, Italy, March 6, 1475; d. at Rome, Feb. 18, 1564. An Italian sculptor, painter, architect, and poet. He came of an ancient but poor Florentine family. He was apprenticed to the painter Ghirlandajo April 1, 1488, and with other boys from the atelier began soon after to study the classical marble sculpture collected by Lorenzo de' Medici in the garden of San Marco. Lorenzo discovered him there, and in 1489 took him into his palace, where he had every opportunity for improvement and study. The Centaur relief in the Casa Buonarroti was made at this time, at the suggestion of Angelo Poliziano. In 1491 he came under the influence of Savonarola, whom he always held in great reverence. In 1492 Lorenzo died, and Michelangelo's intimate relations with the Medici family terminated. In 1493 he made a large wooden crucifix for the prior of San Spirito, and with the assistance of the prior began the profound study of anatomy in which he delighted. Before the expulsion of the Medici he fled to Bologna, where he was soon engaged upon the Arca di San Domenico begun by Niccolo Pisano in 1265, to which he added the well-known kneeling angel of Bologna. He was probably much influenced by the reliefs of Della Quercia around the door of San Petronio; two of these he afterward imitated in the Sistine Chapel. In 1495 he returned to Florence, when he is supposed to have made the *San Giovannino* in the Berlin Museum. From 1496 to 1501 he lived at Rome. To this period are attributed the *Bacchus* of the Bargello and the *Cupid* of the South Kensington Museum. The most important work of this time is the *Pietà di San Pietro* (1498). In 1501 he returned to Florence, and on September 13 began the great *David* of the Signoria, made from a block of marble abandoned by Agostino di Duccio, which was placed in position May 18, 1504. The two roundels of the *Madonna and Child* in Burlington House and the Bargello were probably made then, and also the picture of the *Holy Family* in the Uffizi. In 1503 Piero Soderini, gonfaloniere, projected two frescoes for the Sala Grande of the Palazzo Vecchio. The commission for one was given to Leonardo da Vinci, that for the other to Michelangelo in 1504. For it he prepared the great cartoon of the Battle of Cascina, an incident in the war with Pisa when, on July 28, 1364, a band of 400 Florentines were attacked while bathing by Sir John Hawkwood's English troopers. This cartoon contained 288 square feet of surface and was crowded with nude figures in every position. It had, probably, more influence upon the art of the Renaissance than any other single work. To about this time may be attributed the beginning of his poetic creations, of the multitude of which undoubtedly written a few only have come down to us. In November, 1505, he was called to Rome by Pope Julius II to design his mausoleum, the history of which runs through the entire life of the master. Repeated designs and repeated attempts to carry them out were made, only to be frustrated by the successors of the great Pope. The matter finally ended in the reign of Pope Paul III by the placing

in San Pietro in Vincoli of the statue of Moses surrounded by mediocre works finished by Raffaello da Montelupo and others. The *Two Captives* of the Louvre are part of the work as originally designed. In the spring of 1506 he assisted in the discovery of the *Laocoön* in the palace of Titus. His favorite piece of ancient sculpture was the *Belvedere Torso,* supposed to be a copy of the *Hercules Epitrapezius* of Lysippus. In April, 1506, probably as a result of the intrigues of Bramante, he was forced to abandon Rome for Florence. In the autumn he joined the Pope at Bologna, and made (1506–07) the bronze statue of Julius which stood over the door of San Petronio and was destroyed in 1511. The ceiling of the Sistine Chapel was begun early in 1508, and finished in October, 1512. Pope Julius II died on Feb. 21, 1513, and was succeeded by Cardinal Giovanni de' Medici, son of the great Lorenzo, as Leo X. Michelangelo was diverted from the tomb of Julius by Leo, and employed from 1517 to 1520 in an abortive attempt to build the façade of San Lorenzo in Florence, and in developing the quarries of Carrara and Seravezza. In 1520 he began, by order of Cardinal Giulio de' Medici, the sacristy of San Lorenzo and the tombs of Giuliano and Lorenzo de' Medici with the famous reclining figures on the sarcophagi, perhaps the most thoroughly characteristic of all his works. Pope Leo X was succeeded by Adrian VI in 1521, and he in turn by Giulio de' Medici as Clement VII in 1523. On April 6, 1529, Michelangelo was appointed "governor and procurator-general over the construction and fortification of the city walls" of Florence. On Sept. 21, 1529, occurred his unexplained flight to Venice. He returned November 20 of the same year, and was engaged in the defense of the city until its capitulation, Aug. 12, 1530. Before the end of the year 1534 he left Florence, never to return. The statues of the sacristy, including the *Madonna and Child,* were arranged after his departure. Alessandro Farnese succeeded Clement VII as Pope Paul III, in October, 1534. The *Last Judgment* was begun about Sept. 1, 1535, and finished before Christmas, 1541. Michelangelo's friendship for Vittoria Colonna began c1538. The frescoes of the Pauline Chapel were painted between 1542 and 1549. They represent the conversion of Saint Paul and the martyrdom of Saint Peter. He succeeded Antonio da Sangallo in 1546 in the offices which he held, and became architect of Saint Peter's on Jan. 1, 1547. From this time until his death he worked on the church without compensation. The dome alone was completed with any regard to his plans.

Michelet (mēsh.le), **Jules.** b. at Paris, Aug. 21, 1798; d. at Hyères, France, Feb. 9, 1874. A French historian. He began his literary studies under the guidance of an old bookseller, and in his spare moments helped his father, a printer by trade, in setting type. He went through the Collège Charlemagne, and entered on a higher course of study. In 1821 he graduated with the highest university honors, and was called at once to the chair of history in the Collège Rollin (1821–26). His first works were *Tableau chronologique de l'histoire moderne* (1825), *Tableaux synchroniques de l'histoire moderne* (1826), and *Précis de l'histoire moderne* (1827). He was appointed lecturer at the École Normale in

1827, and published his *Introduction à l'histoire universelle* (1831), *Origines du droit français* (1837), and *Histoire romaine: république* (1839). Michelet began his famous courses of anticlerical, and in particular anti-Jesuit, lectures at the Collège de France in 1838, and wrote in that connection *Des Jésuites* (1843), *Du prêtre, de la femme et de la famille* (1844), and *Du peuple* (1845). The clergy succeeded at last in silencing him, and he retired to a life of study. The publication of his masterpiece, the *Histoire de France* in 16 volumes (1833–67), was interrupted by his *Histoire de la révolution française* (1847–53), *Le Procès des templiers* (1851), and *Légendes démocratiques du Nord* (1854). He wrote, further, *Les Femmes de la révolution* (1854), *L'Oiseau* (1856), *L'Insecte* (1858), *L'Amour* (1859), *La Femme* (1860), *La Mer* (1861), and *La Bible de l'humanité* (1864). Michelet made a last return to history in attempting to bring his great work down to date. He completed but a few volumes of his *Histoire du XIXᵉ siècle* (1872–73).

miching malicho (mich'ing mal'i.kō). A phrase occurring in Shakespeare's *Hamlet* (III.ii) and glossed as "skulking mischief" by Tucker Brooke. The quarto has "munching Mallico." *Miching* is a participle form of the Middle English verb *miche*, meaning "to skulk." The last word may be from the Spanish *malhecho*, i.e., "misdeed." Eric Partridge has suggested that it was a Gypsy word.

Mickle (mik'l), **William Julius.** b. at Langholm, Dumfriesshire, Scotland, Sept. 28, 1735; d. at Forest Hill, London, Oct. 28, 1788. A Scottish poet. He translated the *Lusiad* (1775) and is the reputed author of the song *There's nae luck aboot the hoose.* Among his other works are a Spenserian poem, *The Concubine* (or *Syr Martyn*, 1765), and *Cumnor Hall* (1784), which Sir Walter Scott used as a basis in writing *Kenilworth.*

Micromégas (mē.kro.mā.gàs). A philosophical romance by Voltaire, published in 1752. It was an imitation in French of Jonathan Swift's *Gulliver's Travels.*

Midas (mī'das). In Greek legend, a king of Phrygia, son of Gordius and Cybele. The god Dionysus, from gratitude for kindness shown to his teacher Silenus by Midas, promised to grant whatever the latter might ask. Midas, accordingly, requested that whatever he touched might turn to gold; but when he found that even his food was not excepted, and that he was likely to starve, he prayed that the gift might be taken away, and on bathing in the Pactolus was restored to his natural condition. The sands of the river, however, were ever after full of gold.

Midas. A comedy (c1590) by John Lyly, in which Midas presumably represents Philip II of Spain.

Mid-Channel. A tragedy (1909) by Arthur Wing Pinero about a woman whose marriage fails after she and her husband decide not to have any children.

Middle Ages. A period of about a thousand years, between the close of what is technically considered ancient history and the first definite movements in Europe of the distinctively modern spirit of freedom and enterprise, the Renaissance. Its beginning is synchronous with that of the so-called dark ages,

and it is variously reckoned as extending to the fall of Constantinople (1453), the invention of printing, the Renaissance, or the discovery of America, in the 15th century, or to the Reformation, in the early part of the 16th. The literature of the Middle Ages has certain general characteristics. In the first place, little value was placed on anything that did not serve a moral purpose; most literature was designed to teach. The importance of religion in everyday life and the influence of the church in the Middle Ages were so great that a large part of medieval literature consists of religious writings. Several factors conspired to make medieval literature impersonal: works reproduced by hand often varied from copy to copy because of editing or errors by the scribes; the interest of the people lay more in the work than in the writer; and admiration for authority gave greater weight to works based on authoritative sources than to works claiming to be original. Because the audience for medieval literature was frequently a listening rather than a reading audience, poetry played an especially important role. Middle English literature displayed all of these features and was in addition greatly influenced by the fact that authors were likely to be trilingual after the Norman Conquest, writing in Latin, English, and French.

Middle English. See under **English.**

Middlemarch (mid'l.märch). A novel by George Eliot, published in 1871 in *Blackwood's Magazine,* and in book form in 1872.

Middlesex (mid'l.seks), 1st Earl of. A title of **Sackville, Charles.**

Middleton (mid'l.ton), **Clara.** The heroine of George Meredith's novel *The Egoist.* The book describes her method of escaping from the promise she made to marry Sir Willoughby Patterne, the "egoist."

Middleton, Conyers. b. in Yorkshire, England, Dec. 27, 1683; d. July 28, 1750. An English divine. In 1724 he went to Rome, and in 1729 published the *Letter from Rome* upon pagan beliefs and ceremonies in the Roman Catholic Church. In his *Letter to Waterland* he ridiculed some parts of the Book of Genesis, and showed a skeptical tendency in an *Introductory Discourse* (1747). Of his numerous works the best-known is his *Life of Cicero.*

Middleton, Dr. The father of the heroine in George Meredith's novel *The Egoist.*

Middleton, Sir Hugh. See **Myddleton, Sir Hugh.**

Middleton, Thomas. b. probably at London, 1580; d. at Newington Butts, London, about July, 1627. An English dramatist. He studied at Oxford, entered Gray's Inn c1593, became a playwright c1599, and wrote in conjunction with William Rowley, Anthony Munday, Michael Drayton, John Webster, and others. He arranged lord mayor's shows and court masques, and in 1620 was appointed city chronologer. Among his plays are *The Old Law* with Rowley (printed 1656), *The Mayor of Quinborough* with Rowley (1661), *Blurt, Master Constable* (1602, with Dekker, who probably wrote most of it), *The Phoenix* (1607), *Michaelmas Terme* (1607), *The Family of Love* (licensed 1607), *A Trick to Catch the Old One* (licensed 1607), *Your Five Gallants* (1607), *A Mad World, my Masters* (1608), *The Roaring*

Girl with Dekker (printed 1611), *A Fair Quarrel* with Rowley (1617), *The Changeling* and *The Spanish Gipsy* with Rowley (1623), *More Dissemblers besides Women* (1615), *Women Beware Women* (licensed before 1622, printed 1657), and *A Game at Chess* (1624). The last-named play, an allegory written about the fruitless embassy of Prince Charles (later Charles I) to Spain in an attempt to secure a match with the Spanish infanta, displays an almost virulent anti-Spanish bias; as a result, complaints were officially made and the play was banned from the theaters. However, three editions were printed in the first part of 1625 and the play, though off the stage, continued popular. The date of the following plays is conjectural: *A Chaste Maid in Cheapside* (1611), *No Wit, No Help like a Woman's* (1613), *The Witch* (c1615), *Anything for a Quiet Life*, with Webster (c1621), and *The Widow*, with Ben Jonson and Fletcher (c1616). Middleton also had a small part in writing with Dekker *The Honest Whore* (1st part, 1604). He was the author of the lost plays *Caesar's Fall* (1602), *Randal, Earl of Chester*, and *The Viper and Her Brood* (1606). *The Puritan, or the Widow of Watling Street* (1607), a play sometimes attributed to Shakespeare, may have been written by Middleton. He wrote also about 20 masques, entertainments, and pageants; some miscellaneous verse, including *Microcynicon: Six Snarling Satires* (1599); and various prose pamphlets, including *The Black Book* (1604) and *Father Hubberd's Tale* (1604). Middleton's works were not collected till 1840, when Alexander Dyce's edition appeared.

Middle Years, The. The title of a short story and an autobiographical piece by Henry James, published in 1917.

Midgard (mid′gärd). [Old Norse, **Midhgardhr.**] In Old Norse mythology, the middle earth; this earth, between heaven and hell; the abode of the human race, formed in the midst of Ginnungagap from the body of the giant Ymir, the first created being. Midgard is connected with Asgard, the home of the gods, by the rainbow bridge, Bifrost.

Midgardsorm (mid′gärdz.ôrm). In Old Norse mythology, the great sea-serpent which encircles the earth, offspring of Loki and a giantess. It is slain by Thor.

Midlothian (mid.lō′ᴛʜi.an), **The Heart of.** See **Heart of Midlothian, The.**

Midsummer Night's Dream, A. A comedy by Shakespeare, written in 1595 or 1596, and certainly staged several times within the next four years, although the date of first performance is not known. It is mentioned by Francis Meres in his *Palladis Tamia*, which was issued in 1598, was entered on the Stationers' Register Oct. 8, 1600, and was first published in 1600. It is included in the folio of 1623 with a few added stage directions but no scene markings. The following sources may have been used: for Theseus and Hippolyta, Plutarch's "Life of Theseus" and Chaucer's *Knight's Tale;* for Pyramus and Thisbe and the name Titania, Ovid's *Metamorphoses;* for Robin Goodfellow (Puck) and the ass's head, Scot's *Discovery of Witchcraft* (Stephen Scot made an attack on witchcraft in this work, published in 1584); for Oberon, Robert Greene's *James IV* or the Old

French romance *Huon de Bordeaux* (translated by Berners). However, the fairy legends were well known in Elizabethan England and there is no reason to think Shakespeare needed or used special sources for this background aspect of the play. Though the work is now ranked as one of the best of the comedies, it was not always so highly esteemed (a performance in 1662 merited Pepys's comment: "The most insipid, ridiculous play that ever I saw in my life.").

The Story. To the court of Theseus, Duke of Athens, who is about to marry Hippolyta, come Hermia and her father, Egeus, who insists that she marry Demetrius (who now loves Hermia, but who has earlier avowed love for Hermia's friend Helena, by whom he is still loved). Lysander also loves Hermia, and it is his suit that she favors. Theseus invokes the Athenian law, which gives her four days in which to agree to her father's request; if she persists after that time in her disobedience she must become a nun or be condemned to death. However, she and Lysander arrange to meet that night in a neighboring wood, whence they plan to flee beyond the reach of Athenian law, but she tells her plan to Helena, who tells Demetrius, hoping thus to regain his love. Demetrius follows Hermia and Lysander into the wood, and Helena follows Demetrius. In the wood also, but unbeknownst to them, are fairies who have arrived from India for the wedding of Theseus and Hippolyta. Titania and Oberon, the Queen and King of the fairies, are quarreling about the possession of a changeling boy who has caught Titania's fancy. Oberon, to spite Titania, drops on her eyelids as she sleeps a magic liquid squeezed from a certain flower so that when she awakens she will fall in love with the first creature she sees. This happens to be Bottom, a weaver, one of a group of Athenian artisans who have gone into the wood to rehearse a play in honor of the forthcoming marriage of Theseus and Hippolyta; Puck, Oberon's mischievous servant, has playfully given Bottom the head of an ass. Oberon, having overheard Demetrius berating Helena for following him, seeks to help them out of their difficulty by ordering Puck to anoint Demetrius so that he may fall in love with Helena. But Puck confuses Lysander with Demetrius, and drops the liquid on the eyes of the wrong man; Lysander, upon awakening, sees Helena, and loves her. Seeking to correct the mistake, Oberon himself now anoints Demetrius, who also first sees Helena upon awakening, so that both young men are now in love with Helena, exactly the reverse of the situation at the beginning. Neither Helena nor Hermia has any inkling of what has caused the situation; Hermia upbraids Helena (who, far from wanting the attentions of Lysander, has thought he was making sport of her in offering them). Titania, meanwhile, has been entrapped by the unique (to her) beauty of Bottom's donkey's ears and velvet muzzle; never, in her bewitched eyes, has there been an object of such surpassing beauty. But when Oberon reproaches her for her folly she becomes confused, and yields in the matter of the changeling boy; Oberon thereupon lifts the spell. Puck, by enclosing the human lovers in a dense fog, arranges that Lysander will awaken to love Hermia once more, and Demetrius to love Helena. Theseus and Hippolyta arrive in the wood, discover the couples, and arrange a triple wedding which takes place in the palace. At the ceremony the artisans' play, the "most lamentable comedy" of Pyramus and Thisbe, is presented. After the lovers retire, the fairies dance through the palace, leaving Puck to deliver the Epilogue.

Midsummer Night's Dream, A. A famous overture (1826) by Mendelssohn.

Miggs (migz), **Miss.** In Dickens's *Barnaby Rudge*, a shrewish servant, later a turnkey, who pursues Tappertit with her attentions.

Mikado (mi.kä′dō). In Gilbert and Sullivan's *The Mikado*, the Mikado of Japan. He is remembered for his edict that the "punishment [should] fit the crime."

Mikado, The. A comic opera in two acts by Arthur Sullivan, with a libretto by W. S. Gilbert, produced at London on March 14, 1885.

Milan (mi.lan′, mil′ạn), **Duke of.** In Shakespeare's *Two Gentlemen of Verona*, the father of Silvia.

Milan, Duke of. See also the entries on **Antonio** and **Prospero,** both characters in Shakespeare's *Tempest*.

Milan Decree. A decree issued by Napoleon at Milan, Italy, Dec. 17, 1807, a part of the plan known as the Continental System. It declared the forfeiture of all vessels bound to or from British ports, and of all which paid licenses or duties to Great Britain or had submitted to search by British cruisers.

Mildred (mil′drẹd). The younger daughter of Touchstone in Marston, Chapman, and Jonson's comedy *Eastward Ho!* Touchstone describes her as "of a modest humility and comely soberness" and "of a most hopeful industry." She is snubbed by her proud sister Gertrude because she loves Golding, an up-and-coming young apprentice. When Gertrude is married to the impoverished Sir Petronel Flash, Mildred takes the remains of the wedding feast and goes off quietly to marry Golding. When Gertrude is deceived by her knight and left penniless, Mildred, though not forbearing to remind her of her folly, offers her a place to stay. Mildred was intended to personify the respectable Jacobean tradesman's wife, conceived of typically as helpful to her husband through her thrift and good business sense.

Mildred Rogers (roj′ẽrz). See **Rogers, Mildred.**

Miles (mīlz). Bacon's servant in Robert Greene's play *Friar Bacon and Friar Bungay*.

Milesians (mī.lē′zhạnz). In Old Irish mythology and legend, the fifth and last invaders of Ireland. They are so named because they came to Ireland with the five sons of Mil (Latinized, Milesius), king of Spain. They are regarded as ancestors of the modern Irish. They were at first beaten off by the Tuatha De Danann (the ancient divine race of Ireland), but they finally made a landing and overcame the Tuatha De Danann in two great battles. Three of the five sons of Mil survived: Eremon, who became king of the north of Ireland, Eber, who became king in the south, and Amergin, who was a poet and disdained possessions.

Milesian Tales or **Fables** (mī.lē′zhạn). Short stories of a witty and obscene nature, greatly in vogue among the Greeks and Romans. The name has arisen from a collection of tales by Antonius Diogenes, compiled by Aristides of Miletus; they were translated into Latin by Cornelius Sisenna (119–67 B.C.). These tales are now lost, but the name is still given to stories of a like nature.

Milestones. A drama (1912) by Arnold Bennett and Edward Knoblock.

Mill (mil), **James.** b. at Northwater Bridge, Forfarshire, Scotland, April 6, 1773; d. at Kensington, London, June 23, 1836. An English utilitarian philosopher. He was the son of a shoemaker, and father of John Stuart Mill. He entered Edinburgh University in 1790, and from 1794 to 1798 studied divinity. He was licensed to preach in 1798. He sought literary employment in London in 1802, and in 1806 began the *History of India*, which was finished 10 years later. He also formed a close intimacy with Bentham, whose disciple he became, revising his writings and advancing his principles. The *History of India* appeared in 1817, and became a standard work immediately. In 1819 he entered the India House. His intimacy with Ricardo began in 1811. Other disciples were George Grote, Henry Bickersteth, and John Black. He assisted in establishing the *Westminster Review* in 1824. His *Analysis of the Human Mind* was published in 1829, his *Elements of Political Economy* in 1821.

Mill, John Stuart. b. at London, May 20, 1806; d. at Avignon, France, May 8, 1873. An English philosophical writer, logician, and economist; eldest son of James Mill. He was a precocious child and was put through an extraordinary system of forcing by his father, who took entire charge of his education. He was brought up an agnostic from his infancy and never acquired any religious beliefs. In 1820 he visited France and in 1823 entered the India House as his father's assistant. He became chief examiner in 1856. His first important literary work was the editing of Buchanan's *Treatise upon Evidence* (1825). His *Essays on Unsettled Questions of Political Economy* were written c1830 (published 1844). In 1836 the *London Review*, established in 1835, was amalgamated with the *Westminster Review*, and Mill became practically its superintendent; he was its proprietor from 1837 to 1840. In 1836 he passed through a severe mental crisis, probably as a result of his extraordinary training, and was led to modify the strict utilitarianism of his father's school. His intimacy with Mrs. Taylor (whom he married in 1851) began in 1830. Mill's *Logic*, his first successful work, was published in 1843. His *Political Economy* was published in 1848. His most carefully written work, the *Essay on Liberty*, was published in 1859. He was elected member of Parliament for Westminster in 1865. His book *On the Subjection of Women* was published in 1869; his *Autobiography* appeared in 1873. Among his other publications are *Thoughts on Parliamentary Reform* (1859), *Dissertations and Discussions* (1859–67), *Considerations on Representative Government* (1861), *Utilitarianism* (1863), *Examination of Sir William Hamilton's Philosophy* (1865), *Auguste Comte and Positivism* (1865), *England and Ireland* (1868), *On the Irish Land Question* (1870),

ḍ, d or j; ṣ, s or sh; ṭ, t or ch; ẓ, z or zh; *o*, F. cloche; ü, F. menu; ċh, Sc. loch; ṅ, F. bonbon.

and *Nature, the Utility of Religion, and Theism* (1874).

Millais (mi.lā'), Sir **John Everett.** b. at Southampton, England, June 8, 1829; d. at London, Aug. 13, 1896. An English painter. In 1848, with Holman Hunt, D. G. Rossetti, and others, he founded the association which was afterward known as the Pre-Raphaelite Brotherhood, and began to paint with the precision and attention to detail which characterize that school. He became associate royal academician in 1854, royal academician in 1863, and president of the Royal Academy in 1896. He was created baronet in 1885. In 1883 he was elected to the French Institute. Among his works are *Isabella* (1849), *Christ in the House of his Parents* (1850), *The Huguenot* (1852), *Ophelia* (1852), *The Proscribed Royalist* (1853), *The Order of Release* (1853), *Autumn Leaves* (1856), *Sir Isumbras at the Ford* (1857), *The Black Brunswicker* (1860), *Charlie is my Darling* (1864), *The Minuet* (1866), *Rosalind and Celia* (1868), *The Gambler's Wife* (1869), *The Boyhood of Raleigh* (1870), *Chill October* (1871), *The Northwest Passage* (1874), *Yes or No?* (1875), *Yeoman of the Guard* (1876), *Jersey Lily* (1878), *Bride of Lammermoor* (1878), *Olivia* (1882), *Idyl of 1745* (1884), *Lady Peggy Primrose* (1885), *Dew-drenched Furze* (1890), *Dorothy* (1891), and others. He also designed illustrations for a number of books, including Tennyson's poems and some of Trollope's novels.

Millamant (mil'ạ.mant). The principal female character in William Congreve's comedy *The Way of the World*. She is an incarnation of elegance, indifference, impertinence, and affectation; and, though a brilliant coquette and fine lady, is not without heart. Her acceptance of Mirabell as a husband at the end of the play is considered one of the finest scenes in Restoration comedy.

Miller (mil'ẽr), **Daisy.** The heroine of *Daisy Miller* (1878), a story by Henry James about an American girl abroad whose naïve innocence makes her the victim of scandal.

Miller, Hugh. b. at Cromarty, Scotland, Oct. 10, 1802; committed suicide near Edinburgh, Dec. 23, 1856. A Scottish geologist, editor from 1840 of *The Witness*, an Edinburgh newspaper devoted to the church controversy in Scotland. In his youth he worked as a stonemason. In 1829 he published *Poems, Written in the Leisure Hours of a Journeyman Mason*. In 1834 he became an accountant in the Commercial Bank of Cromarty. His *Scenes and Legends of the North of Scotland*, with a chapter on geology, appeared in 1835. He corresponded with Murchison and Agassiz, and published *The Old Red Sandstone* (1841), *The Footprints of the Creator, or the Asterolepis of Stromness* (1847), *My Schools and Schoolmasters* (1852), and others. *The Testimony of the Rocks*, explaining the six days of creation as six periods, was published in 1857.

Miller, Joe. [Actual name, **Joseph** or **Josias Miller.**] b. 1684; d. at London, 1738. An English actor. The collection of jests known as *Joe Miller's Jests* appeared originally in 1739 as *Joe Miller's Jest Book, or the Wit's Vade Mecum*. It was made by John Mottley and received its name unwarrantably from Joseph Miller, who is popularly said never to have made a joke in his life, and could neither read

nor write. It has been many times enlarged and reprinted. Any stale jest is now known as a "Joe Miller" from the fact that it is supposed to have emanated at some time from this source.

Miller, Thomas. [Called "the Basketmaker."] b. at Gainsborough, England, 1807; d. at London, Oct. 24, 1874. An English poet, novelist, and writer on rural life.

Miller, William. [Called the **"Laureate of the Nursery."**] b. at Bridgegate, Glasgow, in August, 1810; d. there, Aug. 20, 1872. A Scottish woodworker and poet. He contributed poems and songs (1832–53) to *Whistle Binkie*, but is best known for his nursery lyric "Wee Willie Winkie," which appeared in *Scottish Nursery Songs and Other Poems* (1863), the only collected edition of his works.

Miller of Mansfield (manz'fēld), **The.** An old ballad, included in Percy's *Reliques*, concerning a miller who entertains King Henry II, unwittingly, and as a reward is knighted by the king.

Miller of Trompington (trum'ping.tọn). The name of the miller in The Reeve's Tale, in Chaucer's *Canterbury Tales.*

Miller's Tale, The. One of Chaucer's *Canterbury Tales*. Its source is unknown, but the elements of the story were probably in circulation in a number of naughty tales of the time. The grossest of Chaucer's stories, it tells with vivid ribaldry of young Alison's deception of her carpenter husband John with the young student Nicholas; Alison also cruelly dupes Absolon, an amorous parish clerk, who then revenges himself upon her lover. The tale is told out of turn by Robin the Miller, who breaks in noisily while the Host is asking the Monk to speak next, and will not be silenced. He is an engaging drunk:

> But first I make a protestracioun
> That I am dronke, I knowe it by my soun;
> And therfore, if that I misspeke or seye,
> Wyte it the ale of Southwerk, I yow preye . . .

in contrast with the sour-faced Reeve, who quarrels with him over the story. Chaucer describes Robin in the Prologue as "a stout carl," heavy-set and red-bearded, who plays well on the bagpipe:

> His mouth as greet was as a greet forneys.
> He was a Ianglere and a goliardeys,
> And that was most of sinne and harlotryes.

Millin (mil'in), **Sarah Gertrude.** [Maiden name, **Liebson.**] b. at Kimberley, South Africa, March 19, 1889—. A South African novelist and biographer. Her writing is concerned with the racial and colonial problems in South Africa. Author of *Rhodes: A Life* (1933), *General Smuts* (1936), and the novels *The Dark River* (1920), *Middleclass* (1921), *God's Stepchildren* (1924), *Three Men Die* (1934), *What Hath a Man?* (1938), *The Herr Witch Doctor* (1941), and *King of the Bastards* (1950).

Millionairess, The. A play (1936) by George Bernard Shaw.

Mill on the Floss (flos), **The.** A novel by George Eliot, published in 1860.

Milly Bloom (mil'i blŏm'). See **Bloom, Milly.**

Milly Costigan (kos'ti.gạn). See **Costigan, Emily.**

Milly Swidger (swij'ẽr). See **Swidger, Milly.**

Milman (mil'man), **Henry Hart.** b. at London, 1791; d. near Ascot, England, Sept. 24, 1868. An English clergyman. In 1812 he won the Newdigate prize with an English poem on the *Apollo Belvedere* and in 1821 was elected professor of poetry at Oxford. *Fazio*, a drama composed at Oxford, was published in 1815. *Samor*, an epic, appeared in 1818, the *Fall of Jerusalem* in 1820, and the *Martyr of Antioch* in 1822. In 1835 he published translations from Sanskrit poems. His *History of the Jews*, which appeared in 1830, treated them as an Oriental tribe, with little attention to the miraculous element. In 1835 Sir Robert Peel made him canon of Westminster and rector of Saint Margaret's. In 1840 he published the *History of Christianity under the Empire*. Although shunned by the clergy for his unconventional views, he was advanced to the deanery of Saint Paul's in 1849. In 1838 he edited Gibbon, and in 1855 published the *History of Latin Christianity down to the death of Pope Nicholas V*.

Milne (miln), **A. A.** [Full name, **Alan Alexander Milne.**] b. Jan. 18, 1882; d. in Sussex, England, Jan. 31, 1956. An English novelist, poet, and playwright. He is known especially for his children's books in prose, including *Winnie-the-Pooh* (1926) and *The House at Pooh Corner* (1928), and in verse, such as *When We Were Very Young* (1924) and *Now We are Six* (1927). He was assistant editor (1906–14) of *Punch*. His plays include *Wurzel-Flummery* (1917), *Make-Believe* (1918), *Mr. Pim Passes By* (1919), *The Romantic Age* (1920), *The Truth About Blayds* (1921), *The Dover Road* (1922), *The Great Broxopp* (1923), *Ariadne* (1925), *The Ivory Door* (1927), *Toad of Toad Hall* (1930), *Miss Elizabeth Bennet* (1936), *Sarah Simple* (1937), and *Gentleman Unknown* (1938). Author also of *The Day's Play* (1910), *Once on a Time* (1917), *Mr. Pim* (1921), *The Red House Mystery* (1922), *Two People* (1931), *Four Days' Wonder* (1933), *It's Too Late Now* (1939), and *Chloe Marr* (1946).

Milner (mil'nėr), **Miss.** The principal character in Elizabeth Inchbald's *Simple Story*.

Milnes (milz, milnz), **Richard Monckton.** [Title, 1st Baron **Houghton.**] b. at London, June 19, 1809; d. at Vichy, France, Aug. 11, 1885. An English statesman and poet. He graduated at Cambridge (Trinity College) in 1831, and was an intimate there of Alfred Tennyson, Arthur Henry Hallam, and William Makepeace Thackeray. He became a Conservative member of Parliament for Pontefract in 1837, but joined the Liberal Party during the Corn Law struggle, and assisted in passing the copyright act. In 1863 he was created Baron Houghton. He was noted as a patron of letters; his circle included many brilliant authors whose first recognition came from him. He published several volumes of poems and *The Life and Letters of Keats* (1848).

Milo (mī'lō) or **Milon** (mī'lon). b. at Crotona, Magna Graecia, Italy; fl. in the last part of the 6th century B.C. A Greek athlete, famous for his strength. He was six times victor in wrestling at the Olympic Games and six times at the Pythian, and many stories were told of his extraordinary feats of strength, of which the best-known is his carrying a heifer, four years old, on his shoulders through the stadium at Olympia, then slaying it with his fist and eating the whole of it in a day.

He is said to have been eaten by wolves which attacked him while his hands were caught in a cleft tree which he had endeavored to rend.

Milo. In Maurice Hewlett's historical novel *The Life and Death of Richard Yea-and-Nay* (1900), an abbot, the friend and confessor of Richard Coeur-de-Lion, and the supposed teller of the story.

Milor Beefington (mi.lôr' bē'fing.ton). See **Beefington, Milor.**

Milton (mil'ton). A symbolic and mystical poem by William Blake, published in 1804. Returning to earth from Heaven, John Milton corrects the interpretation given to his works, and enters the soul of Blake, who expounds the Christian doctrine of forgiveness.

Milton, John. b. at London, Dec. 9, 1608; d. there, Nov. 8, 1674. An English poet. His father was John Milton, a scrivener. Educated by private tutors and at St. Paul's School, he entered Christ's College, Cambridge, in 1625 (B.A., 1629; M.A., 1632). The years 1632–38 were devoted to study at his father's country estate at Horton. It was at either Cambridge or Horton that he abandoned his destined career as minister for that of poet. The writing of great poetry, he felt, demanded severe intellectual and moral discipline. His poems up to this date, both Latin and English, gave him mastery of nearly all types of lesser poetry (chief poems: *On the Morning of Christ's Nativity*, *L'Allegro*, *Il Penseroso*, *Comus*, *Lycidas*). In 1638 he traveled in Europe, spending the chief part of his time with people in the literary circles of Italy. It was in Italy also that he met Galileo. He returned (1639) to England because civil war threatened, and now abandoned his poetical ambitions to write prose tracts in the cause of liberty as he saw it. His position was extremely liberal. He attacked the episcopal system (*Of Reformation touching Church Discipline* in 1641, and others); advocated divorce (*The Doctrine and Discipline of Divorce* in 1643, and others), reform in education (*Of Education* in 1644), freedom from censorship (*Areopagitica* in 1644, one of the world's most famous writings on this subject), and the right of the people, under the contract theory of government, to execute a tyrant (*Of the Tenure of Kings and Magistrates* in 1649). This last tract's appearance just after the execution of Charles I brought him into Cromwell's government as Secretary for Foreign Tongues. His chief duty was what is now called propaganda. He wrote *Eikonoklastes* (1649) in English in a vain attempt to discredit the very popular *Eikon Basilike*, purportedly written by Charles I; his Latin tract *Pro Populo Anglicano Defensio* (1651) was a successful rebuttal of a Latin defense of Charles I by Claude de Saumaise (Salmasius), a famous European scholar (two other Latin defenses followed). Writing the *Defensio* hastened his blindness, which became total in 1652. In that same year his first wife died. She was Mary Powell, daughter of an Oxfordshire royalist. Milton had married her in 1642, when she was 17. Differences in age (he was then 34), political sympathies, and, doubtless, temperament made the marriage a failure, and after a month she returned to her parents. This desertion was an important contributing factor in his writing on divorce (and the threat of prose-

ḍ, d or j; ṣ, s or sh; ṭ, t or ch; ẓ, z or zh; o, F. cloche; ü, F. menu; ċh, Sc. loch; ṅ, F. bonbon.

cution arising from the first divorce tract contributed to the writing of *Areopagitica*). However, Mary returned to Milton in 1645 and of the marriage three children (all daughters) survived their father, but he does not seem to have been on happy terms with them. In 1656 he married Catherine Woodcock, who died in 1658. His great sonnet *Methought I saw my late espoused Saint* is evidence that this marriage was completely happy. In 1663 he married (apparently again happily) his third wife, Elizabeth Minshull, who survived him. After 1655 he did little official work. Continuing his struggle to the end, he wrote in 1659 several tracts urging a republican form of government. He had become famous (or, in the eyes of some, infamous) as the chief literary defender of the Commonwealth, and it is not known why he escaped punishment at the Restoration. In spite of his public and private calamities he now turned back to poetry. The theme for *Paradise Lost* had been considered as early as 1640, and he had probably begun composing it by 1658. The poem was completed in 1665 and published in 1667. It derives from the Bible plus the body of Christian and Jewish commentary, from the theologians, from classic epics, and from various Renaissance versions of portions of the theme. It brought him little money but won immediate recognition. In 1671 he published *Paradise Regained* and *Samson Agonistes*, the latter being almost certainly his last poem. Partly responsible for the writing of *Paradise Regained* was the suggestion of Thomas Ellwood: "Thou hast said much of Paradise lost, but what hast thou to say of Paradise found?"

mime (mīm). **1.** An imitator; one skilled in mimicry; a mimic; specifically, a mimic actor; a performer in the ancient farces or burlesques called *mimes*.

> Let him go now and brand another man injuriously with the name of Mime, being himselfe the loosest and most extravagant Mime that hath been heard of; whom no lesse then almost halfe the world could serve for stage roome to play the Mime in. (Milton, *Apology for Smectymnuus*.)

> The strolling mimes carried the last, and probably many of the worst, reminiscences of the Roman acting drama across the period of those great migrations which changed the face of the Western world. (A. W. Ward, *Eng. Dram. Lit.*)

2. A dramatic entertainment among the ancient Greeks of Sicily and southern Italy and the Romans, consisting generally of farcical mimicry of real events and persons. The Greek mimes combined spoken dialogue of somewhat simple and familiar character with action; the Roman consisted chiefly of action, often of a coarse and even indecent character, with little speaking.

> This we know in Laertius, that the Mimes of Sophron were of such reckning with Plato, as to take them nightly to read on and after make them his pillow. Scaliger describes a Mime to be a Poem imitating any action to stirre up laughter. (Milton, *Apology for Smectymnuus*.)

Mimir (mē'mir). [Also, **Mimer**.] In Old Norse mythology, a giant who dwelt by the root of the world-tree Yggdrasil at the well of Mimir (the ocean), the source of all wisdom, from which he drank, and thus knew all things, past, present, and future. Odin, to obtain a drink from the well, gave up one of his eyes in exchange. In Wagner's *Ring of the Nibelungs*, he appears as Mime.

Mincing (min'sing). In William Congreve's comedy *The Way of the World*, Millamant's waiting-maid.

Mind, Will, and Understanding. [Also, **Wisdom**.] An English morality play (c1460) by an unknown author. Since it was obviously not intended for popular presentation in the streets of a city or town, it has been suggested that it was designed for a monastic community.

Minerva (mi.nėr'va). In Roman mythology, one of the three chief divinities, the other two being Jupiter and Juno. The chief seat of the cult of all three was the great temple on the Capitoline Hill. Minerva was originally an ancient Italian goddess adopted from the Etruscans by the Romans. She was a goddess of artisans, a more important patronage in Etruria than in Rome. In Roman myth, she was the virgin daughter of Jupiter, the supreme god, and hence was identified, as the Romans came more and more under the influence of Hellenic culture, with the Greek Athena. Like Athena, Minerva was represented in art with a grave and majestic countenance, armed with helmet, shield, and spear, and wearing long full drapery, and on her breast the aegis.

Minerva Press, The. A printing house of London, which, in the 18th century, was noted for its publication of trashy novels.

Minetta (mi.net'a). A flippant waiting-maid in Hannah Cowley's comedy *A Bold Stroke for a Husband*.

Ming (ming). A native Chinese dynasty which overthrew the Mongols in 1368 and ruled China until 1644, when the Manchu (Ch'ing) dynasty succeeded it. The city of Peiping (Peking) as we know it today was laid out by the third Ming emperor in 1403. It was the last great period of purely Chinese power. During the reign of the Ming rulers, European influence began to be felt in China; the Portuguese and the Jesuits obtained footholds, and Canton and Macao came under foreign sway.

Minna Troil (min'a troil'). See under **Troil, Magnus**.

minnesinger (min'e.sing.ėr; German, min'e.zing.ėr). One of a class of German lyric poets and singers of the 12th, 13th, and 14th centuries: so called because love was the chief theme of their songs.

Minola (min'o.la), **Baptista**. See **Baptista Minola**.

Minor, The. A comedy by Samuel Foote, produced at Dublin in 1760. It satirized the Methodists, Dr. Squintum being a caricature of George Whitfield, and his supposed conversion of a bawd, Mrs. Cole, being a coarse slur on Methodism. The plot concerns a trick played upon Sir George, a roué, by his father, Sir William Wealthy.

Minories (mī'nor.iz), **the**. A parish in London, on the left bank of the Thames, not far from the Tower. In old London, the house of the sisters of the Franciscan order without the walls at Oldgate was called the Abbey of Saint Clare. The nuns were called Poor Clares or Minoresses, whence the name Minories.

Minos (mī′nos, -nọs). In Greek legend, a king of Crete and lawgiver of that island; after his death a judge in the lower world. Minos was the son of Zeus and Europa, and husband of Pasiphae, who, enamored of a bull which Minos refused to sacrifice to Poseidon, conceived and bore the Minotaur. Minos had the Labyrinth built to contain the monster.

Minot (mī′nọt), **Laurence.** b. c1300; d. c1352. An English soldier and war poet, author of 11 poems written in Northern English, with an admixture of Midland features which may be due to a copyist. The poems, in various meters, exhibit both rhyme and alliteration. They deal with the period 1333–52, the first glorying in the English victory at Halidon Hill, and the last celebrating the capture of Guînes. Minot was intensely patriotic and loyal to Edward III, whose victories in Scotland, France, and Flanders inspired him. His poetry, preserved in a single manuscript, was discovered by Thomas Tyrwhitt, Chaucerian scholar, and first published (1795) by Joseph Ritson, exposer of literary forgeries, as *Poems on Interesting Events in the Reign of King Edward III*. The best modern edition is that of Joseph Hall (1897).

Minotaur (min′ọ.tôr). In Greek mythology, a monster having a human body and the head of a bull; the offspring of Pasiphae (wife of Minos) and a bull. He was confined in the Cretan Labyrinth and fed with human flesh; he devoured the seven youths and seven maidens whom Minos compelled the Athenians to send him periodically as a tribute. The Minotaur was killed by the hero Theseus, a member of the last company so sent, who escaped from the Labyrinth by the aid of a clew of thread devised by Ariadne, daughter of Minos.

minstrel (min′strẹl). 1. A musician, especially one who sings or recites to the accompaniment of instruments. Specifically, in the Middle Ages, the minstrels were a class who devoted themselves to the amusement of the great in castle or camp by singing ballads or songs of love and war, sometimes of their own composition, with accompaniment on the harp, lute, or other instrument, together with suitable mimicry and action, and also by storytelling, etc. The intermediate class of professional musicians from which the later minstrels sprang appeared in France as early as the 8th century, and was by the Norman conquest introduced into England, where it was assimilated with the Anglo-Saxon gleemen. Everywhere the social importance of the minstrels slowly degenerated, until in the 15th century they had formed themselves generally into guilds of itinerant popular musicians and mountebanks. In England they fell so low in esteem that in 1597 they were classed by a statute with rogues, vagabonds, and sturdy beggars; but in France their guilds were maintained until the revolution.

> Whan the servise was ffynisshed, the kynge Arthur and the Barouns returned in to the paleys, where-as was grete plente of mynstralles, and iogelours, and other.
>   ("Merlin," in *E. E. T. S.*, iii. 454.)

> Ye'll gi'e the third to the minstrel
>   That plays before the king.
> ("Young Akin," in Child's *Ballads*, I. 184.)

> Wake ye from your sleep of death,
> Minstrels and bards of other days!
>   (Scott, *Bard's Incantation*.)

But while the minstrel proper accompanied his lord to the field and shared with him the danger and the honour of his warlike exploits, the connection between him and the humbler kind of entertainer [the jongleur], who was still the servant of the multitude rather than of a particular lord, cannot have been wholly forgotten.
        (A. W. Ward, *Eng. Dram. Lit.*)

Hence—2. Any poet or musician. [Poetical.]

Minstrel, The. An unfinished poem in Spenserian stanzas by James Beattie, published in 1771–74, concerning the education of a poet. Edwin, the poet (who is supposed to represent Beattie) is instructed by the beauties of country life, the great poets of the past, and a knowledge of philosophy and history.

minstrelsy (min′strẹl.si). 1. The art or occupation of minstrels; singing and playing in the manner of a minstrel; lyrical song and music.

> Holliche thanne with his host hizede to here tentes
> With merthe of alle menstracye, and made hem attese.
>   ("William of Palerne," in *E. E. T. S.*, l. 1295.)

>   When every room
> Hath blaz'd with lights and bray'd with minstrelsy.
>   (Shak., *T. of A.*, II.ii.)

Originally . . . the profession of the joculator included all the arts attributed to the minstrels; and accordingly his performance was called his minstrelsy in the reign of Edward II., and even after he had obtained the appellation of a tregetour.   (Strutt, *Sports and Pastimes*.)

2. An assemblage or company of minstrels; a body of singers and players.

> So many maner minstracie at that mariage were.
>   ("William of Palerne," in *E. E. T. S.*, l. 5010.)

> The bride hath paced into the hall—
> Red as a rose is she!
> Nodding their heads before her goes
> The merry minstrelsy.
>   (Coleridge, *Ancient Mariner*.)

3. A collection or body of lyrical songs and ballad poetry, such as were sung by minstrels: as, Scott's "*Minstrelsy* of the Scottish Border."

The body of traditional minstrelsy which commemorated the heroic deeds performed in these wars.   (Prescott, *Ferd. and Isa.*, Int.)

Minto (min′tō), **William.** b. in Alford parish, Aberdeenshire, Scotland, Oct. 10, 1845; d. at Aberdeen, Scotland, March 1, 1893. A Scottish man of letters, editor (1874–78) of the London *Examiner*, and professor of logic and English literature in the University of Aberdeen from 1880. He wrote a *Manual of English Prose Literature* (1872), *Characteristics of English Poets from Chaucer to Shirley* (1874), and several novels.

Mirabeau (mir′ạ.bō; French, mē.rà.bō), Comte **de.** [Title of **Honoré Gabriel Riqueti** or **Riquetti**.] b. at

---

ḍ, d or j; ṣ, s or sh; ṭ, t or ch; ẓ, z or zh; o, F. cloche; ü, F. menu; čh, Sc. loch; ṅ, F. bonbon.

Bignon, near Nemours, France, March 9, 1749; d. at Paris, April 2, 1791. A French revolutionary orator and statesman. He entered (1767) the army, served in Corsica, and rose to the rank of captain of dragoons. His escapades, in which his success in amorous intrigue was not hampered by his disfigurement by smallpox at the age of three, caused his father to have him imprisoned by *lettre de cachet*. He became reconciled with his father and married (1772) according to his father's wishes, but he soon spent the better part of his wife's fortune and again was imprisoned, this time in the Château d'If, near Marseilles. He was moved to the castle of Joux, but, enjoying comparative liberty, escaped (1775) from Pontarlier, nearby, with Mme. de Monnier (Sophie in his notorious letters to her). They went to Holland, where he was arrested (1777); he then spent 42 months in prison at Vincennes. Up to the time of his release, he had written essays and pamphlets, translated English and German books, and kept up a correspondence with Sophie, to whom he dedicated his *Erotica biblion* and other works. To the early period of his life belong the *Essai sur le despotisme* and *Essai sur les lettres de cachet*. After traveling in Switzerland, he went to London (1784–85) and then to Berlin (1785–86). From here he wrote home a series of official reports, *Histoire secrète de la cour de Berlin* (1789), and he also gathered materials for his *De la monarchie prussienne sous Frédéric le Grand* (1788). The result of these writings was to alienate the opinion of those in power in France and to build at the same time his reputation as a scholar.

Mirabel or **Mirabell** (mir′a̧.bel). The principal character in John Fletcher's play *The Wild Goose Chase*. He is a libertine and fashionable rake, gaining his title of "wild goose" from his successful evasion of the marriage noose.

Mirabel, Old. In George Farquhar's comedy *The Inconstant*, a peevish old man with a fondness for his son.

Mirabel, Tommy. The son of Old Mirabel; "the inconstant" in Farquhar's play of that name. He is a gay and generous gentleman, but unstable in his affections.

Mirabell (mir′a̧.bel). In William Congreve's comedy *The Way of the World*, a brilliant and witty fine gentleman who is in love with Millamant and succeeds ingeniously in getting her hand, despite various obstacles in the form of an aunt, legal documents, a discarded love affair, and the insouciance of the lady herself.

Mirabella (mir.a̧.bel′a̧). A fair maiden, in Edmund Spenser's *Faerie Queene*, who had scorned many lovers. She was sentenced in Cupid's court to ride on a wretched jade, "accompanied by a fool, till she had saved as many lovers as she had slain."

Mirabilis (mi.rab′i.lis), **Doctor.** See **Bacon, Roger.**

Miracle on Sinai (sī′nā̧.ī, -nī). A satirical novel by Sir Osbert Sitwell, published in 1933.

miracle plays. See **mystery plays.**

Miranda (mi.ran′da̧). In Shakespeare's *Tempest*, the daughter of Prospero. She is loved by Ferdinand.

Miranda. In Susannah Centlivre's comedy *The Busybody*, an heiress, in love with Sir George Airy.

Miriam (mir′i.a̧m). One of the heroines of D. H. Lawrence's autobiographical novel *Sons and Lovers* (1913).

Mirour de l'omme (mē.rör dė lom). See **Speculum Meditantis.**

Mirror for Magistrates, The. A compilation of poems undertaken by William Baldwin with aid from George Ferrers and others. It was begun and partly printed in 1555, but was stopped by the lord chancellor, Stephen Gardiner. In 1559, after Elizabeth's accession, it was licensed and first issued. It then contained 19 metrical tragedies, or biographies, of men in high place who had come to violent ends, and was an English sequel to John Lydgate's *Falls of Princes* (from Boccaccio). It was republished in 1563, 1574, 1578, and 1587, each time with additions. The "Induction" and "Complaint of Buckingham" which were contributed by Thomas Sackville, Lord Buckhurst, to the edition of 1559, but not published till 1563, are usually considered the best poems in the compilation.

Mirrors of Downing Street (dou′ning), **The.** A study of English statesmen (1921) of the period of World War I and early post-war period by "A Gentleman with a Duster" (Harold Begbie).

Mirror of Modesty, The. A romance by Robert Greene, published in 1584. It tells the story of Susanna and the elders.

Mirror of the World, The. A book translated from a Latin *Speculum vel Imago Mundi* in 1245, for the Duke of Berry, into French verse, which was afterwards turned by a Maistre Gossouin (possibly only a copyist) into French prose. From that prose William Caxton made his translation in 1481 at the request of Hugh Brice, of the Mercers' Company, alderman of London.

Misalliance. A play (1910) by George Bernard Shaw.

Misanthrope (mē.zän.trop), **Le.** A comedy by Molière, produced in 1666. This play is an almost inexhaustible source of allusions, quotations, and proverbial sayings in English literature as well as in French. It is the ideal of French classic comedy.

mise en scène (mēz oń sān). The entire scenery, properties, and detail of an acted play; hence, the surroundings of any event.

Misenus (mī.sē′nus). In Roman legend, a companion of Aeneas.

Miser, The. A comedy by Thomas Shadwell (1672), based upon Molière's *L'Avare*. He noted that his source, published four years earlier, had "not suffer'd" by his reworking of it (apparently he considered that he had actually improved it).

Miser, The. A comedy by Henry Fielding (produced 1733), based upon Molière's *L'Avare* (1668). It is a much better play than Shadwell's adaptation six decades earlier.

Misfortunes of Arthur (är′thėr), **The.** A tragedy written principally by Thomas Hughes, produced in 1587 before Queen Elizabeth. Eight members of the Society of Gray's Inn coöperated with him, and the "triumphs" and dumbshow were devised principally by Francis Bacon.

Mishnah (mish′na̧). A collection of rabbinical discussions on the law of Moses, the object of which was to apply and adapt it to the varying circumstances of life and of the times, and to extend it by logical conclusions and analogies. The word *Mishnah* properly means "repetition," then "instruction," "learning." It was not at first permissible that these discourses should be reduced to writing; they had to be learned by heart, and are called the oral law as opposed to the written law, or the Pentateuch. The beginning of the Mishnah goes back to the time of the Maccabees. It was delivered in the schools orally from generation to generation. At the end of the 2nd century A.D. the patriarch Judah I collected, arranged, and codified the accumulated material in its present shape. The numerous rules and decisions are arranged according to subject in six orders (*sedarim*): (1) seeds (*zeraim*), on agriculture; (2) festivals (*moed*); (3) women (*nashim*), on connubial affairs; (4) damages (*nezikim*), civil and criminal laws; (5) sacrifices (*kodashim*); (6) purifications (*tahoroth*). The six orders are divided into 63 tracts, and these again into chapters. The explanations of or comments on the Mishnah are called *Gemara*, and both together constitute the Talmud.

Misogonus (mi.sog'ọ.nus). A rhymed play variously attributed to Thomas Richards (or Rychards) and Lawrence Johnson (about neither of whom is very much else known). The title page carries the date 1577; it was probably written c1560. It contains songs, and has some changes of meter, but is mainly four-lined stanzas. It is based on the theme of the prodigal son.

Miss Betsy Thoughtless (bet'si thôt'les). [Full title, **The History of Miss Betsy Thoughtless.**] A novel by Eliza Haywood, published in 1751.

Miss in Her Teens: or, The Medley of Lovers. A farce by David Garrick, produced in 1747.

Miss Kilmansegg and Her Precious Leg (kil'mạnseg). A poem by Thomas Hood, of which it has been said that "as a sustained piece of metrical humor, [it] is absolutely unique."

Miss Mole (mōl). A novel by E. H. Young, published in 1930.

Miss Sara Sampson (sär'ạ samp'sọn). A play by Gotthold Ephraim Lessing, written and produced in 1755. With it the so-called "bourgeois tragedy" was introduced into Germany.

Mistake, The. A comedy (1705) by John Vanbrugh, taken in part from Molière's *Le Dépit amoureux* or from Dryden's *An Evening's Love.*

Mistral (mēs.tràl), **Frédéric.** b. at Maillane, Bouches-du-Rhône, France, Sept. 8, 1830; d. there, March 25, 1914. A Provençal poet, belonging to, and considered the leading poet of, the brotherhood of modern Provençal poets known as Les Félibriges. Among his works (in Provençal, with French translations) are *Mirèio* (*Mireille*, 1859), *Calendau* (1867), *Lis Isclo d'or* (*Les Îles d'or*, 1875), *Lou Tresor dou félibrige* (1879–86; a Provençal-French dictionary), *Nerto* (1884), *La Reino-Jano* (1890), *Lou Pouèmo dou Rose* (1897), and a volume of memoirs (1906). In 1904 he received, with José Echegaray, the Nobel prize for literature.

Mistress, The. A "love-cycle" by Abraham Cowley, published in 1647. It shows a considerable influence by John Donne.

Mistress Ford (fōrd). See **Ford, Mistress.**

Mitchel (mich'ẹl), **John.** b. at Dungiven, County Derry, Ireland, Nov. 3, 1815; d. March 20, 1875. An Irish revolutionist, a leader in the "Young Ireland" movement. He was convicted as editor of the *United Irishman* for advocating armed rebellion against England and sentenced to 14 years' banishment in 1848, escaped from Van Diemen's Land (Tasmania) and came to New York in 1854, and lived in the U. S. until 1874, when he returned to Ireland. In 1875 he was elected to Parliament for Tipperary, but was declared ineligible. He wrote *Jail Journal* (1854), *The Last Conquest of Ireland —Perhaps* (1861), and others.

Mitchell (mich'ẹl), **Sir Peter Chalmers.** b. at Dunfermline, Scotland, 1864; d. at London, July 2, 1945. An English zoölogist and author, noted for improvements in the care of animals at the London zoo. His scientific works include *Outlines of Biology* (1894), *The Biological Problem of Today* (1896), *The Nature of Man* (1904), *The Childhood of Animals* (1912), *Evolution and the War* (1915), and *Materialism and Vitalism in Biology* (1930). Author also of *My House in Málaga, My Fill of Days: Reminiscences,* and a biography of Thomas Henry Huxley.

Mitchison (mich'i.sọn), **Naomi.** [Full name, **Naomi Margaret Haldane Mitchison.**] b. at Edinburgh, Nov. 1, 1897—. A British writer. Author of *The Conquered* (1923), *When the Bough Breaks* (1924), *Cloud Cuckoo Land* (1925), *The Laburnum Branch* (poetry, 1926), *Barbarian Stories* (1929), *Comments on Birth Control* (1930), *The Corn King and the Spring Queen* (1931), *The Delicate Fire* (1933), *The Fourth Pig* (1936), *The Kingdom of Heaven* (1939), *The Blood of the Martyrs* (1939), and *The Bull Calves* (1947).

Mite (mīt), **Sir Matthew.** The "nabob" in Samuel Foote's play of that name. He returns from a profitable residence in India with ill-gotten gains, which he uses to annoy and ruin his neighbors.

Mitford (mit'fọrd), **John.** b. at Richmond, Surrey, England, Aug. 13, 1781; d. April 27, 1859. An English writer and clergyman. He became curate of Kelsale, Suffolk, in 1809. From 1834 until 1850 he edited the *Gentleman's Magazine.* He assisted in editing the Aldine edition of British poets, and wrote *Agnes, the Indian Captive,* a poem (1811).

Mitford, Mary Russell. b. at Alresford, Hampshire, England, Dec. 16, 1787; d. at Swallowfield, near Reading, England, Jan. 10, 1855. An English author. Her father, George Mitford, was a physician who squandered his wife's fortune and finally became dependent upon his daughter's earnings. At ten years of age she drew a lottery prize of 20,000 pounds, which her father also spent. In 1810 her *Miscellaneous Poems* appeared, and in 1812 *Blanche of Castile.* In 1820 her father's irregularities obliged her to support herself by literature. *Julian,* a tragedy, was accepted by W. C. Macready and performed at Covent Garden, March 15, 1823. *The Foscari* was produced by Charles Kemble, Nov. 4, 1826, and *Rienzi,* her best tragedy, was produced at Drury Lane, Oct. 9, 1828. The sketches entitled *Our Village* began in the *Lady's Magazine* in 1819, and gained great popularity. *Belford Regis,* a novel,

ḍ, d or j; ṣ, s or sh; ṭ, t or ch; ẓ, z or zh; o, F. cloche; ü, F. menu; ċh, Sc. loch; ṅ, F. bonbon.

was published in 1835, and *Recollections of a Literary Life* in 1852. She also published a number of poems, sonnets, stories of American life, and stories for children.

Mitford, William. b. at London, Feb. 10, 1744; d. at Exbury, England, Feb. 10, 1827. An English historian. The first volume of his *History of Greece*, suggested by Edward Gibbon, appeared in 1784; the work was completed in 1810. Mitford, writing in a period when the French Revolution and its excesses caused high feeling, was a monarchist, and his treatment of the Athenian democracy shows his bias. His work was, however, of such excellence that not until the appearance of the more balanced histories of George Grote and Connop Thirlwall in the 1840's was it superseded. He was a member of Parliament (1785–90, 1796–1806, and 1812–18).

Mithra (mith'rạ) or **Mithras** (mith'rạs). In ancient Persian mythology, the god of light and truth, and an ally of Ahura Mazda in his struggle against evil and darkness. In Vedic mythology, he is Mitra, a sun god, and ruler of the day. His worship was introduced into Rome. After Pompey had wrested Pontus in Asia Minor from the Persians, the worship of Mithra superseded the Dionysia, and was prevalent throughout the Roman Empire. In the 2nd century Mithraism was stronger than Christianity in the Roman Empire. Certain initiatory ceremonies entailed in the worship of Mithra have been reflected in the ceremonies of the secret societies of the Middle Ages, of the Rosicrucians, and of the Freemasons.

Mithridates, King of Pontus (mith.ri.dā'tēz; pon'tus). A tragedy by Nathaniel Lee, produced in 1678.

Mitre (mī'tėr), **The.** A former noted tavern in Mitre Court, off Fleet Street, London. It was a favorite resort of Samuel Johnson.

mixed metaphor. A figurative expression in which two or more metaphors are confused, as in the following quotation:

Where—still to use your lordship's tropes—
The level of obedience slopes
Upward and downward, as the stream
Of hydra faction kicks the beam!
(T. Moore, *To Lord Castlereagh.*)

Mjöllnir (myėl'nir). In Old Norse mythology, the hammer used by Thor against the giants.

M'Lehose (mak'lẹ.hōz), **Agnes.** See **Maclehose, Agnes.**

Mnemosyne (nẹ.mos'i.nē, -moz'-). In Greek mythology, a Titaness, the goddess of memory; daughter of Uranus (Heaven) and Ge (Earth), and mother, by Zeus, of the Muses.

Mnevis (nē'vis). In Egyptian mythology, the sacred bull of Heliopolis.

Moabite Stone (mō'ạ.bīt). A slab of black basalt bearing an inscription in early Semitic characters, which records the victories of Mesha, king of Moab, over the Israelites. It was discovered in 1868, and is the oldest known monument (9th century B.C.) of the Semitic alphabet.

Mob, The. A drama (1914) by John Galsworthy, dealing with a question of international morality.

Mock Doctor, The. [Full title, **The Mock Doctor: or, The Dumb Lady Cur'd.**] A farce by Henry Fielding, acted in 1732 at the Drury Lane, slightly altered from Molière's comedy *Le Médecin malgré lui.*

Mock Doctor, The. The English libretto of Charles Gounod's opera *Le Médecin malgré lui,* by Charles Kenny.

Mockery Gap. A novel by Theodore Francis Powys, published in 1925.

Modern Comedy, A. An omnibus volume by John Galsworthy, published in 1929, which includes *The White Monkey* (1924), *The Silver Spoon* (1926), and *Swan Song* (1928), and two "interludes," *The Silent Wooing* (1925) and *Passersby* (1927). This collective work depicts the fortunes of the Forsyte family in the 20th century.

Modern Husband, The. A comedy (1732) by Henry Fielding.

Modern Love. A sequence of 50 poems by George Meredith, published in 1862. Each poem, consisting of 16 lines, deals with some phase of a passionate but unhappy and discordant marriage which ends in separation. It is supposed that the series of poems reflects Meredith's marriage with Mary Ellen Nicolls.

Modern Lover, A. A novel by George Moore, published in 1883.

Modern Painters. A work on art in five volumes, by John Ruskin (published 1843, 1846, 1856, and 1860). Ruskin sets out to prove that modern landscape painters are greater masters of their art than were the ancients. He bases his case on studies of examples from almost every style in the history of Western art, and stresses the excellence of Joseph Turner as a great contemporary landscape painter. Ruskin deals with the study of nature by artists, and the use of their imagination in portraying what they see. He lauds Turner in this at the expense of such French masters as Poussin and Claude. He believes that the greatest art is that which gives the viewer the greatest number of useful ideas, and establishes certain categories within which these ideas may fall. They are Beauty, Truth, Imitation, Power, and Relation. Ruskin goes into minute detail on technique and the description of scenes from nature, dealing with paint, light, and composition at great length. He praises Tintoretto and Giorgione, but in all his discussions, English painters are supreme.

Modish (mō'dish), **Lady Betty.** In Colley Cibber's comedy *The Careless Husband,* a brilliant coquettish woman of quality, wayward and selfish, but not heartless.

Modo (mō'dō). In Shakespeare's *King Lear,* a fiend ("of murder") mentioned by Edgar (IV.i). The name is taken from Samuel Harsnett's *Popish Impostures.*

Modred (mō'drẹd). [Also, **Mordred.**] In Arthurian romance, the treacherous nephew (or son) of King Arthur, a knight of the Round Table. When Arthur departed for the campaign against Rome, he left both his kingdom and his queen in Modred's care, but Modred seized both in his absence. When Arthur returned he drove Modred out of the kingdom and finally killed him at the battle of Camlan, but was killed himself.

Moerae (mē'rē). The Fates.

Mogridge (mog'rij), **George.** b. at Ashted, near Birmingham, England, Feb. 17, 1787; d. at Hastings, England, Nov. 2, 1854. An English writer, chiefly of juveniles.

Moguls (mō'gulz, mō.gulz'), **Empire of the.** [Also, **Empire of the Mughals.**] A Mohammedan empire in India. It began with Baber, conqueror of Hindustan, 1526, and was at its height under Akbar, Jahangir, Shah Jehan, and Aurung-Zeb. After the death of the last-named (1707), the empire split up and the power passed to the Mahrattas and to the British in 1803. The last (nominal) emperor was deposed in 1857 (d. 1862). The greatness of the Mogul Empire survives in its art and architecture.

Mohammed (mō.ham'ed) or **Mahomet** (mạ.hom'et). [Also: **Mahomed, Muhammad, Mahmoud, Mahmud, Mehemet;** Eng. trans., "*Praised One.*"]. b. at Mecca, Arabia, c570; d. at Medina, Arabia, June 8, 632. The founder of Mohammedanism, or Islam (meaning "surrender," namely, to God). He was the posthumous son of Abdallah by his wife Amina, of the family of Hashim, of the noble tribe of Koreish, and was brought up in the desert among the Banu Saad by a Bedouin woman named Halima. At the age of six he lost his mother, and at eight his grandfather, after which he was cared for by his uncle. As a youth he attended sundry preachings and literary recitations at the annual fair of Okatz at Mecca, which may have awakened his poetical and rhetorical powers and his religious feelings. He came to be known among his people as al-Amin ("the trustworthy or faithful"). It was, in all probability, at the commercial city of Mecca that he first came in contact with Jews and Christians. For some time he was occupied as a shepherd, to which he later refers as being in accordance with his career as a prophet, even as it was with that of Moses and David. When 25 years old he entered the service of the widow Khadijah, and made a successful business journey to Syria, where he had an opportunity to come in frequent contact with Jews and Christians and to increase his knowledge of their religious teachings. He soon married Khadijah, who was 15 years his senior. Of the six children which she bore him, Fatima became the most famous as the only one to carry on Mohammed's line. In 605 he attained some influence in Mecca by settling a dispute about the rebuilding of the Kaaba. The impressions which he had gathered from his contact with Judaism and Christianity, and from Arabic lore, began now strongly to engage his mind. He frequently retired to solitary places, especially to the cave of Mount Hira, north of Mecca. He passed at that time (he was then about 40 years old) through great mental struggles. It must have been during these lonely contemplations that the yearnings for a messenger from God for his people, and the thought that he himself might be destined for this mission, were born in his ardent mind. During one of his reveries, in the month of Ramadan, 610, he heard the voice of the angel Gabriel, who ordered him to recite after him the words which begin the 96th *sura* (chapter) of the Koran. This is known as the Call of Mo-

hammed. After the lapse of some time, the revelations began to follow one another frequently. His own belief in his mission as apostle and prophet of God was now firmly established. The first convert was his wife Khadijah, then followed his cousin Ali, his adopted son Zeid, and his friend Abu-Bakr, afterward his father-in-law and first successor (caliph). Gradually some 50 adherents rallied about him. But after three years' preaching the mass of the Meccans rose against him, so that part of his followers had to flee to Abyssinia for safety in 614. This is termed the first *hejira* (flight). Mohammed in the meanwhile continued his meetings in the house of one of his disciples, in front of the Kaaba, which later became known as the "House of Islam." At one time he offered the Koreish a compromise, admitting some of their gods into his system as intercessors with Allah, the Supreme Being, but, becoming conscience-stricken, he repented of this deed and uncompromisingly asserted the unity of God. The conversion of the hitherto belligerent Hamza and Omar and a few others in 615–616 strengthened his cause. The alarmed Koreish now excommunicated Mohammed and his followers, who were therefore forced to live in retirement. In 620, at the pilgrimage, he won over to his teachings a small party from the northern city of Medina. In Medina, whither a teacher was deputed, the new religion spread rapidly. In 622 more than 70 persons from Medina bound themselves to stand by Mohammed. These invited him to their city to arbitrate their tribal disputes, and in return promised him their support against his Meccan enemies. The Meccans now plotted to kill Mohammed, and he fled on June 20, 622, to Medina. This is known as the Hejira, and marks the beginning of the Mohammedan era. This event formed a turning point in the activity of Mohammed. He was thus far a religious preacher and persuader; he became in his Medinian period a legislator and warrior. He built there in 623 the first mosque, and married Ayesha, the young daughter of Abu-Bakr, his friend and successor. To this period also belongs the vision or dream of the miraculous ride on the winged horse Al Borak to Jerusalem, where he was received by the prophets, and thence ascended to heaven. In 624 the first battle for the faith took place between Mohammed and the Meccans in the plain of Bedr; the latter were defeated. He now changed the direction of prayer (*kibla*) from that of Jerusalem to that of the Kaaba at Mecca, appointed Friday as the day for public worship, and instituted the fast of the month of Ramadan and the tithe or poor rate. Mohammed had at first reached out to the Jews of Medina for recognition and support. These, however, not only refused to recognize him as a prophet, but ridiculed his claims and teaching. He retaliated by accusing them of falsifying the Scriptures and now claimed that God had sent him as the last and the "seal of the prophets" to restore and complete the sacred revelation. As the rift widened, Mohammed took aggressive measures. The Jewish tribe of the Banu Kainuka, settled at Medina, was driven out; while another Jewish tribe, the Banu Kuraiza, all the men, some 600 in number, were executed for their plotting against him with the Meccans. In 625 Mohammed and his followers were defeated by the Meccans in the battle of Ohud.

ḍ, d or j; ṣ, s or sh; ṭ, t or ch; ẓ, z or zh; o, F. cloche; ü, F. menu; ċh, Sc. loch; ṅ, F. bonbon.

The following years were filled with expeditions. One tribe after another submitted to Mohammed, until by late 630 something like a definite Mohammedan state was established, the culmination coming in the conquest of Mecca itself. In the following years Mohammed concluded treaties of peace with the Jews and Christians, who were called on to pay land and poll taxes in return for protection and freedom of worship. This policy was followed by his successors. In 632 the prophet made his last pilgrimage to Mecca, known as the "farewell pilgrimage," or the pilgrimage of the "announcement" of "Islam." In the same year he died while planning an expedition against the frontier of the Byzantine Empire. Mohammed was a little above middle height, of a commanding figure, and is described as being of a modest, tender, and generous disposition. His manner of life was very simple and frugal. He mended his own clothes, and his common diet was bread, dates, and water. But he enjoyed perfumes and the charms of women. His character appears composed of the strongest inconsistencies. He could be tender, kind, and liberal, but on occasion could sanction wholesale political executions. His leadership and vision led him to undertake, with some measure of success, a social revolution in Arabia, where religious unity and allegiance took precedence over the blood ties of tribe and family, and where woman made some progress towards emancipation. With regard to his prophetic claims, it is less difficult to assume that he was sincere throughout, or self-deceived, than that he was throughout an impostor. In his doctrines there is practically nothing original. The legends of the Koran are chiefly drawn from the Old and New Testaments and rabbinical literature, though Mohammed presents them as original revelations by the angel Gabriel.

Mohammedanism. [Also, **Islam**.] A religion named after its founder and prophet, Mohammed. Every true follower of it is called upon to perform certain prescribed rites: to recite the creed, "There is no God but Allah, and Mohammed is his prophet"; to worship God, from the age of seven, five times daily, morning, noon, afternoon, evening, and night, by praying on individual prayer rugs, washing his hands and feet, kneeling, touching his forehead to the ground, and, always, facing to the east; to fast during the month of Ramadan (which is their ninth month); to give prescribed alms to the poor; and, if it is at all possible for him to do so, to make the pilgrimage to Mecca once in his life. It is estimated that there are over 210 million Mohammedans today, most of them in Asia Minor, India, China, and Africa. The word Islam is also often used to refer to the entire Mohammedan world, as well as the religion.

Mohocks (mō′hoks). Ruffians who infested the streets of London about the beginning of the 18th century: so called from the fact that their savagery was supposed to resemble that of the Mohawk (or, in an older form, Mohock) Indians.

Mohun (mön), **Charles.** [Title, 5th Baron **Mohun**.] b. c1675; killed in a duel in Hyde Park, London, Nov. 15, 1712. An English desperado. On Dec. 9, 1692, he was associated with Captain Richard Hill in the murder of William Mountfort, the actor, but he was acquitted after trial by the House of Lords. He was repeatedly engaged in duels, and twice tried for murder and acquitted. In 1701 he was involved in a protracted lawsuit with James Douglas, 4th Duke of Hamilton, over the estate of the Earl of Macclesfield, which resulted in a duel and the death of both parties. This duel figures in Thackeray's *Henry Esmond.*

Moir (moir), **David Macbeth.** [Pseudonym, **Delta**, written Δ.] b. at Musselburgh, Scotland, Jan. 5, 1798; d. at Dumfries, Scotland, July 6, 1851. A Scottish author. Among his works are poems, the tale *Autobiography of Mansie Wauch, Tailor* (1828), and *Sketches of the Poetical Literature of the Past Half-Century* (1851).

Molesworth (mōlz′werth), **Mary Louisa.** [Pseudonym, **Ennis Graham**; maiden name, **Stewart**.] b. at Rotterdam, Netherlands, May 29, 1839; d. at London, July 20, 1921. An English novelist and author of juveniles. As Ennis Graham and under her married name she wrote stories for children, in which she was at her best, and serious novels, in which she was less successful. Among her works are *Lover and Husband* (1869), *She Was Young and He Was Old* (1872), *Cicely* (1874), *Tell Me a Story* (1875), *Carrots* (1876), *The Cuckoo Clock* (1877), *The Tapestry Room* (1879), *Miss Bouverie* (1880), *A Charge Fulfilled* (1887), *Marrying and Giving in Marriage* (1887), *The Third Miss St. Quentin* (1888), *Meg Langholme* (1897), *Miss Mouse and Her Boys* (1897), *The Laurel Walk* (1898), *The Grim House* (1899), *Peterkin* (1902), and *The Story of a Year* (1910).

Molière (mo.lyer). [Pseudonym of **Jean Baptiste Poquelin**.] Baptized at Paris, Jan. 15, 1622; d. there, Feb. 17, 1673. A French dramatist and actor, most famous of French writers of comedies. His works have been translated into a vast number of languages and he is generally ranked among the great dramatists of the world. His father was an upholsterer, as were the male relatives of his mother, Marie Cressé, who died when he was quite young. He received a good education at the Jesuit Collège de Clermont. In 1643, however, he renounced the profession of his father, who had become an upholsterer to the king, and, with Madeleine Béjart and others of her family, formed a troupe of professional actors, the "Illustre Théâtre." It was then he took the name Molière. Unsuccessful in two years of struggles at Paris, Molière and the Béjarts joined a troupe of strolling players, of which he later became the leader. Thirteen years of touring the provinces brought him invaluable experience. He composed several farces, now lost, and two longer plays in Italian style. Returning to Paris, he won the favor of Louis XIV and, after the success of *Les Précieuses ridicules* in 1659, his troupe was firmly established and could resist the attacks of rival authors and actors, and the more threatening hostility occasioned by *Le Tartuffe* (first presented in three acts in 1664, finally permitted to be played in public in 1669), a daring portrayal of religious hypocrisy in that day. The poet's marriage to Armande Béjart, Feb. 20, 1662, was not a happy one. Leading actor of his troupe in comic roles, as well as director, and often summoned to perform before the king or to compose a play for some royal fête, Molière had to work feverishly, and suffered from ill health, but the 28 plays composed between 1659 and 1673 include many masterpieces. Even his death was dramatic, caused by a hemorrhage as the sick actor indomitably played the imaginary invalid, in the fourth performance of *Le Malade imaginaire*. In that play, as in others, his own experience with doctors and with sickness furnished material for his ridicule. He drew from all sources, ancient and modern plays, people and events about him, transforming his borrowings by his skill in adapting them to his purpose. He was the foe of quackery in all its guises. He mocked the bombast of rival actors, demanding that both author and actor follow nature and depict men of their own day. He believed also in the duty of the writer of comedies to correct men while amusing them, and one of his great contributions was to put into the framework of the old farce or comedy of situation true observation of character and manners, exaggerated to be sure, but with a real face behind the mask, and a lesson with the laugh. He exposed unerringly the foibles and vices of his time, but he also laid bare depths of the human soul, and in his mirror the audience of today can see its own frailties and perceive defects of mankind in general. In verse or in prose, sometimes with ballets as an essential part, his plays range from slapstick farce, as in *Les Fourberies de Scapin*, to the thought-provoking study of *Le Misanthrope*. Throughout one finds a complete grasp of comic devices, whether of words, situation, or naïve self-revelation. He satirizes whatever is antisocial or deviates from the golden mean (often mere folly, but sometimes dangerous vices) and, constantly, human gullibility. He has sometimes been criticized for being too matter-of-fact, too materialistic, too bourgeois, lacking idealism, fantasy, and romance. His characters seem too much "of a piece," having one-track minds, lacking the complexity of those of Shakespeare, just as his verse lacks the latter's vivid imagery and soaring fancy. His plays conform usually to the unities and can be presented with a single setting. In addition to still popular farces, such as *Le Mariage forcé* (1664), *L'Amour médecin* (1665), *Le Médecin malgré lui* (1666), and *Les Fourberies de Scapin* (1671), and one-act plays of dramatic criticism, *La Critique de l'École des femmes* and *L'Impromptu de Versailles* (1663), Molière left enduring monuments in *L'École des maris* (1661), *Les Fâcheux* (1661), *L'École des femmes* (1662), *Don Juan* (1665), *Le Misanthrope* (1666), *Amphitryon* (1668), *L'Avare* (1668), *Le Tartuffe* (1669), *Le Bourgeois gentilhomme* (1670), *Les Femmes savantes* (1672), and *Le Malade imaginaire* (1673). His influence was immediately felt in England.

Molina (mō.lē'nä), **Luis.** b. at Cuenca, New Castile, Spain, 1535; d. at Madrid, Oct. 12, 1600. A Spanish Jesuit theologian. He propounded in 1588 the doctrine that the efficacy of divine grace depends simply on the will which accepts it, that grace is a free gift to all, but that the consent of the will is requisite in order that grace may be efficacious. The Dominicans in particular attacked the doctrine; the resultant controversy was eventually suppressed by papal order. His chief work is *Liberi arbitrii cum gratiae donis, divina praescientia, pro-* *videntia, praedestinatione et reprobatione, concordia* (1588).

Molinos (mō.lē'nōs), **Miguel de.** b. at or near Saragossa, Spain, Dec. 21, 1640; d. at Rome, Dec. 29, 1696. A Spanish mystic, founder of the Molinists or Quietists. He was condemned by the Inquisition in 1687 and died in prison. His most noted work is *Guida spirituale* (Spiritual Guide, 1675).

Moll (mol). The daughter of Yellowhammer, the goldsmith, and his blowsy wife Maudlin, in Thomas Middleton's *A Chaste Maid in Cheapside*. She is the "chaste maid" whose love for a gentleman, Touchwood, and enforced engagement to a licentious knight, Whorehound, form the principal basis of the plot.

Moll Cutpurse (kut'pèrs). See **Cutpurse, Moll**; see also **Frith, Mary.**

Moll Flanders (flan'dèrz). [Full title, **The Fortunes and Misfortunes of the Famous Moll Flanders**.] A novel by Daniel Defoe, published in 1722, considered to be one of the first extended works of fiction in English literature to express unmistakably a note of social criticism (in Defoe's case, criticism of the disregard for the demoralizing effect of poverty). Moll Flanders is born in Newgate Prison and, after her mother is transported to Virginia, she becomes a public charge. She is taken into a kind household as a servant and soon finds that her beauty attracts the older son. He seduces her, and she finds that she loves him very much, but the family forces her to marry the unattractive younger son, who wants her for a wife. He soon dies, leaving her with two children. Moll then has a succession of love affairs and marriages, seeking always a life of ease. She first marries a gentleman draper, but he runs away because of financial difficulties. Then she meets and marries a planter from Virginia, and emigrates to America with him. She is very happy and makes a good wife, until she discovers to her horror that her husband is also her own brother (this is revealed to her when she learns that her mother-in-law is, in fact, also her own mother, long since settled in Virginia). Moll decides that she must leave him and her three children, and returns to England. There she has three more affairs, one with a wealthy gentleman who finally rejects her when he turns to religion, one with a banker, and one with an Irish highwayman. All of her lovers have some undeniably good qualities, that attract her to them; by reason of this she manages to retain some of her self-respect, persuading herself that her feelings of true love, however frequently and easily attained, keep her safe from whoredom. After many more misfortunes, however, poverty drives her to theft. She enters a compact with a woman who once had served her as a midwife (she bears twelve children in the novel) and becomes an expert pickpocket. Captured and convicted as a thief, she is sent to Newgate, where she again meets her highwayman. Both repent and decide that, if they are freed, they will lead good and honest lives. They are transported to Virginia, where they fulfill their good intentions and end their lives in honesty and prosperity.

Molly Bloom (mol'i blöm'). See **Bloom, Molly.**

---

d̪, d or j; ṣ, s or sh; t̪, t or ch; z̧, z or zh; o, F. cloche; ü, F. menu; ch, Sc. loch; ṅ, F. bonbon.

Molly Maguires (mạ.gwīrz'). A secret society organized in Ireland about 1843, chiefly for intimidation of the agents of the landlords. The members disguised themselves as women (whence the name).

Molly Seagrim (sē'grim). See **Seagrim, Molly.**

Moloch (mō'lok). [Also, **Molech** (-lek).] In the ancient Canaanite religion, a form of Baal, worshiped among all the ancient Canaanitish and Semitic tribes. The worship of Moloch involved offering of human sacrifices. The Carthaginians sacrificed their first-born children to him. The image was bronze, calf-headed, and had long arms which were slanted to an opening in the breast, through which the victims rolled into the furnace blazing inside. It is said that music of flute and timbrel was played to drown the cries. The worship of Moloch was introduced into Israel at different periods, with its principal place in the valley of Hinnom (it certainly existed under Ahaz, Manasseh, and Amon). The Old Testament mentions children being burned for Moloch (Lev. xviii. 21, xx. 2; 1 Kings, xi. 7; 2 Kings, xxiii. 10; Jer. xxxii. 35). At Carthage the bloody rites of Moloch were officially suppressed by the emperor Tiberius (14–37 A.D.).

Molossus (mọ.los'us). In Greek legend, the son of Neoptolemus and Andromache.

Mommsen (mom'zẹn), **Theodor.** b. at Garding, Schleswig, Nov. 30, 1817; d. at Charlottenburg, Nov. 1, 1903. A German historian. He studied philology and jurisprudence at Kiel. From 1844 to 1847 he traveled in France and Italy, engaged in archaeological studies. In 1848 he was made professor of law at Leipzig, a position which he was obliged to renounce in 1850 in consequence of his participation in the political movements of 1848–49. In 1852 he became professor of Roman law at Zurich. In 1854 he accepted a similar professorship at Breslau, and in 1857 was made professor of ancient history at the University of Berlin. His principal work, one of the classics of historical writing, is his *Römische Geschichte* (vols. 1–3, 5, 1854–56; the fourth volume never appeared). Other works are *Die römische Chronologie bis auf Cäsar* (1858), *Geschichte des römischen Münzwesens* (1860), *Römische Forschungen* (1864–79), *Römisches Staatsrecht* (1871–76), and numerous minor articles and monographs on archaeological subjects and Roman law. As secretary, after 1873, of the Berlin Academy, he was the editor of the great *Corpus inscriptionum latinarum* published (1861 *et seq.*) by that body. He was awarded (1902) the Nobel prize for literature.

Momus (mō'mus). [Also, **Momos** (-mos).] In Greek mythology, the personification of ridicule, censure, and mockery; according to Hesiod, the son of Night.

Mona (mō'nạ). Latin name of Anglesey, in N Wales, and also of the Isle of Man.

Mona Lisa (mō.nạ lē'zạ). [Also, **La Gioconda.**] A portrait by Leonardo da Vinci, in the Louvre, Paris (stolen in August, 1911; recovered in December, 1913). It is said to represent "La Gioconda," the wife of the Florentine Francesco del Giocondo. The painter worked at it for four years, and then proclaimed it unfinished.

Monarchicke Tragedies. Four tragedies (published from 1603 to 1607) by Sir William Alexander. They were *Darius, Croesus, The Alexandrian Tragedy,* and *Julius Caesar.*

Monastery, The. A novel by Sir Walter Scott, published in 1820. *The Abbot* (1820) is a sequel to it.

Monboddo (mon.bod'ō), Lord. [Title of **James Burnett.**] b. in October or November, 1714; d. May 26, 1799. A Scottish judge. He became sheriff of Kincardineshire in 1764, and in 1767 became an ordinary lord of session, on which occasion he assumed the title of Lord Monboddo. He was a pioneer anthropological theorist whose hypotheses were looked upon in his day as eccentric. He conceived of man as primarily a species of animal and studied him as such, as related to the orangutans, and he used the practices of primitive tribes to illustrate social habits. Man's rise to civilization he traced as growing out of his social needs, as did also language. Author of *Of the Origin and Progress of Language* (1773–92) and *Ancient Metaphysics* (1779–99).

Moncrieff (mon.krēf', mọn-), **William Thomas.** b. at London, Aug. 24, 1794; d. in the Charterhouse, London, Dec. 3, 1857. An English dramatist. As manager (1810–19) of the Regency (later Prince of Wales) Theatre, he wrote *Moscow, or the Cossack's Daughter* in 1810; and for the Olympic, where he became manager in 1819, *All at Coventry* (1816). He joined R. W. Elliston at Drury Lane, and wrote *Wanted, a Wife* (May, 1819), *Monsieur Tonson* (September, 1821), and *The Spectre Bridegroom* (July 2, 1821). *Tom and Jerry, or Life in London* was produced at the Adelphi Nov. 26, 1821, and ran continuously for two seasons. *The Cataract of the Ganges,* produced at Drury Lane in 1823, introduced a real waterfall, which was then an innovation. For Charles Mathews the elder he wrote *The Bashful Man* (1824); for the Surrey Theatre, *Old Heads and Young Shoulders* (1830); and for W. J. Hammond of the Strand, *Sam Weller* (July, 1837), adapted from Dickens's *Pickwick Papers.* He became blind in 1843 and was admitted as a brother at the Charterhouse in 1844. He wrote more than 170 plays in all, besides other works. Dickens despised him for stealing and dramatizing his novels almost as rapidly as they came off the presses, and satirized him in *Nicholas Nickleby.*

Money. A comedy by Edward Bulwer-Lytton, first produced on Dec. 8, 1849.

Moneytrap (mun'i.trap). In Sir John Vanbrugh's play *The Confederacy,* a threadbare, rusty, rich moneylender.

Monica (mon'i.kạ), Saint. [Also, **Monnica.**] b. at Tagaste, in northern Africa, 332 or 333; d. at Ostia, Italy, May 4, 387. The mother of Saint Augustine. Married to a pagan, she helped convert him to Christianity. Her prayers and solicitude were also influential in the conversion of Augustine, as he relates in his *Confessions.*

Monimia (mọ.nim'i.ạ). The chief female character in Thomas Otway's play *The Orphan;* an orphan left in charge of old Acasto, and loved by both his sons, Castalio and Polydore. Though married to the former, she became the innocent victim of the latter, and her woes have made the character proverbial as a type of suffering innocence.

fat, fāte, fär, ȧsk, fāre; net, mē, hėr; pin, pīne; not, nōte, mȯve, nôr; up, lūte, pull; ꜰʜ, then;

Moniplies (mun'i.plīz), **Richie.** An honest, pedantic servant of Olifaunt in Sir Walter Scott's novel *The Fortunes of Nigel.*

Monk, The. [Original full title, **Ambrosio, or the Monk.**] A Gothic romance by Matthew Gregory ("Monk") Lewis, published in 1795. A second edition was issued in which many passages considered objectionable in the first edition were omitted. The author gained the sobriquet of "Monk" Lewis from this book. This work combines the supernatural, the horrible, and the indecent in its plot about Ambrosio, the superior of the Capuchins of Madrid. He is seduced by Matilda de Villanegas, a woman driven to blind nymphomania by fiends (in the literal sense), who enters the monastery disguised as a boy. His entire character changes, and he pursues other women with the aid of magic and by murdering. His sins are found out and he is tortured by the Inquisition, finally being sentenced to death. He makes a bargain with the Devil in order to escape, but the Devil destroys him.

Monkbarns (mungk'bärnz), **Laird of.** Jonathan Oldbuck, the antiquary of Sir Walter Scott's novel *The Antiquary.*

Monkhouse (mungk'hous), **Allan.** [Full name, **Allan Noble Monkhouse.**] b. at Durham, England, May 7, 1858; d. at Disley, Cheshire, England, Jan. 10, 1936. An English novelist and playwright. He was literary editor (1902–32) of the Manchester *Guardian.* He was the author of many dramas, most of which were produced by repertory theaters at Birmingham, Manchester, and Liverpool. Among his plays are *Mary Broome* (1912), *Four Tragedies* (1913), *The Education of Mr. Surrage* (1913), *War Plays* (1916), *The Conquering Hero* (1923), *The Grand Cham's Diamond* (1924), *First Blood* (1924), and *Cecilia* (1932). His novels include *A Deliverance* (1898), *Love in a Life* (1903), *Dying Fires* (1912), *Men and Ghosts* (1918), *True Love* (1919), *My Daughter Helen* (1922), *Suburb* (1925), and *Farewell Manchester* (1931).

"Monk" Lewis (mungk' lö'is). See **Lewis, Matthew Gregory.**

Monks (mungks). In Dickens's *Oliver Twist,* Oliver's half brother.

Monk's Tale, The. One of Chaucer's *Canterbury Tales.* A series of 17 "tragedies" (stories of those who have fallen from high estate), told in eight-line stanzas, it contains, among others, the story of Ugolino from Dante, and follows Boccaccio's *De casibus virorum et feminarum illustrium* in a general way. It is unfinished, being stopped by the Knight:

> . . . for litel hevinesse
> Is right y-nough to mochel folk, I gesse.

The Host agrees ("Ye seye right sooth; this monk, he clappeth loude"), and the Monk takes it in good part, being a jovial fellow, no ascetic, but fond of hunting and the other good things of life:

> His heed was balled, that shoon as any glas,
> And eek his face, as he had been anoint.
> He was a lord ful fat and in good point; . . .
> His botes souple, his hors in greet estat.
> Now certeinly he was a fair prelat;
> He was nat pale as a for-pyned goost.
> A fat swan loved he best of any roost.

Monmouth's Rebellion (mon'muths). An unsuccessful rebellion (1685) against James II of England, led by the Duke of Monmouth (the illegitimate son of Charles II), who was defeated, captured, and beheaded. The precipitating cause of the revolt was popular fear of James's known Roman Catholic sympathies.

monologue (mon'ọ.log). That which is spoken by one person alone. Especially: (**a**) A dramatic soliloquy. (**b**) A kind of dramatic entertainment, consisting of recitations, imitations, anecdotes, songs, etc., performed throughout by one person. (**c**) A long speech or harangue uttered by one person, especially in the course of a conversation.

monometer (mọ.nom'ẹ.tẻr). In prosody, a meter consisting of a single measure.

Monomotapa (mō''nō.mō.tä'pä). A name given to an African kingdom said once to have flourished in the lower Zambezi basin. It was often mentioned by early Portuguese writers (whence picked up, under various spellings, by 16th-century English chroniclers) for its gold mines, but all attempts of the Portuguese to colonize the area failed, and most of the accounts of it were so embellished by legend as to be of little historical use.

Monro (mun.rō'), **Harold Edward.** b. at Brussels, Belgium, March 14, 1879; d. at Broadstairs, Kent, England, March 16, 1932. An English poet, critic, and anthologist. He founded the Poetry Society and the *Poetry Review,* a quarterly, in 1911, established (1912) the Poetry Bookshop in a London slum area, in order to bring poetry to the people, and founded (1913) the periodical *Poetry and the Drama,* which was suspended (December, 1914) because of World War I and was reëstablished (1919) as *The Chapbook* and finally discontinued in 1921. Author of *Poems* (1906), *Judas* (1908), *Before Dawn* (1911), *Children of Love* (1914), *Trees* (1916), *Strange Meetings* (1917), *Real Property* (1922), *The Earth for Sale* (1928), and *Elm Angel* (1930), poetry; *Proposals for a Voluntary Nobility* (1907), *Chronicle of a Pilgrimage: Paris to Milan on Foot* (1909), *The Evolution of the Soul* (1917), *Some Contemporary Poets* (1920), and *One Day Awake: A Modern Morality* (1922), prose; and of *Twentieth Century Poetry* (1929), an anthology. Among his single poems are *Every Thing, City, Storm, Solitude, Children of Love, Dog,* and *Man Carrying Bale.*

Monsieur (mẹ.syè'). The Machiavellian brother of the King of France in George Chapman's tragedy *Bussy D'Ambois.*

Monsieur D'Olive (dọ.lēv'). A tragicomedy by George Chapman, published in 1606 and probably written in 1604 or 1605.

Monsieur Thomas (tom'ạs). A play by John Fletcher, written c1616, acted in 1639 as *Father's Own Son,* and printed in that same year. It is based upon the second part of Honoré d'Urfé's *L'Astrée,* a romance published in 1610.

Mons Meg (monz meg). An old cannon in the castle at Edinburgh, made at Mons, Belgium.

Montacute (mon'tạ.kūt) or **Montagu** (mon'tạ.gū), **John de.** See under **Salisbury, (3rd) Earl of.**

Montacute or **Montagu, Thomas de.** See under **Salisbury, (4th) Earl of.**

Montagu (mon'ta.gū), **Basil.** b. at London, April 24, 1770; d. at Boulogne, France, Nov. 27, 1851. An English lawyer and writer. He was educated at the Charterhouse and at Christ's College, Cambridge, where he graduated in 1790. He was admitted to Gray's Inn, and went to London in 1795. He was an intimate of Samuel Coleridge and William Wordsworth. He was called to the bar in 1798, and published in 1801 *A Summary of the Law of Set Off*, and from 1805 to 1807 prepared a *Digest of the Bankruptcy Laws*. In 1825 he exposed the delay and expense of the existing bankruptcy procedure, and in 1835 was made accountant general in bankruptcy. Between 1825 and 1834 he edited the *Works of Lord Bacon*. His *Essays* were published in 1824.

Montagu, Charles. [Title, 1st Earl of **Halifax.**] b. probably at Horton, Northamptonshire, England, April 16, 1661; d. May 19, 1715. An English statesman, financier, and poet. He studied at Westminster and at Cambridge (Trinity College). In 1689 he was returned to the Convention Parliament for Maldon. In March, 1692, he was appointed a lord of the treasury, and induced Parliament to raise a loan of a million in annuities based on new excise duties. This loan was the beginning of the English national debt. Adopting William Patterson's scheme for a national bank, he carried through a bill to raise a loan of 1,200,000 pounds based on a tonnage bill, the subscribers to form a corporation known as the Governor and Company of the Bank of England. On April 30, 1694, he was made chancellor of the exchequer. With the aid of Somers, Locke, Newton, and Halley he reformed the currency in 1695, and for the first time issued the exchequer bills by which the British government gets its first credit from the House of Commons. In 1696 he carried his "general mortgage" scheme, by which a consolidated fund was formed. In 1697 he became prime minister, but resigned in 1699. In 1698 he established the society to which a monopoly of the Indian trade was given. On Dec. 13, 1700, he was created Baron Halifax. He was impeached in 1701 and acquitted, but was not in office during Queen Anne's reign. On Oct. 19, 1714, he was created Earl of Halifax. He served as president of the Royal Society from 1695 to 1698. He was the collaborator of Matthew Prior in *The City Mouse and the Country Mouse* (1687), a parody of John Dryden's *The Hind and the Panther*.

Montagu, Edward Wortley. b. 1713; d. in Italy, 1776. An English author; son of Lady Mary Wortley Montagu. He was the reputed author of *Reflections on the Rise and Fall of Ancient Republics* (1759).

Montagu, Elizabeth. [Maiden name, **Robinson.**] b. at York, England, Oct. 2, 1720; d. at Montagu House, London, Aug. 25, 1800. An English author and social leader. After 1750 she held her salon in Hill Street, Mayfair. The epithet "bluestocking" was first applied to her assemblies. Among her visitors were George, Lord Lyttelton, Edmund Burke, David Garrick, and Sir Joshua Reynolds. Her younger associates included Hannah More and Fanny Burney. In 1760 she contributed three dialogues to Lyttelton's *Dialogues of the Dead*. In 1769 she wrote an essay on the *Genius of Shakespeare* in answer to Voltaire.

Montagu, Lady Mary Wortley. [Maiden name, **Pierrepont.**] Baptized at Covent Garden, London, May 26, 1689; d. in England, Aug. 21, 1762. An English writer; eldest daughter of Evelyn Pierrepont, 5th Earl (later Duke) of Kingston. She privately married (against her father's wishes) Edward Wortley Montagu, grandson of Edward Montagu, 1st Earl of Sandwich, on Aug. 12, 1712. She was a favorite of the Princess of Wales (afterward Queen Caroline). In 1716 Montagu was appointed ambassador to Turkey. He was recalled in October, 1717, but resided in Constantinople until June, 1718. An interesting account of the visit appears in her *Letters*. While at Adrianople she observed the practice of inoculation against smallpox, and she assisted in introducing it into England. She was quite intimate with Alexander Pope, but quarreled with him finally, perhaps because, as some believe, she laughed aloud at a declaration of love from the deformed poet or perhaps because she allowed a parody she had written of one of his poems to circulate. In 1739 she again went abroad, and in 1758 settled at Venice, returning to England in 1762. Her *Letters* appeared in 1763 and 1767.

Montague (mon'ta.gū). In Shakespeare's *Romeo and Juliet*, the family name of Romeo. Montague is Romeo's father and a bitter enemy of Capulet. This feud between the houses of Montague and Capulet plays an important part in the separation of the lovers which leads to the eventual tragedy. However, Montague is reconciled after Romeo and Juliet's deaths, promising to erect a statue of Juliet.

Montague. The "honest man" in John Fletcher and Philip Massinger's play *The Honest Man's Fortune*.

Montague, Lady. In Shakespeare's *Romeo and Juliet*, the mother of Romeo.

Montague, Marquess of. In Shakespeare's *3 Henry VI*, the historical John Neville, Marquis of Montagu, a supporter of York who later joins the Lancastrians under Henry VI and is killed at the battle of Barnet.

Montague Tigg (tig). See **Tigg, Montague.**

Montaigne (mon.tān'; French, môn.teny'), **Michel Eyquem de.** b. at the Château Montaigne, Dordogne, France, Feb. 28, 1533; d. there, Sept. 13, 1592. A French essayist and philosopher. His early education was carried on at home under his father's guidance. After graduating from college at Bordeaux, he studied law. In 1559 he was at the court of Francis II, and in 1571 became attached to the person of Henry III. In this year Montaigne published his friend Étienne La Boétie's translations from the Greek, and in 1572 edited the latter's French verses. In 1580 he traveled in Germany, Switzerland, and Italy. He left Rome in 1581 to become mayor of Bordeaux. Montaigne is chiefly known for his *Essais* (Bordeaux, 1580; the edition of 1588 was the last to be published during the author's lifetime). Mademoiselle de Gournay, a warm admirer of Montaigne who prepared the edition of 1595, did not have access to the copy of his last edition which Montaigne himself had corrected. The famous English translation of 1603, by John Florio, was made from Mademoiselle de Gournay's text. There are many complete modern translations. In his essays, usually considered the best personal essays ever written, Montaigne studies himself as well as the men of the society of his day. He examines everything in a skeptical spirit, is inclined to doubt, and his motto is *Que sais-je?* (What do I know?). Montaigne's ideas and influence are to be traced in many of the best French authors of the 17th and 18th centuries, while outside of France his essays were diligently read by Bacon, Shakespeare, and many succeeding writers.

Montano (mon.tan′ō). The name of Reynaldo in the first quarto *Hamlet*.

Montano. In Shakespeare's *Othello*, the Governor of Cyprus.

Montargis (môṅ.tàr.zhē). A town in C France, in the department of Loiret, on the Loing River ab. 63 mi. SE of Paris. It is the site of ruins of a medieval castle and of a statue of the "Dog of Montargis," which, reputedly, exposed the murderer of its master. According to the legend, when the murderer was accused by the dog's attitude, Charles VIII ordered that a duel be fought between the dog and the accused. The dog won this "judicial combat" and the murderer confessed his crime.

Monte Carlo (mon′tē kär′lō; French, môṅ.te kàr.lō; Italian, mōn′tä kär′lō). A town in the principality of Monaco, situated on the Mediterranean Sea coast between Nice and Menton, adjacent to the town of La Condamine. It is one of the most fashionable resorts on the French Riviera, with a bathing beach and artistic and sports festivals. The famous gambling casino was built in 1879 and enlarged at the end of the 19th century.

Montemayor (mōn′′tä.mä.yor′), **Jorge de.** b. at Montemayor, Portugal, c1520; d. at Turin, Italy, Feb. 26, 1561. A Spanish romancer and poet, author of the pastoral romance *Diana Enamorada*. A soldier during his youth, he was later attached as a musician to the traveling chapel of Prince Philip (later Philip II) of Spain. Some sources have suggested that his principal work (mentioned above) may have been used in translation by Shakespeare in the preparation of *Two Gentlemen of Verona*.

Montesinos (mōn.tä.sē′nōs). A legendary hero of Spanish medieval romance. According to legend, he retired to a cavern at La Mancha, and lived there. In Cervantes's *Don Quixote*, the hero's visit to the cave of Montesinos (book ii, chap. 23) is an important episode.

Montesquieu (mon′tẹs.kū; French, môṅ.tes.kyė), Baron **de la Brède et de.** [Title of **Charles de Secondat.**] b. at the Château de la Brède, near Bordeaux, France, Jan. 18, 1689; d. at Paris, Feb. 10, 1755. A French writer and political philosopher. He was brought up at the College of Juilly, near Meaux, and returned to his native province to study law. In 1714 he was made councilor, and in 1716 president, of the Bordeaux parliament. He was not in sympathy, however, with the duties of his position, and he gradually withdrew from them

and devoted his attention to the study of literature and jurisprudence. In 1721 he won fame in the world of letters with his *Lettres persanes*, in which he criticizes the French society of his time, using the fiction of two Persians who see French life from an alien and therefore fresh viewpoint. For this work he was elected to the French Academy in 1728. The following years were spent in travel, and he visited Austria, Italy, Germany, Switzerland, the Netherlands, and England. After his return to France he devoted his life entirely to literary work. Among his many productions, the two which have contributed most to his renown are the *Considérations sur les causes de la grandeur et de la décadence des Romains* (1734) and *L'Esprit des lois* (1748). The latter played an important role in shaping subsequent political thought.

Montez (mon′tez, mon.tez′), **Lola.** [Original name, **Marie Dolores Eliza Rosanna Gilbert.**] b. at Limerick, Ireland, 1818; d. at Astoria, N. Y., Jan. 17, 1861. An Irish dancer and adventuress. She was married to Captain Thomas James of the British army in 1837, but was divorced by him in 1842. Having taken lessons from a Spanish dancing teacher, she began her public career at London in 1843 under the professional name of Lola Montez, billed as a Spanish dancer. Less than laudatory opinions have been recorded concerning her dancing, but her beauty, charm, and spirit were undeniable. She appeared with great success in various European cities, and at Munich so captivated the elderly King Ludwig of Bavaria that presently (1847) she was his recognized mistress. Having been naturalized and made Baronne de Rosenthal and Comtesse de Landsfeld, by her ascendancy over the monarch she became virtual ruler of the kingdom, displaying moreover great ability and sagacity. This eminence, however, was of short duration. Hostility between liberal and conservative students at the university, the former of whom she had patronized, led to a riot in which her life was threatened. She caused the university to be closed, an action which was among the events leading up to the insurrection which forced Ludwig to abdicate on March 21, 1848. Lola was banished; and, returning to England, she was married to George Trafford Heald in July, 1849. She was summoned for bigamy, but fled to Spain; and in 1851, again in the character of a Spanish dancer, she came to the U. S., opening at New York, and everywhere drawing crowded houses. Her second husband having, it is supposed, died in 1853, in that year she married P. P. Hull, a San Franciscan. She toured Australia (1855–56), returned to the U. S., and before long retired from the stage. From 1859 she devoted herself to aiding outcast women, spending her means and laboring among them until, stricken with paralysis, she died in poverty.

Montezuma (mon.tẹ.zō′mạ). The magnanimous general of the Inca in Dryden and Howard's *The Indian Queen*. He is nearly driven mad by his passion for Orazia, the Inca's daughter, who scorns him.

Montferrers (mont.fer′ėrz), **Lord.** The brother of D'Amville and father of Charlemont, murdered by D'Amville and Borachio in Cyril Tourneur's *The Atheist's Tragedy*.

ḍ, d or j; ṣ, s or sh; ṭ, t or ch; ẓ, z or zh; o, F. cloche; ü, F. menu; ċh, Sc. loch; ṅ, F. bonbon.

Montgomerie (mǫnt.gum'ri, -gum'ę.ri), **Alexander.** b. c1556; d. before 1615. A Scottish poet. His chief work is the allegorical poem *The Cherry and the Slae* (1597). He also wrote *The Flyting betwixt Montgomery and Polwart* (1621).

Montgomery (mǫnt.gum'ri, -gum'ę.ri), 1st Earl of. See **Herbert, Philip.**

Montgomery, James. b. at Irvine, Ayrshire, Scotland, Nov. 4, 1771; d. April 30, 1854. A Scottish poet. In 1792 he entered the office of the *Sheffield Register*, and in 1795 the paper became his property; the name meanwhile had been changed to the *Sheffield Iris*. In 1806 his poems *The Wanderer of Switzerland* and *The Grave* won him recognition. The numerous hymns on which his reputation chiefly rests were collected in 1853.

Montgomery, Jemima. See **Tautphoeus, Baroness von.**

Montgomery, Leslie Alexander. See **Doyle, Lynn.**

Montgomery, Robert. b. at Bath, England, 1807; d. at Brighton, England, Dec. 3, 1855. An English poet. Among his poems are *The Stagecoach* (1827), *Omnipresence of the Deity* (1828), *Satan* (1830), and *The Puffiad* (1830). His work was attacked by the critics, notably by T. B. Macaulay in the *Edinburgh Review* (1830), but his poems, especially *Omnipresence of the Deity*, continued in great popularity.

Montgomery, Sir John. In Shakespeare's *3 Henry VI*, a supporter of Edward, Earl of March. He urges Edward to fight for the throne (IV.vii).

Monticelso (mon.ti.sel'sō), **Cardinal.** A Machiavellian character in John Webster's tragedy *The White Devil*.

Montjoie (môṅ.zhwä). The hill near Paris where Saint Denis was martyred. Before 1789 it was the name of the king at arms. In ancient tournaments "Montjoie" was the cry of the French heralds, and "Montjoie Saint Denis" the war cry of the French in battle. The kings of England had at one time the war cry "Montjoie Saint George." It was last used by the French at the siege of Montargis in 1426. Shakespeare gives the name Montjoy to the French herald in *Henry V*.

Montjoy (mont.joi'). In Shakespeare's *Henry V*, a French herald who asks whether Henry will offer ransom before he is forced to engage in battle with the French army at Agincourt. Later he acknowledges French defeat.

Montmartre (môṅ.màrtr). A hill in N Paris, locality of an old town incorporated since 1860 in the city of Paris as the 18th arrondissement. The hill, which is named either for Saint Denis and his fellow martyrs (*Mons martyrum*) or for an ancient temple to Mars (*Mons martis*), is topped by the basilica of Sacré-Cœur, which stands at the highest point in Paris. The section, once noted for its bohemian inhabitants, is now perhaps best known for its cabarets. The famous Montmartre cemetery is on the W flank of the hill. Height, 420 ft.

Montoni (mon.tō'nē). The villain in Ann Radcliffe's novel *The Mysteries of Udolpho.*

Montrose (mon.trōz'), 5th Earl and 1st Marquis of. Titles of **Graham, James.**

Montsurry (mont.sur'i). The husband of Tamyra, who is loved by both Bussy D'Ambois and Monsieur in George Chapman's tragedy *Bussy D'Ambois.*

Monument, the. A column in London, N of the Thames, near London Bridge. It was erected to commemorate the great fire of 1666, and stands close to the spot where the conflagration started. It is a fluted Roman-Doric column designed by Wren, standing on a square base ornamented with reliefs, and supporting on a pedestal above the capital an urn from which flames issue. The height is 202 ft.

Moody (mö'di). In John Dryden's play *Sir Martin Mar-all*, a swashbuckler.

Moody. The guardian of Peggy, the country girl, in David Garrick's adaptation of William Wycherley's *The Country Wife.*

Moon and Sixpence, The. A novel by W. Somerset Maugham, published in 1919. The character of Charles Strickland, the central figure in the story, is supposedly based on Paul Gauguin, the French post-impressionist painter.

Moonshine (mōn'shīn). In Shakespeare's *Midsummer Night's Dream*, the part played by Starveling, the tailor, in the interpolated play.

Moonstone, The. A novel by Wilkie Collins, published in 1868. This work is generally agreed to be one of the best, as well as the first, of modern detective novels. The novel is composed of sections supposedly written by various of the characters. John Herncastle, an English officer, has murdered three Brahmins in order to obtain a great gem (a yellow diamond) that was set in the forehead of the moon god. He takes it back to England and bequeathes it to his niece, Rachel Verinder, as a present on her 18th birthday. The Moonstone disappears on the same night that she receives it, and three Indian jugglers, who have appeared in the neighborhood, are suspected of the theft. Sergeant Cuff, one of the first detectives in English fiction, comes to attempt to solve the mystery. Two persons know the identity of the thief from the beginning (Rosanna Spearman, whose suicide complicates the mystery, and Rachel Verinder, who refuses to coöperate with the investigation). It is Franklin Blake, the man with whom both are in love. He stole it from Rachel's cabinet at night, but she does not realize that he had secretly been given opium at the time and cannot remember that he took it nor why (he had wished to put it in a safer place). Meanwhile, the Moonstone has been taken from the unconscious Blake by Godfrey Ablewhite, another of Miss Verinder's admirers. He is tracked down by the three Indians who have come for their possession, and finally they murder the villainous Ablewhite. The mystery is explained at last, and Miss Verinder is free to marry Blake, whom she has shielded (though she thought him a criminal) from the beginning.

Moor (mör), **Edward.** b. 1771; d. at London, Feb. 26, 1848. An English writer on Hindu mythology. He published *Hindoo Pantheon* (1810), *Hindoo Infanticide* (1811), *The Gentle Sponge*, a proposal for reducing the interest on the national debt (1829), and *Suffolk Words and Phrases* (1823).

fat, fāte, fär, ȧsk, fāre; net, mē, hėr; pin, pīne; not, nōte, mõve, nôr; up, lūte, půll; ᴛн, then;

Moore (mōr), **Edward.** b. at Abingdon, England, March 22, 1712; d. at South Lambeth, London, March 1, 1757. An English dramatist and fabulist. He failed in business as a linen draper at London, and began as a writer with his *Fables for the Female Sex* in 1744. *The Foundling*, a comedy, was produced at Drury Lane Theatre, London, on Feb. 13, 1748; *Gil Blas*, a comedy, in 1751; and *The Gamester*, in which Garrick appeared (and which he partly wrote), at Drury Lane on Feb. 7, 1753. In 1753 he was made editor of *The World*, a popular paper, which had a number of famous contributors.

Moore, George. b. at Moore Hall, County Mayo, Ireland, 1852; d. Jan. 21, 1933. A British novelist, poet, dramatist, and critic. He published two volumes of verse, *Flowers of Passion* (1877) and *Pagan Poems* (1881). As a critic he was one of the first in England to champion the impressionist school of painters and the naturalistic school in literature. He was associated with Edward Martyn and William Butler Yeats in founding the Irish Literary Theatre (out of which grew the Abbey Theatre) at Dublin, and wrote two plays, *The Strike at Arlingford* (1893) and *The Bending of the Bough* (1900). His other works include *A Modern Lover* (1883), *A Mummer's Wife* (1884), *Parnell and his Ireland* (1887), *Confessions of a Young Man* (1888), *Mike Fletcher* (1889), *Vain Fortune* (1891), *Modern Painting* (1893), *Esther Waters* (1894), *Impressions and Opinions* (1895), *Celibates* (1895), *Evelyn Innes* (1898), *Sister Teresa* (1901; a continuation of *Evelyn Innes*), *The Untilled Field* (1903), *The Lake* (1905), *Hail and Farewell* (a trilogy including *Ave*, 1911; *Salve*, 1912; and *Vale*, 1914), *The Brook Kerith* (1916), *Héloise and Abélard* (1921), *Conversations in Ebury Street* (1924), and *Aphrodite in Aulis* (1931). He was influenced in many of these works by Flaubert, Zola, and Balzac.

Moore, John. b. at Stirling, Scotland, 1729; d. at Richmond, Surrey, England, Jan. 21, 1802. A Scottish physician, novelist, and writer of travels; father of Sir John Moore (1761–1809). His best-known work is the novel *Zeluco* (1786), which Byron attempted to imitate in poetry in his *Childe Harold.*

Moore, Sir John. b. at Glasgow, Nov. 13, 1761; d. at La Coruña, Spain, Jan. 16, 1809. A British general. He was the eldest surviving son of John Moore (1729–1802), author of *Zeluco*. In 1776 he became ensign of the 51st Foot, and he served as captain lieutenant in Nova Scotia during the American Revolutionary War. He became member of Parliament for Linlithgow in 1784, and served in Corsica (1793–94), but displeased Horatio Nelson and Gilbert Elliot because of his friendliness with the Corsicans and was ordered home. In November, 1797, he joined Ralph Abercromby in Ireland. He was made major general in 1798. He fought (1801) in Egypt, and then returned (1803) to England to train troops for the expected invasion of England by Napoleon. In July, 1808, he sailed for Portugal as second in command to Sir Henry Burrard, and by September the entire command was left to him. He entered Spain on Nov. 11, 1808, but, abandoned by the Spaniards and threatened by the actual presence of Napoleon, was obliged to retreat 250 miles to La Coruña.

While the troops were embarking the French attacked them, and, although the British won a brilliant victory, Moore was killed and buried in the citadel during the night of January 16–17. He received a monument in Saint Paul's Cathedral. *The Burial of Sir John Moore*, by Rev. Charles Wolfe, is one of the most popular English poems.

Moore, Thomas. [Pseudonyms: **Thomas Little, Thomas Brown the Younger.**] b. at Dublin, May 28, 1779; d. at Bromham, near Devizes, England, Feb. 25, 1852. Irish poet. He entered Trinity College, Dublin, in 1794, where he was intimate with Robert Emmet. In 1799 he entered the Middle Temple, London, and in 1800 published his translation of *Anacreon*. In 1803 and 1804 he traveled in America. He published his *Odes and Epistles* in 1806 and his *Irish Melodies* from 1807 to 1834, receiving from them about 500 pounds a year. His lampoons on the regent and his favorites were extremely successful, and were collected in 1813 in *The Twopenny Post Bag*. On March 25, 1811, he married Bessie Dyke, an actress, and in the same year his friendship for Byron began. *Lalla Rookh*, for which Longmans agreed to pay 3,000 pounds without having seen it, was published in 1817, *National Airs* in 1815, and *Sacred Songs* in 1816. His prose works, besides the political squibs, are *Life of Sheridan* (1825), *The Epicurean* (1827), *Life of Byron* (1830), *History of Ireland*, and others, besides a number of collections of humorous short papers like *The Fudge Family in Paris*, all under the pseudonym Thomas Brown the Younger. *Moore's Memoirs, Journals, and Correspondence* were published 1853–56 by Earl Russell.

Moore, T. Sturge. b. at Hastings, England, March 4, 1870; d. 1944. An English poet, engraver, and art critic. He made designs for volumes of Yeats's poetry, and his books of criticism include works on Correggio, Dürer, and Blake. In his poetry he relied largely on mythological and classical themes, trying, however, to give them a modern diction and style. His volumes of verse include *The Vinedresser and Other Poems* (1899), *Danaë* (1903), *A Sicilian Idyll* (1911), *The Sea is Kind* (1914), and *Judas* (1923). His prose writings include *Life and Art* (1910) and *Armour for Aphrodite* (1929).

Moorfields (mōr'fēldz). A district of old London, outside the wall, once used as a place of recreation. It received its name from the moor which lay on the N side of the city. Finsbury Square and adjacent streets now cover it.

Moor Fires. A novel by E. H. Young, published in 1916.

Moorgate (mōr'gāt). A postern gate in the old London city wall, built on the moor side of the city in the time of Henry V (c1415). It was rebuilt in 1472 and was pulled down c1750.

Mopsa (mop'sa). In Sir Philip Sidney's romance *Arcadia*, a deformed country girl; the daughter of Dametas.

Mopsa. A shepherdess in Shakespeare's *Winter's Tale*.

Morakanabad (mō.ra.kan'a.bad). The grand vizier of Vathek in William Beckford's tale *Vathek.*

ḍ, d or j; ş, s or sh; ṭ, t or ch; z̧, z or zh; o, F. cloche; ü, F. menu; ċh, Sc. loch; ṅ, F. bonbon.

morality plays. [Also, **moralities.**] Plays developed in the early 15th century, having the didactic purpose of inculcating good behavior in their hearers. Generally speaking, the morality play presents abstract virtues and vices struggling for possession of a man's soul. There is usually a debate between Body and Soul in which the Soul moralizes against the Body, which has led it unwillingly down the road to damnation. Finally, after death, abstractions representing heavenly judgment decide whether Man shall be given mercy or harsh punishment. These heavenly abstractions are often the Four Daughters of God: Mercy and Peace (for salvation), Righteousness and Truth (for damnation). The earliest morality play is *The Pride of Life* (c1400), and others include *The Castle of Perseverance* (c1405), *Mind, Will, and Understanding* (c1460), *Mankynd* (c1475), and the well-known *Everyman* (late 15th century).

Morals of Marcus Ordeyne (mär′kus ôr′den), **The.** A novel (1905) by W. J. Locke.

Moraunt (môr′ônt), **Sir.** See **Morhault, Sir.**

Mordaunt (môr′dant), **Elinor.** [Maiden name, **Evelyn May Clowes.**] b. in Nottinghamshire, England, c1877; d. 1942. An Anglo-Irish novelist, traveler, and writer of short stories and books for children. She lived and traveled in Mauritius, Australia, the Balkans, Italy, and Morocco, writing accounts of most of these areas. She went (1923) around the world for the London *Daily News.* Author of the novels *The Garden of Contentment* (1902), *Ship of Solace* (1911), *The Cost of It* (1912), *Lu of the Ranges* (1913), *Simpson* (1913), *Bellamy* (1914), *The Island* (1914), *The Family* (1915), *The Rose of Youth* (1915), *Shoe and Stocking Stories* (1915), *The Processionals* (1918; American title, *While There's Life*), *The Little Soul* (1921), *Laura Crichton* (1921), *Father and Daughter* (1928; American title, *Too Much Java*), *Full Circle* (1931; American title, *Gin and Bitters*), *Mrs. Van Kleek* (1933), *Prelude to Death* (1936), *Roses in December* (1939), *Death, It Is* (1939), *Return to Spring* (1940), *Hobby House* (1940), *Judge Not* (1940), and *Tropic Heat* (1941). *Sinabada* (1937) is her autobiography.

Mordecai (môr′de.kī, môr.de.kā′ī). [Also, **Mardochai** (mär′dọ.kī, mär.dọ.kā′ī).] In the Bible, according to the book of Esther, a Jew of the tribe of Benjamin, who lived in captivity in the time of Xerxes. He accepted a post at the court in order to be near his cousin and adopted daughter, Esther, who had been elevated to the rank of queen, and with her help frustrated the machinations of Haman against the Jews. In remembrance of this deliverance the feast of Purim is still celebrated by orthodox Jews in the month of Adar (March–April). The resemblance of the names Mordecai and Esther to Marduk and Ishtar has made scholars suspect a Hebrew adaptation of a Babylonian myth in the story.

Mordecai. In George Eliot's novel *Daniel Deronda*, a Jew who believes himself inspired with a mission to elevate and reunite the Jewish people.

Mordred (môr′dred). See **Modred.**

Mordure (môr.dūr′). Another name of the magic sword Excalibur.

More (mōr), **Hannah.** b. at Stapleton, Gloucestershire, England, Feb. 2, 1745; d. at Clifton, England, Sept. 7, 1833. An English religious writer. She was educated by her father, and in 1757 joined her other sisters in establishing a school at Bristol. In 1762 she published *The Search after Happiness*, a pastoral drama. In 1773 and 1774 she visited London, and became an intimate of Garrick and his wife; she also met Joshua Reynolds, Edmund Burke, Samuel Johnson, and Mrs. Elizabeth Montagu. Garrick produced two of her dramas, *Percy* (1777) and *Fatal Falsehood* (1779). In 1782 she published *Sacred Dramas*. After the death (Jan. 20, 1779) of Garrick her religious tendencies became stronger. In 1787 she was attracted by William Wilberforce's agitation against the slave trade, and was much interested in establishing schools among the poor as an antidote to the prevailing atheism. She wrote in 1792 *Village Politics, by Will Chip*, followed by *Cheap Repository Tracts* (1795–98), one of which was "The Shepherd of Salisbury Plain." Some of them were illustrated by John Bewick. The organization which circulated them developed into the Religious Tract Depository in 1799. Her other works are *Thoughts on the Importance of the Manners of the Great to General Society* (1788), *Strictures on the Modern System of Female Education* (1799), *Coelebs in Search of a Wife* (1809), which, in the form of a novel, depicted the corrupt Regency society, and which was a great success, *Practical Piety* (1811), and *Christian Morals* (1813).

More, Henry. b. at Grantham, England, Oct. 12, 1614; d. at Cambridge, England, Sept. 1, 1687. An English philosophical writer. His philosophical works (largely mystical and Platonic) were published in 1678. His chief work in verse is *The Song of the Soul*.

More, Sir Thomas. For the play, see **Sir Thomas More.**

More, Sir Thomas. [Also, Saint **Thomas More.**] b. at London, Feb. 6, 1477 or 1478; executed there, July 6, 1535. An English statesman and author. He was the son of Sir John More, a London barrister, and Agnes, daughter of Thomas Graunger. He began his studies at Saint Anthony's School on Threadneedle Street, London, under Nicholas Holt, but at about the age of 12 or 13 was placed in the household of John Morton, archbishop of Canterbury (later cardinal) and chancellor, where he continued his education until 1492, when he entered Canterbury Hall (later merged in Christ Church), Oxford. He entered New Inn, London, in 1494, and Lincoln's Inn in 1496. In 1499 he met Erasmus in England, and corresponded with him throughout the rest of his life. For four years he considered becoming a priest, during which time, although a layman, he lectured (at the invitation of William Grocyn) on *The City of God* at Saint Lawrence Jewry and lived, without vow, with the monks of the Charterhouse. However, finding himself without a vocation for the life of a priest, he married (c1504) Jane, daughter of John Colt, by whom he had four children: Margaret (b. 1505, married William Roper in 1521), Elizabeth (b. 1506, married William Dauncey in 1525), Cecily (b. 1507, married Giles Heron in 1525), and John

(b. 1509, married Anne Cresacre in 1529). His home was "the old Barge," Bucklesbury, London. He was first elected to Parliament in 1504, where his opposition to Henry VII's extravagant demands for a dowry for his daughter Margaret, lately married to James IV of Scotland, may have necessitated a protective exile; in 1508 he visited the universities of Paris and Louvain. He greeted Henry VIII's coronation in 1509 with exuberant congratulatory Latin. He became under-sheriff of London in 1510. In 1511 his first wife died; in the same year he married Alice Middleton, a widow. In May, 1515, he was sent to Flanders to settle disputes with merchants there, and in August, 1517, to Calais on similar business. Returning in October, he was appointed one of the king's councilors and a judge of the court of requests. In June, 1520, he was with King Henry at the Field of the Cloth of Gold. In 1521 he was knighted and made undertreasurer, in April, 1523, speaker of the House of Commons, in 1524 high steward of Oxford University, and in 1525 high steward of Cambridge University and chancellor of the Duchy of Lancaster. In 1524 he was buying property at Chelsea, where he moved his home from London. On Oct. 26, 1529, he succeeded Thomas Wolsey as chancellor. He opened the Parliament of Nov. 3, 1529, to which Henry complained of the divided allegiance of his clergy; the clergy completely surrendered to the king as "Head of the Church" on May 15, 1532, and on the next day More resigned the chancellorship. An act of Parliament in March, 1534 (25 Henry VIII, 22), fixed the succession in the issue of Anne Boleyn and demanded oaths of agreement to the act. To this More was willing to swear, but the oath as presented to him contained an illegal rider, introduced by Thomas Audley and Cromwell (made legal by a later statute: 26 Henry VIII, 2) which gave the king theological power over the church. To this More refused to swear, but he made no statement against the oath or those who took it. Nevertheless, he was committed to the Tower of London on April 17, 1534, and, though guilty of no word or deed against the king, on July 1, 1535, was charged with silence and convicted of treason for what the court believed he thought. Five days later he was beheaded on Tower Hill. His feast day is July 6; he was beatified by Pope Leo XIII on Dec. 29, 1886, and canonized by Pope Pius XI on May 19, 1935. His literary reputation is based chiefly on the Latin work *Utopia* (published 1516 and first translated into English by Ralph Robinson, 1551), but his English prose style (as evidenced by his *History of Richard III*, a source of Shakespeare's play on the same king) is clear, tough, witty, cadenced, eloquent, and dramatic. Unfortunately his reputation suffers in this respect because much of his writing is concerned with religious controversy, wherein style is not usually looked for, and because many of his pieces have not been reprinted since the collected *English Works* of 1557. The most complete collection of his Latin works is the Frankfort-Leipzig edition of 1689. More's chief writings were: (in Latin) a translation of four dialogues of Lucian, a commentary on the Psalms, a refutation of Luther's charges against Henry VIII, written under the pseudonym of William Ross, 255 epi-

grams, and *Utopia;* (in both English and Latin) the *History of Richard III* and *Treatise on the Passion;* (in English) some schoolboy poetry, a *Life of John Pico*, a commentary on *The Four Last Things*, several theological debates, a *Dialogue of Comfort against Tribulation*, and an autobiographical defense of himself. Besides these, More was in communication with all the important humanists of his day. Of his letters, 218 survive.

More Dissemblers besides Women. A comedy by Thomas Middleton, licensed as "an old play" in 1623, printed in 1657 with *Women Beware Women*, but probably acted in 1615.

More Frightened than Hurt. See under **Duellists, The.**

Morel (mô.rel′), **Paul.** The hero of D. H. Lawrence's autobiographical novel *Sons and Lovers* (1913).

Morell (mô.rel′), **James.** The husband of Candida in George Bernard Shaw's play *Candida.*

Morelove (mōr′luv), **Lord.** The lover of Lady Betty Modish in Colley Cibber's *The Careless Husband.*

Moren (mōr′en), **Countess.** A character in George Chapman's comedy *An Humorous Day's Mirth.*

More of More Hall (mōr). See under **Dragon of Wantley, The.**

Moresby (mōrz′bi), **Louis.** A pseudonym of **Beck, Lily Adams.**

Morgan (môr′gan). In Shakespeare's *Cymbeline*, the assumed name of Belarius.

Morgan. A Welsh surgeon in Tobias Smollett's novels *Roderick Random* and *Peregrine Pickle.*

Morgan, Charles. [Full name, **Charles Langbridge Morgan.**] b. in Kent, England, Jan. 22, 1894—. An English novelist and critic; husband of Hilda Vaughan. He was drama critic (1921 *et seq.*) for the London *Times.* He was awarded the Femina-Vie Heureuse prize (1930) for *Portrait in a Mirror* (1929; published in America under the title *First Love*), the Hawthornden prize (1933) for *The Fountain* (1932), and the James Tait Black Memorial prize (1941) for *The Voyage* (1940). Author also of *The Gun-room* (1919), *My Name is Legion* (1925), *Sparkenbroke* (1936), *The Empty Room* (1941), *Reflections in a Mirror* (1944), *The Judge's Story* (1947), and others, and the play *The Flashing Stream* (1938).

Morgan, Sir Frederick Edgworth. b. Feb. 5, 1894—. An English soldier. In World War II he was chief of staff to Dwight Eisenhower, the supreme allied commander, and planned the invasion of the Continent. He served (1945–46) as deputy to General Walter Bedell Smith and was head of the United Nations Relief and Rehabilitation Administration in Germany. He succeeded (1951) Sir Charles Portal as director of the British atomic energy commission. Author of *Overture to Overlord* (1950), the story of his work in preparing the European invasion.

Morgan, George Campbell. b. at Tetbury, Gloucestershire, England, Dec. 9, 1863; d. 1945. An English Congregational minister. He was the editor of the *Westminster Bible Record* and the *Westminster*

ḍ, d or j; ṣ, s or sh; ṭ, t or ch; ẓ, z or zh; o, F. cloche; ü, F. menu; ċh, Sc. loch; ṅ, F. bonbon.

Pulpit. He published *The Crises of the Christ* (1903), *The Analyzed Bible* (1907), and others.

Morgan, Sydney. [Title: Lady **Morgan;** maiden name, **Sydney Owenson.**] b. at Dublin, c1783; d. at London, April 14, 1859. An Irish novelist; daughter of an Irish actor, and wife (married 1812) of Sir Thomas Charles Morgan. She published a volume of poems and a novel, *St. Clair,* in 1804. *The Wild Irish Girl,* a political novel, made her reputation in 1806. Among her other works are *O'Donnel* (1814), *Florence Macarthy* (1816), *France under the Bourbons* (1817), and its companion *Italy* (1821), both of the latter exciting furious opposition both in England and on the Continent, *Life and Times of Salvator Rosa* (1823), *Woman and Her Master* (1840), *The Book Without a Name* (with Sir T. C. Morgan, 1841), *Luxima, the Prophetess* (1859), *Passages from My Autobiography: an Odd Volume* (1859; this contains, among other things, her letters for the years 1818–19), and others.

Morgan, Sir Thomas Charles. b. at London, c1783; d. there, Aug. 28, 1843. An English surgeon and author; husband of Sydney Morgan. His works include *Sketches of the Philosophy of Life* (1818) and *Sketches of the Philosophy of Morals* (1822).

Morgan, William Frend De. See **De Morgan, William** (Frend).

Morgana (môr.gä′na̞), **Fata.** See under **Morgan le Fay.**

Morgan le Fay (môr′ga̞n le̞ fā′). [Also: **Morgana** (môr.gä′na̞), **Morgaine** (môr.gen′).] In Arthurian romance, a sister of King Arthur. She is a composite and variable character, partaking of the nature of various Old Irish and Brythonic goddesses (especially river goddesses) and mermaids. (The mermaids of modern Breton folklore, for instance, are called Morgans.) She first appeared in Geoffrey of Monmouth's *Vita Merlini* (12th century). Usually she appears as a lake-dweller, versed in healing magic, and lover of many men; often she is the mistress of Avalon. In the later Arthurian romances, however, she appears as a malign sorceress, tempting lovers to be unfaithful, and plotting the death of Arthur. In the medieval French romance *Ogier the Dane,* she receives Ogier in the Isle of Avalon when he is over 100 years of age, and restores him to eternal youth. In the Charlemagne romances she is referred to as Fata Morgana (i.e., the Fairy Morgan). As late as the 19th century the famous mirages in the Strait of Messina were attributed to her, and they are named for her, still being called *fata morgana.*

Morgannwg (môr.gän′u̇g), **Iolo.** See **Williams, Edward.**

Morgawse (môr′gôz). See **Margawse.**

Morgiana (môr.gi.ä′na̞). In the story of "Ali Baba and the Forty Thieves" in *The Arabian Nights' Entertainments,* a slave of Ali Baba. She aids in the concealment of the murder of Cassim (Ali Baba's brother who was killed in the cave) and discovers the robbers, who are brought by their captain, concealed in oil jars, to Ali Baba's house. She kills them by pouring boiling oil into the jars. She recognizes their captain when, as Cogia Houssain,

he dines with Ali Baba, and stabs him as she dances the "dagger dance." Ali Baba shows his gratitude by marrying her to his nephew.

Morglay (môr′glā). The sword of Sir Bevis of Hampton.

Morhault (môr′hôlt), **Sir.** [Also: **Sir Marhaus, Sir Moraunt, Sir Morholt** (môr′hôlt).] In Arthurian romance, the brother of Isolt; a tribute gatherer. He was killed by Tristram, before the latter met Isolt.

Moria (mō′ri.a̞). A character representing folly in Ben Jonson's *Cynthia's Revels.* She is the guardian of two court ladies.

Morier (mō′ri.ėr, mor′i.ā), **James Justinian.** b. 1780; d. at Brighton, England, March 19, 1849. An English novelist, diplomat, and writer of travel books. In 1812 he published *A Journey through Persia, Armenia, and Asia Minor to Constantinople 1808–9.* From 1810 to 1814 he was secretary of embassy at the court of Persia. He published his *Second Journey* in 1818; also a romance, *The Adventures of Hajji Baba of Ispahan* (1824), *The Adventures of Hajji Baba of Ispahan in England* (1828), and *Zohrab the Hostage* (1832).

Morison (mor′i.son), **James Augustus Cotter.** b. at London, 1832; d. Feb. 26, 1888. An English author. He was a positivist in philosophy. He was a contributor to the *Saturday Review,* and published *Life and Times of Saint Bernard* (1863), *The Service of Man: an Essay towards the Religion of the Future* (1887), and others.

Morland (môr′la̞nd), **Catherine.** The principal character in Jane Austen's novel *Northanger Abbey.*

Morland, George. b. at London, June 26, 1763; d. there, Oct. 27, 1804. An English painter, son of a painter and picture dealer. In 1786 he married a sister of James Ward the animal painter. He painted moralities in the manner of Hogarth, also genre and animals, and was noted equally for the brilliancy of his work and the extreme recklessness of his life. His picture *Inside of a Stable* is in the National Gallery.

Morland, Henry. In George Colman the younger's *Heir-at-Law,* the missing and finally reappearing heir to the title and estates of Lord Duberly.

Morleena Kenwigs (môr.lē′na̞ ken′wigz). See **Kenwigs, Morleena.**

Morley, Henry. b. at London, Sept. 15, 1822; d. May 14, 1894. An English author. He was educated at the Moravian school at Neuwied, Germany, and at King's College, London. He practiced medicine from 1844 to 1848. He wrote for *Household Words* and the *Examiner* from 1850 to 1864, and was editor of the latter during part of that time, was professor of English language and literature from 1865 to 1889 at University College, London, held the same position at Queen's College, London, from 1878, and became principal of University Hall in 1882. He wrote *A Defence of Ignorance* (1851), lives of Palissy (1852), Cardan (1854), and Cornelius Agrippa (1856), *Memoirs of Bartholomew Fair* (1857), *English Writers before Chaucer* (1864–67), *First Sketch of English Literature* (1873), and *Library of English Literature.* He edited Boswell's *Life of Johnson* in 1886. He began *English Writers* in 1887; ten volumes had been issued at his death. In 1864–67 a preliminary book with the same title was published, which was afterward merged in the larger work.

Morley, John. [Title, 1st Viscount **Morley of Blackburn.**] b. at Blackburn, Lancashire, England, Dec. 24, 1838; d. at London, Sept. 23, 1923. An English statesman, journalist, editor, critic, and biographer. He was educated at Cheltenham College and at Lincoln College, Oxford. He served on the staff of the *Saturday Review*, and was editor (1867–82) of the *Fortnightly Review*. A liberal in politics and religion, he turned the conservative *Pall Mall Gazette* into a radical organ under his editorship (1880–83). He was a member of Parliament (1883–1908). He was a supporter of Gladstone's Irish and general policy, was chief secretary for Ireland in 1886, was reappointed in 1892, was secretary of state for India (December, 1905–1910), and lord president of the council (1910). He was editor of the English Men of Letters series, writing for it *Edmund Burke* (1867). Author of *Critical Miscellanies* (1871, 1877, 1886, 1908) and *Studies in Literature* (1891), criticism; *Voltaire* (1872), *Rousseau* (1873), *Diderot* (1878), *Richard Cobden* (1881), *Walpole* (1889), *Cromwell* (1900), and *William Ewart Gladstone* (3 vols., 1903), biography; *On Compromise* (1874), a philosophical essay; and *Recollections* (1917).

Morlocks (môr′loks). See under **Time Machine, The.**

Morocco (mọ.rok′ō), **Prince of.** In Shakespeare's *Merchant of Venice*, an unsuccessful suitor of Portia. He chooses the golden casket as the one containing her portrait; it doesn't, and he thus fails to win her.

Morose (mọ.rōs′). In Ben Jonson's comedy *Epicœne, or The Silent Woman*, a melancholy recluse who can bear no sound except that of his own voice. He is eventually driven to distraction by a shrewish wife, who fills his house with her friends.

Morpheus (môr′fẹ.us). In Greek mythology, one of the sons of Hypnos, or Sleep. Morpheus was the bringer of dreams. He is more prominent in literary allusion than in mythology itself, and hence, by extension, is very commonly referred to as the god of sleep.

Morrice (mor′is), **Gil** (or **Childe**). See **Gil Morrice.**

Morrigan (môr′i.ạn). [Also, **Morrigu** (môr′i.ū).] In Old Irish mythology, one of three war goddesses (with Neman and Macha). Sometimes Badb (Old Irish war goddess) is interchangeable with Morrigan; sometimes Badb is identified with Morrigan; sometimes Morrigan is a collective name for all three. Their functions were practically identical. Heads of warriors killed in battle were dedicated to one or the other of the three. They all appeared on the battlefields in the form of ravens, and from this probably came the belief that they ate the flesh of those killed in battle. In the legends, Morrigan admired and loved Cuchulain, worked against him when he spurned her, but was devoted enough to warn him against the battle in which he met death.

Morris (mor′is), **Dinah.** One of the two principal female characters in George Eliot's *Adam Bede.*

She is a factory girl and Wesleyan preacher, with a spiritual clear-sighted nature, and delicate sensitiveness to the condition and wants of others. She is said to be in some particulars a sketch from an aunt of the author, Elizabeth Evans.

Morris, Sir Lewis. b. at Carmarthen, Wales, Jan. 23, 1833; d. at Penrhyn, Wales, Nov. 12, 1907. A Welsh poet and essayist. He was called to the bar in 1861, and practiced law until 1880. He was one of the founders (1893) of the University of Wales. Author of *Songs of Two Worlds* (3 series, 1871, 1874, 1875), *The Epic of Hades* (1877), *Gwen* (1879), *The Ode of Life* (1880), *Songs Unsung* (1883), *Gycia* (1886), *Songs of Britain* (1887), *A Vision of Saints* (1890), and a volume of essays, *The New Rambler* (1905). Morris's poetry was ridiculed by the *Saturday Review* and severely criticized by the *Athenaeum*.

Morris, May. b. at Upton, England, March 25, 1863; d. at Lechdale, England, Oct. 16, 1938. An English embroidery designer and editor; daughter of William Morris. She edited and wrote introductions to her father's collected works (24 vols.). She lectured on embroidery, jewelry, costume, and pattern designing in the U. S. and England, was a designer for the firm of Morris and Company, and was chairman and founder of the Women's Guild of Arts.

Morris, Richard. b. at London, Sept. 8, 1833; d. there, May 12, 1894. An English philologist. He published *The Etymology of Local Names* (1857), *Specimens of Early English* (1867), *Historical Outlines of English Accidence* (1872), *English Grammar* (1874), and edited some of Chaucer's *Canterbury Tales* with notes, and also several texts for the Early English Text Society.

Morris, William. b. at Walthamstow, England, 1834; d. at London, Oct. 3, 1896. An English painter, decorator, designer, manufacturer, printer, poet, and socialist leader. While a student at Oxford he helped establish the *Oxford and Cambridge Magazine*, to which he contributed poems, stories, and essays. At Oxford, too, he began a lifelong friendship with Edward Burne-Jones. Influenced by the writings of John Ruskin and by enthusiasm for the great cathedrals of the Middle Ages, Morris entered an architect's office, but presently turned to painting, studied with Dante Gabriel Rossetti, and in 1857 set up a studio at London with Burne-Jones. Convinced of the ugliness of most furniture and draperies then being manufactured, the two young men set about making all the needed furnishings themselves, designing and building the furniture, designing and dyeing and weaving the textiles. Thus began one of the most significant revolutions in taste of modern times. All his life William Morris was distressed by what he considered to be ugliness, and he might be said to have declared war upon it with the establishment in 1861, with the assistance of Burne-Jones, Rossetti, Ford Madox Brown, and Philip Webb, of the manufacturing and decorating firm at first known as Morris, Marshall, Faulkner and Company, and later as Morris and Company. He revived an interest, almost moribund in England, in textiles and in stained glass; his influence penetrated innumerable homes in that country, in the U. S., and elsewhere, with the furniture, the ceramics, and the wallpapers he designed. Though his glance was backward to the beauties created by medieval craftsmen rather than forward to the functionalism which came to dominate 20th-century design, he prepared the way for the latter by making unprofitable the cheap, meretricious design which had followed the industrialization of the arts and crafts. His principles were propagated by the Arts and Crafts Society (which he founded) and derived support from the Pre-Raphaelite school of painting, in which his friends Rossetti and Burne-Jones were to the fore. In 1890 he took within the scope of his immense energies a revival of the typographical art, founding the Kelmscott Press at Hammersmith, for which he designed type faces, ornamental initials, and borders. Some of the books bearing the Kelmscott imprint were Morris's own writings (he was one of the most prolific writers in 19thcentury England). The Arthurian tales and other medieval legends inspired much of his early writing, such as *The Defense of Guinevere, and Other Poems* (1858); he drew on classical sources for *The Life and Death of Jason* (1867) and *The Earthly Paradise* (1868–71); and as the outcome of two trips to Iceland he made translations of the Norse sagas and wrote the epic poem *Sigurd the Volsung* (1876). It has been pointed out by William Butler Yeats that the protagonists in Morris's poems and romances, whether they be knights and heroes and ladies, or peasants, or workers, are typically healthy, handsome, physically strong, serene men and women, who find the earth and heavens friendly, enjoy life to the full, and come to its end without resentment. In the men and women around him Morris found few who corresponded to his ideal, but rather observed multitudes who were warped physically and mentally, mean, joyless and hopeless. These things, he believed, resulted from unsound social conditions, and the same revulsion against ugliness which caused him to undertake the reform of design in the crafts and manufactures led him to affiliate with the socialist movement in the hope of reforming the design of society. In 1883 he joined the Socialist Democratic Federation; in 1885 he was among those who withdrew from that organization to form the Socialist League; upon the rise in this group of tendencies he disapproved of, he became a member of the Hammersmith Socialist Society. This "great-hearted poet," as Edwin Markham has called him, put all the power of his art into many a poem and song for the workers, and into such prose works, arguing allegorically or directly for Socialism, as *The Dream of John Ball* (1888), *News from Nowhere* (1891), and *Socialism: Its Growth and Outcome* (1893). Among his other books are poetic translations of the *Odyssey* and the *Aeneid; Love is Enough* (a morality play, 1873), *Three Northern Love Songs* (1875), *The House of the Wolfings* (1889), *The Roots of the Mountains* (1890), *The Story of the Glittering Plain* (1890), *The Wood Beyond the World* (1894), *Child Christopher* (1895), *The Well at the World's End* (1896), *The Water of the Wondrous Isles* (1897), and *The Story of the Sundering Flood* (1898).

Morrison (mor'i.sọn), **Arthur.** b. near London, Nov. 1, 1863; d. 1945. An English journalist and novelist. A civil service clerk at London, he began writing for the *National Observer* in 1890, contributing to it the work by which he is best known, *Tales of Mean Streets* (published in book form, 1894). Author of *A Child of the Jago* (1896), *To London Town* (1899), *Cunning Murrell* (1900), and *The Hole in the Wall* (1902), novels; *That Brute Simmons* (1904), *The Dumb Cake* (1907), and *A Stroke of Business* (1907), plays; *Divers Vanities* (1905), *Green Ginger* (1909), and *Fiddle o' Dreams* (1933), short-story collections; *The Painters of Japan* (2 vols., 1911), a critical history of Japanese art; *Martin Hewitt, Investigator* (1894), *Chronicles of Martin Hewitt* (1895), *Adventures of Martin Hewitt* (1896), *The Dorrington Deed-Box* (1897), *The Red Triangle* (1903), and *The Green Eye of Goona* (1904), a detective-story series.

Morrison, George Ernest. [Called "Chinese" Morrison.] b. at Geelong, Victoria, Australia, Feb. 4, 1862; d. at Sidmouth, England, May 30, 1920. An Australian journalist. His first newspaper assignment came in 1883 when the Melbourne *Age* sent him to New Guinea; he was speared by natives and nearly died there. Subsequently he went to Scotland to study medicine, traveled (1887) in the U. S., the West Indies, and Spain, and served as a medical officer in Spain, Morocco (1889–90), and Australia (1890–93). He went to China in 1893 and traveled overland from Shanghai to Rangoon (1894). He was appointed Far Eastern correspondent of the London *Times* in 1895 and thereafter until 1912 covered all major developments in that area. In August, 1912, he became political adviser to the Chinese republic, to which his final service was given at Versailles in 1919. His only published book was *An Australian in China* (1895).

Morte Arthur (môrt är'thẽr). A Middle English alliterative romance (c1360), preserved in the Thornton manuscript (c1435), which was an abridgment of the original, dealing with Arthur's later years, his Roman campaign, his death, and his burial at Glastonbury. It is particularly noted for its vivid and detailed scenes, the parting of Arthur and Guinevere, the fight between Arthur and Modred, and for its use by Malory in his depiction of these events in Book V of the *Morte d'Arthur*. Some scholars have attributed it to the Scottish poet Huchoun, but this attribution is generally rejected.

Morte Arthure (môrt är'thẽr). A Middle English stanzaic poem (c1400) dealing primarily with the romantic exploits of Sir Lancelot, his love for Queen Guinevere, their parting, and his death. It is also concerned with the last battles of Arthur, Modred's treason, and the fatal wound which caused the king's death.

Morte d'Arthur or **Morte Darthur** (môrt där'thẽr). A Middle English collection of prose romances on the life and death of King Arthur and the knights of the Round Table, compiled (c1470) in prison by Sir Thomas Malory, and printed by William Caxton in 1485. Arthur is the natural son of Uther Pendragon and Igerna (or Igraine), and is raised by Sir Ector. While he is still a boy he proves his identity as the king by pulling the magic sword, Excalibur, from a block of stone. Many valiant knights come to his court, forming the Knights of the Round Table, pledged to virtue and chivalry. Arthur marries Guinevere and lives with her and his knights at Camelot, where Sir Lancelot is named the first knight of Christendom. The love story of Tristram (or Tristan) and Isolt appears in this work, as well as the discovery of the Grail by the young son of Lancelot, Sir Galahad. Guinevere's affection for Lancelot, and his love for her, lead their enemies to report rumors of scandal to Arthur, and battle ensues between the two noble knights. Arthur is killed in a battle with the army of the traitorous Modred, and he is carried on a barge to the magic Vale of Avalon. Guinevere enters a convent and Lancelot becomes a holy hermit. Until this century, Malory's work was known only from the printed text of Caxton, who, it is now clear, made a single book out of what Malory had written as a series of separate tales. In 1934 a manuscript, not Malory's own, but closer to it than the printed version, was discovered at Winchester College; it was edited by Eugène Vinaver in 1947.

Morte d'Arthur. A poem by Alfred Tennyson, included later in the *Idylls of the King* under the title *The Passing of Arthur*.

Mortimer (môr′ti.mẻr). See under **Cade, Jack.**

Mortimer, Edmund. In Shakespeare's *1 Henry IV*, a prisoner of Owen Glendower, whose daughter he marries. His sister is Hotspur's wife and he and Glendower join Hotspur against Henry IV. Shakespeare confused the historical Sir Edmund (1376–1409) with his nephew, Edmund, 5th Earl of March.

Mortimer, Edmund, (5th) **Earl of March.** In Shakespeare's *1 Henry VI*, an old nobleman. He tells Richard that he is imprisoned by the Lancastrians because he is the real heir to the throne and Richard is his heir. Shakespeare apparently confused the historical Earl with his uncle, Sir Edmund Mortimer, or with another member of the family.

Mortimer, Lady. In Shakespeare's *1 Henry IV*, the daughter of Owen Glendower and wife of Edmund Mortimer. She can speak only Welsh. Hotspur tries to imitate Mortimer's amorous wooing of his Welsh bride.

Mortimer, Sir Edward. A character in the younger George Colman's *The Iron Chest*.

Mortimer, Sir John and **Sir Hugh.** In Shakespeare's *3 Henry VI*, illegitimate sons of Roger Mortimer and uncles of Richard, Duke of York.

Mortimer, Young Roger. In Christopher Marlowe's tragedy *Edward II*, the upstart young baron who challenges the power of the King when he sees his weakness for his favorite, Gaveston. He makes love to the Queen for the purpose of turning her against her husband, so that he may be deposed with greater ease. Like Shakespeare's Richard III, Mortimer is a hypocrite whose intellectual ability finally turns to vicious cruelty. Inevitably his own arrogance causes his downfall when Edward III, succeeding to the throne, has him imprisoned and executed. Before dying he reflects upon the instability of fortune.

Mortimer Delvile (del′vil). See **Delvile, Mortimer.**

Mortimer his Fall. See **Fall of Mortimer, The.**

Mortimeriados (môr.ti.mer.i.ā′dōz). A poem (1596) by Michael Drayton, the sequel to *Piers Gaveston* (1593), and dealing, like it, with events in the reign of Edward II. It appeared again in 1619, lengthened and renamed *The Barons' Wars.*

Morton (môr′ton). In Shakespeare's *2 Henry IV*, the retainer who brings Northumberland news of Hotspur's death.

Morton, Guy Mainwaring. [Pseudonym, **Peter Traill;** original surname, **Dunstan.**] b. at London, Sept. 9, 1896–. An English novelist and dramatist. With his stepfather, he collaborated on the plays *Fallen Angels* (1924), *After the Theatre* (1924), *By Right of Conquest* (1925), *Salvage* (1926), *The Stranger in the House* (1928), and *Because of Irene* (1929). He was sole author of the play *Tread Softly* (1936), and of the novels *Woman to Woman* (1924), *The Divine Spark* (1926), *The White Hen* (1927), *Great Dust* (1932), *The Angel* (1934), *Not Proven* (1938), *Under the Plane Trees* (1947), and *The Portly Peregrine* (1948).

Morton, Henry. The hero of Sir Walter Scott's *Old Mortality.*

Morton, John. In Shakespeare's *Richard III*, the Bishop of Ely, an adherent of Richmond after having escaped from Richard. The historical Morton became Archbishop of Canterbury in Henry VII's reign and Sir Thomas More lived in his house. More got material from him for his *History of Richard III*, which Shakespeare used as a source for *Richard III.*

Morton, John Madison. b. at Pangbourne, Berkshire, England, Jan. 3, 1811; d. Dec. 19, 1891. An English playwright; son of Thomas Morton (1764–1838). He wrote the very popular *Box and Cox* (1847) upon which Burnand and Sullivan based *Cox and Box* (1867), *Lend Me Five Shillings* (1846), and about 100 other farces.

Morton, Thomas. b. in Durham, England, c1764; d. at London, March 28, 1838. An English dramatist. He wrote *Speed the Plough* (1798), introducing the invisible Mrs. Grundy, *The Blind Girl* (1801), *Town and Country* (1807), *School for Grown Children* (1827), and others.

Morven (môr′ven). A mythical kingdom referred to in the poems of Ossian, as being ruled by Fingal.

Mosaic. A novel by G. B. Stern, published in 1930. It is the concluding panel in her trilogy of Jewish life, *The Rakonitz Chronicles* (1932).

Mosca (mos′ka). In Ben Jonson's play *Volpone, or the Fox*, a parasite, in the sense of the classic drama. His pliancy and presence of mind render him invaluable to his master, Volpone, upon whom he finally turns.

Moschus (mos′kus). fl. in the 2nd century B.C. A Greek bucolic poet of Syracuse. The *Lament for Bion* is traditionally, but doubtfully, ascribed to him; in a like manner he is called the pupil of Bion but this too is dubious. His work, which includes a poem on Europa, is usually printed with that of Bion and Theocritus.

Moses (mō′zes). A Jewish moneylender in Richard Brinsley Sheridan's *School for Scandal.*

ḍ, d or j; ṣ, s or sh; ṭ, t or ch; ẓ, z or zh; o, F. cloche; ü, F. menu; ċh, Sc. loch; ṅ, F. bonbon.

Moth (môth). In Shakespeare's *Love's Labour's Lost*, a witty, knavish page of Armado.

Moth. A fairy in Shakespeare's *Midsummer Night's Dream*.

Moth. In William Cartwright's play *The Ordinary*, a shallow-brained antiquary, whose conversation is mostly disjointed scraps from Chaucer.

Mothe-Fénelon (mot.fān.lôṅ), **François de Salignac de La.** See **Fénelon.**

Mother, The. A novel by Naomi Royde-Smith, published in 1931.

Mother and Other Poems, The. A volume of poetry by Edith Sitwell, published in 1915.

Mother Bombie (bom′bi). A prose comedy by John Lyly, written between 1587 and 1590 and printed in 1594. The chief character is named after a colorful London figure of the day, a fortune teller who had attained considerable notoriety.

Mother Bunch (bunch). See **Bunch, Mother.**

Mother Goose. A name famous in children's literature through various familiar rhymes. It is said that there was a Mrs. Goose, mother-in-law of Thomas Fleet, an early Boston publisher, and that he issued the collection under this title to avenge himself for her persistent and unmelodious chanting of these ditties to his infant son. An apocryphal early edition is said to have borne the title "*Songs for the Nursery; or Mother Goose's Melodies for Children:* printed by T. Fleet at his printing house, Pudding Lane, 1719. Price, two coppers." This story, however, has been discredited in that no copy of such a book has ever been found. Moreover, the concept of a story-telling Mother Goose probably came to America from France, via English nursery lore. Charles Perrault published *Contes de ma mère l'oye* in 1697; but the name was quoted by the satirist Régnier more than a century before. Queen Goosefoot (Reine Pédance or Reine Pédauque), or Bertha with the great foot (who was the mother of Charlemagne), has been suggested as the original of Mother Goose, but there is no substantiation for the idea. The *Contes de ma mère l'oye*, by Charles Perrault, were published under the name of his ten-year-old son, Perrault d'Armancourt. They consist of ten stories, seven of which may be derived from the *Pentamerone*, a 17th-century Italian collection, or from Straparola's *Facetious Nights* (1550).

Mother Hubbard (hub′ạrd). The heroine of an English nursery rhyme, who went to the cupboard to get a bone for her dog and found the cupboard bare. She then made numerous expeditions out to the shops of the neighborhood on errands for the dog, and on each return found him doing something more and more fantastic, through 14 verses. These were first published in 1805 under the title *The Comic Adventures of Old Mother Hubbard and her Dog*, and had instantaneous popularity. Sarah Catherine Martin (1768–1826) was the author. It was immediately pirated by some 26 chapbooks. Old Mother Hubbard herself, however, was a folk character known as early as the 16th century.

Mother Hubberd's Tale (hub′ẽrdz). A poem by Edmund Spenser, published in 1591 in a volume known as *Complaints*, but written much earlier.

It is an intentional imitation of Chaucer's manner. It was also entitled *Prosopopoia.*

Mother of the Gods, The. An epithet of the deity Cybele.

Mother Sawyer (sô′yẽr). See **Sawyer, Mother.**

Mother Shipton (ship′tọn). A mythical prophetess, formerly believed to have foretold (in the reign of Henry VIII) most modern inventions and the end of the world, which her verses claimed would occur in 1881.

Mother Shipton. A comedy by T. T. (Thomas Thomson). Although undated, it probably appeared about 1660. A ballad was written by George Colman the elder in 1771 with this title.

Motherwell (muᴛʜ′ẽr.wẹl, -wel), **William.** b. at Glasgow, Oct. 13, 1797; d. there, Nov. 1, 1835. A Scottish poet and antiquary. He wrote *Minstrelsy Ancient and Modern* (1827) and *Poems Narrative and Lyrical* (1832). "Jeanie Morrison" appears in the latter.

motif (mō.tẽf′; French, mo.tẽf). [Also, **motive.**] A subject or theme for development or treatment, as in art, literature, or music; a dominant idea or feature.

motivation. The act or manner of motivating; the act or process of furnishing with an incentive or inducement to action.

Motley. A volume of verse (1919) by Walter De la Mare.

Motte-Fouqué (mot′fö.kā′), Baron **Friedrich Heinrich Karl de la.** See **Fouqué.**

Motteux (mo.tẽ), **Pierre Antoine.** [Also, **Peter Anthony Motteux.**] b. at Rouen, France, Feb. 25, 1663; murdered at London, Feb. 18, 1718. An English translator and playwright. He was a French Huguenot merchant, at London after 1685, having gone to England on the revocation of the Edict of Nantes. One of his dramas, called *Novelty*, gives a distinct play in each act. He is better known as the translator, with Thomas Urquhart, of Rabelais's works; and he also, with others, translated *Don Quixote.*

Mottley (mot′li), **John.** b. at London, 1692; d. there, Oct. 3, 1750. An English writer. Author of *Joe Miller's Jests, or The Wit's Vade Mecum* (1739), the most famous of all English jestbooks, and of five dramas, *History of Peter the Great* (1739), and *The Lives of Dramatic Authors* (1747).

Mottram (mot′rạm), **R. H.** [Full name, **Ralph Hale Mottram.**] b. at Norwich, England, Oct. 30, 1883—. An English writer. His publications include *Poems Old and New* (1930), *The Headless Hound* (1931), *Early Morning* (1935), *Journey to the Western Front* (1936), *Old England* (1937), *The World Turns Slowly Round* (1942), *Visit of the Princess* (1946), *Buxton the Liberator* (1946), and *The Gentleman of Leisure* (1947).

Mouldy (mōl′di), **Ralph.** In Shakespeare's *2 Henry IV*, a recruit whom Falstaff allows to purchase his freedom.

Moult (mōlt), **Thomas.** b. at Mellor Hall, Derbyshire, England, Sept. 23, 1895—. An English critic, novelist, poet, and anthologist. He was music critic on the Manchester *Guardian*, art and drama critic

---

fat, fāte, fär, ȧsk, fãre; net, mē, hẽr; pin, pīne; not, nōte, mõve, nôr; up, lūte, pull; ᴛʜ, then;

on the *Athenaeum* and the *English Review,* and a sports writer on English and Australian periodicals. He was editor of the annual *Best Poems* (1923–39) and of *Modern Writers and Playwrights* (1929) in the Critical Biographies series. Author of the novels *Snow over Eldon* (1920), *The Comely Lass* (1923), and *Saturday Night* (1931); of the books of poetry *Down Here the Hawthorn* (1921), *Brown Earth* (1922), and *Dear England* (1941); of the critical studies *Barrie* (1928) and *W. H. Davies* (1934); and also of *Bat and Ball, a New Book of Cricket* (1935) and *How We Write Our Poems* (1940).

Moulton, Richard Green. b. at Preston, England, May 5, 1849; d. at Tunbridge Wells, England, Aug. 15, 1924. An English author, critic, and educator, professor in the University of Chicago from 1892 until his retirement in 1919. He was engaged (1874–92) as a lecturer in university extension work in England and America. Among his works are *Shakespeare as a Dramatic Artist* (1885), *Ancient Classical Drama* (1890), *The Literary Study of the Bible* (1896), *A Short Introduction to the Literature of the Bible* (1901), *The Moral System of Shakespeare* (1903), and *World Literature* (1911). He edited *The Modern Reader's Bible* (1895–98), an edition that treats the Bible as literature and indicates, by the usual typographic devices, the poetry, drama, and other literary forms in the Old and New Testaments.

Moultrie (mōl′tri), **John.** b. at London, Dec. 30, 1799; d. at Rugby, England, Dec. 26, 1874. An English poet. He was rector of Rugby from 1828, at the time when Thomas Arnold, who became his friend, was headmaster at the school there. He published *My Brother's Grave* (1837), *The Dream of Life* (1843), and *Sermons* (1853).

Mountain. A name given to the extreme Revolutionary party in the legislatures of the first French Revolution. The name was derived from the fact that they occupied the higher part of the hall. Among the most important members of the group were Robespierre and Danton.

Mountaineers, The. A melodrama taken from *Don Quixote* by George Colman the younger, produced on Aug. 3, 1793, and printed in 1795.

Mountain Meadow. A novel by John Buchan, published in 1941.

Mountebank, The. A novel by William John Locke, published in 1921, dealing with the theme of dual personality.

Mountford (mount′fọrd), **Sir Charles.** The enemy of Sir Francis Acton in Thomas Heywood's tragedy *A Woman Killed with Kindness.* He is freed from prison upon payment of his debt by his enemy, Acton, who is infatuated with his sister, Susan. Unable to bear this obligation, he wishes his sister to free him by dishonoring herself: "What moved my foe To enfranchise me? 'Twas, sister, for your love. . . . And shall he not enjoy it?"

Mountford, Susan. The sister of Sir Charles Mountford in Thomas Heywood's tragedy *A Woman Killed with Kindness.*

Mountstuart Jenkinson (mount′stū″ạrt jeng′kinsọn), **Mrs.** See **Jenkinson, Mrs. Mountstuart.**

Mourning Bride, The. A tragedy by William Congreve, produced in 1697. Several lines from it have become very well known, including "Music hath charms to soothe a savage breast" and the often misquoted "Nor hell a fury, like a woman scorned."

Mourning Garment. [Original title, **Greene's Mourning Garment.**] Novel by Robert Greene, registered in 1590. It is a paraphrase of the parable of the prodigal son.

Mouton (mö.tôṅ), **Michel.** See **Villon, François.**

movement. Action; incident. "The dialogue is written with much vivacity and grace, and with as much dramatic movement as is compatible with only two interlocutors." (Prescott, *Ferdinand and Isabella.*)

Mowbray (mō′brạ). In Shakespeare's *2 Henry IV,* one of the lords opposing Henry.

Mowbray, Thomas. [Titles: Earl of **Nottingham,** 12th Baron **Mowbray,** 1st Duke of **Norfolk.**] d. at Venice, 1399. An English nobleman. He was created Earl of Nottingham in 1383, earl marshal in 1384, and was one of the lord appellants of 1387, but afterward joined the king. He was created Duke of Norfolk in 1397. Having been accused of treason by Henry Bolingbroke, Earl of Hereford (afterward Henry IV), in 1398, he challenged the latter to single combat, and the lists were set at Coventry in presence of Richard II, who banished both disputants on the eve of the contest, Norfolk for life and Hereford for ten years. Shakespeare introduces him in his *Richard II.*

Mowbray, Thomas. In Shakespeare's *Richard II,* the Duke of Norfolk. Bolingbroke accuses him of treason before Richard, and Mowbray, to defend his honor, challenges Bolingbroke to single combat. At the zero hour, Richard calls off the tournament and banishes Bolingbroke for 10 years, and Mowbray for life.

Mowcher (mou′chẻr), **Miss.** In Dickens's *David Copperfield,* a merry talkative dwarf, a hairdresser.

Mowgli (mou′gli). A native boy suckled by wolves and reared among animals of the jungle, in Rudyard Kipling's *Jungle Books.*

Moxon (mok′sọn), **Edward.** b. at Wakefield, Yorkshire, England, in December, 1801; d. at Putney Heath, London, June 3, 1858. An English publisher and poet, remembered as the friend and publisher of great poets. He began (1830) his publishing career with Charles Lamb's *Album Verses,* and brought out works by Tennyson, Browning, Wordsworth, Southey, W. S. Landor, Coventry Patmore, the Disraelis, R. Monckton Milnes, Sheridan Knowles, and others. With all these writers Moxon was on terms of friendship, as well as with John Forster, Harriet Martineau, and Mary Lamb. His own works include *The Prospect and other Poems* (1826), dedicated to Samuel Rogers, *Christmas* (1829), dedicated to Lamb, and *Sonnets* (1835), dedicated to Wordsworth. He married (1833) Lamb's adopted daughter, Emma Isola.

Mozart (mō′tsärt). A biography by Sacheverell Sitwell, published in 1932.

Mr. Apollinax (ạ.pol′i.naks). A short satirical poem by T. S. Eliot, published in 1917.

Mr. Britling Sees It Through (brit'ling). A novel by H. G. Wells, published in 1916. It is the story of the different attitudes taken by Mr. Britling as he becomes aware of the approach of World War I, and how it affects him and his family when England engages in it. As the war grows in violence a young tutor employed by Mr. Britling enters on the side of Germany, while his son, Hugh, enlists and is killed in battle. However, Mr. Britling is presently consoled by the idea that his son and friends are dying for a better world, and he goes forward with renewed faith and optimism.

Mr. Dick (dik). See **Dick, Mr.**

Mr. Fortune's Maggot (fôr'tụnz). A philosophical novel by Sylvia Townsend Warner, published in 1927.

Mr. F.'s Aunt. A character in Dickens's *Little Dorrit*. She is characterized by "extreme severity and grim taciturnity; sometimes by a propensity to offer remarks . . . totally uncalled for by anything said by anybody, and traceable to no association of ideas."

Mr. Gilfil's Love Story (gil'filz). One of George Eliot's *Scenes of Clerical Life*.

Mr. Gilhooley (gil.hö'li). A novel by Liam O'Flaherty, published in 1926.

Mr. H. A play by Charles Lamb. This farce (in two acts) was performed at Drury Lane Theatre, London, in December, 1806, but did not survive the first night of its appearance. In America, however, it was performed with some success. The point of the play is the anxiety of the hero to conceal his name (Hogsflesh) and the way in which all his devices to this end are frustrated by his unhappy destiny.

Mr. Midshipman Easy (ē'zi). A sea story by Frederick Marryat, published in 1836.

Mr. Pim Passes By (pim). A drama (1919) by A. A. Milne.

Mr. Polly (pol'i), **The History of.** See **History of Mr. Polly, The.**

Mrs. Caudle's Curtain Lectures (kô'dlz). A series of sketches by Douglas Jerrold, published (1845) in *Punch*. They take the form of discourses on domestic subjects inflicted by Mrs. Caudle upon Mr. Caudle after they had gone to bed and the curtains were drawn for the night.

Mrs. Craddock (krad'ọk). A novel by W. Somerset Maugham, published in 1902.

Mrs. Dalloway (dal'ọ.wā). A psychological novel (1925) by Virginia Woolf, written in the "stream of consciousness" technique. The novel is practically plotless, all the interest being centered in the characters, in what they think about life, themselves, and each other. London is the setting, and the time is a single day in June, 1923. Two kinds of time are illustrated in the novel: time as the word is ordinarily used to mean passing hours, and time in which the thoughts, events, and feelings of one's past life go through one's mind.

Mrs. Dane's Defence (dānz). A play (1900) by Henry Arthur Jones.

Mrs. Hauksbee (hôks'bẹ). See **Hauksbee, Mrs.**

Mrs. Grundy (grun'di). See **Grundy, Mrs.**

Mrs. Lancelot—A Comedy in Assumptions (lån'sẹ.lọt, -lot). A novel by Maurice Hewlett, published in 1912.

Mrs. Lirriper's Legacy (lir'i.pẹrz). A story by Charles Dickens, a sequel to *Mrs. Lirriper's Lodgings*. It was published in December, 1864.

Mrs. Lirriper's Lodgings. A Christmas tale by Charles Dickens, published in December, 1863. Mrs. Lirriper herself is the narrator of the story, which contains much colorful comment concerning the tribulations of keeping a boarding house in 19th-century London.

Mr. Sludge, the Medium (sluj). A poem (1864) by Robert Browning.

Mrs. Malaprop (mal'ạ.prop). See **Malaprop, Mrs.**

Mrs. Perkins's Ball (pẹr'kin.ziz). One of Thackeray's *Christmas Books*, published in 1847.

Mrs. Siddons (sid'ọnz). A four-act play (1931) about the great English actress Sarah Siddons, by Naomi Royde-Smith.

Mrs. Warren's Profession (wôr'ẹnz). A play (1893) by George Bernard Shaw, included in his *Plays, Pleasant and Unpleasant* (1898). A prostitute, Mrs. Warren plies her trade in order to keep her daughter in comfortable circumstances. The play deals with the revelation of character on the part of both when Mrs. Warren's daughter discovers the nature of her mother's profession. The theme aroused so much controversy that a stage production was not possible until 1902.

Mr. Tasker's Gods (tås'kẹrz). A novel by Theodore Francis Powys, published in 1925.

Mr. Waddington of Wyck (wod'ing.tọn; wik). A novel by May Sinclair, published in 1921.

Mr. Weston's Good Wine (wes'tọnz). A novel by Theodore Francis Powys, published in 1927.

M'Turk (mạk.tẹrk'). In Rudyard Kipling's *Stalky and Co.*, the "gentleman" of the trio (the other two are Stalky and Beetle) about whom the stories revolve. He is the heir to an estate in Ireland.

Mucedorus (mū.sẹ.dō'rus). A play, perhaps by George Peele, Robert Greene, or Thomas Lodge, printed anonymously in 1598 and reprinted with additions in 1610. It was erroneously assigned to Shakespeare by Edward Archer in 1656.

Much (much). [Also, **Much the Miller's Son.**] In *A Lytell Geste of Robyn Hode*, an English ballad included in Ritson's collection, a miller's son. He is a companion to one of the outlaws both in this ballad and in the general body of Robin Hood legend.

Much Ado About Nothing. A comedy by Shakespeare, produced c1598. It may have been written in 1598 or 1599, although some authorities have thought that its verse is earlier in style. It was first printed in 1600, and its registry that year marked the first appearance of Shakespeare's name in the Stationers' Register. The story of Hero is taken with some variations from one of Matteo Bandello's tales, translated into French by Belleforest in his *Histoires tragiques*, which probably was borrowed from the story of Geneura and Ariodantes in the *Orlando Furioso* of Ariosto (itself translated into English by Sir John Harington). The subplot, apparently invented by Shakespeare, concerns the love of Benedick and Beatrice. The constable, Dogberry, and his assistants are also Shakespeare's.

The Story. Claudio and Benedick, officers in the army of Don Pedro, Prince of Arragon, are with him when he visits Leonato, the Governor of Messina. Claudio falls in love with Hero, Leonato's daughter, and despite the scheming of Don John, the vindictive bastard brother of the Prince, the wedding is arranged. Meanwhile, Beatrice, the niece of Leonato, and Benedick bait each other in verbal skirmishes, each professing to oppose the very idea of love or marriage, but are tricked into love for each other when Claudio and Don Pedro contrive that each shall overhear a conversation touching on the love which the other is supposed to feel, but is unwilling to express, for the listener. In the affair of Claudio and Hero, however, things are somewhat less happy. Don John persuades Borachio to converse at midnight through a window with Hero's maid Margaret, who is dressed as Hero, and arranges that Claudio and Don Pedro shall witness the conversation and thereby be brought to suspect the virtue of Hero. The wicked scheme succeeds, and at the wedding ceremony on the following day Claudio and Don Pedro denounce Hero, who swoons (whereupon Friar Francis, convinced of her innocence, persuades her father to announce her death). In the following scene the love of Beatrice and Benedick is declared, and Beatrice lays as a task on Benedick that he should kill Claudio for impugning her cousin Hero's virtue. However, Claudio is not to suffer for his mistrust; Borachio boasts of his exploit, and is arrested by Dogberry and Verges. A repentant Claudio, believing Hero to be dead, agrees to marry Leonato's niece, who, when she is unveiled, turns out to be Hero. Benedick and Beatrice (with some manifestly feigned reluctance on the part of the latter) also marry, and word comes that Don John has been apprehended and is being returned for punishment.

Mucklewrath (muk'l.ràth), **Habakkuk.** In Sir Walter Scott's novel *Old Mortality*, a fanatical preacher and leader of the Covenanters.

Muck-rake, Man with the. A character in the second part of *The Pilgrim's Progress*, shown by the Interpreter to Christiana and her company. John Bunyan describes him as follows: "a man that could look no way but downwards, with a muck-rake in his hand. There stood also one over his head with a celestial crown in his hand, and proffered him that crown for his muck-rake; but the man did neither look up nor regard, but raked to himself the straws, the small sticks, and dust of the floor." The explanation given is that he is a man of the world who prefers things carnal to things celestial.

Muddock (mud'ok), **Joyce Emerson Preston.** [Pseudonym, **Dick Donovan.**] b. at Southampton, England, May 23, 1843; d. Jan. 23, 1934. An English novelist, journalist, and traveler in Australia, China, Japan, Java, the South Sea Islands, Canada, Russia, and Europe. Swiss correspondent for the London *Daily News* and special correspondent for

the *Hour,* he also contributed to the *Strand Magazine, Chambers' Journal, Daily Mail,* and other papers and periodicals. He edited and published *Muddock's Guide to Switzerland* and *Guide to Davos Platz.* Author of *Maid Marian and Robin Hood* (1892), *The "V.C." for Valor* (1895), *Basile the Jester* (1897), *Jim the Penman* (1901), *Sweet "Doll" of Haddon Hall* (1920), and others. Under his pseudonym he wrote more than 50 volumes, among which are *Tracked and Taken* (1890), *Records of Vincent Trill of the Detective Service* (1899), *The Man from Manchester* (1900), *Stories from the Note-Book of a Detective* (1900), and *Pages from an Adventurous Life* (1907).

Mudfog Association (mud'fog). [Full name, **Full Report of the First and Second Meeting of the Mudfog Association for the Advancement of Every Thing.**] A series of satirical pieces by Charles Dickens which appeared (1837–38) in *Bentley's Miscellany.* They were aimed at the British Association for the Advancement of Science.

Mudie (mū'di), **Charles Edward.** b. at Chelsea, London, Oct. 18, 1818; d. at Hampstead, London, Oct. 28, 1890. An English bookseller. In 1842 he founded Mudie's Lending Library, which became the largest circulating library in London. He wrote *Stray Leaves* (1872).

Mug (mug), **Matthew.** A character in Samuel Foote's *The Mayor of Garratt.*

Muggleton (mug'l.ton), **Lodowicke.** b. 1609; d. 1697 or 1698. An English fanatic, founder, conjointly with John Reeve, of the Muggletonians. His doctrines were published in *The Divine Looking-Glass* (1656).

Muggletonians (mug.l.tō'ni.anz). A sect founded (c1651) in England by Lodowicke Muggleton and John Reeve. The members of the sect believed in the prophetic inspiration of its founders, as being the two witnesses mentioned in Rev. xi. 3–6, and held that there is no real distinction between the persons of the Trinity, that God has a human body, and that Elijah was His representative in heaven when He descended to die on the cross. The sect died out c1868.

Muiopotmos, or the Fate of the Butterfly (mö"i.ọ-pot'mos). A poem by Edmund Spenser, in ottava rima, published in 1591 in the volume known as *Complaints.*

Muir (mūr), **Edwin.** b. at Orkney, Scotland, May 15, 1887—. A British novelist, poet, and critic. Author of *The Marionette* (1927), *The Three Brothers* (1931), *Poor Tom* (1932), and translations, with Willa Muir, of the works of Franz Kafka and Hermann Broch. His verse includes *First Poems, Chorus of the Newly Dead, Journeys and Places,* and *The Voyage.* Among his critical works are *Latitudes* (1924), *Transition* (1926), and *The Structure of the Novel* (1928).

Mulberries, The. A club, founded in 1824, in which members regularly contributed a paper, or poem, or conceit bearing upon Shakespeare. Later the club was called the Shakespeare Club. Charles Dickens and W. C. Macready were among its members.

Mulberry Garden. A place of refreshment at London, much frequented by persons of quality in the

17th century. Sir Charles Sedley produced a comedy with this title in 1668, partly taken from Molière's *École des maris.*

Mulberry Hawk (mul′ber″i hôk′), **Sir.** See **Hawk, Sir Mulberry.**

Mulcaster (mul′kas″tẻr), **Richard.** b. at Carlisle, England; d. April 15, 1611. An English philologist. He was made master of Merchant Taylors' School in 1561, and of Saint Paul's School in 1596, and taught Edmund Spenser. He wrote *Positions . . . necessarie for the Training up of Children* (1581), *The First Part of the Elementarie . . . of the Right Writing of our English Tung* (1582), and others.

Mulciber (mul′si.bẻr). In Roman mythology, an epithet of Vulcan, meaning "the Melter."

Mulgrave (mul′grāv), **2nd Earl of.** A title of **Phipps,** Sir **Constantine Henry.**

Mulgrave, 3rd Earl of. A title of **Sheffield, John.**

Müller (mil′ẻr, mul′ẻr; German, mül′ẻr), **Friedrich Max.** See **Max Müller, Friedrich.**

Mulock (mū′lok), **Dinah Maria.** See **Craik, Dinah Maria.**

Mulready (mul.red′i, mul′red″i), **William.** b. at Ennis, County Clare, Ireland, April 1, 1786; d. at London, July 7, 1863. An Irish landscape and figure painter. He was made royal academician in 1816. He painted *The Carpenter's Shop* (1809), *The Barber's Shop* (1811), *Interior of an English Cottage* (1828), *Choosing the Wedding Gown* (1846), and others. In 1840 he furnished the ornamental design for the outside of Rowland Hill's postal envelope, known as the Mulready envelope (it was actually a folded half-sheet of letter paper).

Mulvaney (mul.vā′ni), **Terence.** The gigantic and witty Irishman of Rudyard Kipling's *Soldiers Three,* and the boon companion of Ortheris, a sharp little Cockney, and Learoyd, a saturnine Yorkshireman.

Mumbo Jumbo (mum′bō jum′bō). An idol or bugbear of west African tribes.

mummer. One who mums, or masks himself and makes diversion in disguise; a masker; a masked buffoon; specifically, in England, one of a company of persons who go from house to house performing a mumming play.

Mummer's Wife, A. A novel by George Moore, published in 1885. It is a naturalistic story of a troupe of actors, concentrating on the life of Kate Ede, who is ruined by drink.

mummery. 1. Pantomime as enacted by mummers; a show or performance of mummers.

Your fathers Disdain'd the mummery of foreign strollers.　　　　　　　　　　　　　　(Fenton.)

This festival [of fools] was a religious mummery, usually held at Christmas time.
　　　　　　　　　　(Strutt, *Sports and Pastimes.*)

2. A ceremony or performance considered false or pretentious; farcical show; hypocritical disguise and parade: applied in contempt to various religious ceremonies by people who are of other sects or beliefs.

The temple and its holy rites profan'd
By mumm'ries he that dwelt in it disdain'd.
　　　　　　　　　　(Cowper, *Expostulation.*)

But for what we know of Eleusis and its mummeries, which is quite enough for all practical purposes, we are indebted to none of you ancients, but entirely to modern sagacity.
　　　　　　　　　　(De Quincey, *Secret Societies.*)

mumming play. A primitive folk drama, possibly derived from a spring festival. Versions were acted all over England into the 19th century, but performances now are confined to a few villages. Saint George, the Christian knight, is challenged by the Turkish Knight, a combat occurs, one of them is slain, then a doctor is procured and recites in the form of a jingle the diseases he can cure, finally restoring the dead warrior to life. A collection is then taken. There are various fools also: Father Christmas, Beelzebub, Jack the Sweeper. They speak in rhyming couplets. The situation of death and rebirth is paralleled, of course, by the return of spring to the barren earth. However, nothing is known of such plays before the 18th century and they are probably not older than the 17th.

Mum, Sothsegger (mum sõth′sej.ẻr). [Meaning, "Hush, Truth-teller."] A Middle English alliterative poem, originally attributed to William Langland, supposed author of *Piers Plowman,* and published (1838) as *Richard the Redeless,* but identified as early as the 16th century as *Mum, Sothsegger.* It is in the form of a letter written to Richard II after his imprisonment in 1399, criticizing him for his laxity, weakness, and unfortunate choice of advisers. It ends abruptly in Passus IV. In 1928, a manuscript in the form of a dialogue between Mum and Sothsegger was discovered, in which the two opposites discuss many of the same subjects, although they refer to events of a few years later (1403–06). The main argument of the poem is that a truth-teller is needed to help Richard II formulate his policies. The two fragments show differences of style but, because of the unusualness of the names and the similarity of content, scholars assume some sort of association between the two poems.

Mundus et Infans (mun′dus et in′fanz). An interlude (the title means "The World and the Child") printed by Wynkyn de Worde in 1522, written c1500.

Mungo (mung′gō), **Saint.** See Saint **Kentigern.**

Mungo Malagrowther (mal.a̤.grou′ᵵHẻR), **Sir.** See **Malagrowther, Sir Mungo.**

Munro (mun.rō′), **Charles Kirkpatrick.** [Original name, **Charles Walden Kirkpatrick MacMullan.**] b. at Pertrude, County Antrim, Ireland, Feb. 17, 1889—. A British playwright and essayist. His plays include *Wanderers* (1915), *At Mrs. Beam's* (1921), *The Rumour* (1922), *Storm* (1924), *The Mountain* (1926), *Mr. Eno* (1928), *Veronica* (1930), *Bluestone Quarry* (1931), and *Coronation Time at Mrs. Beam's* (1937). He is author also of the essay collections *The True Woman* (1931) and *Watching a Play* (1933).

Munro, Hector Hugh. [Pseudonym, **Saki.**] b. at Akyab, Burma, Dec. 18, 1870; killed in France, Nov. 13, 1916. A British humorist and satirist. His only serious work, and the only one published under his own name, was *The Rise of the Russian Empire* (1900). He wrote whimsical political articles for the *Westminster Gazette* which were collected and published as *The Westminster Alice* (1902). His initial collection of short stories, which also appeared in the same journal, was published as *Reginald* (1904). He served (1902–08) as the *Morning Post* correspondent in Russia, Paris, and the Balkans. At the outbreak of World War I he enlisted in the 22nd Royal Fusiliers and was killed in action at Beaumont-Hamel. Author of novels and collections of short stories including *Reginald in Russia* (1910), *The Chronicles of Clovis* (1911), *The Unbearable Bassington* (1912), *When William Came* (1913), *Beasts and Super-Beasts* (1914), *The Toys of Peace and Other Papers* (1919), and *The Square Egg and Other Sketches* (1924). His writing, which at times touches fantasy, is often bitterly sarcastic, although it never loses its urbanity.

Munro, Hugh Andrew Johnstone. b. at Elgin, Scotland, Oct. 19, 1819; d. at Rome, March 30, 1885. A Scottish classical scholar. He edited Lucretius (1864) and Horace (1869), and wrote Greek and Latin verse.

Muralto (mū.ral′tō), **Onuphrio.** A fictitious canon of Saint Nicholas at Otranto, from whom Horace Walpole, as William Marshall, professed to translate *The Castle of Otranto*.

Muratorian Fragment or **Canon** (mū.ra̱.tō′ri.a̱n), **The.** A summary of the canonical books of the New Testament, in popular and illiterate language of about the time of Marcus Aurelius.

Murder in the Cathedral. A drama in verse by T. S. Eliot, produced and published in 1935. The plot involves the decision of Saint Thomas à Becket to obey the dictates of God even though this must entail his loss of temporal power and his eventual death (Eliot obtains a striking effect by casting the speeches of his murderers in prose, rather than the blank verse used elsewhere in the play). Choral effects are employed to create atmosphere and give emotional tone to the scenes.

Murdockson (mėr′dǫk.sǫn), **Madge.** See **Wildfire, Madge.**

Murdockson, Meg. In Sir Walter Scott's *Heart of Midlothian*, the woman who steals Effie's baby and gives him to outlaws, then swears that Effie committed child-murder. She is finally hanged as a witch.

Murdstone (mėrd′stōn, -stǫn), **Edward.** In Dickens's *David Copperfield*, a black-haired, violent-tempered, vindictive, cruel man; David Copperfield's stepfather.

Murdstone, Jane. In Dickens's *David Copperfield*, the cold and bitter sister of Edward Murdstone.

Mure (mūr), Sir **William.** b. at Rowallan, Ayrshire, Scotland, 1594; d. 1657. A Scottish poet. A member of the Scottish parliament (1643), he joined the fight against the English; he was wounded (1644) at Marston Moor. He wrote the *True Crucifix for True Catholics* (1629), a version of the Psalms (1639), and others.

Murillo (mū.ril′ō; Spanish, mö.rē′lyō), **Bartolomé Esteban.** b. at Seville, Spain (baptized Jan. 1, 1618); d. there, April 3, 1682. A Spanish painter, chiefly of religious subjects. In 1643 he moved to Madrid, where he came under the influence of Velásquez, then at the zenith of his fame. He returned to Seville in 1645, where he spent several years (1661–74) in painting a series of 11 pictures which at once brought him into notice. Among these are *Moses Striking the Rock*, *Abraham and the Angels*, *The Miracle of the Loaves and Fishes*, *Saint Peter Released from Prison*, and *Saint Elizabeth*. A favorite subject with Murillo was the Virgin of the Conception; the most famous example of this is in the Louvre.

Murphy (mėr′fi), **Arthur.** b. near Elphin, County Roscommon, Ireland, Dec. 27, 1727; d. at London, June 18, 1805. An Irish dramatist. In the period 1752–74 he published the *Gray's Inn Journal* at London. He appeared as actor and dramatist, and was called to the bar in 1762. He wrote *The Apprentice* (1756), *The Upholsterer* (1757), *The Way to Keep Him* (1760), *The Citizen* (1761), *All in the Wrong* (1761), *The School for Guardians* (1767), *Know Your Own Mind* (1777), *Three Weeks after Marriage* (1776), a farce, and translations of Sallust and Tacitus (1793).

Murray (mur′i), **Alexander.** b. at Dunkitterick, Kirkcudbrightshire, Scotland, Oct. 22, 1775; d. at Edinburgh, April 15, 1813. A Scottish philologist. He attended school for a short time in 1788 and, afterward by his own efforts, mastered the English language, the classics, the European languages, Hebrew and other Oriental tongues, and Abyssinian. In 1812 he was chosen professor of Oriental languages at Edinburgh. In 1823 he published *History of the European Languages*.

Murray, Alexander Stuart. b. at Arbirbolt, Scotland, Jan. 8, 1841; d. at London, March 5, 1904. A Scottish archaeologist and author. He was with the British Museum as assistant keeper (1867–86) and keeper (1886–1904) in its department of Greek and Roman antiquities. Author of *A Manual of Mythology* (1873, and numerous editions in England and America), *History of Greek Sculpture* (1880–83), *Handbook of Archaeology* (1892), *Greek Bronzes* (1898), *Excavations in Cyprus* (1900), and *The Sculptures of the Parthenon* (1903).

Murray, Charles. b. in Aberdeenshire, Scotland, 1864; d. there, May 2, 1941. A Scottish poet, engineer, and public official. He spent the greater part of his life in South Africa, where he was secretary of public works (1910–24) for the Union, and director of defense (1917). He retired in 1924 and returned to Scotland.

Murray, David Christie. b. at West Bromwich, Staffordshire, England, April 13, 1847; d. at London, Aug. 1, 1907. An English novelist, journalist, and essayist. He was correspondent for the *Times* and the *Scotsman*, covering the Russo-Turkish War (1877–78). He became interested in the case of Captain Alfred Dreyfus, and defended him in lectures and press articles. Author of *A Life's Atonement* (1879), *Joseph's Coat* (1881), *Val Strange* (1882), *By the Gate of the Sea* (1883), *Rainbow Gold* (1885), and *Aunt Rachel* (1886), novels of Staffordshire life; and of *A Novelist's Notebook* (1887), *The Making of a Novelist* (1894), *My Contemporaries in Fiction* (1897), and *Recollections and Guesses at Truth* (1908), autobiography, criticism, and essays.

ḏ, d or j; ṣ, s or sh; ṭ, t or ch; ẓ, z or zh; *o*, F. cloche; ü, F. menu; čh, Sc. loch; ṅ, F. bonbon.

Murray, Gilbert. [Full name, **George Gilbert Aimé Murray.**] b. at Sydney, Australia, Jan. 2, 1866—. A British classical scholar, widely known for his annotated editions of the Greek tragedies. He was educated at London and at St. John's College, Oxford, and was professor of Greek at Glasgow University (1889–99) and regius professor of Greek at Oxford (1908 *et seq.*). He headed (1923–38) the League of Nations Union. He published *History of Ancient Greek Literature* (1897), two plays, *Carlyon Sahib* (1899) and *Andromache* (1900), *The Rise of the Greek Epic* (1907), *Four Stages of Greek Religion* (1913), and other works, including translations. Among his later works are *The Classical Tradition in Poetry* (1927) and *Aeschylus, Creator of Tragedy* (1940).

Murray, Grenville. [Full name, **Eustace Clare Grenville Murray.**] b. 1824; d. at Passy, France, Dec. 20, 1881. An English journalist and author; natural son of Richard Grenville, 2nd Duke of Buckingham. In 1851 he was attaché at Vienna, in 1852 at Constantinople, and in 1855 consul general at Odessa. His journalistic endeavors were pioneering efforts in society gossip. In 1869 he was publicly horsewhipped by an English nobleman and soon afterward left England. He wrote *The Roving Englishman* (1854–55), *History of the French Press* (1874), and the novels *The Member for Paris* (1871) and *Young Brown* (1874).

Murray, Sir James Augustus Henry. b. at Denholm, Roxburghshire, Scotland, Feb. 7, 1837; d. at Oxford, England, July 26, 1915. A Scottish lexicographer and philologist, editor of the *New English Dictionary.* He was educated at the University of London (B.A., 1873), was assistant master (1854–57) at the Hawick Grammar School, master (1857–62) at Hawick Academy, and master (1870–85) at Mill Hill School, London. He lived (1885 *et seq.*) at Oxford, where he engaged in the work by which he is remembered, and for which he was knighted in 1908. He edited some old Scottish texts (1871–75), contributed to the *Athenaeum*, wrote on "The English Language" for the *Encyclopædia Britannica* (1878), and was the author of *Dialect of the Southern Counties of Scotland* (1873). His chief work was the Philological Society's *A New English Dictionary on Historical Principles* (popularly known as the *Oxford English Dictionary*), to the editorship of which he was appointed in 1879. He planned the work and was responsible for the volumes A–D, H–K, O, P, and T. The first volume of the dictionary was published in 1884, and the final one appeared in 1935, the editorship being shared with Murray by Henry Bradley (1890 *et seq.*) and William Craigie (1901 *et seq.*).

Murray, John. [Original surname, **MacMurray.**] b. at Edinburgh, 1745; d. Nov. 6, 1793. An English publisher, of Scottish birth. He obtained a commission in the Royal Marines in 1762, and in 1768 bought the bookselling business of William Sandby at London. He published the *English Review*, D'Israeli's *Curiosities of Literature*, and other works.

Murray, John. b. Nov. 27, 1778; d. June 27, 1843. An English publisher; son of John Murray (1745–93). He started the *Quarterly Review* (Feb. 1, 1809)

in opposition to the *Edinburgh Review*, an undertaking in which he had the coöperation of Canning, Scott, Heber, Ellis, and Barrow. He published the works of Byron, Crabbe, Moore, Campbell, Irving, and others.

Murray, John. b. at London, April 16, 1808; d. there, April 2, 1892. An English publisher; son of John Murray (1778–1843) and grandson of John Murray (1745–93). Educated at Charterhouse and at Edinburgh University, he entered the family business in 1830, becoming its head in 1843. He was the author of travel handbooks on Holland, Belgium, the Rhine, France, South Germany, and Switzerland, and also wrote *Scepticism in Geology* (1877). He published works of George Borrow, Grote's *History of Greece*, Smith's classical dictionaries, Darwin's *Origin of Species*, Layard's *Nineveh and Its Remains*, works by Lyell, Lockhart, Henry Hallam, Dean Milman, Dean Stanley, and John Lothrop Motley, Livingstone's *Travels*, Maine's *Ancient Law*, and Elwin's *Pope*.

Murray, Sir John. b. at London, June 12, 1884—. An English publisher and editor. He entered (1906) the publishing firm founded by his great-grandfather John Murray (1745–93) and became (1928) its senior partner. He was editor (1928 *et seq.*) of the *Quarterly Review*.

Murry (mur'i), **John Middleton.** b. at London, Aug. 6, 1889—. An English editor and critic; husband of Katherine Mansfield. He was on the staff (1912–14) of the *Westminster Gazette*, and was editor of the *Athenaeum* (1919–21), the *Adelphi* (1923–30), and *Peace News* (1940 *et seq.*). His books include *Still Life* (1916), *Fyodor Dostoevsky* (1917), *Poems* (1919), *The Evolution of an Intellectual* (1920), *The Things We Are* (1922), *Pencillings* (1923), *The Voyage* (1924), *Things to Come* (1928), *God* (1929), *Son of Woman* (1931), *The Necessity of Communism* (1932), *The Life of Katherine Mansfield* (1933; with Ruth E. Mantz), the autobiographical *Between Two Worlds* (1934), *Shakespeare* (1936), *The Necessity of Pacifism* (1937), *Christocracy* (1942), *Adam and Eve* (1944), and *The Free Society* (1947).

Musaeus (mū.zē'us). A legendary Greek poet of Attica, associated with Orpheus (as a pupil or, in some accounts, as a son). To him were attributed various poems connected with the mysteries of Demeter at Eleusis, over which he was said to have presided.

Musaeus. [Surnamed **Grammaticus.**] fl. c5th century A.D. A Greek grammarian, author of a celebrated poem on Hero and Leander. Of this poem 340 verses have been preserved. It was imitated by Marlowe.

Musagetes (mū.saj'ē.tēz). An epithet of Apollo, as the "leader of the Muses."

Musée des Beaux Arts (mü.zā dā bō zàr). See under **Another Time.**

"Muse of Cumberland" (kum'bėr.land), **the.** See **Blamire, Susanna.**

Muses (mū'zez). In Greek mythology, the nine daughters of Zeus and Mnemosyne, who according to the earliest writers were goddesses of memory, then inspiring goddesses of song, and later, divinities presiding over poetry, the sciences, and the arts, while at the same time having as their especial province springs and streams. Originally, they were three; later nine: Clio, the Muse of lyre playing, or of history; Euterpe, of tragedy, lyric poetry, and the double flute; Thalia, of pastoral life and comedy; Melpomene, of lyre playing and tragedy; Terpsichore, of choral dance and song; Erato, of erotic poetry, pantomime, and the lyre; Polymnia or Polyhymnia, of the inspired and stately hymn and religious dance; Urania, of astronomy and celestial poetry; and Calliope, the chief of the Muses, of heroic or epic poetry. The Muses were intimately associated in legend and in art with Apollo, who, as the chief guardian and leader of their company, was called Musagetes.

Muses' Looking-Glass, The. A play by Thomas Randolph, originally acted (1630) under the title of *The Entertainment.* It was printed in 1638.

Musica Antiqua (mū′si.kạ an.tē′kwạ). A collection (1812) of old songs compiled by John Stafford Smith, and containing English and Norman pieces.

Musidora (mū.si.dō′rạ). The coy sweetheart of Damon in James Thomson's *The Seasons.* His delicacy on the occasion of seeing her bathing won her affections. She is the subject of a painting by Thomas Gainsborough, in the National Gallery, London.

Muspellsheim (mŭs′pels.hām). [Also: **Muspel, Muspelheim**; Old Norse, **Muspellsheimr.**] In the Old Norse cosmogony, the realm of fire and warmth in the south. At Ragnarök the Surt (Old Norse *Surtr*), the ruler of Muspellsheim, comes with his flaming sword leading his forces against the gods, and destroys the world with fire.

Musset (mü.se), **Alfred de.** [Full name, **Louis Charles Alfred de Musset.**] b. at Paris, Nov. 11, 1810; d. there, May 1, 1857. A French poet, playwright, and short-story writer. He graduated with high honors from the Collège Henri IV at Paris, and had just completed his 20th year when he published his first volume of poetry, *Contes d'Espagne et d'Italie* (1829). Two more collections of poems established his fame, *Poésies diverses* (1831) and *Le Spectacle dans un fauteuil* (1832). In 1833 he went to Italy with George Sand; but, after an extended trip, fell out with her at Venice, and returned to France alone. His morbid state of mind finds expression in the *Confession d'un enfant du siècle* (1836). During these years (1833–37) De Musset contributed a number of short plays to the *Revue des Deux Mondes;* they have appeared since then as *Comédies et proverbes* (1840). Short stories from the same magazine (1837–39) were also reprinted in book form (1840). In the same year (1840) appeared the first edition of the *Poésies nouvelles.* One of his last publications was a volume of *Contes* (1854). He was received in the French Academy in 1852. His complete works were published in 1860.

Mustapha (mus′tạ.fạ). A tragedy in Senecan style, printed in 1609, by Sir Fulke Greville.

Mustapha Baba (bä′bä). See **Baba, Mustapha.**

Mustard and Pepper. See under **Dinmont, Dandie.**

Mustardseed (mus′tạrd.sēd). A fairy in Shakespeare's *Midsummer Night's Dream.*

Mut (mö̇t). In Egyptian mythology, "the mother," consort of Amen, and a personification of the female principle.

Mutations of the Phoenix. A volume of poetry by Herbert Read, published in 1923.

Mutius (mū′shus). In Shakespeare's *Titus Andronicus,* the youngest son of Titus. He is killed by his father as he attempts to protect Lavinia.

My Brother Jonathan (jon′ạ.thạn). A novel by Francis Brett Young, published in 1928.

Myddleton (mid′l.tọn), Sir **Hugh.** [Also: **Myddelton, Middleton.**] b. c1555; d. Dec. 10, 1631. An English goldsmith, capitalist, and projector of the "New River" water supply of London. He was commissioned to build a canal to bring water into London from New River at Ware, Hampshire. The canal, dug with financial aid from James I after Myddleton had used up his money, was opened in 1613. It was not a financial success until after Myddleton died.

Myers (mī′ėrz), **Frederic William Henry.** b. at Keswick, Cumberland, England, Feb. 6, 1843; d. at Rome, Jan. 17, 1901. An English man of letters and philosophical writer. He studied at Trinity College, Cambridge, taking his degree in 1864, and became a fellow of Trinity in 1865. When the Society for Psychical Research was established in 1882 he was one of its founders, and he remained until his death one of the most important of the workers in this field. With Frank Podmore and Edmund Gurney he published, in 1886, *Phantasms of the Living. Science and a Future Life* appeared in 1893 and *Human Personality and its Survival of Bodily Death* in 1901. He also published poems of considerable merit (collected 1870 and 1882). He wrote *Essays, Classical and Modern* (1883), and *Wordsworth* (1881), a volume in the English Men of Letters series.

My Lady Mary (mãr′i). One of three historical tales in *The Ladies!* (1922), by Lily Adams Beck under the pseudonym E. Barrington.

My Lady of Orange (or′ạnj). A historical novel by Henry Christopher Bailey, published in 1901.

"My Mind to Me a Kingdom Is." The first line of a popular 16th-century song in Percy's *Reliques,* and attributed by Bartlett (*Familiar Quotations*) to Edward Dyer. Ben Jonson refers to it in *Every Man in His Humour.*

My Name is Legion. A novel by Charles Morgan, published in 1925.

My Novel, or Varieties of English Life. A novel by Edward Bulwer-Lytton, published in 1853.

Myrddhin (mir′ꜰH̵in). See **Merlin.**

Myrmidon (mėr′mi.dọn). In Greek mythology, a son of Zeus, in some accounts the reputed ancestor of the Myrmidons.

Myrmidons (mėr′mi.dọnz, -donz). In Greek legend, a warlike tribe of Phthiotis, Thessaly. They were led by Achilles in the Trojan War. According to one account, they were transformed from a horde of ants by Zeus, and performed their warlike duties as relentlessly as ants.

Myrmidons. In Shakespeare's *Troilus and Cressida,* the soldiers of Achilles.

Myrrha (mir'ạ). In Greek mythology, the mother of Adonis. She was transformed into a myrrh tree by the gods, to protect her from her father; and Adonis was born from the trunk of the tree.

Myrsilus (mẽr.sĩ'lus). See **Candaules.**

Myrtilus (mẽr'ti.lus). In Greek legend, a charioteer whose curses, when he was thrown into the sea by Pelops, brought innumerable woes upon the descendants of Pelops.

Myrtle (mẽr'tl). A young gentleman in love with Lucinda, an heiress, in Steele's *The Conscious Lovers.*

Mysie Happer (mĩ'si hap'ẽr). See **Happer, Mysie.**

Mysteries of Udolpho (ū.dol'fō), **The.** A Gothic novel by Ann Radcliffe, published in 1794. The story is set at the end of the 16th century, and revolves about its beautiful young heroine, Emily de St. Aubert. She has a tyrannical guardian, Madame Cheron, who insists that Emily give up her intention of marrying Valancourt, the young man she loves. Madam Cheron takes Emily to the castle of Udolpho in the Apennines, and she herself marries the robber chief Mortoni, who owns the castle. In spite of supernatural obstacles, hidden panels, underground passages, and frightening deeds, Emily escapes to Valancourt and marries him.

Mystery of Edwin Drood (ed'win drŏd'), **The.** An unfinished novel by Charles Dickens, the first number of which was issued in April, 1870. It was to have been completed in 12 monthly parts, but only about six were written when he died. Many books have since been written in an effort to solve its mystery. An edition valuable to students of the subject was edited (1941) by Vincent Starrett. Rosa Bud and Edwin Drood, two young orphans, were betrothed by their fathers before those gentlemen died. Edwin does not love Rosa, but Neville Landless, another orphan, does. John Jasper, Edwin's uncle, has an uncontrollable passion for Rosa, and not knowing that Edwin and she have broken their engagement, he promotes enmity between Edwin and Neville. The young men have a quarrel, and that night Edwin disappears. Neville is blamed but no charges can be proved against him because no body is found. Rosa flies from Jasper in terror, and is aided by Mr. Grewgious (her guardian), Mr. Septimus Crisparkle (a minor canon), and Mr. Tartar (a retired naval officer). Everyone is mystified by the actions of the stranger, Dick Datchery, who seems to be trailing Jasper. Here the fragment breaks off; there is no hint to the solution of the story. Some memorable characters are Mr. Sapsea, auctioneer and mayor; Mr. Honeythunder, a bullying "philanthropist"; Mr. Bazzard, the clerk; and Stony Durdles, the stonemason.

mystery plays. [Also, **miracle plays.**] Plays developed in the 14th and 15th centuries for secular performance but with religious themes. They are the successors of earlier, simpler dramatizations of episodes in the Christian story which were presented in church. As such dramatic presentations grew more elaborate, they passed out of the church into the market-place and the streets of the town and out of the hands of the clergy into those of the guilds. (The word *mystery* in this connection was apparently influenced by the now archaic *mystery*, "a craft or trade."). In a number of larger towns cycles of such plays developed, which were performed on "pageants," movable platforms that were wheeled through the streets. As each platform reached a designated point (at York at one time there were 14), it stopped and the play was presented. Then it moved on and another took its place. The great occasion for these performances was Corpus Christi Day, and most cycles were given then. The particular subjects were often assigned according to the association of a given guild with the event depicted. Thus the York cycle has the shipwrights' guild performing the story of Noah and his ark, the fishermen and mariners doing the ark's voyage, the bakers doing the Last Supper, the vintners performing the miracle of the wedding feast at Cana, and the cooks doing the harrowing of hell. This cycle had 57 pageants at its peak, more than that of any other town. There are four cycles preserved more or less fully, those of York (1415) with 48 plays, Wakefield (best known as the Towneley Plays, 15th century) with 32 plays, Chester (1328) with 25 plays, and the Hegge cycle (in a manuscript of 1468) with 42 plays, as well as two Coventry plays and one each from Norwich and Newcastle. There are three plays in the Digby series (the Digby Plays) of the 15th century. The Beverley cycle of 38 plays (1423) has vanished. The term "miracle play" has also been used to refer to this type of drama, and a technical distinction has sometimes been made between a play concerning an event in the life of Christ as given by the gospels (mystery) and a play concerning the activities of a saint, or a subject taken from the Bible or apocryphal sources (miracle). See also **morality plays.**

mystery story. A short story, novelette, or novel whose primary business it is to pose and solve a mystery. Several closely related kinds of story are usually grouped under this common heading: crime stories, in which the mystery is a crime, and the emphasis is upon that crime; detective stories, in which the mystery is a crime but the emphasis is on solving the crime; mystery stories, in which the mystery may or may not be criminal, and the emphasis is on the effect of that mystery upon those involved in it rather than on the mystery itself or its solution. The best of the crime stories are those in which the reader's sympathy is with the criminal, as in E. W. Hornung's "Raffles" stories, for the success of the crime story depends upon the reader's reluctance to have the criminal apprehended. In the pure detective story, the most successful are those where the detective has so engaged the reader's interest that the solution of the crime is intensely desired. In this genre there are many famous examples. Among the professional and semiprofessional detectives of fiction are Sir Arthur Conan Doyle's "Sherlock Holmes"; Chesterton's "Father Brown"; H. C. Bailey's "Mr. Fortune"; R. Austin Freeman's "Dr. Thorndyke." Dorothy L. Sayers's "Lord Peter Wimsey" is an appealing amateur of detection; "Walter Hartright," in Wilkie Collins's *The Woman in White,* is neither a professional nor an amateur, but simply a man who finds himself involved in a mystery which he feels he must solve. The mystery story that is not in either the crime or the detective class is the most difficult one to define, for often a novel which may not be thought of in this category is basically a mystery story. Practically every book Dickens wrote is a mystery story, or has in it one or more mysteries; even *Pickwick Papers* has its mysteries. *A Tale of Two Cities* derives much of its power from the mystery, and Dickens's unfinished *Mystery of Edwin Drood* is so baffling that, despite many attempts to construct the probable ending which death kept Dickens from writing, no one has brought forth a satisfactory solution. Dickens, however, cannot be classed as a mystery-story writer; rather, he used this arresting form as a means of holding the reader's interest while he conveyed the rest of what he had to say, often a plea for reform of various social evils. Many other writers have used the mystery in the same way, as a vehicle for other matters. In modern mystery stories writers use realistic characterization and psychology to create an atmosphere of fear and suspense. Among those who are most successful in creating real characters, whose terror the reader keenly feels, are Eric Ambler, Geoffrey Household, Helen MacInnes, and Graham Greene. Also, the writers of today's better mystery stories are inclined to base their fictions to some extent on current social and political topics as well as on theft or murder. The two world wars of the 20th century have inspired the mystery tale of espionage, exemplified by Somerset Maugham's *Confidential Agent* and John Buchan's *The Thirty-Nine Steps* and *Greenmantle*. The "tough" school of mystery writers in the United States, perhaps begun by Dashiell Hammett, has achieved a certain popularity and influence. A very large proportion of the output of English and American publishers today is devoted to the mystery story, of one sort or another, besides the many magazines that specialize in mystery fiction. An American mystery-story writer, Ellery Queen (actually, a pseudonym used by two collaborating authors), has compiled a useful bibliography called *The Detective Short Story: A Bibliography.*

My Sword for Lafayette (lä.fȧ.et'). A historical novel by Sir Max Pemberton, published in 1906.

mytacism (mī'tȧ.sizm). A fault of speech or of writing, consisting of a too frequent repetition of the sound of the letter *m*, either by substituting it for others through defect of utterance, or by using several words containing it in close conjunction.

myth (mith). **1.** A traditional story in which the operations of natural forces and occurrences in human history are represented as the actions of individual living beings, especially of men, or of imaginary extra-human beings acting like men; a tale handed down from primitive times, and in form historical, but in reality involving elements of early religious views, as respecting the origin of things, the powers of nature and their workings, the rise of institutions, the history of races and communities, and the like; a legend of cosmogony, of gods and heroes, and of animals possessing wondrous gifts.
2. In a looser sense, an invented story; something purely fabulous or having no existence in fact; an imaginary or fictitious individual or object: as, his wealthy relative was a mere *myth;* his having gone to Paris is a *myth. Myth* is thus often used as a euphemism for *falsehood* or *lie.*

Mytilene (mit.i.lē'nē) or **Mytilini** (mē.tē.lē'nē). See **Lesbos.**

N

Nabbes (nabz), **Thomas.** b. c1605; d. c1641. An English dramatist and poet.

Nabob (nā'bob), **The.** A comedy by Samuel Foote, produced in 1772.

Nabonassar (nab.ō.nas'ȧr), **Era of.** Era sometimes used in ancient chronology, reckoned from the accession (747 B.C.) of the Babylonian ruler Nabonassar. It originated with the Babylonian chroniclers, but was later used to some extent also by the Greeks.

Naboth (nā'both). In the Old Testament, an inhabitant of Jezreel who was put to death by stoning when he refused to part with his vineyard to King Ahab, who coveted it. The family of Ahab was thereupon placed under a curse by Elijah and his dynasty fell from power, from which event stems the phrase "Naboth's Vineyard." 1 Kings, xxi.

Naboth's Vineyard. A piece of property which a superior desires and takes away from one not in a position to prevent the wrong, from Ahab's treatment of Naboth.

Nabugodonosor (nab"ö.gō.don'ō.sọr). Chaucer's name for Nebuchadnezzar in "The Monk's Tale," one of *The Canterbury Tales.*

Naden (nā'den), **Constance Caroline Woodhill.** b. at Edgbaston, Birmingham, England, Jan. 24, 1858; d. at London, Dec. 23, 1889. An English poet, author of *Songs and Sonnets of Springtime* (1881) and *A Modern Apostle and Other Poems* (1887). With Robert Lewins, she was the cofounder of a philosophical system known as hylo-idealism, which sought to reconcile metaphysics and science.

Naggleton (nag'l.ton), **Mr. and Mrs.** Characters appearing (1864–65) in *Punch*, who are always quarreling over trifles.

Naglfar (nä'gl.fär). In Scandinavian mythology, the ship of the giants in Ragnarök.

Nag's Head Tavern. An old London tavern on the corner of Friday Street, not far from the Mermaid and the Mitre, where the consecration of the first Protestant bishop in 1559 was alleged by contemporary opponents of the Anglican Church to have taken place; hence derisively called "the Nag's Head Consecration." The ceremony really took place at the Church of Saint Mary-le-Bow.

Naiads (nā'adz, nī'-). In Greek and Roman mythology, female spirits presiding over springs, rivers, streams, and fountains. The Naiads were represented as beautiful nymphs with their heads crowned with flowers, light-hearted, musical, and beneficent. Their beneficence extends to the life-giving properties of water.

Nailor (nā'lọr), **John.** A follower of Robin Hood, known as "Little John" because of his gigantic stature.

Nairne (nārn), **Carolina.** [Title: Baroness **Nairne**; maiden name, **Oliphant;** sometimes called the **"Flower of Strathearn."**] b. at the house of Gask, Perthshire, Scotland, Aug. 16, 1766; d. there, Oct. 26, 1845. A Scottish poet; daughter of Lawrence Oliphant, a leading Jacobite. In June, 1806, she married William Murray Nairne, who became 5th Lord Nairne. As "Mrs. Bogan of Bogan," she contributed lyrics to the *Scottish Minstrel* (1821–24). After her death her poems were published as *Lays from Strathearn.* Among her songs are *The Land o' the Leal, The Laird of Cockpen, Wha'll be king but Charlie?, Bonnie Charlie's noo awa', Charlie is my Darling,* and *Caller Herrin'.*

Naked Warriors. A volume of poetry by Herbert Read, published in 1919.

Nala (nä'la). In Hindu literature, the king of Nishadha, and husband of Damayanti. The episode of Nala and Damayanti is one of the most celebrated of the *Mahabharata.* It has been translated into English by Milman, and by Sir Edwin Arnold in his *Indian Idylls.*

"Namby Pamby" (nam'bi pam'bi). Nickname of **Philips, Ambrose.**

Name of Action, The. A novel by Graham Greene, published in 1930.

Nan (nan), **The Tragedy of.** A drama (1909) by John Masefield.

Nana (nan'a). The dog who serves, in a manner of speaking, as nurse for the Darling children, Wendy, Michael, and John, in *Peter Pan* (1904), the fairy play by Sir James M. Barrie.

Nancy (nan'si). In Dickens's *Oliver Twist,* the mistress of Bill Sikes, who brutally murders her.

Nanda (nan'da). In Sanskrit mythology, a cowherd, the foster-father of Krishna.

Nanki-Poo (nang'ki.pö'). In Gilbert and Sullivan's *The Mikado,* the son of the Mikado. He assumes the disguise of a wandering minstrel for his courtship of Yum-Yum.

Nanna (nän'nä). In Old Norse mythology, the goddess of flowers and vegetation; wife of Balder. When Balder died, Nanna died of grief and accompanied him to Hel. When Balder returned to earth, Nanna remained in the underworld, but sent flowers to carpet the earth.

Nansen (nän'sẹn), **Fridtjof.** b. near Christiania (now Oslo), Norway, Oct. 10, 1861; d. at Lysaker, Norway, May 30, 1930. A Norwegian arctic explorer. He sailed (June, 1893) from Christiania at the head of an arctic expedition, intending to

drift in a specially constructed vessel, the *Fram,* from the Siberian coast across the North Pole to the coast of Greenland. He returned in 1896, having reached with sledges lat. 86°14′ N., two degrees and 50 minutes further than Lockwood's furthest and the northernmost point reached by man up to that time. Active in the establishment (1905) of a Norwegian government independent of Sweden, he was in 1905 appointed his country's first minister (and later, ambassador) at the Court of St. James, retiring in 1908. He served as professor of oceanography at the university from 1908 and was a member (1910–14) of oceanographic expeditions to the North Atlantic. He was awarded (1922) the Nobel peace prize for his efforts to repatriate (1918 *et seq.*) prisoners of war and for his steps toward alleviating (1921–23) the Russian famine. He wrote *Farthest North* (1897), *The Norwegian North Polar Expedition 1893–96: Scientific Results* (with others, 1900 *et seq.*), *Norway and the Union with Sweden* (1905), *In Northern Mists* (1911), *Russia and Peace* (1923), *Hunting and Adventure in the Arctic* (1925), *Armenia and the Near East* (1928), and others.

Nantes (nants; French, nänt), **Edict of.** An edict issued by Henry IV of France on April 13, 1598. It temporarily ended the religious wars of the country (see also **Revocation of the Edict of Nantes**). The Edict put the Huguenots on an equality with the Catholics in political rights, and certain classes of nobles and citizens of certain towns were allowed freedom of worship, although this was prohibited in Paris and its neighborhood and in episcopal cities. Military and judicial concessions were also made to the Huguenots.

Nanty Ewart (nan'ti ū'ạrt). See **Ewart, Nanty.**

Naoise (nē'shē). [Also: **Naisi** (nä'shē), **Noise** (noi'-).] In Old Irish legend, one of the three sons of Usnach, lover and husband of Deirdre, and one of the best warriors of Ulster. Naoise came upon Deirdre in the forest, where she had been secluded by Conchobar, king of Ulster, so that no man might behold her. The two fell in love, Naoise and his two brothers carried Deirdre off to Scotland, and Conchobar officially banished them forever. Later he sent for them to return with promise of full pardon. But on the first night of their return Conchobar treacherously had Naoise and his two brothers slain.

Napier (nā'pi.ẻr, na.pir'), **Henry Edward.** b. March 5, 1789; d. Oct. 13, 1853. An English author. He wrote *Florentine History* (1846–47) and others.

Napier, John. [Also: **Neper;** title, Laird of **Merchiston** (mẻr'kis.tọn).] b. at Merchiston, near Edinburgh, 1550; d. there, April 4, 1617. A Scottish mathematician, the inventor of logarithms. He was the eldest son of Archibald, the seventh Napier of Merchiston, hereditary justice-general of Scotland. He matriculated at St. Salvator's College, at St. Andrews, in 1563, and probably completed his education at the University of Paris. His *Mirifici logarithmorum canonis descriptio,* in which his discovery was announced, appeared in 1614. Napier's bones or rods, constructed to simplify multiplication and division, were introduced in the *Rabdologia* (1617). The *Constructio,* or method by which the canon was constructed, was published in 1619.

Napier, Macvey. b. at Kirkintilloch, Dumbartonshire, Scotland, April 11, 1776; d. at Edinburgh, Feb. 11, 1847. A Scottish author and editor. In 1829 he succeeded Jeffrey as editor of the *Edinburgh Review*, and he was editor (1830–42) of the 7th edition of the *Encyclopaedia Britannica*.

Napier, Sir William Francis Patrick. b. near Dublin, Dec. 17, 1785; d. at Clapham Park, London, Feb. 10, 1860. A British military historian and general. He was with Sir John Moore in the retreat to La Coruña, and served in the Peninsular campaigns. He entered the military college at Farnham with his brother Charles, and commanded a regiment in the occupation of France until 1819. Retiring on half pay, he began his literary career in 1821. In 1823 his *History of the War in the Peninsula* was begun; it was published between 1828 and 1840.

Napoleon I (na.pō′lẹ.ọn; French, nà.po.lā.ôṅ). [Also: **Napoleon Bonaparte**; French, **Napoléon Bonaparte**; Italian, **Napoleone Buonaparte** (or **Bonaparte**); called le *Petit Caporal*, meaning "the Little Corporal," and **"the Corsican."**] b. at Ajaccio, Corsica, Aug. 15, 1769, or, according to some, at Corte, Jan. 7, 1768; d. at Longwood, St. Helena, May 5, 1821. Emperor of the French (1804–14). He was the son of Charles Marie Bonaparte and Letizia (or Laetitia) Ramolino, and Aug. 15, 1769, is the commonly accepted date of his birth, Jan. 7, 1768, being that of his brother Joseph. It has been said, but without good reason, that these dates were interchanged at the time of Napoleon's admission to the military school of Brienne in 1779, no candidate being eligible after 10 years of age. After his studies at Brienne (1779–84), he attended the military school at Paris (1784–85), and received a lieutenant's commission in the French army in 1785. At first sympathetic, he later opposed the patriot movement under Paoli in Corsica (1792–93), from which he fled; and he commanded the French artillery in the attack on Toulon, which had hoisted the flag of the Bourbons, in the same year. He was promoted to the rank of general in 1794, but was imprisoned shortly thereafter during the Thermidorian reaction. He was soon released, however, and served briefly as an artillery general in Italy. Dropped for insubordination, he received a new appointment as second in command to Barras and subdued the revolt of the sections at Paris in October, 1795, with "a whiff of grapeshot," thus saving the revolutionary government. He married Josephine de Beauharnais on March 9, 1796. Toward the close of this month (March 27) he assumed command at Nice of the French forces in Italy, which he found opposed by the Austrians and the Sardinians. He began his electrifying campaign on April 10, and, after first defeating the Austrians, turned rapidly against the Sardinians, whose defeats forced them to sign the separate convention of Cherasco (April 29). In the following month he began an invasion of Lombardy, and by a brilliant series of victories, including those of Lodi (May 10) and Arcole (November 15–17), expelled the Austrians from their possessions in the north of Italy, receiving the capitula-

tion of Mantua, their last stronghold, on Feb. 2, 1797. Before crossing the Alps into Austrian territory he encouraged nationalist and democratic uprisings in northern Italy, and then dictated preliminaries of peace on April 18. The definitive peace of Campo Formio followed (October 17). By the treaty of Campo Formio northern Italy was reconstructed in the interest of France, which furthermore acquired the Austrian Netherlands and received a guarantee of the left bank of the Rhine. Campo Formio destroyed the coalition against France and put an end to the revolutionary war on the Continent. The only enemy that remained to France was England. At the instance of Bonaparte the willing Directory adopted the plan of attacking the English in India, which involved the conquest of Egypt and raised the vision of a French conquest of the Near and Middle East. Placed at the head of an expedition of about 35,000 men, Bonaparte set sail from Toulon on May 19, 1798, occupied Malta (June 12), disembarked at Alexandria (July 2), and defeated the Mamelukes in the decisive battle of the Pyramids (July 21). He was master of Egypt, but the destruction of his fleet by Nelson in the battle of the Nile (August 1) cut him off from France and doomed his expedition to failure. Utilizing the Sultan's declaration of war, he thereupon undertook the subjugation of Syria, and stormed Jaffa on March 7, 1799. Repulsed at Acre, the defense of which was supported by the English, he commenced a retreat to Egypt on May 21. He inflicted a final defeat on the Turks at Aboukir (July 25), transferred the command in Egypt to Kléber (August 22), and, setting sail with two frigates, arrived in the harbor of Fréjus (October 9). During his absence a new coalition, which included Russia, had been formed against France, and the Directory for a time saw its armies defeated both on the Rhine and in Italy. But before Bonaparte returned the most pressing military danger was over. With the assistance of his brother Lucien, and of Sieyès and Roger-Ducos, he executed the coup d'état of Brumaire, whereby he abolished the sorely discredited Directory and virtually made himself monarch under the title of first consul, holding office for a term of 10 years. He crossed the Alps through the Great St. Bernard Pass in May, 1800, and restored the French ascendancy in Italy by the victory of Marengo (June 14), which, with that won by Moreau at Hohenlinden (December 3), brought about the peace of Lunéville (Feb. 9, 1801). The treaty of Lunéville with the Austrians, which was based on that of Campo Formio, destroyed the coalition and restored peace on the Continent. He concluded the peace of Amiens with England on March 27, 1802. After the peace of Lunéville he returned to the task of the legislative and administrative reconstruction of France, the public institutions of which had been thrown into confusion during the Revolution. To this period belong the ending of the schism and restoration of the Roman Catholic Church by the Concordat (concluded July 15, 1801), the reorganization of education which was to culminate in the erection of the Imperial University (1808), and the establishment of the Legion of Honor (May 19, 1802). The Civil Code became law in 1804, and work continued on the other codes. Meantime, he was made consul for life (Aug. 2, 1802), had the innocent Duc d'Enghien executed (March 21, 1804), was proclaimed hereditary emperor of the French on May 18, 1804 (the coronation ceremony took place Dec. 2, 1804), and was crowned king of Italy (May 26, 1805). In the meanwhile, however, England had been provoked into declaring war (May 18, 1803), and a new coalition consisting of England, Russia, Austria, and Sweden was formed against France in 1805; Spain was allied with France. The victory of Nelson at the battle of Trafalgar (Oct. 21, 1805) followed the failure of the projected invasion of England. Breaking up his camp at Boulogne, Napoleon invaded Austria, occupied Vienna, and defeated (Dec. 21, 1805) the allied Russians and Austrians at Austerlitz. The Russians retired from the contest under a military convention; the Austrians signed the peace of Pressburg (Dec. 26, 1805); and the coalition was destroyed. Fresh intervention in Germany brought about the abolition of the Holy Roman Empire (June, 1806) and the establishment of the Confederation of the Rhine on July 12, 1806. This confederation, which was placed under Napoleon's protection, ultimately embraced nearly all the states of Germany except Austria and Prussia. Its creation, together with other provocation, caused Prussia to mobilize its army in August, and Napoleon presently found himself opposed by another coalition, with Prussia, Russia, and England as its principal members. He crushed the Prussian army at Jena and Auerstädt (October 14), entered Berlin (October 27), fought the Russians and Prussians in the drawn battle of Eylau (Feb. 7–8, 1807), defeated the Russians at the battle of Friedland (June 14), and compelled both Russia and Prussia to conclude peace at Tilsit (July 7 and 9, 1807, respectively). By a secret treaty, Russia now became the ally of France; by the open treaty, Prussia was deprived of nearly half her territory; and Napoleon was now, perhaps, at the height of his power. The imperial title was no empty form. He was the head of a great confederacy of states. He had surrounded the imperial throne with subordinate thrones occupied by members of his own family. His stepson Eugène de Beauharnais was viceroy of the kingdom of Italy in northern and central Italy; his brother Joseph was king of Naples in southern Italy; his brother Louis was king of Holland; his brother Jerome was king of Westphalia; his brother-in-law Murat was grand duke of Berg. The Confederation of the Rhine existed by virtue of his protection, and his troops occupied dismembered Prussia. He directed the policy of most of Europe. England alone, mistress of the seas, appeared to stand between him and universal dominion. England was safe from invasion, but she was vulnerable, he reasoned (though erroneously), through her commerce. Napoleon undertook to bring her to her knees by closing the ports of the Continent to her maritime trade. This policy became known as "the Continental system," and was rationalized by the Berlin decree in 1806 and the Milan decree in 1807. To further this policy of self-blockade he resolved to seize the maritime states of Portugal and Spain. His armies expelled the house of Bra-

ganza from Portugal, and on Nov. 30, 1807, the French entered Lisbon. Under pretense of guarding the coast against the English, he quartered 80,000 troops in Spain, then in 1808 enticed Ferdinand VII and his father Charles IV (who had recently abdicated) to Bayonne, extorted from both a renunciation of their claims, and placed his brother Joseph on the Spanish throne. An uprising of the Spaniards took place, followed by a popular insurrection in Portugal, movements which found response in Germany and especially in Austria. The seizure of Spain and Portugal proved in the end a fatal error. The war which it kindled, known as the Peninsular War, drained him of his resources and placed an enemy in his rear when northern Europe rose against him in 1813. The English in 1808 landed an army in Portugal, whence they expelled the French, and penetrated into Spain. Napoleon, hoping to secure himself against Austria, sought to strengthen the alliance with Czar Alexander at Erfurt (concluded Oct. 12, 1808). He then hastened in person to Spain with 250,000 men, drove out the English, and entered Madrid (Dec. 4, 1808). He was recalled by rumors of trouble in Paris and by the threatening attitude of Austria, against which he precipitated war in April, 1809. He occupied Vienna (May 13), was defeated by Archduke Charles at Aspern and Essling (May 21–22), but defeated him at Wagram (July 5–6), and concluded the peace of Schönbrunn (Oct. 14, 1809). He then divorced Josephine (Dec. 16, 1809), and for reasons of state married Maria Louisa of Austria. He annexed the Papal States in 1809 (the Pope being carried prisoner to France), and Holland in 1810. The refusal of Czar Alexander to carry out strictly the Continental System, which Napoleon himself evaded by the sale of licenses, was the final rift which brought on war with Russia. He crossed the Niemen (June 24, 1812), won the victory of Borodino (September 7), and occupied Moscow (September 14). His proffer of truce was rejected by the Russians, and he was forced by the approach of winter to begin a tardy retreat (October 8). He was overtaken by the harsh winter, and his army dwindled before the cold, hunger, and the enemy. He left the army in command of Murat (December 4) and hastened to Paris. Murat recrossed the Niemen (December 13) with 100,000 men, the remnant of the Grand Army of 600,000 veterans. The loss sustained by Napoleon in this campaign encouraged the defection of Prussia, which formed an alliance with Russia at Kalisch (Feb. 28, 1813). Napoleon defeated the Russians and Prussians at Lützen (May 2) and at Bautzen (May 20–21). Austria declared war (August 12), and Napoleon presently found himself opposed by a coalition of Russia, England, Sweden, Prussia, and Austria, of which the first three had been united since the previous year. He won his last great victory at Dresden (August 26–27), but lost the decisive battle of Leipzig (October 16, 18, and 19). Rejecting moderate peace terms from the Allies, he fought on, at Laon (March 9–10, 1814) and Arcis-sur-Aube (March 20–21), but on March 31 the Allies entered Paris. Napoleon was compelled to abdicate at Fontainebleau (April 11) but was allowed to retain the title of emperor and received the island of Elba as a sovereign principality, and an annual income of two million francs. He arrived in Elba on May 4. The Congress of Vienna convened in September, 1814, for the purpose of restoring and regulating the relations between the powers disturbed by Napoleon. Encouraged by the quarrels which arose at the Congress between the Allies, Napoleon escaped from Elba (Feb. 26, 1815), landed at Cannes (March 1), and entered Paris (March 20), the troops sent against him, including Ney with his corps, having joined his standard. At the return of Napoleon the Allies again took the field. He was finally overthrown at Waterloo (June 18, 1815) and the Allies entered Paris a second time (July 7). After futile attempts to escape to America, he surrendered himself to the British admiral Hotham at Rochefort (July 15). By a unanimous resolve of the Allies he was transported as prisoner of war to St. Helena, where he arrived on Oct. 16, 1815, and where he was detained for the rest of his life. In 1840 Louis Philippe ordered h's remains to be moved to the Hôtel des Invalides, Paris. One of the most remarkable military leaders the world has ever seen, he was also a highly talented administrator, and his conquests had a profound effect on the character of Europe as well as France.

Napoleon III. [Full name, **Charles Louis Napoléon Bonaparte**; known as **Louis Napoleon**; called **Carbonaro** and **Napoléon le Petit**.] b. at Paris, April 20, 1808; d. at Chiselhurst, near London, Jan. 9, 1873. Emperor of the French (1852–70). He was the son of Louis Bonaparte, king of Holland, and Hortense de Beauharnais, and the nephew of Napoleon I. He lived in exile at Arenenberg and Augsburg (1815–30), joined in an unsuccessful revolt (1830–31) against the Pope in the Romagna, made an unsuccessful attempt (1836) to organize a revolution among the French soldiers stationed at Strasbourg, made a descent on France near Boulogne in 1840, was captured, and was imprisoned at Ham until 1846, when he escaped. He was made a member of the National Assembly after the fall of Louis Philippe in 1848, was elected president of the republic (December, 1848), executed the coup d'état of Dec. 2, 1851, was chosen president for 10 years in December, 1851, and after a plebiscite in November, 1852, was proclaimed emperor (Dec. 2, 1852). He married Eugénie de Montijo, a Spanish countess, on Jan. 30, 1853, took part in the Crimean War (1854–56), fought with Sardinia against Austria in 1859, and was present at the battles of Magenta and Solferino, waged war in Mexico (1862–67), declared war against Germany in July, 1870, was taken prisoner at Sedan (September 2), and was imprisoned at Wilhelmshöhe, near Kassel (1870–71). He was later permitted to go to England, where he lived at Chiselhurst (1871–73). He was the author of various political and military works, including *Histoire de Jules César* (1865–66).

Napoleon of Notting Hill (not'ing), **The.** A novel by G. K. Chesterton, published in 1904.

Narcissa (när.sis'a̧). A name given by Pope in his *Moral Essays* to Anne Oldfield (1683–1730), a well-known actress.

Narcissa. A beautiful woman whose early death is commemorated in the third night of Edward

Young's *Night Thoughts*. She is identified with a Miss Lee who married Henry Temple, son of Lord Palmerston, and was the daughter of Young's wife by her first husband. She did in fact die in France but the account in the *Night Thoughts* is unfactual in stating that she was refused burial because she was a Protestant. After the translation of Young's book into French, the belief sprang up that she was buried at midnight in the Botanic Garden at Montpellier. Her supposed grave was discovered, was visited by strangers, and became one of the sights of the town. But in fact Mrs. Temple died at Lyons, and was buried in the Protestant cemetery there.

Narcissus (när.sis'us). In Greek mythology, a beautiful youth who was metamorphosed into a flower. He was indifferent to the love of the wood nymph, Echo, and for this insensibility he was caused by Nemesis to fall in love with his own image reflected in water. Unable to grasp this shadow, he pined away and became the flower which bears his name.

Nares (närz), **Edward.** b. at London, 1762; d. at Biddenden, Kent, England, Aug. 20, 1841. An English scholar, clergyman, and miscellaneous writer. He was educated at Oxford (Christ Church) and took orders in 1792. He married a daughter of the Duke of Marlborough in 1797. He was regius professor of modern history (1813–41) at Oxford.

Nares, Robert. b. at York, England, June 9, 1753; d. at London, March 23, 1829. An English clergyman and author. He was educated at Oxford (Christ Church) and took orders in 1778. He was assistant librarian at the British Museum (1795–1807), and aided in founding *British Critic*, which he edited from 1793 to 1813.

Nariman (nä.rē.män'). In the *Shahnamah*, a warrior of Faridun, killed in his attack upon Sipand, and avenged by Rustam, his great-grandson.

narrative. In prose or poetry, the recounting or relating in order of the particulars of some action, occurrence, or other affair. In simple narrative, as in a newspaper account, the events are told, for the most part, in chronological order. Defoe's *Apparition of Mrs. Veal* (1706) is an early example in English literature of simple narrative. The events of a narrative may also be arranged according to a preconceived design, in which case the order is determined by the plot. Narrative may be said to focus on externals of events, rather than on character or internal action. Until Richardson, English fiction was almost entirely narrative; since then, narrative elements in novels, although never entirely absent, have gradually tended, in the works of many English writers, to become subordinate to character development.

narration. In rhetoric, that part of an oration in which the speaker makes his statement of facts. The narration is to be distinguished from the proposition (prothesis) or statement of the subject. Besides the principal narration or narration proper (the diegesis), ancient rhetoricians distinguished subordinate forms of narration—the catadiegesis, epidiegesis, hypodiegesis, paradiegesis, and prodiegesis.

Narrenschiff (när'en.shif), **Das.** [Eng. trans., "*The Ship of Fools*."] A satirical poem by Sebastian

Brant, published in 1494. It is illustrated with woodcuts by well-known artists of the time. Alexander Barclay's translation (1508) was published in 1509.

Nash (nash), **John.** b. at London, 1752; d. May 13, 1835. An English architect. In London he designed Regent Street, the Haymarket, the terraces in Regent's Park, and others.

Nash, Richard. [Called Beau Nash and the "King of Bath."] b. at Swansea, Wales, Oct. 18, 1674; d. at Bath, England, Feb. 3, 1762. An English leader of fashion and master of ceremonies (1705 *et seq.*) at Bath. He was educated at Oxford (Jesus College), and studied law at the Inner Temple. He conducted the pageant at an entertainment given by the Inns of Court to William III. Much of the success of Bath as a resort of fashionable society was due to his efforts. He was a professional gambler until Parliament enacted (1745) a law against gaming. Goldsmith wrote his life in 1762.

Nash or **Nashe** (nash), **Thomas.** [Pseudonym, **Pasquil.**] b. at Lowestoft, England, 1567; d. c1601. An English satirical pamphleteer, poet, and dramatist. He took the degree of B.A. at Cambridge (Saint John's College) in 1585. His earliest work is a preface to Robert Greene's *Menaphon* (1589); the *Anatomy of Absurdity* appeared in 1589. Using his pseudonym, he entered (1589) the Martin Marprelate controversy on the side of the bishops, and is generally credited with writing *A Countercuffe to Martin Junior, Martins Months Minde,* and *Pasquils Apologie,* though no definite ascription is possible. In 1591 he edited, without authorization, Philip Sidney's poems, and the next year began his long and scurrilous "paper war" with Gabriel Harvey in *Pierce Pennilesse, his supplication to the Devil.* In it he attacked Richard Harvey for criticizing *Menaphon;* Greene's death in degraded circumstances gave fuel to the Harveys' side of the conflict, and the ensuing years saw publication by Nash, in answer to attacks by Harvey, of *Strange Newes of the intercepting certaine Letters* (1592), *Christs Teares over Jerusalem* (1593, a conciliatory effort followed by a renewal of the attack in a new edition in 1594), and *Have with You to Saffronwalden, or Gabriell Harveys Hunt is Up* (1596). The whole affair was ended by the intervention (1599) of John Whitgift, archbishop of Canterbury, who officially suppressed it. Nash wrote a pioneering realistic novel of adventure, *The Unfortunate Traveller, or the Life of Jack Wilton* (1594), a satirical masque, *Summers Last Will and Testament* (1592), and *Lenten Stuffe* (1599, a tongue-in-cheek praise of Yarmouth and the red herring). He is thought to have completed (1596) Christopher Marlowe's play *Dido Queen of Carthage;* the lost play *The Isle of Dogs* (1597), written in collaboration with others, contained material considered seditious and slanderous, for which he was sentenced to the Fleet prison, but he does not appear to have served his sentence.

Nash's Lenten Stuffe (nash'iz len'ten stuf). See **Lenten Stuffe.**

Nasier (nȧ.zyä), **Alcofribas.** Pseudonym of **Rabelais, François.**

Naströnd (näs'trend). In Old Norse mythology, a huge hall in Niflheim, the cold afterworld, drip-

ping with venom, set aside for the punishment of murderers.

Nathan (nā'thạn), **Isaac.** b. at Canterbury, England, 1791; d. in Australia, Jan. 15, 1864. An English composer of songs and operas, for whom George Gordon, Lord Byron, wrote the text for *Hebrew Melodies.* He also composed music to many other poems by Byron, for the operetta *Sweethearts and Wives* (1823), and several comic operas.

Nathan der Weise (nä'tän dėr vī'zẹ). [Eng. trans., *"Nathan the Wise."*] A drama by G. E. Lessing, published in 1779; so called from the name of its principal character. Its theme is religious tolerance, especially in the episode of the three rings, which was taken from Boccaccio. Nathan shows some resemblance to Lessing's friend Moses Mendelssohn.

Nathaniel (nạ.than'yẹl). In Shakespeare's *Taming of the Shrew,* one of Petruchio's servants.

Nathaniel, Sir. A curate in Shakespeare's *Love's Labour's Lost.*

Nathaniel Winkle (wing'kl). See **Winkle, Nathaniel.**

National Gallery. A picture gallery on the N side of Trafalgar Square, London, founded in 1824 by the purchase for the government of the Angerstein collection. The present building was opened in 1838. It was designed by Wilkins, and is in the Greek classical style: its façade is ab. 460 ft. in length. The buildings were altered and enlarged in 1860, 1876, 1887, and 1911. Many important collections have been added, among them the Vernon (1847), Turner (1856), and Peel (1871) collections. The Royal Academy of Arts occupied part of the building for a long time previous to its removal to Burlington House in 1869.

Nationalist Party. In 19th- and early 20th-century British politics, the Irish party formed for the advocacy of Home Rule.

National Library of Scotland. See under **Advocates' Library.**

naturalism. A type of fictional writing that aims to reproduce life with absolute and objective fidelity. It may be called realism pushed to its utmost. Where realistic writers like Galsworthy, Maugham, Waugh, and Aldous Huxley use realism as a means of expressing some personal vision of life, to the naturalistic writers realism often becomes not a means to an end but an end in itself. Perfect adherence to the "scientific" details of living is usually a poor substitute in fiction for the inner vision of a sensitive person, and as a result the naturalistic technique in the hands of any but a very great writer tends to leave the reader unsatisfied, although possibly satiated. George Saintsbury, a critic vehemently opposed to the naturalists, compares that technique to photography as against an artist's drawing, and accuses it of extreme dullness except when relieved by reference to crime and vice, which he says are subjects that of themselves hold a morbid interest for many readers; to mention the unmentionable, Saintsbury says, is the ambition of the school of naturalism. Émile Zola, a French novelist and critic writing in the latter half of the 19th century, established this technique, with the support of a few other writers including Guy de Maupassant. They claimed to derive from Stendhal, through Balzac and Flaubert, although these earlier authors were realists rather than naturalists. Among English writers, Arnold Bennett is sometimes classed as a naturalist, although he is more a follower of Balzac than of Zola. Zola's chief disciples in England were George Moore and George Gissing (although Gissing is sometimes called a realist). George Moore set out to shock the sensibilities of a public unaccustomed to frank, bold treatment of certain aspects of life. Sometimes the result was rather vulgar and crude, as in *A Modern Lover* (1883), but sometimes, too, he succeeded in giving masterly treatment to some neglected or overly sentimentalized subject, as in *Esther Waters* (1894), a powerful novel about the English servant class. George Gissing in *The Nether World* (1889) wrote of the lowest sort of slum existence, a favorite subject with the naturalists, from his own experience in such an environment; but the absolute objectivity upon which Zola insisted could not be achieved by one who loathed and despised (as Gissing actually did) the people of whom he wrote. Naturalism has had a great influence on many kinds of writing, from popular detective stories to the most *avant garde* magazines of experimental writing, and occasionally a novelist embraces it in its entirety, as James Hanley does in *Boy* (1931), a brutal, coarse, and violent story of sea life, and in *The Furys* (1935), a story of the grim misfortunes of a lower-class family in a waterfront city. But this sort of naturalism, derived from material realists like Moore, has attracted fewer good writers than has psychological naturalism, deriving from character analysts like Meredith and Henry James, and reaching its culmination in the stream-of-consciousness novel. These two paths of naturalism are interestingly suggested in Gissing's *New Grub Street* by the two principal characters, both authors; one of these, Biffen, has as his aim "absolute realism in the sphere of the ignobly decent" while the other, Reardon, was "a psychological realist for the more cultivated." Frank Swinnerton (*Nocturne*, *Young Felix*, *The Georgian House*) is a 20th-century follower of Gissing along Biffen's way, although his view of the "ignobly decent" is more cheerful than Gissing's. *The Twentieth Century Novel* by J. W. Beach (1932) discusses the technique of naturalism in George Moore and later writers.

Nature. A morality play by Henry Medwall, printed c1530 by William Rastell and written sometime between 1490 and 1501.

Nature and Art. A romance by Elizabeth Inchbald, published in 1796. It is the story of two brothers of very different characters, and their influence on their own sons. William is a worldly and ambitious man, while Henry, his brother, is a good and honest man who marries beneath him. Henry goes to Africa after he loses his wife, and is shipwrecked on Socotra Island with his infant son. This boy, Henry, is sent to live with his uncle William. He finds that his cousin, the younger William, has become a brutal and villainous judge, who even hangs the woman whom he has seduced.

The profligate William dies miserably after a life of remorse. The young Henry is untouched by the evils of civilization and surmounts all the obstacles that he meets, living a very happy life.

Nature of the Four Elements, The. An interlude probably by John Rastell, printed in 1518. Possibly the first part of a two-part play, it is a primitive study of physics, supposedly dealing with ten "diverse matters" of natural philosophy.

Nausicaa (nô.sik'ä.ạ). In the *Odyssey*, the daughter of Alcinous, king of the Phaeacians. When Odysseus was shipwrecked on the Phaeacian shore, Nausicaa found him and took him to her father's court.

Navarino (nä.vä.rē'nō; Anglicized, nav.ạ.rē'nō), **Battle of.** A battle fought Oct. 20, 1827, in which the English, French, and Russian fleets, united for the protection of Greece, entering the harbor of Navarino (Pylos) under the command of Sir Edward Codrington, annihilated the Turkish-Egyptian fleet.

Nazarene (naz'ạ.rēn). An inhabitant of Nazareth, a town in Galilee, Palestine: a name given (in contempt) to Jesus (with the definite article), and to the early converts to Christianity (Acts, xxiv. 5); hence, a Christian.

Nazarenes. A sect of Jewish Christians which continued to the 4th century A.D. They observed the Mosaic ritual, and looked for a millennium on earth. Unlike the Ebionites, they believed in the divinity of Christ.

Nazarites (naz'ạ.rīts). [Also, **Nazirites**.] Among the ancient Hebrews, religious devotees, set apart to the Lord by a special vow the terms of which are carefully prescribed in Num. vi. They included entire abstinence from wine and other intoxicating liquors, from all cutting of the hair, and from all approach to a dead body. The vow might be taken either for a limited period or for life. They first appear in the time of the Philistine oppression.

Nazi Party (nä'tsi, nat'si). [Popular appellation of the **National Socialist German Workers' Party**; abbreviation, **NSDAP**, from the German **National-sozialistische Deutsche Arbeiterpartei**.] A German political party, founded in 1920 and dominant in Germany from 1933 to 1945 under the leadership of Adolf Hitler. Its program, marking the peak of European totalitarianism as it developed between the two world wars, was based on an extreme nationalism and the embodiment of the principle of leadership (*Führer-prinzip*), the exploitation of the desires and frustrations of large segments of the German population searching for a leader who would bring them some measure of hope out of the despair that followed World War I.

Neaera (nē.ē'rạ). A name of a maiden in classical Latin pastoral poetry. Milton uses the name in *Lycidas*:

> To sport with Amaryllis in the shade,
> Or with the tangles of Neaera's hair. . . .

Neal (nēl), **Daniel.** b. at London, Dec. 14, 1678; d. there, April 4, 1743. An English historian. He was educated at the Merchant Taylors' School and at the universities of Utrecht and Leiden. In 1706 he settled as an independent clergyman at

ḏ, d or j; ş, s or sh; ṭ, t or ch; z̧, z or zh; o, F. cloche; ü, F. menu; c̀h, Sc. loch; ṅ, F. bonbon

London. He wrote *History of New England* (1720) and, his chief work, *History of the Puritans* (4 vols., 1732–38).

Neale (nēl), **Edward Vansittart.** b. at Bath, England, April 2, 1810; d. Sept. 16, 1892. An English Christian Socialist. He founded the first coöperative stores at London and assisted in the establishment of various industrial enterprises on a coöperative basis. He wrote *The Characteristic Features of Some of the Principal Systems of Socialism* (1851), *The Analogy of Thought and Nature Investigated* (1863), *A Manual for Coöperators* (1879), and others. In 1890 a scholarship at Oriel College for the sons of coöperators was founded in his honor.

Neale, John Mason. b. at London, Jan. 24, 1818; d. at East Grinstead, England, Aug. 6, 1866. An English hymnologist and ecclesiastical historian. He belonged to the extreme High Church party, and was burned in effigy in 1857. He founded (1855) the nursing sisterhood of Saint Margaret. His contributions to modern hymnology are notable. He wrote *An Introduction to the History of the Holy Eastern Church* (1850), *Mediaeval Hymns and Sequences* (1851), *Hymns of the Eastern Church* (1863), and others. He also translated the medieval hymn *De contemptu mundi* by Bernard of Cluny, in several parts, beginning "Brief life is here our portion," "Jerusalem the Golden," and others.

Neanderthal Man (nē̩.an'dẽr.täl, -thol; German, nä.än'dẽr.täl). A type of prehistoric man, some of whose skeletal remains were found (1856) in the Neanderthal, a small valley near Düsseldorf, Germany. From extensive study of these and other remains found scattered over Europe, in Palestine, C Asia, and N and SE Africa, he is considered to be a forerunner of modern man, though not a direct ancestor, being of a different species of the genus *Homo.* He was extremely dolichocephalic, short-statured (average height 5 ft. 3 inches), stooped; he had beetling brows, protruding teeth, and a chinless lower jaw. Whether or not he was hairy is conjectural, although most of the restorations show him so. He had a cave, hunting, and flake-tool culture (his tools show a degree of skilled workmanship). The group of Neanderthals called Mousterian had fire, buried their dead, and seem to have had some concept of a life after death. Anthropologists have classified Neanderthal Man into four subgroups, a classification now commonly accepted: (1) the Rhodesian group, named for fossil finds unearthed in Northern Rhodesia. Rhodesian Man is believed to be more closely allied to the anthropoids than the following groups, and is still regarded by a few as a transitional phase, rather than true Neanderthal in type; (2) the Mousterian or Spy group, represented by skulls or skeletons found at Gibraltar (1848), Spy, Neanderthal, La Chapelle, Krapina, and Le Moustier. The Gibraltar skull was not classified as Neanderthal until the type was scientifically established; (3) the Ehringsdorf group, which shows a slight advance over the Mousterian; (4) the fourth group is the closest to modern man, and is known to have been partially contemporary with Cro-Magnon man (possibly the direct antecedent of the modern species). This fourth group

is classified from a skull found at Galilee and other discoveries of the 1920's.

Nebuchadnezzar (neb″ū̩.ḳạd.nez'ạr). [Also: **Nebuchadnezzar II, Nebuchadrezzar** (neb″ū̩.ḳạd-rez'ạr); Babylonian, **Nabu-kuduri-uçur,** meaning "Nebo protect the boundary."] King of Babylonia (605–562 B.C.), the chief ruler of the New Babylonian Empire, and one of the greatest monarchs of the ancient world. The mighty canals and walls with which he surrounded Babylon, his magnificent palace (represented by the modern ruins of al-Kasr, "the castle"), the so-called Hanging Gardens of Semiramis or Hanging Gardens of Babylon, which he constructed for his Median wife Amytis (Amitu), his restoration of many temples, especially Esagila in Babylon and Ezida in Borsippa, were among his major accomplishments. A full description of the buildings he constructed is given by himself in a long inscription comprising 620 lines. There is no mention in the cuneiform inscriptions of Nebuchadnezzar's insanity and eating of grass as related in the Book of Daniel (iv. 26 ff.), but it has a certain parallel in the narrative of Abydenus (preserved by Eusebius), according to which the king once ascended the citadel of his palace and, inspired by a god, announced the fall of his empire.

Neckam (nek'ạm), **Alexander.** [Also, **Necham.**] b. at St. Albans, Hertfordshire, England, in September, 1157; d. at Kempsey, Worcestershire, England, 1217. An English scholar; foster brother of King Richard I. He was educated at St. Albans. In 1180 he was distinguished as a professor at Paris; in 1188 he became an Augustinian canon at Cirencester; and in 1213 he was elected abbot. He wrote scientific and grammatical treatises, Latin poems, theological works, commentaries on Aristotle, and others. In his writings is found the earliest European mention of the magnetic needle as an aid to navigation. His name was punned upon as *Nequam,* meaning "useless" or "wicked."

Necker (ne.ker; Anglicized, nek'ẽr), **Suzanne.** [Maiden name, **Curchod.**] b. at Crassier, Switzerland, 1739; d. at Coppet, Switzerland, in May, 1794. A French writer; wife of Jacques Necker, and a leader in literary circles. She was at one time engaged to the historian Edward Gibbon. She was the mother of Mme. de Staël.

Ned Bratts (ned brats). A poem by Robert Browning, based on one of the episodes in John Bunyan's *Life and Death of Mr. Badman,* concerning a rogue who, after many adventures, finally confessed and was hanged.

Negus (nē'gus), **Francis.** d. at Dallinghoo, Suffolk, England, Sept. 9, 1732. An English soldier, inventor of "negus," a mildly alcoholic compound of wine, water, spices, and sugar.

Neilson (nēl'sọn), **John Shaw.** b. at Penola, South Australia, Feb. 22, 1872; d. at Melbourne, Australia, May 12, 1942. An Australian lyric poet. He attended school for only 30 months, and worked all his life as a common laborer. He nevertheless wrote a group of lyrics which assures him a high place among Australian writers. He published *Collected Poems* (1934).

Neilson, Lilian Adelaide. [Also known as **Lizzie Bland;** original name, **Elizabeth Ann Brown.**] b. at

Leeds, Yorkshire, England, March 3, 1848; d. at Paris, Aug. 15, 1880. An English actress. At the age of 17 she made her debut as Juliet. In 1870 she made a conspicuous success as Amy Robsart at London, and by 1878 she was acknowledged queen of the English stage. She performed in Shakespeare's plays, and also in dramatizations of Scott.

Nekayah (nek′ạ.yạ), **Princess.** The sister of Rasselas, in Samuel Johnson's work of that name.

Neleus (nē′lūs). In Greek mythology, the son of Poseidon and Tyro, founder of Pylus in Messenia, and father of Nestor.

Nelson (nel′sọn), **Horatio.** [Title, Viscount **Nelson.**] b. at Burnham Thorpe, Norfolk, England, Sept. 29, 1758; d. on board the *Victory* at the battle of Trafalgar, Oct. 21, 1805. An English admiral. He entered the navy in 1770, and was made post captain, i.e., captain in rank, at the age of 21, serving in the American Revolutionary War in the West Indies and in Canada. In 1787 he married Frances Nisbet, a widow with a small son. At the declaration of war with France in 1793, he was made captain of the *Agamemnon* in the Mediterranean, serving first under Samuel, Viscount Hood and afterward under Admiral William Hotham. At Calvi (1794), he lost his right eye. In 1793 he convoyed troops from Naples to Toulon, under attack by Napoleon, and while at Naples met Emma Hamilton, wife of the English envoy at Naples. He later (1794) was present at the occupation of Corsica. On Feb. 14, 1797, under Admiral John Jervis (later Earl of St. Vincent), he fought in the battle off Cape St. Vincent, the victory being in large measure due to Nelson's initiative. He had become a commodore (1796) and now was appointed rear admiral (1797). On July 24, 1797, he ventured on a foolhardy attempt to capture Santa Cruz de Tenerife with only a limited crew; the attack failed, and Nelson, his right elbow shattered, lost his arm in a desperate operation. He was invalided home, and rejoined the fleet late in April, 1798. In May, 1798, he was sent by Lord St. Vincent to intercept Napoleon's expedition to Egypt. He failed to catch the French at Toulon but scoured the Mediterranean for them; he found them at last and destroyed the French fleet at anchor in the harbor of Abukir, August 1–2, in the engagement called "the battle of the Nile." He retired to Naples, where he became involved in an intrigue with Emma Hamilton, and through her was induced to use his naval power as a means of restoring the Neapolitan royal family. He became completely a tool of Mrs. Hamilton and was swept into the cesspool of Bourbon politics. He was under orders to aid the Neapolitan king, but so far exceeded his orders as to refuse to obey the orders of his superior officer. In 1800 he returned to England in the company of the Hamiltons and was made vice-admiral and a peer. He had, however, estranged English society by his conduct at Naples and by bringing Emma Hamilton to live in the same house as his wife, who then left him (1801) for good. The battle of Copenhagen was fought April 2, 1801, in order to destroy the coalition of the northern powers, known as the (second) Armed Neutrality. During the battle,

his superior officer, Sir Hyde Parker, gave the order to retire; Nelson, recognizing it as a maneuver leading to defeat, put his telescope to his blind eye and said he could see no such signal. Nelson was made a viscount after Copenhagen. When the war with France broke out again (1803), he was placed in command in the Mediterranean. He kept Toulon blockaded for two years. The French fleet under Admiral P. C. de Villeneuve left Toulon in March, 1805, and sailed to the West Indies with the intention of drawing off the English fleet and returning to support Napoleon's projected invasion of England. Nelson followed, and, after Napoleon's plan had been thwarted by the hesitancy of Villeneuve, fought the French-Spanish fleet off Cape Trafalgar, Oct. 21, 1805. He hoisted the signal "England expects that every man will do his duty" at the beginning of this fight. During the fight a musket ball from the French *Redoutable* struck him in the chest and broke his spine; he was carried below, but before he died heard the news that his opponents were destroyed. He was buried at St. Paul's Cathedral, London. In 1849 the monument to him was erected in Trafalgar Square; the lions at the base, by Sir Edwin Landseer, date from 1867. He left one child, a daughter, Horatia, born in 1801 to Emma Hamilton.

Nelson, Thomas. b. at Edinburgh, Dec. 25, 1822; d. there, Oct. 20, 1892. A Scottish publisher. He entered his father's firm in 1839, and opened a London branch of Thomas Nelson and Sons in 1844. He invented (1850) a rotary press, and was responsible for other improvements in the printing and publishing of books. He initiated (1870) the successful and soon widely imitated Royal Readers. Author of atlases of the world (1859) and of ancient geography (1867).

Nelson Monument. A column and statue in Trafalgar Square, London, commemorative of Horatio Nelson's naval exploits.

Nemea (nē′mẹ.ạ, nẹ.mē′ạ). In ancient geography, a valley in Argolis, Greece, ab. 11 mi. SW of Corinth. It is noted as the site of the Nemean Games, and in legend as the haunt of the Nemean lion, choked to death by Hercules as the first of his 12 labors.

Nemean Games. One of the four national festivals of the ancient Greeks. It was celebrated at Nemea in the 2nd and 4th year of each Olympiad.

Nemesis (nem′ẹ.sis). In Greek mythology, a goddess of law and justice, personifying especially divine retribution for violations of law and justice. Sometimes Nemesis was represented as winged, with the wheel of fortune, or borne in a chariot drawn by griffins. By extension she is popularly regarded as a goddess of the inevitable.

Nemo (nē′mō). The signature of Hablot Knight Browne to the first two of his plates illustrating Charles Dickens's *Pickwick Papers*, which he afterward changed to "Phiz."

Nemo. In Dickens's *Bleak House*, a poor "writer" (that is to say, one who does copying for lawyers). He is discovered to have been an early lover of Lady Dedlock.

Nennius (nen′i.us). fl. 8th or 9th century. Welsh author or compiler of the *Historia Brittonum*, a late 8th-century or early 9th-century chronicle notable for containing the first mention of King Arthur. Nennius is known to have been a pupil of a certain Bishop Elbotus of Bangor.

neologism (nē.ol′ọ.jizm). **1.** A new word or phrase, or a new use of a word.

> Philologists have marked out . . . how ancient words were changed, and Norman neologisms introduced.
>> (Isaac D'Israeli, *Amenities of Literature.*)

2. The use of new words, or of old words in new senses.

> I learnt my complement of classic French
> (Kept pure of Balzac and neologism).
>> (Mrs. Browning, *Aurora Leigh.*)

3. A new doctrine.

Neoplatonists (nē.ọ.plā′tọ.nists). Believers in a system of philosophical and religious doctrines and principles which originated in Alexandria with Ammonius Saccas in the 3rd century, and was developed by Plotinus, Porphyry, Iamblichus, Hypatia, Proclus, and others in the 3rd, 4th, and 5th centuries. The system was composed of elements of Platonism and Oriental beliefs, and in its later development was influenced by the philosophy of Philo, by Gnosticism, and by Christianity. Its leading representative was Plotinus. His views were popularized by Porphyry and modified in the direction of mysticism by Iamblichus. Considerable sympathy with Neoplatonism in its earlier stages was shown by several eminent Christian writers, especially in Alexandria, such as Saint Clement, Origen, and others. The last explicitly Neoplatonic schools were suppressed in the 6th century.

Neoptolemus (nē.op.tol′ē.mus). [Also, **Pyrrhus.**] In Greek legend, a son of Achilles: one of the heroes of the Trojan War. He was one of the band which was concealed in the wooden horse by means of which Troy was captured, slew Priam, hurled the child Astyanax over the wall, and carried off to slavery Andromache, the wife of Hector. He went later to Epirus, where he carried off a granddaughter of Hercules, and plundered the temple of Apollo at Delphi. He married Hermione. At Delphi he was worshiped as a hero, and was said to have protected that shrine from the Goths.

nepenthe (nē.pen′thē). A legendary drug, mentioned in the *Odyssey* as driving away sorrow, and taken as the name of a poem by George Darley.

Neper (nā′pėr), **John.** See **Napier, John.**

Nephele (nef′ē.lē). In Greek legend, the wife of Athamas, and mother of Phrixus and Helle.

Nepos (nē′pos, nep′os), **Cornelius.** b. probably at Verona, Italy; fl. in the 1st century B.C. A Roman historian, a friend of Cicero. He was the author of love poetry, a three-book *Chronica*, anecdotes, and lives of Cicero and Cato, all lost. His only extant work, *De Excellentibus Ducibus Extarum Gentium*, is a section from the *De Viris Illustribus*, a larger work of his now lost.

Neptune (nep′tūn). In Roman mythology, the god of the sea. He was originally a water god and rain giver, and thus associated with the growth of vegetation; but he came to be identified by the Romans with the Greek Poseidon. In art Neptune is usually represented as a bearded man of stately presence, with the trident as his chief attribute, and the horse and the dolphin as symbols.

Nereids (nir′ē.idz). In Greek mythology, sea nymphs, the 50 daughters of Nereus (whence the name) and Doris. The most famous among them were Amphitrite, Thetis, and Galatea. The Nereids were beautiful maidens helpful to voyagers, and constituted the main body of the female, as the Tritons did of the male, followers of Poseidon. They were imagined as dancing, singing, playing musical instruments, wooed by the Tritons, and passing in long processions over the sea seated on hippocamps and other sea creatures. Works of ancient art represent them lightly draped or nude, in poses characterized by undulating lines harmonizing with those of the ocean, and often riding on sea monsters of fantastic forms.

Nereus (nē′rūs). In classical mythology, the ancient sea god.

Neri (nā′rē). See under **Bianchi.**

Nerissa (nē.ris′ạ). In Shakespeare's *Merchant of Venice*, the clever waiting-maid of Portia. When Portia disguises herself as a lawyer, she acts as a clerk.

Nero (nē′rō, nir′ō). [Full name, **Nero Claudius Caesar Drusus Germanicus**; original name, **Lucius Domitius Ahenobarbus.**] b. at Antium, Italy, Dec. 15, 37 A.D.; committed suicide near Rome, June 9, 68. Roman emperor (54–68); son of the consul Domitius Ahenobarbus and Agrippina (daughter of Germanicus Caesar). He was adopted by his stepfather, the Emperor Claudius, in 50, and in 53 married Octavia, the daughter of Claudius by Messalina. In 54 Claudius was poisoned by Agrippina, who caused her son to be proclaimed to the exclusion of Britannicus, the son of Claudius, who was Nero's ward. His former tutors, the philosopher Seneca and Burrus, commander of the pretorian guards, were placed at the head of the government, and the early years of his reign were marked, on the whole, by clemency and justice. He caused his rival, Britannicus, to be removed by poison in 55. In 59 he procured the assassination of his mother, of whose control he had become impatient. Burrus died in 62, whereupon Seneca retired from public life. Freed from the restraint of his former advisers, he gave free rein to a naturally tyrannical and cruel disposition. He divorced Octavia in order to marry Poppaea, who had been his mistress for several years, and shortly afterward put Octavia to death (62). Poppaea ultimately died from the effects of a kick administered by her brutal husband. Having been accused of kindling the fire which in 64 destroyed a large part of Rome, he sought to divert attention from himself by ordering a persecution of the Christians, whom he accused of having caused the conflagration. Traditionally Peter and Paul both died in this persecution. Legend states that Nero, having set the fire, watched it spread while playing music on his lyre: undoubtedly the legendary picture fits Nero's personality, but the legend has taken root in the tradition of Christians, to whom Nero was a monstrous personage. Among others, he put Seneca to death in 65 for his supposed complicity in a plot to replace Nero, and visited (67–68) Greece, where he competed, and was thoroughly victorious, for the prizes as a musician and charioteer in the religious festivals. He was overthrown by a revolt under Galba, and stabbed himself to death with the assistance of his secretary.

Nero, The Tragedy of. A tragedy (printed in 1624) sometimes attributed to Thomas May.

Nero, Emperor of Rome. A tragedy by Nathaniel Lee, produced in 1674. It is filled with rant and violence (the very first scene contains a murder). Its chief contribution to English drama was an interest in gruesome murders, torments, and blood, which passed into Dryden's heroic plays.

Neroni (ne.rō'ni), **Signora Madeline.** [Also, **Madeline Vesey-Neroni.**] One of the principal characters of Anthony Trollope's *Barchester Towers*. She is an utterly selfish woman, but extremely beautiful, and insistent that her beauty be recognized. She has been married to an Italian who never appears in the book, but whose character is explained to have been that of a man who delighted equally in cruelty to his wife (whom he has made a cripple) and in affairs with other women.

Nerthus (ner'thus). [Also, **Hertha.**] An ancient Germanic goddess of fertility and growth; the earth mother, mentioned by Tacitus as being worshiped by seven northerly Germanic tribes. The seat of her worship was an ocean island which has not been identified.

Nesbit (nez'bit), **E.** Pen name of **Bland, Edith Nesbit.**

Nesbit, Norah. In W. Somerset Maugham's novel *Of Human Bondage* (1915), a writer, one of the women in love with the central character, Philip Carey.

Nesbitt (nez'bit), **William.** Kate's husband, and the father of Lydia, Mabel, Dora, and Janet, the hero of E. H. Young's novel *William* (1925).

Nesle (nel), **Blondel de.** See **Blondel.**

Nessus (nes'us). In Greek legend, a centaur slain by Hercules. He carried Deianira, Hercules's wife, across the river Evenus; but when he attempted to abduct her, Hercules shot him with a poisoned arrow. Dying, Nessus declared to Deianira that his bloody shirt would preserve her husband's love, and she took it with her. Later she sent the shirt to Hercules, hoping to speed his return home. Hercules donned it to offer sacrifice; the garment clung to his flesh, which was torn off with it. The messenger, Lichas, who brought the shirt, was cast by the raging hero into the sea, and Deianira hanged herself. Hercules built and ascended a pyre, had it set on fire, and was carried off from it to Olympus.

Nestor (nes'tor). In Greek legend, a king of Pylus; son of Neleus. He was one of the heroes of the Argonaut expedition, and helped hunt the Calydonian boar. He was the wisest and oldest councilor of the Greeks before Troy.

Nestor. In Shakespeare's *Troilus and Cressida,* a Greek commander. Old and greatly venerated by the other warriors, he remarks that adversity is the test of valor (I.iii).

Nettleship (net'l.ship), **Henry.** b. in Northamptonshire, England, May 5, 1839; d. at Oxford, England, July 10, 1893. An English educator and writer. He was assistant master at Harrow from 1868 to 1873 and classical lecturer (1873) at Christ Church, Oxford. He was elected professor of Latin literature at Oxford in 1878.

Neurin (noi'rin). See **Aneurin.**

Neville (nev'il). The name of a family prominent in English history, several of whose members appear as characters in Shakespeare's historical plays, as follows: Anne Neville is Lady Anne in *Richard III;* John Neville is the Marquess of Montague in *3 Henry VI;* a Ralph Neville is the Earl of Westmoreland in *1* and *2 Henry IV* and in *Henry V;* another of the same name and title appears in *3 Henry VI;* a Richard Neville is the Earl of Salisbury in *2 Henry VI;* and another Richard Neville, the famous "Kingmaker," is the Earl of Warwick in *2* and *3 Henry VI.*

Neville, Constance. A young friend of Miss Hardcastle in Oliver Goldsmith's comedy *She Stoops to Conquer.* She is in love with Hastings.

Neville Landless (land'les). See **Landless, Neville.**

Neville's Cross (nev'ilz). A place near Durham, in N England. It was the scene of an English victory over the Scots in 1346.

Nevinson (nev'in.son), **H. W.** [Full name, **Henry Woodd Nevinson.**] b. at Arcadia, Leicestershire, England, 1856; d. at Chipping Campden, Gloucestershire, England, Nov. 9, 1941. An English journalist, essayist, and biographer. He was on the staffs of the *Daily Chronicle* (1897–1903), the *Nation* (1906–23), the *Manchester Guardian,* the *Daily News,* and other journals, reporting wars over a period of three decades, and was wounded (1915) at the Dardanelles. He visited Greece, Crete, Africa (where he exposed the brutalities of the slave trade), Russia, Morocco, India, Spain, Palestine, Berlin, France, Gallipoli, Salonica, Egypt, and the U. S. Author of *Neighbors of Ours* (1895), *In the Valley of Tophet* (1896), *The Thirty Days' War* (1898), *Life of Schiller* (1899), *Ladysmith* (1900), *Books and Personalities* (1905), *A Modern Slavery* (1906), *The Dawn in Russia* (1906), *The New Spirit in India* (1908), *Essays in Freedom* (1909), *Peace and War in the Balance* (1911), *The Growth of Freedom* (1912), *Essays in Rebellion* (1913), and *The Dardanelles Campaign* (1918); *Original Sinners,* short stories (1920); *Changes and Chances* (1923), *More Changes, More Chances* (1925), *Last Changes, Last Chances* (1928), and *Running Accompaniments* (1936), autobiography; *The English* (1928), *England, Voice of Freedom* (1929), *Rough Islanders, or the Natives of England* (1930), and *Goethe—Man and Poet* (1931), biography and criticism.

New Atlantis (at.lan'tis), **The.** An allegorical romance by Francis Bacon; so called from its scene of action, an imaginary island in the ocean. It was written before 1617. The narrator visits the island of Bensalem in the Pacific Ocean, and finds there an ideal state based on Christianity, scientific research, and philosophy. The research college is called Solomon's House. No person ever leaves the island except for the "Merchants of Light," men who go into the world at special times to bring back news of new discoveries and ideas.

New Bath Guide. A satirical poem by Christopher Anstey, published 1766.

Newbery (nū'ber''i), **John.** b. 1713; d. Dec. 22, 1767. An English publisher, the friend of Samuel Johnson, Oliver Goldsmith, and Tobias Smollett. He settled at London in 1744, and was the first publisher of small storybooks for children. Among the famous children's books published by him, some of which he may have written, were *Little Goody Two Shoes, Giles Gingerbread,* and *Mother Goose's Nursery Rhymes.* In 1758 he started the *Universal Chronicle or Weekly Gazette,* in which Johnson's *Idler* essays appeared. The *Public Ledger* was commenced in 1760. The Newbery Medal (1922 *et seq.*), named in his honor, is awarded each year to an American author who has published an outstanding book for children.

Newbolt (nū'bōlt), Sir **Henry John.** b. at Bilston, Staffordshire, England, June 6, 1862; d. April 19, 1938. An English editor, author, and poet. He was admitted to the bar in 1887, and practiced law until 1899. In 1900 he founded the *Monthly Review,* of which he was editor intil 1904. From 1911 to 1921 he was professor of poetry at Oxford. Among his publications are *Taken from the Enemy* (1892), *Mordred, A Tragedy* (1895), *Admirals All* (1897), *The Island Race* (1898), *The Sailing of the Longships* (1902), *Songs of the Sea* (1904) and *Songs of the Fleet* (1910), both with music by Sir Charles Villiers Stanford, *The Year of Trafalgar* (1905), *The New June* (1909), *Songs of Memory and Hope* (1910), *A Naval History of the Great War* (1920), and *Studies Green and Gray* (1926). Newbolt's patriotic sea poems and his scholarly history of Trafalgar made his reputation as a historian of the empire; in 1923 he was appointed official naval historian and under his direction was published the five-volume *Naval Operations* (1920–31), a history covering World War I.

Newcastle (nū'kȧs''l), Duchess of. Title of **Cavendish, Margaret.**

New Chronicles of England and France. A popular prose work by Robert Fabyan, printed by Pynson in 1516, the first of a series of Tudor histories. Its later influence can be seen in Marlowe's *Edward II.*

New College. [Also (formerly), **College of Saint Mary Winton.**] A college of Oxford University, founded 1379.

Newcome (nū'kum), **Barnes.** In Thackeray's novel *The Newcomes,* the brother of Ethel, and Clive Newcome's cousin. He ill-treats his wife, who flees for refuge to her former lover, Lord Highgate.

Newcome, Clive. In Thackeray's novel *The Newcomes,* Colonel Newcome's son, a young artist who eventually marries his cousin Ethel.

Newcome, Colonel. In Thackeray's novel *The Newcomes,* a simple, gallant, and unworldly retired officer, the father of Clive Newcome and the uncle of Ethel and Barnes. He loses his fortune and dies a pensioner in the Charterhouse.

Newcome, Ethel. In Thackeray's novel *The Newcomes,* Colonel Newcome's niece, destined by her grandmother for a brilliant match. In the end she marries her cousin Clive.

Newcomes (nū'kumz), **The.** A novel by William Makepeace Thackeray, published in 1855.

New Custom. A religious interlude with an anti-Papist theme, printed in 1573 and produced c1562. Its author's name is not known.

Newdigate (nū'di.gȧt), Sir **Roger.** b. at Arbury, Warwickshire, England, May 30, 1719; d. there, Nov. 23, 1806. An English scholar and antiquary, the founder (1805) of the annual Newdigate Prize. He was a member of Parliament (1741–47 and 1750–80).

Newdigate Prize. An annual prize for verse at Oxford University. It was founded by Sir Roger Newdigate.

New Forest. A forest region in SW Hampshire, England, covering ab. 144 square miles. The tract was forcibly afforested by William the Conqueror for use as a hunting demesne.

Newgate (nū'gāt). The western gate of London wall by which the Watling Street left the city. It was at first called Westgate, but later Chancellor's Gate. In the reign of Henry I Chancellor's Gate was rebuilt and called Newgate. At about the same time the county of Middlesex was given to the citizens of London, and Newgate was used for prisoners from that county. The use of this locality for a prison continues until the present day, although now only a house of detention is located here. Newgate always had an unsavory reputation, and resisted all efforts at reform. These began as early as the time of Richard Whittington, lord mayor several times in the period 1397–1420, who left a large sum for its improvement. The prison was burned during the Gordon Riots in 1780, and was rebuilt in 1782. It was pulled down in 1902.

Newgate Calendar. A biographical record (1773 *et seq.*) of the most notorious criminals confined in Newgate Prison.

Newgate Prison. A prison located at Newgate, London, destroyed in 1902.

New Grub Street. A novel by George Gissing, published in 1891. It portrays, with a grim realism bordering on naturalism, the life of various members of the 19th-century English lower middle class, especially as seen through the eyes of a writer who belongs to this class. This man, Rearden, an honest craftsman who refuses any compromises that would violate his basic integrity, dies a death of poverty and heartbreak, while his opportunistic acquaintance and rival, Jasper Milvain, who uses his art solely and cynically as a means to commercial success, lives a life of wealth and relative happiness. Biffen, another struggling young writer, loves Rearden's wife, but cannot win her, and commits suicide (Rearden and Biffen may be viewed as illustrating slightly different facets of the same basic problem; both are honest, and both are destined to fail). Jasper Milvain, on the other hand, wins fame, money, and finally, Amy, Rearden's wife.

New Holland. A former name of Australia.

---

fat, fāte, fär, ȧsk, fāre; net, mē, hėr; pin, pīne; not, nōte, mȯve, nôr; up, lūte, pu̇ll; ᴛн, then;

New Inn, or the Light Heart, The. A comedy by Ben Jonson, first played by the King's Servants in 1629, entered on the Stationers' Register in 1631, and published the same year.

New Machiavelli (mak"i.a.vel'i), **The.** A novel by H. G. Wells, published in 1911.

Newman (nū'man), **Ernest.** b. at Liverpool, England, Nov. 30, 1868—. An English music critic. He was a reviewer for the Birmingham *Post* (1906–19) and the London *Times* (1920–39). Author of *Gluck and the Opera* (1895), *Hugo Wolf* (1907), *Wagner as Man and Artist* (1924), *The Unconscious Beethoven* (1927), *Fact and Fiction about Wagner* (1931), *The Life of Richard Wagner* (4 vols., 1933–46), and *Wagner Nights* (1949; American title, *The Wagner Operas*).

Newman, Francis William. b. at London, June 27, 1805; d. at Weston-super-Mare, England, Oct. 4, 1897. An English scholar and miscellaneous writer; brother of John Henry Newman. In 1826 he was graduated from Oxford (Worcester College), and was made fellow of Balliol. In 1840 he was made classical professor in Manchester New College, and was professor (1846–69) of Latin in University College, London. He was a rationalist and opposed in principle to his brother's stand. He was much criticized for his *Contributions chiefly to the Early History of Cardinal Newman* (1891). He wrote *Phases of Faith* (1850), *History of the Hebrew Monarchy* (1847), *The Soul* (1849), *Regal Rome* (1852), *Theism* (1858), *Handbook of Modern Arabic* (1866), *Libyan Vocabulary* (1882), *Politica* (1889), *Economica* (1890), translations from Horace and Homer, and others.

Newman, John Henry. b. at London, Feb. 21, 1801; d. at Edgbaston, near Birmingham, England, Aug. 11, 1890. An English Anglican divine and Roman Catholic cardinal. His father was a banker and young Newman took his degree at Oxford (Trinity College) in 1820. He was elected fellow of Oriel College in 1822. He became curate (1824) of St. Clement's, Oxford, and was tutor (1826) at Oriel. In 1828 he was vicar of Saint Mary's, the university chapel, and in 1831–32 preached before the university. He resigned (1832) his tutorship after a quarrel with the provost over his opposition to religious liberalism and ended a period in which he had come into contact with E. B. Pusey, John Keble, and Richard Hurrell Froude. In 1833 he published *The Arians of the Fourth Century* and in that same year went on an extended trip to the Mediterranean with Froude. There he wrote *Lead, Kindly Light* and other poems which were published (1834) in *Lyra Apostolica*, to which Froude also contributed. He returned to England less than a week before Keble delivered his famous sermon (July 14, 1833) on National Apostasy, considered the beginning of the Oxford Movement. Newman soon became the acknowledged leader of the movement, meant to restore the doctrine of apostolic succession. He soon began writing the *Tracts for the Times*, a series attempting to establish a foundation of doctrine for the Church of England, normally split between High (ceremonial) Church and Low (liberal) Church; these writings gave to the Oxford Movement its alternative name, the Tractarian Movement. The tracts reached their climax in 1841 with the publication of Tract XC, in which Newman adopted the position that the Thirty-Nine Articles, the basic creed of the Church of England, was not in conflict with the basic tenets of Roman Catholicism, but was rather an attempt to correct abuses of those common bases. The tract raised a storm in Oxford, and the Bishop of Oxford ordered the series ended. Newman soon resigned the position he had held (1833–41) as editor of the *British Critic*, and went into seclusion. In 1843 he published a retraction of all criticism he had made of the Roman Catholic Church and resigned his vicarship. He published (1845) *Essay on the Development of Christian Doctrine* and that year was admitted to the Roman Catholic Church. In 1847, at Rome, he was ordained a priest as a member of the Oratorian order, the order founded by Saint Philip (Filippo) Neri. He returned (1847) to England to found, near Birmingham, a branch of the Oratorian Congregation. He attacked (1851) an ex-priest named Achilli in his *Lectures on the Present Position of Roman Catholics*, with the result that he was sued for libel; Newman proved the factual basis of his allegations but was nevertheless found guilty and assessed 100 pounds damage and costs of 12,000 pounds. The entire sum, and more, the surplus being donated to charity, was received in the form of gifts within a short time. In 1854 he went to Dublin to become rector of a Catholic University there, but the position was uncongenial and he returned to England in 1858. He revised a series of lectures he had given at Dublin and published them as one of his most popular and enduring works, *The Idea of a University Defined* (1873); in it he holds that the university's work is not to provide factual knowledge but rather to train the mind. In 1858 he also broached the idea of a Roman Catholic school at Oxford, but the opposition of other members of his church, among whom was H. E. Manning, caused him to drop the idea. In December, 1863, Charles Kingsley reviewed in *Macmillan's Magazine* the *History of England* by J. A. Froude, younger brother of Newman's old friend; in the review Kingsley attacked what he believed to be Newman's stated disregard of the principle of the truth. Newman answered with what is generally considered his greatest work, the *Apologia pro vita sua, or a History of My Religious Opinions* (1864), a beautifully written history of Newman's spiritual life. The result was a tremendous popular acclaim, from both sides, for his brilliant exposition. In 1866 he published his most popular poem, *A Dream of Gerontius*, and in 1870 his logical approach to belief, *A Grammar of Assent*. At this period he was involved in a widespread misunderstanding of his position when he opposed the enunciation of the doctrine of papal infallibility, a matter that was splitting the Roman Catholic Church into warring camps. Newman had no doubt of the correctness of the doctrine, but he questioned the wisdom of its publication at that time; the resultant controversy widened the gap between him and the more liberal Roman Catholic clergy. One result of the quarrel was to cause Pope Pius IX to look askance at Newman. When Newman wrote (1877) an answer to W. E. Gladstone's attack on the church, he addressed it to the Duke of Norfolk, the principal Roman Catholic layman in the country. The letter was brought to the attention of the Vatican, and when Leo XIII ascended the papal throne Newman was appointed (1879) Cardinal of Saint George in Velabro; because of his age he was allowed to remain in England. He was at the same time appointed honorary fellow of his own college, Trinity, an honor hitherto unknown there. Newman retired to Edgbaston to live out his remaining years. Newman, more than any other man, has been credited with the growth of Roman Catholicism in Protestant England and the U. S.; not only his personal appeal but his writing lives on and is responsible for many conversions to Roman Catholicism.

Newman Noggs (nogz). See **Noggs, Newman.**

New Model Army. In English history, the name given to the Parliamentary army from the time of its reorganization in 1645. It was commanded by Sir Thomas Fairfax, and later by Oliver Cromwell.

Newnham College (nūn′ạm). A college for women at Cambridge, England, but not formally connected with Cambridge University (although it has access to all necessary university facilities). It was founded in 1871. The college consists of five halls: Old Hall (originally Newnham Hall), Sidgwick Hall, Clough Hall (so called after its first principal, Anne J. Clough, sister of Arthur Hugh Clough), Peile Hall, and College Hall, used chiefly for dining and for college concerts and debates.

New Pilgrimage, The. A volume of verse (1889) by Wilfrid Scawen Blunt.

New Place. The house of William Shakespeare's (later) residence and death at Stratford-upon-Avon, England. The foundations still remain. It is now believed to have been built c1490. Shakespeare bought it in 1597, paying 60 pounds for it in that year. At that time there were two barns, two gardens, and two orchards belonging to it. Shakespeare afterward enlarged the gardens, and retired there permanently in 1610. The house was torn down in 1759; the site was bought by subscription in 1861.

New Sarum (sãr′um). See **Salisbury.**

New Scotland Yard. See under **Scotland Yard.**

Newsome (nū′sọm), **Chad.** A character in the novel *The Ambassadors* (1903), by Henry James.

New Spirit in Literature, The. Essays by Harold Nicolson, published in 1931.

Newstead Abbey (nū′sted). A building in Nottinghamshire, England, ab. 9 mi. N of Nottingham, in ancient times an abbey. It was founded by Henry II as an atonement for Thomas à Becket's murder in 1170, and was the home of the family of George Gordon, Lord Byron, obtained by Sir John Byron, his ancestor, at the dissolution of the monasteries by Henry VIII in 1540. Numerous relics of Lord Byron are preserved in the house. He undertook to keep it up in 1809, with what remained of his fortune, but was obliged to sell it in 1818.

New Style Calendar. See **Gregorian Calendar.**

New Testament, The. A collection of books, containing the records of the Christian covenant, and forming part of the Christian Bible.

New Timon (tī′mọn), **The.** A satire by Edward Bulwer-Lytton, published in 1847.

Newton (nū′tọn), **Sir Isaac.** b. at Woolsthorpe, near Grantham, Lincolnshire, England, Dec. 25, 1642; d. at Kensington, now a borough of London, March 20, 1727. An English mathematician and natural philosopher. His father, Isaac Newton, was a small freehold farmer, somewhat weak and carefree, who died before his son was born. He matriculated at Cambridge (Trinity College) on June 5, 1661, was elected to a scholarship on April 28, 1664, and graduated in January, 1665. At the university he was especially attracted by the study of Descartes's geometry and Kepler's optics. The method of fluxions first occurred to him in 1665. Newton was a minor fellow of Trinity in 1667, but a few months later, on March 16, 1668, he was admitted as a major fellow. On July 7 of the same year he was created a master of arts. He was made Lucasian professor at Cambridge in October, 1669. He became a fellow of the Royal Society in January, 1671.

Scientific Achievement. There is no example of greater achievement in the history of science than that of Newton who, as a youth during the years 1665–66 in the peaceful village of Woolsthorpe, unaided made the following three great fundamental discoveries in the realm of the physical sciences: first, the mathematical method of fluxions, which is the basis of all modern mathematics and the instrument by which all physical problems involving force and motion are now solved; second, the law of the composition of light, from which he later constructed a real science of optics; third, the law of universal gravitation. Newton's attention was drawn to the subject of gravitation as early as 1665. The story of the fall of the apple was first told by Voltaire, who had it from Mrs. Catharine Barton Conduitt, Newton's niece. This observation merely suggested to Newton that the same law which caused the apple to fall would hold for the moon. Kepler had established the laws of the planetary orbits, and from these laws Newton proved that the attraction of the sun upon the planets varies inversely as the squares of their distances. Measuring the actual deflection of the moon's orbit from its tangent, he found it to be identical with the deflection which would be created by the attraction of the earth, diminishing in the ratio of the inverse square of the distance. The hypothesis that the same force acted in each case was thus confirmed. The success of Newton's work really depended on the determination of the length of a degree on the earth's surface by Jean Picard in 1671 and the universal law of gravitation was completely elaborated by 1685. Albert Einstein's theory of relativity offers a certain degree of refinement to the classical law of gravitation as formulated by Newton.

Publication of the Principia. The first book of the *Principia* or *Philosophiae Naturalis Principia Mathematica* was presented to the Royal Society on April 28, 1686, and the entire work was published in 1687. The *Principia* was published in three different editions during Newton's lifetime and has also been translated into seven different languages. Edmund Halley, who bore the expense of the printing of the *Principia*, is known as the discoverer of Newton. In 1689 Newton sat in Parliament for Cambridge University, and at this time was associated with John Locke; in 1701 he was reëlected. When his friend Charles Montague (afterward Lord Halifax) was appointed chancellor of the exchequer, Newton was made warden of the mint, and in 1699 master of the mint. The reformation of English coinage was largely his work. He was knighted by Queen Anne in 1705.

Method of Fluxions and Work in Optics. The method of fluxions, which Newton had discovered, was employed in part in the calculations for the *Principia,* but did not appear until 1693, when it was published by Wallis. It also appeared as a supplement in 1704 to the first edition of the *Optics.* This work also appeared in four different editions and was translated into foreign languages. Newton discovered that the rays of light when passed through a prism were composed of various colors, known as a spectrum, arranged according to the refrangibility of their wave length. His minor works which were published after his death are *The Chronology of Ancient Kingdoms Amended, Observations upon the Prophecies of Daniel and the Apocalypse of St. John,* and *Arithmetica Universalis.* Newton was all his life interested in alchemy and chemistry. On Feb. 21, 1699, he was elected a foreign associate of the French Academy of Sciences and in 1703 he was elected president of the Royal Society, an office which he held until his death. Newton lies buried in Westminster Abbey, final resting place of England's honored great. In 1946 (four years late due to World War II) the Royal Society of London, Cambridge University (Trinity College), and the Royal Mint commemorated the tercentenary of Isaac Newton's birth. Newton has had a great many interpreters or protagonists, and hence a larger number of commentaries have been issued on his works than on those of any scientist of modern times. See *Memoirs of the Life, Writings and Discoveries of Isaac Newton,* by Sir David Brewster (2 vols., 1855), *Isaac Newton (1642–1727),* by W. J. Greenstreet (1927), *Isaac Newton,* by L. T. Moore (1934), and *Weltfahrt der Erkenntnis, Leben und Werk Isaac Newton,* by Friedrich Dessauer (Zürich, 1945). See also publications for the History of Science Society and the Royal Academy on the occasions, respectively, of a bicentenary evaluation of his work (1927) and of the Newton Tercentenary (1942 and 1946).

Newton, John. b. at London, July 24, 1725; d. there, Dec. 21, 1807. An English clergyman and religious poet. His father was governor of York Fort in Hudson Bay. Newton served in his father's ship before 1742, and was afterward in the navy as an impressed seaman and then a midshipman, and in the slave trade, until 1755, when he was made tide surveyor at Liverpool. Taking up the study of Greek and Hebrew, he was ordained priest in June, 1764, and became curate of Olney, where William Cowper settled c1767. They published the *Olney Hymns* together in 1779. In 1780 he was made rector of Saint Mary Woolnoth, London. Besides many well-known hymns, he wrote *Cardiphonia* (1781) and other religious works, and an *Authentic Narrative* of his early life (1764).

New Trick to Cheat the Devil, A. A play (printed 1639) by Robert Davenport.

New Way to Pay Old Debts, A. A play by Philip Massinger, printed in 1627, and written in 1626. In Sir Giles Overreach, Massinger created one of the great dramatic figures of the English stage. He has risen by his ruthlessness to fortune, employing the gluttonous Justice Greedy and his man, Marrall, as his agents, and reducing his nephew, Wellborn, to poverty. He is the figure of the vulgar Caroline monopolist, living in luxury and determined to be included among the aristocracy through the marriage of his daughter to a peer. However, Lord Lovell, for whom his daughter is intended, contrives that she shall be married to Tom Allworth, whom she loves.

New Wonder, A. [Full title, **A New Wonder: A Woman Never Vext.**] A comedy by William Rowley, printed in 1632. It may be a revision of a lost play by Thomas Heywood.

New Year Letter. A volume of poetry (1941) by W. H. Auden. It consists of the prologue, the title poem (with accompanying prose notes), "The Quest," a "sonnet sequence," and an epilogue. Among the shorter poems included with the notes are those published later (1945) in *Collected Poetry,* "The Diaspora," "Luther," and "Blessed Event."

Nibelungenlied (nē′bẹ.lủng.ẹn.lēt″). [Eng. trans., *"Song of the Nibelungs."*] A Middle High German epic poem, written in its present form by an unknown author in South Germany in the first half of the 13th century. The legends, however, are much earlier, having been handed down orally. Its hero, Siegfried, is a prince who killed the possessors of the hoard of the Nibelungs (a famous golden treasure which cursed all who unrightfully seized it). He wooed Brunhild, a princess of Iceland, for the Burgundian king Gunther, whose sister, Kriemhild, became his wife. He was afterward treacherously slain, and the gold was ultimately sunk in the Rhine. The *Nibelungenlied* is the greatest monument of early German literature. Historical and mythical elements are mingled in it. Wagner's *Ring of the Nibelungs* has taken material more from the Old Norse *Volsunga Saga* and *Elder Edda* than from the German version, the *Nibelungenlied.*

Nibelungs (nē′bẹ.lủngz). [German, **Nibelungen.**] In German legend, originally a race of Northern dwarfs, so called from their king, Nibelung. The name came to be applied to the successive possessors of their fatal golden treasure; hence, to the followers of Siegfried, later to the Burgundians.

Nicanor (ni.kā′nọr). In Shakespeare's *Coriolanus,* the Roman who chats with the Volscian and tells him of the banishment of Coriolanus (IV.iii).

Nicene Councils (nī′sēn, nī.sēn′). Two general ecclesiastical councils which met at Nicaea, in Asia Minor, the first in 325 to deal with the Arian heresy, the second in 787 to consider the question of images.

Nicene Creed. A formal statement of the chief tenets of Christian belief, adopted by the first Nicene Council. Now, usually, a later creed of closely similar form referred to the Council of Constantinople (381) and hence sometimes known

ḍ, d or j; ṣ, s or sh; ṭ, t or ch; ẓ, z or zh; o, F. cloche; ü, F. menu; ch, Sc. loch; ṅ, F. bonbon.

as the "Nicaeno-Constantinopolitan Creed," received universally in the Eastern Church, and, with an addition introduced in the 6th century, accepted generally throughout western Christendom.

Nice Valour, The. [Full title, **The Nice Valour, or the Passionate Madman.**] A comedy by John Fletcher, printed in 1647. In this play is "Hence, all you vain delights," a song which is echoed in some lines of Milton's *Il Penseroso.*

Nice Wanton. An interlude written in 1560 by an unknown author.

Nichol (nik'ọl), **John.** b. Sept. 8, 1833; d. Oct. 11, 1894. A Scottish writer and lecturer. He was professor of English literature in Glasgow University from 1862 to 1889. He published *Fragments of Criticism* (1860), *English Composition* (1879), *Byron* (1880: in the *English Men of Letters* series), *The Death of Themistocles, and Other Poems* (1881), *American Literature: an Historical Review* (1882), and others.

Nicholas (nik'ọ.lạs), **Saint.** d. (probably) Dec. 6, 345 or 352. A bishop of Myra, in Lycia, Asia Minor. He has been adopted as the patron saint of Russia, and is also regarded as the patron saint of seafaring men, thieves, virgins, and children. He is a popular saint of the Greek and Roman churches, and his festival is celebrated December 6. He owes his position as Santa Claus (a corruption of the Dutch Sant Nikolaus) to the legend that he wished to preserve the three daughters of a poor nobleman from dishonor when the father, having no money for marriage portions, was about to force them to support themselves by prostitution. Saint Nicholas threw a purse of gold in at an open window for three nights in succession, thus furnishing a dowry for each daughter. From this incident is said to be derived the custom of placing gifts in the shoes or stockings of children on Saint Nicholas's eve, and attributing the gifts to Santa Claus, whose bulging pack of toys is an extension of the three bags of gold, symbol of Saint Nicholas. The custom has in the U. S. and some other countries been transferred to Christmas.

Nicholas. The young student in Chaucer's *Miller's Tale.*

Nicholas' clerks. See **Saint Nicholas' clerks.**

Nicholas Cully (kul'i), **Sir.** See **Cully, Sir Nicholas.**

Nicholas de Guildford (gil'fọrd). See under **Owl and the Nightingale, The.**

Nicholas Frog (frog). See **Frog, Nicholas.**

Nicholas Gimcrack (jim'krak), **Sir.** See **Gimcrack, Sir Nicholas.**

Nicholas Nickleby (nik'l.bi). A novel by Charles Dickens, first published serially during 1838–39, an excellent example of the spontaneous, loosely organized narrative technique of his early writing. Nicholas is a fine, independent boy who has been left penniless by the death of his father. In his efforts to support his sister, Kate, he approaches his uncle, Ralph Nickleby, but is rebuffed by the miserly old usurer. He finally obtains the position of tutor in Dotheboys Hall, a school run by the malicious and cruel Wackford Squeers. The latter's cruel treatment of the boys, especially of the half-witted Smike, raises Nicholas's anger, and he thrashes Squeers before he leaves, taking Smike with him. He earns a living first by joining a troupe of actors, and then by obtaining a position in the counting house of the Cheeryble brothers. His sister Kate has meanwhile been apprenticed to Madame Mantalini, a dressmaker; however, disaster threatens when her uncle permits her to be seen by the lustful Sir Mulberry Hawk, and stands aside while Hawk proceeds brutally to the task of making her his mistress. Nicholas finds out about the plan, and arrives in time not only to save his sister but also to thrash Hawk. He then meets the lovely Madeline Bray, who is the object of another of Ralph Nickleby's schemes (Ralph plans to force Madeline to marry Gride, his partner in usury). Nicholas and Madeline fall in love, and the enraged Ralph tries to hurt his nephew through the young man's devotion to the half-witted Smike. Smike dies, but Ralph discovers that he was his own son, and hangs himself. Squeers and Gride are both punished for their many wrongs, Nicholas marries Madeline, and Kate marries the Cheerybles' nephew, Frank.

Nicholas Vaux (vôks), **Sir.** See **Vaux, Sir Nicholas.**

Nichols (nik'ọlz), **Beverley.** b. 1899—. An English writer. Author of *Prelude* (1920), *Patchwork* (1921), *Self* (1922), *Crazy Pavements* (1927), *The Star Spangled Manner* (1928), *Evensong* (1932; dramatized with E. Knoblock), *For Adults Only* (1932), *Cry Havoc* (1933), *Green Grows the City* (1939), *Men do not Weep* (1941), and *The Stream that Stood Still.* His plays include *The Stag* (1929), *Avalanche* (1931), and *Floodlight* (1937).

Nichols, John. b. at Islington, near London, Feb. 2, 1745; d. Nov. 26, 1826. An English printer and antiquary. He was an apprentice of William Bowyer. He was editor of and contributor to the *Gentleman's Magazine* from 1778 until his death. His *Memoirs of Bowyer,* begun in 1778, were expanded into the *Literary Anecdotes and Illustrations,* a literary history of the 18th century. He also wrote seven volumes on the court festivities of the reigns of Elizabeth and James I.

Nichols, John Bowyer Buchanan. b. 1859; d. at Lawford, Essex, England, June 2, 1939. An English poet, critic, and anthologist. He was the author of *Inez de Castro,* a Newdigate prize poem, delivered at the Sheldonian Theater, Oxford, June 13, 1883, and published the same year; *The Mourning Bride* (1896) and *Portrait of a Gentleman* (1897), short stories, both contributed to the *Westminster Gazette,* of which he was art critic; and *Poems* (1943). In 1895 he published *Words and Days* (reprinted 1941, with a preface by Logan Pearsall Smith), an anthology of prose and poetry, and in 1903 edited *A Little Book of English Sonnets.*

Nichols, Robert. [Full name, **Robert Malise Bowyer Nichols.**] b. at Shanklin, Isle of Wight, Sept. 6, 1893; d. Dec. 17, 1944. An English poet and dramatist; son of J. B. B. Nichols. Author of *Ardors and Endurances* (1917), *The Assault* (1918), *Aurelia* (1920), and *Fisbo* (1934), poems; *Under the Yew* (1928), a short novel; *Guilty Souls* (1922), *Twenty Below* (1927), and *Wings Over Europe* (1929), plays; and of *The Budded Branch* (1918),

The Smile of the Sphinx (1920), *Fantastica* (1923), and *Golgotha and Company* (1928), prose. He edited an *Anthology of War Poetry: 1914–1918* (1943). Among his best-known poems are *Fulfillment, The Pilgrim, Nearer,* and *By the Wood.*

Nichols, Thomas. b. in Pembrokeshire, Wales, 1820; d. at London, May 14, 1879. An English writer. He was one of the founders of the University of Wales. He published *The Pedigree of the English People* (1868) and others.

Nicias (nish′i.ạs). Executed in Sicily, 413 B.C. An Athenian general and politician, after the death of Pericles (429 B.C.) chief leader of the aristocratic faction at Athens in the Peloponnesian War, opposed by Cleon. He arranged (421) the Peace of Nicias with Sparta, envisaging a 50-year truce, but broken almost immediately. He commanded the unsuccessful expedition against Syracuse (415–413), where he was captured and executed. The failure of the expedition has traditionally been laid to Nicias's extreme caution; he delayed a retreat, because of fear occasioned by an eclipse of the sun, and was stranded when the Athenian fleets were soon afterward defeated.

Nick Bottom (nik bot′ọm). See **Bottom, Nick.**

Nickleby (nik′l.bi), **Kate.** In Dickens's novel *Nicholas Nickleby,* the sister of Nicholas, a charming and attractive girl who is apprenticed to Madame Mantalini, and later thrown in the way of the lustful Sir Mulberry Hawk by her uncle, Ralph Nickleby. She eventually marries Frank Cheeryble.

Nickleby, Mrs. The weak and characterless mother of the hero of Dickens's *Nicholas Nickleby.*

Nickleby, Nicholas. The hero of Dickens's novel *Nicholas Nickleby.*

Nickleby, Ralph. In Dickens's novel *Nicholas Nickleby,* the uncle of Nicholas, a grasping and wicked man.

Nicodemus Boffin (nik.ọ.dē′mus bof′in). See **Boffin, Nicodemus.**

Nicol (nik′ọl), **William.** b. at Dumbretton, in Annan parish, Scotland, c1744; d. probably at Edinburgh, April 21, 1797. A Scottish schoolmaster, friend of Robert Burns, and the "Willie" of Burns's well-known drinking song *Willie Brew'd a Peck o' Maut* (1789).

Nicolas (nik′ọ.lạs), Sir **Nicholas Harris.** [Generally known as Sir **Harris Nicolas.**] b. March 10, 1799; d. near Boulogne, France, Aug. 3, 1848. An English antiquary and historian. He published *Notitia Historica* (1824; republished as *The Chronology of History,* 1833–38), *Synopsis of the Peerage of England* (1825), *History of the Orders of Knighthood of the British Empire* (1841–42), and *Despatches and Letters of Admiral Lord Viscount Nelson* (1844–46).

Nicol Jarvie (nik′ọl jär′vi). See **Jarvie, Nicol.**

Nicoll (nik′ọl), **Robert.** b. at Auchtergaven, Perthshire, Scotland, Jan. 7, 1814; d. near Edinburgh, Dec. 7, 1837. A Scottish poet and editor. He was author of *Il Zingaro* (1833), a passionate love story in prose, and of more than 140 poems, published (1835, 1844) as *Songs and Lyrics.* Among his best-known poems are *We are Brethren a',* *Thoughts of Heaven,* and *Death.*

Nicoll, Sir **William Robertson.** [Pseudonym, **Claudius Clear.**] b. at Lumsden, Scotland, Oct. 10, 1851; d. at London, May 4, 1923. A British author and editor. He was first editor (and also the founder) of the *British Weekly* and the *Bookman* in 1886, and of the *British Monthly* in 1900. Among his works are *Literary Anecdotes of the Nineteenth Century* (1895–96; with T. J. Wise), *James Macdonell* (1890), *Letters on Life* (1901), *A Garden of Nuts* (1905), *The Key of the Blue Closet* (1906), *Life of Ian Maclaren* (1908), and others.

Nicolson (nik′ọl.sọn), **Harold.** b. at Tehran, Persia (now Iran), 1886—. An English diplomat, writer, and critic. He married (1913) V. M. Sackville-West. He was a member of the delegation to the Peace Conference of 1919, and served in embassies at Madrid (1910) and Constantinople (1911), and at legations at Tehran (1925) and Berlin (1927). He joined the editorial staff of the London *Evening Standard* (1930). He served as a National Labour member of Parliament (1935–45), and was parliamentary secretary in the ministry of information (1940–41), and governor of the British Broadcasting Corporation (1941–46). Author of biographies and critical works including *Paul Verlaine* (1921), *Tennyson* (1923), *Byron* (1924), *Swinburne* (1926), *The Development of English Biography* (1927), *Sir Arthur Nicolson, Bart., First Lord Carnock* (1930; published in America under the title *Portrait of a Diplomat*), *The New Spirit in Literature* (1931), *Curzon: The Last Phase* (1934), and *Peacemaking, 1919* (1939). Among his novels are *Sweet Waters* (1921) and *Public Faces* (1932).

Nidhug (nēd′hög). [Also, **Nithhogg.**] In Old Norse mythology, a dragon which lies in Niflheim forever gnawing at the root of Yggdrasil, the world tree.

Niel Blane (nēl blān). See **Blane, Niel.**

Nietzsche (nē′chẹ), **Friedrich Wilhelm.** b. near Lützen, Germany, Oct. 15, 1844; d. at Weimar, Germany, Aug. 25, 1900. A German philologist and philosopher. He was brought up by his widowed mother in an atmosphere of great piety (his father had been a Lutheran minister), and studied theology as well as philology at the universities of Bonn and Leipzig. Both studies were of importance to his career; the first seems to have confirmed him in an aversion to religion which was to be influential in shaping his philosophy; the second for some years (1869–80) gave him his living as professor of classical philology at the University of Basel. During his Leipzig years his thought was deeply colored by the pessimistic philosophy of Arthur Schopenhauer, but at this time also began the close personal friendship with Richard Wagner and the enthusiasm for Wagner's works and purposes which for some years were to mean much to both men. If Schopenhauer completed Nietzsche's disillusion with man as he was, and with the religious and philosophical concepts by which civilized man lived in the 19th century, Wagner confirmed the exciting hope of the rise of the *Übermensch* or Superman. Nietzsche's sensitivity to music had much to do with the identity of thought and purpose which prevailed for a time between the two men, and Wagner considered Nietzsche his most important adherent. But presently the younger man's ardor cooled, and with characteristic intemperance he later compared Wagner's music disparagingly with that of Bizet. Nietzsche's health was always frail; by 1879 his increasing nervous instability and his weakening eyesight led to his resignation from the faculty at Basel, and thereafter for a decade, supported by a small personal income and a small pension from the university, he traveled in vain search of a climate and an environment which would restore his health. Often in pain, he wrote doggedly until 1889, when his mind finally gave way completely. The many corruptions and hypocrisies of Western civilization may be said to have invited the attacks upon traditional religion, philosophy, and social concepts, which multiplied during the 19th century; Nietzsche was among the most outspoken of the critics, and the violence of his attack gave it an influence which in many ways proved unfortunate. Civilization, he said, had come to the end of its possibilities. It had been dominated by the ideal of the good, the true, and the beautiful, which sapped masculine vitality, and by Jewish-Christian ethics. The Jews, he said, when they first appeared in history, were a warlike, conquering people, exalting force, cruel and joyous; these things they considered good, and so did Nietzsche. But after the Jews were enslaved, they made virtues of humility, patience, charity, and peace, which Nietzsche called evil. Christianity merely spread these Jewish ideals, and Socialism threatened to impose them on all mankind. Against these virtues, against classless social and political equality, against mass rule, Nietzsche inveighed in a vigorous rhetorical style and with cryptic, prophetic, and at least apparently profound utterance. Control of society must be wrested from the masses by Supermen; the poor in spirit must be ruled by the proud; the meek must not inherit the earth, but must serve the strong and the ruthless. He foretold that the 20th century would be ensanguined by terrible wars, which he hoped would lead to the rise of tyrants. These ideas naturally fascinated such men as those who a few years later tried to impose Fascism and Nazism on the world; and the detestation of Jews and Jewish influence which Nietzsche's analysis of civilization's sickness could arouse in the minds of such men, contributed to eventuations from which he himself would almost certainly have recoiled. When it is considered that Nietzsche was a frail, sickly, frustrated, neurotic, and poverty-harassed man, Nietzschianism appears in one aspect at least as the end-product of an extreme inferiority complex. Unhappily, the compensation which Nietzsche found in the realm of theory, lay all too readily at hand to be translated into action by another victim of an extreme inferiority complex, Adolf Hitler. All of Nietzsche's works have been translated into English; the most important of them are *Die Geburt der Tragödie* (The Birth of Tragedy, 1872), *Menschliches Allzumenschliches* (Human, All too Human, 1878–80), *Die fröhliche Wissenschaft* (Joyful Wisdom, 1882) *Also sprach Zarathustra* (Thus Spake Zarathustra, 1883–92), and *Jenseits von Gut und Böse* (Beyond Good and Evil, 1886).

Niflheim (nivʹl.hām). [Old Norse, **Niflheimr.**] In the Old Norse cosmogony, the cold world of fog in the north. In the midst was the spring from which flowed ten rivers. One root of the world tree, Yggdrasil, reached into Niflheim, and the dragon, Nidhug, lay there forever gnawing on it.

Niflhel (nifʹl.hel). In Old Norse mythology, the realm of the goddess Hel; the abode of the dead.

Nigel Olifaunt (nīʹjel olʹi.fạnt). See **Olifaunt, Nigel.**

Nigel Wireker (wirʹẹ.kėr). See **Wireker, Nigel.**

Nigger of the Narcissus. A novel by Joseph Conrad, published in 1897 (it was first issued between two covers on Nov. 30, at New York, as *The Children of the Sea: A Tale of the Forecastle*, and two days later at London under the title of entry). It is based on Conrad's own experiences as second mate on a sailing vessel (which actually bore the name *Narcissus*) in 1884; moreover, there actually was a Negro who did die at sea. The book brought Conrad many new admirers, including Henry James, who considered it "the very finest and strongest picture of . . . sea-life that our language possesses." The book tells the thoughts and reflections of the West Indian Negro, James Wait, who is dying of tuberculosis on board the *Narcissus*. It reveals the influence of this man and his fate on every other member of the ship's crew.

Night and Morning. A novel by Edward Bulwer-Lytton, published in 1841.

Night at an Inn, A. A drama of retribution (1917), by Lord Dunsany.

Night Has a Thousand Eyes, The. A poem by Francis Bourdillon. It has been widely anthologized.

Nightingale (nīʹtin.gāl, -ting-), **Florence.** [Called the "**Lady with the Lamp.**"] b. at Florence, Italy, May 15, 1820; d. at London, Aug. 13, 1910. An English philanthropist, nurse, and administrator, noted as a heroine of modern nursing. Early in life she became interested in nursing, and after 1844 she inspected schools and hospitals in England and all parts of Europe. In 1849–50 she spent several months at a Roman Catholic hospital at Alexandria, Egypt, and in 1850–51 trained as a nurse at the Institute of Protestant Deaconesses at Kaiserswerth. After that she studied further at Paris and in 1853 returned to London to take charge of a women's hospital. When news of the suffering of the wounded in the Crimean War reached England in 1854, she volunteered her services and was accepted. At the head of a group of 38 nurses, she reached Scutari in early November, 1854, soon after the battle of Balaklava, and there set up a hospital. She instituted severe sanitary measures intended to reduce the dangers of cholera, typhus, and dysentery; in this she was successful, and by 1855 the death rate had fallen from almost 50 percent to about two percent. Opposition and the inertia of a government at war did not dishearten her; she worked faithfully and hard for her charges, making her rounds at night with lamp in hand, superintending the arrival of new casualties, attending operations, ministering to the wounded and their families, performing all the administrative duties of the head of the hospitals along the Bosporus as well; even when she herself collapsed of fever in May, 1855, she refused to be invalided home. After the war she founded (1860), with a fund donated as a testimonial to her services, the Nightingale Home at St. Thomas's Hospital, for the training of nurses; during the next 30 years she helped in the establishment of several nursing homes in England. Her health so ruined by her war service that she could not participate actively in nursing, she became a consultant on matters of sanitation and the reform of camp hospitals, village sanitary systems, and other projects now comprised in the study of public health. She was an official adviser on sanitation during the American Civil War and the Franco-Prussian War. In 1907 she became the first woman to receive the Order of Merit. She published *The Institution at Kaiserswerth* (1850), *Notes on Hospitals* (1859), *Notes on Nursing* (1860), *Observations on the Sanitary State of the Army in India* (1863), and others.

Nightmare Abbey. A novel by Thomas Love Peacock, published in 1818. Like the author's other works, this has little formal plot; a houseparty is used as a device to bring together various interesting characters, who are used to satirize transcendentalism, Byronism, and pessimism. Mr. Hilary is a very cheerful gentleman; Mr. Toobad and Scythrop Glowry are pessimists; Mr. Flosky is a caricature of Coleridge, and Mr. Cypress of Byron.

Night Must Fall. A melodrama by Emlyn Williams, published in 1935.

Night Thoughts. A meditative poem in nine parts (1742–45) on religion and morality, by Edward Young. Its whole title is *The Complaint, or Night Thoughts on Life, Death, and Immortality.* It is generally considered by critics to be one of the most important blank-verse poems of the 18th century, ranking with Thomson's *Seasons* and Cowper's *The Task.* The first book contains the poet's reflections on life, death, and immortality; the argument of the following seven books is in the form of an exhortation to Lorenzo, a non-believing man of the world, to accept the Faith; the last book is in the form of a vision, entitled "The Consolation," in which the poet offers his views on Judgment Day and eternity.

Night Walker or the Little Thief, The. A comedy by John Fletcher, but licensed in 1633 as "corrected by [James] Shirley." However, it was printed in 1640 as by Fletcher only.

Nike (nī′kē). In Greek mythology, the goddess of victory.

Nile (nīl), **Battle of the.** A name often given to the British naval victory of Aug. 1–2, 1798, over the French, in the Bay of Aboukir.

Nimrod (nim′rod). In the Bible, according to Gen. x., son of Cush, grandson of Ham, famous for his exploits as a hunter, at first ruler of Shinar (or Shumir, i.e., Sumer or South Babylonia), then founder of the Assyrian Tetrapolis (Assur, Nineveh, Rehoboth-Ir, and Calah). Some Assyriologists identify Nimrod with Gilgamesh or Izdubar, the principal hero of the Babylonian Gilgamesh legends, the so-called Nimrod Epic.

Nimrod. Pseudonym of **Apperley, Charles James.**

Nineteen Hundred and Nineteen. A work of verse (1919) by W. B. Yeats, published in *The Tower* (1928). It consists of six short poems concerned generally with the chaotic state of Ireland, morally and politically, as a result of the undeclared war with England: "a drunken soldiery can leave the mother, murdered at her door, to crawl in her own blood, and go scot-free." In a note to the sixth poem Yeats explains the origin of the "horsemen" in Irish legend, and shows how he uses them here as symbols of the worsening times.

Nine Worthies. Nine heroes of ancient legend and medieval chivalric romance. In one of the latter, the *Triumphes des neufs Preux,* the author feigns that there appeared to him in a vision nine heroes, and in a second vision a tenth hero, i.e., Joshua, David, Judas Maccabaeus, Hector, Alexander the Great, Julius Caesar, and then Arthur, Charlemagne, Godfrey of Bouillon, and finally Bertrand du Guesclin. They charge him to undertake the description of their lives and feats, in order that Lady Triumphe, who appears with them, may decide which of them has deserved her crown. The nine heroes of this romance are not infrequently mentioned in English literature. Shakespeare alludes (in *Love's Labour's Lost*) to the Nine Worthies. They also appear in the verses which precede the Low German history of Alexander the Great. They figure in tapestry and paintings. This selection of thrice three heroes may have originated in the Welsh *Triads,* where the three pagan, Jewish, and Christian trinities are enumerated as follows: Hector, Alexander, and Julius Caesar; Joshua, David, and Judas Maccabaeus; Arthur, Charlemagne, and Godfrey de Bouillon. Guy of Warwick is sometimes substituted for Godfrey.

Nine Worthies. In Shakespeare's *Love's Labour's Lost,* the masque presented before Ferdinand, King of Navarre, the Princess of France, and the rest of the court by Costard as Pompey, Sir Nathaniel as Alexander, Moth as Hercules, and Armado as Hector. It is intended as a parody on a pageant familiar to Elizabethans on state occasions.

Ninian (nin′i.an), Saint. fl. c400 A.D. A British missionary among the southern Picts. He built a church at Withern, or Whithorn, in Galloway, Scotland, in 397, and in 420, when driven to Ireland, is said to have founded a monastery at Clonconnor.

Ninon de Lenclos or **L'Enclos** (nē.nôṅ de läṅ.klō). See **Lenclos** or **L'Enclos, Anne.**

Ninus (nī′nus). In Greek legend, the eponymous founder of Nineveh and of the Assyrian Empire; husband of Semiramis, the famous Assyrian queen. She is said to have coaxed Ninus into giving her full power for five days; he did so, and on the second she had him put to death.

Niobe (nī′ọ.bē). In Greek mythology, the daughter of Tantalus and wife of Amphion, king of Thebes. Proud of her numerous progeny, she boasted of them to Leto, who had but two. She was punished by seeing all her children die by the arrows of Apollo and Artemis, the children of Leto. She herself was metamorphosed by Zeus into a stone,

ḍ, d or j; ṣ, s or sh; ṭ, t or ch; z̧, z or zh; o, F. cloche; ü, F. menu; ċh, Sc. loch; ṅ, F. bonbon.

perpetually weeping, and which is still pointed out on Mount Sipylus, near Smyrna. The story is represented in the Niobe Group, attributed to Scopas, now best known from copies in the Uffizi at Florence.

Niord (nyôrd). See **Njord**.

Nipper (nip′ẽr), **Susan.** In Dickens's *Dombey and Son*, a young maid in charge of Florence Dombey, noted for her sharp tongue.

Nirvana (nẽr.van′ạ, nir.vä′nạ). In Buddhism, the final state to which the Buddhist aspires as the highest aim and highest good. In Brahmanism, Nirvana is release from birth, suffering, death, and rebirth, a merging and absorption of the individual with and into the absolute. To Buddha the Nirvana concept was this same ancient concept, triumph over the pain of life, of release and redemption (through enlightenment) from anger, lust, delusion, and ignorance. To seek and attain the wisdom that must be attained before the individual can experience Nirvana is the essence of Buddhist idealism. To some, however, extinction of consciousness is inconceivable except in terms of annihilation of the individual; to these Nirvana means just that: release from life, extinction, annihilation. The true Buddhist maintains, however, that no matter how inconceivable, Nirvana as the supreme and final good of the individual can be reached if one follows the method.

Nisroch (nis′rok). An Assyrian deity, in whose temple at Nineveh Sennacherib was murdered (2 Kings, xix. 37, Isa. xxxvii. 38). The name was formerly derived from Hebrew *nešer* ("eagle"), and the deity is regarded as one of the eagle-headed gods frequently represented on Assyrian sculptures.

Nisus (nī′sus). In Greek legend, a king of Megara who had one purple (or golden) hair (or lock) in his head, on which his life depended. The prophecy was that if it were to be pulled out, he would die. When Nisus was attacked by King Minos of Crete, his daughter Scylla fell in love with Minos, and pulled out the hair. Thus Nisus died; or, in some versions of the legend, weakened and lost the kingdom.

Nisus. In classical legend, a follower of Aeneas and bosom friend of Euryalus, whom he would not abandon to save his own life.

Niven (niv′ẹn), **Frederick John.** b. at Valparaíso, Chile, March 31, 1878; d. at Vancouver, British Columbia, Jan. 30, 1944. An English novelist, poet, journalist, and librarian. He became a librarian, serving for many years in Glasgow and Edinburgh libraries, worked in lumber and railway camps in Canada, writing stories and sketches of his experiences for Glasgow and Dundee newspapers, and served (1914–18) in the ministries of food and information during World War I. Author of *Lost Cabin Mine* (1908), *Island Providence* (1910), *A Wilderness of Monkeys* (1911), *Dead Men's Bells* (1912), *Porcelain Lady* (1913), *Ellen Adair* (1913), *Justice of the Peace* (1914), *The S. S. Glory* (1915), *Hands Up!* (1915), *Two Generations* (1916), *Cinderella of Skookum Creek* (1916), *Sage-Brush Stories* (1917), *Penny Scot's Treasure* (1918), *Lady of the Crossing* (1919), *A Tale That Is Told* (1920), *The Wolfer* (1923), *Treasure Trail* (1923),

Queer Fellows (1927; American title, *Wild Honey*), *The Rich Wife* (1932), *Mrs. Barry* (1933), *Triumph* (1934), *Old Soldier* (1936), *The Maitlands* (1939), *Mine Inheritance* (1940), and *Prelude to Victory* (1941), novels; *Maple-Leaf Songs* (1917) and *A Lover of the Land* (1925), poetry; and of *Canada West* (1930) and *Color in the Canadian Rockies* (1937), nonfiction.

Njord (nyôrd). [Also: **Niord, Njorth** (nyôrth); Old Norse, **Njördhr** (nyẽr′тнẽr).] In Old Norse mythology, the god of the sea; father of Frey and Freya. He and his two children belonged by race to the Vanir, very ancient fertility gods who were later associated with the weather. Njord came as a hostage to Asgard after the war between the Vanir and the Aesir (the high gods). He ruled the wind and calmed the sea, and hence was the god of sailors and fishermen. Njord became identified with the ancient fertility goddess Nerthus, whose cult and characteristics became in turn identical with those of Freya.

Noah (nō′ạ). In the Old Testament, a patriarch, the son of Lamech. With his family and animals of every species, he survived the Deluge. Gen. v.-ix.

Noah Claypole (klā′pōl). See **Claypole, Noah.**

Nobbs (nobz), **Dr.** [Also, **Dr. Nobs.**] The horse of Dr. Dove, the hero of Robert Southey's *The Doctor.*

Nobel (nō.bel′), **Alfred Bernhard.** b. at Stockholm, Oct. 21, 1833; d. at San Remo, Italy, Dec. 10, 1896. A Swedish chemist and engineer. He was educated at St. Petersburg, and studied engineering for a number of years. Among his many inventions are those of dynamite, explosive gelatin, ballistite, and artificial gutta-percha. He acquired large wealth through the manufacture of dynamite and other explosives, and the exploitation of the Baku oil fields. By the terms of his will, the bulk of his fortune was devoted to the establishment of a prize fund, known as the "Nobel gift," the interest of which he proposed to have divided annually into five parts and awarded to the persons who have rendered to humanity the greatest services during the preceding year (or, in exceptional cases, earlier), as follows: (1) by the most important discovery or invention in the physical sciences; (2) by the most important discovery or the greatest improvement in chemistry; (3) by the most important discovery in physiology or medicine; (4) by the most remarkable literary work of an idealistic tendency; and (5) to the person who has done most, or labored best, for the cause of fraternity among different peoples, for the suppression or reduction of standing armies, or for the formation and promotion of peace congresses. The first two prizes are awarded by the Swedish Academy of Sciences, the third by the Caroline Institute of Stockholm, the fourth by the Stockholm Academy, and the fifth by a commission of five members elected by the Norwegian Storthing. The terms of the will have not been strictly observed. Statutes have been drawn up providing that only 60 percent of the income need be used for the Nobel Prizes, and that they need be awarded only once in five years. Provision has also been made for the establishment of Nobel institutes for research work and similar enterprises.

---

fat, fāte, fär, àsk, fãre; net, mē, hẽr; pin, pīne; not, nōte, möve, nôr; up, lūte, pùll; тн, then;

Nobel Prizes. Prizes awarded annually from the bequest of Alfred B. Nobel.

Noble (nō'bl), **Edward.** b. 1857; d. 1941. An English seaman, author of novels and short stories of the sea. Author of *The Edge of Circumstance* (1905), *Fisherman's Gat* (1907; American title, *The Issue*), *The Grain Carriers* (1908), *The Bottle-Fillers* (1915), *Outposts of the Fleet* (1917), *The Naval Side* (1918), *The Mandarin's Bell* (1925), *The Fire of Spring* (1926), *Moving Waters* (1928), and *Pulse of Darkness* (1929).

Noctes Ambrosianae (nok'tēz am.brō.si.ā'nē). A series of papers in the form of dialogues on popular topics, contributed (1822–35) to *Blackwood's Magazine*, chiefly by John Wilson (under the pseudonym Christopher North). They take their name from a public house, Ambrose's, where Wilson met with his friends, and he recorded their conversations in a witty and vivid manner. Often he uses imaginary characters, but Hogg and Maginn are impersonated with great humor.

Nocturnal Reverie. A poem by Anne Finch, Countess of Winchilsea, probably published before 1712. The poem is remembered today largely because of Wordsworth's praise of it in the *Essay Supplementary to the Preface* (1815).

nocturne (nok'tẽrn, nok.tẽrn'). [Also, **notturno**.] In music, a composition, properly instrumental, which is intended to embody the dreamy sentiments appropriate to the evening or the night; a pensive and sentimental melody; a reverie; a serenade. The style of composition and the term are peculiar to the romantic school.

Nocturne. A novel (1917) by Frank Swinnerton.

"Noddy" Boffin (nod'i bof'in). See **Boffin, Nicodemus.**

Noel (nō'el), **Roden Berkeley Wriothesley.** b. Aug. 27, 1834; d. at Mainz, Germany, May 26, 1894. An English poet and critic. Author of *Behind the Veil* (1863), *Beatrice* (1868), *The Red Flag* (1872), *Livingstone in Africa* (1874), *Songs of the Heights and Deeps* (1885), *A Modern Faust* (1888), and *Poor People's Christmas* (1890), volumes of poetry; *The House of Ravensburg* (1877), a poetic drama; *Essays upon Poetry and Poets* (1886), *Philosophy of Immortality* (1882), *Life of Byron* (1890), and editions of Spenser (1887) and Otway (1888), the latter for the *Mermaid* series. *A Little Child's Monument* (1881), written in memory of his son who died at the age of five, is regarded by many as his best poem.

Noel, Thomas. b. at Kirkby-Mallory, Leicestershire, England, May 11, 1799; d. at Brighton, England, May 16, 1861. An English poet. Author of *The Cottage Muse* (1833), *Village Verse* (1841), and *Rymes and Roundelayes* (1841), he is best known for a few single poems, such as *Poor Voter's Song, Pauper's Drive, A Thames Voyage,* and *Rocked in the Cradle of the Deep.*

Noggs (nogz), **Newman.** In Dickens's *Nicholas Nickleby*, a man who has been at one time a gentleman, but who is reduced to serving Ralph Nickleby as clerk and menial servant. He does not, however, condone Nickleby's criminal schemes and is finally able to tell him so.

Noir Fainéant (nwär fā.nā.än'), **Le.** See **Fainéant, Le Noir.**

nom de plume (nôn dẹ plüm). A pseudonym used by a writer instead of his real name; a signature assumed by an author.

No More Music. A novel by Rosamond Lehmann, published in 1939.

No More Parades. A novel (1925) by Ford Madox Ford, a continuation of *Some Do Not* (1924).

No Name. A novel by Wilkie Collins, published in 1862.

Nones (nōnz). A volume of poems (1952) by W. H. Auden. The title is probably intended to be ambiguous, but the obvious primary reference is to the afternoon hour of prayer in a monastery. There is considerable experimentation in this volume with a rhyme scheme where the next-to-the-last syllable of one line rhymes with the last syllable of the preceding or the following line. Among the poems in the collection are the two Phi Beta Kappa poems, "Under Which Lyre," with its concluding "Hermetic Decalogue," and "Music is International." The dedicatory poem to Reinhold and Ursula Niebuhr is of interest especially to those seeking information as to Auden's conception of his role as a poet.

Non-Juror, The. A play by Colley Cibber, produced in 1717. It is an adaptation of Molière's *Tartuffe*, written to support the Hanoverian succession and in opposition to the Roman Catholics. The play was later adapted by Isaac Bickerstaffe as *The Hypocrite* (1768).

nonsense verse. A variety of verse made by taking any words which may occur without reference to forming any connected sense, correct meter, pleasing rhythm, or a grotesque effect being all that is aimed at. In English schools Latin verse composition often begins with nonsense verses, the object being to familiarize the pupil with the quantity of syllables and the metrical forms on their mechanical side before aiming at expression of thought.

Non Sum qualis Eram Bonae sub Regno Cynarae (nōn sùm kwā'lis er'ạm bō'nẹ sub reg'num sin'-ạ.rẹ). The formal title of the most famous of Ernest Dowson's poems. See **Cynara.**

No Popery Riots. See **Gordon Riots.**

Norah Nesbit (nō'rạ, nôr'ạ, nez'bit). See **Nesbit, Norah.**

Nore, the. A sandbank in SE England, lying in the estuary of the river Thames, between Essex and Kent, ab. 4 mi. NE of Sheerness. The name is applied also to the estuary itself.

Norfolk (nôr'fọk), **1st Duke of.** See **Mowbray, Thomas.**

Norfolk, Duke of. In Shakespeare's *3 Henry VI*, a supporter of the Yorkist (White Rose) faction.

Norfolk, (1st) Duke of. In Shakespeare's *Richard III*, the historical John Howard, a supporter of the King. He is killed at Bosworth.

Norfolk, (2nd) Duke of. In Shakespeare's *Henry VIII*, the historical Thomas Howard, a strong opponent of Wolsey. He appears as the Earl of Surrey, son of the 1st Duke of Norfolk, in *Richard III*.

ḍ, d or j; ṣ, s or sh; ṭ, t or ch; ẓ, z or zh; o, F. cloche; ü, F. menu; ċh, Sc. loch; ṅ, F. bonbon.

Norfolk, Duke of. See also under **Mowbray, Thomas** (in Shakespeare).

Norman (nôr'man), Sir **Henry.** b. at Leicester, England, Sept. 19, 1858; d. June 4, 1939. An English journalist and traveler, active on various international research committees during the early development of transoceanic radio. He was graduated from Harvard University, and was on the editorial staff of the *Pall Mall Gazette* and of the London *Daily Chronicle.* In 1902 he founded *World's Work.* He was a Liberal member of Parliament for South Wolverhampton (1900–10), and was assistant postmaster general (1910). Among his publications are *The Real Japan* (1892), *The Peoples and Politics of the Far East* (1895), *All the Russias* (1902), *Motors and Men* (1905), and others. He was knighted in 1906.

Normanby (nôr'man.bi), 1st Marquis of. A title of **Phipps,** Sir **Constantine Henry.**

Norman Conquest. In English history, the conquest of England by William, Duke of Normandy (William the Conqueror). It was begun by and is usually dated from his victory at Senlac (Hastings) in 1066. The leading results were the downfall of the native English dynasty, the union of England and Normandy for a time under one sovereign, and the introduction into England of Norman-French customs and language.

Norman Conquest of England, History of the. The chief historical work of Edward A. Freeman (6 vols., 1867–79).

Norman French. A form of French spoken by the Normans, which became upon the Norman Conquest the official language of the court and of legal procedure, undergoing in England a further development (Anglo-French), until its final absorption in English. Norman French was the language of legal procedure until the reign of Edward III. Many isolated phrases and formulas in this language (Law French) remain unassimilated in archaic use.

Nor Many Waters. A novel by Alec Waugh, published in 1928 and issued in America under the title *Portrait of a Celibate.*

Norna (nôr'na). A kind of sibyl, a character in Scott's novel *The Pirate.* She was Ulla Troil, called Norna of the Fitful Head.

Norns (nôrnz). In Old Norse mythology, the Fates, usually three, whose decrees were irrevocable. They were represented as three virgin goddesses who dwelt at the foot of the world-tree Yggdrasil. Their parallels in other mythologies are the Greek Moirae and the Roman Parcae.

Norris (nor'is), **John.** b. at Collingbourne-Kingston, Wiltshire, England, 1657; d. at Bemerton, Wiltshire, England, 1711. An English clergyman and philosopher, remembered as one of the Cambridge Platonists. He published *An Idea of Happiness* in 1683. The greater part of his poems appeared in 1684. In 1689 he published *Reason and Religion.* Locke's famous *Essay on Human Understanding* excited his opposition, and in the appendix to his *Christian Blessedness* appeared the first published critique of the essay. In 1697 he wrote *An Account of Reason and Faith,* and in 1701 appeared the first volume of his chief work, *An Essay Towards the Theory of the Ideal or Intelligible World;* the second

volume appeared in 1704. It was in this work that he espoused and outlined in detail the metaphysical position of Nicolas de Malebranche (which takes as its basic doctrine the view that the mind of man is able to have external knowledge only through God) as against the materialist position of Locke and his followers.

Norris, Mrs. The interfering aunt of Fanny, the heroine, in Jane Austen's novel *Mansfield Park.*

Norris, William Edward. b. at London, 1847; d. Nov. 19, 1925. An English novelist. He was called to the bar in 1874, but never practiced. Among his novels are *Heaps of Money* (1877), *Mademoiselle de Mersac* (1880), *Matrimony* (1881), *No New Thing* (1883), *My Friend Jim* (1886), *A Bachelor's Blunder* (1886), *Major and Minor* (1887), *The Rogue* (1888), *The Countess Radna* (1893), *The Dancer in Yellow* (1896), *Clarissa Furiosa* (1897), *The Fight for the Crown* (1898), *Giles Ingilby* (1899), *An Octave* (1900), *The Flower of the Flock* (1900), *His Own Father* (1901), *The Credit of the County* (1902), *Lord Leonard the Luckless* (1903), *Nature's Comedian* (1904), *Barham of Beltana* (1905), *Pauline* (1908), *The Perjurer* (1909), *Not Guilty* (1910), and *Trevalion* (1925).

North (nôrth), **Christopher.** Pseudonym of **Wilson, John** (1785–1854).

North, Roger. b. 1653; d. 1734. An English historian. He was attorney general to the queen (Mary, wife of James II). He wrote the abusive *Examen* of White Kennett's *History of England* (1740), and also biographies of his brothers, *A Discourse on the Study of the Laws* (first printed in 1824), and *Memoirs of Music* (first printed in 1846).

North, Sir Thomas. b. c1535; d. c1601. An English translator. His first book was *The Diall of Princes* (1557), originally from an Italian work by Guevara, and now notable chiefly for an ornate style foreshadowing the euphuism of Lyly. He also translated the *Moral Philosophy* of Doni, and an Italian version of a book of Arabian fables, *Kalilah and Dimnah* (1570). His translation of Plutarch (*Lives of the Noble Grecians and Romans*) was taken from the French version of Jacques Amyot, and first appeared in 1579 (there were added *Lives* in subsequent editions in 1595 and 1603). It was from this work that Shakespeare obtained much of his material for *Antony and Cleopatra, Coriolanus,* and *Julius Caesar.*

North and South. A novel by Elizabeth Cleghorn Gaskell, published in 1854–55. It contrasts the people of the North and South of England, also giving a picture of 19th-century worker-employer relations. Margaret Hale comes from a life of luxury and quiet refinement to live in a cotton-spinning town that is racked by a bitter dispute between workers and employers. She strongly advocates a more sympathetic approach by the employers; John Thornton, one of the masters, is attracted to her in spite of her views. She protects him once from the wrath of a mob, and he is so encouraged by this that he proposes to her. Margaret repulses him in contempt, and they become even more hostile to each other when John catches Margaret in what appears to be a compromising situation with another man (who is actually her brother). Margaret then realizes that she loves John, but much misfortune is endured by both before they are brought together.

Northanger Abbey (nôrth'ăn.jẽr). A novel by Jane Austen, written in the period 1797–98, but not published until 1818, the year after the author's death. It is a parody on the Gothic novels popular at the time. Catherine Morland, the daughter of a prosperous clergyman, has acquired a very vivid imagination as a result of having read all of the romantic novels of terror by Mrs. Radcliffe. She is invited to accompany her friends, Mr. and Mrs. Allen, to Bath for a season, and there she meets Henry Tilney and his sister, Eleanor. She and Tilney fall in love and win the approval of Henry's father, General Tilney, because he has been mistakenly told that Catherine is very wealthy. She is invited to Northanger Abbey, the Tilneys' medieval home, where she lets her imagination run riot. She persuades herself that General Tilney is a murderer, that the old house has many secret dungeons and passages, and that she has found a mysterious manuscript, which eventually proves to be only a laundry list. Her other suspicions prove equally groundless. Unfortunately, the general hears another false story to the effect that Catherine is penniless and from a very poor background. He therefore puts her out of the house and forbids her marriage with his son. But Henry, who is very much in love with her, remains faithful and follows her home. There he persuades her to marry him. The general is finally appeased when he learns the truth and when his daughter, Eleanor, marries a peer. A secondary plot involves Catherine's brother, who is engaged to the ill-bred Isabella Thorpe. Isabella breaks her engagement when Captain Tilney, Henry's older brother, pays her attentions; she thereby loses Catherine's friendship, only to discover that the captain was merely amusing himself.

North Briton (brit'ọn). A periodical (1762–63) published at London and conducted by John Wilkes. It was noted for the violence of its attacks on the Bute ministry and (in one instance) on George III.

Northcliffe (nôrth'klif), Viscount. Title of **Harmsworth, Alfred Charles William.**

Northcote (nôrth'kōt), **James.** b. at Plymouth, England, Oct. 22, 1746; d. at London, July 13, 1831. An English historical and portrait painter and author. In 1771 he entered the studio of Joshua Reynolds, and in 1777 went to Italy. He executed pictures for the Boydell Shakespeare gallery, and painted *The Death of Wat Tyler* for the city of London, now in the Guildhall. He wrote a life of Reynolds (1813) and a life of Titian (1830).

Northern Iron, The. A novel by James Owen Hannay under the pseudonym George A. Birmingham, published in 1907. Set in North Ireland in 1798, it presents a realistic description of the unsuccessful Irish rebellion of May, 1798.

Northern Lass, or a Nest of Fools, The. A comedy by Richard Brome, printed in 1632.

Northumberland (nôr.thum'bẽr.lạnd), **Earl of.** See **Siward.**

Northumberland, 9th Earl of. Title of **Percy, Sir Henry** (1564–1632).

Northumberland, (1st) **Earl of.** In Shakespeare's *Richard II*, the elder Henry Percy, who joins Bolingbroke on his return to England, and later orders Richard to Pomfret and his Queen to France. In *1 Henry IV*, he pretends illness to avoid committing himself against Henry IV (Bolingbroke) in battle and is not present at Shrewsbury when his son, Hotspur, is killed. In *2 Henry IV*, he encourages Archbishop Scroop to rebel, but then flees to Scotland. Later it is announced that he has been defeated.

Northumberland, (3rd) **Earl of.** In Shakespeare's *3 Henry VI*, the historical Henry Percy, grandson of Hotspur, a supporter of the King and of the Lancastrian (Red Rose) faction. He is killed at Towton.

Northumberland, Lady. In Shakespeare's *2 Henry IV*, the wife of the (1st) Earl of Northumberland. She advises her husband to flee to Scotland.

Northumberland House. A historic house formerly on the Strand, London. It was dismantled in 1873–74.

Northumbria (nôr.thum'bri.ạ). [Also, **Kingdom of Northumberland.**] The chief Anglian kingdom in England during the Heptarchy, at its greatest extent reaching from the Humber to the Firth of Forth, and from the North Sea W to the Celtic Strathclyde. The Anglian kingdoms of Bernicia in the N (founded by Ida in 547) and Deira (founded a few years later) were united (c600) under Ethelfrith. Christianity was introduced under Edwin (d. 633). Northumbria reached its highest point in the 7th century, as the most powerful kingdom in the island. It was the center of English literature in the 7th and 8th centuries, thereafter playing a secondary role (it contributed relatively little to the brilliant literary and scholarly activity that gained its impetus in S England under King Alfred). It was largely resettled by the Danes in the 9th century, nominally conquered by the Anglo-Saxons in the middle of the 10th century, and thereafter governed by practically independent Danish earls until the period of the Norman conquest. The N portion was ceded (c1000) to Scotland.

Northward Ho! [Also, **Northward Hoe!**] A comedy by Thomas Dekker and John Webster, produced in 1605 and printed in 1607. It was in answer to Chapman, Jonson, and Marston's *Eastward Ho!*

Northwest Passage. A sea passage between the Atlantic and Pacific Oceans, passing N of the mainland of North America, along the Arctic coast, and through the Canadian Arctic Archipelago. It was sought by navigators from the 16th century on, but the first successful passage was made by the Norwegian explorer Roald Amundsen in 1906–09. Because of the freezing of numerous straits, and prolonged and severe winter conditions, the route is not of practical use.

Norton (nôr'tọn), **Caroline Elizabeth Sarah.** [Maiden name, **Sheridan.**] b. 1808; d. June 15, 1877. An English poet and novelist. She was one of "the three graces," daughters of Thomas Sheridan. She published *The Dandies' Rout* (illustrated by her-

---

ḍ, d o˙ j; ṣ, s or sh; ṭ, t or ch; z̧, z or zh; o, F. cloche; ü, F. menu; ċh, Sc. loch; ṅ, F. bonbon.

self at the age of 13), *The Sorrows of Rosalie* (1829), and *The Undying One* (1830). She also wrote *A Voice from the Factories* (1836), *The Lady of La Garaye* (1862), *Lost and Saved* (1863), and *Old Sir Douglas* (1867). She is considered by some to have been the model for the heroine of Meredith's *Diana of the Crossways*.

Norton, Thomas. b. at London, 1532; d. at Sharpenhoe, Bedfordshire, England, 1584. An English lawyer, translator, and author. He wrote (with Sackville) the first English tragedy, *Gorboduc*. He published a *Translation of Calvin's Institutes* (1561), and translated many of the psalms in the Psalter of Sternhold and Hopkins (1561).

Norumbega (nor.um.bē′gạ). An old name of a region on the Atlantic coast of North America, frequently mentioned in maps and writings of the 16th and 17th centuries. It was placed between Cape Breton and Florida, or narrowed to the N part of that region, or more definitely placed within what is now the state of Maine. Various English and French explorers made journeys to Norumbega. It is disputed whether the name is of Indian, Norse, or Spanish origin. The river of Norumbega has been often identified with the Penobscot.

Norval (nôr′vạl), **Young.** In Home's play *Douglas*, the son of Lady Randolph by a previous marriage with Douglas. The part was a favorite one with John Kemble and others, and Macready played it to Mrs. Siddons's Lady Randolph.

Norway (nôr′wā), **Nevil Shute.** See **Shute, Nevil.**

Norwich Festival (nor′ij), **The.** A triennial musical festival at Norwich, England. It was established in 1824.

Nosce Teipsum (nos′kẹ tē′ip.sum). A long poem (1599) by Sir John Davies, concerned with the nature and immortality of the soul.

Nostradamus (nos.trạ.dā′mus). [Original name, **Michel de Notredame** (or **Nostredame**).] b. at St.-Remy, France, Dec. 14, 1503; d. at Salon, near Aix, France, July 2, 1566. A French astrologer and physician, noted as the author of a book of prophecies entitled *Centuries* (1555), which has been the subject of much controversy. It was condemned by the papal court in 1781.

Nostromo: A Tale of the Seaboard (nos.trō′mō). A novel by Joseph Conrad, published in 1904. It is a story of adventure, revolution, and buried treasure in a South American republic.

Note in Music, A. A novel by Rosamond Lehmann, published in 1930.

Notre Dame (nọ.trẹ dȧm). A church at Paris, one of the most imposing and famous of cathedrals. The present structure was begun in 1163, but dates chiefly from the early 13th century.

Nottingham (not′ing.ạm), **Earl of.** See **Mowbray, Thomas.**

Nottingham's Company, Earl of. See **Lord Admiral's Men.**

Noureddin (nö.red.dēn′). See **Nureddin.**

Nourjahad (nör.jȧ.häd′). [Full title, **The History of Nourjahad.**] An oriental romance (1767) by Frances Sheridan.

Nourmahal (nör.mä.häl′). [Also, **Nurmahal.**] The wife of the Mogul emperor Jehangir, who reigned from 1605 to 1627. Her name means "Light of the Palace." The story of his quarrel and reconcilement with her is told in Moore's poem *The Light of the Harem.* She was also called Nourjehan, or "Light of the World."

Nouronihar (nö.ron.i.här′). In William Beckford's *Vathek*, the daughter of Fakreddin, a mischievous girl with whom Vathek falls in love, and who accompanies him to the hall of Eblis.

Nouvelle Héloïse (nö.vel ā.lo.ēz), **La.** [Full title, **Julie ou la Nouvelle Héloïse.**] A novel by Jean Jacques Rousseau, published in 1761. Told chiefly in the form of letters, it recounts the love of a noble young lady, Julie, for Saint-Preux, a man of low rank. A kind of afterpiece depicts Julie's married life with a respectable but prosaic freethinker, M. de Wolmar. Rousseau injects into the novel many of his social views.

Novall (nō′vạl). The seducer of Beaumelle in Massinger and Field's *The Fatal Dowry.*

novel. A fictitious prose narrative or tale, involving some plot of more or less intricacy, and aiming to present a picture of real life in the historical period and society to which the persons, manners, and modes of speech, as well as the scenery and surroundings, are supposed to belong. Its method is dramatic, and the novel may be regarded as a narrative play to the extent that the various persons or characters, upon whose qualities and actions the development and consummation of the plot or motive depend, are brought upon the scene to play their several parts according to their different personalities, disclosing, with the aid of the author's delineation and analysis, diverse aspects of passion and purpose, and contributing their various parts to the machinery of the drama to be enacted among them. The novel may be regarded as representing the third stage of transition in the evolution of fictitious narrative, of which the epic was the first and the romance the second. The novel in its most recent form may be divided, according to its dominant theme or motive, into the philosophical, the political, the historical, the descriptive, the social, and the sentimental novel; to which may be added, as special forms, the novel of adventure, the novel of society, the novel of character, the novel of criticism and satire, the novel of reform, and the military, the nautical, and the sporting novel.

Our Amours can't furnish out a Romance; they'll make a very pretty Novel.
(Steele, *Tender Husband.*)

The novel—what we call the novel—is a new invention. It is customary to date the first English novel with Richardson in 1740.
(S. Lanier, *The English Novel.*)

Novel (nov′ẹl). A character in Wycherley's comedy *The Plain Dealer.* He is a pert coxcomb "who, rather than not rail, will rail at the dead, whom none speak ill of; rather than not flatter, will flatter the poets of the age, whom none will flatter" (ii. 1).

novelette (nov.ẹl.et′). A short novel. "The classical translations and Italian novelette of the age of Elizabeth." (J. R. Green.)

Novelist, The. See under **Another Time.**

Novello (nō.vel'ō), **Ivor.** [Original name, **Ivor Novello Davies.**] b. at Cardiff, Wales, 1893 or 1894; d. at London, March 6, 1951. An English actor, playwright, and composer. Associated as actor-manager with *The Rat* (1924; which he wrote in collaboration with Constance Collier) and his own *The Truth Game* (1928), *Symphony in Two Flats* (1929), *Fresh Fields* (1933), *Murder in Mayfair* (1934), *Comedienne* (1938), and *Ladies into Action* (1939). After appearing (1929–31) in motion pictures in England, he came (1931) to Hollywood as a writer and actor. His musical compositions include the songs *Keep the Home Fires Burning* and *We'll Gather Lilacs* and the musical plays *Tabs* and *The House That Jack Built.*

Novelty Fashion (nov'el.ti fash'on), **Sir.** See **Fashion, Sir Novelty.**

Novum Organum (nō'vum ôr'ga.num). The chief philosophical work of Francis Bacon, written in Latin, and published in 1620. The meaning of the title in English is "new instrument"; Bacon develops in this work the theory that all learning must be based on experience, from which, cumulatively, general conclusions may be reached. This essentially inductive method was in sharp opposition to the deductive methods which were at that time the rule among scholars. One of the most famous passages of the *Novum Organum* is the description of the defects of man's reason, included in the four "Idols." The Idols of the Tribe are defects in all human nature; the Idols of the Cave originate in the individual; the Idols of the Marketplace are errors in society's use of language; and the Idols of the Theatre are errors based on the false doctrines of philosophers, who create their own little worlds, or theaters. By understanding these errors of reason man may, according to Bacon, eliminate them.

No Wit, No Help like a Woman's. A comedy of intrigue by Thomas Middleton, acted c1613–14. Shirley revived it, somewhat altered, in 1638 as *No Wit to a Woman's.* It was not printed till 1657.

Nowell (nō'el), **Robert.** b. in Lancashire, England, c1520; d. at Gray's Inn, London, Feb. 6, 1569. An English lawyer. He is principally remembered for a fund which he established by his will for benefactions to the poor. His brothers and John Towneley were his executors, and left a list of the persons to whom money was paid. This list, which contains important facts regarding Edmund Spenser (who was one of the poor scholars benefited from time to time), was printed by Grosart in 1871.

Noyes (noiz), **Alfred.** b. at Wolverhampton, Staffordshire, England, Sept. 16, 1880—. An English poet. He studied at Oxford, followed the sea for a time, and then established his reputation as a writer. He was professor of modern English literature (1914–23) at Princeton University. Noyes is a professional poet, earning his living by writing poetry, and is therefore not inclined to experiment with forms not familiar to his public. His work is traditional and musical (some of it has been set to music by Samuel Coleridge-Taylor and Edward Elgar) and he has become, in his lifetime, one of the classic English poets. His works include *The Loom of Years* (1902), *The Flower of Old Japan* (1903), *Poems* (1904), *The Forest of Wild Thyme*

(1905), *Drake, an English Epic* (1906), *Forty Singing Seamen* (1907), *William Morris* (1907), *The Magic Casement* (1908), *The Golden Hynde* (1908), *Collected Poems* (1910), *Tales of the Mermaid Tavern* (1913), and the trilogy *The Torch Bearers* (*The Watchers of the Sky*, 1922; *The Book of the Earth*, 1925; *The Last Voyage*, 1930). Best known among his single poems are *The Highwayman* and *The Barrel Organ*. He has also written short stories, novels, critical essays, and other works in prose. *The Unknown God* (1934) is the story of his becoming (1925) a Roman Catholic; his biography *Voltaire* (1936) was revised after objections from the Church.

Nubbles (nub'lz), **Kit.** In Dickens's *Old Curiosity Shop*, a boy employed to help Little Nell at the Old Curiosity Shop, who becomes her staunch friend and protector.

Nudd (nuŦH). See **Lud.**

Numa Pompilius (nū'ma pom.pil'i.us). According to the legends, the second king of Rome (715–673 B.C.). He was the reputed author or founder of many Roman institutions, including the pontifices, salii, flamens, fetiales, vestal virgins, worship of Terminus, and the temple of Janus.

"Nun of Kent," the. See **Barton, Elizabeth.**

Nun's Priest's Tale, The. One of Chaucer's *Canterbury Tales*. Based upon a version of the French *Roman de Renart*, it is the story of Chauntecleer (or Chanticleer), who escaped from the jaws of the fox by his cunning in making the latter open his mouth to speak. It was later modernized by Dryden as *The Cock and the Fox*. Although it follows the convention of the beast fable of the time, with a moral, it is valued by modern readers chiefly for the deftness of its satirical portraits: Chauntecleer is pompous and vain, proud of his learning in astronomy and other subjects, and given to quoting Latin to Pertelote, his favorite among his seven hens, whom he addresses as Madame; she is brisk and pretty, and full of wifely lore, makes light of his nightmare about a fox, and prescribes herbs to purge him of the red choler. Chauntecleer is caught off guard by Dan Russel the fox, who flatters him on his singing, but the cock saves himself at the last minute by a stratagem of his own. The Nun's Priest is mentioned but not described in the Prologue; when it is his turn to tell a tale, the Host chaffs him about the horse, "both foule and lene," on which he rides.

Nureddin (nö.red.dēn'). [Also, **Noureddin;** full name, **Malek-al-Adel Nureddin Mahmoud.**] b. at Damascus, Syria, c1116; d. c1173. Sultan of Syria from c1145. He conquered Egypt and became its sultan, and defeated the Christian armies of the second Crusade.

Nurmahal (nör.mä.häl'). See **Nourmahal.**

Nurse. In Shakespeare's *Romeo and Juliet*, a go-between during the early romance who later (after he is banished) urges Juliet to forget Romeo. A very practical woman, and a major source of comic relief in the play, she has come to be one of the best-known minor characters in Shakespeare.

Nurse. In Shakespeare's *Titus Andronicus*, a witness of the birth to Tamora of Aaron's bastard son, and therefore killed by Aaron.

---

d, d or j; s, s or sh; t, t or ch; z, z or zh; o, F. cloche; ü, F. menu; ċh, Sc. loch; ṅ, F. bonbon.

Nut-Brown Maid, The. An English ballad belonging to the end of the 15th century, preserved in the 16th-century *Arnold's Chronicle* and also included in Percy's *Reliques*. Prior took it for the foundation of his *Henry and Emma*. The "nut-brown maid" proclaims her faithfulness to her lover, who tells her at the end of every second stanza that he is a banished man. By saying (at the end of the intervening stanza) "I love but you alone," her love and meekness prevail; and he consoles her in the end by saying

> Thus have ye won an erles son,
> An not a banysshed man.

Nutmeg Tree, The. A novel by Margery Sharp, published in 1937.

Nuts of Knowledge, The. A book of lyrical poems by George William Russell (Æ), published in 1903.

Nydia (nid'i.a̧). A blind girl in Edward Bulwer-Lytton's *Last Days of Pompeii.*

Nym (nim). In Shakespeare's *Merry Wives of Windsor*, a thief and sharper, the companion of Falstaff; "an amusing creature of whimsey." He also appears with Pistol and Bardolph in *Henry V*. It has been thought that he may be a parody of characters in the Jonsonian humour comedies, since he is constantly referring to his "humour."

Nymphidia (nim.fid'i.a̧). A fairy poem by Michael Drayton, published in 1627, concerning a rupture in the harmony between Queen Mab and King Oberon over Pigwiggin, who has fallen in love with the queen. Proserpine and Lethe heal the breach. The poet asserts that all these doings have been reported to him by Nymphidia, attendant to Queen Mab.

O

Oak (ōk), **Gabriel.** The young countryman who is the hero of Thomas Hardy's novel *Far from the Madding Crowd.*

Oakly (ōk'li), **Charles.** A young man in love with Harriot in the elder George Colman's comedy *The Jealous Wife.*

Oakly, Mrs. The "jealous wife" in the elder George Colman's play of that name.

Oaks, The. A race for three-year-old fillies run annually at Epsom, England, on the Friday after the Derby. It was established in 1779.

Oannes (ō.an'es). In Babylonian mythology, the water god, depicted as having the body of a fish and the head and feet of a man. He appeared out of the Persian Gulf and taught the Babylonians letters, science, and all the arts of their civilization. He was also a fertility god and medicine god, and is identified with Ea of the cuneiform inscriptions.

Oates (ōts), **Titus.** b. at Oakham, 1649; d. at London, July 12, 1705. An English impostor. He studied at Cambridge, and took orders in the Anglican Church, but was deprived of his living for bad conduct. He was expelled from a chaplaincy in the navy as well before he fell in with Israel Tonge, a London clergyman obsessed with the idea that there was a Jesuit conspiracy to take over England. Oates pretended to become a Roman Catholic convert, was accepted in and then thrown out of the Jesuit College of Valladolid, and entered the college at St. Omer, whence he was ejected for bad conduct in 1678. He and Tonge then fabricated a series of documents, based on out-and-out lies or on distortions of truth, purporting to outline a plot, backed by Pope Innocent XI, whereby a general massacre of Protestants, the killing of the king, and the destruction of London were to be put into action. Oates was interviewed by King Charles II in August, 1678, but his evidence was so obviously nonsensical that the king ignored the matter. Oates then made an affidavit before Sir Edmond Berry Godfrey, a magistrate, implicating persons close to the Duke of York (the future James II), who was admittedly a Roman Catholic. Oates was called before the privy council and, during the course of the investigation, some letters from Edward Coleman, secretary to the Duchess of York, to the confessor to Louis XIV of France, were given in evidence. Coleman and others were imprisoned on the basis of statements in the letters, but even then the imposture might have been exposed had not the magistrate, Godfrey, been mysteriously murdered; some investigators of the problem think Oates may have had something to do with the murder. Popular prejudice, however, immediately blamed the murder on the Roman Catholics and during the following year some 35 Roman Catholics were killed after farcical trials, evidence being supplied principally by Oates and other witnesses with conveniently flexible memories; other Roman Catholics were murdered by maddened mobs. It was not until Oates had accused Queen Catherine and her physician, George Wakeman, and they had been acquitted (1679) that the frenzy died down. Oates lost prestige and, after he had called the Duke of York a traitor, was sued and fined (1685) 100,000 pounds. When he could not pay, he was jailed. James came to the throne in 1685; Oates was tried for perjury, found guilty, and sentenced to be pilloried and flogged. He was pardoned (1689) and granted a pension of 300 pounds a year when William III came to the throne, and spent the remainder of his life in sordid intrigues. He became a Baptist in 1698, but he was expelled in 1701 as a hypocrite.

Obadiah (ō.ba̧.dī'a̧). [Also, **Abdias.**] A Hebrew prophet, author of the short prophetic book in the Old Testament which bears his name. His date is uncertain, but is often given as c585 B.C. Of his personality nothing is known. His prophecy is a denunciation of the Edomites.

Obadiah. A "drinking nincompoop" in Sir Robert Howard's *The Committee.*

Obadiah. A canting Quaker in Susannah Centlivre's *A Bold Stroke for a Wife*. The name was frequently conventionally given to Quakers. Steady, in Charles Dibdin's opera *The Quaker*, is called Obadiah in the introduction; and Clever, in J. S. Knowles's *Woman's Wit*, when disguised as a Quaker, calls himself by the same name.

Obadiah. A servant in Laurence Sterne's *Tristram Shandy*.

Obadiah Lismahago (lis.mạ.hā′gō). See **Lismahago, Obadiah.**

Obadiah Slope (slōp). See **Slope, Obadiah.**

Oberland (ō′bėr.land). A novel by Dorothy M. Richardson, published in 1927. It is the ninth section of *Pilgrimage*, a novel sequence in 12 parts.

Oberon (ō′bẹ.rọn). In medieval legend and romance, the king of the fairies. He appears in the old French romance *Huon de Bordeaux* as the son of Julius Caesar and Morgan le Fay, and is thus connected with the Arthurian genealogy. Oberon gave Huon a magic bugle which caused its hearers to laugh uncontrollably. Shakespeare introduces him in *A Midsummer Night's Dream*.

Oberon. The King of the Fairies in an interlude in *James IV*, a comedy by Robert Greene, which is thought perhaps to have influenced Shakespeare.

Oberon. In Shakespeare's *Midsummer Night's Dream*, the King of the Fairies, who quarrels with his wife Titania. It is the magic liquid which he drops into her eyes (and thus causes her to fall in love with the first creature she sees on wakening), and which Puck drops into the eyes of various human participants in the play, that makes possible the various misunderstandings and misdirected affections upon which the plot depends.

Obidicut (ọ.bid′i.kut). In Shakespeare's *King Lear*, a fiend ("of lust") mentioned by Edgar (IV.i).

obiter dictum (ob′i.tėr dik′tum). [Plural, **obiter dicta**.] Something said by the way or incidentally, and not as the result of deliberate judgment; a passing remark; specifically, an incidental opinion given by a judge, in contradistinction from his judicial decision of the essential point.

O'Carolan (ọ.kar′ọ.lạn), **Turlogh.** [Also, **Carolan.**] b. in County Meath, Ireland, c1670; d. March 25, 1738. An Irish minstrel. Blinded in 1684 by smallpox, he was one of the last of the improvising wandering bards, and traveled with a harp from door to door, composing songs named for his hosts.

O'Casey (ọ.kā′si), **Sean.** b. at Dublin, 1884—. An Irish playwright, notably of works dealing with topical social problems. He was born of a poor family, Protestants in the generally Catholic community, and after a short period of formal education went to work at manual jobs. Bitterly resentful of British exploitation of Irish workers, he joined in the transport strike of 1913. Later he became a member of the Irish Citizen Army, of whose uprising in the Easter Rebellion of 1916 he wrote a prose account, although, being in jail at the time, he was not a participant. An outspoken individual of strong convictions in literature as well as in life, O'Casey fought the Abbey Theatre's rejection of his expressionistic play, *The Silver Tassie;* attacked English critics (who did not appreciate his *Within the Gates*) in another play, *The Flying Wasp;* presented controversial matters so frankly that his *The Plough and the Stars* incited a riot when it was

produced. He wrote with a deep understanding of common people, with a socialist's indignation at the poverty of Dublin in particular and at the power of moneyed groups of all kinds. He is noted for his powerful language, vivid opposition of historic events and the common people affected by them, ability to create intensely human character, and moral integrity that expresses itself in irony and indignation of considerable dramatic effect. Several of his works, including *The Shadow of a Gunman* (1923) which depicts the struggle between the Irish Republican Army and the Crown forces in 1920, were written especially for the Abbey Theatre at Dublin. He was awarded (1926) the Hawthornden prize for *Juno and the Paycock* (1924), in which the civil war of 1922 between Irish Free Staters and extremist Irish Republicans is the background for a poor family's hope of an inheritance and its disappointment. *The Plough and the Stars* (1926) deals with the unsuccessful Easter Rebellion of 1916, and *The Silver Tassie* (1928) concerns itself with World War I. His other plays include *Within the Gates* (1933), dealing with the unemployed in England, *Purple Dust* (1940), and *Red Roses for Me* (1946). He has written reminiscences of his life in *I Knock at the Door* (1939), *Pictures in the Hallway* (1941), *Inishfallen, Fare Thee Well* (1949), and *Rose and Crown* (1952).

Occam (ok′ạm), **William of.** See **Ockham, William of.**

Occleve (ok′lēv), **Thomas.** [Also, **Hoccleve.**] b. c1370; d. c1450. English poet. He was the author of a *Complaint*, a *Dialogue*, and *La Male Règle* (1406), all autobiographical, and *Mother of God*, a religious poem, once assigned to Geoffrey Chaucer. His chief work, however, is usually considered to have been *De Regimine Principum* (c1411–12), a long poem on the responsibilities of a prince or ruler, dedicated to Henry, Prince of Wales (later Henry V).

Oceana (ō.shẹ.ā′nạ), **The Commonwealth of.** A philosophical treatise on the theory of civil government, by James Harrington, published in 1656.

Oceanus (ọ.sē′ạ.nus). In the belief of ancient geographers, a swift and unbounded stream that encircled all the world.

Oceanus. In classical mythology, the ocean personified, the husband of Tethys.

Ochiltree (ō′chil.trē, -kil-, och′il-, ok′il-), **Edie.** In Sir Walter Scott's novel *The Antiquary*, a king's beadsman or licensed beggar, called "Blue Gown" from his costume.

Ochino (ō.kē′nō) or **Occhino** (ōk.kē′nō), **Bernardino.** b. at Siena, Italy, 1487; d. at Schlackau, in Moravia, c1565. An Italian reformer. He was a Franciscan and became (1534) a Capuchin. He was named vicar general of the Capuchins in 1538 and 1541. He had become a believer in justification by faith, probably through the influence of Juan de Valdés, and, some of his utterances reflecting this, was called (1542) to Rome to answer to the Inquisition newly established there. Instead he fled to Geneva, where he became a prize convert of John Calvin. He became a minister at Augsburg in 1545, fled to England in 1547 when the forces of the emperor Charles V took the city, and was welcomed at

Canterbury. When Mary Tudor came to the English throne, he returned (1555) to Switzerland, becoming a pastor at Zurich. In 1563 he incurred the anger of the Calvinists by his publication of *Thirty Dialogues*, in which he went counter to doctrine on the subjects of polygamy, divorce, and the Trinity. He was expelled and went to Poland, but was forced to leave there in 1564; he died in Moravia still seeking asylum. He was the author of *A Tragedy or Dialogue of the unjust usurped Primacy of the Bishop of Rome* (1549), thought by some to have influenced John Milton in his writing of *Paradise Lost*.

Ockham (ok′ạm), **William of.** [Also: **Occam**; known as **Doctor Invincibilis, Venerabilis Inceptor, Princeps Nominalium.**] b. at Ockham, Surrey, some time between 1270 and 1300; d. at Munich, c1349. An English scholastic philosopher. A Franciscan, he studied at Oxford and Paris, where he was the pupil of his later great rival Duns Scotus. In 1322 he was present at the Franciscan assembly at Perugia that defended against Pope John XXII the principle of evangelical poverty. He was called to Avignon in 1328 and imprisoned there for heresy, but escaped after a few months (along with several other rebels, including Michael of Cesena, the general of the Franciscans) to Pisa, where he was taken under the protection of the emperor Louis IV. The emperor and the pope were engaged in a struggle concerning the temporal power of the papacy and Ockham contributed to the imperial cause with his *Opus nonaginta Dierum* (1330), an answer to John XXII's attack on Michael of Cesena, and with other polemical writings. He became general of the order after Michael of Cesena's death in 1342. His greatest work, the *Dialogus* (c1343), is an attack on the civil authority of the papacy and includes also arguments against even the spiritual powers claimed by the pope. Ockham's philosophy is a revival of the nominalism of such earlier philosophers as Peter Abelard. He distinguishes between the fact and its name: the individual thing is the reality, the universal (its name or noun) is an abstraction and a generalization, and therefore a subjective and conventional tool. Such abstractions have no actual relation to reality; therefore, intellectual knowledge is not valid; the only true approach to such questions of reality as immortality, the nature of the soul, and the existence of God is through intuition. The principle known as Ockham's razor or the law of parsimony is a consequence of this logic: *Entia non sunt multiplicanda praeter necessitatem* (entities must not be multiplied beyond what is necessary), that is, an argument must be shaved down to its absolutely essential and simplest terms.

Ockley (ok′li), **Simon.** b. at Exeter, England, 1678; d. at Swavesey, Cambridgeshire, England, Aug. 9, 1720. An English Orientalist. His chief work is a *History of the Saracens* (2 vols., 1708–18; vol. 3, 1757).

Ocnus (ok′nus). In Greek mythology, the droll of the underworld and personification of delay or futile effort. He is described as forever plaiting a straw rope, which his ass devours as fast as he makes it: or sometimes he is shown loading the ass with sticks which keep falling off.

O Come, All Ye Faithful. See *Adeste fideles.*

O'Connor (ọ.kon′ọr), **Thomas Power.** [Known as **Tay Pay.**] b. at Athlone, Oct. 5, 1845; d. Nov. 18, 1929. An Irish politician and journalist. A free-lance journalist at London after 1870, he wrote *Lord Beaconsfield: a Biography* (1879), an attack on Benjamin Disraeli that brought him much attention. He entered Parliament in 1880 and served there continuously until his death. He became an active member of the Parnellite party, and was elected president of the Irish National League of Great Britain in 1883. Although he was one of those who deserted Parnell in 1891, he continued home-rule agitation, especially through his writings in papers he founded. He established and edited the *Star*, *Sun*, *Sunday Sun*, and *T. P.'s Weekly*, the latter in 1902 as a literary journal in which he published his observations on life. He was the author of *Gladstone's House of Commons* (1885), *The Parnell Movement* (1886), and other books.

octameter (ok.tam′ẹ.tẻr). In prosody, a verse or period consisting of eight measures. This word is little used, except in the sense of "octapody" by some writers on modern versification who confound *measure* with *foot*.

octave. In versification: 1. A stanza of eight lines; especially, the ottava rima.

> With moneful melodie it continued this octave.
> (Sir P. Sidney, *Arcadia.*)

2. The first two quatrains or eight lines in a sonnet.

> It requires no doubt considerable ingenuity to construct a satisfactory sonnet running upon two rhymes in the octave and two in the sestet.
> (*Athenæum*, No. 3141.)

Octavia (ok.tā′vi.ạ). In Shakespeare's *Antony and Cleopatra*, the rather conventional and matronly wife of Antony. She accepts marriage with Antony in an effort to reconcile him and her brother Octavius, but Antony deserts her for Cleopatra. She also appears in Dryden's *All for Love.*

Octavian (ok.tā′vi.ạn). A 15th-century romance relating to the emperor Augustus (who was born Gaius Octavius, and is often still called Octavian by some sources). There are two English versions from a French original, *Octavien* or *Florent et Lyon.*

Octavian. In the younger George Colman's play *The Mountaineer*, an inspired maniac.

Octavius Caesar (ok.tā′vi.us sē′zạr). In Shakespeare's *Julius Caesar*, one of the triumvirs after Caesar's death and a victorious general in the civil war against Cassius and Brutus. Shakespeare's *Antony and Cleopatra* has him marrying off his sister Octavia to Antony, ridding himself of Lepidus, the other triumvir, and making war on Cleopatra and Antony after the latter has deserted Octavia and fled to Egypt. Defeating Antony at Actium, he then invades Egypt and after the suicides of Antony and Cleopatra is left in control of the Roman Empire. The historical Octavius (63 B.C.–14 A.D.) was Caesar's nephew and became emperor of Rome in 27 B.C.

octavo. [Usually written **8vo.**] A book or pamphlet every section or gathering of which contains eight leaves, each sheet supposed to be one eighth of the sheet printed. When the name of the paper of which the book is made is not specified, an octavo is understood as a medium octavo, 6 by 9½ inches.

October Club, The. A former club of English Tories, very influential in the reign of Anne.

October and Other Poems. A volume of verse (1920) by Robert Bridges.

octosyllabic. In prosody, consisting of eight syllables. "The grave dignity of Vergil's style, its continuous flow and stately melody, are misrepresented in the octosyllabic lines of *Marmion*." (*Edinburgh Review.*)

ode. 1. A lyric poem expressive of exalted or enthusiastic emotion, especially one of complex or irregular metrical form; originally and strictly, such a composition intended to be sung.

> See how from far, upon the eastern road,
> The star-led wisards haste with odours sweet;
> O, run, prevent them with thy humble ode,
> And lay it lowly at his blessed feet!
> (Milton, *Nativity.*)

The Odes of Pindar which remain to us are Songs of Triumph, Victory, or Success in the Grecian Games.   (Congreve, *On the Pindaric Ode.*)

2. The music to which such a poem is set.
3. In ancient prosody, the fourth part of the parabasis of a comedy. Also called the *strophe.*

Ode. A poem by Arthur O'Shaughnessy, originally consisting of seven stanzas, but cut down by Palgrave to its present three. It is considered by some critics to be one of the classics of the last years of the 19th century. It opens with the famous lines:

> We are the music-makers
> And we are the dreamers of dreams.

Ode for Saint Cecilia's Day (sē.sil'yąz). See **Alexander's Feast.**

Ode on a Grecian Urn. A poem (1819) by John Keats, one of the most famous of the works produced by any of the Romantic poets. It was inspired by the ageless beauty of the figures on an ancient Greek urn, and ends with the well-known lines:

> "Beauty is truth, truth beauty,"—that is all
> Ye know on earth, and all ye need to know.

Ode on a Distant Prospect of Eton College. See **Distant Prospect of Eton College.**

Ode on the Athenian Society. An early poem by Jonathan Swift, written in the form of a Pindaric ode, published (1692) in *The Athenian Gazette.* It is the only piece of his early verse that he published.

Ode on the Death of a Favorite Cat, Drowned in a Tub of Gold Fishes. A poem by Thomas Gray (1716–71), referring to a cat owned by Horace Walpole.

Ode on the Morning of Christ's Nativity. A poem (1629) by John Milton, in which the poet develops the theme that Christ was born to redeem fallen man, and "with his father work us a perpetual grace," an idea which he later developed more fully in *Paradise Lost* and *Paradise Regained.* Most critics agree that from the point of view of form, it is one of the most perfect poems in English literature. It consists of 27 eight-line stanzas.

Ode on the Poetical Character. A poem by William Collins, explaining his theories of poetry, elaborating the tradition of which he feels himself a part, and recalling the masters in this tradition. He believed poetry should be imaginative and wild, and that it should be stirred by divine passion. He associated himself with Milton and Shakespeare, rather than with Pope and Dryden.

Ode to England. One of William Collins's best-known poems included in *Odes* (1747).

Ode to the Queen. A poem (1706) by William Congreve. It is of some importance in the study of the development of poetic forms in English because of the section entitled "Discourse," in which he attempts to regularize the discipline of the Pindaric ode.

Ode to the West Wind. A poem (1819) by Percy Bysshe Shelley, written in the same year as Keats's *Ode on a Grecian Urn*, with which work it shares renown as one of the greatest poems of the Romantic Age. It is an unrestrained invocation of the wild West Wind, and closes with the well-known lines:

> The trumpet of a prophecy! O, Wind,
> If Winter comes, can Spring be far behind?

Odin (ō'din). [Also: **Othin, Wodan, Woden.**] In Old Norse mythology, the chief god of the Aesir and lord of Asgard, the home of the Aesir (the high gods). He is a warrior god, and lord of Valhalla, the paradise of heroes slain in battle. He is one-eyed, having given one eye in exchange for one draught from the well of wisdom. Thus he is the source of wisdom, and the patron of culture and of heroes. He is attended by two ravens, his informants, and two wolves, his watchdogs. He is devoured by the Fenis-wolf at Ragnarök, the great battle at the end of the world. Frigga is his consort. His name survives in Wednesday (Woden's day).

O'Dowd (ō.doud'), **Bernard Patrick.** b. at Beaufort, Victoria, Australia, April 11, 1866—. An Australian poet and lawyer. He was assistant librarian of the Victoria Supreme Court (1887–1913), first assistant state parliamentary draftsman (1913–31), and parliamentary draftsman (1931–35). He began publishing pamphlets of verse in 1903, and subsequently built up a reputation as a major poet of intellectualist tendencies, keenly reformist or "socialist" in outlook. His most famous single work is *The Bush* (1912).

O'Dowd, Glorvina. In Thackeray's novel *Vanity Fair*, the sister of Major O'Dowd.

O'Dowd, Major. [Later, **General Sir Michael O'Dowd, K.C.B.**] In Thackeray's novel *Vanity Fair*, a courageous soldier, whose valor and skill in battle provides a sharp contrast to his meekness under the eye of his domineering wife.

O'Dowd, Mrs. [Called **Peggy.**] In Thackeray's novel *Vanity Fair*, a good-humored but strong-minded woman, who exercises absolute control over her husband.

Odysseus (ō.dis'ūs, ō.dis'ē.us). [Latin, **Ulysses, Ulixes.**] In Greek legend, a king of Ithaca, one of the heroes of the Trojan War, especially famous for his wanderings and exploits on the ten-year homeward voyage, related in the *Odyssey.* He was the

ḍ, d or j; ṣ, s or sh; ṭ, t or ch; ẓ, z or zh; o, F. cloche; ü, F. menu; ċh, Sc. loch; ṅ, F. bonbon.

son of Laertes, the husband of Penelope, and the father of Telemachus. His courage, craftiness, strategy, and resourcefulness in all emergencies make him the ideal representative of the Ionic Greeks.

Odyssey (od′i.si). An epic poem, attributed to Homer, in which are celebrated the adventures of Odysseus (Ulysses) during the ten years of wandering, spent in repeated endeavors to return to Ithaca, his native island, after the close of the Trojan War. Some critics, both ancient and modern, who have acknowledged the Homeric origin of the *Iliad*, attribute the *Odyssey* to a different author. These critics believe that the *Odyssey* is a later poem. The *Odyssey* is the only complete surviving example of a whole class of epics, called *Nostoi*, describing the return voyages of various Greek heroes from Troy. It represents Odysseus as being driven by a storm at the outset of his voyage to the coast of Thrace, north of the island of Lemnos. He plundered the town of Ismarus, belonging to the Cicones, where he lost a number of his followers. Next he was driven to the country of the Lotophagi (the Lotus-Eaters) on the coast of Libya; then to the goat island, which lay a day's voyage to the north of the Lotophagi. Leaving behind all his ships except one, he sailed to the neighboring island of the Cyclopes (the W coast of Sicily), where with 12 companions he entered the cave of the one-eyed Cyclops, Polyphemus, a son of Poseidon. Polyphemus devoured six of the intruders, and kept Odysseus and the others prisoners. Odysseus made Polyphemus drunk with wine, put out his one eye with a burning pole, and escaped with the remnant of his companions by concealing himself and them under the bellies of the sheep which the blinded Cyclops let out of his cave (he ran his hands over their backs, but forgot that his enemies might be clinging to their bellies). Thenceforth, however, Odysseus was pursued by the anger of Poseidon, who sought to avenge the injury inflicted on his son. After further adventures, in which he lost all his ships except one, he arrived at the island of Aeaea, inhabited by the sorceress Circe. At her instance he made a journey to Hades, where he consulted the shade of the seer Tiresius. He then sailed by the island of the Sirens (near the W coast of Italy), passed between Scylla and Charybdis, and arrived at Trinacria, the island of Apollo. Here his companions killed some of the sacred oxen belonging to the god, with the result that they were all drowned in a shipwreck after leaving the island. Odysseus escaped with his life to the island of Ogygia, inhabited by the nymph Calypso, with whom he lived eight years. Leaving Ogygia on a raft built with the assistance of the nymph, he was again shipwrecked, but reached the island of the Phaeacians, where he was discovered naked by Nausicaa (the daughter of Alcinous, their king), clothed, and presented at court, where he told his story. He was carried to Ithaca by the hospitable Phaeacians, and after slaying the suitors of his wife Penelope, who had been wasting his property during his absence, was welcomed by his wife and subjects.

Oedipus (ed′i.pus, ē′di-). In Greek legend, a king of Thebes; son of Laius and Jocasta. Because of a prophecy that he would kill his father and marry his mother, the infant Oedipus was taken out and abandoned in the mountains, with a spike through his feet (Oedipus means literally "swollen foot"). He was found, however, by a shepherd who took him to the king of Corinth, and here he was reared as the king's son. When Oedipus was grown and learned that he was destined to kill his father and marry his mother, he ran away from home, heading for Thebes. En route he met Laius in a narrow pass, and killed him in an argument over the right of way. Thus unknowingly Oedipus fulfilled the first half of the prophecy. When he arrived at Thebes, he was confronted with the Sphinx, guessed the riddle of the Sphinx, thereby liberating the city of Thebes from the monster and all future non-guessers from being devoured, and for this he was rewarded with the hand of the queen of Thebes (Jocasta) in marriage. Thus unknowingly he married his mother and fulfilled the second half of the prophecy. The couple lived in happy ignorance for several years, but eventually Oedipus learned the truth, and blinded himself in self-punishment. Jocasta hanged herself. It was this story, or parts of it, which provided the basis of three of Sophocles's greatest tragedies (*Oedipus Rex*, *Antigone*, and *Oedipus at Colonus*); many later writers and composers (even into the 20th century, with Jean Cocteau and Igor Stravinsky) have made adaptations of it.

Oeneus (ē′nūs). In Greek legend, the king of Calydon, husband of Althaea, and father of Meleager and Tydeus.

Oenomaus (en.ọ.mā′us, ē.nọ-). In Greek mythology, a son of Ares and father of Hippodamia, whose suitors he killed until Pelops overcame him by strategy and won her.

Oenone (ẹ.nō′nẹ). In Greek legend, the beloved of Paris before he knew Helen. She was a nymph of Mount Ida, and versed in healing. When Paris received an arrow wound in the Trojan War, he sought her help, but out of jealousy she refused him. When he died she threw herself on his funeral pyre in grief and remorse. Tennyson used her story as the subject of two poems, *Oenone* and *The Death of Oenone*.

Oenone. In George Peele's pastoral comedy *The Arraignment of Paris*, the sweetheart of Paris, to whom he is unfaithful.

O'Faoláin (ọ.fal′ạn), **Seán.** b. at Cork, Ireland, Feb. 22, 1900—. An Irish writer. Author of the short-story collections *Midsummer Night Madness* (1932) and *A Purse of Coppers* (1937), the novels *A Nest of Simple Folk* (1933) and *Come Back to Erin* (1940), the biographies *Constance Markievicz* (1934), *King of the Beggars* (1938; about Daniel O'Connell), *De Valera* (1939), and *The Great O'Neill* (1942), the survey sketch of his people, *The Irish* (1947), and others.

Offa's Dyke (of′ạz). An entrenchment extending from near the mouth of the river Wye N near the border of England and Wales to the mouth of the river Dee. It was built in the 8th century for defense against the Welsh by Offa, king of Mercia.

Of Human Bondage. A novel by W. Somerset Maugham, published in 1915. It is the story of a sensitive young man, Philip Carey, who goes through life with a feeling of inferiority because of a clubfoot. Philip, an orphan, goes to Blackstable to live with his aunt and uncle, Louisa and William Carey, when he is nine. His deformity makes life at school so unbearable that he leaves. Later he goes to Heidelberg, where he learns to appreciate art under the instruction of Hayward. He returns to Blackstable and has his first affair; the woman involved, Emily Wilkinson, is older than Philip. He is then articled to an accountant in London, but leaves to study art in Paris. Philip's ambition in art is lost when he finds that he can never produce any great works. He goes to London to study medicine, and here finds his natural vocation. New problems arise when he meets two women, the waitress Mildred Rogers and the writer Norah Nesbit. His infatuation for Mildred, a worthless girl, leads to his destitution. Philip is aided by Thorpe Athelny, a new friend, and finally inherits a small estate which enables him to pursue his medical studies. He marries Athelny's daughter, Sally, and acquires a small country medical practice.

O'Flaherty (ọ.fla'hėr.ti), **Liam.** b. in the Aran Islands, 1896—. An Irish novelist. His *Thy Neighbor's Wife* (1924) was followed by *The Informer* (1925), which was turned into a screen play which won (1935) the Motion Picture Academy of Arts and Sciences award. Author also of *Mr. Gilhooley* (1926), *The Assassin* (1928), *Famine* (1937), *Land* (1946), *Two Lovely Beasts and Other Stories* (1950), and others.

O'Flaherty, V. C. A play (1915) by George Bernard Shaw, included by most critics among his lesser plays.

Og (og). An Amorite king of Bashan, defeated by the Hebrews. He was a giant. Deut. iii.11.

Og. In Dryden's *Absalom and Achitophel*, a character intended to represent the portly Thomas Shadwell (by allusion to the Biblical Og, mentioned in Deuteronomy as a man of such size as to require a bed nine cubits long by four cubits wide).

Ogier the Dane (ō'ji.ėr). [Danish, **Holger Danske, Olger Dansk** (ôl'gėr dänsk'); French, **Ogier le Danois** (o.zhyā lẹ dả.nwà), **Ogier de Danemarcke** (dẹ dản.màrk).] A national hero of Denmark, celebrated in the ballads, folk songs, and legends of Denmark. The story is that he now lies asleep in the Kronenberg mountain and will wake to rescue his country in time of danger. In the medieval French *chansons de geste*, he is a Danish prince, but one of the paladins of Charlemagne. Ogier, the son of Geoffrey, king of Denmark, is brought up at the court of Charlemagne, and at one period of the romance assumes the crown of Denmark; but he tires of it and returns to Charlemagne, becoming one of his chief paladins. After a successful warlike career, at the age of 100 years he is carried away to the Isle of Avalon by Morgan le Fay, who restores him to youth, with entire forgetfulness of the world, but sends him back after 200 years to defend France. After repelling its invaders and restoring the old spirit of knighthood, he returns to Avalon, where he sleeps, and whence he may again awake and return to defend the right.

Ogilby (ō'gl.bi), **John.** b. at Edinburgh, 1600; d. at London, Sept. 4, 1676. A Scottish poet, translator,

and compiler of atlases. He published *America, being the most accurate Description of the New World* (1671), as well as translations of the *Iliad* and *Odyssey*, Aesop's fables, and others, and three epic poems. He is ridiculed in John Dryden's *MacFlecknoe* and Alexander Pope's *The Dunciad*.

Ogilvie (ō'gl.vi), **John.** b. in Marnoch, Banffshire, Scotland, April 17, 1797; d. at Aberdeen, Scotland, Nov. 21, 1867. A Scottish lexicographer. He compiled *The Imperial Dictionary* (1847–50), *The Comprehensive English Dictionary* (1863), *The Student's English Dictionary* (1865), and *An English Dictionary . . . for the Use of Schools* (1867).

Ogle (ō'gl). A character in Susannah Centlivre's comedy *The Beau's Duel*, who fancies everybody is in love with him.

Ogleby (ō'gl.bi), **Lord.** In David Garrick and the elder George Colman's *The Clandestine Marriage*, a faded and delicate but witty old beau.

Ogygia (ọ.jij'i.ạ). In classical geography, the island of Calypso, referred to in the *Odyssey*. Plutarch says it lies due west, beneath the setting sun.

Oig (oig), **Robin.** See **M'Combich, Robin Oig.**

Oisin (u.shēn'). In Old Irish legend, the son of Fionn mac Cumhal (Finn MacCool) and Sadb (the first wife of Fionn). Oisin was born in the forest and found and brought home by Fionn's famous dog, Bran. He grew up to be one of the most famous of the Fianna (the warriors of Fionn) and was also noted as a poet and musician. Several poems in the Old Irish *Book of Leinster* are said to be his. One of the best-known stories about Oisin is *Oisin in the Land of Youth*, in which Oisin is beguiled off to the typical Celtic fairy otherworld by a fairy woman, and returns 150 years later to find Fionn and the Fianna long dead and hymn-singing Christians in Ireland. William Butler Yeats's *Wanderings of Oisin* also presents this story. The most famous of the Oisin stories, however, is the 13th-century *Colloquoy of the Old Men*, describing the return of the hero to Ireland, his meeting with Saint Patrick, his sojourn with the monks, and the long paganism-versus-Christianity discussion between Oisin and the monks, ending with Oisin's choice of hell (being assured that Fionn was there) over the Christian heaven. James Macpherson's *Ossian* is based on the Oisin legends.

O'Keeffe (ọ.kēf'), **John.** b. at Dublin, Ireland, June 24, 1747; d. at Southampton, England, Feb. 4, 1833. An Irish dramatist. William Hazlitt says he may be called "the English Molière," but posterity has accorded him a somewhat less elevated position in English letters. He wrote comedies and farces, including *Wild Oats* (1791), *The Poor Soldier* (1783), and others. He is best remembered for his song from *Merry Sherwood* "I am a friar of orders grey."

O'Kelly (ọ.kel'i), **Seumas.** b. 1881; d. 1918. An Irish novelist, short-story writer, and playwright. His best-known play is *The Shuiler's Child* (1909). He also wrote *The Bribe* (1913) and *The Parnellite* (1917).

Old Bachelor, The. A comedy by William Congreve, produced in 1693, and acted as late as 1789. It was his first play. Heartwell, the "old bachelor," falls in love with the trollop, Sylvia, formerly Vainlove's mistress, but his "marriage" to her is performed by the disguised Bellamour, Vainlove's friend, who plays the part of a fanatical Puritan preacher, Tribulation Spintext, in order that he may more conveniently cuckold the banker, Fondlewife. Sylvia is truly married finally to Sir Joseph Wittol, a foolish knight, who has offended Vainlove and who takes her to be the wealthy Araminta. Bellamour is in love with Bellinda, but this does not deter him from an escapade with Fondlewife's wife, Laetitia. Another romance ends in the marriage of Araminta and Vainlove. In its original performance, the play had an excellent cast, including Betterton, Mrs. Barry, Mrs. Bracegirdle, and Mrs. Mountfort.

Old Bailey Court (bā′li). The principal criminal court of England. It was on the street named Old Bailey, which runs from Newgate Street to Ludgate Hill. The new Central Criminal Court was opened in 1905.

Old Barnacle (bär′na.kl). See **Barnacle, Young** and **Old.**

Old Beaugard (bō′gärd). See **Beaugard, Old.**

Old Bellair (bel.âr′). See **Bellair, Old.**

Old Bill Barley (bär′li). See **Barley, Old Bill.**

Oldbuck (ōld′buk), **Jonathan.** Laird of Monkbarns and Scottish antiquary (he is an ardent collector of coins and medals), the leading character in Sir Walter Scott's novel *The Antiquary*. He is eccentric and easily irritated, but essentially benevolent.

Old Calabria (ka.lā′bri.a). A novel by Norman Douglas, published in 1928.

Old Captivity, An. A novel by Nevil Shute, published in 1940.

Oldcastle (ōld′kàs′'l), **Sir John.** See under **Falstaff, Sir John;** for the play, see **Sir John Oldcastle.**

Oldcraft (ōld′kràft), **Sir Perfidious.** One of the principal characters in *Wit at Several Weapons*, by John Fletcher and others.

Old Curiosity Shop, The. A novel by Charles Dickens, published in 1840–41. As the story opens, Little Nell and her old grandfather are living in the Old Curiosity Shop, but the grandfather is presently reduced to utter destitution when he gambles away the last of the money borrowed from Quilp, a vicious, dwarflike creature, one of the most terrifying of all of Dickens's villains. Quilp has been happy to loan money to the old man, because of the mistaken notion that he is a miser, and that he has a fortune hidden in the Old Curiosity Shop. When Quilp discovers this to be false, he falls into a towering rage, and Nell and her grandfather are forced to flee from his malice. They wander through the land, working in puppet shows and Mrs. Jarley's Wax Works, and finally settle in a little house next to a church, where Nell tends the graves. Meanwhile the brother of Nell's grandfather has returned from abroad and wishes to help them, but he returns too late. Little Nell has died, and her grandfather follows soon after. The evil Quilp is drowned as he tries to escape the police. Among the other characters are Kit Nubbles, the faithful friend of Nell; Dick Swiveller, a happy-go-lucky fellow; Sampson and Sally Brass, confederates of the villain; and "the Marchioness," the poor little maid-of-all-work of the Brasses.

Old Delabole (del′a.bōl). A novel (1915) by Eden Phillpotts.

Old Dornton (dôrn′ton). See **Dornton, Old.**

Old English. See under **English.**

Old English. A drama (1924) by John Galsworthy.

"Old English Annals." See **Anglo-Saxon Chronicle.**

Old English Baron, The. A story by Clara Reeve, published in 1777, intended to combine the romance and the novel by making the former more probable.

Oldfield (ōld′fēld), **Anne.** b. at London, 1683; d. there, Oct. 23, 1730. An English actress. In 1704 Colley Cibber assigned to her the part of Lady Betty Modish in his *Careless Husband*, and she won immediate success. By 1706 she was held to be the rival of Mrs. Bracegirdle. She was the original representative of 65 characters, the greater part of which belong to genteel comedy. She played tragic parts with great dignity and feeling, but in Lady Betty Modish, Lady Townley, Sylvia, and Mrs. Sullen she was probably never equaled. She lived for some years with Arthur Mainwaring, a wealthy bachelor, by whom she had a son who bore his father's name and surname. Later, after the death of Mainwaring, she was "under the protection" of General Charles Churchill, the son of an elder brother of the Duke of Marlborough, by whom she had also one son.

Old Flame, The. A novel by A. P. Herbert, published in 1925.

Old Fortunatus (fôr.tū.nā′tus). A play by Thomas Dekker, printed in 1600 with the title *The Pleasant History of Old Fortunatus*. The first part was performed in 1596, and no second part is mentioned by Henslowe, although one dating from c1599 appears to have existed. The play as it now exists probably represents the two parts boiled down to one. A portion of it may have been written as early as 1590, judging from allusions in it to the Martin Marprelate controversy.

Old Gobbo (gob′ō). See **Gobbo, Old.**

Old Grimes (grīmz). The title of one of George Crabbe's tales in verse; also, that of a ballad by Albert G. Greene.

Oldham (ōl′dam), **John.** b. at Shipton Moyne, Gloucestershire, England, Aug. 9, 1653; d. at Holme Pierrepoint, Nottinghamshire, England, Dec. 9, 1683. An English satirical poet. His *Four Satires upon the Jesuits* (1679) attracted much attention, coming on the heels of Titus Oates's revelation of the alleged "Popish Plot." He also wrote *Some New Pieces* (1681).

Old Heads and Young Hearts. A play by Dion Boucicault, produced in 1844.

Old Hundredth or **Old Hundred.** A popular psalm tune, first published in the *Genevan Psalter* (c1551–52) edited by Louis Bourgeois. It was originally adapted to Théodore de Bèze's version of the 134th Psalm, but when adopted in England was set to William Kethe's version of the 100th Psalm. It was at first known as the "Hundredth," but in 1696, when Nahum Tate and Nicholas Brady published their "New Version," the word "Old" was used to show that the tune was the one which had been in use in the previous Psalter (Sternhold and Hopkins's of the 16th century). It is now generally sung to the doxology, "Praise God, from whom all blessings flow."

Old Huntsman, The. A volume of verse (1917) by Siegfried Sassoon, the first of his books of anti-war verse.

Old King Cole (kōl). A nursery rhyme, probably connected with the King Cole who, according to the old chroniclers, reigned in Britain in the 3rd century.

Old Ladies, The. A novel (1924) by Hugh Walpole. It is the story of three old women living together, who have no understanding of one another.

Old Lady. In Shakespeare's *Henry VIII*, a companion to Anne Bullen (II.iii). She somewhat resembles the Nurse in *Romeo and Juliet*.

"Old Lady of Threadneedle Street" (thred'nē"dl). A name often applied to the Bank of England.

Old Law, or a New Way to Please You, The. A play published in 1656 as by Philip Massinger, Thomas Middleton, and William Rowley. The original play was probably written by Middleton in 1599 and acted c1600. Rowley may have revised it (c1615) and Massinger again (c1625).

Old Madge (maj). See **Madge, Old.**

Old Madhouse, The. A novel by William De Morgan, published in 1919. Left unfinished at his death, it was completed by his wife, Evelyn De Morgan.

Old Mahon (ma̱.hön', -hōn'). See **Mahon, Old.**

Old Maids. A comedy by J. Sheridan Knowles, produced in 1841.

Old Man. In Shakespeare's *King Lear*, one of Gloucester's tenants. He leads the blinded Earl, and is sent by him for clothes for Tom o' Bedlam (IV.i).

Old Man. In Shakespeare's *Macbeth*, a minor character (III.iv).

Old Man of the Sea, The. In *The Arabian Nights' Entertainments*, an old man who asked to be carried across a brook on the back of Sindbad the sailor, then clung to him and refused to dismount. Sindbad finally managed to smash his head and thus got rid of him. The name is applied, in literary allusion, to any person of whom one cannot get rid.

Old Man's Youth, The. A novel by William De Morgan, published in 1921. Left unfinished at his death, it was completed by his wife, Evelyn De Morgan.

Old Man Taught Wisdom, An. [Full title, **An Old Man Taught Wisdom, or The Virgin Unmask'd.**] A ballad opera by Henry Fielding, produced in 1734 and printed in 1735.

old men's tale. See **old wives' tale.**

Old Mirabel (mir'a̱.bel). See **Mirabel, Old.**

Oldmixon (ōld'mik.sǫn), **John.** b. in Somersetshire, England, 1673; d. at London, July 9, 1742. An English historical writer. He abused Alexander Pope in his *Essay on Criticism in Prose* (1728), and was promptly replied to by a scathing attack in the *Dunciad* (ii. 283). Among his other works are *The British Empire in America* (1708), *Critical History of England* (1724–26), *History of England* (1729–39), and *Memoirs of the Press* (1742).

Old Mole (mōl). A novel by Gilbert Cannan, published in 1914. The story of an old schoolmaster, a student of French and Latin literature, its subtitle is the *Surprising Adventures in England of Herbert Jocelyn Benham, M.A., Sometime Sixth-Form Master*.

Old Mortality. A historical novel about the rising of the Covenanters in 1679, by Sir Walter Scott, published in 1816. It is so called from the epithet given to Robert Paterson, who passed his life in restoring the gravestones of the Covenanters.

Old Nick (nik). A popular euphemism for the Devil. Some early scholars ascribed the origin of the name to the malign Germanic water spirits, the nixes, who lie in wait for human beings and lure them to their drowning, but there is no proof for this speculation.

Old Oaken Bucket, The. A popular poem, of which the original title was *The Bucket*, by Samuel Woodworth, an American poet. A sentimental ballad, it was set to music by Frederick Smith (who used a theme which George Kiallmark had composed for *Araby's Daughter*, by Thomas Moore), and in this form became a familiar 19th-century song. The ballad was written c1818.

"Old Parr" (pär). See **Parr, Thomas.**

"Old Pretender." See **Stuart, James Francis Edward.**

"Old Q." See **Douglas, William** (1724–1810).

Old Sarum (sār'um). See under **Salisbury.**

Old Shepherd. See **Shepherd, Old.**

Old Ships, The. The title poem of a volume of verse by James Elroy Flecker, published in 1915.

Old St. Paul's. A novel by William Harrison Ainsworth, published in 1841.

Old Susan. A poem by Walter De la Mare, opening with the well-known line: "When Susan's work was done, she'd sit. . . ."

Old Testament, The. A collection of books, containing the records of the Mosaic covenant, and forming part of the Christian Bible.

Old Vic (vik), **the.** A London theater, opened in 1818. It was originally called the Coburg Theatre (in honor of Prince Leopold of Coburg, husband of Princess Charlotte). Victoria (not yet queen) paid it a visit, and in 1833 it was renamed the Victoria (whence, affectionately, after a period of years, the Old Vic). In 1914 it was established as a Shakespearian theater, which it has since been. The theater building was reopened in 1950, after damage done during bombing raids in World War II had been repaired.

old wives' tale. [Also, **old men's tale.**] A proverbial expression for any tale of a legendary character, dealing usually with the marvelous.

I am content to drive away the time with an old wives' winter's tale.
          (Peele, *Old Wives' Tale* (ed. Bullen).)

I find all these but dreams, and old men's tales,
To fright unsteady youth.
          (Ford, *'Tis Pity*, I.iii.)

Old Wives' Tale, The. A comedy (1593) by George Peele, acted at Court before Queen Elizabeth. It is based on a number of tales from English folklore;

some critics consider it a satire on the extravagant romances of the time. It may have influenced Milton in his writing of *Comus*.

Old Wives' Tale, The. A novel by Arnold Bennett, published in 1908.

Old World Idylls. A volume of verse (1883) by Austin Dobson.

Olifaunt (ol′i.fant), **Nigel.** [Title, **Lord Glenvarloch.**] The principal character in Sir Walter Scott's *Fortunes of Nigel*.

Oliphant (ol′i.fant), **Carolina.** See **Nairne, Carolina.**

Oliphant, Laurence. b. in Cape Town, 1829; d. at Twickenham, England, Dec. 23, 1888. An English traveler, diplomat, and author. In 1867 he joined a semi-mystical community in America, founded by Thomas Lake Harris, who exercised unbounded influence over him. In 1881, his faith in Harris having been destroyed, he took up the scheme for the colonization of Palestine by the Jews. He published *A Journey to Katmandu* (1852), *The Russian Shores of the Black Sea* (1853), works on the Crimean War, *Minnesota* (1855), *The Narrative of the Earl of Elgin's Mission to China and Japan* (1860), *Piccadilly* (1870), *Altiora Peto*, a novel (1883), *Sympneumataea: Evolutionary Forces now active in Man* (1885), *Massollam* (1886), and *Scientific Religion* (1888).

Oliphant, Margaret Oliphant. [Maiden name, **Wilson.**] b. at Wallyford, Midlothian, Scotland, 1828; d. at London, June 25, 1897. A Scottish novelist and biographical writer. Much of her work appeared in *Blackwood's Magazine*. She wrote various stories of Scottish life, such as *Passages in the Life of Mrs. Margaret Maitland of Sunnyside* (1849), *Zaidee* (1855), *Chronicles of Carlingford* (4 novels, 1861–64), and many other novels. She also published a *Life of Edward Irving* (1862), *Historical Sketches of the Reign of George II* (1869), *The Makers of Florence* (1876), *The Literary History of England, 1790–1825* (1882), *The Makers of Venice* (1888), and *Royal Edinburgh* (1890).

Olivant (ol′i.vant). In the Charlemagne cycle of romances, the magic horn of Orlando, or Roland. It could be heard for a distance of 20 miles. In the French *Song of Roland*, Roland (Orlando) blew it in the pass of Roncesvalles as he lay dying, thus recalling Charlemagne and his army.

Oliver (ol′i.vėr). [French, **Olivier** (o.lē.vyā).] In the Charlemagne cycle of romances, one of the 12 peers of Charlemagne. He was the true friend of Roland, or Orlando.

Oliver. In Shakespeare's *As You Like It*, the elder brother of Orlando. He plots to kill Orlando, who thereupon flees to the forest. Later Oliver is saved from a lion, repents, and marries Celia. In Lodge's *Rosalynde*, from which the plot is taken, he is called Saladyne.

Oliver, George. See **Onions, Oliver.**

Oliver Cob (kob). See **Cob, Oliver.**

Oliver Cockwood (kok′wud), **Sir.** See **Cockwood, Sir Oliver.**

Oliver le Dain (lẹ dān′). A barber and intimate adviser of Louis XI of France, introduced as a character in Sir Walter Scott's novel *Quentin Durward*.

Oliver Martext (mär′tekst), **Sir.** See **Martext, Sir Oliver.**

Oliver Proudfute (proud′fut). See **Proudfute, Oliver.**

Oliver Surface (sėr′fas), **Sir.** See **Surface, Sir Oliver.**

Oliver Twist (twist). A novel by Charles Dickens, published in 1837–38. One of its purposes was to promote reform of the abuses in almshouses. Oliver is born in a workhouse, and all trace of his parentage has presently disappeared. The cruel parish beadle, Bumble, apprentices him to an undertaker, Sowerberry, and the boy soon runs away to London in order to escape such a life. There he falls into the hands of the thief, Fagin, and his confederates, Nancy, Bill Sikes, and the Artful Dodger, a pickpocket. The gang tries to teach the boy how to become a skillful thief, but Oliver is saved from this unpleasant fate by the kind Mr. Brownlow, who cares for the boy until the robbers snatch him back. It now emerges that a mysterious character, Monks, is the chief instigator of the boy's persecution. Oliver has found a new friend in Rose Fleming, and to her Nancy (who is not utterly evil) reveals that Oliver is some relation to Monks and to Rose herself. Nancy is murdered by Bill Sikes for divulging this information, and he is accidentally hanged while trying to escape from his pursuers. Monks is now found and confesses that Oliver is his half brother, and that he has been trying to prevent the boy from receiving any of his father's property. Rose proves to be Oliver's aunt. Oliver is taken in by Mr. Brownlow and is educated by him, while Monks dies in prison.

Olivia (ọ.liv′i.ạ). A principal character in Shakespeare's *Twelfth Night*. She eventually marries Sebastian.

Olivia. In William Wycherley's comedy *The Plain Dealer*, a woman with whom Manly is in love; a detracting, treacherous creature who deceives him vilely.

Olivia. A young Frenchwoman in love with Valentine in Oliver Goldsmith's comedy *The Good-natured Man*.

Olivia. The principal character in Hannah Cowley's *A Bold Stroke for a Husband*.

Olivia Primrose (prim′rōz). See **Primrose, Olivia.**

Ollapod (ol′a.pod), **Doctor.** In the younger George Colman's comedy *The Poor Gentleman*, a warlike apothecary, and also a cornet in a militia troop, noted for his "jumble of physic and shooting" and his harmless prescriptions.

Ollivant (ol′i.vant), **Alfred.** b. 1874; d. Jan. 19, 1927. An English novelist, noted as the author of the dog story *Bob, Son of Battle* (1898; published in England under the title *Owd Bob, the Grey Dog of Kenmuir*). His other works include *Danny* (1902), *The Gentleman* (1908), *The Taming of John Blunt* (1911), *The Royal Road* (1912), *Two Men* (1919), and *One Woman* (1920).

Olney Hymns (ol′ni). A collection of hymns written by William Cowper and John Newton, published in 1779. Cowper's contributions include

Hark, My Soul! It is the Lord and *God Moves in a Mysterious Way.*

Olympia (ọ.lim′pi.ạ). In ancient geography, a valley in Elis, in the Peloponnesus, Greece, situated on the Alpheus River. It is famous as the seat of a celebrated sanctuary of Zeus and of the Olympic Games, the most important of the great public games of classical antiquity. The origins of the sanctuary and of the games are anterior to history; according to tradition the games were reorganized, in obedience to the Delphic oracle, in the 9th century B.C.

Olympic Games (ọ.lim′pik). The greatest of the games or festivals of ancient Greece, held every four years in the plain of Olympia in Elis, in honor of Zeus; also, a modern revival of these games, consisting of international competitions in athletics, held every four years, each time in a different country.

Olympic Theatre. A London theater, opened in 1806. Philip Astley, its original manager, had lost 10,000 pounds by 1813 and Robert Elliston took over, renaming it the Little Drury Lane. He rebuilt it in 1818, but he, too, lost money, and sold it to John Scott in 1824. The theater closed in 1899.

Olympus (ọ.lim′pus). In ancient geography, the name of various mountains, but especially of one (elevation, ab. 9,794 ft.) on the borders of Macedonia and Thessaly, regarded as the especial home of the chief gods of Greek mythology. Hence the word is often used to mean heaven. The Mysian Olympus was on the borders of Mysia, Bithynia, and Phrygia in Asia Minor. Others were in Lydia, Lycia, Cyprus, Laconia, and Elis. There are believed to have been 14 in all.

Om (ōm). A holy or mystic syllable, important in the Hindu and Buddhist religions. Originally it was a syllable of affirmation out of the Vedic incantations and hymns of praise, and could be literally translated as "aye" or "amen." It affirms the universe, and not only affirms, but in itself is the expression of creation and absolute truth. Much of the *Upanishads* treat of the mystic meaning of Om, as summing up in itself all truth. In later Hinduism it is regarded as representing the divine triad: Brahma, the creator, Vishnu, the preserver, and Shiva, the destroyer.

Oman (ō′mạn), Sir **Charles William Chadwick.** b. in India, 1860; d. June 23, 1946. An English historian. He was a fellow of All Souls College, Oxford (1883–1946), and Chichele professor of modern history, Oxford (1905 *et seq.*). Author of *Warwick the Kingmaker* (1891), *A History of the Art of War in the Middle Ages* (1898), *A History of the Peninsular War* (7 vols., 1907–30), *A History of England Before the Norman Conquest* (1910), *The Art of War in the 16th Century* (1937), and others. He was general editor of the eight-volume *History of England.*

Omar (ō′mär, -mạr). [Also, **Omar I;** full name, **Omar ibn al-Khattab** (ō′mär ib′n äl.čhät.täb′).] b. c581; assassinated at Medina, 644. The second Mohammedan caliph (634–644). He was at first an opponent of Islam, but was converted (617) and aided Abu Bakr in his campaigns. His daughter was the third wife of Mohammed. He succeeded Abu

Bakr unopposed and brought Syria, Phoenicia, Persia, Egypt, and Jerusalem under the sway of Islam, thus beginning the real expansion of Moslem power. He was stabbed by Firuz, a Persian slave, but lingered for several days, long enough to appoint the group of six who later selected Othman as the next caliph. Omar took an important part in the first collection of the Koran and instituted the system of making the date of the Hegira the beginning of the Mohammedan calendar. He was the first to assume the title "Commander of the Faithful" (*Emir al-muminin*), and he organized a complete military-religious commonwealth.

Omar Khayyám (ō′mär kī.äm′, ō′mạr). b. at Nishapur, in Khurasan, Persia, c1050; d. there, c1123. A Persian poet, mathematician, and astronomer. Khayyám is an epithet thought to be derived from his father's trade, and meaning "the tentmaker." He studied at Nishapur, having as his companions Hasan ibn-al-Sabbah, afterward the head of the military order of the Assassins, and Nizam-al-Mulk, later vizier of Alp Arslan and Jalal-al-Din (Malik Shah). Having attained power, Nizam-al-Mulk granted Omar Khayyám a yearly pension. Omar was one of the eight learned men appointed by Jalal-al-Din to reform the calendar, the result being the Jalali era, so called from the king's name. "Omar's calendar was very accurate," says Sarton, "probably more so than the Gregorian calendar." He was the author of an Arabic treatise on algebra, including a classification of equations and an examination of Euclid's postulates, but is especially known as a poet from his *Rubáiyát*, or *Quatrains* (in two verses or four hemistichs, of which the first, second, and fourth rhyme), which have been translated by Edward FitzGerald and others. FitzGerald's translation was a rearrangement and editing of the original, since Omar's quatrains, as in all similar Persian poetry, were disconnected and arranged only in the alphabetical order of their first words; FitzGerald made a sequential poem of these quatrains, using some as he found them, combining others, paraphrasing some, and omitting many of Omar's original 500. The result has been a poem, extremely popular with English readers, that catches the spirit of Omar's radical approach to tradition, his praise of hedonism, his railings against the fate that brings all to dust; the spirit is perhaps nearest to that of *Ecclesiastes*, but it has also been compared with the tenor of the writing of Lucretius, Hafiz, Voltaire, Byron, and Swinburne.

O'Meara (ọ.mä′rạ), **Barry Edward.** b. in Ireland, 1786; d. at London, June 3, 1836. An Irish surgeon, physician to Napoleon at St. Helena (1815–18). He was dismissed as a consequence of differences with Sir Hudson Lowe, governor of St. Helena, over the treatment given to Napoleon, with whom O'Meara was intriguing. He published *Napoleon in Exile* (1822) and others.

Ommiads (ọ.mī′adz). [Also, **Omayyads.**] A dynasty of caliphs which reigned at Damascus (661–750 A.D.), the first of whom was Muawiyah, successor to Hasan, the son of Ali. (The Ommiad claim to the caliphate stemmed from Othman, who was Mohammed's son-in-law.) The Ommiads were followed by the Abbassides. The last of the Eastern

Ommiads escaped to Spain and founded (756) the so-called Caliphate of Córdoba. This Western caliphate, and with it the Ommiad dynasty, became extinct in 1031.

Omnium (om'ni.um), **Duke of.** In Trollope's *Framley Parsonage, Phineas Finn,* and *Phineas Redux,* a nobleman of remarkable hauteur and self-confidence: ". . . the Queen might be the queen so long as he was the Duke of Omnium. Their revenues were about the same, with the exception, that the Duke's were his own." He appears also, but less importantly, in several of Trollope's other tales.

Omphale (om'fạ.lē). In Greek legend, a Lydian queen, in whose service Hercules wore women's clothes and did women's work for three years to expiate a murder. Later she became the mistress of Hercules.

On a Girdle. A short lyric poem by Edmund Waller, containing the well-known lines:

> That which her slender waist confined,
> Shall now my joyful temples bind.

On American Taxation. A speech made in Parliament by Edmund Burke in 1774 which made evident his stand for compromise with the rebellious Americans. In reference to the duty on tea, he urged the British, "Do not burden the Americans with taxes."

Once On a Time. A novel by A. A. Milne, published in 1917.

Ondurdis (ôn.dûr'dis). See **Skadi.**

O'Neale (ọ.nēl'), **Redmond.** In Sir Walter Scott's narrative poem *Rokeby,* a gallant page.

O'Neill, or The Rebel (ọ.nēl'). A romance by Edward Bulwer-Lytton, in heroic couplets, published in 1827.

Oneiza (ọ.nā'zạ). The wife of Thalaba in Robert Southey's poem *Thalaba.*

One of Our Conquerors. A novel by George Meredith, published in 1891.

On Heaven and Other Poems. A volume of verse (1916) by Ford Madox Ford, including the lyric "There Shall Be More Joy."

Onions (un'yọnz), **Berta.** [Maiden name, **Ruck.**] b. in Wales, 1878—. A Welsh novelist and short-story writer; wife of Oliver Onions. She illustrated stories, articles, and advertising matter before devoting herself to literature. Author of the novels and collections of short stories *His Official Fiancée* (1914), *The Girls at His Billet* (1916), *In Another Girl's Shoes* (1916), *Three of Hearts* (1917), *Bridge of Kisses* (1920), *Sweet Stranger* (1921), *Arrant Rover* (1921), *The Wrong Mr. Right* (1922), *Sir or Madam?* (1923), *Dancing Star* (1923), *Clouded Pearl* (1924), *Leap Year Girl* (1924), *Lucky in Love* (1924), *The Immortal Girl* (1925), *Kneel to the Prettiest* (1925), *Her Pirate Partner* (1927), *The Maid of a Minx* (1927), *One of the Chorus* (1929; American title, *Joy-Ride*), *Unkissed Bride* (1929), *Offer of Marriage* (1930), *Missing Girl* (1930; American title, *Love-Hater*), *Post-War Girl* (1930), *Wanted on the Voyage* (1930), *Change for Happiness* (1933), *Sudden Sweetheart* (1933), *Eleventh Hour Lover* (1933), *Lad With Wings* (1933), and

Understudy (1933). *A Story-Teller Tells the Truth* (1935) is her autobiography.

Onions, Charles Talbut. b. Sept. 10, 1873—. An English lexicographer and philologist. He joined the staff of the *Oxford English Dictionary* in 1895 and became coeditor in 1914, serving in that position until 1933. He edited the *Shorter Oxford English Dictionary* (1933, 1936, 1945) and the publication *Medium Aevum* (1932 *et seq.*). His publications include *Advanced English Syntax* (1904), *A Shakespeare Glossary* (1911), and revisions of *Sweet's Anglo-Saxon Reader* (1922, 1946, 1949).

Onions, Oliver. [Original name, **George Oliver Onions;** changed legally to **George Oliver.**] b. at Bradford, Yorkshire, England, 1873—. An English novelist. Trained as an artist, he devoted himself to literature after working as a book and poster designer and magazine illustrator. In addition to novels of character, he has written ghost tales, such as *The Painted Face, Widdershins,* and *Ghosts in Daylight.* Among his works are *The Compleat Bachelor* (1901), *The Odd-Job Man* (1903), *Little Devil Doubt* (1906), *The Exception* (1911), *Gray Youth* (1914), *The New Moon* (1918), *The Tower of Oblivion* (1921), *The Spite of Heaven* (1925), the trilogy *Whom God Hath Sundered* (1926; containing *In Accordance With the Evidence, The Debit Account,* and *The Story of Louie*), *The Open Secret* (1930), *The Italian Chest* (1939), *Blood Eagle* (1941), *The Story of Ragged Robin* (1945), and *Poor Man's Tapestry* (1946; awarded the 1947 James Tait Black memorial prize).

onomatopoeia (on.ọ.mat.ọ.pē'ạ). [Also, **onomatopoësis, onomatopoiesis.**] **1.** In philology, the formation of names by imitation of natural sounds; the naming of anything by a more or less exact reproduction of the sound which it makes, or something audible connected with it; the imitative principle in language-making: thus, the verbs *buzz* and *hum* and the nouns *pewit, whippoorwill,* etc., are produced by onomatopoeia. Words thus formed naturally suggest the objects or actions producing the sound.

Onomatopœia [as a word], in addition to its awkwardness, has neither associative nor etymological application to words imitating sounds. (J. A. H. Murray, *9th Ann. Address to Phil. Soc.*)

2. In rhetoric, the use of imitative and naturally suggestive words for rhetorical effect.

On the Consolation of Philosophy. See **De consolatione philosophiae.**

On the Face of the Waters. A novel of the Sepoy Mutiny in India, by Flora Annie Steel, published in 1896.

On the Memory of Mr. Edward King, Drowned in the Irish Seas. A poem (c1637) by John Cleveland, written (as was Milton's *Lycidas*) in sorrow over the death of King, his classmate at Cambridge.

On the Morning of Christ's Nativity. See **Ode on the Morning of Christ's Nativity.**

On the Rocks. A play (1932) by George Bernard Shaw. It deals, rather bitterly, with the problems faced by a socialist prime minister who is kept in

---

fat, fāte, fär, ȧsk, fâre; net, mē, hėr; pin, pīne; not, nōte, mŏve, nôr; up, lūte, pu̇ll; ᴛн, them;

power only by the support of various conservative groups.

On the Staircase. A novel (1914) by Frank Swinnerton.

On This Island. The American title of a collection of verse (1937) by W. H. Auden. See **Look, Stranger!**

Onuphrio Muralto (ō.nö′frē.ō mṳ̄.ral′tō). See **Muralto, Onuphrio.**

opera. A form of extended dramatic composition in which music is an essential and predominant factor; a musical drama, or a drama in music. The opera is one of the chief forms of musical art; on many grounds it is claimed to be the culminating musical form. At least it affords opportunity for the application of nearly every known resource of musical effect. Its historical beginning was doubtless in the musical declamation of the Greeks, especially in connection with their dramatic representations. The idea of a musical drama was perpetuated during the Middle Ages under the humble guise of mysteries or miracle plays, in which singing was an accessory. The modern development began in Italy near the close of the 16th century, when an attempt was made to revive the ancient melodic declamation, an attempt which led directly to the discovery and establishment of monody and harmony in the place of the medieval counterpoint, of the recitative and the aria as definite methods of composition, and of instrumentation as an independent element in musical works. The modern opera involves the following distinct musical constituents, combined in various ways: (a) *recitatives*, musical declamations, mainly epic or dramatic in character, with or without extended accompaniment; (b) *arias, duets,* or *trios,* melodies for one, two, or three voices, constructed in a more or less strict musical form, predominantly lyrical in character, and usually with carefully elaborated accompaniments; (c) *choruses* and *concerted numbers* of various form, in which the dramatic element generally predominates, and which are often wrought into noteworthy climaxes of great musical and dramatic interest; (d) *instrumental elements*, including both accompaniments and independent passages, the former varying from the merest harmonic groundwork for declamation to a detailed instrumental commentary upon the dramatic emotions and situations as they succeed each other, and the latter including overtures, intermezzi, marches, dances, etc., which either introduce, connect, supply, or embellish the links in the chain of dramatic incident. To these may be added dancing, or the ballet, which is introduced either as an incidental diversion or as a component part of the dramatic action itself. In the older operas the successive numbers or movements are sharply separated from each other, while in recent ones the action is continuous except at one or two principal points. In Italy the opera has had an unbroken course of development since before 1600. It began to be diligently cultivated in France and Germany about 1650, and in England somewhat later. Every leading modern composer, except Mendelssohn, has contributed more or less to its literature. Italian operas have tended toward a lyrical extreme, to the neglect of dramatic consistency and truth, while German operas have strongly emphasized the romantic and strictly dramatic elements. French operas have often sought much for comic or spectacular effects. The Wagnerian theory of the opera presents some peculiarities, especially in the obliteration of the distinction between the recitative and the formal aria, in the remarkable elaboration of the orchestral effects, and in the unification of the poetic, musical, dramatic, and scenic elements, though these characteristics were foreshadowed in the works and theories of earlier masters. The maintenance of expensive opera houses, with regular seasons of performances annually, is a matter of governmental appropriation in most European countries. The opera has therefore become a powerful factor in the social and artistic life of many cities. Operas are often described by such qualifying terms as *grand* or *serious, dramatic, comic,* etc. Grand operas have an elaborate plot, and the entire work is set to music; while comic operas frequently contain spoken dialogue. In common speech, *German opera* means opera in German; *Italian opera,* opera in Italian, etc. A *ballad-opera* is a light dramatic work into which ballads or popular songs are arbitrarily introduced.

An Opera is a poetical tale or fiction, represented by vocal and instrumental musick, adorned with scenes, machines, and dancing.
> (Dryden, *Albion and Albanius,* Pref.)

She went from opera, park, assembly, play.
> (Pope, *To Miss Blount,*
> *on her Leaving the Town,* l. 13.)

opéra bouffe (o.pä.rä böf). A comic opera, especially one of an extravagantly humorous character.

operetta. A short opera, generally of a light character and so belonging to the class of comic opera or opéra bouffe.

Ophelia (ọ.fē′li.ạ, ọ.fēl′yạ). In Shakespeare's *Hamlet,* the daughter of Polonius. On her father's advice, she is cautious with respect to Hamlet's tentative overtures of affection, and she takes his apparent madness subsequently as being caused by this. When Hamlet accidentally kills Polonius, she goes mad and drowns herself.

Ophir (ō′fėr). In Old Testament geography, a country whence gold, silver, precious stones, ivory, sandalwood, apes, and peacocks were brought. It was especially noted for its gold. The fleet of Solomon is said to have occupied three years in making a journey to it. It has been variously identified with India, Sumatra, the Malabar Coast, the E coast of Africa, and the S or SE part of Arabia on the Persian Gulf.

Opie (ō′pi), **Amelia.** [Maiden name, **Alderson.**] b. at Norwich, England, Nov. 12, 1769; d. there, Dec. 2, 1853. An English novelist. She published various novels, the first, *Father and Daughter,* appearing in 1801.

Opium-Eater. See **Confessions of an English Opium-Eater.**

Oppenheim (op′ẹn.hīm), **E. Phillips.** [Full name, **Edward Phillips Oppenheim.**] b. at London, 1866; d. on the island of Guernsey, Feb. 3, 1946. An English novelist, noted for stories of suspense and international intrigue, among the most widely read of which is *The Great Impersonation* (1920). Among his more than 100 other books are *A Prince of Sinners* (1903), *Anna the Adventuress* (1904), *The Master Mummer* (1905), *A Maker of History* (1906), *The Long Arm of Mannister* (1910), *Berenice* (1911), and *The Moving Finger* (1911).

Ops (ops). In Roman mythology, a very old harvest and fertility goddess, hence also construed as a goddess of plenty. She was the wife of Saturn and mother of Jupiter. Later the Romans identified her with the Greek Rhea.

Opus Majus (ō′pus mā′jus). A Latin prose work (1267–68) by Roger Bacon. It is a treatise on natural science, logic, grammar, and philosophy, which, in its advocacy of experiment and observation, exhibits Bacon as one of the precursors of modern science.

Opus Minus (ō′pus mī′nus). A prose work in Latin (1267–68) by Roger Bacon.

Orange (or′anj; French, o.räṅzh), **House of.** A European princely family, the former rulers of the principality of Orange (which fell to the House of Nassau in 1530 and later to France, the House of Nassau retaining the title Prince of Orange). William III of England was of this house, as is the present royal family of the Netherlands.

Orange, Prince of. The name given to the historic Prince Maurice of Nassau by Fletcher and Massinger in their play *Sir John van Olden Barnavelt.*

Oran Haut-ton (ō.rän′ ō′tôṅ′), **Sir.** See **Haut-ton, Sir Oran.**

oration. 1. A formal speech or discourse; an eloquent or weighty address. The word is now applied chiefly to discourses pronounced on special occasions, and to academic declamations.

> Upon a set day Herod, arrayed in royal apparel, sat upon his throne, and made an oration unto them. (Acts. xii.21.)

> Orations are pleadings, speeches of counsel, laudatives, invectives, apologies, reprehensions, orations of formaility or ceremoney, and the like.
> (Bacon, *Advancement of Learning.*)

2. A prayer; supplication; petition.

> Finding not onely by his speeches and letters, but by the pitifull oration of a languishing behaviour . . . that despaire began now to threaten him destruction. (Sir P. Sidney, *Arcadia.*)

"Orator Henley" (hen′li). See **Henley, John.**

Orators, The. A comedy by Samuel Foote, performed in 1762.

Orators, The. A volume (1932) of works by W. H. Auden. Four shorter prose pieces and the longer "Journal of an Airman" are dramatic monologues; of the poems (written in what has been described as "rhythmic prose"), four are open letters. Auden's chief concern in this volume seems to be to find a mask from which to speak, a problem which he solved more completely later on. A major problem towards the understanding of several of these early works is private reference: "Private faces in public places Are wiser and nicer Than public faces in private places," says Auden in his dedication to Stephen Spender, but private references interfere with communication.

Orazia (ō.rä′zi.ạ). The proud daughter of the Inca, loved by the great hero, Montezuma, in Dryden and Howard's *The Indian Queen.*

Orbilius Pupillus (ôr.bil′i.us pū.pil′us). A Roman grammarian and schoolmaster, the teacher of Horace. The epithet "plagosus" was given to him by Horace on account of the floggings which his pupils received from him, and the name Orbilius has often since been used in literature for a teacher of this type.

Orcades (ôr′ka.dēz). An ancient name of the Orkney Islands.

Orchard and Vineyard. A volume of poems by V. Sackville-West, published in 1921.

Orchestra, or a Poeme of Dauncing. A long poem (1594) by Sir John Davies, written in rhyme royal.

Orcus (ôr′kus). In Roman mythology, a god of the underworld, identified with the Greek Horcus, god of oaths, who punished perjurers. Orcus was later identified with the Greek underworld god, Hades, and still later with Pluto. The word eventually became synonymous with Hades as a place.

Orczy (ôr′tsi), Baroness. [Title of **Emmuska Orczy.**] b. at Tarnaörs, Hungary, 1865; d. at London, Nov. 12, 1947. An English novelist and playwright. Her novel *The Scarlet Pimpernel* (1905) was dramatized (1905) and scenarized (1934); she continued the Pimpernel series in other books based on the French Revolution, such as *The Triumph of the Scarlet Pimpernel.* She was author also of *A Son of the People* (1906), *Beau Brocade* (1908; dramatized in 1910), *Castles in the Air* (1921), *Nicolette* (1923), *The Divine Folly* (1937), *Will-o′-the-Wisp* (1946), and other novels.

Ordeal of Richard Feverel (rich′ard fev′e.rel), **The.** A novel by George Meredith, published in 1859.

Ordericus Vitalis (ôr.de.rī′kus vī.tā′lis, ôr.der′i.kus vi.tal′is) or **Orderic Vital** (ôr′de.rik ve.täl′). b. at Atcham, near Shrewsbury, England, 1075; d. c1143. An Anglo-Norman historian and Benedictine monk. He wrote in Latin an *Ecclesiastical History,* especially interesting for its account of Normandy and England in the 11th and 12th centuries.

Order of the Bath. See **Bath, Order of the.**

Order of the Garter. See **Garter, Order of the.**

Order of the Thistle. See **Thistle, Order of the.**

Orders in Council. Orders promulgated by the British sovereign with the advice of the privy council; specifically, the orders of 1807, which prohibited neutral trade directly with France or the allies of France. All goods had to be landed in England, pay duties there, and be reëxported under English regulations. These orders bore with especial severity on American commerce.

Ordinary, The. A play (c1635) by William Cartwright.

Orellana (ō.rä.yä′nä), **River of.** A name frequently given, in early books and maps, to the Amazon, in South America.

Orestes (ō.res′tēz). In Greek legend, the son of Agamemnon and Clytemnestra, and brother of Electra. He slew Clytemnestra and her lover Aegisthus, to avenge their murder of his father. Homer presents Orestes as the righteous, dutiful, and praiseworthy avenger of his father's death. The Greek dramatists, however, depict him as being pursued by the Erinyes for the crime of killing his mother. He fled before them till he came to Delphi, was tried by the Areopagus, and won a tied vote. Athena cast the deciding vote in his favor, and henceforth the Erinyes ceased to follow and torment him, and became known as the Eumenides.

Orfeo (ôr.fā′ō). A dramatic pastoral by Politian, produced in 1483. Both the name and theme were widely borrowed by English writers during the next two centuries. It was one of the first pastorals written in Italian, the language of the country in which the dramatic action of such works was traditionally laid.

Orfeo (ôr′fẹ.ō), **Sir.** See **Sir Orfeo.**

Orford (ôr′fọrd), 4th Earl of. Title of **Walpole, Horace.**

Orgilus (ôr′gi.lus). In John Ford's *The Broken Heart*, the betrothed of Penthea, whose brother, Ithocles, makes her marry Bassanes instead.

Orgoglio (ôr.gō′lyō). In Spenser's *Faerie Queene*, a character of great arrogance, representing the Church of Rome. He is the son of earth and wind, and as tall as three men. He captures the Red Cross Knight, but is finally slain by Prince Arthur.

Orgon (ôr.gôn̄). A credulous dupe in Molière's *Tartuffe*. He has an imbecile infatuation for the hypocritical Tartuffe.

Oriana (ō.ri.an′ạ). In the medieval romance *Amadis de Gaul*, the mistress of Amadis; daughter of Lisuarte, a legendary king of Britain. Queen Elizabeth is frequently called "the peerless Oriana" in the adulatory poems of her time.

Oriana. The principal character in John Fletcher's comedy *The Wild Goose Chase*, and in George Farquhar's comedy *The Inconstant*, which is practically the same. She is betrothed to the evasive Mirabel (the "wild goose"), and finally brings him to reason and marries him.

Oriana. In Francis Beaumont and John Fletcher's play *The Woman Hater*, a teasing, tormenting brilliant woman.

Oriana. A ballad by Alfred Tennyson, published in 1830.

Oriana, The Triumphs of. A collection of madrigals in honor of Queen Elizabeth, compiled and published by Thomas Morley in 1601.

Original Chronicle of Scotland (skot′lạnd), **The.** A rhymed chronicle by Andrew of Wyntoun, finished between 1420 and 1424. It begins with the angels, follows with Adam and Eve, and continues down to the author's time. Wyntoun wrote it in nine books in honor of the nine orders of angels.

Origin of Species, The. [Full title, **On the Origin of Species by Means of Natural Selection, or the Preservation of Favoured Races in the Struggle for Life.**] A work by Charles R. Darwin, developing his theory of evolution, published in 1859. It is now generally considered one of the most influential works ever published.

Orion (ō.rī′ọn). In Greek mythology, a giant hunter. There are various legends about him. According to one, he was blinded, with the aid of

Dionysus, by a father whose daughter he had ravished. Sightless, he waded through the sea into the east and regained his sight by opening his eyes to the rays of the rising sun. Later he was slain by Artemis either out of jealousy or, in some versions, accidentally. Another story states that he was killed by a scorpion. After his death he was changed to a constellation, which forever precedes the constellation Scorpio (the Scorpion).

Orlando (ôr.lan′dō). In Shakespeare's *As You Like It*, the younger brother of Oliver, and lover of Rosalind.

Orlando (ôr.län′dō). Italian form of **Roland.**

Orlando: A Biography (ôr.lan′dō). A novel by Virginia Woolf, published in 1928. It is a study (in fantasy) of English life and character from the Elizabethan period down to the 20th century, in which the central figure is both male and female.

Orlando Friscobaldo (fris.kọ̄.bal′dō). See **Friscobaldo, Orlando.**

Orlando Furioso (ôr.län′dō fö.ryō′sō). [Eng. trans., *"Orlando the Mad."*] A metrical romance by Lodovico Ariosto, 40 cantos of which were published in 1515, to which he added five more before his death in 1533. Sir John Harington's English translation was published in 1591. It is a continuation of Matteo Maria Boiardo's *Orlando Innamorato*, but it begins at a point before the end of Boiardo's work. Orlando's madness is occasioned by the falseness of Angelica.

Orlando Furioso. [Full title, **The History of Orlando Furioso, one of the Twelve Peers of France.**] A comedy by Robert Greene, produced probably c1591. It was revived in 1592 and printed in 1594. It was adapted from a translation of Ariosto's poem.

Orlando Innamorato (ēn.nä.mō.rä′tō). [Eng. trans., *"Orlando the Enamored."*] A metrical romance by Matteo Maria Boiardo, on the love of Orlando (Roland) for Angelica. The hero, however, is really Ruggiero. Boiardo left it unfinished in 1494, and Lodovico Ariosto wrote his *Orlando Furioso* as its sequel. Boiardo's poem was remodeled and somewhat denatured by Francesco Berni.

Orleans (ôr.lēnz′, ôr′lẹ.ạnz), **Bastard of.** See **Bastard of Orleans.**

Orleans, Duke of. In Shakespeare's *Henry V*, the historical Charles d'Orléans, the cousin and close companion of the Dauphin. He brags of the French superiority, but is captured at Agincourt.

Orley Farm (ôr′li). A novel by Anthony Trollope, published in 1862.

Orm (ôrm). See under **Ormulum.**

Ormazd (ôr.mäzd′) or **Ormuzd** (ôr.muzd′). See **Ahuramazda.**

Orme (ôrm), **Robert.** b. at Anjengo, Travancore, India, in June, 1728; d. at Great Ealing, near London, Jan. 13, 1801. An English historian of India. He was intimately associated with Robert Clive, succeeded George Pigot as governor of Madras, and was commissary general from 1757 to 1759. In 1759 he returned to London, and between 1763 and 1778 published a three-volume *History of the Military Transactions of the British Nation in Indostan from 1745.*

ḏ, d or j; ṣ, s or sh; ṯ, t or ch; ẕ, z or zh; o, F. cloche; ü, F. menu; ċh, Sc. loch; ṅ, F. bonbon.

Ormerod (ôrm′rod), **Mrs. Sarah.** An old widow, in *Lonesome-Like* (1911), a one-act play of Lancashire life by Harold Brighouse.

Ormond (ôr′mọnd). A novel by Maria Edgeworth, published in 1817.

Ormulum (ôr′mū̇.lum). [Also, **Orrmulum.**] A fragmentary work in 10,000 long unrhymed lines, consisting of paraphrases of passages in the Gospels, rearranged chronologically, together with homilies upon them, composed by Orm (or Orrmin or Orrm) in the first part of the 13th century. Its title derives from his name. He was an Augustinian canon, and it is assumed that he lived in Lincolnshire or Nottinghamshire, but arguments have also been advanced in favor of Ormskirk in Lancashire. The work is excessively tedious and its importance is chiefly linguistic. Orm had a phonetic system of his own, distinguishing the short vowels by doubling the following consonant. The *Ormulum* was first edited from the manuscript by Robert Meadows White in 1852.

Oroonoko (ō.rú.nō′kō). [Full title **Oroonoko, or the Royal Slave.**] A novel by Aphra Behn, published c1678. It is based on facts which became known to her while residing in Surinam and is, for the period, a remarkable condemnation of the cruelties of the slave trade. Oroonoko, the grandson and heir of an African king, falls in love with Imoinda. When the king learns of this, he has Imoinda sold into slavery, for he loves the girl himself. Oroonoko is captured by slave traders and taken to Surinam, where he finds Imoinda. Together they persuade all of the slaves in the colony to revolt. When the deputy governor says he will grant them pardon, the slaves surrender, but he breaks his word and has Oroonoko whipped. Oroonoko kills Imoinda to save her from vengeance and then is executed by the governor's men.

Oroonoko. [Full title, **Oroonoko, or the Royal Slave.**] A tragedy by Thomas Southerne, based on Aphra Behn's novel, and first acted in 1695. The phrase "Pity's akin to love," which is found in this play, has passed into a proverb.

Orphan, or the Unhappy Marriage, The. A tragedy by Thomas Otway, produced in 1680. It is derived from a romance entitled *The English Adventures.* Mrs. Barry acted the orphan, Monimia, one of her best roles, and Betterton was her lover, Castalio.

Orphan Island. A novel (1925) by Rose Macaulay.

Orpheus (ôr′fẹ.us, -fūs). In Greek legend, the son of Apollo, or of a Thracian river god and one of the Muses, and husband of Eurydice. He had the power of charming all animate and inanimate objects with the music of his lyre. When Eurydice died, he descended into Hades to bring her back to life, and, by his compelling music, won permission to conduct her back to earth, but on condition that he never look back to see if she were following until they had passed out of the gates. Orpheus agreed, but his yearning was so great that just as they reached the light he glanced back. He caught a glimpse of Eurydice, but because of the broken taboo she immediately vanished and was lost to him forever. Later he met his death at the hands of infuriated Thracian maenads, either because he was faithful to Eurydice and repulsed them, or at the command of Zeus, because he had worshiped Apollo over Zeus.

Orrery (or′ẹ.ri), **Earl of.** A title held by various members of the **Boyle** family.

Orrm (ôrm) or **Orrmin** (ôr′min). See under **Ormulum.**

Orrmulum (ôr′mū̇.lum). See **Ormulum.**

Orsino (ôr.sē′nō). In Shakespeare's *Twelfth Night,* the Duke of Illyria. He loves Olivia, who discourages him. He finally marries Viola, who secretly loves him and has served him in disguise as a page.

Ortelius (ôr.tē′li.us). [Latinized surname of **Abraham Oertel** (or **Ortell**).] b. at Antwerp, Belgium, 1527; d. there, 1598. A Flemish geographer, considered the greatest of his time next to Mercator. He published an atlas, *Theatrum orbis terrarum* (1570), and others. He went to England in 1577, and it was his encouragement and solicitation that induced Camden to produce his *Britannia.*

Ortheris (ôr′thẹ.ris), **Stanley.** One of the "Soldiers Three" in Kipling's series of stories grouped under that title. He is a brash Cockney, very proud of his marksmanship.

orthius (ôr′thi.us). In ancient prosody, a great foot, consisting of three tetrasemic longs, the first of which forms the arsis, while the other two constitute the thesis.

Orton (ôr′tọn), **Arthur.** [Called the **Tichborne Claimant;** assumed names, **Thomas Castro, Roger Charles Tichborne.**] b. 1834; d. at London, April 1, 1898. An English impostor, central figure in two famous 19th-century trials. He emigrated (1852) from England to Australia, where he took up his father's trade, that of a butcher. In 1866, on the invitation of Lady Tichborne, he returned to England, she having become convinced from descriptions that he was her elder son, who had been lost at sea in 1854. When they met, she became positive of his supposed identity. Lady Tichborne died in 1868, but Orton was received by many others as the missing Tichborne son. The success of his imposture was so great that in 1871 he brought suit for ejectment against the then baronet, the infant heir of Lady Tichborne's younger son. The trial lasted 102 days, after which Orton's counsel asked to have the case dismissed. The sequel was a trial (1873–74) for perjury against Orton, who was sentenced to 14 years' imprisonment. He was released in 1884, and in 1895 published a confession of his fraud in the press.

Ortygia (ôr.tij′i.ạ). An ancient name of **Delos.**

Orville (ôr′vil), **Lord.** The lover of Evelina, in Fanny Burney's novel of that name.

Orwell (ôr′wel, -wẹl). A pseudonym of **Smith, Walter Chalmers.**

Orwell, George. [Pseudonym of **Eric Blair.**] b. at Motihari, in Bengal, India, 1903; d. at London, Jan. 21, 1950. An English novelist and essayist, chiefly known in the U. S. for his satirical novels *Animal Farm* (1946) and *Nineteen Eighty-Four* (1949). The son of a member of the Anglo-Indian civil service, he attended Eton (where he claimed to have learned little) and was later (1922–27) a member of the British constabulary in Burma (where he came to the conclusion that British imperialism was "very largely a racket"). This conviction, plus ill health and a desire to write, led him to return to Europe, and he lived for about 18 months at Paris, supporting himself by washing dishes in restaurants and by various odds and ends of teaching. It was during this period that he wrote *Down and Out in Paris and London* (1933) and *Burmese Days* (1934). By 1935 his works were bringing him an income great enough to permit him to devote full time to writing, and during the next few years he published *A Clergyman's Daughter* (1935), *Keep the Aspidistra Flying* (1936), *The Road to Wigan Pier* (1937), and *Homage to Catalonia* (1938). The last of these derived from his experiences as a member of the Republican army in the Spanish Civil War. He subsequently published *Coming Up for Air* (1939), *Inside the Whale* (1940), *The Lion and the Unicorn: Socialism and the English Genius* (1941), but interrupted his writing to serve during World War II as an overseas broadcaster for the British Broadcasting System and as a part-time factory worker. In 1946 he published *Critical Essays* (issued in the U. S. as *Dickens, Dali, and Others*) and also the satirical *Animal Farm* (published under the same title in the U. S.). *Nineteen Eighty-Four* (published in 1949 in both Great Britain and the U. S.) was his last major work, although he contributed essays and reviews to *Horizon*, the London *Observer*, and *Tribune* almost until the end of his life. Although he is best known in the U. S. for what are obviously to most readers bitter attacks on Russian totalitarianism, he considered himself to be a Marxist and was an adherent of the anti-Stalinist left-wing of the British Labour Party.

Osbaldistone (oz.bôl'dis.ton), **Francis.** The narrator and nominal hero of Sir Walter Scott's *Rob Roy*.

Osbaldistone, Rashleigh. The villain of Sir Walter Scott's *Rob Roy*.

Osborne (oz'born), **Dorothy.** b. at Chicksands, Bedfordshire, England, 1627; d. at Moor Park, Surrey, England, in January, 1695. An English letter writer; wife of Sir William Temple, Jonathan Swift's employer and patron. She wrote Temple a series of letters, published in 1888, 1903, and 1928, notable as containing invaluable descriptions of the time in which she lived. She is buried in Westminster Abbey.

Osborne, Francis. b. at Chicksands, Bedfordshire, England, Sept. 26, 1593; d. at Nether Worton, near Deddington, Oxfordshire, England, Feb. 11, 1659. An English writer and minor official. Author of *Advice to a Son* (part 1, 1656; part 2, 1658), dealing with "Studies," "Love and Marriage," "Travel," "Government," and "Religion," and *Memoirs of the Reigns of Elizabeth and James I* (1658), interesting for its court gossip.

Osborne, George. In Thackeray's *Vanity Fair*, the handsome, selfish husband of Amelia.

Osborne, John. In Thackeray's *Vanity Fair*, the father of George Osborne. He is an arrogant, snobbish man who for a long period refuses to accept Amelia Sedley as his daughter-in-law.

Osborne, Thomas. d. at Islington, London, Aug. 21, 1767. An English bookseller and printer, publisher of Samuel Richardson's *Pamela*. He was attacked verbally by Alexander Pope in the *Dunciad*,

and physically by Samuel Johnson, who gave him a beating for being "impertinent." Apart from his share in issuing, with Charles Rivington, Richardson's first novel, he is remembered by references to him in Johnson's *Pope*, Boswell's *Johnson*, and other contemporary literature.

Oscar (os'kar). In Old Irish legend, a beautiful young warrior combining the ideals of fierceness and gentleness. He was the son of Oisin and the grandson of Fionn mac Cumhal (Finn MacCool).

Osewold the Reeve (oz'wold, -wôld). [Also, **Oswald.**] The Reeve who relates "The Reeve's Tale" in Chaucer's *Canterbury Tales*.

O'Shaughnessy (ọ.shô'ne.si), **Arthur William Edgar.** b. at London, March 14, 1844; d. there, Jan. 30, 1881. An English poet, influenced by D. G. Rossetti and the Pre-Raphaelites. He was an assistant in the natural history division of the British Museum. He published *Epic of Women* (1870), *The Lays of France* (1872), an adaptation of the *Laïs* of Marie de France, *Music and Moonlight* (1874), and *Songs of a Worker* (1881). His ode beginning "We are the music-makers, And we are the dreamers of dreams" has become famous through its partial inclusion (three of seven stanzas) in Francis Turner Palgrave's *Golden Treasury*.

Osiris (ọ.sī'ris). In Egyptian mythology, the god and judge of the dead, and lord of the underworld. He was also believed by the ancient Egyptians to have given them their religious rites, their knowledge of agriculture, and the other arts of civilization. Probably the most widely known myth about Osiris is that he was the son of Geb (earth) and Nut (sky), consort of his sister Isis, that he was killed by his envious brother, Set, cut up into 14 pieces and scattered over Egypt, and avenged by his posthumous son, Horus, who killed Set. Isis recovered the scattered fragments of his body and buried them here and there in Egypt; and each of these places became a center of the Osiris cult. The gods then gave Osiris immortality and made him judge and guardian of the dead. Osiris was originally an ancient fertility god who became associated with the fertility-giving Nile, and because of his death, resurrection, and immortality story, became associated with the setting and forever-rising sun, and thus with Ra, the sun god. His chief center of worship was at Abydos. In art he was portrayed as a bearded human figure in mummy swathing, wearing the crown of Upper Egypt, and bearing in his hands, which protruded from the swathing, the shepherd's crook and the flail (both agricultural symbols).

Osric (oz'rik). In Shakespeare's *Hamlet*, an affected courtier.

Ossa (os'a). A mountain in the E part of Thessaly, Greece, situated NW of Pelion and separated from Olympus on the N by the Vale of Tempe. According to myth, Pelion was piled atop Ossa by the giants when they stormed Olympus. Elevation, ab. 6,400 ft.

Ossian (osh'an, os'i.an). A variant name of Oisin, son of Fionn mac Cumhal (Finn MacCool). To him (under the spelling Ossian) was ascribed the authorship of the poems (*Fingal* and others) published (1760–63) by James Macpherson, but it has now long since been known that Macpherson himself was the author of the bulk of these works, although he did draw upon some ancient Irish sources.

Ossianic (osh.i.an'ik, os.i-). Pertaining to or characteristic of Ossian, or the poems of Ossian. "The Ossianic magniloquence, the Cambyses vein, and the conventional hyperbole of the national speech [Spanish]." (*Edinburgh Rev.*)

Ostler (os'lẽr), **William.** fl. 1601–23. An English actor. He is one of the performers listed in the first folio edition (1623) of Shakespeare's plays.

Ostrogoths (os'trọ.goths). See under **Goths.**

O'Sullivan (ọ.sul'i.van), **Seumas.** Pseudonym of **Starkey, James.**

Oswald (oz'wald, -wôld), Saint. b. c604; killed at the battle of Maserfield, Aug. 5, 642. King of Northumbria (c635–642); son of Ethelfrith. He was banished from Northumbria when his uncle Edwin became king in 617. During his exile he apparently became converted to Christianity in Iona. In 633 Edwin was killed by Caedwalla of Wales and Penda of Mercia, and soon after Oswald defeated Caedwalla at a place called Heavenfield and became king of Northumbria. He reunited Deira and Bernicia with Northumbria and brought the kingdom once more to a position of eminence. He received (635) St. Aidan as a missionary to the Northumbrians and presented him with Lindisfarne as the place to establish a monastery. His death in battle against the pagan Penda made a Christian martyr of him; his festival is celebrated August 5.

Oswald, Saint. d. 992. A bishop of Worcester (later archbishop of York), who with Dunstan, Archbishop of Canterbury, and Ethelwold, Bishop of Winchester, fostered the reform of the church and the revival of learning in England in the mid-10th century.

Oswald. In Shakespeare's *King Lear,* Goneril's steward. He is a haughty, insulting person who, having angered Lear, is struck by him. He is called a "serviceable villain" (IV.vi) by Edgar, who kills him.

Oswald the Reeve. See **Osewold the Reeve.**

Oswald Wycliffe (wik'lif). See **Wycliffe, Oswald.**

Othello (ọ.thel'ō). [Full title, **The Tragedy of Othello, the Moor of Venice.**] A tragedy by Shakespeare, probably written in 1602, first acted in 1604, and printed in 1622 in a quarto and in 1623 in the first folio edition. The folio is better than the quarto, but both were apparently prepared from the Shakespeare manuscript, the folio containing revisions made during the playing. It was based on one of Giraldi's (Cinthio's) romances in the *Hecatommithi* (1565), although there are differences in detail. Shakespeare here concentrates on the betrayal of a good man by a completely wicked man whose evil flows out of the boundless and irrational nature of all evil. With diabolical adroitness Iago links Cassio's utterly innocent activities with the supposed faithlessness of Desdemona, and thus contrives to build in Othello's mind a hideous structure of suspicion. But Iago does not work toward this by plain words; his strategy is marked by disingenuous indirection, leaving Othello always with the suspicion that he (Iago) knows more than he has hinted at. The play, which contains some of the most beautiful poetry in all of Shakespeare, is well plotted and moves at a rapid pace. The double time scheme, by which the actual stage events are spaced within the compass of two days whereas the actual sequence of time for the plot development is several months, contributes to this unity.

The Story. Othello, a Moorish general in the service of Venice, has secretly married Desdemona, a Venetian beauty. While he is explaining their love to her father, Brabantio, and the Senate, news comes that war has broken out in Cyprus and he must leave immediately. Desdemona follows him, accompanied by Othello's ensign, Iago, who is angry that a promotion has been given to Cassio rather than himself. This is the ostensible motive for the course of treachery he immediately starts to follow. He manages to get Cassio drunk and consequently demoted for disorderly behavior; then suggests to him that he approach Othello through Desdemona for reinstatement. At the same time, Iago manages to suggest to Othello that she and Cassio are having an affair. Then, getting Emilia, his wife, to remove a handkerchief from Desdemona's chamber, he contrives that Cassio should give it to his mistress, Bianca, and that Othello should see her sewing upon it. The handkerchief itself has magic in it, as Othello tells Desdemona. It is more than a mere incriminating clue. It now becomes for Othello the symbol of Desdemona's supposed wantonness, for in giving it to Cassio, as he supposes, she has betrayed the scant regard which she attaches to his love. In the last act, Othello is a ruthless avenger, bent (as he now thinks) on preventing Desdemona from betraying other men. Just as he has always done his duty on the field of battle, Othello must do his duty now, even though it breaks his heart. He asks Iago to kill Cassio; the deed is attempted by Iago's dupe Roderigo but fails, and Iago kills Roderigo to avoid betrayal. Othello thereupon goes to Desdemona and smothers her in her bed. But his love for her is not dead, and at this climactic moment he is overwhelmed by a poignant realization of his loss. At the same time, he does not yet suspect the perfidy of Iago and he keeps repeating the ironic refrain, "Honest, honest Iago." Emilia, however, questions Iago and almost instantly perceives the truth, crying "Villainy, villainy!" Meanwhile, letters have been found on Roderigo's body which incriminate Iago. With this, Othello's world collapses, and he bitterly renounces his honor, "But why should honor outlive honesty? Let it go all." After trying, and failing, to kill Iago, he recalls the service he has done on the battlefield and asks that Cassio and the others remaining do him the justice of reporting things honestly as they have happened. With a return to the quiet dignity which is perhaps his most essential characteristic, he says simply that they should, in referring to him, speak of "one that loved not wisely but too well," and one "perplexed in the extreme." He stabs himself and, falling on Desdemona's bed, dies.

Othello. The hero of Shakespeare's tragedy *Othello* (*q.v.*).

Otia Imperialia (ō'shi.a im.pēr.i.ā'li.a). A collection (c1211) of miscellaneous stories, folklore, and other prose writings in Latin by Gervase of Tilbury.

---

fat, fāte, fär, ȧsk, fãre; net, mē, hẽr; pin, pīne; not, nōte, möve, nôr; up, lūte, pùll; ᴛʜ, then;

Otranto (ọ.trän'tō), **The Castle of.** See **Castle of Otranto, The.**

O'Trigger (ọ.trig'ėr), **Sir Lucius.** In Richard Brinsley Sheridan's comedy *The Rivals*, a fortune-hunting Irishman, noted for his pertinacious attachment to the practice of dueling.

ottava rima (ot.tä'vä rē'mä). In prosody, a term designating an eight-line stanza, the last two forming a couplet, each line containing eleven syllables, as originally used by the Italian poets Tasso and Ariosto. Byron uses a modified form (with ten-syllable lines) in his *Beppo* and *Don Juan*.

Otter (ot'ėr), **Captain.** The henpecked husband of Mistress Otter in Jonson's comedy *Epicœne*.

Otter, Mistress. The bullying wife of Captain Otter (who calls her "princess") in Jonson's comedy *Epicœne*.

Otterbourne (ot'ėr.bėrn). [Also, **The Battle** (or **Ballad) of Otterbourne**.] An old ballad, included in Percy's *Reliques*, telling of the battle at Otterburn, near the Scottish border, between the Scots under the Earl of Douglas and the English under Lord Percy. Douglas falls by Percy's sword and Percy is taken prisoner:

> This deed was done at Otterbourne,
>   About the breaking of day:
> Earl Douglas was buried at the braken bush,
>   And the Percy led captive away.

Ottomans (ot'ọ.manz). A branch of the Turks which founded and ruled the Turkish Empire. The Ottoman Turks lived originally in central Asia. Under the reign (1288–1326) of their first sultan, Osman I, they founded a realm in Asia Minor, which was soon extended into Europe. With the capture of Constantinople in 1453 they succeeded to the Byzantine Empire, and their rule, at its height in the 16th century, extended over the greater part of SE Europe and much of W Asia and N Africa. The Ottoman Turks, being Sunnite Mohammedans, used to regard the sultans as caliphs.

Otuel (o.tü.el). The hero of a group of Middle English verse romances in the Charlemagne cycle, all based on French *chansons de geste*. One of Charlemagne's paladins, he is a pagan knight at the start, but is converted to Christianity by the prayers of Charlemagne and his people during a battle (but he kills Roland before he is converted). The oldest version of the romance that survives is in four-stress couplets.

Otuel and Roland (rō'land). A Middle English verse romance of the Otuel group of the Charlemagne cycle, probably a continuation of *Roland and Vernagu*. It continues the story of Otuel with about 1,000 lines telling of Charlemagne's victories over the Saracen Ebrahim and the King of Navarre and ends with Roland's death.

Otway (ot'wā), **Thomas.** b. at Trotton, Sussex, England, March 3, 1652; d. at Tower Hill, London, April 14, 1685. The principal tragic poet of the English classical school. He entered Christ Church, Oxford, in 1669. He fell in love with Mrs. Barry, who appeared in his *Alcibiades*, and she became his evil genius; to escape her he enlisted and served in Flanders, but returned to her. She made his great-

est reputation in his plays. He died in a baker's shop near the sponging-house (a place of enforced residence for debtors awaiting trial) in which his last days were spent. Among his plays are *Alcibiades* (1675), *Don Carlos* (1676), translations of Racine's *Titus and Berenice* (1677), and Molière's *Fourberies de Scapin* (*Cheats of Scapin*, 1677), *Friendship in Fashion* (1678), *Caius Marius* (1680), *The Orphan* (1680), *The Soldier's Fortune* (1681), *Venice Preserved* (1682), and *The Atheist* (1684; a second part of *The Soldier's Fortune*). The reputation of Otway was very high in the 18th century, actually approaching that of Shakespeare.

Ouffle (öfl), **Histoire des imaginations extravagantes de M.** A work by Laurent Bordelon, published in 1710. It is notable as being the book to which Johnson refers in his *Life of Pope* as the prototype of the *Memoirs of Martinus Scriblerus*. The book has been mistakenly ascribed to the Abbé Bourdelot.

Ouida (wē'da). Pseudonym of **Ramée, Marie Louise de la.**

Ould (ōld), **Hermon.** b. at London, Dec. 14, 1886—. An English dramatist, poet, and critic. Among his plays are *Between Sunset and Dawn* (1913), *The Black Virgin* (1922), *Flames in Sunlight* (1928), and *The Meeting* (1936); his verse includes *Candle-Ends* (1921), *In the Country* (1937), and *To One Who Sang* (1942); author also of *John Galsworthy* (1934) and *Shuttle* (1945).

Our Betters. A comedy of manners (1917) by W. Somerset Maugham, a satire of Anglophile American expatriates.

Our Father. See **Lord's Prayer.**

Our Mutual Friend. A novel by Charles Dickens, published in 1865, his last complete and full-length novel.

Our Village. Sketches (1819–32) of village life by Mary Russell Mitford.

Outcast of the Islands, The. A novel (1896) by Joseph Conrad; the outcast's later life is told in *Almayer's Folly*.

Outline of History, The. A popular interpretive historical work by H. G. Wells, published in 1920 and issued in a revised edition in 1931.

Out of the Flame. A volume of verse (1923) by Osbert Sitwell.

Outram (ö'tram), **George.** b. near Glasgow, March 25, 1805; d. Sept. 15, 1856. A Scottish poet and editor. Educated at Edinburgh University, he turned to literary work after failing in the practice of law. He was editor (1837–56) of the Glasgow *Herald*, author of *Lyrics, Legal and Miscellaneous* (1874), and was associated with John Wilson (1785–1854), known as "Christopher North," in the *Dies Boreales* papers.

Out Upon It. A poem (1639) by Sir John Suckling, writing of love in the half-mocking style of the cavalier poet. It opens with the famous lines:

> Out upon it, I have loved
>   Three whole days together!
> And am like to love three more,
>   If it prove fair weather.

ḍ, d or j; ṣ, s or sh; ṭ, t or ch; ẓ, z or zh; o, F. cloche; ü, F. menu; ċh, Sc. loch; ṅ, F. bonbon.

Overbury (ō'vẽr.ber.i, -bẽr.i), Sir **Thomas**. b. at Compton-Scorpion, Warwickshire, England, 1581; poisoned in the Tower of London, Sept. 15, 1613. An English miscellaneous writer. He studied at Queen's College, Oxford (1595–98) and at the Middle Temple, and traveled on the Continent. He became the protégé of Robert Carr, Viscount Rochester (afterward Earl of Somerset), paramour of Lady Essex. Having incurred the enmity of Lady Essex by opposing a marriage between her and Carr, he was by her influence imprisoned in the Tower on April 26, 1613, and poisoned there. He wrote *The Wife* (1614), *Characters* (1614), and *Crumms fal'n from King James's Table*, first printed in 1715.

Overdone (ō'vẽr.dun), **Mistress**. In Shakespeare's *Measure for Measure*, a bawd who is sent to prison.

Overdoo (ō'vẽr.dö), **Adam**. A complacent justice, a prominent character in Ben Jonson's *Bartholomew Fair*.

Overreach (ō'vẽr.rēch), **Sir Giles**. The principal character in Massinger's *A New Way to Pay Old Debts*: a cruel extortioner whose actions are governed by systematic, calculating self-love. He is believed to be based on the historical Sir Giles Mompesson, a man well known in his day for his wealth and greed. He is proud and grasping; but, as his name indicates, finally overreaches himself, and is "outwitted by two weak innocents and gulled by children."

Overruled. A play (1913) by George Bernard Shaw, included by most critics among his lesser works.

Overton (ō'vẽr.ṭon), **Richard**. [Pseudonym, **Martin Marpriest**.] fl. 1642–63. An English pamphleteer and satirist. Much of his work was published anonymously and some of it under the name of "Martin Marpriest," who was put forward as the son of "Martin Marprelate."

Overtures to Death. A volume of verse (1938) by Cecil Day Lewis.

Ovid (ov'id). [Full Latin name, **Publius Ovidius Naso**.] b. at Sulmo, Italy, 43 B.C.; d. at Tomi (now Constana), near the Black Sea, 18 A.D. A Roman poet, one of the leading writers of the Augustan age. He lived at Rome, and was exiled for an unknown cause to Tomi on the Euxine (Black Sea), in Moesia, c9 A.D. His chief works are elegies, and poems on mythological subjects, *Metamorphoses*, *Fasti*, *Ars Amatoria* (Art of Love), *Heroides*, and *Amores*. He was one of the most widely read of the classical authors during the Middle Ages, and was particularly influential in the development of the tradition of courtly love.

Ovoca (ọ.vō'kạ). See **Avoca**.

Owain ab Gruffydd (ō'wän äb grif'iᴛʜ). See **Glendower, Owen**; see also **Owain Cyveiliog**.

Owain Cyveiliog (ku.vä'lyŏg). [Also, **Owain ab Gruffydd** (äb grif'iᴛʜ).] d. 1197. A Welsh prince (of Powys). He was noted as a fighter, and as the author of *The Hirlas Horn*.

Owen (ō'ẹn), **John**. [Latinized, **Audoenus** or **Owenus**.] b. in Wales, c1560; d. 1622. A British Latinist, noted for his Latin epigrams.

Owen, Robert. b. at Newtown, Montgomeryshire, Wales, May 14, 1771; d. there, Nov. 17, 1858. A British manufacturer and educator, a founder of British socialism. Owen's early career was that of a self-made businessman. Leaving home at the age of ten, he made his way first at London and then at Manchester. In 1800 he became manager and part owner of the cotton mills at New Lanark, Scotland, which was during the next quarter of a century the focal point not only of his business affairs but also of his educational, philanthropic, and propagandist activities. With benevolent paternalism he improved the social conditions of the little mill town, and he laid increasing stress on education. He was one of the first to establish an infant school, he inaugurated programs of adult education, and his Institution for the Formation of Character (erected 1809–16) attracted attention in its time equal to that accorded the schools of Pestalozzi and Fellenberg. Owen's success in molding the character of his employees confirmed a long-held conviction of his that "character is universally formed *for* and not *by* the individual." It also encouraged him to believe that industrial society as a whole could be reformed by the application of his principles. He was disappointed, however, with the meager result of his agitation for factory laws, and he turned from legislative measures to what can best be described as communitarian socialism, that is, the proposal to reorganize society, fundamentally but peaceably, on the basis of small experimental communities, numbering from 800 to 2,500 members, combining agriculture with industry, and organizing both production and consumption coöperatively. He elaborated his plans in 1817 and inaugurated a great propagandist effort, which produced widespread discussion, but not the practical test he desired. In 1824 he came to the U. S., purchased the property of the communistic sect of Rappites in southern Indiana, and inaugurated in 1825 the New Harmony Community, which lasted only until 1827. He was greeted with surprising enthusiasm in America, and two speeches he made in 1825 in the Capitol at Washington were attended by Presidents Monroe and J. Q. Adams. The failure of New Harmony cost him the major part of his fortune, however, and his American influence melted away, particularly after a public debate in 1829 designed "to prove that the principles of all religions are erroneous." He returned to England in 1829 and threw himself into the coöperative and labor movements, sponsoring a National Equitable Labour Exchange (1832–34), and a Grand National Consolidated Trades Union (1834). After their failure Owen took up once more his plan for achieving reform through coöperative communities. A succession of propagandist organizations and a number of "social missionaries" disseminated his ideas. Eventually an experimental community was organized, Harmony Hall or Queenwood in Hampshire (1839–45). Its failure marked the final end of Owenism as a separate movement, though the force of his ideas was felt in later movements and though Owen himself continued his propaganda undiminished until his death at the age of 87. Owen is often supposed to have advocated complete community of property, but in fact his views on the matter were never fixed nor very clearly stated. His proposal to use the small experimental community as a lever for complete social reconstruction was the real heart of his doctrine. The basic economic theory of socialism was developed by certain of his radically equalitarian disciples, whose ideas he himself adopted only in the middle period of his career, roughly from 1824 to 1830. His own earlier and later plans implied considerable social stratification. Owen was under constant attack, not only on economic grounds, but also because of his criticisms of organized religion and of the institution of marriage. His opponents acknowledged, however, the disinterestedness of his motives, his fairness in debate, and his personal charm.

Owen, Wilfred. b. at Oswestry, England, March 18, 1893; killed in France, in November, 1918. An English poet. His poems were published posthumously (1920) by his friend Siegfried Sassoon.

Owen Glendower (glen'dör, glen'dou''ér). See **Glendower, Owen.**

Owl and the Nightingale, The. A Middle English poem attributed to one Nicholas de Guildford of Portesham, Dorsetshire, of whom little is known. Its date is disputed: the handwriting of the manuscript is that of the first half of the 13th century, but most scholars are of the opinion that the poem was written before 1200. It is in the form of a debate, closely following the 12th-century law court procedures. The Nightingale has been interpreted by some as championing the cause of the new lyric poetry and the life of the secular world, and the Owl as defending the older forms of religious poetry and the ascetic, monastic life.

Owlglass (oul'glas). See **Eulenspiegel, Till.**

Oxen, The. A poem (1915) by Thomas Hardy, a fanciful retelling of the old tradition that cattle fall on their knees on Christmas Eve at midnight, as supposedly did the ox in the stable of the Nativity.

Oxenham (ok'sen.am, oks'nam), **John.** [Pseudonym of **William Arthur Dunkerley.**] b. at Manchester, Lancashire, England, c1861; d. at Worthing, Sussex, England, Jan. 24, 1941. An English journalist, novelist, and poet. He was on the staff of the *Idler* and *To-Day,* both of which he initiated with Jerome K. Jerome. A prolific writer, he published *Bees In Amber* (1913), *All's Well* (1916), *The King's Highway* (1916), *Hymn for the Men at the Front* (1916), *The Vision Splendid* (1917), *The Fiery Cross* (1917), *Hearts Courageous* (1918), and *Gentlemen—The King!* (1920), poetry; *Everywoman and War* (1916) and *Winds of the Dawn* (1919), essays; *The Cedar Box* (1924), *The Hidden Years* (1925), *Anno Domini* (1932), and several other works on the life of Christ; and 43 novels, including *God's Prisoner* (1898), *Rising Fortunes* (1899), *A Princess of Vascovy* (1900), *John of Gerisau* (1903), *Bondman Free* (1903), *Mr. Joseph Scorer* (1903), *Barbe of Grande Bayou* (1903), *Recollections of Roderick Fyfe* (1927), and *The Hawks of Como* (1928).

Oxford (oks'ford), 1st Earl of. Title of **Harley, Robert.**

Oxford, 17th Earl of. Title of **Vere, Edward de.**

Oxford, Earl of. In Shakespeare's *3 Henry VI,* the historical John de Vere, a supporter of Margaret and the Lancastrians. He is captured at the battle of Tewkesbury. In Shakespeare's *Richard III,* he joins Richmond and fights at Bosworth.

Oxford, Earl of. One of the principal characters in Sir Walter Scott's novel *Anne of Geierstein.*

Oxford, University of. A university at Oxford, England, the older of the two great English universities. It developed in the 12th century, Robert Pullen and the Lombard Vacarius being early teachers of note. It contains the following colleges: University (founded in 1249), Merton (1264), Balliol (between 1263 and 1268), Exeter (1314 and 1565), Oriel (1324 and 1326), Queen's (1340), New (1379), Lincoln (1427 and 1478), All Souls (1437), Magdalen (1458), Brasenose (1509), Corpus Christi (1516), Christ Church (1546), Trinity (1554), Saint John's (1555), Jesus (1571), Wadham (1612), Pembroke (1624), Worcester (1714), Keble (1870), and Hertford (1874). There are four colleges for women: Lady Margaret Hall (1878), Somerville (1879), Saint Hugh's (1886), and Saint Hilda's (1889). Among its affiliated institutions are Saint David's College (at Lampeter), Firth College (at Sheffield), Royal Albert Memorial University College (at Exeter), and University College (at Nottingham). Among the institutions connected with the university are the Bodleian Library, which contains more than 1,500,000 volumes, Radcliffe Library, Ashmolean Museum, and Clarendon Press. University sermons are mostly preached at Saint Mary's Church, a fine old building (of the 15th and 16th centuries) in High Street, which has always been closely connected with the university. The two governing bodies are the Convocation, which includes all who continue members of the university, and the Hebdomadal Council, consisting of the chancellor, vice-chancellor, proctors, and 18 elected members. The ancient house of congregation, once a governing body, is now largely concerned with the granting of degrees.

Oxford Movement. The name sometimes given to a movement in the Church of England toward High Church principles, as against the tendency toward liberalism and rationalism; so called from the fact that it originated (1833–41) in the University of Oxford.

Oxford Street. [Former name, **Tyburn Road.**] The principal commercial thoroughfare between the NW part of London and the City of London. As late as 1729 it was built up only on its N side. It extends from Holborn to the Marble Arch, and contains many of the most important shops in London.

Oxford Tracts. See **Tracts for the Times.**

oxymoron (ok.si.mō'ron). In rhetoric, a figure consisting in adding to a word an epithet or qualification apparently contradictory; in general, close connection of two words seemingly opposed to each other; an expression made epigrammatic or pointed by seeming self-contradictory.

Ozymandias (oz.i.man'di.as). A poem by Shelley, published by Leigh Hunt in *The Examiner* in 1818. It is based on a story recounted by Diodorus Siculus, a Greek historian of the 1st century A.D., who reported the statue of Ozymandias (so called by Diodorus Siculus; the statue was actually that of the Egyptian Pharaoh Ramses (or Rameses) II)

---

d̦, d or j; ș, s or sh; ț, t or ch; z̧, z or zh; o, F. cloche; ü, F. menu; čh, Sc. loch; ń, F. bonbon.

to be the largest in Egypt, and to bear the inscription: "I am Ozymandias, the King of Kings; if any man wishes to know what I am and where I am buried, let him surpass me in some of my achievements." Shelley uses this story to empha-

size how futile and vain such sentiments actually are:

> . . . Round the decay
> Of that colossal wreck, boundless and bare
> The lone and level sands stretch far away.

P

Packard (pak′ard), **Frank Lucius.** b. at Montreal, Canada, 1877; d. at Lachine, Quebec, Canada, Feb. 17, 1942. A Canadian writer, chiefly noted for his Jimmie Dale detective stories. His books include *Pawned*, *The Four Stragglers*, *Greater Love Hath No Man*, *The Beloved Traitor*, *The Night Operator*, and *The Wire Devils*.

Packlemerton (pak′ęl.mėr.tǫn), **Jasper.** A figure in Mrs. Jarley's waxworks in Dickens's *Old Curiosity Shop*. He had murdered 14 wives by tickling the soles of their feet.

Pacolet (pak′ǫ.let). A dwarf in *Valentine and Orson*, in the Charlemagne cycle of romances. The name has been given to other dwarfs in literature. Sir Walter Scott gave it to a character in *The Pirate*, and Steele used it for a familiar spirit in *The Tatler*.

Pactolus (pak.tō′lus). In ancient geography, a small river of Lydia, Asia Minor, a tributary of the Hermus. It was long celebrated for its gold, but its sands had ceased to produce by the time of Augustus. In Greek legend, its golden sands were caused by the touch of Midas.

Paeonia (pē.ō′ni.ą). In ancient geography, a region in the interior of Macedonia.

paean (pē′ąn). Originally, a hymn to a help-giving god, especially Apollo, under the title of *Paean* or *Paeon*, containing the invocation "Io Paean," asking for aid in war or other trouble, or giving thanks for aid received; hence, a war song sung before a battle in honor of Ares, or after a battle as a thanksgiving to Apollo; in later times, a hymn in praise of other gods, or even of mortals; hence, a song of triumph generally; a loud and joyous song.

> With ancient rites,
> And due devotions, I have ever hung
> Elaborate Pæans on thy golden shrine.
> (B. Jonson, *Cynthia's Revels*, V.ii.)

> I sung the joyful Pæan clear,
> And, sitting, burnished without fear
> The brand, the buckler, and the spear—
> Waiting to strive a happy strife.
> (Tennyson, *The Two Voices*.)

Paganini (pä.gä.nē′nē), **Nicolò.** b. at Genoa, Italy, Oct. 27, 1782; d. at Nice, France, May 27, 1840. An Italian violin virtuoso. He first appeared in public in 1793 at Genoa. He commenced his foreign tours in 1797; from 1801 till 1805 he did not play in public; he then resumed his concert tours, and soon after became solo player to the court at Lucca. It was here that he became famous for his execution on the single G-string. From this time his success was remarkable, and his bizarre and mysterious appearance (on and off the stage) added to his fame

(it was currently reported by some credulous persons that he was a son of the devil, whom he was fancied to resemble). He left several sonatas and concertos, but is perhaps best remembered as a composer for his 24 caprices (which were later given piano scores by Liszt and Schumann).

Page (pāj). In Shakespeare's *Merry Wives of Windsor*, the easy husband of Mistress Page.

Page, Anne. In Shakespeare's *Merry Wives of Windsor*, the daughter of the Pages, wooed and finally won by Fenton. She rejects both Slender and Dr. Caius, her parents' choices.

Page, Mistress. In Shakespeare's *Merry Wives of Windsor*, one of the married women to whom Falstaff professes love. She fools him into believing that she responds, but in fact devises the Windsor Forest incident, the climax of all the pranks played on Falstaff.

Page, William. In Shakespeare's *Merry Wives of Windsor*, the young brother of Anne Page. The scene where he appears was first printed in the folio of 1623.

pageant. 1. *Obs.* A scaffold, in general movable (moving on four wheels, as a car or float), on which shows, spectacles, and plays were represented in the Middle Ages; a stage or platform; a triumphal car, chariot, arch, statue, float, or other object forming part of or carried in public shows and processions.

> And bytwene euery of the pagentis went lytell children of bothe kyndes, gloryously and rychely dressyd.   (Sir R. Guylforde, *Pylgrymage*.)

> In 1500, "the cartwryghts [are] to make iiij new wheles to the pagiaunt."   (*York Plays*, Int.)

> The maner of these playes were, every company had his pagiant, or p′te, wᶜʰ pagiants weare a high scafold w′th 2 rowmes, a higher and a lower, upon 4 wheels. In the lower they apparelled themselves, and in the higher rowme they played, beinge all open on the tope, that the behoulders might heare and see them. The places where they played them was in every streete.
> (Quoted in A. W. Ward's *Eng. Dram. Lit.*)

> At certain distances, in places appointed for the purpose, the pageants were erected, which were temporary buildings representing castles, palaces, gardens, rocks, or forests, as the occasion required.
> (Strutt, *Sports and Pastimes*.)

2. The play performed upon such a scaffold or platform; a spectacle; a show; an entertainment; a theatrical exhibition; hence, a procession or parade with stately or splendid accompaniments; a showy display.

Any forein vsing any part of the same craft that

cumyth into this citie to sell any bukes or to take any warke to wurk shall pay to the vp-holding of their padgiant yerelie iiijd.
(Quoted in *York Plays*, Int.)

If you will see a pageant truly play'd, . . .
Go hence a little and I shall conduct you,
If you will mark it.
(Shak., *As You Like It*, III.iv.)

We see the pageants in Cheapside, the lions and the elephants; but we do not see the men that carry them: we see the judges look big, look like lions; but we do not see who moves them.
(Selden, *Table-Talk*.)

In the first pageant, or act, the Deity is represented seated on his throne by himself.
(Strutt, *Sports and Pastimes*.)

Paget (paj'ẹt), **Violet.** [Pseudonym, **Vernon Lee.**] b. 1857; d. Feb. 13, 1935. An English essayist and critic. She wrote much on the art, literature, and drama of Italy, where she lived for many years, and contributed to the principal English reviews. Author of *Studies of the Eighteenth Century in Italy* (1880), *Baldwin* (1886), *Althea* (1894), *Limbo and Other Essays* (1897), *Genius Loci* (1899), *Gospels of Anarchy* (1908), *The Tower of Mirrors* (1914), *Satan, the Waster* (1920), and *The Golden Keys* (1925).

Page to Falstaff (fôl'stȧf). In Shakespeare's *2 Henry IV*, a small boy who serves Falstaff and who talks rather precociously. In *Henry V*, he is the "Boy" who serves Bardolph, Nym, and Pistol, upon whose antics he comments caustically. He is killed by the French while guarding the army supplies of the English.

Pagett, M. P. (paj'ẹt). In Rudyard Kipling's volume *Departmental Ditties*, a meddlesome member of Parliament who spends the shortest possible time in a country, and then proceeds to create a hubbub in London about alleged examples of poor colonial administration. The character is mentioned in several pieces, perhaps most notably in the poem beginning "Pagett, M.P., was a liar, and a fluent liar therewith."

Pahlavi (pä'lạ.vē). [Also, **Pehlevi.**] An Iranian language, important as the medium for post-Avestan religious texts. It is one of the languages classified as Middle Persian and belongs to the western branch of the Iranian group of the Indo-Iranian subfamily of Indo-European languages.

Pain (pān), **Barry Eric Odell.** b. at Cambridge, England, Sept. 28, 1864; d. at Watford, England, May 5, 1928. An English humorist and novelist, author of *Eliza* (1900), *The One Before* (1902), *Eliza Getting On* (1911), *Exit Eliza* (1912), *Eliza's Son* (1913), and others.

Painter (pān'tèr), **William.** b. in Middlesex, England, c1540; d. at London, 1594. An English translator. In 1566 he published the first volume of *The Palace of Pleasure*, containing 60 tales from Livy and the older writers, and from Boccaccio, Bandello, Straparola, and other Italian and French novelists. The second volume was published in 1567, containing 34 tales. In later editions six more tales were added, so that there were 100 stories in all.

Pair of Blue Eyes, A. A novel by Thomas Hardy, published in 1873.

Pakht (päċht). In Egyptian mythology, a lioness-headed goddess, nearly indistinguishable from Bast.

Palace of Honour, The. A poem by Gawain Douglas, written in 1501. It is an imitation of Chaucer's *House of Fame*.

Palace of Pleasure, The. A collection of tales published in two volumes (a third was projected, but never written) by William Painter in 1566–67. Translations of the stories of Livy, Boccaccio, Bandello, and Margaret of Navarre appear here (Painter originally intended to translate only from Livy, but changed his plan and added the later French and Italian stories). The two volumes contain a hundred tales, making this the largest prose work between *Morte d'Arthur* and North's *Plutarch*, and it is the source for the plots of many Elizabethan dramas.

Palaemon (pạ.lē'mon). In Greek mythology, a sea divinity into which Melicertes was metamorphosed when Ino, his mother, fleeing from her husband, Athamus, leaped into the sea with the child Melicertes in her arms.

Palaeologus (pä.lẹ.ol'ọ.gus). [Also, **Paleologus.**] A Byzantine family which furnished the rulers of the Byzantine Empire during nearly the whole period from the accession of Michael in 1261 until the death of Constantine in 1453.

Palamede (pal'ạ.mēd). The young heir in Dryden's *Marriage à la Mode* who has been ordered by his father to marry Melantha, but decides upon his return from abroad that he prefers Doralice, his friend's wife.

Palamedes (pal.ạ.mē'dēz). In Greek legend, one of the Greek warriors in the expedition against Troy. He was killed by the Greeks through the machinations of Odysseus, who contrived that he should appear to have betrayed the Greeks for gold.

Palamon (pal'ạ.mon). In *The Two Noble Kinsmen*, one of the principal characters, the cousin and friend of Arcite.

Palamon and Arcite (är'sīt). Two noble youths the story of whose love for Emelye (or Emilia) has been told by Chaucer in *The Knight's Tale* (derived from Boccaccio's *Il Teseida*), by Dryden in a version of *The Knight's Tale* called *Palamon and Arcite*, by Fletcher and another (perhaps Shakespeare) in a play called *The Two Noble Kinsmen* (1634), and by others. Richard Edwards produced a play (now lost) entitled *Palamon and Arcite* at Christ Church Hall, Oxford, in 1566, in honor of Queen Elizabeth's visit there.

Pale (pāl), **the.** In Irish history, that part of Ireland in which English law was acknowledged, and within which the dominion of the English was restricted, for some centuries after the conquests of Henry II. John distributed the part of Ireland then subject to England into 12 counties palatine, and this region became subsequently known as the Pale, but the limits varied at different times.

Pale Horse. In literary allusion, an embodiment of death. The Pale Horse was shown to Saint John (Rev. vi. 8) in association with the death-dealing agents of sword, famine, and plague.

---

d̦, d or j; ṣ, s or sh; ț, t or ch; z̦, z or zh; o, F. cloche; ü, F. menu; ċh, Sc. loch; ṅ, F. bonbon.

Pales (pā'lēz). In old Italian and Roman mythology, a deity, protector of shepherds and flocks, sometimes regarded as a god and equated by the Romans with Pan or Faunus, and sometimes regarded as a goddess and identified with Vesta. The festival of Pales was the Parilia, celebrated April 21, for the increase of flocks.

Paley (pā'li), **William.** b. at Peterborough, England, in July, 1743; d. May 25, 1805. An English theologian and philosopher. He graduated at Christ's College, Cambridge, in 1763, took holy orders, and in 1766 was chosen a fellow of his college. He vacated his fellowship by marriage in 1776, and retired to the rectory of Musgrave in Westmorland, which had been conferred on him the year before. He was appointed archdeacon of Carlisle in 1782, became a prebendary of Saint Paul's in 1794, was presented to the subdeanery of Lincoln Cathedral, and in 1795 received the rectory of Bishop-Wearmouth. He published *Principles of Moral and Political Philosophy* (1785), *Horae Paulinae, or the Truth of the Scripture History of Saint Paul* (1790), *View of the Evidences of Christianity* (1794), and *Natural Theology* (1802).

Palgrave (pal'grāv, pôl'-), Sir **Francis.** b. at London, in July, 1788; d. at Hampstead (now part of London), July 6, 1861. An English historian. He was the son of a stockbroker named Meyer Cohen, and took his wife's name by royal permission in 1823, when he was admitted to the Church of England. He was called to the bar at the Middle Temple in 1827, and in 1838 was appointed deputy keeper of the public records. He was knighted in 1832. His chief works are *Rise and Progress of the English Commonwealth* (1832) and *History of Normandy and England* (4 vols., 1851–64).

Palgrave, Francis Turner. b. at London, Sept. 28, 1824; d. there, Oct. 24, 1897. An English poet; son of Sir Francis Palgrave. He was educated at the Charterhouse and at Balliol College, Oxford, and was professor of poetry at Oxford (1885–95). He published *Idylls and Songs* (1854), *Essays on Art* (1866), *Hymns* (1867), and *Lyrical Poems* (1871), and edited *Golden Treasury of English Lyrical Poetry* (1861) and *Treasury of Sacred Song* (1889).

Palgrave, William Gifford. b. at London, Jan. 24, 1826; d. at Montevideo, Uruguay, Sept. 30, 1888. An English traveler; son of Sir Francis Palgrave. In 1862–63 he traveled extensively in the interior of Arabia, and in 1865 he was employed by the British government to negotiate for the release of prisoners in Ethiopia. Subsequently he held various British consular positions, and from 1884 was minister to Uruguay. He published *Narrative of a Year's Journey through Central and Eastern Arabia* (1865), *Essays on Eastern Questions* (1872), *Dutch Guiana* (1876), and others.

palimpsest (pal'imp.sest). **1.** A parchment or other writing material from which one writing has been erased or rubbed out to make room for another; hence, the new writing or manuscript upon such a parchment.

Amongst the most curious of the literary treasures we saw are a manuscript of some of St. Augustine's works, written upon a palimpsest of Cicero's "De Republica," etc.
(Greville, *Memoirs*, May 12, 1830.)

2. Any inscribed slab, etc., particularly a monumental brass, which has been turned and engraved with new inscriptions and devices on the reverse side.

A large number of brasses in England are palimpsests, the back of an ancient brass having been engraved for the more recent memorial. (*Encyc. Brit.*)

palindrome (pal'in.drōm). A word, verse, or sentence that reads the same either from left to right or from right to left. The English language has few palindromes. Examples are—"Madam, I'm Adam" (supposed speech of Adam to Eve); "lewd did I live & evil I did dwel" (John Taylor).

　Spun out riddles, and weav'd fiftie tomes
　Of logogriphes and curious palindromes.
　　　(B. Jonson, *An Execration upon Vulcan.*)

palinode (pal'i.nōd). A poetical recantation, or declaration contrary to a former one; a poem in which a poet retracts the invectives contained in a former satire; hence, a recantation in general.

Palinode. The Catholic shepherd in the May Eclogue of Spenser's *Shepherd's Calendar.*

Palinode, A. A poem by Edmund Bolton, included in *England's Helicon* (1600).

Palinurus (pal.i.nū'rus). In Greek legend, the helmsman of Aeneas, who fell asleep, fell overboard, and was drowned off the western coast of Italy.

Palladium (pạ.lā'di.um). In Greek religion, an image of Pallas Athena, on which depended the safety of the city which harbored it. In Greek legend, it was sent by Zeus to Troy. As long as it stood unharmed, Troy could not be taken; after the Greeks stole it, however, Troy fell to them. In Roman legend, Aeneas rescued the sacred image from the burning city of Troy, took it to Italy, and it became established at Rome. It is said to have saved Rome from the sack of the Gauls in 390 B.C. Many cities in both Greece and Italy claimed and disputed the possession of the original.

Pallas (pal'ạs). In Greek mythology, a title of the goddess Athena, in reference to her having killed a Titan or giant named Pallas in the war between the gods and the giants.

Palliser (pal'i.sėr), **Plantagenet.** In the novels of Anthony Trollope, a noble and upright gentleman who appears in *The Small House at Allington, Can You Forgive Her?, Phineas Finn, The Prime Minister,* and *The Duke's Children.* He is heir to the Duke of Omnium, and eventually becomes prime minister.

Pall Mall (pel' mel', pal' mal'). A street in London, leading from Trafalgar Square to the Green Park, famous for its clubs. In the 18th century, it was known for its taverns, which were the scene of meetings of various literary and convivial societies.

Palmer (pä'mėr), **John** (**Leslie**). [Pseudonym (with Hilary Aidan St. George Saunders), **Francis Beeding.**] b. 1885; d. 1944. An English novelist and critic. He was a staff member (1910–15) of the *Saturday Review,* drama critic (1916 *et seq.*) of the *Evening Standard,* and a member from 1920 until 1939 of the permanent secretariat of the League of Nations. Author of novels including *Peter Paragon* (1915), *The King's Men* (1916), *The Happy Fool* (1922). *Looking After Joan* (1923), *Jennifer* (1926), and *Timothy* (1931). His critical works include *The Comedy of Manners*, *Molière* (1930), and a study of Ben Jonson. Under their joint pseudonym he and Saunders wrote many mystery and adventure novels, among them *The Seven Sleepers* (1925), *Death Walks in Eastrepps* (1931), and *Eleven Were Brave* (1941). See also **Beeding.**

Palmer, Roger. [Title, Earl of **Castlemaine.**] b. at Dorney Court, Buckinghamshire, England, Sept. 3, 1634; d. at Oswestry, Shropshire, England, July 21, 1705. An English diplomat and writer. He was raised to the Irish peerage after the Restoration to propitiate his wife, Barbara Villiers, who was the mistress of Charles II, when Charles married (1662) Catherine of Braganza. He was accused in the Popish Plot and acquitted. Later, as James II's envoy to Rome, he acted undiplomatically in respect to certain of the king's favorites and thus angered the Pope. He was excluded from the act of indemnity (1690) and was later banished.

Palmer, Sir Roundell. [Title, 1st Earl of **Selborne.**] b. at Mixbury, England, Nov. 27, 1812; d. at Blackmoor, near Petersfield, England, May 4, 1895. An English jurist and hymnologist. He was solicitor general (1861–63), attorney general (1863–66), British counsel at the Geneva Court of Arbitration (1871–72), and lord chancellor under Gladstone (1872–74, 1880–85). He published *Book of Praise, from the Best English Hymn-writers* (1863) and other works.

Palmerín of England (päl.mä.rēn'). A 16th-century Portuguese romance (known to Edmond Spenser, and reflected in portions of *The Faerie Queene*) concerning the exploits of Palmerín of England, son of Don Duardos (who was the son of Fadrique, King of Britain) and Flerida, daughter of Palmerín de Oliva. Southey published a translation of it (with some modifications) in 1807.

Palmyra (pal.mī'ra). [In the Bible, **Tadmor.**] In ancient geography, a city situated on an oasis in the desert E of Syria, said to have been built by Solomon. It early became an important commercial center, rose to prominence in the reign of Hadrian (c130 A.D.), became a Roman colony c212, became practically independent in the reigns of Valerian and Gallienus under Odenathus, and was the capital of an important kingdom. It became formally independent under Zenobia, who was defeated and captured by Aurelian in 272. Palmyra was destroyed in 273.

Palsgrave (palz'grāv, pôlz'-), **John.** b. at London, c1480; d. there, 1554. An English scholar. He was appointed teacher of French to the Princess Mary, sister of Henry VIII, before her marriage (1514) to Louis XII of France. He remained in her service, returning to England with her when she married (1515) Charles Brandon, 1st Duke of Suffolk. He became tutor to the king's bastard son, Henry Fitzroy, Duke of Richmond, in 1525, went to Oxford in 1531, and was presented with the living of Saint Dunstan's in the East, London, by Thomas, Archbishop Cranmer, in 1533. He wrote a book containing his method of instruction, a grammar and dictionary combined, entitled, *Lesclaircissement de la Langue Francoyse, composé par Maistre Jehan Palsgrave, Angloys, Natif de Londres, et Gradué de Paris*, in 1530. It is a valuable record of the exact state of the French and English languages at the time. In 1540 he published a translation of a Latin play entitled *Acolastus*, by a Dutch schoolmaster, Willem de Volder (Fullonius).

Palsgrave's Company. See **Lord Admiral's Men.**

Paltock (pôl'tok), **Robert.** b. probably at Westminster, London, 1697; d. at Lambeth, London, March 20, 1767. An English lawyer and author. Author of *Peter Wilkins* (c1751), a romantic story of the Robinson Crusoe type, and the *Memoirs of the Life of Parnese, a Spanish Lady* (1751).

Pam (pam). A nickname of the 19th-century British statesman Lord Palmerston, once much used by journalists.

Pamela (pa.mē'la). A character in Sir Philip Sidney's *Arcadia*, whose name (but not its pronunciation) Richardson borrowed for his first novel.

Pamela (pam'e.la). [Full title, **Pamela, or Virtue Rewarded.**] The first of the series of novels written by Samuel Richardson, published in 1740. Pamela Andrews is an extremely virtuous servant whose mistress dies, whereupon Mr. B, the young son and heir of the family, presses his dishonorable advances upon her (she is finally forced to leave the house to escape from him). She shows great wit and cleverness in eluding him, and he eventually grows so enamoured of her that he is willing to overlook her low social position and marry her. The second part of the novel, published in 1741, shows Pamela married to the profligate Mr. B. By her sweetness and virtue she reforms his character. This book is often considered the first modern English novel. It was an immediate and tremendous success. It evoked satirical sketches from several contemporary authors, of which *An Apology for the Life of Mrs. Shamela Andrews* (1741), possibly by Fielding, is one of the best known. Indeed, it so amused Henry Fielding that he was moved to write the history of *Joseph Andrews*, an equally virtuous servingman and the brother of Pamela, which was begun as a caricature but grew into a work of independent character. Fielding's amusement (and that of some other readers) did not stem from any contempt for virtue as such, but from a suspicion that Pamela's "virtue" was used thoughtfully and coldly to trap her master into marriage.

Pancks (pangks). In Dickens's novel *Little Dorrit*, the good little man who is Casby's rent collector, and is blamed by Casby's tenants for the avaricious ruthlessness which is actually that of his employer. He is of great help to the Dorrits, and has the satisfaction in the end of revealing Casby as the wicked hypocrite he actually is.

Pan (pan). In Greek mythology, the god of pastures and flocks. The original seat of his worship was in Arcadia, whence it gradually spread over the rest of Greece. He was represented with the head and body of a man; his lower parts were the hind quarters of a goat, of which animal he bore the horns and ears also. He was fond of music and of dancing with the forest nymphs, and was the inventor of the syrinx, or Panpipes, which he made of reeds. Sudden terror (panic) without visible or reasonable cause was attributed to his influence.

The Romans identified Pan with their own god Inuus, and sometimes also with Faunus.

Panchatantra (pan.chạ.tan'trạ). A celebrated Sanskrit book of fables: the source of the tales known in Europe as Kalilah and Dimnah, or the Fables of Bidpai.

Pandareos (pan.dā'rẹ.os). In Greek legend, a Milesian who stole and gave to Tantalus the golden dog made by Hephaestus.

Pandarus (pan'dạ.rus). In Greek legend, a hero among the Trojans during the siege of Troy, leader of the Lycians. The procurer of this name in medieval romance, and presented by Shakespeare and others, is not the same character.

Pandarus. In Shakespeare's *Troilus and Cressida*, the uncle of Cressida. Troilus, when he discovers that Cressida is Diomedes's mistress, turns upon Pandarus and curses him as a "broker-lackey" (whence the origin of the word "pander").

Pandects of Justinian (pan'dekts; jus.tin'i.ạn). [Also called **The Digest.**] A collection of Roman civil law made by the emperor Justinian I in the 6th century, containing decisions or judgments of lawyers, to which the emperor gave the force and authority of law. This compilation, the most important of the body of Roman civil law, consists of 50 books.

Pandemonium (pan.dẹ.mō'ni.um). A place in Hell invented by Milton in *Paradise Lost*. It is the principal gathering place of the fallen angels.

Pandemos (pan.dē'mos). [Also, **Pandemus.**] An epithet of Aphrodite, in her aspect of the Goddess of Worldly Love.

Pander. In Shakespeare's *Pericles*, the owner of the brothel in Mytilene to which Boult brings Marina. His trade is nearly lost by her persuading his clients to desist from their vice.

Pandion (pan'di.on). In Greek legend, a king of Athens; father of Procne and Philomela, the two girls who were transformed, respectively, into swallow and nightingale.

Pandora (pan.dō'rạ). In Greek mythology, the first woman. She was created by Hephaestus at the command of Zeus in revenge for the theft of fire from heaven by Prometheus. The gods gave her beauty, cunning, and other attributes fitted to bring misfortune to man. She was given to Epimetheus, who accepted the gift in spite of the warnings of Hephaestus. For Pandora carried a box (or jar) which she was forbidden to open. When her curiosity finally won out, however, out flew all the evils of life. Or, according to another version, the blessings of the gods flew out and were lost; only one thing remained in the box: Hope.

Pandosto, the Triumph of Time (pan.dos'tō). A romance by Robert Greene, published in 1588. The second title is *The History of Dorastus and Fawnia;* the later editions give this as the title. Shakespeare based his *Winter's Tale* on this story; the character of Pandosto was the original of Leontes, king of Sicilia, in Shakespeare's play.

Pandrosos (pan'drọ.sos). In Greek mythology, a daughter of Cecrops.

Pandulph (pan'dulf), **Cardinal.** In Shakespeare's *King John*, the papal legate who forces the French

king to break his peace with John. He persuades the Dauphin to invade England, but then vainly tries to make him withdraw when John accepts the Pope's (and Pandulph's) candidate for Archbishop of Canterbury.

Pandulpho (pan.dul'fō). One of the revengers in John Marston's tragedy *Antonio's Revenge*.

panegyric (pan.ẹ.jir'ik). 1. A eulogy, written or spoken, in praise of some person or achievement; a formal or elaborate encomium.

> We give you Thanks, not only for your Presents, but your Compliments too. For this is not so much a making of Presents as Panegyricks.
> (N. Bailey, tr. of *Colloquies* of Erasmus.)

> A stranger preach'd at Euston Church, and fell into a handsome panegyric on my Lord's new building the church. (Evelyn, *Diary*, Sept. 9, 1676.)

2. Praise bestowed on some person, action, or character; laudation: as, a tone of exaggerated *panegyric*.

> Let others . . . bestrew the hearses of the great with panegyric.
> (Goldsmith, *Citizen of the World*, xliii.)

Pangloss (pan'glos), **Doctor.** In Voltaire's *Candide*, an obstinately optimistic philosopher, the tutor of Candide. His favorite maxim is that "all is for the best in this best of all possible worlds."

Pangloss, Doctor. In the younger George Colman's play *The Heir-at-Law*, a pedantic but gay and amusing prig, the tutor of Dick Dowlas. He is a satirical portrait of the mercenary tutor of the period.

Panhellenius (pan.he.lē'ni.us). In Greek mythology, a surname of Zeus.

Pankhurst (pangk'hèrst), **Estelle Sylvia.** b. at Manchester, England, May 5, 1882—. An English feminist and propagandist. She was founder (1914) of the *Workers' Dreadnought*, and was frequently imprisoned and fined for her militant suffragist activities. Author of *The Suffragette* (1912), *Save the Mothers* (1932), *The Life of Emmeline Pankhurst* (1935), and *Education in Ethiopia* (1946).

Pantagruel (pan.tag'rọ̈.el; French, päṅ.tå.grü.el). The King of the Dipsodes and son of Gargantua, in François Rabelais's *History of Gargantua and Pantagruel*. He is able to deal with serious matters in a spirit of broad and somewhat cynical good humor.

Pantaloon (pan.tạ.lön'). [French, **Pantalon** (päṅ.tà.lôṅ); Italian, **Pantalone** (pän.tä.lō'nä).] A traditional character from Italian folk comedy. He was a stock character in Italian comedy by the middle of the 16th century. He usually appears as a bespectacled, beslippered old man, wearing tight trousers which are a combination of pants and stockings. He plays a buffoon part and is the butt of many jokes.

Panthea (pan'thẹ.ạ). The beautiful young heroine of Beaumont and Fletcher's *A King and no King*, loved by both Arbaces and Tigranes.

pantheism (pan'thẹ.izm). 1. *Obs.* The worship of all the gods.
2. The metaphysical doctrine that God is the only substance, of which the material universe and man are only manifestations. It is accompanied with a denial of God's personality.

Pantheon (pan′thē.on, -ǫn). A building at Rome, now the Church of Santa Maria Rotonda, completed by Agrippa in 27 B.C., and consecrated originally to the "divine ancestors" of the Julian family. The lighting of the interior is solely from an open circle, 28 ft. in diameter, at the summit of the dome. The effect is unique and highly imposing. The construction is of concrete, lightly faced with brick, and encrusted (now almost exclusively in the interior) with marble. The dome is practically solid concrete, the familiar system of inset arches being merely one brick deep, and having served as a scaffolding during the erection. Raphael is buried in the Pantheon.

Panthino (pan.thē′nō). In Shakespeare's *Two Gentlemen of Verona*, the servant of Antonio.

pantomime (pan′tǫ.mīm). **1.** One who expresses his meaning by action without words; a player who employs only action—mimicry, gestures, movements, and posturing—in presenting his part. [Obsolete or rare.]

> Betweene the actes, when the players went to make ready for another, there was great silence, and the people waxt weary; then came in these maner of conterfaite vices, they were called Pantomimi. (Puttenham, *Arte of Eng. Poesie.*)

> I would our pantomimes also and stage players would examine themselves and their callings by this rule. (Bp. Sanderson, *Sermon on 1 Cor. vii. 24.*)

> Not that I think those pantomimes
> Who vary action with the times
> Are less ingenious in their art
> Than those who dully act one part.
> (Butler, *Hudibras.*)

2. (*a*) Under the Roman empire, a kind of spectacular play resembling the modern "ballet of action," in which the functions of the actor were confined to gesticulation and dancing, the accompanying text being sung by a chorus; in modern times, any play the plot of which is expressed by mute gestures, with little or no dialogue; hence, expression of anything by gesture alone: as, he made known his wants in *pantomime*.

> In the early days of the Empire tragedy was dissolved into choral music and pantomimic action; and the pantomime, a species of ballet of action, established itself as a favourite class of entertainment. (A. W. Ward, *Eng. Dram. Lit.*)

(*b*) A popular theatrical entertainment of which many are produced in Great Britain about the Christmas season, usually consisting of two parts, the first or burlesque being founded on some popular fable, the effects being heightened by gorgeous scenery and catching music, and the second, or harlequinade, consisting almost wholly of the tricks of the clown and pantaloon and the dancing of harlequin and columbine.

> The brilliancy of the dresses and scenery . . . and the excellence of the music, in the pantomimes, are great improvements upon the humble attempts of the vagrant motion-master. (Strutt, *Sports and Pastimes.*)

Pantomime. A novel by G. B. Stern, published in 1914.

Panurge (pa.nėrj′; French, pȧ.nürzh). In François Rabelais's *History of Gargantua and Pantagruel*, a companion whom Pantagruel picks up at Paris. A roguish libertine, he cannot decide whether to marry, and the investigation of the entire problem of marriage occupies entertainingly the latter part of Rabelais's work.

Panza (pan′zạ; Spanish, pän′thä), **Sancho.** See **Sancho Panza.**

Paolo and Francesca (pä′ō.lō; frän.chäs′kä). A drama by Stephen Phillips, published in 1899. The theme, the love of Paolo Malatesta for his elder brother's wife, Francesca, is a favorite one in literature and has been used by many writers from Dante onward. It inspired a tone poem by Tschaikowsky.

Papal Tyranny in the Reign of King John. Colley Cibber's alteration of Shakespeare's *King John*, produced in 1745.

Paperstamp (pā′pėr.stȧmp), **Mr.** In Thomas Love Peacock's *Melincourt*, a character satirizing Wordsworth.

Paphos (pā′fos). In ancient geography, a city in Cyprus. The celebrated temple of Astarte, or Aphrodite, here was built of unburned brick and wood on a stone foundation measuring 164 by 220 ft. The famous image of the goddess was a baetylus (a conical meteoric stone). The temple stood in a large enclosure whose walls were likewise of sun-dried brick on a massive stone foundation.

parable (par′ạ.bl). An allegorical relation or representation from which a moral is drawn for instruction. It is a species of fable, and differs from the apologue in that it deals with events which, though fictitious, might reasonably have happened in nature. The word is also employed in the English Bible to signify a proverb, a proverbial or notable saying, a thing darkly or figuratively expressed.

> I will open my mouth in a parable; I will utter dark sayings of old. (Ps. lxxviii.2.)

> Shall not all these take up a parable against him, and a taunting proverb against him? (Hab. ii.6.)

> Thou shalt never get such a secret from me but by a parable. (Shak., *T. G. of V.*, II.v.)

Paracelsus (par.ạ.sel′sus). A long poem by Robert Browning, published in 1835–36. One of his earlier works, it won the praise of Wordsworth and Walter Savage Landor. It is based on the life of the 16th-century alchemist. In his poem, Browning conceives of Paracelsus as a man in search of ultimate truth, the secret of the world. After a variety of adventures he eventually comes to his death, finally accepting the Christian faith, and realizing that what he had lacked was not knowledge, but human sympathy.

Paracelsus, Philippus Aureolus. [Original name, **Theophrastus Bombastus von Hohenheim.**] b. at Maria-Einsiedeln, Switzerland, Dec. 17, 1493; d. at Salzburg, Austria, Sept. 23, 1541. A German-Swiss physician and alchemist. He entered the University of Basel at the age of 16, but left without a degree, and spent many years in travel and intercourse with distinguished scholars. He lectured on medicine at Basel from c1526 to 1528, when he was driven from the city by the medical

ḍ, d or j; ṣ, s or sh; ṭ, t or ch; ẓ, z or zh; o, F. cloche; ü, F. menu; ċh, Sc. loch; ṅ, F. bonbon.

corporations, whose methods he had severely criticized. He is important in the history of medicine chiefly on account of the impetus which he gave to the development of pharmaceutical chemistry. He was an opponent of the then-current theory that diseases were caused by imbalance of the humors, or body fluids, holding instead that a disease actually had existence and could be fought by specific remedies. Among the drugs he introduced to medical practice were opium, mercury, sulfur, iron, and arsenic. He was also the author of a visionary and theosophic system of philosophy. The first collective edition of his works appeared at Basel in 1589–91. Among the many legends concerning him is that he kept a small demon in the hilt of his sword.

Paradise Lost. An epic poem by John Milton, published in 12 books in 1667, originally planned as a drama to be entitled "Adam Unparadised." The subject is the fall of man. This is his greatest work, and is generally considered the chief epic in the English language and the poem in which blank verse is used with the most majestic and sonorous effect. It opens *in medias res*, with the fall of the angels, their council for revenge, the election of Satan, and the choosing of a course of covert guile instead of open war. After a slight digression in Book III, Milton opens Book IV with Satan standing on top of Mount Niphrates, pondering his mission. It is in this soliloquy that Milton first clearly portrays Satan as a semiheroic figure. The scene then switches to Eden, where Adam and Eve are shown in all their beautiful innocence (but Eve's interest in her own beauty is emphasized as a foreshadowing of her later fall). Satan approaches Eve in her sleep, but Adam dispels her fears, and Book V begins with the famous morning hymn. The angel Raphael now appears to instruct Adam and Eve, and Books V–VIII are taken up with an epic recapitulation, in which the fall of the angels is traced to the moment of their first revolt, the creation of the world is described, and the philosophic doctrines of Milton, notably the doctrine of free will, are set forth:

> God made thee perfect, not immutable;
> And good he made thee, but to persevere
> He left it in thy power; ordain'd thy will
> By nature free, not over-rul'd by Fate
> Inextricable, or strict necessity.

In Book IX, Satan, in the form of a serpent, enters the garden, finds Eve alone, and flatters her into eating of the forbidden fruit of the Tree of Knowledge. When Adam discovers her trespass he also eats of the fruit (not for self-love, as did Eve, but because of his deep and passionate love of Eve). Immediately after this highly symbolic act of sin, they start to quarrel and are embarrassed at their nakedness. In Book X, God sends his Son to judge Adam and Eve. He does so, but also takes pity on them and clothes them. The progeny of Satan, Sin and Death, become aware of this, and enter the world of man by building a highway over Chaos. When Satan returns to Pandemonium (the chief place of Hell) he boasts of his success, but instead of applause he is greeted by hissing, for God has turned all of the fallen angels into serpents, luring them with the Tree of Knowledge which when

tasted turns into ash and dust. Adam and Eve eventually decide to pray to God for forgiveness, and Christ intercedes for them; God accepts their repentance, but orders them out of Eden. The archangel Michael appears to the fallen pair to do God's bidding, first telling them of God's further plans concerning man (the Flood, and the Birth, Incarnation, Death, Resurrection, and Ascension of Christ) and then leads them out of the garden.

Paradise of Dainty Devices, The. A collection of poems compiled by Richard Edwards and printed in 1576. It was very popular, and went through nine or ten editions before 1606.

Paradise of Fools. In medieval cosmography, that section of Limbo reserved for fools who were not responsible for their behavior.

Paradise Regained. An epic poem by John Milton, published in four books in 1671, in which Christ figures as the epic hero. It opens with Satan's hearing news of the baptism of Christ, followed by a council of the fallen angels, at which Satan is again elected as seducer. Satan appears to Christ in the wilderness in the guise of an old man tempting Him to obtain food by turning stone into bread, but Christ refuses. In the next book Simon, Andrew, and Mary are shown wondering over the disappearance of Christ, and a second council of the damned considers the future tactics of seduction. Glory and honor are chosen by Satan as the materials for the second temptation. First Christ dreams of food, and Satan responds by contriving the vision of a luxurious banquet, but Christ again refuses, saying that He will accept food "thereafter as I like the giver." Satan now offers wealth, but is refused. Satan then shows Christ all the kingdoms of the earth, and offers them to Him if He will but fall down and worship Satan. Satan, in desperation, now carries Christ by force to the pinnacle of a high temple, there expecting Him to fall. But, instead, Satan falls, and Christ remains in his "uneasy station," from which He is carried away to Heaven by the angels.

Paradiso (pä.rä.dē′zō). The third part of Dante's *Divina Commedia.*

paradox (par′ạ.doks). A statement or proposition which at first view seems absurd, or at variance with common sense, or which actually or apparently contradicts some ascertained truth or received opinion, though on investigation or when explained it may appear to be well founded. As a rhetorical figure its use is well exemplified in the first quotation.

> As unknown, and yet well known; as dying, and, behold, we live; as chastened, and not killed; as sorrowful, yet always rejoicing; as poor, yet making many rich; as having nothing, and yet possessing all things.   (2 Cor. vi.9,10.)

> The fraudulent disputation of the sophister tendeth alwayes to one of these five ends or marks: that is, by force of argument . . . to make you . . . to grant some paradox, which is as much to say as an opinion contrary to all mens opinions.
>   (Blundeville, *Arte of Logicke* (1619), vi.4.)

> These are old fond paradoxes to make fools laugh i' the alehouse.   (Shak., *Othello*, II.i.)

> Some of my readers are hardly inclined to think

that the word paradox could once have had no disparagement in its meaning; still less that persons could have applied it to themselves. I chance to have met with a case in point against them. It is Spinoza's "Philosophia Scripturæ Interpres, Exercitatio Paradoxa."
(De Morgan, *Budget of Paradoxes*.)

Paragot (par'ạ.got), **Berzelius Nibbidard.** The quixotic hero, the "vagabond" in William John Locke's novel *The Beloved Vagabond* (1906).

paraphrase (par'ạ.frāz). A restatement of a text or passage, giving the sense of the original in other words, generally in fuller terms and with greater detail, for the sake of clearer and more complete exposition. When the original is in a foreign language, translation and paraphrase may be combined.

All his commands being but a transcript of his own life, and his sermons a living paraphrase upon his practice. (South, *Sermons*.)

In paraphrase, or translation with latitude, the author's words are not so strictly followed as his sense. (Dryden.)

Parasitaster, or the Fawn (par″ạ.si.tas'tẻr). A play by John Marston, acted (c1604) at Blackfriars, London, and printed in 1606.

Parcae (pär'sē). The three Fates of Roman mythology. Originally there was one (named Parca), a birth goddess who decided the destiny of the newborn. She was early equated with the Greek Moirae, and thus the concept became triplicate.

Pardoe (pär'dō), **Julia.** b. at Beverley, Yorkshire, England, 1806; d. Nov. 26, 1862. An English historical and miscellaneous writer.

Pardoner's Tale, The. One of Chaucer's *Canterbury Tales*, an exemplum on avarice. The plot is found in ancient Eastern tales and in the Italian collection *Cento Novelle Antiche*. With great simplicity and power, Chaucer tells the story of three revelers in a tavern who set out to find Death and kill him. They meet an old man who directs them to a certain tree, under which he says Death is sitting, but at the foot of which they find instead a great heap of gold. The youngest is sent to bring bread and wine while the other two guard the treasure; when he returns they murder him, but he has poisoned the wine, and so shortly the others have also met Death. The Pardoner himself has been called one of the best-described knaves in literature. He has long straggling hair, "yelow as wex," and eyes like a hare's:

A vernicle hadde he sowed on his cappe.
His walet lay biforn him in his lappe,
Bret-ful of pardoun come from Rome al hoot.
A voys he hadde as smal as hath a goot.

He carries an assortment of objects, such as a glass of "pigges bones," all purporting to be holy relics, and the prologue to his tale is a long recital of his prowess in selling his spurious absolutions and gulling the ignorant and the superstitious. He finishes the tale with a show of honest piety:

And Iesu Crist, that is our soules leche,
So graunte yow his pardon to receyve;
For that is best; I wol yow nat deceyve . . .

but then immediately offers to sell his pardons to the company.

parenthesis. **1.** An explanatory or qualifying clause, sentence, or paragraph inserted in another sentence or in the course of a longer passage, without being grammatically connected with it. It is regularly included by two upright curves facing each other (also called *parentheses*), or the variant form of them called *brackets*, but frequently by dashes, and even by commas. The quotation from Dryden given below contains a parenthesis.

Your first figure of tollerable disorder is [Parenthesis] or by an English name the [Insertour], and is when ye will seeme, for larger information or some other purpose, to peece or graffe in the middest of your tale an vnnecessary parcell of speach.
(Puttenham, *Arte of Eng. Poesie*.)

Thou shalt be seen
(Though with some short parenthesis between)
High on the throne of wit.
(Dryden, *To Congreve*, l. 52.)

2. The upright curves ( ) collectively, or either of them separately, used by printers and writers to mark off an interjected explanatory clause or qualifying remark: as, to place a word or clause in *parenthesis* or within *parentheses*.

The parentheses ( ), including the square form [ ] also called *crotchets* and now usually *brackets*, were formerly (as in the first quotation under def. 1) used to separate a word or words typographically, where quotation-marks are now used. In phonetic discussions (Ellis, Sweet, etc.) the curves are often used for a similar purpose, to indicate that the letters of the words so enclosed have a fixed phonetic value, according to a system previously explained. The curves are also used to enclose small marks and letters, and figures of reference, in order to make them more distinct to the eye.

Paris (par'is). [Also, **Alexander.**] In Greek legend, the second son of Priam, king of Troy, and Hecuba. Before his birth Hecuba dreamed that she had given birth to a firebrand which caused a conflagration of the city. The dream was interpreted to mean that she would give birth to a son who would bring disaster on Troy. Paris was accordingly exposed on Mount Ida, but was nourished by a she-bear, and found and brought up by the same shepherd who had been entrusted with his exposure. His parentage was accidentally discovered, and he was admitted to the household of Priam. He married the river nymph Oenone, and became celebrated far and wide for his beauty and accomplishments. During the nuptials of Peleus and Thetis, Eris (goddess of discord), who alone among the gods was uninvited, threw a golden apple among the marriage guests with the inscription "To the Fairest." A dispute arose between Hera, Aphrodite, and Athena over who should claim it. Zeus ordered Hermes to take the three goddesses to Paris, then still a shepherd tending his flocks on Mount Ida, to judge which was fairest. To influence his decision, Hera offered him power, Athena martial glory, and Aphrodite the most beautiful of women. So he gave the apple to Aphrodite, who in return helped him carry off Helen, the wife of Menelaus. The abduction of Helen from Sparta gave rise to the Trojan War, during which Paris earned somewhat of a reputation for cowardice. He fought against the Greeks to the end, however, killed Achilles, and was himself fatally wounded by Philoctetes with a poisoned arrow at the taking of Troy.

Paris. In George Peele's comedy *The Arraignment of Paris*, a Trojan shepherd.

Paris. In Shakespeare's *Romeo and Juliet*, a young nobleman to whom Capulet has betrothed his daughter Juliet against her will.

Paris. In Shakespeare's *Troilus and Cressida*, a son of Priam and lover of Helen. He, of course, opposes Hector's suggestion that Helen be returned to the Greeks so that the war may end, and fights with Menelaus, Helen's former husband (V.vii).

Paris. The "Roman actor" in Philip Massinger's play of that name.

Paris, Matthew. b. probably c1200; d. 1259. An English chronicler. His surname probably originated in the circumstance that he studied at the University of Paris. He entered the Benedictine monastery of St. Albans in 1217, was present at the nuptials of Henry III and Eleanor of Provence in 1236, and was sent on a mission to the Benedictine monastery of Holm (Trondheim), Norway, in 1248. He became chronicler of St. Albans on the death of Roger of Wendover in 1236. He enjoyed the favor of Henry III, who admitted him to his table and to private conversations during a visit of a week's duration at St. Albans in March, 1257. His chief works are *Chronica Majora* and *Historia Minor* (also known as *Historia Anglorum*), which is mainly compiled from the first-mentioned work. He also wrote biographies of Edward the Confessor, of some of the abbots of St. Albans, and of various saints.

Paris Garden. A former establishment for bullbaiting and bearbaiting, on the Bankside, London. It is said to have derived its name from one De Paris who built a house there in the reign of Richard II. It was in use at the beginning of Henry VIII's reign, and was afterward fitted up and used for a playhouse also.

Parisian Nights (pạ.rizh′ạn). Collected essays by Arthur Symons, published in 1926.

Parisina (par.i.sē′nạ). A poem by Byron, published in 1816. An overture for it was composed by William Sterndale Bennett in 1835.

Park (pärk), **Mungo.** b. in Selkirkshire, Scotland, Sept. 10, 1771; d. in Africa, probably in 1806. A Scottish explorer in Africa. He visited Benkoelen as assistant surgeon on an East-Indiaman in 1792, contributing on his return a description of eight new Sumatran fishes to the *Transactions* of the Linnean Society. As agent of the African Association he undertook in 1795 to explore the course of the Niger River. Leaving Pisania (now Karantaba), on the Gambia River, in December, 1795, he reached the Niger (being the first European to accomplish that feat) at Ségou in July, 1796, after many adventures, and ascended to Bamako. In 1799 he published a narrative of his journey, entitled *Travels in the Interior of Africa*.

Parker (pär′kẻr), Sir **Gilbert.** [Full name, **Horatio Gilbert George Parker.**] b. at Camden East, Addington, Ontario, Canada, Nov. 23, 1862; d. at London, Sept. 6, 1932. A Canadian journalist, novelist, dramatist, and poet. He worked on the editorial staff of the Sydney (Australia) *Morning Herald*, and subsequently lived (1898–1932) in England, but was buried in Canada at his request. He served as Conservative member of Parliament (1900–18) for Gravesend. During World War I he headed British publicity in the U. S. Author of *Mrs. Falchion* (1893), *The Trail of the Sword* (1894), *When Valmond Came to Pontiac* (1895), *The Battle of the Strong* (1898), *A Ladder of Swords* (1904), *The Weavers* (1907), *The Judgment House* (1913), *You Never Know Your Luck* (1915), *The Money Master* (1915), *The World For Sale* (1916), *No Defence* (1920), *Carnac's Folly* (1922), *The Power and the Glory* (1925), and *Tarboe* (1927), novels; of *Pierre and His People* (1892), *An Adventurer of the North* (1895), *The Lane That Had No Turning* (1900), *Northern Lights* (1909), and *Wild Youth* (1919), short-story collections; of *A Lover's Diary: Songs in Sequence* (1894), poetry; *History of Old Quebec* (1903 with Claude G. Bryan); and *The World in Crucible* (1915), dealing with World War I. He is best remembered for *The Seats of the Mighty* (1896), a historical novel of Quebec, and *The Right of Way* (1901), a psychological novel of dual personality; both were dramatized. His plays include *Faust* (1888) and *The Vendetta* (1889).

Parker, Louis Napoleon. b. 1852; d. in Devonshire, England, Sept. 21, 1944. An English dramatist and composer.

Parker, Martin. b. probably at London, c1600; d. c1656. An English innkeeper, Royalist, and author of broadsides and chapbooks. Author of many ballads, sentimental, comic, and political, of chapbooks such as *A True Tale of Robin Hood* (1632) and *The Nightingale Warbling Forth her Owne Disaster* (1632), and of romances such as *Guy, Earl of Warwick* (1640). He also wrote *A History of that renowned Christian Worthy, King Arthur* (1660). *When the King Enjoys his Own Again* (1643) is regarded as his best ballad.

Parker, Matthew. b. at Norwich, England, Aug. 6, 1504; d. at London, May 17, 1575. Archbishop of Canterbury (1559–75). He graduated at Cambridge (Corpus Christi College) in 1525, and was appointed (1533) chaplain to Queen Anne Boleyn. He was selected to preach at Paul's Cross by Thomas Cromwell. In 1545 he was appointed vice-chancellor of Cambridge. On the accession of the Roman Catholic queen Mary Tudor he resigned, and lost all his preferments. He was consecrated archbishop of Canterbury Dec. 17, 1559. As primate he devoted himself to the organization and discipline of the English Church, and was a firm opponent of Puritanism, attempting to find a middle course for the new Anglican Church between the old dispensation and the democratization demanded by such reformers as Peter Wentworth. The revision of the Thirty-nine Articles (1562) was carried out under his direction, as was the publication (1572) of the Bishops' Bible. He did considerable historical research and published editions of early chroniclers.

Parliament. See **House of Commons** and **House of Lords.**

Parliament, The Mad. See **Mad Parliament, The.**

Parliament of Bees, The. A dramatic entertainment (printed in quarto in 1641) by John Day.

Parliament of Fowls, The. [Also: **The Parlement of Foules, The Assembly of Fowls.**] A stanzaic poem in 700 lines, variously dated between 1374 and 1382, by Chaucer. The poet, after reading the *Dream of Scipio*, goes to sleep and in his dream is conducted by the Roman on Saint Valentine's Day to a park, where the birds are gathered to choose their mates. A royal and two noble eagles make their pleas for a beautiful formel or female eagle. She requests a year's time in which to decide. Modern commentators have sought an allegorical application, most commonly to the suit of Richard II for Anne of Bohemia. The chief literary borrowings to be noted in the poem are from the *Dream of Scipio*, which is summarized at the beginning, and Boccaccio's *Il Teseida*, a long passage in which is closely imitated.

Parliament of Love, The. A play by Philip Massinger, licensed in 1624, and produced by Elizabeth's Men in that year, but not published until 1805.

Parmenides (pär.men′i.dēz). b. at Elea; fl. c450 B.C. A Greek philosopher, head of the Eleatic school. He is believed to have arrived (c450 B.C.) at Athens at the age of 56, which suggests a birthdate of c504 B.C. He wrote his opinions in a didactic poem, *Nature*. His central thought is the unity and permanence of being; there is no not-being or change. A celebrated dialogue of Plato was named from him.

Parnassian (pär.nas′i.ąn). *a.* and *n.* **I.** *a.* Pertaining to Parnassus, or to poetry; also, noting or pertaining to a school of French poets, of the latter half of the 19th century, characterized especially by emphasis on form and by repression of emotion (so called from *Le Parnasse contemporain*, the title of their first collection of poems, published in 1866). **II.** *n.* A poet; also, a member of the Parnassian school of French poets.

Parnassus (pär.nas′us). **1.** A mountain ridge in Greece, ab. 83 mi. NW of Athens, near the ancient Delphi, and situated mainly in ancient Phocis. It was sacred to Apollo, the Muses, Dionysus, and the nymphs, and hence was regarded as the seat of music and poetry. Highest summit, Lycoreia (8,068 ft.). Hence, figuratively—
2. The abiding-place of poetry and home of poets: sometimes used as a name for a collection of poems or of elegant literature.

Not with less glory mighty Dulness crown'd
Shall take through Grub-street her triumphant
  round,
And, her Parnassus glancing o'er at once,
Behold an hundred sons, and each a dunce.
              (Pope, *Dunciad*.)

Parnassus Plays. See **Return from Parnassus, The.**

Parnell (pär.nel′, pär′nel), **Charles Stewart.** b. at Avondale, County Wicklow, Ireland, 1846; d. at Brighton, England, Oct. 6, 1891. An Irish statesman. He was the fourth son of John Henry Parnell (whose ancestors emigrated from England to Ireland in the 17th century) and Delia Tudor Stewart, daughter of Admiral Charles Stewart of the U. S. navy. He studied at Magdalene College, Cambridge, without taking a degree, and was elected to Parliament in 1875. He became the first president of the Irish Land League in 1879, visited (1879–80) the U. S. in the interest of the Irish agitation for home rule, and succeeded William Shaw as leader of the Home Rule Party in 1880. He was imprisoned (1881–82) under the Coercion Act. In 1886 William Ewart Gladstone formed a parliamentary alliance with Parnell, and proposed a Home Rule Bill which secured the support of all the Irish members (85), but caused a split in the Liberal Party and restored Robert Gascoyne-Cecil, Marquis of Salisbury, to power. Toward the close of the session of 1887 the London *Times* sought to discredit Home Rule before the country by publishing a series of articles entitled *Parnellism and Crime*, in which it tried to connect Parnell with the Phoenix Park murders and other assassinations. In support of its allegations it published a number of letters alleged to have been written by Parnell, which were proved, before a committee appointed by Parliament to investigate the *Times* charges, to have been forged by one Richard Pigott. Parnell brought suit for libel against the *Times*, recovering 5,000 pounds in damages. In November, 1890, Captain William Henry O'Shea obtained a grant of divorce from his wife, Parnell (who afterward married Mrs. O'Shea) having figured as the co-respondent in the suit. He was in consequence deposed from the leadership, at the instance of the Liberal leaders, by a majority of his party, but refused to submit, and led a minority until his death.

Parnell, Thomas. b. at Dublin, 1679; d. 1718. A British writer. He was ordained in 1700, was archdeacon of Clogher in 1706, and was presented to the vicarage of Finglas, near Dublin, in 1716. He was a member of the Scriblerus Club and a contributor to both *The Spectator* and *The Guardian*. Among his poems are *The Hermit, Night-Piece on Death, Hymn to Contentment,* and *Allegory on Man.* He translated Homer's *Battle of the Frogs and Mice;* he annotated and wrote the prefatory essay to Alexander Pope's *Iliad* translation. In 1770, Oliver Goldsmith wrote a biography of him.

parody (par′ọ.di). A kind of literary composition in which the form and expression of grave or dignified writings are closely imitated, but are made ridiculous by the subject or method of treatment; a travesty that follows closely the form and expression of its original; specifically, a burlesque imitation of a poem, in which a trivial or humorous subject is treated in the style of a dignified or serious one: also applied to burlesque musical works.

They were satirick poems, full of parodies—that is, of verses patched up from great poets and turned into another sense than their author intended them.
              (Dryden.)

The sublime parody of Cervantes, which cut short the whole race of knights-errant.
          (Prescott, *Ferd. and Isa*.)

Parolles (pạ.rol′es). In Shakespeare's *All's Well That Ends Well*, a braggart whose poltroonery is humorous and droll. One of Shakespeare's best comic parts, he has been called a forerunner of Falstaff, but his boasting dominates him whereas Falstaff's does not. Like Pistol he is pompous and lacks a sense of humor. When exposed, he takes his dishonor calmly and decides to make use of his talents: "There's place and means for every man alive."

paronomasia (par″ọ̄.nọ̄.mā′si.ạ). [Also, **paronomasy.**] In rhetoric, the use of words similar in sound but different in meaning, so as to give a certain antithetical force to the expression; also, the use of the same word in different senses; a play upon words.

> The seeming contradiction of a poor antithesis; . . . the jingle of a more poor paronomasia.
> (Dryden, *To Sir R. Howard.*)

> My learned friend had dined that day with Mr. Swan, the famous punster; and desiring him to give me some account of Mr. Swan's conversation, he told me that he generally talked in the Paronomasia, that he sometimes gave into the Ploce, but that in his humble opinion he shined most in the Antanaclasis. (Addison, *Spectator*, No. 61.)

Parr (pär), **Samuel.** b. at Harrow, England, Jan. 26, 1747; d. at Hatton, England, March 6, 1825. An English scholar. He studied at Harrow, and was at Cambridge for a short time in 1765. From 1767 to 1771 he was chief assistant to Dr. Robert Sumner at Harrow School, and in 1783 was made vicar of Hatton, near Warwick. He was a warm friend of Richard Porson. A determined Whig, he was famous both for the variety of his knowledge and for his dogmatism.

Parr, Thomas. [Called "Old Parr."] d. at London, Nov. 14, 1635. An English centenarian. He was said to have been born in 1483, and hence would have been 152 years old when he died. W. J. Thoms, the editor of *Notes and Queries*, examined the evidence and found it untrustworthy, though Parr was certainly very old and was a celebrity for many years before his death.

Parrhasius (pạ.rā′shi.us). b. at Ephesus; fl. c400 B.C. A Greek painter, considered one of the greatest of antiquity. The anecdotes of Pliny about all the painters of this time indicate extraordinary realism carried to the point of actual illusion. There were many pen-and-ink sketches by Parrhasius still in existence in the time of Pliny. Among his principal works were *The Personification of the Demos of Athens*, probably suggested by Aristophanes; a *Prometheus*, the *Hercules* at Lindus, the *Theseus* at Athens, afterward on the Capitol at Rome, and a *Contest of Ajax and Odysseus for the Weapons of Achilles.*

Parsifal (pär′si.fäl, -fạl; German, pär′zē.fäl) or **Parsival** (pär′si.vạl, -väl). A music drama in three acts by Richard Wagner. The poem was composed by him in 1877, the music in 1879. It was first performed at Bayreuth, July 28, 1882.

Parson Adams (ad′ạmz). See **Adams, Parson.**

Parson Austen's Daughter (ôs′tẹnz). A novel by Helen Ashton about the English novelist Jane Austen, published in 1949.

Parson's Progress, The. A novel by Compton Mackenzie, published in 1923. The second volume of a trilogy, begun in *The Altar Steps* (1922) and concluded in *The Heavenly Ladder* (1924), it deals with the stages in the spiritual development of Mark Lidderdale, an Anglican minister who finally becomes a Roman Catholic priest.

Parson's Tale, The. One of Chaucer's *Canterbury Tales*. A long prose sermon on Penitence, it incorporates a treatise on the Seven Deadly Sins. Each is described, for each a remedy is offered, and the evils attendant upon each are enumerated. Among the many medieval works dealing with such subjects, Chaucer's immediate source has not been discovered. But the sermon on Penitence corresponds to a part of Raymond of Pennaforte's *De Poenitentia* and the material on the Deadly Sins seems derived from the *Summa de Vitiis* of Gulielmus Peraldus. This is one of the two prose sections (hardly tales, especially this one) in *The Canterbury Tales*, the other being *The Tale of Melibeus*. The Parson, as he is described in the general Prologue, is one of Chaucer's most sympathetic characterizations. Though poor in the worldly sense, he is rich "of holy thoght and werk," self-denying, untiring in the care of his flock, kind to the penitent, and hard on the defiant:

> To drawen folk to heven by fairnesse,
> By good ensample, this was his bisinesse:
> But it were any persone obstinat,
> What so he were, of heigh or lowe estat,
> Him wolde he snibben sharply for the nones.
> A bettre preest I trowe that nowher noon is.

Parson Trulliber (trul′i.bėr). See **Trulliber, Parson.**

Partenay (par′tẹ.nā). [Also, **Melusine.**] A Middle English romance in which the hero promises never to look at his wife, a fairy of great beauty, on Saturdays. He breaks this promise, and finds that on that day she turns into a serpent from the waist down. He loses her forever when he repeats the offense.

Parthenia (pär.thē′ni.ạ). In Sir Philip Sidney's *Arcadia*, the wife of Argalus. She assumes the armor of a knight to revenge his death upon his slayer Amphialus.

Parthenon (pär′thẹ.non). The official temple of Athena (as Athena Parthenos, the virgin Athena), at Athens, as protectress of the city and guardian of the Athenian hegemony. It was begun c450 B.C. by Ictinus, under the political direction of Pericles and the artistic presidency of Phidias. The temple is a Doric peripteros of eight by 17 columns, on a stylobate of three steps, measuring on the highest step 101 by 228 ft. The surviving fragments from the pediments and much of the frieze are among the Elgin Marbles in the British Museum, and are considered among the most precious existing sculptures.

Parthenope (pär.then′ọ.pē). In Greek mythology, a Siren said to have been drowned and cast up at Naples, which was anciently called by her name.

Parthians (pär′thi.ạnz). The people of ancient Parthia in Asia. It is suggested that they may originally have been Scythians, or that they may have been of Turkoman linguistic stock. They were skilled horsemen and excelled in fighting on horseback with bows and arrows. The expression "a Parthian shot" means a parting shot or, in modern usage, the last word in an argument. This is in allusion to the custom of the ancient Parthians of shooting at an enemy from horseback with the horse turned away as if in flight.

Partington (pär'ting.tǫn), **Mrs.** The dame of Sydney Smith's anecdote about the housewife who tried to mop a high tide out of her house at Sidmouth. ("The Atlantic beat Mrs. Partington.")

Partlet (pärt'lĕt). See **Pertelote.**

Partonope of Blois (pär.ton'ǫ.pē; blwä). A Middle English romance of 12,000 lines. Partonope travels to a magic city where he falls in love with a fairy, Melior. The fairy insists that Partonope never look at her; he disobeys her twice, and is threatened with an end to his love, but finally marries her.

Partridge (pär'trij). In Henry Fielding's *Tom Jones*, Tom's faithful attendant, formerly a schoolmaster, later a barber. He is remembered best for his naïve excitement on seeing Garrick as Hamlet.

Partridge, Eric Honeywood. b. at Waimata Valley, Gisborne, New Zealand, Feb. 6, 1894—. A British literary critic and lexicographer. He was founder and managing director (1927–31) of the Scholartis Press. Author of *Eighteenth Century English Romantic Poetry* (1924), *The Scene is Changed* (a novel), *Slang To-day and Yesterday: A History and a Study* (1933), *A Dictionary of Slang and Unconventional English* (1937), *The World of Words* (1938), *A Dictionary of Clichés* (1940), *A Dictionary of Abbreviations* (1943), *Usage and Abusage: A Guide to Good English* (1947), *A Dictionary of the Underworld, British and American* (1950), and others.

Parvus (pär'vus), **John.** See **John of Salisbury.**

Parzival (pär'tsi.fäl). The title and legendary hero of an epic poem written c1205 by the German poet Wolfram von Eschenbach, using Chrétien de Troyes's *Conte del Graal* and also local legend. Parzival is the son of Gamuret, prince of Anjou, and Queen Herzeloide of Valois. His father falls in battle, and his mother, to protect him from a like fate, brings him up in the solitude of the forest in ignorance of knightly customs. After many misadventures, however, he arrives at Arthur's court, and ultimately becomes a knight of the Round Table. Afterward, in search of adventures, he rescues Queen Condwiramurs, who becomes his wife, and then arrives at the Castle of the Holy Grail. Here, having neglected certain conditions, he loses the sovereignty of the Grail (which it was possible for him to obtain), and leaves the castle in disgrace. The messenger of the Grail afterward appears at the court of Arthur and rebukes him, and he is banished from the Round Table. At this open shame he renounces his allegiance to God, and wanders about still in search of the Grail. Finally he learns the true nature of God and of the Grail, leads a life of abstinence, and becomes again a member of the Round Table. At the Castle of the Grail he is declared to be now worthy to become the sovereign of the Grail. See under **Perceval.**

Pascal (pas.kal', pas'kạl; French, pȧs.kȧl), **Blaise.** b. at Clermont-Ferrand, Puy-de-Dôme, France, June 19, 1623; d. at Paris, Aug. 19, 1662. A French geometrician, philosopher, and writer. He rose to highest literary excellence in setting forth and defending the doctrines of Port Royal against the Jesuits. Between January, 1656, and March, 1657, over his nom de plume, Louis de Montalte, Pascal wrote 18 letters, professedly to a friend in the provinces; hence the epistles are known as *Les Provinciales*. These letters defending Jansenism are considered classic examples of the use of irony. At the time of his death Pascal was engaged on a work that he was to name *Apologie de la religion catholique*. The notes he had made for it were subsequently found, but in such a scattered and imperfect condition that it was useless to attempt restoring his plan. They were therefore published in 1670 under the title *Pensées de M. Pascal sur la religion et sur quelques autres sujets, qui ont été trouvées après sa mort parmi ses papiers* (usually now called simply *Pensées*). In addition to these works Pascal wrote a *Discours sur la condition des grands, Prière pour demander le bon usage des maladies*, and finally a limited number of letters, addressed among others to Mademoiselle Charlotte de Roannez in 1657.

Pasiphaë (pạ.sif'ạ.ē). In Greek legend, the daughter of Helios, wife of Minos, king of Crete, and mother of Ariadne. She was enamoured of a white bull given to Minos by Poseidon, and by him became the mother of the Minotaur.

Pasquil (pas'kwil). Pseudonym of **Nash** or **Nashe, Thomas.**

Pasquin (pas'kwin). A dramatic satire by Henry Fielding, published in 1736. The subtitle explains that it is the "rehearsal of two plays, viz. a comedy call'd, The Election; and a tragedy call'd, The Life and Death of Common-Sense." In it Fielding hits at the difficulties of having plays produced, the problems presented by an 18th-century audience which tended to divide into cliques pro-author or anti-author, the continuing great popularity of dancers at the expense of serious drama, and epilogues which succeed in compromising the serious intent of the very plays they are appended to.

Passages from the Diary of a Late Physician. A collection of short stories by Samuel Warren, first published in *Blackwood's Magazine*. In 1831 in America (1832 in England) two volumes were published, and in 1838 a third was added.

Passage to India, A. A novel (1924) by E. M. Forster, treating sympathetically the racial tensions existing between the Indians and the British in India.

Passenger to Teheran (te.ẹ.ran', -rän'). A travelbook by V. Sackville-West, published in 1926.

Passfield (pas'fēld), **1st Baron.** Title of **Webb, Sidney James.**

Passing of Arthur, The. The closing poem (1869) in Tennyson's *Idylls of the King*. In it Sir Bedivere speaks of the last battle of Arthur, between Arthur and Modred (in which Modred is killed and Arthur mortally wounded), of his own finally successful attempts to throw the magic sword Excalibur into the lake, of the arm rising from the lake to claim the sword, and of the black barge with the three queens which comes and carries Arthur away. The poem is substantially the same in content as the earlier *Morte D'Arthur* (1842).

Passing of the Third Floor Back, The. A symbolical play (1907) by Jerome K. Jerome, based on his own short story of the same name.

Passionate Elopement, The. A novel (1911) by Compton Mackenzie.

ḍ, d or j; ṣ, s or sh; ṭ, t or ch; ẓ, z or zh; o, F. cloche; ü, F. menu; ċh, Sc. loch; ṅ, F. bonbon.

Passionate Friends, The. A novel by H. G. Wells, published in 1913.

Passionate Pilgrim, A. A collection of stories by Henry James, published in 1875. The title story was originally published in 1871.

Passionate Pilgrim, The. A poetical miscellany, published (1599) by William Jaggard, and attributed by him to William Shakespeare. Of the 21 poems, Shakespeare is known to have written only five; others are by Richard Barnfield, Bartholomew Griffin, Christopher Marlowe, and unknown writers.

Passion Play, The. A dramatic representation of Christ's passion, given at Oberammergau, Bavaria, at regular intervals, performed in fulfilment of a vow made in 1633, when the inhabitants of the village were saved from a plague.

pastiche (pas.tēsh'). A medley; a hotchpotch; a farrago.

Passover (pas'ō''vėr). [Hebrew, **Pesach** (pe'säċh).] A Jewish feast commemorating the exodus of the Jews from Egypt. The eight-day observance begins on the 14th of Nisan (March–April), and is marked by the absence of leavened bread from the diet, cakes of an unleavened dough, called matzoth, being substituted. On each of the first two nights of the observance a ceremonial meal, called *Seder*, is served in the home. At the *Seder* the head of the house reads the story of the Exodus from the Passover *Haggadah*, and various symbolic foods are served in allusion to the hardships endured by the Jews during their captivity in Egypt.

Paston Letters (pas'ton). A series of letters written or received by members of the Paston family, of Paston, Norfolk, England. The series commenced in 1422 and ended in 1509. They are valuable for 15th-century history, and were first published in part by Sir John Fenn in 1787. One of the best editions is by James Gairdner (6 vols., 1904), containing over 1,000 letters and other papers, with notes and other apparatus.

pastoral (pàs'tor.ạl). **1.** A poem describing the life and manners of shepherds, or a poem in which the characters are shepherds or shepherdesses; in general, any poem the subject of which is the country or a country life; a bucolic.

A pastoral is a poem in which any action or passion is represented by its effects on a country life.   (Johnson.)

2. Any work of art of which the subject is rural.

Thou, silent form! dost tease us out of thought
As doth eternity: cold Pastoral!
                    (Keats, *Ode on a Grecian Urn*.)

Patelin (pàt.làn). A conventional character in French comedy. He is a supple, insinuating flatterer, one who tries to accomplish his ends by indirect means. He seems to have had his origin in a 14th-century farce, *L'Avocat Pathelin*.

Pater (pā'tėr), **Walter Horatio.** b. at London, Aug. 4, 1839; d. at Oxford, England, July 30, 1894. An English critic and essayist. He was educated at Oxford and in 1864 became a fellow at Brasenose College there. Pater became with time the center of a cult of devotees of the art and the humanism of the Renaissance, and expounded a theory of art and aesthetics as being in themselves an end of

living. His writing was not easy, but he polished what he wrote to a precise, almost metallic, finish that reflected his intellectual approach to beauty. His writings include *Studies in the History of the Renaissance* (1873), *Marius the Epicurean* (1885), a novel considered his masterpiece, *Imaginary Portraits* (1887), *Appreciations, with an Essay on Style* (1889), *Plato and Platonism* (1893), and *The Child in the House* (1894), as well as *Greek Studies* (1895) and *Gaston de Latour* (1896), published posthumously.

Pater Noster or **Paternoster** (pat'ėr.nos.tėr). See **Lord's Prayer.**

Paternoster Row. A street in London, N of Saint Paul's, long famous as a center of book publishing. It is said to be so named from the prayer books or rosaries formerly sold in it.

Paterson (pat'ėr.son), **William Romaine.** [Pseudonym, **Benjamin Swift.**] b. at Glasgow, July 29, 1871—. An English novelist, essayist, and critic. Under his pseudonym he wrote *Nancy Noon* (1896), *The Tormentor* (1897), *The Destroyer* (1898), *Siren City* (1899), *Nude Souls* (1900), *The Game of Love* (1902), *In Piccadilly* (1903), *The Old Dance-Master* (1911), *What Lies Beneath* (1917), and *Sudden Love, A Tale of Picardy* (1922), fiction. He also wrote *Nemesis of Nations: Studies in History* (1907), *Problems of Destiny* (1935), and *The Passions of Life, Being the Search for an Ideal* (1938).

Pathelin (pàt.làn), **L'Avocat.** See under **Patelin.**

pathetic fallacy. A term first used by Ruskin (in an essay called *The Pathetic Fallacy*) designating the literary device by which external and nonhuman objects are credited with human feelings under certain conditions (for example, a reference to nature mourning, as in Milton's *Lycidas:* "Whom Universal nature did lament").

Pathway, The. An autobiographical novel by Henry Williamson, published in 1928. It is the concluding volume of a tetralogy under the general title *The Flax of Dream.*

Patience (pā'shens). A Middle English alliterative poem (late 14th century) attributed to the author of *The Pearl* and *Cleanness* (or *Purity*). It is a retelling of the Biblical story of Jonah and the whale, in which the poet develops his theme of patience in the face of all adversity, with much concentration on descriptive details.

Patience. In Shakespeare's *Henry VIII*, a gentlewoman to Queen Katherine.

Patience. [Subtitle, **Bunthorne's Bride.**] A comic opera in two acts, with music by Sir Arthur Sullivan and words by W. S. Gilbert, produced at London on April 23, 1881.

Patient Grissell (gri.sel'). A play by Thomas Dekker, Henry Chettle, and William Haughton, produced in 1600, entered on the Stationers' Register in 1600, and published in 1603.

Patmore (pat'mōr), **Coventry.** [Full name, **Coventry Kersey Dighton Patmore.**] b. at Woodford, Essex, England, July 23, 1823; d. at Lymington, Hampshire, England, Nov. 26, 1896. An English poet and writer. He was assistant librarian at the British Museum (1846–66). He published *Poems*

(1844), *Tamerton Church Tower* (1853), *The Angel in the House* (in four parts, 1854–62), *The Unknown Eros, and Other Odes* (1877), *Amelia* (1878), collected poems (1886), *Principle in Art* (1889), *Religio Poetae* (1893), and *Rod, Root, and Flower* (1895).

Patmore, Peter George. b. at Ludgate Hill, London, 1786; d. near Hampstead, London, Dec. 19, 1855. An English author and editor; father of Coventry Patmore. He was associated (1841–53) as contributor and editor with the *New Monthly Magazine*, and others. Author of *Imitations of Celebrated Authors, or Imaginary Rejected Articles* (1826), *My Friends and Acquaintances* (3 vols., 1854), and *Marriage in Mayfair* (1854).

Patmos (pat′mos; Greek, pät′môs). [Also: **Patino** (pä′tē.nō); Italian, **Patmo** (pät′mō).] An island of the Dodecanese, in the Greek *nomos* (department) of Calymnos, situated in the Aegean Sea, ab. 20 mi. SW of Samos. There is a monastery bearing the name of Saint John the Divine, and a cave is pointed out where, according to legend, the apostle saw the visions of the Apocalypse. Area, ab. 22 sq. mi.

"Patriarch of Ferney" (fer.nā′), **the.** See **Voltaire.**

Patrician, The. A novel by John Galsworthy, published in 1911.

Patrick (pat′rik), **Saint.** [Original name, **Sucat;** Latin, **Patricius** (pạ.trish′us).] b., according to tradition, at Nemthur (now Dumbarton), Scotland, c396; d. probably 469. Patron saint of Ireland; son of the deacon Calpurnius, son of Potitus, a priest. After the withdrawal of the Roman garrisons, Calpurnius retired to the country south of the Wall of Severus, where Patrick was captured by the Picts about 411, and sold as a slave into Ireland. After six years he escaped, and, devoting himself to the conversion of Ireland, prepared for the priesthood, spending 12 years in study. About 425 he entered upon his mission. In 432 he was consecrated bishop, and received the pallium in 441. The details of Patrick's mission are obscured but his success in converting, before his death, nearly all of pagan Ireland is clear. He faced persecution and imprisonment at the hands of the native pagan clergy; courageously attacked the pagan idols and proceeded with Christian ceremonies; and organized the church in Ireland by coördinating existing communities of Christians, establishing churches and monasteries, and appointing abbots and bishops to look after the church. Patrick's knowledge of the people he dealt with and of their customs, in addition to his genius for adapting usage to conform to existing circumstances without losing the essential meaning of the usage, were largely responsible for his success. Many legends are told about him, so many (and so sparse is the actual information that has come down) that many believe that everything about his career is legendary. He is said to have explained the Trinity by means of a shamrock he found growing at his feet, and he is often credited with driving the snakes out of Ireland. He wrote a *Confession* and an *Epistle*. He is usually credited also with the authorship of the remarkable poem called variously the *Lorica*, the *Hymn of Saint Patrick, The Cry of the Deer*, or *Faed Fiada*.

Patrick Charteris (chär′tėr.is), **Sir.** See **Charteris, Sir Patrick.**

Patrick Earnscliff (ėrnz′klif). See **Earnscliff, Patrick.**

Patrick's, Dean of Saint. See **Swift, Jonathan.**

Patrick Spens (spens), **Sir.** See **Spens, Sir Patrick.**

Patriots. A three-act play of Irish politics by Lennox Robinson, published in 1912.

Patriot's Progress, The. A novel, dealing with "the vicissitudes of Private John Bullock," by Henry Williamson, published in 1930.

Patroclus (pạ.trō′klus). In the *Iliad*, the intimate friend of Achilles. When the sulky Achilles withdraws from the fight, and the Greek host is in danger of being routed, he lends Patroclus his armor to fight against the Trojans. Patroclus at first succeeds, but at last is met by Hector and slain. Achilles then, to avenge his friend, reappears in the battle, drives the Trojans within their walls, and vanquishes Hector.

Patroclus. In Shakespeare's *Troilus and Cressida*, a Greek commander. He urges his friend Achilles to stop sulking and rejoin the war, but it requires his death at Trojan hands finally to rouse Achilles to action.

Patron, The. A comedy by Samuel Foote, produced in 1764.

Patterne (pat′ern), **Crossjay.** In George Meredith's *The Egoist*, a young and distant relative of the principal character, Sir Willoughby Patterne.

Patterne, Sir Willoughby. The title character of Meredith's *Egoist*, a refined embodiment of masculine self-appreciation.

Patti (pat′i; Spanish, pä′tē), **Adelina.** [Original name, **Adela Juana Maria Patti.**] b. at Madrid, Feb. 10, 1843; d. in Wales, Sept. 27, 1919. An operatic soprano. She was taken to America as a child by her parents, both singers, and first appeared at New York in 1859 and at London in 1861. She was perhaps the most popular singer of the time. Her repertoire contained between 30 and 40 parts, including Linda, Norina, Luisa Miller, Lucia, Violetta, and Zerlina. After she retired (before 1890) from the operatic stage, she appeared often in concert; her rendition of *Home Sweet Home* was famous.

Pattieson (pat′i.sọn), **Peter.** An imaginary schoolmaster, the assumed author of the *Tales of My Landlord*, by Sir Walter Scott. He has a brother, Paul Pattieson, who publishes his manuscripts for his own advantage.

Pattison (pat′i.sọn), **Mark.** b. at Hornby, Yorkshire, England, 1813; d. at Harrogate, Yorkshire, July 30, 1884. An English writer. He graduated at Oxford (Oriel College) in 1837, and became a fellow of Lincoln College in 1839, and later tutor and (1861) rector. He wrote a *Report on Elementary Education in Protestant Germany* (1861) and *Milton* (1879). His essays were collected in 1889.

Paul (pôl), **Herbert Woodfield.** b. 1853; d. Aug. 4, 1935. An English essayist and historian. He was a member of Parliament (1892–99 and 1906–09) and was second civil service commissioner from 1909. He published *Men and Letters* (1901), *Matthew Arnold* (1902), *History of Modern England* (1904–

06), *Lord Acton* (1904), *Life of Froude* (1905), *Stray Leaves* (1906), *Queen Anne* (1906), and others.

Paula Tanqueray (pô'lạ tang'ke̩.rạ). See **Tanqueray, Paula.**

Paul Clifford (klif'ọrd). A novel by Edward Bulwer-Lytton, published in 1830.

Paul Eitherside (ē'ᵗHėr.sīd, ī'-), **Sir.** See **Eitherside, Sir Paul.**

Paul Emanuel (ẹ.man'ū.ẹl). See **Emanuel, Paul.**

Paulet (pô'lẹt), **Sir William.** [Title, 3rd Marquis of **Winchester.**] b. c1535; d. 1598. An English nobleman, chiefly remembered for a curious little work entitled *The Lord Marques Idlenes* (1586). He was one of the commissioners for the trial of Mary, Queen of Scots (1586) and steward of her funeral (1587).

Pauletti (pô.let'i), **Lady Erminia.** See **Hermione, Lady.**

Paulicians (pô.lish'ạnz). A sect probably founded by Constantine of Syria during the latter half of the 7th century. They held the dualistic doctrine that all matter is evil; believed that Christ, having a purely ethereal body, suffered only in appearance; and rejected the authority of the Old Testament and religious ordinances and ceremonies. The sect is said to have become extinct in the 13th century. The name is probably derived from their high regard for the apostle Paul.

Paulina (pô.lī'nạ). In Shakespeare's *Winter's Tale,* the wife of Antigonus and defender of Hermione. She brings Leontes the young Perdita and announces Hermione's death. Years later she produces Hermione before Leontes and there is a reconciliation. Antigonus having died, Leontes persuades Paulina to marry Camillo.

Paulina. A historical novel by Sir Max Pemberton, published in 1922.

Paul Morel (pôl mô.rel'). See **Morel, Paul.**

Paul Pattieson (pat'i.sọn). See under **Pattieson, Peter.**

Paul Pry (prī). A comedy by John Poole, attributed to Douglas Jerrold, produced in 1853. The impudent, meddlesome adventurer who gives his name to the play was drawn from a Thomas Hill, at one time connected with the press.

Paul's Boys. [Also, **Children of Paul's.**] An Elizabethan theatrical company formed from the choirboys of Saint Paul's Cathedral, London.

Paul's Cathedral, Saint. See **Saint Paul's.**

Paul's Cross. A wooden cross near Saint Paul's, London, at which the folkmoot assembled: replaced in the 15th century by a stone cross.

Paul's Letters to His Kinsfolk. A series of letters by Sir Walter Scott, published in 1816, in which the author describes a journey to Brussels, Waterloo, and Paris a few weeks after the Battle of Waterloo.

Paul's Walk. [Also, **Duke Humphrey's Walk.**] The nave of old Saint Paul's, London, which during the latter part of the 15th and the first part of the 16th century became a rendezvous for the transaction of business and for secular amusements of every description. It was frequented by disreputable characters and unemployed men and is frequently alluded to in old plays. A "Paul's man"

was a frequenter of Paul's Walk, and presumably disreputable. The tomb of Duke Humphrey, the son of Henry IV, was said to be located here.

Paul Sweedlepipe (swē'dl.pīp). See **Sweedlepipe, Paul.**

Paulus Pleydell (pôl'us plā'del). See **Pleydell, Paulus.**

Pausanias (pô.sā'ni.ạs). fl. in the 2nd century A.D. A Greek geographer and writer on art. He wrote *Periegesis of Greece,* devoted to a description of Greek antiquities. It is one of the best sources we have on the topography, customs, legends, and history of ancient Greece.

Pax (paks). Pseudonym of **Cholmondeley, Mary.**

Payn (pān), **James.** b. at Cheltenham, England, Feb. 28, 1830; d. at London, March 25, 1898. An English novelist and poet. He became editor of *Chambers's Journal* in 1858, and of the *Cornhill Magazine* in 1882. He published poems (1855), and some 100 novels, including *Lost Sir Massingberd* (1864) and *By Proxy* (1878).

Payne (pān), **John.** b. 1842; d. 1916. An English poet and translator, best known for his translation of *The Arabian Nights' Entertainments* (9 vols., 1882–84).

Paysage Moralisé (pā.zảzh mo.rả.lē.zā). A poem by W. H. Auden, originally published in the volume *Look, Stranger!* (1936) under its first line, "Hearing of harvests rotting in the valley." Its later, formal title indicates its use of landscape to represent symbolically various psychological and social matters.

Peachey Carnahan (pē'chi kär'nạ.han). See **Carnahan, Peachey.**

Peachum (pē'chum). In John Gay's *Beggar's Opera,* a receiver of stolen goods, and the father of Polly Peachum, the principal female character, who marries the highwayman Macheath. In part, at least, he may be taken as a satirical representation of Sir Robert Walpole, who was prime minister at the time of the first performance of *The Beggar's Opera.*

Peachum, Polly. The heroine of Gay's *Beggar's Opera.* She is the bride of Macheath, the leader of a band of highwaymen, and remains constant to him in his troubles, even though learning of his affairs with other charmers.

Peacock (pē'kok), **Thomas Love.** b. at Weymouth, Dorsetshire, England, Oct. 18, 1785; d. at Lower Halliford, near Chertsey, England, Jan. 23, 1866. An English satirical novelist and poet. He was intimately associated with Shelley and Byron, and was literary executor of the former. In 1816 he published *Headlong Hall,* followed by *Melincourt* in 1817. He published *Nightmare Abbey* and *Rhododaphne,* a volume of verse (1818). In 1819 he was made assistant examiner at the India House, and in 1836 he succeeded Mill as chief examiner. *Maid Marian* appeared in 1822, *The Misfortunes of Elphin* in 1829, *Crotchet Castle* in 1831, and *Gryll Grange* in 1860.

Peacock Pie. A volume of poems (1913) for children, by Walter De la Mare.

Pearl, The. A Middle English poem, written in the latter half of the 14th century. A poem of 100 stanzas, each of 12 alliterative lines in an elaborate rhyme scheme, it is an allegory, usually considered an elegiac lament for the unknown poet's two-year-old daughter, although several scholars have given it other interpretations. The dream symbolism of the poem is drawn from the Apocalypse and from the *Roman de la Rose*. As an example of personal poetry lyrically handled it is unequaled in Middle English literature. It is generally considered to be by the same author as *Patience* and *Cleanness* (or *Purity*).

Pearse (pirs), **Patrick Henry**. [Called **Padraic Pearse**.] b. at Dublin, Nov. 10, 1879; d. there, May 3, 1916. An Irish educator, writer, and patriot, a leader in the Easter Rebellion of 1916. Son of an English father and Irish mother, as a boy he dedicated his life to the service and the cause of Ireland. Drawn into the Gaelic Revival, he so mastered that language that he could use it as a literary medium equally with English, and for some years he edited *An Claidheamh Soluis* (The Sword of Light), organ of the Gaelic League.

Pearson (pir′sọn), **John**. b. at Great Snoring, Norfolk, England, Feb. 28, 1613; d. at Chester, England, July 16, 1686. An English bishop and theological writer. He took orders in 1639, and in 1640 was chaplain to Lord Keeper Finch. He was a Royalist chaplain during the English Civil War. A defender of the English church against both Puritans and Roman Catholics, in 1659 he published the *Exposition of the Creed*, one of the monuments of English theology. In 1661 he was one of the commissioners on the review of the liturgy at the Savoy. On April 13, 1662, he was appointed master of Trinity College, Cambridge; and in 1673 he was made bishop of Chester. His defense of the authenticity of the Ignatian epistles (1672) has since been shown to be correct.

Peaseblossom (pēz′blos″ọm). A fairy in Shakespeare's *Midsummer Night's Dream*.

Pecock (pē′kok), **Reginald**. b. probably in Wales, c1395; d. c1460. An English prelate and religious writer. He wrote, among other works, *The Repressor of Overmuch Weeting* (Blaming) *of the Clergy* (c1455) and *The Book of Faith* (c1456). He was bishop of St. Asaph (1444–49) and of Chichester (1450–59), and a privy councilor (1454–57).

Pecksniff (pek′snif). A notorious hypocrite in Dickens's *Martin Chuzzlewit*. He has two daughters: Mercy (Merry), married to Jonas Chuzzlewit, and Charity (Cherry), who is a victim of her own misplaced affection.

Pecorone (pā.kō.rō′nä), **Il**. [Eng. trans., "*The Dunce*."] A collection of 50 tales by Ser Giovanni Fiorentino. He began to write them in 1376, but the book was not published until 1558 at Milan. The stories were mostly drawn from the chronicles of Giovanni Villani. William Painter, in his *Palace of Pleasure*, and subsequent writers are indebted to it.

Pecunia (pē.kū′ni.ạ), **Lady**. See under **Argurion**.

Pedant. In Shakespeare's *Taming of the Shrew*, a teacher who pretends to be Vincentio, the father of Lucentio, and is useful in arranging Lucentio's marriage to Bianca. When the real father of Lucentio appears, he runs away, but he reappears in the happy scene at the end of the play.

pedantry. **1.** The overrating of mere knowledge, especially of matters of learning which are really of minor importance; also, ostentatious or inappropriate display of learning.

Pedantry proceeds from much reading and little understanding. A pedant among men of learning and sense is like an ignorant servant giving an account of a polite conversation. (Steele, *Tatler*.)

Pedantry consists in the use of words unsuitable to the time, place, and company.
(Coleridge, *Biographia Literaria*.)

The more pretentious writers, like Peter of Blois, wrote perhaps with fewer solecisms, but with more pedantry, and certainly lost freedom by straining after elegance.
(Stubbs, *Medieval and Modern History*.)

2. Undue addition to the forms of a particular profession, or of some one line of life.

There is a pedantry in manners, as in all arts and sciences; and sometimes in trades. Pedantry is properly the overrating any kind of knowledge we pretend to. And if that kind of knowledge be a trifle in itself, the pedantry is the greater.
(Swift, *On Good Manners*.)

Pedro (pē′drō, pā′-), **Don**. In Shakespeare's *Much Ado About Nothing*, the Prince of Arragon. He arranges for the marriage of Claudio and Hero, but by the scheme of his bastard brother, Don John, is convinced of Hero's unfaithfulness. Later he makes amends when the truth is discovered. He arranges also for Benedick to overhear that Beatrice is in love with him, and for Beatrice to be similarly entrapped.

Pedro Garcias (gär.thē′äs). See **Garcias, Pedro**.

Peebles (pē′blz), **Peter**. In Sir Walter Scott's *Redgauntlet*, the Scottish plaintiff in a case appealed to Parliament. He is a litigious drunkard and ne'er-do-well.

Peel (pēl), **John**. b. 1776; d. 1854. A British huntsman, of Cumberland, the hero of the famous hunting ballad *D'ye Ken John Peel* (written by Peel's friend John Woodcock Graves).

Peele (pēl), **George**. b. c1557; d. 1596. An English dramatist and poet. His father, James Peele, was a clerk of Christ's Hospital and a writer of pageants. George entered grammar school in 1565, went to Broadgates Hall, Oxford, in 1571, and thence to Christ Church College, Oxford, in 1574, taking the B.A. and M.A. there. He went to London in 1581 but returned to Oxford in 1583 to supervise the performance of some plays. He published *The Arraignment of Paris* (1584), *The Famous Chronicle of King Edward I* (1593), *The Old Wives' Tale* (1593), *David and Bethsabe* (c1593), and *The Battle of Alcazar* (1594). Attributed to him, at least in part, are *Mucedorus*, printed in 1598, and *The Turkish Mahomet and Hiren the Fair Greek* (c1594), a play since lost. He also wrote two pageants honoring the Lord Mayor of London, and one for a tilting tournament in honor of Queen Elizabeth in 1595. A collection of ribald stories published twelve years after his death was called *The Merry Conceited Jests of George Peele*. William Gager applauded Peele in verse as a wit and poet. Robert Greene seems to have had Peele in mind where, in

ḍ, d or j; ṣ, s or sh; ṭ, t or ch; ẓ, z or zh; *o*, F. cloche; ü, F. menu; ċh, Sc. loch; ṅ, F. bonbon.

his *Groatsworth of Wit*, he warned university men against writing for the professional theater. Thomas Nash remarked on Peele's "pregnant dexterity of wit and manifold variety of invention, wherein . . . he goeth a step beyond all that write." Peele excelled as a lyric poet rather than as a dramatist.

Peele Castle. A castle in the Isle of Man, celebrated in a famous poem by Wordsworth.

Peep-Bo (pēp′bō). In Gilbert and Sullivan's *The Mikado*, a young schoolgirl. She is one of the three wards of Ko-Ko (Yum-Yum and Pitti-Sing are the other two). She eventually marries Pish-Tush.

Peeping Tom of Coventry (kuv′ẹn.tri). A man of Coventry, England, celebrated in the legend of Lady Godiva (who rode naked through the streets to free the people from burdensome taxes). He was struck blind for peeking through his window, despite orders that the people should remain behind closed shutters.

Peep o'Day Boys (pēp ọ.dā′). A Presbyterian faction in Northern Ireland (c1785–90), opposed to the Roman Catholic "Defenders." They were closely allied to the Orangemen.

Peer Gynt (pir gint; Norwegian, pär günt). A dramatic poem written in 1867 by Henrik Ibsen. Edvard Grieg composed a symphonic suite, in two series, based upon the poem, which centers on the exploits of Peer Gynt, hero of Norse folk tale, whom Ibsen makes an irresponsible egotist in search of sensation.

Peerybingle (pir′i.bing.gl), **Mrs.** The wife of a carrier in Dickens's *Cricket on the Hearth;* a blithe cheery little woman called "Dot."

Pegasus (peg′ạ.sus). In Greek mythology, the winged horse which sprang from the blood of Medusa when she was slain by Perseus, and later given by Athena to the Muses. With a stroke of his hoof he is said to have caused to well forth, on Mount Helicon in Boeotia, the poetically inspiring fountain Hippocrene. He was ultimately changed into a constellation.

"Pegeen Mike" (peg.ēn′ mīk′). See **Flaherty, Margaret.**

Peggotty (peg′ọ.ti), **Clara.** In Dickens's novel *David Copperfield*, David's homely, devoted nurse, who marries Barkis (Barkis having announced that he "is willin' "). She is the aunt of Little Em'ly.

Peggotty, Dan. In Dickens's novel *David Copperfield*, a retired boatman, the brother of Clara Peggotty.

Peggotty, Ham. In Dickens's novel *David Copperfield*, a cousin of Little Em'ly, with whom he is in love and whom he loses to the wicked Steerforth.

Peggy Heath (peg′i hēth). See **Heath, Peggy.**

Peggy O'Dowd (ọ.doud′). See **O'Dowd, Mrs.**

Pegler (peg′lėr), **Mrs.** In Dickens's novel *Hard Times*, a good and kindly old woman, actually the mother of the scoundrel Bounderby (although this fact is concealed by him in order that he may boast of having risen "from the gutter").

Peg Woffington (peg wof′ing.tọn). A novel by Charles Reade, published in 1853. It is an adaptation of a play, *Masks and Faces*, he had written (1852) with Tom Taylor. It is the story of an episode in the life of the famous actress, Margaret Woffington.

Pehlevi (pā′lẹ.vē). See **Pahlavi.**

Peisistratus (pī.sis′tra.tus). See **Pisistratus.**

Pelagia (pẹ.lā′ji.ạ). A penitent of Antioch, of the 5th century A.D., previously an actress and dancer. A character of the same name, resembling her, is introduced in Charles Kingsley's *Hypatia*.

Pelagians (pẹ.lā′ji.ạnz). The followers of Pelagius, who is believed to have been a British monk of the 4th and early 5th century A.D. They held that there was no original sin through Adam, and consequently no hereditary guilt; that every soul is created by God sinless; that the will is absolutely free; and that the grace of God is universal, but is not indispensable; they rejected infant baptism. Pelagius, however, held to the belief in the Trinity and in the personality of Christ. His views were developed by his pupil Coelestius, but were anathematized by Pope Zosimus in 418. Pelagianism was the principal anthropological heresy in the early church, and was strongly combated by Pelagius's contemporary Augustine.

Pelasgi (pẹ.las′jī). An ancient race inhabiting Greece and the islands and coasts of the Aegean Sea and the eastern Mediterranean in prehistoric times.

Peleus (pē′lūs, pē′lẹ.us). In Greek legend, a king of the Myrmidons in Thessaly; son of Aeacus, husband of the nymph Thetis, and father of Achilles. It was at the wedding of Peleus and Thetis, to which all the gods were invited except the goddess of discord, Eris, that that goddess sent the apple of discord inscribed "To the Fairest." Peleus was one of the heroes of the Calydonian boar hunt, and also took part in the expedition of the Argonauts.

Pelham, or the Adventures of a Gentleman (pel′ạm). A novel (1828) by Edward Bulwer-Lytton.

Pelias (pē′li.ạs). In Greek legend, a son of Poseidon, who usurped the throne of Iolcus in Thessaly from his brother Aeson, and sent Aeson's son Jason to steal the Golden Fleece, an expedition which he intended to be a death errand. But when Jason returned to Iolcus with Medea, Pelias was slain by Medea, through the agency of his own daughters, whom Medea persuaded to cut up and boil their father, with a false prescription for rejuvenation.

Pelican (pel′i.kạn). Original name of the **Golden Hind.**

Pelion (pē′li.ọn). A mountain in Thessaly, N Greece, near the coast, SE of Ossa. It was the legendary home of the Centaurs, and known especially as the dwelling place of Chiron, the wise Centaur who was tutor to Achilles. The two mythical giants known as the Aloadae piled Mount Ossa on Olympus and then Pelion on Ossa in their attempt to reach heaven.

Pell (pel), **Solomon.** In Dickens's *Pickwick Papers*, an attorney (practicing in the "Insolvent Court") who served various of Sam Weller's acquaintances when they found themselves faced with financial difficulties. He was of service to Sam himself in the matter of Sam's "voluntary imprisonment" with Mr. Pickwick.

---

fat, fāte, fär, åsk, fåre; net, mē, hėr; pin, pīne; not, nōte, möve, nôr; up, lūte, půll; ᴛʜ, then;

Pelleas (pel'ę.as), **Sir.** One of the knights of the Round Table, in the Arthurian cycle of romance. He was renowned for his great strength.

Pelleas and Ettarre (e.tär'). One of the *Idylls of the King*, by Alfred Tennyson.

Pellegrin (pel'ę.grin). Pseudonym of **Fouqué,** Baron **Friedrich Heinrich Karl de la Motte-.**

Pelles (pel'ēz), **King.** In Arthurian romance, the king of "a foreign country" and father of Elaine, the mother of Sir Galahad.

Pellinor (pel'i.nōr), **Sir.** [Also, **Pellenore** (pel'ę-nōr).] In the Arthurian cycle of romance, and specifically in some versions of the Grail stories, the custodian of the Grail castle. Another Sir Pellinor was the father of Perceval.

Peloponnesian War (pel''ọ.pọ.nē'zhạn, -shạn). A war between Athens and its allies on one side and the Peloponnesian confederacy under the lead of Sparta and its allies (Boeotia, Phocis, Megara, and others) on the other. It was carried on from 431 to 404 B.C. The Peloponnesian War actually consisted of two wars, the Archidamean War (431–421 B.C.) and the Decelean War (414–404 B.C.), and the uneasy Peace of Nicias between them; the first war is named for Archidamus, then king of Sparta, the second for Decelea, a town in Attica whose seizure by the Spartans signaled the beginning of open warfare once more. The cause of the Peloponnesian War is obscure, but basically it resulted from the reaching of the saturation point in the alliances of both of the chief Greek powers, Athens and Sparta. Athens had built up, following the Persian Wars at the beginning of the 5th century B.C., a great league of city-states around the Aegean Sea, while Sparta had developed a confederacy of land powers covering the Peloponnesus and part of northern Greece. It was thus the clash of a sea power with a land power; Athenian strategy, determined initially by Pericles, was to avoid land battles and to wait for Sparta's military efforts and Athenian raids to exhaust her; Sparta would try to starve Athens out, besieging her, laying the countryside waste, and alienating her allies. The war resulted in the end of Athenian leadership in Greece; for a time Sparta replaced her, but by 370 the weakness of Spartan leadership in government had prevailed and Thebes became the principal city of Greece. Thucydides's history of the Peloponnesian War, down to 411, is the principal and most accurate source.

Pelops (pē'lops). In Greek legend, a son of Tantalus, and grandson of Zeus. He was dismembered by his father and served to the gods as food; but when they discovered the nature of the dish, they restored him to life and wholeness. He won Hippodamia as bride in a chariot race against her father, and became king of Pisa in Elis. He was the father of Atreus and Thyestos. The Peloponnesus is named for him.

Pemberton (pem'bẻr.tọn), Sir **Max.** b. at Birmingham, England, June 19, 1863; d. Feb. 22, 1950. An English author. He was editor of *Cassell's Magazine* (1896–1906). He wrote many novels and short stories. Among his published volumes are *The Impregnable City* (1895), *Queen of the Jesters* (1897), *The Garden of Swords* (1899), *I Crown Thee King* (1902), *Beatrice of Venice* (1904), *The Hundred*

Days (1905), *My Sword for Lafayette* (1906), *Sir Richard Escombe* (1908), *The Show Girl* (1909), *White Motley* (1911), *Captain Black* (1911), *The Virgin Fortress* (1912), *The Great White Army* (1915), *Paulina* (1922), *The Mad King Dies* (1928), and *Sixty Years and After* (1936).

Pembroke (pem'brŭk), Countess of. [Title of **Mary Herbert.**] b. 1561; d. 1621. The sister of Sir Philip Sidney. She was a patroness of many Elizabethan poets and dramatists, and herself translated the French dramatist Robert Garnier's *Marc-Antoine* as *Antonius* (1592). Sidney wrote his *Arcadia* (originally *The Countess of Pembroke's Arcadia*) for her.

Pembroke, Earl of. A title held by various members of the **Herbert** family. See also **Aymer de Valence,** and also **Humphrey** (1391–1447).

Pembroke, Earl of. In Shakespeare's *3 Henry VI*, the historical William Herbert, a Yorkist whom Edward IV orders to secure men for his cause against King Henry.

Pembroke, (1st) Earl of. In Shakespeare's *King John*, the historical William Marshal, 1st Earl of Pembroke and Striguil. He disapproves of submission to the Pope and later joins the other English lords in their defection to the French after Arthur's supposed murder. When these lords find that the French have sworn to kill them after defeating John, they return to his side.

Pembroke College. A college of Cambridge University, founded by the Countess of Pembroke in 1347.

Pembroke College. A college of Oxford University, founded in 1624.

Penates (pę.nā'tēz). In ancient Roman religion, the household gods, who presided over families, and were worshiped in the interior of every dwelling. They had their own place on every hearth, where a fire was kept burning for them. Their worship was associated with that of Vesta, the hearth goddess, and of the Lares.

Pendennis (pen.den'is). A novel by William Makepeace Thackeray, published in 1850: so called from the name of one of its leading characters, Arthur Pendennis, a poet. Major Pendennis, his uncle, is a worldly and courageous old dandy.

Pendennis, Arthur. A successful young writer, the central figure of Thackeray's *Pendennis* and the professed "author" of *The Newcomes*. After some imprudent love affairs, including that with Blanche Amory, he settles down to marriage with his foster sister Laura Bell.

Pendennis, Laura. In Thackeray's novel *The Newcomes*, the wife of Arthur Pendennis. In *Pendennis* she was Laura Bell, Arthur's foster sister, whom he eventually married.

Pendennis, Major. In Thackeray's *Pendennis*, Arthur Pendennis's uncle, a worldly old dandy: a finished portrait of the gentlemanly tuft-hunter.

Pendragon (pen.drag'ọn), **Uther.** See **Uther Pendragon.**

Penelope (pę.nel'ọ.pē). In Greek legend, the wife of Odysseus, famous as a model of the domestic virtues. In the absence of Odysseus, she was beset with importunate suitors. She promised to decide among them as soon as she finished a certain piece of weaving, but to hold them off she unraveled every night what she had woven each day.

Penelophon (pẹ.nel'ọ.fon). See under **Cophetua.**

Pennant (pen'ạnt), **Thomas.** b. at Downing, Flintshire, Wales, June 14, 1726; d. there, Dec. 16, 1798. A British naturalist and antiquary. His works include *British Zoölogy* (1766), *Synopsis of Quadrupeds* (1771; later expanded to *History of Quadrupeds*), *A Tour in Scotland in 1769* (1771), *Tour in Wales* (1778–81), *Arctic Zoölogy* (1784–87), and *Account of London* (1790). He wrote much on the archaeology of Great Britain.

Penruddock (pen.rud'ọk). A character in Richard Cumberland's *The Wheel of Fortune.*

Penfeather (pen'feᴛн.ẽr), **Lady Penelope.** In Sir Walter Scott's novel *St. Ronan's Well,* the haughty, somewhat flighty patroness of the "watering place" (that is to say, St. Ronan's Well itself) about which the story revolves.

Penry (pen'ri), **John.** b. in Brecknockshire, Wales, 1559; hanged at St. Thomas-a-Watering, Surrey, England, May 29, 1593. A British Puritan pamphleteer, noted for his connection with the *Martin Marprelate* tracts (1588–89) attacking the practices and clergy of the Church of England. An earlier pamphlet, published in 1587, was directed against alleged similar abuses within the established church in Wales, and brought Penry a brief term of imprisonment. However, Puritan sentiment rallied to his support and upon his release he and several associates (most notably John Udall and Job Throckmorton) were provided with a clandestine printing press, from which the seven *Martin Marprelate* tracts were issued during the next several months. The tracts aroused a tremendous public outcry, and government action against the alleged principals in the affair was, if not particularly swift by modern standards, exceedingly stern. Udall was arrested in 1590, and Penry was forced to take refuge in Scotland. Two years later he attempted to make his way secretly back into England, was arrested, accused of writing material calculated to incite rebellion, and hanged. Although it is not definitely known even yet who wrote any particular one of the *Martin Marprelate* tracts, there is certainly a strong probability that Penry was their chief author, if not their sole author. The real problem, at the time of the trial and since, has been whether or not Penry's admittedly great share in the responsibility for them could justify a charge of something very close to treason: as a Puritan and a reformer, Penry certainly thought not; equally obviously, however, the government of England, and Queen Elizabeth in particular, could not afford at that time to view any controversy involving the established church as being outside the political realm.

Penseroso (pen.sẹ.rō'sō), **Il.** A poem by John Milton, written c1632. The song "Hence all you Vain Delights," by John Fletcher, in *Nice Valor,* which begins with phrasing similar to Milton's opening, is thought to have influenced the poem.

Penshurst (penz'hẽrst), **2nd Baron.** A title of **Smythe, George Augustus Frederick Percy Sydney.**

Pentameron (pen.tam'ẹ.rọn), **The.** A work by Walter Savage Landor, published in 1837. It is principally an imaginary discussion between Petrarch and Boccaccio on the literature of Italy, including Dante and Vergil.

pentameter (pen.tam'ẹ.tẽr). In ancient prosody, a verse differing from the dactylic hexameter by suppression of the second half of the third and of the sixth foot; a dactylic dipenthemimeres or combination of two catalectic dactylic tripodies, thus:

$$\stackrel{\_}{\smile}\stackrel{\_}{\smile} \mid \stackrel{\_}{\smile}\stackrel{\_}{\smile} \mid \stackrel{\_}{} \quad \| \stackrel{\_}{} \smile\smile \mid \stackrel{\_}{} \smile\smile \mid \stackrel{\_}{}.$$

The first half of the line ended almost without exception in a complete word and often with a pause in the sense. Spondees were excluded from the second half-line. The halves of the line often terminated in words of similar ending and emphasis, generally a noun and its attributive. This meter received its name from a false analysis of some ancient metricians, who explained it as consisting of two dactyls, a spondee, and two anapests. In modern English prosody, a verse having five feet, especially iambic feet.

Pentateuch (pen'tạ.tūk). The first five books of the Old Testament, regarded as a connected group. They are Genesis, Exodus, Leviticus, Numbers, and Deuteronomy. They record the creation, the diffusion of peoples, the formation of the Hebrew nation, and its history through its sojourn in the wilderness. Opinions regarding the authorship of these books differ greatly. Some scholars believe that they, with the book of Joshua, were written substantially by Moses, Joshua, and their contemporaries; others hold that they were compiled at a much later period (in part about the 7th century B.C., or even in postexilic times).

Pentecost (pen'tẹ.kost). [Also, **Whitsunday.**] A Christian feast day commemorating the anniversary of the gift of the Holy Ghost to Christ's disciples subsequent to the Ascension.

Penthea (pen.thē'ạ). The principal female character in John Ford's *The Broken Heart.*

Penthesilea (pen″the.si.lē'ạ). In Greek legend, a queen of the Amazons who aided the Trojans against the Greeks after the death of Hector. She was slain by Achilles.

Pentheus (pen'thūs). In Greek legend, a king of Thebes who was torn to pieces by his mother, Agave, and other maenads because he denied the divinity of Dionysus and had attempted to spy on and stop the orgiastic ceremonies involved in worship of him by the women.

Pentweazel (pent'wē″zl), **Lady.** In Samuel Foote's comedy *Taste,* a kind of Mrs. Malaprop, vain of her lost charms.

People's Palace, The. An institution in East London for the entertainment and instruction of the working population.

Pepita (pe.pē'tạ). A novel by V. Sackville-West, published in 1937.

Peppercul (pep'ẽr.kul). See **Colepepper, Captain John.**

Pepperpot (pep'ẽr.pot), **Sir Peter.** A rich West Indian, in Samuel Foote's play *The Patron.*

Pepys (pēps, peps, pips, pep'is), **Samuel.** b. Feb. 23, 1633; d. May 26, 1703. An English politician and diarist. He was a son of a tailor at London. In 1650 he entered Magdalene College, Cambridge. He married in 1655 and was taken into the house of Sir Edward Montagu (afterward Earl of Sandwich), whose mother had married Pepys's grandfather. His *Diary* was begun Jan. 1, 1660, and is one of the chief sources for information on the Restoration, in which Pepys actively participated. Montagu made him secretary of the generals at sea in March, 1660, and clerk of the acts of the navy in July, 1660. During the plague of 1666 he remained at London. He also assisted in checking (so far as it could be checked) the great fire of the same year. He became secretary of the admiralty in 1673. In 1678–79 he sat as member of Parliament for Harwich, and was twice master of Trinity House. On May 22, 1679, during the hysteria of the Popish Plot, he was sent to the Tower of London as a papist, because of his being close to the Duke of York (later James II). From 1684 to 1686 he was president of the Royal Society. He was dismissed from all his offices after the revolution of 1688 which placed William of Orange on the throne. About 1690 he published *Memoirs relating to the State of the Royal Navy*. His library of 3,000 volumes was bequeathed to Magdalene College, Cambridge. The last entry in the *Diary* was made May 31, 1669; his sight was beginning to fail and he gave up keeping the record. The *Diary* was written in cipher, actually his own adaptation of Thomas Shelton's shorthand system, and was translated by the Reverend John Smith and published, with many omissions, by Richard Griffin Neville, 3rd Baron Braybrooke (who had discovered it in the Pepysian Library), in 1825. In 1875–79 Mynors Bright republished it with much original matter, and in 1893 the whole, except for certain lurid passages which could not be printed, was edited by H. B. Wheatley.

Pepysian Library (pēp′si.ạn, pep′-). The library of Samuel Pepys (containing the cipher manuscript of his *Diary* and a large collection of ballads), bequeathed by him to Magdalene College, Cambridge, England. It is in a separate building, which was approaching completion about the time Pepys determined to bequeath his collection either to Magdalene or to Trinity, and in which (in the former case) he wished it to be deposited. The library came into the possession of the college on the death of his nephew in 1724.

Perceforest (pėr.sẹ.for′ẹst). [Also, **Perceforêt** (persfo.re).] A medieval French historical romance, and the name of its hero. It is set in Britain before the reign of King Arthur.

Perceval (pėr′sẹ.vạl). [Also: **Percival, Percivale** (pėr′si.vạl).] One of the principal heroes in the medieval Arthurian cycle of romance and legend, figuring especially in the search for the Grail. He first appeared in the French poem *Perceval, ou le Conte du Graal* by Chrétien de Troyes c1175, and then passed into the literature of nearly every European nation. The story of Perceval begins with his boyhood in the forest, where he was brought up by his mother ignorant of the ways of knights and warriors or of courtly manners; it goes on to his arrival at King Arthur's court, where he makes one awkward blunder after another, receives in-

struction in knighthood and warfare, and becomes one of the best knights of the Round Table. Perceval's quest for the Holy Grail is the main incident, ending with his being rewarded with a sight of it. The story as told in Wolfram von Eschenbach's *Parzival* lays stress on the courtly training which transforms the simple forest boy into the noble knight, his first failure in the Grail quest, his years of suffering, and final achievement of the sovereignty of the Grail. Almost all versions present the forest boyhood, the gaucheries at court, and the Grail story. Late tellings, however, usually present him as a virgin knight. Thomas Malory's story of Perceval is a condensation of the 13th-century Cistercian *Queste del Saint Graal*. Malory was the source of Tennyson's version in *Idylls of the King*.

Perceval of Gales (pėr′sẹ.vạl; gālz) or **Wales** (wālz), **Sir.** See **Sir Perceval of Gales.**

Percy (pėr′si). A tragedy by Hannah More, produced in 1777. She is supposed to have been assisted by David Garrick in this play.

Percy, George. b. 1580; d. 1632. An English author and colonist. After service in the Low Countries, he sailed for Virginia in the first expedition of James I's reign (1606). On the recall of John Smith (1609), and again after departure of Thomas West, Baron de la Warr (1611), he was appointed deputy governor. According to his *A True Relation of the Proceedings . . . In Virginia* (c1625), John Smith was a braggart and slanderer.

Percy, Sir Henry. [Called **Hotspur.**] b. 1364; killed in the battle of Shrewsbury, England, 1403. An English soldier; son of Henry Percy (1342–1408), 1st Earl of Northumberland. In 1402 he fought with his father at Homildon Hill, and captured the Earl of Douglas. Angered by the refusal of Henry IV to accept Douglas as ransom for his (Percy's) brother-in-law, Edmund Mortimer (whom Henry was holding prisoner), Percy associated himself with Owen Glendower in his war against the king, and was killed at Shrewsbury in 1403. Shakespeare introduces him (on a basis of the accounts in Holinshed) as a gay, jesting, fiery-tempered soldier in his *Henry IV*, first part.

Percy, Sir Henry. [Title: 9th Earl of Northumberland; called "the Wizard Earl."] b. at Tynemouth, England, 1564; d. at Petworth, England, 1632. English nobleman; son of Sir Henry Percy (c1532–85), 8th Earl of Northumberland. His scientific experiments won him his sobriquet. For failure to warn the king against the Gunpowder Plot, he was tried and sentenced to life imprisonment. Released in 1621 after 15 years in prison, he did not reënter public life. George Peele celebrated his installation into the Order of the Garter with *Honour of the Garter* (1593).

Percy, Henry. In Shakespeare's historical plays, three characters, based on historical figures, appear, as follows: the (1st) Earl of Northumberland, father of Hotspur, in *Richard II* and 1 and 2 *Henry IV;* Hotspur, in 1 *Henry IV;* and the (3rd) Earl of Northumberland, grandson of Hotspur, in 3 *Henry VI.*

Percy, Lady. In Shakespeare's 1 *Henry IV*, the wife of Hotspur and sister of Mortimer. In a rather amusing domestic scene she pleads with Hotspur to tell what plans he has in hand. He refuses to talk to her about the rebellion, but she follows him to Wales to join Mortimer and Glendower. In *2 Henry IV* she speaks proudly of her husband, noting that every courtier is affecting his lisp. She urges Northumberland to be avenged for his son's death at Shrewsbury.

Percy, Thomas. b. at Bridgnorth, England, April 13, 1729; d. at Dromore, Ireland, Sept. 30, 1811. An English poet, bishop, and antiquary, editor of the *Reliques of Ancient English Poetry*, known as *Percy's Reliques*. He was the son of a grocer, and graduated from Oxford (Christ Church) in 1750. He was appointed vicar of Easton Maudit, Northamptonshire, in 1753, chaplain to George III in 1769, and bishop of Dromore, Ireland, in 1782. The *Reliques of Ancient English Poetry* appeared in 1765; the first edition contained 176 poems or ballads. It was coarsely, but with some justice, attacked by Joseph Ritson as not being an exact transcription from the original manuscripts. The collection, nevertheless, served as the inspiration for a good deal of the output of the romantic poets of the next century, and it had a notable success in stirring other collectors to work. He also published *Hau Kiou Chooan* (1761; a Chinese novel from the Portuguese), *Miscellaneous Pieces relating to the Chinese* (1762), and *Northern Antiquities* (1770; translated from Paul Henri Mallet).

Percy, Thomas. b. at Southwark, London, Sept. 13, 1768; d. at Ecton, near Northampton, England, May 14, 1808. An English minor poet; nephew of Thomas Percy (1729–1811). He edited the fourth edition of Percy's *Reliques* (1794).

Percy, Thomas. See also **Worcester, Thomas Percy, Earl of.**

Percy Dacier (dā′si.ẽr), **the Honourable.** See **Dacier, the Honourable Percy.**

Percy's Reliques. The popular name of the work formally entitled *Reliques of Ancient English Poetry*, from its editor, Thomas Percy (1729–1811).

Percy Society. An association of English literary scholars and others interested in the authentication and publication of early English ballads and other similar materials. It was founded in 1840, and takes its name from Thomas Percy (1729–1811).

Perdiccas (pẽr.dik′as). Assassinated in Egypt, 321 B.C. One of the generals of Alexander the Great. He became regent in 323, and conquered Cappadocia in 322. A league was formed against him by Ptolemy and others; he moved to attack the allies and was defeated. He was killed by his own soldiers.

Perdita (pẽr′di.ta). In Shakespeare's *Winter's Tale*, the daughter of Leontes and Hermione. Leontes orders that she be abandoned in some desert place, but she is rescued and raised as a shepherdess. Florizel falls in love with her, and she is finally restored to her mother and penitent father. George IV, when he was Prince of Wales, fell in love with Mary Robinson, who played the part at Drury Lane in 1779. She was referred to as Perdita (and he as Florizel) in his correspondence with her.

Perdita. Pseudonym of **Robinson, Mary.**

Peredur (per′e.dür). The title and hero of one of the Arthurian stories in the Welsh *Mabinogion*,

taken (c1200) from one or more earlier French prose romances. It comprises one of the earliest versions of the Perceval-and-the-Grail legend. It is especially interesting in that it substitutes for the usual chalice a platter bearing a man's severed head.

Père Goriot (per go.ryō), **Le.** A novel by Honoré de Balzac, published in 1835.

Peregrine Pickle (per′ẹ.grin pik′l). [Full title, **The Adventures of Peregrine Pickle.**] A novel by Tobias Smollett, published in 1751 and revised in 1758. The work is a series of episodes concerning the adventures of the rascally hero, Peregrine Pickle, on the Continent and in England. Smollett's humor and satiric skill are very much in evidence, but the principal merit of the book is to be found in its excellent characterizations. Pickle is really a bully and a brute, in spite of his witty elegance, and his reckless disregard for principle leads him into duels, imprisonments, and a series of amatory adventures. He finally inherits his father's property and marries Emily Gauntlet, a young lady whom he has pursued from the beginning of the story. A wonderful character drawing is to be found in Commodore Trunnion, an old sea captain married to Peregrine's Aunt Grizzle, who runs his house as though it were a fortress and who enforces discipline with the most abusive of language, but whose sincere kindness and humor endear him to the reader. He is aided in "the garrison" by Lieutenant Hatchway, a one-legged man, and a boatswain, Tom Pipes, who becomes Peregrine's companion in his travels. Scenes such as the trip to the church at Commodore Trunnion's wedding, the dinner party given in the manner of the ancients, and Pipes' attempt to soften Emily's heart (by telling her Peregrine has committed suicide because she rejected him) show Smollett's capacity for combining hilarious incidents with unforgettable characters.

Perez (pē′rez), **Michael.** A character in Francis Beaumont and John Fletcher's play *Rule a Wife and Have a Wife*, known as "the Copper Captain."

Perfidious Oldcraft (pẽr.fid′i.us ōld′kráft), **Sir.** See **Oldcraft, Sir Perfidious.**

Pergamus (pẽr′ga.mus) or **Pergamum** (-mum). The citadel of Troy.

Periander (per.i.an′dẽr). d. 585 B.C. A tyrant of Corinth (625–585 B.C.). Despite almost universal agreement on his despotism, he appears to have acted for the good of Corinth, establishing colonies to the north, promoting trade, extending Corinthian influence, and developing a program of public works. He is usually counted among the Seven Wise Men of ancient Greece.

Pericles (per′i.klēz). b. probably c495 B.C.; d. of the plague at Athens, 429 B.C. An Athenian statesman and orator; son of Xanthippus and a member of the powerful Alcmaeonid family. He entered public life c469, became the leader of the democratic party, and secured the ostracism of Cimon (c459) and later of Thucydides (441). After 444 he was the principal minister of Athens. He aided in the military and naval development of the state, making peace (448) with Persia, seeking an understanding with Sparta, and, that failing, building Athenian defenses for the inevitable struggle. He encouraged art and literature, completed the fortification of Athens and Piraeus, and caused the building of the Parthenon, Propylaea, Odeon, and the other public works that have caused his period of ascendancy to be known as the Golden Age of Athens. He instituted many government reforms, all tending to strengthen Athenian democracy. He commanded in the war against Samos (440–439) and in the first part of the Peloponnesian War (431–429).

Pericles. [Full title, **Pericles, Prince of Tyre.**] A play by Shakespeare, written possibly in 1607 or 1608. It must have been first performed in the interval January, 1606–November, 1608 (probably nearer to the latter date), as we have a report from the Venetian ambassador that he saw it in London in that span of time. It was published in 1609, in quarto in a corrupt and probably unauthorized text, and again in quarto in 1611, 1619, 1630, and 1635. Not in the folio of 1623, it appears first in folio in 1664. It is now generally agreed that Shakespeare did not write the entire play, and it was probably not included in the folio of 1623 for that reason. It has been suggested that Shakespeare took two acts by an inferior playwright and added three more (except possibly for the Gower choruses). George Wilkins, a contemporary writer, produced a novel in 1608 with some passages like the play, and it is barely possible that he was the other writer (although the late George L. Kittredge, among others, looked upon this conjecture as dubious in the extreme). By whomever used, however, it is fairly certain that the sources for the play must have included Gower's *Confessio Amantis*, and *The Patterne of Painefull Adventures*, a prose work published sometime after 1576. In 1660 Betterton acted the play on the Restoration stage (some have thought that it was the first of Shakespeare's works to take the stage again after the Restoration).

The Story. Pericles discovers early in his courtship of the daughter of Antiochus of Antioch that the father and daughter are entangled in an incestuous romance, and is therefore placed in peril of his life by Antiochus. Deputizing his loyal minister, Helicanus, to rule Tyre in his stead, he boards ship for Tarsus, but is cast up on the shores of Pentapolis, the sole survivor of a shipwreck. He participates in a tourney for the hand of Thaisa, daughter of King Simonides of Pentapolis, and marriage follows shortly on the heels of his victory. Thus far, in the first two acts (which Shakespeare is believed not to have written), the play has followed a very straightforward plot, but at this point manifold complications are introduced. Pericles is informed by Helicanus of the death of Antiochus, and the hero therefore sets out at once for Tyre with his wife, who is now with child. A violent storm arises, and Thaisa, terrified, falls into a state of unconsciousness so deep as to simulate death (but having given birth to a daughter a few moments before). Pericles, believing her dead, places her in a chest, and casts the chest into the sea. Thaisa is washed ashore at Ephesus, and restored to consciousness by Cerimon. Convinced that her husband has perished, she enters the temple of Diana as a votaress. Pericles, meanwhile, leaves the daughter, Marina, in Tarsus, with Cleon and his

wife, Dionyza. Sixteen years later Dionyza, violently jealous of a child now become a beautiful woman, seeks to rid herself of Marina by ordering a servant to kill her, but he is frightened off by pirates and Marina is carried off to a brothel in Mytilene. Humbled by her chastity and beauty, the patrons of this establishment leave her untouched, and one of them, Lysimachus, governor of the city, buys her freedom. Pericles now sees Marina's tomb in a dream and sets out to visit it; cast ashore at Mytilene, he recognizes and is joyfully reunited with Marina. Another dream now sends him to Ephesus with Marina, and here he encounters Thaisa. Marina is forthwith married to Lysimachus and it is related that Dionyza and Cleon have been murdered by the Athenians.

Pericles. The Prince of Tyre, the hero of Shakespeare's *Pericles.* He is Apollonius in Gower's *Confessio Amantis*, which retold the *Pantheon* of Godfrey of Viterbo, in itself a reworking of a Latin history by Apollonius. This was an extremely popular work in medieval times and various vernacluuar versions are found in many languages. Possibly his name was suggested by Pyrocles, the much-shipwrecked hero of Sidney's *Arcadia*.

Perigot (per′i.gō). The lover of the "faithful shepherdess" in John Fletcher's pastoral play of that name.

Perillous Chair, the. See **Siege Perilous.**

periodic. In rhetoric: **1.** Of or pertaining to a period or complete sentence; complete in grammatical structure.
2. Denoting that form of sentence in which the sense is incomplete or suspended until the end is reached.

These principles afford a simple and sufficient answer to the vexed question as to the value of the periodic sentence—or sentence in which the meaning is suspended till the end—as compared with the loose sentence, or sentence which could have been brought to a grammatical close at one or more points before the end. (A. S. Hill, *Rhetoric.*)

peripetia (per″i.pe.tī′a). That part of a drama in which the plot is unraveled and the whole concludes; the dénouement.

Peripatetics (per″i.pa.tet′iks). The followers of Aristotle (384–322 B.C.). They were so called from his teaching while walking up and down. Theophrastus succeeded Aristotle as leader of the school. Under later teachers, especially during and after the 1st century B.C., the Peripatetics wrote commentaries and expositions of Aristotle; the school became eclectic and eventually turned to Neoplatonism. In the Middle Ages the word was often used to signify "logicians."

periphrasis (pe.rif′ra.sis). A roundabout way of speaking; a roundabout phrase or expression; the use of more words than are necessary to express the idea; a phrase employed to avoid a common and trite manner of expression; circumlocution.

Then haue ye the fiture Periphrasis, holding somewhat of the dissembler, by reason of a secret intent not appearing by the words, as when we go about the bush.
(Puttenham, *Arte of English Poesie.*)

ḍ, d or j; ş, s or sh; ṭ, t or ch; ẓ, z or zh; o, F. cloche; ü, F. menu; ċh, Sc. loch; ṅ, F. bonbon.

They speak a volume in themselves, saving a world of periphrasis and argument.

(Prescott, *Ferdinand and Isabella*.)

Perissa (pẹ.ris'ạ). In Edmund Spenser's *Faerie Queene*, the youngest of three sisters who were always at odds with each other. She is the sister of Elissa and Medina.

Perjur'd Husband, or the Adventures of Venice, The. A tragicomedy by Susannah Centlivre, produced and printed in 1700. This was her first play.

Perker (pėr'kėr), **Mr.** In Dickens's *Pickwick Papers*, a good-hearted and competent lawyer. It is he who finally arranges for Pickwick's release from the Fleet Prison.

Perkin Warbeck (pėr'kin wôr'bek). A historical play by John Ford, acted at the Phoenix Theatre and published in 1634. The source may have been Bacon's *Life of Henry VII*, which mentions the impostor, Perkin Warbeck. The two kings (Henry VII of England and James IV of Scotland) are contrasted: the former is a shrewd, cool diplomat; the other is emotionally chivalric, readily taken in by Warbeck's charm, and easily persuaded to fight for his claim to the English throne. However, when James finally realizes what pressing Warbeck's claim will cost in terms of English anger, he bids him seek shelter elsewhere.

Perolla and Izadora (pẹ.rol'ạ; iz.ạ.dō'rạ). A tragedy by Colley Cibber, produced in 1705.

peroration (per.ọ.rā'shọn). The concluding part of an oration, in which the speaker recapitulates the principal points of his discourse or argument, and urges them with greater earnestness and force, with a view to make a deep impression on his hearers; hence, the conclusion of a speech, however constructed.

Nephew, what means this passionate discourse,
This peroration with such circumstance?

(Shakespeare, *2 Henry VI*.)

Perplex'd Lovers, The. A comedy by Susannah Centlivre, produced and printed in 1712.

Perrault (pe.rō), **Charles.** b. at Paris, Jan. 12, 1628; d. there, May 16, 1703. A French writer. According to his own testimony, he left the college at Beauvais in consequence of a misunderstanding with one of his professors, but spent the next three or four years in study, especially of the classics. Two odes in eulogy of Louis XIV brought him into favor at court, so that no opposition was raised to his admission to the French Academy, Sept. 22, 1671. His poem *Le Siècle de Louis le Grand*, read before this body on Jan. 27, 1687, expressed incidentally some ideas that were disparaging to the old classics. Between Boileau and Perrault arose then the great literary quarrel concerning the respective merits of the ancients and the moderns, which lasted over a dozen years, and did much to bring Perrault's name into prominence. In the course of their dispute Perrault started in 1688 the publication of his *Parallèle des anciens et des modernes*. He also wrote the two works upon which his literary fame rests, *Les Hommes illustres qui ont paru en France pendant ce siècle* (1696–1701), and *Les Contes de ma mère l'oye* (1697). These "tales of my mother, the goose" are also known simple as *Les Contes de Perrault*. They include 18 fairy tales including "Cinderella,"

"Sleeping Beauty," "Bluebeard," "Little Red Riding-Hood," and "Puss in Boots." These stories were folk material long before Perrault's day, but to him belongs the credit of first giving them in their French form a simple and lasting expression. The remainder of Perrault's writings have not added materially to his literary reputation, and he himself died in relative obscurity.

Persant of India (pėr'sạnt). [Also, **Phosphorus**.] In Arthurian legend and romance, the wonderful knight clad and armed in blue whom Gareth fought against for two hours and overcame. Persant so admired Gareth's prowess that he entertained and rested Gareth and his lady at his pavilion after the battle. He later came to Arthur's court with 100 knights at the feast of Pentecost and swore fealty to Arthur. He is also called Phosphorus; Tennyson, in *Gareth and Lynette*, calls him the Morning Star.

Persephone (pėr.sef'ọ.nē). [Roman, **Proserpine**.] In Greek mythology, the daughter of Zeus and Demeter. She was abducted by Hades and taken to the underworld, where she became his consort. The grieving Demeter sought her daughter everywhere. During this time no vegetation grew upon the earth, and at last the gods consented to let Persephone return to the world. It was discovered, however, that she had eaten one pomegranate seed in the land of the dead, and for this reason she was obliged to remain in the underworld for one third of the year, but could spend the other eight months on earth. This is one of the familiar symbolic vegetation myths of ancient Greece. Demeter and Persephone were interpreted as two aspects of the grain goddess, Persephone representing the new young grain, Demeter the ripened harvest. Persephone is also associated with the mother goddess, Aphrodite, in the fertility myth regarding the vegetation god, Adonis. Adonis dwelt with Persephone under the earth for one third of the year, and spent the other eight months with Aphrodite in the world. Persephone's cult name was Kore, the maiden, and in this aspect she figured in the Eleusinian mysteries. The Romans called her Proserpine and made little or no change in the myth or its interpretation.

Persepolis (pėr.sep'ọ.lis). In ancient geography, one of the capitals of the Persian Empire, ab. 35 mi. NE of what is now Shiraz. It became the capital under Darius I, was captured and burned by Alexander the Great c330 B.C., and is still noted for the ruins of its palaces.

Perseus (pėr'sūs, -sẹ.us). In Greek mythology, the son of Danaë by Zeus as the shower of gold. Forewarned that his daughter's son would kill him, Acrisius (king of Argos and the father of Danaë) set both mother and child adrift on the sea in a chest. The chest came ashore on the island of Sesiphus, where they were cared for. The king of Sesiphus sent Perseus when he was grown to kill the Gorgon Medusa. This Perseus did with the help of the gods, who gave him a magic sword, winged sandals, a cap of invisibility, and a shield which served as a mirror. On his way home he rescued and married Andromeda, and on arriving at Sesiphus, turned its king into stone with the Gorgon's head for mistreating Danaë. The fatal prophecy was fulfilled later when Perseus journeyed to Argos to see his grandfather Acrisius, took part in some games, and accidentally struck and killed him with a discus-throw.

persiflage (pėr′si.fläzh). Light, flippant banter; idle, bantering talk or humor; an ironical, frivolous, or jeering style of treating or regarding a subject, however serious it may be.

I hear of Brougham from Sefton, with whom he passes most of his spare time, to relieve his mind by small talk, persiflage, and the gossip of the day.
(Greville, *Memoirs, March 15, 1831.*)

Persius (pėr′shi.us, -shus). [Full name, **Aulus Persius Flaccus.**] b. at Volaterrae, in Etruria, 34 A.D.; d. 62 A.D. A Roman satirist. His six satires, written in hexameters, are actually homilies advocating the Stoic doctrine; their style is involved and moral.

personification. The act of personifying; specifically, in rhetoric, a figure of speech, or a species of metaphor, which consists in representing inanimate objects or abstract notions as endued with life and action, or possessing the attributes of living beings; prosopopoeia: as, "the floods clap their hands," "the sun rejoiceth as a strong man to run a race," "the mountains and the hills shall break forth into singing," etc.

The sage, the satirist, and the seer . . . veiled his head in allegory; he published no other names than those of the virtues and the vices; and, to avoid personality, he contented himself with personification. (I. D'Israeli, *Amen. of Lit.*)

Persuasion. A novel by Jane Austen, published in 1818, after the death of the author. This work is more definitely a love story than Miss Austen's earlier novels, and reveals more tenderness, greater subtlety in the shading of character, and a less satiric tone. Anne Elliot became engaged to Captain Frederick Wentworth when she was about 19, but broke the engagement on the persuasion of a friend, Lady Russell, who pointed out that the young man had no fortune, but did have a hot temper. Eight years have gone by, and Anne no longer is in the bloom of youth. Her father, Sir Walter Elliot, is forced to rent his home, Kellynch Hall, to Admiral and Mrs. Croft because of his foolish waste of money in maintaining social position. Mrs. Croft is Captain Wentworth's sister. He is therefore once more thrown into contact with Anne, who regrets greatly having broken her engagement to him. He is now wealthy and quite eligible and seems attracted to Louisa and Henrietta Musgrove, sisters-in-law of Mary, Anne's younger sister. Captain Wentworth almost decides to ask Louisa to marry him when she falls from a carriage and is seriously injured; as he was helping her down, he feels responsible for the accident. His proposal of marriage is never made, however, because Louisa becomes engaged to Captain Benwick, a friend of his. He now goes to Bath, where Sir Walter has taken his daughters, because he feels drawn to Anne once more. There he finds that Anne is being courted by her cousin, William Elliot, the heir to Sir Walter's estate, who is having an affair at the same time with Mrs. Clay, the girls' companion, chiefly to keep her from marrying Sir Walter and thus possibly preventing him from inheriting Sir Walter's estate. Anne finds out about the intrigue,

breaks off relations with William, and finds that she is still in love with Captain Wentworth. He learns of her devotion, asks her hand in marriage, and is accepted.

Pertelote (pėr′tẹ.lọt). [Also: **Partlet, Dame Partlet.**] The hen, the favorite wife of Chauntecleer the cock in *Reynard the Fox* and Chaucer's *Nun's Priest's Tale.* The later form of the name, Partlet, became a class name for "hen." Dryden's line "Sister Partlet with her hooded head," in *The Hind and the Panther,* refers to the Roman Catholic nuns.

Pertolepe (pėr.tol′ẹ.pē). [Also, **Hesperus.**] In Arthurian legend and romance, the formidable knight clad and armed in green, who was overcome by Gareth and put under oath to come to Arthur's court and yield to him when called. This he did at the feast of Pentecost, along with all the other knights whom Gareth had overcome on this expedition. He was also called Hesperus; Tennyson calls him the Evening Star.

Perugino (pä.rö.jē′nō). [Original name, **Pietro Vannucci.**] b. at Città della Pieve, Umbria, Italy, 1446; d. 1524. An Italian painter of the Umbrian school, called Perugino from his long residence at Perugia. He has long been known chiefly as having been the master of Raphael. Leading a somewhat wandering life, he was called to Rome by Pope Sixtus IV to assist in the decoration of the Sistine Chapel, and is credited with nine frescoes there. Perhaps his greatest work is the decoration of the Sala del Cambio at Perugia.

Peter (pē′tėr), Saint. [Originally, **Simon.**] One of the 12 apostles, a fisherman, the reputed author of the two New Testament epistles bearing his name.

Peter. In Shakespeare's *Measure for Measure,* a confidant of Vincentio, the Duke of Vienna.

Peter. In Shakespeare's *Romeo and Juliet,* the servant of Juliet's nurse.

Peter. Entries on literary characters having this prename will be found also under the surnames Bullcalf, Davies, Featherstone, Grimes, Pattieson, Peebles, Pepperpot, Plumdamas, Pounce, Poundtext, Quince, Teazle, Thump, Westcott, and Wimsey.

Peter Bell (bel). A poetical tale by William Wordsworth, published in 1819. It was written in 1798, and dedicated to Robert Southey. It tells of the spiritual conversion of Peter Bell, a potter, insensitive to human values and the beauties of life and nature. Bell, about to steal an ass apparently standing alone at a river bank, is given pause when he finds the beast sorrowfully regarding the body of his drowned master. Bell determines to find the home of the poor man and return the ass to his widow at the same time as he tells her of her misfortune, and while traveling there he has the various other experiences which cause him to change his attitude toward life.

Peter Bell the Third. A burlesque poem (1819) by Percy Bysshe Shelley. It strikes bitterly at Wordsworth's desertion of the liberal cause. A parody of the Wordsworthian style, *Peter Bell* by J. H. Reynolds had appeared earlier in 1819, hence Shelley's poem was called by him "the Third."

Peter Ibbetson (ib′ẹt.sọn). A novel (1892) by George Du Maurier.

d, d or j; ṣ, s or sh; ṭ, t or ch; ẓ, z or zh; o, F. cloche; ü, F. menu; ċh, Sc. loch; ṅ, F. bonbon.

Peter Lombard (lom'bärd, -bẹrd; lum'-). See **Lombard, Peter.**

Peter of Langtoft (lang'toft). See **Langtoft, Peter of.**

Peter of Pomfret (pum'frẹt, pom'-). In Shakespeare's *King John*, a prophet who predicts that John will yield up his crown before Ascension Day. He is hanged for this.

Peter Pan (pan). A play (1904) and story (1906) by Sir J. M. Barrie, about an elfish boy who, never growing up, lives perennially in the "Never-never Land" of childhood. See also under **Barrie.**

Peter Simple (sim'pl). A novel by Frederick Marryat, published in 1834. The hero is considered the fool of the family, and is sent off to sea, where he proves his gallantry and courage after many adventures. He finally meets and wins the girl of his heart. Among the notable characters are Captain Savage, Terence O'Brien, the boatswain Chucks, and Captain Kearney.

Peter the Hermit. [Also, **Peter of Amiens.**] b. c1050; d. at the monastery of Neufmontier (Liége), Belgium, July 11, 1115. Hermit and monk, one of the chief preachers of the first Crusade. He led the advance division of the first Crusade as far as Asia Minor in 1096.

Peter the Lombard (lom'bärd, -bẹrd; lum'-). See **Lombard, Peter.**

Petit André (pẹ.tē tän.drā). An executioner in Louis XI's retinue, introduced as a character in the novel *Quentin Durward* by Sir Walter Scott.

Petite Pallace of Pettie his Pleasure (pet'i), A. See under **Pettie, George.**

Petition of Right. An act of Parliament passed in May, 1628, one of the chief documents of the English constitution. It provided that no freeman be required to give any gift, loan, benevolence, or tax without prior approval by act of Parliament; that no freeman be imprisoned or detained contrary to the law of the land; that soldiers or mariners be not billeted in private houses; and that commissions to punish soldiers and sailors by martial law be revoked and no more issued.

Peto (pē'tō). In Shakespeare's *1* and *2 Henry IV*, an associate of Sir John Falstaff.

Petowker (pẹ.tou'kẹr), **Henrietta.** In Dickens's novel *Nicholas Nickleby*, an actress of very limited talents, but very romantic notions. She marries Lillyvick, and abandons him for a captain on half pay when he bores her.

Petrarch (pē'trärk). [Italian, **Francesco Petrarca** (pä.trär'kä); original name, **Petracco** (pä.träk'kō).] b. at Arezzo, Italy, July 20, 1304; d. at Arquà, near Padua, July 19, 1374. An Italian poet, second in importance among Italian poets of the Middle Ages only to Dante. His father belonged to the party of the Bianchi (Whites) and was banished at the same time as Dante; Petrarch remembered seeing the latter in his childhood. The family went to Avignon in 1310, and when about 14 years of age Petrarch went to Montpellier to pursue his studies in law, later shifting to Bologna. He returned to Avignon in 1326, soon after the death of his father, and lived there until 1347. In 1327 he first saw the Laura idealized and celebrated in his sonnets. There have been many theories as to her identity; that gener-

ally received is that she was the daughter of Audibert de Noves, married Hugues de Sade in 1325, and became the mother of 11 children before her death in 1348. This identification has been disputed, but her real identity is unimportant: what is important is the effect she had on Petrarch's lyric poems of unrequited love and consequent melancholy, together with his inner conflict between desire and religious duty. These reactions were distilled into verse of remarkable elegance, clarity of expression, and formal perfection. Petrarch's homage was conventional, and personal relations are not supposed to have existed between the wife of De Sade and the poet. His literary infatuation did not, however, prevent his having by other women a natural son and daughter, born in 1337 and 1343 respectively. He received a canonry at Lombez, at the foot of the Pyrenees, in 1335, serving there under Giacomo Colonna, Bishop of Lombez, and a member of the family in whose service Petrarch performed diplomatic duties for several years. In 1337 he bought a little house at Vaucluse, near Avignon, to which he retired and where he did most of his best works. From the outset of his career he was an avid student of antiquity, his passion for which was evidenced in his Latin works of erudition, such as his collection of biographies *De viris illustribus* (On Famous Men, 1338 *et seq.*), and in his first major work, the Latin epic poem *Africa* (1338–42), celebrating the exploits of Scipio Africanus. Primarily in recognition of the promise shown in the *Africa*, he was crowned poet laureate by the senate in Rome April 8, 1341, he having received on the same day as the invitation to Rome a similar invitation from the University of Paris. In 1347 he built a house at Parma, but resided partly at Vaucluse until 1353, when he settled at Milan. He was patronized by nobles and ecclesiastics, and employed on various diplomatic missions, principally by the Visconti, whom he represented at the court of King John II of France, conducting the marriage of a young Visconti with the daughter of the king. In 1362 he removed to Padua, where he had held a canonry since 1347, and to Venice, in the same year, where he saw Boccaccio for the last time, having first met him in 1350 at Florence. He went to Arquà in 1370, where he died. Posterity remembers him chiefly for his personal utterances, in his *Canzoniere* (collected lyric poems, in Italian) and such Latin works as his *Epistles* (1326–74) and his philosophic-religious treatises *Secretum* (Innermost Thoughts, 1343), *De vita solitaria* (On Solitary Life, 1346–56), *De otio religiosorum* (On Monastic Freedom from Care, 1347–56), and *De remediis utriusque fortunae* (On the Remedies for Good and Bad Fortune, 1350's–1366). An effort to rival Dante in an Italian allegorical and didactic poem, *I Trionfi* (The Triumphs, c1352–74), was unsuccessful. Petrarch forms in a way a bridge between medieval and modern intellectual life. His deep interest in the rediscovery and revival of ancient culture marks him as an immediate forerunner of the humanistic renaissance. The intellectual content of his work and some elements of his poetic form were traditional, but his attitude, in its subjectivity and introspection, in its instability and many-sidedness, anticipates strikingly many later developments, so that he has been termed "the first modern man of letters." Petrarch, rather than Dante or Boccaccio, carried the prestige of Italian literature to the rest of Europe, and he still serves as a model for formal perfection and for harmony of verse and content in poetical expression. The English sonnet, perhaps the principal verse form in the language, stems directly from Petrarch through Henry Howard, Earl of Surrey, and Sir Thomas Wyatt, whose translations of his sonnets appeared early in Elizabeth's reign and inspired in the next 50 years a great flow of English lyric poetry.

Petronel Flash (pet.rǫ.nel′ flash′), **Sir**. See **Flash, Sir Petronel.**

Petronius Arbiter (pẹ.trō′ni.us är′bi.tẻr), **Gaius**. d. probably c66 A.D. A Roman author, often identified with a certain Gaius Petronius mentioned by Tacitus. This Petronius was one of the emperor Nero's companions, formerly proconsul in Bithynia, and was made by the emperor arbiter at his luxurious court in matters of taste. From his title in this post, *Arbiter Elegantiae* (Arbiter of Elegance), stems the identification with the writer. Petronius's influence aroused the jealousy of Tigellinus, prefect of the Praetorian Guard, and he carried tales about Petronius to the emperor. When Petronius subsequently received an order to remain in a sort of house arrest at Cumae, he committed suicide by opening his veins and dying slowly and quietly while his friends feasted about him. The *Satyricon* attributed to him is a vivid and elegantly written portrayal, in alternating prose and verse, of Roman life of the time, existing now only in fragments. Among these the largest is the *Cena Trimalchionis* (Trimalchio's Feast), depicting a feast tendered by a vulgar rich man; the story of the Matron of Ephesus is another of the surviving episodes.

Petruchio (pẹ.trö′ki.ō, -chi.ō). In Shakespeare's *Taming of the Shrew*, a Veronese gentleman who determines to wed and tame the shrew, Katherina. Despite her display of temper on their first meeting, he calls her "passing courteous" and "modest as a dove." By asserting his dominance (in such ways as arriving late and in old clothes for the wedding, refusing to let her stay for the dinner, taking her food and new clothes from her, and making her call the sun the moon) he makes her a gentle and submissive wife. John Fletcher introduces him in a reversed role in *The Woman's Prize, or the Tamer Tamed* as the henpecked husband of a second wife, Maria.

Pettie (pet′i), **George**. b. 1548; d. at Plymouth, Devonshire, England, in July, 1589. An English writer of prose romances. He was the author of a work important for the part it played in developing Elizabethan prose fiction, a collection of 12 tales taken from medieval legend and classical myth and entitled *A Petite Pallace of Pettie his Pleasure, contayning many pretie Hystories by him, set foorth in Comely Colours, and most Delightfully Discoursed* (1576), an imitation of William Painter's *Palace of Pleasure* (1567), and written in the ornate style later further developed by John Lyly. He was also the translator of Guazzo's *Civile Conversation* (1581).

Petty (pet′i), **Sir William**. b. at Romsey, Hampshire, England, May 26, 1623; d. at London, Dec.

16, 1687. An English statistician and political economist. He retired to the Continent on the outbreak of the civil war, returning to England in 1646. In 1651 he was professor of anatomy at Oxford. In 1652 he was appointed physician to the army in Ireland, and c1654 executed by contract a fresh survey, commonly known as the Down Survey, of the forfeited Irish lands granted to soldiers. He bought large tracts of land and established various industries. After the Restoration in 1660 he was knighted. In 1663 he invented a double-bottomed ship. He is best remembered as an economist and early statistician. He criticized the bullionist mercantile theory and stated instead that price is fixed by the labor necessary in production. He was a firm advocate of union with Ireland. He wrote *Treatise of Taxes and Contributions* (1662–85), *Political Arithmetic* (1683 and 1686), *Political Anatomy of Ireland* (1672; printed 1691), and others.

Petulengro (pet.ụ.leng′grō), **Jasper**. In George Borrow's *Romany Rye* and *Lavengro*, a young gypsy chief. The character is drawn from Ambrose Smith, a Norfolk gypsy whom Borrow had once known.

Peveril of the Peak (pev′ẻr.il). A historical novel by Sir Walter Scott, published in 1823.

Phaeacia (fẹ.ā′shạ). An unknown island in Greek legend, inhabited by a seafaring people who were traditionally hospitable to other seafarers. In the *Odyssey*, Odysseus was shipwrecked on its shores while returning from Troy to Ithaca, and was succored and entertained by its king and his daughter, Nausicaa. It is sometimes identified with Corfu.

Phaedra (fē′drạ). In Greek legend, the daughter of king Minos of Crete and Pasiphae; sister of Ariadne, and wife of Theseus, noted for her love for her stepson Hippolytus. She was repulsed by Hippolytus, and accused him to Theseus, thus securing his death. When his innocence became known, she committed suicide. She was the subject of tragedies by Euripides, Seneca, and Racine, and of a lost tragedy by Sophocles.

Phaedrus (fē′drus). fl. in the first half of the 1st century A.D. A Roman fabulist, originally a Macedonian slave. His five books of fables, in verse, are apparently renderings of Aesopian fables current in his day. Phaedrus was the principal medieval source for the fables of Aesop.

Phaer or **Phayer** (făr, fā′ẻr), **Thomas**. b. c1510; d. at Kilgerran, Pembrokeshire, Wales, 1560. An English translator. In 1558 he published his translation of the *Seven First Books of the Eneidos of Virgil*. He had begun the tenth book when he died; nine books were published in 1562. He also wrote on various subjects, including law and medicine.

Phaethon (fā′ẹ.thọn). In Greek mythology, the son of Helios, the sun god. Phaethon longed to drive his father's chariot (the sun) across the sky, but, being unable to check the horses, nearly set the earth on fire. The situation was saved by Zeus, who struck the youth with a thunderbolt. Phaethon fell in flames into the Po (ancient Eridanus) River.

Phalaris (fal′ạ.ris). A tyrant of Agrigentum in Sicily from c570 to c554 B.C., notorious for his cruelty (notably his human sacrifices in a heated brazen bull). The inventor of the bull was the first victim to be roasted alive. The spuriousness of some

ḍ, d or j; ṣ, s or sh; ṭ, t or ch; ẓ, z or zh; o, F. cloche; ü, F. menu; ċh, Sc. loch; ṅ, F. bonbon.

148 epistles which passed under his name was shown by the classical scholar Richard Bentley in his *Epistles of Phalaris* (1697).

Phantom Rickshaw, The. A story of Anglo-Indian life (1888) by Rudyard Kipling.

Phaon (fā′ọn). In Greek legend, a boatman of Mytilene, the favorite of Sappho.

Pharamond (far′ạ.mond). A legendary king of France, noted in the Arthurian cycle of romance. He is said to have been the first king of the Franks, and his reign has been placed between 420 and 428.

Pharamond. In Beaumont and Fletcher's play *Philaster*, a prince betrothed to Arethusa.

Pharaoh (fā′rō, fär′ō, fär′ạ.ō). A title given to the ancient Egyptian kings, meaning "great house." Among those mentioned in the Old Testament are a contemporary of Abraham (Gen. 12–20); the patron and friend of Joseph (Gen. 39–47); the oppressor of the Hebrews, perhaps Ramses II (Ex. 1); the Pharaoh who reigned at the time of the Exodus, perhaps Merneptah (Ex. 12); Pharaoh Necho; Pharaoh Hophra or Apries; Shishak or Sheshonk; and Tirhakah or Tarhaka.

Pharsalia (fär.sā′li.ạ). An epic poem in ten books, by Lucan (Marcus Annaeus Lucanus), on the civil war between Pompey and Caesar.

Phases of English Poetry. A critical study by Herbert Read, published in 1928.

Phases of the Moon, The. A poem by William Butler Yeats, published in *The Wild Swans at Coole* (1919).

Phebe (fē′bẹ). In Shakespeare's *As You Like It*, a shepherdess loved by Silvius. She falls in love with the disguised Rosalind, but finally marries Silvius.

Pheidippides (fī.dip′i.dēz). fl. 490 B.C. An Athenian athlete. When the Persians landed at Marathon, Pheidippides was sent as a courier from Athens to Sparta, asking the latter city's help against the invader. According to Herodotus, he covered the distance of about 150 miles in two days. Pheidippides is sometimes confused with the runner, whose name is not preserved, who brought to Athens the news of the Greek victory at Marathon.

Phenix (fē′niks). See **Phoenix**.

Philander (fi.lan′dẹr). A name often given to lovers in old plays and romances, as in Lodovico Ariosto's *Orlando Furioso* and Francis Beaumont and John Fletcher's *The Laws of Candy*.

Philario (fi.lä′ri.ō). In Shakespeare's *Cymbeline*, an Italian gentleman, the friend who tries to prevent Posthumus and Iachimo from making their wager.

Philanderer, The. A comedy (1893) by George Bernard Shaw, appearing in his *Plays, Pleasant and Unpleasant* (1898). It deals somewhat satirically with the liberated woman depicted in Ibsen's social dramas, but it is not, as some contemporary critics thought, an attack on Ibsen's basic social purpose.

Philaster, or Love Lies a-Bleeding (fi.las′tẹr). A play (1609) by Beaumont and Fletcher.

Philby (fil′bi), **Harry St. John Bridger.** b. at St. John's, Badula, Ceylon, April 3, 1885—. A British explorer in Arabia and Arabic scholar. He made numerous journeys of exploration to central and

south-central Arabia, was adviser to the ministry of interior of Mesopotamia (1920–21), and served as chief British representative in Trans-Jordan (1921–24). His books include *The Heart of Arabia* (1922), *Arabia of the Wahhabis* (1928), *Arabia* (1930), *The Empty Quarter* (1933), *Sheba's Daughters* (1939), *Arabian Days* (1948), and others.

Philemon (fi.lē′mọn, fī-). In Greek legend, a Phrygian who with his wife Baucis offered hospitality to Zeus and Hermes, and were rewarded with the gift of an inexhaustible pitcher.

Philemon. In Shakespeare's *Pericles*, a servant of Cerimon.

Philip II (fil′ip). See under **Philip, King of France**.

Philip, Adventures of. See **Adventures of Philip**.

Philip Baboon (ba.bön′). See **Baboon, Lewis** and **Philip**.

Philip Carey (kãr′i). See **Carey, Philip**.

Philip Faulconbridge (fô′kọn.brij, fôl′-). See **Faulconbridge, Philip**.

Philip, King of France. In Shakespeare's *King John*, the historical Philip II, who supports Arthur's claim to the English throne.

Philippi (fi.lip′ī). In ancient geography, a city in Macedonia, ab. 73 mi. NE of Salonika. It was named after Philip II of Macedon, and is famous as the site of the two battles in 42 B.C., in which Augustus (Octavius) and Mark Antony defeated the republicans under Brutus and Cassius. A Christian church was founded here by Paul, who addressed to the congregation the Epistle to the Philippians.

Philippics (fi.lip′iks), **The.** A group of nine orations of Demosthenes, directed against Philip II of Macedon. In these orations Demosthenes urges his fellow Athenians to resist conquest by Philip. They comprise the first Philippic, urging the sending of a military force to Thrace, delivered in 351 B.C.; three orations in behalf of the city of Olynthus (destroyed by Philip), delivered in 349–348; the oration *On the Peace* (346); the second Philippic (344); the oration *On the Embassy* (343); the speech *On the Chersonese* (341); and the third Philippic (341). The name is also given to a series of 14 orations of Cicero against Mark Antony, delivered in 44–43 B.C. The word "philippic" has come, therefore, to mean any speech of caustic denunciation.

Philip Quarles (kwôrlz, kwärlz). See **Quarles, Philip**.

Philip Quarll (kwôrl, kwärl). [Full title, **The Adventures of Philip Quarll**.] A tale (c1727) modeled on Daniel Defoe's *Robinson Crusoe*, whose author is sometimes identified as Edward Dorrington, otherwise unknown, but possibly a pseudonym of some well-known writer.

Philips (fil′ips), **Ambrose.** [Nicknamed "Namby Pamby."] b. c1675; d. at London, June 18, 1749. An English writer. He was of a Leicestershire family, and was educated at Cambridge (Saint John's College), where he wrote his *Pastorals*, which appeared in the sixth volume of Jacob Tonson's *Miscellanies* (1709), the same volume in which Alexander Pope's *Pastorals* appeared. When Pope's work was ignored by the writer in *The Guardian* who praised Philips highly, Pope began a long series of attacks on Philips, out of sheer jealousy. Philips sided with Joseph Addison in his quarrel with Pope. He went to Ireland as secretary to Archbishop Hugh Boulter, and was a member of the Irish Parliament. His nickname "Namby Pamby" was conferred on him by Henry Carey, and adopted by Pope, who considered it suited to his "eminence in the infantile style." He is best known by his play *The Distrest Mother*, an adaptation of Jean Baptiste Racine's *Andromaque* (1712). Among his other plays are *The Briton* (1722) and *Humfrey, Duke of Gloucester* (1723).

Philips, John. b. at Bampton, Oxfordshire, England, Dec. 30, 1676; d. at Hereford, England, Feb. 15, 1709. An English writer. *The Splendid Shilling*, a burlesque of John Milton's *Paradise Lost*, appeared in 1705. In 1705 he published *Blenheim*, also in imitation of Milton, as an answer for the Tories to Joseph Addison's *Campaign;* it was, however, so overdone that it failed. On Jan. 24, 1708, he published *Cyder*, his most ambitious work, in imitation of Vergil's *Georgics*.

Philips, Katharine. [Called **"the Matchless Orinda"**; maiden name, **Fowler**.] b. at London, Jan. 1, 1631; d. June 22, 1664. An English letter-writer and poet. She was known as "the Matchless Orinda" because of the signature Orinda adopted by her in a correspondence with Sir Charles Cotterel, who used the name of Poliarchus. She also used the name as her usual signature. She translated *Horace* (in part) and *La Mort de Pompée*, two of Pierre Corneille's plays, which, with a number of poems, were published in 1667.

Philipson (fil'ip.sọn). A surname assumed by the Earl of Oxford and his son Arthur de Vere on the occasion of their European exile, in Sir Walter Scott's *Anne of Geierstein*.

Philip Swidger (fil'ip swij'ėr). See **Swidger, Philip.**

Philip the Bastard. See **Faulconbridge, Philip.**

Philip the King. A drama (1914) by John Masefield.

Philip van Artevelde (van är'tẹ.vel.dẹ). A play by Sir Henry Taylor, published in 1834. It was an attempt to revive the traditions of the tragic school of Marlowe and Shakespeare.

Philip Wakem (wā'ḳẹm). See **Wakem, Philip.**

Philisides (fi.lis'i.dēz). In Sir Philip Sidney's *Arcadia*, a shepherd whose name is formed from some of the letters of Sidney's own. In the volume of Edmund Spenser's poems published in 1596 is a collection of laments for Sidney, among which is a *Pastoral Aeglogue upon the Death of Sir Philip Sidney*, in which each shepherd begins his lament with the words "Philisides is dead." It has been attributed to Sir Edward Dyer.

Philistines (fi.lis'tinz, fil'is.tēnz, -tĭnz). In the Old Testament, a people, possibly of Semitic origin but more probably originally from Crete, dwelling in Philistia. They were frequently at war with the Hebrews, and reached their highest power in the reigns of Saul and David.

Philistine (fi.lis'tin, fil'is-). **1.** In Germany, one who has not been trained in a university: so called by the students.
2. A matter-of-fact, commonplace person; a man upon whom one can look down, as of culture inferior to one's own; one of "parochial" intellect; a satisfied person who is unaware of his own lack of culture.

The people who believe most that our greatness and welfare are proved by our being very rich, and who most give their lives and thoughts to becoming rich, are just the very people whom we call Philistines. (M. Arnold, *Sweetness and Light*.)

Phillips (fil'ips), **Samuel.** b. Dec. 28, 1814; d. at Brighton, England, Oct. 14, 1854. An English writer. His first novel, *Caleb Stukely*, appeared (1841) in *Blackwood's Magazine*. In 1845 and 1846 he was political editor of the *Morning Herald*, and he was literary critic of the *Times* (1845–54). *Essays from the Times* was published in 1851.

Phillips, Stephen. b. at Somerton, near Oxford, England, July 28, 1868; d. at Deal, Kent, England, Dec. 9, 1915. An English poet and playwright. He was on the stage from 1886 to 1892. He wrote *Poems* (1897), *Paolo and Francesca* (1899), *Herod* (1900), *Ulysses* (1902), *The Sin of David* (1904), *Nero* (1906), *The Last Heir* (1908), *The New Inferno* (1910), *Pietro of Siena* (1910), *The King* (1912), and others. He was editor of *The Poetry Review*.

Phillis (fil'is). See **Phyllis.**

Phillpotts (fil'pots), **Eden.** [Pseudonym in early works, **Harrington Hext**.] b. at Mount Abu, India, Nov. 4, 1862—. An English novelist. His work includes regional novels of Devonshire, which have been highly regarded, detective stories, historical novels, poems, plays, and short stories. Author of *Down Dartmoor Way* (1895), *Lying Prophets* (1896), *Children of the Mist* (1898), *Sons of the Morning* (1900), *The Good Red Earth* (1901), *The Striking Hours* (1901), *The River* (1902), *My Devon Year* (1903), *The Golden Fetich* (1903), *The American Prisoner* (1904), *The Farm of the Dagger* (1904), *The Secret Woman* (1905), *Knock at a Venture* (1905), *The Portreeve* (1906), *The Sinews of War* (1906; with Arnold Bennett), *The Mother of the Man* (1908), *The Virgin in Judgment* (1908), *The Statue* (1908; with Arnold Bennett), *The Three Brothers* (1909), *Tales of the Tenements* (1910), *Wild Fruit*, poems (1910), *Demeter's Daughter* (1911), *The Beacon* (1911), *Widdecombe Fair* (1913), *Children of Men* (1923), *The Jury* (1927), *Minions of the Moon* (1934), *The Changeling* (1943), and *Through a Glass Darkly* (1951).

Phillpotts, Mary Adelaide Eden. b. at Ealing, England, April 23, 1896—. An English novelist and playwright; daughter of Eden Phillpotts, and collaborator with him on the play *Yellow Sands* (1926). Her novels include *Man, a Fable* (1922), *A Marriage* (1928), *The Growing World* (1934), *The Gallant Heart* (1939), *Our Little Town* (1942), and *The Lodestar* (1946). Author also of the plays *Arachne* (1920), *Akhnaton* (1926), and *Laugh With Me* (1938).

Philo (fī'lō). In Shakespeare's *Antony and Cleopatra*, a friend of Antony.

ḍ, d or j; ṣ, s or sh; ṭ, t or ch; ẓ, z or zh; o, F. cloche; ü, F. menu; ch, Sc. loch; ṅ, F. bonbon.

Philobiblon (fĭ.lō.bib'lon). A treatise on book collecting by Richard Aungerville (also called Richard de Bury), bishop of Durham and chancellor of Edward III. It was finished in 1345, and was printed at Cologne in 1473.

Philoctetes (fil.ok.tē'tēz). In Greek legend, a Greek warrior in the Trojan War, famous as an archer. He was the friend and armorbearer of Hercules, and set fire to the funeral pile of that hero. On his way to the Trojan War, he was wounded either by a serpent or accidentally by one of the poisoned arrows given him by Hercules, and was left to die on Lemnos. It was prophesied, however, that Troy could not be taken without the arrows of Hercules, so haste was made to bring Philoctetes to Troy, and there he was healed. It was Philoctetes who killed Paris. He was the subject of a drama by Sophocles entitled *Philoctetes*.

philology. The love or the study of learning and literature; the investigation of a language and its literature, or of languages and literatures, for the light they cast upon men's character, activity, and history. The word is sometimes used more especially of the study of literary and other records, as distinguished from that of language, which is called *linguistics;* often, on the other hand, of the study of language or of languages.

Philology . . . deals with human speech, and with all that speech discloses as to the nature and history of man.   (Whitney, *Encyc. Brit.*)

Philomel (fil'ō.mel) or **Philomela** (fil.ō.mē'la̤). Associated with Philomela, daughter of King Pandion of Athens, who was fabled to have been turned into a nightingale; hence, the nightingale: used as a proper name: as, "All night long sweet Philomel pours forth her ravishing, delightful song" (Smollett, *Humphry Clinker*).

Philomela (fil.ō.mē'la̤). In Greek legend, the daughter of King Pandion of Athens, and sister of Procne, who was married to Tereus, king of Thrace. Tereus reported that Procne was dead and sent for Philomela. When she arrived, he raped her and cut out her tongue, to prevent her telling. But Philomela embroidered her story and sent the cloth to Procne. In revenge Procne served the flesh of their son to Tereus and fled with her sister. Tereus followed them, but the pair were turned into birds by compassionate gods.

Philomela. A novel by Robert Greene, published in 1592.

Philostrate (fil'os.trāt). In Shakespeare's *Midsummer Night's Dream*, Theseus's master of the revels.

Philotas (fi.lō'tas). A play (printed 1605) by Samuel Daniel.

Philoten (fi.lō'ten). In Shakespeare's *Pericles*, the daughter of Cleon and Dionyza. She is so far surpassed by Marina that the latter's murder is plotted by the jealous parents of the plainer girl. She does not appear on stage. In Lillo's adaptation of the play she instigates the attempt to murder Marina.

Philotus (fi.lō'tus). In Shakespeare's *Timon of Athens*, a servant to one of Timon's creditors.

Phineas Finn (fin'ē.as fin'). A novel by Anthony Trollope, published in 1869. It is one of the works in the so-called Parliamentary series, including also *Phineas Redux* (1873), *The Prime Minister* (1875), and *The Duke's Children* (1880). In *Phineas Finn* the young and penniless Irishman is elected to Parliament, and comes to London. He leaves behind him his young love, Mary Flood-Jones, and soon becomes enamoured of Violet Effingham, Lady Laura Standish, and Madame Max Goesler. He quarrels with the leading members of his party, after becoming secretary for the colonies, resigns, and returns to Mary.

Phineus (fī'nūs, fin'ē.us). In Greek mythology, a suitor of Andromeda, who, at her wedding with Perseus, was turned to stone at sight of the Gorgon's head.

Phipps (fips), Sir **Constantine Henry.** [Titles: 1st Marquis of **Normanby,** 2nd Earl of **Mulgrave.**] b. May 15, 1797; d. at London, July 28, 1863. An English statesman and writer. He published his first novel, *Matilda*, in 1825, and in 1828 *Yes and No*. He was made captain general and governor of Jamaica in 1832, was made lord lieutenant of Ireland in 1835, and was colonial secretary (1839) and home secretary (1839–41), successively, in Lord Melbourne's administration. From 1846 to 1852 he was ambassador at Paris, and later minister at Florence (1854–58), provoking criticism at both posts for meddling in the politics of those states.

Phiz (fiz). Pseudonym of **Browne, Hablot Knight.**

Phlegethon (fleg'ē.thon, flej'-). A fabled river of fire in Hades, the lower world of Greek mythology; hence (*cap.* or *l.c.*), a stream of fire or fiery light (as, "Heaven flows in a fierce phlegethon With the far-flashing wave for a brim"; Eden Phillpotts's *Cherry Stones*, Sea Sunset).

Phoebe (fē'bē). In Greek mythology, a Titaness; daughter of Uranus and Gaea. She was the mother of Leto, and thus the grandmother of Artemis. The name Phoebe became synonymous with the moon in later writings, and hence synonymous both with Artemis and the Roman Diana, as identified with the moon.

Phoenix (fē'niks). [Also, **Phenix.**] A Greek name for the ancient Egyptian mythological bird, the *bennu*, a bird of great beauty which, after living 500 or 600 years in the Arabian wilderness, the only one of its kind, built for itself a funeral pyre of spices and aromatic gums, lighted the pile with the fanning of its wings, was burned upon it, but from its ashes rose new and young. The Phoenix was the Egyptian symbol for the rising sun and the hieroglyph for the sun. In Christian symbolism the Phoenix represents resurrection and immortality. The story exists in Arabia, Persia, and India. It is mentioned in the Old Testament (Job, xxix. 18). In heraldic symbolism the Phoenix is always represented in the midst of flames.

Phoenix. In Greek legend: **a.** a brother or father of Europa and reputed ancestor of the Phoenicians. **b.** son of Amyntor and Hippodamia, and teacher and attendant of Achilles.

Phoenix, The. An Old English poem, preserved in the *Exeter Book* and sometimes attributed to Cynewulf. The first part of the poem is a paraphrase translation of an earlier Latin work, *De Ave Phoenice*, attributed to Lactantius Firmianus, which describes the beauty of the bird, its flights, and its death and rebirth. The second half shows Christian influence, under which the Phoenix becomes a symbol of the righteous Christian life and of Christ, and the myth of the Phoenix becomes an argument for and a symbol of the resurrection.

Phoenix, The. A comedy by Thomas Middleton, printed in 1607. It is founded on a Spanish novel, *The Force of Love*.

Phoenix, the. A London theater near Drury Lane. It was altered (1616) from a pit for fighting cocks and its earlier name was the Cockpit. It was pulled down in 1649 by the Puritans, but not completely destroyed. Plays were staged there, even during Parliamentary rule, until soon after the Restoration, when newer theaters superseded it.

Phoenix and Turtle, The. A poem generally accepted as being by Shakespeare, first published in an appendix to a book called *Love's Martyr*, by Robert Chester, in 1601.

Phoenix Nest, The. A collection of poems published in 1593, edited by "R.S. of the Inner Temple, gentleman." It contains poems by Sir Walter Raleigh, George Peele, Thomas Lodge, Sir Edward Dyer, and Thomas Watson, among others.

Phoenix Park. A famous public park in Dublin, Ireland. It was the scene of the assassination (1882) of Lord Frederick Cavendish and Thomas H. Burke.

Phoenix Too Frequent. A comedy (1946) by Christopher Fry.

Phorbas (fôr'bạs). In Greek legend, son of Lapithes. He freed Rhodes from a plague of serpents. Eventually he was slain by Apollo in a boxing contest.

Phorcyads (fôr.sī'ạdz). [Also: **Phorcides** (fôr'si-dēz), **Phorcids** (-sidz), **Phorkyads** (-ki.adz).] In Greek mythology, the daughters of Phorcus and Ceto. They are depicted as hideous and sharing between them but one tooth and one eye. In the second part of Goethe's *Faust*, Mephistopheles is turned into a Phorcyad.

Phosphorus (fos'fọ.rus). In Greek mythology, the morning star; a son of Astraeus and Eos. It is also the name of the planet Venus when seen in the early dawn. Phosphorus is sometimes depicted as a youth carrying a blazing torch.

Phosphorus. See also **Persant of India.**

Photinus (fọ.tī'nus). The chief minister of Ptolemy in Massinger and Fletcher's *The False One*, who is jealous of Cleopatra.

Phrixus (frik'sus). In Greek mythology, the brother of Helle. He sacrificed to Zeus the ram bearing the golden fleece, which he gave to Aetes.

Phryne (frī'nē). [Original name, **Mnesarete**.] b. in Boeotia; fl. in the middle of the 4th century B.C. An Athenian courtesan. She is supposed to have been the model of the picture *Aphrodite Anadyomene* by Apelles, and of the statue of the Cnidian Aphrodite by Praxiteles. According to legend, she was defended, on a capital charge, by her lover Hyperides; and when he failed to move the judges by his oratory, he bade her uncover her bosom, and

by her beauty moved them to grant her acquittal.

Phrynia (frin'i.ạ). In Shakespeare's *Timon of Athens*, a mistress of Alcibiades.

Phunky (fung'ki), **Mr.** In Dickens's *Pickwick Papers*, Serjeant Snubbins's "junior" in the case of Bardell vs. Pickwick. He is categorized as an "infant barrister," having had only a little more than eight years of experience.

Phyllis (fil'is). In Greek legend, the betrothed of Demophon, metamorphosed into an almond tree.

Phyllis. [Also, **Phillis**.] In pastoral poetry, a conventional name for a maiden.

Physician's Tale, The. [In some older sources, **The Doctor's Tale**.] One of Chaucer's *Canterbury Tales*. The Roman story of Appius and Virginia, it was expanded from the same story in the *Roman de la Rose*, though the account purports to be direct from Livy. The beautiful Virginia, daughter of the centurion Virginius, is slain by her father to keep her from the power of the decemvir Appius Claudius, who has determined to possess her, and this act sets off a people's revolt against Appius. The retelling of classical legends was a favorite literary device of the period. The Physician is described in the Prologue as a man well versed in the works of the classical and medieval medical writers, and also in astrology, well dressed but a moderate spender:

> In sangwin and in pers he clad was al,
> Lyned with taffata and with sendal,
> And yet he was but esy of dispence;
> He kepte that he wan in pestilence.
> For gold in phisik is a cordial,
> Therfore he lovede gold in special.

Physiologus (fiz.i.ol'ọ.gus). A bestiary, or collection of allegorical fables on animals. These were widely read in the Middle Ages. The word was sometimes used as if it were the name of the author. A *Physiologus* ascribed to Epiphanius was published at Rome in 1587. In the Western Church there is reference to a Latin *Physiologus*, ascribed to Saint Ambrose, which was condemned as apocryphal and heretical by Pope Gelasius I in a council of the year 496. There are several Latin manuscripts of such works, but none earlier than the 8th century. They are to be found also in Old High German prose of the 11th century, and in the Old French of Philippe de Thaun at the beginning of the 12th century. Another is of the 13th century, *Le Bestiaire Divin* of Guillaume, Clerc de Normandie. Another is *Le Bestiaire d'Amour* of Richard de Fournival. Traditions taken from the Bestiaries found their way also into the *Speculum Naturale* of Vincent of Beauvais.

Piano Quintet. A novel by Edward Sackville-West, published in 1925.

Piazza, The. An arcade of Covent Garden Market, London.

picaresque (pik.ạ.resk'). Pertaining to or dealing with rogues or picaroons: said of literary productions that deal with the fortunes of rogues or adventurers, and especially of works in Spanish literature about the beginning of the 17th century, of which *Guzmán de Alfarache* was a type.

The rise of the taste for picaresque literature in

Spain towards the close of the 16th century was fatal to the writers of pastoral.

(*Encyclopaedia Britannica*.)

Piccadilly (pik′a̯.dil.i). A great thoroughfare in London between Hyde Park Corner and the Haymarket. The street was named from a house of entertainment (Piccadilly House) which stood in the Haymarket in the time of Charles I. The W portion of Piccadilly was then called Portugal Street.

Piccolomini; or, The First Part of Wallenstein (pik.o̯.lō′mi.ne̯; wol′e̯n.stīn). A tragedy by Samuel Coleridge, published in 1800 and translated from Schiller's *Wallenstein*. The second part appeared in the same year as *The Death of Wallenstein*.

Pickering (pik′ėr.ing), **William**. b. April 2, 1796; d. at London, April 27, 1854. An English publisher. He began (1820) his business at Lincoln's Inn Fields, London, moving to larger quarters at Chancery Lane in 1824, and to Piccadilly in 1842. He became known (1821–31) for his publication of small, finely printed volumes, including the Diamond Classics (24 vols., representing such authors as Shakespeare, Milton, Izaak Walton, Homer, Horace, Vergil, Terence, Cicero, Dante, and Petrarch) and the widely used Aldine Edition of the British Poets (53 vols., including Chaucer, Milton, Dryden, Cowper, Collins, Burns, Gray, Pope, and Swift). In 1830 Pickering adopted the famous Aldine trademark (a dolphin twined round an anchor) of the Italian printer Aldus Manutius, adding to it the phrase "Aldi Discip. Anglvs." He also published Hume, Smollett, Johnson, and other 18th-century authors in the Oxford Classics and brought out Alexander Dyce's scholarly editions of Greene, Peele, and Webster.

Pickle the Spy (pik′l). See **Macdonell, Alastair Ruadh**.

Pickthall (pik′thôl), **Marmaduke (William)**. b. at Chillesford, Suffolk, England, April 7, 1875; d. at St. Ives, Cornwall, England, May 19, 1936. An English journalist, traveler, and novelist. He traveled on the Continent, and in Egypt, Turkey, and Syria, wrote pro-Turkish articles (1913) for the *New Age*, and edited (1920–24) the *Bombay Chronicle*, the *Hyderabad Quarterly Review*, and *Islamic Culture*. Author of *All Fools* (1900), *Said the Fisherman* (1903), *Enid* (1904), *Brendle* (1905), *The House of Islam* (1906), *The Myopes* (1907), *The Children of the Nile* (1908), *The Valley of the Kings* (1909), *Pot-au-Feu* (1911), *Larkmeadow* (1912), *Veiled Women* (1913), *With the Turk in War-Time* (1914), *Tales from Five Chimneys* (1915), *The House of War* (1916), *Knights of Araby* (1917), *Oriental Encounters* (1918), *Sir Limpidus* (1919), *The Early Hours* (1921), *As Others See Us* (1922), and *The Meaning of the Glorious Koran* (1930).

Pickwick (pik′wik), **Samuel**. In Dickens's *Pickwick Papers*, the founder of the Pickwick Club. He is a benevolent, simple-minded gentleman, and becomes the center of a series of farcical adventures.

Pickwick Club. The imaginary club created by Dickens in *The Pickwick Papers*.

"Pickwickian sense" (pik.wik′i.a̯n). A term applied to epithets or words which are not to be understood literally, or even in any ordinary figurative sense. In Dickens's *Pickwick Papers* Blotton is called upon to say whether he used the term "humbug" in its usual sense in speaking of Mr. Pickwick. Mr. Blotton says that he did not, that he "used the word in its Pickwickian sense." Mr. Pickwick then admits that when he said Mr. Blotton acted in "a vile and calumnious manner" he, too, was speaking in the Pickwickian sense.

Pickwick Papers (pik′wik). [Full title, **The Posthumous Papers of the Pickwick Club**.] A story by Charles Dickens, published serially in 1836–37. It takes its name from its chief character, Mr. Samuel Pickwick, the founder of the Pickwick Club. It comprises picaresque and generally hilarious adventures, culminating in the boisterous burlesque of legal chicanery and formality in the Bardell-Pickwick breach-of-promise trial. In describing Mr. Pickwick's subsequent imprisonment in the Fleet, Dickens sounds for the first time in one of his major works the note of social criticism which marks much of his writing.

Pico della Mirandola (pē′kō del′lä mē.rän′dō.lä), Count **Giovanni**. b. Feb. 24, 1463; d. at Florence, Nov. 17, 1494. An Italian humanist and philosopher, one of the leading scholars of the Italian Renaissance. After study that took him through France and Italy and made him master of Greek, Latin, Hebrew, and Arabic and gave him insight into the Cabala, he came (1486) to Rome. There he published a set of 900 propositions in theology, philosophy, mathematics, and other subjects that he was prepared to defend; no answer was forthcoming, but Pope Innocent VIII accused him of heresy and Pico was forced to issue an *Apologia* on the theses. In 1493 Alexander VI cleared him of the taint of heresy. He left (1487) Rome and traveled in Italy, making his base at Florence, where his friends Politian and Marsilius Ficinus lived. He was for some time under Savonarola's influence and appears to have planned to become a missionary preacher, but he died before he could carry out the scheme. He was the author of the *Heptaplus* (1489), a mystical account of the creation, *In Astrologiam*, an attack on astrology, and others.

Picrochole (pē.kro.shol). In François Rabelais's *Gargantua and Pantagruel*, a character supposed by some to represent either Ferdinand II of Aragon or Charles V.

Picture, The. A play by Philip Massinger, licensed in 1629 and printed in 1630. The plot was from one of Matteo Bandello's stories in Painter's *Palace of Pleasure*. The picture is a magical one, and grows brighter or darker according to the behavior of the absent wife it represents.

Picture of Dorian Gray (dō′ri.a̯n grā′), **The**. A novel by Oscar Wilde, published in 1891.

Picture Show. A volume of verse (1920) by Siegfried Sassoon, including the poems "The Dug-Out" and "Everyone Sang."

Picumnus (pi.kum′nus) and **Pilumnus** (pi.lum′nus). In Roman religion, two fertility gods associated with marriage and especially with childbirth. Offerings were made to them after a delivery.

fat, fāte, fär, a̯sk, fāre; net, mē, hėr; pin, pīne; not, nōte, mōve, nôr; up, lūte, pull; ᴛʜ, then;

Pidgin English. In China, West Africa, Australia, and Oceania, a reduction and adaptation of English to the speech habits of native peoples. There are wide local variations. Melanesian Pidgin is used in New Guinea, the Solomons, New Britain, and adjacent groups with only slight changes. Everywhere, Pidgin is more than English badly spoken: it has definite rules of its own. Sounds are derived from English but with changes such as insertion of a vowel between any two adjacent consonants, so that "stop" becomes "si-top," "box" becomes "bok-is." The vocabulary is mainly English, with some borrowing from native languages and some modifications of out-moded British slang, like "gammon," "humbug." Grammar is much changed. Nouns have no plural; verbs no tense, person, or number, but they have new suffixes such as *-im* to form a transitive verb.

Pied Beauty. A poem (1919) by Gerard Manley Hopkins, written in praise of all the things which are composed of many colors in irregular patterns, created by God "whose beauty is past change."

Pied Piper. A novel by Nevil Shute, published in 1941.

Pied Piper of Hamelin (ham′lin). [Also, **Piper of Hamelin** or **Hameln** (hä′meln).] In medieval legend, a magician who in the year 1284, for a stipulated sum of money, freed the town of Hamelin from a plague of rats by playing on his pipe and leading the vermin, which followed the music, into the river where they were drowned. When the townsmen refused to pay the money, the piper returned and, again playing on his magical pipe, led the way through the Bungen-Strasse out of the town, this time followed by 130 children. He led them to a hill called the Koppenberg, into which they all entered and disappeared. The event is recorded in inscriptions on the *Rathaus* (town hall) and elsewhere in the town, and was long regarded as historical. The legend has been told in verse by Robert Browning. He apparently founded it on Verstegan's account in his *Restitution of Decayed Intelligence* (1634). Brandenburg, Lorch, and other towns have a similar tradition, and there are Chinese and Persian legends much resembling it.

Pierce of Exton (pirs; eks′tǫn), **Sir.** See **Exton, Sir Pierce of.**

Pierce Penniless his Supplication to the Devil. A prose satire by Thomas Nash, published in 1592, and containing an attack on Gabriel and Richard Harvey for attacking Robert Greene's *Menaphon*, to which Nash had written a preface. This work is written in the form of a letter to the Devil, complaining about the evils of the time, and covering each of the Seven Deadly Sins. Nash goes into special detail on drunkenness and wrath, and inserts a defense of the theater in the section on sloth.

Piercie Shafton (pir′si shaf′tǫn), **Sir.** See **Shafton, Sir Piercie.**

Pieria (pī.ir′i.ạ), **Pierian Spring, Pierides** (pī.ir′i-dēz). Names relating to Pieria, a district in ancient Thessaly, the fabled home of the Muses (hence called Pierides); also, of or pertaining to the Muses: as, "A little learning is a dangerous thing; Drink deep, or taste not the Pierian spring" (Pope's *Essay on Criticism*, 216).

Piero (pye′rō). The villainous Doge of Venice and father of Mellida in John Marston's double play, *Antonio and Mellida* and *Antonio's Revenge.*

Pierre (pi.er′). A fiery, single-minded revolutionist in Thomas Otway's *Venice Preserved.* He is unable to understand why his friend Jaffeir should be upset when called upon to subordinate love to political honor.

Pierre Heath (hēth). See **Heath, Pierre.**

Pierrot (pē.ẹ.rō′; French, pye.rō). A traditional buffoon from old French pantomime. He dresses in loose white clothes with enormous white buttons, and his face is whitened; he is a gourmand and absolutely without moral sense. The 19th-century Pierrot was created by Gaspard Deburau under the Restoration; previous to this he had been a gayer and more insignificant personage, a cross between a fool and an *ingénu.*

Piers Gaveston (pirz gav′ẹs.tǫn). See **Gaveston, Piers.**

Piers Plowman (pirz′ plou′mạn). [Full title, **The Vision of William Concerning Piers Plowman.**] A Middle English allegorical and satirical poem, generally attributed to William Langland (c1332–c1400), though other authors may have been involved in the original composition of 2,579 lines, as first circulated in 1362, and even more probably in the elaboration of later texts, which by 1393 or thereabouts had grown to 7,353 lines. The number (50 or more) of manuscripts of the poem still preserved is evidence that it was widely circulated in that form before printing came to England, and beginning in 1550 several editions were printed; in the 19th and 20th centuries it has been several times reprinted, either in Middle English versions such as the exhaustive edition prepared by Walter William Skeat in 1886, or in modernized redactions, one of which was also the work of Skeat. The poem, in unrhymed but alliterative verse, relates how the poet in a vision beholds a tower (Truth, or Heaven), a dungeon (Error, or Hell), and a "fair field full of folk" (the world, or more specifically England). Many pilgrims are seeking the way to "Saint Truth," and Piers the plowman offers to guide them if they will help him plow his small farm, which some do, while others shirk. Many religious and moral concepts are allegorically brought into the action under such names as Reason, Conscience, Holy Church, Lady Meed (meaning reward, sometimes in the sense of bribery), Do-Wel, Do-Bet, Do-Best, and so forth. The central thought seems to be that the way to truth (and to heaven) lies in honest work and the observance of Christian precepts; the lesson is plain also that if the workers and poor folk are to find any betterment of their lot, they must achieve it by their own industry, good sense, and resolution, for it will not be conferred upon them by the lords, the rich, the exploiters, the lovers of luxury, the lawyers, the clerics who have grown indifferent and worldly, or the hordes of fraudulent parasites who take the livery of monastic and mendicant orders so that by preying on the people's superstitions they may live without working. In the later portions of the poem, Piers becomes in effect identified with Christ, seeking to guide men to God. The great and abiding interest and historical value of the poem lies in its

ḏ, d or j; ṣ, s or sh; ṯ, t or ch; ẓ, z or zh; o, F. cloche; ü, F. menu; ch, Sc. loch; ṅ, F. bonbon.

vivid, crowded, sharply characterized pictures of life in 14th-century England, when as feudalism began to break down, swarming evils and injustices evoked determination to bring about better times, in the spirit of the deeply pious Catholic Christian social ideals which the poet shared with the plain people of the land.

Piers Plowman's Crede. A Middle English satirical alliterative poem (c1394), after the style of *Piers Plowman.*

Pietro (pye′trō). The usurper of the throne of Genoa in John Marston's tragicomedy *The Malcontent.*

Pietro Comparini (kom.pä.rē′nē). See **Comparini, Pietro.**

Piety in Pattens, or the Handsome Housemaid. A puppet-show droll, produced by Samuel Foote in 1773, played by ingeniously contrived puppets.

Pigeon, The. A comedy (1912) by John Galsworthy. It makes the point that philanthropy and efforts toward the reform of society by well-meaning people cannot solve the problems of people like Ferrand, the vagabond turned philosopher, who are just naturally different from others and cannot fit into the standards of any society.

Pigott Diamond (pig′ọt), **The.** A famous diamond weighing 49 carats, brought to England by Earl Pigott.

Pigwiggen (pig.wig′ẹn). A fairy knight in Michael Drayton's *Nymphidia.* He has a combat with Oberon, who is jealous of him and his love for Queen Mab. The name is also given to a constable mentioned in *Selimus,* a tragedy, vaguely attributable to Robert Greene, published in 1594.

Pilgrim, The. A play by John Fletcher, produced at court in 1621 and printed in 1647. It is based upon a story by Lope de Vega, and was itself adapted in 1700 by Sir John Vanbrugh, with a prologue, epilogue, and masque by Dryden.

Pilgrim, The. A tragedy by Thomas Killigrew, printed in 1664.

Pilgrimage. A sequence of 12 novels by Dorothy M. Richardson, published in omnibus form in 1938. It consists of *Pointed Roofs* (1915), *Backwater* (1916), *Honeycomb* (1917), *The Tunnel* (1919), *Interim* (1919), *Deadlock* (1921), *Revolving Lights* (1923), *The Trap* (1925), *Oberland* (1927), *Dawn's Left Hand* (1931), *Clear Horizon* (1935), and *Dimple Hill* (1938). The work employs the stream-of-consciousness technique.

Pilgrimage of Grace. An insurrection in Yorkshire and Lincolnshire (1536–37), headed by Robert Aske. It was precipitated by the ecclesiastical and political reforms of Henry VIII, especially by the dissolution of the monasteries. The rebels occupied York, where they were joined by Edward Lee, the archbishop of York. Their number having increased to 30,000, they proceeded to Doncaster, where they were induced to disband by the representations of the royal commissioners. Finding themselves deceived, they rose again under Sir Francis Bigod. Martial law was declared in the north, and the rising was suppressed with great severity.

Pilgrim of Eternity, The. A biography of Byron (1925) by John Drinkwater.

Pilgrimage to Parnassus (pär.nas′us), **The.** See **Return from Parnassus, The.**

Pilgrims of the Rhine (rīn). A descriptive work by Edward Bulwer-Lytton, published in 1834.

Pilgrim's Progress. [Full title, **The Pilgrim's Progress From This World to That Which Is to Come.**] An allegory by John Bunyan, published in 1678. It is one of the most popular works in English literature and has been translated into more than a hundred languages. Bunyan's sincerity and his prolonged study of the Bible were undoubtedly largely responsible for the simplicity and discipline of the style, to which much of the power of the book is due. It emphasizes the inescapable responsibility of each individual soul and the futility of merely formal observances. It is also a call to those in danger of compliance with authority when persecution endangers their loyalty. It displays the moral earnestness of Puritanism at its best, without a bigoted exclusion of joy, and is remarkable for its sympathetic portrayal of a great variety of types of religious experience. An epic of man's dealings with man, as well as of the soul's search, through trials and tribulations, for individual salvation, it gave great impetus to contemporary and later religious movements in which simple and unlettered men and women could feel sure of their value in the sight of God. Bunyan wrote it while he was in prison, and he explains that it came to him in a dream. Christian reads that his home, the City of Destruction, will be razed by fire. He cannot persuade his wife and children to come with him, but he packs up and begins his long journey to the Celestial City. He is forced to wander through the Slough of Despond, the Interpreter's House, the Palace Beautiful, the Valley of Humiliation, the Valley of the Shadow of Death, Vanity Fair, Doubting Castle, the Delectable Mountains, and the country of Beulah before finally reaching the Celestial City. The episodes are made real as well as thrilling by the author's appreciation of nature and his vivid character portrayal. Christian meets in his travels Mr. Worldly Wiseman, Faithful, Giant Despair, Hopeful, Talkative, and Mrs. Diffidence. In the second part of the book Christiana, Christian's wife, makes the same journey, with the help of Greatheart, to rejoin her husband.

Pilgrim's Tale, The. A poem thought by William Thynne to have been Chaucer's. He printed it, but it was not published, being objected to by the bishops. It was lost, apparently; and, attention having been directed to it, it was searched for in vain for over 200 years. Thomas Tyrwhitt found part of it, examined it, and it disappeared again. At length it was rediscovered and printed by the Chaucer Society. It is now believed to be by someone acquainted with Chaucer's work, but writing after 1532.

Pillars of Hercules (hẽr′kụ.lēz). In ancient geography, the two opposite promontories Calpe (Gibraltar) in Europe and Abyla in Africa, situated at the E extremity of the Strait of Gibraltar, at the outlet from the Mediterranean into the Atlantic. According to one of several explanations of the name, they were supposed to have been torn asunder by Hercules.

---

fat, fāte, fär, ȧsk, fāre; net, mē, hẽr; pin, pīne; not, nōte, mŏve, nôr; up, lūte, pŭll; ᴛʜ, then;

Pilot, The. [Full title, **The Pilot; or, A Tale of the Sea.**] A melodrama (1825) by Edward Fitzball.

Pilpay (pil′pī). See **Kalilah and Dimnah.**

Pilumnus (pi.lum′nus). See **Picumnus.**

Pinafore (pin′a̱.fŏr). [Full title, **H.M.S. Pinafore, or The Lass that Loved a Sailor.**] An operetta in two acts by Sir Arthur Sullivan, with a libretto by W. S. Gilbert, first performed at the London Opéra Comique Theatre on May 25, 1878.

Pinch (pinch). In Shakespeare's *Comedy of Errors*, a schoolmaster who believes Antipholus and Dromio of Ephesus to be mad, and orders them to be confined.

Pinch, Ruth. In Dickens's *Martin Chuzzlewit*, a pretty little person, unreasonably grateful to the Pecksniffs for their patronage of her brother Tom Pinch.

Pinch, Tom. In Dickens's *Martin Chuzzlewit*, an ungainly, kindhearted man of sterling qualities, in the employment of Mr. Pecksniff.

Pinchbeck (pinch′bek), **Christopher.** b. c1670; d. 1732. A London watchmaker. He invented an alloy which resembled gold, once much used in cheap jewelry. The word "pinchbeck" hence came to be applied to sham or spurious things.

Pinchwife (pinch′wīf), **Mr.** In William Wycherley's comedy *The Country Wife*, the anxious husband of Mrs. Marjory Pinchwife, the "country wife." He tries without success to keep his wife in a state of ignorance.

Pindar (pin′da̱r). b. at Cynoscephalae, near Thebes, Greece, c522 B.C.; d. at Argos, 443 B.C. The greatest of the Greek lyric poets. He resided chiefly at Thebes, but spent about four years at the court of Hieron in Syracuse. Little is known of his life. His work includes 44 *Epinicia* (Victory Odes) to the winners of the Olympian, Pythian, Nemean, and Isthmian games. Many fragments are extant, including *Hymns* (to Persephone, to Fortune, and the like), *Paeans* (to Apollo of Delphi and Zeus of Dodona), *Choral dithyrambs* to Dionysus, *Processional songs, Choral songs for maidens, Choral dance-songs, Encomia* (laudatory odes), *Scolia* (festive songs to be sung at banquets by a *comus* or festive troop), and *Dirges* (to be sung to the flute, with choral dance). The earliest of the *Epinicia* apparently is the 10th Pythian Ode, 502 B.C.; the latest, the 5th Olympian, 452 B.C.

Pindar, Peter. Pseudonym of **Wolcot, John.**

Pindaric (pin.dar′ik). Of or pertaining to Pindar, one of the first of Greek lyric poets (about 522 to 443 B.C.), or resembling or characteristic of his style.

Almighty crowd! thou shortenest all dispute, . . .
Thou leap'st o'er all eternal truths in thy
Pindaric way! (Dryden, *The Medal*, l. 94.)

You will find, by the account which I have already given you, that my compositions in gardening are altogether after the Pindaric manner, and run into the beautiful wildness of nature, without affecting the nicer elegancies of art.
(Addison, *Spectator*, No. 477.)

It was a strange misconception that led people for centuries to use the word Pindaric and irregular

as synonymous terms; whereas the very essence of the odes of Pindar . . . is their regularity.
(*Encyc. Brit.*)

Pindarism (pin′da̱r.izm). Imitation of Pindar.

Pindarism prevailed about half a century, but at last died gradually away, and other imitations supply its place. (Johnson, *Cowley.*)

A sort of intoxication of style—a Pindarism, to use a word formed from the name of the poet on whom, above all other poets, the power of style seems to have exercised an inspiring and intoxicating effect. (M. Arnold, *Study of Celtic Literature.*)

Pindarus (pin′da̱.rus). In Shakespeare's *Julius Caesar*, a servant of Cassius. When Cassius thinks the battle is lost at Philippi, he makes Pindarus stab him.

Pinero (pi.nir′ō), Sir **Arthur Wing.** b. at London, May 24, 1855; d. there, Nov. 3, 1934. An English dramatist, actor, and essayist, noted chiefly for his dramas about social problems, on the pattern established by Henrik Ibsen. The only son of John Daniel Pinero (originally Pinheiro), a Portuguese Jew practicing law in London, he was educated at London schools and at the Birkbeck Institute (later College). He was on the stage (1874–81, 1885), acting in modern roles, and playing Claudius and other Shakespearian parts with Sir Henry Irving. He wrote the following noteworthy plays, among others: *The Magistrate* (1885), *The Schoolmistress* (1886), *Sweet Lavender* (1888), *The Profligate* (1889), *The Second Mrs. Tanqueray* (1893), *The Notorious Mrs. Ebbsmith* (1896), *Trelawney of the Wells* (1898), *The Gay Lord Quex* (1899), *Iris* (1903), *The Thunderbolt* (1908), perhaps his most interesting satire, and *Mid-Channel* (1909). As a critic of his craft, Pinero wrote *Browning as a Dramatist* (1912), *Robert Louis Stevenson as a Dramatist* (1914), and "The Theater in the 'Seventies" (1929, for *The Eighteen Seventies*, a volume edited by H. Granville-Barker). Pinero's reputation as a dramatist has suffered during the past few decades. His satire, highly esteemed by his Victorian contemporaries, is now recognized as being rather timid. He excelled in plot construction, but was unable to create realistic characters. Shaw called him "a humble and somewhat belated follower of the novelists of the middle of the nineteenth century," a judgment now generally accepted by critics.

Pinkerton (ping′kĕr.tọn), **John.** b. at Edinburgh, Feb. 17, 1758; d. at Paris, March 10, 1826. A Scottish historian, antiquary, and miscellaneous writer. He published *Two Dithyrambic Odes on Enthusiasm and Laughter* (1782), an *Essay on Medals* (1784), *Ancient Scottish Poems* (1786), *Dissertation on the Origin and Progress of the Scythians or Goths* (1787), *Enquiry into the History of Scotland* (1790), *Iconographica Scotica* (1797), and others.

Pinkertons, the Miss. In Thackeray's novel *Vanity Fair*, the principals or headmistresses of a school for young ladies at Chiswick Mall.

Pinto (pēn′tö), **Fernão Mendes.** b. near Coimbra, Portugal, c1509; d. near Lisbon, Portugal, July 8, 1583. Portuguese adventurer and traveler in the East (China and Japan). He wrote an account of his travels entitled *Peregrinacão* (1614), a work that was then considered by many to be made up of fabrications but has since been shown to be extremely accurate, considering the limitations of his times. It is now generally recognized as one of the great travel books of all time.

Piozzi (pi.oz′i), **Hester Lynch.** See **Thrale, Mrs.**

Pip (pip). The hero of Dickens's *Great Expectations.* His original full name (which is virtually never used) is Philip Pirrip.

Pipchin (pip′chin), **Mrs.** In Dickens's *Dombey and Son,* a disagreeable old woman, proprietress of an "infantine boarding-house of a very select description" at Brighton, where little Paul Dombey was sent for his health.

Pipe of Tobacco. A poem (1736) by Isaac Hawkins Browne, written in the style of Prior, consisting of a series of stanzas imitating various contemporary poets.

Piper (pī′pėr), **Tom.** One of the six traditional male characters who perform in the English morris dance.

Pipes (pīps), **Tom.** A boatswain who joins Peregrine Pickle on his travels in Tobias Smollett's novel *Peregrine Pickle.*

Pippa Passes (pip′a). A long poem by Robert Browning, published in 1841 as the first of the series *Bells and Pomegranates.* It tells how Pippa, a poor girl who works all year round in the silk mills, inadvertently alters the lives of four people as she walks through the town singing to herself on her one holiday, New Year's Day. The line "God's in his heaven/ All's right with the world" causes Sebald to repent his murder of his sweetheart's husband; the line "Give her but a least excuse to love me" allows Jules the painter to become reconciled with his new wife, Phene; "A king lived long ago" incites the patriot, Luigi, to action (from which he had been nearly dissuaded by his mother), and thus saves him from the police; and finally, the Bishop, on hearing her sing "Suddenly God took me away," repents his evil intentions toward Pippa herself.

Pirandello (pē.rän.del′lō), **Luigi.** b. at Girgenti, Sicily, June 28, 1867; d. at Rome, Dec. 10, 1936. An Italian dramatist and novelist. At the beginning of his literary career, he was chiefly supported by an allowance from his father; but marriage with a woman of his father's choice turned out unhappily; a professorship of Italian literature which he was constrained to accept, and which he held for 24 years (1897–1921), became irksome; and fame eluded him until 1921, when his drama *Sei Personaggi in cerca d'autore* (*Six Characters in Search of an Author*) won international acclaim and established him at once among the principal figures in modern Italian literature. His unique qualities, earlier perceived by a few discerning critics including James Joyce, were thereafter recognized in Italy and abroad. Earlier plays were successfully revived, and Pirandello formed his own theatrical troupe, which produced his works in Europe and America. His most successful later dramatic works were *Enrico IV* (*Henry IV,* 1922) and *Come tu mi vuoi* (*As You Desire Me,* 1930), the last-named being made into a successful motion picture featuring Greta Garbo. His success as a playwright also led to wider appreciation of his novels, the most popular of which are *L'Esclusa* (*The Outcast,* 1901), *Il Fu Mattia Pascal* (*The Late Mattia Pascal,* 1923), *I Vecchi e i giovani* (*The Old and the Young,* 1928), and *Uno, nessuno, centomila* (*One, None, and a Hundred Thousand,* 1933). Of his short stories, numbered by the hundreds, collections in English translation have been published under the titles *Horse in the Moon* (1932), *Better Think Twice about It* (1935), and *The Medals and Other Stories* (1939). In a great many of the short stories and some of the novels, the fantastic form of his plots proves a deterrent to the projection of his ideas, but in the most noted of his plays his philosophy shines through with intriguing clarity. It is not difficult to see how that philosophy, pessimistic and supercilious toward human hopes, aspirations, and capabilities, led to Pirandello being numbered among the intellectuals who embraced fascism. He was decorated by the Italian and the French governments, and in 1934 was awarded the Nobel prize for literature.

Piran Round (pir′an). An ancient open-air theater in Cornwall.

Pirate, The. A romance (1822) by Scott. The action takes place among the Shetland and Orkney Islands in the 17th century.

Pirates of Penzance (pen.zans′), **The.** A comic opera (1879) by W. S. Gilbert and Arthur Sullivan.

Pirithous (pī.rith′ọ.us). In Greek legend, one of the Lapithae; a son of Zeus and a friend of Theseus. The famous battle between the Lapithae and the Centaurs took place on the occasion of his wedding to Hippodamia. Later Pirithous accompanied Theseus to Hades in an attempt to abduct Persephone. Theseus alone escaped; Pirithous was bound to a rock.

Pirithous (pī.rith′ọ.us; in Shakespeare also pī′ri-thös). In *The Two Noble Kinsmen,* an Athenian general.

Pirrip (pir′ip), **Philip.** See under **Pip.**

Pisander (pī.san′dėr). The leader of the rebels in Philip Massinger's *The Bondman.*

Pisanio (pi.zä′ni.ō). In Shakespeare's *Cymbeline,* the servant of Posthumus who, when he receives his master's letter ordering him to kill Imogen, disguises her as a boy and bids her join the Roman army.

Pish-Tush (pish′tush). In Gilbert and Sullivan's *The Mikado,* a nobleman who eventually marries Peep-Bo.

Pisistratus (pī.sis′tra.tus). [Also **Peisistratus.**] b. c605 B.C.; d. 527 B.C. A tyrant of Athens (560, 554–527 B.C.), a friend of Solon. He was opposed in his attempts to control the city by the powerful clan of the Alcmaeonids and their aristocratic allies, who succeeded in having Pisistratus expelled from the city in 560 soon after he had seized power and again in 556. He returned in 554 and thenceforth retained and consolidated his power, leaving his sons Hippias and Hipparchus in control of the city after his death. Pisistratus oriented Athenian diplomacy towards Ionia in an effort to make the Aegean Sea the area of Athenian hegemony. In the latter years of his reign he commissioned a learned body to establish a definitive text of the Iliad and

---

fat, fāte, fär, àsk, fâre; net, mē, hėr; pin, pīne; not, nōte, mōve, nôr; up, lūte, pull; ᴛʜ, then;

the Odyssey; this version is the one from which all subsequent texts of Homer are derived.

Pistol (pis'tǫl). In Shakespeare's *Merry Wives of Windsor*, in *2 Henry IV*, and also in *Henry V*, a bully and swaggerer, a companion of Falstaff. He is the modification of the stock type of Italian comedy, the "Thraso." Shakespeare may have intended him as a satire upon the acting of Edward Alleyn, the well-known Elizabethan tragedian. His bombast also parodies Euphuism, a contemporary literary style.

Pistyl of Susan (pis'til; sö'zạn), **The.** A Middle English poem (14th century), a paraphrase of the story of Susannah and Daniel, told in alliterative verse and attributed by some scholars to Huchoun. The word "pistyl" in the title means "epistle."

Pitt (pit), **William.** [Title, 1st Earl of **Chatham**; called **the Elder Pitt** and the **"Great Commoner."**] b. at Westminster (now part of London), Nov. 15, 1708; d. at Hayes, Kent, England, May 11, 1778. An English statesman and orator. He studied at Trinity College, Oxford, and obtained a cornet's commission in the dragoons (but was dismissed when he published a satire against George II). From the famous pocket borough of Old Sarum, which his family owned, he entered Parliament, as a Whig, in 1735, and in 1746 became vice-treasurer of Ireland in Henry Pelham's administration. He was in the same year promoted to the office of paymaster-general, which he retained under the Duke of Newcastle. Disappointed in his hope of advancement, and also in disagreement with Newcastle over foreign policy, he attacked the government in 1755, and was deprived of office. With considerable reluctance, after Newcastle's resignation, George II asked Pitt to form a government in 1756; the result pleased no one: Pitt lacked knowledge of party politics, and was able neither to hold a working majority nor to revitalize the military effort against France (at this time Pitt was secretary of state under the nominal prime ministership of the Duke of Devonshire; actually Pitt was head of the government). He resigned in April, 1757, but returned in early summer to form a coalition with the Duke of Newcastle, who became premier, with Pitt as secretary of state; this combination was immediately successful: Newcastle held Parliament in line, and Pitt had a free hand in matters of foreign policy. He adopted vigorous measures in prosecution of the Seven Years' War, and the period which followed is one of the most brilliant in English history. Pitt resigned again in 1761, when he failed to receive the support of the rest of the ministry for a war with Spain. He became premier on the fall of Rockingham in 1766, was created Viscount Pitt and Earl of Chatham, but resigned in 1768, owing to ill health. He opposed the stubborn and foolish policy of George III toward the American colonists (to whom, however, he certainly never wished to grant independence; his last appearance in the House of Lords, on April 7, 1778, was in order to protest against the dismemberment of the British Empire by any acknowledgment of their independence).

Pitt, William. [Called **the Younger Pitt**.] b. at Hayes, near Bromley, Kent, England, May 28, 1759; d. at Putney (now part of London), Jan.

23, 1806. An English statesman; second son of William Pitt, 1st Earl of Chatham, and Lady Hester Grenville, daughter of Hester, Countess Temple. He is considered by many to have been the greatest of all English prime ministers. In 1773 he entered Pembroke Hall (now Pembroke College), Cambridge. In 1780 he was called to the bar at Lincoln's Inn and elected member of Parliament for Appleby. On Feb. 26, 1781, he attracted attention with his first speech, in favor of Edmund Burke's plan for various economies in government. In a speech on May 7, 1782, he attacked the existing electoral system and moved an investigation, being defeated by a narrow majority. In July, 1782, he became chancellor of the exchequer and leader of the House of Commons in Shelburne's ministry, which resigned March 31, 1783. On the downfall of "the coalition" of North and Fox, Pitt became prime minister, first lord of the treasury, and chancellor of the exchequer (December, 1783). He faced considerable hostility in Parliament, but had the king and a vast portion of the English electorate behind him; he therefore refused to resign, despite his defeat in early 1784 on measure after measure, and won a clean majority in the election of March, 1784. He thereafter held office until 1801, one of the longest ministries in English history. During this period he was able to introduce major reforms in financing the public debt, in customs duties, and in the administration of India (which he took out of the hands of the East India Company). In the pressing problem of Parliamentary reform, however, he was able to do nothing; and presently he was faced with the urgent question of a British policy toward France. The French Revolution in 1789 was at first regarded with favor in England, and as late as the spring of 1792 Pitt hoped for peace. When finally dragged into the struggle (1792–93), his activity was political rather than military. His policy was frustrated by Napoleon on the Continent, but at home it met with no opposition; by 1799 the largest possible minority in Parliament was 25. At this time, and subsequently, he was the chief architect of great coalitions against Napoleon. His internal administration was extremely severe. Jacobinism was suppressed, and the Habeas Corpus Act repeatedly suspended. His policy in Ireland was based on corruption of the most flagrant sort, but it achieved the immediately useful end of the union of 1800 (which had the effect of quieting for a short time the spirit of revolt that had produced the rising of 1798); however, his attempt to achieve Roman Catholic emancipation was opposed by the king, and he resigned on March 14, 1801. The Addington ministry, which succeeded, was made up of Pitt's supporters. It fell after the failure of the treaty of Amiens, and Pitt's second administration began May 10, 1804. Napoleon's attempted invasion of England failed through the vigilance of Nelson, but the coalition of England, Russia, and Austria, with which Pitt opposed him on the Continent, was wrecked at Ulm and Austerlitz in 1805. Pitt, completely prostrated by these disasters, retired to his villa at Putney (now part of London) on Jan. 11, 1806, and there he died less than two weeks later.

Pittacus (pit'ạ.kus). b. in Lesbos, c650 B.C.; d. c569 B.C. A Greek politician and poet, one of the

ḑ, d or j; ṣ, s or sh; ţ, t or ch; ẓ, z or zh; o, F. cloche; ü, F. menu; ċh, Sc. loch; ṅ, F. bonbon.

Seven Wise Men of ancient Greece. He was chiefly responsible for the overthrow (c611) of the reigning tyrant of Mytilene, and himself became tyrant in 589. His ten-year rule (which ended with voluntary resignation) securely established democratic government in the city.

Pitt Crawley (pit′ krô′li), **Sir** and **Mr.** See under Crawley.

Pitt Diamond, The. A famous diamond of 137 carats, sold by Thomas Pitt (1717) to the Regent of Orléans for about $675,000.

Pitti-Sing (pit′i.sing′). In Gilbert and Sullivan's *The Mikado*, a young schoolgirl. She is one of the three wards of Ko-Ko (Yum-Yum and Peep-Bo are the other two). She eventually marries Pooh-Bah.

Pizarro (pi.zär′ō). An English play, translated from Kotzebue's *Die Spanier in Peru* (1790). It is generally listed with the works of Richard Brinsley Sheridan (who produced it at London in 1799, but certainly did not translate it).

placebo (plā̇.sē′bō). A Latin word meaning "I shall please," occurring in Ps. cxvi 9 ("Placebo Domino in regione vivorum") and used to signify the vesper service for the dead in the church, because in the older services this line was the opening of the first antiphon. It came to mean a flatterer and sycophant, that is, one who came to the services for his own gain. In Chaucer's *Merchant's Tale*, a flattering and obsequious man, brother of January, is given the name.

plagiarism (plā′ji.ȧ.rizm). **1.** The purloining or wrongful appropriation of another's ideas, writings, artistic designs, etc., and giving these forth as one's own; specifically, the offense of taking passages from another's compositions, and publishing them, either word for word or in substance, as one's own; literary theft.

Sir J. Reynolds has been accused of plagiarism for having borrowed attitudes from ancient masters. Not only candour but criticism must deny the force of the charge.   (Walpole, *Anecdotes of Painting*.)

2. A passage or thought thus stolen.

Plagiary (plā′ji.ȧ.ri), **Sir Fretful.** A character in *The Critic*, by Richard Brinsley Sheridan. It is a satirical portrait of Cumberland, said to have been written in revenge for the latter's behavior at the first night of *The School for Scandal*.

Plague Year, A Journal of the. See **Journal of the Plague Year, A.**

Plain, the. In the French legislature at the time of the French Revolution, the floor of the house, occupied by the more moderate party; hence, that party itself, as distinguished from the Mountain, or radical party.

Plain Dealer, The. A comedy by Wycherley, produced in 1674 and printed in 1677. It is modeled in general plot upon Molière's *Le Misanthrope*.

plaint. A lamentation; complaint; audible expression of sorrow; a sad or serious song.

Greet was the pite for to here hem pleyne,
Thurgh whiche pleyntes gan her wo encrease.
            (Chaucer, *Man of Law's Tale*.)
Thy accent will excell
In Tragick plaints and passionate mischance.
            (Spenser, *Colin Clout*.)

Nor Tears can move,
Nor Plaints revoke the Will of Jove.
            (Prior, *Turtle and Sparrow*.)

Plain Tales from the Hills. A collection of 40 short stories (Calcutta, 1888; 3rd edition, London, 1890) by Rudyard Kipling. It was this work which won Kipling his first general recognition outside of India. In it he introduced various characters who were to occur again in later works, and whose names were soon to be known throughout the English-speaking world (perhaps most notably Terence Mulvaney, Ortheris, and Learoyd).

Planché (plän.shā′), **James Robinson.** b. at London, Feb. 27, 1796; d. May 30, 1880. An English dramatist and writer on heraldry and costume. He wrote, translated, or adapted more than 150 burlesques, extravaganzas, pantomimes, and interludes.

Plantagenet (plan.taj′e.net), **Edith.** King Richard's accomplished kinswoman in Sir Walter Scott's *The Talisman*.

Plantagenet, George. See under **Clarence, George, Duke of.**

Plantagenet, Lady Margaret. In Shakespeare's *Richard III*, a young daughter of Clarence who mourns his death.

Plantagenet, Richard. See under **York, (3rd) Duke of.**

Plantagenet Palliser (pal′i.sėr). See **Palliser, Plantagenet.**

Plasher's Mead. American title of **Guy and Pauline.**

Plato (plā′tō). [Original name, **Aristocles.**] b. 428 or 427 B.C.; d. at Athens, 348 or 347 B.C. A Greek philosopher, associate of Socrates ("my elderly friend") until the latter's death, and founder of the Academic School, of which Theaetetus, Eudoxus, and Aristotle were members.

Platonick Lovers, The. A tragicomedy by Sir William D'Avenant, printed in 1635.

Platonism (plā′tō.nizm). **1.** The doctrines, opinions, or philosophy of Plato, or of the Academic school.
2. A Platonic saying or proposition.

The striking Platonisms of Coleridge.
            (R. Choate, *Addresses*.)

"Platonist," the. See **Taylor, Thomas.**

Plausible (plô′zi.bl), **Lord.** In Wycherley's comedy *The Plain Dealer*, an insinuating fop, in love with Olivia.

Plautus (plô′tus). [Full name, **Titus Maccius Plautus.**] b. at Sarsina, Umbria, Italy, c254 B.C.; d. 184 B.C. A Roman comic dramatist. Although he was unquestionably the most famous and most popular of ancient Roman writers of comedy, the details of his life are virtually unknown. It seems reasonably certain that he was intimately connected with the stage from a comparatively early age, if only because of the remarkable knowledge of stage technique manifested in his plays (indeed, his works remain today among the most widely read and enjoyed of the Latin classics). He drew much from Menander and the other dramatists of the Greek New Comedy (including stock characters, such as the clever, unscrupulous slave, and stock situations, involving mistaken identity and carefully contrived misunderstandings between two lovers), but he wrote in the popular idiom of his day. As a result his plays do not merely ape those of the Greeks, but are vigorous, often coarse, always amusing examples of practical stagecraft. His works were read and often adapted by such later writers as Molière, Jonson, and Shakespeare. Of his comedies, 21 (nearly all complete) are extant. Among them are *Amphitruo, Captivi, Aulularia, Trinummus, Rudens, Miles Gloriosus, Mostellaria, Pseudolus,* and *Menaechmi.*

Playboy of the Western World, The. A one-act play (1907) by John Millington Synge. It is the story of Christy Mahon, a farmer's son, who believes that he has killed his father, Old Mahon. He is regarded as a hero by the girls until the father appears, with nothing more serious than a wound in his head, and gives Christy a good licking. Among the other characters in the play are Margaret Flaherty ("Pegeen Mike") and her father, Michael James Flaherty. When first produced at the Abbey Theatre at Dublin, the play led to actual riots (some of the spectators objected to it on the ground that it represented the Irish as glorifying a patricide).

Player Queen, The. A play (1922) by William Butler Yeats.

Players. In Shakespeare's *Hamlet,* the company that comes to play at the Court. They travel because they could not find city employment. The "late innovation" is a Shakespearian reference to contemporary conditions in the London theatrical world, either to the child companies whose popularity had temporarily surpassed that of the adult companies or to the banning of plays in London because of Essex's recent rebellion (1601). They perform the "Murder of Gonzago," in which Hamlet has inserted a few pertinent speeches. Hamlet's advice to the actors (III.iii) is of documentary interest in illustrating the stylized acting of the Elizabethan stage.

Players. In the Induction to Shakespeare's *Taming of the Shrew,* the company represented as about to enact the play itself, for the entertainment of Christopher Sly.

Play of Love, The. An interlude by John Heywood, written in the early 16th century.

Plays for Puritans, Three. See **Three Plays for Puritans.**

Plays, Pleasant and Unpleasant. A collection of plays by George Bernard Shaw, published in 1898, including *The Philanderer, Mrs. Warren's Profession, Arms and the Man, Candida, The Man of Destiny, You Never Can Tell,* and *Widowers' Houses.*

Pleasant Riderhood (plez'ạnt rī'dèr.hụd). See **Riderhood, Pleasant.**

Pleasures of Hope. A poem by Thomas Campbell, published in 1799.

Pleasures of Memory. A poem by Samuel Rogers, published in 1792. The poem is a poetic interpretation of the theory of the association of ideas, based on Hartley's *Essays on the Nature and Principles of Taste* (1790).

Pleasures of the Imagination. A didactic poem in three books by Mark Akenside, published in 1744, later rewritten and published again in 1757. The poem, which aims to "pierce Philosophy's retreats," divides the pleasures of the imagination into the primary pleasures of the sublime and beautiful and the secondary pleasures of the senses, and concludes with a discussion of the various aspects of folly and evil.

Pleiad (plē'ad) or **Pléiade** (plā.yàd). A name given in literature to several groups of seven poets living at the same time, notably to such a group at Alexandria in the time of Ptolemy Philadelphus. These were Lycophron, Theocritus, Aratus, Nicander, Homer, Apollonius of Rhodes, and Callimachus. The name has been applied to other similar groups, especially in the 16th century to that formed by Ronsard with Joachim du Bellay, Antoine de Baïf, Jodelle, Pontus de Thyard, Dorat, and Rémi Belleau. These united in a close league to impose a classical form on French language and literature. They had many followers.

Pleiades (plē'ạ.dēz, plī'-). [Also, **Pleiads** (plē'adz, plī'-).] A cluster of third-magnitude and fainter stars in the constellation Taurus, conspicuous on winter evenings 24 degrees N of the celestial equator, and coming to the meridian at midnight in the middle of November. There were anciently said to be seven Pleiades, although only six were conspicuous to the naked eye, then as now; hence the suggestion of a lost Pleiade. In Greek mythology they were the daughters of Atlas and the nymph Pleione, and were changed into stars either after their death or during their flight from Orion. Literally, Pleiades means "The Weepers"; they are also called the Seven Sisters, and were named Alcyone, Merope, Celaeno, Electra (the usual "missing Pleiade," said to have left her place in order not to see the fall of Troy), Sterope or Asterope, Taygeta, and Maia. These names, with those of the parents, have been applied by astronomers since Ricciolo (1665) to the group (which actually contains several hundred stars, and is upwards of 325 light years distant from the earth).

pleonasm (plē'ọ.nazm). **1.** Redundancy of language; the use of more words than are necessary to express an idea. Pleonasm may be justifiable when the intention is to present thoughts with particular perspicuity or force.

> The first surplusage the Greekes call Pleonasmus (I call him too full speech), and is no great fault: as if one should say, I heard it with mine eares, and saw it with mine eyes, as if a man could heare with his heeles, or see with his nose.
> (Puttenham, *Arte of English Poesie.*)

2. A redundant phrase or expression; an instance of redundancy of language.

> Harsh compositions, pleonasms of words, tautological repetitions.
> (Burton, *Anatomy of Melancholy.*)

Pleydell (plā'del), **Paulus.** In Sir Walter Scott's novel *Guy Mannering,* an Edinburgh lawyer notable for his wit and his distinguished appearance. He is a friend of Mannering.

ḍ, d or j; ṣ, s or sh; ṭ, t or ch; ẓ, z or zh; o, F. cloche; ü, F. menu: ċh. Sc. loch; ṅ, F. bonbon.

Pliable (plī′a.bl). A neighbor of Christian in John Bunyan's *Pilgrim's Progress*. He deserts Christian at the first difficulty.

Pliant (plī′ant), **Dame.** A handsome foolish widow in Ben Jonson's comedy *The Alchemist*. She is finally married to Lovewit.

Pliant, Sir Paul and **Lady.** [Also, **Plyant**.] Characters in Congreve's comedy *The Double Dealer*. Lady Pliant is noted for her easy virtue and awkwardly assumed prudery, and her insolence to her uxorious old husband.

Pliny (plin′i). [Called **Pliny the Elder**; full Latin name, **Gaius Plinius Secundus**.] b. at Novum Comum (now Como), Italy, 23 A.D.; perished in the eruption of Vesuvius, 79 A.D. A Roman naturalist. He went to Rome in his early youth, served in Africa, and was, at the age of 23, commander of a troop of cavalry in Germany. He returned to Rome and studied law, was procurator in Spain under Nero (c70–72), and was charged with other official duties in various parts of the empire. His literary work, which was conducted with extraordinary industry in the intervals of his official labors (scarcely a waking moment of day or night being left unoccupied), extended into the departments of tactics, history, grammar, rhetoric, and natural science. Of his writings, only his *Natural History* (*Historia naturalis*) is extant; it is a scientific encyclopedia, very elaborate and of great value. His death, an account of which is preserved in a letter of the younger Pliny, was the result of his efforts to observe more closely the eruption of Vesuvius and to aid those who were in danger.

Pliny (plin′i). [Called **Pliny the Younger**; full Latin name, **Gaius Plinius Caecilius Secundus**.] b. at Novum Comum (now Como), Italy, 62 A.D.; d. 113. A Roman author; nephew of the elder Pliny. He was a consul in 100, and later (111 or 112) governor of Bithynia and Pontica. He was a friend of Trajan and Tacitus. His *Epistles* and a eulogy of Trajan have been preserved. The most celebrated of his letters is one to Trajan concerning the treatment of the Christians in his province.

Plomer (plö′mẽr), **William (Charles Franklin)**. b. in the northern Transvaal, Africa, Dec. 10, 1903—. A British novelist. Educated at Rugby, he was a farmer in the Stormberg Mountains in South Africa, resided at Johannesburg, and was a trader in Zululand. Author of the novels *Turbott Wolfe* (1926), *Sado* (1931; American title, *They Never Come Back*, 1932), *The Case Is Altered* (1932), *The Invaders* (1934), *Double Lives* (1943), and *D'Arfey's Curious Relations* (1945). His collections of short stories include *I Speak of Africa* (1928), *Paper Houses* (1929), *The Child of Queen Victoria* (1933), and *Visiting the Caves* (1936). He is the author of a biography, *Cecil Rhodes* (1933).

Plornish (plôr′nish), **Mrs.** A plasterer's wife in Dickens's *Little Dorrit*: "a young woman, made somewhat slatternly in herself and her belongings by poverty."

Plornish, Thomas. A plasterer in Dickens's *Little Dorrit*.

plot. 1. The story of a play, poem, novel, or romance, comprising a complication of incidents which are at last unfolded by unexpected means; the intrigue.

If the plot or intrigue must be natural, and such as springs from the very subject, as has been already urged, then the winding-up of the plot, by a more sure claim, must have this qualification, and be a probable consequence of all that went before.

(Le Bossu, tr. in Preface to Pope's *Odyssey*.)
2. Contrivance; deep reach of thought; ability to plan.

> Who says he was not
> A man of much plot
> May repent that false accusation.
> (Sir J. Denham, *Return of Mr. Killegrew*.)

Plot, The. A historical novel by Henry Christopher Bailey, published in 1922. The title refers to the Popish Plot (1678) of Titus Oates, one of the characters, who appears with Charles II, Shaftesbury, Buckingham, Duke of Monmouth, and the Duke of York.

Plotinus (plọ.tī′nus). b. at Lycopolis, Egypt, c204 A.D.; d. in Italy, c270. A Greek philosopher, remembered for the formulation of the basic principles of Neoplatonism. He studied at Alexandria under Ammonius Saccas, and afterward taught philosophy at Rome. His works (called *Enneads*) were edited by Creuzer in 1835. "The relation in which Plotinus stood to his predecessors among the Greek philosophers is very easily stated. He had made himself acquainted with every system, and culled from them all whatever seemed to support his solution of the great problems of thought and existence. Plato is the chief authority and the starting-point in his speculations. But he takes full cognizance of Aristotle, whose system of categories he directly opposes; and he endeavours in all essential points to identify the doctrines of the Old Academy and the Lyceum. To effect this, he is obliged to have recourse to an overstrained latitude of interpretation, sometimes making his own inferences from opinions half expressed, and not unfrequently quoting from memory. Although he is strongly at variance with the Stoics on the grounds of knowledge, treating with great contempt their doctrine of intellectual conception, he borrows a good deal from Chrysippus wherever he can find an agreement even in expression. The older writers also furnished him with suggestive materials. He was acquainted with Anaxagoras, Democritus, Empedocles, Parmenides, and the most ancient Pythagoreans. And he refers directly to the later Peripatetics Aristoxenus and Dicaearchus. He cannot, then, be termed strictly or exclusively a Neo-Platonist."

Plough and the Stars, The. A play (1926) by Sean O'Casey. It is set against a background of the Easter Rebellion of 1916, and takes up in detail its effect on various poor people in Dublin: Nora, who anxiously warns her husband against fighting, loses her expected child as the result of her fear, and goes mad; Covey, who sees that the mere fact of revolution against the English, even if the rising is successful, will not end the slums; Fluther Good and Peter, two "patriots" who spend their energy drinking; a neglected child who dies; and an old shrew who, despite her love of the English, tenderly nurses Nora.

Plougher, The. A poem by Padraic Colum, included in *Wild Earth*, a volume of verse published first in 1909 and revised for American publication in 1916. It is a contrast study of the farmer at his plow and the horse that pulls it, as they pause in the field at sunset.

Plowman's Tale, The. A poem once attributed to Chaucer, appearing in Thynne's 1542 edition (but not in that of 1532). It was apparently written by the author of *Piers Plowman's Crede*, and inserted as a supplementary Canterbury tale. It is frequently confused with both *Piers Plowman's Crede* and *Piers Plowman*. Cast in the form of a conversation between a griffon and a pelican, it is a Lollard denunciation of clerical corruption.

Pluche (plüsh), **Charles Jeames de la.** One of the many pseudonyms of **Thackeray, William Makepeace.**

Pluck (pluk). In Dickens's novel *Nicholas Nickleby*, a servile creature in the service (with his fellow toady Pyke) of Sir Mulberry Hawk.

Plumdamas (plum'da.mas), **Peter.** In Sir Walter Scott's novel *The Heart of Midlothian*, an Edinburgh grocer much given to gossip with and about his neighbors and customers.

Plume (plöm), **Captain.** The "recruiting officer," the principal character in Farquhar's comedy of that name. He is a gay and gallant soldier, irresistible to women, for whom he cares less than for his profession. It was a favorite part with Garrick and Macready.

Plummer (plum'ẽr), **Bertha.** In Dickens's *Cricket on the Hearth*, the blind daughter of Caleb Plummer.

Plummer, Caleb. In Dickens's *Cricket on the Hearth*, a poor and careworn old toymaker. His spirit is crushed with hopeless depression, but he conceals his hardships from his blind daughter Bertha with a pathetic attempt at cheerfulness, and describes his daily life to her as prosperous and happy.

Plunkett (plung'kẹt), **Joseph.** b. in Ireland, 1887; d. at Dublin, 1916. An Irish poet and patriot, active in the Easter Rebellion of 1916 (for which he was executed by the British). He was the author of brief lyric poems, including *Poppies* and *I See His Blood Upon the Rose.*

Plurabelle (plö'ra.bel), **Anna Livia.** See **Anna Livia Plurabelle.**

Plutarch (plö'tärk). b. at Chaeronea, Boeotia, Greece, c16 A.D. A Greek historian, celebrated as the author of 46 "Parallel Lives" (*Plutarch's Lives*) of Greeks and Romans. He also wrote various philosophical, ethical, and other works, grouped as *Opera moralia*. He was a Platonist, but occupied himself chiefly with ethical and religious reflections. "In spite of all exceptions on the score of inaccuracy, want of information, or prejudice, Plutarch's lives must remain one of the most valuable relics of Greek literature, not only because they stand in the place of many volumes of lost history, but also because they are written with a graphic and dramatic vivacity, such as we find in few biographies, ancient or modern."

Plutarch's Lives. A collection of 46 biographies of famous Greeks and Romans by Plutarch.

Pluto (plö'tō). In Greek mythology, a cult name of Hades, god of the infernal regions. The word means "rich one" or "wealth-giver," and thus he is associated with Plutus. Pluto is commonly the name used for him in the Persephone abduction myth. The Romans called him Dis.

Plutus (plö'tus). In Greek mythology, a personification of wealth; a son of Iasion and Demeter, and intimately associated with Irene, goddess of peace, who is often represented in art holding the infant Plutus. Zeus is said to have blinded him in order that he might not bestow his favors exclusively on good men, but should distribute his gifts without regard to merit (however, by some accounts he was later cured and gave wealth only to those who he could see were honest).

Plyant (plī'ant). See **Pliant, Sir Paul** and **Lady.**

Plymouth Brethren (plim'uth). [Also: **Darbyites, Plymouthites** (plim'uth.īts).] A sect of Christians which attracted (1830) notice at Plymouth, England, and later extended over Great Britain, the U. S., and among the Protestants of France, Switzerland, Italy, and elsewhere in Europe.

Pocahontas (pō.ka.hon'tas). b. c1595; d. at Gravesend, England, in March, 1617. An American Indian princess, noted for her alleged rescue of Captain John Smith. Her real name was Matoaka, the Indian term *pocahontas* (playful one) having been used for several of the daughters of Powhatan, leader of the Powhatan confederacy in Virginia. She was supposedly a child of ten years of age when the English first came (1607) to Virginia. According to the narrative of Captain John Smith, she saved his life after his capture (1608) by Powhatan. The veracity of the story is still a subject for dispute among historians. Seized as a prisoner by the English in 1613, she was instructed in the Christian faith and took the name of Rebecca. An English gentleman, John Rolfe, was so smitten with her that he secured permission to marry her from Governor Dale, to whom the connection appeared useful as a means of keeping the good will of the Virginia Indians. The marriage took place in April, 1614, at Jamestown and resulted in an eight-year peace between the English and the Indians. Going to England in 1616, Pocahontas was received as a princess and was presented to the king and queen. She died while making preparations to return to Virginia.

Pocket (pok'ẹt), **Herbert.** In Dickens's *Great Expectations*, a warm-hearted young man who becomes a close friend of Pip. His life is filled with schemes for making a great and quick success, and in the end his dreams are actually realized (with the secret help of Pip) when he becomes a partner in the firm of Clarriker and Company. He marries Clara Barley.

Podmore (pod'mōr), **Frank.** b. Feb. 5, 1856; d. Aug. 15, 1910. An English author. He was educated at Pembroke College, Oxford. He was especially interested in spiritualism and psychical phenomena, and was an active member of the Society for Psychical Research. Among his published works are *Apparitions and Thought-Transference* (1894), *Studies in Psychical Research* (1897), *Modern Spiritualism* (1902), *Robert Owen* (1906), and *The Newer Spiritualism* (1911).

d, d or j; ₷, s or sh; ţ, t or ch; ₴, z or zh; o, F. cloche; ü, F. menu; ch, Sc. loch; ṅ, F. bonbon.

Podsnap (pŏd′snap), **Mr.** In Dickens's *Our Mutual Friend*, a smiling, eminently respectable man, who always knows exactly what Providence means: "And it was very remarkable (and must have been very comfortable) that what Providence meant was invariably what Mr. Podsnap meant. These may be said to have been the articles of faith of a school which the present chapter takes the liberty of calling, after its representative name, Podsnappery."

poem. 1. A written composition in metrical form; a composition characterized by its arrangement in verses or measures, whether in blank verse or in rhyme.

> The first and most necessarie poynt that euer I founde meete to be considered in making of a delectable poeme is this, to grounde it upon some fine inuention. (Gascoigne, *Notes on English Verse*.)

> A poem is not alone any work or composition of the poets in many or few verses; but even one alone verse sometimes makes a perfect poem.
> (Ben Jonson, *Discoveries*.)

> A poem, round and perfect as a star.
> (Alexander Smith, *A Life Drama*.)

2. A written composition which, though not in verse, is characterized by imaginative and poetic beauty in either the thought or the language.

Poema Morale (pō̄.ē′mạ mō̄.rā′lē). A Middle English poem of the early 13th century, concerning the transience of worldly pleasures, cast in 14-syllable rhymed couplets.

Poems and Translations. A volume of verse by J. M. Synge, published posthumously (1910). It contains a collection of his poems (among them "In Kerry" and "On an Island"), translations of Villon and Petrarch, and a section devoted to his theory of poetry.

Poems of Pinchbeck Lyre (pinch′bek līr′). A volume of verse (1931) by Siegfried Sassoon, published anonymously, and parodying the poetry of Humbert Wolfe.

Poems of West and East. A volume by V. Sackville-West, published in 1917.

Poetaster, The. [Full title, **The Poetaster, or His Arraignment.**] A satiric comedy (acted 1601 and printed in quarto in 1602) by Ben Jonson. It was written by Jonson in answer to John Marston's *What You Will* (1600), in which Jonson had been satirized in the character of Lampatho Doria. It is set in Rome, where the poets Horace, Crispinus, Demetrius (representing Jonson, Marston, and Dekker), and Ovid present their works for the delight of the emperor's daughter, Julia, and the Court. Vergil enters in the last act, presumably to represent the standard of poetical excellence. In his presence the two poets, Crispinus and Demetrius, are punished for their plays (the first being made to vomit his "fustian terms" and the second made to wear a cap for being a slanderer). It was in reply to this that Dekker produced his *Satiromastix, or the Untrussing of the Humorous Poet*. In 1603 and 1604, however, Jonson collaborated with both Dekker and Marston.

Poetical Rapsody, A. An anthology (1602) of Elizabethan poetry, edited by Francis Davison and reissued in 1608, 1611, and 1621. It includes 40 "sonnets, odes, elegies, and madrigals" by Davison, 18 pieces by his brother Walter, and about 50 poems by Sidney, Raleigh, Campbell, and other Elizabethan poets.

poetic justice. An ideal distribution of rewards and punishments such as is common in poetry and works of fiction, but seldom exists in real life.

poetic license. A privilege or liberty taken by a poet in using words, phrases, or matters of fact in order to produce a desired effect.

poetics. That branch of criticism which treats of the nature and laws of poetry.

poet laureate. Formerly, a poet who had been publicly crowned with laurel by a sovereign or some other eminent person in recognition of his merits; also, a student in a university who had been so crowned on receiving an honorable degree in grammar, including poetry and rhetoric; now, in Great Britain, a salaried officer of the royal household, of whom no special duty is required, but who formerly was expected to furnish an ode annually for the sovereign's birthday, and to celebrate in verse great national events. The office of poet laureate seems to have existed with interruptions from the time of Edward III or IV, but was first made permanent in 1630.

"Poet of Despair." See **Thomson, James** (1834–82).

Poets' Corner. A space in the E side of the S transept of Westminster Abbey, containing the tablets, statues, busts, or monuments of Shakespeare, Ben Jonson, Chaucer, Milton, Spenser, and other British poets, actors, divines, and great men. Some of them are buried near or under their monuments.

poetry. 1. That one of the fine arts which addresses itself to the feelings and the imagination by the instrumentality of musical and moving words; the art which has for its object the exciting of intellectual pleasure by means of vivid, imaginative, passionate, and inspiriting language, usually though not necessarily arranged in the form of measured verse or numbers.

> By poetry we mean the art of employing words in such a manner as to produce an illusion on the imagination, the art of doing by means of words what the painter does by means of colours.
> (Macaulay, *Milton*.)

> Poetry is itself a thing of God;
> He made his prophets poets; and the more
> We feel of poesie do we become
> Like God in love and power—under-makers.
> (Bailey, *Festus*, Proem.)

> The grand power of Poetry is its interpretative power, by which I mean . . . the power of so dealing with things as to awaken in us a wonderfully full, new, and intimate sense of them, and of our relations with them.
> (M. Arnold, *Maurice de Guérin*.)

> We shall hardly make our definition of poetry, considered as an imitative art, too extended if we say that it is a speaking art of which the business is to represent by means of verbal signs arranged with musical regularity everything for which verbal signs have been invented. (*Encyc. Brit.*)

2. An imaginative, artistic, and metrical collocation of words so marshaled and attuned as to excite or control the imagination and the emotions; the language of the imagination or emotions metrically expressed. In a wide sense poetry comprises whatever embodies the products of the imagination and fancy, and appeals to these powers in others, as well as to the finer emotions, the sense of ideal beauty, and the like. In this sense we speak of the *poetry* of motion.

The essence of poetry is invention: such invention as, by producing something unexpected, surprises and delights.
(Johnson, *Waller*.)

Poetry is not the proper antithesis to prose, but to science. Poetry is opposed to science, and prose to metre. . . . The proper and immediate object of science is the acquirement or communication of truth; the proper immediate object of poetry is the communication of immediate pleasure.
(Coleridge.)

No literary expression can, properly speaking, be called poetry that is not in a certain deep sense emotional whatever may be its subject matter, concrete in its method and its diction, rhythmical in movement, and artistic in form. (*Encyc. Brit.*)

3. Composition in verse; a metrical composition; verse; poems: as, heroic *poetry;* lyric or dramatic *poetry;* a collection of *poetry.*

Oon seyde that Omere made lyes
Feyninge in his poetries.
(Chaucer, *House of Fame*, l. 1477.)

And this young birkie here, . . . will his . . .
poetries help him here?   (Scott, *Rob Roy*.)

Poggio (pod'jō). A character in George Chapman's *The Gentleman Usher* who habitually misuses words, thus winning the title "Cousin Hysteron Proteron." He carries the report of Vincentio's supposed murder to Margaret.

Pogram (pō'grạm), **Elijah.** In Dickens's *Martin Chuzzlewit*, an American, a public benefactor and a member of Congress. Most readers, on both sides of the Atlantic, now find the character an amusing one, but at the time (1843) of the original publication of *Martin Chuzzlewit*, Pogram (and most of the other American characters in the book) were resented by many readers in the U. S.

Poins (poinz, poins). In Shakespeare's *1 and 2 Henry IV*, a dissolute, witty companion of Prince Henry and Falstaff.

Point Counter Point. A novel by Aldous Huxley, published in 1928.

Pointed Roofs. A novel by Dorothy M. Richardson, published in 1915. It is the first section of *Pilgrimage* (1938), a novel sequence in 12 parts employing the stream-of-consciousness technique.

Poiré (pwȧ.rā), **Emmanuel.** See **Caran d'Ache.**

Poirot (pwȧ.rō), **Hercule.** The detective in the works of Agatha Christie.

Polack (pō'lak). A Pole; used in Shakespeare's *Hamlet* (I.i, and elsewhere).

Pole (pōl, pöl), **William de la.** See under **Suffolk,** (4th) **Earl of.**

Polexandre (po.leg.zäṅdr). Romance by Marin Le Roy Gomberville. It was published in 1632, and enjoyed a high reputation. It was the earliest of the heroic romances, and seems to have been imitated by Gautier de Costes de la Calprenède and Georges de Scudéry.

Policraticus (pol.i.krat'i.kus). An extensive treatise by John of Salisbury, finished in 1159, on the principles and practices which ought to govern the behavior of the individual and of the government under which he lives.

Polish (pol'ish), **Mrs.** The vulgar, talkative confidante of Lady Loadstone in Ben Jonson's comedy *The Magnetic Lady.*

Politick Would-be (pol'i.tik wủd'bē), **Sir.** See **Would-be, Sir Politick.**

Polixenes (po.lik'sẹ.nēz). In Shakespeare's *Winter's Tale*, the King of Bohemia, father of Florizel.

Pollard (pol'ạrd), **Alfred William.** b. 1859; d. March 8, 1944. An English bibliographer. He was assistant (1883–1909) in department of printed books in the British Museum, becoming assistant keeper (1909) and keeper (1917). He served as professor of English bibliography (1919–32) at King's College, University of London, and was a director (1930 *et seq.*) of the Early English Text Society. He was the author of *Early Illustrated Books* (1893), *Italian Book Illustrations* (1894), *Fine Books* (1912), and other works, and coauthor of *Census of Shakespeare* (1916). He contributed the chapter on Shakespeare's text to the *Cambridge Companion to Shakespeare Studies* (1934), was chief editor of *Short Title Catalogue of Books Printed in England, Scotland, and Ireland, and of English Books Printed Abroad, 1475–1640* (1926), and edited the Globe *Chaucer* (1898).

Pollente (pol'ent). In Spenser's *Faerie Queene*, a character supposed to represent King Charles IX of France. He is the "cruel sarazin" who holds "bridge Perilous," attacking all who try to cross. He is slain by Sir Artegal.

Pollexfen (pol'iks.fen), **Sir Hargrave.** The villain who abducts Harriet Byron in Samuel Richardson's epistolary novel *Sir Charles Grandison.*

Pollock (pol'ọk), Sir **William Frederick.** b. April 13, 1815; d. Dec. 24, 1888. An English barrister, remembered chiefly as a member of the little society whose debates are celebrated in Alfred Tennyson's *In Memoriam.*

Pollok (pol'ọk), **Robert.** b. at Moorhouse, Renfrewshire, Scotland, 1798; d. at Southampton, England, Sept. 18, 1827. A Scottish religious poet. He was educated at Glasgow University. His chief work, *The Course of Time*, was published in 1827, six months before his death.

Poll Sweedlepipe (pol swē'dl.pīp). See **Sweedlepipe, Paul.**

Pollux (pol'uks). [Also, **Polydeuces.**] In Greek mythology, the twin brother of Castor, one of the Dioscuri.

Polly (pol'i). A ballad opera by John Gay, a sequel to *The Beggar's Opera.* It was ready for the stage in 1728, but was suppressed by the government, some members of which had been satirized in the first opera. Gay published it, however, in 1729.

Polly, Alfred. The hero of H. G. Wells's novel *The History of Mr. Polly* (1910).

ḍ, d or j; ṣ, s or sh; ṭ, t or ch; ẓ, z or zh; o, F. cloche; ü, F. menu; ċh, Sc. loch; ṅ, F. bonbon.

Polly Honeycombe (hun'i.kōm). An English farce, the first play written by George Colman the elder. It was first played in 1760, and was a satire mocking what Colman considered to be the addled readers of sentimental novels (such works, on the pattern of *Pamela*, then attracted the almost feverish devotion of a considerable body of readers).

Polly Peachum (pē'chum). See **Peachum, Polly.**

Polly Toodle (tö'dl). See **Toodle, Polly.**

Polo (pō'lō), **Marco.** b. at Venice, Italy, c1254; d. there, c1324. A Venetian traveler. His father and uncle left Constantinople for the Crimea on a commercial enterprise in 1260. Their business eventually brought them to Bukhara, where they fell in with some envoys of Kublai Khan. They were persuaded to accompany the envoys to Kublai, whom they found either at Cambaluc (Peiping) or at Shangtu, north of the Great Wall. Kublai received them well, and sent them as his envoys to the Pope with a request for one hundred educated men to instruct his subjects in Christianity and in the liberal arts. The brothers arrived at Acre in 1269. They obtained from Gregory X, who had just been elected, two Dominicans who turned back at an early stage of the return journey. The brothers left Acre on the journey in 1271, accompanied by Marco, then 17 years of age. They traveled through Khurasan, up the Oxus to the Pamir, by Kashgar, Yarkand, and Khotan, to Lob Nor, and across the great desert of Gobi to Tangut, thence to Shangtu, where they found Kublai Khan in 1275. They were kindly received, and retained in the public service. Marco rose rapidly in the emperor's favor, and was employed in important missions in various parts of the empire. With his father and uncle, Marco left China in 1292, as escorts of a Mongol bride for the Khan of Persia, and after many adventures reached Venice by way of Sumatra, India, and Persia in 1295. In 1298 Marco was taken prisoner in the battle of Curzola between the Venetians and the Genoese. He was detained for a year at Genoa. Here he dictated in the French language to a fellow captive, Rusticiano of Pisa, an account of his adventures, which ultimately obtained a wide popularity, inasmuch as his report was virtually the only source of material in Europe on central Asia. Much that is apparently fantastic traveler's tales appears in the account, but basically the book is factual.

Polonius (pō.lō'ni.us). In Shakespeare's *Hamlet*, the father of Ophelia, and the King's chamberlain. In the first quarto he is called Corambis. He is an interfering individual, who sends Reynaldo to spy on Laertes in Paris after giving Laertes some rather sententious advice. He orders Ophelia to reject Hamlet and then arranges with Claudius to spy on their meeting. His spying on Hamlet's interview with Gertrude, which he does to obtain more support for his contention that Hamlet is mad, results in his murder by Hamlet, who thinks the noise behind the arras is made by Claudius.

Polton (pōl'ton). The assistant of Dr. John Thorndyke in the detective stories of Richard Austin Freeman.

Polybius (pō.lib'i.us). b. at Megalopolis, Arcadia, Greece, c204 B.C.; d. c122 B.C. A Greek historian. He was in the service of the Achaean League, was taken as a political prisoner to Rome c169, and became a friend of the younger Scipio Africanus. He was released in 151, and was later engaged in settling the affairs of Achaea. He went to Egypt in 181, with his father and Aratus, as an ambassador of the Achaean League. He was the author of a history of Rome from 220 to 146 B.C. in 40 books, five of which, with fragments of others, have been preserved; it is an attempt at accurate re-creation of history, with occasional excursions into such subjects as the art of warfare, the Roman constitution, and the philosophy of history.

Polychronicon (pol.i.kron'i.kon). A chronicle of universal history, by Ranulf Higden, written by him to 1342; a continuation was added to the year 1413. It begins with a sketch of the history of the known world, with lives of Adam, Abraham, and other Biblical characters, and brings its entries down to the time of writing. The original section (to 1342) was translated from Latin into English in 1387 by John de Trevisa.

Polycletus (pol.i.klē'tus) or **Polyclitus** (-klī'tus). [Sometimes called **Polycletus of Sicyon** (sish'i.on, sis'-).] fl. in the last part of the 5th century B.C. A Greek sculptor and architect. He is associated with the high development of abstract proportion which characterizes Greek sculpture.

Polycrates (pō.lik'ra.tēz). Put to death, c522 B.C. A tyrant of Samos from c536 (or 532) to 522. He was a patron of literature and art. He built a large fleet and soon controlled shipping in the eastern Mediterranean, to the annoyance of the Persians. According to Herodotus, Polycrates suggested an alliance with Amasis of Egypt, but Amasis refused on the ground that Polycrates had been too fortunate up to that time and was therefore bound to fall through the envy of the gods. Legend has it that to emphasize his point, Amasis advised Polycrates to attempt to get rid of a valuable possession; Polycrates threw a ring into the sea, only to have it returned in a few days in a fish presented to him by a fisherman. Eventually, Polycrates was trapped into coming to the mainland by Oroetes, satrap of Lydia, and was crucified at Magnesia for his piracies.

Polydeuces (pol.i.dū'sēz). See **Pollux.**

Polydore (pol'i.dōr). In Shakespeare's *Cymbeline*, the name under which Guiderius is raised by Morgan (actually Belarius).

Polydore. The brother of Castalio in Thomas Otway's *The Orphan*, who impersonates Castalio on the latter's wedding night.

Polydorus (pol.i.dō'rus). In Greek legend, the youngest son of Priam, killed by Achilles or Polymestor.

Polynices (pol.i.nī'sēz). In Greek legend, a son of Oedipus and Jocasta, and brother of Eteocles. Polynices and Eteocles agreed to rule Thebes year and year about, but Eteocles refused to descend from the throne at the end of his year. Polynices thereupon sought the aid of Adrastus, and the famous expedition of the Seven against Thebes was made to restore him. The two brothers killed each other in single combat.

Polyolbion (pol.i.ol'bi.on). [Also, **Poly-Olbion.**] A poem by Michael Drayton, published 1613–22. His longest poem, it consists of 30 "songs" filled with antiquarian knowledge. Its full title is not without interest: *Poly-Olbion. A Chorographicall Description of All the Tracts, Rivers, Mountains, Forests, and Other Parts of This Renowned Isle of Great Britain, With Intermixture of the Most Remarkeable Stories, Antiquities, Wonders, Rarities, Pleasures, and Commodities of the Same.*

Polyphemus (pol.i.fē′mus). In Greek legend, a one-eyed giant, the chief of the Cyclopes, and son of Poseidon, celebrated in the *Odyssey.* He kept Odysseus and several of his companions prisoners in his cave and devoured one a day, until the clever Odysseus made him drunk, put out his one eye, and managed to escape with the remnant of his companions by hiding himself and them under the bellies of the ogre's sheep as they passed out of the cave to graze.

polyphonic (pol.i.fon′ik). Capable of being read or pronounced in more than one way: said of a written character. "The particular value to be assigned to each of the polyphonic characters." (Isaac Taylor, *The Alphabet.*)

Polyxena (pọ.lik′sẹ.nạ). In Greek legend, a daughter of Priam and Hecuba, and bride of Achilles. At her marriage to Achilles, the latter was slain by Paris, and the Greeks later sacrificed her to appease his shade. In another story, Polyxena fell in love with the hero Achilles, ran away from Troy to join him in the Greek camp, and killed herself at his death. She was the subject of a lost tragedy by Sophocles, and of the tragedies *Hecuba* by Euripides and *Troades* by Seneca. She is not mentioned by Homer.

Pomfret (pum′frẹt, pom′-), **Countess of.** Title of **Fermor, Henrietta Louisa.**

Pomfret, John. b. 1667; d. in November, 1702. An English poet. He was the author of *The Choice or Wish: A Poem written by a Person of Quality* (1700), a poem very popular in the 18th century.

Pomona (pọ.mō′nạ). In Roman mythology, the protecting goddess of fruit trees.

Pompadour (pom′pạ.dọr, -dör; French, pôṅ.pà.dör), **Marquise de.** [Title of **Jeanne Antoinette Poisson le Normant d'Étioles.**] b. at Paris, Dec. 29, 1721; d. at Versailles, April 15, 1764. The chief mistress of Louis XV of France. A beautiful and witty woman, she became, soon after her marriage to the nephew of her protector, a banker, the toast of middle-class Paris. She met the king at a ball in 1744 and in 1745 became his titular mistress. Until her death, she controlled the king and his internal and foreign policies, examining his mail, checking his appointments to office, and, when her position was threatened, even deliberately supporting his liaisons with other women. She changed the traditional French policy of containment of Austria to one of alliance; the result was the disastrous Seven Years' War. Her desire to lead society caused her to patronize such men as Voltaire, Quesnay, and Boucher, but hand in hand with this went a wild extravagance that brought her enemies in all classes.

Pompeii (pom.pā′ē). An ancient city in Italy, situated on the Bay of Naples ab. 13 mi. SE of Naples, nearly at the foot of Mount Vesuvius. It was a flourishing provincial town, containing many villas. It was severely injured (63 A.D.) by an earthquake, and was totally destroyed (79) by an eruption of Vesuvius. Owing to the preservation of the ruins practically intact to the present day by the layer of ashes and pumice that buried them, the remains of Pompeii afford in many ways the most complete information we possess of Roman material civilization.

Pompeii, The Last Days of. See **Last Days of Pompeii, The.**

Pompey (pom′pi). [Called **Pompey the Great;** full Latin name, **Gnaeus Pompeius Magnus.**] b. 106 B.C.; murdered in Egypt, 48 B.C. A Roman general. He served in the Social War in 89, and as a partisan of Sulla (83–81) in Italy, Sicily, and Africa. He commanded against the Marians in Spain (76–72), aided in suppressing the Servile Insurrection in 71, and was consul with Crassus in 70. He was appointed by the Gabinian Law commander in the war against the pirates, whom he subdued in 67, and by the Manilian Law commander in the East in 66. He ended the war with Mithridates, annexed Syria and Palestine, and was given a triumph at Rome in 61. He formed with Julius Caesar and Crassus the first triumvirate in 60, and was consul (55). Pompey's wife Julia was Caesar's daughter, but her death in 54, followed by that of Crassus in 53, led to an intensification of the differences between Caesar and Pompey. He became the champion of the senate and conservative party, was maneuvered into a position in which he was required to disband his followers, began the civil war with Caesar in 49, and was totally defeated by Caesar at Pharsala in 48. He attempted to seek refuge in Egypt but was killed by one of his old followers as he landed.

Pompey. [Also, **Sextus Pompeius.**] In Shakespeare's *Antony and Cleopatra,* a leader of the rebellion against the triumvirate. When Antony returns from Egypt, Pompey makes peace with him and Octavius and entertains them on his galley. In the war between Antony and Octavius he sides with Antony. In history he was the younger son of Pompey the Great.

Pompey. In Shakespeare's *Measure for Measure,* the clownish servant of Mistress Overdone.

Pompilia (pom.pil′i.ạ). The heroine of Robert Browning's long poem *The Ring and the Book.*

Ponderevo (pon.dẹ.rē′vō), **Edward.** The principal male figure of H. G. Wells's novel *Tono-Bungay.* He is the inventor of the patent medicine Tono-Bungay (a tonic, called by Wells "slightly injurious rubbish"), and is enabled through its tremendous popularity to attain great wealth. At the start of the story he is a poor young chemist, filled with various romantic notions, and some of these (particularly the ones which adapt to the Nietzschean ideal of the Superman) remain with him to the end of his life.

Ponderevo, George. The narrator of H. G. Wells's novel *Tono-Bungay.* He is the nephew of Edward Ponderevo.

Ponsonby (pun′sọn.bi), **William.** b. c1546; d. before September, 1604. An English publisher, remembered for his connection with Edmund Spenser. His

ḍ, d or j; ṣ, s or sh; ṭ, t or ch; ẓ, z or zh; o, F. cloche; ü, F. menu; ch, Sc. loch; ṅ, F. bonbon.

first publication was John Alday's *Praise and Dispraise of Women* (1579); his last was Sir Thomas North's translation of Plutarch's *Lives*. In 1590 he published Spenser's *Faerie Queene* (books I–III; books IV–VI, 1596), also bringing out Spenser's *Complaints* (1591), *Amoretti* (1595), and *Colin Clout's Come Home Again* (1595), and several other volumes by the poet.

Pontifex (pon'ti.feks), **Ernest.** The hero of Samuel Butler's *The Way of All Flesh.*

Pooh-Bah (pö'bä'). In Gilbert and Sullivan's *The Mikado*, a personage characterized as "Lord High Everything Else" (as distinguished from Ko-Ko, the Lord High Executioner). His name has passed into the language to describe a person who is pompous and whose high position is perhaps not fully justified by his talents.

Poole (pöl), **John.** b. c1786; d. at London, in February, 1872. An English playwright. His best-known work is *Paul Pry*, produced at the Haymarket Theatre, London, in 1825. Among his other works are *Deaf as a Post, Little Pedlington and the Pedlingtonians*, a satire (1839), and *A Comic Miscellany* (1845).

Poole, Reginald Lane. b. at London, March 29, 1857; d. at Oxford, England, Oct. 28, 1939. An English historian and educator; grandson of Sophia Lane. He was assistant in the department of manuscripts in the British Museum (1880–81), assistant editor, later joint editor with S. R. Gardiner, and finally sole editor of the *English Historical Review* (1885 *et seq.*), and lecturer on modern history at Jesus College, Oxford (1886–1910).

Poor Gentleman, The. A comedy by George Colman the younger, produced at Covent Garden Theatre, London, in 1801, and printed in 1802.

Poor Relations. A novel (1919) by Compton Mackenzie.

Poor Robin (rob'in). An almanac which first appeared in 1663, and was discontinued in 1828. Robert Herrick is said to have assisted in the first numbers.

Poor Tom (tom). A novel by Edward Muir, published in 1932.

Pope (pōp), **Alexander.** b. at London, May 21, 1688; d. at Twickenham, Middlesex, England, May 30, 1744. An English poet, remembered as perhaps the chief exponent of the heroic couplet in the history of English literary technique, and as one of the outstanding satirists of world literature. He lived much of his life in a villa at Twickenham, near London. Born a Roman Catholic in a country which was at that time violently anti-Catholic, he had an irregular education, but read extensively in English and Latin poets. His *Pastorals*, circulated in manuscript, early attracted the attention of such older writers as William Wycherley. Pope became the close friend of prominent literary and political figures, including in particular Jonathan Swift, Viscount Bolingbroke, and other Tory wits and statesmen. Pope was small in stature and suffered from a spinal ailment, but led a surprisingly active life. His best-known works fall into three periods: The first included *Pastorals* (1709), *An Essay on Criticism* (1711), *The Rape of the Lock* (1712; revised

1714), *Elegy to the Memory of an Unfortunate Lady*, and *Eloisa to Abelard* (1717). The second period was noteworthy for his translations of the *Iliad* (1715–20) and the *Odyssey* (1725–26). The third period included *The Dunciad* (1728; revised 1743), *An Essay on Man* (1733–34), and various ethical epistles and satires, of which particular note may be made of *Epistle IV, Of the Use of Riches* (1731), with account of Timon's villa, and *The Epistle to Dr. Arbuthnot* (1735), with its portrait of Atticus. Pope's quarrels with Joseph Addison and others are notorious, but recent scholarship tends to place the blame less on Pope than formerly, and his reputation is higher now than at any time since the early 19th century. The modern reader will find much of Pope's best writing in the vigorous colloquial style of his satirical and ethical poems.

Pope, Jane. b. 1742; d. 1818. An English actress. She was the original Mrs. Candour in Sheridan's *School for Scandal* and played *Tilburina* in his *Critic.* She appeared with Macklin, playing Portia to his Shylock.

Pope, Thomas. fl. 1586–1603. An English actor of the Elizabethan period. He is mentioned as one of the "principal actors" in the first folio edition of Shakespeare (1623).

Pope-Hennessy (pōp'hen'ę.si), **Una.** [Maiden name, **Birch.**] b. 1876; d. at London, Aug. 16, 1949. An English writer. Author of *Three English Women in America* (1929), *The Aristocratic Journey* (1931), *The Laird of Abbotsford* (1932), *Edgar Allan Poe: A Critical Biography* (1934), *The Closed City* (1938), *Agnes Strickland* (1940), *Durham Company* (1941), *Charles Dickens* (1943), and *A Czarina's Story* (1948).

Popilius Lena (pō.pil'i.us lē'ną). See **Lena, Popilius.**

Popish Impostures. See under **Harsnett, Samuel.**

Popish Plot. In English history, an alleged conspiracy of the Roman Catholics in 1678 to murder Charles II and control the government in the interest of the Roman Catholic Church. The story was chiefly contrived by Titus Oates, and, as the result of circumstantial evidence found by investigators, raised popular hysteria to such heights that many Roman Catholics were killed.

Popple (pop'l), **William.** b. 1701; d. 1764. An English dramatist, author of *The Lady's Revenge: or, The Rover Reclaim'd* (1734) and *The Double Deceit: or, A Cure for Jealousy* (1735).

Porcupine (pôr'kụ.pīn), **Peter.** Pseudonym of **Cobbett, William.**

Porlock (pôr'lok), **Martin.** A pseudonym of **MacDonald, Philip.**

Pornick (pôr'nik), **Ann.** In H. G. Wells's novel *Kipps*, the daughter of a haberdasher in New Romney. She is Kipps's childhood sweetheart, and eventually becomes his wife.

Porphyry (pôr'fi.ri). [Latin, **Porphyrius** (pôr.fir'i.us); original name, **Malchus.**] b. at Tyre, or Batanea (Bashan), c233 A.D.; d. at Rome, c305. A Neo-Platonic philosopher, a disciple of Plotinus, and teacher of philosophy at Rome. He wrote a treatise against the Christians (15 books), a life of Plotinus, a life of Pythagoras, works on Aristotle, commentaries, chronicles, and others. He is credited with originating the Tree of Porphyry, a logical device for analyzing by a succession of dichotomies. His Latin name, meaning "purple," is a punning allusion to his name Malchus, which means "king" in Syrian.

Porsena (pôr′se̯.na̯), **Lars.** [Also, **Porsenna** (pôr-sen′a̯).] In Roman legend, a king of Clusium in Etruria, who gained power over Rome in the 6th century. He was celebrated in the legends of Tarquin, Horatius Cocles, and others.

Porson (pôr′so̯n), **Richard.** b. at East Ruston, Norfolkshire, England, Dec. 25, 1759; d. Sept. 25, 1808. An English classical scholar. He was a child prodigy, whose education at Eton and Cambridge was subsidized by patrons. His *Letters to Archdeacon Travis, on the spurious verse I John V. 7* (1788–89) aroused great interest, but resulted in severe criticism of its author, although its scholarship has been shown to be exemplary. In 1792 he was elected Regis professor of Greek at Cambridge. His brilliant scholarship was displayed in subsequent years in his editions of Euripides and Aeschylus and in his notes on such other Greek writers as Aristophanes and Hesychius. He advanced not only textual criticism but also knowledge of Greek meter.

Porteous Riots (pôr′tyus). Riots at Edinburgh, Scotland, in 1736. They originated in a disturbance at a smuggler's execution, when Captain John Porteous, chief of the city guard, ordered his troops to fire on the crowd. Sixteen or seventeen persons were killed or wounded. Porteous was tried for murder and condemned, but was reprieved, whereupon a mob dragged him from the prison and hanged him, on September 7. This incident is the starting point of Sir Walter Scott's novel *The Heart of Midlothian.*

Porter. In Shakespeare's *Macbeth,* the drunken doorman who admits Macduff and Lennox to Macbeth's castle just as Macbeth has murdered Duncan. He is the only comic character in the tragedy.

Porter (pōr′te̯r), **Anna Maria.** b. at Durham, England, 1780; d. Sept. 21, 1832. An English novelist; sister of Jane Porter. She wrote *Artless Tales* (1793–95), *Walsh Colville* (1797), *Octavia* (1798), *The Lake of Killarney* (1804), *Honor O'Hara* (1826), and *The Barony* (1830).

Porter, Henry. fl. 1596–99. An English dramatist. He was one of the authors for the Admiral's Men and, according to the entries in Philip Henslowe's diary, wrote several plays. The only one surviving is *The Two Angry Women of Abingdon* (c1598), a comedy of English middle-class domestic life, which may have influenced Shakespeare's *Merry Wives of Windsor.*

Porter, Jane. b. at Durham, England, 1776; d. at Bristol, England, May 24, 1850. An English novelist; sister of Anna Maria Porter. She made a great reputation as a romantic novelist. She wrote *Thaddeus of Warsaw* (1803), *The Scottish Chiefs* (1810), *Tales Round a Winter Hearth* (with her sister, 1826), and *The Field of Forty Footsteps* (1828).

Porthos (pôr.tos; Anglicized, pôr′tho̯s). One of the "three Musketeers" in *The Three Musketeers,* and its sequels, by the elder Alexandre Dumas. He is

noted for his great size and strength and his inordinate love of display.

Portia (pôr′sha̯). In Shakespeare's *Julius Caesar,* the wife of Marcus Brutus. She goes insane from anxiety over her husband, and her death (from swallowing fire) is reported (IV.iii).

Portia. In Shakespeare's *Merchant of Venice,* an heiress in love with Bassanio. Portia is noted for her law-court defense of Bassanio's friend Antonio against the demand of Shylock for a pound of flesh from Antonio's body. It is she who (disguised as Balthasar, a learned doctor of law) delivers the famous speech beginning "The quality of mercy is not strain'd" (IV.i), a plea for Shylock's mercy. When Shylock remains adamant, she makes the law a matter of exact scruple: neither more nor less than one pound of flesh shall he have on pain of death.

Portinari (pōr.tē.nä′rē), **Beatrice.** See **Beatrice Portinari.**

Portland Vase (pōrt′la̯nd). An urn of blue transparent cameo-cut glass, ten inches high. It was discovered (c1630) in a sarcophagus near Rome. It is so called from William Henry Cavendish Bentinck, 3rd Duke of Portland, who bought it in 1787 from Sir William Hamilton (its original purchaser in 1770), and placed it in the British Museum in 1810.

Portrait by Caroline. American title of **Winter Comedy.**

Portrait of a Celibate. American title of **Nor Many Waters.**

Portrait of a Lady. A poem by T. S. Eliot, published in *Prufrock* (1917), describing the failure of a possible friendship between an older woman and an unsure young man who, understanding neither the woman nor life itself, can only continue to smile and "go on drinking tea."

Portrait of a Lady, The. A novel by Henry James, published in 1881.

Portrait of a Man with Red Hair. A novel (1925) by Hugh Walpole.

Portrait of the Artist as a Young Man, A. An autobiographical novel by James Joyce, published in 1916. The novel is notable for the author's early utilization of the stream-of-consciousness technique. The hero, Stephen Dedalus, is a sensitive young man who finds all society and nature antagonistic to him. The reader follows the thoughts of Stephen through his sordid childhood, unhappy education, disillusionment about religion, and unrewarding loves. He finally purges himself of all religious and social inhibitions, and decides to isolate himself from society and devote his life to his art. Among the characters are Davin and Lynch, fellow students; Emma, a girl who is loved by Stephen at one point in his life; and Simon and May Dedalus, Stephen's father and mother. This work provides the background for the writer's best-known work, *Ulysses.*

Port-Royal (-roi′a̯l; French, pôr.rwȧ.yȧl). A Cistercian abbey for nuns, ab. 17 mi. SW of Paris. It was founded in 1204, was reformed under the abbess Jacqueline Marie Angélique Arnauld in 1608, was called Port-Royal des Champs after the establishment (1626) of a branch house at Paris (called Port-Royal de Paris), and became noted as a center of Jansenism. The older establishment became famous for its schools and as a center of learning; it was suppressed in 1709. Port-Royal de Paris continued until 1790.

Portunus (pôr.tū'nus) or **Portumnus** (pôr.tum'nus). In Roman mythology, the protecting god of harbors.

Poseidon (pọ.sī'dọn). In Greek mythology, one of the chief Olympian gods; brother of Zeus, and lord of the sea and navigation. Originally, however, he was a god of earthquakes and water. Earthquakes and storms arose when Poseidon shook his trident. He was also a god of horses. Among his more interesting amours were those with Medusa, whence he begot the winged horse, Pegasus, and with Demeter, who turned herself into a horse to escape him. Poseidon, however, turned himself into a stallion and begot by her the wonderful speaking horse, Arion. Other of his offspring were Triton, the giant Orion, and the one-eyed Cyclops, Polyphemus. His consort was the Nereid Amphitrite, and his attendant train was composed of Nereids, Tritons, and sea monsters of every form. In art he is a majestic figure; his most common attributes are the trident, the dolphin, and the horse, which he was reputed to have created during his contest with Athena for supremacy in Attica. The original Roman or Italic Neptune became assimilated to him.

Posthumous Papers of the Pickwick Club (pik'wik), **The.** See **Pickwick Papers.**

Posthumus Leonatus (pŏst.hū'mus lē.ọ.nā'tus). In Shakespeare's *Cymbeline*, the husband of Imogen. His wager as to her fidelity is a turning point of the play.

posy (pō'zi). **1.** A verse of poetry (the term originated as a contraction of "poesy") attached to or inscribed on a ring, knife, or other object; hence, in general, a motto; an epigram; a legend; a short inscription.

And the tente was replenyshed and decked with this posie: After busy labor commeth victorious rest.   (Hall, *Hen. V.*, an. 7.)

We call them [short epigrams] Posies, and do paint them now a dayes vpon the backe sides of our fruite trenchers of wood, or vse them as deuises in rings and armes and about such courtly purposes.   (Puttenham, *Arte of Eng. Poesie.*)

A hoop of gold, a paltry ring
That she did give me, whose posy was
For all the world like cutler's poetry,
Upon a knife, "Love me, and leave me not."
          (Shak., *M. of V.*, V.i.)

2. A bunch of flowers, or a single flower; a nosegay; a bouquet. [Perhaps so called from the custom of sending verses with flowers as gifts.]

And I will make thee beds of roses,
And a thousand fragrant posies.
          (Marlowe, *Passionate Shepherd to his Love.*)

Nature pick'd several flowers from her choice banks,
And bound 'em up in thee, sending thee forth
A posy for the bosom of a queen.
          (Fletcher (and another), *Queen of Corinth*, III.i.)

Y' are the maiden posies,
And so grac't
To be plac't
'Fore damask roses.
          (Herrick, *To Violets.*)

A girl came with violet posies, and two
Gentle eyes, like her violets, freshened with dew.
      (F. Locker-Lampson, *Mr. Placid's Flirtation.*)

potboiler (pot'boi'lẽr). A work of art or literature produced merely "to keep the pot boiling"—that is, for the sake of providing the necessaries of life.

His [Raff's] very fertility is a misfortune; . . . writing pot-boilers has injured the development of a delicate feeling for what is lofty and refined.
          (*Grove's Music Dictionary.*)

Murillo executed a few portraits about the time he was painting pot-boilers for sale at fairs and to sea-captains.   (*The American.*)

Potiphar's Wife (pot'i.färz, -farz). In Old Testament history, the wife of Pharaoh's chieftain, Potiphar. She was enamored of Joseph, slave and steward in Potiphar's household, and tried to seduce him. Joseph refused her advances and in revenge she tore his robe, screamed for help, and accused him of improper advances. Joseph was imprisoned for the alleged crime. In some rabbinical versions of the legend, her false accusation was exposed and Joseph was exonerated.

Pot of Broth, A. A drama (1902) by William Butler Yeats.

Pott (pot), **Mr.** In Dickens's *Pickwick Papers*, the loud-talking but actually pusillanimous editor of the Eatanswill *Gazette*. His last appearance in the story is on the occasion of a fight (more notable for its noise than its effect) with Slurk, his opponent as editor of the *Independent*.

Potterism. A novel (1920) by Rose Macaulay.

Potter's Field. See under **Aceldama.**

Poulters' measure (pōl'tẽrz). A kind of verse combining lines of 12 and 14 syllables.

The commonest sort of verse which we vse now adayes (viz. the long verse of twelue and fourteen sillables) I know not certainly howe to name it, vnlesse I should say that it doth consist of Poulters' measure, which giueth xii. for one dozen and xiiij. for another.   (Gascoigne, *Steele, Glas*, etc.)

The first or the first couple hauing twelue sillables, the other fourteene, which versifyers call powlters measure, because they tallie their wares by dozens.
          (W. Webbe, *Discourse of English Poetrie.*)

Pounce (pouns), **Peter.** A penurious acquaintance of Fanny in Henry Fielding's novel *Joseph Andrews* who rescues her from kidnappers.

Poundtext (pound'tekst), **Peter.** In Sir Walter Scott's novel *Old Mortality*, an "Indulged" preacher (that is, one licensed to preach). He is caught in the fighting of the Covenanters, which comprises the background of the story, but has little heart for it.

Povey (pō'vi), **Samuel.** In Arnold Bennett's *Old Wives' Tale*, the man who falls in love with (and eventually marries) Constance Baines.

---

fat, fāte, fär, àsk, fāre; net, mē, hėr; pin, pīne; not, nōte, mŏve, nôr; up, lūte, pùll; ᴛʜ, then;

Powell (pō'el), **Frederick York.** b. at London, Jan. 14, 1850; d. at Oxford, England, May 8, 1904. An English historian, teacher, and translator. He was lecturer in law (1874–94) at Christ Church, and regius professor of modern history (1894–1904) at Oxford. He was instrumental in founding (1885) the *English Historical Review*, and in establishing (1899) Ruskin College. Author of *Early England to the Norman Conquest* (1876), *Old Stories from British History* (1882), and *History of England from the Earliest Times to the Death of Henry VII* (1885).

Powell (pou'el), **Willie.** Sincere but weak hero of *A Young Man from the South* (1917), novel by Lennox Robinson.

Power (pou'ėr), **Cecil.** A pseudonym of **Allen, Grant.**

Power, Eileen. b. Jan. 9, 1889; d. Aug. 8, 1940. A British economic historian, well known as a scholar and writer for the general public. She was professor of economic history at the London School of Economics (1931–40). Author of *The Paycockes of Coggeshall* (1919), *Medieval English Nunneries* (1922), and *Medieval People* (1924); and joint editor with R. H. Tawney of *Tudor Economic Documents* (1924), with M. Postan of *Studies in the History of English Trade in the 15th Century* (1932), and with J. H. Clapham of *Cambridge Economic History of Europe* (vol. I, 1941).

Power and the Glory, The. A novel by Graham Greene, published in 1940.

Power House, The. A novel by John Buchan, published in 1916.

Power of Love, The. A work by Mary de la Rivière Manley (1720), consisting of six novels: *The Fair Hypocrite*, *The Physician's Stratagem*, *The Wife's Resentment*, *The Husband's Resentment in Two Examples*, *The Happy Fugitive*, and *The Perjured Beauty*.

Powys (pō'is), **John Cowper.** b. at Shirley, Derbyshire, England, Oct. 8, 1872–. An English novelist, poet, and critic; brother of Theodore Francis Powys and Llewelyn Powys. Among his novels are *Wolf Solent* (1929), *A Glastonbury Romance* (1933), *Maiden Castle* (1937), and *Owen Glendower* (1941). His verse includes *Wolfsbane*, *Mandragora*, and *Samphire*. Author also of the philosophical *The Complex Vision*, *The Religion of a Sceptic*, and *In Defense of Sensuality* (1930); the critical works *Visions and Revisions*, *The Meaning of Culture* (1930), and *Rabelais* (1947); an autobiography; and *Morwyn* (1937) and *The Pleasures of Literature* (1938).

Powys, Llewelyn. b. at Dorchester, England, Aug. 13, 1884; d. at Clavadel, Switzerland, Dec. 2, 1939. An English novelist, essayist, and traveler; brother of John Cowper Powys and Theodore Francis Powys. Suffering from tuberculosis, he traveled abroad for his health, visiting Switzerland (1909–14) and Kenya colony, British East Africa (1914–19). He was at New York (1920–25) as a journalist, in Palestine (1928), in the West Indies (1930), and again in Switzerland (1936–39). Author of *Thirteen Worthies* (1923), *Pathetic Fallacy—A Study of Christianity* (1930), *Impassioned Clay* (1931), *Now that the Gods Are Dead* (1932), and *Earth Memories* (1934), critical essays and studies; *Apples Be Ripe*

(1930) and *Love and Death* (1939), novels; *Confessions of Two Brothers* (1916), *Skin for Skin* (1925), and *The Verdict of Bridlegoose* (1926), autobiographies; *Life of Henry Hudson* (1928); *The Cradle of God* (1929) and *A Pagan's Pilgrimage* (1931), descriptions of Palestine; *Ebony and Ivory* (1923) and *Black Laughter* (1924), sketches and stories of African life; *Rats in the Sacristy* (1937) and *A Baker's Dozen* (1940), collected essays.

Powys, Theodore Francis. b. at Shirley, Derbyshire, England, 1875–. An English writer; brother of John Cowper Powys and Llewelyn Powys. His books include *Black Bryony* (1923), *Mark Only* (1924), *Mockery Gap* (1925), *Mr. Tasker's Gods* (1925), *Innocent Birds* (1926), *Mr. Weston's Good Wine* (1927), *The House with the Echo* (1928), *Kindness in a Corner* (1930), *The White Paternoster* (1930), *Unclay* (1931), *The Two Thieves* (1932), and *Goat Green* (1937).

Poynton (poin'ton), **The Spoils of.** See **Spoils of Poynton, The.**

Poyser (poi'zėr), **Martin.** In George Eliot's novel *Adam Bede*, the hearty, generous farmer. Hetty Sorrel is a member of his household during the early portions of the story.

Poyser, Mrs. In George Eliot's novel *Adam Bede*, a vigorous, hard-working countrywoman, keen, clever, and inclined to shrewishness, living with her husband on one of Squire Donnithorne's farms.

P. P., Clerk of this Parish, Memoirs of. A work by John Arbuthnot, a satire on Gilbert Burnet's *History of My Own Time*.

Praed (prād), **Rosa Caroline Mackworth.** [Maiden name, **Prior.**] b. in Queensland, Australia, March 27, 1851; d. at Torquay, England, April 13, 1935. An Australian novelist. Among her books are *An Australian Heroine* (1880), *Nadine* (1882), *The Head Station* (1885), *The Romance of a Station* (1889), and *As a Watch in the Night* (1900).

Praed, Winthrop Mackworth. b. at London, July 26, 1802; d. there, July 15, 1839. An English poet, best known as a writer of light *vers de société*. In 1822 he was a principal contributor to *Knight's Quarterly Magazine*. Called to the bar in the Middle Temple in May, 1829, he was Tory member of Parliament for St. Germans (1830–32), afterward member for Great Yarmouth, and still later for Aylesbury until his death. His collected poems were published in 1864, his prose essays in 1887, and his political poems in 1888.

Praetorian Guard (prē.tō'ri.an). [Also, **Pretorian.**] Roman troops assigned to personal protection of the emperor.

Praise of Folly, The. [Latin, **Encomium Moriae.**] A satirical work by Desiderius Erasmus, published in 1511, directed against the clergy and others.

Praise of Women. A poem at one time erroneously attributed to Chaucer.

Prajapati (pra.jä'pa.tē). In the *Rig-Veda*, an epithet of several gods, applied especially to Savitri, to Soma, and to Indra and Agni. Once in the *Rig-Veda*, and often in the *Atharva-Veda* and *Yajasaneyisanhita* and in the *Brahmanas*, Prajapati is a creator and supreme god over the other gods of the Vedic period. This Prajapati becomes the Brahma of later philosophical speculation. The name is also given to the seven or ten Rishis from whom mankind is descended.

Prakrit (prä′krit). A collective name for the vernacular languages or dialects of northern and central India, especially those of the ancient and medieval periods, as distinguished from the Sanskrit; also, any of these languages or dialects.

Pratt (prat), **Edwin John.** b. at Western Bay, Newfoundland, Feb. 4, 1883—. A Canadian poet. He was professor (1919 *et seq.*) of English at Victoria College of the University of Toronto, and editor of *Canadian Poetry Magazine*. He was awarded the annual governor general's poetry award for *The Fables of the Goats and Other Poems* (1937). Author also of *Newfoundland Verse* (1923), *The Witches' Brew* (1926), *Titans* (1926), *The Iron Door* (1927), *Verses of the Sea* (1930), *Many Moods* (1933), *Dunkirk* (1941), *Still Life* (1943), *They Are Returning* (1945), and *Behind the Log* (1947).

Praxiteles (prak.sit′ẹ.lēz). b. at Athens about the end of the 5th century B.C. A Greek sculptor. His activity lasted until about the time of Alexander the Great, or 336 B.C. Nearly threescore of his works are mentioned in old writers. The characteristics of his work are shown in the statue of Hermes and Dionysus, identified by Pausanias's description. Various figures in modern museums are supposed to be copies of his work. Among them are the *Satyr* of the Capitol (the *Marble Faun* of Hawthorne's novel); a much more beautiful torso discovered in the Palatine, and now in the Louvre; the *Apollino* of the tribune in Florence; and the *Apollo Sauroctonus* of the Vatican. His most celebrated work was the *Aphrodite of Cnidus*, which, next to the *Zeus* of Phidias, was the most admired of the statues of antiquity.

Prayer Book. See **Book of Common Prayer.**

Preacher, The. See **Ecclesiastes.**

Preachers, Order of. See **Dominicans.**

preamble (prē′am.bl). **1.** A preliminary statement; an introductory paragraph or division of a discourse or writing; a preface; prologue; prelude.

This is a long preamble of a tale.
(Chaucer, Prologue to *Wife of Bath's Tale*.)

After this fabulous preamble, they proceeded to handle the matter of fact with logical precision.
(Motley, *History of Netherlands*.)

2. The introductory part of a statute or resolution, which states or indicates the reasons and intent of what follows.

preciosity (presh.i.os′i̇.ti). The quality of being overnice; fastidiousness; excessive refinement.

Precious Bane. A novel by Mary Webb, published in 1924. It was awarded the 1925 Femina-Vie Heureuse prize.

Preedy (prē′di), **George Runnell.** A pseudonym of **Long, Gabrielle Margaret Vere.**

preface (pref′ạs). **1.** A statement or series of statements introducing a discourse, book, or other composition; a series of preliminary remarks, either written or spoken; a prelude. A preface is generally shorter than an introduction, which contains matter kindred in subject, and additional or leading up

to what follows; while a preface is usually confined to particulars relating to the origin, history, scope, or aim of the work to which it is prefixed.

I thoughte it good to speake somewhat hereof, trusting yat the pleasaunt contemplacion of the thing it selfe shal make the length of this preface lesse tedious.
(R. Eden, *First Books on America*, Ep. to Reader.)

Tush, my good lord, this superficial tale
Is but a preface of her worthy praise.
(Shakespeare, *1 Henry VI*, V.v.)

How prologues into prefaces decay,
And these to notes are fritter'd quite away.
(Pope, *Dunciad*.)

2. A title; an introductory or explanatory epithet.

I say he is not worthy
The name of man, or any honest preface,
That dares report or credit such a slander.
(Fletcher (and another), *Love's Pilgrimage*.)

prelude (prē′lūd, prel′ūd). An introductory performance; a preliminary to an action, event, or work of broader scope and higher importance; a preface; presage; foreshadowing.

A strange accident befell him, perchance not so worthy of memory for itself as for that it seemeth to have been a kind of prelude to his final period.
(Sir H. Wotton, *Reliquiae*.)

Are but the needful preludes of the truth.
(Tennyson, *Princess*, Conclusion.)

Prelude, The. A philosophical poem by William Wordsworth, published posthumously in 1850, but written some 50 years earlier.

Preludes. A volume of verse (1876) by Alice Meynell.

Prelude to Adventure, The. A novel by Hugh Walpole, published in 1912.

Pre-Raphaelite Brotherhood (prē.raf′ạ.ẹl.īt). A band of artists, originally consisting of Holman Hunt, D. G. Rossetti, and J. E. Millais (joined later by William Michael Rossetti, Thomas Woolner, F. G. Stephens, and James Collinson), who united in 1848 with a view of adopting a closer study of nature, and as a protest against academic dogma. *The Germ* was started in 1850, but only four numbers were published. Its avowed object was to "enforce and encourage an entire adherence to the simplicity of nature." The principle was applied to the writing of poetry as well as to painting. Ruskin earnestly advocated the school, whose methods he defined as the effort "to paint things as they probably did look and happen, not as, by rules of art developed under Raphael, they might be supposed gracefully, deliciously, or sublimely to have happened." A storm of vituperative criticism raged round the brotherhood for five years, and finally spent itself on their successors. By 1854 the band was practically broken up by divergence of methods.

Press Cuttings. A play (1909) by George Bernard Shaw, included by most critics among his lesser works.

Prester John (pres′tẽr jon). [Meaning "John the Priest" or "John the Presbyter."] A legendary Christian monarch believed, in the 12th century,

---

fat, fāte, fär, ȧsk, fāre; net, mē, hẽr; pin, pīne; not, nōte, mȯve, nôr; up, lūte, pull; ᵺH, then;

to have made extensive conquests and to have established a powerful empire somewhere in Asia "beyond Persia and Armenia," or, according to other accounts, in Africa (Ethiopia). Marvelous tales were told of his victories, riches, and power. Among the marvels reported from Prester John's kingdom were: a fountain from which three drafts ensured everlasting youth and complete lack of poverty and crime, an herb which dispelled demons, ants which mined gold, a magic mirror which revealed plots, and Prester John's couch of sapphire which ensured chastity. Extraordinary letters purporting to have been written by him to the Byzantine emperor Manuel Comnenus and to other potentates were circulated. Pope Alexander III sent him a letter by a special messenger (who never returned). The foundation of the legend is uncertain. Sir John Mandeville gives this account of the name: an emperor of the Orient, who was a Christian, went into a church in Egypt on the Saturday in Whitsun week, where the bishop was ordaining priests. "And he beheld and listend the servyse fulle tentyfly." He then said that he would no longer be called emperor, but priest, and that he would have the name of the first priest of the church, which was John. Since that time he has been called Prester John.

Preston (pres'tọn), **George F.** A pseudonym of **Warren, John Byrne Leicester.**

Preston, Thomas. b. 1537; d. 1598. An English dramatist. In 1583 it is recorded that he went to Scotland and became a favorite of King James VI. He became master of Trinity Hall, Cambridge, in 1584, and vice-chancellor of the university in 1589. He signed a memorandum to Lord Burghley in 1592 in favor of prohibiting plays at Cambridge. For this reason it is somewhat puzzling that his name should be linked to *Cambises*, a highly farcical interlude published between 1569 and 1584, but nevertheless the work is usually attributed to him.

Pretiosa (prẹ.shi.o'sạ). The name adopted by Constanza in her disguise as a "Spanish gypsy" in the play of that name by Thomas Middleton and William Rowley.

Pretorian Guard (prẹ.tō'ri.ạn). See **Praetorian Guard.**

Pretty Lady, The. A novel by Arnold Bennett, published in 1918.

Prettyman (prit'i.man), **Prince.** A whimsical character in *The Rehearsal*, by George Villiers, 2nd Duke of Buckingham, who alternates between being a fisherman and a prince, and is in love with Chloris. His embarrassments are amusing and numerous. He was intended to ridicule Leonidas in John Dryden's *Marriage à la Mode.*

Prévost d'Exiles (prā.vō deg.zēl), Abbé **Antoine François.** [Known as **Abbé Prévost.**] b. at Hesdin, in Artois, French Flanders, April 1, 1697; d. in the forest of Chantilly, France, Nov. 23, 1763. A French novelist. For 30 years he divided his time between the Jesuits' schools, the army, society, and the cloister. Finally he took monastic vows, but fled from the Benedictine monastery at St.-Maur and resided six years in the Netherlands and England. He made a livelihood by means of his pen, and at the outset drew largely upon his own fund of

personal experiences for the subject-matter of his writings. He achieved success with his *Mémoires d'un homme de qualité* (1728–32). Then he wrote *Histoire de M. Cleveland, fils naturel de Cromwell, ou le philosophe anglais* (1732–39), and his celebrated masterpiece, *Histoire du chevalier Des Grieux et de Manon Lescaut* (1733). A periodical publication, *Le Pour et le Contre*, in 20 volumes, extended over seven years, beginning in 1733. He also wrote *Le Doyen de Killerine* (1735), *Histoire de Marguerite d'Anjou* (1740), *Campagnes philosophiques* (1741), *Mémoires pour servir à l'histoire de Malte* (1741), *L'Histoire d'une Grecque moderne* (1741), *Histoire de Guillaume le Conquérant* (1742), *Mémoires d'un honnête homme* (1745), *Histoire générale des voyages* (1745–70), *Manuel lexique* (1750), *Le Monde moral* (1760), *Mémoires pour servir à l'histoire de la vertu* (1762), *Contes, aventures, et faits singuliers* (1764), and *Lettres de mentor à un jeune seigneur* (1764). As a translator he rendered into French works of John Dryden, David Hume, Samuel Richardson, Cicero, and others.

Prewett (prö'it), **Frank.** b. in Canada, Aug. 24, 1893–. A British poet. His volumes of verse include *Poems* (1920) and *Rural Scene* (1924).

Priam (prī'ạm). In Greek legend, the king of Troy at the time of its siege by the Greeks. He was the husband of Hecuba, and the father of 50 sons, including Hector, Paris, and Polydorus, and also of the seeress Cassandra. He perished, by the sword of Neoptolemus, at the capture of Troy.

Priam. In Shakespeare's *Troilus and Cressida*, the King of Troy. He debates with his sons about returning Helen to the Greeks and later pleads with Hector not to fight Achilles.

Priapus (prī.ā'pus). In Greek mythology, a god, a son of Dionysus and Aphrodite, the promoter of fertility of crops, cattle, and women. He is depicted as a faunlike deity with penis always erect. In Rome he was identified with Mutinuus, another fertility god. The first fruits of garden and field were sacrificed to him. In the Middle Ages he became the protector of cattle, herds, shepherds, farmers, and fishermen, and of women in childbirth.

Price (prīs), **Fanny.** The meek heroine of Jane Austen's novel *Mansfield Park.*

Price, Fanny. In W. Somerset Maugham's novel *Of Human Bondage*, a physically unattractive woman who loves Philip Carey, who does not return her love. Unsuccessful in her ambition to become an artist, tired of loneliness, failure, and starvation, she hangs herself, leaving her pathetic possessions to Philip.

Price, Matilda. In Dickens's *Nicholas Nickleby*, the bosom friend of Fanny Squeers. She afterward marries John Browdie. She is alluded to by Miss Squeers in their little unpleasantness as "base degrading 'Tilda."

Price, Richard. b. at Tynton, Glamorganshire, Wales, Feb. 23, 1723; d. at London, April 19, 1791. An English philosophical writer. In 1757 he published *Review of the Principal Questions in Morals*, a statement much resembling that later produced by Immanuel Kant. He is best known as a writer on financial and political questions. As a result of his public support of the American cause in the

Revolutionary War, in 1778 he was invited by the Continental Congress to help in the management of the national finances, but declined.

Price of Money, The. A four-act drama (1906) by Alfred Sutro.

Prichard (prich'ạrd), **Katherine Susannah.** b. at Levuka, Fiji, 1884—. An Australian novelist. She worked as a journalist at Melbourne and London until 1919, when she married and took up residence in West Australia. She is the author of a long series of novels, including *Working Bullocks* (1926), *Coonardoo* (1929), *The Roaring Nineties* (1946), verse, and plays, and journalism supporting the Communist Party of Australia. She also wrote *The Earth Lover* (1932), poems; *The Real Russia* (1934); and a play, *Brumly Innes* (1940).

Pride and Prejudice. A novel by Jane Austen, written in 1796 under the title *First Impressions* and published in 1813. Mr. and Mrs. Bennet have five daughters, and because on their death their property will pass by entail to a male cousin, William Collins, rather than to their daughters, they wish to see the young ladies marry well. Mr. Collins enjoys the patronage of the haughty and wealthy Lady Catherine de Bourgh. Meanwhile, Charles Bingley, a rich young bachelor, has moved into a house near the Bennets and brings with him his friend, Fitzwilliam Darcy, Lady Catherine's nephew. Bingley falls in love with the gentle and pretty Jane, the eldest of the Bennet girls, while the proud and insolent Darcy is attracted, much against his wishes, to Elizabeth, the lively and high-spirited second sister. Elizabeth is offended by his manners and haughtiness and is further prejudiced by a false report about him received from George Wickham, a young officer whose father was steward of the Darcy estate. She also thinks that Darcy and Bingley's sisters have plotted to estrange Jane and Bingley, who have by this time separated. Darcy is therefore angrily rejected by Elizabeth when he proposes, particularly as he does not trouble to hide the fact that his pride is injured by her inferior connections. Darcy writes a letter to Elizabeth explaining his actions and protesting his innocence of having cheated Wickham. Later, on a trip to the north of England with her aunt and uncle, Elizabeth stops at Pemberley, Darcy's home, not realizing that he is there. He produces a much more favorable impression upon Elizabeth, and manages to save the situation when her sister Lydia runs away with the worthless Wickham. He pursues them and, by giving him money, persuades Wickham to marry the girl. Darcy also aids in the reconciliation of Jane and Bingley. When Lady Catherine indignantly reports to her nephew that Elizabeth has refused to promise not to marry him, Darcy proposes again and this time is accepted.

Prideaux (prid'ō), **Humphrey.** b. at Padstow, Cornwall, England, May 3, 1648; d. at Norwich, England, Nov. 1, 1724. An English theological writer, dean of Norwich (1702–24). He wrote *Marmora Oxoniensia ex Arundellianis . . . conflata* (Description of the Arundel Marbles, 1676), *The Validity of the Orders of the Church of England* (1688), *Connection of the Old and New Testaments in the History of the Jews* (1716–18), a number of ecclesiastical tracts, and others.

Pride of Life, The. An English morality play (c1400), known through its prologue summary and the existing 500 lines. It is the earliest extant play of this genre.

Pride's Purge. In English history, the forcible exclusion from the House of Commons, Dec. 6, 1648, of all the members (about 100) who were favorable to compromise with the royal party. This was effected by a military force commanded by Thomas Pride, in execution of orders of a council of Parliamentary officers. The remaining members, about 60, were known as the Rump Parliament.

Priestley (prēst'li), **J. B.** [Full name, **John Boynton Priestley.**] b. at Bradford, Yorkshire, England, 1894—. An English novelist, critic, and playwright. He was United Kingdom delegate (1946–47) to the United Nations Educational, Scientific, and Cultural Organization conferences. His novels include *The Good Companions* (1929), which he dramatized (1931) with E. Knoblock, *Angel Pavement* (1930), *Faraway* (1932), *Let the People Sing* (1939), *Blackout in Gretley* (1942), and *Festival* (1951). Among his plays are *Dangerous Corner* (1932), *Laburnum Grove* (1933), *Time and the Conways* (1937), *I Have Been Here Before* (1937), *Music at Night* (1938), *The Long Mirror* (1940), *An Inspector Calls* (1946), and *The Linden Tree* (1947). He is author also of the commentaries *English Journey* (1934) and *Out of the People* (1941); the autobiographical *Rain Upon Gadshill* (1939); and the critical works *The English Comic Characters* (1925), *The English Novel* (1927), *George Meredith* (1926) and *Peacock* (1927) in the *English Men of Letters* series.

Priestley, Joseph. b. at Fieldhead, near Leeds, Yorkshire, England, March 13, 1733; d. at Northumberland, Pa., Feb. 6, 1804. An English clergyman and natural philosopher, especially celebrated as the discoverer of oxygen. He was the son of a nonconformist cloth-dresser, and was educated at a Dissenters' academy at Daventry. In 1755 he took charge of a small congregation at Needham Market, Suffolk, which was subsidized by both Independents and Presbyterians. In 1761 he was tutor in an academy at Warrington. In 1767 he published the *History of Electricity*, in which "Priestley rings" left on metal by an electrical discharge were explained and an attempt was made to explain the discharge phenomena of a Leyden jar. He adopted Socinian views on religion, and materialistic views on philosophy; Jeremy Bentham took his idea of morality aiming at "the greatest happiness of the greatest number" from Priestley's *Essay on the First Principles of Government* (1768). At this time began his researches in "different kinds of air." About 1772 he became literary companion to William Petty (then Lord Shelburne and later 1st Marquis of Lansdowne), and traveled with him in Holland and Germany, returning to Paris in 1774. In 1774 he announced his discovery of "dephlogisticated air," now called oxygen (after Lavoisier further investigated the gas and recognized in it the significance that Priestley had missed). Although he remained an adherent of the phlogiston theory, he made many important chemical discoveries, isolating such gases as nitrous oxide, carbon monoxide, and ammonia, and decomposing ammonia by electrical means. In 1780 he removed to Birmingham, and became associated with Matthew Boulton, James Watt, and Erasmus Darwin, grandfather of Charles Darwin. He published several works on religion in this period, one of them, *History of the Corruption of Christianity* (1782), being burned (1785) by order of the authorities. For sympathizing with the French Revolution (he had been made a citizen of the French republic) he was attacked in 1791 by a mob, his house was broken into and burned, and his manuscripts and instruments destroyed. In 1794 he removed to America, where he continued his religious writings, his scientific experiments, and his philosophic controversies.

Prig (prig), **Betsey.** A nurse, the friend and "frequent pardner" of Sairey Gamp, in Dickens's *Martin Chuzzlewit.* Their quarrel (originating in Betsey's doubt as to the actual flesh-and-blood existence of Sairey Gamp's friend "Mrs. Harris") is one of the famous comic scenes of English literature.

Primas (prī'măs). fl. 12th century. A scholar and poet, supposed to have come from Orléans, in France. He is the presumed author of some of the 12th- and 13th-century Goliardic verse.

Primrose (prim'rōz), **Charles.** The vicar of Wakefield in Oliver Goldsmith's tale of that name. He is a sincere, humane, and simple-minded man, who preserves his modesty and nobility through hardship and good fortune.

Primrose, Olivia. The daughter of the vicar in Oliver Goldsmith's *Vicar of Wakefield.*

Primrose League. In Great Britain, a league or combination of persons pledged to principles of Conservatism as represented by Benjamin Disraeli, Earl of Beaconsfield, and opposed to the "revolutionary tendencies of radicalism." The object of the league is declared to be "the maintenance of religion, of the constitution of the realm, and of the imperial ascendancy of Great Britain." The scheme of the organization was first discussed at the Carlton Club in October, 1883, and the actual league made its first public appearance at a grand banquet at Freemasons' Tavern in London a few weeks later. The organization of the league is by "habitations" or clubs; these obey the instructions of the Grand Council, and annually send delegates to the Grand Habitation, which is held at London on or near the 19th of April, the anniversary of Disraeli's death. A noteworthy feature is the enrollment of women, or "dames," who take an active part in all the business of the association, having an executive committee and a fund of their own. The name and the symbol of the league are derived from Disraeli's favorite flower.

primrose path. A gay and easy way to evil and hell; used by Ophelia (to Laertes) in Shakespeare's *Hamlet* (I.iii), in contrast to the difficult way to heaven:

Do not as some ungracious pastors do,
Show me the steep and thorny way to heaven,
Whiles, like a puff'd and reckless libertine,
Himself the primrose path of dalliance treads
And recks not his own rede.

Prince Dorus (dō'rus). A poem by Charles Lamb, published in 1811.

Prince Henry's Company. See **Lord Admiral's Men.**

Prince Hohensteil-Schwangau (hō'ĕn.shtīl.shväng'-ou). A poem (1871) by Robert Browning, written in the form of a dramatic monologue, in which the speaker is the Prince (intended by Browning to represent Napoleon III). The poem is considered by some scholars to have been begun around 1859, but much of it was probably written (or rewritten) during the months immediately preceding publication, after the collapse of Napoleon III's Second Empire in 1870. It contains many references to contemporary affairs and people which are obscure to the modern reader; the Prince is shown as somewhat of an opportunist, basing his policies on the expediency of the moment.

Prince of Bohemia (bō.hē'mi.ą). See **Florizel.**

Prince of Verona (vę.rō'ną). See **Escalus.**

Prince's Progress, The. The title poem of a volume of poetry by Christina Rossetti, published in 1866. It is an allegorical poem, describing the journey of a Prince to meet his bride. However, he succumbs to various temptations along the way, and when he reaches his love, he finds her dead.

Princess, The. A narrative poem by Alfred Tennyson, published in 1847. It contains such familiar lyrics as "Sweet and low," "The splendour falls on castle walls," "Tears, idle tears," and "Home they brought her warrior dead."

Princess Casamassima (kas"i.mą.sē'mą), **The.** A novel (1886) by Henry James.

Princesse de Clèves (praṅ.ses dę klev), **La.** A novel by the Countess de la Fayette, published in 1677. The scene is placed in the court of Henry II, but the chief characters are the author herself, her husband, François de la Rochefoucauld, and others of her contemporaries.

Princess Ida, or Castle Adamant (ī'dą; ad'ą.mant). An operetta in three acts by Sir Arthur Sullivan, with a libretto by W. S. Gilbert, produced in 1884. It is a burlesque of Alfred Tennyson's *The Princess.*

Princess of Cleve (klēv), **The.** A tragedy by Nathaniel Lee, produced in 1681 and printed in 1689. It was founded on the Countess de la Fayette's romance.

Princess of France. In Shakespeare's *Love's Labour's Lost,* a visitor to the "little Academe" of the King of Navarre. The King falls in love with her, and thus breaks his vow to deny love for three years.

Princess Street. The principal street of Edinburgh, Scotland.

Principia (prin.sip'i.ą). [Full title, **Philosophiae Naturalis Principia Mathematica,** meaning "The Mathematical Principles of Natural Philosophy."] A work by Sir Isaac Newton, composed chiefly in 1685–86, presented to the Royal Society on April 28, 1686, and first published (in Latin) in 1687 (edited by Edmund Halley). The second edition (1713) was edited by Roger Cotes. It is generally considered to have ushered in the modern age in astronomy, mechanics, and mathematical physics.

Pringle (pring'gl), **Thomas.** b. at Blaiklaw, in Teviotdale, Scotland, Jan. 5, 1789; d. at London, Dec. 5, 1834. A Scottish poet, editor, librarian, and abolitionist. He edited the *Edinburgh Monthly Magazine*, the *Edinburgh Star*, a newspaper, and Constable's *Edinburgh Magazine*, and at Capetown (1820 *et seq.*) the *South African Journal* and the *South African Commercial Advertiser*, until they were suppressed. He returned (1826) to London, where he became prominent in the Anti-Slavery Society. Author of *Ephemerides* (1828), *African Sketches* (1834, a volume of poems including the "Narrative of his Residence in South Africa"). His lyrics *Emigrant's Farewell* (written on leaving England) and *Afar in the Desert*, and the narrative poem *The Bechuana Boy*, are considered his best pieces.

Pringle-Pattison (pring'gl.pat'i.son), **Andrew Seth.** See **Seth, Andrew.**

Prior (prī'or), **Matthew.** b. probably in East Dorset, July 21, 1664; d. at Wimpole (Robert Harley's country seat), Cambridgeshire, Sept. 8, 1721. An English poet and diplomat. He was educated at Westminster under Dr. Richard Busby, and graduated from Cambridge (St. John's College) in 1686. In 1698 he was secretary to William Bentinck, 1st Earl of Portland, in his embassy to France. In 1699 he succeeded John Locke as commissioner of trade and plantations, and became undersecretary of state. In 1701 he was a member of Parliament for East Grinstead. He went as ambassador to Paris in 1712, was the principal negotiator (1713) of the Treaty of Utrecht, which was known derisively as "Matt's Peace," was imprisoned in England (1715–17) during the triumph of the Whigs, and passed most of the rest of his life at his home, Down Hall in Essex, a country house that had been given him by his friend and patron, Robert Harley. He was the author, with his friend Charles Montagu (later Earl of Halifax), of the *Story of the Country-Mouse and the City-Mouse* (1687; a parody on Dryden's *Hind and Panther*). He collected his poems, and they were published in 1709 under the title *Poems on Several Occasions*. While imprisoned, he wrote (1716) *Alma: or the Progress of the Mind.* An epic poem, *Solomon on the Vanity of the World*, was published in 1718. In 1740 two volumes of his poems were published, with (alleged) memoirs, and some of his best poems which had not been printed before. His light verse is noted for its polished grace; he is known also as a wit and epigrammatist. Biographies of Prior have been written by Francis Bickley (1914) and L. G. Wickham Legg (1921).

Prioress's Tale, The. One of Chaucer's *Canterbury Tales*. Narrated by Madame Eglentyne (or Eglantine), it is a retelling of the medieval legend of the Christian child supposed to have been killed by Jews. The child's body is found still singing *O Alma redemptoris*, as he loved to do when he lived, and he relates how the Virgin came to him as he died, bade him continue to sing, and laid a grain upon his tongue saying that when this was removed he could come to Heaven. A monk removes the grain and the child gives up the ghost. (In most versions of this legend the child is miraculously restored to life; Chaucer's ending may go back to the tale of Hugh of Lincoln.) This is a miracle story characteristic of the period, full of tenderness and pathos, and has been called one of Chaucer's best technical achievements (its form is rhyme royal rather than

the more usual couplets of *The Canterbury Tales*). That the Jews performed ritual murders was widely believed, and thus the violence of feeling against the "cursed Jewes" is not so uncharacteristic as it might seem of the gentle prioress. She is described in the Prologue as amiable, elegantly educated and dressed, extremely dainty when she eats, perhaps a bit affected:

> Ful wel she song the service divyne,
> Entuned in hir nose ful semely;
> And Frensh she spak ful faire and fetisly,
> After the scole of Stratford atte Bowe,
> For Frensh of Paris was to hir unknowe.

Above all, she is most soft-hearted:

> She was so charitable and so pitous,
> She wolde wepe, if that she sawe a mous
> Caught in a trappe, if it were deed or bledde.

Priscian (prish'an). [Full Latin name, **Priscianus Caesariensis.**] b. probably at Caesarea, in Mauretania; fl. at Constantinople, c500 A.D. A Latin grammarian. His most famous work is *Institutiones grammaticae*, an 18-book work so popular in the Middle Ages that some 1,000 manuscript versions still exist.

Prisoner of Chillon (shi.lon', shil'on), **The.** A poem by Lord Byron, published in 1816, inspired by the imprisonment of François de Bonnivard in the Castle of Chillon in Switzerland.

Prisoner of Zenda (zen'da), **The.** A novel by Anthony Hope (Hawkins), published in 1894. Rudolf Rassendyl is an English gentleman traveling in Ruritania, who meets the king of that land and finds himself to be identical with the king in appearance. He impersonates the king, and triumphs over a group of villainous conspirators who have plotted a *coup d'état* to remove him from the throne. He falls in love with the Princess Flavia and has a chance to keep the throne and marry her, but he will not take advantage of his position, and leaves the country, his great and courageous deed unknown to any except Flavia and the king himself.

Pritchard (prich'ard), **Hannah.** [Maiden name, **Vaughan.**] b. 1711; d. at Bath, England, in August, 1768. An English actress. She was noted both in tragedy and in comedy, and was Mrs. Siddons's greatest predecessor in the characters of Lady Macbeth and Queen Katharine. She excelled also in characters of intrigue and gaiety, as Lady Betty Modish and Lady Towneley.

Pritchett (prich'et), **V. S.** [Full name, **Victor Sawdon Pritchett.**] b. at Ipswich, Suffolk, England, Dec. 16, 1900—. An English short-story writer and critic. Author of *Marching Spain* (1928), *Clare Drummer* (1929), *The Spanish Virgin* (1930), *Dead Man Leading* (1937), *In My Good Books* (1942), *It May Never Happen* (1945), and *The Living Novel* (1946).

Private Papers of Henry Ryecroft (hen'ri rī'kroft), **The.** A novel by George Gissing, published in 1903. It is largely autobiographical and deals with the problems of a struggling author.

Procne (prok'nē). In Greek legend, the daughter of Pandion, sister of Philomela, and wife of Tereus, by whom she became the mother of Itys. She was turned into a swallow.

Procris (prō′kris). In Greek legend, the wife of Cephalus (a hero of Attica), by whom she was accidentally slain. She was accustomed to overhearing him call upon a breeze to cool him, and thinking it the name of a lover, jealously spied on him. Cephalus, noticing the movement of the bushes which hid her, threw his spear at what he thought was some wild beast, and thus killed his wife.

Procrustes (prō̜.krus′tēz). In Greek legend, a famous Attic robber. He had a bed (named from him the Procrustean bed) upon which his prisoners were tortured: those who were too short he stretched to fit it, and those who were too tall had their limbs cut to the proper length. He was killed by Theseus.

Procter (prok′tèr), **Adelaide Ann.** [Pseudonym, **Mary Berwick.**] b. at London, Oct. 30, 1825; d. there, Feb. 2, 1864. An English poet; daughter of Bryan Waller Procter (Barry Cornwall). She wrote *Legends and Lyrics* (1858–60), which includes "The Lost Chord" (set to music by Sir Arthur Sullivan), and many well-known hymns.

Procter, Bryan Waller. [Pseudonym, **Barry Cornwall.**] b. at Leeds, England, Nov. 21, 1787; d. at London, Oct. 5, 1874. An English poet; father of Adelaide Ann Procter. He was educated at Harrow, and was a schoolmate of Lord Byron and Sir Robert Peel. In 1807 he went to London to study law. In 1820 he began writing under the pseudonym Barry Cornwall, and in 1831 was called to the bar. From 1832 to 1861 he was commissioner of lunacy. He wrote *Dramatic Scenes and Other Poems* (1819), *A Sicilian Story* (1821), *Mirandola* (1821; performed at Covent Garden in 1821), *Flood of Thessaly* (1823), *Effigies Poetica* (1824), *English Songs* (1832), and memoirs of Edmund Kean (1835), Charles Lamb (1866), Ben Jonson (1838), and Shakespeare (1843).

Proculeius (prō.kū̜.lē′us). In Shakespeare's *Antony and Cleopatra*, a friend of Octavius. He is sent to capture Cleopatra at the end of the play, but is frustrated in his purpose when she kills herself.

prodigal son, the. The subject, taken from Luke, xv. 11–32, of many plays written in the mid-16th century. The influence of the French neoclassic writers on early Tudor dramatists is indicated by the popularity of this theme.

proem (prō′em). A preface; introduction; preamble; preliminary observations prefixed to a book or writing.

> In the proheim off hys notabile boke.
> ("Romance of Partenay," in *E.E.T.S.*)

> So glozed the tempter, and his proem tuned.
> (Milton, *Paradise Lost.*)

> Thus much may serve by way of proem;
> Proceed we therefore to our poem.
> (Swift, *Death of Dr. Swift.*)

> The proeme, or preamble, is often called in to help the construction of an act of parliament.
> (Blackstone, *Com.*, I., Int.)

Professor, The. A novel by Charlotte Brontë, published in 1857, after her death. The story is the same one that the writer was to deal with later in *Villette* (the book was published posthumously, but is known to have been written at a relatively early date in the author's career). A young schoolmaster, William Crimsworth, goes to Brussels to teach in a girls' school. There he meets and falls in love with an Anglo-Swiss girl who does not at once return his affection, but is gradually won over by his personality and strength of character.

Profligate, The. A tragedy (1887) by Arthur Wing Pinero.

Progress of Julius, The. A novel by Daphne Du Maurier, published in 1933.

Progress of Poetry, The. A long poem (1754, but not published until 1759) by Thomas Gray. In the form of a Pindaric ode, it traces the development of poetry from Greece to Gray's own day in England. Most critics, from Dr. Johnson onward, considered that he used a superfluity of classical allusions and dazzling images to illustrate his theme.

prolegomenon (prō.le.gom′ę.non). A preliminary observation: chiefly used in the plural, and applied to an introductory discourse prefixed to a book or treatise.

> " 'Tis a pithy prolegomenon," quoth I—and so read on.   (Sterne, *Tristram Shandy.*)

> The mention of the Venetian scholia leads us at once to the Homeric controversy; for the immortal Prolegomena of Wolf appeared a few years after Villoison's publication.
> (*Encyclopaedia Britannica.*)

prolepsis (prō̜.lep′sis). **1.** In rhetoric: **a.** A name sometimes applied to the use of an adjective (or a noun) as objective predicate as if implying an anticipation of the result of the verb's action. **b.** A figure consisting in anticipation of an opponent's objections and arguments in order to preclude his use of them, answer them in advance, or prepare the reader to receive them unfavorably. This figure is most frequently used in the exordium. It is also called **procatalepsis.**
2. An error in chronology, consisting in dating an event before the actual time of its occurrence; an anachronism. "Mr. Errington, called Lord Errington in the dispatches, by a prolepsis we suppose." (*The American.*)

prologue, prolog (prō′log). **1.** The preface or introduction to a discourse or performance; specifically, a discourse or poem spoken before a dramatic performance or play begins; hence, that which precedes or leads up to any act or event.

> Jerom in hise twei prologis on Matheu seith this.
> (Wycliffe, *Prolog* (on Matthew).)

> Think'st thou that mirth and vain delights,
> High feed, and shadow-short'ning nights, . . .
> Are proper prologues to a crown?
> (Quarles, *Emblems.*)

> How this vile World is chang'd! In former Days Prologues were serious Speeches before Plays.
> (Congreve, *Old Batchelor*, Prol.)

> I'll read you the whole, from beginning to end, with the prologue and epilogue, and allow time for the music between the acts.
> (Sheridan, *The Critic*, I. i.)

2. The speaker of a prologue on the stage.

> It is not the fashion to see the lady the epilogue; but it is no more unhandsome than to see the lord the prologue.   (Shak., *As You Like It*, Epil.)

ḏ, d or j; ş, s or sh; ṯ, t or ch; ẕ, z or zh; o, F. cloche; ü, F. menu; ċh, Sc. loch; ṅ, F. bonbon.

The duke is entering; set your faces right,
And bow like country prologues.
(Fletcher (and another), *Noble Gentleman*, III.ii.)

Prometheus (prọ.mē′thẹ.us). In Greek mythology, the son of Iapetus and the ocean nymph Clymene, celebrated as the benefactor of mankind. For deceit practiced upon him by Prometheus in a sacrifice, Zeus denied to man the use of fire; but Prometheus stole it from heaven and brought it to earth in a hollow reed. For this he was chained, by order of Zeus, on a mountain (Caucasus), where daily his liver (which grew again at night) was consumed by an eagle. He was freed by Hercules. To counterbalance the acquisition of fire, Zeus sent woman to confuse mankind, giving Pandora, the first mortal woman, to Prometheus's brother, Epimetheus, for wife. Prometheus warned his brother against the gift, but Epimetheus married her anyway. In a late myth Prometheus is credited with having created mankind.

Prometheus Bound. A tragedy by Aeschylus, of uncertain date. Prometheus, bound to the rocks by order of Zeus for stealing fire from heaven, resists all efforts to subdue his will and purpose, bids defiance to the father of the gods, and disappears in an appalling tempest. It is one of a trilogy, of which the other parts, *Prometheus Unbound* and *Prometheus the Fire-bringer*, have been lost. Elizabeth Barrett Browning published a poetical translation in 1833.

Prometheus Unbound. A lyrical drama by Percy Bysshe Shelley, published in 1820, in which a majestic, courageous, and pure Prometheus is chained to the rock and eternally tortured by the command of Jupiter, symbolic of a vengeful, despotic Deity. Jupiter is overthrown through the power of Prometheus's purity and innate love, and removed from the throne by Demogorgon, the symbol of the primal power of the universe. A golden age ruled by the power of love results, in which each man is free: "king over himself; just, gentle, wise, but man."

Promise. A novel by Ethel Sidgwick, published in 1910.

Promos and Cassandra (prō′mos; kạ.san′drạ). A play by George Whetstone, printed in 1578, but possibly never acted. Shakespeare took the story of *Measure for Measure* from this play, which is in two parts, and which was in turn taken from one of Cinthio's novels. In 1582 Whetstone translated it as a prose novel.

Promptorium Parvulorum, sive Clericorum (promptō′ri.um pär.vụ.lō′rum sī′vē kler.i.kō′rum). An English-Latin dictionary, said to have been the first in use. *Promptorium* should properly be *promptuarium* ("storehouse"), and is so spelled by Wynkyn de Worde in his edition *Promptuarium Parvulorum Clericorum* (1510). The words were collected from various authors by Fratre Galfridus (Geoffrey), called Grammaticus, a preaching friar, a "recluse of Bishop Lynne" in Norfolk. There are several manuscripts, and, besides Wynkyn de Worde, Richard Pynson printed it in 1499 and Julian Notary in 1508.

propaganda. Any kind of institution or organization for propagating a new doctrine or system of doctrines, or for proselyting.

The first attempts at a propaganda of liberty, and the first attempts at a propaganda of nationality, were marked by great excesses and great mistakes. (Stubbs, *Medieval and Modern History*.)

Propertius (prọ.pėr′shus), **Sextus.** b. at Assisi, Italy, c50 B.C.; d. after 16 B.C. A Roman elegiac poet, a friend of Maecenas, Vergil, and Ovid. His poems are largely amatory, celebrating his mistress Cynthia (whose real name was Hostia).

Prophetess, The. A play by John Fletcher and Philip Massinger, licensed in 1622 and printed in 1647.

proscenium (prọ.sē′ni.um). **1.** In the ancient theater, the stage before the scene or back wall.

During his time, from the Proscenium ta'en,
Thalia and Melpomene both vanish'd.
(Colman, *Poetical Vagaries*.)

In Asia Minor some of the theatres have their proscenia adorned with niches and columns, and friezes of great richness.
(J. Fergusson, *History of Architecture*.)

2. In the modern theater, that part of the house which lies between the curtain or drop scene and the orchestra: often used also to mean the curtain and the arch or framework which holds it.

prose. 1. The ordinary written or spoken language of man; language not conformed to poetical measure, as opposed to verse or metrical composition.

"Sire, at o word, thou shalt no lenger ryme." . . .
"I wol yow telle a litel thyng in prose
That oghte liken yow, as I suppose."
(Chaucer, Prol. to *Tale of Melibeus*.)

              Prompt eloquence
Flow'd from their lips, in prose or numerous verse.
(Milton, *P. L.*)

Well, on the whole, plain prose must be my fate: . . .
I'll e'en leave verses to the boys at school.
(Pope, *Imit. of Horace*.)

Prose, however fervid and emotional it may become, must always be directed, or seem to be directed, by the reins of logic. (*Encyc. Brit.*)

Hence—**2.** Commonplace ideas or discourse. (Goodrich.)
3. In liturgics, a hymn sung after the gradual, originating from a practice of setting words to the jubilatio of the alleluia. Such hymns were originally either in the vernacular or in rimed Latin, with rhythms depending, as in modern verse, upon the accent: hence they were called *prosae*, proses, in distinction from *versus*, verses, this latter term being applied only to poetry written in meters depending on quantity as in the ancient classic poets.

Hymns or proses full of idolatry.
(Harmar, tr. of *Beza* (1587).)

On all higher festivals, besides this sequence, the rhythm called the prose, which generally consisted of between twenty and thirty verses, was likewise chanted. (Rock, *Church of our Fathers*.)

Proserpine (prǭ.sėr'pi.nẹ, pros'ėr.pīn). Roman form of **Persephone.**

prosody (pros'ǭ.di). The science of the quantity of syllables and of pronunciation as affecting versification; in a wider sense, metrics, or the elements of metrics, considered as a part of grammar.

Prosody and orthography are not parts of grammar, but diffused like the blood and spirits through the whole. (Ben Jonson, *English Grammar.*)

Prosperity. A poem attributed by William Morris to Chaucer. W. W. Skeat, however, refused to accept it in the canon.

Prospero (pros'pẹ.rō). In Shakespeare's *Tempest,* the rightful Duke of Milan. He is represented as a wise and good magician (not a necromancer or wizard) living in exile on an island with his daughter Miranda. Through his use of magic he makes Ferdinand fall in love with Miranda and prevents Caliban, Stephano, and Trinculo from murdering him. Alonso, the King of Naples, Antonio, the usurping Duke of Milan, and the evil Sebastian are humbled by him, and forgiven when they repent their crimes. He thereupon renounces his magic: "But this rough magic I here abjure" (V.i). This is said after the beautiful speech in which he dissolves the masque presented before the lovers, Ferdinand and Miranda: "These our actors . . . were all spirits and Are melted into air; . . . the great globe itself, Yea, all which it inherit, shall dissolve, And, . . . Leave not a rack behind. We are such stuff As dreams are made on, and our little life Is rounded with a sleep" (IV.i). It has been suggested by some Shakespeare scholars, somewhat poetically perhaps, that this speech marks a valedictory to Shakespeare's career, and that Shakespeare is here also bidding farewell to his art.

Pross (pros), **Solomon.** [Alias **John Barsad.**] A spy and thorough villain in Dickens's novel *A Tale of Two Cities.* He robs his sister, and later becomes a turnkey in a Paris prison.

protagonist (prō.tag'ō.nist). In the Greek drama, the leading character or actor in a play; hence, in general, any leading character.

'Tis charged upon me that I make debauched persons (such as they say my Astrologer and Gamester are) my protagonists, or the chief persons of the drama.
(Dryden, *Mock Astrologer,* Preface.)

Protesilaus (prǭ.tes.i.lā'us). In Greek legend, the first Greek slain in the Trojan War.

Proteus (prō'tẹ.us, prō'tūs). In classical mythology, a sea god, the son of Oceanus and Tethys, who had the power of assuming different shapes. If caught, however, and held fast through all his many changes until he reassumed his own shape, he was compelled to answer questions. In one legend, Menelaus, on his return from Troy, surprised Proteus and held him fast until Proteus revealed to him how to return home.

Proteus. In Shakespeare's *Two Gentlemen of Verona,* one of the "two gentlemen." He is faithless to Julia, his betrothed, and betrays his friend, Valentine, but eventually repents and is happily wedded to Julia at the end of the play.

Prothalamion (prō.thạ.lā'mi.ǫn). A "spousal verse" by Edmund Spenser, published under this name in 1596. It was written on the occasion of the marriage on the same day of Lady Katherine and Lady Elizabeth Somerset, the two daughters of the Earl of Worcester, to Henry Guilford and William Petre.

Prothero (proᴛʜ'ẹ.rō), **George Walter.** b. in Wiltshire, England, Oct. 14, 1848; d. at London, July 10, 1922. An English historian, writer, and editor; brother of Rowland Edmund Prothero. He was university lecturer in history and tutor at King's College, Cambridge (1876–94), professor of history at the University of Edinburgh (1894–99), and lecturer at Cambridge in 1903. In 1899 he succeeded his brother as editor of the *Quarterly Review.* He was coeditor (1901–12) of the *Cambridge Modern History.* Among his publications are *Life and Times of Simon de Montfort* (1877), *Memoir of Henry Bradshaw* (1889), and *British History Reader* (1898).

Prothero, Rowland Edmund. [Title, 1st Baron **Ernle.**] b. at Clifton on Teme, Worcestershire, England, Sept. 6, 1852; d. near Wantage, Berkshire, England, July 1, 1937. An English writer; brother of George Walter Prothero. He was editor of the *Quarterly Review* (1894–99). He was a member of Parliament (1914–19) and president of the Board of Agriculture and Fisheries (1916–19) during World War I. Among his works are *Life and Correspondence of Dean Stanley* (1893; with G. G. Bradley), *Letters and Journals of Lord Byron* (1898–1901), *The Psalms in Human Life* (1903), *Letters of Richard Ford* (1905), *The Pleasant Land of France* (1908), and others.

prototype (prō'tǭ.tīp). A primitive form; an original or model after which anything is formed; the pattern of anything to be engraved, cast, etc.; an exemplar; an archetype.

In many respects [he] deserves to be enniched, as a prototype for all writers, of voluminous works at least. (Sterne, *Tristram Shandy.*)

The square or circular altar, or place of worship, may easily be considered as the prototype of the Sikra surrounded by cells of the Jains.
(J. Fergusson, *History of Indian Architecture.*)

Proudfute (proud'fût), **Magdalen.** In Sir Walter Scott's novel *The Fair Maid of Perth,* the widow of Oliver Proudfute, aroused by her anger at his murder to a much grander nature.

Proudfute, Oliver. In Sir Walter Scott's novel *The Fair Maid of Perth,* a maker of ladies' hats, murdered by mistake when he dons the garb of an acquaintance known for his strength and courage (neither of which is possessed by Proudfute, but to both of which he pretends).

Proudie (prou'di), **Bishop.** In Trollope's Barchester series of novels, the Bishop of Barchester, married to an active and socially troublesome wife.

Proust (prōst), **Marcel.** b. at Paris, July 10, 1871; d. there, Nov. 18, 1922. A French novelist. Author of *À la recherche du temps perdu* (1913–27; 13 to 16 vols., according to the edition; Eng. trans., *Remembrance of Things Past,* 1922–32), his chief work, *Les Plaisirs et les Jours* (1896; Eng. trans., *Pleasures and Regrets,* 1949), and *Pastiches et Mélanges* (1919). Translator of Ruskin's *The Bible*

---

d̯, d or j; ṣ, s or sh; ṭ, t or ch; ẓ, z or zh; o, F. cloche; ü, F. menu; ċh, Sc. loch; ṅ, F. bonbon.

of Amiens (1904) and *Sesame and Lilies* (1906). An invalid from asthma from the age of nine, he was brought up in ease and luxury by his wealthy father. As a young man he frequented the salons of Mme. Arman de Caillavet and others and became known as a dilettante; his first book, published with a preface by Anatole France, bore the marks of the "decadentism" of the period. Following the deaths of his father (1904) and his mother (1905), he retired from society and began work on what was originally planned as a three-volume novel; over the years this developed into the "picture of the death of a society," *À la recherche du temps perdu*. Working in a cork-lined chamber, mostly at night, rarely seeing even his most intimate friends, he labored constantly in what he considered a race against death. The novel had not been completed when he died. A new, three-volume novel, *Jean Santeuil*, reconstructed by an editor from Proust's manuscripts and dating from 1899, was published in 1951.

Prout (prout), **Father.** Pseudonym of **Mahony, Francis.**

proverb. **1.** A short pithy sentence, often repeated colloquially, expressing a well-known truth or a common fact ascertained by experience or observation; a popular saying which briefly and forcibly expresses some practical precept; an adage; a wise saw: often set forth in the guise of metaphor and in the form of rhyme, and sometimes alliterative.

> And trewe is the proverbe that the wise man seith, that "who is fer from his iye is soone foryeten." ("Merlin," in *E. E. T. S.*)

> They said they were an-hungry; sigh'd forth proverbs,
> That hunger broke stone walls, that dogs must eat,
> That meat was made for mouths.
> (Shak., *Cor.*, I.i.)

> What is a proverb but the experience and observation of several ages gathered and summed up into one expression? (South, *Sermons*.)

> The pithy quaintness of old Howell has admirably described the ingredients of an exquisite proverb to be sense, shortness, and salt.
> (I. D'Israeli, *Curios. of Lit.*)

2. A byword; a reproach; an object of scorn or derision.

> I will deliver them . . . to be a reproach and a proverb, a taunt and a curse, in all places whither I shall drive them. (Jer. xxiv. 9.)

> Salisbury was foolish to a proverb.
> (Macaulay, *Hist. Eng.*)

3. In the Scriptures, an enigmatical utterance; a mysterious or oracular saying that requires interpretation.

> To understand a proverb, and the interpretation; the words of the wise, and their dark sayings.
> (Prov. i. 6.)

4. *pl.* [*cap.*] One of the books of the Old Testament, following the Book of Psalms. The full title is Proverbs of Solomon (i. 1). It is a collection of the sayings of the sages of Israel, taking its full title from the chief among them, though it is by no means certain that he is the author of a majority of

them. The original meaning of *mashal*, the Hebrew word translated "proverb," seems to be "a comparison." The term is sometimes translated "parable" in our English Bible; but, as such comparisons were commonly made in the East by short and pithy sayings, the word came to be applied to these chiefly, though not exclusively. They formed one of the most characteristic features of Eastern literature.

5. A dramatic composition in which some proverb or popular saying is taken as the foundation of the plot. Good examples are—"A Door must be either Open or Shut" (Alfred de Musset); "Still Water Runs Deep" (Dion Boucicault). When such dramas are extemporized, as in private theatricals, the proverb employed is often withheld, to be guessed by the audience after the representation.

Proverbial Philosophy. A didactic work in blank verse by M. F. Tupper, published in four series (1839–76).

Proverbs of Alfred. A collection of wise sayings, dating from the Old English period, and long associated with King Alfred. Scholars now generally believe, however, that little if anything in it is attributable to Alfred, and that the collection derived its name simply from the fact that Alfred's name was synonymous with wisdom in the minds of the generations immediately following him.

provincialism. A word or manner of speaking peculiar to a province; a local or dialectal term or expression.

> The inestimable treasure which lies hidden in the ancient inscriptions might be of singular service, particularly in explaining the provincialisms.
> (H. Marsh, translation of *Michaelis*, 1793.)

Provis (prō'vis). See **Magwitch, Abel.**

Provoked Husband, The. A comedy begun by Sir John Vanbrugh, who wrote nearly four acts before his death (1726), under the title *A Journey to London*. It was finished by Colley Cibber, and produced in 1728.

Provoked Wife, The. A comedy by Sir John Vanbrugh, produced in 1697. It was revived in 1726, the year of his death.

Provost. In Shakespeare's *Measure for Measure*, the prison custodian. He sympathizes with Claudio and agrees to execute Barnardine in his stead, but finally sends Angelo the head of another prisoner who has already died.

Prudence (prō'dẹns). See under **Melibeus, The Tale of.**

Prue (prö), **Miss.** In William Congreve's play *Love for Love*, a romping awkward country girl with a well-developed taste for a lover.

Prufrock (prö'frok). [Full title, **Prufrock and Other Observations.**] A collection of poems by T. S. Eliot, published in 1917. It contains "The Love Song of J. Alfred Prufrock," "Portrait of a Lady," and "Mr. Apollinax."

Pry (prī), **Paul.** The title character of a comedy (1825) by John Poole. His name has become a synonym for an officious meddler.

Pryce (prīs), **Richard.** b. at Boulogne, France, 1864; d. at London, 1942. An English novelist and dramatist. Author of *An Evil Spirit* (1887), *The*

Ugly Story of Miss Wetherby (1889), *Just Impediment* (1890), *Miss Maxwell's Affections* (1891), *Elementary Jane* (1897), *Jezebel* (1900), *The Successor* (1904), *Christopher* (1911), *Time and the Woman* (1913), *David Penstephen* (1915), *The Statue in the Wood* (1918), *Romance and Jane Weston* (1924), and *Morgan's Yard* (1932), novels; *Little Mrs. Cummin* and *The Visit* (both 1910), plays; *Helen With the High Hand* (1914), *The Old House* (1920), *Thunder on the Left* (1928), and *Frolic Wind* (1935), plays adapted from novels. With Frederick Fenn, he was coauthor of the plays *A Scarlet Flower* (1903), *Saturday to Monday* (1904), *Op-o'-Me-Thumb* (1904), *His Child* (1906), and *The Love Child* (1921).

Prynne (prin), **William.** b. at Swainswick, near Bath, England, 1600; d. at London, Oct. 24, 1669. An English Presbyterian lawyer, pamphleteer, and statesman. He graduated at Oxford in 1621, entered Lincoln's Inn in the same year, and was afterward called to the bar. In 1633 he published *Histriomastix,* an attack on actors and the stage. For indirectly criticizing the king and queen in this book he was sentenced (1634) by the Star Chamber to imprisonment, fined 5,000 pounds, expelled from his profession, degraded from his university degree, and set in the pillory, where he lost both his ears. He continued his writing from prison and in 1637 lost the stumps of his ears and was branded with S.L., for "seditious libeler," on both cheeks; he preferred to think of the letters as meaning "stigmata laudis," Laud's stigmata, blaming the Anglican prelate for his troubles. In 1640 he was released by the Long Parliament. In 1643 he entered upon the prosecution of Archbishop Laud. His position led him into conflict with Presbyterians and Independents, with Commonwealth advocates and with the army, and with John Milton, whose ideas on divorce he attacked and who answered him in *Colasterion.* On Nov. 7, 1648, he obtained a seat in the House of Commons. He at once took the part of the king, and was included in Pride's Purge (Dec. 6, 1648). He was arrested by John Bradshaw June 30, 1650, and imprisoned. He was released Feb. 18, 1653. He was appointed by Charles II keeper of the records in the Tower. In 1666–70 he published the *Vindication of the Ecclesiastical Jurisdiction of the English Kings.*

psalm (säm). A sacred poem or song, especially one in which expressions of praise and thanksgiving are prominent: usually restricted either to those contained in the Book of Psalms, or to the versifications of these composed for the use of churches, as the Psalms of Tate and Brady, of Watts, etc.

"This Dragon of Dissait, that thou defly hath fourmet:"
So sethe in the sauter the Salme to the end.
                    ("Destruction of Troy," in *E.E.T.S.*)

Euen the name Psalmes will speake for mee, which, being interpreted, is nothing but songes.
                    (Sir P. Sidney, *Apology for Poetrie.*)

They do no more adhere and keep place together than the Hundredth Psalm to the tune of "Green Sleeves." (Shakespeare, *Merry Wives of Windsor.*)

The great organ . . . rolling thro' the court
A long melodious thunder to the sound
Of solemn psalms, and silver litanies.
                    (Tennyson, *Princess.*)

Psalms. [Also, **The Book of Psalms;** sometimes called **Psalter.**] A book of the Old Testament which contains 150 psalms and hymns. The authorship of a large number of the psalms is ascribed traditionally to David. Many of them, however, are supposed to date from the time of the exile or later. The name "Psalter" is usually restricted to those versions or of compends from it which are arranged especially for the services of the church. The translation of the Psalter in the Book of Common Prayer is not that of the Authorized Version, but that of the earlier version of Coverdale's Bible.

Pseudodoxia Epidemica, or an Enquiry into Vulgar Errors (sö.dọ.dok′si.ạ ep.i.dem′i.kạ). [Often called **Vulgar Errors.**] A work by Sir Thomas Browne, published in 1646. Browne here confutes many errors of popular belief. The work is based largely on personal observations and experiments.

pseudonym (sū′dọ.nim). A false name; especially, a fictitious name assumed by an author in order to conceal or veil his identity.

The [Brontë] sisters adopted the pseudonyms Currer, Ellis, and Acton Bell, corresponding to their initials. (L. Stephen, *Dict. National Biog.*)

Psyche (sī′kē). In Greek mythology, a mortal maiden, beloved by Eros, the god of love, who after long tribulation and suffering was accorded her place among the gods as the equal of her god consort. Psyche as personification of the soul came into Greek mythology in the 4th–5th centuries B.C. Psyche as soul symbolized by a butterfly first appeared in the 5th century B.C. Before this the soul was conceived of and depicted either as a bird or as the spirit-double of the individual. For the myth, see **Cupid and Psyche.**

Psyche. A religious poem in 24 cantos, by Joseph Beaumont, published in 1648.

Ptah (ptä). In Egyptian mythology, the chief god and creator, though not one of the oldest. He was the creative force (not solar), the divine builder, the vivifying intellectual power, honored especially at Memphis. He was represented as an idol in human form, holding the divine scepter including the ankh, which was the symbol of life.

P. T. Letters. A series of letters published by Alexander Pope.

Ptolemy (tol′ẹ.mi). [Full Latin name, **Claudius Ptolemaeus.**] b. at Alexandria; flourished in the first half of the 2nd century A.D. An Alexandrian astronomer, geographer, and mathematician. His influence extended to the seventeenth century and was second only to that of Aristotle. His astronomic system is strictly geocentric, the sun, planets, stars, and heavens revolving about the earth, but, though it requires an intricate system to support his theory, the theory explains the phenomena Ptolemy knew; the Copernican system superseded it (16th and 17th centuries) because it was simpler, not because the Ptolemaic system was proved false. He elaborated trigonometry to accommodate astronomy as a mathematical discipline, and catalogued 1,028 stars. In his *Geographical Treatise* he first technically used the terms "parallel" and "meridian." He adopted Posidonio's wrong estimate of the size of the earth; his overestimate in the extent in longitude of Eurasia was one of the factors of Columbus's discovery. His recorded observations (at Canopus) extended from 127 to 151 A.D.

Ptolemy II. [Surnamed **Philadelphus**; Latin, **Ptolemaeus.**] b. in the island of Cos, 309 B.C.; d. 247 B.C. King of Egypt (285–246); son of Ptolemy I. He annexed Phoenicia and Coele-Syria, encouraged commerce, literature, science, and art, and raised the Alexandrian Museum and Library, founded by his father, to importance. He completed the Pharos, and is credited with authorizing the Bible translation known as the Septuagint and the Egyptian history of Manetho.

Public Faces. A novel by Harold Nicolson, published in 1932.

Publius (pub'li.us). In Shakespeare's *Julius Caesar*, a senator who is astonished by the conspiracy against Caesar.

Publius. In Shakespeare's *Titus Andronicus*, the son of Marcus Andronicus.

Puccini (pöt.chē'nē), **Giacomo.** [Full name, **Giacomo Antonio Domenico Michele Secondo Maria Puccini.**] b. at Lucca, Italy, June 22, 1858; d. at Brussels, Belgium, Nov. 29, 1924. An Italian operatic composer, a pupil of Amilcare Ponchielli at the Milan Conservatory. His most important operas are *Manon Lescaut* (1893), *La Bohème* (1896), *Tosca* (1900), and *Madame Butterfly* (1904; revised 1905). *La Fanciulla del West* (*The Girl of the Golden West*) was produced in 1910. His other works include *Il Tabarro* (1918), *Gianni Schicchi* (1918), and *Turandot* (1926). He was considered one of the most talented and original of his school of Italian composers; his work is marked by constant melodic invention and is influenced to some extent by Oriental music.

Pucelle (pü.sel), **Joan la.** See **Joan of Arc.**

Puck (puk). [Also, **Robin Goodfellow.**] In Shakespeare's *Midsummer Night's Dream*, the servant of Oberon. He plays many pranks in the woods near Athens, including changing the head of Bottom to that of an ass. Puck was a mischievous household spirit of English folklore, and Shakespeare transmuted him from a rather malicious sprite, often called Robin Goodfellow, to the gay and joking fairy of the play.

Puck of Pook's Hill. A volume of stories for children (1906) by Rudyard Kipling.

Pudding (pud'ing), **Jack.** A low-comedy character in English folk comedy. Like the parallel character in various European folk comedy, he is named for a hearty dish (he corresponds to the Dutch Pickelhering, German Hanswurst, and others).

Puff (puf). A cowardly servant in David Garrick's *Miss in Her Teens*.

Puff. A humbugging auctioneer in Samuel Foote's *Taste*.

Puff. A publisher and vender of quack medicine in Samuel Foote's *The Patron*.

Puff. A bustling and impudent literary humbug in Richard Brinsley Sheridan's *The Critic*. He is the author of the tragedy rehearsed in the play, and past master in the art of puffing.

Pug (pug). The Devil in man's shape in Ben Jonson's *The Devil Is an Ass*. He gives the title to the play, being made an ass of, much to his mortification.

Pughe (pū), **William Owen.** [Original name, **William Owen.**] b. at Tyn y Bryn, Wales, Aug. 7, 1759; d. June 4, 1835. A Welsh antiquary. He published a Welsh-English dictionary (1793–1803) and, with others, *Myvyrian Archaiology of Wales* (1801–07).

Pullet (pul'et), **Aunt.** A selfish invalid, one of the principal characters in George Eliot's *Mill on the Floss*. She henpecks her husband, whose mission in life seems to be to flatter her and find her pills for her. She is the sister of Aunt Glegg and Mrs. Tulliver.

Pulley, The. A poem (1633) by George Herbert, explaining God's purpose in making man almost completely self-sufficient, but withholding the treasure of perfect rest. It was God's hope that thus, like a pulley, the need for a surcease of fatigue would draw man to God:

> If goodness lead him not, yet weariness
> May toss him to my breast.

Pumblechook (pum'bl.chuk), **Mr.** A pompous old gentleman in Dickens's *Great Expectations*. He is Joe Gargery's uncle, and makes himself peculiarly odious to Pip by his patronage and his offensive habit of springing mathematical problems on him for solution.

pun. An expression in which the use of a word in two different applications, or the use of two different words pronounced alike or nearly alike, presents an odd or ludicrous idea; a play on words that are alike or nearly alike in sound but differ in meaning; a kind of verbal quibble.

A pun can be no more engraven than it can be translated. When the word is construed into its idea, the double meaning vanishes.

> (Addison, *Ancient Medals*.)

A better pun on this word [gay] was made on the Beggar's Opera, which, it was said, made Gay rich, and Rich gay. (Walpole, *Anecdotes of Painting*.)

Punch (punch). A violent-tempered, hump-backed, hooked-nosed puppet, with a squeaking voice, the chief character in the traditional English street puppet show called *Punch and Judy*. He kills his child for squalling, beats his wife (Judy) to death, belabors a policeman, escapes from prison, and outwits the Devil. Punch is the descendant of the *Punchinello* (French, *Polichinelle*) of the Italian *commedia dell' arte;* the part as it first appeared in England is thought to have been created by Silvio Fiorillo, a comedian, c1600. Punch first appeared in France as a puppet in the beginning of the reign of Louis XIV. The origin of Toby, his dog, is uncertain.

Punch. A humorous illustrated journal, published weekly at London. It was founded in 1841.

Puntarvolo (pun.tär'vō.lō). In Ben Jonson's *Every Man Out of His Humour*, a knight affecting excessive romanticism.

Purana (pö.rä'nä). The name of each of 18 Sanskrit works, important in their connection with the later phases of Brahmanism. They contain stories of the gods, interwoven with legendary tales of kings and rishis and other subjects. Though nominally trithe-istic, they are practically polytheistic and yet essentially pantheistic. Their form is in general that of dialogues in which a well-known and inspired sage answers the questions of his disciples. The *Puranas* deal with the mythology and theology of creation, death, and re-creation, the periods of the Manus, genealogies of kings, and the four stages of all human life and effort: love, wealth, righteous-ness, and final liberation from the cycle of birth and rebirth.

Purcell (pėr′sẹl), **Henry.** b. at Westminster, Lon-don, c1658; d. there, Nov. 21, 1695. An English musician and composer. He was admitted as choris-ter in the Chapel Royal, and in 1670 composed an ode for the king's birthday. In 1680 he composed his famous opera, *Dido and Aeneas,* for performance in a school. In 1676 he was a copyist at West-minster Abbey, and composed the music of Dry-den's *Aurengzebe,* and Shadwell's *Epsom Wells* and *The Libertine.* In 1677 he wrote the music to Aphra Behn's tragedy *Abdelazar.* Some of the songs in these compositions are still popular. In 1680 he was the organist of Westminster Abbey, and during the next five or six years composed most of his church music. In 1682 he was organist of the Chapel Royal. In 1683 he began to compose chamber music; and in 1686 wrote the music for Dryden's *Tyrannic Love.* He composed the anthem *Blessed Are They That Fear the Lord,* by command of the king, in 1688, the music for Dryden's *King Arthur* in 1691, and his greatest work, the *Te Deum and Jubilate,* written for Saint Cecilia's Day, in 1694.

Purchas (pėr′chạs), **Samuel.** b. at Thaxted, Essex, England, c1575; d. at London, in September, 1626. An English clergyman and author, known for his travel works. He published *Purchas his Pilgrimage, or Relations of the World and the Religions observed in all Ages and Places* in 1613; a second edition appeared in 1614, much enlarged. Four succeeding volumes, comprising articles from Hakluyt's pub-lications and manuscripts, appeared in 1625 with the general title *Hakluytus Posthumus, or Purchas his Pilgrimes: containing a History of the World, in Sea Voyages and Land Travels by Englishmen and Others.* The fourth edition of *Purchas his Pil-grimage* was later usually sold with the latter work as if it were a succeeding fifth volume, and the five became known as *Purchas's Pilgrims.* The collec-tion is of great historical value. Purchas also pub-lished *Purchas his Pilgrim: Microcosmus, or the History of Man* (1619) and *The King's Tower* (1623; a sermon).

Pure (pūr), **Simon.** In Susannah Centlivre's com-edy *A Bold Stroke for a Wife,* a Pennsylvania Quaker who is intended by the guardian of Ann Lovely, an heiress, to marry her. His name and per-sonality are assumed by Colonel Fainwell in order to win the lady's person and fortune; hence arose the expression "the *real* Simon Pure," as he brings witnesses finally to prove that he was the owner of the name.

Purgatorio (pōr.gä.tō′rē.ō), **Il.** The second part of Dante's *Divina Commedia.*

Puritanism (pū′ri.tạn.iz.ẹm). A movement within the Church of England during the latter half of the 16th century and the first 70 years of the 17th century, leading to the rise of various separatist sects and to profound political changes. The name "Puritans" was first applied scornfully in 1564 to opponents of the Anglican hierarchy's directives in ritualistic matters; and it fell into disuse, in a partisan sense, after the Restoration. Historically, the ground was prepared for Puritanism by Henry VIII's establishment of a national church; by the continuance in that church of doctrines, ceremonies, and organizational forms similar to those of the Roman Catholic Church; by the persecutions under Queen Mary, which caused numerous English Protestants to flee to Geneva and other Calvinistic centers, where they adopted some of the doctrines of Calvinism and conceived an admiration for the Genevan form of church government; by the re-vulsion of virtuous and conscientious people from the licentiousness and profligacy of Tudor and Stuart England; by the absolutist tendencies of James I and Charles I, which bred resistance among all who cherished English liberties; by cumulative resentments against economic and social inequali-ties; and by widespread reading of the Bible, in which an armory of arguments was found for re-form. The first skirmishes between Puritans and the established church regime occurred as early as the reign of Edward VI, when John Hooper, ordained bishop of Gloucester, refused to don the prescribed vestments, and numerous other ministers discarded the surplice, refused to make the sign of the cross in baptism, rejected the use of a ring in the marriage ceremony, and denounced various other "remnants of popery." Elizabeth, always the practical politician, was resolute to use the crown-controlled church to buttress her throne, and per-ceived that an hierarchical establishment, with enforced conformity of doctrine, and with emphasis on ceremony and trappings rather than on preach-ing and discussion, would best serve that end. These things accordingly had been provided for by Acts of Supremacy and of Uniformity in 1559. Nevertheless, opposition to the establishment spread, and even a demand for substitution of the presbyterian for the episcopal form of church gov-ernment. Thomas Cartwright, professor of divinity at Cambridge, first gave bold voice to this program in 1571, and in the following year some of his follow-ers addressed an Admonition to Parliament calling for sweeping reforms. Such things as these only hardened Elizabeth's determination, and in 1583 she established what has been called "a spiritual despotism" by means of an Ecclesiastical Com-mission with unlimited power to prescribe and enforce doctrine, to compel conformity, to deprive ministers of their livings, and to prescribe the re-ligious teachings of schools and colleges. Among other things, all conventicles or gatherings for preachings and Bible reading in homes or other private places were forbidden. At least as early as 1567 small groups began to hold such meetings, and some of these moved toward separatism, under a conviction that neither an episcopal nor a pres-byterian form of church organization was sanc-tioned by Holy Writ. By 1593 there seem to have been fully 20,000 such "Brownists," as they were called (from the chief spokesman of their tenets, Robert Brown). It was one of these groups, settled at Leiden, which supplied the little band of "Pilgrim Fathers" who in 1620 brought Puritanism to America. In 1603, at the accession of James I, the Millenery Petition, so called because it was intended that 1,000 clergymen would sign it (and it did in fact carry the assent of some 800 of them, about a tenth of all the ministers in the realm), was presented to the monarch, asking no change in church government, but again calling for the sweeping elimination of Roman Catholic survivals in doctrine, ceremonies, and the Book of Common Prayer. But when, in January, 1604, James, on the petition of Puritan divines, called the Hampton Court Conference, which included Anglican and Puritan representatives, and the last-named urged a change from episcopal to presbyterian forms, the sovereign ended the parleys with the remark, "No bishop, no king!" It was, however, a suggestion made by the Puritans on this occasion which led to the new translation of the Bible known as the Authorized, or the King James, Version. James never relaxed his opposition; the Ecclesiastical Commission functioned remorselessly; yet Puritanism still spread as Bible reading increased. Great numbers of the small "Geneva Bible" were distributed. The Bible was, in fact, almost the only book known to most of the English people, and its influence on their thought, and on the events especially of the first half of the 17th century, was incalculable. Between the Puritans and Charles I, with his despotic pretensions and his Roman Catholic wife, an increasingly acute struggle was inevitable; it led to the Long Parliament, the Puritan Revolution, the rise of Oliver Cromwell, the beheading of the king, and the dictatorship of Cromwell. Until 1643 probably a majority of Puritans would have been satisfied with doctrinal changes of a Calvinistic tendency, elimination of "popish" ceremonial, and purification of morals and conduct, within an episcopalian church. When the exigencies of the Civil War made it necessary for the English Parliament to accept the Solemn Covenant, Presbyterianism for a time was in the ascendant. But Separatism had grown apace; and Cromwell, finding the Separatists, by that time generally called Independents, his best soldiers, and that he could not have an army without them, successfully opposed all efforts to establish a Presbyterian Church in England, which, by the evidence of events in Scotland, would then have been as intolerant and despotic as ever the Anglican Church was alleged to be. Among the Independents were those who, being of the farming and laboring classes, combined with their revolt against religious formalism and despotism a determination to use the revolution to end economic and social evils and class distinctions, and were therefore known as Levellers. Once in power, Cromwell suppressed these radicals, who had helped greatly to put him in power, with sanguinary ruthlessness. The noble concept of religious tolerance, which from time to time had appeared here and there in the Christian world, found another small root among the Independents. In New England, the Separatist Pilgrims were followed by Puritans still adhering to the Church of England, but these presently, under constraint of new conditions, adopted the Congregational form of organization. Tolerance was no part of the virtues or purposes of their leaders, yet among them tolerance grew, and in historical perspective, rather rapidly. If the term Puritan now evokes the image of a dour, fanatically joyless tribe, most of the earlier Puritans must surely be exempted. As we know by the instances of John Milton and others, they felt free to enjoy music, secular literature, and even dancing, games, sports, and the theater, within limits. The Puritans reprobated intemperance but never banned alcoholic beverages. Gradually, however, the rather grim implications of Calvinism and the intensive study of the Bible, in which, under conditions of struggle and persecution, their attention was not unnaturally drawn most of all to the gloomier and the more sanguinary books, great numbers of the Puritans did become rather glum and even (by modern standards) masochistic. Dancing, especially the village revels around the maypole, and music (excepting solemn hymns), were banned equally with gambling, loose sexual conduct, games and exhibitions, and indeed all pleasures and enjoyments. Identifying Sunday with the Jewish Sabbath, they forbade all but the most necessary work and absolutely all recreation on that day, even mere idle strolling; the day must be given to attendance at church and to prayer and Bible reading at home. Edward Dowden wrote that the Puritans' great fault was a "concept of God as the God of righteousness alone, and not as also the God of joy and beauty and intellectual light." The Puritan was likely to feel himself not only dedicated, but elect. But these people whose aim was "to walk in all the ways which God had made known or should make known to them" also contributed to England and America, and the world at large, qualities of moral earnestness which have flowered in many invaluable ways. In the course of their struggle they forwarded concepts of political liberty and social equality which were nowhere more edifyingly manifested than in the great days of New England liberalism. Moreover by eschewing extravagance in dress and living, by insisting on frugality, by exalting industry and seriousness of mind, Puritanism prepared its adherents to play a large role in the evolution and expansion of mercantilism and capitalism. Despite the reaction against it following the restoration of the monarchy under Charles II, Puritanism persisted as a vital influence in England, having obvious echoes in Methodism, in other nonconformist movements, and even in Chartism.

Puritan Widow, The. [Also, **The Puritan, or the Widow of Watling Street.**] A play published in 1607 and included in the second issue of the third Shakespeare folio (1664) but now not considered his. It has also been attributed to Thomas Middleton, William Rowley, Wentworth Smith, and others.

Purity. See **Cleanness.**

Purple Island, The. An allegorical poem on the human body by Phineas Fletcher, published in 1633.

Purple Land, The. An account of life in South America (1885) by W. H. Hudson.

Pursuit of Psyche (sī'kē). A poem by W. J. Turner, published in 1931.

fat, fāte, fär, åsk, fåre; net, mē, hėr; pin, pīne; not, nōte, mõve, nôr; up, lūte, půll; ᴛʜ, then;

Pusey (pū′zi), **Edward Bouverie.** b. at Pusey, Berkshire, England, Aug. 22, 1800; d. Sept. 14, 1882. An English theologian, a leader in the Oxford Movement (which has sometimes also been called Puseyism). His father's name was originally Bouverie, but the family, of Huguenot origin, became lords of the manor of Pusey, near Oxford, and hence altered its name. In 1819 he entered Christ Church, Oxford, and in 1823 became a fellow of Oriel. He was associated with John Henry Newman and John Keble. In 1828 he was regius professor of Hebrew at Oxford and canon of Christ Church. In 1835 he took part in the tractarian movement, and later was suspended for three years (1843–46) from the function of preaching for publishing *The Holy Eucharist a Comfort to the Penitent.* The practice of confession among the extreme ritualists (that is to say, the extreme "High Church" group) of the Church of England dates from his two sermons on "the entire absolution of the penitent" (1846). Among his works are *Doctrine of the Real Presence* (1855), *The Real Presence* (1857), and *The Minor Prophets* (1860). He was one of the editors of the *Library of Translations from the Fathers* and the *Anglo-Catholic Library.* He endeavored (1865 *et seq.*) to bring about a reunion of the Church of England and the Roman Catholic Church, but he did not follow Newman into Roman Catholicism; moreover, there is no reason to believe that he ever basically questioned the point of view which led him to preach the sermon *Rule of Faith* (1851), which did much to halt withdrawals from the Anglican communion in favor of that of Rome.

Pushkin (pŏsh′kin), **Aleksandr Sergeyevich.** [Also written **Alexander Poushkin.**] b. at Moscow, June 6, 1799; d. at St. Petersburg, Feb. 10, 1837. Russian writer. His mother was a descendant of an Abyssinian general in the service of Peter the Great, but his family, though of the nobility, was impoverished. He attended (1811–17) the lyceum at Tsarskoe Selo and entered the ministry of foreign affairs after finishing school. He embarked on a gay life at St. Petersburg, but in 1820 was exiled to southern Russia for writing an *Ode to Liberty* that came to the attention of the authorities. After a stay at Ekaterinoslav and Kishinev, he again shocked his superiors by joining several secret societies; he was sent to Odessa in 1823, again got into trouble, and was dismissed from the service. He was ordered to live at Mikhailovskoye, near Pskov, but later went to Moscow, where in 1825 he was presented to the new czar, Nicholas I, despite the fact that many of his friends, and perhaps Pushkin himself, were involved in the Decembrist revolt of that year. In 1831 he married Natalia Goncharova, and in 1832 regained his position in the foreign office. His wife's temperament did not match his, and he found moreover that he was being driven deep into debt by her extravagances and love of show. In addition, she gave him cause to be jealous; to defend her name, he fought a duel with her sister's husband's adopted son and was killed. His reputation had grown during the last years of his life and now increased to the point where he was generally recognized as the great Russian romantic poet. Many of his works are concerned with the Caucasus and the Crimea, a region he first visited

in 1820 and to which he returned again and again. Among these are *The Captive of the Caucasus* (1822), *The Fountain of Bakhchisarai* (1822), *The Robber Brothers* (1822), *The Gipsies* (1823–24), all romantic poems in the manner of Byron, and *A Voyage to Arzrum* (1836), a travel account, and a number of lyrics. Pushkin's masterpiece, *Eugene Onegin* (1832), is a tale in verse influenced by Byronic ideas. This, as well as his short story, *The Queen of Spades* (1834), was set to music by Peter Tchaikovsky; Modeste Mussorgsky made an opera of his *Boris Godunov* (1825), a historical drama, Rimsky-Korsakov did the same for *The Golden Cockerel* (1833), and Glinka turned Pushkin's first long poem, *Ruslan and Ludmila* (1820), also into opera. Pushkin's other work includes historical poems, like *Poltava* (1828) and *The Bronze Horseman* (1833); novels like *The Captain's Daughter* (1837) and *Dubrovsky* (1841); plays like *Mozart and Salieri* (1830), *The Stone Guest* (1830), and *Rusalka* (1836); *Folk Tales* (1831–32) and short stories, a group of which he published anonymously in 1831 as *Tales by Belkin.* These latter purported to be by one Ivan Belkin, and Pushkin playfully supplied him with background in a burlesque *History of the Manor of Goryukhino* (1857), in which Belkin appears. He wrote a serious *History of the Pugachev Rebellion of 1773* (1834), a historical event that forms the background of *The Captain's Daughter.*

Puss-in-Boots (pus′in.bŏts′). The title and hero of an English nursery tale, translated in the 18th century from the French *Chat Botté* (1697), by Charles Perrault. This cat, by his cleverness, makes the fortune of his master, a miller's son, saves him from various dangers, and also wins for him high honors and a beautiful wife. Tieck published a German version of the story in 1795 as *Der gestiefelte Kater.*

Puttenham (put′en.am), **George.** d. 1590. An English author; brother of Richard Puttenham. He was educated at Oxford. The *Arte of English Poesie* (1589) has been attributed both to him and to his brother.

Puttenham, Richard. b. c1520; d. c1601. An English author; brother of George Puttenham.

Put Yourself in His Place. A novel by Charles Reade, published in 1870. The title is taken from the favorite saying of Dr. Amboyne, an important character. The story deals with the struggles of Henry Little, an inventor, against the trade unions.

Pwyll (pwil). In Brythonic legend, a local king; husband of Rhiannon. In Brythonic mythology Pwyll was an otherworld deity who exchanged kingdoms and personalities for one year with Arawn, lord and king of the Brythonic otherworld.

Pye (pī), **Henry James.** b. at London, Feb. 20, 1745; d. at Pinner, England, Aug. 11, 1813. An English poet. He was educated at Oxford (Magdalen College), and became a member of Parliament in 1784. In 1790 he succeeded to the poet laureateship. In 1792 he was made a London police magistrate. He was a poet of remarkably limited talents (although not, perhaps, quite as bad in his verses as Byron was to suggest in his well-known blast against contemporary poets laureate) who tried humbly to please the throne with patriotic jingles; his only work of any scope was *Alfred*, an epic, published in 1801.

Pygmalion (pig.mā'li.ọn). In Greek legend, a sculptor and king of Cyprus. He fell in love with an ivory statue which he had made, and at his request Aphrodite gave it life.

Pygmalion. In Greek legend, the brother of Dido.

Pygmalion. A play (1913) by George Bernard Shaw. It deals with the transformation of a Cockney flower girl, Liza Doolittle, who, under the tutelage of Henry Higgins, a professor of phonetics, gains admission to polite society. It was the first of Shaw's plays to be filmed (1939).

Pygmalion and Galatea (gal.ạ.tē'ạ). A fairy comedy by W. S. Gilbert, produced in 1871.

Pyke (pīk). In Dickens's novel *Nicholas Nickleby*, a servile creature in the service (with his fellow toady Pluck) of Sir Mulberry Hawk.

Pylades (pil'ạ.dēz). In Greek legend, a nephew of Agamemnon, friend of Orestes, and husband of Electra.

Pyramus and Thisbe (pir'ạ.mus, thiz'bē). In classical legend, two Babylonian lovers. They were forbidden to see each other by their parents, and talked together through a crack in the garden wall. They finally planned to meet at a certain tomb. Thisbe, who arrived first, was terrified by a lion, fled, and dropped her cloak. Pyramus arrived a few minutes later, found the cloak bloodstained from the lion's mouth (the lion, according to the traditional account, had eaten someone else just before it saw Thisbe), believed Thisbe dead, and killed himself. When Thisbe returned and found her lover dead, she, too, killed herself. Their story is celebrated by Ovid in his *Metamorphoses*, and Shakespeare introduces it (as "Pyramus and Thisby") in the interlude of *A Midsummer Night's Dream*, presented by Bottom, Flute, and the other artisans in honor of the marriage of Theseus and Hippolyta.

Pyrgopolinices (pėr"gọ.pol.i.nī'sēz). A braggart, a character in the comedy *Miles Gloriosus*, by Plautus.

Pyrocles (pir'ọ.klēz). A character in Sir Philip Sidney's *Arcadia*. He disguises himself as a woman, Zelmane.

Pyrocles. The son of Acrates and brother of Cymocles, in Spenser's *Faerie Queene*.

Pyrocles. See also under **Pericles**.

Pyrrha (pir'ạ). In Greek mythology, the wife of Deucalion, who with him survived the Flood and cast stones into the field, from which rose men and women to repeople the earth.

pyrrhic (pir'ik). In prosody, consisting of two short times or syllables: as, a *pyrrhic* foot; composed of or pertaining to feet so constituted: as, *pyrrhic* verse; *pyrrhic* rhythm.

Pyrrho (pir'ō). b. in Elis, Greece, c360 B.C.; d. c270 B.C. A Greek philosopher, the founder of the skeptical school.

Pyrrhus (pir'us). b. c318 B.C.; killed at Argos, Greece, 272 B.C. A king of Epirus, one of the greatest generals of antiquity. He was invited by Tarentum to assist it against Rome, defeated the Romans at Heraclea in 280 and at Asculum in 279, remained in Sicily until 276, and was defeated by the Romans at Beneventum in 275.

Pyrrhus. See also **Neoptolemus**.

Pythagoras (pi.thag'ọ.rạs, pī-). b. in Samos, Greece; d. at Metapontum, in Magna Graecia, c497 B.C. A Greek philosopher and mathematician. He emigrated (c529) to Crotona, in Magna Graecia, and later removed to Metapontum. None of his writings are extant, and it is almost impossible to distinguish between his own theories and those formulated by his followers. However, it was due to Pythagoras that mathematics was raised to the rank of a science, and many early geometrical discoveries have been ascribed to the Pythagorean thinkers. They are considered to have founded the theory of numbers, and the mathematical study of acoustics and music. They have appeared to have been among the very first (if not, in each instance, demonstrably the very first) thinkers to conceive of incommensurable quantities, and of the earth as a globe. Their emphasis on the study of numbers led on the one hand to number mysticism (which is what many modern readers now chiefly associate with Pythagoras and his school), and on the other hand to a quantitative study of nature.

Pytheas (pith'ē.ạs). fl. second half of the 4th century B.C. A Greek navigator and astronomer. He was a native of Massilia (Marseilles), and visited the coasts of Spain, Gaul, and Great Britain. His works, only fragments of which remain, contain our earliest first-hand information concerning northwestern Europe.

Pythia (pith'i.ạ). In Greek religion, the medium and oracular prophetess of Apollo at Delphi.

Pythian Games (pith'i.ạn). One of the four great national festivals of ancient Greece, celebrated once in four years, in honor of Apollo, at Delphi. The most notable feature of the festival was originally a musical competition: the composition and performance of a hymn to the gods. After 582 B.C. athletic and equestrian games were added to the program.

Pythias (pith'i.ạs). See **Damon and Pythias**.

Pythius (pith'i.us). In Greek mythology, a surname of Apollo, as the slayer of the Python.

Python (pī'thon). In Greek mythology, a huge female dragon or serpent born from the mud of the Flood. She guarded the cave and chasm at Delphi and there was killed by Apollo, who thus became henceforth the possessor and motivating deity of the oracle at Delphi. A ritual drama representing the killing of the dragon by the god was annually reënacted there.

---

fat, fāte, fär, ȧsk, fãre; net, mē, hėr; pin, pīne; not, nōte, mõve, nôr; up, lūte, pull; ᴛʜ, then;

Q. Pseudonym of **Quiller-Couch,** Sir **Arthur Thomas.**

Quackleben (kwak'l.bẹn), **Dr. Quentin.** In Sir Walter Scott's novel *St. Ronan's Well,* the "Man of Medicine" who has discovered the healing properties of the waters in "St. Ronan's Well," and therefore looks upon himself as their principal custodian.

quadrivium (kwod.riv'i.um). The collective name of the four branches of mathematics according to the Pythagoreans: arithmetic (treating of number in itself), music (treating of applied number), geometry (treating of stationary number), and astronomy (treating of number in motion). This Pythagorean quadrivium, preceded by the trivium of grammar, logic, and rhetoric, made up the seven liberal arts taught in the schools of the Roman Empire.

Quadroon, The. A novel by Mayne Reid, published in 1856. It was adapted by Dion Boucicault for the play *The Octoroon* (1859).

Quai d'Orsay (kā dôr.sā). A quay along the S bank of the Seine in Paris, on which are situated the department of foreign affairs and the building of the Corps Législatif; hence, in journalistic usage, the French foreign office, or the government in general.

"Quaker Poet." See **Barton, Bernard.**

Quality Street. A play (1901) by Sir James M. Barrie.

quantity. In ancient prosody and metrics, the relative time occupied in uttering a vowel or a syllable; that characteristic of a vowel or a syllable by which it is distinguished as long or short; syllabic measure or time; prosodic length. In ancient Greek and Latin pronunciation a long vowel or syllable occupied nearly, or in deliberate enunciation fully, twice the time of a short vowel or syllable, and the grammarians accordingly assumed the average short vowel or syllable as the prosodic unit (mora), and taught that a long vowel or syllable was equal to two short ones. Some vowels or syllables varied in time between these two limits and were called *common,* admitting of metrical use as either longs or shorts. In certain situations (elision, ecthlipsis) vowels were much shorter in pronunciation than the average short, and, although audible, were disregarded in metrical measurement. A syllable was long either by nature or by position. In the English pronunciation of Latin and Greek, quantity in the proper sense is entirely disregarded, except in so far as the length of the penult affects the accent according to the Latin rule; and English writers use the phrase *false quantity* for a false accentuation. Thus, to pronounce *vec-tī'gal vec'ti-gal* is called a "false quantity," but to pronounce the *a* alike in *păter* and *māter* is not so designated.

> All composed in a metre for Catullus,
> All in quantity, careful of my motion.
> (Tennyson, *Experiments,* Hendecasyllabics.)

Quarles (kwôrlz, kwärlz), **Francis.** b. at Rumford, Essex, England, 1592; d. Sept. 8, 1644. An English poet. He was educated at Christ's College, Cambridge, and became a student at Lincoln's Inn, London. He was city chronologer in 1639. Among his works (largely sacred poems) are *Divine Emblems* (1635), *Hieroglyphics* (1638), and a prose work, *Enchiridion* (1640).

Quarles, John. b. 1624; d. 1665. An English poet and author; son of Francis Quarles.

Quarles, Philip. A character in Aldous Huxley's novel *Point Counter Point* (1928). A novelist, he is generally considered to be an autobiographical portrait of Huxley himself.

quarto (kwôr'tō). [Abbreviated **4to.**] A size of book in which the leaf is one fourth of a described or implied size of paper. The sheet folded twice in cross directions makes the square quarto, or regular quarto; folded twice in the same direction makes the long quarto. A cap quarto is 7 x 8½ inches; demy quarto, 8 x 10½ inches; folio-post quarto 8½ x 11 inches; medium quarto, 9 x 12 inches; royal quarto, 10 x 13 inches. The leaf of a quarto is understood to have a broad and short shape.

> In my library there is a large copy of the Apocrypha, in what may be called elephant quarto, printed for T. Cadell and W. Davies, by Thomas Bensley, 1816.   (*N. and Q.,* 7th ser.)

Quasimodo (kwä.si.mō'dō). A misshapen dwarf, one of the chief characters in Victor Hugo's *Notre Dame de Paris.*

quatorzain (kạ.tôr'zān). A stanza or poem of 14 lines; a sonnet.

> Put out your rush candles, you poets and rimers, and bequeath your crazed quarterzayns to the chandlers; for loe! here he commeth that hath broken your legs.
> (Nash, quoted in *Pierce Penilesse,* Int.)

> His [Drayton's] next publication is Idea's mirror; Amours in Quatorzains, 1594. It contains fifty-one sonnets.   (*N. and Q.,* 6th ser.)

quatrain (kwot'rān). A stanza of four lines rhyming alternately.

> I have chosen to write my poem in quatrains, or stanzas of four in alternate rhyme, because I have ever judged them more noble, and of greater dignity both for the sound and number, than any other verse in use amongst us.
> (Dryden, *Account of Annus Mirabilis.*)

> Who but Landor could have written the faultless and pathetic quatrain?—
> I strove with none, for none was worth my strife;
> Nature I loved, and, next to Nature, Art;
> I warmed both hands before the fire of life;
> It sinks, and I am ready to depart.
> (Stedman, *Vict. Poets.*)

ḍ, d or j; ṣ, s or sh; ṭ, t or ch; ẓ, z or zh; o, F. cloche; ü, F. menu; ch, Sc. loch; ṅ, F. bonbon.

Quebec Bagnet (kwẹ.bek′ bag′net). See under **Bagnet, Mr.** and **Mrs. Joseph.**

Queen. In Shakespeare's *Cymbeline*, the wife of Cymbeline and the mother of Cloten by a former husband. In her efforts to secure the throne for her son, she tries to marry him to Imogen, then tries to poison Imogen, Cymbeline, and Pisanio. She goes mad and confesses her crimes before she dies.

Queen. In Shakespeare's *Richard II*, the historical Isabel of France, Richard's Queen. She overhears a gardener talking about an orchard and comparing his husbandry with that of Bolingbroke. She bids farewell to Richard as he goes to the Tower.

Queen and huntress, Chaste and fair. A poem by Ben Jonson, included in the masque *Cynthia's Revels*. It is a song of praise to Diana or Cynthia, who represents Queen Elizabeth in the masque.

Queen Anne's Men. See **Worcester's Men.**

Queen Elizabeth's Men. An Elizabethan theatrical company, formed by Edmund Tilney, Master of the Revels under Queen Elizabeth. They were the most important company in London from 1583 to 1590.

Queen Mab (mab). An early poem by Shelley, written when he was 18, published in a pirated version in 1813. It tells of the maiden Ianthe's abduction by Queen Mab, and Queen Mab's revelation to Ianthe of the past and future history of the world. The poem was used as a vehicle for Shelley's protests against various social injustices, and contains a bitter denunciation of God by Ahasuerus, the Wandering Jew, the sufferer from God's vengeance. The work is partly written in the irregular verse of Southey's *Thalaba* and partly in blank verse. Parts of it were published in the *Alastor* volume (1816).

Queen Mab. See also **Mab, Queen.**

Queen Mary. A history play in blank verse by Alfred Tennyson, published in 1875. It is part of a series (the others being *Harold* and *Becket*) about the growth of English society.

Queen Mother, The. A play (1860) by Algernon Charles Swinburne. The character of the "Queen Mother" was based on the historical Catherine de' Medici.

Queen of China (chī′nạ), **The.** A volume of poems by Edward Shanks, published in 1919. It was the first winner of the Hawthornden prize.

Queen of Corinth (kor′inth), **The.** A play by Fletcher and Massinger, written c1617 and printed in 1647.

Queen of Cornwall (kôrn′wôl, -wạl), **The.** [Full title, **The Famous Tragedy of the Queen of Cornwall.**] A play (1923) by Thomas Hardy.

Queen of Sicilia (si.sil′yạ, -sil′i.ạ). See **Hermione.**

Queen of the Amazons. See **Hippolyta.**

Queen of the Fairies. See **Titania.**

Queen of the Goths. See **Tamora.**

Queen's Arcadia (är.kā′di.ạ), **The.** An English pastoral play by Samuel Daniel, performed in 1605 at Oxford. The plot is more or less original, though some use was made of Tasso's *Aminta*.

Queensberry (kwēnz′ber″i, -bér.i), 4th Duke of. A title of **Douglas, William** (1724–1810).

Queensberry, 8th Marquis of. [Title of **John Sholto Douglas.**] b. 1844; d. 1900. An English nobleman, notable as the person chiefly responsible for drawing up the rules of boxing now followed in virtually every country of the world. The Queensberry rules were first outlined in 1865, and by 1889 had been standardized and put into effect on both sides of the Atlantic. The Marquis of Queensberry is also of some note from the fact that it was his objection, by way of a public letter written to Oscar Wilde in 1895, to the friendship between the writer and Queensberry's son that precipitated the libel suit which brought about revelation of Wilde's various immoralities.

Queens' College. A college of Cambridge University, founded in 1448 by Margaret of Anjou and refounded in 1465 by Elizabeth Woodville.

Queen's College. A college of Oxford University, founded in 1340 in honor of the consort of Edward III.

Queen's English. See under **King's English.**

Queen's Exchange, The. A comedy by Richard Brome, printed in 1657, and reprinted (1661) with the title *The Royal Exchange*.

Queen's Maries (mä.rēz′), **The.** A popular Scottish ballad relating the death of Mary Hamilton, one of the "Queen's Maries." The Maries are named as "Marie Seaton and Marie Beaton and Marie Carmichael and me" (i.e., Marie Hamilton). They belonged to the four families of Livingston, Fleming, Seaton, and Beaton. These four Maries went to France with Mary Stuart when she was a child of five in 1548, and returned with her to Scotland in 1561. Young Marie Hamilton found a lover at court, became pregnant, and drowned her child at birth. For this she was hanged. Scott's version, published in 1833, was a composite of several older versions. There are 28 versions of the ballad altogether.

Queen's Masque, The. [Also, **Love's Mistress.**] A masque (1634) by Thomas Heywood, originally produced with designs by Queen Henrietta Maria, the wife of Charles I and scenery by Inigo Jones. It was presented three times in a week at the Phoenix Theatre.

Queen's Quair, or the Six Years' Tragedy (kwãr), **The.** A historical novel by Maurice Hewlett, published in 1904. It presents a sympathetic treatment of Mary, Queen of Scots. The title was suggested by *The Kingis Quair*, a poem composed by James I of Scotland. "Quair" means "little book."

Queen's Wake, The. A long poem (1813) by James Hogg, consisting of several verse narratives supposedly sung by rival poets at the wake of Queen Mary.

Queen's Wigs, The. A novel by Naomi Royde-Smith, published in 1934.

Queen Victoria (vik.tō′ri.ạ). A biographical study by Lytton Strachey, published in 1921. Strachey's candid and human portrait of the queen set a new style in biographical writing.

Queer Street. A novel by Edward Shanks, published in 1932.

Quennell (kwen′ẹl), **Peter** (**Courtney**). b. at London, March 9, 1905—. An English novelist, biographer, critic, and poet. He is editor of the *Cornhill Magazine*, and has contributed to magazines including the *Criterion, Life and Letters*, and the *New Statesman and Nation*. Author of biographical and critical works including *Baudelaire and the Symbolists* (1929), *Byron: The Years of Fame* (1936), *Caroline of England* (1940), and *Byron in Italy* (1941). In *Byron: A Self Portrait* (1950), he edited Byron's letters and diaries. He has also written a novel, *The Phoenix-Kind* (1931), *Sympathy and Other Stories* (1933), and volumes of poetry, including *Poems* (1926) and *Inscription on a Fountain Head* (1929).

Quentin Durward (kwen′tĭn dẽr′wₐrd). A novel by Sir Walter Scott, published in 1823. Quentin Durward is an archer of the Scottish Guard, who seeks his fortune in France in the reign of Louis XI.

Quentin Quackleben (kwak′l.bẹn), **Dr.** See **Quackleben, Dr. Quentin.**

quibble. A trivial conceit.

It was very natural, therefore, that the common people, by a quibble, which is the same in Flemish as in English, should call the proposed "Moderation" the "Murderation."

(Motley, *Dutch Republic.*)

Quick (kwik), **John.** b. 1748; d. 1831. An English actor. He joined a provincial company at 14, and came to London in 1767 (he was first at the Haymarket and then at Covent Garden). His vast repertory of comic roles included Justice Shallow in *Henry IV*, Polonius in *Hamlet*, Tony Lumpkin in *She Stoops to Conquer*, and Bob Acres in *The Rivals*. He was the favorite actor of George III.

Quickly (kwik′li), **Mistress.** In Shakespeare's *1* and *2 Henry IV*, and *Henry V*, the simple-minded and garrulous Hostess of the Boar's Head, the tavern where Falstaff and his friends hang out. In *2 Henry IV*, she claims that Falstaff has promised to marry her, and that he owes her 100 pounds. He talks her out of it, even though she will have to pawn the tavern furnishings. Later she goes to prison with Doll Tearsheet for beating up a man. In *Henry V*, it appears that she has married Pistol. She movingly describes the death of Falstaff (II.i).

Quickly, Mistress. In Shakespeare's *Merry Wives of Windsor*, the housekeeper of Dr. Caius. She assists Ann Page's suitors and later plays the Queen of the Fairies. Some critics argue that she is not identical with the Mistress Quickly in the historical plays.

Quiller-Couch (kwil′er.köch′), Sir **Arthur Thomas.** [Pseudonym, **Q.**] b. in Cornwall, England, Nov. 21, 1863; d. 1944. An English man of letters. He was a lecturer in classics at Trinity College, Oxford (1886–87), was on the editorial staff of the *Speaker* from its start until 1899, and in 1912 was appointed King Edward VII professor of English literature at Cambridge University. He was knighted in 1910. Among his publications are *The Splendid Spur* (1889), *The Blue Pavillions* (1891), *The Warwickshire Avon* (1892), *The Delectable Duchy* (1893), *Wandering Heath* (1895), *Poems and Ballads* (1896), *Fairy Tales from Far and Near* (1896), *Adventures in Criticism* (1896), *The Ship of Stars* (1899), *Old Fires and Profitable Ghosts* (1900), *Hetty Wesley* (1903), *Shining Ferry* (1905), *George Eliot* (1906),

The Mayor of Troy (1906), *Major Vigoureux* (1907), *Lady Good-for-Nothing* (1910), *Brother Copas* (1911), *The Vigil of Venus* (1912), and others. In 1897 he was selected to finish Robert Louis Stevenson's uncompleted novel *St. Ives.* He compiled and edited the *Oxford Book of English Verse,* the *Oxford Book of Ballads,* and *The Oxford Book of Victorian Verse.*

Quilp (kwilp). In Dickens's *Old Curiosity Shop,* a malicious and usorious dwarf. He is the principal villain of the book, and one of the most terrifying of all of Dickens's characters.

Quin, James. b. at London, Feb. 24, 1693; d. at Bath, England, Jan. 21, 1766. An English actor. His earliest London appearances were at Drury Lane in small parts, and it was there that he made his first success in 1715 as Bajazet in Nicholas Rowe's *Tamerlane.* The following year he went to Lincoln's Inn Fields Theatre to play Hotspur in *Henry IV,* and continued there for a number of years in such parts as Othello, Lear, Falstaff, the Ghost in *Hamlet,* and Buckingham in *Richard III.* He went to Covent Garden in 1732, returned two years later to Drury Lane to play leading roles in tragedy, and finally went back to Covent Garden, where he ended his career. There in 1748 he played the part of Coriolanus (in James Thomson's adaptation of Shakespeare's *Coriolanus*) in 18th century neoclassical costume. Quin's acting technique was probably learned from Barton Booth, a disciple of Thomas Betterton's school of sonorous oratory, commanding stage presence, and stylized mannerisms. This old-fashioned declamatory manner of Quin's was very different from the naturalistic acting of the rising young David Garrick, of whom Quin remarked that "if the young fellow is right, I and the rest . . . have been all wrong." As Garrick became increasingly popular, the rivalry between the two actors stirred up keen public interest. Whatever coolness their professional competition may have engendered before Quin's retirement in 1751 seems to have passed off in later meetings. Quin visited Garrick often toward the end of his life, and Garrick wrote Quin's epitaph. Quin was a great eater and drinker; his wit was coarse but not venomous; he was ill-tempered, but kind to people in trouble. Tobias Smollett's *Humphry Clinker* has in it a character sketch of Quin.

Quinapalus (kwi.nap′ₐ.lus). In Shakespeare's *Twelfth Night* (I.v), an imaginary authority cited by the clown: "For what says Quinapalus? 'Better a witty fool than a foolish wit.' "

Quinbus Flestrin (kwim′bus fles′trin). See **Flestrin, Quinbus.**

Quince (kwins), **Peter.** In Shakespeare's *Midsummer Night's Dream,* a carpenter. He is stage manager and speaks the Prologue in the interpolated play.

Quintilian (kwin.til′yₐn). [Full Latin name, **Marcus Fabius Quintilianus.**] b. at Calagurris (Calahorra), Spain, c35 A.D.; d. c95 A.D. A Roman rhetorician. He was educated at Rome, returned to his birthplace as a teacher of oratory, and went back to Rome with Galba in 68, and taught oratory there for 20 years. He was patronized by Vespasian and Domitian. His most celebrated work is his *Institutio Oratoria,* which exerted a powerful influ-

ḍ, d or j; ş, s or sh; ţ, t or ch; ẓ, z or zh; *o*, F. cloche; ü, F. menu; ċh, Sc. loch; ṅ, F. bonbon.

ence in its day. It is the most elaborate treatise on education, as well as one of the most important ancient documents of literary criticism.

Quintus (kwin'tus). In Shakespeare's *Titus Andronicus*, one of the four sons of Titus.

quip. A smart sarcastic turn; a sharp or cutting jest; a severe retort; a gibe.

> *Psyi.* Why, what's a quip?
> *Manes.* Wee great girders call it a short saying of a sharpe wit, with a bitter sense in a sweet word.
> (Lyly, *Alexander and Campaspe*, III.ii.)

> If I sent him word again it was not well cut, he would send me word he cut it to please himself. This is called the Quip Modest.
> (Shak., *As You Like It*, V.iv.)

> Haste thee, nymph, and bring with thee
> Jest, and youthful jollity,
> Quips, and cranks, and wanton wiles.
> (Milton, *L'Allegro*, l.72.)

Quip Modest. See under **Retort Courteous.**

Quirinalia (kwir.i.nā'li.a̱). An ancient Roman festival in honor of Quirinus, celebrated Feb. 17, the anniversary of Romulus's supposed apotheosis.

Quirinus (kwir'i.nus). An ancient Italian god of war, later identified with Romulus. He was similar to but not identified with Mars.

Quirk, Gammon, and Snap (kwėrk, gam'on, snap). A firm of rascally solicitors in Samuel Warren's *Ten Thousand a Year.*

Quixote (kwik'sǫt, kẹ.hō'tẹ; Spanish, kē.ᴴō'tä), **Don.** The hero of Cervantes's romance *Don Quixote*, who was inspired by lofty and chivalrous but impracticable ideals.

Quomodo (kwō.mō'dō). In Thomas Middleton's play *Michaelmas Terme*, a woolen draper and usurer, whose amusingly frustrated ambition is to be a landed proprietor.

Quotem (kwōt'ẹm), **Caleb.** A character in *The Review*, by the younger Colman. The character was taken by him from an unsuccessful comic opera, *Caleb Quotem and his Wife, or Paint, Poetry, and Putty*, by Henry Lee. Quotem is a ubiquitous and preternaturally loquacious jack of all trades, as may be seen by the sign over his door: "Quotem, Auctioneer, Plumber, Glazier, Engraver, Apothecary, Schoolmaster, Watchmaker, Sign-Painter, etc., etc. N. B. This is the Parish Clerk's—I cure Agues and Teach the Use of the Globes."

R

Ra (rä). [Also, **Re.**] In Egyptian mythology, the sun god and supreme deity, the protector of men and vanquisher of evil. According to myth, he was the first king of Egypt, and left the world because of the pettiness of mankind. Every night he fights against the hostile serpent of darkness during his journey through the underworld, and reappears victorious every morning. Because Ra, the sun, was the first ruler of Egypt, all subsequent kings ruled "in his image" (each king was called the son of Ra, for the specific purpose of ruling Egypt, which was called the daughter of Ra). The center of his cult was Heliopolis, where he is thought to have displaced a more ancient god. Ra became identified with local gods everywhere in Egypt, and he "loaned himself" to other gods to enhance their power. His symbols were the falcon, the bird that soars into the sun; the dung beetle or scarab, because he rolls a little ball, symbol of the sun as a rolling ball; and the uraeus serpent, symbol of sovereignty. He was commonly depicted as a bearded man crowned with the sun disk.

Rab and His Friends (rab). A story (1859) by John Brown (1810–82) about a Scotch carrier, his wife, and their mastiff, Rab. Rab, the real hero, so grieves after the death of his master and mistress that he has to be shot.

Rabbi Ben Ezra (ben ez'ra̱). A dramatic monologue by Robert Browning, published in *Dramatis Personae* (1864). It opens with the well-known lines: "Grow old along with me,/ The best is yet to be,/ The last of life, for which the first was made." The supposed narrator is based upon the historical figure of Abraham ben Meïr ibn-Ezra, the great Jewish scholar. He discusses the immortality of the soul, and the beauties of old age as contrasted with youth.

Rabbi Busy (biz'i). See **Busy, Zeal-of-the-Land.**

Rabelais (rab'ẹ.lä, rab.ẹ.lä'; French, rȧb.le), **François.** [Pseudonym, **Alcofribas Nasier** (an anagram of his name).] b. at or near Chinon, in Touraine, France, c1494; d. probably at Paris, in April, 1553. A French satirist and humorist. Little is known of his life before 1520, although tradition has it that he lived at Angers from 1515 to 1518 and studied at the Franciscan monastery of La Baumette near that town. Late in 1520 he became a monk in the Franciscan monastery of Puy-Saint-Martin, at Fontenay-le-Comte, in Poitou, where, thanks to the encouragement of a group of erudite lawyers with whom he became associated, and the eminent scholar Guillaume Budé with whom he corresponded, he began the study of Greek. Greek being then in disrepute among the Franciscans, Rabelais moved to a nearby Benedictine convent, the better to pursue his humanistic studies. As secretary to the bishop, Geoffroy d'Estissac, he traveled widely in Poitou, gaining that detailed knowledge of the local terrain, speech, customs, amusements, and legends which was to lend his writings their special popular and realistic flavor. He probably lived at Paris in the period 1528–30 and attended the university there. At the University of Montpellier, where he matriculated and received the degree of bachelor of medicine in 1530, he distinguished himself by his learned commentaries on Greek medical texts. By 1532 he was a practicing physician at Lyons, though he did not receive the doctor's degree until 1537. In 1534 he became physician to Jean du Bellay, bishop of Paris, in whose company he did considerable traveling, including several sojourns at Rome. In 1539 he was engaged as physician to Guillaume du Bellay-Langey, governor of Piedmont. From 1854, when the latter died, to 1546, Rabelais is lost to view. In 1546, his *Tiers Livre* having been condemned by the Sorbonne theologians, he took refuse at Metz. From 1548 to 1550 he was at Rome with Jean du Bellay, now a cardinal.

Literary Works and Viewpoint. Rabelais is best known as the author of *Gargantua and Pantagruel*, one of the world's literary masterpieces, the five books of which appeared from 1532 to 1564, the last posthumously and of debatable authenticity. Each book has a character and emphasis of its own. This epic of men and giants presents a juxtaposition on a vast scale of erudition and popular lore, of serious philosophy and obscene buffoonery, of crass realism and esoteric allegory. His extended discussions of contemporary life and thought, although placed in a framework of unrestrained fantasy, provide a faithful mirror of Renaissance social customs and intellectual interests. In his opposition to war Rabelais assumed, for the most part, the enlightened humanist position represented by Erasmus. His satire of legal practices and his attack on monasticism are applications of his expansive spirit. In the quarrel on the worth of women, which raged in the 1540's, Rabelais took an antifeminist stand. In his detailed treatments of navigation and of mechanical inventions he is to be associated with the forward-looking thinkers who, by about 1600, brought about a fusion of scholarship and the skilled crafts to produce modern science. Readers of Rabelais have usually been impressed by his exuberance, his optimism, and his generally expansive view of the world and man. The best-known English translation is that of Thomas Urquhart and Pierre Motteux (1653–1708).

Rabelais, the English. An epithet given variously to Jonathan Swift, Thomas Amory, and Laurence Sterne.

Rachel Verinder (rā′chel ver′in.dėr). See **Verinder, Rachel.**

Rachel Wardle (wôr′dl), **Miss.** See under **Wardle, Mr.**

Racine (ra.sēn′; French, rȧ.sēn), **Jean Baptiste.** b. at La Ferté-Milon, France, in December, 1639; d. at Paris, April 26, 1699. A French tragic poet and dramatist. He lost his parents at a very early age, and was brought up by his grandparents. His studies, having begun when he was ten years old at the College of Beauvais, were continued at Port-Royal, and finished at the Collège d'Harcourt (1658–59). On graduating, he went to live with a cousin of his, who was in the service of the Duc de Luynes. He was well received in society, and made friends among men of literary bent. His early training in Greek and Latin classics, especially the former, had been very thorough, and his tastes all ran in the direction of intellectual pursuits. He attracted attention in this line for the first time by an ode written for the marriage of Louis XIV, and entitled *La Nymphe de la Seine* (1660). A couple of short comedies, *Amasie* (1660) and *Les Amours d'Ovide* (1661), are among his first attempts as a playwright, and unfortunately are now lost. His friendly

relations with men like Jean de La Fontaine, Nicolas Boileau, and Molière led him to devote himself to writing for the stage; he thus produced a couple of plays, *La Thébaïde* (1664) and *Alexandre* (1665). His first real success as a dramatic poet was scored in *Andromaque* (1667), which is the initial tragedy in a long series of masterpieces. He attempted comedy next in *Les Plaideurs* (1668), but reverted completely to tragedy in *Britannicus* (1669), *Bérénice* (1670), *Bajazet* (1672), *Mithridate* (1673), *Iphigénie* (1674), and *Phèdre* (1677). Racine's enemies conspired against him at this time, and preferred to him a minor poet named Nicolas Pradon, who had written a rival tragedy on Phaedra which they extolled far above Racine's play. The great poet abstained then for a number of years from composing tragedies, but finally, at the request of Madame de Maintenon, wrote two plays of great lyric beauty, dealing with subjects from the Bible: *Esther* (1689) and *Athalie* (1691). Besides the above, Racine composed four hymns that rank among the finest productions in lyric poetry of his day; also an *Abrégé de l'histoire de Port-Royal*, and a few other minor writings. The best edition of Racine's works was made by Paul Mesnard for the *Collection des grands écrivains de la France* (1865–74).

Racket (rak′et), **Mrs.** A character in Hannah Cowley's comedy *The Belle's Stratagem.*

Rackstraw (rak′strô), **Ralph.** In Gilbert and Sullivan's *Pinafore*, an Able Seaman in love with Josephine, the daughter of Captain Corcoran. His name is pronounced (rāf) rather than (ralf), the former being a variant of the name still heard in Great Britain.

Radcliffe (rad′klif), **Ann.** [Maiden name, **Ward.**] b. at London, July 9, 1764; d. there, Feb. 7, 1823. An English novelist. Among her novels are *The Castles of Athlin and Dunbayne* (1789), *A Sicilian Romance* (1790), *The Romance of the Forest* (1791), *The Mysteries of Udolpho* (1794), and *The Italian* (1797). In these, especially in the last three, she used the English scenery and ruins she loved to view as background for romantic tales of villainy and horror that are the archetypes of the so-called Gothic novel. The supernatural terrors in her books are always explained as being attributable to natural causes; although her novels were later surpassed in the multiplication of the mysterious, she remains among the most readable novelists of the genre.

Radcliffe, John. b. at Wakefield, England, 1650; d. near London, Nov. 1, 1714. An English physician, founder of the Radcliffe Library at Oxford. He studied at Oxford, and in 1684 settled at London as a medical practitioner. He obtained great celebrity as a physician, and attended several members of the royal family. He entered Parliament in 1713. He left 40,000 pounds for the building of the library at Oxford which bears his name.

Radcliffe Library. A library, originally medical, connected with Oxford University: founded by John Radcliffe (1650–1714).

Radigund (rad′i.gund). The Queen of the Amazons in Spenser's *Faerie Queene*. She captures Sir Artegall, and forces him to dress like a woman and spin flax. He is rescued by Britomart, who slays Radigund.

Radot (rá.dō).   See **Badinguet**.

Raeburn (rā'-bẽrn), Sir **Henry**. b. at Stockbridge, near Edinburgh, March 4, 1756; d. there, July 8, 1823. A Scottish portrait painter. He was educated at Heriot's Hospital, and at 15 apprenticed to a goldsmith at Edinburgh. From this he passed to miniature painting and to oil painting, entirely self-taught. On the advice of Sir Joshua Reynolds, he studied in Italy, returning to Edinburgh in 1787, where he remained. He painted portraits of Scott, Blair, Robertson, Dugald Stewart, and others. In 1814 he was made associate royal academician, and in 1815 royal academician.

Raffle Buffle (raf'l buf'l), **Sir**.   See **Buffle, Sir Raffle**.

Raffles (raf'lz). A gentleman burglar and chief character in *The Amateur Cracksman* (1899) and other books by E. W. Hornung (1866–1921).

Ragman Roll. A collection of parchments recording the fealty of Scottish nobles, clergy, and gentry to Edward I of England in 1296.

Ragman Roll. A poem printed by Wynkyn de Worde, consisting of a list, in alternate stanzas, of good and bad women.

Ragnar Lodbrok (räg'när lōd'brōk). In Old Norse legend, a Viking, who became king of Denmark and invaded England in the 8th century.

Ragnarök (räg'nä.rẽk). In Old Norse mythology, the final battle of the world between the gods and the evil powers, in which all perish and the universe is consumed by fire. The only survivors are one man and one woman, Lif and Lifthrasir, who sleep safely in Hodmimir's forest through it all, and waken to repeople the earth.

Rahu (rä'hö). In Hindu mythology, the demon who seizes the sun and moon, and thereby occasions their eclipse. In Hindu astronomical treatises the name is applied to the ascending node, the eclipse itself, and especially the moment at which the obscuration begins.

Raigne of King Edward the Third (rān), **The**. See **Edward III.**

Raina (rī'nä). The young Bulgarian girl in love with the heroic Sergius in George Bernard Shaw's *Arms and the Man*.

Rainbow, The. A novel by D. H. Lawrence, published in 1915. Its sequel is *Women in Love* (1920). It deals with the proud and hot-tempered Brangwen family of Nottinghamshire, and tells of three generations of these farmers and craftsmen.

Rakonitz Chronicles (rạ.kon'its), **The**. A trilogy on Jewish life and character by G. B. Stern, published collectively in 1932. It consists of the novels *Tents of Israel* (1924; American title, *The Matriarch*, 1925), *A Deputy Was King* (1926), and *Mosaic* (1930).

Rakshasas (räk'shạ.sạz). In Hindu mythology, a group of evil demons who are inimical to mankind. They play a great part in Hindu belief. They are believed to haunt cemeteries, destroy sacrifices, animate dead bodies, ensnare and even devour human beings and corpses. Some have long arms, some are fat, some thin, some dwarfish, some tall and humpbacked, some have only one eye, some only one ear, some have five feet, or enormous paunches, poisonous projecting teeth, and crooked thighs; occasionally they assume beautiful forms, but their eyes are always vertical slits.

Raleigh (rô'li, rä'li), Sir **Walter**. [Surname as he preferred to spell it, **Ralegh**.] b. at Hayes, Devonshire, England, c1552; executed at London, Oct. 29, 1618. An English courtier, colonizer, and poet. After a short residence at Oriel College, Oxford, he entered the Huguenot army (1569), returning to England before 1576. He joined (1578) his half-brother Sir Humphrey Gilbert in an expedition purportedly to explore and discover; in fact, the ships were to engage in piracy on the Spaniards. They were, however, driven back both in 1578 and 1579 without appreciable gains. Raleigh soon thereafter became attached to the followers of Robert Dudley, Earl of Leicester, the queen's favorite. In 1580, he commanded an English company in Munster, Ireland. On his return he came into great favor at court; according to legend, this was due to his gallant action of spreading his cloak over a puddle so that the queen might not wet her shoes. Actually, his personal charm, good looks, and powerful sponsors at court all probably facilitated his rapid rise. He was granted several estates, a licensing patent, and a woolen-export monopoly (1584). In 1585 he became warden of the stanneries, giving him wide control in the tin mines of the west country, and vice-admiral of Devon and Cornwall; in 1586 he was captain of the guard. In 1584 he was granted a charter of colonization, and sent Philip Amadas and Arthur Barlow to explore the region between Florida and the Carolinas, which he called Virginia in honor of Elizabeth, the "Virgin Queen." In 1585 he despatched a fleet of colonists, who landed on Roanoke Island, but were brought back by Francis Drake the following year. In 1587 another body of emigrants was sent out; they settled on Roanoke Island, but had disappeared when a relief expedition reached the island in 1590; Virginia Dare was born during this unsuccessful colonizing attempt and suffered whatever fate befell the colonists. About 1586 Raleigh introduced the potato in Munster on lands he was granted by the queen; he is also credited with introducing the "drinking" of tobacco, as smoking was then called. In 1588 he took an active part against the Armada. During this period he became a friend of Edmund Spenser, whom he had met in Ireland some years earlier. He introduced Spenser to Elizabeth and persuaded him to publish the *Faerie Queene*. He had, however, gradually fallen out of the queen's favor as she became more and more infatuated with Robert Devereux, 2nd Earl of Essex; despite Raleigh's attempts to succeed the recently deceased Leicester as her principal favorite, he lost out, probably because of the intrigues of the many courtiers who had come to dislike his swaggering manner and who looked upon him as a Devonshire upstart. He stayed away from court for almost four years, but when Essex married he again came into favor. However, for his seduction of and marriage to Elizabeth Throckmorton (or Throgmorton), one of the queen's maids of honor, he was imprisoned (1592) in the Tower. Again barred from court, although granted freedom, Raleigh became the center of a group of poets and scientists, known as the "school of night," that included Christopher Marlowe, Thomas Harriot, George Chapman, Walter Warner, and Matthew Royden, among others. This brilliant group, containing some of the best minds in England, gained notoriety for their free attitude toward such matters as religion, in those days so closely tied to government in the person of the monarch that atheism was tantamount to treason; Marlowe was killed before the Privy Council could examine him on his opinions, but an official investigation was made into Raleigh's beliefs in 1594, the charges eventually dying for lack of decisive evidence. In 1595 he sailed for Trinidad and ascended the Orinoco in an effort to find treasure, but the expedition was fruitless. In 1596 he commanded a squadron under Charles Howard and the Earl of Essex in the expedition which destroyed the Spanish fleet at Cadiz; in 1597 he captured Fayal in the Azores, gaining renown in both expeditions. He again quarreled with Essex, and again fell out of favor at court. In 1600 he was appointed governor of Jersey and in 1601 took part in suppressing Essex's rebellion. He served as captain of the guard at the execution of Essex, but his triumph was shortlived. Elizabeth's death brought to the throne James I, whose policies ran counter to those Raleigh had supported. The background is unclear, but apparently James looked upon Essex as one of his supporters and therefore upon Raleigh as one of his enemies, all the more so since he favored a peaceful conclusion to the troubles with Spain and Raleigh was an exponent of further attacks on the Spaniard. In addition, Raleigh's enemies continued to work against him and Raleigh was probably implicated in one or several of the plots to keep the king from the throne. On the accession of James in 1603, Raleigh was stripped of his honors and estates and charged with a plot to place Arabella Stuart on the throne. He was again imprisoned in the Tower, tried very unfairly in November, 1603, and sentenced to death. The sentence was not carried out, but Raleigh remained a prisoner in the Tower until 1616. In the Tower he devoted himself to chemical experiments, and wrote as much of his *History of the World* as was ever finished. In 1616 he was released to command another expedition to Guiana and the Orinoco, promising not only that he would find gold but also that he would not interfere with the Spaniards; obviously this whole attempt was a move of desperation, Raleigh preferring to stake everything on one last gamble, for if he should find gold the inevitable clash with the Spaniards might be overlooked. The expedition was a failure from the start; ships were lost in storms; his men melted away as the result of disease and desertion; a group got into a fight with the Spaniards and Raleigh's son was killed. On his return, when the Spanish ambassador made an official complaint about the destruction of a Spanish town by Raleigh, the old sentence was invoked, and Raleigh was executed. In addition to the incomplete *History of the World*, which contains a famous apostrophe to Death, he wrote a number of prose works, including accounts of the Azores fight and the discovery of Guiana, and he was the author of several poems: *Cynthia* (which is his longest extant poem and may be a fragment of a much longer work), *The Lie, The Pilgrimage, The Nymph's Reply* (to Marlowe's *The Passionate Shepherd*), the sonnet

appended to the *Faerie Queene* "Methought I saw the grave where Laura lay," and others.

Raleigh, Sir Walter Alexander. b. 1861; d. May 13, 1922. An English essayist and biographer. He was professor of modern literature at University College, Liverpool (1889–1900), of English language and literature at Glasgow University (1900–04), and from 1904 of English literature at Oxford. He published *The English Novel* (1894), *Robert Louis Stevenson* (1895), *Style* (1897), *Milton* (1900), *Wordsworth* (1903), *The English Voyages of the Sixteenth Century* (1906), *Shakespeare* (1907), *Six Essays on Johnson* (1910), and *Romance* (1917).

Ralph (ralf; British also rāf). A grocer's apprentice who becomes the "Grocer Errant," or "Knight of the Burning Pestle," in Beaumont's play of the latter name.

Ralph. The husband of Jane, an industrious young journeyman employed by Simon Eyre in Dekker's *Shoemaker's Holiday*.

Ralph, James. b. at Philadelphia between 1695 and 1705; d. at Chiswick, England, Jan. 24, 1762. An English pamphleteer, historical writer, poet, and playwright. He went to England (1724) with Benjamin Franklin, settled there, and began writing poetry. He became a political journalist in the pay of Frederick Louis, Prince of Wales.

Ralph Mouldy (mōl'di). See **Mouldy, Ralph.**

Ralph Nickleby (nik'l.bi). See **Nickleby, Ralph.**

Ralph Rackstraw (rāf rak'strô). See **Rackstraw, Ralph.**

Ralph Roister Doister (ralf, rāf, rois'tėr dois'tėr). A comedy by Nicholas Udall, probably written before 1553, and acted by the boys at the Chapel Royal or Westminster School. It was licensed and printed in 1566, and is considered to be the first English comedy. The *Miles Gloriosus* of Plautus appears to be its direct forerunner. Many of the Latin comedy character types are here, the principal one being the braggart warrior, Ralph. Dame Custance is a middle-class city lady, vulgar yet always pretending to maintain the proprieties. She holds off several suitors, including the foolish Ralph, by her deft boxing of ears, and is finally reconciled to Goodluck, the man to whom she was originally engaged.

Ramachandra (rä.mạ.chan'drạ). The hero of the Ramayana, and a character in the Mahabharata.

Ramadan (ram.ạ.dän') or **Ramazan** (ram.ạ.zän'). The ninth month of the Mohammedan year. Each day of the entire month is observed as a fast from dawn till sunset.

Ram Alley, or Merry Tricks. A comedy by David Barry, acted c1608 and printed in 1611. Ram Alley led from Fleet Street to the Temple, and formerly secured immunity from arrest; hence it was the resort of sharpers and persons of ill fame of both sexes.

Ramayana (rä.mä'yạ.nạ). One of the two great epics of India, the other being the *Mahabharata*. It is ascribed to a poet Valmiki of the 2nd century B.C., and consists at present of ab. 24,000 couplets, divided into seven books. It is the production of one man, though many parts are later additions, such as those in which Ramachandra is represented as an incarnation of Vishnu, all the episodes in the first book, and the whole of the seventh. It was at first handed down orally, and variously modified in transmission, as afterward when reduced to writing; hence the number of distinct recensions, agreeing for the most part as to contents, but following a different arrangement. One belongs to Benares and the NW; another to Calcutta and Bengal proper; a third to Bombay and W India; while Weber found among the manuscripts of the Berlin Library what seemed to be a fourth. In 1806 and 1810 the text and translation of two books in the Bengal recension were published at Serampore; in 1829–38 A. W. von Schlegel at Bonn published two of the northern, with Latin translation; in 1843–70 the Italian Gorresio published at Paris the complete text of the Bengali recension, with Italian translation. Two complete editions of the text appeared in 1859 in India, one at Bombay, the other at Calcutta. There is an English translation by Griffiths (Benares, 1870–74), following the Bombay edition.

Rambler, The. A periodical, after the style of *The Spectator*, published at London (1750–52) by Samuel Johnson.

Rambouillet (räm.bo͞o.ye), Marquise **de.** [Title of **Catherine de Vivonne.**] b. at Rome, 1588; d. at Paris, 1665. A French social leader, celebrated for her influence on French literature and society through the meetings in her salon.

Rambures (ram.bo͞o′riz; French, räṅ.bor). In Shakespeare's *Henry V*, the Master of the Cross-bows and one of the French lords who boast about the power of the French army before the battle of Agincourt.

Ramée (rà.mā′), **Marie Louise de la.** [Pseudonym, **Ouida.**] b. at Bury Saint Edmunds, England, 1840; d. at Viareggio, Italy, Jan. 25, 1908. English novelist. Her works include *Strathmore* (1865), *Chandos* (1866), *Idalia* (1867), *Under Two Flags* (1867), *Tricotrin* (1868), *A Dog of Flanders* (1872), *Pascarel* (1873), *Ariadne* (1880), *Moths* (1880), *Bimbi* (1882), *In Maremma* (1882), *Princess Napraxine* (1884), *A Rainy June* (1885), *Othmar* (1885), *Don Gesualdo* (1886), *A House Party* (1887), *Guilderoy* (1889), *Ruffino* (1890), *Syrlin* (1890), *The Tower of Taddeo* (1890), *Santa Barbara* (1891), *The New Priesthood* (1893), *The Silver Christ* (1894), *Two Offenders* (1894), *Le Selve* (1896), *The Massarenes* (1897), *Toxin, an Altruist* (1897), *La Stregha* (1899), *The Waters of Edera* (1900), *Critical Studies* (1900), and *Street Dust* (1901).

Raminagrobis (rà.mē.nà.gro.bēs). In François Rabelais's *Gargantua and Pantagruel*, an aged poet. The character was intended to represent Guillaume Crétin, a poet celebrated at that time, but now almost utterly forgotten. Jean de La Fontaine gave the name to a great cat in his *Fables*.

Ramorny (rạ.môr′ni), **Sir John.** In Sir Walter Scott's novel *The Fair Maid of Perth*, the arrogant and dissolute man who serves as "Master of the Horse" to the Duke of Rothsay. He murders Rothsay when Rothsay dismisses him from his service, and is himself hanged on the same day in punishment.

Ramsay (ram′zi), **Allan.** b. at Leadhills, Lanarkshire, Scotland, Oct. 15, 1686; d. at Edinburgh,

Jan. 7, 1758. A Scottish poet. Of very humble birth, he was apprenticed at 15 to a wigmaker at Edinburgh. *The Gentle Shepherd*, a pastoral comedy, his best-known work, was suggested by the critique of Alexander Pope's *Windsor Forest* in the *Guardian*, April 7, 1713. It substituted for the pseudo-pastoral poetry of the time the real life of the Scottish shepherds. It has been called "the first genuine pastoral after Theocritus." He set up a bookshop in High Street and published his collections of poems, *The Tea-Table Miscellany* (English and Scottish songs, 1724–27; the music for these was published in 1763–75) and *The Ever Green*, the precursor of *Percy's Reliques*, containing Scottish songs written before 1600 (1724–27); *Thirty Fables*, partly original (1730), and *Scots Proverbs* (1737).

Ramsay, Andrew Michael. [Called **Chevalier de Ramsay.**] b. at Ayr, Scotland, July 9, 1686; d. at St.-Germain-en-Laye, France, May 6, 1743. A Scottish author. He wrote in French; his chief work is *Les Voyages de Cyrus* (1727).

Ramsay, Margaret. In Sir Walter Scott's *The Fortunes of Nigel*, a watchmaker's daughter. She eventually marries the hero.

Ramsay, Sir William Mitchell. b. at Glasgow, March 15, 1851; d. at Bournemouth, England, April 20, 1939. A Scottish historian and archaeologist. Author of *The Historical Geography of Asia Minor* (1890), *The Church in the Roman Empire* (1893), *Was Christ Born at Bethlehem?* (1898), *The Education of Christ* (1902), *Pauline and Other Studies in Early Christian History* (1906), *The Bearing of Recent Research on the Trustworthiness of the New Testament* (1914), *Asianic Elements in Greek Civilization* (1927), and *The Social Basis of the Permanence of the Roman Empire, traced from the inscriptions of Sterrett and other travellers* (part I, 1938).

Ran (rän). [Old Norse, **Rán.**] In Old Norse mythology, the goddess of the stormy sea; she caught ships in her hands and drowning men in her net.

Randolph (ran′dolf), **Thomas.** b. at Houghton, Daventry, Northamptonshire, England, 1605; d. in March, 1635. An English poet and dramatist, one of the "sons" of Ben Jonson. He wrote the plays *Aristippus, Or, The Joviall Philosopher*, *The Muses' Looking-Glass, a Comedy*, *Amyntas, or the Impossible Dowry*, *The Conceited Pedlar*, *The Jealous Lovers*, and a number of minor poems.

Random (ran′dọm), **Roderick.** In Smollett's *Roderick Random*, a good-humored but unprincipled young Scottish adventurer.

Random Harvest. A novel by James Hilton, published in 1941.

Rands (randz), **William Brighty.** [Called **"the Laureate of the Nursery"**; pseudonyms, **Henry Holbeach** and **Matthew Browne.**] b. 1823; d. 1882. An English writer, known for his children's fairy tales and poems. One of his more noted works is *Lilliput Levee*, illustrated by Millais and Pinwell.

Ranelagh Gardens (ran′ẹ.lạ). Gardens formerly situated near the Thames, in Chelsea, London. They were noted for concerts from c1740 to c1805, and famous as the scene of wild and extravagant entertainments and masquerades. They were closed in 1805, and no trace of them remains today.

Ranger (rān′jẻr). A cynical roué in Wycherley's *Love in a Wood*. He makes love to Christina.

Ranke (räng′kẹ), **Leopold von.** b. at Wiehe, Thuringia, Germany, Dec. 21, 1795; d. at Berlin, May 23, 1886. A German historian. He was educated at Leipzig; became professor extraordinary of history at Berlin in 1825, professor ordinary in 1834, and historiographer of Prussia in 1841; he retired from his professorship in 1871. He is usually regarded as the founder of modern historical study. In place of the older method of reliance on tradition and legend and of the approach based on philosophical or other preconceptions, he substituted recourse to original sources in an effort to reconstruct events as they occurred and without the intervention of subsequent interpretation. His chief works are *Geschichten der romanischen und germanischen Völker von 1494 bis 1535* (1824), *Fürsten und Völker von Düdeuropa im 16. und 17. Jahrhundert* (1827), *Die serbische Revolution* (1829), *Die Verschwörung gegen Venedig im Jahr 1688* (1831), *Die römischen Päpste* (1834–37), *Deutsche Geschichte im Zeitalter der Reformation* (1839–47), *Neun Bücher preussicher Geschichte* (1847–48), *Französische Geschichte, vornehmlich im 16. und 17. Jahrhundert* (1852–61), *Englische Geschichte im 16. und 17. Jahrhundert* (1859–67), *Weltgeschichte* (1880–86), *Geschichte Wallensteins* (1869), *Ursprung des Siebenjährigen Krieges* (1871), *Ursprung der Revolutionskriege 1791 und 1792* (1875), and *Die deutschen Mächte und der Fürstenbund* (1872).

Ransome (ran′sọm), **Arthur.** b. at Leeds, Yorkshire, England, Jan. 18, 1884——. An English writer. Author of *Edgar Allan Poe* (1910), *The Hoof-marks of the Faun* (1911), *The Elixir of Life* (1915), *Six Weeks in Russia* (1919), *The Chinese Puzzle* (1927), and, for children, *Swallows and Amazons* (1930), *Peter Duck* (1932), *Winter Holiday* (1933), *Secret Water* (1939), and *The Picts and the Martyrs* (1943).

Ranulf de Glanville (ran′ulf dẹ glan′vil). See **Glanville, Ranulf de.**

Rape of Lucrece (lö.krēs′), **The.** [Also, **Lucrece.**] A narrative poem by Shakespeare, published in 1594, taken from the Roman story of Lucretia.

Rape of Lucrece, The. A tragedy by Thomas Heywood, published in 1608 and revised in 1636. It was produced in 1612. Possibly it was written in 1607, since the Roman theme may have been suggested by an edition of Shakespeare's *Rape of Lucrece* which appeared in that year; however, Heywood used Livy for the historical material in the play.

Rape of the Lock, The. A mock-heroic poem by Alexander Pope, published in two cantos in 1712 in Barnaby Lintot's *Miscellany*, and in its present form in five cantos in 1714. It is based on an actual incident (the cutting, despite the young lady's protests, of a lock of Arabella Fermor's hair by a young nobleman in love with her). Pope considered that the hue and cry over this matter (the two families became bitterly hostile to each other as a result of it) was a trifle foolish, and attempted to soothe the hurt feelings of all concerned by glorifying the incident, which ends, in Pope's poem, with the lock of hair going to the heavens to shine with the stars.

Rape upon Rape. [Full title, **Rape upon Rape; or, The Justice Caught in his Own Trap.**] A comedy by Henry Fielding, produced in 1730. It was later staged again, as *The Coffee-House Politician.* The play deals with the cruel and venal Justice Squeezum, who is finally betrayed by his own greed.

Raphael (raf′ạ.ẹl, rā′fạ.ẹl). [Also: **Rafael** or **Raffaello** (räf.fä.el′lō); original surname, **Sanzio** or **Santi.**] b. at Urbino, Italy, March 28, 1483; d. at Rome, April 6, 1520. An Italian painter of the Renaissance, still one of the best known, particularly for his madonnas.

Raphael. In Jewish and Christian angelology, one of the seven archangels, the angel of healing. He is the companion and instructor of Tobias in the Book of Tobit; and Milton represents him in *Paradise Lost* as the instructor of Adam and Eve.

Rappoport (rap′ọ.pōrt), **Angelo Solomon.** b. at Baturin, in Little Russia, Sept. 5, 1871; d. June 2, 1950. A British editor and author. He was on the staff (1906) of the *Encyclopaedia Britannica*, and edited *Twentieth Century Russia* (1915–16), the *New Gresham Encyclopedia* (1918–24), and *Illustrated Palestine* (1927–29). He coedited the *British Encyclopedia* (1933). In France at the outbreak of World War II, he was arrested (1940) by the Gestapo for his anti-Nazi writings and interned in concentration camps until 1944. His publications include *Primer of Philosophy* (1903), *Russian History* (1905), *English Drama* (1906), *Home Life in Russia* (1913), *History of Poland* (1915), *Dictionary of Socialism* (1926), *Myths and Legends of Ancient Israel* (3 vols., 1928), *Medieval Legends of Christ* (1934), *The Gauntlet against the Gospel* (1936), and *The Folk-lore of the Jews* (1937).

Raredrench (rär′drench). In Sir Walter Scott's novel *The Fortunes of Nigel*, an apothecary: ". . . as sometimes happens to those of the learned professions, [he] had rather more lore than knowledge."

Rashleigh Osbaldistone (rash′li oz.bôl′dis.tọn). See **Osbaldistone, Rashleigh.**

Raspe (räs′pẹ), **Rudolph Erich.** b. at Hanover, Germany, 1737; d. at Muckross, Ireland, 1794. A German author. He was for a time professor of archaeology and curator of the museum at Kassel, but was charged with stealing medals under his care, and fled to England to avoid prosecution. He was assay master and storekeeper at the Dolcoath mines in Cornwall (1782–88). He then went to Caithness in Scotland, where his "salting" activities to delude Sir John Sinclair into believing he possessed valuable mining properties were exposed, forcing Raspe to flee to Ireland; the incident was the basis for Sir Walter Scott's characterization of Dousterswivel in *The Antiquary*. He wrote some scientific works, but is known chiefly as the compiler of *Baron Munchausen's Narrative of his Marvellous Travels and Campaigns in Russia* (1785), a German translation of which was introduced in Germany by the poet Gottfried August Bürger in 1786.

---

d̤, d or j; ṣ, s or sh; ṭ, t or ch; z̧, z or zh; o, F. cloche; ü, F. menu; c̓h, Sc. loch; ṅ, F. bonbon.

Rasselas (ras'ẹ.lạs). A philosophical romance by Samuel Johnson, published in 1759. Rasselas lives in the Happy Valley, a land where pain and hardship are unknown. He resolves to go out into the world to compare his condition with that of other men, and to seek out the happiest life in existence. With him go his sister Nekayah and the poet Imlac. However, all three become very unhappy when they find that no man is satisfied with his life, and after many adventures and philosophical discussions they all return to the Happy Valley.

Rastell (ras.tel'), **John.** b. at Coventry, England, c1475; d. at London, 1536. An English printer, lawyer, and author. In 1518 he wrote *The Nature of the Four Elements*, an interlude on the principles of moral philosophy. For *The Field of the Cloth of Gold*, another interlude, he contrived a roof for the Banquet Hall out of silken thread interlaced with gold, and thereby gained himself a considerable reputation as a presenter of pageants for ceremonial occasions. He published (c1524) *A Hundred Merry Tales*, which became a standard Elizabethan jest-book, and in the period 1526–29 two interludes, *Gentilness and Nobility* and *Calisto and Melibea*. He also printed works by John Heywood, his son-in-law, and Thomas More, his brother-in-law, especially the famous *Utopia*.

Ratcliff (rat'klif), **Sir Richard.** In Shakespeare's *Richard III*, a follower of the King who leads Richard's various victims to execution. He is killed at Bosworth with Richard.

Ratsey (rat'si), **Gamaliel.** Hanged at Bedford, England, March 26, 1605. An English highwayman. His notoriety is celebrated in several ballads. In carrying out his exploits, Ratsey always wore a mask.

Ratsey's Ghost. [Also, **Ratsei's Ghost.**] A very rare tract, printed without date, but supposed to have been published in 1605. It mentions *Hamlet* by name, and refers to the author and some circumstances of his life. Gamaliel Ratsey, whose exploits are described, is referred to in many other publications of the time.

Rat, the Cat, and Lovel the Dog (luv'ẹl), **The.** The first line of a 15th-century political rhyme, which was followed by the line "Rule all England under the Hog." The three animals in the first line refer to three of the followers of Richard III: Ratcliffe, Catesby, and Lovell. The Hog refers to the figure of a boar in the royal coat of arms, and therefore symbolizes Richard III.

Rattlin (rat'lin), **Jack.** A sailor in Tobias Smollett's novel *Roderick Random*.

Rauf Coilyear (rôf koil'yèr). [Full title, **The Taill of Rauf Coilyear.**] A Middle English verse romance written in Scotland between 1475 and 1500. It tells with some humor how a peasant entertains Charlemagne in disguise, and, unaware that he is not conversing with a man humble as himself, treats the king very boldly.

Ravenscroft (rā'vẹnz.kroft), **Edward.** b. c1650; d. 1697. An English dramatist, at one time a student of law. He was skilled in making popular if trifling farces from borrowed material. In his plays he took passages, style, situations, and whole plots from the works of English, French, Spanish, and Italian writers. *The Citizen Turn'd Gentleman* (1671; reissued as *Mamamouchi*, 1675) and *The Careless Lovers* (1673) derive from Molière. *The English Lawyer* (1678) is a translation of George Ruggle's Latin play *Ignoramus*. *Scaramouch* (1677) is from a Spanish source. Other plays by Ravenscroft include *The Wrangling Lovers* (1677), *King Edgar and Alfreda* (1677), *The London Cuckolds* (1682), *Dame Dobson* (1684), *The Canterbury Guests* (1695), *The Anatomist* (1697), and *The Italian Husband* (1697).

Ravenscroft, Thomas. b. c1590; d. c1633. An English song composer, remembered for *The Whole Booke of Psalmes*, commonly known as *Ravenscroft's Psalter*, containing 100 settings, of which he composed 48. His *Pammelia, Musick's Miscellanie* (1609) is the first such English work; he was the collector also of *Deuteromelia* (1609) and *Melismata* (1611), containing such well-known rounds and catches as *Three Blind Mice, Hold Thy Peace, We Be Soldiers Three*, and *The Three Ravens*.

Ravenshoe (rā'vẹnz.hō). A romance by Henry Kingsley, published in 1862.

Ravenswood (rā'vẹnz.wúd), **Edgar, Master of.** The lover of Lucy Ashton in Scott's *Bride of Lammermoor*. A melancholy and revengeful man, finding her, as he supposes, faithless to him, he bitterly reproaches her, is challenged by her brother, and perishes in a quicksand on his way to the meeting.

Rawdon Crawley (rô'dọn krô'li). See under **Crawley.**

Rawlinson (rô'lin.sọn), **George.** b. at Chadlington, Oxfordshire, England, Nov. 23, 1812; d. at Canterbury, England, Oct. 6, 1902. An English historian, Orientalist, and theologian; brother of Sir H. C. Rawlinson. He held (1861–89) the Camden professorship of ancient history at Oxford, and was canon (1872 *et seq.*) of Canterbury and rector (1888 *et seq.*) of All Hallows, London. Author of *The Five Great Monarchies of the Ancient Eastern World: Chaldea, Assyria, Babylonia, Media, Persia* (1862–67), *The Sixth Great Oriental Monarchy: Parthia* (1873), *The Seventh Great Oriental Monarchy: the Sassanian or New Persian Empire* (1876), *A History of Egypt* (1881), *Phoenicia* (1889), and various theological works.

Rawlinson, Sir Henry Creswicke. b. at Chadlington, Oxfordshire, England, April 11, 1810; d. at London, March 5, 1895. An English Assyriologist and diplomatist. He entered the East India Company's army in 1827, and held various important offices both military and diplomatic, retiring in 1855. In 1859 he was appointed British minister at Teheran, where he remained one year. He became a member of the Council of India in 1858 and again in 1868. He copied, amid great hardships, the trilingual inscription of Darius I (Darius Hystaspis) at Behistun; the transcription, and its interpretation, were published by him from 1846 to 1851. He published *On the Inscriptions of Assyria and Babylonia* (1850), *Outline of the History of Assyria* (1852), and *England and Russia in the East* (1875); and was the joint editor of *Cuneiform Inscriptions of Western Asia* (1861–70), and other collections of inscriptions.

Rawnsley (rônz'li), **Hardwicke Drummond.** b. at Henley-on-Thames, England, Sept. 28, 1851; d.

May 28, 1920. An English clergyman, author, and poet. He was vicar of Wray, Windermere (1878–83), vicar of Crosthwaite, Keswick, and rural dean from 1883, and honorary canon of Carlisle. Among his works are *Valete Tennyson, and Other Poems* (1893), *Literary Associations of the English Lakes* (1894), *Life and Nature at the English Lakes* (1899), *Memories of the Tennysons* (1900), *A Rambler's Notebook at the English Lakes* (1902), *Sermons on the Sayings of Jesus* (1905), *Months at the Lakes* (1906), *A Sonnet Chronicle* (1906), *Round the Lake Country* (1909), and others.

Ray or Wray (rā). **John.** b. at Black Notley, Essex, England, Nov. 29, 1627; d. there, Jan. 17, 1705. An English naturalist, called "the father of English natural history." He traveled (1663–66) on the Continent with Francis Willughby. It is thought that the latter deserves much of the praise which Ray received as the founder of systematic zoölogy. Together they collected many specimens of plant and animal life on which to base a system of classification. Ray occupied himself with the plants: he first used the number of cotyledons as a means of dividing the plant kingdom and adopted the flower as the basis for classification into genera and species. He continued Willughby's work in classifying the animal kingdom, carrying it further than the birds and fishes that Willughby had completed at the time of his death (1672). He published *Catalogus plantarum Angliae* (1670); *A Collection of English Proverbs* (1670, and many later editions); *Methodus plantarum nova* (1628); *Historia plantarum* (1686–1704); *Methodus insectorum* (1705), and many zoölogical works; *The Wisdom of God manifested in the Works of the Creation* (1691); *Miscellaneous Discourses* (1692); etc. The Ray Society was established in 1844 for the purpose of publishing "rare books of established merit" on zoölogy, botany, and other divisions of natural history.

Razor (rā′zọr). An amusing intriguing valet in Sir John Vanbrugh's comedy *The Provoked Wife.*

Re (rā). See **Ra.**

Read (rēd), **Herbert** (**Edward**). b. near Kirbymooreside, Yorkshire, England, Dec. 4, 1893—. An English critic and poet. He was assistant keeper (1922–31) at the Victoria and Albert Museum, and professor of fine arts (1931 *et seq.*) at Edinburgh. Author of *Songs of Chaos* (1915), *Naked Warriors* (1919), *Eclogues* (1919), *Mutations of the Phoenix* (1923), *Reason and Romanticism* (1926), *Phases of English Poetry* (1928), *The Sense of Glory* (1929), *The Meaning of Art* (1931; American title, *The Anatomy of Art*, 1932), *The Innocent Eye* (1933), *The End of a War* (1933), *Poems, 1914–1934* (1935), *Art and Society* (1936), *Poetry and Anarchism; Collected Essays* (1938), *Education through Art* (1943), *A World Within a War* (1944), *A Coat of Many Colours* (1945), and *The Grass Roots of Art* (1947).

Reade (rēd), **Charles.** b. at Ipsden House, Oxfordshire, England, June 8, 1814; d. at London, April 11, 1884. An English novelist and dramatist. He was graduated from Oxford (Magdalen College) in 1835, elected to a Vinerian fellowship at Oxford in 1842, and called to the bar at Lincoln's Inn in 1843. Although Reade wished to be remembered primarily as a dramatist, he is known for his novels, and chiefly for *The Cloister and the Hearth* (1861), which portrays the tragic love story of the parents of Erasmus against the colorful background of the early Renaissance. This masterpiece, like much of Reade's other fiction, was based on his documentary method of compiling data from reliable printed sources and, when possible, from expert testimony and personal experience. It was this method that gave conviction to Reade's novels of purpose and established his reputation as an effective social reformer. Written in the humanitarian tradition of Charles Dickens, these novels are *It is Never Too Late to Mend* (1856), which castigated the separate system of English penal discipline; *Hard Cash* (1863), which revealed the iniquities of English lunacy laws and private lunatic asylums; *Foul Play* (1868), which censured the insurance frauds of ship-scuttlers; *Put Yourself in His Place* (1870), which exposed the terroristic discipline of lawless English trade unions; and *A Woman-Hater* (1877), which assisted Sophia Jex-Blake in her pioneering efforts to break the male monopoly of medicine and open British medical schools to women. Reade's other significant fiction includes two charming portraits, *Peg Woffington* (1853, a reworking of a play, *Masks and Faces*, that he had written with Tom Taylor in 1852) and *Christie Johnstone* (1853), and three energetic psychological novels, *Griffith Gaunt* (1866), *A Terrible Temptation*, wherein Reade, in the guise of Rolfe, describes his literary workshop (1871), and *A Simpleton* (1873).

Reade, William Winwood. b. at Ipsden, Oxfordshire, England, Jan. 30, 1838; d. at Wimbledon, England, April 24, 1875. An English traveler in Africa, and novelist; nephew of Charles Reade.

Reading Gaol (red′ing jāl), **The Ballad of.** See **Ballad of Reading Gaol, The.**

realism. In literature, the picturing of life as it actually is, or as it seems to the carefully observant artist. Reform novels, satires, novels of city life, novels about middle- or lower-class people (except where these are idealized beyond recognition for some philosophical purpose of the writer) tend naturally toward realism, for the artist's aim is usually to reveal the true facts of life. These facts are often of an unpleasant nature, and in the early days of modern realism, when writers embraced this style in active rebellion against romantic or purely artistic ("art for art's sake") styles, the unpleasant facts were stressed to the almost complete exclusion of the pleasant ones. It was this exaggeration of the unsavory aspects of life that made a fastidious critic like George Saintsbury say, "The former adjective [realistic] has rather usurped its name, for killing is not in the least more real than kissing, nor are descriptions of outrage and torture more so than descriptions of dances and Watteau-like picnics." The difference between the romantic and the realistic schools may be seen in Saintsbury's implied equating of a kiss and a Watteau-like picnic, where to a realistic writer the two experiences would perhaps have nothing whatever in common. As for such things as killing, outrage, and torture, as writers broke in this new style of realism so that it sat more comfortably on them, they were able to apply it to the gentler aspects of life as well as to the harsher ones. Today realism has come to mean treating all the varied experiences of life in an unsentimental manner; in its most extreme form, it is naturalism (*q.v.*).

Reason and Romanticism. A volume of literary criticism by Herbert Read, published in 1926.

rebec (rē′bek). A medieval stringed instrument like a violin and played with a bow. One of the musicians in *Romeo and Juliet* is referred to as Hugh Rebeck.

Rebecca (rẹ.bek′ạ). [Also, **Rebekah**.] In the Bible, the sister of Laban, wife of the patriarch Isaac and mother of Esau and Jacob. Gen. xxii, xxiv, etc.

Rebecca. In Sir Walter Scott's novel *Ivanhoe*, a Jewess, the daughter of Isaac of York, a moneylender. She secretly loves Ivanhoe.

Rebecca. A novel by Daphne Du Maurier, published in 1938.

Rebecca and Rowena (rō.wē′nạ). [Full title, **Rebecca and Rowena, a Romance upon Romance, by Mr. Michael Angelo Titmarsh**.] A novel by Thackeray, published in 1850 as a satiric sequel to Scott's *Ivanhoe*. Ivanhoe is shown as the henpecked husband of a shrewish Rowena, and decides to join King Richard in France in order to escape from her. He is with Richard when the king is killed, and is himself left for dead on the field. Wamba carries the news of Ivanhoe's supposed death to Rowena, who immediately marries Athelstane. Ivanhoe recovers, and comes home to find Rowena on the verge of death; with her last breath she exacts from him a promise that he will never marry a Jewess. However, shortly thereafter, Ivanhoe rescues Rebecca, the beautiful Jewess, and marries her immediately upon her conversion to Christianity.

Rebecca West (west). See **West, Rebecca**.

Rebellion, the Great. See **Civil War, English**.

Reboux (rẹ.bö), **Paul.** b. at Paris, May 21, 1877—. A French writer. He is best known for a famous series of parodies of contemporary writers, *À la manière de* (1908; with Charles Muller; later editions in two volumes and augmented with further parodies), called by critics the most successful French literary satire of recent times.

Recorde (rek′ọrd), **Robert.** b. at Tenby, Wales, c1510; d. at London, 1558. A British mathematician and physician. He entered Oxford in 1525, was fellow of All Souls College in 1531, and was physician to Edward VI and Queen Mary Tudor. He wrote *The Grounde of Artes, teachinge the Perfect Worke and Practice of Arithmeticke* (1540), *The Pathway to Knowledge, containing the First Principles of Geometry* (1551), *The Castle of Knowledge* (1551), and the first English book on algebra (1557). Most of his works are in the form of dialogues between the pupil and his master.

recorder. A small flutelike wind instrument of wood with a whistle-shaped mouthpiece and eight holes, much used in Shakespeare's day. In *Hamlet* the courtiers Rosencrantz and Guildenstern are carrying recorders. Guildenstern claims he cannot

play, and Hamlet counters, "It is as easy as lying" (III.ii).

Recruiting Officer, The. A comedy (1706) by George Farquhar.

Rector of Wyck (wik), **The.** A novel by May Sinclair, published in 1925.

Recuyell of the Historyes of Troye (rẹ.ku′yẹl; troi), **The.** [Also, **The Siege of Troy**.] A prose romance translated from the French and printed by William Caxton at Bruges in 1474 or 1475. It was the first book to be printed in English.

redaction (rẹ.dak′shọn). **1.** The act of reducing to order; the act of preparing for publication: said of literary or historical matter.

To work up literary matter and give it a presentable form is neither compiling, nor editing, nor resetting; and the operation performed on it is exactly expressed by redaction.
(F. Hall, *Mod. Eng.*)

2. A work thus prepared; a special form, edition, or version of a work as digested, revised, or rewritten.

In an early redaction of the well-known ballad of Lord Ronald . . . the name of the unfortunate victim to "eels boil'd in brue" is Laird Rowland.
(*N. and Q.*, 6th ser.)

This fresh discovery does not furnish us with the date of the story, but it gives us the date of one of its redactions, and shows it must have existed in the middle of the fourteenth century.
(*Edinburgh Rev.*)

Red Book of Hergest (hèr′gest), **The.** A collection of ancient Welsh tales, 11 of which were translated and included by Lady Charlotte Guest in her *Mabinogion*. It is a manuscript of the 14th century, preserved at Jesus College, Oxford. It contains a chronology from the time of Adam to 1318 A.D. and a chronological history of the Saxons to 1376.

Red Bull, the. A public playhouse built in Clerkenwell, now part of London, about 1604.

Red Cross Knight. The hero of the first book of the *Faerie Queene*, by Edmund Spenser. He typifies holiness and represents the spirit of the Anglican Church. In the complex double allegory of the story he also represents Saint George of England.

"Red Dean," the. See **Johnson, Hewlett**.

Redford (red′fọrd), **John.** fl. c1530. An English poet, musician, and teacher of singing at Saint Paul's. He was the author of *Wit and Science*, an educational interlude.

Redgauntlet (red′gônt″let). A romance (1824) by Scott. Its title character is a fanatical Jacobite of the 18th century.

Red House Mystery, The. A detective novel by A. A. Milne, published in 1922.

Red Knight: A Romance, The. A novel by Francis Brett Young, published in 1921.

Redlaw (red′lô). The principal character of Dickens's story *The Haunted Man*.

Red Lions, The. An exclusive English club, originating in 1839 in a dinner of members of the British Association at the Red Lion, Birmingham.

---

fat, fāte, fär, àsk, fāre; net, mē, hèr; pin, pīne; not, nōte, mōve, nôr; up, lūte, pùll; ᴛH, then;

Redmond O'Neale (red'mǫnd ǭ.nēl'). See **O'Neale, Redmond.**

Red Ridinghood (rī'ding.hůd), **Little.** [French, **Le Chaperon Rouge**; German, **Rothkäppchen.**] A nursery tale of oral tradition all over Europe, but especially common in W Europe. It is about a little girl who forgets her mother's command "to speak to no one whom she meets." She tells a wolf that she is going to her grandmother's cottage with some wine and bread. He reaches the cottage before her, eats her grandmother, and, when Little Red Ridinghood arrives, devours her also. In the German version, *Rothkäppchen*, as recorded by Grimm, a hunter comes and rips open the wolf, and Red Ridinghood and her grandmother are restored to life. This story is familiar to us not only through Grimm, but also through Perrault's French version, *Le Chaperon Rouge.*

Red Rose. The emblem of the House of Lancaster in the Wars of the Roses.

Red Saint, The. A historical novel by Warwick Deeping, published in 1909.

Reds of the Midi (mē.dē'), **The.** An English translation, by Catharine A. Janvier, of the Provençal tale *Li Rouge dóu Miejour*, written by Félix Gras in 1896. It was published in 1898, before the appearance of the original or of its author's French translation, *Les Rouges du Midi.*

reductio ad absurdum (rē.duk'shi.ō ad ab.sèr'dum). A reduction to an absurdity; the proof of a proposition by proving the falsity of its contradictory opposite: an indirect demonstration.

redundant (rē.dun'dǎnt). Using or containing more words or images than are necessary or useful: as, a *redundant* style. "Where the action is redundant, mark those paragraphs to be retrenched." (Watts.)

Redworth (red'wèrth), **Thomas.** In George Meredith's novel *Diana of the Crossways*, the patient and faithful friend of Diana, who marries her at the end of the novel.

Reed (rēd), **Douglas.** b. at London, 1895—. An English journalist and writer. He was engaged (1921 *et seq.*) as a newspaper correspondent, especially for the London *Times*, and established (1946) his own weekly newspaper, *Tidings*. His books include *The Burning of the Reichstag* (1934), *Insanity Fair* (1938), *Nemesis?* (1940), *A Prophet at Home* (1941), *All Our Tomorrows* (1942), *The Next Horizon* (1945), and *Yeoman's Progress* (1946).

Rees (rēs), **Abraham.** b. at Llanbrynmair, Wales, 1743; d. June 9, 1825. A British author. He edited *Chambers's Cyclopaedia* (1776–86) and *Rees's Cyclopaedia* (1802–20).

Reeve (rēv), **Clara.** b. at Ipswich, Suffolk, England, 1729; d. there, Dec. 3, 1807. An English novelist. Beginning (1772) her literary career with *The Phoenix*, a translation of John Barclay's Latin romance, *Argenis*, she also wrote *The Progress of Romance* (1785), a literary history, and *The School for Widows* (1791), a novel. She is remembered for *The Old English Baron, a Gothic Story* (1778), a novel originally published in 1777 as *The Champion of Virtue.* It is a supernatural tale written in the manner of Sir Horace Walpole.

Reeve, Henry. b. at Norwich, England, Sept. 9, 1813; d. in Hampshire, England, Oct. 21, 1895. An English writer. He was registrar of the Privy Council (1843–87), wrote on foreign affairs for the London *Times* (1840–55), and became editor of the *Edinburgh Review* in 1855. He published translations of Alexis de Tocqueville's *Democracy in America* and *France before the Revolution of 1789*, and of F. P. G. Guizot's *Washington.* He published *A Journal of the Reigns of King George IV and King William IV* by Charles Greville in 1875, and sequels to that work in 1885 and 1887. He also published *Royal and Republican France*, a collection of historical essays (1872).

Reeves (rēvz), **Helen Buckingham.** [Pseudonym, **David Lyall**; maiden name, **Mathers**; known as **Helen Mathers.**] b. at Crewkerne, Somersetshire, England, 1853; d. March 11, 1920. An English novelist. Most of her works were signed Helen Mathers. She published *Comin' Thro' the Rye* (1875), *Cherry Ripe* (1877), *My Lady Green Sleeves* (1879), *The Story of a Sin* (1881), *Found Out* (1884), *The Fashion of this World* (1886), *A Man of the Time* (1894), and others.

Reeve's Tale (rēvz), **The.** One of Chaucer's *Canterbury Tales.* He probably took it from Jean de Bove's fabliau *De Gombert et des deux clercs*, but it also forms the sixth tale of the ninth day of Boccaccio's *Decameron.* The Miller of Trompington, Simkin (or Symkyn), undertakes to grind corn for Aleyn and John, two young Cambridge students, steals part of their flour, and is punished by their seduction of his wife and daughter. With this tale Osewold (or Oswald) the Reeve, formerly a carpenter, retaliates with equal ribaldry upon Robin the Miller, who has just recounted the cuckolding of a carpenter. Chaucer apologizes for them both ("the Miller is a cherl, ye knowe wel this; So was the Reve . . ."), but, while the Miller is a hearty, boisterous type, not unlikable, the Reeve (or bailiff) is portrayed as meager and mean:

> The Reve was a sclendre colerik man,
> His berd was shave as ny as ever he can.
> His heer was by his eres round y-shorn.
> His top was dokked lyk a preest biforn.
> Ful longe were his legges, and ful lene,
> Y-lak a staf, ther was no calf y-sene.

Reflections on the French Revolution. See **French Revolution, Reflections on the.**

Reform Bill. In English history, a bill for the purpose of enlarging the number of voters in elections for members of the House of Commons, and of removing inequalities in representation. The first (actually the third offered in two years) of these bills (often called specifically the Reform Bill), passed in 1832 by the Liberals after a violent struggle, disfranchised many rotten boroughs (boroughs with very few or no inhabitants), gave increased representation to the large towns, and enlarged the number of the holders of county and borough franchise. The effect of the second Reform Bill, passed by the Conservatives under Liberal pressure in 1867, was in the direction of a more democratic representation, and the same tendency was further shown in the Franchise Bill passed by the Liberals in 1884, which extended suffrage to nearly all men. In 1918 suffrage was given to all

---

ḍ, d or j; ṣ, s or sh; ṭ, t or ch; ẓ, z or zh; o, F. cloche; ü, F. menu; ċh, Sc. loch; ṅ, F. bonbon.

men and to women over 30; in 1928, all persons over 21 were enfranchised.

refrain. 1. A burden or chorus recurring at regular intervals in the course of a song or ballad, usually at the end of each stanza.

> Everemo "allas?" was his refreyne.
> (Chaucer, *Troilus.*)

2. The musical phrase or figure to which the burden of a song is set. It has the same relation to the main part of the tune that the burden has to the main text of the song.

Refusal, or the Ladies' Philosophy, The. A comedy by Colley Cibber, produced and printed in 1721. It is from Molière's *Les Femmes savantes*, with incidents taken from the South Sea Bubble. Witling is a foolish, improvident fellow, who invests in South Sea stock (as had many other people supposedly anything but foolish); Granger is in love with Sophronia and pretends to be an idealist so as to attract her.

Regan (rē'gan). In Shakespeare's *King Lear*, the second daughter of Lear; the fierce and revengeful wife of Cornwall. She urges Cornwall to put out Gloucester's other eye when he extinguishes the first. In her conduct toward Lear she is mercilessly frank: "Oh, Sir, you are old, Nature in you stands on the very verge Of her confine." She tempts Oswald to betray the contents of Goneril's letter to Edmund, and encourages him in an attempt to murder Gloucester. She makes Edmund her general after Cornwall's death and takes him for her lord, but is poisoned by the jealous Goneril.

Regency. In history, a term that designates the last nine years (1811–20) of the reign of George III of Great Britain; in aesthetics, a term that applies to the culture of that period, including literature, architecture, and the arts of decoration. On the occasion of George III's first lapse into insanity, in 1788, the Prince of Wales, backed by Charles James Fox, claimed the right to assume the regency without parliamentary action. The younger William Pitt maintained that the power to name a regent lay with Parliament. The king's recovery put an end to the debate at that time, but when he became totally insane in 1811, Pitt's view prevailed, and the prince (who was to rule after 1820 as George IV) became regent by Parliamentary action, which circumscribed his powers. His extravagances, his amours, and his treatment of his consort during this period gave point, as did his earlier and later conduct, to Thackeray's characterization of him as "the last and worst of all the Georges." But in addition to his generosity (at the taxpayers' expense) he had audacity, and a flair for making things center about him; moreover, during the years when he waited on the doorstep of power, he played the role of a liberal, favoring Fox and the Whigs generally, though once he was established as virtual monarch, he ruled largely through the Tories, including Castlereagh. The few years of his deputized rule were, however, exciting and crucial years, marked by final British triumph over Napoleon and by a flowering of British letters, art, and architecture.

Regent's Park (rē'jents). One of the largest parks of London, situated in the NW part of London. It is 472 acres in extent, and contains the Zoölogical Gardens.

Regent Street (rē'jent). One of the principal streets of the West End of London, extending from Portland Place to Waterloo Place.

Reggie Fortune (rej'i fôr'chun). See **Fortune, Reggie.**

Regicide, The. [Full title, **The Regicide: or, James the First of Scotland.**] A tragedy by Tobias Smollett. It was published in 1749, but was never acted.

Regillus (rē.jil'us), **Lake.** In ancient geography, a small lake near Rome (perhaps near Frascati). It is traditionally the scene of a victory of the Romans over the Latins c496 B.C. that gave Rome preeminence in Latium.

Reginald Front de Boeuf (rej'i.nald frôn' de bef'), **Sir.** See **Front de Boeuf, Sir Reginald.**

Reginald Wilfer (wil'fer). See **Wilfer, Reginald.**

Regiomontanus (rē"ji.ọ.mon.tā'nus; German, rā"gē-ọ.mon.tä'nus). [Pseudonym (translation into Latin of the German Königsberg, his birthplace) of **Johann Müller.**] b. at Königsberg, in Franconia, June 6, 1436; d. at Rome, July 6, 1476. A German mathematician and astronomer, bishop of Regensburg. In an effort to correct errors in the Alfonsine Tables, a revision of the Ptolemaic planetary tables, he traveled (1462) to Rome to search for better manuscripts and to learn Greek. He wrote a work on trigonometry, the study of which he was later to foster in Germany, but was forced to leave Rome after a quarrel with the papal secretary, George of Trebizond, over the latter's translation of the *Almagest*. He went to Vienna, then to Buda, and then settled at Nuremberg (1471). There, with the financial help of Bernhard Walther, he built an observatory and established a printing press. He made observations of the comet of January, 1472 (later known as Halley's comet), and published a series of calendars as well as an *Ephemeris* covering the years 1474–1506 (said to have been used by Columbus). He was called to Rome in 1472 by Pope Sixtus IV to help in the work of reforming the calendar and died there.

Regnault (re.nyō). A French form of **Rinaldo.**

Regulus (reg'ū.lus), **Marcus Atilius.** d. c250 B.C. A Roman general. He was consul in 267, and as consul again in 256 during the First Punic War defeated the Carthaginian fleet at Ecnomus, invaded Africa, and defeated the Carthaginian army. He was defeated by the Carthaginians under the Spartan general Xantippus in 255 and taken prisoner. According to Roman tradition he was sent by the Carthaginians to Rome with an embassy, in 250, to ask for peace or an exchange of prisoners. He is said to have given his word to return to Carthage and, when his embassy produced no results because he himself advised the senate not to accept the Carthaginian terms, he went back to Africa and was tortured to death. The story is probably a fabrication.

Rehearsal, The. A burlesque tragedy or farce by George Villiers, 2nd Duke of Buckingham, and others, produced in 1671. It was originally intended (1663) to satirize operatic plays by D'Avenant, such as *The Siege of Rhodes*, and Howard and

fat, fāte, fär, ȧsk, fâre; net, mē, hėr; pin, pīne; not, nōte, mōve, nôr; up, lūte, pull; ŦH, then;

Dryden's tragicomedy *The Indian Queen*, as well as the Earl of Orrery's tragedies. By 1671 it was revised to make John Dryden the center of satire in the figure of Mr. Bayes (an allusion to Dryden's laurels as poet laureate) and to travesty his bombastic rhymed plays. In *The Rehearsal*, friends of Bayes attend a rehearsal of his new play; he berates the actors for their poor performance, and tries to explain to them and to the onlookers the ridiculous episodes of the play. Samuel Butler, the author of *Hudibras*, Dr. Thomas Sprat, Martin Clifford, and others assisted Buckingham. R. B. Sheridan's *The Critic* is a similar play, and Andrew Marvell's satire *The Rehearsal Transprosed* is indebted to it.

Rehoboam (rē.ọ̄.bō′ạm). King of Judah (c933–c914 B.C.); son of Solomon. His accession was the signal for the revolt of the ten northern tribes under the leadership of Jeroboam, which resulted in the separation of the Hebrews into two kingdoms, that of Judah and that of Israel. Sheshonk I (Shishak) of Egypt invaded Palestine during Rehoboam's reign.

Reid (rēd), **Forrest.** b. at Belfast, Ireland, 1876; d. 1947. An English novelist, short-story writer, poet, and critic. Author of *The Garden God* (1906), *The Bracnels* (1911), *Following Darkness* (1912; reissued in 1937 as *Peter Fleming*), *The Gentle Lover* (1913), *At the Door of the Gate* (1916), *The Spring Song* (1917), *A Garden By the Sea* (1918), *Pirates of the Spring* (1920), *Uncle Stephen* (1931), *Brian Westby* (1934), and *The Retreat, or the Machinations of Henry* (1936), fiction; *W. B. Yeats* (1915) and *Walter De La Mare* (1929), critical studies; *Retrospective Adventure* (1941), essays and stories; and *Apostate* (1926), and its continuation, *Private Road* (1940), autobiography.

Reid, Mayne. See **Reid, Thomas Mayne.**

Reid, Thomas. b. at Strachan, Kincardineshire, Scotland, April 26, 1710; d. at Glasgow, Oct. 7, 1796. A Scottish philosopher, the principal founder of the Scottish school of philosophy. He opposed the skepticism of John Locke and his followers with a "common-sense" approach that accepted the existence of things and did not attempt to make of them subjective mental phenomena. Similarly, morality in his system was based on an intuitive perception of ethics. He graduated from Marischal College, Aberdeen, in 1726, was librarian there, became pastor at Newmachar, near Aberdeen, in 1737, was appointed professor of philosophy at King's College, Aberdeen, in 1751, and was professor of moral philosophy at Glasgow (1764–81). He wrote an *Essay on Quantity* (1748), *Enquiry into the Human Mind on the Principle of Common Sense* (1764), *Essays on the Intellectual Powers of Man* (1785), and *Essays on the Active Powers of the Human Mind* (1788). His works were edited by Sir William Hamilton.

Reid, Thomas Mayne. [Called **Mayne Reid.**] b. in Ireland, April 4, 1818; d. at London, Oct. 22, 1883. A British novelist. He traveled in the U. S., and served as captain in the U. S. army in the Mexican War. He sailed from New York in 1849 with a party of volunteers to aid in the Hungarian struggle for freedom, but arrived too late to take part in it. He then turned to writing tales of adventure, including *The Rifle Rangers* (1850), *The Scalp Hunt-*

ers (1851), *The Boy Hunters* (1852), *The Bush Boys* (1855), *The Quadroon* (1856), *The War Trail* (1857), *Osceola* (1858), *The Boy Tar* (1859), *The Maroon* (1862), *The Headless Horseman* (1866), *The Castaways* (1870), *The Ocean Waifs* (1871), *The Death Shot* (1874), *The Flag of Distress* (1875), *The Vee Boers* (1880), *Gaspar the Gaucho* (1880), and others.

Reignier, Duke of Anjou (rā.nir′; an′jö). In Shakespeare's *1 Henry VI*, the supporter of the Dauphin and Joan of Arc and assumed King of Naples, Sicily, and Jerusalem. He agrees to the marriage of Margaret, his daughter, with Henry if he can have the territories of Maine and Anjou.

Reign of Terror. In French history, that period of the French Revolution during which the country was under the sway of a faction whose members made the summary execution of persons (regardless of age or sex) who were considered obnoxious to their measures one of the cardinal principles of the government. This period may be said to have begun in March, 1793, when the Revolutionary tribunal was appointed, and to have ended in July, 1794, with the overthrow of Robespierre and his associates.

Reinach (re.nȧk), **Salomon.** b. at St.-Germain-en-Laye, France, Aug. 29, 1858; d. at Paris, Nov. 4, 1932. A French archaeologist, keeper of the National Museum of St.-Germain (1902 *et seq.*). He published *Manuel de philologie classique*, *Traité d'epigraphie grecque*, *Répertoire de la statuaire grecque et romaine*, *Répertoire des vases grecs et étrangers*, *Répertoire de reliefs grecs et romains*, and others. His best-known works are *Apollo: Histoire générale des arts plastiques* (1904) and *Orpheus: Histoire générale des religions* (1909), both translated into English.

Rejected Addresses. A collection of parodies on Wordsworth, Byron, Scott, Moore, Coleridge, and other poets, written by the brothers James and Horace Smith, and published in 1812.

Relapse, or Virtue in Danger, The. A play by Sir John Vanbrugh, produced in 1696. It was a sequel to Colley Cibber's *Love's Last Shift*. Cibber, who had acted the role of the fop, Sir Novelty Fashion, in his own play, desired to repeat his success and Vanbrugh therefore created Lord Foppington, "whom Nature has made no Fool, [but] . . . is very industrious to pass for an Ass."

Relief of Lucknow (luk′nou), **The.** A play (1862) by Dion Boucicault. It contains the famous incident, probably apocryphal, of Jessie Brown and the approach of the column of relieving troops playing "The Campbells Are Coming."

Religio Laici (rē.lij′i.ō lā′i.sī). A polemic poem by John Dryden, published in 1682.

Religio Medici (med′i.sī). A philosophic treatise (1643) by Sir Thomas Browne. It represents one of the important milestones in the development of English prose.

Reliques of Ancient English Poetry. A collection of English popular ballads (1765) gathered and edited by Bishop Thomas Percy.

Rembrandt (rem′brant; Dutch, rem′bränt). [Full name, **Rembrandt Harmenszoon van Rijn** or **Ryn** (här′mẹn.sōn vän rīn).] b. at Leiden, Netherlands, July 15, 1607; d. at Amsterdam, Netherlands

---

ḍ, d ọr j; ş, s or sh; ṭ, t or ch; ẓ, z or zh; ọ, F. cloche; ü, F. menu; ċh, Sc. loch; ṅ, F. bonbon.

(buried Oct. 8, 1669). A Dutch painter and etcher, the chief member of the Dutch school of painting.

Remedy of Love, The. A poem written apparently c1530. It was printed in 1532 in an edition of Geoffrey Chaucer's poems, and long (wrongly) attributed to him.

Remington (rem'ing.ṭon), **Richard.** The hero of H. G. Wells's novel *The New Machiavelli* (1911).

Remonstrance, Grand. In English history, a formal protest passed by the House of Commons on Nov. 22, 1641. It listed the unconstitutional and unwise acts of the reign of Charles I, and demanded remedies.

Remorse. A tragedy in blank verse by Samuel Taylor Coleridge, written in 1797 as *Osorio* and adapted from Schiller's novel *Der Geisterseher*. It is imbued with Coleridge's current political feelings about revolution and unitarianism. It deals with a humane hero who is outlawed by his evil brother. The work was rejected by Sheridan, who had commissioned it, and was later revised. It was produced in 1813 at the Drury Lane.

Remorse of Conscience, The. See **Ayenbite of Inwit, The.**

Remus (rē'mus). In Roman legend, the brother of Romulus.

Renaissance (ren.a̤.zäns', -säns', rē.nā'sans) or **Renascence** (rē.nas'ens). These terms, respectively from the French and from the Latin, and signifying "rebirth," historically identify the period of transition in western Europe from medieval to modern times, and critically refer to the thought, philosophy, art, and spirit of that period. The essence of the Renaissance was the reintroduction into western European thought and aesthetics of the full cultural heritage of Greece and Rome. It was not so much a rebirth as a reëmergence of things lost in the rubble of the Roman world, and little valued during the age of scholasticism, of narrow preoccupation with theology. The close of the Renaissance may be correlated with the end of the 16th century, but to date its beginning is far more difficult. In one view, Saint Francis of Assisi (c1182–1226) is a forerunner of the Renaissance, in that his religion was joyous and he frankly loved nature and creatures. Dante, journeying through a medieval hell, and purgatory, and paradise, pointed to the Renaissance when he chose the pagan and classical Vergil for his guide; the passionate yet urbane Petrarch and the sophisticated Boccaccio are already men of the Renaissance, yet they all died before the dawn of the 15th century (which some take as the beginning of the Renaissance). The Crusades and the journeys of Marco Polo, enlarging the horizon of European man, were factors leading to the Renaissance, as the voyages of Columbus, Vasco de Gama, and Magellan later enriched it. Classic and Hellenistic works of poetry, philosophy, mathematics, and grammar, preserved by the Arabs, came back into Europe with returning Crusaders and through the Moors in Spain. Before the fall of Constantinople in 1453, Moslem pressure on the Byzantine Empire caused numerous scholars to flee to Italy, bringing classical lore and manuscripts. The climate was right for a spring season of the human spirit in Italy in the 15th and 16th centuries. The painters led the way, with the example of Giotto (1276–1336) before them. Many factors made his city, Florence, the center of Renaissance painting and sculpture, but these and other arts flourished also at Rome, Padua, Perugia, Urbino, Ferrara, Mantua, Milan, Bologna, and Venice. No other period of human history has seen such a galaxy of great painters as that which includes Fra Angelico, Pisanello, Masaccio, Fra Filippo Lippi, Piero della Francesca, Pollaiuolo, Mantegna, Jacopo Bellini, Giovanni Bellini, Verrocchio, Botticelli, Perugino, Carpaccio, Giorgione, Fra Bartolommeo, Andrea del Sarto, Correggio, and Tintoretto, all clustering about the supreme figures of Michelangelo, Leonardo da Vinci, Raphael, and Titian. But that caution is called for in fixing both the temporal and the geographic outlines of the Renaissance is illustrated by the fact that in the late 14th and early 15th centuries Flemish painting was ahead of Italian painting in such typically Renaissance characteristics as the trend toward realism, the practice of portraiture, the increase of human interest. The work of such Flemings as the van Eycks, Roger van der Weyden, and Hugo van der Goes greatly influenced Italian painting, as later Italian painting was to influence Flemish artists, including Memling, Matsys, Bosch, the Brueghels, and Rubens, and French artists, and German artists, including Dürer and Holbein. But though the influence of Italian Renaissance sculpture was also felt abroad, nowhere outside Italy were the achievements of Donatello and Ghiberti, Michelangelo and Cellini, Verrocchio and Luca della Robbia even approached. Renaissance architecture also had its origin, and its fullest development, in Florence, Rome, Pavia, Ferrara, Milan, Venice, and other Italian cities. The Gothic style had taken little root in Italy. Yet for nearly a thousand years Italian architects had ignored the remnants and ruins of antiquity with which they were surrounded, or had used them only as quarries for the stone that went into their contemporary creations. However, as the city-states waxed in power and wealth under their forceful ducal rulers, coincidentally with the flowering of the Renaissance, both necessity and the spirit of ostentation called for great palaces and public buildings; the models of antiquity were first drawn upon for these, and presently their influence was felt in ecclesiastical architecture also. The Italians did not, however, return to the noble simplicity of antiquity; Renaissance architecture was no matter of copying, but was an original, creative art, born of an exuberant age. Antiquity was drawn on not so much for form as for decoration, and while many Italian Renaissance structures are of breath-taking beauty, others exhibit the excess of ornament which eventually led to the baroque style. In other countries the Renaissance induced architectural developments growing out of their own conditions, though some traces of Italian influence are found in French chateaus and public buildings and in English palaces. The informing spirit and impulse behind all these visible manifestations was the great stirring of human thought historically known as Humanism. Most Renaissance Humanists remained, sincerely or otherwise, affiliated with the Roman Catholic Church, though Humanism did have something to do with the rise of Protestantism. But many things, the Crusades and voyages, as already noted, the recovery of remnants of classical literature, the unearthing of examples of classical sculpture, the invention of printing, the new cosmology resulting from the theorizing of such men as Copernicus and Galileo, the growth of cities and increase of wealth, gave rise to what has aptly been called Neo-Protagoreanism, remembering that Protagoras said "Man is the measure of all things." There were among the Humanists some who were virtually atheists, but Humanism might be generally defined as a partial diversion of interest from theology and the future life to the present life and to man, accompanied by a vastly increased confidence in man's capacity to understand the universe and the forces of nature, and to work out his destiny. The spirit of Humanism is accordingly best perceived in Renaissance writings, literary and philosophical; among a very numerous company of writers, we need mention only Machiavelli, Erasmus, More, Montaigne, Bacon, and the English dramatists and poets of Elizabeth's and James I's reigns, Renaissance men all of them, and none more so than Shakespeare. Spain is an exception to the general statement that the Renaissance can be considered to have ended with the end of the 16th century. Humanistic thought had little utterance in Spanish save through Cervantes and Lope de Vega, late in the 16th and early in the 17th century. Although Charles V was partial to Italian art, the influence of the Renaissance in painting was slight until the rise of Velásquez, and it persisted as late as the days of Murillo. Later than elsewhere also, there evolved a Spanish Renaissance architecture, showing some Italian influence but largely native in origin. The Renaissance as a whole is often divided into the Early Renaissance, running to about the year 1500; the High Renaissance, defined as the years 1500 to 1530, when the very greatest of the Italian artists were at the peak of their powers, and the patronage of beauty-loving popes and nobles was most generous; and the Late Renaissance, from 1530 to the end of the century.

Renan (r̄e.nän̄), (**Joseph**) **Ernest.** b. at Tréguier, Côtes-du-Nord, France, Jan. 27, 1823; d. at Paris, Oct. 2, 1892. A French philologist and historian. His studies, begun in his native town, were completed at Paris. He was discouraged in the study of theology by the barrenness of the scholastic method then in vogue, and broke sharply with the system. While making his living by teaching, he pursued his studies in comparative philology, and took, one after the other, his university degrees. His works published between 1850 and 1860 attracted much attention, especially for their style. They include his doctor's thesis, *Averröés et l'averroïsme* (1852), *Études d'histoire religieuse* (1857), *De l'origine du langage* (1858), and *Essais de morale et de critique* (1859). Soon after his return from a mission to the East (1861), Renan was called to the chair of Hebrew in the Collège de France; but, as he denied the divinity of Christ, he fell out with the clerical party, and was forced to resign his professorship in 1864. The works he wrote about this time contributed perhaps in greatest measure to his reputation. Foremost among them stands *La Vie de Jésus* (1863), the first book in the series entitled *Histoire*

des origines du christianisme, which includes *Les Apôtres* (1866), *St. Paul et sa mission* (1867), *L'antéchrist* (1873), *Les Évangiles et la seconde génération chrétienne* (1877), *L'Église chrétienne* (1879), and *Marc-Aurèle et la fin du monde antique* (1880). The *Index* was published in 1889, and the natural introduction to the entire series is to be found in an entirely separate work, *Histoire du peuple d'Israël* (1887–94). Renan was also the author of *Questions contemporaines* (1868), *Dialogues philosophiques* (1876), *Drames philosophiques* (1888), and many other works.

Renaud (r̄e.nō). A French form of **Rinaldo.**

Renault (r̄e.nôlt'; French, r̄e.nō). A licentious, egotistical conspirator in Thomas Otway's *Venice Preserved*, who casts aside personal honor in an effort to seduce Belvidera, the wife of Jaffeir, one of his fellow conspirators against the Venetian Senate.

Rendall (ren'dal), **Gerald Henry.** b. at Harrow, Middlesex, England, 1851; d. Jan. 4, 1945. An English classical scholar, headmaster of the Charterhouse School (1897–1911). His writings include *The Cradle of the Aryans* (1889), a translation of the *Meditations* of Marcus Aurelius (1897), and others.

Renegado, or the Gentleman of Venice (ren.ē̲-gä'dō), **The.** A play by Philip Massinger, licensed in 1624 for performance at the Cockpit theater and printed in 1630. The title was changed before James Shirley's *Gentleman of Venice* was produced. The "renegade" is Grimaldi, who is converted to Mohammedanism and then back to Christianity again when the Viceroy of Tunis dismisses him from his service as a pirate.

Rennell (ren'el), **1st Baron.** [Title of **James Rennell Rodd.**] b. Nov. 9, 1858; d. at Ardath, Shamley Green, Surrey, England, July 26, 1941. An English diplomat and writer. He was secretary of legation (1894–1901) at Cairo, councilor of embassy (1901–04) at Rome, minister (1904–08) to Sweden, and ambassador (1908–19) to Italy. He was a delegate (1921, 1923) to the League of Nations, and headed courts of conciliation between Austria and Switzerland (1925) and Italy and Chile (1928).

Renouncement. A poem in sonnet form by Alice Meynell, classed by Dante Gabriel Rossetti as one of the greatest of English sonnets to be written by a woman.

Rent Day, The. A domestic drama by Douglas Jerrold, printed in 1832.

repartee (rep.ar.tē'). 1. A ready, pertinent, and witty reply.

They [wicked men] know there is no drolling with so sour a piece as that [conscience] within them is, for that makes the smartest and most cutting repartees, which are uneasie to bear, but impossible to answer.   (Stillingfleet, *Sermons.*)

There were the members of that brilliant society which quoted, criticised, and exchanged repartees under the rich peacock-hangings of Mrs. Montague. (Macaulay, *Warren Hastings.*)

2. Such replies in general or collectively; the kind of wit involved in making sharp and ready retorts.

As for repartee in particular, as it is the very soul of conversation, so it is the greatest grace of comedy, where it is proper to the characters.

(Dryden, *Mock Astrologer*, Pref.)

You may allow him to win of you at Play, for you are sure to be too hard for him at Repartee. Since you monopolize the Wit that is between you, the Fortune must be his of Course.

(Congreve, *Way of the World*.)

Reply Churlish. See under **Retort Courteous.**

Repressor of Overmuch Weeting [Blaming] of the Clergy, The. A Middle English treatise (c1455) by Reginald Pecock, attempting to refute by logic the doctrines of the Lollards. It is important as a fine example of 15th-century English.

Reprisals, or the Tars of Old England, The. A comedy by Tobias Smollett, produced in 1757.

Reproof Valiant. See under **Retort Courteous.**

Republic, The. A work by Plato, descriptive of a commonwealth drawn according to his ideal.

requiem (rē′kwi.em). **1.** The mass for the dead.

We should profane the service of the dead
To sing a requiem and such rest to her
As to peace-parted souls.

(Shak., *Hamlet*, V.i.)

2. A musical setting of the mass for the dead. The usual sections of such a mass are the Requiem, the Kyrie, the Dies Irae (in several sections), the Domine Jesu Christe, the Sanctus, the Benedictus, the Agnus Dei, and the Lux Aeterna.

3. Hence, in popular usage, a musical service or hymn for the dead.

For pity's sake, you that have tears to shed,
Sigh a soft requiem, and let fall a bead
For two unfortunate nobles.

(Webster, *Devil's Law-Case.*)

Requiem. A poem by Robert Louis Stevenson, containing the well-known lines "Home is the sailor, home from the sea,/And the hunter home from the hill."

Rescue, The. A psychological novel (1920) by Joseph Conrad.

Research Magnificent, The. A novel by H. G. Wells, published in 1915.

resolution. In ancient prosody: (*a*) The use of two short times or syllables as the equivalent for one long; the division of a disemic time into the two semeia of which it is composed. (*b*) An equivalent of a time or of a foot in which two shorts are substituted for a long: as, the dactyl ($-\cup\cup$) or anapest ($\cup\cup-$) is a resolution of the spondee ($--$). The resolution of a syllable bearing the ictus takes its ictus on the first of the two shorts representing the long ($\overset{\smile}{\smile}\cup\cup$ for $\cup\!\!\!\!\diagup$, $\cup\overset{\smile}{\smile}\cup$ for $\cup\!\!\!\!\diagup$).

Respublica (rēz.pub′li.ką). An interlude (1553), probably by Nicholas Udall. It celebrates the accession to the throne of the Roman Catholic Queen Mary ("Bloody Mary"), which occurred in the year that it was written. Respublica has lost Conscience and Honesty under Edward VI, and has fallen under the domination of Policy, Authority, Reformation, and Dishonesty (who are really Avarice, Insolence, Oppression, and Adulation). Respublica and People (the English people)

are saved from these malefactors when four virtues (Mercy, Truth, Peace, and Justice) arrive with Nemesis to turn them out. People speaks with a southwestern dialect, which is interesting as an early example of attempted realism in speech.

Restoration. In English history, the reëstablishment of the English monarchy with the return of King Charles II in 1660; by extension, the whole reign of Charles II, or, often, the period between 1660 and the accession of Queen Anne in 1702.

Restoration. A novel by Ethel Sidgwick, published in 1923.

Retaliation. A poem (1774) by Oliver Goldsmith. It was inspired by Garrick's joking epitaph for Goldsmith:

Here lies poor Goldsmith, for shortness called Noll,
Who wrote like an angel, but talked like poor Poll.

Goldsmith, in replying, took the opportunity to prepare similar epitaphs for various others of his friends, including Edmund Burke and Sir Joshua Reynolds. For Garrick he closed with the following:

. . . a salad; for in him we see
Oil vinegar, sugar, and saltness agree.

Retort Courteous. In Shakespeare's *As You Like It* (V.iv), the first (and now probably the best known) of the seven possible retorts to an insult, or "degrees of the lie," cited by Touchstone as causes of a quarrel. The others, in order, are the Quip Modest, the Reply Churlish, the Reproof Valiant, the Countercheck Quarrelsome, the Lie Circumstantial, and the Lie Direct.

Return from Parnassus (pär.nas′us), **The.** A play in two parts, which, with *The Pilgrimage to Parnassus*, forms a trilogy (often called the *Parnassus Plays*) in this order: *The Pilgrimage to Parnassus; The Return from Parnassus, Part I; The Return from Parnassus, Part II,* subtitled *The Scourge of Simony.* The first play of the trilogy was acted in 1597, the second probably in 1598, and the third in 1601. The three plays are thought to have been written by members of Saint John's College, Cambridge, where they were acted. They are satires, aiming to show the trials and poverty of those who follow the scholarly life; *The Return from Parnassus, Part II* shows the envy of scholars and writers for the professional actors. There are a number of references in the plays to well-known figures of the time. The character Furor Poeticus has been identified as John Marston, Ingenioso as Thomas Nash and Robert Greene. There are allusions to Ben Jonson and Shakespeare. The actors Richard Burbage and Will Kempe appear as characters in their own names.

Return of the Brute. A novel by Liam O'Flaherty, published in 1929.

Return of the Druses (drö′zęz), **The.** A tragedy in blank verse by Robert Browning, published as part of *Bells and Pomegranates* (1843).

Return of the Native, The. One (1878) of the major Wessex novels of Thomas Hardy.

Return of the Prodigal, The. A drama (1905) by St. John Hankin.

Return of the Soldier, The. A novel by Rebecca West, published in 1918.

Reuben Butler (rö′bĕn but′lĕr). See **Butler, Reuben.**

Reuchlin (roiċh′lin), **Johann.** [Grecized, **Capnio.**] b. at Pforzheim, Baden, Dec. 28 (or Feb. 22), 1455; d. at Liebenzell, near Hirschau, Bavaria, June 30, 1522. A German humanist. He opposed, in a formal opinion to the emperor in 1510, the suppression of Jewish books hostile to Christianity, advocated by the converted Jew Johann Pfefferkorn, which involved him in a controversy (1510–16) with the Dominicans and the obscurantists generally. Reuchlin proposed instead that the Jewish communities be required to supply books to support two chairs of Hebrew at every German university; the controversy ended in his victory when an accusation against him at Rome was dropped. He promoted education in Germany by publishing Greek textbooks, and wrote various works on Latin, Greek, and Hebrew, including a Hebrew grammar, *Rudimenta Hebraica* (1506). He published the cabalistic works *De verbo mirifico* (1494) and *De arte cabbalistica* (1494).

Revels, Master of the. See under **Revels Office.**

Revels Office. An official body existing in England from about the middle of the 16th century to the late 17th century, headed by the Master of the Revels, and charged with supervising Court performances of plays and other entertainments. Sir Thomas Cawarden was the first permanent Master. Court Revels were held from Nov. 1 to the beginning of Lent in the time of Henry VIII; under Elizabeth they were concentrated around Christmas; and James I (who greatly enjoyed the theater) lengthened the season again. The office continued after the Restoration, but eventually lost all authority and became extinct. It is presumed that in most cases plays licensed by the Master of the Revels for playing were automatically licensed for printing.

Revenge. A tragedy by Edward Young, produced in 1721.

Revenge for Honour. A tragedy sometimes attributed to George Chapman, published in 1654.

Revenge of Bussy D'Ambois (bü.sē′ däṅ.bwà′), **The.** See **Bussy D'Ambois, The Revenge of.**

Revenger's Tragedy, The. A tragedy by Cyril Tourneur, published in 1607 anonymously but attributed to Tourneur by Archer, a bookseller, and also, toward the end of the 17th century, by Kirkman, a scholar.

Review. A periodical by Daniel Defoe, issued from one to three times a week from 1704 to 1713. It was a precursor of the *Tatler* in its essays, and of other later periodicals in its gossip column and use of a leading article. It comprises a valuable record of political and social thought in its time.

Review, The. A musical farce by George Colman the younger, printed in 1800. It was taken from an unsuccessful comic opera, *Caleb Quotem and his Wife, or Paint, Poetry, and Putty,* by Henry Lee.

Revival of Learning. The Renaissance in its relation to learning.

Revocation of the Edict of Nantes (nants; French, näṅt). A proclamation of Louis XIV of France, Oct. 18, 1685, annulling the Edict of Nantes (1598). It forbade the free exercise of the Protestant religion. Its promulgation was followed by the emigration of ab. 300,000 persons, including artisans, men of science and letters, and others, to the Netherlands, Brandenburg, England, Switzerland, America, and elsewhere.

Revolt of Islam (is′lạm), **The.** A narrative poem (1818) by Shelley. It was first called *Laon and Cythna.*

Revolving Lights. A novel by Dorothy M. Richardson, published in 1921. It is the seventh section of *Pilgrimage* (1938), a novel sequence in 12 parts employing the stream-of-consciousness technique.

Reynaldo (rā.nal′dō). In Shakespeare's *Hamlet,* a servant to Polonius. In the first quarto he is called Montano.

Reynard the Fox (ren′ạrd, rā′nạrd). A medieval beast epic which receives its name from the central character. Other characters are King Noble, the lion, Bruin, the bear, Chanticleer, the cock, Tybert, the cat, Isegrim, the wolf, and many others. Reynard the Fox is not any one book, but several accumulations from classical fables and traditional European animal tales and folk motifs worked into a satire not only on medieval society but on human nature. One of the earliest of such compilations was the Latin poem *Isengrimus* (c1148) by the Fleming Nivardus of Ghent. Various sections of the French *Roman de Renart* appeared in the period of 1175–1205. Most of the Reynard material is of French origin, but the version best known to English readers is the translation made by William Caxton in 1481 from a lost Flemish manuscript, and originally entitled *The Historye of Reynart the Foxe.* Goethe's *Reinecke Fuchs* is a reworking into modern German of an 1180 Low German version. The Bibliotheca Curiosa edition of Caxton's book lists 30 principal editions in English of this beast epic between 1481 and 1884, variously entitled *Historye of Reinard the Foxe, Booke of Raynarde the Foxe, The Shifts of Reynardine, The Crafty Courtier, or Fable of Reynard the Fox, The most delectable History of Reynard the Fox,* and others.

Reynard the Fox. A narrative poem (1920) by John Masefield.

Reynolds (ren′ọldz), Sir **Joshua.** b. at Plympton Earl, Devonshire, England, July 16, 1723; d. at London, Feb. 23, 1792. An English portrait painter. He was educated by his father, a schoolmaster and clergyman. In October, 1740, he went to London and studied under Thomas Hudson. In 1746 he established himself as a portrait painter at London. By invitation of his friend, Commodore (afterward Admiral) Keppel, he sailed for Italy on the *Centurion,* arriving in Rome at the close of 1749. Owing to a cold which he took there, he became deaf and never recovered his hearing. After two years at Rome he visited Parma, Florence, Venice, and other Italian cities. He returned to London in 1752, and was intimately associated with Johnson, Burke, Goldsmith, Garrick, and others. The Literary Club was established at his suggestion in 1764. In 1768 the Royal Academy was founded, with Reynolds as its first president. His annual addresses form its well-known *Discourses.* In 1784, on the death of Allan Ramsay, he was made painter to the king. Reynolds wrote three essays in the *Idler* (1759–60). His most famous works include his portraits of Johnson, Garrick, Sterne and Goldsmith, *The Age of Innocence, Mrs. Siddons as the Tragic Muse, The Infant Hercules, The Strawberry Girl,* and *Garrick Between Tragedy and Comedy.*

Rhadamanthus (rad.ạ.man'thus). In Greek mythology, brother of Minos, king of Crete, and son of Zeus and Europa, who because of his great justice became (with Minos and Aeachus) one of the three judges of the dead in the lower world.

Rhea (rē'ạ). In Greek mythology, the great mother goddess, whose cult was associated with fertility rites. She was a daughter of Uranus (the sky) and Gaea (the earth), wife of Cronus and mother of Zeus, Poseidon, Hades, Hera, Hestia, and Demeter. She was often identified with Cybele, the great Anatolian mother goddess. She was worshiped especially in Crete, where her cult may have originated. At Rome she was identified with Ops.

Rhea Silvia (sil'vi.ạ). [Also, **Ilia.**] In Roman legend, a vestal virgin, mother by Mars of Romulus and Remus.

Rhesus (rē'sus). In Greek legend, a Thracian ally of the Trojans, slain by Odysseus and Diomedes.

rhetoric (ret'ọr.ik). 1. The art of discourse; the art of using language so as to influence others. Rhetoric is that art which consists in a systematic use of the technical means of influencing the minds, imaginations, emotions, and actions of others by the use of language. Primarily, it is the art of oratory, with inclusion of both composition and delivery; secondarily, it also includes written composition and recitation. It is also used in narrower senses, so as to present the idea of composition alone, or the idea of oratorical delivery (elocution) alone. Etymologically, rhetoric is the art, or rather the technics (τέχνη, somewhat different in scope from our *art*), of the rhetor—that is, either the popular (political) orator or the judicial and professional rhetor. Accordingly, ancient writers regarded it mainly as the art of persuasion, and something of this view almost always attaches to the word even in modern use, so that it appears to be more or less inappropriate to use *rhetoric* of mere scientific, didactic, or expository composition. The element of persuasion, or at least of influence of thought, belongs, however, to such composition also in so far as accurate and well-arranged statement of views leads to their adoption or rejection, the very object of instruction involving this. On the other hand, poetry and epidictic oratory chiefly address the imagination and emotions, while the most important branches of oratory (deliberative and judicial oratory) appeal especially to the mind and emotions with a view to influencing immediate action. The theory or science underlying the art of rhetoric, and sometimes called by the same name, is essentially a creation of the ancient Greeks. Rhetoric was cultivated on its more practical side first of all by the earlier rhetors (so-called "sophists") and orators (Empedocles—considered the inventor of rhetoric—Gorgias, Isocrates, etc.), many of whom wrote practical treatises (τέχναι) on the art. The philosophers, on the other hand, among them Aristotle, treated the subject from the theoretical side. The system of rhetoric which finally became estab-

lished, and has never been superseded, though largely mutilated and misunderstood in medieval and modern times, is that founded upon the system of the Stoic philosophers by the practical rhetorician Hermagoras (about 60 B.C.). Its most important extant representatives are Hermogenes (about 165 A.D.) among the Greeks, and Quintilian (about 95 A.D.) among the Latins. This theory recognizes three great divisions of oratory. The art of rhetoric was divided into five parts: invention, disposition, elocution (not in the modern sense, but comprising diction and style), memory (mnemonics), and action (delivery, including the modern elocution).

> With rethorice com forth Musice, a damsel of oure hows.   (Chaucer, *Boëthius.*)

> Generall report, that surpasseth my praise, condemneth my rethoricke of dulnesse for so colde a commendation.
>   (Nash, quoted in Int. to *Pierce Penilesse.*)

> For rhetoric, he could not ope
> His mouth, but out there flew a trope.
>   (Butler, *Hudibras.*)

2. Skill in discourse; artistic use of language.
3. Artificial oratory, as opposed to that which is natural and unaffected; display in language; ostentatious or meretricious declamation.

> Enjoy your dear wit, and gay rhetorick,
> That hath so well been taught her dazzling fence.
>   (Milton, *Comus*, l. 790.)

> Like quicksilver, the rhet'ric they display
> Shines as it runs, but, grasp'd at, slips away.
>   (Cowper, *Progress of Error*, l. 21.)

Rhiannon (rẹ.an'on). In Brythonic legend, the wife of Pwyll, a local king, falsely accused of devouring her own child, and condemned to sit at the gate and tell her story to strangers. Later the child was produced by the foster father who had found and raised him, and Rhiannon was exonerated. In Brythonic mythology, she was the ancient mother goddess, associated with fertility.

Rhoda Fleming (rō'dạ flem'ing). A novel by George Meredith, published in 1865.

Rhode (rōd), **John.** Pseudonym of **Street, Cecil John Charles.**

Rhodes (rōdz), **Cecil John.** b. at Bishop Stortford, Hertfordshire, England, July 5, 1853; d. near Cape Town, South Africa, March 26, 1902. An English colonial statesman. He went (1870) to South Africa for his health, joining an older brother in Natal. The brothers took part in the diamond rush in the Orange Free State in 1871 and soon were among the most prosperous of the diggers. At about this time Rhodes first conceived, as the result of a trip through the country, his dream of a united African empire under the British crown, seeing in South Africa a tremendous source of mineral wealth. For a number of years after 1873, interrupted by illness so serious that he was given less than six months to live, he traveled between South Africa and England, where he studied at Oxford, taking his degree in 1881, in which year he became a member of the Cape assembly. Just before this he concluded the consolidation of a number of the Kimberley diamond mines in the De Beers Company, which, after merger (1888) with the Barnato interests, mo-

---

fat, fāte, fär, ȧsk, fāre; net, mē, hėr; pin, pīne; not, nōte, mŏve, nôr; up, lūte, pu̇ll; ᴛʜ, then;

nopolized South African diamond production and was supposedly the richest company in the world. Rhodes established ties with the Dutch settlers in the colony and with their aid annexed Bechuanaland to the colony in 1884, thus limiting the spread of the Transvaal republic. As resident deputy commissioner of the new territory, Rhodes met with trouble from the Dutch settlers there and from commandoes from the Transvaal; appeals to Paul Kruger, president of the Transvaal, brought only disclaimers, whereupon Rhodes called in troops, established them near the Transvaal border, and forced the withdrawal of the Dutch. By treaty with Lobengula, King of the Matabele, he obtained a great area north of Bechuanaland, known as Rhodesia, and established (1889) the British South Africa Company, of which he was manager. He began at this time to plan the Cape-to-Cairo chain of British possessions that marked the subsequent course of British expansion in Africa. In 1890 he became premier of Cape Colony, becoming, with Dutch aid, virtual dictator. He restricted the native vote by establishing educational and wage qualifications; he encouraged native education, but at the same time, insisting that he was encouraging individual enterprise, encouraged a program of hard work for the native population and made determined efforts to break up the tribal hold on the individual. Rhodes was implicated as the moving spirit behind the Jameson Raid of December, 1895, and in other revolutionary activities of the Uitlanders, as the English settlers in the Transvaal were called; these acts of a prime minister against a friendly nation were deemed reprehensible and Rhodes was forced to resign in January, 1896. He then turned his attention to developing Rhodesia, extending railway and telegraph lines and making a start on exploiting the area's mineral resources. He personally obtained a promise of peace from the rebellious Matabele in 1896, living alone and undefended until the natives came to treat with him, one of the great feats of personal heroism. During the Boer War he was besieged in Kimberley, but he died before the war ended and the peace brought partial realization of his ambitious dreams of a South African union. He left a fortune of six million pounds to public service, part of which went toward establishing the Rhodes Scholarships.

Rhodes, Knights of. See **Hospitalers of Saint John of Jerusalem, Order of the.**

Rhodes, William Barnes. b. Dec. 25, 1772; d. Nov. 1, 1826. An English dramatist, author of *Bombastes Furioso.*

Rhodes Scholarships. A number of scholarships at Oxford University established by the will of Cecil John Rhodes (d. 1902), providing for the support of selected students from the British colonies, Germany, and the States and Territories of the United States.

Rhodophil (rō.dof′il). The flirtatious husband of Doralice in Dryden's *Marriage à la Mode.* He decides that "a foolish marriage vow" should not keep him from wooing Melantha, the fiancée of his friend Palamede.

Rhodopis (rō.dō′pis). [Also, **Doricha.**] A Greek courtesan, a Thracian by birth, said to have been a fellow slave of Aesop. She was taken to Naucratis,

Egypt, where the brother of Sappho fell in love with her and ransomed her. She was attacked by Sappho in a poem. Her real name was Doricha, and Rhodopis, "the rosy-cheeked," was merely an epithet. It was under this name of Doricha that she was mentioned by Sappho.

rhyme. A metrical device in which there is a similarity of final sounds in two or more words. Masculine or male rhymes are those in which the final syllable is accented, while feminine or double rhymes are those in which the final syllable is unaccented. Internal rhyme refers to rhyme within the line, as in Tennyson's "The splendor falls on castle walls."

Rhymed Ruminations. A volume of occasional verse (1941) by Siegfried Sassoon.

Rhyme of the Duchess May. A romantic ballad by Elizabeth Barrett Browning.

Rhymer, Thomas the. See **Thomas the Rhymer.**

rhyme royal. A metrical form consisting of a seven-line stanza, written in iambic pentameter, rhyming *ababbcc.* The name has been said to derive from its original use by James I in *The Kingis Quair,* although some scholars believe it to come from a French form. It was first used in England by Chaucer in *Troilus and Crisyede, The Parliament of Fowls,* and *Complaint unto Pity.*

Rhyming Poem, The. [Also, **The Riming Poem.**] An Old English poem, probably of the 10th century, dated from its appearance in the *Exeter Book.* It is a rhymed account of the cares of worldly existence, using the troubles of a wealthy and powerful man as its example.

Rhys (rēs), **Ernest.** b. at London, July 17, 1859; d. at Chelsea, London, May 25, 1946. An English editor, anthologist, novelist, poet, and critic. He lived in Wales during his early life, returned to London as a young man, abandoned a career as a mining engineer, and devoted himself to literature. He edited the Camelot series (30 vols., 1886–1900), Lyric Poets (10 vols., 1895–1905), and Everyman's Library (1905–40), whose title he originated and which numbered 967 volumes at the time of his retirement, *Readings in Welsh History* (1910), *Readings in Welsh Literature* (1911), *New Golden Treasury* (1914), and *Golden Treasury of Longer Poems* (1921). Author of *A London Rose* (1891), *Welsh Ballads* (1903), *Enid and Geraint* (1905), *Lancelot and Guenevre* (1906), *Lays of the Round Table* (1908), and *Rhymes for Everyman* (1933), poetry and poetic drama; *The Fiddler of Carne* (1901), *The Whistling Maid* (1904), and *Black Horse Pit* (1925), novels; *English Lyric Poetry* (1913) and *Rabindranath Tagore* (1920), studies; *Everyman Remembers* (1931) and *Wales England Wed* (1941), autobiography.

rhythm. In metrics: (*a*) Succession of times divisible into measures with theses and arses; metrical movement. Theoretically, all spoken language possesses rhythm, but the name is distinctively given to that which is not too complicated to be easily perceived as such. Rhythm, so limited, is indispensable in metrical composition, but is regarded as inappropriate in prose, except in elevated style and in oratory, and even in these only in the way of

---

ḍ, d or j; ṣ, s or sh; ṭ, t or ch; ẓ, z or zh; o, F. cloche; ü, F. menu; ċh, Sc. loch; ṅ, F. bonbon.

vague suggestion, unless in certain passages of special character.

> Rhythm . . . is of course governed by law, but it is a law which transcends in subtlety the conscious art of the metricist, and is only caught by the poet in his most inspired moods.   (*Encyc. Brit.*)

(*b*) A particular kind or variety of metrical movement, expressed by a succession of a particular kind or variety of feet: as, iambic *rhythm;* dactylic *rhythm.*

Riah (rī′a), **Mr.** In Dickens's *Our Mutual Friend*, a gentle old Jew in the employment of Fascination Fledgeby, and abominably treated by him.

Rialto (ri.al′tō; Italian, rē.äl′tō), **Bridge of the.** A bridge over the Grand Canal in Venice. It was begun in 1588, and consists of a single graceful arch of marble, about 91 ft. in span, 24½ ft. above the water in the middle, and 72 ft. wide. In the middle there is a short level stretch beneath a large open arch, to which steps ascend from the quay on each side. It is divided into three footways separated by two rows of shops built under arcades.

Ribbon Society. In Irish history, a secret association, formed c1808 in opposition to the Orange organization of the northern Irish counties, and so named from the green ribbon worn as a badge by the members. The primary object of the society was soon merged in a struggle against the landlord class, with the purpose of securing to tenants fixity of tenure, or of inflicting retaliation for real or supposed agrarian oppression. The members were bound together by an oath, had passwords and signs, and were divided locally into lodges.

Ricardo (ri.kär′dō), **David.** b. at London, April 19, 1772; d. at Gatcomb Park, Gloucestershire, England, Sept. 11, 1823. An English political economist. He made a fortune as a stock broker and was able to go into virtual retirement to follow his scientific and economic studies at the age of 25. His chief work is *Principles of Political Economy and Taxation* (1817). He also wrote *The High Price of Bullion a Proof of the Depreciation of Bank-Notes* (1810), *Funding System* (1820; in the *Encyclopaedia Britannica*). He was especially noted for his discussion of the theory of rent. Ricardo is the founder of the classical school of economics, and was followed by economic theorists throughout the 19th century. The best-known of his laws is usually called the "iron law of wages" (it states that, other considerations aside, wages tend to fall to the lowest level that will permit the worker to subsist). His theory of value, extremely influential, is based on the principle that, where competition is free, it is the amount of labor (which is not defined) involved in production that determines the exchange value of a product. Other contributions include theories of rent, taxes, distribution, currency, standards, profits, and foreign trade. Ricardo's theories, in general, tend toward the abstract and take so little account of the human factor that they have been criticized as anti-social, but his establishing of the theoretical approach, notably in the fields of banking and currency, has led to a more scientific study of economics.

Ricardus Tertius (ri.kär′dus tēr′shus). A tragedy (1579) by Thomas Legge, based on events from English history.

Rice (rīs), **James.** b. at Northampton, England, Sept. 26, 1843; d. at Redhill, Surrey, England, April 26, 1882. An English editor and novelist. He was owner and editor (1868–72) of *Once a Week*, London correspondent (1872) of the Toronto *Globe*, and a frequent contributor to *All the Year Round*. With Sir Walter Besant he was the co-author of several novels, including *Ready-Money Mortiboy* (1872), *With Harp and Crown* (1874), *This Son of Vulcan* (1875), *The Golden Butterfly* (1876), *The Monks of Thelema* (1877), *By Celia's Arbor* (1878), *The Chaplain of the Fleet* (1879), and *The Seamy Side* (1881).

Rice, John. fl. 1607–20. An English actor. He acted in Shakespeare's plays and is mentioned in the first folio edition (1623) of Shakespeare's works.

Riceyman Steps (rī′si.man). A novel (1923) by Arnold Bennett.

Rich (rich), **Barnabe.** b. c1540; d. at Dublin, Nov. 10, 1617. An English pamphleteer and writer of romances. He produced (1574 *et seq.*) a considerable body of work, much of it in the involved style and manner of John Lyly. The best known of his many works are *Riche his Farewell to the Militarie Profession* (1581), *A Looking Glass for Ireland* (1599), *The Excellency of Good Women* (1613), *The Honestie of this Age, proving that the World was never Honest Till Now* (1614), and *The Irish Hubbub* (1617). The chief interest of the *Farewell*, which contains eight stories, is its second tale, "The History of Apolonius and Silla," which Shakespeare used as the source for the main plot of *Twelfth Night*.

Rich, John. b. c1682; d. Nov. 26, 1761. An English harlequin, called "the Father of Harlequins," and noted as a pure pantomime player. He played under the name of Lun. He was manager at Lincoln's Inn Fields (1713–32), and then built the first Covent Garden Theatre, which was opened Dec. 7, 1732. During the season of 1718–19 Rich frequently produced French plays and operas at Lincoln's Inn Fields.

Rich, Penelope. See **Devereux, Penelope.**

Richard (rich′ard). Entries on literary characters bearing this prename will be found under the surnames Amlet, Carstone, Feverel, Hannay, Ratcliffe, Remington, Rowan, Scroop, Varney, and Vernon, and also (for three Shakespeare characters) under the titles Cambridge, Gloucester, and York.

Richard I. [Called **Cœur de Lion** or **the Lion-Hearted;** also known as **Richard Yea and Nay.**] b. probably at Oxford, Sept. 8, 1157; d. near Limoges, France, April 6, 1199. King of England (1189–99); third son of Henry II. He was invested with the duchy of Aquitaine in 1169, joined the league between his elder brother Henry and Louis VII of France against his father (1173–74), and became heir apparent on the death of his brother Henry in 1183. He acted with Philip II of France against his father (1188–89), and succeeded to the throne of England, the duchy of Normandy, and the county of Anjou in 1189. He started on the third Crusade in alliance with Philip II of France in 1190, but soon quarreled with Philip. He conquered Cyprus in 1191, arrived at Acre in June, assisted in the capture of Acre in July, defeated the Saracens at Arsuf the same year; retook Jaffa from Saladin in 1192, signed a truce with Saladin in September, and left Palestine in October, having heard that his brother John, in his absence, was plotting to overthrow him. He was taken prisoner in Austria by the margrave Leopold V of Babenberg in December, was discovered in the castle of Dürenstein by Blondel, his faithful minstrel (according to legend), was transferred to the Emperor Henry VI in March, 1193, although the holding of a crusader under duress was illegal, and returned to England on the payment of a very heavy ransom in 1194. Having suppressed the rebellion of his brother John, he turned against John's ally, Philip II, whom he defeated at Gisors in 1195. He built the Château Gaillard in 1197, and was mortally wounded by a bolt from a crossbow while besieging Chaluz, near Limoges. Richard, who spent little of his life in England, being more interested in his French possessions than in those in England, is a well-known figure in English romantic literature, probably as a consequence of his close association with the troubadours (he wrote poetry and was a member of their brotherhood), who magnified his virtues and colorful deeds.

Richard II. b. at Bordeaux, France, Jan. 6, 1367; probably murdered at Pontefract, England, Feb. 14, 1400. King of England 1377–99; son of Edward, the "Black Prince," and grandson of Edward III, whom he succeeded. During his minority the government was conducted by his uncles John of Gaunt, Duke of Lancaster, and Thomas of Woodstock, Duke of Gloucester. A rebellion of the peasants under Wat Tyler was put down in 1381. Richard assumed the government personally in 1389. He was overthrown (1399) by the Duke of Hereford, whom he had banished (1398), was deposed by Parliament, Hereford becoming king as Henry IV, and was probably murdered in prison.

Richard II. [Full title, **The Tragedy of King Richard the Second.**] A historical play by Shakespeare, produced probably in 1595, and published in 1597. The deposition scene unquestionably carried particular significance for Queen Elizabeth (whose right to the throne was questioned by a fair number of her subjects for most of her reign). Understandably, therefore, it was omitted in the first quarto (1597); however, by the time of the fourth quarto (1608) it was restored. The play was also given a special performance at the Globe theater on Feb. 7, 1601, the day before Essex started his rebellion. It was paid for by his supporters, but none of the actors were punished for putting it on. The plot is from Holinshed's *Chronicles* (1587 edition), with one scene between the Queen and the Gardener being Shakespeare's invention. Strongly suggestive in its tone and plotting of Marlowe's works, the play is now nevertheless generally conceded to be Shakespeare's (although certainly influenced by Marlowe, and close in many respects to Marlowe's *Edward II*).

The Story. In the presence of the King, Bolingbroke accuses Mowbray of causing the death of the Duke of Gloucester. It is agreed that each man may defend his honor in a tournament, but just as each is about to attack the other, the King dramatically halts the proceedings and banishes them both. Shortly thereafter, upon the death of John of Gaunt, Bolingbroke's father, Richard seizes his estates in order to finance an Irish campaign. This additional evidence of Richard's disregard for the rights of his nobles arouses the ire of both York and Northumberland, and the latter, with other nobles, goes to join Bolingbroke (who has returned, despite his exile, to claim his dukedom). When Richard returns from Ireland, he learns that his army has dispersed, and his favorites, Bushy and Green, have been executed by Bolingbroke. Richard takes refuge in Flint Castle, and when Bolingbroke meets him there (ostensibly to claim his estates) submits to being taken as a prisoner to London. Before Parliament, he is forced to confess his crimes against the state and, despite the protests of the Bishop of Carlisle, he hands over his crown to Bolingbroke, who is already acting as king. Aumerle, the son of York, has meanwhile plotted against the new ruler. When York discovers this he hastens to inform Bolingbroke, but Aumerle and his mother, York's wife, plead for and are granted clemency. Richard is imprisoned in Pomfret Castle, where he is murdered by Sir Pierce of Exton (who mistakenly believes that Bolingbroke wishes Richard's death). Bolingbroke, however, regrets the murder and vows to lead a Crusade to ease his conscience. In its theme, the play touches a principle which was to tear England apart half a century later: the right, conferred by God, of a king to hold his throne. This right is here examined in a situation in which the king is a poor ruler, but an attractive person, and the usurper, whose abilities may merit the throne, must nevertheless bring "disorder, horror, fear, and mutiny" to England by taking it. As Richard points out, he himself is a traitor to the crown by giving it up, and Bolingbroke is aspiring beyond his reach in accepting the crown.

Richard II. In Shakespeare's *Richard II*, the King of England, a poetic and charming man, but a fatally weak monarch. Unable to follow any decisive course of action, he fails in his royal duties (but with his keen sense of the dramatic, he takes a kind of satisfaction in posing as the wronged and wretched king). With a Narcissism born of egoism and self-pity, he gazes into a mirror:

> . . . was this the face
> That, like the sun, did make beholders wink?
> Was this the face that faced so many follies,
> And was at last outfaced by Bolingbroke?

The punning is typical of his sheer enjoyment of words. Before his death he is pensive and realizes, somewhat like Macbeth, that he can only be happy with being nothing. He has wasted his time and his kingdom is now "Bolingbroke's proud joy."

Richard III. [Nicknamed **"Crouchback."**] b. at Fotheringay, England, Oct. 2, 1452; killed at the battle of Bosworth, Aug. 22, 1485. King of England (1483–85); third son of Richard, 3rd Duke of York, and younger brother of Edward IV. He was known as the Duke of Gloucester before his accession. He served in the battles of Barnet and Tewkesbury in 1471, and invaded Scotland in 1482. On the death of Edward IV in April, 1483, he seized the young Edward V, and caused himself to be proclaimed protector. On June 26, 1483, he assumed the crown,

ḍ, d or j; ṣ, s or sh; ṭ, t or ch; ẓ, z or zh; o, F. cloche; ü, F. menu; c̆h, Sc. loch; ṅ, F. bonbon.

the death in prison of Edward V and his brother, Richard, Duke of York, being publicly announced shortly after. He suppressed the powerful rebellion of Henry Stafford, 2nd Duke of Buckingham, in 1483, and was defeated and slain in the battle of Bosworth by Henry Tudor, Earl of Richmond (see Henry VII). His nickname "Crouchback" was given to him on account of a (probably slight) bodily deformity. Richard, last of the Yorkist kings in the period of the Wars of the Roses, has had a generally bad reputation, but some historians are now supporting the thesis that he was an able ruler who chose ruthless means like many another king.

Richard III. [Full title, **The Tragedy of King Richard the Third.**] A historical play, written by Shakespeare in 1592–93. It was printed anonymously in quarto in 1597; in a 1598 quarto Shakespeare's name appears; other quartos were published in 1602, 1605, 1612, and 1622; it appears also in the folio of 1623. Cibber produced an alteration in 1700, using parts of other Shakespeare plays, which was long considered the only acting version of the text. Cibber himself acted in the role of Richard until 1739. Macready produced a partial restoration in 1821. In 1876 Edwin Booth restored the Shakespeare version with slight changes of arrangement, but no interpolations. The line "Off with his head— so much for Buckingham!" is Cibber's; the most famous line in the play is Richard's "A horse! a horse! my kingdom for a horse!" Shakespeare's sources were Hall and Holinshed, and possibly a work entitled *The True Tragedie of Richard III*, printed in 1594.

The Story. Richard, Duke of Gloucester, having determined to obtain the crown, sets out to dispose of every obstacle, whether a person or a right, which may stand in his way. He manages to get his elder brother, the Duke of Clarence, imprisoned by the dying Edward IV, and orders his murder in the Tower. As the funeral procession of Henry VI passes by, he greets Lady Anne, the widow of Henry's son, and is soundly cursed by her; nevertheless, he proposes to her, and is accepted. Margaret, the widow of Henry VI, Elizabeth, the widow of the now dead Edward IV, and the Duchess of York, the mother of Edward, Clarence, and Richard, all curse the scheming Richard, and mourn the loss of their loved ones. While appearing to arrange the coronation of young Edward (whom he has imprisoned with his younger brother in the Tower), Richard executes Hastings, Rivers, Grey, and Vaughan, supporters of Elizabeth and her son. Buckingham, Richard's supporter, goes to the Guildhall and persuades the citizens to offer Richard the crown. When he is crowned he disposes of all who might oppose him, including the young princes in the Tower. His henchman, Buckingham, having refused to kill the princes, flees to join Richmond, but is murdered on the way. Meanwhile Richmond, the champion of justice, has landed and marches toward London, and at Bosworth Field the two forces meet. On the eve of the battle, Richard sees all the ghosts of his victims, and the following day he is slain by Richmond, who is then crowned as Henry VII, the first Tudor king.

Richard III.   See also **Gloucester, Richard, Duke of.**

Richard III, The History of. See under **Morton, John.**

Richard Babley (bab′li).   See **Dick, Mr.**

Richard Cœur de Lion (kėr′ de lē′on). A Middle English historical verse romance (c1350) of about 800 lines, based on a French romance, which deals very freely with the facts of the king's life and uses much legendary material.

Richard de Bury (de ber′i).   See **Aungerville, Richard.**

Richard Ganlesse (gan′les).   See **Ganlesse, Richard.**

Richard Hurdis; or, The Avenger of Blood (hėr′dis). A romance by William Gilmore Simms, published in 1838 as the first of his series of Border Romances. Its sequel is *Border Beagles* (1840).

Richard Feverel (fev′e.rel).   See **Feverel, Richard.** For the novel, see **Ordeal of Richard Feverel, The.**

Richard of Cirencester (sis′e.tėr, sī′ren.ses.tėr). d. at Westminster, London, c1401. An English Benedictine monk and historian. He wrote an English history (*Speculum Historiale de Gestis Regum Angliae, 447–1066,* edited 1863–69 by J. E. B. Mayor), and long was reputed to be the author of the forgery *De situ Britanniae,* actually by C. J. Bertram (1758).

Richard of Ely (ē′li).   See **Fitzneale** or **Fitznigel, Richard.**

Richard Roe (rō).   See **Roe, Richard.**

"Richards" (rich′ardz).   See **Toodles, Polly.**

Richardson (rich′ard.son), **Dorothy M.** [Married name, **Mrs. Alan Odle.**] b. 1882—. An English novelist, noted for her pioneer employment of the stream-of-consciousness technique in English fiction. Her major work, with the collective title of *Pilgrimage* (1938), consists of 12 novels: *Pointed Roofs* (1915), *Backwater* (1916), *Honeycomb* (1917), *The Tunnel* (1919), *Interim* (1919), *Deadlock* (1921), *Revolving Lights* (1923), *The Trap* (1925), *Oberland* (1927), *Dawn's Left Hand* (1931), *Clear Horizon* (1935), and *Dimple Hill* (1938). She is also author of *The Quakers, Past and Present* (1914).

Richardson, Henry Handel. [Pseudonym of **Henrietta Richardson;** original name, **Ethel Florence Lindesay Richardson;** married name, **Robertson.**] b. at Melbourne, Australia, Jan. 3, 1870; d. at Hastings, Sussex, England, March 20, 1946. An Australian novelist. She was educated at the Presbyterian Ladies' College, Melbourne. She went (c1890) to Leipzig, Germany, to study the piano, studying for three and a half years before concluding that she was not suited to the concert stage. She married (1895) J. G. Robertson, a Scottish student of German literature, who was appointed to the chair of German literature at the University of London, 1903. She lived at London until Robertson's death (1933), then in Sussex. Her outstanding works were *Maurice Guest* (1908) and *The Fortunes of Richard Mahony* (1930). An incomplete autobiography, *Myself When Young,* was published in 1948.

Richardson, Samuel. b. at Derbyshire, England, 1689; d. at London, July 4, 1761. An English novelist, often called the founder of the English domestic novel. He was apprenticed to a stationer at London in 1706, and eventually rose to become printer for the House of Commons. When a boy he was addicted to letter writing, and was employed by young girls to write love letters for them. In 1739 he composed a volume of *Familiar Letters*, which were afterward published as an aid to those incapable of writing their own letters without assistance. From this came *Pamela, or Virtue Rewarded* (1740), a novel in epistolary style telling of the dangers incurred by a virtuous maidservant. The success (and patent absurdity) of the novel called forth a stream of parodies and burlesques, by Henry Fielding among others, and brought from Richardson an unsuccessful sequel. He then wrote his masterpiece, *Clarissa, or the History of a Young Lady*, usually called *Clarissa Harlowe* (first 2 vols., 1747; last 5, 1748), and *The History of Sir Charles Grandison* (1753). His correspondence, with a biography by Anna Letitia Barbauld, was published in 1804. All his novels were published in the form of letters.

Richard the Redeless (rĕd'lĕs). See under **Mum, Sothsegger**.

Richard Varney (vär'ni). See **Varney, Richard**.

Richard Vere (vēr). See **Vere, Richard**.

Richard Vernon (vėr'nọn), **Sir**. See **Vernon, Sir Richard**.

Richard Yea-and-Nay (yā'ạnd.nā'). See **Life and Death of Richard Yea-and-Nay**.

Richelieu (rish'ẹ.lö; French, rē.shẹ.lyė). A play in blank verse by Edward Bulwer-Lytton, first produced on March 7, 1839. William Charles Macready created the part of Richelieu, the great Cardinal, who is here shown contending with a conspiracy to overthrow him.

Richelieu, Cardinal and Duc de. [Titles of **Armand Jean du Plessis**; called **Éminence Rouge**.] b. at Paris, Sept. 9, 1585; d. there, Dec. 4, 1642. A French prelate and statesman. He was educated for the church, became bishop of Luçon in 1607 and secretary of state in 1616, was exiled to Blois (later to Avignon) in 1617, became cardinal in 1622, and was the principal minister (1624–42) of Louis XIII. He vastly increased the power of France among the nations of Europe and strengthened the rule of the crown at home (and thereby lessened the power of the great nobles, who had long since become accustomed to thinking of themselves as the actual masters of France). The chief events in his administration were the destruction of the political power of the Huguenots by the siege and capture of La Rochelle (1627–28), the war in Italy against Spain and Austria (1629–30), the defeat of the partisans of Marie de Médicis in 1630, the suppression of the rising of Montmorency and Gaston of Orléans in 1632, the coöperation of France with Sweden in the Thirty Years' War, the founding of the French Academy in 1635, and the defeat of the Cinq-Mars conspiracy in 1642. His literary remains include religious works, dramas, memoirs, correspondence, and state papers.

Riches. A stage version, still used, of Massinger's *City Madam* (licensed 1632).

Richest Man, The. A novel by Edward Shanks, published in 1923.

Richie Moniplies (rich'i mun'i.plĭz). See **Moniplies, Richie**.

Richings (rich'ingz), **Peter**. b. at London, May 19, 1798; d. at Media, Pa., Jan. 18, 1871. An English actor and manager in the U. S. He came to America in 1821, and made his debut at New York as Harry Bertram in *Guy Mannering*. Captain Absolute (in *The Rivals*) was one of his best roles.

Richmond (rich'mọnd), **Henry Tudor, Earl of**. In Shakespeare's *3 Henry VI*, a young boy who Henry prophesies shall be King one day. In *Richard III*, he lands with an army, bent on dethroning the tyrannical Richard. He defeats Richard at Bosworth and is proclaimed Henry VII. His reign is foreseen as bringing peace to England. The historical Henry VII, first of the Tudor dynasty, unified the Lancastrians and Yorkists by his marriage with Edward IV's daughter, Elizabeth. The phrase "another Richmond," which has come to mean a new adversary, is a reference to the speech of the desperate King in *Richard III* (V.iv):

I think there be six Richmonds in the field;
Five have I slain to-day instead of him.

Richmond, Legh. b. at Liverpool, England, Jan. 29, 1772; d. at Turvey, Bedfordshire, England, May 8, 1827. An English clergyman and religious writer. He is best known from his tracts entitled *Annals of the Poor* (1814: including "The Dairyman's Daughter," "The Young Cottager," "The Negro Servant," and others). He edited *Fathers of the English Church* (1807–12).

Rickman (rik'mạn), **Keith**. A Cockney poet, the hero of May Sinclair's novel *The Divine Fire* (1904). Rickman is believed to represent the poet Ernest Dowson.

Ridd (rid), **John**. The hero of the novel *Lorna Doone*.

Riddell (rid'ẹl), **Charlotte Eliza Lawson**. [Also: Mrs. **J. H. Riddell**; pseudonym in early works, **F. G. Trafford**; maiden name, **Cowan**.] b. Sept. 30, 1832; d. Sept. 24, 1906. An English novelist. She became coproprietor and editor of *St. James's Magazine* in 1867. She wrote *The Head of the Firm* (1892), *A Silent Tragedy* (1893), *A Rich Man's Daughter* (1897), *Footfall of Fate* (1900), *Poor Fellow* (1902), and others.

riddle. A literary device popular in the Old English period. Many poems, in both Latin and English, took the form of a description, narration, or the like, of something the reader was to identify; these poems varied widely in complexity and relative obscurity, as well as literary quality. A collection of about 95 (variously counted because of missing pages, etc.) in Old English is preserved in the *Exeter Book*.

Riddle of the Sands, The. A novel by Erskine Childers, published in 1903.

Riderhood (rī'dėr.hůd), **Pleasant**. In Dickens's *Our Mutual Friend*, Roger (Rogue) Riderhood's daughter: "Upon the smallest of small scales she was an unlicensed pawnbroker, keeping what was popularly called a leaving-shop."

Riderhood, Roger (or **Rogue**). In Dickens's *Our Mutual Friend*, a river thief and longshoreman

ḍ, d or j; ṣ, s or sh; ṭ, t or ch; ẓ, z or zh; o, F. cloche; ü, F. menu; ċh, Sc. loch; ṅ, F. bonbon

Afterward a lock-keeper, he is drowned in the lock in a struggle with Bradley Headstone.

Riders to the Sea. A one-act tragedy (1904) of Irish life by John Millington Synge. The characters include Maurya, an old woman who has lost her husband and four sons to the sea; Bartley, her last son, who goes the way of his father and brothers; and two daughters, Cathleen and Nora. The scene of action is a cottage kitchen on an island off the west of Ireland.

Ridge (rij), **William Pett.** b. c1860; d. 1930. An English writer. Author of the novels *A Son of the State*, *Splendid Brother*, *Love at Paddington*, and *Just Like Aunt Bertha*, he also wrote *London Please* (1925), a collection of four plays with a Cockney background.

Ridley (rid′li), **Nicholas.** b. in Northumberland, England, c1500; burned at Oxford, England, Oct. 16, 1555. An English bishop and Protestant martyr. He was chaplain to Cranmer (with whom he was closely associated in outlining the Thirty-Nine Articles and in preparing the English prayer book) and to Henry VIII. He became bishop of Rochester in 1547, and of London in 1550. He denied the legitimacy of both Elizabeth and Mary, insisting that only Lady Jane Grey could be considered a lawful child of Henry VIII (and hence that only she could claim the throne). He flatly refused to compromise in this position, and was therefore promptly arrested upon Mary's accession (1553) to the throne; two years later he was declared a heretic, tried, and burned at the stake with Latimer.

Riel (ryel), **Hervé.** A Breton sailor who saved (1692) a French naval force from almost certain destruction by guiding it safely into the harbor of St. Malo. For a reward he is believed actually to have requested a discharge from the navy (although Browning in his poem *Hervé Riel* has him asking only for a day's leave to spend with his wife).

Rience (rī′ęns). See **Ryance.**

Rienzi (ri.en′zi). A tragedy by Mary Russell Mitford, published in 1828. It deals with the story of Rienzi, the 14th-century Roman patriot, which the author sees as offering some parallels to the early career of Napoleon.

Rienzi. A historical novel by Edward Bulwer-Lytton, published in 1835. It is based on the story of Cola de Rienzi, who established a government in Italy patterned on the system of the old Roman republic in 1347. Rienzi's government fell after only seven months (it was bitterly opposed by the papacy), and he went into exile. He is often called "the last of the Romans."

Rigaud (ri.gō′). [Also: **Blandois,** and **Lagnier.**] In Dickens's *Little Dorrit*, a sinister-looking, sharp, murderous criminal, formerly a convict at Marseilles. His "moustache went up and his nose went down."

Rigdumfunnidos (rig.dum.fun′i.dos). [Also: **Rigdum-Funnidos, Rigdum Funnidos.**] Lord in waiting at the court of Chrononhotonthologos, in Henry Carey's 18th-century burlesque of that name. Sir Walter Scott jokingly applied this name to John Ballantyne, his printer, as being more mercurial than his brother.

Rightful Heir, The. A play by Edward Bulwer-Lytton, produced in 1869.

Rig-Veda (rig.vā′dạ). See under **Vedas.**

Rima (rē′mạ). An important character, the "bird-girl," in W. H. Hudson's *Green Mansions*. The figure of Rima in Jacob Epstein's memorial to Hudson, in London, roused violent controversy in 1925.

Rime of Sir Thopas (tō′pạs), **The.** One of Chaucer's *Canterbury Tales*, a burlesque on the metrical romances of the day, such as *Guy of Warwick* and *Bevis of Hampton*, and in all probability also a satirical thrust at the Flemish knighthood. It is the first of the two represented as being told by Chaucer himself. Sir Thopas, a knight of Poperyng (Poperinge), in Flanders, and his prowess at various sports, are described in minute and tedious detail. He starts for Fairyland to find an elf queen for his wife and meets a three-headed giant who challenges him to mortal combat but seems to be willing to wait while Sir Thopas goes back home for his armor. At this point the story comes to a standstill, interminable descriptions follow, and soon the courteous Host himself can stand no more. He breaks in, "No more of this, for goddes dignitee." Chaucer thereupon tells *The Tale of Melibeus*, which most modern readers, at least, find more tedious than the Host found Sir Thopas.

Rime of the Ancient Mariner, The. See **Ancient Mariner, The Rime of the.**

Riming Poem, The. See **Rhyming Poem, The.**

Rimini (rē′mē.nē), **Francesca da.** See **Francesca da Rimini.**

Rimini (rim′i.ni), **Story of.** A poem by Leigh Hunt, published in 1816.

Rimor (rīm′ọr), **Thomas.** See **Thomas the Rhymer.**

Rinaldo (ri.nal′dō). [French, **Regnault, Renaud de Montauban.**] A character in medieval romance. He was one of the four sons of Aymon, the cousin of Orlando, and one of the bravest of the knights of Charlemagne. In the French romances he is known under various names.

Rinaldo. In Shakespeare's *All's Well That Ends Well*, the steward of the Countess of Rossillion.

Rinaldo. The younger brother of Fortunio in George Chapman's comedy *All Fools, or All Fools but the Fool.*

Rind (rind). In Norse mythology, one of Odin's wives: the earth's crust personified.

Ring and the Book, The. A poem by Robert Browning, published in 1869. It is based on an incident from Italian history, which Browning became familiar with through a parchment volume purchased in Florence. It deals with the marriage of the haughty Count Guido Franceschini and the gentle Pompilia, the supposed daughter of Violante and Pietro Comparini. When Franceschini discovers her to be actually not their daughter, but a foundling introduced into the Comparini household by Violante, he sets out to get rid of her on a trumped-up charge of adultery, and a trial is begun to settle future ownership of the property that had been Pompilia's when she was presumed to be a Comparini. So great is Guido's cruelty to Pompilia that she flees from him to Rome under the protection of a young priest, Giuseppi Capon-sacchi. Guido follows and institutes another trial, this one to deal with the matter of her alleged adultery. A separation is granted, and Pompilia is sent to a convent. However, since she is with child, she is presently allowed to return home, where, after the birth of a son, she and the Comparinis are murdered by Guido and four hired thugs. For this, finally, Guido is arrested, tried, and hanged. The poem is written in the form of dramatic monologues, through which the event is viewed from the point of view of twelve different participants in it, allowing all the evidence in the case to be offered and balanced. It ends with the Pope's judgment, commending the "warrior-priest" Caponsacchi and proclaiming Pompilia "the rose I gather for the breast of God."

Rink (ringk), **Effie.** In H. G. Wells's *Tono-Bungay*, a typist who is involved with Edward Ponderevo in a passionate love affair. She is an efficient, strong-minded woman (at one point she establishes a typing bureau and manages it with great success), and eventually marries a poet whose weak nature provides her with ample opportunity for the "managing" impulse of her own personality.

Rintherout (rin'thĕr.out), **Jenny.** In Sir Walter Scott's novel *The Antiquary*, a flirtatious servant girl, but withal docile and conscientious in the performance of her duties.

Riquet with the Tuft (ri.ket'). An English translation of *Riquet à la houppe*, title and hero of a fairy tale by Charles Perrault, translated into English in the 18th century. This is, in the main, the same as the typical European folk tale commonly called *Beauty and the Beast*.

Rising Dawn, The. A historical novel by Harold Begbie, published in 1913. It is laid in England, in the 14th century; among the characters are John Ball, John of Gaunt, John Wycliffe, and Geoffrey Chaucer.

Risingham (riz'ing.am), **Bertram.** In Sir Walter Scott's narrative poem *Rokeby*, an adherent of Oswald Wycliffe in his effort to capture Rokeby Castle.

Rising of the Moon, The. A play (1907) by Augusta Gregory (Lady Gregory) in which a police sergeant allows an Irish revolutionist to escape from jail after the latter has won him over with his patriotic idealism.

Risk (risk). A character in the musical farce *Love Laughs at Locksmiths*, by George Colman the younger.

Risorgimento (rē.sôr.jē.men'tō). In 19th-century Italian history, the movement for the national unification of Italy. Italy had not been a political unit from the fall in the 5th century of the Roman Empire in the West until the regional unifications imposed by Napoleon gave added force to the Italian dream of a free and united country. The term Risorgimento seems to have come into use in c1815 to identify the group and movement that developed from the Carbonari under Giuseppe Mazzini and others. However, Mazzini, who was imprisoned for a time in 1830–31 and had to go into exile, operated thereafter through his own organization, *Giovine Italia* (Young Italy), rather than the Carbonari. The second great leader of the Risorgimento, Giuseppe Garibaldi, took his inspiration from Mazzini. The third pillar of Risorgimento, Camillo Benso, Conte di Cavour, derived from the July Revolution in France (1830) a conviction that a constitutional monarchy offered a better hope of measured progress than a republican form of government. The movement and the era of the Risorgimento may be considered to have ended in 1870.

Ristori (rē.stô'rē), **Adelaide.** b. at Venice, Italy, 1821; d. Oct. 9, 1905. An Italian actress. She first appeared in infant roles, but at 13 was already playing "second" ladies. When she was 16, she turned down an offer to be leading lady in a theater, and, wanting more experience, took the post of ingenue in the company of the king of Sardinia. For 18 years she developed her art with this group; and when she and her husband, the Marquis del Grillo, took the Royal Sardinian Company to Paris (1855) her success challenged the supremacy of Rachel, whose quick departure for an American tour was regarded as an artistic retreat. Medea (in Legouvé's tragedy of the same name) became one of her great roles, along with the part of Mary Stuart in Schiller's play. In 1857 she played Lady Macbeth in Italian, at London. In 1875 she played Mary Stuart at New York, and again at New York (1885) she played Lady Macbeth with Edwin Booth. By the beginning of the 20th century she was considered the greatest of tragediennes, and was called the Italian Mrs. Siddons. In her *Memoirs* (published 1907) she wrote a penetrating analysis of her interpretation of Lady Macbeth.

Ritchie (rich'i), Lady **Anne Isabella.** [Maiden name, **Thackeray.**] b. at London, June 9, 1837; d. at Freshwater, Isle of Wight, England, Feb. 26, 1919. An English biographer and novelist; daughter of William Makepeace Thackeray. Author of *The Story of Elizabeth* (1863), *The Village on the Cliff* (1865), *Old Kensington* (1873), *Toilers and Spinsters* (1873), *Bluebeard's Keys* (1874), *Miss Angel* (1875), and *Mrs. Dymond* (1885), novels; *Madame de Sévigné* (1881), *Lord Tennyson and His Friends* (1893), *Portraits and Reminiscences* (1893), *Chapters From Some Memoirs* (1894), *The Blackstick Papers* (1908), and *From the Porch* (1913), criticism, recollections, and essays.

Ritchie, Sir **Lewis Anselm.** [Pseudonym, **Bartimeus;** original name, **L. A. da Costa Ricci.**] b. April 29, 1886—. An English writer. Author of *Naval Occasions* (1914), *The Long Trick* (1917), *Navy Eternal* (1918), *Seaways* (1923), *An Off-Shore Wind* (1936), *Under Sealed Orders* (1938), *Steady As You Go* (1942), *East of Malta, West of Suez* (1943), and *The Turn of the Road* (1946).

Ritson (rit'son), **Joseph.** b. at Stockton, England, Oct. 2, 1752; d. 1803. An English antiquary. Among his works are *Ancient Songs* (1792), *Scottish Songs* (1794), and *Robin Hood* (1795; a collection of ballads).

Rival Fools, The. An alteration of John Fletcher's *Wit at Several Weapons*, produced in 1709 by Colley Cibber.

Rival Ladies, The. A tragicomedy by Dryden, produced in 1664. The plot seems to reflect in part

Scarron's *L'Écolier de Salamanque*, and is of some interest as showing a tendency away from comedy of humour toward the comedy of manners.

Rival Queens, or the Death of Alexander the Great, The. A tragedy by Nathaniel Lee, played in 1677. It is Lee's best-known play. Some of the scenes seem to have been suggested by La Calprenède's novel *Cassandre*, and it was long a favorite with actresses. Cibber produced a "comical tragedy" called *The Rival Queans, with the Humors of Alexander the Great*, in 1710, printed in 1729.

Rivals, The. A tragicomic adaptation of *The Two Noble Kinsmen*, by Sir William D'Avenant, played in 1664, printed in 1668.

Rivals, The. A comedy by Richard Brinsley Sheridan, produced in 1775. It is considered by many to be a better play than *The School for Scandal*, though perhaps less celebrated. Its first performance was not too well received, partly because Sir Lucius O'Trigger was regarded as insulting to the Irish gentry. Sheridan promptly modified the script (Sir Lucius's part was rewritten, the play was shortened, and the dialogue was very much livened up), whereupon it became a great success, and has been hardly less successful in subsequent presentations up to the present day. Sir Anthony Absolute, a choleric gentleman, wishes his son, Captain Absolute, to marry Lydia Languish, but does not know that he (Captain Absolute) has already been wooing her in the character of the impecunious Ensign Beverley (Lydia's romantic notions will not permit her to consider a comfortable marriage with the son of a baronet, whence the need for Absolute's disguise). Mrs. Malaprop, Lydia's aunt, famous for her charming ability to use words improperly, has not looked favorably upon Lydia's marriage to the supposedly impoverished Beverley, and threatens to retain half of Lydia's fortune, as she has the right to do, if Lydia marries without her consent. However, she is quite agreeable to a match with the son of Sir Anthony, and Captain Absolute is thereby forced into a predicament. Should he inform Lydia of the true identity of Beverley? If he does, she may well jilt him in disgust. Meanwhile, Bob Acres, his rival, knows that Beverley has been pursuing Lydia and, urged on by the fiery Sir Lucius O'Trigger, issues a challenge to Beverley through his friend Absolute (not knowing they are the same person). Sir Lucius also challenges Beverley, because he thinks that Lydia is in love with him (he has mistaken love letters from Mrs. Malaprop as being actually from Lydia). There is a highly comic scene when Bob, a coward at heart, considers the danger in fighting Beverley, only to be saved at the last moment by the discovery of Beverley's true identity. He promptly declines to fight and leaves Lydia to Captain Absolute. Things come to a satisfactory conclusion upon the arrival on the scene of Mrs. Malaprop and Lydia; the latter, after abusing her lover for ruining her hopes of a romantic elopement, consents to a marriage.

Rivers (riv'ẽrz), **Earl.** In Shakespeare's *3 Henry VI*, the brother of Elizabeth, Lady Grey, who is later the Queen of Edward IV. In *Richard III*, he

is executed on Richard's order because he has urged the coronation of young Prince Edward.

Rizpah (riz'pạ). A poem by Alfred Tennyson, published in his *Ballads and Other Poems* (1880).

R. L. S. See **Stevenson, Robert Louis.**

Road to Ruin, The. A comedy by Thomas Holcroft, produced in 1792.

Road to Wigan Pier (wig'ạn), **The.** A novel by George Orwell, published in 1937.

Roan Barbary (rōn bär'bạ.ri). In Shakespeare's *Richard II*, the favorite horse of King Richard.

Roaring Girl, The. [Full title, **The Roaring Girl; or, Moll Cut-Purse.**] A comedy by Thomas Dekker and Thomas Middleton. It was produced in 1610, and printed in 1611. The original of the roaring girl was Moll Cut-purse, alias Mary Frith, a notorious London character who dressed and was armed like a man. The roaring girl is the counterpart of the roaring boy, a swaggering type common in the Elizabethan and Jacobean periods.

Robarts (rō'bärts), **Lucy.** In Anthony Trollope's novel *Framley Parsonage*, the young sister of Mark Robarts. She is a girl of independence and beauty (of whom Trollope later wrote "Lucy Robarts is, perhaps, the most natural English girl I ever drew").

Robarts, Mark. In Anthony Trollope's novel *Framley Parsonage*, the vicar of Framley Church and, briefly, a prebendary of Barchester Cathedral. He appears also in *The Last Chronicle of Barset*.

Robarts, Mrs. Fanny. In Anthony Trollope's novel *Framley Parsonage*, the wife of Mark Robarts. She is a woman of extraordinary goodness.

Robert (rob'ẽrt). [Title, Earl of **Gloucester.**] d. Oct. 13, 1147. An illegitimate son of Henry I of England, and an adherent of his half-sister Matilda against his cousin Stephen during their struggle over the crown. Stephen confiscated (1137) his large estates in England and Wales, and Robert joined Matilda in her invasion (1139) of England. He captured Stephen at Lincoln (1141) but fell into the hands of Stephen's followers at Stockbridge and was exchanged for him. He won a victory over Stephen at Wilton (1143), but could not gain the final advantage.

Robert. Entries on literary characters having this prename will be found under the surnames Brakenbury, Bramble, Drury, Dunwoody, Eccles, Faulconbridge, Hand, and Tusher.

Robert I. [Called **Robert le Diable**; English, **"Robert the Devil."**] d. at Nicaea, July 22, 1035. Duke of Normandy (1028–35); younger son of Richard the Good, and father of William the Conqueror. He supported the English against Canute. He made a pilgrimage to Jerusalem, and died on the way back to France. Lodge wrote a life of Robert before 1593, and many legends have collected about his name. He was often identified with a legendary Robert the Devil, who was celebrated in medieval romance.

Robert de Boron (ro.ber dẹ bo.rôṅ). [Also, **Boron.**] fl. probably in the late 12th and early 13th centuries. An Anglo-French or French poet, author of a trilogy in which the legend of the Grail is worked out and connected with the main body of Arthurian legend. Of the three poems, *Joseph d'Arimathie*, *Merlin*, and *Perceval*, only the first and part of the second are still extant. He is said to have composed two versions of the Joseph legend.

Robert Elsmere (elz′mir). A novel (1888) by Mrs. Humphry Ward about an English clergyman whose intellectual doubts force him to abandon strict orthodoxy.

Robert of Brunne (brun). See **Mannyng, Robert.**

Robert of Gloucester (glos′tẽr). fl. in the second half of the 13th century. An English monk, the reputed author of a rhymed *Chronicle of English History*, from the legendary Brut to 1270 A.D., one of the last Old English works.

Roberts (rob′ẽrts), **Cecil Edric Mornington.** b. at Nottingham, England, May 18, 1892—. An English poet, novelist, and journalist. His verse works include *Phyllistrata and other Poems* (1913), *Through Eyes of Youth* (1914), *Youth of Beauty* (1915), *Collected War Poems* (1916), and *Training the Airmen* (1918). Among his plays are the poetic drama *A Tale of Young Lovers* (1922), the comedy *The Right to Kiss* (1926), and *Spears Against Us* (1939). He was author also of the novel *The Chelsea Cherub* (1917) and of *Little Mrs. Manington* (1926), *Havana Bound* (1930), *Victoria Four-Thirty* (1937), *They Wanted to Live* (1938), *And So to Bath* (1939), *One Small Candle* (1942), and *Eight for Eternity* (1948).

Roberts, Morley. b. at London, Dec. 29, 1857; d. June 8, 1942. An English novelist and journalist. For many years he led an adventurous life as a cattleman and railroadman in Australia, the U.S., Canada, and South Africa, and as a sailor in various parts of the world. His works include *The Western Avernus* (1887), *Songs of Energy* (1891), *Red Earth* (1894), *A Son of Empire* (1899), *The Colossus* (1899), *Lord Linlithglow* (1900), *The Plunderers* (1900), *Immortal Youth* (1902), *The Way of a Man* (1902), *The Promotion of the Admiral* (1903), *Rachel Marr* (1903), *A Tramp's Notebook* (1904), *The Idlers* (1905), *The Prey of the Strongest* (1906), *The Blue Peter* (1907), *The Flying Cloud* (1907), *Lady Anne* (1907), *Captain Spink* (1908), *David Bran* (1908), *Midsummer Madness* (1909), *Sea Dogs* (1910), *The Wonderful Bishop* (1910), *Thorpe's Way* (1911), *Four Plays* (1911), and *A Humble Fisherman* (1932).

Robertson (rob′ẽrt.son), **E. Arnot.** [Pen name of Mrs. **Henry Ernest Turner;** maiden name, **Eileen Arbuthnot Robertson.**] b. 1903—. English novelist. Author of *Cullum* (1928), *Three Came Unarmed* (1929), *Four Frightened People* (1931), *Ordinary Families* (1933), *Thames Portrait* (1937), *Summer's Lease* (1940), and *The Signpost* (1943).

Robertson, Henrietta. See **Richardson, Henry Handel.**

Robertson, John Mackinnon. b. on the Isle of Aran, Ireland, Nov. 14, 1856; d. Jan. 5, 1933. An English journalist, politician, and Shakespeare scholar. He was an editorial writer (1878–84) for the Edinburgh *Evening News*, editor (1891–93) of the *National Reformer*, and publisher and editor (1893–95) of the *Free Review*. As a member of Parliament (1906–18), he was parliamentary secretary to the Board of Trade (1911–15). In his Shakespearian scholar-

ship, he tended to eliminate much in the accepted canon as being by other playwrights. Author of *The Baconian Heresy, a Confutation* (1913), *Shakespeare and Chapman* (1917), *The Problem of Hamlet* (1919), *The Shakespeare Canon* (1922–30), *The Problems of the Shakespeare Sonnets* (1926), *History of Free Thought in the 19th Century* (1929), and *Literary Detection* (1931).

Robertson, John Parish. b. at Edinburgh, c1793; d. at Calais, France, Nov. 1, 1843. A Scottish author and traveler.

Robertson, Thomas William. b. at Newark, Nottinghamshire, England, Jan. 9, 1829; d. at London, Feb. 3, 1871. An English dramatist; son of a provincial actor and manager and elder brother of Madge Kendal. In 1864 his first successful drama, *David Garrick*, was produced at the Haymarket with E. A. Sothern in the principal role. Among his other plays are *Society* (1865), *Ours* (1866), *Caste* (1867), *Play* (1868), *School* (1869), and *M. P.* (1870). These plays, far more realistic in their subdued theatricalism than the customary drama of the time, were criticized as "cup-and-saucer" comedy; though their literary merit is slight, they are notable as marking the advent in England of the drama of naturalism.

Robertson, William. b. at Borthwick, Scotland, Sept. 19, 1721; d. near Edinburgh, June 11, 1793. A Scottish historian and clergyman. He became a royal chaplain in 1761, principal of the University of Edinburgh in 1762, and king's historiographer in 1763. His works, which had tremendous influence on the historians of his time and afterward, and which place him in the same rank with Edward Gibbon and David Hume, include *History of Scotland during the Reigns of Mary and James VI* (1759), *History of the Reign of the Emperor Charles V* (1769), *History of America* (1777), *An Historical Disquisition concerning the Knowledge which the Ancients had of India* (1791), and others.

"Robert the Devil" (rob′ẽrt). See **Robert I** (of Normandy).

Robert Tusher (tush′ẽr). See **Tusher, Robert.**

Robespierre (rōbz′pi.ãr, -pir; French, ro.bes.pyer), **Maximilien François Marie Isidore de.** [Called **"the Incorruptible."**] b. at Arras, May 6, 1758; guillotined at Paris, 10th Thermidor, Year 2 (July 28, 1794). A French revolutionist. He was originally a lawyer at Arras, was elected (1789) from Artois to the Third Estate of the States-General, and became the leader of the radicals in the Constituent Assembly, and one of the leading orators in the Jacobin Club. His influence increased after the death (1791) of Mirabeau. He was elected (1792) to the Convention as first Parisian deputy, sitting with the Mountain in opposition to the Girondists. The quarrel between the two parties was held in abeyance during the trial of the king, in which Robespierre declared: "Louis must die, that the nation may live."

Robey (rō′bi), **George.** [Stage name of **George Edward Wade.**] b. Sept. 20, 1869—. An English comic actor. He acted (1891 *et seq.*) chiefly on the variety stage. In motion pictures, he appeared in *Don Quixote, Chu Chin Chow, Southern Roses, Henry V, Waltz Time,* and *The Trojan Brothers.*

ḍ, d or j; ṣ, s or sh; ṭ, t or ch; ẓ, z or zh; o, F. cloche; ü, F. menu; ċh, Sc. loch; ṅ, F. bonbon.

Robin (rob′in). In Shakespeare's *Merry Wives of Windsor*, Falstaff's page. He may be the same person as the Page who appears in *2 Henry IV* with Falstaff and in *Henry V* with Bardolph, Nym, and Pistol.

Robin Adair (ạ.dār′). A song and air. The latter, which first became popular in England in the last half of the 18th century, is the Irish air *Eileen Aroon*. English words were written for it, and there are several versions, all having *Robin Adair* as the refrain. Robert Burns made a Scottish version, but it is not known who wrote the present song. Robin Adair is said to have been a real person of some local interest: a Robert Adair, an ancestor of the later Viscounts Molesworth, lived in County Wicklow in the early part of the 18th century.

Robin and Makyne (mā′kin). A poem by the 15th-century Scottish poet Robert Henryson, telling of the unrequited love of Makyne for Robin the Shepherd. Robin changes his mind, but it is too late and Makyne will have none of him, for, as she says:

> The man that will nocht qwhen he may
> Sall haif nocht qwhen he wald.

"Robin Bluestring" (blö′string). A nickname of **Walpole**, Sir **Robert**.

Robin Goodfellow (gụd′fel″ō). See **Puck**.

Robin Gray (grā), **Auld.** See **Auld Robin Gray**.

Robin Hood (hụd). See **Hood, Robin**.

Robin Hood and Guy of Gisborne (gī; giz′born). One of the better-known ballads in the Robin Hood cycle, included in Percy's *Reliques*, telling of a quarrel between Robin Hood and Little John, as the result of which they part, Little John being captured by the sheriff, and Robin Hood meeting with Guy of Gisborne, who has vowed to kill him. They fight and Robin is the victor. Clad in the clothes of Guy, he comes upon the sheriff and Little John. The sheriff, thinking he is Guy, places him in charge of Little John, whom Robin Hood releases, giving him Guy's bow and arrow, at which point the sheriff flees. Later the quarrel between the two outlaws is smoothed over.

Robin Oig M'Combich (rob′in oig mạ.kum′bi). See **M'Combich, Robin Oig**.

Robinson (rob′in.sọn), **Henry Crabb.** b. at Bury Saint Edmunds, England, March 13, 1775; d. at London, Feb. 5, 1867. An English writer. From 1800 to 1805 he studied at Jena, Weimar, and elsewhere on the Continent, in 1807 was reporter of the *Times* in Spain, and in 1813 was called to the bar. In 1828 he was one of the founders of London University. His *Diary, Reminiscences, and Correspondence*, a brief selection from a hundred volumes he left, was edited in 1869 by Dr. Thomas Sadler; later selections have also been printed. He was a friend of Goethe, Wieland, Wordsworth, Lamb, and other authors.

Robinson, Lennox. [Full name, **Esmé Stuart Lennox Robinson**.] b. at Douglas, County Cork, Ireland, Oct. 4, 1886—. An Irish dramatist, novelist, and theater director. He was the manager (1910–14, 1919–23) and a director (1923 *et seq.*) of the Abbey Theatre at Dublin. His plays, many of which were originally produced at the Abbey, include *The Clancy Name* (1908), *Patriots* (1912), *The Dreamers* (1915), *The Whiteheaded Boy* (1916), *The Lost Leader* (1918), *Crabbed Youth and Age* (1922), *Portrait* (1925), *The Big House* (1926), *Church Street* (1934), *When Lovely Woman* (1936), *Killycreggs in Twilight* (1937), *Roly-Poly* (1942), and *The Lucky Finger* (1949). He is author also of the novel *A Young Man from the South* (1917), the collected short stories *Dark Days* (1918), and the autobiographical *Curtain Up* (1942).

Robinson, Mary. [Maiden name: **Darby**; pseudonym, **Perdita**.] b. at Bristol, England, Nov. 27, 1758; d. Dec. 26, 1800. An English actress, novelist, and poet. She went (1776) on the stage, for which she had previously been prepared by David Garrick, on account of the loss of the property of her husband, Thomas Robinson, a clerk. In her third season she was cast for Perdita in *The Winter's Tale*, and attracted the notice of the Prince of Wales (later George IV). She left the stage for him, but he soon cast her off; his personal bond to her for 20,000 pounds was never paid, but Charles James Fox obtained a pension for her. Her profession being closed to her because of public opinion, she wrote poems and novels under the pseudonym of Perdita. Gainsborough, Reynolds, Romney, and Hoppner were among those who painted her portrait.

Robinson, Richard. d. 1648. An English actor, celebrated as an impersonator of female characters. He appears in the lists of actors of the Shakespeare 1623 and Beaumont and Fletcher 1647 folios. He is known to have acted in Jonson's *Catiline* (1611) and Fletcher's *Bonduca* (1611).

Robinson Crusoe (krö′sō). [Full title, **The Life and Strange Surprizing Adventures of Robinson Crusoe, of York, Mariner**.] A novel by Daniel Defoe, published in 1719. Based on the adventures of Alexander Selkirk, who had lived for five years alone on an uninhabited island, on a book by William Dampier (captain of the expedition that set Selkirk on the island), and on other sources, it was followed by two less successful sequels (1719, 1720). It is one of the great successes of world literature and has evoked many similar works from other writers. Robinson Crusoe runs away from home to ship on a privateer, but is shipwrecked on a small island near the Orinoco River. He builds a hut for himself, plants corn, and finds solace in the Bible. After 24 years he saves the life of a young savage and names him Friday, in honor of the day he finds him. The two live together on the island for a few more years, when they are joined by the captain of a nearby ship. His crew has mutinied, and Crusoe helps to subdue them. He then returns to England. The first sequel, *The Farther Adventures of Robinson Crusoe*, was never as popular as the original; it tells of Crusoe's return to the island and establishment of a Christian colony there. When Friday is killed by cannibals, the grief-stricken Crusoe returns to England. The second sequel, *Serious Reflections . . . of Robinson Crusoe*, was not a story but a moralizing tract.

Robinson Crusoe's Island. An imaginary uninhabited island on the N coast of South America, off the mouth of the Orinoco River, described in Daniel Defoe's tale *Robinson Crusoe*. It is often identified

---

fat, fāte, fär, ȧsk, fāre; net, mē, hėr; pin, pīne; not, nōte, möve, nôr; up, lūte, pụll; ᵺH, then;

with Tobago in the Caribbean Sea or with Más a Tierra in the Juan Fernández group.

Robin Starveling (rob'in stärv'ling). See **Starveling, Robin.**

Robin the Miller. The Miller who recites a tale in Chaucer's *Canterbury Tales.*

Robin Toodle (tö'dl). See **Rob the Grinder.**

Rob Roy (rob roi). A novel by Sir Walter Scott, published in 1818. It deals with the period of the Jacobite uprising of 1715, and its hero is young Frank Osbaldistone, who is banished by his father to the home of his uncle, Sir Hildebrand Osbaldistone. There he meets his six cousins, all men, and his uncle's niece, the lovely Diana Vernon. One of Hildebrand's sons, Rashleigh, has designs upon Diana as well as being involved in a Jacobite plot. Diana and Rob Roy, the great-hearted outlaw, help Frank to defeat the schemes of Rashleigh. Rob Roy is a Scotsman, once a drover, but turned into an outlaw by cruelty and injustice. He befriends Diana, averts the ruin of Frank's father, and kills Rashleigh after the villain has betrayed some Jacobite conspirators to the government. Frank once again enjoys his father's favor, inherits Osbaldistone Hall, and marries Diana. One of Scott's best characters is Frank's servant, Andrew Fairservice.

Rob Roy. See also **Macgregor, Robert.**

Robsart (rob'särt), **Amy.** A character in Sir Walter Scott's novel *Kenilworth.* She is the unacknowledged wife of the Earl of Leicester, and escaping from her place of concealment, follows him to Kenilworth, only to be disowned and sent back to die at the hand of Richard Varney.

Rob the Grinder (rob). [Original name, **Robin Toodle.**] In Dickens's novel *Dombey and Son,* the son of Polly Toodle, educated at the school of the Charitable Grinders (whence his name). He is a vicious lad, willing to steal or spy, as may be most profitable. He is finally taken in hand and set, somewhat doubtfully, on the path of virtue by Miss Tox.

Roc (rok). In Arabian folklore, a bird so huge that it could transport elephants. In *The Arabian Nights' Entertainments,* it carried Sindbad the Sailor out of the Valley of Diamonds; and it appears also in other stories in the *Entertainments.*

Roche (rōsh), **Sir Boyle.** b. 1743; d. at Dublin, June 5, 1807. An Irish politician. He was a member of the Irish Parliament from 1777 until the Union in 1801. He is known chiefly as a perpetrator of Irish bulls, many of them apocryphal; the most famous is his "Why should we put ourselves out of the way to do anything for posterity? What has posterity done for us?"

Roche, Regina Maria. [Maiden name, **Dalton.**] b. in the south of Ireland, c1764; d. at Waterford, Ireland, May 17, 1845. An Irish novelist. She published many romances, the best known of which is *The Children of the Abbey* (1798).

Rochester (roch'es"tėr, -ĕs.tėr), 2nd Earl of. Title of **Wilmot, John.**

Rochester, Edward Fairfax. One of the principal characters in Charlotte Brontë's *Jane Eyre* (1847).

He is the prototype of many of the vigorous, ruthless heroes in the world of fiction since his time.

Rochfort (roch'fort; French, rosh.fôr). The Chief Justice of Dijon in Massinger and Field's *The Fatal Dowry,* and the father of Beaumelle.

Rock Day. See **Distaff's Day, Saint.**

Rocky Road to Dublin, The. Poems (1915) by James Stephens.

rococo (rō.kō'kō). A variety of ornament originating in the style of the period of Louis XIV of France and continuing with constantly increasing exaggeration throughout the period of Louis XV. It is generally a rich assemblage of scrolls and shellwork, wrought into irregular and indescribable forms, often in costly material. The style has interest from its use in a great number of sumptuous European residences, and from its intimate association with a social life of great outward refinement and splendor. Much of the painting, engraving, porcelain work, etc., of the time has great decorative charm. Because the style in its extreme development was often chiefly or purely ostentatious or frivolous, "rococo" has been used attributively in contempt to note anything feebly pretentious and tasteless in art or literature.

The jumble called rococo is, in general, detestable. A parrot seems to have invented the word; and the thing is worthy of his tawdriness and his incoherence.   (Leigh Hunt, *Old Court Suburbs.*)

Roderick (rod'ę.rik), **Vision of Don.** See **Vision of Don Roderick.**

Roderick Dhu (dū). A Highland chieftain, one of the principal characters in Sir Walter Scott's *Lady of the Lake.*

Roderick Hudson (hud'son). Novel by Henry James, published in 1876. It is the story of an American abroad.

Roderick Random (ran'dom). [Full title, **The Adventures of Roderick Random.**] A novel by Tobias Smollett, published in 1748. It is the story of the wild adventures and unprincipled character of its hero, Roderick. His father has disappeared after being disinherited by Roderick's grandfather because of a marriage of which the grandfather disapproved. Roderick is given no money by his grandfather, but is taken under the wing of his uncle, Lieutenant Tom Bowling of the Royal Navy. When his uncle also disappears, he goes to London accompanied by his school friend, the faithful Strap, and there falls into the evil company of cardsharps, harlots, and courtiers. Seized by a press gang, he becomes a sailor; he soon qualifies as surgeon's mate and has many adventures in battle on board the *Thunderer,* a man-of-war. He returns to England after much suffering, takes the position of servant to a wealthy old lady, and falls in love with her niece Narcissa. Carried off to France by smugglers, he meets his uncle again and joins the French army. After he is discharged, he is once again penniless, but his old friend Strap comes to his aid with money that he has inherited. Roderick wastes the money and then tries to marry the wealthy Miss Melinda Goosetrap, but her mother intervenes. After pursuing some other women of fortune, and failing in his efforts to lure them into marriage, he meets Narcissa again and realizes that he still loves her.

ḍ, d or j; ş, s or sh; ţ, t or ch; z̧, z or zh; o, F. cloche; ü, F. menu; ċh, Sc. loch; ṅ, F. bonbon.

Narcissa is carried away by her brother, and in despair Roderick goes to sea once more. While in South America he meets his father, now a wealthy trader who calls himself Don Roderigo. With his aid Roderick is enabled to return to England with a small fortune and marry Narcissa.

Roderick, the Last of the Goths (goths). A narrative poem by Robert Southey, published in 1814.

Roderigo (rod.e̦.rē′gō). In Shakespeare's *Othello*, a foolish gentleman in love with Desdemona. Iago uses him to involve Cassio in a quarrel, hoping the latter will be killed, but then himself stabs Roderigo while he is scuffling with Cassio. The letters incriminating Iago are found on his body.

Rodilardus (rō.di.lär′dus). In Rabelais's *Pantagruel*, a huge cat which attacks Panurge.

Rodin (ro.dȧn), **Auguste**. b. at Paris, in November, 1840; d. 1917. A French sculptor. His best-known works broke with the tradition of the École des Beaux-Arts and were therefore at the time of their first public appearances often the center of bitter controversy. At the age of 14 he entered La Petite École, and later the school of the Gobelins and Barye's classes at the Jardin des Plantes. He executed the famous bust called *The Broken Nose* in 1862–63. Rodin worked as an artisan at Marseilles and Strasbourg, and finally entered the atelier of Carrier-Belleuse. During the Commune he followed Carrier-Belleuse to Belgium, where he remained until 1874. He then went to Italy, where he made a careful study of the works of Donatello and Michelangelo (which study seems to have revealed his own powers to the sculptor himself, now 34 years of age). He returned to Brussels. At the Salon of 1877 he exhibited a figure called *L'Age d'airain* (*The Age of Bronze*), which expressed what he believed to be the right principle of construction of a statue (it was highly naturalistic, so much so that his critics accused him of making a cast from life). His bust of *St.-Jean Baptiste* (*Saint John the Baptist*) established his reputation. Among his other works are another *St.-Jean* (1880), *Creation of Man* (1881), busts of J. P. Laurens and Carrier-Belleuse (1882), Victor Hugo (1884), a statue of Bastien-Lepage (1885), and a monument for the city of Calais in commemoration of the patriotism of Eustache de Saint-Pierre and his companions, who offered themselves as a sacrifice to the demands of Edward III of England, conqueror of the city in 1347. He also received a commission for the bronze doors of the Musée des Arts Décoratifs, of which the subject was taken from the *Inferno* of Dante. This commission was never completed, but several of Rodin's most famous works were modeled for it: *Le Penseur* (*The Thinker*) and statues of Adam and Eve are among the most notable (the latter are now at the Metropolitan Museum of Art, New York; the original of the former remains at Paris). Other outstanding works include *Le Baiser* (*The Kiss*), at the Luxembourg, Paris, and *The Hand of God*, at the Metropolitan Museum of Art.

Rodney Stone (rod′ni stōn′). A novel by Sir Arthur Conan Doyle, published in 1896.

Rodomonte (rō.dō.mōn′tā). A brave though bragging Moorish king in Matteo Boiardo's *Orlando Innamorato* and Lodovico Ariosto's *Orlando Furi-*

oso. The word "rodomontade" is derived from his name. He appears to have originated in the Mezentius of Vergil.

Roe (rō), **Richard**. The name of the imaginary defendant formerly in use in cases of ejectment; John Doe was the plaintiff in such cases.

Roger (roj′ėr). Entries on literary characters having this prename will be found under the surnames Bolingbroke, Coverley, Mortimer, Riderhood, Scatcherd, and Wildrake.

Rogero (rō.jä′rō). In Shakespeare's *Winter's Tale*, a gentleman of Sicilia.

Rogero. See also **Ruggiero.**

Roger of Hoveden (roj′ėr; hov′dẹn, huv′-). [Also: **Hovedon, Howden** (hou′dẹn).] fl. in the latter half of the 12th and the beginning of the 13th century. An English chronicler, author of a Latin chronicle (*Chronica*) of England, first printed in 1596. He was a clerk and a member of the royal household of Henry II, and seems to have been well versed in the law. He served the king in various diplomatic and public affairs, and on Henry's death he probably retired to the collegiate church of Hoveden (Hovedon or Howden), in the East Riding of Yorkshire, and compiled his chronicle, which covers the period 732–1201 (only the period from 1192 being an original source). An English translation by Henry T. Riley appeared in 1853.

Roger of Ware (wãr). The narrator of "The Cook's Tale" in Chaucer's *Canterbury Tales*.

Roger of Wendover (wen′dō″vėr). d. 1236. An English chronicler, a monk of the Abbey of St. Albans and prior of Belvoir. He was the author of that portion of the *Flores historiarum* (a chronicle from which Matthew Paris adapted parts of his *Chronica Majora*) which treats of the period after 1189. The rest is by John de Cella.

Rogers (roj′ėrz), **James Edwin Thorold**. b. at West Meon, Hampshire, England, 1823; d. at Oxford, England, Oct. 12, 1890. An English political economist. He officiated for a time as a clergyman, but afterward renounced his orders. From 1862 to 1868 he was professor of political economy at Oxford, from 1859 until his death he was professor of statistics and economic science at King's College, London, and from 1880 to 1886 he sat in Parliament as an advanced Liberal. He published *History of Agriculture and Prices in England* (1866–87), *Six Centuries of Work and Wages* (1884), *The Economic Interpretation of History* (1888), and others.

Rogers, Mildred. In W. Somerset Maugham's novel *Of Human Bondage*, a selfish and vulgar Cockney waitress.

Rogers, Samuel. b. at Newington Green, London, July 30, 1763; d. at London, Dec. 18, 1855. An English poet. He was educated at the Nonconformist Academy at Newington Green, and entered his father's bank. His house at London was noted as a literary center, and Rogers acted as patron and friend to many men of letters, being almost the literary dictator in England from late in the 18th century until the middle of the 19th. His principal poems are *The Pleasures of Memory* (1792), *An Epistle to a Friend* (1798), *The Voyage of Columbus* (1812), *Jacqueline* (1814), *Human Life* (1819), and *Italy* (1822–28). The last was a failure but when

fat, fāte, fär, ȧsk, fãre; net, mē, hėr; pin, pīne; not, nōte, mōve, nôr; up, lūte, pu̇ll; ᴛʜ, then;

republished (1830) with illustrations by J. M. W. Turner, Thomas Stothard, and Samuel Prout it became very successful. A collection of anecdotes, his *Table-Talk*, was collected through the years by his friend Alexander Dyce and published in 1856; Rogers's own notebook of *Recollections* was edited and published by his nephew William Sharpe in 1859. Because of his age, Rogers refused (1850) the laureateship when Wordsworth died; he suggested that Tennyson be chosen instead.

Roget (rō.zhā′), **Peter Mark.** b. at London, 1779; d. 1869. An English writer and physician. He took his medical degree at Edinburgh in 1798, and practiced as a physician at Manchester and at London. He was for many years secretary of the Royal Society, and was Fullerian lecturer on physiology at the Royal Institution. His chief work is the notable *Thesaurus of English Words and Phrases* (1852), a work for which he collected material for 50 years, and which has been revised and reprinted many times since its first appearance.

Rogue Riderhood (rōg rī′dėr.hůd). See **Riderhood, Roger.**

Rohmer (rō′mėr), **Sax.** [Reputed original name, **Arthur Sarsfield Wade** (or **Ward** or **Warde**).] b. 1886—. An English author of mystery novels. He stated (1930) that his name is not, and never has been, "Arthur S. Ward." He is noted as creator (1913) of the fictional character Dr. Fu Manchu, who appears in such novels as *The Mask of Fu Manchu* (1932), *President Fu Manchu* (1936), and *Shadow of Fu Manchu* (1948). His other books include *The Yellow Claw* (1915), *Tales of Chinatown* (1922), *The Day the World Ended* (1930), and *White Velvet* (1936).

Roi d'Yvetot (rwà dėv.tô), **Le.** [Eng. trans., "*The King of Yvetot.*"] A song by Pierre Jean de Béranger, which appeared in 1813. It alludes to the contented ruler of a very small seigniory, and had a political significance (turning on the fact that the French, at that time returned from Moscow, had begun to weary of glory which cost so much in blood and tears). The ballad of the King of Yvetot, who took "pleasure for his code," was sung by all France. His figure passed into literature as a type of the "*roi bon enfant*" whose reign the French wished to inaugurate.

Rois Fainéants (rwà fe.nä.än), **les.** [Eng. trans., "*the Do-Nothing* or *Sluggard Kings.*"] A name given to King Clovis II of Neustria (d. 656) and his ten successors. They were merely figureheads, each of them being entirely under the management of the mayor of the palace, or major domus, an officer who had charge of the royal household and later of the royal domain. The mayor was originally elected by the nobles, but the office became hereditary in the Austrasian family which came to be known as the Carolingians. The empire of the Merovingians slowly declined in the useless hands of the "Rois Fainéants" until 751, when Pepin the Short usurped the crown, deposing Childeric III.

Roi Soleil (rwà so.ley′), **Le.** See **Louis XIV.**

Rojas (rō′Häs), **Fernando de.** fl. early 16th century. A Spanish dramatist. Author of *Celestina* (*Comedia de Calisto y Melibea*, c1499), a novel written as a

drama and important in the development of Spanish drama.

Rokeby (rōk′bi). A narrative romance in verse (1813) by Scott. It comprises six cantos.

Rokesmith (rōk′smith), **John.** See **Harmon, John.**

Roland (rō′land). [Also: **Rowland;** Danish, **Roeland** (rō′län); French, **Roland** (ro.län); German, **Roland** (rō′länt), **Rudland** (rüd′länt), **Ruland** (rö′länt); Italian, **Orlando;** Portuguese, **Roldão** (rōl-doun′).] In medieval romance, a nephew of Charlemagne, and the most celebrated of his 12 paladins. He was famous for his prowess and for his brave stand against the Saracens and death in the pass at Roncesvalles in 778. This took place when Roland, Oliver, and the French rear guard were cut off from Charlemagne's army. There were no survivors. He had a wonderful horn called Olivant, which he won, together with the sword Durandal (Durindana), from a giant. The horn could be heard at the distance of 20 miles. There are numerous legends concerning Roland. He is said once to have fought for five days with Oliver or Olivier, son of Regnier, Duke of Genoa, another of Charlemagne's paladins. They were equally matched, and neither one gained the advantage; hence the phrase "to give a Roland for an Oliver" means to equal blow for blow. His deeds were first recorded in Turpin's pseudo-chronicle and in the 11th-century *Chanson de Roland*, and later in the works of Pulci, Boiardo, and Ariosto.

Roland, Song of. See **Song of Roland.**

Roland and Vernagu (vėr′na.gū). A Middle English romance in tail-rhyme stanzas, written c1350. It is one of the Otuel group of the Charlemagne cycle, and takes its name from Vernagu, the forty-foot tall Saracen knight who challenges and vanquishes various of Charlemagne's knights, but is himself overcome by Roland.

Roland de Vaux (dė vō′). In Coleridge's *Christabel*, a former friend of Christabel's father.

Roland for an Oliver (ol′i.vėr). A farce by Thomas Morton, founded on Eugène Scribe's *Visite à Bedlam* and *Une Heure de mariage*. It was produced in 1819.

Roland Graeme (grām). See **Graeme, Roland.**

Roland Whately (hwāt′li). American title of **Lonely Unicorn, The.**

Rolland (ro.län), **Romain.** b. at Clamecy, France, Jan. 29, 1866; d. at Vézelay, Switzerland, Dec. 30, 1944. A French novelist, dramatist, and music expert. He is best known for his novels *Jean-Christophe* (10 vols., 1905–13; Eng. trans., 1910–13) and *L'Âme enchantée* (7 vols., 1922–33; Eng. trans., *The Soul Enchanted*, 1925–34). His plays include *Les Loups* (1898; Eng. trans., *The Wolves*, 1937), *Danton* (1900; Eng. trans., 1918), *Le Quatorze Juillet* (1902; Eng. trans., *The Fourteenth of July*, 1918), *Le Jeu de l'amour et de la Mort* (1924; Eng. trans., *The Game of Love and Death*, 1926), and *Robespierre* (1938).

Roll-Call, The. A novel by Arnold Bennett, published in 1919.

Rolle of Hampole (rōl; ham′pōl), **Richard.** b. at Thornton Dale, Yorkshire, England, c1290; d. at Hampole, England, 1349. An English hermit and

d, d or j; ş, s or sh; ţ, t or ch; z, z or zh; o, F. cloche; ü, F. menu; ch, Sc. loch; ń, F. bonbon,

religious writer, known as "the Hermit of Hampole." He was at Oxford as a youth but, repelled by the scholastic philosophy, returned home and devoted himself to the solitary life of contemplation. He wrote many prose treatises, the nature of which has marked him as the first English mystic. They include *Melum Contemplativorum, Incendium Amoris, Emendatio Vitae,* and several works in English. *The Prick of Conscience,* the most popular poem of the 14th century, describing the misery of earth and the glory of heaven, was formerly ascribed to him, but no evidence exists for the attribution.

Roman Actor (rō′man̦), **The.** A play by Philip Massinger, licensed in 1626 and published in 1629. The play is particularly interesting to students of English literature for its defense of the theater and of actors (who were being violently attacked at the time of its first performance by many leading religious figures as a pack of thieving scoundrels, drunkards, and libertines). In Act I, Scene 3, the Roman actor, Paris, argues that the stage is more effective in teaching virtue than philosophy, and that vice is always punished at the end of the play.

romance. **1.** Originally, a tale in verse, written in one of the Romance dialects, as early French or Provençal; hence, any popular epic belonging to the literature of modern Europe, or any fictitious story of heroic, marvelous, or supernatural incidents derived from history or legend, and told in prose or verse and at considerable length: as, the *romance* of Charlemagne; the Arthurian *romances.*

He honoured that hit hade, euer-more after,
As hit is breued in the best boke of romaunce.

  ("Sir Gawayne and the Green Knight," in
      E. E. T. S.)

Upon my bedde I sat upright,
And bad oon reche me a book,
A romaunce, and hit me took
To rede and dryve the night away;
For me thoghte it better play
Than playe either at chesse or tables.
And in this boke were written fables
That clerkes hadde, in olde tyme,
And other poets, put in ryme.

  (Chaucer, *Book of the Duchess.*)

And yf any man demaunde hou certain,
What me shall call thys romans souerain,
Hit name the Romans as of Partenay,
And so som it call certes at this day.

  ("Rom. of Partenay," in *E. E. T. S.*)

Upon these three columns—chivalry, gallantry, and religion—repose the fictions of the middle ages, especially those usually designated as romances. These, such as we now know them, and such as display the characteristics above mentioned, were originally metrical, and chiefly written by natives of the north of France.

  (Hallam, *Introd. to Lit. of Europe.*)

History commenced among the modern nations of Europe, as it had commenced among the Greeks, in romance.   (Macaulay, *History.*)

2. In Spain and other Romanic countries—either (*a*) a short epic narrative poem (historic ballad), or, later, (*b*) a short lyric poem.

The romance . . . is a composition in long verses of fourteen syllables ending with one rhyme,

or assonance, which have been generally, but wrongly, divided into two short lines, the first of which, naturally, is rhymeless.   (*Encyc. Brit.*)

3. A tale or novel dealing not so much with real or familiar life as with extraordinary and often extravagant adventures, as Cervantes's *Don Quixote,* with rapid and violent changes of scene and fortune, as Dumas's *Count of Monte Cristo,* with mysterious and supernatural events, as R. L. Stevenson's *Dr. Jekyll and Mr. Hyde,* or with morbid idiosyncrasies of temperament, as Godwin's *Caleb Williams,* or picturing imaginary conditions of society influenced by imaginary characters, as Fouqué's *Undine.* Special forms of the romance, suggested by the subject and the manner of treatment, are the historical, the pastoral, the philosophical, the psychological, the allegorical, etc.

The narrative manner of Defoe has a naturalness about it beyond that of any other novel or romance writer. His fictions have all the air of true stories.   (Lamb, *Estimate of Defoe.*)

Others were much scandalized. It ["The Pilgrim's Progress"] was a vain story, a mere romance, about giants, and lions, and goblins, and warriors.   (Macaulay, *John Bunyan.*)

Sir Philip Sidney's The Countess of Pembroke's Arcadia, which appeared in 1590, after the author's death, is the most brilliant prose fiction in English of the century, and a genuine pastoral and heroic romance.   (*Encyc. Brit.*)

4. An invention; fiction; falsehood: used euphemistically.

This knight was indeede a valiant gentleman, but not a little given to romance when he spake of himselfe.   (Evelyn, *Diary,* Sept. 6, 1651.)

A Staple of Romance and Lies,
False Tears and real Perjuries.
  (Prior, *An English Padlock.*)

5. A blending of the heroic, the marvelous, the mysterious, and the imaginative in actions, manners, ideas, language, or literature; tendency of mind to dwell upon or give expression to the heroic, the marvelous, the mysterious, or the imaginative.

The splendid phantoms of chivalrous romance, the trophied lists, the embroidered housings, the quaint devices, the haunted forests, the enchanted gardens, the achievements of enamoured knights, and the smiles of rescued princesses.
  (Macaulay, *Milton.*)

The age of Romance has not ceased; it never ceases; it does not, if we think of it, so much as very sensibly decline.
  (Carlyle, *Diamond Necklace.*)

Romance. A novel (1903) by Joseph Conrad and Ford Madox Ford.

Romance of Alexander. See **Alexander, Romance of.**

Romance of the Forest, The. A romance by Ann Radcliffe, published in 1791.

Roman Comique (ro.män̄ ko.mēk). The unfinished history (1651) of a troupe of strolling players, written in the picaresque manner, by Scarron.

Roman de Brut (ro.män̄ de̦ brüt). [Meaning, "Romance of Brutus."] A poetical romance (1155) of 15,000 lines by Wace, an adaptation of Geoffrey of Monmouth's *Historia Regum Britanniae* with additions to the legend of King Arthur from what seems to have been oral tradition, such as the first literary references to the Round Table. An English adaptation of the *Roman de Brut*, Layamon's *Brut*, written c1205, marks the first appearance of the Arthurian legends in English.

Roman de la Rose (ro.män dẹ là rōz). [Eng. trans., "*Romance of the Rose*."] A French poem, begun by Guillaume de Lorris about 1237, and continued 40 or 50 years later by Jean de Meung. The part written by the former poet, extending to more than 4,000 lines, is an allegorical love-vision. Jean de Meung's continuation, some 18,000 lines long, is conceived in a very different spirit. Love, still the central theme, is no longer treated in the courtly tradition of Guillaume, but is analyzed rationalistically; woman, idealized and idolized by the earlier poet, is here made the object of biting satire. A fragmentary English translation, first published in 1532, is in part the work of Chaucer, whose own poetry reflects the strong and lasting influence of the *Roman*.

Roman de Rou (ro.män dẹ rö). [Meaning, "Romance of Rollo."] A history in verse of the dukes of Normandy, beginning with Rollo, the first duke, written by Wace c1160. It was based on a story of the Norman conquest written by William of Poitiers, chaplain to William the Conqueror; Wace did not complete it because he fell into disfavor with Henry II and was replaced by another chronicler.

Roman de Troie (ro.män dẹ trwà). A poem by Benoît de Sainte-Maure, written c1160. It contains the earliest known version of the story of Troilus and Cressida ("Briseide" in Benoît).

romantic. 1. Pertaining to or resembling romance, or an ideal state of things; partaking of the heroic, the marvelous, the supernatural, or the imaginative; chimerical; fanciful; extravagantly enthusiastic: as, *romantic* notions; *romantic* expectations; *romantic* devotion.

> So fair a place was never seen
> Of all that ever charm'd romantic eye.
> (Keats, *Imitation of Spenser*.)

A romantic scheme is one which is wild, impracticable, and yet contains something which captivates the young. (Whately.)

The poets of Greece and Rome . . . do not seem to have visited their great battle-fields, nor to have hung on the scenery that surrounded them with that romantic interest which modern poets do. (Shairp, *Poetic Interpretation of Nature*.)

2. Pertaining to romances or the popular literature of the Middle Ages; hence, improbable; fabulous; fictitious.

> Their feigned and romantic heroes.
> (Dr. J. Scott, *Works*.)

I speak especially of that imagination which is most free, such as we use in romantick inventions. (Dr. H. More, *Immortal. of Soul*.)

3. Wildly or impressively picturesque; characterized by poetic or inspiring scenery; suggesting

thoughts of romance: as, a *romantic* prospect; a *romantic* glen.

> Such dusky grandeur clothed the height
> Where the huge Castle holds its state, . . .
> Mine own romantic town!
> (Scott, *Marmion*.)

Romantic school. A name originally assumed by a number of young poets and critics in Germany— the Schlegels, Novalis, Tieck, and others—to designate a combination of writers whose efforts were directed to the overthrow of the artificial rhetoric and unimaginative pedantry of the French school of poetry. The name is also given to a similar school which arose in France between 20 and 30 years later, and engaged in a long struggle for supremacy with the older classic school; Victor Hugo and Lamartine were among the leaders. In English literature the name is attached to various of the poets of the late 18th and early 19th centuries, perhaps most notably Wordsworth, Keats, Shelley, Coleridge, and Byron. From literature the name passed into music as the designation of a class of musicians having many of the characteristics of the romantic school of authors.

Romany (rom'ạ.ni). See **Gypsies.**

Romany Rye (rī), **The.** An autobiographical work (1857) by George Borrow. It is a sequel to *Lavengro*.

Romaunt of the Rose (rō.mônt'). An incomplete translation of the *Roman de la Rose*, attributed with some uncertainty to Chaucer. In the Prologue to *The Legend of Good Women*, he says that he translated the French poem, but it is probable that much of the version that has come down to us is by another hand.

Romelio (rō.mēl'yō). A rich merchant of Naples, a Machiavellian plotter, in John Webster's tragicomedy *The Devil's Law-Case*.

Romeo (rō'mẹ.ō). The hero of Shakespeare's *Romeo and Juliet*. He is moody at first, then reveals to Benvolio his longing for the haughty Rosaline. When he sees Juliet he is gay and lyrical (even Tybalt gets no harsh words), but his happiness is ruined when he is forced into a duel with Tybalt by the latter's killing of Mercutio. In Friar Laurence's cell he is distracted, threatens suicide, and has to be warned that this would betray his love for Juliet. He must face banishment in accordance with the Prince's edict. He revives at the hope of meeting Juliet but, when he hears she is dead, his own death is his inevitable next thought.

Romeo and Juliet (jöl'yẹt, jö'li.ẹt, jö.li.et'). [Full title, **The Tragedy of Romeo and Juliet.**] A romantic tragedy by Shakespeare, printed in an unauthorized edition in 1597, which is 800 lines shorter than the quarto of 1599, and known to have been produced before 1597. It was written between 1594 and 1596 and the textual critics Dover Wilson and Alfred Pollard have suggested that it is basically a revision of an older play. The legend of the lovers is founded on a tale in the *Novelle* (1476) of Masuccio di Salerno. The story next appears in *La Giulietta* (1535), a tale by Luigi da Porto. It was later reworked by Matteo Bandello, a Dominican monk, who published his version in the *Novelle* (1554). Pierre Boaistuau, a French

---

ḍ, d or j; ṣ, s or sh; ṭ, t or ch; ẓ, z or zh; o, F. cloche; ü, F. menu; c̓h, Sc. loch; ṅ, F. bonbon.

translator, published his version in 1559 and this was later used by Arthur Brooke in his poem *The Tragicall Historye of Romeus and Juliet* (1562), upon which Shakespeare based his play. *Romeo and Juliet* was adapted by Otway in 1680 as *Caius Marius;* in altered form it was the object of a competition in 1750 between Garrick and Anne Bellamy at Drury Lane and Barry and Mrs. Theophilus Cibber at Covent Garden. Indeed, it was not until 1850 (and then as a vehicle for the American actress Charlotte Cushman) that the play was performed as Shakespeare wrote it.

The Story. Romeo, of the Veronese house of the Montagues, falls in love with Juliet, a daughter of the Capulets, when he sees her at Capulet's ball and, despite an age-old feud between the families, the two pledge to be married the following day. However, shortly after their secret marriage by Friar Laurence, Romeo kills the Capulet, Tybalt, who has slain his friend Mercutio, and is consequently banished by the Prince. After one night with Juliet, Romeo leaves. Juliet, meanwhile, takes a potion given her by the Friar, which will cause her to appear dead and thus enable her to escape her parents' insistence that she marry Paris. Romeo returns and, discovering Juliet apparently dead in the tomb, drinks poison. When Juliet awakes and finds him dead, she stabs herself.

Romney (rom'ni, rum'-), **George.** b. at Beckside, Lancashire, England, Dec. 15, 1734; d. at Kendal, Westmorland, England, Nov. 15, 1802. An English painter of portraits and historical subjects. He was apprenticed at first to a woodworker, was a clever musician, and began very early to paint portraits. He established himself at London in 1762, and made some success with his *Death of General Wolfe.* He visited Paris in 1764, and exhibited the *Death of King Edmund* in 1765. This was followed by a sojourn in Italy. He returned to London in 1775, where he took a studio in Cavendish Square and painted a series of famous portraits. He assisted in preparing the Boydell Shakespeare Gallery in 1791. Although left without a rival at the death of Reynolds, he was seized with hypochondria, left London, rejoined his wife and family, whom he had abandoned 30 years before, and spent the remainder of his life in retirement at Kendal.

Romola (rom'ō.lạ). A historical novel (1863) by George Eliot. The title character is a young Florentine woman who, after a marriage with the hedonistic Tito Melema, comes under the influence of Savonarola and through faith and service finds peace.

Romont (rō'mont; French, ro.môn). The faithful friend of Charalois in Massinger and Field's *The Fatal Dowry,* who finds that Charalois's wife has been unfaithful.

Romulus (rom'ụ.lus). In Roman legend, the founder of Rome (753 B.C.) and its first king (753–716). He and his twin brother, Remus, were considered to be sons of Mars and the vestal Rhea Silvia, and thus grandsons of Numitor. Legend has it that they were exposed at birth, suckled by a she-wolf, and fostered by a shepherd, and lived to make themselves known and restore their grandfather to his throne. Romulus was chosen to found a new city (Rome) by bird omens. He was wor-

shiped as a divinity under the name of Quirinus.

Roncesvalles (rōn.thez.Bä′lyäs). [French, **Roncevaux** (rôn.sẹ.vō).] A place in Navarre, Spain, in the Pyrenees ab. 20 mi. NE of Pamplona. It is notable for the defeat near there of Roland and the rear guard of Charlemagne's army, on its return from Spain (according to tradition by the Saracens or Moors, but more probably by forebears of the modern Basques) in 778.

rondeau (ron'dō). A poem in a fixed form, borrowed from the French, and consisting either of 13 lines on two rhymes with an unrhyming refrain, or of ten lines on two rhymes with an unrhyming refrain. It may be written in octosyllabic or decasyllabic measure. The refrain is usually a repetition of the first three or four words, sometimes of the first word only. The order of rhymes in the 13-line rondeau, known technically as the "rondeau of Voiture" (that is Vincent Voiture, 1598–1648), is *aabba; aab* (and refrain); *aabba* (and refrain); that of the ten-line rondeau, known technically as the "rondeau of Villon" (that is, François Villon, 1431–c1461), is *abba; ab* (and refrain); *abba* (and refrain). These are the strict rules; but, as in the case of the sonnet, both in France and England, they are not always observed. There is also a form called the *rondeau redoublé.* It consists of six quatrains, *abab,* on two rhymes. The first four lines form in succession the last lines of the second, third, fourth, and fifth quatrains. At the end of the final quatrain, the first words of the poem are added as an unrhyming and independent refrain. Sometimes the final quatrain is styled the *envoi* or *envoy.*

This sort of writing, called the rondeau, is what I never knew practised in our nation.   (Pope.)

rondel (ron'del). A poem in a fixed form, borrowed from the French, and consisting of 13 lines on two rhymes. It may be written in octosyllabic or decasyllabic measure. The first line is repeated at the close, and the first two lines are repeated as the seventh and eighth lines. Thus, the whole poem, like the rondeau, falls into three divisions or stanzas—two of four, and one of five—arranged as follows: *abba; abab; abbaa.* It is permissible to repeat the first couplet at the close, making the last division *abbaab,* and 14 lines in all. Rondels in English were written by Charles of Orleans, Chaucer, Occleve, Lydgate, and others.

In its origin the rondel was a lyric of two verses, each having four or five lines, rhyming on two lines only. In its eight (or ten) lines, but five (or six) were distinct, the others being made by repeating the first couplet at the end of the second stanza, sometimes in an inverse order, and the first line at the end of its first stanza. The eight-lined rondel is thus to all intents and purposes a triolet. . . . With Charles d'Orléans the rondel took the distinct shape we now assign to it, namely of fourteen lines on two rhymes, the first two lines repeating for the seventh and eighth and the final couplet . . . By the time of Octavien de Saint Gelais (1466–1502) the rondel has nearly become the rondeau as we know it.

(Gleeson White, *Ballades and Rondeaus,* Int.)

Ronsard (rôn.sàr), **Pierre de.** b. at the Château de La Poissonnière, in Vendômois, France, Sept. 11,

1524; d. at the priory of St.-Côme, in Touraine, France, in December, 1585. A French poet, chief of the Pléiade. After a brief stay at the Collège de Navarre at Paris, he became page to Charles, Duke of Orléans, second son of Francis I of France. He spent also a couple of years in the service of James V of Scotland, and then returned to his former post, and was attached to various diplomatic embassies. On his final return to France in 1542, he lost his sense of hearing in consequence of a severe illness. This infirmity compelled him to give up the life at court, and led him to turn all his attention to literary labors. Together with his friend Jean Antoine Baïf, he took up a course of study that extended over seven years (1542–49) and made of him an excellent Greek scholar. The ultimate end he had in view was to regenerate his native tongue, and demonstrate in his own works that the French language was capable of as much power and nobility of expression as it had of acknowledged grace and refinement. About 1552 he began to publish his poetic works: *Odes, Sonnets à Cassandre, Le Bocage, Les Amours,* and others. His greatest success was attained in his *Hymnes* (1555–56), and he became a great favorite with Charles IX, king of France from 1560 to 1574. On the death of his royal patron, Ronsard was gradually relegated to the background; finally he left the court in utter discouragement. The last years of his life (1574–85) were spent in quiet and sad retirement. Ronsard was the father of lyric poetry in France. Perhaps his best-known work is the *Sonnets pour Hélène,* written to Hélène de Surgères, a primarily literary love of the poet's. His great ambition, however, had been to rank as the Homer or Vergil of his country, and in this spirit he undertook to write a long poem, *La Françiade;* he labored on it for 25 years, and finally left it unfinished.

Rood (röd), **the Black.** A cross of gold, supposed to contain a fragment of the true cross, taken to Scotland by the wife of Malcolm III. All trace of it is lost.

Roodee (rö'dē). A meadow near Chester, England, partly surrounded by a Roman wall, and used from early times as a racecourse.

Rookery, The. A former slum, part of St. Giles's, London.

Room With a View, A. A novel by E. M. Forster, published in 1908.

Roper's Row (rō'pėrz). A novel by Warwick Deeping, published in 1929.

Ropes (rōps), **Arthur Reed.** [Pseudonym, **Adrian Ross.**] b. at Lewisham, London, Dec. 2, 1859; d. at Kensington, London, Sept. 11, 1933. English librettist and author of lyrics for musical comedies and operettas such as *San Toy* (1899), *The Merry Widow* (1907), *The Dollar Princess* (1909), *The Count of Luxembourg* (1911), *Monsieur Beaucaire* (1919), *Lilac Time* (1922), and *The Beloved Vagabond* (1927). He published *Short History of Europe* (1889) and other books.

Rory O'More (rō'ri ọ.mōr'). A romantic novel by Samuel Lover, published in 1836.

Rosa Bud (rō'zạ bud). See **Bud, Miss Rosa.**

Rosa Dartle (där'tl). See **Dartle, Rosa.**

Rosader (ros'ạ.dèr). In Thomas Lodge's *Rosalynde* the younger brother of Torrismond the Usurper, and lover of Rosalynde. He became Orlando in Shakespeare's adaptation of the story, *As You Like It.*

Rosalind (roz'ạ.lind). According to some authorities, a name given by Edmund Spenser to Rosa Daniel, the sister of Samuel Daniel. She was supposedly loved by Spenser in her youth, and his complaints of her ill usage of him appear in *The Shepherd's Calendar.* In *The Faerie Queene* he is again said to introduce her under the name of Mirabella. Several other identifications of Rosalind have been made, but final identification remains uncertain.

Rosalind (roz'ạ.lind; in Shakespeare also -lĩnd). In Shakespeare's *As You Like It,* the daughter of the exiled duke, in love with Orlando.

Rosaline (roz'ạ.lin, -lĩn, rō'zạ.lēn). In Shakespeare's *Love's Labour's Lost,* an attendant to the Princess of France. Berowne falls in love with her.

Rosaline. In Shakespeare's *Romeo and Juliet,* a Capulet with whom Romeo is in love at the beginning of the play. She does not appear.

Rosalynde, or Euphues' Golden Legacy (roz'ä.lind; ū'fū.ēz). A prose idyl by Thomas Lodge, first printed in 1590. In part, Shakespeare took his *As You Like It* from it. It is the most famous book of the Euphuist school, with the exception of *Euphues* itself.

Rosamond (roz'ạ.mọnd), **the Fair.** See **Clifford, Rosamond.**

Rosamond's Bower. A subterranean labyrinth in Blenheim Park, Woodstock, England, said to have been built by Henry II for Rosamond Clifford ("the Fair Rosamond").

Rosamond's Pond. Before 1770, a pond in St. James's Park, London, "consecrated to love and elegiac poetry."

Rosamond Vincy (vin'si). See **Vincy, Rosamond.**

Rosamund, Queen of the Lombards (roz'ạ.mund; lom'bärdz). A tragedy by Algernon Charles Swinburne, published in 1899. It tells the story of a queen forced to drink from her father's skull, and her efforts to be avenged for this. An earlier drama (1860) by Swinburne, equally grim but on a different theme, was entitled simply *Rosamund.*

Rosary, The. A novel by Florence Louisa Barclay, published in 1909.

Rosa Timmins (tim'inz). See **Timmins, Rosa.**

Rosaura (rō.zôr'ạ). A woman in love with Count D'Alvarez in James Shirley's *The Cardinal.*

Rosciad (rosh'i.ad), **The.** A poem by Charles Churchill, published in 1761. It is his first published poem, and is a violent satire on various London actors. It was issued anonymously, but its success was so great that Churchill at once acknowledged it.

Roscius (rosh'us), **Quintus.** d. c62 B.C. The greatest of Roman comic actors (whence the appellation "Roscius" applied to some leading English actors of the 17th and 18th centuries, implying preëminence on the stage). He was a native of Solonium, near Lanuvium, in Latium. He was presented by Sulla with a gold ring, the symbol of equestrian rank, and was the instructor and friend of Cicero, who defended him in a lawsuit.

Roscoe (ros'kō), **William.** b. at Liverpool, England, March 8, 1753; d. June 30, 1831. An English historian, poet, and miscellaneous author. His chief works are *Life of Lorenzo de' Medici* (1796) and *Life and Pontificate of Leo X* (1805). He also published poems, pamphlets against the slave trade, and others, including the children's classic *The Butterfly's Ball and the Grasshopper's Feast* (1807).

Roscommon (ros.kom'ọn), 4th Earl of. [Title of **Wentworth Dillon.**] b. in Ireland, c1633; d. at London, Jan. 17, 1685. An English poet, critic, and translator. Educated at Caen and Rome, he traveled in France and Germany, returning to England after the Restoration. In addition to a blank-verse translation of Horace's *Art of Poetry* (1680) and *Essay on Translated Verse* (1684), he translated passages from Horace, Vergil, and Guarini, and paraphrased psalms and prayers. He also translated into English the famous Latin hymn *Dies Irae*. He was the first critic to praise John Milton's *Paradise Lost*.

Rose (rōz). The daughter of Sir Roger Oately, the Lord Mayor of London in Dekker's *The Shoemaker's Holiday*. She is loved by the well-born Lacy, nephew to the Earl of Lincoln, but her father opposes the match because she is too low in rank for Lacy. Nevertheless he wins her and obtains the consent of the King, who argues (somewhat oddly for a Tudor monarch) that "love respects no blood; Cares not for difference of birth or state. The maid is . . . A worthy bride for any gentleman."

Rose, George. [Pseudonym, **Arthur Sketchley.**] b. 1817; d. at London, Nov. 11, 1882. An English humorous writer. He was the author of several plays, but is better known as the author of the *Mrs. Brown Lectures*, written in the character of a garrulous cockney woman.

Rose, John Holland. b. at Bedford, England, 1855; d. March 3, 1942. An English historian, noted chiefly as coeditor of the *Cambridge History of the British Empire*. Author of *The Life of Napoleon* (2 vols., 1902), *William Pitt and National Revival* (1911), *The Mediterranean in the Ancient World* (1933), *Man and the Sea: Stages in Maritime and Human Progress* (1935), and others.

Rose, the. An Elizabethan playhouse on the Bankside, Southwark (now part of London), built in 1588 by Philip Henslowe and his partner John Cholmley. It was a round building with a thatched roof, and with walls apparently built of timber and plaster upon a brick foundation. Shakespeare presumably acted there (with the Lord Admiral's Men).

Rose, the. A tavern in Russell Street, Covent Garden, London, near the theaters, and much frequented about 1667.

Rose and the Ring, The. A fairy tale by W. M. Thackeray, published in 1855. The rose and the ring are magic, and have the power of making their owners (Prince Bulbo and Prince Giglio) appear beautiful. While the Princess Angelica possesses them she also appears lovely, but when she loses them she is revealed as a cross and ugly person. The ridiculous Bulbo eventually marries Angelica,

while the honest Giglio weds Rosalba, a deposed princess.

Rose Aylmer (āl'mėr). A short elegy (1806) by Walter Savage Landor, written on the death of Rose Aylmer, a friend of the poet.

Rose Bradwardine (brad'wạr.dēn). See **Bradwardine, Rose.**

Rosebud (rōz'bud). See **Bud, Miss Rosa.**

Rosedale (rōz'dāl). A play by Lester Wallack, based on Sir Edward Bruce Hamley's novel *Lady Lee's Widowhood*. It was produced in 1863.

Rose Fleming (rōz flem'ing). See **Fleming, Rose.**

Rose Jocelyn (jos'ẹ.lin). See **Jocelyn, Rose.**

Rose Mackenzie (mạ.ken'zi). See **Mackenzie, Rose.**

Rose Mary (mār'i). A poem by Dante Gabriel Rossetti, published (1881) in *Ballads and Sonnets*, concerning the strange powers of a piece of magic beryl (a type of semiprecious stone) in which only the pure in heart can see the truth.

Rosenberg (rōz'ẹn.bėrg), **Isaac.** b. Nov. 25, 1890; d. April 1, 1918. English poet, killed during World War I. His volumes of verse include *Night and Day* (1912), *Moses* (1916), and *Poems* (published posthumously in 1922).

Rosencrantz (rō'zẹn.krants). In Shakespeare's *Hamlet*, an old schoolfellow of Hamlet, sent for, along with Guildenstern, by the King to spy upon him.

Roses, Wars of the. A series of armed contests (1455–85) for the throne of England, between the houses of Lancaster and York; so called because the Yorkists took as their cognizance the white rose, whereupon the Lancastrians adopted the red rose as their badge. No issue of importance to the English people was at stake, and for the most part, both in the countryside and in the towns, they remained aloof from the proceedings. Little injury was inflicted upon the people, rural or urban, while the nobles and their retainers, in mutual slaughter, prepared the way for the near-absolutism of the monarchy under the Tudors and Stuarts. The Lancastrian dynasty came to the throne when Henry of Bolingbroke, Duke of Lancaster and Hereford, son of John of Gaunt, compelled the abdication of Richard II, son of Edward the Black Prince, John of Gaunt's older brother. Bolingbroke assumed the royal title as Henry IV, and was confirmed in it by Parliament in 1399. He was succeeded by his son and his grandson, Henry V and Henry VI. The latter was nine months old at his accession; during his minority the affairs of the kingdom were managed by a council and by a succession of powerful nobles. In 1431 Henry was crowned king of France at Paris, which did not abate French opposition to the English claims. In the hope of bolstering those claims, William de la Pole, 4th Earl of Suffolk, then chief of Henry's counselors, in 1445 arranged his marriage with Margaret of Anjou. When on the latter's advice Henry relinquished the county of Maine to the French, anger turned against Suffolk, who was impeached and murdered. His successor in power was Edmund Beaufort, 2nd Duke of Somerset, of a junior branch of the House of Lancaster, who in view of Henry and Margaret's continued childlessness, had his eye on succession to the crown. But so did Richard, Duke of York, by virtue of descent from the next older brother of John of Gaunt. In 1453 Margaret at last gave Henry an heir, but the struggle between Somerset and York continued, especially during two periods (1453–54, 1455–56) when Henry was insane, and in 1455 York took the field with an army, which on May 22 defeated the Lancastrians at St. Albans, killing Somerset and taking the king prisoner. For a time Richard of York was acknowledged as protector of the realm, but Queen Margaret, who well understood his designs, brought about his ouster. In 1459 York, backed by Richard Neville, 1st Earl of Salisbury, and Richard Neville, Earl of Warwick, renewed the war, but after a victory by Salisbury at Blore Heath on September 23, some of the Yorkist forces deserted, and the duke fled to Ireland while the earls took refuge at Calais. In 1460 they and York returned to England and defeated the royal forces at Northampton on July 10, taking the king prisoner, while the queen fled to Scotland. A general rising of the people in Kent and at London contributed to the Yorkist victory, discontent being rife because of the continued disorders under Henry's weak rule, the drain of the French war, and the persecution of the religious sect known as the Lollards. The Duke of York convened Parliament and urged upon it his claim to the throne, but had to be satisfied with a decision that Henry should continue to be king while he lived, but that York, instead of Henry's son, should be the heir presumptive. Upon this, the Lancastrians rallied, and York was defeated and slain at Wakefield on December 31; Salisbury was taken prisoner and beheaded. The Lancastrian ascendancy was brief; Duke Richard's eldest son, Edward, Earl of March, routed them at Mortimer's Cross on Feb. 2, 1461; he was checked at St. Albans on February 17, but Queen Margaret, commanding the Lancastrians, failed to follow up her advantage, pausing instead to direct bloody reprisals upon captured foes; and the young Yorkist leader pressed forward to London, where the people acclaimed him, and a council of Yorkist nobles named him king, as Edward IV. He had to fight for his throne, but did so successfully at Towton (where fully 120,000 men engaged in the sanguinary melee, with no quarter given) on March 29, 1461, at Hedgely Moor on April 25 of the same year, and at Hexham on May 8, 1464. King Henry was taken prisoner again and confined in the Tower of London. Meanwhile bills of attainder, confiscations of property, and death on the block were the lot of all the principal Lancastrians upon whom King Edward could lay his hands. The Earl of Warwick dominated the early reign of Edward IV, but a progressive divergence of their policies led to Warwick's revolt and capture of the king, whom the earl planned to replace with his brother George, Duke of Clarence. The Yorkist nobles, however, compelled Warwick to liberate Edward, with whom he was nominally reconciled while he fomented rebellions in the north. These Edward energetically put down, and Warwick and Clarence in 1470 fled to France. Warwick now deserted Clarence, made an alliance with Queen Margaret, returned to England with a Lancastrian force and with French aid at a time when Edward

was in the north attending to a fresh revolt, and restored Henry VI to the throne. Edward IV in turn fled to the Netherlands, secured the assistance of Charles the Bold of Burgundy, returned in March, 1471, and captured London, again imprisoning Henry. Warwick was defeated and killed at Barnet on April 14, 1471; Margaret was taken captive, and her son Edward, Henry VI's heir, was killed at Tewkesbury shortly afterward; the unfortunate Henry went to the Tower for the last time, and his death there is not implausibly supposed to have followed upon Edward IV's orders. That monarch reigned until his death in 1483; in his will he named his brother Richard, Duke of Gloucester, as guardian of his son and heir, Edward V, who at that time was 12 years of age. The able and ambitious Gloucester induced certain lords and others to present a petition, impugning Edward V's legitimacy and beseeching Gloucester to take the crown. This he did, with the title of Richard III, moreover sending the young Edward V and his still younger brother, the Duke of York, to the Tower, where they were put to death. This murder of two innocent boys, a crime which historians agree in imputing to their uncle, may have contributed to a revulsion of sentiment against Richard, whose reign had begun auspiciously with his initiation of reforms demanded by the increasingly important mercantile classes. There was a Lancastrian claimant to the throne in the person of the Welsh Henry Tudor, Earl of Richmond. In his behalf Henry Stafford, 2nd Duke of Buckingham, raised a revolt in 1483 and, failing, lost his head. But in 1485 Henry Tudor landed in Wales, gathered support, and defeated Richard at Bosworth Field on August 22. Subsequently marrying Yorkist Edward IV's daughter, Lancastrian Henry VII brought an end to the Wars of the Roses. Under the Lancastrian kings, parliamentary government had made notable advances. This progress was halted by the Wars of the Roses, in which moreover the baronial class, hitherto the chief check upon the monarchy, dissipated its strength, so that the first Tudor monarch found England ripe for the kind of rule that was congenial to his temperament and that of his dynastic successors.

Rosetta Stone (rō.zet'ạ). A slab of black basalt found 1799 near the Rosetta mouth of the Nile. Its inscriptions of pre-Christian origin provided the first key to the interpretation of Egyptian hieroglyphics.

Rosicrucianism (rō.zi.krö'shạn.iz.ẹm). An esoteric and mystical philosophy, with many adherents, usually traced to Christian Rosenkranz, reputed scion of a noble Austrian family, born in 1387. According to some accounts, however, Christian Rosenkranz was a pseudonym of Johann Valentine Andreä, but another version of the story makes Andreä a 16th-century successor of the original leader. Rosenkranz, in any case, seems to have traveled extensively in the Holy Land, Syria, Egypt, and Spain, consulting learned men and studying ancient lore, which after his return to Austria he spent some years collating and arranging, before choosing three companions to whom he imparted his religious, philosophical, and medical learning. Thus was formed the first Society of the

ḍ, d or j; ṣ, s or sh; ṭ, t or ch; ẓ, z or zh; o, F. cloche; ü, F. menu; ċh, Sc. loch; ṅ, F. bonbon.

Rose and Cross (perhaps more often but probably less accurately known as the Society of the Rosy Cross). The Frater I.O., one of Rosenkranz's original comrades, is supposed to have been the first to bring Rosicrucianism to England, and has been credited with curing one of the Earls of Norfolk of leprosy. Early in the 17th century the English mystic Robert Fludd was initiated into the Rosicrucian cult, became magus or chief of the order in that country, and in turn is said to have initiated Francis Bacon, among others. Fludd was succeeded by Sir Kenelm Digby. Another English Rosicrucian of note was Elias Ashmole, who introduced elements of Rosicrucian symbolism into freemasonry.

Rosinante (roz.i.nan'tẹ). [Spanish, **Rocinante** (rō-thē.nän'tä).] In Cervantes's *Don Quixote*, Don Quixote's charger, all skin and bone.

Ross (rôs, ros). In Shakespeare's *Macbeth*, a Scottish thane, who must tell Macduff that his wife and children have been killed on Macbeth's orders.

Ross, Adrian. Pseudonym of **Ropes, Arthur Reed.**

Ross, Alexander. b. in Aberdeenshire, Scotland, April 13, 1699; d. at Lochlee, Forfarshire (now Angus), Scotland, May 20, 1784. A Scottish schoolmaster and poet. He wrote *Helenore, or the Fortunate Shepherdess* (1768), a narrative poem, and a number of songs, including *Wooed an' Married an' a'*, and other poetical pieces in the rural dialect of Aberdeenshire.

Ross, Sir James Clark. b. at London, April 15, 1800; d. at Aylesbury, England, April 3, 1862. An English navigator and arctic explorer. He served with his uncle, Sir John Ross, and with W. E. Parry on their arctic expeditions. He commanded the expedition of the *Erebus* and *Terror* to the antarctic regions (1839–43), discovering Victoria Land and penetrating to lat. 78°10′ S., the farthest point then yet reached in the antarctic regions; and commanded the *Enterprise* in search of Sir John Franklin in 1848. He published *Voyage of Discovery and Research to Southern and Antarctic Regions* (1847). To Sir James Clark Ross is generally given the credit for the discovery (1831) of the position of the north magnetic pole. Several parts of Antarctica are named for him.

Ross, Sir John. b. at Inch, Wigtownshire, Scotland, June 24, 1777; d. at London, Aug. 30, 1856. An English admiral and arctic explorer. He commanded expeditions in search of the Northwest Passage (1818 and 1829–33), and one in search of Sir John Franklin (1850–51). He published *A Voyage of Discovery* (1819), *Narrative of a Second Voyage in Search of a Northwest Passage* (1835), and others.

Ross, Lord. In Shakespeare's *Richard II*, one of the noblemen who join Bolingbroke when he comes to claim his estates.

Rossetti (rọ.set'ẹ), **Christina Georgina.** [Pseudonym, **Ellen Alleyn.**] b. at London, Dec. 5, 1830; d. there, Dec. 29, 1894. An English poet; sister of Dante Gabriel Rossetti. An extremely religious person, she twice refused to marry. Her last years, marred by serious illness, were spent in seclusion, her beauty (she had sat as a model for her brother, Holman Hunt, J. E. Millais, and other of the Pre-Raphaelites) disfigured by goiter. She contributed to *The Germ* as Ellen Alleyn, and wrote *Goblin Market* (1862), *The Prince's Progress* (1866), *Sing-Song, a Nursery Rhyme Book* (1872), *A Pageant and Other Poems* (1881), *Time Flies* (1885), *New Poems* (1896), and a number of religious works on the Benedicite and the minor festivals.

Rossetti, Dante Gabriel. [Full name, **Gabriel Charles Dante Rossetti.**] b. at London, May 12, 1828; d. at Birchington, near Margate, England, April 9, 1882. An English poet and painter. He was the dominant personality of the Pre-Raphaelites, and one of the chief poets of the later romantic school. He has been called "the most profoundly and essentially artistic force there has ever been in England." As a painter he had little formal training, and his draftsmanship was often inferior; his greatest distinction was as a colorist. Among his best oils are *Beata Beatrix*, *Lady Lilith*, and *The Beloved*, all painted between 1860 and 1870. His earliest poems appeared in *The Germ* (1850). Besides his translations from the *Early Italian Poets* (1861), he published two volumes: *Poems* (1870) and *Ballads and Sonnets* (1881). Among his best poems are *The Blessed Damozel*, *Sister Helen*, the sonnet sequence *The House of Life* (notable for the richness of its imagery), and the narrative ballad *The White Ship*.

Rossetti (rọ.set'ẹ), **Maria Francesca.** b. at London, Feb. 17, 1827; d. there, Nov. 24, 1876. An English author and religious worker; sister of Dante Gabriel Rossetti. Deeply religious, she entered (1874) an Anglican sisterhood. Author of *A Shadow of Dante, an Essay Towards Studying Himself, His World, and His Pilgrimage* (1871) and *Letters to My Bible-Class on Thirty-Nine Sundays* (1872).

Rossetti, William Michael. b. at London, Sept. 25, 1829; d. there, Feb. 5, 1919. An English art critic and essayist; brother of Dante Gabriel Rossetti. Educated at King's College, London, he was a civil service clerk (1844–94) in the excise office. He was a member of the Pre-Raphaelite Brotherhood, and editor (1850) of its short-lived organ, *The Germ*. Author of *Fine Art: Chiefly Contemporary* (1867), *Swinburne's Poems and Ballads: A Criticism* (1867), *Lives of Some Famous Poets* (1878), *Life of Keats* (1887), *Dante Gabriel Rossetti as Designer and Writer* (1889), *Memoir of Dante Gabriel Rossetti* (1895), *Some Reminiscences* (1906), *Democratic Sonnets* (1907), *Memoir of Christina Rossetti* (1908), and *Dante and his Convito* (1910). He wrote on art for the *Critic*, the *Spectator*, and the *Encyclopaedia Britannica*.

Rossillion (rō.sil'yọn, ros-), **Countess of.** In Shakespeare's *All's Well That Ends Well*, the mother of Bertram and guardian of Helena, who tries to bring Bertram back when he abandons Helena. George Bernard Shaw thought this the most beautiful of old women's parts.

Rossillion, Count of. See **Bertram.**

Rossini (rōs.sē'nē), **Gioachino Antonio.** b. at Pesaro, Italy, Feb. 29, 1792; d. at Paris, Nov. 13, 1868. An Italian operatic composer. He was of humble birth, and was early apprenticed to a smith. He began to take regular lessons in music, and played the horn in a theater at Bologna when he was about 13. In 1807 he entered a class in counterpoint at the Licero, and a little later studied the cello. In 1808 a cantata by him was performed in public, and before 1823 he had written 20 operas, most of them after 1815, at which time he became director of the San Carlo and Del Fondo theaters at Naples. In 1821 he married Isabella Colbran and went to Vienna (1822), where he had much success in spite of opposition. He visited London in 1823, where he was warmly received, and soon went to Paris, where he was made director of the Théâtre Italien for 18 months. Here he brought out a number of his operas as well as Meyerbeer's *Crociato*. He was retained in the king's service until 1836, when he retired to Bologna and devoted himself to the encouragement of the Liceo. In 1842 his *Stabat Mater* was first given in its complete form. In 1847 he went to Florence, and in 1855 to Paris, where at his villa at Passy he was the center of a brilliant circle till his death. Toward the end of his life he wrote little but piano music. His nearly 40 operas include *Tancredi* (1813), *Elisabetta* (1815), *Il Barbiere di Siviglia* (1816), *Otello* (1816), *La Cenerentola* (1817), *La Gazza Ladra* (1817), *Armida* (1817), *La Donna del Lago* (1819), *Maometto Secondo* (1820), *Zelmira* (1821), *Semiramide* (1823), and *Guillaume Tell* (1829). He also wrote *Mosè in Egitto* (1818; an oratorio), and *Messe Solennelle* (1864).

Rostand (ros.täṅ), **Edmond.** b. at Marseilles, April 1, 1864; d. at Paris, Dec. 2, 1918. A French poet and playwright. He wrote *Les Romanesques* (1894), *La Princesse lointaine* (1895), *La Samaritaine* (1897), *Cyrano de Bergerac* (1897), *L'Aiglon* (1900), *Un Soir à Hernani* (1902), *Les Mots* (1905), *Chantecler* (1907–09), *Le Bois sacré* (1909), and others. Several of these were written for Sarah Bernhardt, who especially liked the role of the Duke of Reichstadt in *L'Aiglon*. *Cyrano*, a part created by the elder Coquelin and played by many leading actors since, is a masterpiece of modern neoromantic drama.

Rota Club (rō'tạ). [Also, **the Coffee Club.**] A London political club, founded in 1659 as a kind of debating society for the dissemination of republican opinions. It met in New Palace Yard "at one Miles's, where was made purposely a large oval table with a passage in the middle for Miles to deliver his coffee." The club was broken up after the Restoration.

Rotherham (roᴛн'ẹr.ạm), **Thomas.** In Shakespeare's *Richard III*, the Archbishop of York. He resigns when he hears that Rivers and Grey have been imprisoned.

Rothermere (roᴛн'ẹr.mir), 1st Viscount. Title of **Harmsworth, Harold Sidney.**

Rothesay (roth'sạ). A royal burgh and resort in W Scotland, county seat of Buteshire, situated on the E coast of the island of Bute, on the Firth of Clyde, ab. 31 mi. W of Glasgow. It is one of the most popular summer resorts in Scotland. The headquarters of the Royal Northern Yacht Club are here. The ruins of Rothesay Castle are near the center of the town. The first cotton mill in Scotland was erected (1779) at Rothesay.

Rothsay (roth'sạ), **Duke of.** In Sir Walter Scott's novel *The Fair Maid of Perth*, a gallant young claimant to the throne of Scotland who falls victim

to the ambitions of those who espouse his cause, and finally dies miserably in prison.

Rotten Row (rot'ẹn rō). A fashionable thoroughfare for equestrians in Hyde Park, London, extending W from Hyde Park Corner for 1½ mi. It was part of the old royal route (which also included what is now the Mall and Birdcage Walk in St. James Park) from the palace of the Plantagenet kings at Westminster to the royal hunting forests and was reserved for royalty, the only other person allowed to use the route being (from his association with the hunting grounds) the Grand Falconer of England.

Rouget de Lisle (rö.zhe dẹ lēl), **Claude Joseph.** [Also, **Rouget de l'Isle.**] b. at Montaigu, Lons-le-Saulnier, France, May 10, 1760; d. at Choisy-le-Roi, near Paris, June 26 or 27, 1836. A French soldier and composer of songs. He wrote a number of songs, and published *Cinquante chants français* (1825) and other works, but is most celebrated as the author of the *Marseillaise* (1792).

Rough Crossing, The. A novel by Sylvia Thompson, published in 1918.

Roughead (ruf'hed), **William.** b. Feb. 13, 1870; d. 1952. A Scottish writer and amateur in criminology. Author of *Rhyme Without Reason* (1901), the series *Notable British Trials* (1906 et seq.), *Malice Domestic* (1928), *Rogues Walk Here* (1934), *Knaves' Looking-Glass* (1935), *Mainly Murder* (1937), *Rascals Revived* (1940), and *The Art of Murder* (1943).

round. [Also: **rondo, rota.**] A short rhythmical song in which the several voices enter at equal intervals of time: distinguished from a *catch* simply in not being necessarily humorous. Rounds have always been very popular in England. The earliest specimen is the famous *Sumer is icumen in*, which dates from the early part of the 13th century, and is the oldest example of counterpoint extant.

> Some jolly shepherd sung a lusty round.
> (Fairfax, tr. of Tasso's *Godfrey of Boulogne*.)

> A Round, a Round, a Round, Boyes, a Round,
> Let Mirth fly aloft, and Sorrow be drown'd.
> (Brome, *Jovial Crew*.)

Roundabout Papers, The. A work by William Makepeace Thackeray, published in 1862.

roundel (roun'dẹl). A form of rondel, specifically applied by Swinburne to a form apparently invented by himself. This consists of nine lines with two refrains, arranged as follows: *aba* (and refrain); *bab; aba* (and refrain)—the refrain, as in the rondeau and rondel, being part of the first line. The measure is unrestricted, and the refrain generally rhymes with the *b* lines.

> Many a himpne for your holy daies
> That highten balades, roundels, virelaies.
> (Chaucer, *Good Women*.)

> All day long we rode
> Thro' the dim land against a rushing wind,
> That glorious roundel echoing in our ears.
> (Tennyson, *Merlin and Vivien*.)

roundelay (roun'dẹ.lā). **1.** Any song in which an idea, line, or refrain is continually repeated.

> *Per.*　It fell upon a holy eve,
> *Wil.*　Hey, ho, hallidaye!

ḍ, d or j; ṣ, s or sh; ṭ, t or ch; ẓ, z or zh; *o*, F. cloche; ü, F. menu; ċh, Sc. loch; ṅ, F. bonbon.

Per. When holy fathers went to shrieve;
Wil. Now ginneth this roundelay.

. . . .
Wil. Now endeth our roundelay.
Cud. Sicker, sike a roundle never heard I none.
(Spenser, *Shep. Cal.*, August.)

Loudly sung his roundelay of love.   (Dryden.)

While linnet, lark, and blackbird gay
Sing forth her nuptial roundelay.
(Scott, *Rokeby.*)

The breath of Winter . . . plays a roundelay
Of death among the bushes and the leaves.
(Keats, *Isabella*, st. 32.)

2. A rondeau.

The roundelay, in which, after each strophe of
the song, a chorus interposes with the same refrain.
(J. Sully, *Sensation and Intuition.*)

3. A dance in a circle; a round or roundel.

The fawns, satyrs, and nymphs did dance their
roundelays.   (Howell.)

As doth the billow there upon Charybdis,
That breaks itself on that which it encounters,
So here the folk must dance their roundelay.
(Longfellow, tr. of Dante's *Inferno.*)

Roundheads (round'hedz). In English history, the
members of the Parliamentarian or Puritan party
during the civil war. They were so called opprobri-
ously by the Royalists or Cavaliers, in allusion to
the Puritans' custom of wearing their hair closely
cut, while the Cavaliers usually wore theirs in
ringlets. The Roundheads were one of the two
great parties in English politics, first formed c1641,
and continued under the succeeding names of
Whigs and Liberals, as opposed to the Cavaliers,
Tories, and Conservatives respectively.

Roundheads, The. [Full title, **The Roundheads:
or, The Good Old Cause.**] A comedy by Aphra
Behn, produced c1681.

Round Table. In Arthurian legend, a table made
by Merlin for Uther Pendragon, who gave it to
the father of Guinevere, from whom Arthur received it with 100 knights as a wedding gift. The
table would seat 150 knights. (In some accounts it
would seat 1,600, in others only 50 or 13.) In
Wace's story, Arthur had it made so that no knight
could take precedence over another. One seat was
called the Siege Perilous because it was death to
any knight to sit upon it unless he were the knight
whose achievement of the Holy Grail was certain.
The romances of the Grail and of the Round Table
are closely connected. There were legends of the
Round Table before the Norman poet Wace mentioned it in 1155, but between 1155 and 1200 several books were collectively called *Romances of the
Round Table.* There is a round wooden board hanging in Winchester Castle, depicting the figure of
Arthur and showing the names of 24 knights, which
is traditionally said to be the original.

Round Table, The. A three-act play, called "a
comic tragedy," by Lennox Robinson, produced in
1922 and published in 1924.

Round the Corner. A novel by Gilbert Cannan,
published in 1913.

Rousard (rö.särd'; French, rö.sår).   The sickly son
of D'Amville in Cyril Tourneur's *The Atheist's
Tragedy.*

Rousseau (rö.sö'), **Jean Jacques.** b. at Geneva,
Switzerland, June 28, 1712; d. at Ermenonville,
near Paris, July 2, 1778. A French writer and
philosopher. He was for one year (1740) the resident tutor of the two children of M. de Mably
(brother of Gabriel Bonnot de Mably and Étienne
Bonnot de Condillac), and wrote for them his first
educational work: *Projet pour l'éducation de M. de
Sainte-Marie.* In 1742 he went to Paris in order to
read before the Académie des Sciences a paper on
a new system of music annotation which he had
invented. He accepted a position as secretary to
the French ambassador to Venice, M. le Comte de
Montaigu, but quarreled with him and returned
to Paris to fight his case before the court there in
October, 1744. It was at that time that he began a
liaison with Thérèse Levasseur, an illiterate and
stupid servant girl who is said to have borne him
five children, and whom he married 20 years later.
Rousseau placed his children in a foundlings' home,
justifying his action by saying that, as illegitimate
children, they would otherwise have been deprived
of many of the privileges other children enjoyed.
In 1749, when the Academy of Dijon had proposed
the question "Did the progress of Sciences and
Letters tend to corrupt or to uplift morals?"
Rousseau answered, condemning civilization in a
most eloquent discourse, in which he stated that
the progress of the arts and sciences had led man
away from the original virtues bestowed upon him
by the Creator, had made him physically and
morally weak, lazy, and vicious, and had induced
him to live an artificial, senseless life, which would
eventually destroy his civilization as it had the
civilizations of Athens and Rome. The Academy
awarded him the prize and he rose to sudden fame.
The following year his charming opera, *Le Devin
du village*, was performed before the French court
at Fontainebleau. Then, answering another question of the Academy of Dijon, he published his
famous *Discours sur l'inégalité des conditions*
(1754), which made him the champion of the
bourgeoisie in all the civilized countries. He returned to Geneva and to Protestantism. Angered
by the article on Geneva which Jean Le Rond
d'Alembert had written for the *Encyclopédie* (and
in which he advocated the establishment of a permanent theater in that city), Rousseau wrote his
Lettre sur les spectacles (1758) condemning the
stage as a dangerous institution. In the *Nouvelle
Héloïse* (1761), a lengthy novel in the form of letters, describing the love of Saint-Preux, a young
teacher of low position, for Julie, a girl of noble
birth, he expresses his opinion on various subjects
including suicide, education, and country life. In
1762 he published the *Contrat social* (*The Social
Contract*), a picture of his ideal government, a
republic in which the rights of the individuals
(*volonté de tous*) are ingeniously protected by those
of the society (*volonté générale*). This book has been
called the Bible of the leaders of the French Revolution, but its theories proved utterly impractical
in application. Just as impractical is Rousseau's
treatise on education, *Émile* (1762), although it
has been said that no other book has had a greater

influence on our educational systems. Rousseau, starting from his conviction that man is born good, maintains that the main concern of the educator is to preserve and develop the original instincts of the child, guide them and develop them away from the nefarious influence of society, until the young man is strong enough morally to act according to his conscience. This book brought upon him the anger of the Sorbonne and of the Genevan Consistory, and Rousseau had to seek refuge at Moûtiers, in the Neuchâtel territory, then under the protection of Frederick the Great. Later, invited by David Hume, he went to England and made his home at Wooton, near Derby (1766). In May, 1767, he was back in France, near Grenoble in Savoie, suffering from what apparently was paranoia. In 1772 he was permitted to return to Paris. There he wrote his *Dialogues*, and also his famous *Confessions*, which he read among his friends in order to justify his conduct. These books were published six years after his death. His last work Rousseau wrote in the peaceful seclusion of Ermenonville. It is *Les Rêveries d'un promeneur solitaire*, often considered his best book and the most representative of his true self. In literature he is considered by many to have been the "father of romanticism."

Rover, The.   A novel by Joseph Conrad, published in 1923.

Rover, or the Banished Cavaliers, The.   A comedy in two parts by Aphra Behn, produced in 1677 (Part I) and 1680 (Part II).

Rowan (rō′an), **Richard.**   In James Joyce's three-act play *Exiles* (1918), an Irish author living in Italy, believed to be a self-portrait.

Rowe (rō), **Nicholas.**   b. at Little Barford, Bedfordshire, England, 1674; d. Dec. 6, 1718. An English dramatist and poet, appointed (1715) poet laureate. He was educated for the bar. His chief tragedies are *The Ambitious Stepmother, Tamerlane* (1702), *The Fair Penitent* (1703), *Ulysses* (1706), *The Royal Convert* (1707), *Jane Shore* (1714), and *Lady Jane Grey* (1715). He also wrote *The Biter* (1704), a comedy. He translated Lucan's *Pharsalia*. His edition (1709) of Shakespeare included a collection of traditions gathered at Stratford by Thomas Betterton; Rowe used his knowledge of the stage to divide the plays into acts and scenes, to indicate exits and entrances, to add a *dramatis personae* to each play, and to amend the many errors of spelling and punctuation in the text.

Rowena (rō.wē′na).   In British legend, the daughter of Hengist, and the wife of the British chieftain Vortigern.

Rowena.   A fair Saxon maiden of royal descent, the ward of Cedric, in Sir Walter Scott's *Ivanhoe*. She marries Ivanhoe.

Rowland (rō′land).   See **Roland.**

Rowland Mallet (mal′et).   See **Mallet, Rowland.**

Rowlands (rō′landz), **Samuel.**   b. c1570; d. in 1630 or shortly thereafter (his last poem was written in that year). An English pamphleteer.

Rowlandson (rō′land.son), **Thomas.**   b. at London, in July, 1756; d. there, April 22, 1827. An English painter, etcher, and caricaturist. It is related that as a schoolboy he drew caricatures and humorous

pictures in the margins of his books. He studied drawing and painting at the Royal Academy and at Paris, where he stayed three years with a wealthy aunt, and as early as 1775 exhibited at the Academy a picture of Delilah visiting the captive Sampson. After 1777 he had a studio in London, executed portraits, and was a regular exhibitor at the Royal Academy until 1781. About that time he began to give rein to his flair for caricature, and presently his name disappeared from the Academy catalogues, but his prints began to flow from the presses, to delight a wider public. His father, a prosperous merchant, lost his substance in speculation, but his aunt gave him a liberal allowance and at her death left him a considerable inheritance, which before long he lost at the gaming tables. His passion for gambling was incurable; as often as he recouped his fortunes, he risked and lost all; he took his losses with equanimity, confident that by a little industry he could again become affluent. Meanwhile his keen eye noted every aspect of life at London and in Bath, and his wit played upon English politics and politicians and held Napoleon up to ridicule. Series of drawings, some of them running for a year or more, later to be collected and reissued, appeared under such titles as *Comforts of Bath, Miseries of Life,* and *Cries of London.* For the *Poetical Magazine* he executed the noted series *Tour of Dr. Syntax in Search of the Picturesque* (1809, reissued 1812), *Tour of Dr. Syntax in Search of Consolation* (1820), and *Tour of Dr. Syntax in Search of a Wife.* He also illustrated some of the works of Goldsmith, Smollett, and Sterne, and a number of other books. Many of his cartoons, which were published in editions of hundreds of copies, were carelessly and garishly executed, but the Dr. Syntax series and some others, as well as his book illustrations, are splendid in color as well as incisive in line. His method was to draw his composition in large outline with a reed pen, afterward applying water colors; he then made copperplate etchings of the pictures, and the prints were colored, to accord with his drawings, by the publisher. Rowlandson's endlessly varied work constituted an invaluable record of English life and society in his time, in town and country, in taverns and at fairs, in high social circles and in the streets of London, a record informed with keen insight, broad and sometimes sardonic humor, sympathy, and sentiment. Some of his drawings also were records of things observed during tours of the Continent, and they include numerous sensitive landscapes. There are collections of Rowlandson drawings in the British Museum and the Victoria and Albert Museum, and the Metropolitan Museum of Art at New York.

Rowley (rou′li), **Samuel.**   An English dramatist of the early 17th century. Only two of his plays exist in print: *When You See Me, You Know Me,* a chronicle play on Henry VIII (1605), and *The Noble Soldier* (1634), probably written with Day and Dekker.

Rowley, William.   b. c1585; d. 1626 (or, according to some authorities, c1642). An English dramatist. He is mentioned as an actor in the Duke of York's Company in 1610, and also acted with Princess Elizabeth's Company at the Cockpit theater in

1623. In 1621 he was writing for this latter company, both alone and with Thomas Middleton. He joined the King's Men in 1625 and did his last work for them. Five of his plays are extant: *A New Wonder: A Woman never Vext* (printed 1632), *A Match at Midnight* (printed 1633), *All's Lost by Lust* (printed 1633), *A Shoemaker a Gentleman* (printed 1638), and *The Birth of Merlin* (printed 1662) which bore Shakespeare's name as co-author when it was printed, although it is now thought that not Shakespeare but possibly Middleton collaborated on it. *The Thracian Wonder* is no longer considered Rowley's, although his name appears on its title page. He was a collaborator on a play for Queen Anne's Men in 1607. He worked with Middleton on *A Fair Quarrel* (printed 1617), *The Spanish Gypsy* (acted c1623, printed 1653), *The Changeling* (acted 1624, published 1653), and *A Game of Chess* (licensed and acted 1624, printed 1625). A play (c1615) that is thought to be a first revision of Middleton's lost play, *The Old Law*, is credited to Rowley. With John Ford and Thomas Dekker he wrote *The Witch of Edmonton* (acted 1623, printed 1658); with Dekker, *Keep the Widow Waking* (now lost); with John Webster, *A Cure for a Cuckold* (printed 1661); and with Thomas Heywood, *Fortune by Land and Sea* (printed 1655). It is thought that Rowley also worked on some of the plays attributed to Beaumont and Fletcher.

Rowley Poems, The. A collection of poems written by Thomas Chatterton and attributed by him to a mythical Thomas Rowley, a priest of the 15th century. He began to write them in 1764. They were declined by Robert Dodsley, the publisher, in 1768, but in 1769 Chatterton succeeded in temporarily deceiving Horace Walpole with them. Thomas Gray, however, discovered the hoax.

Rowson (rou'son), **Susanna.** [Maiden name, **Haswell.**] b. at Portsmouth, England, 1762; d. at Boston, March 2, 1824. An English author, actress, and educator, best known for her story of *Charlotte Temple*. Her husband becoming bankrupt, she went on the stage, appeared at Edinburgh (1792–93), and toured in America (1793–97). She superintended (1797–1822) a school for girls at Boston. Among her publications are *The Inquisitor* (1788), *Charlotte, a Tale of Truth* (1791, titled in later editions *Charlotte Temple*), and *Reuben and Rachel* (1798).

Rowton Heath (rou'ton). The scene, near Chester, England, of a Royalist defeat (1645) by the Parliamentary army.

Roxana (rok.san'a -sā'na). [Also, **Roxane** (rok.san'ē, -sā'nē).] Murdered at Amphipolis, Macedonia, 311 B.C. A Bactrian princess; daughter of Oxyartes. She married (327) Alexander the Great, bore him a posthumous son, who was accepted by the Diadochi (Alexander's generals and successors), sided with Olympias, Alexander's mother, against Cassander, and was put to death with her son by order of Cassander.

Roxana. [Full title, **Roxana, or The Fortunate Mistress.**] A novel by Daniel Defoe, published in 1724. The theme is very similar to that of the author's *Moll Flanders*, an earlier work. Roxana (or Mlle. Beleau) is the daughter of French refugees, raised in England, and married to a London brewer. After five children are born to them, he loses his money and deserts her. Roxana, whose only friend is her maid Amy, is thus forced into a life of adventure. Both she and Amy become the mistresses of the landlord, each having a child by him. He is killed, and they are forced to seek their fortune elsewhere. After traveling through many countries and enjoying the protection of many men, they arrive in Holland, where Roxana marries a Dutch merchant and leads a good life until he finds out about her past. He soon dies and leaves Roxana almost no money. In the end Amy and Roxana are imprisoned for debt and die repentant.

Roxane (rôk.sàn'). The beautiful girl who is beloved by Cyrano de Bergerac.

Roxburghe Club (roks'bér.ọ). A club founded in 1812, at the time of the sale of the library of John, 3rd Duke of Roxburghe. The Rev. Thomas Frognall Dibdin claimed the title of founder. The object of the club was the reprinting of rare pieces of ancient literature.

Royal Academy. [Full name, **Royal Academy of Arts.**] A society founded in 1768 by George III for the establishment of a school of design and the holding of an annual exhibition of the works of living artists. Its first rooms were in Pall Mall, London; thence it removed to Somerset House, later to Trafalgar Square (1834), and it now occupies Burlington House. The society consists of 40 royal academicians, at least 30 associates, and four engravers, of whom two may be academicians. Its first president was Sir Joshua Reynolds.

Royalist, The. A play by Thomas D'Urfey, produced in 1682. Some of the music for it was written by Henry Purcell.

Royall King and the Loyall Subject, The. A play by Thomas Heywood, printed in 1637 but probably acted around 1602. It is based upon a story from Bandello in Painter's *Palace of Pleasure*.

"Royal Oak." See under **Boscobel.**

Royal Road, The. A novel by Alfred Ollivant, published in 1912.

Royal Slave, The. A tragedy (1636) by William Cartwright.

Royal Society. [Full name, **The Royal Society of London for Improving Natural Knowledge.**] An association founded (c1660) at London and incorporated in 1662, the object of which is the advancement of science, especially of the physical sciences. It has held the foremost place among such societies in England, and has always numbered the leaders of British science among its members. Its principal publications are *The Proceedings of the Royal Society* and *The Philosophical Transactions.*

Royal Society Club. A London club, formed about 1709, consisting largely of fellows of the Royal Society.

Royal Spanish Academy. [Spanish, **Real Academia Española.**] An academy founded at Madrid in 1713 by the Duke of Escalona, and established by royal confirmation in 1714, with the object of cultivating and improving the national language.

Royde-Smith (roid'smith'), **Naomi (Gwladys).** An English novelist and playwright. Her plays include *A Balcony* (1926), *Mrs. Siddons* (1931), and *Pri-*

vate Room (1934). She is author also of the novels *The Tortoiseshell Cat* (1925), *The Housemaid* (1926), *Skin-Deep* (1927), *John Fanning's Legacy* (1927), *Children in the Wood* (1928; American title, *In the Wood*), *Summer Holiday, or Gibraltar* (1929; American title, *Give Me My Sin Again*), *The Island* (1930), *The Mother* (1931), *The Delicate Situation* (1931), *Incredible Tale* (1932), *The Bridge* (1932), *David* (1934), *The Queen's Wigs* (1934), *The Altar-Piece* (1939), *Jane Fairfax* (1940), *The Unfaithful Wife* (1941), *Fire-Weed* (1945), and *The State of Mind of Mr. Sherwood* (1947); and of the biographical studies *The Double Heart* (1931) and *The Private Life of Mrs. Siddons* (1933; American title, *Portrait of Mrs. Siddons*).

Rubáiyát (rö′bī.yät, -bi-), **The.** See under **Omar Khayyám.**

Rubens (rö′benz), **Peter Paul.** b. at Siegen, in Westphalia, Germany, June 29, 1577; d. at Antwerp, Belgium, May 30, 1640. A Flemish painter. He was made honorary M.A. at Cambridge, and knighted at Whitehall, March 3, 1630. He painted several pictures in England, and received an order for the decoration of Whitehall. On Dec. 6, 1630, he married Helena Fourment, a niece of his first wife. He was famous as a colorist, and painted historical and sacred subjects, portraits, and landscapes. His pictures are in the Louvre, the Belvedere at Vienna, at Antwerp (including many pictures in churches), in the National Gallery at London, in the Metropolitan Museum at New York, and many other collections. Among his chief works are *The Descent from the Cross* (Antwerp), *Elevation of the Cross* (Antwerp), *Rape of the Sabines* (London), *Venus and Adonis* (Metropolitan, New York), and a number of portraits, notably those of Helena Fourment and of his children.

Rubicon (rö′bi.kon). In ancient geography, a small river in Italy, near Rimini. In the later Roman republic it was the boundary between Italy proper and Cisalpine Gaul. The crossing of it by Julius Caesar, in 49 B.C., took place despite contrary orders to Caesar from the senate, and signalized Caesar's irrevocable decision to proceed against Pompey, which meant civil war. From this event, the phrase "cross the Rubicon" has since come to describe any act or decision of irrevocable import. It has been identified with the Rugone, Uso, and Fiumicino.

Rudabah (rö.dä.bä′). In the *Shahnamah*, the daughter of Mihrab (king of Kabul), wife of Zal, and mother of Rustam. The story of the love of Zal and Rudabah, of the anger of Mihrab, and of the opposition of Sam and Minuchihr is one of the most idyllic portions of the poem.

Ruddigore, or the Witches' Curse (rud′i.gōr). A comic opera (1887) by W. S. Gilbert and Arthur Sullivan.

Rudge (ruj), **Barnaby.** In Dickens's *Barnaby Rudge*, a simple-minded lad who becomes accidentally involved in the Gordon Riots.

Rüdiger (rü′di.ger). In the *Nibelungenlied*, a warrior of King Etzel who, because of an unwitting vow, had to fight against the Burgundians, to whom he had sworn loyalty. He was killed in the fight. Robert Southey used him as the title character of one of his poems.

Rudra (rö′dra). In Hindu mythology, in the *Rig-Veda*, the storm god. He was the sender of diseases and death to the earth, but he also bestowed remedial herbs and had a special power over the cattle. In the *Atharva-Veda* he was invoked as the master of life and death. In post-Vedic mythology, he became the Shiva of the Hindu triad.

Rueful Mating, The. The American title of **Little Red Horses.**

Rugby (rug′bi), **John.** In Shakespeare's *Merry Wives of Windsor*, a servant to Dr. Caius.

Rugby Chapel. A poem by Matthew Arnold, written in November, 1857, in commemoration of his father, Thomas Arnold ("Arnold of Rugby"), who had died 15 years earlier.

Rugby School. One of the most famous of the great English public schools, founded in 1567.

Ruggiero (röd.jä′rō). [English, **Rogero.**] A Saracen knight, one of the most important characters in Matteo Boiardo's *Orlando Innamorato* and in Lodovico Ariosto's *Orlando Furioso*. He becomes a Christian and is baptized for the sake of Bradamante; they marry and become the progenitors of the family of Este, in whose honor the poems were written.

Ruggle (rug′l), **George.** b. 1575; d. 1622. An English author. He wrote the well-known burlesque *Ignoramus* (1615), an attack on the deputy-recorder at Cambridge, and possibly *Club Law* (c1599), another attack on Cambridge officials. He was a fellow of Clare College, Cambridge.

Ruin, The. An Old English poem, of unknown authorship and date, in the *Exeter Book*, describing a ruined city and contrasting its present state with its former splendor. Presumably the city dates from the Roman period (some authorities have conjectured that it is meant to be Bath), and its destruction has taken place at the hands of the Saxon invaders.

Ruin, The. A novel by Edward Sackville-West, published in 1926.

Ruined City. A novel by Nevil Shute, published in 1938.

Ruins and Visions. A volume of poetry by Stephen Spender, published in 1942.

Ruins of Rome, The. A poem (1740) by John Dyer.

Rule a Wife and Have a Wife. A comedy, once extremely popular (staged in 1624; printed in 1640) by John Fletcher.

Rule Britannia! (bri.tan′i.a). An English patriotic air. The words, by James Thomson and David Mallet, and the music, by Thomas Arne, were composed for *The Masque of Alfred*. It was first performed at Maidenhead, at the residence of Frederick, Prince of Wales, in 1740.

Rumour. In the Induction to Shakespeare's *2 Henry IV*, a stage direction reads "Enter Rumour painted full of tongues." He brings false news to Northumberland of Hotspur's victory at Shrewsbury. Rumour was a common figure in the masques.

ḍ, d or j; ṣ, s or sh; ṭ, t or ch; ẓ, z or zh; o, F. cloche; ü, F. menu; ċh, Sc. loch; ṅ, F. bonbon.

Rump Parliament. The remnant of the Long Parliament after Pride's Purge.

"Rumty" (rum'ti). See **Wilfer, Reginald.**

Runaway, The. A play by Hannah Cowley. It was produced by David Garrick, who may have made additions to it, in 1776 and printed the same year.

Runciman (run'si.man), Sir **Walter.** b. at Dunbar, East Lothian, Scotland, 1847; d. Aug. 13, 1937. A British shipowner and writer. Author of *Windjammers and Sea Tramps, The Shellback's Progress, Drake, Nelson, and Napoleon,* the series *Sunbeam Logs,* and other books.

rune. A letter or character of any of various alphabets used by the peoples of northern Europe from an early period to the 11th century, and believed to be derived from a Greek source. Runic inscriptions are found widely on ancient weapons and stone monuments in Scandinavia and the British Isles. The names of the letters were also words in the Germanic languages, often with magic or mysterious connotations, and thus the word rune also means a secret or mystery, or a proverbial or mystic saying or rhyme.

Runic Poem, The. An Old English poem, thought to date from the 8th century or later, consisting of 29 sections, each beginning with the name of a rune and containing a proverb or the like dealing with the magic or other attribute of the opening word. This and the two other extant works of the kind (one in Norwegian and one in Icelandic) are believed to be elaborations of earlier and simpler verses that were designed to help in memorizing the runes.

Runnymede (run'i.mēd). [Also: **Runnemede, Runnimede.**] A meadow on the right bank of the Thames, near Egham in Surrey, England, ab. 21 mi. SW of London. It is noted in English history as the place where the barons forced King John to grant (June 15, 1215) the Magna Charta; Charter Island, in the Thames nearby, may, however, have been the place of actual signing.

Runnymede. Pseudonym of **Disraeli, Benjamin.**

Rupert Johnson (rö'pėrt jon'son). See **Johnson, Rupert.**

Rupert of Hentzau (hent'sou). A novel by Anthony Hope, a sequel to *The Prisoner of Zenda,* published in 1898. In it, the gallant Englishman Rassendyl again saves the king and Flavia from the plots of the villain, Rupert of Hentzau, and again has a chance to take the throne and Flavia, but is killed without having revealed his decision.

Ruritania (rör.i.tā'ni.a). The imaginary country which is the setting of Anthony Hope's novels *The Prisoner of Zenda* and *Rupert of Hentzau.*

Rush (rush), **Friar.** In medieval German folklore, the Devil in the guise of a friar. He used to turn up in monasteries to annoy and seduce the monks. In English folklore he plays a more mischievous and less malignant role: pulling the bungs out of beer or wine barrels and letting the liquid waste was one of his favorite tricks. In Sir Walter Scott's *Marmion* the friar's lantern (will-o'-the-wisp) was called Friar Rush.

Ruskin (rus'kin), **John.** b. at London, Feb. 8, 1819; d. at Brantwood, Coniston, England, Jan. 20, 1900.

An English writer on art and social problems, considered one of England's greatest masters of prose. He entered Christ Church College, Oxford, in 1837, won the Newdigate prize with a poem entitled *Salsette and Elephanta* in 1839, and graduated in 1842, after a year of absence due to illness. He was the son of a rich wine merchant, and Ruskin's formal education was enriched by extensive travel and by private lessons in drawing. In 1843 he published the first volume of *Modern Painters,* written in defense of the landscape painter J. M. Turner, then the target of much criticism. This work created a sensation by the brilliance of its style and the originality of its approach to art. Succeeding volumes followed (II, 1846, III–IV, 1856, V, 1860), together with *The Seven Lamps of Architecture* (1849) and *The Stones of Venice* (3 vols., 1851–53). Together, these works established Ruskin's reputation as an art critic and one of the leading literary figures of the day. He was in the period 1870–71 the first Slade professor of fine arts at Oxford, and served a second period in 1883–85. Several courses of his Oxford lectures were published as *Lectures on Art* (1870), *Lectures on Landscape* (delivered 1871, published 1898), *Aratra Pentelici* (1871), *The Eagle's Nest* (1872), *Ariadne Florentina* (1873–76), and *Val d'Arno* (1874). Ruskin's art and nature interests found further expression in the following books: *The Elements of Drawing* (1857), *The Elements of Perspective* (1859), *The Queen of the Air* (1869), *The Laws of Fésole* (1877–78), *Proserpina* (flowers, 1875–86), *Love's Meinie* (birds, 1873–78), *Deucalion* (geology, 1875–83), *St. Mark's Rest: The History of Venice* (1877–84), *Mornings in Florence* (1875–77), and *The Bible of Amiens* (1880–85). In these works and others Ruskin developed a view of art at once simple and comprehensive: "The art of man is the expression of his rational and disciplined delight in the forms and laws of the creation of which he forms a part. . . . He is the greatest artist who has embodied, in the sum of his works, the greatest number of the greatest ideas." These ideas are, chiefly, truth, beauty, significance. To produce such art the artist must have not only technical mastery of his medium but also a healthy, integrated life, and life integrated and healthy is the basis of all worthy art, whether of the individual, the nation, or the race. Further, Ruskin wanted the power and charm of such art brought within the reach of everybody. "There never was, nor can be, any essential beauty possessed by a work of art, which is not based on the conception of its honored permanence, and local influence, as a part of appointed and precious furniture, either in the cathedral, the house, or the joyful thoroughfare." This conception of the meaning and function of art is the root from which sprang Ruskin's social and economic notions. It seemed to him futile to teach the dependence of art upon sound life, social as well as individual, while society was rushing madly into ways and habits that were unsound, and while an older and simpler order was retreating before the "deforming mechanism and the squalid misery in modern cities." From 1860 onwards, therefore, he turned much of his attention to social and economic studies, becoming a critic of the older order, a prophet of the new, and an experimenter in various schemes of reform. His most important writings in this field are: *A Joy for Ever* (1880; originally entitled *The Political Economy of Art*, 1857), *The Two Paths* (1859), *Unto This Last* (1860–62), *Munera Pulveris* (reissue 1872 of *Essays on Political Economy*, 1862–63), *Sesame and Lilies* (1865), *The Ethics of the Dust* (1866), *The Crown of Wild Olive* (1866), *Time and Tide* (1867), and *Fors Clavigera: Letters to the Workmen and Laborers of Great Britain* (1871–84). His last work is an unfinished autobiography, *Praeterita* (1885–89). The only complete edition of Ruskin's works is the monumental Library Edition in 39 volumes (1903–12). Lives of Ruskin have been written by W. G. Collingwood (1902), by E. A. Cook (2 vols., 1911), by Derrick Leon (1949), and by Peter Quennell (1949).

Russel (rus′el), **Dan.** The Fox in Chaucer's *Nun's Priest's Tale.*

Russell (rus′el), **Elizabeth Mary.** [Titles: Countess **von Arnim,** Countess **Russell;** pseudonym, **Elizabeth;** original name, **Mary Annette Beauchamp.**] b. at Sydney, Australia, 1866; d. at Charleston, S. C., Feb. 9, 1941. An English novelist and society wit; cousin of Katherine Mansfield. She lived in Australia, England, Germany, France, Switzerland, and, from the beginning of World War II until her death, in the U. S. Her first husband was Count Henning August von Arnim (d. 1910), a Prussian on whose 60,000-acre estate she lived for 20 years, and by whom she had five children; her second husband was John Francis Stanley Russell, 2nd Earl Russell, and brother of Bertrand Russell, whom she married in 1916 and from whom she was separated in 1919. Author of *Elizabeth and Her German Garden* (1898), *The Solitary Summer* (1899), and *The Adventures of Elizabeth in Rügen* (1904), semifictional accounts of her life as the wife of a Prussian nobleman. Her other works are satirical society novels, *The Benefactress* (1902), *Princess Priscilla's Fortnight* (1906), *Fräulein Schmidt and Mr. Anstruther* (1907), *The Pastor's Wife* (1914), *Christopher and Columbus* (1919), *In the Mountains* (1920), *Vera* (1921), *The Enchanted April* (1923), *Love* (1925), *Introduction to Sally* (1926), *Expiation* (1929), *Father* (1931), *The Jasmine Farm* (1934), *All the Dogs of My Life* (1936), and *Mr. Skeffington* (1940).

Russell, George William. [Pseudonym, Æ.] b. in Lurgan, County Armagh, Ulster, Ireland, April 10, 1867; d. at Bournemouth, England, July 17, 1935. An Irish poet, essayist, and journalist. He organized agricultural societies, and edited *The Irish Homestead* (1904–23) and *The Irish Statesman* (1923–30). His pseudonym was the result of a typographical error; an article he contributed to *The Irish Theosophist* was signed "Æon," but the last two letters were omitted in error; he thereafter used Æ as a pen name. His poetry includes *Homeward—Songs by the Way* (1894), *The Earth Breath* (1897), *The Divine Vision* (1904), *New Poems* (1904), *Gods of War* (1915), *Midsummer Eve* (1928), *Vale and Other Poems* (1931), and *House of the Titans and Other Poems* (1934). Author of *The Hero in Man*, *Irish Essays* (1906), *The Renewal of Youth* (1911), *The National Being—Some Thoughts on an Irish Policy* (1917), *The Candle of Vision* (1919), and other essays on mysticism and economics. He published the play *Deirdre* (1907), and collaborated on *Literary Ideals in Ireland* and *Ideals in Ireland.*

Russell, Lord John. [Titles: 1st Earl **Russell of Kingston Russell,** Viscount **Amberley;** nicknamed **"Finality John."**] b. at London, Aug. 18, 1792; d. May 28, 1878. An English statesman, orator, and author. He studied at Edinburgh, and entered Parliament in 1813. He began his advocacy of Parliamentary reform in 1819, advocated Roman Catholic emancipation in 1826, and the repeal of the Test Acts in 1828, became paymaster of the forces in 1830, and introduced the Reform Bill in 1831, and was one of its leading champions until its passage in 1832. He became leader of the Whig party in 1834, was home secretary (1835–39), secretary for war and the colonies (1839–41), and prime minister and first lord of the treasury (1846–52). After Palmerston's premature recognition of the coup d'état of Louis Napoleon (Napoleon III), he forced Palmerston to resign. The next year he was forced to resign by Palmerston. He published the anti-Roman Catholic *Durham Letter* in 1850, was foreign secretary and later president of the council (1852–55), and represented England at the Vienna Conference in 1855. He was colonial secretary in 1855 and foreign secretary in the Palmerston-Russell administration (1859–65), acting to keep England neutral during the American Civil War and to establish Italian independence. After Palmerston's death, he was prime minister and first lord of the treasury (1865–66). He was created Earl Russell in 1861. He edited the memorials and correspondence of Charles James Fox (1853–57) and of Thomas Moore (1852–56), and wrote *Life and Times of Fox* (1859–67), *Recollections and Suggestions* (1875), and others.

Russell, Lady. A friend and adviser of the heroine in Jane Austen's novel *Persuasion.*

Russell, William Clark. b. at New York, Feb. 24, 1844; d. at Bath, England, Nov. 8, 1911. An English novelist. He served (1858–66) in the British merchant marine, later using his experiences as a basis for his sea novels. He wrote articles on the sea (1882–89) for the *Daily Telegraph.* Author of *John Holdsworth, Chief Mate* (1875), *Wreck of the Grosvenor* (1877), *My Watch Below* (1882), *Round the Galley Fire* (1883), *The Frozen Pirate* (1887), and *Romance of a Midshipman* (1898), novels; *Dampier* (1889), *Nelson* (1890), and *Collingwood* (1891), naval biographies; and *The Turnpike Sailor, or Rhymes on the Road* (1907), poetry.

Russell, Sir William Howard. b. at Lily Vale, County Dublin, Ireland, March 28, 1820; d. Feb. 10, 1907. A British war correspondent. He covered (for the London *Times*) the Crimean War (1854–55), the Sepoy Mutiny, the American Civil War (1861–62), the Austro-Prussian War (1866), the Franco-Prussian War (1870), and the Zulu War (1879). He founded and edited (1860–1907) the *Army and Navy Gazette.* Author of *The War from the Landing at Galipoli to the Death of Lord Raglan* (1855–56), *My Diary in India* (1860), *My Diary, North and South During the Civil War in America* (1862), *My Diary in the East During the Tour of the Prince and Princess of Wales* (1869), *Hesperothen: a Record of a Ramble in the United States and Canada* (1882), *My Diary During the Last Great*

War (1883), and *The Great War With Russia* (1895). His accounts of the suffering of English soldiers during the Crimean War are credited with inspiring Florence Nightingale in her work, and he was the author of the vivid phrase "the thin red line," first used in his dispatch (Oct. 25, 1854) to the *Times* reporting the action of the British infantry at Balaklava.

Russell Square. A London square which lies to the E of the British Museum.

Rustam (rus'tạm, rûs.täm'). [Also, **Rustum** (-tum).] A hero of the Persian epic, the *Shahnamah*. He was the father of Suhrab (usually spelled Sohrab in English literature). According to the traditional account, on the first day of his life he became as large as a child one year old, and ten nurses were necessary to provide him with milk. While a mere child he killed a raging elephant, and while still a youth he avenged the death of his great-grand-father.

Ruth (rōth). In the Bible, the leading character of the Book of Ruth, a Moabitess who, after the death of her husband, went with Naomi, her mother-in-law, to Bethlehem and there married Boaz; an ancestress of David.

Ruth. A novel by Elizabeth Gaskell, published in 1853.

Rutherford and Son (ruᴛʜ'ėr.fọrd). A realistic drama of family conflict by Katherine Githa Sowerby, published in 1912. It has been translated into many European languages.

Ruth Honeywill (rōth hun'i.wil). See **Honeywill, Ruth.**

Ruth Pinch (pinch). See **Pinch, Ruth.**

Ruthwell Cross (ruth'wel). A cross found among Northumbrian Saxon remains at Ruthwell on the Scottish border. Some of the runic writing on it (inscriptions of the 7th, 8th, and 9th centuries) was effaced when it was toppled. These runes set forth a few couplets of a religious poem on the events sculptured in the two principal compartments of the stone, namely, the washing of Jesus's feet by Mary Magdalene and the glorification of Jesus through his Passion.

Rutland (rut'lạnd), **Edmund, Earl of.** In Shakespeare's *3 Henry VI*, a son of the Duke of York, killed by Clifford to avenge the death of his father.

Rutter (rut'ėr), **Owen.** b. Nov. 7, 1889; d. at Hargrave, London, Aug. 1, 1944. An English novelist and biographer. Author of *British North Borneo* (1922), *Through Formosa* (1923), *The New Baltic States and Their Future* (1925), *Sepia* (1926), *Chandu* (1927), *Lucky Star* (1929), *Pagans of North Borneo* (1929), *Cain's Birthday* (1930), *White Rajah* (1931), *The Monster of Mu* (1932), *If Crab No Walk* (1933), *One Fair Daughter* (1934), *Turbulent Journey: Life of William Bligh* (1936), *The True Story of the Mutiny of the Bounty* (1936), *Regent of Hungary: Admiral Nicholas Horthy* (1939), *Portrait of a Painter: Philip de László* (1939), *The Land of St. Joan* (1941), and *Red Ensign* (1943).

Rutuli (rö'tụ.lī). In Roman legend, a people of Latium. Their capital was Ardea. Turnus, their king, appears in the stories of Aeneas.

"R. W." See **Wilfer, Reginald.**

Ryall (rī'ạl), **William Bolitho.** See **Bolitho, William.**

Ryance (rī'ạns). [Also: **Rience, Ryence.**] In Arthurian legend and romance, a king of North Wales, Ireland, and the many isles, who bearded every knight and king he overcame. He had made for himself a cloak of the beards, and lacking one, sent a messenger to King Arthur demanding his, saying if Arthur would not send him his beard he would come and take it. Arthur sent back a message of defiance and refusal. Later when Ryance came into Arthur's country, he was met and brought as a prisoner to Arthur's court by two of Arthur's knights.

Ryecroft (rī'krôft), **Henry.** The principal character in George Gissing's autobiographical novel *The Private Papers of Henry Ryecroft.*

Rye House Plot (rī). In English history, a conspiracy by some extreme Whigs to kill Charles II and the Duke of York (afterward James II), in June, 1683. It is so called from Rye House in Hertfordshire, the meeting place of the conspirators. Lord William Russell, Algernon Sidney, and Robert Baillie were executed for alleged complicity in it.

Ryence (rī'ẹns). See **Ryance.**

Rymer (rī'mėr), **Thomas.** b. 1641; d. at London, Dec. 14, 1713. An English antiquary. He was called to the bar (1673) at Gray's Inn. In 1692 he succeeded Thomas Shadwell as historiographer royal. On Aug. 26, 1693, he began the great *Foedera*, based on the *Codex Juris Gentium Diplomaticus* of Leibnitz. It is a compilation of all the treaties, conventions, correspondence, and other records relating to the foreign relations of England from 1101 A.D. to his own time. The publication, in 20 volumes, five published posthumously, was completed after his death in 1735. His critical work was good, but he produced an unsuccessful play, *Edgar, or the English Monarch* (1678). He criticized other dramatists somewhat harshly, attacking Beaumont and Fletcher in *The Tragedies of the Last Age* (1677) and denouncing Shakespeare's *Othello* as a "bloody farce" that did not preserve the classical unities in *A Short View of Tragedy* (1692).

Rymer, Thomas. See also **Thomas the Rhymer.**

Ryswick (ris'wik), **Peace of.** [Also, **Treaty of Ryswick.**] A treaty signed at Rijswijk, in the Netherlands, on Sept. 21, 1697, between France on the one side and England, the Netherlands, and Spain on the other. France acknowledged William III as king of England, abandoning the cause of the Stuarts, and restored conquests in Catalonia and in the Spanish Netherlands (except certain "reunited" towns); the Dutch restored Pondichéry to the French; and England and France mutually restored conquests in America. The treaty was ratified by the Empire Oct. 30; France restored its conquests except those in Alsace; the Duke of Lorraine had most of his dominions restored; and a clause prejudicial to the Protestants was inserted, applying to the towns "reunited" by France.

S

Saadi (sä′dē). [Also: **Sadi;** original name, **Muslih-ud-Din.**] b. at Shiraz, Persia, c1184; d. there, c1291. A Persian poet. There is great uncertainty as to many statements concerning his life. He is said to have been educated at Baghdad, to have made the pilgrimage to Mecca 15 times, and to have traveled in parts of Europe and in all the countries between Barbary and India. When near Jerusalem he was captured by the Crusaders and forced to work upon the fortifications of Tripoli, but was ransomed by a citizen of Aleppo, sometimes described as a chief, sometimes as a merchant, who married him to a beautiful (but nagging) daughter. After her death he married again and unhappily. His son and daughter were children of the first wife. The son died in infancy; the daughter lived to become the wife of the poet Hafiz. Saadi is honored as a Mohammedan saint, and his tomb near Shiraz is still visited. He wrote many works in both prose and verse and in both Arabic and Persian, and some authorities have maintained that he was the first poet to write in Hindustani. Among his writings are a *Diwan*, or collection of odes, the *Gulistan* (Rose-Garden), *Bustan* (Flower-Garden), and *Pandnamah* or *Book of Counsel*. Elegance, simplicity, and wit are Saadi's chief merits.

Sabatini (sab.ạ.tē′nẹ), **Rafael.** b. at Jesi, Italy, April 29, 1875; d. at Adelboden, Switzerland, Feb. 13, 1950. An English novelist. Educated in Switzerland and Portugal, he served (1917–18) with the British military intelligence during World War I. His novels of high adventure and historical romance include *The Tavern Knight* (1904), *Bardelys the Magnificent* (1906), *The Sea Hawk* (1915), *Scaramouche* (1921), *Captain Blood* (1922), and *The Black Swan* (1932).

Sabellians (sạ.bel′i.ạnz). A primitive Italian people which included the Sabines and others.

Sabines (sä′bīnz). An ancient people of C Italy, who lived chiefly in the mountains N and NE of Rome. They were defeated by Rome in 290 B.C. and formed subsequently an important ethnic element in the composition of the Romans. The so-called rape of the Sabine women is a notable incident in the legendary history of early Rome. (According to one account of it, Romulus invited the Sabines to a celebration of games, and the Roman youths utilized the occasion to carry off several of the Sabine women for wives). The chief town of the Sabines was Reate (now Rieti).

Sabra (sä′brạ). In the English ballads of *Saint George and the Dragon*, the maiden for whom he slew the dragon, and whom he afterward married.

Sabrina (sạ.brī′nạ). In British legend, the daughter of Locrine. She was drowned in the river Severn (from *Savarina* or *Sabrina*), with her mother, by Locrine's enraged widow, and became its nymph. Milton introduces her in *Comus;* Drayton in his *Polyolbion* and Fletcher in *The Faithful Shepherdess* tell of this transformation.

Sabrina. A Latin name of the river Severn, in Wales and England.

Sacharissa (sak.ạ.ris′ạ). A lady celebrated (c1634–38) by Edmund Waller in his poems. In real life, she was Lady Dorothy Sidney, later to be Countess of Sunderland.

Sachs (zäks), **Hans.** b. at Nuremberg, Germany, Nov. 5, 1494; d. there, Jan. 19, 1576. A German poet, the most celebrated of the meistersingers. He was a most prolific writer. From 1514, when he began to write, to 1567 he had by his own computation composed 4,275 meistersongs, 208 dramas, 1,558 narratives, fables, allegories, and the like, and seven prose dialogues (in all, 6,048 works, a number that was considerably increased in the succeeding two years of his literary activity). His dramas are tragedies, comedies, and carnival plays. Among them are his first tragedies, *Lucretia* (1527) and *Virginia* (1530), and the later ones *Julian der Abtrünnige, Melusine, Klytemnestra, Hürnen Seyfried* (1557); the comedy *Die ungleichen Kinder Evä* (1553); and the carnival play *Das Narrenschneiden*. In the Reformation he arrayed himself on the side of Luther, in praise of whom he wrote, in 1523, his *Wittenbergisch Nachtigall;* from 1524 are four prose dialogues counseling moderation in the religious strife. His literary material is drawn from all available sources of the time; he makes use of the Bible, of ancient history, legends, popular tales, and folk books.

Sackerson (sak′ẹr.sọn). [Also, **Sackarson.**] A famous performing bear seen at Paris Garden in Shakespeare's time. Slender mentions him to Anne Page in *The Merry Wives of Windsor* (I.i).

Sackville (sak′vil), **Charles.** [Titles: Baron **Buckhurst,** 6th Earl of **Dorset,** 1st Earl of **Middlesex.**] b. 1638; d. 1706. An English poet, patron of poets, and courtier. His poems include songs, ballads, and various satires. He was the patron and friend of such poets as Prior and Dryden.

Sackville, Thomas. [Titles: Baron **Buckhurst,** 1st Earl of **Dorset.**] b. at Buckhurst, Sussex, England, 1536; d. at London, April 19, 1608. An English poet and statesman. He entered the Inner Temple, was called to the bar, and was for many years one of Elizabeth's chief and most trusted councilors. It was Sackville who formally informed (1586) Mary, Queen of Scots, that she had been condemned to death. He was made Buckhurst in 1567, and Earl of Dorset at the accession of James I. His poems were the models for some of Spenser's best work, and his "Induction" to the *Mirror for Magistrates* (2nd ed., 1563) is now generally considered the best part of that book. He wrote, with Thomas Norton, the blank-verse tragedy *Gorboduc* (1562), usually classified as the earliest English tragedy.

Sackville-West (sak′vil.west′), **Edward** (**Charles**). b. Nov. 13, 1901—. An English novelist and biographer; nephew of V. Sackville-West. Author of the novels *Piano Quintet* (1925), *The Ruin* (1926),

Mandrake Over The Water-Carrier (1928), *Simpson: A Life* (1931), and *The Sun in Capricorn* (1934). His biographical and critical works include *The Apology of Arthur Rimbaud* (1927) and *A Flame in Sunlight* (1936; American title, *Thomas De Quincey*).

Sackville-West, V. [Full name, **Victoria Mary Sackville-West.**] b. at Knole Castle, Sevenoaks, Kent, England, March 9, 1892—. An English novelist and poet. In *Knole and the Sackvilles* (1922) she wrote an informal chronicle of her ancestors whose prominence dates back to the 16th century, when the family castle was presented by Queen Elizabeth to her lord treasurer, Thomas Sackville; *Passenger to Teheran* (1926) is an account of her travels in Bulgaria, Morocco, Hungary, and Persia with Harold Nicolson, journalist and diplomat, whom she married in 1913. She won (1927) the Hawthornden prize for *The Land* (1926), a verse chronicle, with lyrical interludes, of an English farmer's year. Her verse also includes *Poems of West and East* (1917), *Orchard and Vineyard* (1921), *King's Daughter* (1930), *Collected Poems* (1933), and *Solitude* (1938); among her novels are *Heritage* (1919), *The Dragon in Shallow Waters* (1921), *Grey Wethers* (1923), *Challenge* (1923), *The Edwardians* (1930), *All Passion Spent* (1931), *Family History* (1932), *The Dark Island* (1934), *Saint Joan of Arc* (1936), *Pepita* (1937), and *Grand Canyon* (1942); author also of the collections of short stories *The Heir* (1922) and *Thirty Clocks Strike the Hour* (1932), and of biographies of Aphra Behn and Andrew Marvell (1929); among her other works are *Twelve Days* (1928), *Sissinghurst* (1933), *Some Flowers* (1937), and the essays *Country Notes* (1939), *The Eagle and the Dove* (1943), and *The Garden* (1946).

Sacred and Profane Love: A Novel in Three Episodes. A novel by Arnold Bennett, published in 1905 and issued in revised form (1911) as *The Book of Carlotta*. Together with *Anna of the Five Towns* (1902) and *Leonora* (1903), it comprises the first "Five Towns" trilogy.

Sacred Band. A band of 300 Thebans formed to take part in the wars of the 4th century B.C. against Sparta.

Sacred Nine, The. A poetic epithet of the Muses.

Sacred Wood, The. A collection of critical essays by T. S. Eliot, published in 1920.

Sacripante (sä.krē.pän′tä). A character in the *Orlando Innamorato* of Boiardo and the *Orlando Furioso* of Ariosto.

Saddletree (sad′l.trē), **Bartoline.** In Sir Walter Scott's novel *The Heart of Midlothian*, an Edinburgh saddle-maker who fancies himself to have legal talent. He continually inflicts long discourses on his associates, and fails to understand that he is considered an insufferable bore.

Saddletree, Mrs. In Sir Walter Scott's novel *The Heart of Midlothian*, the wife of Bartoline Saddletree and a relative of Effie Deans (in whose fate she takes a considerable interest).

Sadducees (sad′ū.sēz). A religious and political party in Judea in the last centuries of its existence as a Jewish state. They were the rivals of the Pharisees. The name is probably derived from

Zadok, one of the leaders of the party. The Sadducees were recruited from among the aristocracy and the wealthy class. From them the officers of the state and army were taken. Contrary to the Pharisees, they placed secular interests above those of religion. They did not absolutely reject the tradition and the oral law, but considered only the ordinances which appeared clearly expressed in the Pentateuch as binding, regarding the traditional precepts as subordinate. In like manner they did not exactly deny the immortality of the soul, but repudiated the idea of judgment after death. Owing to this tenet and to their literal interpretation of the Mosaic code, they were very rigorous in the administration of justice. In the last struggle of Judea for independence, the Sadducees mostly sided with Rome. After the fall of Jerusalem, they vanish from history.

Sade (såd), **Donatien Alphonse François,** Comte **de.** [Called Marquis de Sade.] b. 1740; d. 1814. A French soldier, writer, and libertine. He served in the Seven Years' War, but was cashiered and sentenced to prison for his licentious conduct. Much of the rest of his life was spent in prisons in various parts of France, and he died in an insane asylum. His two novels, *Justine* (1791; full title, *Justine; ou, Les Malheurs de la vertu*) and *Juliette* (6 vols., 1797–98; full title, *Histoire du Juliette; ou, Les Prospérités du vice*), were, by reason of their obscenity, the cause of two sojourns in prison by their author. It is from him that sadism (the type of sexual perversion which gratifies itself by inflicting extreme pain upon the person or persons most attractive to the sadist) derives its name and original meaning.

Sad Fortunes of the Reverend Amos Barton (ā′mos bär′ton), **The.** A story by George Eliot. It first appeared in *Blackwood's Magazine* for January and February, 1857, and was afterward included in *Scenes of Clerical Life.*

Sadi (sä′dē). See **Saadi.**

Sadleir (sad′lėr), **Michael.** b. at Oxford, England, Dec. 25, 1888—. An English writer and publisher. He joined (1912) and became a director (1920) of Constable and Company, Ltd., publishers. He was also a member of the British delegation to the peace conference (1919) after World War I and of the secretariat (1920) of the League of Nations. Author of novels and critical works, including *Trollope: A Commentary* (1927), *Trollope: A Bibliography* (1928), *Bulwer and His Wife* (1931), *The Strange Life of Lady Blessington* (1933), *These Foolish Things* (1937), *Fanny by Gaslight* (1940), *Things Past* (1944), and *Forlorn Sunlight* (1947).

Sadler's Wells (sad′lėrz). A London theater that originated on the site of a late 17th-century resort in the vicinity of medicinal springs discovered (1683) on the property of a certain Mr. Sadler (at the time, this was a section not yet included within the densely populated area of the city). The original theater was built during the late 1720's and the first performance took place about 1730. Various later buildings replaced this original one, housing a considerable variety of types of entertainment (Kean appeared there, as did the great clown Grimaldi). In 1931 the building then standing was restored by Lilian Baylis, under whose aegis it be-

fat, fāte, fär, àsk, fāre; net, mē, hėr; pin, pīne; not, nōte, mõve, nôr; up, lūte, pùll; ŦH, then;

came a companion undertaking to the Old Vic (unlike the company of the Old Vic, however, it specializes in ballet and ballad opera).

Sado (sä′dō). A novel by William Plomer, published in 1931. It was issued in America under the title *They Never Come Back* (1932).

Sad Shepherd, The. An unfinished pastoral drama by Ben Jonson (published posthumously in 1641), on the subject of Robin Hood. It was completed by F. G. Waldron in 1783.

Sæhrimnir (sä.rim′nir). In Scandinavian mythology, the boar served and eaten daily at the banquets of Valhalla (its flesh is miraculously restored between the banquets).

Sæmund (sä′mụnd). b. c1055; d. 1133. An Icelandic scholar, long erroneously reputed to be the author of the *Elder* (or *Poetic*) *Edda*.

saga (sä′gạ). An ancient Scandinavian legend or tradition of considerable length, relating either mythical or historical events; a tale; a history: as, the *Volsunga Saga*.

"Sage of Chelsea" (chel′si), **the.** See **Carlyle, Thomas.**

Sagittary (saj′i.tär.i). A monster described in medieval romances of the Trojan War as a terrible archer, a centaur armed with a bow. He is said to have fought on the side of the Trojans, and, with his eyes of fire, to have struck men dead.

Saïd the Fisherman (sä.ēd′). A novel by Marmaduke Pickthall, published in 1903.

Sailing to Byzantium (bi.zan′shi.um, -ti-). A poem (1927) by W. B. Yeats, published in *The Tower* (1928), expressing old age's envy of vital youth, the desire of the soul to be freed from the body, and to live eternally in the remote and sensuous Byzantium.

"Sailor William." [Also, **"the Sailor King."**] A nickname of William IV (of England), who entered the Royal Navy as a midshipman in 1779 and remained formally (although for the most part in an honorary capacity) an officer on active duty until 1827.

Saint (sānt). For geographical and other proper names not found immediately below, see also under **St.** and **Ste.**

Saint Agnes's Eve (ag′nẹs.ẹz). A Christian feast, celebrated on the night of Jan. 20. It is especially a holiday for young maidens. It was supposed possible by various forms of divination for a girl on this night to see the form of her future husband. A narrative poem by John Keats, *The Eve of Saint Agnes*, is based on this tradition. It is also used by Tennyson in *Saint Agnes' Eve*.

Saint Agnes' Eve (ag′nẹs). A poem by Alfred Tennyson, published in 1842.

Saint Alban's (ôl′bạnz). See **St. Alban's.**

Saint Bartholomew (bär.thol′ọ.mū), **Massacre of.** In French history, a massacre of the Huguenots, commencing at Paris on the night of Aug. 23–24 (Saint Bartholomew's Day), 1572. The anti-Huguenot leaders were the Duke of Guise, the queen mother (Catherine de Médicis), and Charles IX. Coligny was the most famous victim, and the total number in France has been estimated at from 20,000 to 30,000. The occasion was the wedding festivities of Henry of Navarre. A religious war followed directly. It is disputed whether the massacre was suddenly caused by the discovery of Huguenot plots or had been long premeditated.

Saint Catharine's College (kath′ạ.rinz). One of the colleges of Cambridge University. It was founded in 1473 by Robert Wodelarke, who was chancellor of the university and provost of King's College.

Saint Cecilia's Day (sẹ.sil′yạz), **Ode for.** See **Alexander's Feast.**

Saint Cecilia's Day, Song for. A lyrical poem (1687) by John Dryden. It is sometimes confused with the *Ode for Saint Cecilia's Day*, better known as *Alexander's Feast*, written ten years later.

Saint Distaff's Day. See **Distaff's Day, Saint.**

Sainte-Beuve (saṅt.bėv), **Charles Augustin.** b. at Boulogne, France, Dec. 23, 1804; d. at Paris, Oct. 13, 1869. A French poet, literary critic, and historian. He began his studies in his native city, and completed them in Paris. On graduation he took a course in medicine, but gave it up a year later. A few book reviews brought him favorable notice in literary circles, and the friendship of Victor Hugo, among others. In 1827 he competed without success for a prize offered by the French Academy for a dissertation on the subject *Tableau de la poésie française au XVIᵉ siècle*. An improved edition of this work appeared in 1843, and is still considered a standard work on the subject and period in question. He was also a contributor to *La Revue de Paris*, *La Revue des Deux Mondes*, *Le Constitutionnel*, *Le Moniteur*, and *Le Temps*. The revolution of 1830 developed his political interest, and he became closely connected with *Le Globe* and *Le National*. His early work embraces some collections of poems, *Poésies de Joseph Delorme* (1829), *Consolations* (1830), and *Pensées d'août* (1837); also a novel, *Volupté* (1832). Of a more serious nature are *L'Histoire de Port-Royal* (1840–42) and *Chateaubriand et son groupe* (1849). His contributions to periodicals include most of his work as a critic. These so-called *Portraits* and *Causeries* have since been collected, and constitute his strongest claim to literary recognition. They are published as *Portraits littéraires* (1st series, 1832–39; 2nd series, 1844), *Portraits de femmes* (1844), *Portraits contemporains* (1846), *Causeries du lundi* (1851–57), *Nouveaux lundis* (1863–72), and *Premiers lundis* (1875). In 1845 Sainte-Beuve was elected to the French Academy. He gave a series of lectures on literary subjects at Lausanne in 1837 and at Liége in 1848. For a brief period thereafter he filled the chair in Latin poetry at the Collège de France. His last work was as an educator as done in connection with the lectureship he held (1857–61) at the École Normale. He was made senator in 1865.

Saint Edmund Hall (sānt ed′mund). One of the colleges of Oxford University. It was founded (c1226) by Edmund Rich, archbishop of Canterbury. Although commonly called Saint Edmund Hall, or Saint Edmund's, Edmund Hall is a more accurate name from the standpoint of history, as it was established before its founder was canonized. It is headed by a principal, who, since 1559, has been appointed by Queen's College, which acquired its property two years earlier. Of the various academic halls that once flourished, Saint Edmund is the only one that still survives, although it is no longer a separate foundation, but dependent on Queen's. As such, it is the only example of a system that is older than any of the college foundations.

Saint Elian's Well (ē'li.ạnz). A celebrated well in Denbighshire, Wales, known as "the head of the cursing wells," and associated with ancient superstition.

Sainte-Maure or **Sainte-More** (sȧṅt.mōr), **Benoît de.** See **Benoît de Sainte-Maure.**

Saint George and the Dragon. An English ballad of unknown date, preserved in several copies in Samuel Pepys's collection of some 2,000 old ballads at Magdalen College, Cambridge. It tells the story of Saint George's arrival in a country being ravaged by a dragon, which is propitiated with the daily sacrifice of a maiden. George comes upon the king's daughter, Sabra, placed before the dragon's cave, awaiting her fate; he questions her, kills the dragon, returns her to her father's house, and after being sent on various ill-intentioned death-errands, returns successful, marries the lady, and takes her home to England. The dragon-slaying episode and the story of George and Sabra is a close rendition of the story of the medieval romance *Bevis of Hampton*. The ballad as preserved in Percy's *Reliques of Ancient English Poetry* is a composite of two black-letter copies in the Pepys collection.

Saint Joan (jōn). A play (1923) by George Bernard Shaw, dealing with the trial and death of Joan of Arc. Shaw presents her as a social rebel who antagonizes both the Roman Catholic church and the English by her visions and her militant assertion of French nationalism. Warwick, a British lord, and Cauchon, the Catholic churchman with whom he debates, reveal the real reasons for their hatred of her. When national loyalty becomes a real and living thing, as it has for the Frenchmen whom Joan has led into battle, feudalism ends, and the power of the lords or king is threatened by a deeper allegiance to the ideal of the state. Cauchon, on the clerical side, sees in her claim of direct inspiration from God a threat to the spiritual supremacy of the church, which claims to be the sole mediator between God and the individual. Therefore to protect their different but equally basic interests, it is necessary that she be condemned to burn at the stake, branded as a witch.

Saint John's College (jonz). One of the colleges of Cambridge University. Dedicated to Saint John the Evangelist, it was founded in 1511 by Lady Margaret (who also founded Christ's College), Countess of Richmond and Derby, and the mother of Henry VII. It is noted for its four courts, of which the fourth is approached across the river Cam by a covered bridge known as the Bridge of Sighs. Its fine library, the gift of John Williams, bishop of London, contains, among other rarities, a copy of the 1540 Cranmer Bible.

Saint John's College. One of the colleges of Oxford University. It was founded in 1555 by Sir Thomas White, a London alderman, and a member of the Merchant Taylors' Company (for which reason it has always had a close connection with the Merchant Taylors' School, some of its best scholarships being restricted to boys of that school).

Saint Juliana (jö.li.an'ạ), **Saint Katherine** (kath'ẹrin), and **Saint Margaret** (mär'gạ.rẹt). See **Katherine Group.**

Saint Margaret's (mär'gạ.rẹts). A historic church in Westminster, London, founded by Edward I and modified by Edward IV. Here Sir Walter Raleigh and William Caxton were buried, and Milton was married. The church contains numerous stained-glass windows and other memorials to the great men who have been associated with it. It is one of the most fashionable churches in modern London, and a "marriage at Saint Margaret's" is a major event of high society.

Saint Mark's (märks). See **Mark, Basilica of Saint.**

Saint Martin's le Grand (mär'tinz lẹ grand). A monastery and church formerly at London, dating from very early times. In the second year of William the Conqueror it was exempted from ecclesiastical and civil jurisdiction. Its site is now occupied by the General Post Office.

Saint Mary le Bow (mār'i lẹ bō). [Also, **Bow Church.**] A church at London, on Cheapside, within the sound of whose celebrated bells all Cockneys are said to be born. It was designed by Wren, and begun in 1671. It stands over the Norman crypt of the older church, which was destroyed by the fire of 1666. The spire (235 ft. high) is especially admired, and has been pronounced the most graceful in outline and appropriate in detail of any erected since the medieval period.

Saint Mary's College. See **Winchester School.**

Saint Mary's the Great. The official university church at Cambridge, England, built between 1487 and 1519. It is in Perpendicular style.

Saint Mary the Virgin. The official university church at Oxford, England. The great tower is surmounted by a superb octagonal spire of 1300, with unusually rich pinnacles at the angles, rising in the form of steps. The existing choir dates from 1460, and the nave from 1488: they exhibit varied types of the Perpendicular. The south porch, with broken pediment and twisted columns, is of the 17th century.

Saint Mary Winton (win'tọn), **College of.** The former name of **New College.**

Saint Nicholas' clerks (nik'ọ.lạs). Highwaymen, a reference to Saint Nicholas as the patron of thieves; used by Gadshill in Shakespeare's *1 Henry IV* (II.i).

Saint Patrick for Ireland (pat'rik). A play by James Shirley, published in 1640 and produced in Ireland. It deals with the Christianizing mission of the saint in Ireland, and touches on the banishing of the serpents (including one in human form, the pagan priest, Archimagus) from the country.

Saint Patrick's Day. A holiday honoring Saint Patrick, the patron saint of Ireland. It falls on March 17, and is observed by the Irish as well as by many descendants of Irish settlers in other countries.

Saint Patrick's Day; or, the Scheming Lieutenant. A farce by Richard Brinsley Sheridan, produced in 1775.

Saint Patrick's Purgatory. In Christian legend, an earthly purgatory or place for the expiation of sins, granted to Saint Patrick by God so that Patrick could show the people how sinners were punished. The traditional entrance to it was a cave on an island in Lough Derg, Ireland. Here a church was built which became a famous place of medieval pilgrimage. The legend was given to the world in a manuscript in Latin, *Purgatorium Patricii*, written c1190 by Henry of Saltrey, an English monk. This purposes to describe a vision seen by an English knight on Lough Derg c1153.

Saint Paul's (pôlz). A cathedral at London, begun 1675, according to the designs of Sir Christopher Wren, in place of the old cathedral of the 11th–13th centuries, which was destroyed in the great fire of 1666. The cathedral was first used for divine service in 1697, and was completed in 1710. In plan and architecture it is akin to Saint Peter's at Rome, but only one half as great in area, and relatively longer and narrower. Its dimensions are 500 by 118 ft.; length of transepts, 250; inner height of dome, 225; height to top of cross, 364; diameter of dome, 112 ft. The exterior is classical, with two stories; the front and transepts are pedimented, and the former is flanked by bell-towers. The upper story on the sides is merely a mask, the actual structure of lofty nave and low aisles being the same as in a medieval cathedral. The dome is magnificent (some consider it to be the most imposing in existence). Its drum is surrounded by a range of Corinthian columns, and it is surmounted by a lantern. The interior is impressive from its size, and is not dwarfed like Saint Peter's by disproportionate size of its classical details. The vaulted crypt, like the church itself, contains many tombs of famous men. The modern reredos, in the Italian Renaissance style, is elaborately sculptured. It suffered no serious damage in World War II.

Saint Paul's Churchyard. The open space surrounding Saint Paul's Cathedral, London.

Saint-Pol (sänt.pôl′; French, san.pol), **Jehane**. A character in Maurice Hewlett's historical novel of the third Crusade, *The Life and Death of Richard Yea-and-Nay* (1900); she is later the Countess of Anjou.

Saint Ronan's Well (rō′nạnz). See **St. Ronan's Well.**

Saints and Sinners. A melodramatic play (1884) by Henry Arthur Jones.

Saintsbury (sānts′bėr.i), **George Edward Bateman.** b. at Southampton, England, Oct. 23, 1845; d. Jan. 28, 1933. An English literary critic and historian. He was educated at Oxford (Merton College), where he graduated in 1867. He was classical master at Elizabeth College, Guernsey (1868–74), and headmaster of the Elgin Educational Institute (1874–76). Soon after 1876 he established himself at London. He published a *Primer of French Literature* (1880), *Dryden* in the English Men of Letters series (1881), *A Short History of French Literature* (1882), *French Lyrics: Selected and Annotated* (1883), *Marlborough* in English Worthies (1885), a

History of Elizabethan Literature (1887), *Essays on English Literature* (1891), *Essays on French Novelists* (1891), *Miscellaneous Essays* (1892), *Corrected Impressions* (1895), *Nineteenth Century Literature* (1896), *The Flourishing of Romance and the Rise of Allegory* (1897), *Sir Walter Scott* (1897), *A Short History of English Literature* (1898), *Matthew Arnold* (1899), *A History of Criticism* (3 vols., 1900–04), *The Earlier Renaissance* (1901), *Loci Critici* (1903), *Minor Caroline Poets* (2 vols., 1905–06), *History of Elizabethan Literature* (1906), *A History of English Prosody* (Vol. I, 1906; Vol. II, 1908; Vol. III, 1910; condensed into *Historical Manual of English Prosody*, 1911), *History of XIX. Century Literature* (1906), and *The Later Nineteenth Century* (1907).

Saint Sepulchre (sep′ul.kėr). A church at Cambridge, England. A Norman building dating from 1101, it is the oldest of the four circular churches still surviving in England.

Saints' Everlasting Rest, The. A devotional work by Richard Baxter, published in 1650.

Saint's Progress. A novel by John Galsworthy, published in 1919. Set in the period of World War I, it offers a sympathetic portrayal of internal conflict in Edward Pierson, a clergyman.

Sairey Gamp (sā′ri gamp), **Mrs.** See **Gamp, Mrs. Sairey.**

Saki (sä′ki). Pseudonym of **Munro, Hector Hugh.**

Sala (sal′ạ), **George Augustus Henry.** b. at London, Nov. 24, 1828; d. Dec. 8, 1895. An English novelist and journalist. He was correspondent of the London *Telegraph* in the U. S. during the Civil War, in France in 1870–71, in Russia in 1876, and in Australia in 1885. Among his works are *A Journey Due North* (1858), the novel *Seven Sons of Mammon* (1862), *My Diary in America in the Midst of War* (1865), *A Journey Due South* (1885), *Things I Have Seen and People I Have Known* (1894), and *Life and Adventures of George Augustus Sala* (1895).

Saladin (sal′ạ.din). [Full name, **Salah-al-Din Yusuf ibn-Ayyub.**] b. at Tikrit, in what is now Iraq, c1138; d. at Damascus, Syria, in March, 1193. Sultan of Egypt and Syria. He became (c1169) vizier in Egypt, suppressed (1171) the Fatimite dynasty, was proclaimed (c1174) sultan, and conquered Damascus and the greater part of Syria. He endeavored to drive the Christians from Palestine, totally defeated (1187) them near Tiberias, taking prisoner Guy de Lusignan (king of Jerusalem), Châtillon (grand master of the Templars), and many others, and captured Acre, Jerusalem, Ashkelon, and other cities. The fall of Jerusalem brought to the scene a powerful army of Crusaders under Richard I (Richard of England the Lion-Hearted) and Philip II of France, which captured (1191) Acre. Richard took Caesarea and Jaffa, and forced (1192) Saladin to accept a truce for three years. Scott introduces Saladin in *The Talisman* disguised as the Arabian physician Adonbec and as Ilderim.

Saladyne (sal.ạ.din, -dīn). See under **Oliver.**

Salanio and Salarino (sạ.lä′ni.ō; sä.lạ.rē′nō). See **Solanio and Salerio.**

ḍ, d or j; ṣ, s or sh; ṭ, t or ch; ẓ, z or zh; o, F. cloche; ü, F. menu; ċh, Sc. loch; ṅ, F. bonbon.

Salathiel (sạ.lā'thi.ẹl). A romance by George Croly, published in 1827. It is a story of the Wandering Jew, here named Salathiel ben Sadi.

Salerio (sạ.ler'i.ō, -lir'-). See **Solanio and Salerio.**

Salisbury (sôlz'ber''i, -bėr.i). [Also, **New Sarum.**] A municipal borough and cathedral town in S England, the county seat of Wiltshire, situated ab. 22 mi. NW of Southampton, ab. 84 mi. SW of London by rail. It was known during the Middle Ages for its woolen manufactures, and at the end of the 14th century was the eighth largest town in England. About 1½ mi. away is Old Sarum, now in ruins, long one of the most notorious "rotten boroughs" in England (it sent two members to Parliament from 1295 to 1832, when the Reform Bill eliminated its franchise, despite the fact that for much of this time it had, literally, no population). The cathedral, considered by many to be the most beautiful of English ecclesiastical monuments, was begun in 1220 and finished in 1260, in a uniform and dignified early Gothic style. Salisbury and its environs have long figured in English literature, and in literary history. The residence of Penelope Devereux, the "Stella" of Sir Philip Sidney's *Astrophel and Stella* is within a few miles of the town, and, in more recent times, it figures in Charles Dickens's *Martin Chuzzlewit* (literary historians believe that the "famous old inn" at which John Westlock entertained Tom and young Martin Chuzzlewit was probably the White Hart, still standing in Salisbury).

Salisbury, Earl of. In Shakespeare's *2 Henry VI*, the historical Richard Neville. He is the enemy of Suffolk, whom he has banished, and also of Cardinal Beaufort, whose death he witnesses. He joins the Duke of York and fights at St. Albans. In *3 Henry VI*, Warwick says that the Yorkist side caused his death at Wakefield.

Salisbury, (3rd) Earl of. In Shakespeare's *King John*, the historical William de Longespée (or Longsword), illegitimate son of Henry II. Disapproving of John's second coronation and suspecting him of responsibility for Arthur's death, he resolves to join the Dauphin, but on learning of the French treachery returns to John.

Salisbury, (3rd) Earl of. In Shakespeare's *Richard II*, the historical John of Montacute (or Montagu), a loyal supporter of Richard. He tries to keep Richard's Welsh troops in order, and later he rebels against Henry IV, but is captured and executed.

Salisbury, (4th) Earl of. In Shakespeare's *Henry V*, the historical Thomas de Montacute (or Montagu). He is present at Agincourt. In *1 Henry VI*, he is killed by a cannon blast.

Salisbury Cathedral. The most beautiful of English churches, built 1220–60, in a uniform and dignified early Gothic style.

Salisbury Court Theatre. An old London theater. It was built in 1629 and became one of the principal playhouses. It was destroyed in 1649, and Duke's Theatre (Dorset Garden Theatre) took its place in 1671.

Salisbury Crags. A range of low cliffs in the SE quarter of Edinburgh, Scotland, on the W slope of Arthur's Seat. They range from 60 to 80 ft. in height.

Salisbury Plain. An extended rolling and elevated district in S England, in Wiltshire, lying between Salisbury and Devizes. Stonehenge, and the remains of many British and Roman camps are found here.

Sallust (sal'ust). [Full Latin name, **Gaius Sallustius Crispus.**] b. at Amiternum, in the country of the Sabines, Italy, c86 B.C.; d. c34 B.C. A Roman historian. He was elected tribune of the people in 52. In 50 he was expelled from the senate by the censors on the ground, according to some, of adultery with Fausta, the daughter of the dictator Sulla and wife of Titus Annius Milo, but more probably for political reasons, inasmuch as he was an active partisan of Caesar. He accompanied Caesar in 46 on his African campaign, at the conclusion of which he was appointed governor of Numidia, a post in which he is said to have amassed a fortune by injustice and extortion. He wrote *Catilina* or *Bellum Catilinarium*, and *Jugurtha* or *Bellum Jugurthinum*, both extant but marked by bias; only fragments exist of a history of Rome covering the period 78–67 B.C.

Sally Brass (sal'i bràs'). See **Brass, Sally.**

Sally (or Salley) in Our Alley. A popular ballad composed (1734) by Henry Carey. Considered trivial by most of Carey's contemporaries, it nevertheless won the praise of Addison and has survived as a popular song to this day (although Carey's original tune has been replaced by one taken from an older ballad).

Sally in Our Alley. A comedy by Douglas Jerrold, produced in 1826.

Sally Lunn (lun). A type of sweet bread, sliced warm and often served at tea time in England. It is named from the woman who is supposed to have originated and first sold it, at Bath in the 1780's.

Salmacida Spolia (sal.mạ.sī'dạ spō'li.ạ). A masque by William D'Avenant and Inigo Jones, performed in 1640 with King Charles and Queen Henrietta Maria in its cast.

Salmacis (sal'mạ.sis). In Greek mythology, the nymph of a fountain in Caria, which was said to make effeminate all who drank of it. In Ovid's *Metamorphoses*, she was united with Hermaphroditus into one bisexual deity.

Salmasius (sal.mā'shus, -zhus), **Claudius.** [Latinized name of **Claude de Saumaise.**] b. at Sémur, Côte-d'Or, France, April 15, 1588; d. Sept. 3, 1653. A French classical scholar. He succeeded his father as a counselor of the parliament of Dijon, but was ultimately deprived of this post because of his Protestant faith. He became (1631) a professor in the University of Leiden, a position which he occupied until his death. He exercised a virtual literary dictatorship throughout western Europe, and his advice was sought even in English and Scottish politics. In 1649 he defended the absolutism of Charles I of England in *Defensio regia pro Carolo I*, which elicited an answer from John Milton. Among his works are editions of Florus (1609), the *Augustan History* (1620), and *Plinianae exercitationes in Solinum* (1629).

Salmoneus (sal.mō'nẹ.us). In Greek mythology and legend, one of the six sons of the wind god,

Aeolus. In later Greek legend, he was a king of Elis who impersonated Zeus, pretending to cause lightning and thunder. He was killed by Zeus for this mockery, with a real thunderbolt.

Salome (sạ.lō'mẹ). In Biblical history, the daughter of Herodias, and wife of Philip the Tetrarch and later of Aristobulus. She caused the death of John the Baptist (the account is that she danced so well before her uncle Herod Antipas that he offered her a boon "unto the half of my kingdom," and Herodias, who had been insulted by John for her marriage to her brother-in-law Herod Antipas, told Salome to demand John's head).

Salome. A tragedy (1892) by Oscar Wilde, dealing with the well-known story of the beheading of John the Baptist at the request of Salome (who is portrayed by Wilde as a dissipated neurotic).

Salomo Sephardo (sạ.lō'mō se.fär'dō). See **Sephardo, Salomo.**

Salteena (sôl.tē'nạ), **Mr.** The hero of Margaret Mary (Daisy) Ashford's story *The Young Visiters, or Mr. Salteena's Plan*, written when the author was nine years old, but not published until 1919.

Saltwater Ballads. A collection of poems (1902) by John Masefield.

Salus (sā'lus). The Roman goddess of health and prosperity: in part identified with the Greek Hygeia.

Salvation Yeo (sal.vā'shọn yā'ọ). See **Yeo, Salvation.**

Sama-Veda (sä'mạ.vā'dạ). See under **Vedas.**

Sam Horrocks (sam hor'ọks). See **Horrocks, Sam.**

Samiasa (sạ.mī'ạ.sạ). In Byron's *Heaven and Earth*, a seraph in love with Aholibamah, the granddaughter of Cain.

Samient (sā'mi.ẹnt). In Spenser's *Faerie Queene*, the lady sent as an ambassador to Queen Adicia by Queen Mercilla. On Adicia's instructions, two knights insulted her, but she was avenged by Sir Artegal. Samient is meant to stand for the emissaries sent by the Dutch to Spain, and there imprisoned.

Sampson (samp'sọn). In Shakespeare's *Romeo and Juliet*, a servant of Capulet.

Sampson, Dominie. A homely and awkward schoolmaster in Sir Walter Scott's novel *Guy Mannering*.

Sampson, John. See **Awdelay** or **Awdeley, John.**

Sampson Brass (bràs). See **Brass, Sampson.**

Sampson Legend (lej'ẹnd), **Sir.** See **Legend, Sir Sampson.**

Sam Slick (sam slik'). See **Sayings and Doings of Samuel Slick, The.**

Samson (sam'sọn). In the Bible, the son of Manoah of the tribe of Dan, and the 15th in order of the "judges," or deliverers, of Israel. His exploits and adventures with the Philistines, the hereditary enemies of his people, are related in the Book of Judges, xiii–xvi. He revealed to Delilah that the secret of his great strength lay in his long hair which he never cut; and she betrayed him to the Philistines by cutting it off in his sleep. Thus they took him, blinded him, and chained him inside their temple. As his hair grew, his great strength re-

turned, and finally he pulled down the temple with his hands upon the heads of his enemies, and perished with them. This is one of the most famous stories in the world, embodying the ancient and worldwide folklore concept of the separable soul or vital power which abides apart in some animal or inanimate object.

Samson Agonistes (ag.ọ.nis'tēz). A tragic drama in blank verse by John Milton, printed in 1671. In its theme and style it reflects Milton's strong antipathy for the works of the various Restoration playwrights which then principally occupied the stage in London; the influence of the Greek and Roman classics, perhaps most obviously of the works of Euripides, is evident. In the opening portion Samson is seen resting before the prison at Gaza, moaning of his fallen state (thus setting the background for the play); in the second portion Manoa, Samson's father, announces that the Philistines have proclaimed a day of thanksgiving for their deliverance from Samson, and outlines his hope of ransoming his son from them (thus beginning the development toward the eventual tragedy); in the third portion we have the debate with Delilah, a woman of dazzling beauty (who is likened to Circe, as the incarnation of sensuality), whose remorse is as false as it is superficially appealing, and who is finally dismissed by the chorus as "a manifest Serpent by her sting—till now conceal'd"; the fourth portion opens with Harapha's summons to Samson to show his strength at the temple of Dagon, which Samson at first refuses, but finally accepts; in the last portion Samson's death is reported, thus crushing the hopes of Manoa, who has returned joyfully hoping for Samson's release.

Samson Carrasco (kạ.ras'kō; Spanish, kär.räs'kō). See **Carrasco, Samson.**

Samuel (sam'ụ.ẹl). A Hebrew prophet. He was the son of Elkanah and Hannah, of the tribe of Ephraim (according to 1 Chron. vi. 27, 34, of the tribe of Levi), and grew up in the sanctuary of Shiloh, under the eyes of the high priest Eli. In his early youth he felt himself called to the exalted vocation of prophet, and obtained a place in the history of Israel second only to that of Moses. He was the preserver of the work of Moses, reuniting the people and averting the threatening decay and internal corruption. After the fall of the sanctuary of Shiloh and the defeat of Israel by the Philistines, Samuel rallied the people in Mizpah, renewed the covenant with Jehovah, and repelled the Philistines. He thus became the religious and political reformer of Israel. To spread a healthy and pure religious life in Israel, he established the so-called schools of prophets, a special feature of which was the cultivation of sacred poetry and song. His sons Joel and Abijah shared with Samuel the management of the affairs of the people. They were disliked, being accused of misusing their power. In addition to this, need for a leader in case of war became more and more felt. This resulted in the demand by the people for Samuel to place a king at the head of the Israelite community. With a heavy heart the aged prophet acceded to the wish of the people, in which he saw the loss of their liberty and independence, and anointed Saul. Saul's disobedience in the war against Amalek caused a rupture between Samuel

---

ḍ, d or j; ṣ, s or sh; ṭ, t or ch; ẓ, z or zh; o, F. cloche; ü, F. menu; ċh, Sc. loch; ṅ, F. bonbon.

and himself, and his virtual deposition. Later Samuel anointed David as king, and this is the last act recorded of him. He died at an advanced age in Ramah. The Biblical books of Samuel owe their title to the circumstances that they begin with the history of the prophet; they were not composed by him, nor does his history form the chief part of their contents. Like the books of Kings, the books of Samuel formed originally one book; the division was introduced in the old Greek and Latin versions. The books of Samuel comprise the history of Israel from the birth of Samuel to the death of David (which, however, is not distinctly recorded in the book), i.e., a period of more than 100 years. The first book relates the birth of Samuel, the establishing of the monarchy in Israel, and the conflict between Saul and David, closing with the death of Saul. The second book gives the history of David's reign.

Samuel Pickwick (pik′wik). See **Pickwick, Samuel**.

Samuel Povey (pō′vi). See **Povey, Samuel**.

Samuel Slick of Slickville. See **Sayings and Doings of Samuel Slick of Slickville, The**.

Samuel Slumkey (slum′ki), **the Honourable.** See **Slumkey, the Honourable Samuel**.

Samuel Titmarsh (tit′märsh). See **Titmarsh, Samuel**.

Sam Weller (sam wel′ẽr). See **Weller, Sam**.

San Celestino (sän chä.les.tē′nō). A historical novel on a religious theme by Monsignor Count Francis Browning Drew Bickerstaffe-Drew under the pseudonym John Ayscough.

Sancho Panza (san′chō pan′za; Spanish, sän′chō pän′thä). The "round, selfish, and self-important" squire of Don Quixote, in Cervantes's satirical romance of that name.

Sanchuniathon (san.kū.nī′a.thon). [Also, **Sanchoniathon** (san.kō.nī′a.thon).] A legendary chronicler of ancient Phoenicia, said to have lived before the Trojan War, whose works (allegedly founded upon records preserved in the temples) Philo Byblius pretended to have translated.

Sandabar (san.da.bär′). The *Mishle Sandabar*, or *Parables of Sandabar*, a medieval collection of tales in Hebrew. They are substantially the same book as the Greek *Syntipas, the Philosopher*, and the Arabic *Romance of the Seven Viziers*. The work was translated into Latin at least early in the 13th century, and became very popular in almost every language of Western Europe under the name of the *Romance of the Seven Sages*.

Sanderson (san′dẽr.son), **Robert.** b. either at Sheffield or Gilthwaite Hall, near Rotherham, Yorkshire, England, Sept. 19, 1587; d. at his palace of Buckden, Huntingdonshire, England, Jan. 29, 1663. An English bishop and writer. He was educated at Lincoln College, Oxford, took orders in 1611, in 1631 was a royal chaplain, and was regius professor of divinity at Oxford (1646–48). At the Restoration (1660) he was created bishop of Lincoln. The *Cases of Conscience*, his most celebrated work, composed of deliberate judgments on points of morality, was published after his death. His *Compendium of Logic* was published in 1618.

Sandford and Merton (sand′ford; mẽr′ton), **History of.** A popular book about education, by Thomas Day, published in 1783–89. It was written to prove that persuasion and gentle guidance are the best means of education, as exemplified in Sandford, a farmer's son. Merton is the rich gentleman's son who is raised in the old school of education by force and pressure, and is a thoroughly disagreeable person.

Sandhurst (sand′hẽrst). A parish in Berkshire, England, ab. 33 mi. SW of London. It is the seat of the Royal Military College, and near it is the Staff College.

Sandra Belloni (san′dra be.lō′ni). A novel by George Meredith, published in 1864. The work originally appeared under the title *Emilia in England*. Its sequel is *Vittoria* (1866).

Sandringham (sand′ring.am). An English royal residence, near the coast of Norfolk, England, N of King's Lynn.

Sandys (sandz), **George.** b. at York, England, 1578; d. at Bexley Abbey, Kent, England, in March, 1644. An English traveler and translator. He was educated at Oxford, and began his travels in 1610. His records were a valuable contribution to early geography and ethnology. In 1615 he published a valuable account of a journey to Greece, Asia Minor, Palestine, and Egypt. He went to Virginia as colonial treasurer in 1621. He built the first water mill, the first ironworks, and the first ship in Virginia. He returned to England in 1624. He subsequently printed various religious works and a translation of Ovid's *Metamorphoses* (1621–26), and paraphrased the Psalms, the Book of Job, Ecclesiastes, and the Lamentations of Jeremiah.

Sandys, Lord. [Also, **Sir William Sandys** (or **Sands**).] In Shakespeare's *Henry VIII*, a courtier.

Sandys, Oliver. [Pseudonym of Mrs. **Marguerite Florence Hélène Evans**; additional pseudonym, Countess **Barcynska**; maiden name, **Jervis**.] b. at Henzada, Burma, 1894—. An English novelist. Her books include *The Garment of Gold, The Green Caravan, Jinks, Mops, Whatagirl, Deputy Pet, Miss Paraffin,* and *Learn to Laugh Again*. As Countess Barcynska, she published *Honeypot, Tesha, Under the Big Top, God and Mr. Aaronson, That Trouble Piece, Joy Comes After, Luck Is a Lady,* and *We Lost Our Way*.

Sandys, Tommy. The title character in Barrie's *Sentimental Tommy*.

Sanglier (sang′gli.ẽr), **Sir.** In Spenser's *Faerie Queene*, a knight who cut off the head of his lady, and is compelled by Sir Artegall always to carry the head before him as a grim token of his crime.

Sanhedrin (san′hē.drin, san′ē-). A body of men, or two distinct bodies, formerly at Jerusalem, having religious and judicial powers and functions. From the Mishna it would appear that the Sanhedrin was a kind of academic body, composed of teachers of the law, and concerned with interpretation of the scriptures; but in the New Testament and in the writings of Josephus it appears to have been a kind of high court, over which a high priest presided. To what extent the Sanhedrin was involved in the trial and death of Jesus Christ is not at all clear.

Jesus certainly appeared before civil authorities, namely Herod and Pilate, and before ecclesiastical authorities, namely Annas and Caiaphas, and it is generally supposed that the latter sat in judgment in his capacity as head of the Sanhedrin; but on the other hand, some scholars assert that the proceedings with respect to Jesus were irreconcilable with the procedures before the Sanhedrin as we know of them from Jewish sources.

Sannazaro (sän.nä.dzä'rō), **Jacopo.** b. at Naples, Italy, July 28, 1458; d. there, April 27, 1530. An Italian poet. He wrote in Italian the first modern pastoral romance, *Arcadia* (1504). He also wrote sonnets, and, in Latin, *De partu virginis* and other poems.

Sansfoy, Sansjoy, and Sansloy (sanz.foi', sanz.joi', sanz.loi'; French, sän.fwà, sän.zhwà, sän.lwà). In Spenser's *Faerie Queene*, three brothers, whose names respectively mean Faithless, Joyless, and Lawless. The first is killed by the Red Cross Knight; the second is defeated by him (but is saved from death by Duessa); the third runs off with Una and kills her lion (this act is thought to represent Queen Mary's bloody suppression of the Protestants).

Sangraal (sang.grāl'). [Also, **Sangreal** (sang'grē.äl).] The Holy Grail. See **Grail.**

Santa Claus or **Santa Klaus** (san'tạ klôz). A corruption of the Dutch name for Saint Nicholas (which is *Sant Nikolaas*). He is identified with Saint Nicholas as the patron saint of children. As dispenser of Christmas gifts he is depicted as a white-bearded, merry, plump little man in a red suit and cap with a huge pack of presents on his back. Traditionally he drives over the rooftops in a reindeer-drawn sleigh, and delivers his gifts via the chimneys.

Santa Maura (sän'tä mou'rä). See **Leukas.**

Sapho and Phao (saf'ō; fā'ō). A comedy (1584) by John Lyly. It is an allegory on the alleged courtship of Elizabeth by the Duke of Alençon.

Sapper (sap'ėr). Pseudonym of **McNeile, Cyril.**

Sapphic stanza (saf'ik). In prosody, a stanza consisting of three Sapphic hendecasyllabics, to the last of which an Adonic ($- \smile \smile | - \smile$) is subjoined. This strophe was one of the most frequent forms of versification in ancient lyric poetry, and was a favorite with Sappho, Alcaeus, and Horace.

Sappho (saf'ō). fl. c600 B.C. A Greek lyric poet. She appears to have been a native of Mytilene, in Lesbos, where she probably spent her life. According to Suidas, her father's name was Scamandronymus, her mother's Cleis. She had a brother, Larichus, who in his youth acted as cupbearer in the prytaneum of Mytilene, an office assigned only to beautiful youths of noble birth. Another brother, Charaxus, a merchant, became enamored of the courtesan and slave Doricha, surnamed Rhodopis, at Naucratis, in Egypt, and purchased her freedom at an immense price. So much is known of the brothers from Sappho's poems. She also mentions a daughter, named Cleis. Her husband's name is said to have been Cercolas or Cercylas of Andros. She was a contemporary of Alcaeus, with whom she maintained friendly relations, and with whom she shared the supremacy of the Aeolian school of lyric poetry. She appears to have given instruction

in the art of versification, and to have been the center of a literary coterie of women. There is no foundation for the story that she threw herself from the Leucadian promontory (Leucas) into the sea, out of love for a beautiful youth, Phaon, who disdained her advances. She wrote nine books of lyric poems, all of which are lost except an ode to Aphrodite and a number of fragments. She was called "the tenth Muse."

Sapsea (sap'sẹ), **Thomas.** [Called "Mr. Sapsea."] In Charles Dickens's unfinished novel *The Mystery of Edwin Drood*, a bustling, loud-talking auctioneer and Cloisterham town official. So impressed by his magnificence was the timid woman he married that she could reply to his proposal only (and with a sigh): "Oh Thou."

Saracens (sar'ạ.sẹnz). A name applied in the Middle Ages to the nomads of the Syro-Arabian desert who harassed the Roman frontiers, afterward applied in a broader sense to all Arabs, and eventually to all Moslems. It finally referred specifically to the Moslems with whom the medieval Christian states were at war, including those encountered in the Crusades.

Saracen's Head. An old London inn that figures in Charles Dickens's novel *Nicholas Nickleby* as the place where the cruel schoolmaster Squeers gathers his unfortunate pupils for their trip to Yorkshire, and also as the place where the Browdies spent their honeymoon. The original inn was torn down in 1868. There is a Saracen's Head also in *The Pickwick Papers*, situated at Towcester (this establishment, called the Pomfret Arms since 1831, still survives).

Sarah Battle (sār'ạ, sā'rạ, bat'l), **Mrs.** See **Battle, Mrs. Sarah.**

Sarah Ormerod (ôrm'rod), **Mrs.** See **Ormerod, Mrs. Sarah.**

Sardanapalus (sär''dạ.nạ.pā'lus). A tragedy by Byron, published in 1821 and acted in 1834 (in an adaptation by Charles Kean). It is the story of the last of the Assyrian kings, conceived of by Byron as a man detesting conquest or tyranny, a champion of free rational inquiry.

Sardanapalus. The Greek name of Assurbanipal, king of Assyria from 668 B.C. to c626 B.C.

Sard Harker (särd här'kėr). A novel (1924) by John Masefield, combining mystery, exotic adventure, and picturesque description.

Sardou (sàr.dö), **Victorien.** b. at Paris, Sept. 7, 1831; d. there, Nov. 8, 1908. A French dramatist, author of numerous popular successes, largely in the field of comedy and satire.

Sarpedon (sär.pē'dọn). In Greek legend, a Lycian prince; a son of Zeus. He was an ally of the Trojans in the Trojan War, during which he fell by the hand of Patroclus. According to one legend, his body was, at the command of Zeus, anointed with ambrosia by Apollo and carried to Lycia for burial. In post-Homeric legend, Sarpedon was a son of Zeus and Europa whom Zeus allowed to live for three generations. This Sarpedon was either confused with the above or said to be his grandfather.

Sarti (sär'tē), **Caterina.** [Called **Tina.**] In George Eliot's tale "Mr. Gilfil's Love-Story," included in

Scenes of Clerical Life, a beautiful young Italian girl who loves, desperately but in vain, the unscrupulous Captain Wybrow. She finally marries Mr. Gilfil, but dies shortly thereafter.

Sartor Resartus (sär'tor rĕ.sär'tus). A satirical work by Thomas Carlyle, published serially (1833–34) in *Fraser's Magazine* and in book form in 1835. It purports to be the work of a certain "Professor Teufelsdröckh," a German teacher of "Things in General," who is used by Carlyle as a means of voicing Carlyle's disillusionment with the society of his day (to the reader who knew German an inkling that Teufelsdröckh might espouse rather unusual views became apparent with the mere reading of his name; it means "Devil's dung" in German). Ostensibly, Teufelsdröckh is concerned with the review of a work on the "Philosophy of Clothes" (the title of the work means, in English, the "Tailor Re-tailored"), but this is simply a device to permit Carlyle to cut through the superficial aspect (or "clothing") of the world and its customs to various basic points of objective truth. It was Carlyle's bitter conviction that practically all institutions and manners of society were corrupted, or fatally compromised, by sham and expedient self-delusion. As his spokesman for this point of view, Teufelsdröckh first tells how, in early life, he fell in love with a beautiful girl, and was persuaded of his immortality by a kiss, only to have her forsake him for a man of wealth. In his subsequent endeavor to find the basic meaning of life he goes through three phases: the Everlasting No, the Center of Indifference, and the Everlasting Yea. By this third phase Carlyle means that the individual should not hope to find truth except in terms of the present, of what is here and now, and that the truth-seeking person has the consequent duty to deal with the world of the present on a basis of absolute and rigorous honesty, shunning that which is illusionary and rejecting that which is spurious.

Sassenach (sas'ę.naċh). In Scotland and some parts of Wales, an Englishman. The word derives from the Gaelic (meaning "Saxon"), and formerly conveyed an implication of dislike or contempt.

Sassoon (sạ.sön'), **Siegfried.** [Full name, **Siegfried Lorraine Sassoon;** pseudonyms: **Saul Kain, Pinchbeck Lyre, Sigmund Sashûn** (sä.shön').] b. Sept. 8, 1886—. An English poet and biographer. His verse includes *Twelve Sonnets* (1911), *The Daffodil Murderer* (1913; published under the pseudonym Saul Kain), *The Old Huntsman* (1917), *Counter-Attack* (1918), *Picture Show* (1920), *Satirical Poems* (1926), *The Heart's Journey* (1928), *Poems of Pinchbeck Lyre* (1931), *Vigils* (1935), and *Rhymed Ruminations*. He is author also of the autobiographical *Memoirs of a Fox-Hunting Man* (1928) which won the Hawthornden prize and James Tait Black memorial prize, *Memoirs of an Infantry Officer* (1930), and *Sherston's Progress* (1936), three volumes which were collected as *Memoirs of George Sherston* (1937). Among his later works are the autobiographical *The Old Century and Seven More Years* (1938), *The Weald of Youth* (1942), and *Siegfried's Journey, 1916–20* (1945), and the biography *Meredith* (1948).

Satan (sā'tạn). The personification of evil; the great adversary of man; the devil, and lord of hell. In Jewish, Christian, and Mohammedan legend, he is the fallen angel who defied God. He is usually depicted as a tailed black demon with horns, cloven hoofs, and sometimes with bat's wings. In medieval church art he is shown as a serpent with a human face. The medieval European gentleman-devil (as typified by Mephistopheles) has pointed ears and a dashing mustache, and wears a long black cape. There are many euphemisms for his name (dating from a time when it was believed that speaking of him might cause him to appear). He is traditionally regarded as the cause of all evil in the world, and temptation to worldly delights is his greatest weapon. In various European folklores, he is so busy that his grandmother has to run hell in his absence; he is given to making contracts with men, taking their souls in exchange for a specific period of wealth or fame or happiness; he is a master musician on bagpipe, fiddle, or banjo, and when the devil plays all are compelled to dance; he leads the witches on their Sabbat.

Satanic School. In 19th-century English literary history, a name first given by Robert Southey to those writers whose works (and political views) were in opposition to what he considered to be the proper principles of morality and the Christian religion. Among the most prominent were Byron, Moore, Shelley, Bulwer-Lytton, Paul de Kock, and Victor Hugo.

satire. A literary work intended to arouse ridicule, contempt, or disgust at abuses and follies of man and his institutions, and aimed at the correction of malpractices by inspiring both indignation and laughter with a mixture of criticism and wit. The models for much satire in English literature were classical writers such as Juvenal, Horace, and Petronius, as well as medieval fabliaux and beast epics. Strong elements of satire are present in Chaucer, in the Prologue to *The Canterbury Tales*, and to mention one, in the "Nun's Priest's Tale." Didactic prose and verse of the following centuries frequently attacked vices and abuses in a satirical manner; however, satire in England probably first became most developed in drama with the plays of Ben Jonson and the later Restoration dramatists. In verse, Dryden sustained both criticism and witty cleverness, particularly in *Absalom and Achitophel*, and pointed the way to the flourishing of satire in the 18th century. Major satirists of that century were Pope, Fielding, and Johnson. Because satire is classical in spirit and usually attacks society and institutions, the Romantic poets, on the whole more interested in the individual, wrote little satire. Byron, however, is a notable exception. Of the 19th-century writers, Thackeray is probably the most prominent satirist. Among 20th-century writers, Shaw, Aldous Huxley, Evelyn Waugh, to name a few, have displayed a marked satiric spirit.

The first and most bitter inuectiue against vice and vicious men was the Satyre.
(Puttenham, *Arte of Eng. Poesie*.)

The one [sort of readers] being ignorant, not knowing the nature of a satire (which is, under feigned private names to note general vices), will

needs wrest each feigned name to a private un-
feigned person.

> (Marston, *Scourge of Villanie*,
> "To Him That Hath Perused Me.")

Adjourn not that virtue unto those years when
Cato could lend out his wife, and impotent Satyrs
write Satyrs against Lust.

> (Sir T. Browne, *Letter to a Friend*.)

**Satiromastix, or the Untrussing of the Humorous
Poet** (sat″i.rọ.mas′tiks). A play by Thomas Dekker, acted in 1601 and printed in 1602. It is Dekker's
answer to Ben Jonson's *Poetaster*, which is thought
to have contained a direct attack on him. There is
a formal plot concerning the times of William II of
England (William Rufus).

Saturn (sat′ẽrn). In Roman mythology, a god of
agriculture, believed to have been a king in the
reign of Janus, who instructed the people in agriculture, gardening, and the like. His reign was sung
by the poets as "the golden age." He became early
identified with the Cronus of the Greeks. Ops, the
personification of wealth and plenty, and sometimes Rhea, the mother goddess, were his consorts.

Saturnalia (sat.ẽr.nā′li.ạ). In Roman religion, the
festival of Saturn, celebrated in the middle of
December as a harvest observance. It was a week
of feasting and mirthful license and enjoyment for
all classes, extending even to the slaves.

Saturninus (sat.ẽr.nī′nus). In Shakespeare's *Titus
Andronicus*, the son of the late emperor of Rome.
When Titus withdraws from the election, Saturni-
nus is chosen emperor. He marries Tamora, Queen
of the Goths. Discovering the body of his brother
Bassianus, he orders Titus's sons executed for his
murder. He kills Titus and is himself killed by
Lucius.

Satyrane (sat′i.rān). The son of a satyr in Spenser's
Faerie Queene. Bred in the woods, he shows the
might and bravery of man in his natural state. He
delivers Una from the satyrs.

Satyricon (sạ.tir′i.kon). See **Euphormionis Satyricon.**

Saul (sôl). fl. c1025 B.C. The first king of the
Hebrews; son of Kish of the tribe of Benjamin. He
was anointed by Samuel after the people demanded
a king. The story of Saul's moody jealousy of his
musician David, of the friendship of David and
Saul's son Jonathan that prevented David from
attacking Saul, and of Saul's consultation with
Samuel's spirit in the cave of the Witch of Endor
combine to make one of the most moving tales in
the Bible. His reign was occupied by wars against
the Philistines, Amalekites, and other Gentile nations. He fell in battle against the Philistines on
Mount Gilboa. He was succeeded by David.

Saul. An oratorio by G. F. Handel, composed in
1738 and produced at London in 1739. It contains
the famous *Dead March*.

Saul. A poem (1845) by Robert Browning, published in his collected works.

Saul Kane (kān). See **Kane, Saul.**

Saul of Tarsus (tär′sus). The name by which Saint
Paul is first referred to in the New Testament.
Acts, vii. 58.

Saumaise (sō.mez′), **Claude de.** See **Salmasius,
Claudius.**

Saunders (sôn′dẽrz, sän′-), **Hilary Aidan St. George.**
See **Beeding, Francis.**

Saunder Simpcox (sôn′dẽr sim′koks). See **Simpcox,
Saunder.**

Savage (sav′ạj), **Captain.** In Frederick Marryat's
novel *Peter Simple*, the stern, but just and very
able, naval officer with whom Peter first serves.
The character was based on that of Thomas Cochrane, the officer under whom Marryat himself
had served as a midshipman, and certain of his
attributes appear in the characters of naval commanders in Marryat's later books.

Savage, Richard. b. at London, c1697; d. at Bristol,
England, Aug. 1, 1743. An English poet. He maintained that he was the illegitimate son of Richard
Savage, 4th Earl Rivers, and the Countess of Macclesfield (but the son born of that connection is
thought actually to have been dead long before the
claim was made). He owes his literary fame to the
life which Samuel Johnson wrote (1744). His life
was disreputable, and he abused the charity of his
friends. During his last years he lived on a pension
allowed him by Alexander Pope, and finally died
miserably in a debtors' prison. He published a
poem on the Bangorian Controversy (1717),
adapted a play (*Woman's a Riddle*) already translated from the Spanish (1717), published *Love in a
Veil* (1719; a comedy), *Sir Thomas Overbury* (1724),
in which he played (very indifferently) the hero,
The Bastard (1728; a poem addressed to his supposed mother), and *The Wanderer* (1729). In 1775
his works were collected and published with Johnson's *Life of Savage* prefixed.

Savile (sav′il), **Sir George.** [Title, Marquis of **Halifax**.] b. Nov. 11, 1633; d. at London, April 5, 1695.
An English statesman, author, and orator. He was
made privy councillor (1672) and in 1680 caused
the rejection of the Exclusion Bill debarring the
Duke of York (later James II), as a papist, from
succeeding to the throne. He was lord privy seal
(1682–85 and 1689), went as an ambassador from
James II to William of Orange, and changed his
allegiance to William. He was the chief of the party
called the "Trimmers" (referring to those who
trimmed their course to events). His pamphlet *The
Character of A Trimmer* (1688) is one of the first
political tracts. His *Advice to a Daughter* was published in 1688 and his *Miscellanies* in 1700.

Savile, Sir Henry. b. near Halifax, England, Nov.
30, 1549; d. at Eton, England, Feb. 19, 1622. An
English classical scholar and mathematician. He
was warden of Merton (Oxford) after 1585, and
provost of Eton after 1596. Besides mathematical
works he published *Rerum Anglicarum scriptores
post Bedam* (1596), an edition of Chrysostom, and
others. He was one of the translators of the Authorized Version (King James Version) of the Bible.
The Savile professorships of geometry and astronomy at Oxford were endowed by him in 1619.

Saviolina (sav″i.ọ.lī′nạ). A character in Ben Jonson's comedy *Every Man Out of His Humour*.

Savonarola (sav″ọ.nạ.rō′lạ; Italian, sä″vō.nä.rō′lä),
Girolamo. b. at Ferrara, Italy, Sept. 21, 1452;
executed at Florence, May 23, 1498. An Italian

ḍ, d or j; ṣ, s or sh; ṭ, t or ch; ẓ, z or zh; o, F. cloche; ü, F. menu; ch, Sc. loch; ṅ, F. bonbon.

moral, political, and religious reformer. He became a Dominican monk at Bologna in 1475, and in 1482 removed to Florence, where he became prior of St. Mark's in 1491. He brought about a religious revival by his denunciation of the vice and corruption prevalent both in the church and in the state, and was one of the chief instruments in the overthrow of the Medici and the restoration of the republic in 1494. He was for a time virtually dictator of Florence, but incurred the enmity of Pope Alexander VI, whom he had denounced, and was in consequence excommunicated in 1497. A series of events tended to diminish his hold on the populace, culminating (April 7, 1498) in a promised ordeal by fire in which one of his disciples intended to test himself against a Franciscan opponent of Savonarola. The huge crowd present was furious when the ordeal was put off by a rain squall and vented its rage on Savonarola. He took refuge in St. Mark's, which was stormed the next day. He was arrested at the altar, and put to death (strangled and then burned) at the instance of the Pope.

Savoy (sa̯.voi'), **the.** A former London palace. On Feb. 12, 1246, a grant of land lying between the "Straunde" and the Thames was made by Henry III to Peter of Savoy, uncle of Queen Eleanor, and he built the palace there. Peter died and left his property to the friars of Montjoy, who sold the palace to Queen Eleanor in 1270. In 1284 she gave it to Edmund, Earl of Lancaster, and later it became the town seat of the dukes of Lancaster. When the Savoy was occupied by John of Gaunt in 1376, it was twice attacked by a mob and again by Wat Tyler's followers in 1381, who completely destroyed the palace. It was rebuilt c1505 as a hospital and endowed by the will of Henry VII, suppressed by Edward VI, refounded by Mary Tudor, and finally dissolved by Elizabeth. The French Protestants had a chapel here from the time of Charles II till c1737: this is the origin of the name Savoy given in the 18th century to the psalm tune now known as *Old Hundredth*. The Savoy Theatre was built near here on the Strand, and opened in 1881 (it was here that the D'Oyly Carte Company first performed the works of Gilbert and Sullivan, whence the epithet "Savoyard" since applied to members of that group). A hotel now covers part of the site of the former palace.

Savoyard (sa.voi.ärd'). See under **Savoy, the.**

Savoy Operas, The. A name for the succession of comic operas by W. S. Gilbert and Arthur Sullivan, produced at the Savoy Theatre, London. Among these were *Patience, Iolanthe, The Mikado, Ruddigore, The Yeomen of the Guard,* and *The Gondoliers.*

Sawles Warde (soul'es wär'de; modernized, sōlz wôrd). See under **Katherine Group.**

Sawyer (sô'yėr), **Bob.** A rollicking, though impecunious, young medical student in Dickens's *Pickwick Papers.*

Sawyer, Mother. The "witch of Edmonton" in the play of that name by John Ford, Thomas Dekker, William Rowley, and others.

Saxnot (säks'nōt). In Germanic mythology, a name of the god of war, appearing in Anglo-Saxon as a son of Woden (Odin).

Saxo Grammaticus (sak'sō gra̯.mat'i.kus). fl. in the 13th century. A Danish historian. Little is known with certainty of his personal history, except that he was a clerk, and that his father and grandfather fought under Waldemar I of Denmark. He had the surname Longus, but is commonly known as Grammaticus because of his fluent style as a writer. His history is written in Latin, and was undertaken at the instance of Archbishop Absalon, whose secretary he probably was. Parts of the work, from internal evidence, were written before 1202; he is supposed to have died shortly after the year 1208. The history consists of 16 books: the first nine are purely legendary; the two following are partly legendary; authentic history begins with the 12th book. The whole ends with the year 1186. The material for the earliest part was provided by oral traditions, myths, legends, and poems, most of which have otherwise been lost, although a few have been preserved in the original Old Norse form. Among others of the kind it contains the Hamlet (Amleth) legend, of which it is the single extant source. The oldest edition is that of Kristiern Pedersen, Paris, 1514.

Saxons (sak'sonz). A Germanic people of the lower Elbe valley, first mentioned by Ptolemy in the 2nd century. They were a marauding people who extended their holdings southward and westward. They first landed in Britain c449 with the Angles and Jutes. Their chief kingdom in England was Wessex, in the middle Thames valley and the regions adjoining it to the south and west. When Northumbria, most powerful of the Anglian kingdoms of the north, fell to the Danes in the middle of the 9th century, it was this Saxon kingdom which took the lead as the chief non-Danish power in England, and in the later 9th century, under King Alfred, it produced a considerable body of scholarly literature.

Saxon Shore. That portion of the E and S British coast which was exposed to forays of Saxon pirates at the time of the Roman occupation. The Saxon Shore was guarded by a force of Roman soldiers, whose commander enjoyed the title of Comes Litoris Saxonici, or Count of the Saxon Shore, and whose jurisdiction extended from Sussex to Norfolk.

Say (sā), **Lord.** In Shakespeare's *2 Henry VI*, the Lord Treasurer. Cade captures him and accuses him of various crimes against the populace. He is executed and his head put on a pole.

Sayers (sā'ėrz, sārz), **Dorothy L.** [Full name, **Dorothy Leigh Sayers.**] b. 1893—. An English writer of detective fiction, poetry, drama, and essays. Her detective novels, featuring Lord Peter Wimsey, include *Whose Body?* (1923), *Strong Poison* (1930), *Hangman's Holiday* (1933), *Murder Must Advertise* (1933), *The Nine Tailors* (1934), *Gaudy Night* (1935), *Busman's Honeymoon* (1937), and *In the Teeth of the Evidence* (1939). Among her collections of essays are *Begin Here* (1940), *The Mind of the Maker* (1941), *Unpopular Opinions* (1946), and *Creed or Chaos?* (1947). Author also of *Op. 1* (1916), in verse, and of the plays *The Zeal of Thy House* (1937), *The Devil to Pay* (1939), and *The Just Vengeance* (1946). Her translation of Dante's *Inferno* appeared in 1949.

fat, fāte, fär, ȧsk, fâre; net, mē, hėr; pin, pīne; not, nōte, mõve, nôr; up, lūte, pull; ᴛʜ, then;

Sayings and Doings of Samuel Slick of Slickville, The. [Also, **The Clockmaker.**] A series of sketches (1837–40) by the Canadian writer T. C. Haliburton, about a shrewd and humorous Yankee clockmaker and peddler.

Scaevola (sē'vọ.lạ, sev'ọ-), **Gaius Mucius.** A Roman hero. According to legend, when Lars Porsena was besieging Rome in 509 B.C., Scaevola, concealing a dagger about his person, went to the king's camp with the intention of putting him to death, but killed instead a royal secretary whom he mistook for Porsena. He was threatened with death by fire unless he revealed the details of a conspiracy which he said had been formed at Rome for the purpose of assassinating Porsena, whereupon he thrust his right hand into a sacrificial fire burning on an altar hard by, and permitted the flames utterly to consume the flesh and bones. This extraordinary demonstration of disregard for physical pain so excited the admiration of Porsena that he ordered Scaevola to be released. The story, which is perhaps as widely known as the one about the Spartan boy who remained impassive while a fox devoured his entrails, probably stems from an etiological legend hinging upon the name Scaevola, which means "left-handed."

Scala (skä'lä), **Bartolomeo della.** See under **Escalus.**

Scala, Cane Grande della or **Can Francesco della.** [Called **Can Grande.**] b. at Verona in 1291; d. at Treviso, July 22, 1329. A sovereign prince of Verona and chief of the Ghibellines in Lombardy. He was appointed imperial vicar of Verona by the emperor Henry VII. He was the most illustrious of his line, and conquered Vicenza, Padua, and Treviso. He is famous as the patron of Dante.

scald or **skald** (skald, skôld). An ancient Scandinavian poet; one who composed poems in honor of distinguished men and their achievements, and recited and sang them on public occasions. The scalds of the Norsemen answered to the bards of the Britons or Celts.

So proudly the Scalds raise their voices of triumph,
As the Northmen ride over the broad-bosomed
  billow.   (W. Motherwell, *Battle-flag of Sigurd.*)

I heard his scalds strike up triumphantly
Some song that told not of the weary sea.
    (William Morris, *Earthly Paradise*, I.18.)

Scale of Perfection. A Middle English prose work of the late 14th century by Walter Hilton, written for a nun who had become a recluse. It describes the weaknesses of the flesh, the means of overcoming them, and the quiet ecstasy of the mystic experience, reflecting the influence of Richard Rolle of Hampole.

Scales (skālz), **Gerald.** In Arnold Bennett's novel *The Old Wives' Tale*, the man with whom one of the heroines, Sophia, elopes.

Scales, Lord. In Shakespeare's *2 Henry VI*, the commander of the Tower who is solicited for aid during the rebellion of Cade. In *1 Henry VI*, a messenger reports that he has been captured at Patay.

Scaliger (skal'i.jẽr), **Joseph Justus.** b. at Agen, France, Aug. 5, 1540; d. at Leiden, Jan. 21, 1609. A Protestant scholar; son of J. C. Scaliger. He studied at Bordeaux and Paris, traveled in Italy, England, and Scotland, lectured (1572–74) in Geneva, lived with his patron Louis de Chastaigner, Lord of La Roche Pozay, and became (1593) professor at Leiden. By his *De emendatione temporum* (1583) and *Thesaurus temporum* (1606) he became the founder of modern chronology. He edited Catullus, Propertius, Tibullus, and others, doing pioneer work in modern textual criticism of the classics. His *Opuscula varia* were edited by J. Casaubon in 1610.

Scaliger, Julius Caesar. b. 1484; d. 1558. An Italian philologist. He abandoned an early career as a soldier because of his health, received training as a physician, and settled in France, where he presently concerned himself with various matters of scholarship and literary criticism (although he was also a practicing physician). His most famous work is his *Poetics* (1561).

Scamander (skạ.man'dẽr). [Also: **Xanthus;** modern Turkish, **Menderes, Küçük Menderes.**] In ancient geography, a river in Mysia, Asia Minor. It rose near Mount Ida and emptied into the Hellespont near Troy. According to legend its water made the hair a beautiful color and for this reason Venus, Minerva, and Juno bathed in it in preparation for the contest before Paris for the golden apple. Length, ab. 60 mi.

Scandinavians. The natives or inhabitants of Scandinavia (Norway, Sweden, Denmark, and Iceland).

scansion (skan'shọn). The measuring of a verse by feet in order to see whether the quantities are duly observed.

Scapin (skạ.pañ; Anglicized, skä'pin). The wily intriguing valet in Molière's comedy *Les Fourberies de Scapin*, a model for similar characters in many 17th-century English comedies.

Scaramouche (skar'ạ.mösh; French, skȧ.rȧ.mösh). The French name of the old Italian stock comedy character, Scaramuccia. The character was introduced into France c1640 by an Italian actor, Tiberio Fiurelli (1608–96). The name was applied to the titular hero of a tremendously popular novel written by Raphael Sabatini in 1921, but Sabatini's Scaramouche is in most respects the reverse of the blustering clown originally associated with the name.

Scarborough (skär'bur''ọ, -bẽr.ọ). A municipal borough, seaport, and seaside resort in NE England, in the North Riding of Yorkshire, on the North Sea ab. 36 mi. NE of York, ab. 230 mi. N of London by rail. The ruins of its ancient castle, founded in 1136, are situated on a promontory NE of the town. Piers Gaveston was captured here in 1312.

Scarlet (skär'lẹt), **Will.** In the English Robin Hood ballad cycle, one of the chief companions of Robin Hood. His name also occurs as Scadlock, Scarlock, and Scathlock. In one of the ballads he is mentioned as Robin Hood's nephew.

Scarron (skȧ.rôn), **Paul.** b. at Paris, 1610; d. there, Oct. 14, 1660. A French burlesque poet and dramatist. As a result of a serious accident (c1638), he was for much of his life a paralytic, deprived of the use of his lower limbs. At about the same time as

ḍ, d or j; ṣ, s or sh; ṭ, t or ch; ẓ, z or zh; o, F. cloche; ü, F. menu; ċh, Sc. loch; ṅ, F. bonbon.

this accident his father died, leaving him without any share in the patrimony. He obtained some pensions and sought besides to help himself along by means of his pen. He attempted the burlesque style, and made a success of it in his first publication, *Le Typhon, ou la Gigantomachie* (1644). His style of writing became at once the fashion; this made the more acceptable his comedies *Jodelet, ou le maître valet* and *Les Trois Dorothée, ou Jodelet soufleté* (1645), and his farce *Scènes du capitan Matamore et de Boniface pédant* (1647). In 1648 he began the publication of *Virgile travesti*. Then he wrote some stinging pamphlets, among others *La Mazarinade*, and scored a great success with his *Roman comique* (1651). The following year Scarron married Françoise d'Aubigné, who later became Madame de Maintenon. During the last period of his life he wrote several short stories, *Nouvelles tragi-comiques* (1654), one of which (*L'Hypocrite*) underlies Molière's *Tartuffe*, and composed also his best comedies, *Don Japhet d'Arménie* (1653), *L'Écolier de Salamanque* (1654), and *Le Marquis ridicule* (1656), and two plays, *La Fausse Apparence* and *Le Prince corsaire* (1662), which appeared posthumously.

Scarus (skar′us). In Shakespeare's *Antony and Cleopatra*, a friend of Antony. He describes the flight of Cleopatra's fleet at Actium, and remains loyal to Antony.

Scatcherd (skach′ėrd), **Lady.** In Anthony Trollope's novel *Doctor Thorne* and very briefly in *Framley*, the unassuming, industrious wife of Sir Roger Scatcherd, loyal to her husband, but ill at ease in her position as the wife of a baronet.

Scatcherd, Mary. [Married name, **Tomlinson.**] In Anthony Trollope's novel *Doctor Thorne*, the sister of Sir Roger Scatcherd. She is seduced by young Henry Thorne, who is therefore murdered by Roger (at this time still a simple stonemason).

Scatcherd, Sir Louis Philippe. In Anthony Trollope's novel *Doctor Thorne*, the heir of Sir Roger Scatcherd, who strives (but fails) to make a gentleman of him. He has inherited all his father's vices, and none of his strength: "he had begun life by being dissipated without being generous; and at the age of twenty-one he had already suffered from delirium tremens. . . . His voice [was] a cross between that of an American trader and an English groom."

Scatcherd, Sir Roger. One of the principal characters in Anthony Trollope's novel *Doctor Thorne*. A greedy and brutal man, he has forced his way upward from the humble position of a stonemason to a position of wealth and power, and has been made a baronet. He eventually dies of alcoholism.

scenario (sẹ.när′i.ō, -nä′ri-). **1.** A skeleton libretto of a dramatic work, giving the general movement of the plot and the successive appearances of the principal characters.
2. The plot itself of such a work.

scene. 1. A stage; the place where dramatic pieces and other shows are performed or exhibited; that part of a theater in which the acting is done.

Giddy with praise, and puff'd with female pride,
She quits the tragic scene.
(Churchill, *Rosciad.*)

Our scene precariously subsists too long
On French translation and Italian song.
(Pope, Prol. to Addison's *Cato*, 1. 41.)

2. The place in which the action of a play is supposed to occur; the place represented by the stage and its painted slides, hangings, etc.; the surroundings amid which anything is set before the imagination.

In fair Verona, where we lay our scene.
(Shak., *R. and J.*, Prol.)

Asia, Africa, and Europe are the several scenes of his [Vergil's] fable.
(Addison, *Spectator*, No. 357.)

3. One of the painted slides, hangings, etc., used on the stage of a theater to give an appearance of reality to the action of a play. These are of several kinds, and are known, according to their forms and uses, as *flats, drops, borders* or *soffits*, and *wings*.

By Her Majesty's Command no Persons are to be admitted behind the scenes.
(Quoted in Ashton's *Social Life in Reign of Queen Anne*.)

4. A division of a play or of an act of a play, generally so much as represents what passes between the same persons in the same place; also, some particular incident or situation represented in the course of a play.

At last, in the pump-and-tub scene, Mrs. Grudden lighted the blue-fire, and all the unemployed members of the company came in . . . in order to finish off with a tableau.
(Dickens, *Nicholas Nickleby*.)

Behind the scenes, back of the visible stage; out of sight of the audience; among the machinery of the theater; hence, having information or knowledge of affairs not apparent to the public.

You see that the world is governed by very different personages to what is imagined by those who are not behind the scenes. (Disraeli.)

Carpenter's scene, a short scene played near the footlights, while more elaborate scenery is being set behind.—**Set scenes,** scenes on the stage of a theater made up of many parts mounted on frames which fit into each other, as an interior with walls, doors, windows, fireplace, etc., a garden with built-up terraces, etc.

Scenes of Clerical Life. A series of three tales by George Eliot, published in 1857. The first is *The Sad Fortunes of the Reverend Amos Barton*. It deals with an untutored and tactless clergyman who wins the affection of his parishioners through his misfortunes and because of the sweetness of his wife Milly. The second is *Mr. Gilfil's Love-Story*, the tale of Maynard Gilfil, a man whose nature is warped by an unhappy love. The third story is *Janet's Repentance*, and deals with one man's fight for religious belief in the industrial community of Milby.

Schamir (shä.mēr′). [Also, **Shamir.**] A mysterious worm which, according to Persian and other legends adopted by the Jews and woven around the legends of Solomon, was able to cut through the hardest stone (supposedly Solomon built the Temple with the aid of the Schamir, the stones of which were not hewn by human hands).

Scheherazade (shẹ.her.ạ.zä′dẹ). [Also: **Shahrazad, Sheherazade.**] In *The Arabian Nights' Entertainments*, the daughter of the grand vizier and wife of the sultan of India. The tales which she told him each night were of such great interest that he postponed taking her life from day to day in order to hear more, and finally repealed the law condemning to death each morning his bride of the previous night. It was this story that inspired Rimsky-Körsakov's symphonic suite *Scheherazade* (Opus 35).

Schelling (shel′ing), **Friedrich Wilhelm Joseph von.** b. at Leonberg, Würtemberg, Jan. 27, 1775; d. at Ragatzt, Switzerland, Aug. 20, 1854. A German philosopher. He was educated at Tübingen, became professor at Jena in 1798, and at Würzburg in 1803, and occupied various official positions at Munich (1806–41). He also lectured at various times at Stuttgart and Erlangen, and was lecturer (1841–46) at the University of Berlin. Schelling, the philosopher of the romantic school, associated with Fichte, the Schlegels (he married Caroline Schlegel after she was divorced by her husband), and Goethe, began as a disciple of Fichte, but afterward chose his material from so diametrically opposed a thinker as Hegel to develop his own concepts; his philosophy is his own despite the apparent borrowing. The ideal, in his view, is a development of the real; mind or consciousness, as well as the absolute, is part of nature, and all existence is a unity, the various levels of which need explanation and correlation. Schelling thus attempted to find a middle ground between the realists and the transcendentalists. His works include *Der Erste Entwurf eines Systems der Naturphilosophie* (1799), *Der transcendentale Idealismus* (1800), *Darstellung meines Systems der Philosophie* (1801), *Bruno* (1802), *Philosophie und Religion* (1804), and *Menschliche Freiheit* (1809). His collected works were published in 14 volumes (1856–61).

Schiff (shif), **Sydney.** See **Hudson, Stephen.**

Schiller (shil′ẻr), **Johann Christoph Friedrich von.** b. at Marbach, Germany, Nov. 10, 1759; d. at Weimar, Germany, May 9, 1805. A German poet, dramatist, and historian. His literary career began in 1781 with the publication of the tragedy *Die Räuber*, the plan of which he had conceived as early as 1778. He was not able to find a publisher, and was obliged to print the work at his own expense, but the following year it was successfully produced at Mannheim. His second drama, which finally appeared in 1783, after having been twice rejected by the theater direction at Mannheim, was *Fiesco* (full title, *Die Verschwörung des Fiesco zu Genua: republikanisches Trauerspiel*). At Bauerbach he lived until July, 1783, under the name of Dr. Ritter, engaged upon a third tragedy which he at first called *Luise Millerin*, but which was published in 1784 under the name of *Kabale und Liebe*. In 1783 he returned to Mannheim to accept the position of theater poet with a stipend of 300 florins, for which he was to furnish three plays a year. To eke out his support he founded a journal called *Die rheinische Thalia*. His connection with the theater lasted only until November, 1784, when he resigned. In 1785, with the advice and assistance of Christian Gottfried Körner, the father of the

poet Karl Theodor Körner, he left Mannheim for Leipzig, where he arrived in April. Shortly thereafter he moved to the little village of Gohlis, nearby, and then, that same year, accompanied Körner to Dresden; here, and in the village of Loschwitz, where his friend had a villa, he lived until 1787. In 1786 three lyrical poems had appeared in the *Thalia:* "Freigeisterei der Leidenschaft," "Resignation," and "An die Freude," the last written at Gohlis. In the garden house at Loschwitz he completed the drama *Don Carlos*, begun at Mannheim and finally published in 1787. Unlike the preceding dramas, which are all in prose, this, like its successors, is written in iambic pentameter. To the Dresden period belongs, further, a novel that was never completed, called *Der Geisterseher*. In 1787, having grown tired of his life at Dresden, he removed to Weimar, and then in 1789 to Jena. In 1788 appeared his first historical work, the *Geschichte des Abfalls der Niederlande*. Belonging also to this early time at Weimar are the poems *Die Götter Griechenlands* and *Die Künstler*. In 1789 he was called as professor extraordinary of history, but without a stipend, to the University of Jena. The succeeding year (1790) he married Charlotte von Lengefeld, having previously been granted, on his application, a small stipend by the Duke of Weimar. During 1790–93 appeared his second historical work, the *Geschichte des dreissigjährigen Kriegs*. In 1794 falls the beginning of the intimate association with Goethe, which had a marked influence upon both poets. In 1795, with the coöperation of Goethe, he founded the journal *Die Horen*, which was continued down to 1798. In 1796 the annual *Der Musenalmanach* was begun under his editorship; it was published until 1800. In it appeared the satiric epigrams, the famous *Xenien*, written in collaboration with Goethe, and a number of his most celebrated poems, among them "Der Handschuh," "Der Ring des Polykrates," "Ritter Toggenburg," "Der Taucher," "Die Kraniche des Ibykus," "Der Gang nach Eisenhammer," "Der Kampf mit dem Drachen," "Das Eleusische Fest," and (1800) "Das Lied von der Glocke," the most popular of all his poems. In 1799 another drama had been completed, and the following year it was revised for publication. This is the trilogy *Wallenstein*, which consists of the prelude *Wallensteins Lager, Die Piccolomini*, a drama in five acts, and *Wallensteins Tod*, also in five acts. In 1798, further, he gave up his professorship at Jena and went back to Weimar, which was henceforth his home. The succeeding years were characterized by extraordinary dramatic productiveness. The tragedy *Maria Stuart* appeared in 1801. *Die Jungfrau von Orleans*, which he called "a romantic tragedy," followed in 1802. This same year he was ennobled by the emperor Francis II. In 1803 appeared also *Die Braut von Messina*, with the subtitle *Die feindlichen Brüder: Trauerspiel mit Chören;* and finally, in 1804, the drama *Wilhelm Tell*. Still another tragedy, *Demetrius*, was left uncompleted at his death. His death in 1805 resulted from a lung disease of many years' duration. His life may be divided into three periods. The first is that of his youth from 1759 to 1785 when he moved to Leipzig: in this period fall the "Storm and Stress" dramas *Die Räuber, Fiesco,* and

---

ḍ, d or j; ṣ, s or sh; ṭ, t or ch; ẓ, z or zh; o, F. cloche; ü, F. menu; ċh, Sc. loch; ṅ, F. bonbon.

Kabale und Liebe, and the lyric poems published in his *Anthologie* of 1782. A second period is that of scientific production, in reality a time of research, from 1785 down to his intimate association with Goethe in the publication of the *Horen:* in this period fall, most especially, *Don Carlos*, his historical works, and several philosophical and aesthetic treatises, the principal among them being that on *Naive und sentimentalische Dichtung*. A third and last period is from 1794 until his death in 1805. This is the time of his greatest productivity: in it fall the best of his poems, of which there are many besides the ballads mentioned, and the most important of his dramas.

Schism, Great. Forty years' division (1378–1417) between different parties in the Roman Catholic Church, which adhered to different popes. The end of the so-called Babylonian Captivity at Avignon came in 1378 when Gregory XI returned to Rome. He died soon afterward, however, and the Roman populace, fearful that the papacy would again leave Rome, demanded the election of an Italian as pope. The conclave elected Urban VI, who soon proved unsuitable. Asserting that the election had been forced from them by threat of force, a number of the cardinals met (August, 1378) at Angani, nullified Urban's election, and chose in his place Clement VII, who in 1379 established his court at Avignon. The Avignon papacy was supported, primarily for political reasons, by France, Castile, Aragon, Naples, and Scotland. Clement was succeeded by Benedict XIII; Urban by Boniface IX, Innocent VII, and Gregory XII. Within the church the conciliar movement, maintaining that the pope was subject to the decisions of a general council, gained strength as it became apparent that the Schism would continue. At the Council of Pisa (1409) both Gregory XII and Benedict XIII were declared deposed and Alexander V was elected. Alexander died in 1410 and John XXIII was chosen in his place. Since both the popes at Avignon and at Rome refused to resign, there were now three claimants for the tiara and, despite the general adherence to John XXIII, a further step was felt to be needed. In 1414 John reluctantly called the Council of Constance and Martin V was chosen pope; Gregory XII resigned in response to the Council's call, both John XXIII and Benedict XIII refused to give up their claims and had to be deposed, but the Great Schism was ended.

Schlegel (shlā′gel), **August Wilhelm von.** b. at Hanover, Germany, Sept. 8, 1767; d. at Bonn, Germany, May 12, 1845. A German poet and critic; brother of Friedrich von Schlegel. He studied at Göttingen, and was subsequently a tutor for three years at Amsterdam. Returning thence to Germany, he devoted himself wholly to literature until 1798, when he was made professor of literature and aesthetics at the University of Jena. He had founded, with his brother Friedrich Schlegel, the critical journal *Athenaeum*, which became the organ of the romantic school in Germany. In 1801 he left Jena for Berlin, where in 1803–04 he delivered lectures on literature. After 1804 he traveled extensively, and was in France, Italy, Austria, and Sweden, the greater part of the time in the company of Madame de Staël. In 1818 he was made professor of aesthetics and literature at the Univer-

sity of Bonn. He was several times in France, and in 1823 in England, engaged in Oriental studies. He wrote distichs, romances, sonnets, odes, and elegies. His first volume of poems appeared in 1800. His tragedy *Ion* (1803), which was produced at Weimar, was not successful. His work as a critic, and particularly as a translator, is of especial importance. His *Spanisches Theater* appeared in 1803–09; *Vorlesungen über dramatische Kunst und Litteratur*, delivered originally at Vienna, were published in the period 1809–11; his translation of Shakespeare, afterward continued by Dorothea Tieck and Wolf von Baudissin, appeared between 1797 and 1810. From 1823 to 1830 he published the *Indische Bibliothek* a periodical devoted to Oriental languages, and printed several Sanskrit texts. His complete works were published at Leipzig (1846–47) in 12 volumes.

Schlegel, Caroline Albertine Dorothee. [Maiden name, **Michaelis;** married names, **Böhmer, Schlegel, Schelling;** often called **Caroline Schlegel-Schelling.**] b. at Göttingen, Germany, Sept. 2, 1763; d. at Maulbronn, Germany, Sept. 7, 1809. A German romanticist. She was a central figure of the Jena group, not through literary works (of which she produced none) but through her personality and correspondence. After the death (1788) of her first husband, the physician Franz Wilhelm Böhmer, she led a turbulent life, mainly at Mainz while that city was occupied by the French and under siege by the Prussians. She was subsequently (1795) married to August Wilhelm von Schlegel, whose home at Jena became a focus of early German romanticism mainly through her influence. She was divorced in 1803 and married Schelling, whom she followed to Munich.

Schlegel, Dorothea. [Maiden name, **Mendelssohn.**] b. at Berlin, Oct. 24, 1763; d. at Frankfort on the Main, Germany, Aug. 3, 1839. A German writer; daughter of Moses Mendelssohn and wife of Friedrich von Schlegel. Her original prename was Veronika, but when Schlegel preferred Dorothea she adopted that. She was married to Simon Veit when she met Schlegel; she left her husband to live with Schlegel. She was the original of the heroine in Schlegel's *Lucinde*. She retold the old French story of *Lothar und Maller* (1805) and wrote in imitation of Goethe's *Wilhelm Meister* her novel *Florentin* (1801).

Schlegel, Friedrich von. b. at Hanover, Germany, March 10, 1772; d. at Dresden, Germany, Jan. 12, 1829. A German author and critic; brother of August Wilhelm von Schlegel. He studied at Göttingen and Leipzig and was for a short time (1800–02) an instructor at Jena. At Paris, where he went to study Oriental languages, he edited the magazine *Europa*. As a result of his Paris studies he brought out his treatise *Über die Sprache und Weisheit der Indier* (1808). At Vienna, where he settled in 1808, he became secretary of the state chancery. He was ennobled by the Pope, and was legation counselor with the Austrian delegation at the Frankfort Diet. Schlegel's real significance lies in his connection with German romanticism. He was the virtual founder of the German romantic school, the precepts for which he laid down in the *Athenaeum*, which he and his brother edited. He had actually arrived at these ideas through his studies of Greek culture, on which he wrote several brilliant essays. His own artistic creations include the so-called novel *Lucinde* (1799) and the tragedy *Alarcos* (1802).

Schliemann (shlē′män), **Heinrich.** b. at Neu-Buckow, in Mecklenburg-Schwerin, Germany, Jan. 6, 1822; d. at Naples, Italy, Dec. 27, 1890. A German archaeologist and traveler. He acquired considerable wealth as a merchant, and traveled extensively in Europe and in the East. He became especially famous, however, for his explorations of Greek sites and antiquities. From 1870 to 1882 he explored the site of ancient Troy, making many discoveries, and began similar work in 1876 at Mycenae, in 1881 at Orchomenus, and in 1884 at Tiryns. He wrote *La Chine et le Japon* (1866), *Ithaka, der Peloponnesus und Troja* (1869), *Trojanische Altertümer* (1874), *Mykenä* (1878), *Ilios* (1881), *Orchomenos* (1881), *Reise in der Troas* (1881), *Troja* (1883), and *Tiryns* (1886).

Scholar-Gypsy, The. A poem (1853) by Matthew Arnold, in which he incorporates the Oxford legend of the poor scholar who gave up the "sick hurry" of ordinary life to wander with the Gypsies.

scholasticism (skọ.las′ti.sizm). The Aristotelian teaching of the medieval schools and universities, and similar teaching in Roman Catholic institutions in modern times, characterized by acknowledgment of the authority of the church, by being largely, if not wholly, based upon the authority of the church fathers, of Aristotle, and of Arabian commentators, and by its stiff and formal method of discussion. It consisted of two distinct and independent developments, the one previous the other subsequent to the discovery of the extra-logical works of Aristotle in the last part of the 12th century. Scholasticism should be considered as arising about 1000 A.D., and is separated by a period of silence from the few writers between the cessation of the Roman schools and the lowest ebb of thought (such as Isidorus, Rhabanus, Gerbert, writers directly or indirectly under Arabian influence, Scotus Erigena and other Irish monks, the English Alcuin, with his pupil Fridigisus, etc.), writers marked by great ignorance, by a strong tendency to materialize abstractions, by a disposition to adopt opinions quite arbitrarily, but also by a certain freedom of thought. The first era of scholasticism was occupied by disputes concerning nominalism and realism. It naturally falls into two periods, since the disputants of the 11th century took simple and extreme ground on one side or the other, the nominalistic rationalist Berengarius being opposed by the realistic prelate Lanfranc, the Platonizing nominalist Roscellin by the mystical realist Anselm; while in the 12th century the opinions were sophisticated by distinctions until they cease to be readily classified as nominalistic and realistic. The scholastics of the latter period included Peter Abelard (1079–1142); Gilbert of Poitiers (died 1154), one of the few writers of the 12th century ever quoted in the 13th; Peter Lombard (died 1164), compiler of the four books of "Sentences," or opinions of the fathers, which was the peg on which much later speculation was hung as commentary; and John of Salisbury (died 1180), an

elegant and readable author. For more than a generation after his death the schoolmen were occupied with studying the works of Aristotle and the Arabians, without producing anything of their own. Then began the second era of scholasticism, and this divides itself into three periods. During the first, which extended to the last quarter of the 13th century, Alexander of Hales (died 1245), Albertus Magnus (1193–1280), and Saint Thomas Aquinas (died 1274) set up the general framework of the scholastic philosophy, while Petrus Hispanus (perhaps identical with Pope John XXI, who died 1277) wrote the standard textbook of logic for the remainder of the Middle Ages, and Vincent of Beauvais (died about 1264) made an encyclopedia which is still found in every library of pretension. During this period the University of Paris received a thorough organization, and thought there became exclusively concentrated upon theology. The second period, which lasted for about a century, was the great age of scholastic thought, and it may be doubted whether the universities of western Europe have at any subsequent time been so worthy of respect as when Duns Scotus (died 1308) and his followers were working up the realistic conception of existence, while "Durus" Durandus (died 1332), Occam (died about 1349), and Buridanus (died after 1350) were urging their several nominalistic theories, and other writers, now so forgotten that it is useless to name them, were presenting other subtle propositions commanding serious examination. During this period the scholastic forms of discussion were fully elaborated—methods cumbrous and inelegant, but enforcing exactitude, and conformed to that stage of intellectual development. The third period, extending to the time of the extinction of scholasticism, early in the 16th century, presented somewhat different characters in different countries. It was, however, everywhere marked by the formal perfectionment of systems, and attention to trivial matters, with decided loss of vitality of thought. Among the innumerable writers of this time may be mentioned Albert of Saxony (14th century), Pierre d′Ailly (1350–1425), Gerson (1363–1429), and Eckius, adversary of Luther.

scholiast (skō′li.ast). One who makes scholia; a commentator; an annotator; especially, an ancient grammarian who annotated the classics.

The title of this satire, in some ancient manuscripts, was "The Reproach of Idleness"; though in others of the scholiasts it is inscribed "Against the Luxury and Vices of the Rich."
(Dryden, tr. of Persius's *Satires*, iii., Arg.)

The Scholiasts differ in that.
(Congreve, *On the Pindaric Ode*, note.)

scholium (skō′li.um). [Plural, **scholia, scholiums.**] A marginal note, annotation, or remark; an explanatory comment; specifically, an explanatory remark annexed to a Latin or Greek author by an early grammarian. Explanatory notes inserted by editors in the text of Euclid's *Elements* were called scholia, and the style of exposition resulting from this was considered by later writers so admirable that they deliberately left occasion for and inserted scholia in their own writings. A geometrical scholium is, therefore, now an explanation or reflection inserted into a work on geometry in such

---

ḍ, d or j; ṣ, s or sh; ṭ, t or ch; ẓ, z or zh; o. F. cloche; ü, F. menu; ċh, Sc. loch; ñ, F. bonbon.

a way as to interrupt the current of mathematical thought.

School for Scandal, The. A comedy by Richard Brinsley Sheridan, produced at the Drury Lane Theatre, London, May 8, 1777.

schoolman. A master in one of the medieval universities or other schools; especially, a Christian Peripatetic of the Middle Ages; a scholastic.

The Schoolmen reckon up seven sorts of Corporal Alms, and as many of Spiritual.
(Stillingfleet, *Sermons*, II.vii.)

If you want definitions, axioms, and arguments, I am an able school-man.
(Steele, *Lying Lover*, I.i.)

There were days, centuries ago, when the schoolmen fancied that they could bring into class and line all human knowledge, and encroach to some extent upon the divine, by syllogisms and conversions and oppositions. (Stubbs, *Medieval and Modern Hist.*)

Schoolmaster, The. [Also, **The Scholemaster.**] A treatise on education by Roger Ascham, published in 1570 by his widow. It was the result of a conversation between the author and Sir Richard Sackville, who asked him to put in writing "the chief points of this our talk . . . for the good bringing up of children and young men." The whole title is *The Scholemaster, a plaine and perfite way of teachyng children to understand write and speake in Latin tong.* It was many times reprinted.

Schoolmistress, The. A poem by William Shenstone, published in 1742. It originally had a ludicrous turn, and Shenstone expressly says: "I have added a ludicrous index purely to show (fools) that I am in jest." In a later edition, however, the "ludicrous index" was omitted and many took the poem to be a serious work.

School of Abuse, A. A volume attacking the theater, by Stephen Gosson, published in 1579.

Schopenhauer (shō′pẹn.hou.ėr), **Arthur.** b. at Danzig, Feb. 22, 1788; d. at Frankfort on the Main, Germany, Sept. 21, 1860. A German philosopher. His father was a well-to-do merchant, and appears to have had some hope that his son would follow him in a mercantile career (it was certainly with this end in view that Arthur was placed, in 1805, in the office of a merchant at Hamburg). However, the young man's outlook on life had already been formed to some extent by an awareness of the basic incompatibility of his parents (their marriage was unhappy almost from its outset, and there can be no doubt that the constant awareness of this had an unsettling effect on young Arthur); thus, when his father died a few months later in the year 1805, and as soon as he had become of age he gave up the idea of a business career, and studied first at Göttingen and then at Berlin and Jena. His first major work was his doctoral thesis, a monograph entitled *Über die vierfache Wurzel des Satzes vom zureichenden Grunde (On the Fourfold Root of the Principle of Sufficient Reason)*, which was published in 1813. His principal work, *Die Welt als Wille und Vorstellung (The World as Will and Idea)*, appeared in 1819. In 1820 he settled as docent at the University of Berlin but, having failed to obtain a professorship, withdrew (1831) to private life at Frankfort on the Main, where he subsequently lived. His

other works are *Über den Willen in der Natur* (On the Will in Nature, 1836), which was directed against the professional philosophy of the day (for most of his life, Schopenhauer went unrecognized by contemporary scholars in Germany, and his bitterness against them revealed itself here), and *Die beiden Grundprobleme der Ethik* (The Two Fundamental Problems of Ethics, 1841). A collection of his minor essays was published (1851) under the title *Parerga und Paralipomena*. His complete works appeared at Leipzig (1873–74) in six volumes. Schopenhauer's name has been irrevocably linked with a philosophy of pessimism, and no one who has read all of his works will seriously question the justice of this linking. Although the basis of his thinking entailed an acceptance of some aspects of Platonic idealism (in that all seemingly material things are an objectification of idea), he was utterly incapable of seeing even momentary beauty or joy in the world except at the highest level of Platonic idealism, which is the level of aesthetics, and particularly of music (in his view, the aesthetic experience was the first means of escape from the passions and frustrations of the ordinary, or phenomenal, world). Unlike the Buddhists (to whom Schopenhauer was greatly drawn, and with whom he finally agreed that the end of life, the salvation of man, can be attained only through asceticism, through denial of the self and its passions) Schopenhauer did not simply accept the existence of evil; he made it a necessary part of his philosophy by his twin concepts of the world as idea and the world as will, the latter being conceived of as a force which constantly negates the former and which must finally be overcome in the last of the three steps toward salvation. However, although his logic thus offers a way toward salvation, it is not a road very many can hope to travel; most human beings will remain the victims of the will, which is, by definition, insatiable in its drive (thus, logically, what are thought of as happiness or joy in the phenomenal world become negative values: they represent simply the absence of pain, or the momentary satisfaction of the will). In Schopenhauer's mind there could be no doubt as to the horrible nature of such a world as this. It is, by his logic, necessarily the worst of all possible worlds because, clearly, if it were any worse than it is no one at all would be willing to live in it, and mass suicide would be the result).

Schreiner (shrī′nėr), **Olive** (**Emilie Albertina**). [Pseudonym, **Ralph Iron.**] b. c1863; d. 1920. A South African author. She became known in England with her book *The Story of an African Farm*, which she published in 1883 under the pseudonym Ralph Iron. She also published *Dreams* (1890), *Dream Life and Real Life* (1893), *The Political Situation* (1895; written jointly with her husband), *Trooper Peter Halket of Mashonaland* (1897), *An English South African's View of the Situation* (1898), *Woman and Labor* (1911), and others.

Schubert (shō′bėrt), **Franz Peter.** b. at Vienna, Jan. 31, 1797; d. there, Nov. 19, 1828. An Austrian composer. When little over 10 years old he was first soprano in the choir of Lichtenthal, the parish in which he was born, and had composed songs and violin solos. He was educated in music at Vienna. In 1818 he became teacher of music in the Ester-

fat, fāte, fär, ȧsk, fāre; net, mē, hėr; pin, pīne; not, nōte, mȯve, nȯr; up, lūte, pŭll; ᴛн, then;

házy family, at Budapest, but soon returned to Vienna, and lived there for a time with Mayrhofer the poet. In 1819 his song the *Schäfers Klagelied* was performed in public at Vienna. In 1825 he made a tour with his friend Vogl, who sang Schubert's songs from *The Lady of the Lake* to the latter's accompaniments. He next directed his attention to dramatic music. By 1827 his prospects had decidedly brightened, and he composed ceaselessly, surpassing his former achievements, and having many demands from foreign publishers; but poverty and hard work had already weakened his system, and in 1828 he succumbed to an attack of typhoid fever. The number of his compositions is large, including several operas, cantatas, ten symphonies, many sonatas, masses, marches, quartets, and fantasias, and more than 500 songs, in which he reached the highest level of song writing. Among the songs are *Erlkönig, The Wanderer, The Trout, Who Is Sylvia?*, and *Hark, Hark, the Lark*.

science fiction. A type of literature which narrates, in terms of contemporary scientific knowledge, fantastic adventures which, typically, take place in imaginary lands; during voyages into space, time, and other dimensions; or in the aftermath of some new scientific or mechanical discovery. Various works by Jules Verne and H. G. Wells are considered to be the precursors of this type of fiction. In recent years, with the publication of several specialized magazines, science fiction has become increasingly popular, and today many authors handle advanced theories of physics in order to make convincing their increasingly fantastic stories.

Scio (shē'ō). Italian name of **Chios**.

Scipio (sip′i.ō). [Called **Scipio the Elder**; full name, **Publius Cornelius Scipio Africanus**.] b. c236 B.C.; d. probably 183 B.C. A Roman general. He served at the Ticinus (Ticino) River and Cannae, became edile in 212, was appointed to the chief command in Spain as proconsul in 210, defeated Hasdrubal in 209, completed the conquest of Spain in 206, was elected consul, with Sicily as his province, in 205, invaded Africa in 204, defeated Syphax and Hasdrubal (son of Gisco) in 203, defeated Hannibal at Zama in 202, and negotiated the treaty with Carthage ending the second Punic War in 201. He was censor in 199 and consul in 194, and accompanied his brother in the campaign against Antiochus in 190.

Sciron (sī′ron). In Greek legend, a robber who frequented the region near Megara, and forced strangers passing by to wash his feet. While they were doing so he would kick them off the rocks into the sea, where they were devoured by a turtle. When Theseus passed by, he hurled Sciron himself into the sea, and his bones are said to form the high cliffs which still exist in the region.

Scogan (skō′gạn), **Henry**. [Also, **Scoggin** (skog′in).] b. c1361; d. 1407. English poet and scholar. He was a friend of Chaucer (some of his poems were long thought to be actually by Chaucer) and tutor to the sons of Henry IV (whence the suggestion made by some authorities that Shakespeare was referring to him in *2 Henry VI*; however, from the context of the play, it is clear that Shakespeare was

thinking of the famous jester, even though he put him a century before his time).

Scogan, John. [Also, **Scoggin**.] fl. c1480. A person said to have been the favorite jester of Edward IV, now chiefly remembered from a work known as *Scogan's Jests*, compiled and published by a certain Andrew Boorde (or Borde) in 1526. Some sources, including the *Dictionary of National Biography*, are inclined to suspect that he may have been a fictional character, invented as something upon which to hang the collection of witticisms now attributed to him. There is an allusion to him (but within the wrong century) in Shakespeare's *2 Henry IV*.

Scone (skön), **The Stone of.** See **Stone of Scone**.

scop (skop). In the Old English period, a minstrel or professional poet (also called a *gleeman*), who went from one court to another as an entertainer, performing to the accompaniment of a harp and presenting songs, often of his own composition, in honor of the kings he visited or in celebration of battles and other events, contemporary or of the past. In some instances, a scop was attached to a royal household to perform these functions, somewhat like a poet laureate. The poems of the early scops had typically a four-stress line, of uneven length, and made much use of the kenning for embellishment and emphasis. In *Widsith* a scop recounts his adventures; in several parts of *Beowulf*, notably after the defeat of Grendel, the performance of the scop is described.

Scornful Lady, The. A comedy of domestic life, by Beaumont and Fletcher. It was written c1609, performed c1613, and published in 1616. From the reference in it to various names of importance in the period 1612–13 it is thought that the version now extant represents a revision, at least in part, of the original. In 1783 it was altered by Cooke and produced as *The Capricious Lady*.

Scot (skot), **Alexander.** See **Scott, Alexander**.

Scot or **Scott** (skot), **Michael.** b. probably before 1180; d. before 1235. A Scottish schoolman, who attained posthumous fame as a wizard and magician. He is said to have studied at Oxford and Paris, and to have learned Arabic at Toledo. On the invitation of the emperor Frederick II he superintended a translation of Aristotle and his commentators from Arabic into Latin. His original works deal with astrology, alchemy, and the occult sciences. The chief are *Super auctorem spherae* (Bologna, 1495; Venice, 1631), *De sole et luna* (in *Theatrum chimicum*, Strasbourg, 1622), and *De physiognomia et de hominis procreatione*. According to a tradition followed by Sir Walter Scott in *The Lay of the Last Minstrel*, he was buried in Melrose Abbey. He has been identified by Boece with Sir Michael Scot of Balwearie, and by Camden with a Cistercian monk of Cumberland.

Scot, Reginald. d. 1599. An English author. He studied at Hart Hall, Oxford, and afterward lived at Smeeth. He wrote a book against the persecution of witches, entitled *Discoverie of Witchcraft* (1584), which was burned by order of James I.

Scotichronicon (skō.ti.kron′i.kon), **The.** A Scottish chronicle written partly by John of Fordun, who brought the chronicle down to 1153, and partly by

Walter Bower (1385–1449), who brought it to 1436. An abridgment of the work written by Walter Bower was known as the *Book of Cupar;* it was never printed.

Scotists (skō'tists). The followers of the scholastic Duns Scotus. Their fundamental doctrine was that distinctions which the mind inevitably draws are to be considered as real, although they do not exist apart from their relations to the mind. Such distinctions were called "formal," the abstractions thence resulting "formalities," and those who insisted upon them "formalists" or "formalizers" (Middle Latin *formalizantes*).

Scotland (skot'lạnd). [French, **Écosse**; Latin, **Caledonia**; medieval Latin, **Scotia**; sometimes called **North Britain**; nickname, **"Land of Cakes."**] A country occupying the N part of the island of Great Britain, and forming an integral part of the United Kingdom of Great Britain and Northern Ireland. Its capital is Edinburgh, and its largest city, Glasgow. The mainland, which extends from lat. 54°38′ to 58°41′ N., and from long. 1°45′ to 6°14′ W., is bounded by the Atlantic on the W and N, the North Sea on the E, and England and the Irish Sea on the S. The country is divided generally into the Highlands in the N and W, the Central Lowlands, and the Southern Uplands in the S and E. The chief indentations of the coast are the Moray Firth, Firths of Tay and Forth, Solway Firth, and Firth of Clyde. The highest mountains are the Grampians, ab. 4,000 ft. (Ben Nevis, the highest mountain in Great Britain, 4,406 ft.). The chief river systems are those of the Spey, Tay, Forth, Tweed, and Clyde. There are many mountain lakes, including Lochs Tay, Awe, Lomond, and Katrine. The principal islands are the Orkney Islands, Shetland Islands, and the Inner and Outer Hebrides. Scotland has important commerce, valuable mines of iron and coal (though both are declining), fisheries, flourishing iron, cotton, woolen, linen, and jute manufactures, shipbuilding industries, whiskey distilleries, and others. The country accounts for about half of all British shipbuilding tonnage in normal years, the principal centers being along the banks of the river Clyde. About a fourth of the total area of the country is under cultivation or in permanent pasture. Another half of the total area is in rough grazing land. Sheep raising is an important activity, but has been declining of late years in the Highlands. The most famous cultivated district is that lying S of the Firth of Forth in the counties of West Lothian, Midlothian, and East Lothian. The principal Scottish crop is oats, with more than half of the total cultivated area being devoted to it. A form of combined subsistence agriculture and fishing, known as "crofting," is practiced by the scattered inhabitants along the coasts of the northern Highland counties. Scotland has 33 counties. It has been represented since 1918 by 74 members in the House of Commons; and the peerage, to which no additions have been made since 1707, but which still numbers 86 members, appoints 16 peers at the opening of each Parliament to sit in the House of Lords, in which, however, 50 of the other Scottish peers have seats as holders of British titles. The great majority of the Scots are Presbyterians (mostly of the Established Church, Free Church, or United Presbyterian Church); there are also Roman Catholics, Episcopalians, Congregationalists, and other denominations. Gaelic (a Celtic language) was spoken by 7,069 persons, mostly in the Highland counties of Argyllshire, Inverness-shire, Ross and Cromarty, and Sutherland, in 1931. An additional 130,080 persons were found to speak both Gaelic and English. Capital, Edinburgh; area, 29,797 sq. mi.; pop. 5,095,969 (1951)

History. The original inhabitants were Celts. Scotland was invaded by the Romans under Agricola in the 1st century. A wall between the rivers Clyde and Forth was built under Antoninus and Septimius Severus. Invasions of Roman Britain by the Picts and Scots took place in the 4th and 5th centuries. In the 6th century a kingdom was founded by the Dalriad Scots (who came from Ireland); there was a settlement of Angles in the southeast; and the conversion of the Picts was begun by Saint Columba. A union of Picts and Scots into a kingdom (called Scotia in medieval Latin) was effected in the 9th century. From the 8th century to the 11th there were raids by the Norsemen, and settlements were made by them especially in the Orkneys and Shetlands. King Malcolm II achieved the conquest of Lothian in 1018. In the struggles between England and Scotland, the latter was invaded by William the Conqueror, but no territory was lost. The kingdom prospered in the 12th and 13th centuries, especially under the three Alexanders. The death of Margaret, the Maid of Norway, granddaughter of Alexander III, led to a notable dispute about the succession, and to the interference of Edward I of England in Scottish affairs. In the contest between Bruce and Baliol, in which Edward was virtually arbitrator, Baliol was chosen king in 1292. He paid homage to Edward, but afterward renounced his allegiance, and a war followed which was really a struggle on Edward's part for sovereignty and on Scotland's for independence. Scotland was invaded by Edward in 1296. The Scots under Wallace were victorious at Stirling in 1297, but were defeated at Falkirk in 1298. On the death of Wallace in 1305, Robert Bruce succeeded as national leader, and was crowned king in 1306. The independence of Scotland was secured by the victory of Bannockburn in 1314, and was recognized by Edward III in 1328. Robert II (who succeeded in 1371), the son of Bruce's daughter, was the first sovereign of the Stuart dynasty. In 1513 the Scots under James IV invaded England and suffered a disastrous defeat at Flodden, September 9. The following are important among subsequent events: reign of Mary, Queen of Scots (1542–67); introduction of the Reformation (1560); invasion by the English under Somerset and defeat at Pinkie (1547); accession of James VI, king of Scotland, to the throne of England as James I (1603); success of the Covenanters against Charles I (1639–40); persecution of the Covenanters under Charles II and James II; legislative union of the two kingdoms of England and Scotland (1707); Jacobite insurrections (1715 and 1745–46).

Scotland Yard. A short street in London, near Trafalgar Square, formerly the site of the London police headquarters, now removed to New Scotland Yard, on the Thames Embankment; hence, a name for the London police.

Scots Wha Hae wi' Wallace Bled (skots hwä hā wi wol'ạs bled). [Also, **Bannockburn.**] A patriotic song by Robert Burns.

Scott (skot), **Alexander.** [Also, **Scot.**] b. c1525; d. 1584. A Scottish author of satirical and amatory verse. Of his 36 poems, critics regard as his best *The Lament of the Maister of Erskyn* (1547), *A New Year Gift to Quene Mary* (1562), and *The Justing at the Drum*, a satire on tournament conventions. Scott's poetry was published, in whole or in part (frequently expurgated), in 1724, 1770, 1802 (in Sibbald's *Chronicle of Scottish Poetry*), 1821, 1874–81, 1882, 1887, and 1895.

Scott, Clement. b. at London, Oct. 6, 1841; d. there, June 25, 1904. An English journalist, playwright, and drama critic. He also published several volumes of poems.

Scott, Hugh Stowell. [Pseudonym, **Henry Seton Merriman.**] b. at Newcastle, England, May 9, 1862; d. at Melton, near Woodbridge, England, Nov. 19, 1903. An English novelist. He published his first novel anonymously, and the others under his pseudonym. Author of *Young Mistley* (1888), *The Phantom Future* (1889), *Prisoners and Captives* (1891), *From One Generation to Another* (1892), *With Edged Tools* (1894), *The Grey Lady* (1895), *The Sowers* (1896), *Raden's Corner* (1898), *Isle of Unrest* (1900), *The Velvet Glove* (1901), *Barlasch of the Guard* (1902), and *The Last Hope* (1904).

Scott, John. See **Scott of Amwell, John.**

Scott, Michael. b. at Glasgow, Oct. 30, 1789; d. there, Nov. 7, 1835. A Scottish novelist, writer of sea stories, among them *Tom Cringle's Log.*

Scott, Michael. See also **Scot, Michael.**

Scott, Robert Falcon. b. at Devonport, England, June 6, 1868; d. in Antarctica (lat. 79°40′ S., long. 169°23′ E.), about March 27, 1912. An English naval officer and explorer. He entered the navy in 1882, was promoted to captain in 1904, and commanded the national antarctic expeditions of 1900–04 and 1910–12. With four companions he reached the South Pole (Jan. 17–18, 1912), but all perished on the return journey. He published an account of his first voyage in *The Voyage of the Discovery* (1905); and an account of the last expedition, compiled from his diaries, was issued as *Scott's Last Expedition* in 1913.

Scott, Sir Walter. b. at Edinburgh, Aug. 15, 1771; d. at Abbotsford, Scotland, Sept. 21, 1832. A Scottish poet and novelist. Both the Scotts and his mother's folk, the Rutherfords, were old Border families, long established in that turbulent region of warfare, feuds, and romantic legends; and the young Walter Scott, though lame as a result of illness in infancy, was indefatigable in exploring the Border, eagerly listening to old tales which he stored in a remarkably retentive memory, during every vacation and holiday he could take from his studies at the University of Edinburgh and in his father's law office. The Romantic Movement, mainly of German origin but having the powerful support of Scotland's Robert Burns as well as of Scott's English contemporaries the Lake Poets, was in the air, and as a youth Walter Scott mastered German, French, and Italian, the better to breathe that atmosphere which accorded so well with the spirit of Border traditions and minstrelsy. His admission to the bar in 1792 did not diminish either his antiquarian or his literary interests. In 1796 he published, anonymously, translations of ballads by the German Gottfried August Bürger and in 1799 his translation of Goethe's *Götz von Berlichingen* appeared. In that year also Scott's former schoolmate James Ballantyne reissued the Bürger translations in the same volume with some original ballads by Scott, with the title *Apology for Tales of Terror*. Meanwhile Scott was busily editing an extensive collection of historical and romantic ballads, which appeared in 1802 as *Minstrelsy of the Scottish Border*. Responsive to the suggestion of a lady admirer of this collection, Scott produced his own first major work, *The Lay of the Last Minstrel*, a narrative poem, published with great success in 1805. In 1797 he had married; in 1799 he was made a sheriff-deputy of Selkirkshire, at 300 pounds a year, with duties too light to interfere with the literary career upon which he now definitely decided. In 1805 he also became a partner in James Ballantyne's printing business, for which he edited scholarly editions of John Dryden, Jonathan Swift, and other writers, while composing his own lengthy martial poem, *Marmion* (1808). But a quarrel with *Marmion's* publisher, Constable, led Scott to finance an expansion of the Ballantyne business, under an arrangement with another publisher. The auspices seemed good for this new alliance when Scott's next long poem, *The Lady of the Lake*, was enthusiastically received by the reading public in 1810. But although Scott's opinion of his own business ability was high, he was actually quite inept in that field. The Ballantyne firm was waterlogged with debts and unsold books beyond salvage while Scott's next three poems, *The Vision of Don Roderick* (1811), *Rokeby* (1813), and *The Bridal of Triermain* (1813), aroused only tepid interest among readers who were at this time hailing the genius of another Scottish poet, Lord Byron. Frankly ambitious to live in the grand manner which he thought suitable to the scion of an old Border family, Scott had already begun to accumulate the property along the Tweed where he was to build the imposing mansion he named Abbotsford. In 1812 he was appointed clerk of the sessions court, still retaining his post as sheriff-deputy, and having from these two positions an income of 1,600 pounds per annum. In 1813 he withdrew from the Ballantyne firm, assuming its debts; in 1814 he completed a novel which he had begun and abandoned years before, and this work Constable, with whom he became reconciled, brought out under the title *Waverley*. Because Scott feared that novel writing would seem beneath the dignity of a clerk of court, this work, instantly successful, was issued anonymously; and finding that public speculation concerning "the Great Unknown" helped sales, he persisted in this anonymity through the publication of successive works of fiction until 1826, although the secret of his authorship gradually became widely known. In fact it was in recognition of his genius as a writer of fiction, no less than in acknowledgment of his stature as a poet and as the author of such works as *Border Antiquities of England and Scotland* (1814–17) and *Provincial Antiquities of Scotland* (1819–26), that Scott was created a baronet in 1820. He had returned to narrative poetry with *The Lord of the Isles* (1815), but *Harold the Dauntless* (1817) was his last work in that sort. The novels which now appeared in quick succession were at first concerned with Scottish themes; such were *Guy Mannering* (1815), *The Antiquary*, *The Black Dwarf*, and *Old Mortality* (1816), *Rob Roy* and *The Heart of Midlothian* (1818), *The Bride of Lammermoor* and *The Legend of Montrose* (1819); but beginning with *Ivanhoe* (1820), which found its plot in 12th-century England, Scott ranged farther afield in place and time. No writer can always be at his best; nevertheless Scott's great following was seldom disappointed as his tireless pen gave them *The Monastery* and *The Abbot* (1820), *Kenilworth* (1821), *The Pirate*, *The Fortunes of Nigel*, and *Peveril of the Peak* (1822), *Quentin Durward* (1823), *St. Ronan's Well* and *Redgauntlet* (1824), and *The Betrothed* and *The Talisman* (1825). *St. Ronan's Well* was a novel of manners; all of the others were historical romances. In 1825 England experienced a financial crisis; the house of Constable crashed. Scott's earnings, of course, had been great, but he had built Abbotsford at great cost and lived on a lavish scale. The Ballantyne debts had not been fully liquidated; the crash left him overwhelmed with obligations, but refusing to resort to bankruptcy he set himself to pay them all (and they totaled 130,000 pounds) by his pen. Since 1817 he had often been painfully ill, and his last years were marked by much suffering. But indomitably he turned out fiction: *Woodstock* (1826), the two series of *Chronicles of the Canongate*, including *The Highland Widow*, *The Two Drovers*, and *The Surgeon's Daughter* (1827), and *The Fair Maid of Perth* and *Aunt Margaret's Mirror* (1828), *Anne of Geierstein* (1829), *Tales of a Grandfather* (stories for children, 1828–30), *Count Robert of Paris* and *Castle Dangerous* (1832); dramas: *The Doom of Dervorgoil* and *Auchindrane, or the Ayrshire Tragedy;* and miscellaneous works such as a *Life of Napoleon Buonaparte* (1827), a *History of Scotland* (1829–30), and *Letters on Demonology and Witchcraft* (1830). In February, 1830, he suffered a stroke of apoplexy; in 1831 his mental powers began to fail. On a vessel provided by the British government he made a leisurely tour of Mediterranean lands, at peace in the belief (which was not true) that his debts were fully paid; he returned to die at his beloved Abbotsford; and, from the continued earnings of his books, the debts were indeed finally liquidated. The long poems which first brought fame to Sir Walter Scott have long been out of fashion, but many of them still make exciting reading, for the young and indeed for any extrovert, by virtue of their clarity, their vivid description of natural scenes, and their swift and spirited narrative, especially when the theme is martial; not without justification has the battle scene in *Marmion* been compared with the *Iliad*. A handful of his shorter poems, such as *Lochinvar*, hold an undiminished place among ballads and lyrics in English. As a novelist, Scott must be recognized as one of the major influences in modern literature. He originated the historical novel; and if the vogue

of romanticism comes and goes it can never, while his works remain in print, cease to challenge writers to emulation, or fail to delight a large public. His plots and his characters alike may be said to lack subtlety, but his actions seldom lack excitement, and his principal actors (kings and nobles, yeomen and peasants, queens and gentle maidens) never lack flesh and blood and a share of the universal passions and sentiments. They come alive, and readers at once understand them, know them as they know their neighbors, and enter into their problems, sorrows, and triumphs with comprehension and sympathy. Scott himself has recorded that time and again his carefully worked-out plots were disrupted when some character he had created, or some situation he had contrived, took command of his imagination; some of his novels are ill-constructed successions of scenes, but they are lively and exciting scenes. His invention was as inexhaustible as the energy which enabled him to complete 23 novels in 14 years, while discharging his official duties, carrying a load of business details, and holding practically open house for the great and the humble who flocked to Abbotsford to see him. He had an immense influence not only on British, but on German, French, and American literature, and the end of that influence is not yet.

Scott, William Bell. b. at Edinburgh, Sept. 12, 1811; d. at Penkill Castle, Ayrshire, Scotland, Nov. 22, 1890. A Scottish artist and poet.

Scottish Chiefs (skot′ish), **The.** A romance by Jane Porter, published in 1810. It is based on early Scottish history. Wallace and Robert the Bruce figure largely in the story, which opens in the late 13th century and closes with the battle of Bannockburn.

Scottish Highlands. See **Highlands, the.**

Scottish school. A group of philosophical writers of Scotland beginning with Francis Hutcheson (1694–1747). They were intuitionalists in morals, and opposed Locke in regard to innate ideas.

Scott of Amwell (am′wel), **John.** b. at Bermondsey, London, Jan. 9, 1730; d. at Ratclif, London, Dec. 12, 1783. A Scottish poet and essayist. Largely self-educated, he began his writing career by contributing poetry (1753–58) to the *Gentleman's Magazine*, later (1760) publishing his best-known work, *Amwell*, a descriptive poem. His other works are *Four Elegies* (1760), *Four Moral Eclogues* (1778), *Observations on the State of the Parochial and Vagrant Poor* (1773), and *Critical Essays* (1785). Scott's collected *Poetical Works* appeared in 1782. Although appreciated in his own time he is virtually unknown today.

Scotus (skō′tus), **John Duns.** See **Duns Scotus, John.**

"Scourge of Princes." See **Aretino, Pietro.**

Scrap of Paper, A. A play adapted from Sardou's *Les Pattes de mouche* (1861) by Palgrave Simpson. Charles Mathews produced an adaptation, by himself, in 1867 as *Adventures of a Love Letter*.

Scriblerus Club (skrib.lē′rus). A club of writers at London, founded by Swift in 1714 after the breaking up of "The Brothers" in 1713. Among the members were Pope, Arbuthnot, Bolingbroke,

Gay, and others. The object of the club was to satirize literary incompetence; it was not political.

"Scrogie" Touchwood (skrō′ji tuch′wŭd). See **Touchwood, P. S.**

Scrooge (skrōj), **Ebenezer.** The central character in Dickens's *Christmas Carol.* He is "a squeezing, wrenching, grasping, scraping, clutching, covetous old sinner," but is visited by spirits on Christmas Eve, and changed by his experiences into a worthy, kindly man.

Scroop (skrōp), **Lord.** In Shakespeare's *Henry V,* a traitor who with Cambridge and Grey plots to murder the King. He is discovered (it is not explained how) and given a warrant for his death which he believes at first to be a commission for the French campaign. He had been one of Henry's most trusted counsellors.

Scroop, Richard. In Shakespeare's *1* and *2 Henry IV,* the historical Richard le Scrope, Archbishop of York. He joins Hotspur's rebellion in *1 Henry IV* but is not present at the crucial battle. In *2 Henry IV,* he is tricked into making an armistice and dismissing his forces, after which he is arrested. He supports the justice of the rebellion even though Prince John censures him for using his authority to subvert the English people.

Scroop, Sir Stephen. In Shakespeare's *Richard II,* a supporter of Richard who reports the death of Bushy and Green.

Scrope (skrōp), **Edward.** The Bishop of Princhester, the principal character of H. G. Wells's *The Soul of a Bishop.* He suffers from increasing doubts as to the validity of the religion he serves, and at the close of the story withdraws from the church entirely.

Scrub (skrub). In *The Beaux' Stratagem* by Farquhar, an amusing valet; a favorite character with Garrick.

Scrymgeour (skrim′jėr), (Mrs.) **Helen.** In H. G. Wells's novel *Tono-Bungay,* a woman novelist, slight in stature and of a not unpleasing plumpness, with whom Edward Ponderevo has a very brief romance.

Scudamour (skud′a.mör), **Sir.** In Spenser's *Faerie Queene,* the knightly lover of Amoret.

Scudéry (skü.dā.rē), **Madeleine de.** b. at Le Havre, France, 1607; d. at Paris, June 2, 1701. A French novelist and poet. On her parents' death she was brought up by an uncle, and when he died she went to Paris with her brother Georges. Naturally bright and clever, she was not slow to assert her ability in the literary circle of the Hôtel de Rambouillet. When these famous gatherings broke up as a gradual result of the internal troubles that attended the minority of Louis XIX, Mademoiselle de Scudéry was able to command her own salon, meeting every Saturday. Her first novel, *Ibrahim, ou l'illustre Bassa,* appeared in 1641 under her brother's name. Encouraged by its success, she affixed her own signature to the two works for which she is best known, *Artamène, ou le grand Cyrus* (1650) and *Clélie, histoire romaine* (1656). In these novels she has introduced under assumed names a great many of her contemporaries; in the former she speaks of herself as Sapho. Victor Cousin

discovered the complete key to all her characters. In addition to these works, Mademoiselle de Scudéry published *Almahide, ou l'esclave reine* (1660), *Célinde* (1661), *Les Femmes illustres, ou harangues héroïques* (1665), *Mathilde d'Aguilar, histoire espagnole* (1665), *La Promenade de Versailles, ou histoire de Célanire* (1669), and finally *Le Discours de la gloire* (1671), which won for the first time the academic prize for French eloquence founded by Jean-Louis Guez de Balzac.

Scylla (sil′a). In Greek mythology, a sea monster, said once to have been a beautiful sea nymph changed by Circe into a hideous six-headed, 12-footed monster. She was represented as the perilous rock Scylla, opposite the whirlpool Charybdis, in the Strait of Messina.

Scylla. In Greek mythology, the daughter of Nisus of Megara, who cut from her father's head the lock of hair on which his life depended.

Scythrop (skī′thrŏp). In Thomas Love Peacock's *Nightmare Abbey,* a biting caricature of Shelley.

Sea and the Mirror, The. A work by W. H. Auden, who characterizes it as "a commentary on Shakespeare's *The Tempest.*" It was published (1944) with his "For the Time Being." The preface, comments by Prospero and the minor characters, and the postscript are in verse; the soliloquy of Caliban to the audience is in Auden's "rhythmic prose."

Sea Captain. In Shakespeare's *Twelfth Night,* the captain of the ship wrecked on the Illyrian coast. He promises to present Viola, disguised as a page, to Orsino, the Duke.

Sea Captain. See also **Shipmaster.**

Sea Captain, The. A historical novel by Henry Christopher Bailey, published in 1914.

seacoast of Bohemia (bọ.hē′mi.ạ). See **Bohemia, seacoast of.**

Seacole (sē′kōl). In Shakespeare's *Much Ado About Nothing,* the Second Watchman, who arrests Borachio and Conrade.

Seafarer, The. An Old English poem of the early 8th century, preserved in the *Exeter Book.* It has been interpreted as either a dialogue between an old sailor and a young boy or a monologue of the old sailor, in which both the troubles and the joys of a life at sea are expressed, concluding with a brief contemplation of life after death and the transience of worldly joys.

Sea-Fever. A short poem by John Masefield, opening with the often quoted lines: "I must down to the seas again, to the lonely sea and the sky,/And all I ask is a tall ship and a star to steer her by."

Seagrim (sē′grim), **Molly.** A girl whom Tom Jones seduces and later defends, in Fielding's novel *Tom Jones.*

Sea Horses. A novel of sea life by Francis Brett Young, published in 1925.

Seaman (sē′mạn), Sir **Owen.** b. at London, Sept. 18, 1861; d. there, Feb. 2, 1936. An English poet, humorist, and editor. He was appointed professor of literature at the Durham College of Science, Newcastle, in 1890, joined the staff of *Punch* in 1897, became its subeditor in 1902, and became editor in chief in 1906. His best work consists of parodies of other poets. He wrote *Horace at Cam-*

ḍ, d or j; ş, s or sh; ṭ, t or ch; ẓ, z or zh; o, F. cloche; ü, F. menu; ċh, Sc. loch; ń, F. bonbon.

bridge (1894), *The Battle of the Bays* (1896), *In Cap and Bells* (1899), *Borrowed Plumes* (1902), *A Harvest of Chaff* (1904), and *Interludes of an Editor* (1929).

Search (sẽrch), **Edward.** Pseudonym of **Tucker, Abraham.**

Seasons, The. A poem in blank verse, in four parts, by James Thomson (1700–48). "Winter" was published in 1726, "Summer" in 1727, "Spring" in 1728, the whole (including "Autumn" and a "Hymn to Nature") in 1730. The work is important as being the first major English poem to treat nature in the manner later developed by the romantic school.

Seasons, The. [German title, **Die Jahreszeiten.**] An oratorio by Franz Josef Haydn, produced at Vienna in 1801. The words are by Van Swieten, after James Thomson's poem of the same title.

Seb (seb). In Egyptian mythology, the father of Osiris, and god of the earth.

Sebastian (sẹ.bas'chạn), Saint. b. possibly at Narbonne, in Gaul; shot to death by archers at the order of Diocletian, c288 A.D. A Roman soldier and Christian martyr, revered as a protector against pestilence. Little is actually known about either his life or death, the legend being that he did not die from the wounds inflicted by the arrows, but recovered and was finally killed by blows from a club. However, beginning with the religious paintings of the Renaissance, he has been portrayed in works of art as a young man pierced with arrows.

Sebastian. [Portuguese, **Sebastião** (sā.bạsh-tyouň').] b. 1554; killed in the battle of Alcazarquivir, in Morocco, Aug. 4, 1578. King of Portugal (1557–58). He was a posthumous son of Prince John, and succeeded his grandfather, John III. During his minority (ending in 1568) Portugal was under the regency of his grandmother, Catherine of Austria, and his uncle Henry, who succeeded him as king. Sebastian, educated by the Jesuits, looked upon himself as a crusader for Christendom and resolved to crusade against the Moors in North Africa; he lived an ascetic life and, though the House of Aviz lacked an heir, refused to marry. As a result, after his successor's death, control of Portugal went to his uncle, Philip II of Spain (whose motives in helping Sebastian fit out his disastrous final expedition may not have been entirely without self-interest). Sebastian led an expedition against Morocco in 1578, in which he was defeated and slain. Soon after the battle rumors began to arise that he was not dead, and in 1584, 1594, and 1598 impostors appeared claiming the crown. The last was hanged at Sanlúcar de Barrameda in Spain in 1603. The belief of the people in these impostors arose from the popularity of Sebastian and their firm faith in his reappearance. As late as 1808 in Portugal and 1838 in Brazil, his name was used as a rallying cry. John Dryden and others wrote plays about him.

Sebastian. In Shakespeare's *Tempest*, the brother of the King of Naples.

Sebastian. In Shakespeare's *Twelfth Night*, the twin brother of Viola.

Sebastian. The younger son of D'Amville in Cyril Tourneur's *The Atheist's Tragedy*.

Sebastian, Duke. See **Duke Sebastian.**

Sebek (seb'ek). In Egyptian mythology, the crocodile-headed god, seemingly a double of Set, the god of evil.

Second Blooming, The. A novel by W. L. George, published in 1914.

Second Coming, The. A poem by William Butler Yeats, published in *Michael Robartes and the Dancer* (1921), using much the same mythological basis as *Sailing to Byzantium* and *Byzantium*, although following a more logical and concrete development of images and thought. Yeats here expresses the idea that Christianity is just one of the many cycles of the experience of man, characterizing it as a "stony sleep." He speculates upon the second coming, wondering "what rough beast, its hour come round at last, slouches towards Bethlehem to be born?"

Second Jungle Book, The. See under **Jungle Books.**

Second Maiden's Tragedy, The. A play of unknown authorship, at one time attributed to George Chapman and also to William Shakespeare. On a basis of internal evidence, it has also been suggested that it may have been a collaborative work by Philip Massinger and Cyril Tourneur. It was licensed in 1611 and first printed in 1824. It probably owes its existence to the success of Francis Beaumont and John Fletcher's *Maid's Tragedy*, though the plot is entirely different.

Second Mrs. Tanqueray (tang'kẹ.rạ), **The.** A play (1893) by Arthur Wing Pinero. One of Pinero's most successful works, it tells the story of a "woman with a past" who, in order to save her stepdaughter, reveals that the man she (the stepdaughter) is thinking of marrying is, in fact, her own former lover. She thus saves the girl from a tragic misstep, but loses her good name in the girl's eyes as a result.

Second Nun's Tale, The. One of Chaucer's *Canterbury Tales*. It is a tale of the martyrdom of Saint Cecilia and her husband Valerian, and was taken from the *Legenda Aurea* of Jacobus a Voragine. There was a French version of this by Jehan de Vignay, c1300, Caxton's *Golden Legend* in 1483, and a Latin version by Simeon Mefaphrastes. The preamble to Chaucer's poem contains 14 or 15 lines translated from the 33rd canto of Dante's *Paradiso*, or perhaps from their original in some Latin prayer or hymn.

Second Part of King Henry the Fourth, The. See **Henry IV** (*Part Two*).

Second Part of King Henry the Sixth, The. See **Henry VI** (*Part Two*).

Secondsight (sek'ọnd.sīt), **Solomon.** Pseudonym of **McHenry, James.**

Secret Agent, The. A novel (1907) by Joseph Conrad.

Secret Battle, The. A novel by A. P. Herbert, published in 1919.

Secret City, The. A novel by Hugh Walpole, published in 1919. A sequel to *The Dark Forest* (1916), it is based on the author's years (1914–16) with the Russian Red Cross during World War I. It was awarded the James Tait Black memorial prize.

Secret Love. See **Maiden Queen, The.**

fat, fāte, fär, ȧsk, fãre; net, mē, hẽr; pin, pīne; not, nōte, mõve, nôr; up, lūte, půll; ᴛн, then;

Secret Places of the Heart, The. A novel (1922) by H. G. Wells.

Secrets. A volume of verse (1924) by William H. Davies.

Sedgemoor (sej'mŏr). A locality in Somersetshire, England, near Bridgwater. Here the Royalists under Louis de Durfort de Duras, Earl of Feversham, defeated (July 6, 1685) the forces of James Scott, Duke of Monmouth. The battle (which has been called the last battle in England) resulted in the overthrow and capture of Monmouth.

Sedley (sed'li), **Amelia.** The sweet but foolish daughter of a broken-down London stockbroker, in Thackeray's *Vanity Fair.* She is the antithesis of Becky Sharp.

Sedley, Sir Charles. b. in Kent, England, 1639; d. Aug. 20, 1701. An English wit, poet, and dramatist. His first comedy, *The Mulberry Garden,* was published in 1668. He also wrote *Antony and Cleopatra* (1677), *Bellamira* (1687), *Beauty the Conqueror* (1702), *The Grumbler* (1702), and *The Tyrant King of Crete* (1702). He sat in Parliament for New Romney, and took an active part in politics. His life was scandalous, and he is remembered as excusing himself for the part he took in the Revolution by saying that, "as James II had made his [Sedley's] daughter a countess, he could do no less than endeavour to make the king's daughter a queen."

Sedley, John. In Thackeray's novel *Vanity Fair,* the father of Amelia Sedley. He first appears in the story as a prosperous businessman, but suffers a catastrophic financial reverse and is never again able to do more than eke out a bare living.

Sedley, Joseph or **Jos.** The collector of Boggley Wallah (a fictitious station in India), in Thackeray's *Vanity Fair;* brother of Amelia Sedley. He is a fat, sensual, but timid dandy, and falls a victim to Becky Sharp.

Sedley, Mrs. In Thackeray's novel *Vanity Fair,* the mother of Amelia Sedley. She is a woman of bustling affection and an unfortunate tendency for meddling in the affairs of her daughter.

Seeds of Time, The. A volume of verse (1921) by John Drinkwater.

Seege of Troye (sēj; troi). The earliest Middle English romance (c1300) on the popular theme of the fall of Troy, of unknown authorship, written for recitation in the northeast Midlands and composed of about 2,000 lines. It tells the story from Jason's capture of the Golden Fleece to the destruction of Troy.

Seeley (sē'li), **Sir John Robert.** b. at London, 1834; d. Jan. 13, 1895. An English historian. He became professor of Latin in University College, London, in 1863, and in 1869 professor of modern history at Cambridge. *Ecce Homo, or Survey of the Life and Work of Jesus Christ,* his most celebrated work, appeared anonymously in 1865. His other works are an edition of Livy, *Lectures and Essays* (1870), *Life and Times of Stein* (1878), *Natural Religion* (1882), *The Expansion of England* (1883), *Short History of Napoleon I* (1885), and others.

Sege of Melayne (sēj; me̞.lān'), **The.** A Middle English verse romance of the Otuel group of the

Charlemagne cycle, written in the 14th century. It tells how the army of the Christians, faced by almost certain defeat, is finally victorious when the Archbishop Turpin reproaches the Virgin for allowing things to have come to such a pass. Here the archbishop is the hero, rather than Charlemagne or Roland.

Sejanus His Fall (se̞.ja'nus). A tragedy by Ben Jonson, acted in 1603 and published in 1605. It is said that Shakespeare played in it.

Selborne (sel'bȯrn, -bôrn). A parish in Hampshire, England: the locale of Gilbert White's *Natural History and Antiquities of Selborne.*

Selborne, 1st Earl of. Title of **Palmer, Sir Roundell.**

Selden (sel'de̞n), **John.** b. at Salvington, Sussex, Dec. 16, 1584; d. at London, Nov. 30, 1654. An English jurist, antiquary, Orientalist, and author. At about 16 years of age he entered Hart Hall, Oxford, and in 1602 Clifford's Inn, London; in 1604 he transferred to the Inner Temple. He was intimately associated with Ben Jonson, Michael Drayton, Edward Littleton, Henry Rolle, Edward Herbert, and Thomas Gardener. He was first employed by Sir Robert Cotton to copy and abridge parliamentary records in the Tower. He established a large and lucrative practice, but his chief reputation was made as a writer and scholar. In 1610 he published *England's Epinomis* and *Jani Anglorum, Facies Altera,* which treated of English law down to Henry II. These were followed by *Titles of Honour* (1614), *Analecton Anglo-Britannicon* (1615), and *De Diis Syriis* (1617), the latter, an inquiry into polytheism, establishing his reputation as an Oriental scholar. The *History of Tithes,* published in 1618, was suppressed. He was the instigator of the "protestation" of Dec. 18, 1621, and was committed to the Tower. In 1623 he entered Parliament as member for Lancaster, was prominent in the impeachment proceedings against George Villiers, 1st Duke of Buckingham, and in 1628 helped to draw up and carry the Petition of Right. In 1629 he was imprisoned for his opposition to the imposition of the tonnage and poundage charges, and after his release in 1631 opposed the granting of ship money. In 1635 he dedicated his *Mare Clausum* to the king (Charles I), and seems to have inclined to the court party. He was returned to the Long Parliament (1640) for the University of Oxford, and was a member of the committee which impeached (1641) Archbishop Laud. In 1645 he declined the mastership of Trinity Hall, Cambridge. Besides the works mentioned, he was the author of *De jure naturali et gentium juxta disciplinam Ebraeorum* (1640), *Privileges of the Baronage of England When They Sit in Parliament* (1642), and *Table Talk,* his best-known work (1689), a collection of his sayings edited by his secretary, Richard Milward.

Selene (se̞.lē'nē). In Greek mythology, the goddess of the moon, daughter of Hyperion and Thea. She had no cult.

Seleucids (se̞.lö'sidz). [Also, **Seleucidae** (se̞.lö'si.dē).] A royal dynasty in Syria which reigned from 312 B.C. to c64 B.C.; descended from Seleucus I (Seleucus Nicator).

d, d or j; s̬, s or sh; t̬, t or ch; z̬, z or zh; o, F. cloche; ü, F. menu; ch, Sc. loch; ṅ, F. bonbon.

Seleucus (sē̩.lö′kus, -lū′-). In Shakespeare's *Antony and Cleopatra*, the treasurer of Cleopatra.

Seleucus. In James Shirley's *The Coronation*, the supposed son of Eubulus, but in reality Leonatus, the king of Epirus.

Selim (sē′lim, se.lēm′). The hero of Byron's poem *The Bride of Abydos*.

Selincourt (sel′in.kōrt), **Basil de.** b. 1876—. An English critic, essayist, and scholar; brother of Ernest de Selincourt; husband (married 1908) of Anne Douglas Sedgwick. Author of *Giotto* (1905), *William Blake* (1909), *Walt Whitman* (1914), *The English Secret* (1923), *Pomona, or the Future of English* (1926), *The Enjoyment of Music* (1928), and *Towards Peace* (1932).

Selincourt, Ernest de. b. at Streatham, England, Sept. 24, 1870; d. at Kendal, Westmorland, England, May 22, 1943. An English poet and biographer, chiefly known for his collection and editing of the correspondence of William and Dorothy Wordsworth; brother of Basil de Selincourt. He was professor of English language and literature (1908–35) and vice-principal (1931–35) at Birmingham University. His works include the biography *Dorothy Wordsworth* (1933), *Oxford Lectures on Poetry* (1934), *The Letters of William and Dorothy Wordsworth* (1935–41), and *Wordsworthian and Other Studies* (1947).

Seljuks (sel.jöks′). The name of several Turkish dynasties which reigned in C and W Asia from the 11th to the 13th century. After conquering Persia, Togrul Beg, the grandson of the founder of the dynasty, who belonged to the orthodox Mohammedan sect of the Sunnites, rescued (1055) the Abbasside caliph at Baghdad from his Shiite lieutenant, and was nominated "commander of the faithful." He was succeeded (1063) by his nephew Alp Arslan, who took Syria and Palestine from the Fatimite caliph of Egypt, and defeated (1071) and captured the Byzantine emperor Romanus IV, who purchased his release by the cession of a large part of Anatolia or Asia Minor. Alp Arslan was followed (1072) by his son Malik Shah, on whose death in 1092 the succession was disputed. The ensuing civil war resulted in the partition of the empire among four branches of the Seljuk family, of which the principal dynasty ruled in Persia, and three younger dynasties at Kerman, Damascus, and Konya respectively. The last named, whose sultanate was called Roum (meaning "of the Romans"), outlasted the others; it was superseded by the Ottomans at the end of the 13th century.

Selkirk (sel′kė̇rk), **Alexander.** [Also, **Selcraig** (sel′krāg).] b. at Largo, Fifeshire, Scotland, 1676; d. on the ship *Weymouth*, Dec. 12, 1721. A Scottish sailor, the supposed original of Daniel Defoe's Robinson Crusoe. He was engaged in buccaneering exploits in the south seas, and in 1703 was sailing master of a galley under William Dampier. In 1704 he was at his own request put ashore on one of the islands of the Juan Fernández group, and remained there alone four years. His *Life and Adventures* were published by Howell in 1829, and he is the subject of a poem by William Cowper.

Selwyn College (sel′win). A college of Cambridge University, founded 1882 to meet the wants of students of the Church of England unable to attend the more expensive colleges.

Sembal (sem′ba̩l). A novel by Gilbert Cannan, published in 1922 as a sequel to his *Pugs and Peacocks* (1920).

Semele (sem′e̩.lē). In Greek mythology, the daughter of Cadmus and Harmonia, and mother by Zeus of Dionysus. She was tricked by the jealous Hera into importuning Zeus to allow her to behold him in his godly glory, and was consumed by lightning. Zeus saved the unborn infant Dionysus from her ashes, and in later years Dionysus brought her out of Hades and made her immortal.

Semiramis (sē̩.mir′a̩.mis). [Assyrian, **Sammu-ramat.**] In Assyrian legend, the wife of Ninus, the founder of Nineveh. She was the daughter of the Syrian goddess Derketo, and was endowed with surpassing beauty and wisdom. She beguiled Ninus into making her queen for five days, had him killed, assumed the government of Assyria, and built the city of Babylon with its hanging gardens. She conquered Persia, Egypt, Ethiopia, and Libya, and organized a campaign against India. Some of the exploits of Semiramis are identical with those attributed to the goddess Ishtar, and she was identified with Ishtar in a fertility aspect. The historical original of these legends was possibly Sammu-ramat. She is the only Assyrian queen whose name is recorded on the monuments.

Semitic (sē̩.mit′ik). A large group of related languages spoken in an irregular area reaching from Cape Blanc on the Atlantic Ocean to the Suez Canal and on into Arabia. Semitic-speaking peoples occupy a large area of the W Sudan in Mauritania and N French Sudan, a broad strip along the Mediterranean coast in Algeria, Tunisia, N Libya, and Egypt, and a belt running S from Egypt into the Anglo-Egyptian Sudan, N Ethiopia, and N French Equatorial Africa. According to the conventional classification, Semitic is considered as one of the five language families of modern Africa, along with Hamitic, Sudanic, Bantu, and Khoisan. Like Hamitic and Indo-European it is inflective, employs sex gender, and lacks semantic tone and noun classes. Semitic has been introduced into Africa in at least four different periods. Geez or Ethiopic, the ancient language of Ethiopia, dates from an unknown period, and ceased to be a spoken language at the beginning of the 10th century; it is represented today by derivative languages such as Amharic, Gurage, Harari, Tigre, and Tigrinya, spoken in N Ethiopia. Punic was introduced into N Africa by Carthaginian colonists in the 5th century, but is now extinct. Arabic has been spread through Mohammedan contacts since the 7th century, and accounts for the major part of the area in which Semitic languages are spoken. Hebrew is spoken in N Africa by the Sephardim, descendants of Jews expelled from Spain and Portugal at the end of the 15th century.

Sempill (sem′pil), **Francis.** [Also, **Semple** (sem′pl).] b. at Lochwinnoch, Renfrewshire, Scotland, c1616; d. at Paisley, Scotland, March 12, 1682. A Scottish balladist, wit, and author of papers on political and social questions. Among the many Scottish ballads attributed to him are *Maggie Lauder*, *The Blythsome Bridal*, *Hallow Fair*, and *She Rose and*

---

fat, fāte, fär, ȧsk, fāre; net, mē, hėr; pin, pīne; not, nōte, mȯve, nôr; up, lūte, pu̇ll; ᴛʜ, then;

Let Me In. His chief work (an autobiographical poem), *The Banishment of Poverty by James Duke of Albany,* deals in semihumorous fashion with his own financial and other difficulties, representing poverty as the author's constant and inseparable companion.

Sempill, Robert. [Also, **Semple.**] b. c1530; d. 1595. A Scottish soldier, balladist, and humorous and satirical poet. He lived at Paris (c1544–72), fleeing (Aug. 24, 1572) on the outbreak of the Saint Bartholomew's Massacre, and was afterward resident at Edinburgh. He was violently opposed to Mary, Queen of Scots, and the Roman Catholics. Author of *Ane Complaint upon Fortoun* (1581), *The Legend of the Bischop of St. Androis Lyfe* (1584), *Sege of the Castel of Edinburgh* (1573), and other poems, ballads, and satires. His poems, preserved in manuscript form at London and Edinburgh, have been published in different collections.

Sempill, Robert. [Also, **Semple.**] b. at Beltrees, Lochwinnoch, Renfrewshire, Scotland, c1595; d. probably c1665. A Scottish poet; father of Francis Sempill (c1616–82). He is best known as the author of *The Life and Death of the Piper of Kilbarchan, or the Epitaph of Habbie Simson* (c1640), a richly humorous poem. He also expanded *A Pick-Tooth for the Pope, or a Packman's Pater Noster Set Down in a Dialogue betwixt a Packman and a Priest,* an anticlerical satire in verse begun by his father, Sir James Sempill (1566–1626).

Sempronia (sem.prō'ni.ạ). A dabbler in politics in Ben Jonson's *Catiline's Conspiracy.*

Sempronius (sem.prō'ni.us). In Shakespeare's *Timon of Athens,* one of the lords who refuse to help Timon.

Sempronius. In Shakespeare's *Titus Andronicus,* a kinsman of Titus.

Sempronius. In Joseph Addison's tragedy *Cato,* a Roman senator and adherent of Caesar, to whom he betrays Cato.

Seneca (sen'ẹ.kạ), **Lucius Annaeus.** [Called **Seneca the Younger.**] b. at Corduba (now Córdoba), Spain, c4 B.C.; d. at his villa near Rome, 65 A.D. A Roman Stoic philosopher. While still a child, he was brought by his parents to Rome, where he presently studied rhetoric and philosophy and rose to prominence in early manhood as a pleader of causes. He was a senator under Caligula. In the first year (41) of the reign of Caligula's successor, Claudius, he was banished to Corsica at the instigation of the empress Messalina, who accused him of improper intimacy with Julia, the daughter of Germanicus. He was recalled in 49 through the influence of Agrippina, the new wife of Claudius, who entrusted him with the education of her son Nero. On the accession of his pupil in 54 he obtained virtual control of the government, which he exercised in concert with Sextus Afranius Burrus, prefect of the Praetorian Guard. The restraint which his counsel imposed on the emperor made his tenure of power precarious, and on the death of Burrus in 62 he petitioned for permission to retire from the court. The permission was withheld; nevertheless, he largely withdrew from the management of affairs. He was ultimately charged with complicity in the conspiracy of Gaius Calpurnius Piso, and took his own life in obedience to the order of Nero. His writings consist of the prose works *De ira, De consolatione ad Helviam matrem liber, De consolatione ad Polybium liber, Liber de consolatione ad Marciam, De providentia liber, De animi tranquilitate, De constantia sapientis, De clementia ad Neronem Caesarem libri duo, De brevitate vitae ad Paulinum liber, De vita beata ad Gallionem, De otio aut secessu sapientis, De beneficiis libri septem, Epistolae ad Lucilium, Apocolocyntosis,* and *Quaestionum naturalium libri septem;* and the tragedies *Hercules, Troades, Phoenissae* or *Thebais, Medea, Phaedra* or *Hippolytus, Oedipus, Agamemnon, Thyestes, Hercules Oetaeus,* and according to some, *Octavia.*

Senecan tragedy. A term applied to Elizabethan tragedy based upon the theme of revenge, influenced by the nine tragedies of the Roman Lucius Annaeus Seneca. Principally, three Senecan themes were taken over by the Elizabethans: the inconstancy of fortune, as in his *Troades;* commission of a horrible crime and its attendant evils, as in *Thyestes, Medea,* and *Agamemnon;* and advocation of a life of simplicity, poverty, and chastity, as in *Hercules Oetaeus* and *Hippolytus.* The main character may take his revenge on the person doing the original wrong or upon his descendants; he may use accomplices; he may claim to be mad; and he may reflect rhetorically on the broad topics of life, death, and fate, as he prepares to take his revenge. The Elizabethans, who conceived of revenge as a form of private justice, contrasted instant retaliation with long-harbored resentment. Other Senecan characteristics adopted by the Elizabethan dramatists were ghosts, who appear in the prologue and to spur on the revenger; the detailed study of a passion, such as ambition, love, jealousy, or pride; a structure based upon rising and falling action in five acts; and dialogue in the first scene to explain previous action. Early Elizabethan Senecan tragedies, such as Sackville and Norton's *Gorboduc,* were outright imitations of Seneca, but later, with Kyd, who fixed the formula of the ghost, the revenge, and plenty of blood, the revenger became a Machiavellian villain, as in his *Spanish Tragedy,* one of the most popular of the type. It is interesting to note that the villain was frequently a Spaniard, because of the popular Elizabethan belief that all Spaniards were masters of hypocritical dissimulation. Iago, in Shakespeare's *Othello,* is a refined version of such a villain. In the plays of Tourneur, such as *The Revenger's Tragedy,* the plot becomes considerably more complicated and the ethics of Stoicism, as in the original Senecan tragedies, tend to be submerged in cynical pessimism.

Senior, Duke. See **Duke Senior.**

Senior (sēn'yọr), **Nassau William.** b. at Compton, Berkshire, England, Sept. 26, 1790; d. at Kensington, London, June 4, 1864. An English political economist and critic. He was professor of political economy at Oxford, and was a member of the education commission of 1857. He published *An Outline of the Science of Political Economy* (1836), a lecture on the *Production of Wealth* (1849), *American Slavery* (1856), *Suggestions on Popular Education* (1861), *Essays on Fiction* (1864), and *Historical and Philosophical Essays* (1865).

ḍ, d or j; ṣ, s or sh; ṭ, t or ch; ẓ, z or zh; o, F. cloche; ü, F. menu; ċh, Sc. loch; ṅ, F. bonbon.

Sennacherib (se̱.nak′e̱.rib). [Assyrian, **Sin-ahe-erba.**] King of Assyria (705–681 B.C.); son and successor of Sargon II. Sennacherib was one of the great Assyrian monarchs, and well known in Biblical history. In English literature, his story provides the basis of Byron's *Destruction of Sennacherib*. He was first engaged, like his father, in many bloody wars against the Babylonian and Elamite alliance, the hereditary foe of Assyria. These ended with the capture and destruction of Babylon in 689, and the defeat of Elam in 691 B.C. Of his further expeditions, which according to Greek and cuneiform accounts reached as far as Cilicia in Asia Minor, where he is supposed to have founded the city of Tarsus, may be mentioned that against Phoenicia and Palestine known from the Old Testament. The expedition was provoked by the coalition of Phoenicia, Palestine, and the principalities of Syria with Egypt, Mesopotamia's rival for supremacy in Asia, and its object was to isolate Egypt. The bulk of the Assyrian army met (701 B.C.) the forces of the coalition at Eltekeh (Assyrian, Altaku). The battle seems to have been indecisive. The siege of Jerusalem had to be given up because of a pestilence which broke out in the Assyrian army. Like Sargon, Sennacherib engaged in much building, and endeavored generally to promote the welfare of the country. His reign was of special importance for the history of the city of Nineveh, which, after having long been neglected, was again raised by him to the dignity of a capital, and restored to unprecedented splendor and glory. While praying in a temple he was murdered by two of his sons, who fled to Armenia (Urartu).

Sense and Sensibility. A novel by Jane Austen, written during 1797–98 and published in 1811. It is the story of two sisters, daughters of Mrs. Henry Dashwood; Elinor has sense, and Marianne has sensibility. On Mr. Dashwood's death, his money has passed to Mrs. Dashwood's stepson, John, so that Mrs. Dashwood and her daughters are obliged to seek modest quarters in Devonshire. Meanwhile, Elinor has met and fallen in love with Edward Ferrars, John's brother-in-law, and Marianne with John Willoughby, an attractive scoundrel. John leads Marianne to believe that he is in love with her, but when the girls visit London, she receives a cruel letter from him informing her that he is going to marry a wealthy woman. She is heartbroken, and makes no attempt to conceal her grief and distress. Her sister's love story is no more fortunate. Edward has been engaged for four years to Lucy Steele, a shrewd and selfish girl, and will not sully his honor (as he sees it) by breaking the engagement. When Edward's mother learns of the engagement, she disinherits him and settles all her fortune on Robert, the younger son, whereupon the avaricious Lucy abandons Edward for the brother with the better prospects. Edward is thus left free to marry Elinor, who has concealed her unhappiness and borne all her troubles with resignation. Marianne comes to realize that her overly romantic nature is bringing her unhappiness, and she finally determines to marry Colonel Brandon, an older and more serious admirer.

Sensitive Plant, The. A poem (1820) by Percy Bysshe Shelley.

sentimental comedy. A type of drama popular in the late 17th and early 18th centuries, and associated particularly with Sir Richard Steele (who was the first and the best-known of the writers to specialize in it). It is characterized by a tendency to moralize, and by heroes and heroines of a remarkable gentility (as opposed to the coarseness of the principal figures in many of the plays of the Restoration).

sentimentalism. A tendency to be swayed by sentiment; affected sensibility or sentiment; mawkish susceptibility; specifically, the philosophy of Rousseau and others, which gave great weight to the impulses of a susceptible heart. The French Revolution, with its terror, was regarded as in some measure the consequence of this philosophy, which thenceforward fell more and more into contempt. At present, the fact that it was a deliberately defended attitude of mind is almost forgotten, the current of sentiment running now strongly the other way. "Eschew political sentimentalism." (Disraeli, *Coningsby*.)

Sentimental Journey through France and Italy, A. A work by Laurence Sterne, two volumes of which were published shortly before his death in 1768.

Sentimental Tommy. A novel (1896) by Sir J. M. Barrie: a sequel is *Tommy and Grizel* (1900).

Sephardim (se.fär′dim). Spanish-Portuguese Jews, as distinguished from Ashkenazim, or German-Polish Jews.

Sephardo (se.fär′dō), **Salomo.** In George Eliot's *The Spanish Gipsy*, a Jewish astrologer.

Sepher-haz-Zohar (se′fer.häz′zō′här). See **Zohar.**

Sephestia (se.fes′ti.a̱). In Robert Greene's romance *Menaphon*, the banished daughter of King Damocles, beloved by the shepherd Menaphon. While disguised as the shepherdess Samela, she is also the object of the passion of her father, her husband Maximus, and her son Pleusidippus.

Sepoy Mutiny (sē′poi). A revolt of the Sepoy troops in British India in the transference of the administration of India from the East India Company to the crown.

September. A novel by Frank Swinnerton, published in 1919.

September Massacres. A series of murders perpetrated by the extreme revolutionaries at Paris, Sept. 2–6, 1792, the victims being royalists and constitutionalists confined in prison. The massacres were undertaken by the Commune of Paris, and were occasioned by the consternation felt over the approach of the Prussians, whose avowed object was to restore the king. Similar executions took place at other cities.

September, 1913. A poem by William Butler Yeats, written in 1913 and published (1914) in *Responsibilities*. The poem mourns the death of "romantic Ireland":

> Romantic Ireland's dead and gone,
> It's with O'Leary in the grave.

septenarius (sep.te̱.nā′ri.us). In Latin prosody, a verse consisting of seven feet. The name is used especially for the trochaic tetrameter catalectic (*versus quadratus*), which in the older Latin writers admits a spondee or anapest in the first, third, and

---

fat, fāte, fär, a̱sk, fāre; net, mē, hér; pin, pīne; not, nōte, mȯve, nôr; up, lūte, pull; ᴛʜ, then;

fifth, as well as in the second, fourth, and sixth places, and for the iambic tetrameter catalectic.

Septimus Crisparkle (sep'ti.mus kris'pär.kl). See **Crisparkle, Septimus.**

Septimus Harding (här'ding). See **Harding, Septimus.**

Septuagint (sep'tū.a.jint). A Greek version of the Hebrew Scriptures made, according to tradition, by about 70 translators; usually expressed by the symbol LXX ("the Seventy"). The legend is that it was made by 72 persons, six from each of the 12 tribes, in 72 days. It is said by Josephus to have been made in the reign and by the order of Ptolemy II (Ptolemy Philadelphus), king of Egypt, c270 or 280 B.C. It is supposed, however, by modern critics that this version of the several books is the work not only of different hands but of separate times. It is probable that at first only the Pentateuch was translated, and that the remaining books were translated at intervals thereafter; however, the entire translation is believed to have been completed by the 2nd century B.C. The Septuagint is written in the Hellenistic (Alexandrine) dialect, and is linguistically of great importance from its effect upon the diction of the New Testament, and as the source of a large part of the religious and theological vocabulary of the Greek fathers, and (through the Old Latin version of the Bible and the influence of this on the Vulgate) of that of the Latin fathers also, and of all western nations to the present day. In the Greek Church the Septuagint has been in continuous use from the earliest times (although other Greek versions were anciently also in circulation) and it is the Old Testament still used in that church. The Septuagint contains the books afterward placed in the Apocrypha and the pseudepigraphia intermingled among the other books. It is the version which agrees with most of the citations in the New Testament.

sequel. The continuation of the narrative which began in a preceding section.

Seraphim and Other Poems. A volume of poems (1838) by Elizabeth Barrett Browning.

Serapis (se.rā'pis). An ancient deity of Egyptian origin, whose worship was officially promoted under the Ptolemies and was introduced into Greece and later to Rome. Serapis was the dead Apis bull, honored under the attributes of Osiris; he was lord of the underworld and identified with the Greek Hades. His worship was a combination of Egyptian and Greek cults, and was favored by the Ptolemies for political reasons.

Sergeant (sär'jant), **Emily Frances Adeline.** b. at Ashbourne, Derbyshire, England, July 4, 1851; d. at Bournemouth, Hampshire, England, Dec. 4, 1904. An English novelist and poet. The daughter of a Methodist minister, she was at one time a member of the Church of England, became an agnostic and a Fabian Socialist, and finally became a Roman Catholic. Author of more than 90 novels, among them *Dicky and His Friends* (1879), *Una's Crusade* (1880), *Jacobi's Wife* (1882), *Beyond Recall* (1883), *An Open Foe* (1884), *No Saint* (1886), *Seventy Times Seven* (1888), *Esther Denison* (1889), *Story of a Penitent Soul* (1892), *The Idol Maker* (1897), *This Body of Death* (1901), *A Soul Apart*

(1902), and *Beneath the Veil* (1903). She also wrote *Poems* (1866), and *Roads to Rome* (1901), an account of her conversion.

Sergius (sėr'ji.us). A dashing, recklessly courageous soldier in George Bernard Shaw's *Arms and the Man.*

Serlio (ser'lyō), **Sebastiano.** b. at Bologna, Italy, Sept. 6, 1473; d. at Fontainebleau, France, 1554. An Italian architect and theater designer. His *Architectura*, published in 1551, was translated into English in 1611 and describes his idea of a theater and its sets, based upon the Roman theaters. These sets were adapted by Inigo Jones for court performances, and also appeared in the private playhouses of the early 17th century in England.

Serpentine (sėr'pen.tīn), **The.** An artificial pond in Hyde Park, London, made by order of Queen Caroline.

serpentine verse. A metrical form in which each line begins and ends with the same word. It is so called because of the old representations of the serpent with his tail in his mouth, signifying eternity (since it has neither beginning nor end).

Servetus (sėr.vē'tus), **Michael.** [Latinized name of **Miguel Serveto.**] b. at probably Tudela (he gave both Tudela and Villanova as his birthplace), Spain, 1511; burned at Geneva, Switzerland, Oct. 27, 1553. A Spanish controversialist and physician. He studied law at Saragossa and Toulouse, and afterward visited Italy in the train of Juan de Quintaña, confessor to Charles V. He published at Haguenau in 1531 an essay directed against the doctrine of the Trinity, entitled *De trinitatis erroribus*, which attracted considerable attention. It was revised and reprinted under the title of *Dialogorum de trinitate libri duo* in 1532. In 1535 he was at Lyons editing scientific works for the printing firm of Trechsel. He removed in 1536 to Paris, where, according to his own statement, he graduated in medicine and lectured on geometry and astrology. He afterward studied theology at Louvain. After practicing medicine for short periods at Avignon and Charlieu, and after further study in medicine at Montpellier, he settled in 1541 as a medical practitioner at Vienne. He is credited with the discovery of the pulmonary circulation of the blood. In 1553 he published *Christianismi restitutio*, which caused him to be arrested by order of the inquisitor general at Lyons. He escaped, but was apprehended at the instance of John Calvin at Geneva on his way to Naples, and was burned after a trial for heresy lasting from Aug. 14 until Oct. 26, 1553.

Servilius (sėr.vil'i.us). In Shakespeare's *Timon of Athens,* one of Timon's servants.

Sesame and Lilies. A collection of essays (1865) by John Ruskin.

Sesostris (se.sos'tris). In Greek legend, a king of Egypt, said to have conquered vast areas in Asia and Africa. His legendary exploits are said to be founded on the deeds of Ramses II and others.

sestet (ses'tet). The two concluding stanzas of a sonnet, consisting of three lines each; the last six lines of a sonnet. "Milton . . . frequently disregards the law which makes separate sections of octave and sestet, and welds the two." (*Athenaeum*, No. 3253.)

sestina (ses.tē′nạ). A poem in fixed form, borrowed from the French, and said to have been invented by the Provençal troubadour Arnaut Daniel (13th century). It consisted originally of six stanzas of six unrhymed lines, with a final triplet or half-stanza, also unrhymed—all the lines being of the same length. The terminal words of stanzas 2 to 6 were the same as those of stanza 1, but arranged differently; and they were repeated in the triplet or envoy, partly at the end and partly in the middle of the lines. The modern sestina is written on two or three rhymes, and the formula for a two-rhymed sestina is thus given in the *Vers Français et leur Prosodie* of the best French authority, M. de Gramont: 1, 2, 3, 4, 5, 6; 6, 1, 5, 2, 4, 3; 3, 6, 4, 1, 2, 5; 5, 3, 2, 6, 1, 4; 4, 5, 1, 3, 6, 2; 2, 4, 6, 5, 3, 1; triplet 2, 4, 6 at the end, and 1, 3, 5 at the beginning of the lines. In stanza 1, lines 1, 3, and 4 rhyme, and 2, 5, and 6 rhyme. Sestinas were written in Italy by Dante and Petrarch, in Spain and Portugal by Cervantes and Camões, and in England by Drummond of Hawthornden (1585–1649). Swinburne (in *Poems and Ballads*, 2d ser.) has achieved a double sestina.

A sestina is a poem written neither in rhyme nor blank verse, but in so-called six-line stanzas, each one of which has to take the last word of the stanza preceding it, and twist it about into some new and fantastic meaning. (*Athenaeum*, No. 3141.)

sestine (ses′tin). In prosody, the same as *sestina*.

The day was so wasted that onely his riming
Sestine, delivered by one of great account among
them, could obtain favor to bee heard.
(Sir P. Sidney, *Arcadia*, iv.)

Sestos (ses′tọs). [Also, **Sestus**.] In ancient geography, a town in the Chersonesus Thracica, situated on the European shore of the Hellespont, opposite Abydos. It is noted as the residence of Hero in the legend of Hero and Leander, and as the place of debarkation of the army of Xerxes in his invasion of Europe.

Set (set). [Also: **Seth** (seth); Greek, **Typhon**.] In Egyptian mythology, the brother, opponent, and slayer of Osiris. He was the god of darkness, night, and evil. Originally, he was a war god who insured victories for Egypt, only much later did he become the personification of evil. With the division of Egypt among the gods, Upper Egypt was assigned to Set, Lower Egypt to Horus. He was called Typhon by the Greeks. In Egyptian art he is shown with a strange animal's head, having a pointed muzzle and high, square ears.

Setebos (set′ẹ.bos). A supposed Patagonian god, mentioned by Caliban in Shakespeare's *Tempest*, and by Browning in *Caliban upon Setebos*.

Seth (seth), **Andrew**. [Later known as **Andrew Seth Pringle-Pattison**.] b. at Edinburgh, Dec. 20, 1856; d. near Selkirk, Scotland, Sept. 1, 1931. Scottish philosophical writer, professor of logic and metaphysics at the University of Edinburgh from 1891. He was appointed professor of logic and philosophy at University College, Cardiff, in 1883, and of logic, rhetoric, and metaphysics at St. Andrews in 1887. In 1898 he assumed the name of Pringle-Pattison (in order to meet the provisions of a bequest). Among his works are *The Development from Kant to Hegel* (1882), *Scottish Philosophy* (1885), *Hegelianism and Personality* (1887), *Man's Place in the Cosmos* (1897), *Two Lectures on Theism* (1897), *The Philosophical Radicals* (1907), and *The Idea of Immortality* (1922).

Seth Bede (bēd). See **Bede, Seth**.

Seton-Watson (sē′tọn.wot′sọn), **Robert William**. b. Aug. 20, 1879; d. on Skye, Scotland, July 25, 1951. A British historian, expert on central Europe and the Balkans. Professor of central European history (1922–45) at the University of London, he was the founder of the magazine *New Europe* (1916) and joint editor, with Sir Bernard Pares, of the *Slavonic Review* (1922–49). Among his works are *The Southern Slav Question* (1911), *Europe in the Melting Pot* (1919), *Slovakia Then and Now* (1931), *Treaty Revision* (1934), *Britain in Europe, 1789–1914* (1937), *Britain and the Dictators* (1938), and *From Munich to Danzig* (1939).

setting. The mounting of a play or an opera for the stage; the equipment and arrangement of scenery, costumes, and properties; the mise en scène.

Settle (set′l), **Elkanah**. b. at Dunstable, England, Jan. 1, 1648; d. in the Charterhouse, London, Feb. 12, 1724. An English poet and playwright. He was a fellow of Trinity College, Oxford, and wrote and edited many political pamphlets in the time of Charles II. He offended John Dryden, who thereupon published a pamphlet attacking him (Dryden was assisted in writing the pamphlet by John Crowne and Thomas Shadwell). Settle criticized and "answered" all Dryden's political poems in retaliation, and the fashionable literary world at once took sides, Settle being the favorite among the younger Cambridge and London men. He has been immortalized by the ridicule of Dryden and Alexander Pope, being the Doeg of *Absalom and Achitophel* and appearing in the *Dunciad*. Later he was made city poet, and composed verses to be recited at the pageants; he was the last to hold that office. Among his plays are *Cambyses, King of Persia* (1666), *The Empress of Morocco* (1671 and 1673), *Love and Revenge* (1675), *Pastor Fido, or the Faithful Shepherd* (1677; a pastoral drama, being an alteration of Sir R. Fanshawe's translation from Guarini), *Fatal Love, or the Forced Inconstancy* (1680), *The Female Prelate, or the History of the Life and Death of Pope Joan* (1680), *The Heir of Morocco, with the Death of Gayland* (produced 1682, printed 1694), *Distressed Innocence, or the Princess of Persia* (1691), *The World in the Moon* (1697; a comic opera), *The City Ramble, or the Playhouse Wedding* (1711), and *The Ladies' Triumph* (1718; a comic opera).

Seven against Thebes (thēbz), **Expedition of the.** In Greek legend, an expedition by the heroes Adrastus, Polynices, Tydeus, Amphiaraus, Hippomedon, Capaneus, and Parthenopaeus against Thebes, to overthrow the usurping king Eteocles and restore the throne to Polynices. All perished except Adrastus. The legend provides the basis for a tragedy by Aeschylus, exhibited 468 B.C.

Seven Bishops, Case of the. A famous English trial in 1688. Archbishop William Sancroft of Canterbury and six bishops (Thomas Ken of Bath and

Wells, John Lake of Chichester, William Lloyd of St. Asaph, Jonathan Trelawny of Bristol, Francis Turner of Rochester and Ely, Thomas White of Peterborough) were arraigned on a charge of libel in protesting, in a petition to James II, against his order that his "declarations for liberty of conscience" be read in the churches. They were acquitted on the day (June 30) that the invitation was sent to William of Orange (William III) to land in England.

Seven Champions of Christendom. In medieval tales, the seven national saints, Saint Denis of France, Saint Anthony of Italy, Saint James of Spain, Saint George of England, Saint Andrew of Scotland, Saint Patrick of Ireland, and Saint David of Wales. Their exploits are celebrated in many ballads, plays, and other forms of literature, notably in the *Famous History of the Seven Champions of Christendom*, by Richard Johnston, a romance entered on the Stationers' Register in 1596; a second part was brought out in 1608, and a third in 1616.

Seven Champions of Christendom. A play by John Kirke, licensed in 1638 and probably acted in 1636. It is in prose and verse.

Seven Cities, Island of the. A fabled island which, in the 14th and 15th centuries, was supposed to exist in the Atlantic W of Europe. It was said to have been peopled by seven bishops who, with many followers, had been driven out of Spain by the invasion of the Moors. In 1475 and later, the kings of Portugal granted privileges to discover and govern it. The geographers of the time frequently called it Antilla or Antillia.

Seven Deadly Sins. Pride, Envy, Anger, Lechery, Covetousness (or Avarice), Gluttony, and Sloth. Discussions of these sins formed a large part of medieval theological tracts and sermon literature, and they are represented in Chaucer's *Parson's Tale* and in *Piers Plowman.* Spenser also uses them as the basis of part of his allegory in *The Faerie Queene.*

Seven Deadly Sins of London, The. A pamphlet by Thomas Dekker, published in 1606.

Seven Dials. A small area in London, near St. Martin's Lane, out of which stem seven small streets, once the focal point of an area famous for its slums, depravity, and crime. It is mentioned frequently in 19th-century English journalism, and also in the works of Dickens (it was near Seven Dials that Dr. Mantalini was last seen alive in *Nicholas Nickleby*).

Seven for a Secret. A love story by Mary Webb, published in 1922.

Seven Hills of Rome, the. The seven hills (the Aventine, Caelian, Capitoline, Esquiline, Palatine, Quirinal, and Viminal) on and about which the ancient city of Rome was built.

Seven Lamps of Architecture, The. A treatise on architecture by John Ruskin, published in 1849. The author defends what he considers to be the noblest period of architecture, the Gothic, on the basis of an aesthetic that is inextricably intertwined with morality. The work was influential in giving a national form to 19th-century English art. The seven lamps that burn on the altar of art are Sacrifice, Truth, Power, Beauty, Life, Memory, and Obedience. According to Ruskin, these are reflected in the creation of all good art.

Seven Sages. Seven men of ancient Greece, famous for their practical wisdom. A list commonly given is made up of Thales of Miletus, Solon of Athens, Bias of Priene, Chilo of Sparta, Cleobulus of Rhodes, Periander of Corinth, and Pittacus of Mitylene.

Seven Seas, The. A volume of verse by Rudyard Kipling, published in 1896. It is named for the North and the South Atlantic, the North and the South Pacific, the Arctic, the Antarctic, and the Indian oceans.

Seven Sisters. A poetical name of the Pleiades.

Seven Sleepers of Ephesus (ef'ẹ.sus). In Christian legend, seven Christian youths who concealed themselves in a cavern near Ephesus, and were walled in during the persecution of Christians under Decius (249–251 A.D.). They fell asleep there, and did not awaken till two or three hundred years later, when Christianity had become the religion of the empire under Theodosius II. The Mohammedan version of the story mentions a little dog who guarded them during this time.

Seven Wise Masters. [Also, **Seven Sages.**] An old collection of tales, of Eastern origin, which has undergone many transformations. It is the story of a king who is dissuaded from executing his son (falsely accused by one of his queens of making improper advances to her) by his son's seven instructors, each of whom tells a tale which shows the dangers of hasty judgment and postpones the execution. At the end of seven days and seven stories, the young prince himself tells a story which reveals that he has, in fact, refused the queen's advances, and the queen is put to death in his stead.

Seven Wonders of the World. The seven most remarkable structures of ancient times. These were the Egyptian pyramids, the Mausoleum erected by Artemisia at Halicarnassus, the Temple of Artemis at Ephesus, the hanging gardens at Babylon, the Colossus at Rhodes, the statue of Zeus by Phidias in the great temple at Olympia, and the Pharos or lighthouse at Alexandria. The walls of Babylon sometimes replace the last.

Severn (sev'ẽrn), **Joseph.** b. 1793; d. at Rome, Aug. 3, 1879. An English portrait and figure painter, noted for his close friendship with Keats.

Severus (sẹ.vir'us), **Wall of.** A wall built c208 A.D by the emperor Lucius Septimius Severus, between the river Tyne and Solway Firth in Britain, as a defense against northern inroads. It followed the line of the fortifications of Hadrian.

Sévigné (sã.vē.nyã), Marquise (or Madame) **de.** [Maiden name, **Marie de Rabutin-Chantal.**] b. at Paris, Feb. 6, 1626; d. at Grignan, Drôme, France, April 18, 1696. A French epistolary writer. In 1644 she was married to Henri, Marquis de Sévigné, who was killed in a duel in 1651. Their union produced two children, a daughter, Françoise Marguerite, and a son, Charles. The former married in 1669 François d'Adhémar, Comte de Grignan, who occupied an administrative position in southern France. Madame de Grignan accompanied her husband to his home, while her mother spent her time either at Paris or at her country seat, Les Rochers, in Brittany. It was this separation that occasioned the famous correspondence from mother to daughter which ranks as one of the finest achievements of its type in French literature. As everything of daily interest is recorded by Madame de Sévigné for her daughter's benefit, these letters are valuable from a historical point of view as well as for the charm of their expression.

Sèvres (sevr). A town in N France, in the department of Seine-et-Oise, on the Seine River ab. 2 mi. SW of Paris. It is celebrated for its porcelain manufactures (established at Vincennes in 1745, removed to Sèvres in 1756, and acquired by the state in 1759), which are exported to many countries. The first treaty between the Allies and Turkey, superseded by the 1923 Treaty of Lausanne, was signed here in 1920. The museum of ceramics was damaged in World War II.

Seward (sō'ạrd), **Anna.** [Called the **"Swan of Lichfield."**] b. at Eyam, Derbyshire, England, 1747; d. at Lichfield, Staffordshire, England, March 25, 1809. An English poet. In 1782 she published her poetical novel *Louisa;* this was followed by *Sonnets* (1799) and the *Life of Dr. Darwin* (1804). She was associated with Samuel Johnson, Erasmus Darwin, and others, and her letters, in which she imitated Johnson, were published in six volumes (1811–13). She bequeathed the publication of her poems to Sir Walter Scott. They were issued in three volumes in 1810.

Sewell (sō'ẹl), **Anna.** b. at Yarmouth, England, March 30, 1820; d. at Norwich, England, April 25, 1878. An English writer, author of *Black Beauty, the Autobiography of a Horse* (1877). A highly popular work, it was translated into most of the European languages and went through many editions. She also wrote *Walks with Mamma, Homely Ballads, Mother's Last Words,* and stories for children in prose and verse.

Sextus Pompeius (seks'tus pom.pē'us). **See Pompey.**

Sextus Tarquinius (tär.kwin'i.us). In Roman legend, the son of Tarquinius Superbus, whose rape of Lucretia led to the fall of the Tarquins.

Seymour (sē'mōr), **Beatrice Kean.** [Maiden name, **Stapleton.**] An English novelist. Her novels include *Invisible Tides* (1919), *Intrusion* (1921), *The Hopeful Journey* (1923), *The Romantic Tradition* (1925; American title, *Unveiled*), *The Last Day* (1926), *Three Wives* (1927), *Youth Rides Out* (1928), *False Spring* (1929), *But Not for Love* (1930), *Maids and Mistresses* (1932), *Daughter to Philip* (1933), *Interlude for Sally* (1934), *The Happier Eden* (1937), *The Unquiet Field* (1940), and *Family Group* (1947).

Seyton (sē'ton). In Shakespeare's *Macbeth,* an officer attending Macbeth. He reports the death of Lady Macbeth.

Seyton, Catherine. An attendant of Mary, Queen of Scots, in Sir Walter Scott's novel *The Abbot.*

Sforza (sfôr'tsä), **Francesco.** b. 1401; d. 1466. An Italian condottiere. He married Bianca Maria Visconti, the natural daughter of Filippo Maria Visconti, Duke of Milan, on whose death (1447) without male heirs he procured his own elevation as duke (1450), after overthrowing the Ambrosian

republic set up by the Milanese. He widened the realm held by the Milanese duchy, ruling over Lombardy and Genoa.

Sforza, Ludovico. The "Duke of Milan" in Philip Massinger's tragedy of that name. Like Shakespeare's Othello, he is enmeshed in tragedy by his unjustified suspicions of his wife, taking her coldness upon his return from a trip as a proof of infidelity and believing the jealous accusations of his relations and of his favorite, Francisco.

Sganarelle (zgà.nà.rel). A comic character out of ancient comedy, frequently introduced by Molière in his plays, and invested by him with different traits and peculiarities according to the necessities of the subject. He first appears in *Sganarelle, ou le cocu imaginaire* (1660), and after that in many other plays: in *Don Juan, ou le festin de Pierre* (where he is the Leporello of the opera *Don Giovanni*), in *L'Amour médecin, Le Médecin malgré lui, Le Médecin volant, L'École des maris, Le Mariage forcé,* and others. The Sganarelle to which most frequent allusion is made is that in *Le Médecin magré lui,* where he uses many expressions which have become proverbial, such as his often reiterated "*Nous avons changé tout cela*" (We have changed all that).

Shabby Genteel Story, A. A tale by Thackeray, first printed serially in *Fraser's Magazine* in 1840. It appeared in book form in 1852. It was subsequently included, as a prologue, with *The Adventures of Philip.*

Shadow (shad'ō), **Simon.** In Shakespeare's *2 Henry IV,* a man pressed into military service by Falstaff.

Shadow and Substance. A play (1934) by Paul Vincent Carroll, drawing upon the author's own background as a schoolteacher in Ireland. O'Flingsley, a teacher, has written an anticlerical book which incites a mob. The book and O'Flingsley's conception of a teacher's responsibilities to his pupils have led to the vexation of his superior, Canon Skerritt, who rigidly adheres to orthodoxy in religion while neglecting its spirit. Torn between them is O'Flingsley's servant-girl, Brigid, who dies while protecting him from the mob. She represents Carroll's idea of a true Christian, the simple person who has direct communication with God and who is truly humble and sympathetic to her fellow men. The play was intended by Carroll as an attack on the domination of Irish schools by the clergy.

Shadowgraph, The. A volume of poems by Edward Shanks, published in 1925.

Shadow-Line, The. A novel (1917) by Joseph Conrad.

Shadow of a Gunman, The. A play (1923) in two acts by Sean O'Casey.

Shadow of the Glen, The. A comedy (1903) by John Millington Synge. Nora Burke, an Irish peasant woman, is deceived by her husband, an old man, into believing he is dead. She thereupon confesses several indiscretions to a tramp who comes by (which the "dead" husband hears), and then goes off to fetch Michael Dara, a young neighbor. The husband sits up for some whiskey while she is gone, but plays dead again upon her return, and listens as she outlines to the sympathetic Michael her story of her husband's shortcomings. Her insults finally cause him to leap up and drive her out of the house; Michael, previously a suitor, has no desire to be involved in the quarrel, and sits down to a drink with her husband. Nora goes off with the tramp.

Shadrach (shā'drak). In the Bible, a companion of Daniel: one of the three (Shadrach, Meshach, Abednego) thrown into the fiery furnace of Nebuchadnezzar. Dan. iii. 12–30.

Shadwell (shad'wel), **Charles.** See under **Shadwell, Thomas.**

Shadwell, Thomas. b. in Norfolk, England, c1642; d. at London, Nov. 20, 1692. An English playwright and poet laureate. He was educated at Cambridge and the Inner Temple, but deserted the law for literature. He is chiefly remembered for his quarrel with John Dryden, who revenged Shadwell's attack upon him in *The Medal of John Bayes* (1682) by mercilessly satirizing him in *MacFlecknoe, or a Satire on the True-Blue-Protestant Poet,* T. S., and as "Og" in the second part of *Absalom and Achitophel.* Shadwell, a Whig who scoffed at Catholicism, naturally aroused the antagonism of Dryden, who was a Tory and a Catholic. He succeeded Dryden, however, as poet laureate and historiographer royal in 1689 (when Dryden would not take the oath to William III), notwithstanding his predecessor's satire in *MacFlecknoe:*

> The rest to some fain meaning make pretence,
> But Shadwell never deviates into sense.

Shadwell was heavy, but not so dull as Dryden saw fit to depict him. His plays are coarse and witty. Among them are *The Sullen Lovers, or the Impertinents* (1668), *The Humorist* (1671), *The Tempest* (1667, based upon an opera of D'Avenant and Dryden), *Psyche* (1675, a dramatic opera), *Epsom Wells* (1673), *The Virtuoso* (1676), *The Libertine* (1676), *The True Widow* (1679, a comedy to which Dryden wrote an epilogue in 1678, before their quarrel), *The Lancashire Witches and Tegue o' Divelly, the Irish Priest* (1682), *The Squire of Alsatia* (1688), *Bury Fair* (1689), *The Amorous Bigotte* (1690), and *The Volunteers* (1693). His opera, *The Tempest,* is a romantic adaptation of Shakespeare's play and is interesting for its elaborate staging and songs, particularly "Arise ye Subterranean Winds." An entirely fanciful setting distinguishes *Psyche,* his second opera. Aside from *The Sullen Lovers,* where he satirizes the love-and-honor dilemma characteristic of Dryden's tragicomic plots, his own style of comedy is Jonsonian in conception. *The Humorists* centers around a rather pure and tender couple, Raymund and Theodosia, with various of Jonson's "humour" types surrounding them. *Epsom Wells* is essentially nonheroic, stressing the importance of a proper marriage and exalting in characteristically Restoration fashion the art of cuckolding. *The Virtuoso* satirizes affectations of the day in Jonsonian fashion, although not with the same power. *The Squire of Alsatia* pretends to a moral purpose while presenting a realistic picture of rascality in a disreputable corner of London, with the foul-mouthed obscenity that sometimes mars Jonson himself. His later plays tend toward the sentimental as in *Bury Fair.* His son, Charles Shadwell, was the author of several plays sometimes confounded with Thomas Shadwell's. They are *The*

Fair Quaker of Deal (1710), *The Humours of the Navy* (1710), *The Humours of the Army* (1713), *The Hasty Wedding* (1717), and others.

Shaftesbury (shàfts'ber"i, -bèr.i), 1st Earl of. [Title of **Anthony Ashley Cooper;** additional title, 1st Baron **Ashley.**] b. at Wimborne St. Giles, Dorsetshire, England, July 22, 1621; d. at Amsterdam, Jan. 21, 1683. An English statesman. A member (1640) of Parliament, at first he supported the cause of Charles I, but in 1644 went over to the Parliamentary side, was appointed field-marshal with the command of a brigade of horse and foot Aug. 3, 1644, and took an active part in the struggle, capturing Corfe Castle April, 1646. He was an adherent of Cromwell in the parliaments of 1653 and 1654, but soon broke with him. He remained an active supporter of Parliament against the army, supporting the Rump Parliament and eventually becoming reconciled with Monck. He was one of the commissioners to Charles II at Breda, sustaining during this journey an injury that left him with a chronic abscess. He became a privy councillor at the Restoration and held several official posts, including that of chancellor of the exchequer (1661–72). He was a member of the "Cabal" ministry (1667) and became lord chancellor in 1672. He supported (1673) the Test Act, with the result that he was dismissed (Sept. 9, 1673). He became thereafter the leader of the antiroyal faction, and was a prominent supporter of the anti-Roman Catholic agitation. He was jailed (1677) for a year when he objected to the proroguing of Parliament for more than a year. In the "Popish Plot" period following the allegations of Titus Oates in 1678 he took a leading part in attacking the Roman Catholics. He supported Monmouth, the king's illegitimate son, against the claims of the Duke of York (later James II) to the throne, was arrested in 1681, indicted for high treason, and released by a Whig jury on bail. Recognizing that the chances for a successful rebellion were slight, he fled to Holland in 1682, where he died. He was active in colonial affairs and was one of the nine to whom Carolina was granted March 24, 1663. It was at his suggestion that John Locke drew up a constitution for that colony (1669). Dryden, who made him the Achitophel of *Absalom and Achitophel,* drew a very unflattering picture of him, as did Macaulay, but later historians have shown him as the first real Parliamentary leader in English history.

Shaftesbury, 3rd Earl of. [Title of **Anthony Ashley Cooper;** called Lord **Ashley.**] b. at London, Feb. 26, 1671; d. at Naples, Italy, Feb. 15, 1713. An English moralist. Author of *Characteristics of Men, Manners, Opinions, and Times* (1711; revised ed., 1713). In this are included a "Letter Concerning Enthusiasm," "Sensus Communis: an Essay Concerning Wit and Humour," and "An Enquiry Concerning Virtue."

Shaftesbury, 7th Earl of. [Title of **Anthony Ashley Cooper;** called Lord **Ashley.**] b. at London, April 28, 1801; d. at Folkestone, Kent, England, Oct. 1, 1885. An English philanthropist. He entered Parliament as Lord Ashley in 1826, and succeeded to the earldom on the death of his father in 1851. He was a promoter of many philanthropic projects, and

---

d̦, d or j; ș, s or sh; ț, t or ch; z̦, z or zh; o, F. cloche; ü, F. menu; c̆h, Sc. loch; n̦, F. bonbon.

was president of the British and Foreign Bible Society, the Evangelical Alliance, and others.

Shafton (shaf'tọn). A false friend of Sir Francis Acton in Thomas Heywood's *A Woman Killed with Kindness*.

Shafton, Sir Piercie. In Sir Walter Scott's novel *The Monastery*, a would-be gallant. He claims to be a very fashionable cavalier.

Shagpat (shag'pat). See under **Shaving of Shagpat, The.**

Shahnamah (shä.nä.mä'). [Eng. trans., "*Book of Kings*."] The great Persian epic of Firdausi, written c1010 A.D. It had been begun by the poet Dakiki, who completed some 1,000 verses before his death. It is chiefly concerned with the Rustam legend. There is also a *Shahnamah* in Turkish, recounting the history of all the kings of the East. When Bajazet II, to whom it was dedicated, ordered its abridgment from 300 to 80 volumes, the author emigrated in humiliation to Khurasan.

Shahrazad (shä.rä.zäd'). See **Scheherazade.**

Shairp (shärp), **John Campbell.** b. at Houston, Linlithgowshire, Scotland, July 30, 1819; d. at Ormsary, Argyllshire, Scotland, Sept. 18, 1885. A British literary critic and poet. From 1846 to 1857 he was a master at Rugby, and became in 1861 professor of Latin at St. Andrews, in 1868 principal of the United College, St. Andrews, and in 1877 professor of poetry at Oxford. He published *Kilmahoe* (1864), *Studies in Poetry and Philosophy* (1868), *Culture and Religion* (1870), *Poetic Interpretation of Nature* (1877), and *Aspects of Poetry* (1881). He wrote a biography of Robert Burns (1879) for the *English Men of Letters* series.

Shakespeare (shāk'spir), **William.** [Also: **Shakespear, Shakspere, Shaxper,** and many other forms.] b. at Stratford-on-Avon, England, in April, 1564 (baptized April 26); d. there, April 23, 1616 (buried April 25). An English poet and playwright, considered by many to have been the greatest dramatist in world history. More is known of his life than of most of the playwrights of his day, but the facts are fewer than we could wish. He was the first son and the third child of John Shakespeare, a glover and worker in leather, and Mary Arden, co-heiress of Robert Arden, a small landowner of Snitterfield. His parents were possessed of a little property, and the father held various public offices (constable, alderman, and high bailiff) at Stratford; but their prosperity did not survive the poet's boyhood. Where or when Shakespeare was educated is not known. The "small Latine, and lesse Greeke" attributed to him by Jonson could have been learned inexpensively in the excellent Stratford Grammar School. A bond was given on Nov. 28, 1582, to protect the Bishop of Worcester, who had issued a license for the marriage of Shakespeare and Anne Hathaway of Stratford after one asking of the banns. A child, Susanna, was christened on May 26, 1583, and early in 1585, twins, Hamnet and Judith. He joined his parents in 1589 in a suit against John Lambert. The date of Shakespeare's arrival at London is unknown, but by 1592 he was an experienced actor and had enough skill as a playwright to be a dangerous rival to the university wits. One of these, Robert

Greene, attacked him as "an upstart crow, beautified with our feathers" who "supposes he is as well able to bombast out a blank verse as the best of you" (i.e., as a player presumptuously turned playwright). "Divers of worship" acted in his behalf, however, and Greene's editor, Henry Chettle, apologized in print before the end of the year. The meager records of the time do not tell what company he first acted with or wrote for, but by 1594 he had been associated as actor or author with Pembroke's, Strange's, and possibly the Queen's and Sussex's players. While the theaters were closed by the plague in 1593 and 1594, Shakespeare published *Venus and Adonis* and *The Rape of Lucrece*, both dedicated to the Earl of Southampton; the later dedication mentions his patron's favor. In the reshuffling of companies when the plague ended, Shakespeare became a sharer, with Burbage and others, in a company under the patronage of the Lord Chamberlain. He is one of the three payees for the company for performances at court in the winter of 1594. He continued as sharer and chief playwright for this company, known after 1603 as the King's Men, until his retirement from the stage about 1610 or 1612. From 1594 the growth of his fame may be measured by his increasing prosperity and by the uses publishers made of his name, putting it, after 1597, on most of the editions of his plays and even on plays he had not written, and publishing a number of plays in defective versions surreptitiously obtained. The first manifestation of Shakespeare's prosperity was his revival in 1596 of an earlier petition of his father for a grant of arms. A manuscript in the College of Arms preserves a sketch of the arms (or on a bend sable a spear of the first steeled argent, with a falcon bearing a spear as the crest) granted in 1596 to John Shakespeare in recognition of services of his ancestors to Henry VII; another manuscript notes John's public service under Elizabeth as "justice of peace," "bailiff, officer, and chief of the town of Stratford-upon-Avon." The grant was confirmed and extended in 1599. In 1597 Shakespeare purchased the substantial freehold house of New Place at Stratford. In the next two years he incurred heavy expenses while joining with Burbage and others in the construction of the Globe playhouse, of which he became one-tenth owner. Thenceforth, his earnings as actor and writer were supplemented by his profits from the playhouse. In 1602 he bought valuable property at Old Stratford from Combe, to which in 1610 he added 20 acres. Also in 1602 he purchased a cottage in Chapel Lane, Stratford, and in 1605 a share of the Stratford tithes. It was not until 1613 that he acquired private holdings at London by the purchase of a house in fashionable Blackfriars. These records of Shakespeare's business affairs beginning in 1596, the year in which his son Hamnet died, show his concern for his family and for his own and their future in Stratford. They also make it seem likely that he had been regularly in touch with Stratford during the early years in London. The Quiney papers of 1598, on the other hand, are evidence that townspeople recognized in Shakespeare a substantial citizen. After 1594, literary allusions to the dramatist and his works increase rapidly. Meres in 1598 placed him on a level with

fat, fāte, fär, àsk, fāre; net, mē, hèr; pin, pīne; not, nōte, möve, nôr; up, lūte, pùll; ᵵн, then;

the best writers of Greece and Rome, and in 1603 Camden ranked him with Sidney, Spenser, and Jonson. As soon as King James reached London he assumed the patronage of Shakespeare's company, thereafter called the King's Men, and Shakespeare's name heads the list of actors licensed as Grooms of the King's Chamber. In this capacity he waited on the Spanish ambassador in 1604. For some time before 1596, Shakespeare owned taxable property in St. Helen's, Bishopsgate. A petition of late November, 1596, by William Wayte of Southwark indicates that he had left St. Helen's and probably was living near the Swan in Paris Garden, where his company may have been acting. The owner of the Swan, Francis Langley, along with Shakespeare, Dorothy Soer, and Anna Lee, is charged with having threatened injury or death to Wayte, who asks that they be bound over to keep the peace. About 1602 Shakespeare must have lived at the corner of Monkwell and Silver Streets, St. Olave's Parish, in the house of Christopher Mountjoy, a prosperous Huguenot tire-maker (a maker of women's headdresses of silk, silver and gold thread, and jewels), who solicited him to arrange a marriage between Mountjoy's daughter Mary and Stephen Belott, his apprentice. The marriage took place in 1604, and Shakespeare and others gave signed depositions about it in 1612. John Shakespeare died in 1601. In 1607 Susanna married John Hall, a physician at Stratford, and Shakespeare's brother Edmund, an actor, died and was buried in St. Saviour's Church, Southwark. His mother died in 1608, and his two remaining brothers, Gilbert and Richard, in 1612 and 1613. In February, 1616, his daughter Judith married Thomas Quiney, a vintner of Stratford. The marriage created new conditions which seem to have necessitated changes in Shakespeare's will, for in March he gave it a final revision. On April 23, 1616, he died, after what John Ward, vicar at Stratford (1662–81), describes as a merry meeting with Ben Jonson and Michael Drayton. His grave is in the chancel of Holy Trinity Church, Stratford, and above it is a monumental bust, ascribed to Gerard Johnson, that was erected as early as 1623. His widow, Anne, survived him seven years. Judith Quiney's three sons died without offspring, and Susanna Hall's daughter Elizabeth, who married first Thomas Nash and second Sir John Bernard, also died without issue. Such books and papers as may have been at Stratford were included in the bequest to John and Susanna Hall. Perhaps some of them were among the things forcibly removed from New Place by bailiffs in 1637. There is little reason to think any play manuscripts were involved, for as the plays had been written they had been bought by the acting companies. The use of Shakespeare's rough drafts in the printing of several quartos in his lifetime and several plays in the First Folio after his death indicates that his company secured the rough drafts as well as the fair copies and retained both. Ownership of a play by an acting company carried with it the right of sale for publication, so that at his death Shakespeare did not possess the manuscripts of his unprinted plays or share any financial interest in the copyrights of those that had been published. It was not Shakespeare's heirs but the King's Men

who permitted the publication of the First Folio and benefited by the sale of hitherto unpublished plays. Shakespeare's poems are *Venus and Adonis* (entered in the Stationers' Register 1593), *The Rape of Lucrece* (1594), *The Phoenix and Turtle* (published in Robert Chester's *Love's Martyr*, 1601), *The Passionate Pilgrim* (1599; most of the verses not by Shakespeare), the sonnets (not published till 1609, but conjectured to have been written 1593–1603), and *A Lover's Complaint* (published with the sonnets; authorship doubtful). The sonnets are 154 in number and were provided with a dedication by the publisher, Thomas Thorpe, to "Mr. W.H.," their "only begetter," about whom controversy has raged. In the following list of plays, the dates of composition are given as accurately as can be determined, but some of the dates are disputed, and the probable revision of several plays makes dating difficult. The present tendency is to push the composition of the early plays back two or three years. *Henry VI* (three parts, 1589–91), *Richard III* (1592–93), *Comedy of Errors* (1592–94), *Titus Andronicus* (1593–94), *Taming of the Shrew* (1593–94), *Two Gentlemen of Verona* (1594–95), *Love's Labour's Lost* (1594–95; possibly revised 1597), *Romeo and Juliet* (1594–96), *Richard II* (1595–96), *Midsummer Night's Dream* (1595–96), *King John* (1596–97), *Merchant of Venice* (1596–97), *Merry Wives of Windsor* (1597–1601), *Henry IV* (two parts, 1597–98), *Much Ado About Nothing* (1598–99), *Henry V* (1598–99), *Julius Caesar* (1599–1600), *As You Like It* (1599–1600), *Twelfth Night* (1599–1600), *Hamlet* (1600–01), *Troilus and Cressida* (1598–1601), *All's Well That Ends Well* (1602–04), *Othello* (1602), *Measure for Measure* (1604–05), *King Lear* (1605), *Macbeth* (1605–06), *Antony and Cleopatra* (1606–07), *Coriolanus* (1607–08), *Timon of Athens* (1605–08), *Pericles* (1607–08), *Cymbeline* (1609–10), *Winter's Tale* (1610–11), *Tempest* (1611–12), *Henry VIII* (1612–13), *Two Noble Kinsmen* (1612–13). All but *Pericles* and *Two Noble Kinsmen* were printed in the First Folio. In *Henry VIII* and *Two Noble Kinsmen*, John Fletcher was probably a collaborator. Some 140 lines in the manuscript play, *The Booke of Sir Thomas More*, may be Shakespearian. Munday, Chettle, Dekker, and perhaps Heywood, had each a share in the play; a fifth hand, that of a playhouse scribe, is unidentified. The revised version of one scene, in a sixth hand, is thought to be by Shakespeare because the ideas and verse resemble his and the handwriting is strikingly similar to that of his six incontestable signatures. Another passage (21 lines) may be by Shakespeare, but it is in the hand of the theatrical scribe. The date of composition is put between 1593 and 1605, with strong support for 1600. The second issue of the Third Folio (1664) included for the first time *Pericles* and six plays not now considered Shakespearian: *The London Prodigal* (1605), *Thomas Lord Cromwell* (1602), *Sir John Oldcastle* (1619), *The Puritan Widow* (1607), *Locrine* (1595), and *A Yorkshire Tragedy* (1608). Quarto title-pages of these six had already named Shakespeare or "W.S." as the author. Scenes in *Edward the Third* have been attributed to him, as have several other plays, the most puzzling of which is *The History of Cardenio*. Half of Shakespeare's plays were printed separately in quarto form in his lifetime. In 1619 William Jaggard (who in 1599 and 1612 had incurred Shakespeare's displeasure by using his name on the title page of *The Passionate Pilgrim*) and Thomas Pavier began to publish a quarto series of Shakespeare's plays—some with false dates. In 1623, Jaggard and Blount published the first collected edition, the First Folio; the Second Folio appeared in 1632; the Third Folio, in 1663 (reissued in 1664 with seven additional plays); and the Fourth Folio, in 1685. Rowe produced the first edited text of the plays in 1709. Among the many later editions may be mentioned that of Pope (1723–25), Theobald (1733), Hanmer (1743–44), Warburton (1747), Johnson (1765), Capell (1768), Johnson and Steevens (1773), Malone (1790), first American edition (1795), Bowdler's expurgated edition (1818), Knight (1839–42), Collier (1842–44), Halliwell (1853–65), Dyce (1857), White (1857–65), Cambridge (1863–66), Globe (1864), Dyce (1875), Hudson (1880–81), Oxford (1892), Neilson (1906), Kittredge (1936), Alexander (1951), Arden (1899–1924), New Cambridge (1921 *et seq.*), New Arden (1951 *et seq.*). Variorum editions have been edited by Reed (1803), Boswell (1821), and Furness (continued after his death by H. H. Furness, Jr., and since his death under the auspices of the Modern Language Association of America. The intensity of interest in Shakespeare has led to the production of many forgeries, notably those of Ireland, Collier, and Cunningham. It has even led to some question of Shakespeare's authorship, the chief candidates being Francis Bacon, Edward Dyer, and the Earls of Oxford, Derby, and Rutland. Lacking any documentary support, the rival claims tend to cancel each other.

"Shakespeare-Baconian controversy." See **Baconian Theory.**

Shakespeare's Cliff. [Also, **Hay Cliff.**] A cliff in SE England, in Kent, ab. 2 mi. W of Dover. It is traditionally considered to be the locale of one of the climactic scenes of *King Lear*. Height, 350 ft.

Shakuntala (shạ.kùn'tạ.lä). The heroine of the great drama of Kalidasa.

Shalford (shal'fọrd), **Edwin.** In H. G. Wells's novel *Kipps*, the owner of the Folkestone Drapery Bazaar, to whom Kipps is apprenticed at the start of the story.

Shallow (shal'ō). A solemn, insignificant country justice in Shakespeare's *Merry Wives of Windsor* and *2 Henry IV*. He has fictitious memories of having been a roaring blade in his youth. In *2 Henry IV*, when Hal denounces Falstaff, Shallow loses both his hope of advancement and his loan of 1,000 pounds to Falstaff, who had promised him the favor of the new King. In *The Merry Wives*, he threatens a suit against Falstaff for his tricks and tries to secure the hand of Anne Page for Slender, his cousin. He is usually considered a satire on Sir Thomas Lucy, by tradition the author's old Stratford enemy, but doubt has been cast on the identification and even on the enmity. The Shakespeare scholar J. Leslie Hotson thought he might be Justice William Gardiner, who was involved with Shakespeare in a lawsuit brought by William Wayte, a theater owner.

Shalott (shạ.lot), **The Lady of.** See **Lady of Shalott, The.**

Shamir (shä.mēr'). See **Schamir.**

Shandean (shan'di.ạn). Denoting or characterized by the attitudes or behavior of Tristram Shandy or of his immediate relatives, as described by Laurence Sterne in his novel *Tristram Shandy*.

Shandon (shan'dọn), **Captain.** A witty, sweet-tempered, but intemperate literary hack who lives in the Fleet Prison: a character in William Makepeace Thackeray's *Pendennis*. His original was William Maginn.

Shandy (shan'di), **Captain.** See **Toby, Uncle.**

Shandy, Tristram. See **Tristram Shandy.**

Shandy, Walter. In Sterne's *Tristram Shandy*, the father of Tristram. His innumerable theories and whimsies fill the considerable part of the novel which precedes the birth of the nominal hero.

Shanks (shangks), **Edward** (**Richard Buxton**). b. at London, June 11, 1892—. An English writer and journalist, first to win (1919) the Hawthornden prize for imaginative literature, with *Queen of China and Other Poems* (1919). He was assistant editor (1919–22) on the London *Mercury*, and chief editorial writer (1928–35) on the *Evening Standard*. Author of *Songs* (1915), *Poems* (1916), *The Old Indispensables* (1919), *The People of the Ruins* (1920), *The Island of Youth and Other Poems* (1921), *First Essays on Literature* (1923), *The Richest Man* (1923), *Bernard Shaw* (1924), *The Shadowgraph* (1925), *The Beggar's Ride* (1926), *Second Essays on Literature* (1927), *Queer Street* (1932), *The Enchanted Village* (1933), *Tom Tiddler's Ground* (1934), *My England* (1938), *Rudyard Kipling* (1939), *Elizabeth Goes Home* (1942), *The Night Watch for England* (1943), and *The Dogs of War* (1948).

Shan Van Voght (shôn van voit). A rousing song (composed 1798) long associated with the movement for Irish independence from England (". . . Ireland shall be free / From the centre to the sea!"). It was composed at the time of an abortive rising against the British (the Irish hoped to secure effective aid from the French, but failed, and many leaders of the revolt hastily emigrated from Ireland).

Sharp (shärp'), **Becky** (or **Rebecca**). The central character in William Makepeace Thackeray's novel *Vanity Fair*: a friendless girl, "with the dismal precocity of poverty," whose object it is to rise in the world. She is agreeable, cool, selfish, and entirely unmoral; "small and slight of person, pale, sandy-haired, and with green eyes, habitually cast down, but very large, odd, and attractive when they looked up."

Sharp, James. b. at Castle Banff, Scotland, May 4, 1618; murdered on Magus Muir, near St. Andrews, Scotland, May 3, 1679. A Scottish prelate, archbishop of St. Andrews (1661–79). In 1643 he was chosen a regent of philosophy in Saint Leonard's College, St. Andrews, and in 1648 he was appointed minister of Crail in Fife. He was a leader of the Resolutioners (the moderate party) against the Protesters. In 1657 he went to London to counteract the influence of the Protesters with the Protector, Oliver Cromwell. In February, 1660, he visited London again to watch the movements of

George Monck. He was well received by Monck and was sent to Charles II, at Breda, ostensibly to advocate the Presbyterian cause. He was in confidential communication with Charles and Edward Hyde, Earl of Clarendon, assisted in the restoration of Episcopacy in Scotland, and for his desertion of the Presbyterian cause was appointed archbishop of St. Andrews in August, 1661. When John Maitland, Earl of Lauderdale, became supreme as secretary of Scottish affairs, Sharp cooperated in passing the National Synod Act of 1663, the first step in subjecting the church to the crown. In 1667, with John Leslie, 7th Earl of Rothes, he was the governing power in Scotland. Their tyranny and cruelty provoked a rising of the Covenanters. On July 10, 1668, an unsuccessful attempt to assassinate him was made by James Mitchell, a preacher; Mitchell escaped, but was captured in 1674. He made a private confession on being promised leniency, but was condemned through Sharp's vindictive insistence on punishment. Sharp was murdered by a number of Covenanters while on his way to St. Andrews.

Sharp, Luke. Pseudonym of **Barr, Robert.**

Sharp, Margery. b. 1905—. An English novelist. Her books include *Rhododendron Pie, Fanfare for Tin Trumpets, The Flowering Thorn, The Nutmeg Tree* (1937), *Harlequin House* (1939), *The Stone of Chastity* (1940), *Cluny Brown* (1944), *Britannia Mews* (1946), *The Foolish Gentlewoman* (1948), and *Lise Lillywhite* (1951).

Sharp, Rebecca. See **Sharp, Becky.**

Sharp, Timothy. The "lying valet" in David Garrick's play of that name.

Sharp, William. [Pseudonym, **Fiona Macleod.**] b. at Paisley, Scotland, Sept. 12, 1855; d. in Sicily, Dec. 12, 1905. A Scottish poet, critic, and editor, one of the leading figures in the Celtic renaissance of the late 19th century. He traveled for his health in Australia, Canada, Scotland, France, Germany, Greece, Italy, and the U. S., and returned to Britain to be employed as a law clerk at Glasgow and a bank clerk at London. He wrote under his own name, and, after 1894, as Fiona Macleod, a fictitious personality, supposed to be a Highland poetess and his cousin; the secret was kept until after his death, Sharp refusing to divulge it during his lifetime. He contributed to the *Pall Mall Gazette* and was art critic for the Glasgow *Herald*, and edited the *Canterbury Poets* series and an anthology, *Lyra Celtica* (with his wife and first cousin, Elizabeth Amelia Sharp). Under his own name he wrote lives of Rossetti (1882), Shelley (1887), Heine (1888), Browning (1890), and Joseph Severn (1892), *Human Inheritance* (1882), *Earth's Voices* (1884), *Romantic Ballads and Poems of Fantasy* (1886), *Sospiri di Roma* (1891), *Flower o' the Vine* (1894), and *Sospiri d'Italia* (1906), poetry; *Fellowe and His Wife* (1892), *Wives in Exile* (1896), and *Silence Farm* (1899), novels; *Progress of Art in the Century* (1902) and *Literary Geography* (1904), criticism. Under his pseudonym he published *Pharais: A Romance of the Isles* (1894), *The Mountain Lovers* (1895), *The Sin-Eater* (1895), *The Hill of Dream* (1896), *The Washer of the Ford* (1896), *Green Fire* (1896), *The Dominion of Dreams* (1899), *Divine Adventure* (1900), and *Winged Destiny* (1904), mys-

tical works in prose and verse; and two plays, *The House of Usna* and *The Immortal Hour* (both 1900).

Sharper (shär′pėr). A character in William Congreve's *The Old Bachelor*. It is he who says: "Thus grief still treads upon the heels of pleasure— Marry'd in haste, we may repent at leisure."

Shavian (shā′vi.an). Denoting or characterized by the attitudes or qualities, especially attitudes or qualities of satiric wit, generally associated with George Bernard Shaw or his written works.

Shaving of Shagpat (shag′pat), **The.** A story by George Meredith, published in 1856. It is a tale about an enchanter, Shagpat, who controls a city by means of the power he holds over the king through a single magic hair on his (Shagpat's) head. The hero of the story becomes a barber and cuts this hair, using much magic and ingenuity to accomplish the feat, and thus to deliver the city from Shagpat.

Shaw (shô), **Flora Louise.** [Title, Lady **Lugard.**] b. at Dublin, 1851; d. at Abinger Common, Surrey, England, Jan. 25, 1929. A British journalist, novelist, and writer of books for juveniles. She served on the staff of the *Pall Mall Gazette*, and later on the London *Times*, becoming the head of its colonial department. She traveled in South America, Australia, and Canada, and reported the second Klondike gold rush in 1898. She worked for the Belgian refugees in World War I and founded the Lady Lugard Hospitality Commission. Author of *Castle Blair* (1878), *Hector* (1883), *A Sea Change* (1885), *Colonel Chiswick's Campaign* (1886), and *A Tropical Dependency* (1905).

Shaw, George Bernard. b. at Dublin, July 26, 1856; d. at Ayot St. Lawrence, England, Nov. 2, 1950. An Irish-English playwright, novelist, critic, and socialist agitator and pamphleteer. His father was a government clerk on a meager salary; his mother, a woman of culture and courage, largely supported the family by teaching music. To enlarge her earnings she moved to London, whither in 1876 George Bernard, having quit school at the age of 14, and having for some years worked for a pittance as a rent collector, followed her. He had determined on a literary career, but during his first London decade his income by the pen hardly totaled a good week's salary, and he was supported by both parents while he wrote his five novels, namely *Immaturity, The Irrational Knot, Love among the Artists, Cashel Byron's Profession,* and *An Unsocial Socialist.* Some of these first appeared serially in socialist periodicals of small circulation; several of them had a later vogue. A speech by Henry George in 1882 gave Shaw that awareness of the importance of economics in human affairs which colored his outlook thereafter, so that he could aptly say that in his works economic knowledge "played as important a part as the knowledge of anatomy does in the works of Michael Angelo." From listening to Henry George it was a step to reading Karl Marx and Friedrich Engels; in 1884 Shaw became one of the founders of the Fabian Society, dedicated to promoting socialism by gradual and peaceful methods, and for several years thereafter, a voluntary, unpaid orator, he preached his creed in the streets and parks of London. During those years he became the friend of William

---

ḍ, d or j; ṣ, s or sh; ṭ, t or ch; ẓ, z or zh; o, F. cloche; ü, F. menu; ćh, Sc. loch; ṅ, F. bonbon.

Morris, Edward Carpenter, Sidney and Beatrice Webb, and other socialist leaders. Of even more importance to his career was the friendship of William Archer, critic, dramatist, and translator and champion of Henrik Ibsen. Archer aroused Shaw's enthusiasm for the modern purposeful drama, procured him employment as a critic, at first in the field of music, and advised him to write plays instead of novels. As music critic of the London *Star* (1888–89), Shaw used the pseudonym Corno di Bassetto; filling the like post on the *World* (1890–94), he familiarized the cultured English public with the initials G.B.S. In 1895 he became, and for some years continued, drama critic for the *Saturday Review*. Vigorous and provocative, his critical writings were especially influential in widening the English audience for the music dramas of Richard Wagner and the plays of Henrik Ibsen, and his two small books *The Quintessence of Ibsenism* (1891) and *The Perfect Wagnerite* (1898) were also well received in the U. S. Meanwhile his career as a playwright had its small beginnings when *Widowers' Houses*, a play dealing with slum life and landlordism, matters which he had observed at first hand as a rent collector, was produced by the Independent Theatre; the year was 1892. His next play, *The Philanderer*, written in 1893, waited many years for a showing on any stage. In that same year Shaw really hit his stride with the writing of *Mrs. Warren's Profession*, which, dealing with the economic bases of prostitution, was of course banned by the English censor. It was, however, put on privately by the Stage Society of London in 1902, and in 1905 was successfully produced by Arnold Daly at New York. Not until 1924 was a public presentation of *Mrs. Warren's Profession* permitted in England. For his fame and later fortune Shaw, in fact, owed comparatively little to the British public, but much to the enthusiasm of American and Continental (especially German) actors and playgoers. *Arms and the Man*, a lively satire on military life, was produced at London in 1894, but had a longer run at New York, where Richard Mansfield produced it in the same year. *Candida* saw the stage at London in 1897, but became a sensational success only when played by Arnold Daly at New York in 1903. *You Never Can Tell* had its first showing at London in 1900, for a short run. Shaw was not the man to take rebuffs passively; if censors wouldn't permit, if producers wouldn't produce, if playgoers wouldn't attend his plays, perhaps readers would read them, especially if he added to their interest by provocative introductions expounding his unconventional, radical ideas. That he was right was proved by the success, in Britain and America, of the book *Plays Pleasant and Unpleasant* (1898), the pleasant plays being *Arms and the Man*, *Candida*, *The Man of Destiny*, and *You Never Can Tell*; the unpleasant titles being *Widowers' Houses*, *The Philanderer*, and *Mrs. Warren's Profession*. Thereafter Shaw's challenging, mocking, eloquent prefaces were enjoyed by his following almost as much as the plays themselves. It was the financial returns of a long run of *The Devil's Disciple* as produced by Richard Mansfield at New York in 1897 (two years before its first staging at London) that enabled Shaw to drop reviewing, to concentrate on writing plays.

The following year, moreover, he married an **Irish**-woman of independent means, Charlotte Payne-Townshend. In 1900 *The Devil's Disciple, Caesar and Cleopatra* (first produced at London in 1899), and *Captain Brassbound's Conversion* (written for Ellen Terry in 1899 but not produced until 1906) were published as *Three Plays for Puritans*. That year saw the publication also of *John Bull's Other Island*, written at the request of William Butler Yeats for the Irish Literary Theatre, and produced in 1904. The Abbey Theatre at Dublin, successor to the Irish Literary Theatre, first produced *The Showing Up of Blanco Posnet* in 1909, after it had been banned by the censor in England. In the early 1900's H. Granville-Barker undertook to win decisive acceptance for Shaw on the English stage, and before the outbreak of World War I his position, and his world-wide fame, were securely established. All told, the Shavian canon includes 47 plays, of which, in addition to those already mentioned, the better known are (with the dates of their publication): *Man and Superman* (1903), *The Doctor's Dilemma* (1906), *Major Barbara* (1907), *Getting Married* (1908), *Misalliance* (1910), *Fanny's First Play* (1911), *Androcles and the Lion* (1912), *Pygmalion* (1912), *Great Catherine* (1913), *O'Flaherty, V.C.* (1915), *Heartbreak House* (1917), *Back to Methusaleh* (1921), *Saint Joan* (1923), and *The Apple Cart* (1929). Among his less-known works, all of which were published and produced, are *The Admirable Bashville* (based on Shaw's novel *Cashel Byron's Profession*), *How He Lied to Her Husband, Passion. Poison and Petrifaction, The Fascinating Foundling, The Glimpse of Reality, Press Cuttings, The Dark Lady of the Sonnets, Overruled, The Music Cure, The Inca of Perusalem, Augustus Does His Bit, Annajanska, Jitta's Atonement* (translated from the German of Siegfried Trebitsch), *Too True To Be Good, The Village Wooing, On the Rocks, The Six of Calais, The Simpleton of the Unexpected Isles, The Millionairess, Geneva,* and *In Good King Charles' Golden Days.* In 1925 Shaw was awarded the Nobel prize for literature; the money that went with it was, he said, in his case, "a life belt thrown to a man who has already reached shore," so he used it to establish an institution for the study of Scandinavian literature in Great Britain. Down the years Shaw contributed many an essay or article, incisive and witty, to Fabian publications, and some of his many public speeches, always at once pithy and mirth-provoking, were published as pamphlets. His early critical writings have been collected, and his letters to Ellen Terry, with whom he seems to have been more than a little in love, have also been published. He never hedged on his radicalism (which is set forth most explicitly in *The Intelligent Woman's Guide to Socialism and Capitalism*, 1928), his pacifism, his vegetarianism, his opposition to vivisection, or his conviction of the superiority of the Irish to the English; but though he irritated reactionaries and bewildered stodgy souls, and during World War I was widely unpopular for his criticisms of British policy, his international fame enabled him always to speak his mind, and he had warm friends even among the aristocrats and plutocrats whom he satirized and excoriated. He knew what he was doing when he called himself a greater dramatist than Shake-

---

fat, fāte, fär, ȧsk, fâre; net, mē, hėr; pin, pīne; not, nōte, mȯve, nôr; up, lūte, pṳll; ᴛʜ, then;

speare: it not only made people talk about him, but it underlined, for the discerning, his thesis that even the greatest works of dramatic genius written before the rise of social science could not be as important as any reasonably good play composed in the light of modern social-scientific knowledge. Shaw has been called "a cart-tail orator in the theatre," a teacher and a propagandist who employed the resources of dramatic art to preach and promote his ideas. He had a faculty of "scenting out the other half of the truth," and his usual approach was to stand some conventional concept on its head, to capture public attention by some outrageous proposition, and to press home his argument with the weapons of paradox and wit, but also on occasion with a high eloquence full of moral purpose and passion. It has been said that he created no characters but only types and symbols, yet many among his *dramatis personae* (for instance, the four persons in *Candida*, and the titular figure in *Saint Joan*) are actually to many readers and playgoers poignantly human characters who seem to be mere types and symbols only because the actions in which they are involved turn not upon small personal passions, but upon moral or intellectual problems or large public or social issues. And Shaw, for all his didacticism, was very much an artist; his language is often beautifully cadenced, and it is conceded that he surpassed all other modern dramatists in scintillant dialogue full of unexpected twists and turns, in this respect emulating but surpassing such earlier Irish playwrights as George Farquhar, Oliver Goldsmith, Richard Brinsley Sheridan, and Oscar Wilde. Shaw's best plays have worn well, and have continued to fascinate successive generations of playgoers. In 1952, 60 years after its first production, *Widowers' Houses* was well received by New York audiences, and that same year saw the revival of, among others, *Candida*, *Caesar and Cleopatra*, and *Too True To Be Good*, as well as the first New York production of *The Millionairess*.

Shaw, T. E. See **Lawrence, Thomas Edward.**

She. A novel by H. Rider Haggard, published in 1887.

Shearing (shir'ing), **Joseph.** A pseudonym of **Long, Gabrielle Margaret Vere.**

Sheba (shē'bạ). In the Bible, a grandson of Cush (Gen. x. 7); a descendant of Jokshan (x. 28); also, a grandson of Abraham and Keturah (xxv. 3). Either of the two latter is construed as the eponymous ancestor of the Sabaeans, natives of the region called Sheba, who were, according to Biblical and classical notices, the most important people of S Arabia. From this country there came a queen to test Solomon's wisdom (1 Kings, x. 1). In Arabic legend the Queen of Sheba's name is Balkis. She bore a son to Solomon. From this son the Ethiopians claim descent.

Sheep-Shearing, The. A pastoral play by George Colman the elder, produced in 1777.

Sheffield (shef'ēld), **John.** [Titles: 3rd Earl of **Mulgrave,** 1st Duke of **Buckingham and Normanby.**] b. April 7, 1648; d. Feb. 24, 1721. An English statesman and poet, the patron of John Dryden. He commanded under Charles II against the

Dutch, and in the expedition for the relief of Tangier (1680). He was banished (1682) from court for courting Princess Anne, who, when she became queen (1702), restored him as lord privy seal to the privy council, from which he had been dismissed (1696) for opposition to William III. He was again forced to resign (1705) his appointment by the Whigs. He was lord president of the council (1710–14). He wrote *Essay upon Poetry* (1682), which was lauded by his friend Alexander Pope; *Essay upon Satyr* (1680), attributed to Dryden (who was thrashed by the hirelings of John Wilmot, Earl of Rochester, for it), and other poetical works.

Sheherazade (shẹ.her.ạ.zä'dẹ). See **Scheherazade.**

Sheil (shēl), **Richard Lalor.** b. at Drumdowney, County Tipperary, Ireland, Aug. 17, 1791; d. at Florence, Italy, May 25, 1851. An Irish politician, orator, and dramatist. He studied law at Lincoln's Inn, and was admitted to the Irish bar in 1814, but devoted himself for some years to literature. In 1814 his drama *Adelaide, or the Emigrants* was brought out at Crow Street Theatre, Dublin. *The Apostate* (1817) confirmed his reputation, and was followed by *Bellamira* (1818), *Evadne* (1819, based on Shirley's *The Traitor* and Massinger's *The Fatal Dowry*), *The Huguenot* (1822), and *Montini* (1820). In 1823 he was one of the founders of the Catholic Association. He supported Daniel O'Connell's agitation until Catholic emancipation was granted in 1829. In 1830 he was member of Parliament for Milborne Port, Somersetshire; and in 1831 was returned for Louth, and later for Tipperary and Dungarvan. He was vice-president of the Board of Trade (1838–41) in Lord Melbourne's ministry, in 1846 master of the mint under Lord John Russell, and in 1850 British minister at Florence.

Sheldon (shel'dọn), **Gilbert.** b. at Stanton, Staffordshire, England, 1598; d. 1677. An English prelate, archbishop of Canterbury (1663–77). In 1626 he became warden of All Souls' College, Oxford, and in 1648 was removed by Parliament, although he was later reinstated. He was appointed (1660) bishop of London; the Savoy Conference took place at his house. He was chancellor of Oxford (1667 *et seq.*) and built and endowed the Sheldonian Theatre there.

Sheldonian Theatre (shel.dō'ni.ạn). A theater at Oxford University, England, built by Archbishop Gilbert Sheldon (Sir Christopher Wren, architect) in 1664–69, in which the "Encænia," or annual commemoration of founders (with the reading of prize poems and essays and conferring of honorary degrees), is held.

Shelley (shel'i), **Mary Wollstonecraft.** [Maiden name, **Godwin.**] b. at London, Aug. 30, 1797; d. Feb. 1, 1851. An English author; daughter of William Godwin and Mary Wollstonecraft, and second wife of Percy Bysshe Shelley. She went (1814) to the Continent with Shelley and married him there (1816). She returned to England in 1823 with her son. Her chief work is a romance, *Frankenstein* (1818), one of the great horror stories of literature, originating in Byron's proposition that he himself, Polidori (Byron's physician), and Shelley and his wife should each write a ghost-story. She also wrote *Valperga* (1823), a historical novel; *The Last Man* (1826), a tale of the future; *Lodore*

(1835), *Falkner* (1837), and other novels; *Journal of a Six Weeks' Tour* (1814), and *Rambles in Germany and Italy* (1844). She edited Shelley's poems, letters, essays, and other works, supplying invaluable notes.

Shelley, Percy Bysshe. b. at Field Place, near Horsham, Sussex, England, Aug. 4, 1792; drowned off Viareggio, Italy, July 8, 1822. An English poet; son and heir of Timothy (after 1815 Sir Timothy) Shelley. He attended Sion House Academy (1802–04) and Eton (1804–10), and entered University College, Oxford, in October, 1810, but was expelled along with Thomas Jefferson Hogg on March 25, 1811, for refusing to acknowledge or deny the authorship of *The Necessity of Atheism* (1811). At Edinburgh, on Aug. 28, 1811, he married Harriet Westbrook, 16-year-old daughter of a retired London coffee-house keeper, and thus completed his estrangement from his father. In February-March, 1812, in Ireland, he campaigned actively for reform. The remainder of 1812 and 1813 he spent in Devonshire, in Wales, and at London. In 1813 he printed privately his first important poem, *Queen Mab.* His violent love for Mary Godwin, daughter of William Godwin and Mary Wollstonecraft, whom he met in April, 1814, led to his elopement with Mary on July 28, 1814. Their six-weeks' trip to Switzerland is chronicled in Mary's *Journal of a Six Weeks' Tour* (1814). Their subsequent poverty and social isolation in London were relieved by an annuity of 1,000 pounds upon the death of his grandfather, Sir Bysshe Shelley, in January, 1815. At Bishopsgate, near Windsor Forest, he wrote *Alastor* (1816). During May-August, 1816, he lived near Geneva, Switzerland, in daily association with George Gordon, Lord Byron. After Harriet Westbrook's suicide by drowning in November, 1816, he married Mary Godwin on December 30, and in March, 1817, moved to Marlow, where he wrote *Laon and Cythna* (1818). The custody of his children by Harriet (Ianthe and Charles) was denied Shelley in March, 1817, by decision of the lord chancellor in a suit initiated by the Westbrooks. Shelley's intimate friends during these years were Thomas Jefferson Hogg, Thomas Love Peacock, Leigh Hunt, and Horace Smith; he also knew John Keats. His health took him to Italy in March, 1818. Here, though stricken by the death of two children (Clara and William), he was to write his greatest poems. His intimacy with Byron was renewed at Venice in August, 1818. The winter of 1818–19 at Naples, the spring of 1819 at Rome, the summer near Leghorn, and the autumn at Florence (where Percy Florence was born on November 12) were followed by a migration in January, 1820, to Pisa; here Shelley put down roots as he had never done elsewhere. The Pisa circle included the Italians Vaccà, Pacchiani, and Emilia Viviani, the Greek exile Prince Alexander Mavrocordato, and Thomas Medwin, Mr. and Mrs. Mason, John and Maria Gisborne (at Leghorn), Edward and Jane Williams. Byron settled at Pisa on Nov. 1, 1821, and Edward John Trelawny arrived in January, 1822. In May, 1822, the Shelleys and Williamses took a house near Lerici, on the Gulf of Spezia, for a summer of sailing. When returning from Leghorn on July 8, Shelley and Williams were drowned when their yacht sank in a storm. Shelley's body was cremated on August 16 under the supervision of Trelawny and in the presence of Byron and Leigh Hunt. His ashes were buried in the Protestant Cemetery at Rome.

Works and Evaluation. Shelley's chief long poems are *Queen Mab* (1813), *Laon and Cythna* (1818; revised and reissued as *The Revolt of Islam*), *Alastor* (1816), *Prometheus Unbound* (1820), *The Cenci* (a tragedy, 1819), *Epipsychidion* (1821), *Adonais* (1821), and *The Triumph of Life* (incomplete; 1824). Important but of lesser value are *Rosalind and Helen* (1819), *Julian and Maddalo* (1824), *The Masque of Anarchy* (1832), *Peter Bell the Third* (1839), *The Witch of Atlas* (1824), *Oedipus Tyrannus* (1820), and *Hellas* (1822). Short poems include *Hymn to Intellectual Beauty, Ozymandias, Stanzas Written in Dejection, near Naples, Ode to the West Wind, The Cloud, To a Skylark,* and *Ode to Liberty.* Mary Shelley published his *Posthumous Poems* in 1824, and the *Poetical Works* in 1839. Shelley's letters and prose works are also important, especially *A Defence of Poetry* (1840), the *Essay on Christianity* (1859), and *A Philosophical View of Reform* (1920). The prose works were collected and edited by Mrs. Shelley as *Essays, Letters from Abroad, &c.* (1840). As a lyric poet Shelley is perhaps unrivaled in English literary history. He was an idealist, a philosopher, rebel, and reformer, and both in prose and verse expressed with singular completeness the revolutionary and more progressive aspects of his time. His belief in humanity and its ultimate approach towards perfectibility through truth and love is a constant theme which finds its fullest expression in *Prometheus Unbound.*

Shenstone (shen'stŏn, -stọn), **William.** b. at Halesowen, England, Nov. 13, 1714; d. there, Feb. 11, 1763. An English poet. He was educated at Pembroke College, Oxford. His best-known poem is *The Schoolmistress.* Besides this, which gained for him the title of "the water-gruel bard" from Horace Walpole, he published *Poems* (1737), *The Judgment of Hercules* (1741), and others.

Sheol (shē'ōl). In ancient Jewish religion, the dark underworld dwelling place of the dead. The original is in the Authorized Version rendered as the "grave," "hell," or "pit"; in the revised version of the Old Testament the word *Sheol* is substituted. It was not originally conceived of as a place of punishment, but it gradually became equated with the Gehenna and the hell of the New Testament, and has been used colloquially for the abode of evil and condemned spirits.

Shepherd. In Shakespeare's *1 Henry VI*, the father of Joan of Arc.

Shepherd, Old. In Shakespeare's *Winter's Tale*, the reputed father of Perdita, but who actually has found her on the shore and has brought her up as his daughter. He is condemned to death by Polixenes for permitting Florizel's infatuation with her and flees with the lovers to Sicilia.

Shepherd, The. A volume of verse (1922) by Edmund Blunden.

"Shepherd," the. See **Stiggins, the Reverend Mr.**

"Shepherd Kings." See **Hyksos.**

"Shepherd Lord," the. See **Clifford, Henry de.**

---

fat, fāte, fär, àsk, fãre; net, mē, hèr; pin, pīne; not, nōte, mŏve, nôr; up, lūte, pùll; ᴛʜ, then;

Shepherd of Banbury (ban'ber''i, -bėr.i). A title assumed by one John Claridge in publishing (1744) a collection of rules for predicting weather changes. The Shepherd of Banbury's rules attained great popularity, and passed through many editions.

Shepherd of Salisbury Plain (sôlz'ber''i, -bėr.i), **The.** A popular moral tale by Hannah More. It is a tract aimed at the supposed "immoralities" of the poor.

Shepherd's Calendar, The. A pastoral poem in 12 eclogues by Edmund Spenser, published in 1579. Each eclogue represents a different month of the year, and is written in a different meter. Colin Clout (the name assumed by Spenser) laments the coldness of his love, Rosalind, praises Elysa (Queen Elizabeth), and discusses religion, contemporary mores, and the state of poetry.

Shepherd's Calendar, The. A volume of verse (1827) by John Clare.

Shepherd's Hunting, The. A poem (1615) by George Wither, written while the author was imprisoned in the Marshalsea as a result of his publication of *Abuses Stript and Whipt*. It is divided into five pastoral poems, in which the poet defends his controversial satire during the course of a supposed conversation with his friend Willy (William Browne of Tavistock, whose *Shepherd's Pipe* Wither greatly admired).

Shepherd's Pipe, The. A series of eclogues, published in 1614, by William Browne (c1591–c1643), of Tavistock.

Shepherd's Week, The. A series of six burlesque pastoral poems by John Gay, published in 1714. They are written in the form of eclogues, and were originally intended to mock the works of Ambrose Philips.

Sheppard (shep'ard), **Elizabeth Sara.** b. at Blackheath, London, c1830; d. at Brixton, London, March 13, 1862. An English novelist. Among her books are *Charles Auchester* (1853), *Counterparts* (1854), *My First Season, by Beatrice Reynolds* (1855), and *Rumour* (1858).

Sheppard, John. [Called **Jack.**] b. at Stepney, England, 1702; hanged at Tyburn Prison, London, Nov. 16, 1724. An English robber. He was a carpenter by trade, and began (c1720) his career of robbery. He was of a generous disposition, and was very popular. His portrait was painted by Sir John Thornhill; a pantomime, *Harlequin Sheppard*, was produced at Drury Lane; Daniel Defoe wrote a narrative about him in 1724; and a novel by W. H. Ainsworth, *Jack Sheppard*, was published in 1839. He made two remarkable escapes from Newgate, once, with the aid of his preceptor in crime Edgeworth Bess (Bess Lyon), from the condemned cell, but after many vicissitudes was finally captured in an ale-house while drunk.

Sheppey (shep'i). A tragedy (1933) by W. Somerset Maugham about a sweepstakes winner, who, believing in Christian charity, gives his winnings to the poor. He is deemed to be mad, however, since no sane man would give his money to the poor: "A sane man takes money from the poor. . . ."

Sheraton (sher'a.ton), **Thomas.** b. at Stockton-on-Tees, England, 1751; d. at London, 1806. An English furniture maker and designer.

Shere Khan (shir kän). In Rudyard Kipling's Mowgli stories, the lame tiger. He claims Mowgli as his prey at the outset of the stories, and finally meets his death through Mowgli's efforts.

Sheridan (sher'i.dan), **Frances.** [Maiden name, **Chamberlaine.**] b. in Ireland, 1724; d. at Blois, France, 1766. A British novelist and dramatist; wife of Thomas Sheridan (1719–88) and mother of Richard Brinsley Sheridan. Among her novels are *Memoirs of Miss Sidney Bidulph* (1761) and *Nourjahad* (1788; afterward dramatized). She wrote two comedies, *The Discovery* (1763; the principal role was played by David Garrick) and *The Dupe* (1764).

Sheridan, Lady Helen Selina. [Titles: Countess of **Dufferin,** Countess of **Gifford**; pseudonym, **Impulsia Gushington.**] b. 1807; d. at Highgate, London, June 13, 1867. An Irish beauty and poet; granddaughter of Richard Brinsley Sheridan. She married (1825) Price Blackwood, later Baron Dufferin, and after his death (1841) married (1862) George Hay, Earl of Gifford. She was the mother of Frederick Temple Hamilton-Temple Blackwood, 1st Marquis of Dufferin and Ava. Under her pseudonym she wrote *Lispings from Low Latitudes* (1863); she also wrote a play, *Finesse, or a Busy Day in Messina* (acted at London, 1863). Much of her poetry was published anonymously; a collected edition of her *Songs, Poems, and Verses* (1894) was brought out by her son. Two of her best poems, *Lament of the Irish Emigrant* and *Terence's Farewell*, are to be found in many anthologies of Irish and English poetry.

Sheridan, Richard Brinsley (**Butler**). b. at Dublin, in autumn of 1751 (baptized Nov. 4, 1751, but precise birthday uncertain); d. at London, July 7, 1816. A British dramatist, orator, and statesman; son of Thomas Sheridan (1719–88), an Irish actor and theater manager, and Frances Sheridan, novelist and playwright. Educated at Harrow, in 1770 he moved with his family from London to Bath, scene of his romantic courtship of Elizabeth Linley, "the Maid of Bath," already famed for her captivating beauty and singing in her father's concerts. After their romantic elopement and marriage in 1773, Sheridan turned to the London theater for a livelihood. Within a single year (1775), Covent Garden Theatre productions of his first comedy, *The Rivals, Saint Patrick's Day* (short farce), and *The Duenna* (light opera) established his popularity and versatility as a dramatic author. In 1776 he succeeded David Garrick as manager of the Drury Lane Theatre, acquiring first Garrick's share, then main control of the property, chiefly through partnerships and mortgages. *The School for Scandal* (1777) and *The Critic* (1779) confirmed his supremacy in the comedy of manners and in dramatic satire. Among lesser Drury Lane productions, he had a shaping hand in *A Trip to Scarborough* (1777), altered from Sir John Vanbrugh's comedy, *The Relapse; The Camp* (1778), "a Musical Entertainment," of disputed, but probably composite, authorship; *Robinson Crusoe, or, Harlequin Friday* (1781), a widely popular pantomime; and *Pizarro* (1799), a melodramatic tragedy, "taken from the German Drama of Kotzebue and adapted to the English Stage" with spectacular success.

d, d or j; ş, s or sh; ţ, t or ch; z, z or zh; o, F. cloche; ü, F. menu; ċh, Sc. loch; ṅ, F. bonbon.

Political Career. Sheridan's long political career began in 1780, when he entered Parliament as Whig member for Stafford. Under Charles James Fox he became undersecretary for foreign affairs in 1782, and he was secretary to the treasury in 1783, but the younger William Pitt's advent as prime minister relegated the Whigs to the ranks of the opposition. Sheridan's fame as a political orator rose dramatically with his speeches against Warren Hastings. His "Begum speech" (1787), which held the House of Commons spellbound for over five hours, and his opening speech (1788) at the trial of Hastings roused unprecedented enthusiasm in Parliament and among the public. As a liberal and independent statesman, he early sympathized with the American and French revolutionists, but deplored crimes committed in the name of liberty, and later denounced Napoleon. Constantly absorbed in public affairs, he had neither time nor temperament to regulate the finances of Drury Lane, virtually his sole source of income, and his costly venture in rebuilding this theater (1794) ended with the fatal Drury Lane fire of 1809. Debts and dissipations were ruinous. Save for a brief post as treasurer of the navy (1806–07), he lacked the emoluments of office. In 1812, unable to meet the expenses of standing again for Parliament, he had to abandon his public career of over 30 years.

Private Life and Later Years. In private, as in political life, Sheridan early became conspicuous. As youthful champion of the Maid of Bath, he fought two duels with an obnoxious suitor; at 26, he was elected to Dr. Johnson's Literary Club, and, at 29, to Brooks's Club, fashionable Whig center. In society he was a brilliant and magnetic figure, and long stood high in the favor and confidence of the prince regent (later George IV). However, with the decline of his fortunes and health, Sheridan's last years were tragic. He died in bitter suffering and obscurity. In dramatic contrast were the public honors thereupon quickly bestowed. The popular verdict linked him with Fox, Burke, and Pitt, while Byron's *Monody* eulogized the full sweep of his genius. Sheridan's burial in the Poets' Corner of Westminster Abbey, near Garrick, accorded him dramatic and poetical justice.

Sheridan, Thomas. b. at Quilca, near Dublin, 1719; d. at Margate, England, Aug. 14, 1788. An Irish actor, elocutionist, and author; father of Richard Brinsley Sheridan. He first went on the stage at Dublin in 1743 and at London in 1744, and played with David Garrick in 1745. He was manager of a Dublin theater for ten years, and of Drury Lane after his son bought out Garrick there. He wrote a *General Dictionary of the English Language* (1780), *Life of Swift* (1784; whose works he edited in 17 volumes), and works on education.

Sheriff of Nottingham (not'ing.am). The officer who represents Norman law in the Robin Hood stories, and who is usually outwitted by Robin and his men.

Sherlock (shėr'lok), **Thomas.** b. at London, 1678; d. July 18, 1761. An English prelate; son of William Sherlock.

Sherlock, William. b. at London, 1641; d. at Hampstead, London, June 19, 1707. An English clergyman. He was suspended from clerical office in 1689 for refusing to take the oath of allegiance to William and Mary, but later submitted, and was made dean of Saint Paul's in 1691. He published *The Case of Resistance of the Supreme Powers* (1684), *Doctrine of the Trinity* (1690), and others.

Sherlock Holmes (hōmz). A fictional detective in the works of Sir Arthur Conan Doyle. He appears in the novels *A Study in Scarlet* (1887), *The Sign of Four* (1890), *The Hound of the Baskervilles* (1902), and *The Valley of Fear* (1915), and in the collections of short stories (56 tales in all) *The Adventures of Sherlock Holmes* (1892), *The Memoirs of Sherlock Holmes* (1894), *The Return of Sherlock Holmes* (1905), *His Last Bow* (1917), and *The Case Book of Sherlock Holmes* (1927). Holmes's spare figure, his hunting cap and pipe, his magnifying glass, his violin, and, above all, his hypodermic needle are among the most famous attributes in English literature. The Holmes rooms at 221B, Baker Street, London, shared for a time with his friend and chronicler, Dr. Watson, were made real in the dramatization of the Holmes story by William Gillette, whose characterization has added such reality to Holmes that many believe him actually to have lived. The Holmes myth has been fostered by later imitators, especially by the members of the Baker Street Irregulars, an organization of Holmes enthusiasts. The Holmes process of reconstruction of a crime from small clues closely observed began a vogue in the detective story.

Sherriff (sher'if), **Robert Cedric.** b. at Kingston-on-Thames, England, June 6, 1896—. An English dramatist and novelist. Among his plays are *Journey's End* (1929), *Badger's Green* (1930), *Windfall* (1933), *St. Helena* (1935, in collaboration with Jeanne de Casalis), *Miss Mabel* (1948), *Home at Seven* (1950), and the motion-picture scenarios *The Road Back* (1932), *The Invisible Man* (1933), *Goodbye, Mr. Chips* (1936), *The Four Feathers* (1938), *Lady Hamilton* (1941), *This Above All* (1942), *Odd Man Out* (1945), and *Quartet* (1948). He is the author also of the novels *The Fortnight in September* (1931), *Greengates* (1936), *The Hopkins Manuscript* (1939), and *Another Year* (1946).

Sherston's Progress (shėr'stonz). An autobiographical narrative by Siegfried Sassoon, published in 1936.

Sherwood (shėr'wŭd), **Mary Martha.** [Maiden name, **Butt.**] b. at Stanford, Worcestershire, England, May 6, 1775; d. at Twickenham, Middlesex, England, Sept. 22, 1851. An English author. She went to India in 1804 with her husband, and there became interested in missionary work. She is chiefly known, however, for her works for children, among which are *Little Henry and His Bearer*, *The History of Susan Gray*, and *The History of the Fairchild Family.*

Sherwood Forest. A forest in Nottinghamshire, England, ab. 14 mi. N of Nottingham. Formerly an extensive area, it was the principal scene of the legendary exploits of Robin Hood.

She Stoops to Conquer, or the Mistakes of a Night. A comedy by Oliver Goldsmith, one of the best of its period, first played on March 15, 1773, and printed in 1774.

Shetland Islands (shet'land). [Also, **Zetland Islands**.] A group of islands in N Scotland, in the Atlantic Ocean between 50 and 60 mi. NE of the Orkney Islands. The group contains ab. 100 islands, of which 23 are inhabited. The surface is generally hilly and rocky, rising to a maximum elevation of 1,475 ft. at Ronas Hill, on Mainland island. The principal island is Mainland; others include Unst, Yell, Fetlar, Bressay, Whalsay, Papa Stour, and Foula. The Shetland Islands form the county of Shetland. The islands are noted for their breed of ponies. Cattle and sheep also are raised, and oats and potatoes are grown. The herring fishery is the main industry, but whaling is also conducted from several of the many sea inlets. Knitting of woolen goods is an important home industry. The islands were acquired by Scotland in 1469. Area, 551 sq. mi.

Shewing-up of Blanco Posnet (blang'kō poz'net), **The**. [Also, **The Showing Up of Blanco Posnet**.] A comedy (1909) by George Bernard Shaw, in which the essential moral goodness of the chief character is revealed under the stress of crisis (a theme which Shaw had used 12 years earlier in *The Devil's Disciple*).

She Would if She Could. A comedy by George Etherege, produced in 1668. It was very successful in its day.

Shiel (shēl), **M. P.** [Full name, **Matthew Phipps Shiel**.] b. at Montserrat, West Indies, July 21, 1865; d. at Chichester, Sussex, England, Feb. 17, 1947. An English journalist and novelist. A noted writer of fantasy, he was the author of *The Yellow Danger* (1898), *The Purple Cloud* (1901), *Unto the Third Generation* (1903), *The White Wedding* (1907), *The Dragon* (1913), *The Lord of the Sea* (1924), *Children of the Wind* (1924), *How the Old Woman Got Home* (1927), *Here Comes the Lady* (1928), *Cold Steel* (1929), *The Black Box* (1930), *Dr. Krasinski's Secret* (1930), *The Invisible Voices* (1936), and *The Young Men Are Coming* (1937). His other novels include *Prince Zaleski* (1895), *The Isle of Lies* (1909), and *The Last Miracle* (1906). He published *Poems* in 1936.

Shift (shift). An impudent beggar who pretends to be a disbanded soldier, in Ben Jonson's *Every Man Out of His Humour*.

Shift. An attorney's clerk, a mimic, appearing as Smirk, an auctioneer, in Samuel Foote's play *The Minor*.

Shimei (shim'ē.ī). In Dryden's *Absalom and Achitophel*, the name given to a character satirizing the man who was then Lord Mayor of London:

> The council violent, the rabble worse,
> The Shimei taught Jerusalem to curse.

By Jerusalem Dryden meant the reader to understand London.

Shipman's Tale, The. One of Chaucer's *Canterbury Tales*. The story is from the first tale of the eighth day of Boccaccio's *Decameron*. Several lines at the beginning of this tale make clear that it was originally assigned to a woman, presumably the Wife of Bath, and was then transferred to the Shipman. A rather involved fabliau of a merchant both cuckolded and robbed by a wily monk, it is less colorful than the Shipman himself, apparently

something of a pirate, a navigator without equal "from Hulle to Cartage," rough and merry:

> And, certeinly, he was a good felawe.
> Ful many a draughte of wyn had he y-drawe
> From Burdeux-ward, whyl that the chapman sleep.
> Of nyce conscience took he no keep . . .
> Hardy he was, and wys to undertake;
> With many a tempest hadde his berd been shake.

Shipmaster. [Also, **Sea Captain**.] In Shakespeare's *2 Henry VI*, the captor of the Duke of Suffolk.

Ship Money. In old English law, a charge or tax imposed by the king upon seaports and trading towns, requiring them to provide and furnish warships, or to pay money for that purpose. It fell more or less into disuse, but was not formally abolished until 1641. Charles II attempted to extend it to all counties in 1634. The attempt to revive it met with strong opposition, notably in the famous resistance to it by John Hampden, and was one of the proximate causes of the English Civil War. It was abolished by statute 17 Charles I. c. 2 (1641).

Ship of Fools, The. A translation by Alexander Barclay, made in 1508 and published in 1509, of Sebastian Brant's *Narrenschiff*. It is believed to be the first English book in which mention is made of the New World.

Shipton (ship'ton), **Mother**. [Maiden name, **Ursula Southiel**.] b. near Knaresborough, Yorkshire, England, in July, 1488; d. c1559. A semi-legendary English prophetess. She is said to have married Toby Shipton, a builder. According to tradition, she was the child of Agatha Shipton and the devil, and author of *Mother Shipton's Prophecies*. No evidence actually exists of her really having lived. The earliest reference to her is in 1641, at least 80 years after her reputed death; a biography, *The Life and Death of Mother Shipton* (1684) by Richard Head, and another soon afterward, apparently were built up from the many chapbooks in circulation about her prophecies. So convincing were these predictions that the London fire of 1666 was held to have been foreseen by her; predictions of the fate of certain members of the court of Henry VIII were probably written after the fact. She had, according to tradition, reported that the end of the world would occur in 1881, and much of rural England was upset as a result when 1881 arrived; this prophecy was, however, one of the several forged by Charles Hindley, who published (1862) a supposedly contemporary biography of the seeress.

Shipwreck, The. A descriptive poem in three cantos by William Falconer, published in 1762. Revised versions were published in 1764 and 1769. The poem deals with the story of the wreck of a ship off the coast of Greece.

Shirburne Ballads (shir'burn). A collection of ballads found in an early 17th-century manuscript at Shirburne (or Shirbourne) Castle, in Oxfordshire.

Shirley (shėr'li). A novel by Charlotte Brontë, published in 1849 under the pseudonym of Currer Bell. It is set in Yorkshire at the beginning of the 19th century, and tells the story of the fight waged by Robert Moore, the owner of a factory, to install machinery. This precipitates an outburst of violence by the workers, but Moore is able finally to show them that the change will, in the long run, mean more work rather than less, and will provide a better standard of living for all. There is a considerable historical background for this aspect of the story; almost from the start of the Industrial Revolution working people in England feared the effect of machines on their jobs. Moore proposes to Shirley Keeldar, an impulsive young lady of wealth (this is connected indirectly with his plans to convince the workers of the rightness of his course), but she rejects him. He finally marries the quiet and gentle Caroline Helstone, who has always adored him, and whom he comes to love. Shirley marries the tutor, Louis Moore, a man of spirit and intelligence that matches her own. Charlotte Brontë modeled her picture of Shirley on her sister, Emily.

Shirley, James. b. at London, Sept, 18, 1596; d. there, in October, 1666. An English dramatist. He was educated at Merchant Taylors' School, at St. John's College, Oxford, and at Catherine Hall, Cambridge. Afterwards he took orders in the Anglican Church and was appointed to a living at St. Albans which he gave up on joining the Roman Catholic Church. He remained at St. Albans (1623–25) as master of the grammar school but gave up teaching in 1625 to become a playwright. Settling in London at Gray's Inn, he soon became prominent in Court circles. It is said that Charles I took enough interest in him to furnish the plot for *The Gamester* (acted 1634, published 1637). He composed an impressive masque, *The Triumph of Peace*, in 1634, which was offered at Court by the Inns of Court. For several years (1637–40) he lived in Ireland, writing for the theater in Dublin. Upon his return to England he wrote until the theaters were closed by act of Parliament in 1642. His plays were published in 1653, 1655, and 1659, and he contributed the prefatory address to the 1647 Beaumont and Fletcher folio of which he was editor. In his latter years he returned to teaching and assisted John Ogilby, once manager of the Dublin Theatre, in translating the classics. In the course of his playwriting career he wrote about 40 plays, of which 31 survive. He is said to have died with his wife as the result of fright and exposure during the Great Fire of London. Among his plays are *Love Tricks, or the School of Compliment* (1625, published in 1631), *The Wedding* (1629), *The Witty Fair One* (1628, published in 1633), *The Maid's Revenge* (1626, published in 1639), *The Brothers* (1626), *The Grateful Servant* (licensed in 1629, under the title of *The Faithful Servant*, and printed in 1630), *The Traitor* (1631), *Love's Cruelty* (1631), *The Changes, or Love in a Maze* (1632), *The Bird in a Cage* (1633), *Hyde Park* (1632), *The Ball* (licensed Nov. 16, 1632, and printed 1639 as the joint work of George Chapman and Shirley although probably all Shirley's work), *The Coronation* (licensed Feb. 6, 1635, as "a play by Shirley," but the title page of the first edition in 1640 gives it to John Fletcher, who had died ten years before; Shirley claimed it as his), *The Lady of Pleasure* (1635, generally considered his best comedy of manners), *Saint Patrick for Ireland* (1640), *The Humorous Courtier* (1640), *The Imposture* (1640, published in 1652), *The Cardinal* (1641, published in 1653), and *The Sisters* (1652). In 1659 Shirley

published, together, *Honoria and Mammon* and *The Contentions of Ajax and Ulysses for the Armour of Achilles.* The first piece was a revision of his own interlude called *The Contention of Honour and Riches.* He also wrote *Manductio, or a Leading of Children by the Hand through the Principles of Grammar* (1660). He revised for the stage a number of Fletcher's plays. His attempts to write Elizabethan tragedy are pallid, for he did not have the qualities requisite for great poetic tragedy. He did his best work in romantic plays of the Fletcherian type and in frothy comedies of manners that foreshadowed Restoration comedy. His verse is fluent, technically competent, but inclined to prosiness except in his songs.

Shirley, John. b. c1366; d. at London, Oct. 21, 1456. An English traveler and collector of manuscripts, especially those of Geoffrey Chaucer and John Lydgate.

Shiva (shē′va). [Also, **Siva**.] The third god of the Hindu triad, in the later mythology regarded as the destroyer, with Brahma as the creator and Vishnu as the preserver. The Shaivas, or Shiva-worshipers, assign to him the first place in the triad, identifying him with creation and reproduction as well as destruction, and so constituting him the Supreme Being. In modern Hinduism Shiva is a development of the Vedic storm god, Rudra, by the addition of many characteristics from popular religion. The name Shiva, "the auspicious," was at first an epithet of Rudra, in his aspect of protector and increaser of cattle, and gradually it supplanted the name Rudra itself. There are more than 1,000 names and epithets for Shiva: Mahadeva is the most frequent. He is depicted with four arms, five faces, and three eyes, one in his forehead. The third eye is so destructive as to annihilate gods or men at a glance. His throat is dark blue from the poison which would have destroyed the world had he not swallowed it. He wears sometimes a deerskin, sometimes a tigerskin, sometimes an elephant's skin. His attributes are a trident, a bow, a club, an hourglass-shaped drum, a noose, the rat, and the elephant. His wife or consort is Devi; his sons are Ganesha and Karttikeya. His residence is Kailas, one of the loftiest peaks of the Himalayas. He is especially worshiped at Benares.

Shoemaker's Holiday, or the Gentle Craft, The. A comedy by Thomas Dekker. It was published anonymously in 1600 and played in 1599. Dekker took the story from *The Gentle Craft* (1597) by Thomas Deloney. Simon Eyre, the shoemaker, is a sympathetic and realistic portrait of the London tradesman who was rising to a position of civic importance during the later years of Queen Elizabeth's reign. Simon is proud of his vocation, his apprentices, and his wife. When he becomes sheriff of London, his first thoughts are for the welfare of his wife and his workmen. When he becomes Lord Mayor and entertains the King at dinner, he gives another banquet on the same day for his fellow craftsmen in London and proclaims that every Shrove Tuesday shall be a shoemaker's holiday. Paralleling this realism is a double love story. The characters concerned are Simon's journeyman Ralph and his new wife Jane; and Rose, daughter of Simon's predecessor as Lord Mayor, and Lacy, nephew of the Earl of Lincoln. Jane, upon a false report that Ralph has been killed in the wars, yields to the suit of Hammon, a wealthy citizen who has tried unsuccessfully to win the hand of Rose. Hammon loses Jane when Ralph, wounded but alive, appears just as Hammon and Jane are entering the church to be married. Meanwhile, Lacy's uncle, to avoid an unsuitable match between his gentleman nephew and middle-class Rose, has separated the lovers by procuring Lacy a military command abroad. Lacy deserts his post and returns home, finding employment in Simon's shop. He and Rose marry, despite the opposition of Lacy's uncle, who appeals to the King to divorce them. The King, honoring true love, approves the union between Lacy and Rose, whom he describes as "young, well-born, fair, virtuous, A worthy bride for any gentleman." As a further sign of favor, he knights Lacy. The play is a reflection of attitudes toward caste during the Elizabethan era, when the rising middle class began to merge with the older class of gentlemen. The King's actions are consonant with the Tudor policy of utilizing the merchant-tradesman class as a check upon the provincial nobility.

Shops and Houses. A novel by Frank Swinnerton, published in 1918.

Shore (shōr), **Jane.** b. at London, c1445; d. 1527. Mistress of King Edward IV. While still a girl she married William Shore, a citizen of London. After her intrigue with the king began (c1470) she lived in the greatest luxury, and after his death she became the mistress of William, Baron Hastings, who was beheaded by Richard III, June 13, 1483. Richard imprisoned Jane Shore (largely out of malice, but with a great show of virtuous indignation), robbed her house, accused her of witchcraft, and obliged her to do penance for unchastity at Saint Paul's Cross. She afterward became the mistress of Thomas Grey, 1st Marquis of Dorset. The agonizing details of her death in a ditch from starvation are without authority, though an old ballad cites them with great precision.

Shoreditch (shōr'dich). A metropolitan borough in N and E London, in the County of London, situated immediately N of the City of London, ab. ½ mi. NE of Liverpool Street station, London. It forms part of the East End of London, and suffered heavy war damage during World War II. It has now been largely rebuilt. Shoreditch is noted for its furniture manufactures, carried on in many small workshops, each one performing a specialized operation. The furniture is commonly moved from shop to shop by wheelbarrow.

Short (shôrt), **Bob.** A pseudonym allegedly used by Alexander Pope in his contributions to the *Guardian*, Nos. 91 and 92.

Shorter (shôr'tẽr), **Clement King.** b. at London, July 19, 1858; d. Nov. 19, 1926. An English journalist and critic. He was editor of the *Illustrated London News* (1891–1900), of the *Sketch* (1893–1900), which he had founded, and of the *English Illustrated Magazine* (1893–1900). From 1900 he was editor of the *Sphere*, which he also founded, and of the *Tatler*. Among his publications are *Charlotte Brontë and Her Circle* (1896), *Victorian Literature* (1897), *Charlotte Brontë and Her Sisters*

(1905), *George Borrow* (1905), *Immortal Memories* (1908), and others.

Shorthouse (shôrt'hous), **Joseph Henry.** b. at Birmingham, England, Sept. 9, 1834; d. at Edgbaston Park, Birmingham, March 4, 1903. An English novelist. Author of *John Inglesant* (privately printed, 1880; published in 1881), which brought him instant success when it was praised by W. E. Gladstone, T. H. Huxley, and Cardinal Manning; *The Little Schoolmaster Mark* (1883), *Sir Percival* (1886), *The Countess Eve* (1888), *Blanche, Lady Falaise* (1891), and other novels; *A Teacher of the Violin* (1888), short stories; and *The Platonism of Wordsworth* (1882) and *The Royal Supremacy* (1899), essays.

Short Parliament. In English history, the fourth Parliament of Charles I, which sat from April 13 to May 5, 1640. Called by the king to support a campaign against the Scottish Covenanters, it refused to make any grants until its grievances had been answered, and it was dissolved. It was followed in November by the Long Parliament.

short story. A brief piece of fiction, usually narrative in form. The modern short story may range in length from approximately 500 words (called, by some, the "short, short" story) to approximately 7,500 words. A length of approximately 5,000 words is perhaps now most common, and stories of more than 10,000 words often tend to take on the character of the short novel.

Short View of the Immorality and Profaneness of the English Stage, A. An attack (1698) on the stage by Jeremy Collier. He laid the blame for the "immorality" of the stage chiefly against Dryden, Wycherley, Congreve, Vanbrugh, D'Urfey, and Otway (a list including those now generally considered to have been the best of the Restoration dramatists). He disliked the profanity then fairly general in many stage conversations, and also what he regarded (with some justice) as a generally unflattering portrait of the clergy.

Shottery (shot'ẽr.i). A village in Warwickshire, noted as the residence of Anne Hathaway, Shakespeare's wife.

Showing Up of Blanco Posnet (blang'kō poz'nẹt), **The.** See **Shewing-up of Blanco Posnet, The.**

Shropshire (shrop'shir). [In writing often shortened as **Salop** (without a period).] An inland county in W England. It is bounded on the N by Cheshire and the detached portion of Flintshire (Wales), on the E by Staffordshire, on the SE and S by Worcestershire, on the S by Worcestershire, Herefordshire, and Radnorshire (Wales), and on the W by Montgomeryshire (Wales). The N part of the county is generally rolling; in the S part it is more rugged and elevated, reaching 1,792 ft. in the Clee Hills. Most of the county is drained by the river Severn and its tributaries. Shropshire is largely an agricultural county with more than half the acreage in permanent pasture. Dairying is important, and it is famous for its breed of sheep. The name of the county is derived from an ancient tribal name, the Scrobsaetan, being the only Mercian shire which has kept a tribe name. County seat, Shrewsbury; area, ab. 1,400 sq. mi.

ḍ, d or j; ṣ, s or sh; ṭ, t or ch; ẓ, z or zh; o, F. cloche; ü, F. menu; ċh, Sc. loch; ṅ, F. bonbon

Shropshire Lad, A. A volume of verse (1896) by A. E. Housman, containing the well-known lyrics "When I was One-and-Twenty" and "With Rue My Heart is Laden."

Shute (shöt), **Nevil.** [Full name, **Nevil Shute Norway.**] b. at London, Jan. 17, 1899——. An English writer and aeronautical engineer. He became associated (1924) with an airship construction company, and helped to design and build the airship *R-100*, in which he made (1930) a round-trip flight from England to Montreal as technical representative. His novels include *So Disdained* (1928; published in the U. S. as *The Mysterious Aviator*), *Lonely Road* (1932), *Kindling* (1938), *Ordeal* (1939), *Landfall* (1940), *Pied Piper* (1942), *Pastoral* (1944), *Most Secret* (1945), *The Chequer Board* (1947), *Round the Bend* (1950), *The Legacy* (1950), and *The Far Country* (1952).

Shuter (shö′tėr), **Edward.** b. 1728; d. Nov. 1, 1776. An English actor, said by David Garrick to be the greatest comic genius he had ever known. Among his original creations were Papillon in *The Liar*, Old Hardcastle in *She Stoops to Conquer*, and Sir Anthony Absolute in *The Rivals*.

Shylock (shī′lok). In Shakespeare's *Merchant of Venice*, a Jew, one of the principal characters. He lends Bassanio 3,000 ducats on condition that if they are not repaid at the promised time he shall be allowed to cut a pound of flesh from the body of Antonio, Bassanio's friend and surety. He claims the forfeiture, but is defeated by Portia, who reminds him that he loses his life if he sheds one drop of blood or takes more or less than his lawful pound of flesh. Down to the time of Charles Macklin the part was played by the low comedian, and was grotesque to buffoonery. He transformed it from "the grimacings of low comedy to the solemn sweep of tragedy," and made Shylock a vengeful, inexorable moneymaker.

Sibylline Books or **Sibylline Oracles** (sib′i.lēn, -lĭn). In Roman history, a collection of oracular utterances, written in Greek hexameters, containing directions as to the worship of the gods and the policy of the Romans, which were kept with great care at Rome. According to legend, these books were bought by Tarquinius Superbus from the Cumaean sibyl, who at first offered him nine books; when he refused them six she burned three, and offered him the remaining six at the original price; when he again refused, she burned three more, and offered him the remaining three, still at the original price, and these he bought.

Sibylline Leaves. A volume of verse (1817) by Samuel Taylor Coleridge.

Sibyls (sib′ilz). In ancient mythology, certain old women reputed to possess special powers of prophecy or divination and intercession with the gods in behalf of those who resorted to them. Heraclitus, in the 6th century B.C., mentioned one prophetess named Sibyl, whose legend spread to various localities; by c350 B.C. she was mentioned as many. Different writers mention from one to ten sibyls, enumerated as the Persian, Libyan, Delphian, Cimmerian, Erythraean, Samian, Cumaean, Hellespontine or Trojan, Phrygian, and Tiburtine. Of these the most celebrated was the Cumaean sibyl (of Cumae in Italy), whose story is that she appeared

before Tarquin the Proud and offered him nine books for sale. He refused to buy them, whereupon she burned three, and offered the remaining six at the original price. He again refused them; she destroyed three more, and offered the remaining three at the price she had asked for the nine. Tarquin, astonished, bought the books, which were found to contain directions as to the worship of the gods and the policy of the Romans. These Sibylline Books, or books professing to have this origin, written in Greek hexameters, were kept with great care at Rome, and consulted only by direction of the senate. They were destroyed at the burning of the Temple of Jupiter in 83 B.C. Fresh collections were made, which were finally destroyed soon after 400 A.D. The 14 or 15 Sibylline Oracles referred to by the Christian fathers, and still extant, belong to early ecclesiastical literature, and are a mixture of Jewish, Hellenistic, and later Christian material. In composition they seem to date from the 2nd century B.C. to the 3rd century A.D.

Sicelides (si.sel′i.dēz). A pastoral play by Phineas Fletcher, written in 1614 and printed in 1631.

Sicilian Bull (si.sil′yạn). A bronze bull made as an instrument of torture by Perillus for the use of the Sicilian tyrant Phalaris. As with many such instruments, legend has it that its first victim was the inventor, Perillus.

Sicilian Vespers. A name given to the massacre (1282) of the French in Sicily by the Sicilians. It is so called from its commencement at vespers on Easter Monday.

Sicinius Velutus (si.sin′i.us vẹ.lö′tus, -lū′-). In Shakespeare's *Coriolanus*, a tribune of the people. Junius Brutus is the other.

Sick Man of Europe. [Also, **Sick Man of the East.**] A name given to the former Turkish empire, in allusion to the steady deterioration of its power and to the growing corruption of its government. It was first used by Czar Nicholas I of Russia in a conversation (1853) with the British ambassador Sir George Hamilton Seymour. For obvious reasons, the term has not been used since the regime of Mustapha Kemal, after World War I.

Siculus (sik′ụ.lus), **Diodorus.** See **Diodorus.**

Siddhartha (si.där′thạ) or **Siddharta** (-tạ), Prince. See **Buddha.**

Siddons (sid′ọnz), **Sarah.** [Maiden name, **Kemble;** commonly called Mrs. **Siddons.**] b. at Brecknock, Wales, July 5, 1755; d. at London, June 8, 1831. An English tragic actress; daughter of Roger Kemble, a theater manager. She was educated at the schools of the towns in which Kemble's company played, and married (Nov. 26, 1773) William Siddons, an actor. She made her first appearance at London in 1775 as Portia. In 1777 she returned to the provinces, and in 1782 appeared at Drury Lane Theatre, London, with extraordinary success as Isabella in Thomas Southerne's *Fatal Marriage*. Thereafter she was the acknowledged queen of the English theater. In 1785 she first appeared as Lady Macbeth, her greatest role, and in 1788 appeared as Queen Katharine in her brother John's revival of *Henry VIII*. In 1803 her brother bought a share of Covent Garden Theatre, and she joined his company, playing there until she left the stage,

June 29, 1812, after a remarkable career in her profession. She made a great impression as Jane Shore, as Belvidera in Thomas Otway's *Venice Preserved*, as Zara in Congreve's *The Mourning Bride*, and as Queen Elinor in Shakespeare's *King John*.

Siddons, Scott. b. in India, 1844; d. at Paris, Nov. 19, 1896. An English actress; great-grand-daughter of Sarah Siddons.

Sidgwick (sij'wik), **Ethel.** b. at Rugby, England, Dec. 20, 1877—. An English novelist. Author of the novels *Promise* (1910), *Herself* (1912), *Succession* (1913), *A Lady of Leisure* (1914), *Duke Jones* (1914), *The Accolade* (1915), *Hatchways* (1916), *Jamesie* (1917), *Madam* (1921), *Restoration* (1923), *Laura* (1924), *When I Grow Rich* (1928), *The Bells of Shoreditch* (1928), and *Dorothy's Wedding* (1931).

Sidgwick, Henry. b. at Skipton, Yorkshire, England, May 31, 1838; d. at Cambridge, England, Aug. 28, 1900. An English philosopher and teacher. Educated at Rugby and Trinity College, Cambridge, he was associated (1859 *et seq.*) with Trinity as fellow, lecturer, and professor (1883–1900) of moral philosophy. A follower of J. S. Mill and Jeremy Bentham, he nevertheless held that the goodness of an action is in the pleasure it produces, distinguishing further between egoism and altruism as means to this pleasure; his ethics thus becomes a form of intentional utilitarianism. He was a founder of the Society for Psychical Research, of which he was president (1882–85, 1888–93). Opposed to religious tests, and in favor of admitting women to college degrees, he resigned his fellowship and his membership (1890–98) in the Trinity senate in protest against prevailing policies. He married (1876) Arthur J. Balfour's sister, Eleanor Mildred, who was later vice-president and president of Newnham, the Cambridge University college for women, which her husband helped to found. Author of *The Methods of Ethics* (1874), *Principles of Political Economy* (1883), *Outlines of the History of Ethics* (1886), *The Elements of Politics* (1891), *Practical Ethics* (1898), *Lectures on the Ethics of T. H. Green, Spencer, and Martineau* (1902), *Philosophy: Its Scope and Relations* (1902), *The Development of European Polity* (1903), *Miscellaneous Essays and Addresses* (1904), and *Lectures of Kant* (1905).

Sidney or **Sydney** (sid'ni), **Algernon.** b. at Penshurst, Kent, England, c1622; beheaded at London, Dec. 7, 1683. An English politician and patriot. He served in the Parliamentary army, being wounded at Marston Moor in 1644. He was elected (1646) to Parliament, where he took rank as one of the leaders of the Independents. He became governor of Dublin and lieutenant general of horse in Ireland (1647), but remained in retirement (1653–59) because of his objection to the power given to Cromwell. He became councilor of state in 1659, and was peace commissioner between Denmark and Sweden (1659–60). He lived on the Continent after the Restoration until 1677, and, being known to be a supporter of Monmouth, was arrested on the discovery of the Rye House Plot (with which he had no connection) in June, 1683, and condemned to death for high treason. He wrote *Discourses Concerning Government* (1698), and others.

Sidney, Sir **Philip.** b. at Penshurst, Kent, England, Nov. 30, 1554; d. at Arnhem, Holland, Oct. 17, 1586. An English soldier, statesman, and poet, and critic; brother of Mary Herbert, Countess of Pembroke. Educated (1568–71) at Christ Church, Oxford, he made the grand tour (1572–75), traveling in France, Flanders, Germany, Hungary, and Italy. He served in Parliament (1581) for Kent. Knighted in 1583, he was a favorite, at various times, of Queen Elizabeth. He was appointed (1585) governor of Flushing, and was shot (Sept. 22, 1586) at the Battle of Zutphen, where, suffering pangs of thirst, according to a story that well illustrates (whatever its truth) the esteem in which he was held as a gracious knight and a chivalrous gentleman, he gave the water he had called for and was about to drink to a wounded soldier, saying, "Thy necessity is greater than mine." Author of *Arcadia* (written 1580–83; published 1590), a combination of prose romance and poetry, *Apologie for Poetrie* (published 1595, in two editions, one entitled *Defence of Poesie*), historically important as the first good example of English literary criticism, and *Astrophel and Stella* (1591), a series of 11 songs and 108 sonnets addressed to Penelope Devereux (wife of Robert Rich, with whom she was unhappy). Despite this feverish literary attachment to Stella, to whom he continued to address sonnets even after his marriage, he married (1583) Frances Walsingham, daughter of Elizabeth's secretary of state. The *Arcadia*, written for his sister's amusement, was used by William Shakespeare, James Shirley, Edmund Spenser, Francis Beaumont and John Fletcher, and many others, in the Elizabethan and later periods, as source material for plays, poems, and stories; the *Apologie* was an answer to the *Schoole of Abuse* (1579), an attack on plays and poetry by Stephen Gosson, a clergyman; Sidney's sonnets anticipated and influenced those by Shakespeare.

Sidney Sussex College (sus'eks). A college of Cambridge University, founded 1595 by the Countess of Sussex.

Sidonia (si.dō'ni.ạ). In Benjamin Disraeli's novels *Coningsby* and *Tancred*, a wealthy and intelligent banker, who uses the wisdom he has gained in the East to solve the problems of the West.

Sidrophel (sid'rọ.fel). A character in Samuel Butler's *Hudibras*, probably intended to represent William Lilly, the astrologer.

Siege of Corinth (kor'inth), **The.** A narrative poem by Byron, published in 1816.

Siege of Damascus (dạ.mas'kus), **The.** A tragedy (1720) by John Hughes.

Siege of Jerusalem (jẹ.rö'sạ.lẹm), **The.** A Middle English romance in alliterative verse, dealing with Titus's siege of Jerusalem and stressing the battle scenes.

Siege of Rhodes (rōdz), **The.** A play by Sir William D'Avenant, first brought out as a musical and spectacular entertainment in 1656. In 1662, when it was again produced, in a much elaborated form and with a great deal more music, a second part was added; both were printed in 1663. It is important as being practically the first opera produced in England. Matthew Locke, Henry Lawes, and Henry Cooke provided the music.

Siege of Troy (troi), **The.** See **Recuyell of the Historyes of Troye.**

Siege Perilous (per′i.lus). [Also, **The Perillous Chair.**] A vacant seat at the Round Table, in Arthurian romance, which could be filled only by the predestined finder of the Holy Grail. Any other who sat in it paid for the act with his life. When the proper time came the name of Sir Galahad was found on it.

Siegfried (sēg′frēd; German, zēk′frēt). [Also, **Sigfrid.**] The hero of the Middle High German *Nibelungenlied.* The legend is that he became invulnerable when he killed and bathed in the blood of the dragon Fafnir, except for one spot, where a leaf fell on his shoulder. He won the treasure of the Nibelungs, and became their king, and fought against the Danes and Saxons in behalf of Gunther, king of the Burgundians. He married Kriemhild, Gunther's sister, and helped Gunther win Brünhild for wife. Brünhild discovered the vulnerable spot of Siegfried, and out of jealousy brought about his death. Siegfried's story parallels that of Sigurd of the Icelandic *Volsunga Saga* and *Elder Edda.* He is also the hero of Wagner's opera cycle *The Ring of the Nibelungs.*

Sieveking (sēv′king), **Lancelot de Giberne.** [Known as **Lance Sieveking.**] b. at Harrow, England, March 19, 1896—. An English writer and dramatist. He served with the Royal Air Force during World War I, and was a prisoner of war (1917–18). He was owner and editor (1919–22) of *The New Cambridge,* and joined (1924) the British Broadcasting Corporation, for which he produced the first televised play (1927). Author of *Dressing-Gowns and Glue* (1919), *Gladstone Bags and Marmalade* (1920), *The Cud* (1922), *Stampede* (1924), *Bats in the Belfry* (1926), *The Perfect Witch* (1935), *Silence in Heaven* (1936), *North American Binocular* (1948), and *A Tomb with a View* (1950).

Sif (sēf). In Old Norse mythology, the wife of Thor.

Sigismund Alvan (sij′is.mund, sig′-, al′van). See **Alvan, Sigismund.**

Sigmund (sig′mund). In the Icelandic *Elder Edda* and the *Volsunga Saga,* the youngest son of Volsung. Sigmund alone was able to draw Odin's sword out of the great oak that grew in his father's hall, and he was the only survivor of the treacherous slaughter of the Volsungs. Sigmund escaped and lived to avenge his father, and his brothers and their warriors, the Volsungs. Sigmund was the father of Sigurd.

signature. 1. A letter or figure placed by the printer at the foot of the first page of every section or gathering of a book. The letters begin with A, the figures with 1, and follow in regular order on succeeding sections. They are intended to aid the binder in folding, collating, and arranging the sections consecutively. In early printed books the signature mark was often repeated on the 3rd, 5th, and 7th pages of a section of 16 pages as an additional safeguard for the folder: as, A on 1st page, A i on 3rd, A ii on 5th, and A iv on 7th page. Hence—**2.** A sheet; especially, in bookbinders' use,

a sheet after it has been folded and is ready to be gathered.

Signy (sig′ni). In William Morris's *Sigurd the Volsung,* the sister of Sigmund.

Sigurd the Volsung (sig′ėrd; vol′sŭng). [Full title, **The Story of Sigurd the Volsung and the Fall of the Niblungs** (nēb′lŭngz).] An epic poem by William Morris, published in 1876, based upon the *Volsunga Saga,* and consisting of four books. It is considered his most important narrative poem, and reveals very clearly his discontent with contemporary civilization. It tells the story of Sigmund in the first book, and the story of his son Sigurd in the following two; the fall of the Niblungs is described in the fourth book. It deals with the love of Sigurd and Brynhild, the success of Grimhild, queen of the Niblungs, in tricking Sigurd (who loves Brynhild) into marrying her daughter Gudrun, and Brynhild into marrying Gudrun's brother Gunnar. When Brynhild learns of the deception she causes Gunnar to kill Sigurd, then kills herself to join him in death. Gudrun then marries Atli (Attila of the Huns), provoking him to destroy the Niblungs to avenge Sigurd. She then kills Atli and herself.

Sigyn (sē′gün). In Norse mythology, the wife of Loki.

Sikes (sīks), **Bill.** In Dickens's *Oliver Twist,* a brutal thief, housebreaker, and murderer. He persecutes Oliver, and kills Nancy, who has befriended Oliver.

Silas Marner (sī′las mär′nėr). [Full title, **Silas Marner, the Weaver of Raveloe** (rav′e̤.lō).] A novel by George Eliot, published in 1861. When he was young Silas Marner had been driven from his town because of a false accusation of theft. He comes to Raveloe and lives a life of seclusion as a weaver, delighting only in counting over the slowly growing hoard of gold obtained from his trade over the course of 15 years. Meanwhile, Godfrey Cass, son of a local squire, carries the guilty secret of having married and abandoned a dissipated woman of the lower class. Godfrey's brother, Dunstan, steals Silas Marner's gold to pay some debts, and on his way home with the stolen money takes a fatal fall into an old quarry where his body lies undiscovered. One night Godfrey's wife, on her way to force her husband to acknowledge her and his child, loses her way and dies in the snow. The child wanders to the cottage of Silas Marner. He comes to love the little girl, whose golden hair reminds him of his lost gold, and through the mediation of a friend, Mrs. Dolly Winthrop, is allowed to keep the foundling, Eppie. She grows up happily, loving Dolly's son, Aaron. Godfrey, meanwhile, has married Nancy Lammeter. Although the pair have no children together, he conceals the fact that Eppie is his daughter. When the old quarry is eventually drained, Duncan's skeleton is found at the bottom of it with Marner's stolen gold. Godfrey then confesses to his father the story of Duncan's debts, and reveals that Eppie is his child. Silas unselfishly advises Eppie to claim her father and the heritage which is hers, but she prefers to stay with the old man and marry Aaron Winthrop.

Silas Wegg (weg). See **Wegg, Silas.**

Silence (sī′lens). In Shakespeare's *2 Henry IV,* a dull country justice.

Silent Woman, The. See **Epicoene, or the Silent Woman.**

Silenus (sī.lē'nus). In Greek mythology, a forest god, depicted as a shaggy, full-bearded old man, with horse ears, and sometimes horse legs, usually drunk, and often riding on an ass or on a wine-vessel. He was reported to be extraordinarily wise, and if caught could be made to reveal his wisdom and give answers to questions. The Phrygian king Midas is said to have plied Silenus with wine and questions and received astounding answers; but nobody learned what Silenus told Midas, except that it would be better never to be born. In the 6th century B.C. Silenus became associated with Dionysus and thereafter appeared in the Dionysian frolics and processions attended by troops of satyrs. He became credited with being the foster father and boon companion of Dionysus. The term *sileni* (plural) is applied to a group of woodland spirits or semi-deities, who were much confused with the satyrs, whom they resembled, except that the sileni were old and were differentiated from the goat-like satyrs by their horselike characteristics. They, too, were characterized as wise, drunk, and prophetic. They were credited with being wonderful musicians, and with having taught Dionysus the secrets of the vine and wine-making. Socrates was compared to Silenus is wisdom and irony.

Silhouettes. A volume of verse (1892) by Arthur Symons.

Silius (sil'i.us). In Shakespeare's *Antony and Cleopatra*, an officer under Ventidius.

Silkworm (silk'wẽrm), **Sir Diaphanous.** A courtier "of a most elegant thread," in Ben Jonson's comedy *The Magnetic Lady.*

Silures (si.lö'rēz, sil'ū.rēz). An ancient people of Britain, formerly dwelling in the hills of what is now SE Wales, at the period of the Roman conquest. The geological term Silurian is derived from this tribal name.

"Silurist" (si.lö'rist, sil'ū.rist), **the.** See **Vaughan, Henry.**

Silver (sil'vẽr), **Long John.** See **Long John Silver.**

Silverado Squatters (sil.vẹ.rä'dō), **The.** An autobiographical narrative by Robert Louis Stevenson, published in 1883. In it he describes a trip to California, on which he was accompanied by his wife and son.

Silver Box, The. A social problem play (1906) by John Galsworthy.

Silver-Fork School. In English fiction, a nickname given to a group of novelists, including Theodore Hook, Frances Trollope, and Lady Blessington, who laid great stress on matters of etiquette.

Silver King. A melodrama (1882) by Henry Arthur Jones.

Silver Spoon, The. A novel by John Galsworthy, published in 1926. This work, which traces the fortunes of the Forsyte family, was later included in *A Modern Comedy* (1929).

Silver Tassie, The. A play (1928) by Sean O'Casey.

Silvia (sil'vi.ạ). In Shakespeare's *Two Gentlemen of Verona*, the daughter of the Duke of Milan, loved by Valentine.

Silvia or **Sylvia** (sil'vi.ạ). The forsaken mistress of Vainlove in William Congreve's *The Old Bachelor.*

Silvia or **Sylvia.** The daughter of Justice Balance in George Farquhar's comedy *The Recruiting Officer.*

Silvius (sil'vi.us). In Shakespeare's *As You Like It*, a shepherd in love with Phebe.

Simeon of Durham (sim'ẹ.ọn; dur'ạm). [Also, **Symeon.**] d. c1130. An English chronicler, author of a history of the church of Durham, and a history of the kings of Northumbria, both in Latin.

simile (sim'i.lẹ). In rhetoric, the comparing or likening of two things having some strong point or points of resemblance, both of which are mentioned and the comparison directly stated; a poetic or imaginative comparison; also, the verbal expression or embodiment of such a comparison.

> *Tra.* O, sir, Lucentio slipp'd me like his greyhound,
> Which runs himself and catches for his master.
> *Pet.* A good swift simile, but something currish.
> (Shakespeare, Taming of the Shrew.)

> In this Simily wee have himselfe compar'd to
> Christ, the Parlament to the Devill.
> (Milton, Eikonoklastes.)

> In Argument
> Similies are like Songs in Love:
> They much describe; they nothing prove.
> (Prior, Alma.)

Simkin (sim'kin). A miller, the subject of "The Reeve's Tale" in Chaucer's *Canterbury Tales.*

Simnel (sim'nẹl), **Lambert.** b. c1475; d. c1537. A pretender to the throne of England, personating Edward, Earl of Warwick. Warwick, who was the surviving Yorkist claimant to the throne, had been imprisoned (1485) when Henry VII (Henry Tudor) became king. Originally it had been planned to have Simnel appear as one of the young princes who had been killed by Richard III in the Tower, since their claim was prior to that of Warwick's; however, a rumor to the effect that Warwick had died caused a change in plans and the Yorkists, taking Simnel to Ireland, put him forward as Warwick, supposedly escaped from the Tower. He was crowned, as Edward VI, in Dublin on May 24, 1487. Meanwhile, Henry had become cognizant of the Yorkists' plot and, to forestall trouble in London, exhibited the real Warwick in the streets (he was not executed until 1499). In June, 1487, the Yorkists, supported by German and Irish troops (which lost them any chance they might have had of support from the English), landed in Lancashire and attacked the royal troops under Henry at Stoke-on-Trent (June 16, 1487). The Yorkists were routed, their leaders died in the field, and Simnel was captured. Realizing that the youth was only a pawn in the game, Henry spared his life. Simnel is said to have become a scullion and later a falconer in the king's service.

Simon (sī'mon). A comic figure in Thomas Middleton's *The Mayor of Quinborough.* He is the main character of the subplot, and by his election to the Mayor's office gives the play its title.

Simon. Entries on literary characters having this prename will also be found under the surnames Dedalus, Glover, Pure, Shadow, and Tappertit.

ḍ, d or j; ṣ, s or sh; ṭ, t or ch; z̧, z or zh; o, F. cloche; ü, F. menu; ċh, Sc. loch; ṅ, F. bonbon.

Simon. See also Saint **Peter.**

Simon Eyre (ār). A London shoemaker (based on a historical figure of the same name), in Thomas Dekker's comedy *The Shoemaker's Holiday*, who becomes lord mayor of London. Dekker got the story from Thomas Deloney's *The Gentle Craft*, a eulogy of the shoemaker's trade. Eyre is proud of his vocation: "Prince am I none, yet am I nobly born, as being the sole son of a shoemaker." His spirit is that of the rising tradesman, proud of himself even though he is not a gentleman in the Elizabethan sense, and speaks of his apprentices as "pillars of his profession."

Simonides (sī.mon′i.dēz). In Shakespeare's *Pericles*, the King of Pentapolis and father of Thaisa. He calls Pericles a traitor to test him before he consents to his marriage to Thaisa.

Simonides of Ceos (sē′os). b. at Iulis, island of Keos (Ceos), Greece, 556 B.C.; d. at Syracuse, c469 or 467 B.C. A Greek poet. He lived in Athens, Thessaly, and Syracuse, spending the last years of his life at the court of Hiero of Syracuse. His poetry, including epigrams, lyrics, epitaphs, threnodies, and other forms, is among the best of ancient Greece. His elegies on the heroes of Marathon and Thermopylae are especially famous.

Simon Pure (sī′mon pūr). See **Pure, Simon.**

Simon the Jester. A novel by William John Locke, published in 1910.

Simony (sī′mō.ni), **Dr.** A character in Samuel Foote's play *The Cozeners*, supposed to be intended for Dr. William Dodd, who was afterward executed (though for forgery, not for simony).

Simpcox (sim′koks), **Saunder.** In Shakespeare's *2 Henry VI*, an impostor who pretends to be lame until he is whipped and runs away. His wife is also present and is whipped with him.

Simple (sim′pl). In Shakespeare's *Merry Wives of Windsor*, a servant of Slender.

Simple, Peter. The hero of a novel of the same name by Frederick Marryat, published in 1837.

Simple Simon (sī′mon). The title and hero of an old English nursery rhyme, and also of an Elizabethan chapbook which includes it. Simon seems to have been a popular synonym for any simpleton, and as such probably antedates the rhyme. Simple Simon performed the traditionally silly acts of trying to buy pies without money, fishing for a whale in his mother's pail, and looking for plums on a thistle. There existed also a 17th-century tune entitled *Simple Simon*, and a later 17th-century ballad entitled *Simple Simon's Misfortunes.*

Simple Story, A. A romance by Elizabeth Inchbald, written in 1777 but not published until 1791.

Simpleton of the Unexpected Isles, The. A play (1935) by George Bernard Shaw, included by most critics among his lesser works.

Simplicissimus (zim.plē.tsis′ē.mus). A German satirical weekly founded in 1896 by Albert Langen, a publisher at Munich. The contributing artists included Theodor Thomas Heine, Olaf Gulbransson, Ferdinand von Reznicek, and Wilhelm Schulz, while Karl Kraus and Ludwig Thoma were represented with literary contributions. The high standards established by the caricatures drawn for *Sim-*

plicissimus and *Die Jugend*, also at Munich, tended to force an improvement in such drawings in comparable German publications in other cities, as in the Berlin *Kladderadatsch* (founded in 1848).

Simpson (simp′son), **Evan John.** [Pseudonym, **Evan John.**] b. 1901; d. 1953. An English historical novelist and dramatist. Author, under his pseudonym, of *King Charles I* (1933), *Two Kingdoms* (1935), *Crippled Splendor* (1938), and *King's Masque* (1941); *Plus Ça Change* (1935), *Prelude to Massacre* (1937), and *The King's March* (1937), plays; and *Lofoten Letter* (1941), a personal narrative.

Simpson—A Life. A novel by Edward Sackville-West, published in 1931.

Sims (simz), **George Robert.** [Pseudonym, **Dagonet.**] b. at London, Sept. 2, 1847; d. there, Sept. 4, 1922. An English poet, journalist, novelist, and dramatist. Author of *Dagonet Ballads* (1879, 1882); *Crutch and Toothpick* (1879) and *The Lights of London* (1881), plays; *Blue-Eyed Susan* (1892) and *The Dandy Fifth* (1898), musical comedies; *How the Poor Live* (1883), *Rogues and Vagabonds* (1885), and *Land of Gold* (1888), poetry; also *Dorcas Dene, Detective* (1897), *Once upon a Christmas Time* (1898), and *My Life* (1917).

Sim Tappertit (sim tap′ėr.tit). See **Tappertit, Sim.**

Simurgh (sē.mùrg′). [Also, **Simurg.**] A huge bird of ancient Persian folklore and mythology. He was believed to have seen and survived three destructions of the world, and to possess all the wisdom of all the ages. In the *Shahnamah*, this huge bird cared for and reared the infant Zal.

Sinbad the Sailor (sin′bad). See **Sindbad the Sailor.**

Sinclair (sin.klār′, sin′klär, sing′-), **Catherine.** b. at Edinburgh, April 17, 1800; d. at Kensington, London, Aug. 6, 1864. A Scottish novelist and writer. She was supervisor of a charitable institution for widows of officers of the army and navy. She wrote *Modern Accomplishments* (1836), *Modern Society* (1836), *Modern Flirtations* (1841), and *Beatrice* (of which more than 40,000 copies were sold within 16 months of its publication in 1852).

Sinclair, May. b. c1865; d. 1946. A British novelist, a pioneer in the use of the stream-of-consciousness technique in fiction. Author of the novels *Audrey Craven* (1897), *Mr. and Mrs. Nevill Tyson* (1898), *Two Sides of a Question* (1901), *The Divine Fire* (1904), *The Helpmate* (1907), *Kitty Tailleur* (1908; American title, *The Immortal Moment*), *The Creators* (1910), *The Flaw in the Crystal* (1912), *The Combined Maze* (1913), *The Three Sisters* (1914), *Tasker Jevons* (1916; American title, *The Belfry*), *The Tree of Heaven* (1917), *Mary Olivier* (1919), *Mr. Waddington of Wyck* (1921), *Life and Death of Harriett Frean* (1922), *A Cure of Souls* (1924), *Arnold Waterlow* (1924), *The Rector of Wyck* (1925), and *The History of Anthony Mainwaring* (1927). Her collections of short stories include *The Judgment of Eve* (1908), *Uncanny Stories* (1923), and *The Intercessor and Other Stories* (1931). Author of the narrative poem *The Dark Night* (1924) and the biographical study *The Three Brontës* (1912).

Sindbad the Sailor (sind′bad). [Also, **Sindbad the Sailor.**] The chief character in the story of that title in *The Arabian Nights' Entertainments*. He is a wealthy citizen of Baghdad, called "the sailor" because of his seven wonderful voyages, in which he discovers a roc's egg and the Valley of Diamonds, escapes twice from the man-eating Anthropophagi, is buried alive, kills the Old Man of the Sea (who got on his back and would not dismount), and is the bearer of a letter and gifts from the King of the Indies to Harun-al-Rashid, caliph of Baghdad, who sends Sindbad back with his acknowledgment of the letter. During this last voyage he finds a valley filled with the dead bodies of elephants, from which he obtains much ivory.

"Single-speech Hamilton" (ham'il.tǫn). See **Hamilton, William Gerard.**

Singleton (sing'ɡl.tǫn), **Captain.** See **Captain Singleton.**

Sinister Street. A novel in two parts (Part I, 1913; Part II, 1914) by Compton Mackenzie. Part I was first entitled *Youth's Encounter*. The two-part novel is followed by *Guy and Pauline* (1915), *Sylvia Scarlett* (1918), and *Sylvia and Michael* (1919). It deals with the difficult lives of Michael and Stella Fane, the illegitimate children of educated, wealthy people.

Sinjohn (sin'jǫn), **John.** Pseudonym of **Galsworthy, John.**

sink-a-pace. See **galliard.**

Sinklo (singk'lō). In Shakespeare's *3 Henry VI*, one of the keepers. Humphrey is the other. The name derives from that of John Sincler, an actor of Shakespeare's day, who is indicated by the stage directions in the folio of 1623 to have played the part.

Sinn Fein (shin fān). A concept, policy, and party in modern Irish affairs; a name derived from the slogan *"Sinn féin amháin"* ("Ourselves alone"), implying self-reliance. The concept had roots in 19th-century Ireland, and the Gaelic League, founded in 1893, had made the use of Irish products and patronage of Irish industry a corollary of its work in reviving the use of the Gaelic language, although conditions then and later kept the Irish in the main tied to the English market. Other roots of Sinn Fein went back to the German Friedrich List in the 1830's and to the Hungarian Francis Deak in the 1840's. These several strands were drawn together by Arthur Griffith, one of a minority of Irish intellectuals who saw the Irish national cause dwindling into impotence as a result of the Irish Parliamentary Party's decline following the death of Charles Stewart Parnell. In 1904 Griffith established for this group a weekly paper, *The United Irishman*, in which he first published "The Resurrection of Hungary," later issued as a pamphlet, relating how Francis Deak, after the failure of Kossuth in 1848, had rallied the Hungarian people to a constitutional policy based on assertion of Hungary's status as a separate kingdom under the same crown as Austria. The feasibility of such a policy in Ireland was Griffith's thesis, and the first step in such a direction was the organization of the National Council, which held its first convention at Dublin, in November, 1905, adopting a policy proposed by Griffith: "National self-development through the recognition of the duties and

rights of citizenship on the part of the individual, and by the aid and support of all movements originating from within Ireland, instinct with national tradition, and not looking outside Ireland for the accomplishment of their aims." In 1906 Griffith further elucidated his thesis in a widely circulated pamphlet, *The "Sinn Féin" Policy*, and in 1909 he launched a daily newspaper under the name *Sinn Féin*. The National Council fell apart because of personal antagonisms, but Sinn Fein clubs arose to urge the boycott of English goods, the support of home industries (making use of the ideas of Friedrich List), and the convening of a National Assembly, to be composed of members of the General Council of County Councils, with representatives of urban councils, rural councils, poor law boards, and harbor boards, which should become the government of the country. Griffith based his politics on the Act of Renunciation, by which the British Parliament in 1783 had conceded that the king, lords, and commons of Ireland were the legitimate government of Ireland, and had renounced any claim to legislate for that country. The Sinn Fein policy made way slowly in a country politically dominated by the Irish Parliamentary Party, especially when that party accepted the Home Rule Bill passed at Westminster in 1912. A faction of Ulster Protestants, landlords, and British army officers formed the Ulster Volunteers and threatened rebellion if the Home Rule measure were implemented, and King George V withheld his assent. The secret revolutionary organization, the Irish Revolutionary Brotherhood (I.R.B.), which had existed since the 1850's, thereupon countered the Ulster Volunteers by forming the Irish Volunteers. The sudden outbreak of World War I caused the hasty reënactment of Home Rule, with, however, a clause suspending its operation until after the war, but the I.R.B., with the support and financial backing of its affiliate in America, the United Brotherhood (the Clan-na-Gael) immediately began planning a rebellion, which broke out in Easter Week, 1916. The I.R.B. and the Clan had backed Sinn Fein, and the I.R.B. leaders were mostly members of that organization, but Griffith was not privy to the plan for insurrection, and Easter Week was in no sense a "Sinn Fein rebellion." But after the execution of the principal leaders of the rebellion, and the imprisonment in Britain of most of their followers, the men who succeeded to leadership of the I.R.B. perceived the availability of the Sinn Fein organization as a cover for a renewed revolutionary campaign. Following release of the prisoners in July, 1917, a Sinn Fein convention in October elected Eamon De Valera, senior surviving I.R.B. officer, as president, and essayed to set up a provisional government. Sinn Fein clubs arose throughout the country; shipments of food to Britain, which threatened a new Irish famine, were halted; arbitration courts were set up; and British administration was partly superseded by Irish. In May, 1918, on the basis of an alleged German plot (of which no satisfactory proof has yet been adduced), the principal known Sinn Fein leaders were arrested, with the result that Michael Collins and other I.R.B. leaders secured full control of Sinn Fein. World War I ended as suddenly as it began, and when the British government set parliamentary elections for December, 1918, the Sinn Fein for the first time became technically a full-fledged political party. To 21 Unionists and seven Nationalists, Sinn Fein elected 73 members of the British Parliament, all of whom were pledged to refuse to attend that body but to set up a parliament at Dublin. In January, 1919, this body, known as Dáil Éireann, met at Dublin; but as for most of the 73 members, the clerk as he read off their names had to add, "Imprisoned by the English." Nevertheless, Dáil Éireann again proclaimed Irish independence, and organized a national administration as best it could. In February, De Valera escaped from prison and proceeded to the U. S., where he rallied great support for the Irish Republic, of which he was popularly styled President (though he was in fact only president of the executive council). In September, the British government "proclaimed" Dáil Éireann; in November, Collins's men captured every Royal Irish Constabulary barracks in the land; in the spring of 1920 the British government loosed on Ireland the forces known as the "Black and Tans" and the Auxiliaries, and for a year and a half savage warfare raged. In December the British Parliament passed the Government of Ireland Act, setting up parliaments in northern and southern Ireland, with a Council for Ireland to act in matters of common agreement. In the elections of May, 1921, this scheme was accepted in the North, but in the South Sinn Fein captured 124 of 128 seats (in June the "Parliament of Southern Ireland" met—with four members attending). Accordingly, in July, British Prime Minster Lloyd George held a conference with De Valera and Sir James Craig, prime minister of Northern Ireland. This was abortive, but in October a second conference was held, which De Valera refused to attend, laying upon Collins and Griffith the onus of accepting the inevitable compromise, the treaty establishing the Irish Free State, which in January, 1922, Dáil Éireann by a rather narrow margin ratified.

Sin of David, The. A drama (1904) by Stephen Phillips.

Sinon (sī′nọn). In Greek legend, a Greek warrior in the Trojan War. When the wooden horse was presented to the Trojans, Sinon pretended to be a deserter, made up a long story about the horse, and induced them to haul it inside the walls. At night he opened the horse and let out the Greek soldiers within it, and took part in the destruction of the city.

Sion College (sī′ọn, zī′ọn). A London college, founded in 1623 as a college and almshouse. In 1884 the almshouse was abolished, and in 1886 a new building was formally opened. It is situated toward the east end of the Victoria Embankment. It contains one of the most valuable theological libraries in Great Britain.

Sir Aldingar (ôl′ding.gär). A Middle English ballad concerning a false steward who sought to take away the honor of his queen. In the ballad with this title from Percy's *Reliques* the queen's name is Elinore, the wife of Henry II, but the story is a very widespread one.

Sir Amadas (am′ạ.dạs). A Middle English romance which tells of a knight who spends his last penny in order to bury a friend. The spirit of the friend helps him regain his fortune and protects his wife and children.

Sir Anthony Love, or The Rambling Lady (an′thọ.ni, -tọ-, luv′). A comedy (1690) by Thomas Southerne.

Sirat (si.rät′), **Al.** See Al Sirat.

Sir Charles Grandison (gran′di.sọn). [Full title, **The History of Sir Charles Grandison.**] A novel told in letters by Samuel Richardson, published in 1753. Harriet Byron, a beautiful young lady, comes to London, where she is surrounded by many admirers. Among these is the unscrupulous and vain Sir Hargrave Pollexfen, who proposes to her and is refused. Outraged at this blow to his pride, Sir Hargrave captures her after a masquerade and carries her off to wed her by force. The coach in which they travel is stopped by Sir Charles Grandison, who rescues the lady and promptly falls in love with her. However, they are unable to marry because Sir Charles is half-engaged to Clementina della Porretta, a beautiful and exotic young Italian girl. He has not married her because of the difference in their religions, but hastens to Italy when he hears that in her unhappiness she is going mad. However, to 18th-century English readers, there was really no choice between a nice English girl and an Italian Catholic, however beautiful, and Sir Charles is enabled to follow his heart with honor when Clementina decides that she cannot marry a heretic. He returns to London to wed Harriet.

Sir Cleges (klē′jẹs). A Middle English romance based on a folk theme. It concerns a man who is told he must share any reward he gets with selfish officials, and thereupon asks for twelve strokes of the lash.

Sir Courtly Nice (kôrt′li nīs′). [Full title, **Sir Courtly Nice; or, It Cannot Be.**] A comedy by John Crowne, produced at the Drury Lane in 1685. It was adapted from a Spanish work by Agustín Moreto at the request of Charles II, and named from the principal character, an insignificant but self-important fop.

Sir Degare (deg′ạ.rē). [Also, **Sir Degore** (deg′ọ.rē).] A Middle English metrical romance (early 14th century), consisting of 900 lines, concerning the adventures of Sir Degare, the abandoned bastard son of an English princess and a knight, in search of his father.

Sir Degrevant (deg′rẹ.vạnt). A Middle English romance in which a vassal is wronged by his lord, but eventually marries the lord's daughter and inherits his lands.

Sir Eglamour (eg′lạ.mör). A Middle English romance concerning a patient wife who is plotted against but finally achieves happiness.

Siren Land. A novel by Norman Douglas, published in 1911.

Sirens (sī′rẹnz). In Greek mythology, a group of sea nymphs who by their singing fascinated those who sailed past their island, and lured them to their death. In art they are often represented as hideous, malevolent, and monstrous, with the head, arms, and breasts of a young woman, and the wings and lower body (or sometimes only the feet) of a bird. Homer mentions two Sirens; three are often depicted; but they are usually thought of as a large group. Odysseus passed them safely by sealing the ears of his companions with wax and lashing himself to the mast. Orpheus saved the Argonauts from their enchantment by singing even more enchantingly. The Sirens were doomed to die when mortals could resist them (they leaped into the sea and became rocks). In early belief they were thought of as accompanying the souls of the dead from earth to Hades. That they grieve, singing, for the dead is a poetic allusion. In Attic comedy they took on erotic roles.

Sir Ferumbras (fèr.um'brạs). A Middle English verse romance of the Ferumbras group of the Charlemagne cycle, generally considered to be the best Middle English work in the cycle. It tells the part of the Ferumbras story that starts with the arrival of that Saracen hero in Spain (a subject covered also by the second part of *The Sowdone of Babylone*), and is of bibliographical interest as one of the very few medieval romances that have survived in the author's autograph.

Sir Fopling Flutter (fop'ling flut'ẽr). See **Man of Mode.**

Sir Gawain and the Green Knight (gä'win; -wän). See **Gawain and the Green Knight, Sir.**

Sir George Tressady (jôrj tres'ạ.di). A novel (1896) by Mrs. Humphry Ward, a sequel to *Marcella.*

Sir Giles Goosecap (jīlz gös'kap). A comedy, probably by George Chapman, published anonymously in 1606.

Sir Gowther (gou'thẽr). A Middle English romance telling the story of Robert the Devil.

Sir Harry Wildair (har'i wīl'dār). A comedy (1701) by George Farquhar, a sequel to his *Constant Couple.*

Siris (sī'ris). A work by Bishop George Berkeley, published in 1744. It is an extraordinary series of inquiries and philosophical reflections concerning his favorite panacea, tar water, which he distilled at Cloyne.

Sir Isenbras (ī'zẹn.bras) or **Isumbras** (iz'um.bras). See **Isenbras, Sir.**

Sirius (sir'i.us). [Also, **Dog Star.**] A white double star, the brightest in the sky. It is ¾ magnitude brighter than Canopus, the next brightest; its magnitude is minus 1.6. It is situated in the mouth of the dog. The companion star is remarkable for its immense density, about 40,000 times that of water.

Sir John Oldcastle (ōld'kás.'l). A play published in two parts in 1619 in a false folio (supposedly actually of 1600), now believed to be the work of Anthony Munday, Michael Drayton, and others. It was once attributed to Shakespeare (being therefore included in the second issue of the folio of 1664). It may have been written to vindicate the memory of the real Oldcastle, who was a leader of the Lollards during the reign of Henry V, and whose descendants were understandably irked that his name should be linked to Shakespeare's Falstaff (who was originally named Oldcastle).

Sir John Van Olden Barnavelt (van ōl'dẹn bär'na-velt). A tragedy (1619) by John Fletcher and, probably, Philip Massinger. It is based on historical events in the history of Holland during Fletcher's day.

Sir Landeval (lan'dẹ.val). A Middle English romance based on the *Lay le Freine* of Marie de France. Its story is almost the same as that found in Thomas Chestre's *Sir Launfal*, in which a fairy princess weds a knight on condition that he never mention her.

Sir Launcelot Greaves (lôn'sẹ.lot, län'-, grēvz). [Full title, **The Adventures of Sir Launcelot Greaves.**] A burlesque romance (1760–61) by Tobias Smollett, in the mode of Cervantes' *Don Quixote.*

Sir Launfal (lôn'fạl). A Middle English romance based on the French *Lay le Freine* of Marie de France. It is supposed to have been written (c1430) by Thomas Chestre, and tells the story of a Knight of the Round Table who marries a fairy princess but is not allowed to mention her. He breaks this promise and almost loses her, but is finally pardoned.

Sir Martin Mar-all, or the Feigned Innocence (mär'tin mär'ôl''). A comedy by Dryden, produced in 1667 and printed in 1668. Dryden adapted it from the Duke of Newcastle's translation of Molière's *L'Étourdi*, with additions from Quinault's *L'Amant indiscret.* The principal character, Sir Martin Marall, is a foolish knight who regularly commits blunders against his own interest whenever he is not advised by his servant Warner. No other play of Dryden's was so well known to his contemporaries as this one.

Sir Orfeo (ôr'fẹ.ō). A Middle English minstrel's poem (c1320), in which the classical story of Orpheus and Eurydice is retold in medieval terms and in the fashion of a Breton lay. Orfeo, when his queen, Heurodis, is carried off by the king of the magical land of the dead, wanders distracted through the world for ten years, comes finally to the land of the dead, and regains his queen by his skill on the harp. They return to their kingdom, which has been held for Orfeo by his faithful steward. A ballad of later date, *King Orfeo*, which deals with the same theme, is included as No. 19 in Child's collection.

Sir Patrick Spens (spens). A Scottish popular ballad about a knight sent by the king on a mission to Norway and lost with all his crew on the voyage home.

Sir Perceval of Gales (pèr'sẹ.val; gālz) or **Wales** (wälz). A Middle English romance in 16-line stanzas, written c1375. This is the only romance of Perceval in the vernacular. Perceval, left fatherless, is reared by his mother in the forest, and then taken to Arthur's court. He defeats the Red Knight, rescues the Lady Lufamour, and marries her. He finally achieves knighthood. The theme of the Grail is not mentioned in this version.

Sir Roger de Coverley (roj'ẽr dẹ kuv'ẽr.li). See **Coverley, Sir Roger de.**

Sir Thomas More (mōr). A chronicle play, based on the life of More as told in Hall's *Chronicles.* Parts of it have been attributed to Shakespeare on the basis of handwriting, as well as to Munday and Dekker, by W. W. Greg and others, who have examined the manuscript, the form in which it remained until the 19th century. If the handwriting could be proven to be Shakespeare's, the knowledge would be a valuable aid in determining the authorship of other manuscripts. The insurrection scenes in this play bear a similarity to Jack Cade's rebellion in Shakespeare's *2 Henry VI*, and the tone of the scene in which More entertains the Lord Mayor, and of his speech on degree after his fall from favor is much like Shakespeare. Chambers dates the play about 1596; but Shücking, on the basis of its similarity to the work of Shakespeare, dates it 1604–05.

Sir Thomas Wyatt (wī′ạt), **The Famous History of.** A play formerly attributed only to John Webster and Thomas Dekker, but now believed to have involved the collaboration also of Henry Chettle and William Smith. It was printed in 1607, and appears to be taken in large part from a play called *Lady Jane*.

Sir Triamour (trī′ạ.mör). A Middle English romance dealing with the persecution of a loyal wife by a treacherous steward.

Sir Tristrem (tris′trem). A Middle English version of the Tristram legend, written in the north of England c1300. (The extant manuscript, which exhibits a mixture of Northern and Southeast Midland dialect forms, is apparently not the original.) The romance, written in an unusual eleven-line stanza, is of inferior workmanship: the episodes are sometimes poorly motivated and the transitions often so abrupt as to be bewildering. It has been suggested that the poem is the work of a minstrel telling a story already well known to his audience.

Sister Helen (hel′en). A poem (1870) by Dante Gabriel Rossetti, cast in the form of a dialogue between a woman, her brother, and an unidentified third person. The woman destroys her unfaithful lover by melting a wax image of him, and consequently loses her own soul.

Sisters, The. A comedy by James Shirley, licensed in April, 1652. It was one of the last productions of the pre-Restoration drama.

Sister Teresa (te.rē′sạ). A novel by George Moore, published in 1901. A continuation of his *Evelyn Innes* (1898), it is a character study of an opera singer. Evelyn becomes Sister Teresa, a nun.

Sistine Chapel (sis′tēn). A papal private chapel in the Vatican, constructed by Pope Sixtus IV, for whom it was named ("Sistine" is an adjectival rendering of "Xystus," an older form of Sixtus). It was built in 1473, and is in plan a rectangle 157½ by 52½ ft., and 59 ft. high. Architecturally it is not particularly notable, but it has long been world famous for the paintings which cover its walls and vault, including works by Perugino, Botticelli, Luca Signorelli, Ghirlandaio, and above all the pictures by Michelangelo of *The Creation*, *The Deluge*, and *The Last Judgment*. The singing of the papal choir of the chapel (the Pontifical Choir) has also long been celebrated, and its archives contain a remarkable collection of illumi-

nated manuscript works of the composers of the 15th and 16th centuries.

Sisyphus (sis′i.fus). In Greek mythology, a son of Aeolus, brother of Athamas, and husband of the Pleiad Merope. He was the founder of Ephyra (later Corinth). According to Homer, he was the craftiest of all men. He was condemned in the lower world to roll a huge stone up a hill, without ceasing, which when he reached the top always rolled down again. The reason for this punishment is variously given as rape, revealing secrets of the gods, or killing guests to whom he owed hospitality. A long series of tricks and crimes comprise his life story.

Sita (sē′tạ). The heroine of the Hindu epic, the *Ramayana*, and a popular goddess of the Hindu pantheon. The wife of Rama, she was abducted and taken to Lanka (Ceylon) by the demon Ravana, and rescued by Rama and his armies. In spite of all threats, she preserved her virtue, later proved it by ordeal, and is therefore regarded by the Hindus as the great example of wifely chastity. She is the goddess of agriculture and horticulture.

Sitwell (sit′wel, -wel), **Edith.** b. at Scarborough, England, 1887—. An English poet and critic; sister of Sir Osbert Sitwell and Sacheverell Sitwell. Her books include *The Mother and Other Poems* (1915), *Twentieth Century Harlequinade* (1916), *Clowns' Houses* (1918), *The Wooden Pegasus* (1920), *Façade* (1922), *Bucolic Comedies* (1923), *The Sleeping Beauty* (1924), *Elegy on Dead Fashions* (1926), *Gold Coast Customs* (1929), *Alexander Pope* (1930), *Bath* (1932), *Five Variations on a Theme* (1933), *The English Eccentrics* (1933), *Aspects of Modern Poetry* (1934), *Victoria of England* (1936), the novel *I Live under a Black Sun* (1937), the anthology, *Look! The Sun* (1941), *Green Song* (1944), *A Song of the Cold* (1945), *Fanfare for Elizabeth* (1946), and *Gardeners and Astronomers* (1953).

Sitwell, Sir Osbert. [Full name, **Francis Osbert Sacheverell Sitwell.**] b. at London, Dec. 6, 1892—. An English novelist, essayist, poet, and biographer; brother of Edith Sitwell and Sacheverell Sitwell. Educated at Eton, he served with the Coldstream Guards in World War I. Author of *Argonaut and Juggernaut* (1919), *Who Killed Cock Robin?* (1921), *Out of the Flame* (1923), *Triple Fugue and Other Stories* (1924), *Before the Bombardment* (1926), *England Reclaimed* (1927), *The Man Who Lost Himself* (1929), *Dumb Animal and Other Stories* (1930), *Dickens* (1932), *Miracle on Sinai* (1933), *Penny Foolish* (1935), *Those Were the Days* (1938), *Two Generations* (1940), and *A Place of One's Own* (1942); he also wrote a series of family memoirs, including *Left Hand, Right Hand* (1944), *The Scarlet Tree* (1946), and *Laughter in the Next Room* (1948).

Sitwell, Sacheverell. b. 1897—. An English poet, critic, and essayist; brother of Edith Sitwell and Osbert Sitwell. His works include *Southern Baroque Art* (1924), *German Baroque Art* (1924), *The Gothick North* (1929), *Mozart* (1932), *Canons of Giant Art* (1933), *Liszt* (1936), *Dance of the Quick and the Dead* (1936), *Narrative Pictures* (1937), *Old Fashioned Flowers* (1939), *Poltergeists* (1940), *Valse des Fleurs* (1941), *The Hunters and the Hunted* (1947), and *Morning, Noon and Night in London* (1948).

---

fat, fāte, fär, ạsk, fāre; net, mē, hėr; pin, pīne; not, nōte, mȯve, nôr; up, lūte, pu̇ll; ᴛʜ, then;

Siva (shē'vạ). See **Shiva.**

Siward (sö'ạrd). [Title: Earl of **Northumberland;** called **"Siward the Strong."**] d. 1055. A Danish soldier in England. He is introduced as a character in Shakespeare's *Macbeth,* where he leads an army of 10,000 English soldiers sent by Edward the Confessor. His son, Young Siward, is killed in a fight with Macbeth.

Six Articles, Act of. In English history, an act passed in 1539. It asserted (1) transubstantiation; (2) the sufficiency of communion in one kind; (3) celibacy of the clergy; (4) the maintenance of vows of chastity; (5) the continuation of private masses; and (6) auricular confession. The penalty for denying the first was death; for the rest, forfeiture of property for the first offense, death for the second.

Six of Calais (kạ.lā'. kal'ā) **The.** A play (1934) by George Bernard Shaw, included by most critics among his lesser works.

Skạdi (skä'dē). [Also: **Ondurdis; Old Norse, Ondurdis, Skadhi, Skathi.**] In Old Norse mythology, a giantess; the daughter of the frost giant, and the wife of the sea god Njord. Three nights she dwelt with Njord at his abode, on condition that he spend nine with her in the land of the frost giants, where she hunted with bow and snowshoes. This is interpreted as representing the northern three-month summer and nine-month winter. As Ondurdis she was the snowshoe goddess.

Skanda (skan'dạ). [Also, **Karttikeya.**] In Hindu mythology, the god of war and the planet Mars; the younger of the two sons of Shiva. He is called the god of war because he is commander in chief of the armies of good demons, whom he leads against those who are evil, especially against those who seek to overcome and enslave the gods. His most common name is Skanda, but he is also called Karttikeya, meaning "Son of the Krittikas," because his foster mothers are the six Krittikas, or Pleiades. He is represented as having six faces, so that he may be nursed by the six nurses. In the south of India he is not worshiped as presiding over war, but as Subrahmanya, "the very pious or sacred one." Subrahmanya and his two wives are believed to grant children, and to thwart and cast out devils.

Skeat (skēt), **Walter William.** b. at London, Nov. 21, 1835; d. at Cambridge, England, Oct. 6, 1912. An English scholar, critic, and editor, a specialist in Old and Middle English. Educated at King's College School and at Christ's College, Cambridge, he was chief founder (1873) and president, until 1896, of the English Dialect Society. He was a founder also of the Chaucer and New Shakespeare societies, and professor of Anglo-Saxon (1878–1912) at Cambridge University. He edited *Lancelot of the Laik* (1865), *Piers Plowman* (1866), *Lay of Havelock* (1868), Chatterton's *Poems* (1871), *Specimens of English* (1871), the *Anglo-Saxon Gospels* (1871–87), *Shakespeare's Plutarch* (1875), Aelfric's *Lives of the Saints* (1881–1900), *English Etymological Dictionary* (1879–82), *Chaucer* (7 vols., 1894–97), and a large amount of material on etymology, dialects, magic, spelling, and place names.

Skeggs (skegz), **Carolina Wilhelmina Amelia.** One of the town ladies who imposed upon the innocent family of the Vicar of Wakefield, in Oliver Goldsmith's novel of that name.

Skeggs, The Honourable Wilhelmina Amelia. One of the many pseudonyms of **Thackeray, William Makepeace.**

Skelton (skel'tọn), **John.** b. c1460; d. at Westminster, London, June 21, 1529. An English scholar and poet. He was a protégé of Henry VII, a noted scholar, and the tutor of Henry VIII. He took holy orders in 1498, and for 25 years was rector of Diss in Norfolk (he was suspended from this office for marrying). He wrote *The Bowge of Court, The Boke of Phyllyp Sparrow, Magnificence, The Tunning of Elinor Rummyng, The Garland of Laurel, Colin Clout,* a satire on the clergy, and *Why Come Ye Not to Court?,* a satire on Wolsey. He was the hero of a book of "merye" tales.

Skerrett (sker'ẹt). A novel by Liam O'Flaherty, published in 1932.

sketch. **1.** A brief, slight, or hasty delineation; a rapid or offhand presentation of the essential facts of anything; a rough draft; an outline.

> The first schetse of a comedy, called *The Paradox.*
> (Dr. Pope, *Life of Bishop Ward,* 1697.)

> However beautiful and considerable these Antiquities are, yet the Designs that have been taken of them hitherto have been rather Sketches, they say, than accurate and exact Plans.
> (T. Hollis, in Ellis's *Lit.*)

> Boyish histories
> Of battle, bold adventure . . . and true love
> Crown'd after trial; sketches rude and faint,
> But where a passion yet unborn perhaps
> Lay hidden.   (Tennyson, *Aylmer's Field.*)

2. A short and slightly constructed play or literary composition.

> We always did a laughable sketch entitled *Billy Button's Ride to Brentford,* and I used to be Jeremiah Stitchem, a servant of Billy Button's, that comes for a "sitiation."
> (Mayhew, *London Labour and London Poor.*)

Sketches by Boz (bōz, boz). A collection of stories by Charles Dickens, published 1835–36. The work is a series of impressions and character essays about London and the people of the city.

Sketchley (skech'li), **Arthur.** Pseudonym of **Rose, George.**

Sketch of a Sinner. A novel by Frank Swinnerton, published in 1929.

Skewton (skū'tọn), **the Honourable Mrs.** In Dickens's *Dombey and Son,* the mother of the cold and haughty Edith, Dombey's second wife.

Skidbladner (skid'bläd.nėr). In Old Norse mythology, the ship of Frey. It could travel on sea, on land, or through the air, and is construed as representing the clouds.

Skimpole (skim'pōl), **Harold.** A self-seeking sentimentalist and aesthete in Dickens's *Bleak House.* He was drawn from Leigh Hunt, who was, understandably, offended by the likeness.

Skin-Deep. A novel by Naomi Royde-Smith, published in 1927. It has the secondary title *Portrait of Lucinda, with a Prolog and Epilog from the London Adventure of Arabell Holdenbrook.*

ḍ, d or j; ṣ, s or sh; ṭ, t or ch; ẓ, z or zh; o, F. cloche; ü, F. menu; ċh, Sc. loch; ń, F. bonbon.

Skinfaxi (shēn′fä.ksē). In Scandinavian mythology, the shining horse which draws the chariot of the sun.

Skinner (skin′ẽr), **John.** b. at Birse, Aberdeenshire, Scotland, 1721; d. June, 1807. A Scottish clergyman and poet. He was educated at Marischal College, Aberdeen, took orders in the Scottish Episcopal Church, and had a charge at Longside, Aberdeenshire. He was persecuted for Jacobitism. He is known by his songs, collected in 1809; of these *Tullochgorum* was called by Burns "the best Scotch song Scotland ever saw." In 1788 he published an *Ecclesiastical History of Scotland.*

Skiold (skyōld) or **Skjöld** (skyẽld). In Norse mythology, the son of Odin, and a mythical king of Denmark.

Skirnir (skir′nir). In Old Norse mythology, the messenger of the gods, especially of Frey.

Sladen (slā′dẹn), **Douglas Brooke Wheelton.** b. at London, Feb. 5, 1856; d. at Hove, Sussex, England, Feb. 12, 1947. An English editor, teacher, and novelist. Educated at Cheltenham College and at Trinity College, Oxford, he planned and edited (1897–99) the first *Who's Who* and the *Green Book.*

Slammer (slam′ẽr), **Doctor.** In Dickens's *Pickwick Papers,* a military surgeon whose honor (and feelings) are affronted by Mr. Jingle's flirtation at a ball with an elderly (and wealthy) widow whom he has picked out for himself. He challenges Mr. Jingle to a duel, but is brushed aside; the next morning he sends a fellow-officer to press the challenge again, and Mr. Winkle (whose suit, unbeknownst to him, Jingle had been wearing) accepts it, having been himself sufficiently in his cups the night before to suspect that he might be the offending party. As the duel is about to take place, however, Dr. Slammer observes that his opponent is a stranger, and the affair ends in exchanges of mutual esteem.

Slawkenbergius (slô.kẹn.bẽr′ji.us), **Hafen.** An imaginary author, noted for the length of his nose; referred to in Laurence Sterne's *Tristram Shandy.* A story professedly by him is introduced in the work.

Slay-Good (slā′gụd), **Giant.** A giant in the second part of Bunyan's *Pilgrim's Progress.* He is killed by Greatheart.

Sleary (slir′i). In Dickens's *Hard Times,* the kindhearted owner of a circus in Coketown.

Sleek (slēk), **Aminadab.** A hypocritical character in Morris Barnett's comedy *The Serious Family.*

Sleeping Beauty. [French, **La Belle au bois dormant;** German, **Dornröschen;** English, also, **Little Briar Rose.**] A generic title for a widespread European folk tale featuring the fatal prophecy at the birth of a child, the magic sleep, and disenchantment by a kiss. The story is probably best known to English readers through translations of Perrault's *La Belle au bois dormant,* and the version in Grimm's collection, *Dornröschen,* or *Little Briar Rose.* The story is that a certain king invites 12 wise women to a feast to celebrate the birth of a daughter, but neglects to invite the 13th. At the feast the slighted one appears and predicts that in her 15th year the little princess will prick her finger on a spindle and die. The curse is mitigated by one of the other wise women, however, who says she will not die, but will sleep 100 years. In spite of the destruction and hiding of spindles throughout the land, all comes to pass as the 13th wise woman prophesied. All the inmates of the palace share the magic slumber, until after 100 years a young prince arrives, breaks through the briar thicket which has grown up around the castle, and wakens the princess with a kiss. Tennyson takes this story for the subject of his poem *The Day-Dream.*

Sleeping Beauty, The. A volume of verse (1924) by Edith Sitwell.

Sleep of Prisoners, The. A religious play (1951) by Christopher Fry, presenting various Biblical episodes in the form of dreams by war prisoners in a bombed church.

Sleipnir (slāp′nir). In Old Norse mythology, the eight-legged steed of Odin. Sleipnir was the horse which carried Hermod to Hel.

Slender (slen′dẽr). In Shakespeare's *Merry Wives of Windsor,* a provincial gentleman, cousin to Shallow. He is an inimitable official booby, in love with "sweet Anne Page."

Slick (slik), **Sam.** Pseudonym of **Haliburton, Thomas Chandler.**

Slipslop (slip′slop), **Mrs.** In Fielding's novel *Joseph Andrews,* Lady Booby's slatternly maid, who, like Lady Booby, is irresistibly attracted to Joseph.

Sloane (slōn), **Sir Hans.** b. at Killyleagh, County Down, Ireland, April 16, 1660; d. at London, Jan. 11, 1753. A British physician and naturalist. He resided in Jamaica (1687–89), and was chief physician to Christ's Hospital, London (1694–1730) and physician-general to the army (1714 *et seq.*), president of the College of Physicians (1719–35), and physician to the king from 1727. In the latter year he succeeded Sir Isaac Newton as president of the Royal Society. His works include an account of his voyage to Jamaica and of the natural products of that island, generally called *Natural History of Jamaica* (1707–25; whole title, *Voyage to the Islands Madeira, Barbados, Nieves, St. Christopher's, and Jamaica, with the Natural History, etc., of the Last*); a catalogue of the plants of Jamaica; and many papers in the *Philosophical Transactions.* His library (50,000 vols. and over 3,000 manuscripts) and collections were bequeathed to the nation on condition that 20,000 pounds (much less than their value) should be paid to his heirs; they formed the nucleus of the British Museum.

Sloane Museum, The. The library and collections of Sir Hans Sloane, bequeathed to the English nation. They formed a nucleus of the British Museum.

Slocombe (slō′kọm), **George Edward.** b. at Bristol, England, March 8, 1894—. An English historian, journalist, and critic. He was chief foreign correspondent (1920–31) of the London *Daily Herald,* and foreign editor (1932–34) of the *Evening Standard.* Author of *A History of Poland* (1916; reprinted 1939), *Gaucheries* (1922), *Paris in Profile* (1928), *Henry of Navarre* (1931), *The Heart of France* (1934), *Crisis in Europe* (1934), *Don John of Austria* (1935), *The Dangerous Sea* (1936), *A Mirror to Geneva* (1937), *Rebels of Art: Manet to Matisse*

(1939), *Conquest of the Mediterranean* (1943), the autobiographical *The Tumult and the Shouting* (1936), and the novels *Dictator* (1932), *Men in Arms* (1936), and *Escape into the Past* (1943).

Slop (slop), **Doctor.** In Laurence Sterne's novel *Tristram Shandy*, Mrs. Shandy's attendant physician, who breaks Tristram's nose at his birth. He is described as having "a breadth of back and a sesquipedality of belly which might have done honour to a serjeant in the Horse-Guards."

Slope (slōp), **Obadiah.** In Anthony Trollope's *Barchester Towers*, the unctuous, scheming chaplain of Bishop Proudie.

Slough of Despond, The. In Bunyan's *Pilgrim's Progress*, a "miry slough . . . whither the scum and filth that attends conviction for sin doth continually run . . . many fears, and doubts, and discouraging apprehensions, which all of them get together, and settle in this place," in which Christian, falling in, struggles in vain until drawn out by Help.

Slowboy (slō'boi), **Tilly.** In Dickens's *Cricket on the Hearth*, an awkward nurse employed by Mr. Peerybingle. She is constantly surprised at being so well treated, and has a genius for bumping the baby's head.

Sludge (sluj), **Dickon.** [Called **Flibbertigibbet.**] In Scott's *Kenilworth*, a mischievous urchin.

Slumkey (slum'ki), **the Honourable Samuel.** In Dickens's *Pickwick Papers*, a candidate for Parliament from Eatanswill.

Sly (slī), **Christopher.** A tinker in the Induction to Shakespeare's *Taming of the Shrew*. He is found in a drunken sleep by a nobleman, who has him taken to his own home, as a jest; and when he wakes he is made to believe that he is the lord of the manor, just recovered from 15 years of insanity. The "Taming of the Shrew" is played for his entertainment before his illusion is broken.

Small House at Allington (al'ing.ton), **The.** A novel by Anthony Trollope, published in two volumes in 1864.

small quarto. A square octavo; a book having eight leaves to a sheet but the shape of a quarto.

Smalls. [Also: **smalls, Little-Go.**] In the great English universities, a colloquial term for the examinations comprising a first preliminary to the complete body of examinations required for a degree. See also **Greats.**

Smallways (smôl'wāz), **Albert Peter.** [Called "Bert" **Smallways.**] The hero of H. G. Well's novel *The War in the Air.* He is one of the indomitable Cockneys considered to have provided Wells with some of his favorite heroes.

Smallweed (smôl'wēd), **Grandfather.** In Dickens's *Bleak House*, an old man, the grandfather of young Smallweed (called "Chickweed"): "in a helpless condition as to his lower and nearly so as to his upper limbs." He enjoys throwing his pillows at his even more feeble wife; both are then shaken up and settled by their granddaughter Judy.

Smart (smärt), **Christopher.** b. at Shipbourne, Kent, England, April 11, 1722; d. at London, May 21, 1771. An English poet. He entered Cambridge (Pembroke Hall) in 1739, and was elected a fellow in 1745. He became a hack writer and contributed to several periodicals. In the lucid intervals between fits of insanity, or rather of religious mania, for which he was confined (1756–58) in an asylum, he wrote the poem *A Song to David*, published in 1763, which was omitted from his collected works, perhaps as being proof definite of his insanity; actually it is one of the masterpieces of 18th-century poetry. He also wrote *The Hilliad* (1753), a poetical translation of Phaedrus (1765), a prose translation of Horace (1756), and metrical versions of the Psalms and Parables.

Smectymnuus (smek.tim'nū.us). The professed author of a controversial tract against episcopacy, written in 1641 in answer to Bishop Joseph Hall. The name is made up from the initials of the names of the authors: *S*tephen *M*arshall, *E*dmund *C*alamy, *T*homas *Y*oung, *M*atthew *N*ewcomen, *W*illiam *S*purstow. Bishop Hall's reply to it was answered by John Milton, and the answer to that was again attacked by Milton in 1642.

Smedley (smed'li), **Francis (Edward).** b. at Great Marlow, England, Oct. 4, 1818; d. at London, May 1, 1864. An English novelist, editor for a time of *Sharpe's London Magazine.* He wrote *Frank Fairleigh* (1850) *Lewis Arundel, or the Railroad of Life* (1852), and *Harry Coverdale's Courtship* (1855). His books were illustrated by George Cruikshank and Hablot Knight Browne ("Phiz").

Smee (smē). In J. M. Barrie's *Peter Pan*, one of the pirates.

Smelfungus (smel.fung'gus). A name given by Laurence Sterne to Tobias Smollett, on account of the pessimistic tone of Smollett's *Travels.*

Smellie (smel'i), **William.** b. at Edinburgh, 1740; d. there, June 24, 1795. A Scottish printer and author. He edited the first edition of the *Encyclopaedia Britannica* (1768–71), and is understood to have been largely responsible for the plan of that work and to have been the principal compiler. He also wrote *Philosophy of Natural History* (1790–99).

Smerdis (smėr'dis). [Also, **Bardiya.**] Killed c523 B.C. Younger brother of Cambyses II of Persia. Cyrus made him governor of the provinces in the east just before he died. Cambyses, about to set out on a campaign against Egypt, and fearing that Smerdis might usurp the throne, had him put to death secretly. This was not generally known and a Pseudo-Smerdis arose the next spring.

Smike (smīk). In Dickens's *Nicholas Nickleby*, a poor, homeless, persecuted boy, abused by Squeers, afterward befriended by Nicholas Nickleby, and finally discovered to be Ralph Nickleby's son.

Smile of the Sphinx, The. A volume of short stories by Robert Nichols, published in 1920.

Smiles (smīlz), **Samuel.** b. at Haddington, Scotland, Dec. 23, 1812; d. at Kensington, London, April 16, 1904. A Scottish author and physician. After practicing (1832–38) at Haddington he abandoned medicine to devote himself to literature. He was editor (1838–42) of the Leeds *Times*. Author of *Physical Education* (1837), *Character* (1871), *Thrift* (1875), *Duty* (1880), and *Life and Labour* (1887), inspirational essays; *Life of George Stephenson* (1857), *Lives of the Engineers* (5 vols., 1861–65), *George Moore: Merchant and Philanthropist* (1878),

---

d̦, d or j; ṣ, s or sh; ṭ, t or ch; z̧, z or zh; o, F. cloche; ü, F. menu; ċh, Sc. loch; ṅ, F. bonbon.

Robert Dick: Geologist and Botanist (1879), *Josiah Wedgwood* (1894), biographies; *History of Ireland Under England* (1844), *The Huguenots in England and Ireland* (1867), and *The Huguenots in France* (1874), history; his *Autobiography* appeared in 1905. He is best known for his *Self-Help* (1859), which puts forth the philosophy that perseverance and courage always lead to success. Immensely popular, the book went through many editions and was translated into a score of languages, both European and Oriental.

Smintheus (smin'thŭs). In Greek mythology, a surname of Apollo.

Smith (smith), **Adam.** b. at Kirkcaldy, Fife, Scotland, June 5, 1723; d. at Edinburgh, July 17, 1790. A Scottish moralist and political economist. He was a student at Glasgow (1737–40) and Oxford (1740–46). In 1748 he gave a series of public lectures at Edinburgh on English literature, with such success that the course was repeated the two following years, supplemented in one of these years by a course in jurisprudence and political economy. In 1751 he was elected to the chair of logic at Glasgow, which he exchanged for that of moral philosophy at the same university in 1752. His lectures on moral philosophy were divided into four parts: natural theology, ethics, jurisprudence, and political economy. His ethical views were published in 1759 in the *Theory of Moral Sentiments*, a work which brought him immediate recognition as one of the foremost of contemporary writers. He resigned his professorship in 1764 and spent the next three years traveling on the Continent as tutor and companion to young Henry Scott, 3rd Duke of Buccleuch. While in France his fame, and the sponsorship of his friend and countryman David Hume, brought him into intimate relations with Voltaire, Turgot, d'Alembert, d'Holbach, Quesnay and the Physiocrats, and other leaders of the French Enlightenment. Returning to Scotland in 1766, he lived for several years in studious retirement at Kirkcaldy, working on *An Inquiry into the Nature and Causes of the Wealth of Nations*, which appeared in 1776, and which was the first systematic formulation of classical English economics. In 1778 he was appointed commissioner of customs for Scotland, and took up his residence at Edinburgh, where he lived until his death. Besides the two works mentioned above, he was the author of *Considerations Concerning the First Formation of Languages*, appended to the sixth edition (1790) of the *Moral Sentiments*, and of three essays on the history of science, published by his executors in 1795 under the title *Essays on Philosophical Subjects.*

Smith, Albert Richard. b. at Chertsey, Surrey, England, May 24, 1816; d. at London, May 23, 1860. An English novelist and writer of extravaganzas. Among his works are *Blanche Heriot* (1842), a drama; *A Month at Constantinople* (1850), *Mont Blanc* (1852), and *To China and Back* (1859), entertainments; dramatizations of Charles Dickens's *Cricket on the Hearth* (1845) and *Battle of Life* (1846); *Adventures of Mr. Ledbury and His Friend Jack Johnson* (1844), *Adventures of Jack Holyday, with Something about His Sister* (1844), *Fortunes of the Scattergood Family* (1845), *Struggles and Adventures of Christopher Tadpole at Home and Abroad*

(1848), and *The Pottleton Legacy, a Story of Town and Country Life* (1849), novels.

Smith, Alexander. b. at Kilmarnock, Scotland, Dec. 31, 1830; d. at Wardie, near Edinburgh, Jan. 5, 1867. A Scottish poet, a member of the "spasmodic" school. He wrote *A Life Drama and Other Poems* (1853) and *War Sonnets* (with Sydney Dobell, 1855). His chief prose works are *Dreamthorp; Essays Written in the Country* (1863), *A Summer in Skye* (1865), and *Alfred Hagart's Household* (1866).

Smith, Charlotte. [Maiden name, **Turner.**] b. at London, May 4, 1749; d. at Tilford, Surrey, England, Oct. 28, 1806. An English novelist, poet, and translator. Author of *Emmeline, or the Orphan of the Castle* (1788), *Celestina* (1792), *Desmond* (1792), *The Old Manor House* (1793), *The Banished Man* (1794), and *The Young Philosopher* (1798), novels; and of *Sonnets* (1784) and the poem *Beachy Head* (1807). She also translated (1785) the French novel *Manon Lescaut* (1731) by Abbé Prévost, and accounts of several famous trials from *Les Causes Célèbres* which appeared (1786) as *The Romance of Real Life.*

Smith, Dodie. [Former pseudonym, **C. L. Anthony.**] An English writer. Her plays include *Autumn Crocus* (1930), *Service* (1932), *Touch Wood* (1933), *Call It a Day* (1935), *Bonnet over the Windmill* (1937), and *Dear Octopus* (1938). Author of the novel *I Capture the Castle* (1949). She wrote under the name of C. L. Anthony up to 1935.

Smith, Lady Eleanor Furneaux. b. at Birkenhead, Cheshire, England, 1902; d. at London, Oct. 20, 1945. An English journalist and novelist, a specialist in the lore of the Gypsies; daughter of Frederick Edwin Smith, 1st Earl of Birkenhead. Author of *Red Wagon* (1930), *Flamenco* (1931), *Ballerina* (1932), *Christmas Tree* (1933; later called *Seven Trees*), *Tzigane* (1935; American title, *Romany*), *Portrait of a Lady* (1936), *The Spanish House* (1938), *Lovers' Meeting* (1940), and *The Man in Grey* (1941), novels; *Satan's Circus* (1932), a collection of short stories; and her autobiography, *Life's a Circus* (1939).

Smith, George. b. at London, March 19, 1824; d. at Byfleet, near Weybridge, Surrey, England, April 6, 1901. An English publisher. He joined the firm of Smith, Elder, and Company, founded by his father, George Smith (1789–1846), with Alexander Elder, and upon the death of his father in 1846 became its head. Among the authors whose works he published were John Ruskin, Charlotte Brontë, William Makepeace Thackeray, Anthony Trollope, Elizabeth Gaskell, Wilkie Collins, Robert Browning and Mrs. Browning, Leigh Hunt, Matthew Arnold, Sir Leslie Stephen, and Mrs. Humphry Ward. In 1859 he started the *Cornhill Magazine*, with Thackeray as editor, and in 1865 founded the *Pall Mall Gazette*. His most noted publication was the monumental *Dictionary of National Biography* (1885–1901; supplement and index volume, 1901–03).

Smith, George Barnett. b. 1841; d. Jan. 2, 1909. An English journalist and writer. Among his works are *Poets and Novelists* (1875), lives of Shelley (1877), Gladstone (1879), Sir Robert Peel (1881), John Bright (1881), Victor Hugo (1885), and Queen

Victoria (1886), and *William I and the German Empire* (1889).

Smith, Goldwin. b. at Reading, Berkshire, England, Aug. 13, 1823; d. at Toronto, Canada, June 7, 1910. An English journalist and historian. Educated at Eton and at Magdalen College, Oxford, he served as professor of law (1846–67) and regius professor of modern history (1858–66) at Oxford. He visited (1864) America, supporting the North during the Civil War. He left England in 1868 to become professor of English and constitutional history (1868–71) at Cornell University, lived (1871 *et seq.*) in Canada, engaging in political journalism, contributing to the *Nation*, editing the *Canadian Monthly* (1872–74), and founding *The Week* (1884) and *The Bystander*. Author of *Modern History* (1861), *The Empire* and *Does the Bible Sanction American Slavery?* (both 1863), *Cowper* (1881), *Jane Austen* (1890), *Canada and the Canadian Question* (1891), *William Lloyd Garrison* (1892), *The United States—A Political History* (1893), *Guesses at the Riddle of Existence* (1897), *Commonwealth or Empire?* (1902), and *Irish History and the Irish Question* (1905). He wrote his *Reminiscences* (1912).

Smith, Harriet. The protégée of Emma in Jane Austen's novel *Emma*.

Smith, Henry. [Also: **Henry Gow, Hal o' the Wynd.**] An armorer who is the hero of Sir Walter Scott's novel *The Fair Maid of Perth*.

Smith, Horace (or **Horatio**). b. at London, Dec. 31, 1779; d. at Tunbridge Wells, England, July 12, 1849. An English poet and novelist; brother of James Smith (1775–1839) and associated with him in *Rejected Addresses* (1812). He wrote *Brambletye House* (1826) and other novels.

Smith, John. b. at Willoughby, Lincolnshire, England, 1580; d. at London, June 21, 1631. An English adventurer, president (1608–09) of the colony of Virginia. He was the eldest son of George Smith, a tenant farmer. Little is known of his life, except through his own writings, which are largely eulogistic of himself and of questionable authority. He studied at the free schools of Alford and Louth, and at the age of 15 was apprenticed to a trade, but ran away and served under Peregrine Bertie, Lord Willoughby, in the Netherlands and elsewhere. He afterward served in Hungary and Transylvania against the Turks, and was captured and sent into slavery, but escaped to Russia and ultimately returned to England, probably about 1605. He accompanied the expedition, consisting of three vessels and 105 men, which left London on Dec. 19, 1606, under the command of Christopher Newport, for the purpose of establishing a colony in Virginia. He professed to have been kept under arrest during part of the voyage, on suspicion of aiming to usurp the government and make himself king. The colonists sighted the Virginia coast (Cape Henry) April 26, 1607. The same day they opened the sealed orders which they carried with them providing for the local government of the colony. The orders named a council of seven members, including John Smith (although for the present he was not allowed to take his seat), which was to elect an annual president, and which ultimately chose Edward Maria Wingfield. The settlement of Jamestown began in May, 1607. Smith's energy in exploring the neighboring rivers, and his success in obtaining supplies from the Indians, soon secured for him admission to his place on the council. While on a voyage of exploration up the James in 1607 he was captured by the Indians and brought before Powhatan, who after a six weeks' captivity sent him back to Jamestown. It was at this time that his life was allegedly saved by Pocahontas. When he returned to Jamestown, he found the colonists reduced to 40 men, but they were presently reinforced by the arrival of Captain Nelson with 140 immigrants. Smith explored the coast of Chesapeake Bay as far as the mouth of the Patapsco River (June–July) and the head of the Chesapeake (July–September, 1608). On Sept. 10, 1608, he was elected president of the colony. Insubordination and Indian uprisings were overcome by Smith's tact and energy, but false accounts of his administration were sent home by his enemies. A new charter was obtained by the proprietors in England (the London Company); Thomas West, Lord De La Warr, was made governor; and three commissioners were empowered to manage the affairs of the colony until the arrival of the governor. The commissioners sailed in 1609 with over 500 emigrants in nine ships, one of which, the *Sea Venture*, was shipwrecked off the Bermudas. The warrant of the new commission was lost in the shipwreck, with the result that Smith retained his presidency and enforced his authority over the newcomers, who were composed largely of the riff-raff of London. While on an exploring expedition he was severely wounded by the explosion of his powder-bag, and returned to London in the autumn of 1609. He subsequently conducted (1614) an expedition fitted out by some London merchants to the coast of New England, which he explored from Penobscot to Cape Cod. In 1615 he started on a similar voyage, but was captured by the French. He escaped the same year, and the remainder of his life was spent in vain endeavors to procure financial support for the establishment of a colony in New England. He obtained the promise of 20 ships in 1617, and received the title of Admiral of New England, which he bore until his death. The expedition, however, never sailed. He wrote *A True Relation . . .* (1608), *A Map of Virginia . . .* (1612), *A Description of New England* (1616), *New England's Trials* (1620), *The Generall Historie of Virginia, New England, and the Summer Isles* (1624), *An Accidence for Young Seamen* (1626), *The True Travels . . .* (1630), and *Advertisements for the Inexperienced Planters of New England* (1631).

Smith, Logan Pearsall. b. at Milville, N. J., Oct. 18, 1865; d. at London, March 2, 1946. An English essayist and literary critic. He was a resident (1888–1944) of England and a naturalized British subject (after 1913). He was noted for his brilliantly polished style, especially in his short, pithy essays. Author of *The Youth of Parnassus* (1895), *Trivia* (1902), *Life and Letters of Sir Henry Wotton* (1907), *Songs and Sonnets* (1909), *The English Language* (1912), *Words and Idioms* (1925), *On Reading Shakespeare* (1933), *Reperusals and Recollections* (1936), *Unforgotten Years* (1939), *Milton and His Modern Critics* (1940), and other works. He published a collection of earlier writings in *All Trivia* (1934).

ḍ, d or j; ş, s or sh; ṭ, t or ch; ẓ, z or zh; o, F. cloche; ü, F. menu; ch, Sc. loch; ṅ, F. bonbon.

Smith, Sarah. See **Stretton, Hesba.**

Smith, Sydney. b. at Woodford, Essex, England, June 3, 1771; d. at London, Feb. 22, 1845. An English clergyman, wit, and essayist. He was educated at Winchester and at New College, Oxford, took orders (1796), and was curate of Nether Avon on Salisbury Plain. He lived in Edinburgh from 1798 to 1803, and then went to London. While in Edinburgh he was one of the founders of the *Edinburgh Review*, its first editor (1802), and one of its chief contributors for 20 years. From 1804 to 1808 he was one of the lecturers on moral philosophy at the Royal Institution, London, teaching the principles of Dugald Stewart, under whom he had studied at Edinburgh. These lectures were published in 1850. In 1806 he was presented to the living of Foston-le-Clay, Yorkshire, where there had been no clergyman for 150 years; he lived there (1814–28) as a village priest. In 1828 he was presented to a prebend in Bristol Cathedral and in 1829 to the living of Combe-Florey in Somerset; in 1831 he was canon residentiary of St. Paul's. He was noted as a brilliant critic, and as a talker and a wit. That he never became a bishop has been laid to his humor and to his inability to compromise with what he saw as the truth. He was very much in favor of reform of Parliament but opposed to extension of the ballot. His sayings are among the most brilliant attributed to any person in English history. T. B. Macaulay calls him "the greatest master of ridicule that has appeared among us since Swift"; others make similar comparisons with Voltaire; but Smith had not the bitterness of either. His chief works are *Letters on the Subject of the Catholics, by Peter Plymley* (1807–08: advocating Catholic emancipation and Parliamentary reform); sixty-five articles from the *Edinburgh Review*, republished in 1839; *Wit and Wisdom* (edited by Duyckinck, 1856); and a number of volumes of speeches, sermons, and letters on questions of the day. His life was published by his daughter, Lady Holland (1855; including his letters).

Smith, Walter Chalmers. [Pseudonyms: **Herman Knott, Orwell.**] b. at Aberdeen, Scotland, Dec. 5, 1824; d. Sept. 20, 1908. A Scottish poet. Author of *The Bishop's Walk* (1861), *Olrig Grange* (1872), *Borland Hall* (1874), *Hilda among the Broken Gods* (1878), *North Country Folk* (1883), *Kildrostan* (1884), *A Heretic* (1890), and other volumes of descriptive and narrative poetry.

Smith, Wayland. See **Wayland Smith.**

Smith, William. [Called **"Gentleman Smith."**] b. 1730; d. 1819. An English actor. After being expelled from Cambridge, he took up acting and first appeared on the stage in 1753 at Covent Garden. In 1774 he went to the Drury Lane, where he created the role of Charles Surface in Sheridan's *School for Scandal*. He also played Macbeth opposite Mrs. Siddons's Lady Macbeth, and alternated *Hamlet* and *Richard III* with Garrick.

Smith, Sir William. b. at London, 1813; d. there, Oct. 7, 1893. An English classical and Biblical scholar; brother of Philip Smith. He studied at University College (London), and kept terms at Gray's Inn, but abandoned law in order to devote himself to the study of classical literature. He was editor of the *Quarterly Review* from 1867 until his death. He edited *Dictionary of Greek and Roman Antiquities* (1842), *Dictionary of Greek and Roman Biography and Mythology* (3 vols., 1849), *Dictionary of Greek and Roman Geography* (2 vols., 1854–57), *Dictionary of the Bible* (1860–65), and a Latin-English Dictionary (1855); and was joint editor of *Dictionary of Christian Antiquities* (1875–80) and *Dictionary of Christian Biography* (4 vols., 1877–87). He wrote or edited various classical textbooks, historical manuals, and others.

Smith, William Robertson. b. at Keig, Aberdeenshire, Scotland, Nov. 8, 1846; d. at Cambridge, England, March 31, 1894. A Scottish Biblical scholar and Orientalist. In 1870 he was appointed Hebrew professor in the Free Church College at Aberdeen. A keen ecclesiastical controversy arose out of certain of his writings, the question at issue being the extent of liberty in matters of Biblical criticism and interpretation permissible in an evangelical church. His contributions to the ninth edition of the *Encyclopaedia Britannica*, especially the article *Bible*, published in 1875, led to a series of attempts to convict him of heresy. These were unsuccessful, largely owing to the attraction of a powerful personal influence, as well as to the skillful conduct of his defense; but in 1881 he was removed from his chair without being deprived of his emoluments, which, however, he declined to continue to accept. The ground assigned by the assembly for this action was that "they no longer considered it safe or advantageous for the church that Professor Smith should continue to teach in one of her colleges." From 1881 he was associated as joint editor of the *Encyclopaedia Britannica* with Thomas Spencer Baynes, after whose death in 1887 he was sole editor. He was lord almoner's professor of Arabic at Cambridge University (1883–86), librarian of the university (1886–89), and professor of Arabic (1889–94). He published *The Old Testament in the Jewish Church* (1881), *The Prophets of Israel, and Their Place in History* (1882), *Kinship and Marriage in Early Arabia* (1885), *The Religion of the Semites* (1889), and others.

Smithfield. A locality in London, north of Saint Paul's, long famous for its cattle market and as the scene of Bartholomew Fair. It was the scene of Wat Tyler's death (1381), and the place where many Protestants suffered death at the stake in the reign of Mary Tudor.

Smith's Prizes. Two prizes at the University of Cambridge, England, founded by Robert Smith (1689–1768), a mathematician and astronomer. From 1769 to 1882 they were awarded to the students proceeding B.A. who were most successful in a special examination in mathematics. From 1883 they have been awarded to writers of the best essays on any subject in mathematics or natural philosophy.

Smith the Weaver. In Shakespeare's *2 Henry VI*, a follower of Jack Cade.

Smolkin (smol′kin). A fiend mentioned in Shakespeare's *King Lear*.

Smollett (smol′et), **Tobias George.** b. at Dalquhurn, near Bonhill, in the vale of Leven, Dumbartonshire, Scotland, in March, 1721; d. at Il Giardino, in Antignano, near Leghorn, Italy, Sept. 17,

1771. An English novelist. Descended from a well-known Scottish family, he was educated at the Dumbarton grammar school and at Glasgow University. In 1736 he was apprenticed to prominent surgeons at Glasgow, but he went to London in 1739. For some two years he served as surgeon's second mate on board the *Chichester*, and he accompanied the ill-starred expedition (1741) against the Spanish at Cartagena. In 1744 he was a practicing surgeon on Downing Street, London. Although engaging in some medical practice and publishing (1752) a medical essay after obtaining his M.D., Smollett turned increasingly to multifarious literary activities: some of his lyrics were published with musical settings in the 1740's; he was a frustrated writer of plays; he published satires in the manner of Alexander Pope, translated *Gil Blas*, and achieved success in 1748 with *Roderick Random*, his first novel, famous for its nautical scenes and characters. Other novels were *Peregrine Pickle* (1751, revised 1758), *Ferdinand Count Fathom* (1753), *Sir Launcelot Greaves* (1760–61), and *Humphry Clinker*, generally considered to be his finest work (1771). Smollett also succeeded as an able and popular historian with his *Complete History of England* (1757–58) and *Continuation* of the same (1760–65). A translation of *Don Quixote*, for which he was responsible, appeared in 1755. In 1756 he was a leader in founding the important *Critical Review*, and he contributed heavily to it until 1763, when, owing to failing health and the death of his daughter, he and Mrs. Smollett traveled to Nice. Returning to England he published in 1766 his *Travels*, distinguished by their authenticity, style, and self-revelation. In 1769 he published the satire *The Adventures of an Atom*, ostensibly about Japan but actually attacking conditions in England under George III. Smollett's violent temper, aggravated by colossal labor and bad health, involved him in regrettably vitriolic controversy and libelous satire. These excesses he repeatedly confessed and regretted. His emotional ebullience led, on the other hand, to notable and repeated generosity to needy friends. As a writer, Smollett must be granted a secure place, along with Richardson, Fielding, and Sterne, as a distinguished 18th-century novelist. He displayed great originality in the art of grotesque caricature in his presentation of eccentric types, and nautical types in particular, as seen in *Roderick Random* and in *Peregrine Pickle*. In *Humphry Clinker* he developed the possibilities of the epistolary novel. Despite certain indelicacies which offended the Victorians, and despite his nondramatic picaresque pattern and limited psychological treatment of character, Smollett displayed the great gifts of narrative gusto, significant satire, masterly prose, and, with all these, a rare power of provoking laughter.

Smorltork (smôrl′tôrk, smôl′tôk), **Count.** In Charles Dickens's *Pickwick Papers*, a foreign nobleman visiting England (he proposes to stay all of three weeks) in order to gather information for a book about England. Pickwick and his companions are introduced to him at a party. He was based upon the actual figure of Count Moskau, who did write a book about England based upon an amount of research hardly greater than that which Smorltork proposed to invest in his project.

Smythe (smĭŦH, smĭth), **George Augustus Frederick Percy Sydney.** [Titles: 7th Viscount **Strangford,** 2nd Baron **Penshurst.**] b. at Stockholm, April 13, 1818; d. at Bradgate Park, near Leicester, England, Nov. 23, 1857. An English statesman, poet, and essayist. He was a member of Parliament (1841, 1847–52) and foreign undersecretary of state (1845–46) in Robert Peel's second administration. At first a member of Disraeli's Young England Party, he left it to follow Peel; he is the "Coningsby" of Disraeli's novel of that name. His duel (1852) with Colonel Frederick Romilly at Weybridge was the last in England. Author of *Historic Fancies* (1844), a volume of prose and poetry, essays (1845) on George Canning and Earl Grey, *Angela Pisani* (1875), and many articles (1847–52) in the *Morning Chronicle* and other papers.

Snagsby (snagz′bi), **Mr.** A mild, bald, timid man, very retiring and unassuming, in the law-stationery business, in Dickens's *Bleak House*. He is in great fear of his domineering wife, and usually prefaces his remarks with "Not to put too fine a point upon it." He feels great pity for little Jo, and helps him until the boy dies.

Snagsby, Mrs. In Dickens's novel *Bleak House*, the nagging wife of Mr. Snagsby. She suspects her husband of a tremendous variety of things, none of which are ever defined, but which nevertheless impel her to make life difficult for him. She is eventually, and somewhat bluntly, straightened out by Inspector Bucket.

Snailsfoot (snālz′fŭt), **Bryce.** In Sir Walter Scott's novel *The Pirate*, a clever little peddler, whose vulgarity is matched only by his wit: ". . . his are the true flourishes of eloquence, in the course of which men snip the cloth an inch too short."

Snake (snāk), **Mr.** A malicious character in Richard Brinsley Sheridan's *School for Scandal.*

Snare (snâr). In Shakespeare's *2 Henry IV*, one of the two sheriff's officers (Fang is the other) sent to arrest Falstaff in Mistress Quickly's suit.

Snark, Hunting of the. See **Hunting of the Snark.**

Snark, The. An imaginary beast in Lewis Carroll's poem *The Hunting of the Snark* (1876).

Sneak (snēk), **Jerry.** A foolish, good-natured henpecked husband in Samuel Foote's play *The Mayor of Garratt.*

Sneer (snir). A disagreeable critic in Richard Brinsley Sheridan's play *The Critic.*

Sneerwell (snir′wel), **Lady.** A beautiful widow, a scandal-monger, in Richard Brinsley Sheridan's *School for Scandal.*

Snell (snel), **Hannah.** b. 1723; d. 1792. An English woman adventurer. A biographical work was published over her name in 1750, in which it was alleged that she had enlisted as a marine in 1745 and had actually received a pension for wounds received at Pondichéry. Some portion of what she claimed as her adventures is now believed almost certainly to be true, but there can be no doubt that the truth was embellished with a considerable amount of fancy.

Snevellicci (snä.ve̞.lē′chē̞), **Miss.** An actress, engaged in Mr. Vincent Crummles's theatrical troupe, "who could do anything, from a medley dance to

ḑ, d or j; ş, s or sh; ṭ, t or ch; ẓ, z or zh; o, F. cloche; ü, F. menu; ċh, Sc. loch; ṅ, F. bonbon.

Lady Macbeth"; a character in Dickens's *Nicholas Nickleby*.

Snevellicci, Mr. In Dickens's novel *Nicholas Nickleby*, the father of Miss Snevellicci. He has "been in the acting profession ever since he . . . played the ten-year-old imps in the Christmas pantomime." He is a man of imposing appearance, but no very great skill, and an unfortunate fondness for the bottle.

Snevellicci, Mrs. In Dickens's novel *Nicholas Nickleby*, the mother of Miss Snevellicci.

Snob Papers, The. See **Book of Snobs, The.**

Snobs of England, by One of themselves, The. The original title (the one used when the work was published serially in *Punch*) of Thackeray's **Book of Snobs.**

Snodgrass (snod'grās), **Mr. Augustus.** A member of the famous Pickwick Club, with a turn for poesy, in Dickens's *Pickwick Papers*.

Snorri Sturluson (snôr'ē stör'lù.sôn). [Also: **Snorri** or **Snorre** (snôr'ā) or **Snorro** (snôr'ō) **Sturleson** (stör'le.sôn).] b. at Hvamm, Iceland, 1179; assassinated on his estate, Reykjaholt, Iceland, Sept. 23, 1241. An Icelandic historian and high legal officer in Iceland. He twice visited Norway. He was the author of the *Heimskringla* ("Sagas of the Norwegian Kings"; Eng. trans by Laing), and the reputed author of the *Younger Edda*.

Snout (snout), **Tom.** In Shakespeare's *Midsummer Night's Dream*, a tinker who is cast in the part of the father of Pyramus in the interpolated play. However, he finally plays the part of the wall.

Snowdoun (snō'dun), **Knight of.** A title assumed by James V of Scotland in Scott's poem *The Lady of the Lake*. Under this disguise he meets Ellen Douglas, the "Lady of the Lake," and vanquishes Roderick Dhu in single combat.

Snowe (snō), **Lucy.** The principal character in Charlotte Brontë's novel *Villette*.

"Snow King," the. See **Gustavus Adolphus.**

Snubbin (snub'in). In Dickens's *Pickwick Papers*, the lawyer for the defense (that is, for Mr. Pickwick) in the case of Bardell vs. Pickwick.

Snuffe (snuf), **Languebeau.** A hypocritical Puritan preacher in Cyril Tourneur's *The Atheist's Tragedy*. His willingness to compromise his supposedly unimpeachable integrity by arranging a marriage of convenience for D'Amville convinces the latter of the rightness of atheism.

Snuffy Davie (dā'vi). [Also, **Davie Wilson.**] In Sir Walter Scott's novel *The Antiquary*, according to a story told by Jonathan Oldbuck, the fortunate purchaser of a copy of Caxton's *Game at Chess* for two groschen.

Snug (snug). In Shakespeare's *Midsummer Night's Dream*, a joiner who plays the part of the Lion in the interpolated play.

Social Climbers, The. A play (1927) by Romer Wilson (Mrs. Edward J. O'Brien).

Social Contract, The. See under **Rousseau, Jean Jacques.**

Society for Pure English, The. [Abbreviation, **S.P.E.**] A society established in 1913 for the purpose of observing current usage and other matters pertaining to the English language. It has included in its membership some of the principal scholars and writers of the modern period, and has issued (through its *Tracts*) a body of valuable linguistic material.

sock. A light shoe worn by the ancient actors of comedy; hence, comedy, in distinction from tragedy, which is symbolized by the buskin.

Where be the sweete delights of learnings treasure,
That wont with Comick sock to beautefie
The painted Theaters?
    (Spenser, *Tears of the Muses*, **1.**176.)

Then to the well-trod stage anon,
If Jonson's learned sock be on,
Or sweetest Shakespeare, Fancy's child,
Warble his native wood-notes wild.
    (Milton, *L'Allegro*, **1.**132.)

Socrates (sok'ra.tēz). b. at Athens c470 B.C.; d. there, 399. A Greek philosopher. He was the son of Sophroniscus, a sculptor, and of Phænarete, a midwife. He at first adopted his father's art; in the time of Pausanias a group of draped Graces, by him, is said still to have stood on the approach to the Acropolis. He soon, however, devoted himself entirely to the pursuit of philosophy, and became famous through the persistence and skill with which, in conversation with the sophists and with everyone who would yield himself to the dialogue, he conducted the analysis of philosophical and ethical ideas ("the Socratic method"). This analysis consisted of a directed sequence of questions; the answers ideally would indicate that the knowledge of the subject belonged to all and that a good teacher could evoke the best from his disciples. He was above all a searcher after a knowledge of virtue (which indeed he identified with knowledge), and was in himself the noblest exponent of the ethical life of the Greeks. In the Peloponnesian War, he served at Potidaea (431), Delium (424), and Amphipolis (422), was president of the prytanes in 406, and opposed the Thirty Tyrants. He is the chief character in the dialogues of Plato, in which his teachings are set forth (greatly modified by Plato's own views), and is the subject of the *Memorabilia* of Xenophon. Socrates himself left no writings. His most famous pupils were Plato, Xenophon, and Alcibiades. He was bitterly attacked by Aristophanes as a sophist and innovator, and drew upon himself by his mode of life and the character of his opinions the enmity of many others. In 399 he was accused of impiety (the introduction of new gods) and of corrupting the youth; he defended himself in a famous speech which enraged rather than conciliated his judges, was condemned, and drank hemlock in his prison, surrounded by his disciples. Socrates was not a prepossessing figure; his indifference to his outward appearance was well known throughout Athens. His marriage to the shrewish Xanthippe resulted in many apocryphal tales.

So Disdained. A novel by Nevil Shute, published in 1928.

Sodom (sod'ọm). In Biblical geography, one of the cities of the Vale of Siddim, destroyed with Gomorrah and other cities of the plain on account of its wickedness in the time of Abraham and Lot (Gen. xviii–xix). According to tradition its site is covered by the Dead Sea, but geologists now consider this to be highly improbable.

Sohar (sō.här′). See **Zohar.**

Soho (sō′hō). A portion of W London comprising the area N of Piccadilly Circus to Oxford Street, bounded on the west by Regent Street and on the east by Charing Cross Road. It is traversed from N to S by Wardour Street. During the 19th century and earlier it was famous as the residence of many of England's greatest literary figures, including Blake, Dryden, and De Quincey. It retains today many of the foreign restaurants for which it has long been famous with Londoners, but has ceased to have any particular importance for the writers living in it (Wardour Street, for example, is now largely given over to the offices of various film companies).

Soho Square. A square in London, south of Oxford Street, made in the reign of Charles II, and once called King's Square.

Sohrab and Rustum (sō′räb; rös′tum). A poem (1853) by Matthew Arnold, based on a tale he read in a translation of the *Shahnamah*, concerning the battle between Sohrab and Rustum (Sohrab's father), the identity of each unknown to the other. At a crucial point in the battle, Sohrab hears his antagonist utter the name "Rustum," and, realizing the situation, he hesitates and is felled. Before he dies he reveals his identity to his father.

Sohrab and Rustum. See also **Rustam.**

Solanio and Salerio (sō.lä′ni.ō; sạ.ler′i.ō, -lir′-). [Also, **Salanio and Salarino.**] Two minor characters in Shakespeare's *Merchant of Venice*. They play roles in incidents involving Lorenzo and Antonio.

Soldier, The. A poem by Rupert Brooke, published (1914) as part of the sonnet sequence *1914*. It opens with the lines:

If I should die, think only this of me;
That there's some corner of a foreign field
That is forever England. . . .

Soldier's Fortune, The. [Also, **The Souldier's Fortune.**] A comedy by Thomas Otway, produced in 1680, based on Molière's *L'École des maris* and Scarron's *Le Roman Comique.* The figure of Sir Jolly Jumble was probably suggested by Dryden's Pandarus in *Troilus and Cressida.*

Soldiers Three. A collection of seven short stories (Calcutta, 1888) by Rudyard Kipling. It deals with the adventures, and reminiscences, of three soldiers in the British Army in India: Terence Mulvaney (an Irishman), Stanley Ortheris (a Cockney), and John Learoyd (a Lancashireman).

Soldiers Three and Other Stories. A collection of stories (1895) by Rudyard Kipling. It comprises the contents of three smaller books: *Soldiers Three* (1888), *The Story of the Gadsbys* (1888), and *In Black and White* (1888). All three of the lesser books were originally published at Calcutta.

solecism (sol′ẹ.sizm). **1.** A gross deviation from the settled usages of grammar; a gross grammatical error, such as "I *done* it" for "I *did* it."

Whatever you meddle with, except when you make solecisms, is grammar still.
(Milton, *Ans. to Salmasius.*)

The offences against the usage of the English language are—(1) Barbarisms, words not English; (2) Solecisms, constructions not English; (3) Improprieties, words or phrases used in a sense not English. (A. S. Hill, *Rhetoric.*)

2. Loosely, any small blunder in speech.

Think on't, a close friend,
Or private mistress, is court rhetoric;
A wife, mere rustic solecism.
(Massinger, *Guardian,* I.i.)

They [the inhabitants of London] are the modern Solœci, and their solecisms have furnished much food for laughter. This kind of local reproach is not common, but it is not unprecedented.
(*N. and Q.*, 7th ser.)

Solemn League and Covenant. In Scottish history, one of certain bonds of agreement signed by the Scottish Presbyterians for the defense or promotion of their religion, especially the "National Covenant" of 1638, or the "Solemn League and Covenant" of 1643 (entered into with England).

soliloquy (sọ.lil′ọ.kwi). **1.** A talking to one's self; a discourse or talk by a person who is alone, or which is not addressed to any one even when others are present.

2. A written composition containing such a talk or discourse, or what purports to be one.

Soliloquies; or, holy self-conferences of the devout soul, upon sundry choice occasions.
(Bp. Hall, *Soliloquies*, Title.)

The whole Poem is a Soliloquy.
(Prior, *Solomon*, Pref.)

Soliman and Perseda (sol′i.man; pẻr′sẹ.dạ). [Also, **Solyman and Perseda.**] A tragedy (utilizing the device of a play within a play) written c1589, probably by Thomas Kyd, although George Peele has also been suggested. It is an elaboration of the play within a play in Kyd's *Spanish Tragedy.*

Solinus (sọ.lī′nus). In Shakespeare's *Comedy of Errors,* the Duke of Ephesus.

Solomon (sol′ọ.mọn). King of Israel (c973–c933 B.C.); son of David and Bathsheba. He was the youngest son of David, but, through the influence of his mother and of Nathan, was made his heir. Under him Israel became a great power, and he, himself, became famous for his wealth, his luxury, and his wisdom, the last, according to the Biblical account, a special gift of God. His great work was the building of the temple. He is the reputed author of *Proverbs*, *The Song of Songs*, and *Ecclesiastes* in the Biblical canon; and of *The Wisdom of Solomon* in the *Apocrypha.* He was in alliance, political and commercial, with Hiram of Tyre and with other powers, and extended Israelitish commerce to all parts of the known world. The name of Solomon, who was supposed to have possessed extraordinary magical powers, plays an important part in Eastern and thence in European legends. According to one tradition, the Ethiopians are descended from him through a son born to him by the Queen of Sheba. Solomon's great harem was in keeping with his status as a great prince.

ḍ, d or j; ṣ, s or sh; ṭ, t or ch; ẓ, z or zh; o, F. cloche; ü, F. menu; ċh, Sc. loch; ň, F. bonbon.

Solomon. [Full title, **Solomon on the Vanity of the World.**] An epic poem by Matthew Prior, published in 1718, although written earlier. It is cast in heroic couplets, and written in the form of a soliloquy which expresses the pessimistic notion that "in vain We lift up our presumptious Eyes/to what our Maker to their ken denies."

Solomon. Entries on literary characters having this prename will be found under the surnames Daisy, Eagle, Flint, Gills, Pell, and Pross.

Solomons, Esq., Junior (sol'ọ.mọnz), **Ikey.** One of the many pseudonyms of **Thackeray, William Makepeace.**

Solon (sō'lọn). b. c638 B.C.; d. c559. An Athenian lawgiver. He encouraged the Athenians to regain possession of Salamis from Megara; he avoided the legal injunction not to mention the name of Salamis by pretending to be mad and reciting a poem on the subject in the market place. In 594 he became archon and was charged with various reforms. He improved the condition of the debtors, divided the population into four "classes," and reorganized the Boule, the popular assembly, and the council of the Areopagus. He traveled in Cyprus and the East to avoid the criticism leveled against these reforms. After 10 years he returned, and soon afterward saw his friend Pisistratus become tyrant of Athens.

Solyman and Perseda (sol'i.man; pẽr'sẹ.dạ). See **Soliman and Perseda.**

Solyman the Magnificent. The magnanimous infidel antagonist of Alphonso, the Christian warrior, in Sir William D'Avenant's *Siege of Rhodes.*

Soma (sō'mạ). In Vedic mythology, the personification and god of the soma plant and its sap. This plant (*Sarcostemma viminalis* or *Asclepia acida*) was in Vedic times collected by moonlight and carried to the place of sacrifice, where the priests crushed the stalks between stones, sprinkled them with water, and placed them on a sieve whence the acid juice trickled into a vessel. It was allowed to ferment, and offered in libations to the gods, or drunk by the Brahmans. In the myths it was brought from the sky by an eagle and guarded by the Gandharvas. The soma juice was regarded in Vedic times as conferring eternal life and vigor on its drinkers, whether gods or men, and was a favorite propitiatory offering. The personification of the sacred soma as a god, Soma, was regarded as the lord of plants and stars and of the moon, all-powerful, all-pervading, healing all diseases, and lord of all other gods.

Some Chinese Ghosts. A collection of stories (1887) by Lafcadio Hearn.

Somehow Good. A novel (1908) by William De Morgan; the title is from the familiar lines from *In Memoriam.*

Somers (sum'ẽrz), **Will.** See **Summer, Will.**

Somerset (sum'ẽr.set), (2nd) **Duke of.** In Shakespeare's *2 Henry VI*, the historical Edmund Beaufort, brother of John Beaufort. He carries on a fight with the Duke of York, begun by his brother. Made Regent of France, he later reports that he has lost the English territories. He is killed at St. Albans.

Somerset, (4th) **Duke of.** In Shakespeare's *3 Henry VI*, the historical Edmund Beaufort, son of the

2nd Duke. He joins Warwick against Edward IV, sends Richmond to Brittany for security, and is captured and executed at the battle of Tewkesbury.

Somerset, Earl of. In Shakespeare's *1 Henry VI*, John Beaufort, who later becomes Duke. He tries to maintain peace between Gloucester and the Bishop of Winchester but quarrels with the Duke of York.

Somerset House. A palace in the Strand, London, built (1549) by the Protector, Edward Seymour, Duke of Somerset. Later it was crown property. It was demolished in 1775, but has been rebuilt and is used for government offices (Registrar General, Inland Revenue, Exchequer, and others). It is now perhaps best known for the fact that in it may be found one of the most complete sets of birth and death records in the world (every birth and death in the United Kingdom is supposedly entered in its files).

Somers Islands (sum'ẽrz). A former name of **Bermuda.**

Somervile (sum'ẽr.vil), **Sir John.** In Shakespeare's *3 Henry VI*, a supporter of the Yorkist faction.

Somerville (sum'ẽr.vil), **Edith Anna Œnone.** b. on Corfu, 1861—. An Irish novelist. She collaborated (1887–1915) with her cousin Violet Florence Martin, until the latter's death, on picturesque stories of Irish manners; these novels include *An Irish Cousin*, *The Real Charlotte*, *All on the Irish Shore*, and *Stray-Aways.* Singly she wrote *The Big House of Inver* (1925), *The States through Irish Eyes* (1930), and the biography of her great-grandfather Charles Kendal Bushe, chief justice of Ireland, under the title *An Incorruptible Irishman.*

Somerville, William. b. at Edstone, Warwickshire, England, 1675; d. there, July 17, 1742. An English poet. He was educated at Winchester and New College, Oxford. He wrote *The Chase* (1735), *Hobbinol, or the Rural Games* (1740), and *Field Sports* (1742), poems on country diversions.

Something Is Bound to Happen. See **Doom Is Dark and Deeper than Any Sea-Dingle.**

Somme le Roi (som lẹ rwà). [Original title, *Somme des Vices et Vertues* (som dā vēs e ver.tü).] A religious treatise in French, written in England in 1279. It was intended to instruct the clergy as well as the laity and achieved a wide circulation. A Middle English translation was made under the title *The Book of Vices and Virtues.*

Somnium Scipionis (som'ni.um sip.i.ō'nis). See **Dream of Scipio, The.**

Somnus (som'nus). The Roman counterpart of the Greek Hypnos.

Sompnour's Tale (sump'nẽrz), **The.** See **Summoner's Tale, The.**

song. 1. A short poem intended for singing, or set to music; a ballad or lyric. A song is properly distinguished by brevity, free use of rhythmic accent and rhyme, more or less division into stanzas or strophes, often with a refrain or burden, comparative directness and simplicity of sentiment, and a decidedly lyrical manner throughout.

Out on you, owls! nothing but songs of death?
(Shak., *Rich. III.*, IV.iv.)

fat, fāte, fär, àsk, fãre; net, mē, hẽr; pin, pīne; not, nōte, mǒve, nôr; up, lūte, pùll; тн, then;

The bard who first adorn'd our native tongue
Tun'd to his British lyre this ancient song.
(Dryden, *To the Duches of Ormond
with Pal. and Arc.*)

Perhaps it may turn out a sang,
Perhaps turn out a sermon.
(Burns, *Epistle to a Young Friend.*)

2. A particular melody or musical setting for such a poem, for either one or several voices (in the latter case usually called a *part-song* or *glee*). Songs are generally written in song form, but are often irregular also. They usually contain but a single movement, and have an accompaniment of a varying amount of elaboration. They are classified as *folk songs*, which spring up more or less unconsciously among the common people, or *art songs*, which are deliberately composed by musicians; as *strophic*, when made up of a movement repeated for the several strophes, or *composed through*, when the music varies with the successive strophes; or they are named by reference to their general subject or style, as *rustic, patriotic, national, martial, naval, nuptial, hunting, bacchanalian,* etc.

Song. A poem from *Aglaura*, by Sir John Suckling, well known for the opening line: "Why so pale and wan, fond lover?"

Songe to Ælla (al'ạ). A poem (c1768) by Thomas Chatterton, first published as the work of Thomas Rowley, the fictitious 15th-century monk, invented by Chatterton to serve as author of Chatterton's own works. The deception was exposed by Thomas Tyrwhitt in an essay published in 1777.

Song for Saint Cecilia's Day (sẹ.sil'yạz). See **Saint Cecilia's Day, Song for.**

Song of Canute (kạ.nūt'), **The.** [Also, **Cnut's Song** (knöts).] A song, the first four lines of which are recorded in the *Liber Eliensis* (early 12th century), which ascribes its composition to King Canute as he was being rowed to the church at Ely. It has been described as the earliest surviving example of Middle English verse.

Song of Roland (rō'lạnd). A Middle English paraphrase of the French *Chanson de Roland*, written c1450 in 1,049 four-stress lines rhymed in couplets. It suffers by comparison with the French masterpiece.

Song of Solomon (sol'ọ.mọn). [Also: **Canticles, Song of Songs, The Songs.**] One of the books of the Old Testament. Until the 19th century it was universally ascribed to Solomon, but critics now regard it as of later date. Its allegorical interpretation as a song of God's love is more common than its acceptance as a type of Oriental love poem.

Song of the Shirt. A poem of social protest by Thomas Hood.

Song of the Three Holy Children. An addition to the Book of Daniel, found in the Septuagint and in the Apocrypha, purporting to be the prayer and song of the three Hebrews in the fiery furnace.

Songs of Chaos. Poems by Herbert Read, published in 1915.

Songs of Experience. A volume of mystical poetry by William Blake, published in 1794 with hand-colored copperplate engravings by the author.

The work includes the noted poem *Tiger! Tiger! burning bright.*

Songs of Innocence. A volume of mystical poetry by William Blake, published in 1789 with hand-colored copperplate engravings by the author.

Song, To Celia (sēl'yạ). See **To Celia.**

sonnet (son'ẹt). **1.** A song; a ballad; a short poem.

I have a sonnet that will serve the turn.
(Shak., *T.G. of V.,* III.ii.)

Teach me some melodious sonnet,
Sung by flaming tongues above.
(R. Robinson, *Come, Thou Fount of Every Blessing.*)

Specifically—**2.** A short poem in fixed form, limited to 14 lines with a prescribed disposition of rhymes. The form is of Italian origin, and is generally written in decasyllabic or five-foot measure (but it may be written in octosyllabics). There are two types of sonnet in English literature: the first, in point of time, usually called the Petrarchan sonnet, consists of a major group of eight lines or two quatrains, and a minor group of six lines or two tercets. The quatrains are arranged thus: *abba; abba;* the tercets, either *cdcdcd,* or *cdecde.* In modern French examples the order of the tercets is generally *ccdede.* The second form of sonnet, later in development but more often used in English verse, is the Elizabethan or Shakespearian sonnet, consisting of three quatrains and a couplet, with the rhyme scheme *ababcdcdefefgg.*

sonnets (of Shakespeare). Sonnets (154 in number) written by Shakespeare, probably between 1593 and 1603, published in 1609. It would seem from the contents that the bulk of the sonnets were written to a man and the remaining to a woman (the Dark Lady), but, although there have been various theories, no one has been able to identify these people. The poems are referred to by their first lines, among the best-known of which are: "When to the sessions of sweet silent thought," "When I have seen by time's fell hand defaced," and "Let me not to the marriage of true minds."

Sonnets from the Portuguese (pōr'tụ.gēz, -gēs). A series of sonnets by Elizabeth Barrett Browning, published in 1850. They were written during a period of seven years, and are considered by some scholars to have been inspired by her love for her husband. The basis for the title of the series is generally assumed to have been a sequence addressed to "Catarina" by the great 16th-century Portuguese poet Luiz de Camões (or Camoens).

Son of the Soil, A. Pseudonym of **Fletcher, Joseph Smith.**

Sons and Lovers. An autobiographical novel by D. H. Lawrence, published in 1913.

Sons of the Sword. A novel by Margaret Louisa Woods, published in 1901.

Soothsayer. In Shakespeare's *Antony and Cleopatra*, a seer who tells Charmian and Iras that they will outlive Cleopatra.

Soothsayer. A character in Shakespeare's *Cymbeline*. He foretells success to the Romans and interprets Posthumus's vision.

Soothsayer. In Shakespeare's *Julius Caesar*, an old man who warns Caesar to "beware the Ides of March."

Sophia Baines (sọ.fī'ạ bānz'). See **Baines.**

Sophia Western (wes'tẽrn). See **Western, Sophia.**

Sophocles (sof'ọ.klēz). b. at Colonus, near Athens, c496 B.C.; d. 406 B.C. One of the three great tragic poets of Greece, ranked with Aeschylus and Euripides. He defeated Aeschylus for the tragic prize in 468, and was defeated by Euripides in 441; he never fell below second place in the competitions. He was one of the Athenian generals in the Samian War (440). He added the third actor to the drama, and made various changes in the chorus. His extant tragedies of the more than 120 he wrote include *Œdipus Tyrannus* (or *Oedipus Rex*), *Oedipus at Colonus, Antigone, Electra, Philoctetes, Ajax,* and *Maidens of Trachis;* fragments of others exist.

Sophonisba (sof.ọ.niz'bạ). d. c204 B.C. Carthaginian woman; daughter of Hasdrubal, son of Gisco. She was betrothed to the Numidian prince Masinissa, but was afterward married in 206 B.C., for political reasons, to Syphax, the rival Numidian ruler. Her husband was defeated by Masinissa, who acted as an ally of the Romans while Syphax was an ally of the Carthaginians, in the second Punic War. Sophonisba fell into the hands of the conqueror, who married her, but was compelled by Scipio to reject her. She committed suicide by poison sent by Masinissa to prevent her from falling into the hands of the Romans. She has been the subject of many tragedies.

Sophonisba. A tragedy by James Thomson, produced in 1730. It contains the line "O Sophonisba! Sophonisba, O!" whose bathos has been remembered when most of Thomson's more solid work has been ignored. This line was parodied in Fielding's *Tom Thumb.*

Sophonisba, or Hannibal's Overthrow (han'i.bạlz). A tragedy by Nathaniel Lee, produced in 1675.

Sophonisba, or the Wonder of Women. A tragedy by John Marston, produced in 1602.

Sophronia (sọ.frō'nē.ä). A character in Torquato Tasso's *Jerusalem Delivered.*

Sophy (sō'fi), **The.** A play by Sir John Denham, acted in 1641 at Blackfriars, and printed in 1642.

Sophy Crewler (krö'lẽr). See under **Crewler.**

Sophy Wackles (wak'lz), **Miss.** See **Wackles, Miss Sophy.**

Soranzo (sọ.ran'zō). The husband of Annabella in John Ford's *'Tis Pity She's a Whore.*

Sordello (sôr.del'ō; Italian, sôr.del'lō). b. at Goito, near Mantua, Italy, c1180; d. c1255. A Provençal poet or troubadour. He was attached for a time to the household of the chief of the Guelph party in the march of Treviso, and later entered the service of Raymond Berenger, the last count of Provence of the house of Barcelona. At that time the Italian language did not enjoy social or intellectual favor, and Sordello wrote in the Provençal language. He gradually became in popular tradition a hero of romance, a *preux chevalier,* and an Italian knight errant. Many fables were woven about his name (it was even said that the sovereignty of Mantua had been bestowed upon him). He owes his repu-

tation principally to Dante's mention of him; he introduces him as the main character of two cantos of the *Purgatorio.* Nothing survives of his prose or his Italian poems, but about 34 Provençal poems still exist and are included in François Raynouard's *Choix de poésies originales des troubadours* and his *Lexique roman.*

Sordello. A poem (1840) by Robert Browning. Its action takes place in northern Italy in the 13th century.

Sordido (sôr'di.dō). An avaricious farmer in Jonson's *Every Man Out of His Humour.* He tries to hang himself to avoid paying taxes for the support of his neighbors, but is cut down by them before he suffers harm.

Sorrel (sor'ẹl), **Hetty.** A pretty, vain, and pleasure-loving dairymaid in George Eliot's novel *Adam Bede;* she is Adam's first love.

Sorrell and Son (sọ.rel', sor'ẹl). A novel by Warwick Deeping, published in 1925.

Sothern (suᴛʜ'ẽrn), **Edward Askew.** b. at Liverpool, England, April 1, 1826; d. at London, Jan. 20, 1881. An English actor, known for his comic roles. He made his first professional appearance in 1849, on the island of Jersey, first acted in the U. S. in 1852, and in 1858 made his mark in the character of the imbecilic Lord Dundreary in Taylor's *Our American Cousin.*

Sot-Weed Factor, The. [Full title, **The Sot-Weed Factor: or, a Voyage to Maryland.**] A satirical poem that appeared over the name "Ebenezer Cook" (a pseudonym, but of whom no one yet knows). It was published at London in 1708.

Soul and Body. [Also, **The Address of the Soul to the Body.**] An Old English poem, of unknown authorship and date, dealing with punishment and reward after death, a theme widely treated in medieval literature. It comprises two parts: in the first (of which two versions survive, one in the *Vercelli Book* and one in the *Exeter Book*) the soul of a wicked person visits the dead body to reproach it for the sins which sent the soul to hell; in the second (preserved, though not complete, in the *Vercelli Book*) the body of the righteous person is praised by the returning soul.

Souldier's Fortune (sōl'jẽrz), **The.** See **Soldier's Fortune, The.**

Soul of a Bishop, The. A novel (1917) by H. G. Wells. It tells the story of Edward Scrope, bishop of a diocese in the industrial Midlands of England, whose religious misgivings finally culminate in formal withdrawal from the church.

Soul's Tragedy, A. A two-part drama (1846) in blank verse by Robert Browning, part of *Bells and Pomegranates.*

Soutar (sö'tạr), **Andrew.** b. 1879; d. at St. Austell, Cornwall, England, Nov. 24, 1941. An English novelist and dramatist. Author of *Chosen of the Gods* (1909), *Island of Test* (1910), *Broken Ladders* (1910), *Magpie House* (1913), *Charity Corner* (1915; American title, *Honor of His House*), *Green Orchard* (1916), *The Imperfect Lover* (1919), *Neither Do I Condemn Thee* (1924), *This Frail Woman* (1924), *Dear Fools* (1927), *Consider Your Verdict* (1928), *"Not Mentioned"* (1930), *The Devil's Triangle* (1931), *Strange Bedfellows* (1931), *The Golden Win-*

---

fat, fāte, fär, ȧsk, fãre; net, mē, hẽr; pin, pīne; not, nōte, möve, nôr; up, lūte, pu̇ll; ᴛʜ, then;

dows (1932), *Silent Thunder* (1932), *Opportunity* (1932), *Tomorrow Is Yesterday* (1933), *Kharduni* (1933), *Coward's Castle* (1934), *Night of Horror* (1934), *Secret Ways* (1934), and *Salome Had a Sister* (1939). He wrote *If We But Knew* (1928), a play, and various one-act plays and scenarios.

South (south), **Marty.** In Thomas Hardy's *The Woodlanders*, a young woman who is secretly in love with the hero, Giles Winterborne.

South, Robert. b. at Hackney, near London, 1633; d. at London, July 8, 1716. An English divine. He was made prebendary of Westminster in 1663, canon in Oxford in 1670, and rector of Islip in 1678. A strong believer in the Church of England, he opposed both Roman Catholics and dissenters. He engaged (1693–94) in a heated controversy concerning the Trinity with William Sherlock; the feeling aroused was so bitter that the king ordered the discussion suppressed. South is known also for his sermons, published in 1692.

Southampton (south.amp'ton, -hamp'-), 3rd Earl of. [Title of **Henry Wriothesley.**] b. Oct. 6, 1573; d. in the Netherlands, Nov. 10, 1624. An English politician and soldier, a friend and patron of William Shakespeare, who dedicated to him *Venus and Adonis*, and *The Rape of Lucrece*. He was a patron also of several other writers, including Thomas Nash and John Florio. He accompanied Robert Devereux, 2nd Earl of Essex, on the expeditions of 1596 and 1597, and in 1598 married Essex's cousin, Elizabeth Vernon, a marriage that brought down on his head the ire of Queen Elizabeth. He sponsored the performance of Shakespeare's *Richard II*, a play revolving about the deposition of an incompetent king, just before the ill-fated rebellion of Essex (1601) and, being otherwise implicated in the plot, was sentenced to death. The sentence was commuted to life imprisonment, and he was released (1603) on the accession of James I. He was deeply interested in colonization, and was a member of the council of the Virginia Company, whose expedition (1605) he helped to finance. He was treasurer of the company from 1620 to 1624.

Southampton, Sir. See **Bevis of Hampton.**

Southcott (south'kot), **Joanna.** b. in Devonshire, England, 1750; d. Dec. 27, 1814. An English religious fanatic, originally a domestic servant. She became a Methodist, and, probably sincerely convinced that she had supernatural gifts, dictated prophecies in rhyme, proclaimed herself to be the woman mentioned in the Apocalypse (chapter xii), and, although 64 years old, affirmed that she was to be delivered of "Shiloh," the second Messiah. She died soon after the date on which the birth was to take place. Her sect numbered over 100,000 at its peak (a charge of up to a guinea being made to enroll each new member), and is still not entirely extinct. She wrote *Strange Effects of Faith* (1801), *The True Explanation of the Bible* (1804–10), *The Book of Wonders* (1813–14), and others.

Southdown (south'doun), **Dowager Countess of.** In Thackeray's novel *Vanity Fair*, a wealthy, autocratic, meddlesome old woman. She is Pitt Crawley's mother-in-law.

Southdown, Earl of. In Thackeray's novel *Vanity Fair*, the "late husband" of the Dowager Countess of Southdown. He occurs in the novel only through his widow's references to him. He was "an epileptic and simple-minded nobleman."

Southdown, (4th) **Earl of.** In Thackeray's novel *Vanity Fair*, an amiable but not very clever young man who is bilked of his money by one of Becky Sharp's schemes. He is the son of the Dowager Countess of Southdown.

Southerne (suth'ern), **Thomas.** b. in County Dublin, Ireland, 1660; d. May 22, 1746. A British dramatist. Among his plays are *The Loyal Brother, or the Persian Prince* (1682), *The Fatal Marriage, or the Innocent Adultery* (1694, based on Aphra Behn's novel *The Nun*, and later retitled *Isabella*), *Oroonoko, or the Royal Slave* (1696, also based on a Behn novel), *Sir Anthony Love, or the Rambling Lady* (1691), and others.

Southey (south'i, suth'i), **Caroline Ann.** [Maiden name, **Bowles.**] b. at Lymington, Hampshire, England, Oct. 7, 1786; d. there, July 20, 1854. An English poet and author; second wife of Robert Southey, whom she married in 1839. Among her works are the poems *Ellen Fitzarthur* (1820) and *The Widow's Tale* (1822). Her collected poems were published in 1867. Among her prose works are *Chapters on Churchyards* (1829) and *Selwyn in Search of a Daughter* (1835). Her correspondence with Southey, beginning when she submitted *Ellen Fitzarthur* to him and culminating in their marriage, is her best-known work.

Southey, Robert. b. at Bristol, England, Aug. 12, 1774; d. at Greta Hall, near Keswick, England, March 21, 1843. An English poet and prose writer, one of the so-called Lake poets. He went to Westminster School, but was expelled in 1792 for an essay on "Flogging" in the *Flagellant*, a school magazine. He was refused admittance to Christ Church, Oxford, on account of this essay, but was admitted to Balliol. He made the acquaintance of Samuel Taylor Coleridge in 1794, and formed with him the scheme of an ideal colony, "Pantisocracy," to be established on the Susquehanna in America. He traveled in Spain and Portugal (1795–96), held for a short time a government sinecure, and settled down to literary work in 1803 at Greta Hall, near Keswick, where he collected a large library and wrote with great regularity. He was made poet laureate in 1813 and pensioned by the government. Southey replaced his early republicanism with a vigorous Toryism; he contributed to the *Quarterly Review;* he wrote a *Vision of Judgment* (1821) so abjectly worshipful of the Tories and George III that Byron parodied it in his own poem of the same title (1822). In 1839 he married his second wife, Caroline Bowles, but soon became (1839) demented, dying afterward of softening of the brain. His chief poems are *Joan of Arc* (1796), *Thalaba, the Destroyer* (1801), *Madoc* (1805), *The Curse of Kehama* (1810), *Roderick, the Last of the Goths* (1814), and *A Vision of Judgment* (1821). His prose works, considered by many to be far better than his romantic epics, include *History of Brazil* (1810), *Life of Nelson* (1813), *Life of John Wesley* (1820), *History of the Expedition of Orsua and Crimes of Aguirre* (1821), *History of the Peninsular War* (1823), *Book of the Church* (1824), and *Sir Thomas More* (1829). Southey wrote several shorter poems of great popul.irity, such as *The Battle of Blenheim, The Cataract of Lodore, The Inchcape Rock,* and *The Holly Tree.* He edited *The Pilgrim's Progress,* with a life of John Bunyan (1830), wrote *The Doctor* (1834–37), in which the children's story *The Three Bears* appears, and edited William Cowper's works, with his life (1833–37). He also translated *Amadis de Gaul* (1805), *Palmerin of England* (1807), Espriella's *Letters from England* (1807), and *Chronicle of the Cid* (1808). His *Common-Place Book* was edited in 1849–51, and his letters in 1856.

South Kensington Museum (ken′zing.t̯on, -sing-), **The.** A museum, now the Victoria and Albert Museum, at Brompton, London, opened 1857. It contains several museums, the National Gallery of British Art, the Royal College of Science, the National Art Training Schools, libraries, etc.

South Sea Bubble. A financial scheme whereby the South Sea Company (incorporated 1711) assumed a large part of the British national debt in return for an annual fixed sum and a monopoly of British trade with the Pacific islands and South America. It collapsed in 1720.

Southwark (suṭʜ′ärk, south′wärk). A metropolitan borough in SE London, in the County of London, situated on the S bank of the river Thames. The chief London hop markets have been located here for many years. Southwark is comparatively unusual among London boroughs in that high ground rents have long made it necessary for structures to be of more than the two or three stories usual in many parts of the city in order for them to yield a reasonable return on the investment of the landlord.

Southwell (south′wel, -wel̯), **John.** In Shakespeare's *2 Henry VI,* a priest who conjures up a spirit for the Duchess of Gloucester.

Southwell, Robert. b. in Norfolk, England, c1561; executed at Tyburn, London, Feb. 21, 1595. An English poet and Jesuit martyr. He was educated at Paris, and in 1578 was received into the Society of Jesus. In 1586 he returned to England. In 1589 he became domestic chaplain to Ann Howard, Countess of Arundel (it was at about this time that he wrote *Consolations for Catholics* and most of his poems). In 1592 he was betrayed to the authorities; he was tortured, closely imprisoned for three years, and was finally tried at Westminster and executed. In addition to the work cited above, he wrote *Saint Peter's Complaint* (it is his longest poem), and *The Burning Babe,* much admired by Ben Jonson and others since.

South Wind. A novel by Norman Douglas, published in 1917. The work does not have a plot, in the formal sense, but moves forward through the developing characterization of various people on the imaginary island of Nepenthe in the Mediterranean Sea. They are, almost without exception, people whose moral standards and actions would be viewed askance or, in some cases, utterly condemned in ordinary society, and the book portrays the effect they have on Thomas Heard, a gentle English clergyman who has long been bishop of an Anglican diocese in central Africa. He arrives on the island and meets Monsignor Francesco, a sensual cynic; Van Koppen, an American millionaire;

Miss Wilberforce, a frustrated Englishwoman; Ernest Eames, a historian; and Madame Steynlin, who takes a Russian religious fanatic for her lover.

Southwold (south′wōld), **Stephen.** [Pseudonyms, **Neil Bell, Paul Martens.**] b. at Southwold, Suffolk, England, 1887—. An English novelist and writer of books for juveniles. Under his own name he published *In Between Stories* (1923), *Twilight Tales* (1925), *Listen Children! Stories for Spare Moments* (1926), *Once Upon-A-Time Stories* (1927), *Listen Again, Children!* (1928), *Happy Families* (1929), and (all in 1930) *Fiddlededee, Hey, Diddle Diddle, The Hunted One, The Jumpers, Tales Quaint and Queer, The Last Bus, The Welsh Rabbit, Tick-Tock Tales, The Longest Lane, True Tales of an Old Shellback, The Sea Horses, Tales of Forest Folk,* and *Three by Candlelight.* As Neil Bell he wrote the novels *Life and Andrew Otway* (1931), *Precious Porcelain* (1931), *The Marriage of Simon Harper* (1932), *The Disturbing Affair of Noel Blake* (1932), *The Lord of Life* (1933), *Bredon and Sons* (1934), *The Son of Richard Cardon* (1935), *Crocus* (1936), *The Testament of Stephen Fane* (1937), *So Perish the Roses* (1940), *Desperate Pursuit* (1941), and *Tower of Darkness* (1942). As Paul Martens he wrote *Death Rocks the Cradle* (1933), a mystery novel, and *The Truth about My Father* (1934).

Sovereign of the Seas, The. The largest of the early English war-ships (100 guns), launched 1637 at Woolwich.

Sowdone of Babylone (sou′d̯on; bab′i.lon̯), **The.** A Middle English verse romance of the Ferumbras group of the Charlemagne cycle, written c1400. It tells first how Laban (or Balan), the sultan of Babylon, with the help of his son, Ferumbras, sacks Rome and seizes various holy relics. A second portion of the romance deals with the later adventures of Ferumbras in Spain.

Sowerberry (sou′ér.ber.i). In Dickens's *Oliver Twist,* a casket maker to whom Oliver is apprenticed.

Sowerby (sō′ér.bi), **Katherine Githa.** [Married name, **Mrs. John Kendall.**] An English dramatist, author of the play *Rutherford & Son* (1912). Her other works include *Before Breakfast* (1912), *A Man and Some Women* (1914), *Sheila* (1917), *The Stepmother* (1924), and *The Policeman's Whistle* (1934).

Sowerby, Mr. In Anthony Trollope's *Framley Parsonage,* the squire of Chaldicotes, who lives on other people's money.

Spaconia (spa.kō′ni.a̯). A woman in love with Tigranes in Beaumont and Fletcher's play *A King and No King.*

Spalding (spôl′ding), **William.** b. at Aberdeen, Scotland, May 22, 1809; d. Nov. 16, 1859. A Scottish critic, philosopher, and miscellaneous writer.

Spanish Armada. See **Armada, Spanish.**

Spanish Armada, The. The so-called tragedy rehearsed by Mr. Puff in Richard Brinsley Sheridan's *The Critic.*

Spanish Barber, or the Fruitless Precaution, The. A comedy by George Colman the elder, taken from *Le Barbier de Séville* of Beaumarchais, and produced at London in 1777.

---

fat, fāte, fär, a̯sk, fāre; net, mē, hėr; pin, pīne; not, nōte, mōve, nôr; up, lūte, pull; ᴛʜ, then;

Spanish Curate, The. A play by John Fletcher and Philip Massinger, licensed in 1622 and printed in 1647.

Spanish Decretals. See **Isidorian Decretals.**

Spanish Fryar (frī'ạr), **The.** [Full title, **The Spanish Fryar; or, The Double Discovery.**] A comedy (produced 1680) by John Dryden. It is based on Molière's *L'École des femmes* and *Le Médecin malgré lui.*

Spanish Gold. An adventure novel, with an Irish setting, by James Owen Hannay under the pseudonym George A. Birmingham, published in 1908.

Spanish Gypsy (jip'si), **The.** A play by Thomas Middleton (with William Rowley), acted in 1623 and printed in 1653.

Spanish Gypsy, The. A poem by George Eliot, published in 1868.

Spanish Lady, The. A historical novel by Margaret Louisa Woods, published in 1927.

Spanish Moor's Tragedy, The. A play attributed to Thomas Dekker, John Day, and William Haughton, licensed in 1600. No copies of it are now known to exist, but some scholars have conjectured that it may have been an adaptation of *Lust's Dominion.*

Spanish Tragedy, The. [Subtitle, **Hieronimo (or Jeronimo) Is Mad Again!**] A play by Thomas Kyd, sometimes considered the continuation of another play usually called *The First Part of Hieronimo.* It was licensed in 1592 and printed, possibly illegally, in that year. A revision of doubtful authorship was written, probably in 1597; Kyd himself may have written it. The use of madness, murder, revenge, and the supernatural make this play one of the typical Senecan tragedies of the Elizabethan era. Lorenzo, nephew of the King of Spain, and Horatio, son of the Marshal of Spain, Hieronimo, take as prisoner of war Balthazar, son of the Portuguese viceroy. Balthazar falls in love with Bel-imperia, sister of Lorenzo, and for political reasons Lorenzo supports Balthazar's suit. But Bel-imperia, Lorenzo discovers, loves Horatio. One night Lorenzo and Balthazar surprise the lovers in Hieronimo's arbor and kill Horatio. Hieronimo, upon discovering the murder, wildly plots vengeance with Bel-imperia. He arranges to present before the court a play in which he, Bel-imperia, Lorenzo, and Balthazar are performers, and in course of which the two murderers are killed. Bel-imperia and Hieronimo then take their own lives. In addition to the conventions of Senecan tragedy (a chorus, a ghost, and a revenge theme) Kyd's play, in comparison with other plays of his time, has more interesting, compact, and vigorous action, and a more complex moral theme. Hieronimo, crying out for justice in an unjust world, is an important character type, being both villain and hero. His revenge is a crime in terms of the rules of society, although he has a moral right to punish the villains. The play contains much verbal imitation of Seneca, especially his *Thyestes.* The famous speech "O eyes, no eyes, but fountains fraught with tears" was parodied by contemporaries, yet many dramatists borrowed the versatility and dynamics of the florid style. In the best speeches, such as the opening speech of the Ghost, Hieronimo's soliloquies, and the love scene between Bel-imperia and Horatio, the style is ranting but undeniably exciting. The moral theme that sin will inevitably be punished is taken up by other writers such as Marlowe in *Dr. Faustus.* Hieronimo, the avenger, foreshadows Shakespeare's Hamlet and Tourneur's Vendice. Such plays as *Hamlet, King Lear,* and *Macbeth* are further related in episodes, characterization, and devices to Kyd's work. John Marston, in particular, is a follower of Kyd.

Sparagus Garden, or Tom Hoyden of Taunton Dean (spar'ạ.gus; tom hoi'dẹn; tôn'tọn dēn), **The.** A comedy by Richard Brome, acted in 1635 and printed in 1640.

Sparkish (spär'kish). A foppish gallant in William Wycherley's *The Country Wife.* He is supposed to marry Alithea, but loses her to Harcourt through his bumbling arrogance.

Sparkler (spärk'lẹr), **Edmund.** In Dickens's novel *Little Dorrit,* a high-born, somewhat empty-headed young man who marries Fanny Dorrit. He eventually secures a high post in the Circumlocution Office.

Sparsit (spär'sit), **Mrs.** In Charles Dickens's novel *Hard Times,* a lady of high family who serves as Josiah Bounderby's housekeeper. She is anxious to marry Bounderby for his money, and when Bounderby marries Louisa Gradgrind bends every effort to provoke dissension between them.

"spasmodic school." A group of British authors of the middle of the 19th century, including Philip Bailey, George Gilfillan, and Alexander Smith, whose writings were considered to be distinguished by an overstrained and unnatural style. The name, however, properly has a much more extensive scope, being exemplified more or less in nearly all times and countries, both in literature and in art.

The so-called spasmodic school of poetry, whose peculiarities first gained for it a hasty reputation, and then, having suffered under closer critical examination, it almost as speedily dropped out of mind again.   (*Encyc. Brit.*)

S.P.E. Abbreviation of the **Society for Pure English.**

Spec. (spek), **Mr.** One of the many pseudonyms of **Thackeray, William Makepeace.**

Spectator, The. An English periodical, published daily from March 1, 1711, to Dec. 6, 1712. It comprised 555 numbers, of which 274 were by Joseph Addison (including the *Sir Roger de Coverley* papers and critiques on *Paradise Lost*), 236 by Richard Steele, one by Alexander Pope (*The Messiah,* No. 378), and 19 by John Hughes. Eustace Budgell also contributed to it. Addison killed Sir Roger de Coverley in Number 517, "that nobody else might murder him." *The Spectator* was revived by Addison in 1714.

Speculum Meditantis (spek'ū.lum med.i.tan'tis). [Also, **Mirour de l'omme.**] A poem (c1376–78) by John Gower, written in French, consisting of 30,000 lines in which the conflict between the seven vices and virtues is carefully described, concluding with the discovery that since man is corrupt, he must turn to the Virgin Mary for intercession and help. In describing the various groups of men, he presents a detailed picture of late medieval life.

ḍ, d or j; ş, s or sh; ṭ, t or ch; ẓ, z or zh; o, F. cloche; ü, F. menu; ċh, Sc. loch; ṅ, F. bonbon.

Spedding (sped'ing), **James.** b. at Mirehouse, near Bassenthwaite, England, in June, 1808; d. from an injury, at St. George's Hospital, London, March 9, 1881. An English editor, noted especially for his editing of the works of Francis Bacon. From 1835 until 1841 he was a clerk in the Colonial Office, and in 1842 was appointed private secretary of Alexander Baring, Baron Ashburton, in America. From 1857 to 1874 he published *Works, Life, and Letters of Bacon.* In 1878 he published *Account of the Life and Times of Bacon,* and in 1881 *Studies in English History.*

Speed (spēd). In Shakespeare's *Two Gentlemen of Verona,* a servant of Valentine.

Speed, John. b. at Farrington, Cheshire, England, 1552; d. at London, July 28, 1629. An English antiquary. He wrote *History of Great Britain under the Conquests of the Romans, Saxons, Danes, and Normans* (1611) and *Theater of the Empire of Great Britain* (1611), a series of 54 maps of England.

Speed the Plough. A comedy by Thomas Morton, produced in 1800. It contains a reference to Mrs. Grundy, as the bigoted busybody her name has come to represent, in the question (put in country dialect) of one of the chief characters: "What will Mrs. Grundy zay?"

Speke (spēk), **John Hanning.** b. at Jordans, Somersetshire, England, May 4, 1827; d. at Bath, England, Sept. 18, 1864. An English explorer in Africa. After military and scientific service in India, he accompanied Sir R. F. Burton to the great central African lakes (1858), and crossed the continent with James Augustus Grant from Zanzibar over Lake Victoria and down the Nile to Egypt (1860–63). He discovered Lake Victoria and its affluent, the Kagera, or Alexandra Nile, the main source of the Nile. He published *Journal of the Discovery of the Source of the Nile* (1863).

spells. Combinations of words, written or spoken, supposed to be endowed with magical power; incantations; charms. These formed an important part of Old English popular literature. Those in one group preserved from the 10th and 11th centuries are notable for their variety of pattern, their use of repetition (single words or refrains) for metrical as well as mnemonic purposes, and the holdover of pagan elements along with the Christian ("The Anglo-Saxon Charms," by F. Grendon, in *The Journal of American Folk-Lore* (1909); vol. 22, pp. 105–237). They include incantations to the earth, and against snakes, wens, poisonous plants, and stitch in the side.

Spence (spens), **Joseph.** b. at Kingsclere, Hampshire, England, April 25, 1699; drowned at Byfleet, Surrey, England, Aug. 20, 1768. An English critic. His chief works are *Essay on Pope's Odyssey* (1726), *Polymetis* (a work on Roman art and poetry, 1747), and a volume of anecdotes, observations, and characters of books and men.

Spence, Thomas. b. at Newcastle, Northumberland, England, June 21, 1750; d. at London, Sept. 8, 1814. A London bookseller and economist, known as one of the first to advocate the nationalization of land. *The Real Rights of Man,* a paper he submitted (1775) to the Royal Philosophical Society, proposed that parish inhabitants should form a corporation in which all land should be vested. Rent was to be collected by parish officers, and, after deducting expenses, to be distributed among inhabitants. Besides rent, he proposed that there should be no tax. His efforts to obtain wide distribution of this paper brought about his expulsion by the Royal Philosophical Society. The paper, however, was republished with additions under the title *The Meridian Sun of Liberty* (1796) and again by H. M. Hyndman as *The Nationalization of Land in 1775 and 1882* (1882). His views are challenged by Thomas Malthus in the fifth edition of the *Principle of Population.* He also devised a new phonetic system explained in *The Grand Repository of the English Language.* He issued many pamphlets during his lifetime and acquired a number of disciples who called themselves Spenceans and organized (1816) a Society of Spencean Philanthropists.

Spencer (spen'sėr), **Captain.** The gallant young adventurer whose heart is given to Bess Bridges, a tavern maid, in Thomas Heywood's *The Fair Maid of the West.*

Spencer, Herbert. b. at Derby, England, April 27, 1820; d. at Brighton, England, Dec. 8, 1903. An English philosopher, founder of the system named by himself the synthetic philosophy. He was educated by his father, a schoolmaster at Derby, and by his uncle, the Rev. Thomas Spencer, rector of Hinton. He was articled to a civil engineer in 1837, but in 1845 abandoned engineering and devoted himself to literature. He was assistant editor of the *Economist* (1848–53), and in 1882 visited the U. S. where he gave a number of lectures. His first effort in the field of general literature (he had previously published a number of professional papers in the *Civil Engineers' and Architects' Journal*) was a series of letters to the *Nonconformist* on *The Proper Sphere of Government,* which appeared in 1842 and was reprinted in pamphlet form in the following year. In 1855 (four years before the appearance of Charles Darwin's *Origin of Species*) he published his *Principles of Psychology,* which is based on the principle of evolution. The first edition of *Principles of Psychology* had little influence, but the second edition (2 vols., 1870, 1872) has had a great influence on psychology. It contained his statement of evolutionary association, asserting, in effect, that the associate law of frequency operated phylogenetically as well as ontogenetically; thus, the reflexes of lower animals formed the instincts of higher animals. This view influenced William James, and through him helped shape American functionalism. In 1860 he issued a prospectus of his *System of Synthetic Philosophy,* in which, beginning with the first principles of knowledge, he proposed to trace the progress of evolution in life, mind, society, and morality. His works include *Social Statics, or the Conditions Essential to Human Happiness Specified* (1850), *Over-Legislation* (1854), *Essays* (1857–74), *Education: Intellectual, Moral, and Physical* (1861), *Classification of the Sciences* (1864), *Illustrations of Universal Progress* (1864), *The Study of Sociology* (1873), *Descriptive Sociology* (1874–82: compiled under his direction by James Collier, D. Duncan, and Richard Sheppig), *Progress: Its Law and Course* (1881), *The Philosophy of Style* (1882), *The Man versus the State* (1884), *The Factors of Organic Evolution* (reprinted in 1887 from the *Nineteenth Century*), and others. The series announced in 1860 under the general title *A System of Synthetic Philosophy* was published as follows: Vol. I, *First Principles* (1862); Vols. II, III, *The Principles of Biology* (1863 and 1867); Vols. IV, V, *The Principles of Psychology* (1870–72); Vols. VI, VII, VIII, *The Principles of Sociology* (1877: vol. VI includes *The Data of Sociology, The Inductions of Sociology,* and *The Domestic Relations;* vol. VII includes *Ceremonial Institutions*, 1879, *Political Institutions*, 1882, and *Ecclesiastical Institutions*, 1885; vol. VIII was published in 1897); Vols. IX, X, *The Principles of Morality or of Ethics* (vol. IX includes *The Data of Ethics*, 1879, *Induction of Ethics*, 1892, and vol. X contains *Justice*, 1891, and *Negative Beneficence and Positive Beneficence*, 1893).

Spencer, William Robert. b. 1769; d. at Paris, 1834. An English poet. He spent the last ten years of his life at Paris. His principal poems are *vers de société* and ballads, among the latter that of *Beth Gelert, or the Grave of the Grey-Hound.*

Spender (spen'dẽr), **John Alfred.** b. at Bath, Somersetshire, England, 1862; d. at Farnborough, Kent, England, June 21, 1942. An English journalist, historian, and biographer. He was editor (1886–90) of the Hull *Eastern Morning News,* and a staff member (1892–93) of the *Pall Mall Gazette.* He was with the *Westminster Gazette* from its founding (1893), as assistant editor (1893–96) and editor (1896–1922). Author of *The Comments of Bagshot* (1907), *The Indian Scene* (1912), *Foundations of British Policy* (1917), *Life of Sir H. Campbell-Bannerman* (1923), *The Changing East* (1926), *Fifty Years of Europe* (1933), *A Short History of Our Times* (1934), *The Government of Man* (1938), and *New Lamps and Ancient Lights* (1940); two volumes of memoirs, *Life, Journalism and Politics,* were published in 1927.

Spender, Stephen (Harold). b. May 28, 1909—. An English poet, critic, and essayist. He founded, with Cyril Connolly, the magazine *Horizon.* His books include *Poems* (1933), *Vienna* (1934), *The Destructive Element* (1935), *The Burning Cactus* (1936), *Forward from Liberalism* (1937), *The New Realism* (1939), *Poems for Spain* (1939), *The Still Center* (1939), *The Backward Sun* (1940), *Ruins and Visions* (1942), *Life and the Poet* (1942), and others. Author of the verse drama *Trial of a Judge* (1938).

Spenlow (spen'lō), **Dora.** The frail "child-wife" of David Copperfield, in Dickens's *David Copperfield.*

Spenlow, Francis. In Dickens's novel *David Copperfield,* the father of Dora Spenlow. He is a proctor of the firm of Spenlow and Jorkins.

Spenlow and Jorkins (jôr'kinz). In Dickens's novel *David Copperfield,* the firm to which David is articled. The phrase "Spenlow and Jorkins" has passed into the language as a means of referring to a partnership or other undertaking in which one principal blames his own harshness on the other (from Mr. Spenlow's custom of telling his employees that he would be only too happy to grant their various requests, but that the cold and implacable Mr. Jorkins "wouldn't hear of it." In fact, it was Mr. Spenlow who "wouldn't hear of it," and Mr.

Jorkins was being used simply as a means of shifting the blame).

Spens (spens), **Sir Patrick.** The subject of a Scottish ballad, of which 18 versions are recorded. According to one of these, Sir Patrick (a sailor, the best that sailed upon the sea) was sent to Norway by the king of Scotland, to conduct the king's daughter to be queen of Norway. The vessel sank off the Orkneys in a storm.

Spenser (spen'sẽr), **Alice.** See under **Amaryllis.**

Spenser, Edmund. b. at London, c1552; d. at Westminster (now part of London), Jan. 13, 1599. An English poet. He was educated at the Merchant Taylors' School, London, and at Pembroke College, Cambridge (1569–76), where he associated with Gabriel Harvey, Edward Kirke, and other men of note. Afterward, he became intimate with Sir Philip Sidney and Robert Dudley, 1st Earl of Leicester, who did much for him. In 1580 he went to Ireland as secretary to Lord Grey of Wilton. Until about 1588 he was resident usually at or near Dublin. Prominent among the men of letters there who were his close friends were Geoffrey Fenton and Lodowick Bryskett. From 1588 to 1598 he resided chiefly on his estate at Kilcolman in Munster in the southwestern part of Ireland. He returned to London with Sir Walter Raleigh in 1589 with the first three books of the *Faerie Queene,* which he published there in 1590, dedicating the work to Queen Elizabeth. In 1591 he returned to Kilcolman Castle, and on June 11, 1594, he married Elizabeth Boyle. In his *View of Ireland* (written c1596; published 1633) Spenser advocates the necessity of severe measures to reform Ireland. Kilcolman Castle was burned by the Irish rebels in 1598, and Spenser fled with his family to Cork, whence he went to London, where he died about four weeks later. He was buried near Geoffrey Chaucer in Westminster Abbey. His first poems, translations from Petrarch and Joachim du Bellay, were published in John van der Noodt's *Theatre* (1569). His chief poems are *The Shepherd's Calendar* (1579), *The Faerie Queene* (1590–96), *Daphnaïda* (1591), *Complaints,* including "Tears of the Muses," "Mother Hubbard's Tale," and others (1591), *Colin Clout's Come Home Again, Astrophel, Amoretti,* and *Epithalamion* (1595), and *Four Hymns* and *Prothalamion* (1596).

Spenserian (spen.sir'i.ạn). Of or pertaining to the English poet Edmund Spenser; specifically, denoting the style of versification adopted by Spenser in his *Faerie Queene.* It consists of a strophe of eight decasyllabic lines and an Alexandrine, with three rhymes, the first and third line forming one, the second, fourth, fifth, and seventh another, and the sixth, eighth, and ninth the third. It is the stateliest of English measures, and is used by Thomson in his *Castle of Indolence,* by Byron in his *Childe Harold,* etc.

Sphinx (sfingks). In Greek legend, a monster having a winged lion's body and a woman's head and bust. It was thought to have frequented a high rock near the gate of Thebes and waylaid passersby, asking them: "What creature walks on four legs in the morning, on two at noon, and on three in the evening?" And she devoured all those who could not answer the riddle. When Oedipus came to Thebes, he answered correctly: "Man, who crawls on all fours as a babe, walks upright in his prime, and needs a cane in old age." The Sphinx thereupon perished (or killed herself), and Oedipus entered Thebes as deliverer of the people from the monster.

Spinoza (spi.nō′zạ), **Baruch** (or **Benedict**). b. at Amsterdam, Netherlands, Nov. 24, 1632; d. at The Hague, Netherlands, Feb. 21, 1677. A Dutch philosopher, the greatest modern exponent of pantheism. His parents were members of the Jewish community of Amsterdam, a community largely consisting of persons who had fled Spain or Portugal, or descendants of such persons. Spinoza's family occupied an important position in the group. He received rabbinical training in a school for Jewish boys, and, in addition, pursued secular studies (Latin, mathematics, and probably scholastic philosophy) in a school established in 1652 by Franz van den Enden. The latter was suspected of atheism, which added to the suspicions directed upon Spinoza. The religious situation in Amsterdam was complex, and the Jewish community was confronted by many difficulties. Spinoza was suspected of heresy, and on July 27, 1656, was publicly condemned and excommunicated. After this he lived in various places, earning his living by tutoring and by grinding lenses. He lived with a friend (a Remonstrant) just outside of Amsterdam until about the beginning of 1661, when they removed to the village of Rhynsburg, near Leiden. In 1664 he went to Voorburg, a suburb of The Hague, and in 1670 took up his residence at The Hague itself. An attempt upon his life was made at Amsterdam in 1656. In 1673 he was offered a professorial post at Heidelberg, but he refused it as a disturbing influence in his way to a peaceful life. He was a student of the philosophy of Descartes, and his metaphysical speculations have the Cartesian philosophy as their point of departure. He died of tuberculosis, his end being probably hastened by his grinding of lenses. Spinoza was noted for the charm and simplicity of his manners. In the highest sense of the term, he was a gentleman and received the admiring and unswerving loyalty of his friends. However austere in his manner of living, he was capable of deep feeling. Aristocratic in spirit, he nevertheless had a passionate longing for human welfare, unity, and peace. There are few indeed who would deny today that Spinoza must rank with the very greatest philosophical minds. He was a person of profound religious conviction. In view of this, and because of the conditions of his age, the incessant conflicts of theological doctrines pointed to a problem that, for Spinoza, was of the utmost theoretical and practical urgency. It is reasonable to think that his philosophical work was motivated by his desire to solve the problem. It is of great significance, for an understanding of Spinoza's philosophy, even on its technical side, that in 1665 he seems to have postponed completion of the *Ethica ordine geometrico demonstrata* (the mature statement of his philosophical position, published posthumously) in order to compose the *Tractatus theologico-politicus* (published in 1670). The latter work was designed to serve the cause of religious and political freedom by distinguishing between religious faith and the speculative interpretations of the faith. Traditional theological doctrines had arisen by a process of interaction between philosophical speculation and Scripture, leading to the fallacy of identifying the purport of the latter with theological doctrine. The Bible, he declared, leaves Reason absolutely free, has nothing in common with philosophy, and its essential object is the inculcation of piety and obedience. There is, indeed, a universal religion. To it belong "only such dogmas as are absolutely required to attain obedience to God." In these dogmas the real meaning of revelation is to be found. Philosophical speculation is a matter of the intellect, not of the imagination and its anthropomorphic analogies, and its sole function is the articulated display of the nature of being, of truth. The bitter divisions of mankind are due neither to the articles of a universal religion, nor to philosophy, but to theological doctrines with their inadequacies due to the confusion of images with ideas, and still more to the identification of such doctrines with the moral teaching of Scripture. Theological speculation, as such, is a matter of freedom of thought. But it should not be confused with religious faith, and political power should not be enlisted in support of theological speculative positions. To have mankind come to understand all this would insure unity, peace, and freedom. It is notable that the mature exposition of Spinoza's philosophy, a masterpiece of metaphysics, is called the *Ethics*. Its towering structure is the intellectual complementation of the counsels of piety and obedience forming the content of universal faith. Part I has the title "Concerning God." The concluding Part V is called "Of the Power of the Intellect, or of Human Liberty." As the teachings of universal faith enjoin love of and obedience to God and love of one's neighbor, so the truths of metaphysics, the articulated intellectual revelation of the nature of reality itself, culminate in the intellectual love of God, the vision of the eternal, and the recognition of man's participation therein.

Spiritual Quixote (kẹ.hō′tẹ), **The.** [Full title, **The Spiritual Quixote; or, the Summer's Ramble of Mr. Geoffrey Wildgoose** (jef′ri wīld′gōs).] A novel by Richard Graves, published in 1772. It recounts, in a satirical vein, the adventures of Geoffrey Wildgoose, a convert to Methodism, who is accompanied on his missionary activities by Jerry Tugwell, the village cobbler.

Spitalfields (spit′ạl.fēldz). A quarter in London, N of the Tower of London, long noted as a seat of silk manufacture, which was introduced by French refugees expelled in 1685, on the revocation of the Edict of Nantes. It once belonged to the Priory of Saint Mary Spital, founded in 1197.

Spleen, The. A poem by Matthew Green, published in 1796. It extols the virtues of a meditative life.

Spoils of Poynton (poin′tọn), **The.** A novel (1879) by Henry James.

spondee (spon′dē). In prosody, a foot consisting of two long times or syllables, one of which constitutes the thesis and the other the arsis: it is accordingly tetrasemic and isorrhythmic. The spondee is principally used as a substitute for a dactyl or an anapest. In the former case it is a *dactyl spondee* (⌣— for ⌣ ⌣), in the latter an anapestic spondee

(— ⌣ for ⌣). An *irrational spondee* represents a trisemic foot, trochee, or iambus (⌣ — for ⌣ ⌣, or — ⌣ for ⌣ ⌣). It is found in the even places of trochaic lines and in the odd places of iambic lines, also in logaoedic verses, especially as representing the initial trochee ("basis"). A foot consisting of two spondees is called a *dispondee*.

Sporus (spō'rus). A favorite of the emperor Nero. He was a beautiful youth of slave parentage, and is said to have possessed a striking resemblance to Nero's wife Poppaea Sabina. After her death in 65 A.D., Nero had him castrated and dressed as a woman, and gave him the name of Sabina, publicly going through the ceremony of marriage with him in Greece in 67. Sporus fled with Nero from Rome on the insurrection of Galba in the following year, and was reputedly present at his suicide. He was afterward intimate with the emperor Otho, a former companion in debauchery of Nero, and ultimately committed suicide under Vitellius to avoid the indignity of appearing under degrading circumstances as a girl on the stage.

Spottiswoode (spot'is.wŭd), **Alicia Ann.** b. at Spottiswoode, Lauder, Scotland, 1801 (or 1810); d. 1890 (or March 12, 1900). A Scottish composer and poet. She married (1836) Lord John Scott (1809–60), and again assumed her maiden name when she succeeded to the Spottiswoode estate in 1870. She composed the music for *Annie Laurie*, *Douglas*, *Tender and True*, *The Comin' o' the Spring*, and many other popular songs.

Sprat (sprat), **Jack.** See **Jack Sprat.**

Sprat, Thomas. b. in Dorsetshire, England, 1635; d. at Bromley, England, May 20, 1713. An English prelate, bishop of Rochester (1684 *et seq.*). He was a member of James II's ecclesiastical commission. He wrote a history of the Royal Society, an account of the Rye House Plot, poems, and others.

Spreading the News. A comedy (1904) by Augusta Gregory (Lady Gregory).

Spring (spring), **Howard.** b. at Cardiff, Wales, Feb. 10, 1889—. A British novelist. Author of *Shabby Tiger* (1934), *Rachel Rosing* (1935), *My Son! My Son!* (1938; published in England as *O Absalom*), *Fame Is the Spur* (1940), *Hard Facts* (1944), *Dunkerley's* (1946), and *There Is No Armour* (1948). He also wrote the autobiographical *Heaven Lies about Us* (1939), *In the Meantime* (1942), *And Another Thing* (1946), and *The Houses In Between* (1951).

Spring, The. A poem by Thomas Carew contrasting the warmth and tenderness of the spring season, which wakens the birds and causes "all things smile," with the coldness of his beloved:

    Only she doth carry
    June in her eyes, in her heart January.

Spring Garden (spring). A place of refreshment in St. James's Park, London, much frequented in the 17th century.

sprung rhythm. A type of meter associated with the poetry of Gerard Manley Hopkins, who explains it thus: "Sprung Rhythm . . . is measured by feet of from one to four syllables, and for particular effects any number of weak or slack [unaccented] syllables may be used. It has one stress, which falls on the only syllable, if there is only one, or if there are more, then . . . on the first, and so gives rise to four sorts of feet. . . . And there will be four corresponding natural rhythms; but nominally the feet are mixed and any one may follow any other." Scansion of a work in this meter is not a line-by-line process as in regular rhythm but involves the whole stanza as one line. Hopkins, in a letter to Bridges concerning his poem *The Deutschland*, said he used sprung rhythm because "it is nearest to the rhythm of prose, that is the native and natural rhythm of speech, the least forced, the most rhetorical, and emphatic of all possible rhythms, combining as it seems to me opposite and, one would have thought incompatible, excellences."

Spurgeon (sper'jon), **Charles Haddon.** b. at Kelvedon, Essex, England, June 19, 1834; d. at Menton, France, Jan. 31, 1892. An English Baptist preacher. He was educated at Colchester and Maidstone, and became usher in a private school at Cambridge. In 1851 he became pastor of the Baptist church at Waterbeach, 5 mi. from Cambridge, while retaining his place as usher. He accepted a call to the pastorate of the New Park Street Baptist Church in Southwark, London, in 1853, removing with his congregation in 1861 to a large new edifice, the Tabernacle, in Newington, London. He was also the founder of a pastors' college, schools, almshouses, and an orphanage; and he edited a monthly magazine, *The Sword and the Trowel*. He opposed the doctrine of baptismal regeneration and was also an opponent of modern Biblical criticism as being destructive of true orthodoxy. Among his works are *The Treasury of David: Exposition of the Book of Psalms* (1870–85), *Feathers for Arrows, or Illustrations for Preachers and Teachers* (1870), *Lectures to My Students* (1875–77), *Commenting and Commentaries: together with a Catalogue of Biblical Commentaries and Expositions* (1876), *John Ploughman's Pictures: More of His Plain Talk* (1880), and 50 volumes of his very popular sermons.

Spurio (spū'ri.ō). The illegitimate son of the Duke in Cyril Tourneur's *The Revenger's Tragedy*.

Spurs, Battle of the. See **Battle of the Spurs.**

Square (skwâr). In Henry Fielding's novel *Tom Jones*, one of Tom's and Blifil's instructors, who is actually a great hypocrite. See also **Thwackum.**

Squeamish (skwē'mish), **Lady.** A character in William Wycherley's *The Country Wife*.

Squeamish, Lady. A character in Thomas Otway's *Friendship in Fashion*.

Squeers (skwirz), **Fanny.** In Dickens's novel *Nicholas Nickleby*, the unprepossessing daughter of Wackford Squeers. From her mother she inherited "a voice of harsh quality"; from her father she derived "a remarkable expression of the right eye, something akin to having none at all."

Squeers, Master Wackford. In Dickens's novel *Nicholas Nickleby*, the bumptious son of Wackford Squeers. However, "as his chief amusement was to tread upon the other boys' toes in his new boots. his flow of spirits was rather disagreeable than otherwise."

Squeers, Mr. Wackford. The cruel and ignorant schoolmaster of Dotheboys Hall, in Yorkshire; a character in Dickens's *Nicholas Nickleby*.

ḍ, d or j; ṣ, s or sh; ṭ, t or ch; ẓ, z or zh; o, F. cloche; ü, F. menu; ċh, Sc. loch; ṅ, F. bonbon.

Squint (skwint), **Lawyer.** In Oliver Goldsmith's *Citizen of the World*, a very plausible, personable, and adaptable man, the politician *par excellence*. He is able to contrive a "seasonable thought" upon any subject that may come up.

Squintum (skwin'tum), **Dr.** In Samuel Foote's *The Minor*, a nonconformist clergyman. He is a satire on the well-known 18th-century Methodist, George Whitefield. The choice of the name "Squintum" was doubtless suggested by the fact that Whitefield had a cast in one eye.

Squire (skwīr), **J. C.** [Full name, Sir **John Collings Squire**; pseudonym in early writings, **Solomon Eagle**.] b. at Plymouth, England, April 2, 1884—. An English journalist, editor, and critic. He founded and edited (1919–34) the London *Mercury*. Among his books are *Imaginary Speeches* (1912), *The Three Hills and Other Poems* (1913), *The Birds, and Other Poems* (1919), *Collected Parodies* (1921), *Essays on Poetry* (1924), *Apes and Parrots* (1928), *Sunday Mornings* (1930), *The Honeysuckle Bee* (1937), and *Water Music* (1939). In collaboration with John L. Balderston, he wrote the play *Berkeley Square* (1928).

Squire Allworthy (ôl'wėr″ᴛʜi). See **Allworthy, Squire.**

Squire Hardcastle (härd'kȧs″l). See **Hardcastle, Squire.**

Squire of Alsatia (al.sā'shȧ), **The.** A comedy by Thomas Shadwell, produced in 1688. There is a comic contrast of two fathers and two sons patterned on that in Terence's *Adelphi;* use was also made of Molière's *L'École des maris*, and the fourth act is modeled on his *L'Avare*. It was Shadwell's purpose to show how an easy-going father produces good qualities in a son and a strict one produces the opposite.

Squire of Dames. In Spenser's *Faerie Queene*, a young nobleman who is set a one-year task by his lady, Columbell, to help women in distress. At the end of the year, after he has helped 300 women, she sends him on a three-year mission, to exact 300 pledges of chastity from various ladies. He is, however, able to exact only three, one of them from a courtesan, the second from a nun, and the third from a peasant girl.

Squire of Low Degree, The. A Middle English verse romance of the early 14th century, concerning a low-born squire and his love for the daughter of the king of Hungary. After seven years, during which time the squire is imprisoned, presumed dead, and mourned by the princess, the king consents to their marriage.

Squire's Tale, The. One of Chaucer's *Canterbury Tales*. It is an Eastern romance told by the Squire "who left half told the story of Cambuscan bold," which John Milton wished Musaeus or Orpheus could finish. Edmund Spenser tried to finish it in the fourth book of *The Faerie Queene*. Cambuscan (or Cambyuskan) is a king of Tartary who receives from the king of Arabia magical birthday gifts of extraordinary power, a ring, a glass, a sword, and a brazen horse. Canace, his daughter, wears the ring, which enables the wearer to understand the language of birds, and hears the story of a falcon deserted by her lover. The poet promises to tell

also the adventures of the king and of his two sons, Camballo and Algarsife, but the tale is broken off. The Squire is the gay young son of the Knight (who tells the first tale):

> A lovyere, and a lusty bacheler,
> With lokkes crulle, as they were leyd in presse.
> Of twenty yeer of age he was, I gesse. . . .
> Singinge he was, or floytinge, al the day;
> He was as fresh as is the month of May.
> So hote he lovede, that by nightertale
> He sleep namore than dooth a nightingale.
> Curteys he was, lowly, and servisable,
> And carf biform his fader at the table.

Squire Sullen (sul'ẹn). See **Sullen, Squire.**

Squire Western (wes'tẽrn). See **Western, Squire.**

Stabat Mater (stäbät mä'ter, stā'bat mä'tẽr). In the Roman Catholic liturgy, a sequence on the Virgin Mary at the crucifixion, written c1300 by Jacobus de Benedictis (Jacopone da Todi). It is so called from the first words of the Latin text, *Stabat mater*, "The mother (of Jesus) was standing." It has also been ascribed to Pope Innocent III and others, and was probably modeled on older hymns such as the *staurotheotokia* of the Greek Church. It is sung after the Epistle on the feast of the Seven Dolours of the Blessed Virgin Mary, on the Friday before Good Friday, and on the third Sunday in September. Music for it has been written by Palestrina, Pergolesi, Rossini, Haydn, Dvořák, and others.

Stables (stā'blz), **William Gordon.** b. at Aberchirder, Marnoch, Banffshire, Scotland, May 21, 1840; d. at Reading, Berkshire, England, May 10, 1910. A Scottish writer of books for young people. As an assistant surgeon (1863–71) in the Royal Navy and in the merchant service he visited India, Africa, and the South Seas. Author of more than 100 books, among them *Wild Adventures in Wild Places* (1881), *The Cruise of the Snowbird* (1882) and its sequel, *Wild Adventures round the Pole* (1883), *The Hermit Hunter of the Wilds* (1889), *Westward with Columbus* (1889), *Kidnapped by Cannibals* (1899), and *In Regions of Perpetual Snow* (1904), adventure stories for boys; *Friends in Fur* (1877) and *Our Friend the Dog* (1884), animal stories; and *'Twixt Daydawn and Light* (1898) and *On War's Red Ride* (1900), historical novels.

Staël (stäl), **Mme. de.** [Full name, **Anne Louise Germaine Necker**, Baronne **de Staël-Holstein**.] b. at Paris, April 22, 1766; d. there, July 14, 1817. French writer; daughter of Jacques Necker. As a child she enjoyed in her own home the society of men like Buffon, Marmontel, Grimm, and Gibbon, who were all personal friends of her father. She especially admired Jean Jacques Rousseau, and devoted to him her first serious essay, *Lettres sur le caractère et les écrits de J. J. Rousseau* (1788). In 1786 she was married to the Baron of Staël-Holstein, ambassador from Sweden to France; he died in 1802. Madame de Staël was in Germany (1803–04), and met both Goethe and Schiller at Weimar. In 1805 she took a short trip to Italy. In 1800 she published one of her best works, *De la littérature considerée dans ses rapports avec les institutions sociales*. In 1802 appeared her novel *Delphine*, and in 1807 *Corinne*. She returned to Germany in 1808 to finish *De l'Allemagne*, her best-known work. The first edition (Paris, 1810) was destroyed, presumably at the instigation of Napoleon (who consistently evinced a spirit of what can only be called petty enmity toward her). She also wrote *Considérations sur la révolution française* (1818). Other works by her, published posthumously, are *Dix années d'exil* and *Essais dramatiques* (1821), and finally her *Œuvres inédites* (1836).

Stafford (staf'ọrd), **Edward, Henry,** and **Humphrey.** Historical figures in Shakespeare's plays. See under **Buckingham, Duke of.**

Stafford, Lord. In Shakespeare's *3 Henry VI*, a supporter of the Yorkist faction.

Stafford, Sir Humphrey and **William.** In Shakespeare's *2 Henry VI*, brothers, members of an armed force which tries to stop the rebel, Jack Cade, and his men. The two Staffords are killed.

Stage Defended, The. A tract (1726) by John Dennis, written in answer to Law's *Absolute Unlawfulness of the Stage-Entertainment.*

"Stagirite" (stạ.jĭ'rīt). See **Aristotle.**

Stahl (stäl), **Jacob.** The architect hero of three novels by John Davys Beresford, *The Early History of Jacob Stahl* (1911), *A Candidate for Truth* (1912), and *The Invisible Event* (1915).

St. Albans (sānt ôl'bạnz). An English monastery of the Benedictine order, at what is now the city of St. Albans, in Hertfordshire, founded by King Offa of Mercia in 793 on the site where Saint Alban is said to have been martyred c300. In the 13th century it became noted as a center of historical writing because of the work of a series of chroniclers, including Roger of Wendover and Matthew Paris.

St. Albans, Viscount. A title of **Bacon, Francis.**

St. Aldegonde (ôl'dẹ.gọnd, al'-), **Lord.** In Benjamin Disraeli's novel *Lothair*, the witty and agreeable young heir to a dukedom. He avows himself an ardent believer in a republican form of government, being "opposed to all privileges and all orders of men except dukes, who [are] a necessity."

Stalky (stô'ki, stôl'-). The principal figure in Rudyard Kipling's *Stalky and Co.* He is the strategist and tactician who conceives the plots and guides the trio in their various escapades.

Stalky and Co. A collection of stories for boys by Rudyard Kipling, serialized in 1899 and since published several times in book form. The stories deal with the adventures of three boys in an English school: Stalky, who is the leader in their various escapades; M'Turk, who is the gentleman of the trio; and Beetle, who is now generally considered to be Kipling's autobiographical portrait of himself.

Stamboul Train (stam.bôl'). A novel by Graham Greene, published in 1932.

Standard, Battle of the. Victory gained by the English, led by Archbishop Thurstan, over the Scots under King David, near Northallerton, Yorkshire, in 1138: so called from the English banner.

Stanhope (stan'ọp), **Lady Hester Lucy.** b. at London, March 12, 1776; d. at Djoun, in what is now Lebanon, June 23, 1839. A daughter of Charles Stanhope, 3rd Earl Stanhope, niece of William Pitt, and from 1803 the head of Pitt's household and his private secretary. She attended his deathbed. In February, 1810, she left England and established a small satrapy at Djoun in the Lebanon mountains. In 1832 Ibrahim Pasha, when about to invade Syria, was obliged to secure her neutrality. Her *Memoirs, as Related by Herself in Conversation with Her Physician* (Dr. Meryon) were published in 1845, and later (1846) the *Memoirs* were supplemented by her *Travels.*

Stanhope, Philip Dormer. [Title: 4th Earl of Chesterfield; pseudonym, **Geffery Broadbottom.**] b. at London, Sept. 22, 1694; d. there, March 24, 1773. An English statesman, orator, wit, and patron of letters. Whig member of Parliament for St. Germans (1715–23) and for Lostwithiel (1722–25), he succeeded to his father's title in 1726, entering the House of Lords. He served as ambassador (1728–32) to The Hague, lord high steward (1730), again ambassador to The Hague (1744), lord lieutenant of Ireland (1745–46), and secretary of state (1746–48), before quitting politics because of growing deafness. His name long a synonym for fine manners and worldliness, he is best remembered as the recipient of Johnson's stinging letter (Feb. 7, 1755) which killed the system of literary patronage as the author of the *Letters to His Son* (1774) written to his illegitimate son, Philip (1732–68), and intended to educate the youth in the ways of the world, and for his friendship with Alexander Pope, Jonathan Swift, and Henry St. John, Viscount Bolingbroke. A leader of the House of Lords opposition to George II, he denounced the government in letters to the press written under the name Geffery Broadbottom.

Stanhope, Philip Henry. [Titles: 5th Earl **Stanhope;** designated by the courtesy title Lord **Mahon** before his accession to the earldom.] b. Jan. 30, 1805; d. at Bournemouth, England, Dec. 24, 1875. An English historian and politician; grandson of Charles Stanhope, 3rd Earl Stanhope. He wrote *History of England from the Peace of Utrecht to the Peace of Versailles* (1836–53), *The War of Succession in Spain* (1832); lives of Belisarius, Condé, Joan of Arc, and William Pitt; and a *History of England, Comprising the Reign of Anne until the Peace of Utrecht* (1870).

Stanley (stan'li), **Arthur Penrhyn.** b. at Alderley, Cheshire, England, Dec. 13, 1815; d. at London, July 18, 1881. An English divine, historian, and theological writer. He was a tutor at Oxford (1843–51), canon of Canterbury (1851–56), and professor of ecclesiastical history at Oxford (1856–63). He was appointed dean of Westminster in 1863 and entered office in 1864. He traveled in Egypt and Palestine (1852–53), in Russia in 1857, in Egypt and Palestine with the Prince of Wales in 1862, and in America in 1878. His works include *Life and Correspondence of Thomas Arnold* (1844), *Sermons on the Apostolic Age* (1847), *Commentary on the Epistles to the Corinthians* (1855), *Memorials of Canterbury* (1855), *Sinai and Palestine* (1856), *Lectures on the History of the Eastern Church* (1861), *History of the Jewish Church* (1863–76), *Historical Memorials of Westminster Abbey* (1868), *Essays on Church and State* (1870), *Church of Scotland* (1872), and *Christian Institutions* (1881).

Stanley, Lord. In Shakespeare's *Richard III*, a lord attending Richard. He is mistrusted by Rich-

---

ḍ, d or j; ṣ, s or sh; ṭ, t or ch; ẓ, z or zh; o, F. cloche; ü, F. menu; čh, Sc. loch; ṅ, F. bonbon.

ard because his wife is the mother (by Henry Tudor) of Richmond. Richard keeps Stanley's son, George, as hostage when Richmond lands in England, and on the eve of Bosworth Stanley tells Richmond he cannot openly help him. However, he also refuses to help Richard. In one quarto and folio he is called the Earl of Derby.

Stanley, Sir Hubert. An impoverished squire in Thomas Morton's comedy *A Cure for the Heart Ache* (1797). The well-known phrase "Approbation from Sir Hubert Stanley is praise indeed" occurs in Act v, scene 2.

Stanley, Sir John. In Shakespeare's *2 Henry VI*, the escort of the Duchess of Gloucester when she goes into exile.

Stanley, Sir William. In Shakespeare's *3 Henry VI*, a member of the Yorkist faction.

Stanley, Thomas. b. in Hertfordshire, England, 1625; d. at London, April 12, 1678. An English translator, poet, and miscellaneous writer, author of a *History of Philosophy* (1655–62).

Stanley Ortheris (ôr'the̱.ris). See **Ortheris, Stanley.**

Stannard (stan'ạrd), **Henrietta Eliza Vaughan.** [Pseudonyms: **Violet Whyte, John Strange Winter;** maiden name, **Palmer.**] b. at York, England, Jan. 13, 1856; d. at Putney, London, Dec. 14, 1911. An English novelist, short-story writer, and journalist. She began her literary career in 1874, writing sketches and serial novels of military life for the *Family Herald*, using first the pseudonym Violet Whyte and then John Strange Winter, a name she had used for a character in her first book. Author of *Cavalry Life* (1881), *Regimental Legends* (1883), *Bootles' Baby: A Story of the Scarlet Lancers* (1885), *Army Society* (1886), *Bootles' Children* (1888), *Grip* (1896), *The Man I Loved* (1901), *Uncle Charles* (1902), and *Love and Twenty* (1905). *Bootles' Baby*, a best seller in its day, sold more than two million copies.

St. Anne (sānt an'), **Earl of.** A character in George Chapman's *Monsieur D'Olive* who, in rather macabre taste, retains the body of his dead countess in his chamber because he cannot bear to leave her. He is cured of this peculiar behavior by Vandome, who has him act as his agent in making love to Eurione. The latter bears a certain resemblance to the Earl's dead wife, and the Earl presently finds himself in love with her. He thereupon buries his wife and welcomes Eurione: "The grace and fashion of my other wife, You have reviv'd her to my loving thoughts."

Stanyhurst (stan'i̱.hèrst), **Richard.** b. at Dublin, 1547; d. at Brussels, 1618. An Irish miscellaneous author and translator; an uncle of Archbishop Usher. He was educated at University College, Oxford, and studied law at Furnival's Inn. Later he became the chaplain of Albert, Archduke of Austria, the governor of the Spanish Netherlands. He translated the first four books of Vergil's *Aeneid*, printed with translations of four of the Psalms at Leiden in 1582, and the next year at London. He also wrote the description of Ireland in Holinshed's *Chronicles*, a life of Saint Patrick (1587), and others.

stanza. In versification, a series of lines arranged in a fixed order of sequence as regards their length, metrical forms, or rhymes, and constituting a typi-

cal group, or one of a number of similar groups, composing a poem or part of a poem. *Stanza* is often used interchangeably with *strophe*—strophe, however, being used preferably of ancient or quantitative, and stanza of modern or accentual and rhymed poetry. In the latter the stanza often consists of lines identical in form throughout, the arrangement of rhymes alone defining the group of lines. Such a stanza is not properly a strophe. A couplet is not regarded as a stanza, and a triplet is rarely so designated. Abbreviated *st.*

> Horace . . . confines himself strictly to one sort of verse, or stanza, in every Ode.
> (Dryden, *Misc.*, Pref.)

Staple Inn (stā'pl). One of the old Inns of Chancery, situated in Holborn, London. In one of its courtyards Mr. Snagsby was wont to walk on pleasant summer days in Dickens's *Bleak House*, and Mr. Grewgious, in the same novel, lived in one of the houses in its second quadrangle.

Staple of News, The. A comedy (1625) by Ben Jonson.

Stapleton (stā'pl.ton) or **Stapylton** (-pil-), **Sir Robert.** d. 1669. An English soldier, translator, dramatist, and poet. He was a student at Douai, but was converted to Protestantism, and became gentleman usher to King Charles II. He translated Juvenal and Musaeus, and wrote three plays, *The Slighted Maid* (acted in 1663), *The Stepmother* (acted in 1663), and *Hero and Leander*, based on Musaeus (printed in 1669).

Star and Garter, The. A famous tavern formerly standing in Pall Mall, London.

Star Chamber. In English history, a former court of civil and criminal jurisdiction at Westminster, London. It was constituted in view of offenses and controversies most frequent at the royal court, or affecting the interests of the crown, such as maintenance, fraud, libel, conspiracy, or riots resulting from faction or oppression, but freely took jurisdiction of other crimes and misdemeanors, and administered justice by arbitrary authority instead of according to the common law. Such a jurisdiction was exercised at least as early as the reign of Henry VI, the tribunal then consisting of the privy council. A statute passed under Henry VII authorized a committee of the council to exercise such a jurisdiction, and this tribunal grew in power (although successive statutes from the time of Edward IV were enacted to restrain it) until it fell into disuse in the latter part of the reign of Henry VIII. In 1640 the court of Star Chamber was abolished by an act reciting that "the reasons and motives inducing the erection and continuance of that court [of Star Chamber] do now cease."

Stareleigh (stär'li), **Mr. Justice.** In Dickens's *Pickwick Papers*, the judge who presided in the ludicrous breach-of-promise case of Bardell vs. Pickwick.

Stark (stärk), **Freya Madeleine.** b. at Paris, —. An English writer and traveler, especially in the Arab countries. She was associated (1939 *et seq.*) with the British Ministry of Information. Her travel books include *Baghdad Sketches* (1933), *The Valleys of the Assassins* (1934), *The Southern Gates of Arabia* (1936), *Seen in the Hadhramaut* (1939), *A Winter*

---

fat, fāte, fär, ȧsk, fāre; net, mē, hėr; pin, pīne; not, nōte, mŏve, nôr; up, lūte, pŭll; ᴛʜ, then;

in Arabia (1940), *Letters from Syria* (1942), *East Is West* (1945), and *Perseus in the Wind* (1948); she wrote *The Freya Stark Story* (1953).

Starkey (stär′ki), **James.** [Pseudonym, **Seumas O'Sullivan.**] b. at Dublin, 1879—. An Irish poet, active in the Irish literary revival. He has contributed to the *Irish Homestead* and *The United Irishman*, and has been editor of *The Dublin Magazine* since 1923. His verse includes *The Twilight People* (1905), *Verses, Sacred and Profane* (1908), *Selected Lyrics* (1910), *Poems* (1912), *Requiem* (1917), *Poems* (1923), *Twenty-five Lyrics* (1933), *Personal Talk* (1936), and *Collected Poems* (1940). His essays include *Impressions* (1912), *Mud and People* (1917), and *Common Adventures* (1926).

Starveling (stärv′ling), **Robin.** In Shakespeare's *Midsummer Night's Dream*, a tailor who is cast in the part of the mother in the interpolated play. He actually has no lines to speak and plays Moonshine instead.

Statius (stā′shus), **Publius Papinius.** b. c45 A.D.; d. c96. A Roman poet, court poet to Domitian. He wrote the epics *Thebais* and *Achilleis* (unfinished), and the collection *Silvae.*

Stator (stā′tôr). See **Jupiter Stator.**

Statue and the Bust, The. A long poem (1855) by Robert Browning, based on the story of the love of Duke Ferdinando de' Medici and a woman kept prisoner by her jealous husband in the Palazzo Riccardi in Florence. (A tangible memento of this love affair exists today in Florence in the form of a statue of Ferdinando in the Piazza dell' Annunziata, facing the lady's window.) In Browning's version the lovers plan to flee Florence together, but delays intrude upon their plans, and they presently come to believe that their love was just a passing infatuation. Browning castigates the lovers for this inability to be true to their passion, despite obstacles. The poem seemed to some readers to advocate adultery (in fact, it simply advocates a steadfastness of purpose and an honest acceptance of love), which scandalized and offended many of Browning's 19th-century admirers.

Staunton (stän′ton), **Sir George.** [Also called **Gentle Geordie.**] The seducer of Effie Deans in Sir Walter Scott's *Heart of Midlothian.*

stave. A stanza; a verse; a metrical division.

Of eleuen and twelue I find none ordinary *staues* vsed in any vulgar language.
(Puttenham, *Arte of Eng. Poesie.*)

Chant me now some wicked stave,
Till thy drooping courage rise.
(Tennyson, *Vision of Sin.*)

Stead (sted), **William Thomas.** b. at Embleton, Northumberland, England, July 5, 1849; drowned in the sinking of the *Titanic*, April 15, 1912. An English journalist. He was appointed editor of the *Northern Echo* (at Darlington) in 1871, and in 1880 assistant editor of the *Pall Mall Gazette*, of which he later was editor (1883–89). In 1890 he founded the *Review of Reviews*, of which he was the editor and publisher.

Steed (stēd), **Henry Wickham.** b. Oct. 10, 1871; d. in Oxfordshire, England, Jan. 13, 1956. An English journalist. He was correspondent at Vienna (1902–

13) for the London *Times*, of which he was later foreign editor (1914–19) and editor (1919–22). He was owner and editor (1923–30) of the *Review of Reviews*, and a lecturer (1925–38) on central European history at King's College, London. Author of *The Hapsburg Monarchy* (1913), *Through Thirty Years* (1924), *The Real Stanley Baldwin* (1930), *Hitler: Whence and Whither?* (1934), *The Doom of the Hapsburgs* (1937), *Our War Aims* (1939), *The Fifth Arm* (1940), *That Bad Man* (1942), and *Words on the Air* (1946).

Steel (stēl), **Flora Annie.** [Maiden name, **Webster.**] b. at Harrow, England, April 2, 1847; d. April 12, 1929. An English novelist. In 1867 she went to India, where she was connected with government schools in the Punjab for a number of years. Many of her stories deal with Anglo-Indian life. Among her publications are *Tales of the Punjab* (1894), *The Potter's Thumb* (1895), *Red Rowans* (1895), *On the Face of the Waters* (1896), *In the Tideway* (1897), *Voices in the Night* (1900), *India* (1906; with Mortimer Menpes), *Sovereign Remedy* (1906), *India through the Ages* (1908), and *The Gift of the Gods* (1911).

Steele (stēl), **Sir Richard.** [Pseudonyms: **Isaac Bickerstaff, Nestor Ironside.**] b. at Dublin, in March, 1672; d. near Carmarthen, Wales, Sept. 1, 1729. British essayist, dramatist, and politician; companion of Addison at the Charterhouse School, and later at Oxford. He did not graduate, but entered the army (1694), serving as a trooper under the Duke of Ormonde, and becoming a captain. He was gazetteer (1707–10) and later member of Parliament, but was expelled for seditious language in *The Crisis.* He was knighted and held various offices under George I. He was a member of the Kit-Kat Club, and in 1707 is said first to have met Swift; by 1710 their relations became strained, and in 1719 he quarreled with Addison. He was extremely careless in money matters, warm-hearted and impulsive. He founded and edited *The Tatler* (1709–11), under the name of Isaac Bickerstaff, and next to Addison was chief contributor to *The Spectator* (1711–12). He founded and was chief contributor to *The Guardian* in 1713, employing the pseudonym Nestor Ironside. To attack the Tory ministry he started *The Englishman* in October, 1713: his later ventures, *Town Talk*, *The Tea Table*, and *Chit Chat*, were unsuccessful. In his most famous political periodical, *The Plebeian* (1718), he opposed Addison on Sunderland's Peerage Bill. His last venture was *The Theatre* (January–April, 1720); about this time he was patentee of Drury Lane. In 1714 he wrote *An Apology* for himself and his writings. He was an ardent Whig, and in 1710 lost his gazetteership on the accession of the Tories to power. He wrote the treatise *The Christian Hero* (1701; a manual of religious ethics) and the comedies (which were written with the avowed purpose of reforming the morals of the age) *The Funeral* (1701), *The Lying Lover* (1704), *The Tender Husband* (1705), and *The Conscious Lovers* (1722).

Steel Glass, The. A satire in blank verse by George Gascoigne, written in 1576. It is the first English satire in blank verse, and holds up a mirror "true as steel" to the vices of his countrymen (the allusion being to the early mirrors made of polished metal).

Steelyard (stēl′yärd, stil′yạrd). A place in London, formerly comprising great warehouses, called before the reign of Edward IV Gildhalla Teutonicorum ("Gildhall of the Germans"), where, until expelled in 1597, the merchants of the Hanseatic League had their English headquarters. By extension, the term came to be applied also to the company of merchants themselves. The merchants of the Steelyard were bound by almost monastic guild rules under a separate jurisdiction from the rest of London, were exempt from many exactions and restrictions, and for centuries controlled most of the foreign trade of England.

Steen (stēn), **Marguerite.** b. at Liverpool, England —. An English novelist. She retired from school teaching to become an actress, and performed briefly (1921–23) on the stage with Fred Terry, brother of Ellen Terry. Among her novels are *Gilt Cage* (1927), *The Reluctant Madonna* (1929), *Unicorn* (1931), *The Wise and Foolish Virgins* (1932), *Matador* (1934), *The Tavern* (1935), *The Lost One* (1937), *Family Ties* (1939), *The Sun Is My Undoing* (1941), *Bell Timson* (1946), and *Twilight on the Floods* (1949).

Steenie (stē′ni). A name given by James I of England to the Duke of Buckingham, on account of a fancied resemblance to Saint Stephen.

Steenson (stēn′sọn), **Maggie.** In Sir Walter Scott's novel *Redgauntlet*, the wife of Wandering Willie.

Steenson, Willie. See **Wandering Willie.**

Steerforth (stir′fôrth, -fọrth), **James.** The most prominent youth at Salem House, in Dickens's *David Copperfield;* a friend and protector of David Copperfield, but afterward the lover and betrayer of Little Em'ly.

Steevens (stē′vẹnz), **George.** b. at Stepney, London, May 10, 1736; d. at Hampstead, London, Jan. 22, 1800. An English Shakespeare scholar. He was educated at Eton and at King's College, Cambridge. He published *Twenty of the Plays of Shakespeare* (1766), and with Samuel Johnson edited Shakespeare in 1773. His own edition (with Reed) of Shakespeare, in which he adopted "the expulsion of useless and supernumerary syllables, etc.," supplying what he thought necessary, appeared in 1793 and 1803, and was an authority till Malone's *Variorum Shakespeare* (edited, after Malone's death, by Boswell in 1821) took its place. His life was marked by constant quarrels stemming from his habit of making anonymous attacks upon his friends in the newspapers, and from his bad temper.

Stella (stel′ạ). Jonathan Swift's name for Esther Johnson, to whom he is thought to have been secretly married in 1716.

Stella. Sir Philip Sidney's name for **Devereux, Penelope.**

Stella Maris (mā′ris). A sentimental novel by William John Locke, published in 1913.

Stendhal (sten′däl; French, staṅ.däl). [Pseudonym of **Marie Henri Beyle.**] b. at Grenoble, France, Jan. 23, 1783; d. at Paris, March 23, 1842. A French novelist and critic. After serving in the French armies under Napoleon, he lived in Italy (1814–21), where he was later a member (1830 *et seq.*) of the French consular service. His two best-known novels, *Le Rouge et le noir* (1930) and *La Chartreuse de Parme* (1839), are considered by many novelists and critics to be predecessors of the 20th-century psychological novel. He was the author also of lives of Napoleon, Haydn, Mozart, Rossini, and Metastasio. Among his other works are *Histoire de la peinture en Italie* (1817), *Racine et Shakespeare* (1823–25), and *Armance* (1827).

Stentor (sten′tôr). In Greek legend, a Greek herald before Troy, who, in Homer's *Iliad*, had a voice as loud as those of 50 men together. The adjective "stentorian" is derived from his name.

Stephano (ste.fä′nō). A messenger in Shakespeare's *Merchant of Venice.*

Stephano (stef′ạ.nō). In Shakespeare's *Tempest*, a drunken butler who plots with Caliban to murder Prospero. He is the master of the ship in Dryden and D'Avenant's version.

Stephen (stē′vẹn), **Saint.** In New Testament history, a deacon of the church at Jerusalem, stoned to death by the people. He was the first Christian martyr, and his day is celebrated in the Roman Catholic and Anglican churches on December 26. In England Saint Stephen's day is known as Boxing Day, because Christmas boxes, or presents of money, are then given to employees.

Stephen. [Also: **Stephen of Blois.**] b. at Blois, France, 1105; d. Oct. 25, 1154. King of England (1135–54). He was the son of the Earl of Blois and Adela, daughter of William the Conqueror. He obtained the countship of Boulogne by marriage with Matilda, daughter of Count Eustace. Although he had sworn to secure the succession of his cousin, the empress Matilda (who was the daughter of Henry I of England, and thus, like Stephen, a grandchild of William the Conqueror) and her son, he went to England on the death of Henry I, in 1135, and, with the help of his brother, Henry, bishop of Winchester, was elected and crowned (December 26). In two charters he undertook to observe the laws and his subjects' liberties. His defective title was the cause of outbreaks in 1136 and 1137. David, king of Scotland, Matilda's uncle, invaded Yorkshire, but his advance was checked at the Battle of the Standard in 1138. Matilda landed in England in 1139, and the country was plunged in civil war. This continued till 1153, when the treaty of Wallingford gave Stephen permission to reign until his death and secured the succession to Henry (Henry II), the son of Matilda.

Stephen, Sir James. b. at London, Jan. 3, 1789; d. at Koblenz, Germany, Sept. 14, 1859. English historical writer. He was educated at Cambridge (Trinity Hall) and Lincoln's Inn. He was undersecretary for the colonies (1834–47). In 1849 he was appointed regius professor of modern history at Cambridge. He published *Essays in Ecclesiastical History* and *Lectures on the History of France.*

Stephen, Sir James Fitzjames. b. March 3, 1829; d. March 11, 1894. An English jurist; son of Sir James Stephen (1789–1859). He was educated at Eton, at King's College, London, and at Trinity College, Cambridge, where he graduated in 1851.

In 1854 he was called to the bar at the Inner Temple. From 1879 to 1891 he was judge of the High Court of Justice. He published *General View of the Criminal Law of England* (1863), *Digest of the Law of Evidence* (1876), and *History of the Criminal Law of England* (1883).

Stephen, James Kenneth. [Called **J. K. S.**] b. Feb. 25, 1859; d. Feb. 3, 1892. An English poet and scholar. Educated at Eton and at King's College, Cambridge, of which he became (1885) a fellow. Author of *International Law* (1884), an essay that won him the fellowship, *Living Languages* (1891), *Lapsus Calami* (1891), and *Quo, Musa, Tendis?* (1891), the last two volumes being collections of light verse.

Stephen, Sir Leslie. b. at Kensington, London, Nov. 28, 1832; d. there, Feb. 22, 1904. An English man of letters; son of Sir James Stephen (1789–1859). He was educated at Eton, at King's College, London, and at Trinity Hall, Cambridge, where he took the degree B.A. in 1854. He was editor of the *Cornhill Magazine* (1871–82) and editor of the *Dictionary of National Biography* (1885–91), latterly in association with Sidney Lee, who succeeded him. He published *The Playground of Europe* (1871), *Hours in a Library* (1874–79), *History of English Thought in the Eighteenth Century* (1876), *Life of Henry Fawcett* (1885), and others. He was knighted in 1902.

Stephen Blackpool (blak'pŏl). See **Blackpool, Stephen.**

Stephen Dedalus (ded'a̱.lus, dĕ'da̱-). See **Dedalus, Stephen.**

Stephen Guest (gest). See **Guest, Stephen.**

Stephens (stē've̱nz), **James.** b. at Dublin, in February, 1882; d. at London, Dec. 26, 1950. An Irish poet and novelist, author of fantasies and tales based on old Gaelic legends. His published poems include *Insurrections* (1909), *The Hill of Vision* (1912), *Songs From the Clay* (1915), *The Rocky Road to Dublin* (1915), *Green Branches* (1916), *A Poetry Recital* (1925), *Strict Joy* (1931), *Kings and the Moon* (1938), and *Collected Poems* (1941); author also of the novels *The Charwoman's Daughter* (1912), which appeared in America under the title *Mary, Mary,* and *The Crock of Gold* (1912), *Here Are Ladies* (1913), *The Demi-Gods* (1914), *Reincarnation* (1918), *Deirdre* (1923), and *In the Land of Youth* (1924); and of *Etched in Moonlight* (1928), short stories.

Stephen Scroop (skrŏp), **Sir.** See **Scroop, Sir Stephen.**

Stepsons of France. A volume of short stories by P. C. Wren, published in 1917.

Steps to the Temple. [Full title, **Steps to the Temple, with Other Delights of the Muses.**] A volume of verse by Richard Crashaw, printed in 1646, and divided into two sections, the first dealing with secular themes, the second with religious themes. It is particularly noted for its religious poems, including "The Weeper," "The Tear," "Hymn of the Nativity, Sung by the Shepherds," and "A Hymn to the Name and Honor of the Admirable Saint Teresa."

Sterling (stėr'ling), **Fanny.** The daughter of the newly rich Sterlings in Garrick and Colman's comedy *The Clandestine Marriage.*

Sterling, John. b. at Kames Castle, Buteshire, Scotland, July 20, 1806; d. at Ventnor, Isle of Wight, England, Sept. 18, 1844. An English poet and author, known as a friend of Carlyle. He studied at Glasgow and Cambridge (but left without a degree); went to London and purchased the *Athenaeum* in 1828, but soon gave it up; and in 1834 became curate at Hurstmonceaux, where Julius Hare was vicar. He wrote *Arthur Coningsby* (1833), *Poems* (1839), *Strafford* (1843), *Essays and Tales* (edited by Hare, 1848), and *The Onyx Ring* (reprinted from *Blackwood's* in 1856). His life was written by Carlyle (1851).

Stern (stėrn), **G. B.** [Full name, **Gladys Bronwyn Stern.**] b. at London, June 17, 1890—. An English novelist, dramatist, journalist, and short-story writer. Educated at Notting Hill High School, London, and at the Royal Academy of Dramatic Art. She is best known for *The Rakonitz Chronicles* (1932), a trilogy on Jewish life and character consisting of *Tents of Israel* (1924; issued in America in 1925 under the title *The Matriarch;* dramatized in 1931), *A Deputy Was King* (1926), and *Mosaic* (1930). Author also of *Pantomime* (1914), *See-Saw* (1914), *Twos and Threes* (1916), *Grand Chain* (1917), *Children of No Man's Land* (1919; American title, *Debatable Ground*), *Larry Munro* (1920; American title, *The China Shop*), *The Room* (1922), *The Back Seat* (1923), *The Happy Meddler* (1926; in collaboration with Geoffrey Lisle Holdsworth), *The Dark Gentleman* (1927), *Debonair* (1928; dramatized in 1930), *Little Red Horses* (1932; American title, *The Rueful Mating*), *Another Part of the Forest* (1941), *Ten Days of Christmas* (1950), and other novels; of the play *The Man Who Pays the Piper* (1931); and of *Smoke Rings* (1923), *Jack A' Manory* (1927), and *The Slower Judas* (1929), collected short stories.

Sterne (stėrn), **Laurence.** b. at Clonmel, Ireland, Nov. 24, 1713; d. at London, March 18, 1768. A British novelist. The son of an English subaltern stationed in Ireland and an Irish mother, his early years were spent following his father's regiment. From 1723 to c1731 he was in school near Halifax, Yorkshire. He received his B.A. from Jesus College, Cambridge, in 1737 and shortly afterward took holy orders, apparently more for economic than for religious reasons. In 1738 he received the living of Sutton on the Forest, near York. In 1741 he married Elizabeth Lumley, with whom he was never compatible. He upset his wife, at one time, to the point of temporary insanity, by his "small, quiet attentions" to various ladies and by his taking part in the carousals of the "Demoniacks" at Skelton Castle, home of John Hall-Stevenson, author of *Crazy Tales* (1762). In 1759 he published *A Political Romance,* a satire that gave him the impetus to write *Tristram Shandy,* the first two books of which probably appeared late in the same year, though dated 1760. The remaining seven volumes were published at irregular intervals between 1760 and 1767. Because of its eccentric humor, whimsicality, and indecorum, the novel won an immediate success, and Sterne was lionized in London. The first two volumes of *Sermons of Mr. Yorick* also appeared in 1760. Consumption, from which Sterne had long suffered, caused him to go to France in 1762, and again to France and Italy in 1765. During his last winter at London he indulged in his famous sentimental affair with Eliza Draper, young wife of an official of the East India Company, to whom he wrote letters (after her departure for Bombay) and a journal which is known as *The Bramine's Journal*. The latter exists in manuscript (in the British Museum); the *Letters of Yorick to Eliza* were published in 1775. He published two of the projected four volumes of *A Sentimental Journey through France and Italy* in 1768, shortly before his death. His chief works are *The Life and Opinions of Tristram Shandy, Gent.* (9 vols., 1760–67), *A Sentimental Journey through France and Italy* (1768), and *Sermons* (1760–69). Several volumes of his letters were published in 1775. There were numerous forgeries, imitations, and continuations of his novels and letters.

Sternhold (stĕrn'hōld), **Thomas.** b. near Blakeney, Gloucestershire, England, c1500; d. in August, 1549. An English writer, joint author with John Hopkins of a metrical version of the Psalms (first edition c1547; enlarged as *The Whole Book of Psalms*, 1561).

Steuart (stū'ạrt). See **Stuart.**

Stevenson (stē'vẹn.sọn), **John Hall.** b. 1718; d. 1785. An English poet, remembered as a friend of Laurence Sterne. He is the original of Eugenius in *Tristram Shandy* and wrote a continuation in 1769 of *The Sentimental Journey.*

Stevenson, Robert Louis. [Sometimes called **R.L. S.**; full original name, **Robert Lewis Balfour Stevenson**; Samoan name, **Tusitala** ("teller of tales").] b. at Edinburgh, Nov. 13, 1850; d. at Apia, Samoa, Dec. 4, 1894. A Scottish poet, essayist, and novelist; son of Thomas Stevenson, a meteorologist and engineer. A sickly child, he was educated in Edinburgh schools and, after studying engineering for a time, went to Edinburgh University, and was called to the bar (1875) but never practiced. He had already begun writing, studying the style of others carefully, and contributing to magazines. In 1876 he made a trip to the Continent and in 1878, in his first published book, described it in *An Inland Voyage.* The work entitled *Travels with a Donkey in the Cévennes* (1879) is also an account of his journeying. He had met Mrs. Osbourne in France and, in 1879, hearing that she was ill in California, he traveled in steerage across the Atlantic and then, in the worst sort of accommodations, across the U. S. They were married in 1880 and returned to Scotland later that year. His health, injured by the rigorous trip to America, grew worse, and, after vain sojourns at resorts in Europe, he emigrated (1887) to America. Despite his ill health, including several illnesses that threatened to carry him off, he had written in this period *Silverado Squatters* (1883), an account of his life in a California mining camp, the essays collected in *Virginibus Puerisque* (1881) and *Familiar Studies of Men and Books* (1882), the stories of *The New Arabian Nights* (1882), *Treasure Island* (1883), an extremely popular book into which he crowded all the adventurous happenings he thought should go into a

story of piracy (including a picture of his friend W. E. Henley as Long John Silver), *A Child's Garden of Verses* (1885), *The Body Snatcher* (1885), *Prince Otto* (1885), *The Strange Case of Dr. Jekyll and Mr. Hyde* (1886), *Kidnapped* (1886), and other stories. He stayed at Saranac Lake for a time, writing *The Master of Ballantrae* (1888) and contributing monthly essays to *Scribner's Magazine.* In 1888 he went again to the West Coast, to embark on a schooner for the South Seas. He touched at the Marquesas, Tahiti, Honolulu, Molokai, the Gilberts, and finally at Samoa on Dec. 25, 1889. During the last five years of his life, except for one trip to Sydney, New South Wales, in 1890, to publish his famous defense of Father Damien of Molokai, he lived in Samoa, on his estate "Vailima" as a planter and chief of the natives. To this period belong *A Footnote to History: Eight Years of Trouble in Samoa* (1892), *The Wrecker* (1892; with his stepson Lloyd Osbourne), *Island Nights' Entertainment* (1893), *Catriona* (1893), and *The Ebb Tide* (1894; with Osbourne). He was dictating *The Weir of Hermiston* (unfinished) when he died suddenly of apoplexy. His plays, unsuccessful, include four written with W. E. Henley: *Beau Austin, Deacon Brodie, Admiral Guinea,* and *Robert Macaire.* With his wife, he wrote *The Dynamiter* (1885), and, in addition to those mentioned above, *The Wrong Box* (1889) with Lloyd Osbourne. *St. Ives* (1897) was completed by Authur Quiller-Couch. Sidney Colvin, his friend since 1873, edited his *Letters,* published in 1895.

Stevenson, William. d. after 1533. An English scholar and writer, known to have been a fellow of Christ's College, Cambridge. He is believed to be the "Master S." who wrote *Gammer Gurton's Needle.*

St. Evrémonde (saṅ.tev.rā.mônd'), **Charles.** See **Darnay, Charles.**

Stewart (stū'ạrt). See also **Stuart.**

Stewart, Alan Breck. See **Breck, Alan.**

Stewart, Dugald. b. at Edinburgh, Nov. 22, 1753; d. there, June 11, 1828. A Scottish philosopher. He was a pupil of Thomas Reid at Glasgow University in 1771, conjoint professor of mathematics in 1775, and professor of moral philosophy in 1785, and retired from active service in 1810. His chief works are *Elements of the Philosophy of the Human Mind* (3 vols., 1792, 1814, 1827), *Outlines of Moral Philosophy* (1793), *Philosophical Essays* (1810), a dissertation for the supplement of the *Encyclopaedia Britannica* entitled "General View of the Progress of Metaphysical, Ethical, and Political Philosophy since the Revival of Letters" (1815–21), and *Philosophy of the Active and Moral Powers* (1828).

Stewart, Henry. See **Darnley, Lord.**

Stewart, John Innes. [Pseudonym, **Michael Innes.**] b. near Edinburgh, Sept. 30, 1906—. A Scottish writer of detective fiction. He is the author of *Seven Suspects* (1936), *Hamlet, Revenge!* (1937), *Lament for a Maker* (1938), *The Spider Strikes* (1939), *A Comedy of Terrors* (1940), *The Secret Vanguard* (1941), and *Appleby on Ararat* (1941).

Stewart, Robert. [Titles: Viscount **Castlereagh;** 2nd Marquess of **Londonderry.**] b. June 18, 1769;

committed suicide Aug. 12, 1822. A British statesman, notable for his achievements as foreign secretary in the period 1812–22. He urged the desirability of comparatively lenient terms for France after
the fall of Napoleon, and advocated strongly that
Great Britain should adhere to Metternich's international policy of maintaining an equilibrium of
power between the chief nations of Europe.

Stewart of the Glens, James. In Robert Louis
Stevenson's *Kidnapped* and *Catriona*, a Jacobite
partisan, based on a personage from actual history.
He is imprisoned and later executed for the murder
of Colin Campbell, the King's factor, a crime he
did not commit, through the power of the Campbells and as a result of their hatred for the Stewarts.

Steyne (stīn), **Marquis of.** In Thackeray's *Vanity
Fair*, a cynical old nobleman and man of the world,
who is soundly thrashed by Rawdon Crawley for
his attentions to Becky Sharp, Rawdon's wife.

stichomythia (stik.ọ.mith′i.ạ). A type of rapid
dialogue in verse, in which two speakers dispute
in alternate lines. It is a classical Greek convention,
but was used occasionally in the mystery plays and
by Shakespeare in *Richard III.*

Stiggins (stig′inz), **the Reverend Mr.** [Called "the
Shepherd."] In Dickens's *Pickwick Papers*, a
hypocritical and intemperate clergyman.

Still (stil), **John.** b. at Grantham, Lincolnshire,
England, c1543; d. Feb. 26, 1608. An English
prelate. He was dean of Bocking, canon of Westminster, master of Saint Johns (1574) and Trinity
(1577) colleges, vice-chancellor of Cambridge, and
bishop of Bath and Wells (1593–1608). He may
have been the author of the comedy *Gammer Gurton's Needle*, though William Stevenson is more
probably the author, and John Bridges is sometimes given credit for the play. He made a large
fortune in lead mines discovered in the Mendip
Hills.

Still Center, The. A volume of poems by Stephen
Spender, published in 1939.

Stillingfleet (stil′ing.flēt), **Edward.** b. at Cran-
borne, Dorsetshire, England, April 17, 1635; d. at
Westminster (now part of London), March 27,
1699. An English prelate and theologian. He graduated at Cambridge (St. John's College), in 1652,
was chaplain to Charles II, and dean (1678) of St.
Paul's; and was made bishop of Worcester in 1689.
Among his works are *Irenicum* (1659), *Origines
Sacrae* (1662), *Unreasonableness of Separation*,
Origines Britannicae (1685), works against the
noncomformists and Roman Catholics, and others.

Stirling (stėr′ling), **Earl of.** Title of **Alexander,
Sir William.**

Stirling-Maxwell (stėr′ling.maks′wel, -wẹl), **Sir William.** b. near Glasgow, March 8, 1818; d. at Venice, Jan. 15, 1878. A Scottish author. In 1876 he
married Caroline Norton, a famous 19th-century
English beauty and one of the three granddaughters
of Richard Brinsley Sheridan. He became (1876)
chancellor of Glasgow. His works include *Annals
of the Artists of Spain* (3 vols., 1848), *The Cloister
Life of Charles V* (1852), *Velasquez and his Works*
(1855), and *Don John of Austria* (1883; privately
printed earlier).

St. James's Palace (jām′ziz). A palace in London,
adapted as a royal residence by Henry VIII, enlarged by Charles I, damaged by fire in 1809, and
since restored. Though no longer occupied by the
sovereign, it gives its name officially to the British
court. The picturesque brick gate toward St.
James's Street and the interesting presence chamber date from Henry VIII, as does the chapel,
which is known as the Chapel Royal. The apartments of state are splendidly decorated.

St. James's Park. A public park of 87 acres, in
London, E of Green Park. It originally consisted
of fields acquired by Henry VIII in exchange for
lands in Suffolk. The Hospital of St. James, which
owned it, was pulled down, and St. James's Palace
was erected on its site. It is the first of a series of
parks extending from near the Thames at Whitehall
to Kensington Palace, 2½ mi. E and W.

St. John (sānt jon; in Great Britain usually sin′jọn),
Henry. See **Bolingbroke,** Viscount.

St. John's Wood. A quarter in the northwestern
part of London, now chiefly residential. It is the
site of Lord's Cricket Ground.

Stoics (stō′iks). The disciples of the philosopher
Zeno, who founded the school c308 B.C. He taught
that men should be free from passion, unmoved by
joy or grief, and submit without complaint to the
unavoidable necessity by which all things are governed. The Stoics are proverbially known for the
sternness and austerity of their doctrines, and for
the influence which their tenets exercised over
some of the noblest spirits of antiquity, especially
among the Romans. Their system appears to have
been an attempt to reconcile a theological pantheism and a materialist psychology with a logic
which seeks the foundations of knowledge in the
representations or perceptions of the senses, and a
morality which claims as its first principle the absolute freedom of the human will. The Stoics teach
that whatever is real is material; that matter and
force are the two ultimate principles; and that
matter is of itself motionless and unformed, though
capable of receiving all motions and all forms.
Force is the active, moving, and molding principle,
and is inseparably joined with matter; the working
force in the universe is God, whose existence as a
wise, thinking being is proved by the beauty and
adaptation of the world. The supreme end of life, or
the highest good, is virtue, that is, a life conformed
to nature, the agreement of human conduct with the
all-controlling law of nature, or of the human with
the divine will; not contemplation, but action, is
the supreme problem for man; virtue is sufficient
for happiness, but happiness or pleasure should
never be made the end of human endeavor. The
wise man alone attains to the complete performance
of his duty; he is without passion, although not
without feeling; he is not indulgent but just toward
himself and others; he alone is free; he is king and
lord, and is inferior in inner worth to no other rational being.

Stoke Poges (stōk pō′jis). A village in Bucking-
hamshire, England, the burial place of Thomas
Gray. He composed there his *Elegy Written in a
Country Churchyard.*

Stoker Haslett (stō′kėr haz′lẹt). A collection of
short stories by James Hanley, published in 1932.

Stolen Heiress, or the Salamanca Doctor Outplotted (sal.ạ.mang′kạ), **The.** A comedy by Susannah Centlivre, produced in 1702 as *The Heiress.* It was adapted from Thomas May's comedy *The Heir.*

Stonehenge (stōn′henj). A circular grouping of stones standing in Salisbury Plain, S England, ab. 10 mi. N of Salisbury. The huge stones, many of them now fallen or carried away for building purposes, originally stood in three concentric rings, the outer ab. 100 ft. in diameter, the inner (the "horse shoe") incomplete and open to the east; the standing stones, 16 ft. high and 6 to 7 ft. thick in the outer ring, were topped by others in a lintel construction. A separate stone, the so-called sun stone or Friar's Heel, stands outside the outer circle at a point where a viewer in the center of the inner circle will see the sun rise at the summer solstice. This construction is first mentioned by Nennius (9th century A.D.) and since then many conjectures have been made as to the significance and original purpose of Stonehenge, the early hypotheses of its being a burial place or a commemorative monument giving place in the 18th century to the theory that it was somehow connected with Druid worship; the matter is still subject to archaeological study and debate.

Stone of Scone (skön). [Also, **Coronation Stone.**] A famous stone, formerly at Scone, Scotland, upon which the Scottish kings sat at coronation: now beneath the coronation chair in Westminster Abbey.

Stones of Venice. A treatise on art (1851) by John Ruskin.

Stony Durdles (dèr′dlz). See **Durdles, Stony.**

Stork, King. In Aesop's Fables, a stork sent by Jupiter to eat up the frogs who complained of King Log.

Storm and Stress. [A translation of the German *Sturm und Drang,* alluding to a drama by Klinger, "Sturm und Drang."] A name given to a period in German literary history (c1770 to 1790) influenced by a group of younger writers whose works were characterized by passion and reaction from the old methods.

Storm and Treasure. A romantic historical novel by Henry Christopher Bailey, published in 1910.

Story of an African Farm, The. A novel (1883) by Olive Schreiner, published under the pseudonym Ralph Iron.

Story of Rimini (rim′i.ni). See **Rimini, Story of.**

Story of the Country-Mouse and the City-Mouse, The. A satirical poem (1687) by Matthew Prior and Charles Montagu, burlesquing Dryden's *The Hind and the Panther.*

Story of the Gadsbys (gadz′biz), **The.** A volume of eight loosely connected stories (Calcutta, 1888) by Rudyard Kipling. Its contents were included with "Soldiers Three" and "In Black and White" in *Soldiers Three and other Stories* (London, 1895).

Stow (stō), **John.** b. at London, c1525; d. there, April 6, 1605. An English historian and antiquary. In 1565 he published *A Summarie of Englysche Chronicles,* and in 1580 his *Annales, or Generale Chronicle of England from Brute until the Present Yeare of Christ 1580.* However, Stow is best known

for his *Survey of London* (1598), long the standard authority on old London. Through the patronage of Archbishop Matthew Parker he was able to print the *Flores Historiarum* of Matthew of Westminster (1567), the *Chronicle* of Matthew Paris (1571), and the *Historia Brevis* of Thomas Walsingham (1574). In 1604 he was authorized by James I to collect "amongst our loving subjects their voluntary contributions and kind gratuities."

Strabo (strā′bō). b. at Amasia, Pontus, c63 B.C.; d. c24 A.D. A Greek geographer. He traveled extensively, and wrote a geographical work, in 17 books, describing Europe (Books III–X), Asia (XI–XVI), and Egypt and North Africa (XVII). He also wrote a history now completely lost.

Strachey (strā′chi), **Lytton.** [Full name, **Giles Lytton Strachey.**] b. at London, March 1, 1880; d. at Inkpen, Berkshire, England, Jan. 21, 1932. An English biographer, critic, and essayist. He was educated at Trinity College, Cambridge, where he won (1902) the chancellor's English medal with his poem *Ely.* With J. M. Keynes, Roger Fry, Virginia Woolf, Clive Bell, and others, he was a member of the noted "Bloomsbury group" of writers and artists. His brilliant character studies inaugurated a new school of biography during the post-World War I era. Author of *Landmarks in French Literature* (1912), *Eminent Victorians* (1918), *Queen Victoria* (1921; awarded the James Tait Black memorial prize, and considered by many to be the best biography of Victoria yet written), *Books and Characters—French and English* (1922), *Pope* (1925), *Elizabeth and Essex* (1928), *Portraits in Miniature* (1931), and *Characters and Commentaries* (1933).

Stradivari (strä.dē.vä′rē), **Antonio.** [Latinized, **Antonius Stradivarius** (strad.i.vār′i.us).] b. at Cremona, Italy, c1644; d. there, Dec. 18, 1737. Italian maker of violins, the most celebrated of the masters of the art. He was a pupil of Nicolo Amati. His best violins were made in the period c1700–25.

Strafford (straf′ọrd), **1st Earl of.** [Title of Sir Thomas Wentworth.] b. at London, April 13, 1593; executed at London, May 12, 1641. An English statesman. He entered Parliament in 1614, and was an opponent of the policy of James I, and until 1628–29 of that of Charles I. He was too moderate, however, in his opposition, and lost his Parliamentary leadership to John Eliot and Edward Coke, who were nearer to the temper of the members in their determined stand against the king. In 1628 he was raised to the peerage, became president of the council of the north in 1628, was made a privy councillor in 1629, was appointed lord deputy of Ireland (1632) and arrived there (1633), subduing the country with his "Thorough" policy. By 1639 he had become the chief adviser of Charles I. In 1640 he was made earl of Strafford and lord lieutenant of Ireland. He raised an Irish army to use against the Scottish Presbyterians but could not use it. He commanded the English army against the Scots in 1640, but was defeated. He was recalled to London, was impeached by the Long Parliament, and was condemned by a bill of attainder, reluctantly signed by the king in place of the untenable impeachment. The charges against him stated that he had suggested to the king the use of the Irish army against what he claimed to be a subversive Parliament.

Strafford. A tragedy by Robert Browning, relating to Thomas Wentworth, 1st Earl of Strafford. It was written for W. C. Macready, at his own request, and he played the title role on its production in 1837.

Strand, the. One of the chief thoroughfares of London, extending southeast from Fleet Street to Charing Cross.

Strange Case of Dr. Jekyll and Mr. Hyde (jek′il, jē′kil; hīd), **The.** See **Dr. Jekyll and Mr. Hyde.**

Strange's Men (strān′jez). See **Lord Chamberlain's Men.**

Strange Story, A. A novel by Edward Bulwer-Lytton, published during 1862 in *All the Year Round*.

Strangford (strang′fǫrd), 7th Viscount. A title of **Smythe, George Augustus Frederick Percy Sydney.**

Strap (strap). [Full name, **Hugh Strap.**] In Tobias Smollett's *Roderick Random*, a faithful follower of the hero, who treats him shabbily.

Straparola (strä.pä.rō′lä), **Giovanni Francesco.** [Full surname, **Straparola da Caravaggio.**] b. near the end of the 15th century; d. 1557. An Italian novelist. He published *Sonetti, strambotti, epistole e capitole* (1508), but is best remembered by his collection of stories called *Tredici piacevoli notti*, drawn from many sources and published at Venice in two series in 1550 and 1554. Many editions were issued, and the book has been a storehouse from which succeeding writers have obtained plots and other material. Shakespeare and Molière are indebted to it, one of the stories is in Painter's *Palace of Pleasure*, and there have been several French translations. The stories are told on separate nights by a party of ladies and gentlemen enjoying the cool air at Murano (on the outskirts of Venice), and are frequently called *Straparola's Nights*.

Stratford-on-Avon (strat′fǫrd.on.ā.vǫn, av′ǫn). [Also: **Stratford-upon-Avon, Stratford.**] A municipal borough and market town in C England, in Warwickshire, situated on the river Avon, at the N end of the Cotswolds, ab. 8 mi. SW of Warwick, ab. 101 mi. NW of London by rail. It is famous as the birthplace of William Shakespeare. It contains the Church of the Holy Trinity (Early English and Perpendicular styles), with the tomb of Shakespeare; the house where it is thought that Shakespeare was born; and the New Place, the site of the house built by Sir Hugh Clopton in the time of Henry VII, and bought by Shakespeare in 1597. Shakespeare's supposed birthplace is now national property and has been suitably restored. The low gabled exterior and the interior rooms preserve their 16th-century character. A Shakespeare Museum has been formed in the house. The Shakespeare Memorial Building (built by popular subscription from the U. S. and Britain) includes a theater in which the annual Shakespeare Festival takes place, a gallery, and a library. The Shakespeare fountain was erected in 1887 by George W. Childs. Nearby is Shottery, with Anne Hathaway's cottage.

Strato (strā′tō). In Shakespeare's *Julius Caesar*, a servant of Brutus. He is the only one who consents to hold the sword on which Brutus kills himself (V. v).

Strawberry Hill (strô′ber″i hil). Horace Walpole's country house, near Twickenham, Surrey, England. He made the house into a miniature castle in the style of the "Gothic" then popular. He gave Kitty Clive a small house near it, which he called Cliveden, sometimes "Little Strawberry Hill."

Street (strēt), **Cecil John Charles.** [Pseudonym, **John Rhode.**] b. 1884—. An English author, best known for his crime and mystery stories in which his fictional character Dr. Priestley appears. Under his pseudonym he wrote *Dr. Priestly's Quest* (1926), *The Ellerby Case* (1927), *Murders in Praed Street* (1928), *The Tragedy at the Unicorn* (1928), *The House on Tollard Ridge* (1929), *Murder at Bratton Grange* (1929), *Peril at Cranbury Hall* (1930), *Dr. Priestley Investigates* (1930), *Tragedy on the Line* (1931), *Dead Men at the Folly* (1932), *Dr. Priestley Lays a Trap* (1933), *Poison for One* (1934), *The Corpse in the Car* (1935), *Hendon's First Case* (1935), *Shot at Dawn* (1935), *Death at Breakfast* (1936), *Murder at the Motor Show* (1936), *Death Sits on the Board* (1937), *The Harvest Murder* (1937), *Body Unidentified* (1938), *Death on the Boat Train* (1940), *Murder at Lilac Cottage* (1940), *Signal for Death* (1941), *Death at the Helm* (1941), *They Watched by Night* (1941), and *The Fourth Bomb* (1942), murder and detective novels. Under his own name, he is the author of serious works in biography and history, including *The Administration of Ireland in 1921* (1921), *Ireland in 1921* (1922), *Rhineland and Ruhr* (1923), *Hungary and Democracy* (1923), *East of Prague* (1924), *The Treachery of France* (1924), *Lord Reading* (1928), *The Case of Constance Kent* (1928; in the Famous Trials series), and *President Masaryk* (1930).

Strephon (stref′ǫn). A shepherd in Sir Philip Sidney's *Arcadia*. In English poetry it is often a conventional name of a lover.

Strether (strē′thėr, streth′ėr), **Lewis Lambert.** In Henry James's novel *The Ambassadors*, the Boston gentleman who is sent to Europe as the first "ambassador" to bring back the son of Mrs. Newsome.

Stretton (stret′ǫn), **Hesba.** [Pseudonym of **Sarah Smith.**] b. 1832; d. 1911. An English novelist and writer of books for juveniles. She published *Jessica's First Prayer* (1866) and *Bede's Charity.*

Strickland (strik′lạnd), **Agnes.** b. Aug. 19, 1796; d. July 8, 1874. An English historical writer. Her chief works are *Lives of the Queens of England* (12 vols., 1840–48; written in collaboration with her sister), *Lives of the Queens of Scotland* (8 vols., 1850–59), *Bachelor Kings of England* (1861), and *Lives of the Seven Bishops* (1866). She also edited *Letters of Mary Queen of Scots* (1843), and wrote several novels.

Strickland, Charles. The hero of W. Somerset Maugham's novel *The Moon and Sixpence* (1919). The novel is supposedly a fictional portrayal of the life of the French painter Paul Gauguin.

Strife. A drama (1909) by John Galsworthy, dealing with the conflict between capital and labor.

Strindberg (strind′bėrg; Swedish, strēnd′bery′), **August.** b. at Stockholm, Jan. 22, 1849; d. there, May 14, 1912. A Swedish dramatist and novelist, a leader of modern Swedish literature. Among his plays are *Mäster Olof* (1872), *Gillets hemlighet* (1880), *Fadren* (1887), *Fröken Julie* (1888), *Gläubiger* (1889), *Till Damaskus* (3 parts, 1898–1904), and a series of historical dramas, including *Gustavus Wasa* (1899), *Erik XIV* (1899), *Gustavus Adolphus* (1900), and *Carl XII* (1901). He wrote also the novels *Röda rummet* (1879); *Det nya riket* (1882), which provoked so much criticism that the author left Sweden for a number of years; *Svenska folket i helg och söken* (1882); *Giftas* (1884); *Die Beichte eines Thoren* (1893); *Inferno* (1897); written after one of his periodical attacks of insanity; *Einsam* (1903), an autobiographical novel; *Die Gotischen Zimmer* (1904); and other volumes, many of them concerned with difficult relationships between men and women, a subject which had a degree of familiarity to the three-times-divorced Stringberg. He has been called "the Shakespeare of Sweden."

Strode (strōd), **Ralph.** fl. 1350–1400. An English scholastic philosopher, Oxford teacher of philosophy and logic, and colleague of John Wycliffe, with whom he disagreed on theological questions. Author of *Consequentiae* and *Obligationes*, fragmentary treatises published in 1477 and 1507, and of *Logica*, a work that has not survived. Various poems have been attributed to him; the Merton College 15th-century catalogue notes say that "he was a noble poet and author of an elegiac work." In his dedication of *Troilus and Criseyde*, Chaucer couples his name (calling him the "philosophical Strode") with that of John Gower. Sir Israel Gollancz regarded Strode as the possible author of *The Pearl, Patience, Cleanness* (or *Purity*), and *Sir Gawain and the Green Knight*, but this attribution has not been found convincing by others.

Strode, William. b. near Plympton, Devonshire, England, 1602; d. at Oxford, England, March 11, 1645. An English poet, preacher, and dramatist. Educated at Westminster and at Christ Church, Oxford, he served as chaplain to Richard Corbet, Oxford bishop and poet. Author of *The Floating Island*, a tragi-comedy acted (Aug. 29, 1636) by the Christ Church students before Charles I and Queen Henrietta; and several short lyrics, of which the best-known are *To a Lady Taking Off her Veil, Melancholy Opposed, The Commendation of Music, On Westwell Downs,* and *On Chloris Walking in the Snow.*

St. Ronan's Well (sānt rō'nạnz). A novel by Sir Walter Scott, published in 1824.

Strong (strông), **Captain Edward.** [Called **"the Chevalier Strong."**] In Thackeray's novel *Pendennis,* a hearty military man who is much given to telling stories of his adventures. He is the close friend of Sir Francis Clavering.

Strong, Dr. In Dickens's *David Copperfield,* the kindly old scholar who is headmaster of the school attended by David while he is living under the care of Miss Betsey Trotwood.

Strong, L. A. G. [Full name, **Leonard Alfred George Strong.**] b. 1896—. An English novelist and poet. His verse includes *Dublin Days* (1923) and *Call to the Swan* (1936). Among his novels are *Dewer Rides* (1929), *The Jealous Ghost* (1930), *The Garden* (1931), *The Brothers* (1932; American title, *Broth-*

ers), *Sea Wall* (1933), *The Bay* (1941), *Othello's Occupation* (1945), and *Travellers* (1945).

strophe (strō'fē). In ancient prosody: (a) A system the metrical form of which is repeated once or oftener in the course of a poem; also, a stanza in modern poetry. In a narrower sense—(b) The former of two metrically corresponding systems, as distinguished from the latter or *antistrophe.* (c) The fourth part of the parabasis and first part of the epirrhematic syzygy. It is hymnic in character, as opposed to the scoptic tone of the epirrhema.

Structure of the Novel, The. A critical study by Edwin Muir, published (1928) as No. 6 in the *Hogarth Lectures on Literature* series. It discusses "novels of action and character," the "dramatic novel," "time and space," "the chronicle," and "the period novel and later developments."

Struldbrugs (struld'brugz). The immortal inhabitants of Luggnagg, an imaginary land described in Swift's *Gulliver's Travels.*

Struther (struᴛн'ėr), **Jan.** [Pseudonym of **Joyce Maxtone Placzek;** maiden name, **Anstruther.**] b. at London, June 6, 1901; d. at New York, July 20, 1953. An English novelist and poet. Author of *Betsinda Dances and Other Poems* (1931), *Sycamore Square and Other Verses* (1932), *Try Anything Twice* (1938), *Mrs. Miniver* (1939), *The Glassblower and Other Poems* (1940), *Letters from Great Britain* (1941), and *A Pocket Full of Pebbles* (1945).

Strutt (strut), **Joseph.** b. in Essex, England, Oct. 27, 1749; d. at London, Oct. 16, 1802. An English engraver and antiquary. He published *The Regal and Ecclesiastical Antiquities of England* (1773), *Horda-Angel-Cynnan* (1774), *Biographical Dictionary of Engravers* (1785–86), *Complete View of the Dress and Habits of the People of England* (1796–99), and *The Sports and Pastimes of the People of England* (1801).

Strype (strīp), **John.** b. at Stepney, now part of London, Nov. 1, 1643; d. at Hackney, now part of London, Dec. 11, 1737. An English biographer and historical writer. His works fill 13 folio volumes. They include *Memorials of Archbishop Cranmer* (1694), *Annals of the Reformation in England* (4 vols., 1709–31), an edition of Stow's *Survey of London* (1720), *Ecclesiastical Memorials* (3 vols., 1721), and lives of Sir Thomas Smith, John Aylmer, John Cheke, Edmund Grindal, Matthew Parker, and John Whitgift.

Stuart or **Stewart** or **Steuart** (stū'ạrt). A royal family of Scotland and England. It was descended from a family which for several generations held the office of high steward of Scotland (whence the name). Walter, the sixth high steward, married Margaret, daughter of Robert Bruce, and on the death of Margaret's brother David II in 1371, the only child of this marriage succeeded as Robert II. The Stuart sovereigns of Scotland were Robert II, Robert III, James I, James II, James III, James IV, James V, Mary, Queen of Scots, and James VI. James IV married Margaret, daughter of Henry VII of England, and on the failure of direct heirs at the death of Elizabeth, the last of Henry VIII's descendants in 1603, James VI of Scotland, Margaret's great-grandson, succeeded to the throne of England as James I. The Stuart sovereigns of England and Scotland jointly were James I, Charles I, Charles II, James II, Mary (consort of William III), and Anne. For many years after the Hanoverians came to the English throne, the Stuart (Jacobite) pretenders maintained their claim to the crown, but after 1745 they took no overt action. The Hanoverian claim came through Sophia, mother of George I, who was a granddaughter of James I.

Stuart, Charles Edward Louis Philip Casimir. [Often referred to as **Charles Edward**; called **"the Young Pretender"** or **"Bonnie Prince Charlie"** or **"the Young Chevalier"** or **"the Young Adventurer."**] b. at Rome, Dec. 31, 1720; d. there, Jan. 31, 1788. An English prince, claimant to the throne after 1766 as grandson of James II; eldest son of James Francis Edward Stuart and Princess Clementina, daughter of James Sobieski. A dashing young soldier, he was a favorite figure of the Jacobites, who saw in him the romantic hope of their cause. He sailed for Scotland July 13, 1745, to head an insurrection for the recovery of the British crown for his father, and landed in the Hebrides. The Highlanders flocked to his standard, and he marched to Edinburgh (September 11), defeated the forces sent against him at Prestonpans (September 21), captured Carlisle, and marched upon London; but after reaching Derby (December 4) he was forced to retreat, and was utterly routed at Culloden, April 16, 1746. The prince, after hiding in the Highlands for several months, escaped to Brittany, disguised as a sewing woman in the company of Flora MacDonald, daughter of one of his supporters. In 1748, by the Treaty of Aix-la-Chapelle ending the War of the Austrian Succession, he was expelled from France and, as the Count of Albany, traveled about Europe. His followers began to desert his cause as a result of his open liaison with Clementina Walkinshaw, who was, they claimed, spying on him to the benefit of George III; he would not give her up, and moreover had taken to drink and displayed an ungovernable temper. His mistress left him in 1760, after she had given birth to a daughter, Charlotte (1753–89), and he married (1772) Louisa von Stolberg, known as the Countess of Albany, but she too left him in 1780. He lived at Florence and at Rome with his daughter until his death. "Bonnie Prince Charlie" is commemorated in many Highland ballads and songs.

Stuart, Francis. See **Bothwell, Sergeant.**

Stuart, Henry. See **Darnley, Lord.**

Stuart, James Francis Edward. [Often referred to as **James Edward**; title, Prince of **Wales**; also called **"the Chevalier de St. George"** or **"the Old Pretender."**] b. at St. James's Palace, June 10, 1688; d. at Rome, Jan. 1, 1766. An English prince, pretender to the throne after 1701 as James III; only son of James II of England and Mary of Modena. The events that led within the year to the overthrow of the Stuarts were in process when he was born and it was widely rumored in England, even before that day, that he was not actually a royal child, that the reported pregnancy of the queen was part of a Jesuit plot to insure the succession of a Roman Catholic prince rather than the Protestant Princess Mary, that the king at 54

was too old to sire a child and that the queen (though only 30) was past the childbearing period; there is, however, no doubt that he was the child of the king and queen. Two days before his father fled from the kingdom (Dec. 11–12, 1688), the infant and his mother were sent to France. On his father's death, he was proclaimed king of England (James III) and Scotland (James VIII) by Louis XIV, September, 1701, although he had been excluded from the succession by act of Parliament; he was, moreover, attainted in 1702. The English and French being on opposite sides in the War of the Spanish Succession, he was sent with a French force to Scotland in 1706, but the expedition was unable to land because of the weather. He served in the French army, distinguishing himself at Oudenarde (1708) and Malplaquet (1709). In 1714 George I was called to succeed Anne on the English throne, destroying James Edward's wishful belief that he would be called upon when she died leaving no heir. In 1715, therefore, he countenanced the unsuccessful Jacobite uprising in Scotland under the Earl of Mar, appearing there in person in the latter part of the year and setting up court at Scone. But his appearance was a mistake; he alienated his troops and early in 1716 had to return to France, the rebellion broken. Eventually he settled at Rome, where he married (1719) Princess Clementina Sobieski, daughter of John Sobieski. She bore him two sons, Charles Edward, the Young Pretender, and Henry Benedict Stuart, later Cardinal York. His wife left him in 1724, but they were reconciled in 1726 and lived together until her death in 1735, but the incident lost more followers for James. In 1727 he received a pension from the pope, and until 1745 was heartened by occasional plots to give him the English throne, but after the failure of Charles Edward in the uprising of 1745 Jacobite hopes were, for all practical purposes, ended.

Stuart, John Patrick Crichton-. [Title, 3rd Marquis of **Bute.**] b. at Mountstuart, Scotland, Sept. 12, 1847; d. Oct. 9, 1900. An English author and official. Born a Presbyterian, he abandoned that faith for the Roman Catholic, and in so doing probably suggested to Benjamin Disraeli the plot of *Lothair* (1870). He was appointed mayor of Cardiff (1890), and lord lieutenant of Buteshire in 1892, the year he began his six-year term as rector of St. Andrew's University. He translated into English the breviary (1879), the orders of service for the greater church festivals, and wrote *The Language of the Natives of Teneriffe* (1891).

Stuart, Mary. See **Mary, Queen of Scots.**

Stuart-Wortley (stū′art.wêrt′li), Lady **Emmeline Charlotte Elizabeth.** b. May 2, 1806; d. at Beirut, in what is now Lebanon, in November, 1855. An English poet, dramatist, and traveler. She traveled in the Netherlands, Germany, Italy, Turkey, Hungary, Palestine, and the U. S. Among her many works are *London at Night* (1834), *Travelling Sketches in Rhyme* (1835), *The Knight and the Enchantress* (1835), *The Village Churchyard* (1835), *Fragments and Fancies* (1837), *Hours at Naples* (1837), and *Impressions of Italy* (1837), volumes of poetry; *Eva* (1840), *Alphonso Algarves* (1841), and *Angiolina del Albino, or Truth and Treachery*

(1841), poetic dramas; *Moonshine* (1843) and *Ernest Mountjoy* (1844), comedies; *Sketches of Travel in America* (1853), and her last work, *A Visit to Portugal and Madeira* (1854). She edited (1837, 1840) *The Keepsake*, to which Alfred Tennyson contributed his *Saint Agnes*, later called *Saint Agnes' Eve.*

Stubbs (stubz), **Philip.** [Also, **Stubbes.**] fl. 1580–90. An English Puritan and pamphleteer, remembered for his *Anatomie of Abuses* (1583), a violent attack on the theater and other aspects of the cultural life of the day which offended his fanatically moral sensibilities.

Stubbs, William. b. at Knaresborough, Yorkshire, England, June 21, 1825; d. at Cuddesdon, Oxfordshire, England, April 22, 1901. An English historian. He studied at Oxford (Christ Church), graduating in 1848. He was appointed regius professor of modern history at Oxford in 1866, curator of the Bodleian Library in 1868, canon of Saint Paul's in 1879, and bishop of Chester in 1884, and was translated to the see of Oxford in 1889. He was the author of *The Constitutional History of England in its Origin and Development* (1874–78), *The Early Plantagenets* (1876: *Epochs of Modern History* series), and *Seventeen Lectures on the Study of Mediaeval and Modern History and Kindred Subjects* (1886); and edited Benedict of Peterborough's *Gesta Regis Henrici Secundi Benedicti Abbatis: Chronicles of the Reigns of Henry II and Richard I, 1169–92* (1867), *Select Charters and Other Illustrations of English Constitutional History, from the Earliest Times to the Reign of Edward the First* (1870), *Memoriale Fratris Walteri de Coventria: The Historical Collections of Walter of Coventry: Edited from the MS. in the Library of Corpus Christi College, Cambridge* (1872–73), *Memorials of Saint Dunstan, Archbishop of Canterbury* (1874), *Radulfi de Diceto Decani Ludoniensis Opera Historica: The Historical Works of Master Ralph de Diceto, Dean of London* (1876), *The Historical Works of Gervase of Canterbury: Vols. I and II, The Chronicle of the Reigns of Stephen, Henry II, and Richard I by Gervase, the Monk of Canterbury* (1879–80), *Chronicles of the Reigns of Edward I and Edward II* (1882–83), and others.

Stucco House, The. A novel by Gilbert Cannan, published in 1918.

Students, The. A play printed in 1762, said by John Genest to be "professedly *Love's Labour's Lost* adapted to the stage," but it does not seem ever to have been acted.

Studies in Seven Arts. A critical work by Arthur Symons, published in 1906.

Study in Scarlet, A. The first of the Sherlock Holmes adventures by Arthur Conan Doyle, published in 1887.

Stukeley (stūk′li). In George Peele's play *The Battle of Alcazar*, an English adventurer (the historical Sir Thomas Stucley or Stukely), killed in the battle.

Stukeley, William. b. at Holbeach, Lincolnshire, England, Nov. 7, 1687; d. at London, March 3, 1765. An English antiquary. He published some 20 works on the antiquities of England, especially on Stonehenge (1740) and other reputed Druid remains.

Sturgeon (stėr′jon), **Major.** A character in Samuel Foote's play *The Mayor of Garratt.*

Sturluson (stör′lụ.sôn) or **Sturleson** (-le-), **Snorri.** See **Snorri Sturluson.**

Sturm und Drang (shtůrm ůnt dräng). See **Storm and Stress.**

Stutly (stut′li), **Will.** In the Robin Hood ballad cycle, one of Robin Hood's band in Sherwood Forest. He was taken by the sheriff, and was about to be hanged, when Robin Hood and his men arrived and rescued him at the very foot of the gallows.

Stymphalides (stim.fal′i.dēz). In Greek legend, a flock of fierce birds near Lake Stymphalus. Heracles killed them as one of his twelve labors.

Styx (stiks). In Greek mythology, one of the five rivers surrounding Hades, over which the souls of the dead had to pass. It was so sacred that the gods swore by it. Styx was also the name of a river in Arcadia, whose waters were believed to be poisonous and to flow to the underworld. The Arcadians swore by it.

Styx. In Greek mythology, a daughter of Oceanus, the goddess of the river Styx, by whom the most solemn oaths were sworn.

Subtilis (sub′ti.lis), **Doctor.** See **Duns Scotus, John.**

Subtle (sut′l). The title character, a knavish cheat, in Ben Jonson's *Alchemist.*

Subtle. A sharper in Samuel Foote's comedy *The Englishman in Paris.*

Succession, a Comedy of the Generations. A novel by Ethel Sidgwick, published in 1913. It is the sequel to her novel *Promise* (1910).

Such Things Are. A tragedy (1787) by Elizabeth Inchbald, based on the life of the prison reformer John Howard (1726–90), who is represented by the character Haswell.

Suckling (suk′ling), **Sir John.** b. at Whitton, Middlesex, England (baptized Feb. 10, 1609); supposed to have committed suicide at Paris, c1642. An English Royalist (Cavalier) poet and man of fashion at the court of Charles I. His father was a comptroller of the household of Charles I. In 1623 he entered Trinity College, Cambridge, and fought (1631–32) in the Marquis of Hamilton's troop in Gustavus Adolphus's army. Returning to court just as the masques had passed their splendor, he wrote plays adapted to the scenery which the taste for them had developed. *Aglaura* was produced in 1637, and *Brennoralt*, under the name of its first draft, *The Discontented Colonel*, appeared in quarto in 1640. When the war with the Scottish Covenanters began (1639), he raised a troop of 100 horse for the king. In May, 1641, he was implicated in a plot for the liberation of the Earl of Strafford, was charged with high treason, and fled from England. He is best known from his lyric poems and ballads, such as "Why so pale and wan, fond lover?" from *Aglaura*, and "Out upon it, I have loved three whole days together." Suckling has been noted as the typical Cavalier, dashing, rich, a bit of a ladies' man, and a daring gambler;

---

fat, fāte, fär, àsk, fāre; net, mē, hèr; pin, pīne; not, nōte, mōve, nôr; up, lūte, pùll; ᴛʜ, then;

he is said to have invented cribbage and was noted as a card player and bowler.

Suddlechop (sud'l.chop), **Benjamin.** In Sir Walter Scott's novel *The Fortunes of Nigel*, a barber of remarkable versatility: "he could . . . draw a cup of beer as well as a tooth, tap a hogshead as well as a vein, and wash with a draft of good ale the moustaches which his art had just trimmed."

Suddlechop, Ursula. In Sir Walter Scott's novel *The Fortunes of Nigel*, the wife of Benjamin Suddlechop. She is known for her ability to keep a secret (unless compelled by a "sufficient bribe" to do otherwise) and is in great demand as a go-between in various matters of the heart.

Sudermann (zö'dėr.män), **Hermann.** b. at Matzicken, in East Prussia, Dec. 9, 1857; d. at Berlin, Nov. 21, 1928. A German playwright and novelist who enjoyed enormous popularity around the end of the 19th century. Many critics consider that his best work is to be found in his early novel, *Frau Sorge* (1887; Eng. trans., *Dame Care*, 1891). *Der Katzensteg* (1889) was much read at the time, but attracts few modern readers. Late in life he returned to narrative writing with *Litauische Geschichten* (1917) and the three novels *Der tolle Professor* (1926; Eng. trans., *The Mad Professor*, 1928), *Die Frau des Steffen Tromholt* (1927; Eng. trans., *The Wife of Steffen Tromholt*, 1929), and *Purzelchen* (1928; Eng. trans., *The Dance of Youth*, 1930). Of his plays, the two that brought him greatest fame were *Die Ehre* (1889) and *Heimat* (1893; Eng. trans., *Magda*, 1896).

Sue (sö; French, sü), **Eugène.** [Pseudonym of **Marie Joseph Sue.**] b. at Paris, Dec. 10, 1804; d. at Annecy, Savoie, France, July 3, 1857. A French novelist. His sponsors were Prince Eugène Beauharnais and the empress Josephine; from the former he took the name Eugène, which he prefixed to Sue to form his nom de plume. After a short stay at the Lycée Bonaparte in Paris, he took up painting and then medicine. He spent six years in the navy as a surgeon, falling heir to his father's large estate on his return to France in 1830. Chance led him to write his first novel, *Plick et Plock* (1831), and he was encouraged by its success to publish *Atar-Gull* (1831), *La Salamandre* (2 vols., 1832), *La Coucaratcha* (4 vols., 1832–34), and *La Vigie de Koat-Ven* (1833). For the subject matter of all these works he drew largely upon his store of personal reminiscences and experiences. A great deal of sound information on naval matters is found embodied in his *Histoire de la marine française* (1835–37). Dropping gradually into the general style of novel, he published *Arthur* (1838), *Le Marquis de Létorière* (1839), *Mathilde* (1841), and *Le Morne au diable* (1842). In a more erudite strain he composed two historical novels, *Latréaumont* (1837) and *Jean Cavalier* (1840). He exerted a profound influence by the views to which he gave expression in his two most popular works, *Les Mystères de Paris* (1842–43) and *Le Juif errant* (1844–45). The change of government drove him into exile in 1852, and he spent the remainder of his life at Annecy. In addition to the works mentioned above, he wrote a few plays and a number of other novels.

Sue Bridehead (sö brīd'hed).   See **Bridehead, Sue.**

Suetonius (swē.tō'ni.us).   [Full name, **Gaius Suetonius Tranquillus.**] fl. in the first part of the 2nd century A.D. A Roman biographer and historian. He was private secretary to Hadrian (c119–121), and was a friend of the younger Pliny, whom he accompanied to Bithynia in 112. His chief work is *Lives of the Caesars*, which contains biographies (of an anecdotal character) of the first 12 caesars, including Julius. It is important on account of its revelations concerning the private life of the emperors. Fragments of his *De grammaticis* and of other works are extant.

Suffolk (suf'ọk), (1st) **Duke of.** In Shakespeare's *Henry VIII*, the historical Charles Brandon. He is present in a number of scenes including the coronation of Anne, the arraignment of Cranmer, and the christening of Princess Elizabeth.

Suffolk, (4th) **Earl of.** In Shakespeare's *1 Henry VI*, the historical William de la Pole, a Lancastrian supporter who captures Margaret at Angiers. He arranges her marriage with Henry and becomes her lover. In *2 Henry VI*, he is created (1st) Duke and attains greater power, managing the imprisonment of Gloucester and the banishment of the Duchess of Gloucester. He himself is banished and later killed by Walter Whitmore.

Suhrab (sö.räb').   See **Rustam.**

Sullen (sul'ẹn), **Mrs.** The gay, youthful wife of the drunken Squire Sullen, in George Farquhar's comedy *The Beaux' Stratagem.*

Sullen, Squire. The drunken husband of the heroine in George Farquhar's comedy *The Beaux' Stratagem.*

Sullen Lovers, The. [Full title, **The Sullen Lovers; or, The Impertinents.**] A comedy (1668) by Thomas Shadwell, based on Molière's *Le Misanthrope.* The prologue censures Dryden's lovers, saying that he presents a "swearing, drinking, whoring ruffian for a lover" and "an impudent, ill-bred tomrig for a mistress."

Sullivan (sul'i.vạn), Sir **Arthur Seymour.** b. at London, May 13, 1842; d. there, Nov. 22, 1900. An English composer and conductor. He was choir boy in the chapel royal, won the Mendelssohn scholarship in 1856, studied at Leipzig (1858–61), was principal (1876–81) of the National Training School for Music, and became (1888) president of the Birmingham and Midland Institution. In 1867 he and George Grove discovered at Vienna a number of lost pieces by Franz Schubert, including the *Rosamunde* music. He is famous for his operettas for which W. S. Gilbert wrote the librettos (1871 et seq.). Among those composed with others are *Cox and Box* (1867; with F. C. Burnand), *The Zoo* (1875; with B. Rowe), *Ivanhoe* (1891; libretto by Julian Sturgis), and *Haddon Hall* (1892; with S. Grundy). He composed many songs (including *Orpheus with his Lute, The Lost Chord, Arabian Love Song, O Fair Dove, O Fond Dove,* and *If Doughty Deeds*); the oratorios *The Prodigal Son* (1869), *The Light of the World* (1873), and *The Martyr of Antioch* (1880); incidental music for *The Tempest, The Merchant of Venice, The Merry Wives of Windsor, Macbeth,* and *Henry VIII,* and for Wills's *Olivia;* part-songs, anthems, services,

---

ḍ, d or j; ṣ, s or sh; ṭ, t or ch; ẓ, z or zh; o, F. cloche; ü, F. menu; ċh, Sc. loch; ṅ, F. bonbon.

hymn-tunes (including *Onward, Christian Soldiers*, cantatas, a symphony in E, and music for Longfellow's *Golden Legend*.

Sullivan, Timothy Daniel. b. at Bantry, County Cork, Ireland, 1827; d. at Dublin, March 31, 1914. An Irish poet and journalist. He served in Parliament for many years, representing County Westmeath, Dublin, and County Donegal. He was a contributor (1854–84) to *The Nation*, and its owner and editor (1884–1900). He was lord mayor of Dublin (1886–87). Author of *Dunboy* (1868), *Green Leaves* (1879), *Lays of the Land League* (1887), *Poems* (1888), *Prison Poems and Lays of Tullamore* (1888), *Blanaid and Other Irish Poems, Historical and Legendary* (1892), *Evergreen* (1907), and other volumes of poetry. He also wrote *Recollections of Troubled Times in Irish Politics* (1905).

Sumer is icumen in (sŭm'ėr is i.kŭm'ẹn in). [Also, **Cuckoo Song**.] A Middle English folk song, perhaps the most famous of Middle English lyrics, preserved in a single manuscript in the British Museum. The accompanying music is of considerable importance, since the song is the earliest known example of a six-part round (or circular canon). It is usually thought to have been composed c1240, but some have argued for a later date, c1300.

Summer (sum'ėr), **Will.** [Also: **Summers** or **Somers**.] A jester of Henry VIII. His effigy is at Hampton Court, and his portrait, by Holbein, at Kensington. Several fools in old plays are called by his name.

Summer Holiday, or Gibraltar (ji.brôl'tạr). A novel by Naomi Royde-Smith, published in 1929. It was issued in America under the title *Give Me My Sin Again*.

Summers (sum'ėrz), **Montague.** [Full name, **Alphonsus Joseph-Mary Augustus Montague Summers**.] b. April 10, 1880; d. 1948. An English clergyman and author, considered an authority on witchcraft and demonology, as well as in the field of Restoration drama. His numerous books include *Poems* (1907), *Jane Austen, An Appreciation* (1919), *The History of Witchcraft and Demonology* (1926), *Horrid Mysteries* (1927), *The Vampire, His Kith and Kin* (1928), *The Werewolf* (1933), *The Black Mass* (1936), *A Popular History of Witchcraft* (1937), and *Six Ghost Stories* (1937). Among his critical works are *Architecture and the Gothic Novel* (1931), *The Playhouse of Pepys* (1935), *The Gothic Achievement* (1939), and *A Bibliography of the Gothic Novel* (1940).

Summers (or **Summer**) **Islands** (sum'ėrz). Former names of **Bermuda**.

Summer's Night. A novel by Sylvia Thompson, published in 1932.

Summerson (sum'ėr.sọn), **Esther.** The illegitimate daughter of Lady Dedlock and Captain Hawdon, and ward of Mr. Jarndyce, who calls her "Dame Durden"; one of the principal characters in Dickens's *Bleak House*. She is the narrator of a large part of the story, and finally marries the doctor, Alan Woodcourt.

Summoner's Tale (sum'ọn.ėrz), **The.** [Also, **The Sompnour's Tale**.] One of Chaucer's *Canterbury Tales*. The Summoner's business was to summon delinquents to the ecclesiastical courts. "The Friar's Tale" is aimed at the summoner and throws him into a furious rage. He in his turn tells how a hypocritical friar is humiliated. The tale, at bottom merely a coarse anecdote, has been skillfully expanded with witty dialogue and satirical characterization. Chaucer describes the Summoner as having a red, pimpled face, with eyes close together, sly but stupid:

> For sawcefleem he was, with eyen narwe.
> As hoot he was, and lecherous, as a sparwe;
> With scalled browes blake, and piled berd;
> Of his visage children were aferd.

Sun in Capricorn (kap'ri.kôrn), **The.** A novel by Edward Sackville-West, published in 1934.

Sun Is My Undoing, The. A historical novel by Marguerite Steen, published in 1941.

Sunium (sö'ni.um) or **Sunium Promontorium** (prom-ọn.tō'ti.um). In ancient geography, the promontory at the SE extremity of Attica, Greece, in modern times known as Cape Colonna or Sounion. It contains the ruins of a temple of Athena, with a large statue, long a famous landmark from the sea.

Sunnites (sun'īts). [Also, **Sunnis** (sŭn'iz).] A Mohammedan sect comprising the greater part of the Moslem world, usually claiming to be the traditional or orthodox sect. They recognize the first three caliphs as legitimate successors of Mohammed, and accept six books of the *Sunna*, or "rule," which purport to contain the verbal utterances of Mohammed, in contradistinction to the Koran, the written revelation. The Sunnites are opposed by the Shiites, who hold that Ali was the first legitimate successor of Mohammed. They also have five books of traditions, differing from those of the Sunnites. In the course of time many differences of practice have grown up. The Mohammedans of Turkey, Arabia, N Africa, and India are mostly Sunnites, those of Iran and many in India being Shiites.

Sun's Darling, The. A "moral masque" by John Ford and Thomas Dekker, licensed in 1624 and published in 1656.

Superhuman Antagonists, The. A volume of poetry by Sir William Watson, published in 1919.

Supple (sup'l). A character in Colley Cibber's comedy *The Double Gallant*.

Supple. The spiritual adviser and boon companion of Squire Western in Henry Fielding's novel *Tom Jones*.

Supplicants. In Scottish history, those who protested, about 1637–38, against Laud's policy in Scotland: known later as Covenanters.

Supposes, The. A comedy (produced in 1566), based on Ariosto's *I Suppositi*, as translated by George Gascoigne. It was later used as the subplot for Shakespeare's *Taming of the Shrew*. It is one of the earliest of English prose comedies.

Supremacy, Act of. In English history: **1.** A statute of 1534 (26 Hen. VIII, c. 1) which proclaimed that Henry VIII was the supreme head of the English Church. **2.** A statute of 1558–59 (1 Eliz., c. 1) vesting spir-

---

fat, fāte, fär, ȧsk, fāre; net, mē, hėr; pin, pīne; not, nōte, mȯve, nôr; up, lūte, pụll; ᴛʜ, then;

itual authority in the crown, to the exclusion of all foreign jurisdiction.

Surface (sẽr'fạs), **Charles.** A gay and amiable rake in R. B. Sheridan's *School for Scandal.*

Surface, Joseph. A malicious hypocrite in R. B. Sheridan's *School for Scandal,* the elder brother of the reckless Charles. He is called "the Tartuffe of sentiment."

Surface, Sir Oliver. The rich uncle of Charles and Joseph Surface in Sheridan's *School for Scandal.*

Surgeon's Daughter, The. A short novel by Sir Walter Scott, published in 1827.

Surly (sẽr'li). A dour friend of Epicure Mammon who scoffs at alchemy in Jonson's *The Alchemist.* He warns Dame Pliant against the cheating of Face and Subtle, but is brazenly outfaced by them in the presence of her brother, Kastril.

Surly. A kind of "plain dealer" in John Crowne's *Sir Courtly Nice.* He is the antithesis of Sir Courtly, and one of the most repulsive figures in the whole range of English comedy.

Surrey (sur'i), **Earl of.** See **Howard, Henry.**

Surrey, (1st) Duke of. In Shakespeare's *Richard II,* the historical Thomas Holland, also 3rd Earl of Kent. He defends Aumerle against a charge of treason, joins the rebellion against Henry IV, and is captured and killed. He is also referred to in the play as Kent (V. vi).

Surrey, Earl of. In Shakespeare's *2 Henry IV,* the historical Thomas Fitzalan, a supporter of the King.

Surrey, Earl of. In Shakespeare's *Henry VIII,* the historical Thomas Howard, a gentleman of the court. He opposes Wolsey and avenges the death of Buckingham.

Surrey, Earl of. In Shakespeare's *Richard III,* the historical Thomas Howard, later the 2nd Duke of Norfolk, a supporter of Richard.

Surtees (sẽr'tēz), **Robert Smith.** b. at Durham, England, 1803; d. at Brighton, England, March 16, 1864. An English lawyer, journalist, and writer of humorous and sporting novels. Educated at Durham grammar school and apprenticed to a lawyer, he practiced law for a time at London, later turning to journalism, and contributing to the *Sporting Magazine.* With Rudolph Ackermann he began (1831) the *New Sporting Magazine,* in the pages of which his fictional Cockney grocer, John Jorrocks, first appeared. Author of *The Horseman's Manual* (1831); and of *Jorrocks' Jaunts and Jollities, or the Hunting, Shooting, Racing, Driving, Sailing, Eating, Eccentric and Extravagant Exploits of That Renowned Sporting Citizen, Mr. John Jorrocks* (1838), *Handley Cross* (1843), *Hillingdon Hill, a Tale of Country Life* (1845), *Mr. Sponge's Sporting Tour* (1853), *Ask Mamma* (1858), and *Mr. Facey Romford's Hounds* (1865), humorous novels.

Surtr (sõr'tẽr). In Old Norse mythology, a fire giant.

Surveyor. In Shakespeare's *Henry VIII,* the surveyor to the Duke of Buckingham. He swears that his master threatened Henry's life.

Surya (sõr'yạ). The Hindu sun god and personification of the sun. He is believed to move on a car drawn by four (or seven) ruddy horses. Surya is the preserver of all things and the vivifier of men. He is still worshiped in parts of India, and his festival, the *Suryapuja,* is still observed in the spring.

Susan Mountford (sõ'zạn mount'fọrd). See **Mountford, Susan.**

Susan Nipper (nip'ẽr). See **Nipper, Susan.**

Susanna (sõ.zan'ạ). Wife of Joachim, the subject of The History of Susanna, one of the books of the Apocrypha (an addition to the Book of Daniel). The subject of her surprise by two of the elders while in her bath has been frequently used by painters (perhaps most notably by Rembrandt and Rubens). The story of Daniel's cross-examination of the elders and his demonstration of the falsity of their accusation has been called the first detective story.

Suspense. A novel (1925) by Joseph Conrad, left unfinished at the author's death.

Suspicious Husband, The. A comedy (1747) by Benjamin Hoadly.

Sussex (sus'ẹks). A maritime county in SE England. It nearly corresponds to the early kingdom of Sussex, one of the Saxon kingdoms during the Heptarchy, which was founded by Ælla (who landed here in 477), and came under the supremacy of Wessex c685. It was the scene of the landing of William the Conqueror and of the battles of Hastings, or Senlac (1066), and Lewes (1264).

Sussex Gorse. A novel (1916) by Sheila Kaye-Smith, depicting the struggle with the soil.

Sutra (sõ'trạ). In Sanskrit, literally a "thread" or "string," hence, a brief rule, or book of such rules, so named because each rule was a short line, or because the collection was a string of rules. There are four groups of *Sutras* of c500 to 200 B.C.: the *Sharutasutras,* treating especially of ritual, and the *Grihyasutras* and *Dharmasutras,* which are, respectively, rules for family worship and domestic ceremonies and rules for conventional social customs, and a fourth group which treats of magic and astronomy.

Sutro (sõ'trō), **Alfred.** b. at London, Aug. 7, 1863; d. in Surrey, England, Sept. 11, 1933. An English playwright and translator. His plays include *The Cave of Illusion* (1900), *Carrots* (1900), *Arethusa* (1903), *The Walls of Jericho* (1904), *The Perfect Lover* (1905), *The Fascinating Mr. Vanderveldt* (1906), *John Glayde's Honour* (1907), *The Builder of Bridges* (1908), *The Laughing Lady* (1922), *The Desperate Lovers* (1927), and *Living Together* (1929). He translated Maurice Maeterlinck's *Wisdom and Destiny* and *The Life of the Bee.*

Svengali (sven.gä'li). The hypnotist in George Du Maurier's *Trilby.*

Swain (swän), **Charles.** [Called "the Manchester Poet."] b. at Manchester, England, Jan. 4, 1801; d. Sept. 22, 1874. An English poet. He wrote *Dryburgh Abbey* (1832).

Swan, the. A London playhouse built in 1594 on the Bankside, on the south bank of the Thames. A well-known drawing of the Swan, one of the very few in existence of Elizabethan theaters, shows a

---

ḍ, d or j; ṣ, s or sh; ṭ, t or ch; ẓ, z or zh; ọ, F. cloche; ü, F. menu; ċh, Sc. loch; ṅ, F. bonbon.

circular building with three galleries of three tiers each. A forestage or apron stage comes forward into the pit yard, and halfway back columns support the "shadow" or roof of the stage. It had no inner stage, but merely two doors leading into the dressing rooms. Above the stage were six boxes, including an upper stage, a room for distinguished spectators, and one for musicians. After 1620, it was used for prize fights, and by 1632 a contemporary source referred to it as "fallen to decay."

"Swan of Avon" (ā'vŏn, av'ŏn), **the.** In Jonson's *To the Memory of Shakespeare*, a reference to Shakespeare, who was born at Stratford-on-Avon. The phrase has since passed into the language, and is now widely used and generally accepted as denoting Shakespeare.

"Swan of Lichfield" (lich'fēld), **the.** See **Seward, Anna.**

Swan Song. A novel by John Galsworthy, published in 1928. A continuation of the author's portrayal of the Forsyte family, it was later included in *A Modern Comedy* (1929).

Swaran (swä'rän). A character in *Fingal*, one of the "poems of Ossian" by the Scottish poet Macpherson. Swaran is the Scandinavian king of Lochlin, invader of Ireland.

Swedenborg (swē'dĕn.bôrg; Swedish, svä'dĕn.bôry'), **Emanuel.** [Original surname, **Svedberg** or **Swedberg.**] b. at Stockholm, Jan. 29, 1688; d. at London, March 29, 1772. A Swedish scientist and seer, whose theological writings contain the doctrines of the New Church. He was educated at Uppsala University, and later pursued his scientific studies abroad, devoting more than 12 years, at different times, to study in England, the Netherlands, France, Germany, and Italy. In 1716 he published Sweden's first scientific journal, *Daedalus Hyperboreus*, and was appointed by the king to the Royal Board of Mines. While serving as engineer under Charles XII at the siege of Fredrikshald, his ingenuity was the key factor in making possible the transport of a number of small ships of war 16 miles overland to frustrate the Danish blockade. In 1719 he took his seat in the Swedish House of Nobles, where he played an active part in the revival of his country's war-wrecked economy.

Scientific Achievements. For 25 years he served on the Board of Mines, making valuable contributions to the improvement of mining and smelting methods, based on extensive investigation of the industry in Germany and Bohemia. During this period he published scientific works in many fields, including chemistry, physics, mathematics, astronomy, geology, engineering, mining, metallurgy, anatomy, and physiology, the most important being *Opera Philosophica et Mineralia* (1734), *Oeconomia regni animalis* (1740), and *Regnum animale* (1744–45). Among his most noteworthy scientific achievements were an airplane design (the first based on the principle of stationary wings for support with a separate mechanism for propulsion), a theory that the planets of our solar system were originally part of the sun's body and a formulation of a nebular hypothesis antedating Kant and Laplace, and the localization of the motor centers

in the brain cortex. Unfortunately, a great number of his scientific works remained unpublished until long after his death, so that his genius is only now beginning to be recognized by scientists.

Contributions as Religious Thinker. At the age of 55 he underwent a religious crisis which culminated in a vision of the Lord, and the belief that he was called to reveal a new Christian doctrine. He resigned from the Board of Mines and devoted the last 25 years of his life to Biblical studies and theological writings, the most important of which are the *Arcana Coelestia* (8 vols., 1749–56), *Heaven and Hell* (1758), *Divine Love and Wisdom* (1763), and *The True Christian Religion* (1771). Though Swedenborg himself remained a Lutheran and had no idea of founding a new ecclesiastical body, after his death his English disciples established themselves as a "dissenting sect."

Sweedlepipe (swē'dl.pīp), **Paul** (or **Poll**). In Dickens's *Martin Chuzzlewit*, a bird-fancier and "easy shaver," Mrs. Gamp's landlord.

Sweet (swēt), **Henry.** b. at London, Sept. 15, 1845; d. at Oxford, England, April 30, 1912. An English philologist and phonetician. In 1901 he was appointed reader in phonetics at Oxford. His works include editions of Old and Middle English texts, Old and Middle English readers and primers, *A History of English Sounds from the Earliest Period* (1874), *A Handbook of Phonetics* (1877), *A Primer of Spoken English* (1890), *A Primer of Phonetics* (1890), *A New English Grammar* (1892–98), *A Student's Dictionary of Anglo-Saxon* (1897), *The Practical Study of Languages* (1899), *A History of Language* (1900), and others.

Sweet Waters. A novel by Harold Nicolson, published in 1921.

Sweet William's Farewell to Black-eyed Susan (wil'yạmz; sō'zạn). See **Black-eyed Susan.**

Swidger (swij'ẽr), **George.** In Dickens's tale *The Haunted Man*, the brother-in-law of Milly Swidger. He dies from the dreadful effect of Redlaw ("the haunted man").

Swidger, Milly. In Dickens's tale *The Haunted Man*, the gentle, kind-hearted wife of the college gatekeeper. She is the only one of all the characters in the story who is not affected by the dreadful influence of Redlaw ("the haunted man"), and it is only through her that he and his victims are finally restored to sanity.

Swidger, Philip. In Dickens's tale *The Haunted Man*, the father-in-law of Milly Swidger.

Swidger, William. In Dickens's tale *The Haunted Man*, the husband of Milly Swidger. He and his father are only saved from Redlaw ("the haunted man") through the quiet goodness of Milly.

Swift (swift), **Benjamin.** Pseudonym of **Paterson, William Romaine.**

Swift, Jonathan. [Called **Dean Swift.**] b. at Dublin, Nov. 30, 1667; d. there, Oct. 19, 1745. An English satirist and man of letters. His grandfather, Thomas Swift, vicar of Goodrich in Herefordshire, was defiantly loyal to Charles I. Swift matriculated at Trinity College, Dublin, in 1682, leaving with only a degree *speciali gratia* in 1686. In 1688, owing to the Revolution, he went to England, and in 1689 became amanuensis or secretary to Sir William

Temple (who had known Swift's family in Ireland) at Moor Park, near Farnham. Swift disliked his subordinate position, and returned to Dublin in about a year. In 1692 he received the degree of M.A. at Oxford, took orders in 1695, and in 1695 obtained the prebend of Kilroot, County Antrim, Ireland. In 1696, tired of obscurity, he returned to Sir William Temple, and remained with him till his death in January, 1699. During these years of quiet Swift not only read much, but had a brief experience at court which gave him a useful insight into politics. In 1697 he wrote *A Tale of a Tub* and the *Battle of the Books* (both published in 1704); he also published Temple's letters (1700–03). He became vicar of the rustic parish of Laracor near Dublin, with two incidental small livings, in 1700. In 1696 he had proposed marriage to Jane Waring ("Varina") of Belfast, who refused him on account of her ill health and his poverty. When he obtained the living of Laracor, in 1700, she looked more favorably on marriage. He broke off the match by making impossible and insulting conditions. He published the Whig tract *A Discourse on the Dissensions between the Nobles and Commons in Athens and Rome* in 1701. At Laracor he was joined by Esther Johnson ("Stella," born in 1681), whom Swift had known at Moor Park, and who, with Rebecca Dingley as companion, lived near his house but never in it except as guests or during his absences. In 1708 he wrote the pamphlets *The Sentiments of a Church of England Man, A Project for the Advancement of Religion,* the ironical *Argument against Abolishing Christianity,* and his witty poem *Baucis and Philemon.* He was at London for a longer or shorter period nearly every year from 1701 to 1710. In 1710 he abandoned the Whigs and went over to the Tories: a full account of this is given in the *Journal to Stella,* a volume of the letters he wrote (1710–13) to Esther Johnson and Rebecca Dingley, which depicted not only everyday life in London but also the political maneuverings of the period. In November, 1710, he began to write for the *Examiner,* a Tory journal, and had a chief hand in forming a political-literary "Society of Brothers." In July, 1711, he left the *Examiner,* but continued to write Tory pamphlets (*The Conduct of the Allies* and *Remarks on the Barrier Treaty*). He was appointed by Queen Anne dean of Saint Patrick's, Dublin, in 1713. He was intimately associated with Edward Harley, 2nd Earl of Oxford, and Henry St. John, Viscount Bolingbroke, and was a friend of Richard Steele, Joseph Addison, Alexander Pope, John Arbuthnot, William Congreve, Thomas Parnell, and John Gay; Arbuthnot and Pope were joined with Swift in an imaginary "Scriblerus Club," out of which came many of the ideas for *Gulliver.* Some of his best work belongs to this period, the last four years of the reign of Queen Anne. After the fall of the Tories in 1714 Swift retired to Dublin. While he was living at London, Esther Vanhomrigh, the "Vanessa" of his poem *Cadenus and Vanessa,* had fallen in love with him. In 1714 her mother died, and she followed Swift to Ireland, to a house at Celbridge not far from Dublin. Gossip then said, and the tradition has persisted and been supported by some scholars, that "Stella" was privately Swift's wife and "Vanessa" his mistress. There is no certainty on either

point. Vanessa died in 1723; Stella survived her. Swift devoted himself fiercely to the condition of Ireland and Irish politics, and in 1720 published his *Proposal for the Universal Use of Irish Manufactures,* urging the disuse of English goods by the Irish. A patent for supplying Ireland with copper coins had been granted to William Wood, who was to share a large expected profit with the Duchess of Kendal, the mistress of George I. In 1724 Swift attacked this abuse in letters signed "M. B. Drapier," collected as the *Drapier's Letters,* which raised his popularity to a passion in Ireland. Returning to England in 1726, he was recalled on account of "Stella's" illness, but she did not die till 1728. In 1726 he published *Travels into Several Remote Nations of the World . . . by Lemuel Gulliver,* later known as *Gulliver's Travels,* his greatest work, and in 1729 his *Modest Proposal for Preventing the Children of Poor People in Ireland from Being a Burden to their Parents,* his ironical suggestion being that they should be fattened and eaten. In his later years his brain became diseased, and he was alternately in a state of torment or one of apathy. He was declared insane in 1742, but lived till 1745. He was buried in Saint Patrick's Cathedral, Dublin. Among his other works are *Predictions for the ensuing year* (1708; a playful attack upon astrology in the person of John Partridge, the almanac-maker, in which Swift assumed the character of an almanac-maker and the name of Isaac Bickerstaff, Astrologer), *A Proposal for Correcting, Improving, and Ascertaining the English Tongue* (1712; the only work to which he ever put his name), *History of the Last Four Years of Queen Anne* (not published till 1758), a number of volumes of miscellanies with Arbuthnot, Pope, Gay, and others, *A Complete Collection of Genteel and Ingenious Conversation* (1738), *Verses on the Death of Doctor Swift. Written by Himself* (1739), and *Directions to Servants* (1745).

Swinburne (swin′bẽrn), **Algernon Charles.** b. at London, April 5, 1837; d. there, April 10, 1909. An English poet and man of letters. He was educated at Eton and Oxford (Balliol College), entering the university in 1856 and leaving it in 1860 without a degree. Though Swinburne wrote impressionistic criticism, as well as tragedies in the Greek and Elizabethan tradition, he was primarily a great lyric poet, whose work was characterized by power of imagination, fervor, metrical skill, and inventiveness. The sea, freedom, the ideal republic which was to spring from spiritual progress, children, great men, as well as his love of literature and old stories, are among the favorite sources of the poet's inspiration. He published *The Queen-Mother and Rosamond* (1860), *Atalanta in Calydon* (1865), *Chastelard* (1865), *Poems and Ballads* (1866; this volume was severely criticized for its alleged sensuality and paganism, both in England and in America, where it bore the title *Laus Veneris, and Other Poems and Ballads;* Swinburne replied to the criticism with *Notes on Poems and Reviews,* 1866), *William Blake* (1868), *Songs before Sunrise* (1871), *Under the Microscope* (1872; an answer to Robert Buchanan's attack on "the fleshly school"), *Bothwell* (1874), *Essays and Studies* (1875), *George Chapman* (1875), *Erechtheus* (1876), *A Note on Charlotte*

Brontë (1877), *Poems and Ballads: Second Series* (1878), *A Study of Shakespeare* (1880), *The Heptalogia* (1880), *Songs of the Springtides* (1880), *Studies in Song* (1880), *Mary Stuart* (1881), *Tristram of Lyonesse* (1882), *A Century of Roundels* (1883), *A Midsummer Holiday and Other Poems* (1884), *Marino Faliero* (1885), *Miscellanies* (1886), *A Study of Victor Hugo* (1886), *Locrine* (1887), *A Study of Ben Jonson* (1889), and *Poems and Ballads: Third Series* (1889). The best poems are contained in the various series of *Poems and Ballads* and in *Songs before Sunrise*. Among the later works are *Studies in Prose and Poetry* (1894), *The Tale of Balen* (1896), *Rosamund, Queen of the Lombards* (1899), *Love's Cross-Currents* (a novel, 1905), and *The Duke of Gandia* (1908).

Swing (swing), **Captain.** A fictitious name signed to various threatening letters in England, about 1830, especially to letters addressed to the users of threshing machines, which were obnoxious to the old-fashioned threshers.

Swinnerton (swin'ẽr.tọn), **Frank (Arthur).** b. at Wood Green, Middlesex, England, Aug. 12, 1884—. An English novelist and critic. His works include *The Merry Heart* (1909), *The Young Idea* (1910), *The Casement* (1911), *The Happy Family* (1912), *R. L. Stevenson: A Critical Study* (1914), *Nocturne* (1917), *Shops and Houses* (1918), *September* (1919), *Coquette* (1921), *The Three Lovers* (1922), *Young Felix* (1923), *The Elder Sister* (1925), *A Brood of Ducklings* (1928), *Sketch of a Sinner* (1929), *The Georgian House* (1932), *Elizabeth* (1934), *The Georgian Literary Scene* (1935), *Swinnerton: An Autobiography* (1937), *The Fortunate Lady* (1941), *Thankless Child* (1942), *English Maiden* (1946), *The Cats and Rosemary* (1948), and *Faithful Company* (1948).

Swiss Family Robinson (rob'in.sọn). [German title, **Der schweizerische Robinson.**] Romance by J. R. Wyss. The scene is laid on a desert island about 1800. It was originally published under its German title in four volumes (1812–27).

Swithin (swiᴛʜ'in), **Saint.** [Also, **Swithun.**] b. near Winchester, England, probably c800; d. 862. A bishop of Winchester. It is said he performed many miraculous cures after his death, and he was translated with great ceremonial on July 15, 971. He was not regularly canonized, but received his title of saint on his translation. His legend is that when his remains were moved to a new cathedral, he showed his protest by causing 40 days of rain: hence the saying that if it rains on Saint Swithin's Day (July 15) it will rain for 40 days more.

Swiveller (swiv'ẹl.ẽr), **Dick.** A happy-go-lucky, devil-may-care fellow in Dickens's *Old Curiosity Shop.*

Sybaris (sib'ạ.ris). In ancient geography, a city of Magna Graecia, S Italy, situated near the Gulf of Tarentum in lat. 39°41' N., long. 16°28' E. The modern town of Terranova di Sibari is near the site. It was founded (720 B.C.) by Achaean colonists. It· was celebrated for its wealth, and its inhabitants were proverbial for their luxury (whence the epithet "Sybarite"). It was destroyed (510 B.C.) by the inhabitants of Crotona. A second Sybaris arose upon the ruins of the first, but it never flourished, and was finally merged in the Athenian

colony of Thurii (443 B.C.), which was built in the neighborhood. Herodotus is said to have been one of the colonists.

Sybil (sib'il). A political novel by Benjamin Disraeli, published in 1845. It describes the two "nations" of England (the rich and the poor) in the early 19th century. The heroine is the daughter of a Chartist, and the hero, Charles Egremont, is a "Tory democrat," as well as the son of a cruel landlord.

Sybil Warner (wôr'nẽr). See **Warner, Sybil.**

Sycorax (sik'ọ.raks). A witch, the mother of Caliban in Shakespeare's *Tempest;* in Dryden and D'Avenant's version, his sister.

Sydney (sid'ni), **Algernon.** See **Sidney, Algernon.**

Sydney Carton (kär'tọn). See **Carton, Sydney.**

Sykes (sīks), **Ella Constance.** d. March 23, 1939. An English traveler, author of works on Persia. She traveled in Persia (1894–96) and in Chinese Turkistan (1915) with her brother, Sir Percy Molesworth Sykes. Author of *Through Persia on a Side-Saddle* (1898), *The Story Book of the Shah, or Legends of Old Persia* (1901), *Persia and Its People* (1910), and *A Home-Help in Canada* (1912), and coauthor with her brother of *Through Deserts and Oases of Central Asia* (1920).

Sykes, Sir Percy Molesworth. b. 1867; d. at London, June 11, 1945. An English soldier and author; brother of Ella Constance Sykes. He traveled (1893–1918) in Persia and Baluchistan, holding several government positions. His organization (1916) of the South Persia Rifles helped to hold Persia against possible German or Turkish attack. His books include *Ten Thousand Miles in Persia* (1902), *The Glory of the Shia World*, *History of Persia*, *History of Exploration* (1934), *The Quest for Cathay* (1937), and *History of Afghanistan*. He was coauthor with his sister of *Through Deserts and Oases of Central Asia* (1920).

syllabus (sil'ạ.bus). A compendium containing the heads of a discourse, the main propositions of a course of lectures, etc.; an abstract; a table of statements contained in any writing, of a scheme of lessons, or the like.

All these blessings put into one syllabus have given to baptism many honourable appellatives in Scripture and other divine writers.
(Jer. Taylor, *Works*, ed. 1835.)

Turning something difficult in his mind that was not in the scholastic syllabus.
(Dickens, *Our Mutual Friend.*)

Sylvander (sil.van'dẽr). The name under which Robert Burns corresponded with Mrs. Agnes Maclehose ("Clarinda"). The letters were published in 1802, afterward suppressed, and republished in 1845.

"Sylvanus Urban, Gent." (sil.vā'nus ẽr'ban). See under **Cave, Edward.**

Sylva, or a Discourse of Forest Trees (sil'vạ). A report on the condition of timber in the English dominions, by John Evelyn, published in 1664.

Sylvester (sil.ves'tẽr), **Josuah.** b. in Kent, England, 1563; d. at Middelburg, Netherlands, Sept. 28, 1618. An English poet. He translated into English verse the *Divine Weeks and Works* (1590, 1592, 1598–99, 1604, 1605–06) of Seigneur du Bartas, French diplomat and religious poet.

Sylvester Daggerwood (dag′ẽr.wŭd). A "whimsical interlude" (actually a prelude to another drama on the playbill) by George Colman the younger, produced in 1796. There are but two characters: Sylvester Daggerwood, a strolling player, and Fustian, a Grub Street playwright.

Sylvia (sil′vi.ạ). See also **Silvia**.

Sylvia and Michael (mī′kẹl). A novel by Compton Mackenzie, published in 1919. It continues the adventures of his hero and heroine in *Sinister Street* (1913) and *Sylvia Scarlett* (1918).

Sylvia Scarlett (skär′lẹt). A novel by Compton Mackenzie, published in 1918.

Sylvia's Lovers. A novel by Elizabeth Gaskell, published in 1863.

symbolism. 1. The investing of things with a symbolic meaning or character; the use of symbols. **2.** Symbolic character. **3.** An exposition or comparison of symbols or creeds.

Symeon of Durham (sim′ẽ.ọn; dur′ạm). See **Simeon of Durham.**

Symkyn (sim′kin). See under **Reeve's Tale, The.**

Symonds (sim′ọndz), **John Addington.** b. at Bristol, England, Oct. 5, 1840; d. at Rome, April 19, 1893. An English man of letters. He published *An Introduction to the Study of Dante* (1872), *Studies of the Greek Poets* (1873–76), and *Sketches in Italy and Greece* (1874). His best-known work, *The Renaissance in Italy*, consists of five parts: *The Age of the Despots* (1875), *The Revival of Learning* (1877), *The Fine Arts* (1877), *Italian Literature* (1881), and *The Catholic Reaction* (1886). He also wrote *Life of Shelley* (1878), *Sketches and Study in Italy* (1879), *Italian Byways* (1883), *Shakespeare's Predecessors in the English Drama* (1884), *Wine, Woman, and Song* (1884; an essay on the Latin songs of the 12th-century students), *Life of Sir Philip Sidney* (1886), *Life of Ben Jonson* (1886), *Life of Michelangelo* (1892), and several volumes of verse. He translated the sonnets of Michelangelo and Campanella (1878), and the autobiography of Benvenuto Cellini (1887).

Symons (sim′ọnz), **Arthur.** b. at Milford Haven, Wales, Feb. 28, 1865; d. at Wittersham, England, Jan. 22, 1945. A British poet, author, and critic, influential in spreading appreciation in England of the French symbolists and decadents. His works include *An Introduction to the Study of Browning* (1886), *Days and Nights* (1889), *Silhouettes* (1892), *London Nights* (1895), *Amoris Victima* (1897), *Studies in Two Literatures* (1897), *The Symbolist Movement in Literature* (1900), *Images of Good and Evil* (1900), *Collected Poems* (1901), *Plays, Acting, and Music* (1903), *Cities* (1903), *Studies in Prose and Verse* (1904), *Spiritual Adventures* (1905), *The Fool of the World* (1906), *Studies in Seven Arts* (1906), *William Blake* (1907), *Cities of Italy* (1907), *The Romantic Movement in English Poetry* (1909), *Tragedies* (1916; includes *The Harvesters, The Death of Agrippina,* and *Cleopatra in Judaea*), *Tristan and Iseult* (1917), *Color Studies in Paris* (1918), *Iseult of Brittany* (1920), *Cesare Borgia*

(1920), *Charles Baudelaire* (1921), *Parisian Nights* (1926), *Dramatis Personae* (1926), *Studies in Strange Souls* (1929), the autobiographical *Confessions* (1930), and *A Study of Walter Pater* (1932).

Sympathy and Other Stories. A collection by Peter Quennell, published in 1933.

Symplegades (sim.pleg′ạ.dēz). In Greek legend, two rocky cliffs at the entrance to the Black Sea. The ancients believed that they clashed together in order to crush any vessel that tried to pass between them. Legend has it that Jason's ship, the *Argo*, got safely through by sending a pigeon first, and slipping through quickly while the rocks were opening for the bird.

Symposium (sim.pō′zi.um), **The.** A work by Plato, consisting of an account given by Aristodemus of a banquet at the house of the tragic poet Agathon after one of his victories. At the banquet, together with other less famous persons, Socrates, the physician Eryximachus, Aristophanes, and (in the latter part of the work) Alcibiades, discuss the nature and praise of Eros (love).

syncopation. The contraction of a word by taking a letter, letters, or a syllable from the middle, as in the seamen's *fo′c′sle* for *forecastle;* especially, such omission of a short vowel between two consonants.

The time has long past for such syncopations and compressions as gave us arbalist, governor, pedant, and proctor, from arcubalista, gubernator, paedagogans, and procurator.

        (F. Hall, *Mod. Eng.*, note.)

syncope (sing′kọ.pē). The contraction of a word by elision; an elision or retrenchment of one or more letters or a syllable from the middle of a word, as in *ne'er* for *never.*

synecdoche (si.nek′dọ.kē). In rhetoric, a figure or trope by which the whole of a thing is put for a part, or a part for the whole, as the genus for the species, or the species for the genus, etc.: as, for example, a fleet of ten *sail* (for *ships*); a master employing new *hands* (for *workmen*).

Then againe if we vse such a word (as many times we doe) by which we driue the hearer to conceiue more or lesse or beyond or otherwise then the letter expresseth, and it be not by vertue of the former figures Metaphore and Abase and the rest, the Greeks then call it Synecdoche.

        (Puttenham, *Arte of Eng. Poesie.*)

Synge (sing), **John Millington.** b. near Dublin, in 1871; d. there, March 24, 1909. An Irish dramatist and poet. A graduate of Trinity College, Dublin (1892), he spent much time in Paris and elsewhere on the Continent and in the west of Ireland. He was associated with William Butler Yeats, who induced him to live in the Aran Islands and to leave literary criticism for creative writing about the Irish people, and who, with Lady Augusta Gregory, joined him in the founding (1904) and in the direction of the Abbey Theatre, Dublin. His writings, among the most influential in the Irish literary revival, deal with Irish peasant life. Besides two descriptive works, *The Aran Islands* (1907) and *Kerry and Wicklow,* his chief writings are his plays, which include *Riders to the Sea* (1905), *In the Shadow of the Glen* (1905), *The Well of the Saints* (1905), *The Playboy of the Western World* (1907),

---

ḍ, d or j; ṣ, s or sh; ṭ, t or ch; ẓ, z or zh; o, F. cloche; ü, F. menu; ċh, Sc. loch; ṅ, F. bonbon.

The Tinker's Wedding (1907), and *Deirdre of the Sorrows* (1910; unfinished).

Synge and the Ireland of His Time. A critical study of John Millington Synge by William Butler Yeats, published in 1911.

Synod of Whitby (hwit′bi). See **Whitby, Synod of.**

synopsis (si.nop′sis). A summary or brief statement giving a general view of some subject; a compendium of heads or short paragraphs so arranged as to afford a view of the whole or of principal parts of a matter under consideration; a conspectus.

That the reader may see in one view the exactness of the method, as well as the force of argument, I shall here draw up a short synopsis of this epistle.
(Warburton, *On Pope's Essay on Man.*)

I am now upon a methodical Synopsis of all

British Animals excepting Insects, and it will be a general Synops. of Quadrupeds.
(Ray, in Ellis's *Lit. Letters.*)

Syntax (sin′taks), **Dr.** A pious and amiable clergyman in William Combe's *Tour of Dr. Syntax in Search of the Picturesque* and its sequels.

Syphax (sī′faks). A Numidian ally of Cato, and eventually one of his betrayers, in Addison's tragedy *Cato.*

Syrinx (sir′ingks). In Greek mythology, a nymph who fled from Pan and prayed for help during the pursuit. She was transformed into a bed of reeds, just as Pan seized her. He found seven reeds in his hand, which gave forth a musical sound under his gasp of frustration. These he bound together into the instrument called the pipes of Pan (or syrinx).

T

Tabard (tab′ạrd), **the.** An ancient London hostelry, made famous by Chaucer as the house at which his pilgrims assembled before starting for Canterbury. It was situated on the High Street of Southwark, near the Kent Road. Stow says in 1598 that it was then "amongst the most ancient" of the "fair inns for receipt of travellers." It received its name from its sign, which was a tabard, or sleeveless coat. It was originally the property of the Abbey of Hyde. In 1866 the inn was condemned, and shortly afterward demolished and a freight depot of what was later the London, Midland, and Scottish Railway built on the spot. Until shortly before its destruction the inn was marked by an inscription (not ancient) which said "This is the Inne where Sir Jeffrey Chaucer and twenty pilgrims lay in their journey to Canterbury anno 1383." A small inn called the Tabard now stands near the old site. The Host of the Tabard was Harry Bailey.

Tabitha (tab′i.thạ). See **Dorcas.**

Tabitha Bramble (bram′bl). See **Bramble, Tabitha.**

Table Talk. A name given to various collections of essays. Perhaps the most notable works so entitled are those of Luther, of John Selden (published in 1689, after his death, by his amanuensis), of Hazlitt (1821–57), and of Coleridge (published by his son in 1835, and republished in 1884). Dyce published in 1856 *Recollections of the Table Talk of Samuel Rogers;* and Cowper added a poetical dialogue entitled *Table Talk* to a volume of poems published in 1782.

Tabley (tab′li), 3rd Baron **de.** Title of **Warren, John Byrne Leicester.**

Tacitus (tas′i.tus), **Cornelius.** b. c55 A.D.; d. probably after 117. A Roman historian, noted also as an orator. He was praetor in 88 and consul in 97. He was a friend of the younger Pliny. His extant works include *Dialogus de oratoribus*, an "attempt to demonstrate and explain the decay of oratory in the imperial period, in the form of a dialogue between literary celebrities of the time of Vespasian"; a biography of his father-in-law Julius Agricola

(*De vita et moribus Julii Agricolae*); the *Germania*, a celebrated ethnographical work on the Germans; the *Historiae*, a narrative of events in the reigns of Galba, Otho, Vitellius, Vespasian, Titus, and Domitian, of which only the first four books and the first half of the fifth book survive; and the *Annales*, a history of the Julian dynasty from the death of Augustus. Of the last work only the first four books and parts of the fifth and sixth have come down to us.

Tackleton (tak′l.tọn), **Mr.** A character in Dickens's *Cricket on the Hearth.* He is a toy merchant who has mistaken his vocation in life, and, "cramped and chafing in the peaceable pursuit of toy-making," becomes at last the implacable enemy of children.

Tadmor (tad′môr). See **Palmyra.**

Taffy (taf′i). A nickname for any Welshman: from the Welsh pronunciation of Davy, nickname for David, Saint David being the patron saint of Wales and David a common prename in that country.

Taglioni (tä.lyō′nē), **Maria.** b. at Stockholm, 1804; d. at Marseilles, France, April 23, 1884. A ballet dancer, one of the most celebrated of the early 19th century in London. She first appeared as a première danseuse in June, 1822. Her most celebrated parts were in *La Bayadère, La Sylphide*, and *La Fille du Danube.*

Tagore (tạ.gōr′), Sir **Rabindranath.** [Also written **Ravindranatha Thakura.**] b. at Calcutta, India, 1861; d. 1941. A Hindu philosopher and artist, awarded (1913) the Nobel prize for literature. His writings have found great popularity in India and abroad. He founded Santiniketan (Visna-Bharati University, Bolpur, 1901) and made it an Indian art center and a school of international culture. His talents were expressed in a wide range of artistic activity, as a novelist, dramatist, poet, essayist, and painter, and he also contributed to Indian philosophical and political thought. Among his best-known works are *Gitanjali* (1912), *Gardener* (1913), *The Crescent Moon* (1913), *Sacrifice and Other Plays* (1917), *Broken Ties* (1924), and *Red Oleander* (1924); among his topical and autobiographical writings are *Nationalism* (1917), *My Reminiscences* (1917), *The Home and the World* (1919), *Glimpses of Bengal* (1923), and *The Religion of Man* (1931).

tailed rhyme. See **end-rhyme.**

Taillefer (tä.yẹ.fer). Killed at the battle of Hastings (or Senlac), England, 1066. A Norman trouvère in the invading army of William the Conqueror. Having obtained permission from William to strike the first blow, he rode ahead of the Norman forces, singing of Charlemagne and Roland; he felled two Englishmen before he was overcome.

Tailor. In Shakespeare's *Taming of the Shrew*, a character who brings a dress for Katherina which is refused by Petruchio.

Tailors of Tooley Street (tö'li), **Three.** See **"Three Tailors of Tooley Street."**

Tain Bo Cuailgne (tä'ẹn bō köl'nyẹ, kö'lẹ). [English, **Cattle Raid of Cooley.**] An Old Irish epic tale recounting the marauding expedition of Queen Medb of Connacht into Ulster to steal the famous brown bull of the hills of Cuailgne. This raid is sometimes referred to as the War for the Brown Bull. The *Tain Bo Cuailgne* is the most ancient and most famous epic of all western Europe. Besides the details of the raid, in which Cuchulain defended Ulster single-handed against the amassed forces of Medb and fought the tragic fight against his beloved comrade Ferdiad, the *Tain Bo Cuailgne* includes, in flashbacks, the whole boyhood life and youthful exploits of Cuchulain. The *Tain Bo Cuailgne* is thought to have been first written down in the 7th century, but the material is centuries older than that. The oldest extant manuscript of the tale is contained in the Old Irish manuscript called the *Book of the Dun Cow* (before 1106), so called because it is written on the hide of a dun cow. Another version, taken from this, is in the 12th-century *Book of Leinster*, and a later redaction is contained in the 14th-century *Yellow Book of Lecan.*

Taine (tān; French, ten), **Hippolyte Adolphe.** b. at Vouziers, Ardennes, France, April 21, 1828; d. at Paris, March 5, 1893. A French historian, philosopher, and critic, one of the founders of genetic criticism and a forerunner of French naturalism. He graduated with the highest honors from the Collège Bourbon at Paris, and was admitted to the École Normale in 1848. After a brilliant career there and two dull years of teaching in provincial *lycées*, he established himself as a writer at Paris, took his doctor's degree (1853) with a brilliant thesis on La Fontaine's fables, and in the next ten years made himself the leading literary critic of his gifted generation. His *Histoire de la littérature anglaise* (1856–65) brought him international recognition. In 1864 he became professor of aesthetics at the École des Beaux Arts. After the defeat of 1871 he devoted most of his intellectual effort to a long investigation of the historical sources of his country's collapse, published (1875–90) as *Les Origines de la France contemporaine*. His other writings include monographs on Livy (1854), Carlyle (1864), and John Stuart Mill (1864), studies in aesthetics (*Philosophie de l'art*, 1865; *L'Idéal dans l'art*, 1867), works of philosophy (*Les Philosophes classiques du XIXᵉ siècle en France*, 1856; *De l'intelligence*, 1870),

several volumes of travel notes, and three of miscellaneous critical essays. All of his books illustrate his celebrated thesis that given a knowledge of a man's heredity, environment, and historical moment, we can define and explain his particular genius. The University of Oxford conferred upon Taine the honorary degree of LL.D. in 1871, and the French Academy elected him to membership, Nov. 14, 1878.

Taj Mahal (täzh' mạ.häl', täj'). A mausoleum erected just E of Agra, India, by Shah Jehan for his favorite wife. It was begun c1630 and completed c1648. It stands on a platform of white marble 18 ft. high and 313 ft. square, with tapering cylindrical minarets 133 ft. high at the angles. The mausoleum itself is in plan 186 ft. square with the corners cut off; it consists without of two tiers of keel-shaped arches, with a great single-arched porch in the middle of each side. The structure is crowned by a pointed and slightly bulbous dome, 58 ft. in diameter and ab. 210 ft. in exterior height, flanked by four octagonal kiosks. The interior is occupied by four domed chambers in the corners and a large arcaded octagon in the middle, all connected by corridors. In the central chamber stand two cenotaphs enclosed by a remarkable openwork rail in marble. No light is admitted to the interior except through the delicately pierced marble screens which fill all the windows. The decoration is enriched by mosaic inlaying in stone of flower motifs and arabesques, much of it in agate, bloodstone, and jasper.

Talbot (tôl'bọt, tal'-), **Catherine.** b. in May, 1721; d. 1770. An English writer. She was the lifelong friend of Samuel Johnson, and imitated his literary style. She wrote No. 30 of the *Rambler.*

Talbot, John. In Shakespeare's *1 Henry VI*, the son of Lord Talbot.

Talbot, Lord. In Shakespeare's *1 Henry VI*, the commander of the English army. He is captured at Patay through Fastolfe's cowardice, escapes from the Countess of Auvergne, and with his son is surrounded and killed near Bordeaux.

Talbot, Mary Anne. [Called **"the British Amazon."**] b. 1778; d. 1808. An English woman adventurer. She served as a drummer boy against the French in 1792, shortly thereafter becoming a cabin boy on the *Le Sage*. She was wounded in action on June 1, 1794. In later life she was a servant of Robert S. Kirby, who tells her story in *The Wonderful Museum* (volume 2, 1804). The tale of her life, unlike that of the well-known Hannah Snell, is known to be substantially true in all its details.

Talbot Twysden (twiz'dẹn). See **Twysden, Talbot.**

tale. A narrative, oral or written (in prose or verse), of some real or imaginary event or group of events; a story, either true or fictitious, having for its aim to please or instruct, or to preserve more or less remote historical facts; more especially, a story displaying embellishment or invention.

> With a tale forsooth he commeth vnto you; with a tale which holdeth children from play, and old men from the chimney corner.
> (Sir P. Sidney, *Apol. for Poetrie*.)

> Life is as tedious as a twice-told tale
> Vexing the dull ear of a drowsy man.
> (Shak., *K. John*, III.iv.)

ḍ, d or j; ṣ, s or sh; ṭ, t or ch; ẓ, z or zh; o, F. cloche; ü, F. menu; ċh, Sc. loch; ṅ, F. bonbon.

Mine is a tale of Flodden Field,
And not a history.
                    (Scott, *Marmion*, v.34.)

Tale of a Tub, A. A comedy by Ben Jonson, licensed in 1633, but written somewhat earlier. Inigo Jones is satirized in the character of Vitruvius Hoop.

Tale of a Tub, A. An allegorical religious satire by Jonathan Swift, written in 1697 and published in 1704. Three brothers, Peter (the Roman Catholic Church), Jack (the dissenters), and Martin (the Anglican Church), each receive a coat from their father before he dies, but he warns them in his will that they must never change the coats in any way. The coats symbolize Christian faith. The three brothers, however, lock the will up and proceed to ignore its provisions. Peter makes the first changes by adding all sorts of laces and bows to his coat to keep in fashion; the other two brothers quarrel with him about this, but also decorate their coats. Jack soon is looked upon with disfavor by Martin, and these two separate. When the will is brought out again, Peter persists in keeping his laces and bows, Jack throws away not just the trimming but also parts of the coat, while Martin pulls off what he can without seriously harming his coat. Martin is thus the only brother dealt with favorably, but even he comes under the scorn of the author at times. The title was chosen because it was the practice for seamen to throw a tub into the sea to divert whales from attacking the ship. Swift intended his satire to be the tub, drawing attacks by the critics of the age on his work and away from the church and state.

Tale of Chloe (klō′ē̤), **The.** A novel by George Meredith, published in 1879.

Tale of Gamelyn (gam′ẹ.lin), **The.** See **Gamelyn, The Tale of.**

Tale of Melibeus (mel.i.bē′us), **The.** See **Melibeus, The Tale of.**

Tale of Mystery, A. A melodrama (1802) by Thomas Holcroft, adapted from a contemporary French work. It is the first English play to be designated as a melodrama.

Tale of Two Cities, A. A novel by Charles Dickens. It first appeared serially (April–November, 1859) in *All the Year Round*. It is probably the most famous of all novels about the French Revolution.

Tales in Verse. A poetical work by George Crabbe, published in 1812.

Tales of a Grandfather. A collection of historical stories, comprising a popular history of Scotland to 1746, by Sir Walter Scott, published in four series (1827–30).

Tales of Fashionable Life. See **Fashionable Tales.**

Tales of My Landlord. A collective name for four series of the Waverley novels by Sir Walter Scott. The first series comprised *Old Mortality* and *The Black Dwarf;* the second *The Heart of Midlothian;* the third *The Bride of Lammermoor* and *A Legend of Montrose;* and the fourth *Count Robert of Paris* and *Castle Dangerous.*

Tales of the Crusaders. A collective name for the novels *The Talisman* and *The Betrothed* by Sir Walter Scott.

Tales of the Genii. A series of tales published by James Ridley in 1764, under the pseudonym Sir Charles Morell, as a translation from the Persian of "Horam the Son of Asmar."

Tales of the Hall. A work in verse by George Crabbe, published in 1819.

Tales of the Irish Peasantry. A work by Anna Maria Hall, published in 1840.

Talfourd (tal′fẽrd, tôl′-), Sir **Thomas Noon.** b. 1795; d. March 13, 1854. An English jurist and dramatic poet, remembered also as a friend of Charles Dickens. As member of Parliament (1835–41, 1847 *et seq.*) he advocated the international copyright bill which he introduced. In 1849 he became judge of the court of common pleas. His best-known work is the classical tragedy *Ion* (produced 1836). His other plays include *Athenian Captive* (1838), *Glencoe* (1840), and *The Castilian* (1853). He published also *Life and Letters of Lamb* (1837), *Final Memorials of Charles Lamb* (1849–50), travels, a history of Greek literature, and other works.

Taliesin (tal.i.es′in). A legendary, perhaps mythical, Celtic bard of the 6th century. The poems ascribed to him are of considerably later date.

Talisman, The. A romance of the Crusades (1825) by Sir Walter Scott.

Talkative (tô′ka̤.tiv). A character in John Bunyan's *Pilgrim's Progress.*

Tallyho (tal.i.hō′), Sir **Toby.** A roistering character in Samuel Foote's play *The Englishman Returned from Paris.*

Talmud (tal′mud). A monumental work which contains the Jewish traditional or oral laws and regulations of life explanatory of the written law of the Pentateuch as applied to the various and varying conditions and circumstances of life, and developed by logical conclusions, analogies, and combination of passages. To a lesser degree the Talmud contains comments on the historical, poetical, and ethical portions of the Scriptures, in a homiletical spirit. This latter part is called Hagada or Agada (from *nagad*, to say, make known; narrative, tale), while the former, or legislative, part, is called Halacha (from *halach*, to go, walk; the path or way of life as ruled and governed by the law). The Talmud may be externally divided into the Mishnah and Gemara. The relation of one to the other is that of exposition to thesis. The Mishnah gives a simple statement of a law or precept; the Gemara presents the discussion and debate on it. The authors of the Mishnah are called Tenaim (doctors); they were preceded by the Sopherim (scribes). The activity of the Tenaim began in the time of the Maccabees, and their rules and decisions, nearly 4,000 in number, were codified and arranged according to subjects by Rabbi Judah I or Judah ha-Nasi (patriarch 190–220 A.D.). The authors of the Gemara are called Amoraim (from *amar*, to say; speakers). The discussions of the Amoraim in the schools of Palestine (especially at Tiberias) were codified in the 4th century in the Jerusalem Talmud; the discussions of the Amoraim of the schools of Babylonia were codified in the course of the 5th and 6th centuries in the Babylonia Talmud. The Mishnah is composed in Hebrew ("post-Biblical," or "New Hebrew"), the Gemara mainly in Aramaic. Neither the Jerusalem nor the Babylonia Talmud contains the complete Gemara to the entire Mishnah. But the Babylonia Talmud is about four times as voluminous as that of Jerusalem. The Babylonia Talmud obtained greater popularity and authority among the Jews than that of Jerusalem, and is always meant when the Talmud is spoken of without a qualification. Its 63 tracts are usually printed in 12 folio volumes on 2,947 pages. The Mishnah is besides separately printed in six volumes, according to its division into six orders or *sedarim;* and also the portions of the Hagada under the title of *Ain Yakob.*

Talos (tā′los). In Greek legend: **1.** The inventive nephew of Daedalus, by whom he was slain.
2. A man of brass made by Hephaestus for Minos, to guard Crete.

Talus (tā′lus). An iron man, the attendant of Sir Artegall and executor of Justice, a character in Edmund Spenser's *Faerie Queene* (Book V).

Tamarisk Town. A novel (1919) by Sheila Kaye-Smith.

Tamburlaine (tam′bẽr.lān). A tragedy in two parts, by Christopher Marlowe, acted in 1587 and 1588, and entered on the Stationers' Register and printed in 1590. It is his earliest play, and the first in which blank verse of such lyric quality was introduced on the public stage. From among many contemporary accounts of the life of Tamerlane (Timur or Timur-Leng), who lived at the time of Chaucer, Marlowe chose as his chief source George Fortescue's *Forest* (1571), which contained a translation of Pedro Maxia's Spanish biography of the Asiatic conqueror. Marlowe also knew a Latin biography, Perondinus's *Magni Tamerlain Scytharum Imperatoris Vita* (1553), and Ortelius's *Theatrum Orbis Terrarum* (1584), a geography that provided him with exotic place names. The play tells the story of Tamburlaine, a Scythian shepherd, whose ruthless ambition defeats all enemies except death. In Part 1, Tamburlaine persuades the Persian general Theridamas to conspire with him for the conquest of the King of Persia. He defeats not only the king but the king's brother, Cosroe, who hoped to use Tamburlaine to get the crown for himself. Then the erstwhile shepherd, having attained "the sweet fruition of an earthly crown," goes on to defeat his strongest opponent, Bajazet, the ruler of Turkey. Tamburlaine keeps the defeated Bajazet and his wife Zabina in a cage, heaping on them such indignities that they end their enslavement by dashing out their brains. Zenocrate, beautiful daughter of the Soldan of Egypt and beloved of Tamburlaine, begs him to spare Egypt; but despite her pleas he conquers that country, too, slaughtering the virgins of Damascus who are stationed before the city to intercede for its salvation. Part 2 continues Tamburlaine's conquests, the most famous scene being his victorious entry into Babylon in a chariot drawn by kings he has defeated. But then he suffers a terrible blow in the death of Zenocrate. This goads him to still greater frenzy and brutality until at last he dies, still undefeated, falling upon the bier of his adored Zenocrate. The play and its hero exemplify many Renaissance characteristics.

Tamburlaine is an exaggerated Machiavellian man, a glorious and audacious villain-hero. He epitomizes the Renaissance egotist, totally lacking the courtly and Christian virtues of humility, piety, patience, moderation, and compassion. While these virtues were being celebrated by Spenser (from whose unpublished *Faerie Queene,* Book I, Marlowe may have borrowed some passages) Marlowe was creating a new type of character possessed of a fascination similar to Milton's Satan. Tamburlaine is no crass materialist. Although he destroys kings and defies divinity in pursuit of his ambitions, he does not conquer so much for wealth and power as for the intellectual satisfaction of toppling the established order. Tamburlaine combines a typical Renaissance devotion to beauty with a cruelty capable of such ugly deeds as the slaughter of the Damascan virgins. Like the hero's character, the language of the play is a mixture of sharply contrasting styles, combining florid bombast and exquisite poetry. Although contemporaries scoffed at *Tamburlaine,* they soon imitated the bombastic rhetoric of its hero. The play was very popular. Edward Alleyn, who played the title role in the original production of Part 1, made such a success with it that the public demanded a second part.

Tamerlane (tam′ẽr.lān). A play by Nicholas Rowe, produced c1701. Tamerlane, though supposed to be the Tamburlaine of Marlowe's play, is made a calm philosophic prince, with poetical allusion to William III, so that it was played for many years on the 4th and 5th of November, the anniversaries of the birth and of the landing of William III. Bajazet, his opponent, is meant to represent Louis XIV. George Frederick Handel composed the music for a libretto by Piovene, called *Tamerlano;* it was produced at London in 1724.

Taming of the Shrew, The. A comedy by Shakespeare, printed in 1623 and probably rewritten (especially the Petruchio-Kate and Sly scenes) from an earlier play printed in 1594. The Bianca subplot appears to have been based largely on Gascoigne's *Supposes.* The earlier play was probably not by Shakespeare, but by someone else writing for Pembroke's company in 1588–89; another hypothesis has it that the earlier play is a version adapted by the Earl of Pembroke's players after the play had been sold to another company.
The Story. In the Induction, Christopher Sly is found in a drunken sleep by a nobleman who decides to have some fun with him. Sly is taken to the nobleman's house, treated lavishly, and persuaded (with some difficulty) that he is himself a nobleman just recovered from 15 years of insanity. For his entertainment a group of strolling players present "The Taming of the Shrew": Baptista Minola has two daughters, the hot-tempered, cantankerous Katherina, and the sweet and gentle Bianca. Baptista will not allow the younger to wed until Katherina has found a husband. Petruchio resolves to woo her, partly to help his friend Hortensio gain Bianca, and partly for Katherina's large dowry. At their first meeting she rails at him, but he pretends that he finds her soft-spoken and gentle, and commences his taming of her. He arrives late at the wedding, riding on a tired nag and dressed in disreputable clothes. He embarrasses her at the ceremony, refuses to let her stay for the wedding dinner,

ḍ, d or j; ṣ, s or sh; ṭ, t or ch; ẓ, z or zh; o, F. cloche; ü, F. menu; čh, Sc. loch; ń, F. bonbon.

takes her to his country house, where his cruelty to his servants forces her to defend them, gives her nothing to eat, tosses in bed all night so that she can get no sleep, and sends her new clothes away. After these and other pranks she is so exhausted and bewildered that she is quite submissive. Meanwhile young Lucentio, in the guise of a tutor, has won Bianca; Hortensio, the disappointed rival, consoles himself with a rich widow. At Lucentio's wedding feast, Petruchio easily wins a wager that he has the most docile and obedient wife of any husband in the room.

Tamora (tam'ō.ra̱). In Shakespeare's *Titus Andronicus*, the Queen of the Goths. Taken a prisoner by Titus, with her three sons, she plots with her lover, Aaron, to avenge the sacrifice of her eldest son. Titus, in turn, avenges the death of his sons, the rape and mutilation of his daughter, and the loss of his own hand, first by serving Tamora a pie in which her sons' bodies have been baked, and then by killing her.

Tam o'Shanter (tam' ō.shan'tèr). A rollicking poem (1791) by Robert Burns, generally considered to be one of his best works. It tells the story of the encounter of a Scottish farmer with the "Auld One" and his attendant witches, and of Tam's wild ride homeward by night, pursued by the witches, after his market-day potations.

Tamyra (ta̱.mī'ra̱). The wife of the Count of Montsurry, beloved by Bussy D'Ambois in George Chapman's tragedy *Bussy D'Ambois*. She is also loved by Monsieur, brother of the King of France, and the jealous Monsieur reveals her meetings with Bussy to her husband, thus setting the stage for the eventual murder of Bussy.

Tanagra (tan'a̱.gra̱, ta̱.nag'ra̱). In ancient geography, a town of Boeotia, Greece, situated near the Asopus River, ab. 24 mi. NW of Athens. A victory was gained here in 457 B.C. by the Spartans over the Athenians and their allies. Its extensive necropolis has made this obscure town famous, for from it came (c1874) the first of the terra-cotta figurines which drew attention to the antiquities of this type. Such figurines, previously ignored, have since been eagerly sought and found in great quantities, not only at Tanagra but upon a great number of sites in all parts of the Greek world.

Tanaquil (tan'a̱.kwil). In Roman legend, the wife of Tarquinius Priscus, fifth king of Rome.

Tanaquil. A British princess. Edmund Spenser uses the name with reference to Queen Elizabeth in the *Faerie Queene*.

Tancred (tang'krẹd). d. at Antioch, 1112. A Norman soldier, one of the chief heroes of the first Crusade (1096–99). He was the son of Otho the Good and Emma, sister of Robert Guiscard. He joined the crusading army under his cousin, Bohemund of Tarentum, son of Robert Guiscard. He distinguished himself at the taking of Nice and Tarsus, the siege of Antioch, the capture of Jerusalem, and the battle of Ascalon. He became prince of Galilee and later of Edessa, extending his conquests, and by his actions making enemies of the Byzantines and his fellow Latin barons. In the complex struggle among the Christian princes of the east for power and lands, he maintained himself by grasping opportunity as it came. His virtues and achievements are celebrated in Torquato Tasso's *Jerusalem Delivered*.

Tancred and Gismund (jiz'mund), **The Tragedy of.** See **Gismond of Salerne in Love.**

Tancred, or The New Crusade. A novel by Benjamin Disraeli, published in 1847.

Tannahill (tan'a̱.hil), **Robert.** b. at Paisley, Scotland, June 3, 1774; committed suicide, May 17, 1810. A Scottish poet. His best-known lyrics are in such songs as *The Flower of Dunblane* and *Gloomy Winter's Noo Awa*.

Tanner (tan'ẽr). The ostensible hero of George Bernard Shaw's *Man and Superman*. Although he attempts to flee his ward, Ann, who is in love with him, he is eventually caught by her in the Sierra Nevada mountains.

Tanner of Tamworth (tam'wẽrth), **The.** An old ballad, included in Percy's *Reliques*, telling of the encounter between a tanner and Edward IV, the tanner's mistaking Edward for a highwayman, their exchange of horses, and finally the revelation of the king's identity. The tanner, instead of being hanged as he has feared, is rewarded with 300 marks a year and a manor at Plumpton Park.

Tannhäuser (tän'hoi.zẽr). A Middle High German lyric poet of the 13th century. He belonged to the Salzburg family of Tanhusen. From c1240 to 1270 he led a wandering life in which he lived at the Bavarian, Austrian, and other courts, and visited the Far East. He was a minnesinger and writer, particularly, of dance songs. A German ballad of the 16th century has preserved the memory of the historical Tannhäuser. This first describes his parting with Lady Venus, with whom he has been for a year in the Venusberg. He makes a visit of penance to Rome and asks for absolution, but Pope Urban declares that as little as the papal staff can grow green and flower, so little can he have God's mercy. In despair he goes away. On the third day, however, the papal staff begins to bud, and the Pope sends out in search of him; but Tannhäuser has gone back to the Venusberg. The legend of Tannhäuser is the subject of the opera of the same name by Richard Wagner.

Tanqueray (tang'kẹ.ra̱), **Paula.** The title character in Pinero's *Second Mrs. Tanqueray.*

Tanqueray, The Second Mrs. See **Second Mrs. Tanqueray, The.**

Tantalus (tan'ta̱.lus). In Greek mythology, a son of Zeus and king of Mount Sipylus in Lydia. For revealing the secrets of the gods, or for some other affront to them, such as requesting immortality, or serving them human flesh, he was condemned to stand in Tartarus up to his chin in water under a loaded fruit tree, the fruit and water retreating whenever he sought to satisfy his hunger or thirst. From his name is derived the word "tantalize."

Taoism (tä'ō.iz.ẹm). A Chinese philosophy and religious cult. The founder of Taoism is traditionally Lao-Tze (born c604 B.C.), to whom has long been attributed the text on which Taoism is based (but which is now thought to postdate Lao-Tze by some 300 years). Literally, Tao means "the Way." The Way is the way of nature, the effortless succession of natural events. And the individual's concern is the relation of man to the universe in all its physical, human, spiritual, and supernatural aspects. The essence of the whole doctrine is non-effort. Through noncompetition, withdrawal, rather than self-assertion, the individual attains wisdom, serenity, spiritual power. A favorite aphorism of Taoism is that water always seeks the lowest level yet has power to wear away the solid stone. Man too must abstain from effort, abandon ambition, repudiate worldly affairs, and seek the inner mystical experience. Politics and the social virtues are to be despised, for he who follows the Way is beyond the civil and social code, on the grounds that perfection requires no rules of conduct. There is an emphasis and metaphysic in Taoism which causes the busyness and pretentiousness of practical life to seem empty and insubstantial. The Taoist cult, though based on the Taoist philosophy, differs noticeably from it. It embraces a great body of indigenous folkloristic beliefs and practices antedating the philosophy by hundreds of years. It recognizes an enormous pantheon comprised of ancient and local gods, spirits, and powers, and a multiplicity of heavens and hells. There are thousands of Taoist temples and shrines throughout China which function through the agency of more thousands of priests, monks, nuns, diviners, and magicians. The true cultist believes in divination and relies on a legion of talismans and charms. The rites associated with birth, puberty, marriage, and death are important and meticulously observed. He is a student of physiology that he may attune his body to the acquirement of energy and serenity; and he is a student of chemistry, for the search for the pill of immortality does not cease. A "master of heaven" heads the cult (likened by many observers to a pope); the first took office in the 1st century A.D. This man was a famous alchemist, who was believed to have found the elixir of immortality by virtue of powers received direct from Lao-Tze himself. All subsequent masters of heaven are considered to have been his descendants. Taoism is a living religion in China today and its cult devotees are still concerned with rediscovering the pill of immortality and with enhancing individual vital essence by meditation and by breathing and sexual exercises. On the other hand, the morale of the cult has disintegrated to the extent that both the priests and those in monasteries devoted to seeking the Way, know less of their own discipline and lore than in times past.

Tapley (tap'li), **Mark.** In Dickens's *Martin Chuzzlewit*, Martin's servant and traveling companion, a light-hearted, merry fellow, who takes constant credit to himself for being jolly under the most adverse circumstances.

Tappertit (tap'ẽr.tit), **Sim** (or **Simon**). A character in Dickens's *Barnaby Rudge*. He is a ridiculously conceited and pompous apprentice, very proud of his figure, and in love with Dolly Varden. Dolly, however, marries Joe Willet, and Sim weds a widow.

Taprobane (tạ.prob'ạ.nē). A fabulous island in the dominion of Prester John, in which, according to Sir John Mandeville, there were huge ants as large as hounds, guarding hills of gold and working in

them, finding and storing the pure gold. The name was used also by the ancient Greeks for the island (the existence of which was known to their geographers) now known as Ceylon.

Tara (tar'ạ). A village in County Meath, Ireland, ab. 20 mi. NW of Dublin. The hill of Tara (ab. 500 ft. high) was famous in the early history of Ireland as the royal residence of the ancient Irish kings. In the Old Irish mythical chronicles, Tara was named for a mythical queen Tea, because it was given to her as dowry and burial place. The original Irish form of the word was *Teamuir*, translated as Tea's house or fort. The etymology is false, but the legend remains. In 1843 it was the scene of a large mass meeting in favor of repeal of the Act of Union uniting Great Britain and Ireland.

Tarboe: The Story of a Life (tär'bō). A novel by Sir Gilbert Parker, published in 1927.

Targum (tär'gum). A name applied to the Chaldean (i.e., Aramaic) paraphrases of the Old Testament. They developed out of the oral translations and paraphrases of the passages of Scripture read in the synagogues, a custom which probably arose after Aramaic had replaced Hebrew as the common tongue. The most popular Targum is that which passes under the name of Onkelos, which originated probably in the 3rd century A.D. in Babylonia; the name is supposed to be a corruption of Aquila (Akylos), the celebrated convert and author of a Greek version of the Old Testament, to whom it was ascribed. It gives in general a faithful translation of the Hebrew text. Another Targum is attributed to Jonathan ben Uzziel, a disciple of Hillel, which is more free in its rendering of the original; while the so-called Jerusalem Targum ("pseudo-Jonathan") is more of a homiletical paraphrase than a translation. None of these Targums is in its present shape a complete version of the Old Testament.

Tarka the Otter (tär'kạ). [Full title, **Tarka the Otter, His Joyful Water-life and Death in the Country of the Two Rivers.**] An animal story by Henry Williamson, published in 1927. It was awarded the Hawthornden prize in 1928.

Tarlton (tärl'ṭon), **Richard.** d. at London, 1588. An English clown and comic actor. He is said to have been brought to London from Shropshire, and to have been a "prentice in his youth" in the city of London, later a "water-bearer." He was enrolled (1583) as one of the 12 of Queen Elizabeth's Men, and became a kind of court jester as well. He was celebrated for his extemporaneous rhymes and for his "jigs" (comic songs with a dance), which he invented. His popularity and audacity were both unbounded. He fell into disgrace and was dismissed from court for scurrilous reflections upon Robert Dudley, 1st Earl of Leicester, and Sir Walter Raleigh. He then kept a tavern in Paternoster Row. He wrote *The Seven Deadly Sins*, a play which appears to have been the result of his real or pretended repentance of his irregularities. The second part, extant in manuscript form, was once thought to be a sketch for a performance similar to the Italian *commedia dell' arte*, but it is now known to be a summary of the episodes and a cue sheet. A collection of jokes and humorous anecdotes compiled in the 1590's was attributed to him as *Tarl-*

ḍ, d or j; ṣ, s or sh; ṭ, t or ch; ẓ, z or zh; o, F. cloche; ü, F. menu; ċh, Sc. loch; ṅ, F. bonbon.

ton's Jests, though the material is much older. He is said to have been the person Shakespeare had in mind in writing about "poor Yorick," in *Hamlet.*

Tarpeia (tär.pē'ạ). In Roman legend, daughter of the governor of the citadel of Rome on the Capitoline Hill. She betrayed the fortress to the Sabines in return for "what they wore on their left arms." She meant their gold bracelets, but as they entered they cast their shields upon her (which they also bore on their left arms) and she was crushed to death. The Tarpeian Rock was named for her.

Tarquinius Priscus (tär.kwin'i.us pris'kus). In Roman legend, the fifth king of Rome (616–578 B.C.), the son of a Greek colonist at Tarquinii in Etruria. He settled at Rome, became guardian of the sons of Ancus Marcius, his predecessor, and succeeded the latter. He is said to have built the original cloacae (i.e., the sewers), the Circus Maximus, and the Capitoline Temple.

Tartar (tär'tạr). In Dickens's unfinished novel *The Mystery of Edwin Drood,* a boyhood friend of Crisparkle who is very much drawn to Rosa Bud. It has been suggested that Dickens intended him to play a major part in the latter part of the book, and probably finally to marry Rosa.

Tartarin (tár.tà.raṅ). A gasconading humbug, the principal character in Alphonse Daudet's *Tartarin de Tarascon, Tartarin sur les Alpes,* and *Port Tarascon.* He is a satire on the typical character attributed to southern France.

Tartars (tär'tạrz). [Also, **Tatars.**] All the peoples who swarmed over certain parts of Asia and Europe in the 13th century under Mongol leadership have in times past been called Tatars; but the Turkic-speaking Tatars proper are now distinguished from the Mongols. The Tatars are those peoples speaking a language of the northwestern branch of Turkic, living principally near the Volga River, in the Tatar Autonomous Soviet Socialist Republic, in smaller numbers in the Molotov, Saratov, and Gorki regions, in the Astrakhan region, and in SW Siberia, all in the U.S.S.R. Their total number was ab. three million in 1946. The Volga Tartars formed the Kazan khanate in 1438, after the breakup of the Golden Horde. Kazan then became a center of Mohammedan culture, which it long remained despite Russian conquest in 1552. The term Tartars is also loosely used for any of the Turkic and Mongol peoples.

Tartarus (tär'tạ.rus). A deep and sunless abyss, according to Homer and also to earlier Greek mythology, situated far below Hades. Here Zeus imprisoned the rebel Titans. Later poets describe Tartarus as the place in which the wicked are punished. Sometimes the name is synonymous with Hades, for the lower world in general.

Tartuffe (tár.tüf). [Also, **Tartufe.**] A comedy by Molière, produced at the Comédie Française in 1667. Tartuffe is a hypocritical wretch who palms himself off on an honest and refined family, tries to drive the son away, marry the daughter, corrupt the wife, and ruin and imprison the father. He almost succeeds. Matthew Medbourne translated and adapted it in 1670.

Task, The. A descriptive poem in six parts by William Cowper, published in 1785. It is written in blank verse and consists of over 5,000 lines. Its original impetus came from Lady Austen's request in July, 1783, that Cowper write a blank-verse poem about anything ("write upon that sofa!"). The six books are entitled respectively "The Sofa," "The Time Piece," "The Garden," "The Winter Evening," "The Winter Morning Walk," and "The Winter Walk at Noon." The most notable parts of the poem are those in which Cowper describes rural scenery and various country characters.

Tasker Jevons (tas'kẻr jev'ọnz). A novel (1916) of World War I by May Sinclair; published in America under the title *The Belfry.*

Tasman (täs'män), **Abel Janszoon** (or **Janszon** or **Janszen**). b. probably at Hoorn, The Netherlands, c1602; d. at Batavia, in October, 1659. A Dutch navigator. He sailed from Batavia in August, 1642, in command of an exploring expedition to Australia, under the auspices of Anton Van Diemen, governor general of the Dutch East Indies. He discovered Tasmania (which he named Van Diemen's Land) in November, 1642, New Zealand in December, 1642, part of the Friendly Islands (Tonga) in 1643, and returned to Batavia in June, 1643. His circumnavigation of Australia proved it to be an island. In a second voyage (1644) he discovered the Gulf of Carpentaria.

Tasso (täs'sō), **Torquato.** b. at Sorrento, Italy, March 11, 1544; d. at Rome, April 25, 1595. An Italian poet. He was educated at the Jesuit schools at Naples, Rome, and Bergamo. His father, Bernardo Tasso, was involved in the political troubles of the prince of Salerno, his patron, and joined the prince in Rome; but, that city becoming unsafe for him, he accepted shelter at Pesaro, the court of the duke of Urbino, where his son Torquato was taught with the son of the duke. In 1557 Torquato went to study law at Padua. He was influenced by his father's writings and not by his advice to study a profession that, unlike letters, would leave him free of patronage, and in 1562, while still at Padua, published *Rinaldo.* It was successful, and, his father ceasing his opposition to a literary career, Tasso went to Bologna to study philosophy and literature. He returned to Padua shortly after, and by 1565 was attached to the service of the House of Este, the glories of which he celebrated in *Jerusalem Delivered;* Rinaldo was said to be of that family. He was well received at court, and was encouraged to finish the epic *Goffredo* (later called *Gerusalemme Liberata*), which he had begun at Bologna. In 1570 Cardinal Luigi d'Este, his patron, went to Paris, taking Tasso with him. There he met Pierre de Ronsard, the rest of the Pléiade, and other distinguished men. He left the cardinal after his return on account of a difference in religious opinion, but was received by Duke Alfonso d'Este of Ferrara, who loaded him with favors. He produced his *Aminta* in 1573, and had written 18 cantos of *Goffredo* in 1574, when he was seized with fever. After this his mind was not clear; he became quarrelsome, worried himself about the orthodoxy of his poem, and became subject to delusions, dreading accusations of heresy and assassination or poison. At length he was placed in a convent at Ferrara for medical treatment. He escaped and fled to his sister in the disguise of a shepherd. She cared for him, and in 1578 the duke received him again; but his delusions continued, and he wandered from place to place (to Mantua, Turin, and elsewhere), finally returning to Ferrara. There he became so violent in accusing the duke of a design to poison him that he was placed in an insane asylum. After he had remained there for seven years he was released, on the personal promise of the Prince of Mantua that Alfonso should not again be exposed to his insane attacks. A theory was at one time current that Tasso was shut up in an asylum on account of his aspirations for the hand of Leonora d'Este, the duke's sister; Goethe's play was based on this supposition. *Goffredo* was published at Venice during the time of Tasso's seclusion, but it was very inaccurately printed, and in 1581 a revised edition was printed at Parma, with its present title *Gerusalemme Liberata (Jerusalem Delivered)*. He remained a year at Mantua, wrote *Torrismondo* (1586), and again resumed his wanderings. He had many friends eager to help him, but he was broken in health and spirit. His *Gerusalemme Conquistata*, much inferior to the *Gerusalemme Liberata*, was published in 1593. Two years later he died at Rome, whither he had been summoned by Pope Clement VIII to be crowned poet laureate; the ceremony was never performed, owing to his illness. The *Gerusalemme Liberata*, an epic dealing with the First Crusade and the freeing of Jerusalem from the Moslems, has been translated into many languages; it is one of the masterpieces of European literature and places the author among the best of the Italian writers.

Taste. A comedy (1752) by Samuel Foote.

Tat (tät). See **Thoth.**

Tatars (tä′tạrz). See **Tartars.**

Tate (tāt), **Nahum.** b. at Dublin, 1652; d. at London, Aug. 12, 1715. An English poet and playwright, appointed poet laureate in 1692. He was associated with Nicholas Brady in a poetical version of the Psalms (1696), and wrote various poems and plays, especially adaptations of Elizabethan plays. With John Dryden he wrote the second part of *Absalom and Achitophel.*

Tate Gallery. An art gallery at London. The building, designed in the classic style by Sidney R. J. Smith, and fronting on the river Thames about half a mile above the Houses of Parliament, was presented to the British people, and opened to the public by the Prince of Wales (later King Edward VII), July 21, 1897. Sir Henry Tate gave the building and with it 65 pictures and two important bronzes. To these are added, by act of the president and council of the Royal Academy, the works bought with the Chantrey Bequest Fund. George Frederick Watts presented 22 of his most important paintings and one piece of sculpture to form the Watts collection. The Vernon collection of 53 pictures has been added. From time to time representative works by British artists are acquired. It occupies the site of the old Millbank Penitentiary.

Tatler, The. A periodical founded by Richard Steele in 1709, and discontinued in 1711. Joseph Addison wrote 41 papers; Addison and Steele together 34. Steele wrote a much larger number alone.

Tattersall's (tat′ẽr.sôlz, -sạlz). A sporting establishment and auction mart for horses, at London, opened c1770 by Richard Tattersall (1724–95).

Tattle (tat′l). In William Congreve's *Love for Love,* a vain, impertinent beau, boasting of his amours, yet priding himself on his secrecy.

Tattycoram (tat.i.kō′rạm). [Original name, **Harriet Beadle.**] A foundling in Dickens's *Little Dorrit.* She is by nature passionate and headstrong.

Tauchnitz (touch′nits), Baron **Christian Bernhard von.** b. at Naumburg, Germany, Aug. 25, 1816; d. Aug. 14, 1895. A German publisher. He founded (1837) his own publishing firm (Bernhard Tauchnitz, at Leipzig) and in 1841 began the publication of his *Collection of British Authors* (the *Tauchnitz Edition*), to which were subsequently added *Collection of German Authors* in English translation (1868 *et seq.*) and the *Students' Tauchnitz Edition* (1886 *et seq.*).

Taurus (tô′rus). An ancient constellation and sign of the zodiac, between Aries and Gemini, representing the forward part of a bull. It contains the reddish star Aldebaran (α Tauri) of the first magnitude, and the striking groups of the Pleiades and Hyades.

Taurus. In Shakespeare's *Antony and Cleopatra,* Octavius's commander at Actium.

tautology (tô.tol′ọ.ji). **1.** Repetition of the same words conveying the same idea, in the same immediate context.
2. The repetition of the same thing in different words; the useless repetition of the same idea or meaning: as, "they did it successively one after the other"; "both simultaneously made their appearance at one and the same time." Tautology is repetition without addition of force or clearness, and is disguised by a change of wording; it differs from the repetition which is used for clearness, emphasis, or effect, and which may be either in the same or in different words.

> How hath my unregarded language vented
> The sad tautologies of lavish passion!
> (Quarles, *Emblems.*)

> I wrote him an humble and very submissive Letter, all in his own stile: that is, I called the Library a venerable place; the Books sacred reliques of Antiquity, etc., with half a dozen tautologies.
> (Humphrey Wanley, in Ellis's *Lit. Letters.*)

Tautphoeus (tout′fė.ůs), Baroness **von.** [Original name, **Jemima Montgomery.**] b. in Ireland, Oct. 23, 1807; d. at Munich, Nov. 12, 1893. An Irish novelist. She published *Cyrilla, Quits, At Odds, The Initials,* and others.

Tawney (tô′ni), **Richard Henry.** b. at Calcutta, India, 1880—. An English educator and economist. Early in his teaching career he became interested in problems of education of the working class, and he served on the executive board (1905–47) and as president (1928–44) of the Workers Educational Association. While holding the chair of economic history at the University of London, he served on several important government boards and commissions. He is the author, among other works, of *The Agrarian Problem in the Sixteenth Century, The Acquisitive Society, Education, the Socialist Policy,*

ḍ, d or j; ṣ, s or sh; ṭ, t or ch; ẓ, z or zh; *o,* F. cloche; ü, F. menu; ċh, Sc. loch; ṅ, F. bonbon.

Religion and the Rise of Capitalism, Equality, and *Land and Labour in China,* and he collaborated in the writing of *English Economic History* and of *Tudor Economic Documents.*

Taylor (tā′lọr), **Ann.** [Maiden name, **Martin.**] b. June 20, 1757; d. at Ongar, Essex, England, June 4, 1830. An English author of manuals, and books for young people. Among her works are *Advice to Mothers* (no date), *Maternal Solicitude for a Daughter's Best Interests* (1813), *Practical Hints to Young Females, or the Duties of a Wife, a Mother, and a Mistress of a Family* (1815), *Reciprocal Duties of Parents and Children* (1818), *Retrospection, a Tale* (1821), *Itinerary of a Traveller in the Wilderness* (1825), and *Correspondence between a Mother and Her Daughter at School* (1817).

Taylor, Ann. b. at London, Jan. 30, 1782; d. at Nottingham, England, Dec. 20, 1866. An English poet, hymn writer, and author of books for young people; daughter of Ann Taylor (1757–1830). Coauthor with her sister, Jane, of *Original Poems for Infant Minds* (2 vols., 1804–05), *Rhymes for the Nursery* (1806), *Rural Scenes* (1806), *City Scenes* (1809), *Hymns for Infant Minds* (1810), *Incidents of Childhood* (1821), and *The Linnet's Life* (1822). Author of *The Wedding among the Flowers* (1808), *The Convalescent; 12 Letters on Recovery from Sickness* (1839), *Seven Blessings for Little Children* (1844), *Memoir of the Rev. Joseph Gilbert* (1853), and *Autobiography and Other Memorials* (1874).

Taylor, Billy. See **Billy Taylor.**

Taylor, Sir Henry. b. near Durham, England, Oct. 18, 1800; d. at Bournemouth, England, March 27, 1886. An English dramatic poet and critic. He obtained an appointment in the colonial office in 1824, retiring in 1872. He became editor of the *London Magazine* in 1824. His chief dramas are *Isaac Comnenus* (1827), *Philip van Artevelde* (1834), *Edwin the Fair* (1842), and *The Virgin Widow* (1850). Among his other works are *The Statesman* (1836), *Notes from Life* (1847), *The Eve of the Conquest, and Other Poems* (1847), and *Notes from Books* (1849).

Taylor, Isaac. b. at Lavenham, Suffolk, England, Aug. 17, 1787; d. at Stanford Rivers, Essex, England, June 28, 1865. An English author; son of Ann Taylor (1757–1830). He studied art, but ultimately adopted literature as a profession. Among his works are *The Natural History of Enthusiasm* (1829), *Saturday Evening* (1832), *Natural History of Fanaticism* (1833), *Spiritual Despotism* (1835), *The Physical Theory of Another Life* (1836), *Ancient Christianity* (1839), *Restoration of Belief* (1855), and *Spirit of Hebrew Poetry* (1861).

Taylor, Jane. b. at London, Sept. 23, 1783; d. at Ongar, Essex, England, April 13, 1824. An English poet and author; daughter of Ann Taylor (1757–1830). Conjointly with her sister Ann Taylor (1782–1866) she wrote *Original Poems for Infant Minds, Hymns for Infant Minds,* and other works. Among her independent works are *Display* (1815) and *Essays in Rhyme on Morals and Manners* (1816). *Rhymes for the Nursery* (1806), written with her sister, included Jane's poem "Twinkle, Twinkle, Little Star."

Taylor, Jeremy. b. at Cambridge, England (baptized Aug. 15, 1613); d. at Lisburn, Ireland, Aug. 13, 1667. An English bishop and celebrated theological writer. He was the son of a barber, and was educated at Caius College, Cambridge, being elected a fellow of his college in 1633. He was afterward appointed to a fellowship at All Souls, Oxford, by Archbishop William Laud. He became rector of Uppingham, in Rutlandshire, in 1638. He was also chaplain in ordinary to the king, and when the English Civil War broke out he joined the royalists, losing thereby his parish. He was captured in Wales in 1645, imprisoned for a time, and then released. Subsequently he supported himself by teaching in a school he operated in Wales and by becoming private chaplain to Richard Vaughan, 2nd Earl of Carbery. The earl's home, Golden Grove, is commemorated in Taylor's devotional manual, *The Golden Grove* (1655), and in two books of sermons (1651, 1653) preached there. One of his best sermons was preached at the funeral of Lady Carbery in 1650. Taylor appears also to have visited London during this period, because he is supposed to have been given a watch and several jewels by Charles I just before his execution. He is mentioned also prominently in John Evelyn's diary, and apparently was imprisoned several times for short periods. In 1658 he obtained a lectureship at Lisburn, Ireland, through Evelyn's help, and after the Restoration was appointed bishop of Down and Connor and also of Dunmore. He became a member of the Irish privy council as well. Taylor's years as bishop were occupied with struggles with the Presbyterians of his region, who objected to Episcopal supervision, and with the Roman Catholics, who objected to attending Protestant services. Taylor is noted for his rich, clear, imaginative style, which has been praised by many critics. His principal works, in addition to *The Golden Grove,* are *The Liberty of Prophesying* (1647), a work on religious toleration, *The Rule and Exercises of Holy Living* (1650), *The Rule and Exercises of Holy Dying* (1651), and *The Worthy Communicant* (1660), devotional works, *Ductor Dubitantium, or The Rule of Conscience* (1660), dedicated to Charles II as a manual of "case histories meant to be an encyclopedia of casuistic reasoning," and *Dissuasive from Popery* (2 parts, 1664, 1667).

Taylor, John. [Known as **"the Water Poet."**] b. in Gloucestershire, England, Aug. 24, 1580; d. at London, in December, 1653. An English poet. By occupation he was a waterman on the Thames, and afterward gave of wine duties for the Tower of London lieutenant. At the outbreak of the English Civil War he became a Royalist, and kept a tavern at Oxford; at the time of his death he kept the Crown Tavern in Phoenix Alley, Longacre, London. His writings are valuable illustrations of the manners of his age, not only in England but also in Scotland and on the Continent, where he traveled. He wrote many poetical and prose works, first collected in 1630, which were once very popular. His complete works, comprising about 140 separate titles, were edited by Charles Hindley in 1872.

Taylor, John Edward. b. at Ilminster, Somersetshire, England, Sept. 11, 1791; d. at Cheetham, near Manchester, England, Jan. 6, 1844. An English journalist. He wrote for London papers and for the Manchester *Gazette*. Charged by John Greenwood, conservative industrialist, with having written a paper that led to the burning of the Manchester Exchange, he called Greenwood "a liar, a slanderer, and a scoundrel," and was indicted (1819) for libel, but acquitted. He founded (1821) the Manchester *Guardian* and edited it until his death. Under Taylor's editorship, the *Guardian* established the reputation it still enjoys as one of the world's most influential independent newspapers. Outspoken in denouncing the violence of the authorities at the "Peterloo Massacre" (Aug. 16, 1819), he wrote *Notes and Explanations, Critical and Explanatory, on the Papers relative to the Internal State of the Country, recently presented to Parliament, with a Reply to Pamphlet in Defence of the Manchester Magistrates and Yeomanry for their Share in the Catastrophe of Peterloo* (1819).

Taylor, Joseph. d. at Richmond, England, in November, 1652. An English actor. He was the successor of Richard Burbage in *Hamlet* and *Othello*, and is supposed to have been the original Iago. It is said that Shakespeare personally instructed him in the playing of Hamlet, and the remembrance of this performance enabled Sir William D'Avenant to give the traditions of Shakespeare's directions; however, he seems not to have joined the King's Men until 1619, three years after Shakespeare's death.

Taylor, Meadows. [Full name, **Philip Meadows Taylor.**] b. at Liverpool, England, Sept. 25, 1808; d. at Menton, France, May 13, 1876. An Anglo-Indian administrator, journalist, and novelist. He was an officer in the army of one of the native rulers, and also a correspondent (1840–53) for the London *Times*. Author of *Confessions of a Thug* (1839), *Tippoo Sultaun* (1840), a tale of the Mysore War, *Tara* (1863), a story of the establishment of the Mahratta power, *Ralph Darnell* (1865), dealing with Robert Clive, and *Seeta* (1872), a story of the Sepoy Mutiny. *A Noble Queen* (1878) was published in book form after his death, after having been serialized in the *Indian Mail*. His *Story of My Life* (2 vols., 1877; reprinted, 1920) was edited by his daughter.

Taylor, Thomas. [Sometimes called **"the Platonist."**] b. at London, May 15, 1758; d. Nov. 1, 1835. An English classical scholar and miscellaneous author. He studied three years at St. Paul's School, and afterward received instruction from private teachers. He was for a time a bank clerk, and then a teacher in private schools, and spent the last 40 years of his life in studious retirement. He made translations, almost universally derided by the scholars of his day, of Plato, Aristotle, Pausanias, and various Neoplatonists.

Taylor, Tom. b. near Sunderland, England, Oct. 19, 1817; d. at Wandsworth, England, July 12, 1880. An English dramatist, editor of *Punch* from 1874 to 1880. He studied at Glasgow University and at Trinity College, Cambridge, and for two years was professor of English at University College, London. He was called to the bar in 1846, and in 1854 was appointed secretary of the board of health. He wrote or adapted over 100 plays, among which are *Still Waters Run Deep*, *Victims*, *An Unequal Match*, *The Overland Route*, *The Contested Election*, *To Parents and Guardians*, *Twixt Axe and Crown*, *Joan of Arc*, *Lady Clancarty*, *Anne Boleyn*, and, with Charles Reade, *Masks and Faces*, *Two Loves and a Life*, and *The King's Rival*. His most famous plays are *Our American Cousin* (1858), in which Lord Dundreary appears, and *The Ticket of Leave Man* (1863), notable for the relentless detective Hawkshaw. He wrote a life of B. R. Haydon, edited the *Autobiographical Recollections* of C. R. Leslie, and wrote *Leicester Square, Its Associations and Its Worthies* (1874) and others.

Tay Pay (tā pā). See **O'Connor, Thomas Power.**

Tchaikovsky (chĭ.kôf′ski), **Peter Ilich.** [Also: **Chaikovski, Tschaikovsky, Tschaikowsky.**] b. at Votkinsk, government of Perm, May 7, 1840; d. at St. Petersburg (now Leningrad), Nov. 6, 1893. Russian composer. He obtained (1859) a position in the ministry of justice, but after a trip to western Europe gave up his post (1863) to study at the newly founded St. Petersburg Conservatory of Music. Anton Rubinstein was his teacher of orchestration there and, after Tchaikovsky's graduation in 1866, obtained for him a post at the Moscow Conservatory under his brother, Nikolai Rubinstein. In 1878, assured of an annuity from Nadejda von Meck, a wealthy patroness (whom he was never to meet), he resigned his teaching position to devote himself entirely to composition. Though a homosexual (as his letters to his brother Modest indicate), he ventured (July, 1877) into an ill-starred marriage with a Conservatory pupil, Antonina Miliukova; by October, he had had a nervous breakdown, attempted suicide, and left her for good; she later became insane and died (1917) in an asylum. Tchaikovsky now overcame his fear of audiences and took up conducting; much to his surprise, he liked it, and traveled widely, visiting England in 1881 and 1889. In 1891 he came to New York at the invitation of the New York Symphony Society, and conducted a number of his own compositions, appearing at the opening of the Music Hall (now Carnegie Hall). He died of cholera soon after finishing and conducting his Sixth Symphony. Tchaikovsky was a firm adherent of the western school of composition and was not at all attached to the Russian nationalist school; his music, however, makes much of Russian themes and is distinctly Slavic in character, as well as being, at times, very personal. Of his six symphonies, the Fourth (F minor), the Fifth (E minor), and the Sixth (B minor, the Symphonie Pathétique), are best known. His violin concerto (D major) and his first piano concerto (B flat minor) are in the standard repertoire; his second and third piano concertos (in G and E flat) are seldom played. Tchaikovsky's 11 operas (10 complete) include *Eugene Onegin* (after Pushkin's poem, first presented 1879), *Pique-Dame* (*The Queen of Spades*, 1890), *Iolanthe, Joan of Arc*, and *Vakula the Smith*. His ballets, *The Swan Lake, The Sleeping Beauty*, and *The Nutcracker*, and the orchestral suites taken from them, are far more popular than his operas. Tchaikovsky's orchestral works, including *Marche Slave*, the *Ouverture Solennelle* (*1812 Overture*), *Capriccio Italienne*, the *Romeo and Juliet* overture-fantasia, *Francesca da Rimini, Manfred*, and the suite *Mozartiana*, remain concert favorites. Among the most hackneyed of dinner-ensemble pieces are the second movement,

ḍ, d or j; ş, s or sh; ṭ, t or ch; ẓ, z or zh; o, F. cloche; ü, F. menu; ċh, Sc. loch; ń, F. bonbon.

Andante Cantabile, from his D major quartet, and the song "None but the lonely heart" (*Nur wer die Sehnsucht kennt*). Well-known to students of piano are such pieces as the *Dumka* and *Troika*. His chamber music includes three string quartets and a piano trio; he also wrote a serenade for strings.

Teague (tāg, tēg). A character in Sir Robert Howard's play *The Committee*. He is a faithful Irishman, a character said by Charles Dibdin to have been copied from Howard's own Irish servant. "Teague" became a half-contemptuous name for an Irishman in the 17th-century plays and novels; it appears in the famous ballad *Lillibullero*.

Tearsheet (tār'shēt), **Doll.** In Shakespeare's *2 Henry IV*, Falstaff's mistress. She quarrels with Pistol (II.iv). Later she is taken to prison. Her death is announced by Pistol in *Henry V*.

Tears of the Muses. A poem by Edmund Spenser, included in his volume *Complaints* (1591).

Teazle (tē'zl), **Lady.** A gay and imprudent country-bred girl in Richard Brinsley Sheridan's *School for Scandal*.

Teazle, Sir Peter. The forgiving husband of Lady Teazle in Richard Brinsley Sheridan's *School for Scandal*.

Tehuti (te.hö'tē). See **Thoth.**

Telamon (tel'ạ.mon). In Greek legend, son of Aeacus, brother of Peleus, and father of Ajax.

Telegonus (tẹ.leg'ọ.nus). In Greek legend: **1.** A son of Proteus, slain by Hercules. **2.** A son of Odysseus and Circe. He killed Odysseus and married Penelope.

Telemachus (tẹ.lem'ạ.kus). An Asiatic monk, famous for his attempt in 404 A.D. to stop the gladiatorial shows. He sprang into the arena and endeavored to separate the gladiators, but was stoned to death by the spectators. He was proclaimed a martyr by the emperor Honorius, and his act and death led to the abolition of the exhibitions.

Telemachus. In Greek legend, the son of Odysseus and Penelope, prominent in the *Odyssey*. He went (attended by Athena), in search of his father, and joined the latter, on his return to Ithaca, in slaying the suitors of Penelope.

Télémaque (tā.lā.màk), **Aventures de.** [Eng. trans., "*Adventures of Telemachus*."] A romance by Fénelon, published in 1699. Founded on the legendary history of Telemachus, it is one of the classics of French literature.

Telephus (tel'ẹ.fus). In Greek legend, a son of Hercules and king of Mysia. The Greeks landed on his shores on their way to Troy; Telephus resisted them, and was wounded by Achilles.

Tell (tel), **William.** A legendary hero of Switzerland in the struggle for independence of the cantons Schwyz, Uri, and Unterwalden with Albert of Austria (the German emperor Albert I). The story is that Tell, who was the head of the independent confederates, refused to salute the cap which Gessler, the Austrian governor, had placed on a pole in the market place of Altdorf as a symbol of imperial authority. For his refusal he was ordered to place an apple on the head of his little son and shoot it off. Tell did so, and revealed another arrow with which he had intended to shoot Gessler if he had killed his son. For this defiance he was taken across the lake to be imprisoned, but in the confusion caused when a storm came up he shot Gessler, escaped, and afterward liberated his country. The principal source of the life and deeds of Tell is the *Chronicon Helveticum* (Swiss Chronicle) of Aegidius Tschudi (1505–72), which gives 1307 as the date of the Tell incident. Based principally upon Tschudi is Schiller's drama *Wilhelm Tell* (1804). The legend of William Tell is of ancient Germanic origin. The earliest extant version of the story of the skillful archer who shoots an apple from his son's head is in the Old Norse *Vilkina Saga*. The story of the famous shot of the archer Egil (a brother of Volund) is here related: at the command of King Nidung an apple is placed upon the head of the three-year-old son of Egil, who is then made to shoot, and strikes it directly in the middle with his first arrow. When asked why he had taken two other arrows when only one shot was allowed, he replied boldly, "In order to shoot the king if I had injured the child." Another version is found in Saxo Grammaticus's 13th-century *Historia Danica* and the story is also told in English balladry of William of Cloudesley.

Tell-Truth (tel'trŏth), **Paul.** Pseudonym of **Carey, George Saville.**

Tellus (tel'us). In Roman mythology, goddess and personification of the earth. Her worship included fertility sacrifices, such as a cow with calf. Like many other earth deities, she was also associated with rites for the dead.

Temora (tem'ọ.rạ). One of the poems of Ossian, published in 1763.

Temperley (tem'pėr.li), **Harold William Vazeille.** b. at Cambridge, England, April 20, 1879; d. there, July 11, 1939. An English historian. He was a British representative at the Paris peace conference (1919), and contributed (1920–24) to the *History of the Paris Peace Conference*. He edited (13 vols., 1926–38), with George P. Gooch, *British Documents on the Origins of the War*. He was professor of modern history (1931–39) at Cambridge, and was appointed (1938) master of Peterhouse (Saint Peter's College). His works include *Life of George Canning* (1905), *Frederic the Great and Kaiser Joseph* (1915), *The Foreign Policy of Canning, 1822–27* (1925), and *England and the Near East—The Crimea* (1936). He was coauthor with A. J. Grant of *Europe in the Nineteenth and Twentieth Centuries* (1927) and subsequent revisions.

Tempest (tem'pẹst), Dame **Mary Susan.** [Maiden name, **Etherington**; known as **Marie Tempest.**] b. at London, July 15, 1866; d. there, Oct. 14, 1942. An English actress. She made her debut (1885) in the operetta *Boccaccio*, and spent her early career in musical comedy. She appeared (1899 *et seq.*) in straight comedy, playing the main role in *Becky Sharp*. She became noted as a player in both England and the U. S. She appeared (1936) with Ignace Paderewski in her only motion picture, *The Moonlight Sonata*. She was created (1937) a Dame of the British Empire.

Tempest, The. A play by Shakespeare, written and first performed in 1611 or 1612, and first printed in the folio of 1623. It was his last finished play.

fat, fāte, fär, àsk, fāre; net, mē, hėr; pin, pīne; not, nōte, mŏve, nôr; up, lūte, pùll; ᴛн, then;

The subject was taken from a pamphlet, *A Discovery of the Bermudas, Otherwise Called the Isle of Devils*, by "one Jourdan, who probably returned from Virginia" (1610). Shakespeare also used Richard Rich's ballad *News from Virginia* (1610), William Strachey's *A True Repertory of the Wracke and Redemption of Sir Thomas Gates, upon and from the Islands of the Bermudas* (in manuscript, 1610), and *A True Declaration of the Estate of the Colonie in Virginia* (1610).

The Story. Prospero, whose brother, Antonio, with the aid of Alonso, King of Naples, has usurped his rightful claim to the duchy of Milan and set him adrift in a boat with his lovely daughter, Miranda, now, twelve years later, is living not unhappily with Miranda on an enchanted tropical isle. Prospero has used his knowledge of the art of magic to release the airy spirit Ariel, who had been imprisoned in a tree, and to force the brutish Caliban, son of the witch Sycorax, to serve him. Learning, with the help of Ariel, that his former enemies are sailing near the island, Prospero summons a tempest to force them into his power, and they presently reach the shore from their wrecked ship in separate groups. Ferdinand, the son of the King of Naples, wanders to the cave of Prospero and, there meeting Miranda, falls in love with her, and she with him. Meanwhile, most of the other survivors (who believe Ferdinand to be dead) are lulled to sleep by Ariel's music, but Antonio and Sebastian, Alonso's brother, remain awake and plot the murder of Alonso. Ariel, however, prevents this by awakening the others just in time. Another group from the ship, Stephano, a drunken butler, and Trinculo, a jester, have met Caliban and have given him some of their liquor, which delights and bemuses him. Caliban offers to serve them, suggesting that they should murder Prospero and seize the island, and that Stephano should then marry Miranda. But Ariel has overheard these plotters too, and warns Prospero, who, with Ariel's aid, sets out to punish and reward all according to their just deserts. To punish Alonso and Antonio, Prospero and Ariel set before the hungry men a magnificent banquet which vanishes each time they try to eat. Ariel, disguised as a harpy, then rebukes Alonso for his crimes against Prospero. Prospero next presents a graceful masque before the now betrothed Ferdinand and Miranda, but suddenly interrupts it when he remembers Caliban's plot. These conspirators, however, are easily distracted by the gaudy clothes Ariel has hung upon a line, and run away howling as spirits in the shape of dogs chase them around the island. The other group of conspirators are now led by Ariel's music to the cave of Prospero, where Prospero reveals his identity and demands the return of his dukedom. He shows the repentant Alonso Ferdinand and Miranda playing chess; the other conspirators return, sore from the pinching they have received; Prospero renounces his magic, setting free Ariel and Caliban, who says he will try to be wiser and to seek for grace. The entire group plans to sail for Naples with "calm seas, auspicious gales" on the following day. Because *The Tempest* is Shakespeare's final comedy, some critics have interpreted the role of Prospero as Shakespeare bidding farewell to his own art. In some respects, this is a tenable

interpretation, although other critics deny its plausibility. But whether or not *The Tempest* is a conscious conclusion to Shakespeare's career, the play is, in a way, a summation of his work. The themes of reconciliation and concord, which appear throughout Shakespeare's dramas, are nowhere more ideally worked out than here. The conspiracies are never actually dangerous, because Prospero and Ariel never allow them to reach fruition; yet Prospero happily renounces his supernatural power to return to normal society. The play abounds in contrasts: Ariel and Caliban; delicate music and crude jesting (by Trinculo and Stephano); love and discord; storm and calm. The poetry in the play ranks with Shakespeare's best, and even the ugly Caliban is given some beautiful lines:

> The isle is full of noises,
> Sounds and sweet airs that give delight and hurt not.
> Sometimes a thousand twangling instruments
> Will hum about mine ears.
>   (III.ii).

Tempest, The. [Full title, **The Tempest; or, The Enchanted Island.**] An operatic play adapted in 1667 by Sir William D'Avenant and John Dryden from Shakespeare's *Tempest*.

Templars (tem'plarz). [Also: **Knights Templars, Knights of the Temple.**] A military order, whose name was taken from the early headquarters of the order in the Crusaders' palace at Jerusalem (the so-called Temple of Solomon); with the Knights Hospitalers and the Teutonic Knights one of the three great medieval Christian military groups. The order was founded at Jerusalem c1118, and was confirmed by the Pope in 1128. Its special aim was protection to pilgrims on the way to the holy shrines, and the distinguishing garb of the knights was a white mantle with a red cross. The order took a leading part in the conduct of the Crusades, and spread rapidly, acquiring great wealth and influence in Spain, France, England, and other countries in Europe. Its chief seats in the East were Jerusalem, Acre, and Cyprus, and in Europe a foundation called Le Temple, then just outside Paris. The members comprised knights, men-at-arms, and chaplains; they were grouped in commanderies, with a preceptor at the head of each province, and a grand master at the head of the order. The Templars were accused of heresy, immorality, and other offenses by Philip IV of France in 1307, and the order was suppressed (1312) by the Council of Vienne.

Temple (tem'pl), **Charlotte.** See **Charlotte Temple.**

Temple, Miss. In Charlotte Brontë's novel *Jane Eyre*, a governess. Her sweet and gentle personality enables her finally to become the "good genius" of everyone immediately connected with her.

Temple, the. A religious edifice of the Jews at Jerusalem. There were three buildings successively erected on the same spot, and called, from the names of their builders, the Temple of Solomon, the Temple of Zerubbabel, and the Temple of Herod. The first was built by Solomon, and was destroyed (c586 B.C.) by Nebuchadnezzar. The second was built by the Jews on their return (c537 B.C.) from the captivity, and was pillaged or partly destroyed several times, especially by Antiochus IV (Antiochus Epiphanes), Pompey, and Herod. The third, the largest and most magnificent of the three, was begun by Herod the Great, and was completely destroyed at the capture of Jerusalem by the Romans (70 A.D.). Various attempts have been made toward the restoration of the first and the third of these temples, but scholars are not agreed in respect to architectural details. The ornament and design were in any case of severe and simple character, though rich materials were used. The successive temples all consisted of a combination of buildings, comprising courts separated from and rising one above another, and provided also with chambers for the use of the priests and for educational purposes. The enclosure of Herod's temple covered 19 acres. It comprised an outer court of the gentiles, a court of the women, a court of Israel, a court of the priests, and the temple building with the holy place, and within all (entered only once a year, and only by the high priest) the holy of holies. Within the court of the priests were the great altar and the laver; within the holy place, the golden candlestick, the altar of incense, and the table for the showbread; and within the holy of holies, the ark of the covenant and the mercy seat.

Temple, the. A lodge at London of the religious and military establishment of the Middle Ages known as the Templars. The first settlement of the Templars at London was in Holborn, where in 1118 they built a house which must have stood near what is now the NE corner of Chancery Lane. They removed to the New Temple in the Strand in 1184. When the order was suppressed (1308) in the reign of Edward II, their house was given by the king to the Earl of Pembroke; it went next to the Earl of Lancaster, and at his death reverted to the crown. In 1338 it went to the Knights Hospitalers, at Clerkenwell, who leased part of it in 1346 to students of the common law, and on the site of the London Temple the two Inns of Court called the Middle Temple and Inner Temple now stand; they have ever since been occupied by barristers, and are the joint property of the Societies of the Inner and of the Middle Temple, which have the right of calling candidates to the degree of barrister. The Inner Temple is so called because it is within the precincts of the City of London, the Middle Temple because it was between the Inner and Outer Temple. The Outer Temple remained in the possession of the bishop of Exeter when the remainder was leased, and was afterward converted into the Exeter Buildings.

Temple, Sir **William.** b. at London, 1628; d. at Moor Park, Surrey, England, Jan. 27, 1699. An English diplomat, statesman, and author. He was educated at Cambridge, and entered Parliament in 1660. He concluded a treaty with the Bishop of Munster in 1665, became minister at Brussels in 1665, and negotiated the treaty of the Triple Alliance with Holland and Sweden against France in 1668, but found that this was reversed by Charles II's secret agreement (1670) with Louis XIV, and retired to Ireland. He was ambassador at The Hague (1668–71), and negotiated a peace with the Netherlands in 1674 after the two-year war. He was ambassador to the Congress of Nijmwegen (1679), having previously arranged the marriage

(1677) of Princess Mary, daughter of James II, and William of Orange (later William III). He formed a plan for a privy council in 1679, and became one of its chief members, but withdrew from public life in 1681 when the plan came to nothing. He lived thereafter in Ireland and in Surrey, his secretary (1689 *et seq.*) being Jonathan Swift. He took no part in the revolution that brought William and Mary to the throne. He wrote *An Essay on the Present State and Settlement of Ireland* (1668), *The Empire* (1671), *Observations upon the United Provinces* (1672), *Essay upon Government* (written 1671, published 1680), *Trade in Ireland* (1673), *Miscellanies,* including poems (1679 and 1692), *Memoirs* (1691 and 1709), and *Introduction to the History of England* (1695). Temple's Epicurean philosophy is set forth in his essays in a polished style much admired by writers in the following century (many of whom took him as their pattern). His essay, *Of Ancient and Modern Learning,* bringing the question of progress into doubt, began a literary controversy in England that evoked Swift's *Battle of the Books.*

Temple Bar. A famous gateway before the Temple at London, which formerly divided Fleet Street from the Strand. According to ancient custom, when the sovereign visited the City, he asked permission of the Lord Mayor to pass it. In its last form it was a rather ugly archway built by Christopher Wren in 1670. It spanned the street with an elliptical arch flanked by two small arches over the footways, and had a second story in which were four niches with statues of sovereigns, and a curved pediment above. It was removed in 1878, and reerected at Waltham Cross, Hertfordshire. It is now represented by a monument called the Temple Bar Memorial, a tall pedestal with statues of Queen Victoria and the Prince of Wales (later Edward VII) in niches at the sides, surmounted by the griffin and arms of the city of London.

Temple Bar Memorial, The. A monument which replaced the old Temple Bar, removed 1878.

Temple Beau, The. A comedy by Henry Fielding, produced in 1730.

Temple Gardens. Gardens of the Temple, London, separated from the Thames by the Victoria Embankment.

Temple of Fame, The. A poem by Alexander Pope, published in 1715.

Temple of Glass, The. A poem by John Lydgate, partly in imitation of Chaucer's *House of Fame.*

Tenant of Wildfell Hall (wĭld'fel)**, The.** A novel by Anne Brontë, published (1848) under the pseudonym Acton Bell.

Tender Husband, or the Accomplished Fools, The. A comedy by Sir Richard Steele, produced in 1705, based on Molière's *Le Sicilien.* Possibly Addison aided in its composition; he certainly wrote the epilogue.

Tennant (ten'ạnt)**, William.** b. at Anstruther, Fife, Scotland, May 15, 1784; d. near Dollar, Clackmannanshire, Scotland, Oct. 14, 1848. A Scottish poet. His chief work is the mock-heroic poem *Anster Fair* (1812). He also wrote *The Thane of Fife* (1822) and others.

Tennent (ten'ẹnt), Sir **James Emerson.** [Original name, **James Emerson.**] b. at Belfast, Ireland, April 7, 1804; d. at London, March 6, 1869. A British traveler, politician, and author. He was returned as member of Parliament for Belfast in 1832, and was colonial secretary at Ceylon (1845–50), and permanent secretary of the Board of Trade (1852–67). He published *Picture of Greece* (1826), *Letters from the Aegean* (1829), *History of Modern Times* (1830), *Christianity in Ceylon* (1850), *Ceylon, Physical, Historical, and Topographical* (1859), and others.

Tenniel (ten'yẹl), Sir **John.** b. at London, 1820; d. Feb. 25, 1914. An English artist and cartoonist. He was a member (1851–1901) of the staff of *Punch*. He illustrated *Alice's Adventures in Wonderland* and *Through the Looking Glass*. He was knighted in 1893.

Tennyson (ten'i.sọn), **Alfred.** [Title: 1st Baron **Tennyson;** commonly called **Alfred, Lord Tennyson.**] b. at Somersby, Lincolnshire, England, Aug. 6, 1809; d. at Aldworth House, near Haslemere, Surrey, England, Oct. 6, 1892. An English poet, laureate of England (1850 *et seq.*). He was the son of George Clayton Tennyson, vicar of Great Grimsby and rector of Somersby and Enderby. He published with his brother Charles a collection of juvenile poems (*Poems by Two Brothers*) in 1827, and was a student at Trinity College, Cambridge (1828–31), with Arthur H. Hallam, Richard Monckton Milnes, R. C. Trench, and others, where he wrote the prize poem *Timbuctoo* (1829). He lived at various places till 1850, when he married Emily Sellwood, after an engagement lasting nearly 20 years, and settled at Twickenham; he afterward lived at Aldworth (Sussex), and from 1853 at Farringford (Isle of Wight). He received a state pension in 1845, succeeded William Wordsworth as poet laureate in 1850, and was raised to the peerage in 1884. He lived a secluded life, and died of old age after a short and painless illness. He was buried in the Poets' Corner, near Geoffrey Chaucer, in Westminster Abbey. He wrote *Poems, Chiefly Lyrical* (1830; including *Mariana, Recollections of the Arabian Nights*, and *The Ballad of Oriana*), *Poems* (1832; including *The Lady of Shalott, The Miller's Daughter, Œnone, The Palace of Art, The May Queen, The Lotus Eaters*, and *A Dream of Fair Women*), *Poems* (1842; including *Ulysses, Two Voices, The Talking Oak, Morte d'Arthur, The Gardener's Daughter*, and *Locksley Hall*), *The Princess* (1847, 1850), a work on the emancipation of women notable for its songs ("Tears, idle tears," "The splendor falls on castle walls," "Home they brought her warrior dead," "Sweet and low") and ridiculed by W. S. Gilbert in *Princess Ida; In Memoriam* (1850), a collection of elegiac poetry, written between 1833 (when his friend and prospective brother-in-law Hallam died) and 1850, which was very popular as a searching for the meaning of death and immortality and which probably brought Tennyson the laureateship, *Ode on the Death of the Duke of Wellington* (1852), *Charge of the Light Brigade, Maud*, and other poems (1855), *Idylls of the King* (1859–85), a romantic retelling of the Arthurian legends, *A Welcome to the Princess Alexandra* (1863), *Enoch Arden and Other Poems*

(1864), *The Golden Supper* (1869), *The Window, or the Songs of the Wrens*, with music by Sir Arthur Sullivan (1871), *Queen Mary* (a drama, 1875), *Harold* (a drama, 1876), *The Falcon* (a short play, acted 1879, published 1884), *The Cup* (a short play, acted 1881, published 1884), *The Promise of May* (acted 1882, published 1886), *Becket* (a drama, 1884), *The Lover's Tale* (1879; including as its fourth part *The Golden Supper*), *Ballads and Other Poems* (1880), *Tiresias and Other Poems* (partly new, 1885), *Locksley Hall Sixty Years After* (1886), *Demeter and Other Poems* (1889, including "Crossing the Bar"), *The Death of Œnone, Akbar's Dream, and Other Poems* (1892), and *The Foresters, Robin Hood, and Maid Marian* (a drama, 1892). Tennyson's reputation as a poet, attacked on various grounds by the late Victorian poets and critics, particularly because of his conservatism and his lack of adequate discernment of artistic values as well as on several other counts, has recently risen again.

Tennyson, Charles. See **Turner, Charles Tennyson.**

Tennyson, Frederick. b. 1807; d. at Kensington, London, Feb. 26, 1898. An English poet; brother of Alfred Tennyson. He published a volume of poems entitled *Days and Hours* (1854), and also *Isles of Greece* (1890) and *Daphne and Other Poems* (1891). He was author of some of the verse in the collection (chiefly by Charles and Alfred Tennyson) *Poems by Two Brothers* (1827).

Tennyson, Hallam. [Title, 2nd Baron **Tennyson.**] b. at Twickenham, England, Aug. 11, 1852; d. Dec. 2, 1928. An English author and colonial governor; son of Alfred Tennyson. He was private secretary to his father, governor and commander in chief of South Australia (1899–1902), first acting governor general of the Commonwealth of Australia (1902), and governor general of Australia (1902–03). He published *Alfred, Lord Tennyson: a Memoir* (1897) and edited *Tennyson and his Friends* (1911).

Tennyson, Lionel Hallam. [Title, 3rd Baron **Tennyson.**] b. Nov. 7, 1889—. An English soldier and author; son of Hallam Tennyson and grandson of Alfred Tennyson. Author of *From Verse to Worse* (1933) and others.

Ten Thousand a Year. A novel (1839–41) by Samuel Warren, about a conceited shopman, Tittlebat Titmouse, who inherits a large estate.

Tents of Israel (iz'rā.ẹl). A novel by G. B. Stern, published in 1924 and issued in America under the title *The Matriarch* (1925). It is the first volume in her trilogy of Jewish life, *The Rakonitz Chronicles* (1932). *The Matriarch* was dramatized in 1931.

tercet (tẽr'set). In poetry, a group of three rhyming lines; a triplet.

Terence (ter'ẹns). [Full Latin name, **Publius Terentius Afer.**] b. at Carthage, c185 B.C.; d. c159. A Roman comic poet and dramatist. He wrote six comedies: *Andria, Hecyra, Heautontimoroumenos, Eunuchus, Phormio*, and *Adelphi*, all cast in the style of Menander. His comedies were acted by grammar schools and universities in England in the 16th and 17th centuries, and served as models for comedies such as *Ralph Roister Doister* and *Gammer Gurton's Needle*. Such plays as Gascoigne's *The Supposes* were based on plot incidents

ḍ, d or j; ṣ, s or sh; ṭ, t or ch; ẓ, z or zh; o, F. cloche; ü, F. menu; ċh, Sc. loch; ṅ, F. bonbon.

from Plautus and Terence. The Terentian comedies known to most Renaissance English readers were the *Heautontimoroumenos*, *Eunuchus*, and *Adelphi*.

Terence Mulvaney (mul.vā′ni). See **Mulvaney, Terence.**

Teresa (tẹ.rē′sạ), Saint. See Saint **Theresa.**

Teresa D'Acunha (tạ.rä′sạ dä.kön′yạ). See **Acunha, Teresa D'.**

Tereus (tir′ẹ.us). In Greek legend, a king of Thrace; son of Ares. He married Procne and Philomela, and was transformed into a hoopoe (or hawk) for mistreating them.

Termagaunt (tẽr′mạ.gônt). [Also, **Termagant.**] A name given to the god of the Saracens in the medieval romances, moralities, and folk dramas. He was popularly believed by Christians to be a blustering, bullying Mohammedan god. The word "termagant" is now commonly applied to a noisy, scolding woman.

Terpander (tẽr.pan′dẽr). b. at Antissa, Lesbos, Greece; fl. mid-7th century B.C. A Greek musician and poet. He was undoubtedly a historical person, but very little is known about him, and some of what is told may be legend rather than fact. He is said to have won the laurel for music at the Carnean Games in 676 B.C., and to have been summoned to Sparta c650 B.C., in conformity with a revelation by the oracle at Delphi, to bring about peace between contending groups in that city-state. He has been called the father both of Greek classical music and of lyric poetry, and it seems certain that he was in fact a poet, a composer, and a player of stringed instruments. Strabo wrote that to the four strings which the lyre formerly had Terpander added three more; but others understand that his innovation was in the form of the *nome*, or ode recited to music, which he divided into seven parts, where previously there were four. Terpander has in fact been credited with the origination of musical notation, but this is considered very doubtful. He was, in any case, the earliest Greek musician of whom we have even fragmentary historical knowledge.

Terpsichore (tẽrp.sik′ọ.rē). In Greek mythology, one of the Muses, the patroness of lyric poetry, the choral dance, and the dramatic chorus developed from it. In the last days of the Greek religion her attributions became restricted chiefly to the province of lyric poetry. In art this Muse is usually represented as bearing a lyre.

Terra (ter′ạ). In Roman mythology, a goddess personifying the earth.

Terrible Meek, The. A drama (1911) by Charles Rann Kennedy.

Terrible Temptation, A. A novel by Charles Reade, published in 1871.

Terror, Reign of. See **Reign of Terror.**

Terry (ter′i), Dame **Ellen Alicia** (or **Alice**). b. at Coventry, England, Feb. 27, 1848; d. July 21, 1928. An English actress. She made her first appearance on the stage with Charles Kean's company in 1856 in the parts of Mamillius in *The Winter's Tale* and Prince Arthur in *King John*. She appeared in London in 1863 as Gertrude in *The Little Treasure*. In 1864 she married George Frederick Watts and

left the stage, but reappeared in 1866 after separating from him. In 1867 she made her first appearance with Henry Irving, and was associated with him in all his successful Shakespearian productions, and as Camma in Tennyson's *The Cup* and Rosamonde in his *Becket*. From 1868 to 1874 she retired to live with E. W. Godwin, her two children being born in this period. After her divorce from Watts, she married (1877) C. C. Wardell; they separated in 1881; in 1907 she married James Usselmann (stage name James Carew), but again the marriage failed and they parted in 1910. She visited America eight times, seven with Irving. Her Beatrice, Viola, Juliet, and other Shakespearian roles were remarkable for their charm. Her memoirs, *The Story of My Life*, appeared in 1908. She carried on a notable correspondence with George Bernard Shaw.

Tertium Quid (tẽr′shum kwid). In Browning's *The Ring and the Book*, the third and closing section, in which judgment is rendered on the matter of the story (the opinions of the two sides into which it has split Rome are dealt with in the first two sections).

Tertullian (tẽr.tul′yạn). [Full Latin name, **Quintus Septimius Florens Tertullianus.**] b. at Carthage, in Africa, c160 A.D.; d. c230. An ecclesiastical writer, one of the fathers of the Latin Church. He became converted to Christianity (c192), lived in Rome and Carthage, and became a Montanist (c203). His chief work is his *Apologeticus*, a defense of Christianity called forth by the persecutions under Septimius Severus. Among his other works are *Ad Martyres*, *De Baptismo*, *De Poenitentia*, *De Spectaculis*, *De Patientia*, *De Praescriptione*, *Adversus Marcionem*, *De Virginibus velandis*, and *Adversus Praxean*. His writing is marked by vigorous Latin, some of it epigrammatic and now proverbial: "Certum est quia impossibile est," "Semen est sanguis Christianorum."

terza rima (ter′tsạ rē′mạ). A form of verse in iambic rhythm used by the early Italian poets. In it the lines consist of ten or eleven syllables, and are arranged in sets of three that are closely connected. The middle line of the first tercet rhymes with the first and third lines of the second tercet, the middle line of the second tercet rhymes with the first and third lines of the third tercet (*aba*, *bcb*, *cdc*), and so on. At the end of the poem or canto there is an extra line which has the same rhyme as the middle line of the preceding tercet. In this form of verse Dante's *Divina Commedia* is written. The most conspicuous example of its use in English literature is Byron's *Prophecy of Dante*.

Tessa (tes′ạ). In George Eliot's novel *Romola*, Tito's second wife.

Tess of the D'Urbervilles (tes; dẽr′bẽr.vilz). [Full title, **Tess of the D'Urbervilles: a Pure Woman.**] A tragic novel (1891) by Thomas Hardy: the story of a village girl who kills her betrayer after having been repudiated by her husband. Mrs. Minnie Maddern Fiske appeared in 1897 in a dramatization of this story.

Testament of Cresseid (kres′id), **The.** See **Cresseid, The Testament of.**

Testament of Love. A prose work, by Thomas Usk but wrongly attributed by Thomas Speght to

Chaucer. Purporting to be written by a prisoner in danger of being hanged (Usk was executed in 1388), it is a political allegory, full of obscurities, in which Usk attempts to justify his conduct.

Tethys (tē′this). A sea goddess of Greek mythology; daughter of sky and earth. She became the consort of ocean, and mother of all the rivers and 3,000 oceanids.

Tetrachordon (tet.rạ.kôr′don). A work by Milton about marriage and the evils of divorce. The title (taken from the Greek) means "Four Strings," in allusion to the principal sections of the Bible that refer to marriage (there are two in the Old Testament and two in the New Testament).

tetrameter (te.tram′ẹ.tẽr). In prosody, a verse or period consisting of four measures. A trochaic, iambic, or anapestic tetrameter consists of four dipodies (eight feet). A tetrameter of other rhythms is a tetrapody, or period of four feet. The name is specifically given to the trochaic tetrameter catalectic. An example of the acatalectic tetrameter is:

Ŏnce ŭpŏn ă/mĭdnĭght drēarў,//
ās Ĭ pŏndĕred/wēak ănd wēarў.
(Poe, *The Raven.*)

Tetterby (tet′ẽr.bi), **Adolphus.** In Dickens's tale *The Haunted Man*, a poor newsvender who comes under the baleful influence of Redlaw ("the haunted man") and is saved, with his family, only through the aid of Milly Swidger.

Teubner (toib′nẽr), **Benediktus Gotthelf.** b. at Grosskraussnigt, Germany, June 16, 1784; d. at Leipzig, Germany, Jan. 21, 1856. A German publisher, founder (1824) of the firm of B. G. Teubner, at Leipzig, which specialized at first in low-priced Greek and Roman classics. His sons-in-law and successors extended the firm's activities to popular publications in many fields of philosophy, science, art, literature, and history. Its best-known product is the collection *Aus Natur und Geisteswelt* (1898 et seq.).

Teucer (tū′sẽr). Either of two heroes of Greek legend. One was the first king of Troy. Another was the son of Telamon and half brother of Ajax; noted as an archer. After his banishment by Telamon, he was said to have founded Salamis in Cyprus.

Teufelsdröckh (toi′fẹls.drẽk), **Herr.** A German philosopher, the central character and pretended author of Thomas Carlyle's *Sartor Resartus.* He is an eccentric Professor of Things in General at the University of Weissnichtwo.

Tewkesbury Chronicle (tūks′bẽr.i), **The.** A chronicle of ecclesiastical history kept (1066–1263) at the Abbey of Tewkesbury.

Thackeray (thak′ẹ.ri), **William Makepeace.** [Pseudonyms: **Mr. Brown; George Savage Fitz-Boodle; Major Goliah Gahagan; Charles Jeames de la Pluche; Michael Angelo Titmarsh; Charles James Yellowplush; The Fat Contributor; The Honourable Wilhelmina Amelia Skeggs; Ikey Solomons, Esq., Junior; Mr. Spec.; Miss Tickletoby; T. T.; Launcelot Wagstaff; Théophile Wagstaff,** and others.] b. at Calcutta, India, July 18, 1811; d. at London, Dec. 24, 1863. An English novelist and satirist. The son of a high official in the service of the East India Company, Thackeray was brought to England in 1817 after his father's death. He received the education of a gentleman at Charterhouse School and Trinity College, Cambridge, but he did not distinguish himself in formal studies at either institution. Having left the university without a degree in 1830, he passed the ensuing winter at Weimar. On his return to England he undertook to read for the bar at the Middle Temple, but he soon abandoned the law to dabble in journalism and art. In 1833 he lost the bulk of his 20,000-pound inheritance through the failure of a Calcutta agency house. Reduced from affluence almost to penury, he removed to Paris, where for three years he sought unsuccessfully to make himself a painter. He married Isabella Shawe in 1836 and the following year returned to England to try his fortune as a writer. He had already gained some recognition as a contributor to the *Times* and *Fraser's Magazine* and as the author of *The Paris Sketch Book*, when his wife lost her mind after the birth of her third child in 1840. She lived until 1894 without recovering her sanity. Though Thackeray continued to write voluminously after the breakup of his home, producing such stories as *The Great Hoggarty Diamond* (1841) and *Barry Lyndon* (1844) and such travel narratives as *The Irish Sketch Book* (1843) and *Notes of a Journey from Cornhill to Grand Cairo* (1846), it was not until the appearance of "The Snobs of England" in *Punch* during 1846–47 and above all of the monthly parts of *Vanity Fair* during 1847–48 that he became famous. He consolidated his reputation with three other major novels, *Pendennis* (1848–50), *The Newcomes* (1853–55), and his great historical romance, *The History of Henry Esmond* (1852), while he amused his readers with a series of Christmas books, the best of which is *The Rose and the Ring* (1854). Lectures on *The English Humourists* (1851) and *The Four Georges* (1855) made him personally known to admirers both in England and in the U. S., which he visited in 1852–53 and 1855–56. The fees that he received for these performances, for such later novels as *The Virginians* (1857–59) and *Philip* (1861–62), and for his editorship of *The Cornhill Magazine* (1860–62) enabled him to leave his daughters substantially the same fortune that he had inherited as a young man; but apart from his familiar essays contributed to *The Cornhill Magazine*, collected as *The Roundabout Papers*, and his unfinished romance *Denis Duval* (1864), the writing of his last years is markedly inferior to that of his prime.

Thaddeus of Warsaw (thad′ẹ.us; wôr′sô). A historical romance of Poland (1803), by Jane Porter.

Thais (thā′is). fl. in the last part of the 4th century B.C. An Athenian courtesan; mistress of Alexander the Great. She is alleged (undoubtedly erroneously) to have incited him to set fire to Persepolis. She was afterward mistress of the King of Egypt.

Thaisa (thā.is′ạ, thā′i.sạ). In Shakespeare's *Pericles*, the daughter of Simonides and wife of Pericles.

Thalaba the Destroyer (thal′ạ.bạ). A descriptive poem (1801) by Robert Southey.

Thales (thā′lēz). b. at Miletus, Asia Minor, c640 B.C.; d. c546. A Greek philosopher, astronomer, and geometer, one of the seven wise men of ancient Greece, and the earliest of the Ionian natural philosophers. He regarded water as the principle of all things. He is said to have predicted an eclipse of the sun for May 28, 585 B.C.; and to him were attributed various discoveries in geometry and astronomy. His reputation as an abstract philosopher, it is said, brought the criticism that he was impractical; according to the story, he then went into the olive-oil business and made a fortune. He is memorable, not only for his actual discoveries, but for being the first to base a philosophy on natural phenomena alone without recourse to the supernatural.

Thalia (thạ.lī′ạ). In Greek mythology, the Muse of comedy and of idyllic poetry. In later art she is generally represented with a comic mask, a shepherd's crook, and a wreath of ivy.

Thaliard (thal′yạrd). In Shakespeare's *Pericles*, a lord of Antioch.

Thames (temz). [Also: **Isis**; Latin, **Tamesa, Tamesis.**] Principal river in Great Britain, in S and SE England. It rises on the E slope of the Cotswold Hills, near Cirencester, in Gloucestershire. It flows mainly E, forming a part of the whole of the following boundaries: Gloucestershire-Wiltshire, Berkshire-Oxfordshire, Berkshire-Buckinghamshire, Middlesex-Surrey, and Essex-Kent. Broadening into a considerable estuary, it flows into the North Sea. For part of its course to its junction with the river Thame it is called also the Isis. The chief places on its banks are Oxford, Abingdon, Reading, Great Marlow, Windsor, Eton, Staines, Chertsey, Kingston-on-Thames, Richmond, Brentford, London, Gravesend, and Sheerness. The principal tributaries are the rivers Cherwell, Thame, Colne, Lea, and Roding on the N, and the Kennet, Mole, and Medway on the S. Above London it passes through some of the richest agricultural country in England; below London it is one of the greatest arteries of shipping in the world. It is navigable for ocean-going vessels to London Bridge; it is tidal to Teddington. Length to Sheerness, ab. 228 mi.; width at London Bridge, 900 ft.; at Gravesend, half a mile.

Thames Embankment, the. [Also, **the Embankment.**] A broad drive with sidewalks, constructed 1864–70 in London along the north bank of the Thames from Blackfriars Bridge to Westminster.

Thamyris (tham′i.ris). In Greek legend, a Thracian singer. He boasted that he could surpass the Muses, and for this presumption was deprived by them of his sight and of the power of singing.

Thanatos (than′ạ.tos). In Greek mythology, the personification of Death, brother of Sleep.

Thane of Cawdor (kô′dọr). See **Cawdor, Thane of.**

Thane of Fife (fīf). See under **Macduff.**

Thane of Glamis (glämz, glä′mis). See **Glamis, Thane of.**

Theagenes and Chariclea (thē.aj′ẹ.nēz; kar.i.klē′ạ). [Also, **Aethiopica.**] Ancient romance by Heliodorus, written in the 4th century. It recounts the loves and adventures of Theagenes, a Thessalian, and Chariclea, the daughter of Persina, queen of Ethiopia. It was rendered into English prose by Thomas Underdown, and into French by Jacques Amyot.

theater or **theatre.** **1.** A building appropriated to the representation of dramatic spectacles; a playhouse. The most usual American spelling, except in the names of some actual theater buildings, is *theater*. The spelling *theatre* is more common in England. The former spelling appears in Cotgrave (1611), Minsheu (1617, 1625), Sherwood (1632), Bullokar (1641), Cockeram (1642), Blount (1670), Holyoke (1677), Hexham (1678), etc. The spelling *theatre* appears to have obtained currency in the latter part of the 17th century and since (Coles, 1708, Johnson, 1755; both *theater* and *theatre* in Bailey, 1727, etc.), owing to the constant and direct association of the word with the modern F. *théâtre* (itself a false form in respect to accent). Among the Greeks and Romans theaters were among the most important and the largest public edifices, very commonly having accommodation for from 10,000 to 40,000 spectators. The Greek and Roman theaters resembled each other in their general distribution, the Roman theater being developed from the Greek with the modifications, particularly about the orchestra and the stage, due to the difference from the Greek of Roman dramatic ideals. The auditorium, including the orchestra, was commonly in general plan a segment of a circle, usually a half-circle in Roman examples, greater than a half-circle in Greek, and was not, unless very exceptionally, covered by a roof or awning. It was termed *cavea* by the Romans and κοῖλον by the Greeks. The seats were all concentric with the orchestra, and were intersected by diverging ascents or flights of steps, which divided the auditorium into wedge-shaped compartments (*cunei*, κερκῖδες), and also by one longitudinal passage or more. The stage of the Roman theater formed the chord of the segment, and was called the *scena* (σκηνή). The Greek theater of the great dramatic period in the 5th century B.C. had no stage, the action taking place in the orchestra, or space below the seats, in which actors and chorus figured together, the orchestra proper being a circle in the center of which stood the *thymele*, or altar of Dionysus. The Romans appropriated the orchestra for the seats of the senators. The later Greek theaters had stages, at first wholly beyond the circle of the orchestra; but under the Roman domination in Greece the stage of nearly all the Greek theaters was moved forward until at last it occupied the position adopted by the Romans themselves. Besides these essential parts there were the λογεῖον, *proscenium*, or *pulpitum*, the stage proper, and the *postscenium*, or structure behind the stage, in which parts the Greek and Roman theaters differed considerably. Almost all surviving Greek theaters were profoundly modified in Roman times, but the original disposition can still be followed in several, as those of Epidaurus and Sicyon. Scenery, in the modern sense of the word, was little employed, but the stage machinery became elaborate with the advance of time. In the early days of the modern theater the buildings were only partially roofed, and the stage but scantily if at all provided with scenery. The interior of the theaters of the present day is usually constructed on a horseshoe or semicircular plan, with several tiers of galleries round the walls. The stage has a slight downward slope from the back, and is furnished with movable scenes, which give an air of reality to the spectacle which was unsought in the ancient theater.

As for their theaters in halfe circle, they came to be by the great magnificence of the Romain princes and people somptuously built with marble & square stone in forme all round, & were called Ampitheaters, wherof as yet appears one amōg the anciēt ruines of Rome.

(Puttenham, *Arte of Eng. Poesie*.)

The world by some, & that not much amisse,
Vnto a Theater comparèd is,
Vpon which stage the goddes spectatours sitt,
And mortals act their partes as best doth fitt.

("Times' Whistle," in *E. E. T. S.*)

As in a theater the eyes of men,
After a well grac'd Actor leaues the Stage,
Are idely bent on him that enters next.

(Shak., *Rich. II* (fol. 1623), V.ii.)

Sceaw-stow. A Theater, a Shew-place, a behold-ing-place.

(Verstegan, *Restitution of Decayed Intelligence* (ed. 1628).)

2. A room, hall, or other place, with a platform at one end, and ranks of seats rising stepwise as the tiers recede from the center, or otherwise so arranged that a body of spectators can have an unobstructed view of the platform. Places of this description are constructed for public lectures, academic exercises, anatomical demonstrations, surgical operations before a class, etc.: as, an operating *theater*.

Stately theatres,
Bench'd crescent-wise. In each we sat, we heard
The grave Professor. (Tennyson, *Princess*.)

3. A place rising by steps or gradations like the seats of a theater.

Shade above shade, a woodie Theatre
Of stateliest view.

(Milton, *P. L.* (1st ed.), iv. 141.)

Helps the ambitious hill the heavens to scale,
Or scoops in circling theatres the vale.

(Pope, *Moral Essays*.)

4. A place of action or exhibition; a field of operations; the locality or scene where a series of events takes place or may be observed; scene; seat: as, the *theater* of war.

Men must know that in this theatre of man's life it is reserved only for God and angels to be lookers on. (Bacon, *Advancement of Learning*.)

This City was for a long time the Theatre of Contention between the Christians and Infidels.

(Maundrell, *Aleppo to Jerusalem*.)

5. The drama; the mass of dramatic literature; also, theatrical representation; the stage: as, a history of the French *theater*.

But now our British theatre can boast
Drolls of all kinds, a vast, unthinking host!

(Addison, Prol. to Steele's *Tender Husband*.)

Theatre, The. The first London theater. It was a wooden building erected by James Burbage, the father of Richard Burbage, in 1576–77, on the site of the priory of Saint John the Baptist, Shoreditch, which had been destroyed during the Reformation.

It was taken down in 1598, and the Globe, Bankside, was built from the materials.

Theatre Royal, The. The Drury Lane Theatre, London.

Thebes (thēbz). [Also: **Diospolis Magna;** Old Testament name, **No;** Latin, **Thebae**.] A city of ancient Egypt, situated on both sides of the Nile, ab. 480 mi. S of the site of modern Cairo. Thebes proper was on the E bank, and the Libyan suburb (Pathyris or Memnonia) on the W bank. The village of Luxor now stands on the site. The remains of antiquity here are of great interest. The Colossi, or statues of Memnon as commonly called, are two huge seated figures, originally monolithic, of Amenhotep III (15th–14th century B.C.), standing, with others now ruined, before the ruined temple of that king. They are ab. 50 ft. high, and are raised on sandstone pedestals measuring ab. 10 ft. They are much weather-beaten and broken by earthquake shocks, but have suffered still more from vandalism. The northernmost figure is the famed vocal statue of Memnon, which is said to have emitted a sound when touched by the rays of the rising sun. The temple of Ramses I and Seti I, or of Amen-Ra, is entered by a dromos, or passage, of sphinxes between two pylons, the second of which is followed by a similar dromos before the fine prostyle colonnade, whose columns are of the early type resembling stalks bound together. The portal opens on a columned hall surrounded by chambers, beyond which lies a large hall with four columns, preceding the now ruined sanctuary. On both sides of the main temple there are other halls and rooms; those on the west may have formed part of the royal palace. The sculptures, which refer to Ramses I, Seti I, and Ramses II, are of high interest. The tomb of Seti I (d. 1292 B.C.), No. 17 of the Tombs of the Kings (commonly called Belzoni's tomb, from its discoverer), is, like its fellows, a rock-cut tomb. At its entrance, which is a mere shaft in the face of the cliff, a long, steep stair descends, followed by a narrow passage, another stair, and another passage, at the end of which there was a deep pit, the continuation of the passage beyond which was walled up, stuccoed, and painted over with scenes continuing those on the side walls. Beyond is a first hall with four pillars, elaborately sculptured and painted; then another hall, and a series of passages by which is reached the great hall, 27 ft. square, with six pillars. A vaulted chamber 19 by 30 ft. continues this hall, and contained the alabaster sarcophagus of the king. Other columned chambers flank this one, and still other passages and chambers extend on a lower level into the mountain, the total length open being 470 ft., and the depth below the entrance 180. The sculptures, historical, mythological, and ceremonial, with particular reference to the rites of royal burial, are exceedingly remarkable. With allowance for endless differences of detail, this may be taken as a type of the Tombs of the Kings. The Tombs of the Queens, Temple of Ramses III, Memnonium, Temple of Luxor, Temple of Karnak, obelisks, and sphinxes are also noteworthy. Thebes is first mentioned in the XIth dynasty. It supplanted Memphis as the great Egyptian center, was at its peak in the XVIIIth, XIXth, and XXth dynasties (Thutmose III, Amenhotep

III, Seti, Ramses II, Ramses III), was afterward supplanted by cities of the Delta, and declined under the Ptolemies.

Thebes. [Modern Greek, **Thevai**; Latin, **Thebae**.] In ancient geography, the chief city of Boeotia, in Greece. It is said to have been founded by Cadmus (hence Cadmea, the citadel), and is famous in connection with Amphion, Sethus, Laius, and Oedipus, and the expeditions of the Seven against Thebes and of the Epigoni. It was early settled by the Boeotians from Thessaly, quarreled with Athens at the end of the 6th century B.C., was allied with the Persians in the Persian War, and was defeated by Athens at Oenophyta in 456. Thebes was the bitter enemy of Athens in the Peloponnesian War, had a severe struggle with Sparta in the battle of Coronea in 394, had to yield to Sparta, 382–379; defeated Sparta at Leuctra in 371, and at Mantinea in 362, and held the hegemony in Greece under the leadership of Epaminondas. The city took part in the Sacred War, was allied with Athens in the defeat at Chaeronea in 338, and was severely treated by Philip II of Macedon; it rebelled in 335, but was retaken by Alexander and destroyed. It was rebuilt by Cassander, but lapsed into insignificance under the Roman Empire. In the Middle Ages it was again an important city, noted for its silk manufactures, and was plundered by the Normans of Sicily and others. It was the reputed birthplace of Tiresias, Amphion, Hercules, and Bacchus.

Thélème (tā.lem′), **Abbey of.** In the *Gargantua* of François Rabelais, an imaginary abbey under the rule of free will, situated in Thelema by the Loire River. The customs in force there were to be in direct opposition to those of any convent in existence. The one rule of its order was "do what you wish."

Themis (thē′mis). An ancient Greek goddess, originally a sort of earth goddess; daughter of Uranus and Gaea (sky and earth). She was the mother by Zeus of the Horae and the Fates and of Prometheus. Early mythology says that she received the oracle of Delphi from Gaea, and the prophetic gift remained one of her attributes, for she warned her son Prometheus of what was in store for him. Later she became a sort of abstract personification of law, custom, and justice.

Thenot (then′ǫt). In Spenser's *Shepherd's Calendar*, a wise old shepherd who tells young Cuddy the fable of the oak and the bramble (the old oak shades the bramble from the sun, wherefor the bramble urges the master of the field to cut it down; but when it is felled, the bramble is exposed to the bitter winds of winter from which the oak had sheltered it). The oak is supposed to represent Thenot, and the bramble is the brash young Cuddy.

Thenot. In John Fletcher's *The Faithful Shepherdess*, a shepherd in love with Corin. His esteem for her is based on his admiration of her faithfulness to her dead lover, and when she pretends to a love for him (Thenot) he is utterly disillusioned.

Theobald (thē′ǫ.bôld, tib′ạld), **Lewis.** b. at Sittingbourne, Kent, England, 1688; d. Sept. 18, 1774. An English playwright, translator, Shakespeare commentator, and historical writer. He published *Shakespeare Restored* (1726), in which, with some justice, he attacked Alexander Pope for his edition (1725) of the plays; he edited Shakespeare (1733),

his edition being one of the best early redactions. He was the original King of Dullness in Pope's *Dunciad*, in revenge for *Shakespeare Restored*.

Theocritus (thē.ok′ri.tus). b. at Syracuse; lived in the 3rd century B.C. A Greek idyllic poet, credited with being the inventor of pastoral poetry. He lived in Syracuse, Cos, and Alexandria. His idyls represent the life of herdsmen, shepherds, and fishermen.

Theodore and Honoria (thē′ǫ.dōr; hǫ.nō′ri.ạ). A poem by Dryden, based on an episode from Boccaccio's *Decameron*.

Theodoric (thē.od′ǫ.rik) or **Theoderic** (thē.od′ėr.ik). [Called **Theodoric the Great**; known in legend as **Dietrich von Bern**.] b. in Pannonia, c454; d. Aug. 30, 526. A king of the Ostrogoths (East Goths); son of the Amaling prince Theodemer. He passed his boyhood as a hostage at Constantinople, with his father invaded Moesia in 473, and succeeded his father (c474). He started on the invasion of Italy late in 488, repeatedly defeated the Gepidae, and defeated Odoacer at the Isonzo (Aug. 28, 489), at Verona (September 30), and on the Adda (Aug. 11, 490). On Feb. 27, 493, a peace was concluded according to which the two kings were to live together in Italy, Odoacer as the military subordinate of Theodoric. But in March Odoacer was slain by Theodoric at a banquet, and the latter became the sole ruler in Italy and the founder of the East-Gothic power there with its capital at Ravenna. He introduced many reforms. He put to death Boethius and Symmachus. In medieval German romance, in which he figured as a legendary hero, he is celebrated as Dietrich von Bern (*q.v.*).

Theophilus (thē.of′i.lus). The persecutor of the Christians in Dekker and Massinger's *The Virgin Martyr*.

Theophilus Bird (bėrd). See **Bird, Theophilus.**

Theophrastus (thē.ǫ.fras′tus). b. at Eresus, Lesbos, c372 B.C.; d. c287 B.C. A Greek philosopher, a disciple of Aristotle, whom he succeeded as head of the Peripatetic school. He wrote on the *History of Plants*, and other botanical works, but is best remembered for his 30 short *Characters*, vivid vignettes of such types as The Flatterer, The Grumbler, and The Boastful Man. His scientific-philosophical work is, however, important in the development of scientific thought.

Theophrastus. Pseudonym of **Creech, William.**

Theophrastus Such (such), **The Impressions of.** A series of essays by George Eliot, published in 1879.

Theramenes (thē.ram′ẹ.nēz). Executed 404 B.C. An Athenian politician and military commander. He was one of the leaders in the establishment (411 B.C.) of the oligarchic rule of the 400, which he later opposed, served at Cyzicus, Arginusae, and elsewhere, and was instrumental in procuring the condemnation of the Athenian generals after Arginusae. He was one of the negotiators (405–404 B.C.) for peace with Sparta, became one of the 30 tyrants, and was forced to drink poison through the influence of Critias.

Theresa or **Teresa** (tẹ.rē′sạ, -zạ; Spanish, tä.rä′sä), Saint. [Spanish, **Teresa de Ávila**.] b. at Ávila, Spain, March 28, 1515; d. at Alba de Tormes, Spain, 1582. A Spanish saint and author. She entered the Car-

fat, fāte, fär, ȧsk, fāre; net, mē, hėr; pin, pīne; not, nōte, mȯve, nôr; up, lūte, pull; ᵺ, then;

melite order in 1534, began the Carmelite reform (Discalced Carmelites) in 1562, and became famous for her mystical experiences. Her works, including *El Camino de la perfección* (Way of Perfection) and *El Castillo interior* (Castle of the Soul), were published in 1587.

Thérèse Defarge (tā.rez' dẹ.färzh'). See **Defarge, Thérèse.**

Thermidor (thẻr'mi.dôr; French, ter.mē.dôr). The name adopted in 1793 by the National Convention of the first French republic for the 11th month of the year. It consisted of 30 days, beginning in the years 1 to 7 on July 19, and in 8 to 13 on July 20.

Thermopylae (thẻr.mop'i.lē). In ancient geography, a narrow pass from Thessaly to Locris, between Mount Oeta and a marsh bordering the Maliacus Sinus (Gulf of Lamia). The configuration of the land has been somewhat changed in modern times. Through it passed the only road from N to S Greece. Here occurred (480 B.C.) one of the most famous conflicts of the Persian Wars. A small army of Greeks under the Spartan Leonidas defended the pass against a vast army under Xerxes. Their position was betrayed, and Leonidas sent away his troops, except for 300 Spartans and 700 Thespians, who remained and were slain. Here, too, in 279 or 278 B.C., the allied Greeks attempted unsuccessfully to prevent the passage of the Gauls under Brennus; and here, in 191 B.C., the Romans under Glabrio defeated Antiochus III of Syria. The place was also noted for its hot salt springs.

Thersites (thẻr.sī'tēz). In Greek legend, the most impudent of the Greeks assembled before Troy. He assailed the name of Agamemnon and was beaten by Odysseus (Ulysses). When he taunted Achilles, Achilles killed him. Shakespeare introduces him in *Troilus and Cressida*. His bawdiness is contrasted with Troilus's romantic nature, and he acts as a Chorus. Possibly he was meant to be Marston, alluding to a current controversy in London.

Thersites or **Thersytes** (thẻr.sī'tēz). An interlude written c1537 for performance at Oxford.

These Lynnekers (lin'ẹ.kẻrz). A novel (1916) by J. D. Beresford, dealing with family life and revolt against its restraints.

These Twain. A novel by Arnold Bennett, published in 1916, the final volume in the second "Five Towns" trilogy, or "Clayhanger" series.

Theseus (thē'sös, thē'sẹ.us). In Greek legend, the chief hero of Attica; son of Aegeus, king of Athens. While Theseus was still an infant, Aegeus hid his sandals and sword under a rock and told the mother that when the boy was strong enough to lift the rock, to send him to him at Athens. When he reached the age of 16, Theseus lifted the rock, and then set out for Athens, where he was recognized and acknowledged by Aegeus. He captured the Marathonian bull, and when the Athenians sent their tribute of youths and maidens to Minos, he went with them and slew the Minotaur with the help of Ariadne, daughter of Minos, who fell in love with him. She gave him a sword, and a clew of thread with which he found his way through the Labyrinth. He sailed away with Ariadne, but abandoned her on the island of Naxos. After this came the incident of the black and white sails,

when Theseus forgot to hoist the white sails on the journey home as a sign to his father that he still lived, and Aegeus drowned himself. Theseus thereupon became king of Athens in his father's place. He accompanied Hercules to fight against the Amazons. He was one of the Argonauts, took part in the Calydonian boar hunt, and performed other marvelous exploits. He was slain by Lycomedes, king of Skyros.

Theseus. In Shakespeare's *Midsummer Night's Dream,* the Duke of Athens, engaged to marry Hippolyta. He also appears in *The Two Noble Kinsmen.*

thesis (thē'sis). [Plural, **theses** (-sēz).] An essay or dissertation upon a specific or definite theme, as an essay presented by a candidate for a diploma or degree, as for that of doctor.

> Then comes the struggle for degrees,
> With all the oldest and ablest critics;
> The public thesis and disputation.
>
> (Longfellow, *Golden Legend*, vi.)

Thespian Maids (thes'pi.ạn), **The.** The Muses.

Thespis (thes'pis). fl. in the middle of the 6th century B.C. An Attic poet, the reputed founder of tragic drama. He is said to have introduced monologues and perhaps dialogues into the dithyrambic choruses, which until then had responded as a unit to the leader.

Thetis (thē'tis). In Greek mythology, the chief of the Nereids, and mother by Peleus of Achilles. She was beloved of the gods but given to Peleus, a mortal, because of the prophecy that her son would outshine his father. It was to the wedding of Thetis and Peleus that Eris sent the apple of discord.

They Never Come Back. American title of **Sado.**

Thibault (tē.bō), **Jacques Anatole.** See **France, Anatole.**

Thierry and Theodoret (ti.er'i; thẹ.od'ọ.ret). A play by John Fletcher and Francis Beaumont, possibly with Philip Massinger as collaborator, published in 1621. The 1621 edition was anonymous, one in 1648 gave Fletcher's name, but a 1649 edition listed Beaumont also. Swinburne conjectured that a third hand was in the play and Massinger has been generally accepted.

Thing Happens, The. See under **Back to Methuselah.**

Things We Are, The. A novel by John Middleton Murry, published in 1922.

Third Estate. [French, **Tiers État** (tyer zā.tà).] In France, that portion of the nation which belonged neither to the nobility, nor the clergy (the two privileged classes), nor the peasantry. It consisted chiefly of the burghers who sent representatives to the States-General. The name was made famous by the struggles of the representatives of this order in the last French States-General for power equal to that of both the other orders, and their final assumption of supreme authority, consummating the French Revolution.

Third Part of King Henry the Sixth, The. See **Henry VI** (*Part Three*).

Thirkell (thẻr'kẹl), **Angela Margaret.** [Maiden name, **Mackail.**] b. Jan. 30, 1890—. An English novelist. Her novels, set in Anthony Trollope's

---

ḍ, d or j; ṣ, s or sh; ṭ, t or ch; ẓ, z or zh; o, F. cloche; ü, F. menu; ċh, Sc. loch; ṅ, F. bonbon.

imaginary Barsetshire and portraying the contemporary English middle class, include *August Folly* (1936), *Coronation Summer* (1937), *Summer Half* (1937), *The Brandons* (1939), *Cheerfulness Breaks In* (1940), *Northbridge Rectory* (1941), *Marling Hall* (1942), *Peace Breaks Out* (1947), *Private Enterprise* (1947), and *Love among the Ruins* (1948).

Thirlwall (thẽrl'wôl), **Connop.** b. at Stepney, London, Feb. 11, 1797; d. at Bath, England, July 27, 1875. An English historian, critic, and prelate. He was bishop of St. David's (1840–74). His chief work is a *History of Greece* (1835–44).

Thirteenth Caesar, The. A volume of verse (1924) by Sacheverell Sitwell.

Thirty Clocks Strike the Hour. Collected short stories by V. Sackville-West, published in 1932.

Thirty-Nine Steps, The. A novel by John Buchan, published in 1915. It is a story of mystery and suspense, of which the central character is the adventurous Richard Hannay. He learns of a German plot to invade England, and when his informant, Scudder, is killed by a secret group called the Black Stone, he realizes his own life is endangered. He flees to Scotland, pursued by the Black Stone and hunted by the police, who suspect him of murdering Scudder. He tries to figure out a way to tell Scotland Yard about his discovery, but knows they will not believe him unless he has some evidence. When Karolides, a Greek diplomat, is killed, Hannay realizes that a small black book which has come into his hands must contain valuable information and evidence. However, the clues it offers are concealed in a cryptic reference to thirty-nine steps and a high tide at 10:17 P.M. Hannay ultimately finds the site of the intended invasion by searching the coast until he finds a cove where the tide is high at 10:17, and where a house has thirty-nine steps leading to the water. The Black Stone agents are found in the house and captured by the police.

Thirty Tyrants. An aristocratic body which usurped the government of Athens (404–403 B.C.). The most notable was Critias. They were expelled by the democratic party under the lead of Thrasybulus.

Thirty Years' War. A religious and political war in central Europe which involved Germany and various other countries. It was caused by the friction between the Protestants and Roman Catholics in the Holy Roman Empire; the immediate occasion was the infringement by the court of Austria of the rights of the Bohemian Protestants, who in May, 1618, rose in revolt under the lead of Count Heinrich von Thurn. In 1619 the Emperor Matthias died, and was succeeded in the Hapsburg dominions and as emperor by Ferdinand II, but Frederick V, the Winter King, elector of the Palatinate, was chosen as a rival king by the Bohemians. In November, 1620, the Catholic League defeated Frederick at the White Mountain; in 1622 Tilly and the Catholic League were victorious at Wimpfen and Höchst; in 1625 Christian IV of Denmark became the leader of the Protestants; in 1626 Tilly defeated Christian IV at Lutter am Barenberge, and Wallenstein, the Imperialist general, defeated Mansfeld at Dessau. In 1629 the Edict of Restitution was issued by Ferdinand II. In 1630 Wallen-

stein was dismissed, and Gustavus Adolphus of Sweden became the Protestant leader. The events of 1631 were the storming of Magdeburg by Tilly and the victory of Gustavus at Breitenfeld; of 1632, the successes of Gustavus, the reëntry of Wallenstein to the Imperialist service, and the victory and death of Gustavus at Lützen (November 16). By now the war's complexion had changed from one of religious struggle to one of outright political effort to destroy the power of the Hapsburgs by winning land in the empire. In 1634 Wallenstein was murdered, and the Imperialists won a victory over the Swedes at Nördlingen. In 1635, the treaty of Prague was signed between Saxony and Ferdinand II, and France, under the lead of Richelieu, entered the war on the Protestant side. The victory of the Swedes at Wittstock in 1636 was followed by the death of Ferdinand II. He was succeeded by Ferdinand III in 1637. The victory of the Swedes near Leipzig in 1642 was succeeded in 1643, 1644, and 1645, by a series of generally French and Swedish victories under Condé, Turenne, and Torstenson. In 1648 the war was terminated by the treaty of Westphalia. In general the Protestants were strong in northern Germany, the Roman Catholics in southern Germany. Spain was the chief ally of the emperor; France, Sweden, and Denmark were the principal allies of the Protestants. The main profits of the war fell to France and Sweden. Germany suffered severely in loss of life, property, and morale, and the Holy Roman Empire became thereafter a minor factor in European politics.

Thisbe (thiz'bē). In classical legend, a maiden of Babylon, loved by Pyramus. The two made love secretly through a hole in the wall between their houses, their parents being opposed. Pyramus killed himself when he saw blood which he mistakenly believed to be Thisbe's. See also **Pyramus and Thisbe.**

Thistle, Order of the. A Scottish order of knighthood, conferred on noblemen of Scotland.

Thistlewood (this'l.wŭd), **Arthur.** b. at Tupholme, near Lincoln, England, 1770; d. on the gallows at Newgate, London, May 1, 1820. An English anarchist. Always an exponent of extreme violence, Thistlewood plotted several revolutions, none of which succeeded. Apparently unbalanced (after, but not necessarily because of, reading Thomas Paine's works), he joined the revolutionary Spencean Society, and organized (1816) a public demonstration at Spa Fields; the proposed revolution failed. Imprisoned but acquitted, he plotted the assassination of Robert Stewart, Viscount Castlereagh, and other ministers (this plot being known as the Cato Street Conspiracy, so called from the loft at which they stored their arms), but was betrayed, probably by George Edwards, a fellow conspirator, tried, and found guilty of high treason. He was hanged and publicly decapitated, but not quartered (although the law then still provided for quartering in cases of high treason).

Thistlewood Conspiracy. See **Cato Street Conspiracy.**

Thom (tom), **William.** b. at Aberdeen, Scotland, c1798; d. at Hawkhill, Dundee, Scotland, Feb. 29, 1848. A Scottish poet. He worked as a weaver (1814 *et seq.*) at Dundee, Newtyle, Aberdeen, Inverurie, and London; like Burns, he was for a short time lionized by society and literary lights at London. Author of *Rhymes and Recollections of a Handloom Weaver* (1844). Some of his best poems are *The Blind Boy's Pranks, The Mitherless Bairn, The Maniac Mother's Dream, The Overgate Orphan, Autumn Winds, Bonnie May, Yon Bower, The Wedded Waters,* and *Jeanie's Grave.*

Thomas (tom′ạs), Saint. [Also, **Didymus.**] One of the 12 apostles; according to tradition, an evangelist in Parthia and India, where he suffered martyrdom. His skepticism when he first heard of the Resurrection of Christ, and his expressed wish to see the actual marks of the Crucifixion on the body of Christ, have given rise to the term "doubting Thomas," used to describe anyone who is needlessly or inordinately skeptical of a proposal or stated fact.

Thomas. In Shakespeare's *Measure for Measure,* the head of an order of friars. He permits the Duke of Vienna to disguise himself as a friar of the order so that he may spy on Angelo.

Thomas. Entries on literary characters having this prename will also be found under the surnames Aimwell, Allworthy, Balderstone, Bertram, Chiffinch, Clifford, Gargrave, Gradgrind, Grey, Grimes, Horner, Lovell, Mowbray, Plornish, Redworth, Rotherham, Sapsea, Vaughan, and Wart.

Thomas, Dylan Marlais. b. at Swansea, South Wales, Oct. 27, 1914; d. at New York, Nov. 9, 1953. A British poet. His education consisted of training at the Swansea Grammar school, after which he did hack journalistic work and documentary script writing. His poetry has its roots primarily in the culture of Wales and, despite his lack of knowledge of the Welsh language, he manages to convey its rhythms and word patterns. Wales also provided him with much of his nature imagery, expressed in a style somewhat involuted but with a tremendous intensity and clarity of image. His books include *Twenty-Five Poems* (1936), *Map of Love* (1939), *The World I Breathe* (1939), *Portrait of the Artist as a Young Dog* (1940), *Deaths and Entrances* (1946), *Collected Poems . . . 1934–1953* (1953), *The Doctor and the Devils* (1953), and *Under Milkwood* (1953).

Thomas, Edward. b. 1878; d. at Arras, France, 1917. An English poet. He started his literary career as a writer for the Manchester *Guardian,* but under the influence of Robert Frost he began to write serious poetry. His themes, like those of Frost, are simple and rustic. *Poems* (1917) was dedicated to Frost; the volume *Last Poems* was published posthumously in 1919. His collected poems, with an introduction by Walter De la Mare, were published in 1922. Aldous Huxley has described the atmosphere of Thomas's poems as "a nameless emotion of quiet happiness shot through with melancholy."

Thomas à Becket (ạ bek′ẹt), Saint. [Also: Saint **Thomas Becket,** Saint **Thomas of London.**] b. at London, c1118; killed in Canterbury Cathedral, Canterbury, England, Dec. 29, 1170. An English ecclesiastic. The son of a well-to-do merchant, he was trained originally to be a notary, and entered

(c1142) the household of Theobald, then archbishop of Canterbury. In this service he distinguished himself, and, following the accession of Henry II, he was appointed (1155) chancellor, after having studied law on the Continent under Theobald's patronage. As chancellor, Thomas was close to Henry II and had much influence with him; he proved himself a brilliant and devoted minister and a courageous knight. Despite his protests, he was appointed by Henry to succeed (1162) Theobald as archbishop of Canterbury. Once he had been invested with his office, he abandoned the courtly ways appropriate to a chancellor for those of a man of the church; and while previously he had loyally taken the part of Henry, he now concentrated on furthering the cause of the church. Since the aims of state and church were often at variance, Thomas à Becket was inevitably involved in many disputes with Henry, finding himself again and again in opposition to the sovereign. Disagreement between them broke out in 1164, over the Constitutions of Clarendon. These were drawn up by Henry to codify the allegiance of the church to the state; Thomas at first refused to accept them at all, but was urged by Pope Alexander III to submit. However, he drew up counter rules, in which he insisted that clerics were to be tried in ecclesiastical councils, even for secular misdemeanors. He also asserted the belief that clergy of any rank should be responsible to higher authorities only within the church, the only overlord of an archbishop being a pope. Henry's persecution of Thomas having now become very active, Thomas removed himself to the Continent, where he won the Pope's annulment of the Constitutions of Clarendon. In Thomas's absence, Henry had his son Henry (d. 1183) crowned king of England by the archbishop of York, an attempt to circumvent a possible excommunication and also an open breach of tradition; at the same time Henry divided his continental holdings between his sons Geoffrey and Richard, the youngest, John (Lackland), receiving no portion. This act led to further dispute between Henry and Thomas after the latter's return to England when it had seemed that a reconciliation had been effected. Thomas's attempt to excommunicate the bishops involved in the crowning roused Henry, who was in Normandy when he heard of it, to further exasperation. The king's rashly expressed desire to be relieved from the power of this "turbulent priest" was overheard and acted upon by four overeager knights. On Dec. 29, 1170, Richard le Breton, Reginald Fitzurse, Hugh de Morville, and William Tracy assaulted Thomas within the cathedral and murdered him. Upon his death, Thomas was almost immediately idealized as a martyr, and Henry was forced to make many of the concessions toward the freedom of the church which the archbishop had tried to achieve. Thomas was canonized in 1172, and two years later the king did public penance at his tomb. He remained a popular saint all through the Middle Ages; the Trinity Chapel of Canterbury, to which his bones had been transferred in 1220, was the goal of many pilgrimages (including the fictional one of Geoffrey Chaucer's *Canterbury Tales*). T. S. Eliot's verse play *Murder in the Cathedral* (1935) was written about his martyrdom.

ḏ, d or j; ṣ, s or sh; ṭ, t or ch; ẓ, z or zh; o, F. cloche; ü, F. menu; ċh, Sc. loch; ň, F. bonbon.

Thomas a Kempis (ą kem′pis). [Also: **Thomas Hammerken** (or **Hamerken** or **Hemerken**); also, **Thomas Hämmerlein**.] b. at Kempen, Germany, c1380; d. near Zwolle, Netherlands, July 25, 1471. A German mystic and ascetic writer, generally regarded as the author of *De imitatione Christi* (*Imitation of Christ*, 1486). He entered the Augustinian convent Agnetenberg, near Zwolle, in 1407, and became subprior in 1423 and again in 1447.

Thomas Aquinas (ą.kwī′nąs), Saint. See **Aquinas, Saint Thomas.**

Thomas Beverly (bev′ẽr.li). See under **Mayor of York.**

Thomasin Yeobright (tom′ą.sin yō′brīt). See **Yeobright, Thomasin.**

Thomas, Lord Cromwell (krom′wel, -wel; krum′-). [Also, **The Life and Death of Thomas, Lord Cromwell**.] A play published in 1602 and included in the second issue of the third Shakespeare folio (1664), but now considered not to be Shakespeare's.

Thomas Muskerry (mus.ker′i, mus′ker.i). A play (1910) by Padraic Colum.

Thomas of Britain. fl. c1185. An Anglo-Norman poet. He wrote his *Roman de Tristan* for Queen Eleanor, wife of Henry II of England. He is thought also to have been the Thomas who wrote a version of the King Horn legend.

Thomas of Clarence (klar′ęns). See **Clarence, Thomas of.**

Thomas Percy, Earl of Worcester (pẽr′si; wus′tẽr). See **Worcester, Thomas Percy, Earl of.**

Thomas the Rhymer. [Also: **Thomas of Erceldoune** (ẽr′sęl.dön), **Thomas of Earlston** (ẽrlz′tọn), **Thomas Rymer, Thomas Rimor, Thomas Learmont** (lär′mọnt); called **"True Thomas."**] fl. c1220–97. A Scottish poet, noted in folklore and legend as a prophet and a guide to the mysterious halls beneath the Eildon Hills. According to the popular story, the queen of the elves came to him as he sat under the Eildon tree, and carried him to elfland, where they lived in happiness for seven years, at the end of which time she brought him back to the Eildon tree and told him of many things that were to happen in the wars between England and Scotland. He was called "True Thomas" from the truth of these prophecies. He finally disappeared in a forest, following a hart and hind, and was seen no more. *The Romance and Prophecies of Thomas of Erceldoune*, edited by Murray for the Early English Text Society (1875), was ascribed to him, but was actually written more than 100 years after his death. Sir Walter Scott also attributed to him the poem *Sir Tristrem*, a 13th-century romance, which he edited from the Auchinleck manuscript in 1804, and the Middle English romance *Sir Launfal* has also been called his, but is now generally credited to Thomas Chestre. There are five versions of the Scottish popular ballad *Thomas Rymer*, which tell the story of Thomas and the queen of elfland, collected by Child in his *English and Scottish Popular Ballads*. This same story is told also of Ogier the Dane and Morgan le Fay.

Thomists (tō′mists). The followers of Thomas Aquinas. He held two sources of knowledge, faith and reason; the doctrines of unconditional pre-

destination and efficacious grace; and a physical as well as a moral efficacy; and denied the doctrine of the immaculate conception. His theology, embodied in his great work *Summa theologiae*, was based on a philosophical system rather than on either the Bible or the traditional teaching of the church. It was an attempt to reconcile Aristotelian philosophy with the Christian faith. It is of very high authority in the Roman Catholic Church, and its influence is great even outside of that church.

Thompson (tomp′sọn, tom′-), **Francis.** b. at Preston, Lancashire, England, Dec. 18, 1859; d. in a London hospital, Nov. 13, 1907. An English poet and essayist. He was educated at Ushaw College, near Durham, and studied (1876–82) at Owens College, Manchester. Between 1882 and 1888 he made several unsuccessful attempts as book agent, shoemaker, soldier, errand boy, and match seller, to earn a living, finally going to London, where, driven by the misery of extreme poverty, he became an opium addict. He was reduced to starvation, and attempted (1888) suicide, but he also composed his first poems, some of which were published by Wilfred Meynell in his magazine, *Merry England*. Thompson spent the rest of his life in the home of Wilfred and Alice Meynell, receiving care from them or in hospitals and monasteries to which they sent him. Author of *Poems* (1893), containing his famous "The Hound of Heaven," *Sister Songs* (1895), and *New Poems* (1897); and of the prose works *Health and Holiness* (1905), *Life of Saint Ignatius Loyola* (1909), *Essay on Shelley* (1909), and *Life of John Baptist de la Galle* (1911). Among his best-known poems are *Daisy, To a Snowflake, Arab Love-Song, All's Vast, The Poppy, The Sun, A Fallen Yew, Any Saint,* and *In No Strange Land.*

Thompson, Sylvia. b. Sept. 4, 1902—. An English novelist and lecturer. Author of *The Rough Crossing* (1918), *A Lady in Green Gloves* (1924), *The Hounds of Spring* (1925), *The Battle of the Horizons* (1928), *Chariot Wheels* (1929), *Winter Comedy* (1931; American title, *Portrait by Caroline*), *Summer's Night* (1932), *Helena* (1933; American title, *Unfinished Symphony*), *Breakfast in Bed* (1934), *Golden Arrow* (1935), *A Silver Rattle* (1935), *Third Act in Venice* (1936), *Recapture the Moon* (1937), *The Adventure of Christopher Columin* (1939), and *The Gulls Fly Inland* (1941).

Thomson (tom′sọn), **James.** b. at Ednam, Roxburghshire, Scotland, Sept. 11, 1700; d. near Richmond, England, Aug. 27, 1748. A British poet. He was educated at Edinburgh, and studied for the church, was private tutor for a short time, and held several sinecure offices. He wrote *The Seasons* (*Winter*, 1726; *Summer*, 1727; *Spring*, 1728; *Autumn*, 1730), generally held to be the first considerable treatment of nature in the manner of the later Romantic School as opposed to the personifying methods of the classical group. He also wrote *The Castle of Indolence* (1748), in Spenserian stanzas and acclaimed by critics not only as Thomson's best work, but as the best use of the stanza since Spenser, and *Ode to the Memory of Sir Isaac Newton* (1727), *Liberty* (1734–36), and the plays *Sophonisba* (1730; containing the famous line which killed the piece after the critics had burlesqued it sufficiently, "O Sophonisba, Sophonisba O," parodied by everyone as "O Jemmy Thomson, Jemmy Thomson O") and *Agamemnon* (1738), the masque *Alfred*, in conjunction with David Mallet (1740), which contains the song "Rule Britannia," claimed by Mallet but usually ascribed to Thomson, and *Tancred and Sigismunda* (1745). Thomson's popularity has waned, but it is said that at one time every home had at least three books: the Bible, *Pilgrim's Progress*, and *The Seasons*.

Thomson, James. [Pseudonym: **B. V.**, i.e., **Bysshe Vanolis** (from Shelley's middle name and an anagram of Novalis); called the **"Poet of Despair."**] b. at Port Glasgow, Scotland, Nov. 23, 1834; d. at London, June 3, 1882. A Scottish poet. He was an army schoolteacher in Ireland when he fell in love, but the death of his sweetheart in 1853 drove him into a deep pessimism, unrelieved by recourse to narcotics and drink. He became a lawyer's clerk in 1862, later came to America as a mining agent, was a war correspondent in Spain, and during the last years of his life worked as a journalist. He is best known as the author of *The City of Dreadful Night* (1874, 1880), one of the most impressive poems in English in its sustained note of melancholy. He also wrote *Vane's Story, A Voice from the Nile* (1884), and *Shelley, a Poem* (1885).

Thomson, William. See **Kelvin,** 1st Baron.

Thopas (tō′pạs), **Sir.** See **Rime of Sir Thopas, The.**

Thor (thôr, tôr). [German, **Donar;** Icelandic, **Thorr.**] In Old Norse mythology, the god of thunder. He was the son of Odin, the supreme god. He was the champion of the gods, the friend of mankind, and the enemy of the giants. He always carried a heavy hammer, called the Crusher, which returned to his hand of itself; and he possessed a girdle which had the virtue of renewing his strength. Thursday is named for him (Thor's day).

Thornbury (thôrn′bėr.i), **George Walter.** b. at London, 1828; d. there, June 11, 1876. An English writer. Among his works are *Lays and Legends* (1851), *The Buccaneers, or Monarchs of the Main* (1855), *Shakespeare's England* (1856), *Art and Nature at Home and Abroad* (1856), *Songs of the Cavaliers and Roundheads* (1857), *Every Man His Own Trumpeter* (1858), *Life in Spain* (1860), *British Artists from Hogarth to Turner* (1861), and *Life of J. M. W. Turner* (1861).

Thorndike (thôrn′dĭk), **Dame Sybil.** b. at Gainsborough, England, 1882—. An English actress. She appeared in Shakespearian plays in the U. S. (1903–07) and at the Old Vic, London (1914–18), and afterward added roles from other dramatists to her repertoire.

Thorndyke (thôrn′dĭk), **Dr. John.** In the stories of Richard Austin Freeman, a criminal lawyer and amateur detective.

Thornhill (thôrn′hil), **Sir William.** A character in Oliver Goldsmith's *Vicar of Wakefield*. He assumes the name of Mr. Burchell, and is the good genius of the story.

Thorpe (thôrp), **Dr.** Lossie's father, in William De Morgan's novel *Joseph Vance* (1906).

Thorpe, Isabella. In Jane Austen's novel *Northanger Abbey*, the eldest daughter of Mrs. Thorpe. She is a great beauty, and her two sisters (both somewhat plain) manage to attract admirers simply by aping her dress and manner.

Thorpe, John. In Jane Austen's novel *Northanger Abbey*, the eldest son of Mrs. Thorpe. He is a stout, not very attractive young man, who perversely fears that unless he wears the garb of a groom he will be "too handsome."

Thorpe, Lossie. The heroine of William De Morgan's novel *Joseph Vance* (1906).

Thorpe, Mrs. In Jane Austen's novel *Northanger Abbey*, a girlhood friend and schoolmate of Mrs. Allen. She is an amiable woman, but perhaps too indulgent as a mother.

Those Barren Leaves. A novel (1925) by Aldous Huxley: satire on a literary house-party.

Thoth (thoth, tōt). [Also: **Tat, Tehuti, Thot.**] In Egyptian mythology, originally a moon god, later the god and inventor of speech and hieroglyphics or letters, of the reckoning of time and measurements, and the god of wisdom. He was the scribe of the gods, and kept the records of the dead in a book, which he read at the time of judgment. The cynocephalous ape and the ibis were sacred to him. He is represented as a human figure, usually with the head of an ibis, and frequently with the moon disk and crescent. In Hellenistic times the Greeks identified him with their Hermes.

Thoughts in a Garden. A poem by Andrew Marvell (1621–78).

Thousand and One Days, The. A series of Persian tales, modeled on the *A Thousand and One Nights*.

Thousand and One Nights, A. See **Arabian Nights' Entertainments, The.**

Thrale (thrāl), **Mrs.** [Name commonly used in referring to **Hester Lynch Piozzi;** maiden name, **Salusbury.**] b. at Bodville, Caernarvonshire, Wales, Jan. 16, 1741; d. at Clifton, England, May 2, 1821. An English writer, a friend of Samuel Johnson. She was well educated in Latin and Greek and the modern languages. In 1763 she married Henry Thrale, a brewer of Southwark. In 1764 she met Dr. Johnson, beginning an intimacy which lasted for 20 years, Johnson living with the Thrales and traveling with them. Her husband died on April 4, 1781, and on July 25, 1784, she married Gabriel Piozzi, an Italian musician. Johnson became angry with her on hearing of the marriage and they were still estranged when he died later in the same year. Her anecdotes of and correspondence with Dr. Johnson are second in interest only to Boswell's *Life.*

Thraso (thrā′sō). A soldier in Terence's *Eunuchus* whose boasting has given us the term "thrasonical" for any braggart, particularly one who pretends to military prowess but is, in actual conduct, very unmartial, or even cowardly. This stock character, varying from a three-dimensional version such as Falstaff to a "humour" character in Jonson's comedy *Petronel Flash*, was a favorite of Elizabethan comedy.

Threadneedle Street (thred′nē″dl). A prominent commercial street in the City of London which leads out from the Bank of England.

Three Bears. An English nursery tale written by Robert Southey (but attributed by him to his

Uncle William). It was frequently retold and modified in the 19th century (sometimes with a little girl named Silverhair for heroine) but is also familiar under the title *Goldilocks and the Three Bears*. The story is that a little girl disobeys her mother and walks into the forest. She comes to a little house which she enters. There she sits in the three kinds of chairs (too hard, too soft, and just right), tastes the three bowls of porridge (too hot, too cold, and just right) and devours the third, tries the three beds, and falls asleep in the smallest one, which belongs to the baby bear. The three bears come home and discover all that she has done. When they find her in the little bed, she wakes up and runs home terrified. One of the features of the story is that it is read to children in three tones of voice, representing the father bear, the mother bear, and the baby bear.

Three Brontës (bron'tĕz), **The.** A biographical study by May Sinclair, published in 1912.

Three Brothers, The. A novel by Edwin Muir, published in 1931.

Three Calenders (kal'ẹn.dẽrz), **the.** See **Calenders, the Three.**

Three Clerks, The. A novel by Anthony Trollope, published in 1858.

Three Graces, the. See **Graces, the Three.**

Three Hours after Marriage. A play by Alexander Pope, John Arbuthnot, and John Gay, produced in 1717. It was Colley Cibber's ridicule of this play in his part of Bayes in *The Rehearsal* which was the occasion of the quarrel between him and Pope.

Three Kings of Cologne (kọ.lōn'). See **Cologne, Three Kings of.**

Three Lovers, The. A psychological novel by Frank Swinnerton, published in 1922.

Three Men in a Boat. A humorous account of a holiday excursion (1889) by Jerome K. Jerome.

Three Musketeers, The. [French, **Les Trois Mousquetaires.**] A novel by Alexandre Dumas *père*, published in 1844. The scene is laid in France in the time of Richelieu. The three musketeers are Athos, Porthos, and Aramis, but D'Artagnan, an adventurous young Gascon, is the principal character. The four appear also in the sequels *Twenty Years After* (*Vingt ans après*) and *Ten Years After, or the Vicomte de Bragelonne* (*Dix Ans Plus Tard, ou le Vicomte de Bragelonne*).

Three Plays for Puritans. A volume (1901) of plays by George Bernard Shaw. It includes *The Devil's Disciple, Captain Brassbound's Conversion,* and *Caesar and Cleopatra.*

Three Pretty Men. A novel (1916) by Gilbert Cannan; published in America under the title *Three Sons and a Mother.*

Three Score and Ten. A novel by Alec Waugh, published in 1929.

Three Sisters, The. A novel (1914) by May Sinclair: a study of feminine psychology.

Three Sons and a Mother. See **Three Pretty Men.**

"Three Tailors of Tooley Street" (tö'li). A phrase designating an act of startling effrontery, especially of audacious effrontery. It originated with a petition submitted to Parliament in 1827, during the ministry of George Canning, urging certain reforms desired by three men who had held a meeting in Tooley Street, Southwark, London. The petition began with the words: "We, the people of England. . . ."

Three Wives. A novel by Beatrice Kean Seymour, published in 1927.

threnody (thren'ọ.di). A song of lamentation; a dirge; especially, a poem composed for the occasion of the funeral of some personage.

Through the Looking Glass. A novel by Charles Lutwidge Dodgson (writing under the pseudonym Lewis Carroll), published in 1872. A sequel to *Alice's Adventures in Wonderland* (1865), it continues the dream encounters of Alice. In this book she is transported into the world behind the mirror, where she meets with a set of animated chessmen, talks with Humpty Dumpty and Tweedle-Dum and Tweedle-Dee, and finds a checkerboard landscape which keeps moving, so that only by running can one stay in the same place. Dodgson's famous nonsense poem, *Jabberwocky*, occurs in this book. Critics have pointed out that the encounters of the story are plotted as a chess problem.

Thrums (thrumz). The scene of many of Sir James Barrie's stories, especially *A Window in Thrums* and *The Little Minister:* it represents Kirriemuir, Barrie's birthplace, near Dundee, Scotland.

Thrush and the Nightingale, The. A Middle English poem, considered by scholars to have been composed in the south of England during the last quarter of the 13th century. It follows the debate form particularly popular in French and Latin poetry, although using more dramatic devices than did most of its models. Some critics have tried to relate it to *The Owl and the Nightingale,* but the only connection is the form (although the present poem does not have a narrative opening) and the device of the two feathered antagonists.

Thrym (thrim). In Old Norse mythology, the giant who stole Mjöllnir, the hammer of Thor.

Thucydides (thụ.sid'i.dēz). b. probably 471 B.C.; d. c401 B.C. A Greek historian. He was a native of Athens, belonged to a family which claimed blood relationship with Miltiades and Cimon, is said to have been a pupil of Antiphon of Rhamnus and of Anaxagoras, and possessed an ample fortune, part of which was invested in gold mines in Thrace, opposite Thasos. In 424 he commanded an expedition sent to the assistance of Amphipolis against Brasidas, but failed to prevent the capture of the city, and in consequence went into exile (whether enforced or voluntary is unknown), from which he returned 20 years later, in 403. He was commonly supposed by the ancients to have died a violent death soon after, probably at Athens. He began a *History of the Peloponnesian War,* which he did not live to finish, the narrative ending in 411, seven years before the end of the war. The Greek text was first printed by Aldus at Venice in 1502.

thula (thö'lạ). A metrical list of names, characteristic of Icelandic and other Germanic literature, and in Old English (specifically, in the 7th-century poem *Widsith*) constituting the earliest known poetic form in the language. These lists served as a mnemonic or allusive device and were often arranged in alliterative patterns. There are three thulas in *Widsith*, one of kings, one of tribes, and one of heroes.

Thule (thū'lē). The name given by Pytheas of Marseilles to a region or island north of Great Britain, the position of which has been for more than two thousand years the subject of investigation and a matter of controversy. Of the voyage of Pytheas, who was probably nearly contemporaneous with Alexander the Great, nothing is known with certainty, since none of his writings have been preserved. It is, on the whole, most probable that he followed the east coast of Great Britain (of whose size he got a very much exaggerated idea), and that he obtained information in regard to the groups of islands lying still further north—namely, the Orkneys and Shetland—which he embraced under the general name of *Thule*. From what he is believed to have said in regard to the length of the day in Thule at the summer solstice, it is evident that, as he is known to have been a skilled astronomer, he thought that this land was situated on or near the arctic circle. The Romans frequently added to Thule the designation of *Ultima* (the Furthest Thule), and, from classic times down to the present day, *Thule*, besides remaining a subject for voluminous controversy among geographical critics, has been in constant use by poets and others as designating some unknown, far-distant, northern, or purely mythical region, or even some goal, not necessarily geographical, sought to be attained. This use of *Thule* and *Ultima Thule* runs through the literature of all the cultivated languages of Europe.

> Where the Northern Ocean, in vast whirls,
> Boils round the naked melancholy isles
> Of furthest Thule.   (Thomson, *Autumn.*)

> This ultimate dim Thule.   (Poe, *Dream-Land.*)

Thump (thump), **Peter.** In Shakespeare's *2 Henry VI*, an apprentice to Horner. He accuses his master of treasonous speech and in a fight with sandbags kills him. The King believes the outcome to be an indication of God's power and justice (II.iii).

Thunderbolt, The. A comedy (1910) by Arthur Wing Pinero.

Thunderer, the. An epithet of Zeus (Jove).

Thunderer, the. A name given to the London *Times.*

Thurio (thū'ri.ō). In Shakespeare's *Two Gentlemen of Verona*, a rival to Valentine for Silvia. He is foolish and cowardly. Proteus pretends to be wooing Silvia for him after Valentine has been banished, and in the final act Thurio claims Silvia, but gives her up as soon as Valentine challenges him.

Thurston (thėrs'ṭon), **E. Temple.** [Full name, **Ernest Charles Temple Thurston.**] b. Sept. 23, 1879; d. March 19, 1933. An English novelist, dramatist, and poet; husband of Katherine Cecil Thurston. Author of *The Apple of Eden* (1905), *Traffic—the Story of a Faithful Woman* (1906), *The Evolution of Katherine* (1907), *Sally Bishop* (1908), *City of Beautiful Nonsense* (1909), *The Greatest Wish in the World* (1910), *The Garden of Resurrection—the Love Story of an Ugly Man* (1911), *The Open Window* (1913), *Richard Furlong* (1913), *The Antagonists* (1914), *Achievement* (1914), *The Pas-*

sionate Crime (1915), *The Five-Barred Gate* (1916), *Enchantment* (1917), *World of Wonderful Reality* (1920), *The Green Bough* (1921), *The Miracle* (1922), *May Eve* (1924), and *A Hank of Hair* (1932), novels; *The Realist* (1906), *Thirteen* (1912), and *The Rossetti* (1926), collected short stories; *Red and White Earth* (1902), *The Greatest Wish* (1913), *Always Tell Your Wife* (1913), *Driven* (1914), *The Cost* (1914), *The Wandering Jew* (1920), *A Roof and Four Walls* (1923), *Judas Iscariot* (1923), *The Blue Peter* (1924), and *Charmeuse* (1930), plays; and *Poems* (1895), *Summer 1917* (1917), and *Poems 1918–1923* (1923).

Thurston, Katherine Cecil. [Maiden name, **Madden.**] b. at Cork, Ireland; d. there, Sept. 5, 1911. A British novelist; wife (married 1901) of E. Temple Thurston, from whom she was divorced in 1910. She published *The Circle* (1903), *John Chilcote, M.P.* (1904; American title, *The Masquerader*; dramatized 1905 by E. Temple Thurston), *The Gambler* (1906), *The Fly on the Wheel* (1908), and *Max* (1910).

Thwackum (thwak'um). In Fielding's *Tom Jones*, one of a pair of tutors (the other being named Square) in whom Fielding satirizes the theological pedantry of education. Square holds by the natural virtue of man; Thwackum deduces everything from original sin.

Thyestes (thī.es'tēz). In Greek legend, son of Pelops, brother of Atreus, and father of Aegisthus by his own sister. Thyestes seduced the wife of Atreus and attempted his life. In revenge Atreus slew the sons of Thyestes and served them up to their father to eat. Aegisthus, however, survived this slaughter.

Thyreus (thī'rē.us). In Shakespeare's *Antony and Cleopatra*, a follower whom Octavius sends to Cleopatra to persuade her to desert Antony.

Thyrsis (thėr'sis). A herdsman in the *Idylls* of Theocritus; a shepherd in the *Eclogues* of Vergil; in later literature, a rustic or shepherd.

Thyrsis. An elegiac poem (1861) by Matthew Arnold, in commemoration of the death of his close friend Arthur Hugh Clough. It ranks as one of the greatest elegies in English.

Tibbs (tibz), **Beau.** In *The Citizen of the World*, a series of essays by Oliver Goldsmith, a pathetic boaster who talks of his familiarity with the nobility and pretends to be a man of fashion, in spite of the fact that he is poor and unknown.

Tibullus (ti.bul'us), **Albius.** b. c54 B.C.; d. 18 B.C. A Roman elegiac poet. He was patronized by Messala, whom he accompanied in a campaign to Aquitania. He wrote the first two of the books extant under his name.

Tichborne Claimant (tich'bôrn, -bọrn). See **Orton, Arthur.**

Tickell (tik'el), **Thomas.** b. at Bridekirk, Cumberland, England, 1686; d. at Bath, England, April 23, 1740. An English poet. In 1708 he graduated from Queen's College, Oxford. He was a friend of Addison, and through him in 1717 was appointed undersecretary of state. His poem on *The Prospect of Peace* appeared in 1713, and a poem, *Kensington Gardens*, in 1722. He contributed to the *Spectator* and *Guardian*, and wrote the elegy on Addison prefixed to his edition of Addison's works in 1721. He translated the first book of the *Iliad*, which Pope suspected was done by Addison, and wrote the ballad *Colin and Lucy*.

Ticket-of-Leave Man, The. A play by Tom Taylor, produced in 1863. It is from the French play *Léonard*, by Édouard Brisbarre and Eugène Nus. It is perhaps most interesting to modern readers for its inclusion of the detective Hawkshaw.

Tickletoby (tik'l.tō.bi), **Miss.** One of the many pseudonyms of **Thackeray, William Makepeace.**

Tiger Lily. An Indian princess who protects Peter and his young friends, in Sir James M. Barrie's play *Peter Pan*.

Tigg (tig), **Montague.** In Dickens's novel *Martin Chuzzlewit*, an audacious rascal who nearly succeeds in besting the greedy, scheming Jonas Chuzzlewit at his own blackmailing game, but is murdered by Jonas. He has, unlike Jonas, a certain rakish charm, and carries out his various ventures with the utmost aplomb (at one point, he reverses his name and as Tigg Montague sets himself up as the head of the Anglo-Bengalee Assurance Company, an enterprise utterly without assets and existing solely for the financial benefit of Tigg).

Tigranes (tī.grā'nēz). In Beaumont and Fletcher's play *A King and No King*, the king of Armenia, who is captured by Arbaces.

Tilburina (til.bū.rī'na). The daughter of the governor of Tilbury Fort, a character in the tragedy rehearsed in Richard Brinsley Sheridan's *The Critic*: a type in which the sorrows of the tragic heroine are burlesqued.

Till Eulenspiegel (til oi'len.shpē.gel). See **Eulenspiegel, Till.**

Tillietudlem (til.i.tud'lem). In Sir Walter Scott's novel *Old Mortality*, the baronial castle of Lady Margaret Bellenden.

Tillotson (til'ot.son), **John.** b. at Sowerby, Yorkshire, England, in October, 1630; d. Nov. 22, 1694. An English prelate and theological writer. He was dean of Canterbury and of Saint Paul's, and became archbishop of Canterbury in 1691.

Tilly Slowboy (til'i slō'boi). See **Slowboy, Tilly.**

Tilney (til'ni). The name of the family living at Northanger Abbey in Jane Austen's novel of that name. It consists of General Tilney (the father), Captain Tilney and Henry (his sons), and Eleanor (his daughter). Henry is the hero of the story.

Timandra (ti.man'dra). In Shakespeare's *Timon of Athens*, a mistress of Alcibiades.

Tim Cratchit (tim krach'it). See **Cratchit, Tim.**

Time. In Shakespeare's *Winter's Tale*, Time acts as Chorus, bridging the gap (16 years) between Acts III and IV.

Time Importuned. A volume of poetry by Sylvia Townsend Warner, published in 1928.

Time Machine, The. A novelette (1895) by H. G. Wells. With *The War of the Worlds* (1898) it holds an assured place as one of the classics of English "science fiction." It opens with the Time Traveller explaining to the narrator his theory of Time as the Fourth Dimension, and shortly thereafter showing

him a model of a machine by which he proposes to travel in time. A few days later he reports to the narrator on his first voyage: he has ventured forward to the year 802701 A.D., and finds the valley of the Thames turned into a tremendous and beautifully kept garden, apparently inhabited only by the exquisite Eloi, a delicately formed, timid people who seem to have no interest in him (except for the little Weena, whom he saves from drowning). But very soon, through the disappearance at their hands of his Time Machine, he learns of the existence of the Morlocks, the other race into which humankind has differentiated. The Morlocks, presumably descended from a servant class, provide the Eloi with food and clothing, but prey upon them also for their meat. The Time Traveller enters their subterranean establishment and manages, after several adventures (during one of which Weena is killed), to get possession again of the Time Machine, and leaps forward again in time, reaching on this occasion a point so far in the future that the earth has ceased its motion, and the sun has dimmed to a dull red sphere. The Time Traveller returns with word of all this, but is not believed by his friends, and departs again to secure evidence of his travels. From this second voyage, however, he never returns. Specialists in this type of fiction have pointed out on numerous occasions how cleverly Wells manages in this story to avoid the pitfalls to which, by its very nature, the theme of time travel is subjected: (1) the Time Traveller voyages into the future, but never the past, and Wells thus evades the need to explain how his hero can participate in an earlier moment of a historical sequence which includes him as a portion of a later moment without introducing elements which will alter the course of history (in its simplest form, this problem becomes obvious if one asks the question "What if, through accident, the Time Traveller should set in motion a series of actions that resulted finally in the death of one of his own ancestors?"); and (2) by not having the Time Traveller return from his second voyage, on which he proposed to get evidence of his time travel, Wells avoids the problem of explaining what would be the effect on contemporary society of artifacts from a very much more advanced culture (for example, how could one logically explain the existence in a given year, as a result of time travel, of something which wasn't supposed to be invented until many centuries in the future? How, in other words, can something be both known in the present and invented in the future?).

Times, The. A leading British newspaper, published in London, founded in 1785 under the title *The London Daily Universal Register*. The present name was adopted in 1788.

Times Literary Supplement, The. A weekly periodical of reviews and comment on various literary matters. It was established in 1902.

Time to Dance, A. A volume of verse (1935) by Cecil Day Lewis, expressing "the conflict between the past and the future of the individual."

Time Traveller. See under **Time Machine, The.**

Timias (tim'i.as). In Spenser's *Faerie Queene*, the squire of Prince Arthur, supposed to represent Sir Walter Raleigh.

---

fat, fāte, fär, ȧsk, fāre; net, mē, hėr; pin, pīne; not, nōte, mȯve, nôr; up, lūte, pu̇ll; ᵺн, then;

Tim Linkinwater (tim ling′kin.wô.tẻr, -wot.ẻr). See **Linkinwater, Tim.**

Timmins (tim′inz), **Fitzroy.** In Thackeray's tale *A Little Dinner at Timmins,* the young barrister who is persuaded by his socially ambitious wife to agree to a "little dinner" which is far beyond what he can afford.

Timmins, Rosa. In Thackeray's tale *A Little Dinner at Timmins,* the pretty wife of Fitzroy Timmins. She fancies herself as a poet, and has a burning desire to be recognized socially (preferring "Tymmyns" as a spelling of her name on the grounds that it suggests a relationship with an old and distinguished family).

Timoleon (ti.mō′lẹ.ọn, tī-). b. at Corinth; d. 337 or 336 B.C. A Greek general and statesman. He was sent from Corinth to aid Syracuse against Dionysius the Younger and Hicetas in 344, delivered Syracuse from Dionysius the Younger in 343, reorganized the city and the Greek power in Sicily, and defeated the Carthaginians at the Crimisus River.

Timoleon. A Greek general who assists the Sicilians in their war against Carthage in Philip Massinger's *The Bondman.*

Timon (tī′mọn). In Shakespeare's *Timon of Athens,* the noble Athenian who is the hero of the play. Although he is at first a trusting and warm-hearted person, the ingratitude of his friends (when he loses his fortune) causes a violent reaction in him and he becomes a bitter misanthrope, only occasionally revealing glimpses of his former goodness, as in his touching words to Flavius. The historical Timon lived in the last part of the 5th century B.C.

Timon of Athens (ath′ẹnz). [Full title, **The Life of Timon of Athens.**] A tragedy by Shakespeare, probably all by his hand, although some scholars have doubted it. It was written between 1605 and 1608, was printed in the folio of 1623, and was adapted by Shadwell. There is no record of performance before 1678 and this was Shadwell's adaptation (not until 1851 was there a performance of Shakespeare's play). The sources for the play were Plutarch's *Lives,* Lucian's *Timon, the Misanthrope,* Painter's *Palace of Pleasure,* and probably also an anonymous earlier play entitled *Timon* (c1585).

The Story. Timon is a kindly and good Athenian, but perhaps a trifle too lavish as a host. When he suddenly discovers that he is deeply in debt, he asks his friends, whom he has so frequently entertained, for help. They, however, are only "feast-won" and refuse him. As a final gesture, Timon invites them all to a banquet at which he serves only warm water, and this he throws in their faces. Bitterly denouncing all mankind, Timon then retreats to a cave, where he lives on roots grubbed from the earth nearby. One day in his digging he discovers buried treasure, and when he learns that the great captain Alcibiades is preparing to attack Athens, he shares his gold with him. Apemantus, the professional misanthrope, visits him, as well as a number of thieves, artists, and others, all anxious now to flatter him, and thus perhaps to secure some of his gold. Flavius, his faithful steward, is the only one to whom Timon speaks kindly, but he too

is finally sent away and, as Alcibiades enters Athens, news comes that Timon has died alone by the sea.

Timotheus (ti.mō′thẹ.us, -moth′ẹ.us; tī-). d. c354 B.C. An Athenian naval commander; son of Conon. He conquered Corfu in 375 B.C., and took Samos from the Persians in 365.

Timothy Crabshaw (tim′ọ.thi krab′shô). See **Crabshaw, Timothy.**

Timothy Sharp (shärp). See **Sharp, Timothy.**

Tina Sarti (tē′nä sär′tē). See **Sarti, Caterina.**

Tindal (tin′dạl), **Matthew.** b. at Beer-Ferrers, Devonshire, England, c1656; d. at Oxford, England, Aug. 16, 1733. An English deist. He studied at Lincoln College, Oxford. In 1685 he joined the Roman Catholic Church, but returned in 1688 to the Church of England. He published *An Essay of Obedience to the Supreme Powers* (1694), and *The Rights of the Christian Church asserted against the Romish and all other priests who claim an independent power over it* (1706–09). His defense of the theory of state control of the church led to the proscription of the work, Dec. 12, 1707. He continued to defend his deistic position, and in 1730 published *Christianity as Old as the Creation, or the Gospel a Republication of the Religion of Nature,* a work recognized as the "Bible" of deism. The work was translated into German by J. Lorenz Schmidt in 1741, and had great influence on German theology. Tindal called himself a "Christian deist."

Tindal or **Tindale** (tin′dạl), **William.** See **Tyndale, William.**

Tinker Bell (ting′kẻr bel). A very small fairy in Sir James M. Barrie's play *Peter Pan.* Peter's loyal friend, she risks her own life in order to save him from the cruel Captain Hook. She is not seen or heard on the stage, except as a faint light and a tinkling sound.

Tinker's Wedding, The. A comedy (1909) by John Millington Synge, satirizing the Irish clergy. It was never staged in Ireland (despite Synge's insistence that his countrymen should have enough humor to be able to laugh at themselves). It tells the story of the effort of Michael Byrne and Sarah Casey, living together but unmarried, to legalize their association. As payment to the local priest, Michael agrees to give 10 shillings and a gallon can, but his tippling mother makes off with the can, leaving three whiskey bottles in its place. The priest is so enraged upon finding the bottles that he refuses to perform the marriage, whereupon Michael and Sarah toss him into a ditch.

Tintagel Head (tin.taj′ẹl). A promontory in SW England, in Cornwall, ab. 5 mi. NW of Camelford. The ruins of the famous castle which is one of the legendary birthplaces of King Arthur may still be seen here. Elevation, ab. 300 ft.

Tintern Abbey (tin′tẻrn). A ruined medieval abbey in Monmouthshire, England, situated on the river Wye ab. 17 mi. NW of Bristol. The ivy-clad church, dating from the middle of the 13th century, is one of the most picturesque of English ruins, and was celebrated in verse by William Wordsworth. The vaulting is gone, but otherwise it is well preserved. It retains most of its window tracery, and has a fine west portal of two cusped arches, and a single very large window, a typical English feature, in each of the main and transept façades. The monastic buildings survive in part.

Tinto (tin′tō), **Dick.** A light-hearted artist who is supposed to relate Sir Walter Scott's novel *The Bride of Lammermoor* to Peter Mattieson.

Tintoretto (tin.tọ.ret′ō; Italian, tēn.tō.rät′tō). [Also: **Tintoret** (tin′tọ.ret); original name, **Jacopo Robusti,** called Tintoretto from the trade of his father, a dyer.] b. at Venice, Sept. 16, 1518; d. there, May 31, 1594. A Venetian painter. He entered the atelier of Titian, with whom it does not appear that he stayed very long. From Titian he went to Andrea Schiavone. In 1546 he received his first important order, for the decoration of the choir of Santa Maria dell'Orto. The compositions were over 50 ft. high. They brought him a considerable reputation and a commission to paint the *Miracle of Saint Mark*, now in the Accademia delle Arti at Venice. In 1560 Tintoretto began decorations for the Scuola di San Rocco and the doge's palace. The famous *Crucifixion* of the Scuola di San Rocco dates from this time. In 1576 he painted the ceiling of the great hall. In 1560 also he seems to have taken the place of Titian as court painter at Venice. The great conflagrations of 1574 and 1577 threw much of the work of restoration into the hands of Tintoretto. The work accomplished by him on these commissions includes the great *Paradise* (1589–90).

"Tiny Tim" (tim). See **Cratchit, Tim.**

Tipkin (tip′kin), **Biddy.** A romantic character in Richard Steele's *The Tender Husband.*

Tippoo Sahib (ti′pö sä′hib). [Also, **Tipu Saib.**] b. 1749; killed at the storming of Seringapatam, May 4, 1799. Sultan of Mysore (1782–99). He was distinguished in the Mahratta war (1775–79), and defeated Braithwaite on the Colerun in 1782. After he succeeded his father in 1782, he gained several successes in the war with the British, and concluded peace in 1784. He attacked Travancore (1789–90), and provoked the second Mysore war, was defeated by Charles Cornwallis at Arikera in 1791, and concluded peace and ceded about half of his dominions to the British in 1792. He intrigued against the British who renewed the war in 1799. He was killed defending his capital.

Tipuca (tip′ụ.kạ). Pseudonym of **Wilson, T. P. Cameron.**

Tiresias (tī.rē′si.ạs). In Greek legend, a blind Theban seer. He was said to have been blinded by Athena, whom he saw bathing. The goddess relented, but was unable to restore his sight, and so gave him instead the vision of the seer and understanding of bird and animal languages. Another legend states that he was blinded for revealing the secrets of the gods. At the suggestion of Circe, Odysseus descended into Hades to ask him how to return to Ithaca.

Tirocinium (tī.rọ.sin′i.um). A poem (1785) by William Cowper, attacking the public schools (which were, and are, in England the great private schools, most notably Eton, Harrow, Rugby, and Winchester).

Tisiphone (ti.sif′ọ.nē). In Greek mythology, one of the Erinyes, or Furies.

'Tis Pity She's a Whore. A tragedy by John Ford, written c1628 and printed in 1633. It deals (somewhat like Fletcher's *A King and No King*) with an incestuous relationship between a brother and sister, but Ford, unlike Fletcher, does not mitigate the expectation of disaster by a last-minute revelation that there is actually no blood kinship between the lovers. Giovanni and Annabella both recognize the perilous nature of their passion, but the promptings of a friar, who is their confessor, are of no avail against what Giovanni considers to be fate: "'Tis my destiny That you must either love or I must die."

Titan (tī′tạn). A classical name for the sun personified.

Titania (ti.tā′ni.ạ). In Shakespeare's *Midsummer Night's Dream*, the Queen of the Fairies. Shakespeare is said to have been the first to give this name to the queen of the fairies, although Ovid used it as an epithet of Diana.

Titanic (tī.tan′ik). A transatlantic steamship of the White Star Line, which, on her maiden voyage, collided with an iceberg S of Newfoundland at 11:40 P.M. on April 14, 1912, and sank about 2:20 the next morning. The ship was the largest built up to that time, and had been considered almost unsinkable. According to the official English report, issued after investigation of the disaster, she had on board 2,224 persons, of whom 711 were rescued from lifeboats (20 in number, of which three were lost) and rafts by the Cunard Line steamship *Carpathia* in answer to a radio call.

Titans (tī′tạnz). In Greek mythology, the old pre-Olympic gods; children of Uranus and Gaea (heaven and earth). There were six male Titans (Oceanus, Coeus, Crius, Hyperion, Japetus, and Cronus), and six female (Theia, Rhea, Themis, Mnemosyne, Phoebe, and Tethys). They were imprisoned by their father Uranus from their birth, but, after mutilating and dethroning him, were delivered by Cronus. Zeus, son of Cronus, compelled him to disgorge his elder brothers and sisters, whom he had swallowed at their birth. A terrible war between the Titans and the Olympian gods then ensued; and the Titans (except Oceanus) were thrust into Tartarus, under guard of the hundred-armed giants.

Titans and Gods. A volume of verse (1922) by F. V. Branford.

Tithonus (ti.thō′nus). In Greek mythology, a prince of Troy; son of Laomedon and brother of Priam. He was beloved by Eos, who besought the gods to give him immortality. This they did, but Eos had forgotten to include eternal youth in the request, and in his extreme old age Tithonus withered away and was finally metamorphosed into a grasshopper.

Titian (tish′ạn). [Italian name, **Tiziano Vecelli** or **Vecellio**; surnamed **Da Cadore** and **Il Divino** (meaning "The Divine").] b. at Pieve di Cadore, Friuli, Italy, c1477; d. at Venice, Aug. 27, 1576. A Venetian painter. He first studied painting at his native place, and at nine or ten years of age went to Venice and was put to study with Giovanni Bellini. He does not seem to have been influenced by any of the foreign schools. In the period 1507–08 he worked as collaborator with Giorgione in the decoration of the exterior of the Fondaco de' Tedeschi at Venice; these frescoes have been destroyed. In 1511 Titian was at work at the school of Padua with Campagnola, who was his assistant. He returned to Venice in 1512, and in 1513 sought to obtain an order for a battlepiece for the council hall, and applied for the first vacancy as broker at the Fondaco, a privilege already accorded to Bellini and Carpaccio. About this time he declined an invitation to work at Rome for the Pope. On the death of Bellini he became his successor as broker at the Fondaco and as portrait painter to the doges. In 1516 he went to Ferrara at the invitation of Alphonso d'Este, and painted several pictures, some of which are now in various public and private collections. From this time he was occupied with commissions from various royal and private clients until 1523, when he returned to Venice to paint the portrait of the new doge, Andrea Gritti, and the fresco over the landing of the doge's palace, *Saint Christopher Carrying the Christ Child*, which still remains. About this time he married, and in 1530 was left a widower with three children. In 1532 Titian was called to Bologna by Charles V, who had come to meet the Pope. He became painter to the emperor, and enjoyed his friendship. This relation led him in 1546 to Rome, where he met Michelangelo and became acquainted with the works of Raphael and the Greeks. He was at this time 69 years old. In 1547 he was summoned to Augsburg by the emperor, and there he painted many portraits. His court life was brilliant and profitable. In 1549 he was again at Venice, and in 1550 returned to Augsburg. His life from this time forward is a succession of honors and triumphs. He succeeded to the favor of Philip on the death of Charles V. He died of the plague at the age of 99. Among his chief paintings, besides many representations of the Magdalen, Venus, Danaë, the Madonna, and the Holy Family, are *Sacred and Profane Love* (Rome), *Bacchus and Ariadne* (London), *Ecce Homo* (Vienna), *Entombment of Christ* (Louvre), *Tribute Money* (Dresden); *Martyrdom of Saint Lawrence, Saint Peter Martyr, Last Supper, Christ Crowned with Thorns* (Louvre); *Bella di Tiziano* (Titian's Mistress; Palazzo Pitti, Florence), *Venus of the Tribune* (Uffizi, Florence), *L'Homme au Gant* (Louvre), *Knight of Malta* (Madrid), and *Titian and his Mistress* (Louvre).

Titinius (ti.tin′i.us, tī-). In Shakespeare's *Julius Caesar*, a friend of Brutus and Cassius. He meets Brutus's forces at Philippi, but Cassius thinks he is taken prisoner by the enemy and kills himself. Titinius stabs himself on finding Cassius's body.

title. A prefixed designating word, phrase, or combination of phrases; an initial written or printed designation; the distinguishing name attached to a written production of any kind: as, the *title* of a book, a chapter or section of a book, etc.; the *title* of a poem. The title of a book in the fullest sense includes all the matter in the title page preceding the author's name or whatever stands in place of it. It may be either a single word or a short phrase, or be divided into a leading and a subordinate title connected by *or;* or it may be extended by way of description to the larger part of a closely printed page, according to a practice formerly very common. The title by which a book is quoted, however, is nearly always the shortest form that will serve to designate it distinctively. For bibliographical purposes, especially in the cases of old, rare, and curious books, the entire title page, word for word and point for point, is regarded as the title, and when copied the actual typography is often indicated, as by a vertical bar after each word which ends a line, etc.

"They live by selling titles, not books, and if that carry off one impression, they have their ends." (Dryden, *Life of Lucian.*)

Titmarsh (tit′märsh), **Michael Angelo.** The name under which William Makepeace Thackeray wrote, in *Fraser's Magazine*, his *Paris Sketch Book* and others.

Titmarsh, Samuel. The narrator and hero of Thackeray's *Great Hoggarty Diamond.* He is an honest but somewhat naïve young man employed as a clerk in a commercial house known as the Independent West Diddlesex. He receives the "Great Hoggarty Diamond" as a gift from his aunt, and is forthwith thrust into a level of society and a way of life more fashionable and more expensive than he has hitherto known. At the end of the story, after the manager of the Independent West Diddlesex embezzles the assets of the firm, Samuel is held to be liable, and is enabled to start a new and happier life only after, and as a result of, pawning the diamond.

Titmouse (tit′mous), **Tittlebat.** One of the principal characters in Samuel Warren's novel *Ten Thousand a Year:* a vulgar shopman in Oxford Street, London.

Tito Melema (tē′tō me.lä′mạ). See **Melema, Tito.**

Tittlebat Titmouse (tit′l.bat tit′mous). See **Titmouse, Tittlebat.**

Titurel (tit′ụ.rel). A hero of the legend of the Holy Grail in Wagner's opera *Parzival.* He was the great-grandfather of Parzival. It is also the title of an unfinished poem by Wolfram von Eschenbach, of which the 6,000-verse continuation by the poet Albrecht (c1270) is known as *Der jüngere Titurel.*

Titus (tī′tus). In Shakespeare's *Timon of Athens*, a servant of one of Timon's creditors.

Titus Andronicus (an.dron′i.kus). [Full title, **The Tragedy of Titus Andronicus.**] A tragedy, produced probably in 1593 or 1594, variously attributed to Christopher Marlowe, Thomas Kyd, and William Shakespeare. However, it was published with Shakespeare's plays in the first folio (1623) and on that ground is generally accepted as one of Shakespeare's plays, though Edward Ravenscroft, who published a revision in 1687, reported that he had heard that Shakespeare merely touched up the play "by a private Author." If it was new in 1594, it was crude for such a date, but possibly Ravenscroft was right (one other reference makes it earlier, 1584–89). Its sources were Seneca's *Thyestes* and *Troades*, and Ovid's *Metamorphoses;* the murderous Moor (Aaron) and his white wife (in Shakespeare's play, Tamora) was a common theme of the day.

The Story. Titus, a victorious Roman general, brings home as his captives Tamora, Queen of the Goths, and her three sons, the eldest of whom

ḍ, d or j; g, s or sh; ṭ, t or ch; ẓ, z or zh; *o*, F. cloche; ü, F. menu; čh, Sc. loch; ṅ, F. bonbon.

(Alarbus) is sacrificed by Titus's sons. Saturninus, the new emperor, and Bassianus, his brother, both claim the hand of Titus's daughter, Lavinia, but Saturninus renounces Lavinia and marries Tamora, who, with her lover, Aaron the Moor, is determined to be revenged on Titus for the death of her son. Her two remaining sons, Demetrius and Chiron, meet Bassianus and Lavinia in the woods. They kill Bassianus, throw his body into a pit, ravish Lavinia, and cut off her hands and tongue. Titus's sons Quintus and Martius fall into the pit and are accused of murdering Bassianus. Aaron informs Titus that they will be pardoned if Titus cuts off one of his hands and sends it as ransom. Aaron, however, returns the hand along with the heads of the two sons. Titus, driven mad, takes revenge by killing Demetrius and Chiron, and serving them baked in a pie to Tamora. He kills Lavinia, Mutius (his youngest son, who is trying to protect his sister), then Tamora, and is himself killed by Saturninus, whom Lucius, the last remaining son, then kills. Aaron, meanwhile, has been captured and is condemned by Lucius, now the new emperor, to be set breast-deep in earth until he starves to death.

Titus Andronicus. The hero of Shakespeare's *Titus Andronicus* (q.v.).

Titus and Vespasian (ves.pā′zhạn). A Middle English religious romance, written in the late 14th century. The stories of Christ, Judas, and Pilate are combined with the tale of Vespasian being miraculously cured of leprosy by means of Saint Veronica's veil.

Titus Lartius (lär′shi.us, -shus). In Shakespeare's *Coriolanus*, a Roman general who opposes the Volscians.

Titus Livius (liv′i.us). Latin name of **Livy**.

Tityus (tit′i.us). In Greek mythology, the giant son of Zeus or of Gaea, and father of Europa. He assaulted Leto at the instigation of Hera and was killed by Apollo, her son. In Hades his punishment was to be extended on the ground (the story is that he covered nine acres) while vultures gnawed his liver.

Tiu or **Tiw** (tē′ö). See **Tyr**.

To Althea, from Prison (al′thẹ.ạ). A poem by Richard Lovelace expressing the idea that true liberty cannot be chained or fettered, because it consists in the freedom of love and the free soul. Its last stanza contains the well-known lines:

> Stone walls do not a prison make,
> Nor iron bars a cage. . . .

Tobit (tō′bit), **Book of.** One of the apocryphal books of the Old Testament, so called from the name of one of its leading characters. The original text of the story was in Hebrew, but the extant Hebrew text is taken from a Chaldee text preserved in the Bodleian Library. It is believed to have been written no earlier than the time of Hadrian (76–138 A.D.). The story is that Tobit was a pious Jew in captivity at Nineveh, who took it upon himself to bury the Hebrew dead at night in defiance of civil bans. In time he became blind, miserable, and impoverished, and sent his son Tobias to a distant city to collect a loan. Tobias set out on the journey with his little dog and in company with a young

man whom he hired as guide. This, unbeknownst to Tobias, was the archangel Raphael, who because of the piety of Tobit had come to help them. After several adventures, they arrived at the city and went to the house of the brother of Tobit, Tobias's uncle. Here Tobias fell in love with his cousin Sara and prepared to marry her. Sara, however, had attracted the demon Asmodeus, and Asmodeus had killed all her seven previous bridegrooms on their wedding night. Nevertheless, with the help of his traveling companion, Tobias became the lucky eighth, the demon was exorcised, and the marriage was consummated, after which Asmodeus was powerless against them. They collected the loan for his father, and the four (Tobias, Sara, the fellow traveler, and the little dog) returned to Nineveh, and magically restored sight to Tobit. Tobit and Tobias then offered the helpful companion half of the money collected, whereupon Raphael revealed himself, praised Tobit for his piety in burying the dead, and vanished.

Toby (tō′bi). Punch's dog, in the English Punch and Judy puppet shows. He wears bells to frighten off Satan.

Toby, Uncle. [Also called **Captain Shandy**.] The uncle of Tristram Shandy, in Laurence Sterne's novel of that name; one of its chief characters. He is a retired captain, famous for his military pedantries, sentimentality, modesty, and gallantry. The Widow Wadman tries to captivate him.

Toby Belch (belch), **Sir.** See **Belch, Sir Toby**.

Toby, M. P. Pseudonym of **Lucy**, Sir **Henry**.

Toby Tallyho (tal.i.hō′), **Sir.** See **Tallyho, Sir Toby**.

Toby Veck (vek). See **Veck, Toby**.

To Celia (sēl′yạ). [Full title, **Song, to Celia**.] A famous poem by Ben Jonson, opening with the lines: "Drink to me only with thine eyes,/ And I will pledge with mine." It is based on four letters from Philostratus, a Greek writer (c170–245 A.D.). In letter 24 he says: "Drink to me with thine eyes only. Or if thou wilt, putting the cup to thy lips, fill it with kisses, and so bestow it upon me." And again in letter 25, he says: "I, as soon as I behold thee, thirst, and taking hold of the cup, do not, indeed, apply that to my lips for drink, but thee."

Tocqueville (tok′vil; French, tok.vēl′), **Alexis Charles Henri Clérel de.** b. at Paris, July 29, 1805; d. at Cannes, France, April 16, 1859. A French statesman and writer. His studies, begun at Metz, were completed by a course in law at Paris. He took his final degree in 1826, and then spent a year or more traveling in Italy and Sicily. On his return to France he occupied a post in the law court at Versailles. But jurisprudence was not altogether suited to his tastes, and on April 2, 1831, he left France for the U. S., whither he was sent by his government for the purpose of studying the penitentiary system. He did not limit himself, however, to this special field, but extended his observations also to the social and political institutions and customs of the new country. The following year he published in France, together with his friend and traveling companion, Gustave de Beaumont, the result of their official investigations, under the title *Du système pénitentiaire aux États-Unis et de son application en France*. This important work at-

---

fat, fāte, fär, ȧsk, fāre; net, mē, hėr; pin, pīne; not, nōte, mōve, nôr; up, lūte, pùll; ᴛʜ, then;

tracted much attention, and was crowned by the French Academy. From the notes that he had taken in a private capacity while on his visit to the U. S., he wrote his masterpiece, *De la démocratie en Amérique* (2 vols., 1835–40), which remains today a classic interpretation by a foreign observer of the American republican system and a democratic society. Its success secured his admission to the French Academy (Dec. 23, 1841). After several years of public life (1839–51), he retired in order to devote his entire time to travel and writing. Besides the works already mentioned, he wrote a number of pamphlets on various subjects, also *Histoire philosophique du règne de Louis XV* (1846), and the first volume of the work left unfinished at his death, *L'Ancien régime et la révolution* (1856). A paper entitled *État social et politique de la France* was translated into English by John Stuart Mill and published in the April, 1834, number of the *Westminster Review*. De Tocqueville's complete works were edited (1860–65) by his friend de Beaumont.

To Daffodils. A poem by Robert Herrick in the first stanza of which he beseeches the daffodils to stay awhile longer. He concludes the poem by comparing the shortness of human life to the short blooming of the daffodil:

> We have short time to stay as you;
> We have as short a spring;
> As quick a growth to meet decay,
> As you or anything.

Todgers (toj'ėrz), **Mrs.** In Dickens's novel *Martin Chuzzlewit*, the owner and manager of a commercial boarding-house, who has a "soft heart" for Mr. Pecksniff. Mercy and Charity Pecksniff are taken to stay at her establishment by their father, and when Mercy's marriage to Jonas Chuzzlewit reaches the point of hopeless impasse Mrs. Todgers proves to be Mercy's only true friend in London.

To His Coy Mistress. A poem (1681) by Andrew Marvell which relies heavily on various metaphysical conceits ("vegetable love," "time's winged chariot," and the "grave") to convey the first theme of "let us love now" and the second more serious theme of the onrush of time and its effects on both life and love. The lines "The grave's a fine and private place,/ But none I think do there embrace" are often quoted as an example of metaphysical wit.

Tolbooth (tōl'bȯth), **Edinburgh.** In Sir Walter Scott's novel *The Heart of Midlothian*, the building in Edinburgh containing the prison, and the site of the Porteous Riots. A "tolbooth" was originally a simple stall or other structure at which taxes were paid; with the growth of Edinburgh and certain other cities it came to mean the principal building of the city government, often including the prison. Byron refers to the Edinburgh Tolbooth in *English Bards and Scotch Reviewers* in his satirical recounting of the "duel" between the critic Francis Jeffrey and the poet Thomas Moore (it was discovered, when the police interrupted the affair, that neither pistol contained a bullet):

> The Tolbooth felt defrauded of his charms
> If Jeffrey died, except within her arms.

Told by an Idiot. A novel (1923) by Rose Macaulay.

To Let. A novel by John Galsworthy, published in 1921. It was later included in *The Forsyte Saga* (1922).

Tolstoy (tol.stoi', tol'stoi), Count **Leo** (or **Lev**) **Nikolayevich.** [Also, **Tolstoi.**] b. in the government of Tula, Russia, Aug. 28, 1828; d. at Astapova, Nov. 20, 1910. Russian novelist, social reformer, and religious mystic. He was educated at the University of Kazan, and served in the army in the Caucasus and in the Crimean war, being appointed commander of a battery in 1855. He took part in the battle of the Chernaya, defended against the storming of Sevastopol, and after the battle was sent as a special courier to St. Petersburg. He retired at the end of the campaign. After the liberation of the serfs he lived on his estates, working with and relieving the peasants, and also devoting himself to study. After 1876 he experienced a religious transformation, rejecting Orthodox doctrine for that of Christian love, which involved the principle of not resisting evil but of taking it in and transforming it. Many converts were attracted to the new sect by Tolstoy's own writings on his conversion and experiences. The stories regarding his life have almost assumed the proportions of myth. His chief novels are *War and Peace* (1865–68: a picture of Russian society 1805–15) and *Anna Karenina* (1875–78). Among his other works are *Sevastopol* (1853–55), *The Cossacks* (composed while in the army, published 1863), *Ivan Ilyich* (1886), *Two Pilgrims*, *Childhood* (1852), *Boyhood* (1854), and *Youth* (1856), *My Religion* (1885), *My Confession* (1884), *A Commentary on the Gospel* (1881), *Life*, *The Kreutzer Sonata* (1890), *War* (1892), *What Is Art?* (1897–98), *Resurrection* (1900), and *The End of the Age* (1906).

To Lucasta on Going to the Wars (lö.kas'tạ). A poem by Richard Lovelace in which the poet implores his lady to forgive him for leaving her to go to war because "I could not love thee, Dear, so much,/ Loved I not Honour more."

Tom (tom). Entries on literary characters having this prename will be found under the surnames Allworth, Bowling, Brown, Codlin, Folio, Gradgrind, Hickathrift, Jones, Pinch, Piper, Pipes, Snout, Tulliver, and Tusher.

Tom a Lincoln (ạ ling'kọn). An anonymous 16th-century prose romance, based upon earlier materials of which, for the most part, no record has survived. It tells the story of an illegitimate son of King Arthur, who is reared as the son of a poor shepherd. When Arthur is informed of his identity (Tom meanwhile having become a powerful outlaw) he makes him the commander of a great army (but does not actually acknowledge Tom as his son until he is on his deathbed).

Tom-All-Alones (tom'ôl'ạ.lōnz). In Dickens's novel *Bleak House*, the incredible slum in which Jo the crossing sweeper lived.

Tom and Jerry, or Life in London (jer'i; lun'dọn). A novel by Pierce Egan, published serially in 1821–22, which contains the adventures of Jerry Hawthorn, Corinthian Tom, and Bob Logic. It was illustrated by George Cruikshank, and was very popular.

ḍ, d **or** j; ṣ, s or sh; ṱ, t or ch; ẓ, z or zh; o, F. cloche; ü, F. menu; ċh, Sc. loch; ṅ, F. bonbon.

Tomb of Burns (bẽrnz), **The.** A poem by Sir William Watson, published in 1903.

Tom Brown at Oxford (tom broun; oks'fǫrd). A story by Thomas Hughes, published in 1861. It is a continuation of *Tom Brown's School Days.*

Tom Brown's School Days. A story by Thomas Hughes, published in 1856. It describes life at Rugby School under the headmastership of Thomas Arnold (father of Matthew Arnold).

Tom Gate. A gate of Christ Church College, Oxford, completed (1682) by Christopher Wren.

Tom Jones (jōnz). [Full title, **The History of Tom Jones, a Foundling.**] A novel by Henry Fielding, published in 1749. It is probably the first novel conceived and developed in accordance with a definite artistic plan and is generally considered one of the masterpieces of English literature. Each of the 18 books in this novel opens with a diverting and extremely well written essay which explains the author's purpose. The plot is very complex. Squire Allworthy lives with his sister Bridget, a spinster, and returns home one night from a long visit to find an infant lying on his bed. He names the foundling Tom Jones, taking the last name from that of a young servant in his home, Jenny Jones, who is suspected of being the baby's mother. A married schoolmaster, Mr. Partridge, is accused of being the father, and he is dismissed and leaves town, as does Jenny. Soon after this Bridget marries Captain Blifil, a fortune-hunter; they have a son, and shortly afterwards the captain dies. The two boys are brought up together, taught by Thwackum and Square; Tom's many misdemeanors are always found out and reported by them and Master Blifil, who has taken a strong dislike to Tom. Tom's only friend is Mr. Western, a neighbor, who has a lovely daughter, Sophia. Tom is injured in saving her life one day, and while he recuperates at her home, the two young people fall in love. Unfortunately, Tom falls out of Squire Allworthy's favor as a result of one of his lapses, a love affair with Molly Seagrim, a gamekeeper's daughter. Young Blifil also takes every opportunity to misrepresent Tom's actions. The squire sends Tom away, and Blifil thinks that he can now marry Sophia himself. Tom has many adventures on the road after he leaves home, including a love affair with Jenny Jones, now the wife of Captain Waters. When someone tells him that Jenny is thought to be his mother, Tom is horror-stricken. Meanwhile, Sophia is aghast at the idea of marrying Blifil, and when her father and aunt try to force her to do so, she flees to London with Mrs. Honour, her maid. She takes refuge in the home of a friend, Lady Bellaston. Sophia and Tom are here able to meet once more, and Tom convinces her that he loves her deeply. Her father has by this time traced her and comes to take her home. Tom receives word that Squire Allworthy is coming with Blifil to London, where Sophia will be forced to marry Blifil, and in his fear and consternation goes to the home of a friend, Mrs. Fitzpatrick, but encounters her jealous husband at the door. The two men fight a duel, and Fitzpatrick is wounded, apparently gravely. Tom is taken to prison on a charge of murder and is visited by Mrs. Waters (Jenny Jones) and Partridge, the schoolmaster, whom he

has met on his travels. Jenny then reveals to Squire Allworthy and Blifil, as well as to Mr. Western, that she is not Tom's mother, but that he is the son of Bridget, now dead, and a student whom Squire Allworthy had befriended. As Fitzpatrick recovers from his wound, Tom is released and permitted to marry Sophia, Blifil's treachery through the years comes to light, and Tom is made the true heir of the squire.

Tomkis or **Tomkys** (tom'kis), **Thomas.** b. c1597; d. c1614. A scholar of Trinity College, author of the play *Albumazar* (acted in 1614, printed in 1615) and *Lingua, or the Combat of the Tongue and the Five Senses for Superiority* (acted c1602, printed in 1607). (The latter has also been attributed to Antony Brewer.) He is always spoken of as Tomkis, though his father's name was Tomkins.

Tomlinson (tom'lin.sǫn), **H. M.** [Full name, **Henry Major Tomlinson.**] b. at London, 1873—. An English novelist and journalist, known for his sea stories. He was a war correspondent (1914–17) in Belgium and France, and literary editor (1917–23) of the *Nation* and the *Athenaeum*. Author of *The Sea and the Jungle* (1912), *Old Junk* (1918), *London River* (1921), *Waiting for Daylight* (1922), *Tidemarks* (1924), *Under the Red Ensign* (1926), *Gallions Reach* (1927), *Between the Lines* (1928), *All Our Yesterdays* (1930), *The Snows of Helicon* (1933), *Mars His Idiot* (1935), *All Hands* (1937), *The Day Before* (1940), *The Wind Is Rising* (1941), *The Turn of the Tide* (1945), and *Morning Light* (1946).

Tomlinson, Mary. See **Scatcherd, Mary.**

Tommy (tom'i). [In full, **Tommy Atkins** (at'kinz).] A popular name for an English soldier, comparable to the American "doughboy" or "GI." It derives from the use in the early 19th century of the name "Thomas Atkins" on various specimen forms prepared by the military authorities to show how such forms should be filled in. The full name "Tommy Atkins" is also used for the rank and file collectively.

Tommy and Grizel (gri.zel'). A novel by Sir James M. Barrie, published in 1900.

Tommy Atkins (at'kinz). See **Tommy.**

Tommy Mirabel (mir'ạ.bel). See **Mirabel, Tommy.**

Tommy Sandys (sandz). See **Sandys, Tommy.**

Tommy Traddles (trad'lz). See **Traddles, Tommy.**

Tom o'Bedlam (tom ọ.bed'lạm). Formerly, in England, a popular name for a lunatic. "Bedlam" was the colloquial name for the hospital of Saint Mary of Bethlehem, at London, an insane asylum which for a period was so overcrowded that many inmates, uncured but considered harmless, were dismissed and turned beggars. In Shakespeare's *King Lear*, Edgar pretends to be one of these mendicants, calling himself "Poor Tom."

Tom Quad (kwod). The quadrangle of Christ Church College, Oxford.

Tom's. A former London coffee house frequented in the 18th century by many famous personages.

Tom Thumb (tom thum). An old English nursery tale, about a diminutive boy (no larger than a man's thumb) in the days of King Arthur. His very small size leads to various extraordinary adventures, such as being accidentally swallowed by a cow, being mistaken for a mouse, and the like.

Tom Thumb. "A little hero with a great soul" as Fielding describes him in *Tom Thumb the Great.*

Tom Thumb the Great. [Full title, **The Tragedy of Tragedies; or, The Life and Death of Tom Thumb the Great.**] A satirical burlesque (1730) by Henry Fielding. Henry Carey's *Chrononhotonthologos* was imitated from it in part. The original title was *Tom Thumb: A Tragedy,* but it was produced with the title given above and after the third edition that title was used. Fielding in ascribing the work to "H. Scriblerus Secondus" harks back to the satire of Arbuthnot, Pope, and Gay, *The Memoirs of Martinus Scriblerus.* The object of Fielding's satire was the foolish diction of contemporary and Restoration plays, particularly heroic tragedy. He parodies other plays by citing, in footnotes, passages from them by which, he alleges, the absurd lines of Tom Thumb have been inspired. The ridicule extends to the characters as well as the verse. King Arthur is "a passionate sort of King, husband to Queen Dollallolla, of whom he stands a little in fear; father to Huncamunca, whom he is very fond of, and in love with Glumdalca." Tom Thumb, whose diminutiveness burlesques the grandiose heroic hero, has "a great Soul somewhat violent in his Temper, which is a little abated by his love for Huncamunca." Critics as well as playwrights come in for a share of the satire.

Tom Tiddler's Ground (tid′lėrz). A novel by Edward Shanks, published in 1934.

Tono-Bungay (tō′no.bung′gā). A novel (1909) by H. G. Wells.

Tonson (ton′sọn), **Jacob.** b. c1656; d. 1736. An English bookseller. He published some of Thomas Otway's and Nahum Tate's plays, was John Dryden's publisher in 1679 and later, issuing the noted *Miscellany* (1684–1708), and published Nicholas Rowe's edition of Shakespeare in 1709. He purchased and published Milton's *Paradise Lost,* was founder and secretary (c1700 *et seq.*) of the Kit-Cat Club, and managed a bookshop in the Strand where the *Spectator* was planned by Joseph Addison and Richard Steele.

Tonstall (tun′stạl), **Cuthbert. See Tunstall, Cuthbert.**

Tony Lumpkin (tō′ni lump′kin). **See Lumpkin, Tony.**

Tony Weller (wel′ėr). **See under Weller, Sam.**

Toodle (tö′dl), **Mr.** In Dickens's *Dombey and Son,* a stoker, husband of Polly Toodle, Paul Dombey's nurse, and sire of Robin Toodle. He is known as "The Biler."

Toodle, Polly. [Called (by the Dombeys) "**Richards.**"] In Dickens's novel *Dombey and Son,* the woman hired to care for little Paul Dombey, and discharged for taking him with her when she visits her family (whence the child is exposed to "society which [is] not to be thought of without a shudder"). She is the mother of Rob the Grinder.

Toodle, Robin. See Rob the Grinder.

Tooke (tůk), **Horne.** [Full name: **John Horne Tooke;** original name, **John Horne.**] b. at Westminster, London, June 25, 1736; d. at Wimbledon,

England, March 18, 1812. An English politician and philologist. He was educated at Eton and Cambridge, and was vicar at New Brentford until 1773. He began (c1765) his political career as a Liberal, engaged in controversies with John Wilkes (whom he originally supported) and Junius, and was the chief founder of the "Society for Supporting the Bill of Rights" in 1769. He opposed the American war, and was imprisoned for libel (1777–78) for attempting to raise money for the relatives of the Americans "murdered at Lexington and Concord." He assumed the name of Tooke in 1782, adopting the surname of a friend and benefactor. In 1794 he was tried for high treason as a suspected sympathizer with the French revolutionaries and acquitted. He was a member of Parliament (1801–02), but was excluded later as a clergyman, a bill specially being passed to bar him. His chief work is the philological treatise *Epea Pteroenta, or The Diversions of Purley* (2 parts, 1786, 1805). He also wrote various political pamphlets, including *Petition of an Englishman* (1765), *Two Pair of Portraits* (1788), and others.

Toole (töl), **John Lawrence.** b. at London, March 12, 1832; d. at Brighton, England, July 30, 1906. An English comedian. His first public appearance was at the Haymarket Theatre, London, in 1852, and he appeared at the St. James Theatre in 1854. In 1858 he became leading comedian at the Adelphi, and after five years engagements followed at the Queen's Theatre, the Gaiety, and other principal theaters. He made a tour of America in 1874 and of the Australian colonies in 1890. In 1879 he became manager of the Folly Theatre, later (1882) renamed Toole's Theatre, and managed it until his retirement in 1895. Among the best known of his roles are Paul Pry, Caleb Plummer in *The Cricket on the Hearth,* the Artful Dodger, and Uncle Dick in *Uncle Dick's Darling.*

Too True to Be Good. A play (1932) by George Bernard Shaw, constructed as a moral allegory on the theme of man's moral bankruptcy.

Toots (töts), **Mr. P.** In Dickens's novel *Dombey and Son,* a likable, very friendly person, who is, however, somewhat deficient in intelligence (it is said of him that "when he began to have whiskers, [he] left off having brains"). He is remembered for his comment "It's of no consequence," which he makes on every occasion of disappointment or disaster.

Topas (tō′pạs), **Sir. See under Feste.**

Tophet (tō′fẹt). [Also, **Topheth** (tō′fẹth).] In Biblical geography, a place at the SE extremity of Gehenna or the Valley of Hinnom, S of Jerusalem. It is said that here those Jews who practiced idolatry sacrificed their children to Moloch, and that for this reason the whole valley became the place where the city's rubbish was burned, and a symbol and a name for the place of torment in a future life.

Toplady (top′lạ.di), **Augustus Montague.** b. at Farnham, Surrey, England, Nov. 4, 1740; d. at London, Aug. 14, 1778. An English clergyman, controversialist, and sacred poet. He was an earnest Calvinist and an opponent of John Wesley and Methodism. He published *The Doctrine of Absolute Predestination Stated and Asserted* (1769), *The*

ḍ, d or j; ṣ, s or sh; ṭ, t or ch; ẓ, z or zh; o, F. cloche; ü, F. menu; ċh, Sc. loch; ṅ, F. bonbon.

Church of England Vindicated from the Charge of Arminianism (1769), *Historic Proof of the Doctrinal Calvinism of the Church of England* (1774), *Poems on Sacred Subjects* (1775), and *Psalms and Hymns* (1776). He wrote several other volumes of hymns and sacred poems. He is best known as the author of the hymn *Rock of Ages.*

Topographia Hibernica (top.ọ.graf′i.ạ hi.bẻr′ni.kạ). [Eng. trans., *Topography of Ireland.*] A prose treatment in Latin of the geography of Ireland by Giraldus Cambrensis, written in 1187.

Topsy, M.P. (top′si). A novel by A. P. Herbert, published in 1929. It is the sequel to *The Trials of Topsy* (1928).

Tor (tôr), **Sir.** In Malory's *Morte d'Arthur*, a knight of the Round Table.

Torfrida (tôr′fri.dạ). In Charles Kingsley's novel *Hereward the Wake*, the wife of Hereward. She is loyal to him throughout the period of his desperate struggle with the Norman invaders, but is forsaken by him at the end for the Lady Elfrida, through whom Hereward has been able to arrange a peace with William I (William the Conqueror).

Tories (tō′riz). In English history, the more conservative of the two great political parties which arose late in the 17th century.

Torquemada (tôr.kwẹ.mä′dạ; Spanish, tôr.kä.mä′- ᴛʜä), **Tomás de.** b. c1420; d. 1498. A Dominican prior, made by Ferdinand and Isabella first inquisitor general for Castile in 1483. He organized the Inquisition in Spain, and became infamous for the severity with which he administered his office. The number of his victims who suffered death is sometimes placed at nearly 9,000, but is probably nearer 2,000. He forwarded the plan for the expulsion of the Jews from Spain in 1492.

Torquilstone (tôr′kwil.stōn). In Scott's *Ivanhoe*, the castle of Front de Bœuf.

Torquil the Oak (tôr′kwil). In Sir Walter Scott's novel *The Fair Maid of Perth*, the wise and very courageous man who is the foster father of Conachar (Eachin MacIan). He refuses to accept his confession of cowardice, believing that the young man is the victim of an evil spell, and makes very clear his own valor and loyalty with the words: "See now, my Chief . . . and judge my thoughts toward thee—others might give thee their own lives and that of their sons—I sacrifice to thee the honour of my house."

Torre (tôr), **Sir.** In Tennyson's "Lancelot and Elaine," one of the *Idylls of the King*, the brother of Elaine.

Torregiano (tôr.rä.jä′nō). b. 1472; d. 1522. A Florentine sculptor, perhaps best known as the sculptor who broke Michelangelo's nose in a quarrel (c1491). For many years he served in the papal army under Cesare Borgia. About 1503 he went to England, where he won great reputation and made the tomb of Henry VII in Westminster Abbey which Francis Bacon called "one of the stateliest and daintiest monuments in Europe." He afterward wandered to Spain, and is said to have died of starvation in a prison at Seville.

Torrent of Portingale (tor′ẹnt; pôr′ting.gãl). A Middle English romance closely resembling *Sir Egla-*

mour, and dealing, like it, with the theme of the patient and suffering wife.

Torres Vedras (tôr′rẹzh vä′drạsh), **Lines of.** Lines of fortifications in Portugal extending from near Torres Vedras (a town about 26 mi. NW of Lisbon) to the Tagus River. They were defended by the Anglo-Portuguese forces under Wellington against the French under Masséna, October, 1810–March, 1811, in the Peninsular War. Length of longest line, 29 mi.

Torricelli (tôr.rē.chel′lē), **Evangelista.** b. at Piancaldoli, Italy, Oct. 15, 1608; d. at Florence, Italy, Oct. 25, 1647. An Italian physicist and mathematician. He was the friend and amanuensis of Galileo, who had become blind, and his successor as professor at Florence. He discovered the principle of the barometer in 1643, made other mathematical and physical discoveries, and improved the microscope. His barometer, still known as the Torricellian tube, consisted of a column of liquid in a tube open at one end; the open end was placed in a container of the same liquid and the atmospheric pressure supported the column in the tube; variations in pressure resulted in the falling or rising of the column. His *Opera geometrica* were first published in 1644, and appeared in a three-volume modern edition in 1919.

Tortoiseshell Cat, The. A novel by Naomi Royde-Smith, published in 1925.

To the Lighthouse. A novel by Virginia Woolf, published in 1927.

To the Memory of My Beloved Master, William Shakespeare. An elegiac poem by Ben Jonson, written upon the death of Shakespeare, whom Jonson calls "Soul of the age, the applause, delight, the wonder of our stage." Later in the poem Jonson refers to him as "sweet swan of Avon," which came into popular use as an epithet for Shakespeare. It is Jonson's reference in this poem to Shakespeare's "small Latin and less Greek" which has given rise to the conjectures as to the extent of Shakespeare's schooling. However, some scholars take the phrase to mean simply that Shakespeare didn't rely as heavily as some of his contemporaries on classical sources for his themes.

To the North. A novel by Elizabeth Bowen, published in 1932.

To the Virgins, to Make Much of Time. A poem (1648) by Robert Herrick, expressing the Cavalier sentiment that one is foolish to spurn the pleasures of the moment, for "this same flower that smiles to-day/ To-morrow will be dying." It is well known for its opening line "Gather ye rosebuds while ye may."

Tottel (tot′l), **Richard.** d. 1594. An English printer and compiler, now best remembered for the work entitled *Tottel's Miscellany.*

Tottel's Miscellany (tot′lz). The title usually given to the first regular Elizabethan collection of English miscellaneous verse. It was issued in June, 1557, by Richard Tottel, with the title *Songes and Sonettes*, and was probably edited by Nicholas Grimald. It contained the songs and sonnets of Sir Thomas Wyatt and Henry Howard, Earl of Surrey, Grimald, and others. A second edition, omitting

Grimald, appeared in the same year, and eight editions had been issued by 1587.

Touchstone (tuch'stŏn). In Shakespeare's *As You Like It*, an "allowed fool." He is wise in his facetiousness, a fool by profession, not an unconscious clown.

Touchstone. A shrewd, honest goldsmith in *Eastward Ho!* by Ben Jonson, George Chapman, and John Marston.

Touchwood (tuch'wŭd). The lover of the chaste maid, Moll, in Thomas Middleton's comedy *A Chaste Maid in Cheapside*.

Touchwood, Lady. A brilliant and shameless woman in William Congreve's *The Double Dealer*, in love with her husband's nephew Mellefont.

Touchwood, Lady. A simple countrywoman, in Hannah Cowley's *The Belle's Stratagem*, whose husband tries to keep her away from the world.

Touchwood, Lord. The husband of the faithless Lady Touchwood in William Congreve's *The Double Dealer*.

Touchwood, P. S. [Called **"Scrogie" Touchwood**.] In Sir Walter Scott's novel *St. Ronan's Well*, a fussy, meddlesome old man, whose wealth has permitted him the luxuries of travel and interfering in the affairs of his friends.

Tourguenieff (tŏr.gā'nyif), **Ivan Sergeyevich.** See **Turgenev, Ivan Sergeyevich.**

Tourneur (tèr'nèr), **Cyril.** [Also: **Turner** or **Turnour**.] b. c1584; d. in Ireland, Feb. 28, 1626. An English tragic poet. He was a member of Edward Cecil's expedition to Cadiz in 1625 and was one of the sick put ashore at Kinsale on the return of the expedition; he died soon afterward. He published in 1600 an obscure allegorical poem, and in 1613 an elegy on the death of Prince Henry, son of James I. His chief fame rests on two tragedies: *The Revenger's Tragedy* (1607) and *The Atheist's Tragedy, or the Honest Man's Revenge* (1611).

Tower Hill. A hill in London, near the Tower of London, formerly the scene of execution of political offenders.

Tower of Babel (bā'bel, bab'el). See **Babel, Tower of.**

Tower of London (lun'don). An ancient palacecitadel of London. It is situated on the Thames at the SE angle of the old walled City of London. The Roman wall ran through the site. It consists of a large and irregular agglomeration of buildings of different periods, enclosed within battlemented and moated walls. While a stronghold of some kind existed earlier on the site, the recorded history of the Tower begins with William the Conqueror, and the chief buildings are the work of the Norman kings and Henry III. No important additions were made after Edward I. When it ceased to be a royal residence it became famous as a state prison, and is now nominally a national arsenal. The royal mint was located there in the Middle Ages. The Tower has four gates, the Iron, Water, and Traitors' gates on the side toward the Thames, and the Lions' Gate at the SW angle. In the middle of the enclosure rises the square and lofty White Tower, the keep of the medieval fortress. It is characterized by its four tall angle-turrets with modern crowning.

In the White Tower is the venerable Chapel of Saint John, with heavy cylindrical pillars, round arches, and rude capitals; it is unsurpassed as an example of the earliest type of Norman architecture. In the halls above is shown an admirable collection of medieval arms and armor. The buildings of the inner enclosure include 12 towers, with many of which are associated memories of historic captives, executions, and crimes. In the Record of Wakefield Tower are kept the crown jewels of England. In the Chapel of Saint Peter ad Vincula, in the NW angle, and the little cemetery adjoining, are buried most of the noted persons who suffered death within the Tower precincts or on Tower Hill. The buildings are for the most part severely plain, in rough masonry of small stones, their great interest lying almost wholly in their many associations. The Tower Warders (or Yeomen Warders) wear a costume very similar to that of the Yeomen of the Guard, called Beefeaters, but are in fact a distinct (and very much older) corps, whose members leave the Tower only on state occasions of the utmost solemnity (for example, to escort the crown to Westminster at a coronation).

Towneley Plays (toun'li). [Also, **Wakefield Plays**.] A cycle of 32 mystery plays performed on Corpus Christi Day at Wakefield, England, during the 14th and 15th centuries. We know them from a manuscript (c1460) long kept at Towneley Hall. First in the cycle are simple plays probably of the late 14th century, then five plays corrupted from the York cycle with others possibly composed in the early 15th century, and finally a most brilliant achievement by an unknown writer called by scholars the Wakefield Master, who added the final group and possibly touched up others. The 13 plays attributed to him are distinguished by a nine-line stanza with anapestic meter and a verse scheme of rhyming quatrain, couplet, and triplet.

Townley (toun'li), **Lord.** The "provoked husband" in Sir John Vanbrugh and Colley Cibber's play of that name.

Townshend (toun'zend), **Charles.** [Title, 2nd Viscount **Townshend**.] b. 1674; d. at Raynham, Norfolk, England, June 21, 1738. An English statesman, originally a Tory and later a Whig. He was plenipotentiary with the Duke of Marlborough in the negotiations with the Netherlands (1709), and ambassador at The Hague (1709–11), but fell into disgrace as a result of his part in the making of the Barrier treaty. With the accession of George I, he became secretary of state (1714–16) in the north, and put down (1715) the Jacobite rebellion. He was dismissed through the intrigues of James Stanhope, but when Stanhope fell from grace with the bursting of the South Sea Bubble he and his brother-in-law Robert Walpole came back into power. He became president of the council in 1720, and secretary of state in 1721. He quarreled with Walpole, whose ability was too great for Townshend to cope with, and resigned in 1730. Townshend's last years were spent in agricultural experiments, his introduction of turnips into wide cultivation and his expounding of crop rotation being landmarks in English farming history.

Towwouse (tou'wouz), **Mrs.** A shrewish woman in Henry Fielding's novel *Joseph Andrews*.

Tox (toks), **Miss.** [Full name, **Lucretia Tox.**] In Dickens's novel *Dombey and Son*, a kindly spinster, disappointed in her dream of becoming the second wife of Mr. Dombey. She proves to be his only true friend when disaster strikes, and secretly serves him to the very last. At the end of the book she has embarked upon the seemingly hopeless task of reforming Rob the Grinder.

Toxophilus: The Schools and Partitions of Shooting (tok.sof′i.lus). A treatise (1545) relating to archery, written by Roger Ascham.

Toynbee (toin′bē), **Arnold Joseph.** b. at London, April 14, 1889—. An English historian; nephew of Paget Toynbee. He served (1915–19) in the political intelligence and other departments of the Foreign Office during World War I, was a member (1946) of the British delegation to the peace conference at Paris, and was director (1943–46) of the research department at the Foreign Office. He was professor of Byzantine and modern Greek language, literature, and history (1919–24) and of international history (1925 *et seq.*) at the University of London. Author of *Nationality and the War* (1915), *Greek Historical Thought* (1924), and *A Study of History* (1934–39) in six volumes but incomplete, the first five of which were abridged (1946) by D. C. Somervell.

Toynbee, Paget. b. at Wimbledon, Surrey, England, Jan. 20, 1855; d. May 13, 1932. An English philologist, author, and critic. He was best known as a Dante scholar. Among his publications are *Specimens of Old French, with Notes and Glossary* (1892), *Dictionary of Proper Names and Notable Matters in the Works of Dante* (1898), *Dante Alighieri* (1900), *Dante Studies and Researches* (1902), and *Dante in English Literature from Chaucer to Cary* (1909).

Toynbee Hall. A clublike college in Whitechapel, London, founded 1885 to provide education and recreation for the poor districts of London.

To You, Mr. Chips. A novel by James Hilton, published in 1938.

tract. A short treatise, discourse, or dissertation; especially, a brief printed treatise or discourse on some topic of practical religion. "The church clergy at that time are allowed to have written the best collection of tracts against popery." (Swift, *The Presbyterians' Plea of Merit*.)

Tract No. 90. The last of the *Tracts for the Times*, written by Newman. It attempts to reconcile the Thirty-Nine Articles of the Church of England with the doctrines of the Council of Trent. It resulted in Newman's entering the Roman Catholic Church.

Tracts for the Times. [Also, **Oxford Tracts.**] A series of 90 pamphlets, published at Oxford from 1833 to 1841, the doctrines of which formed the basis of the Oxford School (whence developed the Oxford Movement). The tracts consisted of extracts from the High-Church divines of the 17th century and the church fathers, with contributions by J. H. Newman, R. H. Froude, E. B. Pusey, John Keble, and Isaac Williams. In the last of the series, Tract No. 90, Dr. (afterward Cardinal) Newman took the ground that the Thirty-Nine Articles of the Church of England are in large part susceptible of an inter-

pretation not inconsistent with the doctrines of the Council of Trent. This tract was condemned by a number of bishops and heads of colleges, and a part of the Tractarians (among them Newman in 1845) entered the Roman Catholic Church, others remaining with Pusey and Keble in the Church of England, and maintaining the principles of sacramental efficacy and apostolic authority within that communion.

Tracy Tupman (trā′si tup′man). See **Tupman, Tracy.**

Traddles (trad′lz), **Tommy.** In Dickens's *David Copperfield*, the good and loyal friend of David at school and in later life. He is contrasted with Steerforth, whose brilliance and charm are a mask for selfishness and lack of integrity. Tommy's talent for the cultivation of difficulties leads him to marry one of the "ten daughters of a poor curate."

tradition. A statement, opinion, or belief, or a body of statements or opinions or beliefs, that has been handed down from age to age by oral communication; knowledge or belief transmitted without the aid of written memorials.

> Roselayn is a place where are the Cisterns called Solomon's, supposed, according to the common tradition hereabouts, to have been made by that great King, as a part of his recompence to King Hiram. (Maundrell, *Aleppo to Jerusalem*.)

> Nobody can make a tradition; it takes a century to make it. (Hawthorne, *Septimius Felton*.)

Trafalgar (tra.fal′gar), **Battle of.** The greatest British naval victory in the Napoleonic wars, gained off Cape Trafalgar, Spain, Oct. 21, 1805. The British fleet numbered 27 ships of the line and four frigates under Horatio Nelson (Cuthbert Collingwood second in command); the French-Spanish fleet numbered 33 ships of the line and five frigates under Pierre de Villeneuve. The latter lost 20 ships; Nelson and the Spanish admiral Federico de Gravina were killed and Villeneuve was taken prisoner.

Trafalgar Square. One of the principal squares in London, ab. 1½ mi. SW of Saint Paul's. It contains the Nelson monument and the site of Charing Cross; the National Gallery faces on it.

Trafford (traf′ord), **F. G.** Pseudonym of **Riddell, Charlotte Eliza Lawson.**

tragedy. 1. A dramatic poem or composition representing an important event or series of events in the life of some person or persons, in which the diction is grave and dignified, the movement impressive and stately, and the catastrophe unhappy; that form of the drama which represents a somber or a pathetic character involved in a situation of extremity or desperation by the force of an unhappy passion. Types of these characters are found in Shakespeare's Lady Macbeth and Ophelia, Rowe's Jane Shore, and Scott's Master of Ravenswood. Tragedy originated among the Greeks in the worship of the god Dionysus or Bacchus. A Greek tragedy consisted of two parts—the dialogue, which corresponded in its general features to the dramatic compositions of modern times; and the chorus, the tone of which was lyrical rather than dramatical, and which was meant to be sung, while the dialogue was to be recited.

fat, fāte, fär, àsk, fâre; net, mē, hèr; pin, pīne; not, nōte, mõve, nôr; up, lūte, pùll; ᴛн, then;

Tragedie is for to seyn a certeyn storie . . .
Of him that stood in greet prosperitee,
And is yfallen out of heigh degree
Into miserie, and endeth wrecchedly.
And they ben versifyed comounly
Of six feet, which men clepe exametrown.
In prose eek ben endyted many oon,
And eek in metre, in many a sondry wyse.

        (Chaucer, *Prol.* to *Monk's Tale.*)

Life is a tragedy, wherein we sit as spectators a while, and then act our own part in it.

        (Swift, *To Mrs. Moore, Dec. 27, 1727.*)

Over what tragedy could Lady Jane Grey have wept, over what comedy could she have smiled?

        (Macaulay, *Lord Bacon.*)

"The Bride of Lammermoor," which almost goes back to Æschylus for a counterpart as a painting of Fate, leaving on every reader the impression of the highest and purest tragedy.

        (Emerson, *Walter Scott.*)

2. [*cap.*] Tragedy personified, or the Muse of tragedy.

    Sometime let gorgeous Tragedy
    In sceptred pall come sweeping by.

        (Milton, *Il Penseroso,* l.97.)

3. A fatal event; a dreadful calamity.

But I shall laugh at this a twelve-month hence,
That they who brought me in my master's hate,
I live to look upon their tragedy.

        (Shak., *Rich. III.,* III.ii.)

    The day came on that was to do
        That dreadful tragedy.

        ("Sir Hugh le Blond," in Child's *Ballads.*)

Tragedy. The twelve works entitled tragedies by Shakespeare are entered in this book under their short titles. They are: *Antony and Cleopatra, Coriolanus, Hamlet, Julius Caesar, King Lear, Macbeth, Othello, Richard II, Richard III, Romeo and Juliet, Titus Andronicus,* and *Troilus and Cressida.*

Tragedy of an Elderly Gentleman. See under **Back to Methuselah.**

Tragedy of Caesar and Pompey (sē'zạr; pom'pi), **The.** See **Caesar and Pompey, The Tragedy of.**

Tragedy of Chabot, Admiral of France (shà.bō'), **The.** See **Chabot, Admiral of France.**

Tragedy of Dido, Queen of Carthage (dī'dō; kär'thạj), **The.** See **Dido, Queen of Carthage, The Tragedy of.**

Tragedy of Mr. Arden of Feversham (är'dẹn; fev'ẹr-shạm). See **Arden of Feversham, Tragedy of Mr.**

Tragedy of Nan (nan), **The.** See **Nan, The Tragedy of.**

Tragedy of Tragedies, The. See **Tom Thumb the Great.**

Tragic Comedians, The. A novel by George Meredith, published in 1880. It is based on the tragic love affair of the German socialist Ferdinand Lasalle, who appears in the novel as Sigismund Alvan, and Helene von Dönniges, who figures as Clotilde von Rüdiger.

tragicomedy (traj.i.kom'ẹ.di). A dramatic composition in which serious and comic scenes are blended; a composition partaking of the nature of both tragedy and comedy, and of which the event is not unhappy, as Shakespeare's *Measure for Measure.*

Neither the admiration and commiseration, nor the right sportfulnes, is by their mungrell Tragycomedie obtained.

        (Sir P. Sidney, *Apol. for Poetrie.*)

Such acts and scenes hath this tragi-comedy of love.

        (Burton, *Anat. of Mel.*)

Tragicomedy of Virtuous Octavia (ok.tā'vi.ạ), **The.** A play (1598) by Samuel Brandon, in imitation of Samuel Daniel's *Cleopatra.*

Traherne (trạ.hẽrn'), **Thomas.** b. at Hereford, England, c1637; d. at Teddington, England, in September, 1674. An English clergyman, writer, and metaphysical poet. He studied at Oxford in 1656 and became a rector of Credwell, in Herefordshire, in 1657. His poems were discovered in manuscript in a bookstall in 1896 and A. B. Grosart meant to include them in an edition of Henry Vaughan's work, but died before he could complete the work. Bertram Dobell showed that they were the work of Traherne and not of Vaughan. His *Poetical Works* were edited by Dobell in 1906, his *Centuries of Meditation* in 1908, and his *Poems of Felicity,* edited by H. I. Bell, were published in 1910.

Traill (trāl), **Henry Duff.** b. 1842; d. 1900. An English journalist, biographer, and poet. His biographies are a life of Sir John Franklin (1896) and one of William III. He wrote *Recaptured Rhymes* (1882) and *Saturday Songs* (1890), two volumes of satiric verse. He is also author of *The New Lucian* (1884) and *Number Twenty* (1892).

Traill, Peter. Pseudonym of **Morton, Guy Mainwaring.**

Traitor, The. A tragic drama by James Shirley, staged in 1631 and printed in 1635. It is based on a historical episode involving one of the de' Medicis.

Traitors' Gate. The Southwark end of London Bridge, where after 1577 the heads of persons executed for treason were exhibited.

Trajan (trā'jạn). [Full Latin name, **Marcus Ulpius Trajanus;** surnamed **Dacicus** and **Parthicus.**] b. in Italica, Spain, c53 A.D.; d. at Selinus, Cilicia, July or August, 117. A Roman emperor (98–117). He entered the army at an early age, served as military tribune in various provinces, marched from Spain to Germany (c89), was made consul (91) and by Nerva consular legate in Germany, and was adopted by Nerva, and succeeded him in January, 98. He developed the defenses of the empire on the northeastern frontier, built many roads and other improvements, founded the institution of *alimenta* (for rearing poor children in Italy), and encouraged various reforms. He conducted (c101–106) a successful war against the Dacians under Decebalus, and annexed Dacia to the empire; the Column of Trajan at Rome commemorates this conquest. He incorporated (114) Damascus, and part of Arabia, into the empire, and carried on an unsuccessful war with the Parthians (114–116). There were revolts in the eastern part of the empire and among the Jews in the last part of his reign, but he died before he could organize a campaign to put down the rebels.

Tramping Methodist, The. A novel (1908) by Sheila Kaye-Smith.

Tranio (trā′ni.ō, trä′-). In Shakespeare's *Taming of the Shrew*, a servant of Lucentio.

transition. In rhetoric, a passing from one subject to another.

> So here the archangel paused
> Betwixt the world destroy'd and world restored . . .
> Then, with transition sweet, new speech resumes.
> (Milton, *P.L.*, xii.5.)

Transition. Studies in contemporary literature by Edwin Muir, published in 1926.

Transome (tran′sọm), **Harold.** In George Eliot's novel *Felix Holt*, the eventual heir to the Transome estate. He is a young man of pleasing appearance, and basically honorable, but his opinion of himself is perhaps a trifle too high.

Transome, Mr. In George Eliot's novel *Felix Holt*, the paralytic, dim-witted husband of Mrs. Arabella Transome.

Transome, Mrs. Arabella. In George Eliot's novel *Felix Holt*, the mother of Harold Transome. She is a haughty, handsome woman, whose personality has been hopelessly embittered by a sin committed during the time of her early married life.

Trap, The. A novel by Dorothy M. Richardson, published in 1925. It is the eighth section of *Pilgrimage* (1938), a novel sequence in 12 parts employing the stream-of-consciousness technique.

Trapbois (trap′boiz). In Sir Walter Scott's *Fortunes of Nigel*, an old miser living in Alsatia (a portion of London once known for its thieves and other criminals).

Trappists (trap′ists). A monastic body, a branch of the Cistercian order. It is named for the village of Soligny-la-Trappe, in the department of Orne, France, where the Abbey of La Trappe was founded in 1140 by Rotrou, Count of Perche. The abbey soon fell into decay, and was governed for many years by titular or commendatory abbots. Armand Le Bouthillier de Rancé, who had been commendatory abbot of La Trappe from his boyhood, became its actual abbot in 1664, and thoroughly reformed and reorganized the order. The rules of the order are noted for their extreme austerity, and require extended fasts, severe manual labor, almost perpetual silence, abstinence from meat and fish, and rigorous asceticism in general. The order was repressed in France during the Revolutionary and Napoleonic periods. There are branch monasteries in France, Belgium, Great Britain, Italy, and elsewhere in Europe, and in the U.S., as well as in Canada.

Traveling Man, The. A drama (1910) by Augusta Gregory (Lady Gregory).

Traveller, The. A poem by Oliver Goldsmith, published in 1765. The first of his signed poems, it is dedicated to his brother, and is expressive of a patriotism able, without compromising itself, to see certain merits in other countries.

Travels in Arabia Deserta (a̤.rā′bi.a̤ dẹ.zẹr′ta̤). See **Arabia Deserta, Travels in.**

Travels of Sir John Mandeville (man′dẹ.vil). A famous 14th-century book of travels. The author calls himself John (or Jehan de) Mandeville, or John Maundevylle, knight of St. Aubin or St. Albans, England, and says that, leaving England on Michaelmas Day, 1322 (or 1332), he visited Turkey, Armenia, Tartary, Persia, Syria, Arabia, Egypt, Libya, Ethiopia, Chaldea, Amazonia, and India. The book is, however, a compilation intended as a guide to pilgrims to the Holy Land, based upon William of Boldensele (1336) and Friar Odoric of Pordenone (1330). It is full of wild travelers' tales and marvels: the Phoenix and people with no heads and eyes in their shoulders appear along with accounts of the Pyramids and other actualities. The original was in French, and the oldest manuscript is in that language, dated 1371. The *Travels* was translated into Latin and several times into English. The earliest of the English manuscripts are from shortly after 1400. It is now believed that the author was a physician of Liége known as John of Burgundy or John With the Beard (Jehan à la Barbe), exiled for some reason from England, who died in 1372. Another theory attributes the work to Jean d'Outremeuse, a writer of Liége.

Travers (trav′ẻrz). In Shakespeare's *2 Henry IV*, a retainer of Northumberland who brings the news of Hotspur's defeat.

Travers, Pamela L. b. in Queensland, Australia, 1904—. A British actress and writer (especially of books for young people). She began her literary career by contributing verse to the *Irish Statesman*, and lived in the U. S., Australia, Ireland, Russia, and England, where she played many Shakespearian roles. Author of such works as *Mary Poppins* (1934; translated into Swedish, Italian, German, and Czech), *Mary Poppins Comes Back* (1935), *Happy Ever After* (1940), *Aunt Sass* (1941); and also of *Moscow Excursion* (1935) and *I Go by Sea, I Go by Land* (1941), travel books.

travesty (trav′ẹs.ti). In literature, a burlesque treatment or setting of a subject which had originally been handled in a serious manner; hence, by extension, any burlesque or ludicrous imitation, whether intentional or not; a grotesque or absurd resemblance. Travesty is in strict use to be distinguished from parody: in the latter the subject matter and characters are changed, and the language and style of the original are humorously imitated; in *travesty* the characters and the subject matter remain substantially the same, the language becoming absurd or grotesque.

> The extreme popularity of Montemayor's "Diana" not only caused many imitations to be made of it, . . . but was the occasion of a curious travesty of it for religious purposes.
> (Ticknor, *Span. Lit.*)

> He was driven to find food for his appetite for the marvellous in fantastic horrors and violent travesties of human passion.
> (E. Dowden, *Shelley*.)

> One of the best of the many amusing travesties of Carlyle's style, a travesty which may be found in Marmaduke Savage's "Falcon Family," where one of the "Young Ireland" party praises another for having "a deep no-meaning in the great heart of him."
> (R. H. Hutton, *Modern Guides*.)

Traxalla (trak′sạ.lạ). The general of the usurping Queen of Mexico, Zempoalla, in Dryden and Howard's *The Indian Queen*.

Treasure Island. A novel by Robert Louis Stevenson, published in 1883. In 1740, Jim Hawkins and his mother, who manage the Admiral Benbow Inn, acquire a lodger named Bill Bones, an old seaman who is pursued by some pirates. Blind Pew, Black Dog, and other villains finally find Bones, and he dies. Jim takes an old treasure map, which the pirates covet, from Bones's sea chest. Squire Trelawney and Doctor Livesey decide to fit out a ship, the *Hispaniola*, and go with Jim to find the treasure once buried by Captain Flint. The ship's cook, Long John Silver, is aware of the purpose of the voyage and leads the crew to mutiny. Jim, who knows their plot but has not been able to tell his friends, smuggles himself ashore with the pirates and meets Ben Gunn, a member of Captain Flint's old pirate crew, marooned on the island three years before. Meanwhile, the doctor and Squire Trelawney discover the mutineers' plans. They battle the pirates, and repulse them. During another fight, Jim steals out to the *Hispaniola*, kills the man left to guard her, and sets the ship drifting to a safe, secret place. When he returns to the island he finds that Doctor Livesey has surrendered the map to save the lives of those loyal to him. Jim is taken by the pirates, but is saved from their wrath by Long John Silver. When the pirates fail to find the gold where the map shows it to be (for Ben Gunn has dug it up and hidden it elsewhere), they turn on Long John and Jim; but the doctor and the squire save them. The survivors return to England, Silver managing to escape through the devices of Ben Gunn, and divide the rescued treasure.

Treatise of Human Nature, A. A lengthy philosophical work composed by David Hume in his early manhood, and issued in sections during the period 1739–40.

Treatise on the Astrolabe (as′trọ.lāb), **The.** See **Astrolabe, The Treatise on the.**

Trebonius (trẹ.bō′ni.us). In Shakespeare's *Julius Caesar*, a conspirator who (with Brutus) opposes the killing of Antony. At the time of the assassination of Caesar, he leads Antony away from the scene.

Tree (trē), Sir **Herbert Beerbohm.** [Known as Sir Herbert Tree.] b. at London, Dec. 17, 1853; d. there July 2, 1917. An English actor and theatrical manager; half-brother of Max Beerbohm. He first appeared on the stage in 1878, adapted the surname Tree (a translation of the "bohm" in his name), managed the Haymarket Theatre, London (1887–96), and was subsequently manager of His Majesty's Theatre, London. His productions, especially of poetic drama, were considered the leading theatrical events of their day and Tree was acclaimed as the leader of the English theater.

Treece (trēs), **Henry.** b. 1912—. A British poet. He served as a pilot in the Royal Air Force during World War II. Author of *Thirty-Eight Poems* (1940), *Towards a Personal Armageddon* (1941), and *Invitation and Warning* (1942).

Tree of Heaven, The. A novel by May Sinclair, published in 1917.

Tree of the Universe. See **Yggdrasil.**

Trelawney (trẹ.lô′ni), **Edward John.** b. at London, Nov. 13, 1792; d. near Worthing, England, Aug. 13, 1881. An English adventurer, a friend of Byron and Shelley. He helped recover the bodies of Shelley and his companion, Edward Williams, after they drowned; he arranged for Shelley's cremation and it was he who took Shelley's heart from the pyre. He accompanied Byron to Greece and served in the war of independence. He later became a social lion at London. He wrote *Recollections of the Last Days of Shelley and Byron* (1858), rewritten as *Records of Shelley, Byron, and the Author* (1878).

Trench (trench), **Richard Chenevix.** b. at Dublin, Sept. 9, 1807; d. at London, March 28, 1886. A British prelate, philologist, and poet. He was graduated from Cambridge (Trinity College), became dean of Westminster in 1856, and was archbishop of Dublin (1864–84). Among his works are *The Story of Justin Martyr* (1835), *Sabbation* (1838), *Poems from Eastern Sources* (1842), *Study of Words* (1851), *English Past and Present* (1855), *Select Glossary of English Words* (1859), and *Lectures on Medieval Church History* (1878).

Trenchard (tren′chạrd), **Asa.** The title role of Tom Taylor's *Our American Cousin.* Though intended for the principal part, it was soon overshadowed by that of Lord Dundreary.

Trent (trent), **Council of.** A council (usually reckoned as the 18th ecumenical council) held (with several prorogations and suspensions) at Trent, in the Tyrol, Dec. 13, 1545, to Dec. 4, 1563. It condemned the leading doctrines of the Reformation concerning the Bible, original sin, and justification. Its decrees were confirmed by Pope Pius IV, Jan. 26, 1564. He also published in that year the Tridentine Profession of Faith.

Trent, Fred. In Dickens's *Old Curiosity Shop*, the brother of Little Nell.

Trespasser, The. A novel by D. H. Lawrence, published in 1912.

Tressel (tres′ẹl). In Shakespeare's *Richard III*, an attendant to Lady Anne.

Tressilian (tre.sil′yạn), **Edmund.** In Sir Walter Scott's novel *Kenilworth*, a brave and devoted man, who loves Amy Robsart but is unable to prevent her murder.

Trevelyan (trẹ.vel′yạn), **George Macaulay.** b. Feb. 16, 1876—. An English historian and biographer; third son of Sir George Otto Trevelyan. He served as regius professor of modern history (1927–40) at Cambridge, and as master (1940–51) of Trinity College, Cambridge. Among his works are *Garibaldi's Defense of the Roman Republic* (1907), *Garibaldi and the Thousand* (1909), *Garibaldi and the Making of Italy* (1911), *British History in the Nineteenth Century, 1782–1901* (1922), *History of England* (1926), *England under Queen Anne* (3 vols., 1930, 1932, 1934), *The English Revolution, 1688* (1938), *English Social History* (1942), and the biographies *The Life of John Bright* (1913), *Grey of Fallodon* (1937), and *Sir George Otto Trevelyan: A Memoir* (1932).

Trevelyan, Sir George Otto. b. at Rothley Temple, Leicestershire, England, July 20, 1838; d. at Wall-

ḍ, d or j; ṣ, s or sh; ṭ, t or ch; ẓ, z or zh; *o*, F. cloche; ü, F. menu; ċh, Sc. loch; ṅ, F. bonbon.

ington, Northumberland, England, Aug. 17, 1928. An English historian and statesman; nephew of Thomas Babington Macaulay. He served as a Liberal member of Parliament (1865–86), civil lord of admiralty (1868–70), parliamentary secretary to the admiralty (1881), chief secretary for Ireland (1882–84), and secretary for Scotland (1886, 1892–95). Author of two satires, *Horace at the University of Athens* (1861) and *The Ladies in Parliament* (1867). His major work is the *Life and Letters of Lord Macaulay* (1876). He also wrote *Cawnpore* (1865), *The Early History of Charles James Fox* (1880), and *The American Revolution* (6 vols., 1899–1914).

Trevet (trev'ẹt), **Nicholas.** See **Trivet, Nicholas.**

Trevisa (trẹ.vē'sạ), **John de.** b. in Cornwall, England, c1326; d. c1412. An English translator, vicar of Berkeley. He completed in 1387 the translation of Ranulph Higden's *Polychronicon* into English, and in 1398 the *De Proprietatibus Rerum* of Bartholomew Anglicus, as well as other Latin works, and possibly the Bible.

Trial of a Judge. A poetic drama (1938) by Stephen Spender.

Trial of Jesus, The. A passion play (1925) by John Masefield.

Trials of Topsy (top'si), **The.** A novel by A. P. Herbert, published in 1928. Its sequel is *Topsy, M.P.* (1929).

Triamond (trī'ạ.mọnd). In Spenser's *Faerie Queene*, the son of Agape and brother to Diamond and Priamond. He opposes Cambell in the tournament, but afterwards they vow friendship, and eventually Triamond wins the hand of Canace, Cambell's sister.

Triamour (trī'ạ.mọr), **Sir.** See **Sir Triamour.**

tribrach (trī'brak). In prosody, a foot comprised of three short syllables.

Tribulation Wholesome (trib.ū.lā'shọn hōl'sọm). See **Wholesome, Tribulation.**

Trick to Catch the Old One, A. A comedy by Thomas Middleton, printed in 1608 and acted c1607.

Trilby (tril'bi). A novel by George Du Maurier, published in 1894. It deals with artists' life in the Latin Quarter of Paris. It was dramatized (1895) by Paul Potter. Trilby O'Ferrall, the heroine, is by occupation a laundress and also a model in the artists' quarter. She is gay, generous, and friendly, and is famous for the possession of the most beautiful foot in Paris. Her comradeship with the three artists, Taffy, the Laird (a Scotchman), and Little Billee, who all love her more or less, forms the theme of the story. Svengali, a musical genius, gains control of her hypnotically, and by means of this power develops her voice and transforms her into a celebrated prima donna.

trilogy (tril'ọ.ji). Originally, in the Greek drama, a series of three tragedies, each forming a complete part or stage in a historical or poetical narrative; hence, any literary, dramatic, or operatic work consisting of a sequence of three parts, each complete and independent save in its relation to the general theme. Thus, the name trilogy is given by

some to Shakespeare's *Henry VI*, and to Schiller's *Wallenstein*.

Trim (trim), **Corporal.** A military servant of Uncle Toby in Laurence Sterne's *Tristram Shandy*.

Trimalchio (tri.mal'ki.ō). In the *Satiricon* of Petronius Arbiter, a rich and ignorant parvenu who gives a feast. An account of this feast forms one of the largest of the fragments of which the work now consists.

trimeter (trim'ẹ.tẽr). In prosody, a verse or period consisting of three measures. A trochaic, iambic, or anapestic trimeter consists of three dipodies (six feet); a trimeter of other rhythms is a hexapody, or period of six feet. The name is specifically given to the iambic trimeter,

$$\smile\_\smile\_ / \smile\_\smile\_ / \smile\_\smile\smile,$$

regularly with penthemimeral or hepthemimeral caesura. This is the usual verse of the dialogue of the ancient Greek drama.

Trimmers. An English group which (1680–90) followed the Marquis of Halifax in trimming between the Whigs and the Tories.

Trimurti (trē.mör'tē). The Hindu triad, consisting of Brahma as the creator, Vishnu as the preserver, and Shiva as the destroyer. This is regarded as a threefold manifestation of the one supreme spirit.

Trinacria (tri.nā'kri.ạ). An old name of Sicily, referring to the three promontories Pachynus, Peloris, and Lilybaeum.

Trincalo (tring'kạ.lō) or **Trinculo** (-kụ.lō). A farmer, the principal character in Thomas Tomkis's *Albumazar*.

Trinculo (tring'kụ.lō). In Shakespeare's *Tempest*, a jester who, with Stephano and Caliban, plans to murder Prospero.

Trinity College. The largest college of Cambridge University, England, founded by Henry VIII in 1546 by the union of several older foundations. The beautiful gateway on the street is mainly of the time of Henry VIII. The great court, 340 by 280 ft., is bounded on the north by the chapel and on the west by the hall. The chapel is of the Tudor period, with fine woodcarving and portrait sculptures. The cloister court is arcaded on three sides and on the fourth is bounded by the handsome classical library built by Christopher Wren. There are several other comparatively modern courts.

Trinity College. A college of Oxford University, England, founded by Sir Thomas Pope in 1554 upon the site of an old college of the priors of Durham which had been founded in 1286. The Renaissance chapel, built in 1694, has a plain exterior with large round-arched windows, and possesses a fine altarpiece and a beautiful carved screen.

Trinity College. [Also, **University of Dublin.**] The leading educational institution of Ireland, founded in 1591 by Queen Elizabeth.

Trinity Hall. A college of Cambridge University, occupied chiefly by students of law: founded 1350.

Trinity Homilies. A collection (c1200) of homilies, apparently based upon older collections of religious prose.

Trinobantes (trin.ọ.ban'tēz). A people which, in the early history of Britain, occupied the unforested parts of what now comprises Essex and Middlesex.

Trinovant (trī'nō.vant). See under **Troynovant**.

triolet (trē'ō.let). A poem in fixed form, borrowed from the French, and allied to the rondel and rondeau. It consists of eight lines on two rhymes, and is generally written in short measures. The first pair of lines are repeated as the seventh and eighth, while the first is repeated as the fourth. Representing the repeated lines by capital letters the rhyme scheme would thus be *A,B,a,A,a,b,A,B*. In humorous examples a fresh sense is often skilfully given to the fourth line. The first French triolet is said to have been by Adam le Roi (end of 13th century). Triolets were written in England as early as 1651 by Patrick Carey, whose efforts Sir Walter Scott published in 1820.

Tripartite Chronicle. See **Cronica Tripartita**.

Triple Entente. An unwritten accord between France, Russia, and Great Britain, formed at the beginning of the 20th century and designed to offset the power of the Triple Alliance (Germany, Austria, Italy).

triplet. In prosody, a sequence of three rhyming lines, sometimes introduced as a variation in a work otherwise utilizing heroic couplets.

Trip to Calais (ka.lā', kal'ā, kal'is), **A.** A comedy (1776) by Samuel Foote, in which he undertook to ridicule (as the character Lady Kitty Crocodile) the notorious Duchess of Kingston (Elizabeth Chudleigh Pierrepont). She secured the prohibition of the play, and he altered it and produced it as *The Capuchin;* but his health broke down under an indictment for criminal assault, procured by an agent of the duchess, and he died not long after.

Triptolemus (trip.tol'ē̯.mus). In Greek mythology, a favorite of Demeter. He was considered to be the inventor of the plow and a patron of agriculture. He was honored in the Eleusinian mysteries as an agricultural figure. His symbol was an ear of wheat.

Triptolemus Yellowley (yel'ō.li). See **Yellowley, Triptolemus**.

Trip to Scarborough (skär'bur"ō, -bėr.ō), **A.** An alteration by Richard Brinsley Sheridan of Sir John Vanbrugh's *The Relapse* (1696), produced in 1777.

Tristan (tris'tän, -tạn). [Also: **Tristans** (-täns, -tạnz), **Tristant** (-tänt, -tạnt), **Tristanz** (-tänz, -tạnz), **Tristram** (-trạm), **Tristan** (-trạn), **Tristrant** (-trạnt), **Tristranz** (-trạnz), **Tristrem** (-trẹm), **Tritan, Tritans, Tritanz, Trustram, Trystan, Trystrem, Trystren**.] The hero of a body of medieval legend and romance of whom the original was Drust, son of an 8th-century king of the Picts. His native land was Loonois (later Lothian, in Scotland) which Malory corrupted into Lyoness. His story passed from Scotland into Wales, where Drust became Drystan or Trystan, the lover of Esyllt (later Isolt, Isolde, or Iseult), the wife of King Mark. Fragments of this old Welsh version survive in a 16th-century text, *Ystoria Trystan.* From Wales to Cornwall was an easy step, and Cornish *conteurs* localized the legend around the castle of Tintagel. From Cornwall the legend passed into Brittany and was known there as early as 1000 A.D. Breton *conteurs* greatly influenced the material, and it became the popular property of French troubadours. The second Isolt (Isolt of the White Hands), whom Tristan married in Brittany, is taken from a famous

Arabic romance popular in Europe in the Middle Ages (which *conteur* first added this material is unknown). The amalgamation of ancient Celtic legend and Arabic romance plus the coloring of the French cult of courtly love gave the world one of its immortal and best-known love stories. The countless oral versions of the tale recited by Welsh, Norman, Breton, and German *conteurs* cannot be estimated. The earliest extant version is the Anglo-Norman *Roman de Tristan par Thomas* written in the late 12th century for Eleanor, wife of Henry II. A Norse monk translated this text in 1226 for the king of Norway. A condensed and inferior English version, *Sir Tristrem,* was made c1300. The *Tristan und Isolde* of Gottfried von Strassburg was based on the Anglo-Norman narrative. Eventually the Tristan legend became attached to the Arthurian cycle and the story can be found in full in Malory's *Morte d'Arthur,* where the hero is called Sir Tristram of Lyoness. It is best known to modern readers through Swinburne's *Tristram of Lyonesse,* Tennyson's *The Last Tournament,* Matthew Arnold's *Tristram and Iseult,* Wagner's opera *Tristan und Isolde,* Maurice Hewlett's *Forest Lovers* (based on Malory), and E. A. Robinson's *Tristram.*

Tristan. See also **Tristram of Lyonesse, Sir.**

Tristan L'Hermite (trĕs.tän ler.mēt'). In Sir Walter Scott's novel *Quentin Durward,* the hangman of the French king Louis (and greatly esteemed by that monarch for his loyalty). His grim visage accurately reflects the grimness of his nature.

Tristram and Iseult (tris'trạm; i.sölt'). A poem by Matthew Arnold, published in 1852, the first modern version of this Arthurian legend, in which Tristram is shown on his deathbed, tended by his wife, Iseult of Brittany. He dreams of his youth and his love for Iseult of Ireland, who comes to him in a vision; after a short but intense conversation with her, he dies.

Tristram of Lyonesse (lī.ọ.nes'), **Sir.** One of the most celebrated knights of the Round Table in Malory's *Morte d'Arthur.* His love for Isolt, the wife of King Mark of Cornwall, forms the main theme of the story. He was born in the open country, where his mother, who died shortly after, was in great sorrow; hence she gave him the name Tristram, from *triste,* meaning "sorrowful." See also **Tristan.**

Tristram Shandy (shan'di). [Full title, **The Life and Opinions of Tristram Shandy, Gentleman.**] A novel (9 vols., 1760–67) by Laurence Sterne. It is named after its hero. The first volume introduces Walter Shandy and his brother the Captain (Uncle Toby), Slop, and Yorick. Corporal Trim is prominent in the second volume; the third and fourth contain a good deal on the subject of noses and Slawkenbergius; the sixth contains the episode of Le Fevre; and the Widow Wadman is introduced in the eighth.

Tristrem (tris'trẹm), **Sir.** See **Sir Tristrem.**

Tritan (trē'tạn) or **Tritans** (-tạns) or **Tritanz** (-tạnz). See **Tristan.**

trite. Used till so common as to have lost its novelty and interest; commonplace; worn out; hackneyed; stale. "So trite a quotation that it almost demands an apology to repeat it." (Goldsmith, *English Clergy*.)

Triton (trī'tọn). In Greek mythology, a gigantic son of Poseiden and Amphitrite who dwelt at the bottom of the sea. In the later mythology Tritons appear as a class of minor sea deities, figuring with Nereids in the train of the greater sea gods. They were conceived as having human figures from the waist up combined with those of fish from the waist down. A common attribute of the Tritons is a shell-trumpet, which they blow to raise or calm storms.

Triumph of Life, The. An unfinished allegorical poem by Percy Bysshe Shelley (the poet was working on it at the time of his death).

Triumph of Peace, The. A masque by James Shirley, presented at Court in 1613 with scenery by Inigo Jones.

Triumph of the Philistines, The. A play (1895) by Henry Arthur Jones.

Triumphs of Oriana (ō.ri.an'ạ), **The.** See **Oriana, The Triumphs of.**

Trivet (triv'ẹt), **Nicholas.** [Also, **Trevet.**] b. c1258; d. c1328. An English chronicler, author of *Annales sex Regum Angliae qui a Comitibus Andegavensibus originem traerunt*, a history covering the years 1136–1307. A Dominican friar, he was the writer also of many theological and philosophical works.

Trivia, or the Art of Walking the Streets of London. A burlesque poem by John Gay, published in 1716.

trivium (triv'i.um). [Plural, **trivia.**] In the schools of the Middle Ages, the first three liberal arts (grammar, rhetoric, and logic)—the other four (namely, arithmetic, music, geometry, and astronomy) being termed quadrivium.

trochee (trō'kē). In prosody, a foot of two syllables, the first long or accented and the second short or unaccented. The trochee of modern or accentual versification consists of an accented followed by an unaccented syllable. The trochee of Greek and Latin poetry ($-$ / $\smile$) consists of a long time or syllable, forming the thesis (or metrically accented part of the foot), succeeded by a short as arsis, and is accordingly trisemic and diplasic. Its resolved form is the (trochaic) tribrach ($\smile\smile$ / $\smile$). In the even places of a trochaic line an irrational trochee or spondee is frequently substituted for the normal trochee ($-$ $-$ for $-$ $\smile$), as also in the so-called "basis" of logaoedic verse. The irrational trochee may take an apparently anapestic form ($\smile$ $\smile$ $-$ for $-$ $-$ for $-$ $\smile$). This foot receives its names of trochee (running) and choree or choreus (dancing) from its rapid movement and fitness to accompany dances.

Troil (troil), **Magnus.** A magnate (or "udaller") of Zetland in Sir Walter Scott's novel *The Pirate*. His daughters Minna and Brenda are the principal female characters.

Troilus (troi'lus, trō'i.lus). In Shakespeare's *Troilus and Cressida*, the youngest son of Priam and lover of Cressida. He is faithful, open, and chivalric, and when he witnesses Cressida's unfaithfulness, is broken-hearted and vows to kill Diomedes (who, however, escapes).

Troilus and Cressida (kres'i.dạ). [Full title, **The Tragedy of Troilus and Cressida.**] A tragedy written sometime in the period 1598–1601 by Shakespeare, date of first performance unknown. It was published in 1609 in quarto, and appears in the first folio (1623). It was not paged in that edition, apparently having been withdrawn for a time because of some difficulty over its ownership. Dryden's version of it (with Cressida much altered) was staged in 1679 with Betterton as Troilus and Mrs. Betterton as Andromache. A few revivals were staged of this version, but the original Shakespeare play did not receive another performance until 1907. The principal source is Chaucer's *Troilus and Criseyde*. Of all of the versions of the story of Troilus and Cressida which have been written, Shakespeare's is for many modern readers one of the least satisfactory. His Cressida is at best a thoughtless flirt, at worst a selfish wanton, and Troilus's sorrow at her betrayal of their love thereby loses dignity (to lose one's true love is one thing, but to lose a passing bed-mate, however pleasing she may have been, is quite another, and Cressida's behavior certainly suggests that she was never more than the latter). For this reason, among others, this work is usually grouped with Shakespeare's "problem plays." We see here a world without love, honor, or nobility of character; the atmosphere is one of degeneracy and corruption, from the commanders on either side down to the vulgar and cynical Thersites.

The Story. In Troy, during the Trojan War, Troilus, the youngest son of King Priam, has fallen deeply in love with Cressida. Pandarus, her uncle, helps them arrange meetings and otherwise encourages the romance, and they pledge eternal faithfulness. Meanwhile, Calchas, Cressida's father, who has deserted Troy for the Greeks, persuades the Greek commanders to exchange one of their prisoners for Cressida. Cressida parts reluctantly from her lover, but she does not remain long forlorn; very soon we see her in dalliance with various of the Greek commanders, and she even gives to Diomedes, as she embraces him, the token of love that Troilus had given her at the time of their parting. Troilus, in the Greek camp under a safe conduct from Ulysses, witnesses this betrayal of their love by Cressida, and is broken-hearted. He vows to kill Diomedes, but the fight between them at the end of the play ends indecisively. The other part of the plot concerns the Greek decision to redouble their efforts to end the war. In a council meeting, Ulysses arouses the spiritless and weary commanders and, when a challenge to personal combat comes from the Trojan warrior Hector, he suggests giving it to Ajax instead of Achilles, who is moodily sulking in his tent. The fight between Hector and Ajax ends in a truce, and the two armies feast together. On the following day, however, the fighting continues and, when Hector kills Patroclus, Achilles is aroused to avenge his friend. Coming upon Hector resting without his armor, Achilles treacherously kills him. The day ends with defeat for the Trojans.

Troilus and Cressida. A play by Thomas Dekker and Henry Chettle, acted in 1599.

Troilus and Cressida, or Truth Found too Late. A play by John Dryden, printed in 1677, in which he undertook to "correct" what he "opined was in all probability" one of "Shakespeare's first Endeavours on the Stage."

Troilus and Criseyde (in Chaucer usually trō′i.lus; kri.sā′dẹ). A long romance in rhyme royal by Chaucer, written c1385 and based on Boccaccio's *Il Filostrato*. There are additions which reflect his reading of Boccaccio's *Il Filocolo*, Benoît de Sainte-Maure's *Roman de Troie*, Guido delle Colonne's *Historia Troiana* (a Latin prose redaction of Benoît), Joseph of Exeter's poetical paraphrase of Dares Phrygius, Boethius's *De Consolatione Philosophiae*, and other works. Benoît and Guido had told of Briseida's faithlessness to Troilus. Boccaccio invented Troilo's falling in love with Criseida (as the names are spelled in Italian), and his wooing and winning of her with the aid of Pandaro. While Chaucer's poem is much indebted to the *Filostrato*, his own contribution is vastly greater, reshaping Boccaccio's rather simple story into what has been described as the first psychological novel. Particularly noteworthy is the subtle and complex character of Criseyde. Robert K. Root's critical edition of *The Book of Troilus and Criseyde* (1926) is based on a careful study of the 16 surviving manuscripts.

Trois Echelles (trwä zā.shel). An executioner in the service of Louis XI of France. Sir Walter Scott introduces him in *Quentin Durward*.

Trois Mousquetaires (trwä mös.kẹ.ter), **Les.** See **Three Musketeers, The.**

Trojan Cycle (trō′jạn), **The.** A group of legends or poems relating to the Trojan War.

Trojan War. In Greek legend, a war waged for ten years by the confederated Greeks under the lead of Agamemnon, king of Mycenae and Argolis, against the Trojans and their allies, for the recovery of Helen, wife of Menelaus (king of Sparta or Lacedaemon), who had been carried off by Paris, son of the Trojan king Priam. The Trojan War is celebrated in the *Iliad* and its end is the point of departure for the *Odyssey*. The Trojan War of history probably took place c1200 B.C.

Trollope (trol′ọp), **Anthony.** b. at London, April 24, 1815; d. at Harting, Sussex, England, Dec. 6, 1882. An English novelist; son of Frances Trollope (1780–1863), and brother of Thomas Adolphus Trollope. The family fortunes being impaired, he was raised in a kind of shabby gentility, and in 1834 he became a postal clerk, and continued to serve the British post office until 1867, being during most of those years a roving inspector in Ireland and England, also on occasion traveling abroad in an official capacity, all of which widened his opportunities for observation of life and people, and contributed finally to his literary achievement. His early novels laid in Irish scenes, *The Macdermots of Ballycloran* (1847) and *The Kellys and the O'Kellys* (1848), won scant attention, and an attempt at historical fiction, *La Vendée* (1850), was a dismal failure. He attained his first great success when he wrote *The Warden* (1855). This was the first of the famous Barsetshire series, Barsetshire being a fictitious county, and Barset an imagined cathedral city (very possibly modeled on Winchester) in the south of England. In the books of this series, *Barchester Towers* (1857), *Doctor Thorne* (1858), *Framley Parsonage* (1861), *The Small House at Allington* (1864), and *The Last Chronicle of Barset* (1867), in addition to *The Warden*, many of the same characters reappear, the most famous being Mrs. Proudie, Lady Glencora, Mr. Slope, and Dr. Stanhope. In another series of his books, *Can You Forgive Her?* (1864), *Phineas Finn: the Irish Member* (1869), *The Eustace Diamonds* (1873), *Phineas Redux* (1874), *The Prime Minister* (1876), and *The Duke's Children* (1880), the connecting thread is the British Parliament. Other Trollope novels are *The Three Clerks* (1857), *The Bertrams* (1859), *Castle Richmond* (1860), *Orley Farm* (1861–62), *The Struggles of Brown, Jones, and Robinson* (1862), *Rachel Ray* (1863), *The Belton Estate* (1865), *Miss Mackenzie* (1865), *The Claverings* (1867), *Nina Balatka* (1867), *Linda Tressel* (1868), *He Knew He Was Right* (1869), *The Vicar of Bullhampton* (1870), *Sir Harry Hotspur of Humblethwaite* (1871), *Lady Anna* (1874), *Harry Heathcote* (1874), *The American Senator* (1877), *Is He Popenjoy?* (1878), *John Caldigate* (1879), *An Eye for an Eye* (1879), *Cousin Henry* (1879), *Ayala's Angel* (1881), *Dr. Wortle's School* (1881), *The Fixed Period* (1882), *Kept in the Dark* (1882), *Marion Fay* (1882), and (posthumously published) *An Old Man's Love* (1884). In addition Trollope published a satirical work, *The Way We Live Now* (1875), lives of Cicero and of Thackeray, and accounts of his travels in the West Indies, North America, South Africa, and Australia. In 1865 Trollope assisted in founding the *Fortnightly Review;* after his retirement from the postal service in 1867 he edited *St. Paul's Magazine*, which lasted little more than three years; and he contributed to *Blackwood's*, the *Cornhill Magazine*, and other periodicals. He visited the U. S. in 1868, partly in the interest of plans for international copyright. In that same year he tried, unsuccessfully, for a seat in Parliament. His autobiography, posthumously published in 1883, reveals some of the secrets of his voluminous literary output: he rose early every morning, and wrote approximately 250 words every quarter hour for two and a half hours. A keen observer, with an eye especially for human foibles, Trollope recorded the comedy of the English middle class in the mid-Victorian era.

Trollope, Frances. [Maiden name, **Milton.**] b. at Stapleton, near Bristol, England, March 10, 1780; d. at Florence, Italy, Oct. 6, 1863. An English novelist and writer of travel works; mother of Anthony Trollope and Thomas Adolphus Trollope. In the fall of 1827 she sailed for New Orleans; she spent 25 eventful months in frontier Cincinnati, creating sensational tableaux for a museum and rearing a fantastic building, the "Bazaar," and 16 months of extreme poverty in the eastern U. S. In March, 1832, seven months after her return to England, she published *Domestic Manners of the Americans*, widely read in England and in the U. S., where the book was fiercely attacked. It remains, however, a classic of American travel. Its success launched her at 52 upon a prolific career as a writer of novels and travel books. Notable among her 34 novels are *Jonathan Jefferson Whitlaw, The Vicar of Wrexhill, The Widow Barnaby,* and *Petticoat Government*, which last foreshadows her son Anthony's famous novels of English cathedral-town life.

ḍ, d or j; ş, s or sh; ṭ, t or ch; ẓ, z or zh; o, F. cloche; ü, F. menu; çh, Sc. loch; ṅ, F. bonbon.

Trollope, Frances Eleanor. [Maiden name, Ternan.] An English novelist; second wife of Thomas Adolphus Trollope. She wrote a number of novels, among them *Aunt Margaret's Trouble*, *The Sacristan's Household*, and *That Unfortunate Marriage*. With her husband she wrote *Homes and Haunts of the Italian Poets* (1881).

Trollope, Thomas Adolphus. b. April 29, 1810; d. at Clifton, England, Nov. 11, 1892. An English writer; brother of Anthony Trollope. He went to Italy in 1843, and resided in Florence till 1873, when he went to Rome. About 1890 he returned to England. He wrote *A Summer in Brittany* (1840), *A Summer in Western France* (1841), *Impressions of a Wanderer* (1850), *The Girlhood of Catherine de' Medici* (1856), *A Decade of Italian Women* (1859; *Vittoria Colonna* was included in this), *Tuscany in 1849 and in 1859* (1859), *Filippo Strozzi* (1860), *Paul V the Pope and Paul the Friar* (1860), *A Lenten Journey in Umbria* (1862), *A History of the Commonwealth of Florence* (1865), *The Papal Conclaves as They Were and as They Are* (1876), *Life of Pope Pius the Ninth* (1877), *A Peep Behind the Scenes at Rome* (1877), *Sketches from French History* (1878), and *What I Remember* (1887). He wrote also a number of novels, among them *La Beata*, *Lindisfarn Chase*, *Diamond Cut Diamond*, and *The Garstangs of Garstang Grange*.

Trompart (trom′pärt). In Spenser's *Faerie Queene*, the squire of Braggadocchio. He is characterized as a cunning knave.

Trompington (trum′ping.ton), **Miller of.** See **Miller of Trompington**; see also **Reeve's Tale**.

trope (trōp). In rhetoric, a figurative use of a word; a word or expression used in a different sense from that which properly belongs to it, or a word changed from its original signification to another for the sake of giving spirit or emphasis to an idea, as when we call a stupid fellow an ass, or a shrewd man a fox. Tropes are chiefly of four kinds: metaphor, metonymy, synecdoche, and irony; but to these may be added allegory, prosopopoeia, hyperbole, antonomasia, and some others. Tropes are included under figures in the wider sense of that word. In a narrower sense, a trope is a change of meaning, and a figure any ornament except what becomes so by such change.

> Is not the trope of music, to avoid or slide from the close or cadence, common with the trope of rhetoric, of deceiving expectation?
> (Bacon, *Advancement of Learning*, ii.)

> Wee acknowledge and beleeve the Catholick reformed Church, and if any man be dispos'd to use a trope or figure, as Saint Paul once did in calling her the common Mother of us all, let him doe as his owne rethorick shall perswade him.
> (Milton, *On Def. of Humb. Remonst.*)

> Your occasional tropes and flowers suit the general coarseness of your style as tambour sprigs would a ground of linsey-woolsey.
> (Sheridan, *Critic*, I.i.)

> Tropes are good to clothe a naked truth,
> And make it look more seemly.
> (Tennyson, *Queen Mary*, III.iv.)

Trophee (trō.fē′, trō′fē). A writer referred to by Chaucer in *The Monk's Tale*. Nothing is now known of either the man or his supposed works. According to Lydgate, Chaucer made a translation of a book, *Trophe*, and "gave it the name of Troilus and Criseyde." It has been conjectured that the common noun "tropaea, trophea," meaning victory columns, was applied to Guido because of his epithet "delle Colonne" (Guido was author of the *Historia Troiana*, which was one of Chaucer's sources for *Troilus and Criseyde*). But the matter is very uncertain.

Trophonius (trō.fō′ni.us). A legendary Greek architect, reputed to have been the son of Erginus, king of Orchomenus, or of Apollo. He is said to have built, with his brother Agamedes, the temple of Apollo at Delphi. He was celebrated as a hero after his death, and had an oracle in a cave near Lebadea in Boeotia.

Trossachs or **Trosachs** (tros′aks). A valley in the Highlands of W Perthshire, Scotland, between Lochs Katrine and Achray, celebrated by Sir Walter Scott in *The Lady of the Lake*.

Trotcosey (trot.kō′zi). In Sir Walter Scott's novel *The Antiquary*, an ancient abbey frequently mentioned by Jonathan Oldbuck, Laird of Monkbarns, since the house of Monkbarns stood on its lands.

Trotter (trot′ėr), **Catherine.** Maiden name of **Cockburn, Catherine.**

Trotter, Job. In Dickens's *Pickwick Papers*, the servant and bosom crony of Jingle.

"Trotty" (trot′i). See **Veck, Toby.**

Trotwood (trot′wůd), **Betsey.** The eccentric but kindhearted great-aunt of David Copperfield, in Dickens's novel *David Copperfield*.

troubadour (trö′ba.dör). One of a class of early poets who first appeared (as trouvères) in France. The troubadours were considered the inventors of a species of lyrical poetry, characterized by an almost entire devotion to the subject of chivalric love, and generally very complicated in regard to meter and rhyme. They flourished from the 11th to the latter part of the 13th century, principally in the south of France, Catalonia, Aragon, and northern Italy. The most renowned among the troubadours were knights who cultivated music and poetry as a polite accomplishment; but the art declined, and in its later days was chiefly cultivated by an inferior class of minstrels.

Troublesome Raigne (or **Reign**) **of King John, The.** See **King John** (1588).

trouvère (trö.vär′). [Also, **trouveur.**] One of the medieval poets of northern France, whose productions partake of a narrative or epic character, and thus contrast broadly with the lyrical, amatory, and more polished effusions of the troubadours. The works of the trouvères include the chansons de geste, the fabliaux, poems of the Round Table cycle, the *Romance of the Rose*, *Reynard the Fox*, etc.

> It is to the North of France and to the Trouvères that we are to look for the true origins of our modern literature.   (Lowell, *Study Windows*.)

Troy (troi). [Also: **Ilium**; Latin, **Troia, Troja.**] Ancient city in Asia Minor, famous in Greek legend as the capital of Priam and the object of the siege by the allied Greeks under Agamemnon. The site of this Homeric city was generally believed in antiquity to be identical with that of the Greek Ilium (the modern Hissarlik); and this view has been supported in later times most notably by Heinrich Schliemann, whose explorations (1871 *et seq.*) at Hissarlik laid bare remains of a series (nine) of ancient towns, one above the other, at least one of which is universally admitted to be prehistoric. The third and later the second from the bottom he identified with the Homeric town, those levels showing the effects of a conflagration and massive ruins. On the other hand, some scholars regarded the situation of Ilium as irreconcilable with Homer's description of Troy, and preferred a site in the neighborhood of the later Bunárbashi, holding Schliemann's results to be inconclusive. More recent investigations indicate, however, that Schliemann was correct about the site, but that the sixth or, more probably, the seventh level was ancient Ilium.

Troy, Sergeant. A principal character in Thomas Hardy's novel *Far from the Madding Crowd.*

Troy Book. A poem by John Lydgate, written between 1412 and 1420. It consists of 30,117 lines in decasyllabic couplets, based on Guido delle Colonne's Latin history. In the section dealing with Troilus and Cressida, grateful mention is made of his "master," Chaucer.

Troyes (trwä), **Chrétien (or Chrestien) de.** See **Chrétien (or Chrestien) de Troyes.**

Troynovant (troi'nọ.vant). A name given to London in the early chronicles, as the city of the Trinovantes. In Layamon's *Brut* it is given as Trinovant.

Truce of God. A suspension of private feuds which was observed, chiefly in the 11th and 12th centuries, in France, Italy, England, and elsewhere. The terms of such a truce usually provided that such feuds should cease on all the more important church festivals and fasts, or from Thursday evening to Monday morning, or during the period of Lent, or the like. This practice, introduced by the church during the Middle Ages to mitigate the evils of private war, fell gradually into disuse as the rulers of the various countries became more powerful.

True Chronicle History of King Leir . . . (lir), **The.** See **King Leir.**

True Heart, The. A novel by Sylvia Townsend Warner, published in 1929.

True Relation of Such Occurrences and Accidents of Noate as Hath Hapned in Virginia since the First Planting of That Collony, A. An account of Virginia exploration and the Jamestown settlement by Captain John Smith (1580–1631), published at London in 1608.

"True Thomas" (tom'ạs). See **Thomas the Rhymer.**

True Tragedie of Richard III, The. An anonymous play (1594) based on English history, which may have served as a source for Shakespeare's *Richard III.*

True Tragedie of Richard Duke of York . . . , The. A play published in 1595 and once thought to be by Marlowe with Shakespeare's additions. It is now thought to be a poor rendition of *3 Henry VI,* possibly written down by an actor who played War-

wick and Clifford or by a prompter who knew the plot.

Truewit (trö'wit). A scholar and gentleman, the expositor of the other characters in Ben Jonson's *Epicoene.*

Trulliber (trul'i.bẹr), **Parson.** In Henry Fielding's novel *Joseph Andrews,* a coarse and brutal curate represented as lacking all the virtues that Parson Adams possessed.

Trumper (trum'pẹr), **Victor Thomas.** b. at Sydney, Australia, Nov. 2, 1877; d. there, June 28, 1915. An Australian cricketer, considered by some the greatest batsman of his generation. He played 402 innings in first-class matches for 17,150 runs at an average of just over 45. He reached his peak with the Australian team in England (1902).

Trumpet-Major, The. A novel by Thomas Hardy, published in 1880.

Trumpington (trum'ping.tọn), **Miller of.** See **Miller of Trompington;** see also **Reeve's Tale.**

Trunnion (trun'yọn), **Commodore Hawser.** The kindhearted uncle of Peregrine Pickle, in Tobias Smollett's novel *Peregrine Pickle.*

Trustram (trus'trạm). See **Tristan.**

Trusty Eckhardt (ek'härt), **the.** See **Eckhardt.**

Truth. See **Flee from the Press.**

Tryan (trī'ạn), **Reverend Edgar.** In George Eliot's tale "Janet's Repentance," included in *Scenes of Clerical Life,* a noble-spirited clergyman through whose efforts Janet Dempster is saved from hopeless despair.

Trystan (tris'tän) or **Trystrem** (-trẹm) or **Trystren** (-trẹn). See **Tristan.**

Try the Sky. A novel by Francis Stuart, published in 1933.

Tschaikovsky or **Tschaikowsky** (chī.kôf'ski). See **Tchaikovsky.**

T. T. One of the many pseudonyms of **Thackeray, William Makepeace.**

Tuatha De Danann (tö.ä'hạ dä dạ.nän'). In Old Irish mythology, literally, "the people of the goddess Dana (or Danu)." They were the tall, beautiful, immortal, divine race of Ireland. Dagda, the good, was their king. In the mythological chronicles, especially in the *Book of Invasions,* they were descendants of the Nemedians (legendary people from Scythia, the third people to invade Ireland) of whom surviving remnants fled to Greece after their defeat, there became so learned and skilled in magic and druidism as to be called the Tuatha De Danann, and returned to Ireland, the fourth invading people. They descended on Ireland from the sea out of a great mist and conquered the Fomorians, according to the *Book of Invasions,* in the 15th century B.C. They in turn were defeated by the Milesians, and disappeared into the hills and mounds of Ireland, gradually became referred to as *aes side,* "the people of the mounds," and eventually came to be regarded as the fairies of modern Irish folklore.

Tubal (tū'bạl). In Shakespeare's *Merchant of Venice,* a Jewish friend of Shylock.

Tubal-Cain (tū'bạl-kān'). In the Bible, the third son of Lamech, the Cainite. He was the first smith,

ḍ, d or j; ṣ, s or sh; ṭ, t or ch; ẓ, z or zh; o, F. cloche; ü, F. menu; ċh, Sc. loch; ṅ, F. bonbon.

a worker in brass and iron, according to Gen. iv. 22.

Tucca (tuk′a̤), **Captain.** A bragging bully in Ben Jonson's *Poetaster*. Thomas Dekker introduces him in his *Satiromastix*, but without the success which attended Jonson's character.

Tuck (tuk), **Friar.** A vagabond monk in the English Robin Hood cycle of ballads and a character in the morris dances and May Day plays. Sir Walter Scott introduces him in *Ivanhoe* as the "holy clerk of Copmanhurst."

Tucker (tuk′ẽr), **Abraham.** [Pseudonym, **Edward Search.**] b. at London, Sept. 2, 1705; d. Nov. 20, 1774. An English metaphysician and moralist. He wrote under his pseudonym *The Light of Nature Pursued* (4 vols., 1768, and 3 vols. edited after his death; edited again by H. P. Mildmay, 1805).

Tucker, Charlotte Maria. [Pseudonym, **A.L.O.E.**] b. in Middlesex, England, May 8, 1821; d. at Amritsar, India, Dec. 2, 1893. An English writer of religious works and books for young people. Her pseudonym consists of the initials of the phrase "A Lady of England." When she was 54 years old she went as a missionary to India, and worked there for 18 years. She wrote more than 50 volumes.

Tudor (tū′dọr). An English dynasty, descended on the male side from Owen Tudor, who married Henry V's widow, Catherine of Valois, and on the female side from John of Gaunt, son of Edward III, through the Beauforts. It comprised the sovereigns Henry VII, Henry VIII, Edward VI, Mary, and Elizabeth.

Tuileries (twē′le̤.riz; French, twēl.rē), **Palace of the.** A royal residence formerly existing at Paris, connected with the Louvre by wings. In 1518 Francis I bought a house here for his sister Margaret of Navarre. It was demolished in 1564 by Catherine de Médicis, who began the erection of the Tuileries, which was enlarged by Henry IV and Louis XIV. The palace, the scene of many of the most memorable events attending the overthrow of the ancient French monarchy, was invaded by the mob June 20, and stormed by the mob Aug. 10, 1792, and was the seat of the Convention. It was taken by the people July 29, 1830, and Feb. 24, 1848, and was burned by the Commune in 1871, the ruins not being removed till 1883. Nothing remains except the pavilions at the two extremities, which have been restored and now form a rich architectural termination to the two extended arms of the Louvre. Its history as a royal residence came to an end with the battle of Sedan (1870) and the departure of the empress Eugénie. The Jardin des Tuileries, a popular promenade, was enlarged in 1889, and now covers the site of the palace. The Quai des Tuileries existed at a very early period as the road to St.-Cloud. The wall of Charles V terminated at the Tour du Bois, between the Louvre and the Tuileries. Outside of this wall were the tile yards or *tuileries*, mentioned as early as 1274.

Tulkinghorn (tul′king.hôrn), **Mr.** An attorney in Dickens's *Bleak House*. He cruelly persecutes Lady Dedlock when he finds out about her early love affair; he is finally murdered by her French maidservant.

Tullia (tul′i.a̤). In Roman legend, a daughter of Servius Tullius. As wife of Lucius Tarquinius, she rode to the senate house to greet her husband as king, and on her return drove over the dead body of her father, whom Tarquinius had murdered.

Tullius Aufidius (tul′i.us ô.fid′i.us). See **Aufidius, Tullius.**

Tulliver (tul′i.vẽr), **Maggie.** In George Eliot's *Mill on the Floss*, the miller's daughter and principal character. Her generous impulsiveness exposes her to the condemnation of the unsympathetic. Her deep love for her brother Tom (whose character is the opposite of hers) is the main theme of the story. Though he ruins her happiness by his blind hatred of the man she loves, she persists in her loyalty, which Tom comes to appreciate only just before they are both drowned in a flood of the river Floss.

Tulliver, Mr. In George Eliot's novel *The Mill on the Floss*, the father of Maggie Tulliver. He is a miller who is finally led to ruin and tragedy by his passion for engaging in lawsuits.

Tulliver, Mrs. In George Eliot's novel *The Mill on the Floss*, the mother of Maggie Tulliver. She is an attractive, even-tempered woman, but utterly lacking in a sense of humor. See also under **Dodson.**

Tulliver, Tom. In George Eliot's novel *The Mill on the Floss*, the brother of Maggie Tulliver.

Tulloch (tul′ọch, -ọk), **John.** b. in Perthshire, Scotland, 1823; d. at Torquay, England, Feb. 13, 1886. A Scottish Presbyterian theologian, educator, and author. He became principal of Saint Mary's College, St. Andrews, in 1854, and served as one of Queen Victoria's chaplains. His works include *Theism* (1855), *Leaders of the Reformation* (1859), *English Puritanism and Its Leaders* (1861), *Beginning Life* (1862), *The Christ of the Gospels and the Christ of Modern Criticism* (1864), *Rational Theology and Christian Philosophy* (1872), *The Christian Doctrine of Sin* (1876), *Modern Theories in Philosophy and Religion* (1884), *Movements of Religious Thought in the 19th Century* (1885), and others.

Tullochgorum (tul.ọch.gō′rum). A song by John Skinner, called by Burns "the best Scotch song Scotland ever saw."

Tully (tul′i). The Anglicized form of Tullius, formerly generally used as the name of the Roman orator, philosopher, and statesman (Marcus Tullius) Cicero.

Tumble-Down Dick: or, Phaeton in the Suds (fā′e̤.tọn). A farce by Henry Fielding which ridicules the popular 18th-century pantomime. Its general theme may be understood from the subtitle: "A Dramatick Entertainment of Walking, in Serious and Foolish Characters [i.e., pantomimes]; Interlarded with Burlesque, Grotesque, Comic Interludes, call'd Harlequin a Pick-Pocket . . . Being ('tis hop'd) the last Entertainment that will ever be exhibited on any Stage. Invented by the Ingenious Monsieur Sans Esprit. The Musick compos'd by the Harmonious Signior Warblerini. And the Scenes painted by the Prodigious Mynheer Van Bottom-Flat." *The Fall of Phaeton*, a popular pantomime, was a particular object of Fielding's satire.

Tunbelly Clumsy (tun′bel′′i klum′zi), **Sir.** See **Clumsy, Sir Tunbelly.**

---

fat, fāte, fär, a̤sk, fāre; net, mē, hẽr; pin, pīne; not, nōte, mȯve, nôr; up, lūte, pu̇ll; ᴛʜ, then;

Tunnel, The. A novel by Dorothy M. Richardson, published in 1919. It is the fourth section of *Pilgrimage* (1938), a novel sequence in 12 parts employing the stream-of-consciousness technique.

Tunning of Elynour Rumming (el'i.nọr rum'ing), **The.** A poem by John Skelton in which is described the various people that gather at the alehouse of Elynour Rumming to drink her brew. It is thought to have been directly influenced by Chaucer's *Wife of Bath's Tale*, and to a lesser degree by his *Nun's Priest's Tale.*

Tunstall (tun'stạl), **Cuthbert.** [Also, **Tonstall**.] b. at Hatchford, Yorkshire, England, in 1474; d. at Lambeth Palace, London, 1559. An English prelate. A brilliant student at Oxford, Cambridge, and Padua, he was a friend of Erasmus and Thomas More. After taking orders, he was advanced rapidly in the church and acted several times as ambassador for Henry VIII. In 1522 he was appointed bishop of London and in 1530 succeeded Thomas Wolsey as bishop of Durham. When Henry VIII broke with the Roman Catholic Church, Tunstall adopted a passive role, not approving or supporting the reforms, but obeying the law once it was in force. He became (1537) president of the council of the north, and under Edward VI remained a reluctant participant in the Reformation in England. In 1550 he was implicated in the events leading to the fall of the Protector, Edward Seymour, Duke of Somerset, and was accused (1551) of treason. Though the charge was dropped, he was deprived (1552) of his offices and kept in custody. With the accession of the Roman Catholic Mary Tudor, he again assumed the bishopric of Durham, but took no part in the persecution of the Protestants. He refused (1559) to take the oath of supremacy of Elizabeth or to assist at the consecration of Matthew Parker as archbishop of Canterbury and was once more deprived of his offices and placed in custody.

Tupman (tup'mạn), **Tracy.** In Dickens's *Pickwick Papers*, a member of the famous Pickwick Club. He is notable for his too susceptible disposition.

Tupper (tup'ẽr), **Martin Farquhar.** b. at London, July 17, 1810; d. in Surrey, England, Nov. 29, 1889. An English poet. He was called to the bar at Lincoln's Inn in 1835, but soon abandoned law in order to devote himself to literature. His chief work is *Proverbial Philosophy* (four series, 1839–76), a once very popular collection of moral statements in blank verse. His Whig ballads and poems also enjoyed a considerable popularity.

Turberville or **Turbervile** (tẽr'bẽr.vil), **George.** b. in Dorsetshire, England, c1540; d. c1610. An English poet, translator, and writer on hunting. Among his works are *Epitaphs, Epigrams, Songs and Sonets* (1567) and *The Booke of Faulconrie* (1575). He is of some importance for his early use (1567) of blank verse in translating Ovid.

Turbott Wolfe (tẽr'bọt wulf). A novel by William Plomer, published in 1926.

Turgenev (tör.gä'nyif), **Ivan Sergeyevich.** [Also: **Tourguenieff, Turgeneff, Turgeniev.**] b. at Orel, Russia, Nov. 9, 1818; d. at Bougival, near Paris, Sept. 3, 1883. A Russian novelist. Born of a landowning family in Orel province, he was educated at Moscow and St. Petersburg, and in 1838 went to Berlin to study philosophy and the classics. About 1840 he received an appointment in the Russian ministry of the interior. He began to publish poems in 1841, and his first story, *Andrei Kolosov*, appeared in 1844. He contributed to the cause of the emancipation of the serfs through his *A Sportsman's Sketches* (or *Annals of a Sportsman*) which appeared in the years following 1847. The first of these appeared in English in 1847 in the *Contemporary Review;* they were also published in French and German, and appeared in book form in 1852. In 1852 some remarks on Russian officialdom made in an obituary letter on Gogol led to his being deprived of his official position, imprisoned, and afterward banished to his estate in Orel, in the interior of Russia. In 1854 he was allowed to return, and in later life lived at Baden-Baden and Paris, with short visits to Russia and elsewhere. He never married, but his love for the singer Pauline Viardot-Garcia led him to live near her and to follow her on her tours. He created much personal antagonism by his analysis of political parties, and was misunderstood by those he was most in sympathy with; the epithet "Nihilist," which he applied to narrowly revolutionary tendencies, was applied to all socialistic and democratic tendencies by the Russian government. In later years, however, this misunderstanding disappeared and popular opinion was in his favor. His novels, forming together a sort of social history of Russia from the 1830's to the 1870's, are *Rudin* (1855), *A Nest of Gentlefolk* (1858), *On the Eve* (1860), *Fathers and Sons* (1862: in this, generally considered his finest novel, the epithet Nihilist is introduced and defined), *Smoke* (1867), and *Virgin Soil* (1876). Among his short stories, some of them classed with the best ever written for their atmosphere and characterization, are *Punin and Baburin, First Love, Asya, A Lear of the Steppe*, and *Clara Milich*. He also wrote *Senilia* (1883: a collection of philosophic pieces), an essay on Don Quixote and Hamlet, plays (including *A Month in the Country*, 1850, and *A Provincial Lady*, 1851), and others.

Turk Gregory (tẽrk greg'ọ.ri). In Shakespeare's *1 Henry IV* (V.iii), Falstaff says, "Turk Gregory never did such deeds in arms as I have done this day." This is a double reference to the sultan of Turkey and to Pope Gregory VII, who made war on Henry IV of Germany.

Turkish Mahomet and Hiren the Fair Greek (mạhom'ẹt; hī'rẹn), **The.** A play (c1594), now lost, attributed to George Peele.

Turnbull Street (tẽrn'bul). See **Turnmill Street.**

Turner (tẽr'nẽr), **Charles Tennyson.** b. at Sowerby, Yorkshire, England, July 4, 1808; d. April 25, 1879. An English poet; brother of Alfred Tennyson. He collaborated with Alfred in *Poems by Two Brothers* (1827) and published several volumes of sonnets. In 1830 he adopted the name Turner by the terms of a will of his great-uncle.

Turner or **Turnour** (tẽr'nẽr), **Cyril.** See **Tourneur, Cyril.**

Turner, John Hastings. b. at London, Dec. 16, 1892—. An English dramatist and novelist. His plays include *Account Rendered* (1913), *Iris Inter-*

venes (1915), *A Breath of Fresh Air* (1917), *Back Again* (1919), *The Sea Urchin* (1925), *The Spot on the Sun* (1927), and *For the Defence* (1935). He also wrote the novels *The Affairs of Men* (1932) and *Bear, Mouse and Waterbeetle* (1938).

Turner, Joseph Mallord William. b. at London, April 23, 1775; d. there, Dec. 19, 1851. An English landscape painter. The son of a barber at London, his education was meager, but he devoted himself to drawing at a very early age. In 1789 he entered the school of the Royal Academy, and for a short time worked with Sir Joshua Reynolds. In 1790 he exhibited a *View of the Archbishop's Palace, Lambeth,* at the Royal Academy. He was made associate of the Royal Academy in 1799, and royal academician in 1802. Before the latter date he was more noted for his water-color painting. Between 1795 and 1799 he sent 39 works to the academy exhibitions. In 1808 he was professor of perspective at the academy. He visited Scotland in 1800, and the Continent c1802 and in 1804. In 1803 he exhibited six foreign subjects, among them the famous *Calais Pier.* From 1807 to 1819 he produced his *Liber Studiorum.* In 1818 he went to Scotland to make the illustrations for Scott's *Provincial Antiquities.* In 1819 he visited Italy for the first time. The visit was followed by increased brilliancy of color, as in *The Golden Bough* and *The Fighting Téméraire.* In 1816 he illustrated Whitaker's *History of Richmondshire* (pub. 1823), in 1824 *The Rivers of England,* in 1830 Rogers's *Italy,* and in 1833–35 *The Rivers of France.* In 1828 he again visited Italy. His first Venetian picture appeared at the academy in 1833. In 1839 he exhibited *The Fighting Téméraire,* in 1840 *The Slave Ship,* and in 1842 *The Burial of Wilkie at Sea.* He continued to exhibit till 1850.

Turner, Sharon. b. at London, Sept. 24, 1768; d. there, Feb. 13, 1847. An English historian. His chief works are *History of England from the Earliest Period to the Norman Conquest* (4 vols., 1799–1805), and *History of England from the Norman Conquest to 1509* (1814–29).

Turner, W. J. [Full name, **Walter James Redfern Turner.**] b. at Melbourne, Australia, Oct. 13, 1889—. A British poet, critic, and novelist. He was music critic (1916 *et seq.*) of the *New Statesman and Nation,* drama critic (1919–23) of the London *Mercury,* literary editor (1920–23) of the London *Daily Herald,* and music critic (1923 *et seq.*) of the London *Daily Express.* Author of the volumes of poetry *The Hunter and Other Poems* (1916), *The Dark Fire* (1918), *The Dark Wind* (1920), *Paris and Helen* (1921), *In Time Like Glass* (1921), *Landscape of Cytherea* (1923), *Pursuit of Psyche* (1931), *Songs and Incantations* (1936), and *Selected Poems* (1939). His novels include *The Aesthetes* (1927) and *The Duchess of Popocatepetl* (1939). Among his critical and biographical works are *Music and Life* (1921), *Orpheus* (1926), *Beethoven* (1927), *Wagner* (1933), *Berlioz* (1934), and *Mozart* (1938).

Turnmill Street (tẽrn′mil). [Also, **Turnbull Street.**] A street in Clerkenwell, London, mentioned in Elizabethan plays, once notorious for low taverns and lodgings.

Turn of the Screw, The. A story of supernaturalism by Henry James, published in 1898 in his volume *The Two Magics.* The tale was dramatized as *The Innocents* (1950).

Turnus (tẽr′nus). In Roman legend, the king of the Rutulians, in Italy, at the period of the arrival of the Trojans under Aeneas.

Turpin (tẽr′pin; French, tür.paṅ). d. c794. An archbishop of Reims, long supposed to be the author of a history of Charlemagne (which is now known actually to have been composed in the 11th or 12th century).

Turpin (tẽr′pin), **Richard.** [Called **Dick Turpin.**] b. 1706; executed 1739. An English highwayman. The popular account of his famous ride to York on his mare "Black Bess" is not mentioned in the Newgate Calendar.

Turveydrop (tẽr′vi.drop), **Mr.** A fatuous character, a "model of deportment," in Dickens's *Bleak House.*

Tusculum (tus′kū.lum). In ancient geography, a city in Latium, Italy, situated in the Alban Hills ab. 13 mi. SE of Rome, near the modern Frascati. According to tradition its chief, Mamilius, joined Tarquinius Superbus against the Romans. Later it was allied with Rome. Under the republic and empire it contained villas of many Romans (Lucullus, Pompey, Brutus, and Cicero). It was destroyed near the end of the 12th century. Its ruins contain a Roman amphitheater and a theater.

Tusher (tush′ẽr), **Dr. Robert.** In Thackeray's novel *Henry Esmond,* the vicar of Castlewood. Through servility and flattery he strives to be liked by all who have the power to help or hurt him.

Tusher, Mrs. In Thackeray's novel *Henry Esmond,* the wife of Dr. Robert Tusher.

Tusher, Tom. In Thackeray's *Henry Esmond,* and briefly in *The Virginians,* an obsequious clergyman. He is the son of Dr. Robert Tusher, whom he succeeds as vicar of Castlewood, and from whom he derives the convenient ability to be most friendly with those who have it in their power to advance his career ("honest Tom never gave up a friend as long as he was the friend of a great man"). He eventually marries Beatrix Esmond, and through her influence finally becomes a bishop.

Tusitala (tö.sē.tä′lä). The Samoan name of **Stevenson, Robert Louis.**

Tussaud's Waxworks (tu.sōz′), **Madame.** A collection of waxworks representing notable persons and various curiosities, on the Marylebone Road, London, near Baker Street Station. It was established (1802) by a Swiss woman who had learned to model at Paris, and after an imprisonment during the French Revolution brought her collection to London (a few of the figures still on exhibition are said to have been modeled by her).

Tusser (tus′ẽr), **Thomas.** b. at Rivenhall, Essex, England, c1524; d. at London, about April, 1580. An English poet. He was a chorister of Saint Paul's, studied at Eton and was at King's College, Cambridge, spent ten years at court, and then settled on a farm in Suffolk. He wrote *A Hundred Good Points of Good Husbandry* (1557) and *Five Hundred Points of Good Husbandry United to as Many of Good Wiferie* (1573).

fat, fāte, fär, ȧsk, fãre; net, mē, hẽr; pin, pīne; not, nōte, mōve, nôr; up, lūte, pūll; ᴛн, then;

Tut-ankh-amen (töt.ängk.ä′mẹn). [Also: **Tutenkh-amon**; original name, **Tut-ankh-Aton** (-ä′tọn).] fl. c1355 B.C. A pharaoh of Egypt, of the XVIIIth dynasty. In childhood he was married to a daughter of Ikhnaton (or Akhenaton). He is thought to have been at his accession about 12 years of age, and to have ruled, nominally, for about six years. He is now among the best-known of all pharaohs only for the reason that his tomb, discovered in 1922 by Howard Carter, turned out to be the most instructive Egyptian find as yet made. All other known interments of Egyptian kings and queens of early times, whether in pyramids or in rock tombs in the Valley of the Kings, had been plundered. It is known that a like attempt was made on the tomb of Tut-ankh-amen, but was interrupted when the robbers had made off with only a few gold vessels. Carter uncovered the steps leading to his tomb, which, for all that it was certainly inferior to others, yielded a wealth of artistic treasure that dazzled the world of that day. Excavation of the tomb was completed in 1926. Most of the treasure was removed to the national museum at Cairo.

Tutivillus (tū.ti.vil′us). In medieval demonology, a demon who was said to collect all the fragments of words which the priests had skipped over or mutilated in the performance of the service, and to carry them to hell. He figures in various English mystery plays.

Tutor to Rutland (rut′lạnd). In Shakespeare's _3 Henry VI_, the companion of Rutland. He begs Clifford not to slay his charge.

Tvashtri (tväsh′trē). [Also, **Tvashtar** (-tär).] In later Hindu mythology, one of the Adityas, but in the ancient Vedic mythology the divine builder and artisan of the Hindu pantheon. He forged the thunderbolts of Indra and fashioned the drinking cup of the gods. He bestowed offspring and formed husband and wife for each other, even from the womb.

Twa Dogs, The. A poem (1786) by Robert Burns in which Caesar, the gentleman's dog ("Keepit for his honour's pleasure"), and Luath, the plowman's work collie, discuss their respective masters, deciding at the end of the poem that they are better off as dogs.

Tweedledum and Tweedledee (twē.dl.dum′; twē-dl.dē′). A phrase in a satirical squib by Byrom (1692–1763) alluding to the differences between the adherents of Handel and of Buononcini.

> Strange all this difference should be
> 'Twixt Tweedledum and Tweedledee.

Tweedledum and Tweedledee. Twin brothers of identical appearance in _Through the Looking-Glass_ by Lewis Carroll (C. L. Dodgson). They recite _The Walrus and the Carpenter_ to Alice, and fight a duel, armored with pots and pans, which is interrupted by a huge bird.

Tweedsmuir (twēdz′mūr), 1st Baron. Title of **Buchan**, Sir **John.**

Twelfth Day. See **Epiphany.**

Twelfth Night. An English secular celebration on January 5, the eve of Epiphany; not widely observed today. The festivities traditionally included the presentation of plays and it is from this custom that Shakespeare's _Twelfth Night_, written for such an occasion, takes its title.

Twelfth Night. [Full title, **Twelfth Night; or What You Will.**] A comedy by Shakespeare, first acted in 1602 and printed in the folio of 1623. The Olivia-Orsino and Viola-Sebastian plots are from the tale "Apolonius and Silla" in Barnabe Riche's _Farewell to the Militarie Profession_ (1581). Cinthio's _Hecatommithi_ has been suggested as Riche's source for this, but Belleforest's French version (1571) of a short novel by Bandello (1554) is more likely. The subplot of Malvolio, Maria, Sir Andrew Aguecheek, and Toby Belch is Shakespeare's own.

The Story. The Duke of Illyria, Orsino, is courting the wealthy countess Olivia with the aid of his page Cesario, who is really the beautiful Viola disguised as a man (and who has been shipwrecked on the coast of Illyria and thus separated from her twin brother, Sebastian). Olivia refuses the advances of Orsino and falls in love with Cesario (Viola), who has herself fallen in love with Orsino. In the household of Olivia, drunken Sir Toby Belch, Sir Andrew Aguecheek, the clown Feste, Fabian, and Maria plot to trick the stern and melancholy Malvolio by leading him to believe that Olivia is in love with him. They contrive that he shall discover a letter apparently written by Olivia (but actually penned by Maria) which will sustain his amorous hopes, and, as the letter suggests, he appears before the astonished Olivia in yellow stockings, crossed garters, and a constant smile. Because of his strange antics, he is believed insane and, in confinement as a madman, is subjected to further teasing by Feste until finally Olivia releases him. Meanwhile, Sebastian has arrived in Illyria, and Olivia, believing him to be the page, persuades him to marry her. After much confusion resulting from mistaking the twins, Orsino discovers his love for the lovely Viola (whom he too has hitherto thought to be a man) and decides to marry her.

Twelve-Pound Look, The. A comedy (1910) by J. M. Barrie about a pompous husband whose pleasure at his success in high society is spoiled by his wife's discontent with her marriage to him. She saves 12 pounds to buy a typewriter, so that she may obtain a job and live independently, but he realizes that he has been a fool before she actually goes away. However, the typewriter remains in their home as a warning of her restlessness, and he has learned to shudder at the thought of another "twelve-pound look."

Twelve Sonnets. Poems by Siegfried Sassoon, published in 1911.

Twelve Stories and a Dream. A collection of short stories by H. G. Wells, published in 1903.

Twentieth Century Harlequinade. A volume of poems by Edith Sitwell, published in 1916.

Twickenham (twik′ẹn.ạm). A municipal borough in SE England, in Middlesex, situated on the river Thames ab. 12 mi. SW of Waterloo Station, London. It has a river frontage of ab. 9 mi. on the Thames. Its manor belongs to the crown. Twickenham contains many villas, and was once the residence of Alexander Pope.

ḍ, d or j; ṣ, s or sh; ṭ, t or ch; ẓ, z or zh; o, F. cloche; ü, F. menu; ċh, Sc. loch; ṅ, F. bonbon.

Twin Rivals, The. A comedy by Farquhar, produced in 1702.

Twitcher (twich'ẽr), **Jemmy.** A treacherous highwayman in John Gay's *Beggar's Opera*. As a nickname the term was applied to John Montagu, 4th Earl of Sandwich, by the newspapers in the latter part of the 18th century on account of notable irregularities in his conduct.

Two Angry Women of Abingdon (ab'ing.dọn), **The.** A comedy (c1598) by Henry Porter, thought to have influenced Shakespeare in writing *The Merry Wives of Windsor*.

Two Drovers, The. A tale (1827) by Sir Walter Scott: one of the *Chronicles of the Canongate*.

Two Foscari (fōs'kä.rē), **The.** A tragedy (1821) by Byron. It deals with the Venetian doge, Foscari, who in doing his duty must sentence his own son to death.

Two Gentlemen of Verona (vẹ.rō'nạ), **The.** A comedy by Shakespeare, written in 1594 or 1595 and first printed in the folio of 1623. There is no record, however, of any performance until 1672, in the reign of Charles II. Parts of the story are identical with that of the shepherdess Filismena in Montemayor's *Diana*, translated in manuscript by Young (or Yonge) in 1582. Another possible source is *Felix and Philiomena* (staged in 1584, but now lost), which appears also to have been based on *Diana*.

The Story. Valentine, one of the two Veronese gentlemen of the title, travels to the court of Milan, where he falls in love with the Duke's daughter, Silvia. His friend Proteus, the other gentleman of Verona, pledges constant faithfulness to his beloved Julia before departing for Milan, but there he, too, falls in love with Silvia. Determined to have her for himself, he betrays the confidence of his friend by informing the Duke that Valentine is about to elope with his daughter. Valentine is thereupon banished and joins a band of robbers. Proteus continues his courting of Silvia, who rejects both him and her father's choice, the foolish Thurio. Meanwhile, Julia has arrived, disguised as a page, and offers her services to Proteus. When Silvia, in search of Valentine, flees her father's court, Proteus and his page follow her and rescue her from robbers. As Proteus is in the act of pressing (perhaps too ardently) his suit with Silvia, Valentine appears and, because Proteus is so overcome with remorse, even offers to yield Silvia to Proteus. However, at this point the page faints, Proteus recognizes her as Julia, and realizes that she, rather than Silvia, is his true love. The Duke and Thurio arrive, but because Thurio is too cowardly to fight Valentine for Silvia, the Duke gives her to the "gentleman of Verona."

Two Kings of Brentford (brent'fọrd), **the.** See **Brentford, the Two Kings of.**

Two Noble Kinsmen, The. A play attributed by some to Shakespeare on the basis of the Stationer's Register for 1634 (but this lists John Fletcher as coauthor with Shakespeare), probably written in the period 1612–13 (which would place it after *The Tempest*, usually considered Shakespeare's "last play," if, in fact, this work can be grouped with the body of Shakespeare's plays) and first staged c1619. It was published in 1634 in a good

text and included in 1679 in the second folio of Beaumont and Fletcher's plays. D'Avenant produced a version of it as *The Rivals* in 1664.

The Story. The principal source for the play was Chaucer's *Knight's Tale*, which tells the story of Palamon and Arcite ("the two noble kinsmen"), who fight for Thebes against Theseus, are captured and imprisoned, fall in love with Emilia (sister of Hippolyta, the wife of Theseus), and (now out of prison) are discovered by Theseus as they fight each other for the right to woo her. Theseus is at first disposed to condemn them both to death, but substitutes (at the behest of Hippolyta and Emilia) another sentence: Palamon and Arcite must within a month's time each secure three knights and then engage in a tourney for the hand of Emilia. The victor will marry her; the loser will be beheaded. In the tourney, Arcite (who has prayed to Mars) is victorious over Palamon (who has prayed to Venus), but just as Palamon is about to be executed word arrives that Arcite has been mortally hurt by a fall from his horse, and as he dies he surrenders Emilia to Palamon (whom Theseus now spares from death). The story differs from Chaucer's only in its subplot, wherein Palamon is enabled to escape from prison by the Jailer's Daughter, who has fallen in love with him, but who shortly removes herself from further important involvement in the play by going mad for fear her father may be punished for her action and Palamon may be devoured by wolves.

Two on a Tower. A novel by Thomas Hardy, published in 1882.

Two People. A novel by A. A. Milne, published in 1931.

Two Virtues, The. A four-act comedy (1913) by Alfred Sutro.

Two Years Ago. A novel by Charles Kingsley, published in 1857.

Twysden (twiz'dẹn), **Talbot.** In Thackeray's *The Adventures of Philip*, an insufferable snob who, despite his very limited means, seeks to make his home a much-frequented address by the great and powerful people of the day. He is immune to insult by those he considers to be his superiors in society, but extremely "resolute in not knowing unfortunate people."

Tybalt (tib'ạlt). In Shakespeare's *Romeo and Juliet*, the nephew of Lady Capulet. He is a quarrelsome young man who wishes to fight with Romeo upon discovering him in the street. When Romeo, knowing that Juliet is Tybalt's cousin, refuses to fight, Mercutio accepts the challenge and is mortally wounded by a thrust of Tybalt when Romeo interferes. Romeo in remorse attacks Tybalt and kills him. Tybalt is referred to as Prince or King of Cats in allusion to the tale of *Reynard the Fox*, where Tibert (or Tybalt) is Prince of Cats.

Tyburn (tī'bẽrn). In old London, a tributary of the Thames which rose in the clay beds at the foot of Hampstead Heath. It passed through what is now Regent's Park, and thence through Green Park, Buckingham Palace gardens, and St. James's Park to the Thames. There was a place of execution on the Tyburn near what is now the Marble Arch, Hyde Park.

---

fat, fāte, fär, ȧsk, fãre; net, mē, hẽr; pin, pīne; not, nōte, mŏve, nôr; up, lūte, pũll; ᴛʜ, then;

Tyburnia (tī.bėr′ni.ạ). A fashionable quarter of London, north of Hyde Park: named from the former Tyburn.

Tyburn Road (tī′bėrn). See **Oxford Street.**

Tyburn Tree. Before 1783, the public gallows in London.

Tyche (tī′kē). In Greek mythology, the goddess of fortune: corresponding to the Roman Fortuna.

Tydides (ti.dī′dēz). Diomedes, son of Tydeus.

Tyler (tī′lėr), **Wat** (or **Walter**). [Also, **Helier.**] Killed at Smithfield, London, June 15, 1381. The leader of a revolt of peasants in England in 1381. He is said to have killed a tax gatherer who insulted his daughter, and with Jack Straw to have led the men of Kent and Essex to London. While treating with Richard II at Smithfield, he was killed by Lord Mayor Walworth.

Tyndale or **Tindal** or **Tindale** (tin′dạl), **William.** b. in Gloucestershire, England, c1484; executed at Vilvorde, near Brussels, Belgium, Oct. 6, 1536. An English reformer, and translator of the Bible. He studied at Oxford and Cambridge, was ordained priest c1521, and was for a time chaplain and domestic tutor in the family of Sir John Walsh, Little Sodbury, Gloucestershire. Having exposed himself to persecution on account of his professions of sympathy with the new learning, he left England for the Continent in 1524, and after a visit to Luther at Wittenberg settled at Cologne, whence, however, he was presently expelled. He took refuge at Worms, where he published his octavo edition of the New Testament in 1525. His translation of the Pentateuch appeared at Marburg in 1530. His movements between 1526 and 1530 are uncertain; after 1530 he lived chiefly at Antwerp. He was arrested (May 24, 1535) at the insistence of Henry VIII, was imprisoned in the castle of Vilvorde, near Brussels, and after a protracted trial for heresy was strangled (Oct. 6, 1536), his body being burned at the stake. Among his other works are *Parable of the Wicked Mammon* (1528), *Obedience of a Christian Man* (1528), and *Practice of Prelates* (1530).

Tyndaridae (tin.dar′i.dē). Castor and Pollux, by one account the sons of Leda and Tyndareus.

Tynewald (tīn′wold), **The.** The independent bicameral parliament of the Isle of Man.

Typhon (tī′fọn). [Also, **Typhoeus** (tī.fē′ūs).] In Greek mythology, as Typhoeus, the personification of violent windstorms. As Typhon, a huge monster and father of monsters (e.g., the Chimera, the Nemean lion, the Sphinx, and others). He battled with Zeus, was overcome, and was buried by Zeus under Mount Etna (or in Tartarus).

Typhon. See also **Set.**

Typhoon. A short tale by Joseph Conrad, published in 1902.

Tyr (tir). [Also: **Tiu, Tiw.**] In Old Norse mythology, the god of war and victory; son of Odin. He is the same as the Teutonic Tiu or Tiw. He is represented with one hand, the other having been bitten off by the wolf Fenris, in whose mouth he

had placed it as a pledge. Tuesday is named for him.

Tyrannick Love, or the Royal Martyr. A tragedy in rhymed couplets by Dryden, produced in 1669 and printed in 1670.

Tyre (tīr), **Prince of.** See **Pericles.**

Tyrold (tir′ọld), **Sir Hugh.** The uncle of the heroine in Fanny Burney's *Camilla.*

Tyrrel (tir′ẹl), **Francis.** In Sir Walter Scott's novel *St. Ronan's Well,* the half-brother of Etherington, in love with Clara Mowbray. It has been thought that he was born a bastard, but it is discovered that he is, in fact, not only legitimate but also the rightful heir to the earldom of Etherington.

Tyrrel, Sir James. In Shakespeare's *Richard III,* a supporter of Richard. He is ordered to kill the Princes in the Tower, but hires two murderers to do the deed for him.

Tyrrell (tir′ẹl), **George.** b. at Dublin, Feb. 6, 1861; d. at Storrington, Sussex, England, July 15, 1909. An Irish theologian. Influenced by the writings of Newman, he entered the Roman Catholic Church in 1879, and in 1880 joined the Society of Jesus. His modernist views, however, especially as shown in his *Letter to a Professor of Anthropology* (afterward republished as *A Much Abused Letter*), brought him into collision with the order, and led to his expulsion in 1906. A little later his criticism of the Pope's encyclical *Pascendi Gregis* caused him to be virtually excommunicated.

Tyrrell or **Tyrel**, **Sir James.** Executed at Tower Hill, London, May 6, 1502. An English nobleman, remembered as the confessed murderer of Edward V and his brother Richard, Duke of York.

Tyrtaeus (tėr.tē′us). fl. in the middle of the 7th century B.C. A Greek elegiac poet of Sparta, said to have been a native of Attica. According to tradition, the Spartans who were at war with the Messenians were commanded by the oracle to take a leader from among the Athenians. The latter, not wishing to aid the Spartans, sent Tyrtaeus, a lame schoolmaster of no reputation; but by his songs he so inspired his followers that they obtained the victory. Fragments of his poems are extant.

Tyrwhitt (tir′it), **Thomas.** b. at London, March 29, 1730; d. there, Aug. 15, 1786. An English literary critic. He studied at Oxford, and was elected a fellow of Merton in 1755, but in 1762 abandoned his academic career in order to become clerk of the House of Commons. He resigned his clerkship in 1768, and devoted himself to literature. He wrote *Observations on Some Passages of Shakespeare* (1766), and prepared excellent editions of Chaucer's *Canterbury Tales* (1775–78) and Aristotle's *Poetics* (1794). He is chiefly known for his work in connection with the "Rowley Poems," which he demonstrated to be a forgery by Chatterton.

Tytler (tīt′lėr), **Patrick Fraser.** b. at Edinburgh, Aug. 30, 1791; d. at Great Malvern, England, Dec. 24, 1849. A Scottish historian. His chief work is a *History of Scotland* (9 vols., 1828–43). Among his other works are *Lives of Scottish Worthies* (1831–33) and *Progress of Discovery on the Northern Coasts of America* (1832).

---

d̦, d or j; ș, s or sh; ț, t or ch; z̦, z or zh; o, F. cloche; ü, F. menu; c̦h, Sc. loch; ṅ, F. bonbon.

U

Ubu Roi (ü.bü rwà). A satiric comedy (final version, 1896) by Alfred Jarry. Originally written (1888) when the author was 15 as a lampoon of his mathematics teacher, but expanded for the stage and played by actors wearing grotesque masks and speaking in false voices, its fantastic technique, anarchistic philosophy, and obscene language caused a riot at the first performance. *Ubu* is a travesty of the complacent bourgeois. The play was later much admired by the surrealists.

Udall (ū'dạl), **John.** [Also, **Uvedale.**] b. c1560; d. in the Marshalsea Prison, London, 1592. An English nonconformist, one of the writers for the Marprelate press. He published a very able pamphlet, *Diotrephes* (*The State of the Church of Englande*) in 1588, the first answer to John Bridges's *A Defence of the Government Established in the Church of England for Ecclesiastical Matters*, and was summoned before the Court of High Commission and finally deprived of his living at Newcastle and imprisoned at Southwark. He then printed a work called *A Demonstration of the Truth of that Discipline which Christ hath Prescribed.* This book was declared seditious, and he was sentenced to death in February, 1591. Efforts were made by Sir Walter Raleigh and others for his release, but just when they were successful he was taken ill in prison and died. He also wrote *The Key to the Holy Tongue*, the first Hebrew grammar in English, printed at Leiden in 1593.

Udall, Nicholas. [Also, **Uvedale.**] b. in Hampshire, England, 1505; d. 1556. An English dramatist and Latin scholar. He was headmaster at Eton in 1534, and of Westminster School (c1554–56). He was the author of the first extant English comedy, *Ralph Roister Doister*. In 1542 he published his translation of the *Apothegms* of Erasmus; he also translated (1542–45) Erasmus's paraphrase on Luke. His *Flowers for Latin-speaking, Selected and Gathered out of Terence and the Same Translated into English* (1533) was frequently printed as a grammar-school text for the use of young students of Latin, who were taught to embellish their style by choice bits taken out of the comedies of Terence. He was probably also the author of *Respublica*, an interlude.

udaller (ū'dạl.ẻr, ö'-). A proprietor of land in the north of Scotland in line from an old Norse grant. In Sir Walter Scott's novel *The Pirate*, Magnus Troil is "the Udaller of Jarlshof."

Udolpho (ū.dol'fō). See **Mysteries of Udolpho, The.**

Ulfilas (ul'fi.lạs). [Also: **Ulfila** (ul'fi.lạ), **Ulphilas, Wulfila.**] b. c311; d. at Constantinople, c381. Bishop to the Goths and translator of the Bible. His parents were Christians of Cappadocian origin. At the Synod of Antioch (341), he was consecrated bishop of the Arian Visigoths, who lived to the north of the lower Danube. In 348, persecuted and driven out of this region by Athanaric, Ulfilas and his people, with the permission of the emperor Constantius II, emigrated to Moesia, in the neighborhood of Nicopolis. From their new home they are consequently frequently called Moesogoths and their language Moesogothic. Ulfilas died at Constantinople, where he had gone to defend the doctrines of Arianism. He preached in Greek, Latin, and Gothic. He translated the Bible into Gothic from a Greek original, but is said to have omitted the Books of Kings. For his translation he invented a written alphabet by supplementing the Greek alphabet in necessary instances from the Gothic runes. His translation, which from internal evidence shows the work of several hands, and was, doubtless, in part done by others under his supervision, has been preserved only in a fragmentary form: in all there are the greater part of the Gospels, a large portion of the Epistles, and scraps of the Old Testament. The principal manuscript is the so-called Codex Argenteus of the University Library at Uppsala, Sweden, which is written in silver characters on a purple ground. Fragments of other manuscripts are preserved at Wolfenbüttel, Germany, and at Milan and Turin, Italy. The Gothic translation of the Bible is the oldest extant literary monument in the Germanic languages. It has been many times published.

Ulixes (ū.lik'sēz). See **Odysseus.**

Ullin's Daughter (ul'inz), **Lord.** See **Lord Ullin's Daughter.**

Ulpian (ul'pi.ạn) [Full Latin name, **Domitius Ulpianus.**] Murdered c228 A.D. A Roman jurist, of Phoenician descent. He held office from the time of Septimius Severus, was banished by Heliogabalus, and was a praetorian prefect under Alexander Severus; his reduction of the privileges of the Praetorian Guard eventually caused them to kill him. He wrote many commentaries and other legal works (*Ad edictum, Ad Sabinum*, and others), largely used in the *Digest*, forming about one half of that work.

Ulric (ul'rik). In Byron's *Werner*, the son of the hero.

Ulrica (ul'ri.kạ). In Sir Walter Scott's novel *Ivanhoe*, the witch who sets fire to the castle of Torquilstone and dies there.

Ulster Cycle (ul'stẻr). A cycle of Old Irish legend and romance, preserved in manuscripts dating from the 7th and 8th centuries, but depicting the Ireland and Irish heroes of the 1st century A.D. and the civilization and culture of pagan Ireland of centuries before that. It is so called because it celebrates the exploits of Ulster heroes. Cuchulain is the central figure. The *Tain Bo Cuailgne* is the principal text. Among many others are *The Wooing of Emer* (how Cuchulain won his wife), *Bricriu's Feast* (how Cuchulain won the champion's portion over the heroes of Ulster), *The Tragic Death of Aife's Only Son* (how Cuchulain unknowingly killed his own son), and the *Exile of the Sons of Usnach* (which tells the famous Deirdre story).

---

fat, fāte, fär, àsk, fāre; net, mē, hẻr; pin, pīne; not, nōte, mȯve, nôr; up, lūte, pull; ᴛʜ, then;

Ultima Thule (ul'ti.mạ thū'lē). See **Thule.**

Ulysses (ū.lis'ēz). In Shakespeare's *Troilus and Cressida,* one of the Greek commanders. He makes the speech on degree (I.iii) in an attempt to bring order to the Greeks. He also suggests that Achilles be made jealous of Ajax so as to get him into battle again. He goes with Troilus to see Cressida and tries to comfort him when Troilus sees her with Diomedes.

Ulysses. A poem by Alfred Tennyson.

Ulysses. A drama (1902) by Stephen Phillips.

Ulysses. A novel by James Joyce, published at Paris in 1922. Consisting of 18 sections based on correspondences to episodes in the Homeric myth, it presents the following counterparts among its chief characters: Leopold Bloom (Ulysses), Molly Bloom, his wife (Penelope), and Stephen Dedalus (Telemachus). The entire action takes place within the span of a single day (June 16, 1904) at Dublin. The novel, widely regarded as one of the greatest produced in the 20th century, is notable for its employment of the stream-of-consciousness technique on a massive scale. This method, in addition to other devices used by Joyce, influenced the technique of novelists including John Dos Passos, Virginia Woolf, Thomas Wolfe, and William Faulkner. *Ulysses* was banned from the U. S. from 1920 until 1933 on the ground of alleged obscenity; a federal court decision ended the ban after many years of litigation. The book begins at 8 A.M. Stephen Dedalus is shown as a young teacher living in an old tower above Dublin Bay with two friends. They are Buck Mulligan and Haines, dissipated and insecure medical students. At 10:00 Stephen gives a lesson at Mr. Deasy's School for Boys. He remembers his own awkward youth and unhappy life with his parents, and it is apparent that he is unhappy with his life and companions. At 11:00 Stephen walks along the beach, carried away by his own turbulent and lonely thoughts. At this point the work reverts to 8 A.M. when Leopold Bloom, the Ulysses of the novel, rises. He prepares breakfast for his wife Molly, meditating unhappily on her affair with Blazes Boylan. At 10:00 he goes to the post office, where he receives a letter from Martha Clifford, with whom he is carrying on an intrigue. After enjoying the sensuous leisure of a public bath, Bloom attends the funeral of Paddy Dignam with Stephen's father. While there Bloom remembers his own son, Rudy, who died at the age of eleven, and it is revealed that Bloom has been searching for a spiritual son ever since then. At noon he goes to a newspaper office to arrange for some advertisements, and his path is crossed by Stephen, who has quit his job at the school, and who invites all present to go to a local pub with Stephen. Stephen and Bloom do not meet here. At 1:00 Bloom has lunch in a pub, and at 2:00 goes to the public library to the newspaper files. There he passes Dedalus and his roommates discussing Shakespeare's private life, but again they do not meet. After wandering through the Dublin streets, Bloom has dinner at 4:00 with Stephen's father and uncle, and realizes that his wife, Molly, is entertaining her lover, Blazes, at his home. After more wandering Bloom arrives at the beach at about 8:00, and is the witness to the

exhibitionism of a young girl, Gerty MacDowell. (This corresponds to Homer's Nausicaa episode.) At 10:00 Bloom goes to a hospital to visit a friend who has just had a baby, and there he finally meets Stephen Dedalus. The young man is very rapidly becoming drunk, and Bloom decides to follow him to see that he does not get into any trouble. They go together to a brothel at midnight. Stephen gets into a fight with two soldiers when he leaves, and Bloom takes him home to care for him. There they drink chocolate and recall various parts of their lives; this section is written in the form of a catechism. Stephen goes home at last, and Bloom lies in bed, telling Molly about the day's adventures. He finally falls asleep, and Molly's thoughts, told in a stream-of-consciousness monologue, form one of the most famous parts of the book. She thinks about Blazes, her latest lover, about her childhood, courtship, and married life. The book ends on a high note with Molly asserting her belief in the passion of life by recalling her first surrender to love.

Ulysses. See also **Odysseus.**

Umbriel (um'bri.el). A dusky sprite in Alexander Pope's *Rape of the Lock.*

Una (ū'nạ). A "lovely ladie," the personification of truth, in Edmund Spenser's *Faerie Queene.* She is ultimately united to Saint George, the Red Cross Knight, who has slain the dragon in her behalf. In her wanderings she is followed by a lion who has been tamed by her gentleness and purity.

Unbearable Bassington (bås'ing.tọn), **The.** A novel by H. H. Munro (Saki), published in 1912.

Uncanny Stories. A collection of tales and short stories by May Sinclair, published in 1923.

Uncle Anyhow. A three-act comedy (1919) by Alfred Sutro.

Uncle Silas (sī'lạs). A novel of the supernatural by J. S. Le Fanu, published in 1864.

Uncle Toby (tō'bi). See **Toby, Uncle.**

"Uncle Tom" (tom). See **Balderstone, Thomas.**

Uncommercial Traveller, The. A volume of sketches by Charles Dickens, first published serially in his own magazine, *All the Year Round,* in 1860.

Undergrowth. A novel by Francis Brett Young, written in collaboration with his brother, Edward, and published in 1913.

Underhill (un'dėr.hil), **Evelyn.** b. in Staffordshire, England, 1874; d. at London, June 15, 1941. An English novelist and poet. Author of *The Grey World* (1904), *The Lost Word* (1907), and *The Column of Dust* (1909), novels; *Immanence* (1912) and *Theophanies* (1916), volumes of poetry; *Mysticism, a Study in the Nature and Development of Man's Spiritual Consciousness* (1911), *The Mystic Way, a Psychological Study in Christian Origins* (1913), *Practical Mysticism—A Little Book for Normal People* (1914), *Mysticism and War* (1915), *Essentials of Mysticism* (1920), *The Life of the Spirit and the Life of To-Day* (1922), *Mystics of the Church* (1925), *Concerning the Inner Life* (1926), *Man and the Supernatural* (1927), *The House of the Soul* (1929), *The Golden Sequence—A Fourfold Study of the Spiritual Life* (1932), *Mixed Pasture— Twelve Essays and Addresses* (1933), *The School*

ḍ, d or j; ṣ, s or sh; ṭ, t or ch; ẓ, z or zh· o. F. cloche; ü, F. menu; ċh, Sc. loch; ṅ, F. bonbon.

of Charity, Meditations on the Christian Creed (1934), *Worship* (1936), *The Spiritual Life—Four Broadcast Talks* (1937), *The Mystery of Sacrifice* (1938), and *Fruits of the Spirit* (1942).

Under Milkwood (milk'wŭd). "A Play for Voices" (1953) by Dylan Thomas, written in a combination of prose, poetry, and song. It shows the life of a Welsh town on a Spring day, starting before dawn and ending with the "rain of dusk" just before nightfall. Captain Cat is the central voice of the cast of 63 voices, and other important voices are those of the Reverend Eli Jenkins, Willy Nilly, and Polly Garter. It is linked to a work the author wrote some years earlier, *Quite Early One Morning.*

Under the Greenwood Tree. A novel by Thomas Hardy, published in 1872. It tells the story of Fancy Day, a young schoolmistress. She is loved by Dick Dewy but accepts an offer of marriage from the vicar, Arthur Maybold. However, she presently realizes that she really loves Dick, and they finally marry.

Under Western Eyes. A novel (1911) by Joseph Conrad.

Under-wood. The title under which Ben Jonson's miscellaneous poems were grouped in the folio of 1616. His famous tribute to Shakespeare was included with them.

Underwoods. A volume of miscellaneous poems by Robert Louis Stevenson, published in 1887. Stevenson adapted his title from Jonson's *Under-wood.*

Undine (ŭn.dē'nḝ). The title and heroine of a romance by Baron de la Motte Fouqué, published in German in 1811. Undine is a water spirit who is endowed with a soul by her marriage with a mortal. When her husband fell in love with another, Undine went home to the sea, but returned on his wedding night to deliver a death-bringing kiss. Paracelsus used the term "undine" generically to designate a class of water spirits who might obtain souls only by marrying mortals and bearing children.

Undying Fire, The. A novel (1919) by H. G. Wells.

Unfortunate Traveller, The. An adventure tale by Thomas Nash, published in 1594. It is the earliest example of the picaresque romance in English. Jacke Wilton is a page at the court of Henry VIII, and displays a great love for mischief. He travels through Europe, meeting many famous men of the day, such as Erasmus, Thomas More, and Luther. He falls in love with a courtesan in Italy, and runs off with her, but is captured. He lives through the plague, then returns to England, having finally married his Italian sweetheart.

Uniformity, Act of. In English history: **1.** An act of Parliament, passed in 1549, which provided for uniformity of religious service.
2. An act of Parliament passed in 1662. It obliged holders of church livings to be ordained by a bishop, to assent to the Book of Common Prayer, to renounce the Covenant, to declare the unlawfulness of bearing arms against the sovereign, and to make oath of canonical obedience. Many clergymen, the Nonconformists, resigned their benefices rather than sign.

Union of the Noble and Illustre Famelies of Lancastre and York (lang'k̬as.tẽr; yôrk), **The.** See under **Hall, Edward.**

unity. The principle by which a uniform tenor of story and propriety of representation is preserved in literary compositions; conformity in a composition to this principle; a reference to some one purpose or leading idea, or to the main proposition, in all the parts of a discourse or composition. The so-called Aristotelian law of *unity of time, of place, and of action* (called 'the unities') in a drama was the fundamental rule or general idea from which the French classical dramatic writers and critics derived, or to which they referred, all their practical rules for the construction of a drama. This law demanded that there should be no shifting of the scene from place to place, that the whole series of events should be such as might occur within the space of a single day, and that nothing should be admitted irrelevant to the development of the single plot.

> The author has not observed a single unity in his whole play. (Addison, *Sir Timothy Tittle.*)

> The writers of plays have what they call unity of time and place, to give a justness to their representation. (Steele, *Spectator,* No. 358.)

> The so-called unities of time and place are purely fictitious principles, to either of which it may be convenient to adhere in order to make the unity of an action more distinctly perceptible, and either of which may with equal propriety be disregarded in order to give the action probability.
> (A. W. Ward, *Introd. to Eng. Dram. Lit.*)

Universal Gallant, The. A comedy (1735) by Henry Fielding.

University College. 1. The oldest college of Oxford University, established in 1280. (There is a legend that it was founded in 872 by King Alfred.)
2. A nonsectarian London college founded in 1828. It is now part of the University of London.

University of Dublin. See **Trinity College.**

University Wits. A group of young writers of the Elizabethan period who had studied at either Oxford or Cambridge. The group, mainly dramatists and pamphleteers, included Marlowe, Nash, Greene, Lodge, and Harvey.

Unknown Goddess, The. A volume of verse (1925) by Humbert Wolfe.

Unnatural Combat, The. A play by Philip Massinger, acted c1619 and printed in 1639. It is a horror tragedy dealing with a theme of incest forced by a father on his daughter.

Unreason, Abbot of. See **Abbot of Misrule.**

Unrest. A novel by Warwick Deeping, published in 1916.

Unsocial Socialist, An. A novel (1883) by George Bernard Shaw.

Unto This Last. A series of essays on political economy by John Ruskin, published serially in the *Cornhill Magazine* in 1860 (but publication was abruptly halted before the end by Thackeray, then editor of the magazine, as a result of the hostility of reviewers and many readers to the views Ruskin was espousing). Ruskin himself considered the work

---

fat, fāte, fär, ȧsk, fãre; net, mē, hẽr; pin, pīne; not, nōte, mŏve, nôr; up, lūte, púll; ᴛʜ, then;

to be the "truest, rightest, most serviceable" thing he ever wrote.

Upanishads (ŏ.pan'i.shadz, ö.pä'ni.shädz). Philosophical treatises or metaphysical commentaries attached to the *Brahmanas*. They are probably the oldest speculative treatises of the Hindus; the oldest is believed to antedate 500 B.C. The word means "sitting close to" and refers to a group sitting around a teacher. The *Upanishads* discuss the origin of the universe, the nature of deity, the nature of the soul, and the relationship between spirit and matter. Their fundamental tenet is that the inner self of the individual should be identified with the universal self or soul. The ancient Vedic literature first became known outside of India through the *Upanishads*. They were translated first (1657) from Sanskrit into Persian, then the most widely read language of the East, and thus became generally accessible. Twelve of them were translated by Friedrich Max Müller, with introductions and notes, in the *Sacred Books of the East*.

Upon Julia's Clothes (jŏl'yăz). A poem (1648) by Robert Herrick in which he speaks of the beauty of his beloved when she dresses in her silks:

> Whenas in silks my Julia goes,
> Then, then, methinks how sweetly flows
> The liquefaction of her clothes.

Urania (ū.rā'ni.ą). In Greek mythology, the Muse of astronomy and celestial forces.

Uranus (ū'rą.nus, ū.rā'nus). In Greek mythology, the god and personification of the sky. He was both son and consort of Gaea or Ge (the earth), and by her the father of the Titans, Cyclopes, and others. He feared his children and confined them in Tartarus; but on the instigation of Gaea, Cronus, the youngest of the Titans, overthrew and dethroned him.

Urchard (ėr'kạrd, -kärd), Sir **Thomas**. See **Urquhart, Sir Thomas**.

Urfé (dür.fā), Honoré d'. b. at Marseilles, 1567; d. in Spain, June 1, 1625. A French writer. He is principally remembered as the author of *L'Astrée* (1610–27), a very long novel of pastoral setting and complex love affairs entailing long analyses of tender passion. The style became the fashion of the age in the novel and in drama.

Urfey (dėr'fi), Thomas d'. See **D'Urfey, Thomas**.

Urganda (ėr.gan'dą). A fairy and enchantress in the medieval French and Spanish romances of *Amadis of Gaul*.

Ur-Hamlet (ur'ham''lẹt). The name given by scholars to a lost pre-Shakespearian play. (Ur means "source.") The existence of such a play is shown by such evidence as a reference in Greene's *Menaphon* (1589), a performance in June, 1594, which was not a new play, Thomas Lodge's allusion to the Ghost in 1596, and in Dekker's *Satiromastix* (1601), where a character says "My name's Hamlet revenge" and mentions Paris Garden, where the old *Hamlet* probably was acted in 1596. Possibly this play was by Kyd; some scholars maintain that it is merely a bad version of the final play.

Uriah (ū.rī'ą). [Also, **Urias** (ū.rī'ạs].) In the Bible, a Hittite officer in the army of David; husband of Bathsheba. David ordered Joab, his general, to secure Uriah's death by abandoning him in the heart of battle. 2 Sam. xi.

Uriah Heep (hēp). See **Heep, Uriah**.

Uriel (ū'ri.ẹl). One of the seven archangels of Christian legend. He is spoken of in 2 Esdras as the good angel. He has been conceived to be an angel of light, and his station to be in the sun. He is introduced by Milton in *Paradise Lost*, and by Longfellow in the *Golden Legend*.

Urizen (ūr'i.zẹn). In the mystical poems of William Blake, a puritanical giant, who is identified with some aspects of the Old Testament Jehovah.

Urn-Burial. See **Hydriotaphia**.

Urquhart (ėr'kạrt, -kärt), Sir **Thomas**. [Also, **Urchard**.] b. 1611; d. 1660. A Scottish Royalist, author, and translator. He possessed estates in Cromarty, was educated at King's College, Aberdeen, and traveled, having a good knowledge of foreign tongues. He was declared a rebel by Parliament, took arms on the king's side, fought in the battle of Worcester, and, though sent a prisoner to London, had some liberty. He escaped, and died abroad (during a fit of laughter, it is said, on hearing of the Restoration). He published several works, but is best known for his spirited but not literal translation of Rabelais (1653, 1693), completed by P. A. Motteux.

Ursula (ėr'sụ.lą), Saint. d. possibly in the 3rd or the 5th century. In Christian legend, a British saint and martyr who (with 11,000 other virgins) was said to have been put to death by an army of Huns near Cologne. In the first part of the 12th century, in digging foundations for new walls, the citizens of Cologne found a large number of bones in the cemetery of the old Roman town of Colonia Agrippina. These were announced by Elizabeth of Schönau, a visionary nun, as the relics of the 11,000 virgins, and for many years were so venerated. Bones of men and children, however, were found among them, and the remains are now considered to be those of Roman colonists. The Church of Saint Ursula of Cologne is, nevertheless, still visited by thousands of believers. One matter-of-fact explanation of the 11,000 reduces them to one in the person of a Saint "Undecemilla." Although the version of the legend put forth by Geoffrey of Monmouth is one of the best known, it is so filled with conflicts and other obvious errors as to be of little use in establishing a basis of fact concerning Ursula's life. In order to account for all the details in the legend, some scholars have advanced the probability that there were two separate massacres, one in the 3rd century and one in the 5th, and that later accounts have drawn from both.

Ursula. In Shakespeare's *Much Ado About Nothing*, one of Hero's gentlewomen.

Ursula Suddlechop (sud'l.chop). See **Suddlechop, Ursula**.

Urswick (ėrz'wik), **Christopher**. b. at Furness, England, 1448; d. March 25, 1522. An English cleric and diplomat who held several minor ecclesiastical positions while an adviser to Henry VII, and was elected (1495) dean of Windsor.

Urswick, Christopher. In Shakespeare's *Richard III*, a priest who is sent with a message to Richmond (IV.v).

ḍ, d or j; ṣ, s or sh; ṭ, t or ch; ẓ, z or zh; o, F. cloche; ü, F. menu; ċh, Sc. loch; ṅ, F. bonbon.

usage. The established or customary mode of employing a particular word, phrase, or construction; current locution.

The more closely one looks into usage, the firmer must be one's conviction that its adjudications have greatly more of freedom and elasticity than find countenance with mere word-fanciers.
(F. Hall, *Modern English*, Preface.)

Usher (ush'ẽr), **James.** See **Ussher, James.**

Usk (usk), **Thomas.** b. at London; executed at Newgate, London, 1388. An English poet and politician. Usk was an ardent supporter of John de Northampton while the latter was attempting to reform London city government and morals during his term as mayor. When de Northampton fell with the defeat of John of Gaunt's party and was imprisoned for sedition, Usk betrayed him. Later (1388) Usk was condemned to death for his treacheries Author of *The Testament of Love*, a prose allegory in which Usk tries to justify his conduct. The work was formerly believed to have been written by Chaucer, but later scholarship correctly attributed it to Usk.

Usnach (ûsh'nạ). [Also, **Usnech** (-nẹ).] In Old Irish legend, a famous warrior of Ulster. He was the father of three even more famous sons, who eloped with Deirdre to Scotland and were treacherously slain on their return. Of these Naoise was the lover and husband of Deirdre. A hill (modern Usney) in the center of Ireland is named for Usnach.

Ussher (ush'ẽr), **James.** [Also, **Usher.**] b. at Dublin, Jan. 4, 1581; d. at Reigate, Surrey, England, March 21, 1656. A British prelate, theologian, and scholar. He took the degree of M.A. at Trinity College, Dublin, in 1600, was regius professor of divinity there (1607–20), and chancellor of Saint Patrick's Cathedral, Dublin, in 1605, was appointed bishop of Meath in 1621, and became archbishop of Armagh and primate of Ireland in 1625. He was on a visit to England at the outbreak of the English Civil War, and took sides with Charles I, with the result that he lost nearly all his property in Ireland, with the exception of his library. He was a preacher to the Society of Lincoln's Inn, London, from 1647 until shortly before his death. His most notable work is *Annales Veteris et Novi Testamenti* (1650–54), in which he proposed a scheme of Biblical chronology, long printed in marginal notation in the Authorized Version, that determined the date of the Creation to be 4004 B.C. Later investigations disproving his chronology have tended unfairly to cast a shadow over his other works, which display a profound scholarship.

Utgard-Loki (öt'gärd-lō'kẹ). In Norse mythology, the chief of the giants. His dwelling place was Utgard.

Uther and Igraine (ū'thẽr; i.grān'). A novel by Warwick Deeping, published in 1903 and issued in revised form in 1927.

Uther Pendragon (pen.drag'ǫn). A legendary king of Britain; reputed father of King Arthur of the Round Table. Pendragon was a title, meaning "chief dragon" (i.e. "chief war leader"), which was used by a number of ancient British and Welsh chieftains who claimed primacy over lesser chieftains, and sovereignty over those peoples. It is said that their standards displayed the semblance of a dragon. Nothing really is known of Uther (probably a historical person whose story has been overlaid by myth and legend), but he is represented as the father by Igerna of Arthur.

Utilitarianism. A philosophical work (1863) by John Stuart Mill, in which he introduced and explained the system of ethics since associated with him.

Utopia (ụ.tō'pi.ạ). A political romance by Sir Thomas More, published in Latin in 1516; so called from an imaginary island, the seat of an ideal commonwealth. The name itself means "no place." The original title was *De Optimo Reipublicae Statu, deque Nova Insula Utopia*. It was translated in 1551 by Ralph Robinson, and by Bishop Gilbert Burnet in 1683. The name Utopia has given rise to the adjective "utopian" with the meaning of "impracticable" or "ideal," especially as applied to schemes for the advancement of social conditions. Utopian literature, a genre widely used for the expression of social criticism, occurs in the literatures of many peoples throughout the ages.

Utrecht (ū'trekt), **Peace of.** [Also, **Treaty of Utrecht.**] A peace concluded in 1713, through several separate treaties, between France on one side and Great Britain, the Netherlands, Prussia, Savoy, and Portugal on the other, and acceded to by Spain. With the subsequent treaties of Rastatt and Baden (1714), it put an end to the War of the Spanish Succession. Philip V (of Bourbon) was confirmed as king of Spain (furthering England's desire to see that the crowns of France and Spain should never be united) and France recognized the Protestant succession in England. Prussia was recognized as a kingdom. Great Britain received Newfoundland, Nova Scotia, and other areas in North America from France, and Gibraltar and Minorca from Spain, with the right to send African slaves to Spanish America. The Spanish Netherlands, Sardinia, Milan, and Naples were ceded to Austria. Savoy received Sicily from Spain. Prussia received Neuchâtel and part of Gelderland, and renounced its claims to Orange. Portugal received additional territory in South America.

Uvedale (ūv'dāl). See **Udall.**

Uzziel (u.zī'ẹl, uz'i.ẹl). One of the principal angels (his name means "strength of God"). Milton refers to him in *Paradise Lost* (Book IV) as the angel next in power to Gabriel.

---

fat, fāte, fär, ȧsk, fãre; net, mē, hẽr; pin, pīne; not, nōte, möve, nôr; up, lūte, pull; ᴛн, then;

Vachell (vă'chel), **Horace Annesley.** b. at Sydenham, Kent, England, Oct. 30, 1861; d. at Bath, England, Jan. 10, 1955. An English novelist, playwright, and essayist. Among his novels are *Romance of Judge Ketchum* (1894), *Quinney's* (1914; dramatized 1915), *Whitewash* (1920), *Vicar's Walk* (1933), and *Quinney's for Quality* (1938). His plays include *Her Son* (1907; also published as a novel), *Jelf's* (1912), *Searchlights* (1915), *The Case of Lady Camber* (1915), *Who Is He* (1915), *Fishpingle* (1916), *Count X* (1921), and *Plus Fours* (1923). He is author also of the essay collections *My Vagabondage* (1936) and *Little Tyrannies* (1940), and of *A Writer's Autobiography* (1937).

vade mecum (vā'dē mē'kum). A book or other thing that a person carries with him as a constant companion; a pocket companion; a manual; a handbook. "One boracho or leathern bottle of Tours . . . Panurge filled for himself, for he called that his vademecum." (Urquhart, tr. of Rabelais.)

Vainlove (vān'luv). In William Congreve's comedy *The Old Bachelor*, a capricious rake.

Vaishyas (vīsh'yaz). [Also, **Vaisyas**.] In the Sanskrit designation of castes, the third caste, the folk, ranking below the Brahmans, or priests, and the Kshatriyas, or warriors.

Valence (val'ens), **Sir Aymer De.** In Sir Walter Scott's novel *Castle Dangerous*, a haughty young nobleman, but withal brave and courteous, who serves as deputy to the governor of Douglas Castle.

Valentine (val'en.tīn). In Shakespeare's *Titus Andronicus*, a kinsman of Titus.

Valentine. In Shakespeare's *Twelfth Night*, a gentleman attending on Orsino, Duke of Illyria.

Valentine. In Shakespeare's *Two Gentlemen of Verona*, one of the "two gentlemen." He is the lover of Silvia.

Valentine. A light-hearted spendthrift in John Fletcher's *Wit without Money*.

Valentine. A young gentleman truly and deeply in love with Christina in Wycherley's *Love in a Wood*. He almost loses her to the rake Ranger.

Valentine. The principal character, a young rake in love with Angelica in Congreve's *Love for Love*. Betterton was famous in this part, with Mrs. Bracegirdle as Angelica.

Valentine. A romantic young lover in Goldsmith's comedy *The Good-natured Man*. He falls in love with Olivia, when sent to get his sister from France, and brings her home as his sister.

Valentine and Orson (ôr'son). A romance of the Charlemagne cycle, which was written during the reign of Charles VIII, and first printed in 1495 at Lyons. Valentine and Orson were twins, born in a forest. Orson was carried off and reared by a bear, and became rough and uncouth. Valentine was taken by his uncle, King Pepin, and grew up a courtier and knight. The point of the story lies in the affinity between twins, in that the two (knight and bear boy) recognize each other in the forest years later.

Valentine Bulmer (bul'mer). See **Bulmer, Valentine**.

Valentinian (val.en.tin'i.an, -tin'yan). A tragedy by John Fletcher, written c1612, produced before 1618, and printed in 1647. It is based upon Urfé's *Astrée* (published 1610), and probably also upon Procopius's *De Bello Vandalico*. Although the play takes its name from Valentinian, the Roman emperor, the central characters are Maximus and Aëcius, two friends whose loyalty to one another is strained by the fact that Valentinian has raped Lucina, Maximus's wife, and she has killed herself, causing Maximus to vow vengeance upon Valentinian, whereas his friend, although a critic of Valentinian, puts loyalty to his ruler first.

Vale of Avalon (av'a.lon). See **Avalon**.

vale of tears. See under **Baca, Valley of**.

Valère (và.ler'). The principal character in Susannah Centlivre's play *The Gamester*.

Valeria (va.lir'i.a). In Shakespeare's *Coriolanus*, a friend of Virgilia.

Valeria. A girl with a mania for biological research in Susannah Centlivre's *The Basset-Table*.

Valerian (va.lir'i.an). The husband of Saint Cecilia, who appears with her as a character in Chaucer's *Second Nun's Tale*.

Valerio (va.lir'i.ō). A young gallant who has been secretly married to a beautiful but poor gentlewoman in George Chapman's *All Fools, or All Fools but the Fool*.

Valerius (va.lir'i.us). In *The Two Noble Kinsmen*, a Theban nobleman.

Valéry (và.lā.rē), **Paul Ambroise.** b. at Sète, France, Oct. 30, 1871; d. at Paris, Aug. 20, 1945. A French poet and philosopher. His books of poetry are *La Jeune Parque* (1917), *Odes* (1920), *Le Cimetière marin* (1920; Eng. trans., *The Graveyard by the Sea*, 1932), *Album de vers anciens* (1920), and *Charmes* (1922). His philosophical papers include *Introduction à la méthode de Léonardo da Vinci* (1895; Eng. trans., 1929), *La Soirée avec M. Teste* (1896; Eng. trans., *An Evening with Mr. Teste*, 1925), *Eupalinos* (1923), *Variété* (5 vols., 1924, 1929, 1936, 1938, 1944; Eng. trans., *Variety*, 1927, and *Variety, Second Series*, 1938), and *Regards sur le monde actuel* (1931; Eng. trans., *Reflections on the World of Today*, 1948). Educated at Montpellier for the law, he moved to Paris in 1891 and joined Stéphane Mallarmé's group, but renounced poetry after some early successes. He married Mallarmé's daughter, and supported his family by work at the war ministry (1897–1900) and at the Havas news agency. In 1917 he returned to poetry with the publication of *La Jeune Parque* and from that time until his death was a major literary figure.

---

d̠, d or j; s̠, s or sh; t̠, t or ch; z̠, z or zh; o, F. cloche; ü, F. menu; ch, Sc. loch; n̊, F. bonbon.

Valhalla (val.hal′ạ). [Also, **Walhalla**.] In Old Norse mythology, the abode of Odin in Asgard, a warrior's paradise to which only those went who were slain in battle. Its roof was made of polished shields upheld by spears. Troops of heroes issued daily from its 540 doors to delight themselves in battle, and returned to drink and feast and hear heroic tales at evening, when Odin was the host and the Valkyries bore about the mead horns.

Vali (vä′lē). In Old Norse mythology, one of the high gods; a son of Odin. He was born for the purpose of killing Hoder, who killed Balder. He is construed as a personification of light, especially of the light that lingers as spring days grow longer.

Valiant-for-Truth (val′yạnt.fọr.trŏth′). One of Christian's companions in the second part of John Bunyan's *Pilgrim's Progress*.

Valjean (vȧl.zhäṅ), **Jean**. The principal character in Victor Hugo's *Les Misérables*.

Valkyries (val.kir′iz, val′ki.riz). [Also: **Valkyrs**; German, **Walküren**; Old Norse, **Valkyrja**.] In Old Norse mythology, the company of handmaidens of Odin, usually said to number nine, though the number varies. They were believed to serve at the banquets at Valhalla, but are best known as "the choosers of the slain," being sent forth by Odin to every battle. They ride through the air, and with their spears designate which heroes shall fall, afterward conducting the slain to Valhalla. In the *Volsunga Saga* Brynhild, the daughter of Odin, is one of them, as also in Wagner's *Die Walküre*.

Valley of Humiliation. The scene of the contest between Christian and Apollyon, in John Bunyan's *Pilgrim's Progress*.

Valley of the Shadow of Death. The valley traversed by Christian after his contest with Apollyon in John Bunyan's *Pilgrim's Progress*. Bunyan took the name from Psalms, xxiii.4.

Vanbrugh (van′bru), Dame **Irene**. b. at Heavitree, Exeter, Devonshire, England, Dec. 2, 1872; d. at London, Nov. 30, 1949. An English actress; wife of Dion Boucicault (1859–1929), son of the dramatist, whom she married in 1901.

Vanbrugh (van.brö′, van′bru), Sir **John**. b. 1664; d. at London, March 26, 1726. An English dramatist and architect. He studied the arts in France and spent some time (1690–92) in French prisons as an English spy. After 1697 he joined William Congreve in the management of a theater which was not successful; the Haymarket theater which he built (1705) was architecturally imposing but acoustically poor. He was comptroller of the board of works (1702–12, 1715) and from 1704 to his death was Clarenceux king of arms, chief of the College of Heralds for South England (from 1715 to 1718 he acted as Garter king of arms), but his ridicule of the heraldic procedures in *Aesop* (1697) caused him to be disliked by the heralds. He built Castle Howard in Yorkshire (1701–14), a leading example of the Palladian style of architecture; Blenheim Palace in Oxfordshire (1705 *et seq.*), a sprawling mansion built as a tribute to the Duke of Marlborough (and completed without Vanbrugh's aid by the Duchess of Marlborough, who disliked him); and several other country houses. Vanbrugh wrote *The Relapse* (1697), a sequel to

Colley Cibber's *Love's Last Shift*; *Aesop* (in two parts, published in 1697), an adaptation of Edmond Boursault's French play; *The Provok'd Wife* (1697), a play giving rise to Jeremy Collier's allegation that all Vanbrugh's heroes were libertines and beginning a controversy in which Vanbrugh did not hold his own; *The Pilgrim* (1700); *The False Friend* (1702); *The Confederacy* (1705); *A Journey to London* (unfinished, but completed by Cibber as *The Provok'd Husband*, 1728); and others. Unlike Congreve's plays, where the comedy comes out of witty observation of manners, Vanbrugh's comedy relies largely on devices. Although his work occasionally has a moral quality, as in *The Confederacy* (based upon Dancourt's *Les Bourgeoises à la Mode*), for the most part it displays the immoral qualities of the Restoration. His last plays deteriorated into farce, generally based on French models.

Vance (vans), **Joseph**. See **Joseph Vance**.

Vancouver (van.kö′vẹr), **George**. b. c1758; d. near London, May 10, 1798. A British navigator. He served under Captain James Cook in his second and third voyages, and commanded an expedition to the Pacific (1791–95), on which he explored the Strait of Juan de Fuca, the Gulf of Georgia, and the shores of Vancouver Island, which he circumnavigated. He left a narrative of his voyage which was published by his brother under the title *Voyage of Discovery to the North Pacific Ocean and Round the World* (3 vols. and atlas, 1798).

Vandals (van′dạlz). An ancient Germanic tribe which first migrated from the Baltic region into Hungary as early as 170 A.D. In the first half of the 5th century they ravaged Gaul, Spain, and N Africa. They took Carthage (c435) and in 455 they sacked Rome itself, with great damage to the accumulated treasures of art and literature (whence the term "vandalism"). The Vandals founded a kingdom in Africa, with Carthage as its capital, which took in also the great islands of the W Mediterranean, including Sicily. In 533 the Romans captured Carthage, and the Vandals, as an ethnic unit, vanished from history.

Vanderdecken (van′dẹr.dek.ẹn). The captain of the Flying Dutchman in the English version of that legend. He was condemned to sail round the Cape of Good Hope forever.

Van Diemen's Land (van dē′mẹnz). A former name of Tasmania. Abel Tasman (for whom it is now named), its discoverer in 1642, named the island for the sponsor of his expedition, Anton van Diemen, governor general of the Dutch East India Company's settlements.

Vandome (van.dōm′). A young man in love with Countess Marcellina in George Chapman's *Monsieur D'Olive*.

Van Druten (van drö′tẹn), **John** (**William**). b. at London, June 1, 1901—. An English playwright. Author of the plays *Young Woodley* (1928; published as a novel, 1929), *Diversion* (1928), *After All* (1929), *London Wall* (1931), *There's Always Juliet* (1931), *Behold We Live* (1932), *The Distaff Side* (1933), *Flowers of the Forest* (1934), *Leave Her to Heaven* (1940), *Old Acquaintance* (1940), *The Damask Cheek* (1942; in collaboration with Lloyd Morris), *The Voice of the Turtle* (1943), *I Remember*

Mama (1944), *The Druid Circle* (1947), *Bell, Book, and Candle* (1950), and *I've Got Sixpence* (1952). He wrote the autobiographical *The Way to the Present* (1938).

Vandyke or **Van Dyck** (van.dĭk'), Sir **Anthony.** b. at Antwerp, Belgium, March 22, 1599; d. at London, Dec. 9, 1641. A Flemish painter, best known as a portraitist. He was a pupil of Rubens, whom he assisted in some of his greatest compositions. He was in England (1620–21), in Italy (1621–25), later at Antwerp, and after 1632 chiefly in England. In 1632 he was knighted and made court painter to Charles I. Among his best-known works are *Crucifixions* (especially one at Mechelen), *Elevation of the Cross* (Courtrai), *Saint Augustine in Ecstasy* (Antwerp), portraits of Charles I and members of his family, and of various other prominent Englishmen of the time.

Vanessa (va.nes'a). Jonathan Swift's poetical name for his friend Esther Vanhomrigh; composed of the first syllable of her surname and Essa for Esther.

Vanhomrigh (van.um'ri), **Esther.** b. Feb. 14, 1690; d. 1723. The Vanessa of Jonathan Swift's *Cadenus and Vanessa* (1712–13; published 1726). He made her acquaintance in 1708. She became his pupil, fell in love with him, and followed him to Ireland in 1714. She is said to have died of a broken heart because of his failure to return her love (although he was a devoted friend).

Vanir (vä'nir). [Old Norse, **Vanr.**] In Old Norse mythology, a class of gods originally at war with the Aesir, but later received by them into Asgard. Njörd, Frey, and Freya were Vanir, and usually Nerthus is numbered as one of them. They were all fertility gods, who later were construed as weather deities and protectors of crops. The mythical war between the Aesir and the Vanir probably had its origin in the subordination of an older fertility cult to the newer cult of Odin.

Vanity Fair. A fair described in John Bunyan's *Pilgrim's Progress*. It was held by Beelzebub, Apollyon, and Legion in the town of Vanity, and at the fair kingdoms, honors, titles, and all sorts of pleasures could be bought. The phrase is often used as a synonym for the present world and its worldliness.

Vanity Fair. A novel by William Makepeace Thackeray, which appeared (1847–48) in monthly parts. A novel of English society in the early years of the 19th century, it is generally considered one of the best of all English novels; the amoral heroine, Becky Sharp, is probably Thackeray's greatest creation. Its title is taken from the fair in Bunyan's *Pilgrim's Progress*.

Vanity of Human Wishes, The. A poem by Samuel Johnson, published in 1749, modeled upon the *Tenth Satire* of Juvenal, and considered one of the most important of Johnson's poetical works.

Vanolis (va.nō'lis), **Bysshe.** Pseudonym of **Thomson, James** (1834–82).

vapours. 1. A hectoring or bullying style of language or conduct, adopted by ranters and swaggerers with the purpose of bringing about a real or mock quarrel.

They are at it [quarrelling] still, sir; this they call vapours. (Ben Jonson, *Bartholomew Fair.*)

2. A disease of nervous debility in which strange images seem to float hazily before the eyes, or appear as if real; hence, hypochondriacal affections; depression of spirit; dejection; spleen; "the blues": a term much affected in the 18th century, but now rarely used.

Some call it the fever on the spirits, some a nervous fever, some the vapours, and some the hysterics. (Fielding, *Amelia.*)

Caused by a dearth of scandal, should the vapours Distress our fair ones—let them read the papers. (Garrick, Prol. to Sheridan's *School for Scandal.*)

But really these thick walls are enough to inspire the vapours if one never had them before.
(Miss Burney, *Cecilia.*)

Varden (vär'den), **Dolly.** A notable character in Dickens's *Barnaby Rudge;* daughter of Gabriel Varden, a prosperous locksmith. She is a pert and attractive girl.

Varden, Gabriel. In Dickens's *Barnaby Rudge*, a locksmith, the father of Dolly.

Varina (va.rī'na). A name given by Jonathan Swift to Miss Waring, the sister of an old college friend.

variorum (vär.i.ō'rum). Denoting an edition of some work in which the notes of different commentators are inserted: as, a *variorum* edition of Shakespeare.

Varney (vär'ni), **Richard.** The villainous master of the horse to the Earl of Leicester, in Sir Walter Scott's *Kenilworth.*

Varrius (var'i.us). In Shakespeare's *Antony and Cleopatra*, a friend of Pompey.

Varrius. In Shakespeare's *Measure for Measure*, a friend of the Duke. The Duke merely speaks to him, and he was not listed in the folio of 1623.

Varro (var'ō). In Shakespeare's *Julius Caesar*, a servant of Brutus.

Varro. In Shakespeare's *Timon of Athens*, two servants of a usurer, who sends them to collect a debt from Timon. They are both called by the name of their master (who does not appear).

Varuna (vä'rö.na). In Sanskrit, literally, the encompasser of the universe; in the *Rig-Veda*, creator and supreme god of the cosmos. To him belong especially the waters, the night, and the west. He is associated with the moon in E Bengal, and is widely worshiped by fishermen. At marriages he is invoked for fertility. He is the noblest character of the Vedic pantheon. He is both a punisher and forgiver of sins, but is merciful even to the guilty.

Vasari (vä.zä'rē), **Giorgio.** b. at Arezzo, Italy, July 30, 1511; d. at Florence, Italy, June 27, 1574. An Italian architect, painter, and writer on art. He painted many pictures at Florence, Rome, and elsewhere, and constructed part of the Uffizi Palace. He is best known from his biographies of artists (*Vite de' più eccellenti architetti, pittori, e scultori italiani*, 1550; enlarged 1568).

Vasco da Gama (väsh'kö da gu'ma). See **Gama, Vasco da.**

Vashti (vash'tī). In the Bible, the proud queen of Ahasuerus, mentioned in the Book of Esther.

---

d̦, d or j; ş, s or sh; ț, t or ch; z̧, z or zh; o, F. cloche; ü, F. menu; ch̓, Sc. loch; ṅ, F. bonbon.

Vathek (vath′ek). An Oriental romance by William Beckford, published in 1787. Its title is taken from the name of the hero. It was written in French; and the English translation was not by the author, but by a person (actually his friend Samuel Henley) whom he declared to be a stranger. This translation was published anonymously in 1786, before the French original.

Vatican (vat′i.kạn). A hill in Rome, on the right bank of the Tiber, opposite the Pincian. On it are Saint Peter's and the Vatican Palace.

Vatican City. A city-state, an enclave in Rome, Italy, whose ruler is the Pope (bishop of Rome and chief of the Roman Catholic hierarchy). The state (established by the Lateran Treaty of Feb. 11, 1929, between the Italian government and the Papal See, which ended a quarrel going back to 1870, when Italy absorbed the States of the Church) comprises 108.7 acres adjoining and including the Vatican Palace; several places outside Vatican City itself, such as Castel Gandolfo and a number of Roman churches, are administered by Vatican City. The head of the civil government is a governor. The Vatican state is fully independent and exchanges diplomatic representatives with other governments.

Vatican Palace. The chief residence of the Popes since 1377. It is supposed to contain some 11,000 rooms, halls, chapels, etc.

vaudeville (vōd′vil). **1.** The name given by Oliver Basselin, a French poet of the 15th century, to his convivial songs composed in the valley of the Vire, which became very popular throughout France.

Vaudeville, a countrey ballade, or song; a Roundelay or Virelay: so tearmed of Vaudevire, a Norman towne wherin Olivier Bassel, the first inuēter of them, liued; also a vulgar proverb, a countrey or common saying.   (Cotgrave.)

Hence—**2.** In modern French poetry, a light, gay song, frequently embodying a satire, consisting of several couplets with a refrain or burden, sung to a familiar air, and often introduced into theatrical pieces; a song popular with the common people, and sung about the streets; a ballad; a topical song. Hence—**3.** A light kind of dramatic entertainment, combining pantomime with dialogue and songs, which obtained great popularity about the middle of the 18th century. At present any short, light piece, usually comic, with songs and dances intermingled with the dialogue, is called a *vaudeville*.

Vaudois (vō.dwȧ). See **Waldenses.**

Vaughan (vôn), **Hannah.** Maiden name of **Pritchard, Hannah.**

Vaughan, Henry. [Known as "the Silurist."] b. at Newton-by-Usk, Brecknockshire, Wales, April 17, 1622; d. at Scethrog, Wales, April 23, 1695. A Welsh metaphysical poet. His epithet was derived from the Silures, the inhabitants of South Wales in ancient times. He wrote *Poems* (1646), *Olor Iscanus* (1651), and *Silex Scintillans* (1650–55). His mystical poetry, far more than his secular poems, make him important. Such poems as *The Retreat, The World,* and the one beginning "They are all gone into the world of light" place him in the first rank of the followers of George Herbert and influenced such later poets as William Wordsworth.

Vaughan, Hilda. [Married name, **Morgan.**] b. at Builth, Brecknockshire, Wales, 1892—. A Welsh novelist; wife (married 1923) of Charles L. Morgan. Author of novels of Welsh life and character and stories of theatrical life, including *The Battle to the Weak* (1925), *Here Are Lovers* (1926), *The Invader* (1928), *Her Father's House* (1930), *The Soldier and the Gentlewoman* (1932; dramatized 1933), *A Thing of Nought* (1935), *The Curtain Rises* (1935), *Harvest Home* (1937), *She, Too, Was Young* (1938; a play), and *Fair Woman* (1942).

Vaughan, Robert. b. 1795; d. at Torquay, England, June 15, 1868. An English clergyman and historian. In 1845 he founded the *British Quarterly Review*, of which he remained editor for 20 years. He wrote *Protectorate of Oliver Cromwell* (1838), *History of England under the House of Stuart* (1840), *Revolutions in England* (1859–63), and others.

Vaughan, Sir Thomas. In Shakespeare's *Richard III*, an enemy of Richard who is executed with Rivers and Grey.

Vaughan, William. b. at Golden Grove, Carmarthenshire, Wales, 1577; d. there, in August, 1641. An English traveler and poet. He purchased (1616) land in Newfoundland, settling it with colonists, and visiting it in 1622 and later. Author of *The Spirit of Detraction* (1611), defending himself against charges in connection with his wife's death by lightning, a Latin poem (1625) celebrating the marriage of Charles I to Henrietta Maria, *The Golden Fleece* (1626), a combination of prose and poetry, *The Newlanders Cure* (1630), dealing with diseases peculiar to Newfoundland, *The Church Militant* (1640), and *The Soul's Exercise* (1641).

Vaumont (vō′mont), **Count.** The husband of Countess Marcellina in George Chapman's comedy *Monsieur D'Olive*.

Vaux (vō), **Roland de.** See **Roland de Vaux.**

Vaux (vôks), **Sir Nicholas.** In Shakespeare's *Henry VIII*, a gentleman of the court who is put in charge of Buckingham when he is arrested.

Vaux, Sir William. In Shakespeare's *2 Henry VI*, a messenger who announces that Cardinal Beaufort is dying.

Vaux (vôks, vōks, vôz), **Thomas.** [Title, 2nd Baron **Vaux of Harrowden.**] b. 1510; d. in October, 1556. An English lyric poet and courtier. Some of his poems appear in *Tottel's Miscellany* (1557) and the *Paradise of Dainty Devices* (1576); among them are *The Aged Lover Renounceth Love; A Lover, Disdained, Complaineth; Of a Contented Mind,* and *No Pleasure without Some Pain.*

Vauxhall Gardens (voks′hôl″, vok′sôl″). [Original name, **Foukes Hall;** later, **Fox Hall.**] A once-popular and fashionable London resort, formerly situated on the Thames above Lambeth. The gardens were laid out in 1661, and were at first known as the New Spring Gardens at Fox Hall to distinguish them from the Old Spring Gardens at Whitehall. They were finally closed in 1859, and the site was built over.

Veck (vek), **Toby.** [Called "Trotty."] In Dickens's story *The Chimes,* the principal character, a porter and runner of errands.

Vedas (vā′dạz, vē′-). The books containing the sacred writings of Hinduism. There are four principal collections of hymns, prayers, and ritualistic instructions, setting forth the mythology, the religious philosophy, and the holy lore of Hinduism. And although the total Vedas comprise some 100 books in all, including commentaries, glosses, and appendices, these basic four are: the *Rig-Veda*, the *Sama-Veda*, the *Yajur-Veda*, and the *Atharva-Veda*.

Vega (Bā′gä), **Garcilaso de la.** See **Garcilaso de la Vega.**

Vega, Lope de. [Full name: **Lope Félix de Vega Carpio**; often called simply **Lope.**] b. at Madrid, Nov. 25, 1562; d. there, Aug. 27, 1635. A Spanish dramatist and poet. He was educated at the Jesuit college of Madrid and at the University of Alcalá, was in the service of the Bishop of Ávila, and secretary to the Duke of Alva, and was twice married. He was obliged to live away from Madrid for several years on account of a duel. He joined the Spanish Armada in 1588, and returned to Madrid in 1590, and was soon known as a dramatic writer. He had previously, during his exile, written for the theater in Valencia. He was the inventor of a witty character known as the "gracioso," a parody of the heroic character of the play, which passed first to the French and from that to all other modern theaters. He entered the church (c1612), after the death of his second wife, and took (c1614) priest's orders. His plays fall into three classes: the first, called "Comedias de Capa y Espada" (cloak and sword dramas), the second class consisted of "Comedias Heroicas" or "Historiales," and the third of dramas founded on domestic life. He also wrote epics, romances, lyrics, pastorals, and prose novels. The number of works written by him has been placed as high as 1800 plays and 400 *autos* (of which fewer than 500 survive), besides the various prose and verse works not intended for the stage. He wrote poems on Francis Drake and Mary, Queen of Scots, but it is as the founder of Spanish drama that he is remembered.

Veil, The. A volume of verse (1921) by Walter De la Mare.

Veiled Prophet of Khorassan (kō′rạ.san, kō.rạ.san′), **The.** The first part of the poem *Lalla Rookh* by Thomas Moore; so called from the chief character, Mokanna.

Veitch (vēch), **John.** b. at Peebles, Scotland, Oct. 24, 1829; d. there, Sept. 3, 1894. A Scottish philosophical writer and historian, professor of logic, rhetoric, and metaphysics at St. Andrews (1860–64) and of logic and rhetoric at Glasgow (1864–94). He wrote *The Tweed, and Other Poems* (1875), *The Feeling for Nature in Scottish Poetry* (1887), *Merlin, and Other Poems* (1889), *The History and Poetry of the Scottish Border* (1893), *Dualism and Monism* (1895), and others.

Velásquez or **Velázquez** (vä.läs′keth), **Diego.** [Full name, **Diego Rodríguez de Silva y Velásquez.**] b. at Seville, Spain (baptized June 6, 1599); d. at Madrid, Aug. 7, 1660. A Spanish painter. He was a pupil of Herrera el Viejo and of Pacheco, whose daughter he married. He was patronized by Philip IV, became court painter (c1623), visited Italy (1629–31), and for 18 years painted portraits, landscapes, and historical and genre subjects at

Madrid. From 1652 to 1660 he was quartermaster general of the king's household, and he died from over-fatigue in the preparations for the marriage of Louis XIV and the infanta Maria Theresa. Among his principal works in his earlier manner are *The Water-Carrier of Seville* (Apsley House) and *The Adoration of the Shepherds* (National Gallery, London). Among his other works are *Los Borrachos*, *Las Meninas*, *Las Hilanderas*, *The Expulsion of the Moriscos*, and *Forge of Vulcan* (Madrid Museum); *Joseph's Coat* (Escorial); *Saint John the Evangelist* (London); *Boar Hunt*, *Lot and his Daughters*, *The Surrender of Breda*, and a *Crucifixion* (in the Prado). His famous portraits include those of Philip IV, of which he painted about 40, Innocent X Quevedo (Apsley House), Admiral Pulido Pareja (National Gallery, London), Olivares, Prince Baltasar Carlos, and a series of portraits of jesters and dwarfs. His genius was not fully known till about the beginning of the 19th century, when the royal pictures were collected in the Prado Museum.

Velutus (vẹ.lö′tus, -lū′-), **Sicinius.** See **Sicinius Velutus.**

Vendémiaire (väṅ.dā.myer). The name adopted in 1793 by the National Convention of the first French republic for the first month of the year. It consisted of 30 days, beginning in the years 1, 2, 3, 5, 6, 7 with September 22; in 4, 8, 9, 10, 11, 13, 14 with September 23; and in 12 with September 24. The republican calendar came into use on the 14th Vendémiaire, year 2 (Oct. 5, 1793). It was on 13th Vendémiaire, year 4 (Oct. 5, 1795), that Napoleon's "whiff of grapeshot" broke up a Parisian demonstration against the Convention.

Vendice (ven′dis). The "revenger" against the lustful Duke and his corrupt family in *The Revenger's Tragedy* by Cyril Tourneur. He assumes various disguises, in one of which he is hired to kill the personage which he has assumed in the other.

Veneering (vẹ.nir′ing), **Anastasia.** In Dickens's novel *Our Mutual Friend*, the wife of Hamilton Veneering. She is in perfect agreement with him in his ambition for social greatness.

Veneering, Hamilton. In Dickens's novel *Our Mutual Friend*, a man anxious to impress everyone with his importance and his wealth (the former negligible; the latter very new). He buys his way into Parliament (through the purchase of "Pocket Breaches," a rotten borough of the type eliminated by the Reform Bill of 1832) and seeks to make his house and table popular with the widest possible number of important people.

Venetia (vẹ.nē′shạ). A novel by Benjamin Disraeli, published in 1837.

Venice (ven′is), **Duke of.** In Shakespeare's *Merchant of Venice*, the judge presiding at the trial of Antonio. He pardons Shylock on the terms suggested by Antonio.

Venice, Duke of. In Shakespeare's *Othello*, the ruler of Venice. He tries to persuade Brabantio to accept Othello as his son-in-law, and orders Othello to take charge of the expedition to Cyprus.

Venice Preserv'd, or a Plot Discovered. A tragedy by Thomas Otway, produced and printed in 1682. The plot is from a work by C. V. de St. Réal. This

---

ḍ, d or j; ṣ, s or sh; ṭ, t or ch; ẓ, z or zh; o, F. cloche; ü, F. menu; čh, Sc. loch; ṅ, F. bonbon.

play was highly regarded in the 18th century, Johnson remarking that its author "conceived forcibly and drew originally by consulting nature in his own breast."

Venn (ven), **Diggory.** In Thomas Hardy's novel *The Return of the Native*, a simple man who humbly adores Thomasin Yeobright, and whose suit is at first refused by her, but eventually accepted.

Venn, John. b. 1834; d. 1923. An English writer and lecturer on moral science. Among his works are *The Logic of Chance* (1866), *On Some of the Characteristics of Belief, Scientific and Religious* (1870), *Symbolic Logic* (1881), and *The Principles of Empirical or Inductive Logic* (1889).

Ventidius (ven.tid'i.us, -tid'jus). In Shakespeare's *Antony and Cleopatra*, one of Antony's generals.

Ventidius. In Shakespeare's *Timon of Athens*, a false friend of Timon.

Ventidius. In Dryden's *All for Love*, a loyal, honest officer who represents to Antony the impropriety of his passion for Cleopatra.

Venus (vē'nus). In Roman mythology, the goddess of grace and love. Originally she was an Italic goddess of gardens and growth, and only at a comparatively late period became identified with the Greek goddess of love, Aphrodite. In medieval times her name became synonymous with earthly love as contrasted with spiritual love.

Venus, Mr. In Dickens's *Our Mutual Friend*, a one-time ally of Silas Wegg, who finally confesses a blackmail plot to Mr. Boffin.

Venus and Adonis (a.don'is). A narrative poem by Shakespeare, published in 1593.

Venusberg (vē'nus.bėrg). [Eng. trans., "*Mountain of Venus*."] A mountain, probably in the Hörselberge, a group between Eisenach and Gotha, Germany, within whose caverns (the Hörselloch), according to medieval legend, Venus held her court with heathen splendor and revelry. Of those who, charmed by music and sensuous allurements, entered her abode, none ever returned except Tannhäuser.

Veranilda (ver.a.nil'da). A historical novel by George Gissing, published in 1904. It deals with the Roman Empire at the time of the invasions by the Goths.

Verbruggen (vėr.brug'en), **John.** d. c1707. An English actor. He was the original Oronooko in Thomas Southerne's play, and so famous as Alexander that he was sometimes called by that name.

Verbruggen, Susanna. b. c1667; d. 1703. An English actress. Colley Cibber celebrated her in his *Apology*.

Vercelli Book (ver.chel'lē). A manuscript collection (c1000 A.D.) of Old English poetry, plus legends and homilies. The poems it contains are *Andreas, The Fates of the Apostles*, one version of *Soul and Body* (the other is in the *Exeter Book*), *The Dream of the Rood, Elene*, and a homiletic fragment. It was discovered by Friedrich Blume at Vercelli, Italy, in 1822, and has been retained there in the cathedral library.

Vercingetorix (vėr.sin.jet'ō.riks). Executed c45 B.C. A chief of the Arverni in Gaul, the leader of the great rebellion against the Romans in 52 B.C. He gained various successes against Caesar, but was besieged by him at Alesia and surrendered in 52. He was exhibited in Caesar's triumph at Rome in 46, and then by Caesar's order beheaded.

Verdi (ver'dē), **Giuseppe.** b. at Roncole, Italy, Oct. 10, 1813; d. at Milan, Jan. 27, 1901. An Italian operatic composer. He received his musical education at Busseto and Milan, was appointed organist at Roncole when only 10 years old, settled in Milan in 1838, and lived in later life in Genoa and at his villa Sta. Agata (near Busseto). He was a member of the Italian Parliament for a short time in 1860, and was chosen senator in 1875, but never attended a sitting. His chief operas are *Nabucodonosor* or *Nabucco* (1842), *I Lombardi* (1843), *Ernani* (1844), *I due Foscari* (1844), *Attila* (1846), *Macbeth* (1847; revised 1865), *Luisa Miller* (1849), *Rigoletto* (1851), *Il Trovatore* (1853), *La Traviata* (1853), *Les Vêpres Siciliennes* (1855), *Simon Boccanegra* (1857; revised 1881), *Un Ballo in maschera* (1859), *La Forza del destino* (1862), *Don Carlos* (1867), *Aïda* (1871), *Otello* (1887), and *Falstaff* (1893). His other works include *Inno delle Nazioni* (1862), *Requiem Mass* (1874), sacred compositions, a quartet, and others.

Vere (vir), **Arthur De.** See **De Vere, Arthur.**

Vere, Sir **Aubrey** and **Aubrey Thomas de.** See **de Vere.**

Vere, Edward de. [Title, 17th Earl of **Oxford;** called Lord **Bulbeck.**] b. April 12, 1550; d. at Newington, Middlesex, England, June 24, 1604. An Elizabethan soldier, poet, and patron of poets and players. He married (1571) Anne Cecil, daughter of Lord Burghley. In September, 1579, he insulted Sir Philip Sidney by calling him "a puppy," a duel being prevented only by the interference of Queen Elizabeth. In October, 1586, he acted as judge at the trial of Mary, Queen of Scots, and in 1588 he served as a volunteer against the Spanish Armada. His poems were included after his death in the *Paradise of Dainty Devices* (1576), the *Phoenix Nest* (1593), and *England's Parnassus* and *England's Helicon* (both 1600); among the best known are *Of the Mighty Power of Love, Who Taught Thee First to Sigh?, If Women Could be Fair, Of the Birth and Bringing Up of Desire, What Cunning Can Express?*, and the epigram "Were I a king, I could command content." He is one of the several writers held by some to be the author of Shakespeare's works.

Vere, Isabella. The heroine of Sir Walter Scott's novel *The Black Dwarf*.

Vere, John de. See under **Oxford,** (13th) **Earl of.**

Vere, Richard. The Laird of Ellieslaw in Sir Walter Scott's novel *The Black Dwarf*, a haughty, selfish, and dissimulating man.

Vere de Vere, Lady Clara. See **Lady Clara Vere de Vere.**

Verges (vėr'jęz). In Shakespeare's *Much Ado About Nothing*, a "headborough" (a minor constable), assistant to Dogberry.

Vergil or **Virgil** (vėr'jil). [Full Latin name, **Publius Vergilius Maro.**] b. in Andes, near Mantua, Cisalpine Gaul, Oct. 15, 70 B.C.; d. at Brundisium, Italy, Sept. 21, 19 B.C. A Roman epic, didactic, and idyllic poet. He studied at Cremona, Mediolanum,

Neapolis, and Rome, where he devoted himself to rhetoric, philosophy, and poetry. In 41 his paternal estate near Mantua, where he had grown up, was confiscated for the benefit of the soldiery which had assisted Octavian in the civil war against Brutus and Cassius; but he was later indemnified through the intercession of Maecenas. He enjoyed the friendship and patronage of Asinius Pollio, Maecenas (to whom he was introduced about 40), and Octavian (later Augustus). He was an intimate friend of Horace, whom he introduced to Maecenas. About 37 B.C. he settled at Rome; his later years were spent chiefly in Campania. His works include the *Eclogues* or *Bucolics* (written 42–37) and the *Georgics* (written about 37–30), poems celebrating rural life, and the *Aeneid*, an epic on Aeneas, and the great Latin poem, second only to Homer in the classical epic. The first printed edition of Vergil appeared at Rome about 1469.

Vergil or **Virgil, Polydore.** b. at Urbino, Italy, c1470; d. there, c1555. An Italian-English ecclesiastic and historian. He was sent to England as deputy collector of Peter's pence by the Pope in 1501, was presented to an English living in 1503, and in 1504 was appointed the bishop of Hereford's proxy on his translation to the see of Bath and Wells. He was collated to the prebend of Scamblesby in Lincolnshire in 1507, was naturalized in 1510, and was collated to the prebend of Oxgate in Saint Paul's in 1513. He was imprisoned for a short time (c1515) on the charge of slandering Thomas Wolsey. He returned (c1550) to Italy. His chief work is *Historiae Anglicae libri xxvi* (1534; a 27th book was added in the 3rd ed., 1555).

Verinder (ver'in.dèr), **Rachel.** The heroine of Wilkie Collins's mystery novel *The Moonstone.*

Verisopht (ver'i.sôft), **Lord Frederick.** In Dickens's *Nicholas Nickleby,* a foppish, ineffectual nobleman.

Verlaine (ver.len), **Paul.** b. at Metz, France, March 30, 1844; d. at Paris, Jan. 8, 1896. A French poet. He at first belonged to the Parnassians, but afterward became one of the most noted of the symbolists and the so-called decadents. Following, in part, the example of Villon, he used his misfortunes in prison and hospital as a theme for his poems and prose works. He lectured on poetry in England in 1893. Among his works are *Poèmes saturniens* (1865), *Sagesse* (1881), *Jadis et naguère* (1885), *Romances sans paroles* (1887), *Bonheur* (1891), and *Mes hôpitaux* (1891).

Vermeer (vėr.mār'), **Jan.** [Also, **Jan van der Meer.**] b. at Delft, Netherlands, 1632; d. there, 1675. A Dutch painter.

Verne (vėrn; French, vern), **Jules.** b. at Nantes, France, Feb. 8, 1828; d. at Amiens, France, March 24, 1905. A French novelist. He was educated at Nantes, and afterward studied law at Paris, but ultimately devoted himself to literature. After turning out a number of moderately successful plays, he struck a new vein in his scientific romances, which gained a world-wide popularity. They include *Cinq semaines en ballon* (*Five Weeks in a Balloon,* 1863), *Voyage au centre de la terre* (*Journey to the Center of the Earth,* 1864), *De la terre à la lune* (*A Trip to the Moon,* 1865), *Vingt mille lieues sous les mers* (*Twenty Thousand Leagues*

under the Sea, 1870), *L'Île mystérieuse* (*The Mysterious Island,* 1870), *Voyage autour du monde en quatre-vingts jours* (*Round the World in Eighty Days,* 1872), *Michel Strogoff* (1876), and *Le Rayon vert* (1882).

Vernon (vėr'non). In Shakespeare's *1 Henry VI,* an adherent of the Duke of York. He quarrels with Basset, a supporter of the Lancastrian faction, and both ask for single combat, but are refused.

Vernon, Diana (or **Di**). A high-spirited girl with a love for manly sports, the heroine of Scott's *Rob Roy.* She is aided by Rob Roy in her struggle against the plots of the villainous Rashleigh, and eventually marries Francis, the young hero.

Vernon, Sir Richard. In Shakespeare's *1 Henry IV,* one of the rebels. He tells Hotspur of the royal army approaching "all plumed like estridges . . . As full of spirit as the month of May," and describes Hal vaulting on his horse "As if an angel dropped down from the clouds To turn and wind a fiery Pegasus" (IV.i).

Vernon Whitford (hwit'fọrd). See **Whitford, Vernon.**

Veronica (vẹ.ron'i.kạ), **Saint.** In Christian legend, a woman of Jerusalem, said to have died at Rome, who reputedly gave to Jesus on his way to Calvary a handkerchief to wipe his brow. He took it, and upon it was miraculously left an impression of his face. She is commemorated on February 4th.

verse. 1. In prosody: (*a*) A succession of feet (colon or period) written or printed in one line; a line: as, a poem of three hundred *verses;* hence, a type of metrical composition, as represented by a metrical line; a meter. A verse may be catalectic, dimeter, trimeter, iambic, dactylic, rhymed, unrhymed, alliterative, etc.

> He made of ryme ten vers or twelve.
> (Chaucer, *Book of the Duchess.*)

> They . . . thought themselues no small fooles, when they could make their verses goe all in ryme as did the schooles of Salerne.
> (Puttenham, *Arte of Eng. Poesie.*)

(*b*) A type of metrical composition, represented by a group of lines; a kind of stanza: as, Spenserian *verse;* hence, a stanza: as, the first *verse* of a (rhymed) hymn.

> Now, good Cesario, but that piece of song . . .
> Come, but one verse.
> (Shak., *T. N.,* II.iv.)

> A young lady proceeded to entertain the company with a ballad in four verses.
> (Dickens, *Oliver Twist.*)

> A stanza—often called a *verse* in the common speech of the present day—may be a group of two, three, or any number of lines.
> (S. Lanier, *Sci. of Eng. Verse.*)

(*c*) A specimen of metrical composition; a piece of poetry; a poem. [Rare.]

> This verse be thine, my friend.
> (Pope, *Epistle to Jervas.*)

(*d*) Metrical composition in general; versification; hence, poetical composition; poetry, especially as involving metrical form: opposed to *prose.*

ḍ, d or j; ṣ, s or sh; ṭ, t or ch; ẓ, z or zh; o, F. cloche; ü, F. menu; ċh, Sc. loch; ṅ, F. bonbon.

To write, to th' honour of my Maker dread,
Verse that a Virgine without blush may read.
(Sylvester, tr. of Du Bartas's *Weeks*.)

Who says in verse what others say in prose.
(Pope, *Imit. of Horace*, II.i.202.)

2. (*a*) A succession of words written in one line; hence, a sentence, or part of a sentence, written, or fitted to be written, as one line; a stich or stichos. It was a custom in ancient times to write prosaic as well as metrical books in lines of average length. This custom was continued especially in writing the poetical books of the Bible, which, though not metrical in form, are composed in balanced clauses, and in liturgical forms taken from or similar to these.
Hence—(*b*) In liturgics, a sentence, or part of a sentence, usually from the Scriptures, especially from the Book of Psalms, said alternately by an officiant or leader and the choir or people; specifically, the sentence, clause, or phrase said by the officiant or leader, as distinguished from the response of the choir or congregation; a versicle. In the hour-offices a verse is especially a sentence following the responsory after a lesson. In the gradual the second sentence is called a *verse*, and also that following the alleluia. Also *versus*.
(*c*) In church music, a passage or movement for a single voice or for soloists, as contrasted with *chorus;* also, a soloist who sings such a passage.
(*d*) A short division of a chapter in any book of Scripture, usually forming one sentence, or part of a long sentence or period. The present division of verses in the Old Testament is inherited, with modifications, from the masoretic division of verses (*pesūqīm*), and has been used in Latin and other versions since 1528. The present division of verses in the New Testament was made by Robert Stephanus, on a horseback journey from Paris to Lyons, in an edition published in 1551. In English versions the verses were first marked in the Geneva Bible of 1560.

versification. The act, art, or practice of composing poetic verse; the construction or measure of verse or poetry; metrical composition.

Donne alone . . . had your talent; but was not happy enough to arrive at your versification.
(Dryden, *Essay on Satire*.)

Bad versification alone will certainly degrade and render disgustful the sublimest sentiments.
(Goldsmith, *Poetry Distinguished from Other Writing*.)

The theory that versification is not an indispensable requisite of a poem seems to have become nearly obsolete in our time. (*Encyc. Brit.*)

Vertumnus (vér.tum'nus). [Also, **Vortumnus**.] An ancient Etruscan deity taken over by the Romans. Little is known of him except that he came to be regarded as presiding over gardens and orchards, and was worshiped as the god of the changing seasons.

Verulamium (ver.ū.lā'mi.um). A Latin name of St. Albans, England.

Verulam of Verulam (ver'ū.lạm, -ŭ-), 1st Baron. A title of **Bacon, Francis.**

Very Hard Cash. See **Hard Cash.**

Very Woman, or the Prince of Tarent (tar'ẹnt), **A.** A comedy printed in 1655 as the work of Philip Massinger. It was probably written by Fletcher and revised by Massinger.

Vesey (vē'zi), **Elizabeth.** b. c1715; d. near London, 1791. An Irish lady of literary tastes, remembered as a leader of the London "Bluestocking" circle. Her chief ambition, to bring leading society and literary personalities to her drawing room, was realized before 1770; until 1784 her famous parties, held on alternate Tuesdays, were attended by Samuel Johnson and the other celebrated members of Johnson's group. She began (1786) to fail mentally, and by February, 1789, was in a state of imbecility. Hannah More addressed to her the poem, *Conversation*, beginning, "Vesey, of verse the judge and friend."

Vesey-Neroni (vē'zi.nẹ.rō'ni), **Madeline.** See **Neroni, Signora Madeline.**

Vespucci (ves.pö'chẹ; Italian, vās.pöt'chē), **Amerigo.** [Latinized, **Americus Vespucius.**] b. at Florence, Italy, c1451; d. at Seville, Spain, Feb. 22, 1512. An Italian navigator; son of Nastugio Vespucci, a notary of Florence. He received his education from his uncle, a Dominican friar, and became a clerk in the commercial house of the Medici family. He was sent to Spain by his employers about 1490 and some years after appears to have entered the service of the commercial house of Juonato Berardi at Seville, of which he became a member in 1495. This house fitted out Columbus's second expedition (1493), and it has been suggested that Vespucci may have accompanied Columbus's first or second expedition, although the supposition is unsupported by any proof. Vespucci himself claims to have accompanied at least four expeditions to the New World. Two of these sailed from Spain by order of King Ferdinand in May, 1497, and May, 1499, respectively; the other two were dispatched from Portugal by King Emanuel in May, 1501, and June, 1503. The first expedition, in which he would appear to have held the post of astronomer, left Cádiz May 10 or 20, 1497, and after touching at the Canaries came "at the end of twenty-seven days upon a coast which we thought to be that of a continent." If this expedition is authentic, Vespucci reached the continent of America a week or two earlier than the Cabots and about 14 months earlier than Columbus. His account of these expeditions was contained in a diary said to have been written after his fourth voyage, and entitled *Le Quattro Giornate*, no portion of which is extant. He also wrote several letters to his former schoolfellow Soderini, gonfalonier of Florence, one of which remains in a Latin translation printed at St.-Dié in 1507. The German geographer Martin Waldseemüller (Hylacomylus), who made use of this letter in his *Cosmographiae Introductio*, published at St.-Dié in the same year, was the first to suggest the name America for the new continent, in honor of Amerigo Vespucci.

Vesta (ves'tạ). The hearth goddess of the ancient Romans, equivalent to the Greek Hestia. She presided over both the private family hearth or altar, and the central altar of the city, the tribe, or the state. She was worshiped along with the Penates at every meal, when the family assembled round the altar or hearth, which was in the center of the house. Aeneas was said to have carried the sacred fire (her symbol) from Troy, and to have brought it to Italy, and it was preserved at Rome by the state in the sanctuary of the goddess which stood in the Forum. There was no image of Vesta; she was represented entirely by the fire. This fire was watched by six virgins, called "vestals," who prevented it from going out. If it did, it was rekindled by friction. Her festival, the Vestalia, was observed June 9–15, during which time her sanctuary was cleaned.

Vestris (ves'tris), **Madame.** See **Mathews, Lucia Elizabeth.**

Vholes (vōlz). In Dickens's *Bleak House*, one of the lawyers participating in the case of Jarndyce vs. Jarndyce.

Vicar of Bray (brā), **The.** A well-known song, long attributed to a soldier of George I. A version dating from Queen Anne's time has been found.

Vicar of Wakefield (wāk'fēld), **The.** A novel by Oliver Goldsmith, published in 1766. It has appeared in numerous editions and in several dramatizations.

Vicar's Daughter, The. A novel by E. H. Young, published in 1928. It is the story of a vicar unjustly suspected of being the father of a young woman in his household.

Vice Versa. A novel by T. A. Guthrie, published in 1882. It tells the story of Mr. Bultitude, who is changed into the physical form of his son, while his son becomes the father.

Vichy-Chamrond (vē.shē.shäṅ.rôṅ), **Marie de.** See **Deffand, Marquise du.**

Vicinal Way (vis'i.nạl), **The.** An old Roman road in Britain, by which produce was formerly brought from farms in Essex to London.

Victor and Cazire (vik'tọr; kạ.zir'). The pen names which Percy Bysshe Shelley and Elizabeth Shelley used in their joint publication of *Original Poetry* (1810).

Victoria (vik.tō'ri.ạ). [Full name, **Alexandrina Victoria.**] b. at Kensington Palace, London, May 24, 1819; d. at Osborne House, Isle of Wight, Jan. 22, 1901. Queen of Great Britain and Ireland, and empress of India. She was the only child of Edward Augustus, Duke of Kent, fourth son of George III, and was educated under the direction of her mother, Mary Louisa Victoria, daughter of Francis Frederick, Duke of Saxe-Coburg-Saalfeld, and of the Duchess of Northumberland. On the death of William IV, the third son of George III, she succeeded to the throne, June 20, 1837. She was crowned June 28, 1838, and married Albert, Prince of Saxe-Coburg-Gotha (who died Dec. 14, 1861), on Feb. 10, 1840. Her favorite residences were Balmoral Castle (in the Highlands of Aberdeenshire, Scotland), Osborne (Isle of Wight), and Windsor. She assumed the title of Empress of India in 1876. The jubilee of her reign was celebrated in 1887, and her diamond jubilee (60 years) in 1897. (For the leading events in her reign, see the article on England.) She was author in part of *Leaves from the Journal of Our Life in the Highlands* (private printing, 1867; publicly issued, 1868) and *More Leaves from the Journal of a Life in the Highlands*

(1883). She supervised the preparation of lives of the Prince Consort by Charles Grey (1867) and Theodore Martin (1875–80).

Victoria. In Roman mythology, victory personified.

Victoria and Albert Museum (al'bèrt). A museum at London, formerly known (1857–99) as the South Kensington Museum. It has departments relating to architecture, sculpture, painting, ceramics, woodwork, metalwork, textiles, engraving, illustration and design, and Indian art. It also has a library and extension division. The collections illustrate the fine and applied arts of all periods.

Victoria Tower. The tall tower on the Houses of Parliament, London.

Victories of Love, The. See under **Angel in the House, The.**

Victory. A novel (1915) by Joseph Conrad.

Vidar (vē'där). [Also: **Vidharr, Vitharr.**] In Old Norse mythology, a powerful god; son of Odin and the giantess Grid. At Ragnarok he killed the Fenris wolf.

Vienna (vi.en'ạ), **Congress of.** A congress of the principal European powers for settling the affairs of Europe, held at Vienna from September, 1814, to June, 1815. It was begun soon after the first abdication of Napoleon and the restoration of the Bourbons to the throne of France, and it closed, after an interruption, caused by Napoleon's return, ten days before the Battle of Waterloo ended Napoleon's "Hundred Days." Among the persons present at the Congress were the monarchs of Russia, Prussia, Austria, Denmark, Bavaria, and various smaller German states, Wellington and Castlereagh of Great Britain, Talleyrand of France, Nesselrode of Russia, Hardenberg of Prussia, Metternich of Austria, and Stein of Russia. The principal decisions were in the hands of the four major powers (Austria, Prussia, Russia, and Great Britain) and the larger group never met as a whole, though its members were called upon for minor decisions. Eventually Talleyrand, as the representative of the French Bourbon king, Louis XVIII, was admitted to the inner circle. The chief stipulations were: the retention by France of the limits existing at the outbreak of the Revolution; the restoration of the Austrian monarchy without Belgium, Breisgau, and W Galicia, but with the addition of Lombardy-Venetia, Dalmatia, the Tyrol, and other territory; the restoration of the Prussian monarchy without most of the territory taken in 1807 to form the duchy of Warsaw, and minus Ansbach and Bayreuth (ceded to Bavaria), but with the addition of more than half of Saxony, extensive territories in the region of the Rhine, and Swedish Pomerania; the formation of the German Confederation of 39 states under the hegemony of Austria (replacing the defunct Holy Roman Empire); the creation of a new kingdom of Poland under the ruling Russian dynasty; the establishment of the kingdom of the Netherlands, including Holland and Belgium; the retention of Norway (ceded by Denmark in 1814) by Sweden; the retention of Finland (acquired from Sweden in 1809) by Russia; the restoration of the Sardinian monarchy with the annexation of Genoa; the restoration of

---

ḍ, d or j; ṣ, s or sh; ṭ, t or ch; ẓ, z or zh; o, F. cloche; ü, F. menu; ċh, Sc. loch; ṅ, F. bonbon.

the States of the Church, Avignon and Venaissin being left to France; the reconstitution of the Swiss Confederation with enlarged limits; the retention by Great Britain of Cape Colony, Ceylon, part of Surinam (Dutch Guiana), Mauritius, Tobago, Malta, Helgoland, and others; the establishment of a British protectorate over the Ionian Islands; the restoration of the Bourbons and other former dynasties in Spain, Tuscany, and Modena. Also arising from the Congress, though not actually a part of its official activities, were the Holy Alliance (agreed to later in 1815) and a continuation of the wartime Quadruple Alliance. The Concert of Europe, a term often used to describe the agreement among the great powers to act only after conference, and specifically used of their general policy regarding Turkey and the Balkans, was an outgrowth of the Quadruple Alliance. The Congress system, despite numerous strains on its existence, lasted until the revolutionary period of 1848–49.

Vienna, Duke of. See **Vincentio, Duke of Vienna.**

Vigiles (vij'i.lēz). In ancient Rome, a corps of police and firemen under military discipline.

Vigils. A volume of verse (1935) by Siegfried Sassoon.

Vigny (vē.nyē), **Alfred Victor, Comte de.** b. at Loches, in Touraine, France, March 27, 1799; d. at Paris, Sept. 17, 1863. A French poet, dramatist, and novelist. At the age of 16 he entered the army, and he was promoted to captain in 1823. During various periods of inactivity in his military career he pursued his studies; as early as 1815 he composed a couple of essays, *La Dryade* and *Syméta*. His first collection of poems appeared in 1822 as *Poëmes antiques et modernes.* That same year he published *Le Trappiste*, and *Eloa, ou la sœur des anges* in 1824. Then came his last work of Biblical character, *Le Déluge*, and his first work in the new romantic vein, *Dolorida*. He published his great historical novel *Cinq-Mars* in 1826, and resigned from the army in 1828 because of ill health. As a dramatist he translated Shakespeare's *Othello* and *Merchant of Venice* into French verse, wrote an original historical drama, *La Maréchale d'Ancre*, and finally produced his best piece of work in this line, *Chatterton* (1835). This drama is related in its subject to *Stello, ou les diables bleus* (1832), in which De Vigny defined the position of a poet in modern society. Another work, in which a warrior's position is similarly defined, appeared as *Servitude et grandeur militaires* (1835). Among the last publications during the author's lifetime was a series of *Poëmes philosophiques* (1843). He spent the last 20 years of his life in retirement, and left several works unpublished at the time of his death. He was admitted to the French Academy on May 8, 1845.

Vile Bodies. A novel by Evelyn Waugh, published in 1930.

Vili (vē'lē). In Norse mythology, a brother of Odin.

Village, The. A long poem (1783) by George Crabbe, written partly as a realistic response to Goldsmith's romantically portrayed *Deserted Village.*

Village Coquette, The. A short comedy, with songs, by Charles Dickens, published in 1836.

Village Wooing, The. A play (1934) by George Bernard Shaw, included by most critics among his lesser works.

villanelle (vil.ạ.nel'). A poem in a fixed form borrowed from the French, and allied to the virelay. It consists of 19 lines on two rhymes, arranged in six stanzas, the first five of three lines, the last of four. The first and third line of the first stanza are repeated alternately as last lines from the second to the fifth stanza, and they conclude the sixth stanza. Great skill is required to introduce them naturally. The typical example of the villanelle is one by Jean Passerat (1534–1602), beginning "J'ai perdu ma tourtourelle."

> Who ever heard true Grief relate
> Its heartfelt Woes in "six" and "eight"?
> Or felt his manly Bosom swell
> Within a French-made Villanelle?
> (A. Dobson.)

Villa Rubein (vil'ạ rö.bān'). A novel by John Galsworthy, published (1900) under the pseudonym John Sinjohn. It is the story of a poor painter with radical views.

Villette (vi.let'). A novel by Charlotte Brontë, published in 1853. "Villette" is the city of Brussels, where Lucy Snowe goes to teach in a girls' boarding school run by Madame Beck. Lucy has neither wealth nor beauty, but proves that she can make her way in the world through her strength of character. She fosters the romance of John Bretton, an English doctor, and Paulina Home, while she herself is attracted to the bitter and despotic professor Paul Emanuel. He changes under her influence to a kind and generous man, and leaves her in charge of her own school in Brussels when he has to make a trip to the West Indies.

Villiers (vil'yẽrz), **George.** See **Buckingham,** 1st and 2nd Dukes of.

Villon (vē.yôn), **François.** [Original name perhaps **François de Montcorbier** (or **Corbier** or **Corbeuil** or **des Loges**); also known as **Michel Mouton.**] b. at Paris, 1431; d. after 1463. A French poet. Law court records and his writings are the chief sources of information concerning his life. Because of the protection afforded him by certain Bourbons, it is surmised that he may have been distant kin to that royal house. But he was born in humble circumstances, and after his father's death he was reared by Guillaume de Villon, canon of the Church of Saint-Benoît-le-Bestourné, whom he called "more than father" and whose name he took. His patron saw him through the Sorbonne, where he took the degrees of B.A. in 1449 and M.A. in 1452; at that time degrees were easily granted and Villon, by his own account, spent little time studying but much time roistering with the notoriously unruly students, drinking, wenching, brawling, engaging in petty thievery, and fighting the police. He seems to have taken clerical orders but never to have held a benefice. In 1455 he fatally stabbed a priest, undoubtedly in self-defense; Villon's punishment was banishment from France. He left Paris but not France, and roamed the countryside with a gang of ruffians, amusing them and celebrating their deeds and ways in numerous ballads in their special slang, known as *le jargon*. Villon at this time was already famous and had friends in high places, who presently managed to have his banishment revoked. Returning to Paris, he also returned to his former company and old ways, and presently was involved in an affray, for which he blamed Catherine de Vaucelles, following which he thought it discreet to flee his beloved city again. During this second period of exile the authorities, rounding up a criminal gang, came upon facts connecting Villon with a recent large-scale robbery. At this time he wrote a poem, *Le Dit de la naissance Marie*, dedicated apparently to a daughter of Charles, Duc d'Orléans. Charles d'Orléans himself was a poet, and seems to have become Villon's protector at this time. In or about 1457 Villon is known to have taken part in a contest of poets held by his Bourbon patron at Blois. In 1461 a church in the archdiocese of Orléans was burglarized; the archbishop of Orléans accused Villon, secured his conviction, and had him imprisoned all summer. Fortunately for the poet, 1461 also saw the accession to the French throne of Louis XI, and Villon was liberated in the course of a general amnesty proclaimed by the new monarch. He returned to Paris in 1462; with no great delay he was again convicted of theft and imprisoned. With the help, apparently, of influential personages, he was released, only to be convicted the following year of attempted murder, a charge of which for once he was innocent. He was sentenced to be hanged, but successfully appealed the case and was let off with a decree of ten years' banishment from Paris. Rabelais wrote that Villon thereafter found refuge at London, and there are other stories, but actually nothing is known of his movements after 1463 and it is generally supposed that he died shortly after his last escape from the gallows. Villon's principal poetical works can be dated by his misadventures with the law. We have seen that after his first arrest and banishment he wrote his ballads for thieves and ruffians in *le jargon*. After his second arrest he composed his poem to the Orleanist princess, and after his release through her or her father's good offices he wrote the *Little* (or *Lesser*) *Testament*. It was in the archbishop of Orléans's dungeon that he composed the *Dialogue Between the Heart and Body of François Villon;* it was after his rescue from that harrowing experience that he put together his *Grand* (or *Great*) *Testament;* and the *Epitaph of Villon*, also known as *Ballad of the Hanged*, was the fruit of his meditations when the noose threatened his neck at Paris. During the reign of classical ideals in the French literature of the 17th and 18th centuries, he was little regarded in his native land and almost unknown beyond its borders. He has since come to be regarded as the fountainhead of modern French poetry and acknowledged moreover as one of the great poets of all times. Villon seems preeminently to deserve the appellation "a genius." In the eyes of the law a criminal; in the view of the world a failure; socially, by the most generous estimate, an irresponsible wastrel, in him a great passion for life and a clear-eyed, searing honesty that did not spare himself were wedded to a spontaneous gift for lyrical utterance hardly ever surpassed. Boisterously humorous and mercilessly satiric, he

could also be compassionate, as in the poem commiserating the lot of the chimney sweeps, and tenderly pious, as in the lines to the Blessed Virgin, written at his mother's request. The *Little* and the *Grand Testaments* are alike compositions in eight-line stanzas, interspersed with ballades and rondeaus, all alive with passion, ribaldry, piety, patriotism, pity, rebellion, contrition, and a pervading concern with death. The first extensive English translation of Villon was published in 1874, and the first modern definitive edition in French appeared in 1892. Dante Gabriel Rossetti, Algernon Charles Swinburne, and Andrew Lang have been among Villon's English translators, and Rossetti's version of the most famous of all Villon's poems, the *Ballade of Dead Ladies*, is especially effective, with its rendering of the haunting last line of each stanza, *Mais où sont les neiges d'antan?*, as "But where are the snows of yesteryear?"

Vincent Crummles (vin'sent krum'lz). See **Crummles, Vincent.**

Vincentio (vin.sen'shi.ō). In Shakespeare's *Taming of the Shrew*, an old gentleman of Pisa, Lucentio's father.

Vincentio, Prince. The hero of George Chapman's *The Gentleman Usher*. He is secretly in love with Margaret, as is his father.

Vincentio, Duke of Vienna (vi.en'a). In Shakespeare's *Measure for Measure*, the reigning duke.

Vincent of Beauvais (vin'sent; bō.vā'). A Dominican monk of the 13th century, whose work the *Speculum Majus*, an encyclopedic summation of all medieval knowledge, is referred to by Chaucer in the Prologue to *The Legend of Good Women*.

Vinci (vēn'chē; Anglicized, vin'chi), **Leonardo** (or **Lionardo**) **da.** b. at Anchiano in the community of Vinci, near Florence, Italy, April 15, 1452; d. at Cloux, near Amboise, France, May 2, 1519. Italian painter, sculptor, musician, engineer, and scientist, considered by many to have been the first man of the modern age to anticipate what science and invention would achieve in man's struggle against nature. He anticipated Galileo's and Newton's discoveries, and man's conquest of the air. He was the illegitimate son of Ser Piero da Vinci, a noted lawyer at Florence, and Caterina, a country girl of Anchiano. After a boyhood spent in his father's house at Vinci, he entered (c1469) Andrea Verrocchio's workshop at Florence. There he learned many crafts: painting, goldsmithing and casting of monuments, construction, and engineering. In 1472 he was accepted in the painters' guild, but he still remained Verrocchio's coworker. His most important surviving works of this period are the angel in Verrocchio's painting of the *Baptism of Christ* (now in the Uffizi, Florence), the *Annunciations* (Uffizi and Louvre, Paris), the unfinished panels of *Saint Jerome* (Vatican, Rome) and of the *Adoration of the Magi* (Uffizi), commissioned by the monks of San Donato di Scopeto in 1481. In 1482 da Vinci entered the service of Lodovico Sforza, Duke of Milan, with whom he remained for 17 years until the end of the Sforza regime in 1499. His great paintings of this period are the *Madonna of the Rocks* (Louvre), ordered by the Confraternity of the Conception, and the *Last Supper*, painted on the wall of the refectory of the Convent Santa Maria delle Grazie for the Duke of Milan. This latter work has become world famous as a masterpiece of pictorial invention and psychological interpretation. Leonardo worked on it from 1495 to 1497, using oil tempera which after some years cracked. Further damage resulted through warfare and faulty restoration. The painting is now under expert care to avoid further damage. Leonardo worked through all his Milanese years on the great equestrian statue of Francesco Sforza, but the monument was never cast in bronze. When the French captured Milan (1499), French archers destroyed the model. Leonardo was also engaged in architectural and engineering tasks, both military and civil. He planned cities and fortifications, designed pageants, built the first revolving stage, and worked on projects for the diversion of rivers, developing a canal system with locks which are still in operation. He studied mathematics with Luca Pacioli, and designed the illustrations for a book (*De Divina Proportione*) written by this famous mathematician. "There is no certainty," Leonardo said, "where you cannot apply one of the mathematical sciences." He filled his notebooks with mathematical, anatomical, botanical, and geophysical observations; with studies in optics, hydraulics, mechanics, both practical and theoretical, with precepts for painters, and with philosophical reflections. Of his notebooks more than 7,000 pages are preserved. All are written in left-handed mirror script. This storehouse of knowledge, in its original form illegible to the general reader, has been carefully studied, transcribed, and edited during the past century. In 1500 Leonardo returned to Florence, and in 1502 he became military engineer for Cesare Borgia, for whom he drew maps of strategic zones which are the first examples of modern cartography. He designed such weapons as an armored tank, guided projectiles, and breechloading cannons. He studied the flight of birds and designed flying machines, conceiving the problem of flight in the modern sense of aerodynamic reciprocity. At Florence from 1500 to 1506 he painted the panel of *Saint Anne* (Louvre) and the portrait of *Mona Lisa* (or *La Gioconda*), famous and much discussed for the smile which gives it life; great for the simplicity and dignity of composition and for the mountain landscape which opens the background into infinite distances. Leonardo and Michelangelo were commissioned to paint frescoes in the Council Hall of Florence, but only the cartoons were completed, and these were later destroyed. We have, however, a record of them in a sketch which Peter Paul Rubens made of the middle scene of Leonardo's *Battle of Anghiari*. In 1507 Leonardo returned to Milan in the service of the French king. More and more interested in scientific problems, he left many paintings to be finished by his pupils: thus Ambrosio de'Predis finished another version of the *Madonna of the Rocks* (National Gallery, London). In 1513, at the age of 61, Leonardo went to Rome, but he did not get the support he expected from Cardinal de' Medici, a relative of the Pope. The Pope listened to secret and false accusations by enemies and forbade Leonardo the use of the hospital for dissections. While Michelangelo and Raphael executed their great frescoes in the Vatican, Leonardo lived in seclusion until Francis I requested him to come to France as "first painter and engineer to the King." Accepting this offer in 1516 Leonardo left Italy forever. Accompanied by his faithful pupil, Francisco Melzi, he spent the last four years of his life in the little castle of Cloux, near Amboise. He painted only one more panel, *Saint John* (Louvre), but was engaged in architectural and canal-engineering projects. He again staged a great festival with a repetition of the scenery of Milan in 1490. He was honored and admired, received many distinguished guests, and was frequently visited by the enthusiastic King Francis I. See *The Notebooks of Leonardo da Vinci*, edited by Edward MacCurdy (1948), *Paragone*, by Irma Richter (1949), *Leonardo da Vinci*, by Kenneth Clark (1939), *Leonardo the Florentine*, by Rachel A. Taylor (1927), *The Renaissance*, by Walter Pater (1893), and *Leonardo da Vinci, A Study in Psychosexuality*, by Sigmund Freud (1947).

Vincy (vin'si), **Rosamond.** One of the principal female characters in George Eliot's novel *Middlemarch*. She marries Dr. Lydgate, who is eventually corrupted by her selfishness and greed.

Vinegar Bible, The. An edition printed (2 volumes, 1716–17) at the Clarendon Press, Oxford, with the heading to Luke xx the "Parable of the *Vinegar*" instead of the "Parable of the *Vineyard*."

Viner (vī'nėr), **Charles.** b. at Salisbury, England, 1678; d. at Aldershot, England, June 5, 1756. An English jurist, founder of the Vinerian common-law professorship, scholarships, and fellowships at Oxford University. He published *A General Abridgment of Law and Equity* (23 vols., 1742–53).

Viola (in Shakespeare, vī'ọ.lạ). In Shakespeare's *Twelfth Night*, the principal female character, twin sister of Sebastian. She assumes a page's disguise and the name of Cesario when she arrives in Illyria. She wins the heart of, and eventually marries, the duke whose service she enters as a page (meanwhile having been embarrassed by the attentions of the Countess Olivia, who falls in love with her in her guise as a page).

Viola (vī'ọ.lạ, vī.ō'lạ). A principal character in Francis Beaumont and John Fletcher's *The Coxcomb*.

Violante Comparini (vē.ō.län'tä kōm.pä.rē'nē). See under **Comparini, Pietro.**

Violenta (vī.ọ.len'tạ). In Shakespeare's *All's Well That Ends Well*, a Florentine woman, friend of the Widow.

Viper (vī'pèr), **Docter.** A character in Samuel Foote's play *The Capuchin*. Under this name the author severely castigated an Irish clergyman named Jackson, in the pay of Elizabeth Chudleigh Pierrepont, called the Duchess of Kingston, as a revenge for the suppression of Foote's play *The Trip to Calais*.

virelay (vir'e.lā). An old French form of poem, in short lines, running on two rhymes; also, a succession of stanzas on two rhymes, and of indeterminate length, the rhyme of the last line of each becoming the rhyme of the first couplet in the next, thus: *a, a, b, a, a, b, a, a, b; b, b, c, b, b, c, b, b, c;*

c, c, d, c, c, d, c, c, d; etc. In a nine-line lay the rhyme-order is as follows: *a, a, b, a, a, b, a, a, b.* The *virelai nouveau* is written on two rhymes throughout; and the lines of the first couplet reappear alternately at irregular intervals throughout the poem, concluding it in reverse order. No rhyme should be repeated. This form has been written in English but sparingly. Except by example, it is difficult to explain it. Here is the beginning of one:

> Good-bye to the Town!—good-bye!
> Hurrah! for the sea and the sky!
> In the street the flower-girls cry;
> In the street the water-carts ply;
> And a fluter, with features a-wry,
> Plays fitfully, "Scots, wha hae"—
> And the throat of that fluter is dry;
> Good-bye to the Town!—good-bye!
> And over the roof-tops nigh
> Come a waft like a dream of the May,—etc.

The next paragraph closing with:

> Hurrah! for the sea and the sky!
> (A. Dobson, *July.*)

> Of swich matere made he many layes,
> Songes, compleintes, roundels, virelayes.
> (Chaucer, *Franklin's Tale.*)

Virelay. Round, Freeman's Song.
(Cotgrave, 1611.)

Virelay, a roundelay, Country-ballad, or Freemans song.
(Blount, 1670.)

> And then the band of flutes began to play,
> To which a lady sung a virelay.
> (Dryden, *Flower and Leaf.*)

Virgil (vẽr'jil). See **Vergil.**

Virgilia (vẽr.jil'i.a). In Shakespeare's *Coriolanus,* the wife of Coriolanus. She, with her son and Volumnia, persuade Coriolanus to spare Rome.

virginal. An early form of stringed keyboard instrument, much used in 16th-century England, in which the strings were plucked by pins fastened to wooden jacks. This instrument developed into the harpsichord and spinet.

Virgin Fortress, The. A historical novel by Sir Max Pemberton, published in 1912.

Virginia (vẽr.jin'ya). In Roman legend, the daughter of Virginius, a centurion, who was slain by her father to keep her from the lust of the decemvir Appius Claudius (449 B.C.). This act led to the overthrow of the decemvirate.

Virginia. See also under **Physician's Tale, The.**

Virginia, New England, and the Summer Isles. See **Generall Historie of Virginia, New-England, and the Summer Isles.**

Virginians, The. A novel by William Makepeace Thackeray, published in 1857–59. It is a sequel to *Henry Esmond.*

Virginius (vẽr.jin'yus). A tragedy by J. Sheridan Knowles, produced in 1820.

Virginius. See also under **Physician's Tale, The.**

Virgin Martyr, The. A tragedy by Philip Massinger and Thomas Dekker, licensed in 1620 and printed in 1622.

"Virgin Queen," the. An epithet of Queen Elizabeth.

Virgo (vẽr'gō). An ancient constellation, between Leo and Libra, and the sixth sign of the zodiac. The figure represents a young girl in a robe holding a spike of grain in her left hand, a palm leaf in her right. The constellation has been identified everywhere with harvest and fertility goddesses: the Babylonian Ishtar, Assyrian Belit, Greek Persephone, and others. The constellation contains the white first-magnitude star Spica.

Virtuoso, The. A comedy (1676) by Thomas Shadwell.

Vishnu (vish'nö). One of the three principal gods of the Hindu pantheon, the preserver of the triad (with Brahma as creator and Shiva as destroyer). He is a very popular deity, and his votaries worship him as the supreme one of the three. Vishnu's preserving and restoring power is believed to have been manifested to the world in ten different incarnations, called avatars. Two of these incarnations, Rama and Krishna, are specially honored and worshiped. He is usually portrayed as having four arms, holding a conch shell, the disc of the sun, a club, and a lotus. Sometimes he is seated on a lotus with his wife Lakshmi beside him.

Visigoths (viz'i.goths). See under **Goths.**

Vision of Don Roderick (don rod'e.rik). A narrative poem by Sir Walter Scott, published in 1811.

Vision of Judgment, A. A poem by Robert Southey, published in 1821.

Vision of Judgment, The. A burlesque (1822) by Byron of Robert Southey's *A Vision of Judgment,* in which Southey had apotheosized George III. Byron mercilessly pilloried the Tories, Southey, and the dead king.

Vision of Mirza (mẽr'za), **The.** An allegory by Joseph Addison, published in *The Spectator,* No. 159. It is a vision of human life, seen as a broken and ruined bridge along which people walk.

Vision of Piers Plowman (pirz plou'man), **The.** See **Piers Plowman.**

Vision of the Twelve Goddesses, The. A masque by Samuel Daniel, presented at Hampton Court in 1604 by Queen Anne and her ladies.

Vision of William Concerning Piers Plowman (pirz' plou'man), **The.** See **Piers Plowman.**

Vitalis (vī.tā'lis) or **Vital** (vē.täl'), **Ordericus** (or **Orderic**). See **Ordericus Vitalis.**

Vita Nuova (vē'tä nwô'vä). [Eng. trans., *"New Life."*] A work by Dante, finished probably c1292. It consists of several types of song symmetrically arranged and interspersed by commentaries in prose. Much of it can be read as romantic autobiography, as a record of Dante's love for Beatrice; but in its deeper and more general sense it is a lyrical, philosophical, and theological analysis of the "new" or "marvelous" life of love in all its forms from romantic passion through Platonic, "courtly," and artistic love to the divine infusion of supernatural charity.

Vitruvius Pollio (vi.trö'vi.us pol'i.ō), **Marcus.** [Called **Vitruvius.**] b. at Verona, Italy; fl. 1st century B.C. A Roman architect and engineer, a military engineer under Caesar and Augustus. His treatise on architecture, in ten books (*De architectura*), dedicated to Augustus, is the only surviving Roman treatise on the subject. He seems to have been an unsuccessful architect; his book, however, was well known to Pliny, and on it was based almost all the earlier theory and practice of Renaissance and pseudoclassical architecture.

Vittoria (vi.tō′ri.a̤). A novel by George Meredith, published in 1866. It is a sequel to *Sandra Belloni*.

Vittoria Corombona (kō.rôm.bō′nä). See **Corombona, Vittoria,** and **White Devil, The.**

Vitus (vī′tus), Saint. fl. late 3rd century. A Christian saint, a martyr under Diocletian. His festival is celebrated June 15. At Ulm and Ravensburg and other places in Germany it was believed in the 17th century that good health could be secured for a year by dancing before his image at his festival, and bringing gifts; whence it is said that Saint Vitus's dance came to be confounded with chorea, a nervous disorder, and he was invoked against it.

Vivian (viv′i.a̤n). [Also: **Viviane, Vivien.**] In the Arthurian cycle of romance, an enchantress, the mistress of Merlin. She brought up Lancelot in her palace, which was situated in or under a magical lake; hence her epithet of Lady of the Lake. Tennyson has used the subject of her subjugation of Merlin in his "Merlin and Vivien" in the *Idylls of the King.*

Vivian, Herbert. b. April 3, 1865; d. April 18, 1940. An English travel writer, biographer, and journalist. He was special correspondent (1898–99) for the *Morning Post* and correspondent (1899–1900, 1918) for the *Daily Express*, and editor (1890) of *The Whirlwind.* Author of *Servia—The Poor Man's Paradise* (1897), *Tunisia and the Modern Barbary Pirates* (1899), *Abyssinia: Through the Lion-Land to the Court of the Lion of Judah* (1901), *The Servian Tragedy, with Some Impressions of Macedonia* (1904), *Italy at War* (1917), *Myself Not Least, Being the Personal Reminiscences of "X"* (1923), *Secret Societies, Old and New* (1927), *Life of the Emperor Charles of Austria* (1932), *Kings in Waiting* (1933), and *Fascist Italy* (1936).

Vivian Grey (grā). A brilliant early novel (1826–27) by Benjamin Disraeli.

Vivonne (vē.von), **Catherine de.** See **Rambouillet, Marquise de.**

Vizetelly (viz.e̤.tel′i), **Frank.** b. at London, Sept. 26, 1830; d. in the Sudan, c1883. An English newspaper artist and war correspondent; brother of Henry Richard Vizetelly. He was a traveling correspondent and illustrator for the *Pictorial Times*, war correspondent (1859–83) for the *Illustrated London News*, and one of the founders and editor (1857–59) of *Le Monde Illustré.* His reports and sketches, from Solferino (1859), Sicily (1860), Spain, America, Sadowa (1866), and Egypt, appeared in the *Illustrated London News.* It is believed that he was killed during the massacre of Hicks Pasha and his army.

Vizetelly, Henry Richard. b. at London, July 30, 1820; d. at Heatherlands, Farnham, England, Jan. 1, 1894. An English engraver, journalist, and publisher; brother of Frank Vizetelly (1830–c1883). He established (1843) the *Pictorial Times* and

founded (June, 1855) the *Illustrated Times*, and was Paris correspondent (1865–72) and Berlin correspondent (1872) for the *Illustrated London News.* He translated and published (1867–90) novels by French and Russian authors, including Flaubert, Daudet, Gogol, Dostoyevsky, and Tolstoy, and was fined (1888, 1889) and imprisoned (1889) for three months for publishing Zola's works. He was the author of *Wines of the World* (1875), *Facts about Sherry* (1876), *Champagne* (1879), and *Port and Madeira* (1880), as well as *Berlin under the New Empire* (1879) and *Paris in Peril* (1882; with his son, Ernest).

Vogelweide (fō′gel.vī.de̤), **Walther von der.** See **Walther von der Vogelweide.**

Vogler (fō′glėr), **Georg Joseph.** [Called **Abt** (or **Abbé**) **Vogler.**] b. at Würzburg, Germany, June 15, 1749; d. at Darmstadt, May 6, 1814. A German organist, composer, and writer on music. He was kapellmeister successively at Mannheim (1755–78), Stockholm (1786–99), and Darmstadt (1807–14), and conductor of schools of music at those cities. A priest (ordained 1773), he traveled widely, demonstrating, especially on a portable organ or "orchestrion" he invented, his method of simplified organ construction. His compositions include operas, orchestral and piano music, and masses and other church music. Browning's dramatic monologue *Abt Vogler,* published in *Dramatis Personae* (1864), shows the musician "after he has been extemporizing upon the musical instrument of his invention."

Voice in the Wilderness, The. A novel by Richard Blaker, published in 1922.

Voice of the Turtle, The. A romantic comedy (1943) by John Van Druten.

Vokes (vōks), **Rosina.** b. at London, 1858; d. near Torquay, England, Jan. 27, 1894. An English actress. She first appeared in the English provinces in pantomime with her brother Fred and her sisters Victoria and Jessie. In 1870, with Fawdon Vokes, who assumed the name, they made a success at London as "the Vokes family." They were also very successful in America, where they appeared annually for many years.

Volpone, or the Fox (vol.pō′nē). A comedy by Ben Jonson, played in 1606 and printed in 1607. The theme treated in this "humour comedy" is greed. Volpone and his confederate Mosca (the Fly) delude three avaracious Venetians into believing that Volpone is dying and will leave a large fortune to some fortunate heir. The three who vie for Volpone's favor are Corvino, a merchant; Corbaccio, an elderly gentleman; and Voltore, an advocate. Volpone, lustful for Corvino's wife, Celia, has Mosca persuade Corvino that a beautiful woman in his bed will cure him and win his gratitude. Corvino consents to have Celia laid beside Volpone, who woos her with the lyrical "Come, my Celia, let us prove, While we can, the sports of love." But Bonario, who has been secreted by the malicious Mosca in Volpone's bedroom to hear his father, old Corbaccio, disinherit him in Volpone's favor, rushes out of hiding in time to save Celia's virtue. He hales the two rogues to court, but there they outface his indignation and the suspicions of the advocates. Corvino, to avoid public exposure of his part in the affair, perjures himself; and Voltore, the advocate, turns the case against Bonario for attacking a bedridden man. Further to taunt their greedy dupes, the two rascals pretend that Volpone has died leaving the sought-after fortune to Mosca. For a while the two, in disguise, enjoy the discomfiture of the disappointed competitors for the fortune. But then Mosca turns against Volpone, who, when his guilt is revealed, in turn ruins Mosca. A subplot concerning three typically English characters somewhat spoils the technical perfection of the play, but it lightens the dark atmosphere of Jonson's bleak tale of villainy. To emphasize the bestiality of his characters, Jonson names them from the animal world: the fox, the fly, the vulture, the crow, and others. Not even the innocent characters, Celia and Bonario, are treated with much compassion. Justice is represented as blind and foolish. The satire in *Volpone* is so bitter as to make it almost a tragedy rather than a comedy.

Volscius (vol′shus), **Prince.** A young lover in the comedy *The Rehearsal*, by the Duke of Buckingham and others. He is intended to mock the character of Comely in Howard's *The English Monsieur*, and also the love-and-honor debates frequent in the heroic tragicomedy of the Restoration; unable to decide between love and honor, which he identifies respectively with his right and left boots, he finally goes off with one boot on and one off.

Volsunga Saga (vol′sung.ga̤ sä′ga̤). [Old Norse, **Völsunga-saga.**] An Old Icelandic prose saga. Its central hero is Sigurd, equated to the Siegfried of the *Nibelungenlied*. It was probably compiled about the 12th–13th centuries. Its material was based largely on old heroic poems, some of which are preserved in the second section of the *Elder Edda*. It, and not the *Nibelungenlied*, is the source of Wagner's *Ring of the Nibelungs*.

Voltaire (vol.tār′; French, vol.ter). [Assumed name of **François Marie Arouet;** called the **"Patriarch of Ferney."**] b. at Paris, Nov. 21, 1694; d. there, May 30, 1778. A French writer. He took the name of Voltaire, the origin of which is still in dispute, in 1718, a short time after the performance of his tragedy *Œdipe*. His father, a notary connected with the tribunal of the Châtelet, was a man of some wealth. Young Arouet was one of the most brilliant pupils of the Collège Louis-le-Grand (then in the hands of the Jesuits). Before he was out of college he began writing poetry. His wit, as well as the influence of his godfather, the Abbé de Châteauneuf, secured for him an introduction into the most aristocratic circles of Parisian society. The freedom of his utterances soon brought him into trouble. Between 1716 and 1726 he was thrice exiled from Paris and twice imprisoned in the Bastille. He was first imprisoned in 1717 for having written verses against the regent, Philippe d'Orléans (1674–1723). His second imprisonment was the result of a quarrel with a dissolute young nobleman, the Chevalier de Rohan. He was soon liberated, however, and at once went to England, where he remained over two years (1726–29). While in England he published his epic poem on Henry the Fourth, *La Henriade*, the first edition

of which was dedicated to the queen of England. He returned to France in 1729, and won success with the *Histoire de Charles XII* in 1731 and with *Zaïre* in 1732. In 1734 he took up his residence with the Marquise du Châtelet in the chateau of Cirey in Champagne, where he resided most of the time until that lady's death in 1749. In 1745 he became royal historiographer and the following year "a gentleman of the king's bedchamber." He was also elected at this time to the French Academy. After Madame du Châtelet's death he returned to Paris, but soon left France for Prussia, where Frederick the Great, who had always admired him, had often requested him to take up his residence. There he remained from July, 1750, to March, 1753. Voltaire and Frederick parted bitter enemies, and the writer was arrested on his way through Frankfort on the Main, at the request of the king's representative. During his stay at Berlin and Potsdam he had completed and published one of his most important works, *Le Siècle de Louis XIV*. His return to France was followed by a period of wandering caused by the refusal of the arbitrary government of Louis XV to allow him to come to Paris. He finally settled at Geneva (1755), whence in 1759 he moved to Ferney, a large estate only a few miles distant, which he purchased and where he lived until 1778. Much of his time was given to the defense and protection of the victims of religious intolerance and fanaticism. He thus spent about three years getting justice done to the family and memory of a Protestant, Jean Calas, who had been put to death upon a false accusation of killing one of his sons to prevent his turning Roman Catholic. He was also constantly at work revising his earlier published writings, issuing numerous pamphlets, both in prose and verse, in favor of freedom of thought, and carrying on an extensive correspondence. Early in 1778, during the reign of Louis XVI, he returned to Paris, where he was received with great enthusiasm. The fatigue of the journey and the excitement of his reception proved too much for his weakened frame, and he died at Paris.

Important Works and Evaluation. His most important works are: tragedies, *Œdipe, Brutus, Zaïre* (considered the best), *Mérope, Mahomet, Alzire,* and *Tancrède;* poems, *La Henriade, Épître à Uranie, La Mort d'Adrienne Lecouvreur, Discours sur l'homme, La Loi naturelle, Le Désastre de Lisbonne, Le Mondain,* and *La Pucelle;* history, *Histoire de Charles XII, Essai sur les mœurs et l'esprit des nations, Le Siècle de Louis XIV,* and *Histoire de Russie sous Pierre le Grand;* philosophy, *Lettres philosophiques, Traité de métaphysique, Traité de la tolérance,* and *Dictionnaire philosophique;* literary criticism, *Essai sur la poésie epique, Temple du goût,* and *Commentaire sur Corneille;* fiction, *Candide, La Princesse de Babylone, L'Ingénu, L'Homme aux quarante écus,* and *Zadig;* and miscellanies which fill a very large number of volumes. His correspondence, which is enormous, is considered as fine as that of Madame de Sévigné. The important editions of his works are the Édition de Kehl (Kehl, 72 vols., 1784 *et seq.*), Beuchot's edition (Paris, 72 vols., 1829 *et seq.*), and Moland's edition (Paris, 52 vols., 1883 *et seq.*). Georges Bengesco is the author of a bibliography of Voltaire's works, in four volumes; G. Lanson (*Vol-*

taire, Paris, 1910) has written the best biography of the man and estimate of his work. The outstanding trait of Voltaire is a feverish intellectual curiosity. He delved into natural science and in the social theories as they were then being discussed as well as into the more formal genres of literature. He laid the foundations of modern historical method, and established almost single-handed modern historical criticism, both in the field of art and letters and in the field of moral philosophy. He always regarded himself, however, as a man of letters. He is thus an excellent example of a man who is interesting to the historian, since he is probably the most representative figure of the Age of the Enlightenment; to the historian of ideas, since he took part in every intellectual movement of that time; and to the literary critic, since his constant preoccupation was turned to seeking an adequate literary form in which to cast the ideas of his time. His production, which is enormous, is distinguished by its variety (epic, light verse, philosophical verse, drama, history, tales, dialogues, essays, philosophical writings) and by its clear and lucid expression.

Voltemand (vol′tẹ.mand). In Shakespeare's *Hamlet,* a courtier.

Volumnia (vọ.lum′ni.ạ). In Shakespeare's *Coriolanus,* the mother of Coriolanus. She is a powerful woman who exerts great influence over her son. Her arguments persuade Coriolanus to give up his plan to attack Rome, and as a result she wins a "happy victory to Rome," but loses her son, who is killed by his Volscian allies under Aufidius (V.iii,vi).

Volumnius (vọ.lum′ni.us). In Shakespeare's *Julius Caesar,* a boyhood friend who refuses to hold the sword for Brutus's suicide.

Volunteers, or, The Stock Jobbers, The. A comedy (produced 1692) by Thomas Shadwell, remembered for the two characters of General Blunt and Colonel Hackwell.

Vortigern (vôr′ti.gẽrn). A legendary British king of the middle of the 5th century who, according to Bede, invited the Jutes under Hengist and Horsa to Britain to aid the Britons against the Picts and Scots.

Vortigern and Rowena (rọ.wē′nạ). A play written in 1796 by William Henry Ireland, and assigned by him, with his other forgeries, to Shakespeare.

Vox Clamantis (vǒks klạ.man′tis). An allegorical poem in Latin, by John Gower. It is written in 10,000 lines and contains a vivid description of the Peasants' Revolt of 1381.

Voyage, The. A novel by John Middleton Murry, published in 1924.

Voyage, The. A novel by Charles Morgan, published in 1940.

Voyage Out, The. A novel (1915) by Virginia Woolf.

Voynich (voi′nich), **Ethel Lilian.** [Maiden name, **Boole.**] b. 1864—. An English novelist. She wrote *The Gadfly* (1897), *Jack Raymond* (1901), *Olive Latham* (1904), *Put Off Thy Shoes* (1945), and others.

Voysey Inheritance (voi′zi), **The.** A drama (1905) by Granville-Barker.

Vulcan (vul′kạn). In Roman mythology, the god of fire, especially volcanic fire. Originally an independent, and not benevolent, deity, he became completely identified with the Greek Hephaestus, and as such patron of metallurgy and handicrafts. He was the son of Jupiter and Juno, or of Juno alone, and was originally considered to have been born with deformed feet (according to late myths, however, his lameness came from his having been hurled from heaven by Jupiter in a fit of anger). He was the divine artificer and the creator of all that was mechanically wonderful. On earth various volcanoes, as Lemnos and Etna, were held to be his workshops. He had the power of conferring life upon his creations, and was thus the author of Pandora and of the golden dogs of Alcinous.

Vulgar Errors. See **Pseudodoxia Epidemica, or an Enquiry into Vulgar Errors.**

Vulgate (vul′gāt). A Latin version of the Bible long accepted as the authorized version of the Roman Catholic Church. It was prepared by Jerome about the close of the 4th century, partly by translation from the original, partly by revision of prior Latin versions. It gradually came into general use between the 6th and 9th centuries. The Anglo-Saxon translations were made from it, and also Wycliffe's English version, while other English versions from Tyndale's onward have been much influenced by it. The Vulgate was the first book printed (c1455). The Council of Trent (1546) ordered that the "old and vulgate edition," approved by the "usage of so many ages," should be the only Latin version used in "public lectures, disputations, sermons, and expositions." Authorized editions were afterward published under Pope Sixtus V in 1590 and Clement VIII in 1592–93. The latter, or Clementine edition, is at present the accepted standard of the Roman Catholic Church, and is the basis of the Douay Bible. In 1907 Pope Pius X entrusted to the Benedictine order the task of preparing a revision of the Vulgate. The religious terminology of the languages of W Europe has been in great part derived from or influenced by the Vulgate.

Vye (vī), **Eustacia.** The principal female character in Thomas Hardy's novel *The Return of the Native.*

Wace (wās, wäs). [Also: **Eustace;** erroneously called **Robert Wace.**] b. on the island of Jersey, c1100; d. c1175. A Norman poet. He received a prebend at Bayeux under Henry II, and was attached to the court. He wrote two poetical romances, the *Roman de Brut* and the *Roman de Rou,*

as well as several saints' lives in verse and a poem entitled *La Conception Nostre Dame.*

Wacht am Rhein (väċht äm rīn), **Die.** [English title, **The Watch on the Rhine.**] A German song, with words by Max Schneckenburger (1840), music by Karl Wilhelm (1854). It enjoyed great vogue in the Franco-Prussian War (1870–71), becoming a national song. Other composers also wrote music for it.

Wackford Squeers (wak'fǫrd skwîrz), **Mr.** See **Squeers, Mr. Wackford** and **Master Wackford.**

Wackles (wak'lz). The name of a mother and her daughters, characters in Dickens's novel *The Old Curiosity Shop.*

Wackles, Jane. In Dickens's novel *The Old Curiosity Shop,* a sister of Sophy Wackles.

Wackles, Melissa. In Dickens's novel *The Old Curiosity Shop,* a sister of Sophy Wackles.

Wackles, Miss Sophy. In Dickens's novel *The Old Curiosity Shop,* a young lady who, with her two sisters, keeps a small school for girls. She is the youthful love of Dick Swiveller, who breaks off with her when he has hopes that he may someday marry Little Nell, wherefore eventually (to Dick's mortification) she marries a market gardener.

Waddell (wo.del'), **Helen.** b. at Tokyo, May 31, 1889—. A British author. Author of *The Wandering Scholars* (1927), *Peter Abelard* (1933), *Beast and Saints* (1934), *The Desert Fathers* (1936), and others.

Wade (wād), **George Edward.** See **Robey, George.**

Wade, Miss. In Dickens's novel *Little Dorrit,* an odd woman whose full story is not told until the second half of the novel, but who appears, voicing her bitter discontent with everything, in the first part, and presently persuades Tattycoram to run away with her.

Wade's Boat (wādz). A mythical boat referred to by Chaucer in "The Merchant's Tale" in *The Canterbury Tales.* Wade is mentioned a number of times in medieval literature, but it is not possible to reconstruct from these references the story that Chaucer knew.

Wadham College (wod'ǎm). A college of Oxford University, founded in 1612 by Nicholas Wadham.

Wadman (wod'mǎn), **Widow.** A character in Laurence Sterne's *Tristram Shandy.* She is a widow with a tender feeling for Uncle Toby.

Wages of Virtue, The. A romantic novel by P. C. Wren, published in 1916.

Wagg (wag), **Mr.** In Thackeray's novel *Pendennis,* and earlier in *Vanity Fair,* a fashionable writer, wit, and man-about-town, whose amiable good nature is fatally compromised by his snobbery and essential vulgarity: "He had the soul of a butler who had been brought from his pantry to make fun in the drawing-room." He is somewhat more fully developed as a character in *Pendennis* than in *Vanity Fair,* where he is simply the servile hanger-on of Lord Steyne.

Waggoner, The. A poem by William Wordsworth, written in 1805, and published with a dedication to Charles Lamb in 1819.

Wagner (wag'nėr; German, väg'nėr). Faust's famulus, a pedant, in Goethe's *Faust.* He also appeared in Christopher Marlowe's *Dr. Faustus,* with some of the same characteristics. The character is early attached to Faust, appearing in the *Faustbuch,* as the chapbook containing the story is called.

Wagner, Richard. [Full name, **Wilhelm Richard Wagner.**] b. at Leipzig, Germany, May 22, 1813; d. at Venice, Feb. 13, 1883. A German composer and poet. His father died six months after his birth, and, nine months later, his mother married Ludwig Geyer. That Wagner was the natural son of Geyer, a Jewish actor, has been the subject of considerable speculation but of no satisfactory proof. Of Wagner's numerous early compositions the most important are his *Symphony in C* (1832), two operas, *Die Feen* (1834) and *Das Liebesverbot* (1836), and the *Faust Overture* (1840). From 1833 to 1839 Wagner lived a precarious existence as conductor of one small opera company after another. In 1836 he married Minna Planer, an actress. In 1839 he traveled to Paris, with his unfinished grand opera, *Rienzi,* in the hope of conquering the French operatic stage. All his efforts proved futile. He completed *Rienzi* in 1840, and *Der Fliegende Holländer,* a somber work which is a truer product of Wagner's characteristic artistry than the derivative *Rienzi,* in 1841. Performances of these two works at Dresden led to Wagner's appointment as court *Kapellmeister* (choirmaster) there in 1843. *Tannhäuser* was produced at Dresden in 1845 under Wagner's direction, but was not well received. The third act especially was bewildering to the opera public of that day. *Lohengrin,* which has proved to be his most popular work, was completed in 1848. Accused of active participation in the abortive Dresden revolution of 1849, Wagner was forced to flee from Germany. The exact extent of his revolutionary activities has long been debated, particularly because Wagner's own unreliable autobiography, *Mein Leben* (published posthumously in 1911), beclouds the issue. It now seems certain, however, that he had an active part in the supervision of the revolutionary troop movements. In the succeeding three years, Wagner suspended creative composition and devoted himself to a detailed theoretical exposition of the new art form which had been gradually crystallizing in his mind, the word-tone-drama, an organic synthesis of poetry, music, and stage action, in which all the set patterns of opera were discarded in favor of a continuous flow of melodic dialogue carefully synchronized with the action, and supported by a rich orchestral commentary in which leitmotifs constituted the chief unifying principle. Details of this theory are to be found in the essays *Das Kunstwerk der Zukunft* (1850) and *Oper und Drama* (1851). By 1852, Wagner had completed the poems of his major work, *Der Ring des Nibelungen,* a cycle of three full-length music dramas (*Die Walküre, Siegfried,* and *Götterdämmerung*) preceded by the shorter *Das Rheingold.* The texts of all these were constructed according to the unique prosodic principles he had expounded in *Oper und Drama.* The music to *Das Rheingold* was finished in 1854. *Die Walküre,* which is the most complete artistic realization of these theories, was completed in 1856. His inspiration for the impassioned love music in this work, as well as in *Tristan und Isolde,* was

---

ḍ, d or j; ṣ, s or sh; ṭ, t or ch; ẓ, z or zh; o, F. cloche; ü, F. menu; ċh, Sc. loch; ṅ, F. bonbon.

Mathilde Wesendonck, the wife of a wealthy Zurich merchant, who befriended the Wagners and in 1857 invited them to live permanently on the Wesendonck estate. In a little over a year, however, the untenable situation had reached a crisis, and Wagner separated from his wife and left Zurich for Venice. Under the spell of his renunciation of Mathilde and the pessimistic doctrines of Schopenhauer, he completed *Tristan und Isolde* (1859). Wagner's enthusiastic acceptance of Schopenhauer's metaphysics of music brought about a significant shift in his concept of the role of music in the music drama, with the result that in *Tristan und Isolde* and all succeeding works the music is considerably more independent and the exact synthesis of word and tone formerly required is no longer a central factor. In 1861 a revised *Tannhäuser* was produced at Paris and gave rise to the famous Jockey Club scandal which kept the audience in a turmoil throughout most of the performance. Wagner had interrupted the composition of his *Nibelungen* cycle in 1857, at the end of the second act of *Siegfried*, and, uncertain whether it would ever be completed and performed, he published the poems in 1862. At possibly the darkest period of his life, Wagner was dramatically rescued by young Ludwig II, shortly after the latter had ascended the Bavarian throne. He called Wagner to Munich in 1864, and relieved him of all concern save for the completion and production of his works. *Tristan und Isolde* was given a fine première performance at Munich in 1865, and *Die Meistersinger*, a somewhat romanticized picture of 16th-century Nuremberg, in 1868. Court intrigue, mounting expenses, Ludwig's eccentricities, and Wagner's tactlessness soon led to trouble and Wagner was forced to leave Munich for Switzerland in 1865, though continuing to enjoy a generous annuity. With him went Cosima, the daughter of Franz Liszt, wife of Hans von Bülow. They were married in 1870 at Lucerne, after the death of Wagner's estranged wife, Minna (and Bülow's divorce of Cosima). From this union there were three children, Isolde, Eva, and Siegfried, all born before their parents' marriage. Wagner moved to Bayreuth in northern Bavaria in 1872, where he supervised the erection of his Festival Theater, in which the first complete performances of the *Ring* dramas, an event which commanded world-wide attention, were given in 1876. In 1882, Wagner completed his last work, *Parsifal*, which he called a Consecrational Festival Play. It was given the same year at Bayreuth. Wagner died the following year in his suite in the Palazzo Vendramini at Venice.

Wagstaff (wag'staf), **Launcelot** and **Théophile.** Two of the many pseudonyms of **Thackeray, William Makepeace.**

Wain (wān), **Charles's.** In astronomy, the seven brightest stars in the constellation Ursa Major, or the Great Bear. Two of the stars are known as "the pointers," because, being nearly in a straight line with the polestar, they direct an observer to it. This combination of stars has also been called the Plow, the Great Dipper, the Northern Car, and sometimes the Butcher's Cleaver.

Wait, James. The Negro in Conrad's *The Nigger of the Narcissus.*

Wakefield (wāk'fēld), **Harry.** In Sir Walter Scott's tale *The Two Drovers*, the English drover. He is killed by the Scottish drover, Robin Oig M'Combich.

Wakefield Master. See under **Towneley Plays.**

Wakefield Plays. See **Towneley Plays.**

Wakem (wā'kem), **Philip.** One of the principal characters in George Eliot's novel *The Mill on the Floss*, a deformed youth in love with Maggie Tulliver.

Walcot (wol'kọt, wôl'-), **Charles Melton.** b. at London, 1816; d. at Philadelphia, May 13, 1868. An English actor.

Waldegrave (wôl'grāv), **Robert.** b. at Blockley, Worcestershire, England, c1554; d. at London, 1604. An English Puritan printer, original publisher of the *Martin Marprelate* tracts. He began (1578) his London publishing business with *A Castell for the Soule*, later printing (1588–89) the controversial *Marprelate* tracts. He was (1590–1603) at Edinburgh as the royal printer, where he published books by John Napier, James VI (afterward James I of England), John Penry, Alexander Hume, Thomas Cartwright, and William Alexander. In 1603 he returned to England and reëstablished his London business. Waldegrave also published pirated editions of Sir Philip Sidney's *Arcadia* (1599), Thomas Tusser's *500 Points of Good Husbandry* (1599), and Robert Southwell's *Saint Peter's Complaint* (1600).

Waldemar Fitzurse (wôl'dẹ.mär fits.ẻrs'). See **Fitzurse, Waldemar.**

Waldengarver (wôl'dẹn.gär.vẻr). See **Wopsle, Mr.**

Waldenses (wol.den'sēz). [Also: **Leonists, Waldensians** (wôl.den'si.ạnz); French, **Vaudois, Vaudois des Alpes.**] Members of a reforming body of Christians, followers of Peter Waldo (Valdo) of Lyons, formed c1170. Their chief seats were in the Alpine valleys of Piedmont, Dauphiné, and Provence: hence the French name *Vaudois des Alpes*, or *Vaudois*. The Waldenses, refused recognition by the papacy, drifted into heresy and, when it arose in the 16th century, joined the Reformation movement. They were often severely persecuted, and were the object of several crusades.

Waldhere (wäld'her''e). [Also, **Waldere.**] A manuscript consisting of two fragments of an Old English poem, discovered in Copenhagen in 1860. The first of the fragments is a dialogue between Hildegund, a princess of Burgundy, and Waldhere (Walter) of Aquitaine, who are both prisoners of Attila, ruler of the Huns. The second fragment gives the end of a speech by Gunther, new king of the Franks, and the reply of Waldhere. In the complete story (which is known from other sources), Waldhere and Hildegund, after various fights with the men of Attila, manage to escape and are married.

Wales (wālz). [Welsh, **Cymru;** Latin, **Cambria.**] A titular principality of Great Britain, part of the United Kingdom. It is bounded by the Irish Sea on the N, the English counties of Cheshire, Shropshire, Herefordshire, and Gloucestershire on the E, the Bristol Channel on the S, and St. George's Channel on the W. Its surface is largely mountainous, reaching 3,560 ft. in Snowdon, the highest point in S Britain. It is noted for mineral wealth, producing iron, coal, copper, lead, zinc, slate, and limestone. The N and NW sections of Wales (Anglesey, the valleys of North Wales, and the Lleyn peninsula) raise many sheep and beef cattle. The SW part is important for dairy cattle and pigs. The C portion of the country is mostly in rough hill pasture for sheep. The Vale of Glamorgan is an area of mixed farming. The Welsh Borderland (with England), or Welsh Marches, is mainly an area of permanent pasture where many cattle and sheep are raised. The country is divided into North Wales, containing the counties Anglesey, Caernarvonshire, Denbighshire, Flintshire, Merionethshire, and Montgomeryshire; and South Wales, containing the counties Brecknockshire, Cardiganshire, Carmarthenshire, Glamorganshire, Pembrokeshire, and Radnorshire. South Wales is highly industrialized, with a great coal field and large iron and steel works, chemical plants, and other heavy industries. The inhabitants of Wales are largely of Welsh stock, and the Welsh language is commonly spoken by about 40 percent of the population. The ancient inhabitants were the Celtic tribes Ordovices, Demetae, and Silures. Wales was not subdued by the Romans; maintained prolonged struggles with the Anglo-Saxons; was made tributary by Athelstan, Harold II, and William the Conqueror; and after repeated efforts was subdued (1276–84) by Edward I, and united to England. An unsuccessful rebellion, under Owen Glendower, broke out in 1400. The principality was incorporated with England in 1536.

Walford (wôl′fọrd), **Lucy Bethia.** [Maiden name, **Colquhoun.**] b. at Portobello, Scotland, April 17, 1845; d. 1915. A Scottish novelist. Her works include *Mr. Smith* (1874), *Pauline* (1877), *The Baby's Grandmother* (1885), *A Mere Child* (1888), *One of Ourselves* (1900), *Charlotte* (1902), *The Stay-at-Homes* (1903), *Leonore Stubbs* (1908), *Recollections of a Scottish Novelist* (1910), and others.

Walhalla (väl.häl′ä). See **Valhalla.**

Walker (wô′kẽr), **John.** b. at Colney Hatch, Middlesex, England, March 18, 1732; d. at London, Aug. 1, 1807. An English actor and lexicographer. After leaving (1768) the stage, he became a teacher of elocution at London. His best-known work is *Critical Pronouncing Dictionary and Exposition of the English Language* (1791; this was the first dictionary after Thomas Sheridan's of 1780 in which pronunciation was systematically recorded). He also published a *Rhyming Dictionary* (1775 and subsequent editions to the present day).

Wall (wôl). In Shakespeare's *Midsummer Night's Dream,* the wall that separates Pyramus and Thisby (Thisbe) in the interpolated play. It is represented (with spoken lines) by Snout, the tinker.

Wallace (wol′ạs), **Alfred Russel.** b. at Usk, Monmouthshire, England, Jan. 8, 1823; d. at Broadstone, Dorsetshire, England, Nov. 7, 1913. An English scientist, independent discoverer of the theory of natural selection. He was influenced by the naturalist Henry Walter Bates, whom he accompanied (April, 1848–March, 1850) on an exploring trip to the Amazon, and by T. R. Malthus' book, *On Population.* While in the Malay Archipelago (1854–62), working independently of Charles Darwin, he discovered the principle of natural selection, reaching the same conclusions that Darwin had formulated and was ready to announce. Wallace sent a statement of his views to Darwin; with each worker insisting on giving credit to the other, the problem was solved by the publication of a joint paper, read (July 1, 1858) before the Linnaean Society of London, in which the theory was presented as a joint discovery. Wallace distinguished two regions in the East Indies, separated by a narrow belt of water (called Wallace's Line), with distinct differences in animal life on either side of the line. Author of *Travels on the Amazon and Rio Negro* and *Palm Trees of the Amazon* (both 1853), *The Malay Archipelago* (1869), *Contributions to the Theory of Natural Selection* (1870), *On Miracles and Modern Spiritualism* (1875), *Geographical Distribution of Animals* (1876), *Tropical Nature* (1878), *Island Life* (1880), *Land Nationalization* (1882), *Darwinism* (1889), *The Ice Age and Its Work* (1894), *Method of Organic Evolution* (1896), *Vaccination—A Delusion* (1898), *Man's Place in the Universe* (1903), *My Life* (1905), *Is Mars Habitable?* (1907), *The World of Life* (1910), *Social Environment and Moral Progress* (1912), and *The Revolt of Democracy* (1913).

Wallace, Bryan. b. in England, 1906—. An English screen writer; son of Edgar Wallace and his first wife, Iva Maud Caldecott.

Wallace, Sir **Donald Mackenzie.** b. Nov. 11, 1841; d. at Lymington, Hampshire, England, Jan. 10, 1919. A British writer and traveler in Russia, foreign editor (1891–99) of the London *Times.* He wrote *Russia* (1877), *Egypt and the Egyptian Question* (1883), and *The Web of Empire* (1902), and for a short time in 1899 edited the tenth edition (1902–03) of the *Encyclopaedia Britannica.*

Wallace, Edgar. [Full name, **Richard Horatio Edgar Wallace.**] b. at Greenwich, London, April 1, 1875; d. at Hollywood, Calif., Feb. 10, 1932. An English writer of mystery and adventure novels. He married (1900) Iva Maud Caldecott, and after their divorce (1918) married (1921) his former secretary, Ethel Violet King. A private in the British army, he fought in the Boer War, and was a war correspondent (1899–1902) for Reuter's Agency, the *Daily News,* and the *Daily Mail.* He was the author of more than 150 novels, more than 300 short stories, 20 or more plays, and other works, dictating or writing at phenomenal speed. Among his books are *The Four Just Men* (1905), *Angel Esquire* (1908), *Sanders of the River* (1911), *The Clue of the Twisted Candle* (1916), *The Green Archer* (1923), *A King By Night* (1926), *The Terrible People* (1926), *The Murder Book of J. G. Reeder* (1929), *Mr. Commissioner Sanders* (1930), *Red Aces—Being Three Cases of Mr. Reeder* (1930), and *Mr. Reeder Returns* (1932), novels; *The Forest of Happy Dreams* (1914), *M'Lady* (1921), *The Ringer* (1926), *The Yellow Mask* (1927), *The Man Who Changed His Name* (1928), *The Squeaker* (1928), *The Flying Squad* (1928), *Persons Unknown* (1929), *The Calendar* (1929), and *On the Spot* (1931), plays; *People* (1929) and *My Hollywood Diary* (1932), autobiography. He had completed one scenario before his death, *King Kong.*

Wallace, Sir **William.** [Also: **Walays, Wallensis.**] b. c1272; executed at London, Aug. 23, 1305. A

Scottish patriot and national hero. He was out-lawed in early life, became a leader of a party of insurgents against the rule of Edward I of England in 1297, and totally defeated the English at the battle of Stirling Bridge Sept. 11, 1297. He devastated several counties in northern England, was made guardian of Scotland, and was defeated by Edward I at Falkirk July 22, 1298. He carried on a guerrilla warfare for several years, went to France and Rome to attempt to gain aid for the Scottish cause, was betrayed to the English near Glasgow Aug. 3, 1305, was taken to London, and was tried, condemned for treason, and hanged, drawn, and quartered.

Wallace, William. b. at Greenock, Scotland, July 3, 1860; d. 1940. A Scottish composer. His most important compositions are six symphonic poems for orchestra: *The Passing of Beatrice, Sister Helen, Amboss oder Hammer, Greeting to the New Century, Sir William Wallace,* and *François Villon.* He wrote many other musical works and several books, including *On the Threshold of Music* (1908), *The Musical Faculty* (1914), and *A Study of Wagner* (1925).

Wallack (wol'ạk), **Henry John.** b. at London, 1790; d. at New York, Aug. 30, 1870. An actor on the London and New York stage. After attaining a reputation in England, he made his first American appearance (1819) at Baltimore, and made his New York debut in 1821; in 1824 he became leading man at the Chatham Garden Theatre at New York. In England in the periods 1828–32 and 1834–36, he was during the latter time stage manager and leading man at Covent Garden, London, subsequently filling similar posts at the National Theatre (New York) beginning in 1837.

Waller (wol'ẽr), **Edmund.** b. at Coleshill, Hertfordshire, England, March 3, 1606; d. at Beaconsfield, England, Oct. 21, 1687. An English poet. He entered Parliament in 1621, when he was only 16. In 1631 he married a rich woman, found himself in legal difficulties because of the marriage, and was fined; his wife died in 1634. He was a member of the Long Parliament and a supporter of the king, in whose favor he concocted the "Waller Plot" in 1643, a plan to keep London loyal to the king; the plot was discovered and Waller gave evidence against his companions, who were executed while his own punishment was a fine and banishment. He lived in France, traveled through Switzerland and Italy with John Evelyn, and returned (1652) to England after Parliament revoked the sentence of banishment. After the Restoration he again sat in Parliament (1661–87). Among his poems are a panegyric on Cromwell, a lament for Cromwell's death, congratulations on Charles II's return, a number of early poems to "Sacharissa" (Lady Dorothy Sidney, whom he wooed after his first wife's death), a group of lyrics including *Go, Lovely Rose* and *On a Girdle,* the longer *St. James's Park* (1661), and *Divine Poems* (1685). Waller's poetry is not marked by warmth but by an elegance that covers his lack of originality; he is credited with popularizing the heroic couplet.

Walling (wol'ing), **Robert Alfred John.** b. at Exeter, England, Jan. 11, 1869; d. at Plympton, Devonshire, England, Sept. 4, 1949. An English

journalist and writer, notably of detective stories. He was the editor of the *Western Independent* at Plymouth. His books include *The Man with the Squeaky Voice* (1930), *The Corpse with the Dirty Face* (1936), and *The Corpse with the Grimy Glove* (1938).

Wall of Antoninus (an.tǫ.nī'nus). See under **Antoninus Pius.**

Wall of Severus (sẹ.vir'us). See **Severus, Wall of.**

Walls of Jericho (jer'i.kō), **The.** A four-act play (1904) by Alfred Sutro.

Walmsley (wômz'li), **Leo.** b. at Shipley, Yorkshire, England, Sept. 29, 1892–. An English novelist. Author of *The Silver Blimp* (1921) and *Toro of the Little People* (1926), books for children. His novels include *Three Fevers* (1932; filmed as *Turn of the Tide*), *The Phantom Lobster* (1933), *Foreigners* (1935), *Sally Lunn* (1937), the autobiographical *Love in the Sun* (1939), *Fishermen at War* (1941), *So Many Loves* (1944), and *Master Mariner* (1948).

Walpole, Horace (or **Horatio**). [Title, 4th Earl of Orford.] b. at London, Oct. 5, 1717; d. there, March 2, 1797. An English author; third surviving son of Sir Robert Walpole. He was educated at Eton and at King's College, Cambridge. On leaving Cambridge he traveled (1739–41) with Thomas Gray in France and Italy. In 1741 he was elected to Parliament, where he remained until 1768. His political career was largely devoted to furthering the interests of his cousin, Henry Seymour Conway. His income, which averaged about 5,000 pounds a year, came from several sinecures to which he had been appointed by his father. In 1747 he moved to a small house, Strawberry Hill (on the Thames near Twickenham), which he began to remodel in 1749 in the neo-Gothic style; his last addition was built in 1790. On Dec. 5, 1791, he succeeded as 4th Earl of Orford. Strawberry Hill is a landmark in English taste, since it influenced (dubiously) architectural style in the English-speaking world for upwards of a century and a half. Walpole, an ardent collector, filled his house with pictures, books, and curiosities that made it one of the showplaces of England. The contents of Strawberry Hill were sold at auction in 1842 in two celebrated sales that took 32 days. In 1757 Walpole opened the Strawberry Hill Press with Gray's two Pindaric *Odes.* This was perhaps the most famous private press ever to be operated in England. Thirty-four books of varying size and importance were printed at it and 77 single sheets of verses, title pages, and the like. Walpole was the author of five pioneer works, *Aedes Walpolianae* (1747), which was a description of his father's great collection of pictures at Houghton in Norfolk, *A Catalogue of the Royal and Noble Authors of England* (1758), *Anecdotes of Painting in England* (1763–71), a romance entitled *The Castle of Otranto* (1765), and *Historic Doubts on the Life and Reign of Richard III* (1768). Though *The Castle of Otranto* was immensely popular for upwards of a century as the first "Gothic romance," Walpole's literary fame today depends mostly upon his letters, which are regarded as the best in the language. They and his memoirs of his times, which he wrote secretly from 1751 to 1791 and which he arranged to be published many years after his death, furnish the fullest picture we have of 18th-century life in

England. There have been many editions of Walpole's letters, the first being included in *The Works of Lord Orford* (1798). The two most recent are those of Paget and Helen Toynbee (19 vols., 1903–26), and the *Yale Edition of Horace Walpole's Correspondence*, edited by W. S. Lewis, which were in 1950 in progress of publication.

Walpole, Sir Hugh. [Full name, **Hugh Seymour Walpole.**] b. at Auckland, New Zealand, 1884; d. at Keswick, Cumberland, England, June 1, 1941. An English novelist and critic. He began his literary career as a book reviewer for the London *Standard*. Author of the novels *The Wooden Horse* (1909), *Maradick at Forty* (1910), *The Prelude to Adventure* (1912), *Fortitude* (1913); *The Duchess of Wrexe* (1914), *The Green Mirror* (1917), and *The Captives* (1920; awarded James Tait Black memorial prize), a trilogy; *Jeremy* (1919), *Jeremy and Hamlet* (1923), and *Jeremy at Crale* (1927), a trilogy; *The Dark Forest* (1916) and its sequel, *The Secret City* (1919; awarded James Tait Black memorial prize); a tetralogy, "The Herries Chronicles," including *Rogue Herries* (1930), *Judith Paris* (1931), *The Fortress* (1932), and *Vanessa* (1933); *The Thirteen Travelers* (1921), *The Young Enchanted* (1922), *The Cathedral* (1922), *The Old Ladies* (1924), *Portrait of a Man with Red Hair* (1925), and *Hans Frost* (1929); of *The Young Huntress* (1933) and *The Haxtons* (1939), plays; of *Joseph Conrad* (1916), *The Art of James Branch Cabell* (1920), *The English Novel* (1925), *Reading* (1926), *Anthony Trollope* (1928), and *My Religious Experience* (1928), critical works; and of collections of short stories, including *Head in Green Bronze* (1938).

Walpole, Sir Robert. [Title: 1st Earl of **Orford**; nicknamed **"Robin Bluestring"** and **"the Grand Corrupter."**] b. at Houghton, Norfolk, England, Aug. 26, 1676; d. there, March 18, 1745. An English statesman. He was educated at Eton and Cambridge, entered Parliament in 1701, became a member of the council to Prince George in 1705 and secretary at war in 1708, and became one of the Whig leaders. He was treasurer of the navy and manager of the Sacheverell impeachment in 1710, was accused of corruption, expelled from Parliament, and sent to the Tower in 1712, was returned to Parliament in 1713, became paymaster general in 1714, and was prime minister (first lord of the treasury and chancellor of the exchequer) 1715–17. In 1717 he worked out a sinking fund to reduce the national debt. Walpole had warned of the danger of the South Sea speculation; he became paymaster general in 1720, and, on the breaking of the South Sea Bubble (1720), was called to take charge of the desperate financial situation. He was again first lord of the treasury and chancellor of the exchequer in 1721 and from then until 1742 was the leading political figure in England, actually the first prime minister in the modern sense. With Charles Townshend as secretary of state he set forth on a policy directed toward building prosperity while avoiding war. Townshend resigned in 1730 after a quarrel with Walpole and thereafter he stood alone. He reduced duties, paid out subsidies, cut the land tax, and in general attempted to base the economy on a free flow of goods. He shifted the center of gravity in government from the House of Lords to the House of Commons, began the trend of government from the hands of the king to those of the prime minister, and made the prime minister actual chief of the government by a calculated policy of rewards and punishments based on loyalty. Eventually his methods led to a united front of opposition to him and, first forced into the War of the Austrian Succession (1739) by the war party and then criticized for the lack of military success, he resigned in 1742.

Walpole, Sir Spencer. b. at London, Feb. 6, 1839; d. in Sussex, England, July 7, 1907. An English government official, essayist, and historian. He was inspector of fisheries for England and Wales, governor (1882–93) of the Isle of Man, and secretary (1893–99) to the post office. Author of *History of England from 1815 to 1856* (6 vols., 1878–90), *Life of Lord John Russell* (1889), *A History of Twenty-Five Years: 1856–80* (4 vols., 1904–08), *Studies in Biography* (1906), and *Essays: Political and Biographical* (1908). He also wrote a biography (1874) of his grandfather, Spencer Perceval.

Walpurgis Night (väl.pûr′gis). The night before May 1. In German folklore, witches are said to ride on this night on broomsticks, goats, and the like, to some appointed rendezvous, especially the Brocken, highest peak in the Harz Mountains, where they observe their witches' Sabbat with their master the devil. Goethe utilizes this belief in *Faust*.

Walsh (wôlsh), **William.** b. 1663; d. March 18, 1708. An English poet, a friend of John Dryden and Alexander Pope.

Walsingham (wôl′sing.am), **Thomas.** d. c1422. An English historian and monk, author of a history of England (*Brevis Historia*) from Edward I to Henry V, and a history of Normandy.

Walter (wôl′tėr). Entries on literary characters having this prename will be found under the surnames Blunt, Carling, Elliot, Gay, Herbert, Shandy, Whitmore, and Whorehound.

Walter, John. b. probably at Battersea, London, Feb. 23, 1776; d. at London, July 28, 1847. An English journalist. He served as comanager (1797–1803), manager (1803 *et seq.*), editor (1803–10), and coeditor (1811 *et seq.*, with John Stoddart, Thomas Barnes, and John Thaddeus Delane) of the London *Times*. He was a member of Parliament (1832–37, 1841). Noted for his opposition (1834, 1837) to the English and Irish poor laws, he frequently offended the government, suffering financial loss as a result by his frank and independent criticism of policy, but at the same time building the reputation of his newspaper. He was the first (1805) to send special correspondents abroad to report foreign news and the first to feature the leading article.

Walter, John. b. at Printing House Square, London, 1818; d. at Bear Wood, Berkshire, England, Nov. 3, 1894. An English journalist; son of John Walter (1776–1847). He was associated (1840–47) with the London *Times*, and its chief owner (1847 *et seq.*); John Thaddeus Delane, Thomas Chenery, and George Earle Buckle were editors during his management. He was a member of Parliament (1847–65, 1868–85). He devised and introduced (1869) the Walter printing press, enabling one machine to turn out 12,000 copies an hour.

d, d or j; ş, s or sh; ţ, t or ch; z̧, z or zh; o, F. cloche; ü, F. menu; ċh, Sc. loch; ṅ, F. bonbon.

Walter, Master. The hunchback in James Sheridan Knowles's *The Hunchback.* He is the guardian of Julia, and is discovered to be her father.

Walter Lorraine (lô.rān'). In Thackeray's *Pendennis,* and referred to in *The Newcomes,* the first novel written by Pendennis.

Walters (wôl'tẽrz), **John.** b. 1759; d. at Efenechtyd, Wales, June 28, 1789. A Welsh poet and translator. Author of sermons, *Translated Specimens of Welsh Poetry in English Verse* (1772), *Ode on the Immortality of the Soul* (1776), *Life, an Elegy* (1776), and *Poems with Notes* (1780). At the request of the Society of Royal British Bowmen, he edited (1778) a reprint of *Toxophilus,* Roger Ascham's famous work on archery. His *Poems with Notes* is commonly called *Bodleian Poems,* for they were composed while the author was an Oxford student and an assistant librarian at the Bodleian Library.

Waltham Abbey (wôl'tạm, -thạm). A restored abbey church in the town of Waltham Abbey, Essex. The original abbey was founded by King Harold.

Walther von der Vogelweide (väl'tẽr fon dẽr fō'gẽl-vī.dẹ). b. probably in Austria (date unknown); d. at Würzburg, Germany, after 1227. A Middle High German lyric poet, the greatest of the period. He was of noble family, as his title "Herr" indicates, but poor. His youth was spent at Vienna, at the court of Duke Frederick I. After the death of his patron in 1198, he lived the life of a wandering singer, and traveled through a great part of Germany and the countries adjoining. He was not only with the Babenberg princes in Austria, whither he subsequently returned, but also at the courts of Thuringia, Meissen, Bavaria, and Carinthia; and in turn was with the emperors Philip of Swabia, Otto IV, and Frederick II. The last-named gave him a fief, it is supposed at Würzburg. His career as a poet began about 1187; the last poem which can be dated is a song in encouragement of the crusade (the fifth Crusade) of Frederick II in 1227. His poems are love songs, political songs or *Sprüche,* and religious songs, the last written in his later years. He is the principal minnesinger and the most gifted lyric poet of medieval Germany.

Walton (wôl'tọn), **Izaak.** [Called "the Father of Angling."] b. at Stafford, England, Aug. 9, 1593; d. at Winchester, England, Dec. 15, 1683. English author. He was a shopkeeper in London until the English Civil War, when he retired. Walton is famous from his work *The Compleat Angler, or the Contemplative Man's Recreation* (1653; 5th edition, 1676, with continuation on fly-fishing by Charles Cotton), a series of dialogues on the joys of fishing with many digressions, anecdotes, and quotations, one of the monuments of English literature. He also wrote lives of John Donne, Henry Wotton (with *Reliquiae Wottonianae*), Richard Hooker, George Herbert, and Robert Sanderson.

Walton, Sir John. The defender of Douglas Castle in Sir Walter Scott's novel *Castle Dangerous.*

Wamba (wom'bạ). In Scott's *Ivanhoe,* a jester who risks his life to save his master, Cedric the Saxon.

Wanderer, The. An Old English poem of 115 lines of the early 8th century, preserved in the *Exeter Book.* Except for the opening and closing lines it is a monologue by a man who has lost his lord, telling of the trials of exile and recalling the joys of the days of comradeship in the hall of his lord. Throughout runs the sentiment that it is the true hero and wise man who knows how to keep his sorrow within his heart.

Wanderer, The. A poem (1729) by Richard Savage, in five cantos, containing moral reflections upon the life of man.

Wandering Jew. In medieval legend (specifically according to a story by Matthew Paris, dating from the 13th century) a servant of Pilate, by name Cartaphilus, who gave Jesus a blow when he was led out of the palace to execution. In a later story he was a cobbler, named Ahasuerus, who refused Jesus permission to sit down and rest when he passed his house on the way to Golgotha. Both legends agree in the sentence pronounced by Jesus on the offender, "Thou shalt wander on the earth till I return." A prey to remorse, he has since wandered from land to land without being able to find a grave. He is introduced in Edgar Quinet's *Ahasuerus,* by Chamisso, A. W. Schlegel, Lenau, H. C. Andersen, George Croly (in his novel *Salathiel*), Eugène Sue (in his novel *Le Juif errant*), and others. He is alleged to have appeared in different cities and countries through the centuries, the last such allegation being made in England in 1830.

Wandering Lovers, The. A play attributed to John Fletcher and Philip Massinger, licensed in 1623.

Wandering of Oisin (u.shēn'), **The.** A long narrative poem (1889) by W. B. Yeats. Yeats stated that the "poem is founded upon the Middle Irish dialogues of S. Patrick and Oisin and a certain Gaelic poem of the last century." The poem may be said to illustrate the conflict between dream and reality, imagination and fact.

Wanderings of Cain (kān), **The.** A tale in verse projected as a collaborative effort, but never finished, by Coleridge and Wordsworth. Coleridge wrote the second canto in the early part of 1798 (Wordsworth was to have written the first canto, but did not complete it, and the fragment which exists is wholly Coleridge's).

Wandering Willie (wil'i). [Full name, **Willie Steenson.**] In Sir Walter Scott's novel *Redgauntlet,* a blind fiddler who is devoted to the Redgauntlet family.

Wapping (wop'ing). An ecclesiastical district in E London, in the County of London, in Stepney metropolitan borough, situated along the N bank of the river Thames below the Tower of London, ab. 2 mi. SE of Fenchurch Street Station.

Warbeck (wôr'bek), **Perkin.** b. c1474; executed at London, Nov. 23, 1499. A pretender to the English crown, possibly a Fleming by birth. He claimed to be Richard, Duke of York, son of Edward IV, actually slain in the Tower in 1483. In 1491 he arrived at Cork, as assistant to a silk merchant. The Yorkist atmosphere there made it possible for him to be considered one of the Yorkist heirs to the throne and he soon went to France, where he was recognized as Duke of York by the court. He made an unsuccessful landing in Kent in 1495, was acknowledged by James IV of Scotland in 1496, unsuccessfully invaded England with the Scots in

1496, went to Ireland, and made a descent upon Cornwall in 1497, but was captured. He escaped from the Tower in 1498 but was retaken, and was condemned and executed in 1499. He was made the subject of a tragedy by John Ford, called *The Chronicle History of Perkin Warbeck* (1634), and also of a play by Charles Macklin, the actor, called *King Henry VII, or the Popish Impostor* (1716). Another, called *The Pretender*, was written by Joseph Elderton, an attorney, but never acted.

War Between the States. See **Civil War.**

Warburton (wôr′bėr″tọn, -bėr.tọn), **Eliot.** [Full name, **Bartholomew Elliott George Warburton.**] b. near Tullamore, Ireland, 1810; d. at sea, Jan. 4, 1852. An Irish traveler and novelist. He traveled in the East, and perished in the burning of the steamship *Amazon*. He published *The Crescent and the Cross* (1844), *Memoir of Prince Rupert* (1849), *Reginald Hastings* (1850; a novel), and *Darien* (1852; a novel).

Warburton, John. b. in February, 1682; d. 1759. An English antiquary. He published a number of maps, and *Vallum Romanum, or the History and Antiquities of the Roman Wall* (1753) and others. He made a large collection of manuscripts, engravings, books, and similar antiquities, but is principally known to posterity as the master of a careless cook who burned a large number of valuable plays as waste paper (hence the entries in dramatic catalogues, "Burned by Mr. Warburton's servant").

Warburton, William. b. at Newark, England, Dec. 24, 1698; d. at Gloucester, England, June 7, 1779. An English prelate, theological controversialist, and critic. He was made bishop of Gloucester in 1759. His works include *The Alliance between Church and State* (1736), *The Divine Legation of Moses Demonstrated* (1738–41: the last part posthumous, 1788), *Julian* (concerning the attempt to rebuild the temple at Jerusalem, 1750), *Principles of Natural and Revealed Religion* (1753), *View of Bolingbroke's Posthumous Writings* (1754), *Doctrine of Grace* (1762). He edited Shakespeare's plays (1747), and, as Alexander Pope's literary executor, issued Pope's works (1751).

Ward (wôrd), **Edward.** [Frequently called **Ned Ward.**] b. in Oxfordshire, England, 1667; d. at London, June 20, 1731. A London innkeeper, satirist, and poet. He published (1691 *et seq.*) satires on the church, the Whigs, the government, and various phases of London life. Because of his attacks on the administration, Ward had to stand in the pillory on at least two occasions in 1705. Author of more than 80 works in realistic verse and prose, of which the most important are *The London Spy* (18 parts, 1698–1703), *Hudibras Redivivus* (12 parts, 1705–07), a burlesque poem in the style and manner of the 17th-century Samuel Butler, and a metrical translation of *Don Quixote* (2 vols., 1711–12).

Ward, Mrs. Humphry. [Maiden name, **Mary Augusta Arnold.**] b. at Hobart Town, Tasmania, 1851; d. March 24, 1920. An English novelist; granddaughter of Thomas Arnold. Her works include the novels *Miss Bretherton* (1884), *Robert Elsmere* (1888; a defense of the "higher criticism" against orthodoxy that became a great success after being reviewed by W. E. Gladstone), *David Grieve*

(1892), *Marcella* (1894), *Story of Bessie Costrell* (1895), *Sir George Tressady* (1896), *Helbeck of Bannisdale* (1898), *Eleanor* (1900), *Lady Rose's Daughter* (1903), *The Marriage of William Ashe* (1905), *Fenwick's Career* (1906), *William Thomas Arnold, Journalist and Historian* (1907), *The Testing of Diana Mallory* (1908), *Marriage à la Mode* (1909), *Canadian Born* (1910), *The Case of Richard Meynell* (serially, 1910–11), and *The Coryston Family* (1913); biographical and critical works; and a translation of *Amiel's Journal* (1885).

Ward, Nathaniel. [Pseudonym, **Theodore de la Guard.**] b. at Haverhill, England, in 1578; d. in England, c1652. An English preacher and author. He emigrated to Massachusetts in 1634, was a Puritan pastor at Ipswich (Agawam), and returned to England in 1646, holding a pastorate in Essex after 1648. He was the author of the satirical work *The Simple Cobler of Aggawam* (1647), a discussion of politics, religion, women, and other matters; he also drew up a legal code in Massachusetts, enacted in 1641, the first to be established in New England.

Ward, Robert Plumer. b. at Mayfair, London, March 19, 1765; d. at London, Aug. 13, 1846. An English lawyer, essayist, and novelist. He was a member of Parliament (1802–06, 1807–23), and held (1805–23) several offices in the government. He added Plumer to his name upon his second marriage (1828), to Mrs. Plumer Lewin. Author of *History of the Law of Nations in Europe from the Greeks and Romans to Grotius* (1795), *Pictures of the World at Home and Abroad* (1839), works on law and politics (1801, 1837, 1838), and three society novels, *Tremaine, or the Man of Refinement* (1825), *De Vere, or the Man of Independence* (1827), and *De Clifford, or the Constant Man* (1841).

Warden (wôr′dẹn), **Henry.** In Sir Walter Scott's novels *The Monastery* and *The Abbot*, an elderly Protestant clergyman whose zealousness involves him in various difficulties, and eventually compels him to take refuge in Avenel Castle.

Warden, The. A novel by Anthony Trollope, published in 1855. It is the first in the Barsetshire series.

Wardle (wôr′dl), **Mr.** A hospitable, kindly, bustling old gentleman, the owner of Manor Farm, Dingley Dell, and the host and friend of the Pickwick Club; a character in Dickens's *Pickwick Papers*. His family comprises Miss Rachel Wardle (his old but girlish sister, who elopes with Alfred Jingle), his very deaf old mother, and his daughters Isabella and Emily. Joe (the "Fat Boy") is in his employ.

Wardour (wôr′dėr), **Isabella** and **Sir Arthur.** The heroine and her father in Sir Walter Scott's novel *The Antiquary*.

Wardour Street. A street running from north to south in Soho, London, once known for its dealers in bric-a-brac which was, or was supposed to be, antique. The street is now largely given over to the offices of various motion-picture companies, but the term "Wardour Street" has survived in literature to describe dialogue or descriptive passages which seek an "authentic" effect of early times through the use of archaisms.

Waring (wār′ing). A poem by Robert Browning, published in 1842 in *Dramatic Romances*. It was

---

ḍ, d or j; ṣ, s or sh; ṭ, t or ch; ẓ, z or zh; o, F. cloche; ü, F. menu; ċh, Sc. loch; ṅ, F. bonbon.

suggested by the sudden departure for New Zealand of Alfred Dormett, a young poet.

War in the Air, The. A novel (1908) by H. G. Wells. It describes the fantastic adventures of Albert Peter ("Bert") Smallways, an irrepressible Cockney bicycle mechanic who is accidentally carried aloft and across the North Sea in a balloon, and shot down over Germany by gunners who believe him to be actually Butteridge, a famous English designer of flying machines. He is taken aboard the *Vaterland*, the flagship of a great fleet with which the Germans are about to embark on a conquest first of America and then of the world. He is forced to surrender Butteridge's plans for an advanced type of flying machine (but manages to make rough sketches first), witnesses the "Battle of the North Atlantic" and the bombing of New York, and is presently caught (as a witness from the ground) in the climactic battle of the war, the "Battle of Niagara" between the German and Asiatic fleets of airships. When it is learned that he has copies of the Butteridge plans, he is rushed to the President of the United States, but it is too late: the world is now irretrievably caught by disaster. People are dying by the millions of a plague known as the "Purple Death," and no vestige of orderly government can hope long to survive. Smallways manages to cross the Atlantic, and make his way back to London, where he rescues his sweetheart Edna Bunthorne from one of the strong-arm chieftains who have arisen out of the chaos, and makes himself leader in his stead.

Warner (wôr'nėr), **Adam.** In Bulwer-Lytton's historical novel *The Last of the Barons*, a principal character of the fictional plot set against the historical background. He is a poor philosopher, interested in various types of scientific inquiry, and eventually killed as a result of public suspicion that he is a "dabbler in black magic."

Warner, Sybil. In Bulwer-Lytton's historical novel *The Last of the Barons*, the beautiful daughter of Adam Warner, loved but forsaken by Lord Hastings. She meets her death with her father.

Warner, Sylvia Townsend. b. 1893—. An English fiction writer and poet. Her verse includes *The Espalier* (1925) and *Time Importuned* (1928). She is author of the novels *Lolly Willowes* (1926), *Mr. Fortune's Maggot* (1927), *The True Heart* (1929), *Elinor Barley* (1930), *Opus 7* (1931; novel in verse), *After the Death of Don Juan* (1938), and *The Corner That Held Them* (1948); and also of the collected short stories *The Salutation* (1932), *A Garland of Straw* (1943), and *Museum of Cheats* (1947).

Warner, William. b. in Oxfordshire, England, c1558; d. in March, 1609. An English poet. He wrote a rhymed history of England, *Albion's England* (1586), and *Menaechmi* (a comedy translated from Plautus, registered in 1594 and published in 1595); Shakespeare's *Comedy of Errors* was derived from this.

Warning for Fair Women, A. A tragedy (1599) by an unknown author, which, like *Arden of Feversham*, was based on a contemporary crime. It was probably acted by the Lord Chamberlain's Men.

War of the Worlds, The. A novel (1898) by H. G. Wells, now generally considered to be one of the

first authentic "science-fiction" novels in the history of English letters. It describes an invasion of the earth (in Wells's book, however, the attack is restricted to England) by beings from Mars. Both the Martians and their "Fighting Machines" reach the earth in great cylinders, some 90 feet in diameter, and through their dreadful "Heat-Ray" succeed in defeating every force brought to bear against them. The tide is finally turned against them, and they all perish, not as a result of English guns, but from the effects of the disease germs of the earth, to which they are fatally susceptible.

Warren (wôr'ẹn, wor'ẹn), **John Byrne Leicester.** [Title: 3rd Baron **de Tabley;** pseudonyms, **George F. Preston, William Lancaster.**] b. in Cheshire, England, April 26, 1835; d. at Ryde, Isle of Wight, Nov. 22, 1895. English poet and dramatist. Author of *Ballads and Metrical Sketches* (1860), *The Threshold of Atrides* (1861), *Glimpses of Antiquity* (1862), *Eclogues and Monodramas* (1864), *Studies in Verse* (1865), *Philoctetes* (1866), *Orestes* (1868), *Searching the Net* (1873), *The Soldier's Fortune* (1876), and *Poems Dramatic and Lyrical* (2 vols., 1893, 1895).

Warren, Samuel. b. in Denbighshire, Wales, May 23, 1807; d. at London, July 29, 1877. A British novelist and legal writer. His chief work was the once extremely popular novel *Ten Thousand a Year* (published in *Blackwood's Magazine* 1839–41).

Warrington (wôr'ing.tọn, wor'-), **George.** A friend of Pendennis in William Makepeace Thackeray's novel of that name. His family (several generations earlier) appears in *The Virginians*. The George Warrington in the latter novel is the twin brother of Henry Esmond Warrington.

Wars of the Roses. See **Roses, Wars of the.**

Wart (wôrt), **Thomas.** In Shakespeare's *2 Henry IV*, a recruit in Falstaff's army.

Warton (wôr'tọn), **Joseph.** b. at Dunsfold, Surrey, England, in April, 1722; d. at Wickham, Hampshire, England, Feb. 23, 1800. An English poet, critic, clergyman, and schoolmaster; son of Thomas Warton (c1688–1745), and brother of Thomas Warton (1728–90). He held (1743 *et seq.*) various church posts, and was second master (1755–63) and headmaster (1766–93) of Winchester. Author of *The Enthusiast, or the Lover of Nature* (1744), *Odes on Various Subjects* (1746), and *Essay on the Genius and Writings of Pope* (2 vols., 1756, 1782). In his poetry and essays, he was an opponent of the canons of "correctness" observed by Alexander Pope, and is therefore considered one of the principal critical forerunners of the Romantic Movement in England. Among his best poems are *The Dying Indian, The Enthusiast,* and *Ode to Fancy.*

Warton, Thomas. b. c1688; d. at Basingstoke, Hampshire, England, Sept. 10, 1745. An English poet and schoolmaster; father of Joseph Warton and Thomas Warton (1728–90). He was professor of poetry (1718–28) at Oxford, and vicar of Basingstoke and master of the Basingstoke Grammar School from 1723 to 1745. Author of *Poems on Several Occasions* (1748); among them are "Ode to Sleep" and "Retirement, An Ode."

Warton, Thomas. b. at Basingstoke, England, Jan. 9, 1728; d. May 21, 1790. An English critic and poet laureate, professor of poetry (1757–67) and of history (1785–90) at Oxford; son of Thomas Warton (1688–1745), and brother of Joseph Warton. He became poet laureate in 1785. His chief works are a *History of English Poetry* (3 vols., 1774–81), *Pleasures of Melancholy* (1747), *Observations on the Poetry of Spenser* (1754), and editions of Theocritus, the Greek Anthology, and the minor poems of Milton. He was a leader of the critics of Thomas Chatterton's poems as forgeries. Warton's poetry reflects his interest in Gothic ruins and he is generally considered an early precursor of the romantic Gothic revival.

Warwick (wôr′ik, wor′ik). A British lord in Shaw's *Saint Joan.*

Warwick, Diana. The heroine of Meredith's *Diana of the Crossways,* an Irish beauty and wit supposed to have been modeled to some extent upon Mrs. Caroline Norton.

Warwick, Earl of. In Shakespeare's *2 Henry IV, Henry V,* and *1 Henry VI,* the historical Richard de Beauchamp. In *2 Henry IV,* he is a counsellor to the King and reassures him about the rebellion and the behavior of the Prince. In *Henry V,* he is a leader of the English forces in France. In *1 Henry VI,* he plucks a white rose, indicating that he favors Richard Plantagenet.

Warwick, Earl of. In Shakespeare's *2* and *3 Henry VI,* the historical Richard Neville, called "the Kingmaker," a member of the Yorkist faction. In *2 Henry VI,* he is convinced that Gloucester was murdered, accuses Suffolk, and later fights on the winning side at the first battle of St. Albans. In *3 Henry VI,* he at first supports Edward but, when he learns that Edward has married Lady Grey instead of Lady Bona, he joins the Lancastrians, captures Edward, and returns Henry VI to the throne. He is killed at Barnet.

Warwick, Edward, Earl of. In Shakespeare's *Richard III,* a young son of the Duke of Clarence, eventually imprisoned by Richard.

Warwick, Mrs. See **Warwick, Diana.**

Washington Square. A novel by Henry James, published in 1880.

Waste. A drama (1907) by Granville-Barker.

Waste Land, The. A poem in five parts by T. S. Eliot, published in 1922. The theme of the poem is the sterility and confusion of the 20th century. The symbolism, deriving from pagan fertility myths and the legend of the Grail, is projected against the "Waste Land," a barren country under the rule of an impotent king. The first part, *The Burial of the Dead,* presents spring and summer as forces making the world awaken to its inadequacies and desolation. *The Game of Chess* shows people preoccupied with modern superficiality and oblivious to the heritage of the past. *The Fire Sermon* sets forth the squalor of the contemporary scene. *Death by Water* translates the drowning of a Phoenician sailor into a redemptive symbol. *What the Thunder Said* presents the fall of modern Europe caused by a lack of spiritual values. The poem, full of esoteric allusion and one of the most controversial of its time, exerted a profound influence on the poets of the following generation.

Watchman, The. A journal "of public affairs" of which ten numbers appeared in the spring of 1796. Coleridge was its editor, and by the impartiality of his attacks on both William Godwin and Pitt soon managed to alienate both his radical and conservative readers. This fact, added to the "drudgery" of regular editorial work, soon persuaded Coleridge to abandon the project.

Watch on the Rhine (rīn), **The.** See **Wacht am Rhein, Die.**

Water Babies, The. A fairy tale by Charles Kingsley, published in 1863. A little chimneysweep, Tom, runs away from his cruel employer, Mr. Grimes, falls into a river, and is turned into a water baby. He meets all sorts of undersea creatures and has many amusing adventures.

Waterfall, The. A poem by Henry Vaughan, published in 1655.

Waterloo (wô′tẽr.lö, wot′ẽr-; wô.tẽr.lö′, wot.ẽr-; Flemish, vä.tẽr.lö′). A town in C Belgium, in the province of Brabant, ab. 9 mi. S of Brussels: headquarters of the Duke of Wellington in the Battle of Waterloo.

Waterloo Bridge. A bridge over the Thames at London, designed and built (1811–17) by John Rennie. It was officially opened on the second anniversary of the battle of Waterloo.

Waterloo Place. A square in London, between Carlton House Terrace and Regent Street. In its center is the Crimean War monument.

"Water Poet," the. See **Taylor, John** (1580–1653).

Watling Street (wot′ling). An ancient Roman military highway, extending from the English Channel coast of Kent, in SE England, NW to Chester, in W England. It commenced at Dover, passed through Canterbury to London, and thence went by St. Albans, Dunstable, Stony Stratford, and other points, passing along the boundary line of the present counties of Leicestershire and Warwickshire, to Wroxeter on the river Severn, and then N to Chester. It had a number of branch roads diverging from it.

Watson (wot′son), **Dr.** (**John H.**). In the Sherlock Holmes stories of Arthur Conan Doyle, Holmes's friend, companion, and chronicler.

Watson, Henry Brereton Marriott. b. at Caulfield, Melbourne, Australia, Dec. 20, 1863; d. Oct. 30, 1921. A British author. He was assistant editor of *Black and White* and of the *Pall Mall Gazette.* He published many novels and short stories, among which are *Lady Faintheart* (1890), *The Web of the Spider* (1891), *Diogenes of London* (1893), *Galloping Dick* (1896), *The Heart of Miranda* (1897), *The Adventurers* (1898), *The Princess Xenia* (1899), *Chloris of the Island* (1900), *Hurricane Island* (1904), *The Privateers* (1907), *The Castle by the Sea* (1909), and *Alise of Astra* (1910).

Watson, John. b. at Glasgow, Feb. 25, 1847; d. at Kingston, Ontario, Canada, Jan. 27, 1939. A Scottish philosophical writer, professor of moral philosophy (1872–1924) in Queen's University, Kingston, Ontario. In 1872 he was appointed professor of logic, metaphysics, and ethics, and, upon the division of the chair, to the position from which he retired as professor emeritus. He published *Kant*

---

d, d or j; s, s or sh; t, t or ch; z, z or zh; o, F. cloche; ü, F. menu; ch, Sc. loch; ṅ, F. bonbon.

and His English Critics (1881), *Schelling's Transcendental Idealism* (1882), *The Philosophy of Kant* (1888), *Comte, Mill, and Spencer* (1895), *Hedonistic Theories* (1895), *An Outline of Philosophy* (1898), *The Philosophical Basis of Religion* (1907), *The Philosophy of Kant Explained* (1908), and others.

Watson, John. [Pseudonym, **Ian Maclaren.**] b. at Manningtree, Essex, England, Nov. 3, 1850; d. at Mount Pleasant, Iowa, May 6, 1907. A Scottish clergyman, religious writer, and novelist. He traveled and lectured (1896, 1899, 1907) in Canada and the U. S., dying in Iowa on his last lecture tour. Under his pseudonym he was the author of some highly successful stories of Scottish life and character, including *Beside the Bonnie Brier Bush* (1894), *Days of Auld Lang Syne* (1895), *Kate Carnegie and Those Ministers* (1897), *Afterwards and Other Stories* (1898), *Rabbi Saunderson* (1899), *The Young Barbarians* (1901), *His Majesty Baby* (1902), *St. Judith* (1907), and *Graham of Claverhouse* (1908). Under his own name he wrote various religious works.

Watson, Richard. b. at Heversham, Westmorland, England, 1737; d. July 2, 1816. An English prelate, theological writer, and chemist. He was regius professor of divinity at Cambridge (1771 *et seq.*) and bishop of Llandaff (1782). He wrote an *Apology for Christianity* (1776, in answer to Edward Gibbon), an *Apology for the Bible* (1796, in answer to Thomas Paine), and others. He was a chemical experimenter and suggested (1787) gunpowder improvements reported to have saved the government 100,000 pounds a year.

Watson, Thomas. b. probably at London, c1557; d. there, in September, 1592. An English poet and translator. Author of Latin translations of the *Antigone* (1581), of Sophocles, and of the *Amyntas* (1585) of Tasso. In English he wrote *Hecatompathia, or Passionate Century of Love* (1592), a collection of so-called sonnets (although each contains 18 lines), and *Teares of Fancie* (1593), a true sonnet sequence. He wrote, in both Latin and English, an *Eglogue* (1590) on the death of his patron, Sir Francis Walsingham. Watson's work shows his thorough knowledge of Latin, Greek, French, and Italian literature. Of his poems, those beginning "If Cupid were a child," "Ev'ry singing bird that in the wood rejoices," "I saw the object of my pining thought," "In clouds she shines," and "If Jove himself be subject unto love" are characteristic of his talent. Watson is the "Amyntas" of Edmund Spenser's poetic allegory *Colin Clout's Come Home Again.*

Watson, Sir William. [Full name, **John William Watson.**] b. at Wharfedale, Yorkshire, England, Aug. 2, 1858; d. at Ditchling Common, Sussex, England, Aug. 11, 1935. An English poet. His poem *Wordsworth's Grave* (1890) drew attention to him, and in 1892 he received a civil pension of 200 pounds rendered vacant by the death of Tennyson. His *Lachrymae Musarum* (1892) was the finest elegy written on the death of the latter. He also wrote *Ode on the Day of the Coronation of King Edward VII* (1902) and *The Tomb of Burns* (1903). He had previously published *Love Lyrics, The Prince's Quest, Epigrams of Art, Life, and Nature;* and he also published *The Eloping Angels* (1893), *Excursions in Criticism, Odes and Other Poems* (1894),

The Purple East (1896), *The Hope of the World* (1897), *For England* (1903), *Sable and Purple* (1910), *The Heralds of the Dawn* (1912), *The Man Who Saw and Other Poems Arising Out of the War* (1917), *The Superhuman Antagonists* (1919), and others. The often violent political opinions expressed in his poetry are thought to have prevented his appointment to the laureateship after Alfred Austin's death in 1913.

Watsons, The. An unfinished novel by Jane Austen, written c1805. Emma Watson is raised by an aunt. When her aunt remarries, Emma returns to her family in a small village in Surrey, to find that her sisters are engaged principally in trying to catch husbands. She meets Lady Osborne and her son; also Tom Musgrave, something of a roué, and Mr. Howard, a clergyman, who was presumably intended eventually to be Emma's husband.

Watt (wot), **James.** b. at Greenock, Scotland, Jan. 19, 1736; d. at Heathfield, near Birmingham, England, Aug. 25, 1819. A British mechanician, inventor, and civil engineer. He was apprenticed to an instrument-maker in London in 1755, became mathematical-instrument maker to the University of Glasgow in 1757, began experiments in improving the steam engine about 1760 after he had repaired the university's working model of Thomas Newcomen's engine, and invented the condensing steam engine in 1765 and obtained a patent in 1769. Many other improvements were devised later and patented. He formed a partnership with Matthew Boulton in Birmingham and began the manufacture of steam engines in 1775. The watt, a unit of power, is named for him. Watt is the hero of a completely apocryphal story in which he obtained insight into the motive power of steam by watching, as a child, the lid of a teakettle move up and down.

Watt, Robert. b. at Stewarton, Ayrshire, Scotland, in May, 1774; d. March 12, 1819. A Scottish physician and bibliographer.

Watteau (wä.tō'; French, vȧ.tō), **Jean Antoine.** b. at Valenciennes, France, Oct. 10, 1684; d. at Nogent-sur-Marne, France, July 18, 1721. A French genre painter. He studied with Gillot at Paris in 1702, and later with Audran. He was unusually successful with subjects representing conventional shepherds and shepherdesses, fêtes champêtres, rustic dances, and the like. The style of female dress represented in many of them, consisting of a sacque with loose pleats hanging from the shoulders, was long known as the "Watteau." Ten of his pictures are in the Louvre, and specimens are in all the principal galleries of Europe.

Watts (wots), **Alaric Alexander.** b. at London, March 16, 1797; d. there, April 5, 1864. An English poet and journalist. He founded the *United Service Gazette* in 1833, and edited it until 1847 (he established more than 20 other journals between 1842 and 1847). His works include *Poetical Sketches* (1822) and *Lyrics of the Heart* (1850). He edited *The Literary Souvenir* (1824–38), *Poetical Album* (1828–29), *Cabinet of British Art* (1835–38), and other similar works.

Watts, Isaac. b. at Southampton, England, July 17, 1674; d. at Theobalds, Hertfordshire, England, Nov. 25, 1748. An English nonconformist theologian, hymn writer, and author, pastor (1700 *et seq.*) of an Independent church at London. He is best known for his sacred poems, *Horae Lyricae* (1706), *Hymns* (1707), *Psalms of David* (1719), *Psalms, Hymns, and Spiritual Songs* (in many editions), and *Divine and Moral Songs for Children* (1720). He also wrote *Logic* (1725), *Improvement of the Mind* (1741), catechisms, and philosophical and theological works. In addition to his hymns and paraphrases of the psalms (including "O God, our help in ages past"), Watts is famous as the author of "How doth the little busy bee," one of his pioneering instructive poems for children.

Watts, Thomas. b. at London, 1811; d. there, Sept. 9, 1869. An English author.

Watts-Dunton (wots.dun'ton), **Theodore.** [Full name, **Walter Theodore Watts-Dunton.**] b. at St. Ives, Huntingdonshire, England, Oct. 12, 1832; d. at Putney, London, June 7, 1914. An English poet, critic, and novelist. Born Watts, he added his mother's maiden name to his own in 1897. He studied science at Cambridge, and then qualified in law, which he practiced at London, later giving it up for literature. He contributed to the *Examiner*, the *Athenaeum*, Chambers's *Encyclopedia of English Literature*, and the *Encyclopaedia Britannica*. Watts-Dunton was a close friend of George Borrow, Alfred, Lord Tennyson, Dante Gabriel Rossetti, and Algernon Charles Swinburne; the last-named lived with him in his home for 30 years. Author of *Poetry* (1885), *The Coming of Love* (1897), *Aylwin* (1898), *Christmas at the Mermaid* (1902), *The Renascence of Wonder* (1903), and *Studies of Shakespeare* (1910). *Vesprie Towers*, a novel, *Old Familiar Faces*, a book of memories, and *Poetry and the Renascence of Wonder* were published in 1916. As much interested in Gypsy life and folklore as George Borrow, he edited Borrow's *Lavengro* (1893) and *The Romany Rye* (1900).

Wat Tyler's Rebellion (wot tī'lèrz). A revolt (1381) of peasants of Essex and Kent, who marched on London and took possession of the city under the leadership of Wat Tyler.

Waugh (wô), **Alec.** [Full name, **Alexander Raban Waugh.**] b. at London, July 8, 1898—. An English novelist and travel writer; elder son of Arthur Waugh and brother of Evelyn Waugh. Author of a novel of English public school life, *The Loom of Youth* (1917), and of *The Lonely Unicorn* (1922; American title, *Roland Whately*), *Card Castle* (1924), *Kept* (1925), *Love in These Days* (1926), *Nor Many Waters* (1928; American title, *Portrait of a Celibate*), *Three Score and Ten* (1929), *So Lovers Dream* (1931), *The Balliols* (1934), *Eight Short Stories* (1937), *No Truce with Time* (1941), *His Second War* (1944), *Unclouded Summer* (1948), and *The Lipton Story* (1950).

Waugh, Arthur. b. at Midsomer Norton, Somersetshire, England, Aug. 24, 1866; d. at London, June 27, 1943. An English critic, editor, and publisher; father of Alec Waugh and Evelyn Waugh. He was London correspondent (1892–97) for the New York *Critic*, literary consultant (1895–1902) for Kegan Paul and Company, and director (1902–30) and chairman (1926–36) of Chapman and Hall, London publishers. He was assistant editor of the *New Review* and book critic for the *Daily Telegraph*.

He edited the works of Charles Lamb, Johnson's *Lives of the Poets* (6 vols., 1896), the Pamphlet Library (1898), and the Biographical Edition (1902–03) of Dickens's novels. Author of *Gordon in Africa* (1888), *Alfred, Lord Tennyson* (1892), *Robert Browning* (1900), *Reticence of Literature* (1915), *Tradition and Change* (1919), *A Hundred Years of Publishing* (1930), and *One Man's Road* (1931).

Waugh, Edwin. [Called "the Lancashire Burns."] b. at Rochdale, Lancashire, England, Jan. 29, 1817; d. at New Brighton, Cheshire, England, April 30, 1890. An English printer and poet. He began his literary career by contributing to the Manchester *Examiner* prose sketches of Lancashire life later published as *Sketches of Lancashire Life and Localities* (1855), and also wrote *Factory Folk during the Cotton Famine*, *The Chimney Corner*, *Tufts of Heather*, *Irish Sketches*, and *Rambles in the Lake Country*. His *Lancashire Poems and Songs* (1859) went through many editions, and in 1889 was included as part of an 11-volume edition of his works. Of his individual poems, he is best known for *Come whoam to the childer an' me* (1856).

Waugh, Evelyn. [Full name, **Evelyn Arthur St. John Waugh.**] b. at Hampstead, London, 1903—. An English novelist; younger son of Arthur Waugh and brother of Alec Waugh. Author of *Decline and Fall* (1928), *Vile Bodies* (1930), *Black Mischief* (1932), *A Handful of Dust* (1934), *Waugh in Abyssinia* (1936), *Scoop* (1938), *Put Out More Flags* (1942), *Brideshead Revisited* (1945), *The Loved One* (1948), *Scott-King's Modern Europe* (1948), *Helena* (1950), and *Men at Arms* (1952), and of the studies *Rossetti: A Critical Biography* (1928) and *Edmund Campion* (1935).

Waverley (wā'vèr.li). [Full title, **Waverley, or 'Tis Sixty Years Since.**] A novel by Sir Walter Scott, the first of the Waverley Novels, published in 1814. Its hero, Waverley, is a young Englishman involved in the Scottish Jacobite uprising of 1745.

Waverley Dramas. A series of eight dramas founded on Sir Walter Scott's Waverley Novels. They were produced (1818–24) at Edinburgh and seven of them were published there in 1823.

Waverley Novels. A series of 32 novels and tales written by Sir Walter Scott; so named from *Waverley* (1814), the first of the series. They were published anonymously "by the author of Waverley" till 1825, when the author disclosed the identity of the "Great Unknown" (who by then was generally known) in the introduction of the first series of *Chronicles of the Canongate*.

Waves, The. A psychological novel by Virginia Woolf, published in 1931.

Way Home, The. A novel by Henry Handel Richardson (Mrs. Henrietta Robertson), published in 1925. It is the second volume of the trilogy *The Fortunes of Richard Mahony* (1930).

Wayland Smith. [Also: **Wayland the Smith, Weland Smith.**] In English folklore, a supernatural smith who once dwelt at an old stone mountain near Ashdown in Berkshire. If a horse had cast a shoe, it was only necessary to lead him thither, place a piece of money on the stone, and retire for a time. Upon returning the money would be gone and the horse shod. The legend of Wayland, the wonderful smith, is common and ancient Germanic property. In the Anglo-Saxon *Beowulf*, a precious piece of armor is called *Wēlandes geweorc* (Weland's work). He is equated to Volund, the Old Norse divine smith, and his deeds are the subject of the *Völundar Kvidha* (Lay of Volund) in the Old Icelandic *Elder Edda*. In the Old Norse *Vilkina Saga*, he was taught his mysterious skill by the smith Mimir. Swedish legend locates his grave near Siseback in Scania. Scott introduces him as a character in *Kenilworth*. He is the ostensible "narrator" of a charming, quasi-historical tale for children in Rudyard Kipling's *Puck of Pook's Hill*.

Wayland Wood. A wood near Watton, England, the legendary scene of the murder of the Children in the Wood.

Way of All Flesh, The. A novel by Samuel Butler, published in 1903. The history of the Pontifex family is traced down to Ernest, son of the bullying Theobald and Christina. They repress him in every possible way during his unhappy childhood, and as a young man he gets into trouble when he makes advances to a respectable girl whom he believes to be a prostitute. He is put in prison, and after his release marries Ellen, a maidservant. However, he is freed from this bond by finding that Ellen is already married. He then inherits enough money from an aunt to enable him to devote his life to literary pursuits. The work presents a good, if bitter, picture of English middle-class society in the late 19th century.

Way of the World, The. A comedy by William Congreve, produced in 1700. This is considered by many to be the finest comedy of manners and one of the best of all English comedies. By the time it appeared the other Restoration dramatists, such as George Etherege, were turning more toward sentimentality, and Jeremy Collier had already attacked the immorality of the Restoration plays. Congreve's play, although it makes use of many of the devices, situations, and characters typical of Restoration comedies, is neither realistic nor coarse. Perhaps for this reason, it was not well received. The hero, Mirabell, is a departure from the usual hero of Restoration comedy in being, to some degree, honorable and trustworthy. Minor characters like the vulgar country squire, Witwoud, and Waitwell, the intriguing servant, are perhaps even better depicted than the major ones. The characters are artificial in the extreme, and the success of production depends largely upon subtle, precise interpretation by the actors of the brilliantly witty dialogue. One of the most wittily written characters is old Lady Wishfort, who controls the fortune of Mrs. Millamant, the charming, if affected, heroine who is pursued by Mirabell. Mirabell has professed love for Lady Wishfort, who is the obstacle in his chase of Millamant, and is having an affair with Lady Wishfort's daughter, Mrs. Fainall. His double duplicity is revealed to Lady Wishfort by the villainess of the piece, Mrs. Marwood, whose love Mirabell has rejected. She is Fainall's mistress, and conspires with him to get possession of Mrs. Fainall's and Millamant's fortunes. After much involved action, Mrs. Marwood is discredited, Mirabell is found to control Mrs. Fainall's property,

and Lady Wishfort agrees to the marriage of Millamant and Mirabell.

Wayward Man, The. A novel by St. John Ervine, published in 1927.

Weakest Goeth to the Wall, The. A play (printed 1600), sometimes attributed to John Webster and Thomas Dekker.

Wealth of Nations, The. A very influential work on economics by Adam Smith, published in 1776 (having previously been offered as a series of lectures in Glasgow). In it Smith outlined the system of laissez-faire economics, based upon an absolutely free economy, with which his name has since been associated.

We Are Not Alone. A novel by James Hilton, published in 1937.

Wearin' of the Green, The. A popular Irish folk ballad, supposed to have originated during the last decade of the 18th century. It tells of the abuses wrought by the British in Ireland:

> The shamrock is forbid by law to grow
> 　on Irish ground.
> Saint Patrick's day no more we'll keep
> His color can't be seen
> For there's a bloody law agin the wearin'
> 　of the Green.

Weather in the Streets, The. A novel by Rosamond Lehmann, published in 1936.

Weavers, The. A novel by Sir Gilbert Parker, published in 1907.

Webb (web), **Beatrice.** [Maiden name, **Potter.**] b. in the Cotswold Hills, Gloucestershire, England, Jan. 22, 1858; d. at Liphook, Hampshire, England, April 30, 1943. An English Socialist, writer on economics and sociology, and an intellectual leader of the Labour Party. She married (1892) Sidney James Webb, who was later named 1st Baron Passfield, but she refused the designation Lady Passfield. She was a member (1905–09) of the Royal Commission on Poor Law and Unemployment, and collaborated with her husband and two other members of the Commission on the authorship of the minority report (1909) proposing strong liberalizing of the poor law, and conducted a campaign on its behalf until 1912. They were both prominent in the organization of the Fabian Society and the Labour Party, the founding (1913) of the *New Statesman*, and the plan for establishing the London School of Economics and Political Science. She was coauthor with her husband of *The History of Trade Unionism* (1894), *Industrial Democracy* (1897), *The State and the Doctor* (1910), *Consumers' Co-operative Movement* (1921), *Decay of Capitalist Civilization* (1921), *English Poor Law History* (3 vols., 1927–29), *Soviet Communism: A New Civilization?* (1936), and *The Truth About Soviet Russia* (1942). She was author of *My Apprenticeship* (1936) and of *Our Partnership* (published posthumously, 1948).

Webb, Mary. [Maiden name, **Mary Gladys Meredith.**] b. in Shropshire, England, March 25, 1881; d. Oct. 8, 1927. An English novelist. Author of the novels *The Golden Arrow* (1916), *Gone to Earth* (1917), *The House in Dormer Forest* (1920), *Seven for a Secret* (1922), and *Precious Bane* (1924; awarded the Femina-Vie Heureuse prize, 1925).

These five novels, all set in Shropshire, attained their greatest popularity after her death, when they were issued in reprints with introductions by John Buchan, Stanley Baldwin, G. K. Chesterton, and others. Among her other works are *Armour Wherein He Trusted* (1929), an unfinished novel, and a volume of poems and essays, *The Spring of Joy* (1929).

Webb, Sidney James. [Title, 1st Baron **Passfield**.] b. at London, July 13, 1859; d. at Liphook, Hampshire, England, Oct. 13, 1947. An English writer on sociology and economics, a founder of the Fabian Society; husband of Beatrice Webb. He was during the early Labour governments connected with the War Office and the Colonial Office, and was a member (1912–27) of the economics faculty of London University. His chief works include *Socialism in England* (1890), *The London Programme* (1892), and *London Education* (1904). With his wife, with whom he was associated in such activities as the founding of the Fabian Society and the contribution of material (with G. B. Shaw) to *Fabian Essays* (1889), he wrote *The History of Trade Unionism* (1894, 1911), *Industrial Democracy* (1897), *Problems of Modern Industry* (1898), *History of Liquor Licensing* (1903), *The Parish and the County* (1906), *The Manor and the Borough* (1907), *The Break-up of the Poor Law and the Public Organisation of the Labour Market, Being the Minority Report of the Poor Law Commission* (1909), *English Poor Law Policy* (1910), *The State and the Doctor* (1910), and *The Prevention of Destitution* (1911).

Webley (web'li), **Everard.** A Fascist leader, founder of the Brotherhood of British Freemen, an English Fascist society, in Aldous Huxley's satirical novel *Point Counter Point* (1928). The character is believed to be a portrait of Sir Oswald Mosley.

Webster (web'stėr), **Augusta.** [Maiden name, **Julia Augusta Davies.**] b. at Poole, Dorsetshire, England, Jan. 30, 1837; d. at Kew, near London, Sept. 5, 1894. An English poet, dramatist, novelist, and translator. Author of *Blanche Lisle and Other Poems* (1860), *Lilian Gray* (1864), *Lesley's Guardians* (1864), *Dramatic Studies* (1866), *Portraits* (1870), and *Mother and Daughter* (1895), works in prose and verse; and of *The Auspicious Day* (1872), *Disguises* (1879), and *The Sentence* (1887), poetic dramas. She translated into English verse the *Prometheus Bound* (1866) of Aeschylus and the *Medea* (1868) of Euripides, and wrote essays on translating poetry.

Webster, John. d. before 1634. An English dramatist, noted for his tragedies. A John Webster appears as a member in the records of the Merchant Taylors' Company, but whether this was the dramatist Webster, his father, or someone else by the same name is not clear. There is also a John Webster listed in a group of English actors playing in Germany (1596). The dramatist Webster is referred to in the past tense in Thomas Heywood's *Hierarchie of the Angels* (1635), so it is assumed that he died before then. He assisted Thomas Dekker, Michael Drayton, Thomas Middleton, and others in writing plays (c1602) for Philip Henslowe. He published, with Dekker, *Northward Ho!* (1607), *Westward Ho!* (1607), and, possibly with additional collaborators, *The History of Sir Thomas Wyat*

(1607). *The Weakest Goeth to the Wall* (1600) has been attributed to him but his authorship is not generally accepted. His finest plays are *The White Devil* (acted c1611, printed 1612) and *The Duchess of Malfi* (acted c1613, printed 1623). He also wrote *The Devil's Law Case* (1623), a city pageant, *Monuments of Honour* (1624), and *Appius and Virginia* (probably a revision of a play by Thomas Heywood and not printed until 1654). Attributed to Webster and William Rowley is *A Cure for a Cuckold*. He added to Marston's *The Malcontent* (1604), and several other plays are believed to contain his work.

Wedderburn (wed'ėr.bėrn), **James.** b. at Dundee, Scotland, c1495; d. in France, 1553. A Scottish poet and dramatist, author of anti-Roman Catholic ballads; brother of John Wedderburn and Robert Wedderburn. Author of *The Beheading of John the Baptist* (1539–40), a tragedy, and *Dionysus the Tyrant*, a comedy (1539–40), satires on practices in the Roman Catholic Church. With his brothers, John and Robert, he wrote several satirical ballads later published in book form as *Ane Compendious Booke of Godly and Spirituall Songs* (1567). Charged with heresy, he escaped to France.

Wedderburn, John. b. at Dundee, Scotland, c1500; d. in England, 1546. A Scottish poet, author of anti-Roman Catholic ballads; brother of James Wedderburn and Robert Wedderburn. Charged with heresy for writing ballads attacking the Roman Catholic Church, he escaped (1540) to Wittenberg. He returned (1542) to Scotland, continuing to write and publish his so-called Dundee Psalms. He fled (1546) to England.

Wedderburn, Robert. b. at Dundee, Scotland, c1510; d. there, c1557. A Scottish poet, author of anti-Roman Catholic ballads; brother of James Wedderburn and John Wedderburn. He joined his brothers in writing the ballads that brought a charge of heresy and fled (c1534) to Paris and later to Wittenberg. Returning to Scotland in 1546, he was made vicar of Dundee.

Wedding, The. A tragicomedy by James Shirley, acted c1629 and printed in 1633.

Wedding Day, The. A comedy by Elizabeth Inchbald, produced in 1794.

Wedgwood (wej'wud), **Josiah.** b. at Burslem, England, July 12, 1730; d. at Etruria, near Newcastle-under-Lyme, England, Jan. 3, 1795. An English potter, noted especially for his copies of classical vases and other antiquities.

Wedmore (wed'mōr). A place in Somersetshire, England, ab. 8 mi. W of Wells. Here a peace was concluded (878) between Guthrum, king of the Danes, and Alfred the Great. The latter secured Wessex and the S part of Mercia; the region lying in general N of Watling Street and the Thames valley fell to the Danes.

Weelkes (wēlks), **Thomas.** b. probably between 1570 and 1580; d. at London, Nov. 30, 1623. An English madrigal writer. In 1600 he was organist of Winchester College, and in 1608 organist of Chichester Cathedral.

Weena (wē'na). See under **Time Machine, The.**

"Weeping Philosopher." A name given to **Heraclitus.**

ḍ, d or j; ṣ, s or sh; ṭ, t or ch; ẓ, z or zh; o, F. cloche; ü, F. menu; ċh, Sc. loch; ṅ, F. bonbon.

Wegg (weg), **Silas.** A wooden-legged seller of fruit and printed ballads in Dickens's *Our Mutual Friend,* employed by Mr. Boffin, whose education has been neglected, to read to him out of "old familiar Decline-and-Fall-off-the-Rooshan-Empire," with an occasional drop into poetry. Wegg turns out to be a rascal, who tries to blackmail his kindly employer.

Weir (wir), **Harrison William.** b. at Lewes, Sussex, England, May 5, 1824; d. in Kent, England, Jan. 3, 1906. An English artist and writer of animal stories. He was wood engraver (1842–1906) with the *Illustrated London News,* and also worked for the *Field* and *Pictorial Times,* and exhibited paintings of birds and animals at the Society of British Artists, the Royal Academy, and the British Institution. He illustrated the works of others, such as J. G. Wood's *Illustrated Natural History* (1853), and his own works, including *Every Day in the Country* (1883), *Animal Stories* (1885), *Our Cats and All About Them* (1889), and *Our Poultry and All About Them* (1903).

Weirds (wirdz). See **Wyrdes.**

Weird Sisters. See **Witches.**

Weir of Hermiston (wir; hếr′mis.ṭon). An unfinished novel by Robert Louis Stevenson, published in 1896.

Weissnichtwo (vīs′niċht.vō). An imaginary city in Thomas Carlyle's *Sartor Resartus.* The name means "Don't-Know-Where."

Weland Smith (wā′land). See **Wayland Smith.**

Well-Beloved, The. A novel by Thomas Hardy, published serially in 1892, revised in 1897.

Weller (wel′ếr), **Sam.** A servant of Mr. Pickwick in Dickens's *Pickwick Papers,* an impudent and witty fellow with an immense fund of humor, a merry heart, and an inexhaustible devotion to his master. His father, Tony Weller, is an apoplectic, pimple-nosed, Cockney coachman, full of good nature and kindliness, with a dread of "widders" and a great admiration for his son Sam and Mr. Pickwick. His "second wentur" is a scolding, slovenly woman, devoted to religious matters.

Weller, Tony. In Dickens's *Pickwick Papers,* the father of Sam Weller.

Wellington (wel′ing.ṭon), 1st Duke of. [Title of **Arthur Wellesley;** also, **Wesley;** called **"the Iron Duke."**] b. at Dublin (or in Meath), Ireland, April 29 (or May 1), 1769; d. at Walmer Castle, England, Sept. 14, 1852. British general and statesman; son of Garrett Wellesley, 1st Earl of Mornington, and younger brother of Richard Colley Wellesley, Marquis of Wellesley. He was educated at Eton and at the military college of Angers, and entered the army as ensign in 1787. He was elected to the Irish Parliament in 1790, served in the Netherlands (1794–95), and was made a colonel in 1796 and sent to India. He took part in the victory of Malaveli and the attack on Seringapatam in 1799, was appointed governor of Mysore, defeated the chieftain Doondiah in 1800, and became major general in 1802. He was commander of the expedition to restore the Peshwa in 1803, defeated the Mahrattas at Assaye (September 23) and Argaum (November) in 1803, negotiated peace in 1803, and was knighted and returned from India in 1805. He took part in the expedition to Hanover in 1805, entered the British House of Commons in 1806, was secretary for Ireland in 1807, and served in the expedition against Copenhagen in 1807. He was made lieutenant general and commander of the forces in the Peninsula in 1808, gained the victory of Vimeiro (Aug. 21, 1808), returned to England after the Convention of Cintra, and was again Irish secretary in 1809 and again commander in chief in the Peninsula (April, 1809). He gained the victory of Talavera in 1809, and was made Viscount Wellington in the same year, fortified the lines of Torres Vedras, repulsed the French at Busaco in 1810, gained the victory of Fuentes d'Onoro in 1811, stormed Ciudad Rodrigo and Badajoz in 1812, gained the victory of Salamanca in 1812, occupied Madrid, besieged Burgos unsuccessfully in 1812, gained the victory of Vitoria in 1813, won various battles in the Pyrenees, captured San Sebastian and Pamplona in 1813, and invaded France and won the victories of Orthez and Toulouse in 1814. In 1814 he was made Duke of Wellington. He was ambassador at Paris (1814–15) and plenipotentiary at the Congress of Vienna (1815). Wellington gained the victory of Quatre-Bras (June 16, 1815) though obliged to retire immediately afterward, and commanded with Gebhard Leberecht von Blücher at Waterloo (June 18, 1815). He negotiated the restoration of the Bourbons and the peace of Paris in 1815, was commander in chief of the army of occupation in France (1815–18), and attended the congresses of Aix-la-Chapelle in 1818 and Verona in 1822. He became master general of the ordnance in 1818, and member of the cabinet, was made ambassador to Russia in 1826, became commander in chief of the army in 1827, and was prime minister (1828–30). Roman Catholic emancipation was carried in his administration, but he opposed parliamentary reform. He was foreign secretary (1834–35), and a member of the cabinet (1841–46). In 1848 he was again active in organizing the forces to protect London during the Chartist disturbances.

Well of St. Keyne (kān), **The.** An ironically humorous ballad by Southey. It is based upon the old tale of a well in Cornwall, the waters of which have the power of giving to whichever one of a newly married couple first drinks of them lifelong mastery over the other. In Southey's poem the husband hastens to the well immediately after the service, only to learn that his wife has taken a bottle of the water to the wedding, and has already sipped it.

Well of the Saints, The. A tragicomedy (1905) by John Millington Synge about two beggars, a man and a woman, miraculously (but, in the event, unhappily) cured of blindness by a saint.

Wells (welz), **Charles Jeremiah.** [Pseudonym, **H. L. Howard.**] b. probably at London, c1799; d. at Marseilles, France, Feb. 17, 1879. An English poet and lawyer, friend of John Keats, William Hazlitt, and Leigh Hunt. He practiced law (1820–30) at London, and was professor of English (1840 *et seq.*) at Quimper, in Brittany. Author of *Stories after Nature* (1822), *Joseph and His Brethren* (1824), a dramatic poem, and *Claribel* (1845), a prose tale. The value of *Stories after Nature* and of *Joseph and His Brethren* was recognized by D. G. Rossetti and A. C. Swinburne in February, 1875, shortly after

Wells burned all his manuscripts. Now accepted as a masterpiece of its kind and praised for its closeness to Elizabethan style, *Joseph and His Brethren* was published under his pseudonym.

Wells, George Philip. b. in England, c1895—. An English biologist, teacher, and scientific writer; eldest son of H. G. Wells and his second wife, Amy Catherine Robbins Wells. Coauthor, with his father and Julian Huxley, of *The Science of Life* (1929–30) and *Evolution—Fact and Theory* (1932).

Wells, H. G. [Full name, **Herbert George Wells.**] b. at Bromley, Kent, England, Sept. 21, 1866; d. at London, Aug. 13, 1946. An English novelist, journalist, historian, and scientific and sociological writer. He was graduated (B.S., 1880) with honors from London University, became a teacher, and then turned to journalism and to writing fiction. A prolific author, he devoted the larger part of his early output to imaginative scientific and social romances including *The Time Machine* (1895), *The Island of Dr. Moreau* (1896), *The Wheels of Chance* (1896), *The Invisible Man* (1897), *Thirty Strange Stories* (1897), *The War of the Worlds* (1898), *Tales of Space and Time* (1899), *When the Sleeper Wakes* (1899), *The Food of the Gods* (1904), *A Modern Utopia* (1905), *In the Days of the Comet* (1906), and *The War in the Air* (1908). His novels of the succeeding period dealt chiefly with individual character and contemporary social problems. Among them are *Love and Mr. Lewisham* (1900), *Kipps* (1905), *Tono-Bungay* (1908), *Ann Veronica* (1909), *The History of Mr. Polly* (1910), *The New Machiavelli* (1911), *Marriage* (1912), *The Passionate Friends* (1913), *The Wife of Sir Isaac Harman* (1914), *The Research Magnificent* (1915), *Mr. Britling Sees It Through* (1916), and *Joan and Peter* (1918). One of his outstanding works is *The Outline of History* (1920; revised ed., 1931), a general and interpretive account that was very popular despite the criticisms of professional historians. In collaboration with his son George Philip Wells, and Julian Huxley, he wrote *The Science of Life* (1929–30). Among his many other works are *The Sea Lady* (1902), *Twelve Stories and a Dream* (1903), *The Country of the Blind* (1911), *Bealby* (1915), *The Soul of a Bishop* (1917), *The Undying Fire* (1919), *The Salvaging of Civilization* (1921), *Men Like Gods* (1923), *The Dream* (1924), *The World of William Clissold* (1926), *Mr. Blettsworthy on Rampole Island* (1928), *The King Who Was a King* (1929), *The Autocracy of Mr. Parham* (1930), *The Work, Wealth, and Happiness of Mankind* (1932), *The Shape of Things To Come* (1933), *The Bulpington of Blup* (1933), *Experiment in Autobiography* (1934), *The Anatomy of Frustration* (1936), *World Brain* (1938), *Apropos of Dolores* (1938), *The Brothers* (1938), *All Aboard for Ararat* (1940), *The New World Order* (1940), *Guide to the New World* (1941), *Phoenix* (1942), and *You Can't Be Too Careful* (1942).

Welsh Honeymoon, The. A one-act drama (1917) by Jeannette Marks which, together with *The Merry, Merry Cuckoo*, won the prize in the Welsh National Theatre Competition.

"Welsh Shakespeare," the. See **Williams, Edward.**

Wemmick (wem′ik), **John.** A kind-hearted but apparently flinty little clerk in Dickens's *Great Expectations*. He has a little home at Walworth, which

looks like a battery with mounted guns, where he devotes himself to his deaf old father, whom he calls "Aged P."

Wendoll (wen′dol, -dọl). The false friend of Frankford in Thomas Heywood's tragedy *A Woman Killed with Kindness*. He commits adultery with Mistress Frankford, thus betraying the friend who has given him shelter in his home. Frankford does not punish him, however, since he could not damn any man "unto a fearfull judgment."

Wendy Darling (wen′di där′ling). See **Darling, Wendy.**

Wenham (wen′ạm), **Mr.** In Thackeray's *Vanity Fair*, a disagreeable follower of the Marquis of Steyne.

Wentworth (went′werth), **Captain Frederick.** The hero of Jane Austen's novel *Persuasion*.

Wentworth, Sir **Thomas.** See **Strafford,** 1st Earl of.

Werner (ver′nẹr). A tragedy by Byron, published in 1823; so called from the name of its hero, a mysterious and morbid character. Macready produced this play in 1830, and Werner was considered one of his most powerful parts.

Wesley (wes′li, wez′-), **Charles.** b. at Epworth, Lincolnshire, England, Dec. 28, 1708; d. at London, March 29, 1788. An English Methodist clergyman and hymn writer; brother of John Wesley. He was educated at Westminster School and at Christ Church, Oxford. He accompanied his brother John to Georgia (1735–36).

Wesley, John. b. at Epworth, Lincolnshire, England, June 28, 1703; d. at London, March 2, 1791. An English clergyman, famous as the founder of Methodism. He was educated at Charterhouse School and at Christ Church, Oxford, became a fellow of Lincoln College in 1726, and was curate to his father (1727–29). In the latter year he settled at Oxford, where he became the leader of a band of young men conspicuous for their religious earnestness; they were somewhat derisively called "methodists" from the regularity and strict method of their lives and studies. He went to Georgia as a missionary in 1735, returning to England in 1738. At first he was allied with the Moravians, but soon abandoned all ecclesiastical traditions and established the Methodist Church. In 1739 he began open-air preaching. The first Methodist conference was held in 1744.

Wessex (wes′ẹks). The chief Saxon kingdom in England during the Heptarchy (Essex and Sussex were the other two). It was the nucleus during the early 9th century and under King Alfred of the consolidated kingdom of England. The settlement of the Saxons on the coast of what is now Hampshire took place in 495, and the kingdom spread N and W to what are now Berkshire, Wiltshire, and Dorsetshire. Wessex obtained the overlordship in Britain in the first part of the 9th century, was reduced in power by the Danes, and under Alfred's successors developed into the kingdom of England. It played a dominant role in the development of Old English literature and Anglo-Saxon scholarship. It was an earldom in the 10th and 11th centuries, comprising the territory S of the Thames. After 1066, when William the Conqueror defeated the Saxons, the term "Wessex" largely disappeared from use until 1874, when Thomas Hardy revived it. In his novel *Far from the Madding Crowd* he applied this name vaguely to the territory once ruled by Alfred the Great. The popularity of Hardy's Wessex novels brought the word back into common use, even though it does not appear on the map of England.

Wessex Poems and Other Verses. A volume of verse (1898) by Thomas Hardy.

West (west), **Gilbert.** b. 1703; d. at Wickham, Kent, England, March 26, 1756. An English poet and translator. Author of *Imitations of Spenser* (1739), *Institution of the Order of the Garter*, a dramatic poem, *Observations on the Resurrection* (1747), and *Odes of Pindar, with Several Other Pieces in Prose and Verse, Translated from the Greek, with a Dissertation on the Olympic Games* (1749).

West, Rebecca. [Pseudonym of **Cicily Isabel Fairfield.**] b. at Kerry, Ireland, Dec. 21, 1892—. A British journalist, novelist, and critic, whose pseudonym is derived from the heroine's name in Ibsen's *Rosmersholm*. On the staff (1912) of the *Clarion* as a political writer; contributor to *The New Yorker*. Her first book, *Henry James* (1916), was followed by the novels *The Return of the Soldier* (1918), *The Judge* (1922), and *War Nurse* (1930); with David Low she collaborated on *The Modern Rake's Progress* (1934); author also of *D. H. Lawrence, an Elegy* (1930), *Ending in Earnest* (1931), *Saint Augustine* (1933), *The Harsh Voice* (1935), *The Thinking Reed* (1936), *Black Lamb and Grey Falcon* (1942), and *The Meaning of Treason* (1948).

Westall (wes'tôl), **William (Bury).** b. at Blackburn, Lancashire, England, Feb. 7, 1834; d. Sept. 9, 1903. An English journalist and novelist. After beginning (1870) his career as a journalist at Dresden and Geneva, he met Kropotkin, Stepniak, and other Russian anarchists, and translated Stepniak's *Russia under the Czars*. Author of many novels and stories of adventure, including *Tales and Traditions of Saxony and Lusatia* (1877), *The Old Factory* (1881), *Larry Lohengrin* (1881), *Red Ryvington* (1882), *The Phantom City* (1886), *Witch's Curse* (1893), *Sons of Belial* (1895), *Her Two Millions* (1897), *With the Red Eagle* (1897), and *Dr. Wynne's Revenge* (1903).

Westcott (west'kǫt), **Peter.** The troubled hero of *Fortitude* (1913) and *The Young Enchanted* (1922), novels by Hugh Walpole.

West End, the. The aristocratic residential section of London.

Western (wes'tèrn), **Sophia.** The heroine of Henry Fielding's novel *Tom Jones*, a very bright and attractive character. After many adventures, she marries Tom.

Western, Squire. In Henry Fielding's novel *Tom Jones*, a foxhunting squire of ungoverned and brutal temper, the father of the fair Sophia.

West Indian (in'di.ạn), **The.** A comedy (1770) by Richard Cumberland, considered his best play. Garrick brought it out in 1771.

Westlock (west'lok), **John.** In Dickens's novel *Martin Chuzzlewit*, a good friend of Tom Pinch, who eventually marries Ruth Pinch.

Westminster (west'min.stèr). A former city, now a metropolitan borough, in W and SW London, in the County of London, situated on the N bank of the river Thames. It is noted for Westminster Abbey, around which it grew up, and for the Houses of Parliament, Buckingham Palace, Saint James's Palace, Albert Hall, the National Galleries, and others. Westminster was the chief crossing place of the Thames before London Bridge was built; Westminster Abbey was built nearby. It was a center of wealth and culture from the early Middle Ages onward. The adjoining palace (now the Houses of Parliament) built by the Norman kings helped to make this the political heart of the country. Many of the government buildings are located here, especially in Whitehall and in Downing Street. Covent Garden, the principal market for imported fruit and vegetables, is here. Westminster may be considered to be part of the West End of London. Until 1878 Westminster was separated from the City of London by Temple Bar (an archway across Fleet Street).

Westminster, Abbot of. In Shakespeare's *Richard II*, a conspirator with Aumerle against Bolingbroke.

Westminster Abbey. A church in Westminster, London, founded on the site of an earlier church by Edward the Confessor, and rebuilt in the 13th century by Henry III and Edward I. The highly ornate chapel of Henry VII, at the east end, was added by that king in the early 16th century. The dimensions, including the chapel, are 513 by 75 ft.; length of transepts, 200 ft.; height of vaulting, 102 ft. The square west towers were designed by Sir Christopher Wren. The north transept façade has three portals, an arcade, and a large wheel window. Henry VII's chapel has nave and aisles, and five radiating chapels in the chevet; it is a notable example of florid Perpendicular style, especially remarkable for the fan tracery and pendants of its ceiling. Its rich stalls are appropriated to the knights and squires of the Bath; over each are suspended a sword and a banner. The abbey is world-famous as the chief burial place of Great Britain's distinguished men. The south transept constitutes the famous Poets' Corner; it contains memorials to a large number of the names honored in English literature. The choir chapels contain medieval and Renaissance monuments; in Henry VII's chapel is the monument to that king, in metal, by Torregiano. Several other kings and princes are buried in this chapel, and in that of Edward the Confessor, which occupies the extremity of the choir. The chapter house is octagonal, with central column. The cloisters also contain tombs.

Westminster Hall. A structure at London, adjoining the Houses of Parliament on the west, forming part of the ancient palace of Westminster. It was begun by William II (William Rufus), burned at the end of the 13th century, and restored by Edward II and Richard II. It has a magnificent framed hammer-beam roof (reinforced by steel after World War I) in a single span 68 ft. wide; the length is 290 ft. and the height 92 ft. Here sat some of the first English Parliaments; here, until George IV, the coronation festivities were held; and here Charles I was condemned, and Cromwell saluted as Lord Protector. The hall now serves as a vestibule to the Houses of Parliament. Below it on the east is the crypt of Saint Stephen, or Church of Saint Mary Undercroft, a vaulted Gothic chapel, in architecture and decoration somewhat resembling the lower chapel of the Sainte Chapelle at Paris: the rich cloisters were built by Henry VIII. The roof of the hall was slightly damaged during enemy air action in World War II.

Westminster Palace. A former royal residence in Westminster, London. A palace is supposed to have existed at Westminster in the reign of Canute (1017–35). Its importance, however, begins with Edward the Confessor (1044–66). Various additions were made by his successors until Henry III (1216–72), in whose reign work was constantly in progress. His palace was richly decorated with pictures in oil (according to Horace Walpole, the first recorded use of that medium). It was repeatedly visited by royalty, and not used again until July 18, 1821, when George IV spent the night before his corona-tion there. The entire palace [...]

taking with him Salvation Yeo, an old sea dog who had gone with Oxenham on his ill-fated voyage. Oxenham's small daughter, whom Yeo vowed to protect, has been lost somewhere in South America, and all his future actions are directed by the hope that someday he will find her again. While they are in Ireland, Amyas captures a Spaniard named Don Guzman de Soto, and brings him home to Devon. There Don Guzman sees Rose Salterne, and they fall in love. The Spaniard escapes to Caracas, with the help of Eustace, Amyas's villainous cousin, taking Rose with him. Amyas and Frank vow re-venge, and they sail with the other young adorers of Rose and Salvation Yeo, to rescue Rose. They reach Caracas after many adventures, and have to fight their way to shore. Rose tells Frank and Amyas that she loves Guzman, and they consent to leave her there, but the evil Eustace, filled with jealous love for Rose, tells her that he will turn her over to the Inquisition if she does not go with him. She refuses, and when Frank is captured by the Spaniards in [...] hand-to-hand battle, both are tor-[tured ...] the proponents of the Inquis-[ition ...] horrible act after he has [...] ars to avenge their [...] ny corner of the [...] by Spanish [...] South [...]

[...] longer taken seriously by scholars. (subtitled "or What You Will.") See also **Twelfth Night**. answering this [...] possibility

Wheel of Fortune, The. A play (1795) by Richard Cumberland, in which J. P. Kemble was very suc-cessful in the role of the reformed misanthrope, Penruddock.

When Ghost Meets Ghost. A novel by William De Morgan, published in 1914.

When I Grow Rich. A novel by Ethel Sidgwick, published in 1928.

When I Was One-and-Twenty. A poem by A. E. Housman, included in *The Shropshire Lad* (1896). The poet describes in it the foolhardiness of early youth ("I was one-and-twenty,/ No use to talk to me"). But he learns by bitter experience that an old [...]

[...] country. [...] age to invent better weapons for his [...] obligations of a scientist to use [...] insoluble problems [...] particular [...] against Napoleon's method of putting down a rising

"whiff of grapeshot." A phrase referring originally to Napoleon's method of putting down a rising in Paris, in 1795. Napoleon, then still only a relatively unknown artillery officer, confronted the rioters with a battery of cannon, and the mob dispersed. Carlyle took the phrase as th[e] title of one of his chapters in his monumental *F[rench] Revolution*.

Whigs (hwigz). The more i[...] English parties which arose [...]

While Paris Laughed. [...] by Leonard Merrick. A [...]

Whipperginny (hwip'er [...]) (1923) by Robert Gr[aves ...]

Whiskerandos (hwis[...] character in the [...] Brinsley Sheridan [...] type.

at, fāte, fär, ask, fâre; net, mē, hėr; pin, pine; not, nōte, mȯ[...]

The Abbess of Vlaye (1904), *Starvecrow Farm* (1905), *Chippinge Borough* (1906), *Laid Up in Lavender* (1907), *The Wild Geese* (1908), and *Ovington's Bank* (1922).

W. H., Mr.   See under **Herbert, William.**

Whately (hwāt′li), **Anne.** See under **Hathaway, Anne.**

Whately, Richard. b. at London, Feb. 1, 1787; d. at Dublin, Oct. 1, 1863. An English prelate. In 1805 he entered Oxford (Oriel College), graduating in 1808. In 1819 he published *Historic Doubts Relative to Napoleon Bonaparte.* He became Bampton lecturer in 1822, principal of St. Albans Hall in 1825, professor of political economy at Oxford in 1829, and archbishop of Dublin in 1831. About 1815 his treatise on logic and that on rhetoric were contributed to the *Encyclopaedia Metropolitana.* In 1837 he wrote *Christian Evidences,* and he edited Bacon's *Essays* in 1856 and Paley in 1859. He advocated Catholic emancipation and unsectarian education, and helped to relieve the Irish famine. Among his numerous other works are *The Use and Abuse of Party Feeling in Matters of Religion* (1822), *Essays on Some of the Peculiarities of the Christian Religion* (1825), *Elements of Logic* (1826), *Elements of Rhetoric* (1828), and *Essays on Some of the Difficulties in the Writings of the Apostle Paul* (1828).

What Every Woman Knows. A comedy (1908) by Sir J. M. Barrie.

What Happened to the Corbetts (kôr′bẹts). A novel by Nevil Shute, published in 1939.

What Maisie Knew (mā′zi). A novel by Henry James, published in 1897. It is the story of a little girl whose parents, the Faranges, are divorced. She finds a friend in the sentimental old Mrs. Wix, and acquires a knowledge beyond her years concerning adult problems.

What the Thunder Said. The fifth section of T. S. Eliot's poem *The Waste Land,* described by Eliot in his notes as employing three themes: "the journey to Emmaus, the approach to the Chapel Perilous . . . , and the present decay of Eastern Europe."

What Will He Do with It? A novel by Edward Bulwer-Lytton, published in 1858.

What You Will. A comedy by John Marston, written in 1601 and published in 1607. The n that Shakespeare was in any wa play in *Twelfth Night* *Will*") is no l

What Y

man was right when he said "Give crowns and pounds and guineas,/ But not your heart away," and so says at the end of the poem "And I am two-and-twenty,/ And oh, 'tis true, 'tis true."

When the Sleeper Wakes. A novel by H. G. Wells, published in 1899.

Where Angels Fear to Tread. A novel by E. M. Forster, published in 1905.

Where There Is Nothing. A five-act play (1902) by William Butler Yeats.

Whetstone (hwet′stōn), **George.** b. at London, c1544; d. c1587. An English playwright, poet, and writer of prose tales. He wrote one play, an early romantic comedy, *Promos and Cassandra,* published and possibly acted in 1578, based on a tale in Cinthio's *Hecatommithi.* Shakespeare may have used this as his source for the plot of *Measure for Measure.*

Whewell (hū′ẹl), **William.** b. at Lancaster, England, May 24, 1794; d. at Cambridge, England, March 6, 1866. An English scientist and philosopher. He entered Cambridge (Trinity College) in 1812. In 1817 he was elected fellow, and in 1818 mathematical lecturer. From 1828 to 1832 he was professor of mineralogy, and from 1838 to 1855 Knightsbridge professor of moral philosophy. In 1841 he became master of Trinity College. His works include *Astronomy and General Physics Considered with Reference to Natural Theology* (1833), *History of the Inductive Sciences* (1837), *Philosophy of the Inductive Sciences* (1840), *Elements of Morality* (1845), *On the History of Moral Philosophy in England* (1852), *Plurality of Worlds, Platonic Dialogues for English Readers* (1859–61), and *Lectures on Political Economy* (1862).

Which Side Am I Supposed to Be On? A poem by W. H. Auden included in *The Orators* (1932). A war setting, frequent in Auden's poetry, is here used to telling advantage in the creation of a situation combining frontier fighting, espionage, and World War I trench warfare into a unity for the symbolic presentation of an ambiguous moral and soci situation. Conventional morality in questioned, and such seeming raised as the moral his knowle

bule to the Houses of Parliament. Below it on the east is the crypt of Saint Stephen, or Church of Saint Mary Undercroft, a vaulted Gothic chapel, in architecture and decoration somewhat resembling the lower chapel of the Sainte Chapelle at Paris: the rich cloisters were built by Henry VIII. The roof of the hall was slightly damaged during enemy air action in World War II.

Westminster Palace. A former royal residence in Westminster, London. A palace is supposed to have existed at Westminster in the reign of Canute (1017–35). Its importance, however, begins with Edward the Confessor (1042–66). Various additions were made by his successors until Henry III (1216–72), in whose reign work was constantly in progress. His palace was richly decorated with pictures in oil (according to Horace Walpole, the first recorded use of that medium). It was repeatedly visited by fire, and in 1512 (reign of Henry VIII) all the living apartments were destroyed. It was then abandoned by royalty, and not used again until July 18, 1821, when George IV spent the night before his coronation there. The entire palace, except Westminster Hall, was burned in 1834.

Westminster Palace. The London Houses of Parliament.

Westminster Review, The. A periodical founded in 1823 by Jeremy Bentham as an "organ of philosophic radicalism." It had on its staff at various times some of the principal figures of English letters.

Westminster School. A preparatory school at Westminster, London. It was established in Westminster Abbey by Henry VIII, and was reëstablished by Elizabeth.

Westmoreland (west′mōr.land), (1st) **Earl of.** In Shakespeare's *1* and *2 Henry IV* and *Henry V*, the historical Ralph Neville (1365–1425), 1st Earl of Westmorland, a loyal adherent of the King. He is a leader of the royal forces, in *Henry IV* against the rebels and in *Henry V* against the French.

Westmoreland, Earl of. In Shakespeare's *3 Henry VI*, the historical Ralph Neville (c1404–84), a member of the Lancastrian faction.

Westward for Smelts. A collection of stories on the plan of Boccaccio's *Decameron*, except that the storytellers are fishwives going up the Thames in a boat. It was written by "Kinde Kit of Kingstone" c1603, and reprinted by the Percy Society.

Westward Ho! A comedy by John Webster and Thomas Dekker, produced in 1604 and printed in 1607.

Westward Ho! [Full title, **Westward Ho! or the Voyages and Adventures of Sir Amyas Leigh** (ā′mi̇̄as lē).] A novel by Charles Kingsley, published in 1855. Amyas Leigh is the young hero of the book. He misses the opportunity to sail with John Oxenham to the New World, but manages to become a member of the crew that journeys with Drake on the first English voyage around the world. When he returns to his home in Devon he once again meets fair Rose Salterne, the young and sought-after daughter of the mayor. Frank, Amyas's brother, also loves her, and they vow that they will protect her no matter who wins her hand in marriage. Amyas then sails to Ireland against the Spanish,

taking with him Salvation Yeo, an old sea dog who had gone with Oxenham on his ill-fated voyage. Oxenham's small daughter, whom Yeo vowed to protect, has been lost somewhere in South America, and all his future actions are directed by the hope that someday he will find her again. While they are in Ireland, Amyas captures a Spaniard named Don Guzman de Soto, and brings him home to Devon. There Don Guzman sees Rose Salterne, and they fall in love. The Spaniard escapes to Caracas, with the help of Eustace, Amyas's villainous cousin, taking Rose with him. Amyas and Frank vow revenge, and they sail with the other young adorers of Rose and Salvation Yeo, to rescue Rose. They reach Caracas after many adventures, and have to fight their way to shore. Rose tells Frank and Amyas that she loves Guzman, and they consent to leave her there, but the evil Eustace, filled with jealous love for Rose, tells her that he will turn her over to the Inquisition if she does not go with him. She refuses, and when Frank is captured by the Spaniards in a hand-to-hand battle, both are tortured and killed by the proponents of the Inquisition. Amyas learns of this horrible act after he has once again set sail, and swears to avenge their deaths by seeking out Guzman in any corner of the earth. Meanwhile, they are attacked by Spanish ships and are forced to beach on the coast of South America. Amyas decides to search for the famous lost city of Manoa, with its marvelous treasures. He has the ship burnt so that there may be no turning back, and the men start a three-year trek into the wilderness. They never find the city, but they do find a young native queen named Ayancanora who falls in love with Amyas and follows him through the jungles, protecting the crew from many dangers for his sake. They finally reach New Granada and capture a Spanish ship, in which they sail home. On the way, Salvation Yeo discovers to his joy that Ayancanora is the long-lost daughter of Oxenham. After remaining at home for a while with his mother and Ayancanora, Amyas once more longs to go to sea, and he joins the famous expedition on its way to fight the Spanish Armada. He wins much renown by his brave deeds, but he is most bitter when he sees that Don Guzman's ship is among the Spanish vessels. Suddenly a storm comes up and Amyas is forced to watch his revenge being taken from him. He becomes reconciled to God's judgment when Guzman's ship is torn apart by the storm. Yeo is killed by lightning and Amyas is blinded. Back home again, Amyas comes under the tender influence of Ayancanora, and falls in love with her. They are married and live a happy life.

Weyburn (wā′bėrn), **Matthew.** Aminta's lover in George Meredith's *Lord Ormont and His Aminta.*

Weyman (wā′man), **Stanley John.** b. at Ludlow, Shropshire, England, 1855; d. April 10, 1928. An English novelist. Among his novels are *The House of the Wolf* (published serially in 1887, and in book form in 1890), *Francis Cludde* (1891), *The New Rector* (1891), *A Gentleman of France* (1893), *Under the Red Robe* (1894), *My Lady Rotha* (1894), *From the Memoirs of a Minister of France* (1895), *The Red Cockade* (1895), *The Man in Black* (1896), *For the Cause* (1897), *Shrewsbury* (1897), *The Castle Inn* (1898), *Sophia* (1900), *Count Hannibal* (1901), *In Kings' Byways* (1902), *The Long Night* (1903),

The Abbess of Vlaye (1904), *Starvecrow Farm* (1905), *Chippinge Borough* (1906), *Laid Up in Lavender* (1907), *The Wild Geese* (1908), and *Ovington's Bank* (1922).

W. H., Mr. See under **Herbert, William.**

Whately (hwāt′li), **Anne.** See under **Hathaway, Anne.**

Whately, Richard. b. at London, Feb. 1, 1787; d. at Dublin, Oct. 1, 1863. An English prelate. In 1805 he entered Oxford (Oriel College), graduating in 1808. In 1819 he published *Historic Doubts Relative to Napoleon Bonaparte.* He became Bampton lecturer in 1822, principal of St. Albans Hall in 1825, professor of political economy at Oxford in 1829, and archbishop of Dublin in 1831. About 1815 his treatise on logic and that on rhetoric were contributed to the *Encyclopaedia Metropolitana.* In 1837 he wrote *Christian Evidences,* and he edited Bacon's *Essays* in 1856 and Paley in 1859. He advocated Catholic emancipation and unsectarian education, and helped to relieve the Irish famine. Among his numerous other works are *The Use and Abuse of Party Feeling in Matters of Religion* (1822), *Essays on Some of the Peculiarities of the Christian Religion* (1825), *Elements of Logic* (1826), *Elements of Rhetoric* (1828), and *Essays on Some of the Difficulties in the Writings of the Apostle Paul* (1828).

What Every Woman Knows. A comedy (1908) by Sir J. M. Barrie.

What Happened to the Corbetts (kôr′bẹts). A novel by Nevil Shute, published in 1939.

What Maisie Knew (mā′zi). A novel by Henry James, published in 1897. It is the story of a little girl whose parents, the Faranges, are divorced. She finds a friend in the sentimental old Mrs. Wix, and acquires a knowledge beyond her years concerning adult problems.

What the Thunder Said. The fifth section of T. S. Eliot's poem *The Waste Land,* described by Eliot in his notes as employing three themes: "the journey to Emmaus, the approach to the Chapel Perilous . . . , and the present decay of Eastern Europe."

What Will He Do with It? A novel by Edward Bulwer-Lytton, published in 1858.

What You Will. A comedy by John Marston, written in 1601 and published in 1607. The possibility that Shakespeare was in any way answering this play in *Twelfth Night* (subtitled *"or What You Will"*) is no longer taken seriously by scholars.

What You Will. See also **Twelfth Night.**

Wheel of Fortune, The. A play (1795) by Richard Cumberland, in which J. P. Kemble was very successful in the role of the reformed misanthrope, Penruddock.

When Ghost Meets Ghost. A novel by William De Morgan, published in 1914.

When I Grow Rich. A novel by Ethel Sidgwick, published in 1928.

When I Was One-and-Twenty. A poem by A. E. Housman, included in *The Shropshire Lad* (1896). The poet describes in it the foolhardiness of early youth ("I was one-and-twenty,/ No use to talk to me"). But he learns by bitter experience that an old man was right when he said "Give crowns and pounds and guineas,/ But not your heart away," and so says at the end of the poem "And I am two-and-twenty,/ And oh, 'tis true, 'tis true."

When the Sleeper Wakes. A novel by H. G. Wells, published in 1899.

Where Angels Fear to Tread. A novel by E. M. Forster, published in 1905.

Where There Is Nothing. A five-act play (1902) by William Butler Yeats.

Whetstone (hwet′stŏn), **George.** b. at London, c1544; d. c1587. An English playwright, poet, and writer of prose tales. He wrote one play, an early romantic comedy, *Promos and Cassandra,* published and possibly acted in 1578, based on a tale in Cinthio's *Hecatommithi.* Shakespeare may have used this as his source for the plot of *Measure for Measure.*

Whewell (hū′ẹl), **William.** b. at Lancaster, England, May 24, 1794; d. at Cambridge, England, March 6, 1866. An English scientist and philosopher. He entered Cambridge (Trinity College) in 1812. In 1817 he was elected fellow, and in 1818 mathematical lecturer. From 1828 to 1832 he was professor of mineralogy, and from 1838 to 1855 Knightsbridge professor of moral philosophy. In 1841 he became master of Trinity College. His works include *Astronomy and General Physics Considered with Reference to Natural Theology* (1833), *History of the Inductive Sciences* (1837), *Philosophy of the Inductive Sciences* (1840), *Elements of Morality* (1845), *On the History of Moral Philosophy in England* (1852), *Plurality of Worlds,* *Platonic Dialogues for English Readers* (1859–61), and *Lectures on Political Economy* (1862).

Which Side Am I Supposed to Be On? A poem by W. H. Auden included in *The Orators* (1932). A war setting, frequent in Auden's poetry, is here used to telling advantage in the creation of a situation combining frontier fighting, espionage, and World War I trench warfare into a unity for the symbolic presentation of an ambiguous moral and social situation. Conventional morality in particular is questioned, and such seemingly insoluble problems raised as the moral obligations of a scientist to use his knowledge to invent better weapons for his country.

"whiff of grapeshot." A phrase referring originally to Napoleon's method of putting down a rising against the government of the Convention, in Paris, in 1795. Napoleon, then still only a relatively unknown artillery officer, confronted the rioters with a battery of cannon, and the mob dispersed. Carlyle took the phrase as the title of one of his chapters in his monumental *French Revolution.*

Whigs (hwigz). The more liberal of the two great English parties which arose late in the 17th century.

While Paris Laughed. A collection of stories (1918) by Leonard Merrick.

Whipperginny (hwip′ẹr.gin.i). A volume of verse (1923) by Robert Graves.

Whiskerandos (hwis.kẹr.an′dōz), **Don Ferolo.** A character in the tragedy rehearsed in Richard Brinsley Sheridan's *The Critic:* a burlesque tragedy type.

---

fat, fāte, fär, àsk, fâre; net, mē, hèr; pin, pīne; not, nōte, mōve, nôr; up, lūte, pùll; ᴛʜ, then;

Whiskers. In Dickens's novel *The Old Curiosity Shop*, the skittish pony owned by Mr. Garland and much loved by Kit Nubbles.

Whistlecraft (hwis'l.kràft), **William and Robert.** Pseudonym of **Frere, John Hookham.**

Whistler (hwis'lẽr), **Laurence.** b. 1912—. An English poet and biographer. Author of *Four Walls* (1934), which won the king's gold medal for the best book of poetry to appear in England in 1934, *The Emperor Heart* (1937), *In Time of Suspense* (1940), and *Sir John Vanbrugh: Architect and Dramatist* (1938), a critical study.

Whitaker (hwit'ạ.kẽr), **Joseph.** b. at London, May 4, 1820; d. at Enfield, Middlesex, England, May 15, 1895. An English publisher and editor, founder of *Whitaker's Almanack.* He founded (1849) the *Penny Post*, a church monthly, and the *Bookseller* (1858), a trade organ, and edited (1756–59) the *Gentleman's Magazine.* He is best known for his highly successful *Almanack*, first published in 1868, and for his useful bibliographical work, *Reference Catalogue of Current Literature* (1874; many editions).

Whitaker's Almanack. An annual publication established by Joseph Whitaker in 1868. It differs from the ordinary American almanac in that it contains a tremendous body of information pertaining to the British royal family, peerage, and various government departments, but it includes also the type of material which Americans have become accustomed to finding in their almanacs. It is still published, and has a very wide circulation throughout the British Commonwealth of Nations.

Whitby (hwit'bi), **Synod** (or **Council**) **of.** An ecclesiastical council held (664) at Whitby, England, under the leadership of the king of Northumbria, to decide the Easter and tonsure questions. It resulted in the triumph of the Roman party as against the Celtic, a decision which was to affect the course of English ecclesiastical affairs for centuries. By its orientation of Anglo-Saxon culture away from Celtic scholarship and toward that of the Continent it also had an effect on the literature first of Northumbria and then of all of England.

White (hwīt), **Babington.** Pseudonym of **Braddon, Mary Elizabeth.**

White, Gilbert. b. at Selborne, Hampshire, England, July 18, 1720; d. there, June 26, 1793. An English naturalist. He was educated at Oriel College, Oxford, and became a fellow there, and was curate at Selborne and elsewhere. He is famous for his *Natural History and Antiquities of Selborne* (1789).

White, Henry Kirke. b. at Nottingham, England, March 21, 1785; d. at Cambridge, England, Oct. 19, 1806. An English poet. He published a volume of poems in 1803, and in 1804 secured a sizarship at Saint John's College, Cambridge, where he died from overstudy. His *Remains* and biography were published by Robert Southey in 1807.

White, Joseph Blanco. b. at Seville, Spain, July 11, 1775; d. at Liverpool, England, May 20, 1841. An English author and clergyman. In 1800 he was ordained a Roman Catholic priest. In 1810 he went to England and took orders in the Church of England, but afterward became a Unitarian. He edited

El Español at London (1810–14), and wrote *Letters from Spain* (1822), *Evidence against Catholicism* (1825), *Poor Man's Preservative against Popery* (1825), *Second Travels of an Irish Gentleman in Search of a Religion* (1833), and the famous sonnet *Night.*

White Blackbird, The. A play by Lennox Robinson, produced in 1925 and published in 1926.

Whiteboys (hwīt'boiz). [Also called **Levelers.**] An illegal agrarian association, formed (c1761) in Ireland. The members of the association assembled at night with white frocks over their other clothes, threw down fences and leveled enclosures, and destroyed the property of harsh landlords or their agents, the Protestant clergy, the tithe collectors, and any others whom the organization found obnoxious.

Whitechapel (hwīt'chap″ẹl). A district comprising three wards of Stepney metropolitan borough in E London, in the County of London. It forms part of the East End of London, and is inhabited by the poorer classes (much of London's Jewish population lives here). It takes its name from Whitechapel Road.

White Company. A band of assassins organized at Toulouse in the Albigensian crusade in the 13th century by "the ferocious Folquet" (the troubadour Folquet de Marseille, who had become bishop of Toulouse). He marched at their head, massacring all who were suspected of favoring heretical opinions. This company joined the army of Simon de Montfort when he besieged Toulouse. The name was also assumed by a band of freebooters (the "Grand Companies") led by Bertrand du Guesclin in 1366, from the white cross which each wore on his shoulder. Bertrand was ransomed from English captivity for the purpose of ridding France of these adventurers. He placed himself at their head and led them out of the country into Spain against Pedro the Cruel. The name was also given, probably on account of their equipment, to another band of adventurers led by Sir John Hawkwood, who ravaged the northern part of Italy with them in the 14th century.

White Company, The. A historical romance (1891) by A. Conan Coyle, based on the career of du Guesclin's band.

White Devil, or Vittoria Corombona (vi.tō'ri.ạ kor-ọm.bō'nạ), **The.** A tragedy by John Webster, published in 1612 and acted c1611 at the Red Bull theater. The plot is based upon the stormy life of Vittoria Accoramboni, Duchess of Bracciano (c1557–85). Despite echoes in the play of Shakespeare and Montaigne, of Sir Philip Sidney's *Arcadia* and Stefano Guazzo's *La Civile Conversatione*, it is a work of Webster's individual genius. It is a departure from the popular plays of the day that were written down to the taste of the pit audience, being as literary as Shakespeare's *Love's Labour's Lost;* yet it is one of the few Elizabethan plays that can still hold the interest of an audience today. Its story of crime and violence is complicated, hinging upon the love between Brachiano and Vittoria Corombona. Vittoria's brother Flamineo contrives a liaison between the two, which is eagerly entered into by Brachiano in spite of the warnings of his brother-in-law, Francisco, Duke of Florence, and of Cardinal Monticelso, uncle of Vittoria's husband, Camillo. Flamineo plots and executes Camillo's murder. Vittoria is brought to trial for adultery and murder. Francisco and Monticelso, sitting in judgment upon her, are confounded by Vittoria's poise and wit. She is condemned to banishment in a house of religious women. Brachiano's love for her survives all Francisco's efforts to destroy it, and, against Flamineo's advice to incite the Duke no farther, the lovers flee to Brachiano's palace in Padua. After much intrigue and violence, including Flamineo's murder of his innocent brother Marcellus, Francisco and Monticelso manage to have Brachiano killed by a poisoned helmet. At the play's end, Flamineo, Vittoria, and her Moorish attendant Zanche are stabbed to death. The world in which Webster's characters move is neither just nor noble nor moral nor reasonable. Flamineo goes to his death saying: "To prate were idle. I remember nothing. There's nothing of so infinite vexation As man's own thought." Vittoria feels that her soul "is like to a ship in a black storm, Is driven I know not whither." Webster enhances his somber theme by the use of ghosts, dumb shows, and a great number of horrid stage deaths.

Whitefield (hwĭt′fēld), **George.** b. at Gloucester, England, Dec. 27, 1714; d. at Newburyport, Mass., Sept. 30, 1770. An English clergyman, celebrated as a pulpit orator, one of the founders of Methodism. He was educated at Gloucester and Oxford, became associated at Oxford with the Methodists, and was ordained deacon in 1736. He visited Georgia in 1738, returning to England in the same year to be ordained a priest. He began open-air preaching at Bristol with great effect, and again visited America (1739–41), preaching in New England, New York, Georgia, and elsewhere. He separated from Wesley on doctrinal points in 1741 (Whitefield retaining his rigid Calvinism and Wesley leaning toward Arminianism), preached throughout Great Britain, was in America for the third time (1744–48, and several times later), and became chaplain to the Countess of Huntingdon. He returned to America for the last time in 1769, and died there.

Whitefriars (hwīt′frī″ạrz). A district in E central London, in the City of London and the County of London. It is named from the convent of an order of Carmelites, established in Fleet Street in 1241. The first monastery of the order in England was founded by Ralph Freshburne near Aterwich, Northumberland, in 1224. In 1580 the Whitefriars' Monastery was given up to a company of players, and known as Whitefriars' Theatre. See also **Alsatia.**

Whitehall (hwīt′hôl). In modern London, the main thoroughfare between Trafalgar Square and the Houses of Parliament. It is lined with the offices of various government departments, whence it has come to be used in an extended sense to mean the government of Great Britain, as in the line "feeling in Whitehall runs high." The street derives its name from a palace, the residence of the archbishop of York, that once stood on a portion of the ground it now traverses.

Whitehall Palace. A palace in London, originally built in the reign of Henry III: partly destroyed by fire in 1615.

White Hart Inn. A tavern in Southwark, mentioned in Shakespeare's *2 Henry VI* (IV.viii) by Jack Cade, perhaps as his headquarters.

Whitehead (hwĭt′hed), **Alfred North.** b. at Ramsgate, England, Feb. 15, 1861; d. at Cambridge, Mass., Dec. 30, 1947. An English philosopher and mathematician. He was a lecturer (1885–1911) on mathematics at Trinity College at Cambridge, reader (1911–14) in geometry at University College, and professor (1914–24) at the Imperial College of Science and Technology of the University of London. He came to America as professor (1924–36) of philosophy at Harvard. Whitehead's philosophy, stemming from a base in mathematics, is idealistic; knowledge of the absolute in God is the aim of his thought. Author of *A Treatise on Universal Algebra* (1898), *The Principles of Natural Knowledge* (1919), *Science and the Modern World* (1925), *Process and Reality, an Essay in Cosmology* (1929), *Adventures of Ideas* (1933), *Nature and Life* (1934), and *Religion in the Making* (1926). He collaborated with Bertrand Russell on the monumental *Principia Mathematica* (3 vols., 1910–13).

Whitehead, Charles. b. at London, 1804; d. at Melbourne, Australia, 1862. An English poet and writer. He published *The Solitary* (1831) and *Autobiography of Jack Ketch* (1834). The *Pickwick Papers* were written by Charles Dickens at his suggestion. In 1857 he went to Melbourne.

Whitehead, William. b. at Cambridge, England, 1715; d. at London, April 14, 1785. An English poet, the successor of Colley Cibber as poet laureate. He was educated at Winchester and Cambridge (Clare Hall). In 1742 he became a fellow of Clare, and in 1757 poet laureate. He wrote the tragedies *A Roman Father* (1750) and *Creusa* (1754), the comedy *A School for Lovers* (1762), and others.

Whiteheaded Boy, The. A three-act Irish comedy by Lennox Robinson, published in 1920.

White Horse of Uffington (uf′ing.tọn) or **of Berkshire** (bẽrk′shir). A huge figure of a horse (374 ft. long) made by cutting away the turf on an escarpment of the Chalk Downs near Wantage, Berkshire, England, and near Uffington castle. Traditionally it is said to commemorate the battle of Ashdown (871) when Alfred the Great defeated the Danes. Actually it is now believed to be much more ancient, possibly having been cut by Belgic settlers from Gaul, who fled from Roman rule. The horse was a religious symbol of the Belgic Gauls.

Whiteing (hwī′ting), **Richard.** b. at London, July 27, 1840; d. June 29, 1928. An English author and journalist. He was writer and correspondent for a number of leading English newspapers. Among his publications are *No. 5 John Street* (1899), *Paris of To-day* (1900), *The Yellow Van* (1903), *Ring in the New* (1906), and *Little People* (1909).

White Lady. In German folklore, a spectral woman clothed in white, a benevolent revenant who appears to certain people to warn or reward them. She is usually associated with some noble family, and is commonly interpreted as an ancestress. In some parts of Germany she is identified with

Berchta. The White Lady of the Hohenzollerns appeared periodically to foretell the death of some member of the family or to announce some event of importance to Germany. The Hapsburg family of Austria had a similar ancestral lady who foretold disaster. She appears in English literature as Scott's "White Lady of Avenel," in *The Monastery.*

White Lady of Avenel (ăv'nęl). A beautiful spirit, garbed entirely in white, introduced by Sir Walter Scott in his novel *The Monastery,* and appearing also in *The Abbot.* She is the guardian spirit of the House of Avenel.

White Monkey, The. A novel by John Galsworthy, published in 1924. A continuation of the author's record of the Forsyte family, it was later included in *A Modern Comedy* (1929). It portrays the restlessness of a certain class of young English people after World War I.

White Peacock, The. A novel by D. H. Lawrence, published in 1911.

White Rabbit. In Carroll's *Alice's Adventures in Wonderland,* the rabbit whom Alice follows down a hole, and who leads her into the first portion of her marvelous adventures.

White Rose of Raby (rā'bi). An epithet of Cecily or Cicely Neville, mother of Edward IV and Richard III of England; so called from the family home, Raby Castle, in Durham.

White's. A noted club in St. James's Street, London, established 1698 as a chocolate house.

White Ship, The. A poem by Dante Gabriel Rossetti, published in *Ballads and Sonnets* (1881).

White Stallion, The. A volume of verse (1924) by Frederick V. Branford.

White Steed, The. A play (produced at New York in 1939) by Paul Vincent Carroll.

White Surrey (sur'i). In Shakespeare's *Richard III,* a favorite horse of Richard.

White Tower. The oldest part of the Tower of London.

Whitford (hwit'fŏrd), **Vernon.** A principal character in George Meredith's novel *The Egoist.*

Whitlock (hwit'lok), **Elizabeth.** [Maiden name, **Kemble.**] b. 1761; d. 1836. An English actress; sister of Sarah Siddons.

Whitmore (hwit'mōr, -môr), **Walter.** A character in Shakespeare's *2 Henry VI* who, in revenge for losing an eye in a sea battle, beheads his prisoner, Suffolk (IV.i).

Whitsunday (hwit'sun"dā, -sun.dā). See **Pentecost.**

Whittington (hwit'ing.tọn), **Richard.** b. c1358; d. in March, 1423. A Lord Mayor of London. He was a son of a Gloucestershire knight who died an outlaw in 1360. In 1393 he was an alderman and sheriff of London, and he was chosen mayor in 1397, 1406, 1419. In 1416 he was elected member of Parliament for London. A legend of c1600 depicts him as going up to London, to seek his fortune, and becoming a scullion to a merchant in whose house he received cruel treatment. He bought a cat for a penny and sent it "on a venture" over the sea. It was sold for a great sum in a rat-ridden country which had no cats, and Whittington's fortune was made. Even-

tually he married the merchant's daughter, and three times became Lord Mayor of London. How this story became associated with the historical Whittington is unknown. It was a popular and widespread tale all over Europe in the 13th century and was known as early as the 12th. W. A. Clouston cites Breton, Bohemian, Danish, French, German, Italian, Norwegian, Portuguese, and Russian versions of it. There was also a 13th-century Persian tale identical in plot for which scholars postulate a still unfound Indian (probably Buddhist) original.

Whole Contention betweene . . . Lancaster and Yorke . . . (lang'kạs.tėr; yôrk), **The.** See under **Henry VI** (*Part Three*).

Wholesome (hōl'sọm), **Tribulation.** A Puritan minister in Jonson's *The Alchemist.* He wishes to possess the philosopher's stone, in order that he may be enabled to convert base metals into gold, with which he proposes to bribe the authorities to permit the return from exile of the other members of his sect.

Whorehound (hōr'hound), **Sir Walter.** The profligate Welsh knight in Thomas Middleton's comedy *A Chaste Maid in Cheapside.*

Whore of Babylon (bab'i.lọn), **The.** An allegorical play by Thomas Dekker, published in 1607 and written possibly in 1600, with revisions in 1605 or 1607.

Whymper (hwim'pėr), **Edward.** b. at London, April 27, 1840; d. at Chamonix, France, Sept. 16, 1911. An English book illustrator and alpinist. He toured the Alps (1860), making sketches, and climbed Mont Pelvoux in 1861. He almost lost his life in the descent after climbing (1865) the Matterhorn, the first time the peak was achieved. He was the first to climb Mount Chimborazo in Ecuador (1880) and other Andean peaks. He visited Greenland, Ecuador, and Canada, collecting plants, making sketches, and studying the effects of atmospheric pressure on human beings, and invented a special tent for mountain climbers. He illustrated his own books which recount his experiences and observations, *Scrambles in the Alps in the Years 1860–69* (1871), *Travels Amongst the Great Andes of the Equator* (1892), *Chamonix and Mt. Blanc* (1896), and *Zermatt and the Matterhorn* (1897).

Whyte (hwīt), **Violet.** A pseudonym of **Stannard, Henrietta Eliza Vaughan.**

Whyte-Melville (hwīt'mel'vil), **George John.** b. near St. Andrews, Scotland, June 19, 1821; d. in a foxhunting accident in the Vale of the White Horse, Berkshire, England, Dec. 5, 1878. An English soldier and novelist. Among his novels, notably of foxhunting, steeplechasing, and similar sports, are *Digby Grand* (1853), *Kate Coventry* (1856), *The Interpreter* (1858), *Holmby House* (1860), *Good for Nothing* (1861), *The Queen's Marys* (1862), *The Gladiators* (1863), *The White Rose* (1868), *Sarchedon* (1871), *Satanella* (1873), *Uncle John* (1874), *Katerfelto* (1875), *Roy's Wife* (1878), and *Black but Comely* (1879).

Wicked Bible. An edition printed in 1632 in which the word *not* is omitted from the seventh commandment.

Wickfield (wik'fēld), **Agnes.** In Dickens's *David Copperfield,* the daughter of Miss Betsey Trotwood's solicitor, in whose home David lives while he continues his education at Canterbury. After the death of his first wife, Dora Spenlow, David realizes his mistake in never recognizing the true worth of Agnes, and he marries her.

Wickham (wik'ạm), **Anna.** b. at Wimbledon, Surrey, England, 1884—. An English poet. Among her volumes of poetry are *The Contemplative Quarry* (1920), *The Man with a Hammer* (1921), and *The Little Old House* (1922).

Wickliffe or **Wiclif** (wik'lif), **John.** See **Wycliffe, John.**

Widow. In Shakespeare's *All's Well That Ends Well*, a Florentine woman with whom Helena lodges, the mother of Diana.

Widow. In Shakespeare's *Taming of the Shrew*, the woman who marries Hortensio.

Widow, The. A comedy by Thomas Middleton, written c1608 and revised c1615, printed in 1652, and then attributed by the publisher to Ben Jonson, John Fletcher, and Middleton.

Widow Barnaby (bär'nạ.bi). A novel by Frances Trollope, published in 1839.

Widow Blackacre (blak'ā"kẻr). See **Blackacre, Widow.**

Widow Damply (dam'pli). See **Damply, Widow.**

Widowers' Houses. A comedy (1892) by George Bernard Shaw, published in *Plays, Pleasant and Unpleasant* (1898), about the evils of slum ownership. Shaw said that he had here turned several acts of a "well-made play of the Parisian type" written several years earlier with William Archer into "a grotesque realistic exposure of slum landlordism, municipal jobbery, and the pecuniary and matrimonial ties between them and the pleasant people with 'independent' incomes who imagine that such sordid matters do not touch their own lives."

Widow Green (grēn). See **Green, Widow.**

Widow in the Bye Street, The. A long narrative poem (1912) by John Masefield, telling of the devotion of a mother to her son Jimmy, and the cruel coldness of the girl Jimmy loves.

Widow's Tears, The. A comedy by George Chapman, produced c1605 and published in 1612. Its main plot is based upon a story in Petronius's *Satyricon*.

Widow Wadman (wod'mạn). See **Wadman, Widow.**

Widsith (wēd'sēth, usually modernized as wid'sith). An Old English poem of the 7th century, incorporating three thulas (metrical name lists) of the 6th century: one of kings, one of tribes, and one of heroes. The author of *Widsith*, which is included in the *Exeter Book*, is unknown. His poem of 143 lines deals with the life of an ideal scop, whose name (which means "one who wanders far and wide") gives name to the poem as well. Standard editions of the poem include that of R. W. Chambers (1912), now out of date, but unquestionably the best exemplification of 19th-century scholarship in this field, and that of Kemp Malone (1936).

Wieland (vē'länt), **Christoph Martin.** b. near Biberach, Germany, Sept. 5, 1733; d. at Weimar, Germany, Jan. 20, 1813. A German poet and novelist. His father was a pastor, and the poet's early works (*Die Natur der Dinge,* 1751; *Anti-Ovid,* 1752) show this didactic and religious influence. It was largely for this reason that J. J. Bodmer invited him to Zurich, where he continued in this vein with the Biblical epic *Der geprüfte Abraham* (1753) and the poem *Empfindungen des Christen* (1755), directed at the frivolity of the Anacreontic poets. With his return to Biberach, where he was given a minor position in the government, his attitude changed completely; he associated with Count Stadion, who introduced him to foreign writers of a more rationalistic sort. On the model of Cervantes's *Don Quixote* he wrote his first novel, *Don Sylvio von Rosalvo* (1765). On reading Voltaire, he became interested in Shakespeare and produced the first German translation of Shakespeare; between 1762 and 1766 he put into German prose 22 of the plays, a feat of momentous importance for German literature. The period 1766–67 saw the appearance of what is generally considered to be his greatest novel, *Die Geschichte des Agathon,* the first of the so-called Bildungsromane, of which Goethe's *Wilhelm Meister* is the classic example. In 1769 he was made professor of philosophy and literature at the University of Erfurt. His pedagogical book, *Der goldene Spiegel* (1772), caused him to be called to Weimar as tutor to the young dukes Charles August and Constantine; thus he was for the rest of his life one of the famous Weimar group that later included Goethe, Herder, and Schiller. Two of his later works deserve special mention: a satire on small-town life, *Die Abderiten* (1774), and the verse epic *Oberon* (1780). He also did valuable service to German literature with his review, *Der teutsche Merkur* (1773–1810).

Wife, The. A play by James Sheridan Knowles, brought out in 1833. Charles Lamb wrote the prologue and epilogue.

Wife for a Month, A. A play by John Fletcher, acted in 1624 and printed in 1647. It is similar in theme to Beaumont and Fletcher's *The Maid's Tragedy.*

Wife of Bath's Tale (bàths), **The.** One of Chaucer's *Canterbury Tales.* It is a skillful adaptation of the widespread folk tale of the Loathly Lady who cannot return to her original beautiful form until a knight is found who will marry her. In Chaucer's version, she offers the knight the choice of having her ugly and faithful or fair and free to follow her inclinations. Dryden modernized the tale and changed it unwarrantably. Variants and analogues of this tale are known in Sanskrit, Turkish, Kaffir, Old Irish, and Icelandic, in the Gawain stories of the Arthurian cycle, the English and Scottish traditional ballads, and in Gower's *Confessio Amantis.* In the prologue, which is twice as long as the tale itself, Alice, the Wife, vigorously expounds her somewhat unorthodox views on marriage and men. She maintains that the "sovereignty" of the woman (which she has won by various means from each of her five husbands) is the secret of success in marriage. This thesis is supported by the tale she tells, in which, when the reluctant knight has promised obedience, the hag becomes a young bride, beautiful and faithful. *The Wife of Bath's Tale* is the first of what is usually called, after Kittredge, the "marriage group." She is described in the Prologue as prosperous and well-traveled, somewhat deaf, and rather gaudy in dress as well as temperament:

> Hir hosen weren of fyn scarlet reed,
> Ful streite y-teyd, and shoes ful moiste and newe.
> Bold was hir face, and fair, and reed of hewe.
> She was a worthy womman al hir lyve;
> Housbondes at chirche-dore she hadde fyve,
> Withouten other companye in youthe;
> But therof nedeth nat to speke as nouthe. . . .
> In felaweschip wel coude she laughe and carpe.
> Of remedies of love she knew per-chaunce,
> For she coude of that art the olde daunce.

Wife of Sir Isaac Harman (ī'zạk här'mạn), **The**. A novel (1914) by H. G. Wells.

Wife of Usher's Well (ush'ẽrz). A popular Scottish border ballad on the revenant theme. The three sons of a widow who lives by Usher's Well have been drowned at sea. They return one winter night to visit their mother. She knows they are from the other world because they wear in their hats green birch leaves, which have been plucked from trees growing by the gates of Paradise. The homely comfort of the mother making the sons' beds and sitting beside them in the night is broken at cockcrow, when the sons have to hurry back to the land of the dead.

Wife's Lament, The. An Old English poem, preserved in the *Exeter Book*, written in the form of a monologue, in which a wife tells of the woes inflicted upon her by her husband's enemies after her husband is driven out of the country.

Wiglaf (wē'läf, sometimes modernized as wig'läf). The faithful thane of Beowulf, his sole companion at the time of his death.

Wilberforce (wil'bẽr.fôrs), **William**. b. at Hull, England, Aug. 24, 1759; d. at London, July 29, 1833. An English philanthropist, statesman, and orator, famous as an opponent of the slave-trade. He was graduated at Cambridge (St. John's College), and in 1780 became member of Parliament for Hull. He was intimately associated with William Pitt. About 1787 he met Thomas Clarkson, and began to agitate the slavery question with the support of Pitt, who, in 1788, in the absence of Wilberforce, introduced the question in Parliament. In 1792 Wilberforce carried in the House of Commons a measure for gradual abolition, which was thrown out by the Lords. Immediate abolition of the trade was secured in 1807. He then directed his energies to the end of destroying slavery as an institution, and was one of the founders of the Anti-Slavery Society. The Emancipation Bill, abolishing slavery completely, was passed in 1833, a month after the death of Wilberforce. Wilberforce was also a champion of Catholic emancipation, a supporter of missionary societies, and an educational reformer. He wrote *A Practical View of the Prevailing Religious System of Professed Christians* (1797) and others.

Wild (wīld), **Jonathan**. b. c1682; hanged at Tyburn, London, May 24, 1725. An English robber. While in prison for debt, he became acquainted with a number of criminals and on his release became a receiver of stolen goods. He developed a system of returning the goods to their owners for the rewards, paying his thieves a commission. He gathered about

him a large organization that planned and carried out crimes and eliminated, by informing against them, those criminals who would not coöperate. For a time it was convenient for the officials to permit his bold depredations, but at last he was arrested, tried, and condemned. He is the subject of Henry Fielding's *Life of Mr. Jonathan Wild the Great* (1743) and of a novel (1725) by Daniel Defoe.

Wildair (wil'dār), **Sir Harry**. A gay, spirited man of fashion in George Farquhar's *Constant Couple* and in its sequel *Sir Harry Wildair*. The part was created by Robert Wilks and afterward played by David Garrick, but Peg Woffington played it so brilliantly that the latter resigned it to her.

Wild Boar of Ardennes (är.den'). In Scott's *Quentin Durward*, an epithet of William de la Marck.

Wilde (wīld), **Oscar**. [Full name, **Oscar Fingal O'Flahertie Wills Wilde**.] b. at Dublin, Oct. 16, 1856; d. at Paris, Nov. 30, 1900. An Irish poet, dramatist, and novelist. He was educated at Trinity College, Dublin, and at Magdalen College, Oxford, where he won prizes and honors, and founded the "aesthetic movement," characterized by a certain flamboyant air, a detached manner, and the "art for art's sake" philosophy, associated with his name and later burlesqued by W. S. Gilbert and Arthur S. Sullivan in *Patience*. He was accused, tried, and found guilty of homosexual practices, and sentenced to imprisonment (1895–97) with hard labor; he was released (May, 1897), physically, spiritually, and financially ruined. He lived thereafter at Paris under the name Sebastian Melmoth. One of the great wits of his time, he was the author of *Vera, or The Nihilists* (1880), *The Duchess of Padua* (1883), *Salome* (1893; written originally in French; Eng. trans., 1894), *Lady Windermere's Fan* (1893), *A Woman of No Importance* (1894), *The Importance of Being Earnest* (1899), and *An Ideal Husband* (1899), plays; *Ravenna* (1878), a prize poem, *Poems* (1881), and *The Ballad of Reading Gaol* (1898), an anonymously published record of his prison experience, poetry; *The Happy Prince and Other Tales* (1888), *A House of Pomegranates* (1891), two collections of fairy tales; *The Picture of Dorian Gray* (1891), a novel, *Lord Arthur Savile's Crime and Other Stories* (1891), *Intentions* (1891), and *The Soul of Man Under Socialism* (1895); *De Profundis*, another work written in prison, was published in part in 1905; the remainder still in manuscript is at the British Museum, where it is to be opened on Jan. 1, 1960.

Wild Earth. A volume of verse by Padraic Colum, published in England in 1909, and later revised for its American publication in 1916.

Wildfell Hall (wīld'fel), **The Tenant of**. See **Tenant of Wildfell Hall, The**.

Wildfire (wīld'fīr), **Madge**. In Sir Walter Scott's novel *The Heart of Midlothian*, a gypsy's daughter who becomes insane after having been seduced and deserted by George Robertson. Her real name is Madge Murdockson.

Wild Gallant, The. A comedy (1663) by John Dryden, supposedly modeled upon the Spanish comedy of intrigue. Some of its scenes were later mocked in *The Rehearsal*, by the Duke of Buckingham and others.

Wild Goose Chase, The. A comedy by John Fletcher, acted in 1621 and printed in 1652. The wild goose, Mirabel, just returned from the wars and a succession of mistresses, asserts his freedom from women by repudiating his engagement to Oriana, with whom he had been in love previously. He is, of course, captured by her in the end.

Wilding (wīl'ding). The principal character in James Shirley's *The Gamester*, played by David Garrick in his version *The Gamesters*.

Wilding. "The liar" in Samuel Foote's play of that name.

Wilding, Mistress. The wife of Wilding in James Shirley's *The Gamester*. She cures her husband of his disregard for her, and of his passion for his witty niece Penelope, by pretending that he has been cuckolded.

Wild Oats: or, The Strolling Gentleman. A comedy by John O'Keeffe, produced in 1791.

Wildrake (wīl'drāk), **Roger.** In Sir Walter Scott's novel *Woodstock*, a rakish supporter of the Stuart cause, much given to wenching and drinking, but loyal to his King. He brings Charles II the first word of his restoration to the throne, and thereby wins himself a modest pension.

Wilfer (wil'fėr), **Bella.** In Dickens's novel *Our Mutual Friend*, a beautiful but, in the early portion of the story, somewhat selfish girl (thought to have been modeled on Maria Beadnell, Dickens's first love). She is supposed to marry John Harmon, according to the terms of old Mr. Harmon's will, and is very much put out by the discovery of John's supposed death to think that she has become a widow without being a bride; however, in the end, and without learning his identity until very late in the story, she marries John in his disguise as John Rokesmith.

Wilfer, Lavinia. [Called "**Lavvy**"; nicknamed **the** "**Irrepressible**."] In Dickens's novel *Our Mutual Friend*, the younger sister of Bella Wilfer.

Wilfer, Mrs. In Dickens's novel *Our Mutual Friend*, the mother of Bella Wilfer (thought to have been modeled on Dickens's own mother). She plays a relatively slight part in the story, but is one of the most memorable of Dickens's more picturesque characters with her unvarying suspicions of persecution and premonitions of disaster (against which, even inside her house, she ties up her head in a handkerchief and wears gloves).

Wilfer, Reginald. [Called (by his wife) "**R. W.**"; (in his office) "**Rumty.**"] In Dickens's novel *Our Mutual Friend*, the husband of Mrs. Wilfer. He is a constant object of Mrs. Wilfer's indignation, and has had to be content with a very modest role in life: "What might have been is not what is."

Wilfrid Wycliffe (wil'frid wik'lif). See **Wycliffe, Wilfrid.**

Wilful Witwoud (wil'ful wit'wụd), **Sir.** See **Witwoud, Sir Wilful.**

Wilkes (wilks), **John.** b. at London, Oct. 17, 1727; d. there, March 2, 1797. An English politician, publicist, and political agitator. He was educated at the University of Leiden, entered Parliament in 1757, and established the *North Briton* in 1762, in which he attacked the Bute ministry. For his

No. 45, criticizing George III (1763), he was imprisoned, but was soon released, and became a popular hero. A scandalous *Essay on Woman*, printed for private circulation, was seized, and Wilkes was expelled from Parliament (1764). He went to France, was tried in his absence, and was outlawed for non-appearance. In 1768 he returned, and was elected to Parliament for Middlesex; was imprisoned on the old charge, and was expelled from Parliament (1769). He was several times reelected, but each time declared ineligible, with the result that he became a martyr in the eyes of the populace. In 1770 he was released and elected alderman of London. In 1771 he became sheriff, and in 1774 lord mayor. In the same year he was again elected to Parliament and allowed to take his seat, remaining a member until 1790. The resolutions invalidating his former elections were expunged in 1782. Wilkes, who led a dissolute private life, nevertheless became the symbol of personal liberty and, supporting such causes as those of the American colonies, was supported by Edmund Burke and Junius; Parliamentary reform and freedom of the press were two tangible results of his activities.

Wilkins (wil'kinz), **William Henry.** b. in Somersetshire, England, Dec. 23, 1860; d. Dec. 22, 1905. An English historian, biographer, and novelist. While at Lund, Sweden, he discovered the correspondence that passed between Sophia Dorothea, wife of George I, and her lover, Count Philipp Königsmark, and published it in two volumes in 1900. Author of *The Romance of Isabel, Lady Burton* (1897), based on new material, *The Love of an Uncrowned Queen* (1900), *Caroline the Illustrious* (1901), and *Mrs. Fitzherbert and George IV* (1905). Among his other works are *The Alien Invasion* (1892), *Saint Michael's Eve* (1892), *The Green Bay Tree* (1894), and *A Queen of Tears* (1904).

Wilkins Micawber (mi.kô'bėr). See **Micawber, Wilkins.**

Wilkinson (wil'kin.sọn), **Sir John Gardner.** b. at Hardendale, Westmorland, England, Oct. 5, 1797; d. at Llandovery, Wales, Oct. 29, 1875. An English Egyptologist. He was educated at Oxford (Exeter College), and after 1821 spent many years in Egypt in archaeological explorations. His works include *Materia Hieroglyphica* (1828), *Topography of Thebes and General View of Egypt* (1835), *Manners and Customs of the Ancient Egyptians* (3 vols., 1837–41), *Modern Egypt and Thebes* (1843; later reissued as *Handbook for Travellers in Modern Egypt*), *Dalmatia and Montenegro* (1848), *Architecture of Ancient Egypt* (1850), *Popular Account of the Ancient Egyptians* (1854), *The Egyptians in the Time of the Pharaohs* (1857), and others.

Wilkinson, Tate. b. Oct. 27, 1739; d. Nov. 16, 1803. An English actor. He was a pupil and associate of Samuel Foote, and a noted mimic. He played with success at London and Dublin, but preferred the provinces. After a time he grew weary of his wandering life and bought the lesseeship of the York circuit, which he conducted for more than 30 years. Many actors and actresses who were afterward successful on the London stage owed their first encouragement to him, among others Roger Kemble, Charles Mathews, and Sarah Siddons. Foote satirized him as Shift in *The Minor* (1760).

---

fat, fāte, fär, ȧsk, fãre; net, mē, hėr; pin, pīne; not, nōte, mõve, nôr; up, lūte, pụll; ᴛʜ, then;

Will (wil). Entries on characters from literature and folklore having this prename will be found under the surnames Boniface, Hazard, Honeycomb, Ladislaw, Scarlet, Stutly, and Wimble.

Willard (wil′ard), **Edward S.** b. in Wales, 1853; d. 1915. An English actor, remembered for his portrayal of villains in various melodramas.

Willet (wil′et), **Joe.** In Dickens's *Barnaby Rudge*, the son of the pig-headed landlord of the Maypole Inn. After a succession of mishaps, he marries Dolly Varden.

Willet, John. In Dickens's *Barnaby Rudge*, the landlord of the Maypole Inn.

William (wil′yam). In Shakespeare's *As You Like It*, a country bumpkin in love with Audrey.

William. A novel by E. H. Young, published in 1925.

William. Entries on literary characters having this prename will also be found under the surnames Ashton, Brandon, Catesby, Collins, Dobbin, Dorrit, Falder, Fondlove, Glansdale, Guppy, Lucy, Marck, Nesbitt, Page, Sandys, Stafford, Stanley, Swidger, Thornhill, and Vaux.

William I. [Surnamed **the Conqueror, the Norman, and the Bastard.**] b. at Falaise, Normandy, in 1027 or 1028; d. at St.-Gervais, near Rouen, Sept. 9, 1087. King of England (1066–87). He was the natural son of Robert the Devil, Duke of Normandy, and Arletta, daughter of Fulbert, a tanner of Falaise. He succeeded to the duchy on the death of his father without legitimate issue in 1035. With the assistance of his suzerain, Henry I, King of France, he put down a formidable rising of his vassals in the battle of Val-es-Dunes, near Caen, in 1047. In a war which broke out between Henry and Geoffrey, Count of Anjou, the next year, he sided with the former, and took possession of the important border fortresses of Alençon and Domfront. He visited, in 1051, his childless kinsman Edward the Confessor of England, from whom he afterward claimed to have received a promise of the succession to the English throne. In 1053 he married Matilda of Flanders, a descendant of Alfred the Great. He repelled an invasion by the allied armies of Henry, Geoffrey of Anjou, and Theobald of Blois at Mortemer in 1054. Soon after he exacted the homage of Geoffrey of Anjou, and in 1058, by the victory of Varaville, repelled a second invasion headed by the French king. In 1063 he acquired Maine, which extended his southern frontier almost to the Loire. Probably in 1064, Harold, Earl of Wessex, was shipwrecked on the coast of Normandy and fell into the hands of William, who compelled him to take an oath whereby he bound himself to assist the duke in obtaining the succession in England. Edward died January 5, and Harold, in defiance of the oath, procured his own election as king by the witan. William, on the other hand, obtained a bull from Pope Alexander II, which declared him to be the rightful heir to the throne. He landed at Pevensey Sept. 28, 1066, overthrew Harold (who fell in battle) at Senlac (or Hastings), October 14, and was crowned at Westminster Dec. 25, 1066. But the conquest of England was only partial; it was completed four years later (in 1070) by the suppression of the last of a succession of

English risings in the north and southwest. William exacted the homage of Malcolm III of Scotland in 1072. He put down (1075–76) a rebellion of the Norman barons in England, who thenceforth remained quiet. The rest of his reign was occupied with almost continuous wars on the Continent against the King of France and rebellious vassals, and with quarrels with members of his own family, especially with his son Robert, who headed a revolt in Normandy (1077–80), and with his half-brother Odo, bishop of Bayeux, who was imprisoned on account of his intrigues. William died of internal injuries received from the plunging of his horse in the burning cinders in the town of Mantes, which he had captured while engaged with Philip I of France in a war concerning Vexin. William made few changes in the English law; indeed, he renewed, with some additions, the "law of Edward the Confessor." However, his introduction of continental feudalism was destined to exercise an enduring social and political influence. He took care to prevent the Norman barons whom he planted on English soil from becoming formidable rivals of the crown by scattering their estates, by maintaining popular courts by the side of the manorial courts, and by requiring an oath of fealty from all landowners, thereby eliminating an essential and dangerous feature of continental feudalism, the exclusive dependence of a vassal on his lord (*Gemot of Salisbury*, 1086). He abolished the four great earldoms, which had threatened the integrity of the kingdom in preceding reigns, and restricted the jurisdictions of the earl to a single shire, which became the largest political division, and the government of which was practically exercised by the sheriff, who was appointed by the king. In 1086 he completed the *Doomsday* (or *Domesday*) *Book*, a census of the wealth of England. He also reorganized the English Church with the assistance of Lanfranc whom he appointed archbishop of Canterbury. He separated the spiritual from the temporal courts, and secured the authority of the crown against papal encroachments.

William II. [Surnamed **Rufus.**] b. c1056; d. Aug. 2, 1100. King of England (1087–1100); third (second surviving) son of William I and Matilda of Flanders. He was the favorite son of his father, to whom he remained loyal when his elder brother Robert raised the standard of rebellion in Normandy. In accordance with the dying request of his father, he was elected to the English throne by the witan, through the influence of Lanfranc, Sept. 26, 1087, while Robert succeeded in Normandy. A revolt of the Norman barons in England broke out in favor of Robert in 1088. William gained the support of the fyrd, or national militia, by promising the repeal of the forest laws, the reduction of taxes, and good government generally to his English subjects, and the rebellion was suppressed in 1090. He carried on a war in Normandy (1090–91) against his brother Robert, who was compelled to accept a disadvantageous peace. He invaded Scotland in 1091, when he exacted the homage of Malcolm III. In 1093 he appointed Anselm, abbot of Bec, archbishop of Canterbury; but presently became involved in a dispute concerning investitures with the new primate, who abandoned the kingdom in 1097. In 1094, during a second invasion of Normandy, he found his brother supported by Philip I of France, and secured the safe retreat of his army only by a bribe to the latter. In 1096 he took possession of Normandy as a pledge for funds advanced to Robert, who in that year joined the Crusade. The duchy remained in William's hands until his death. He conquered Maine (1098–99). He was killed, possibly accidentally, by an arrow shot by Walter Tyrrel (or Tirel), while hunting in the New Forest.

William III.   b. at The Hague, Nov. 4, 1650; d. at Kensington, March 8, 1702. King of England (1689–1702), and stadholder of the United Netherlands (1672–1702). He was the son of William II, stadholder of the United Netherlands, and Mary, daughter of Charles I of England, and was styled Prince of Orange before his accession to the English throne. His father died before his birth. As the head of the house of Orange he became the leader of the democratic monarchical party in opposition to the aristocratic republican party headed by Jan de Witt. The invasion of Holland by the armies of Louis XIV in 1672 caused the overthrow of the aristocratic republican party, and in the same year the office of stadholder, which had been abolished on the death of his father, was restored in his favor. He saved Amsterdam by opening the dikes, and succeeded in forming a coalition against Louis XIV which compelled that monarch to conclude the peace of Nijmegen (1678). He married in 1677 Mary, elder daughter of the Duke of York (who later ascended the English throne as James II). About 1686 he placed himself at the head of the constitutional opposition in England against the absolute and Romanizing policy of James; and, in answer to an invitation signed by the "seven patriots" (the earls of Devonshire, Shrewsbury, and Danby, the Bishop of London, Henry Sidney, Lord Lumley, and Admiral Russell), landed at Torbay, Nov. 5, 1688. James fled to France December 22, and William summoned a convention which met Jan. 22, 1689, and settled the crown on William and Mary, who accepted the Declaration of Right, and were proclaimed Feb. 13, 1689. The revolution was effected in England without serious opposition, but James had many adherents in Scotland and Ireland. With the assistance of Louis XIV, he landed at Kinsale, Ireland, March 14, 1689. War was declared against France May 7, 1689; the Jacobite rising in Scotland ended with the battle of Killiecrankie July 27, 1689; and James was defeated in person by William at the battle of the Boyne in Ireland July 1, 1690. In 1692 occurred the massacre of Glencoe, wiping out the Highland opposition to William. On his accession to the English throne, William began the organization of the Grand Alliance (of the United Netherlands, the Holy Roman Empire, England, Spain, Brandenburg, and Savoy) against France, which was completed in 1690. A victory of the allied English and Dutch fleets over the French at La Hogue May 19, 1692, frustrated a projected invasion of England. William, who commanded the Allies in Flanders, was defeated by Marshal Luxembourg at Steenkerke Aug. 3, 1692. Queen Mary died Dec. 28, 1694; thenceforth William reigned alone. The peace of Ryswick put an end to the war with France in 1697. During the rest of his

reign his foreign policy was chiefly directed to preserving the balance of power in Europe by preventing the Spanish monarchy from being united either to France or to Austria. With this end in view, he negotiated the Partition Treaties, to satisfy the various adherents of the claimants to the Spanish succession. When Louis XIV, in violation of treaty obligations, recognized the bequest of Charles II to Philip of Anjou (Philip V), William formed the Grand Alliance of 1701, and took the initiative in the events leading to the War of the Spanish Succession. He died, in consequence of a fall from his horse, before the commencement of hostilities, leaving no heirs, but with the succession settled, by act of Parliament (1701), on James I's granddaughter Sophia of Hanover and her line. His reign, although disturbed by Jacobite intrigues and the treachery of officials high in station (such as that alleged to Marlborough), witnessed the rise of England to a position of prominence in European politics, and marks the beginning of government by party, the Whigs and Tories appearing as distinct entities during his reign.

William IV.   b. at Windsor, Aug. 21, 1765; d. June 20, 1837. King of England (1830–37); third son of George III. He entered the navy as a midshipman c1779, was created duke of Clarence in 1789, entered (c1791) into a liaison with Dorothea Jordan, an actress, which was not ended until he married Adelaide of Saxe-Meiningen in 1818, and became heir presumptive to the throne on the death of Frederick Augustus, Duke of York, in 1827. In the same year he was appointed lord high admiral, an office which he was shortly compelled to resign on account of his arbitrary conduct and his refusal to consult with his council. He acceded to the throne on the death of his brother, George IV, June 26, 1830. The chief event of his reign was the passage, through his threat to create new peers, of the Reform Bill (1832). He was succeeded by his niece Victoria.

William and Margaret (mär′ga.ret). [Also, **Margaret's Ghost.**] A ballad (1723) by David Mallet.

William Marshall, Gent. (mär′shal). The pseudonym under which Horace Walpole wrote *The Castle of Otranto.*

William of Champeaux (shän.pō′). See **Guillaume de Champeaux.**

William of Cloudeslie (kloudz′li). An archer, the subject of an English popular ballad.

William of Deloraine (del.ọ.rān′). See **Deloraine, William of.**

William of Malmesbury (mämz′bėr.i). b. c1095; d. at Malmesbury, Wiltshire, England, c1142. An English historian and monk, librarian of the monastery at Malmesbury, of which he refused to become abbot. His chief works are *Gesta Regum Anglorum* (Chronicle of the Kings of England) and *Historia Novella* (Modern History), a continuation of the *Gesta*, bringing the history down to 1142 (these books are valuable sources for the history of England, particularly for the reigns of Henry I and Stephen); *Gesta Pontificum Anglorum* (History of the Prelates of England); *Antiquitas Glastoniensis Ecclesiae* (History of the Church at Glastonbury); lives of Saint Patrick, Saint Dunstan, Saint Wulfstan (from the Anglo-Saxon); several books of miracles; and the *Itinerary of John Abbot of Malmesbury to Rome* (John Leland mentions this work, but it is lost).

William of Newburgh (nū'bur.ọ). b. at or near Bridlington, Yorkshire, England, 1136; d. 1198. An English historian. His *Historia Rerum Anglicarum*, which covers the period from 1066 to 1198, is of especial value for the reign of Henry II, and is distinguished by William's conception of his book as history, rather than as a mere chronicle.

William of Ockham or **Occam** (ok'ạm). See **Ockham, William of.**

William of Palerne (pạ.lèrn'). A Middle English alliterative romance of about 5,500 lines, written in the 14th century. It tells how a prince of Spain, changed into a werewolf by a wicked stepmother, protects William, prince of Apulia, and enables him to marry Melchior, daughter of the Roman emperor. William's identity is finally revealed, and the stepmother is compelled to undo her evil magic and restore the Spanish prince to his true form.

William of Shoreham (shōr'ạm). b. at Shoreham, Kent, England; fl. in the first part of the 14th century. An English monk of Leeds priory. He translated (c1327) the Psalms of David into English prose, and wrote a number of religious poems.

William of Wykeham (wik'ạm). See **Wykeham, William of.**

Williams (wil'yạmz), **Caleb.** See **Caleb Williams.**

Williams, Edward. [Known in Wales as **Iolo Morgannwg**; called the **"Welsh Shakespeare."**] b. at Llancarvan, Glamorganshire, Wales, 1746; d. Dec. 18, 1826. A Welsh poet. He was one of the editors of *Myvyrian Archaiology* (1801), collecting and transcribing many of the manuscripts. Author of *Poems, Lyric and Pastoral* (2 vols.; 1794).

Williams, Emlyn. b. at Mostyn, Flintshire, Wales, Nov. 26, 1905—. A British actor and playwright. Author of the plays *A Murder Has Been Arranged* (1930), *Night Must Fall* (1935), *He Was Born Gay* (1937), *The Corn Is Green* (1938), and *The Light of Heart* (1940). He has appeared in such motion pictures as *Major Barbara* and *The Stars Look Down*, and has directed a number of pictures.

Williams, Michael. In Shakespeare's *Henry V*, a soldier who encounters King Henry disguised as an English gentleman before the battle of Agincourt. He challenges the King upon the latter's defending his faithfulness to his troops. Fluellen bears his glove, given as a pledge, and comes to blows with him.

Williams, Valentine. b. Oct. 20, 1883—. An English mystery-story writer. His works include *The Man with the Club Foot* (1918), *The Secret Hand* (1921), and *Masks Off at Midnight* (1934).

Williamson (wil'yạm.sọn), **Henry.** b. 1897—. An English novelist. His first books, *The Beautiful Years* (1921), *Dandelion Days* (1922), *The Dream of Fair Women* (1924), and *The Pathway* (1928), form a tetralogy published as *The Flax of Dream*. He is author also of *The Lone Swallows* (1922), *The Old Stag* (1926), *Tarka the Otter* (1927; awarded the 1928 Hawthornden prize), *The Patriot's Progress* (1930), *The Children of Swallowford* (1939), *The*

Sun in the Sands (1944), and *The Phasian Bird* (1948).

William Tell (tel). A drama by J. Sheridan Knowles, produced (1825) by W. C. Macready.

William the Clerk. fl. 1208–26. An Anglo-Norman romantic poet.

Willie Powell (wil'i pou'ẹl). See **Powell, Willie.**

Willie Steenson (stēn'sọn). See **Wandering Willie.**

Willis (wil'is), **Hal.** A pseudonym of **Forrester, Charles Robert.**

Willis's Rooms. A later name of Almack's assembly rooms, London.

Willoughby or **Willobie** (wil'ọ.bi), **Henry.** b. c1574; d. before June 30, 1596. An English soldier. He is believed to have been the author of a poem in 72 cantos, *Willobie his Avisa, or the True Picture of a Modest Maid and of a Chast and Constant Wife* (1594), the sole general interest of which is its reference (the earliest in print) to Shakespeare, who is probably the friend later called "W.S." Henry Willobie, who appears as the hero and as one of the rejected admirers of Avisa, tells his troubles to a mildly sympathetic "W.S." The *Avisa* was reprinted in 1596, 1605, 1609, and 1635, and, more recently, in 1880, 1886, and 1904.

Willoughby, Sir Hugh. b. probably at Risley, Derbyshire, England; d. 1554. An English navigator. He commanded an expedition (1553–54) to the arctic regions in the ships *Bona Esperanza*, *Edward Bonaventure*, and *Bona Confidentia*. Willoughby and 62 companions perished on the coast of Lapland, in winter quarters, probably of scurvy. Richard Chancellor, in the *Bonaventure*, had parted company with the others in a storm, and so escaped. Willoughby's *Journal* was later found with the remains of the party.

Willoughby, John. A reprobate who deceives Marianne Dashwood in Jane Austen's novel *Sense and Sensibility*.

Willoughby, Lord. In Shakespeare's *Richard II*, a deserter of the King and later a member of Bolingbroke's party.

Willoughby Patterne (wil'ọ.bi pat'èrn), **Sir.** See **Patterne, Sir Willoughby.**

Wills (wilz), **William Gorman.** b. in County Kilkenny, Ireland, 1828; d. at London, Dec. 13, 1891. A British dramatist. His works include *The Man o' Airlie* (1867), *Hinko* (1871), *Charles I* (1872), *Eugene Aram* (1873), *Olivia* (1873), *Mary Queen of Scots* (1874), *Buckingham* (1875), *Jane Shore* (1876), *Vanderdecken* (1878), *Ninon* (1880), *William and Susan* (1880), *Faust* (1885), and *Claudian* (1885). He also wrote several novels, among them *Notice to Quit* and *The Wife's Evidence*, and a number of ballads, of which *I'll Sing Thee Songs of Araby* is best known.

Will's Coffee House (wilz). A coffee house in Russell Street, London, named after its proprietor, whose first name was William. It was the resort of gamblers, poets, and wits in the time of John Dryden, when it was also known as "The Wits' Coffee House." It was on the corner of Bow Street.

Wilmot (wil'mọt), **John.** [Title: 2nd Earl of Rochester.] b. at Ditchley, Oxfordshire, England,

---

ḍ, d or j; ṣ, s or sh; ṭ, t or ch; ẓ, z or zh; o, F. cloche; ü, F. menu; ċh, Sc. loch; ṅ, F. bonbon.

April 10, 1647; d. at Woodstock, Oxfordshire, July 26, 1680. An English Restoration wit and satirist, notorious for his dissolute life and for the obscenity of his literary productions. After traveling in France and Italy, he returned to the court, where he soon became a favorite of Charles II and of various court ladies and their waiting women. His works were published in 1691, 1696, 1741, and in other editions, many of them expurgated.

Wilmot, Robert. fl. 1568–1608. An English dramatist, clergyman, and member of the Inner Temple. With others he wrote *Tancred and Gismund* (1591).

Wilson (wil'sǫn), **Davie.** See **Snuffy Davie.**

Wilson, J. Arbuthnot. A pseudonym of **Allen, Grant.**

Wilson, John. b. April 5, 1595; d. at Westminster (now part of London), Feb. 22, 1674. An English composer of songs and ballads. It is thought that he appeared as a singer in various performances of *Much Ado About Nothing.* He was named (1635) one of the king's musicians. He set to music Shakespeare's *Take O Take Those Lips Away,* but the best known of his songs is *In the Merry Month of May.*

Wilson, John. [Pseudonym, **Christopher North.**] b. at Paisley, Scotland, May 18, 1785; d. at Edinburgh, April 3, 1854. A Scottish essayist, poet, and novelist. From 1817 he was one of the principal contributors to *Blackwood's Magazine.* He was professor of moral philosophy (1820 *et seq.*) at the University of Edinburgh. He wrote the poems *Isle of Palms* (1812) and *City of the Plague* (1816), and the tales *Lights and Shadows of Scottish Life* (1822), *Trials of Margaret Lindsay* (1823), and *The Foresters* (1825). The *Noctes Ambrosianae,* his best-known work, a collection of essays on literature and politics, of verse and character sketches, of philosophy and nonsense, was written mainly by him, with J. G. Lockhart and James Hogg (the Ettrick Shepherd to Wilson's Christopher North) also contributing; it appeared originally in *Blackwood's.* The *Recreations of Christopher North* were reprints of magazine articles.

Wilson, John. b. at Glasgow, 1802; d. 1868. A Scottish printer and author, remembered chiefly as author of *Treatise on Grammatical* (later changed to *English*) *Punctuation* (1826), the first standard study of the subject.

Wilson, John Dover. b. at London, July 13, 1881—. An English Shakespeare scholar and educator. He was professor (1924–35) of education at the University of London, and professor (1936–45) of rhetoric and English literature at Edinburgh. Author of *The Essential Shakespeare* (1932), *The Manuscript of Shakespeare's Hamlet and the Problems of Its Transmission* (1934), *What Happens in Hamlet* (1935), and *The Fortunes of Falstaff* (1943). He compiled *Life in Shakespeare's England* (1911). He has been editor of the *New Shakespeare* (1921 *et seq.*) since the death of his coeditor, Arthur Quiller-Couch, with whom he edited the comedies.

Wilson, John Mackay. b. at Tweedmouth, Berwick-upon-Tweed, England, Aug. 15, 1804; d. there, Oct. 2, 1835. A Scottish poet, editor, and author of tales. He became editor (1832) of the Berwick *Advertiser,* after experiencing hard times as a

London printer and going through the provinces as a lecturer on literary topics. Author of *The Poet's Progress* and *The Border Patriots,* poems; *The Gowrie Conspiracy* (1829) and *Margaret of Anjou,* dramas; *The Enthusiast* (1834), a metrical tale; and, his chief work, *Tales of the Borders,* consisting of 73 stories originally issued (Nov. 8, 1834, *et seq.*) as a weekly series in 48 numbers; among the best of them are "The Vacant Chair," "Tibbie Fowler," "My Black Coat," and "The Poor Scholar."

Wilson, Margaret Oliphant. See **Oliphant, Margaret Oliphant.**

Wilson, Mrs. Alison. In Sir Walter Scott's novel *Old Mortality,* the venerable housekeeper at Milnwood. Her economical and benevolently tyrannical nature permits her one day of celebration a year, a formal banquet for the Laird and his wife, which she spends six months preparing for and six months laying things away after.

Wilson, Robert. d. 1600. An English actor of Shakespeare's time. He was one of the Earl of Leicester's players in 1574, and belonged to the Queen's Company in 1583. *Three Ladies of London,* attributed to him, is sometimes indicated as a possible source of the Shylock plot in *The Merchant of Venice.*

Wilson, Robert. b. 1579; d. 1610. An English dramatic writer. He is frequently confounded with the actor.

Wilson, Sir Robert Thomas. b. at London, 1777; d. there, May 9, 1849. An English general and author. He commanded the Lusitanian Legion and a Spanish brigade in the Peninsular War, was British military commissioner at the Russian and allied headquarters (1812–14), and was later a member of Parliament and governor of Gibraltar (1842–49). He wrote *History of the British Expedition to Egypt* (1802), *Inquiry into the Present State of the Military Force of the British Empire* (1804), *Sketch of the Campaigns in Poland* (1811), *Military and Political Power of Russia* (1817), *Narrative of Events during the Invasion of Russia 1812* (1860), *Diary* (1861), and others.

Wilson, Romer. [Pseudonym of Mrs. **Edward J. O'Brien;** maiden name, **Florence Roma Muir Wilson.**] b. 1891; d. at Lausanne, Switzerland, Jan. 11, 1930. An English novelist. She married (1923) Edward J. O'Brien, American short-story anthologist. Author of the novels *Martin Schüler* (1918), *If All These Young Men* (1919), *The Death of Society* (1921; awarded the Hawthornden prize), *The Grand Tour of Alphonso Marichaud* (1923), *Dragon's Blood* (1926), *Latter-Day Symphony* (1927), and *Tender Advice* (1935). She also wrote the play *The Social Climbers* (1927), and *All Alone* (1928), a life of Emily Brontë.

Wilson, Thomas. d. 1581. An English statesman and writer. He lived on the Continent during the reign of Mary Tudor, and was imprisoned and tortured at Rome on account of alleged heresy in his works on *Logic* and *Rhetoric,* but escaped. He was in favor during the reign of Elizabeth, and held various offices: envoy to the Low Countries in 1576, secretary of state in 1577, and dean of Durham in 1579. Among his works are *The Rule of Reason, Containing the Art of Logic* (1551), *The*

Art of Rhetoric (1553), and *A Discourse upon Usury* (1572).

Wilson, T. P. Cameron. [Pseudonym, **Tipuca.**] b. in England, 1889; d. March 23, 1918. An English poet, author also of one novel and of various articles under the pseudonym of Tipuca. His verse writing was published posthumously in 1919 under the title *Magpies in Picardy.* He was killed in action during World War I.

Wilson, William. b. in Perthshire, Scotland, Dec. 25, 1801; d. at Poughkeepsie, N. Y., Aug. 25, 1860. A Scottish poet, publisher, bookseller, editor, and essayist. He was editor (1823–26) of the Dundee *Literary Olio,* contributing to it a large amount of prose and poetry, moved (1826) to Edinburgh, where he contributed to the *Literary Journal,* and came (1832) to the U. S., settling at Poughkeepsie, N. Y., where he opened a bookselling and publishing business. He wrote prose and verse for leading American periodicals, also sending material to Scottish journals and magazines. A collected edition of his poetry appeared in 1869.

Wimble (wim′bl), **Will.** One of the characters drawn by Joseph Addison in *The Spectator:* a good-natured country gentleman "extremely well versed in all the little handicrafts of an idle man."

Wimsey (wim′zi), **Lord Peter.** The hero of a series of detective novels by Dorothy L. Sayers.

Winchester (win′ches″tèr, -chẹs.tèr), 3rd Marquis of. Title of **Paulet,** Sir **William.**

Winchester, Bishop of. In Shakespeare's *1 Henry VI,* the historical Henry Beaufort, a son of John of Gaunt and great-uncle of Henry VI. He quarrels with Gloucester, the Protector, who accuses him of having Henry V murdered. He crowns Henry VI in Paris and later appears as a Cardinal (V.i). In *2 Henry VI,* he joins York, Suffolk, and others in accusing Gloucester of misdeeds and having him imprisoned. Gloucester is murdered, apparently on his orders, and he repents for this on his deathbed (III.iii).

Winchester, Bishop of. See also under **Gardiner.**

Winchester School. [Also, **Saint Mary's College.**] An important English public school, founded in Winchester (1393) by William of Wykeham.

Winchilsea (win′chil.si), **Countess of.** Title of **Finch, Anne.**

Wind Among the Reeds, The. A volume of verse (1899) by W. B. Yeats, including "The Lover Tells of the Rose of His Heart" and "The Secret Rose."

Windhover, The. A poem by Gerard Manley Hopkins, written in 1877 and published with his other works in 1918. It is subtitled "To Christ our lord," whom Hopkins refers to as "O my chevalier" at the end of the second stanza. Hopkins thought (1879) the poem "the best thing I ever wrote."

Winding Stair, The. A volume of verse (1929) by W. B. Yeats, including "In Memory of Eva Gore-Booth and Con Markiewicz," "A Dialogue of Self and Soul," "The Crazed Moon," and "Byzantium."

Windsor Castle (win′zọr). A residence of the royal family of Great Britain, at Windsor, in Berkshire. The castle consists of buildings enclosing, or situated within, two wards or courts, with a large Round Tower topping an artificial mound in the center. According to Froissart, it was anciently believed that this mound was the site of the hall which sheltered King Arthur's Round Table, and it seems probable that it was in fact a place of some importance in Celtic Britain. Moreover it is certain that there was a stronghold at Windsor in Saxon times; but it was William the Conqueror who, attracted by the proximity of a great forest full of game, made it the chief royal seat in England and began the construction which was added to by other monarchs during the following centuries. When Edward III established (c1346) the Order of the Garter, he enlarged the Round Tower to be its place of assembly. Around the castle lies the Home Garden, from which the Long Walk extends southward to the Great Garden. Seen from the beautifully landscaped gardens and surrounding terraces, the long battlemented walls, broken by the Norman Gateway and by several towers and dominated by the central donjon, are very impressive. The east side of the quadrangle is occupied by the royal family's private apartments, and the north side by state apartments. There are also apartments for guests, a deanery, cloisters, accommodations for canons, a guard room, and quarters for military pensioners. The notable Chapel of Saint George and the Albert Chapel face the lower ward. The former, begun by Edward IV and completed by Henry VIII, is one of the most beautiful structures in the Perpendicular style in all England. The wide interior has double transepts and elaborate fan vaulting. The choir is bordered by the ornately carved stalls of the Knights of the Garter, each adorned with the owner's arms and banner. Over an admired reredos at the east end of this chapel, a great stained-glass window commemorates the late Prince Albert, Queen Victoria's consort. To him also is dedicated the Albert Chapel, to the east of Saint George's. This is a restoration, by Victoria, of a structure begun by Henry VII; under it, since the time of George III, are royal tombs. The interior of the Albert Chapel is decorated very lavishly, encrusted with varicolored marble and adorned with sculpture, mosaics, gilding, and precious stones. The stained-glass windows present Scriptural subjects and scenes from the history of the Saxe-Coburg-Gotha family to which Prince Albert belonged. Toward the east end of the building is a cenotaph of that prince in the form of an altar-tomb. Victoria and Albert are interred, however, in a mausoleum built by Victoria at nearby Frogmore, a structure of modified Byzantine architecture, octagonal in plan, surmounted by a lantern and ornamented with a series of arcades. Saint George's Hall, another feature of the castle, contains many portraits of British sovereigns, and a wealth of pictures, including many Van Dycks, is to be seen in the Waterloo chamber or great dining room, in the council chamber, in the state drawing room, in the old ballroom, and in the library, where moreover there is a great collection of notable drawings, including many by Raphael, Michelangelo, and Leonardo da Vinci, and scores of portraits in sepia and chalk by Holbein the Younger of persons eminent at the court of Henry VIII. The private apartments contain one of the most splendid collections of porcelain, especially of Sèvres ware, in existence.

Windsor Forest. A pastoral poem (1713) by Alexander Pope.

Wings of the Dove, The. A novel by Henry James, published in 1902.

Winifred (win′i.frẹd). The young wife of Security in Chapman, Marston, and Jonson's *Eastward Ho!*

Winifred Jenkins (jeng′kinz), **Mrs.** See **Jenkins, Mrs. Winifred.**

Winkle (wing′kl), **Nathaniel.** A member of the famous Pickwick Club, afterward married to Miss Arabella Allen; a character in Dickens's *Pickwick Papers.* His pretensions as a sportsman are not borne out by events.

Winner and Waster. See **Good Short Debate Between Winner and Waster.**

Winslow Boy (winz′lō), **The.** A drama (1946) by Terence Rattigan about a naval cadet who has been charged with theft, and his father's struggles, despite official inertia, to clear his name.

Winter (win′tẽr), **John Strange.** A pseudonym of Stannard, Henrietta Eliza Vaughan.

Winterblossom (win′tẽr.blos.ọm), **Mr.** In Sir Walter Scott's novel *St. Ronan's Well*, a gentleman "of taste." In his youth he has spent a small legacy in the manner befitting a gentleman, and he now lives on a small income in a fashion which permits him to dine well and with congenial companions (he serves as "perpetual president of the table d'hote at the Well").

Winter Comedy. A novel by Sylvia Thompson, published in 1931 and issued in America under the title *Portrait by Caroline.*

Winter's Tale, The. A play by Shakespeare, produced c1611, printed in the folio of 1623. It was founded on Robert Greene's *Pandosto.* Except for *The Tempest*, it is the last of Shakespeare's works to be written by himself alone (*Henry VIII* and *The Two Noble Kinsmen* are both later than either this or *The Tempest*, but for these Shakespeare had a collaborator). The play was revised in the Restoration, and Garrick produced it as *Florizel and Perdita.*
The Story. Leontes, King of Sicilia, unjustifiably accuses his wife, Hermione, of having a love affair with his friend, Polixenes, King of Bohemia, who is visiting the court at Sicilia. Leontes tries unsuccessfully to poison Polixenes, who flees to safety; Hermione is imprisoned, and shortly thereafter gives birth to a daughter. At the trial of Hermione, the king refuses to believe the Delphian oracle, which has stated that Hermione is innocent. The king orders the baby to be abandoned; word comes of the death of the king's son, Mamillius; and Paulina, a lady at court, reports the death of Hermione. Meanwhile, the baby, Perdita, is discovered on the Bohemian "coast" by an old shepherd, who raises her to young womanhood. Sixteen years later, Florizel, the son of Polixenes, meets her and falls in love with her but, because of the opposition of his father to a marriage, flees with her to Sicilia. There the identity of Perdita is discovered, to the joy of Leontes (who has long since regretted his distrust of his wife), and

Polixenes, who has followed his son, is reconciled to his old friend. Leontes, however, grieves for his wife (whom he thinks dead), but Paulina offers to show him a lifelike statue of her, which turns out to be the actual Hermione. The play ends happily with the betrothal of Florizel and Perdita.

Winthrop (win′thrọp), **Dolly.** One of the principal female characters in George Eliot's *Silas Marner.*

Wintringham (win′tring.ạm), **Tom.** [Full name, **Thomas Henry Wintringham.**] b. at Grimsby, Lincolnshire, England, May 15, 1898; d. 1949. An English writer and soldier. He served (1916–18) with the British air force in France during World War I, was in Spain (1936–37) as a war correspondent, and became commander (1937) of the British battalion of the International Brigade during the Spanish Civil War. He was a founder (1940) of the Osterley Park Training School for the Home Guard. Author of *English Captain* (1939), *New Ways of War* (1940), *Armies of Freemen* (1940), *Politics of Victory* (1941), *People's War* (1942), *Weapons and Tactics* (1943), and *Your M.P.* (1945).

Wireker (wir′ẹ.kẽr), **Nigel.** fl. 1190. An English monk and satirist. He was the author of a prose treatise, *On the Corruptions of the Church* (*Contra curiales et officiales*, c1193), and of a satirical poem attacking clerical hypocrisy and corruption, *The Mirror of Fools* (*Speculum stultorum*, c1180). The *Mirror* was exceedingly popular in the 14th and 15th centuries, and is cited in Chaucer's *Nun's Priest's Tale.*

Wisdom. See **Mind, Will, and Understanding.**

Wisdom of Solomon (sol′ọ.mọn), **Book of the.** [Also: **Wisdom, Book of Wisdom.**] One of the deuterocanonical books of the Old Testament; it is placed in the Apocrypha of the Authorized Version but appears as a canonical book in the Roman Catholic Bible. Tradition ascribes its authorship to Solomon; but by most modern Protestant theologians it is attributed to an Alexandrian Jew of the 1st or 2nd century B.C. The shorter title "Wisdom," or "Book of Wisdom," is commonly applied to this book.

Wise (wīz), **Thomas James.** b. at Gravesend, England, Oct. 7, 1859; d. at Hampstead, London, May 13, 1937. An English bibliographer, bibliophile, and literary forger. He edited with Sir Edmund Gosse the letters and works of Swinburne and unpublished writings of Browning, Landor, Rossetti, and others, and compiled bibliographies of Tennyson, Swinburne, Wordsworth, Coleridge, Ruskin, the Brontës, Byron, and others. One of the most famous collectors in England, Wise was demonstrated (in a pamphlet written by John Carter and Graham Pollard, 1934) to have distributed a number of patent forgeries to collectors who trusted his judgment in such matters.

Wiseman (wīz′man), **Mr. Worldly.** See **Worldly Wiseman, Mr.**

Wiseman (wīz′mạn), **Nicholas Patrick Stephen.** b. at Seville, Spain, Aug. 2, 1802; d. at London, Feb. 15, 1865. An English theologian and Roman Catholic cardinal. His influence on the Roman Catholic revival in England (stemming from the Oxford Movement) was great, and he had a prominent rôle in allaying the suspicion, with his *Appeal to the English People*, that an attempt was being made to bring England within the orbit of the Roman Catholic Church. Among his works are *Horae Syriacae* (1828), *The Connection between Science and Revealed Religion* (1836), *Lectures on the Catholic Church* (1836), and *The Real Presence* (1836). He also wrote the historical novel *Fabiola, or the Church of the Catacombs* (1854).

Wise-Woman of Hogsdon (hogz'dǫn), **The.** A comedy by Thomas Heywood, printed in 1638 and acted c1603. The "wise woman" is the central character of the play and manipulates the various episodes.

Wishfort (wish'fôrt), **Lady.** A decayed belle in Congreve's *Way of the World;* one of his most effective characters.

Wit and Science. An allegorical interlude by John Redford, acted by Paul's Boys c1530.

Wit at Several Weapons. A comedy written c1609 and published in 1647. The writers were John Fletcher and probably various others, among whom have been suggested Beaumont, Middleton, and Rowley.

Witch, The. A play by Thomas Middleton, written probably c1616. It was first printed in 1778 from a manuscript. The stage directions and opening words of the witches' songs in Act III, Scene 3, and Act V, Scene 2, are identical with those found in Shakespeare's *Macbeth* (probably the words from the Shakespeare folio of 1623 were taken by some actor or playwright and fitted into this play after its original writing).

Witches. [Also, **Weird Sisters.**] In Shakespeare's *Macbeth*, three supernatural women. They appear in the first scene, setting the atmosphere of the play. They hail Macbeth as Thane of Glamis, Thane of Cawdor, and "King hereafter" (I.iii). When Macbeth learns immediately afterward that he is indeed to become Thane of Cawdor, their words seem prophetic, and his ambitions are soon raised to a feverish pitch as his mind dwells upon the possibility of the throne being his. Their prophecies upon the second occasion of his consulting them are ambiguous and suggest a security which is not real. The characters are derived from the Scandinavian Norns, or Goddesses of Fate, probably by way of the Anglo-Saxon Wyrdes.

Witches' Sabbath. The same as **Walpurgis Night.**

Witchett (wich'ęt), **Hawkins.** Original name of **Cowell, Joseph Leathley.**

Witch of Atlas (at'lạs), **The.** A poem by Percy Bysshe Shelley.

Witch of Edmonton (ed'mǫn.tǫn), **The.** A tragicomedy by William Rowley, Thomas Dekker, and John Ford, and others, produced at Court in 1621 and published in 1658. The play was intended to have topical significance in that it alluded to Elizabeth Sawyer's execution on a charge of witchcraft. The "heroine" sells herself to the Devil (in the guise of a black dog).

Witch of Endor (en'dǫr). See **Endor.**

Witenagemot (wit'ę.na̤.gę.mōt'). The great national parliament or council, in the Anglo-Saxon period of English history.

Wither (wiᴛʜ'ėr) or **Withers** (wiᴛʜ'ėrz), **George.** b. at Brentworth, Hampshire, England, June 11, 1588; d. at London, May 2, 1667. An English poet. He was educated at Magdalen College, Oxford. In 1639 he was a Royalist captain of horse in an expedition against the Scotch Covenanters; in 1642 he had become a Puritan and a major in the Parliamentary army, and was afterward made by Cromwell master of the statute office and "major general of the horse and foot of the County of Surrey." After the Restoration he was obliged to give up the fortune accumulated in these offices, and was imprisoned by Parliament, but released in 1663. Among his poems are *The Shepherd's Hunting* (1614), *Fidelia* (1615), *The Motto* (1618), *Fair Virtue, or the Mistress of Philarete* (1622), *Hymns and Songs of the Church* (1623), *Emblems* (1634), *Hallelujah* (1641), a satire *Abuses Stript and Whipt* (1613; for which he was imprisoned, as he was for *The Motto*), and a translation of the Psalms of David. His best-known lyric is "Shall I, wasting in despair."

Within the Gates. An expressionistic play (1933) by Sean O'Casey. In the allegorical figures of the Young Whore, a miserable outcast from society (and meant by O'Casey as a symbol of all people abandoned or rejected by society); the Bishop, who fathered her, and then forgot her; the Down-and-Outs, who are the poor people; and the Dreamer, who represents the imaginative power of humanity, O'Casey was attempting to create a parable of modern life.

With Rue My Heart Is Laden. A poem by A. E. Housman, contained in *The Shropshire Lad* (1896).

Wititterly (wi.tit'ėr.li), **Mr. and Mrs.** In Dickens's novel *Nicholas Nickleby*, a pair of insufferable snobs, who boast constantly (and irrelevantly) about their grand friends.

Wits, The. A comedy by Sir William D'Avenant, produced in 1633 and printed in 1636. It was revived after the Restoration, and is frequently mentioned by Samuel Pepys.

"Wits' Coffee House," the. See under **Will's Coffee House.**

Wittol (wit'ôl), **Sir Joseph.** A foolish knight in William Congreve's *The Old Bachelor*. He is duped into marrying the bawdy Sylvia, believing her to be Araminta, a wealthy heiress.

Witty and Witless. An interlude by John Heywood, written in the early part of the 16th century.

Witty Fair One, The. A comedy by James Shirley, acted in 1626 and published in 1633.

Wit Without Money. A play by John Fletcher, acted c1614 and printed in 1639. The two main characters, Lady Heartwell and Valentine, are somewhat like "humour" characters in that their personalities are marked by strong prejudices: the one hates men and refuses a second marriage after losing her husband; the other holds property or money in contempt and looks only to his own merits (rather unusual for a Jacobean character) for success. Eventually, in persuading Lady Heartwell again to accept men, Valentine falls in love with her himself, and has to overcome his prejudice against her wealth.

ḑ, d or j; ṣ, s or sh; ṭ, t or ch; ẓ, z or zh; o, F. cloche; ü, F. menu; ċh, Sc. loch; ṅ, F. bonbon.

Witwoud (wit'wŭd), **Sir Wilful.** A coarse and not very clever, but likeable, country squire in William Congreve's *The Way of the World.*

Wives and Daughters. An unfinished novel by Elizabeth Gaskell, published serially, 1864–66.

"Wizard Earl," the. See **Percy,** Sir Henry (1564–1632).

Wizard of the North. A name given to Sir Walter Scott.

Wodan (wō'dạn) or **Woden** (wō'dẹn). See **Odin.**

Wodehouse (wŏd'hous), **P. G.** [Full name, **Pelham Grenville Wodehouse.**] b. Oct. 15, 1881–. An English writer of humorous novels. His earliest books, *The Pothunters* (1902), *A Prefect's Uncle* (1903), and *Tales of St. Austin's* (1903) were for younger readers. He became well known with *Psmith in the City* (1910), and used the same character in *Psmith, Journalist* (1915), and *Leave it to Psmith* (1923); *The Inimitable Jeeves* (1924), *Very Good, Jeeves* (1930), and *The Code of the Woosters* (1938) involve Bertie Wooster and his valet Jeeves; Stanley Featherstonehaugh Ukridge is the central character of *Ukridge* (1924) and Mr. Mulliner of *Meet Mr. Mulliner* (1927) and *Mulliner Omnibus* (1935); the inhabitants of Blandings Castle and Lord Emsworth are the leading characters of *Blandings Castle* (1935), *Lord Emsworth and Others* (1937), and *Full Moon* (1947). He collaborated with Guy Bolton on the musical *Cabaret Girl* (1922) and the play *Anything Goes* (1935), and was coauthor with Ian Hay of the play *Leave it to Psmith* (1930). Wodehouse is famous for the complex situations in which he involves his slightly "barmy" Beans and Crumpets, as he terms the inhabitants of his fictional world.

Woffington (wof'ing.tọn), **Margaret.** [Called **Peg Woffington.**] b. at Dublin, Oct. 18, c1714; d. at Teddington, Middlesex, England, March 28, 1760. An Irish actress, the daughter of a bricklayer. She appeared as Polly Peachum, with a company of children, in *The Beggar's Opera* when only ten years old, and made her first appearance as a mature actress at Dublin in 1737 as Ophelia. Until 1740 she played a wide range of parts there; in that year she appeared as Sir Harry Wildair in *The Constant Couple.* Her success in this part led to her first appearance at Covent Garden Theatre, playing this same role. Her success was great; her singing and the "finish" of the male characters she assumed made the fortunes of the theaters where she played. She lived for some time with David Garrick and Charles Macklin, and Garrick was reported (but without foundation) to have married her. She attempted to atone for her many and notorious love affairs by her charities, though the almshouses at Teddington said to have been founded by her are actually of much earlier date. She was seized with paralysis while playing Rosalind in *As You Like It* on May 3, 1757, and never appeared on stage again. Her characterizations of "refined ladies" such as Millamant in Congreve's *The Way of the World* were especially good. Charles Reade wrote a novel about her, *Peg Woffington.*

Wolcot (wŭl'kọt), **John.** [Pseudonym, **Peter Pindar.**] b. near Kingsbridge, Devonshire, England, in May, 1738; d. at London, Jan. 14, 1819. An English satirist. In early life he was a physician and was made physician general of the island of Jamaica. He returned to England and was ordained in 1760, but resumed the practice of medicine in a few years at Truro and other places. He removed to London with John Opie in 1781, and became noted for his coarse but witty satires on George III, James Boswell, and the Royal Academy. He was blind for some years before his death. Among his works are *Lyrical Odes to the Royal Academicians* (published first in 1782 and afterward every year till about 1814), *Bozzy and Piozzi* (1786), *The Lousiad* (1785–95), and *The Apple Dumplings and a King.* He painted landscapes also, and a series of his pictures was engraved by Aiken in 1797.

Wolfe (wŭlf), **Charles.** b. at Dublin, Dec. 14, 1791; d. at Cork, Ireland, Feb. 21, 1823. A British clergyman and poet. He wrote *The Burial of Sir John Moore.* His *Poetical Remains,* with a memoir by John Russell, were published in 1825.

Wolfe, Humbert. b. at Milan, Italy, Jan. 5, 1885; d. at London, Jan. 5, 1940. An English poet, critic, satirist, and translator. He entered (1908) the civil service, served in the Ministry of Munitions during World War I, and was afterward a secretary in the Ministry of Labour. He contributed to the *Westminster Gazette, Saturday Review,* and *Encyclopaedia Britannica.* Author of *London Sonnets* (1920), *Shylock Reasons with Mr. Chesterton* (1920), *Kensington Gardens* (1924), *Lampoons* (1925), *The Unknown Goddess* (1925), *Humoresque* (1926), *News of the Devil* (1926), *Cursory Rhymes* (1927), *Requiem* (1927), *Veni Creator!* (1927), *The Silver Cat* (1928), *This Blind Rose* (1928), *Troy* (1928), *Early Poems* (1930), *The Uncelestial City* (1930), *Snow* (1931), and *Kensington Gardens in War-Time* (1940), poetry; *Circular Saws* (1923), short stories; *Now a Stranger* (1933), *Portraits by Inference* (1934), and *The Upward Anguish* (1938), autobiography; *Reverie of a Policeman,* a poetic play (1933; performed at London, 1936); *Labour Supply and Regulation* (1923), *The Craft of Verse* (1928), *Dialogues and Monologues* (1928), *Notes on English Verse Satire* (1929), *Tennyson* (1930), *George Moore* (1931), *Signpost to Poetry—An Introduction to the Study of Verse* (1931), and *Romantic and Unromantic Poetry* (1933), critical essays and studies; and *Others Abide* (1927) and *Homage to Meleager* (1929), verse translations from the *Greek Anthology.* He also translated (1931) Edmond Fleg's *Wall of Weeping* and in 1934 brought out a translation of Ronsard's *Sonnets for Helen.*

Wolf Solent (wŭlf sō'lẹnt). A novel by John Cowper Powys, published in 1929.

Wollstonecraft (wŭl'stọn.kråft), **Mary.** See **Godwin, Mary.**

Wolsey (wŭl'zi), **Thomas.** b. at Ipswich, England, probably in 1475; d. at Leicester, England, Nov. 29, 1530. An English statesman and cardinal. He was educated at Magdalen College, Oxford, studied divinity, became rector of Lymington in 1500, and was successively chaplain to Henry Deane, archbishop of Canterbury, to Sir Richard Nanfan, and to Henry VII. He was sent by Henry VII on a diplomatic mission to the emperor Maximilian, was made dean of Lincoln in 1509, and became, after the accession of Henry VIII, almoner in 1509 and privy councilor in 1511. He was put in charge of planning the invasion of France (1513) and accompanied the king on the expedition. In 1513 he was appointed bishop of Tournai, but was not able to possess the see; in 1514 he became bishop of Lincoln and in the same year was made archbishop of York, becoming a cardinal the next year. In 1515 also, he became lord chancellor, having become by this time the most influential person in the kingdom. Wolsey actively carried out the king's policy of the centering of power in the monarchy and was his principal instrument in foreign affairs. The struggle between the French and the Holy Roman Empire was approaching its climax and Wolsey used English power, which had brought England far up in the world since the advent of the Tudors in 1485, to maintain the balance between the two. At first England's ties were with France, but after Charles V, nephew of Henry's queen Catherine of Aragon, became emperor, Wolsey threw England's strength to Charles's side, partly because the Netherlands, England's important commercial neighbor, was in the hands of the empire. He had negotiated marriage treaties both with the French and with Charles for Mary Tudor (later Queen Mary I), Henry's eldest daughter, and the latter match seemed likely to come to actuality. However, Charles, who had agreed to military alliances with England in 1521 and 1522, avoided the decision to marry, failed to support Wolsey's candidacy for the papacy in 1521 and 1524, and, using England as a tool, secured supremacy on the Continent by defeating Francis I of France at Pavia (1525). Wolsey had borrowed heavily in England to support this unsuccessful foreign policy and its military alliances, and this, combined with his arrogance and his actually regal style of living, made him many enemies at home. When Henry decided to divorce Catherine of Aragon, Wolsey was induced to support the case and obtained from the Pope the right to a trial of the matter in England. But Cardinal Campeggio was sent to try it, superseding Wolsey, and the decision in the case, in the face of Catherine's attitude, was dragged out; appeal was made to Rome but, since Catherine was Charles V's aunt and since Charles held Italy, the Pope refused to grant the divorce. The long delay brought Wolsey the enmity of Anne Boleyn, whose influence over the king told against the cardinal, and in 1529 he was stripped of all his offices, excepting the archbishopric of York. Accused of treason, Wolsey was arrested in November, 1530, but died on his way to London.

Wolsey, Thomas, Cardinal. One of the major characters in Shakespeare's *Henry VIII.*

Woman Hater, The. A play by Francis Beaumont and John Fletcher, published anonymously in 1607 and written c1606.

Woman Hater, The. A novel by Charles Reade, published in 1877.

Woman in the Moon, The. A comedy (c1584) in blank verse by John Lyly. It satirizes the supposedly unpredictable nature of women.

Woman in White, The. A long and involved mystery story (1860) by Wilkie Collins.

Woman Is a Weathercock, A. A comedy by Nathan Field, produced in 1610 with the author in the cast.

Woman Killed with Kindness, A. A play by Thomas Heywood, acted in March, 1603, and printed in 1607. It is a domestic tragedy, set in Yorkshire, and centering around the establishment of Frankford, whose wife, Alice has been unfaithful to him with a friend, Wendoll, whom Frankford has taken in because of his poverty. Their guilt is revealed to Frankford by a servant, and he implies his suspicions as they play a game of cards. Finally he catches them sleeping together but does not exact punishment: "I would not damn two precious souls, Bought with my Saviour's blood— with all their scarlet sins upon their backs."

Woman of No Importance, A. A comedy (1893) by Oscar Wilde.

Woman's Prize, or The Tamer Tamed, The. A comedy by John Fletcher, acted at Court in 1633 (but probably earlier elsewhere) and printed in 1647. It assumes that the audience is familiar with Shakespeare's *Taming of the Shrew*, and inverts the theme of woman-taming utilized in that play by taking up the story of Petruchio after the supposed death of Kate, and his subsequent marriage to the hitherto gentle Maria. She turns his life into an uproar, until he pretends to be dead and is brought to "life" by her tears of sorrow.

Woman Who Did, The. A novel by Grant Allen, published in 1895. The heroine, a woman of high principles but advanced ideas, decides that marriage as an institution is barbaric and irreconcilable with the emancipation of woman. Believing in free love, she puts her theory into practice in real life, with tragic results. The work was a sensation because of its (for that period) daring views.

Women and God. A novel by Francis Stuart, published in 1930.

Women Beware Women. A tragedy by Thomas Middleton, written c1620 and printed in 1657.

Women in Love. A novel by D. H. Lawrence, published in 1920.

Women Pleased. A tragicomedy (c1620) by John Fletcher.

Wonder! A Woman Keeps a Secret, The. A comedy by Susannah Centlivre, produced and printed in 1714.

Wondrous Tale of Alroy (al'roi), **The.** A novel by Benjamin Disraeli, published in 1833.

Wood (wud), **Anthony.** [Called **Anthony à Wood.**] b. at Oxford, England, Dec. 17, 1632; d. there, Nov. 29, 1695. An English antiquary. He was educated at Oxford. He wrote *Historia et Antiquitates Universitatis Oxoniensis* (written in English and translated into Latin for the University Press in 1674). He was dissatisfied with the translation and afterward rewrote his English manuscript, and it was published after his death in two volumes, the first as *The History and Antiquities of the Colleges and Halls of the University of Oxford, with a Continuation to the Present Time by John Gutch*, with *Fasti* (Annals) *Oxoniensis* (1786–90), the second as *The History and Antiquities of the University of*

Oxford (1792–96). He also wrote *Athenae Oxoniensis: an Exact History of All the Writers and Bishops Who Have Had Their Education in the University of Oxford from 1500 to 1690*, with *Fasti*. Two volumes of this were printed (1691–92) before his death; the third he prepared, and it appeared in the second edition in 1721. He also wrote *Modus Salium: a Collection of Pieces of Humour* (1751) and *The Ancient and Present State of the City of Oxford* (1773).

Wood, Edward Frederick Lindley. See **Halifax, 1st Earl of.**

Wood, Mrs. Henry. [Maiden name, **Ellen Price.**] b. at Worcester, England, Jan. 17, 1814; d. Feb. 10, 1887. An English novelist. Among her novels are *East Lynne* (1861; several times dramatized), *The Channings* (1862), *Mrs. Halliburton's Troubles* (1862), and *The Shadow of Ashlydyat* (1863). She also published anonymously *The Johnny Ludlow Tales* (1874–80). In 1867 she became editor of *The Argosy*.

Woodcock (wŭd′kok), **Adam.** In Sir Walter Scott's novel *The Abbot*, the English falconer at Avenel Castle. He is a bold man, inclined to think highly of his capacities as a wit and prankster.

Woodcourt (wŭd′kōrt), **Allan.** The lover of Esther Summerson in Dickens's *Bleak House*. He is a young and sympathetic doctor of very high principles.

Wooden Horse, The. A novel (1909) by Hugh Walpole.

Wooden Pegasus (peg′a̤.sus), **The.** The title poem of a volume of verse (1920) by Edith Sitwell.

Woodhouse (wŭd′hous), **Mr.** Emma's father in Jane Austen's novel *Emma*.

Woodlanders, The. A novel by Thomas Hardy, published in 1887.

Woods (wŭdz), **Margaret Louisa.** [Maiden name, **Bradley.**] b. at Rugby, Warwickshire, England, 1856; d. at Thurley, Surrey, England, Nov. 29, 1945. An English novelist, poet, and dramatist. Author of *A Village Tragedy* (1887), *The Vagabonds* (1894), *Sons of the Sword* (1901), *The King's Revoke* (1905), *The Invader* (1907; revised, 1922), *A Poet's Youth* (1924), and *The Spanish Lady* (1927), novels. Her *Esther Vanhomrigh* (1891), a historical romance, deals with Swift's Vanessa. She also wrote *Lyrics and Ballads* (1889), *Wild Justice* (a poetic drama, 1896), *Poems New and Old* (1907), *Pastels under the Southern Cross* (1911), *Collected Poems and Plays* (1913–14), and *Come unto These Yellow Sands* (1914). Among her poems are *The May Morning and the Old Man, Marlborough Fair*, and *High Tide on Victoria Embankment*.

Woodsmoke. A novel by Francis Brett Young, published in 1924.

Woods of Westermain (wes′tėr.mān), **The.** A poem by George Meredith, published (1883) in *Poems and Lyrics of the Joy of the Earth*.

Woodstock (wŭd′stok). An Elizabethan chronicle play (in the tradition of the morality) by an unknown author, first printed from the manuscript in 1870. It is based on events from the reign of Richard II, and it is possible that both Marlowe

and Shakespeare were familiar with it when they wrote, respectively, *Edward II* and *Richard II*.

Woodstock. A romance (1826) of the 17th century, by Sir Walter Scott.

Woodvile (wŭd′vil). In Shakespeare's *1 Henry VI*, a Lieutenant of the Tower (of London).

Woodville (wŭd′vil), **Elizabeth.** See under **Grey, Lady.**

Woolf (wŭlf), **Leonard Sidney.** b. at London, Nov. 25, 1880—. An English political scientist; husband of Virginia Woolf. He served (1904–11) in the Ceylon civil service, and founded (1917) the Hogarth Press. He was literary editor (1923–30) of *The Nation*, and joint editor (1931 *et seq.*) of *Political Quarterly*. He wrote *The Village in the Jungle* (1913), *International Government* (1916), *Co-operation and the Future of Industry* (1918), *Socialism and Co-operation* (1921), *Essays* (1927), *Imperialism and Civilization* (1928), a survey of contemporary social and political trends of thought, *After the Deluge* (2 vols., 1931, 1939), and others.

Woolf, Virginia. [Full name, **Adeline Virginia Woolf.**] b. at London, 1882; d. a suicide by drowning, at Lewes, Sussex, England, March 28, 1941. An English novelist, short-story writer, critic, and essayist; daughter of Sir Leslie Stephen, sister of Vanessa Stephen (Mrs. Clive Bell), and wife of Leonard Woolf, whom she married in 1912. Author of *The Voyage Out* (1915), *Night and Day* (1919), *Jacob's Room* (1922), *Mrs. Dalloway* (1925), *To the Lighthouse* (1927), *Orlando* (1928), *The Waves* (1931), *The Years* (1937), and *Between the Acts* (1941), novels; *Two Stories* (1917; with Leonard Woolf), *Kew Gardens* (1919), *The Mark on the Wall* (1919), and *Monday or Tuesday* (1921), short stories; *Flush* (1933), a fictionalized biography of Elizabeth Barrett Browning's spaniel, and *Roger Fry* (1940), a biography of the English artist and art critic; *The Common Reader* (1925; 2nd series, 1932), *A Room of One's Own* (1929), *Beau Brummell* (1930), *On Being Ill* (1930), *Letter to a Young Poet* (1932), *Reviewing* (1939), and *The Death of the Moth* (1942), critical essays and studies. In 1922 and 1923 she translated, with S. S. Koteliansky, works on Dostoevski and Tolstoy. With her husband she was a member of the London "Bloomsbury" group (which included J. M. Keynes, Roger Fry, Clive and Vanessa Bell, Arthur Waley, E. M. Forster, and others); with him she founded (1917) the Hogarth Press, which began as a small enterprise bringing out limited editions of unknown authors and soon became a large publishing firm.

Woolner (wŭl′nėr), **Thomas.** b. at Hadleigh, Suffolk, England, Dec. 17, 1825; d. at London, Oct. 7, 1892. An English sculptor and poet. He was a member of the Pre-Raphaelite Brotherhood, and many of his poems first appeared in *The Germ*. He was professor of sculpture at the Royal Academy (1877–79). Among his statues are *Puck, Titania, Eros, Constance and Arthur, Elaine, Ophelia, Achilles and Pallas;* statues of Macaulay, Lord Frederick Cavendish, Lord Palmerston, and others; and busts of Tennyson, Carlyle, Darwin, Gladstone, and others. His poems include *My Beautiful Lady* (1863), *Pygmalion* (1881), *Silenus* (1884), and *Tiresias* (1886).

Woolwich (wŭl'ich, -ij). A metropolitan borough in SE London, in the County of London, situated S of the river Thames, ab. 9 mi. E of Charing Cross Station. The district was originally an area of barren heath. Woolwich is noted for its arsenal and a royal military academy for engineering and artillery. Woolwich became an important naval station and dockyard in the 16th century; the dockyard was closed in 1869.

Woolwich Bagnet (bag'net). See under **Bagnet, Mr. and Mrs. Joseph.**

Wopsle (wop'sl), **Mr.** [Stage name, **Waldengarver.**] In Dickens's novel *Great Expectations*, a close friend of the Gargery family. He had thought at one time that his vocation was in the Church (and became a parish clerk), but decides finally that he is destined to be an actor. However, a single appearance in the role of Hamlet is sufficient to indicate that his place in the world of the theater is not to be that of a star, and he is thereafter relegated to the humble role of a super.

Worcester (wŭs'tẽr). A county borough, market town, and manufacturing center in W England, county seat of Worcestershire, situated on the river Severn ab. 22 mi. SW of Birmingham, ab. 121 mi. NW of London by rail. It has manufactures of gloves (the principal industry), porcelain, Worcestershire sauce, vinegar, and others. It is one of the largest hops-marketing centers in England, and is surrounded by large fruit orchards and berry fields. The cathedral dates in its present form chiefly from the 13th century. It measures 450 by 78 ft.; length of west transepts, 78 ft. each; height of vaulting, 67 ft. The Three Choirs Festival, the oldest musical festival of its kind in the world, is held here in the cathedral every third year, in rotation with Hereford and Gloucester. Worcester was an ancient British settlement and a Roman military station. The final victory of the English Civil War was gained here by Cromwell over the Scottish Royalists under Charles II, Sept. 3, 1651.

Worcester, Thomas Percy, Earl of. In Shakespeare's *1 Henry IV*, the hot-headed younger brother of Northumberland. Suspicious of the King, he fails to tell Hotspur of the King's offer to pardon the rebels.

Worcester's Men. [Later name, **Queen Anne's Men.**] An Elizabethan and Jacobean theatrical company. Under the patronage of the 3rd Earl of Worcester, later of his son, and finally of Queen Anne, the wife of James I, it played at the Boar's Head and Curtain theaters. By 1609 it was playing usually at the Red Bull and the Curtain, and from 1617 to 1619 at The Cockpit theater. After the Queen's death in 1619 the company dissolved. Thomas Heywood, in particular, wrote plays for it.

Worcester College. A college of Oxford University, incorporated in 1714.

Worde (wôrd), **Wynkyn de.** [Original name, **Jan van Wynkyn.**] b. in Alsace; d. c1535. An English printer. He went to England (1476) as an assistant of William Caxton, and in 1491 became his successor. He lived in Fleet Street, London, from c1500.

Words upon the Window-Pane, The. A one-act play (1934) by William Butler Yeats. It deals with incidents from the life of Jonathan Swift, whose spirit is invoked as the prototype of spokesmen for Irish independence.

Wordsworth (wẽrdz'wẽrth), **Christopher.** b. at Lambeth, London, Oct. 30, 1807; d. at Lincoln, England, March 21, 1885. An English prelate and author. He was headmaster of Harrow (1836–44) and canon of Westminster (1844 *et seq.*), and became bishop of Lincoln in 1868. He wrote *Athens and Attica* (1836), *Ancient Writings Copied from the Walls of Pompeii* (1837), *Greece, Pictorial, Descriptive, and Historical* (1839), *Theophilus Anglicanus* (1843), *On the Canon of the Scriptures* (1848), *Memoirs of William Wordsworth* (1851), notes on the New Testament and the Bible, controversial works, and various theological and other works.

Wordsworth, Dorothy. b. at Cockermouth, Cumberland, England, Dec. 25, 1771; d. at Grasmere, Westmorland, England, Jan. 25, 1855. An English writer; younger sister and constant companion of William Wordsworth. She traveled with her brother in France, Germany, Switzerland, Scotland, and the Lake District, recording her impressions in journals and diaries; her Alfoxden and Grasmere *Journals* (1798 *et seq.*), her *Recollections of a Tour Made in Scotland* (1803), her *Journal of a Mountain Ramble* describing a walking trip (November, 1805) in the Lake District, and other accounts of her travels and impressions are important because of their fine style and their value to students and biographers of Wordsworth. She also wrote a few short poems, among them *Christmas Rhyme, Address to a Child,* and *The Cottager to her Infant,* that are included in some editions of Wordsworth's *Poetical Works.* She never completely recovered from a severe mental and physical illness that began in April, 1829. Her *Journals* were published in various forms in 1874, 1889, 1897, 1904, and 1924.

Wordsworth, Dorothy. [Called **Dora;** married name, **Mrs. Edward Quillinan.**] b. at Grasmere, Westmorland, England, Aug. 6, 1804; d. there, July 9, 1847. An English author; daughter of William Wordsworth. Author of *A Journal of a Few Months' Residence in Portugal and Glimpses of the South of Spain* (1847), dedicated to her parents.

Wordsworth, William. b. at Cockermouth, Cumberland, England, April 7, 1770; d. at Rydal Mount, Westmorland, England, April 23, 1850. An English poet, poet laureate (1843–50). He was educated at Hawkshead and at Saint John's College, Cambridge, where he graduated in 1791. He traveled on the Continent in 1790, and traveled and lived in France (1791–92), where he fell in love with Annette Vallon, the daughter of a French surgeon; a daughter, Anne Caroline, was born of the liaison in December, 1792, but Wordsworth, who had gone to England for more funds with which to live, was unable to return to France because of the outbreak of war. Wordsworth had been deeply sympathetic with the aims of the republican revolutionaries, but the war between England and France precipitated a struggle within him between his sympathy for the principles of the

ḑ, d or j; ṣ, s or sh; ṭ, t or ch; ẓ, z or zh; o, F. cloche; ü, F. menu; ċh, Sc. loch; ṅ, F. bonbon.

Revolution and his feelings of patriotism. Outwardly, at least, he was unable to show his sympathy for France and a period of despondency and pessimism ensued; he turned to the philosophy of William Godwin before experiencing a revulsion from politics that led him to a concept of the harmony of man with nature and of man's existence as a natural rather than a political being. He may have paid a brief visit to France, at the risk of his neck, in 1793 to see his daughter; he did correspond with Annette, who was later married (1816). Wordsworth received a legacy in 1795 and settled, with his sister Dorothy, at Racedown, in Dorsetshire. His friendship with Samuel Taylor Coleridge led Wordsworth to remove to Alfoxden in Somersetshire to be near him; the contact with Coleridge determined Wordsworth's career, for, under the influence of Coleridge and the writings of David Hartley, Wordsworth developed the philosophy that he expressed in his poems. In 1798 the two friends published a collection of their poems, *Lyrical Ballads with a Few Other Poems*, in which the revolt from the artificialities of the poetry of the day was provided with leadership in an explanatory preface and in the poems themselves and which acted as the manifesto of the Romantic poets. Wordsworth went to the Continent in 1798 and lived at Goslar, Germany, returned to England in 1799, and settled at Dove Cottage, Grasmere, in the Lake District, whence he later removed to Rydal Mount (1813). In 1802, after visiting France and making a final settlement with Annette Vallon, Wordsworth married Mary Hutchinson. During the next few years he turned vigorously against the radicalism of the day, partly as the result of the events in France where the republican excesses and the subsequent rise of Napoleon aroused in him feelings of antagonism and uneasiness concerning his own beliefs, partly as the result of his growing circle of conservative acquaintances, including Robert Southey and Walter Scott. He was appointed distributor of stamps in 1813, traveled in Scotland (1801, 1803, 1814, 1832) and the Continent (1820, 1837), but in general lived quietly and somewhat secludedly at Rydal Mount for the remainder of his life. Wordsworth's last years, which saw his appointment as poet laureate in 1843 to succeed Southey, were marked by extreme political conservatism; he opposed parliamentary reform, the secret ballot, Roman Catholic emancipation, and other liberal reforms. His works include *An Evening Walk* (1793), *Descriptive Sketches* (1792), *Lyrical Ballads* (1798), which includes Coleridge's *The Ancient Mariner* and Wordsworth's *Lines Composed a Few Miles above Tintern Abbey*, *Poems in Two Volumes* (1807), which includes his *Ode on Intimations of Immortality* and a number of well-known sonnets, *The Convention of Cintra* (1809), a prose work on international politics, *The Excursion* (1814), meant to be part of a larger poetical autobiography to be entitled *The Recluse*, but which was never finished, a collected edition of his poems (1815), *The White Doe of Rylstone* (1815), *Peter Bell* and *The Waggoner* (1819), *The River Duddon* (1820), a group of sonnets, *Ecclesiastical Sketches* (1822), *Memorials of a Tour on the Continent* (1822), *Yarrow Revisited and Other Poems* (1835), collected *Sonnets* (1838), *The Borderers; a*

Tragedy (1842; written about 1796), *Poems, Chiefly of Early and Late Years* (1842), *The Prelude* (1850; finished in 1805), and others. Wordsworth's place in the forefront of the English Romantic poets is undisputed. His stated philosophical approach, to write poetry in "a selection from the real language of men in a state of vivid sensation," resulted in a number of poems notable in the revolt from the extravagances of meter and language indulged in by his predecessors and contemporaries; such poems as *Tintern Abbey* and *Intimations of Immortality* are successful blendings of clarity of language and neo-Platonic philosophy, expressed with a simplicity until then unachieved in poetry and subjected at the time to severe criticism for their "unpoetic" nature. Wordsworth failed often, for his subject matter (as in *The Idiot Boy*) often led him to bucolic bathos, but his successes, as in his sonnets, which rank with Milton's, place him high among English poets.

Workers in the Dawn. A novel by George Gissing, published in 1880.

Workhouse Ward. A comedy (1907) by Augusta Gregory (Lady Gregory) about two poor men, Mike McInnerney and Michael Miskill, both in the workhouse and inseparable because of their actual delight in quarreling with each other. When Mike's sister attempts to improve his condition by taking him to her farm, he tries to bring Michael along, and, failing in this, decides to remain in the workhouse with his friend. When she leaves they gleefully resume quarreling.

World, The. A poem (1655) by Henry Vaughan, perhaps the most famous of all of Vaughan's works. It is written in the form of a vision, in which religion, representing all virtues, is identified with eternity.

Worldly Wiseman (wèrld'li wīz'man), **Mr.** In John Bunyan's *Pilgrim's Progress*, a man who has worldly knowledge but is devoid of spiritual insight.

World of William Clissold (wil'yam klis'ọld), **The.** A novel by H. G. Wells, published in 1926.

Worms (wèrmz; German, vôrms), **Diet of.** An imperial diet, famous in the history of the Reformation, opened by the Emperor Charles V at Worms, Germany, Jan. 28, 1521. On March 6 Luther was cited to appear before the diet, and he arrived at Worms on April 16. On April 17 and 18 he appeared before the diet, and on the latter day refused to recant and defended his position. His determination was expressed in the famous words, "Here I stand. I cannot do otherwise. God help me, Amen." Luther, who had attended under a safe-conduct, was ordered to leave and was placed under the imperial ban.

Worthies of England, History of the. A biographical work by Thomas Fuller, generally considered to be his best work, published after his death, in 1662.

Wortle's School (wèrt'lz, wôrt'lz), **Dr.** A novel by Anthony Trollope, published in 1881. Dr. Wortle, as the proprietor of a private school patronized by the nobility, engages for an assistant master Mr. Peacocke. Mr. Peacocke and his wife are very efficient, but the townspeople find some mystery about their marriage. Actually, Mr. Peacocke married his wife when her first husband, a drunkard, was still alive. Dr. Wortle supports the case of the Peacockes against the townspeople and the bishop, and finally the death of the first husband calms the scandal.

Wortley Montagu (wẽrt′li mon′ta̤.gū, mun′-), **Edward** and Lady **Mary.** See **Montagu.**

Wotton (wot′on), Sir **Henry.** b. in Kent, England, 1568; d. at Eton, England, in December, 1639. An English diplomat and author. He was educated at Winchester and Oxford, and went to the Continent in 1588, where he remained until 1595. In 1595 he became secretary to the Earl of Essex. He was special envoy from Tuscany to James VI of Scotland, English ambassador to Venice and Germany, and in 1624 provost of Eton College. He wrote poems, various Latin pamphlets, *The Elements of Architecture,* and *State of Christendom.* The *Reliquiae Wottonianae* (1651) contains most of his works.

Would-be (wŭd′bē), Sir **Politick** and **Lady.** An amusingly important politician and his pedantic wife, in Jonson's *Volpone.*

Wounds of Civil War, The. A tragedy by Thomas Lodge, produced c1588 and printed in 1594. It is an imitation of Marlowe's *Tamburlaine,* but applied to Roman history and with some incidents suggestive of Shakespeare's *Henry VI.*

Wraxall (rak′sôl), Sir **Nathaniel William.** b. at Bristol, England, April 8, 1751; d. at Dover, England, Nov. 7, 1831. An English historical writer. He went to Bombay, in the service of the East India Company, in 1769, remained in India till 1772, spent a number of years in travel, and entered Parliament in 1780. He was the author of *Memoirs of the Kings of France of the Race of Valois* (1777), *History of France* (1785), and several volumes of contemporary memoirs (among them *Historical Memoirs of My Own Time, 1772–1784,* published in 1815). His own *Memoirs* were published in 1836.

Wray (rā), **John.** See **Ray** or **Wray, John.**

Wrayburn (rā′bẽrn), **Eugene.** A light-hearted, sarcastic, flippant, clever young attorney, the rival of Bradley Headstone, and nearly murdered by him; a character in Dickens's *Our Mutual Friend.* He is afterward married to Lizzie Hexam.

Wren (ren), Sir **Christopher.** b. at East Knoyle, Wiltshire, England, Oct. 20, 1632; d. at Hampton Court, near London, Feb. 25, 1723. An English architect. He was educated at Westminster School and at Wadham College, Oxford, and was made professor of astronomy at Gresham College in 1657, Savilian professor of astronomy at Oxford in 1660, and deputy surveyor general of public works in 1661. He designed the fortifications of Tangier in 1663, was created president of the Royal Society in 1680, and designed Saint Paul's Cathedral, London. Among his other designs were the cloister and chapel of Brasenose College, Oxford (1656), and the central spire of Lichfield Cathedral (1662–69). He was appointed on a committee for the survey of Old Saint Paul's (1663), and designed Pembroke College Chapel, Cambridge (1663–65). He was surveyor at Greenwich (1663–67), and designed the Sheldonian Theatre, Oxford

(1664–69). On Oct. 4, 1666, he was appointed on a committee with May, Pratt, and others, to survey the ruins of London after the great fire, and to make plans for the reconstruction of the burned district, was appointed surveyor general of all the royal works in 1669, and built Mary-le-Bow, Cheapside (1667–71), Temple Bar, in Fleet Street, the "Monument" (202 ft. high; 1671–81), Saint Bride, in Fleet Street (1671–80), Saint Stephen's, Walbrook (1677–79), Drury Lane Theatre, the Royal Observatory at Greenwich (1675), and Hampton Court Palace for King William III (1690). He built the Royal Naval Hospital (1692–1716), giving his services without compensation. In 1706 he remodeled Saint Stephen's Chapel for the enlarged membership (Scottish) of Parliament; in 1709–10 Marlborough House, in Pall Mall; and in 1713 designed the towers of Westminster Abbey (largely, however, built under the supervision of his assistant).

Wren, Jenny. See **Cleaver, Fanny.**

Wren, P. C. [Full name, **Percival Christopher Wren.**] b. in Devonshire, England, 1885; d. at Auberley, Gloucestershire, England, Nov. 23, 1941. An English author. Educated at Oxford, he traveled widely throughout the world, and saw service with the British cavalry, the French Foreign Legion, and, in World War I, with the Indian Army in East Africa. Author of *Dew and Mildew* (1912), *Father Gregory* (1913), *Smoke and Sword* (1914), *Driftwood Spars* (1915), *The Wages of Virtue* (1916), *The Young Stagers* (1917), *Stepsons of France* (1917), *Beau Geste* (1924), *Beau Sabreur* (1926), *Beau Ideal* (1928), *Good Gestes* (1929), *Soldiers of Misfortune* (1929), *The Mammon of Righteousness* (1930), *Mysterious Ways* (1930), *Spring Glory* (1931), *Valiant Dust* (1932), *Port o' Missing Men* (1934), *Bubble Reputation* (1936), *The Fort in the Jungle* (1936), *Rough Shooting* (1938), *Cardboard Castle* (1938), *Paper Prison* (1939), *A Mixed Bag* (1939), *None Are So Blind* (1939), *The Disappearance of General Jason* (1940), *Two Feet From Heaven* (1940), and *The Uniform of Glory* (1941).

Wright (rīt), **Thomas.** b. near Ludlow, England, April 23, 1810; d. at London, Dec. 23, 1877. An English antiquary and historian. He was one of the founders of the Percy, Camden, and Shakespeare societies, and the British Archaeological Association. He directed the excavation of Uriconium (near modern Wroxeter, in Shropshire). His numerous works include *Early English Poetry,* in black letter (1836), an edition of Geoffrey of Monmouth's *Life of Merlin* (with Michel, 1838), and *Queen Elizabeth and her Times,* a series of original letters (1838). He edited *Political Songs of England* (1839), *Reliquiae Antiquae* (with Halliwell, 1839), *Political Ballads* (1841), Map's Latin poems (1841), *The Vision and Creed of Piers Plowman* (1842), *Biographia Literaria* (1842), *The Chester Plays* (1843–47), *Anecdota Literaria* (1844), and *The Archaeological Album* (1845). He also wrote *Essays on Subjects Connected with the Literature, Popular Superstitions, and History of England in the Middle Ages* (1846); edited *The Canterbury Tales* (1847–51), *Early Travels in Palestine* (1848), and various editions of Early English works; wrote

England under the House of Hanover, Illustrated from the Caricatures and Satires of the Day (1848; a new edition in 1868, entitled *Caricature History of the Georges*), *History of Ireland* (1848–52), *Narratives of Sorcery and Magic* (1851), *The Celt, the Roman, and the Saxon* (1852), *Universal Pronouncing Dictionary and Expositor of the English Language* (1852–56), *History of Scotland* (1852–57), *Wanderings of an Antiquary* (1854), *Dictionary of Obsolete and Provincial English* (1857), *A Volume of Vocabularies* (1857), *History of King Arthur and the Knights of the Round Table*, compiled from Malory (1858), *History of France* (1858–62), *Les Cent Nouvelles nouvelles* (medieval tales, 1858), descriptions of Uriconium, *Political Poems and Songs Relating to English History* (1859–61), *Essays on Archaeological Subjects* (1861), *Domestic Manners and Sentiments in England during the Middle Ages* (1862); edited Giraldus Cambrensis (1863); wrote *History of Caricature and Grotesque* (1865); translated, at the author's request, Napoleon's *Vie de Jules César* (1865–66); and wrote *Womankind in Western Europe* (1869), *Uriconium* (1872), and *Anglo-Latin Satirical Poets of the Twelfth Century* (1877).

Wright, William Aldis. b. at Beccles, Suffolk, England, Aug. 1, 1831; d. at Trinity College, Cambridge, England, May 19, 1914. An English scholar. He was educated (1849–54) at Trinity College, Cambridge, of which he was librarian (1863–70), bursar (1870–95), and vice-master (1888–1914). He edited Bacon's *Essays* (1862) and *Advancement of Learning* (1869), Milton's *Poems* (1903), Roger Ascham's *English Works* (1904), and the *Journal of Philology* (1868–1913). His greatest contribution to scholarship was as a Shakespearian scholar: with William George Clark he was coeditor of the first volume of the *Cambridge Shakespeare*, and sole editor of volumes 2 to 9; he also edited the *Globe Shakespeare* (1864) and the *Clarendon Press Shakespeare* (1868–72, 1874–97); a friend and the literary executor of Edward Fitzgerald, he edited the latter's *Letters and Literary Remains* (7 vols., 1889–1903).

Wriothesley (rot′sli), **Henry.** See **Southampton,** 3rd Earl of.

Wriothesley, Sir **Thomas.** See under Lord **Chancellor.**

Wulf and Eadwacer (wŭlf; ā′ạd.wäk″ẽr). See **Eadwacer.**

Wulfila (wŭl′fi.lạ). See **Ulfilas.**

Wulfstan (wŭlf′stän). d. 1023. A bishop of London (996–1002) and of Worcester (1002–16), and archbishop of York (1002–23), famous for his homilies, especially the *Sermo Lupi ad Anglos,* in which Wulfstan fiercely blames the troubled days (it was delivered in 1014, when the Danes were raiding the coasts) on the wickedness of the people and urges them to repent.

Wuthering Heights (wuTH′ẽr.ing hīts). A novel (1846) of extraordinary power and atmosphere, by Emily Brontë (but published under the pseudonym Ellis Bell).

Wyatt (wī′ạt), Sir **Thomas.** For the play, see Sir **Thomas Wyatt, The Famous History of.**

Wyatt or **Wyat** (wī′ạt), Sir **Thomas.** b. in Kent, England, 1503; d. at Sherborne, Dorsetshire, England, Oct. 11, 1542. An English diplomat and poet, sent by Henry VIII on various diplomatic missions. He wrote the first English sonnets, and his poems were printed with Surrey's in 1557.

Wyatt, Sir **Thomas.** b. c1520; executed at London, April 11, 1554. Son of Sir Thomas Wyatt (1503–42). He commanded at Boulogne, joined with the Duke of Suffolk in favor of Lady Jane Grey and against Queen Mary (1553–54), and led the men of Kent against London in February, 1554, but was captured. Webster and Dekker wrote a play on the subject, called *The Famous History of Sir Thomas Wyatt.* It was printed in 1607.

Wybrow (wī′brō), **Captain Anthony.** In George Eliot's *Mr. Gilfil's Love Story,* a selfish young dandy, whose exquisite appearance conceals a fatally weak nature.

Wycherley (wich′ẽr.li), **William.** b. at Clive, near Shrewsbury, England, c1640; d. at London, Jan. 1, 1716. An English dramatist. He went to France when quite young, and mingled in the society of the *précieuses* at the Hôtel de Rambouillet. On returning he went to Oxford and later to the Middle Temple and studied law, became a courtier at the court of Charles II, and was imprisoned several years for debt after the death of his first wife, the Countess of Drogheda, whose fortune involved him in litigation. James II set him free, gave him a pension, and paid his debts out of admiration for his play *The Plain Dealer.* In 1715 he married again, but died shortly after. He wrote the plays *Love in a Wood* (1672), *The Gentleman Dancing Master* (1672), *The Country Wife* (1673), and *The Plain Dealer* (1677).

Wych Street (wich). A London street near Clement's Inn. It was a haunt of the notorious Jack Sheppard.

Wycliffe (wik′lif), **John.** [Also: **Wiclif, Wickliffe, Wyclif.**] b. at Spreswel (thought to be either Hipswell or Barford), near Richmond, Yorkshire, England, c1324; d. at Lutterworth, Leicestershire, England, Dec. 31, 1384. An English religious reformer, called "the Morning Star of the Reformation." He was a fellow, and later (1360) master, of Balliol College, Oxford, and became rector of Fillingham, Lincolnshire, probably in the next year, and in 1368 of Ludgershall, Buckinghamshire, and in 1374 of Lutterworth. (The warden of Canterbury Hall 1365–67 was probably another John Wycliff, of Merton, Oxford, vicar of Mayfield; there is much confusion between the early lives of these two.) He went with John of Gaunt as royal ambassador to confer with papal nuncios at Bruges in 1374, was a popular preacher at London, and was summoned before Convocation in 1377 as an enemy of Rome on account of his attacks on the inordinate arrogance and wealth and power of the higher clergy (this blow was really aimed at John of Gaunt). The Pope signed five bulls against him, authorizing his imprisonment. The beginning of the Great Schism, due to the election of Clement VII, in place of Urban VI, induced him to throw off his allegiance to the papacy. He opposed the doctrine of transubstantiation at Oxford in 1380, and was condemned by the university; and his party was opposed and persecuted by Courtenay (archbishop of Canterbury) and others in 1382. He went back to Lutterworth, where he wrote ceaselessly and fearlessly against papal claims, and in opposition to mere formalism. On Dec. 28, 1384, he was seized with paralysis while hearing Mass, and died in a few days. In 1428 his bones were exhumed, burned, and their ashes cast into the Swift, by order of the Synod of Constance. He made the first complete translation of the Bible into English (c1382) from the Vulgate, assisted by Nicholas of Hereford. The latter translated the Old Testament and the apocryphal books to about the third chapter of the Book of Baruch. Wycliffe certainly translated the Gospels (probably c1360), and presumably all the rest. He wrote many tracts and sermons: *De Juramento Arnaldi, Trialogus, De Officio Pastorali, De Ecclesia, De Benedicta Incarnatione, De Dominio Divino, De Civili Dominio,* and others. His works were edited (1882–92) by the Wyclif Society.

Wycliffe, Oswald. In Sir Walter Scott's long narrative poem *Rokeby*, the principal figure in the plot against Philip of Mortham.

Wycliffe, Wilfrid. In Sir Walter Scott's long narrative poem *Rokeby*, the son of Oswald Wycliffe.

Wykeham (wik'am), **William of.** b. at Wykeham, Hampshire, England, 1324; d. 1404. An English statesman and prelate, bishop of Winchester from 1367. He was chancellor of England (1368–71, 1389–91), and founded Winchester School and New College at Oxford. In 1404 he finished rebuilding the nave of Winchester cathedral, died, and was buried in the chantry.

Wynd (wīnd), **Hal o' the.** See **Smith, Henry.**

Wyndham (win'dam), Sir **Charles.** b. 1837; d. Jan. 12, 1919. An English actor and theater manager. He studied medicine, but preferred the stage. He

went to the U. S. in 1862, and first appeared at Washington. He then served for some time as surgeon in the 19th army corps. He made his first appearance at London in 1868, returned to America the next year, and was thereafter successful on both sides of the Atlantic. From 1876 he managed the Criterion at London, and he opened Wyndham's Theatre and the New Theatre, London. He was knighted in 1902. He was particularly known for the role of David Garrick in Taylor's play of that name.

Wynkyn de Worde (wing'kin de wôrd). See **Worde, Wynkyn de.**

Wynne (win), **Ellis.** b. probably at Harlech, Wales, 1671; d. at Llanfairfechan, Wales, in July, 1734. A Welsh author. He translated (1701) Taylor's *Holy Living* (1650) into Welsh, and was editor (1710) of the *Welsh Prayer-Book*, but is chiefly noted for his *Visions of the Sleeping Bard* (1703), an allegory in three parts; this work, recognized as the great prose classic of Wales, reached its 27th edition in 1898; it was translated into English by George Borrow in 1860, and by R. Gwyneddon Davies in 1897.

Wyntoun (win'tun), **Andrew of.** b. about the middle of the 14th century; date of death unknown. A Scottish chronicler, canon regular of the priory of St. Andrews and prior of St. Serf's, Loch Leven (1395). His *Oryginale Cronykil of Scotland,* in rhymed eight-syllabled verse, was finished between 1420 and 1424 (edited by D. Laing, 1872–79).

Wyrdes (wirdz). [Also, **Weirds.**] In Anglo-Saxon legend, the fates, three sisters who controlled the destinies of men. They are identified with the Old Norse Norns. Today they survive in Scottish folklore as witches and prophesiers. The Witches, or Weird Sisters, in Shakespeare's *Macbeth* are their direct descendants.

X

Xanadu (zan'a.dö). A place referred to by Samuel Taylor Coleridge in *Kubla Khan* as the site of the "stately pleasure-dome." In the Hakluyt Society's edition of *Purchas his Pilgrimes* (1906, vol. xl, p. 231), in the section "Marco Polo," mention is made of Xandu, with descriptions of the countryside, the park, and the "goodly house of pleasure" of "Chan Cublay." Scholars working from Coleridge's notebooks have been able to establish that he had access to a version of this work before the composition of the poem.

Xanthus (zan'thus). In ancient geography, a city in Lycia, Asia Minor, situated on the Scamander (or Xanthus) River near its mouth. It was besieged and destroyed by the Persian general Harpagus c545 B.C., and again by the Romans under Brutus, in 43 or 42 B.C. Important antiquities were discovered (c1838) there by Fellows. Among them is the so-called Nereid monument, a cella with a beautiful Ionic peristyle, dating from the middle of the 4th century B.C. The chief frieze, on the basement, represents a battle of cavalry and foot

soldiers; the second frieze illustrates a siege; the third frieze, on the cella, is sculptured with sacrificial and feasting scenes; the fourth frieze, on the entablature, shows hunting episodes and homage to an official personage. The principal parts of the monument have been transported to the British Museum.

Xanthus. See also **Scamander.**

Xavier (zā'vi.ėr, zav'i.ėr), Saint **Francis** (or **Francisco**). [Also, **Javier;** called the **"Apostle of the Indies."**] b. at the castle of Xaviero, in Navarre, Spain, April 7, 1506; d. on the island of Sancian (or St. John), off Macao, China, Dec. 2, 1552. A Spanish Jesuit missionary. He was educated at the University of Paris, and was one of the founders of the Society of Jesus. He went to Italy in 1536, and labored there for several years; went to Lisbon in 1540, and sailed from there in 1541 on a Portuguese mission to the East Indies; arrived at Goa in 1542; labored in western and southern India, Malacca, the Moluccas, and Japan; and died on his way to undertake a mission to China. His letters

---

d, d or j; ş, s or sh; ţ, t or ch; z, z or zh; o, F. cloche; ü, F. menu; ch, Sc. loch; ṅ, F. bonbon.

were edited in 1795. He was canonized in 1622.

Xenocrates (zē.nok'rạ.tēz). fl. 396–314 B.C. A Platonic philosopher, the successor of Speusippus as head of the Academy, over which he presided for 25 years.

Xenophanes (zē.nof'ạ.nēz). b. at Colophon, Asia Minor, c570 B.C.; d. c480 B.C. A Greek philosopher, the founder of the Eleatic school. He settled at Elea in Italy c536 B.C. Fragments of his elegies and his didactic poem *On Nature* have been preserved.

Xenophon (zen'ọ.fọn). b. at Athens, c430 B.C.; d. after 357 B.C. A Greek historian and essayist, a disciple of Socrates. He joined the expedition of Cyrus the Younger in 401, and after the battle of Cunaxa and the murder of the Greek generals became the chief leader of the 10,000 Greeks in their march to the Black Sea. He later entered the Lacedaemonian service, fought on the Spartan side at the battle of Coronea in 394, was banished from Athens, settled at Scillus, near Olympia, and spent his last years probably at Corinth. He wrote the *Anabasis, Hellenica* (in 7 books), the romance *Cyropaedia, Memorabilia of Socrates* (a defense of

his master's memory), essays on hunting and horsemanship, *Symposium, Revenues of Athens, Hiero, Agesilaus,* and others.

Xerxes (zėrk'sēz). A tragedy by Colley Cibber, produced in 1699.

Xerxes I. [Old Persian, **Khsayarsha;** in the Bible, **Ahasuerus.**] b. c519 B.C.; assassinated 465 or 464 B.C. A king of Persia; son of Darius Hystaspes. He succeeded to the throne in 486 or 485, assembled a large army for the conquest of Greece, bridged the Hellespont, traversed Thrace, Macedonia, and Thessaly, was resisted (480) at Thermopylae, and burned Athens. He was defeated (480) at Salamis, and returned to Asia Minor. His generals were defeated (479) at Plataea and Mycale, but continued the war with Greece.

Ximena (Hē.mä'nä). In Spanish legend, the wife of the Cid, Spanish epic and ballad hero.

Ximena (zi.mē'nạ). [Full title, **Ximena: or, The Heroik Daughter.**] An adaptation of Corneille's *Le Cid* by Colley Cibber, produced in 1712 and printed in 1718.

Xury (zö'ri). A servant of Robinson Crusoe; a character in Daniel Defoe's romance of that name.

Yahoos (yä'höz). The name given by Swift, in *Gulliver's Travels,* to a fictional race of brutes having the form of man and all his degrading passions. They are placed in contrast with the Houyhnhnms, or horses endowed with reason, the whole being designed as a satire on the human race.

Yajur-Veda (yuj'ûr.vä'dạ). See under **Vedas.**

Yama (yä'mạ). In Hindu mythology, the lord and judge of the dead. In the *Rig-Veda,* Yama and his sister Yami were the first human pair; hence Yama was the first man to die, and as such became deified as god of the dead. He is depicted as green in color, garbed in red, carrying the noose with which he snares the dying, and riding on a buffalo.

Yankee Doodle (yang'kẹ dö'dl). An American patriotic song, sung to a traditional tune. Its authorship (c1755) has been traditionally ascribed to Dr. Richard Schuckburgh, a British surgeon in the French and Indian Wars, who wrote the verses to ridicule the tattered colonial troops. It became a favorite with the Yankees themselves and was played at the time of Cornwallis's surrender in 1781. A folk parody of the song, not the air, was *The Yankee's Return from Camp.* The tune is first found in print as an English country-dance tune in James Aird's *Selection of Scotch, English, Irish, and Foreign Airs* (1782); but its ultimate origin is still unknown.

Yankees (yang'kẹz). **1.** Citizens of New England. **2.** By extension, natives of the U. S.; chiefly a European and Latin American use. **3.** Soldiers of the Union armies: so called by the Confederates during the Civil War (1861–65). **4.** Soldiers of the armies of the U. S. who served in the western European theater of operations in

World Wars I and II: so called chiefly by the British and the French, who frequently contracted the term to "Yanks."

Yardley Oak (yärd'li), **The.** A poem (1791) by William Cowper, written in blank verse.

Yarrow Water (yar'ō). [Also, **Yarrow.**] A stream in S Scotland, in Selkirkshire. It rises on the Dumfriesshire-Selkirkshire boundary, ab. 10 mi. NE of Moffat, and flows NE, traversing the Loch of the Lowes and St. Mary's Loch, to a confluence with Ettrick Water ab. 2 mi. SW of Selkirk. Wordsworth wrote three poems on it. Length, ab. 15 mi.

Yates (yāts), **Edmund Hodgson.** b. at Edinburgh, July 3, 1831; d. May 20, 1894. An English journalist and novelist. He retired from a position in the London general post office in 1872, lectured in the U. S. (1872–73), and went as special correspondent of the New York *Herald* to Vienna, St. Petersburg, and elsewhere (1873–75). He was connected with various periodicals, including *Our Miscellany* and the London *Daily News,* was editor of *Temple Bar* till 1867, when he became editor of *Tinsley's Magazine,* founded and edited the London *World* with Grenville Murray in 1874, and was London correspondent of the New York *Tribune* for a number of years before his death. As a columnist (1855 *et seq.*) for the *Illustrated Times,* Yates inaugurated the column of paragraphs about personalities; later, in *The World,* he conducted the first of the "society" papers, journals based on the interest of others in the activities of the prominent. He was expelled from the Garrick Club for some criticism he penned of William Makepeace Thackeray (1858) and was jailed for several weeks (1885) for a libel on Lord Lonsdale. Among his novels are *For*

---

fat, fāte, fär, ȧsk, fāre; net, mē, hėr; pin, pīne; not, nōte, mȯve, nôr; up, lūte, pu̇ll; ᴛʜ, then;

Better, for Worse (1863), *Broken to Harness* (1864), *Running the Gauntlet* (1866), *Kissing the Rod* (1866), *The Black Sheep* (1867), *Wrecked in Port* (1869), *Castaway* (1872), *A Waiting Race* (1872), and *The Yellow Flag* (1872). In 1885 he published *Edmund Yates: his Recollections and his Experiences.*

Years, The. A novel by Virginia Woolf, published in 1937.

Yeast: a Problem. A novel by Charles Kingsley, published in 1851, originally a serial in *Fraser's Magazine* in 1848. This is the author's first novel, and it is more a sociological tract than a work of fiction. There is little plot, and the main "action" consists of dialogue between the characters concerning the regeneration of England. The central character is Launcelot Smith.

Yeats (yāts), **William Butler.** b. at Dublin, June 13, 1865; d. in France, Jan. 28, 1939. An Irish poet, dramatist, and critic. He was one of the founders of the Irish Literary Theatre (1898) and of the National Theatre Society at Dublin, and was identified with the movement for the revival of Irish national literature. His works include *The Celtic Twilight* (1893), *Poems* (1895), *The Secret Rose* (1897), *The Wind among the Reeds* (1899), *Ideas of Good and Evil* (1903), *In the Seven Woods* (1903), *Stories of Red Hanrahan* (1904), *The Green Helmet* (1910), *John Millington Synge and the Ireland of His Time* (1911), and *The Cutting of an Agate* (1912). His plays include *The Countess Kathleen* (1892), *The Land of Heart's Desire* (1894), *The Shadowy Waters* (1900), *Cathleen ni Houlihan* (1902), *The Pot of Broth* (1902), *The Hour Glass and Other Plays* (1903), *On Baile's Strand* (1904), *Deirdre* (1907), *Plays for an Irish Theatre* (1912), and others, including translations of *Oedipus the King* and *Oedipus at Colonna.* After having been, in his youth, a member of the *Yellow Book* group of artists and writers, he turned in his middle period, especially after his marriage (1917) to Georgie Lees, whose occult activities as a medium convinced him of a link to the spirit world, to a more elaborate, more mystic symbolism; in *The Vision* (1925), a prose work, he discussed aspects of spiritualism. His late work is distinguished by its use of an extremely concise self-contained set of symbols to set forth his more austere realization of poetic truths, at the same time still embodying, as in his early works, the elements of Irish mythology; among these works are *The Wild Swans at Coole* (1917), *The Tower* (1927), and *The Winding Stair* (1929), all books of verse. There have appeared *Collected Poems* (1933), *Collected Plays* (1934), and *Last Poems and Plays.* He was awarded (1923) the Nobel prize in literature.

Yeats-Brown (yāts'broun'), **Francis.** b. at Genoa, Italy, Aug. 15, 1886; d. Dec. 19, 1944. An English soldier, traveler, and author. He saw service in India (1906–13) and in France and Mesopotamia (1914–15), winning the Distinguished Flying Cross, was held by the Turks as a prisoner of war (1915–18), and retired (1925) from the army. He traveled widely in India, Europe, Canada, and the U.S. Author of *Caught by the Turks* (1919), *Bengal Lancer* (1930; American title, *Lives of a Bengal Lancer*), *Golden Horn* (1932), *Dogs of War* (1934),

Lancer at Large (1936), *Yoga Explained* (1937), *European Jungle* (1939), *The Army's First Fifteen Months of the War* (1941), *Pageant of India* (1942), and *Fighting India* (1945).

Yellow Book. An English magazine, published (1894–97) quarterly in book form. It had an influence disproportionate to the brevity of its career. At that time French novels, which were apt to seem daring to English readers, were often published in yellow paper covers, and the title *Yellow Book* intimated that this magazine, which was yellow-covered, inclined more toward Continental artistic freedom than toward Victorian proprieties. The American novelist Henry Harland was its literary editor, but it was the designs of its art editor, Aubrey Beardsley, that most compellingly attracted the attention of the *fin-de-siècle* cognoscenti. The magazine was in the nature of a demonstration by the believers in "art for art's sake," but although its contents included much work by such figures as Beardsley, Oscar Wilde, and Ernest Dowson, it also numbered among its contributors Henry James, George Moore, John Davidson, and Edmund Gosse, and gave early encouragement to such men, then young, as Richard Le Gallienne, William Butler Yeats, H. G. Wells, and Arnold Bennett.

Yellowley (yel'ō.li), **Barbara.** In Sir Walter Scott's novel *The Pirate*, the penny-pinching sister of Triptolemus Yellowley.

Yellowley, Triptolemus. In Sir Walter Scott's novel *The Pirate*, an impractical agriculturist. He was believed by his mother to be destined for greatness (on the basis of a dream during her pregnancy that she would be delivered of a plow drawn by three oxen), and was originally intended for the ministry.

Yellowplush (yel'ō.plush), **Charles James.** One of the many pseudonyms of **Thackeray, William Makepeace.**

Yendys (yen'dis), **Sydney.** Pseudonym of **Dobell, Sydney Thompson.**

Yeo (yā'ō), **Salvation.** One of the principal characters in Charles Kingsley's *Westward Ho!*

Yeobright (yō'brīt), **Clym.** In Thomas Hardy's novel *The Return of the Native*, a man blinded by his love for Eustacia Vye. She marries him, but only in the hope of persuading him to take her to Paris.

Yeobright, Thomasin. In Thomas Hardy's novel *The Return of the Native*, the cousin of Clym Yeobright. She is a sweet and gentle girl, who eventually marries Diggory Venn.

Yeoman's Tale, The. See Canon's Yeoman's Tale, The.

Yeomen of the Guard. A military corps established by King Henry VII of England in 1485 as a personal bodyguard for the sovereigns of that country. On the occasion of its founder's coronation in that same year, it stood by him 50 strong; when his son and successor Henry VIII found it desirable to put up an imposing front when meeting Francis I of France, he increased the corps to 600 men, who in 1520 accompanied him to the Field of the Cloth of Gold. Thereafter the number of the yeomen dwindled, and in 1669 was stabilized by Charles II

---

d, d or j; ṣ, s or sh; ṭ, t or ch; ẓ, z or zh; o, F. cloche; ü, F. menu; ċh, Sc. loch; ṅ, F. bonbon

at 100 men plus a captain, a lieutenant, an ensign or standard-bearer, a clerk of the roster, and four corporals. When kings ceased to accompany their troops to battlefronts (the last English sovereign to do so being George II at the battle of Dettingen in 1743) and when violence went out of fashion as a means of determining succession to the throne, any real need for such a body as the Yeomen of the Guard ceased, but the corps has been continued for its symbolic interest and ceremonial usefulness. Under the later Georges and until 1848, many appointments to the Guards were purchased by civilians, but since that year membership (except as to the captain) has been restricted to veterans of the British army or marines, generally men who have won citations. The captain is now generally a member of the nobility, appointed by the lord chamberlain. The Yeomen's uniform derives from Tudor times; it has undergone variations, but now consists of a red tunic ornamented with purple facings and gold lace; red knee-breeches, red stockings, black shoes with colorful rosettes, a flat hat, and an Elizabethan ruff at the neck; they carry ornamental halberds and swords. Officers, however, wear a dress going back no farther than the Napoleonic wars. In 1605 it was members of the Yeomen of the Guard who seized Guy Fawkes in connection with the Gunpowder Plot, and in modern times the chief function of the corps, other than parading, is a symbolic search of the cellars of the Houses of Parliament for gunpowder at the opening of each session. Yeomen of the Guard, characteristically tall and robust men, are popularly known as Beefeaters because formerly their superior physical powers were sustained by especially generous rations of "the roast beef of Old England."

Yeomen of the Guard. A comic opera by Gilbert and Sullivan, first performed in 1888.

Yggdrasil (ig′drạ.sil). [Also: **Igdrasil, Iggdrasill, Ygdrasil; Tree of the Universe;** Icelandic, **Yggdra Syll.**] The world tree of Old Norse mythology, the ash tree which binds together heaven, earth, and hell. Its branches spread over the earth and reach above the heavens. Its three roots are fed by three springs: one in Asgard, one in Niflheim, the other Mimir's well.

Yguerne (i.gėrn′). See **Igerna.**

Ymir (ē′mir). [Also, **Aurgelmir.**] In Old Norse mythology, a mighty sea giant, the first created being, who arose through the interworking of heat and cold in Ginnungagap, the primeval abyss. He was slain by Odin and his brothers Vili and Ve, and hurled into Ginnungagap. His flesh became the land, his bones the mountains, his blood lakes and streams, his hair the forests, his skull the heavens, and his brains the clouds.

Yniol (in′i.ọl). In "Geraint and Enid," one of Tennyson's *Idylls of the King,* the father of Enid.

Yonder. A novel by E. H. Young, published in 1912.

Yonge (yung), **Charlotte Mary.** b. at Otterbourne, Hampshire, England, Aug. 11, 1823; d. there, March 24, 1901. An English novelist, writer of historical romances and books for young people. She began (1842) her literary career by contributing sketches to the *Magazine for the Young,* and

edited the *Monthly Packet* (1851–98), a periodical for juveniles. Author of *Abbey Church* (1844), *The Heir of Redclyffe* (1853), *The Little Duke* (1854), *Heartsease* (1854), *The Lances of Lynwood* (1855), *The Daisy Chain* (1856), *The Pigeon Pie* (1860), *Countess Kate* (1862), *The Trial* (1864), *The Prince and the Page* (1865), *The Clever Woman of the Family* (1865), *The Dove in the Eagle's Nest* (1866), *The Chaplet of Pearls* (1868), *The Caged Lion* (1870), *The Pillars of the House* (1873), *Stories from Greek, Roman, and German History for Children* (1873–78), and *Magnum Bonum* (1879), novels and stories. She also wrote nonfiction, including *Kings of England* (1848), *Landmarks of History* (1852–57), *Pioneers and Founders* (1873), *Life of Bishop Patteson* (1873), *The Book of Golden Deeds* (1874), *History of France* (1879), *Life of Hannah More* (1888), and *Life of the Prince Consort* (1889). In all, she wrote more than 160 works, which were popular despite the author's didactic purpose, she being intent on conveying moral ideals and High-Church concepts in her writing.

Yorick (yôr′ik, yor′ik). In Shakespeare's *Hamlet,* the king's jester whose skull is found by the Gravediggers and is apostrophized by Hamlet.

Yorick. Pseudonym of Laurence Sterne in *A Sentimental Journey.*

Yorick. A humorous parson who claims descent from Shakespeare's Yorick, in Laurence Sterne's *Tristram Shandy.*

York (yôrk). [Latin, **Eboracum, Eburacum.**] City and county borough, market town, and manufacturing center in N central England, in the West Riding of Yorkshire, situated on the river Ouse ab. 188 mi. N of London by rail. It is noted for its chocolate manufactures, and formerly had a woolen industry, begun c1330. York has been the seat of an archbishopric since the 7th century. The cathedral (York Minster) is one of the chief English cathedrals, of Norman foundation, but entirely rebuilt in subsequent medieval periods. The interior was severely damaged by a fire set by a pyromaniac in 1829. The south transept, built in the first half of the 13th century, displays three tiers of arcades, increasing in size upward, and the gable is almost entirely occupied by a rose window. The square towers of the much-paneled west front date from the 15th century, as does the massive central tower; the choir and Lady chapel date from the 14th. The interior is highly impressive from its size and height. The elaborate vaulting is of wood. A massive sculptured rood screen separates the nave from the choir. The window, in Perpendicular style, which fills almost the whole east end, measures 78 by 33 ft., being surpassed only by that at Gloucester. The north transept contains the celebrated group of lancets known as the Five Sisters. The cathedral possesses more old glass (14th and 15th centuries) than any other in England. Among its tombs that of Archbishop Grey (1255) is the most remarkable. The dimensions are 525 by 110 ft.; length of transepts, 222 ft.; height of vaulting, 100 ft.; of western towers, 201 ft. The octagonal chapter house, without central pillar, is of exceptional beauty. The city walls make an almost complete circuit of the city; a footpath runs along the top. The walls date from the time of Edward III, and are pierced by four principal gates (there being a total of six). Mickle-gate Bar is one of the six medieval city gates. It is a high, square, battlemented tower, with bartizans on the angles, whose arch spans the roadway. Besides the cathedral there are several interesting churches, Saint Mary's Abbey, and a castle. The ancient 14th-century Guildhall was destroyed by enemy action in World War II (in 1942) and is now in ruins. York was the capital of Britain during the Roman occupation, was visited by Hadrian, and was the place of death of Lucius Septimius Severus and Constantius I (Constantius Chlorus). In York Constantine was proclaimed emperor. It was the terminus of Ermine Street, an ancient Roman road from London. Later it was the capital of Northumbria and Deira, and an important Danish city. It was an early seat of learning. It was taken by William the Conqueror in 1068, revolted and was retaken by him in 1069, was the meeting place of several parliaments, and was besieged and taken (1644) by the Parliamentarians in the English Civil War.

York, Archbishop of. Several archbishops of York appear in Shakespeare's plays. See **Rotherham, Thomas; Scroop, Richard;** and **Wolsey, Thomas.**

York, Duchess of. In Shakespeare's *Richard II,* the wife of York and mother of Aumerle. She begs Henry to pardon her son's treason.

York, Duchess of. In Shakespeare's *Richard III,* the mother of Edward IV and Clarence, whose deaths she laments with Margaret and Queen Elizabeth. She joins the chorus of cursing women who hate Richard.

York, (1st) Duke of. In Shakespeare's *Richard II,* Edmund of Langley (the historical Edmund de Langley). At first a supporter of Richard, he is left as Lord Protector during Richard's absence in Ireland. As soon as Bolingbroke demonstrates his power, however, he adheres to him, and later he reveals the part of his son Aumerle in the plot against Bolingbroke. Some critics consider York weak, indecisive, or even a sycophant; others consider him correct in his extreme loyalty to the crown, whether held by Richard or Henry.

York, (2nd) Duke of. In Shakespeare's *Henry V,* a cousin to the King. He is killed at Agincourt. In *Richard II,* he is the Duke of Aumerle, son of the Duke of York.

York, (3rd) Duke of. In Shakespeare's *1 Henry VI,* the historical Richard Plantagenet, head of the house of York. He picks a white rose in the Temple Garden, indicating his opposition to the house of Lancaster. As regent in France, he fails to aid Talbot and condemns Joan of Arc to death. In *2 Henry VI,* he claims his right to the throne and, with the support of Warwick and Salisbury, wins the battle at St. Albans and there kills Clifford. In *3 Henry VI,* he makes peace, being promised the succession to the throne at the King's death. Gloucester urges him to break his oath, and he is captured and killed by the Lancastrians at Wakefield.

York, Richard, (5th) Duke of. In Shakespeare's *Richard III,* a young boy, son of Edward IV, who is murdered in the Tower by Richard.

Yorke (yôrk), **Henry.** See **Green, Henry.**

Yorke, Philip. [Title, 2nd Earl of **Hardwicke.**] b. March 19, 1720; d. at London, May 16, 1790. An English author and politician. He was a member of Parliament (1741–64) and a member (1764 *et seq.*) of the House of Lords. He served as high steward (1764–90) of Cambridge University. He was co-author, with his brother, of the *Athenian Letters, or the Epistolary Correspondence of an Agent of the King of Persia Residing at Athens during the Peloponnesian War* (privately printed, 1741; published 1798), a work treating historical events and characters in a fictional but realistic manner. Exceedingly popular in its day, it went through several editions, was twice translated into French, and was published in pirated editions.

Yorke, Stephen. Pseudonym of **Linskill, Mary.**

York Plays (yôrk). A cycle of 48 mystery plays performed by the crafts or mysteries of York, England, on Corpus Christi Day, in the 14th, 15th, and 16th centuries. Each guild gave a play, usually one appropriate in some way to its trade or craft. The earliest mention of them is in 1378, by which time they had already been established some years. The plays are the largest extant English cycle, covering Biblical history from the creation to judgment day. They were printed in 1885 by Lucy Toulmin Smith from manuscripts, dating from 1475, in the library of Lord Ashburnham. The best known of the plays is the Noah episode, in which the shrewish wife argues about entering the ark and eventually strikes Noah, after complaining that he might have revealed his plans before she decided to go to town.

Yorkshire Tragedy (yôrk′shir), **A.** A play produced and printed in 1608, founded on an event which occurred in 1604. It was formerly attributed to Shakespeare, as his name appeared in full on the title page in the 1608 edition, and it was included in the second issue of the third Shakespeare folio (1664), but is not now considered his.

You Never Can Tell. A comedy (written 1895–96) by George Bernard Shaw, published in his *Plays, Pleasant and Unpleasant* (1898).

"Young." Entries on literary characters whose names are commonly preceded by "Young" will be found under the names Barnacle, Bellair, Blight, Cato, Fashion, Loveless, Marcius, Marlow, Mortimer, Norval, and Siward.

Young (yung), **Andrew.** b. at Edinburgh, April 23, 1807; d. there, Nov. 30, 1889. A Scottish poet. His verse, which originally appeared in periodicals, was published (1876) in *The Scottish Highlands and Other Poems.* Of his many hymns, his best known is *There Is a Happy Land* (1838).

Young, Arthur. b. in Suffolk, England, Sept. 11, 1741; d. at London, April 20, 1820. An English traveler and agricultural writer. He was engaged (unsuccessfully) in farming, and was appointed secretary of the Board of Agriculture in 1793. He is best known for his accounts of travels in England, Wales, and Ireland, and especially in France (1787–89). His works include *A Farmer's Tour through the East of England* (1770–71), *A Course of Experimental Agriculture* (1770), *The Farmer's Calendar* (1771), *Political Arithmetic* (1774), *A Tour in Ireland* (1780), and *Travels in France,* his chief work

---

ḏ, d or j; ṣ, s or sh; ṭ, t or ch; ẓ, z or zh; o, F. cloche; ü, F. menu; ċh, Sc. loch; ṅ, F. bonbon.

(1792–94). He edited *Annals of Agriculture* (1784 et seq.).

Young, Charles Mayne. b. at London, Jan. 10, 1777; d. at Brighton, England, June 28, 1856. An English actor. His greatest success was in J. P. Kemble's celebrated revival of *Julius Caesar* in 1812. His farewell benefit occurred at Covent Garden, London, on May 31, 1832, when he appeared as Hamlet and, in his honor, Charles Mathews appeared as Polonius and W. C. Macready as the Ghost.

Young, Edward. b. at Upham, near Winchester, England, in June, 1683; d. April 5, 1765. An English poet. He was educated at Oxford, and in 1730 became rector of Welwyn in Hertfordshire. His chief poem is *Night Thoughts* (1742–45; title, *The Complaint: or, Night Thoughts on Life, Death, and Immortality*), the principal work of the somber "graveyard school" of 18th-century poetry. He also wrote satires under the title *Love of Fame, the Universal Passion* (1725–28), and the dramas *Busiris* (1719) and *The Revenge* (1721).

Young, E. H. [Full name, **Emily Hilda Young.**] b. in Northumberland, England, 1880—. An English novelist. She was awarded (1931) the James Tait Black memorial prize for *Miss Mole* (1930). Author also of *A Corn of Wheat* (1910), *Yonder* (1912), *Moor Fires* (1916), *The Bridge Dividing* (1922; republished in 1927 as *The Misses Mallett;* issued in U. S. as *The Mallets*), *William* (1925), *The Vicar's Daughter* (1928), *Jenny Wren* (1932), and *Celia* (1937).

Young, Francis Brett. b. 1884—. An English novelist. He was a ship's doctor (1906–08) in the Far East, and served as medical officer in East Africa during World War I. His novels include *Undergrowth* (1913; in collaboration with Edward Young), *Deep Sea* (1914), *The Dark Tower* (1914), *The Iron Age* (1916), *Crescent Moon* (1918), *The Young Physician* (1919), *The Tragic Bride* (1920), *The Red Knight* (1921), *Pilgrim's Rest* (1922), *Woodsmoke* (1924), *Portrait of Clare* (1924; American title, *Love Is Enough*), which won the James Tait Black memorial prize, *Cold Harbor* (1924), *Sea Horses* (1925), *The Key of Life* (1928), *My Brother Jonathan* (1928), *Black Roses* (1929), *The Cage Bird and Other Stories* (1933), *They Seek a Country* (1937), *Dr. Bradley Remembers* (1938), *The City of Gold* (1939), *Mr. Lucton's Freedom* (1940), *Cotswold Honey* (1940), *A Man about the House* (1942), and *The Island* (1944). Author also of the plays *Captain Swing* (1919) and *The Furnace* (1928), and the book of poetry *Five Degrees South* (1917).

Young, Sir George. b. at Formosa Fishery, Berkshire, England, Sept. 13, 1837; d. there, July 4, 1930. An English educational administrator and writer. He served as charity commissioner (1882–1903) under the Endowed Schools Acts, and as chief commissioner (1903–06). As secretary to the Bessborough Commission on the Irish Land Acts, he was entirely responsible for drawing up the report on the Irish Land Acts, characterized by W. E. Gladstone as the "very ablest." His best-known translation is *The Dramas of Sophocles Rendered in English Verse, Dramatic and Lyric* (1888). He was author of *An English Prosody* (1928), *Homer and the Greek Accents* (1920), and *The Political and*

Occasional Poems of Winthrop Mackworth Praed (1888).

Young, William. See under **Adams, Parson.**

Young Admiral, The. A romantic comedy by James Shirley, licensed in 1633, acted at Court in that year, and printed in 1637.

"Young Adventurer," the. See **Stuart, Charles Edward.**

Young Archimedes (är.ki.mē′dēz), **The.** A short story by Aldous Huxley, published in 1924.

"Young Chevalier," the. See **Stuart, Charles Edward.**

Young Clifford (klif′ọrd). See under **Clifford, Lord.**

Young Enchanted, The. A novel by Hugh Walpole, published in 1922. It continues the characterization of Peter Westcott, the hero of *Fortitude* (1913).

Young Felix (fē′liks). A novel by Frank Swinnerton, published in 1923.

Young Idea—A Comedy of Environment, The. A novel of autobiographical interest by Frank Swinnerton, published in 1910.

Young Lovers, The. A historical novel by Henry Christopher Bailey, published in 1917.

Young Lucius (lō′shus). In Shakespeare's *Titus Andronicus*, the son of Lucius.

Young Man from the South, A. A psychological novel by Lennox Robinson, published in 1917.

Young Physician, The. A novel by Francis Brett Young, published in 1919.

"Young Pretender," the. See **Stuart, Charles Edward.**

"Young Roscius" (rosh′us). See **Betty, William Henry West.**

Young Visiters, The. [Full title, **The Young Visiters, or Mr. Salteena's Plan.**] A novel written by Margaret Mary (Daisy) Ashford at the age of nine and published in 1919.

Young Waters (wô′tẹrz, wot′ẹrz). A Scottish ballad, included in Percy's *Reliques*, telling of the jealousy of the King, who causes Young Waters to be killed upon discovering his Queen's admiration for the youth.

Youth Rides Out. A novel by Beatrice Kean Seymour, published in 1928.

Youwarkee (yö′ạr.kē, yö.wär′kē). The winged maiden, a Gawrie, whom Peter Wilkins marries in Robert Paltock's romance *Peter Wilkins.*

Yule (yöl), **Sir Henry.** b. near Edinburgh, in May, 1820; d. at London, Dec. 30, 1889. A British military engineer in India, and Orientalist. Among his works are *A Narrative of the Mission Sent to the Court of Ava* (1858; he was secretary of this mission), *Cathay and the Way Thither* (1866), a translation of Marco Polo (2 vols., 1871; revised ed., 1875), articles on Central Asia and the Chinese empire, with A. C. Burnell *Hobson-Jobson; Being a Glossary of Anglo-Indian Colloquial Words and Phrases* (1886), and notes to the Hakluyt Society's reprint of the diary of William Hedges (1887).

Yum-Yum (yum′yum). In Gilbert and Sullivan's *The Mikado*, the ward of Ko-Ko.

Ywain and Gawain (ē′wän; gä′win). A Middle English verse romance (c1350), telling of the exploits of Ywain, assisted by the magical aid of Lunet, in which he wins the widow Alundyne but forgets her when at the urging of Gawain he goes to seek glory. During the course of his adventures he and Gawain fight, each unaware of the other's identity, but upon discovering each other they are reconciled. Again with Lunet's help, Ywain and his wife, Alundyne, are also reconciled. The story is a somewhat condensed adaptation of the *Yvain* of Chrétien de Troyes.

Z

Zabina (zạ.bī′nạ). In Christopher Marlowe's tragedy *Tamburlaine*, the wife of Bajazet, ruler of Turkey.

Zachary Fungus (zak′ạ.ri fung′gus). See **Fungus, Zachary.**

Zadkiel (zad′ki.ẹl). In Jewish rabbinical lore, the archangel associated with the planet Jupiter.

Zadkiel. Pseudonym of **Lilly, William.**

Zadok (zā′dok). A character in John Dryden's *Absalom and Achitophel*, representing Archbishop William Sancroft.

Zagreus (zā′grẹ.us). A divine child of Orphic mythology, later identified with Dionysus. The story is that Zeus, in serpent form, begat Zagreus on Persephone, and intended to bestow on him unlimited power. Hera, in jealousy, induced the Titans to do away with the boy. First they beguiled him to them with toys, then killed and devoured him. Athena managed to save the child's heart; this Zeus swallowed and thus was enabled to rebeget Zagreus in the new Dionysus, son of Semele.

Zanga (zang′gạ). The principal character in Edward Young's *Revenge*.

Zangwill (zang′gwil, -wil), **Israel.** b. at London, Feb. 24, 1864; d. Aug. 1, 1926. An English novelist, poet, and playwright. He was prominently identified with Zionism, especially after the death of Theodor Herzl, but after World War I sought for another area but Palestine for the settlement of the Jews, believing the Palestinian question too much complicated by Britain's counter-promises. He was the author of *The Big Bow Mystery* (1891), *Children of the Ghetto* (1892), *Merely Mary Ann* (1893), *Ghetto Tragedies* (1893), *The King of the Schnorrers* (1894), *Without Prejudice* (1896), *Dreamers of the Ghetto*, a series of sketches of great Jewish thinkers (1898), *They That Walk in Darkness* (1899), *The Mantle of Elijah* (1900), *The Grey Wig* (1903), *Blind Children*, a book of verse (1903), *The Celibates' Club* (1905), *The Melting Pot* (1908), *Italian Fantasies* (1910), *The War for the World* (1916), *The Voice of Jerusalem* (1921), and *We Moderns* (1926). In his novels and plays (some adapted from novels), he attempted a realistic description of Jewish life.

Zanoni (zạ.nō′ni). A romance by Edward Bulwer-Lytton, published in 1842. It is a fantastic horror story about a man who is granted immortality on condition of never yielding to any feeling of human sympathy. However, after five thousand years he sacrifices himself for love of a woman.

Zanzis (zan′zis). An unknown writer referred to by Chaucer in *Troilus and Criseyde* (IV, 414): "And ek, as writ Zanzis, that was ful wys."

Zapolya (zạ.pol′yạ). A tragic drama in blank verse by Coleridge, written in 1816 and published in 1817. It is acknowledged to be based in large part upon Shakespeare's *Winter's Tale*. It did not seem to the management of the Drury Lane theater to have sufficient merit to make its production advisable.

Zara (zä′rạ). A character in William Congreve's play *The Mourning Bride*. It is she who says: "Heaven has no rage like love to hatred turned, Nor hell a fury like a woman scorned."

Zara. A tragedy adapted from Voltaire's *Zaïre* (itself fashioned after Shakespeare's *Othello*) by Aaron Hill.

Zarah (zä′rä). See **Fenella.**

Zarathustra or **Zarathushtra** (zar.ạ.thös′trạ). See **Zoroaster.**

Zayn (zīn), **Prince.** See **Al Asnam, Prince Zayn.**

Zeal (zēl), **Arabella** and **Dorcas.** Characters in Charles Shadwell's play *The Fair Quaker of Deal*.

Zeal-of-the-Land Busy (biz′i). See **Busy, Zeal-of-the-Land.**

Zekiel Homespun (zēk′yẹl hōm′spun). See **Homespun, Zekiel.**

Zempoalla (zem.pọ.al′ạ, zem.pō′lạ). The villainous Queen of Mexico who falls passionately in love with Montezuma, her general, in Dryden and Howard's *The Indian Queen*.

Zend (zend). A name formerly and erroneously given to the language of the *Avesta*, which is actually an ancient form of Iranian or Persian. The word *zand*, meaning "commentary," became attached to the title of the book, and was misconstrued as referring to the language.

Zeno (zē′nō). b. at Citium, in Cyprus; d. c264 B.C. A Greek philosopher, founder of the Stoic school of philosophy. He studied philosophy under the Cynics at Athens, and founded his school, eclectic in its efforts to reach a consistent system, there at the Stoa Poecile ("Painted Porch"), whence its name.

Zenobia (zẹ.nō′bi.ạ). d. after 274 A.D. Queen of Palmyra; wife of Odenathus, ruler of Palmyra. She was joint ruler in her husband's lifetime, and succeeded him (c267) as regent for her son and as queen. Under the cloak of a Roman alliance, she stationed her armies throughout the East, in Asia Minor, Syria, Mesopotamia, and Egypt; on Aurelian's accession, she openly defied Rome. Her armies were defeated by Aurelian in 271, Palmyra was besieged and taken in 272, and she was captured and brought to Rome to grace Aurelian's triumph. She was afterward pensioned and given an estate by the Romans.

ḍ, d or j; ṣ, s or sh; ṭ, t or ch; ẓ, z or zh; o, F. cloche; ü, F. menu; ċh, Sc. loch; ṅ, F. bonbon.

Zenocrate (zẹ.nok'rạ.tē). In Christopher Marlowe's tragedy *Tamburlaine*, the wife of Tamburlaine and the daughter of the Soldan of Egypt. She is captured by Tamburlaine, is wooed lavishly by him, and falls in love with him.

Zephon (zē'fon). A cherub in John Milton's *Paradise Lost*. He is made the "guardian angel of Paradise."

Zephyr (zef'ir). [Also, **Zephyrus** (zef'i.rus).] In Greek mythology, a personification of the west wind, poetically regarded as the mildest and gentlest of all the winds. He sometimes figures as the husband of Iris. The Romans identified Favonius, their west wind, with him.

Zerbino (dzer.bē'nō). The Prince of Scotland in the *Orlando Furioso* of Lodovico Ariosto.

Zetland Islands (zet'lạnd). See **Shetland Islands**.

Zeugma (zōg'mạ). In ancient geography, a town on the right bank of the Euphrates, opposite the modern Birecik, noted as a place of passage across the Euphrates.

Zeus (zös). In Greek mythology, king of the gods, the supreme deity, omnipresent and all-powerful, generally looked upon as the son of Cronus and Rhea, and held to have dethroned and succeeded his father. Specifically, he was a sky god and controlled all celestial phenomena, as rains, snows, and tempests, heat and cold, thunder and lightning. His sister and consort was Hera. Zeus was worshiped widely in Greece, but the most renowned of his sanctuaries were those of Olympia in Elis and Dodona in Epirus. By numerous paramours he was the father of Athena, the Horae, the Moirae, the Muses, and the Graces. He was the father of the twin gods Apollo and Artemis, of Ares, Hermes, Hebe, Aphrodite, and Persephone. Among the many heroes fathered by Zeus were Hercules, Perseus, and the twin heroes Castor and Pollux. The oak and the eagle were sacred to him. The Romans identified their Jupiter with Zeus, and the Zeus myths became an accretion to the ancient Jupiter mythology.

Zeuxis (zök'sis). b. at Heraclea, in Lucania or in Macedonia; fl. at the close of the 5th century B.C. A Greek painter. He formed his style at Athens under the influence of Apollodorus, worked at various other cities, and finally settled at Ephesus. Among his principal works were *Zeus on His Throne Surrounded by Gods*, *Eros Crowned with Roses* (in the temple of Aphrodite at Athens), the *Marsyas* (in the temple of Concord at Rome), the *Centaur Family* (described by Lucian), the *Alcmene of the Argentines*, *Hercules as a Child*, the *Helena* (in the temple of Lucanian Hera), and the *Boy with Grapes*.

Zimmern (zim'ẽrn), **Helen.** b. at Hamburg, Germany, March 25, 1846; d. Jan. 11, 1934. An English author, translator, and art critic. She was a correspondent for various English, German, and Italian periodicals. Her works include *Life and Philosophy of Schopenhauer* (1876), *Life and Works of Lessing* (1878), *Sir Laurence Alma-Tadema* (1886), *Hansa Towns* (1889), *Irish Element in Mediaeval Culture* (1891), *Italy of the Italians* (1906), and various translations.

Zimri (zim'rī). In the Bible, a king of Israel, overthrown by Omri (c887 B.C.) after a very short reign. 1 Kings, xvi. 10–18.

Zimri. A character in John Dryden's *Absalom and Achitophel* who represents George Villiers, 2nd Duke of Buckingham.

Zohar (zō'här). [Also: **Sepher-haz-Zohar, Sohar**; Eng. trans., "*Book of Splendor*" or "*Book of Light*."] A cabalistic work in the form of a commentary on the Pentateuch. It is ascribed traditionally to the 2nd century A.D., but by many is thought to have been written much later, probably in the 13th century.

Zoilus (zō'i.lus). fl. in the 4th century B.C. A Greek rhetorician; called *Homeromastix* (Scourge of Homer) from his severe criticisms of Homer, whose works had too much of the fabulous for Zoilus's taste. His name came to be applied to any carping critic.

Zola (zō'lạ, zọ.lä'; French, zo.là), **Émile.** b. at Paris, April 2, 1840; d. there, Sept. 29, 1902. A French novelist. He studied at the Lycée Saint-Louis, but took no degree. From 1860 to 1862 he lived in great poverty, and finally entered Hachette's bookstore as a packing clerk. He studied the details of publishing until the close of the year 1865, but devoted to writing all the time that was his own. In 1864 he published his first work, *Contes à Ninon*, followed in 1874 by the *Nouveaux contes à Ninon*. In 1865 appeared *La Confession de Claude*, and then other separate novels, as *Le Vœu d'une morte* (1866), *Les Mystères de Marseille* (1867), *Thérèse Raquin* (1867), and *Madeleine Férat* (1868); he also published a number of short stories (1882–84). From 1871 to 1893 Zola published, under the collective title *Les Rougon-Macquart*, 20 novels: *La Fortune des Rougons* (1871), *La Curée* (1872), *La Ventre de Paris* (1873), *La Conquête de Plassans* (1874), *La Faute de l'abbé Mouret* (1875), *Son excellence Eugène Rougon* (1876), *L'Assommoir* (1877), *Une Page d'amour* (1878), *Nana* (1880), *Pot-Bouille* (1882), *Au bonheur des dames* (1883), *La Joie de vivre* (1884), *Germinal* (1885), *L'Œuvre* (1886), *La Terre* (1887), *Le Rêve* (1888), *La Bête humaine* (1890), *L'Argent* (1891), *La Débâcle* (1892), and *Le Docteur Pascal* (1893). His *Trilogy of the Three Cities* includes *Lourdes* (1894), *Rome* (1896), and *Paris* (1898). His writings in criticism include *Mes haines* (1866), *Mon salon* (1866), *Édouard Manet* (1867), *La République française et la littérature* (1879), *Le Roman expérimental* (1880), *Le Naturalisme au théâtre* (1881), *Nos auteurs dramatiques* (1881), *Les Romanciers naturalistes* (1881), *Une Campagne* (1881), and *Documents littéraires, études et portraits* (1881). Some of his novels have been dramatized, as *L'Assommoir* (1879), *Le Ventre de Paris* (1887), *Renée* (1887; adapted from *La Curée*), and *Germinal* (1888). Zola became the leader of the school of naturalism in France, bringing to his novels a minuteness of description that balked at nothing in an effort to build up an accurate picture of the life of his time. He was anticlerical, antimonarchist, and antimilitary in the crises that shook France in the 1890's. On Feb. 23, 1898, he was sentenced to a year's imprisonment and the payment of a fine of 3,000 francs for libeling the court-martial which tried and acquitted Major Esterhazy in the Dreyfus affair. The newspaper article which brought the libel proceedings was *J'accuse*, written in the form of a letter which appeared (Jan. 13, 1898) in the Parisian journal *Aurore*. The sentence was annulled by the court of cassation. He was again tried and sentenced to 12 months' imprisonment and the payment of a fine. He left France for England before notification of judgment in order to secure a retrial later, but soon returned.

Zophiel (zō′fi.ẹl). A cherub in John Milton's *Paradise Lost*.

Zoroaster (zō.rọ.as′tẻr). [Greek form of the Persian name **Zarathushtra** or **Zarathustra**.] fl. probably in the 6th century B.C. An ancient Iranian religious reformer, founder of Zoroastrianism. Nothing definite is known of his life; 660–583 are the dates most usually given for his birth and death, but 630, 570, or even 1000 B.C. are also given as his birth date. He is said to have converted to his belief, when he was in his 40's, King Vishtaspa, who is usually identified with Hystaspes, the father of Darius the Great. All tradition, by which his birth is placed in western or in eastern Iran, which tells of his career, or concerning his death, is much later and appears to have been modified by sectarian differences or by the simple passage of time. His own extant writing, if any, is preserved in the *Gathas*, hymns appearing in the Avesta. Zoroaster, objecting to the multiplicity of gods carried into Iran by the Aryan migrants from India, conceived of the universe as consisting of two opposing principles: one, personified as Ahura Mazda (Ormuzd), was the essence of good; the other was the essence of evil. Everything in the universe partakes of the fight between the two and it is the duty of man, for his own salvation and to secure increase of crops and cattle, to oppose the evil and hold to the good. The reformer was unable to eliminate polytheism, but the subordination of the numerous gods to the dual principle tended to establish belief in one supreme being; the nature gods were enrolled on the side of good as archangels (Amesha Spentas), the demons (daevas) aided the evil. Certain substances, such as fire, earth, and water, are pure; the belief that Zoroastrians are fire-worshipers is widespread but springs from the erroneous conclusion that fire is worshiped, whereas it is rather venerated as a manifestation of good emanating from Ahura Mazda. In the final judgment, all souls will be tried and the forces of evil will be defeated; the good will thereafter reign triumphant, Ahura Mazda having conquered with their aid. Much of this is later addition to Zoroaster's basic doctrine, the Magi, priests of Zoroastrianism, having molded the religion during its spread throughout the Near East and transformed it from a pure doctrine of good and evil to a religious system known as Mazdaism. Between the conquest of Persia by Alexander the Great (330 B.C.) and the advent of the Sassanid kings of the 3rd century A.D., the religion seems to have been dormant, except for the mystical offshoot known as Mithraism which spread through the Roman world. After several centuries of reflorescence under the Sassanids, Zoroastrianism was subdued by the spread of Mohammedanism, a crusading religion that overran Persia in the 7th century, and, though a number of worshipers remain in Iran, the principal existing center of Zoroastrianism is among the Parsis of India, whither it was carried by refugees from Islam.

Zuleika (zö.lā′kä). A favorite woman's name in Persian poetry. Potiphar's wife was also named Zuleika.

Zuleika Dobson (zö.lē′kạ dob′sọn). A satirical novel by Max Beerbohm, published in 1911. It concerns life at Oxford University and the demoralizing effect that the charming and clever Zuleika has on the faculty and students.

Zulema (zö.lē′mạ). A villainous Moorish plotter in Dryden's *The Conquest of Granada*.

ḍ, d or j; ṣ, s or sh; ṭ, t or ch; ẓ, z or zh; o, F. cloche; ü, F. menu; ċh, Sc. loch; ṅ, F. bonbon.